YEARBOOK 2016

# INTERNATIONAL
# FINANCIAL STATISTICS

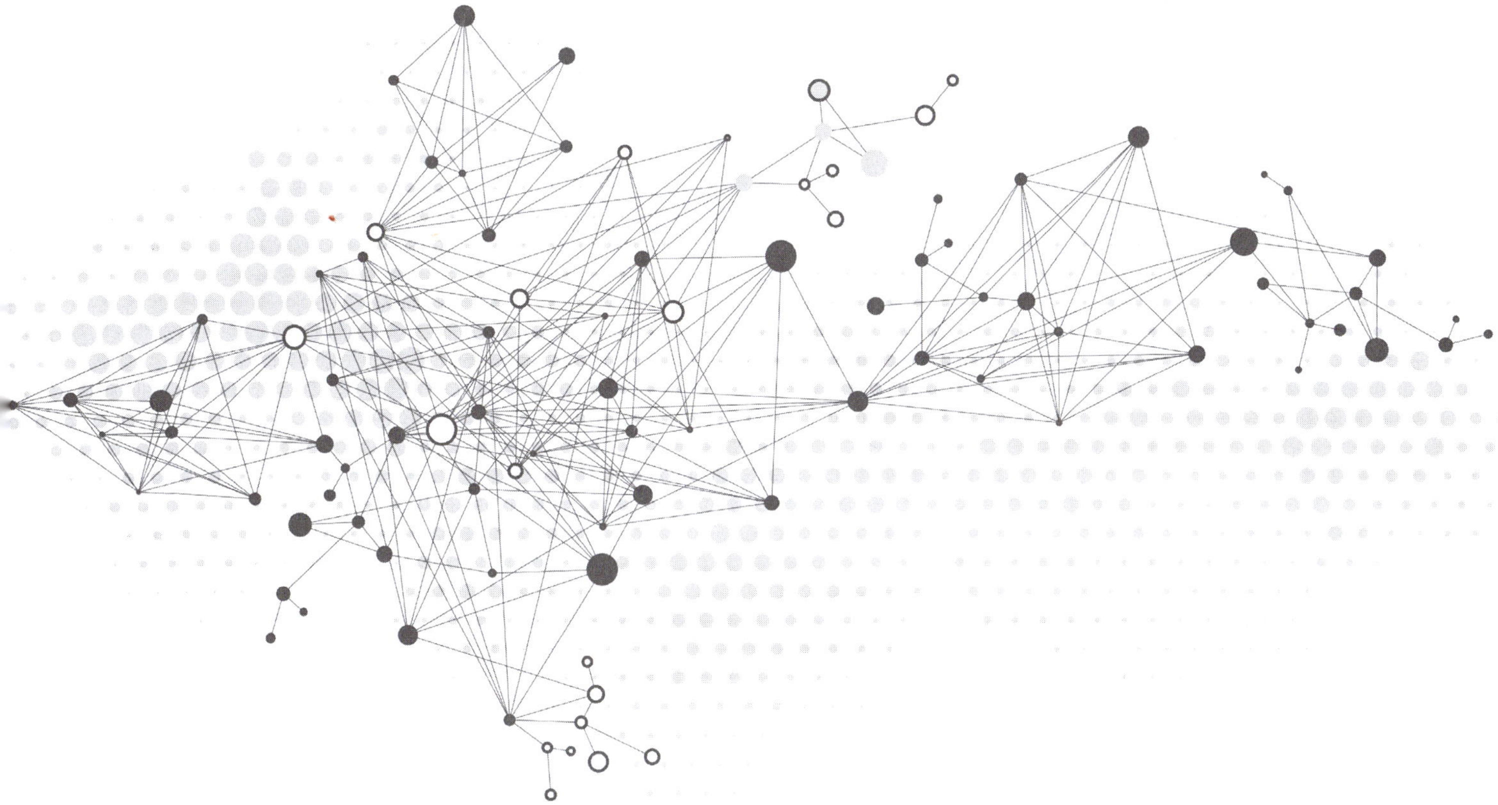

INTERNATIONAL MONETARY FUND

# INTERNATIONAL FINANCIAL STATISTICS

Vol. LXIX, 2016
Prepared by the IMF Statistics Department
Louis Marc Ducharme, Director

For information related to this publication, please:
    fax the Statistics Department at (202) 623-6460,
    or write Statistics Department
        International Monetary Fund
        Washington, D.C. 20431
    or e-mail your query to **tickets@imfdata.uservoice.com**
For copyright inquiries, please fax the Editorial Division at (202) 623-6579.
For purchases only, please contact Publication Services (see information below).

*International Financial Statistics* (IFS) is a standard source of statistics on all aspects of international and domestic finance. IFS publishes, for most countries of the world, current data on exchange rates, international liquidity, international banking, money and banking, interest rates, prices, production, international transactions (including balance of payments and international investment position), government finance, and national accounts. Information is presented in tables for specific countries and in tables for area and world aggregates. IFS is published monthly and annually.

**Address orders to:**
International Monetary Fund
Attention: Publication Services
P.O. Box 92780
Washington, D.C. 20090
U.S.A.
Telephone: (202) 623-7430
Telefax: (202) 623-7201
E-mail: publications@imf.org
Internet: http://www.imf.org

ISSN 0250-7463
ISBN 978-1-51352-138-1

---

**POSTMASTER:** Send address changes to International Financial Statistics, Publication Services, 700 19th St., N.W., Washington, D.C. 20431. Postage for periodicals paid at Washington, D.C. USPS 049-610

MIX
Paper from
responsible sources
FSC® C010236

# Contents

"Country" in this publication does not always refer to a territorial entity that is a state as understood by international law and practice; the term also covers the euro area, the Eastern Caribbean Currency Union, and some nonsovereign territorial entities, for which statistical data are provided internationally on a separate basis.

** Monetary data for these countries are based on the Standardized Report Forms (SRF).

# Selection of Statistical Publications

### International Financial Statistics (IFS)
Acknowledged as a standard source of statistics on all aspects of international and domestic finance, IFS publishes, for most countries of the world, current data on exchange rates, international liquidity, international banking, money and banking, interest rates, prices, production, international transactions (including balance of payments and international investment position), government finance, and national accounts. Information is presented in tables for specific countries and in tables for area and world aggregates. IFS is published monthly and annually. Price: Subscription price is US$890 a year (US$578 to university faculty and students) for twelve monthly issues and the yearbook. Single copy price is US$114 for a monthly issue and US$180 for a yearbook issue.

### Balance of Payments Statistics Yearbook (BOPSY)
Balance of Payments Statistics Yearbook (BOPSY): Contains two sections; World and Regional Tables, and Country Tables. The first section presents 21 world and regional tables for major components of the balance of payments, net International Investment Position (IIP), and total financial assets and total liabilities for the IIP. The second section provides detailed tables on balance of payments statistics for 191 economies and IIP data for 150 economies. Price: US$161.

### Direction of Trade Statistics (DOTS)
Quarterly issues of this publication provide, for 160 countries, tables with current data (or estimates) on the value of imports from and exports to their most important trading partners. In addition, similar summary tables for the world, industrial countries, and developing countries are included. The yearbook provides, for the most recent seven years, detailed trade data by country for approximately 184 countries, the world, and major areas. Price: Subscription price is US$260 a year (US$222 to university faculty and students) for the quarterly issues and the yearbook. Price for a quarterly issue only is US$43 and the yearbook only is US$115.

### Government Finance Statistics Yearbook (GFSY)
This annual publication provides detailed data on transactions in revenue, expense, net acquisition of assets and liabilities, other economic flows, and balances of assets and liabilities of general government and its subsectors. The data are compiled according to the framework of the 2001 Government Finance Statistics Manual, which provides for several summary measures of government fiscal performance. Price: US$107.

## CD-ROM Subscriptions
International Financial Statistics (IFS), Balance of Payments Statistics (BOPS), Direction of Trade Statistics (DOTS), and Government Finance Statistics (GFS) are available on CD-ROM by annual subscription. The CD-ROMs incorporate a Windows-based browser facility, as well as a flat file of the database in scientific notation. Price of each subscription: US$250 a year for single-user PC license (US$125 for university faculty and students). Network and redistribution licenses are negotiated on a case-by-case basis. Please visit www.imfbookstore.org/onlineServicePricing.asp for information.

## Subscription Packages
### Combined Subscription Package
The combined subscription package includes all issues of IFS, DOTS, GFS, and BOPSY. Combined subscription price: US$1,418 a year (US$1,068 for university faculty and students). Expedited delivery available at additional cost; please inquire.

### Combined Statistical Yearbook Subscription
This subscription comprises BOPSY, IFSY, GFSY, and DOTSY at a combined rate of US$563. Because of different publication dates of the four yearbooks, it may take up to one year to service an order. Expedited delivery available at additional cost; please inquire.

## IFS, BOPS, DOTS, GFS on the Internet
The Statistics Department of the Fund is pleased to make available to users the International Financial Statistics (IFS), Balance of Payments Statistics (BOPS), Direction of Trade Statistics (DOTS), and Government Finance Statistics (GFS) databases through the new, easy-to-use data.IMF.org online service. New features include Data Portals, which provide quick access to predefined tables, maps, graphs, and charts aimed at visualizing many common data searches. Data.IMF.org lets you create a basic custom-built data query using the Query tool which offers great flexibility to create larger and more complex queries. Once you have defined your query, you can structure the table the way you want it, and then convert your data into a chart or download it. A number of personalization options are available in the "My profile" section such as accessing your favorites and saved queries. Free registration for My profile can be obtained by clicking on the Sign In or Register link on the data.IMF.org home page.

## Address orders to
Publication Services, International Monetary Fund, PO Box 92780, Washington, DC 20090, USA
Telephone: (202) 623-7430   Fax: (202) 623-7201   E-mail: publications@imf.org
Internet: http://www.imfbookstore.org

**Note:** Prices include the cost of delivery by surface mail. Expedited delivery is available for an additional charge.

# Introduction

## Table of Contents

## 1. Overview

The Fund's principal statistical publication, *International Financial Statistics* (*IFS*), has been published monthly since January 1948. In 1961, the monthly was supplemented by a yearbook, and in 1991 and 2000, respectively, IFS was introduced on CD-ROM and the Internet.

IFS contains country tables for most Fund members, as well as for Anguilla, Aruba, the Central African Economic and Monetary Community (CEMAC), Curaçao, the currency union of Curaçao and Sint Maarten, the Eastern Caribbean Currency Union (ECCU), the euro area, Montserrat, the former Netherlands Antilles, Sint Maarten, the West African Economic Monetary Union (WAEMU), West Bank and Gaza, and some nonsovereign territorial entities for which statistics are provided internationally on a separate basis. Also, selected series are drawn from the country tables and published in area and world tables. The country tables normally include data on a country's exchange rates, Fund position, international liquidity, monetary statistics, interest rates, prices, production, labor, international transactions, government accounts, national accounts, and population. Selected series, including data on Fund accounts, international reserves, and international trade, are drawn from the country tables and published in world tables as well.

The monthly printed issue of IFS reports current monthly, quarterly, and annual data, while the yearbook reports 12 observations of annual data. Most annual data on the CD-ROM and Internet begin in 1948; quarterly and monthly data generally begin in 1957; most balance of payments data begin in 1970.

The following sections describe conceptual and technical aspects of various data published in IFS. The reader will find more detailed descriptions—about coverage, deviations from the standard methodologies, and discontinuities in the data—in the footnotes in the individual country and world tables in the monthly and yearbook issues of IFS, in the Print_Me file on the CD-ROM, and in the PDF pages on the Internet. (Where references are made in this introduction to notes in monthly issues, they refer to notes files on the CD-ROM and Internet as well.)

## 2. Exchange Rates and Exchange Rate Arrangements

Exchange rates in IFS are classified into three broad categories, reflecting the role of the authorities in determining the rates and/or the multiplicity of the exchange rates in a country. The three categories are the **market rate**, describing an exchange rate determined largely by market forces; the **official rate**, describing an exchange rate determined by the authorities—sometimes in a flexible manner; and the **principal**, **secondary**, or **tertiary rate**, for countries maintaining multiple exchange arrangements.

In IFS, exchange rates are expressed in time series of national currency units per SDR (the unit of account for the Fund) and national currency units per U.S. dollar, or vice versa.

The exchange rates in SDRs are classified and coded as follows:

Series **aa** shows the end-of-period national currency value of the SDR, and series **ac** shows the end-of-period SDR value of the national currency unit.

Series **sa**, **sb**, **sc**, and **sd**—provided on the country table for the United States—show the SDR value of U.S. dollars. Series **sa** and **sc** refer to end-of-period values of U.S. dollars per SDR and SDRs per U.S. dollar, respectively, while series **sb** and **sd** are geometric averages of values within the period.

The exchange rates in U.S. dollars are classified and coded as follows:

Series **ae** shows end-of-period national currency units per U.S. dollar, and series **ag** shows end-of-period U.S. dollars per unit of national currency.

Series **rf** shows period-average national currency units per U.S. dollar, and series **rh** shows period-average U.S. dollars per unit of national currency. Series **rf** and **rh** data are the monthly average of market rates or official rates of the reporting country. If those are not available, they are the monthly average rates in New York. Or if the latter are not available, they are estimates based on simple averages of the end-of-month market rates quoted in the reporting country.

The country tables contain two of the U.S. dollar series—either **ae** and **rf** or **ag** and **rh**—depending on the form in which the exchange rate is quoted.

Reciprocal relationships are the following:

The end-of-period rates **aa** and **ac**, **ae** and **ag**, and **sa** and **sc** are reciprocals of each other. The period-average SDR rates in terms of the U.S. dollar (**sb** and **sd**) are also reciprocals of each other, because they are calculated as geometric averages. Other period average rates (**rf** and **rh**) are calculated as arithmetic averages and are not reciprocals.

The relationship between trade figures in IFS and exchange rates is the following:

All trade figures in IFS are converted from national currency values to U.S. dollars and from U.S. dollar values to national currency, using series **rf**. Conversions are based on the data available for the shortest period, and these data are summed to obtain data for longer periods. Conversion is based on longer period rates of only the difference, if any, between the longer period data and the sum of the shorter period data. The country table notes in the monthly issues identify the exchange rates used.

For members maintaining dual or multiple exchange rate systems, which often reflect wide ranges of exchange rates in effect in a country, lines **w**, **x**, and **y** are presented. Notes on the tables in the monthly issues for these countries describe the current exchange rate systems and identify the exchange rates shown.

### Effective Exchange Rates

The country tables, euro area tables, and world tables provide measures of effective exchange rates, compiled by the IMF's Research Department, Strategy, Policy, and Review Department, Statistics Department, and area departments.

A **nominal** effective exchange rate index represents the ratio (expressed on the base 2010=100) of an index of a currency's period-average exchange rate to a weighted geometric average of exchange rates for the currencies of selected countries and the euro area. A **real effective** exchange rate index represents a nominal effective exchange rate index adjusted for relative movements in national price or cost indicators of the home country, selected countries, and the euro area.

### Line ahx

For ease of comparison between the nominal effective exchange rate index and the real effective exchange rate index, the average exchange rate expressed in terms of U.S. dollars per unit of each of the national currencies (line **ah**) is also given as an index form based on 2010=100 (line **ahx**). In both cases of the indices, an increase in the index reflects an appreciation. Because of certain data-related limits, particularly where Fund estimates have been used, data users need to exercise considerable caution in interpreting movements in nominal and real effective exchange rates.

The Fund publishes calculated effective exchange rates data only for countries that have given their approval. Please note that similar indices that are calculated by country authorities could cause different results.

### Lines nel and rel

These series are published starting with the March 2010 issue of IFS. The **nel** and **rel** series are the nominal and real effective exchange rates based on relative unit labor cost for the advanced economies based on a basket of 36 countries and euro area as a group. These 36 advanced economies include Australia, Austria, Belgium, Canada, Cyprus, Czech Republic, Denmark, Estonia, Finland, France, Germany, Greece, Hong Kong SAR, Iceland, Ireland, Israel, Italy, Japan, Korea, Latvia, Lithuania, Luxembourg, Malta, Netherlands, New Zealand, Norway, Portugal, Singapore, Slovak Republic, Slovenia, Spain, Sweden, Switzerland, Taiwan Province of China, United Kingdom, and United States.

The main source for the unit labor cost data is from the OECD Analytical Database (quarterly unit labor cost in manufacturing). However, for Australia, Hong Kong SAR, Singapore, and Israel, the unit labor cost data are provided by IMF staff (annual data interpolated into higher frequencies). The source for the United States' quarterly unit labor cost data is the Bureau of Labor Statistics.

### Lines nec and rec

The nec and rec series are the nominal and real effective exchange rates based on relative consumer prices. The weights used in the calculation take account of each country's trade in both *manufactured* goods and *primary* products with its partner, or competitor, countries.

For *manufactured* goods, trade by type of good and market is distinguished in the database. So it is possible to allow at a disaggregated level for competition among various exporters in a foreign market (i.e., third-market competition) as well as that arising from bilateral trade links.

For *primary* products, the weights assigned depend principally on a country's role as a global supplier or buyer of the product. Trade in crude petroleum, petroleum, and other energy products is excluded. For some countries that depend heavily on tourism, bilateral exports of tourism services averaged over 2004–06 are also included in calculating the competitiveness weights.

From January 2006 onwards, the line **nec** index is weighted based on disaggregate trade data for manufactured goods and primary products covering the three-year period 2004–06. Before that, the weights are for the three-year span 1999–01. The series based on the old weights and the new weights are linked by splicing at December 2004, and the reference base is shifted to 2010=100.

The real effective exchange rate index in line **rec** is derived from the nominal effective exchange rate index, adjusted for relative changes in consumer prices. Consumer price indices, often available monthly, are used as a measure of domestic costs and prices for these countries. This practice typically reflects the use of consumer prices by the reference and partner, or competitor, countries in compiling these indices.

For countries where multiple exchange rates are in effect, Fund staff estimates of weighted average exchange rates are used in many cases. A weighted average exchange rate is constructed as an average of the various exchange rates, with the weights reflecting the share of trade transacted at each rate. For countries where a weighted average exchange rate cannot be calculated, the principal rate, generally line **ahx**, is used.

The notes to the country tables in the monthly issues provide information about exceptions in the choice of the consumer price index (generally line 64) and the period average exchange rate index (generally line **ahx**). For a relatively small number of countries, notes in the country tables in the monthly issues indicate 1) where alternative price indices, such as the wholesale/producer price index or a weighted average of several price indices, are used; 2) where data constraints have made it necessary to use weighting schemes based on aggregate bilateral non-oil trade data; and 3) where trade in services (such as tourism) has been taken into account.

The world table section of this introduction provides a description of the effective exchange rates tables. In addition, a Fund working paper entitled "A Primer on the IMF's Information Notice System" (WP/97/71), distributed in May 1997, provides background on the concepts and methodology underlying the effective exchange rates. Another Fund working paper "New Rates from New Weights" (WP/05/99), provides background on the methodology underlying the new weights.

### SDR Value

Before July 1974, the value of the SDR (unit of account for the Fund) was fixed in terms of U.S. dollars. Over time, the value changed as follows: SDR 1 = U.S. dollar 1 through November 1971; SDR 1 = U.S. dollar 1.08571 from December 1971 through January 1973; and SDR 1 = U.S. dollar 1.20635 from February 1973 through June 1974.

Since July 1974, the Fund has determined the value of the SDR daily on the basis of a basket of currencies, with each currency being assigned a weight in the determination of that value. The currencies in the basket are valued at their market exchange rates for the U.S. dollar. The U.S. dollar equivalents of each currency are summed to yield the rate of the SDR in terms of the U.S. dollar. The rates for the SDR in terms of other currencies are derived from the market exchange rates of these currencies for the U.S. dollar and the U.S. dollar rate for the SDR.

Although the method of calculating the U.S. dollar/SDR exchange rate has remained the same, the currencies' number and weight have changed over time. Their amount in the SDR basket is reviewed every five years.

From July 1974 through June 1978, the currencies in the basket were of the countries that averaged more than 1 percent share in world exports of goods and services from 1968–72. This established a basket of 16 currencies. Each currency's relative weight was broadly proportionate to the country's exports but modified for the U.S. dollar to reflect its real weight in the world economy. To preserve the continuity of valuation, the amount of each of the 16 currencies was such that on June 28, 1974 the value of SDR 1 = U.S. dollar 1.20635.

From July 1978 through December 1980, the composition of the basket was changed on the basis of updated data for 1972–76. The weights of some currencies were also changed. The amount of each of the 16 currencies in the revised basket was such as to ensure that the value of the SDR in terms of any currency on June 30, 1978 was exactly the same in the revised valuation as in the previous valuation.

Since January 1, 1981, the value of the SDR has been determined based on the currencies of the five member countries having the largest exports of goods and services during the five-year period ending one year before the date of the latest revision to the valuation basket. Broadly reflecting the currencies' relative importance in international trade and finance, the weights are based on the value of the exports of goods and services of the members issuing these currencies and the balances of their currencies officially held by members of the Fund.

From January 1981 through December 1985, the currencies and currency weights of the five members having the largest exports of goods and services during 1975–79 were the U.S. dollar, 42 percent; deutsche mark, 19 percent; French franc, Japanese yen, and pound sterling, 13 percent each.

From January 1986 through December 1990, reflecting the period 1980–84, the weights had changed to U.S. dollar, 42 percent; deutsche mark, 19 percent; Japanese yen, 15 percent; French franc and pound sterling, 12 percent each.

From January 1991 through December 1995, reflecting the period 1985–89, the weights were U.S. dollar, 40 percent; deutsche mark, 21 percent; Japanese yen, 17 percent; French franc and pound sterling, 11 percent each.

On January 1, 1996, the weights were U.S. dollar, 39 percent; deutsche mark, 21 percent; Japanese yen, 18 percent; French franc and pound sterling, 11 percent each.

On January 1, 1999, the currency amount of deutsche mark and French francs were replaced with equivalent amounts of euros, based on the fixed conversion rates between those currencies and the euro, announced on December 31, 1998 by the European Council. The weights in the SDR basket were changed to U.S. dollar, 39 percent; euro, 32 percent (in replacement of the 21 percent for the deutsche mark and 11 percent for the French franc), Japanese yen, 18 percent; and pound sterling, 11 percent.

On January 1, 2001, the weights had changed to U.S. dollar, 45 percent; euro, 29 percent; Japanese yen, 15 percent; and pound sterling, 11 percent.

On January 1, 2006, the weights had changed to U.S. dollar, 44 percent; euro, 34 percent; Japanese yen and pound sterling, 11 percent each.

After the latest round of five-yearly review of the currencies of the SDR basket, effective January 1, 2011, the updated weights are U.S. dollar 41.9 percent; euro, 37.4 percent; Japanese yen, 9.4 percent; and pound sterling, 11.3 percent.

### World Tables on Exchange Rates

Tables A and B on exchange rates, described below, are presented in IFS.

Table A of exchange rates gives the monthly, quarterly, and annual SDR rates in terms of U.S. dollars and reciprocals of these rates.

Table B provides, in terms of national currency units per SDR, end-of-period rates for the currencies of Fund members.

### Method of Deriving IFS Exchange Rates

For countries that have introduced new currencies, the rates shown in IFS for the period before the introduction of the most recent currency may be used as conversion factors—they may be used to convert national currency data in IFS to U.S. dollar or SDR data. In such cases, the factors are constructed by chain linking the exchange rates of the old and the new currencies. The basis used is the value of the new currency relative to the old currency, as established by the issuing agency at the time the new currency was introduced. Footnotes about the introduction of new currencies are to be found on individual country tables in the monthly issues of IFS.

For countries that are members of the euro area, the exchange rates shown are expressed in national currency units per SDR or per U.S. dollar through 1998, and in euros per SDR or per U.S. dollar thereafter.

A detailed description of the derivation of the exchange rates in IFS, as well as technical issues associated with these rates, is contained in the *IFS Supplement on Exchange Rates*, No. 9 (1985).

# 3. Fund Accounts

Data on members' Fund accounts are presented in the Fund Position section in the country tables and in four world tables. Terms and concepts of Fund Accounts and the time series in the country and world tables are explained below. More detailed information on member countries' transactions with and position in the Fund are available on the IMF external website at www.imf.org/external/fin.htm

The IMF quota increase under the Fourteenth General Review of Quotas is reflected in the following Fund Accounts for those members that have made their quota payments: Quota, Reserve Tranche Position, Fund Holdings of Currency, SDR Holdings. It is also reflected in the international liquidity and central bank data. The details regarding the associated change can be found in the IMF Press Release No. 16/25, data January 27, 2016. Link to Press Release http://www.imf.org/external/np/sec/pr/2016/pr1625a.htm

### Terms and Concepts in Fund Accounts

### Quota

When a country joins the Fund, it is assigned a quota that fits into the structure of existing quotas. Quotas are considered in the light of the member's economic characteristics, and taking into account quotas of similar countries. The size of the member's quota determines, among other things, the member's voting power, the size of its potential access to Fund resources, and its share in allocations of SDRs.

Quotas ar e reviewed at intervals of not more than five years. The reviews take account of changes in the relative economic positions of members and the growth of the world economy. Initial subscriptions, and normally subscriptions associated with increases in quotas, are paid mainly in the member's own currency, and a smaller portion, not exceeding 25 percent, is paid in reserve assets (SDRs or other members' currencies that are acceptable to the Fund).

### General Resources Account

The General Resources Account (GRA) resources consist of the currencies of Fund member countries, SDRs, and gold. These resources are received in the form of subscriptions (which are equal to quotas), borrowings, charges on the use of the Fund's resources, income from investments, and interest on the Fund's holdings of SDRs. Subscriptions are the main source of funds.

### Borrowing Arrangements

Borrowings are regarded as a temporary source of funds. To supplement its quota resources, the Fund has the authority to borrow the currency of any member from any source with the consent of the issuer.

### Positions in the Fund

The Fund normally determines the currencies that are used in transactions and operations with members. Each quarter, the Fund prepares a financial transactions plan, in which it indicates the amounts of particular currencies and SDRs to be used during the relevant period. The Fund selects the currencies of members with strong balance of payments and reserve positions. It also seeks to promote, over time, balanced "**positions in the Fund**."

The effects of Fund transactions and operations are summarized in the Fund's **holdings of members' currencies** and in two other measures, namely, **reserve position in the Fund** and total **Fund credit and loans outstanding**. (See world table in the monthly printed copy of IFS and the yearbook, entitled Fund Accounts: Position to Date, and also the Fund Position section in the country tables.)

These measures are defined as follows:

The Fund's **holdings of a member's currency** reflect, among other things, the transactions and operations of the Fund in that currency. This concept is used in calculating the amounts that a member can draw on the Fund under tranche policies and in respect to certain of its obligations to the Fund.

**Total Fund credit and loans outstanding** (.2tl.) represents the sum of (1) the use of Fund credit within the GRA and (2) outstanding loans under the SAF, PRGT, and the Trust Fund.

## SDRs

SDRs are unconditional reserve assets created by the Fund to supplement existing reserve assets. SDRs have been allocated by the IMF to members that are participants in the SDR Department at the time of allocation in proportion to their quotas in the IMF. Six allocations totaling SDR 21.4 billion have been made by the Fund in 1970, 1971, 1972, 1979, 1980, and 1981. In addition, a general allocation of SDR 161.2 billion was made on August 28, 2009, and a special allocation of SDR 21.5 billion was made on September 9, 2009.

The Fund cannot allocate SDRs to itself but receives them from members through various financial transactions and operations. Entities authorized to conduct transactions in SDRs are the Fund itself, participants in the SDR Department, and other "prescribed holders."

The SDR can be used for a wide range of transactions and operations, including for acquiring other members' currencies, settling financial obligations, making donations, and extending loans. SDRs may also be used in swap arrangements and as security for the performance of financial obligations. Forward as well as spot transactions may be conducted in SDRs.

## World Tables on Fund Accounts

Beginning with the March 2010 issue of IFS, four world tables on Fund accounts are presented in IFS, as described below. The rest of the Fund accounts tables which used to be published in IFS will no longer be updated, but historical data are accessible on the CD-ROM or Internet.

The table Fund Accounts: Position to Date reports latest monthly data on members' Fund positions, including quota, reserve tranche position, lending to the Fund, total Fund credit and loans outstanding, Fund holdings of currencies, and positions in the SDR Department.

The table Total Fund Credit and Loans Outstanding (.2tl.) relates to the outstanding use of Fund resources under the GRA and to outstanding loans under the SAF, PRGF, and Trust Fund.

The table SDR Holdings (.1b.s) shows holdings of SDRs by members and includes a foot table showing SDR holdings by all participants, the IMF, other holders, and the world.

The table Reserve Position in the Fund (.1c.s) relates to members' claims on the Fund.

### Pamphlet on Fund Accounts

A more detailed description of the Fund accounts is contained in the *IMF Financial Operations*.

## 4. International Liquidity

Data on international liquidity are presented in the country tables and in world tables on reserves. The international liquidity section in the country tables comprises lines for total reserves minus gold, gold holdings, other foreign assets and foreign liabilities of the monetary authorities, and foreign accounts of other financial institutions. The euro area section for international liquidity covers assets of the European Central Bank (ECB) and the national central banks (NCBs) of the countries that have adopted the euro (details below).

### Total Reserves (Minus Gold) and Gold Holdings

Total Reserves Minus Gold (line 1 l.d) is the sum of the items Foreign Exchange, Reserve Position in the Fund, and the U.S. dollar value of SDR holdings by monetary authorities. Monetary authorities comprise central banks and, to the extent that they perform monetary authorities' functions, currency boards, exchange stabilization funds, and treasuries.

Official Gold Holdings (lines 1ad and 1and) are expressed in millions of fine troy ounces and valued, according to national practice, in U.S. dollars.

Under Total Reserves Minus Gold, the line for Foreign Exchange (1d.d) includes monetary authorities' claims on nonresidents in the form of foreign banknotes, bank deposits, treasury bills, short- and long-term government securities, ECUs (for periods before January 1999), and other claims usable in the event of balance of payments need.

For IFS yearbook users, this background information on foreign exchange is particularly useful: Before December 1971, when the U.S. dollar was at par with the SDR, foreign exchange data were compiled and expressed in terms of U.S. dollars at official par values. Conversions from national currencies to U.S. dollars from December 1971 through January

1973 were calculated at the cross rates reflecting the parities and central rates agreed to in December 1971. From February 1973 through June 1974, foreign exchange was valued at the cross rates of parities or central rates for countries having effective parities or central rates, and at market rates for the Canadian dollar, Irish pound, Italian lira, Japanese yen, and pound sterling. Beginning in July 1974, foreign exchange is valued at end-of-month market rates or, in the absence of market rate quotations, at other prevailing official rates.

## Total Reserves for the Euro Area

Total reserves for the euro area and individual euro area countries are based on the statistical definition of international reserves adopted by the ECB's Statistics Committee in December 1998. Defined on a euro area-wide residency basis, they include reserve assets denominated only in currencies of non-euro area countries. All positions with residents of other euro area countries and with the ECB are excluded from reserve assets.

For the euro area countries, Total Reserves minus Gold (line 1 l.d) is defined in accordance with the sixth edition of the *Balance of Payments and International Investment Position Manual* (which mainly clarifies the treatment in the fifth edition, but also contains a new appendix concerning currency unions). It includes the monetary authorities' holdings of SDRs, reserve position in the Fund, and foreign exchange, including financial derivative claims on non-euro area countries. It excludes claims among euro area countries and all euro-denominated claims on non-euro area countries. Total reserves of the euro area comprise the reserve holdings of the NCBs and ECB. Definitions of reserves at the national and euro area levels are harmonized.

### Other Foreign Assets and Foreign Liabilities of the Central Bank

Time series, where significant, are also provided in international liquidity sections on other foreign assets and other foreign liabilities of the central bank.

Other Assets (line 3..d) usually comprises claims on non-residents that are of limited usability in the event of balance of payments need, such as balances under bilateral payments agreements and holdings of inconvertible currencies. (Claims on nonresidents under Other Assets (line 3..d) are included in line 11.)

Other Liabilities (line 4..d) comprises foreign liabilities of the central bank other than use of Fund credit (GRA), SAF, PRGF, and Trust Fund loans outstanding and SDR allocations. Positions with the Fund are reported separately, in SDRs, in the Fund position section of the country tables.

### Foreign Accounts of the Rest of the Financial Corporations

Where significant, foreign accounts of financial corporations other than the central bank are reported. The measures provided are normally U.S. dollar equivalents of time series

reported in the appropriate monetary statistics sections as follows: line 7a.d is derived from line 21; line 7b.d is derived from line 26c; line 7e.d is derived from line 41; and line 7f.d is derived from line 46c. Sometimes the measures are reported directly in U.S. dollars and may differ slightly in coverage.

In addition for some countries, summary data are provided on the foreign accounts of special or international license banks that operate locally but are not presently covered in the monetary statistics section. Their foreign assets are reported as line 7k.d, and their foreign liabilities as line 7m.d, when available (although 7m.d is not shown separately if it is equal to line 7k.d).

### World Tables on Reserves

World tables on reserves report all country table time series on reserves, other than gold at national valuation, and present totals for countries, country groups, and the world.

Also provided is a table on total reserves, with gold valued at SDR 35 per ounce. A foot table to that table reports total reserves of all countries, including gold valued both at SDR 35 per ounce and at market prices. And the yearbook includes a world table on the ratio of nongold reserves (line 1 l.d) to imports (line 71..d), expressed in terms of the number of weeks of imports covered by the stock of nongold reserves.

Except for the world table on gold holdings in physical terms, world tables on reserves are expressed in SDRs. Foreign exchange holdings are expressed in SDRs by converting the U.S. dollar values shown in the country tables on the basis of the end-period U.S. dollar/SDR rate.

Similarly, a foot table to the world table on gold indicates gold holdings valued at SDR 35 per ounce and at market prices for all countries, the IMF, the ECB, the Bank for International Settlements (BIS), and the world. A simple addition of the gold held by all of these holders would involve double-counting, because most of the gold deposited with the BIS is also included in countries' official gold reserves. IFS therefore reports BIS gold holdings net of gold deposits, and negative figures for BIS gold holdings are balanced by forward operations. This foot table also provides data on the U.S. dollar price of gold on the London market, the U.S. dollar/SDR rate, and the end-period derived market price of gold in terms of SDRs.

## 5. Monetary Statistics

Beginning with the April 2009 issue of IFS, there are two presentations of monetary statistics. The first presentation is the new presentation of monetary statistics published in the *IFS Supplement on Monetary and Financial Statistics*, which was discontinued in March 2009. The second presentation is the traditional, albeit outdated, presentation published in IFS.

Statistics on the accounts of financial corporations are given in monetary statistics sections 10 through 50 in the country tables and in world tables, described in the world table section of this introduction.

## 5.1 New Presentation

This presentation is for those countries that are regularly reporting monetary data in accordance with the methodology of the IMF's *Monetary and Financial Statistics Manual* (*MFSM*), 2000 and *Monetary and Financial Statistics Compilation Guide* (*MFSCG*), 2008. For the majority of these countries, the data are transmitted on standardized report forms (SRFs) for the assets and liabilities of a country's central bank (Form 1SR), other depository corporations (Form 2SR), and other financial corporations (Form 4SR), as well as for a country's monetary aggregates (Form 5SR).

### *Central Bank*

The central bank data are presented as a Central Bank Survey (section 10) in each country table in IFS. Major accounts on the asset side are Net Foreign Assets (line 11n), which is disaggregated as Claims on Nonresidents (line 11) less Liabilities to Nonresidents (line 16c), and domestic assets disaggregated as Claims on Other Depository Corporations (line 12e), Net Claims on Central Government (line 12an), and Claims on Other Sectors (line 12s). Net Claims on Central Government is disaggregated as Claims on Central Government (line 12a) less Liabilities to Central Government (line 16d). Claims on Other Sectors is disaggregated into Claims on Other Financial Corporations (line 12g), Claims on State and Local Government (line 12b), Claims on Public Nonfinancial Corporations (line 12c), and Claims on Private Sector (line 12d).

Major accounts on the liability side are Monetary Base (line 14), Other Liabilities to Other Depository Corporations (line 14n), Deposits and Securities Excluded from the Monetary Base (line 14o), Loans (line 16l); Financial Derivatives (line 16m), Shares and Other Equity (line 17a), and Other Items (Net) (line 17r). Monetary Base is disaggregated into Currency in Circulation (line 14a), Liabilities to Other Depository Corporations (line 14c), and Liabilities to Other Sectors (line 14d). Deposits and Securities Excluded from the Monetary Base is disaggregated into Deposits Included in Broad Money (line 15), Securities Other than Shares Included in Broad Money (line 16a), Deposits Excluded from Broad Money (line 16b), and Securities Other than Shares Excluded from Broad Money (line 16s).
Memo item: Total Assets (line 10ra) refers to the total gross financial and nonfinancial assets of the central bank. Figures may differ from those published by official sources due to differing accounting treatments such as consolidation adjustments and provision/depreciation netting.

### *Other Depository Corporations*

Data for other depository corporations are presented in an Other Depository Corporations Survey (section 20) in each country table in IFS. Other depository corporations comprise financial corporations that incur liabilities that are included in the national definition of broad money. Major accounts on the assets side are Net Foreign Assets (line 21n), which is disaggregated as Claims on Nonresidents (line 21) less Liabilities

to Nonresidents (line 26c), and domestic assets disaggregated as Claims on Central Bank (line 20), Net Claims on Central Government (line 22an), and Claims on Other Sectors (line 22s). Claims on Central Bank is disaggregated into Currency (line 20a), Reserve Deposits and Securities (line 20b), and Other Claims (line 20n). Net Claims on Central Government is disaggregated as Claims on Central Government (line 22a) less Liabilities to Central Government (line 26d). Claims on Other Sectors is disaggregated into Claims on Other Financial Corporations (line 22g), Claims on State and Local Government (line 22b), Claims on Public Nonfinancial Corporations (line 22c), and Claims on Private Sector (line 22d).

Major accounts on the liability side are Liabilities to Central Bank (line 26g), Transferable Deposits Included in Broad Money (line 24), Other Deposits Included in Broad Money (line 25), Securities Other than Shares Included in Broad Money (line 26a), Deposits Excluded from Broad Money (line 26b), Securities Other Than Shares Excluded from Broad Money (line 26s), Loans (line 26l), Financial Derivatives (line 26m), Insurance Technical Reserves (line 26r), Shares and Other Equity (line 27a), and Other Items (Net) (line 27r).
Memo item: Total assets (line 20ra) refers to the total gross financial and nonfinancial assets of other depository corporations. Figures may differ from those published by official sources due to differing accounting treatments such as consolidation adjustments and provision/depreciation netting.

### *Depository Corporations*

Data for the central bank and other depository corporations are consolidated into a Depository Corporations Survey (section 30). Major accounts on the assets side are Net Foreign Assets (line 31n), which is disaggregated as Claims on Nonresidents (line 31) less Liabilities to Nonresidents (line 36c), and Domestic Claims (line 32) disaggregated as Net Claims on Central Government (line 32an) and Claims on Other Sectors (line 32s). Net Claims on Central Government is disaggregated as Claims on Central Government (line 32a) less Liabilities to Central Government (line 36d). Claims on Other Sectors is disaggregated into Claims on Other Financial Corporations (line 32g), Claims on State and Local Government (line 32b), Claims on Public Nonfinancial Corporations (line 32c), and Claims on Private Sector (line 32d).

Major accounts on the liability side are Broad Money Liabilities (line 35l), Deposits Excluded from Broad Money (line 36b), Securities Other than Shares Excluded from Broad Money (line 36s), Loans (line 36l), Financial Derivatives (line 36m), Insurance Technical Reserves (line 36r), Shares and Other Equity (line 37a), and Other Items (Net) (line 37r). Broad Money Liabilities is disaggregated into Currency Outside Depository Corporations (line 34a), Transferable Deposits (line 34), Other Deposits (line 35), and Securities Other than Shares (line 36a).

Standard relationships between the lines in the Depository Corporation Survey and lines in the Central Bank Survey (section 10) and Other Depository Corporations Survey (section 20) are as follows:

Net Foreign Assets (line 31n) equals the sum of foreign asset lines 11 and 21 less the sum of foreign liability lines 16c and 26c.

Net Claims on Central Government (line 32an) equals the sum of lines 12a and 22a, less the sum of lines 16d and 26d.

Claims on Other Sectors (line 32s) equals the sum of lines 12s and line 22s. Line 32g, line 32b, line 32c, and line 32d are equal to the sums of lines 12g and 22g, lines 12b and 22b, lines 12c and 22c, and lines 12d and 22d, respectively.

Broad Money Liabilities (line 35l) equals the sum of Currency Outside Depository Corporations—line 34a (line 14a less line 20a) and lines 14d, 15, 16a, 24, 25, and 26a.

Deposits Excluded from Broad Money (line 36b) equals the sum of lines 16b and 26b.

Securities Other than Shares Excluded from Broad Money (line 36s) equals the sum of lines 16s and 26s.

Loans (line 36l) equals the sum of lines 16l and 26l.

Financial Derivatives (line 36m) equals the sum of lines 16m and 26m.

Insurance Technical Reserves (line 36r) equals the same as line 26r.

Shares and Other Equity (line 37a) equals the sum of lines 17a and 27a.

Other Items (Net) (line 37r) equals the sum of lines 17r and 27r plus a consolidation adjustment that arises from differences in the accounting records of the central bank and other depository corporations.

Section 30 also includes Broad Money Liabilities, Seasonally Adjusted (line 35l.b).

## Other Financial Corporations

Data for other financial corporations are presented in an Other Financial Corporations Survey (section 40) in some country tables in IFS. This subsector comprises financial corporations that do not incur liabilities included in the national definition of broad money, but that engage in financial intermediation (other financial intermediaries) or provide financial services other than financial intermediation (financial auxiliaries).

Major accounts on the assets side are Net Foreign Assets (line 41n), which is disaggregated as Claims on Nonresidents (line 41) less Liabilities to Nonresidents (line 46c), and domestic assets disaggregated as Claims on Depository Corporations (line 40), Net Claims on Central Government (line 42an), and Claims on Other Sectors (line 42s). Net Claims on Central Government is disaggregated as Claims on Central Government (line 42a) less Liabilities to Central Government (line 46d). Claims on Other Sectors is disaggregated into Claims on State and Local Government (line 42b), Claims on Public Nonfinancial Corporations (line 42c), and Claims on Private Sector (line 42d).

Major accounts on the liability side are Deposits (line 46b), Securities Other than Shares (line 46s), Loans (line 46l), Financial Derivatives (line 46m), Insurance Technical Reserves (line 46r), Shares and Other Equity (line 47a), and Other Items (Net) (line 47r).

Memo item: Total Assets (line 40ra) refers to the total gross financial and nonfinancial assets of other financial corporations. Figures may differ from those published by official sources due to differing accounting treatments such as consolidation adjustments and provision/depreciation netting.

## Financial Corporations

Data for the depository corporations and other financial corporations are consolidated into a Financial Corporations Survey (section 50). Major accounts on the assets side are Net Foreign Assets (line 51n), which is disaggregated as Claims on Nonresidents (line 51) less Liabilities to Nonresidents (line 56c), and Domestic Claims (line 52) disaggregated as Net Claims on Central Government (line 52an) and Claims on Other Sectors (line 52s). Net Claims on Central Government is disaggregated as Claims on Central Government (line 52a) less Liabilities to Central Government (line 56d). Claims on Other Sectors is disaggregated into Claims on State and Local Government (line 52b), Claims on Public Nonfinancial Corporations (line 52c), and Claims on Private Sector (line 52d).

Major accounts on the liability side are Currency Outside Financial Corporations (line 54a), Deposits (line 55l), Securities Other than Shares (line 56a), Loans (line 56l), Financial Derivatives (line 56m), Insurance Technical Reserves (line 56r), Shares and Other Equity (line 57a), and Other Items (Net) (line 57r).

Standard relationships between the lines in the Financial Corporation Survey and lines in the Depository Corporations Survey (section 30) and Other Financial Corporations Survey (section 40) are as follows:

Net Foreign Assets (line 51n) equals the sum of foreign asset lines 31 and 41 less the sum of foreign liability lines 36c and 46c.

Net Claims on Central Government (line 52an) equals the sum of lines 32a and 42a, less the sum of lines 36d and 46d.

Claims on Other Sectors (line 52s) equals the sum of lines 32s, excluding line 32g, and line 42s. Line 52g, line 52b, line 52c, and line 52d are equal to the sums of lines 32b and 42b, lines 32c and 42c, and lines 32d and 42d, respectively.

Currency Outside Financial Corporations (line 54a) equals Currency Outside Depository Corporations (line 34a) less currency holdings of other financial corporations.

Deposits (line 55l) equals the sum of lines 34, 35, 36b, and 46b, less deposits that other financial corporations hold in depository corporations.

Securities Other than Shares (line 56a) equals the sum of lines 36a, 36s, and 46s, less securities other than shares issued by depository corporations and held by other financial corporations.

Loans (line 56l) equals the sum of lines 36l and 46l, less loans from depository corporations to other financial corporations.

Financial Derivatives (line 56m) equals the sum of lines 36m and 46m, less financial derivatives of depository corporations with other financial corporations.

Insurance Technical Reserves (line 56r) equals the sum of lines 36r and 46r, less insurance technical reserves of depository corporations with other financial corporations.

Shares and Other Equity (line 37a) equals the sum of lines 37a and 47a.

Other Items (Net) (line 57r) equals the sum of lines 37r and 47r plus a consolidation adjustment that arises from relatively minor differences in the accounting records of depository corporations and other financial corporations.

## Monetary Aggregates

Broad money is shown in line 59m. Broad money components that represent liabilities of sectors other than the financial corporations sector are also shown. These consist of Currency Issued by Central Government (line 59m.a), Deposits in Nonfinancial Corporations (line 59m.b) and Securities Issued by Central Government (line 59m.c).

Countries may compile data for narrower definitions of monetary aggregates, as well as data for broad money. These data are shown in series for M0 (line 19mc), M1 (line 59ma), M2 (line 59mb), M3 (line 59mc), and M4 (line 59md). Data for more than one variant of a particular monetary aggregate—for example, M1 (line 59ma) and M1A (line 59maa)—may be shown. These aggregates are compiled according to national definitions and vary across countries.

Monetary aggregates that have been seasonally adjusted are also shown. For example, M3 Seasonally Adjusted is shown in line 59mcc. These data are those that have been seasonally adjusted and reported by a country. Broad Money Liabilities, Seasonally Adjusted (line 35l.b) are compiled by the Fund using the same seasonal adjustment procedures to Broad Money Liabilities (line 35l) for each country.

### 5.1.1 Monetary Statistics for the Euro Area

The European Economic and Monetary Union (EMU) began in January 1999, following which new definitions of statistical aggregates were created. The euro area aggregated series follow a changing composition principle. That is, data for the euro area refers to its actual membership in the respective reference period. Thus, the accession of a new member state, starting with Greece in 2001, creates breaks in the euro area aggregated time series. The 11 original member states were Austria, Belgium, Finland, France,

Germany, Ireland, Italy, Luxembourg, Netherlands, Portugal, and Spain. Greece joined in January 2001, Slovenia in January 2007, Cyprus and Malta in January 2008, the Slovak Republic in January 2009, Estonia in January 2010, Latvia in January 2014, and Lithuania in January 2015.

Further details on methodology are available on the European Central Bank website and, for depository corporations, in the ECB publication "Manual on MFI balance sheet statistics."

## Residency Criteria

Monetary statistics are compiled on the basis of both a national residency criterion, described in the 6th edition of the Balance of Payments and International Investment Position Manual, and a euro area -wide residency criterion, based on the euro area membership in the respective reference period.

In the application of the euro area-wide residency criterion, all institutional units that are resident in the euro area (but not necessarily in the same country) are treated as domestic residents, while all units outside the euro area as nonresidents. For example, claims on government under the national residency criterion include only claims on the government of the same country, whereas claims on government under the euro area-wide residency criterion include claims on the governments of all euro area countries. Further, as a result of the expansion of the euro area, starting in January 2001 with Greece, all institutional units resident in those countries that join the euro area became residents of the euro area, causing breaks in stock series.

The European Central Bank (ECB) is a resident of the euro area but not of an individual country. Thus, the ECB is a resident unit under the euro area-wide residency criterion, but a foreign unit for all countries when the national residency criterion is applied.

The monetary statistics in the tables for each euro area country are presented for both national and euro area-wide residency criteria.

### Euro Banknotes and Coins

The euro banknotes are issued by the Eurosystem as a whole, comprising the ECB and the national central banks (NCBs) of the euro area countries. According to the accounting regime chosen by the Eurosystem (ECB Decision ECB/2010/29, as amended), a share of 8 percent of the total value of euro banknotes put into circulation is allocated to the balance sheet of the ECB each month. The remaining 92 percent is allocated among the NCBs on a monthly basis, whereby each NCB of the Eurosystem records "banknotes issued" on its balance sheet in proportion to its share in the ECBs capital. In the ECB Decision, this allocation procedure is referred to as the banknote allocation key. The allocations are revised each time a new country joins the euro area.

The euro coins are issued by the central government of each euro area country, so that the total issuance of coins is not artificially allocated to individual countries as in the case of banknotes. The ECB approves the volume of coins issued by each country. As an accounting convention, issuance of coins is recorded as currency issued by the NCB, with a balance sheet contra-entry in Other Items (Net).

For those countries in which legacy banknotes and coins remain redeemable, the outstanding stock of legacy currencies is excluded from monetary aggregates beginning in 2003.

## 5.2 Old Presentation

This presentation refers to the old presentation of monetary statistics and is for those countries that do not use the SRFs for reporting monetary data. The presentation of these countries will be changed to the new presentation when the countries implement the reporting of SRF-based data.

### Monetary Authorities

Monetary authorities' data (section 10) in IFS generally consolidate the accounts of the central bank with the accounts of other institutions that undertake monetary functions. These functions include issuing currency, holding international reserves, and conducting Fund account transactions. Data on monetary authorities measure the stock of reserve money comprising currency in circulation, deposits of the deposit money banks, and deposits of other residents, apart from the central government, with the monetary authorities.

Major aggregates of the accounts on the asset side are foreign assets (line 11) and domestic assets (line 12*). Domestic assets are broken down into Claims on Central Government (line 12a), Claims on Deposit Money Banks (line 12e), and, if sizable, Claims on State and Local Governments (line 12b); Claims on Nonfinancial Public Enterprises (line 12c); Claims on the Private Sector (line 12d); Claims on Other Banking Institutions (line 12f), and Claims on Nonbank Financial Institutions (line 12g).

In some countries, where insufficient data are available to provide disaggregations of claims on governmental bodies other than the central government, a classification of Claims on Official Entities (line 12bx) is used. In addition, in countries where insufficient data are available to provide disaggregations of claims on other banking institutions and nonbank financial institutions, a classification of Claims on Other Financial Institutions (line 12f) is used.

The principal liabilities of monetary authorities consist of Reserve Money (line 14); Other Liabilities to Deposit Money Banks (line 14n), comprising liabilities of the central bank to deposit money banks that are excluded from Reserve Money; Liabilities of the Central Bank: Securities (line 16ac); Foreign Liabilities (line 16c); Central Government Deposits (line 16d); and Capital Accounts (line 17a). Other liabilities, if sizable are

Time, Savings, and Foreign Currency Deposits (line 15), Restricted Deposits (line 16b), and Liabilities to Nonbank Financial Institutions (line 16j).

### Deposit Money Banks

Deposit money banks comprise commercial banks and other financial institutions that accept transferable deposits, such as demand deposits. Deposit money banks' data (section 20) measure the stock of deposit money.

Major aggregates of the accounts on the assets side are Reserves (line 20), comprising domestic currency holdings and deposits with the monetary authorities; Claims on Monetary Authorities: Securities (line 20c), comprising holdings of securities issued by the central bank; Other Claims on Monetary Authorities (line 20n), comprising claims on the central bank that are excluded from Reserves; Foreign Assets (line 21); and Claims on Other Resident Sectors (lines 22*), as described in the preceding section on monetary authorities (lines 12*).

The principal liabilities consist of Demand Deposits (line 24); Time, Savings, and Foreign Currency Deposits (line 25); Money Market Instruments (line 26aa); Bonds (line 26ab); Restricted Deposits (line 26b), Foreign Liabilities (line 26c); Central Government Deposits (line 26d); Credit from Monetary Authorities (line 26g); Liabilities to Other Banking Institutions (line 26i); Liabilities to Nonbank Financial Institutions (line 26j); and Capital Accounts (line 27a).

### Monetary Survey

Monetary authorities' and deposit money banks' data are consolidated into a monetary survey (section 30). The survey measures the stock of narrow Money (line 34), comprising transferable deposits and currency outside deposit money banks, and the Quasi-Money (line 35) liabilities of these institutions, comprising time, savings, and foreign currency deposits.

Standard relationships between the monetary survey lines and the component lines in sections 10 and 20 are as follows:

Foreign Assets (Net) (line 31n) equals the sum of foreign asset lines 11 and 21, less the sum of foreign liability lines 16c and 26c.

Claims on Central Government (Net) (line 32an) equals claims on central government (the sum of lines 12a and 22a), less central government deposits (the sum of lines 16d and 26d), plus, where applicable, the counterpart entries of lines 24..i and 24..r (private sector demand deposits with the postal checking system and with the Treasury).

Claims on State and Local Governments (line 32b) equals the sum of lines 12b and 22b. Note that, for some countries, lack of sufficient data to perform the standard classifications of claims on governmental bodies excluding the central government has resulted in the use of the alternative classification "claims on official entities" (line 32bx), which is the sum of lines 12bx and 22bx. These series may therefore include state and local governments, public financial institutions, and non-financial public enterprises.

Claims on Nonfinancial Public Enterprises (line 32c) equals the sum of lines 12c and 22c.

Claims on Private Sector (line 32d) equals the sum of lines 12d and 22d.

Claims on Other Banking Institutions (line 32f) equals the sum of lines 12f and 22f.

Claims on Nonbank Financial Institutions (line 32g) equals the sum of lines 12g and 22g.

Domestic Credit (line 32) is the sum of lines 32an, 32b, 32c, 32d, 32f, and 32g even when, owing to their small size, data for lines 32b, 32c, 32f, and 32g are not published separately. Thus, the data for line 32 may be larger than the sum of its published components.

Money (line 34) equals the sum of currency outside deposit money banks (line 14a) and demand deposits other than those of the central government (lines 14d, 14e, 14f, 14g, and 24) plus, where applicable, lines 24..i and 24..r.

Quasi-Money (line 35) equals the sum of lines 15 and 25, comprising time, savings, and foreign currency deposits of resident sectors other than central government.

The data in line 34 are frequently referred to as M1, while the sum of lines 34 and 35 gives a broader measure of money similar to that which is frequently called M2.

Money Market Instruments (line 36aa) equals the sum of lines 16aa and 26aa.

Bonds (line 36ab) equals the sum of lines 16ab and 26ab.

Liabilities of Central Bank: Securities (line 36ac) equals the outstanding stock of securities issued by the monetary authorities (line 16ac) less the holdings of these securities by deposit money banks (line 20c).

Restricted Deposits (line 36b) equals the sum of lines 16b and 26b.

Long-Term Foreign Liabilities (line 36cl) equals the sum of lines 16cl and 26cl.

Counterpart Funds (line 36e) equals the sum of lines 16e and 26e.

Central Government Lending Funds (line 36f) equals the sum of lines 16f and 26f.

Liabilities to Other Banking Institutions (line 36i) is equal to line 26i.

Liabilities to Nonbank Financial Institutions (line 36j) equals the sum of lines 16j and 26j.

Capital Accounts (line 37a) equals the sum of lines 17a and 27a.

These monetary survey lines give the full range of IFS standard lines. Some of them are not applicable to every country,

whereas others may not be published separately in sections 10 and 20, because the data are small. Unpublished lines are included in Other Items (Net) (lines 17r and 27r) but are classified in the appropriate monetary survey aggregates in section 30.

Exceptions to the standard calculations of monetary survey aggregates are indicated in the notes to the country tables in the monthly issues. Exceptions also exist in the standard presentation of the consolidation of financial institutions, e.g., for Japan, Nicaragua, the United Kingdom, and the United States.

Section 30 also includes Money, Seasonally Adjusted (line 34..b) and Money plus Quasi-Money (line 35l), which is the sum on lines 34 and 35.

## Other Banking Institutions

Section 40 contains data on the accounts of other banking institutions. This subsector comprises institutions that do not accept transferable deposits but that perform financial intermediation by accepting other types of deposits or by issuing securities or other liabilities that are close substitutes for deposits. This subsector covers such institutions as savings and mortgage loan institutions, post-office savings institutions, building and loan associations, finance companies that accept deposits or deposit substitutes, development banks, and offshore banking institutions.

The major aggregates in this section are claims on the various sectors of the economy (lines 42*), as described in the preceding paragraphs, and quasi-monetary liabilities (line 45), largely in the form of time and savings deposits.

## Banking Survey

Where reasonably complete data are available for other banking institutions, a banking survey (section 50) is published. It consolidates data for other banking institutions with the monetary survey and thus provides a broader measure of monetary liabilities.

The sectoral classification of assets in the banking survey follows the classification used in the monetary survey, as outlined in the description for that section.

## Nonbank Financial Institutions

For a few countries, data are shown on the accounts of nonbank financial institutions, such as insurance companies, pension funds, and superannuation funds. Given the nature of their liabilities, these institutions generally exert minimal impact on the liquidity of a given economy. However, they can play a significant role in distributing credit from the financial sector to the rest of the economy.

## Financial Survey

Where reasonably complete data are available for nonbank financial institutions, a financial survey is published. It consolidates data for nonbank financial institutions with the banking survey and thus provides a broader measure of credit from the financial sector to the rest of the economy.

The sectoral classification of assets in the financial survey follows the classification used in the monetary and banking surveys, as outlined in the description for that section.

## 6. Interest Rates

Data are presented in the Interest Rates section in the country tables and in the world tables on national and international interest rates.

Central Bank Policy Rate (line 60) is the target rate used by the central bank to conduct monetary policy. The monetary policy instrument varies across countries and is described in the country notes.

Discount Rate (line 60a) is the rate at which the central banks lend or discount eligible paper for other depository corporations, typically shown on an end-of-period basis.

Money Market Rate (line 60b) is the rate on short-term lending between financial institutions.

Treasury Bill Rate (line 60c) is the rate at which short-term securities are issued or traded in the market.

Deposit Rate (line 60l) usually refers to rates offered to resident customers for demand, time, or savings deposits. Often, rates for time and savings deposits are classified according to maturity and amounts deposited. In addition, other depository corporations may offer short- and medium-term instruments at specified rates for specific amounts and maturities; these are frequently termed "certificates of deposit." For countries where savings deposits are important, a Savings Rate (line 60k) is also published.

Lending Rate (line 60p) is the other depository corporations rate that usually meets the short- and medium-term financing needs of the private sector. This rate is normally differentiated according to creditworthiness of borrowers and objectives of financing.

Government Bond Yield (line 61*) refers to one or more series representing yields to maturity of government bonds or other bonds that would indicate longer term rates.

Interest rates for foreign-currency-denominated instruments and additional interest rates offered and charged by the central bank are also published for countries where such instruments are important.

Quarterly and annual interest rate data are arithmetic averages of monthly interest rates reported by the countries.

The country notes in the monthly issues carry a brief description of the nature and characteristics of the rates reported and of the financial instrument to which they relate.

A typical series from each of these groups is included in the world tables on national interest rates.

### Euro Area Interest Rates

The Eurosystem Marginal Lending Facility Rate (line 60) is the rate at which other monetary financial institutions (MFIs) obtain overnight liquidity from NCBs, against eligible assets. The terms and conditions of the lending are identical throughout the euro area. The Eurosystem Refinancing Rate (line 60r), Interbank Rate (Overnight) (line 60a), and Interbank Rate (Three-Month) (line 60b) are also provided on the euro area table.

A new set of harmonized MFI interest rate statistics is compiled for the euro area MFIs, covering euro-denominated deposits and loans vis-à-vis nonfinancial sectors (other than government) resident in the euro area. The ECB *Manual on MFI Interest Rate Statistics* (ECB: October 2003) describes compilation procedures for interest rates on household and corporate customers' deposits and lending—both for stocks and new business. Interest rates on new business cover all business during the reference month in which new agreements with customers resulted from a first-time contract or new negotiation of existing deposits and loans. The two series for interest rates on bad loans and loans for debt restructuring are not included within the MFI interest rate statistics.

Deposit Rate, Households–Stock (line 60lhs) is the volume-weighted average interest paid on outstanding amounts of euro-denominated deposits from households with an agreed maturity up to and including two years. Deposit Rate, Households–New Business (line 60lhn) is the comparable rate for new business with an agreed maturity up to and including one year. Deposit Rate, Corporations–Stock (line 60lcs) is the volume-weighted average interest paid on outstanding amounts of euro-denominated deposits from nonfinancial corporations with an agreed maturity up to and including two years. Deposit Rate, Corporations–New Business (line 60lcn) is the rate for new business with an agreed maturity up to and including one year. Repos (Repurchase Agreements) (line 60lcr) is the counterpart of cash received against securities/gold sold under a firm commitment to repurchase the securities/gold at a fixed rate on a specified date. The repo series includes holdings by households and nonfinancial corporations. At the euro area level, about 40 percent of repos are held by households. Repos are not applicable for most countries. Data are available only for France, Italy, Greece, Spain, and the euro area.

Lending Rate, Households–Stock (line 60phs) is the volume-weighted average interest charged on outstanding amounts of euro-denominated loans to households with an agreed maturity up to and including one year. Lending Rate, Households–New Business (line 60pns) is the rate for new business loans at a floating rate or up to and including a one-year interest rate fixation. Lending Rate, Households–House Purchase, Stock (line 60phm) is the volume-weighted average interest charged on outstanding amounts of euro-denominated loans to households for purchasing or improving housing with a maturity of five years or more. Lending Rate, Households–House Purchase, New Business (line 60phn) is the rate for new business for loans with fixed interest rates between five and ten years. Lending Rate, Corporations–Stock (line 60pcs) is the volume-weighted average interest charged on outstanding amounts of euro-denominated loans to nonfinancial corporations with an agreed maturity up to and including one year. Lending Rate, Corporations–New Business (line 60pcn) is the rate for new business for loans over 1 million euros at a floating rate or up to and including a one-year interest rate fixation.

### World Table on International Interest Rates

The world table on international interest rates reports London interbank offer rates on deposits denominated in SDRs, U.S. dollars, euros, Japanese yen, and Swiss francs and Paris interbank offer rates on deposits denominated in pounds sterling. Monthly data are averages of daily rates. The table includes the premium or discount on three-month forward rates of currencies of the major industrial countries against the U.S. dollar.

This table also reports the SDR interest rate and the rate of remuneration. Monthly data are arithmetic averages of daily rates. Interest is paid on holdings of SDRs, and charges are levied on participants' cumulative allocations. Interest and charges accrue daily at the same rate and are settled quarterly in SDRs. As a result, participants who have SDR holdings above their net cumulative allocations receive net interest, and those with holdings below their net cumulative allocations pay net charges. Other official holders of SDRs—including the Fund's General Resources Account—receive interest on their holdings and pay no charges because they receive no allocations.

The Fund also pays quarterly remuneration to members on their creditor positions arising from the use of their currencies in Fund transactions and operations. This is determined by the positive difference between the remuneration norm and the average daily balances of the member's currency in the General Resources Account.

Effective August 1, 1983, the weekly SDR interest rate has been based on the combined market interest rate. That rate is calculated by multiplying the yield on the financial instrument of each component currency of the SDR by the value in terms of SDRs of the currency in the basket. As of January 1, 2006, the pertinent yields (on the financial instrument of each component currency in the SDR basket, expressed as an equivalent annual bond yield) include: the three-month Eurepo rate (60c); the rate on Japanese Government thirteen-week financing bills (60c); the three-month U.K. Treasury bills (60cs); and the rate on three-month U.S. Treasury bills (60cs). These series are shown in the table.

The combined market rate is calculated each Friday and enters into effect each Monday. The interest rate on the SDR is 100 percent of the combined market rate, rounded to two nearest decimal places. The rate of remuneration, effective February 2, 1987, is 100 percent of the rate of interest on the SDR.

## 7. Prices, Production, and Labor

This section (lines 62 through 67) covers domestic prices, production, and labor market indicators. The index series are compiled from reported versions of national indices and, for some production and labor series, from absolute data.

There is a wide variation between countries and over time in the selection of base years, depending upon the availability of comprehensive benchmark data that permit an adequate review of weighting patterns. The series are linked by using ratio splicing at the first annual overlap, and the linked series are shifted to a common base period 2010=100.

For industrial production, the data are seasonally adjusted if an appropriate adjusted series is available. Seasonally adjusted series are indicated in the descriptor and also described in the country notes in the monthly issues.

### Share Prices

Indices shown for Share Prices (line 62) generally relate to common shares of companies traded on national or foreign stock exchanges. Monthly indices are obtained as simple arithmetic averages of the daily or weekly indices, although in some cases mid-month or end-of-month quotations are included.

All reported indices are adjusted for changes in quoted nominal capital of companies. Indices are, in general, base-weighted arithmetic averages with market value of outstanding shares as weights.

### Producer Price Index or Wholesale Price Index

Indices shown for Producer or Wholesale Prices (line 63) are designed to monitor changes in prices of items at the first important commercial transaction. Where a choice is available, preference is given to the Producer Price Index (PPI), because the concept, weighting pattern, and coverage are likely to be more consistent with national accounts and industrial production statistics. In principle, the PPI should include service industries, but in practice it is limited to the domestic agricultural and industrial sectors. The prices should be farm-gate prices for the agricultural sector and ex-factory prices for the industrial sector.

The Wholesale Price Index (WPI), when used, covers a mixture of prices of agricultural and industrial goods at various stages of production and distribution, inclusive of imports and import duties. Preference is given to indices that provide broad coverage of the economy. The indices are computed using the Laspeyres formula, unless otherwise indicated in the country notes in the monthly issues.

Subindices are occasionally included for the PPI or the WPI.

### Consumer Price Index

Indices shown for Consumer Prices (line 64) are the most frequently used indicators of inflation and reflect changes in the cost of acquiring a fixed basket of goods and services by the average consumer. Preference is given to series having wider geographical coverage and relating to all income groups, provided they are no less current than more narrowly defined series.

Because the weights are usually derived from household expenditure surveys (which may be conducted infrequently), information on the year to which the weights refer is provided in the country table notes in the monthly issues. The notes also provide information on any limitations in the coverage of commodities for pricing, income groups, or their expenditures in the chosen index. The Laspeyres formula is used unless otherwise indicated in the country notes.

For the European Union (EU) countries, a harmonized index of consumer prices (HICP) (line 64h) is shown. It is compiled according to methodological and sampling standards set by the European Commission. Owing to institutional differences among the EU member countries, the HICP excludes expenditure on certain types of goods and services. Examples are medical care and services of owner-occupied dwellings.

### Wage Rates or Earnings

Indices shown for Wages Rates or Earnings (line 65) represent wage rates or earnings per worker employed per specified time period. Where establishment surveys are the source, the indices are likely to have the same coverage as the Industrial Production Index (line 66) and the Industrial Employment Index (line 67). Preference is given to data for earnings that include payments in kind and family allowances and that cover salaried employees as well as wage earners. The indices either are computed from absolute wage data or are as reported directly to the Fund.

### Industrial Production

Indices shown for Industrial Production (line 66) are included as indicators of current economic activity. For some countries the indices are supplemented by indicators (such as data on tourism) relevant to a particular country.

Generally, the coverage of industrial production indices comprises mining and quarrying, manufacturing and electricity, and gas and water, according to the UN International Standard Industrial Classification (ISIC). The indices are generally compiled using the Laspeyres formula.

For many developing countries the indices refer to the production of a major primary commodity, such as crude petroleum. For most of the OECD countries, Industrial Production data are sourced from the OECD database, as indicated in the country notes. It should be noted that there may be differences for annual data between seasonal adjusted and unadjusted series. These differences are the result of OECD calculation methodology, which is based on two different calculation methods, namely the frequency method and the proxy method. The frequency method is the annual average of the adjusted 12 months data while the proxy method uses the annual data of the unadjusted series for the seasonally adjusted series.

### Labor

Labor market indicators refer to the levels of the Labor Force (line 67d), Employment (line 67e), Unemployment (line 67c), and the Unemployment Rate (line 67r). Data on labor market statistics cover the economically active civilian population. They are provided by the International Labor Organization (ILO), which

publishes these data in its *Yearbook of Labour Statistics* and its Laborsta database, http://laborsta.ilo.org. The concept of employment and unemployment conforms to the recommendations adopted by the ILO: Thirteenth International Conference of Labor Statisticians, Geneva, 1982. In addition, indices of employment in the industrial sector (line 67) are provided for 49 countries. For the euro area, EUROSTAT provides the data. Supplemental sources are also available on the industrial countries' websites.

## 8. International Transactions

Summary statistics on the international transactions of a country are given in lines 70 through 79. A section on external trade statistics (lines 70 through 76) provides data on the values (lines 70 and 71), volumes (lines 72 and 73), unit values (lines 74 and 75), and prices (line 76) for exports and imports. A section follows on balance of payments statistics (lines 78 through 79).

### External Trade

Merchandise Exports f.o.b. (line 70) and Imports c.i.f. (line 71) are, in general, customs statistics reported under the general trade system, in accordance with the recommendations of the UN International Merchandise Trade Statistics: Concepts and Definitions, 1998. For some countries, data relate to the special trade system. The difference between general and special trade lies mainly in the treatment of the recording of the movement of goods through customs-bonded storage areas (warehouses, free areas, etc.).

Many countries use customs data on exports and imports as the primary source for the recording of exports and imports of goods in the balance of payments. However, customs data and the entries for goods in the balance of payments may not be equal, owing to differences in definition. These differences may relate to the following:

- the coverage of transactions (e.g., the goods item in the balance of payments often includes adjustments for certain goods transactions that may not be recorded by customs authorities, e.g., parcel post),

- the time of recording of transactions (e.g., in the balance of payments, transactions are to be recorded when change of ownership occurs, rather than the moment goods cross the customs border, which generally determines when goods are recorded in customs based trade statistics), and

- some classification differences (e.g., in the balance of payments, goods for processing are not included as part of goods transactions).

The data for Merchandise Imports f.o.b. (line 71.v) are obtained directly from statistical authorities.

Details of commodity exports are presented for commodities that are traded in the international markets and have an impact on world market prices.

Data for petroleum exports are presented only for 12 oil exporting countries. For a number of these countries, data estimated by Fund staff are derived from available data for the volume of production. They are also derived from estimates for prices that are, in part, taken from *Petroleum Intelligence Weekly* and other international sources. The country table notes in the monthly issues provide details of these estimates.

For a number of countries where data are uncurrent or unavailable, additional lines show data, converted from U.S. dollars to national currency, from the Fund's *Direction of Trade Statistics* quarterly publication (*DOTS*). Exports and imports data published in DOTS include reported data, updated where necessary with estimates for the current periods. The introduction of DOTS gives a description of the nature of the estimates.

Indices for Volume of Exports (line 72) and Volume of Imports (line 73) are either Laspeyres or Paasche. For nine countries, as indicated in the country notes, export volume indices are calculated from reported volume data for individual commodities weighted by reported values.

Indices for Unit Value of Exports (line 74) and Unit Value of Imports (line 75) are Laspeyres, with weights derived from the data for transactions. For about seven countries, also as indicated in the country notes, export unit values are calculated from reported value and volume data for individual commodities. The country indices are unit value indices, except for a few, which are components of wholesale price indices or based on specific price quotations.

Indices for export and import prices are compiled from survey data for wholesale prices or directly from the exporter or importer (called "direct pricing"). They are shown in line 76, where available. Indices based on direct pricing are generally considered preferable to unit value indices, because problems of unit value bias are reduced.

A more detailed presentation of trade statistics is presented in the *IFS Supplement on Trade Statistics*, No. 15 (1988).

## Balance of Payments and International Investment Position Statistics

Starting August 2012, the balance of payments and international investment position (IIP) lines are presented based on the methodology and presentation of the sixth edition of the *Balance of Payments and International Investment Position Manual* (*BPM6*) published by the IMF in 2009. Earlier issues of the IFS presented balance of payments and IIP data based on the fifth edition of the *Balance of Payments Manual* (*BPM5*).

Data reported to the IMF on a *BPM5* basis are re-arranged to a *BPM6* presentational basis, for publication purposes. Beginning July 2015, migrants' transfers are removed from the capital account resulting in their inclusion in net errors and omissions. Beginning in the September 2015 edition of the *IFS*, the IMF started redisseminating official *BPM6*-basis data for all years for which an economy has reported such data.

Where official *BPM6*-based data are not reported for publication, the IMF has converted data reported on a *BPM5*-basis using a standardized conversion framework. Information on this framework is available in a paper presented to the IMF's Committee on Balance of Payments Statistics (BOPCOM-14/05) posted on the IMF's website.

### Lines for Balance of Payments

In IFS, balance of payments data are shown in an analytic presentation (i.e., the components are classified into five major data categories, which the Fund regards as useful for analyzing balance of payments developments in a uniform manner). In the analytic presentation, the components are arrayed to highlight the financing items (the reserves and related items). The standard presentation, as described in the BPM6, provides the structural framework within which balance of payments statistics are compiled. Both analytic and standard presentations are published in the *Balance of Payments Statistics Yearbook*.

In the publication, current, capital, and financial accounts are labeled "*". This means that Exceptional financing items have been excluded from specific current, capital, and financial account components.

Current Account (line 109bx) is the sum of the balance on goods, services and primary income (line 1y9bx), plus secondary income: credit (line 1d9ca), minus secondary income: debit (line 1d9da).

Goods, credit (exports) (line 1a9cx) and Goods, debit (imports) (line 1a9dx) are both measured on the "free-on-board" (f.o.b.) basis—that is, by the value of the goods at the border of the exporting economy. For imports, this excludes the cost of freight and insurance incurred beyond the border of the exporting economy. The goods item covers general merchandise, net exports of goods under merchanting, and nonmonetary gold.

Services, credit (exports) (line 1b9cx) and Services, debit (imports) (line 1b9dx) comprise manufacturing services on physical inputs owned by others; maintenance and repair services n.i.e.; transport; travel; construction; insurance and pension services; financial services; charges for the use of intellectual property n.i.e.; telecommunications, computer, and information services; other business services; personal, cultural, and recreational services; and government goods and services n.i.e.

Balance on Goods & Services (line 1z9bx) is calculated as goods, credit (exports) (line 1a9cx), minus goods, debit (imports) (line 1a9dx), plus services, credit (exports) (line 1b9cx), minus services, debit (imports) (line 1b9dx).

Primary income: credit (line 1c9cx) and Primary income: debit (line 1c9dx) comprise (1) compensation of employees, (2) investment income (consisting of direct investment income, portfolio investment income, other investment income, and investment income on reserve assets), and (3) other primary income.

Balance on gds., serv., & pri.inc. (i.e., Balance on goods, services, and primary income) (line 1y9bx) is the sum of the Balance on goods & services (line 1z9bx), plus primary income: credit (line 1c9cx), minus primary income: debit (line 1c9dx).

Secondary income: credit (line 1d9ca) comprise all current transfers received by the reporting economy, except those received by the economy to finance the balance of payments needs. The latter are included in Exceptional financing (line 409la) (see below). Secondary income comprises (1) transfers of general government and (2) transfers of financial corporations, nonfinancial corporations, households, and NPISHs.

Secondary income: debit (line 1d9da) comprises all current transfers paid by the reporting economy.

Capital Account (line 209ba) is the balance on the capital account (capital account: credit, minus capital account: debit). Capital account: credit (line 209ca) covers (1) disposal of nonproduced nonfinancial assets and (2) capital transfers receivable. It does not include debt forgiveness and intergovernmental grants that are classified under Exceptional financing. Capital account: debit (line 209da) covers (1) acquisition of nonproduced nonfinancial assets and (2) capital transfers payable.

Financial Account (line 309na) is the sum of net transactions in direct investment (line 3a9aa minus line 3a9la), portfolio investment (line 3b9aa minus line 3b9la), fin. der. & empl. stk. ops. (ESOs): net (i.e., financial derivatives (other than reserves) and employee stock options) (line 3c9na), and other investment (line 3d9aa minus line 3d9la). In the rows that pertain to transactions in assets and liabilities, increases are shown as positive figures (without a plus sign), and decreases are shown as negative figures (with a negative sign).

Direct investment: assets (line 3a9aa) and Direct investment: liabilities (line 3a9la) represent financial account transactions in direct investment. Direct investment includes equity and investment fund shares, and debt instruments associated with various intercompany transactions between affiliated enterprises. Excluded are flows of direct investment capital liabilities for exceptional financing, such as debt-for-equity swaps. Portfolio investment: assets (line 3b9aa) and Portfolio investment: liabilities (line 3b9la) include transactions with nonresidents in securities of any maturity (such as equity and investment fund shares and debt securities) other than those included in direct investment, reserve assets, and exceptional financing.

Equity & investment fund shares (lines 3baaa and 3bala) include shares, stocks, participation, and similar documents (such as American depository receipts) that denote ownership of equity.

Debt securities (lines 3bbaa and 3bbla) cover long and short-term debt instruments with the characteristic feature of negotiability.

Fin. der. & empl. stk. ops. (ESOs) : net (i.e., financial derivatives (other than reserves) and employee stock options) covers financial instruments that are linked to other specific financial instruments, indicators, or commodities, and through which specific financial risks (such as interest rate risk, foreign exchange risk, equity and commodity price risks, credit risk, etc.) can, in their own right, be traded in financial markets. The IFS presents net information as well as gross asset and liability information: Fin. der. & ESOs: assets (line 3c9aa) and Fin. der. & ESOs: liabilities (line 3c9la). Owing to the unique nature of financial derivatives, and the manner in which some institutions record transactions, some countries can provide only net transactions data.

Reserves and Related Items (line 4z9na) is calculated as reserve assets (line 3e9aa) minus credit and loans from the IMF (line 3dcla) minus exceptional financing (line 409la). Reserve assets (line 3e9aa) consist of external assets that are readily available to and controlled by monetary authorities for meeting balance of payments financing needs, for intervention in exchange markets to affect the currency exchange rate, and for other related purposes. Reserve assets comprise monetary gold, special drawing rights, reserve position in the IMF, other reserve assets (consisting of currency and deposits, securities, financial derivatives, and other claims).

Credit and loans from the IMF (line 3dcla) include purchases and repurchases in the credit tranches of the Fund's General Resource Account, and net borrowings under the IMF facilities and the Trust Funds.

Exceptional financing (line 409la) includes any other transactions undertaken by the authorities to meet the balance of payments needs, as an alternative to, or in conjunction with, the use of reserve assets and credit and loans from the IMF.

A more detailed presentation of balance of payments data for use in cross-country comparisons is published in the *Balance of Payments Statistics Yearbook*.

## Lines for International Investment Position

The IIP data are presented in lines 809aa through 8dzla. An economy's IIP is a balance sheet of the stock of external financial assets and liabilities. The coverage of the various components of IIP is similar to that of the corresponding components under the balance of payments. The IIP at the end of a specific period reflects not only the sum of balance of payments transactions over time, but also price changes, exchange rate changes, and other changes in the volume of financial assets and liabilities.

## Availability of Official[1] BPM6 Basis Balance of Payments and International Investment Position Data

| Country Code | Name | BOP BPM6 basis start date | IIP BPM6 basis start date | Country Code | Name | BOP BPM6 basis start date | IIP BPM6 basis start date |
|---|---|---|---|---|---|---|---|
| 914 | Albania | Q12013 | 2008 | 258 | Guatemala | Q12008 | Q12013 |
| 614 | Angola | 2009 | 2009 | 654 | Guinea-Bissau | 2007 | 2007 |
| 911 | Armenia, Republic of | Q11993 | Q11997 | 944 | Hungary | Q11995 | Q11995 |
| 193 | Australia | Q11995 | Q11989 | 176 | Iceland | Q11995 | Q11995 |
| 122 | Austria | Q12006 | Q12006 | 534 | India | Q12009 | Q12006 |
| 912 | Azerbaijan, Republic of | Q12013 | | 536 | Indonesia | Q12010 | Q12013 |
| 513 | Bangladesh | Q12005 | Q12005 | 433 | Iraq | Q12013 | 2012 |
| 316 | Barbados | 2011 | 2010 | 178 | Ireland | Q12014 | Q12014 |
| 913 | Belarus | Q12000 | Q11999 | 436 | Israel | Q12015 | Q12015 |
| 124 | Belgium | Q12008 | Q12008 | 136 | Italy | Q12008 | Q12008 |
| 339 | Belize | Q12011 | | 343 | Jamaica | Q12011 | Q12009 |
| 638 | Benin | 2011 | 2011 | 158 | Japan | Q11996 | 1996 |
| 319 | Bermuda | Q12006 | Q12013 | 439 | Jordan | Q12010 | Q42010 |
| 514 | Bhutan | Q12006 | Q12007 | 916 | Kazakhstan | Q12000 | Q12000 |
| 963 | Bosnia and Herzegovina | Q12007 | 2005 | 826 | Kiribati | Q12006 | Q12007 |
| 223 | Brazil | Q12010 | Q12001 | 542 | Korea, Republic of | Q11980 | Q11994 |
| 516 | Brunei Darussalam | Q12010 | | 967 | Kosovo, Republic of | Q12013 | Q12013 |
| 918 | Bulgaria | Q12010 | Q12010 | 443 | Kuwait | 2009 | 2009 |
| 748 | Burkina Faso | Q12011 | Q12011 | 917 | Kyrgyz Republic | Q12014 | Q12014 |
| 618 | Burundi | 2005 | 2005 | 941 | Latvia | Q12000 | Q12000 |
| 156 | Canada | Q11981 | Q11981 | 946 | Lithuania | Q12004 | Q12004 |
| 228 | Chile | Q12009 | Q12009 | 137 | Luxembourg | Q12002 | Q12002 |
| 924 | China, P.R.: Mainland | Q12005 | Q12011 | 962 | Macedonia, FYR | Q11998 | Q12003 |
| 532 | China, P.R.: Hong Kong | Q11998 | Q12000 | 676 | Malawi | 2003 | 2002 |
| 546 | China, P.R.: Macao | 2002 | | 548 | Malaysia | Q12010 | Q12005 |
| 233 | Colombia | Q12000 | Q12000 | 556 | Maldives | 2011 | |
| 238 | Costa Rica | Q12009 | Q42010 | 678 | Mali | 2005 | 2005 |
| 662 | Côte d'Ivoire | 2011 | 2011 | 181 | Malta | Q12004 | Q12008 |
| 960 | Croatia | Q12000 | Q12001 | 867 | Marshall Islands | 2005 | 2010 |
| 354 | Curaçao | Q42010 | | 684 | Mauritius | Q12013 | |
| 355 | Curaçao & Sint Maarten | Q42010 | | 868 | Micronesia, Fed. Sts of | 2009 | 2009 |
| 423 | Cyprus | Q12008 | Q12008 | 921 | Moldova | Q12011 | |
| 935 | Czech Republic | Q12008 | Q12008 | 943 | Montenegro | Q12013 | |
| 128 | Denmark | Q12013 | Q12013 | 686 | Morocco | Q12014 | Q12013 |
| 243 | Dominican Republic | Q12010 | Q12009 | 688 | Mozambique | Q11996 | 2006 |
| 253 | El Salvador | Q11976 | Q11996 | 518 | Myanmar | Q12013 | Q12013 |
| 939 | Estonia | Q12009 | Q12009 | 558 | Nepal | | Q12012 |
| 163 | Euro Area | Q12014 | Q12014 | 138 | Netherlands | Q12004 | Q22003 |
| 819 | Fiji | Q12005 | Q12005 | 196 | New Zealand | Q12000 | Q12000 |
| 172 | Finland | Q12005 | Q12005 | 278 | Nicaragua | Q12005 | Q12005 |
| 132 | France | Q11999 | Q11999 | 692 | Niger | 2011 | 2011 |
| 915 | Georgia | Q12000 | Q12000 | 142 | Norway | Q12012 | Q12012 |
| 134 | Germany | Q11991 | Q12008 | 564 | Pakistan | Q12005 | Q12014 |
| 652 | Ghana | Q12011 | 2010 | 565 | Palau | 2005 | 2005 |
| 174 | Greece | Q12009 | Q12008 | 566 | Philippines | Q12005 | Q12011 |

[1] Official BPM6-basis availability reflects an economy's own reported BPM6-basis data included in this publication. Data for earlier periods for these economies and for economies not yet providing official BPM6-basis estimates are IMF converted BPM5-basis estimates. The splice point between official BPM6-basis estimates and IMF converted BPM5-basis estimates is marked at the series level on economy specific tables with the "†" symbol.

| Availability of Official[1] BPM6 Basis Balance of Payments and International Investment Position Data | | | | | | | |
| --- | --- | --- | --- | --- | --- | --- | --- |
| Country Code | Name | BOP BPM6 basis start date | IIP BPM6 basis start date | Country Code | Name | BOP BPM6 basis start date | IIP BPM6 basis start date |
| 964 | Poland | Q12004 | Q12004 | 732 | Sudan | Q12010 | 2005 |
| 182 | Portugal | Q11999 | Q11999 | 144 | Sweden | Q12011 | Q12008 |
| 968 | Romania | Q12005 | Q12005 | 146 | Switzerland | Q11999 | Q11999 |
| 922 | Russian Federation | Q12000 | Q12004 | 923 | Tajikistan | Q12014 | Q12014 |
| 714 | Rwanda | 2013 | 2013 | 738 | Tanzania | Q12010 | |
| 862 | Samoa | Q12005 | | 578 | Thailand | Q12005 | Q12005 |
| 716 | São Tomé and Príncipe | Q11997 | Q42014 | 537 | Timor-Leste, Dem.Rep.of | Q12015 | Q12015 |
| 456 | Saudi Arabia | Q12005 | 2007 | 742 | Togo | 2011 | 2011 |
| 722 | Senegal | 2005 | 2005 | 866 | Tonga | Q12011 | Q12010 |
| 942 | Serbia, Republic of | Q12007 | Q42013 | 186 | Turkey | Q12005 | 1996 |
| 718 | Seychelles | Q12007 | | 869 | Tuvalu | 2001 | 2001 |
| 576 | Singapore | Q11995 | Q12001 | 746 | Uganda | Q12001 | Q11999 |
| 352 | Sint Maarten | Q42010 | | 926 | Ukraine | Q12005 | Q12010 |
| 936 | Slovak Republic | Q12004 | Q12004 | 112 | United Kingdom | Q11999 | Q11999 |
| 961 | Slovenia | Q12008 | Q12008 | 111 | United States | Q11999 | Q11976 |
| 813 | Solomon Islands | Q12006 | Q12006 | 846 | Vanuatu | Q12010 | Q12010 |
| 199 | South Africa | Q12002 | 1998 | 299 | Venezuela, Rep. Bol. | Q12005 | Q12005 |
| 733 | South Sudan, Rep. of | 2014 | | 582 | Vietnam | Q12013 | |
| 184 | Spain | Q11999 | Q42012 | 487 | West Bank and Gaza | 2000 | Q42013 |
| 524 | Sri Lanka | Q12012 | Q12011 | 754 | Zambia | Q12005 | 2006 |

[1] Official BPM6-basis availability reflects an economy's own reported BPM6-basis data included in this publication. Data for earlier periods for these economies and for economies not yet providing official BPM6-basis estimates are IMF converted BPM5-basis estimates. The splice point between official BPM6-basis estimates and IMF converted BPM5-basis estimates is marked at the series level on economy specific tables with the "†" symbol.

## 9. Government Finance

The section on Government Finance Statistics (GFS) presents statistics on government finance, for the broadest institutional coverage available. These summary statistics usually cover cash flows of the budgetary central government and/or accrual operations of the consolidated general government (i.e., operations of budgetary central government, extrabudgetary units, social security funds, and state and local governments). The coverage of these high-frequency data may not necessarily include all existing government units. Rather, these data provide a timely indicator of fiscal stance. For data relating to a fiscal year ending other than December 31, the tables present the data within the calendar year for which the greatest number of monthly observations exist.

Starting with the August 2007 issue of IFS, data are presented in the analytical framework of the *Government Finance Statistics Manual* 2001 (*GFSM 2001*). Data are presented in a Statement of Government Operations (line a1 through a2m) supplemented by Balance Sheet information (line a6 through a6m4) where available, and/or a Statement of Sources and Uses of Cash (line c1 through c2m). For some countries, in the absence of a Statement of Government Operations (i.e.,

in the absence of accrual data), IFS will include only data in the Statement of Sources and Uses of Cash. To establish a time series, the cash data previously reported for publication in the IFS were converted to the GFSM 2001 framework, using broad migration rules, as described below.

The data for lines a1 through a2m are flows reported on an accrual basis, while lines c1 through c2m are flows reported on a cash basis. The GFS lines for the Statement of Government Operations and the Statement of Sources and Uses of Cash broadly correspond to each other but with variation in the terminology used to distinguish cash from accrual flows. These aggregates can be described as follows:

Revenue/Cash receipts from operating activities (line a1/c1) comprise all transactions that increase the net worth of government. This aggregate comprises four main components, namely: taxes (line a11/c11); social contributions (line a12/c12); grants (line a13/c13); and other revenue/receipts (line a14/c14). Revenue/cash receipts are shown net of refunds and other adjustment transactions. For data converted from the previous IFS reporting format, cash receipts from operating activities include receipts from sales of nonfinancial assets, if these were not reported separately, enabling reclassification.

Expense/Cash payments for operating activities (line a2/c2) comprises all transactions that decrease the net worth of government. This aggregate includes eight main components in the Statement of Government Operations and seven main components in the Statement of Sources and Uses of Cash. These components are as follows: compensation of employees (a21/c21); use/purchase of goods and services (a22/c22); consumption of fixed capital (a23 – only reported in the accrual statement); interest (a24/c24); subsidies (a25/c25); grants (a26/c26); social benefits (a27/c27); and other expense/payments (a28/c28). For data converted from the previous IFS reporting format, cash payments from operating activities include the purchases of nonfinancial assets, if these were not reported separately, enabling reclassification. For the converted data, expense also includes lending minus repayments for policy purposes because this item was not reported separately in the previous reporting format used in the IFS.

The net operating balance (line anob) is calculated as the difference between revenue (a1) and expense (a2), while the net cash inflow from operating activities (ccio) is calculated as the difference between cash receipts from (c1) and payments for (c2) operating activities.

The net acquisition of nonfinancial assets/net cash outflow from investments in nonfinancial assets (a31/c31) is calculated as the difference between the acquisition/ purchases of nonfinancial assets (a31.1/C31.1) and the disposal/sales of nonfinancial assets (a31.2/c31.2). For data converted from the previous IFS reporting format, sales and purchases of nonfinancial assets are included in cash receipts from (c1) and payments for (c2) operating activities, if these were not reported separately.

Net lending/borrowing (anlb) is calculated as the net result of the net operating balance (anob) and the net acquisition of nonfinancial assets (a31). The cash equivalent, namely the cash surplus/deficit (ccsd), is calculated as the net result of the net cash inflow from operating activities (ccio) and the net cash outflow from investments in nonfinancial assets (c31).

The financing of the net lending/borrowing or cash surplus/deficit is reflected as the sum of net acquisition of financial assets (a32) and net incurrence of liabilities (a33/c33). Because of the focus on the changes in the stock of cash, the Statement of Sources and Uses of Cash presents the net acquisition of financial assets with a split between transactions in financial assets excluding cash (c32x) and net change in stock of cash (cncb). For data converted from the previous IFS reporting format, the net change in stock of cash is included in net incurrence of liabilities (c33), if these were not reported separately.

All financial assets and liabilities are classified according to the type of financial instrument and the residence of the debtor/creditor. The classification of these flows is consistent with the classification of instruments used in the Balance Sheet. Where residency information is not available, the dis-

tinction is based on the currency in which the debt instruments are denominated. For data that were converted from the previous IFS reporting format, information on the net acquisition of financial assets other than cash is not available separately. In the previous IFS reporting format, these data were included in either lending minus repayments or net incurrence of liabilities. If the net change in stock of cash was not reported separately, this item has been included in the net incurrence of liabilities (c33) because data were not separately available in the previous IFS reporting format.

The GFSM 2001 Balance Sheet presents the stock of net worth (a6), comprising the stock of nonfinancial assets (a61), financial assets (a62), and liabilities (a63). The stocks of financial assets and liabilities are presented according to the instruments used and the residency of the holder. Consistent with the recommendations of the 2008 SNA, the stock of liabilities (a63) includes Special Drawing Rights, where held by general government units (rather than by the monetary authority). The corresponding transactions should be included under the net incurrence of liabilities (a33/c33).

Debt is defined as a subset of the liabilities of the reporting government and excludes shares and other equity and financial derivatives.

Data for outstanding debt (lines a6m3, a6m35, and a6m4) relate to the direct and assumed debt of the reporting level of government according to market, face, and nominal values respectively, and exclude any liabilities guaranteed by the government. The distinction between domestic and foreign liabilities (lines a631 and a632) is based on the residence of the lender, where identifiable. Otherwise, it is based on the currency in which the debt instruments are denominated.

In the Statement of Sources and Uses of Cash, outstanding debt data are reported as memorandum item: gross debt (line c63).

Unless otherwise stated in individual country notes in the monthly issues, data are as reported for IFS. In some cases, data are derived from unpublished worksheets and are therefore not attributed to a specific source.

Quarterly and monthly data, when available, may not add up to the annual data, owing to differences in coverage and/or methodology. The country notes in the monthly issues will indicate these differences.

More extensive data for use in cross-country comparisons are published in the quarterly *Government Finance Statistics Database and Browser on CD-ROM (1990 – present GFSM 2001* format). When countries do not report data for IFS but provide data for the GFSY, these annual data—in summary form—are published in IFS.

## 10. National Accounts and Population

The summary data for national accounts are compiled according to the *System of National Accounts (SNA)*. Gross Domestic Product (GDP) is presented in IFS as the sum of final expenditures, following the presentation of either the 1993 or 2008 SNA, as well as the *European System of Accounts (2010 ESA)*.

The national accounts lines shown in the country tables are as follows:

Household Consumption Expenditure, including Non-profit Institutions Serving Households (NPISHs) (line 96f), Government Consumption Expenditure (line 91f), Gross Fixed Capital Formation (line 93e), Changes in Inventories (line 93i) (formerly Increase/Decrease(-) in Stocks), Exports of Goods and Services (line 90c), and Imports of Goods and Services (line 98c).

Household Consumption Expenditure, including Non-profit Institutions Serving Households (NPISHs) (line 96f) consists of the expenditure incurred by resident households and resident NPISHs on individual consumption goods and services. Government Consumption Expenditure (line 91f) consists of expenditure incurred by general government on both individual-consumption goods and services and collective-consumption services.

Gross Fixed Capital Formation (line 93e) is measured by the total value of a producer's acquisitions, less disposals, of fixed assets during the accounting period, plus certain additions to the value of nonproduced assets (such as subsoil assets or major improvements in the quantity, quality, or productivity of land). Changes in Inventories (line 93i) (including work-in-progress) consist of changes in (1) stocks of outputs that are still held by the units that produced them before the outputs are further processed, sold, delivered to other units, or used in other ways and (2) stocks of products acquired from other units that are intended to be used for intermediate consumption or for resale without further processing.

Exports of Goods and Services (line 90c) consist of sales, barter, gifts, or grants of goods and services from residents to nonresidents. Imports of Goods and Services (line 98c) consist of purchases, barter, or receipts of gifts or grants of goods and services by residents from nonresidents. Gross Domestic Product (GDP) (line 99b) is the sum of consumption expenditure (of households, NPISHs, and general government), gross fix ed capital formation, changes in inventories, and exports of goods and services, less the value of imports of goods and services.

Net Primary Income from Abroad (line 98.n) is the difference between the total values of the primary incomes receivable from, and payable to, nonresidents. Gross National Income (line 99a) is derived by adding net primary income from abroad to GDP.

Gross National Income (GNI) (line 99a) is derived by adding Net Primary Income from Abroad (line 98.n) to GDP. Gross National Disposable Income (GNDI) (line 99i) is derived by adding Net Current Transfers from Abroad (line 98t) to GNI, and Gross Saving (line 99s) is derived by deducting

final consumption expenditure (lines 96f + 91f) from GNDI. Consumption of Fixed Capital (line 99cf) is shown for countries that provide these data.

The country table notes in the monthly issues provide information on which countries have implemented the 2008 SNA or the 2010 ESA.

The national accounts lines generally do not explicitly show the statistical discrepancies between aggregate GDP compiled from expenditure flows as against GDP compiled from the production or income accounts (or from a mixture of these accounts). Hence, in some cases, the components of GDP that are shown in IFS may not add up exactly to the total.

For countries that publish quarterly seasonally adjusted data, the data in IFS in the monthly issues are also on a seasonally adjusted basis (codes ending with c or r). For the United States, Japan, Canada, South Africa, Argentina, and Mexico, quarterly data are shown at annual rates, which the country authorities provide as such.

Lines 99b.p and 99b.r are measures of GDP volume at reference year value levels. In the past, these series used a common reference year (e.g., 1990) for publication. With the June 1999 issue, these series are published on the same reference year(s) as reported by the national compilers. The code p indicates data that are not seasonally adjusted, whereas code r indicates data that are seasonally adjusted.

Lines 99bvp and 99bvr are GDP volume indices that are presented on a standard 2010 reference year and are derived from the GDP volume series reported by national compilers. For this calculation the data series provided by national compilers are linked together (if there is more than one series) to form a single time series. The earliest overlapping year from the different reference year series is used to calculate the link factors. Chain-linked GDP volume measures are provided for the following countries: Australia, Austria, Belgium, Canada, China,P.R.:Hong Kong, China,P.R.:Macao, Croatia, Cyprus, Czech Republic, Denmark, Estonia, Euro Area, Finland, France, Germany, Greece, Iceland, Ireland, Italy, Israel, Japan, Latvia, Lithuania, Luxembourg, Netherlands, Nicaragua, Norway, Poland, Portugal, Serbia, Slovak Republic, Slovenia, Spain, Sweden, Switzerland, United Kingdom, and United States.

The GDP Deflator (lines 99bip or 99bir) are not direct measurements of prices but are derived implicitly: the GDP series at current prices is divided by constant price GDP series referenced to 2010. The latter series is constructed by multiplying the 2010 current price GDP level by the GDP volume index (2010=100). The deflator is expressed in index form with 2010=100.

Data on Population are provided by the Population Division of the Department of Economic and Social Affairs of the United Nations. These data represent mid-year estimates and are revised every two years.

# 11. World Tables

Besides the world tables on exchange rates, members' Fund positions and transactions, international reserves, and interest rates—discussed earlier in this introduction—IFS also brings together country data on money, consumer prices, values and unit values of countries' exports and imports, and wholesale prices and unit values (expressed in U.S. dollars) of principal world trade commodities. Tables on balance of payments are found in the *Balance of Payments Statistics Yearbook, Part 2*.

Tables showing totals or averages of country series may report data for selected countries and countries' territories only.

## Country Groups

Countries whose data are included in **world** totals and averages are arrayed into two main groups—advanced economies and emerging and developing economies. The **Advanced Economies** group also shows separate data for the euro area. The **Emerging and Developing Economies** group is further divided into area subgroups for Sub-Saharan Africa, Developing Asia, Europe, the Middle East and North Africa, and the Western Hemisphere, where Europe is subdivided into Central and Eastern Europe, and Commonwealth of Independent States (CIS).

The country composition of the world is all countries and territories for which the topic series are available in the IFS files. The country compositions of the world and its subgroups are by in large aligned with those published in the IMF's *World Economic Outlook (WEO)*. Note that some economies are not included in the WEO exercise, but report data to IFS; they are included in the IFS groups.

Data for subgroups fuel export-earnings countries and nonfuel export-earnings countries are shown as memorandum items. Fuel export-earnings countries are defined as those countries whose fuel exports represent a minimum of 50 percent of their total exports. The calculations presently used to determine which countries meet the above criteria are based on 2008–12 averages.

## Area and World Indices

Area and world indices are obtained as weighted averages of country indices. (Refer to IFS World Tables Methodologies.)

Weights are normally updated at about five-year intervals—following international practice—to reflect changes in the importance of each country's data with the data of all other countries. The standard weight base years used are 1953, 1958, 1963, 1970, 1975, 1980, 1984–86, 1990, 1995, 2000, 2005, and 2010. The corresponding time spans to which the weights are applied are 1948–55, 1955–60, 1960–68, 1968–73, 1973–78, 1978–83, 1983–88, 1988–93, 1993–98, 1998–03, 2003–08 and 2008 onward.

Separate averages are calculated for each time span, and the index series are linked by the splicing at overlap years and shifted to the reference base 2010=100.

## Calculation of Area Totals and Averages

The calculation of area totals and averages in the world tables takes account of the problem that data for some countries are not current and may have gaps. Area estimates are made when data are available for countries whose combined weights represent at least 60 percent of the total country weights.

Area totals or averages are estimated by assuming that the rate of change in the unreported country data is the same as the rate of change in the weighted total or average of the reported country data for that area. These estimates are made for the area totals and averages only; separate country estimates are not calculated.

The world totals and averages are made from the calculated and estimated data for the two main groups—advanced economies and emerging and developing economies. A world total or average will only be calculated when totals or averages are available for both these country groups.

## Calculation of Individual World Tables

*International Reserves*: Country series on international reserves begin generally with their appropriate dates and are complete monthly time series; therefore, earlier period estimates are not required. When current data of a few countries of an area are not reported, the area total is estimated by carrying forward the last reported country figure.

*Broad Money (and Monetary Base*, which is available in the yearbook): Percent changes are based on end-of-month data (over a 12-month period). When there is more than one version or definition of broad money (money plus quasi money for non-SRF countries) and monetary base (reserve money for non-SRF countries) over time, different time series are chained through a ratio splicing technique. When actual stock data needed for the growth rate calculation are missing, no percent change is shown in the world table. The data for *Broad Money* for the euro area is based on the M3 growth rates calculated by the ECB on the basis of adjusted flows rather than a simple comparison of end-of-period levels.

*Ratio of Monetary Base to Broad Money* (available in the yearbook): The measures of monetary base (reserve money for non-SRF countries) and broad money (money plus quasi money for non-SRF countries) used in calculating this ratio are end-of-year data.

*Income Velocity of Broad Money* (available in the yearbook): The measure of income in this table is IFS data on GDP. The data for broad money (money plus quasi-money for non-SRF countries) are annual averages of the highest frequency data available. The ratio is then converted into an index number with a base year of 2010.

| Tables | Calculation Method | Weights Used | Publication* |
|---|---|---|---|
| Consumer Prices | Weighted geometric average | PPP value of GDP | MYC |
| Producer prices/wholesaleprices | Weighted geometric average | PPP value of GDP | Y |
| Industrial Production | Weighted geometric average | Value added in industry | MYC |
| Wages | Weighted geometric average | Value added in industry | Y |
| Employment | Weighted geometric average | Value added in industry | Y |
| GDP volume | Weighted geometric average | PPP value of GDP | Y |
| GDP deflator | Weighted geometric average | PPP value of GDP | Y |
| Gross capital formation as percent of GDP | Weighted arithmetic average | PPP value of GDP | Y |
| Final consumption expenditure as percent of GDP | Weighted arithmetic average | PPP value of GDP | Y |
| Exports, f.o.b. | Summation | No weights required | MYC |
| Imports, c.i.f. | Summation | No weights required | MYC |
| Export unit value | Weighted arithmetic average | Exports value in U.S. dollars | MYC |
| Import unit value | Weighted arithmetic average | Imports value in U.S. dollars | MYC |
| Terms of trade | Export unit values are divided by import unit values | No weights required | Y |

*M: Monthly; Y: Yearbook; C: CD-Rom.

*Real Effective Exchange Rate Indices*: This table shows two real effective exchange rate indices. The first real effective exchange rate index is based on relative unit labor cost (line rel). It covers 26 advanced economies and euro area. The second real effective exchange rate index is based on relative consumer prices (line rec). The real and nominal effective exchange rates are also shown in the country tables.

*Producer/Wholesale Prices* (world table available in the yearbook): Data are those prices reported in lines 63* in the country tables. The percent changes are calculated from the index number series.

*Consumer Prices*: Data are those prices reported in lines 64* in the country tables. The percent changes are calculated from the index number series. The calculation of area totals and averages include Argentina's CPI. The data for Argentina are officially reported data. The IMF has, however, issued a declaration of censure and called on Argentina to adopt remedial measures to address the quality of the official CPI-

GBA data. Alternative data sources have shown considerably higher inflation rates than the official data since 2007. In this context, the Fund is also using alternative estimates of CPI inflation for the surveillance of macroeconomic developments in Argentina.

*Industrial Production*: This table presents non-seasonally adjusted indices on industrial production for 30 industrial countries, together with an aggregate index for the group. The data are those shown in the country tables as either Industrial Production (lines 66..*) or Manufacturing Production (lines 66ey*), the asterisk representing a wildcard.

*Wages* (world table available in the yearbook): This table presents indices computed either from absolute wage data or from the wage indices reported to the Fund for the industrial sector for 21 industrial countries. The data are those shown in the country tables as Wage Rates or Earnings (line 65).

*Employment* (world table available in the yearbook): This table presents indices computed from indices of employment or number of persons employed as reported by the countries for the industrial sector for 20 industrial countries. The data are those shown in the country tables as Employment (lines 67 or 67ey).

*Exports and Imports*: Data are published in U.S. dollars, as reported, if available, by the countries. Otherwise, monthly data in national currency, published in the country tables (lines 70... and 71...), are converted to U.S. dollars using the exchange rate **rf**. For quarterly and annual data, conversions are made using the trade-weighted average of the monthly exchange rates.

*Export Unit Values/Export Prices* and *Import Unit Values/Import Prices*: Data are the index numbers reported in the country tables expressed in U.S. dollars at rate **rf**. The country indices are typically unit value data (lines 74 and 75). However, for some countries, they are components of wholesale price indices or are derived from specific price quotations (lines 76, 76.x, and 76aa). World estimates are made when data are available for countries whose combined weights represent at least 60 percent of the total country weights.

*Terms of Trade* (world table available in the yearbook): Data are index numbers computed from the export and import unit value indices and shown in the appropriate world table. The percent changes are calculated from the index number series. The countrycoverage within the areas for the export and import unit values is not identical, leading to a small degree of asymmetry in the terms of trade calculation.

*GDP Volume Measures* (world table available in the yearbook): Data are derived from those series reported in lines 99bvp and 99bvr in the country tables. The percent changes are calculated from index numbers. The calculation of area totals and averages include Argentina's GDP Volume series. The data for Argentina are officially reported data. The IMF has, however, issued a declaration of censure and called on Argentina to adopt remedial measures to address the quality of the official GDP data. Alternative data sources have shown significantly lower real growth than the official data since 2008. In this context, the Fund is also using alternative estimates of GDP growth for the surveillance of macroeconomic developments in Argentina.

*GDP Deflator* (world table available in the yearbook): Data are derived from those series reported in lines 99bip in the country tables. The percent changes are calculated from index numbers.

*Gross Capital Formation as Percentage of GDP* (world table available in the yearbook): Data are the percent share of gross capital formation in GDP at current market prices. Gross capital formation comprises Gross Fixed Capital Formation and Increase/Decrease (-) in Stocks (lines 93e and 93i, respectively.

*Final Consumption Expenditure as a Percentage of GDP* (world table available in the yearbook): Data are the percent share of final consumption expenditure in GDP at current market prices, which comprises Government Consumption and Private Consumption (91f and 96f, respectively).

*Commodity Prices*: Data are obtained primarily from the Energy and Commodities Surveillance Unit of the IMF's Research Department, from *Commodity Price Data* of the World Bank, from *Monthly Commodity Price Bulletin* of the UNCTAD, and from a number of countries that produce commodities that are significantly traded in the international markets. Data derived from the last source are reported in the country tables. The market price series (lines 76) are expressed as U.S. dollars per quantity units and refer to values often used in the respective commodity markets. For comparison purposes, indices of unit values (lines 74) at base 2010=100 are provided. The accompanying notes to the table (located in the back of the printed copies) provide information specific to each commodity series, including data sources, grades, and quotation frequency.

## 12. Country Codes and IFS Line Numbers

Each IFS time series carries a unique identification code. For publication purposes, the code has been truncated to a three-digit country code and to a five-digit subject code, referred to as the IFS line number.

Line numbers apply uniformly across countries¬—that is, a given line number measures the same economic variable for each country, subject to data availability. The line numbers take the form of two numerics followed by three alphabetic codes (NNaaa). The two numerics are the section and subsection codes, the first two alphabetic codes are the classification codes, and the last alphabetic code is the qualification code. Any of these positions may be blank: for publication purposes, blanks in the first or final positions are omitted, whereas embedded blanks are represented by a period. The line numbers are part of the descriptor stub in the country tables.

Data expressed in units of money (values or prices) are ordinarily expressed in national currency and in natural form, that is, without seasonal adjustment. For these data the qualification code is blank.

Transformation of these data is denoted by various qualification codes. For data that are not seasonally adjusted, qualification codes are *d* for U.S. dollar values, *s* for SDR values, and *p* for constant national currency values. For data that are seasonally adjusted for IFS, codes are *f* for U.S. dollar values, *u* for SDR values, and *b* for national currency values. For data that are seasonally adjusted by national compilers, codes are *c* for national currency values and *r* for constant national currency values.

The qualification codes are also used to distinguish separate groups of deposit money banks or other financial institutions when data for separate groups are given.

## 13. Symbols, Conventions, and Abbreviations

The abbreviation "ff.," often used on the title page of the printed copies of IFS, means "following."

Entries printed in bold on the country page of the monthly book refer to updates and revisions made since the publication of the preceding issue of IFS.

Italic midheadings in the middle of the pages of the monthly book and yearbook identify the units in which data are expressed and whether data are stocks (end of period), flows (transactions during a period), or averages (for a period).

(—) Indicates that a figure is zero or less than half a significant digit.

(....) Indicates a lack of statistical data that can be reported or calculated from underlying observations.

(†) Marks a break in the comparability of data, as explained in the relevant notes in the monthly and yearbook. In these instances, data after the symbol do not form a consistent series with those for earlier dates. The break symbols not explained in the country table notes can show a point of splice, where series having different base years are linked. A case would be the series described in the section of this introduction on prices, production, and labor. They can also point out a change in magnitude for high-inflation countries, as described in the section on electronic products.

(e) In superscript position after the figure marks an observation that is an estimate.

(f) In superscript position after the figure marks an observation that is forecast.

(p) In superscript position after the figure marks that data are in whole or in part provisional or preliminary.

Standard source codes, listed in the footnotes, refer with some exceptions to the following data sources:

(A) Annual report of the central bank

(B) Bulletin of the central bank

(C) Customs department of a country

(E) OECD

(L) International Labor Organization

(M) Ministry or other national source

(N) National bureau or other national source

(S) Statistical office

(U) United Nations

(V) Eurostat

The CD-ROM supports text messages to indicate breaks in the data. The time series observations with footnotes are highlighted in bold blue type within the IFS Data Viewer. When the cursor is moved over the footnoted cell, a small window will be displayed with the footnoted text.

These footnotes/comments provide meaningful information about the specific observation, e.g., butt splicing, ratio splicing, extrapolation, estimations, etc.

Because of space limits in the phototypesetting of descriptor stubs on the country tables and table headings of world tables, abbreviations are sometimes necessary. While most are self-explanatory, the following abbreviation in the descriptors and table headings should be noted:

n.i.e. = Not included elsewhere.

Of which: Currency Outside DMBs = Of which: Currency Outside Deposit Money Banks.

Househ.Cons.Expend., incl.NPISHs = Household

Consumption Expenditure, including Nonprofit Institutions Serving Households.

Use of Fund Credit (GRA) = Use of Fund Credit (General Resources Account).

Fin. der. & empl. stk. ops. (ESOs) = Financial derivatives and employee stock options.

Data relating to fiscal years are allocated to calendar years to which most of their months refer. Fiscal years ending June 30 are allocated to that calendar year. For instance, the fiscal year from July 1, 1999 to June 30, 2000 is shown as calendar year 2000.

For countries that have reported semiannual transactions data, the data for the first half of a year may be given in the monthly book in the column for the second quarter of that year. And those for the second half may be given in the column for the fourth quarter. In these instances, no data are shown in the columns for the first and third quarters.

## 14. CD-ROM and Internet Account Subscriptions

The IFS is available on CD-ROM and the Internet. It contains:

(1) all time series appearing on IFS country tables;

(2) all series published in the IFS world tables;

(3) the following exchange rate series as available for all Fund members, plus Aruba and the Netherlands Antilles: aa, ac, ae, af, ag, ah, b, c, de, dg, ea, eb, ec, ed, g, rb, rd, rf, rh, sa, sb, sc, sd, wa, wc, we, wf, wg, wh, xe, xf, ye, yf, nec, rec, aat, aet, rbt, rft, neu, reu, and ahx (for an explanation of series af, ah, de, dg, rb, and rd, see *IFS Supplement on Exchange Rates*, No. 9 (1985));

(4) Fund accounts time series, denominated in SDR terms, for all countries for which data are available, though some series are not published in the IFS monthly book (2af, 2al, 2ap, 2aq, 2as, 2at, 2ej, 2ek, 2en, 2eo, 2f.s, 1c.s, 2tl, 2egs, 2eb, 2h.s, 1bd, 1b.s, 2dus, 2krs, 2ees, 2kxs, 2eu, 2ey, 2eg, 2ens, 2ehs, 2eqs, 2ers, 2ets, 2kk, 2lk, 2kl, 2ll, 1ch, and 1cj) and in percentages (2tlp, 2fz, and 1bf); and

(5) balance of payments and international investment position series (109bx to 8dzla) for all countries for which data are available, though some series are not published in the IFS monthly book.

All series in IFS contain publication code F except for the euro data lines that contain the code W.

A partner country code may sometimes be included in the control field. When it exists, it usually is shown in the IFS printed copy either in the italic midheading (see Real Effective Exchange Rate Indices table) or in the notes (see Commodity Prices table notes). Occasionally, the partner country code attached to a commodity price refers to a market (e.g., the London Metals Exchange) rather than the country of origin.

In the IFS monthly and yearbook, data expressed in national currency for countries that have undergone periods of high inflation (e.g., Zimbabwe) are presented in different magnitudes on the same printed line. Users may refer to midheaders on country pages for an indication of the magnitude changes. The practice of expressing different magnitudes on the same line was adopted to prevent early-period data from disappearing from the printed tables. On the CD-ROM and the Internet (CSV format), the data are stored in a scientific notation with six significant digits for all time periods. Therefore, historical as well as current data may be viewed when using the display choices available on the CD-ROM and the Internet.

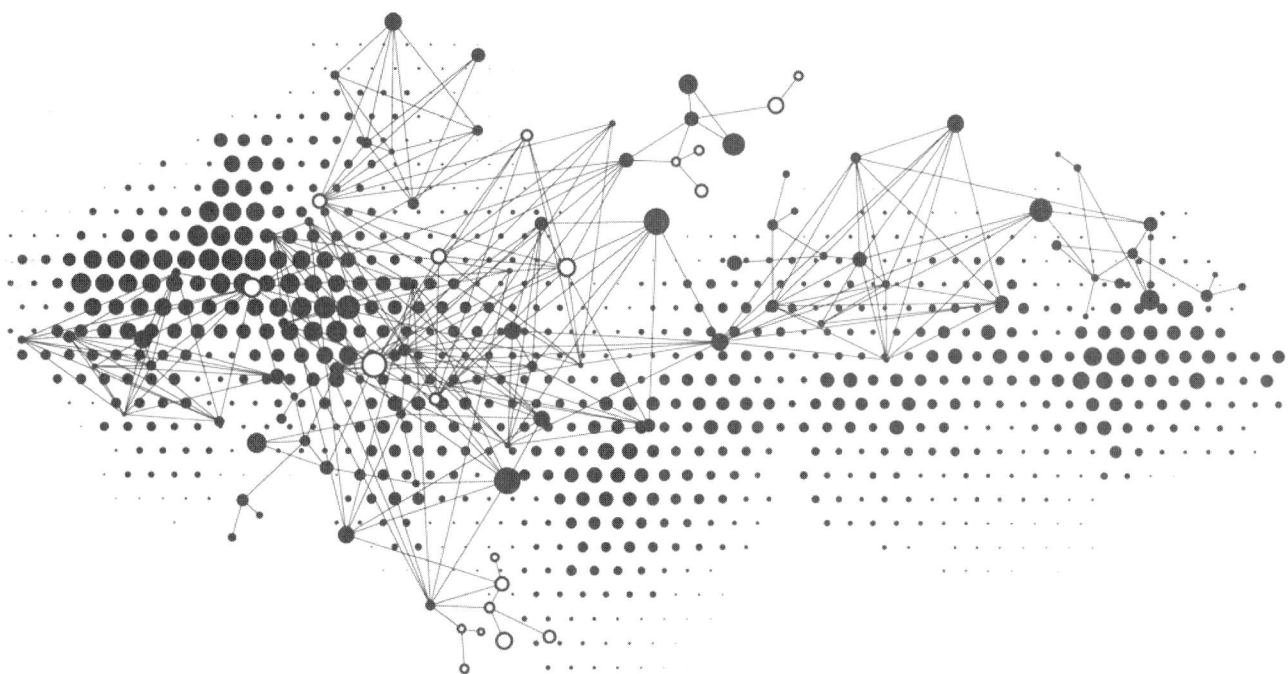

# World

*and*

# Area Tables

# Exchange Rates

A. SDR Rates: 1995–2012

| | Jan. | Feb. | Mar. | Apr. | May | June | July | Aug. | Sep. | Oct. | Nov. | Dec. | I | II | III | IV | Year |
|---|---|---|---|---|---|---|---|---|---|---|---|---|---|---|---|---|---|
| **sa** US Dollars per SDR (End of Period) | | | | | | | | | | | | | | | | | |
| 2000 | 1.35288 | 1.33928 | 1.34687 | 1.31921 | 1.32002 | 1.33728 | 1.31335 | 1.30480 | 1.29789 | 1.27934 | 1.28197 | 1.30291 | 1.34687 | 1.33728 | 1.29789 | 1.30291 | 1.30291 |
| 2001 | 1.29779 | 1.29248 | 1.26065 | 1.26579 | 1.25423 | 1.24565 | 1.25874 | 1.28823 | 1.28901 | 1.27808 | 1.26608 | 1.25673 | 1.26065 | 1.24565 | 1.28901 | 1.25673 | 1.25673 |
| 2002 | 1.24204 | 1.24163 | 1.24691 | 1.26771 | 1.29066 | 1.33046 | 1.32248 | 1.32751 | 1.32269 | 1.32163 | 1.32408 | 1.35952 | 1.24691 | 1.33046 | 1.32269 | 1.35952 | 1.35952 |
| 2003 | 1.37654 | 1.37085 | 1.37379 | 1.38391 | 1.41995 | 1.40086 | 1.39195 | 1.37727 | 1.42979 | 1.43178 | 1.44878 | 1.48597 | 1.37379 | 1.40086 | 1.42979 | 1.48597 | 1.48597 |
| 2004 | 1.48131 | 1.48007 | 1.48051 | 1.45183 | 1.46882 | 1.46622 | 1.45776 | 1.46073 | 1.46899 | 1.49878 | 1.53590 | 1.55301 | 1.48051 | 1.46622 | 1.46899 | 1.55301 | 1.55301 |
| 2005 | 1.52484 | 1.53199 | 1.51083 | 1.51678 | 1.47495 | 1.45661 | 1.45186 | 1.45984 | 1.44946 | 1.44580 | 1.42414 | 1.42927 | 1.51083 | 1.45661 | 1.44946 | 1.42927 | 1.42927 |
| 2006 | 1.44540 | 1.43503 | 1.44085 | 1.47106 | 1.49418 | 1.47937 | 1.48386 | 1.48852 | 1.47637 | 1.48004 | 1.50773 | 1.50440 | 1.44085 | 1.47937 | 1.47637 | 1.50440 | 1.50440 |
| 2007 | 1.49015 | 1.50472 | 1.51019 | 1.52418 | 1.51286 | 1.51557 | 1.53122 | 1.53263 | 1.55665 | 1.57188 | 1.59018 | 1.58025 | 1.51019 | 1.51557 | 1.55665 | 1.58025 | 1.58025 |
| 2008 | 1.59527 | 1.61055 | 1.64450 | 1.62378 | 1.62069 | 1.63362 | 1.62088 | 1.56988 | 1.55722 | 1.48830 | 1.48797 | 1.54027 | 1.64450 | 1.63362 | 1.55722 | 1.54027 | 1.54027 |
| 2009 | 1.50596 | 1.46736 | 1.49507 | 1.49783 | 1.54805 | 1.55223 | 1.55333 | 1.56606 | 1.58437 | 1.61018 | 1.61018 | 1.56769 | 1.49507 | 1.55223 | 1.58437 | 1.56769 | 1.56769 |
| 2010 | 1.55419 | 1.53258 | 1.51824 | 1.51112 | 1.47433 | 1.47890 | 1.51852 | 1.50891 | 1.55619 | 1.57179 | 1.52578 | 1.54003 | 1.51824 | 1.47890 | 1.55619 | 1.54003 | 1.54003 |
| 2011 | 1.56194 | 1.57305 | 1.58550 | 1.62096 | 1.60077 | 1.60045 | 1.59900 | 1.60936 | 1.56162 | 1.58590 | 1.55156 | 1.53527 | 1.58550 | 1.60045 | 1.56162 | 1.53527 | 1.53527 |
| 2012 | 1.55108 | 1.55602 | 1.54909 | 1.55055 | 1.51026 | 1.51755 | 1.50833 | 1.52201 | 1.54219 | 1.54057 | 1.53481 | 1.53692 | 1.54909 | 1.51755 | 1.54219 | 1.53692 | 1.53692 |
| 2013 | 1.54134 | 1.51483 | 1.49920 | 1.50924 | 1.49877 | 1.50396 | 1.51474 | 1.51528 | 1.53408 | 1.54354 | 1.53521 | 1.54000 | 1.49920 | 1.50396 | 1.53408 | 1.54000 | 1.54000 |
| 2014 | 1.53420 | 1.54740 | 1.54563 | 1.54969 | 1.54078 | 1.54589 | 1.53131 | 1.51838 | 1.48258 | 1.47833 | 1.46424 | 1.44881 | 1.54563 | 1.54589 | 1.48258 | 1.44881 | 1.44881 |
| 2015 | 1.40980 | 1.40739 | 1.37949 | 1.40642 | 1.39050 | 1.40639 | 1.39470 | 1.40380 | 1.40374 | 1.39687 | 1.37217 | 1.38573 | 1.37949 | 1.40639 | 1.40374 | 1.38573 | 1.38573 |
| 2016 | 1.38050 | 1.38131 | 1.40882 | 1.41733 | 1.40288 | | | | | | | | 1.40882 | | | | |
| **sb** US Dollars per SDR (Period Average, geometric) | | | | | | | | | | | | | | | | | |
| 2000 | 1.37068 | 1.34485 | 1.34286 | 1.33915 | 1.31082 | 1.33062 | 1.32348 | 1.30836 | 1.29409 | 1.28650 | 1.28276 | 1.29440 | 1.35274 | 1.32681 | 1.30859 | 1.28788 | 1.31879 |
| 2001 | 1.30203 | 1.29353 | 1.27989 | 1.26764 | 1.26217 | 1.25028 | 1.25125 | 1.27495 | 1.28593 | 1.27882 | 1.26827 | 1.26279 | 1.29178 | 1.26001 | 1.27063 | 1.26994 | 1.27304 |
| 2002 | 1.25276 | 1.24463 | 1.25009 | 1.25669 | 1.27713 | 1.30065 | 1.33033 | 1.32103 | 1.32182 | 1.31765 | 1.33109 | 1.34003 | 1.24916 | 1.27803 | 1.32439 | 1.32956 | 1.29485 |
| 2003 | 1.36538 | 1.37045 | 1.37004 | 1.36908 | 1.40825 | 1.41481 | 1.39832 | 1.38494 | 1.39628 | 1.43198 | 1.43391 | 1.46743 | 1.36862 | 1.39723 | 1.39317 | 1.44435 | 1.40058 |
| 2004 | 1.49108 | 1.49645 | 1.47301 | 1.46088 | 1.45118 | 1.46565 | 1.47273 | 1.46495 | 1.46450 | 1.47952 | 1.51377 | 1.54036 | 1.48681 | 1.45922 | 1.46739 | 1.51101 | 1.48098 |
| 2005 | 1.52868 | 1.51752 | 1.52527 | 1.51043 | 1.49728 | 1.46737 | 1.44970 | 1.46691 | 1.46601 | 1.44540 | 1.42714 | 1.43121 | 1.52382 | 1.49158 | 1.46085 | 1.43456 | 1.47733 |
| 2006 | 1.44694 | 1.43561 | 1.43904 | 1.45121 | 1.48877 | 1.47800 | 1.47768 | 1.48701 | 1.48160 | 1.47347 | 1.48967 | 1.50787 | 1.44052 | 1.47258 | 1.48209 | 1.49027 | 1.47124 |
| 2007 | 1.49470 | 1.49713 | 1.50755 | 1.51981 | 1.51753 | 1.51132 | 1.52911 | 1.52942 | 1.54370 | 1.55839 | 1.58643 | 1.57584 | 1.49978 | 1.51622 | 1.53406 | 1.57351 | 1.53065 |
| 2008 | 1.58395 | 1.58555 | 1.63220 | 1.63623 | 1.62378 | 1.61907 | 1.63086 | 1.58486 | 1.55559 | 1.51474 | 1.48299 | 1.52094 | 1.60041 | 1.62634 | 1.59014 | 1.50613 | 1.58010 |
| 2009 | 1.52045 | 1.48565 | 1.48314 | 1.49418 | 1.52073 | 1.54492 | 1.55192 | 1.56021 | 1.57783 | 1.58958 | 1.59989 | 1.58217 | 1.49632 | 1.51980 | 1.56328 | 1.59053 | 1.54205 |
| 2010 | 1.56494 | 1.53811 | 1.52745 | 1.51717 | 1.47982 | 1.46829 | 1.50415 | 1.51779 | 1.52697 | 1.56994 | 1.56192 | 1.53561 | 1.54342 | 1.48828 | 1.51627 | 1.55575 | 1.52571 |
| 2011 | 1.54662 | 1.56288 | 1.58012 | 1.59855 | 1.59758 | 1.59907 | 1.59463 | 1.60591 | 1.57475 | 1.57308 | 1.56645 | 1.54607 | 1.56314 | 1.59840 | 1.59171 | 1.56182 | 1.57868 |
| 2012 | 1.53597 | 1.54921 | 1.54071 | 1.54301 | 1.53095 | 1.51541 | 1.50619 | 1.51276 | 1.53811 | 1.54038 | 1.52956 | 1.53865 | 1.54195 | 1.52975 | 1.51896 | 1.53619 | 1.53169 |
| 2013 | 1.53538 | 1.52705 | 1.50317 | 1.50401 | 1.49945 | 1.51403 | 1.50363 | 1.51854 | 1.52305 | 1.53939 | 1.53013 | 1.53834 | 1.52181 | 1.50582 | 1.51505 | 1.53595 | 1.51962 |
| 2014 | 1.53548 | 1.53976 | 1.54750 | 1.54817 | 1.54760 | 1.53727 | 1.54129 | 1.52623 | 1.49914 | 1.48631 | 1.46694 | 1.45685 | 1.54091 | 1.54434 | 1.52212 | 1.46998 | 1.51904 |
| 2015 | 1.42072 | 1.41235 | 1.38505 | 1.38391 | 1.40450 | 1.40472 | 1.39599 | 1.40238 | 1.40628 | 1.40611 | 1.38235 | 1.38563 | 1.40596 | 1.39768 | 1.40154 | 1.39132 | 1.39911 |
| 2016 | 1.38187 | 1.39302 | 1.39514 | 1.40879 | 1.41125 | | | | | | | | 1.39000 | | | | |
| **sc** SDRs per US Dollar (End of Period) | | | | | | | | | | | | | | | | | |
| 2000 | .73917 | .74667 | .74246 | .75803 | .75757 | .74779 | .76141 | .76640 | .77048 | .78165 | .78005 | .76751 | .74246 | .74779 | .77048 | .76751 | .76751 |
| 2001 | .77054 | .77371 | .79324 | .79002 | .79731 | .80280 | .79445 | .77626 | .77579 | .78243 | .78984 | .79572 | .79324 | .80280 | .77579 | .79572 | .79572 |
| 2002 | .80513 | .80403 | .80198 | .78883 | .77480 | .75162 | .75615 | .75329 | .75603 | .75664 | .75524 | .73555 | .80198 | .75162 | .75603 | .73555 | .73555 |
| 2003 | .72646 | .72947 | .72791 | .72259 | .70425 | .71385 | .71842 | .72608 | .70614 | .69843 | .69024 | .67296 | .72791 | .71385 | .70614 | .67296 | .67296 |
| 2004 | .67508 | .67564 | .67544 | .68879 | .68082 | .68203 | .68599 | .68459 | .68074 | .66721 | .65108 | .64391 | .67544 | .68203 | .68074 | .64391 | .64391 |
| 2005 | .65581 | .65275 | .66189 | .65929 | .67799 | .68652 | .68877 | .68501 | .68991 | .69166 | .70218 | .69966 | .66189 | .68652 | .68991 | .69966 | .69966 |
| 2006 | .69185 | .69685 | .69404 | .67978 | .66926 | .67596 | .67392 | .67181 | .67734 | .67566 | .66325 | .66472 | .69404 | .67596 | .67734 | .66472 | .66472 |
| 2007 | .67107 | .66458 | .66217 | .65609 | .66100 | .65982 | .65307 | .65247 | .64241 | .63618 | .62886 | .63281 | .66217 | .65982 | .64241 | .63281 | .63281 |
| 2008 | .62686 | .62090 | .60809 | .61585 | .61702 | .61214 | .61695 | .63699 | .64217 | .67191 | .67206 | .64924 | .60809 | .61214 | .64217 | .64924 | .64924 |
| 2009 | .66403 | .68149 | .66887 | .66763 | .64597 | .64423 | .64378 | .63855 | .63117 | .62897 | .62105 | .63788 | .66887 | .64423 | .63117 | .63788 | .63788 |
| 2010 | .64342 | .65249 | .65866 | .66176 | .67827 | .67618 | .65854 | .66273 | .64260 | .63622 | .65540 | .64934 | .65866 | .67618 | .64260 | .64934 | .64934 |
| 2011 | .64023 | .63571 | .63072 | .61692 | .62470 | .62482 | .62539 | .62137 | .64036 | .63056 | .64451 | .65135 | .63072 | .62482 | .64036 | .65135 | .65135 |
| 2012 | .64471 | .64267 | .64554 | .64493 | .66214 | .65896 | .66298 | .65703 | .64843 | .64911 | .65155 | .65065 | .64554 | .65896 | .64843 | .65065 | .65065 |
| 2013 | .64879 | .66014 | .66702 | .66259 | .66721 | .66491 | .66018 | .65994 | .65186 | .64786 | .65138 | .64935 | .66702 | .66491 | .65186 | .64935 | .64935 |
| 2014 | .65181 | .64625 | .64699 | .64529 | .64902 | .64688 | .65304 | .65860 | .67450 | .67644 | .68295 | .69022 | .64699 | .64688 | .67450 | .69022 | .69022 |
| 2015 | .70932 | .71054 | .72491 | .71103 | .71917 | .71104 | .71700 | .71235 | .71238 | .71589 | .72877 | .72164 | .72491 | .71104 | .71238 | .72164 | .72164 |
| 2016 | .72438 | .72395 | .70981 | .70555 | .71282 | | | | | | | | .70981 | | | | |
| **sd** SDRs per US Dollar (Period Average, geometric) | | | | | | | | | | | | | | | | | |
| 2000 | .72957 | .74358 | .74468 | .74674 | .76288 | .75153 | .75559 | .76431 | .77275 | .77730 | .77957 | .77256 | .73924 | .75369 | .76418 | .77647 | .75827 |
| 2001 | .76803 | .77308 | .78132 | .78887 | .79229 | .79982 | .79920 | .78435 | .77765 | .78197 | .78847 | .79189 | .77412 | .79365 | .78702 | .78743 | .78552 |
| 2002 | .79824 | .80345 | .79994 | .79574 | .78301 | .76885 | .75169 | .75698 | .75653 | .75893 | .75127 | .74625 | .80054 | .78246 | .75506 | .75213 | .77229 |
| 2003 | .73239 | .72969 | .72990 | .73042 | .71010 | .70681 | .71515 | .72205 | .71619 | .69833 | .69739 | .68146 | .73066 | .71570 | .71779 | .69235 | .71399 |
| 2004 | .67066 | .66825 | .67888 | .68452 | .68909 | .68229 | .67901 | .68262 | .68283 | .67589 | .66060 | .64920 | .67258 | .68529 | .68148 | .66181 | .67523 |
| 2005 | .65416 | .65897 | .65562 | .66206 | .66788 | .68149 | .68980 | .68171 | .68212 | .69185 | .70070 | .69871 | .65625 | .67043 | .68453 | .69708 | .67690 |
| 2006 | .69111 | .69657 | .69491 | .68908 | .67169 | .67659 | .67674 | .67249 | .67495 | .67867 | .67129 | .66319 | .69419 | .67908 | .67472 | .67102 | .67970 |
| 2007 | .66903 | .66794 | .66333 | .65798 | .65897 | .66167 | .65397 | .65384 | .64780 | .64169 | .63035 | .63458 | .66676 | .65954 | .65186 | .63552 | .65332 |
| 2008 | .63133 | .63070 | .61267 | .61116 | .61585 | .61764 | .61318 | .63097 | .64284 | .66018 | .67431 | .65749 | .62484 | .61488 | .62888 | .66395 | .63287 |
| 2009 | .65770 | .67311 | .67425 | .66926 | .65758 | .64728 | .64436 | .64094 | .63378 | .62910 | .62504 | .63204 | .66831 | .65798 | .63968 | .62872 | .64849 |
| 2010 | .63900 | .65015 | .65468 | .65912 | .67576 | .68107 | .66483 | .65885 | .65489 | .63697 | .64024 | .65121 | .64791 | .67192 | .65951 | .64278 | .65545 |
| 2011 | .64657 | .63985 | .63286 | .62557 | .62595 | .62536 | .62710 | .62270 | .63502 | .63570 | .63838 | .64680 | .63974 | .62563 | .62825 | .64028 | .63344 |
| 2012 | .65105 | .64549 | .64905 | .64808 | .65319 | .65989 | .66393 | .66105 | .65015 | .64919 | .65378 | .64992 | .64853 | .65370 | .65835 | .65096 | .65287 |
| 2013 | .65130 | .65486 | .66526 | .66489 | .66691 | .66049 | .66506 | .65853 | .65658 | .64961 | .65354 | .65005 | .65711 | .66409 | .66004 | .65106 | .65806 |
| 2014 | .65126 | .64945 | .64620 | .64592 | .64616 | .65050 | .64881 | .65521 | .66705 | .67281 | .68169 | .68641 | .64897 | .64753 | .65698 | .68028 | .65831 |
| 2015 | .70387 | .70804 | .72200 | .72259 | .71200 | .71188 | .71634 | .71307 | .71110 | .71118 | .72341 | .72170 | .71126 | .71547 | .71350 | .71874 | .71474 |
| 2016 | .72366 | .71787 | .71677 | .70983 | .70859 | | | | | | | | .71943 | | | | |

# Exchange Rates

| | | 2004 | 2005 | 2006 | 2007 | 2008 | 2009 | 2010 | 2011 | 2012 | 2013 | 2014 | 2015 |
|---|---|---|---|---|---|---|---|---|---|---|---|---|---|
| | | | | | | **B. Market, Official, or Principal Rate** *National Currency Units per SDR: End of Period (aa)* | | | | | | | |
| **Advanced Economies** | | | | | | | | | | | | | |
| Euro Area euro | 163 | 1.1402 | 1.2116 | 1.1423 | 1.0735 | 1.1068 | 1.0882 | 1.1525 | 1.1865 | 1.1649 | 1.1167 | 1.1933 | 1.2728 |
| Cyprus pound | 423 | .66004 | .69234 | .66058 | .62860 | .... | .... | .... | .... | .... | .... | .... | .... |
| Estonian kroon | 939 | 17.815 | 18.896 | 17.875 | 16.811 | 17.105 | 17.033 | 18.035 | .... | .... | .... | .... | .... |
| Latvian lats | 941 | .8014 | .8476 | .8064 | .7648 | .7624 | .7666 | .8239 | .8352 | .8161 | .7931 | .... | .... |
| Lithuanian litas | 946 | 3.9361 | 4.1595 | 3.9572 | 3.7250 | 3.7747 | 3.7706 | 4.0193 | 4.0982 | 4.0052 | 3.8651 | 4.1127 | .... |
| Maltese lira | 181 | .49470 | .51841 | .49005 | .46084 | .... | .... | .... | .... | .... | .... | .... | .... |
| Slovak koruna | 936 | 44.255 | 45.662 | 39.484 | 36.140 | 32.939 | .... | .... | .... | .... | .... | .... | .... |
| Slovenian tolar | 961 | 273.71 | 289.33 | 273.70 | .... | .... | .... | .... | .... | .... | .... | .... | .... |
| Australian dollar | 193 | 1.9936 | 1.9480 | 1.9012 | 1.7925 | 2.2233 | 1.7479 | 1.5153 | 1.5117 | 1.4771 | 1.7372 | 1.7664 | 1.8967 |
| Canadian dollar | 156 | 1.8692 | 1.6644 | 1.7531 | 1.5614 | 1.8862 | 1.6407 | 1.5414 | 1.5675 | 1.5295 | 1.6386 | 1.6805 | 1.9179 |
| Czech Republic koruna | 935 | 34.733 | 35.143 | 31.406 | 28.568 | 29.798 | 28.795 | 28.877 | 30.613 | 29.286 | 30.637 | 33.082 | 34.399 |
| Danish krone | 128 | 8.491 | 9.039 | 8.517 | 8.020 | 8.140 | 8.136 | 8.645 | 8.821 | 8.698 | 8.336 | 8.869 | 9.465 |
| Hong Kong dollar | 532 | 12.072 | 11.080 | 11.696 | 12.328 | 11.938 | 12.158 | 11.973 | 11.922 | 11.912 | 11.940 | 11.236 | 10.740 |
| Icelandic krona | 176 | 94.80 | 90.02 | 107.81 | 97.74 | 185.73 | 195.80 | 177.18 | 188.39 | 198.25 | 177.95 | 183.85 | 179.58 |
| Israeli new sheqel | 436 | 6.6904 | 6.5789 | 6.3561 | 6.0776 | 5.8561 | 5.9180 | 5.4656 | 5.8663 | 5.7373 | 5.3453 | 5.6344 | 5.4071 |
| Japanese yen | 158 | 161.70 | 168.61 | 178.95 | 180.15 | 139.78 | 144.32 | 125.44 | 119.32 | 133.02 | 162.16 | 174.78 | 166.98 |
| Korean won | 542 | 1,607.5 | 1,445.8 | 1,398.8 | 1,479.3 | 1,940.0 | 1,825.6 | 1,747.6 | 1,768.3 | 1,645.4 | 1,625.3 | 1,592.7 | 1,624.8 |
| Macao pataca | 546 | 12.439 | 11.416 | 12.044 | 12.696 | 12.295 | 12.522 | 12.345 | 12.289 | 12.271 | 12.300 | 11.576 | 11.063 |
| New Zealand dollar | 196 | 2.1618 | 2.0975 | 2.1312 | 2.0417 | 2.6625 | 2.1722 | 1.9985 | 1.9905 | 1.8737 | 1.8776 | 1.8506 | 2.0236 |
| Norwegian krone | 142 | 9.380 | 9.676 | 9.418 | 8.549 | 10.782 | 9.061 | 9.025 | 9.196 | 8.561 | 9.363 | 10.765 | 12.208 |
| Pound sterling | 112 | .8041 | .8301 | .7664 | .7888 | 1.0566 | .9680 | .9837 | .9930 | .9740 | .9351 | .9282 | .9351 |
| Singapore dollar | 576 | 2.5373 | 2.3786 | 2.3071 | 2.2775 | 2.2168 | 2.2001 | 1.9828 | 1.9969 | 1.8804 | 1.9486 | 1.9143 | 1.9593 |
| Swedish krona | 144 | 10.273 | 11.375 | 10.327 | 10.135 | 12.030 | 11.156 | 10.333 | 10.574 | 9.997 | 9.893 | 11.209 | 11.697 |
| Swiss franc | 146 | 1.7574 | 1.8785 | 1.8358 | 1.7786 | 1.6384 | 1.6155 | 1.4470 | 1.4445 | 1.4087 | 1.3729 | 1.4330 | 1.3748 |
| US dollar | 111 | 1.5530 | 1.4293 | 1.5044 | 1.5803 | 1.5403 | 1.5677 | 1.5400 | 1.5353 | 1.5369 | 1.5400 | 1.4488 | 1.3857 |
| **Emerging & Dev. Economies** | | | | | | | | | | | | | |
| **Emerging & Developing Asia** | | | | | | | | | | | | | |
| Bangladesh taka | 513 | 94.33 | 94.63 | 103.90 | 108.37 | 106.16 | 108.59 | 108.96 | 125.67 | 122.72 | 119.74 | 112.93 | 108.78 |
| Bhutan, ngultrum | 514 | 67.688 | 64.410 | 66.562 | 62.286 | 74.634 | 73.180 | 69.009 | 81.768 | 84.188 | 95.321 | 91.755 | 91.910 |
| Brunei dollars | 516 | 2.5377 | 2.3789 | 2.3075 | 2.2778 | 2.2171 | 2.2001 | 1.9897 | 1.9969 | 1.8804 | 1.9547 | 1.9143 | 1.9593 |
| Cambodian riel | 522 | 6,254.0 | 5,877.2 | 6,103.4 | 6,319.4 | 6,279.7 | 6,529.4 | 6,238.7 | 6,201.0 | 6,140.0 | 6,152.3 | 5,903.9 | 5,614.3 |
| Chinese yuan | 924 | 12.853 | 11.534 | 11.747 | 11.543 | 10.527 | 10.705 | 10.199 | 9.674 | 9.667 | 9.398 | 8.865 | 8.995 |
| Fiji dollar | 819 | 2.5547 | 2.4939 | 2.5036 | 2.4511 | 2.7170 | 3.0234 | 2.8021 | 2.7950 | 2.7470 | 2.9228 | 2.8798 | 2.9477 |
| Indian rupee | 534 | 67.688 | 64.410 | 66.562 | 62.286 | 74.634 | 73.180 | 69.009 | 81.768 | 84.188 | 95.321 | 91.755 | 91.910 |
| Indonesian rupiah | 536 | 14,427 | 14,050 | 13,570 | 14,884 | 16,866 | 14,736 | 13,846 | 13,922 | 14,862 | 18,771 | 18,023 | 19,116 |
| Kiribati, Aust.dollar | 826 | 1.9936 | 1.9480 | 1.9012 | 1.7925 | 2.2233 | 1.7479 | 1.5153 | 1.5117 | 1.4771 | 1.7372 | 1.7664 | 1.8967 |
| Lao, P.D. Rep., kip | 544 | 16,115 | 15,355 | 14,587 | 14,769 | 13,058 | 13,301 | 12,411 | 12,318 | 12,276 | 12,363 | 11,732 | 11,325 |
| Malaysian ringgit | 548 | 5.9014 | 5.4026 | 5.3128 | 5.2251 | 5.3355 | 5.3686 | 4.7487 | 4.8776 | 4.7003 | 5.0535 | 5.0636 | 5.9476 |
| Maldivian rufiyaa | 556 | 19.879 | 18.295 | 19.256 | 20.227 | 19.715 | 20.066 | 19.712 | 23.659 | 23.615 | 23.731 | 22.312 | 21.354 |
| Mongolian togrog | 948 | 1,877.6 | 1,745.1 | 1,752.6 | 1,848.8 | 1,952.3 | 2,261.9 | 1,935.0 | 2,143.8 | 2,139.5 | 2,547.3 | 2,731.9 | 2,765.9 |
| Myanmar kyat | 518 | 8.51 | 8.51 | 8.51 | 8.51 | 8.51 | 8.51 | 8.51 | 8.51 | 1,314.01 | 1,521.52 | 1,494.45 | 1,806.99 |
| Nepalese rupee | 558 | 111.51 | 105.84 | 106.96 | 100.42 | 119.60 | 116.70 | 110.34 | 131.28 | 134.90 | 152.63 | 143.97 | 148.27 |
| Papua New Guinea kina | 853 | 4.8532 | 4.4250 | 4.5588 | 4.4830 | 4.1239 | 4.2370 | 4.0688 | 3.2910 | 3.2322 | 3.7288 | 3.7582 | 4.1676 |
| Philippine peso | 566 | 87.383 | 75.847 | 73.914 | 65.424 | 73.140 | 72.672 | 67.584 | 67.441 | 63.309 | 68.398 | 64.642 | 65.359 |
| Samoa tala | 862 | 4.1513 | 3.9504 | 4.0397 | 4.0426 | 4.4736 | 3.9095 | 3.5982 | 3.6158 | 3.5057 | 3.6099 | 3.5106 | 3.5984 |
| Solomon Islands dollar | 813 | 11.659 | 10.828 | 11.458 | 12.109 | 12.322 | 12.643 | 12.420 | 11.297 | 11.284 | 11.332 | 10.661 | 11.175 |
| Sri Lanka rupee | 524 | 162.45 | 145.95 | 162.03 | 171.80 | 174.27 | 179.32 | 170.87 | 174.87 | 195.44 | 201.36 | 189.86 | 199.63 |
| Thai baht | 578 | 60.662 | 58.643 | 54.227 | 53.284 | 53.752 | 52.235 | 46.434 | 48.655 | 47.078 | 50.533 | 47.757 | 50.009 |
| Tongan pa'anga | 866 | 2.9689 | 2.9439 | 3.0088 | 2.9816 | 3.2863 | 2.9849 | 2.7859 | 2.6493 | 2.6687 | 2.8092 | 2.8303 | 3.0597 |
| Vanuatu vatu | 846 | 165.44 | 160.55 | 160.19 | 157.80 | 173.43 | 153.52 | 143.45 | 143.64 | 140.98 | 149.84 | 148.82 | 153.15 |
| Vietnamese dong | 582 | 24,502 | 22,748 | 24,152 | 25,464 | 26,149 | 28,126 | 29,156 | 31,977 | 32,011 | 32,395 | 30,781 | 30,334 |
| **Europe** | | | | | | | | | | | | | |
| **Emerging & Developing Europe** | | | | | | | | | | | | | |
| Albanian lek | 914 | 143.87 | 148.04 | 141.62 | 130.99 | 135.41 | 150.20 | 160.16 | 165.10 | 162.68 | 156.86 | 166.95 | 174.31 |
| Bosnia & Herzegovina conv.marka | 963 | 2.2300 | 2.3696 | 2.2341 | 2.0995 | 2.1646 | 2.1284 | 2.2542 | 2.3207 | 2.2783 | 2.1840 | 2.3339 | 2.4894 |
| Bulgarian lev | 918 | 2.2300 | 2.3696 | 2.2342 | 2.1036 | 2.1368 | 2.1385 | 2.2682 | 2.3207 | 2.2802 | 2.1853 | 2.3303 | 2.4806 |
| Croatian kuna | 960 | 8.7541 | 8.9095 | 8.3921 | 7.8783 | 7.9409 | 7.9784 | 8.5753 | 8.9351 | 8.8016 | 8.5455 | 9.1306 | 9.6887 |
| Hungarian forint | 944 | 279.99 | 305.26 | 288.27 | 272.77 | 289.43 | 294.84 | 321.33 | 369.51 | 339.55 | 332.13 | 375.43 | 397.19 |
| Kosovo euro | 967 | .... | .... | .... | .... | 1.1068 | 1.0882 | 1.1525 | 1.1865 | 1.1649 | 1.1167 | 1.1933 | 1.2728 |
| Macedonian denar | 962 | 69.990 | 74.120 | 69.879 | 65.828 | 67.096 | 66.886 | 71.325 | 72.978 | 71.699 | 68.728 | 73.252 | 78.120 |
| Montenegro euro | 943 | 1.1402 | 1.2116 | 1.1423 | 1.0735 | 1.1068 | 1.0882 | 1.1525 | 1.1865 | 1.1649 | 1.1167 | 1.1933 | 1.2728 |
| Polish zloty | 964 | 4.6441 | 4.6613 | 4.3786 | 3.8479 | 4.5620 | 4.4684 | 4.5648 | 5.2466 | 4.7638 | 4.6385 | 5.0813 | 5.4059 |
| Romanian leu | 968 | 4.5141 | 4.4419 | 3.8627 | 3.8817 | 4.3654 | 4.6029 | 4.9350 | 5.1267 | 5.1602 | 5.0129 | 5.3415 | 5.7476 |
| Serbian dinar | 942 | 89.97 | 103.22 | 90.23 | 84.90 | 96.88 | 104.61 | 122.09 | 124.15 | 132.45 | 128.02 | 144.10 | 154.16 |
| Turkish new lira | 186 | 2.0803 | 1.9224 | 2.1197 | 1.8502 | 2.3496 | 2.3373 | 2.3736 | 2.9070 | 2.7386 | 3.2897 | 3.3626 | 4.0328 |
| **CIS** | | | | | | | | | | | | | |
| Armenian dram | 911 | 754.51 | 643.44 | 546.85 | 480.74 | 472.45 | 592.41 | 559.71 | 592.26 | 620.27 | 624.69 | 688.14 | 670.35 |
| Azerbaijan manat | 912 | 1.5229 | 1.3129 | 1.3109 | 1.3358 | 1.2338 | 1.2590 | 1.2288 | 1.2075 | 1.2065 | 1.2081 | 1.1364 | 2.1609 |
| Belarusian rubel | 913 | 3,370.0 | 3,075.8 | 3,219.4 | 3,397.5 | 3,388.6 | 4,488.3 | 4,620.1 | 12,819.5 | 13,171.4 | 14,645.4 | 17,168.4 | 25,731.6 |
| Georgian lari | 915 | 2.8342 | 2.5620 | 2.5778 | 2.5151 | 2.5676 | 2.6428 | 2.7302 | 2.5644 | 2.5462 | 2.6739 | 2.7000 | 3.3187 |
| Kazakhstani tenge | 916 | 201.89 | 191.49 | 191.06 | 190.10 | 186.05 | 232.74 | 227.15 | 227.83 | 231.68 | 237.25 | 264.19 | 471.16 |
| Kyrgyz som | 917 | 64.643 | 59.030 | 57.353 | 56.097 | 60.715 | 69.122 | 72.534 | 71.367 | 72.852 | 75.840 | 85.315 | 105.176 |
| Moldovan leu | 921 | 19.352 | 18.340 | 19.414 | 17.887 | 16.019 | 19.285 | 18.717 | 17.986 | 18.540 | 20.108 | 22.623 | 27.241 |
| Russian ruble | 922 | 43.094 | 41.138 | 39.613 | 38.789 | 45.254 | 47.414 | 46.935 | 49.430 | 46.680 | 50.403 | 81.508 | 100.996 |
| Tajik somoni | 923 | 4.7165 | 4.5727 | 5.1548 | 5.4754 | 5.3169 | 6.8524 | 6.7809 | 7.3056 | 7.3225 | 7.3521 | 7.6901 | 9.6865 |
| Ukrainian hryvnia | 926 | 8.239 | 7.218 | 7.597 | 7.980 | 11.860 | 12.518 | 12.261 | 12.267 | 12.285 | 12.309 | 22.846 | 33.258 |

# Exchange Rates

B. Market, Official, or Principal Rate
National Currency Units per SDR: End of Period (aa)

| | | 2004 | 2005 | 2006 | 2007 | 2008 | 2009 | 2010 | 2011 | 2012 | 2013 | 2014 | 2015 |
|---|---|---|---|---|---|---|---|---|---|---|---|---|---|
| **Middle East,N.Africa & Pakistan** | | | | | | | | | | | | | |
| Afghanistan afghani | 512 | 74.886 | 72.050 | 74.994 | 78.570 | 80.310 | 76.409 | 69.717 | 75.290 | 80.135 | 87.226 | 83.770 | 94.299 |
| Algerian dinar | 612 | 112.77 | 104.88 | 107.05 | 105.61 | 109.64 | 114.02 | 115.42 | 116.77 | 120.04 | 120.35 | 127.36 | 148.46 |
| Bahrain, Kingdom of, dinar | 419 | .58393 | .53741 | .56566 | .59418 | .57914 | .58945 | .57905 | .57726 | .57788 | .57904 | .54475 | .52103 |
| Djibouti franc | 611 | 276.00 | 254.01 | 267.36 | 280.84 | 273.74 | 278.61 | 273.70 | 272.85 | 273.14 | 273.69 | 257.48 | 246.27 |
| Egyptian pound | 469 | 9.5221 | 8.1929 | 8.5805 | 8.6974 | 8.4778 | 8.5837 | 8.9208 | 9.2376 | 9.6914 | 10.6922 | 10.3490 | 10.8198 |
| Iranian rial | 429 | 13,656 | 12,993 | 13,875 | 14,668 | 15,133 | 15,652 | 15,944 | 17,141 | 18,843 | 38,152 | 39,318 | 41,752 |
| New Iraqi dinar | 433 | 2,281.4 | 2,125.3 | 1,993.3 | 1,920.0 | 1,805.2 | 1,834.2 | 1,801.8 | 1,796.3 | 1,792.0 | 1,795.6 | 1,689.3 | 1,637.9 |
| Jordan dinar | 439 | 1.1011 | 1.0134 | 1.0666 | 1.1204 | 1.0924 | 1.1131 | 1.0934 | 1.0900 | 1.0912 | 1.0934 | 1.0287 | .9839 |
| Kuwaiti dinar | 443 | .45767 | .41735 | .43499 | .43141 | .42504 | .44961 | .43213 | .42765 | .43225 | .43435 | .42421 | .42057 |
| Lebanese pound | 446 | 2,341.2 | 2,154.6 | 2,267.9 | 2,382.2 | 2,322.0 | 2,363.3 | 2,321.6 | 2,314.4 | 2,316.9 | 2,321.6 | 2,184.1 | 2,089.0 |
| Libyan dinar | 672 | 1.9324 | 1.9324 | 1.9324 | 1.9324 | 1.9324 | 1.9324 | 1.9324 | 1.9324 | 1.9324 | 1.9324 | 1.9324 | . . . . |
| Mauritanian ouguiya | 682 | 399.42 | 386.77 | 407.11 | 399.61 | 402.78 | 410.72 | 434.29 | 442.93 | 465.74 | 460.46 | 452.96 | 469.69 |
| Moroccan dirham | 686 | 12.762 | 13.220 | 12.722 | 12.189 | 12.473 | 12.322 | 12.870 | 13.168 | 12.962 | 12.552 | 13.101 | 13.727 |
| Rial Omani | 449 | .59713 | .54955 | .57844 | .60761 | .59223 | .60278 | .59214 | .59031 | .59095 | .59213 | .55707 | .53281 |
| Pakistan rupee | 564 | 91.82 | 85.51 | 91.65 | 96.74 | 121.83 | 132.10 | 132.00 | 138.13 | 149.29 | 162.74 | 145.55 | 145.32 |
| Qatar riyal | 453 | 5.6530 | 5.2025 | 5.4760 | 5.7521 | 5.6066 | 5.7064 | 5.6057 | 5.5884 | 5.5944 | 5.6056 | 5.2737 | 5.0441 |
| Saudi Arabian riyal | 456 | 5.8238 | 5.3526 | 5.6340 | 5.9259 | 5.7760 | 5.8788 | 5.7751 | 5.7573 | 5.7635 | 5.7750 | 5.4330 | 5.1965 |
| Sudanese pound | 732 | 3.8923 | 3.2950 | 3.0288 | 3.2436 | 3.3639 | 3.5113 | 3.8230 | 4.1097 | 6.8102 | 8.7715 | 8.6526 | 8.4423 |
| Syrian pound | 463 | 17.433 | 16.044 | 16.887 | 17.738 | 17.290 | 17.597 | 17.287 | 17.233 | 17.252 | 17.287 | 16.263 | 15.555 |
| Tunisian dinar | 744 | 1.8627 | 1.9487 | 1.9514 | 1.9290 | 2.0176 | 2.0651 | 2.2144 | 2.3018 | 2.3831 | 2.5359 | 2.6965 | . . . . |
| U.A.Emirates dirham | 466 | 5.7034 | 5.2490 | 5.5249 | 5.8035 | 5.6566 | 5.7573 | 5.6558 | 5.6383 | 5.6443 | 5.6557 | 5.3208 | 5.0891 |
| Yemen,Rep.,Yemeni rial | 474 | 288.66 | 278.82 | 298.62 | 315.32 | 308.18 | 325.01 | 329.26 | 328.24 | 330.27 | 330.93 | 311.33 | 297.78 |
| **Sub-Saharan Africa** | | | | | | | | | | | | | |
| Angolan kwanza | 614 | 133.54 | 115.46 | 120.75 | 118.56 | 115.78 | 140.15 | 142.67 | 146.27 | 147.28 | 150.25 | 149.03 | 187.51 |
| Benin,CFA franc | 638 | 747.90 | 794.73 | 749.30 | 704.15 | 725.98 | 713.83 | 756.02 | 778.32 | 764.10 | 732.49 | 782.77 | 834.92 |
| Botswana pula | 616 | 6.648 | 7.879 | 9.074 | 9.491 | 11.581 | 10.461 | 9.920 | 11.554 | 11.949 | 13.431 | 13.785 | 15.569 |
| Burkina Faso, CFA franc | 748 | 747.90 | 794.73 | 749.30 | 704.15 | 725.98 | 713.83 | 756.02 | 778.32 | 764.10 | 732.49 | 782.77 | 834.92 |
| Burundi franc | 618 | 1,717.4 | 1,425.9 | 1,506.9 | 1,767.2 | 1,911.5 | 1,922.0 | 1,898.7 | 2,083.6 | 2,376.2 | 2,382.4 | 2,249.4 | 2,243.4 |
| Cameroon, CFA franc | 622 | 747.90 | 794.73 | 749.30 | 704.15 | 725.98 | 713.83 | 756.02 | 778.32 | 764.10 | 732.49 | 782.77 | 834.92 |
| Cape Verde escudo | 624 | 125.73 | 133.60 | 125.96 | 118.37 | 122.04 | 120.00 | 127.09 | 130.84 | 128.45 | 123.14 | 131.59 | 140.35 |
| Cent.African Rep.,CFA franc | 626 | 747.90 | 794.73 | 749.30 | 704.15 | 725.98 | 713.83 | 756.02 | 778.32 | 764.10 | 732.49 | 782.77 | 834.92 |
| Chad, CFA franc | 628 | 747.90 | 794.73 | 749.30 | 704.15 | 725.98 | 713.83 | 756.02 | 778.32 | 764.10 | 732.49 | 782.77 | 834.92 |
| Comorian franc | 632 | 560.92 | 596.05 | 561.97 | 528.11 | 544.49 | 535.37 | 567.02 | 583.74 | 573.08 | 549.37 | 587.08 | 626.19 |
| Congo, Dem.Rep., congo franc | 636 | 689.7 | 616.4 | 757.4 | 794.8 | 984.7 | 1,415.1 | 1,409.3 | 1,398.1 | 1,406.6 | 1,425.3 | 1,339.4 | 1,284.2 |
| Congo, Rep., CFA franc | 634 | 747.90 | 794.73 | 749.30 | 704.15 | 725.98 | 713.83 | 756.02 | 778.32 | 764.10 | 732.49 | 782.77 | 834.92 |
| Côte d'Ivoire,CFA franc | 662 | 747.90 | 794.73 | 749.30 | 704.15 | 725.98 | 713.83 | 756.02 | 778.32 | 764.10 | 732.49 | 782.77 | 834.92 |
| Eq. Guinea, CFA franc | 642 | 747.90 | 794.73 | 749.30 | 704.15 | 725.98 | 713.83 | 756.02 | 778.32 | 764.10 | 732.49 | 782.77 | 834.92 |
| Eritrean nakfa | 643 | 21.412 | 21.975 | 23.130 | 24.296 | 23.682 | 24.103 | 23.678 | 23.605 | 23.630 | 23.678 | 22.275 | . . . . |
| Ethiopian birr | 644 | 13.436 | 12.408 | 13.202 | 14.539 | 15.334 | 19.818 | 25.489 | 26.419 | 27.948 | . . . . | . . . . | . . . . |
| Gabon, CFA franc | 646 | 747.90 | 794.73 | 749.30 | 704.15 | 725.98 | 713.83 | 756.02 | 778.32 | 764.10 | 732.49 | 782.77 | 834.92 |
| Gambian dalasi | 648 | 46.084 | 40.212 | 42.194 | 35.618 | 40.882 | 42.235 | 43.720 | 46.427 | 52.132 | 58.381 | 65.602 | . . . . |
| Ghanaian cedi | 652 | 1.4061 | 1.3050 | 1.3894 | 1.5335 | 1.8700 | 2.2239 | 2.2697 | 2.3804 | 2.8894 | 3.3880 | 4.6363 | 5.2588 |
| Guinea franc | 656 | 3,516 | 6,443 | 8,493 | 6,601 | 7,988 | 7,692 | 9,328 | 10,850 | 10,715 | 10,789 | 10,468 | 11,100 |
| Guinea-Bissau, CFA franc | 654 | 747.90 | 794.73 | 749.30 | 704.15 | 725.98 | 713.83 | 756.02 | 778.32 | 764.10 | 732.49 | 782.77 | 834.92 |
| Kenya shilling | 664 | 120.12 | 103.43 | 104.40 | 99.04 | 119.70 | 118.86 | 124.36 | 130.60 | 132.18 | 132.92 | 131.12 | 141.78 |
| Lesotho loti | 666 | 8.74 | 9.04 | 10.49 | 10.76 | 14.33 | 11.57 | 10.21 | 12.50 | 13.07 | 16.15 | 16.78 | 21.54 |
| Liberian dollar | 668 | 84.64 | 80.75 | 89.51 | 98.77 | 98.58 | 110.52 | 110.11 | 111.31 | 111.43 | 127.05 | 119.53 | . . . . |
| Malagasy ariary | 674 | 2,903.2 | 3,087.0 | 3,029.8 | 2,823.4 | 2,865.5 | 3,064.3 | 3,305.1 | 3,450.5 | 3,489.7 | 3,443.6 | 3,762.2 | 4,433.2 |
| Malawi kwacha | 676 | 169.19 | 176.92 | 209.63 | 221.73 | 216.56 | 228.88 | 232.24 | 251.40 | 515.06 | 669.83 | 682.07 | . . . . |
| Mali, CFA franc | 678 | 747.90 | 794.73 | 749.30 | 704.15 | 725.98 | 713.83 | 756.02 | 778.32 | 764.10 | 732.49 | 782.77 | 834.92 |
| Mauritian rupee | 684 | 43.802 | 43.831 | 51.656 | 44.589 | 48.912 | 47.486 | 46.803 | 45.024 | 46.914 | 46.322 | 45.968 | 49.732 |
| Mozambique, metical | 688 | 29.351 | 34.564 | 39.069 | 37.642 | 39.277 | 45.761 | 50.174 | 41.928 | 45.723 | 46.323 | 48.680 | 63.605 |
| Namibia dollar | 728 | 8.743 | 9.040 | 10.486 | 10.762 | 14.332 | 11.570 | 10.213 | 12.502 | 13.066 | 16.154 | 16.779 | 21.541 |
| Niger, CFA franc | 692 | 747.90 | 794.73 | 749.30 | 704.15 | 725.98 | 713.83 | 756.02 | 778.32 | 764.10 | 732.49 | 782.77 | 834.92 |
| Nigerian naira | 694 | 205.54 | 184.38 | 192.97 | 186.42 | 204.18 | 234.50 | 232.02 | 242.98 | 241.80 | 242.18 | 245.83 | 272.99 |
| Rwanda franc | 714 | 880.34 | 791.41 | 825.39 | 860.00 | 860.85 | 895.53 | 915.47 | 927.52 | 970.42 | 1,031.92 | 1,006.02 | 1,035.70 |
| São Tomé & Príncipe dobra | 716 | 15,692 | 17,051 | 19,668 | 22,696 | 23,455 | 26,360 | 28,237 | 29,070 | 28,539 | 27,358 | 29,236 | 31,184 |
| Senegal, CFA franc | 722 | 747.90 | 794.73 | 749.30 | 704.15 | 725.98 | 713.83 | 756.02 | 778.32 | 764.10 | 732.49 | 782.77 | 834.92 |
| Seychelles rupee | 718 | 8.513 | 7.860 | 8.715 | 12.625 | 25.480 | 17.491 | 18.709 | 21.071 | 19.983 | 18.597 | 20.340 | 18.229 |
| Sierra Leonean leone | 724 | 4,321.9 | 4,191.4 | 4,474.0 | 4,705.4 | 4,685.9 | 6,044.5 | 6,465.1 | 6,721.0 | 6,661.2 | 6,708.8 | 7,176.4 | 7,814.3 |
| South African rand | 199 | 8.743 | 9.040 | 10.486 | 10.762 | 14.332 | 11.570 | 10.213 | 12.502 | 13.066 | 16.154 | 16.779 | 21.541 |
| South Sudanese pound | 733 | . . . . | . . . . | . . . . | . . . . | . . . . | . . . . | . . . . | 4.5290 | 4.5339 | 4.5430 | 4.2740 | 23.0324 |
| Swaziland lilangeni | 734 | 8.743 | 9.040 | 10.486 | 10.762 | 14.332 | 11.570 | 10.213 | 12.502 | 13.066 | 16.154 | 16.779 | 21.541 |
| Tanzanian shilling | 738 | 1,619.7 | 1,665.8 | 1,898.0 | 1,789.0 | 1,972.0 | 2,080.1 | 2,241.0 | 2,413.0 | 2,415.5 | 2,431.0 | 2,500.3 | 2,977.3 |
| Togo, CFA franc | 742 | 747.90 | 794.73 | 749.30 | 704.15 | 725.98 | 713.83 | 756.02 | 778.32 | 764.10 | 732.49 | 782.77 | 834.92 |
| Uganda shilling | 746 | 2,700.0 | 2,596.8 | 2,619.8 | 2,682.2 | 3,002.3 | 2,978.2 | 3,554.9 | 3,824.3 | 4,128.1 | 3,893.1 | 4,017.6 | 4,679.6 |
| Zambian new kwacha | 754 | 7.4099 | 5.0153 | 6.6294 | 6.0758 | 7.4430 | 7.2750 | 7.3862 | 7.8560 | 7.9099 | 8.4894 | 9.2619 | 15.2180 |
| **Western Hemisphere** | | | | | | | | | | | | | |
| Anguilla, E.Caribbean dollar | 312 | 4.1931 | 3.8590 | 4.0619 | 4.2667 | 4.1587 | 4.2328 | 4.1581 | 4.1452 | 4.1497 | 4.1580 | 3.9118 | 3.7415 |
| Antigua & Barbuda, E.Car.dollar | 311 | 4.1931 | 3.8590 | 4.0619 | 4.2667 | 4.1587 | 4.2328 | 4.1581 | 4.1452 | 4.1497 | 4.1580 | 3.9118 | 3.7415 |
| Argentine peso | 213 | 4.5954 | 4.3050 | 4.5764 | 4.9446 | 5.2877 | 5.9259 | 6.0924 | 6.5771 | 7.5278 | 10.0115 | 12.3294 | 18.1531 |
| Aruban florin | 314 | 2.7799 | 2.5584 | 2.6929 | 2.8286 | 2.7571 | 2.8062 | 2.7567 | 2.7481 | 2.7511 | 2.7566 | 2.5934 | 2.4805 |
| Bahamian dollar | 313 | 1.5530 | 1.4293 | 1.5044 | 1.5803 | 1.5403 | 1.5677 | 1.5400 | 1.5353 | 1.5369 | 1.5400 | 1.4488 | 1.3857 |
| Barbados dollar | 316 | 3.1060 | 2.8585 | 3.0088 | 3.1605 | 3.0805 | 3.1354 | 3.0801 | 3.0705 | 3.0738 | 3.0800 | 2.8976 | 2.7715 |
| Belize dollar | 339 | 3.1060 | 2.8585 | 3.0088 | 3.1605 | 3.0805 | 3.1354 | 3.0801 | 3.0705 | 3.0738 | 3.0800 | 2.8976 | 2.7715 |
| Bolivia, boliviano | 218 | 12.502 | 11.491 | 12.005 | 12.042 | 10.813 | 11.005 | 10.765 | 10.609 | 10.620 | 10.641 | 10.011 | 9.575 |
| Brazilian real | 223 | 4.1211 | 3.3443 | 3.2152 | 2.7978 | 3.5984 | 2.7284 | 2.5962 | 2.8538 | 3.1481 | 3.6249 | 3.8483 | 5.4102 |
| Chilean peso | 228 | 869.42 | 734.94 | 804.00 | 783.52 | 969.00 | 793.93 | 721.30 | 800.58 | 735.57 | 806.59 | 879.98 | 980.18 |
| Colombian peso | 233 | 3,746.0 | 3,264.8 | 3,348.0 | 3,141.2 | 3,385.7 | 3,204.7 | 3,064.5 | 2,982.6 | 2,722.7 | 2,960.7 | 3,466.2 | 4,364.3 |
| Costa Rican colon | 238 | 712.23 | 709.89 | 779.12 | 787.12 | 855.57 | 886.12 | 789.99 | 785.81 | 781.06 | 772.16 | 781.52 | 746.08 |
| Dominica, E.Caribbean dollar | 321 | 4.1931 | 3.8590 | 4.0619 | 4.2667 | 4.1587 | 4.2328 | 4.1581 | 4.1452 | 4.1497 | 4.1580 | 3.9118 | 3.7415 |

# Exchange Rates

| | | 2004 | 2005 | 2006 | 2007 | 2008 | 2009 | 2010 | 2011 | 2012 | 2013 | 2014 | 2015 |
|---|---|---|---|---|---|---|---|---|---|---|---|---|---|
| | | | | | | B. Market, Official, or Principal Rate | | | | | | | |
| | | | | | | *National Currency Units per SDR: End of Period (aa)* | | | | | | | |
| **Western Hemisphere(Cont.)** | | | | | | | | | | | | | |
| Dominican peso | 243 | 48.313 | 49.851 | 50.422 | 53.837 | 55.115 | 57.034 | 58.408 | 59.555 | 62.037 | 65.989 | 64.309 | 63.267 |
| Salvadoran colon | 253 | 13.589 | 12.506 | 13.164 | 13.827 | 13.477 | 13.717 | 13.475 | 13.434 | 13.448 | 13.475 | 12.677 | 12.125 |
| Grenada, E.Caribbean dollar | 328 | 4.1931 | 3.8590 | 4.0619 | 4.2667 | 4.1587 | 4.2328 | 4.1581 | 4.1452 | 4.1497 | 4.1580 | 3.9118 | 3.7415 |
| Guatemalan quetzal | 258 | 12.033 | 10.877 | 11.470 | 12.059 | 11.975 | 13.086 | 12.345 | 11.985 | 12.134 | 12.092 | 11.004 | 10.605 |
| Guyana dollar | 336 | 310.21 | 286.21 | 302.38 | 321.58 | 316.14 | 318.63 | 313.40 | 312.81 | 313.92 | 317.63 | 299.18 | 286.15 |
| Haitian gourde | 263 | 57.821 | 61.459 | 56.553 | 58.129 | 61.330 | 65.873 | 61.419 | 62.911 | 65.401 | 67.578 | 67.729 | 78.567 |
| Honduran lempira | 268 | 28.937 | 27.006 | 28.426 | 29.859 | 29.104 | 29.622 | 29.099 | 29.244 | 30.680 | 31.720 | 31.167 | 30.995 |
| Jamaica dollar | 343 | 95.43 | 92.02 | 100.84 | 111.24 | 123.56 | 140.04 | 131.83 | 132.60 | 142.26 | 163.31 | 165.73 | 166.33 |
| Mexican peso | 273 | 17.494 | 15.404 | 16.369 | 17.171 | 20.853 | 20.472 | 19.030 | 21.479 | 19.995 | 20.138 | 21.324 | 23.844 |
| Montserrat, E.Caribbean dollar | 351 | 4.1931 | 3.8590 | 4.0619 | 4.2667 | 4.1587 | 4.2328 | 4.1581 | 4.1452 | 4.1497 | 4.1580 | 3.9118 | 3.7415 |
| Nicaraguan gold córdoba | 278 | 25.359 | 24.506 | 27.083 | 29.871 | 30.571 | 32.671 | 33.700 | 35.275 | 37.079 | 39.011 | 38.536 | 38.701 |
| Panamanian balboa | 283 | 1.5530 | 1.4293 | 1.5044 | 1.5803 | 1.5403 | 1.5677 | 1.5400 | 1.5353 | 1.5369 | 1.5400 | 1.4488 | 1.3857 |
| Paraguayan guarani | 288 | 9,706.3 | 8,747.1 | 7,807.8 | 7,703.7 | 7,616.6 | 7,227.1 | 7,043.7 | 6,816.5 | 6,591.5 | 6,967.0 | 6,702.6 | 8,046.8 |
| Peruvian new sol | 293 | 5.0962 | 4.9024 | 4.8073 | 4.7344 | 4.8357 | 4.5298 | 4.3252 | 4.1391 | 3.9191 | 4.3043 | 4.3247 | 4.7260 |
| St.Kitts & Nevis, E.Car. dollar | 361 | 4.1931 | 3.8590 | 4.0619 | 4.2667 | 4.1587 | 4.2328 | 4.1581 | 4.1452 | 4.1497 | 4.1580 | 3.9118 | 3.7415 |
| St.Lucia, E.Caribbean dollar | 362 | 4.1931 | 3.8590 | 4.0619 | 4.2667 | 4.1587 | 4.2328 | 4.1581 | 4.1452 | 4.1497 | 4.1580 | 3.9118 | 3.7415 |
| St. Vinc. & Grens., E.Car. dollar | 364 | 4.1931 | 3.8590 | 4.0619 | 4.2667 | 4.1587 | 4.2328 | 4.1581 | 4.1452 | 4.1497 | 4.1580 | 3.9118 | 3.7415 |
| Surinamese dollar | 366 | 4.2164 | 3.9162 | 4.1296 | 4.3378 | 4.2280 | 4.3033 | 4.2274 | 5.0664 | 5.0718 | 5.0820 | 4.7811 | 5.5429 |
| Trinidad & Tobago dollar | 369 | 9.7838 | 9.0191 | 9.4956 | 10.0207 | 9.7026 | 9.9917 | 9.8922 | 9.8497 | 9.8859 | 9.9584 | 9.2618 | 8.9370 |
| Uruguayan peso | 298 | 40.922 | 34.445 | 36.707 | 33.975 | 37.506 | 30.769 | 30.945 | 30.549 | 29.815 | 32.939 | 35.254 | 41.396 |
| Venezuelan bolivar | 299 | 2.9787 | 3.0686 | 3.2299 | 3.3928 | 3.3070 | 3.3658 | 3.9941 | 6.5852 | 6.5923 | 9.6777 | 9.1046 | 8.7082 |

# Fund Accounts: Position to Date

*(As of May 31, 2016 and Expressed in Millions of SDRs)*

| | | Quota | Reserve Tranche Position | Lending to the Fund (GRA) | Total Fund Credit and Loans Outstanding | | | Fund Holdings of Currency | | SDR Department | | |
| | | | | | Total Amount | Outstanding Purchases (GRA) | Outstanding Loans (PRGT) | Amount | Percent of Quota | Net Cumulative Allocation | Holdings of SDR | |
| | | | | | | | | | | | SDR Holdings | Percent of Allocation |
| | | (1) | (2) | (3) | (4) | (5) | (6) | (7) | (8) | (9) | (10) | (11) |
|---|---|---|---|---|---|---|---|---|---|---|---|---|
| World............................ | 001 | 471,571.1 | 45,880.1 | 31,668.1 | 54,476.8 | 48,011.1 | 6,465.7 | 473,709.3 | 100.5 | 204,177.4 | 204,177.4 | 100.0 |
| Advanced Economies... | 110 | 292,382.7 | 26,395.4 | 24,895.5 | 30,650.5 | 30,650.5 | — | 296,641.2 | 101.5 | 128,629.7 | 117,144.6 | 91.1 |
| Euro Area | | | | | | | | | | | | |
| Austria......................... | 122 | 3,932.0 | 460.9 | 328.0 | — | — | — | 3,471.1 | 88.3 | 1,736.3 | 1,624.4 | 93.6 |
| Belgium....................... | 124 | 6,410.7 | 219.9 | 720.4 | — | — | — | 6,190.9 | 96.6 | 4,323.3 | 3,841.9 | 88.9 |
| Cyprus......................... | 423 | 303.8 | 85.1 | 31.4 | 792.0 | 792.0 | — | 1,010.8 | 332.7 | 132.8 | 59.2 | 44.6 |
| Estonia........................ | 939 | 243.6 | 51.6 | — | — | — | — | 192.0 | 78.8 | 62.0 | 24.6 | 39.7 |
| Finland........................ | 172 | 2,410.6 | 294.0 | 200.2 | — | — | — | 2,116.6 | 87.8 | 1,189.5 | 1,123.1 | 94.4 |
| France......................... | 132 | 20,155.1 | 2,388.5 | 1,695.4 | — | — | — | 17,766.7 | 88.1 | 10,134.2 | 7,319.1 | 72.2 |
| Germany...................... | 134 | 26,634.4 | 3,116.4 | 2,321.6 | — | — | — | 23,518.0 | 88.3 | 12,059.2 | 11,902.9 | 98.7 |
| Greece......................... | 174 | 2,428.9 | 572.8 | — | 11,305.9 | 11,305.9 | — | 13,162.0 | 541.9 | 782.4 | 5.7 | .7 |
| Ireland........................ | 178 | 3,449.9 | 806.8 | — | 3,772.8 | 3,772.8 | — | 6,416.0 | 186.0 | 775.4 | 651.1 | 84.0 |
| Italy............................ | 136 | 15,070.0 | 377.8 | 1,243.2 | — | — | — | 14,692.3 | 97.5 | 6,576.1 | 5,109.0 | 77.7 |
| Latvia.......................... | 941 | 332.3 | .1 | — | — | — | — | 332.3 | 100.0 | 120.8 | 120.8 | 100.0 |
| Lithuania..................... | 946 | 441.6 | — | — | — | — | — | 441.6 | 100.0 | 137.2 | 137.3 | 100.0 |
| Luxembourg................. | 137 | 1,321.8 | 231.1 | 89.5 | — | — | — | 1,090.7 | 82.5 | 246.6 | 244.5 | 99.1 |
| Malta.......................... | 181 | 168.3 | 45.9 | .8 | — | — | — | 122.4 | 72.7 | 95.4 | 87.5 | 91.7 |
| Netherlands................. | 138 | 8,736.5 | 254.0 | 827.8 | — | — | — | 8,482.5 | 97.1 | 4,836.6 | 4,510.3 | 93.3 |
| Portugal...................... | 182 | 2,060.1 | 465.5 | — | 14,779.8 | 14,779.8 | — | 16,374.4 | 794.8 | 806.5 | 535.5 | 66.4 |
| Slovak Republic............ | 936 | 1,001.0 | 153.4 | 2.9 | — | — | — | 847.6 | 84.7 | 340.5 | 179.3 | 52.7 |
| Slovenia...................... | 961 | 586.5 | 156.2 | 1.8 | — | — | — | 430.4 | 73.4 | 215.9 | 162.5 | 75.3 |
| Spain.......................... | 184 | 9,535.5 | 468.2 | 613.4 | — | — | — | 9,067.3 | 95.1 | 2,827.6 | 2,769.4 | 97.9 |
| Australia..................... | 193 | 6,572.4 | 69.0 | 392.5 | — | — | — | 6,503.8 | 99.0 | 3,083.2 | 2,808.8 | 91.1 |
| Canada........................ | 156 | 11,023.9 | 975.2 | 698.5 | — | — | — | 10,048.8 | 91.2 | 5,988.1 | 5,695.5 | 95.1 |
| Czech Republic.............. | 935 | 2,180.2 | 342.6 | 6.5 | — | — | — | 1,837.6 | 84.3 | 780.2 | 457.2 | 58.6 |
| Denmark...................... | 128 | 3,439.4 | 65.9 | 287.9 | — | — | — | 3,373.5 | 98.1 | 1,531.5 | 1,450.7 | 94.7 |
| Iceland........................ | 176 | 321.8 | 69.8 | — | — | — | — | 252.0 | 78.3 | 112.2 | 111.7 | 99.6 |
| Israel........................... | 436 | 1,920.9 | 32.2 | 44.5 | — | — | — | 1,888.8 | 98.3 | 883.4 | 845.4 | 95.7 |
| Japan.......................... | 158 | 30,820.5 | 3,719.5 | 4,981.5 | — | — | — | 27,101.5 | 87.9 | 12,285.0 | 12,387.2 | 100.8 |
| Korea.......................... | 542 | 8,582.7 | 693.5 | 591.5 | — | — | — | 7,889.2 | 91.9 | 2,404.4 | 1,816.0 | 75.5 |
| New Zealand................ | 196 | 1,252.1 | 129.5 | 56.2 | — | — | — | 1,122.7 | 89.7 | 853.8 | 776.1 | 90.9 |
| Norway........................ | 142 | 3,754.7 | 229.9 | 347.4 | — | — | — | 3,524.8 | 93.9 | 1,563.1 | 1,271.8 | 81.4 |
| San Marino.................. | 135 | 49.2 | 12.2 | — | — | — | — | 37.0 | 75.3 | 15.5 | 8.8 | 56.4 |
| Singapore.................... | 576 | 3,891.9 | 630.7 | 117.8 | — | — | — | 3,261.6 | 83.8 | 744.2 | 744.3 | 100.0 |
| Sweden........................ | 144 | 4,430.0 | 81.2 | 390.0 | — | — | — | 4,348.8 | 98.2 | 2,249.0 | 2,116.8 | 94.1 |
| Switzerland.................. | 146 | 5,771.1 | 12.9 | 978.0 | — | — | — | 5,758.2 | 99.8 | 3,288.0 | 3,273.7 | 99.6 |
| United Kingdom............ | 112 | 20,155.1 | 3,531.9 | 1,672.4 | — | — | — | 16,623.3 | 82.5 | 10,134.2 | 7,113.8 | 70.2 |
| United States............... | 111 | 82,994.2 | 5,651.4 | 6,224.6 | — | — | — | 77,344.0 | 93.2 | 35,315.7 | 35,858.6 | 101.5 |
| Emerging & Dev. Econ.. | 200 | 179,188.4 | 19,484.7 | 6,772.6 | 23,826.4 | 17,360.6 | 6,465.7 | 177,068.1 | 98.8 | 75,461.0 | 54,080.4 | 71.7 |
| Emerging & Dev. Asia.. | 505 | 61,652.5 | 9,156.8 | 3,296.0 | 1,061.3 | 318.6 | 742.8 | 52,814.8 | 85.7 | 18,300.1 | 14,012.6 | 76.6 |
| Bangladesh................... | 513 | 1,066.6 | 134.0 | — | 643.3 | — | 643.3 | 932.7 | 87.4 | 510.4 | 971.3 | 190.3 |
| Bhutan........................ | 514 | 20.4 | 4.5 | — | — | — | — | 15.9 | 77.7 | 6.0 | 6.0 | 100.0 |
| Brunei Darussalam......... | 516 | 301.3 | 35.2 | — | — | — | — | 266.3 | 88.4 | 203.5 | 216.5 | 106.4 |
| Cambodia..................... | 522 | 175.0 | 21.9 | — | — | — | — | 153.1 | 87.5 | 83.9 | 88.3 | 105.3 |
| China, P.R.: Mainland..... | 924 | 30,482.9 | 5,066.2 | 2,362.7 | — | — | — | 25,416.7 | 83.4 | 6,989.7 | 7,442.8 | 106.5 |
| Fiji............................... | 819 | 98.4 | 23.7 | — | — | — | — | 74.7 | 75.9 | 67.1 | 44.0 | 65.7 |
| India........................... | 534 | 13,114.4 | 1,725.2 | 800.7 | — | — | — | 11,389.3 | 86.8 | 3,978.3 | 1,065.6 | 26.8 |
| Indonesia..................... | 536 | 4,648.4 | 787.8 | — | — | — | — | 3,860.6 | 83.1 | 1,980.4 | 1,118.6 | 56.5 |
| Kiribati........................ | 826 | 5.6 | — | — | — | — | — | 5.6 | 100.0 | 5.3 | 5.4 | 101.3 |
| Lao People's Dem. Rep... | 544 | 105.8 | 13.2 | — | — | — | — | 92.6 | 87.5 | 50.7 | 37.8 | 74.7 |
| Malaysia...................... | 548 | 3,633.8 | 523.2 | 50.7 | — | — | — | 3,110.6 | 85.6 | 1,346.1 | 821.9 | 61.1 |
| Maldives...................... | 556 | 21.2 | 4.8 | — | 1.6 | — | 1.6 | 16.4 | 77.3 | 7.7 | 3.6 | 46.2 |
| Marshall Islands,Rep..... | 867 | 3.5 | — | — | — | — | — | 3.5 | 100.0 | 3.3 | 3.4 | 101.1 |
| Micronesia, Fed.Sts........ | 868 | 5.1 | — | — | — | — | — | 5.1 | 100.0 | 4.8 | 6.2 | 129.6 |
| Mongolia..................... | 948 | 72.3 | 5.4 | — | — | — | — | 66.9 | 92.5 | 48.8 | 42.9 | 88.0 |
| Myanmar..................... | 518 | 516.8 | — | — | — | — | — | 516.8 | 100.0 | 245.8 | 1.7 | .7 |
| Nepal.......................... | 558 | 156.9 | 16.0 | — | 69.2 | — | 69.2 | 140.9 | 89.8 | 68.1 | 4.1 | 6.1 |
| Palau.......................... | 565 | 3.1 | — | — | — | — | — | 3.1 | 100.0 | 3.0 | 3.0 | 101.1 |
| Papua New Guinea........ | 853 | 131.6 | .5 | — | — | — | — | 131.2 | 99.7 | 125.5 | 9.1 | 7.3 |
| Philippines................... | 566 | 2,042.9 | 269.4 | 29.9 | — | — | — | 1,773.5 | 86.8 | 838.0 | 846.5 | 101.0 |
| Samoa......................... | 862 | 16.2 | 1.8 | — | 10.4 | — | 10.4 | 14.4 | 88.7 | 11.1 | 10.3 | 93.2 |
| Solomon Islands............ | 813 | 20.8 | 3.2 | — | 9.7 | — | 9.7 | 17.7 | 84.9 | 9.9 | 5.6 | 56.3 |
| Sri Lanka..................... | 524 | 578.8 | 47.9 | — | 310.1 | 310.1 | — | 841.0 | 145.3 | 395.5 | 3.9 | 1.0 |
| Thailand...................... | 578 | 3,211.9 | 460.4 | 52.0 | — | — | — | 2,751.5 | 85.7 | 970.3 | 974.8 | 100.5 |
| Timor-Leste.................. | 537 | 25.6 | 4.4 | — | — | — | — | 21.3 | 83.0 | 7.7 | 3.4 | 44.0 |
| Tonga.......................... | 866 | 13.8 | 3.4 | — | — | — | — | 10.4 | 75.1 | 6.6 | 5.4 | 81.5 |
| Tuvalu......................... | 869 | 2.5 | .6 | — | — | — | — | 1.9 | 75.7 | 1.7 | 1.1 | 64.3 |
| Vanuatu....................... | 846 | 23.8 | 4.2 | — | 17.0 | 8.5 | 8.5 | 28.1 | 118.1 | 16.3 | 1.4 | 8.4 |
| Vietnam....................... | 582 | 1,153.1 | — | — | — | — | — | 1,153.1 | 100.0 | 314.8 | 267.9 | 85.1 |
| Europe........................ | 170 | 34,077.1 | 2,624.0 | 1,027.6 | 9,355.1 | 8,802.5 | 552.6 | 40,255.9 | 118.1 | 14,805.4 | 9,527.9 | 64.4 |
| Emer. & Dev. Europe.. | 903 | 15,365.7 | 847.6 | 227.5 | 731.2 | 728.6 | 2.6 | 15,246.8 | 99.2 | 6,109.2 | 2,786.2 | 45.6 |
| Albania....................... | 914 | 139.3 | 26.0 | — | 214.2 | 211.6 | 2.6 | 324.9 | 233.3 | 46.5 | 142.5 | 306.9 |
| Bosnia and Herzegovina | 963 | 169.1 | — | — | 403.7 | 403.7 | — | 572.8 | 338.7 | 160.9 | .5 | .3 |
| Bulgaria...................... | 918 | 896.3 | 98.1 | — | — | — | — | 798.2 | 89.1 | 610.9 | 611.6 | 100.1 |
| Croatia........................ | 960 | 717.4 | .2 | — | — | — | — | 717.2 | 100.0 | 347.3 | 304.9 | 87.8 |
| Hungary...................... | 944 | 1,940.0 | 299.2 | — | — | — | — | 1,640.8 | 84.6 | 991.1 | 12.1 | 1.2 |
| Kosovo........................ | 967 | 82.6 | 20.1 | — | 113.3 | 113.3 | — | 175.8 | 212.8 | 55.4 | 44.6 | 80.5 |
| Macedonia, FYR............ | 962 | 140.3 | — | — | — | — | — | 140.3 | 100.0 | 65.6 | 3.8 | 5.7 |
| Montenegro................. | 943 | 60.5 | 14.9 | — | — | — | — | 45.7 | 75.5 | 25.8 | 18.1 | 70.1 |
| Poland......................... | 964 | 4,095.4 | 229.5 | 227.5 | — | — | — | 3,865.9 | 94.4 | 1,304.6 | 313.0 | 24.0 |
| Romania...................... | 968 | 1,811.4 | — | — | — | — | — | 1,811.4 | 100.0 | 984.8 | 358.1 | 36.4 |
| Serbia, Republic of........ | 942 | 654.8 | 46.8 | — | — | — | — | 608.0 | 92.9 | 445.0 | 11.0 | 2.5 |
| Turkey......................... | 186 | 4,658.6 | 112.8 | — | — | — | — | 4,545.8 | 97.6 | 1,071.3 | 966.1 | 90.2 |

# Fund Accounts: Position to Date

*(As of May 31, 2016 and Expressed in Millions of SDRs)*

| | | Quota | Reserve Tranche Position | Lending to the Fund (GRA) | Total Fund Credit and Loans Outstanding — Total Amount | Total Fund Credit and Loans Outstanding — Outstanding Purchases (GRA) | Total Fund Credit and Loans Outstanding — Outstanding Loans (PRGT) | Fund Holdings of Currency — Amount | Fund Holdings of Currency — Percent of Quota | SDR Department — Net Cumulative Allocation | SDR Department — Holdings of SDR — SDR Holdings | SDR Department — Holdings of SDR — Percent of Allocation |
|---|---|---|---|---|---|---|---|---|---|---|---|---|
| | | (1) | (2) | (3) | (4) | (5) | (6) | (7) | (8) | (9) | (10) | (11) |
| CIS | 901 | 18,711.4 | 1,776.3 | 800.1 | 8,624.0 | 8,073.9 | 550.0 | 25,009.1 | 133.7 | 8,696.2 | 6,741.7 | 77.5 |
| Armenia | 911 | 128.8 | — | — | 296.0 | 159.9 | 136.1 | 288.7 | 224.1 | 88.0 | 8.4 | 9.5 |
| Azerbaijan, Rep. of | 912 | 391.7 | 57.8 | — | — | — | — | 333.9 | 85.2 | 153.6 | 95.9 | 62.4 |
| Belarus | 913 | 681.5 | — | — | — | — | — | 681.5 | 100.0 | 368.6 | 371.8 | 100.9 |
| Georgia | 915 | 210.4 | — | — | 88.4 | 80.0 | 8.4 | 290.4 | 138.0 | 144.0 | 144.1 | 100.1 |
| Kazakhstan | 916 | 1,158.4 | 198.2 | — | — | — | — | 960.2 | 82.9 | 343.7 | 348.3 | 101.4 |
| Kyrgyz Republic | 917 | 88.8 | — | — | 132.1 | — | 132.1 | 88.8 | 100.0 | 84.7 | 129.1 | 152.3 |
| Moldova | 921 | 172.5 | — | — | 315.4 | 133.3 | 182.1 | 305.8 | 177.3 | 117.7 | 3.4 | 2.9 |
| Russia | 922 | 12,903.7 | 1,479.4 | 800.1 | — | — | — | 11,424.3 | 88.5 | 5,671.8 | 4,822.4 | 85.0 |
| Tajikistan | 923 | 174.0 | — | — | 91.3 | — | 91.3 | 174.0 | 100.0 | 82.1 | 22.2 | 27.0 |
| Turkmenistan | 925 | 238.6 | 40.9 | — | — | — | — | 197.8 | 82.9 | 69.8 | 29.0 | 41.5 |
| Ukraine | 926 | 2,011.8 | — | — | 7,700.8 | 7,700.8 | — | 9,712.6 | 482.8 | 1,309.4 | 501.2 | 38.3 |
| Uzbekistan | 927 | 551.2 | — | — | — | — | — | 551.2 | 100.0 | 262.8 | 266.1 | 101.2 |
| Mid.East, N.Afr.& Pak. | 440 | 30,713.2 | 3,109.8 | 1,048.6 | 7,972.8 | 7,607.1 | 365.7 | 35,212.3 | 114.6 | 17,997.1 | 14,616.3 | 81.2 |
| Afghanistan, Islamic Rep. | 512 | 323.8 | .2 | — | 53.8 | — | 53.8 | 323.6 | 99.9 | 155.3 | 83.0 | 53.4 |
| Algeria | 612 | 1,959.9 | 188.1 | — | — | — | — | 1,771.8 | 90.4 | 1,198.2 | 898.5 | 75.0 |
| Bahrain, Kingdom of | 419 | 395.0 | 136.2 | — | — | — | — | 258.8 | 65.5 | 124.4 | 64.7 | 52.1 |
| Djibouti | 611 | 31.8 | 5.1 | — | 19.9 | — | 19.9 | 26.7 | 84.0 | 15.2 | 1.9 | 12.7 |
| Egypt | 469 | 2,037.1 | 273.4 | — | — | — | — | 1,763.8 | 86.6 | 898.5 | 565.3 | 62.9 |
| Iran, I.R. of | 429 | 3,567.1 | 517.5 | — | — | — | — | 3,049.7 | 85.5 | 1,426.1 | 1,536.7 | 107.8 |
| Iraq | 433 | 1,663.8 | 290.0 | — | 891.3 | 891.3 | — | 2,265.2 | 136.1 | 1,134.5 | 25.7 | 2.3 |
| Jordan | 439 | 343.1 | .4 | — | 1,268.1 | 1,268.1 | — | 1,610.8 | 469.5 | 162.1 | 84.4 | 52.1 |
| Kuwait | 443 | 1,933.5 | 155.5 | 50.8 | — | — | — | 1,779.0 | 92.0 | 1,315.6 | 1,327.2 | 100.9 |
| Lebanon | 446 | 266.4 | 34.7 | — | — | — | — | 231.7 | 87.0 | 193.3 | 192.3 | 99.5 |
| Libya | 672 | 1,573.2 | 408.2 | — | — | — | — | 1,165.0 | 74.1 | 1,072.7 | 1,623.8 | 151.4 |
| Mauritania | 682 | 128.8 | 16.1 | — | 76.6 | — | 76.6 | 112.7 | 87.5 | 61.7 | 1.2 | 1.9 |
| Morocco | 686 | 894.4 | 147.0 | — | — | — | — | 747.4 | 83.6 | 561.4 | 550.5 | 98.1 |
| Oman | 449 | 544.4 | 155.8 | — | — | — | — | 388.7 | 71.4 | 178.8 | 98.5 | 55.1 |
| Pakistan | 564 | 2,031.0 | .1 | — | 3,960.0 | 3,960.0 | — | 5,990.9 | 295.0 | 988.6 | 463.8 | 46.9 |
| Qatar | 453 | 735.1 | 201.2 | — | — | — | — | 533.9 | 72.6 | 251.4 | 271.3 | 107.9 |
| Saudi Arabia | 456 | 9,992.6 | 455.7 | 997.8 | — | — | — | 9,536.9 | 95.4 | 6,682.5 | 5,746.3 | 86.0 |
| Somalia | 726 | 44.2 | — | — | 111.5 | 96.2 | 15.3 | 140.5 | 317.8 | 46.5 | 18.3 | 39.4 |
| Sudan | 732 | 169.7 | — | — | 220.6 | 161.4 | 59.2 | 331.1 | 195.1 | 178.0 | 125.2 | 70.3 |
| Syrian Arab Republic | 463 | 293.6 | — | — | — | — | — | 293.6 | 100.0 | 279.2 | 282.2 | 101.1 |
| Tunisia | 744 | 545.2 | 121.1 | — | 1,230.0 | 1,230.0 | — | 1,654.1 | 303.4 | 272.8 | 45.0 | 16.5 |
| United Arab Emirates | 466 | 752.5 | 3.6 | — | — | — | — | 749.4 | 99.6 | 568.4 | 542.5 | 95.4 |
| Yemen, Republic of | 474 | 487.0 | — | — | 140.9 | — | 140.9 | 487.0 | 100.0 | 232.3 | 68.1 | 29.3 |
| Sub-Saharan Africa | 603 | 16,586.4 | 1,416.0 | 29.9 | 4,744.2 | 94.6 | 4,649.5 | 15,265.9 | 92.0 | 8,769.7 | 5,915.4 | 67.5 |
| Angola | 614 | 740.1 | 113.6 | — | 64.4 | 64.4 | — | 691.1 | 93.4 | 273.0 | 228.3 | 83.6 |
| Benin | 638 | 123.8 | 17.9 | — | 86.8 | — | 86.8 | 105.9 | 85.5 | 59.2 | 28.3 | 47.8 |
| Botswana | 616 | 197.2 | 53.6 | — | — | — | — | 143.6 | 72.8 | 57.4 | 58.4 | 101.7 |
| Burkina Faso | 748 | 120.4 | 22.8 | — | 144.5 | — | 144.5 | 97.6 | 81.1 | 57.6 | 19.9 | 34.6 |
| Burundi | 618 | 154.0 | 19.7 | — | 77.0 | — | 77.0 | 134.4 | 87.2 | 73.8 | 13.9 | 18.8 |
| Cameroon | 622 | 276.0 | 1.0 | — | 70.3 | — | 70.3 | 275.0 | 99.6 | 177.3 | 15.4 | 8.7 |
| Cape Verde | 624 | 11.2 | .4 | — | — | — | — | 10.8 | 96.4 | 9.2 | .8 | 8.9 |
| Central African Rep. | 626 | 111.4 | .4 | — | 68.5 | — | 68.5 | 111.0 | 99.6 | 53.4 | .1 | .1 |
| Chad | 628 | 140.2 | 3.1 | — | 45.4 | — | 45.4 | 137.2 | 97.8 | 53.6 | .1 | .1 |
| Comoros | 632 | 17.8 | 2.8 | — | 12.1 | — | 12.1 | 15.0 | 84.3 | 8.5 | 8.6 | 100.7 |
| Congo, Dem. Rep. of | 636 | 1,066.0 | — | — | 263.1 | — | 263.1 | 1,066.0 | 100.0 | 510.9 | 306.1 | 59.9 |
| Congo, Republic of | 634 | 84.6 | .6 | — | 8.0 | — | 8.0 | 84.0 | 99.3 | 79.7 | 70.3 | 88.3 |
| Côte d'Ivoire | 662 | 650.4 | 82.4 | — | 758.0 | — | 758.0 | 568.0 | 87.3 | 310.9 | 132.9 | 42.7 |
| Equatorial Guinea | 642 | 157.5 | 4.9 | — | — | — | — | 152.6 | 96.9 | 31.3 | 21.2 | 67.6 |
| Eritrea | 643 | 15.9 | — | — | — | — | — | 15.9 | 100.0 | 15.2 | 3.7 | 24.4 |
| Ethiopia | 644 | 300.7 | 7.5 | — | 143.7 | — | 143.7 | 293.3 | 97.5 | 127.9 | 53.7 | 42.0 |
| Gabon | 646 | 216.0 | 16.5 | — | — | — | — | 199.5 | 92.4 | 146.7 | 117.4 | 80.0 |
| Gambia, The | 648 | 62.2 | 9.3 | — | 32.0 | — | 32.0 | 52.9 | 85.1 | 29.8 | 7.6 | 25.5 |
| Ghana | 652 | 738.0 | 92.5 | — | 616.0 | — | 616.0 | 645.6 | 87.5 | 353.9 | 164.6 | 46.5 |
| Guinea | 656 | 214.2 | 26.9 | — | 161.2 | — | 161.2 | 187.4 | 87.5 | 102.5 | 118.7 | 115.9 |
| Guinea-Bissau | 654 | 28.4 | 3.9 | — | 13.6 | — | 13.6 | 24.5 | 86.3 | 13.6 | 8.8 | 64.9 |
| Kenya | 664 | 542.8 | 13.3 | — | 602.3 | — | 602.3 | 529.5 | 97.6 | 259.6 | 27.2 | 10.5 |
| Lesotho | 666 | 69.8 | 12.6 | — | 49.8 | — | 49.8 | 57.2 | 82.0 | 32.9 | 37.0 | 112.5 |
| Liberia | 668 | 258.4 | 32.3 | — | 115.7 | — | 115.7 | 226.1 | 87.5 | 124.0 | 153.6 | 123.9 |
| Madagascar | 674 | 122.2 | .1 | — | 80.5 | — | 80.5 | 122.1 | 99.9 | 117.1 | 53.7 | 45.9 |
| Malawi | 676 | 138.8 | 2.4 | — | 112.4 | — | 112.4 | 136.4 | 98.2 | 66.4 | 8.6 | 13.0 |
| Mali | 678 | 186.6 | 33.3 | — | 94.1 | — | 94.1 | 153.3 | 82.1 | 89.4 | 43.9 | 49.2 |
| Mauritius | 684 | 142.2 | 41.3 | — | — | — | — | 101.0 | 71.1 | 96.8 | 89.9 | 92.8 |
| Mozambique | 688 | 227.2 | 28.4 | — | 170.0 | — | 170.0 | 198.8 | 87.5 | 108.8 | 41.6 | 38.2 |
| Namibia | 728 | 191.1 | .1 | — | — | — | — | 191.0 | 100.0 | 130.4 | 4.8 | 3.7 |
| Niger | 692 | 131.6 | 25.1 | — | 106.3 | — | 106.3 | 106.5 | 80.9 | 62.9 | 29.6 | 47.0 |
| Nigeria | 694 | 2,454.5 | 175.5 | — | — | — | — | 2,279.1 | 92.9 | 1,675.4 | 1,499.7 | 89.5 |
| Rwanda | 714 | 160.2 | 20.0 | — | 3.3 | — | 3.3 | 140.2 | 87.5 | 76.8 | 57.1 | 74.3 |
| São Tomé & Príncipe | 716 | 14.8 | — | — | 2.9 | — | 2.9 | 14.8 | 100.0 | 7.1 | .3 | 4.4 |
| Senegal | 722 | 323.6 | 42.3 | — | 92.2 | — | 92.2 | 281.3 | 86.9 | 154.8 | 65.8 | 42.5 |
| Seychelles | 718 | 22.9 | 3.5 | — | 30.2 | 30.2 | — | 49.6 | 216.6 | 8.3 | 5.3 | 64.2 |
| Sierra Leone | 724 | 207.4 | — | — | 182.6 | — | 182.6 | 207.4 | 100.0 | 99.5 | 107.5 | 108.1 |
| South Africa | 199 | 3,051.2 | 420.5 | 29.9 | — | — | — | 2,630.7 | 86.2 | 1,785.4 | 1,492.5 | 83.6 |
| South Sudan, Republic of | 733 | 246.0 | — | — | — | — | — | 246.0 | 100.0 | 105.4 | 2.1 | 2.0 |
| Swaziland | 734 | 78.5 | 6.6 | — | — | — | — | 71.9 | 91.7 | 48.3 | 48.7 | 100.9 |
| Tanzania | 738 | 397.8 | 59.7 | — | 236.3 | — | 236.3 | 338.1 | 85.0 | 190.5 | 40.2 | 21.1 |
| Togo | 742 | 146.8 | 18.9 | — | 68.1 | — | 68.1 | 127.9 | 87.1 | 70.3 | 22.9 | 32.6 |
| Uganda | 746 | 361.0 | — | — | — | — | — | 361.0 | 100.0 | 173.1 | 47.2 | 27.3 |
| Zambia | 754 | 978.2 | — | — | 170.6 | — | 170.6 | 978.2 | 100.0 | 469.1 | 301.4 | 64.2 |
| Zimbabwe | 698 | 706.8 | .3 | — | 62.1 | — | 62.1 | 706.5 | 100.0 | 272.2 | 92.6 | 34.0 |

# Fund Accounts: Position to Date

*(As of May 31, 2016 and Expressed in Millions of SDRs)*

| | | Quota | Reserve Tranche Position | Lending to the Fund (GRA) | Total Fund Credit and Loans Outstanding | | | Fund Holdings of Currency | | SDR Department | Holdings of SDR | |
| | | | | | Total Amount | Outstanding Purchases (GRA) | Outstanding Loans (PRGT) | Amount | Percent of Quota | Net Cumulative Allocation | SDR Holdings | Percent of Allocation |
| | | (1) | (2) | (3) | (4) | (5) | (6) | (7) | (8) | (9) | (10) | (11) |
|---|---|---|---|---|---|---|---|---|---|---|---|---|
| West.Hemisphere | 205 | 36,159.2 | 3,178.0 | 1,370.5 | 692.9 | 537.8 | 155.1 | 33,519.3 | 92.7 | 15,588.7 | 10,008.2 | 64.2 |
| Antigua and Barbuda | 311 | 20.0 | .1 | — | 34.6 | 34.6 | — | 54.6 | 272.8 | 12.5 | — | .2 |
| Argentina | 213 | 2,117.1 | .2 | — | — | — | — | 2,116.9 | 100.0 | 2,020.0 | 2,053.0 | 101.6 |
| Bahamas, The | 313 | 182.4 | 19.3 | — | — | — | — | 163.1 | 89.4 | 124.4 | 54.1 | 43.5 |
| Barbados | 316 | 94.5 | 12.6 | — | — | — | — | 82.0 | 86.7 | 64.4 | 49.7 | 77.2 |
| Belize | 339 | 26.7 | 6.2 | — | — | — | — | 20.5 | 76.7 | 17.9 | 20.0 | 111.9 |
| Bolivia | 218 | 171.5 | 8.9 | — | — | — | — | 162.6 | 94.8 | 164.1 | 166.7 | 101.6 |
| Brazil | 223 | 11,042.0 | 875.2 | 799.8 | — | — | — | 10,166.9 | 92.1 | 2,887.1 | 2,596.8 | 89.9 |
| Chile | 228 | 1,744.3 | 38.8 | 122.3 | — | — | — | 1,705.5 | 97.8 | 816.9 | 541.0 | 66.2 |
| Colombia | 233 | 2,044.5 | 39.1 | — | — | — | — | 2,005.4 | 98.1 | 738.3 | 715.0 | 96.8 |
| Costa Rica | 238 | 369.4 | 71.3 | — | — | — | — | 298.1 | 80.7 | 156.5 | 85.1 | 54.4 |
| Dominica | 321 | 11.5 | — | — | 10.8 | — | 10.8 | 11.5 | 99.9 | 7.8 | .6 | 7.9 |
| Dominican Republic | 243 | 477.4 | 64.6 | — | 27.4 | 27.4 | — | 440.1 | 92.2 | 208.8 | 5.2 | 2.5 |
| Ecuador | 248 | 347.8 | 28.5 | — | — | — | — | 319.3 | 91.8 | 288.4 | 17.7 | 6.1 |
| El Salvador | 253 | 287.2 | — | — | — | — | — | 287.2 | 100.0 | 163.8 | 165.6 | 101.1 |
| Grenada | 328 | 16.4 | 1.2 | — | 22.4 | — | 22.4 | 15.2 | 92.8 | 11.2 | 4.9 | 43.9 |
| Guatemala | 258 | 428.6 | 54.6 | — | — | — | — | 374.0 | 87.3 | 200.9 | 121.0 | 60.2 |
| Guyana | 336 | 181.8 | — | — | .9 | — | .9 | 181.8 | 100.0 | 87.1 | 1.9 | 2.2 |
| Haiti | 263 | 81.9 | .1 | — | 47.2 | — | 47.2 | 81.8 | 99.9 | 78.5 | 68.0 | 86.6 |
| Honduras | 268 | 249.8 | 38.7 | — | — | — | — | 211.1 | 84.5 | 123.8 | 53.8 | 43.5 |
| Jamaica | 343 | 382.9 | 27.4 | — | 473.8 | 473.8 | — | 829.4 | 216.6 | 261.6 | 178.0 | 68.0 |
| Mexico | 273 | 8,912.7 | 894.6 | 448.4 | — | — | — | 8,018.2 | 90.0 | 2,851.2 | 1,448.1 | 50.8 |
| Nicaragua | 278 | 260.0 | 32.5 | — | 57.5 | — | 57.5 | 227.5 | 87.5 | 124.5 | 91.5 | 73.5 |
| Panama | 283 | 376.8 | 54.4 | — | — | — | — | 322.4 | 85.6 | 197.0 | 128.2 | 65.1 |
| Paraguay | 288 | 201.4 | 46.9 | — | — | — | — | 154.6 | 76.7 | 95.2 | 95.7 | 100.5 |
| Peru | 293 | 1,334.5 | 30.4 | — | — | — | — | 1,304.2 | 97.7 | 609.9 | 531.2 | 87.1 |
| St. Kitts and Nevis | 361 | 12.5 | 1.0 | — | — | — | — | 11.5 | 92.2 | 8.5 | 4.7 | 55.7 |
| St. Lucia | 362 | 21.4 | 1.5 | — | 8.7 | — | 8.7 | 19.9 | 92.9 | 14.6 | 11.8 | 81.1 |
| St. Vincent & Grens | 364 | 11.7 | .5 | — | 9.7 | 2.1 | 7.6 | 13.3 | 113.5 | 7.9 | — | .4 |
| Suriname | 366 | 128.9 | 9.2 | — | — | — | — | 119.7 | 92.9 | 88.1 | 28.2 | 32.1 |
| Trinidad and Tobago | 369 | 469.8 | 138.2 | — | — | — | — | 331.6 | 70.6 | 321.1 | 242.2 | 75.4 |
| Uruguay | 298 | 429.1 | 94.5 | — | — | — | — | 334.6 | 78.0 | 293.3 | 215.1 | 73.3 |
| Venezuela, Rep. Bol. | 299 | 3,722.7 | 587.8 | — | — | — | — | 3,134.9 | 84.2 | 2,543.3 | 313.2 | 12.3 |
| **Memorandum Items** | | | | | | | | | | | | |
| Export Earnings: Fuel | 080 | 47,202.6 | 5,396.2 | 1,848.7 | 1,150.1 | 955.7 | 194.4 | 42,764.3 | 90.6 | 26,152.7 | 20,231.0 | 77.4 |
| Export Earn.: Nonfuel | 092 | 131,985.8 | 14,088.5 | 4,923.9 | 22,676.3 | 16,404.9 | 6,271.3 | 134,303.8 | 101.8 | 49,308.3 | 33,849.4 | 68.6 |

# Total Fund Credit & Loans Outstanding

2tl

*Expressed in Millions of SDRs*

| | | 2004 | 2005 | 2006 | 2007 | 2008 | 2009 | 2010 | 2011 | 2012 | 2013 | 2014 | 2015 |
|---|---|---|---|---|---|---|---|---|---|---|---|---|---|
| World | 001 | 62,139.8 | 34,714.3 | 13,666.7 | 9,833.1 | 21,492.8 | 42,062.9 | 60,439.4 | 92,585.5 | 95,808.6 | 90,073.6 | 75,334.3 | 57,333.8 |
| Advanced Economies | 110 | 16.8 | — | — | — | 1,095.3 | 1,378.8 | 10,988.5 | 42,477.5 | 54,398.2 | 64,860.3 | 55,388.7 | 33,546.2 |
| Euro Area | 163 | — | — | — | — | — | — | 9,131 | 40,095 | 53,886 | 64,348 | 55,152 | 33,546 |
| Austria | 122 | — | — | — | — | — | — | — | — | — | — | — | — |
| Belgium | 124 | — | — | — | — | — | — | — | — | — | — | — | — |
| Cyprus | 423 | — | — | — | — | — | — | — | — | — | 223 | 371 | 693 |
| Estonia | 939 | — | — | — | — | — | — | — | — | — | — | — | — |
| Finland | 172 | — | — | — | — | — | — | — | — | — | — | — | — |
| France | 132 | — | — | — | — | — | — | — | — | — | — | — | — |
| Germany | 134 | — | — | — | — | — | — | — | — | — | — | — | — |
| Greece | 174 | — | — | — | — | — | — | 9,131 | 17,542 | 18,941 | 23,281 | 20,017 | 12,718 |
| Ireland | 178 | — | — | — | — | — | — | — | 11,050 | 16,543 | 19,466 | 11,822 | 3,773 |
| Italy | 136 | — | — | — | — | — | — | — | — | — | — | — | — |
| Latvia | 941 | — | — | — | — | 535 | 714 | 982 | 982 | — | — | — | — |
| Lithuania | 946 | 16.8 | — | — | — | — | — | — | — | — | — | — | — |
| Luxembourg | 137 | — | — | — | — | — | — | — | — | — | — | — | — |
| Malta | 181 | — | — | — | — | — | — | — | — | — | — | — | — |
| Netherlands | 138 | — | — | — | — | — | — | — | — | — | — | — | — |
| Portugal | 182 | — | — | — | — | — | — | — | 11,503 | 18,402 | 21,379 | 22,942 | 16,363 |
| Slovak Republic | 936 | — | — | — | — | — | — | — | — | — | — | — | — |
| Slovenia | 961 | — | — | — | — | — | — | — | — | — | — | — | — |
| Spain | 184 | — | — | — | — | — | — | — | — | — | — | — | — |
| Czech Republic | 935 | — | — | — | — | — | — | — | — | — | — | — | — |
| Iceland | 176 | — | — | — | — | 560.0 | 665.0 | 875.0 | 1,400.0 | 511.9 | 511.9 | 236.9 | — |
| Israel | 436 | — | — | — | — | — | — | — | — | — | — | — | — |
| Korea | 542 | — | — | — | — | — | — | — | — | — | — | — | — |
| Emerging & Dev. Economies | 200 | 62,123.0 | 34,714.3 | 13,666.7 | 9,833.1 | 20,397.5 | 40,684.1 | 49,450.9 | 50,108.1 | 41,410.4 | 25,213.3 | 19,945.6 | 23,787.5 |
| Emerging & Developing Asia | 505 | 7,411.7 | 6,479.3 | 670.5 | 665.6 | 712.3 | 1,124.3 | 1,511.8 | 1,673.6 | 2,109.4 | 1,924.0 | 1,439.6 | 1,263.9 |
| Bangladesh | 513 | 148.5 | 215.8 | 316.7 | 316.7 | 445.1 | 430.3 | 400.6 | 317.3 | 278.8 | 461.3 | 504.2 | 653.4 |
| Bhutan | 514 | — | — | — | — | — | — | — | — | — | — | — | — |
| Cambodia | 522 | 62.7 | 56.8 | — | — | — | — | — | — | — | — | — | — |
| China, P.R.: Mainland | 924 | — | — | — | — | — | — | — | — | — | — | — | — |
| Fiji | 819 | — | — | — | — | — | — | — | — | — | — | — | — |
| India | 534 | — | — | — | — | — | — | — | — | — | — | — | — |
| Indonesia | 536 | 6,237.0 | 5,462.2 | — | — | — | — | — | — | — | — | — | — |
| Kiribati | 826 | — | — | — | — | — | — | — | — | — | — | — | — |
| Lao People's Dem. Rep. | 544 | 24.6 | 20.5 | 18.3 | 16.3 | 13.6 | 10.0 | 6.3 | 3.2 | .9 | — | — | — |
| Malaysia | 548 | — | — | — | — | — | — | — | — | — | — | — | — |
| Maldives | 556 | — | 4.1 | 4.1 | 4.1 | 2.6 | 5.6 | 10.3 | 10.3 | 10.3 | 6.7 | 2.6 | 1.7 |
| Mongolia | 948 | 28.5 | 24.5 | 20.4 | 16.1 | 13.0 | 116.0 | 128.3 | 125.9 | 103.2 | 42.2 | 1.9 | — |
| Myanmar | 518 | — | — | — | — | — | — | — | — | — | — | — | — |
| Nepal | 558 | 14.3 | 14.3 | 28.5 | 49.9 | 49.9 | 48.5 | 74.1 | 71.3 | 64.5 | 54.5 | 46.0 | 71.7 |
| Palau | 565 | — | — | — | — | — | — | — | — | — | — | — | — |
| Papua New Guinea | 853 | 41.4 | — | — | — | — | — | — | — | — | — | — | — |
| Philippines | 566 | 486.9 | 272.1 | — | — | — | — | — | — | — | — | — | — |
| Samoa | 862 | — | — | — | — | — | — | 5.8 | 5.8 | 5.8 | 11.6 | 11.6 | 10.4 |
| Solomon Islands | 813 | — | — | — | — | — | — | 6.2 | 12.5 | 12.6 | 12.8 | 12.0 | 10.1 |
| Sri Lanka | 524 | 189.3 | 266.8 | 162.4 | 159.0 | 109.5 | 460.1 | 851.2 | 1,119.1 | 1,633.3 | 1,334.9 | 861.3 | 499.5 |
| Thailand | 578 | — | — | — | — | — | — | — | — | — | — | — | — |
| Timor-Leste | 537 | — | — | — | — | — | — | — | — | — | — | — | — |
| Tonga | 866 | — | — | — | — | — | — | — | — | — | — | — | — |
| Tuvalu | 869 | .... | .... | .... | .... | — | — | — | — | — | — | — | — |
| Vietnam | 582 | 178.6 | 142.3 | 120.1 | 103.5 | 78.7 | 53.8 | 29.0 | 8.3 | — | — | — | — |
| Europe | 170 | 19,774.0 | 13,160.5 | 8,862.3 | 5,410.8 | 13,522.0 | 30,028.4 | 35,911.3 | 35,258.0 | 26,774.4 | 12,014.0 | 7,220.5 | 9,413.1 |
| Emerging & Dev. Europe | 903 | 15,689.3 | 11,649.1 | 7,723.8 | 4,588.5 | 9,801.6 | 20,050.7 | 22,806.3 | 22,031.3 | 16,167.0 | 6,532.1 | 2,177.3 | 753.9 |
| Albania | 914 | 62.4 | 64.3 | 61.5 | 57.0 | 52.3 | 45.6 | 37.6 | 29.9 | 23.2 | 16.4 | 57.7 | 129.3 |
| Bosnia and Herzegovina | 963 | 70.0 | 43.4 | 13.5 | 1.5 | — | 182.6 | 338.2 | 338.2 | 416.8 | 389.8 | 454.9 | 416.4 |
| Bulgaria | 918 | 762.0 | 461.8 | 226.6 | — | — | — | — | — | — | — | — | — |
| Croatia | 960 | — | — | — | — | — | — | — | — | — | — | — | — |
| Hungary | 944 | — | — | — | — | 4,215.0 | 7,637.0 | 7,637.0 | 7,637.0 | 4,416.8 | — | — | — |
| Kosovo | 967 | — | — | — | — | — | — | 18.8 | 18.8 | 97.0 | 94.6 | 85.3 | 100.4 |
| Macedonia, FYR | 962 | 40.3 | 43.5 | 37.0 | — | — | — | — | 197.0 | 197.0 | 197.0 | 123.1 | — |
| Montenegro | 943 | — | — | — | — | — | — | — | — | — | — | — | — |
| Poland | 964 | — | — | — | — | — | — | — | — | — | — | — | — |
| Romania | 968 | 285.4 | 182.6 | 68.9 | — | — | 6,088.0 | 9,800.0 | 10,569.0 | 9,261.8 | 5,210.0 | 1,328.9 | 96.1 |
| Serbia, Republic of | 942 | 621.0 | 606.3 | 162.5 | — | — | 1,021.1 | 1,321.0 | 1,367.7 | 1,192.4 | 624.3 | 127.5 | 11.7 |
| Turkey | 186 | 13,848.3 | 10,247.3 | 7,153.7 | 4,530.0 | 5,534.4 | 5,076.3 | 3,653.7 | 1,873.7 | 562.1 | — | — | — |
| CIS | 901 | 4,084.6 | 1,511.4 | 1,138.6 | 822.3 | 3,720.4 | 9,977.7 | 13,105.0 | 13,226.7 | 10,607.4 | 5,481.8 | 5,043.2 | 8,659.2 |
| Armenia | 911 | 140.1 | 123.4 | 108.8 | 99.9 | 87.5 | 374.3 | 481.0 | 539.0 | 505.0 | 379.7 | 305.1 | 299.0 |
| Azerbaijan, Republic of | 912 | 134.2 | 114.5 | 89.2 | 65.2 | 51.4 | 39.4 | 29.8 | 18.8 | 10.3 | 3.9 | 1.3 | — |
| Belarus | 913 | 5.8 | — | — | — | — | 1,831.6 | 2,269.5 | 2,269.5 | 1,965.9 | 885.8 | 54.7 | — |
| Georgia | 915 | 171.3 | 162.5 | 157.1 | 159.2 | 298.8 | 501.6 | 682.1 | 644.0 | 484.1 | 233.0 | 146.2 | 94.0 |
| Kazakhstan | 916 | — | — | — | — | — | — | — | — | — | — | — | — |
| Kyrgyz Republic | 917 | 133.2 | 124.5 | 108.4 | 94.8 | 106.8 | 106.6 | 114.7 | 118.4 | 124.0 | 131.6 | 127.8 | 135.8 |
| Moldova | 921 | 81.4 | 66.8 | 93.8 | 101.0 | 108.8 | 98.2 | 212.6 | 308.7 | 398.2 | 384.0 | 364.7 | 335.6 |
| Russia | 922 | 2,293.8 | — | — | — | — | — | — | — | — | — | — | — |
| Tajikistan | 923 | 78.7 | 88.9 | 29.4 | 29.4 | 9.8 | 26.1 | 65.3 | 78.3 | 104.4 | 104.4 | 101.8 | 94.0 |
| Ukraine | 926 | 1,033.7 | 830.9 | 551.9 | 272.9 | 3,057.3 | 7,000.0 | 9,250.0 | 9,250.0 | 7,015.6 | 3,359.4 | 3,941.4 | 7,700.8 |
| Uzbekistan | 927 | 12.5 | — | — | — | — | — | — | — | — | — | — | — |

# Total Fund Credit & Loans Outstanding

| | | 2004 | 2005 | 2006 | 2007 | 2008 | 2009 | 2010 | 2011 | 2012 | 2013 | 2014 | 2015 |
|---|---|---|---|---|---|---|---|---|---|---|---|---|---|
| | | | | | | *Expressed in Millions of SDRs* | | | | | | | |
| **Middle East, N.Africa & Pakistan** | 440 | **2,944.3** | **2,247.1** | **2,006.2** | **1,558.8** | **3,436.9** | **5,357.0** | **7,044.4** | **7,158.3** | **5,992.9** | **4,710.0** | **5,314.9** | **7,504.8** |
| Afghanistan, Islamic Rep. of | 512 | — | — | — | 35.8 | 58.4 | 69.7 | 75.4 | 87.4 | 96.9 | 88.6 | 75.8 | 61.3 |
| Algeria | 612 | 414.0 | — | — | — | — | — | — | — | — | — | — | — |
| Bahrain, Kingdom of | 419 | — | — | — | — | — | — | — | — | — | — | — | — |
| Djibouti | 611 | 13.6 | 13.1 | 12.0 | 10.2 | 11.3 | 10.1 | 7.9 | 10.7 | 22.3 | 22.3 | 21.3 | 20.3 |
| Egypt | 469 | — | — | — | — | — | — | — | — | — | — | — | — |
| Iran, I.R. of | 429 | — | — | — | — | — | — | — | — | — | — | — | — |
| Iraq | 433 | 297.1 | 297.1 | 297.1 | — | — | — | 772.5 | 1,069.6 | 1,069.6 | 958.1 | 460.5 | 928.4 |
| Jordan | 439 | 217.5 | 165.3 | 105.2 | 55.4 | 17.9 | 7.6 | 5.1 | 5.1 | 255.8 | 682.0 | 937.8 | 1,332.0 |
| Lebanon | 446 | — | — | — | 50.8 | 76.1 | 76.1 | 63.4 | 38.1 | 12.7 | — | — | — |
| Mauritania | 682 | 58.2 | 48.5 | — | 8.4 | 10.3 | 10.3 | 32.4 | 54.5 | 75.9 | 85.1 | 83.0 | 79.8 |
| Morocco | 686 | — | — | — | — | — | — | — | — | — | — | — | — |
| Pakistan | 564 | 1,207.9 | 1,044.0 | 972.0 | 874.1 | 2,825.4 | 4,780.9 | 5,672.3 | 5,500.1 | 4,010.9 | 2,331.3 | 2,463.0 | 3,600.0 |
| Somalia | 726 | 112.0 | 112.0 | 112.0 | 112.0 | 112.0 | 112.0 | 112.0 | 112.0 | 111.9 | 111.5 | 111.5 | 111.5 |
| Sudan | 732 | 381.7 | 362.6 | 344.3 | 305.1 | 263.6 | 256.8 | 253.0 | 246.2 | 241.4 | 236.6 | 229.6 | 224.2 |
| Syrian Arab Republic | 463 | — | — | — | — | — | — | — | — | — | — | — | — |
| Tunisia | 744 | — | — | — | — | — | — | — | — | — | 98.8 | 787.9 | 1,002.8 |
| Yemen, Republic of | 474 | 242.25 | 204.50 | 163.67 | 107.08 | 61.88 | 33.50 | 50.54 | 34.79 | 95.67 | 95.67 | 144.42 | 144.42 |
| **Sub-Saharan Africa** | 603 | **4,108.6** | **3,638.0** | **1,631.1** | **1,688.7** | **2,188.0** | **3,385.5** | **3,492.8** | **4,341.7** | **4,900.0** | **5,057.2** | **4,891.6** | **4,832.0** |
| Angola | 614 | | | | | | | 572.6 | 773.0 | 858.9 | 687.1 | 357.9 | 110.9 |
| Benin | 638 | 42.0 | 36.9 | 1.8 | 2.6 | 14.6 | 24.8 | 35.4 | 56.4 | 77.2 | 87.2 | 92.9 | 86.9 |
| Burkina Faso | 748 | 73.8 | 72.4 | 23.2 | 23.7 | 35.3 | 70.4 | 83.6 | 94.1 | 138.4 | 139.8 | 137.7 | 146.6 |
| Burundi | 618 | 26.4 | 40.7 | 55.0 | 62.2 | 75.9 | 58.0 | 71.2 | 83.0 | 88.0 | 91.2 | 90.7 | 83.2 |
| Cameroon | 622 | 214.7 | 190.3 | 5.3 | 10.6 | 15.9 | 111.4 | 111.4 | 110.6 | 109.0 | 106.7 | 103.2 | 80.9 |
| Cape Verde | 624 | 6.2 | 8.6 | 8.6 | 8.5 | 8.0 | 7.0 | 5.6 | 3.8 | 2.2 | 1.0 | .2 | — |
| Central African Rep. | 626 | 28.4 | 25.1 | 28.0 | 31.2 | 40.9 | 50.0 | 58.7 | 58.7 | 65.6 | 64.2 | 69.0 | 72.9 |
| Chad | 628 | 61.8 | 55.5 | 45.0 | 35.3 | 26.4 | 18.2 | 10.9 | 5.8 | 3.1 | 1.3 | 13.7 | 45.4 |
| Comoros | 632 | — | — | — | — | 3.3 | 6.8 | 6.0 | 9.6 | 9.7 | 12.8 | 12.8 | 12.6 |
| Congo, Dem. Rep. of | 636 | 526.8 | 553.5 | 553.5 | 511.5 | 424.8 | 510.2 | 209.8 | 308.8 | 308.8 | 308.8 | 308.8 | 281.3 |
| Congo, Republic of | 634 | 18.7 | 18.5 | 23.6 | 23.6 | 24.8 | 27.2 | 17.5 | 21.1 | 19.5 | 16.3 | 12.8 | 8.9 |
| Côte d'Ivoire | 662 | 200.5 | 138.8 | 99.7 | 109.8 | 122.3 | 224.4 | 248.5 | 399.3 | 512.3 | 609.8 | 719.0 | 777.6 |
| Equatorial Guinea | 642 | — | — | — | — | — | — | — | — | — | — | — | — |
| Ethiopia | 644 | 118.0 | 112.1 | — | — | — | 107.0 | 187.2 | 187.2 | 187.2 | 187.2 | 183.8 | 158.4 |
| Gabon | 646 | 64.4 | 47.6 | 37.8 | 15.6 | 1.7 | — | — | — | — | — | — | — |
| Gambia, The | 648 | 15.9 | 14.6 | 11.8 | 4.0 | 8.0 | 18.2 | 20.2 | 22.5 | 31.7 | 32.2 | 30.1 | 34.1 |
| Ghana | 652 | 301.6 | 291.7 | 105.5 | 105.5 | 105.5 | 173.1 | 254.6 | 363.2 | 461.3 | 440.2 | 419.1 | 542.4 |
| Guinea | 656 | 78.5 | 61.1 | 47.9 | 40.9 | 45.9 | 37.6 | 30.9 | 27.1 | 37.2 | 55.6 | 119.1 | 142.8 |
| Guinea-Bissau | 654 | 10.2 | 8.0 | 5.5 | 3.3 | 5.6 | 6.3 | 2.4 | 7.2 | 7.2 | 7.2 | 10.8 | 13.6 |
| Kenya | 664 | 66.1 | 111.1 | 101.9 | 170.2 | 163.4 | 287.4 | 270.7 | 456.5 | 581.6 | 695.5 | 656.9 | 609.8 |
| Lesotho | 666 | 24.5 | 24.5 | 24.2 | 22.4 | 19.3 | 15.4 | 18.3 | 19.4 | 42.0 | 51.7 | 50.6 | 49.8 |
| Liberia | 668 | 223.7 | 223.6 | 223.1 | 222.7 | 557.0 | 568.5 | 28.8 | 37.7 | 49.5 | 64.3 | 101.9 | 115.7 |
| Madagascar | 674 | 145.4 | 148.6 | 19.2 | 27.1 | 63.5 | 64.4 | 63.2 | 61.0 | 56.3 | 49.4 | 67.0 | 85.8 |
| Malawi | 676 | 59.5 | 52.6 | 12.9 | 19.6 | 80.9 | 80.9 | 94.8 | 94.3 | 117.7 | 125.4 | 121.7 | 117.4 |
| Mali | 678 | 93.2 | 76.4 | 5.3 | 8.0 | 26.0 | 28.0 | 31.9 | 60.3 | 65.1 | 90.2 | 93.0 | 95.4 |
| Mauritius | 684 | — | — | — | — | — | — | — | — | — | — | — | — |
| Mozambique | 688 | 127.0 | 109.8 | 6.5 | 9.7 | 9.7 | 109.1 | 123.2 | 122.2 | 120.7 | 118.8 | 116.7 | 178.8 |
| Namibia | 728 | — | — | — | — | — | — | — | — | — | — | — | — |
| Niger | 692 | 87.2 | 89.3 | 17.6 | 25.4 | 32.9 | 36.2 | 39.4 | 36.4 | 43.5 | 49.3 | 76.2 | 107.8 |
| Nigeria | 694 | — | — | — | — | — | — | — | — | — | — | — | — |
| Rwanda | 714 | 59.4 | 53.9 | 2.9 | 5.1 | 7.4 | 9.7 | 9.7 | 9.3 | 8.6 | 7.4 | 5.6 | 3.7 |
| São Tomé & Príncipe | 716 | 1.9 | 2.2 | 2.7 | 1.6 | 2.5 | 2.8 | 3.2 | 3.2 | 3.6 | 3.9 | 3.2 | 3.1 |
| Senegal | 722 | 131.5 | 103.8 | 17.3 | 17.3 | 41.6 | 106.3 | 138.3 | 136.3 | 132.8 | 129.3 | 117.8 | 93.6 |
| Seychelles | 718 | — | — | — | — | — | 6.2 | 11.9 | 20.2 | 23.8 | 27.2 | 28.3 | 29.2 | 30.6 |
| Sierra Leone | 724 | 126.0 | 134.4 | 23.1 | 23.1 | 34.5 | 46.7 | 73.4 | 79.0 | 78.8 | 83.1 | 109.7 | 182.6 |
| South Africa | 199 | — | — | — | — | — | — | — | — | — | — | — | — |
| South Sudan, Republic of | 733 | .... | .... | .... | .... | .... | .... | .... | .... | — | — | — | — |
| Swaziland | 734 | — | — | — | — | — | — | — | — | — | — | — | — |
| Tanzania | 738 | 272.3 | 239.6 | 8.4 | 11.2 | 11.2 | 210.1 | 229.7 | 228.3 | 226.4 | 298.7 | 280.6 | 236.8 |
| Togo | 742 | 17.4 | 9.8 | 5.4 | 1.1 | 31.2 | 58.0 | 86.5 | 95.3 | 95.3 | 94.1 | 86.0 | 74.4 |
| Uganda | 746 | 123.3 | 91.7 | 6.0 | 6.0 | 6.0 | 6.0 | 5.8 | 4.8 | 3.6 | 2.4 | 1.2 | .2 |
| Zambia | 754 | 573.3 | 413.6 | 27.5 | 55.0 | 62.0 | 219.9 | 256.2 | 271.3 | 263.6 | 251.9 | 228.8 | 185.3 |
| Zimbabwe | 698 | 188.8 | 77.3 | 75.0 | 74.9 | 73.8 | 73.8 | 71.1 | 71.1 | 66.2 | 65.1 | 63.8 | 62.5 |
| **Western Hemisphere** | 205 | **27,884.5** | **9,189.4** | **496.4** | **509.2** | **538.2** | **788.8** | **1,490.6** | **1,676.4** | **1,633.8** | **1,508.2** | **1,079.1** | **773.8** |
| Antigua and Barbuda | 311 | — | — | — | — | — | — | 20.3 | 27.0 | 43.9 | 63.3 | 51.5 | 38.0 |
| Argentina | 213 | 9,073.0 | 6,655.7 | — | — | — | — | — | — | — | — | — | — |
| Barbados | 316 | — | — | — | — | — | — | — | — | — | — | — | — |
| Belize | 339 | — | — | — | — | — | 4.7 | 4.7 | 4.7 | 2.9 | .6 | — | — |
| Bolivia | 218 | 197.7 | 170.6 | 9.7 | — | — | — | — | — | — | — | — | — |
| Brazil | 223 | 16,116.7 | — | — | — | — | — | — | — | — | — | — | — |
| Chile | 228 | — | — | — | — | — | — | — | — | — | — | — | — |
| Colombia | 233 | — | — | — | — | — | — | — | — | — | — | — | — |
| Costa Rica | 238 | — | — | — | — | — | — | — | — | — | — | — | — |
| Dominica | 321 | 5.9 | 8.1 | 9.3 | 7.7 | 9.7 | 12.5 | 11.8 | 10.0 | 9.4 | 7.6 | 6.6 | 11.3 |
| Dominican Republic | 243 | 131.3 | 280.2 | 305.4 | 346.5 | 319.6 | 488.9 | 739.9 | 848.0 | 775.8 | 646.3 | 345.3 | 82.1 |
| Ecuador | 248 | 186.8 | 54.7 | 15.1 | — | — | — | — | — | — | — | — | — |
| El Salvador | 253 | — | — | — | — | — | — | — | — | — | — | — | — |
| Grenada | 328 | 5.9 | 5.9 | 6.3 | 4.9 | 8.4 | 14.7 | 18.9 | 18.7 | 18.4 | 18.1 | 20.4 | 21.2 |
| Guatemala | 258 | — | — | — | — | — | — | — | — | — | — | — | — |
| Guyana | 336 | 56.7 | 63.6 | 37.1 | 37.1 | 37.1 | 37.1 | 36.1 | 31.5 | 24.1 | 16.7 | 9.3 | 2.8 |
| Haiti | 263 | 6.1 | 23.5 | 28.1 | 35.7 | 67.3 | 105.0 | 8.2 | 16.4 | 31.1 | 37.7 | 41.0 | 48.0 |
| Honduras | 268 | 125.7 | 117.6 | 20.3 | 20.3 | 20.3 | 20.3 | 19.3 | 16.3 | 12.2 | 8.1 | 4.1 | 1.0 |
| Jamaica | 343 | .6 | — | — | — | — | — | 509.9 | 541.8 | 541.8 | 543.2 | 460.1 | 477.8 |
| Mexico | 273 | — | — | — | — | — | — | — | — | — | — | — | — |

# Total Fund Credit & Loans Outstanding

| 2tl | | 2004 | 2005 | 2006 | 2007 | 2008 | 2009 | 2010 | 2011 | 2012 | 2013 | 2014 | 2015 |
|---|---|---|---|---|---|---|---|---|---|---|---|---|---|
| **Western Hemisphere(Cont.)** | | | | | | *Expressed in Millions of SDRs* | | | | | | | |
| Nicaragua............................... | 278 | 159.5 | 140.5 | 41.8 | 53.7 | 72.1 | 95.9 | 108.7 | 118.4 | 110.0 | 99.3 | 84.9 | 65.7 |
| Panama................................. | 283 | 23.3 | 16.7 | 10.0 | 3.3 | — | — | — | — | — | — | — | — |
| Paraguay................................ | 288 | — | — | — | — | — | — | — | — | — | — | — | — |
| Peru...................................... | 293 | 66.9 | 40.1 | 13.4 | — | — | — | — | — | — | — | — | — |
| St. Kitts and Nevis.................... | 361 | — | — | — | — | — | 2.2 | 2.2 | 24.4 | 44.8 | 47.9 | 33.5 | 6.4 |
| St. Lucia................................. | 362 | — | — | — | — | — | — | 6.9 | 12.3 | 12.3 | 12.3 | 11.7 | 9.5 |
| St. Vincent & Grens.................. | 364 | — | — | — | — | 3.7 | 7.5 | 3.7 | 7.1 | 7.1 | 7.1 | 10.8 | 10.1 |
| Suriname................................ | 366 | — | — | — | — | — | — | — | — | — | — | — | — |
| Trinidad and Tobago.................. | 369 | — | — | — | — | — | — | — | — | — | — | — | — |
| Uruguay................................. | 298 | 1,728.4 | 1,612.2 | — | — | — | — | — | — | — | — | — | — |
| Venezuela, Rep. Bol.................. | 299 | — | — | — | — | — | — | — | — | — | — | — | — |

# Total Reserves minus Gold

*Millions of SDRs: End of Period*

| | | 2004 | 2005 | 2006 | 2007 | 2008 | 2009 | 2010 | 2011 | 2012 | 2013 | 2014 | 2015 |
|---|---|---|---|---|---|---|---|---|---|---|---|---|---|
| World | 001 | 2,489,735 | 3,071,310 | 3,527,945 | 4,275,265 | 4,813,618 | 5,447,638 | 6,264,294 | 6,939,269 | 7,420,818 | 7,874,535 | 8,272,388 | 8,135,312 |
| Advanced Economies | 110 | 1,397,533 | 1,492,975 | 1,530,606 | 1,571,212 | 1,657,337 | 1,938,110 | 2,181,072 | 2,423,597 | 2,615,149 | 2,682,913 | 2,848,502 | 3,029,862 |
| Euro Area (Incl. ECB) | 163 | 136,490 | 129,236 | 130,953 | 136,242 | 141,999 | 180,408 | 194,959 | 206,287 | 216,368 | 214,910 | 226,115 | 240,936 |
| Austria | 122 | 5,060 | 4,785 | 4,660 | 6,764 | 5,786 | 5,176 | 6,227 | 7,156 | 7,959 | 8,100 | 9,763 | 9,163 |
| Belgium | 124 | 6,672 | 5,766 | 5,838 | 6,571 | 6,050 | 10,147 | 10,714 | 11,671 | 12,102 | 11,778 | 11,476 | 11,800 |
| Cyprus | 423 | 2,518 | 2,932 | 3,753 | 3,872 | † 400 | 508 | 334 | 328 | 292 | 246 | 245 | 241 |
| Estonia | 939 | 1,151 | 1,360 | 1,849 | 2,065 | 2,574 | 2,534 | 1,660 | † 127 | 187 | 198 | 295 | 293 |
| Finland | 172 | 7,870 | 7,361 | 4,317 | 4,470 | 4,531 | 6,194 | 4,758 | 5,118 | 5,500 | 6,084 | 6,056 | 6,020 |
| France | 132 | 22,739 | 19,418 | 28,351 | 28,926 | 21,826 | 29,747 | 36,233 | 31,663 | 35,285 | 33,019 | 34,199 | 39,829 |
| Germany | 134 | 31,437 | 31,582 | 27,710 | 28,050 | 28,006 | 38,225 | 40,450 | 43,594 | 43,868 | 43,744 | 42,977 | 42,221 |
| Greece | 174 | 767 | 354 | 376 | 399 | 223 | 992 | 850 | 813 | 826 | 922 | 1,295 | 1,580 |
| Ireland | 178 | 1,823 | 545 | 479 | 493 | 566 | 1,238 | 1,196 | 902 | 911 | 911 | 1,047 | 1,442 |
| Italy | 136 | 17,939 | 17,852 | 17,058 | 17,962 | 24,079 | 29,196 | 30,963 | 32,037 | 32,857 | 32,971 | 32,916 | 33,941 |
| Latvia | 941 | 1,231 | 1,562 | 2,894 | 3,514 | 3,264 | 4,230 | 4,712 | 3,906 | 4,627 | 4,932 | † 2,051 | 2,324 |
| Lithuania | 946 | 2,262 | 2,603 | 3,759 | 4,782 | 4,078 | 4,095 | 4,114 | 5,156 | 5,347 | 5,096 | 5,870 | † 1,082 |
| Luxembourg | 137 | 192 | 169 | 145 | 91 | 217 | 466 | 485 | 587 | 567 | 569 | 536 | 501 |
| Malta | 181 | 1,759 | 1,803 | 1,979 | 2,395 | † 239 | 339 | 348 | 326 | 448 | 380 | 425 | 410 |
| Netherlands | 138 | 6,861 | 6,287 | 7,181 | 6,499 | 7,451 | 11,399 | 11,994 | 13,199 | 14,347 | 14,670 | 13,326 | 12,514 |
| Portugal | 182 | 3,332 | 2,434 | 1,372 | 796 | 850 | 1,566 | 2,371 | 1,286 | 1,429 | 1,804 | 3,361 | 4,595 |
| Slovak Republic | 936 | 9,284 | 10,425 | 8,406 | 11,411 | 11,592 | † 442 | 467 | 556 | 532 | 599 | 961 | 1,308 |
| Slovenia | 961 | 5,662 | 5,651 | 4,677 | † 620 | 564 | 616 | 602 | 541 | 509 | 519 | 617 | 540 |
| Spain | 184 | 7,977 | 6,771 | 7,194 | 7,265 | 8,059 | 11,613 | 12,432 | 21,392 | 23,113 | 23,006 | 27,260 | 32,025 |
| Australia | 193 | 23,054 | 29,345 | 35,528 | 15,674 | 19,926 | 24,846 | 25,103 | 27,867 | 29,192 | 32,302 | 35,073 | 33,585 |
| Canada | 156 | 22,169 | 23,062 | 23,261 | 25,940 | 28,422 | 34,597 | 37,011 | 42,763 | 44,482 | 46,637 | 51,480 | 57,512 |
| China, P.R.: Hong Kong | 532 | 79,549 | 86,928 | 88,519 | 96,590 | 118,466 | 163,150 | 174,444 | 185,828 | † 206,420 | 202,032 | 226,694 | 258,854 |
| Czech Republic | 935 | 18,196 | 20,521 | 20,727 | 21,863 | 23,797 | 26,253 | 27,213 | 25,839 | 28,801 | 36,232 | 37,330 | 46,292 |
| Denmark | 128 | 25,166 | † 23,040 | 19,758 | 20,588 | 26,272 | 47,389 | 47,728 | 53,202 | 56,046 | 55,909 | 50,256 | 45,404 |
| Iceland | 176 | 674 | 725 | 1,530 | 1,632 | 2,282 | 2,432 | 3,701 | 5,504 | 2,658 | 2,702 | 2,830 | 3,589 |
| Israel | 436 | 17,446 | 19,632 | 19,379 | 18,047 | 27,601 | 38,663 | 46,043 | 48,769 | 49,389 | 53,107 | 59,429 | 65,363 |
| Japan | 158 | 536,952 | 583,707 | 584,739 | 602,933 | 655,317 | 652,065 | 689,266 | 819,512 | 798,446 | 803,388 | 849,670 | 871,035 |
| Korea | 542 | 128,136 | 147,150 | 158,789 | 165,892 | 130,590 | 172,185 | 189,276 | 198,177 | 210,295 | 221,850 | 247,641 | 262,064 |
| New Zealand | 196 | 4,473 | 6,222 | 9,352 | 10,914 | 7,175 | 9,947 | 10,859 | 11,081 | 11,440 | 10,596 | 10,948 | 10,608 |
| Norway | 142 | 28,530 | 32,874 | 37,784 | 38,500 | 33,078 | 31,166 | 34,284 | 32,175 | 33,740 | 37,846 | 44,727 | 41,463 |
| San Marino | 135 | 229 | 243 | 318 | 410 | 459 | 504 | 292 | 223 | 250 | 350 | 271 | .... |
| Singapore | 576 | 72,354 | 81,132 | 90,434 | 102,987 | 112,955 | 119,661 | 146,428 | 154,714 | 168,580 | 177,184 | 177,141 | 178,631 |
| Sweden | 144 | 14,268 | 15,456 | 16,470 | 17,114 | 16,813 | 27,339 | 27,639 | 28,676 | 29,617 | 39,282 | 39,829 | 38,834 |
| Switzerland | 146 | 35,735 | 25,396 | 25,322 | 28,144 | 29,255 | 62,640 | 145,114 | 181,981 | 309,489 | 322,051 | 348,881 | 409,141 |
| Taiwan Province of China | 528 | 155,658 | 177,216 | 176,913 | 171,056 | 189,387 | 222,109 | 248,050 | 251,127 | 262,323 | 270,656 | 289,189 | 307,442 |
| United Kingdom | 112 | 25,719 | 26,914 | 27,053 | 30,981 | 28,793 | 35,532 | 44,379 | 51,634 | 57,645 | 60,002 | 66,053 | 85,894 |
| United States | 111 | 48,866 | 37,840 | 36,462 | 37,668 | 43,244 | 76,366 | 78,824 | 89,178 | 90,528 | 86,710 | 82,170 | 76,883 |
| Emerging & Dev. Economies | 200 | 1,092,202 | 1,578,334 | 1,997,339 | 2,704,053 | 3,156,280 | 3,509,528 | 4,083,222 | 4,515,672 | 4,805,669 | 5,191,622 | 5,423,885 | 5,105,449 |
| Emerging & Developing Asia | 505 | 597,364 | 805,083 | 987,467 | 1,346,086 | 1,650,074 | 1,966,854 | 2,362,430 | 2,629,279 | 2,724,498 | 3,038,369 | 3,257,955 | 3,042,479 |
| Bangladesh | 513 | 2,043 | 1,936 | 2,530 | 3,280 | 3,694 | 6,518 | 6,860 | 5,543 | 7,828 | 11,405 | 15,037 | 19,501 |
| Bhutan | 514 | 257 | 327 | 362 | 442 | 497 | 568 | 651 | 514 | 621 | 644 | 859 | 796 |
| Brunei Darussalam | 516 | 315 | 344 | 341 | 422 | 488 | 866 | 1,015 | 1,620 | 2,138 | 2,207 | 2,396 | 2,317 |
| Cambodia | 522 | 607 | 667 | 769 | 1,143 | 1,488 | 1,819 | 2,114 | 2,247 | 2,777 | 2,933 | 3,883 | 4,967 |
| China, P.R.: Mainland | 924 | 395,683 | 574,779 | 710,245 | 968,379 | 1,265,531 | 1,541,149 | 1,861,054 | 2,086,140 | 2,167,400 | 2,493,213 | 2,663,681 | 2,414,030 |
| China, P.R.: Macao | 546 | 3,500 | 4,680 | 6,070 | 8,372 | 10,342 | 11,705 | 15,407 | 22,163 | 10,801 | 10,484 | 11,350 | 13,632 |
| Fiji | 819 | 311 | 225 | 208 | 334 | 209 | 363 | 467 | 542 | 599 | 611 | 632 | 662 |
| India | 534 | 81,515 | 92,302 | 113,492 | 168,953 | 160,633 | 169,154 | 178,748 | 176,702 | 176,058 | 179,541 | 209,451 | 241,253 |
| Indonesia | 536 | 22,506 | 23,187 | 27,322 | 34,790 | 32,200 | 40,546 | 60,329 | 69,394 | 70,815 | 62,574 | 75,121 | 74,523 |
| Lao People's Dem. Rep. | 544 | 144 | 164 | 218 | 337 | 408 | 388 | 457 | 483 | 520 | 469 | 604 | 753 |
| Malaysia | 548 | 42,422 | 48,877 | 54,595 | 63,926 | 59,177 | 60,874 | 68,105 | 85,835 | 89,649 | 86,652 | 79,080 | 67,819 |
| Maldives | 556 | 133 | 132 | 156 | 197 | 158 | 176 | 237 | 227 | 207 | 248 | 433 | 415 |
| Micronesia, Fed. States of | 868 | 35 | 35 | 31 | 31 | 26 | 36 | 36 | 49 | 50 | 55 | 79 | 98 |
| Mongolia | 948 | 125 | 233 | 388 | 507 | 365 | 826 | 1,426 | 1,482 | 2,557 | 1,361 | 1,063 | 900 |
| Myanmar | 518 | 433 | 539 | 821 | 1,955 | 2,414 | 3,350 | 3,712 | 4,562 | 4,531 | .... | .... | .... |
| Nepal | 558 | 942 | 1,049 | 1,287 | 1,275 | 1,596 | 1,766 | 1,907 | 2,365 | 2,802 | 3,437 | 4,160 | 5,728 |
| Papua New Guinea | 853 | 407 | 502 | 931 | 1,300 | 1,268 | 1,633 | 1,969 | 2,772 | 2,557 | 1,802 | 1,555 | 1,221 |
| Philippines | 566 | 8,446 | 11,143 | 13,311 | 19,118 | 21,550 | 24,739 | 35,494 | 43,829 | 47,809 | 49,148 | 49,735 | 53,375 |
| Samoa | 862 | 55 | 57 | 54 | 60 | 57 | 106 | 136 | 109 | 110 | 111 | 97 | 101 |
| Solomon Islands | 813 | 51 | 66 | 69 | 76 | 58 | 93 | 173 | 269 | 305 | 319 | 322 | 357 |
| Sri Lanka | 524 | 1,373 | 1,854 | 1,812 | 2,139 | 1,603 | 2,944 | 4,357 | 4,070 | 4,150 | 4,293 | 5,049 | 4,722 |
| Thailand | 578 | 31,335 | 35,466 | 43,400 | 53,929 | 70,547 | 86,422 | 108,784 | 109,029 | 112,776 | 104,759 | 104,398 | 109,160 |
| Timor-Leste | 537 | 117 | 107 | 56 | 146 | 137 | 159 | 264 | 301 | 575 | 446 | 215 | 316 |
| Tonga | 866 | 36 | 33 | 32 | 41 | 45 | 61 | 68 | 93 | 99 | 101 | 110 | 113 |
| Vanuatu | 846 | 40 | 47 | 70 | 76 | 75 | 95 | 105 | 113 | 119 | 116 | 127 | 194 |
| Vietnam | 582 | 4,534 | 6,332 | 8,897 | 14,858 | 15,510 | 10,491 | 8,095 | 8,819 | 16,639 | 16,414 | 23,598 | 20,387 |
| Europe | 170 | 174,256 | 254,313 | 359,617 | 493,889 | 471,817 | 490,594 | 538,932 | 554,782 | 588,514 | 587,217 | 507,742 | 490,822 |
| Emerging & Dev. Europe | 903 | 82,378 | 110,350 | 131,985 | 159,740 | 163,175 | 184,166 | 201,438 | 206,615 | 225,558 | 238,324 | 235,657 | 224,188 |
| Albania | 914 | 874 | 982 | 1,176 | 1,332 | 1,506 | 1,476 | 1,604 | 1,559 | 1,637 | 1,761 | 1,797 | 2,226 |
| Bosnia and Herzegovina | 963 | 1,563 | 1,782 | 2,440 | 3,190 | 2,908 | 2,889 | 2,835 | 2,703 | 2,787 | 3,161 | 3,275 | 3,384 |
| Bulgaria | 918 | 5,651 | 5,626 | 7,274 | 10,427 | 10,917 | 10,925 | 10,013 | 9,934 | 11,953 | 11,906 | 12,822 | 14,998 |
| Croatia | 960 | 5,639 | 6,157 | 7,636 | 8,653 | 8,412 | 9,501 | 9,177 | 9,434 | 9,634 | 11,537 | 10,646 | 10,801 |
| Hungary | 944 | 10,252 | 12,980 | 14,309 | 15,168 | 21,936 | 28,114 | 29,122 | 31,708 | 28,958 | 30,123 | 28,921 | 23,828 |
| Kosovo | 967 | .... | .... | .... | 602 | 579 | 530 | 550 | 483 | 721 | 716 | 626 | 677 |
| Macedonia, FYR | 962 | 583 | 860 | 1,164 | 1,318 | 1,247 | 1,308 | 1,279 | 1,519 | 1,645 | 1,613 | 1,864 | 1,616 |
| Montenegro | 943 | 53 | 143 | 288 | 436 | 283 | 365 | 361 | 256 | 298 | 379 | 457 | 529 |
| Poland | 964 | 22,745 | 28,591 | 30,824 | 39,846 | 38,503 | 48,430 | 57,675 | 60,345 | 67,275 | 66,387 | 66,580 | 65,954 |
| Romania | 968 | 9,412 | 13,904 | 18,656 | 23,537 | 23,936 | 25,998 | 28,156 | 27,968 | 26,782 | 29,098 | 27,032 | 25,378 |

# Total Reserves minus Gold

2016, International Monetary Fund : *International Financial Statistics Yearbook*

| 1l s | | 2004 | 2005 | 2006 | 2007 | 2008 | 2009 | 2010 | 2011 | 2012 | 2013 | 2014 | 2015 |
|---|---|---|---|---|---|---|---|---|---|---|---|---|---|
| | | | | | | | Millions of SDRs: End of Period | | | | | | |
| **Emerging & Dev. Europe(Cont.)** | | | | | | | | | | | | | |
| Serbia, Republic of | 942 | 2,637 | 3,938 | 7,742 | 8,791 | 7,221 | 9,421 | 8,256 | 9,690 | 8,839 | 9,612 | 7,849 | 7,741 |
| Turkey | 186 | 22,968 | 35,388 | 40,476 | 46,438 | 45,724 | 45,209 | 52,410 | 51,015 | 65,028 | 72,030 | 73,789 | 67,056 |
| **CIS** | 901 | 91,878 | 143,963 | 227,632 | 334,149 | 308,642 | 306,428 | 337,494 | 348,167 | 362,956 | 348,892 | 272,085 | 266,635 |
| Armenia | 911 | 353 | 468 | 713 | 1,050 | 913 | 1,278 | 1,212 | 1,259 | 1,171 | 1,462 | 1,028 | 1,281 |
| Azerbaijan, Republic of | 912 | 692 | 824 | 1,662 | 2,704 | 4,199 | 3,421 | 4,162 | 6,692 | 7,338 | 9,351 | 10,109 | 4,540 |
| Belarus | 913 | 483 | 795 | 710 | 2,501 | 1,744 | 3,082 | 2,228 | 3,915 | 3,780 | 3,206 | 2,362 | 1,980 |
| Georgia | 915 | 249 | 335 | 619 | 861 | 961 | 1,346 | 1,470 | 1,836 | 1,869 | 1,833 | 1,863 | 1,819 |
| Kazakhstan | 916 | 5,456 | 4,257 | 11,799 | 9,984 | 11,603 | 13,217 | 16,378 | 16,400 | 14,400 | 12,420 | 15,056 | 14,791 |
| Kyrgyz Republic | 917 | 340 | 399 | 508 | 701 | 748 | 953 | 1,041 | 1,109 | 1,238 | 1,363 | 1,246 | 1,179 |
| Moldova | 921 | 303 | 418 | 515 | 844 | 1,086 | 944 | 1,115 | 1,280 | 1,634 | 1,830 | 1,487 | 1,266 |
| Russia | 922 | 77,790 | 123,064 | 196,469 | 295,365 | 267,323 | 265,772 | 288,037 | 295,680 | 316,592 | 304,937 | 234,240 | 230,806 |
| Tajikistan | 923 | 101 | 118 | 116 | 25 | 67 | 111 | 211 | 188 | 194 | 299 | 122 | 47 |
| Ukraine | 926 | 6,111 | 13,285 | 14,521 | 20,115 | 19,997 | 16,302 | 21,641 | 19,807 | 14,741 | 12,192 | 4,571 | 8,925 |
| **Middle East, N.Africa & Pakistan** | 440 | 138,635 | 282,966 | 367,525 | 489,725 | 608,755 | 599,217 | 665,892 | 732,956 | 842,123 | 912,587 | 955,293 | 881,288 |
| Afghanistan, Islamic Rep. of | 512 | .... | .... | .... | .... | 1,578 | 2,233 | 2,711 | 3,432 | 3,893 | 4,183 | 4,611 | 4,497 |
| Algeria | 612 | 27,847 | 39,393 | 51,791 | 69,810 | 92,999 | 95,070 | 105,592 | 119,081 | 124,468 | 126,436 | 123,976 | 104,405 |
| Bahrain, Kingdom of | 419 | 1,250 | 1,382 | 1,861 | 2,669 | 2,545 | 2,453 | 3,304 | 2,960 | 3,386 | 3,472 | 4,175 | .... |
| Djibouti | 611 | 60 | 62 | 80 | 84 | 114 | 154 | 162 | 159 | 162 | 276 | 271 | 263 |
| Egypt | 469 | 9,191 | 14,419 | 16,260 | 19,103 | 20,916 | 20,574 | 21,825 | 9,715 | 7,565 | 8,836 | 8,279 | 9,585 |
| Iraq | 433 | 5,038 | 8,469 | 13,249 | 19,805 | 32,421 | 28,148 | 32,699 | 39,566 | 44,722 | 49,424 | 43,405 | 36,797 |
| Jordan | 439 | 3,391 | 3,673 | 4,468 | 4,773 | 5,559 | 7,456 | 8,478 | 7,469 | 5,263 | 8,587 | 10,560 | 10,942 |
| Kuwait | 443 | 5,307 | 6,201 | 8,353 | 10,543 | 11,110 | 12,928 | 13,790 | 16,802 | 18,795 | 19,060 | 22,166 | 20,401 |
| Lebanon | 446 | 7,556 | 8,317 | 8,892 | 8,170 | 13,143 | 18,564 | 20,463 | 21,977 | 24,195 | 23,862 | 27,296 | 27,968 |
| Libya | 672 | 16,541 | 27,642 | 39,411 | 50,248 | 59,933 | 62,975 | 64,703 | 68,260 | 77,042 | 74,803 | 61,494 | .... |
| Mauritania | 682 | 22 | 45 | 124 | 125 | 122 | 144 | 176 | 316 | 618 | .... | .... | .... |
| Morocco | 686 | 10,519 | 11,326 | 13,521 | 15,265 | 14,351 | 14,542 | 14,909 | 12,592 | 10,548 | 11,816 | 13,578 | 16,059 |
| Oman | 449 | 2,316 | 3,049 | 3,333 | 6,027 | 7,519 | 7,784 | 8,457 | 9,357 | 9,369 | 10,357 | 11,227 | 12,660 |
| Pakistan | 564 | 6,310 | 7,020 | 7,673 | 8,887 | 4,671 | 7,220 | 9,315 | 9,463 | 6,664 | 3,348 | 8,150 | 12,867 |
| Qatar | 453 | 2,187 | 3,178 | 3,578 | 5,959 | 6,265 | 11,718 | 19,883 | 10,551 | 21,160 | 27,014 | 29,496 | 26,340 |
| Saudi Arabia | 456 | 17,573 | † 108,467 | 150,249 | 193,296 | 287,125 | 261,336 | 288,775 | 352,170 | 427,130 | 470,969 | 505,187 | 444,520 |
| Sudan | 732 | 862 | 1,307 | 1,103 | 872 | 908 | 698 | 673 | 125 | 125 | 125 | 125 | 125 |
| Syrian Arab Republic | 463 | .... | 12,137 | 10,946 | 10,766 | 11,077 | 11,098 | 12,640 | .... | .... | .... | .... | .... |
| Tunisia | 744 | 2,534 | 3,104 | 4,502 | 4,968 | 5,745 | 7,053 | 6,142 | 4,855 | 5,438 | 4,732 | 4,994 | .... |
| United Arab Emirates | 466 | 11,932 | 14,700 | 18,358 | 48,878 | 20,577 | 16,651 | 21,289 | 24,275 | 30,604 | 44,287 | 54,130 | 67,599 |
| West Bank and Gaza | 487 | .... | .... | 209 | 225 | 331 | 318 | 345 | 324 | .... | .... | .... | .... |
| Yemen, Republic of | 474 | 3,648 | 4,279 | 4,993 | 4,882 | 5,266 | 4,424 | 3,811 | 2,898 | 3,948 | 3,431 | .... | .... |
| **Sub-Saharan Africa** | 603 | 40,001 | 57,269 | 76,289 | 92,231 | 101,977 | 102,518 | 104,329 | 116,845 | 131,296 | 132,358 | 128,736 | 119,327 |
| CEMAC (incl. BEAC hqtrs.) | 758 | 2,003 | 3,599 | 5,908 | 7,554 | 10,168 | 9,156 | 8,869 | 10,237 | 11,406 | 11,832 | 10,567 | 7,317 |
| Cameroon | 622 | 534 | 664 | 1,141 | 1,839 | 2,004 | 2,345 | 2,365 | 2,083 | 2,200 | 2,255 | 2,187 | 2,552 |
| Central African Rep. | 626 | 96 | 97 | 83 | 52 | 79 | 134 | 118 | 101 | 103 | 126 | 179 | 154 |
| Chad | 628 | 143 | 158 | 416 | 604 | 874 | 393 | 411 | 619 | 752 | 768 | 743 | 266 |
| Congo, Rep. of | 634 | 77 | 512 | 1,224 | 1,376 | 2,514 | 2,428 | 2,888 | 3,674 | 3,611 | 3,406 | 3,400 | 1,603 |
| Equatorial Guinea | 642 | 608 | 1,471 | 2,039 | 2,434 | 2,877 | 2,074 | 1,524 | 1,989 | 2,861 | 2,965 | 2,006 | 870 |
| Gabon | 646 | 286 | 468 | 740 | 777 | 1,249 | 1,271 | 1,127 | 1,405 | 1,530 | 1,950 | 1,711 | 1,345 |
| WAEMU (Incl. BCEAO hqtrs.) | 759 | 4,666 | 4,334 | 4,900 | 6,097 | 6,054 | 7,702 | 7,678 | 7,889 | 7,886 | 7,922 | 7,941 | 7,981 |
| Benin | 638 | 409 | 458 | 606 | 765 | 820 | 784 | 779 | 578 | 464 | 451 | 501 | 528 |
| Burkina Faso | 748 | 425 | 307 | 369 | 651 | 602 | 827 | 694 | 623 | 667 | 408 | 205 | 187 |
| Côte d'Ivoire | 662 | 1,082 | 956 | 1,195 | 1,594 | 1,463 | 2,084 | 2,353 | 2,811 | 2,556 | 2,755 | 3,091 | 3,403 |
| Guinea Bissau | 654 | 46 | 56 | 55 | 71 | 81 | 108 | 102 | 143 | 107 | 121 | 198 | 240 |
| Mali | 678 | 548 | 598 | 644 | 688 | 696 | 1,023 | 873 | 898 | 873 | 848 | 594 | 450 |
| Niger | 692 | 161 | 175 | 247 | 375 | 458 | 418 | 494 | 438 | 660 | 758 | 885 | 750 |
| Senegal | 722 | 881 | 830 | 887 | 1,050 | 1,040 | 1,354 | 1,330 | 1,267 | 1,354 | 1,463 | 1,407 | 1,452 |
| Togo | 742 | 230 | 134 | 249 | 277 | 378 | 449 | 464 | 504 | 287 | 329 | 350 | 414 |
| Angola | 614 | 885 | 2,237 | 5,716 | 7,085 | 11,601 | 8,716 | 12,824 | 18,750 | 21,741 | 21,286 | 19,416 | 17,373 |
| Botswana | 616 | 3,645 | 4,414 | 5,313 | 6,195 | 5,920 | 5,552 | 5,120 | 5,264 | 4,963 | 5,017 | 5,745 | 5,446 |
| Burundi | 618 | 42 | 70 | 87 | 112 | 173 | 205 | 215 | 191 | 200 | 213 | 218 | 98 |
| Cabo Verde | 624 | 90 | 122 | 169 | 231 | 235 | 254 | 248 | 221 | 245 | 309 | 353 | 357 |
| Comoros | 632 | 67 | 60 | 62 | 74 | 73 | 96 | 94 | 101 | 126 | 113 | 118 | 144 |
| Congo, Dem. Rep. of | 636 | 152 | 92 | 103 | 114 | 50 | 660 | 844 | 826 | 1,062 | 1,090 | 1,075 | 877 |
| Eritrea | 643 | 22 | 20 | 17 | 22 | 38 | 57 | 74 | 75 | .... | .... | .... | .... |
| Ethiopia | 644 | 964 | 729 | 577 | 816 | 565 | 1,136 | .... | .... | .... | .... | .... | .... |
| Gambia, The | 648 | 54 | 69 | 80 | 90 | 76 | 143 | 131 | 145 | 154 | 137 | 110 | .... |
| Ghana | 652 | 1,047 | 1,226 | 1,389 | 1,256 | 1,149 | 2,160 | 3,093 | 3,572 | 3,492 | 3,409 | .... | .... |
| Guinea | 656 | 71 | 67 | .... | .... | .... | .... | .... | 67 | 101 | 113 | 202 | 180 |
| Kenya | 664 | 978 | 1,259 | 1,606 | 2,123 | 1,869 | 2,455 | 2,805 | 2,778 | 3,716 | 4,285 | 5,460 | 5,447 |
| Lesotho | 666 | 323 | 363 | 438 | 635 | 631 | 753 | 695 | 599 | 669 | 685 | 739 | 652 |
| Liberia | 668 | 12 | 18 | 48 | 76 | 104 | 238 | 303 | 334 | 324 | 320 | 344 | .... |
| Madagascar | 674 | 324 | 337 | 388 | 536 | 638 | 626 | 664 | 739 | 685 | 504 | 534 | 600 |
| Malawi | 676 | 82 | 111 | 89 | 137 | 158 | 95 | 200 | 129 | 145 | 268 | 416 | .... |
| Mauritius | 684 | 1,034 | 937 | 844 | 1,127 | 1,131 | 1,390 | 1,586 | 1,682 | 1,846 | 2,169 | 2,495 | 2,856 |
| Mozambique | 688 | 728 | 737 | 768 | 914 | 1,024 | 1,339 | 1,402 | 1,608 | 1,802 | 2,040 | 2,078 | 1,740 |
| Namibia | 728 | 222 | 218 | 299 | 567 | 839 | 1,308 | 1,101 | 1,164 | 1,136 | 981 | 813 | 1,218 |
| Nigeria | 694 | 10,918 | 19,786 | 28,117 | 32,485 | 34,411 | 28,553 | 22,674 | 22,935 | 30,194 | 29,498 | 25,310 | 22,087 |
| Rwanda | 714 | 203 | 284 | 292 | 350 | 387 | 474 | 528 | 684 | 552 | 695 | 736 | 743 |
| São Tomé & Príncipe | 716 | 13 | 19 | 23 | 25 | 40 | 43 | 31 | 34 | 34 | 41 | 44 | 52 |
| Seychelles | 718 | 22 | 39 | 75 | 26 | 41 | 122 | 166 | 182 | 200 | 277 | 321 | 387 |
| Sierra Leone | 724 | 81 | 119 | 122 | 137 | 143 | 258 | 266 | 286 | 311 | 346 | 415 | 448 |
| South Africa | 199 | 8,462 | 12,999 | 15,326 | 18,724 | 19,856 | 22,477 | 24,789 | 27,744 | 28,626 | 29,132 | 30,554 | 30,034 |
| South Sudan, Republic of | 733 | .... | .... | .... | .... | .... | .... | .... | 904 | 834 | 615 | 288 | 166 |
| Swaziland | 734 | 208 | 171 | 248 | 490 | 488 | 612 | 491 | 391 | 482 | 495 | 477 | 395 |
| Tanzania | 738 | 1,478 | 1,433 | 1,502 | 1,827 | 1,859 | 2,214 | 2,535 | 2,427 | 2,637 | 3,035 | 3,030 | 2,939 |

# Total Reserves minus Gold

Millions of SDRs: End of Period

| 1l s | | 2004 | 2005 | 2006 | 2007 | 2008 | 2009 | 2010 | 2011 | 2012 | 2013 | 2014 | 2015 |
|---|---|---|---|---|---|---|---|---|---|---|---|---|---|
| **Sub-Saharan Africa(Cont.)** | | | | | | | | | | | | | |
| Uganda | 746 | 842 | 940 | 1,204 | 1,620 | 1,494 | 1,910 | 1,757 | 1,705 | 2,061 | 2,167 | 2,289 | 2,099 |
| Zambia | 754 | 217 | 392 | 478 | 690 | 711 | 1,207 | 1,360 | 1,514 | 1,979 | 1,743 | 2,125 | 2,142 |
| Zimbabwe | 698 | 144 | 68 | 103 | 91 | 49 | 524 | 475 | 429 | 374 | 308 | 251 | 233 |
| **Western Hemisphere** | **205** | **141,947** | **178,704** | **206,441** | **282,121** | **323,658** | **350,345** | **411,639** | **481,810** | **519,237** | **521,091** | **574,160** | **571,534** |
| ECCU (incl. ECCB hqtrs.) | 309 | 408 | 420 | 463 | 484 | 494 | 572 | 643 | 696 | 767 | 792 | 1,004 | 1,152 |
| Anguilla | 312 | 22 | 28 | 28 | 28 | 27 | 24 | 26 | 24 | 26 | 27 | 33 | 35 |
| Antigua and Barbuda | 311 | 77 | 89 | 95 | 91 | 90 | 82 | 89 | 96 | 105 | 132 | 205 | 257 |
| Dominica | 321 | 27 | 34 | 42 | 38 | 36 | 48 | 49 | 53 | 62 | 57 | 70 | 91 |
| Grenada | 328 | 78 | 66 | 66 | 70 | 68 | 82 | 77 | 79 | 78 | 98 | 117 | 143 |
| Montserrat | 351 | 9 | 10 | 10 | 9 | 8 | 9 | 11 | 16 | 21 | 26 | 31 | 37 |
| St. Kitts and Nevis | 361 | 51 | 50 | 59 | 61 | 72 | 87 | 110 | 159 | 171 | 196 | 226 | 208 |
| St. Lucia | 362 | 85 | 81 | 89 | 97 | 93 | 112 | 134 | 139 | 151 | 125 | 178 | 229 |
| St. Vincent & Grenadines | 364 | 48 | 49 | 52 | 55 | 54 | 56 | 73 | 58 | 72 | 88 | 109 | 120 |
| Argentina | 213 | 12,160 | 19,016 | 20,542 | 28,275 | 29,121 | 29,402 | 32,294 | 28,156 | 25,974 | 18,275 | 20,028 | 16,898 |
| Aruba | 314 | 190 | 191 | 225 | 235 | 393 | 369 | 369 | 350 | 392 | 346 | 386 | 512 |
| Bahamas, The | 313 | 434 | 410 | 307 | 294 | 369 | 644 | 678 | 697 | 551 | 524 | 603 | 646 |
| Barbados | 316 | 373 | 422 | 423 | 531 | 479 | 556 | 541 | 529 | 546 | 442 | 436 | .... |
| Belize | 339 | 31 | 50 | 76 | 69 | 108 | 142 | 154 | 188 | 262 | 336 | 315 | |
| Bolivia | 218 | 562 | 929 | 1,738 | 2,882 | 4,497 | 4,838 | 5,282 | 6,455 | 7,586 | 8,300 | 9,305 | 8,372 |
| Brazil | 223 | 33,781 | 37,253 | 56,605 | 113,547 | 125,201 | 151,410 | 186,396 | 228,205 | 240,459 | 231,308 | 249,146 | 255,587 |
| Chile | 228 | 10,299 | 11,845 | 12,890 | 10,655 | 14,979 | 16,128 | 18,062 | 27,312 | 27,091 | 26,678 | 27,911 | 27,879 |
| Colombia | 233 | 8,624 | 10,346 | 10,168 | 13,142 | 15,243 | 15,786 | 18,030 | 20,443 | 23,712 | 27,765 | 32,032 | 33,270 |
| Costa Rica | 238 | 1,237 | 1,618 | 2,070 | 2,603 | 2,466 | 2,594 | 3,005 | 3,098 | 4,461 | 4,760 | 4,977 | 5,653 |
| Curaçao & Sint Maarten | 355 | .... | .... | .... | .... | .... | .... | 820 | 840 | 738 | 719 | 972 | 970 |
| Dominican Republic | 243 | 527 | 1,344 | 1,505 | 1,917 | 1,739 | 2,271 | 2,499 | 2,662 | 2,296 | 3,038 | 3,340 | 3,786 |
| Ecuador | 248 | 689 | 1,199 | 990 | 1,782 | 2,427 | 1,833 | 932 | 1,084 | 703 | 2,161 | 2,405 | 1,505 |
| El Salvador | 253 | 1,128 | 1,204 | 1,212 | 1,334 | 1,585 | 1,829 | 1,668 | 1,401 | 1,825 | 1,608 | 1,677 | 1,977 |
| Guatemala | 258 | 2,206 | 2,563 | 2,602 | 2,613 | 2,897 | 3,166 | 3,660 | 3,801 | 4,115 | 4,547 | 4,875 | 5,420 |
| Guyana | 336 | 149 | 176 | 186 | 198 | 231 | 403 | 508 | 522 | 562 | 509 | 461 | 434 |
| Haiti | 263 | 121 | 153 | 244 | 368 | 457 | 671 | 1,228 | 1,225 | 1,408 | 1,590 | 1,356 | 1,383 |
| Honduras | 268 | 1,269 | 1,628 | 1,747 | 1,600 | 1,606 | 1,331 | 1,734 | 1,791 | 1,624 | 1,936 | 2,369 | 2,692 |
| Jamaica | 343 | 1,189 | 1,518 | 1,541 | 1,189 | 1,151 | 1,324 | 1,624 | 1,486 | 1,299 | 1,181 | 1,707 | 2,103 |
| Mexico | 273 | 41,301 | 51,813 | 50,698 | 55,124 | 61,759 | 63,526 | 78,093 | 93,789 | 104,373 | 113,917 | 131,779 | 125,174 |
| Netherlands Antilles | 353 | 267 | 382 | 329 | 418 | 532 | 553 | .... | .... | .... | .... | .... | |
| Nicaragua | 278 | 430 | 509 | 613 | 698 | 741 | 1,003 | 1,168 | 1,233 | 1,228 | 1,294 | 1,571 | 1,799 |
| Panama | 283 | 406 | 847 | 887 | 1,225 | 1,574 | 1,932 | 1,763 | 1,501 | 1,605 | 1,849 | 2,783 | 2,438 |
| Paraguay | 288 | 752 | 908 | 1,131 | 1,558 | 1,847 | 2,449 | 2,686 | 3,224 | 2,965 | 3,608 | 4,603 | 4,084 |
| Peru | 293 | 7,841 | 9,515 | 11,123 | 16,995 | 19,653 | 20,420 | 27,693 | 30,748 | 40,536 | 41,833 | 42,231 | 43,597 |
| Suriname | 366 | 83 | 88 | 143 | 234 | 365 | 381 | 391 | 461 | 576 | 479 | 396 | 205 |
| Trinidad and Tobago | 369 | 2,040 | 3,471 | 4,378 | 4,236 | 6,130 | 5,854 | 6,237 | 6,778 | 6,373 | 6,883 | 8,211 | 7,444 |
| Uruguay | 298 | 1,615 | 2,151 | 2,051 | 2,604 | 4,124 | 5,121 | 4,963 | 6,702 | 8,843 | 10,565 | 12,110 | 11,279 |
| Venezuela, Rep. Bol. | 299 | 11,832 | 16,735 | 19,554 | 15,312 | 21,489 | 13,844 | 8,530 | 6,468 | 6,442 | 3,921 | 5,147 | 4,564 |

# Nongold Reserves/Imports

| 1rl s | | 2004 | 2005 | 2006 | 2007 | 2008 | 2009 | 2010 | 2011 | 2012 | 2013 | 2014 | 2015 |
|---|---|---|---|---|---|---|---|---|---|---|---|---|---|
| | | | | | | | *Weeks of Imports* | | | | | | |
| World.............................. | 001 | **21.4** | **21.3** | **22.4** | **24.8** | **23.6** | **35.4** | **32.9** | **30.4** | **32.5** | **34.0** | **33.4** | **35.9** |
| Advanced Economies............... | 110 | **16.3** | **14.4** | **13.7** | **13.2** | **12.1** | **19.0** | **17.7** | **16.8** | **18.5** | **19.0** | **18.7** | **21.6** |
| Euro Area................................. | 163 | 8.2 | 6.2 | 5.8 | 5.4 | 4.7 | 8.3 | 7.6 | 6.7 | 7.5 | 7.4 | 7.3 | 8.7 |
| Austria.................................. | 122 | 3.6 | 3.0 | 2.8 | 3.5 | 2.6 | 3.1 | 3.3 | 3.1 | 3.7 | 3.8 | 4.3 | 4.5 |
| Belgium................................. | 124 | 1.9 | 1.3 | 1.3 | 1.3 | 1.0 | 2.3 | 2.2 | 2.0 | 2.2 | 2.1 | 1.9 | 2.2 |
| Cyprus.................................. | 423 | 35.9 | 34.6 | 42.5 | 36.6 | 3.0 | 5.2 | 3.1 | 3.0 | 3.2 | 3.1 | 2.7 | 3.1 |
| Estonia................................. | 939 | 11.2 | 9.9 | 12.2 | 11.3 | 12.8 | 20.3 | 10.8 | .6 | .8 | .9 | 1.2 | 1.5 |
| Finland................................. | 172 | 12.5 | 9.4 | 4.9 | 4.5 | 3.9 | 8.3 | 5.5 | 4.9 | 5.7 | 6.3 | 5.9 | 7.2 |
| France.................................. | 132 | 4.1 | 2.9 | 4.1 | 3.8 | 2.4 | 4.3 | 4.8 | 3.5 | 4.2 | 3.9 | 3.9 | 5.1 |
| Germany............................... | 134 | 3.5 | 3.0 | 2.4 | 2.2 | 1.9 | 3.4 | 3.1 | 2.8 | 3.0 | 2.9 | 2.7 | 2.9 |
| Greece.................................. | 174 | 1.1 | .5 | .4 | .4 | .2 | 1.1 | 1.0 | 1.0 | 1.0 | 1.2 | 1.5 | 2.4 |
| Ireland................................. | 178 | 2.4 | .6 | .5 | .5 | .5 | 1.6 | 1.6 | 1.1 | 1.1 | 1.1 | 1.1 | 1.5 |
| Italy.................................... | 136 | 4.1 | 3.4 | 3.0 | 2.9 | 3.4 | 5.7 | 5.1 | 4.6 | 5.4 | 5.5 | 5.3 | 6.0 |
| Latvia.................................. | 941 | 14.2 | 13.5 | 19.8 | 19.0 | 16.6 | 36.9 | 33.9 | 20.2 | 23.0 | 23.5 | 9.2 | 12.0 |
| Lithuania.............................. | 946 | 14.7 | 12.5 | 15.1 | 16.1 | 10.4 | 18.2 | 14.1 | 12.9 | 13.4 | 11.7 | 12.6 | 2.8 |
| Luxembourg........................... | 137 | .9 | .7 | .6 | .3 | .7 | 2.0 | 1.8 | 1.8 | 1.9 | 1.9 | 1.7 | 1.9 |
| Malta................................... | 181 | 37.2 | 35.2 | 38.0 | 43.7 | 3.4 | 5.7 | 4.9 | 3.5 | 4.5 | 4.1 | 3.9 | 4.6 |
| Netherlands........................... | 138 | 2.0 | 1.5 | 1.6 | 1.3 | 1.2 | 2.4 | 2.2 | 2.1 | 2.3 | 2.3 | 2.0 | 2.2 |
| Portugal............................... | 182 | 5.5 | 3.4 | 1.6 | .9 | .7 | 1.8 | 2.5 | 1.2 | 1.6 | 1.9 | 3.3 | 5.0 |
| Slovak Republic...................... | 936 | 24.6 | 21.4 | 13.9 | 15.1 | 12.5 | .6 | .6 | .5 | .5 | .6 | .9 | 1.3 |
| Slovenia............................... | 961 | 26.0 | 21.4 | 15.9 | 1.7 | 1.3 | 2.1 | 1.8 | 1.4 | 1.4 | 1.4 | 1.5 | 1.5 |
| Spain................................... | 184 | 2.5 | 1.7 | 1.7 | 1.6 | 1.5 | 3.3 | 3.2 | 4.7 | 5.7 | 5.5 | 5.8 | 7.6 |
| Australia............................... | 193 | 17.0 | 17.4 | 20.0 | 7.8 | 8.0 | 12.2 | 10.0 | 9.1 | 8.9 | 10.7 | 11.2 | 11.6 |
| Canada................................. | 156 | 6.4 | 5.3 | 5.1 | 5.5 | 5.4 | 8.5 | 7.3 | 7.3 | 7.5 | 7.8 | 8.1 | 9.5 |
| China, P.R.: Hong Kong.............. | 532 | 23.7 | 21.6 | 20.7 | 21.6 | 24.4 | 38.3 | 32.3 | 30.7 | 32.7 | 30.9 | 31.4 | 35.7 |
| Czech Republic....................... | 935 | 20.5 | 20.0 | 17.4 | 15.2 | 13.4 | 20.3 | 17.2 | 13.6 | 16.3 | 20.1 | 18.2 | 23.6 |
| Denmark............................... | 128 | 30.4 | 23.6 | 18.4 | 17.4 | 19.3 | 48.1 | 46.0 | 44.0 | 48.5 | 45.5 | 38.2 | 38.7 |
| Iceland................................. | 176 | 15.3 | 11.8 | 23.5 | 22.0 | 32.4 | 55.0 | 75.6 | 90.9 | 44.5 | 45.2 | 40.7 | 48.7 |
| Israel................................... | 436 | 32.9 | 31.0 | 30.1 | 25.1 | 32.7 | 64.0 | 60.2 | 51.3 | 52.4 | 56.8 | 59.3 | 72.5 |
| Japan................................... | 158 | 95.4 | 84.2 | 78.9 | 79.9 | 68.8 | 96.6 | 79.7 | 76.6 | 72.1 | 77.3 | 78.8 | 96.8 |
| Korea................................... | 542 | 46.1 | 40.9 | 40.2 | 38.2 | 24.0 | 43.4 | 35.6 | 30.2 | 32.3 | 34.5 | 35.5 | 43.3 |
| New Zealand.......................... | 196 | 15.3 | 17.2 | 27.4 | 28.5 | 16.9 | 32.1 | 27.3 | 23.7 | 24.2 | 21.0 | 19.4 | 20.9 |
| Norway................................. | 142 | 47.5 | 44.0 | 46.0 | 39.4 | 29.3 | 36.8 | 35.5 | 28.3 | 30.9 | 33.7 | 38.3 | 39.5 |
| Singapore............................. | 576 | 35.7 | 30.1 | 29.6 | 32.2 | 28.3 | 39.7 | 37.7 | 33.8 | 35.5 | 38.0 | 36.4 | 43.4 |
| Sweden................................ | 144 | 11.4 | 10.3 | 10.1 | 9.2 | 8.0 | 18.5 | 14.9 | 13.1 | 14.4 | 19.7 | 18.8 | 20.5 |
| Switzerland........................... | 146 | 26.2 | 15.8 | 15.0 | 15.1 | 13.5 | 34.6 | 69.6 | 73.8 | 131.1 | 134.5 | 134.7 | 170.5 |
| Taiwan Province of China.......... | 528 | 74.8 | 72.1 | 68.2 | 64.0 | 63.0 | 103.7 | 79.0 | 71.2 | 77.4 | 80.3 | 79.5 | 96.9 |
| United Kingdom...................... | 112 | 4.5 | 3.9 | 3.6 | 4.1 | 3.6 | 6.0 | 6.3 | 6.5 | 7.1 | 7.4 | 7.5 | . . . . |
| United States......................... | 111 | 2.6 | 1.6 | 1.5 | 1.5 | 1.6 | 3.9 | 3.2 | 3.1 | 3.1 | 3.0 | 2.6 | 2.4 |
| Emerging & Dev. Economies...... | 200 | **35.4** | **39.2** | **43.8** | **50.9** | **46.7** | **66.9** | **59.9** | **53.4** | **54.7** | **57.1** | **56.0** | **58.2** |
| Emerging & Developing Asia..... | 505 | **46.7** | **48.2** | **52.7** | **63.2** | **61.8** | **89.2** | **76.9** | **68.0** | **66.9** | **72.0** | **72.4** | **74.3** |
| Bangladesh............................ | 513 | 13.1 | 11.2 | 13.2 | 15.6 | 13.2 | 25.8 | 21.1 | 13.0 | 16.3 | 30.0 | . . . . | . . . . |
| Bhutan................................. | 514 | 51.0 | 62.9 | 67.6 | 69.1 | 73.6 | 87.4 | 61.0 | 39.4 | 50.0 | 56.7 | 79.9 | 49.0 |
| Cambodia.............................. | 522 | 15.4 | 12.6 | 12.7 | 17.7 | 18.3 | 25.4 | 24.9 | 19.3 | 20.2 | 18.1 | 21.7 | 24.9 |
| China, P.R.: Mainland................ | 924 | 56.9 | 64.7 | 70.2 | 83.2 | 89.6 | 125.1 | 106.7 | 95.6 | 95.3 | 102.4 | 102.2 | 103.5 |
| China, P.R.: Macao................... | 546 | 81.3 | 88.9 | 104.0 | 128.2 | 154.4 | 206.5 | 223.8 | 227.8 | 97.2 | 82.8 | 75.9 | 92.6 |
| Fiji...................................... | 819 | 17.4 | 10.4 | 9.0 | 15.2 | 7.4 | 20.5 | 20.6 | 19.8 | 21.2 | 17.3 | 15.7 | 16.2 |
| India.................................... | 534 | 66.0 | 48.0 | 49.7 | 60.7 | 40.1 | 53.6 | 40.9 | 30.4 | 28.7 | 30.9 | 34.1 | 44.2 |
| Indonesia.............................. | 536 | 33.0 | 22.8 | 26.5 | 30.7 | 20.2 | 35.2 | 35.7 | 31.3 | 29.6 | 26.9 | 31.8 | 37.6 |
| Lao People's Dem. Rep.............. | 544 | 16.3 | 13.8 | 16.1 | 26.0 | 23.3 | 21.7 | 17.8 | 16.0 | 13.6 | 12.4 | 13.8 | 14.1 |
| Malaysia............................... | 548 | 32.5 | 31.8 | 32.6 | 35.9 | 30.3 | 40.1 | 33.1 | 36.6 | 36.5 | 33.7 | 28.5 | 27.8 |
| Maldives............................... | 556 | 16.8 | 13.2 | 13.2 | 14.8 | 9.2 | 14.9 | 17.4 | 12.4 | 10.6 | 11.5 | 16.4 | 15.8 |
| Mongolia.............................. | 948 | 9.9 | 14.6 | 20.4 | 19.7 | 8.1 | 31.6 | 34.8 | 18.1 | 30.3 | 17.1 | 15.3 | 17.1 |
| Myanmar.............................. | 518 | 16.1 | 21.0 | 25.3 | 49.5 | 45.4 | 62.8 | 62.5 | 40.4 | 39.6 | . . . . | . . . . | . . . . |
| Nepal................................... | 558 | 39.2 | 37.2 | 42.1 | 35.7 | 40.2 | 39.3 | 29.9 | 35.3 | 41.3 | 46.0 | 42.8 | 64.7 |
| Papua New Guinea................... | 853 | 19.6 | 21.6 | 31.8 | 36.2 | 28.5 | 41.6 | 39.9 | 45.2 | 37.2 | 32.1 | . . . . | . . . . |
| Philippines............................ | 566 | 16.1 | 17.6 | 19.3 | 27.2 | 28.5 | 44.0 | 49.2 | 54.6 | 58.0 | 60.0 | 54.5 | 54.9 |
| Samoa.................................. | 862 | 28.9 | 22.7 | 19.2 | 21.8 | 18.2 | 42.2 | 39.2 | 27.2 | 28.5 | 27.3 | . . . . | . . . . |
| Solomon Islands...................... | 813 | 34.2 | 26.6 | 25.0 | 21.9 | 15.0 | 29.1 | 34.7 | 45.3 | 49.1 | 47.6 | 48.6 | 55.0 |
| Sri Lanka.............................. | 524 | 13.9 | 15.6 | 13.8 | 15.6 | 9.2 | 23.9 | 25.8 | 16.0 | 17.3 | 19.1 | 19.4 | 17.9 |
| Thailand............................... | 578 | 26.8 | 22.3 | 26.0 | 31.4 | 31.5 | 52.3 | 47.1 | 38.0 | 36.0 | 33.6 | 34.5 | 39.0 |
| Tonga.................................. | 866 | 27.4 | 20.2 | 21.4 | 23.8 | 21.6 | 34.4 | 34.2 | 38.6 | 39.8 | 40.8 | 37.8 | 39.6 |
| Vanuatu................................ | 846 | 25.1 | 23.5 | 25.0 | 27.0 | 19.1 | 26.3 | 29.4 | 29.7 | 32.0 | 30.1 | 31.6 | 36.1 |
| Vietnam................................ | 582 | 11.6 | 12.9 | 15.7 | 20.1 | 15.4 | 12.2 | 7.7 | 6.8 | 11.6 | 10.3 | 12.0 | 9.0 |
| Europe.................................. | 170 | **24.8** | **27.9** | **33.4** | **37.1** | **27.7** | **43.0** | **38.3** | **31.3** | **33.3** | **32.3** | **27.2** | **31.8** |
| Emerging & Dev. Europe.......... | 903 | **19.3** | **20.5** | **21.2** | **21.3** | **17.6** | **28.6** | **26.0** | **21.8** | **24.9** | **25.1** | **22.6** | **23.7** |
| Albania................................. | 914 | 30.6 | 27.9 | 30.1 | 26.1 | 23.0 | 26.6 | 28.0 | 23.1 | 26.8 | 28.8 | 25.9 | 37.1 |
| Bulgaria................................ | 918 | 31.5 | 23.0 | 24.5 | 28.5 | 23.6 | 37.8 | 31.5 | 24.3 | 29.2 | 27.8 | 27.8 | 37.6 |
| Croatia................................. | 960 | 27.5 | 24.7 | 27.8 | 27.5 | 21.9 | 36.5 | 36.7 | 33.2 | 37.1 | 44.1 | 35.6 | 37.8 |
| Hungary............................... | 944 | 13.9 | 14.1 | 14.5 | 13.2 | 16.5 | 29.4 | 26.6 | 25.1 | 24.5 | 24.3 | 21.0 | 18.8 |
| Macedonia, FYR...................... | 962 | 16.1 | 19.8 | 24.2 | 20.8 | 14.6 | 21.2 | 18.7 | 17.3 | 20.2 | 19.5 | 19.3 | 18.2 |
| Poland................................. | 964 | 20.9 | 21.1 | 19.3 | 20.5 | 15.0 | 26.4 | 25.9 | 23.1 | 27.5 | 26.0 | 22.6 | 24.3 |
| Romania............................... | 968 | 23.3 | 25.5 | 28.6 | 27.8 | 23.1 | 39.1 | 36.4 | 29.3 | 30.5 | 31.7 | 26.1 | 26.2 |
| Turkey................................. | 186 | 19.0 | 22.5 | 22.7 | 22.4 | 18.1 | 26.2 | 22.6 | 16.9 | 22.0 | 22.9 | 23.0 | 23.3 |
| CIS...................................... | 901 | **41.9** | **48.2** | **61.8** | **70.3** | **48.4** | **76.3** | **65.1** | **51.2** | **50.7** | **48.2** | **40.0** | **56.1** |
| Armenia................................ | 911 | 21.1 | 19.7 | 25.4 | 26.3 | 16.5 | 31.5 | 25.6 | 23.9 | 21.9 | 26.7 | 17.6 | 28.4 |
| Azerbaijan, Republic of.............. | 912 | 15.9 | 14.5 | 24.7 | 38.9 | 46.9 | 45.6 | 50.5 | 54.8 | 60.8 | 69.9 | 82.9 | 34.8 |
| Belarus................................. | 913 | 2.4 | 3.5 | 2.5 | 7.2 | 3.5 | 8.8 | 5.1 | 6.8 | 6.5 | 6.0 | 4.4 | 4.7 |
| Georgia................................ | 915 | 10.9 | 10.0 | 13.2 | 13.6 | 12.2 | 24.4 | 22.4 | 20.8 | 18.6 | 18.3 | 16.3 | 17.0 |
| Kazakhstan............................ | 916 | 31.9 | 17.6 | 38.3 | 24.7 | 24.2 | 37.9 | 54.6 | 43.6 | 32.6 | 21.6 | 27.5 | 35.3 |
| Kyrgyz Republic...................... | 917 | 29.2 | 26.9 | 23.1 | 23.8 | 14.7 | 25.6 | 25.9 | 20.8 | 17.7 | 18.0 | 16.4 | 20.9 |

|  |  | 2004 | 2005 | 2006 | 2007 | 2008 | 2009 | 2010 | 2011 | 2012 | 2013 | 2014 | 2015 |
|---|---|---|---|---|---|---|---|---|---|---|---|---|---|
| **1rl s** |  |  |  |  |  |  | *Weeks of Imports* |  |  |  |  |  |  |
| **CIS(Cont.)** |  |  |  |  |  |  |  |  |  |  |  |  |  |
| Moldova | 921 | 13.8 | 13.6 | 15.0 | 18.8 | 17.8 | 23.5 | 23.2 | 19.7 | 25.0 | 26.7 | 21.1 | 22.9 |
| Russia | 922 | 58.6 | 66.3 | 85.6 | 98.9 | 67.4 | 107.1 | 85.4 | 67.4 | 68.5 | 65.0 | 52.1 | 77.9 |
| Ukraine | 926 | 17.0 | 27.3 | 25.2 | 27.3 | 18.7 | 29.3 | 28.5 | 19.1 | 13.9 | 12.7 | 6.3 | 17.1 |
| **Middle East,N.Africa & Pakistan** | 440 | **34.1** | **52.0** | **63.3** | **70.8** | **64.8** | **74.9** | **72.7** | **69.5** | **73.5** | **75.5** | **72.4** | **70.1** |
| Algeria | 612 | 125.3 | 147.4 | 192.8 | 209.1 | 188.7 | 197.0 | 210.3 | 201.0 | 197.5 | 184.4 | 160.1 | 145.7 |
| Bahrain, Kingdom of | 419 | 13.7 | 10.9 | 13.8 | 19.1 | 18.9 | 27.4 | 27.0 | 18.6 | 18.2 | 21.4 | 22.6 | .... |
| Djibouti | 611 | 18.7 | 16.7 | 18.6 | 14.5 | 15.9 | 27.9 | 30.8 | 24.9 | 22.3 | 39.5 | 25.5 | 21.3 |
| Egypt | 469 | 57.8 | 54.1 | 61.4 | 58.0 | 34.3 | 37.3 | 33.0 | 13.2 | 9.2 | 11.9 | 10.2 | 10.6 |
| Iraq | 433 | 19.1 | 26.7 | 49.6 | 75.6 | 78.7 | 62.0 | 59.6 | 64.5 | 62.7 | 64.9 | 55.4 | 51.0 |
| Jordan | 439 | 33.7 | 26.0 | 30.5 | 29.0 | 26.6 | 41.8 | 45.0 | 32.3 | 20.3 | 31.7 | 34.7 | 39.4 |
| Kuwait | 443 | 33.9 | 29.2 | 37.9 | 40.6 | 35.8 | 53.0 | 48.7 | 53.3 | 55.1 | 52.1 | 53.8 | 46.1 |
| Lebanon | 446 | 63.5 | 64.2 | 72.1 | 54.8 | 62.8 | 91.3 | 88.8 | 87.0 | 90.8 | 90.6 | 97.3 | 109.3 |
| Libya | 672 | 211.2 | 338.0 | 510.4 | 613.3 | 524.6 | 513.4 | 493.5 | 681.2 | 267.7 | 221.9 | 243.8 | .... |
| Mauritania | 682 | 1.9 | 2.3 | 8.3 | 7.2 | 5.1 | 7.8 | 7.3 | 10.2 | 17.6 | .... | .... | .... |
| Morocco | 686 | 47.7 | 40.5 | 44.1 | 39.2 | 27.1 | 36.1 | 33.7 | 22.7 | 18.8 | 20.7 | 22.3 | 30.8 |
| Oman | 449 | 21.1 | 25.7 | 23.9 | 31.0 | 26.3 | 35.5 | 34.2 | 31.6 | 25.4 | 24.2 | 28.8 | 31.4 |
| Pakistan | 564 | 28.4 | 20.6 | 20.1 | 22.4 | 8.8 | 18.6 | 19.7 | 17.2 | 12.1 | 6.0 | 12.9 | 21.2 |
| Qatar | 453 | 29.4 | 23.5 | 17.0 | 20.9 | 18.0 | 38.3 | 68.5 | 37.7 | 67.0 | 80.0 | 72.9 | 58.2 |
| Saudi Arabia | 456 | 31.7 | 135.6 | 168.4 | 176.1 | 199.7 | 223.0 | 216.4 | 213.7 | 219.4 | 224.3 | 218.9 | 183.4 |
| Sudan | 732 | 17.1 | 14.4 | 10.7 | 8.5 | 7.8 | 5.9 | 5.4 | 1.1 | 1.1 | 1.0 | 1.0 | 1.1 |
| Tunisia | 744 | 16.0 | 17.5 | 23.4 | 21.4 | 18.7 | 29.9 | 22.1 | 16.2 | 17.8 | 15.6 | 15.2 | .... |
| United Arab Emirates | 466 | 13.4 | 12.9 | 14.4 | 30.3 | 9.3 | 9.0 | 10.3 | 9.5 | 11.1 | 14.5 | 15.6 | 21.2 |
| Yemen, Republic of | 474 | 73.9 | 59.1 | 64.3 | 47.1 | 40.0 | 39.3 | 31.5 | 23.1 | 26.3 | 22.0 | .... | .... |
| **Sub-Saharan Africa** | 603 | **26.8** | **29.0** | **33.3** | **35.0** | **31.3** | **39.3** | **32.3** | **28.2** | **32.9** | **33.0** | **29.3** | **29.2** |
| **CEMAC** |  |  |  |  |  |  |  |  |  |  |  |  |  |
| Cameroon | 622 | 16.7 | 17.1 | 28.3 | 32.5 | 28.0 | 43.2 | 37.5 | 24.5 | 27.0 | 27.2 | 21.7 | 27.6 |
| Central African Rep. | 626 | 50.9 | 41.9 | 32.2 | 17.2 | 21.1 | 40.1 | 38.6 | 29.1 | 29.8 | 40.3 | .... | .... |
| Chad | 628 | 12.1 | 12.3 | 24.1 | 27.6 | 36.8 | 13.9 | 13.2 | 18.3 | 23.1 | 20.5 | 16.0 | 8.7 |
| Congo, Rep. of | 634 | 6.2 | 28.3 | 46.2 | 43.4 | 64.1 | 66.3 | 77.4 | 56.4 | 55.5 | 49.6 | 41.3 | 14.9 |
| Equatorial Guinea | 642 | 45.0 | 83.5 | 78.9 | 84.4 | 58.9 | 32.5 | 21.4 | 26.5 | 38.1 | 33.9 | 23.3 | .... |
| Gabon | 646 | 17.1 | 23.6 | 33.6 | 29.6 | 38.6 | 41.2 | 30.3 | 30.6 | 33.7 | 40.3 | 41.5 | 31.9 |
| **WAEMU** |  |  |  |  |  |  |  |  |  |  |  |  |  |
| Benin | 638 | 36.8 | 33.5 | 38.6 | 30.9 | 28.7 | 41.2 | 41.8 | 17.1 | 16.8 | 16.8 | .... | 16.1 |
| Burkina Faso | 748 | 27.0 | 18.1 | 21.9 | 31.9 | 23.9 | 32.3 | 25.8 | 19.3 | 15.6 | 7.9 | 4.6 | .... |
| Côte d'Ivoire | 662 | 18.5 | 12.1 | 16.1 | 19.6 | 14.9 | 24.2 | 24.0 | 33.4 | 20.9 | 17.5 | 21.7 | 24.7 |
| Guinea Bissau | 654 | 38.8 | 34.6 | 38.8 | 53.4 | 32.6 | 43.3 | 41.4 | 44.0 | 34.2 | 40.4 | .... | .... |
| Mali | 678 | 32.5 | 28.8 | 27.7 | 25.9 | 16.7 | 33.6 | 20.4 | 21.1 | 23.7 | 18.4 | 11.3 | 10.2 |
| Niger | 692 | 17.3 | 13.8 | 20.3 | 26.8 | 21.6 | 22.7 | 18.2 | 19.3 | 29.3 | 31.9 | 29.6 | 27.1 |
| Senegal | 722 | 24.9 | 19.3 | 20.1 | 20.2 | 14.6 | 24.3 | 24.0 | 18.8 | 18.4 | 19.3 | 17.5 | 20.3 |
| Togo | 742 | 21.1 | 9.4 | 18.0 | 18.4 | 20.0 | 18.7 | 37.3 | 22.4 | 12.8 | 12.6 | .... | .... |
| Botswana | 616 | 91.0 | 101.5 | 134.7 | 125.2 | 91.0 | 96.2 | 71.9 | 57.6 | 48.8 | 47.7 | 53.6 | 61.8 |
| Burundi | 618 | 19.4 | 19.5 | 15.8 | 28.7 | 34.4 | 41.6 | 33.8 | 20.3 | 21.3 | 21.0 | 21.4 | 9.7 |
| Cabo Verde | 624 | 16.8 | 20.7 | 24.4 | 25.3 | 22.8 | 29.2 | 26.8 | 18.6 | 25.5 | 34.1 | 40.6 | 45.7 |
| Comoros | 632 | 63.0 | 45.2 | 42.2 | 44.0 | 33.3 | 46.0 | 39.8 | 29.2 | 33.6 | 31.6 | .... | .... |
| Congo, Dem. Rep. of | 636 | 6.2 | 3.0 | 2.9 | 3.2 | .9 | 13.8 | 15.0 | 12.0 | 13.9 | 13.9 | 12.5 | 10.2 |
| Ethiopia | 644 | 27.1 | 13.3 | 8.5 | 11.6 | 5.5 | 12.1 | .... | .... | .... | .... | .... | .... |
| Gambia, The | 648 | 19.0 | 19.7 | 24.2 | 23.1 | 18.7 | 38.4 | 35.0 | 34.5 | 32.3 | 31.5 | .... | .... |
| Ghana | 652 | 20.8 | 17.0 | 16.1 | 12.8 | 9.0 | 21.8 | 22.5 | 22.6 | 20.5 | 21.3 | .... | .... |
| Guinea | 656 | 8.3 | 6.0 | — | .5 | .1 | 6.3 | 4.3 | 2.5 | 3.5 | 4.2 | 7.2 | .... |
| Kenya | 664 | 17.4 | 15.2 | 17.2 | 19.4 | 13.5 | 19.6 | 18.6 | 15.0 | 18.2 | 21.0 | 22.4 | 24.4 |
| Lesotho | 666 | 18.0 | 19.1 | 22.9 | 30.0 | 24.9 | 31.0 | 25.3 | 32.9 | 33.5 | 23.9 | 25.2 | 24.1 |
| Madagascar | 674 | 15.6 | 14.7 | 17.4 | 18.2 | 13.4 | 16.1 | 21.0 | 22.5 | 22.0 | 12.6 | 12.4 | 13.6 |
| Malawi | 676 | 7.1 | 7.1 | 5.8 | 8.2 | 5.7 | 3.8 | 7.4 | 4.2 | 5.0 | 7.6 | 11.3 | .... |
| Mauritius | 684 | 30.1 | 22.1 | 18.2 | 23.8 | 19.5 | 30.4 | 29.0 | 26.1 | 27.5 | 32.2 | 33.5 | 42.9 |
| Mozambique | 688 | 28.9 | 22.8 | 20.9 | 24.6 | 20.5 | 29.0 | 29.1 | 20.3 | 16.6 | 16.2 | 13.5 | 15.1 |
| Namibia | 728 | 7.1 | 5.9 | 7.2 | 10.3 | 12.8 | 16.5 | 13.5 | 14.0 | 12.4 | 10.4 | .... | .... |
| Nigeria | 694 | 62.2 | 69.0 | 82.2 | 71.0 | 65.0 | 68.6 | 41.0 | 28.4 | 67.6 | 53.0 | .... | .... |
| Rwanda | 714 | 57.6 | 49.0 | 41.7 | 39.0 | 27.3 | 31.5 | 30.2 | 30.7 | 26.7 | 33.6 | 32.3 | .... |
| São Tomé & Príncipe | 716 | 24.5 | 27.9 | 25.1 | 25.9 | 27.9 | 33.6 | 22.3 | 20.7 | 19.2 | 23.7 | 19.2 | 25.2 |
| Seychelles | 718 | 3.6 | 4.3 | 7.8 | 2.5 | 3.2 | 12.3 | 13.4 | 13.8 | 14.9 | 20.2 | 21.1 | 28.1 |
| Sierra Leone | 724 | 29.0 | 26.0 | 24.2 | 25.2 | 21.5 | 40.4 | 27.4 | 13.3 | 15.5 | 17.1 | 19.9 | 21.9 |
| South Africa | 199 | 12.7 | 15.5 | 15.4 | 17.4 | 15.6 | 24.7 | 21.1 | 18.2 | 18.4 | 21.8 | 22.0 | 24.0 |
| Swaziland | 734 | 8.7 | 6.7 | 10.0 | 21.8 | 22.7 | 30.7 | 23.1 | 16.0 | 19.8 | 25.9 | .... | .... |
| Tanzania | 738 | 43.8 | 32.4 | 27.7 | 28.1 | 21.0 | 28.7 | 26.4 | 18.1 | 18.7 | 19.8 | 19.0 | 20.6 |
| Uganda | 746 | 39.2 | 34.1 | 36.8 | 38.1 | 26.4 | 36.6 | 30.0 | 29.7 | 31.5 | 35.2 | 33.9 | 31.8 |
| Zambia | 754 | 8.1 | 11.3 | 12.2 | 14.1 | 11.4 | 26.0 | 20.5 | 16.6 | 18.0 | 13.7 | 16.8 | 18.3 |
| Zimbabwe | 698 | 5.3 | 2.2 | 3.5 | 2.9 | 1.3 | 14.7 | 10.0 | 7.8 | 6.8 | 5.7 | 4.5 | 4.2 |
| **Western Hemisphere** | 205 | **25.4** | **25.0** | **25.5** | **30.6** | **28.2** | **41.5** | **37.4** | **35.5** | **37.3** | **36.1** | **37.3** | **39.6** |
| **ECCU** |  |  |  |  |  |  |  |  |  |  |  |  |  |
| Anguilla | 312 | 16.9 | 15.5 | 15.2 | 9.4 | 7.8 | 11.5 | 13.2 | 12.7 | 13.9 | 14.7 | 16.2 | 15.8 |
| Antigua and Barbuda | 311 | .... | 12.6 | 11.1 | 10.3 | 8.9 | 9.5 | 14.2 | 16.3 | 15.8 | 20.5 | 28.0 | 37.9 |
| Dominica | 321 | 15.2 | 15.5 | 19.6 | 16.1 | 11.6 | 17.4 | 17.7 | 18.7 | 23.6 | 22.3 | 22.9 | 30.1 |
| Grenada | 328 | 25.1 | 14.7 | 15.7 | 15.7 | 14.5 | 22.9 | 19.6 | 19.1 | 18.5 | 21.3 | 26.3 | 29.1 |
| Montserrat | 351 | 25.5 | 24.4 | 25.1 | 25.4 | 15.9 | 25.1 | 29.8 | 38.6 | 45.2 | 50.0 | 56.9 | 69.3 |
| St. Kitts and Nevis | 361 | 22.3 | 17.7 | 18.5 | 18.3 | 17.7 | 24.0 | 32.5 | 51.5 | 59.6 | 62.8 | 62.1 | 53.6 |
| St. Lucia | 362 | 15.8 | 12.6 | 11.8 | 12.6 | 11.3 | 16.9 | 17.8 | 16.6 | 17.7 | 16.7 | 24.1 | 29.0 |
| St. Vincent & Grenadines | 364 | 17.3 | 15.0 | 15.2 | 13.8 | 11.7 | 13.7 | 17.0 | 14.0 | 16.5 | 19.5 | 22.1 | 26.6 |
| Argentina | 213 | 43.8 | 49.3 | 47.0 | 52.0 | 40.6 | 61.3 | 53.8 | 30.2 | 30.3 | 19.8 | 23.1 | 20.4 |
| Aruba | 314 | 17.6 | 13.8 | 16.9 | 17.4 | 27.7 | 26.2 | 27.6 | 21.8 | 24.9 | 21.3 | 23.1 | 31.6 |
| Bahamas, The | 313 | 18.4 | 13.7 | 10.0 | 9.9 | 12.5 | 19.5 | 18.8 | 16.3 | 12.0 | 12.5 | 12.0 | .... |
| Barbados | 316 | 21.3 | 19.6 | 20.9 | 25.5 | 20.4 | 30.8 | 27.8 | 23.4 | 24.2 | 20.1 | 18.9 | .... |
| Belize | 339 | 4.8 | 6.3 | 8.7 | 8.2 | 10.3 | 16.6 | 16.0 | 14.8 | 17.0 | 22.5 | 25.2 | .... |

# Nongold Reserves/Imports

| | | 2004 | 2005 | 2006 | 2007 | 2008 | 2009 | 2010 | 2011 | 2012 | 2013 | 2014 | 2015 |
|---|---|---|---|---|---|---|---|---|---|---|---|---|---|
| 1rl s | | | | | | | *Weeks of Imports* | | | | | | |
| **Western Hemisphere(Cont.)** | | | | | | | | | | | | | |
| Bolivia............................ | 218 | 24.6 | 29.5 | 48.3 | 68.5 | 70.9 | 86.8 | 75.7 | 65.0 | 70.7 | 71.2 | 67.3 | 63.6 |
| Brazil............................ | 223 | 41.1 | 35.7 | 46.2 | 73.7 | 55.0 | 92.3 | 77.9 | 76.9 | 84.1 | 75.7 | 78.5 | 103.0 |
| Chile............................ | 228 | 33.5 | 26.9 | 26.3 | 18.6 | 19.4 | 31.8 | 25.0 | 29.6 | 27.4 | 26.6 | 29.0 | 32.0 |
| Colombia............................ | 233 | 41.6 | 36.3 | 30.5 | 32.6 | 31.1 | 39.1 | 35.5 | 29.9 | 32.3 | 37.4 | 37.7 | 44.3 |
| Costa Rica............................ | 238 | 12.1 | 12.3 | 14.1 | 16.5 | 12.9 | 18.4 | 17.7 | 15.2 | 20.4 | 21.3 | 21.8 | 26.4 |
| Dominican Republic.................... | 243 | 6.9 | 12.0 | 11.7 | 12.1 | 8.6 | 16.0 | 13.5 | 12.2 | 10.5 | 14.7 | .... | 14.4 |
| Ecuador............................ | 248 | 6.8 | 8.7 | 6.4 | 10.8 | 10.3 | 9.9 | 3.6 | 3.6 | 2.2 | 6.4 | 6.5 | 5.0 |
| El Salvador............................ | 253 | 14.4 | 13.1 | 12.4 | 12.6 | 13.0 | 20.6 | 15.6 | 11.1 | 14.2 | 12.0 | 12.0 | 13.7 |
| Guatemala............................ | 258 | 22.8 | 21.6 | 20.0 | 18.1 | 18.1 | 25.6 | 24.3 | 20.9 | 22.1 | 25.3 | 24.6 | 26.0 |
| Guyana............................ | 336 | 18.5 | 16.6 | 16.3 | 15.4 | 14.1 | 28.3 | 29.1 | 23.6 | 22.5 | 23.3 | 19.5 | 20.2 |
| Haiti............................ | 263 | 7.5 | 7.8 | 10.2 | 18.0 | 15.8 | 25.8 | 31.3 | 32.4 | 35.5 | 37.4 | 27.4 | .... |
| Honduras............................ | 268 | 24.3 | 24.9 | 24.0 | 19.4 | 14.6 | 17.7 | 19.6 | 16.0 | 13.7 | 16.9 | 19.2 | 20.6 |
| Jamaica............................ | 343 | 25.5 | 25.3 | 22.7 | 15.3 | 11.9 | 22.2 | 25.0 | 18.3 | 16.0 | 15.2 | 22.0 | 29.9 |
| Mexico............................ | 273 | 16.1 | 16.6 | 14.8 | 15.3 | 15.2 | 21.0 | 19.8 | 20.3 | 21.4 | 22.8 | 23.6 | 21.7 |
| Netherlands Antilles.................... | 353 | 12.5 | 14.5 | 11.7 | 13.5 | 13.8 | 17.3 | .... | .... | .... | .... | .... | .... |
| Nicaragua............................ | 278 | 15.7 | 14.6 | 16.0 | 16.0 | 13.8 | 23.8 | 22.1 | 19.0 | 16.8 | 18.4 | 20.2 | 22.0 |
| Panama............................ | 283 | 9.1 | 15.1 | 14.4 | 14.6 | 13.9 | 20.2 | 15.4 | 10.6 | 10.3 | 11.4 | .... | .... |
| Paraguay............................ | 288 | 19.6 | 17.8 | 14.5 | 21.8 | 16.4 | 28.8 | 21.4 | 20.9 | 20.6 | 23.8 | 28.5 | 28.8 |
| Peru............................ | 293 | 53.8 | 48.8 | 48.7 | 59.4 | 52.7 | 79.5 | 73.7 | 65.4 | 78.8 | 80.7 | 74.5 | .... |
| Suriname............................ | 366 | 11.4 | 7.9 | 12.5 | 17.3 | 19.2 | 22.9 | 22.7 | 22.1 | 23.4 | 17.9 | 15.0 | 7.6 |
| Trinidad and Tobago.................... | 369 | 33.9 | 45.3 | 50.0 | 45.3 | 51.3 | 68.4 | 76.8 | 56.9 | 56.2 | 62.1 | 70.7 | 82.6 |
| Uruguay............................ | 298 | 41.9 | 41.2 | 33.7 | 37.4 | 36.9 | 67.2 | 46.1 | 50.4 | 66.4 | 77.0 | 83.7 | 89.4 |
| Venezuela, Rep. Bol.................... | 299 | 57.3 | 51.8 | 45.5 | 27.3 | 34.7 | 27.8 | 20.2 | 13.5 | 11.8 | 6.8 | 8.7 | 8.2 |

# SDR Holdings

*Millions of SDRs: End of Period*

| | | 2004 | 2005 | 2006 | 2007 | 2008 | 2009 | 2010 | 2011 | 2012 | 2013 | 2014 | 2015 |
|---|---|---|---|---|---|---|---|---|---|---|---|---|---|
| World | 001 | 21,473.9 | 21,470.5 | 21,483.5 | 21,475.7 | 21,447.7 | 204,074.9 | 204,286.2 | 204,072.0 | 204,177.4 | 204,177.4 | 204,177.4 | 204,177.4 |
| Advanced Economies | 110 | 15,547.5 | 12,726.4 | 13,785.7 | 14,043.3 | 14,202.5 | 129,847.2 | 129,731.4 | 126,586.3 | 125,724.6 | 125,792.0 | 125,527.2 | 126,110.7 |
| Euro Area | | | | | | | | | | | | | |
| Austria | 122 | 103.10 | 102.59 | 126.30 | 147.40 | 198.37 | 1,750.53 | 1,747.54 | 1,689.71 | 1,671.89 | 1,780.71 | 1,594.09 | 1,624.31 |
| Belgium | 124 | 225.28 | 219.90 | 361.98 | 385.23 | 369.81 | 4,405.78 | 4,408.38 | 4,233.87 | 4,243.62 | 4,137.13 | 4,038.75 | 4,067.29 |
| Cyprus | 423 | 2.51 | 2.92 | 2.72 | 2.21 | 1.78 | 119.37 | 122.08 | 139.52 | 115.31 | 113.66 | 109.70 | 101.82 |
| Estonia | 939 | .05 | .05 | .06 | .06 | .06 | 62.03 | 62.03 | 62.03 | 62.03 | 62.03 | 62.04 | 62.05 |
| Finland | 172 | 106.72 | 113.27 | 128.40 | 153.72 | 155.19 | 1,201.71 | 1,195.41 | 1,118.76 | 1,125.26 | 1,125.64 | 1,126.08 | 1,123.41 |
| France | 132 | 563.26 | 614.38 | 629.89 | 629.62 | 626.92 | 9,717.51 | 9,739.85 | 9,558.59 | 9,490.46 | 9,185.30 | 9,371.43 | 9,422.93 |
| Germany | 134 | 1,326.98 | 1,323.65 | 1,335.86 | 1,368.05 | 1,426.90 | 12,184.18 | 12,187.67 | 11,896.91 | 11,652.16 | 11,478.94 | 11,959.22 | 11,930.72 |
| Greece | 174 | 17.41 | 20.33 | 19.61 | 17.42 | 15.46 | 694.20 | 609.06 | 553.20 | 553.50 | 554.67 | 553.99 | 258.62 |
| Ireland | 178 | 57.33 | 61.64 | 63.11 | 63.60 | 63.74 | 752.21 | 717.00 | 635.52 | 641.26 | 650.00 | 651.18 | 650.94 |
| Italy | 136 | 93.14 | 159.88 | 180.62 | 209.42 | 169.75 | 6,005.19 | 6,200.67 | 5,982.00 | 6,153.58 | 6,125.86 | 6,130.70 | 5,994.36 |
| Latvia | 941 | .10 | .10 | .11 | .11 | .24 | 119.11 | 121.17 | 94.24 | 101.92 | 120.82 | 120.82 | 120.82 |
| Lithuania | 946 | .06 | .05 | .07 | .07 | .07 | 137.31 | 137.31 | 137.31 | 137.31 | 137.31 | 137.31 | 137.30 |
| Luxembourg | 137 | 9.83 | 11.43 | 12.23 | 12.76 | 13.41 | 243.23 | 243.34 | 243.83 | 244.10 | 244.25 | 244.43 | 244.49 |
| Malta | 181 | 30.77 | 32.10 | 34.04 | 37.85 | 11.68 | 95.98 | 95.85 | 90.70 | 91.04 | 89.47 | 84.51 | 87.51 |
| Netherlands | 138 | 500.82 | 500.95 | 521.56 | 620.81 | 662.70 | 4,886.30 | 4,871.11 | 4,739.35 | 4,660.58 | 4,560.07 | 4,569.88 | 4,716.10 |
| Portugal | 182 | 66.25 | 71.98 | 75.31 | 77.89 | 79.53 | 833.29 | 833.28 | 792.57 | 793.29 | 792.64 | 792.79 | 793.03 |
| Slovak Republic | 936 | .88 | .90 | .93 | .97 | 1.00 | 341.62 | 341.79 | 324.81 | 326.40 | 354.73 | 323.05 | 322.72 |
| Slovenia | 961 | 7.18 | 8.13 | 8.25 | 7.97 | 7.66 | 198.13 | 198.18 | 208.64 | 207.57 | 196.71 | 207.01 | 207.10 |
| Spain | 184 | 213.96 | 232.11 | 222.69 | 233.46 | 144.92 | 2,959.05 | 2,933.13 | 2,664.23 | 2,686.57 | 2,791.42 | 2,710.75 | 2,755.17 |
| Australia | 193 | 125.50 | 135.11 | 132.68 | 121.91 | 113.02 | 3,097.75 | 3,093.65 | 3,017.98 | 2,951.20 | 3,107.26 | 2,946.46 | 3,016.57 |
| Canada | 156 | 595.19 | 627.61 | 640.25 | 642.88 | 643.56 | 5,875.85 | 5,879.16 | 5,840.11 | 5,695.99 | 5,633.06 | 5,634.89 | 5,700.44 |
| Czech Republic | 935 | 3.41 | 8.24 | 11.03 | 12.73 | 13.76 | 794.44 | 794.89 | 750.42 | 750.87 | 751.16 | 751.54 | 751.68 |
| Denmark | 128 | 28.77 | 78.13 | 227.07 | 211.86 | 207.84 | 1,520.50 | 1,521.44 | 1,461.57 | 1,467.91 | 1,467.30 | 1,422.98 | 1,451.18 |
| Iceland | 176 | .08 | .03 | .08 | .11 | .28 | 92.73 | 73.47 | 463.23 | 8.92 | 5.37 | 5.52 | 111.72 |
| Israel | 436 | 9.77 | 13.04 | 12.76 | 10.55 | 8.56 | 785.51 | 859.30 | 826.90 | 830.66 | 999.47 | 782.24 | 849.00 |
| Japan | 158 | 1,827.75 | 1,808.24 | 1,869.06 | 1,919.61 | 1,968.71 | 13,375.01 | 13,392.96 | 12,860.97 | 12,954.62 | 13,071.29 | 13,042.37 | 13,023.79 |
| Korea | 542 | 21.14 | 30.54 | 35.93 | 43.45 | 55.58 | 2,389.16 | 2,298.65 | 2,252.17 | 2,293.99 | 2,266.18 | 2,264.89 | 2,337.19 |
| New Zealand | 196 | 21.99 | 24.08 | 22.14 | 17.98 | 14.57 | 854.66 | 854.93 | 828.26 | 818.36 | 846.05 | 875.54 | 872.47 |
| Norway | 142 | 232.31 | 214.85 | 301.22 | 232.57 | 283.48 | 1,600.22 | 1,594.47 | 1,523.46 | 1,501.57 | 1,486.66 | 1,481.75 | 1,506.17 |
| San Marino | 135 | .56 | .66 | .80 | .97 | 1.13 | 16.69 | 16.70 | 15.37 | 15.37 | 15.46 | 15.46 | 15.47 |
| Singapore | 576 | 188.86 | 199.57 | 210.34 | 221.75 | 240.25 | 980.38 | 991.84 | 867.78 | 872.74 | 873.27 | 873.98 | 874.26 |
| Sweden | 144 | 134.80 | 123.47 | 256.70 | 256.69 | 198.72 | 2,290.79 | 2,287.29 | 2,203.04 | 2,136.95 | 2,156.04 | 2,099.44 | 2,166.80 |
| Switzerland | 146 | 45.50 | 41.86 | 182.72 | 156.92 | 148.93 | 3,439.08 | 3,242.06 | 3,209.31 | 3,028.43 | 3,130.14 | 3,070.05 | 3,403.47 |
| United Kingdom | 112 | 211.29 | 200.59 | 263.03 | 227.93 | 290.81 | 9,149.50 | 9,167.60 | 9,504.94 | 9,620.52 | 9,648.08 | 9,621.64 | 9,552.89 |
| United States | 111 | 8,774.97 | 5,744.05 | 5,896.10 | 5,996.79 | 6,064.13 | 36,878.21 | 36,898.15 | 35,794.96 | 35,818.62 | 35,833.86 | 35,850.78 | 35,856.95 |
| | | | | | | | | | | | | | |
| Emerging & Dev. Economies | 200 | 4,759.2 | 7,329.1 | 4,464.3 | 4,347.3 | 4,658.9 | 70,934.0 | 69,912.5 | 67,260.5 | 65,762.6 | 65,240.3 | 64,343.9 | 62,281.5 |
| Emerging & Developing Asia | 505 | 974.8 | 1,061.7 | 909.9 | 958.4 | 1,091.0 | 17,606.8 | 17,406.4 | 16,675.5 | 16,382.5 | 16,480.3 | 16,472.6 | 16,885.0 |
| Bangladesh | 513 | .80 | .65 | .88 | .49 | 1.37 | 458.33 | 428.30 | 477.99 | 414.56 | 638.99 | 682.03 | 881.30 |
| Bhutan | 514 | .27 | .30 | .33 | .38 | .42 | 6.42 | 6.42 | 6.43 | 6.43 | 6.43 | 6.43 | 6.43 |
| Brunei Darussalam | 516 | 8.81 | 10.17 | 11.20 | 12.04 | 12.73 | 216.33 | 216.38 | 216.46 | 216.48 | 216.49 | 216.51 | 216.51 |
| Cambodia | 522 | .05 | .17 | .12 | .14 | .07 | 68.50 | 68.46 | 68.39 | 68.37 | 68.36 | 68.35 | 88.34 |
| China, P.R.: Mainland | 924 | 803.01 | 875.38 | 710.00 | 754.39 | 778.59 | 7,979.64 | 8,015.75 | 7,722.15 | 7,388.76 | 7,255.35 | 7,215.95 | 7,421.57 |
| Fiji | 819 | 5.35 | 5.59 | 5.94 | 6.39 | 6.86 | 67.06 | 51.10 | 51.09 | 51.09 | 51.08 | 51.08 | 51.08 |
| India | 534 | 3.24 | 3.15 | .64 | 2.07 | 1.78 | 3,297.14 | 3,297.07 | 2,884.84 | 2,886.38 | 2,887.50 | 2,888.77 | 2,889.00 |
| Indonesia | 536 | 1.58 | 4.91 | 12.13 | 5.85 | 21.88 | 1,762.58 | 1,762.19 | 1,761.57 | 1,761.37 | 1,761.26 | 1,761.11 | 1,761.00 |
| Kiribati | 826 | .01 | .01 | .01 | .01 | .01 | 5.34 | 5.34 | 5.34 | 5.35 | 5.39 | 5.39 | 5.39 |
| Lao People's Dem. Rep. | 544 | 9.90 | 9.86 | 9.78 | 9.79 | 9.80 | 51.07 | 51.07 | 51.07 | 51.07 | 51.07 | 51.07 | 51.07 |
| Malaysia | 548 | 128.18 | 137.16 | 142.13 | 145.21 | 147.02 | 1,355.00 | 1,355.66 | 1,285.31 | 1,285.83 | 1,286.16 | 1,286.64 | 1,286.83 |
| Maldives | 556 | .32 | .32 | .33 | .36 | .40 | 7.77 | 7.63 | 6.97 | 6.89 | 6.82 | 6.77 | 6.46 |
| Marshall Islands, Rep. of | 867 | — | — | — | — | — | 3.33 | 3.33 | 3.33 | 3.34 | 3.36 | 3.36 | 3.36 |
| Micronesia, Fed. States of | 868 | 1.22 | 1.25 | 1.29 | 1.35 | 1.39 | 6.20 | 6.20 | 6.21 | 6.23 | 6.23 | 6.23 | 6.23 |
| Mongolia | 948 | .03 | .01 | — | .01 | .04 | 48.75 | 47.23 | 45.46 | 44.11 | 43.22 | 42.93 | 42.91 |
| Myanmar | 518 | .03 | .16 | .14 | .25 | .05 | 72.27 | 1.68 | .62 | .31 | 1.13 | 1.90 | 1.77 |
| Nepal | 558 | 6.23 | 6.15 | 6.00 | 5.73 | 5.41 | 63.71 | 60.84 | 57.96 | 51.17 | 41.17 | 32.59 | 22.59 |
| Palau | 565 | — | — | — | — | — | 2.96 | 2.96 | 2.96 | 2.97 | 2.99 | 2.99 | 2.99 |
| Papua New Guinea | 853 | .47 | .02 | .04 | .06 | .07 | 116.22 | 10.06 | 9.56 | 9.42 | 9.33 | 9.22 | 9.16 |
| Philippines | 566 | .65 | .59 | 1.55 | .47 | 6.91 | 727.93 | 727.78 | 728.13 | 838.26 | 845.98 | 846.30 | 846.43 |
| Samoa | 862 | 2.43 | 2.46 | 2.52 | 2.58 | 2.64 | 12.60 | 12.60 | 12.61 | 12.65 | 12.65 | 12.65 | 11.49 |
| Solomon Islands | 813 | — | — | .01 | — | .01 | 9.26 | 9.26 | 9.26 | 9.40 | 9.40 | 8.51 | 8.58 |
| Sri Lanka | 524 | .12 | 1.06 | 1.80 | 4.31 | 1.27 | 12.80 | 1.60 | 2.87 | 2.52 | 10.09 | 6.32 | 4.86 |
| Thailand | 578 | .66 | .43 | .57 | .12 | 85.23 | 971.48 | 972.00 | 973.32 | 973.82 | 974.14 | 974.59 | 974.78 |
| Timor-Leste | 537 | — | — | — | — | — | 7.73 | 7.73 | 7.73 | 7.75 | 7.75 | 7.10 | 7.10 |
| Tonga | 866 | .24 | .28 | .34 | .41 | .48 | 7.07 | 7.08 | 7.09 | 7.09 | 7.09 | 7.09 | 7.09 |
| Tuvalu | 869 | .... | .... | .... | .... | — | — | 1.26 | 1.26 | 1.26 | 1.26 | 1.26 | 1.26 |
| Vanuatu | 846 | .93 | .99 | 1.08 | 1.19 | 1.30 | 1.58 | 1.55 | 1.49 | 1.53 | 1.52 | 1.50 | 1.42 |
| Vietnam | 582 | .29 | .61 | 1.05 | 4.81 | 5.32 | 267.70 | 267.85 | 268.02 | 268.08 | 268.04 | 267.99 | 267.97 |
| | | | | | | | | | | | | | |
| Europe | 170 | 206.4 | 172.6 | 183.1 | 188.4 | 276.5 | 12,580.3 | 11,988.8 | 11,390.1 | 10,913.2 | 10,522.5 | 10,345.8 | 10,303.3 |
| Emerging & Dev. Europe | 903 | 166.3 | 142.1 | 131.8 | 152.3 | 211.4 | 5,271.7 | 4,758.2 | 4,122.3 | 3,661.9 | 3,265.9 | 3,098.6 | 3,081.3 |
| Albania | 914 | 64.90 | 8.75 | 5.99 | 1.22 | 4.70 | 50.40 | 50.71 | 49.97 | 54.02 | 66.98 | 73.73 | 136.51 |
| Bosnia and Herzegovina | 963 | .32 | .23 | .25 | .17 | .18 | 2.69 | .01 | .48 | 1.98 | 1.25 | 2.23 | 1.52 |
| Bulgaria | 918 | 8.45 | .70 | .71 | .66 | 4.20 | 610.88 | 610.89 | 610.92 | 611.11 | 611.59 | 611.59 | 611.58 |
| Croatia | 960 | .03 | .18 | .11 | .19 | .15 | 303.14 | 303.16 | 303.20 | 304.22 | 304.99 | 304.95 | 304.92 |
| Hungary | 944 | 37.56 | 44.62 | 49.22 | 52.83 | 35.16 | 943.42 | 749.64 | 548.53 | 237.21 | 13.76 | 12.86 | 12.36 |
| Kosovo | 967 | | | | | | 55.37 | 55.18 | 54.91 | 54.34 | 53.34 | 52.34 | 51.17 |
| Macedonia, FYR | 962 | .49 | .55 | 1.98 | .92 | .89 | 58.08 | .81 | .49 | 1.04 | 2.98 | 3.57 | 3.78 |
| Montenegro | 943 | — | — | — | .12 | .29 | 26.15 | 26.16 | 26.19 | 26.23 | 26.34 | 26.35 | 26.35 |
| Poland | 964 | 45.17 | 54.43 | 59.24 | 63.75 | 70.59 | 1,339.25 | 1,302.91 | 1,170.83 | 1,126.09 | 1,063.10 | 987.22 | 946.67 |

# SDR Holdings

| | | 2004 | 2005 | 2006 | 2007 | 2008 | 2009 | 2010 | 2011 | 2012 | 2013 | 2014 | 2015 |
|---|---|---|---|---|---|---|---|---|---|---|---|---|---|
| | | | | | | | *Millions of SDRs: End of Period* | | | | | | |
| **Emerging & Dev. Europe(Cont.)** | | | | | | | | | | | | | |
| Romania | 968 | .36 | .38 | .25 | .32 | 78.86 | 900.87 | 686.86 | 384.37 | 98.02 | 24.93 | 13.44 | 8.58 |
| Serbia, Republic of | 942 | .03 | 21.16 | 5.87 | .51 | 1.40 | 12.30 | 1.92 | 1.67 | 178.78 | 119.79 | 44.23 | 11.80 |
| Turkey | 186 | 9.02 | 11.07 | 8.13 | 31.59 | 14.95 | 969.14 | 969.93 | 970.71 | 968.81 | 976.89 | 966.15 | 966.12 |
| **CIS** | 901 | **40.1** | **30.5** | **51.3** | **36.2** | **65.1** | **7,308.6** | **7,230.6** | **7,267.8** | **7,251.3** | **7,256.6** | **7,247.1** | **7,222.0** |
| Armenia | 911 | 7.70 | 7.12 | 9.28 | 6.08 | 1.89 | 79.50 | 21.74 | 37.15 | 20.64 | 1.23 | 4.31 | 2.06 |
| Azerbaijan, Republic of | 912 | 9.36 | 9.74 | 10.26 | 6.41 | 1.05 | 151.71 | 153.63 | 153.67 | 154.22 | 154.16 | 153.59 | 153.57 |
| Belarus | 913 | .01 | .02 | .03 | .03 | .63 | 368.95 | 368.65 | 372.84 | 369.28 | 371.20 | 371.80 | 371.80 |
| Georgia | 915 | 7.22 | .71 | .60 | 9.37 | 7.99 | 139.53 | 144.42 | 145.42 | 143.98 | 144.09 | 143.98 | 144.09 |
| Kazakhstan | 916 | .79 | .81 | .84 | .87 | .90 | 344.56 | 344.56 | 344.56 | 345.63 | 348.32 | 348.32 | 348.31 |
| Kyrgyz Republic | 917 | 12.80 | 3.69 | 22.13 | 8.74 | 35.88 | 103.38 | 111.50 | 115.32 | 120.90 | 128.60 | 124.82 | 132.83 |
| Moldova | 921 | .05 | .01 | .12 | .10 | .10 | 2.28 | .23 | .58 | 1.03 | 4.16 | .82 | 12.75 |
| Russia | 922 | .55 | 3.95 | 4.75 | .49 | .51 | 5,675.19 | 5,677.78 | 5,683.80 | 5,686.85 | 5,688.86 | 5,691.27 | 5,692.06 |
| Tajikistan | 923 | .85 | 3.80 | 2.34 | 2.29 | 10.16 | 69.86 | 69.82 | 69.76 | 69.75 | 69.74 | 69.73 | 22.21 |
| Turkmenistan | 925 | — | — | — | — | — | 69.82 | 69.82 | 69.82 | 69.82 | 69.82 | 69.81 | 69.81 |
| Ukraine | 926 | .75 | .70 | .99 | 1.78 | 5.59 | 40.55 | 5.17 | 11.66 | 5.98 | 10.36 | 2.58 | 6.37 |
| Uzbekistan | 927 | .02 | .01 | .01 | .01 | .46 | 263.25 | 263.25 | 263.25 | 263.25 | 266.08 | 266.08 | 266.08 |
| **Middle East,N.Africa & Pakistan** | 440 | **1,974.0** | **1,973.8** | **2,031.7** | **1,891.5** | **1,924.6** | **18,474.3** | **18,287.8** | **17,833.7** | **17,332.3** | **16,991.2** | **16,688.0** | **16,253.4** |
| Afghanistan, Islamic Rep. of | 512 | .04 | .03 | .03 | .12 | .02 | 128.47 | 128.39 | 128.27 | 126.26 | 117.94 | 105.09 | 90.56 |
| Algeria | 612 | .80 | 2.44 | 3.15 | 1.99 | 6.46 | 1,075.61 | 1,073.34 | 1,074.05 | 1,074.33 | 1,074.51 | 1,074.77 | 1,074.86 |
| Bahrain, Kingdom of | 419 | .58 | 1.68 | 3.77 | 6.43 | 9.07 | 127.60 | 127.79 | 128.10 | 128.58 | 129.63 | 129.69 | 129.72 |
| Djibouti | 611 | .64 | .02 | .55 | .03 | .06 | 13.05 | 10.87 | 9.21 | 8.30 | 8.29 | 7.37 | 6.29 |
| Egypt | 469 | 106.38 | 70.70 | 80.14 | 84.61 | 70.21 | 833.05 | 818.64 | 819.19 | 819.52 | 821.49 | 827.17 | 836.11 |
| Iran, I.R. of | 429 | 273.91 | 274.66 | 275.76 | 282.19 | 283.32 | 1,535.53 | 1,535.81 | 1,536.27 | 1,540.79 | 1,551.87 | 1,551.98 | 1,536.63 |
| Iraq | 433 | 296.12 | 293.58 | 291.65 | 88.43 | 92.93 | 1,159.86 | 1,151.87 | 1,135.82 | 1,121.96 | 1,008.04 | 501.56 | 67.95 |
| Jordan | 439 | 1.08 | .43 | .84 | 1.39 | 2.09 | 146.72 | 146.59 | 146.45 | 143.35 | 138.67 | 123.49 | 98.59 |
| Kuwait | 443 | 117.07 | 128.70 | 137.79 | 146.15 | 152.03 | 1,442.43 | 1,443.39 | 1,445.35 | 1,446.01 | 1,446.01 | 1,446.98 | 1,447.23 |
| Lebanon | 446 | 21.19 | 22.00 | 23.17 | 22.82 | 21.89 | 209.81 | 208.95 | 192.61 | 192.36 | 192.29 | 192.32 | 192.33 |
| Libya | 672 | 475.41 | 494.88 | 523.12 | 558.29 | 584.69 | 1,603.57 | 1,605.80 | 1,609.28 | 1,613.60 | 1,622.46 | 1,623.23 | 1,623.62 |
| Mauritania | 682 | .02 | .10 | .03 | .04 | .09 | .12 | .05 | .99 | 2.27 | 1.45 | .93 | .84 |
| Morocco | 686 | 77.41 | 55.09 | 34.98 | 20.22 | 12.51 | 486.90 | 482.18 | 401.44 | 283.01 | 245.37 | 558.41 | 550.47 |
| Oman | 449 | 8.98 | 10.32 | 11.10 | 11.84 | 12.83 | 185.50 | 185.61 | 175.09 | 175.87 | 175.23 | 175.30 | 175.33 |
| Pakistan | 564 | 157.76 | 151.02 | 143.28 | 136.06 | 118.55 | 880.60 | 798.90 | 686.22 | 599.26 | 552.11 | 520.16 | 485.52 |
| Qatar | 453 | 23.45 | 25.41 | 26.83 | 28.07 | 29.33 | 268.16 | 268.32 | 268.70 | 268.83 | 271.14 | 271.24 | 271.29 |
| Saudi Arabia | 456 | 334.08 | 384.64 | 425.25 | 456.32 | 477.25 | 6,970.97 | 6,912.76 | 6,704.62 | 6,415.21 | 6,263.61 | 6,266.26 | 6,498.00 |
| Somalia | 726 | — | — | — | — | — | 18.59 | 18.51 | 18.39 | 18.36 | 18.33 | 18.31 | 18.29 |
| Sudan | 732 | — | .04 | — | — | — | 125.76 | 125.62 | 125.39 | 125.33 | 125.29 | 125.24 | 125.21 |
| Syrian Arab Republic | 463 | 36.58 | 36.58 | 36.57 | 36.57 | 36.57 | 279.19 | 279.18 | 279.18 | 280.04 | 282.20 | 282.20 | 282.20 |
| Tunisia | 744 | 6.01 | 1.53 | .86 | 1.25 | 3.38 | 241.80 | 241.78 | 241.84 | 241.87 | 239.43 | 191.40 | 122.83 |
| United Arab Emirates | 466 | 3.49 | 6.73 | 8.13 | 8.68 | 11.08 | 541.03 | 541.25 | 541.25 | 542.06 | 542.21 | 542.42 | 542.52 |
| Yemen, Republic of | 474 | 33.03 | 13.18 | 4.72 | — | .27 | 200.03 | 182.17 | 165.40 | 165.17 | 163.23 | 152.53 | 76.97 |
| **Sub-Saharan Africa** | 603 | **388.9** | **342.5** | **344.5** | **345.0** | **365.4** | **7,758.9** | **7,868.7** | **7,492.0** | **7,356.7** | **7,516.6** | **7,229.3** | **6,940.8** |
| CEMAC (incl. BEAC hqtrs.) | 758 | 16.35 | 3.88 | 15.23 | 4.96 | 4.94 | 473.67 | 466.15 | 452.35 | 244.12 | 243.41 | 241.66 | 239.61 |
| Cameroon | 622 | .43 | 1.49 | 3.08 | 3.03 | 2.96 | 155.46 | 17.62 | 16.23 | 15.26 | 15.16 | 15.16 | 15.15 |
| Central African Rep. | 626 | 1.58 | .08 | .47 | .48 | .02 | 2.76 | 2.78 | 2.78 | 2.76 | 2.75 | .98 | .39 |
| Chad | 628 | .04 | .05 | .06 | .06 | .06 | 2.71 | 2.73 | .06 | .05 | .05 | .05 | .05 |
| Congo, Rep. of | 634 | 4.66 | 1.70 | .13 | .11 | .14 | 70.06 | 70.06 | 70.06 | 70.23 | 70.23 | 69.99 | 69.99 |
| Equatorial Guinea | 642 | .44 | .44 | .44 | .44 | .46 | 25.94 | 25.94 | 21.01 | 21.16 | 21.16 | 21.15 | 21.15 |
| Gabon | 646 | 4.03 | .08 | .58 | .42 | .30 | 132.81 | 132.81 | 132.81 | 132.80 | 132.80 | 132.80 | 132.80 |
| WAEMU (Incl. BCEAO hqtrs.) | 759 | 6.41 | 2.48 | 1.26 | .77 | 2.14 | 699.69 | 700.75 | 700.28 | 794.29 | 948.20 | 791.54 | 861.44 |
| Benin | 638 | .02 | .12 | .03 | .07 | .05 | 49.70 | 49.75 | 49.71 | 49.70 | 49.69 | 49.68 | 43.83 |
| Burkina Faso | 748 | .11 | .14 | .02 | .08 | .05 | 48.09 | 48.17 | 48.15 | 48.14 | 48.14 | 48.13 | 37.07 |
| Côte d'Ivoire | 662 | .13 | .45 | .67 | .36 | .78 | 272.70 | 273.04 | 272.87 | 272.82 | 272.79 | 272.75 | 233.70 |
| Guinea Bissau | 654 | .44 | .40 | .34 | .03 | .05 | 11.89 | 12.39 | 12.39 | 12.39 | 12.38 | 12.38 | 12.38 |
| Mali | 678 | .40 | .19 | .03 | .05 | .05 | 73.38 | 73.44 | 73.39 | 73.38 | 73.37 | 73.35 | 68.55 |
| Niger | 692 | .60 | .21 | .08 | .04 | .96 | 54.29 | 54.28 | 54.27 | 54.26 | 54.26 | 54.25 | 47.46 |
| Senegal | 722 | 4.71 | .96 | .04 | .07 | .11 | 130.39 | 130.32 | 130.21 | 130.18 | 130.16 | 130.13 | 107.70 |
| Togo | 742 | .01 | .01 | .05 | .07 | .08 | 59.24 | 59.35 | 59.30 | 59.28 | 59.28 | 59.26 | 47.65 |
| Angola | 614 | .15 | .15 | .16 | .16 | .17 | 271.52 | 266.31 | 256.05 | 247.23 | 238.19 | 231.69 | 228.73 |
| Botswana | 616 | 34.42 | 35.58 | 36.91 | 38.44 | 39.56 | 92.86 | 92.98 | 87.00 | 85.58 | 85.68 | 85.74 | 85.76 |
| Burundi | 618 | .23 | .19 | .22 | .24 | .10 | 66.65 | 73.22 | 79.01 | 84.04 | 82.32 | 81.76 | 39.28 |
| Cabo Verde | 624 | .02 | .02 | — | .07 | .15 | 8.22 | 6.73 | 4.99 | 3.38 | 1.82 | 1.07 | .82 |
| Comoros | 632 | — | — | — | .01 | — | 6.67 | 8.22 | 9.79 | 11.35 | 14.46 | 11.47 | 11.21 |
| Congo, Dem. Rep. of | 636 | 3.54 | .96 | .17 | 2.08 | 3.88 | 390.76 | 353.20 | 352.51 | 352.31 | 352.19 | 352.03 | 324.49 |
| Eritrea | 643 | — | — | — | — | — | 3.66 | 3.63 | 3.58 | 3.61 | 3.72 | 3.71 | 3.70 |
| Ethiopia | 644 | .33 | .13 | .04 | .06 | .03 | 17.46 | 97.41 | 97.27 | 97.24 | 97.21 | 93.84 | 68.41 |
| Gambia, The | 648 | .48 | .11 | .97 | .15 | .07 | 24.61 | 24.60 | 24.57 | 24.37 | 23.36 | 21.24 | 17.40 |
| Ghana | 652 | 13.34 | .77 | .78 | .37 | .29 | 290.51 | 291.31 | 280.48 | 259.29 | 238.13 | 216.92 | 174.07 |
| Guinea | 656 | — | .01 | — | 7.72 | 1.57 | 82.21 | 75.43 | 61.45 | 78.47 | 96.82 | 160.32 | 145.48 |
| Kenya | 664 | .39 | .01 | .33 | .11 | 1.98 | 223.66 | 206.80 | 11.01 | 5.95 | 19.76 | 8.97 | 10.51 |
| Lesotho | 666 | .40 | .31 | .14 | 3.97 | 3.59 | 31.26 | 34.16 | 35.32 | 37.90 | 47.52 | 46.48 | 45.71 |
| Liberia | 668 | — | — | — | — | 14.18 | 128.49 | 136.68 | 145.62 | 157.46 | 173.20 | 178.53 | 185.94 |
| Madagascar | 674 | .12 | .03 | .03 | .02 | .14 | 97.69 | 96.50 | 94.14 | 89.84 | 83.73 | 70.81 | 59.05 |
| Malawi | 676 | .77 | .74 | .45 | .02 | .05 | 1.23 | 1.05 | .28 | .58 | 5.66 | 6.55 | 3.66 |
| Mauritius | 684 | 17.53 | 17.97 | 18.31 | 18.54 | 18.82 | 99.94 | 99.81 | 99.91 | 99.95 | 99.97 | 100.00 | 100.01 |
| Mozambique | 688 | .05 | .16 | .15 | .11 | .07 | 108.66 | 108.48 | 107.51 | 106.04 | 104.09 | 101.97 | 78.88 |
| Namibia | 728 | .02 | .02 | .02 | .02 | .02 | 130.41 | 130.41 | 5.27 | 5.11 | 5.02 | 4.90 | 4.84 |
| Nigeria | 694 | .27 | .29 | .28 | .55 | .77 | 1,518.15 | 1,675.21 | 1,675.19 | 1,675.17 | 1,675.16 | 1,675.15 | 1,675.12 |
| Rwanda | 714 | 19.45 | 18.13 | 15.19 | 15.23 | 20.40 | 83.51 | 83.47 | 83.10 | 82.42 | 81.28 | 79.46 | 77.58 |
| São Tomé & Principe | 716 | — | .03 | .04 | .01 | .02 | 6.48 | 3.78 | 3.77 | .46 | .33 | .46 | .31 |
| Seychelles | 718 | — | — | — | .01 | — | 7.84 | 7.63 | 6.77 | 6.44 | 6.13 | 5.80 | 5.48 |
| Sierra Leone | 724 | 32.82 | 22.93 | 19.44 | 19.41 | 19.73 | 120.94 | 119.59 | 116.40 | 111.80 | 107.19 | 107.96 | 107.52 |
| South Africa | 199 | 222.82 | 222.87 | 222.94 | 223.04 | 223.11 | 1,788.16 | 1,788.15 | 1,788.14 | 1,788.14 | 1,788.17 | 1,788.20 | 1,788.20 |

# SDR Holdings

| | | 2004 | 2005 | 2006 | 2007 | 2008 | 2009 | 2010 | 2011 | 2012 | 2013 | 2014 | 2015 |
|---|---|---|---|---|---|---|---|---|---|---|---|---|---|
| | | | | | | *Millions of SDRs: End of Period* | | | | | | | |
| **Sub-Saharan Africa(Cont.)** | | | | | | | | | | | | | |
| South Sudan, Republic of | 733 | . . . . | . . . . | . . . . | . . . . | . . . . | . . . . | . . . . | . . . . | 76.25 | 77.15 | 77.14 | 2.14 |
| Swaziland | 734 | 2.47 | 2.48 | 2.49 | 2.51 | 2.55 | 44.41 | 44.41 | 44.41 | 44.56 | 48.73 | 48.74 | 48.74 |
| Tanzania | 738 | .05 | .49 | .04 | .10 | .02 | 158.72 | 158.33 | 156.79 | 154.78 | 152.49 | 134.28 | 90.52 |
| Uganda | 746 | .43 | .80 | .06 | .17 | .13 | 143.66 | 143.37 | 142.24 | 141.00 | 139.78 | 48.54 | 47.47 |
| Zambia | 754 | 16.00 | 11.00 | 8.87 | 6.17 | 6.87 | 406.73 | 405.98 | 402.40 | 394.60 | 382.84 | 359.66 | 316.15 |
| Zimbabwe | 698 | — | .02 | — | — | — | 230.45 | 164.91 | 164.45 | 93.03 | 92.90 | 92.73 | 92.63 |
| **Western Hemisphere** | 205 | **1,215.1** | **3,778.5** | **995.1** | **963.9** | **1,001.3** | **14,513.8** | **14,360.9** | **13,869.2** | **13,777.8** | **13,729.7** | **13,608.1** | **11,899.0** |
| ECCU (incl. ECCB hqtrs.) | 309 | 1.56 | 1.55 | 1.68 | 1.71 | 2.48 | 61.65 | 41.99 | 39.49 | 36.09 | 33.98 | 31.02 | 27.61 |
| Antigua and Barbuda | 311 | .01 | .01 | .01 | .01 | .01 | 12.51 | .31 | .44 | .46 | .01 | .09 | .11 |
| Dominica | 321 | .03 | .01 | .01 | .04 | .02 | 7.01 | 6.28 | 4.33 | 1.76 | 1.09 | 1.04 | .57 |
| Grenada | 328 | .01 | .01 | .11 | .08 | .83 | 10.65 | 10.64 | 10.39 | 10.07 | 9.85 | 8.07 | 6.83 |
| St. Kitts and Nevis | 361 | — | — | — | — | — | 8.51 | 8.49 | 8.21 | 7.62 | 6.84 | 6.02 | 5.66 |
| St. Lucia | 362 | 1.50 | 1.52 | 1.55 | 1.59 | 1.61 | 15.43 | 15.53 | 15.41 | 15.44 | 15.42 | 15.41 | 14.02 |
| St. Vincent & Grenadines | 364 | — | — | — | — | — | 7.55 | .74 | .71 | .73 | .78 | .39 | .42 |
| Argentina | 213 | 564.49 | 3,104.08 | 320.55 | 320.62 | 320.67 | 2,022.33 | 2,022.18 | 2,053.04 | 2,053.07 | 2,053.08 | 2,053.10 | 2,053.08 |
| Bahamas, The | 313 | .02 | .01 | .01 | .06 | .04 | 114.19 | 114.16 | 114.12 | 18.49 | 38.03 | 54.16 | 54.12 |
| Barbados | 316 | .04 | .01 | .02 | .07 | .04 | 56.35 | 56.33 | 56.31 | 56.50 | 56.49 | 56.49 | 56.48 |
| Belize | 339 | 1.64 | 1.76 | 1.93 | 2.15 | 2.31 | 20.17 | 20.12 | 20.08 | 20.04 | 20.02 | 20.02 | 20.02 |
| Bolivia | 218 | 26.56 | 26.75 | 26.75 | 26.80 | 27.48 | 164.91 | 164.91 | 164.91 | 165.42 | 166.68 | 166.68 | 166.70 |
| Brazil | 223 | 2.67 | 20.19 | 5.56 | 1.32 | .72 | 2,887.42 | 2,889.30 | 2,591.45 | 2,593.47 | 2,594.75 | 2,596.22 | 2,596.68 |
| Chile | 228 | 33.88 | 36.63 | 36.06 | 33.64 | 36.86 | 731.72 | 789.95 | 790.78 | 788.21 | 744.75 | 745.01 | 763.09 |
| Colombia | 233 | 116.51 | 120.71 | 128.47 | 138.98 | 148.42 | 755.35 | 751.39 | 742.83 | 736.06 | 732.62 | 723.54 | 714.50 |
| Costa Rica | 238 | .09 | .03 | .02 | .07 | .19 | 132.87 | 132.59 | 132.54 | 132.52 | 132.51 | 132.50 | 132.49 |
| Dominican Republic | 243 | 1.02 | .39 | 16.26 | 62.37 | 23.36 | 175.82 | 76.46 | 12.10 | 13.21 | 1.33 | 4.82 | 5.57 |
| Ecuador | 248 | 36.09 | 15.24 | 5.05 | 15.41 | 17.03 | 16.90 | 16.19 | 15.05 | 15.75 | 18.12 | 17.88 | 17.75 |
| El Salvador | 253 | 24.98 | 24.98 | 24.98 | 24.98 | 25.01 | 163.83 | 163.81 | 163.80 | 164.30 | 165.56 | 165.56 | 165.56 |
| Guatemala | 258 | 5.14 | 4.58 | 3.75 | 2.75 | 2.27 | 174.35 | 173.64 | 173.52 | 174.10 | 175.63 | 175.60 | 175.59 |
| Guyana | 336 | 4.60 | .34 | 1.06 | .30 | .02 | 2.49 | 1.33 | 2.43 | 1.18 | 4.37 | 1.58 | 1.75 |
| Haiti | 263 | .12 | 8.61 | 5.19 | 4.74 | 4.56 | 68.92 | 68.88 | 68.84 | 68.83 | 68.82 | 68.81 | 68.80 |
| Honduras | 268 | .06 | .20 | — | .06 | .06 | 104.78 | 103.63 | 100.44 | 96.35 | 92.26 | 88.10 | 84.95 |
| Jamaica | 343 | .05 | — | .19 | .21 | .05 | 221.01 | 214.07 | 205.73 | 199.44 | 192.27 | 185.80 | 180.68 |
| Mexico | 273 | 299.23 | 311.57 | 320.62 | 294.84 | 337.10 | 2,886.66 | 2,808.20 | 2,660.24 | 2,689.74 | 2,669.17 | 2,528.29 | 2,554.71 |
| Nicaragua | 278 | .32 | .22 | .26 | .08 | .09 | 104.92 | 104.86 | 114.49 | 106.11 | 95.36 | 118.92 | 99.73 |
| Panama | 283 | .56 | .76 | .85 | .56 | .50 | 171.07 | 171.00 | 170.90 | 170.87 | 170.85 | 170.83 | 170.81 |
| Paraguay | 288 | 86.04 | 88.21 | 91.61 | 27.62 | 28.69 | 110.35 | 110.44 | 110.58 | 110.61 | 110.64 | 110.67 | 110.68 |
| Peru | 293 | .23 | .34 | .61 | 2.35 | 5.82 | 524.09 | 524.16 | 524.37 | 526.34 | 531.11 | 531.21 | 531.25 |
| Suriname | 366 | 1.21 | 1.06 | .84 | .57 | .36 | 80.67 | 80.65 | 80.62 | 80.61 | 81.28 | 81.27 | 45.27 |
| Trinidad and Tobago | 369 | 1.73 | 2.60 | 2.00 | .56 | .71 | 275.51 | 275.52 | 275.63 | 275.68 | 275.71 | 275.77 | 275.78 |
| Uruguay | 298 | .78 | 4.37 | .72 | .23 | 2.65 | 245.67 | 245.58 | 245.63 | 245.67 | 245.69 | 245.73 | 245.74 |
| Venezuela, Rep. Bol. | 299 | 5.48 | 3.32 | .01 | .90 | 13.84 | 2,239.80 | 2,239.59 | 2,239.28 | 2,239.16 | 2,258.64 | 2,258.57 | 579.63 |

# Reserve Position in the Fund

1c s

Millions of SDRs: End of Period

| | | 2004 | 2005 | 2006 | 2007 | 2008 | 2009 | 2010 | 2011 | 2012 | 2013 | 2014 | 2015 |
|---|---|---|---|---|---|---|---|---|---|---|---|---|---|
| World | 001 | 55,786.2 | 28,561.2 | 17,507.2 | 13,732.9 | 25,100.9 | 38,676.1 | 48,808.0 | 98,262.0 | 103,244.4 | 97,508.3 | 81,735.9 | 63,453.5 |
| Advanced Economies | 110 | 45,100.0 | 21,712.1 | 12,509.2 | 9,326.1 | 18,105.6 | 27,442.9 | 34,529.9 | 73,913.8 | 77,645.2 | 73,202.3 | 60,635.4 | 46,121.4 |
| Euro Area | | | | | | | | | | | | | |
| Austria | 122 | 602.32 | 275.67 | 164.08 | 123.44 | 235.02 | 375.48 | 469.77 | 860.84 | 1,100.07 | 1,032.05 | 826.62 | 597.58 |
| Belgium | 124 | 1,478.63 | 777.89 | 412.09 | 302.10 | 637.39 | 764.73 | 1,188.68 | 2,231.22 | 2,360.07 | 2,226.16 | 1,797.25 | 1,281.36 |
| Cyprus | 423 | 47.28 | 21.73 | 14.07 | 9.50 | 17.47 | 28.35 | 31.85 | 81.92 | 83.22 | 83.22 | 83.24 | 81.10 |
| Estonia | 939 | .01 | .01 | .01 | .01 | .01 | .01 | .01 | .01 | 8.18 | 13.18 | 14.18 | 14.20 |
| Finland | 172 | 405.99 | 198.27 | 110.66 | 82.90 | 161.05 | 270.10 | 367.44 | 541.87 | 667.98 | 616.81 | 496.76 | 359.79 |
| France | 132 | 3,453.00 | 2,013.94 | 941.91 | 713.39 | 1,473.55 | 2,341.52 | 2,979.99 | 5,073.61 | 5,513.45 | 5,168.96 | 4,002.99 | 2,968.18 |
| Germany | 134 | 4,419.30 | 2,436.60 | 1,301.50 | 883.61 | 1,546.70 | 2,485.15 | 4,005.99 | 6,891.18 | 7,514.64 | 7,118.46 | 5,336.84 | 4,032.18 |
| Greece | 174 | 270.60 | 117.72 | 85.16 | 54.03 | 104.73 | 170.77 | 170.95 | 240.74 | 240.82 | 240.91 | 240.99 | 241.03 |
| Ireland | 178 | 269.23 | 123.25 | 87.28 | 55.34 | 106.29 | 156.22 | 153.69 | 258.53 | 258.61 | 258.66 | 258.70 | 258.70 |
| Italy | 136 | 2,384.59 | 1,230.20 | 649.28 | 464.99 | 986.90 | 1,170.51 | 1,595.44 | 3,806.20 | 4,050.29 | 3,782.59 | 3,069.77 | 2,175.39 |
| Latvia | 941 | .06 | .06 | .06 | .06 | .06 | .06 | .06 | .06 | .06 | .06 | .06 | .06 |
| Lithuania | 946 | .02 | .02 | .03 | .03 | .03 | .03 | .03 | .03 | .03 | .03 | .03 | .03 |
| Luxembourg | 137 | 89.66 | 40.65 | 29.01 | 18.72 | 36.10 | 52.10 | 66.10 | 224.12 | 224.34 | 204.83 | 161.66 | 119.92 |
| Malta | 181 | 40.26 | 40.26 | 40.26 | 40.26 | 40.26 | 33.13 | 30.97 | 45.82 | 47.86 | 51.60 | 45.10 | 30.73 |
| Netherlands | 138 | 1,717.59 | 833.83 | 459.18 | 341.71 | 705.55 | 1,018.66 | 1,342.65 | 2,493.67 | 2,657.34 | 2,520.15 | 2,022.97 | 1,421.75 |
| Portugal | 182 | 283.34 | 141.61 | 76.44 | 57.17 | 107.07 | 215.07 | 231.10 | 271.72 | 271.76 | 271.80 | 241.85 | 207.89 |
| Slovak Republic | 936 | — | — | — | 3.00 | 31.00 | 67.78 | 91.44 | 184.64 | 194.94 | 208.64 | 187.54 | 124.92 |
| Slovenia | 961 | 77.26 | 36.12 | 24.36 | 15.93 | 30.09 | 42.09 | 74.29 | 118.45 | 124.95 | 133.03 | 121.33 | 81.38 |
| Spain | 184 | 1,014.29 | 525.99 | 265.20 | 202.05 | 422.32 | 497.24 | 859.36 | 1,896.15 | 2,068.77 | 1,924.04 | 1,583.49 | 1,119.71 |
| Australia | 193 | 1,098.71 | 543.00 | 284.28 | 214.46 | 421.66 | 696.66 | 715.68 | 1,398.68 | 1,616.86 | 1,575.83 | 1,287.48 | 1,000.70 |
| Canada | 156 | 2,149.58 | 980.30 | 553.45 | 418.49 | 811.07 | 1,546.40 | 1,984.28 | 2,523.98 | 2,841.84 | 3,062.69 | 2,529.21 | 1,962.26 |
| China, P.R.: Hong Kong | 532 | | | | | | | | 23 | 40 | 44 | 41 | 33 |
| Czech Republic | 935 | 263.97 | 126.56 | 74.08 | 53.33 | 104.98 | 153.98 | 226.83 | 432.55 | 455.15 | 485.75 | 443.23 | 343.90 |
| Denmark | 128 | 542.81 | 216.00 | 147.61 | 107.98 | 209.48 | 413.48 | 536.18 | 864.08 | 984.75 | 923.71 | 742.90 | 579.97 |
| Iceland | 176 | 18.58 | 18.59 | 18.59 | 18.59 | 18.59 | 18.63 | 18.66 | 18.71 | 18.74 | 18.75 | 18.75 | 18.75 |
| Israel | 436 | 298.26 | 141.17 | 81.79 | 60.65 | 114.30 | 184.30 | 207.11 | 359.93 | 384.51 | 425.54 | 432.04 | 329.45 |
| Japan | 158 | 4,371.38 | 2,013.20 | 1,285.35 | 882.77 | 1,725.95 | 2,751.25 | 2,992.34 | 11,189.15 | 8,887.15 | 9,197.40 | 8,253.64 | 6,834.47 |
| Korea | 542 | 507.68 | 213.97 | 292.71 | 196.67 | 376.41 | 628.41 | 665.41 | 1,670.29 | 1,811.20 | 1,631.37 | 1,313.57 | 1,007.97 |
| New Zealand | 196 | 305.45 | 115.26 | 79.18 | 59.88 | 113.74 | 173.84 | 177.26 | 324.82 | 355.83 | 393.22 | 360.50 | 278.91 |
| Norway | 142 | 559.24 | 210.92 | 137.61 | 112.64 | 194.19 | 403.19 | 391.00 | 941.69 | 1,007.95 | 912.91 | 733.64 | 569.30 |
| San Marino | 135 | 4.10 | 4.10 | 4.10 | 4.10 | 4.10 | 4.10 | 4.10 | 5.45 | 5.45 | 5.45 | 5.45 | 5.45 |
| Singapore | 576 | 283.42 | 121.84 | 86.45 | 56.72 | 112.99 | 166.93 | 193.08 | 542.53 | 593.41 | 672.37 | 562.37 | 433.95 |
| Sweden | 144 | 842.47 | 371.96 | 211.10 | 162.46 | 300.80 | 462.70 | 729.50 | 1,130.85 | 1,262.86 | 1,168.40 | 936.42 | 708.15 |
| Switzerland | 146 | 1,153.85 | 571.23 | 302.33 | 227.33 | 441.84 | 761.60 | 740.73 | 2,176.25 | 1,998.34 | 1,673.00 | 1,416.96 | 1,162.73 |
| United Kingdom | 112 | 3,562.4 | 1,627.8 | 939.6 | 696.2 | 1,525.8 | 2,125.9 | 3,176.3 | 5,498.1 | 5,766.5 | 5,189.1 | 3,698.1 | 3,028.9 |
| United States | 111 | 12,584.7 | 5,622.4 | 3,350.4 | 2,685.6 | 4,988.1 | 7,262.5 | 8,111.6 | 19,592.6 | 22,227.0 | 19,967.5 | 17,368.9 | 12,707.5 |
| | | | | | | | | | | | | | |
| Emerging & Dev. Economies | 200 | 10,686.2 | 6,849.0 | 4,998.0 | 4,406.9 | 6,995.4 | 11,233.1 | 14,278.1 | 24,348.1 | 25,599.2 | 24,306.1 | 21,100.5 | 17,332.1 |
| Emerging & Developing Asia | 505 | 4,024.7 | 2,272.4 | 1,639.0 | 1,293.7 | 2,509.7 | 4,539.1 | 6,648.4 | 10,471.8 | 9,860.6 | 9,178.3 | 8,039.7 | 6,617.0 |
| Bangladesh | 513 | .21 | .23 | .25 | .28 | .30 | .31 | .41 | .41 | .49 | .49 | .57 | .57 |
| Bhutan | 514 | 1.02 | 1.02 | 1.02 | 1.02 | 1.02 | 1.02 | 1.02 | 1.02 | 1.02 | 1.02 | 1.02 | 1.02 |
| Brunei Darussalam | 516 | 58.29 | 32.27 | 24.58 | 14.56 | 13.67 | 13.67 | 13.67 | 13.67 | 13.67 | 13.67 | 13.67 | 13.67 |
| Cambodia | 522 | | | | | | | | | | | | |
| China, P.R.: Mainland | 924 | 2,138.08 | 973.02 | 718.50 | 531.81 | 1,318.41 | 2,795.06 | 4,153.59 | 6,373.44 | 5,318.99 | 4,584.11 | 3,931.18 | 3,281.64 |
| Fiji | 819 | 15.26 | 15.31 | 15.49 | 15.69 | 15.81 | 16.01 | 16.25 | 16.39 | 16.46 | 16.54 | 16.61 | 16.68 |
| India | 534 | 917.09 | 630.97 | 365.61 | 273.42 | 527.94 | 912.06 | 1,548.35 | 2,555.38 | 2,924.21 | 2,820.66 | 2,293.38 | 1,780.67 |
| Indonesia | 536 | 145.50 | 145.50 | 145.50 | 145.50 | 145.50 | 145.50 | 145.50 | 145.50 | 145.50 | 145.50 | 145.50 | 145.50 |
| Kiribati | 826 | | | | | | | | | | | | |
| Lao People's Dem. Rep. | 544 | | | | | | | | | | | | .02 |
| Malaysia | 548 | 499.76 | 199.43 | 129.55 | 97.94 | 205.99 | 282.19 | 305.89 | 549.33 | 564.43 | 631.05 | 650.50 | 553.20 |
| Maldives | 556 | 1.55 | 1.55 | 1.55 | 1.55 | 1.55 | 1.55 | 1.55 | 2.00 | 2.00 | 2.00 | 2.00 | 2.00 |
| Marshall Islands, Rep. of | 867 | — | — | — | — | — | — | — | — | — | — | — | — |
| Micronesia, Fed. States of | 868 | .001 | .001 | .001 | .001 | .001 | .001 | .001 | .001 | .001 | .001 | .001 | .001 |
| Mongolia | 948 | .12 | .14 | .14 | .14 | .14 | .14 | .14 | .14 | .14 | .14 | .14 | .14 |
| Myanmar | 518 | | | | | | | | | | | | |
| Nepal | 558 | — | — | — | — | — | — | .02 | .02 | .02 | .02 | .02 | .02 |
| Palau | 565 | .12 | .12 | .12 | .12 | — | — | — | — | — | — | .45 | .45 |
| Papua New Guinea | 853 | .43 | .44 | .44 | .44 | .44 | .44 | .44 | .44 | .44 | .44 | .45 | .45 |
| Philippines | 566 | 87.43 | 87.49 | 87.55 | 87.60 | 87.66 | 87.71 | 162.79 | 307.51 | 347.76 | 385.70 | 393.85 | 316.54 |
| Samoa | 862 | .69 | .69 | .69 | .69 | .69 | .69 | .69 | .69 | .69 | .69 | .69 | .69 |
| Solomon Islands | 813 | .55 | .55 | .55 | .55 | .55 | .55 | .55 | .55 | .55 | .55 | .55 | .55 |
| Sri Lanka | 524 | 47.86 | 47.86 | 47.86 | 47.86 | 47.86 | 47.86 | 47.86 | 47.86 | 47.86 | 47.86 | 47.86 | 47.86 |
| Thailand | 578 | 106.56 | 131.59 | 95.36 | 70.27 | 137.97 | 230.07 | 245.07 | 452.83 | 471.71 | 523.18 | 536.41 | 450.51 |
| Timor-Leste | 537 | .001 | .001 | .001 | .001 | .001 | .001 | .001 | .001 | .001 | .001 | .651 | .651 |
| Tonga | 866 | 1.71 | 1.71 | 1.71 | 1.71 | 1.71 | 1.71 | 1.71 | 1.71 | 1.71 | 1.71 | 1.71 | 1.71 |
| Tuvalu | 869 | . . . . | . . . . | . . . . | . . . . | — | — | .43 | .43 | .43 | .43 | .43 | .43 |
| Vanuatu | 846 | 2.50 | 2.50 | 2.50 | 2.50 | 2.50 | 2.50 | 2.50 | 2.50 | 2.50 | 2.50 | 2.50* | 2.50 |
| Vietnam | 582 | .01 | .01 | .01 | .01 | .01 | .01 | .01 | .01 | .01 | .01 | .01 | .01 |
| | | | | | | | | | | | | | |
| Europe | 170 | 948.6 | 630.1 | 545.2 | 556.9 | 1,086.9 | 1,748.5 | 1,797.8 | 3,646.1 | 4,200.6 | 3,921.3 | 3,260.6 | 2,588.7 |
| Emerging & Dev. Europe | 903 | 946.7 | 493.0 | 356.8 | 320.1 | 402.9 | 519.1 | 568.2 | 1,001.1 | 1,125.3 | 1,067.2 | 915.4 | 725.5 |
| Albania | 914 | 3.4 | 3.4 | 3.4 | 3.4 | 3.4 | 3.4 | 3.4 | 3.4 | 6.2 | 6.2 | 6.2 | 6.2 |
| Bosnia and Herzegovina | 963 | | | | | | | | | | | | |
| Bulgaria | 918 | 32.85 | 33.00 | 33.14 | 33.32 | 33.53 | 33.71 | 33.92 | 34.10 | 34.10 | 34.10 | 34.10 | 34.10 |
| Croatia | 960 | .16 | .16 | .16 | .16 | .16 | .16 | .16 | .16 | .16 | .16 | .17 | .20 |
| Hungary | 944 | 346.26 | 134.56 | 91.05 | 71.68 | 73.83 | 73.83 | 73.83 | 73.83 | 73.83 | 73.83 | 73.84 | 73.84 |
| Kosovo | 967 | | | | | | 14 | 14 | 14 | 14 | 14 | 14 | 14 |
| Macedonia, FYR | 962 | — | — | — | — | — | — | — | — | — | — | — | — |
| Montenegro | 943 | — | — | — | 6.60 | 6.60 | 6.60 | 6.60 | 6.60 | 6.60 | 6.60 | 6.60 | 6.60 |

# Reserve Position in the Fund

| 1c s | | 2004 | 2005 | 2006 | 2007 | 2008 | 2009 | 2010 | 2011 | 2012 | 2013 | 2014 | 2015 |
|---|---|---|---|---|---|---|---|---|---|---|---|---|---|
| | | | | | | | *Millions of SDRs: End of Period* | | | | | | |
| **Emerging & Dev. Europe(Cont.)** | | | | | | | | | | | | | |
| Poland | 964 | 451.33 | 209.17 | 116.28 | 92.23 | 172.62 | 274.45 | 323.30 | 756.10 | 877.44 | 819.37 | 667.49 | 477.55 |
| Romania | 968 | — | — | — | — | — | — | — | — | — | — | — | — |
| Serbia, Republic of | 942 | — | — | — | — | — | — | — | — | — | — | — | — |
| Turkey | 186 | 112.78 | 112.78 | 112.78 | 112.78 | 112.78 | 112.78 | 112.78 | 112.78 | 112.78 | 112.78 | 112.78 | 112.78 |
| **CIS** | 901 | **1.9** | **137.1** | **188.4** | **236.7** | **684.1** | **1,229.4** | **1,229.7** | **2,644.9** | **3,075.3** | **2,854.1** | **2,345.3** | **1,863.2** |
| Armenia | 911 | — | — | — | — | — | — | — | — | — | — | — | — |
| Azerbaijan, Republic of | 912 | .01 | .01 | .01 | .05 | .08 | .13 | .13 | .13 | .13 | .13 | .13 | .13 |
| Belarus | 913 | .02 | .02 | .02 | .02 | .02 | .02 | .02 | .02 | .02 | .02 | .02 | .02 |
| Georgia | 915 | .01 | .01 | .01 | .01 | .01 | .01 | .01 | .01 | .01 | .01 | .01 | .01 |
| Kazakhstan | 916 | .01 | .01 | .01 | .01 | .01 | .01 | .01 | .01 | .01 | .01 | .01 | 15.53 |
| Kyrgyz Republic | 917 | — | — | — | — | — | — | — | — | — | — | — | — |
| Moldova | 921 | .01 | .01 | .01 | .01 | .01 | .01 | .01 | .01 | .01 | .01 | .01 | .01 |
| Russia | 922 | 1.83 | 137.04 | 188.33 | 236.64 | 683.92 | 1,229.23 | 1,229.45 | 2,644.72 | 3,075.11 | 2,853.88 | 2,345.04 | 1,847.51 |
| Tajikistan | 923 | — | — | — | — | — | — | — | — | — | — | — | — |
| Turkmenistan | 925 | — | — | — | — | — | — | — | — | — | — | — | — |
| Ukraine | 926 | — | — | — | — | .02 | .02 | .02 | .02 | .02 | .02 | .02 | .02 |
| Uzbekistan | 927 | .01 | .01 | .01 | .01 | .01 | .01 | .01 | .01 | .01 | .01 | .01 | .01 |
| **Middle East,N.Africa & Pakistan** | 440 | **3,898.5** | **2,528.2** | **1,664.0** | **1,456.8** | **2,031.8** | **2,563.9** | **2,663.7** | **5,078.8** | **5,650.8** | **5,470.9** | **4,847.2** | **4,121.0** |
| Afghanistan, Islamic Rep. of | 512 | | | | | | | | | | | | .19 |
| Algeria | 612 | 85.08 | 85.08 | 85.08 | 85.08 | 85.08 | 85.08 | 255.68 | 390.18 | 413.78 | 454.78 | 468.78 | 392.78 |
| Bahrain, Kingdom of | 419 | 70.84 | 71.20 | 71.20 | 71.20 | 71.20 | 71.20 | 71.20 | 71.20 | 71.20 | 71.20 | 71.20 | 71.20 |
| Djibouti | 611 | 1.10 | 1.10 | 1.10 | 1.10 | 1.10 | 1.10 | 1.10 | 1.10 | 1.10 | 1.10 | 1.10 | 1.10 |
| Egypt | 469 | — | — | — | — | — | — | — | — | — | — | — | — |
| Iran, I.R. of | 429 | — | — | — | — | .01 | .01 | .01 | .01 | .01 | .01 | .01 | .01 |
| Iraq | 433 | 171.10 | 171.10 | 171.10 | 171.10 | 171.10 | 171.10 | 171.10 | 171.10 | 171.10 | 171.10 | 171.10 | 171.10 |
| Jordan | 439 | .09 | .14 | .20 | .26 | .26 | .31 | .31 | .33 | .33 | .33 | .38 | .38 |
| Kuwait | 443 | 458.94 | 208.82 | 120.38 | 90.82 | 173.77 | 253.77 | 253.77 | 426.45 | 454.95 | 504.55 | 510.13 | 437.33 |
| Lebanon | 446 | 18.83 | 18.83 | 18.83 | 18.83 | 18.83 | 18.83 | 18.83 | 34.68 | 34.68 | 34.68 | 34.68 | 34.68 |
| Libya | 672 | 395.51 | 395.51 | 395.51 | 395.51 | 395.53 | 379.64 | 241.83 | 295.83 | 295.83 | 295.83 | 295.83 | 295.83 |
| Mauritania | 682 | — | — | — | — | — | — | — | — | — | — | .03 | .03 |
| Morocco | 686 | 70.44 | 70.44 | 70.45 | 70.45 | 70.45 | 70.45 | 70.45 | 70.45 | 70.45 | 70.45 | 70.46 | 70.46 |
| Oman | 449 | 63.68 | 24.24 | 18.07 | 12.43 | 13.63 | 35.63 | 43.63 | 73.78 | 75.08 | 83.08 | 84.08 | 78.92 |
| Pakistan | 564 | — | — | — | — | .12 | .12 | .12 | .12 | .12 | .12 | .12 | .12 |
| Qatar | 453 | 86.36 | 34.66 | 23.43 | 17.12 | 33.32 | 51.32 | 62.32 | 94.22 | 98.42 | 105.42 | 103.00 | 96.62 |
| Saudi Arabia | 456 | 2,253.1 | 1,333.7 | 606.3 | 462.7 | 898.7 | 1,286.6 | 1,286.6 | 3,167.0 | 3,662.9 | 3,351.3 | 2,706.3 | 2,161.1 |
| Somalia | 726 | — | — | — | — | — | — | — | — | — | — | — | — |
| Sudan | 732 | .01 | .01 | .01 | .01 | .01 | .01 | .01 | .01 | .01 | .01 | .01 | .01 |
| Syrian Arab Republic | 463 | .01 | .01 | .01 | .01 | .01 | .01 | .01 | .01 | .01 | .01 | .01 | .01 |
| Tunisia | 744 | 20.22 | 20.22 | 20.25 | 20.25 | 20.25 | 20.25 | 56.25 | 56.25 | 56.25 | 56.25 | 56.39 | 56.46 |
| United Arab Emirates | 466 | 203.16 | 93.04 | 62.02 | 39.97 | 78.42 | 118.42 | 130.42 | 226.02 | 244.62 | 270.62 | 273.62 | 252.62 |
| Yemen, Republic of | 474 | — | — | .01 | .01 | .01 | .01 | .01 | .01 | .01 | .01 | .01 | .01 |
| **Sub-Saharan Africa** | 603 | **119.7** | **102.8** | **95.5** | **91.1** | **101.9** | **105.6** | **117.4** | **149.4** | **222.6** | **297.2** | **316.9** | **308.8** |
| CEMAC (incl. BEAC hqtrs.) | 758 | 1.81 | 1.90 | 1.94 | 2.15 | 2.28 | 2.41 | 2.50 | 10.20 | 10.28 | 10.34 | 10.59 | 10.89 |
| Cameroon | 622 | .65 | .70 | .72 | .79 | .82 | .84 | .87 | .90 | .93 | .96 | .99 | 1.01 |
| Central African Rep. | 626 | .16 | .16 | .16 | .16 | .16 | .20 | .23 | .26 | .26 | .26 | .29 | .36 |
| Chad | 628 | .28 | .28 | .28 | .28 | .28 | .28 | .28 | 2.93 | 2.93 | 2.93 | 2.93 | 3.01 |
| Congo, Rep. of | 634 | .54 | .54 | .54 | .58 | .58 | .58 | .58 | .58 | .58 | .58 | .58 | .59 |
| Equatorial Guinea | 642 | — | — | — | — | — | — | — | 4.93 | 4.93 | 4.93 | 4.93 | 4.93 |
| Gabon | 646 | .18 | .22 | .24 | .35 | .45 | .51 | .54 | .61 | .66 | .69 | .88 | 1.00 |
| WAEMU (Incl. BCEAO hqtrs.) | 759 | 29.49 | 29.81 | 30.13 | 30.47 | 30.74 | 31.11 | 31.46 | 31.78 | 32.02 | 32.26 | 32.41 | 32.61 |
| Benin | 638 | 2.19 | 2.19 | 2.19 | 2.19 | 2.19 | 2.19 | 2.19 | 2.24 | 2.30 | 2.35 | 2.38 | 2.40 |
| Burkina Faso | 748 | 7.31 | 7.33 | 7.37 | 7.39 | 7.42 | 7.44 | 7.47 | 7.52 | 7.54 | 7.58 | 7.64 | 7.70 |
| Côte d'Ivoire | 662 | .59 | .64 | .69 | .72 | .76 | .80 | .84 | .89 | .94 | 1.00 | 1.00 | 1.07 |
| Guinea Bissau | 654 | — | — | — | .01 | .05 | .09 | .13 | .21 | .25 | .29 | .32 | .34 |
| Mali | 678 | 8.97 | 9.14 | 9.34 | 9.58 | 9.69 | 9.89 | 10.00 | 10.00 | 10.00 | 10.00 | 10.00 | 10.00 |
| Niger | 692 | 8.56 | 8.61 | 8.61 | 8.61 | 8.61 | 8.64 | 8.64 | 8.64 | 8.64 | 8.64 | 8.64 | 8.64 |
| Senegal | 722 | 1.53 | 1.57 | 1.60 | 1.64 | 1.68 | 1.71 | 1.79 | 1.82 | 1.88 | 1.88 | 1.88 | 1.88 |
| Togo | 742 | .33 | .33 | .33 | .33 | .33 | .33 | .41 | .45 | .47 | .53 | .55 | .58 |
| Angola | 614 | — | — | — | — | — | — | — | — | — | — | — | — |
| Botswana | 616 | 20.50 | 7.41 | 6.25 | 4.43 | 8.48 | 11.35 | 13.55 | 27.28 | 28.08 | 31.28 | 31.28 | 27.28 |
| Burundi | 618 | .36 | .36 | .36 | .36 | .36 | .36 | .36 | .36 | .36 | .36 | .36 | .36 |
| Cabo Verde | 624 | — | .02 | .02 | .02 | .02 | .02 | .02 | .02 | .02 | .42 | .42 | .42 |
| Comoros | 632 | .54 | .54 | .54 | .54 | .54 | .54 | .54 | .54 | .58 | .58 | .58 | .58 |
| Congo, Dem. Rep. of | 636 | — | — | — | — | — | — | — | — | — | — | — | — |
| Eritrea | 643 | .01 | .01 | .01 | .01 | .01 | .01 | .01 | .01 | .01 | .01 | .01 | .01 |
| Ethiopia | 644 | 7.19 | 7.19 | 7.33 | 7.37 | 7.44 | 7.51 | 7.51 | 7.51 | 7.51 | 7.51 | 7.51 | 7.51 |
| Gambia, The | 648 | 1.48 | 1.48 | 1.48 | 1.48 | 1.48 | 1.48 | 1.54 | 1.54 | 1.54 | 1.54 | 1.54 | 1.54 |
| Ghana | 652 | — | — | — | — | — | — | — | — | — | — | .12 | .21 |
| Guinea | 656 | .08 | .08 | .08 | .08 | .08 | .08 | .08 | .08 | .08 | .08 | .08 | .08 |
| Kenya | 664 | 12.70 | 12.74 | 12.78 | 12.80 | 12.83 | 12.89 | 12.96 | 13.00 | 13.01 | 13.29 | 13.29 | 13.29 |
| Lesotho | 666 | 3.56 | 3.60 | 3.62 | 3.61 | 3.61 | 3.61 | 3.61 | 3.61 | 3.71 | 3.80 | 3.81 | 3.84 |
| Liberia | 668 | .03 | .03 | .03 | .03 | .03 | .03 | .03 | .03 | .03 | .03 | .03 | .03 |
| Madagascar | 674 | .03 | .03 | .03 | .03 | .03 | .03 | .03 | .03 | .03 | .05 | .07 | .07 |
| Malawi | 676 | 2.29 | 2.29 | 2.31 | 2.31 | 2.33 | 2.42 | 2.42 | 2.42 | 2.44 | 2.44 | 2.44 | 2.44 |
| Mauritius | 684 | 21.88 | 17.51 | 10.50 | 7.04 | 13.15 | 13.15 | 22.05 | 31.54 | 33.65 | 37.74 | 38.47 | 32.17 |
| Mozambique | 688 | .01 | .01 | .01 | .01 | .01 | .01 | .01 | .01 | .01 | .01 | .03 | .03 |
| Namibia | 728 | .06 | .07 | .08 | .08 | .08 | .08 | .08 | .08 | .08 | .08 | .08 | .08 |
| Nigeria | 694 | .14 | .14 | .14 | .14 | .14 | .14 | .14 | .14 | .14 | .14 | .14 | .14 |
| Rwanda | 714 | — | — | — | — | — | — | — | — | — | — | — | — |
| São Tomé & Príncipe | 716 | — | — | — | — | — | — | — | — | — | — | — | — |
| Seychelles | 718 | — | — | — | — | — | — | — | .53 | .53 | .53 | .53 | .53 |
| Sierra Leone | 724 | .02 | .02 | .02 | .02 | .02 | .02 | .02 | .02 | .02 | .02 | .02 | .02 |

# Reserve Position in the Fund

| 1c s | | 2004 | 2005 | 2006 | 2007 | 2008 | 2009 | 2010 | 2011 | 2012 | 2013 | 2014 | 2015 |
|---|---|---|---|---|---|---|---|---|---|---|---|---|---|
| **Sub-Saharan Africa(Cont.)** | | | | | *Millions of SDRs: End of Period* | | | | | | | | |
| South Africa | 199 | .57 | .69 | .95 | 1.20 | 1.34 | 1.46 | 1.62 | 1.82 | 42.09 | 108.30 | 126.67 | 157.81 |
| South Sudan, Republic of | 733 | .... | .... | .... | .... | .... | .... | .... | .... | 29.52 | 29.52 | 29.52 | — |
| Swaziland | 734 | 6.56 | 6.56 | 6.56 | 6.56 | 6.56 | 6.56 | 6.56 | 6.56 | 6.56 | 6.56 | 6.56 | 6.56 |
| Tanzania | 738 | 10.00 | 10.00 | 10.00 | 10.00 | 10.00 | 10.00 | 10.00 | 10.00 | 10.00 | 10.00 | 10.00 | 10.00 |
| Uganda | 746 | — | — | — | — | — | — | — | — | — | — | — | — |
| Zambia | 754 | .02 | .02 | .02 | .02 | .02 | .02 | .02 | .02 | .02 | .02 | .02 | .02 |
| Zimbabwe | 698 | .33 | .33 | .33 | .33 | .33 | .33 | .33 | .33 | .33 | .33 | .33 | .33 |
| **Western Hemisphere** | 205 | **1,694.7** | **1,315.5** | **1,054.3** | **1,008.4** | **1,264.9** | **2,276.0** | **3,050.8** | **5,002.0** | **5,664.5** | **5,438.4** | **4,636.0** | **3,696.5** |
| ECCU (incl. ECCB hqtrs.) | 309 | .60 | .60 | .60 | .60 | .60 | .60 | .63 | .65 | .65 | .65 | .65 | .65 |
| Antigua and Barbuda | 311 | .01 | .01 | .01 | .01 | .01 | .01 | .03 | .05 | .05 | .05 | .05 | .05 |
| Dominica | 321 | .01 | .01 | .01 | .01 | .01 | .01 | .01 | .01 | .01 | .01 | .01 | .01 |
| Grenada | 328 | — | — | — | — | — | — | — | — | — | — | — | — |
| St. Kitts and Nevis | 361 | .08 | .08 | .08 | .08 | .08 | .08 | .08 | .08 | .08 | .08 | .08 | .08 |
| St. Lucia | 362 | .01 | .01 | .01 | .01 | .01 | .01 | .01 | .01 | .01 | .01 | .01 | .01 |
| St. Vincent & Grenadines | 364 | .50 | .50 | .50 | .50 | .50 | .50 | .50 | .50 | .50 | .50 | .50 | .50 |
| Argentina | 213 | .16 | .20 | .20 | .20 | .20 | .20 | .20 | .20 | .20 | .20 | .20 | .20 |
| Bahamas, The | 313 | 6.26 | 6.26 | 6.26 | 6.26 | 6.26 | 6.26 | 6.26 | 6.26 | 6.26 | 6.26 | 6.26 | 6.26 |
| Barbados | 316 | 5.15 | 5.30 | 5.45 | 5.58 | 5.64 | 5.74 | 5.81 | 5.81 | 5.81 | 5.81 | 5.81 | 5.81 |
| Belize | 339 | 4.24 | 4.24 | 4.24 | 4.24 | 4.24 | 4.24 | 4.24 | 4.24 | 4.24 | 4.24 | 4.24 | 4.24 |
| Bolivia | 218 | 8.87 | 8.87 | 8.87 | 8.87 | 8.87 | 8.87 | 8.87 | 8.87 | 8.87 | 8.87 | 8.87 | 8.87 |
| Brazil | 223 | — | — | — | — | .14 | 605.83 | 1,322.42 | 1,949.68 | 2,266.26 | 2,071.43 | 1,653.94 | 1,237.75 |
| Chile | 228 | 287.04 | 131.39 | 74.99 | 55.91 | 108.41 | 183.11 | 183.11 | 391.53 | 450.06 | 415.98 | 338.05 | 261.77 |
| Colombia | 233 | 285.80 | 285.80 | 285.80 | 285.80 | 285.80 | 258.67 | 168.68 | 240.73 | 255.28 | 281.34 | 287.39 | 242.44 |
| Costa Rica | 238 | 20.00 | 20.00 | 20.00 | 20.00 | 20.02 | 20.02 | 20.02 | 20.02 | 20.02 | 20.02 | 20.02 | 20.02 |
| Dominican Republic | 243 | — | — | — | — | — | — | — | — | — | — | — | — |
| Ecuador | 248 | 17.15 | 17.15 | 17.15 | 17.15 | 17.15 | 17.15 | 17.15 | 28.53 | 28.53 | 28.53 | 28.53 | 28.53 |
| El Salvador | 253 | — | — | — | — | — | — | — | — | — | — | — | — |
| Guatemala | 258 | — | — | — | — | — | — | — | — | — | — | — | — |
| Guyana | 336 | — | — | — | — | — | — | — | — | — | — | — | — |
| Haiti | 263 | .07 | .07 | .07 | .07 | .07 | .07 | .07 | .07 | .07 | .07 | .07 | .07 |
| Honduras | 268 | 8.63 | 8.63 | 8.63 | 8.63 | 8.63 | 8.63 | 8.63 | 8.63 | 8.63 | 8.63 | 8.63 | 8.63 |
| Jamaica | 343 | — | — | — | — | — | — | — | — | — | — | — | — |
| Mexico | 273 | 578.31 | 415.76 | 226.31 | 211.31 | 397.86 | 613.06 | 686.06 | 1,577.28 | 1,826.05 | 1,758.72 | 1,432.98 | 1,114.98 |
| Nicaragua | 278 | — | — | — | — | — | — | — | — | — | — | — | — |
| Panama | 283 | 11.86 | 11.86 | 11.86 | 11.86 | 11.86 | 11.86 | 11.86 | 11.86 | 11.86 | 11.86 | 11.86 | 11.86 |
| Paraguay | 288 | 21.48 | 21.48 | 21.48 | 21.48 | 21.48 | 21.48 | 21.48 | 21.48 | 21.48 | 21.48 | 21.48 | 21.48 |
| Peru | 293 | — | — | — | — | — | 122.00 | 122.00 | 198.50 | 210.50 | 232.50 | 240.10 | 200.15 |
| Suriname | 366 | 6.12 | 6.12 | 6.12 | 6.12 | 6.12 | 6.12 | 6.12 | 6.12 | 6.12 | 6.12 | 6.12 | — |
| Trinidad and Tobago | 369 | 111.09 | 49.90 | 34.41 | 22.43 | 39.68 | 60.23 | 72.23 | 104.33 | 110.63 | 122.63 | 124.63 | 104.63 |
| Uruguay | 298 | — | — | — | — | — | — | 63.02 | 95.32 | 101.12 | 111.12 | 114.32 | 96.32 |
| Venezuela, Rep. Bol. | 299 | 321.90 | 321.90 | 321.90 | 321.90 | 321.90 | 321.90 | 321.90 | 321.90 | 321.90 | 321.90 | 321.90 | 321.90 |

# Foreign Exchange

*Millions of SDRs: End of Period*

| | | 2004 | 2005 | 2006 | 2007 | 2008 | 2009 | 2010 | 2011 | 2012 | 2013 | 2014 | 2015 |
|---|---|---|---|---|---|---|---|---|---|---|---|---|---|
| World | 001 | 2,413,499 | 3,022,553 | 3,491,824 | 4,242,723 | 4,769,342 | 5,208,202 | 6,015,823 | 6,646,940 | 7,125,866 | 7,585,776 | 8,000,561 | 7,883,808 |
| Advanced Economies | 110 | 1,336,742 | 1,458,396 | 1,503,948 | 1,547,424 | 1,624,716 | 1,780,502 | 2,016,453 | 2,222,537 | 2,411,219 | 2,483,358 | 2,661,778 | 2,857,630 |
| Euro Area (Incl. ECB) | 163 | 116,674 | 116,948 | 122,330 | 128,580 | 131,126 | 124,011 | 134,495 | 135,571 | 143,167 | 143,388 | 157,319 | 177,269 |
| Austria | 122 | 4,355 | 4,407 | 4,369 | 6,493 | 5,353 | 3,050 | 4,009 | 4,606 | 5,187 | 5,287 | 7,343 | 6,941 |
| Belgium | 124 | 4,968 | 4,768 | 5,064 | 5,884 | 5,043 | 4,976 | 5,117 | 5,206 | 5,499 | 5,415 | 5,408 | 6,100 |
| Cyprus | 423 | 2,468 | 2,908 | 3,737 | 3,860 | † 380 | 359 | 179 | 106 | 93 | 49 | 52 | 58 |
| Estonia | 939 | 1,151 | 1,360 | 1,849 | 2,065 | 2,574 | 2,472 | 1,598 | † 65 | 117 | 123 | 219 | 217 |
| Finland | 172 | 7,357 | 7,050 | 4,078 | 4,233 | 4,215 | 4,722 | 3,195 | 3,457 | 3,707 | 4,341 | 4,427 | 4,495 |
| France | 132 | 18,723 | 16,789 | 26,779 | 27,583 | 19,725 | 17,688 | 23,513 | 17,031 | 19,747 | 17,801 | 19,780 | 26,248 |
| Germany | 134 | 25,691 | 27,822 | 25,072 | 25,799 | 25,033 | 23,556 | 24,257 | 24,806 | 24,702 | 25,146 | 25,681 | 26,258 |
| Greece | 174 | 479 | 216 | 271 | 328 | 103 | 127 | 70 | 19 | 32 | 126 | 500 | 1,080 |
| Ireland | 178 | 1,496 | 360 | 328 | 374 | 396 | 330 | 326 | 17 | 2 | 3 | 137 | 532 |
| Italy | 136 | 15,461 | 16,462 | 16,228 | 17,288 | 22,922 | 22,020 | 23,167 | 22,249 | 22,653 | 23,062 | 22,994 | 24,854 |
| Latvia | 941 | 1,231 | 1,562 | 2,894 | 3,514 | 3,264 | 4,111 | 4,590 | 3,812 | 4,525 | 4,811 | † 1,930 | 2,203 |
| Lithuania | 946 | 2,262 | 2,603 | 3,758 | 4,782 | 4,077 | 3,958 | 3,977 | 5,018 | 5,210 | 4,958 | 5,732 | † 944 |
| Luxembourg | 137 | 93 | 117 | 104 | 59 | 168 | 171 | 176 | 119 | 98 | 120 | 130 | 137 |
| Malta | 181 | 1,688 | 1,730 | 1,904 | 2,317 | † 187 | 210 | 221 | 189 | 309 | 239 | 295 | 292 |
| Netherlands | 138 | 4,642 | 4,952 | 6,200 | 5,536 | 6,083 | 5,494 | 5,780 | 5,966 | 7,029 | 7,590 | 6,733 | 6,376 |
| Portugal | 182 | 2,982 | 2,220 | 1,220 | 661 | 664 | 518 | 1,307 | 222 | 364 | 739 | 2,326 | 3,594 |
| Slovak Republic | 936 | 9,283 | 10,424 | 8,405 | 11,407 | 11,560 | † 32 | 34 | 46 | 11 | 35 | 450 | 860 |
| Slovenia | 961 | 5,578 | 5,606 | 4,644 | † 596 | 526 | 376 | 329 | 214 | 176 | 189 | 288 | 251 |
| Spain | 184 | 6,749 | 6,013 | 6,706 | 6,829 | 7,492 | 8,156 | 8,640 | 16,832 | 18,358 | 18,291 | 22,702 | 27,935 |
| Australia | 193 | 21,829 | 28,666 | 35,111 | 15,337 | 19,391 | 21,051 | 21,294 | 23,450 | 24,624 | 27,619 | 30,839 | 29,568 |
| Canada | 156 | 19,424 | 21,454 | 22,067 | 24,878 | 26,967 | 27,175 | 29,147 | 34,399 | 35,944 | 37,942 | 43,316 | 49,849 |
| China, P.R.: Hong Kong | 532 | 79,549 | 86,928 | 88,519 | 96,590 | 118,466 | 163,150 | 174,444 | 185,804 | † 206,380 | 201,988 | 226,653 | 258,821 |
| Czech Republic | 935 | 17,929 | 20,386 | 20,642 | 21,797 | 23,679 | 25,305 | 26,191 | 24,656 | 27,595 | 34,995 | 36,136 | 45,196 |
| Denmark | 128 | 24,595 | † 22,746 | 19,383 | 20,268 | 25,855 | 45,455 | 45,671 | 50,876 | 53,593 | 53,518 | 48,090 | 43,372 |
| Iceland | 176 | 655 | 706 | 1,511 | 1,613 | 2,263 | 2,321 | 3,608 | 5,022 | 2,630 | 2,678 | 2,806 | 3,458 |
| Israel | 436 | 17,138 | 19,478 | 19,284 | 17,976 | 27,478 | 37,693 | 44,976 | 47,583 | 48,174 | 51,682 | 58,215 | 64,184 |
| Japan | 158 | 530,753 | 579,886 | 581,585 | 600,130 | 651,622 | 635,939 | 672,880 | 795,462 | 776,604 | 781,119 | 828,374 | 851,177 |
| Korea | 542 | 127,607 | 146,906 | 158,460 | 165,651 | 130,158 | 169,168 | 186,312 | 194,254 | 206,190 | 217,953 | 244,063 | 258,718 |
| New Zealand | 196 | 4,146 | 6,083 | 9,250 | 10,836 | 7,047 | 8,919 | 9,826 | 9,928 | 10,266 | 9,357 | 9,712 | 9,457 |
| Norway | 142 | 27,739 | 32,448 | 37,345 | 38,155 | 32,601 | 29,163 | 32,298 | 29,710 | 31,231 | 35,447 | 42,511 | 39,387 |
| San Marino | 135 | 224 | 239 | 314 | 405 | 454 | 483 | 271 | 202 | 230 | 329 | 250 | .... |
| Singapore | 576 | 71,882 | 80,811 | 90,137 | 102,709 | 112,602 | 118,514 | 145,243 | 153,303 | 167,114 | 175,639 | 175,704 | 177,323 |
| Sweden | 144 | 13,290 | 14,960 | 16,002 | 16,695 | 16,313 | 24,586 | 24,622 | 25,342 | 26,217 | 35,958 | 36,793 | 35,959 |
| Switzerland | 146 | 34,536 | 24,783 | 24,836 | 27,760 | 28,664 | 58,439 | 141,132 | 176,596 | 304,462 | 317,247 | 344,394 | 404,575 |
| United Kingdom | 112 | 21,946 | 25,085 | 25,850 | 30,057 | 26,976 | 24,256 | 32,035 | 36,631 | 42,258 | 45,165 | 52,733 | 73,313 |
| United States | 111 | 27,507 | 26,474 | 27,216 | 28,985 | 32,191 | 32,226 | 33,814 | 33,791 | 32,482 | 30,909 | 28,950 | 28,319 |
| Emerging & Dev. Economies | 200 | 1,076,757 | 1,564,156 | 1,987,877 | 2,695,299 | 3,144,626 | 3,427,700 | 3,999,371 | 4,424,403 | 4,714,646 | 5,102,418 | 5,338,783 | 5,026,178 |
| Emerging & Developing Asia | 505 | 592,365 | 801,749 | 984,919 | 1,343,834 | 1,646,473 | 1,944,714 | 2,338,381 | 2,602,138 | 2,698,262 | 3,012,717 | 3,233,449 | 3,018,984 |
| Bangladesh | 513 | 2,042 | 1,935 | 2,529 | 3,279 | 3,692 | 6,060 | 6,431 | 5,064 | 7,413 | 10,766 | 14,354 | 18,619 |
| Bhutan | 514 | 255 | 326 | 361 | 441 | 495 | 561 | 643 | 507 | 614 | 636 | 852 | 789 |
| Brunei Darussalam | 516 | 248 | 302 | 306 | 396 | 461 | 636 | 785 | 1,390 | 1,907 | 1,977 | 2,166 | 2,087 |
| Cambodia | 522 | 607 | 667 | 769 | 1,143 | 1,488 | 1,750 | 2,045 | 2,179 | 2,708 | 2,864 | 3,815 | 4,879 |
| China, P.R.: Mainland | 924 | 392,742 | 572,930 | 708,817 | 967,093 | 1,263,434 | 1,530,374 | 1,848,885 | 2,072,045 | 2,154,692 | 2,481,373 | 2,652,534 | 2,403,327 |
| China, P.R.: Macao | 546 | 3,500 | 4,680 | 6,070 | 8,372 | 10,342 | 11,705 | 15,407 | 22,163 | 10,801 | 10,484 | 11,350 | 13,632 |
| Fiji | 819 | 290 | 204 | 186 | 312 | 186 | 280 | 400 | 475 | 531 | 543 | 564 | 595 |
| India | 534 | 80,594 | 91,668 | 113,126 | 168,678 | 160,104 | 164,945 | 173,902 | 171,262 | 170,247 | 173,833 | 204,269 | 236,583 |
| Indonesia | 536 | 22,359 | 23,037 | 27,164 | 34,638 | 32,033 | 38,638 | 58,421 | 67,487 | 68,908 | 60,667 | 73,214 | 72,616 |
| Lao People's Dem. Rep. | 544 | 134 | 154 | 209 | 327 | 398 | 337 | 406 | 432 | 469 | 418 | 553 | 702 |
| Malaysia | 548 | 41,794 | 48,540 | 54,323 | 63,683 | 58,824 | 59,237 | 66,443 | 84,001 | 87,799 | 84,735 | 77,143 | 65,979 |
| Maldives | 556 | 131 | 130 | 154 | 195 | 156 | 166 | 227 | 218 | 198 | 239 | 424 | 407 |
| Micronesia, Fed. States of | 868 | 34 | 34 | 30 | 29 | 25 | 29 | 30 | 43 | 44 | 49 | 73 | 91 |
| Mongolia | 948 | 125 | 233 | 388 | 507 | 364 | 777 | 1,379 | 1,436 | 2,513 | 1,318 | 1,020 | 856 |
| Myanmar | 518 | 433 | 539 | 821 | 1,954 | 2,413 | 3,278 | 3,710 | 4,561 | 4,531 | .... | .... | .... |
| Nepal | 558 | 935 | 1,043 | 1,281 | 1,269 | 1,590 | 1,702 | 1,846 | 2,307 | 2,751 | 3,396 | 4,127 | 5,705 |
| Papua New Guinea | 853 | 406 | 502 | 931 | 1,299 | 1,268 | 1,517 | 1,959 | 2,762 | 2,547 | 1,792 | 1,546 | 1,211 |
| Philippines | 566 | 8,358 | 11,055 | 13,222 | 19,030 | 21,455 | 23,923 | 35,059 | 42,794 | 46,623 | 47,917 | 48,495 | 52,212 |
| Samoa | 862 | 52 | 54 | 50 | 57 | 53 | 92 | 123 | 95 | 96 | 98 | 84 | 88 |
| Solomon Islands | 813 | 51 | 66 | 69 | 76 | 57 | 83 | 163 | 259 | 296 | 309 | 313 | 347 |
| Sri Lanka | 524 | 1,325 | 1,805 | 1,762 | 2,086 | 1,554 | 2,884 | 4,307 | 4,019 | 4,099 | 4,235 | 4,995 | 4,669 |
| Thailand | 578 | 31,228 | 35,334 | 43,304 | 53,859 | 70,323 | 85,220 | 107,567 | 107,603 | 111,330 | 103,261 | 102,887 | 107,734 |
| Timor-Leste | 537 | 117 | 107 | 56 | 146 | 137 | 152 | 256 | 293 | 567 | 438 | 207 | 308 |
| Tonga | 866 | 34 | 31 | 30 | 39 | 43 | 52 | 59 | 85 | 90 | 92 | 101 | 104 |
| Vanuatu | 846 | 36 | 44 | 66 | 72 | 71 | 91 | 101 | 109 | 115 | 112 | 123 | 190 |
| Vietnam | 582 | 4,534 | 6,332 | 8,896 | 14,853 | 15,505 | 10,224 | 7,827 | 8,551 | 16,371 | 16,546 | 23,330 | 20,119 |
| Europe | 170 | 173,101 | 253,510 | 358,889 | 493,144 | 470,454 | 476,598 | 525,479 | 540,079 | 573,733 | 573,109 | 494,471 | 478,266 |
| Emerging & Dev. Europe | 903 | 81,265 | 109,715 | 131,496 | 159,267 | 162,561 | 178,375 | 196,112 | 201,492 | 220,771 | 233,991 | 231,643 | 220,381 |
| Albania | 914 | 806 | 970 | 1,166 | 1,327 | 1,498 | 1,422 | 1,550 | 1,506 | 1,577 | 1,688 | 1,718 | 2,083 |
| Bosnia and Herzegovina | 963 | 1,563 | 1,782 | 2,440 | 3,190 | 2,908 | 2,886 | 2,835 | 2,702 | 2,785 | 3,160 | 3,272 | 3,382 |
| Bulgaria | 918 | 5,610 | 5,592 | 7,240 | 10,393 | 10,880 | 10,281 | 9,368 | 9,289 | 11,308 | 11,260 | 12,176 | 14,352 |
| Croatia | 960 | 5,639 | 6,157 | 7,636 | 8,653 | 8,412 | 9,198 | 8,873 | 9,131 | 9,330 | 11,232 | 10,341 | 10,496 |
| Hungary | 944 | 9,869 | 12,801 | 14,169 | 15,044 | 21,827 | 27,097 | 28,299 | 31,086 | 28,647 | 30,035 | 28,834 | 23,742 |
| Kosovo | 967 | .... | .... | .... | 602 | 579 | 460 | 480 | 414 | 652 | 649 | 559 | 612 |
| Macedonia, FYR | 962 | 582 | 859 | 1,162 | 1,317 | 1,246 | 1,250 | 1,278 | 1,518 | 1,644 | 1,610 | 1,860 | 1,612 |
| Montenegro | 943 | 53 | 143 | 288 | 429 | 276 | 333 | 328 | 223 | 266 | 346 | 424 | 496 |
| Poland | 964 | 22,249 | 28,327 | 30,648 | 39,690 | 38,260 | 46,816 | 56,049 | 58,418 | 65,271 | 64,504 | 64,925 | 64,530 |
| Romania | 968 | 9,411 | 13,903 | 18,656 | 23,537 | 23,857 | 25,097 | 27,469 | 27,584 | 26,684 | 29,073 | 27,019 | 25,369 |
| Serbia, Republic of | 942 | 2,637 | 3,916 | 7,737 | 8,791 | 7,220 | 9,409 | 8,254 | 9,689 | 8,660 | 9,492 | 7,805 | 7,729 |

# Foreign Exchange

2016, International Monetary Fund : *International Financial Statistics Yearbook*

| 1d s | | 2004 | 2005 | 2006 | 2007 | 2008 | 2009 | 2010 | 2011 | 2012 | 2013 | 2014 | 2015 |
|---|---|---|---|---|---|---|---|---|---|---|---|---|---|
| **Emerging & Dev. Europe(Cont.)** | | | | | | | | | | | | | |
| Turkey | 186 | 22,846 | 35,264 | 40,355 | 46,294 | 45,597 | 44,127 | 51,327 | 49,932 | 63,946 | 70,941 | 72,710 | 65,977 |
| **CIS** | 901 | 91,836 | 143,795 | 227,392 | 333,877 | 307,893 | 298,223 | 329,367 | 338,587 | 352,963 | 339,118 | 262,828 | 257,885 |
| Armenia | 911 | 345 | 461 | 703 | 1,044 | 911 | 1,199 | 1,190 | 1,222 | 1,150 | 1,461 | 1,024 | 1,279 |
| Azerbaijan, Republic of | 912 | 683 | 814 | 1,652 | 2,698 | 4,198 | 3,270 | 4,008 | 6,538 | 7,183 | 9,197 | 9,956 | 4,386 |
| Belarus | 913 | 483 | 795 | 710 | 2,501 | 1,744 | 2,713 | 1,859 | 3,543 | 3,410 | 2,835 | 1,990 | 1,608 |
| Georgia | 915 | 242 | 334 | 618 | 852 | 953 | 1,207 | 1,326 | 1,690 | 1,725 | 1,689 | 1,719 | 1,675 |
| Kazakhstan | 916 | 5,455 | 4,256 | 11,798 | 9,983 | 11,602 | 12,872 | 16,034 | 16,056 | 14,054 | 12,072 | 14,708 | 14,428 |
| Kyrgyz Republic | 917 | 327 | 395 | 486 | 692 | 713 | 850 | 930 | 994 | 1,117 | 1,234 | 1,121 | 1,046 |
| Moldova | 921 | 303 | 418 | 515 | 844 | 1,086 | 942 | 1,115 | 1,279 | 1,633 | 1,826 | 1,486 | 1,253 |
| Russia | 922 | 77,788 | 122,923 | 196,276 | 295,128 | 266,639 | 258,868 | 281,130 | 287,351 | 307,830 | 296,394 | 226,204 | 223,267 |
| Tajikistan | 923 | 101 | 114 | 114 | 23 | 57 | 41 | 141 | 119 | 124 | 229 | 53 | 24 |
| Ukraine | 926 | 6,110 | 13,284 | 14,520 | 20,113 | 19,991 | 16,262 | 21,636 | 19,795 | 14,735 | 12,182 | 4,568 | 8,919 |
| **Middle East,N.Africa & Pakistan** | 440 | 132,763 | 278,464 | 363,829 | 486,376 | 604,798 | 578,179 | 644,940 | 710,044 | 819,140 | 890,125 | 933,757 | 860,913 |
| Afghanistan, Islamic Rep. of | 512 | . . . | . . . | . . . | . . . | 1,578 | 2,105 | 2,582 | 3,303 | 3,766 | 4,065 | 4,506 | 4,406 |
| Algeria | 612 | 27,761 | 39,305 | 51,702 | 69,723 | 92,907 | 93,910 | 104,263 | 117,617 | 122,980 | 124,907 | 122,432 | 102,938 |
| Bahrain, Kingdom of | 419 | 1,178 | 1,309 | 1,786 | 2,591 | 2,465 | 2,254 | 3,105 | 2,761 | 3,187 | 3,271 | 3,974 | . . . |
| Djibouti | 611 | 59 | 61 | 78 | 82 | 113 | 140 | 150 | 149 | 152 | 267 | 263 | 256 |
| Egypt | 469 | 9,084 | 14,349 | 16,180 | 19,019 | 20,846 | 19,741 | 21,007 | 8,896 | 6,746 | 8,015 | 7,452 | 8,749 |
| Iraq | 433 | 4,571 | 8,004 | 12,786 | 19,546 | 32,157 | 26,817 | 31,376 | 38,259 | 43,428 | 48,244 | 42,733 | 36,558 |
| Jordan | 439 | 3,390 | 3,673 | 4,467 | 4,771 | 5,556 | 7,309 | 8,331 | 7,322 | 5,120 | 8,448 | 10,436 | 10,843 |
| Kuwait | 443 | 4,731 | 5,863 | 8,095 | 10,306 | 10,784 | 11,232 | 12,093 | 14,930 | 16,894 | 17,109 | 20,209 | 18,516 |
| Lebanon | 446 | 7,516 | 8,276 | 8,850 | 8,128 | 13,103 | 18,336 | 20,236 | 21,750 | 23,968 | 23,635 | 27,069 | 27,741 |
| Libya | 672 | 15,670 | 26,752 | 38,492 | 49,294 | 58,953 | 60,992 | 62,856 | 66,355 | 75,133 | 72,885 | 59,575 | . . . |
| Mauritania | 682 | 22 | 45 | 124 | 125 | 122 | 144 | 176 | 315 | 616 | . . . | . . . | . . . |
| Morocco | 686 | 10,371 | 11,200 | 13,415 | 15,175 | 14,268 | 13,985 | 14,356 | 12,121 | 10,194 | 11,501 | 12,949 | 15,438 |
| Oman | 449 | 2,244 | 3,015 | 3,304 | 6,002 | 7,493 | 7,563 | 8,228 | 9,108 | 9,118 | 10,099 | 11,008 | 12,406 |
| Pakistan | 564 | 6,152 | 6,869 | 7,530 | 8,751 | 4,552 | 6,339 | 8,516 | 8,776 | 6,064 | 2,796 | 7,629 | 12,381 |
| Qatar | 453 | 2,077 | 3,118 | 3,528 | 5,914 | 6,202 | 11,398 | 19,553 | 10,188 | 20,793 | 26,637 | 29,122 | 25,972 |
| Saudi Arabia | 456 | 14,986 | † 106,749 | 149,218 | 192,377 | 285,749 | 253,078 | 280,575 | 342,299 | 417,052 | 461,354 | 496,215 | 435,861 |
| Sudan | 732 | 862 | 1,307 | 1,103 | 872 | 908 | 572 | 547 | — | — | — | — | — |
| Syrian Arab Republic | 463 | . . . | 12,100 | 10,910 | 10,729 | 11,041 | 10,818 | 12,360 | . . . | . . . | . . . | . . . | . . . |
| Tunisia | 744 | 2,508 | 3,082 | 4,481 | 4,947 | 5,722 | 6,791 | 5,844 | 4,557 | 5,140 | 4,436 | 4,746 | . . . |
| United Arab Emirates | 466 | 11,725 | 14,600 | 18,288 | 48,829 | 20,488 | 15,992 | 20,617 | 23,508 | 29,817 | 43,475 | 53,314 | 66,804 |
| West Bank and Gaza | 487 | . . . | . . . | 209 | 225 | 331 | 318 | 345 | 324 | 432 | 445 | 464 | 419 |
| Yemen, Republic of | 474 | 3,615 | 4,266 | 4,988 | 4,882 | 5,266 | 4,224 | 3,628 | 2,732 | 3,783 | 3,268 | . . . | . . . |
| **Sub-Saharan Africa** | 603 | 39,492 | 56,823 | 75,849 | 91,795 | 101,509 | 94,654 | 96,343 | 109,204 | 123,717 | 124,544 | 121,190 | 112,077 |
| CEMAC (incl. BEAC hqtrs.) | 758 | 1,985 | 3,593 | 5,891 | 7,547 | 10,161 | 8,680 | 8,400 | 9,775 | 11,152 | 11,578 | 10,315 | 7,066 |
| Cameroon | 622 | 533 | 662 | 1,137 | 1,836 | 2,000 | 2,188 | 2,347 | 2,066 | 2,183 | 2,238 | 2,171 | 2,536 |
| Central African Rep. | 626 | 94 | 97 | 83 | 52 | 79 | 131 | 115 | 98 | 100 | 123 | 178 | 154 |
| Chad | 628 | 142 | 157 | 415 | 604 | 873 | 390 | 408 | 617 | 749 | 765 | 740 | 263 |
| Congo, Rep. of | 634 | 72 | 510 | 1,223 | 1,375 | 2,513 | 2,357 | 2,817 | 3,604 | 3,540 | 3,335 | 3,330 | 1,533 |
| Equatorial Guinea | 642 | 608 | 1,471 | 2,038 | 2,433 | 2,876 | 2,048 | 1,498 | 1,963 | 2,835 | 2,939 | 1,980 | 844 |
| Gabon | 646 | 281 | 467 | 739 | 776 | 1,248 | 1,138 | 994 | 1,272 | 1,397 | 1,817 | 1,577 | 1,211 |
| WAEMU (Incl. BCEAO hqtrs.) | 759 | 4,630 | 4,301 | 4,869 | 6,066 | 6,021 | 6,971 | 6,946 | 7,157 | 7,060 | 6,942 | 7,117 | 7,087 |
| Benin | 638 | 407 | 456 | 604 | 763 | 818 | 733 | 727 | 526 | 412 | 399 | 449 | 482 |
| Burkina Faso | 748 | 417 | 299 | 361 | 644 | 595 | 771 | 638 | 568 | 611 | 352 | 149 | 143 |
| Côte d'Ivoire | 662 | 1,081 | 955 | 1,194 | 1,593 | 1,461 | 1,810 | 2,080 | 2,537 | 2,282 | 2,481 | 2,817 | 3,168 |
| Guinea Bissau | 654 | 46 | 55 | 54 | 71 | 81 | 96 | 89 | 131 | 94 | 108 | 185 | 227 |
| Mali | 678 | 539 | 588 | 635 | 678 | 686 | 940 | 790 | 815 | 789 | 764 | 511 | 372 |
| Niger | 692 | 152 | 167 | 238 | 367 | 448 | 355 | 431 | 375 | 597 | 695 | 822 | 694 |
| Senegal | 722 | 874 | 827 | 885 | 1,049 | 1,038 | 1,222 | 1,197 | 1,135 | 1,222 | 1,331 | 1,275 | 1,342 |
| Togo | 742 | 230 | 134 | 249 | 277 | 377 | 389 | 404 | 445 | 228 | 269 | 290 | 366 |
| Angola | 614 | 885 | 2,237 | 5,715 | 7,085 | 11,601 | 8,445 | 12,558 | 18,494 | 21,494 | 21,048 | 19,184 | 17,145 |
| Botswana | 616 | 3,591 | 4,371 | 5,270 | 6,152 | 5,872 | 5,448 | 5,014 | 5,150 | 4,850 | 4,900 | 5,628 | 5,333 |
| Burundi | 618 | 42 | 69 | 86 | 111 | 172 | 138 | 141 | 112 | 115 | 130 | 136 | 58 |
| Cabo Verde | 624 | 90 | 122 | 169 | 231 | 235 | 246 | 241 | 216 | 241 | 306 | 351 | 356 |
| Comoros | 632 | 66 | 59 | 62 | 74 | 72 | 89 | 86 | 91 | 114 | 98 | 106 | 133 |
| Congo, Dem. Rep. of | 636 | 149 | 91 | 103 | 112 | 47 | 270 | 491 | 473 | 710 | 738 | 723 | 553 |
| Eritrea | 643 | 22 | 20 | 17 | 22 | 38 | 54 | 70 | 71 | . . . | . . . | . . . | . . . |
| Ethiopia | 644 | 956 | 722 | 569 | 809 | 558 | 1,111 | . . . | . . . | . . . | . . . | . . . | . . . |
| Gambia, The | 648 | 52 | 67 | 78 | 89 | 74 | 117 | 105 | 119 | 128 | 112 | 87 | . . . |
| Ghana | 652 | 1,034 | 1,226 | 1,389 | 1,255 | 1,149 | 1,870 | 2,802 | 3,291 | 3,233 | 3,170 | . . . | . . . |
| Guinea | 656 | 71 | 66 | . . . | . . . | . . . | . . . | . . . | 6 | 22 | 16 | 42 | 34 |
| Kenya | 664 | 965 | 1,246 | 1,593 | 2,110 | 1,854 | 2,219 | 2,585 | 2,754 | 3,697 | 4,251 | 5,438 | 5,423 |
| Lesotho | 666 | 319 | 359 | 434 | 627 | 624 | 718 | 658 | 560 | 627 | 634 | 689 | 603 |
| Liberia | 668 | 12 | 18 | 48 | 76 | 90 | 109 | 166 | 188 | 166 | 147 | 166 | . . . |
| Madagascar | 674 | 324 | 337 | 388 | 536 | 638 | 529 | 568 | 645 | 595 | 420 | 463 | 541 |
| Malawi | 676 | 79 | 108 | 86 | 135 | 155 | 92 | 196 | 126 | 142 | 260 | 407 | . . . |
| Mauritius | 684 | 995 | 902 | 815 | 1,101 | 1,099 | 1,277 | 1,464 | 1,551 | 1,712 | 2,031 | 2,356 | 2,723 |
| Mozambique | 688 | 728 | 737 | 768 | 914 | 1,024 | 1,230 | 1,294 | 1,501 | 1,696 | 1,936 | 1,976 | 1,661 |
| Namibia | 728 | 222 | 218 | 299 | 567 | 839 | 1,178 | 971 | 1,158 | 1,131 | 976 | 808 | 1,213 |
| Nigeria | 694 | 10,918 | 19,786 | 28,116 | 32,484 | 34,410 | 27,035 | 20,999 | 21,260 | 28,518 | 27,823 | 23,634 | 20,411 |
| Rwanda | 714 | 183 | 266 | 277 | 335 | 367 | 390 | 444 | 601 | 469 | 614 | 656 | 666 |
| São Tomé & Príncipe | 716 | 13 | 19 | 23 | 25 | 40 | 36 | 27 | 30 | 33 | 41 | 43 | 52 |
| Seychelles | 718 | 22 | 39 | 75 | 26 | 41 | 114 | 158 | 175 | 193 | 270 | 315 | 381 |
| Sierra Leone | 724 | 48 | 96 | 103 | 118 | 123 | 137 | 146 | 170 | 199 | 239 | 307 | 340 |
| South Africa | 199 | 8,238 | 12,775 | 15,102 | 18,500 | 19,632 | 20,688 | 22,999 | 25,954 | 26,796 | 27,236 | 28,639 | 28,088 |
| South Sudan, Republic of | 733 | . . . | . . . | . . . | . . . | . . . | . . . | — | 904 | 728 | 509 | 181 | 164 |
| Swaziland | 734 | 199 | 162 | 239 | 481 | 479 | 561 | 440 | 340 | 431 | 440 | 421 | 340 |
| Tanzania | 738 | 1,468 | 1,423 | 1,492 | 1,816 | 1,849 | 2,045 | 2,367 | 2,260 | 2,472 | 2,872 | 2,886 | 2,839 |

# Foreign Exchange

| 1d s | | 2004 | 2005 | 2006 | 2007 | 2008 | 2009 | 2010 | 2011 | 2012 | 2013 | 2014 | 2015 |
|---|---|---|---|---|---|---|---|---|---|---|---|---|---|
| | | | | | | | *Millions of SDRs: End of Period* | | | | | | |
| **Sub-Saharan Africa(Cont.)** | | | | | | | | | | | | | |
| Uganda | 746 | 842 | 940 | 1,204 | 1,620 | 1,493 | 1,766 | 1,614 | 1,563 | 1,920 | 2,027 | 2,240 | 2,052 |
| Zambia | 754 | 201 | 381 | 470 | 684 | 704 | 800 | 954 | 1,111 | 1,585 | 1,360 | 1,765 | 1,825 |
| Zimbabwe | 698 | 143 | 68 | 102 | 91 | 49 | 293 | 310 | 265 | 280 | 215 | 158 | 140 |
| **Western Hemisphere** | 205 | **139,037** | **173,610** | **204,391** | **280,149** | **321,392** | **333,556** | **394,227** | **462,939** | **499,795** | **501,923** | **555,915** | **555,938** |
| ECCU (incl. ECCB hqtrs.) | 309 | 406 | 418 | 461 | 482 | 490 | 510 | 601 | 656 | 731 | 758 | 973 | 1,124 |
| Anguilla | 312 | 22 | 28 | 28 | 28 | 27 | 24 | 26 | 24 | 26 | 27 | 33 | 35 |
| Antigua and Barbuda | 311 | 77 | 89 | 95 | 91 | 90 | 69 | 88 | 96 | 105 | 131 | 205 | 257 |
| Dominica | 321 | 27 | 34 | 42 | 38 | 36 | 41 | 43 | 48 | 60 | 55 | 69 | 91 |
| Grenada | 328 | 78 | 66 | 66 | 70 | 68 | 72 | 67 | 68 | 68 | 88 | 109 | 136 |
| Montserrat | 351 | 9 | 10 | 10 | 9 | 8 | 9 | 11 | 16 | 21 | 26 | 31 | 37 |
| St. Kitts and Nevis | 361 | 50 | 50 | 59 | 61 | 72 | 78 | 101 | 151 | 164 | 189 | 220 | 202 |
| St. Lucia | 362 | 84 | 80 | 88 | 96 | 91 | 96 | 118 | 124 | 135 | 109 | 162 | 215 |
| St. Vincent & Grenadines | 364 | 48 | 48 | 52 | 55 | 54 | 48 | 72 | 57 | 71 | 86 | 108 | 119 |
| Argentina | 213 | 11,595 | 15,912 | 20,221 | 27,954 | 28,800 | 27,379 | 30,272 | 26,103 | 23,921 | 16,221 | 17,975 | 14,845 |
| Aruba | 314 | 190 | 191 | 225 | 235 | 393 | 369 | 369 | 350 | 392 | 346 | 386 | 512 |
| Bahamas, The | 313 | 428 | 404 | 300 | 288 | 362 | 524 | 558 | 577 | 526 | 480 | 543 | 586 |
| Barbados | 316 | 368 | 417 | 417 | 526 | 474 | 494 | 479 | 467 | 484 | 380 | 374 | .... |
| Belize | 339 | 25 | 44 | 69 | 62 | 101 | 112 | 117 | 130 | 164 | 237 | 312 | 291 |
| Bolivia | 218 | 526 | 893 | 1,702 | 2,846 | 4,461 | 4,664 | 5,108 | 6,282 | 7,412 | 8,125 | 9,129 | 8,196 |
| Brazil | 223 | 33,778 | 37,233 | 56,599 | 113,546 | 125,200 | 147,917 | 182,185 | 223,664 | 235,599 | 226,642 | 244,896 | 251,753 |
| Chile | 228 | 9,978 | 11,677 | 12,779 | 10,565 | 14,834 | 15,213 | 17,089 | 26,130 | 25,852 | 25,517 | 26,828 | 26,854 |
| Colombia | 233 | 8,222 | 9,939 | 9,753 | 12,717 | 14,809 | 14,772 | 17,110 | 19,460 | 22,721 | 26,751 | 31,021 | 32,313 |
| Costa Rica | 238 | 1,217 | 1,598 | 2,050 | 2,583 | 2,446 | 2,441 | 2,852 | 2,945 | 4,309 | 4,608 | 4,825 | 5,501 |
| Curaçao & Sint Maarten | 355 | .... | .... | .... | .... | .... | .... | 820 | 840 | 738 | 719 | 972 | 970 |
| Dominican Republic | 243 | 526 | 1,343 | 1,489 | 1,855 | 1,716 | 2,095 | 2,423 | 2,650 | 2,282 | 3,037 | 3,336 | 3,781 |
| Ecuador | 248 | 635 | 1,167 | 968 | 1,750 | 2,393 | 1,799 | 898 | 1,040 | 658 | 2,114 | 2,358 | 1,459 |
| El Salvador | 253 | 1,103 | 1,179 | 1,187 | 1,309 | 1,560 | 1,665 | 1,504 | 1,238 | 1,661 | 1,442 | 1,512 | 1,812 |
| Guatemala | 258 | 2,201 | 2,559 | 2,599 | 2,611 | 2,895 | 2,992 | 3,487 | 3,627 | 3,941 | 4,371 | 4,700 | 5,245 |
| Guyana | 336 | 145 | 176 | 185 | 198 | 231 | 400 | 506 | 520 | 561 | 504 | 459 | 432 |
| Haiti | 263 | 121 | 144 | 239 | 363 | 453 | 602 | 1,159 | 1,156 | 1,339 | 1,521 | 1,287 | 1,314 |
| Honduras | 268 | 1,260 | 1,619 | 1,739 | 1,591 | 1,597 | 1,218 | 1,622 | 1,682 | 1,519 | 1,835 | 2,272 | 2,599 |
| Jamaica | 343 | 1,189 | 1,518 | 1,541 | 1,189 | 1,151 | 1,103 | 1,410 | 1,281 | 1,100 | 988 | 1,521 | 1,922 |
| Mexico | 273 | 40,423 | 51,085 | 50,151 | 54,618 | 61,024 | 60,026 | 74,598 | 89,551 | 99,857 | 109,489 | 127,818 | 121,505 |
| Netherlands Antilles | 353 | 267 | 382 | 329 | 418 | 532 | 553 | .... | .... | .... | .... | .... | .... |
| Nicaragua | 278 | 430 | 509 | 613 | 698 | 741 | 899 | 1,063 | 1,118 | 1,122 | 1,199 | 1,452 | 1,699 |
| Panama | 283 | 394 | 834 | 875 | 1,212 | 1,561 | 1,749 | 1,580 | 1,318 | 1,422 | 1,667 | 2,600 | 2,255 |
| Paraguay | 288 | 645 | 798 | 1,018 | 1,509 | 1,797 | 2,317 | 2,554 | 3,092 | 2,833 | 3,475 | 4,471 | 3,952 |
| Peru | 293 | 7,840 | 9,515 | 11,122 | 16,993 | 19,648 | 19,774 | 27,047 | 30,025 | 39,799 | 41,070 | 41,460 | 42,865 |
| Suriname | 366 | 76 | 81 | 136 | 228 | 358 | 294 | 304 | 375 | 489 | 392 | 308 | 160 |
| Trinidad and Tobago | 369 | 1,927 | 3,418 | 4,341 | 4,213 | 6,090 | 5,519 | 5,889 | 6,398 | 5,986 | 6,485 | 7,811 | 7,063 |
| Uruguay | 298 | 1,614 | 2,146 | 2,050 | 2,603 | 4,122 | 4,876 | 4,655 | 6,361 | 8,496 | 10,209 | 11,750 | 10,937 |
| Venezuela, Rep. Bol. | 299 | 11,505 | 16,410 | 19,232 | 14,989 | 21,153 | 11,282 | 5,969 | 3,907 | 3,880 | 1,340 | 2,566 | 3,662 |

# Gold (Million Fine Troy Ounces)

| | | 2004 | 2005 | 2006 | 2007 | 2008 | 2009 | 2010 | 2011 | 2012 | 2013 | 2014 | 2015 |
|---|---|---|---|---|---|---|---|---|---|---|---|---|---|
| | | | | | | | Millions of Ounces: End of Period | | | | | | |
| World.......................................... | 001 | 1,010.70 | 991.30 | 979.57 | 963.35 | 963.92 | 980.79 | 991.54 | 1,003.31 | 1,018.58 | 1,024.14 | 1,029.82 | 1,052.44 |
| Advanced Economies................ | 110 | 761.55 | 744.64 | 733.57 | 716.96 | 708.25 | 704.72 | 704.50 | 705.61 | 706.44 | 706.92 | 706.81 | 706.71 |
| Euro Area (Incl. ECB)................... | 163 | 390.00 | 375.86 | 365.21 | 353.69 | 349.21 | 347.18 | 346.96 | 346.85 | 346.69 | 346.57 | 346.72 | 346.87 |
| Austria....................................... | 122 | 9.89 | 9.73 | 9.28 | 9.00 | 9.00 | 9.00 | 9.00 | 9.00 | 9.00 | 9.00 | 9.00 | 9.00 |
| Belgium...................................... | 124 | 8.29 | 7.32 | 7.32 | 7.32 | 7.32 | 7.32 | 7.31 | 7.31 | 7.31 | 7.31 | 7.31 | 7.31 |
| Cyprus........................................ | 423 | .47 | .47 | .47 | .47 | .45 | .45 | .45 | .45 | .45 | .45 | .45 | .45 |
| Estonia....................................... | 939 | .01 | .01 | .01 | .01 | .01 | .01 | .01 | .01 | .01 | .01 | .01 | .01 |
| Finland....................................... | 172 | 1.58 | 1.58 | 1.58 | 1.58 | 1.58 | 1.58 | 1.58 | 1.58 | 1.58 | 1.58 | 1.58 | 1.58 |
| France........................................ | 132 | 95.98 | 90.85 | 87.44 | 83.69 | 80.13 | 78.30 | 78.30 | 78.30 | 78.30 | 78.30 | 78.30 | 78.31 |
| Germany..................................... | 134 | 110.38 | 110.21 | 110.04 | 109.87 | 109.72 | 109.53 | 109.34 | 109.19 | 109.04 | 108.90 | 108.81 | 108.70 |
| Greece........................................ | 174 | 3.46 | 3.47 | 3.59 | 3.62 | 3.62 | 3.62 | 3.59 | 3.59 | 3.60 | 3.61 | 3.62 | 3.62 |
| Ireland....................................... | 178 | .18 | .18 | .18 | .18 | .19 | .19 | .19 | .19 | .19 | .19 | .19 | .19 |
| Italy........................................... | 136 | 78.83 | 78.83 | 78.83 | 78.83 | 78.83 | 78.83 | 78.83 | 78.83 | 78.83 | 78.83 | 78.83 | 78.83 |
| Latvia......................................... | 941 | .25 | .25 | .25 | .25 | .25 | .25 | .25 | .25 | .25 | .25 | .21 | .21 |
| Lithuania.................................... | 946 | .19 | .19 | .19 | .19 | .19 | .19 | .19 | .19 | .19 | .19 | .19 | .19 |
| Luxembourg................................ | 137 | .07 | .07 | .07 | .07 | .07 | .07 | .07 | .07 | .07 | .07 | .07 | .07 |
| Malta.......................................... | 181 | — | — | .01 | .02 | .01 | .01 | — | .01 | .01 | .01 | — | — |
| Netherlands................................ | 138 | 25.00 | 22.34 | 20.61 | 19.98 | 19.69 | 19.69 | 19.69 | 19.69 | 19.69 | 19.69 | 19.69 | 19.69 |
| Portugal..................................... | 182 | 14.86 | 13.42 | 12.30 | 12.30 | 12.30 | 12.30 | 12.30 | 12.30 | 12.30 | 12.30 | 12.30 | 12.30 |
| Slovak Republic........................... | 936 | 1.13 | 1.13 | 1.13 | 1.13 | 1.13 | 1.02 | 1.02 | 1.02 | 1.02 | 1.02 | 1.02 | 1.02 |
| Slovenia..................................... | 961 | .24 | .16 | .16 | .10 | .10 | .10 | .10 | .10 | .10 | .10 | .10 | .10 |
| Spain......................................... | 184 | 16.83 | 14.72 | 13.40 | 9.05 | 9.05 | 9.05 | 9.05 | 9.05 | 9.05 | 9.05 | 9.05 | 9.05 |
| Australia..................................... | 193 | 2.56 | 2.57 | 2.57 | 2.57 | 2.57 | 2.57 | 2.57 | 2.57 | 2.57 | 2.57 | 2.57 | 2.57 |
| Canada....................................... | 156 | .11 | .11 | .11 | .11 | .11 | .11 | .11 | .11 | .11 | .10 | .10 | .05 |
| China, P.R.: Hong Kong............... | 532 | .07 | .07 | .07 | .07 | .07 | .07 | .07 | .07 | .07 | .07 | .07 | .07 |
| Czech Republic............................ | 935 | .44 | .44 | .43 | .43 | .42 | .42 | .41 | .40 | .37 | .35 | .34 | .32 |
| Denmark..................................... | 128 | 2.14 | 2.14 | 2.14 | 2.14 | 2.14 | 2.14 | 2.14 | 2.14 | 2.14 | 2.14 | 2.14 | 2.14 |
| Iceland....................................... | 176 | .06 | .06 | .06 | .06 | .06 | .06 | .06 | .06 | .06 | .06 | .06 | .06 |
| Israel.......................................... | 436 | — | — | — | — | — | — | — | — | — | — | — | — |
| Japan......................................... | 158 | 24.60 | 24.60 | 24.60 | 24.60 | 24.60 | 24.60 | 24.60 | 24.60 | 24.60 | 24.60 | 24.60 | 24.60 |
| Korea......................................... | 542 | .45 | .46 | .42 | .46 | .46 | .46 | .46 | 1.75 | 2.71 | 3.36 | 3.36 | 3.36 |
| New Zealand............................... | 196 | — | — | — | — | — | — | — | — | — | — | — | — |
| Norway....................................... | 142 | — | — | — | — | — | — | — | — | — | — | — | — |
| San Marino.................................. | 135 | — | — | — | — | — | — | — | — | — | — | — | .... |
| Singapore................................... | 576 | 4.10 | 4.10 | 4.10 | 4.10 | 4.10 | 4.10 | 4.10 | 4.10 | 4.10 | 4.10 | 4.10 | 4.10 |
| Sweden...................................... | 144 | 5.96 | 5.41 | 5.10 | 4.78 | 4.40 | 4.04 | 4.04 | 4.04 | 4.04 | 4.04 | 4.04 | 4.04 |
| Switzerland................................. | 146 | 43.54 | 41.48 | 41.48 | 36.82 | 33.44 | 33.44 | 33.44 | 33.44 | 33.44 | 33.44 | 33.44 | 33.44 |
| United Kingdom........................... | 112 | 10.04 | 9.99 | 9.97 | 9.98 | 9.98 | 9.98 | 9.98 | 9.98 | 9.98 | 9.98 | 9.98 | 9.98 |
| United States.............................. | 111 | 261.59 | 261.55 | 261.50 | 261.50 | 261.50 | 261.50 | 261.50 | 261.50 | 261.50 | 261.50 | 261.50 | 261.50 |
| | | | | | | | | | | | | | |
| Emerging & Dev. Economies...... | 200 | 139.01 | 137.24 | 137.03 | 138.52 | 148.23 | 174.48 | 180.47 | 191.61 | 204.94 | 215.57 | 223.96 | 251.86 |
| Emerging & Developing Asia..... | 505 | 46.85 | 44.67 | 43.72 | 43.36 | 44.03 | 65.57 | 66.06 | 68.01 | 69.31 | 69.88 | 69.94 | 92.80 |
| Bangladesh.................................. | 513 | .11 | .11 | .11 | .11 | .11 | .11 | .43 | .43 | .43 | .43 | .44 | .44 |
| Brunei Darussalam........................ | 516 | — | — | — | — | — | — | — | .06 | .10 | .15 | .15 | .15 |
| Cambodia.................................... | 522 | .40 | .40 | .40 | .40 | .40 | .40 | .40 | .40 | .40 | .40 | .40 | .40 |
| China, P.R.: Mainland................... | 924 | 19.29 | 19.29 | 19.29 | 19.29 | 19.29 | 33.89 | 33.89 | 33.89 | 33.89 | 33.89 | 33.89 | 56.66 |
| China, P.R.: Macao...................... | 546 | — | — | — | — | — | — | — | — | — | — | — | — |
| Fiji............................................. | 819 | — | — | — | — | — | — | — | — | — | — | — | — |
| India.......................................... | 534 | 11.50 | 11.50 | 11.50 | 11.50 | 11.50 | 17.93 | 17.93 | 17.93 | 17.93 | 17.93 | 17.93 | 17.93 |
| Indonesia.................................... | 536 | 3.10 | 3.10 | 2.35 | 2.35 | 2.35 | 2.35 | 2.35 | 2.35 | 2.38 | 2.51 | 2.51 | 2.51 |
| Lao People's Dem. Rep................. | 544 | .12 | .15 | .21 | .21 | .29 | .29 | .29 | † .29 | .29 | .29 | .29 | .... |
| Malaysia...................................... | 548 | 1.17 | 1.17 | 1.17 | 1.17 | 1.17 | 1.17 | 1.17 | 1.17 | 1.17 | 1.17 | 1.15 | 1.23 |
| Maldives..................................... | 556 | — | — | — | — | — | — | — | — | — | — | — | — |
| Micronesia, Fed. States of............. | 868 | — | — | — | — | — | — | — | — | — | — | — | — |
| Mongolia..................................... | 948 | .03 | — | .21 | .24 | .11 | .03 | .06 | .11 | .12 | .13 | .09 | .07 |
| Myanmar..................................... | 518 | .23 | .23 | .23 | .23 | .23 | .23 | .23 | .23 | .23 | .... | .... | .... |
| Nepal......................................... | 558 | .15 | .13 | — | — | — | .05 | .05 | .05 | .07 | .12 | .16 | .20 |
| Papua New Guinea....................... | 853 | .06 | .06 | .06 | .06 | .06 | .06 | .06 | .06 | .06 | .06 | .06 | .06 |
| Philippines.................................. | 566 | 7.12 | 4.97 | 4.62 | 4.23 | 4.95 | 4.99 | 4.95 | 5.12 | 6.20 | 6.22 | 6.28 | 6.30 |
| Samoa........................................ | 862 | .... | .... | .... | .... | .... | .... | .... | .... | .... | .... | .... | .... |
| Solomon Islands........................... | 813 | .... | .... | .... | .... | .... | .... | .... | .... | .02 | .02 | .02 | .02 |
| Sri Lanka.................................... | 524 | .17 | .17 | .17 | .17 | .17 | .68 | .35 | .32 | .44 | .74 | .74 | .72 |
| Thailand..................................... | 578 | 2.70 | 2.70 | 2.70 | 2.70 | 2.70 | 2.70 | 3.20 | 4.90 | 4.90 | 4.90 | 4.90 | 4.90 |
| Timor-Leste................................ | 537 | — | — | — | — | — | — | — | — | — | — | — | — |
| Tonga......................................... | 866 | .... | .... | .... | .... | .... | .... | .... | .... | .... | .... | .... | .... |
| Vanuatu...................................... | 846 | .... | .... | .... | .... | .... | .... | .... | .... | .... | .... | .... | .... |
| Vietnam...................................... | 582 | — | — | — | — | — | — | — | — | — | — | — | — |
| | | | | | | | | | | | | | |
| Europe........................................ | 170 | 27.52 | 28.16 | 29.00 | 30.39 | 32.89 | 37.39 | 42.16 | 48.47 | 57.73 | 67.24 | 74.48 | 81.91 |
| Emerging & Dev. Europe.......... | 903 | 12.40 | 12.50 | 12.49 | 12.43 | 12.43 | 12.49 | 12.48 | 15.10 | 20.41 | 25.63 | 25.97 | 25.56 |
| Albania....................................... | 914 | .07 | .07 | .07 | .07 | .05 | .05 | .05 | .05 | .05 | .05 | .05 | .05 |
| Bosnia and Herzegovina.............. | 963 | — | — | — | — | — | .04 | .03 | .06 | .06 | .10 | .10 | .10 |
| Bulgaria...................................... | 918 | 1.28 | 1.28 | 1.28 | 1.28 | 1.28 | 1.28 | 1.28 | 1.28 | 1.28 | 1.29 | 1.29 | 1.29 |
| Croatia....................................... | 960 | — | — | — | — | — | — | — | — | — | — | — | — |
| Hungary..................................... | 944 | .10 | .10 | .10 | .10 | .10 | .10 | .10 | .10 | .10 | .10 | .10 | .10 |
| Kosovo....................................... | 967 | .... | .... | .... | — | — | — | — | — | — | — | — | — |
| Macedonia, FYR.......................... | 962 | .20 | .22 | .22 | .22 | .22 | .22 | .22 | .22 | .22 | .22 | .22 | .22 |
| Montenegro................................ | 943 | — | — | .04 | — | — | — | — | — | — | — | — | — |
| Poland........................................ | 964 | 3.31 | 3.31 | 3.31 | 3.31 | 3.31 | 3.31 | 3.31 | 3.31 | 3.31 | 3.31 | 3.31 | 3.31 |
| Romania..................................... | 968 | 3.38 | 3.37 | 3.37 | 3.33 | 3.33 | 3.33 | 3.33 | 3.33 | 3.33 | 3.33 | 3.33 | 3.33 |
| Serbia, Republic of..................... | 942 | .34 | .42 | .38 | .39 | .41 | .42 | .42 | .46 | .49 | .52 | .56 | .58 |
| Turkey........................................ | 186 | 3.73 | 3.73 | 3.73 | 3.73 | 3.73 | 3.73 | 3.73 | 6.28 | 11.56 | 16.71 | 17.01 | 16.57 |

# Gold (Million Fine Troy Ounces)

| 1ad | | 2004 | 2005 | 2006 | 2007 | 2008 | 2009 | 2010 | 2011 | 2012 | 2013 | 2014 | 2015 |
|---|---|---|---|---|---|---|---|---|---|---|---|---|---|
| | | | | | | *Millions of Ounces: End of Period* | | | | | | | |
| CIS | 901 | **15.11** | **15.66** | **16.51** | **17.96** | **20.46** | **24.90** | **29.68** | **33.37** | **37.31** | **41.62** | **48.51** | **56.35** |
| Armenia | 911 | — | — | — | — | — | — | — | — | — | — | — | — |
| Azerbaijan, Republic of | 912 | — | — | — | — | — | — | — | — | — | .64 | .97 | .97 |
| Belarus | 913 | .20 | .40 | .50 | .27 | .43 | .74 | 1.13 | 1.21 | 1.37 | 1.43 | 1.36 | 1.35 |
| Georgia | 915 | — | — | — | — | — | — | — | — | — | — | — | — |
| Kazakhstan | 916 | 1.83 | 1.92 | 2.16 | 2.24 | 2.31 | 2.27 | 2.16 | 2.64 | 3.71 | 4.62 | 6.17 | 7.13 |
| Kyrgyz Republic | 917 | .08 | .08 | .08 | .08 | .08 | .08 | .08 | .08 | .10 | .12 | .13 | .14 |
| Moldova | 921 | — | — | — | — | — | — | — | — | — | — | — | — |
| Russia | 922 | 12.44 | 12.44 | 12.91 | 14.48 | 16.71 | 20.87 | 25.36 | 28.39 | 30.79 | 33.28 | 38.84 | 45.48 |
| Tajikistan | 923 | .03 | .04 | .05 | .05 | .07 | .07 | .06 | .15 | .20 | .17 | .28 | .40 |
| Ukraine | 926 | .52 | .78 | .81 | .84 | .85 | .87 | .89 | .90 | 1.14 | 1.36 | .76 | .88 |
| Middle East,N.Africa & Pakistan | 440 | **39.15** | **39.12** | **39.12** | **39.56** | **45.99** | **45.99** | **45.96** | **45.08** | **45.89** | **46.35** | **48.00** | **48.95** |
| Afghanistan, Islamic Rep. of | 512 | .... | .... | .... | .... | .70 | .70 | .70 | .70 | .70 | .70 | .70 | .70 |
| Algeria | 612 | 5.58 | 5.58 | 5.58 | 5.58 | 5.58 | 5.58 | 5.58 | 5.58 | 5.58 | 5.58 | 5.58 | 5.58 |
| Bahrain, Kingdom of | 419 | .15 | .15 | .15 | .15 | .15 | .15 | .15 | .15 | .15 | .15 | .15 | .15 |
| Egypt | 469 | 2.43 | 2.43 | 2.43 | 2.43 | 2.43 | 2.43 | 2.43 | 2.43 | 2.43 | 2.43 | 2.43 | 2.43 |
| Iraq | 433 | .19 | .19 | .19 | .19 | .19 | .19 | .19 | .19 | .96 | 1.36 | 2.89 | 2.89 |
| Jordan | 439 | .41 | .41 | .41 | .46 | .41 | .41 | .41 | .41 | .45 | .50 | .62 | 1.33 |
| Kuwait | 443 | 2.54 | 2.54 | 2.54 | 2.54 | 2.54 | 2.54 | 2.54 | 2.54 | 2.54 | 2.54 | 2.54 | 2.54 |
| Lebanon | 446 | 9.22 | 9.22 | 9.22 | 9.22 | 9.22 | 9.22 | 9.22 | 9.22 | 9.22 | 9.22 | 9.22 | 9.22 |
| Libya | 672 | 4.62 | 4.62 | 4.62 | 4.62 | 4.62 | 4.62 | 4.62 | 3.75 | 3.75 | 3.75 | 3.75 | .... |
| Mauritania | 682 | .01 | .01 | .01 | .01 | .01 | .01 | .01 | .01 | .01 | .... | .... | .... |
| Morocco | 686 | .71 | .71 | .71 | .71 | .71 | .71 | .71 | .71 | .71 | .71 | .71 | .71 |
| Oman | 449 | — | — | — | — | — | — | — | — | — | — | — | — |
| Pakistan | 564 | 2.10 | 2.10 | 2.10 | 2.10 | 2.10 | 2.10 | 2.07 | 2.07 | 2.07 | 2.07 | 2.07 | 2.07 |
| Qatar | 453 | .04 | .02 | .02 | .40 | .40 | .40 | .40 | .40 | .40 | .40 | .40 | .40 |
| Saudi Arabia | 456 | 4.60 | 4.60 | 4.60 | 4.60 | 10.38 | 10.38 | 10.38 | 10.38 | 10.38 | 10.38 | 10.38 | 10.38 |
| Syrian Arab Republic | 463 | .83 | .83 | .83 | .83 | .83 | .83 | .83 | .... | .... | .... | .... | .... |
| Tunisia | 744 | .22 | .22 | .22 | .22 | .22 | .22 | .22 | .22 | .22 | .22 | .22 | .... |
| United Arab Emirates | 466 | — | — | — | — | — | — | — | — | — | — | — | .24 |
| Yemen, Republic of | 474 | .05 | .05 | .05 | .05 | .05 | .05 | .05 | .05 | .05 | .05 | .... | .... |
| Sub-Saharan Africa | 603 | **6.52** | **6.53** | **6.55** | **6.56** | **6.56** | **6.54** | **6.54** | **6.55** | **6.59** | **6.65** | **6.78** | **6.72** |
| CEMAC (incl. BEAC hqtrs.) | 758 | .23 | .23 | .23 | .23 | .23 | .... | .... | .... | .... | .... | .... | .... |
| Cameroon | 622 | .03 | .03 | .03 | .03 | .03 | .... | .... | .... | .... | .... | .... | .... |
| Central African Rep. | 626 | .01 | .01 | .01 | .01 | .01 | .... | .... | .... | .... | .... | .... | .... |
| Chad | 628 | .01 | .01 | .01 | .01 | .01 | .... | .... | .... | .... | .... | .... | .... |
| Congo, Rep. of | 634 | .01 | .01 | .01 | .01 | .01 | .... | .... | .... | .... | .... | .... | .... |
| Equatorial Guinea | 642 | .... | .... | .... | .... | .... | .... | .... | .... | .... | .... | .... | .... |
| Gabon | 646 | .01 | .01 | .01 | .01 | .01 | .... | .... | .... | .... | .... | .... | .... |
| WAEMU (Incl. BCEAO hqtrs.) | 759 | 1.17 | 1.17 | 1.17 | 1.17 | 1.17 | 1.17 | 1.17 | 1.17 | 1.17 | 1.17 | 1.17 | .... |
| Benin | 638 | — | — | — | — | — | — | — | — | — | — | — | — |
| Burkina Faso | 748 | — | — | — | — | — | — | — | — | — | — | — | — |
| Côte d'Ivoire | 662 | — | — | — | — | — | — | — | — | — | — | — | — |
| Guinea Bissau | 654 | — | — | — | — | — | — | — | — | — | — | — | — |
| Mali | 678 | — | — | — | — | — | — | — | — | — | — | — | — |
| Niger | 692 | — | — | — | — | — | — | — | — | — | — | — | — |
| Senegal | 722 | — | — | — | — | — | — | — | — | — | — | — | — |
| Togo | 742 | — | — | — | — | — | — | — | — | — | — | — | — |
| Burundi | 618 | — | — | — | — | — | — | — | — | — | — | — | — |
| Cabo Verde | 624 | — | — | — | — | — | — | — | — | — | — | — | — |
| Comoros | 632 | — | — | — | — | — | — | — | — | — | — | — | — |
| Congo, Dem. Rep. of | 636 | — | — | — | — | — | — | — | — | — | — | — | — |
| Eritrea | 643 | — | — | — | — | — | — | — | — | — | .... | .... | .... |
| Ethiopia | 644 | — | — | — | — | — | — | .... | .... | .... | .... | .... | .... |
| Ghana | 652 | .28 | .28 | .28 | .28 | .28 | .28 | .28 | .28 | .28 | .28 | .... | .... |
| Guinea | 656 | — | — | .02 | — | .01 | .01 | .01 | .01 | .01 | .01 | .01 | .08 |
| Kenya | 664 | — | — | — | — | — | — | — | — | — | — | — | — |
| Malawi | 676 | .01 | .01 | .01 | .01 | .01 | .01 | .01 | .01 | .01 | .01 | .01 | .... |
| Mauritius | 684 | .06 | .06 | .06 | .06 | .06 | .13 | .13 | .13 | .13 | .13 | .25 | .29 |
| Mozambique | 688 | .06 | .10 | .10 | .10 | .10 | .08 | .08 | .08 | .12 | .18 | .18 | .16 |
| Namibia | 728 | — | — | — | — | — | — | — | — | — | — | — | — |
| Nigeria | 694 | .69 | .69 | .69 | .69 | .69 | .69 | .69 | .69 | .69 | .69 | .69 | .69 |
| Rwanda | 714 | — | — | — | — | — | — | — | — | — | — | — | — |
| South Africa | 199 | 3.98 | 3.99 | 3.99 | 4.00 | 4.01 | 4.01 | 4.02 | 4.02 | 4.02 | 4.02 | 4.03 | 4.03 |
| South Sudan, Republic of | 733 | .... | .... | .... | .... | .... | .... | | | | | | |
| Zambia | 754 | — | — | — | — | — | — | — | — | — | — | — | — |
| Zimbabwe | 698 | .03 | .... | .... | .02 | .01 | .... | .... | | | | | .02 |
| Western Hemisphere | 205 | **18.98** | **18.76** | **18.64** | **18.66** | **18.76** | **18.98** | **19.75** | **23.50** | **25.42** | **25.45** | **24.76** | **21.48** |
| Argentina | 213 | 1.77 | 1.76 | 1.76 | 1.76 | 1.76 | 1.76 | 1.76 | 1.98 | 1.98 | 1.98 | 1.98 | 1.98 |
| Aruba | 314 | .10 | .10 | .10 | .10 | .10 | .10 | .10 | .10 | .10 | .10 | .10 | .10 |
| Bahamas, The | 313 | — | — | — | — | — | — | — | — | — | — | — | — |
| Barbados | 316 | — | — | — | — | — | — | — | — | — | — | — | — |
| Bolivia | 218 | .91 | .91 | .91 | .91 | .91 | .91 | 1.14 | 1.36 | 1.36 | 1.37 | 1.37 | 1.37 |
| Brazil | 223 | 1.08 | 1.08 | 1.08 | 1.08 | 1.08 | 1.08 | 1.08 | 1.08 | 2.16 | 2.16 | 2.16 | 2.16 |
| Chile | 228 | .01 | .01 | .01 | .01 | .01 | .01 | .01 | .01 | .01 | .01 | .01 | .01 |
| Colombia | 233 | .33 | .33 | .22 | .22 | .22 | .22 | .22 | .33 | .33 | .33 | .33 | .11 |
| Costa Rica | 238 | — | — | — | — | — | — | — | — | — | — | — | — |
| Curaçao & Sint Maarten | 355 | .... | .... | .... | .... | .... | .... | .42 | .42 | .42 | .42 | .42 | .42 |
| Dominican Republic | 243 | .02 | .02 | .02 | .02 | .02 | .02 | .02 | .02 | .02 | .02 | .02 | .02 |
| Ecuador | 248 | .85 | .85 | .84 | .84 | .84 | .85 | .85 | .85 | .85 | .85 | .38 | .38 |
| El Salvador | 253 | .42 | .25 | .23 | .23 | .23 | .23 | .23 | .23 | .23 | .23 | .22 | .04 |
| Guatemala | 258 | .22 | .22 | .22 | .22 | .22 | .22 | .22 | .22 | .22 | .22 | .22 | .22 |
| Haiti | 263 | — | — | — | — | — | — | — | — | — | — | .06 | .06 | .06 |

# Gold (Million Fine Troy Ounces)

|  |  | 2004 | 2005 | 2006 | 2007 | 2008 | 2009 | 2010 | 2011 | 2012 | 2013 | 2014 | 2015 |
|---|---|---|---|---|---|---|---|---|---|---|---|---|---|
| **1ad** |  | | | | | | *Millions of Ounces: End of Period* | | | | | | |
| **Western Hemisphere(Cont.)** | | | | | | | | | | | | | |
| Honduras | 268 | .02 | .02 | .02 | .02 | .02 | .02 | .02 | .02 | .02 | .02 | .02 | .02 |
| Jamaica | 343 | — | — | — | — | — | — | — | — | — | — | — | — |
| Mexico | 273 | .14 | .11 | .09 | .12 | .20 | .28 | .23 | 3.41 | 4.00 | 3.96 | 3.95 | 3.90 |
| Netherlands Antilles | 353 | .42 | .42 | .42 | .42 | .42 | .42 | .... | .... | .... | .... | .... | .... |
| Nicaragua | 278 | — | — | — | — | — | — | — | — | — | — | — | — |
| Paraguay | 288 | — | — | — | — | .02 | .02 | .02 | .02 | .26 | .26 | .26 | .26 |
| Peru | 293 | 1.11 | 1.11 | 1.11 | 1.11 | 1.11 | 1.11 | 1.11 | 1.11 | 1.11 | 1.11 | 1.11 | 1.11 |
| Suriname | 366 | .02 | .03 | .03 | .04 | .05 | .06 | .06 | .07 | .07 | .03 | .04 | .04 |
| Trinidad and Tobago | 369 | .06 | .06 | .06 | .06 | .06 | .06 | .06 | .06 | .06 | .06 | .06 | .06 |
| Uruguay | 298 | .01 | .01 | .01 | .01 | .01 | .01 | .01 | .01 | .01 | .01 | .01 | — |
| Venezuela, Rep. Bol. | 299 | 11.49 | 11.47 | 11.48 | 11.47 | 11.46 | 11.60 | 11.76 | 11.76 | 11.76 | 11.82 | 11.61 | 8.77 |
| **Memorandum Items** | | | | | | | | | | | | | |
| **Gold Holdings at SDR 35 per Ounce** | | | | | | | | | | | | | |
| **(1a.s)** | | | | | | | *Millions of SDRs: End of Period* | | | | | | |
| World | 001 | 35,374 | 34,696 | 34,285 | 33,717 | 33,737 | 34,328 | 34,704 | 35,116 | 35,650 | 35,845 | 36,044 | 36,836 |
| All Countries | 010 | 31,520 | 30,866 | 30,471 | 29,942 | 29,977 | 30,772 | 30,974 | 31,403 | 31,898 | 32,287 | 32,577 | 33,550 |
| of which: ECB | 168 | 863 | 810 | 720 | 633 | 600 | 564 | 564 | 565 | 565 | 565 | 566 | 568 |
| IMF | 992 | 3,620 | 3,620 | 3,620 | 3,620 | 3,620 | 3,382 | 3,167 | 3,167 | 3,167 | 3,167 | 3,167 | 3,167 |
| BIS | 993 | 234 | 209 | 193 | 155 | 140 | 174 | 563 | 546 | 585 | 391 | 300 | 119 |
| **Gold Holdings at Market Prices** | | | | | | | | | | | | | |
| **(1ams)** | | | | | | | *Millions of SDRs: End of Period* | | | | | | |
| World | 001 | 285,050 | 355,803 | 413,926 | 508,268 | 544,302 | 680,368 | 904,921 | 1,000,515 | 1,102,803 | 801,021 | 857,228 | 805,056 |
| All Countries | 010 | 253,989 | 316,532 | 367,881 | 451,358 | 483,628 | 609,897 | 807,658 | 894,729 | 986,737 | 721,518 | 774,778 | 733,252 |
| of which: ECB | 168 | 6,954 | 8,307 | 8,693 | 9,545 | 9,688 | 11,184 | 14,714 | 16,098 | 17,477 | 12,625 | 13,467 | 12,414 |
| IMF | 992 | 29,173 | 37,127 | 43,710 | 54,576 | 58,410 | 67,028 | 82,571 | 90,223 | 97,955 | 70,764 | 75,311 | 69,207 |
| BIS | 993 | 1,888 | 2,144 | 2,336 | 2,334 | 2,264 | 3,443 | 14,692 | 15,564 | 18,111 | 8,740 | 7,139 | 2,597 |
| **Gold Prices and SDR Rates:** | | | | | | | *End of Period* | | | | | | |
| US Dollars per Oz.(London)(c..) | 112 | 438.00 | 513.00 | 635.70 | 833.75 | 869.75 | 1,087.50 | 1,405.50 | 1,531.00 | 1,664.00 | 1,204.50 | 1,206.00 | 1,060.00 |
| US Dollars per SDR (sa.) | 111 | 1.5530 | 1.4293 | 1.5044 | 1.5803 | 1.5403 | 1.5677 | 1.5400 | 1.5353 | 1.5369 | 1.5400 | 1.4488 | 1.3857 |
| SDRs per Ounce (g..) | 112 | 282.03 | 358.92 | 422.56 | 527.61 | 564.67 | 693.70 | 912.64 | 997.22 | 1,082.68 | 782.14 | 832.41 | 764.94 |

# Total Reserves

1 s (w/ Gold at SDR 35 per Oz)

*Millions of SDRs: End of Period*

| | | 2004 | 2005 | 2006 | 2007 | 2008 | 2009 | 2010 | 2011 | 2012 | 2013 | 2014 | 2015 |
|---|---|---|---|---|---|---|---|---|---|---|---|---|---|
| World | 001 | 2,525,110 | 3,106,006 | 3,562,230 | 4,308,982 | 4,847,355 | 5,481,965 | 6,298,998 | 6,974,385 | 7,456,469 | 7,910,380 | 8,308,431 | 8,172,147 |
| Advanced Economies | 110 | 1,424,187 | 1,519,038 | 1,556,281 | 1,596,306 | 1,682,126 | 1,962,775 | 2,205,730 | 2,448,293 | 2,639,875 | 2,707,655 | 2,873,240 | 3,054,597 |
| Euro Area (Incl. ECB) | 163 | 150,140 | 142,391 | 143,735 | 148,621 | 154,221 | 192,559 | 207,103 | 218,426 | 228,502 | 227,040 | 238,250 | 253,077 |
| Austria | 122 | 5,406 | 5,125 | 4,985 | 7,079 | 6,101 | 5,491 | 6,542 | 7,471 | 8,274 | 8,415 | 10,078 | 9,478 |
| Belgium | 124 | 6,962 | 6,022 | 6,095 | 6,827 | 6,306 | 10,403 | 10,970 | 11,927 | 12,358 | 12,034 | 11,732 | 12,056 |
| Cyprus | 423 | 2,534 | 2,949 | 3,770 | 3,888 | † 416 | 524 | 350 | 344 | 308 | 262 | 261 | 257 |
| Estonia | 939 | 1,152 | 1,360 | 1,849 | 2,065 | 2,574 | 2,534 | 1,660 | † 127 | 187 | 198 | 295 | 293 |
| Finland | 172 | 7,925 | 7,416 | 4,372 | 4,525 | 4,587 | 6,249 | 4,813 | 5,173 | 5,555 | 6,139 | 6,111 | 6,075 |
| France | 132 | 26,098 | 22,597 | 31,412 | 31,855 | 24,630 | 32,487 | 38,974 | 34,404 | 38,026 | 35,759 | 36,939 | 42,570 |
| Germany | 134 | 35,301 | 35,440 | 31,561 | 31,896 | 31,846 | 42,059 | 44,277 | 47,416 | 47,685 | 47,555 | 46,786 | 46,025 |
| Greece | 174 | 888 | 476 | 502 | 526 | 350 | 1,118 | 976 | 939 | 952 | 1,048 | 1,422 | 1,707 |
| Ireland | 178 | 1,829 | 551 | 485 | 499 | 572 | 1,245 | 1,203 | 918 | 909 | 918 | 1,054 | 1,449 |
| Italy | 136 | 20,698 | 20,611 | 19,817 | 20,721 | 26,838 | 31,955 | 33,722 | 34,796 | 35,616 | 35,730 | 35,675 | 36,700 |
| Latvia | 941 | 1,240 | 1,570 | 2,902 | 3,523 | 3,273 | 4,239 | 4,720 | 3,915 | 4,635 | 4,941 | † 2,058 | 2,331 |
| Lithuania | 946 | 2,268 | 2,609 | 3,765 | 4,788 | 4,084 | 4,102 | 4,120 | 5,162 | 5,354 | 5,102 | 5,876 | † 1,088 |
| Luxembourg | 137 | 195 | 171 | 148 | 93 | 220 | 469 | 488 | 589 | 569 | 572 | 539 | 504 |
| Malta | 181 | 1,759 | 1,803 | 1,979 | 2,396 | † 239 | 340 | 348 | 326 | 448 | 380 | 425 | 410 |
| Netherlands | 138 | 7,736 | 7,069 | 7,902 | 7,198 | 8,140 | 12,088 | 12,683 | 13,888 | 15,036 | 15,359 | 14,015 | 13,203 |
| Portugal | 182 | 3,852 | 2,904 | 1,802 | 1,226 | 1,281 | 1,996 | 2,802 | 1,717 | 1,859 | 2,234 | 3,791 | 5,025 |
| Slovak Republic | 936 | 9,323 | 10,465 | 8,446 | 11,450 | 11,631 | † 477 | 503 | 592 | 568 | 634 | 996 | 1,343 |
| Slovenia | 961 | 5,671 | 5,656 | 4,683 | † 624 | 567 | 620 | 605 | 545 | 513 | 523 | 620 | 543 |
| Spain | 184 | 8,566 | 7,286 | 7,663 | 7,582 | 8,376 | 11,930 | 12,749 | 21,709 | 23,430 | 23,323 | 27,576 | 32,342 |
| Australia | 193 | 23,143 | 29,434 | 35,618 | 15,764 | 20,015 | 24,935 | 25,193 | 27,957 | 29,282 | 32,392 | 35,163 | 33,675 |
| Canada | 156 | 22,173 | 23,066 | 23,265 | 25,944 | 28,426 | 34,601 | 37,015 | 42,766 | 44,486 | 46,641 | 51,483 | 57,513 |
| China, P.R.: Hong Kong | 532 | 79,551 | 86,931 | 88,521 | 96,593 | 118,468 | 163,152 | 174,446 | 185,830 | † 206,422 | 202,034 | 226,696 | 258,856 |
| Czech Republic | 935 | 18,212 | 20,536 | 20,742 | 21,878 | 23,812 | 26,268 | 27,227 | 25,853 | 28,814 | 36,244 | 37,342 | 46,303 |
| Denmark | 128 | 25,241 | † 23,115 | 19,833 | 20,663 | 26,347 | 47,464 | 47,803 | 53,277 | 56,120 | 55,984 | 50,331 | 45,478 |
| Iceland | 176 | 676 | 727 | 1,532 | 1,634 | 2,284 | 2,435 | 3,703 | 5,506 | 2,660 | 2,704 | 2,832 | 3,591 |
| Israel | 436 | 17,446 | 19,632 | 19,379 | 18,047 | 27,601 | 38,663 | 46,043 | 48,769 | 49,389 | 53,107 | 59,429 | 65,363 |
| Japan | 158 | 537,813 | 584,568 | 585,600 | 603,794 | 656,178 | 652,926 | 690,127 | 820,373 | 799,307 | 804,249 | 850,531 | 871,896 |
| Korea | 542 | 128,152 | 147,166 | 158,804 | 165,908 | 130,607 | 172,201 | 189,292 | 198,238 | 210,390 | 221,968 | 247,759 | 262,181 |
| New Zealand | 196 | 4,473 | 6,222 | 9,352 | 10,914 | 7,175 | 9,947 | 10,859 | 11,081 | 11,440 | 10,596 | 10,948 | 10,608 |
| Norway | 142 | 28,530 | 32,874 | 37,784 | 38,500 | 33,078 | 31,166 | 34,284 | 32,175 | 33,740 | 37,846 | 44,727 | 41,463 |
| San Marino | 135 | 229 | 243 | 318 | 410 | 459 | 504 | 292 | 223 | 250 | 350 | 271 | . . . . |
| Singapore | 576 | 72,354 | 81,132 | 90,434 | 102,987 | 112,955 | 119,661 | 146,428 | 154,714 | 168,580 | 177,184 | 177,141 | 178,631 |
| Sweden | 144 | 14,476 | 15,645 | 16,649 | 17,281 | 16,967 | 27,481 | 27,781 | 28,817 | 29,759 | 39,424 | 39,970 | 38,976 |
| Switzerland | 146 | 37,259 | 26,847 | 26,773 | 29,432 | 30,426 | 63,810 | 146,285 | 183,152 | 310,659 | 323,221 | 350,052 | 401,310 |
| Taiwan Province of China | 528 | 156,134 | 177,693 | 177,389 | 171,532 | 189,864 | 222,586 | 248,527 | 251,602 | 262,799 | 271,133 | 289,666 | 307,918 |
| United Kingdom | 112 | 26,071 | 27,264 | 27,402 | 31,330 | 29,142 | 35,881 | 44,728 | 51,983 | 57,994 | 60,352 | 66,402 | 86,243 |
| United States | 111 | 58,022 | 46,994 | 45,615 | 46,820 | 52,396 | 85,519 | 87,977 | 98,331 | 99,680 | 95,863 | 91,322 | 86,036 |
| Emerging & Dev. Economies | 200 | 1,097,068 | 1,583,138 | 2,002,135 | 2,708,901 | 3,161,468 | 3,515,634 | 4,089,538 | 4,522,379 | 4,812,842 | 5,199,167 | 5,431,724 | 5,114,265 |
| Emerging & Developing Asia | 505 | 599,004 | 806,647 | 988,998 | 1,347,604 | 1,651,615 | 1,969,148 | 2,364,742 | 2,631,659 | 2,726,924 | 3,040,815 | 3,260,403 | 3,045,727 |
| Bangladesh | 513 | 2,047 | 1,940 | 2,534 | 3,284 | 3,698 | 6,522 | 6,875 | 5,558 | 7,843 | 11,421 | 15,052 | 19,517 |
| Bhutan | 514 | 257 | 327 | 362 | 442 | 497 | 568 | 651 | 514 | 621 | 644 | 859 | 796 |
| Brunei Darussalam | 516 | 315 | 344 | 341 | 422 | 488 | 866 | 1,015 | 1,622 | 2,141 | 2,212 | 2,401 | 2,323 |
| Cambodia | 522 | 621 | 681 | 783 | 1,157 | 1,502 | 1,833 | 2,128 | 2,261 | 2,791 | 2,947 | 3,897 | 4,981 |
| China, P.R.: Mainland | 924 | 396,358 | 575,454 | 710,920 | 969,055 | 1,266,206 | 1,542,335 | 1,862,240 | 2,087,326 | 2,168,586 | 2,494,399 | 2,664,867 | 2,416,013 |
| China, P.R.: Macao | 546 | 3,500 | 4,680 | 6,070 | 8,372 | 10,342 | 11,705 | 15,407 | 22,163 | 10,801 | 10,484 | 11,350 | 13,632 |
| Fiji | 819 | 311 | 225 | 208 | 334 | 209 | 363 | 467 | 542 | 599 | 611 | 632 | 662 |
| India | 534 | 81,917 | 92,704 | 113,895 | 169,356 | 161,036 | 169,782 | 179,375 | 177,330 | 176,685 | 180,169 | 210,079 | 241,880 |
| Indonesia | 536 | 22,615 | 23,296 | 27,404 | 34,872 | 32,282 | 40,628 | 60,411 | 69,476 | 70,899 | 62,662 | 75,208 | 74,610 |
| Lao People's Dem. Rep. | 544 | 144 | 164 | 218 | 337 | 408 | 388 | 457 | 483 | 520 | 469 | 604 | 753 |
| Malaysia | 548 | 42,462 | 48,918 | 54,636 | 63,967 | 59,218 | 60,915 | 68,146 | 85,876 | 89,690 | 86,693 | 79,120 | 67,862 |
| Maldives | 556 | 133 | 132 | 156 | 197 | 158 | 176 | 237 | 227 | 207 | 248 | 433 | 415 |
| Micronesia, Fed. States of | 868 | 35 | 35 | 31 | 31 | 26 | 36 | 36 | 49 | 50 | 55 | 79 | 98 |
| Mongolia | 948 | 126 | 233 | 395 | 516 | 368 | 827 | 1,429 | 1,486 | 2,561 | 1,365 | 1,066 | 902 |
| Myanmar | 518 | 441 | 547 | 829 | 1,963 | 2,422 | 3,358 | 3,720 | 4,570 | 4,539 | . . . . | . . . . | . . . . |
| Nepal | 558 | 947 | 1,053 | 1,287 | 1,275 | 1,596 | 1,768 | 1,909 | 2,367 | 2,804 | 3,441 | 4,166 | 5,734 |
| Papua New Guinea | 853 | 410 | 505 | 933 | 1,302 | 1,270 | 1,636 | 1,971 | 2,775 | 2,559 | 1,804 | 1,558 | 1,223 |
| Philippines | 566 | 8,695 | 11,317 | 13,473 | 19,266 | 21,723 | 24,913 | 36,123 | 44,008 | 48,026 | 49,366 | 49,955 | 53,596 |
| Samoa | 862 | 55 | 57 | 54 | 60 | 57 | 106 | 136 | 109 | 110 | 111 | 97 | 101 |
| Solomon Islands | 813 | 51 | 66 | 69 | 76 | 58 | 93 | 173 | 269 | 305 | 319 | 322 | 357 |
| Sri Lanka | 524 | 1,379 | 1,860 | 1,818 | 2,144 | 1,609 | 2,968 | 4,369 | 4,081 | 4,165 | 4,319 | 5,075 | 4,747 |
| Thailand | 578 | 31,430 | 35,561 | 43,495 | 54,024 | 70,641 | 86,516 | 108,896 | 109,201 | 112,947 | 104,930 | 104,570 | 109,331 |
| Timor-Leste | 537 | 117 | 107 | 56 | 146 | 137 | 159 | 264 | 301 | 575 | 446 | 215 | 316 |
| Tonga | 866 | 36 | 33 | 32 | 41 | 45 | 61 | 68 | 93 | 99 | 101 | 110 | 113 |
| Vanuatu | 846 | 40 | 47 | 70 | 76 | 75 | 95 | 105 | 113 | 119 | 116 | 127 | 194 |
| Europe | 170 | 175,219 | 255,298 | 360,632 | 494,953 | 472,968 | 491,902 | 540,408 | 556,478 | 590,535 | 589,570 | 510,349 | 493,689 |
| Emerging & Dev. Europe | 903 | 82,812 | 110,787 | 132,422 | 160,175 | 163,610 | 184,603 | 201,875 | 207,144 | 226,272 | 239,221 | 236,566 | 225,082 |
| Albania | 914 | 877 | 985 | 1,178 | 1,334 | 1,508 | 1,478 | 1,605 | 1,561 | 1,639 | 1,763 | 1,799 | 2,228 |
| Bosnia and Herzegovina | 963 | 1,563 | 1,782 | 2,440 | 3,190 | 2,908 | 2,890 | 2,836 | 2,705 | 2,789 | 3,165 | 3,278 | 3,387 |
| Bulgaria | 918 | 5,696 | 5,670 | 7,319 | 10,472 | 10,962 | 10,970 | 10,058 | 9,979 | 11,998 | 11,951 | 12,867 | 15,043 |
| Croatia | 960 | 5,639 | 6,157 | 7,636 | 8,653 | 8,412 | 9,501 | 9,177 | 9,434 | 9,634 | 11,537 | 10,646 | 10,801 |
| Hungary | 944 | 10,256 | 12,984 | 14,313 | 15,172 | 21,940 | 28,117 | 29,126 | 31,712 | 28,961 | 30,126 | 28,924 | 23,832 |
| Kosovo | 967 | . . . . | . . . . | . . . . | 602 | 579 | 530 | 550 | 483 | 721 | 716 | 626 | 677 |
| Macedonia, FYR | 962 | 590 | 867 | 1,171 | 1,325 | 1,254 | 1,316 | 1,287 | 1,526 | 1,653 | 1,621 | 1,872 | 1,623 |
| Montenegro | 943 | 53 | 143 | 289 | 436 | 283 | 365 | 361 | 256 | 298 | 379 | 457 | 529 |
| Poland | 964 | 22,861 | 28,706 | 30,939 | 39,962 | 38,619 | 48,546 | 57,791 | 60,461 | 67,391 | 66,503 | 66,696 | 66,070 |
| Romania | 968 | 9,530 | 14,022 | 18,774 | 23,654 | 24,053 | 26,115 | 28,273 | 28,085 | 26,899 | 29,215 | 27,149 | 25,494 |
| Serbia, Republic of | 942 | 2,649 | 3,952 | 7,756 | 8,805 | 7,236 | 9,436 | 8,271 | 9,706 | 8,856 | 9,631 | 7,869 | 7,762 |
| Turkey | 186 | 23,098 | 35,519 | 40,607 | 46,569 | 45,855 | 45,340 | 52,541 | 51,235 | 65,433 | 72,615 | 74,385 | 67,636 |

# Total Reserves

| 1 s (w/ Gold at SDR 35 per Oz) | | 2004 | 2005 | 2006 | 2007 | 2008 | 2009 | 2010 | 2011 | 2012 | 2013 | 2014 | 2015 |
|---|---|---|---|---|---|---|---|---|---|---|---|---|---|
| | | | | | | | *Millions of SDRs: End of Period* | | | | | | |
| CIS | 901 | 92,407 | 144,511 | 228,210 | 334,778 | 309,358 | 307,299 | 338,533 | 349,334 | 364,262 | 350,349 | 273,783 | 268,607 |
| Armenia | 911 | 353 | 468 | 713 | 1,050 | 913 | 1,278 | 1,212 | 1,259 | 1,171 | 1,462 | 1,028 | 1,281 |
| Azerbaijan, Republic of | 912 | 692 | 824 | 1,662 | 2,704 | 4,199 | 3,421 | 4,162 | 6,692 | 7,338 | 9,374 | 10,143 | 4,574 |
| Belarus | 913 | 490 | 809 | 728 | 2,510 | 1,760 | 3,108 | 2,268 | 3,958 | 3,828 | 3,256 | 2,410 | 2,027 |
| Georgia | 915 | 249 | 335 | 619 | 861 | 961 | 1,346 | 1,470 | 1,836 | 1,869 | 1,833 | 1,863 | 1,819 |
| Kazakhstan | 916 | 5,520 | 4,324 | 11,875 | 10,062 | 11,684 | 13,296 | 16,454 | 16,493 | 14,530 | 12,582 | 15,272 | 15,041 |
| Kyrgyz Republic | 917 | 343 | 402 | 511 | 704 | 751 | 956 | 1,044 | 1,112 | 1,242 | 1,367 | 1,250 | 1,184 |
| Moldova | 921 | 303 | 418 | 515 | 844 | 1,086 | 944 | 1,115 | 1,280 | 1,634 | 1,830 | 1,487 | 1,266 |
| Russia | 922 | 78,226 | 123,499 | 196,921 | 295,872 | 267,908 | 266,503 | 288,925 | 296,673 | 317,670 | 306,102 | 235,600 | 232,398 |
| Tajikistan | 923 | 103 | 119 | 118 | 27 | 70 | 114 | 212 | 194 | 201 | 305 | 132 | 61 |
| Ukraine | 926 | 6,129 | 13,312 | 14,549 | 20,144 | 20,027 | 16,333 | 21,672 | 19,839 | 14,781 | 12,239 | 4,597 | 8,956 |
| **Middle East,N.Africa & Pakistan** | 440 | 140,005 | 284,335 | 368,894 | 491,109 | 610,365 | 600,827 | 667,500 | 734,534 | 843,729 | 914,209 | 956,973 | 883,001 |
| Afghanistan, Islamic Rep. of | 512 | .... | .... | .... | .... | 1,603 | 2,258 | 2,735 | 3,456 | 3,917 | 4,208 | 4,636 | 4,522 |
| Algeria | 612 | 28,042 | 39,588 | 51,986 | 70,006 | 93,194 | 95,266 | 105,787 | 119,277 | 124,663 | 126,632 | 124,171 | 104,601 |
| Bahrain, Kingdom of | 419 | 1,255 | 1,387 | 1,867 | 2,674 | 2,551 | 2,458 | 3,309 | 2,965 | 3,392 | 3,477 | 4,180 | .... |
| Djibouti | 611 | 60 | 62 | 80 | 84 | 114 | 154 | 162 | 159 | 162 | 276 | 271 | 263 |
| Egypt | 469 | 9,276 | 14,504 | 16,345 | 19,188 | 21,001 | 20,659 | 21,910 | 9,800 | 7,651 | 8,922 | 8,364 | 9,670 |
| Iraq | 433 | 5,045 | 8,475 | 13,256 | 19,812 | 32,428 | 28,155 | 32,705 | 39,573 | 44,755 | 49,471 | 43,506 | 36,898 |
| Jordan | 439 | 3,406 | 3,688 | 4,483 | 4,789 | 5,573 | 7,471 | 8,493 | 7,484 | 5,279 | 8,604 | 10,582 | 10,988 |
| Kuwait | 443 | 5,396 | 6,290 | 8,442 | 10,631 | 11,199 | 13,017 | 13,879 | 16,891 | 18,883 | 19,149 | 22,255 | 20,490 |
| Lebanon | 446 | 7,879 | 8,640 | 9,214 | 8,492 | 13,466 | 18,887 | 20,786 | 22,300 | 24,518 | 24,185 | 27,619 | 28,291 |
| Libya | 672 | 16,703 | 27,804 | 39,572 | 50,410 | 60,095 | 63,137 | 64,865 | 68,391 | 77,173 | 74,935 | 61,625 | .... |
| Mauritania | 682 | 22 | 46 | 125 | 126 | 123 | 144 | 177 | 316 | 618 | .... | .... | .... |
| Morocco | 686 | 10,544 | 11,350 | 13,546 | 15,290 | 14,375 | 14,567 | 14,933 | 12,617 | 10,572 | 11,841 | 13,603 | 16,084 |
| Oman | 449 | 2,316 | 3,049 | 3,333 | 6,027 | 7,519 | 7,784 | 8,457 | 9,357 | 9,369 | 10,357 | 11,267 | 12,660 |
| Pakistan | 564 | 6,383 | 7,093 | 7,746 | 8,961 | 4,744 | 7,293 | 9,388 | 9,535 | 6,736 | 3,421 | 8,222 | 12,939 |
| Qatar | 453 | 2,188 | 3,179 | 3,579 | 5,973 | 6,279 | 11,732 | 19,897 | 10,565 | 21,174 | 27,028 | 29,510 | 26,354 |
| Saudi Arabia | 456 | 17,734 | † 108,628 | 150,410 | 193,456 | 287,488 | 261,699 | 289,138 | 352,534 | 427,493 | 471,332 | 505,551 | 444,884 |
| Sudan | 732 | 862 | 1,307 | 1,103 | 872 | 908 | 698 | 673 | 125 | 125 | 125 | 125 | 125 |
| Tunisia | 744 | 2,542 | 3,112 | 4,510 | 4,976 | 5,753 | 7,061 | 6,150 | 4,862 | 5,445 | 4,740 | 5,001 | .... |
| United Arab Emirates | 466 | 11,932 | 14,700 | 18,358 | 48,878 | 20,577 | 16,651 | 21,289 | 24,275 | 30,604 | 44,287 | 54,130 | 67,607 |
| West Bank and Gaza | 487 | .... | .... | 209 | 225 | 331 | 318 | 345 | 324 | 432 | 445 | 464 | 419 |
| Yemen, Republic of | 474 | 3,649 | 4,280 | 4,995 | 4,884 | 5,268 | 4,426 | 3,812 | 2,900 | 3,950 | 3,433 | .... | .... |
| **Sub-Saharan Africa** | 603 | 40,229 | 57,497 | 76,518 | 92,461 | 102,206 | 102,747 | 104,558 | 117,074 | 131,527 | 132,591 | 128,974 | 119,562 |
| CEMAC (incl. BEAC hqtrs.) | 758 | 2,011 | 3,607 | 5,916 | 7,562 | 10,176 | 9,156 | 8,869 | 10,237 | 11,406 | 11,832 | 10,567 | 7,317 |
| Cameroon | 622 | 535 | 665 | 1,142 | 1,840 | 2,005 | 2,345 | 2,365 | 2,083 | 2,200 | 2,255 | 2,187 | 2,552 |
| Central African Rep. | 626 | 96 | 98 | 84 | 53 | 79 | 134 | 118 | 101 | 103 | 126 | 179 | 154 |
| Chad | 628 | 143 | 158 | 416 | 605 | 874 | .... | .... | .... | .... | .... | .... | .... |
| Congo, Rep. of | 634 | 77 | 512 | 1,224 | 1,376 | 2,514 | 2,428 | 2,888 | 3,674 | 3,611 | 3,406 | 3,400 | 1,603 |
| Equatorial Guinea | 642 | 608 | 1,471 | 2,039 | 2,434 | 2,877 | 2,074 | 1,524 | 1,989 | 2,861 | 2,965 | 2,006 | 870 |
| Gabon | 646 | 286 | 468 | 741 | 777 | 1,249 | 1,271 | 1,127 | 1,405 | 1,530 | 1,950 | 1,711 | 1,345 |
| WAEMU (Incl. BCEAO hqtrs.) | 759 | 4,707 | 4,375 | 4,941 | 6,138 | 6,095 | 7,743 | 7,719 | 7,930 | 7,927 | 7,963 | 7,982 | .... |
| Benin | 638 | 409 | 458 | 606 | 765 | 820 | 784 | 779 | 578 | 464 | 451 | 501 | 528 |
| Burkina Faso | 748 | 425 | 307 | 369 | 651 | 602 | 827 | 694 | 623 | 667 | 408 | 205 | 187 |
| Côte d'Ivoire | 662 | 1,082 | 956 | 1,195 | 1,594 | 1,463 | 2,084 | 2,353 | 2,811 | 2,556 | 2,755 | 3,091 | 3,403 |
| Guinea Bissau | 654 | 46 | 56 | 55 | 71 | 81 | 108 | 102 | 143 | 107 | 121 | 198 | 240 |
| Mali | 678 | 548 | 598 | 644 | 688 | 696 | 1,023 | 873 | 898 | 873 | 848 | 594 | 450 |
| Niger | 692 | 161 | 175 | 247 | 375 | 458 | 418 | 494 | 438 | 660 | 758 | 885 | 750 |
| Senegal | 722 | 881 | 830 | 887 | 1,050 | 1,040 | 1,354 | 1,330 | 1,267 | 1,354 | 1,463 | 1,407 | 1,452 |
| Togo | 742 | 230 | 134 | 249 | 277 | 378 | 449 | 464 | 504 | 287 | 329 | 350 | 414 |
| Angola | 614 | 885 | 2,237 | 5,716 | 7,085 | 11,601 | 8,716 | 12,824 | 18,750 | 21,741 | 21,286 | 19,416 | 17,373 |
| Botswana | 616 | 3,645 | 4,414 | 5,313 | 6,195 | 5,920 | 5,552 | 5,120 | 5,264 | 4,963 | 5,017 | 5,745 | 5,446 |
| Burundi | 618 | 42 | 70 | 87 | 112 | 173 | 205 | 215 | 192 | 200 | 213 | 218 | 98 |
| Cabo Verde | 624 | 90 | 122 | 169 | 231 | 235 | 254 | 248 | 221 | 245 | 309 | 353 | 357 |
| Comoros | 632 | 67 | 60 | 62 | 74 | 73 | 96 | 94 | 101 | 126 | 113 | 118 | 144 |
| Congo, Dem. Rep. of | 636 | 152 | 92 | 103 | 114 | 50 | 660 | 844 | 826 | 1,062 | 1,090 | 1,075 | 877 |
| Eritrea | 643 | 22 | 20 | 17 | 22 | 38 | 57 | 74 | 75 | .... | .... | .... | .... |
| Ethiopia | 644 | 964 | 729 | 577 | 816 | 565 | 1,136 | .... | .... | .... | .... | .... | .... |
| Gambia, The | 648 | 54 | 69 | 80 | 90 | 76 | 143 | 131 | 145 | 154 | 137 | 110 | .... |
| Ghana | 652 | 1,057 | 1,236 | 1,399 | 1,265 | 1,159 | 2,170 | 3,103 | 3,581 | 3,502 | 3,418 | .... | .... |
| Guinea | 656 | 71 | 67 | .... | .... | .... | .... | .... | 67 | 101 | 113 | 203 | 183 |
| Kenya | 664 | 978 | 1,259 | 1,606 | 2,123 | 1,869 | 2,455 | 2,805 | 2,778 | 3,716 | 4,285 | 5,460 | 5,447 |
| Lesotho | 666 | 323 | 363 | 438 | 635 | 631 | 753 | 695 | 599 | 669 | 685 | 739 | 652 |
| Liberia | 668 | 12 | 18 | 48 | 76 | 104 | 238 | 303 | 334 | 324 | 320 | 344 | .... |
| Madagascar | 674 | 324 | 337 | 388 | 536 | 638 | 626 | 664 | 739 | 685 | 504 | 534 | 600 |
| Malawi | 676 | 83 | 111 | 89 | 138 | 158 | 96 | 200 | 129 | 146 | 269 | 416 | .... |
| Mauritius | 684 | 1,036 | 940 | 846 | 1,129 | 1,134 | 1,394 | 1,590 | 1,687 | 1,850 | 2,173 | 2,504 | 2,866 |
| Mozambique | 688 | 731 | 741 | 772 | 918 | 1,028 | 1,342 | 1,405 | 1,611 | 1,806 | 2,047 | 2,084 | 1,746 |
| Namibia | 728 | 222 | 218 | 299 | 567 | 839 | 1,308 | 1,101 | 1,164 | 1,136 | 981 | 813 | 1,218 |
| Nigeria | 694 | 10,942 | 19,810 | 28,141 | 32,509 | 34,435 | 28,577 | 22,699 | 22,959 | 30,218 | 29,522 | 25,334 | 22,111 |
| Rwanda | 714 | 203 | 284 | 292 | 350 | 387 | 474 | 528 | 684 | 552 | 695 | 736 | 743 |
| São Tomé & Principe | 716 | 13 | 19 | 23 | 25 | 40 | 43 | 31 | 34 | 34 | 41 | 44 | 52 |
| Seychelles | 718 | 22 | 39 | 75 | 26 | 41 | 122 | 166 | 182 | 200 | 277 | 321 | 387 |
| South Africa | 199 | 8,601 | 13,139 | 15,466 | 18,864 | 19,996 | 22,618 | 24,929 | 27,885 | 28,767 | 29,273 | 30,695 | 30,175 |
| South Sudan, Republic of | 733 | .... | .... | .... | .... | .... | .... | .... | — | 834 | 615 | 288 | 166 |
| Swaziland | 734 | 208 | 171 | 248 | 490 | 488 | 612 | 491 | 391 | 482 | 495 | 477 | 395 |
| Tanzania | 738 | 1,478 | 1,433 | 1,502 | 1,827 | 1,859 | 2,214 | 2,535 | 2,427 | 2,637 | 3,035 | 3,030 | 2,939 |
| Uganda | 746 | 842 | 940 | 1,204 | 1,620 | 1,494 | 1,910 | 1,757 | 1,705 | 2,061 | 2,167 | 2,289 | 2,099 |
| Zambia | 754 | 217 | 392 | 478 | 690 | 711 | 1,207 | 1,360 | 1,514 | 1,979 | 1,743 | 2,125 | 2,142 |
| Zimbabwe | 698 | 145 | 68 | 103 | 92 | 49 | 524 | 475 | 429 | 374 | 308 | 251 | 234 |

# Total Reserves

| 1 s (w/ Gold at SDR 35 per Oz) | | 2004 | 2005 | 2006 | 2007 | 2008 | 2009 | 2010 | 2011 | 2012 | 2013 | 2014 | 2015 |
|---|---|---|---|---|---|---|---|---|---|---|---|---|---|
| | | *Millions of SDRs: End of Period* | | | | | | | | | | | |
| Western Hemisphere................. | 205 | 142,611 | 179,361 | 207,093 | 282,774 | 324,314 | 351,010 | 412,330 | 482,633 | 520,127 | 521,982 | 575,026 | 572,286 |
| ECCU (incl. ECCB hqtrs.)................ | 309 | 408 | 420 | 463 | 484 | 494 | 572 | 643 | 696 | 767 | 792 | 1,004 | 1,152 |
| Anguilla........................................ | 312 | 22 | 28 | 28 | 28 | 27 | 24 | 26 | 24 | 26 | 27 | 33 | 35 |
| Antigua and Barbuda.................. | 311 | 77 | 89 | 95 | 91 | 90 | 82 | 89 | 96 | 105 | 132 | 205 | 257 |
| Dominica...................................... | 321 | 27 | 34 | 42 | 38 | 36 | 48 | 49 | 53 | 62 | 57 | 70 | 91 |
| Grenada........................................ | 328 | 78 | 66 | 66 | 70 | 68 | 82 | 77 | 79 | 78 | 98 | 117 | 143 |
| Montserrat................................... | 351 | 9 | 10 | 10 | 9 | 8 | 9 | 11 | 16 | 21 | 26 | 31 | 37 |
| St. Kitts and Nevis...................... | 361 | 51 | 50 | 59 | 61 | 72 | 87 | 110 | 159 | 171 | 196 | 226 | 208 |
| St. Lucia....................................... | 362 | 85 | 81 | 89 | 97 | 93 | 112 | 134 | 139 | 151 | 125 | 178 | 229 |
| St. Vincent & Grenadines............ | 364 | 48 | 49 | 52 | 55 | 54 | 56 | 73 | 58 | 72 | 88 | 109 | 120 |
| Argentina..................................... | 213 | 12,222 | 19,077 | 20,604 | 28,337 | 29,183 | 29,463 | 32,356 | 28,225 | 26,044 | 18,344 | 20,098 | 16,968 |
| Aruba............................................ | 314 | 194 | 195 | 228 | 239 | 396 | 372 | 372 | 353 | 395 | 349 | 390 | 516 |
| Bahamas, The................................ | 313 | 434 | 410 | 307 | 294 | 369 | 644 | 678 | 697 | 551 | 524 | 603 | 646 |
| Barbados....................................... | 316 | 373 | 422 | 423 | 531 | 479 | 556 | 541 | 529 | 546 | 442 | 436 | .... |
| Belize........................................... | 339 | 31 | 50 | 76 | 69 | 108 | 136 | 142 | 154 | 188 | 262 | 336 | 315 |
| Bolivia.......................................... | 218 | 594 | 961 | 1,770 | 2,914 | 4,529 | 4,869 | 5,321 | 6,503 | 7,634 | 8,348 | 9,353 | 8,419 |
| Brazil........................................... | 223 | 33,819 | 37,291 | 56,643 | 113,585 | 125,239 | 151,448 | 186,434 | 228,243 | 240,534 | 231,384 | 249,221 | 255,663 |
| Chile............................................ | 228 | 10,299 | 11,845 | 12,890 | 10,655 | 14,980 | 16,128 | 18,062 | 27,313 | 27,091 | 26,678 | 27,911 | 27,879 |
| Colombia...................................... | 233 | 8,636 | 10,357 | 10,175 | 13,149 | 15,251 | 15,794 | 18,037 | 20,455 | 23,724 | 27,777 | 32,044 | 33,274 |
| Costa Rica.................................... | 238 | 1,238 | 1,618 | 2,070 | 2,603 | 2,466 | 2,594 | 3,005 | 3,098 | 4,461 | 4,760 | 4,978 | 5,653 |
| Curaçao & Sint Maarten.............. | 355 | .... | .... | .... | .... | .... | .... | 835 | 855 | 753 | 734 | 986 | 985 |
| Dominican Republic..................... | 243 | 528 | 1,344 | 1,505 | 1,918 | 1,740 | 2,272 | 2,500 | 2,662 | 2,296 | 3,039 | 3,341 | 3,787 |
| Ecuador........................................ | 248 | 718 | 1,229 | 1,020 | 1,812 | 2,457 | 1,862 | 961 | 1,114 | 732 | 2,191 | 2,418 | 1,518 |
| El Salvador................................... | 253 | 1,143 | 1,213 | 1,220 | 1,342 | 1,593 | 1,837 | 1,676 | 1,410 | 1,833 | 1,616 | 1,685 | 1,979 |
| Guatemala.................................... | 258 | 2,214 | 2,571 | 2,610 | 2,621 | 2,905 | 3,174 | 3,668 | 3,808 | 4,123 | 4,555 | 4,883 | 5,428 |
| Guyana.......................................... | 336 | 149 | 176 | 186 | 198 | 231 | 403 | 508 | 522 | 562 | 509 | 461 | 434 |
| Haiti.............................................. | 263 | 121 | 153 | 244 | 368 | 457 | 671 | 1,228 | 1,225 | 1,408 | 1,592 | 1,358 | 1,385 |
| Honduras...................................... | 268 | 1,269 | 1,629 | 1,748 | 1,601 | 1,607 | 1,332 | 1,735 | 1,792 | 1,624 | 1,937 | 2,369 | 2,693 |
| Jamaica......................................... | 343 | 1,189 | 1,518 | 1,541 | 1,189 | 1,151 | 1,324 | 1,624 | 1,486 | 1,299 | 1,181 | 1,707 | 2,103 |
| Mexico.......................................... | 273 | 41,306 | 51,816 | 50,702 | 55,128 | 61,766 | 63,536 | 78,101 | 93,908 | 104,513 | 114,056 | 131,917 | 125,311 |
| Netherlands Antilles.................... | 353 | 282 | 396 | 344 | 433 | 546 | 568 | .... | .... | .... | .... | .... | .... |
| Nicaragua..................................... | 278 | 430 | 509 | 613 | 698 | 741 | 1,003 | 1,168 | 1,233 | 1,228 | 1,294 | 1,571 | 1,799 |
| Panama......................................... | 283 | 406 | 847 | 887 | 1,225 | 1,574 | 1,932 | 1,763 | 1,501 | 1,605 | 1,849 | 2,783 | 2,438 |
| Paraguay....................................... | 288 | 752 | 908 | 1,131 | 1,558 | 1,848 | 2,449 | 2,687 | 3,225 | 2,974 | 3,617 | 4,612 | 4,093 |
| Peru.............................................. | 293 | 7,880 | 9,554 | 11,162 | 17,034 | 19,692 | 20,459 | 27,732 | 30,787 | 40,575 | 41,872 | 42,270 | 43,636 |
| Suriname....................................... | 366 | 84 | 89 | 144 | 236 | 366 | 383 | 393 | 464 | 579 | 481 | 397 | 207 |
| Trinidad and Tobago.................... | 369 | 2,042 | 3,473 | 4,380 | 4,238 | 6,133 | 5,857 | 6,239 | 6,780 | 6,375 | 6,886 | 8,214 | 7,446 |
| Uruguay........................................ | 298 | 1,616 | 2,151 | 2,051 | 2,604 | 4,125 | 5,122 | 4,964 | 6,702 | 8,843 | 10,566 | 12,110 | 11,280 |
| Venezuela, Rep. Bol..................... | 299 | 12,234 | 17,136 | 19,956 | 15,713 | 21,890 | 14,250 | 8,942 | 6,880 | 6,853 | 4,334 | 5,553 | 4,871 |

**Memorandum Items**
(with Gold at SDR 35 per Ounce)(1..s)

| | | 2004 | 2005 | 2006 | 2007 | 2008 | 2009 | 2010 | 2011 | 2012 | 2013 | 2014 | 2015 |
|---|---|---|---|---|---|---|---|---|---|---|---|---|---|
| | | *Millions of SDRs: End of Period* | | | | | | | | | | | |
| World........................................... | 001 | 2,525,110 | 3,106,006 | 3,562,230 | 4,308,982 | 4,847,355 | 5,481,965 | 6,298,998 | 6,974,385 | 7,456,469 | 7,910,380 | 8,308,431 | 8,172,147 |

(with Gold at Market Prices)(1m.s)

| | | *Millions of SDRs: End of Period* | | | | | | | | | | | |
|---|---|---|---|---|---|---|---|---|---|---|---|---|---|
| World........................................... | 001 | 2,774,786 | 3,427,113 | 3,941,871 | 4,783,533 | 5,357,920 | 6,128,006 | 7,169,216 | 7,939,784 | 8,523,622 | 8,675,556 | 9,129,616 | 8,940,368 |

# Monetary Base

14 x

*Percent Change over Previous Year*

| | | 2004 | 2005 | 2006 | 2007 | 2008 | 2009 | 2010 | 2011 | 2012 | 2013 | 2014 | 2015 |
|---|---|---|---|---|---|---|---|---|---|---|---|---|---|
| **Advanced Economies** | | | | | | | | | | | | | |
| Euro Area | 163 | 8.8 | 12.2 | 10.3 | 31.5 | 20.7 | −4.6 | −.3 | 42.3 | 9.2 | −23.0 | −4.3 | 35.0 |
| Australia | 193 | 2.2 | 6.1 | 5.2 | 15.4 | 16.0 | −1.0 | 2.9 | 5.1 | 5.8 | 7.0 | 6.1 | 7.6 |
| Canada | 156 | 4.8 | 3.1 | 5.7 | 4.7 | 5.3 | 8.8 | −.9 | 5.5 | 4.5 | 4.6 | 5.0 | 8.3 |
| China, P.R.: Hong Kong | 532 | .8 | −3.7 | 4.9 | 7.5 | 58.2 | 99.5 | 2.9 | 3.5 | 13.1 | 3.2 | 7.1 | 18.3 |
| Czech Republic | 935 | −3.7 | −.5 | −4.8 | −3.1 | 11.7 | 8.7 | 2.3 | 1.9 | .4 | 36.9 | 4.8 | 20.1 |
| Denmark | 128 | −7.3 | 15.6 | −2.0 | 3.8 | 28.1 | −1.1 | −8.9 | 19.2 | 90.1 | −30.0 | −21.2 | 29.7 |
| Iceland | 176 | 177.6 | −5.3 | 27.7 | 192.5 | −29.4 | 33.3 | −17.9 | −32.4 | 28.1 | 3.3 | 95.7 | 79.6 |
| Israel | 436 | 23.6 | 12.5 | 13.9 | −12.0 | −.1 | 3.8 | 15.0 | 6.7 | −3.2 | 2.8 | 26.4 | −6.1 |
| Japan | 158 | 3.8 | .9 | −18.7 | 1.3 | 5.5 | 4.5 | 3.5 | 14.2 | 10.7 | 45.8 | 36.7 | 29.1 |
| Korea | 542 | −4.8 | 11.5 | 19.9 | 8.7 | 15.0 | 4.5 | 10.0 | 7.4 | 10.4 | 18.0 | 12.0 | 12.5 |
| New Zealand | 196 | 6.3 | 13.2 | 202.9 | −4.8 | 9.4 | 1.3 | −8.7 | .... | .... | .... | .... | .... |
| Singapore | 576 | 5.7 | 7.2 | 10.1 | 8.9 | 21.6 | 6.5 | 11.5 | 12.1 | 7.2 | 31.4 | −13.7 | 10.0 |
| Sweden | 144 | .1 | 1.7 | 1.1 | 1.7 | 178.7 | −11.7 | −60.8 | 5.9 | 4.8 | −12.4 | −8.7 | 47.3 |
| Switzerland | 146 | −3.1 | −3.0 | 5.7 | 6.1 | 63.1 | 10.0 | −5.8 | 164.3 | 45.3 | 11.4 | 3.3 | 20.1 |
| United Kingdom | 112 | 6.9 | 2.9 | 54.8 | 13.6 | 34.9 | 106.1 | −1.9 | 14.9 | 49.5 | 8.7 | 1.1 | 4.2 |
| United States | 111 | 4.3 | 4.3 | 2.5 | 1.0 | 109.5 | 15.4 | 1.5 | 35.8 | .2 | 38.6 | 6.7 | −8.9 |
| **Emerging & Dev. Economies** | | | | | | | | | | | | | |
| **Emerging & Developing Asia** | | | | | | | | | | | | | |
| Bangladesh | 513 | 7.8 | 25.4 | 37.9 | 11.4 | 17.7 | 17.8 | 21.8 | 15.7 | 17.0 | 4.3 | 14.9 | 15.2 |
| Bhutan | 514 | 11.4 | 38.1 | −3.5 | 18.2 | 8.7 | 41.4 | 22.1 | −22.3 | −9.6 | 14.6 | 58.3 | −25.7 |
| Brunei Darussalam | 516 | 9.1 | 9.0 | 1.3 | 4.6 | 15.9 | −4.0 | 7.4 | 52.8 | 8.3 | 2.9 | 1.2 | 5.2 |
| Cambodia | 522 | −26.8 | −1.6 | 28.3 | 48.4 | 21.6 | 43.3 | 17.3 | 7.8 | 18.1 | 13.0 | 23.8 | 11.7 |
| China, P.R.: Mainland | 924 | 11.4 | 9.3 | 20.8 | 30.6 | 27.3 | 11.4 | 28.7 | 21.2 | 12.3 | 7.4 | 8.5 | −6.0 |
| China, P.R.: Macao | 546 | 14.8 | 7.5 | 20.2 | 18.6 | 12.2 | 85.3 | 15.3 | 20.1 | 33.2 | −19.1 | 29.9 | 15.7 |
| Fiji | 819 | −13.2 | 2.2 | 24.3 | 39.7 | −31.2 | 50.5 | 22.0 | 19.6 | 11.4 | 7.5 | 4.2 | 8.4 |
| India | 534 | 16.3 | 14.9 | 18.5 | 30.4 | 9.7 | 14.7 | 22.1 | 12.3 | 4.6 | 10.7 | 9.4 | 14.3 |
| Indonesia | 536 | 24.3 | 30.9 | 28.3 | 26.5 | −2.9 | 17.2 | 5.2 | 25.2 | 14.9 | 18.1 | 11.4 | 3.7 |
| Lao People's Dem. Rep. | 544 | 16.2 | 18.0 | 37.2 | 58.8 | 20.2 | 32.0 | 48.7 | .... | .... | .... | .... | .... |
| Malaysia | 548 | 10.0 | 5.1 | 10.6 | 9.8 | 7.2 | −20.0 | 11.8 | 57.3 | 9.9 | 9.4 | 7.7 | 10.1 |
| Maldives | 556 | 25.7 | 1.0 | 15.0 | 27.8 | 23.0 | 14.1 | −1.3 | 24.5 | 8.4 | 17.7 | 29.8 | −17.8 |
| Mongolia | 948 | 17.0 | 19.7 | 35.8 | 40.1 | 18.4 | 44.1 | 27.0 | 43.2 | 30.5 | 53.9 | 5.0 | −28.1 |
| Myanmar | 518 | 29.3 | 24.5 | 28.0 | 27.8 | 9.3 | 25.8 | 22.2 | 17.0 | 25.4 | 20.1 | 4.2 | 25.9 |
| Nepal | 558 | 15.4 | 9.1 | 14.3 | 11.2 | 30.3 | 20.7 | 6.5 | 33.0 | 6.9 | 31.8 | 5.4 | 30.8 |
| Papua New Guinea | 853 | 30.2 | 7.4 | 21.7 | 61.8 | −12.0 | 11.9 | 11.1 | 61.7 | 17.6 | .5 | 37.1 | −2.1 |
| Philippines | 566 | 9.8 | 9.3 | 53.8 | 18.0 | 13.3 | 9.0 | 6.9 | 18.1 | 11.5 | 30.5 | 20.6 | 6.2 |
| Samoa | 862 | 15.8 | 3.4 | −2.2 | 26.1 | 9.9 | 57.3 | 13.1 | −31.4 | 3.7 | 21.6 | 11.7 | 13.9 |
| Solomon Islands | 813 | 72.1 | 20.1 | 6.4 | −6.1 | −2.4 | 62.8 | 76.1 | 31.4 | 23.8 | −1.0 | −10.1 | 23.5 |
| Sri Lanka | 524 | 20.6 | 15.7 | 21.3 | 10.2 | 1.4 | 13.4 | 18.9 | 21.4 | 9.9 | .8 | 18.2 | 16.5 |
| Thailand | 578 | 12.4 | 5.1 | 2.2 | 7.8 | 11.4 | 6.2 | 12.9 | 9.9 | 9.7 | 5.5 | 5.5 | 2.5 |
| Timor-Leste | 537 | −5.1 | −4.0 | 30.0 | 147.0 | 25.9 | 120.4 | −2.7 | −37.0 | 189.7 | −14.4 | 71.4 | 45.5 |
| Tonga | 866 | 59.6 | −14.9 | 12.5 | 15.4 | −1.7 | 28.2 | 15.4 | 33.0 | 21.6 | 3.6 | 15.1 | 13.4 |
| Vanuatu | 846 | 9.7 | 12.1 | 33.5 | 11.2 | 5.4 | 1.5 | 18.4 | 6.5 | 9.4 | 18.0 | 9.9 | 20.4 |
| Vietnam | 582 | 16.1 | 23.6 | 32.2 | 36.8 | 20.0 | 11.4 | 4.1 | 18.9 | 25.4 | 6.1 | 18.7 | 19.3 |
| **Europe** | | | | | | | | | | | | | |
| **Emerging & Developing Europe** | | | | | | | | | | | | | |
| Albania | 914 | 11.2 | 11.0 | 9.8 | 4.9 | 19.1 | 4.8 | −.5 | 2.2 | 2.7 | 3.5 | 8.1 | 15.3 |
| Armenia | 911 | 12.9 | 55.4 | 39.4 | 47.1 | 5.3 | 13.8 | 1.6 | 29.2 | 5.6 | 28.7 | −2.8 | 3.9 |
| Bosnia and Herzegovina | 963 | 24.2 | 22.6 | 27.3 | 23.2 | −8.4 | −1.0 | 4.4 | −.9 | −.8 | 10.3 | 9.4 | 8.8 |
| Bulgaria | 918 | 24.4 | 10.7 | 19.1 | 35.0 | −.3 | −4.9 | 3.2 | 8.4 | 17.5 | 1.3 | 6.1 | 40.2 |
| Croatia | 960 | 19.9 | 20.6 | 16.7 | 5.2 | −12.7 | 5.9 | −.1 | 11.4 | −1.7 | † .3 | −.1 | 1.2 |
| Hungary | 944 | 16.8 | 36.4 | 4.0 | −10.8 | 5.3 | −13.8 | 9.3 | 24.4 | −6.9 | 8.5 | 140.1 | −6.5 |
| Kosovo | 967 | 19.8 | 34.9 | −3.2 | 18.3 | 17.7 | 81.0 | −32.0 | −.3 | 42.6 | 61.9 | −35.7 | 8.9 |
| Macedonia, FYR | 962 | 1.5 | 25.1 | 19.9 | 21.9 | 15.8 | 8.0 | 3.9 | 9.2 | 4.1 | −3.9 | 25.9 | −1.2 |
| Montenegro | 943 | 28.6 | 147.4 | 130.9 | 46.4 | −23.4 | −9.2 | 15.9 | −25.3 | 14.5 | 34.7 | 30.5 | 26.2 |
| Poland | 964 | 6.1 | 5.9 | 23.1 | 16.7 | 24.8 | 4.3 | 1.9 | −1.8 | 22.7 | −2.6 | 16.0 | 11.3 |
| Romania | 968 | 39.3 | 62.1 | 55.7 | 41.3 | 3.3 | 2.4 | 6.7 | 11.7 | −6.9 | 19.8 | −.5 | 8.3 |
| Serbia, Republic of | 942 | 28.2 | 67.3 | 60.6 | 10.2 | 17.5 | 4.2 | .6 | 13.4 | 2.8 | 3.0 | −3.8 | 8.5 |
| Turkey | 186 | 32.0 | 40.7 | 28.3 | 9.0 | 27.8 | .9 | 22.5 | 39.1 | 29.8 | 38.6 | 12.6 | 18.8 |
| **CIS** | | | | | | | | | | | | | |
| Armenia | 911 | 12.9 | 55.4 | 39.4 | 47.1 | 5.3 | 13.8 | 1.6 | 29.2 | 5.6 | 28.7 | −2.8 | 3.9 |
| Azerbaijan, Republic of | 912 | 61.3 | 6.3 | 130.8 | 68.3 | 44.2 | −1.1 | 32.9 | 30.2 | 25.6 | 10.6 | .6 | −36.3 |
| Belarus | 913 | 41.9 | 73.7 | 19.8 | 38.4 | 11.7 | −11.5 | 49.5 | 84.1 | 61.6 | 13.4 | 13.8 | 14.9 |
| Georgia | 915 | 46.9 | 16.2 | 26.3 | 41.0 | −8.5 | 14.2 | 11.0 | 39.4 | 12.2 | 22.5 | 12.8 | 9.9 |
| Kazakhstan | 916 | 82.3 | 12.5 | 131.0 | −2.5 | 4.2 | 60.7 | 5.0 | 10.3 | 1.9 | −2.2 | 20.8 | 39.2 |
| Kyrgyz Republic | 917 | 21.8 | 61.4 | 13.6 | 38.9 | 11.3 | 18.3 | 17.4 | 13.3 | 18.7 | 12.2 | −10.4 | 9.5 |
| Moldova | 921 | 39.8 | 31.7 | −1.7 | 59.3 | 25.6 | −12.5 | 8.9 | 21.8 | 19.7 | 27.0 | 6.3 | 7.1 |
| Russia | 922 | 24.3 | 22.4 | 41.5 | 33.7 | 1.2 | 15.9 | 26.6 | 5.5 | 14.0 | 6.6 | 7.9 | −2.5 |
| Tajikistan | 923 | 67.2 | 60.7 | 24.4 | 41.3 | 29.5 | 38.9 | 15.7 | 27.9 | 18.4 | 18.3 | 13.2 | 16.0 |
| Ukraine | 926 | 34.1 | 53.9 | 17.5 | 46.0 | 31.6 | 4.4 | 15.8 | 6.3 | 6.4 | 20.3 | 8.5 | .8 |
| **Middle East, N. Africa & Pakistan** | | | | | | | | | | | | | |
| Afghanistan, Islamic Rep. of | 512 | .... | .... | .... | 26.0 | 36.7 | 26.7 | 35.7 | 25.7 | 3.6 | 14.9 | 13.6 | 2.6 |
| Algeria | 612 | −.1 | 1.6 | 13.9 | 28.8 | 11.4 | 15.0 | 18.2 | 19.9 | 18.2 | 11.6 | 12.9 | 11.7 |
| Bahrain, Kingdom of | 419 | 4.4 | 25.4 | 9.0 | 106.9 | −2.8 | 7.8 | 19.9 | −10.4 | 20.4 | −1.3 | 17.4 | −11.1 |
| Djibouti | 611 | −5.1 | .7 | 27.2 | 4.0 | 21.8 | 7.5 | 25.9 | 4.9 | 12.1 | 21.4 | 16.0 | 1.4 |
| Egypt | 469 | 18.6 | 46.7 | 38.0 | 19.4 | −10.5 | 1.8 | 12.5 | −22.0 | 3.3 | 51.3 | 13.6 | 23.5 |
| Iran, I.R. of | 429 | 14.5 | 22.3 | 37.3 | 41.1 | 31.3 | 11.7 | 32.0 | 2.2 | .... | .... | .... | .... |
| Iraq | 433 | .... | 16.9 | 27.0 | 64.4 | 48.8 | 5.6 | 20.4 | 10.2 | 8.3 | 12.6 | −9.6 | −12.6 |
| Jordan | 439 | 3.2 | 18.4 | 20.7 | 7.9 | 23.4 | −.2 | 7.8 | 9.6 | 1.7 | 9.1 | 16.7 | 1.8 |
| Kuwait | 443 | −12.2 | 36.0 | 42.2 | 17.0 | −35.5 | 124.0 | 27.7 | 28.6 | 18.3 | 18.0 | 6.6 | −14.9 |

# Monetary Base

| | | 2004 | 2005 | 2006 | 2007 | 2008 | 2009 | 2010 | 2011 | 2012 | 2013 | 2014 | 2015 |
|---|---|---|---|---|---|---|---|---|---|---|---|---|---|
| | | | | | | | Percent Change over Previous Year | | | | | | |
| **Middle East,N.Africa & Pakistan(Cont.)** | | | | | | | | | | | | | |
| Lebanon | 446 | 3.3 | −2.1 | −3.9 | 1.5 | 31.1 | 36.4 | 14.6 | 19.2 | 10.6 | 6.2 | 19.2 | 12.2 |
| Libya | 672 | 46.3 | 45.0 | 15.1 | 47.7 | 59.6 | 19.5 | 14.3 | 17.9 | 9.4 | 18.4 | −7.1 | −10.5 |
| Mauritania | 682 | .... | −2.7 | 23.4 | 14.2 | 15.3 | 15.3 | .5 | 39.9 | 19.3 | .... | .... | .... |
| Morocco | 686 | 12.4 | 13.7 | 13.8 | 13.8 | 4.9 | −3.8 | −.4 | 5.9 | .7 | 5.0 | .1 | 10.2 |
| Oman | 449 | 13.7 | 4.5 | 38.2 | 69.9 | 66.9 | −31.8 | 59.2 | −18.4 | 36.5 | 6.4 | 24.5 | 70.0 |
| Pakistan | 564 | 20.0 | 9.8 | 21.0 | 14.8 | 6.3 | 14.0 | 16.6 | 7.5 | 16.8 | 12.1 | 2.0 | 25.0 |
| Qatar | 453 | 31.1 | 37.1 | 23.0 | 201.9 | −22.9 | 94.4 | 100.0 | −66.0 | 46.1 | −3.3 | 23.1 | −10.2 |
| Saudi Arabia | 456 | 11.4 | 10.8 | 19.2 | 7.1 | 24.0 | 12.3 | 9.3 | 21.5 | 22.9 | .7 | 11.8 | 8.1 |
| Sudan | 732 | 28.2 | 38.7 | 25.6 | 13.2 | 22.6 | 28.3 | 19.1 | 27.1 | 44.5 | 19.9 | 16.0 | 22.5 |
| Syrian Arab Republic | 463 | 25.2 | 7.7 | 9.7 | 16.1 | 17.7 | 13.9 | 7.0 | −6.5 | .... | .... | .... | .... |
| Tunisia | 744 | 16.7 | 11.2 | 14.7 | 13.8 | 21.5 | 19.0 | −8.3 | 7.6 | 7.7 | 9.0 | 22.2 | 3.3 |
| United Arab Emirates | 466 | 29.5 | 19.3 | 32.4 | 207.1 | −36.4 | 9.7 | 11.4 | 2.9 | 12.1 | 18.3 | 9.7 | 18.1 |
| West Bank and Gaza | 487 | 10.7 | 1.8 | † −8.7 | 39.1 | 59.0 | 9.1 | −11.2 | −12.9 | 8.2 | .3 | 5.5 | 10.8 |
| Yemen, Republic of | 474 | 14.4 | 21.4 | 16.5 | 12.3 | 7.4 | 10.9 | 7.6 | 13.5 | 13.9 | 1.8 | .... | .... |
| **Sub-Saharan Africa** | | | | | | | | | | | | | |
| CEMAC | 758 | 17.7 | 27.0 | 23.0 | 17.7 | 17.3 | 5.7 | 25.2 | 6.6 | 26.0 | −8.5 | 18.7 | −13.3 |
| Cameroon | 622 | 17.2 | −.1 | 27.4 | 30.4 | .4 | 8.3 | 13.6 | −2.9 | 8.5 | −7.4 | 8.6 | 11.8 |
| Central African Rep. | 626 | 15.2 | 17.3 | −14.8 | −18.5 | 21.2 | 28.0 | 2.3 | 8.2 | −2.4 | 16.4 | 23.6 | −1.8 |
| Chad | 628 | 9.2 | 30.8 | 55.3 | 7.6 | 22.9 | −8.0 | 22.0 | 13.7 | 9.0 | 10.7 | 21.4 | −8.6 |
| Congo, Rep. of | 634 | 21.1 | 69.3 | 22.2 | 21.9 | 44.1 | −10.0 | 16.3 | 37.1 | 17.6 | −14.6 | 44.0 | −30.6 |
| Equatorial Guinea | 642 | 27.4 | 77.4 | 5.6 | 27.0 | −9.9 | 54.9 | 19.2 | 16.4 | 106.5 | −12.6 | 16.1 | −32.8 |
| Gabon | 646 | 23.0 | 44.4 | 20.7 | 11.5 | 36.1 | −3.8 | 10.3 | 27.7 | 4.5 | −9.4 | −.9 | 10.1 |
| WAEMU | 759 | 1.5 | 3.7 | 7.0 | 19.2 | 10.8 | 15.8 | 12.5 | 9.0 | −1.7 | 10.1 | 13.1 | 16.0 |
| Benin | 638 | −18.9 | 33.3 | 12.8 | 7.4 | 47.5 | −4.3 | .3 | 1.2 | .1 | 18.2 | 27.9 | −.8 |
| Burkina Faso | 748 | −26.4 | −16.3 | .8 | 42.9 | 14.9 | 17.3 | −9.3 | −1.8 | 5.7 | −4.2 | 14.2 | 23.4 |
| Côte d'Ivoire | 662 | 20.6 | 1.7 | 8.6 | 25.2 | 3.8 | 24.3 | 19.4 | 15.4 | −6.2 | 9.8 | 13.3 | 17.6 |
| Guinea Bissau | 654 | 61.4 | 35.3 | −11.1 | 20.9 | 15.7 | 2.0 | 19.7 | 45.7 | −12.4 | 5.3 | 61.0 | 25.9 |
| Mali | 678 | −15.1 | 14.8 | −2.8 | 4.0 | 5.3 | 10.1 | .6 | 18.0 | 14.0 | 1.2 | −4.4 | 6.9 |
| Niger | 692 | 11.8 | 6.5 | 18.3 | 25.6 | −1.5 | 28.7 | 30.3 | 2.8 | 33.4 | 5.2 | 33.0 | .7 |
| Senegal | 722 | 10.3 | −1.7 | 11.8 | 17.3 | — | 17.2 | 14.1 | −4.6 | −9.4 | 23.3 | 6.7 | 27.6 |
| Togo | 742 | 31.1 | −19.7 | 54.1 | 12.0 | 21.1 | 10.3 | 31.2 | 20.5 | −19.2 | 2.1 | −6.0 | 48.1 |
| Angola | 614 | 55.9 | 66.4 | 1.1 | 60.1 | 62.2 | 75.5 | 14.9 | 19.6 | 4.4 | 15.2 | .... | .... |
| Botswana | 616 | 27.3 | 20.4 | 164.3 | 18.7 | 8.8 | −.4 | 12.2 | −31.2 | −4.7 | −15.4 | −8.5 | 18.6 |
| Burundi | 618 | 37.1 | 32.6 | 6.8 | 16.0 | 24.7 | 26.6 | 6.0 | .7 | 16.1 | 23.6 | 17.0 | −8.6 |
| Cabo Verde | 624 | 6.9 | 14.4 | 3.5 | 10.0 | 8.0 | 3.4 | −3.4 | −5.7 | 33.3 | 17.9 | 19.1 | 2.1 |
| Comoros | 632 | −1.6 | −1.4 | −1.0 | 6.2 | 10.7 | 17.1 | 5.8 | 15.1 | 18.8 | −14.9 | 18.5 | 17.2 |
| Congo, Dem. Rep. of | 636 | 69.7 | 14.5 | 54.1 | 37.5 | 33.6 | 23.6 | 30.7 | 29.7 | 6.5 | 15.4 | 12.2 | 13.9 |
| Eritrea | 643 | 6.3 | 7.4 | 4.7 | 17.7 | 26.6 | 23.0 | 16.8 | 9.8 | 18.3 | 35.3 | 18.5 | .... |
| Gambia, The | 648 | 28.2 | −3.0 | 24.3 | −4.3 | 5.7 | 9.3 | 10.5 | 12.3 | 6.9 | 28.1 | 11.9 | .... |
| Ghana | 652 | 17.6 | 7.0 | 36.2 | 36.6 | 27.8 | 39.1 | 34.5 | 30.9 | 36.0 | 33.9 | 45.2 | 4.8 |
| Guinea | 656 | 35.8 | 14.5 | 104.0 | 5.7 | 16.4 | 75.1 | 61.3 | 7.2 | −12.1 | 15.5 | 14.5 | 1.9 |
| Kenya | 664 | 15.5 | 6.1 | 16.3 | 25.9 | 4.2 | 11.2 | 22.4 | 14.5 | 17.2 | 7.3 | 18.5 | 5.5 |
| Lesotho | 666 | 7.8 | 31.3 | −7.3 | 1.0 | 4.6 | 41.4 | 3.2 | .1 | 14.7 | 25.2 | 13.7 | .7 |
| Liberia | 668 | 62.3 | 27.1 | 30.9 | 35.7 | 32.2 | 21.9 | 34.8 | 56.5 | 3.0 | −1.5 | 4.3 | −2.2 |
| Madagascar | 674 | 20.1 | 10.6 | 13.3 | 31.3 | 13.6 | 3.6 | 15.3 | 25.6 | 9.8 | −6.1 | 14.1 | 9.6 |
| Malawi | 676 | 30.7 | 14.7 | 4.4 | 25.7 | 33.2 | 39.8 | 13.9 | 27.5 | 54.6 | 38.6 | 35.3 | .... |
| Mauritius | 684 | 18.3 | 4.8 | 7.7 | 10.9 | 9.1 | 17.3 | 25.1 | 7.4 | 9.0 | 18.5 | 9.0 | 8.3 |
| Mozambique | 688 | 20.2 | 16.8 | 20.9 | 20.9 | 7.8 | 27.3 | 29.2 | 8.5 | 19.7 | 15.7 | 20.5 | 29.0 |
| Namibia | 728 | 13.9 | 10.8 | 11.6 | 7.5 | 42.7 | 8.7 | 26.9 | 69.9 | −9.5 | −.8 | 35.7 | −5.0 |
| Nigeria | 694 | 6.3 | 4.5 | 29.6 | 20.6 | 32.4 | 7.1 | 14.3 | 49.8 | 27.5 | 40.0 | 14.4 | −2.0 |
| São Tomé & Príncipe | 716 | −25.5 | 76.6 | 43.9 | 37.6 | 18.9 | 22.3 | −7.9 | −.7 | 28.6 | 29.4 | 23.2 | 37.5 |
| Seychelles | 718 | 82.6 | 3.4 | 32.7 | −23.1 | .6 | 15.7 | 34.7 | −2.7 | 6.9 | 15.4 | 13.9 | 9.5 |
| Sierra Leone | 724 | 11.4 | 23.8 | 10.7 | 19.3 | 15.5 | 21.2 | 34.8 | 12.6 | 22.1 | 17.0 | 30.9 | 10.7 |
| South Africa | 199 | 14.8 | 11.8 | 20.6 | 14.7 | 8.7 | 4.0 | 9.3 | 15.2 | 11.2 | 9.8 | 7.3 | 9.0 |
| South Sudan, Republic of | 733 | .... | .... | .... | .... | .... | .... | .... | .... | 7.7 | −1.5 | 48.6 | 154.8 |
| Swaziland | 734 | 9.8 | 2.9 | 14.1 | 33.9 | 24.4 | 38.3 | −10.2 | 52.1 | .7 | 6.0 | −.8 | 15.4 |
| Tanzania | 738 | 21.1 | 28.5 | 17.1 | 24.9 | 21.1 | 32.2 | 16.2 | 17.6 | 10.1 | 11.1 | 17.5 | 15.6 |
| Uganda | 746 | 20.5 | 13.7 | 16.7 | 25.8 | 24.8 | 13.2 | 32.0 | 14.7 | 20.4 | 1.2 | 29.0 | 10.0 |
| Zambia | 754 | 32.3 | 19.2 | 42.5 | 9.4 | 29.6 | 2.4 | 51.6 | −22.6 | 51.5 | 21.1 | 31.1 | 22.2 |
| **Western Hemisphere** | | | | | | | | | | | | | |
| ECCU | 309 | 13.8 | −5.5 | 12.4 | 9.0 | −2.8 | 3.4 | 13.8 | 13.2 | 6.6 | 12.0 | 18.7 | 8.4 |
| Anguilla | 312 | 3.2 | 15.9 | 8.0 | 13.0 | −10.1 | 3.5 | −6.0 | −8.3 | 11.3 | 2.3 | 11.4 | 1.8 |
| Antigua and Barbuda | 311 | 3.4 | 5.9 | 10.9 | 2.0 | −5.2 | .2 | 10.8 | 18.0 | 6.4 | 16.8 | 36.4 | 5.3 |
| Dominica | 321 | −7.0 | 4.9 | 19.8 | 6.5 | −14.8 | 11.9 | 7.7 | 14.8 | 13.8 | 3.4 | 11.1 | 24.7 |
| Grenada | 328 | 40.0 | −22.9 | 3.6 | 15.8 | −5.2 | −5.0 | −1.2 | 15.2 | −1.0 | 23.2 | 3.7 | 7.2 |
| Montserrat | 351 | −8.3 | −1.8 | 4.6 | −2.3 | −24.9 | 23.7 | 19.4 | 54.2 | 27.7 | 28.3 | −1.7 | 29.2 |
| St. Kitts and Nevis | 361 | 21.9 | −8.7 | 24.4 | 7.8 | 5.8 | 25.6 | 22.0 | 37.3 | −4.1 | 17.0 | 9.3 | −3.1 |
| St. Lucia | 362 | 19.8 | −11.7 | 13.0 | 8.3 | 5.4 | 4.9 | 9.7 | 3.9 | 14.3 | −8.0 | 30.2 | 16.6 |
| St. Vincent & Grenadines | 364 | 6.0 | 1.9 | 12.7 | 18.7 | −1.8 | −18.8 | 52.8 | −14.3 | 14.1 | 25.8 | 17.7 | 7.8 |
| Argentina | 213 | 20.7 | 1.2 | 42.8 | 23.1 | 17.6 | 18.6 | 32.9 | 24.0 | 41.0 | 28.5 | 19.2 | 43.8 |
| Aruba | 314 | 4.9 | 1.2 | 16.6 | 6.8 | 51.1 | 5.7 | 10.4 | −19.2 | 34.9 | −9.0 | 5.0 | 20.0 |
| Bahamas, The | 313 | 31.7 | −8.1 | −1.5 | 16.2 | −3.8 | 7.4 | 19.4 | 6.1 | 2.3 | −3.7 | 14.1 | −.5 |
| Barbados | 316 | −28.7 | .7 | 19.7 | 36.6 | 1.6 | −5.7 | −15.4 | 16.3 | .... | .... | .... | .... |
| Belize | 339 | 13.0 | 11.1 | 25.9 | 4.6 | 13.9 | 11.9 | −2.7 | 14.2 | 19.2 | 16.0 | 24.2 | 24.4 |
| Bolivia | 218 | 15.0 | 16.7 | 45.4 | 46.9 | 21.9 | 22.4 | 15.6 | 32.3 | 19.0 | 9.9 | 6.4 | 11.1 |
| Brazil | 223 | 4.7 | 7.7 | 12.6 | 21.8 | −17.4 | 11.3 | 131.8 | 10.8 | −13.6 | 13.1 | −4.5 | 8.4 |
| Chile | 228 | 12.1 | −64.6 | 16.3 | 7.8 | 15.2 | 8.3 | 20.6 | 24.1 | 15.1 | 11.0 | −6.5 | 11.8 |
| Colombia | 233 | 15.9 | 18.4 | 18.5 | 19.9 | 11.7 | 9.3 | 13.5 | 14.4 | 10.0 | 15.3 | 7.0 | 18.4 |
| Costa Rica | 238 | 10.6 | 29.2 | 30.8 | 19.8 | −1.9 | 5.1 | 1.9 | 14.8 | 16.4 | 18.8 | 5.1 | 9.2 |
| Dominican Republic | 243 | 12.1 | 61.0 | −1.3 | 14.3 | 2.9 | 3.0 | 12.0 | 7.7 | 1.7 | 11.0 | 15.3 | 4.4 |
| Ecuador | 248 | 14.9 | 48.2 | 12.4 | 34.6 | 47.7 | −1.6 | −6.4 | 11.8 | 36.9 | 43.7 | −4.6 | −30.8 |
| El Salvador | 253 | −6.5 | −1.1 | 3.2 | 22.2 | 2.6 | 2.1 | −1.0 | −6.4 | −4.3 | 10.3 | .7 | 5.2 |

# Monetary Base

| | | 2004 | 2005 | 2006 | 2007 | 2008 | 2009 | 2010 | 2011 | 2012 | 2013 | 2014 | 2015 |
|---|---|---|---|---|---|---|---|---|---|---|---|---|---|
| **Western Hemisphere(Cont.)** | | | | | | *Percent Change over Previous Year* | | | | | | | |
| Guatemala | 258 | 10.1 | .6 | 15.2 | .7 | 19.6 | 13.8 | 4.6 | 9.1 | 6.2 | 10.1 | 4.4 | 4.5 |
| Guyana | 336 | 8.8 | 12.7 | 4.6 | 7.5 | 7.1 | 24.1 | 27.6 | 7.0 | 15.2 | 1.5 | 9.4 | 7.1 |
| Haiti | 263 | 10.8 | 11.1 | 9.4 | 9.1 | 17.8 | 11.6 | 43.9 | 2.9 | 9.0 | −3.9 | 12.8 | 25.4 |
| Honduras | 268 | 32.3 | 30.1 | 12.4 | −.1 | 1.1 | 7.8 | 34.3 | 8.5 | −.4 | 10.7 | 16.3 | 10.5 |
| Jamaica | 343 | 13.0 | 6.3 | 15.4 | 4.7 | 30.1 | 20.1 | −2.7 | 9.4 | −8.6 | 32.2 | 112.6 | 5.3 |
| Mexico | 273 | 12.0 | 11.7 | 18.4 | 10.0 | 16.7 | 9.4 | 9.7 | 10.1 | 10.8 | 8.5 | 15.8 | 16.8 |
| Nicaragua | 278 | −1.5 | 3.7 | 11.0 | 3.5 | 11.3 | 31.8 | 25.0 | 6.4 | −1.5 | 14.9 | 17.7 | 14.8 |
| Panama | 283 | 2.5 | 2.4 | 3.6 | 19.9 | 1.7 | 23.1 | −6.5 | 3.8 | 2.2 | −5.3 | 13.4 | 13.2 |
| Paraguay | 288 | 15.0 | 3.8 | 7.9 | 33.5 | 14.4 | 30.4 | 3.5 | 19.1 | 10.0 | 6.0 | 17.4 | 14.1 |
| Peru | 293 | 5.4 | 30.3 | 2.9 | 27.4 | 22.8 | −9.1 | 73.4 | −10.7 | 25.4 | 7.9 | 2.8 | 24.5 |
| Suriname | 366 | 17.5 | 7.9 | 33.3 | 30.6 | 11.9 | 31.6 | 13.8 | 7.9 | 34.6 | −.6 | −8.5 | 18.4 |
| Trinidad and Tobago | 369 | −3.2 | 44.5 | 15.6 | 12.3 | 42.2 | 38.4 | 13.1 | 15.8 | 17.2 | 9.2 | .9 | −13.9 |
| Uruguay | 298 | 10.6 | 55.4 | 10.3 | 16.4 | 29.3 | 6.5 | 16.2 | 17.3 | 26.7 | 12.9 | 1.4 | 7.2 |
| Venezuela, Rep. Bol. | 299 | 31.8 | 36.6 | 89.8 | 48.0 | 27.9 | 24.5 | 23.0 | 50.1 | 43.0 | 67.3 | .... | .... |

# Broad Money

| | | 2004 | 2005 | 2006 | 2007 | 2008 | 2009 | 2010 | 2011 | 2012 | 2013 | 2014 | 2015 |
|---|---|---|---|---|---|---|---|---|---|---|---|---|---|
| | | | | | | *Percent Change over Previous Year* | | | | | | | |
| **Advanced Economies** | | | | | | | | | | | | | |
| Euro Area | 163 | 6.6 | 7.3 | 10.1 | 11.6 | 7.7 | −.3 | 1.1 | 1.7 | 3.5 | 1.0 | 3.8 | 4.7 |
| Australia | 193 | 11.4 | 8.5 | 15.1 | 18.2 | 17.0 | 3.2 | 10.1 | 8.0 | 7.3 | 6.7 | 7.0 | 6.2 |
| Canada | 156 | 5.5 | 9.8 | 12.6 | −25.3 | 15.1 | .... | .... | .... | .... | .... | .... | .... |
| China, P.R.: Hong Kong | 532 | 7.3 | 3.5 | 16.2 | 18.8 | 4.2 | 5.2 | 7.4 | 9.8 | 7.8 | 9.5 | 8.9 | 6.6 |
| Czech Republic | 935 | 7.4 | 11.0 | 13.0 | 16.1 | 13.6 | .2 | 1.9 | 2.8 | 4.8 | 5.8 | 5.9 | 8.0 |
| Denmark | 128 | 2.7 | 14.4 | 11.5 | 17.2 | 7.0 | 4.5 | 7.9 | −5.9 | 2.0 | −9.4 | 14.1 | 9.9 |
| Iceland | 176 | 16.4 | 26.2 | 60.1 | 5.8 | 32.2 | 2.5 | −10.0 | 5.7 | −4.6 | 4.7 | 8.7 | 6.7 |
| Israel | 436 | 7.2 | 10.0 | 6.9 | −21.9 | 14.0 | 5.8 | 2.9 | 11.4 | 6.7 | 8.4 | 12.1 | 4.2 |
| Japan | 158 | .6 | .5 | −.7 | .6 | .7 | 2.1 | 1.7 | 2.9 | 2.2 | 3.5 | 3.0 | 3.1 |
| Korea | 542 | 6.3 | 7.0 | 12.5 | 10.8 | 12.0 | 9.9 | 6.0 | 5.5 | 4.8 | 4.6 | 8.1 | 8.2 |
| New Zealand | 196 | 3.5 | 9.5 | 11.3 | 11.1 | 10.4 | −.6 | 8.4 | .... | .... | .... | .... | .... |
| Norway | 142 | 7.5 | 11.4 | 16.3 | .... | .... | .... | .... | .... | .... | .... | .... | .... |
| Singapore | 576 | 6.2 | 6.2 | 19.4 | 13.4 | 12.0 | 11.3 | 8.6 | 10.0 | 7.2 | 4.3 | 3.3 | 1.5 |
| Sweden | 144 | 3.4 | 16.5 | 15.0 | 18.6 | 2.7 | .5 | 3.5 | 6.6 | 3.4 | 3.8 | 4.2 | 6.6 |
| Switzerland | 146 | 2.9 | 6.8 | 4.6 | 3.3 | 4.0 | 7.6 | 5.5 | 11.2 | 13.0 | 4.1 | 4.6 | .1 |
| United Kingdom | 112 | 9.8 | 13.8 | 14.1 | 15.8 | 17.8 | −.1 | 4.0 | −4.4 | .8 | 2.1 | −2.5 | 1.9 |
| United States | 111 | 5.8 | 8.1 | 9.0 | 11.8 | 8.2 | 5.0 | −2.7 | 6.7 | 5.0 | 4.4 | 5.2 | 3.6 |
| **Emerging & Dev. Economies** | | | | | | | | | | | | | |
| **Emerging & Developing Asia** | | | | | | | | | | | | | |
| Bangladesh | 513 | 14.2 | 15.8 | 20.2 | 13.6 | 16.4 | 20.3 | 21.1 | 16.9 | 17.0 | 14.9 | 15.6 | 14.9 |
| Bhutan | 514 | 16.2 | 13.0 | 18.7 | 11.8 | 26.2 | 25.8 | 16.6 | 4.4 | 5.8 | 3.7 | 25.9 | 3.9 |
| Brunei Darussalam | 516 | 15.8 | −4.5 | 2.1 | 6.7 | 9.6 | 9.7 | 4.8 | 10.1 | .9 | 1.5 | 3.2 | −1.8 |
| Cambodia | 522 | 28.8 | 15.8 | 40.5 | 61.8 | 5.4 | 35.6 | 21.3 | 3.9 | 39.4 | 16.0 | 29.6 | 15.1 |
| China, P.R.: Mainland | 924 | 14.9 | 16.7 | 22.1 | 16.7 | 17.8 | 28.4 | 18.9 | 17.3 | 14.4 | 13.6 | 11.0 | 13.3 |
| China, P.R.: Macao | 546 | 8.9 | 12.2 | 24.5 | 9.8 | 2.3 | 11.8 | 14.5 | 22.6 | 25.9 | 17.7 | 10.4 | −3.0 |
| Fiji | 819 | 9.5 | 15.2 | 22.3 | 8.3 | −6.5 | −.1 | 3.5 | 11.5 | 5.9 | 19.0 | 10.4 | 13.9 |
| India | 534 | 16.7 | 15.6 | 21.6 | 22.3 | 20.5 | 18.0 | 17.8 | 16.1 | 11.0 | 14.8 | 10.6 | 10.6 |
| Indonesia | 536 | 8.7 | 16.3 | 14.9 | 19.3 | 14.9 | 13.0 | 15.4 | 16.4 | 15.0 | 12.8 | 11.9 | 9.0 |
| Lao People's Dem. Rep. | 544 | 21.6 | 7.9 | 26.7 | 38.7 | 18.3 | 32.4 | 39.1 | .... | .... | .... | .... | .... |
| Malaysia | 548 | 12.7 | 8.8 | 13.6 | 7.9 | 10.5 | 7.7 | 7.3 | 14.6 | 8.8 | 7.4 | 6.3 | 3.0 |
| Maldives | 556 | 31.4 | 10.6 | 18.9 | 24.1 | 21.8 | 14.4 | 14.6 | 20.0 | 4.9 | 18.4 | 14.7 | 13.7 |
| Micronesia, Fed. States of | 868 | −.1 | 1.6 | −8.5 | 4.6 | 3.2 | 16.3 | −.1 | 3.9 | 13.9 | 8.1 | 33.3 | −8.3 |
| Mongolia | 948 | 20.4 | 34.6 | 34.8 | 56.3 | −5.5 | 26.9 | 62.5 | 37.0 | 18.8 | 24.2 | 12.4 | −5.5 |
| Myanmar | 518 | 32.1 | 27.3 | 27.3 | 29.9 | 14.9 | 30.6 | 42.5 | 30.4 | 31.7 | 33.6 | 20.0 | 30.7 |
| Nepal | 558 | 13.1 | 9.7 | 17.0 | 18.5 | 38.8 | 29.6 | 9.6 | 18.7 | 14.9 | 21.7 | 16.1 | 24.4 |
| Papua New Guinea | 853 | 14.8 | 29.5 | 38.9 | 27.8 | 7.8 | 21.9 | 10.2 | 17.3 | 10.9 | 6.7 | 3.4 | 8.0 |
| Philippines | 566 | 10.7 | 6.8 | 23.5 | 9.6 | 10.0 | 8.6 | 10.9 | 5.3 | 7.0 | 29.3 | 12.4 | 9.2 |
| Samoa | 862 | 8.3 | 15.6 | 13.8 | 11.0 | 7.4 | 8.9 | 6.4 | −6.1 | −1.6 | 6.4 | 9.6 | 6.0 |
| Solomon Islands | 813 | 17.7 | 46.1 | 26.4 | 21.7 | 8.0 | 16.8 | 13.3 | 25.8 | 17.4 | 12.4 | 5.6 | 15.0 |
| Sri Lanka | 524 | 19.6 | 19.0 | 17.9 | 16.5 | 8.4 | 18.7 | 15.8 | 19.1 | 17.5 | 16.7 | 13.4 | 17.8 |
| Thailand | 578 | 5.6 | 6.1 | 8.1 | 6.2 | 9.2 | 6.8 | 11.0 | 15.1 | 10.4 | 7.3 | 4.7 | 4.4 |
| Timor-Leste | 537 | 6.9 | 18.3 | 28.2 | 43.9 | 34.1 | 39.3 | 9.9 | 9.3 | 26.2 | 22.9 | 19.9 | 7.1 |
| Tonga | 866 | 13.9 | 22.1 | 6.8 | 12.0 | 3.5 | −2.4 | 6.3 | −1.5 | 12.7 | 3.1 | 8.9 | 16.2 |
| Vanuatu | 846 | 9.9 | 11.6 | 7.0 | 16.0 | 13.4 | .5 | −6.0 | 1.3 | −.6 | −5.5 | 8.6 | 11.4 |
| Vietnam | 582 | 31.0 | 30.9 | 29.7 | 49.1 | 20.7 | 26.2 | 29.7 | 11.9 | 24.5 | 21.4 | 19.7 | 14.9 |
| **Europe** | | | | | | | | | | | | | |
| **Emerging & Developing Europe** | | | | | | | | | | | | | |
| Albania | 914 | 13.5 | 14.1 | 16.0 | 13.7 | 7.7 | 6.8 | 12.5 | 9.2 | 5.0 | 2.3 | 4.0 | 1.9 |
| Bosnia and Herzegovina | 963 | 24.0 | 18.6 | 24.2 | 20.7 | 4.1 | 2.2 | 7.2 | 5.8 | 3.4 | 7.9 | 7.3 | 8.0 |
| Bulgaria | 918 | 23.1 | 23.9 | 26.9 | 31.3 | 8.9 | 4.2 | 6.3 | 12.2 | 8.4 | 8.9 | 1.1 | 8.8 |
| Croatia | 960 | 9.3 | 10.6 | 18.1 | 18.3 | 4.4 | −.6 | 12.6 | 1.6 | 3.2 | † −14.6 | .9 | 4.7 |
| Hungary | 944 | 11.5 | 14.7 | 13.8 | 11.0 | 8.7 | 3.6 | 4.3 | 6.7 | −4.6 | 7.8 | 2.5 | 5.8 |
| Kosovo | 967 | 36.6 | 20.3 | 5.5 | 23.4 | 23.2 | 10.8 | 13.5 | 8.8 | 7.1 | 17.2 | −3.9 | 6.0 |
| Macedonia, FYR | 962 | 16.5 | 15.7 | 24.8 | 29.9 | 11.8 | 5.7 | 12.1 | 9.5 | 4.4 | 5.2 | 10.6 | 6.9 |
| Montenegro | 943 | 22.5 | 83.4 | 119.2 | 98.8 | −10.1 | −9.0 | 3.2 | 1.9 | 7.9 | 5.0 | 10.0 | 12.1 |
| Poland | 964 | 2.5 | 15.0 | 16.0 | 13.4 | 18.6 | 8.1 | 8.8 | 12.5 | 4.5 | 6.2 | 8.2 | 9.1 |
| Romania | 968 | 48.4 | 20.0 | 14.1 | 33.8 | 17.5 | 9.0 | 6.8 | 6.5 | 2.8 | 8.8 | 8.4 | 9.4 |
| Serbia, Republic of | 942 | 31.9 | 42.2 | 38.7 | 42.1 | 9.7 | 21.5 | 12.9 | 10.3 | 9.4 | 4.6 | 8.7 | 7.2 |
| Turkey | 186 | 20.8 | 35.8 | 22.2 | 15.2 | 24.9 | 12.7 | 18.5 | 15.2 | 10.4 | 21.2 | 11.2 | 16.5 |
| **CIS** | | | | | | | | | | | | | |
| Armenia | 911 | 22.3 | 27.8 | 32.9 | 42.3 | 2.4 | 15.1 | 11.8 | 23.7 | 19.5 | 14.8 | 8.3 | 10.8 |
| Azerbaijan, Republic of | 912 | 47.5 | 22.1 | 86.8 | 71.7 | 44.0 | −.3 | 24.3 | 32.1 | 20.7 | 15.0 | 11.8 | −1.1 |
| Belarus | 913 | 47.8 | 42.2 | 39.3 | 40.0 | 26.3 | 23.1 | 31.9 | 121.2 | 45.1 | 19.8 | 23.9 | 36.5 |
| Georgia | 915 | 40.0 | 27.9 | 42.7 | 46.4 | 7.9 | 7.7 | 30.1 | 14.5 | 11.4 | 24.5 | 13.8 | 19.3 |
| Kazakhstan | 916 | 69.8 | 25.2 | 78.1 | 25.9 | 35.4 | 19.5 | 13.3 | 15.0 | 7.9 | 10.2 | 10.5 | 34.3 |
| Kyrgyz Republic | 917 | 32.1 | 9.9 | 50.2 | 35.4 | 7.7 | 22.2 | 21.1 | 14.9 | 23.8 | 22.8 | 3.0 | 14.9 |
| Moldova | 921 | 38.1 | 34.4 | 23.6 | 39.8 | 15.9 | 3.2 | 13.6 | 10.6 | 20.8 | 26.5 | 5.1 | −3.0 |
| Russia | 922 | 33.7 | 36.4 | 40.4 | 40.6 | 14.3 | 17.3 | 24.6 | 20.9 | 12.1 | 15.7 | 15.5 | 19.7 |
| Tajikistan | 923 | 41.7 | 59.7 | 45.4 | 80.2 | −2.1 | 40.7 | 18.6 | 33.1 | 19.6 | 19.7 | 7.1 | 18.7 |
| Ukraine | 926 | 31.9 | 54.4 | 34.5 | 51.7 | 30.2 | −5.5 | 22.7 | 14.7 | 12.8 | 17.6 | 5.3 | 3.9 |
| **Middle East, N. Africa & Pakistan** | | | | | | | | | | | | | |
| Afghanistan, Islamic Rep. of | 512 | .... | .... | .... | 42.4 | 31.4 | 33.0 | 26.9 | 21.3 | 8.8 | 9.4 | 8.3 | 3.3 |
| Algeria | 612 | 10.0 | 8.8 | 19.5 | 23.9 | 15.7 | 3.4 | 12.3 | 17.9 | 8.7 | 8.2 | 16.7 | 2.1 |
| Bahrain, Kingdom of | 419 | 4.1 | 22.0 | 14.9 | 39.3 | 19.7 | 5.8 | 10.5 | 3.4 | 4.1 | 8.2 | 6.5 | 2.9 |
| Djibouti | 611 | 13.9 | 11.3 | 11.2 | 8.6 | 20.6 | 17.5 | 12.2 | −4.5 | 15.0 | 6.9 | 6.5 | 19.0 |
| Egypt | 469 | 14.4 | 11.5 | 15.0 | 19.1 | 10.5 | 9.5 | 12.4 | 6.7 | 12.3 | 18.9 | 15.8 | 18.6 |
| Iran, I.R. of | 429 | 28.7 | 32.8 | 36.4 | 33.9 | 11.9 | 27.0 | 24.6 | 20.2 | .... | .... | .... | .... |
| Iraq | 433 | .... | 3.7 | 33.8 | 37.1 | 35.2 | 26.7 | 31.2 | 20.7 | 4.1 | 15.9 | 3.6 | −9.0 |
| Jordan | 439 | 10.5 | 21.4 | 12.8 | 12.4 | 21.1 | 24.3 | 9.2 | 2.7 | −2.0 | 14.2 | 7.3 | 5.3 |

# Broad Money

| 35L x | | 2004 | 2005 | 2006 | 2007 | 2008 | 2009 | 2010 | 2011 | 2012 | 2013 | 2014 | 2015 |
|---|---|---|---|---|---|---|---|---|---|---|---|---|---|
| | | | | | | *Percent Change over Previous Year* | | | | | | | |
| **Middle East,N.Africa & Pakistan(Cont.)** | | | | | | | | | | | | | |
| Kuwait | 443 | 12.3 | 12.0 | 21.7 | 19.1 | 15.8 | 13.4 | 3.0 | 8.2 | 6.5 | 9.8 | 3.7 | 1.4 |
| Lebanon | 446 | 10.1 | 4.5 | 7.8 | 12.4 | 14.8 | 19.6 | 12.1 | 5.5 | 7.0 | 6.9 | 5.9 | 5.1 |
| Libya | 672 | 13.8 | 29.0 | 14.1 | 38.0 | 49.2 | 17.4 | −.6 | 24.0 | 12.6 | 6.3 | −.3 | 12.5 |
| Mauritania | 682 | .... | 14.3 | 15.7 | 18.9 | 13.7 | 15.5 | 11.1 | 21.6 | 10.5 | .... | .... | .... |
| Morocco | 686 | 8.9 | 15.4 | 18.9 | 18.8 | 12.8 | 5.8 | 7.2 | 7.3 | 4.3 | 4.0 | 6.2 | 5.3 |
| Oman | 449 | 4.0 | 21.3 | 24.6 | 37.4 | 23.3 | 4.7 | 11.3 | 12.2 | 10.7 | 8.5 | 12.0 | 14.2 |
| Pakistan | 564 | 20.5 | 17.2 | 14.5 | 19.7 | 5.7 | 14.8 | 15.1 | 12.0 | 17.0 | 14.7 | 10.6 | 13.0 |
| Qatar | 453 | 20.8 | 42.9 | 39.6 | 39.5 | 19.7 | 16.9 | 23.1 | 17.1 | 22.9 | 19.6 | 10.6 | 3.4 |
| Saudi Arabia | 456 | 17.3 | 13.2 | 20.4 | 20.1 | 18.0 | 10.8 | 5.2 | 13.3 | 16.5 | 8.4 | 11.8 | 2.9 |
| Sudan | 732 | 30.2 | 43.4 | 32.2 | 10.8 | 16.3 | 23.8 | 26.3 | 17.7 | 39.1 | 13.1 | 17.0 | 20.9 |
| Syrian Arab Republic | 463 | 10.7 | 11.4 | 7.3 | 12.4 | 25.2 | 8.6 | 13.5 | −7.8 | .... | .... | .... | .... |
| Tunisia | 744 | 11.3 | 11.0 | 11.6 | 12.4 | 14.8 | 12.5 | 11.3 | 9.3 | 7.7 | 6.9 | 7.9 | 5.4 |
| United Arab Emirates | 466 | 23.8 | 30.5 | 23.2 | 41.7 | 19.2 | 9.8 | 6.2 | 5.0 | 4.4 | 22.5 | 8.0 | 5.6 |
| West Bank and Gaza | 487 | 4.3 | 3.9 | 6.1 | 20.4 | 13.2 | 6.0 | 9.6 | 4.0 | 6.8 | 10.7 | 7.2 | 10.4 |
| Yemen, Republic of | 474 | 14.6 | 14.4 | 26.1 | 17.0 | 13.2 | 12.8 | 11.8 | .4 | 22.0 | 13.7 | .... | .... |
| **Sub-Saharan Africa** | | | | | | | | | | | | | |
| CEMAC | 758 | 10.3 | 17.9 | 19.3 | 12.4 | 18.4 | 6.2 | 23.8 | 18.2 | 16.4 | 6.4 | 6.4 | −1.3 |
| Cameroon | 622 | 7.5 | 5.7 | 8.1 | 14.9 | 14.0 | 8.2 | 13.8 | 10.1 | −.1 | 11.4 | 13.2 | 8.8 |
| Central African Rep. | 626 | 13.1 | 18.3 | −4.6 | −6.3 | 18.4 | 11.7 | 16.1 | 13.8 | 1.6 | 5.6 | 14.6 | 5.3 |
| Chad | 628 | 3.1 | 32.9 | 49.9 | 5.7 | 26.4 | −4.6 | 25.3 | 14.2 | 13.4 | 8.6 | 26.5 | −4.7 |
| Congo, Rep. of | 634 | 20.1 | 34.4 | 47.1 | 16.6 | 33.0 | 4.9 | 32.0 | 38.1 | 19.8 | 1.1 | 13.7 | −11.7 |
| Equatorial Guinea | 642 | 32.9 | 36.9 | 12.7 | 40.4 | 30.7 | 29.9 | 33.5 | 7.7 | 57.8 | 7.3 | −14.1 | −10.9 |
| Gabon | 646 | 9.7 | 32.7 | 14.3 | 7.5 | 10.8 | 3.4 | 20.7 | 27.1 | 10.0 | 10.9 | −2.6 | .4 |
| WAEMU | 759 | 5.5 | 8.0 | 11.1 | 18.2 | 9.0 | 14.7 | 15.7 | 10.7 | 9.8 | 10.5 | 14.6 | 15.3 |
| Benin | 638 | −9.3 | 22.3 | 18.1 | 19.8 | 26.6 | 8.0 | 7.1 | 8.2 | 6.2 | 17.4 | 17.9 | 7.3 |
| Burkina Faso | 748 | −8.3 | −4.3 | 10.3 | 23.9 | 12.3 | 22.3 | 19.3 | 13.7 | 16.9 | 10.9 | 10.5 | 18.4 |
| Côte d'Ivoire | 662 | 9.8 | 7.7 | 10.3 | 23.6 | 5.7 | 17.2 | 18.2 | 10.7 | 6.9 | 11.4 | 16.0 | 19.1 |
| Guinea Bissau | 654 | 42.8 | 20.3 | 5.3 | 24.9 | 29.5 | 6.9 | 24.4 | 55.9 | −11.9 | 14.9 | 30.7 | 26.8 |
| Mali | 678 | −2.5 | 9.6 | 8.2 | 8.7 | 1.1 | 14.6 | 12.2 | 15.6 | 15.3 | 6.0 | 8.3 | 13.8 |
| Niger | 692 | 20.2 | 6.6 | 16.2 | 23.2 | 11.9 | 18.7 | 21.6 | 6.0 | 31.4 | 10.0 | 25.6 | 4.0 |
| Senegal | 722 | 13.1 | 8.2 | 11.9 | 12.7 | 1.8 | 11.4 | 13.7 | 6.8 | 6.8 | 7.9 | 11.4 | 13.3 |
| Togo | 742 | 18.2 | 2.0 | 22.7 | 16.8 | 18.2 | 16.0 | 16.3 | 15.6 | 9.1 | 7.0 | 13.0 | 20.3 |
| Angola | 614 | 37.0 | 60.5 | 57.3 | 38.6 | 66.2 | 62.6 | 13.2 | 34.4 | 8.4 | 15.3 | .... | .... |
| Botswana | 616 | 10.7 | 14.4 | 9.0 | 31.5 | 21.5 | −1.3 | 10.7 | 4.4 | 10.0 | 8.4 | 4.6 | 19.9 |
| Burundi | 618 | 10.4 | 24.4 | 23.1 | 4.6 | 33.0 | 16.8 | 21.3 | 5.5 | 15.4 | 12.1 | 12.2 | 1.6 |
| Cabo Verde | 624 | 10.6 | 15.8 | 18.0 | 10.7 | 7.6 | 3.5 | 5.4 | 4.6 | 6.3 | 11.4 | 7.4 | 6.2 |
| Comoros | 632 | −2.9 | 7.1 | 12.5 | 9.6 | 11.5 | 13.3 | 19.4 | 9.6 | 16.0 | 2.8 | 8.1 | 17.1 |
| Congo, Dem. Rep. of | 636 | 81.9 | 23.3 | 56.5 | 50.6 | 55.1 | 56.2 | 34.8 | 21.5 | 20.7 | 18.7 | 14.7 | 9.4 |
| Eritrea | 643 | 11.7 | 10.7 | 5.8 | 12.1 | 15.9 | 15.7 | 15.6 | 14.6 | 14.4 | 16.5 | .... | .... |
| Ethiopia | 644 | 19.3 | 18.6 | 20.0 | 22.2 | 23.4 | .... | .... | .... | .... | .... | .... | .... |
| Gambia, The | 648 | 22.5 | 8.0 | 26.6 | 6.8 | 18.2 | 14.8 | 17.8 | 11.2 | 7.3 | 14.6 | 9.0 | .... |
| Ghana | 652 | 27.3 | 19.5 | 39.3 | 36.8 | 39.2 | 24.7 | 31.9 | 34.0 | 25.1 | 19.5 | 37.3 | 25.6 |
| Guinea | 656 | 36.5 | 33.4 | 94.4 | −12.3 | 38.4 | 18.6 | 85.3 | 18.2 | −5.4 | 14.0 | 12.3 | 19.6 |
| Kenya | 664 | 13.5 | 9.9 | 17.0 | 20.4 | 15.5 | 16.5 | 22.4 | 19.2 | 14.4 | 12.8 | 17.0 | 14.2 |
| Lesotho | 666 | 3.4 | 9.1 | 35.3 | 16.4 | 19.7 | 17.7 | 14.5 | 1.6 | 7.0 | 21.2 | 4.0 | 12.6 |
| Liberia | 668 | 45.7 | 34.1 | 34.6 | 42.4 | 42.6 | 43.4 | 28.5 | 38.7 | −.1 | 26.2 | 2.1 | 9.0 |
| Madagascar | 674 | 25.2 | 2.2 | 26.4 | 20.9 | 12.8 | 11.3 | 9.7 | 16.7 | 7.1 | 4.2 | 11.7 | 15.2 |
| Malawi | 676 | 29.7 | 16.2 | 16.4 | 36.6 | 62.6 | 24.6 | 33.1 | 35.7 | 22.9 | 35.1 | 18.0 | .... |
| Mauritius | 684 | 18.9 | 6.6 | 9.5 | 15.3 | 14.6 | 2.4 | 6.9 | 6.4 | 8.2 | 5.8 | 8.7 | 10.2 |
| Mozambique | 688 | 5.9 | 27.0 | 23.3 | 24.2 | 20.3 | 32.6 | 24.6 | 7.8 | 29.4 | 16.3 | 22.2 | 26.1 |
| Namibia | 728 | 16.1 | 9.8 | 29.6 | 10.2 | 17.9 | 63.2 | 8.0 | 11.9 | 6.3 | 12.4 | 7.8 | 10.2 |
| Nigeria | 694 | 20.7 | 22.6 | 36.4 | 64.2 | 58.5 | 17.2 | 6.8 | 13.0 | 16.8 | 12.4 | 5.0 | 2.4 |
| Rwanda | 714 | 30.0 | 18.0 | .... | .... | .... | .... | .... | .... | .... | .... | .... | .... |
| São Tomé & Príncipe | 716 | 1.0 | 45.4 | 31.5 | 34.3 | 36.9 | 8.2 | 25.1 | 10.5 | 18.4 | 15.8 | 16.8 | 13.2 |
| Seychelles | 718 | 14.0 | 1.7 | 3.0 | −8.0 | 28.0 | 7.8 | 13.7 | 4.4 | −2.3 | 25.8 | 25.8 | 3.0 |
| Sierra Leone | 724 | 20.2 | 31.1 | 21.7 | 17.1 | 26.5 | 34.5 | 24.2 | 29.6 | 22.0 | 10.7 | 22.3 | 11.7 |
| South Africa | 199 | 13.2 | 20.7 | 22.6 | 23.9 | 14.7 | 1.8 | 6.9 | 8.3 | 5.2 | 5.9 | 7.3 | 10.3 |
| South Sudan, Republic of | 733 | .... | .... | .... | .... | .... | .... | .... | .... | 34.4 | −1.6 | 21.7 | 116.5 |
| Swaziland | 734 | 10.3 | 9.7 | 25.1 | 21.5 | 15.4 | 26.8 | 7.9 | 5.5 | 10.0 | 15.9 | 3.9 | 13.6 |
| Tanzania | 738 | 13.5 | 34.8 | 21.5 | 20.5 | 19.8 | 17.7 | 25.4 | 18.2 | 12.6 | 9.8 | 15.6 | 18.8 |
| Uganda | 746 | 8.8 | 17.2 | 16.9 | 22.0 | 30.8 | 17.5 | 38.1 | 12.4 | 14.9 | 9.5 | 15.2 | 11.7 |
| Zambia | 754 | 32.0 | 3.3 | 44.0 | 25.3 | 23.2 | 7.7 | 29.9 | 21.7 | 17.9 | 20.8 | 12.6 | 35.2 |
| Zimbabwe | 698 | 229.3 | 532.7 | 1,453.0 | 60,376.3 | 39,072,195,251.7 | .... | .... | .... | .... | .... | .... | .... |
| **Western Hemisphere** | | | | | | | | | | | | | |
| ECCU | 309 | 11.2 | 7.5 | 11.2 | 10.6 | 3.3 | −1.7 | 2.2 | 3.0 | 6.2 | 4.3 | 5.5 | 4.1 |
| Anguilla | 312 | 18.9 | 30.2 | 11.2 | 14.7 | −4.7 | −2.5 | −2.0 | −1.6 | 1.0 | 2.9 | .7 | 3.8 |
| Antigua and Barbuda | 311 | 6.1 | 8.8 | 11.6 | 11.4 | 3.3 | −9.8 | .2 | 1.5 | 2.6 | 1.3 | 1.4 | .2 |
| Dominica | 321 | 6.6 | 5.5 | 11.2 | 10.2 | 5.6 | 10.1 | 2.6 | 2.6 | 11.3 | 3.0 | 5.0 | 3.5 |
| Grenada | 328 | 20.2 | −6.2 | 2.3 | 12.2 | 5.1 | 3.3 | 3.2 | .4 | −5.0 | 3.8 | 6.2 | 7.3 |
| Montserrat | 351 | 8.7 | 4.1 | 6.6 | 4.3 | .5 | 12.1 | .9 | 11.4 | 17.7 | −5.4 | 10.7 | 1.3 |
| St. Kitts and Nevis | 361 | 16.4 | 6.8 | 14.5 | 11.2 | .2 | 4.9 | 6.4 | 9.7 | 12.0 | 11.0 | 10.7 | 4.9 |
| St. Lucia | 362 | 8.0 | 12.5 | 17.4 | 6.9 | 7.7 | 3.0 | 1.8 | 3.2 | 3.3 | 3.0 | 2.8 | 5.4 |
| St. Vincent & Grenadines | 364 | 4.7 | 4.0 | 4.8 | 8.0 | 4.1 | −2.0 | 2.7 | 2.2 | 4.9 | 6.7 | 8.7 | 4.2 |
| Argentina | 213 | 21.4 | 21.5 | 20.3 | 24.5 | 8.1 | 17.0 | 33.1 | 26.0 | 34.8 | 27.1 | 29.9 | 39.6 |
| Aruba | 314 | 2.6 | 6.4 | 2.9 | 3.0 | 16.6 | 5.7 | −.3 | .1 | 8.2 | −3.8 | 5.7 | 9.5 |
| Bahamas, The | 313 | 9.2 | 10.8 | 7.8 | 10.5 | 5.3 | 1.7 | 2.7 | 1.9 | −.3 | .9 | .5 | −.2 |
| Barbados | 316 | 11.7 | 16.9 | 3.8 | 20.9 | 1.2 | .6 | .... | .... | .... | .... | .... | .... |
| Belize | 339 | 13.2 | 6.6 | 16.5 | 15.4 | 13.3 | 6.4 | −.1 | 5.3 | 11.0 | 1.4 | 7.9 | 7.6 |
| Bolivia | 218 | −7.3 | 17.1 | 24.0 | 26.2 | 22.7 | 11.8 | 14.8 | 22.5 | 20.8 | 17.5 | 14.2 | 12.6 |
| Brazil | 223 | 16.6 | 18.5 | 18.0 | 18.7 | 17.8 | 16.3 | 15.8 | 18.5 | 15.9 | 8.9 | 13.5 | 9.7 |
| Chile | 228 | 9.6 | 11.2 | 19.2 | 18.8 | .2 | −4.7 | 7.7 | 22.9 | 10.3 | 11.7 | 8.7 | 9.2 |
| Colombia | 233 | 19.2 | 17.6 | 18.0 | 17.4 | 18.5 | 8.1 | 11.5 | 18.9 | 16.1 | 13.7 | 9.2 | 11.4 |

# Broad Money

2016, International Monetary Fund : *International Financial Statistics Yearbook*

| 35L x | | 2004 | 2005 | 2006 | 2007 | 2008 | 2009 | 2010 | 2011 | 2012 | 2013 | 2014 | 2015 |
|---|---|---|---|---|---|---|---|---|---|---|---|---|---|
| **Western Hemisphere(Cont.)** | | *Percent Change over Previous Year* | | | | | | | | | | | |
| Costa Rica.................................. | 238 | 22.8 | 27.7 | 22.8 | 20.5 | 17.5 | 8.0 | .6 | 6.7 | 10.0 | 8.7 | 14.0 | 3.7 |
| Dominican Republic..................... | 243 | 15.7 | 7.4 | 6.0 | 17.1 | 5.4 | 13.5 | 12.3 | 12.6 | 10.0 | 11.9 | 9.3 | 12.1 |
| Ecuador...................................... | 248 | 30.9 | 19.7 | 13.1 | 18.4 | 23.6 | 8.1 | 18.7 | 16.7 | 16.0 | 13.7 | 11.4 | .... |
| El Salvador.................................. | 253 | 3.6 | 3.9 | 10.5 | 17.4 | −1.2 | 2.2 | .1 | −2.3 | 1.0 | 2.2 | .2 | 6.6 |
| Guatemala................................... | 258 | 10.8 | 13.7 | 13.0 | 10.3 | 8.5 | 11.3 | 9.1 | 7.2 | 9.4 | 9.5 | 7.9 | 9.1 |
| Guyana....................................... | 336 | 9.7 | 6.0 | 17.0 | 13.0 | 12.2 | 10.5 | 15.8 | 13.3 | 12.9 | 5.7 | 3.6 | −7.8 |
| Haiti........................................... | 263 | 5.4 | 17.8 | 3.1 | 11.5 | 12.8 | 13.6 | 26.1 | 6.8 | 7.2 | 7.6 | 7.7 | 23.8 |
| Honduras..................................... | 268 | 18.1 | 17.3 | 21.6 | 16.6 | 4.9 | .6 | 9.8 | 12.4 | 7.0 | 8.3 | 13.1 | 7.8 |
| Jamaica....................................... | 343 | 19.5 | 9.6 | 10.0 | 2.4 | 8.7 | 5.4 | 5.8 | 5.2 | −2.1 | 17.2 | 20.4 | 15.6 |
| Mexico........................................ | 273 | 13.0 | 10.0 | 6.7 | 10.1 | 8.9 | 11.5 | 12.8 | 10.0 | 10.1 | 8.3 | 12.2 | 12.3 |
| Netherlands Antilles...................... | 353 | 11.5 | 5.3 | 13.4 | 12.3 | 6.5 | 17.6 | .... | .... | .... | .... | .... | .... |
| Nicaragua.................................... | 278 | 17.2 | 9.8 | 8.4 | 18.5 | 7.3 | 14.3 | 21.7 | 12.6 | 15.4 | 18.3 | 15.4 | 19.0 |
| Panama....................................... | 283 | 8.3 | 8.7 | 22.5 | 15.9 | 14.1 | 10.3 | 11.1 | 8.4 | 11.2 | −11.7 | 34.3 | 4.4 |
| Paraguay..................................... | 288 | 15.1 | 11.1 | 10.7 | 29.9 | 34.6 | 21.0 | 19.0 | 16.1 | 11.8 | 20.9 | 15.0 | 13.6 |
| Peru........................................... | 293 | 3.3 | 17.1 | 12.1 | 24.1 | 22.9 | 2.7 | 21.7 | 9.6 | 13.8 | 19.0 | 6.0 | 12.8 |
| Suriname..................................... | 366 | 31.1 | 10.8 | 27.6 | 29.2 | 21.1 | 15.0 | 10.7 | 21.4 | 21.3 | 11.0 | 5.4 | 11.8 |
| Trinidad and Tobago..................... | 369 | 19.2 | 26.7 | 19.7 | 11.6 | 16.4 | 17.3 | 1.0 | .8 | 20.8 | 3.2 | 7.2 | 1.1 |
| Uruguay...................................... | 298 | −3.0 | — | 11.6 | 3.8 | 28.6 | −2.6 | 22.1 | 18.0 | 10.0 | 19.2 | 19.3 | 23.8 |
| Venezuela, Rep. Bol...................... | 299 | 50.0 | 47.4 | 72.7 | 33.9 | 28.8 | 23.3 | 23.5 | 49.2 | 53.3 | 58.8 | .... | .... |

# Ratio of Monetary Base to Broad Money

| | | 2004 | 2005 | 2006 | 2007 | 2008 | 2009 | 2010 | 2011 | 2012 | 2013 | 2014 | 2015 |
|---|---|---|---|---|---|---|---|---|---|---|---|---|---|
| | | | | | | | *Percent* | | | | | | |
| **Advanced Economies** | | | | | | | | | | | | | |
| Euro Area | 163 | 10.5 | 10.9 | 11.0 | 12.7 | 14.2 | 13.7 | 13.6 | 18.9 | 20.0 | 15.3 | 14.0 | 18.0 |
| Australia | 193 | 5.2 | 5.1 | 4.7 | 4.6 | 4.5 | 4.3 | 4.1 | 3.9 | 3.9 | 3.9 | 3.9 | 3.9 |
| China, P.R.: Hong Kong | 532 | 8.6 | 8.0 | 7.2 | 6.5 | 9.9 | 18.8 | 18.0 | 16.9 | 17.8 | 16.8 | 16.5 | 18.3 |
| Czech Republic | 935 | 42.4 | 38.0 | 32.0 | 26.7 | 26.2 | 28.5 | 28.6 | 28.4 | 27.2 | 35.2 | 34.8 | 38.7 |
| Denmark | 128 | 8.8 | 8.9 | 7.8 | 6.9 | 8.3 | 7.8 | 6.6 | 8.4 | 15.6 | 12.1 | 8.3 | 9.8 |
| Iceland | 176 | 8.5 | 6.4 | 5.1 | 14.1 | 7.5 | 9.8 | 9.0 | 5.7 | 7.7 | 7.6 | 13.6 | 23.0 |
| Israel | 436 | 16.8 | 17.2 | 18.3 | 20.6 | 18.0 | 17.7 | 19.8 | 18.9 | 17.2 | 16.3 | 18.4 | 16.5 |
| Japan | 158 | 11.2 | 11.2 | 9.2 | 9.2 | 9.7 | 9.9 | 10.1 | 11.2 | 12.1 | 17.0 | 22.6 | 28.3 |
| Korea | 542 | 4.1 | 4.2 | 4.5 | 4.4 | 4.5 | 4.3 | 4.5 | 4.6 | 4.8 | 5.4 | 5.6 | 5.8 |
| New Zealand | 196 | 3.2 | 3.3 | 9.0 | 7.7 | 7.6 | 7.8 | 6.6 | .... | .... | .... | .... | .... |
| Norway | 142 | 9.0 | 9.0 | 6.5 | .... | .... | .... | .... | .... | .... | .... | .... | .... |
| Singapore | 576 | 10.5 | 10.6 | 9.8 | 9.4 | 10.2 | 9.8 | 10.1 | 10.2 | 10.2 | 12.9 | 10.8 | 11.7 |
| Sweden | 144 | 8.4 | 7.3 | 6.5 | 5.5 | 15.0 | 13.2 | 5.0 | 5.0 | 5.0 | 4.2 | 3.7 | 5.1 |
| Switzerland | 146 | 7.5 | 6.8 | 6.9 | 7.1 | 11.1 | 11.3 | 10.1 | 24.0 | 30.9 | 33.1 | 32.7 | 39.2 |
| United Kingdom | 112 | 2.7 | 2.5 | 3.4 | 3.3 | 3.8 | 7.8 | 7.3 | 8.8 | 13.1 | 13.9 | 14.5 | 14.8 |
| United States | 111 | 8.6 | 8.3 | 7.8 | 7.0 | 13.6 | 14.9 | 15.5 | 19.8 | 18.9 | 25.0 | 25.4 | 22.4 |
| **Emerging & Dev. Economies** | | | | | | | | | | | | | |
| **Emerging & Developing Asia** | | | | | | | | | | | | | |
| Bangladesh | 513 | 15.0 | 16.3 | 18.7 | 18.3 | 18.5 | 18.1 | 18.2 | 18.0 | 18.0 | 16.4 | 16.3 | 16.3 |
| Bhutan | 514 | 49.3 | 60.2 | 48.9 | 51.7 | 44.6 | 50.1 | 52.4 | 39.0 | 33.4 | 36.9 | 46.4 | 33.1 |
| Brunei Darussalam | 516 | 13.2 | 15.0 | 14.9 | 14.6 | 15.5 | 13.5 | 13.9 | 19.3 | 20.7 | 21.0 | 20.6 | 22.0 |
| Cambodia | 522 | 62.6 | 53.2 | 48.6 | 44.5 | 51.3 | 54.2 | 52.5 | 54.4 | 46.1 | 44.9 | 42.9 | 41.6 |
| China, P.R.: Mainland | 924 | 24.3 | 22.7 | 22.5 | 25.2 | 27.2 | 23.6 | 25.5 | 26.4 | 25.9 | 24.5 | 23.9 | 19.9 |
| China, P.R.: Macao | 546 | 4.4 | 4.3 | 4.1 | 4.4 | 4.9 | 8.1 | 8.1 | 8.0 | 8.4 | 5.8 | 6.8 | 8.1 |
| Fiji | 819 | 18.8 | 16.7 | 17.0 | 21.9 | 16.1 | 24.3 | 28.6 | 30.7 | 32.3 | 29.1 | 27.5 | 26.2 |
| India | 534 | 22.1 | 22.0 | 21.4 | 22.8 | 20.8 | 20.2 | 20.9 | 20.2 | 19.1 | 18.4 | 18.2 | 18.8 |
| Indonesia | 536 | 19.9 | 22.4 | 25.1 | 26.6 | 22.5 | 23.3 | 21.3 | 22.8 | 22.8 | 23.9 | 23.8 | 22.6 |
| Lao People's Dem. Rep. | 544 | 30.0 | 32.8 | 35.5 | 40.7 | 41.3 | 41.2 | 44.0 | .... | .... | .... | .... | .... |
| Malaysia | 548 | 8.0 | 7.7 | 7.5 | 7.7 | 7.4 | 5.5 | 5.8 | 7.9 | 8.0 | 8.1 | 8.2 | 8.8 |
| Maldives | 556 | 48.4 | 44.2 | 42.7 | 44.0 | 44.4 | 44.3 | 38.2 | 39.6 | 40.9 | 40.7 | 46.0 | 33.3 |
| Mongolia | 948 | 27.7 | 24.7 | 24.8 | 22.3 | 27.9 | 31.7 | 24.8 | 25.9 | 28.5 | 35.3 | 33.0 | 25.1 |
| Myanmar | 518 | 80.0 | 78.3 | 78.7 | 77.4 | 73.6 | 70.9 | 60.8 | 54.5 | 52.0 | 46.7 | 40.6 | 39.1 |
| Nepal | 558 | 30.2 | 30.0 | 29.3 | 27.5 | 25.8 | 24.0 | 23.3 | 26.2 | 24.3 | 26.4 | 23.9 | 25.1 |
| Papua New Guinea | 853 | 22.2 | 18.5 | 16.2 | 20.5 | 16.7 | 15.3 | 15.5 | 21.3 | 22.6 | 21.3 | 28.2 | 25.6 |
| Philippines | 566 | 14.8 | 15.2 | 18.9 | 20.4 | 21.0 | 21.0 | 20.3 | 22.7 | 23.7 | 23.9 | 25.7 | 24.9 |
| Samoa | 862 | 22.6 | 20.2 | 17.4 | 19.8 | 20.2 | 29.2 | 31.1 | 22.7 | 23.9 | 27.4 | 27.9 | 30.0 |
| Solomon Islands | 813 | 58.4 | 48.0 | 40.4 | 31.1 | 28.1 | 39.2 | 60.9 | 63.6 | 67.1 | 59.1 | 50.3 | 54.0 |
| Sri Lanka | 524 | 20.0 | 19.4 | 20.0 | 18.9 | 17.7 | 16.9 | 17.4 | 17.7 | 16.6 | 14.3 | 14.9 | 14.8 |
| Thailand | 578 | 10.4 | 10.3 | 9.8 | 9.9 | 10.1 | 10.1 | 10.2 | 9.8 | 9.7 | 9.5 | 9.6 | 9.4 |
| Timor-Leste | 537 | 10.0 | 8.1 | 8.2 | 14.1 | 13.3 | 21.0 | 18.6 | 10.7 | 24.5 | 17.1 | 24.4 | 33.2 |
| Tonga | 866 | 37.1 | 25.9 | 27.2 | 28.1 | 26.7 | 35.1 | 38.0 | 51.4 | 55.4 | 55.7 | 58.9 | 57.4 |
| Vanuatu | 846 | 13.9 | 13.9 | 17.4 | 16.7 | 15.5 | 15.7 | 19.7 | 20.7 | 22.8 | 28.5 | 28.9 | 31.2 |
| Vietnam | 582 | 28.5 | 26.9 | 27.4 | 25.2 | 25.0 | 22.1 | 17.7 | 18.8 | 19.0 | 16.6 | 16.4 | 17.1 |
| **Europe** | | | | | | | | | | | | | |
| **Emerging & Developing Europe** | | | | | | | | | | | | | |
| Albania | 914 | 35.5 | 34.5 | 32.7 | 30.1 | 33.3 | 32.7 | 28.9 | 27.1 | 26.5 | 26.8 | 27.9 | 31.5 |
| Bosnia and Herzegovina | 963 | 48.2 | 49.8 | 51.1 | 52.1 | 45.9 | 44.4 | 43.3 | 40.6 | 38.9 | 39.8 | 40.5 | 40.8 |
| Bulgaria | 918 | 41.4 | 36.9 | 34.7 | 35.6 | 32.6 | 29.8 | 28.9 | 27.9 | 30.3 | 28.1 | 29.5 | 38.1 |
| Croatia | 960 | 31.7 | 34.6 | 34.2 | 30.4 | 25.4 | 27.1 | 24.1 | 26.4 | 25.1 | † 29.5 | 29.2 | 28.2 |
| Hungary | 944 | 26.3 | 31.3 | 28.6 | 23.0 | 22.3 | 18.5 | 19.4 | 22.6 | 22.1 | 22.2 | 52.1 | 46.0 |
| Kosovo | 967 | 15.4 | 17.2 | 15.8 | 15.2 | 14.5 | 23.7 | 14.2 | 13.0 | 17.3 | 23.9 | 16.0 | 16.4 |
| Macedonia, FYR | 962 | 24.0 | 25.9 | 24.9 | 23.4 | 24.2 | 24.8 | 22.9 | 22.9 | 22.8 | 20.9 | 23.8 | 22.0 |
| Montenegro | 943 | 18.4 | 24.8 | 26.1 | 19.2 | 16.4 | 16.4 | 18.4 | 13.5 | 14.3 | 18.4 | 21.8 | 24.5 |
| Poland | 964 | 19.0 | 17.4 | 18.5 | 19.1 | 20.1 | 19.3 | 18.1 | 15.8 | 18.6 | 17.0 | 18.2 | 18.6 |
| Romania | 968 | 17.0 | 22.9 | 31.2 | 33.0 | 29.0 | 27.2 | 27.2 | 28.5 | 25.8 | 28.4 | 26.1 | 25.8 |
| Serbia, Republic of | 942 | 46.1 | 54.3 | 62.8 | 48.7 | 52.2 | 44.7 | 39.8 | 41.0 | 38.5 | 37.9 | 33.6 | 34.0 |
| Turkey | 186 | 17.5 | 18.1 | 19.0 | 18.0 | 18.4 | 16.5 | 17.1 | 20.6 | 24.2 | 27.7 | 28.1 | 28.6 |
| **CIS** | | | | | | | | | | | | | |
| Armenia | 911 | 46.9 | 57.0 | 59.8 | 61.8 | 63.5 | 62.8 | 57.0 | 59.6 | 52.6 | 59.1 | 53.0 | 49.7 |
| Azerbaijan, Republic of | 912 | 55.4 | 48.2 | 59.5 | 58.4 | 58.4 | 57.9 | 61.9 | 61.1 | 63.5 | 61.1 | 55.0 | 35.5 |
| Belarus | 913 | 27.1 | 33.1 | 28.5 | 28.1 | 24.4 | 17.9 | 20.3 | 16.9 | 18.8 | 17.8 | 16.3 | 13.8 |
| Georgia | 915 | 56.5 | 51.4 | 45.4 | 43.8 | 37.1 | 39.4 | 33.6 | 40.9 | 41.2 | 40.6 | 40.2 | 37.1 |
| Kazakhstan | 916 | 35.0 | 31.5 | 40.8 | 31.6 | 24.3 | 32.7 | 30.3 | 29.1 | 27.5 | 24.4 | 26.6 | 27.6 |
| Kyrgyz Republic | 917 | 63.8 | 93.7 | 70.9 | 72.8 | 75.2 | 72.8 | 70.5 | 69.5 | 66.6 | 60.9 | 53.0 | 50.5 |
| Moldova | 921 | 48.5 | 47.5 | 37.8 | 43.1 | 46.7 | 39.6 | 37.9 | 41.8 | 41.4 | 41.5 | 42.0 | 46.4 |
| Russia | 922 | 45.0 | 40.4 | 40.7 | 38.7 | 34.3 | 33.9 | 34.4 | 30.1 | 30.6 | 28.2 | 26.3 | 21.4 |
| Tajikistan | 923 | 78.0 | 78.5 | 67.2 | 52.7 | 69.7 | 68.8 | 67.1 | 64.5 | 63.9 | 63.1 | 66.8 | 65.3 |
| Ukraine | 926 | 42.8 | 42.6 | 37.2 | 35.8 | 36.2 | 40.0 | 37.7 | 35.0 | 33.0 | 33.8 | 34.8 | 33.8 |
| **Middle East, N. Africa & Pakistan** | | | | | | | | | | | | | |
| Afghanistan, Islamic Rep. of | 512 | .... | .... | 66.2 | 58.6 | 60.9 | 58.0 | 62.0 | 64.3 | 61.2 | 64.3 | 67.4 | 66.9 |
| Algeria | 612 | 33.3 | 31.1 | 29.6 | 30.8 | 29.6 | 33.0 | 34.7 | 35.3 | 38.4 | 39.6 | 38.3 | 41.9 |
| Bahrain, Kingdom of | 419 | 16.9 | 17.3 | 16.4 | 24.4 | 19.8 | 20.2 | 21.9 | 19.0 | 22.0 | 20.1 | 22.1 | 19.1 |
| Djibouti | 611 | 16.2 | 14.6 | 16.7 | 16.0 | 16.2 | 14.8 | 16.6 | 18.3 | 17.8 | 20.2 | 22.0 | 18.7 |
| Egypt | 469 | 28.7 | 37.8 | 45.3 | 45.4 | 36.8 | 34.2 | 34.2 | 25.0 | 23.0 | 29.3 | 28.7 | 29.9 |
| Iran, I.R. of | 429 | 23.0 | 21.2 | 21.3 | 22.5 | 26.4 | 23.2 | 24.6 | 20.9 | .... | .... | .... | .... |
| Iraq | 433 | 82.2 | 92.7 | 88.0 | 105.5 | 116.1 | 96.8 | 88.8 | 81.1 | 84.3 | 82.0 | 71.5 | 68.7 |
| Jordan | 439 | 26.2 | 25.6 | 27.4 | 26.3 | 26.7 | 21.5 | 21.2 | 22.6 | 23.5 | 22.5 | 24.4 | 23.6 |
| Kuwait | 443 | 7.8 | 9.5 | 11.1 | 10.9 | 6.1 | 12.0 | 14.8 | 17.6 | 19.6 | 21.1 | 21.7 | 18.2 |
| Lebanon | 446 | 43.4 | 40.7 | 36.3 | 32.8 | 37.4 | 42.7 | 43.6 | 49.3 | 51.0 | 50.6 | 57.0 | 60.8 |

# Ratio of Monetary Base to Broad Money

|  |  | 2004 | 2005 | 2006 | 2007 | 2008 | 2009 | 2010 | 2011 | 2012 | 2013 | 2014 | 2015 |
|---|---|---|---|---|---|---|---|---|---|---|---|---|---|
|  |  |  |  |  |  |  | *Percent* |  |  |  |  |  |  |
| **Middle East,N.Africa & Pakistan(Cont.)** |  |  |  |  |  |  |  |  |  |  |  |  |  |
| Libya | 672 | 77.8 | 87.5 | 88.2 | 94.4 | 101.0 | 102.8 | 118.1 | 112.3 | 109.2 | 121.7 | 113.4 | 90.2 |
| Mauritania | 682 | .... | 44.2 | 47.2 | 45.3 | 45.9 | 45.8 | 41.5 | 47.7 | 51.5 | .... | .... | .... |
| Morocco | 686 | 30.6 | 30.2 | 28.9 | 27.7 | 25.7 | 23.4 | 21.7 | 21.4 | 20.7 | 20.9 | 19.7 | 20.6 |
| Oman | 449 | 17.1 | 14.7 | 16.3 | 20.2 | 27.4 | 17.8 | 25.5 | 18.5 | 22.9 | 22.4 | 24.9 | 37.1 |
| Pakistan | 564 | 32.7 | 30.7 | 32.4 | 31.1 | 31.3 | 31.1 | 31.5 | 30.2 | 30.1 | 29.4 | 27.2 | 30.0 |
| Qatar | 453 | 10.9 | 10.5 | 9.2 | 19.9 | 12.8 | 21.3 | 34.7 | 10.1 | 12.0 | 9.7 | 10.8 | 9.3 |
| Saudi Arabia | 456 | 17.3 | 16.9 | 16.7 | 14.9 | 15.7 | 15.9 | 16.5 | 17.7 | 18.7 | 17.4 | 17.4 | 18.2 |
| Sudan | 732 | 47.8 | 46.2 | 43.9 | 44.9 | 47.3 | 49.0 | 46.2 | 49.9 | 51.8 | 54.9 | 54.5 | 55.2 |
| Syrian Arab Republic | 463 | 48.0 | 46.4 | 47.5 | 49.0 | 46.1 | 48.4 | 45.6 | 46.3 | .... | .... | .... | .... |
| Tunisia | 744 | 17.7 | 17.8 | 18.2 | 18.5 | 19.6 | 20.7 | 17.0 | 16.8 | 16.8 | 17.1 | 19.3 | 19.0 |
| United Arab Emirates | 466 | 22.0 | 20.2 | 21.7 | 47.0 | 25.0 | 25.0 | 26.2 | 25.7 | 27.6 | 26.6 | 27.1 | 30.3 |
| West Bank and Gaza | 487 | 15.1 | 14.8 | 12.8 | 14.8 | 20.8 | 21.3 | 17.3 | 14.5 | 14.7 | 13.3 | 13.1 | 13.1 |
| Yemen, Republic of | 474 | 48.6 | 51.5 | 47.6 | 45.7 | 43.3 | 42.6 | 41.0 | 46.3 | 43.3 | 38.7 | .... | .... |
| **Sub-Saharan Africa** |  |  |  |  |  |  |  |  |  |  |  |  |  |
| CEMAC | 758 | 51.4 | 55.4 | 57.1 | 59.9 | 59.3 | 59.0 | 59.7 | 53.8 | 58.3 | 50.2 | 56.0 | 49.1 |
| Cameroon | 622 | 49.9 | 47.2 | 55.7 | 63.2 | 55.6 | 55.7 | 55.5 | 48.9 | 53.2 | 44.1 | 42.3 | 43.5 |
| Central African Rep. | 626 | 77.8 | 77.2 | 68.9 | 59.9 | 61.3 | 70.3 | 61.9 | 58.8 | 56.6 | 62.3 | 67.2 | 62.7 |
| Chad | 628 | 78.1 | 76.8 | 79.6 | 81.1 | 78.9 | 76.1 | 74.1 | 73.8 | 70.9 | 72.2 | 69.3 | 66.5 |
| Congo, Rep. of | 634 | 70.4 | 88.7 | 73.7 | 77.1 | 83.6 | 71.7 | 63.2 | 62.8 | 61.6 | 52.0 | 65.9 | 51.8 |
| Equatorial Guinea | 642 | 74.6 | 96.6 | 90.5 | 81.9 | 56.5 | 67.3 | 60.1 | 65.0 | 85.0 | 69.2 | 93.6 | 70.6 |
| Gabon | 646 | 42.7 | 46.5 | 49.1 | 51.0 | 62.6 | 58.2 | 53.2 | 53.5 | 50.8 | 41.5 | 42.2 | 46.3 |
| WAEMU | 759 | 45.1 | 43.4 | 41.8 | 42.1 | 42.8 | 43.2 | 42.0 | 41.4 | 37.0 | 36.9 | 36.4 | 36.7 |
| Benin | 638 | 44.1 | 48.0 | 45.9 | 41.1 | 47.9 | 42.5 | 39.8 | 37.2 | 35.1 | 35.4 | 38.4 | 35.4 |
| Burkina Faso | 748 | 41.4 | 36.2 | 33.1 | 38.1 | 39.0 | 37.4 | 28.5 | 24.6 | 22.3 | 19.2 | 19.9 | 20.7 |
| Côte d'Ivoire | 662 | 47.0 | 44.4 | 43.7 | 44.2 | 43.5 | 46.1 | 46.6 | 48.6 | 42.6 | 42.0 | 41.0 | 40.5 |
| Guinea Bissau | 654 | 85.0 | 95.6 | 80.7 | 78.1 | 69.8 | 66.6 | 64.1 | 59.9 | 59.6 | 54.6 | 67.3 | 66.8 |
| Mali | 678 | 52.5 | 55.0 | 49.4 | 47.3 | 49.3 | 47.4 | 42.4 | 43.3 | 42.8 | 40.9 | 36.1 | 33.9 |
| Niger | 692 | 55.7 | 55.6 | 56.6 | 57.8 | 50.8 | 55.1 | 59.1 | 57.3 | 58.2 | 55.7 | 59.0 | 57.1 |
| Senegal | 722 | 40.1 | 36.4 | 36.4 | 37.9 | 37.2 | 39.1 | 39.2 | 35.0 | 29.7 | 34.0 | 32.5 | 36.6 |
| Togo | 742 | 36.5 | 28.8 | 36.1 | 34.6 | 35.5 | 33.7 | 38.1 | 39.7 | 29.4 | 28.0 | 23.3 | 28.7 |
| Angola | 614 | 37.6 | 38.9 | 25.0 | 28.9 | 28.2 | 30.5 | 30.9 | 27.5 | 26.5 | 26.5 | .... | .... |
| Botswana | 616 | 25.7 | 27.1 | 65.7 | 59.3 | 53.1 | 53.6 | 54.3 | 35.8 | 31.0 | 24.2 | 21.1 | 20.9 |
| Burundi | 618 | 34.2 | 36.5 | 31.7 | 35.1 | 32.9 | 35.7 | 31.2 | 29.7 | 29.9 | 33.0 | 34.4 | 31.0 |
| Cabo Verde | 624 | 29.5 | 29.2 | 25.6 | 25.4 | 25.5 | 25.5 | 23.3 | 21.1 | 26.4 | 27.9 | 31.0 | 29.8 |
| Comoros | 632 | 79.8 | 73.6 | 64.7 | 62.7 | 62.3 | 64.3 | 57.0 | 59.9 | 61.3 | 50.8 | 55.6 | 55.7 |
| Congo, Dem. Rep. of | 636 | 56.0 | 52.0 | 51.2 | 46.8 | 40.3 | 31.9 | 30.9 | 33.0 | 29.1 | 28.3 | 27.7 | 28.8 |
| Eritrea | 643 | 31.6 | 30.7 | 30.4 | 31.9 | 34.8 | 37.0 | 37.4 | 35.8 | 37.0 | 43.0 | .... | .... |
| Gambia, The | 648 | 42.5 | 38.1 | 37.4 | 33.6 | 30.0 | 28.6 | 26.8 | 27.0 | 26.9 | 30.1 | 30.9 | .... |
| Ghana | 652 | 38.4 | 34.4 | 33.6 | 33.6 | 30.8 | 34.4 | 35.0 | 34.2 | 37.2 | 41.7 | 44.1 | 36.8 |
| Guinea | 656 | 57.4 | 49.3 | 51.7 | 62.3 | 52.4 | 77.4 | 67.4 | 61.1 | 56.8 | 57.5 | 58.6 | 49.9 |
| Kenya | 664 | 20.2 | 19.5 | 19.4 | 20.2 | 18.2 | 17.4 | 17.4 | 16.8 | 17.2 | 16.3 | 16.5 | 15.3 |
| Lesotho | 666 | 23.5 | 28.3 | 19.4 | 16.8 | 14.7 | 17.7 | 15.9 | 15.7 | 16.8 | 17.4 | 19.0 | 17.0 |
| Liberia | 668 | 61.2 | 58.0 | 56.4 | 53.8 | 49.8 | 42.3 | 44.4 | 50.1 | 51.7 | 40.3 | 41.2 | 36.9 |
| Madagascar | 674 | 42.6 | 46.1 | 41.4 | 44.9 | 45.2 | 42.1 | 44.2 | 47.6 | 48.8 | 44.0 | 44.9 | 42.7 |
| Malawi | 676 | 38.7 | 38.2 | 34.2 | 31.5 | 25.8 | 29.0 | 24.8 | 23.3 | 29.3 | 30.1 | 34.4 | .... |
| Mauritius | 684 | 12.6 | 12.4 | 12.2 | 11.7 | 11.2 | 12.8 | 15.0 | 15.1 | 15.2 | 17.1 | 17.1 | 16.8 |
| Mozambique | 688 | 30.3 | 27.8 | 27.3 | 26.6 | 23.8 | 22.8 | 23.7 | 23.9 | 22.1 | 22.0 | 21.7 | 22.2 |
| Namibia | 728 | 7.8 | 7.9 | 6.8 | 6.6 | 8.0 | 5.4 | 6.3 | 9.5 | 8.1 | 7.2 | 9.0 | 7.8 |
| Nigeria | 694 | 34.2 | 29.2 | 27.7 | 20.4 | 17.0 | 15.5 | 16.6 | 22.0 | 24.1 | 30.0 | 32.6 | 31.3 |
| São Tomé & Príncipe | 716 | 40.0 | 48.6 | 53.2 | 54.5 | 47.3 | 53.5 | 39.4 | 35.4 | 38.4 | 42.9 | 45.3 | 55.0 |
| Seychelles | 718 | 21.9 | 22.3 | 28.7 | 24.0 | 18.9 | 20.2 | 24.0 | 22.4 | 24.5 | 22.4 | 20.3 | 21.6 |
| Sierra Leone | 724 | 43.4 | 41.0 | 37.3 | 38.0 | 34.7 | 31.3 | 33.9 | 29.5 | 29.5 | 31.2 | 33.4 | 33.1 |
| South Africa | 199 | 7.8 | 7.2 | 7.1 | 6.6 | 6.2 | 6.4 | 6.5 | 6.9 | 7.3 | 7.6 | 7.6 | 7.5 |
| South Sudan, Republic of | 733 | .... | .... | .... | .... | .... | .... | .... | 97.1 | 77.8 | 77.9 | 95.1 | 111.8 |
| Swaziland | 734 | 15.3 | 14.3 | 13.1 | 14.4 | 15.5 | 16.9 | 14.1 | 20.3 | 18.6 | 17.0 | 16.2 | 16.5 |
| Tanzania | 738 | 31.7 | 30.2 | 29.1 | 30.2 | 30.5 | 34.3 | 31.8 | 31.6 | 30.9 | 31.2 | 31.7 | 30.9 |
| Uganda | 746 | 34.9 | 33.9 | 33.8 | 34.9 | 33.3 | 32.1 | 30.7 | 31.3 | 32.8 | 30.3 | 33.9 | 33.4 |
| Zambia | 754 | 34.3 | 39.6 | 39.1 | 34.2 | 35.9 | 34.2 | 39.9 | 25.4 | 32.6 | 32.7 | 38.0 | 34.4 |
| **Western Hemisphere** |  |  |  |  |  |  |  |  |  |  |  |  |  |
| ECCU | 309 | 15.8 | 13.9 | 14.1 | 13.9 | 13.1 | 13.7 | 15.3 | 16.8 | 16.9 | 18.1 | 20.4 | 21.2 |
| Anguilla | 312 | 11.5 | 10.3 | 10.0 | 9.8 | 9.3 | 9.8 | 9.4 | 8.8 | 9.7 | 9.6 | 10.6 | 10.4 |
| Antigua and Barbuda | 311 | 14.5 | 14.1 | 14.0 | 12.8 | 11.7 | 13.0 | 14.4 | 16.8 | 17.4 | 20.0 | 26.9 | 28.3 |
| Dominica | 321 | 16.4 | 16.3 | 17.6 | 17.0 | 13.7 | 14.0 | 14.7 | 16.4 | 16.8 | 16.8 | 17.8 | 21.4 |
| Grenada | 328 | 19.1 | 15.7 | 15.9 | 16.4 | 14.8 | 13.6 | 13.0 | 15.0 | 15.6 | 18.5 | 18.1 | 18.0 |
| Montserrat | 351 | 24.7 | 23.3 | 22.9 | 21.4 | 16.0 | 17.7 | 20.9 | 28.9 | 31.4 | 42.6 | 37.8 | 48.3 |
| St. Kitts and Nevis | 361 | 13.6 | 11.6 | 12.6 | 12.2 | 12.9 | 15.5 | 17.7 | 22.2 | 19.0 | 20.0 | 19.8 | 18.3 |
| St. Lucia | 362 | 17.9 | 14.1 | 13.5 | 13.7 | 13.4 | 13.7 | 14.7 | 14.8 | 16.4 | 14.7 | 18.5 | 20.5 |
| St. Vincent & Grenadines | 364 | 17.0 | 16.6 | 17.9 | 19.7 | 18.6 | 15.4 | 22.9 | 19.2 | 20.9 | 24.6 | 26.6 | 27.6 |
| Argentina | 213 | 44.0 | 36.7 | 43.5 | 43.1 | 46.9 | 47.5 | 47.4 | 46.7 | 48.8 | 49.4 | 45.4 | 46.7 |
| Aruba | 314 | 19.5 | 18.6 | 21.1 | 21.8 | 28.3 | 28.3 | 31.3 | 25.3 | 31.5 | 29.8 | 29.6 | 32.5 |
| Bahamas, The | 313 | 15.2 | 12.6 | 11.5 | 12.1 | 11.0 | 11.7 | 13.6 | 14.1 | 14.5 | 13.9 | 15.7 | 15.7 |
| Belize | 339 | 19.0 | 19.8 | 21.4 | 19.4 | 19.5 | 20.5 | 19.9 | 21.6 | 23.2 | 26.6 | 30.6 | 35.4 |
| Bolivia | 218 | 29.2 | 29.2 | 34.2 | 39.8 | 39.5 | 43.3 | 43.6 | 47.0 | 46.3 | 43.3 | 40.4 | 39.8 |
| Brazil | 223 | 17.1 | 15.6 | 14.9 | 15.2 | 10.7 | 10.2 | 20.5 | 19.2 | 14.3 | 14.8 | 12.5 | 12.3 |
| Chile | 228 | 18.0 | 5.7 | 5.6 | 5.1 | 5.8 | 6.6 | 7.4 | 7.5 | 7.8 | 7.8 | 6.7 | 6.8 |
| Colombia | 233 | 21.7 | 21.8 | 21.9 | 22.4 | 21.1 | 21.4 | 21.7 | 20.9 | 19.8 | 20.1 | 19.7 | 20.9 |
| Costa Rica | 238 | 40.4 | 40.9 | 43.6 | 43.3 | 36.2 | 35.2 | 35.7 | 38.4 | 40.6 | 44.4 | 40.9 | 43.1 |
| Dominican Republic | 243 | 27.1 | 40.7 | 37.9 | 36.9 | 36.1 | 32.7 | 32.6 | 31.2 | 28.9 | 28.6 | 30.2 | 28.1 |
| Ecuador | 248 | 9.4 | 11.6 | 11.5 | 13.1 | 15.7 | 14.2 | 11.2 | 10.8 | 12.7 | 16.1 | 13.8 | .... |
| El Salvador | 253 | 26.4 | 25.1 | 23.5 | 24.4 | 25.4 | 25.3 | 25.0 | 24.0 | 22.7 | 24.5 | 24.6 | 24.3 |
| Guatemala | 258 | 32.6 | 28.8 | 29.4 | 26.8 | 29.6 | 30.2 | 29.0 | 29.5 | 28.6 | 28.8 | 27.8 | 26.7 |
| Guyana | 336 | 28.2 | 29.9 | 26.8 | 25.5 | 24.3 | 27.3 | 30.1 | 28.4 | 29.0 | 27.8 | 29.4 | 34.1 |

# Ratio of Monetary Base to Broad Money

| | | 2004 | 2005 | 2006 | 2007 | 2008 | 2009 | 2010 | 2011 | 2012 | 2013 | 2014 | 2015 |
|---|---|---|---|---|---|---|---|---|---|---|---|---|---|
| **39abi** | | | | | | | Percent | | | | | | |
| **Western Hemisphere(Cont.)** | | | | | | | | | | | | | |
| Haiti | 263 | 53.4 | 50.4 | 53.4 | 52.3 | 54.6 | 53.7 | 61.2 | 58.9 | 60.0 | 53.6 | 56.1 | 56.8 |
| Honduras | 268 | 37.3 | 41.4 | 38.3 | 32.8 | 31.6 | 33.9 | 41.4 | 40.0 | 37.2 | 38.1 | 39.1 | 40.1 |
| Jamaica | 343 | 16.4 | 15.9 | 16.7 | 17.1 | 20.4 | 23.3 | 21.4 | 22.3 | 20.8 | 23.4 | 41.4 | 37.7 |
| Mexico | 273 | 14.7 | 14.9 | 16.6 | 16.6 | 17.7 | 17.4 | 16.9 | 17.0 | 17.1 | 17.1 | 17.7 | 18.4 |
| Nicaragua | 278 | 51.7 | 48.9 | 50.0 | 43.7 | 45.3 | 52.2 | 53.6 | 50.6 | 43.2 | 42.0 | 42.8 | 41.3 |
| Panama | 283 | 7.1 | 6.6 | 5.6 | 5.8 | 5.2 | 5.8 | 4.9 | 4.7 | 4.3 | 4.6 | 3.9 | 4.2 |
| Paraguay | 288 | 46.3 | 43.2 | 42.2 | 43.3 | 36.8 | 39.7 | 34.5 | 35.4 | 34.8 | 30.5 | 31.2 | 31.3 |
| Peru | 293 | 41.3 | 45.9 | 42.2 | 43.3 | 43.3 | 38.3 | 54.7 | 44.5 | 49.1 | 44.5 | 43.1 | 47.6 |
| Suriname | 366 | 27.0 | 26.3 | 27.5 | 27.8 | 25.7 | 29.4 | 30.2 | 26.8 | 29.8 | 26.7 | 23.1 | 24.5 |
| Trinidad and Tobago | 369 | 18.3 | 20.9 | 20.2 | 20.3 | 24.8 | 29.2 | 32.7 | 37.6 | 36.4 | 38.6 | 36.3 | 30.9 |
| Uruguay | 298 | 8.2 | 12.8 | 12.6 | 14.1 | 14.2 | 15.6 | 14.8 | 14.7 | 17.0 | 16.1 | 13.7 | 11.8 |
| Venezuela, Rep. Bol | 299 | 35.0 | 32.4 | 35.6 | 39.4 | 39.1 | 39.4 | 39.3 | 39.5 | 36.8 | 38.8 | . . . . | . . . . |

# Income Velocity of Broad Money

| 39adi | | 2004 | 2005 | 2006 | 2007 | 2008 | 2009 | 2010 | 2011 | 2012 | 2013 | 2014 | 2015 |
|---|---|---|---|---|---|---|---|---|---|---|---|---|---|
| | | | | | | | | *Index Numbers: 2010=100* | | | | | |
| **Advanced Economies** | | | | | | | | | | | | | |
| Euro Area | 163 | 120 | 115 | 111 | 105 | 99 | 97 | 100 | 101 | 99 | 99 | 100 | 97 |
| Australia | 193 | 129 | 128 | 120 | 111 | 103 | 102 | 100 | 99 | 96 | 93 | 89 | 85 |
| Canada | 156 | 103 | 100 | 93 | 133 | 121 | .... | .... | .... | .... | .... | .... | .... |
| China, P.R.: Hong Kong | 532 | 125 | 129 | 119 | 109 | 109 | 100 | 100 | 99 | .... | .... | .... | .... |
| Czech Republic | 935 | 131 | 125 | 119 | 112 | 104 | 101 | 100 | 99 | 95 | 91 | 89 | 87 |
| Denmark | 128 | 151 | 139 | 132 | 117 | 113 | 103 | 100 | 108 | 108 | 121 | 107 | 101 |
| Iceland | 176 | 155 | 135 | 95 | 103 | 88 | 88 | 100 | 99 | 109 | 110 | 107 | 110 |
| Israel | 436 | 79 | 76 | 76 | 105 | 97 | 96 | 100 | 96 | 96 | 94 | 86 | 87 |
| Japan | 158 | 110 | 109 | 111 | 111 | 108 | 99 | 100 | 94 | .... | .... | .... | .... |
| Korea | 542 | 120 | 118 | 110 | 107 | 102 | 96 | 100 | 100 | 98 | 98 | 94 | 91 |
| New Zealand | 196 | 122 | 119 | 113 | 107 | 105 | 107 | 100 | .... | .... | .... | .... | .... |
| Norway | 142 | 100 | 100 | 96 | .... | .... | .... | .... | .... | .... | .... | .... | .... |
| Singapore | 576 | 120 | 123 | 115 | 117 | 105 | 95 | 100 | 96 | .... | .... | .... | .... |
| Sweden | 144 | 135 | 120 | 112 | 100 | 100 | 97 | 100 | 97 | 95 | 94 | 93 | 93 |
| Switzerland | 146 | 112 | 108 | 109 | 112 | 112 | 103 | 100 | 92 | .... | .... | .... | .... |
| United Kingdom | 112 | 151 | 139 | 129 | 118 | 102 | 99 | 100 | 108 | .... | .... | .... | .... |
| United States | 111 | 119 | 117 | 114 | 107 | 101 | 93 | 100 | 97 | 96 | 95 | 94 | 94 |
| **Emerging & Dev. Economies** | | | | | | | | | | | | | |
| **Emerging & Developing Asia** | | | | | | | | | | | | | |
| Bangladesh | 513 | 112 | 108 | 116 | 117 | 115 | 107 | 100 | 97 | 97 | 96 | 93 | 91 |
| Bhutan | 514 | 129 | 120 | 126 | 125 | 107 | 95 | 100 | 115 | 133 | 120 | 118 | .... |
| Brunei Darussalam | 516 | 103 | 129 | 145 | 138 | 139 | 97 | 100 | 111 | 113 | 106 | 110 | .... |
| Cambodia | 522 | 208 | 216 | 178 | 129 | 147 | 111 | 100 | 106 | 83 | 78 | 66 | .... |
| China, P.R.: Mainland | 924 | 119 | 118 | 113 | 119 | 119 | 101 | 100 | 100 | .... | .... | .... | .... |
| China, P.R.: Macao | 546 | 76 | 77 | 76 | 86 | 95 | 87 | 100 | 107 | 99 | 101 | 98 | 84 |
| Fiji | 819 | 123 | 115 | 99 | 94 | 103 | 96 | 100 | 101 | 100 | 91 | 92 | .... |
| India | 534 | 122 | 120 | 115 | 109 | 102 | 99 | 100 | 100 | .... | .... | .... | .... |
| Indonesia | 536 | 80 | 83 | 87 | 86 | 94 | 94 | 100 | 98 | 94 | 92 | 91 | 91 |
| Lao People's Dem. Rep. | 544 | 208 | 221 | 202 | 162 | 159 | 123 | 100 | .... | .... | .... | .... | .... |
| Malaysia | 548 | 98 | 104 | 100 | 104 | 108 | 93 | 100 | 97 | 95 | 93 | 95 | 96 |
| Maldives | 556 | 135 | 114 | 126 | 120 | 119 | 106 | 100 | 100 | 103 | 97 | 93 | .... |
| Mongolia | 948 | 155 | 148 | 146 | 116 | 162 | 126 | 100 | 96 | 106 | 113 | .... | .... |
| Nepal | 558 | 135 | 135 | 128 | 120 | 97 | 91 | 100 | 97 | 94 | 86 | 84 | .... |
| Philippines | 566 | 109 | 113 | 101 | 101 | 103 | 99 | 100 | 102 | 104 | 88 | 86 | 83 |
| Sri Lanka | 524 | 91 | 90 | 91 | 95 | 108 | 100 | 100 | 98 | .... | .... | .... | .... |
| Thailand | 578 | 101 | 104 | 107 | 109 | 106 | 99 | 100 | 91 | 96 | 94 | 91 | 90 |
| Tonga | 866 | 104 | 92 | 100 | 91 | 96 | 99 | 100 | 111 | 101 | .... | .... | .... |
| Vanuatu | 846 | 89 | 84 | 89 | 85 | 86 | 90 | 100 | 103 | 106 | 117 | .... | .... |
| Vietnam | 582 | 181 | 162 | 145 | 114 | 123 | 109 | 100 | 114 | .... | .... | .... | .... |
| **Europe** | | | | | | | | | | | | | |
| **Emerging & Developing Europe** | | | | | | | | | | | | | |
| Albania | 914 | 118 | 112 | 105 | 101 | 105 | 104 | 100 | 96 | 94 | 93 | 92 | .... |
| Bosnia and Herzegovina | 963 | 130 | 120 | 112 | 103 | 110 | 107 | 100 | 98 | 97 | 92 | 85 | .... |
| Bulgaria | 918 | 139 | 128 | 115 | 105 | 110 | 105 | 100 | 97 | 91 | 84 | 85 | 80 |
| Croatia | 960 | 138 | 134 | 124 | 115 | 119 | 114 | 100 | 100 | 96 | † 112 | 111 | 108 |
| Georgia | 915 | 191 | 177 | 147 | 124 | 129 | 113 | 100 | 102 | 99 | 82 | 78 | .... |
| Hungary | 944 | 132 | 123 | 116 | 111 | 108 | 101 | 100 | 98 | 104 | 101 | 106 | 105 |
| Macedonia, FYR | 962 | 156 | 146 | 127 | 111 | 112 | 106 | 100 | 97 | 92 | 91 | 91 | 91 |
| Poland | 964 | 138 | 127 | 118 | 116 | 106 | 103 | 100 | 96 | 96 | 92 | 90 | 86 |
| Romania | 968 | 119 | 115 | 121 | 109 | 114 | 102 | 100 | 100 | 102 | 101 | 99 | 96 |
| Serbia, Republic of | 942 | 199 | 169 | 143 | 115 | 123 | 106 | 100 | 101 | 97 | 100 | 93 | 88 |
| Turkey | 186 | 162 | 139 | 133 | 128 | 116 | 103 | 100 | 103 | 101 | 93 | 93 | 89 |
| **CIS** | | | | | | | | | | | | | |
| Armenia | 911 | 176 | 162 | 144 | 120 | 133 | 102 | 100 | 88 | 78 | 78 | 76 | 71 |
| Azerbaijan, Republic of | 912 | 140 | 169 | 135 | 119 | 117 | 104 | 100 | 93 | 81 | 75 | 68 | .... |
| Belarus | 913 | 173 | 158 | 138 | 121 | 128 | 110 | 100 | 82 | 100 | 103 | 99 | 81 |
| Kazakhstan | 916 | 144 | 150 | 113 | 111 | 106 | 89 | 100 | 110 | 113 | 120 | 125 | 91 |
| Kyrgyz Republic | 917 | 153 | 149 | 112 | 103 | 126 | 111 | 100 | 113 | 99 | 92 | 101 | 93 |
| Moldova | 921 | 141 | 123 | 118 | 101 | 103 | 96 | 100 | 104 | 92 | 83 | 88 | 98 |
| Russia | 922 | 165 | 153 | 135 | 118 | 131 | 105 | 100 | 100 | 99 | 92 | 85 | 82 |
| Tajikistan | 923 | 171 | 125 | 111 | 85 | 120 | 99 | 100 | 91 | 92 | 86 | 91 | .... |
| Ukraine | 926 | 158 | 131 | 120 | 105 | 106 | 108 | 100 | 105 | 101 | 89 | 92 | 110 |
| **Middle East,N.Africa & Pakistan** | | | | | | | | | | | | | |
| Algeria | 612 | 111 | 125 | 118 | 105 | 107 | 93 | 100 | 103 | 106 | 100 | 89 | .... |
| Bahrain, Kingdom of | 419 | 140 | 137 | 141 | 118 | 118 | 99 | 100 | .... | .... | .... | .... | .... |
| Djibouti | 611 | 105 | 100 | 98 | 99 | 94 | 87 | .... | .... | .... | .... | .... | .... |
| Egypt | 469 | 84 | 83 | 83 | 84 | 91 | 97 | 100 | 107 | 107 | 110 | .... | .... |
| Iran, I.R. of | 429 | 146 | 137 | 122 | 117 | 123 | 103 | 100 | .... | .... | .... | .... | .... |
| Iraq | 433 | 144 | 191 | 186 | 158 | 165 | 108 | 100 | 110 | 108 | 102 | .... | .... |
| Jordan | 439 | 105 | 95 | 101 | 102 | 108 | 95 | 100 | 102 | .... | .... | .... | .... |
| Kuwait | 443 | 116 | 140 | 143 | 133 | 140 | 95 | 100 | 119 | 128 | 118 | 107 | .... |
| Lebanon | 446 | 104 | 100 | 95 | 95 | 98 | 96 | .... | .... | .... | .... | .... | .... |
| Libya | 672 | 93 | 100 | 104 | 88 | 75 | 47 | .... | .... | .... | .... | .... | .... |
| Mauritania | 682 | .... | 100 | 134 | 112 | 115 | 92 | .... | .... | .... | .... | .... | .... |
| Morocco | 686 | 141 | 127 | 117 | 106 | 104 | 102 | 100 | 97 | 97 | 99 | 95 | .... |
| Oman | 449 | 126 | 130 | 125 | 103 | 121 | 92 | 100 | 103 | 105 | 99 | 92 | .... |
| Pakistan | 564 | 85 | 84 | 86 | 81 | 91 | 102 | 100 | 110 | 103 | 100 | 101 | 98 |
| Qatar | 453 | 122 | 119 | 117 | 110 | 133 | 96 | 100 | 116 | 106 | 94 | 89 | .... |
| Saudi Arabia | 456 | 125 | 139 | 130 | 117 | 123 | 88 | 100 | 113 | .... | .... | .... | .... |

# Income Velocity of Broad Money

| 39adi | | 2004 | 2005 | 2006 | 2007 | 2008 | 2009 | 2010 | 2011 | 2012 | 2013 | 2014 | 2015 |
|---|---|---|---|---|---|---|---|---|---|---|---|---|---|
| | | | | | | | | Index Numbers: 2010=100 | | | | | |
| **Middle East,N.Africa & Pakistan(Cont.)** | | | | | | | | | | | | | |
| Sudan............................. | 732 | 162 | 141 | 123 | 128 | 123 | 115 | 100 | 98 | 92 | 98 | .... | .... |
| Syrian Arab Republic.......... | 463 | 98 | 104 | 110 | 116 | 112 | 106 | 100 | .... | .... | .... | .... | .... |
| Tunisia........................... | 744 | 110 | 119 | 116 | 113 | 109 | 103 | 100 | .... | .... | .... | .... | .... |
| United Arab Emirates.......... | 466 | 107 | 100 | 100 | 82 | 84 | 65 | 100 | .... | .... | .... | .... | .... |
| Yemen, Republic of............. | 474 | 91 | 100 | 98 | 96 | 102 | 88 | .... | .... | .... | .... | .... | .... |
| **Sub-Saharan Africa** | | | | | | | | | | | | | |
| CEMAC | | | | | | | | | | | | | |
| Cameroon........................ | 622 | 131 | 130 | 129 | 118 | 110 | 107 | 100 | 97 | 105 | 102 | | |
| Central African Rep............ | 626 | 109 | 100 | 114 | 128 | 119 | 112 | .... | .... | .... | .... | | |
| Chad.............................. | 628 | 100 | 100 | 71 | 68 | 62 | 56 | .... | .... | .... | .... | | |
| Congo, Rep. of.................. | 634 | 98 | 100 | 84 | 67 | 65 | 55 | .... | .... | .... | .... | | |
| Equatorial Guinea.............. | 642 | 91 | 100 | 104 | 85 | 89 | 46 | .... | .... | .... | .... | | |
| Gabon............................ | 646 | 110 | 100 | 96 | 97 | 104 | 84 | .... | .... | .... | .... | | |
| WAEMU........................... | 759 | 100 | 100 | 96 | .... | .... | .... | .... | .... | | | | |
| Benin............................. | 638 | 168 | 148 | 134 | 120 | 107 | 103 | 100 | 96 | .... | | | |
| Burkina Faso.................... | 748 | 133 | 149 | 127 | 106 | 100 | 111 | 100 | 93 | .... | | | |
| Côte d'Ivoire.................... | 662 | 165 | 158 | 144 | 122 | 127 | 113 | 100 | 85 | .... | | | |
| Guinea Bissau................... | 654 | 183 | 167 | 158 | 139 | 122 | 117 | 100 | 68 | .... | | | |
| Mali............................... | 678 | 95 | 95 | 97 | 96 | 108 | 102 | 100 | 91 | .... | | | |
| Niger.............................. | 692 | 137 | 149 | 137 | 120 | 126 | 111 | 100 | 98 | .... | | | |
| Senegal.......................... | 722 | 117 | 117 | 112 | 110 | 118 | 108 | 100 | 97 | .... | | | |
| Togo.............................. | 742 | 152 | 162 | 138 | 124 | 122 | 111 | 100 | 90 | .... | | | |
| Angola............................ | 614 | 99 | 100 | 86 | 78 | 66 | .... | .... | .... | .... | .... | | |
| Botswana........................ | 616 | 110 | 103 | 110 | 95 | 89 | 86 | 100 | 107 | 103 | 107 | 117 | |
| Burundi.......................... | 618 | 90 | 117 | 103 | 111 | 108 | 106 | 100 | 107 | 111 | 112 | 115 | 115 |
| Cabo Verde...................... | 624 | 105 | 95 | 91 | 103 | 106 | 103 | 100 | 102 | .... | .... | | |
| Comoros......................... | 632 | 150 | 144 | 136 | 129 | 122 | 113 | 100 | .... | .... | .... | | |
| Congo, Dem. Rep. of.......... | 636 | 109 | 192 | 155 | 122 | 109 | 114 | 100 | 103 | 101 | 94 | | |
| Ethiopia.......................... | 644 | 97 | 100 | 103 | 110 | 129 | .... | .... | .... | .... | .... | | |
| Gambia, The..................... | 648 | 152 | 145 | 118 | 119 | 109 | 106 | 100 | 90 | 92 | 88 | .... | |
| Guinea............................ | 656 | 100 | 100 | 64 | .... | .... | .... | .... | .... | .... | .... | | |
| Kenya............................. | 664 | 127 | 129 | 126 | 118 | 118 | 113 | 100 | 100 | 99 | 120 | 117 | |
| Lesotho........................... | 666 | 138 | 138 | 113 | 113 | 113 | 104 | 100 | 113 | 112 | 102 | 108 | |
| Madagascar...................... | 674 | 96 | 116 | 108 | 104 | 108 | 101 | 100 | .... | .... | .... | | |
| Malawi........................... | 676 | 175 | 172 | 192 | 169 | 123 | 116 | 100 | .... | .... | .... | | |
| Mauritius......................... | 684 | 102 | 101 | 103 | 102 | 100 | 101 | 100 | 101 | 100 | 101 | 98 | 92 |
| Mozambique..................... | 688 | 144 | 134 | 129 | 140 | 134 | 108 | 100 | 103 | 90 | 86 | 78 | .... |
| Namibia.......................... | 728 | 169 | 166 | 150 | 155 | 149 | 98 | 100 | 98 | 109 | 113 | 122 | |
| Nigeria........................... | 694 | 113 | 117 | 110 | 74 | 55 | 48 | 100 | 102 | 99 | 98 | 104 | |
| Rwanda........................... | 714 | 99 | 100 | .... | .... | .... | .... | .... | .... | .... | .... | | |
| Seychelles........................ | 718 | 60 | 64 | 69 | 93 | 96 | 112 | 100 | 108 | 130 | 113 | 102 | |
| Sierra Leone..................... | 724 | 149 | 138 | 133 | 131 | 119 | 99 | 100 | 96 | 101 | 119 | 108 | |
| South Africa..................... | 199 | 120 | 112 | 103 | 94 | 93 | 96 | 100 | 103 | .... | .... | | |
| Swaziland........................ | 734 | 104 | 100 | 97 | 86 | 87 | 73 | .... | .... | .... | .... | | |
| Tanzania......................... | 738 | 115 | 98 | 90 | 112 | 114 | 112 | 100 | 102 | 107 | 116 | 111 | |
| Uganda........................... | 746 | 142 | 139 | 135 | 129 | 114 | 119 | 100 | 100 | 111 | 113 | .... | |
| Zambia........................... | 754 | 108 | 125 | 109 | 92 | 83 | 100 | 100 | 99 | 97 | 99 | 102 | |
| Zimbabwe........................ | 698 | 116 | 100 | .... | .... | .... | .... | .... | .... | .... | .... | | |
| **Western Hemisphere** | | | | | | | | | | | | | |
| ECCU.............................. | 309 | 103 | 104 | 105 | 105 | 106 | 103 | 100 | 99 | 95 | 94 | 94 | .... |
| Anguilla.......................... | 312 | 113 | 99 | 111 | 121 | 126 | 103 | 100 | 112 | 107 | 106 | 111 | .... |
| Antigua and Barbuda.......... | 311 | 100 | 102 | 104 | 106 | 107 | 107 | 100 | 98 | 102 | 100 | 101 | .... |
| Dominica......................... | 321 | 117 | 110 | 106 | 104 | 108 | 104 | 100 | 100 | 91 | 89 | 88 | .... |
| Grenada.......................... | 328 | 94 | 116 | 114 | 110 | 114 | 103 | 100 | 101 | 109 | 110 | 109 | .... |
| Montserrat....................... | 351 | 105 | 111 | 110 | 111 | 117 | 108 | 100 | 103 | 87 | 87 | 83 | .... |
| St. Kitts and Nevis............. | 361 | 110 | 112 | 114 | 111 | 118 | 109 | 100 | 96 | 86 | 82 | 80 | .... |
| St. Lucia......................... | 362 | 114 | 107 | 103 | 104 | 99 | 96 | 100 | 100 | 98 | 98 | 97 | .... |
| St. Vincent & Grenadines...... | 364 | 94 | 96 | 101 | 105 | 103 | 102 | 100 | 97 | 95 | 92 | 86 | .... |
| Argentina........................ | 213 | 95 | 93 | 95 | 95 | 112 | 106 | 100 | 101 | .... | .... | .... | |
| Aruba............................. | 314 | 128 | 126 | 127 | 133 | 120 | 104 | 100 | .... | .... | .... | .... | |
| Bahamas, The.................... | 313 | 132 | 130 | 124 | 118 | 111 | 102 | 100 | 98 | .... | .... | .... | |
| Barbados......................... | 316 | 105 | 100 | 105 | 91 | 91 | 91 | .... | .... | .... | .... | .... | |
| Belize............................. | 339 | 131 | 129 | 121 | 111 | 104 | 96 | 100 | 101 | 96 | 98 | 96 | .... |
| Bolivia............................ | 218 | 146 | 138 | 132 | 118 | 112 | 101 | 100 | 98 | 92 | 88 | 83 | 74 |
| Brazil............................. | 223 | 136 | 127 | 118 | 112 | 108 | 100 | 100 | 93 | 85 | 86 | 86 | 84 |
| Chile.............................. | 228 | 88 | 90 | 90 | 84 | 87 | 94 | 100 | 89 | 86 | 82 | 81 | 79 |
| Colombia......................... | 233 | 131 | 123 | 118 | 112 | 105 | 103 | 100 | 96 | 88 | 83 | 81 | 77 |
| Costa Rica....................... | 238 | 103 | 94 | 93 | 91 | 89 | 89 | 100 | 102 | 101 | 102 | 96 | .... |
| Dominican Republic............ | 243 | 82 | 86 | 95 | 99 | 107 | 98 | 100 | 100 | 97 | 93 | 93 | 90 |
| Ecuador.......................... | 248 | 134 | 127 | 126 | 116 | 114 | 107 | 100 | 98 | 93 | 89 | 85 | .... |
| El Salvador....................... | 253 | 100 | 105 | 103 | 95 | 102 | 97 | 100 | 111 | 113 | 113 | 116 | 112 |
| Guatemala....................... | 258 | 107 | 102 | 100 | 104 | 108 | 101 | 100 | 104 | 101 | 99 | 98 | 97 |
| Guyana........................... | 336 | 68 | 68 | 65 | 68 | 66 | 64 | 100 | 101 | 99 | .... | .... | |
| Haiti.............................. | 263 | 114 | 116 | 133 | 133 | 134 | 127 | 100 | 106 | 107 | 111 | .... | |
| Honduras......................... | 268 | 104 | 101 | 93 | 90 | 97 | 101 | 100 | 100 | 100 | 97 | 93 | 94 |
| Jamaica.......................... | 343 | 81 | 83 | 85 | 93 | 97 | 98 | 100 | 102 | 111 | 103 | 92 | 85 |
| Mexico............................ | 273 | 116 | 114 | 120 | 119 | 117 | 103 | 100 | 100 | .... | .... | | |
| Nicaragua........................ | 278 | 80 | 84 | 113 | 110 | 123 | 111 | 100 | 104 | 102 | 93 | 92 | .... |
| Panama........................... | 283 | 106 | 106 | 96 | 101 | 104 | 102 | 100 | 110 | 115 | 146 | 119 | .... |
| Paraguay......................... | 288 | 157 | 158 | 159 | 142 | 122 | 99 | 100 | 99 | 92 | 84 | 81 | .... |
| Peru.............................. | 293 | 137 | 129 | 132 | 119 | 107 | 107 | 100 | 102 | .... | .... | .... | .... |
| Suriname......................... | 366 | 96 | 104 | 120 | 104 | 103 | 99 | 100 | 98 | 94 | .... | .... | .... |

# Income Velocity of Broad Money

| | | 2004 | 2005 | 2006 | 2007 | 2008 | 2009 | 2010 | 2011 | 2012 | 2013 | 2014 | 2015 |
|---|---|---|---|---|---|---|---|---|---|---|---|---|---|
| **39adi** | | | | | | *Index Numbers: 2010=100* | | | | | | | |
| **Western Hemisphere(Cont.)** | | | | | | | | | | | | | |
| Trinidad and Tobago...................... | **369** | 149 | 141 | 136 | 144 | 158 | 93 | 100 | 114 | 93 | 95 | . . . . | . . . . |
| Uruguay........................................ | **298** | 86 | 93 | 93 | 104 | 94 | 108 | 100 | 97 | 96 | 88 | 83 | 71 |
| Venezuela, Rep. Bol...................... | **299** | 140 | 136 | 102 | 95 | 102 | 86 | 100 | 89 | 70 | 61 | . . . . | . . . . |

# National Interest Rates

|  |  | 2004 | 2005 | 2006 | 2007 | 2008 | 2009 | 2010 | 2011 | 2012 | 2013 | 2014 | 2015 |
|---|---|---|---|---|---|---|---|---|---|---|---|---|---|
|  |  | | | | | Central Bank Policy Rates (60) *(End of period in percent per annum)* | | | | | | | |
| **Advanced Economies** | | | | | | | | | | | | | |
| Euro Area | 163 | 2.00 | 2.25 | 3.50 | 4.00 | † 2.50 | 1.00 | 1.00 | 1.00 | .75 | .25 | .05 | .05 |
| Slovak Republic | 936 | 4.00 | 3.00 | 4.75 | 4.25 | .... | .... | .... | .... | .... | .... | .... | .... |
| Australia | 193 | 5.25 | 5.50 | 6.25 | 6.75 | 4.35 | 3.74 | 4.75 | 4.30 | 3.03 | 2.50 | 2.50 | 2.00 |
| Canada | 156 | 2.50 | 3.25 | 4.25 | 4.25 | 1.50 | .25 | 1.00 | 1.00 | 1.25 | 1.25 | 1.25 | .75 |
| Denmark | 128 | 2.00 | 2.25 | 3.50 | 4.00 | 3.50 | 1.00 | .75 | .75 | — | — | — | — |
| Israel | 436 | 3.90 | 4.50 | 5.00 | 4.00 | 2.50 | 1.00 | 2.00 | 2.75 | 2.00 | 1.00 | .25 | .10 |
| Korea | 542 | 3.25 | 3.75 | 4.50 | 5.00 | 3.00 | 2.00 | 2.50 | 3.25 | 2.75 | 2.50 | 2.00 | 1.50 |
| New Zealand | 196 | 6.50 | 7.25 | 7.25 | 8.25 | 5.00 | 2.50 | 3.00 | 2.50 | 2.50 | 2.50 | 3.50 | 2.50 |
| Norway | 142 | 3.75 | 4.25 | 5.50 | 6.25 | 4.00 | 1.75 | 2.00 | 1.75 | 1.50 | 1.50 | 1.25 | .75 |
| Singapore | 576 | 1.46 | 3.19 | 3.32 | .98 | .44 | .31 | .20 | .18 | .18 | .21 | .... | .... |
| Sweden | 144 | 2.00 | 1.50 | 2.50 | 3.50 | 2.00 | .50 | .50 | 1.91 | 1.14 | .75 | — | −.35 |
| Switzerland | 146 | 1.25 | 1.50 | 2.50 | 3.25 | 1.00 | .75 | .75 | .25 | .25 | .25 | .25 | −.25 |
| United Kingdom | 112 | 4.75 | 4.50 | 5.00 | 5.50 | 2.00 | .50 | .50 | .50 | .50 | .50 | .50 | .50 |
| United States | 111 | 2.25 | 4.25 | 5.25 | 4.25 | .13 | .13 | .13 | .13 | .13 | .13 | .13 | .38 |
| **Emerging & Dev. Economies** | | | | | | | | | | | | | |
| **Emerging & Developing Asia** | | | | | | | | | | | | | |
| Bangladesh | 513 | 5.00 | 5.00 | 5.00 | 5.00 | 5.00 | 5.00 | 5.00 | 5.00 | 5.00 | 5.00 | 5.00 | 5.00 |
| Fiji | 819 | 1.75 | 2.25 | 4.25 | .... | .... | .... | † 2.50 | .50 | .50 | .50 | .50 | .50 |
| Indonesia | 536 | 7.43 | 12.75 | 9.75 | 8.00 | 9.25 | 6.50 | 6.50 | 6.00 | 5.75 | 7.50 | 7.75 | 7.50 |
| Malaysia | 548 | 2.70 | 3.00 | 3.50 | 3.50 | 3.25 | 2.00 | 2.75 | 3.00 | 3.00 | 3.00 | 3.25 | 3.25 |
| Mongolia | 948 | .... | .... | .... | 8.40 | 9.75 | 10.00 | 11.00 | 12.25 | 13.25 | 10.50 | 12.00 | 13.00 |
| Nepal | 558 | 5.50 | 6.00 | 6.25 | 6.25 | 6.50 | 6.50 | 7.00 | 7.00 | 8.00 | 8.00 | 8.00 | 7.00 |
| Papua New Guinea | 853 | 7.00 | 6.00 | 6.00 | 6.00 | 8.00 | 7.00 | 7.00 | 7.75 | 6.75 | 6.25 | 6.25 | 6.25 |
| Philippines | 566 | 6.84 | 7.14 | 7.59 | 6.83 | 5.56 | .... | 4.10 | 4.60 | 3.60 | 3.52 | 3.69 | 4.00 |
| Thailand | 578 | 2.00 | 4.00 | 5.00 | 3.25 | 2.75 | 1.25 | 2.00 | 3.25 | 2.75 | 2.25 | 2.00 | 1.50 |
| Vietnam | 582 | 5.00 | 5.00 | 6.50 | 6.50 | 10.25 | 8.00 | 9.00 | 15.00 | 9.00 | 7.00 | 6.50 | 6.50 |
| **Europe** | | | | | | | | | | | | | |
| **Emerging & Developing Europe** | | | | | | | | | | | | | |
| Albania | 914 | 5.25 | 5.00 | 5.50 | 6.25 | 6.25 | 5.25 | 5.00 | 4.75 | 4.00 | 3.00 | 2.25 | 1.75 |
| Bulgaria | 918 | 2.37 | † 2.05 | 3.26 | 4.58 | 5.77 | .55 | .18 | .22 | .03 | .02 | .02 | .01 |
| Turkey | 186 | 18.00 | 13.50 | 17.50 | 15.96 | 15.63 | 6.50 | 1.63 | 5.00 | 5.00 | 3.50 | 7.50 | 7.25 |
| **CIS** | | | | | | | | | | | | | |
| Armenia | 911 | 3.75 | 3.50 | 4.75 | 5.75 | 7.25 | 5.00 | 7.25 | 8.00 | 8.00 | 7.75 | 8.50 | 8.75 |
| Azerbaijan, Republic of | 912 | 7.00 | 9.00 | 9.50 | 13.00 | 8.00 | 2.00 | 3.00 | 5.25 | 5.00 | 4.75 | 3.50 | 3.00 |
| Belarus | 913 | 17.00 | 11.00 | 10.00 | 10.00 | 12.00 | 13.50 | 10.50 | 45.00 | 30.00 | 23.50 | 20.00 | 25.00 |
| Georgia | 915 | .... | .... | .... | .... | 8.00 | 5.00 | 7.50 | 6.75 | 5.25 | 3.75 | 4.00 | 8.00 |
| Kazakhstan | 916 | .... | 8.00 | 9.00 | 11.00 | 10.50 | 7.00 | 7.00 | 7.50 | 5.50 | 5.50 | 5.50 | 16.00 |
| Kyrgyz Republic | 917 | 4.00 | 4.13 | 3.15 | 8.79 | 15.22 | .90 | 5.50 | 13.61 | 2.64 | 4.17 | 10.50 | 10.00 |
| Moldova | 921 | 14.50 | 12.50 | 14.50 | 16.00 | 14.00 | 5.00 | 7.00 | 9.50 | 4.50 | 3.50 | 6.50 | 19.50 |
| Russia | 922 | .... | .... | .... | .... | .... | .... | .... | 5.25 | 5.50 | 5.50 | 17.00 | 11.00 |
| Tajikistan | 923 | .... | .... | .... | .... | .... | .... | .... | 23.80 | 18.00 | 17.30 | 18.67 | 17.50 |
| **Middle East, N. Africa & Pakistan** | | | | | | | | | | | | | |
| Bahrain | 419 | .... | .... | .... | 4.00 | .75 | .50 | .50 | .50 | .50 | .50 | .50 | .75 |
| Iraq | 433 | 6.00 | 7.00 | 16.00 | 20.00 | 15.00 | 7.00 | 6.00 | 6.00 | 6.00 | 6.00 | 6.00 | 6.00 |
| Jordan | 439 | 2.25 | 4.50 | 5.25 | 4.75 | 4.00 | 2.50 | 2.00 | 2.25 | 4.00 | 3.50 | 2.75 | 1.50 |
| Qatar | 453 | 2.60 | 4.50 | 5.50 | 5.50 | 5.50 | 5.50 | 5.50 | 4.50 | 4.50 | 4.50 | 4.50 | 4.50 |
| Saudi Arabia | 456 | 2.25 | 4.25 | 4.70 | 4.00 | 1.50 | .25 | .25 | .25 | .25 | .25 | .25 | .50 |
| **Sub-Saharan Africa** | | | | | | | | | | | | | |
| Angola | 614 | .... | .... | .... | .... | .... | .... | .... | 10.50 | 10.25 | 9.75 | 9.00 | 11.00 |
| Gambia, The | 648 | 33.00 | 19.00 | 14.00 | 15.00 | 16.00 | 14.00 | 15.00 | 14.00 | 12.00 | 20.00 | 22.00 | 23.00 |
| Ghana | 652 | 18.50 | 15.50 | 12.50 | 13.50 | 17.00 | 18.00 | 13.50 | 12.50 | 15.00 | 16.00 | 21.00 | 26.00 |
| Kenya | 664 | .... | .... | 10.00 | 8.75 | 8.50 | 7.00 | 6.00 | 18.00 | 11.00 | 8.50 | 8.50 | 11.50 |
| Mauritius | 684 | .... | .... | 8.50 | 9.25 | 6.75 | 5.75 | 4.75 | 5.40 | 4.90 | 4.65 | 4.65 | 4.40 |
| São Tomé & Príncipe | 716 | 14.50 | 18.20 | 28.00 | 28.00 | 28.00 | 16.00 | 15.00 | 15.00 | 14.00 | 14.00 | 12.00 | 10.00 |
| Sierra Leone | 724 | .... | .... | .... | .... | .... | .... | .... | 20.00 | 20.00 | 10.00 | 10.00 | 9.50 |
| South Africa | 199 | 7.50 | 7.00 | 9.00 | 11.00 | 11.50 | 7.00 | 5.50 | 5.50 | 5.00 | 5.00 | 5.75 | 6.25 |
| **Western Hemisphere** | | | | | | | | | | | | | |
| Bahamas, The | 313 | 5.75 | 5.25 | 5.25 | 5.25 | 5.25 | 5.25 | 5.25 | 4.50 | 4.50 | 4.50 | 4.50 | 4.50 |
| Belize | 339 | 12.00 | 12.00 | 12.00 | 12.00 | 12.00 | 12.00 | 18.00 | 11.00 | 11.00 | 11.00 | 11.00 | 11.00 |
| Brazil | 223 | 17.75 | 18.00 | 13.25 | 11.25 | 13.75 | 8.75 | 10.75 | 11.00 | 7.25 | 10.00 | 11.75 | 14.25 |
| Chile | 228 | 2.25 | 4.50 | 5.25 | 6.00 | 8.25 | .50 | 3.12 | 5.25 | 5.00 | 4.50 | 3.00 | 3.35 |
| Colombia | 233 | 6.50 | 6.00 | 7.50 | 9.50 | 9.50 | 3.50 | 3.00 | 4.75 | 4.25 | 3.25 | 4.50 | 5.75 |
| Costa Rica | 238 | .... | .... | 8.97 | 5.52 | 10.00 | 9.00 | 6.50 | 5.00 | 5.00 | 3.75 | 5.25 | 2.25 |
| Dominican Republic | 243 | 7.00 | 10.00 | 8.00 | 7.00 | 9.50 | 4.00 | 5.00 | 6.80 | 5.00 | 6.25 | 6.25 | 5.00 |
| Guatemala | 258 | .... | 4.25 | 5.00 | 6.50 | 7.25 | 4.50 | 4.50 | 5.50 | 5.00 | 5.00 | 4.00 | 3.00 |
| Guyana | 336 | 6.00 | 6.00 | 6.75 | 6.50 | 6.75 | 6.75 | 6.25 | 5.50 | 5.25 | 5.00 | 5.00 | 5.00 |
| Honduras | 268 | .... | 7.00 | 6.00 | 7.50 | 7.75 | 4.50 | 4.50 | 5.50 | 7.00 | 7.00 | 7.00 | 6.25 |
| Mexico | 273 | .... | .... | .... | .... | 8.25 | 4.50 | 4.50 | 4.50 | 4.50 | 3.50 | 3.00 | 3.25 |
| Paraguay | 288 | .... | .... | .... | .... | .... | .... | .... | 7.25 | 5.50 | 6.00 | 6.75 | 5.75 |
| Peru | 293 | 3.00 | 3.25 | 4.50 | 5.00 | 6.50 | 1.25 | 3.00 | 4.25 | 4.25 | 4.00 | 3.50 | 3.75 |
| Suriname | 366 | 14.00 | 14.00 | 14.00 | 10.00 | 9.00 | 9.00 | 9.00 | 9.00 | 9.00 | 9.00 | 12.50 | 12.50 |
| Uruguay | 298 | .... | .... | .... | .... | 7.75 | 6.25 | 6.50 | 8.75 | 9.00 | 9.25 | 9.25 | 9.25 |

# National Interest Rates

| | | 2004 | 2005 | 2006 | 2007 | 2008 | 2009 | 2010 | 2011 | 2012 | 2013 | 2014 | 2015 |
|---|---|---|---|---|---|---|---|---|---|---|---|---|---|
| | | | | | | Central Bank Discount Rates (60.a) | | | | | | | |
| | | | | | | *(End of period in percent per annum)* | | | | | | | |
| **Advanced Economies** | | | | | | | | | | | | | |
| Euro Area | 163 | 3.00 | 3.25 | 4.50 | 5.00 | 3.00 | 1.75 | 1.75 | 1.75 | 1.50 | .75 | .30 | .30 |
| Cyprus | 423 | 5.50 | 4.25 | 4.50 | 5.00 | .... | .... | .... | .... | .... | .... | .... | .... |
| Latvia | 941 | 4.00 | 4.00 | 5.00 | 6.00 | 6.00 | 4.00 | 3.50 | 3.50 | 2.50 | .25 | .... | .... |
| Malta | 181 | 3.00 | 3.25 | 3.75 | 4.00 | .... | .... | .... | .... | .... | .... | .... | .... |
| Slovenia | 961 | 5.00 | 5.00 | 4.50 | .... | .... | .... | .... | .... | .... | .... | .... | .... |
| China, P.R.: Hong Kong | 532 | 3.75 | 5.75 | 6.75 | 5.75 | .50 | .50 | .50 | .50 | .50 | .50 | .50 | .75 |
| Iceland | 176 | 10.25 | 12.00 | 15.25 | 15.25 | 22.00 | 14.55 | 5.50 | 5.75 | 7.00 | 7.00 | 6.25 | 7.50 |
| Israel | 436 | 3.98 | 4.60 | 5.13 | 4.08 | 2.53 | 1.01 | 2.02 | 2.79 | 2.02 | 1.01 | .25 | .10 |
| Japan | 158 | .10 | .10 | .40 | .75 | .30 | .30 | .30 | .30 | .30 | .30 | .30 | .30 |
| Korea | 542 | 2.00 | 2.00 | 2.75 | 3.25 | 1.75 | 1.25 | 1.25 | 1.50 | 1.25 | 1.00 | 1.00 | .75 |
| United States | 111 | 3.25 | 5.25 | 6.25 | 4.75 | .50 | .50 | .75 | .75 | .75 | .75 | .75 | 1.00 |
| **Emerging & Dev. Economies** | | | | | | | | | | | | | |
| **Emerging & Developing Asia** | | | | | | | | | | | | | |
| China, P.R.: Mainland | 924 | 3.33 | 3.33 | 3.33 | 3.33 | 2.79 | 2.79 | 3.25 | 3.25 | 3.25 | 3.25 | 3.25 | † 2.90 |
| Fiji | 819 | 2.25 | 2.75 | 5.25 | 9.25 | 6.32 | 3.50 | 3.00 | 1.00 | 1.00 | 1.00 | 1.00 | 1.00 |
| India | 534 | 6.00 | 6.00 | 6.00 | 6.00 | 6.00 | 6.00 | 6.00 | 6.00 | 9.00 | 8.75 | 9.00 | 7.75 |
| Lao People's Dem. Rep | 544 | 20.00 | 20.00 | 20.00 | 12.67 | 7.67 | 4.75 | 4.33 | .... | .... | .... | .... | .... |
| Maldives | 556 | 18.00 | 18.00 | † 12.00 | 13.00 | 13.00 | 13.00 | † 16.00 | 16.00 | 16.00 | 12.00 | 10.00 | 10.00 |
| Myanmar | 518 | 10.00 | 10.00 | 12.00 | 12.00 | 12.00 | 12.00 | 12.00 | 12.00 | 10.00 | 10.00 | 10.00 | 10.00 |
| Nepal | 558 | 1.50 | 1.50 | 1.50 | 1.50 | 1.50 | 1.50 | 1.50 | 1.50 | 1.50 | 1.00 | 1.00 | 1.00 |
| Papua New Guinea | 853 | 12.67 | 9.67 | 8.13 | 7.38 | 7.00 | 6.92 | 6.00 | 6.35 | 6.42 | 23.56 | 36.50 | 36.50 |
| Philippines | 566 | 6.64 | 6.63 | 5.40 | 3.73 | 4.80 | 3.92 | 3.88 | 4.35 | 3.90 | 3.51 | 3.72 | 4.08 |
| Sri Lanka | 524 | 15.00 | 15.00 | 15.00 | 15.00 | 15.00 | 15.00 | 15.00 | 15.00 | 15.00 | 15.00 | 15.00 | 15.00 |
| Thailand | 578 | 3.50 | 5.50 | 6.50 | 3.75 | 3.25 | 1.75 | 2.50 | 3.75 | 3.25 | 2.75 | 2.50 | 2.00 |
| Vanuatu | 846 | 6.50 | 6.25 | 6.00 | 6.00 | 6.00 | 6.00 | 6.00 | 6.00 | 6.00 | 5.50 | 5.25 | 1.85 |
| **Europe** | | | | | | | | | | | | | |
| **Emerging & Developing Europe** | | | | | | | | | | | | | |
| Croatia | 960 | 4.50 | 4.50 | 4.50 | 9.00 | 9.00 | 9.00 | 9.00 | 7.00 | 7.00 | 7.00 | .... | .... |
| Hungary | 944 | 9.50 | 6.00 | 8.00 | 7.50 | 10.00 | 6.25 | 5.75 | 7.00 | 5.75 | 3.00 | 2.10 | 1.35 |
| Macedonia, FYR | 962 | 6.50 | 6.50 | 6.50 | 6.50 | 6.50 | 6.50 | † 5.00 | 4.00 | 3.75 | 3.50 | 3.25 | 3.25 |
| Romania | 968 | 20.27 | 9.59 | 8.56 | 7.46 | 9.75 | 9.33 | 6.67 | 6.21 | 5.31 | 4.81 | 3.31 | 1.92 |
| Turkey | 186 | 38.00 | 23.00 | 27.00 | 25.00 | 25.00 | 15.00 | 14.00 | 17.00 | 13.50 | 10.25 | 9.00 | 9.00 |
| **CIS** | | | | | | | | | | | | | |
| Kyrgyz Republic | 917 | 4.80 | 6.20 | 4.73 | 13.19 | 18.26 | 1.08 | 6.60 | 16.33 | 3.19 | .... | 11.50 | 12.00 |
| **Middle East,N.Africa & Pakistan** | | | | | | | | | | | | | |
| Algeria | 612 | 4.00 | 4.00 | 4.00 | 4.00 | 4.00 | 4.00 | 4.00 | 4.00 | 4.00 | 4.00 | 4.00 | 4.00 |
| Egypt | 469 | 10.00 | 10.00 | 9.00 | 9.00 | 11.50 | 8.50 | 8.50 | 9.50 | 9.50 | 8.75 | 9.75 | 9.75 |
| Jordan | 439 | 3.75 | 6.50 | 7.50 | 7.00 | 6.25 | 4.75 | 4.25 | 4.50 | 5.00 | 4.50 | 4.25 | 3.75 |
| Kuwait | 443 | 4.75 | 6.00 | 6.25 | 6.25 | 3.75 | 3.00 | 2.50 | 2.50 | 2.00 | 2.00 | 2.00 | 2.25 |
| Lebanon | 446 | 20.00 | 12.00 | 12.00 | 12.00 | 12.00 | 10.00 | 10.00 | 10.00 | 10.00 | 10.00 | 10.00 | 10.00 |
| Libya | 672 | 4.00 | 4.00 | 4.00 | 4.00 | 5.00 | 3.00 | 3.00 | 3.00 | 3.00 | 3.00 | 3.00 | .... |
| Mauritania | 682 | 11.00 | 14.00 | 14.00 | 12.00 | 12.00 | 9.00 | 9.00 | 9.00 | 9.00 | .... | 9.00 | .... |
| Morocco | 686 | 3.25 | 3.25 | 3.25 | 3.25 | 3.32 | 3.31 | 3.25 | 3.25 | 3.04 | 3.00 | 2.92 | 2.50 |
| Oman | 449 | 7.50 | 7.50 | 7.50 | 7.50 | 7.50 | 7.50 | 7.50 | 7.50 | 7.50 | 7.50 | 7.50 | 7.50 |
| Pakistan | 564 | 7.50 | 9.00 | 9.50 | 10.00 | 15.00 | 12.50 | 14.00 | 12.00 | 9.50 | 10.00 | 9.50 | 6.50 |
| Syrian Arab Republic | 463 | 5.00 | 5.00 | 5.00 | 5.00 | 5.00 | 5.00 | 5.00 | .... | .... | .... | .... | .... |
| **Sub-Saharan Africa** | | | | | | | | | | | | | |
| CEMAC | 758 | 6.00 | 5.50 | 5.25 | 5.25 | 4.75 | 4.25 | 4.00 | 4.00 | 4.00 | 3.25 | 2.95 | 2.45 |
| Cameroon | 622 | 6.00 | 5.50 | 5.25 | 5.25 | 4.75 | 4.25 | 4.00 | 4.00 | 4.00 | 3.25 | 2.95 | 2.45 |
| Central African Rep. | 626 | 6.00 | 5.50 | 5.25 | 5.25 | 4.75 | 4.25 | 4.00 | 4.00 | 4.00 | 3.25 | 2.95 | 2.45 |
| Chad | 628 | 6.00 | 5.50 | 5.25 | 5.25 | 4.75 | 4.25 | 4.00 | 4.00 | 4.00 | 3.25 | 2.95 | 2.45 |
| Congo, Rep. of | 634 | 6.00 | 5.50 | 5.25 | 5.25 | 4.75 | 4.25 | 4.00 | 4.00 | 4.00 | 3.25 | 2.95 | 2.45 |
| Equatorial Guinea | 642 | 6.00 | 5.50 | 5.25 | 5.25 | 4.75 | 4.25 | 4.00 | 4.00 | 4.00 | 3.25 | 2.95 | 2.45 |
| Gabon | 646 | 6.00 | 5.50 | 5.25 | 5.25 | 4.75 | 4.25 | 4.00 | 4.00 | 4.00 | 3.25 | 2.95 | 2.45 |
| Angola | 614 | 104.17 | 57.92 | 17.88 | 17.88 | 19.57 | 25.35 | 29.17 | 21.67 | 20.00 | 19.19 | 9.92 | 11.00 |
| Botswana | 616 | 14.25 | 14.50 | 15.00 | 14.50 | 15.00 | 10.00 | 9.50 | 9.50 | 9.50 | 7.50 | 7.50 | 6.00 |
| Burundi | 618 | 14.50 | 14.50 | 11.07 | 10.12 | 10.08 | 10.00 | 11.25 | 14.34 | 13.77 | 12.50 | 8.00 | .... |
| Cabo Verde | 624 | 8.50 | 8.50 | 8.50 | 8.50 | 7.50 | 7.50 | 7.50 | 7.25 | 8.75 | 8.75 | 6.75 | 6.75 |
| Comoros | 632 | 3.55 | 3.59 | 4.34 | 5.36 | 5.36 | 2.21 | 1.93 | 2.37 | 1.73 | 1.59 | 1.60 | 1.40 |
| Gambia, The | 648 | .... | .... | .... | .... | .... | .... | .... | 10.95 | 18.54 | 19.08 | .... | |
| Lesotho | 666 | 13.00 | 13.00 | 10.76 | 12.82 | 14.05 | 10.66 | 9.52 | 9.28 | 9.37 | 9.18 | 10.25 | 10.49 |
| Malawi | 676 | 25.00 | 25.00 | 20.00 | 15.00 | 15.00 | 15.00 | 13.00 | 13.00 | 25.00 | 25.00 | 25.00 | 27.00 |
| Mozambique | 688 | 9.95 | 9.95 | 9.95 | 9.95 | 9.95 | 9.95 | 9.95 | 9.95 | 9.95 | 9.95 | 9.95 | 9.95 |
| Nigeria | 694 | 15.00 | 13.00 | 10.00 | 9.50 | 9.75 | 6.00 | 6.25 | 12.00 | 12.00 | 12.00 | 13.00 | 11.00 |
| Rwanda | 714 | 14.50 | 12.50 | 12.50 | 12.50 | 6.56 | 6.27 | 5.47 | 6.53 | 7.46 | 3.99 | 2.77 | 2.36 |
| Swaziland | 734 | 7.50 | 7.00 | 9.00 | 11.00 | 11.00 | 6.50 | 5.50 | 5.50 | 5.00 | 5.00 | 5.25 | 5.75 |
| Tanzania | 738 | 14.42 | 19.33 | 20.07 | † 16.40 | 15.99 | 3.70 | 7.58 | 12.00 | 12.00 | 16.00 | 16.00 | 16.00 |
| Uganda | 746 | 16.15 | 14.36 | 16.30 | 14.68 | 19.42 | 9.65 | 11.97 | 29.00 | 17.00 | 15.50 | 15.00 | 22.00 |
| Zambia | 754 | 16.68 | 14.81 | 8.79 | 11.73 | 14.49 | 8.39 | 7.17 | 9.71 | 10.38 | 12.13 | 17.23 | 16.87 |
| **Western Hemisphere** | | | | | | | | | | | | | |
| ECCU | 309 | 6.50 | 6.50 | 6.50 | 6.50 | 6.50 | 6.50 | 6.50 | 6.50 | 6.50 | 6.50 | 6.50 | 6.50 |
| Anguilla | 312 | 6.50 | 6.50 | 6.50 | 6.50 | 6.50 | 6.50 | 6.50 | 6.50 | 6.50 | 6.50 | 6.50 | 6.50 |
| Antigua and Barbuda | 311 | 6.50 | 6.50 | 6.50 | 6.50 | 6.50 | 6.50 | 6.50 | 6.50 | 6.50 | 6.50 | 6.50 | 6.50 |
| Dominica | 321 | 6.50 | 6.50 | 6.50 | 6.50 | 6.50 | 6.50 | 6.50 | 6.50 | 6.50 | 6.50 | 6.50 | 6.50 |
| Grenada | 328 | 6.50 | 6.50 | 6.50 | 6.50 | 6.50 | 6.50 | 6.50 | 6.50 | 6.50 | 6.50 | 6.50 | 6.50 |
| Montserrat | 351 | 6.50 | 6.50 | 6.50 | 6.50 | 6.50 | 6.50 | 6.50 | 6.50 | 6.50 | 6.50 | 6.50 | 6.50 |
| St. Kitts and Nevis | 361 | 6.50 | 6.50 | 6.50 | 6.50 | 6.50 | 6.50 | 6.50 | 6.50 | 6.50 | 6.50 | 6.50 | 6.50 |
| St. Lucia | 362 | 6.50 | 6.50 | 6.50 | 6.50 | 6.50 | 6.50 | 6.50 | 6.50 | 6.50 | 6.50 | 6.50 | 6.50 |
| St. Vincent & Grenadines | 364 | 6.50 | 6.50 | 6.50 | 6.50 | 6.50 | 6.50 | 6.50 | 6.50 | 6.50 | 6.50 | 6.50 | 6.50 |

# National Interest Rates

| | | 2004 | 2005 | 2006 | 2007 | 2008 | 2009 | 2010 | 2011 | 2012 | 2013 | 2014 | 2015 |
|---|---|---|---|---|---|---|---|---|---|---|---|---|---|
| | | | | | | Central Bank Discount Rates (60.a) *(End of period in percent per annum)* | | | | | | | |
| **Western Hemisphere(Cont.)** | | | | | | | | | | | | | |
| Aruba......................................... | **314** | 5.00 | 5.00 | 5.00 | 5.00 | 5.00 | 3.00 | 1.00 | 1.00 | 1.00 | 1.00 | 1.00 | 1.00 |
| Barbados.................................... | **316** | 7.50 | 10.00 | 12.00 | 12.00 | 10.00 | 7.00 | 7.00 | 7.00 | 7.00 | 7.00 | 7.00 | 7.00 |
| Bolivia....................................... | **218** | 6.00 | 5.25 | 5.25 | 6.50 | 13.00 | 3.00 | 3.00 | 4.00 | 4.00 | 4.50 | 3.30 | 2.50 |
| Brazil......................................... | **223** | 24.55 | 25.34 | 19.98 | 17.85 | 20.48 | 15.17 | 17.30 | 17.55 | 13.59 | 16.49 | 18.27 | 21.00 |
| Chile.......................................... | **228** | 2.25 | 4.50 | 5.25 | 6.00 | 8.25 | .50 | 3.12 | 5.25 | 5.00 | 4.50 | 3.00 | 3.35 |
| Colombia.................................... | **233** | 11.25 | 10.75 | 9.50 | 11.50 | 11.50 | 5.50 | 5.00 | 6.75 | 6.50 | 5.25 | 6.50 | 7.75 |
| Ecuador...................................... | **248** | 10.23 | 9.96 | 9.54 | † 10.72 | 9.14 | 9.19 | 8.68 | 8.17 | 8.17 | 8.17 | 8.19 | 9.12 |
| Paraguay.................................... | **288** | 20.00 | 20.00 | 20.00 | 20.00 | 20.00 | 20.00 | 20.00 | 20.00 | 20.00 | 20.00 | 20.00 | 20.00 |
| Peru........................................... | **293** | 3.75 | 4.00 | 5.25 | 5.75 | 7.25 | 2.05 | 3.80 | 5.05 | 5.05 | 4.80 | 4.30 | 4.30 |
| Trinidad and Tobago.................... | **369** | 7.00 | 8.00 | 10.00 | 10.00 | 10.75 | 7.25 | 5.75 | 5.00 | 4.75 | 4.75 | 5.25 | 6.75 |
| Uruguay...................................... | **298** | 10.00 | 10.00 | 10.00 | 10.00 | 20.00 | 20.00 | 20.00 | 20.00 | 20.00 | 30.00 | 30.00 | 30.00 |
| Venezuela, Rep. Bol...................... | **299** | 28.50 | 28.50 | 28.50 | 28.50 | 33.50 | 29.50 | 29.50 | 29.50 | 29.50 | 29.50 | 29.50 | 29.50 |

# National Interest Rates

|  |  | 2004 | 2005 | 2006 | 2007 | 2008 | 2009 | 2010 | 2011 | 2012 | 2013 | 2014 | 2015 |
|---|---|---|---|---|---|---|---|---|---|---|---|---|---|
| | | | | | | | Money Market Rates (60b) *(Period averages in percent per annum)* | | | | | | |
| **Advanced Economies** | | | | | | | | | | | | | |
| Euro Area | 163 | 2.05 | 2.12 | 3.01 | 3.98 | 3.78 | .70 | .48 | .82 | .06 | .05 | .05 | −.24 |
| Estonia | 939 | 2.50 | 2.38 | 3.16 | 4.87 | 6.66 | 5.93 | 1.57 | .... | .... | .... | .... | .... |
| Finland | 172 | 2.11 | 2.18 | 3.08 | 4.28 | 4.63 | 1.23 | .81 | 1.39 | .57 | .22 | .21 | −.02 |
| Germany | 134 | 2.05 | 2.09 | 2.84 | 3.86 | 3.82 | .63 | .38 | .81 | .26 | .... | .... | .... |
| Ireland | 178 | 2.13 | 2.40 | 3.64 | 4.71 | 2.99 | .48 | .81 | 1.14 | .11 | .21 | .02 | −.19 |
| Italy | 136 | 2.10 | 2.18 | 3.09 | 4.29 | 4.67 | 1.28 | 1.02 | 2.73 | 2.12 | .... | .... | .... |
| Latvia | 941 | 3.25 | 2.49 | 3.24 | 5.07 | 4.09 | 3.92 | .73 | .31 | .24 | .07 | .... | .... |
| Lithuania | 946 | 1.53 | 1.97 | 2.76 | 4.18 | 3.95 | .88 | .22 | .75 | .14 | .12 | .07 | .02 |
| Slovak Republic | 936 | 3.82 | 3.02 | 4.83 | 4.25 | 3.73 | .... | .... | .... | .... | .... | .... | .... |
| Slovenia | 961 | 4.40 | 3.73 | 3.38 | 4.08 | 4.27 | .90 | .57 | 1.18 | .33 | .13 | .13 | −.07 |
| Spain | 184 | 2.04 | 2.09 | 2.83 | 3.85 | 3.85 | .68 | .45 | 1.02 | .27 | .15 | .12 | −.08 |
| Australia | 193 | 5.25 | 5.46 | 5.81 | 6.39 | 6.67 | 3.28 | 4.35 | 4.69 | 3.70 | 2.74 | 2.50 | 2.11 |
| Canada | 156 | 2.25 | 2.66 | 4.02 | 4.34 | 2.96 | .39 | .60 | 1.00 | 1.00 | 1.00 | 1.00 | .63 |
| China, P.R.: Hong Kong | 532 | .13 | 4.25 | 3.94 | 1.88 | .23 | .13 | .13 | .13 | .06 | .06 | .13 | .08 |
| Czech Republic | 935 | 2.39 | 1.99 | 2.32 | 3.17 | 4.04 | 2.13 | 1.30 | 1.19 | .98 | .45 | .36 | .31 |
| Iceland | 176 | 6.22 | 9.05 | 12.41 | 13.96 | 16.05 | 11.15 | 6.92 | 3.94 | 4.80 | 5.35 | 5.17 | 5.00 |
| Japan | 158 | — | — | .12 | .47 | .46 | .11 | .09 | .08 | .08 | .08 | .07 | .07 |
| Korea | 542 | 3.65 | 3.33 | 4.19 | 4.77 | 4.78 | 1.98 | 2.16 | 3.09 | 3.08 | 2.59 | 2.34 | 1.65 |
| New Zealand | 196 | 5.77 | 6.76 | 7.30 | 7.93 | 7.55 | 2.82 | 2.61 | 2.50 | 2.46 | 2.47 | 3.09 | 3.08 |
| Norway | 142 | 2.17 | 2.26 | 3.12 | 4.84 | 6.06 | .... | .... | .... | .... | .... | .... | .... |
| Singapore | 576 | 1.05 | 2.30 | † 3.32 | 2.25 | .80 | .27 | .14 | .09 | .09 | .05 | .14 | .50 |
| Sweden | 144 | 2.28 | 1.85 | 2.37 | 3.66 | 4.38 | .77 | .67 | 2.07 | 1.66 | 1.07 | .52 | −.25 |
| Switzerland | 146 | .55 | .63 | 1.94 | 2.00 | .01 | .05 | .04 | .07 | −.02 | .01 | −2.00 | −1.00 |
| United Kingdom | 112 | 4.29 | 4.70 | 4.77 | 5.67 | 4.68 | .53 | .48 | .52 | .48 | .45 | .41 | .39 |
| United States | 111 | 1.35 | 3.21 | 4.96 | 5.02 | 1.93 | .16 | .18 | .10 | .14 | .11 | .09 | .13 |
| **Emerging & Dev. Economies** | | | | | | | | | | | | | |
| **Emerging & Developing Asia** | | | | | | | | | | | | | |
| Bangladesh | 513 | 5.91 | 9.46 | 11.26 | 7.37 | 10.24 | 4.39 | 8.06 | 11.15 | 12.82 | 7.78 | 7.14 | 6.20 |
| China,P.R.:Macao | 546 | .27 | 4.09 | 3.91 | 3.27 | .30 | .11 | .25 | .38 | .31 | .24 | .26 | .24 |
| Fiji | 819 | .89 | 1.28 | 4.42 | 5.00 | 1.25 | 1.31 | 1.00 | .... | .... | .... | .... | .... |
| India | 534 | .... | .... | .... | 15.29 | 11.55 | 4.49 | 6.51 | 8.80 | 9.34 | 8.58 | 8.64 | 8.14 |
| Indonesia | 536 | 5.38 | 6.78 | 9.18 | 6.02 | 8.48 | 7.16 | 6.01 | 5.62 | 4.01 | 4.83 | 5.85 | 5.83 |
| Malaysia | 548 | 2.70 | 2.72 | 3.38 | 3.50 | 3.47 | 2.12 | 2.45 | 2.88 | 2.99 | 2.99 | 3.10 | 3.21 |
| Papua New Guinea | 853 | 7.79 | 4.36 | 3.29 | 3.00 | 5.50 | 7.67 | 7.00 | 6.98 | 7.67 | 6.75 | 6.75 | 6.75 |
| Philippines | 566 | 7.05 | 7.31 | 7.84 | 7.02 | 5.48 | 4.54 | 4.20 | 4.56 | 4.03 | 2.38 | 2.23 | 2.53 |
| Sri Lanka | 524 | 8.87 | 10.15 | 12.89 | 30.88 | 21.22 | 11.67 | 9.02 | 8.15 | 10.11 | 8.76 | 6.62 | 6.35 |
| Thailand | 578 | 1.23 | 2.62 | 4.64 | 3.75 | 3.28 | 1.21 | 1.25 | 2.80 | 2.89 | 2.54 | 2.00 | 1.59 |
| Vanuatu | 846 | 5.50 | 5.50 | 5.50 | 5.50 | 5.78 | 5.61 | 5.50 | 5.50 | 5.50 | 5.08 | 4.96 | 2.20 |
| **Europe** | | | | | | | | | | | | | |
| **Emerging & Developing Europe** | | | | | | | | | | | | | |
| Bulgaria | 918 | 1.95 | † 2.02 | 2.79 | 4.03 | 5.16 | 2.01 | .18 | .20 | .10 | .02 | .03 | .01 |
| Croatia | 960 | 5.08 | 3.25 | 2.46 | 5.11 | 6.08 | 7.53 | 1.01 | 1.04 | 1.25 | .51 | .... | .... |
| Poland | 964 | 5.67 | 5.34 | 4.10 | 4.42 | 5.75 | 3.18 | 3.08 | 4.10 | 4.66 | 3.01 | 2.48 | 1.66 |
| Romania | 968 | 20.01 | 8.99 | 8.34 | 7.55 | 11.37 | 10.92 | 5.44 | 4.80 | 4.55 | 3.58 | 1.85 | .69 |
| Serbia, Republic of | 942 | 12.86 | 20.51 | 16.51 | 10.31 | 15.55 | 11.01 | 13.10 | 11.04 | 11.89 | 9.11 | 8.59 | 3.86 |
| **CIS** | | | | | | | | | | | | | |
| Armenia | 911 | 4.18 | 3.17 | 4.34 | 4.47 | 6.75 | 6.25 | 6.58 | 7.69 | 8.68 | 8.23 | 8.15 | 13.80 |
| Georgia | 915 | 11.87 | 7.71 | 9.46 | 7.42 | † 14.77 | 5.55 | 5.45 | 7.64 | 5.59 | 3.94 | 3.85 | 5.97 |
| Kyrgyz Republic | 917 | 4.00 | 1.01 | 2.12 | 4.29 | 13.39 | 2.89 | .... | 11.31 | 7.74 | 6.05 | 18.50 | 11.23 |
| Moldova | 921 | † 13.21 | 6.26 | 9.38 | 12.35 | 16.01 | 10.93 | 5.58 | 8.44 | 5.43 | 6.95 | 8.74 | .... |
| Russia | 922 | 3.33 | 2.68 | 3.43 | 4.43 | 5.48 | 7.78 | 3.07 | 3.93 | 5.50 | 6.10 | 8.52 | 12.82 |
| Ukraine | 926 | 6.34 | 4.16 | 3.58 | 2.27 | 13.71 | 12.64 | 3.42 | 7.11 | 12.15 | 4.50 | 12.81 | 21.88 |
| **Middle East,N.Africa & Pakistan** | | | | | | | | | | | | | |
| Afghanistan, Islamic Rep. of | 512 | .... | .... | 2.50 | 5.65 | .... | .... | 2.01 | .20 | .... | .... | .... | .... |
| Algeria | 612 | 1.64 | 1.43 | 2.05 | 3.13 | 3.27 | 3.68 | 3.22 | 2.14 | .47 | 1.57 | 2.24 | .91 |
| Bahrain, Kingdom of | 419 | 1.74 | 3.63 | 5.25 | 5.12 | 3.09 | 1.82 | .38 | .60 | .... | .... | .... | .... |
| Jordan | 439 | 2.18 | 3.59 | 5.55 | 5.70 | 4.94 | 3.33 | 2.19 | 2.56 | 3.62 | 4.10 | 3.16 | 2.29 |
| Kuwait | 443 | 2.14 | 2.83 | 5.62 | 4.88 | 2.80 | 1.60 | .91 | .94 | .81 | .65 | 1.04 | 1.14 |
| Libya | 672 | 4.00 | .... | .... | .... | .... | .... | .... | .... | .... | .... | .... | .... |
| Morocco | 686 | 2.39 | 2.78 | 2.58 | 3.31 | 3.37 | 3.26 | 3.29 | 3.29 | 3.19 | 3.06 | 2.94 | 2.51 |
| Oman | 449 | .66 | 2.25 | 3.40 | 1.47 | .29 | .08 | .10 | .11 | .17 | .12 | .13 | .19 |
| Pakistan | 564 | 2.70 | 6.83 | 8.89 | 9.30 | 12.33 | 11.96 | 11.69 | 12.47 | 10.45 | 8.81 | 9.24 | 6.98 |
| Qatar | 453 | 2.09 | 3.13 | 4.77 | 4.38 | 1.06 | 2.09 | 1.70 | .46 | .76 | .77 | .64 | .89 |
| Saudi Arabia | 456 | .... | .... | .... | .... | .... | .... | .74 | .69 | .92 | .95 | .94 | .88 |
| Tunisia | 744 | 5.00 | 5.00 | 5.07 | 5.24 | 5.21 | 4.30 | 4.43 | 4.03 | 3.77 | 4.59 | 4.82 | 4.71 |
| **Sub-Saharan Africa** | | | | | | | | | | | | | |
| Congo, Dem. Rep of | 636 | .... | .... | .... | 17.40 | 23.50 | 66.50 | 15.50 | 11.50 | 1.50 | 1.38 | 1.38 | 1.73 |
| Ghana | 652 | 15.73 | 14.70 | 10.57 | 12.00 | 15.64 | 21.50 | 13.56 | 10.71 | 14.48 | 17.57 | 21.81 | 24.16 |
| Madagascar | 674 | 16.50 | 16.50 | 14.50 | 11.00 | 11.50 | 9.50 | 9.50 | 9.50 | .... | .... | .... | .... |
| Mauritius | 684 | 1.33 | 2.45 | 5.59 | 8.52 | 7.52 | 4.63 | 3.07 | 2.33 | 1.82 | 1.85 | 1.65 | 1.36 |
| Mozambique | 688 | 9.87 | 6.35 | 15.25 | 15.15 | 12.84 | 8.66 | 10.24 | 14.06 | 5.79 | 3.24 | 3.18 | 3.66 |
| Namibia | 728 | 6.93 | 6.93 | 7.12 | 8.61 | 9.37 | 7.75 | .... | .... | .... | .... | .... | .... |
| Rwanda | 714 | 11.02 | 8.28 | 8.26 | 7.21 | 7.14 | 8.81 | 6.89 | 7.05 | 9.22 | 8.73 | 5.59 | 3.63 |
| South Africa | 199 | 7.15 | 6.62 | 7.19 | † 9.22 | 11.32 | 8.15 | 6.19 | 5.29 | 5.07 | 4.79 | 5.45 | 5.82 |
| Swaziland | 734 | 4.12 | 3.47 | 4.40 | 6.67 | 8.17 | 5.40 | 3.85 | 2.85 | 2.47 | 2.08 | 2.14 | 2.27 |
| Zimbabwe | 698 | 129.58 | .... | .... | .... | .... | .... | .... | .... | .... | .... | .... | .... |

# National Interest Rates

| | | 2004 | 2005 | 2006 | 2007 | 2008 | 2009 | 2010 | 2011 | 2012 | 2013 | 2014 | 2015 |
|---|---|---|---|---|---|---|---|---|---|---|---|---|---|
| | | | | | | | Money Market Rates (60b) | | | | | | |
| | | | | | | | *(Period averages in percent per annum)* | | | | | | |
| **Western Hemisphere** | | | | | | | | | | | | | |
| ECCU | 309 | 4.67 | 4.01 | 4.76 | 5.24 | 4.92 | 6.03 | 6.37 | 5.68 | 5.04 | 6.28 | 6.19 | 6.44 |
| Anguilla | 312 | 4.67 | 4.01 | 4.76 | 5.24 | 4.92 | 6.03 | 6.36 | 5.68 | 5.19 | 6.28 | 6.19 | 6.44 |
| Antigua and Barbuda | 311 | 4.67 | 4.01 | 4.76 | 5.24 | 4.92 | 6.03 | 6.36 | 5.68 | 5.04 | 6.28 | 6.19 | 6.44 |
| Dominica | 321 | 4.67 | 4.01 | 4.76 | 5.24 | 4.92 | 6.03 | 6.33 | 5.68 | 5.04 | 6.28 | 6.19 | 6.44 |
| Grenada | 328 | 4.67 | 4.01 | 4.76 | 5.24 | 4.94 | 6.03 | 6.36 | 5.68 | 5.19 | 6.28 | 6.19 | 6.44 |
| Montserrat | 351 | 4.67 | 4.01 | 4.76 | 5.24 | 4.92 | 6.03 | 6.36 | 5.68 | 5.19 | 6.23 | 6.19 | 6.44 |
| St. Kitts and Nevis | 361 | 4.67 | 4.01 | 4.76 | 5.24 | 4.92 | 6.03 | 6.37 | 5.68 | 5.04 | 6.28 | 6.19 | 6.44 |
| St. Lucia | 362 | 4.67 | 4.01 | 4.76 | 5.24 | 4.92 | 6.03 | 6.36 | 5.68 | 5.04 | 6.28 | 6.19 | 6.44 |
| St. Vincent & Grenadines | 364 | 4.67 | 4.01 | 4.76 | 5.24 | 4.92 | 6.03 | 6.36 | 5.68 | 5.19 | 6.28 | 6.19 | 6.44 |
| Argentina | 213 | 1.96 | 4.11 | 7.20 | 8.67 | 10.07 | 10.23 | 9.09 | 9.98 | 9.79 | 13.10 | 17.90 | 22.01 |
| Aruba | 314 | .11 | .51 | 2.27 | 2.53 | .45 | .05 | .05 | .05 | .05 | .05 | .05 | .05 |
| Bolivia | 218 | 4.05 | 3.53 | 3.80 | 4.27 | 7.68 | 3.55 | .90 | 1.87 | .67 | 1.59 | 4.21 | 1.58 |
| Brazil | 223 | 16.24 | 19.12 | 15.28 | 11.98 | 12.36 | 10.06 | 9.80 | 11.66 | 8.48 | 8.18 | 10.86 | 13.37 |
| Chile | 228 | 1.88 | 3.48 | 5.02 | 5.36 | 7.11 | 1.95 | 1.40 | 4.67 | 5.01 | 4.93 | 3.76 | 3.06 |
| Colombia | 233 | 7.01 | 6.18 | 6.49 | 8.66 | 9.72 | 5.65 | 3.15 | 4.03 | 5.01 | 3.41 | 3.85 | 4.69 |
| Dominican Republic | 243 | 36.76 | 12.57 | 10.60 | 8.24 | 12.24 | 8.08 | 6.25 | 8.29 | 8.07 | 6.07 | 6.45 | 5.90 |
| Guatemala | 258 | 6.16 | 6.54 | 6.56 | .... | .... | .... | .... | .... | .... | .... | .... | .... |
| Jamaica | 343 | 12.79 | 10.96 | 9.37 | 9.04 | 10.78 | 8.79 | 5.44 | 3.59 | 4.70 | 5.26 | 6.71 | 3.31 |
| Mexico | 273 | 7.15 | 9.59 | 7.51 | 7.66 | 8.28 | 5.93 | 4.91 | 4.82 | 4.79 | 4.28 | 3.52 | 3.32 |
| Panama | 283 | 1.90 | 3.13 | 5.06 | 5.05 | 2.57 | .42 | .28 | .30 | .25 | .81 | .90 | .25 |
| Paraguay | 288 | 1.33 | 2.29 | 8.33 | 3.93 | 4.50 | 8.94 | 1.85 | 7.70 | 6.63 | 6.25 | 6.28 | 6.30 |
| Peru | 293 | 3.00 | 3.34 | 4.51 | 4.99 | 6.54 | 1.24 | 2.98 | 4.24 | 4.24 | 4.09 | 3.80 | 3.77 |
| Uruguay | 298 | 3.57 | 1.25 | 1.60 | 4.11 | 9.80 | 8.60 | 6.31 | 7.58 | 8.82 | 10.28 | 10.94 | 11.78 |
| Venezuela, Rep. Bol | 299 | 4.38 | 2.62 | 5.26 | 8.72 | 11.09 | 10.03 | 5.36 | 4.93 | .82 | 1.61 | 6.37 | 3.37 |

# National Interest Rates

Treasury Bill Rates (60c)
(Period averages in percent per annum)

| | | 2004 | 2005 | 2006 | 2007 | 2008 | 2009 | 2010 | 2011 | 2012 | 2013 | 2014 | 2015 |
|---|---|---|---|---|---|---|---|---|---|---|---|---|---|
| **Advanced Economies** | | | | | | | | | | | | | |
| Euro Area | | | | | | | | | | | | | |
| Belgium | 124 | 1.97 | 2.02 | 2.73 | 3.80 | 3.63 | .58 | .32 | .78 | .07 | .02 | .02 | −.24 |
| Cyprus | 423 | 4.44 | 4.34 | 2.56 | 3.59 | .... | .... | .... | .... | .... | .... | .... | .... |
| France | 132 | 2.02 | 2.07 | 2.89 | 3.86 | 3.62 | .65 | .38 | .69 | .05 | .04 | .06 | −.20 |
| Germany | 134 | 2.00 | 2.03 | 3.08 | 3.81 | .... | .... | .... | .... | .... | .... | .... | .... |
| Greece | 174 | 2.27 | 2.33 | 3.44 | 4.45 | 4.81 | 1.62 | 1.35 | 2.01 | 1.11 | .54 | .48 | .17 |
| Italy | 136 | 2.08 | 2.17 | 3.18 | 4.04 | 3.76 | .96 | 1.13 | 2.79 | 1.90 | .86 | .42 | .05 |
| Latvia | 941 | 3.43 | 2.56 | 4.13 | 4.23 | 6.99 | 10.42 | 2.22 | 1.12 | .54 | .... | .... | .... |
| Lithuania | 946 | 2.25 | 2.36 | 2.95 | 4.23 | 5.35 | 8.54 | 2.80 | 2.40 | 1.33 | .61 | .... | .... |
| Malta | 181 | 2.94 | 3.18 | 3.49 | 4.25 | 4.44 | 1.78 | .82 | 1.23 | .99 | .58 | .... | .... |
| Slovenia | 961 | 4.17 | 3.66 | 3.30 | 3.90 | 3.88 | 1.14 | .55 | 1.09 | 1.10 | .... | .... | .... |
| Spain | 184 | 2.17 | 2.19 | 3.26 | 4.07 | 3.71 | 1.00 | 1.69 | 3.04 | 2.66 | 1.17 | .39 | .05 |
| Australia | 193 | .... | .... | .... | .... | .... | 3.15 | 4.44 | 4.56 | 3.49 | .... | .... | .... |
| Canada | 156 | 2.22 | 2.73 | 4.03 | 4.15 | 2.39 | .35 | .60 | .92 | .97 | .97 | .91 | .50 |
| China, P.R.: Hong Kong | 532 | .07 | 3.65 | 3.29 | 1.96 | .05 | .07 | .28 | .22 | .05 | .11 | .04 | .04 |
| Czech Republic | 935 | 2.26 | 1.95 | 2.14 | 2.84 | 3.62 | 1.29 | .95 | .83 | .62 | .... | .... | .... |
| Iceland | 176 | 6.04 | 8.80 | 13.41 | 15.13 | 17.88 | 11.38 | 6.65 | 4.28 | 5.56 | 6.19 | 6.03 | 5.93 |
| Israel | 436 | 4.29 | 5.21 | 4.98 | 4.61 | 2.05 | 1.86 | 2.44 | 2.59 | 1.81 | .88 | .25 | .15 |
| Japan | 158 | — | — | .42 | .55 | .36 | .12 | .13 | .10 | .09 | .06 | −.01 | −.02 |
| New Zealand | 196 | 5.85 | 6.52 | 7.05 | 7.55 | 7.01 | 2.83 | 2.78 | 2.55 | 2.46 | 2.39 | 3.24 | 2.99 |
| Singapore | 576 | .96 | 2.06 | 2.96 | 2.35 | .91 | .34 | .34 | .29 | .27 | .... | .... | .... |
| Sweden | 144 | 2.11 | 1.72 | 2.33 | 3.55 | 3.91 | .40 | .50 | 1.65 | 1.25 | .93 | .42 | −.29 |
| Switzerland | 146 | .37 | .71 | 1.36 | 2.16 | 1.33 | — | .03 | −.14 | −.31 | −.10 | −.13 | −1.03 |
| United Kingdom | 112 | 4.43 | 4.55 | 4.65 | 5.52 | 4.30 | .53 | .50 | .49 | .31 | .30 | .38 | .44 |
| United States | 111 | 1.37 | 3.15 | 4.72 | 4.41 | 1.46 | .16 | .13 | .06 | .09 | .06 | .04 | .06 |
| **Emerging & Dev. Economies** | | | | | | | | | | | | | |
| **Emerging & Developing Asia** | | | | | | | | | | | | | |
| Bangladesh | 513 | .... | .... | 7.52 | 7.61 | 6.01 | 6.29 | 4.50 | 3.88 | 10.77 | 8.67 | 7.18 | 5.76 |
| Fiji | 819 | 1.52 | 1.94 | 7.45 | 4.55 | .22 | 6.07 | 3.45 | 2.20 | .57 | .15 | 1.17 | 1.19 |
| Lao People's Dem. Rep. | 544 | 20.37 | 18.61 | 18.34 | 18.36 | 12.26 | 9.52 | 7.97 | .... | .... | .... | .... | .... |
| Malaysia | 548 | 2.40 | 2.48 | 3.23 | 3.43 | 3.39 | 2.05 | 2.58 | 2.92 | 3.04 | 3.00 | 3.12 | 3.12 |
| Maldives | 556 | .... | .... | .... | 5.50 | 6.00 | 6.00 | 4.90 | 5.44 | 7.26 | 8.94 | 8.18 | 6.83 |
| Nepal | 558 | 2.40 | 2.20 | 1.98 | 3.59 | 4.72 | 6.35 | 6.82 | .80 | .74 | .08 | .13 | .48 |
| Papua New Guinea | 853 | 8.85 | 3.81 | 4.01 | 4.67 | 6.19 | 7.08 | 4.64 | 4.14 | 2.74 | 2.15 | 3.97 | 5.27 |
| Philippines | 566 | 7.32 | 6.13 | 5.29 | 3.38 | 5.17 | 4.16 | 3.51 | 1.34 | 1.50 | .29 | 1.22 | 1.74 |
| Solomon Islands | 813 | 6.00 | 4.53 | † 3.41 | 3.17 | 3.20 | 4.00 | 3.71 | 2.53 | 1.42 | .40 | .23 | .47 |
| Sri Lanka | 524 | 7.71 | 9.03 | 10.98 | 16.60 | 18.91 | 12.93 | 8.57 | 7.63 | 12.10 | 10.68 | 6.60 | 6.65 |
| Thailand | 578 | 1.30 | 2.67 | 4.66 | 3.48 | 3.19 | 1.24 | 1.44 | 2.87 | 2.97 | 2.57 | 2.07 | 1.61 |
| Vietnam | 582 | 5.69 | 6.13 | 4.73 | 4.15 | 12.13 | 8.04 | 11.15 | 12.35 | 8.82 | 6.64 | 5.04 | 4.23 |
| **Europe** | | | | | | | | | | | | | |
| **Emerging & Developing Europe** | | | | | | | | | | | | | |
| Albania | 914 | 6.79 | 5.52 | 5.49 | 5.93 | 6.24 | 6.27 | 5.83 | 5.46 | 5.15 | 4.21 | 3.11 | 2.40 |
| Bulgaria | 918 | 2.64 | 2.23 | † 2.58 | 3.79 | 4.06 | 4.67 | 2.56 | 1.25 | .... | .40 | 1.21 | .... |
| Hungary | 944 | 11.32 | 6.95 | 6.87 | 7.67 | 8.90 | 8.48 | 5.37 | 6.02 | 6.90 | 4.18 | 2.17 | 1.16 |
| Montenegro | 943 | 10.39 | 6.03 | 1.28 | .52 | .49 | 3.18 | 3.20 | 2.66 | 4.73 | 3.25 | 1.35 | .64 |
| Poland | 964 | 6.60 | 4.90 | 4.19 | 4.70 | 6.27 | 4.56 | 3.93 | 4.46 | .... | .... | .... | .... |
| Romania | 968 | .... | .... | .... | 7.11 | 10.42 | 10.90 | 7.21 | 7.32 | 6.27 | 4.89 | 3.86 | 2.46 |
| Serbia, Republic of | 942 | 21.17 | 14.58 | 10.24 | 4.42 | 9.61 | 10.34 | 14.16 | 11.51 | 12.32 | 9.04 | 7.67 | 3.89 |
| **CIS** | | | | | | | | | | | | | |
| Armenia | 911 | 5.27 | 4.05 | 4.87 | 6.09 | 7.69 | 9.42 | 10.59 | 9.53 | 9.80 | 9.30 | 7.80 | 12.90 |
| Azerbaijan, Republic of | 912 | 4.62 | 7.52 | 10.04 | 10.64 | 10.48 | 3.31 | 1.83 | 2.28 | 2.43 | 1.89 | 1.89 | .... |
| Georgia | 915 | 19.16 | 11.62 | .... | .... | .... | 5.98 | 9.55 | 9.68 | 6.76 | 5.16 | 6.17 | 8.78 |
| Kazakhstan | 916 | 3.28 | 3.28 | 3.28 | 7.01 | .... | .... | .... | .... | .... | .... | .... | .... |
| Kyrgyz Republic | 917 | 6.37 | 6.82 | 6.63 | † 8.67 | 19.53 | 6.37 | 11.07 | 13.39 | 8.98 | 7.91 | 11.13 | 13.48 |
| Moldova | 921 | 12.29 | 3.75 | 7.43 | 13.52 | 18.89 | 11.82 | 7.13 | 11.71 | 6.26 | 5.57 | 6.76 | 20.58 |
| **Middle East, N.Africa & Pakistan** | | | | | | | | | | | | | |
| Algeria | 612 | .87 | .75 | 2.14 | .96 | .33 | .67 | .31 | .21 | .49 | .25 | .29 | .50 |
| Bahrain, Kingdom of | 419 | 1.56 | 3.57 | 5.04 | 4.86 | 2.53 | 1.06 | .83 | .96 | 1.21 | .85 | .79 | .... |
| Egypt | 469 | 9.90 | 8.57 | 9.53 | 6.85 | 11.37 | 9.84 | 9.28 | 13.95 | 12.96 | 11.00 | 11.65 | 11.34 |
| Iraq | 433 | 5.33 | 7.07 | 9.49 | 21.00 | 17.67 | 7.43 | † 8.94 | 9.49 | 6.15 | .... | .... | .... |
| Kuwait | 443 | 1.75 | 1.99 | .... | .... | .... | .92 | .64 | .83 | .... | .... | .... | .... |
| Lebanon | 446 | 5.25 | 5.22 | 5.22 | 5.22 | 5.21 | 4.91 | 4.10 | 3.93 | 4.35 | 4.44 | 4.44 | 4.44 |
| Mauritania | 682 | 7.22 | 11.84 | 11.50 | 10.43 | 11.09 | 8.66 | 8.55 | 2.68 | 3.33 | .... | 3.45 | .... |
| Pakistan | 564 | 2.49 | 7.18 | 8.54 | 8.99 | 11.37 | 12.52 | 12.55 | 13.12 | 11.00 | 9.32 | 9.89 | 7.12 |
| Saudi Arabia | 456 | .... | .... | .... | .... | .... | .... | .38 | .33 | .39 | .49 | .52 | .47 |
| Yemen, Republic of | 474 | 13.84 | 14.89 | 15.65 | 15.86 | 15.20 | 13.47 | 20.92 | 22.87 | 22.17 | 16.66 | .... | .... |
| **Sub-Saharan Africa** | | | | | | | | | | | | | |
| Burundi | 618 | 14.95 | 7.92 | 8.84 | .... | .... | .... | .... | .... | .... | .... | .... | .... |
| Cabo Verde | 624 | 6.42 | 4.07 | 2.70 | 3.41 | 3.41 | 3.52 | 3.89 | 3.96 | 4.18 | 3.39 | 1.51 | 1.15 |
| Ethiopia | 644 | .56 | .25 | .08 | .93 | .68 | .... | .... | .... | .... | .... | .... | .... |
| Gambia, The | 648 | 30.75 | 22.50 | 14.14 | 13.46 | 13.32 | 14.33 | 13.16 | 11.81 | 12.46 | .... | .... | .... |
| Ghana | 652 | 16.57 | 14.89 | 9.95 | 9.66 | 16.96 | 23.76 | 13.28 | 10.40 | 17.79 | 20.82 | 22.57 | 23.61 |
| Kenya | 664 | 2.96 | 8.44 | 6.81 | 6.80 | 7.70 | 7.38 | 3.60 | 8.72 | 12.58 | 8.93 | 8.93 | 10.93 |
| Lesotho | 666 | 8.52 | 7.23 | 6.87 | 7.81 | 9.75 | 7.75 | 6.24 | 5.35 | 5.46 | 5.30 | 5.99 | 6.31 |
| Madagascar | 674 | 12.95 | 18.84 | 21.16 | 11.84 | 8.81 | 7.62 | 9.33 | 9.58 | 6.92 | 6.64 | 8.43 | 8.96 |
| Malawi | 676 | 28.58 | 24.40 | 19.27 | 13.95 | 11.29 | 10.15 | 7.16 | 6.56 | 14.33 | 29.56 | 20.66 | 23.90 |
| Mozambique | 688 | 12.37 | 9.10 | 15.05 | 15.16 | 13.76 | 10.59 | 11.99 | 15.24 | 5.27 | 4.13 | 5.33 | .... |
| Namibia | 728 | 7.78 | 7.09 | 7.26 | 8.59 | 9.64 | 8.19 | 6.46 | 5.62 | 5.54 | 5.42 | 5.81 | .... |
| Nigeria | 694 | 14.34 | 7.63 | 9.99 | 6.85 | 8.20 | 3.79 | 3.85 | 9.70 | 13.64 | 10.85 | 10.50 | 9.40 |

# National Interest Rates

Treasury Bill Rates (60c)
*(Period averages in percent per annum)*

| | | 2004 | 2005 | 2006 | 2007 | 2008 | 2009 | 2010 | 2011 | 2012 | 2013 | 2014 | 2015 |
|---|---|---|---|---|---|---|---|---|---|---|---|---|---|
| **Sub-Saharan Africa(Cont.)** | | | | | | | | | | | | | |
| Rwanda | 714 | 12.52 | 8.35 | 9.86 | † 7.24 | .... | .... | 7.44 | 6.70 | 9.82 | 9.54 | 4.93 | 3.77 |
| Seychelles | 718 | 3.17 | 3.34 | 3.70 | 3.92 | 7.07 | 12.97 | 3.04 | 4.23 | 10.74 | 3.93 | 3.64 | 9.08 |
| Sierra Leone | 724 | 26.14 | 22.98 | 17.71 | 18.41 | 15.48 | 10.47 | 17.21 | 24.45 | 22.40 | 8.05 | 2.37 | 2.06 |
| South Africa | 199 | 7.53 | 6.91 | 7.34 | 9.12 | 10.81 | 7.85 | 6.42 | 5.49 | 5.29 | 5.08 | 5.80 | 6.05 |
| South Sudan, Republic of | 733 | .... | .... | .... | .... | .... | .... | .... | .... | 3.00 | 3.00 | 3.00 | 3.00 |
| Swaziland | 734 | 7.94 | 7.08 | 7.54 | 9.03 | 10.77 | 7.93 | 6.60 | 6.07 | 6.87 | 6.31 | 6.43 | 6.44 |
| Tanzania | 738 | 8.35 | 10.67 | 11.64 | 13.38 | 8.11 | 7.14 | 3.87 | 6.37 | 12.71 | 12.34 | 12.08 | 8.80 |
| Uganda | 746 | 9.02 | 8.50 | 8.12 | 9.05 | 9.08 | 7.10 | 5.01 | 14.61 | 15.70 | 9.92 | 10.23 | 15.83 |
| Zambia | 754 | 12.60 | 16.32 | 10.37 | 11.95 | 13.47 | 15.39 | 6.28 | 9.55 | 10.13 | 11.44 | 15.36 | 19.02 |
| **Western Hemisphere** | | | | | | | | | | | | | |
| ECCU | | | | | | | | | | | | | |
| Antigua and Barbuda | 311 | 7.00 | 7.00 | 6.52 | 6.33 | 6.02 | 6.38 | 6.25 | 6.50 | 5.88 | 5.00 | 5.00 | .... |
| Dominica | 321 | 6.40 | 6.40 | 6.40 | 6.40 | 6.40 | 6.40 | 6.40 | 6.40 | 4.35 | 2.81 | 1.82 | .... |
| Grenada | 328 | 5.50 | 5.50 | 6.25 | 6.38 | 6.25 | 6.33 | 6.21 | 5.94 | 6.00 | 5.96 | 6.00 | 6.00 |
| St. Kitts and Nevis | 361 | 7.00 | 7.00 | 7.00 | 7.00 | 7.00 | 6.85 | 6.75 | 6.75 | 6.75 | .... | .... | .... |
| St. Lucia | 362 | † 5.50 | 4.48 | 5.17 | † 5.65 | 5.60 | 5.20 | 4.50 | 4.45 | 5.10 | 6.00 | 6.00 | 6.00 |
| St. Vincent & Grenadines | 364 | 4.60 | 4.85 | 5.62 | 5.75 | 5.56 | 5.67 | 4.92 | 4.16 | 3.96 | 3.43 | 2.85 | 5.82 |
| Bahamas, The | 313 | .56 | .14 | .87 | 2.66 | 2.73 | 2.62 | 2.28 | 1.25 | .24 | .30 | .53 | .68 |
| Barbados | 316 | 1.20 | 4.62 | 5.96 | 5.65 | 4.20 | 3.76 | 3.30 | 3.41 | 3.50 | 3.40 | 3.20 | 2.82 |
| Belize | 339 | 3.22 | 3.22 | 3.22 | 3.22 | 3.22 | 3.22 | 3.04 | 2.42 | 2.09 | 1.49 | .47 | .11 |
| Bolivia | 218 | 7.41 | 4.96 | 4.56 | 6.04 | 8.31 | 2.86 | .07 | .46 | .52 | 1.09 | 1.98 | .57 |
| Brazil | 223 | 17.14 | 18.76 | 14.38 | 11.50 | 13.68 | 9.70 | 10.93 | 11.66 | 8.07 | 8.99 | 11.54 | 14.16 |
| Guyana | 336 | 3.62 | 3.79 | 3.95 | 3.94 | 3.99 | 4.31 | 3.87 | 2.48 | 1.73 | 1.32 | 1.57 | 1.84 |
| Jamaica | 343 | 15.47 | 13.39 | 12.79 | 12.56 | 15.89 | 19.95 | 9.26 | 6.59 | 6.62 | 7.29 | 8.29 | 6.59 |
| Mexico | 273 | 6.82 | 9.20 | 7.19 | 7.19 | 7.68 | 5.43 | 4.40 | 4.24 | 4.24 | 3.75 | 3.00 | 2.98 |
| Netherlands Antilles | 353 | 3.86 | 3.52 | 5.39 | 6.04 | 4.40 | 1.35 | .... | .... | .... | .... | .... | .... |
| Trinidad and Tobago | 369 | 4.77 | 4.86 | 6.07 | 6.91 | 7.01 | 2.69 | .85 | .53 | .37 | .16 | .10 | .47 |
| Uruguay | 298 | 14.75 | 4.14 | 4.54 | 7.11 | 10.05 | 11.87 | 9.06 | 8.77 | 9.40 | 11.37 | 14.36 | 13.47 |

# National Interest Rates

Deposit Rates (60l)
except for United States (60lc) and Euro Area and its member countries (60lhn)
*(Period averages in percent per annum)*

| | | 2004 | 2005 | 2006 | 2007 | 2008 | 2009 | 2010 | 2011 | 2012 | 2013 | 2014 | 2015 |
|---|---|---|---|---|---|---|---|---|---|---|---|---|---|
| **Advanced Economies** | | | | | | | | | | | | | |
| Euro Area | 163 | 1.90 | 1.97 | 2.67 | 3.79 | 4.34 | 2.01 | 2.11 | 2.60 | 2.76 | 1.97 | 1.33 | .79 |
| Austria | 122 | 1.91 | 1.96 | 2.73 | 3.86 | 4.27 | 1.56 | 1.08 | 1.65 | 1.25 | .73 | .58 | .38 |
| Cyprus | 423 | 4.39 | 4.52 | 3.99 | 4.08 | 5.08 | 4.43 | 3.95 | 4.08 | 4.39 | 2.94 | 2.55 | 1.76 |
| Estonia | 939 | 2.16 | 2.13 | 2.84 | 4.37 | 5.72 | 4.82 | 1.11 | 1.27 | .67 | .42 | .51 | .50 |
| Finland | 172 | 1.96 | 2.06 | 2.92 | 4.12 | 4.54 | 1.46 | 1.52 | 2.00 | 1.50 | 1.08 | 1.08 | .97 |
| France | 132 | 2.06 | 2.15 | 2.76 | 3.77 | 4.17 | 1.68 | 1.60 | 2.10 | 1.92 | 1.63 | 1.68 | 1.39 |
| Germany | 134 | 1.93 | 1.91 | 2.61 | 3.75 | 4.13 | 1.38 | 1.10 | 1.40 | 1.16 | .72 | .58 | .37 |
| Greece | 174 | 2.29 | 2.23 | 2.86 | 3.95 | 4.87 | 2.74 | 3.25 | 4.17 | 4.77 | 3.66 | 2.34 | 1.46 |
| Ireland | 178 | 1.91 | 2.00 | 2.64 | 3.81 | 4.48 | 3.61 | 2.93 | 3.17 | 3.54 | 2.67 | 1.92 | 1.27 |
| Italy | 136 | 1.52 | 1.45 | 1.65 | 2.25 | 2.79 | 2.02 | 1.33 | 1.95 | 3.25 | 2.71 | 2.04 | 1.47 |
| Latvia | 941 | 3.27 | 2.78 | 3.53 | 6.06 | 6.34 | 8.04 | 1.87 | .51 | .37 | .13 | .... | .... |
| Lithuania | 946 | 1.22 | † 2.40 | 2.97 | 5.40 | 7.65 | 4.81 | 1.71 | .... | .... | .... | .... | .... |
| Luxembourg | 137 | 1.78 | 1.86 | 2.56 | 3.58 | 3.93 | .77 | .60 | 1.03 | .64 | .50 | .32 | .35 |
| Malta | 181 | 2.63 | 2.71 | 3.03 | .... | .... | .... | .... | .... | .... | .... | .... | .... |
| Netherlands | 138 | 2.31 | 2.34 | 2.98 | 3.90 | 4.37 | 2.60 | 2.37 | 2.61 | 2.74 | 2.07 | 1.85 | 1.74 |
| Portugal | 182 | 1.82 | 1.87 | 2.50 | 3.67 | 4.21 | 1.99 | 1.71 | 3.52 | 3.01 | 2.13 | 1.59 | .77 |
| Slovak Republic | 936 | .... | .... | .... | .... | .... | 1.49 | 1.75 | 1.97 | 2.09 | 1.57 | 1.53 | 1.69 |
| Slovenia | 961 | .... | .... | 2.17 | 3.36 | 4.31 | 2.52 | 1.82 | 2.15 | 2.31 | 1.86 | .98 | .37 |
| Spain | 184 | 1.96 | 2.07 | 2.75 | 3.88 | 4.63 | 2.48 | 2.41 | 2.62 | 2.65 | 1.52 | .85 | .42 |
| Australia | 193 | 3.85 | 3.89 | 4.06 | 4.53 | 4.73 | 3.08 | 4.21 | 4.34 | 3.92 | 3.25 | 2.90 | 2.30 |
| Canada | 156 | .78 | .79 | 1.83 | 2.08 | 1.50 | .10 | .20 | .48 | .48 | .55 | .55 | .08 |
| China, P.R.: Hong Kong | 532 | .03 | 1.26 | 2.70 | 2.42 | .45 | .01 | .01 | .01 | .01 | .01 | .01 | .01 |
| Czech Republic | 935 | 1.28 | 1.17 | 1.19 | 1.32 | 1.61 | 1.27 | 1.08 | 1.04 | 1.02 | .86 | .70 | .53 |
| Iceland | 176 | 4.85 | .... | .... | .... | .... | .... | .... | .... | .... | .... | .... | .... |
| Israel | 436 | 3.51 | 3.66 | 4.31 | 3.50 | 2.31 | 1.11 | 1.85 | 2.48 | 1.92 | † 1.08 | .57 | .45 |
| Japan | 158 | .08 | .27 | .68 | .81 | .59 | .43 | .50 | .46 | .48 | .54 | .42 | .41 |
| Korea | 542 | 3.87 | 3.72 | 4.50 | 5.17 | 5.87 | 3.48 | 3.86 | 4.15 | 3.70 | 2.89 | 2.54 | 1.81 |
| New Zealand | 196 | 5.77 | 6.68 | 6.92 | 7.78 | 7.55 | 4.04 | 4.58 | 4.27 | 4.11 | 3.83 | 4.01 | 3.73 |
| Norway | 142 | 1.48 | 1.83 | 2.83 | 4.86 | 5.50 | 2.28 | .... | .... | .... | .... | .... | .... |
| San Marino | 135 | 1.44 | 1.35 | 2.13 | 2.63 | 2.23 | .96 | .71 | 1.08 | .... | .... | .... | .... |
| Singapore | 576 | .40 | .44 | .57 | .53 | .42 | .29 | .21 | .17 | .14 | .14 | .14 | .17 |
| Sweden | 144 | 1.00 | .79 | .... | .... | .... | .... | .... | .... | .... | .... | .... | .... |
| Switzerland | 146 | .21 | .52 | 1.40 | 2.13 | † .16 | .08 | .08 | .03 | .03 | .03 | .02 | −.18 |
| United States | 111 | 1.56 | 3.51 | 5.15 | 5.27 | 2.97 | .56 | .31 | .30 | .28 | .... | .... | .... |
| **Emerging & Dev. Economies** | | | | | | | | | | | | | |
| **Emerging & Developing Asia** | | | | | | | | | | | | | |
| Bangladesh | 513 | 5.80 | 5.53 | 5.99 | 6.99 | 7.55 | 7.81 | 7.21 | 8.84 | 10.22 | 11.72 | 9.80 | 8.24 |
| Brunei Darussalam | 516 | 1.04 | 1.01 | 1.04 | 1.17 | .88 | .70 | .47 | .40 | .23 | .28 | .30 | .34 |
| Cambodia | 522 | 1.79 | 1.92 | 1.84 | 1.90 | 1.91 | 1.66 | 1.26 | 1.34 | 1.33 | 1.34 | 1.42 | 1.42 |
| China, P.R.: Mainland | 924 | 2.25 | 2.25 | 2.52 | 4.14 | 2.25 | 2.25 | 2.75 | 3.50 | 3.00 | 3.00 | 2.75 | 1.50 |
| China,P.R.:Macao | 546 | .08 | 1.58 | 2.85 | 2.85 | 1.10 | .03 | .02 | .05 | .06 | .04 | .05 | .04 |
| Fiji | 819 | 1.72 | 1.83 | 5.56 | 7.04 | 2.75 | 4.91 | 5.41 | 3.75 | 2.42 | 2.07 | 1.86 | 2.52 |
| Indonesia | 536 | 6.44 | 8.08 | 11.41 | 7.98 | 8.49 | 9.28 | 7.02 | 6.93 | 5.95 | 6.26 | 8.75 | 8.34 |
| Lao People's Dem. Rep. | 544 | 7.85 | 4.75 | 5.00 | 5.00 | 4.67 | 3.25 | 3.00 | .... | .... | .... | .... | .... |
| Malaysia | 548 | 3.00 | 3.00 | 3.15 | 3.17 | 3.13 | 2.08 | 2.50 | 2.91 | 2.98 | 2.97 | 3.05 | 3.13 |
| Maldives | 556 | 6.50 | 6.50 | 6.50 | 6.50 | 6.50 | 6.50 | † 4.05 | 4.17 | 3.73 | 3.81 | 4.14 | 4.12 |
| Micronesia, Fed. States of | 868 | 1.02 | 1.62 | 2.04 | 2.54 | 2.47 | 1.29 | .91 | .59 | .42 | .53 | .54 | .56 |
| Mongolia | 948 | 14.15 | 13.00 | 13.01 | 13.46 | † 11.39 | 13.28 | 11.86 | 10.47 | 11.27 | 12.05 | 12.31 | 12.98 |
| Myanmar | 518 | 9.50 | 9.50 | 11.38 | 12.00 | 12.00 | 12.00 | 12.00 | 11.33 | 8.00 | 8.00 | 8.00 | 8.00 |
| Nepal | 558 | 2.65 | 2.25 | 2.25 | 2.25 | 2.40 | 2.50 | 3.63 | .... | .... | .... | .... | .... |
| Papua New Guinea | 853 | 1.73 | .85 | .98 | 1.06 | 1.31 | 2.32 | 1.38 | .92 | .49 | .33 | .33 | .43 |
| Philippines | 566 | 6.18 | 5.56 | 5.29 | 3.70 | 4.49 | 2.74 | 3.22 | 3.39 | 3.16 | 1.66 | 1.23 | 1.59 |
| Samoa | 862 | 4.39 | 4.35 | 4.87 | 6.44 | 6.06 | 4.81 | 2.70 | 2.29 | 2.47 | 2.88 | 3.02 | 2.48 |
| Solomon Islands | 813 | 1.10 | .76 | .69 | .68 | .95 | 4.15 | 3.29 | 2.00 | .86 | .29 | .25 | .31 |
| Sri Lanka | 524 | 5.07 | 5.64 | 6.80 | 9.08 | 10.89 | 10.61 | 6.90 | 6.43 | 8.67 | 10.23 | 7.50 | 5.99 |
| Thailand | 578 | 1.00 | 1.88 | 4.44 | 2.88 | 2.48 | 1.04 | 1.01 | 2.28 | 2.80 | 2.88 | 1.96 | 1.42 |
| Timor-Leste | 537 | .79 | .79 | .80 | .78 | .80 | .83 | .81 | .85 | .91 | .90 | .85 | .78 |
| Tonga | 866 | 5.85 | 5.90 | 6.58 | 6.77 | 6.53 | 5.26 | 4.03 | 3.92 | 2.82 | 2.73 | 2.84 | 3.10 |
| Vanuatu | 846 | 1.71 | 2.00 | 1.94 | 1.31 | 1.25 | 1.25 | 1.58 | 1.50 | 1.31 | 1.25 | 1.10 | 1.42 |
| Vietnam | 582 | 6.17 | 7.15 | 7.63 | 7.49 | 12.73 | 7.91 | 11.19 | 13.99 | 10.50 | 7.14 | 5.76 | 4.75 |
| **Europe** | | | | | | | | | | | | | |
| **Emerging & Developing Europe** | | | | | | | | | | | | | |
| Albania | 914 | 6.61 | 5.09 | 5.23 | 5.66 | 6.80 | 6.77 | 6.42 | 5.86 | 5.42 | 4.16 | 1.91 | 1.39 |
| Bosnia and Herzegovina | 963 | 3.72 | 3.56 | 3.69 | 3.56 | 3.49 | 3.60 | 3.16 | 2.80 | 3.18 | 3.01 | 2.66 | 2.06 |
| Bulgaria | 918 | 3.05 | 3.08 | 3.17 | 3.68 | 4.44 | 6.18 | 4.08 | 3.37 | 3.08 | 2.41 | 1.66 | .61 |
| Croatia | 960 | 1.87 | 1.71 | 1.72 | 2.34 | 2.82 | 3.20 | 1.76 | 1.70 | 1.88 | 1.52 | .... | .... |
| Hungary | 944 | 9.09 | 5.17 | 7.45 | 6.81 | 9.92 | 5.82 | 4.92 | 6.19 | 5.29 | 2.46 | 1.42 | .87 |
| Kosovo | 967 | 2.75 | 3.12 | 3.11 | 4.00 | 4.42 | 3.98 | 3.38 | 3.62 | 3.72 | 2.40 | 1.11 | 1.15 |
| Macedonia, FYR | 962 | 6.54 | † 5.23 | 4.66 | 4.88 | 5.89 | 7.05 | 7.07 | 5.91 | 5.09 | 4.42 | 3.70 | 2.89 |
| Montenegro | 943 | 4.87 | 4.84 | 5.06 | 5.08 | † 3.82 | 3.81 | 3.70 | 3.13 | 3.26 | 2.91 | 2.14 | 1.46 |
| Poland | 964 | 3.75 | 2.79 | 2.20 | .... | .... | .... | .... | .... | .... | .... | .... | .... |
| Romania | 968 | 11.54 | 6.42 | 4.77 | 6.70 | 9.51 | 11.99 | 7.31 | 6.30 | 5.51 | 4.55 | 3.02 | 1.89 |
| Serbia, Republic of | 942 | 3.60 | 3.71 | 5.06 | 4.08 | 7.32 | 5.06 | 11.33 | 9.76 | 10.57 | 7.92 | 6.81 | .... |
| Turkey | 186 | 24.26 | 20.40 | 21.65 | 22.56 | 22.91 | 17.65 | 15.27 | 14.22 | 16.35 | 15.76 | 16.77 | 14.92 |
| **CIS** | | | | | | | | | | | | | |
| Armenia | 911 | 4.90 | 5.81 | 5.84 | 6.25 | 6.63 | 8.65 | 8.95 | 9.25 | 9.57 | 10.16 | 10.43 | 14.15 |
| Azerbaijan, Republic of | 912 | 9.18 | 8.52 | 10.58 | 11.56 | 12.22 | 12.20 | 11.64 | 10.87 | 10.22 | 9.89 | 9.17 | 9.00 |
| Belarus | 913 | 12.72 | 9.23 | 7.68 | 8.31 | 8.53 | 10.68 | 9.09 | 13.31 | 22.30 | 20.26 | 18.58 | .... |

# National Interest Rates

| | | 2004 | 2005 | 2006 | 2007 | 2008 | 2009 | 2010 | 2011 | 2012 | 2013 | 2014 | 2015 |
|---|---|---|---|---|---|---|---|---|---|---|---|---|---|
| | | | | | | Deposit Rates (60l) | | | | | | | |
| | | | | | except for United States (60lc) and Euro Area and its member countries (60lhn) | | | | | | | | |
| | | | | | | *(Period averages in percent per annum)* | | | | | | | |
| **CIS(Cont.)** | | | | | | | | | | | | | |
| Georgia............................... | 915 | 7.07 | 7.48 | 10.13 | 10.19 | 11.24 | 10.81 | 10.06 | 11.54 | 10.71 | 9.73 | 8.43 | 8.91 |
| Kyrgyz Republic..................... | 917 | 1.48 | 1.74 | 1.59 | 2.96 | 2.56 | 3.17 | 2.00 | 2.25 | 2.55 | 2.24 | 2.71 | 2.69 |
| Moldova.............................. | 921 | 15.12 | 13.22 | 11.88 | 15.01 | 17.93 | 14.94 | 7.67 | 7.57 | 7.63 | 7.23 | 5.72 | 11.97 |
| Russia................................. | 922 | 3.79 | 3.99 | 4.08 | 5.14 | 5.76 | 8.58 | 6.01 | 4.44 | 5.53 | 5.59 | 6.04 | 9.20 |
| Tajikistan............................ | 923 | 10.17 | 10.15 | 9.52 | 10.99 | 9.37 | 7.58 | 8.65 | 8.24 | 7.67 | 6.58 | 5.49 | 4.23 |
| Ukraine............................... | 926 | 7.80 | 8.57 | 7.57 | 8.12 | 9.95 | 13.76 | 10.56 | 7.90 | 12.96 | 10.78 | 12.10 | 13.01 |
| **Middle East,N.Africa & Pakistan** | | | | | | | | | | | | | |
| Algeria................................ | 612 | 3.65 | 1.94 | 1.75 | 1.75 | 1.75 | 1.75 | 1.75 | 1.75 | 1.75 | 1.75 | 1.75 | 1.75 |
| Bahrain, Kingdom of.............. | 419 | 1.54 | 3.14 | 4.37 | 4.49 | 1.65 | 1.58 | 1.23 | 1.02 | 1.08 | 1.06 | .98 | .99 |
| Djibouti............................... | 611 | .88 | .75 | .69 | 4.53 | 2.96 | 1.67 | 1.72 | 1.78 | 2.34 | 2.03 | 1.24 | .... |
| Egypt.................................. | 469 | 7.73 | 7.23 | 6.02 | 6.10 | 6.58 | 6.49 | 6.23 | 6.74 | 7.64 | 7.68 | 6.92 | 6.91 |
| Iran, I.R. of.......................... | 429 | 11.70 | 11.78 | 11.56 | 11.60 | 13.30 | 13.14 | 11.94 | 11.16 | 14.81 | 14.76 | 16.94 | .... |
| Iraq.................................... | 433 | 8.00 | 6.56 | 6.62 | 10.43 | 10.54 | 7.82 | 6.06 | 5.91 | 5.87 | 5.75 | .... | .... |
| Jordan................................ | 439 | 2.49 | 2.91 | 4.62 | 5.45 | 5.46 | 4.94 | 3.53 | 3.40 | 3.77 | 4.85 | 4.52 | 3.50 |
| Kuwait................................ | 443 | 2.65 | 3.47 | 4.92 | 5.45 | 4.81 | 2.83 | 2.34 | 2.16 | 2.04 | 2.02 | 2.02 | 2.03 |
| Lebanon.............................. | 446 | 7.37 | 8.15 | 7.98 | 7.97 | 7.70 | 7.32 | 6.20 | 5.88 | 5.77 | 5.83 | 5.91 | 5.98 |
| Libya.................................. | 672 | 2.08 | 2.13 | 2.50 | 2.50 | 2.50 | 2.50 | 2.50 | 2.50 | 2.50 | 2.50 | 2.50 | .... |
| Mauritania........................... | 682 | 8.00 | 8.00 | 8.00 | 8.00 | 8.00 | 8.00 | 8.00 | 8.00 | 5.81 | .... | .... | .... |
| Morocco.............................. | 686 | 3.61 | 3.52 | 3.67 | 3.67 | 3.91 | 3.81 | 3.69 | 3.76 | 3.83 | 3.91 | 3.89 | 3.80 |
| Oman.................................. | 449 | 2.32 | 3.30 | 4.00 | 4.14 | 4.48 | 4.14 | 3.37 | 2.80 | 2.62 | 2.39 | 2.02 | 1.93 |
| Pakistan.............................. | 564 | 1.63 | 2.60 | 4.17 | 5.31 | 6.92 | 8.68 | 8.15 | 8.23 | 7.98 | 7.17 | 7.27 | 5.97 |
| Qatar.................................. | 453 | 3.20 | 3.19 | 4.23 | 4.43 | 2.97 | 4.24 | 2.90 | 1.75 | 1.67 | 1.42 | 1.35 | 1.61 |
| Syrian Arab Republic.............. | 463 | 6.00 | 9.00 | 9.00 | 8.36 | 8.12 | 6.35 | 6.22 | .... | .... | .... | .... | .... |
| West Bank and Gaza............... | 487 | 1.12 | 2.24 | 2.97 | 3.02 | .81 | .40 | .29 | .53 | .46 | .62 | .83 | .95 |
| Yemen, Republic of................ | 474 | 13.00 | 13.00 | 13.00 | 13.00 | 13.00 | 10.67 | 18.67 | 20.00 | 19.50 | 15.25 | .... | .... |
| **Sub-Saharan Africa** | | | | | | | | | | | | | |
| CEMAC................................ | 758 | 5.00 | 4.92 | 4.33 | 4.25 | 3.75 | 3.25 | 3.25 | 3.25 | 3.25 | 3.21 | 2.60 | 2.45 |
| Cameroon........................ | 622 | 5.00 | 4.92 | 4.33 | 4.25 | 3.75 | 3.25 | 3.25 | 3.25 | 3.25 | 3.21 | 2.60 | 2.45 |
| Central African Rep............. | 626 | 5.00 | 4.92 | 4.33 | 4.25 | 3.75 | 3.25 | 3.25 | 3.25 | 3.25 | 3.21 | 2.60 | 2.45 |
| Chad............................... | 628 | 5.00 | 4.92 | 4.33 | 4.25 | 3.75 | 3.25 | 3.25 | 3.25 | 3.25 | 3.21 | 2.60 | 2.45 |
| Congo, Rep. of................... | 634 | 5.00 | 4.92 | 4.33 | 4.25 | 3.75 | 3.25 | 3.25 | 3.25 | 3.25 | 3.21 | 2.60 | 2.45 |
| Equatorial Guinea.............. | 642 | 5.00 | 4.92 | 4.33 | 4.25 | 3.75 | 3.25 | 3.25 | 3.25 | 3.25 | 3.21 | 2.60 | 2.45 |
| Gabon............................. | 646 | 5.00 | 4.92 | 4.33 | 4.25 | 3.75 | 3.25 | 3.25 | 3.25 | 3.25 | 3.21 | 2.60 | 2.45 |
| WAEMU.............................. | 759 | 3.50 | 3.50 | 3.50 | 3.50 | 3.50 | 3.50 | 3.50 | 3.50 | 3.50 | 3.50 | 3.50 | 3.50 |
| Benin.............................. | 638 | 3.50 | 3.50 | 3.50 | 3.50 | 3.50 | 3.50 | 3.50 | 3.50 | 3.50 | 3.50 | 3.50 | 3.50 |
| Burkina Faso..................... | 748 | 3.50 | 3.50 | 3.50 | 3.50 | 3.50 | 3.50 | 3.50 | 3.50 | 3.50 | 3.50 | 3.50 | 3.50 |
| Côte d'Ivoire..................... | 662 | 3.50 | 3.50 | 3.50 | 3.50 | 3.50 | 3.50 | 3.50 | 3.50 | 3.50 | 3.50 | 3.50 | 3.50 |
| Guinea Bissau.................... | 654 | 3.50 | 3.50 | 3.50 | 3.50 | 3.50 | 3.50 | 3.50 | 3.50 | 3.50 | 3.50 | 3.50 | 3.50 |
| Mali................................ | 678 | 3.50 | 3.50 | 3.50 | 3.50 | 3.50 | 3.50 | 3.50 | 3.50 | 3.50 | 3.50 | 3.50 | 3.50 |
| Niger............................... | 692 | 3.50 | 3.50 | 3.50 | 3.50 | 3.50 | 3.50 | 3.50 | 3.50 | 3.50 | 3.50 | 3.50 | 3.50 |
| Senegal............................ | 722 | 3.50 | 3.50 | 3.50 | 3.50 | 3.50 | 3.50 | 3.50 | 3.50 | 3.50 | 3.50 | 3.50 | 3.50 |
| Togo............................... | 742 | 3.50 | 3.50 | 3.50 | 3.50 | 3.50 | 3.50 | 3.50 | 3.50 | 3.50 | 3.50 | 3.50 | 3.50 |
| Angola................................ | 614 | 15.44 | 13.40 | 4.50 | 6.76 | 6.54 | 7.59 | 12.76 | 6.31 | 3.60 | 3.15 | 3.53 | 3.31 |
| Botswana............................ | 616 | 9.85 | 9.25 | 8.87 | 8.62 | 8.67 | 7.47 | 5.60 | 5.15 | 3.61 | 3.11 | 2.53 | 2.50 |
| Cabo Verde.......................... | 624 | 3.46 | 3.38 | † 4.43 | 3.29 | 3.81 | 2.88 | 3.11 | 3.35 | 3.79 | 4.17 | 3.48 | 2.87 |
| Comoros.............................. | 632 | 3.50 | 3.00 | 2.50 | 2.50 | 2.50 | 1.88 | 1.75 | 1.75 | 1.75 | 1.75 | 1.75 | 1.75 |
| Congo, Dem. Rep. of.............. | 636 | .... | .... | .... | 14.39 | 7.80 | 16.08 | 16.77 | 13.36 | 7.72 | 4.71 | 4.01 | 3.66 |
| Ethiopia.............................. | 644 | 3.38 | 3.46 | 3.56 | 4.11 | 4.68 | .... | .... | .... | .... | .... | .... | .... |
| Gambia, The......................... | 648 | 22.00 | 17.33 | 12.67 | 12.89 | 12.87 | 15.50 | 14.63 | 11.75 | 11.50 | 13.44 | 16.51 | .... |
| Ghana................................. | 652 | 13.63 | 10.16 | 8.89 | 8.90 | 11.29 | 17.06 | 12.88 | 8.91 | 10.05 | 12.35 | 12.90 | 13.34 |
| Guinea................................ | 656 | 8.85 | 14.35 | 17.50 | 17.50 | 17.50 | 17.50 | 17.50 | 17.50 | 16.73 | 15.62 | 13.13 | 6.69 |
| Kenya................................. | 664 | † 2.43 | 5.08 | 5.14 | 5.16 | 5.30 | 5.97 | 4.56 | 5.63 | 11.57 | 8.64 | 8.37 | 9.19 |
| Lesotho............................... | 666 | 4.24 | 3.95 | 4.54 | 6.46 | 7.64 | 4.85 | 3.68 | 2.70 | 2.85 | 2.85 | 2.73 | 2.34 |
| Liberia................................ | 668 | 3.84 | 3.43 | 3.44 | 3.77 | 4.00 | 4.11 | 3.54 | 3.03 | 3.50 | 3.87 | 4.16 | 4.05 |
| Madagascar.......................... | 674 | 15.19 | 18.75 | 22.30 | 16.50 | 11.50 | 11.50 | 10.50 | 10.65 | 10.50 | 10.75 | 12.40 | 15.00 |
| Malawi................................ | 676 | 13.73 | 10.92 | 11.00 | 5.97 | 3.50 | 3.50 | 3.60 | 4.11 | 11.08 | 18.41 | 13.17 | 11.59 |
| Mauritius............................ | 684 | 8.15 | 7.25 | 9.55 | 11.77 | 10.11 | 8.45 | 8.35 | 7.11 | 6.23 | 6.81 | 6.78 | 6.09 |
| Mozambique......................... | 688 | 9.90 | 7.80 | 10.37 | 11.85 | 10.98 | 9.52 | 9.68 | 12.98 | 11.43 | 8.80 | 8.58 | 8.53 |
| Namibia............................... | 728 | 6.35 | 6.24 | 6.30 | 7.55 | 8.38 | 6.24 | 5.00 | 4.28 | 4.21 | 3.98 | 4.25 | 4.71 |
| Nigeria................................ | 694 | 13.70 | 10.53 | 9.74 | 10.29 | 11.97 | 13.30 | 6.52 | 5.70 | 8.41 | 7.95 | 9.34 | 9.15 |
| Rwanda............................... | 714 | 9.39 | 8.01 | 8.29 | 6.77 | 6.72 | 8.54 | 7.10 | 7.96 | 10.04 | 8.58 | 7.76 | 7.59 |
| São Tomé & Príncipe............... | 716 | 11.49 | † 12.14 | 10.75 | 12.75 | 12.75 | 11.92 | 11.12 | 12.36 | 12.89 | † 9.38 | 3.38 | .... |
| Seychelles............................ | 718 | 3.55 | 3.72 | 2.46 | 3.07 | 3.97 | 9.77 | 2.86 | 2.08 | 3.30 | 3.43 | 2.33 | 3.16 |
| Sierra Leone......................... | 724 | 11.17 | 11.80 | 11.14 | 10.79 | 10.59 | 9.72 | 9.47 | 10.31 | 10.39 | 8.91 | 6.61 | 4.49 |
| South Africa......................... | 199 | 6.55 | 6.04 | 7.14 | 9.15 | † 11.61 | 8.54 | 6.47 | 5.67 | 5.44 | 5.15 | 5.80 | 6.15 |
| South Sudan, Republic of......... | 733 | .... | .... | .... | .... | .... | .... | .... | .... | 1.15 | 1.31 | 1.39 | .11 |
| Swaziland............................ | 734 | 4.63 | 4.01 | 4.93 | 7.05 | 8.17 | 5.40 | 3.85 | 2.85 | 2.47 | 2.08 | 2.14 | 2.27 |
| Tanzania.............................. | 738 | 4.20 | 4.73 | 6.73 | 8.68 | 8.25 | 7.97 | 6.57 | 6.78 | 9.51 | 9.82 | 9.86 | 9.90 |
| Uganda............................... | 746 | 7.74 | 8.79 | 9.09 | 9.26 | 10.67 | 9.75 | 7.69 | 13.02 | 16.23 | 11.84 | 10.81 | 12.77 |
| Zambia................................ | 754 | 11.51 | 11.19 | 10.33 | 9.22 | 6.55 | 7.09 | 7.40 | 7.02 | 7.00 | 6.49 | 7.88 | 8.99 |
| **Western Hemisphere** | | | | | | | | | | | | | |
| ECCU.................................. | 309 | 3.76 | 3.54 | 3.46 | 3.44 | 3.48 | 3.50 | 3.47 | 3.41 | 3.27 | 3.07 | 2.84 | 2.36 |
| Anguilla........................... | 312 | 4.83 | 4.81 | 4.87 | 4.69 | 4.74 | 4.72 | 3.89 | 3.57 | 4.07 | 3.87 | 3.73 | 3.47 |
| Antigua and Barbuda.......... | 311 | 4.12 | 3.86 | 3.83 | 3.52 | 3.54 | 3.48 | 3.37 | 3.38 | 3.16 | 3.04 | 2.89 | 2.47 |
| Dominica.......................... | 321 | 3.26 | 3.15 | 3.33 | 3.26 | 3.20 | 3.20 | 3.26 | 3.20 | 3.10 | 3.05 | 2.87 | 2.45 |
| Grenada........................... | 328 | 3.32 | 2.87 | 2.95 | 3.13 | 3.23 | 3.27 | 3.08 | 3.11 | 2.86 | 2.64 | 2.40 | 1.83 |
| Montserrat........................ | 351 | 2.29 | 2.52 | 2.67 | 2.55 | 2.52 | 2.69 | 2.60 | 2.42 | 2.37 | 2.04 | 1.93 | 1.36 |
| St. Kitts and Nevis.............. | 361 | 4.54 | 4.51 | 4.56 | 4.60 | 4.55 | 4.59 | 4.59 | 4.47 | 4.27 | 3.74 | 3.18 | 2.72 |
| St. Lucia........................... | 362 | 3.05 | 2.83 | 2.95 | 3.10 | 3.26 | 3.25 | 3.32 | 3.49 | 3.06 | 2.93 | 2.80 | 2.27 |
| St. Vincent & Grenadines...... | 364 | 3.30 | 2.89 | 2.92 | 2.82 | 2.79 | 2.94 | 2.86 | 2.99 | 2.88 | 2.73 | 2.64 | 2.12 |

# National Interest Rates

| | | 2004 | 2005 | 2006 | 2007 | 2008 | 2009 | 2010 | 2011 | 2012 | 2013 | 2014 | 2015 |
|---|---|---|---|---|---|---|---|---|---|---|---|---|---|
| | | | | | | Deposit Rates (60l) | | | | | | | |
| | | | | | except for United States (60lc) and Euro Area and its member countries (60lhn) | | | | | | | | |
| | | | | | | *(Period averages in percent per annum)* | | | | | | | |
| **Western Hemisphere(Cont.)** | | | | | | | | | | | | | |
| Argentina | 213 | 2.61 | 3.76 | 6.42 | 7.97 | 11.05 | 11.60 | 9.17 | 10.68 | 12.02 | 14.85 | 20.42 | 21.17 |
| Aruba | 314 | 4.26 | 3.94 | 3.89 | 4.03 | 3.62 | 3.35 | 2.58 | 1.68 | 1.54 | 1.63 | 2.18 | 1.95 |
| Bahamas, The | 313 | 3.83 | 3.22 | 3.36 | 3.69 | 3.92 | 3.78 | 3.44 | 2.63 | 2.01 | 1.68 | 1.42 | 1.41 |
| Barbados | 316 | 2.54 | 3.18 | 4.60 | 5.13 | 4.46 | 2.87 | 2.67 | 2.68 | 2.56 | 2.51 | 2.51 | 1.32 |
| Belize | 339 | 7.42 | 7.71 | 8.16 | 8.32 | 8.46 | 8.37 | 7.76 | 6.44 | 4.41 | 3.59 | 2.90 | 2.60 |
| Bolivia | 218 | 7.42 | 4.93 | 4.03 | 3.55 | 4.66 | 3.44 | 1.05 | 1.40 | 1.63 | 1.74 | 2.95 | 1.41 |
| Brazil | 223 | 15.42 | 17.63 | 13.93 | 10.58 | 11.66 | 9.28 | 8.87 | 10.99 | 7.91 | 7.81 | 10.02 | 12.62 |
| Chile | 228 | 1.94 | 3.93 | 5.11 | 5.61 | 7.49 | 2.05 | 1.75 | 5.29 | 5.79 | 5.17 | 3.92 | 3.61 |
| Colombia | 233 | 7.80 | 7.01 | 6.28 | 8.01 | 9.74 | 6.15 | 3.66 | 4.26 | 5.36 | 4.17 | 4.09 | 4.58 |
| Costa Rica | 238 | 9.51 | 10.14 | 9.77 | 6.35 | 4.15 | 6.96 | 5.32 | 4.01 | 4.74 | 3.88 | 3.32 | 2.37 |
| Dominican Republic | 243 | 21.12 | 13.86 | 9.83 | 6.96 | 10.35 | 7.81 | 4.86 | 7.87 | 7.49 | 6.02 | 6.73 | 6.56 |
| Ecuador | 248 | 4.16 | 3.59 | 4.22 | † 5.26 | 4.87 | 4.78 | 3.90 | 3.84 | 3.89 | 3.89 | 4.03 | 4.38 |
| El Salvador | 253 | 3.34 | 3.44 | 4.39 | 4.71 | 4.21 | 4.48 | 2.87 | 1.76 | 2.52 | 3.40 | 3.78 | 4.24 |
| Guatemala | 258 | 4.19 | 4.35 | 4.50 | 4.76 | 5.08 | 5.58 | 5.45 | 5.24 | 5.29 | 5.45 | 5.48 | 5.47 |
| Guyana | 336 | 2.68 | 2.59 | 2.54 | 2.47 | 2.37 | 2.32 | 2.27 | 1.94 | 1.52 | 1.13 | 1.07 | 1.11 |
| Haiti | 263 | 18.54 | † 4.62 | 7.81 | 5.92 | 2.15 | 1.13 | .74 | .28 | .45 | .68 | 2.61 | 4.29 |
| Honduras | 268 | 11.09 | 10.90 | 9.33 | 7.78 | 9.49 | 10.82 | 9.81 | 8.18 | 8.93 | 11.65 | 10.82 | 9.70 |
| Jamaica | 343 | 7.98 | 7.50 | 7.04 | 7.14 | 7.56 | 6.97 | 6.35 | 3.86 | 3.53 | 3.66 | 5.27 | 4.90 |
| Mexico | 273 | 2.70 | 3.46 | 3.30 | 3.21 | 3.04 | 2.01 | 1.21 | .96 | 1.08 | 1.33 | .84 | .59 |
| Netherlands Antilles | 353 | 2.92 | 2.78 | 2.78 | 2.73 | 2.29 | 2.16 | . . . . | . . . . | . . . . | . . . . | . . . . | . . . . |
| Nicaragua | 278 | 4.72 | 4.03 | 4.87 | 6.08 | 6.57 | 6.01 | 2.99 | 1.85 | 1.00 | 1.01 | 1.05 | 1.05 |
| Panama | 283 | 2.23 | 2.70 | 3.83 | 4.76 | 3.53 | 3.49 | 3.04 | 2.32 | 2.14 | 2.12 | 2.16 | 2.14 |
| Paraguay | 288 | 5.11 | 1.66 | 6.72 | 5.00 | 3.08 | 1.46 | 1.21 | 4.03 | 3.92 | 4.24 | 4.31 | 3.51 |
| Peru | 293 | 2.42 | 2.59 | 3.21 | 3.23 | 3.51 | 2.83 | 1.54 | 2.33 | 2.46 | 2.32 | 2.31 | 2.29 |
| Suriname | 366 | 8.34 | 7.27 | 6.63 | 6.42 | 6.34 | 6.38 | 6.17 | 6.39 | 6.79 | 7.09 | 7.35 | 7.53 |
| Trinidad and Tobago | 369 | 2.79 | 2.20 | 4.79 | 5.90 | 7.37 | 3.42 | 1.51 | 1.50 | 1.50 | 1.50 | 1.50 | 1.50 |
| Uruguay | 298 | 6.20 | 2.84 | 1.83 | 2.36 | 3.23 | 4.40 | 4.17 | 4.55 | 4.45 | 4.65 | 4.90 | 5.60 |
| Venezuela, Rep. Bol | 299 | 12.60 | 11.63 | 10.26 | 10.71 | 16.15 | 16.41 | 14.80 | 14.59 | 14.51 | 14.50 | 14.68 | 14.89 |

# National Interest Rates

| | 2004 | 2005 | 2006 | 2007 | 2008 | 2009 | 2010 | 2011 | 2012 | 2013 | 2014 | 2015 |

Lending Rates (60p) except for Euro Area and its member countries (60pns)
*(Period averages in percent per annum)*

**Advanced Economies**

| | Code | 2004 | 2005 | 2006 | 2007 | 2008 | 2009 | 2010 | 2011 | 2012 | 2013 | 2014 | 2015 |
|---|---|---|---|---|---|---|---|---|---|---|---|---|---|
| Euro Area | 163 | 6.78 | 6.69 | 7.20 | 7.99 | 8.53 | 7.43 | 5.86 | 5.22 | 5.36 | 5.54 | 5.51 | 5.11 |
| Austria | 122 | 5.28 | 5.00 | 5.51 | 6.30 | 6.82 | 5.04 | 4.74 | 5.01 | 4.80 | 4.76 | 4.96 | 4.87 |
| Belgium | 124 | 6.48 | 6.32 | 6.56 | 6.98 | 7.03 | 6.15 | 5.78 | 5.98 | 6.21 | 5.96 | 4.81 | 3.93 |
| Cyprus | 423 | .... | .... | .... | .... | 7.19 | 7.49 | 6.82 | 6.83 | 7.05 | 6.89 | 5.88 | 4.69 |
| Estonia | 939 | 5.66 | 4.93 | 5.03 | 6.46 | 8.55 | 9.39 | 7.76 | 6.12 | 5.75 | 5.36 | 4.76 | 4.48 |
| Finland | 172 | 4.90 | 4.04 | 4.46 | 5.62 | 5.79 | 3.51 | 3.25 | 3.78 | 3.75 | 3.99 | 3.98 | 4.21 |
| France | 132 | 5.29 | 4.84 | 5.97 | 7.28 | 8.13 | 7.46 | 6.66 | 6.04 | 6.25 | 5.82 | 6.07 | 6.05 |
| Germany | 134 | 5.12 | 5.16 | 5.40 | 5.96 | 5.97 | 4.96 | 3.87 | 3.68 | 3.99 | 5.17 | 4.95 | 5.08 |
| Ireland | 178 | 5.19 | 4.98 | 5.53 | 6.52 | 6.75 | 4.28 | 5.39 | 5.88 | 6.11 | 6.66 | 7.62 | 9.04 |
| Italy | 136 | 10.40 | 10.08 | 10.49 | 10.50 | 10.85 | 9.73 | 7.49 | 5.72 | 6.04 | 5.96 | 5.82 | 5.20 |
| Latvia | 941 | 7.45 | 6.11 | 7.29 | 10.91 | 11.85 | 16.23 | 9.56 | 6.39 | 5.52 | 5.92 | .... | .... |
| Lithuania | 946 | 5.74 | † 5.27 | 5.11 | 6.86 | 8.41 | 8.39 | 5.99 | .... | .... | .... | .... | .... |
| Luxembourg | 137 | 3.56 | 3.45 | 3.97 | 4.82 | 4.98 | 2.69 | 2.29 | 2.35 | 2.23 | 2.24 | 2.15 | 2.03 |
| Malta | 181 | 5.32 | 5.51 | 5.65 | 6.24 | 5.89 | 4.47 | 4.60 | 4.75 | 4.70 | .... | .... | .... |
| Netherlands | 138 | 7.80 | 7.30 | 7.94 | 8.71 | 9.66 | 10.01 | 5.75 | 3.21 | .... | .... | .... | .... |
| Portugal | 182 | 7.65 | 7.57 | 7.64 | 7.92 | 8.35 | 6.12 | 6.26 | 7.80 | 8.14 | 8.41 | 7.78 | 6.60 |
| Slovak Republic | 936 | .... | .... | .... | .... | .... | 8.14 | 7.61 | 13.58 | 13.52 | 12.48 | 10.82 | 8.50 |
| Slovenia | 961 | 5.12 | 5.56 | 6.30 | 6.82 | 7.41 | 5.47 | 4.71 | 5.09 | 5.02 | 5.04 | 5.01 | 4.37 |
| Spain | 184 | 8.06 | 7.97 | 8.73 | 9.89 | 11.02 | 10.72 | 7.36 | 5.96 | 6.96 | 6.76 | 6.14 | 4.50 |
| Australia | 193 | 8.85 | 9.06 | 9.41 | † 8.20 | 8.91 | 6.02 | 7.28 | 7.74 | 6.98 | 6.18 | 5.95 | 5.58 |
| Canada | 156 | 4.00 | 4.42 | 5.81 | 6.10 | 4.73 | 2.40 | 2.60 | 3.00 | 3.00 | 3.00 | 3.00 | 2.78 |
| China, P.R.: Hong Kong | 532 | 5.00 | 7.75 | 7.75 | 6.75 | 5.00 | 5.00 | 5.00 | 5.00 | 5.00 | 5.00 | 5.00 | 5.00 |
| Czech Republic | 935 | 6.03 | 5.78 | 5.59 | 5.79 | 6.25 | 5.99 | 5.89 | 5.72 | 5.41 | 4.97 | 4.64 | 4.28 |
| Denmark | 128 | .... | .... | .... | .... | .... | .... | .... | .... | .... | .... | .... | .... |
| Iceland | 176 | 12.02 | 14.78 | 17.91 | 19.29 | 20.14 | 18.99 | 10.26 | 7.70 | 8.32 | 8.15 | 7.74 | 7.61 |
| Israel | 436 | 7.11 | 7.55 | 7.76 | 6.91 | 5.74 | 4.38 | 5.25 | 5.92 | 5.23 | † 4.19 | 3.59 | 3.45 |
| Japan | 158 | 1.77 | 1.68 | 1.66 | 1.88 | 1.91 | 1.72 | 1.60 | 1.50 | 1.41 | 1.30 | 1.22 | .... |
| Korea | 542 | 5.90 | 5.59 | 5.99 | 6.55 | 7.17 | 5.65 | 5.51 | 5.76 | 5.40 | 4.64 | 4.26 | 3.53 |
| New Zealand | 196 | 7.10 | 7.76 | 8.19 | 8.61 | 8.94 | 6.66 | 6.26 | 6.11 | 5.82 | 5.53 | 5.80 | 5.76 |
| Norway | 142 | 4.04 | 4.04 | 4.70 | 6.65 | 7.28 | 4.28 | .... | .... | .... | .... | .... | .... |
| San Marino | 135 | 7.14 | 7.18 | 6.71 | 7.58 | 7.89 | 5.74 | 5.38 | 5.92 | .... | .... | .... | .... |
| Singapore | 576 | 5.30 | 5.30 | 5.31 | 5.33 | 5.38 | 5.38 | 5.38 | 5.38 | 5.38 | 5.38 | 5.35 | 5.35 |
| Sweden | 144 | 4.00 | 3.31 | .... | .... | .... | .... | .... | .... | .... | .... | .... | .... |
| Switzerland | 146 | 3.20 | 3.12 | 3.03 | 3.15 | † 3.34 | 2.75 | 2.73 | 2.72 | 2.69 | 2.69 | 2.69 | 2.68 |
| United Kingdom | 112 | 4.38 | 4.65 | 4.64 | 5.51 | 4.68 | .64 | .50 | .50 | .50 | .50 | .50 | .... |
| United States | 111 | 4.34 | 6.19 | 7.96 | 8.05 | 5.09 | 3.25 | 3.25 | 3.25 | 3.25 | 3.25 | 3.25 | 3.26 |

**Emerging & Dev. Economies**
**Emerging & Developing Asia**

| | Code | 2004 | 2005 | 2006 | 2007 | 2008 | 2009 | 2010 | 2011 | 2012 | 2013 | 2014 | 2015 |
|---|---|---|---|---|---|---|---|---|---|---|---|---|---|
| Bangladesh | 513 | 10.40 | 10.62 | 11.66 | 12.64 | 12.89 | 13.33 | 12.22 | 13.32 | 13.94 | 13.59 | 12.95 | 11.71 |
| Bhutan | 514 | 15.00 | 14.00 | 14.00 | 14.00 | 13.75 | 13.75 | 14.00 | 14.00 | 14.00 | 14.00 | 14.15 | 13.75 |
| Brunei Darussalam | 516 | 5.50 | † 5.50 | 5.50 | 5.50 | 5.50 | 5.50 | 5.50 | 5.50 | 5.50 | 5.50 | 5.50 | 5.50 |
| China, P.R.: Mainland | 924 | 5.58 | 5.58 | 6.12 | 7.47 | 5.31 | 5.31 | 5.81 | 6.56 | 6.00 | 6.00 | 5.60 | 4.35 |
| China,P.R.:Macao | 546 | 6.01 | 7.05 | 8.76 | 7.81 | 5.43 | 5.25 | 5.25 | 5.25 | 5.25 | 5.25 | 5.25 | 5.25 |
| Fiji | 819 | 7.17 | 6.78 | 7.35 | 9.01 | 8.00 | 7.85 | 7.49 | 7.47 | 6.97 | 6.10 | 5.76 | 5.79 |
| India | 534 | 10.92 | 10.75 | 11.19 | 13.02 | 13.31 | 12.19 | † 8.33 | 10.17 | 10.60 | 10.29 | 10.25 | 10.01 |
| Indonesia | 536 | 14.12 | 14.05 | 15.98 | 13.86 | 13.60 | 14.50 | 13.25 | 12.40 | 11.80 | 11.66 | 12.61 | 12.66 |
| Lao People's Dem. Rep. | 544 | 29.25 | 26.83 | 30.00 | 28.50 | 24.00 | 24.78 | 22.61 | .... | .... | .... | .... | .... |
| Malaysia | 548 | . 6.05 | 5.95 | 6.49 | 6.41 | 6.08 | 5.08 | 5.00 | 4.92 | 4.79 | 4.61 | 4.59 | 4.59 |
| Maldives | 556 | † 13.00 | 13.00 | 13.00 | 13.00 | 13.00 | 13.00 | † 10.38 | 10.20 | 10.48 | 11.14 | 11.42 | 11.10 |
| Micronesia, Fed. States of | 868 | 15.38 | 16.38 | 15.62 | 14.03 | 14.38 | 15.38 | 15.13 | 14.35 | 14.32 | 14.83 | 15.83 | 15.93 |
| Mongolia | 948 | 31.47 | 30.57 | 26.93 | 21.83 | 20.58 | 21.67 | 20.07 | 16.61 | 18.11 | 18.48 | 19.03 | 19.56 |
| Myanmar | 518 | 15.00 | 15.00 | 16.08 | 17.00 | 17.00 | 17.00 | 17.00 | 16.33 | 13.00 | 13.00 | 13.00 | 13.00 |
| Nepal | 558 | 8.50 | 8.13 | 8.00 | 8.00 | 8.00 | 8.00 | 8.00 | .... | .... | .... | .... | .... |
| Papua New Guinea | 853 | 13.25 | 11.47 | 10.57 | 9.78 | 9.20 | 10.09 | 10.45 | 10.81 | 10.82 | 10.13 | 9.38 | 8.73 |
| Philippines | 566 | 10.08 | 10.18 | 9.78 | 8.69 | 8.75 | 8.57 | 7.67 | 6.66 | 5.68 | 5.77 | 5.53 | 5.58 |
| Samoa | 862 | 11.23 | 11.43 | 11.72 | 12.65 | 12.66 | 12.08 | 10.72 | 9.96 | 9.86 | 10.20 | 9.98 | 9.39 |
| Solomon Islands | 813 | 14.29 | 14.12 | 13.92 | 14.12 | 14.44 | 15.26 | 14.43 | 13.17 | 11.28 | 10.77 | 10.91 | 10.48 |
| Thailand | 578 | 5.50 | 5.79 | 7.35 | 7.05 | 7.04 | 5.96 | 5.94 | 6.91 | 7.10 | 6.96 | 6.77 | 6.56 |
| Timor-Leste | 537 | 15.54 | 16.65 | 16.55 | 15.05 | 13.11 | 11.17 | 11.03 | 11.04 | 12.21 | 12.41 | 12.87 | 13.50 |
| Tonga | 866 | 11.59 | 11.38 | 11.97 | 12.16 | 12.46 | 12.47 | 11.54 | 11.37 | 10.03 | 9.66 | 8.95 | 8.33 |
| Vanuatu | 846 | 7.61 | 7.47 | 8.25 | 8.16 | 5.29 | 5.50 | 5.50 | 5.50 | 6.05 | 5.00 | 4.69 | 3.63 |
| Vietnam | 582 | 9.72 | 11.03 | 11.18 | 11.18 | 15.78 | 10.07 | 13.14 | 16.95 | 13.47 | 10.37 | 8.67 | 7.12 |

**Europe**
**Emerging & Developing Europe**

| | Code | 2004 | 2005 | 2006 | 2007 | 2008 | 2009 | 2010 | 2011 | 2012 | 2013 | 2014 | 2015 |
|---|---|---|---|---|---|---|---|---|---|---|---|---|---|
| Albania | 914 | 11.76 | 13.08 | 12.94 | 14.10 | 13.02 | 12.66 | 12.82 | 12.43 | 10.88 | 9.83 | 8.66 | 8.70 |
| Bosnia and Herzegovina | 963 | 10.28 | 9.61 | 8.01 | 7.17 | 6.98 | 7.93 | 7.89 | 7.43 | 7.33 | 7.04 | 6.64 | 5.79 |
| Bulgaria | 918 | 8.87 | 8.66 | 8.89 | 10.00 | 10.86 | 11.34 | 11.14 | 10.63 | 9.71 | 9.05 | 8.28 | 7.48 |
| Croatia | 960 | 11.75 | 11.19 | 9.93 | 9.33 | 10.07 | 11.55 | 10.38 | 9.68 | 9.48 | 9.25 | .... | .... |
| Hungary | 944 | 12.82 | 8.54 | 8.08 | 9.09 | 10.18 | 11.04 | 7.59 | 8.32 | 9.00 | 6.30 | 4.45 | 2.90 |
| Kosovo | 967 | 14.77 | 14.00 | 14.57 | 14.06 | 13.79 | 14.09 | 13.97 | 13.30 | 12.24 | 10.90 | 9.29 | 7.69 |
| Macedonia, FYR | 962 | 12.44 | † 12.13 | 11.29 | 10.23 | 9.68 | 10.07 | 9.48 | 8.87 | 8.50 | 8.04 | 7.46 | 7.08 |
| Montenegro | 943 | .... | .... | 11.15 | 9.20 | 9.24 | 9.36 | 9.53 | 9.69 | 9.56 | 9.39 | 9.41 | 8.93 |
| Poland | 964 | 7.56 | 6.83 | 5.48 | .... | .... | .... | .... | .... | .... | .... | .... | .... |
| Romania | 968 | 25.61 | 19.60 | 13.98 | 13.35 | 14.99 | 17.28 | 14.07 | 12.13 | 11.33 | 10.52 | 8.47 | 6.77 |
| Serbia, Republic of | 942 | 15.53 | 16.83 | 16.56 | 11.13 | 16.13 | 11.78 | 17.30 | 17.17 | 18.20 | 17.07 | 14.81 | .... |

**CIS**

| | Code | 2004 | 2005 | 2006 | 2007 | 2008 | 2009 | 2010 | 2011 | 2012 | 2013 | 2014 | 2015 |
|---|---|---|---|---|---|---|---|---|---|---|---|---|---|
| Armenia | 911 | 18.63 | 17.98 | 16.53 | 17.52 | 17.05 | 18.76 | 19.20 | 17.75 | 17.23 | 15.99 | 16.41 | 17.59 |
| Azerbaijan, Republic of | 912 | 15.72 | 17.03 | 17.86 | 19.13 | 19.76 | 20.03 | 20.70 | 18.99 | 18.35 | 18.21 | 17.86 | 17.53 |
| Belarus | 913 | 16.91 | 11.36 | 8.84 | 8.58 | 8.55 | 11.68 | 9.22 | 13.58 | 19.49 | 19.13 | 18.74 | .... |

# National Interest Rates

| | | 2004 | 2005 | 2006 | 2007 | 2008 | 2009 | 2010 | 2011 | 2012 | 2013 | 2014 | 2015 |
|---|---|---|---|---|---|---|---|---|---|---|---|---|---|
| | | \multicolumn{12}{c}{Lending Rates (60p) except for Euro Area and its member countries (60pns)} |
| | | \multicolumn{12}{c}{(Period averages in percent per annum)} |
| **CIS(Cont.)** | | | | | | | | | | | | | |
| Georgia | 915 | 22.09 | 17.55 | 17.06 | 17.09 | 18.04 | 17.87 | 15.85 | 15.00 | 14.81 | 13.59 | 11.91 | 12.49 |
| Kyrgyz Republic | 917 | 29.27 | 26.60 | 23.20 | † 25.83 | 25.69 | 26.36 | 23.11 | 25.27 | 23.90 | 21.73 | 22.36 | 24.25 |
| Moldova | 921 | 20.94 | 19.26 | 18.13 | 18.83 | 21.06 | 20.54 | 16.36 | 14.44 | 13.42 | 12.29 | 11.01 | 14.15 |
| Russia | 922 | 11.44 | 10.68 | 10.43 | 10.03 | 12.23 | 15.31 | 10.82 | 8.46 | 9.10 | 9.47 | 11.14 | 15.72 |
| Tajikistan | 923 | 20.31 | 23.28 | 24.16 | 22.96 | 23.59 | 22.62 | 23.40 | 22.46 | 21.09 | 24.33 | 24.53 | 25.84 |
| Ukraine | 926 | 17.40 | 16.17 | 15.17 | 13.90 | 17.49 | 20.86 | 15.87 | 15.95 | 18.39 | 16.65 | 17.72 | 21.82 |
| **Middle East,N.Africa & Pakistan** | | | | | | | | | | | | | |
| Afghanistan, Islamic Rep. of | 512 | .... | .... | 17.97 | 18.14 | 14.92 | 15.00 | 15.69 | 15.15 | 15.00 | 15.08 | 15.00 | 15.00 |
| Algeria | 612 | 8.00 | 8.00 | 8.00 | 8.00 | 8.00 | 8.00 | 8.00 | 8.00 | 8.00 | 8.00 | 8.00 | 8.00 |
| Bahrain, Kingdom of | 419 | 7.90 | 7.82 | 7.98 | 8.27 | 8.22 | † 7.94 | 7.25 | 6.79 | 6.04 | 5.94 | 5.87 | 5.16 |
| Djibouti | 611 | 11.36 | 11.36 | 11.63 | 10.94 | 11.38 | 11.45 | 10.44 | 11.49 | 11.99 | 11.94 | 12.69 | .... |
| Egypt | 469 | 13.38 | 13.14 | 12.60 | 12.51 | 12.33 | 11.98 | 11.01 | 11.03 | 12.00 | 12.29 | 11.71 | 11.63 |
| Iran, I.R. of | 429 | 16.65 | 16.00 | 14.00 | 12.00 | 12.00 | 12.00 | 12.00 | 11.00 | 11.00 | 11.00 | 14.00 | .... |
| Iraq | 433 | 13.28 | 13.65 | 14.48 | 19.47 | 19.50 | 15.63 | 13.33 | 13.61 | 13.03 | 13.13 | .... | .... |
| Jordan | 439 | 8.26 | 7.61 | 8.18 | 8.68 | 9.03 | 9.25 | 9.02 | 8.71 | 8.78 | 9.01 | 8.99 | 8.48 |
| Kuwait | 443 | 5.64 | 7.50 | 8.58 | 8.54 | 7.61 | 6.16 | 4.91 | 5.19 | 4.98 | 4.56 | 4.27 | 4.28 |
| Lebanon | 446 | 10.81 | 10.64 | 10.26 | 10.26 | 9.96 | 9.57 | 8.34 | 7.53 | 7.25 | 7.35 | 7.27 | 7.09 |
| Libya | 672 | 6.08 | 6.13 | 6.33 | 6.00 | 6.00 | 6.00 | 6.00 | 6.00 | 6.00 | 6.00 | 6.00 | .... |
| Mauritania | 682 | 21.00 | 23.08 | 24.00 | 23.50 | 20.33 | 19.50 | 17.00 | 17.00 | 17.00 | .... | .... | .... |
| Morocco | 686 | 11.50 | 11.50 | .... | .... | .... | .... | .... | .... | .... | .... | .... | .... |
| Oman | 449 | 7.57 | 7.07 | 7.40 | 7.29 | 7.10 | 7.44 | 6.84 | 6.19 | 5.65 | 5.41 | 5.08 | 4.76 |
| Qatar | 453 | 6.99 | 6.65 | 7.18 | 7.43 | 6.84 | 7.04 | 7.27 | 5.49 | 5.38 | 5.11 | 4.96 | 4.44 |
| Syrian Arab Republic | 463 | 7.50 | 8.00 | 8.00 | 10.17 | 10.19 | 10.01 | 9.90 | .... | .... | .... | .... | .... |
| West Bank and Gaza | 487 | 6.92 | 7.34 | 7.73 | 7.98 | 7.19 | 6.19 | 6.24 | 6.79 | 6.97 | 7.52 | 6.41 | 6.80 |
| Yemen, Republic of | 474 | 18.50 | 18.00 | 18.00 | 18.00 | 18.00 | 18.00 | 23.83 | 25.00 | 24.50 | 22.08 | .... | .... |
| **Sub-Saharan Africa** | | | | | | | | | | | | | |
| Angola | 614 | 82.33 | 67.72 | 19.51 | 17.70 | 12.53 | 15.68 | 22.54 | 18.76 | 16.66 | 15.81 | 16.38 | 16.88 |
| Botswana | 616 | 15.75 | 15.74 | 16.46 | 16.22 | 16.54 | 13.76 | 11.46 | 11.00 | 11.00 | 10.19 | 9.00 | 7.95 |
| Burundi | 618 | 18.25 | 18.45 | 17.07 | 16.84 | 16.52 | 14.08 | 12.42 | 13.23 | 14.32 | 15.15 | 15.67 | 15.33 |
| Cabo Verde | 624 | 12.69 | 12.29 | † 9.86 | 10.55 | 9.99 | 10.98 | 11.04 | 9.81 | 9.90 | 10.52 | 10.89 | 10.41 |
| Comoros | 632 | 11.00 | 11.00 | 10.50 | 10.50 | 10.50 | 10.50 | 10.50 | 10.50 | 10.50 | 10.50 | 10.50 | 10.50 |
| Ethiopia | 644 | 7.00 | 7.00 | 7.00 | 7.50 | 8.00 | .... | .... | .... | .... | .... | .... | .... |
| Gambia, The | 648 | 36.50 | 34.92 | 29.75 | 27.92 | 27.00 | 27.00 | 27.00 | 28.00 | 28.00 | 28.00 | 28.50 | .... |
| Kenya | 664 | † 12.53 | 12.88 | 13.64 | 13.34 | 14.02 | 14.80 | 14.37 | 15.05 | 19.72 | 17.31 | 16.51 | 16.09 |
| Lesotho | 666 | 12.38 | 11.72 | 12.16 | 14.13 | 16.19 | 13.00 | 11.22 | 10.43 | 10.12 | 9.92 | 10.34 | 10.59 |
| Liberia | 668 | 18.10 | 17.03 | 15.50 | 15.05 | 14.40 | 14.19 | 14.24 | 13.75 | 13.52 | 13.49 | 13.50 | 13.61 |
| Madagascar | 674 | 25.50 | 27.00 | 29.50 | 45.00 | 45.00 | 45.00 | 49.00 | 52.50 | 60.00 | 60.00 | 60.00 | 60.00 |
| Malawi | 676 | 36.83 | 33.08 | 32.25 | 27.72 | 25.28 | 25.25 | 24.63 | 23.75 | 32.33 | 46.01 | 44.29 | 44.39 |
| Mauritius | 684 | 21.00 | 21.04 | 21.08 | 21.87 | 11.54 | 9.25 | 8.88 | 8.92 | 8.67 | 8.50 | 8.50 | 8.50 |
| Mozambique | 688 | 22.08 | 19.47 | 18.56 | 19.52 | 18.31 | 15.68 | 16.26 | 19.10 | 16.81 | 15.32 | 14.80 | 14.87 |
| Namibia | 728 | 11.39 | 10.61 | 11.18 | 12.88 | 13.74 | 11.12 | 9.72 | 8.73 | 8.65 | 8.29 | 8.70 | 9.32 |
| Nigeria | 694 | 19.18 | 17.95 | 16.90 | 16.94 | 15.48 | 18.36 | 17.59 | 16.02 | 16.79 | 16.72 | 16.55 | 16.85 |
| Rwanda | 714 | 16.48 | 16.08 | 16.07 | 16.11 | 16.51 | 15.77 | 16.94 | 16.73 | 16.49 | 16.93 | 17.66 | 17.03 |
| São Tomé & Príncipe | 716 | 29.77 | 31.20 | 29.30 | 32.40 | 32.40 | 31.11 | 28.87 | 26.95 | 26.17 | † 23.28 | 15.90 | .... |
| Seychelles | 718 | 9.99 | 9.77 | 10.05 | 10.89 | 11.81 | 15.35 | 12.70 | 11.19 | 12.19 | 12.29 | 11.65 | 12.36 |
| Sierra Leone | 724 | 22.08 | 24.58 | 24.00 | 25.00 | 24.50 | 22.17 | 21.25 | 21.00 | 21.00 | 20.56 | 19.41 | 18.73 |
| South Africa | 199 | 11.29 | 10.63 | 11.17 | 13.17 | 15.13 | 11.71 | 9.83 | 9.00 | 8.75 | 8.50 | 9.13 | 9.42 |
| South Sudan, Republic of | 733 | .... | .... | .... | .... | .... | .... | .... | .... | 14.71 | 14.10 | 12.71 | 12.55 |
| Swaziland | 734 | 11.29 | 10.63 | 11.17 | 13.17 | 14.83 | 11.38 | 9.75 | 9.00 | 8.75 | 8.50 | 8.63 | 9.04 |
| Tanzania | 738 | 14.14 | 15.25 | 15.65 | 16.07 | 14.98 | 15.03 | 14.55 | 14.96 | 15.46 | 15.83 | 16.26 | 16.10 |
| Uganda | 746 | 20.60 | 19.65 | 18.70 | 19.11 | 20.45 | 20.96 | 20.17 | 21.83 | 26.31 | 23.25 | 21.53 | 22.60 |
| Zambia | 754 | 30.73 | 28.21 | 23.15 | 18.89 | 19.06 | 22.06 | 20.92 | 18.84 | 12.15 | 9.52 | 11.57 | 13.25 |
| **Western Hemisphere** | | | | | | | | | | | | | |
| ECCU | 309 | 10.93 | 10.49 | 10.19 | 9.84 | 9.71 | 10.00 | 10.13 | 10.02 | 9.47 | 9.25 | 9.30 | 9.15 |
| Anguilla | 312 | 10.99 | 10.38 | 10.04 | 9.76 | 9.51 | 9.27 | 11.38 | 9.30 | 9.38 | 9.08 | 9.09 | 9.05 |
| Antigua and Barbuda | 311 | 11.96 | 11.39 | 10.89 | 10.44 | 10.43 | 10.07 | 11.00 | 10.91 | 10.16 | 9.95 | 10.07 | 9.83 |
| Dominica | 321 | 8.94 | 9.92 | 9.50 | 9.17 | 9.06 | 10.02 | 9.46 | 8.84 | 9.04 | 9.07 | 8.94 | 8.67 |
| Grenada | 328 | 10.18 | 10.07 | 9.85 | 9.76 | 9.53 | 10.99 | 10.58 | 10.69 | 9.73 | 9.27 | 9.19 | 8.96 |
| Montserrat | 351 | 10.95 | 10.56 | 10.48 | 10.40 | 9.89 | 9.04 | 8.73 | 8.56 | 8.16 | 8.00 | 8.02 | 7.82 |
| St. Kitts and Nevis | 361 | 10.25 | 10.03 | 9.30 | 9.28 | 8.70 | 8.75 | 8.62 | 9.45 | 8.73 | 8.78 | 9.28 | 9.30 |
| St. Lucia | 362 | 11.07 | 10.61 | 10.78 | 10.12 | 10.08 | 10.58 | 10.62 | 10.00 | 9.50 | 9.08 | 9.00 | 8.86 |
| St. Vincent & Grenadines | 364 | 9.69 | 9.58 | 9.73 | 9.61 | 9.52 | 9.19 | 9.17 | 9.14 | 9.41 | 9.44 | 9.15 | 9.30 |
| Argentina | 213 | 6.78 | 6.16 | 8.63 | 11.05 | 19.47 | † 15.66 | 10.56 | 14.09 | 14.06 | 17.15 | 24.01 | 24.92 |
| Aruba | 314 | 11.58 | 11.53 | 11.33 | 11.01 | 11.23 | 10.77 | 10.65 | 9.66 | 9.18 | 8.73 | 8.23 | 8.25 |
| Bahamas, The | 313 | 6.00 | 5.54 | 5.50 | 5.50 | 5.50 | 5.50 | 5.50 | 5.06 | 4.75 | 4.75 | 4.75 | 4.75 |
| Barbados | 316 | 8.33 | 9.17 | 10.29 | 10.76 | 10.03 | 9.20 | 8.70 | 8.70 | 8.70 | 8.70 | 8.38 | 8.06 |
| Belize | 339 | 13.94 | 14.26 | 14.21 | 14.33 | 14.14 | 14.08 | 13.88 | 13.36 | 12.44 | 11.57 | 10.82 | 10.32 |
| Bolivia | 218 | 14.47 | 16.62 | 11.89 | 12.86 | 13.87 | 12.36 | 9.91 | 10.92 | 11.13 | 11.05 | 9.69 | 8.07 |
| Brazil | 223 | 54.93 | 55.38 | 50.81 | 43.72 | 47.25 | 44.65 | 39.99 | 43.88 | 36.64 | 27.39 | 32.01 | 43.96 |
| Chile | 228 | 5.13 | 6.68 | 8.00 | 8.67 | 13.26 | 7.25 | 4.75 | 9.03 | 10.06 | 9.26 | 8.10 | 5.51 |
| Colombia | 233 | 15.08 | 14.56 | 12.89 | 15.38 | 17.18 | 13.01 | 9.38 | 11.22 | 12.59 | 10.99 | 10.87 | 11.45 |
| Costa Rica | 238 | 23.43 | 24.66 | 22.19 | 12.80 | 15.83 | 19.72 | 17.09 | 16.15 | 18.21 | 15.19 | 14.90 | 14.23 |
| Dominican Republic | 243 | 32.63 | 24.11 | 19.48 | 15.83 | 19.95 | 18.14 | 12.14 | 15.55 | 15.48 | 13.59 | 13.90 | 14.88 |
| Ecuador | 248 | 9.95 | 9.62 | 9.81 | .... | .... | .... | .... | .... | .... | .... | .... | .... |
| El Salvador | 253 | 6.30 | 6.87 | 7.53 | 7.81 | 7.87 | 9.32 | 7.62 | 5.99 | 5.60 | 5.74 | 5.99 | 6.17 |
| Guatemala | 258 | 13.81 | 13.03 | 12.76 | 12.84 | 13.39 | 13.85 | 13.34 | 13.43 | 13.49 | 13.60 | 13.77 | 13.23 |
| Guyana | 336 | 14.54 | 14.54 | 14.54 | 14.61 | 14.58 | 14.54 | 14.54 | 14.45 | 13.86 | 13.50 | 12.83 | 12.83 |
| Haiti | 263 | 48.00 | † 22.25 | 26.37 | 23.08 | 17.81 | 17.33 | 17.48 | 11.61 | 8.93 | 8.72 | 10.77 | 12.92 |
| Honduras | 268 | 19.88 | 18.83 | 17.44 | 16.61 | 17.94 | 19.45 | 18.86 | 18.56 | 18.45 | 20.08 | 20.61 | 20.66 |
| Jamaica | 343 | 18.14 | 17.36 | 17.64 | 17.20 | 16.83 | 16.43 | 20.45 | 19.51 | 17.63 | 17.72 | 17.22 | 16.98 |
| Mexico | 273 | 7.44 | 9.70 | 7.51 | 7.56 | 8.71 | 7.07 | 5.29 | 4.92 | 4.73 | 4.25 | 3.55 | 3.42 |

# National Interest Rates

| | | 2004 | 2005 | 2006 | 2007 | 2008 | 2009 | 2010 | 2011 | 2012 | 2013 | 2014 | 2015 |
|---|---|---|---|---|---|---|---|---|---|---|---|---|---|
| | | | | | Lending Rates (60p) except for Euro Area and its member countries (60pns) | | | | | | | | |
| | | | | | *(Period averages in percent per annum)* | | | | | | | | |
| **Western Hemisphere(Cont.)** | | | | | | | | | | | | | |
| Netherlands Antilles.................... | 353 | 10.56 | 9.60 | 9.28 | 9.36 | 8.41 | 7.51 | . . . . | . . . . | . . . . | . . . . | . . . . | . . . . |
| Nicaragua...................................... | 278 | 13.49 | 12.10 | 11.58 | 13.04 | 13.17 | 14.04 | 13.32 | 10.54 | 11.99 | 14.98 | 13.54 | 12.05 |
| Panama........................................ | 283 | 8.82 | 8.67 | 8.39 | 8.25 | 8.16 | 8.25 | 7.74 | 6.91 | 6.91 | 6.59 | 6.83 | 7.46 |
| Paraguay...................................... | 288 | 33.54 | 29.91 | 30.14 | 25.02 | 25.81 | 28.26 | 26.04 | † 17.40 | 17.16 | 19.27 | 21.19 | 19.74 |
| Peru............................................. | 293 | 24.67 | 25.53 | 23.93 | 22.86 | 23.67 | 21.04 | 18.98 | 18.68 | 19.24 | 18.14 | 15.74 | 16.11 |
| Suriname...................................... | 366 | 20.44 | 17.40 | 15.64 | 13.77 | 12.20 | 11.65 | 11.59 | 11.76 | 11.74 | 11.98 | 12.28 | 12.62 |
| Trinidad and Tobago.................... | 369 | 9.31 | 9.10 | 10.92 | 11.75 | 12.44 | 11.94 | 9.28 | 7.97 | 7.71 | 7.50 | 7.50 | 8.18 |
| Uruguay....................................... | 298 | 23.68 | 13.61 | 9.25 | 8.94 | 12.45 | 15.28 | 10.33 | 9.78 | 11.20 | 12.43 | 15.53 | 15.84 |
| Venezuela, Rep. Bol...................... | 299 | 18.50 | 16.81 | 15.48 | 17.11 | 22.37 | 19.89 | 18.35 | 17.15 | 16.38 | 15.90 | 17.21 | 19.40 |

# National Interest Rates

| | | 2004 | 2005 | 2006 | 2007 | 2008 | 2009 | 2010 | 2011 | 2012 | 2013 | 2014 | 2015 |
|---|---|---|---|---|---|---|---|---|---|---|---|---|---|
| | | \multicolumn{12}{c}{Government Bond Yields (61)} | | | | | | | | | | | |

**Government Bond Yields (61)**
*(Average yields to maturity in percent per annum)*

| | | 2004 | 2005 | 2006 | 2007 | 2008 | 2009 | 2010 | 2011 | 2012 | 2013 | 2014 | 2015 |
|---|---|---|---|---|---|---|---|---|---|---|---|---|---|
| **Advanced Economies** | | | | | | | | | | | | | |
| Euro Area | 163 | 4.14 | 3.44 | 3.86 | 4.33 | 4.36 | 4.03 | 3.78 | 4.31 | 3.05 | 3.01 | 2.28 | 1.27 |
| Austria | 122 | 4.13 | 3.39 | 3.80 | 4.30 | 4.36 | 3.94 | 3.23 | 3.32 | 2.37 | 2.01 | 1.49 | .75 |
| Belgium | 124 | 4.15 | 3.43 | 3.82 | 4.33 | 4.42 | 3.90 | 3.46 | 4.23 | 3.00 | 2.41 | 1.71 | .84 |
| Cyprus | 423 | 5.80 | 5.16 | 4.13 | 4.48 | 4.60 | 4.60 | 4.60 | 5.79 | 7.00 | 6.50 | 6.00 | 4.54 |
| Estonia | 939 | 4.39 | 3.98 | 4.30 | 5.63 | 8.16 | 7.78 | 5.97 | .... | .... | .... | .... | .... |
| Finland | 172 | 4.11 | 3.35 | 3.78 | 4.29 | 4.29 | 3.74 | 3.01 | 3.01 | 1.88 | 1.86 | 1.45 | .72 |
| France | 132 | 4.10 | 3.41 | 3.80 | 4.30 | 4.23 | 3.65 | 3.12 | 3.32 | 2.54 | 2.20 | 1.67 | .84 |
| Germany | 134 | 4.04 | 3.35 | 3.76 | 4.22 | 3.98 | 3.22 | 2.74 | 2.61 | 1.50 | 1.57 | 1.16 | .50 |
| Greece | 174 | 4.26 | 3.59 | 4.07 | 4.50 | 4.80 | 5.17 | 9.09 | 15.75 | 22.50 | 10.05 | 6.93 | 9.81 |
| Ireland | 178 | 4.08 | 3.33 | 3.77 | 4.31 | 4.53 | 5.23 | 5.74 | 9.60 | 6.17 | 3.79 | 2.37 | 1.18 |
| Italy | 136 | 4.26 | 3.56 | 4.05 | 4.49 | 4.68 | 4.31 | 4.04 | 5.42 | 5.49 | 4.32 | 2.89 | 1.71 |
| Latvia | 941 | 4.86 | 3.88 | 4.13 | 5.28 | 6.43 | 12.35 | 10.34 | 5.91 | 4.57 | 3.34 | 2.51 | .96 |
| Lithuania | 946 | 4.50 | 3.70 | 4.08 | 4.55 | 5.61 | 14.00 | 5.57 | 5.16 | 4.83 | 3.83 | 2.79 | 1.38 |
| Luxembourg | 137 | 2.84 | 2.41 | 3.30 | 4.46 | 4.61 | 4.23 | 3.17 | 2.92 | 1.75 | 1.85 | 1.34 | .37 |
| Malta | 181 | 4.69 | 4.56 | 4.32 | 4.72 | 4.81 | 4.54 | 4.19 | 4.49 | 4.13 | 3.36 | 2.61 | 1.49 |
| Netherlands | 138 | 4.09 | 3.37 | 3.78 | 4.29 | 4.23 | 3.69 | 2.99 | 2.99 | 1.93 | 1.96 | 1.45 | .69 |
| Portugal | 182 | 4.14 | 3.44 | 3.92 | 4.42 | 4.52 | 4.21 | 5.40 | 10.24 | 10.55 | 6.29 | 3.75 | 2.42 |
| Slovak Republic | 936 | 5.03 | 3.52 | 4.41 | 4.49 | 4.72 | 4.71 | 3.87 | 4.42 | 4.55 | 3.19 | 2.07 | .89 |
| Slovenia | 961 | 4.68 | 3.81 | 3.85 | 4.53 | 4.61 | 4.38 | 3.83 | 4.97 | 5.81 | 5.81 | 3.27 | 1.71 |
| Spain | 184 | 4.10 | 3.39 | 3.79 | 4.31 | 4.37 | 3.98 | 4.25 | 5.44 | 5.85 | 4.56 | 2.72 | 1.74 |
| Australia | 193 | 5.59 | 5.34 | 5.59 | 5.99 | 5.82 | 5.04 | 5.37 | 4.88 | 3.38 | 3.70 | 3.66 | 2.71 |
| Canada | 156 | 5.08 | 4.39 | 4.30 | 4.34 | 4.04 | 3.89 | 3.66 | 3.21 | 2.33 | 2.72 | 2.60 | 2.02 |
| Czech Republic | 935 | 4.05 | 3.61 | 3.68 | 4.65 | 4.30 | 3.98 | 3.89 | 3.70 | 2.12 | 2.20 | .67 | .49 |
| Denmark | 128 | 4.31 | 3.40 | 3.81 | 4.29 | 4.28 | 3.59 | 2.93 | 2.73 | 1.40 | 1.75 | 1.33 | .69 |
| Iceland | 176 | 3.88 | 3.73 | 4.32 | 4.96 | 4.30 | 4.30 | 3.49 | 2.95 | 2.28 | 2.55 | 3.20 | 2.66 |
| Japan | 158 | 1.50 | 1.36 | 1.73 | 1.65 | 1.45 | 1.34 | 1.15 | 1.12 | .84 | .70 | .53 | .35 |
| Korea | 542 | 4.45 | 4.66 | 5.07 | 5.43 | 5.79 | 5.10 | 4.59 | 4.11 | 3.43 | 3.16 | 2.98 | 2.11 |
| New Zealand | 196 | 5.98 | 5.98 | 6.01 | 6.81 | 6.17 | 4.66 | 4.86 | 4.02 | 3.11 | 3.52 | 4.02 | 3.01 |
| Norway | 142 | 3.60 | 3.28 | 3.93 | 4.78 | 4.35 | 3.32 | 2.77 | 2.56 | 1.57 | 1.92 | 1.76 | .97 |
| Singapore | 576 | 3.23 | 2.92 | 3.36 | 2.88 | 2.78 | 2.37 | 2.37 | 2.09 | 1.46 | 2.06 | 2.36 | 2.44 |
| Sweden | 144 | 4.43 | 3.38 | 3.71 | 4.17 | 3.89 | 3.25 | 2.89 | 2.61 | 1.59 | 2.12 | 1.72 | .72 |
| Switzerland | 146 | 2.38 | 1.96 | 2.49 | 3.11 | 2.15 | 1.97 | 1.67 | .74 | .56 | 1.25 | .38 | −.04 |
| United Kingdom | 112 | 4.88 | 4.41 | 4.50 | 5.01 | 4.59 | 3.65 | 3.62 | 3.14 | 1.92 | 2.39 | 2.57 | 1.90 |
| United States | 111 | 4.27 | 4.29 | 4.79 | 4.63 | 3.67 | 3.26 | 3.21 | 2.79 | 1.80 | 2.35 | 2.54 | 2.14 |
| **Emerging & Dev. Economies** | | | | | | | | | | | | | |
| **Emerging & Developing Asia** | | | | | | | | | | | | | |
| Bangladesh | 513 | .... | .... | .... | .... | .... | 10.14 | 8.86 | 9.49 | 11.60 | 12.13 | 11.49 | 9.44 |
| Fiji | 819 | 2.55 | 2.74 | 5.75 | 6.87 | 5.91 | 8.13 | .... | .... | 4.00 | 4.00 | † 4.58 | 5.17 |
| India | 534 | .... | † 6.96 | 7.66 | 7.97 | 7.85 | 6.95 | 7.85 | 8.37 | 8.29 | 8.15 | 8.56 | 7.77 |
| Malaysia | 548 | 4.09 | 3.57 | 4.01 | 3.57 | 3.73 | 3.59 | 3.52 | 3.45 | 3.25 | 3.42 | 3.69 | 3.67 |
| Maldives | 556 | .... | .... | .... | .... | .... | 8.00 | 8.00 | 8.00 | 8.00 | † 7.73 | † 2.40 | 2.40 |
| Myanmar | 518 | 9.00 | 9.00 | 12.00 | 12.00 | 12.00 | 12.00 | 12.00 | 12.00 | 9.00 | 9.00 | 9.00 | 9.00 |
| Nepal | 558 | 6.63 | 6.50 | 6.13 | 6.00 | 6.00 | 6.00 | 6.00 | 6.00 | 6.00 | 6.00 | 6.00 | 6.00 |
| Papua New Guinea | 853 | .... | 8.00 | 8.17 | 8.42 | 9.24 | 11.66 | 10.86 | 8.95 | 9.06 | 8.13 | 10.15 | 10.79 |
| Samoa | 862 | 13.50 | 13.50 | 13.50 | .... | .... | .... | .... | .... | .... | .... | .... | .... |
| Solomon Islands | 813 | 4.60 | † 2.99 | 3.24 | 3.24 | 3.24 | 3.24 | 3.24 | 3.24 | 3.24 | 3.24 | 3.24 | 3.24 |
| Thailand | 578 | 4.86 | 5.00 | 5.39 | 4.60 | 4.56 | 3.91 | 3.60 | 3.69 | 3.53 | 3.80 | 3.57 | 2.73 |
| Vanuatu | 846 | 8.50 | 8.50 | 8.50 | 8.58 | 8.50 | 8.45 | 8.24 | 7.91 | 7.64 | 7.82 | 7.81 | 7.80 |
| **Europe** | | | | | | | | | | | | | |
| **Emerging & Developing Europe** | | | | | | | | | | | | | |
| Bulgaria | 918 | 5.36 | 3.87 | 4.18 | 4.54 | 5.38 | 7.22 | 6.00 | 5.36 | 4.50 | 3.47 | 3.35 | 2.49 |
| Hungary | 944 | 8.19 | 6.60 | 7.12 | 6.74 | 8.24 | 9.12 | 7.28 | 7.64 | 7.89 | 5.92 | 4.81 | 3.43 |
| Poland | 964 | 6.90 | 5.22 | 5.23 | 5.48 | 6.07 | 6.12 | 5.78 | 5.96 | 5.00 | 4.03 | 3.52 | 2.70 |
| Romania | 968 | .... | .... | 7.23 | 7.14 | 7.70 | 9.69 | 7.34 | 6.65 | 5.69 | 4.25 | 2.21 | 1.27 |
| **CIS** | | | | | | | | | | | | | |
| Armenia | 911 | 8.21 | 5.18 | 5.86 | 6.56 | 8.32 | 11.86 | 13.88 | 13.80 | 14.30 | 13.20 | 9.82 | 14.41 |
| Kyrgyz Republic | 917 | .... | .... | .... | .... | .... | 9.00 | 18.90 | 16.00 | 14.53 | 13.40 | 14.42 | 15.70 |
| Russia | 922 | .... | 7.84 | 6.74 | 6.52 | 7.53 | 10.06 | 7.57 | 7.71 | .... | .... | .... | .... |
| **Middle East,N.Africa & Pakistan** | | | | | | | | | | | | | |
| Morocco | 686 | 5.67 | 5.35 | 4.04 | 3.65 | .... | .... | 4.34 | 4.36 | 4.57 | .... | 4.30 | 4.01 |
| Pakistan | 564 | 4.63 | 6.19 | 8.47 | 9.50 | 11.66 | 12.73 | 13.05 | 13.36 | 11.73 | 10.49 | 11.87 | 7.72 |
| **Sub-Saharan Africa** | | | | | | | | | | | | | |
| Botswana | 616 | 10.07 | 9.49 | 11.60 | 10.73 | 10.19 | 8.63 | 7.69 | 7.44 | 5.67 | 5.01 | 4.21 | 3.67 |
| Ethiopia | 644 | 3.91 | 3.98 | 4.00 | 4.00 | 4.00 | .... | .... | .... | .... | .... | .... | .... |
| Ghana | 652 | 21.50 | 20.54 | 16.42 | 12.71 | 14.89 | .... | 15.14 | 13.43 | 20.41 | 18.24 | 24.34 | 23.52 |
| Namibia | 728 | 12.11 | 10.89 | 9.61 | 10.02 | 10.02 | 10.02 | .... | .... | .... | .... | .... | .... |
| Seychelles | 718 | 6.58 | 6.00 | 6.89 | 7.14 | 7.32 | 8.75 | 8.06 | 9.00 | .... | .... | 5.50 | 5.50 |
| South Africa | 199 | 9.53 | 8.07 | 7.94 | 7.99 | 9.10 | 8.70 | 8.62 | 8.52 | 7.90 | 7.72 | 8.25 | 8.17 |
| **Western Hemisphere** | | | | | | | | | | | | | |
| Mexico | 273 | 9.54 | 9.42 | 8.39 | 7.79 | 8.31 | 7.96 | 7.11 | 6.65 | 5.60 | 5.68 | 6.01 | 5.99 |
| Netherlands Antilles | 353 | 7.09 | 6.46 | 6.75 | 7.32 | 5.66 | 4.82 | .... | .... | .... | .... | .... | .... |
| Venezuela, Rep. Bol | 299 | 15.57 | 12.93 | 7.81 | 9.55 | 14.47 | 12.84 | 15.53 | 17.52 | 16.76 | 15.26 | 16.12 | 15.39 |

# International Interest Rates

| | | 2004 | 2005 | 2006 | 2007 | 2008 | 2009 | 2010 | 2011 | 2012 | 2013 | 2014 | 2015 |
|---|---|---|---|---|---|---|---|---|---|---|---|---|---|
| | | **London Interbank Offer Rates on US Dollar Deposits** | | | | | | | | | | | |
| | | (11160lda, 60ldb, 60ldc, 60ldd, 60lde, 60ldf) | | | | | | | | | | | |
| | | *(Period averages in percent per annum)* | | | | | | | | | | | |
| Overnight............................ | 111 | 1.40 | 3.25 | 5.02 | 5.15 | 2.31 | .23 | .23 | .16 | .15 | .13 | .10 | .13 |
| One-Month........................... | 111 | 1.50 | 3.38 | 5.09 | 5.25 | 2.67 | .33 | .27 | .23 | .24 | .19 | .16 | .20 |
| Three-Month......................... | 111 | 1.62 | 3.56 | 5.19 | 5.30 | 2.91 | .69 | .34 | .34 | .43 | .27 | .24 | .32 |
| Six-Month............................. | 111 | 1.79 | 3.76 | 5.27 | 5.25 | 3.05 | 1.12 | .52 | .51 | .69 | .41 | .34 | .48 |
| One-Year............................... | 111 | 2.12 | 4.02 | 5.32 | 5.12 | 3.08 | 1.57 | .92 | .83 | 1.01 | .68 | .58 | .79 |
| | | **London Interbank Offer Rates on Three-Month Deposits (60ea)** | | | | | | | | | | | |
| | | (Euro rate relates to Euribor) | | | | | | | | | | | |
| | | *(Period averages in percent per annum)* | | | | | | | | | | | |
| Euro...................................... | 163 | 2.11 | 2.18 | 3.08 | 4.28 | 4.63 | 1.23 | .81 | 1.39 | .57 | .22 | .15 | −.02 |
| Swiss Franc........................... | 146 | .47 | .80 | 1.52 | 2.55 | 2.58 | .38 | .19 | .12 | .07 | .02 | −.22 | −.75 |
| Japanese Yen........................ | 158 | .05 | .06 | .30 | .79 | .92 | .48 | .23 | .19 | .19 | .15 | .12 | .09 |
| Pound Sterling...................... | 112 | 4.64 | 4.76 | 4.85 | 6.00 | 5.51 | 1.21 | .70 | .87 | .83 | .51 | .55 | .57 |
| | | **London Interbank Offer Rates on Six-Month Deposits (60eb)** | | | | | | | | | | | |
| | | (Euro rates relates to Euribor) | | | | | | | | | | | |
| | | *(Period averages in percent per annum)* | | | | | | | | | | | |
| Euro...................................... | 163 | 2.15 | 2.24 | 3.23 | 4.35 | 4.72 | 1.45 | 1.08 | 1.64 | .83 | .34 | .24 | .05 |
| Japanese Yen........................ | 158 | .06 | .07 | .37 | .86 | 1.00 | .67 | .43 | .34 | .33 | .24 | .16 | .13 |
| Swiss Franc........................... | 146 | .59 | .87 | 1.66 | 2.65 | 2.69 | .50 | .27 | .18 | .15 | .08 | −.15 | −.69 |
| Pound Sterling...................... | 112 | 4.77 | 4.76 | 4.92 | 6.04 | 5.59 | 1.42 | .97 | 1.16 | 1.09 | .60 | .68 | .72 |
| | | **SDR Interest Rate (99260s) and Rate of Remuneration (99260r)** | | | | | | | | | | | |
| | | *(Period averages in percent per annum)* | | | | | | | | | | | |
| SDR Interest Rate.................. | 992 | 1.84 | 2.60 | 3.69 | 4.05 | 2.56 | .39 | .29 | .40 | .11 | .08 | .08 | .05 |
| United States (3-Mo.T-Bill Rate)..... | 111 | 1.39 | 3.21 | 4.85 | 4.45 | 1.37 | .14 | .13 | .05 | .08 | .05 | .03 | .... |
| United Kingdom (3-Mo.T-Bill Rate) | 112 | 4.44 | 4.59 | 4.67 | 5.60 | 4.35 | .54 | .50 | .49 | .31 | .30 | .38 | .44 |
| Eurepo (3-Mo. Interbank Rate)....... | 163 | 2.046 | 2.123 | 3.006 | 3.981 | 3.783 | .695 | .481 | .816 | .064 | .046 | .055 | −.244 |
| Japan (13-Wk. Fin. Bill Rate)......... | 158 | — | — | .42 | .55 | .36 | .12 | .13 | .10 | .09 | .06 | −.01 | −.02 |
| Rate of Remuneration................. | 992 | 1.84 | 2.60 | 3.69 | 4.05 | 2.56 | .39 | .29 | .40 | .11 | .08 | .08 | .05 |

# Real Effective Exchange Rate Indices

| | | 2004 | 2005 | 2006 | 2007 | 2008 | 2009 | 2010 | 2011 | 2012 | 2013 | 2014 | 2015 |
|---|---|---|---|---|---|---|---|---|---|---|---|---|---|
| | | | | | | | (2010=100) | | | | | | |
| | | | | | | | Based on Relative Unit Labor Costs (...rel) | | | | | | |
| **Advanced Economies** | | | | | | | | | | | | | |
| Euro Area | 163 | 94.4 | 93.7 | 93.6 | 98.4 | 105.9 | 105.1 | 100.0 | 98.2 | 93.5 | 98.0 | 98.7 | 89.9 |
| Austria | 122 | 105.9 | 106.5 | 104.6 | 104.1 | 100.6 | 99.4 | 100.0 | 100.0 | 99.2 | 100.9 | 101.2 | 97.9 |
| Belgium | 124 | 97.0 | 97.5 | 100.1 | 102.3 | 103.8 | 103.5 | 100.0 | 100.0 | 99.1 | 102.0 | 103.2 | 100.0 |
| Finland | 172 | 109.2 | 109.4 | 104.1 | 100.1 | 101.4 | 102.9 | 100.0 | 100.0 | 98.9 | 100.4 | 101.1 | 97.3 |
| France | 132 | 96.0 | 95.9 | 97.9 | 100.8 | 101.4 | 99.3 | 100.0 | 101.0 | 100.4 | 104.5 | 106.8 | 104.8 |
| Germany | 134 | 100.6 | 97.4 | 94.0 | 94.9 | 99.4 | 101.3 | 100.0 | 96.1 | 94.1 | 97.0 | 97.2 | 92.4 |
| Greece | 174 | 101.1 | 96.9 | 99.9 | 102.4 | 100.9 | 101.1 | 100.0 | 99.7 | 90.3 | 85.5 | 84.8 | 81.8 |
| Ireland | 178 | 130.8 | 139.8 | 140.4 | 137.9 | 137.1 | 116.9 | 100.0 | 91.4 | 87.5 | 89.5 | 89.5 | 83.6 |
| Italy | 136 | 87.5 | 89.8 | 91.1 | 95.1 | 100.7 | 101.0 | 100.0 | 107.2 | 107.6 | 109.2 | 108.8 | 103.7 |
| Luxembourg | 137 | 97.2 | 97.6 | 100.3 | 101.8 | 103.2 | 103.4 | 100.0 | 99.8 | 99.0 | 101.5 | 102.6 | 100.4 |
| Netherlands | 138 | 102.6 | 100.9 | 100.4 | 101.0 | 105.3 | 103.8 | 100.0 | 99.9 | 98.1 | 100.0 | 99.9 | 95.2 |
| Portugal | 182 | 98.0 | 100.5 | 101.9 | 101.8 | 101.3 | 99.1 | 100.0 | 100.9 | 94.7 | 93.1 | 92.5 | 89.4 |
| Spain | 184 | 89.5 | 92.7 | 95.5 | 101.0 | 106.2 | 104.9 | 100.0 | 96.6 | 90.8 | 89.0 | 86.3 | 81.9 |
| Australia | 193 | 71.2 | 76.7 | 79.3 | 88.1 | 87.0 | 80.8 | 100.0 | 111.6 | 118.1 | 114.0 | 109.0 | 103.9 |
| Canada | 156 | 78.0 | 85.1 | 92.7 | 98.9 | 96.8 | 89.3 | 100.0 | 102.5 | 101.3 | 98.5 | 92.7 | 85.0 |
| Denmark | 128 | 102.9 | 104.8 | 104.8 | 104.4 | 106.8 | 106.7 | 100.0 | 96.6 | 96.1 | 99.1 | 101.5 | 99.6 |
| China, P.R.:Hong Kong | 532 | 116.8 | 112.3 | 109.7 | 105.4 | 100.9 | 102.0 | 100.0 | 98.8 | 105.3 | 107.7 | 109.4 | 119.5 |
| Israel | 436 | 80.8 | 82.7 | 84.4 | 88.2 | 97.3 | 91.0 | 100.0 | 101.5 | 98.3 | 105.1 | 107.3 | 110.1 |
| Japan | 158 | 99.4 | 91.1 | 82.9 | 74.5 | 81.7 | 98.5 | 100.0 | 108.0 | 109.0 | 88.1 | 80.7 | 77.3 |
| Korea | 542 | 108.5 | 127.8 | 136.3 | 136.1 | 107.3 | 91.7 | 100.0 | 95.1 | 98.5 | 105.3 | 112.0 | 115.5 |
| New Zealand | 196 | 94.2 | 103.5 | 99.6 | 106.5 | 99.0 | 88.8 | 100.0 | 102.0 | 102.6 | 107.1 | 112.4 | 109.0 |
| Norway | 142 | 78.5 | 83.9 | 90.8 | 96.9 | 97.5 | 92.8 | 100.0 | 107.1 | 110.4 | 109.7 | 105.0 | 96.6 |
| Singapore | 576 | 74.8 | 76.1 | 81.0 | 85.1 | 91.1 | 88.8 | 100.0 | 108.1 | 116.5 | 122.6 | 127.1 | 132.2 |
| Sweden | 144 | 112.6 | 106.6 | 101.2 | 105.6 | 106.8 | 103.5 | 100.0 | 97.0 | 98.4 | 100.4 | 95.5 | 89.3 |
| Switzerland | 146 | 88.2 | 88.9 | 88.1 | 86.7 | 90.0 | 94.8 | 100.0 | 114.7 | 115.9 | 116.6 | 119.7 | 133.6 |
| United Kingdom | 112 | 113.2 | 113.2 | 116.3 | 118.8 | 101.4 | 93.3 | 100.0 | 100.7 | 104.8 | 101.2 | 106.9 | 114.3 |
| United States | 111 | 112.5 | 109.3 | 109.1 | 102.3 | 99.7 | 105.0 | 100.0 | 94.1 | 97.9 | 100.4 | 102.6 | 117.7 |
| | | | | | | | (2010=100) | | | | | | |
| | | | | | | | Based on Relative Consumer Prices (..rec) | | | | | | |
| **Selected Countries** | | | | | | | | | | | | | |
| Algeria | 612 | 102.2 | 97.8 | 97.6 | 96.4 | 100.7 | 99.5 | 100.0 | 99.4 | 104.8 | 103.3 | 105.4 | 100.9 |
| Antigua and Barbuda | 311 | 107.1 | 110.3 | 108.2 | 98.4 | 92.7 | 96.6 | 100.0 | 98.4 | 104.1 | 102.1 | 99.5 | 109.9 |
| Armenia | 911 | 70.5 | 78.7 | 85.4 | 97.5 | 105.9 | 97.9 | 100.0 | 100.1 | 96.8 | 98.0 | 101.8 | 104.9 |
| Australia | 193 | 84.5 | 87.1 | 86.3 | 91.3 | 89.8 | 87.3 | 100.0 | 107.1 | 109.8 | 105.2 | 100.1 | 92.9 |
| Bahamas, The | 313 | 102.9 | 100.7 | 99.1 | 95.2 | 95.0 | 101.9 | 100.0 | 96.6 | 99.6 | 98.4 | 98.6 | 110.1 |
| Bahrain, Kingdom of | 419 | 118.1 | 111.3 | 113.8 | 106.4 | 98.0 | 102.4 | 100.0 | 93.3 | 95.9 | 98.4 | 100.7 | 111.5 |
| Belize | 339 | 100.5 | 99.7 | 99.9 | 94.9 | 94.5 | 98.6 | 100.0 | 90.0 | 91.7 | 90.6 | 91.2 | 99.0 |
| Bolivia | 218 | 89.0 | 85.0 | 84.2 | 85.1 | 96.2 | 105.2 | 100.0 | 101.9 | 107.2 | 113.1 | 122.1 | 141.7 |
| Brazil | 223 | 58.2 | 71.0 | 79.2 | 85.1 | 88.8 | 88.2 | 100.0 | 103.5 | 93.1 | 87.9 | 87.0 | 73.3 |
| Bulgaria | 918 | 82.5 | 82.6 | 86.3 | 91.3 | 99.8 | 104.1 | 100.0 | 102.7 | 100.7 | 102.0 | 101.4 | 98.2 |
| Burundi | 618 | 79.4 | 87.4 | 90.7 | 85.7 | 88.5 | 97.4 | 100.0 | 99.3 | 102.2 | 102.2 | 106.4 | 121.4 |
| Cameroon | 622 | 101.5 | 98.9 | 100.3 | 101.3 | 104.4 | 106.7 | 100.0 | 100.2 | 96.7 | 99.5 | 100.8 | 97.8 |
| Canada | 156 | 84.0 | 89.5 | 94.5 | 97.7 | 95.3 | 90.7 | 100.0 | 102.0 | 101.7 | 98.4 | 92.1 | 84.0 |
| Central African Republic | 626 | 91.3 | 90.7 | 94.2 | 95.4 | 102.8 | 104.9 | 100.0 | 99.0 | 99.2 | 102.3 | 128.0 | 168.5 |
| Chile | 228 | 87.9 | 94.2 | 98.4 | 95.9 | 97.3 | 94.9 | 100.0 | 100.4 | 103.6 | 102.9 | 93.9 | 95.2 |
| China, P.R.: Mainland | 924 | 84.7 | 84.3 | 85.6 | 88.9 | 97.1 | 100.4 | 100.0 | 102.7 | 108.4 | 115.3 | 119.0 | 131.6 |
| Colombia | 233 | 74.1 | 83.6 | 82.0 | 91.2 | 94.9 | 90.7 | 100.0 | 102.1 | 106.8 | 103.7 | 96.4 | 75.6 |
| Congo, Democratic Republic of | 636 | 138.5 | 135.6 | 149.2 | 144.9 | 144.6 | 827.2 | 100.0 | 105.7 | 118.8 | 119.1 | 120.8 | 139.7 |
| Costa Rica | 238 | 81.7 | 82.1 | 82.7 | 84.0 | 87.2 | 89.0 | 100.0 | 102.3 | 107.7 | 112.5 | 108.2 | 118.4 |
| Côte d'Ivoire | 662 | 101.5 | 100.9 | 100.0 | 101.9 | 106.7 | 106.4 | 100.0 | 102.0 | 97.9 | 102.2 | 103.2 | 98.7 |
| Croatia | 960 | 92.9 | 94.4 | 96.3 | 97.0 | 101.5 | 102.6 | 100.0 | 97.9 | 96.1 | 97.4 | 96.3 | 93.4 |
| Czech Republic | 935 | 77.2 | 81.7 | 86.2 | 88.9 | 102.6 | 98.4 | 100.0 | 102.2 | 99.1 | 97.1 | 91.4 | 89.9 |
| Denmark | 128 | 99.0 | 98.0 | 97.7 | 98.7 | 100.6 | 103.5 | 100.0 | 99.4 | 97.1 | 98.2 | 98.7 | 95.2 |
| Dominica | 321 | 105.8 | 102.1 | 100.2 | 97.0 | 98.1 | 103.0 | 100.0 | 94.4 | 94.6 | 94.1 | 93.4 | 97.9 |
| Dominican Republic | 243 | 77.6 | 103.9 | 98.2 | 99.8 | 100.4 | 100.0 | 100.0 | 100.7 | 100.9 | 98.5 | 96.4 | 98.5 |
| Ecuador | 248 | 109.2 | 104.2 | 102.6 | 95.9 | 94.9 | 102.3 | 100.0 | 98.4 | 102.5 | 104.7 | 107.8 | 122.5 |
| Equatorial Guinea | 642 | 80.9 | 83.0 | 84.2 | 88.3 | 95.9 | 99.0 | 100.0 | 103.6 | 99.7 | 103.8 | 105.3 | 98.2 |
| Euro Area | 163 | 105.7 | 103.4 | 102.5 | 104.8 | 108.0 | 109.3 | 100.0 | 99.5 | 94.3 | 98.3 | 98.4 | 89.9 |
| Austria | 122 | 101.8 | 101.3 | 100.5 | 101.3 | 102.0 | 102.8 | 100.0 | 100.5 | 98.8 | 101.0 | 102.3 | 99.6 |
| Belgium | 124 | 99.0 | 99.3 | 98.9 | 99.7 | 103.1 | 103.3 | 100.0 | 101.0 | 98.8 | 100.4 | 99.7 | 95.1 |
| Cyprus | 423 | 98.1 | 97.8 | 97.5 | 97.2 | 102.4 | 105.8 | 100.0 | 100.7 | 97.5 | 97.9 | 95.4 | 89.3 |
| Finland | 172 | 104.1 | 101.8 | 100.7 | 102.4 | 104.6 | 105.7 | 100.0 | 100.0 | 97.1 | 99.3 | 100.6 | 96.6 |
| France | 132 | 101.8 | 101.3 | 100.9 | 101.6 | 102.9 | 103.1 | 100.0 | 99.4 | 96.4 | 97.7 | 97.1 | 92.4 |
| Germany | 134 | 104.6 | 102.8 | 102.0 | 103.8 | 104.4 | 105.1 | 100.0 | 99.2 | 95.6 | 98.2 | 98.6 | 93.4 |
| Greece | 174 | 93.4 | 93.7 | 94.5 | 96.0 | 98.8 | 100.1 | 100.0 | 100.7 | 97.6 | 96.8 | 94.7 | 89.5 |
| Ireland | 178 | 99.8 | 99.8 | 101.7 | 107.5 | 112.5 | 107.2 | 100.0 | 100.1 | 95.4 | 97.4 | 96.2 | 88.6 |
| Italy | 136 | 101.8 | 100.6 | 100.2 | 101.1 | 102.6 | 103.8 | 100.0 | 100.0 | 98.2 | 99.9 | 99.5 | 95.0 |
| Latvia | 941 | 83.8 | 82.2 | 84.8 | 91.5 | 101.4 | 107.1 | 100.0 | 102.0 | 98.8 | 98.8 | 100.2 | 99.0 |
| Luxembourg | 137 | 98.4 | 98.2 | 98.8 | 99.7 | 101.6 | 102.6 | 100.0 | 100.8 | 98.6 | 100.7 | 100.3 | 96.6 |
| Malta | 181 | 98.9 | 98.4 | 98.8 | 99.6 | 98.0 | 104.8 | 100.0 | 99.7 | 96.5 | 98.1 | 97.9 | 93.2 |
| Netherlands | 138 | 101.8 | 101.0 | 99.9 | 100.6 | 101.8 | 103.8 | 100.0 | 99.6 | 96.9 | 99.9 | 99.9 | 95.8 |
| Portugal | 182 | 100.1 | 100.1 | 100.5 | 101.9 | 102.7 | 102.2 | 100.0 | 100.9 | 99.5 | 99.6 | 98.5 | 95.9 |
| Slovak Republic | 936 | 73.7 | 75.6 | 80.2 | 88.9 | 97.3 | 103.7 | 100.0 | 101.2 | 100.7 | 102.2 | 101.9 | 98.5 |
| Spain | 184 | 95.5 | 96.5 | 97.9 | 99.6 | 102.3 | 102.5 | 100.0 | 100.6 | 98.4 | 100.1 | 98.8 | 94.1 |
| Fiji | 819 | 116.0 | 116.2 | 113.7 | 115.6 | 118.7 | 104.8 | 100.0 | 103.4 | 106.6 | 107.6 | 106.6 | 110.4 |
| Gabon | 646 | 97.7 | 98.7 | 95.2 | 99.7 | 103.1 | 103.9 | 100.0 | 98.6 | 96.5 | 98.2 | 102.8 | 99.4 |
| Gambia, The | 648 | 93.1 | 98.9 | 98.3 | 107.1 | 113.5 | 103.1 | 100.0 | 92.4 | 90.1 | 83.4 | 76.1 | 75.8 |
| Georgia | 915 | 83.3 | 87.6 | 92.9 | 96.2 | 110.5 | 104.8 | 100.0 | 109.3 | 111.3 | 107.7 | 106.9 | 99.8 |
| Ghana | 652 | 93.7 | 102.3 | 107.7 | 107.0 | 101.9 | 93.8 | 100.0 | 95.0 | 89.0 | 89.6 | 69.5 | 70.4 |
| Grenada | 328 | 101.1 | 101.6 | 102.2 | 100.0 | 101.0 | 101.0 | 100.0 | 97.9 | 98.7 | 98.2 | 94.7 | 96.4 |

# Real Effective Exchange Rate Indices

| Selected Countries(Cont.) | | 2004 | 2005 | 2006 | 2007 | 2008 | 2009 | 2010 | 2011 | 2012 | 2013 | 2014 | 2015 |
|---|---|---|---|---|---|---|---|---|---|---|---|---|---|
| | | | | | | | (2010=100) | | | | | | |
| | | | | | | | Based on Relative Consumer Prices (..rec) | | | | | | |
| Guyana | 336 | 88.3 | 90.4 | 92.4 | 95.0 | 95.3 | 101.2 | 100.0 | 97.7 | 100.9 | 101.1 | 100.8 | 109.7 |
| Hungary | 944 | 92.3 | 94.2 | 89.9 | 100.2 | 103.9 | 97.8 | 100.0 | 100.0 | 97.7 | 96.6 | 92.3 | 89.1 |
| Iceland | 176 | 135.9 | 152.8 | 142.1 | 149.9 | 117.8 | 95.2 | 100.0 | 101.4 | 101.0 | 105.7 | 112.7 | 115.3 |
| Iran, I.R. of | 429 | 65.9 | 68.5 | 71.9 | 75.2 | 85.5 | 97.1 | 100.0 | 109.3 | 123.2 | 122.3 | 91.9 | 103.8 |
| Israel | 436 | 88.7 | 86.7 | 86.4 | 87.2 | 97.2 | 95.2 | 100.0 | 101.2 | 96.2 | 102.5 | 103.3 | 103.1 |
| Japan | 158 | 103.8 | 97.4 | 88.2 | 81.0 | 87.7 | 98.8 | 100.0 | 101.7 | 100.6 | 80.3 | 75.1 | 70.1 |
| Lesotho | 666 | 91.5 | 94.0 | 91.9 | 90.7 | 82.5 | 87.8 | 100.0 | 100.6 | 94.7 | 84.7 | 79.1 | 73.7 |
| Macedonia, FYR | 962 | 102.0 | 99.5 | 99.4 | 98.9 | 103.1 | 102.8 | 100.0 | 101.6 | 101.1 | 103.4 | 103.2 | 100.8 |
| Malawi | 676 | 98.4 | 99.7 | 96.3 | 94.1 | 97.1 | 106.3 | 100.0 | 96.7 | 79.0 | 66.8 | 72.6 | 83.2 |
| Malaysia | 548 | 92.0 | 91.9 | 95.0 | 97.0 | 97.6 | 94.8 | 100.0 | 100.4 | 100.1 | 100.6 | 99.9 | 91.9 |
| Mexico | 273 | 103.4 | 107.8 | 108.1 | 106.9 | 105.2 | 92.1 | 100.0 | 100.4 | 97.5 | 103.5 | 102.4 | 92.1 |
| Moldova | 921 | 77.0 | 78.7 | 81.1 | 87.7 | 104.6 | 106.5 | 100.0 | 105.9 | 110.2 | 107.7 | 104.4 | 100.8 |
| Morocco | 686 | 104.7 | 102.1 | 102.6 | 101.7 | 102.2 | 104.3 | 100.0 | 97.7 | 95.8 | 97.5 | 97.6 | 97.9 |
| Netherlands Antilles | 353 | 102.9 | 100.6 | 99.0 | 96.4 | 96.1 | 100.1 | .... | .... | .... | .... | .... | .... |
| New Zealand | 196 | 99.8 | 105.3 | 97.6 | 104.0 | 97.0 | 91.3 | 100.0 | 104.1 | 107.8 | 111.4 | 115.0 | 109.0 |
| Nicaragua | 278 | 96.7 | 95.8 | 96.3 | 94.2 | 97.8 | 107.1 | 100.0 | 96.0 | 98.0 | 98.3 | 98.9 | 103.9 |
| Nigeria | 694 | 74.9 | 85.5 | 91.5 | 89.6 | 99.1 | 92.1 | 100.0 | 100.3 | 111.4 | 118.8 | 127.1 | 126.1 |
| Norway | 142 | 93.7 | 97.3 | 97.2 | 97.7 | 97.8 | 95.2 | 100.0 | 100.6 | 100.3 | 98.9 | 94.0 | 86.3 |
| Pakistan | 564 | 93.7 | 96.7 | 99.4 | 98.1 | 94.5 | 95.1 | 100.0 | 102.8 | 104.4 | 102.3 | 109.7 | 119.8 |
| Papua New Guinea | 853 | 88.1 | 88.4 | 88.4 | 83.8 | 95.2 | 102.9 | 100.0 | 108.7 | 128.1 | 127.0 | 123.5 | 131.0 |
| Paraguay | 288 | 80.0 | 74.9 | 84.6 | 93.1 | 107.1 | 98.2 | 100.0 | 111.8 | 110.1 | 115.8 | 119.4 | 117.2 |
| Phillipines | 566 | 75.1 | 79.0 | 87.3 | 94.5 | 97.3 | 95.7 | 100.0 | 100.7 | 105.6 | 109.8 | 109.4 | 116.6 |
| Poland | 964 | 85.6 | 95.5 | 97.5 | 101.0 | 110.7 | 94.1 | 100.0 | 98.6 | 96.0 | 96.7 | 97.3 | 94.0 |
| Romania | 968 | 81.5 | 96.1 | 103.0 | 111.7 | 106.1 | 98.1 | 100.0 | 102.9 | 96.7 | 101.2 | 101.5 | 97.7 |
| Russian Federation | 922 | 72.5 | 79.4 | 87.3 | 92.0 | 98.3 | 91.7 | 100.0 | 104.9 | 106.5 | 108.4 | 99.2 | 81.9 |
| St. Kitts and Nevis | 361 | 97.0 | 95.3 | 98.9 | 97.7 | 95.7 | 102.9 | 100.0 | 101.7 | 101.9 | 102.0 | 106.2 | 109.7 |
| St. Lucia | 362 | 102.7 | 102.2 | 102.1 | 98.8 | 97.8 | 99.8 | 100.0 | 96.8 | 100.1 | 100.8 | 103.2 | 108.1 |
| St. Vincent & Grens | 364 | 99.2 | 101.0 | 99.9 | 96.4 | 95.9 | 102.0 | 100.0 | 95.9 | 101.7 | 99.6 | 99.6 | 111.3 |
| Samoa | 862 | 88.5 | 88.3 | 88.0 | 89.2 | 93.3 | 101.0 | 100.0 | 100.9 | 102.9 | 104.7 | 104.7 | 109.4 |
| Saudi Arabia | 456 | 103.5 | 100.5 | 98.9 | 96.0 | 93.6 | 100.2 | 100.0 | 96.6 | 99.6 | 102.4 | 105.4 | 118.6 |
| Sierra Leone | 724 | 91.1 | 91.7 | 94.7 | 95.6 | 102.1 | 103.5 | 100.0 | 100.6 | 117.3 | 126.9 | 130.7 | 142.4 |
| Singapore | 576 | 91.3 | 89.9 | 91.2 | 91.7 | 96.7 | 96.7 | 100.0 | 105.5 | 110.4 | 113.4 | 112.9 | 110.6 |
| Solomon Islands | 813 | 87.2 | 89.2 | 95.3 | 93.4 | 100.6 | 107.6 | 100.0 | 103.1 | 112.6 | 121.1 | 128.1 | 134.5 |
| South Africa | 199 | 97.6 | 98.9 | 94.9 | 89.3 | 79.4 | 86.6 | 100.0 | 97.9 | 92.6 | 82.8 | 77.6 | 77.2 |
| Sweden | 144 | 108.9 | 104.7 | 104.1 | 105.6 | 103.5 | 93.4 | 100.0 | 106.2 | 105.7 | 106.9 | 100.9 | 94.1 |
| Switzerland | 146 | 94.1 | 93.0 | 90.8 | 87.0 | 91.0 | 94.5 | 100.0 | 109.8 | 106.5 | 104.5 | 104.9 | 113.3 |
| Togo | 742 | 99.5 | 100.5 | 98.9 | 99.4 | 104.9 | 106.5 | 100.0 | 100.7 | 96.7 | 98.8 | 100.0 | 92.9 |
| Trinidad and Tobago | 369 | 74.9 | 76.5 | 79.5 | 81.6 | 86.9 | 94.7 | 100.0 | 99.0 | 107.0 | 111.1 | 117.0 | 129.5 |
| Tunisia | 744 | 112.0 | 106.6 | 105.5 | 102.4 | 101.7 | 100.5 | 100.0 | 98.2 | 96.7 | 94.9 | 94.8 | 99.7 |
| Uganda | 746 | 97.9 | 102.3 | 102.4 | 105.6 | 109.2 | 107.3 | 100.0 | 95.8 | 109.0 | 110.9 | 114.3 | 105.6 |
| Ukraine | 926 | 91.7 | 100.9 | 106.1 | 106.5 | 116.1 | 97.4 | 100.0 | 100.3 | 102.8 | 99.6 | 78.3 | 73.7 |
| United Kingdom | 112 | 119.8 | 119.5 | 121.5 | 125.7 | 110.1 | 96.5 | 100.0 | 101.5 | 106.8 | 105.8 | 113.7 | 121.8 |
| United States | 111 | 110.9 | 109.4 | 108.7 | 103.6 | 99.5 | 104.0 | 100.0 | 95.1 | 98.0 | 99.1 | 101.2 | 113.8 |
| Uruguay | 298 | 69.5 | 78.1 | 79.2 | 79.4 | 87.0 | 89.3 | 100.0 | 102.0 | 105.2 | 112.1 | 110.2 | 114.3 |
| Venezuela, Rep. Bol. | 299 | 53.1 | 52.2 | 55.2 | 60.6 | 74.1 | 98.1 | 100.0 | 71.8 | 86.8 | 84.8 | 128.3 | 302.2 |
| Zambia | 754 | 64.9 | 79.3 | 103.8 | 95.6 | 110.1 | 94.5 | 100.0 | 97.4 | 100.6 | 104.2 | 100.0 | 90.9 |

# Production and Labor Indices

## Industrial Production

Index Numbers (2010=100): (66..i)

| | Code | 2004 | 2005 | 2006 | 2007 | 2008 | 2009 | 2010 | 2011 | 2012 | 2013 | 2014 | 2015 |
|---|---|---|---|---|---|---|---|---|---|---|---|---|---|
| Advanced Economies | 110 | 101.2 | 103.4 | 106.7 | 109.8 | 107.3 | 92.6 | 100.0 | 102.0 | 102.3 | 102.6 | 104.9 | 105.6 |
| **Euro Area** | | | | | | | | | | | | | |
| Austria | 122 | 86.7 | 90.4 | 97.4 | 102.9 | 104.9 | 93.2 | 100.0 | 106.1 | 107.5 | 107.7 | 108.1 | 109.9 |
| Belgium | 124 | 82.4 | 85.4 | 90.6 | 96.7 | 100.1 | 90.1 | 100.0 | 104.0 | 101.8 | 102.8 | 103.7 | 103.4 |
| Cyprus | 423 | 101.1 | 101.8 | 102.8 | 106.0 | 109.4 | 100.7 | 100.0 | 92.9 | 83.5 | 72.3 | 72.3 | 74.7 |
| Estonia | 939 | 86.5 | 96.0 | 105.5 | 112.3 | 106.6 | 81.0 | 100.0 | 119.9 | 121.2 | 126.2 | 131.1 | 128.2 |
| Finland | 172 | 99.9 | 100.0 | 109.6 | 114.7 | 115.6 | 94.7 | 100.0 | 101.7 | 99.6 | 96.5 | 94.7 | 93.9 |
| France | 132 | 111.9 | 111.5 | 112.4 | 113.7 | 110.3 | 95.8 | 100.0 | 102.6 | 100.3 | 99.6 | 98.8 | 100.8 |
| Germany | 134 | 92.0 | 95.0 | 100.5 | 107.1 | 108.1 | 89.3 | 100.0 | 107.9 | 106.7 | 107.7 | 109.8 | 110.4 |
| Greece | 174 | 121.4 | 119.4 | 121.7 | 124.4 | 118.6 | 105.3 | 100.0 | 90.9 | 87.7 | 86.8 | 88.3 | 89.4 |
| Ireland | 178 | 87.5 | 90.9 | 93.7 | 98.6 | 96.5 | 92.2 | 100.0 | 99.6 | 98.1 | 95.9 | 116.0 | 136.4 |
| Italy | 136 | 114.4 | 112.4 | 115.9 | 118.8 | 115.0 | 93.5 | 100.0 | 100.3 | 94.2 | 91.4 | 90.3 | 92.0 |
| Latvia | 941 | 95.3 | 102.1 | 108.7 | 109.9 | 106.4 | 87.1 | 100.0 | 109.0 | 115.8 | 114.7 | 113.5 | 117.6 |
| Luxembourg | 137 | 116.6 | 118.1 | 120.6 | 120.3 | 114.2 | 95.9 | 100.0 | 102.2 | 96.9 | 93.9 | 97.6 | 99.5 |
| Malta | 181 | 103.2 | 97.5 | 104.6 | 112.0 | 107.2 | 92.2 | 100.0 | 100.0 | 106.1 | 100.0 | 94.4 | 100.2 |
| Netherlands | 138 | 93.4 | 93.7 | 95.6 | 99.5 | 100.2 | 93.0 | 100.0 | 99.5 | 99.0 | 99.5 | 96.7 | 93.8 |
| Portugal | 182 | 112.5 | 108.6 | 111.9 | 111.8 | 107.3 | 98.4 | 100.0 | 99.1 | 93.0 | 93.4 | 94.9 | 96.6 |
| Slovak Republic | 936 | 71.6 | 69.9 | 78.5 | 91.1 | 95.5 | 83.2 | 100.0 | 106.3 | 116.8 | 123.3 | 127.1 | 135.2 |
| Slovenia | 961 | 93.7 | 98.0 | 104.4 | 111.9 | 113.7 | 93.5 | 100.0 | 102.1 | 101.5 | 100.3 | 101.9 | 107.4 |
| Spain | 184 | 119.0 | 119.8 | 124.5 | 127.0 | 117.8 | 99.2 | 100.0 | 98.6 | 92.3 | 90.7 | 92.0 | 95.0 |
| Australia | 193 | 95.6 | 96.7 | 97.2 | 98.5 | 100.3 | 98.7 | 100.0 | 101.2 | 104.5 | 106.7 | 111.5 | 113.2 |
| Canada | 156 | 109.5 | 111.7 | 111.0 | 110.1 | 106.9 | 95.3 | 100.0 | 103.7 | 104.8 | 106.1 | 111.0 | 109.4 |
| China, P.R.:Hong Kong | 532 | 84.8 | 112.0 | 114.4 | 112.8 | 105.3 | 96.5 | 100.0 | 100.7 | 99.9 | 100.0 | 99.6 | 98.1 |
| Czech Republic | 935 | 87.2 | 90.6 | 98.1 | 108.6 | 106.6 | 92.1 | 100.0 | 105.9 | 105.0 | 104.9 | 110.1 | 115.2 |
| Denmark | 128 | 113.1 | 116.3 | 120.1 | 117.1 | 115.2 | 98.1 | 100.0 | 101.8 | 101.9 | 102.4 | 103.2 | 104.5 |
| Iceland | 176 | 47.7 | 53.6 | 62.6 | 63.0 | 85.4 | 88.6 | 100.0 | 112.1 | 117.1 | 112.4 | 113.6 | 124.4 |
| Israel | 436 | 77.1 | 80.5 | 87.5 | 92.4 | 98.5 | 92.6 | 100.0 | 102.6 | 106.6 | 106.8 | 108.5 | 110.8 |
| Japan | 158 | 104.6 | 106.1 | 110.7 | 113.8 | 110.1 | 87.0 | 100.0 | 97.1 | 97.7 | 96.9 | 98.7 | 98.1 |
| Korea | 542 | 67.6 | 71.8 | 77.9 | 83.3 | 86.1 | 86.0 | 100.0 | 105.9 | 106.8 | 106.8 | 107.8 | 107.5 |
| New Zealand | 196 | 102.7 | 102.8 | 101.7 | 105.2 | 103.5 | 96.5 | 100.0 | 97.6 | 97.6 | 98.6 | 101.1 | 98.3 |
| Norway | 142 | 113.5 | 113.5 | 111.0 | 109.7 | 110.2 | 105.9 | 100.0 | 95.0 | 96.7 | 94.1 | 96.1 | 97.5 |
| Singapore | 576 | 64.8 | 70.9 | 79.3 | 84.0 | 80.4 | 77.1 | 100.0 | 107.6 | 107.9 | 109.8 | 112.7 | 106.9 |
| Sweden | 144 | 104.7 | 107.3 | 110.6 | 114.5 | 111.4 | 91.4 | 100.0 | 105.9 | 103.7 | 98.6 | 94.2 | 96.8 |
| Switzerland | 146 | 81.1 | 83.8 | 91.4 | 100.6 | 102.8 | 96.0 | 100.0 | 103.6 | 106.3 | 107.1 | 108.6 | 105.9 |
| United Kingdom | 112 | 108.7 | 107.9 | 108.6 | 108.9 | 106.1 | 96.9 | 100.0 | 99.4 | 96.7 | 95.9 | 97.2 | 98.4 |
| United States | 111 | 102.1 | 105.5 | 107.9 | 110.6 | 106.8 | 94.7 | 100.0 | 103.0 | 105.9 | 108.0 | 112.0 | 113.5 |

## Wages

Index Numbers (2010=100): (65, 65ey, 65..c)

| | Code | 2004 | 2005 | 2006 | 2007 | 2008 | 2009 | 2010 | 2011 | 2012 | 2013 | 2014 | 2015 |
|---|---|---|---|---|---|---|---|---|---|---|---|---|---|
| Advanced Economies | 110 | 88.5 | 90.8 | 92.5 | 95.0 | 97.1 | 97.8 | 100.0 | 101.4 | 102.7 | 103.6 | 104.9 | 106.7 |
| **Euro Area** | | | | | | | | | | | | | |
| Austria | 122 | 85.9 | 87.8 | 90.2 | 92.4 | 95.3 | 98.5 | 100.0 | 102.0 | 105.3 | 108.0 | 110.6 | 113.0 |
| Belgium | 124 | 84.2 | 86.3 | 88.4 | 90.2 | 93.2 | 96.6 | 100.0 | 104.0 | 106.6 | 106.7 | 106.1 | 106.2 |
| Finland | 172 | 82.3 | 85.6 | 87.7 | 90.8 | 95.1 | 98.3 | 100.0 | 102.7 | 106.0 | 107.5 | 108.7 | 110.3 |
| France | 132 | 86.3 | 88.7 | 91.2 | 93.6 | 96.6 | 97.5 | 100.0 | 105.0 | 108.0 | 109.6 | 111.2 | 112.9 |
| Germany | 134 | 91.0 | 92.3 | 93.4 | 94.9 | 97.5 | 100.6 | 100.0 | 102.9 | 106.3 | 109.5 | 112.5 | 116.1 |
| Greece | 174 | 87.3 | 88.6 | 90.5 | 95.2 | 99.6 | 99.3 | 100.0 | 95.2 | 87.3 | 78.5 | 78.9 | 78.2 |
| Ireland | 178 | 86.9 | 93.1 | 94.7 | 100.2 | 98.1 | 99.0 | 100.0 | 99.2 | 101.4 | 98.2 | 102.0 | 102.4 |
| Italy | 136 | 85.1 | 87.7 | 90.5 | 93.0 | 95.0 | 97.9 | 100.0 | 101.7 | 103.2 | 104.7 | 105.9 | 107.2 |
| Netherlands | 138 | 88.7 | 89.5 | 91.1 | 92.6 | 96.0 | 98.8 | 100.0 | 101.1 | 102.9 | 104.5 | 106.1 | 107.8 |
| Portugal | 182 | 86.6 | 88.0 | 88.7 | 93.3 | 96.0 | 100.0 | 100.0 | 97.1 | 88.4 | 86.6 | 85.9 | 88.5 |
| Slovak Republic | 936 | 68.3 | 74.5 | 80.9 | 86.9 | 94.0 | 96.8 | 100.0 | 102.2 | 104.7 | 107.1 | 111.6 | 114.8 |
| Slovenia | 961 | 74.7 | 77.4 | 81.1 | 85.9 | 93.1 | 96.3 | 100.0 | 102.0 | 102.0 | 101.9 | 103.0 | 103.8 |
| Spain | 184 | 80.1 | 82.9 | 86.5 | 90.1 | 94.1 | 99.4 | 100.0 | 100.2 | 102.2 | 104.0 | 102.5 | 95.5 |
| Australia | 193 | 75.6 | 79.8 | 82.8 | 86.7 | 90.2 | 95.5 | 100.0 | 104.8 | 109.6 | 113.7 | 117.4 | 119.3 |
| Canada | 156 | 91.4 | 93.8 | 93.6 | 98.6 | 100.4 | 95.3 | 100.0 | 103.2 | 106.1 | 106.1 | 107.0 | 111.8 |
| China, P.R.: Hong Kong | 532 | 90.8 | 90.8 | 93.8 | 96.4 | 101.0 | 98.9 | 100.0 | 104.9 | 114.0 | 117.5 | 123.9 | 129.6 |
| Czech Republic | 935 | 73.2 | 76.9 | 81.9 | 87.8 | 94.7 | 97.8 | 100.0 | 102.5 | 105.0 | 104.9 | 108.0 | 110.9 |
| Denmark | 128 | 82.5 | 84.9 | 87.5 | 90.9 | 94.9 | 97.8 | 100.0 | 101.8 | 103.4 | 104.7 | 106.1 | 107.6 |
| Iceland | 176 | 66.6 | 71.1 | 77.9 | 84.9 | 91.8 | 95.4 | 100.0 | 106.8 | 115.1 | 121.6 | 128.7 | 137.9 |
| Japan | 158 | 101.7 | 102.4 | 103.0 | 103.0 | 102.2 | 99.4 | 100.0 | 99.8 | 99.8 | 99.0 | 99.2 | 99.6 |
| Korea | 542 | 71.6 | 77.4 | 81.8 | 87.1 | 90.1 | 91.8 | 100.0 | 100.5 | 106.5 | 111.5 | 115.7 | 119.0 |
| New Zealand | 196 | 84.7 | 87.3 | 90.1 | 93.0 | 96.4 | 98.3 | 100.0 | 102.0 | 103.9 | 105.6 | 107.4 | 109.1 |
| Norway | 142 | 76.2 | 79.1 | 82.4 | 87.6 | 92.5 | 96.5 | 100.0 | 104.5 | 109.1 | 113.1 | 116.1 | 119.3 |
| Sweden | 144 | 83.0 | 85.5 | 88.1 | 91.1 | 94.9 | 96.9 | 100.0 | 102.7 | 106.1 | 108.6 | 111.0 | 113.9 |
| Switzerland | 146 | 91.7 | 92.6 | 93.7 | 95.2 | 97.1 | 99.2 | 100.0 | 101.0 | 101.8 | 102.6 | 103.3 | 103.7 |
| United Kingdom | 112 | 82.2 | 86.0 | 90.1 | 94.5 | 97.8 | 97.7 | 100.0 | 102.4 | 103.8 | 105.0 | 106.2 | 108.9 |
| United States | 111 | 86.8 | 89.0 | 90.3 | 92.8 | 95.4 | 98.0 | 100.0 | 101.7 | 102.5 | 103.7 | 105.1 | 107.0 |

## Employment

Index Numbers (2010=100): (67, 67ey, 67..c, 67e, 67eyc)

| | Code | 2004 | 2005 | 2006 | 2007 | 2008 | 2009 | 2010 | 2011 | 2012 | 2013 | 2014 | 2015 |
|---|---|---|---|---|---|---|---|---|---|---|---|---|---|
| Advanced Economies | 110 | 102.4 | 103.2 | 104.4 | 105.1 | 104.8 | 100.5 | 100.0 | 100.8 | 101.6 | 102.1 | 103.2 | 104.7 |
| **Euro Area** | | | | | | | | | | | | | |
| Austria | 122 | 93.6 | 94.1 | 95.9 | 98.0 | 99.6 | 99.1 | 100.0 | 101.0 | 101.8 | 102.2 | 102.3 | 103.1 |
| Finland | 172 | 126.7 | 114.7 | 115.7 | 116.8 | 115.3 | 104.8 | 100.0 | 99.4 | 98.5 | 96.8 | 91.6 | 90.7 |
| France | 132 | 115.9 | 113.2 | 111.4 | 110.0 | 107.7 | 102.6 | 100.0 | 99.5 | 98.9 | 97.7 | 96.5 | 95.5 |
| Germany | 134 | 96.0 | 96.0 | 98.1 | 100.2 | 101.5 | 101.3 | 100.0 | 101.9 | 102.6 | 103.5 | 104.2 | 104.9 |
| Greece | 174 | 101.8 | 101.3 | 103.1 | 103.9 | 105.0 | 103.8 | 100.0 | 92.4 | 84.4 | 80.3 | 80.8 | 82.4 |
| Ireland | 178 | 121.1 | 119.6 | 120.9 | 121.9 | 117.4 | 105.6 | 100.0 | 98.0 | 95.4 | 98.0 | 97.4 | 101.2 |
| Italy | 136 | 101.0 | 99.6 | 101.1 | 101.7 | 102.5 | 100.8 | 100.0 | 100.3 | 100.0 | 98.2 | 98.5 | 99.2 |

# Production and Labor Indices

| Advanced Economies(Cont.) | | 2004 | 2005 | 2006 | 2007 | 2008 | 2009 | 2010 | 2011 | 2012 | 2013 | 2014 | 2015 |
|---|---|---|---|---|---|---|---|---|---|---|---|---|---|
| Netherlands | 138 | 98.4 | 97.4 | 99.1 | 101.4 | 102.9 | 102.6 | 100.0 | 99.1 | 99.4 | 98.5 | 97.6 | 98.6 |
| Portugal | 182 | 100.0 | 116.5 | 112.3 | 110.2 | 109.1 | 102.9 | 100.0 | 99.0 | 95.6 | 93.1 | 93.3 | 94.5 |
| Slovak Republic | 936 | 100.9 | 103.0 | 106.9 | 103.3 | 106.0 | 101.1 | 100.0 | 101.9 | 108.2 | 108.2 | 109.8 | 112.6 |
| Slovenia | 961 | 100.4 | 98.2 | 99.4 | 101.6 | 103.5 | 101.4 | 100.0 | 97.2 | 96.3 | 94.3 | 94.7 | 95.7 |
| Spain | 184 | 92.7 | 98.9 | 107.0 | 110.3 | 109.8 | 102.3 | 100.0 | 98.1 | 93.6 | 84.0 | 94.0 | 96.8 |
| Australia | 193 | 106.2 | 104.4 | 103.1 | 105.0 | 106.8 | 102.0 | 100.0 | 96.8 | 96.8 | 94.1 | 94.1 | 90.5 |
| Canada | 156 | 126.6 | 124.5 | 123.3 | 119.1 | 113.7 | 101.0 | 100.0 | 101.5 | 102.2 | 101.7 | 101.0 | 101.4 |
| Czech Republic | 935 | 104.3 | 104.6 | 106.6 | 107.4 | 104.8 | 93.2 | 100.0 | 108.0 | 104.8 | 103.9 | 106.6 | 108.2 |
| Denmark | 128 | 103.3 | 102.0 | 104.1 | 103.9 | 105.7 | 102.6 | 100.0 | 99.6 | 98.8 | 98.8 | 99.5 | 100.9 |
| Iceland | 176 | 98.5 | 96.9 | 102.2 | 106.9 | 107.4 | 100.6 | 100.0 | 100.2 | 101.1 | 104.3 | 106.3 | 109.6 |
| Israel | 436 | 92.7 | 94.3 | 97.2 | 101.1 | 103.1 | 98.2 | 100.0 | 101.5 | 102.3 | 102.6 | 102.7 | 102.6 |
| Japan | 158 | 100.8 | 100.9 | 101.9 | 102.6 | 103.6 | 101.2 | 100.0 | 99.3 | 98.5 | 97.1 | 96.2 | 96.2 |
| Korea | 542 | 103.7 | 102.5 | 100.7 | 99.7 | 98.4 | 95.3 | 100.0 | 101.6 | 101.9 | 103.9 | 107.5 | 111.4 |
| New Zealand | 196 | 115.7 | 111.5 | 110.7 | 108.9 | 106.9 | 99.8 | 100.0 | 101.0 | 96.4 | 98.0 | 100.1 | 102.3 |
| Norway | 142 | 90.8 | 91.4 | 94.2 | 97.5 | 100.3 | 100.1 | 100.0 | 101.5 | 103.4 | 104.1 | 104.8 | 105.4 |
| Sweden | 144 | 120.4 | 117.5 | 117.3 | 117.0 | 116.6 | 102.5 | 100.0 | 102.1 | 99.3 | 97.2 | 94.7 | 95.0 |
| Switzerland | 146 | 99.1 | 99.5 | 101.5 | 104.6 | 107.5 | 101.3 | 100.0 | 99.9 | 100.0 | 99.0 | 103.7 | 102.9 |
| United Kingdom | 112 | 99.7 | 101.1 | 102.2 | 102.9 | 103.4 | 101.1 | 100.0 | 100.2 | 101.8 | 102.9 | 105.8 | 107.8 |
| United States | 111 | 100.9 | 102.9 | 104.7 | 105.9 | 105.3 | 100.7 | 100.0 | 101.2 | 103.0 | 104.7 | 106.7 | 108.9 |

# Producer Prices/Wholesale Prices

2016, International Monetary Fund : *International Financial Statistics Yearbook*

*Percent Change over Previous Year; Calculated from Indices*

| | | 2004 | 2005 | 2006 | 2007 | 2008 | 2009 | 2010 | 2011 | 2012 | 2013 | 2014 | 2015 |
|---|---|---|---|---|---|---|---|---|---|---|---|---|---|
| **World** | 001 | **6.0** | **5.8** | **5.1** | **4.7** | **9.2** | **−3.9** | **5.6** | **7.9** | **2.7** | **1.6** | **2.2** | **−1.8** |
| **Advanced Economies** | 110 | **4.0** | **4.8** | **4.2** | **3.3** | **7.4** | **−6.0** | **4.2** | **6.4** | **1.1** | **.3** | **.4** | **−4.6** |
| Euro Area | 163 | 2.2 | 4.4 | 5.5 | 2.6 | 6.3 | −5.0 | 2.6 | 5.7 | 2.8 | −.2 | −1.6 | −2.7 |
| Austria | 122 | 4.9 | 2.1 | 2.9 | 4.1 | 6.4 | −7.4 | 5.0 | 8.3 | 2.4 | −1.1 | −1.9 | −3.7 |
| Belgium | 124 | 3.8 | 5.3 | 6.0 | 2.7 | 6.3 | −8.6 | 7.9 | 8.9 | 3.7 | −.5 | −3.5 | −5.0 |
| Cyprus | 423 | 5.5 | 4.9 | 5.2 | 3.4 | 10.8 | −1.7 | 3.8 | 5.1 | 6.7 | −2.1 | −2.9 | −5.0 |
| Estonia | 939 | 2.9 | 2.1 | 4.5 | 8.3 | 7.2 | −.5 | 3.3 | 4.4 | 2.3 | 4.1 | −1.6 | −2.0 |
| Finland | 172 | 1.6 | 3.8 | 5.7 | 4.0 | 5.6 | −6.4 | 4.2 | 6.4 | 3.1 | .2 | −1.3 | −3.2 |
| France | 132 | 2.1 | 3.1 | 3.2 | 2.1 | 4.6 | −4.7 | 2.5 | 4.6 | 2.3 | — | −1.4 | −1.6 |
| Germany | 134 | 1.6 | 4.3 | 5.4 | 1.3 | 5.5 | −4.2 | 1.5 | 5.3 | 1.6 | −.1 | −1.0 | −1.9 |
| Greece | 174 | 3.5 | 5.9 | 7.3 | 4.1 | 10.0 | −5.8 | 6.1 | 7.4 | 4.9 | −.7 | −.8 | −5.8 |
| Ireland | 178 | −2.4 | −.1 | .4 | −2.3 | −1.3 | .7 | .1 | .5 | 1.8 | −.4 | −1.3 | 5.4 |
| Italy | 136 | 2.7 | 4.0 | 5.6 | 3.5 | 4.8 | −4.7 | 3.0 | 4.7 | 3.6 | −1.1 | −1.5 | −2.6 |
| Latvia | 941 | 8.6 | 7.8 | 10.3 | 16.1 | 11.7 | −4.7 | 3.1 | 7.7 | 3.7 | 1.5 | .4 | −1.0 |
| Lithuania | 946 | 7.7 | 13.4 | 7.2 | 6.0 | 17.4 | −16.4 | 11.3 | 14.7 | 4.1 | −3.0 | −4.4 | −8.9 |
| Luxembourg | 137 | 9.0 | 8.1 | 7.4 | 9.4 | 9.0 | −8.3 | 3.7 | 8.6 | 2.5 | −2.6 | −3.0 | −1.1 |
| Netherlands | 138 | 3.8 | 6.6 | 5.2 | 4.6 | 6.8 | −10.7 | 8.6 | 10.2 | 3.2 | −1.3 | −2.0 | −6.5 |
| Portugal | 182 | 2.6 | 3.3 | 4.4 | 2.8 | 5.2 | −3.8 | 3.7 | 5.8 | 3.2 | .1 | −1.2 | −3.0 |
| Slovak Republic | 936 | 3.4 | 4.7 | 8.4 | 2.1 | 6.1 | −2.6 | −2.8 | 2.7 | 2.0 | −.9 | −3.4 | −3.0 |
| Slovenia | 961 | 4.4 | 2.8 | 2.4 | 5.5 | 5.6 | −.4 | 2.0 | 3.8 | 1.0 | .3 | −1.1 | −.5 |
| Spain | 184 | 3.4 | 4.7 | 5.4 | 3.6 | 6.5 | −3.4 | 3.7 | 6.9 | 3.8 | .6 | −1.0 | −2.4 |
| Australia | 193 | 4.0 | 6.0 | 7.9 | 2.3 | 8.3 | −5.4 | 1.9 | 3.4 | −.5 | 1.1 | 3.1 | .3 |
| Canada | 156 | 3.2 | 1.6 | 2.3 | 1.5 | 4.3 | −3.5 | 1.5 | 6.9 | 1.1 | .4 | 2.5 | −.8 |
| China, P.R.: Hong Kong | 532 | 2.3 | −7.9 | 2.2 | 3.0 | 5.6 | −1.7 | 6.0 | 8.3 | .1 | −3.1 | −1.7 | −2.7 |
| Czech Republic | 935 | 5.7 | 3.0 | 1.6 | 4.2 | 4.2 | −3.1 | 1.2 | 5.6 | 2.1 | .8 | −.8 | −3.2 |
| Denmark | 128 | 2.1 | 4.1 | 7.4 | 1.9 | 12.7 | −10.4 | 7.4 | 8.6 | 2.3 | 1.6 | −1.0 | −3.7 |
| Israel | 436 | 5.4 | 6.2 | 5.7 | 3.5 | 9.6 | −6.3 | 4.0 | 7.8 | 4.3 | .4 | −1.4 | −5.9 |
| Japan | 158 | 1.3 | 1.7 | 2.2 | 1.7 | 4.6 | −5.3 | −.1 | 1.5 | −.9 | 1.3 | 3.2 | −2.2 |
| Korea | 542 | 6.1 | 2.1 | .9 | 1.4 | 8.5 | −.2 | 3.8 | 6.7 | .7 | −1.6 | −.5 | −4.0 |
| New Zealand | 196 | 2.9 | 5.4 | 5.2 | 3.6 | 10.0 | −2.4 | 3.9 | 4.0 | .4 | 2.3 | −1.7 | −1.4 |
| Norway | 142 | 11.7 | 16.5 | 12.8 | — | 22.9 | −.8 | 18.3 | 16.3 | 2.8 | .6 | −1.4 | −8.1 |
| Singapore | 576 | 5.1 | 9.7 | 5.0 | .3 | 7.5 | −13.9 | 4.7 | 8.4 | .5 | −2.7 | −3.3 | −15.3 |
| Sweden | 144 | 2.1 | 5.2 | 5.4 | 3.7 | 5.6 | −1.0 | 1.4 | 2.8 | −.3 | −2.6 | 1.0 | −.9 |
| Switzerland | 146 | 1.2 | .8 | 2.1 | 2.4 | 3.4 | −2.1 | −.1 | −1.1 | −.5 | .3 | −.8 | −3.7 |
| United Kingdom | 112 | 1.0 | 1.9 | 2.0 | 2.3 | 6.8 | .5 | 2.7 | 4.8 | 2.1 | 1.3 | — | −1.7 |
| United States | 111 | 6.2 | 7.3 | 4.7 | 4.8 | 9.8 | −8.8 | 6.8 | 8.8 | .6 | .6 | .9 | −7.2 |
| **Emerging & Dev. Economies** | 200 | **10.6** | **8.1** | **7.0** | **7.7** | **13.6** | **.2** | **8.3** | **10.6** | **5.8** | **4.2** | **5.6** | **3.7** |
| **Emerging & Developing Asia** | 505 | **7.4** | **6.9** | **7.5** | **6.2** | **11.9** | **.2** | **7.7** | **8.5** | **5.6** | **4.3** | **4.0** | **−2.1** |
| India | 534 | 6.6 | 4.7 | 4.7 | 4.9 | 8.7 | 2.4 | 9.6 | 8.9 | 8.1 | 6.3 | 3.9 | −2.7 |
| Indonesia | 536 | 8.5 | 16.6 | 12.4 | 14.7 | 27.0 | −1.8 | 4.9 | 7.4 | 5.1 | 5.9 | 9.3 | 4.4 |
| Malaysia | 548 | 7.0 | 6.9 | 6.7 | 5.5 | 10.2 | −7.3 | 5.6 | 9.6 | .1 | −1.7 | 1.4 | −4.8 |
| Philippines | 566 | 12.0 | 9.1 | 9.4 | .8 | 4.1 | −1.4 | −5.0 | .9 | −.5 | −7.6 | −.9 | −6.6 |
| Sri Lanka | 524 | 12.6 | 11.5 | 11.7 | 24.4 | 24.9 | −4.2 | 11.2 | .... | .... | .... | .... | .... |
| Thailand | 578 | 6.7 | 9.1 | 7.1 | 3.2 | 12.4 | −3.8 | 9.4 | 5.5 | 1.0 | .3 | .1 | −4.1 |
| **Europe** | 170 | **17.0** | **12.7** | **9.4** | **9.9** | **16.5** | **−2.4** | **10.1** | **14.9** | **6.9** | **2.4** | **5.7** | **6.9** |
| **Emerging & Dev. Europe** | 903 | **10.8** | **4.9** | **6.1** | **4.7** | **8.9** | **1.4** | **5.5** | **8.8** | **4.8** | **1.5** | **3.2** | **.6** |
| Bulgaria | 918 | 6.0 | 6.9 | 12.3 | 7.6 | 10.7 | −6.6 | 8.7 | 9.4 | 4.2 | −1.6 | −1.2 | −1.9 |
| Croatia | 960 | 3.5 | 3.0 | 2.7 | 3.5 | 8.3 | −.5 | 4.3 | 6.4 | 7.0 | .4 | −2.7 | −3.9 |
| Hungary | 944 | 3.5 | 4.7 | 6.5 | 2.3 | 3.6 | 6.4 | 4.2 | 5.4 | 4.1 | .7 | −.4 | −1.0 |
| Poland | 964 | 7.0 | .9 | 2.2 | 2.2 | 2.6 | 3.4 | 2.2 | 7.5 | 3.2 | −1.3 | −1.5 | −2.2 |
| Romania | 968 | 19.1 | 10.5 | 6.7 | 6.4 | 12.7 | 2.5 | 4.4 | 7.1 | 5.4 | 2.1 | −.1 | −2.2 |
| Turkey | 186 | 14.6 | 5.9 | 8.3 | 6.3 | 12.7 | 1.2 | 8.5 | 11.1 | 6.1 | 4.5 | 10.2 | 5.3 |
| **CIS** | 901 | **22.2** | **19.7** | **12.2** | **14.5** | **23.4** | **−5.9** | **14.1** | **20.2** | **8.7** | **3.1** | **7.6** | **12.1** |
| Armenia | 911 | −13.3 | 7.7 | .9 | .6 | 2.2 | 7.1 | 22.6 | 7.7 | 7.0 | 4.7 | 8.5 | −.8 |
| Belarus | 913 | 24.1 | 12.1 | 8.3 | 16.3 | 14.7 | 14.5 | 13.4 | 71.4 | 76.1 | 13.6 | 12.8 | 16.8 |
| Georgia | 915 | 4.6 | 7.5 | 10.8 | 11.6 | 9.8 | −5.5 | 11.3 | 12.8 | 1.6 | −2.0 | 2.9 | 8.7 |
| Kazakhstan | 916 | 16.7 | 23.7 | 18.5 | 10.9 | 36.8 | −22.1 | 25.2 | 27.2 | 3.5 | −.3 | 9.5 | −20.5 |
| Kyrgyz Republic | 917 | 8.8 | 3.1 | 15.9 | 11.8 | 25.3 | 11.3 | 23.1 | 21.8 | −2.1 | −6.1 | .2 | 9.1 |
| Russia | 922 | 23.4 | 20.6 | 12.4 | 14.1 | 21.4 | −7.2 | 12.2 | 17.7 | 6.8 | 3.3 | 6.1 | 12.4 |
| Ukraine | 926 | 20.5 | 16.8 | 9.6 | 19.5 | 35.5 | 6.6 | 20.9 | 19.1 | 3.7 | −.1 | 17.1 | 36.0 |
| **Middle East, N.Africa & Pakistan** | 440 | **8.4** | **7.0** | **5.9** | **9.0** | **15.0** | **−.5** | **9.3** | **9.6** | **3.7** | **3.2** | **2.5** | **−.9** |
| Egypt | 469 | 17.1 | 5.3 | 7.0 | 10.0 | 21.1 | −5.6 | 12.6 | 14.8 | 2.5 | 3.4 | 4.3 | .... |
| Iran, I.R. of | 429 | 12.6 | 12.4 | 9.2 | 10.6 | −35.4 | 9.2 | 10.4 | 37.9 | 24.7 | 37.3 | 17.2 | 7.0 |
| Jordan | 439 | 6.0 | 9.5 | 15.8 | 9.1 | 56.2 | −16.7 | −2.4 | 14.7 | 4.7 | −2.6 | −1.7 | −9.7 |
| Kuwait | 443 | .4 | 4.4 | 2.1 | 3.9 | 6.5 | .1 | 4.5 | 3.8 | 2.1 | 3.5 | 2.4 | 3.0 |
| Pakistan | 564 | 8.4 | 8.7 | 8.5 | 8.2 | 25.3 | 7.3 | 21.3 | 18.8 | 7.1 | 7.8 | 4.8 | −2.5 |
| Saudi Arabia | 456 | 3.1 | 2.9 | 1.2 | 5.7 | 9.0 | −3.0 | 4.3 | 4.2 | 2.2 | 1.5 | .6 | −1.0 |
| Syrian Arab Republic | 463 | .9 | 2.8 | 4.0 | 3.8 | 6.5 | 26.1 | .... | .... | .... | .... | .... | .... |
| **Sub-Saharan Africa** | 603 | **2.3** | **2.9** | **7.6** | **9.8** | **14.2** | **1.0** | **6.1** | **15.1** | **4.3** | **3.9** | **9.6** | **4.3** |
| Central African Rep. | 626 | −.5 | 2.2 | .... | .... | .... | .... | .... | .... | .... | .... | .... | .... |
| Algeria | 612 | 4.4 | 3.5 | 2.4 | 3.1 | 9.3 | 3.4 | 3.1 | 2.1 | 2.6 | .2 | 1.0 | 2.3 |
| Morocco | 686 | −17.9 | 9.1 | 5.9 | 1.8 | 18.0 | −15.1 | 6.4 | 14.8 | 2.9 | −1.9 | −2.8 | −4.6 |
| South Africa | 199 | 2.3 | 3.6 | 7.7 | 10.9 | 14.3 | 3.7 | 2.3 | 12.0 | .7 | 6.0 | 7.4 | 3.6 |
| Tunisia | 744 | 2.6 | 4.3 | 7.0 | 3.4 | 12.1 | 2.0 | 3.1 | 6.4 | 6.5 | 3.0 | 3.2 | 5.1 |
| **Western Hemisphere** | 205 | **10.0** | **6.2** | **4.8** | **6.2** | **11.8** | **2.9** | **7.1** | **9.3** | **6.0** | **6.2** | **8.3** | **9.7** |
| Argentina | 213 | 7.7 | 8.5 | 10.9 | 11.8 | 14.5 | 6.3 | 15.1 | 13.8 | 12.2 | 16.3 | 26.5 | .... |
| Brazil | 223 | 10.5 | 5.6 | .8 | 5.6 | 13.7 | −.2 | 5.7 | 9.4 | 5.9 | 5.9 | 4.6 | 6.0 |
| Chile | 228 | 2.5 | 5.4 | 7.0 | 6.7 | 16.7 | −.3 | −2.0 | 5.9 | .... | −3.9 | .2 | −6.9 |
| Colombia | 233 | 5.2 | 3.1 | 4.2 | 1.0 | 7.2 | 1.9 | 1.7 | 5.5 | .3 | −1.4 | 3.2 | 6.6 |
| Costa Rica | 238 | 15.5 | 13.7 | 13.0 | 13.7 | 22.6 | 6.1 | 1.7 | 8.4 | 3.9 | 2.5 | 4.1 | 1.3 |
| Ecuador | 248 | 9.1 | 14.6 | 12.0 | 5.2 | 17.9 | −18.6 | 17.1 | 19.4 | 2.0 | 1.1 | −2.0 | −20.8 |

# Producer Prices/Wholesale Prices

|  |  | 2004 | 2005 | 2006 | 2007 | 2008 | 2009 | 2010 | 2011 | 2012 | 2013 | 2014 | 2015 |
|---|---|---|---|---|---|---|---|---|---|---|---|---|---|
|  |  | *Percent Change over Previous Year; Calculated from Indices* | | | | | | | | | | | |
| **Western Hemisphere(Cont.)** | | | | | | | | | | | | | |
| El Salvador | 253 | 6.6 | 9.1 | 4.7 | 4.7 | 16.6 | −11.6 | 4.7 | 11.2 | 2.8 | .1 | −1.7 | −8.0 |
| Mexico | 273 | 8.6 | 4.7 | 5.6 | 4.4 | 7.1 | 4.5 | 4.2 | 5.2 | 4.6 | 1.4 | 2.7 | 2.9 |
| Panama | 283 | 4.4 | 5.6 | 6.1 | 5.3 | 15.8 | −6.7 | 3.9 | 11.9 | 4.7 | .1 | −1.6 | −5.7 |
| Paraguay | 288 | 5.8 | 9.0 | 7.1 | 3.7 | 13.0 | −.3 | 6.5 | 12.6 | 3.2 | .5 | 2.9 | 1.9 |
| Peru | 293 | 5.2 | 2.3 | 3.2 | 2.5 | 8.9 | −1.8 | 1.8 | 6.3 | 1.8 | .4 | 1.8 | 1.8 |
| Trinidad and Tobago | 369 | 3.5 | 2.3 | 4.6 | 6.9 | 10.0 | 4.4 | 2.7 | 2.8 | 4.1 | 1.9 | 2.0 | . . . . |
| Uruguay | 298 | 14.7 | −2.6 | 5.9 | 11.8 | 16.9 | 2.1 | 7.6 | 15.9 | 6.4 | 3.5 | 10.9 | 6.8 |
| Venezuela, Rep. Bol | 299 | 30.5 | 17.9 | 13.4 | 19.1 | 24.3 | 29.3 | 26.7 | 22.1 | 15.8 | 37.5 | 57.2 | 145.9 |

# Indices

|  |  | 2004 | 2005 | 2006 | 2007 | 2008 | 2009 | 2010 | 2011 | 2012 | 2013 | 2014 | 2015 |
|---|---|---|---|---|---|---|---|---|---|---|---|---|---|
|  |  | *Index Numbers: 2010=100* | | | | | | | | | | | |
| World | 001 | 77.5 | 82.0 | 86.1 | 90.2 | 98.5 | 94.7 | 100.0 | 107.9 | 110.8 | 112.5 | 115.0 | 112.9 |
| Advanced Economies | 110 | 84.2 | 88.3 | 92.0 | 95.0 | 102.1 | 95.9 | 100.0 | 106.4 | 107.6 | 107.9 | 108.3 | 103.3 |
| Emerging & Dev. Economies | 200 | 65.2 | 70.4 | 75.3 | 81.1 | 92.1 | 92.3 | 100.0 | 110.6 | 117.0 | 122.0 | 128.9 | 133.7 |
| Sub-Saharan Africa | 603 | 67.2 | 69.2 | 74.5 | 81.7 | 93.3 | 94.2 | 100.0 | 115.1 | 120.0 | 124.6 | 136.6 | 142.5 |
| Asia | 505 | 67.8 | 72.5 | 77.9 | 82.7 | 92.6 | 92.8 | 100.0 | 108.5 | 114.6 | 119.5 | 124.2 | 121.6 |
| Europe | 170 | 59.0 | 66.5 | 72.7 | 79.9 | 93.1 | 90.8 | 100.0 | 114.9 | 122.9 | 125.8 | 133.0 | 142.2 |
| Middle East,N.Africa & Pakist | 440 | 64.7 | 69.2 | 73.3 | 79.9 | 91.9 | 91.5 | 100.0 | 109.6 | 113.6 | 117.2 | 120.2 | 119.0 |
| Western Hemisphere | 205 | 68.6 | 72.9 | 76.4 | 81.1 | 90.7 | 93.3 | 100.0 | 109.3 | 115.8 | 123.0 | 133.2 | 146.2 |

# Consumer Prices

| | | 2004 | 2005 | 2006 | 2007 | 2008 | 2009 | 2010 | 2011 | 2012 | 2013 | 2014 | 2015 |
|---|---|---|---|---|---|---|---|---|---|---|---|---|---|
| | | *Percent Change over Previous Year; Calculated from Indices* | | | | | | | | | | | |
| **World** | 001 | **3.6** | **3.7** | **3.6** | **3.7** | **5.8** | **2.4** | **3.6** | **4.8** | **3.8** | **3.6** | **3.2** | **2.8** |
| **Advanced Economies** | 110 | **2.0** | **2.3** | **2.3** | **2.2** | **3.4** | **.1** | **1.5** | **2.7** | **1.9** | **1.3** | **1.4** | **.3** |
| Euro Area | 163 | 2.1 | 2.2 | 2.2 | 2.1 | 3.3 | .3 | 1.6 | 2.7 | 2.5 | 1.4 | .4 | — |
| Austria | 122 | 2.1 | 2.3 | 1.4 | 2.2 | 3.2 | .5 | 1.8 | 3.3 | 2.5 | 2.0 | 1.6 | .9 |
| Belgium | 124 | 2.1 | 2.8 | 1.8 | 1.8 | 4.5 | −.1 | 2.2 | 3.5 | 2.8 | 1.1 | .3 | .6 |
| Cyprus | 423 | 2.3 | 2.6 | 2.5 | 2.4 | 4.7 | .4 | 2.4 | 3.3 | 2.4 | −.4 | −1.4 | −2.1 |
| Estonia | 939 | 3.0 | 4.1 | 4.4 | 6.6 | 10.4 | −.1 | 3.0 | 5.0 | 3.9 | 2.8 | −.1 | −.5 |
| Finland | 172 | .2 | .9 | 1.6 | 2.5 | 4.1 | — | 1.2 | 3.4 | 2.8 | 1.5 | 1.0 | −.2 |
| France | 132 | 2.1 | 1.7 | 1.7 | 1.5 | 2.8 | .1 | 1.5 | 2.1 | 2.0 | .9 | .5 | — |
| Germany | 134 | 1.7 | 1.5 | 1.6 | 2.3 | 2.6 | .3 | 1.1 | 2.1 | 2.0 | 1.5 | .9 | .2 |
| Greece | 174 | 2.9 | 3.5 | 3.2 | 2.9 | 4.2 | 1.2 | 4.7 | 3.3 | 1.5 | −.9 | −1.3 | −1.7 |
| Ireland | 178 | 2.2 | 2.4 | 3.9 | 4.9 | 4.1 | −4.5 | −.9 | 2.6 | 1.7 | .5 | .2 | −.3 |
| Italy | 136 | 2.2 | 2.0 | 2.1 | 1.8 | 3.4 | .8 | 1.5 | 2.7 | 3.0 | 1.2 | .2 | — |
| Latvia | 941 | 6.2 | 6.7 | 6.5 | 10.1 | 15.4 | 3.5 | −1.1 | 4.4 | 2.2 | — | .6 | .2 |
| Lithuania | 946 | 1.2 | 2.6 | 3.7 | 5.7 | 10.9 | 4.4 | 1.3 | 4.1 | 3.1 | 1.0 | .1 | −.9 |
| Luxembourg | 137 | 2.2 | 2.5 | 2.7 | 2.3 | 3.4 | .4 | 2.3 | 3.4 | 2.7 | 1.7 | .6 | .5 |
| Malta | 181 | 2.8 | 3.0 | 2.8 | 1.3 | 4.3 | 2.1 | 1.5 | 2.7 | 2.4 | 1.4 | .3 | 1.1 |
| Netherlands | 138 | 1.2 | 1.7 | 1.2 | 1.6 | 2.5 | 1.2 | 1.3 | 2.3 | 2.5 | 2.5 | 1.0 | .6 |
| Portugal | 182 | 2.4 | 2.3 | 2.7 | 2.8 | 2.6 | −.8 | 1.4 | 3.7 | 2.8 | .3 | −.3 | .5 |
| Slovak Republic | 936 | 7.5 | 2.7 | 4.5 | 2.8 | 4.6 | 1.6 | 1.0 | 3.9 | 3.6 | 1.4 | −.1 | −.3 |
| Slovenia | 961 | 3.6 | 2.5 | 2.5 | 3.6 | 5.7 | .9 | 1.8 | 1.8 | 2.6 | 1.8 | .2 | −.5 |
| Spain | 184 | 3.0 | 3.4 | 3.5 | 2.8 | 4.1 | −.3 | 1.8 | 3.2 | 2.4 | 1.4 | −.1 | −.5 |
| Australia | 193 | 2.3 | 2.7 | 3.5 | 2.3 | 4.4 | 1.8 | 2.8 | 3.3 | 1.8 | 2.4 | 2.5 | 1.5 |
| Canada | 156 | 1.9 | 2.2 | 2.0 | 2.1 | 2.4 | .3 | 1.8 | 2.9 | 1.5 | .9 | 1.9 | 1.1 |
| China, P.R.: Hong Kong | 532 | −.3 | .8 | 2.0 | 2.0 | 4.3 | .6 | 2.3 | 5.3 | 4.1 | 4.4 | 4.5 | 3.0 |
| Czech Republic | 935 | 2.8 | 1.8 | 2.5 | 2.9 | 6.4 | 1.0 | 1.4 | 1.9 | 3.3 | 1.4 | .3 | .3 |
| Denmark | 128 | 1.2 | 1.8 | 1.9 | 1.7 | 3.4 | 1.3 | 2.3 | 2.8 | 2.4 | .8 | .6 | .5 |
| Iceland | 176 | 3.2 | 4.0 | 6.7 | 5.1 | 12.7 | 12.0 | 5.4 | 4.0 | 5.2 | 3.9 | 2.0 | 1.6 |
| Israel | 436 | −.4 | 1.3 | 2.1 | .5 | 4.6 | 3.3 | 2.7 | 3.5 | 1.7 | 1.5 | .5 | −.6 |
| Japan | 158 | — | −.3 | .2 | .1 | 1.4 | −1.3 | −.7 | −.3 | — | .4 | 2.7 | .8 |
| Korea | 542 | 3.6 | 2.8 | 2.2 | 2.5 | 4.7 | 2.8 | 3.0 | 4.0 | 2.2 | 1.3 | 1.3 | .7 |
| New Zealand | 196 | 2.3 | 3.0 | 3.4 | 2.4 | 4.0 | 2.1 | 2.3 | 4.4 | .9 | 1.3 | .9 | .3 |
| Norway | 142 | .5 | 1.5 | 2.3 | .7 | 3.8 | 2.2 | 2.4 | 1.3 | .7 | 2.1 | 2.0 | 2.2 |
| Singapore | 576 | 1.7 | .4 | 1.0 | 2.1 | 6.5 | .6 | 2.8 | 5.3 | 4.5 | 2.4 | 1.0 | −.5 |
| Sweden | 144 | .4 | .5 | 1.4 | 2.2 | 3.4 | −.5 | 1.2 | 3.0 | .9 | — | −.2 | — |
| Switzerland | 146 | .8 | 1.2 | 1.1 | .7 | 2.4 | −.5 | .7 | .2 | −.7 | −.2 | — | −1.1 |
| United Kingdom | 112 | 1.3 | 2.0 | 2.3 | 2.3 | 3.6 | 2.2 | 3.3 | 4.5 | 2.8 | 2.6 | 1.5 | .1 |
| United States | 111 | 2.7 | 3.4 | 3.2 | 2.9 | 3.8 | −.4 | 1.6 | 3.2 | 2.1 | 1.5 | 1.6 | .1 |
| **Emerging & Dev. Economies** | 200 | **6.2** | **5.9** | **5.6** | **6.1** | **9.6** | **5.1** | **6.1** | **7.3** | **6.0** | **6.3** | **5.4** | **5.7** |
| **Emerging & Developing Asia** | 505 | **4.1** | **3.6** | **4.1** | **5.4** | **7.4** | **2.7** | **5.6** | **6.4** | **4.5** | **4.9** | **3.6** | **2.6** |
| Bangladesh | 513 | 7.6 | 7.0 | 6.8 | 9.1 | 8.9 | 5.4 | 8.1 | 10.7 | 6.2 | 7.5 | 7.0 | 6.2 |
| Bhutan | 514 | −18.1 | 5.3 | 5.0 | 5.2 | 8.3 | 4.4 | 7.0 | 8.8 | 10.9 | 7.0 | 8.2 | 4.5 |
| Brunei Darussalam | 516 | .8 | 1.2 | .2 | 1.0 | 2.1 | 1.0 | .4 | 2.0 | .5 | .4 | −.2 | −.4 |
| Cambodia | 522 | 3.9 | 6.3 | 6.1 | 7.7 | 25.0 | −.7 | 4.0 | 5.5 | 2.9 | 2.9 | 3.9 | 1.2 |
| China, P.R.: Mainland | 924 | 3.9 | 1.8 | 1.5 | 4.8 | 5.9 | −.7 | 3.3 | 5.4 | 2.6 | 2.6 | 2.0 | 1.4 |
| China, P.R.: Macao | 546 | 1.0 | 4.4 | 5.2 | 5.6 | 8.6 | 1.2 | 2.8 | 5.8 | 6.1 | 5.5 | 6.0 | 4.6 |
| Fiji | 819 | 2.8 | 2.4 | 2.5 | 4.8 | 7.7 | 3.2 | 3.7 | 7.3 | 3.4 | 2.9 | .5 | 1.4 |
| India | 534 | 3.8 | 4.2 | 6.1 | 6.4 | 8.4 | 10.9 | 12.0 | 8.9 | 9.3 | 10.9 | 6.6 | 4.9 |
| Indonesia | 536 | 6.2 | 10.5 | 13.1 | 6.4 | 9.8 | 4.8 | 5.1 | 5.4 | 4.3 | 6.4 | 6.4 | 6.4 |
| Lao People's Dem. Rep | 544 | 10.5 | 7.2 | 6.8 | 4.5 | 7.6 | — | 6.0 | 7.6 | 4.3 | 6.4 | 4.1 | 1.3 |
| Malaysia | 548 | 1.5 | 3.0 | 3.6 | 2.0 | 5.4 | .6 | 1.7 | 3.2 | 1.7 | 2.1 | 3.1 | 2.1 |
| Maldives | 556 | −1.7 | 1.3 | 2.1 | 7.4 | 12.3 | 4.0 | 6.6 | 12.8 | 12.1 | 2.3 | 2.1 | 1.0 |
| Mongolia | 948 | 8.2 | 12.7 | 5.1 | 9.0 | 25.1 | 6.3 | 10.1 | 9.5 | 15.0 | 8.6 | 13.0 | 5.8 |
| Myanmar | 518 | 4.5 | 9.4 | 20.0 | 35.0 | 26.8 | 1.5 | 7.7 | 5.0 | 1.5 | 5.5 | 5.5 | 10.8 |
| Nepal | 558 | 2.8 | 6.8 | 6.9 | 5.7 | 9.9 | 11.1 | 9.3 | 9.3 | 9.5 | 9.0 | 8.4 | 7.9 |
| Papua New Guinea | 853 | 2.2 | 1.8 | 2.4 | .9 | 10.8 | 6.9 | 6.0 | 4.4 | 4.5 | 5.0 | 5.2 | 6.0 |
| Philippines | 566 | 4.8 | 6.5 | 5.5 | 2.9 | 8.3 | 4.2 | 3.8 | 4.6 | 3.2 | 3.0 | 4.1 | 1.4 |
| Samoa | 862 | 16.3 | 1.9 | 3.7 | 5.6 | 11.6 | 6.3 | .8 | 5.2 | 2.0 | .6 | −.4 | .7 |
| Solomon Islands | 813 | 7.0 | 7.3 | 11.2 | 7.7 | 17.3 | 7.1 | 1.1 | 7.3 | 5.9 | 5.4 | 5.2 | −.6 |
| Sri Lanka | 524 | 7.6 | 11.6 | 10.0 | 15.8 | 22.6 | 3.5 | 6.2 | 6.7 | 7.5 | 6.9 | 3.3 | .9 |
| Thailand | 578 | 2.8 | 4.5 | 4.6 | 2.2 | 5.5 | −.8 | 3.3 | 3.8 | 3.0 | 2.2 | 1.9 | −.9 |
| Timor-Leste | 537 | 3.2 | 1.1 | 3.9 | 10.3 | 9.1 | .7 | 6.8 | 13.5 | 11.8 | 11.2 | .4 | .6 |
| Tonga | 866 | 11.0 | 8.3 | 6.4 | 5.9 | 10.4 | 1.4 | 3.6 | 6.3 | 1.2 | .7 | 2.5 | −1.0 |
| Vanuatu | 846 | 1.4 | 1.2 | 2.0 | 4.0 | 4.8 | 4.3 | 2.8 | .9 | 1.4 | 1.4 | .8 | 2.5 |
| Vietnam | 582 | 7.8 | 8.3 | 7.4 | 8.3 | 23.1 | 7.1 | 8.9 | 18.7 | 9.1 | 6.6 | 4.1 | .9 |
| **Europe** | 170 | **9.3** | **9.6** | **7.8** | **8.0** | **12.1** | **8.4** | **6.4** | **7.8** | **6.2** | **5.3** | **6.1** | **10.4** |
| **Emerging & Dev. Europe** | 903 | **7.6** | **6.6** | **5.9** | **6.0** | **8.0** | **4.9** | **5.4** | **5.3** | **5.8** | **4.1** | **3.4** | **2.6** |
| Albania | 914 | 2.3 | 2.4 | 2.4 | 2.9 | 3.4 | 2.3 | 3.6 | 3.5 | 2.0 | 1.9 | 1.6 | 1.9 |
| Bulgaria | 918 | 6.3 | 5.0 | 7.3 | 8.4 | 12.3 | 2.8 | 2.4 | 4.2 | 3.0 | .9 | −1.4 | −.1 |
| Croatia | 960 | 2.1 | 3.3 | 3.2 | 2.9 | 6.1 | 2.4 | 1.0 | 2.3 | 3.4 | 2.2 | −.2 | −.5 |
| Hungary | 944 | 6.8 | 3.6 | 3.9 | 7.9 | 6.1 | 4.2 | 4.9 | 3.9 | 5.7 | 1.7 | −.2 | −.1 |
| Macedonia, FYR | 962 | .9 | .2 | 3.2 | 2.3 | 8.3 | −.7 | 1.5 | 3.9 | 3.3 | 2.8 | −.3 | −.3 |
| Poland | 964 | 3.6 | 2.1 | 1.1 | 2.4 | 4.3 | 3.8 | 2.7 | 4.3 | 3.6 | 1.0 | .1 | −1.0 |
| Romania | 968 | 11.9 | 9.0 | 6.6 | 4.8 | 7.8 | 5.6 | 6.1 | 5.8 | 3.3 | 4.0 | 1.1 | −.6 |
| Serbia, Republic of | 942 | 11.0 | 16.1 | 11.7 | 6.4 | 12.4 | 8.1 | 6.1 | 11.1 | 7.3 | 7.7 | 2.1 | 1.4 |
| Turkey | 186 | 10.6 | 10.1 | 9.6 | 8.8 | 10.4 | 6.3 | 8.6 | 6.5 | 8.9 | 7.5 | 8.9 | 7.7 |
| **CIS** | 901 | **10.5** | **12.2** | **9.4** | **9.7** | **15.7** | **11.3** | **7.1** | **9.9** | **6.4** | **6.2** | **8.3** | **17.1** |
| Armenia | 911 | 7.0 | .6 | 2.9 | 4.4 | 8.9 | 3.4 | 8.2 | 7.7 | 2.6 | 5.8 | 3.0 | 3.7 |
| Azerbaijan, Republic of | 912 | 6.7 | 9.7 | 8.4 | 16.6 | 20.8 | 1.4 | 5.7 | 7.9 | 1.0 | 2.4 | 1.4 | 4.2 |
| Belarus | 913 | 18.1 | 10.3 | 7.0 | 8.4 | 14.8 | 12.9 | 7.7 | 53.2 | 59.2 | 18.3 | 18.1 | 13.5 |
| Georgia | 915 | 5.7 | 8.2 | 9.2 | 9.2 | 10.0 | 1.7 | 7.1 | 8.5 | −.9 | −.5 | 3.1 | 4.0 |

# Consumer Prices

| | | 2004 | 2005 | 2006 | 2007 | 2008 | 2009 | 2010 | 2011 | 2012 | 2013 | 2014 | 2015 |
|---|---|---|---|---|---|---|---|---|---|---|---|---|---|
| **CIS(Cont.)** | | | | | | | | | | | | | |
| Kazakhstan | 916 | 6.9 | 7.6 | 8.6 | 10.8 | 17.2 | 7.3 | 7.1 | 8.3 | 5.1 | 5.8 | 6.7 | 6.6 |
| Kyrgyz Republic | 917 | 4.1 | 4.4 | 5.6 | 10.2 | 24.5 | 6.9 | 8.0 | 16.5 | 2.7 | 6.6 | 7.5 | 6.5 |
| Moldova | 921 | 12.5 | 11.8 | 12.9 | 12.1 | 12.9 | −.1 | 7.4 | 7.6 | 4.6 | 4.6 | 5.1 | 9.7 |
| Russia | 922 | 10.9 | 12.7 | 9.7 | 9.0 | 14.1 | 11.7 | 6.8 | 8.4 | 5.1 | 6.8 | 7.8 | 15.5 |
| Tajikistan | 923 | 7.1 | 7.1 | 10.0 | 13.1 | 20.5 | 6.4 | 6.4 | 12.4 | 5.8 | 5.0 | 6.1 | 5.7 |
| Ukraine | 926 | 9.0 | 13.6 | 9.1 | 12.8 | 25.2 | 15.9 | 9.4 | 8.0 | .6 | −.3 | 12.2 | 48.7 |
| **Middle East,N.Africa & Pakistan** | 440 | **7.8** | **7.6** | **8.5** | **7.7** | **15.8** | **7.6** | **7.0** | **9.8** | **10.8** | **12.6** | **7.9** | **6.1** |
| Afghanistan, Islamic Rep. of | 512 | .... | 12.7 | 7.3 | 8.5 | 30.6 | −8.3 | .9 | 10.2 | 7.2 | 7.7 | 4.6 | −1.5 |
| Algeria | 612 | 4.0 | 1.4 | 2.3 | 3.7 | 4.9 | 5.7 | 3.9 | 4.5 | 8.9 | 3.3 | 2.9 | 4.8 |
| Bahrain, Kingdom of | 419 | 2.4 | 2.6 | 2.0 | 3.3 | 3.5 | 2.8 | 2.0 | −.4 | 2.8 | 3.3 | 2.7 | 1.8 |
| Djibouti | 611 | 3.1 | 3.1 | 3.5 | 5.0 | 12.0 | 1.7 | 4.0 | 5.1 | 3.7 | 2.4 | 2.9 | .... |
| Egypt | 469 | 11.3 | 4.9 | 7.6 | 9.3 | 18.3 | 11.8 | 11.3 | 10.1 | 7.1 | 9.4 | 10.1 | 10.4 |
| Iran, I.R. of | 429 | 14.8 | 13.4 | 11.9 | 17.2 | 25.5 | 13.5 | 10.1 | 20.6 | 27.4 | 39.3 | 17.2 | 13.7 |
| Jordan | 439 | 3.4 | 3.5 | 6.3 | 5.4 | 14.9 | −.7 | 5.0 | 4.2 | 4.5 | 4.8 | 2.9 | −.9 |
| Kuwait | 443 | 1.2 | 4.1 | 3.1 | 5.5 | 10.6 | 4.6 | 4.5 | 4.9 | 3.2 | 2.7 | 2.9 | 3.3 |
| Libya | 672 | −2.2 | 2.7 | 1.5 | 6.3 | 10.4 | 2.5 | 2.8 | 15.5 | 6.1 | 2.6 | .... | .... |
| Mauritania | 682 | 10.4 | 12.1 | 6.2 | 7.3 | 7.3 | 2.2 | 6.3 | 5.6 | 4.9 | 4.1 | 3.5 | .5 |
| Morocco | 686 | 1.5 | 1.0 | 3.3 | 2.0 | 3.7 | 1.0 | 1.0 | .9 | 1.3 | 1.9 | .4 | 1.6 |
| Oman | 449 | .8 | 1.9 | 3.2 | 6.0 | 12.1 | 3.9 | 3.2 | 4.1 | 2.9 | 1.2 | 1.0 | .1 |
| Pakistan | 564 | 7.4 | 9.1 | 7.9 | 7.6 | 20.3 | 13.6 | 13.9 | 11.9 | 9.7 | 7.7 | 7.2 | 2.5 |
| Qatar | 453 | 6.8 | 8.8 | 11.8 | 13.8 | 15.1 | −4.9 | −2.4 | 1.9 | 1.9 | 3.1 | 3.1 | 1.9 |
| Saudi Arabia | 456 | .3 | .7 | 2.2 | 4.2 | 9.9 | 5.1 | 5.3 | 5.8 | 2.9 | 3.5 | 2.7 | 2.2 |
| Sudan | 732 | 8.4 | 8.5 | 7.2 | 8.0 | 14.3 | 11.2 | 13.2 | 22.1 | 37.4 | 30.0 | 36.9 | 16.9 |
| Syrian Arab Republic | 463 | 4.4 | 7.2 | 10.0 | 3.9 | 15.7 | 2.9 | 4.4 | 4.8 | 36.7 | .... | .... | .... |
| Tunisia | 744 | 3.6 | 2.0 | 4.5 | 3.4 | 4.9 | 3.5 | 4.4 | 3.5 | 5.1 | 5.8 | 4.9 | 4.9 |
| Yemen, Republic of | 474 | 12.5 | 11.8 | 10.8 | 7.9 | 19.0 | 5.4 | 11.2 | 19.5 | 9.9 | 11.0 | 8.1 | .... |
| **Sub-Saharan Africa** | 603 | **7.3** | **9.2** | **7.2** | **6.9** | **12.8** | **8.9** | **7.0** | **9.0** | **8.9** | **6.3** | **6.2** | **6.5** |
| CEMAC | | | | | | | | | | | | | |
| Cameroon | 622 | .2 | 2.0 | 5.1 | .9 | 5.3 | 3.0 | 1.3 | 2.9 | 2.9 | 1.9 | 1.9 | 2.7 |
| Central African Rep. | 626 | −2.1 | 2.9 | 6.7 | .9 | 9.3 | 3.5 | 1.5 | 1.3 | 5.8 | 1.5 | 25.3 | 37.1 |
| Chad | 628 | −5.4 | 7.9 | 8.0 | −9.0 | 10.3 | 10.0 | −2.1 | −3.7 | 14.0 | .1 | 1.7 | 3.7 |
| Congo, Rep. of | 634 | 2.4 | 3.1 | 6.5 | 2.7 | 7.3 | 5.3 | 5.0 | 1.3 | 3.9 | 6.0 | .1 | 5.1 |
| Equatorial Guinea | 642 | 4.2 | 5.6 | 4.4 | 2.8 | 6.6 | 4.7 | 7.8 | 2.5 | 1.0 | 1.2 | 4.8 | 11.7 |
| Gabon | 646 | .4 | 3.7 | −1.4 | 5.0 | 5.3 | 1.9 | 1.5 | 1.3 | 2.7 | .5 | 4.7 | .6 |
| WAEMU | 759 | .6 | 4.3 | 2.3 | 2.3 | 7.4 | .4 | 1.4 | 3.9 | 2.4 | 1.6 | −.1 | 1.0 |
| Benin | 638 | .9 | 5.4 | 3.8 | 1.3 | 7.9 | 2.2 | 2.3 | 2.7 | 6.8 | 1.0 | −1.1 | .3 |
| Burkina Faso | 748 | −.4 | 6.4 | 2.3 | −.2 | 10.7 | 2.6 | −.8 | 2.8 | 3.8 | .5 | −.3 | 1.0 |
| Côte d'Ivoire | 662 | 1.5 | 3.9 | 2.5 | 1.9 | 6.3 | 1.0 | 1.2 | 4.9 | 1.3 | 2.6 | .5 | 1.2 |
| Guinea Bissau | 654 | .9 | 3.3 | 2.0 | 4.6 | 10.5 | −1.7 | 2.5 | 5.0 | 2.1 | 1.2 | −1.5 | 1.4 |
| Mali | 678 | −3.1 | 6.4 | 1.5 | 1.4 | 9.2 | 2.5 | 1.1 | 2.9 | 5.4 | −.6 | .9 | 1.4 |
| Niger | 692 | .3 | 7.8 | — | .1 | 11.3 | .6 | .8 | 2.9 | .5 | 2.3 | −.9 | 1.0 |
| Senegal | 722 | .5 | 1.7 | 2.1 | 5.9 | 5.8 | −2.2 | 1.2 | 3.4 | 1.4 | .7 | −1.1 | .1 |
| Togo | 742 | .4 | 6.8 | 2.2 | 1.0 | 8.7 | 3.3 | 1.8 | 3.6 | 2.6 | 1.8 | .2 | 1.8 |
| Angola | 614 | 43.5 | 23.0 | 13.3 | 12.2 | 12.5 | 13.7 | 14.5 | 13.5 | 10.3 | 8.8 | 7.3 | 10.3 |
| Botswana | 616 | 6.9 | 8.6 | 11.6 | 7.1 | 12.7 | 8.0 | 6.9 | 8.5 | 7.5 | 5.9 | 4.4 | 3.1 |
| Burundi | 618 | 7.9 | 13.5 | 2.8 | 8.3 | 24.1 | 11.0 | 6.4 | 9.7 | 18.0 | 8.0 | 4.4 | 5.6 |
| Cabo Verde | 624 | −1.9 | .4 | 5.4 | 4.4 | 6.8 | 1.0 | 2.1 | 4.5 | 2.5 | 1.5 | −.2 | .1 |
| Comoros | 632 | 4.5 | 3.0 | 3.4 | 4.5 | 1.7 | 4.4 | 3.4 | 1.8 | 1.8 | 2.3 | .6 | −8.1 |
| Congo, Dem. Rep. of | 636 | 4.0 | 21.3 | 13.1 | 16.9 | 17.3 | 2.8 | 7.1 | 15.3 | 9.7 | 1.6 | .... | .... |
| Ethiopia | 644 | 3.3 | 12.9 | 12.3 | 17.2 | 44.4 | 8.5 | 8.1 | 33.2 | 22.8 | 8.1 | 7.4 | 10.1 |
| Gambia, The | 648 | 14.2 | 4.8 | 2.1 | 5.4 | 4.4 | 4.6 | 5.0 | 4.8 | 4.3 | 5.7 | 5.9 | .... |
| Ghana | 652 | 12.6 | 15.1 | 10.9 | 10.7 | 16.5 | 19.3 | 10.7 | 8.7 | 9.2 | 11.6 | 15.5 | 17.1 |
| Guinea | 656 | .... | 31.4 | 34.7 | 22.8 | 18.4 | 4.7 | 15.5 | 21.4 | 15.2 | 11.9 | 9.7 | 8.2 |
| Kenya | 664 | 11.6 | 10.3 | 14.5 | 9.8 | 26.2 | 9.2 | 4.0 | 14.0 | 9.4 | 5.7 | 6.9 | 6.6 |
| Lesotho | 666 | 5.0 | 3.4 | 6.1 | 8.0 | 10.7 | 7.4 | 3.6 | 5.0 | 6.1 | 4.9 | 5.3 | 3.2 |
| Liberia | 668 | 7.8 | 10.8 | 7.3 | 11.4 | 17.5 | 7.4 | 7.3 | 8.5 | 6.8 | 7.6 | 9.8 | .... |
| Madagascar | 674 | 13.8 | 18.5 | 10.8 | 10.3 | 9.2 | 9.0 | 9.2 | 9.5 | 6.4 | 5.8 | 6.1 | 7.4 |
| Malawi | 676 | 11.4 | 15.4 | 14.0 | 8.0 | 8.7 | 8.4 | 7.4 | 7.6 | 21.3 | 27.3 | 23.8 | 21.9 |
| Mauritius | 684 | 4.7 | 4.9 | 8.9 | 8.8 | 9.7 | 2.5 | 2.9 | 6.5 | 3.9 | 3.5 | 3.2 | 1.3 |
| Mozambique | 688 | 12.7 | 7.2 | 13.2 | 8.2 | 10.3 | 3.3 | 12.7 | 10.4 | 2.7 | 4.3 | 2.6 | 3.6 |
| Namibia | 728 | 4.1 | 2.3 | 5.0 | 6.5 | 9.1 | 9.5 | 4.9 | 5.0 | 6.7 | 5.6 | 5.4 | 3.4 |
| Nigeria | 694 | 15.0 | 17.9 | 8.2 | 5.4 | 11.6 | 11.5 | 13.7 | 10.8 | 12.2 | 8.5 | 8.1 | 9.0 |
| Rwanda | 714 | 12.3 | 9.0 | 8.9 | 9.1 | 15.4 | 10.4 | 2.3 | 5.7 | 6.3 | 4.2 | 1.8 | 2.5 |
| São Tomé & Príncipe | 716 | 13.3 | 17.2 | 23.1 | 18.5 | 32.0 | 17.0 | 13.3 | 14.3 | 10.6 | 8.1 | 7.0 | 5.3 |
| Seychelles | 718 | 3.9 | .9 | −.4 | 5.3 | 37.0 | 31.8 | −2.4 | 2.6 | 7.1 | 4.3 | 1.4 | 4.0 |
| Sierra Leone | 724 | 14.2 | 12.1 | 9.5 | 11.7 | −35.8 | 9.3 | 16.6 | 16.2 | 12.9 | 10.3 | 7.3 | 8.0 |
| South Africa | 199 | 1.4 | 3.4 | 4.6 | 7.1 | 11.5 | †7.1 | †4.3 | 5.0 | 5.7 | 5.4 | 6.4 | 4.6 |
| South Sudan, Republic of | 733 | .... | .... | .... | .... | .... | 5.0 | 1.2 | 47.3 | 45.1 | — | 3.3 | 50.2 |
| Swaziland | 734 | 3.4 | 4.8 | 5.3 | 8.1 | 12.7 | 7.4 | 4.5 | 6.1 | 8.9 | 5.6 | 5.7 | 5.0 |
| Tanzania | 738 | 4.7 | 5.0 | 7.3 | 7.0 | 10.3 | 12.1 | 6.2 | 12.7 | 16.0 | 7.9 | 6.1 | 5.6 |
| Uganda | 746 | 3.7 | 8.4 | 7.3 | 6.1 | 12.1 | 13.0 | 4.0 | 18.7 | 14.0 | 5.5 | 4.3 | 5.2 |
| Zambia | 754 | 18.0 | 18.3 | 9.0 | 10.7 | 12.4 | 13.4 | 8.5 | 6.4 | 6.6 | 7.0 | 7.8 | 10.1 |
| Zimbabwe | 698 | 282.4 | 302.1 | 1,096.7 | 24,411.0 | .... | .... | 3.0 | 3.3 | 3.9 | 1.6 | −.2 | −2.4 |
| **Western Hemisphere** | 205 | **6.2** | **5.4** | **4.2** | **4.2** | **6.4** | **5.8** | **5.5** | **6.2** | **5.5** | **6.4** | **7.6** | **10.1** |
| Anguilla | 312 | 4.4 | 4.6 | 8.4 | 5.1 | 6.8 | −.7 | 1.0 | 4.7 | 1.4 | .1 | −.3 | −1.0 |
| Dominica | 321 | 2.4 | 1.7 | 2.6 | 3.2 | 6.3 | — | 3.2 | 2.4 | 1.4 | — | .8 | −.7 |
| Grenada | 328 | 2.2 | 3.5 | 4.3 | 3.9 | 8.0 | −.3 | 3.4 | 3.0 | 2.4 | — | −.9 | −1.4 |
| St. Kitts and Nevis | 361 | 2.3 | 3.4 | 8.5 | 4.5 | 5.3 | 2.0 | .5 | 5.8 | .8 | 1.1 | .2 | −2.3 |
| St. Lucia | 362 | 1.5 | 3.9 | 2.3 | 3.1 | 7.2 | −1.7 | 3.3 | 2.8 | 4.2 | 1.5 | 3.5 | −1.0 |
| St. Vincent & Grenadines | 364 | 3.0 | 3.7 | 3.0 | 6.9 | 10.1 | .4 | 1.5 | 3.2 | 2.6 | .8 | .2 | −1.7 |
| Argentina | 213 | 4.4 | 9.6 | 10.9 | 8.8 | 8.6 | 6.3 | 10.8 | 9.5 | 10.0 | 10.6 | .... | .... |
| Aruba | 314 | 2.5 | 3.4 | 3.6 | 5.4 | 9.0 | −2.1 | 2.1 | 4.4 | .6 | −2.4 | .4 | .5 |

# Consumer Prices

2016, International Monetary Fund : *International Financial Statistics Yearbook*

|  |  | 2004 | 2005 | 2006 | 2007 | 2008 | 2009 | 2010 | 2011 | 2012 | 2013 | 2014 | 2015 |
|---|---|---|---|---|---|---|---|---|---|---|---|---|---|
|  |  | *Percent Change over Previous Year; Calculated from Indices* | | | | | | | | | | | |
| **Western Hemisphere(Cont.)** | | | | | | | | | | | | | |
| Bahamas, The | 313 | 1.0 | 1.6 | 2.4 | 2.5 | 4.5 | 2.1 | 1.3 | 3.2 | 2.0 | .3 | 1.5 | 1.9 |
| Barbados | 316 | 1.4 | 6.1 | 7.3 | 4.0 | 8.1 | 3.6 | 5.8 | 9.4 | 4.5 | 1.8 | 1.9 | −1.1 |
| Belize | 339 | 3.1 | 3.6 | 4.2 | 2.3 | 6.4 | −1.1 | 5.6 | −3.6 | 1.3 | .5 | 1.2 | −.9 |
| Bolivia | 218 | 4.4 | 5.4 | 4.3 | 8.7 | 14.0 | 3.3 | 2.5 | 9.8 | 4.6 | 5.7 | 5.8 | 4.1 |
| Brazil | 223 | 6.6 | 6.9 | 4.2 | 3.6 | 5.7 | 4.9 | 5.0 | 6.6 | 5.4 | 6.2 | 6.3 | 9.0 |
| Chile | 228 | 1.1 | 3.1 | 3.4 | 4.4 | 8.7 | .1 | 1.4 | 3.3 | 3.0 | 1.8 | 4.4 | 4.3 |
| Colombia | 233 | 5.9 | 5.0 | 4.3 | 5.5 | 7.0 | 4.2 | 2.3 | 3.4 | 3.2 | 2.0 | 2.9 | 5.0 |
| Costa Rica | 238 | 12.3 | 13.8 | 11.5 | 9.4 | 13.4 | 7.8 | 5.7 | 4.9 | 4.5 | 5.2 | 4.5 | .8 |
| Dominican Republic | 243 | 51.5 | 4.2 | 7.6 | 6.1 | 10.6 | 1.4 | 6.3 | 8.5 | 3.7 | 4.8 | 3.0 | .8 |
| Ecuador | 248 | 2.7 | 2.4 | 3.0 | 2.3 | 8.4 | 5.2 | 3.6 | 4.5 | 5.1 | 2.7 | 3.6 | 4.0 |
| El Salvador | 253 | 4.5 | 4.7 | 4.0 | 4.6 | 6.7 | 1.1 | .9 | 5.1 | 1.7 | .8 | 1.1 | −.7 |
| Guatemala | 258 | 7.6 | 9.1 | 6.6 | 6.8 | 11.4 | 1.9 | 3.9 | 6.2 | 3.8 | 4.3 | 3.4 | 2.4 |
| Guyana | 336 | 4.7 | 6.9 | 6.6 | 12.3 | 8.1 | 2.9 | 2.1 | 5.0 | 2.4 | 1.8 | .9 | −1.0 |
| Haiti | 263 | 22.8 | 15.7 | 13.1 | 8.5 | 15.5 | — | 5.7 | 8.4 | 6.3 | 5.9 | 4.6 | 9.0 |
| Honduras | 268 | 8.1 | 8.8 | 5.6 | 6.9 | 11.4 | 5.5 | 4.7 | 6.8 | 5.2 | 5.2 | 6.1 | 3.2 |
| Jamaica | 343 | 13.6 | 15.3 | 8.6 | 9.3 | 22.0 | 9.6 | 12.6 | 7.5 | 6.9 | 9.3 | 8.3 | 3.7 |
| Mexico | 273 | 4.7 | 4.0 | 3.6 | 4.0 | 5.1 | 5.3 | 4.2 | 3.4 | 4.1 | 3.8 | 4.0 | 2.7 |
| Netherlands Antilles | 353 | 1.4 | 4.1 | 3.1 | 3.0 | 6.9 | 1.8 | . . . . | . . . . | . . . . | . . . . | . . . . | . . . . |
| Nicaragua | 278 | 8.5 | 9.6 | 9.1 | 11.1 | 19.8 | 3.7 | 5.5 | 8.1 | 7.2 | 7.1 | 6.0 | 4.0 |
| Panama | 283 | .2 | 3.2 | 2.1 | 4.2 | 8.8 | 2.4 | 3.5 | 5.9 | 5.7 | 4.0 | 2.6 | .1 |
| Paraguay | 288 | 4.3 | 6.8 | 9.6 | 8.1 | 10.2 | 2.6 | 4.7 | 8.3 | 3.7 | 2.7 | 5.0 | 3.1 |
| Peru | 293 | 3.7 | 1.6 | 2.0 | 1.8 | 5.8 | 2.9 | 1.5 | 3.4 | 3.7 | 2.8 | 3.2 | 3.6 |
| Suriname | 366 | 10.0 | 9.9 | 11.3 | 6.4 | 14.7 | −.2 | 6.9 | 17.7 | 5.0 | 1.9 | 3.4 | 6.9 |
| Trinidad and Tobago | 369 | 3.7 | 6.9 | 8.3 | 7.9 | 12.0 | 7.0 | 10.5 | 5.1 | 9.3 | 5.2 | 5.7 | 4.7 |
| Uruguay | 298 | 9.2 | 4.7 | 6.4 | 8.1 | 7.9 | 7.1 | 6.7 | 8.1 | 8.1 | 8.6 | 8.9 | 8.7 |
| Venezuela, Rep. Bol | 299 | 21.7 | 16.0 | 13.7 | 18.7 | 31.4 | 27.1 | 28.2 | 26.1 | 21.1 | 40.6 | 62.2 | 121.7 |

# Indices

|  |  | 2004 | 2005 | 2006 | 2007 | 2008 | 2009 | 2010 | 2011 | 2012 | 2013 | 2014 | 2015 |
|---|---|---|---|---|---|---|---|---|---|---|---|---|---|
|  |  | *Index Numbers: 2010=100* | | | | | | | | | | | |
| World | 001 | 79.9 | 82.9 | 85.9 | 89.1 | 94.3 | 96.5 | 100.0 | 104.8 | 108.8 | 112.8 | 116.4 | 119.6 |
| Advanced Economies | 110 | 89.0 | 91.0 | 93.2 | 95.2 | 98.4 | 98.5 | 100.0 | 102.7 | 104.6 | 106.0 | 107.5 | 107.8 |
| Emerging & Dev. Economies | 200 | 68.9 | 73.0 | 77.1 | 81.9 | 89.7 | 94.3 | 100.0 | 107.3 | 113.7 | 120.9 | 127.4 | 134.8 |
| Emerging & Developing Asia | 505 | 75.6 | 78.3 | 81.5 | 85.9 | 92.2 | 94.7 | 100.0 | 106.4 | 111.2 | 116.7 | 120.8 | 124.0 |
| Europe | 170 | 60.6 | 66.5 | 71.7 | 77.4 | 86.7 | 94.0 | 100.0 | 107.8 | 114.5 | 120.6 | 127.9 | 141.3 |
| Middle East,N.Africa & Pakist | 440 | 59.7 | 64.2 | 69.6 | 75.0 | 86.8 | 93.4 | 100.0 | 109.8 | 121.7 | 137.0 | 147.8 | 156.8 |
| Sub-Saharan Africa | 603 | 60.8 | 66.4 | 71.2 | 76.1 | 85.9 | 93.5 | 100.0 | 109.0 | 118.7 | 126.2 | 134.0 | 142.8 |
| Western Hemisphere | 205 | 73.6 | 77.6 | 80.8 | 84.2 | 89.6 | 94.8 | 100.0 | 106.2 | 112.1 | 119.2 | 128.3 | 141.2 |

# Exports, f.o.b.

| | | 2004 | 2005 | 2006 | 2007 | 2008 | 2009 | 2010 | 2011 | 2012 | 2013 | 2014 | 2015 |
|---|---|---|---|---|---|---|---|---|---|---|---|---|---|
| | | | | | | | *Billions of US Dollars* | | | | | | |
| World | 001 | 9,085.3 | 10,374.7 | 11,998.9 | 13,837.9 | 16,005.6 | 12,421.7 | 15,120.8 | 18,053.7 | 18,102.0 | 18,476.6 | 18,663.1 | 16,215.8 |
| Advanced Economies | 110 | 6,435.6 | 7,038.1 | 7,939.5 | 9,022.9 | 10,022.0 | 7,850.4 | 9,270.9 | 10,750.4 | 10,533.6 | 10,677.5 | 10,818.1 | 9,589.8 |
| Euro Area | | | | | | | | | | | | | |
| Austria | 122 | 111.7 | 117.7 | 130.4 | 157.3 | 173.4 | 130.8 | 144.9 | 169.5 | 158.8 | 166.5 | 169.2 | 145.9 |
| Belgium | 124 | 307.7 | 335.7 | 366.7 | 431.8 | 471.9 | 371.4 | 407.1 | 476.0 | 446.6 | 467.8 | 474.1 | 401.2 |
| Cyprus | 423 | 1.1 | 1.5 | 1.4 | 1.5 | 1.7 | 1.3 | 1.5 | 2.0 | 1.8 | 2.1 | 1.9 | 1.9 |
| Estonia | 939 | 5.9 | 7.7 | 8.8 | 11.0 | 12.5 | 9.1 | 11.6 | 16.7 | 16.1 | 16.3 | 16.0 | 12.9 |
| Finland | 172 | 60.9 | 65.2 | 77.3 | 90.1 | 96.9 | 62.9 | 69.5 | 79.1 | 73.1 | 74.4 | 74.3 | 59.7 |
| France | 132 | 422.2 | 443.6 | 490.7 | 550.5 | 608.9 | 476.1 | 517.0 | 585.3 | 558.6 | 568.5 | 568.1 | 493.8 |
| Germany | 134 | 909.2 | 977.9 | 1,122.1 | 1,323.8 | 1,451.4 | 1,120.7 | 1,261.6 | 1,476.9 | 1,408.4 | 1,451.6 | 1,492.5 | 1,326.8 |
| Greece | 174 | 16.6 | 18.4 | 21.5 | 26.6 | 31.3 | 25.1 | 28.2 | 33.9 | 35.5 | 36.2 | 36.0 | 28.7 |
| Ireland | 178 | 104.2 | 107.9 | 109.0 | 122.3 | 127.0 | 119.2 | 118.9 | 127.0 | 117.8 | 115.3 | 118.6 | 122.1 |
| Italy | 136 | 353.4 | 372.9 | 417.2 | 500.2 | 545.0 | 406.7 | 446.9 | 523.3 | 501.5 | 517.6 | 528.1 | 458.5 |
| Latvia | 941 | 3.9 | 5.1 | 5.9 | 7.9 | 9.3 | 7.2 | 8.9 | 12.0 | 12.7 | 13.3 | 13.6 | 11.5 |
| Lithuania | 946 | 9.3 | 11.8 | 14.2 | 17.2 | 23.8 | 16.5 | 20.7 | 28.1 | 29.6 | 32.6 | 32.4 | 25.5 |
| Luxembourg | 137 | 12.2 | 12.7 | 14.0 | 16.4 | 17.7 | 12.9 | 14.3 | 16.8 | 14.0 | 14.1 | 15.1 | 13.1 |
| Malta | 181 | 2.6 | 2.4 | 2.7 | 3.0 | 3.6 | 2.9 | 3.7 | 5.3 | 5.7 | 5.2 | 4.8 | 3.8 |
| Netherlands | 138 | 318.0 | 349.8 | 399.6 | 472.7 | 545.9 | 431.7 | 492.7 | 569.5 | 554.7 | 567.7 | 574.3 | 471.1 |
| Portugal | 182 | 33.1 | 32.2 | 42.9 | 50.2 | 57.6 | 44.3 | 48.7 | 59.6 | 58.3 | 62.8 | 64.1 | 55.4 |
| Slovak Republic | 936 | 27.6 | 32.0 | 41.9 | 57.8 | 71.1 | 55.2 | 63.9 | 78.9 | 79.8 | 85.2 | 85.8 | 75.4 |
| Slovenia | 961 | 15.9 | 17.9 | 21.3 | 26.9 | 29.6 | 22.6 | 24.7 | 29.2 | 27.1 | 28.6 | 30.5 | 26.6 |
| Spain | 184 | 182.1 | 191.0 | 213.3 | 248.9 | 277.7 | 220.8 | 246.3 | 298.5 | 286.2 | 311.0 | 318.9 | 277.4 |
| Australia | 193 | 86.4 | 105.8 | 123.3 | 141.1 | 187.3 | 154.0 | 212.3 | 271.7 | 256.7 | 253.0 | 241.2 | 188.4 |
| Canada | 156 | 304.5 | 360.7 | 388.3 | 420.3 | 456.4 | 314.0 | 387.5 | 452.1 | 454.8 | 458.4 | 469.9 | 409.0 |
| China, P.R.: Hong Kong | 532 | 259.3 | 289.3 | 316.8 | 344.5 | 362.7 | 318.5 | 390.1 | 428.7 | 442.8 | 459.0 | 473.7 | 465.1 |
| Czech Republic | 935 | 67.2 | 78.0 | 95.1 | 122.8 | 146.4 | 113.2 | 133.0 | 162.9 | 157.2 | 162.3 | 175.0 | 158.6 |
| Denmark | 128 | 75.6 | 81.9 | 90.7 | 101.6 | 115.9 | 91.8 | 95.8 | 111.9 | 106.1 | 111.4 | 110.5 | 94.2 |
| Iceland | 176 | 2.9 | 2.9 | 3.2 | 4.3 | 5.2 | 4.1 | 4.6 | 5.3 | 5.1 | 5.0 | 5.0 | 4.7 |
| Israel | 436 | 38.6 | 42.8 | 46.8 | 54.1 | 60.8 | 47.9 | 58.4 | 67.6 | 63.2 | 66.6 | 68.6 | 63.6 |
| Japan | 158 | 565.7 | 594.9 | 646.7 | 714.2 | 782.0 | 580.7 | 769.8 | 822.6 | 798.6 | 714.6 | 690.2 | 624.8 |
| Korea | 542 | 253.8 | 284.4 | 325.5 | 371.5 | 422.0 | 363.5 | 466.4 | 555.2 | 547.9 | 559.6 | 572.7 | 526.8 |
| New Zealand | 196 | 20.6 | 21.9 | 22.9 | 28.1 | 30.9 | 24.8 | 32.3 | 37.5 | 37.4 | 41.1 | 40.7 | 34.3 |
| Norway | 142 | 82.5 | 103.8 | 122.1 | 136.4 | 171.8 | 116.8 | 130.7 | 160.3 | 161.0 | 153.1 | 142.3 | 103.4 |
| Singapore | 576 | 198.6 | 229.6 | 271.8 | 299.3 | 338.2 | 269.8 | 351.9 | 409.5 | 408.4 | 410.2 | 405.3 | 346.6 |
| Sweden | 144 | 123.3 | 130.9 | 147.9 | 169.0 | 183.9 | 131.0 | 158.1 | 187.2 | 172.7 | 167.6 | 162.5 | 139.5 |
| Switzerland | 146 | 117.8 | 126.1 | 141.7 | 164.8 | 191.4 | 166.5 | 185.8 | 223.2 | 214.0 | 217.1 | 227.6 | 210.9 |
| Taiwan Province of China | 528 | 173.9 | 197.8 | 223.7 | 246.4 | 255.1 | 203.7 | 274.6 | 308.3 | 301.0 | 305.4 | 313.8 | 280.5 |
| United Kingdom | 112 | 348.3 | 382.8 | 446.3 | 440.5 | 468.3 | 356.5 | 410.1 | 478.2 | 474.6 | 476.9 | 477.6 | .... |
| United States | 111 | 818.8 | 901.1 | 1,026.0 | 1,148.2 | 1,287.4 | 1,056.0 | 1,278.5 | 1,480.3 | 1,545.7 | 1,579.0 | 1,623.4 | 1,504.6 |
| | | | | | | | | | | | | | |
| Emerging & Dev. Economies | 200 | 2,665.1 | 3,359.6 | 4,089.5 | 4,852.1 | 6,033.7 | 4,608.9 | 5,900.6 | 7,369.5 | 7,639.2 | 7,874.0 | 7,919.3 | 6,691.1 |
| Emerging & Developing Asia | 505 | 1,057.6 | 1,306.0 | 1,612.9 | 1,961.1 | 2,301.1 | 1,936.3 | 2,533.5 | 3,064.7 | 3,235.2 | 3,426.2 | 3,598.6 | 3,411.1 |
| Bangladesh | 513 | 6.6 | 7.2 | 9.1 | 10.2 | 11.8 | 12.4 | 14.2 | 19.8 | 27.7 | 22.4 | .... | .... |
| Bhutan | 514 | .2 | .3 | .4 | .7 | .5 | .5 | .6 | .7 | .5 | .5 | .6 | .6 |
| Cambodia | 522 | 2.8 | 3.2 | 3.8 | 4.4 | 4.7 | 4.2 | 5.1 | 7.0 | 8.2 | 9.1 | 10.8 | 12.0 |
| China, P.R.: Mainland | 924 | 593.3 | 762.0 | 969.4 | 1,217.8 | 1,428.7 | 1,201.8 | 1,578.3 | 1,899.2 | 2,048.9 | 2,210.2 | 2,343.2 | 2,284.5 |
| China, P.R.: Macao | 546 | 2.8 | 2.5 | 2.6 | 2.5 | 2.0 | 1.0 | .9 | .9 | 1.0 | 1.1 | 1.2 | 1.3 |
| Fiji | 819 | .7 | .7 | .7 | .8 | .9 | .6 | .8 | 1.1 | 1.2 | 1.1 | 1.2 | 1.2 |
| India | 534 | 76.6 | 99.6 | 121.8 | 150.0 | 194.5 | 164.9 | 226.4 | 303.0 | 296.8 | 314.7 | 322.5 | 267.7 |
| Indonesia | 536 | 70.8 | 87.0 | 103.5 | 118.0 | 139.6 | 119.6 | 158.1 | 200.6 | 188.5 | 182.7 | 176.3 | 150.4 |
| Lao People's Dem. Rep. | 544 | .4 | .6 | .9 | .8 | 1.1 | 1.1 | 1.7 | 2.2 | 2.3 | 2.3 | 2.7 | 2.3 |
| Malaysia | 548 | 125.7 | 140.9 | 160.6 | 176.0 | 199.4 | 157.2 | 198.6 | 228.1 | 227.5 | 228.3 | 234.1 | 199.9 |
| Maldives | 556 | .1 | .1 | .1 | .1 | .1 | .1 | .1 | .1 | .2 | .2 | .1 | .1 |
| Mongolia | 948 | .9 | 1.1 | 1.5 | 1.9 | 2.5 | 1.9 | 2.9 | 4.8 | 4.4 | 4.3 | 5.8 | 4.7 |
| Myanmar | 518 | 2.4 | 3.8 | 4.5 | 6.3 | 6.9 | 6.7 | 8.7 | 9.2 | 8.9 | 11.2 | 11.3 | 6.0 |
| Nepal | 558 | .8 | .8 | .8 | .9 | .8 | .9 | .8 | .9 | .9 | .8 | .9 | .7 |
| Papua New Guinea | 853 | 2.6 | 3.3 | 4.2 | 4.7 | 5.7 | 4.4 | 5.7 | 6.9 | 6.3 | 6.0 | 8.8 | 8.4 |
| Philippines | 566 | 39.7 | 41.3 | 47.4 | 50.5 | 49.5 | 38.4 | 51.5 | 48.3 | 52.1 | 56.6 | 62.1 | 58.6 |
| Samoa | 862 | — | — | — | — | — | — | — | — | — | — | .... | .... |
| Solomon Islands | 813 | .1 | .1 | .1 | .2 | .2 | .2 | .2 | .4 | .5 | .5 | .5 | .4 |
| Sri Lanka | 524 | 5.8 | 6.3 | 6.9 | 7.7 | 8.1 | 7.1 | 8.3 | 10.6 | 9.8 | 10.4 | 11.2 | 10.5 |
| Thailand | 578 | 96.2 | 110.2 | 130.6 | 153.9 | 175.9 | 151.9 | 193.4 | 220.2 | 227.8 | 224.9 | 225.2 | 211.0 |
| Tonga | 866 | — | — | — | — | — | — | — | — | — | — | — | — |
| Vanuatu | 846 | — | — | — | .1 | .1 | .1 | — | .1 | .1 | — | .1 | .1 |
| Vietnam | 582 | 26.0 | 31.7 | 39.6 | 48.3 | 62.7 | 57.1 | 71.7 | 94.5 | 115.5 | 132.5 | 149.6 | 162.1 |
| Europe | 170 | 557.8 | 685.1 | 840.9 | 1,031.2 | 1,329.9 | 941.1 | 1,153.1 | 1,470.1 | 1,484.7 | 1,498.3 | 1,494.3 | 1,162.9 |
| Emerging & Dev. Europe | 903 | 250.9 | 294.7 | 355.6 | 444.4 | 539.2 | 427.6 | 490.5 | 590.7 | 587.0 | 627.5 | 664.3 | 593.7 |
| Albania | 914 | .6 | .7 | .8 | 1.1 | 1.4 | 1.1 | 1.6 | 2.0 | 2.0 | 2.3 | 2.4 | 1.9 |
| Bulgaria | 918 | 9.9 | 11.7 | 15.1 | 18.6 | 22.5 | 16.4 | 20.6 | 28.2 | 26.7 | 29.5 | 30.9 | 25.8 |
| Croatia | 960 | 8.0 | 8.8 | 10.4 | 12.4 | 14.1 | 10.5 | 11.8 | 13.4 | 12.3 | 11.9 | 13.7 | 12.8 |
| Hungary | 944 | 54.9 | 62.2 | 74.2 | 94.0 | 107.5 | 84.6 | 94.8 | 110.9 | 103.0 | 108.4 | 112.4 | 100.4 |
| Macedonia, FYR | 962 | 1.7 | 2.0 | 2.4 | 3.4 | 3.9 | 2.7 | 3.4 | 4.5 | 4.0 | 4.3 | 4.9 | 4.5 |
| Montenegro | 943 | .6 | .5 | .6 | .6 | .6 | .4 | .4 | .6 | .5 | .5 | .4 | .4 |
| Poland | 964 | 73.8 | 89.3 | 109.6 | 136.4 | 169.5 | 136.6 | 159.8 | 188.7 | 181.8 | 202.6 | 218.9 | 199.4 |
| Romania | 968 | 23.5 | 27.7 | 32.3 | 40.0 | 49.5 | 40.6 | 49.4 | 62.7 | 57.9 | 65.9 | 69.9 | 60.6 |
| Turkey | 186 | 63.2 | 73.5 | 85.5 | 107.3 | 132.0 | 102.1 | 113.9 | 134.9 | 152.5 | 151.8 | 157.6 | 144.0 |
| CIS | 901 | 262.1 | 335.9 | 418.3 | 504.3 | 686.1 | 439.0 | 572.0 | 765.5 | 784.0 | 758.3 | 717.0 | 480.2 |
| Armenia | 911 | .7 | 1.0 | 1.0 | 1.2 | 1.1 | .7 | 1.0 | 1.3 | 1.4 | 1.5 | 1.5 | 1.5 |
| Azerbaijan, Republic of | 912 | 3.6 | 4.3 | 13.0 | 21.3 | 30.6 | 21.1 | 26.5 | 34.5 | 32.6 | 31.7 | 30.3 | 14.5 |
| Belarus | 913 | 13.8 | 16.0 | 19.7 | 24.3 | 32.6 | 21.3 | 25.3 | 41.4 | 46.1 | 37.2 | 36.1 | 26.7 |
| Georgia | 915 | .6 | .9 | .9 | 1.2 | 1.5 | 1.1 | 1.7 | 2.2 | 2.4 | 2.9 | 2.9 | 2.2 |
| Kazakhstan | 916 | 20.6 | 28.3 | 38.8 | 48.4 | 72.0 | 43.2 | 57.2 | 83.3 | 88.6 | 81.9 | 79.1 | 45.7 |

# Exports, f.o.b.

| | | 2004 | 2005 | 2006 | 2007 | 2008 | 2009 | 2010 | 2011 | 2012 | 2013 | 2014 | 2015 |
|---|---|---|---|---|---|---|---|---|---|---|---|---|---|
| | | | | | | *Billions of US Dollars* | | | | | | | |
| **CIS(Cont.)** | | | | | | | | | | | | | |
| Kyrgyz Republic | 917 | .7 | .7 | .9 | 1.3 | 1.9 | 1.7 | 1.8 | 2.3 | 2.0 | 2.1 | 1.9 | 1.4 |
| Moldova | 921 | 1.0 | 1.1 | 1.1 | 1.3 | 1.6 | 1.3 | 1.5 | 2.2 | 2.2 | 2.4 | 2.3 | 2.0 |
| Russia | 922 | 183.2 | 243.8 | 297.5 | 346.5 | 466.3 | 297.2 | 392.7 | 515.4 | 527.4 | 523.3 | 497.8 | 340.3 |
| Ukraine | 926 | 32.7 | 34.2 | 38.4 | 49.3 | 67.0 | 39.7 | 51.4 | 68.4 | 68.8 | 63.3 | 53.9 | 38.1 |
| **Middle East,N.Africa & Pakistan** | 440 | **460.6** | **631.1** | **768.3** | **866.4** | **1,215.4** | **830.3** | **1,053.8** | **1,381.2** | **1,456.9** | **1,475.8** | **1,391.0** | **906.5** |
| Algeria | 612 | 32.2 | 46.4 | 54.8 | 59.5 | 79.1 | 45.2 | 57.8 | 73.7 | 72.6 | 65.5 | 61.2 | 35.1 |
| Bahrain, Kingdom of | 419 | 7.6 | 10.2 | 12.2 | 13.6 | 17.3 | 11.9 | 15.4 | 19.7 | 20.5 | 17.5 | 20.5 | 11.2 |
| Djibouti | 611 | — | | .1 | .1 | .1 | .1 | .1 | .1 | .1 | .1 | .1 | .1 |
| Egypt | 469 | 7.7 | 10.7 | 13.7 | 16.2 | 26.2 | 23.1 | 26.4 | 30.5 | 29.4 | 28.5 | 24.7 | 19.1 |
| Iran, I.R. of | 429 | 41.7 | 56.3 | 77.0 | 83.0 | 113.7 | 78.8 | 101.3 | 130.5 | 95.5 | 82.0 | 88.8 | 63.0 |
| Jordan | 439 | 3.9 | 4.3 | 5.2 | 5.7 | 7.8 | 6.5 | 7.0 | 8.0 | 7.9 | 7.9 | 8.4 | 7.8 |
| Kuwait | 443 | 28.6 | 44.9 | 56.4 | 62.7 | 87.5 | 54.0 | 66.6 | 102.1 | 114.5 | 114.1 | 100.8 | 55.2 |
| Lebanon | 446 | 2.2 | 2.3 | 2.8 | 3.6 | 4.5 | 4.2 | 5.0 | 4.3 | 4.5 | 4.1 | 4.5 | 4.0 |
| Libya | 672 | 20.4 | 31.4 | 40.3 | 47.0 | 62.1 | 37.2 | 46.1 | 18.0 | 59.0 | 44.0 | 21.0 | 10.2 |
| Morocco | 686 | 9.9 | 11.2 | 12.7 | 15.3 | 20.3 | 14.1 | 17.8 | 21.6 | 21.4 | 22.0 | 23.8 | 21.9 |
| Oman | 449 | 13.3 | 18.7 | 21.6 | 24.1 | 37.7 | 28.1 | 36.6 | 47.1 | 53.2 | 56.4 | 52.8 | 34.7 |
| Pakistan | 564 | 13.4 | 16.1 | 16.9 | 17.8 | 20.3 | 17.5 | 21.4 | 25.4 | 24.6 | 25.1 | 24.7 | 22.1 |
| Qatar | 453 | 18.7 | 25.8 | 34.1 | 44.5 | 67.3 | 48.0 | 74.8 | 114.4 | 133.0 | 136.9 | 131.3 | 77.9 |
| Saudi Arabia | 456 | 126.0 | 180.7 | 211.3 | 233.3 | 313.4 | 192.3 | 251.1 | 364.7 | 388.4 | 375.9 | 342.3 | 202.2 |
| Sudan | 732 | 3.8 | 4.8 | 5.7 | 8.9 | 11.7 | 8.3 | 11.4 | 9.7 | 4.1 | 7.1 | 5.5 | 3.0 |
| Syrian Arab Rep. | 463 | 7.4 | 8.7 | 10.9 | 11.5 | 15.4 | 10.9 | 14.0 | 10.0 | 4.0 | 3.0 | .... | .... |
| Tunisia | 744 | 9.7 | 10.5 | 11.7 | 15.2 | 19.3 | 14.4 | 16.4 | 17.8 | 17.0 | 17.1 | 16.8 | 14.1 |
| United Arab Emirates | 466 | 91.0 | 117.3 | 142.5 | 154.0 | 239.2 | 185.0 | 220.0 | 285.0 | 300.0 | 365.0 | 359.0 | 265.0 |
| Yemen, Republic of | 474 | 4.1 | 5.6 | 6.7 | 6.3 | 7.6 | 6.3 | 8.5 | 10.8 | 8.5 | 9.5 | .... | .... |
| **Sub-Saharan Africa** | 603 | **138.0** | **188.9** | **215.2** | **256.4** | **330.1** | **239.5** | **315.5** | **403.9** | **398.7** | **399.7** | **391.6** | **304.2** |
| Angola | 614 | 13.5 | 24.1 | 31.9 | 44.4 | 63.9 | 40.8 | 50.6 | 67.3 | 71.1 | 68.2 | 59.2 | 33.2 |
| Benin | 638 | .6 | .6 | .7 | 1.0 | 1.3 | .4 | .4 | 1.4 | 1.4 | 1.2 | .... | .6 |
| Botswana | 616 | 3.5 | 4.4 | 4.5 | 5.2 | 5.0 | 3.5 | 4.7 | 5.9 | 6.0 | 7.6 | 7.8 | 6.1 |
| Burkina Faso | 748 | .5 | .5 | .6 | .6 | .7 | .9 | 1.3 | 2.4 | 2.2 | 2.4 | 2.5 | .... |
| Burundi | 618 | — | .1 | .1 | .1 | .1 | .1 | .1 | .1 | .1 | .1 | .1 | .1 |
| Cameroon | 622 | 2.4 | 2.9 | 3.6 | 4.2 | 5.3 | 3.5 | 3.9 | 4.5 | 4.6 | 4.5 | 5.2 | 3.8 |
| Cabo Verde | 624 | — | | | | | | | .1 | .1 | .1 | .1 | .1 |
| Central African Rep. | 626 | .1 | .1 | .2 | .2 | .2 | .1 | .1 | .1 | .1 | .1 | .... | .... |
| Chad | 628 | 2.2 | 3.1 | 3.4 | 3.7 | 4.3 | 2.7 | 3.4 | 4.6 | 3.9 | 4.5 | 4.2 | 2.9 |
| Congo, Rep. of | 634 | 3.4 | 4.7 | 6.1 | 5.6 | 8.3 | 6.1 | 8.2 | 11.5 | 11.0 | 9.8 | 8.6 | 4.6 |
| Côte d'Ivoire | 662 | 6.9 | 7.7 | 8.5 | 8.7 | 10.4 | 10.3 | 10.3 | 10.9 | 10.9 | 13.7 | 12.6 | 11.2 |
| Equatorial Guinea | 642 | 4.6 | 7.1 | 8.2 | 10.2 | 15.9 | 9.1 | 10.0 | 13.5 | 15.5 | 14.0 | 11.6 | .... |
| Ethiopia | 644 | .6 | .9 | 1.0 | 1.3 | 1.6 | 1.5 | 2.2 | 3.0 | 3.2 | 3.0 | 4.5 | 3.8 |
| Gabon | 646 | 3.7 | 5.1 | 5.5 | 6.3 | 9.5 | 5.5 | 8.7 | 9.8 | 7.7 | 9.5 | 9.0 | 5.1 |
| Gambia, The | 648 | — | | | | | | | | | | .... | .... |
| Ghana | 652 | 2.5 | 2.8 | 3.7 | 4.3 | 5.3 | 5.8 | 8.0 | 12.8 | 12.0 | 13.7 | 12.5 | 9.6 |
| Guinea | 656 | .7 | .9 | .9 | 1.2 | 1.3 | 1.0 | 1.5 | 1.4 | 1.4 | 1.3 | 1.4 | .... |
| Guinea-Bissau | 654 | .1 | .1 | .1 | .1 | .1 | .1 | .1 | .2 | .1 | .2 | .... | .... |
| Kenya | 664 | 2.7 | 3.3 | 3.4 | 4.1 | 5.0 | 4.5 | 5.1 | 5.8 | 6.1 | 5.9 | 6.0 | 5.9 |
| Lesotho | 666 | .7 | .7 | .7 | .8 | .9 | .7 | .8 | .8 | .7 | .9 | .9 | .8 |
| Madagascar | 674 | 1.0 | .9 | 1.0 | 1.3 | 1.7 | 1.1 | 1.1 | 1.3 | 1.2 | 2.0 | 2.1 | 2.3 |
| Malawi | 676 | .5 | .5 | .5 | .7 | .9 | 1.1 | 1.1 | 1.4 | 1.2 | 1.2 | 1.3 | 1.4 |
| Mali | 678 | 1.0 | 1.1 | 1.6 | 1.6 | 2.1 | 1.8 | 2.0 | 2.4 | 2.2 | 2.6 | 2.1 | 2.5 |
| Mauritius | 684 | 2.0 | 2.1 | 2.3 | 2.2 | 2.4 | 1.9 | 2.3 | 2.6 | 2.6 | 2.9 | 3.1 | 2.7 |
| Namibia | 728 | 2.6 | 2.8 | 3.6 | 4.5 | 5.4 | 5.1 | 5.3 | 5.4 | 5.5 | 5.7 | .... | .... |
| Niger | 692 | .4 | .5 | .5 | .7 | .9 | .6 | .6 | .9 | 1.5 | 1.6 | 1.5 | 1.1 |
| Rwanda | 714 | .1 | .1 | .1 | .2 | .3 | .2 | .3 | .5 | .5 | .6 | .7 | .... |
| Senegal | 722 | 1.0 | 1.1 | 1.0 | 1.2 | 2.0 | 1.8 | 2.1 | 2.4 | 2.4 | 2.4 | 2.6 | 2.3 |
| Seychelles | 718 | .3 | .3 | .4 | .4 | .4 | .4 | .4 | .5 | .5 | .6 | .5 | .4 |
| Sierra Leone | 724 | .1 | .2 | .2 | .2 | .2 | .2 | .3 | .3 | 1.1 | 1.9 | 1.6 | .7 |
| South Africa | 199 | 46.1 | 51.6 | 58.2 | 69.8 | 84.6 | 62.6 | 81.8 | 96.9 | 87.4 | 83.5 | 91.2 | 81.7 |
| Swaziland | 734 | 2.0 | 1.8 | 1.8 | 1.9 | 1.7 | 1.5 | 1.6 | 1.9 | 1.9 | 1.9 | .... | .... |
| Tanzania | 738 | 1.5 | 1.7 | 1.7 | 2.0 | 2.7 | 2.4 | 3.5 | 4.4 | 5.1 | 5.1 | 5.0 | 4.9 |
| Togo | 742 | .6 | .7 | .6 | .7 | .9 | .8 | .6 | 1.1 | 1.0 | 1.1 | .... | .... |
| Uganda | 746 | .8 | 1.0 | 1.2 | 2.0 | 2.7 | 3.0 | 3.1 | 2.4 | 2.9 | 2.8 | 2.7 | 2.7 |
| Zambia | 754 | 1.6 | 2.2 | 3.7 | 4.6 | 5.1 | 4.3 | 7.2 | 8.8 | 9.4 | 10.6 | 9.7 | 7.0 |
| Zimbabwe | 698 | 1.9 | 1.9 | 2.0 | 2.4 | 2.2 | 2.3 | 3.2 | 3.5 | 3.8 | 3.6 | 3.4 | 2.7 |
| **Western Hemisphere** | 205 | **461.9** | **560.3** | **667.3** | **758.0** | **887.7** | **678.0** | **860.6** | **1,072.3** | **1,083.4** | **1,087.6** | **1,053.5** | **895.9** |
| Anguilla | 312 | | | | | | | | | | | | |
| Argentina | 213 | 34.6 | 40.4 | 46.6 | 55.8 | 70.6 | 56.1 | 64.7 | 84.3 | 75.2 | 83.0 | 71.9 | 59.7 |
| Aruba | 314 | .1 | .1 | .1 | .1 | .1 | .1 | .1 | .2 | .2 | .2 | .1 | .1 |
| Bahamas, The | 313 | .5 | .6 | .7 | .5 | .6 | .6 | .6 | .9 | .8 | .8 | .7 | .... |
| Barbados | 316 | .3 | .4 | .4 | .4 | .4 | .4 | .4 | .5 | .6 | .5 | .5 | .5 |
| Belize | 339 | .2 | .2 | .3 | .3 | .3 | .2 | .3 | .3 | .3 | .3 | .3 | .... |
| Bolivia | 218 | 2.1 | 2.8 | 3.9 | 4.5 | 7.1 | 4.9 | 6.2 | 8.1 | 10.3 | 11.2 | 12.3 | 8.3 |
| Brazil | 223 | 96.7 | 118.5 | 137.8 | 160.6 | 197.9 | 153.0 | 201.9 | 256.0 | 242.6 | 242.2 | 225.1 | 191.1 |
| Chile | 228 | 32.5 | 41.3 | 58.7 | 67.7 | 66.5 | 52.0 | 69.0 | 80.0 | 79.7 | 77.9 | 74.5 | 64.1 |
| Colombia | 233 | 16.2 | 21.1 | 24.4 | 29.8 | 38.3 | 32.8 | 39.7 | 56.5 | 59.6 | 58.7 | 54.8 | 35.6 |
| Costa Rica | 238 | 6.3 | 7.0 | 8.2 | 9.4 | 9.6 | 8.7 | 9.3 | 10.2 | 11.2 | 11.5 | 11.2 | 9.5 |
| Dominica | 321 | — | — | — | — | — | — | — | — | — | — | — | |
| Dominican Republic | 243 | 1.3 | 1.4 | 1.9 | 2.6 | 2.4 | 1.7 | 2.7 | 3.7 | 4.1 | 4.5 | 4.7 | .... |
| Ecuador | 248 | 7.8 | 10.1 | 12.7 | 13.9 | 18.8 | 13.9 | 17.4 | 22.3 | 23.8 | 24.8 | 25.7 | 18.3 |
| El Salvador | 253 | 3.3 | 3.4 | 3.5 | 4.0 | 4.6 | 3.8 | 4.5 | 5.0 | 5.3 | 5.5 | 5.3 | 5.5 |
| Grenada | 328 | — | — | — | — | — | — | — | — | — | — | | |
| Guatemala | 258 | 2.9 | 3.5 | 3.7 | 4.5 | 5.4 | 3.8 | 5.9 | 7.2 | 7.1 | 7.0 | 7.4 | 7.2 |
| Guyana | 336 | .6 | .6 | .6 | .7 | .8 | .8 | .9 | 1.1 | 1.4 | 1.4 | 1.2 | 1.1 |
| Haiti | 263 | .4 | .5 | .5 | .5 | .5 | .6 | .6 | .8 | .8 | .9 | 1.0 | .... |

# Exports, f.o.b.

| | | 2004 | 2005 | 2006 | 2007 | 2008 | 2009 | 2010 | 2011 | 2012 | 2013 | 2014 | 2015 |
|---|---|---|---|---|---|---|---|---|---|---|---|---|---|
| | | | | | | *Billions of US Dollars* | | | | | | | |
| **Western Hemisphere(Cont.)** | | | | | | | | | | | | | |
| Honduras......................................... | 268 | 1.6 | 1.9 | 2.1 | 2.1 | 2.9 | 2.3 | 2.7 | 3.9 | 4.4 | 3.9 | 4.1 | 3.9 |
| Jamaica.......................................... | 343 | 1.4 | 1.5 | 1.9 | 2.1 | 2.5 | 1.3 | 1.3 | 1.6 | 1.7 | 1.6 | 1.4 | 1.2 |
| Mexico........................................... | 273 | 189.1 | 213.9 | 250.4 | 272.1 | 291.8 | 229.7 | 298.1 | 349.6 | 370.9 | 380.1 | 397.7 | 380.8 |
| Netherlands Antilles...................... | 353 | .5 | .6 | .7 | .7 | 1.1 | .8 | .8 | .... | .... | .... | .... | .... |
| Nicaragua....................................... | 278 | .8 | .9 | 1.0 | 1.2 | 1.5 | 1.4 | 1.8 | 2.3 | 2.6 | 2.4 | 2.6 | 2.4 |
| Panama.......................................... | 283 | .9 | 1.0 | 1.1 | 1.2 | 1.2 | .9 | .8 | .... | .... | .... | .... | .... |
| Paraguay........................................ | 288 | 2.9 | 3.2 | 3.5 | 4.7 | 6.4 | 5.1 | 6.5 | 7.8 | 7.3 | 9.5 | 9.6 | 8.4 |
| Peru.............................................. | 293 | 12.8 | 17.4 | 23.8 | 27.9 | 31.5 | 26.9 | 35.6 | 46.1 | 45.6 | 41.5 | 37.9 | 34.0 |
| St. Lucia......................................... | 362 | .1 | .1 | .1 | .1 | .1 | .2 | .2 | .3 | .2 | .2 | .2 | .2 |
| St. Vincent & Grens........................ | 364 | — | — | — | — | .1 | — | — | — | — | — | — | — |
| Suriname........................................ | 366 | .7 | .8 | 1.1 | 1.3 | 1.7 | 1.4 | 1.9 | 2.3 | 2.7 | 2.4 | 2.1 | 1.6 |
| Trinidad and Tobago...................... | 369 | 6.5 | 9.9 | 12.1 | 13.2 | 18.6 | 9.2 | 11.2 | 14.9 | 13.0 | 12.8 | 11.6 | 7.3 |
| Uruguay......................................... | 298 | 2.9 | 3.4 | 4.0 | 4.5 | 6.4 | 5.4 | 6.7 | 8.0 | 8.6 | 8.8 | 9.5 | 7.7 |
| Venezuela, Rep. Bol........................ | 299 | 34.0 | 51.9 | 59.2 | 69.2 | 95.0 | 57.6 | 65.7 | 92.8 | 97.9 | 88.8 | 74.7 | 37.2 |

# Imports, c.i.f.

| | | 2004 | 2005 | 2006 | 2007 | 2008 | 2009 | 2010 | 2011 | 2012 | 2013 | 2014 | 2015 |
|---|---|---|---|---|---|---|---|---|---|---|---|---|---|
| | | | | | | | *Billions of US Dollars* | | | | | | |
| World | 001 | 9,384.2 | 10,697.0 | 12,295.0 | 14,140.2 | 16,331.0 | 12,548.9 | 15,251.8 | 18,199.0 | 18,251.1 | 18,521.0 | 18,685.3 | 16,343.5 |
| Advanced Economies | 110 | 6,904.2 | 7,722.4 | 8,755.7 | 9,811.6 | 10,973.6 | 8,314.3 | 9,848.7 | 11,521.1 | 11,317.6 | 11,327.9 | 11,481.1 | 10,103.3 |
| Euro Area | | | | | | | | | | | | | |
| Austria | 122 | 113.3 | 119.9 | 130.9 | 156.8 | 176.2 | 136.1 | 150.6 | 182.3 | 169.7 | 172.6 | 171.4 | 147.4 |
| Belgium | 124 | 286.4 | 319.1 | 353.0 | 413.1 | 466.4 | 354.7 | 391.3 | 466.8 | 439.5 | 451.9 | 455.4 | 380.2 |
| Cyprus | 423 | 5.7 | 6.3 | 6.9 | 8.7 | 10.8 | 7.9 | 8.6 | 8.8 | 7.4 | 6.4 | 6.8 | 5.7 |
| Estonia | 939 | 8.3 | 10.2 | 11.9 | 15.1 | 16.1 | 10.2 | 12.3 | 17.7 | 18.1 | 18.5 | 18.3 | 14.5 |
| Finland | 172 | 50.7 | 58.5 | 69.4 | 81.8 | 92.2 | 60.9 | 68.8 | 84.2 | 76.6 | 77.6 | 76.8 | 60.4 |
| France | 132 | 447.5 | 490.6 | 546.5 | 631.4 | 715.8 | 560.5 | 608.7 | 712.9 | 667.3 | 673.4 | 669.2 | 563.3 |
| Germany | 134 | 715.7 | 780.4 | 922.3 | 1,056.0 | 1,186.7 | 926.2 | 1,056.2 | 1,256.2 | 1,164.6 | 1,192.8 | 1,209.3 | 1,052.1 |
| Greece | 174 | 56.1 | 57.8 | 67.3 | 84.9 | 96.7 | 74.1 | 69.2 | 68.1 | 63.7 | 62.4 | 64.2 | 48.3 |
| Ireland | 178 | 61.4 | 71.5 | 76.4 | 87.0 | 84.9 | 62.6 | 60.7 | 67.2 | 63.2 | 66.0 | 70.7 | 71.5 |
| Italy | 136 | 355.2 | 384.8 | 442.6 | 511.9 | 563.4 | 414.7 | 487.0 | 558.8 | 489.1 | 477.3 | 470.5 | 407.9 |
| Latvia | 941 | 7.0 | 8.6 | 11.4 | 15.2 | 15.8 | 9.3 | 11.1 | 15.4 | 16.1 | 16.8 | 16.8 | 13.9 |
| Lithuania | 946 | 12.4 | 15.5 | 19.4 | 24.4 | 31.3 | 18.3 | 23.4 | 31.8 | 32.0 | 34.8 | 35.2 | 28.2 |
| Luxembourg | 137 | 17.0 | 17.9 | 19.7 | 22.6 | 25.8 | 19.2 | 21.7 | 26.3 | 24.2 | 23.9 | 23.5 | 19.3 |
| Malta | 181 | 3.8 | 3.8 | 4.1 | 4.5 | 5.7 | 4.8 | 5.7 | 7.4 | 7.9 | 7.5 | 8.1 | 6.4 |
| Netherlands | 138 | 283.9 | 310.6 | 358.5 | 421.1 | 495.1 | 382.3 | 440.0 | 507.8 | 500.6 | 513.1 | 508.2 | 419.1 |
| Portugal | 182 | 49.2 | 53.4 | 65.6 | 76.4 | 94.7 | 71.7 | 75.6 | 82.5 | 72.3 | 75.1 | 77.7 | 66.5 |
| Slovak Republic | 936 | 30.5 | 36.2 | 47.3 | 62.2 | 74.1 | 56.6 | 66.0 | 81.4 | 79.0 | 83.6 | 83.4 | 74.9 |
| Slovenia | 961 | 17.6 | 19.6 | 23.0 | 29.5 | 34.0 | 24.1 | 26.3 | 31.4 | 28.4 | 29.4 | 30.1 | 25.8 |
| Spain | 184 | 257.6 | 287.6 | 326.0 | 385.0 | 417.0 | 290.7 | 315.5 | 362.8 | 325.8 | 333.9 | 351.5 | 304.3 |
| Australia | 193 | 109.4 | 125.3 | 139.3 | 165.3 | 200.3 | 165.5 | 201.6 | 243.7 | 260.9 | 242.1 | 236.9 | 208.4 |
| Canada | 156 | 279.9 | 322.4 | 359.0 | 390.2 | 419.0 | 330.9 | 403.9 | 464.8 | 476.3 | 475.8 | 480.0 | 436.3 |
| China, P.R.: Hong Kong | 532 | 271.1 | 299.5 | 334.7 | 367.6 | 388.5 | 347.3 | 433.1 | 483.6 | 504.4 | 523.6 | 544.1 | 522.0 |
| Czech Republic | 935 | 71.6 | 76.3 | 93.4 | 118.5 | 142.2 | 105.3 | 126.6 | 152.1 | 141.5 | 144.3 | 154.2 | 141.3 |
| Denmark | 128 | 66.9 | 72.5 | 84.2 | 97.4 | 109.2 | 80.4 | 83.2 | 96.4 | 92.3 | 98.4 | 99.1 | 84.5 |
| Iceland | 176 | 3.6 | 4.6 | 5.1 | 6.1 | 5.6 | 3.6 | 3.9 | 4.8 | 4.8 | 4.8 | 5.2 | 5.3 |
| Israel | 436 | 42.9 | 47.1 | 50.3 | 59.0 | 67.7 | 49.3 | 61.2 | 75.8 | 75.4 | 74.9 | 75.5 | 65.0 |
| Japan | 158 | 454.5 | 514.9 | 579.6 | 619.7 | 762.6 | 550.5 | 692.4 | 854.1 | 885.6 | 832.4 | 811.9 | 648.3 |
| Korea | 542 | 224.5 | 267.6 | 309.4 | 356.9 | 435.3 | 323.1 | 425.2 | 524.4 | 519.6 | 515.6 | 525.5 | 436.5 |
| New Zealand | 196 | 23.5 | 26.9 | 26.7 | 31.5 | 34.0 | 25.2 | 31.8 | 37.3 | 37.8 | 40.4 | 42.5 | 36.6 |
| Norway | 142 | 48.5 | 55.5 | 64.3 | 80.4 | 90.3 | 69.0 | 77.3 | 90.8 | 87.3 | 90.0 | 88.1 | 75.7 |
| Singapore | 576 | 163.9 | 200.0 | 238.7 | 263.2 | 319.8 | 245.8 | 310.8 | 365.8 | 379.7 | 373.0 | 366.2 | 296.7 |
| Sweden | 144 | 100.8 | 111.6 | 127.7 | 153.5 | 169.0 | 120.3 | 148.5 | 174.7 | 164.1 | 159.7 | 159.5 | 136.3 |
| Switzerland | 146 | 110.3 | 119.8 | 132.0 | 153.2 | 173.3 | 147.6 | 166.9 | 196.8 | 188.6 | 191.7 | 195.1 | 172.9 |
| Taiwan Province of China | 528 | 168.1 | 182.6 | 203.0 | 219.6 | 240.7 | 174.6 | 251.5 | 281.4 | 270.7 | 269.9 | 274.2 | 228.7 |
| United Kingdom | 112 | 460.1 | 508.6 | 588.1 | 621.8 | 644.1 | 486.0 | 562.7 | 638.6 | 646.5 | 645.4 | 663.3 | .... |
| United States | 111 | 1,525.4 | 1,735.1 | 1,918.1 | 2,020.4 | 2,169.5 | 1,605.3 | 1,969.2 | 2,265.9 | 2,336.5 | 2,329.1 | 2,412.5 | 2,315.3 |
| Emerging & Dev. Economies | 200 | 2,494.6 | 2,995.0 | 3,566.0 | 4,366.1 | 5,410.0 | 4,278.2 | 5,462.8 | 6,755.2 | 7,017.4 | 7,282.4 | 7,292.0 | 6,317.4 |
| Emerging & Developing Asia | 505 | 1,033.4 | 1,242.2 | 1,466.9 | 1,748.9 | 2,137.0 | 1,798.1 | 2,460.6 | 3,087.4 | 3,253.3 | 3,377.7 | 3,391.2 | 2,951.5 |
| Bangladesh | 513 | 12.6 | 12.9 | 15.0 | 17.3 | 22.5 | 20.6 | 26.1 | 34.0 | 38.4 | 30.5 | .... | .... |
| Bhutan | 514 | .4 | .4 | .4 | .5 | .5 | .5 | .9 | 1.0 | 1.0 | .9 | .8 | 1.2 |
| Cambodia | 522 | 3.2 | 3.9 | 4.7 | 5.3 | 6.5 | 5.8 | 6.8 | 9.3 | 11.0 | 13.0 | 13.5 | 14.4 |
| China, P.R.: Mainland | 924 | 561.2 | 660.2 | 791.8 | 956.2 | 1,131.6 | 1,004.2 | 1,396.2 | 1,742.9 | 1,818.2 | 1,949.3 | 1,963.1 | 1,680.8 |
| China, P.R.: Macao | 546 | 3.5 | 3.9 | 4.6 | 5.4 | 5.4 | 4.6 | 5.5 | 7.8 | 8.9 | 10.1 | 11.3 | 10.6 |
| Fiji | 819 | 1.4 | 1.6 | 1.8 | 1.8 | 2.3 | 1.4 | 1.8 | 2.2 | 2.3 | 2.8 | 3.0 | 2.9 |
| India | 534 | 99.8 | 142.8 | 178.5 | 228.7 | 320.8 | 257.2 | 350.1 | 464.4 | 489.7 | 465.5 | 462.9 | 393.7 |
| Indonesia | 536 | 55.0 | 75.7 | 80.6 | 93.1 | 127.5 | 93.8 | 135.3 | 176.9 | 191.0 | 186.4 | 178.2 | 142.7 |
| Lao People's Dem. Rep. | 544 | .7 | .9 | 1.1 | 1.1 | 1.4 | 1.5 | 2.1 | 2.4 | 3.1 | 3.0 | 3.3 | 3.9 |
| Malaysia | 548 | 105.3 | 114.4 | 131.1 | 146.2 | 156.3 | 123.8 | 164.6 | 187.5 | 196.4 | 205.9 | 208.9 | 176.0 |
| Maldives | 556 | .6 | .7 | .9 | 1.1 | 1.4 | 1.0 | 1.1 | 1.5 | 1.6 | 1.7 | 2.0 | 1.9 |
| Mongolia | 948 | 1.0 | 1.2 | 1.5 | 2.1 | 3.6 | 2.1 | 3.3 | 6.5 | 6.7 | 6.4 | 5.2 | 3.8 |
| Myanmar | 518 | 2.2 | 1.9 | 2.5 | 3.2 | 4.3 | 4.3 | 4.8 | 9.0 | 9.2 | 12.0 | 16.2 | 15.9 |
| Nepal | 558 | 1.9 | 2.1 | 2.4 | 2.9 | 3.2 | 3.7 | 5.1 | 5.4 | 5.4 | 6.0 | 7.3 | 6.4 |
| Papua New Guinea | 853 | 1.7 | 1.7 | 2.3 | 3.0 | 3.6 | 3.2 | 4.0 | 4.9 | 5.5 | 4.5 | .... | .... |
| Philippines | 566 | 42.3 | 47.0 | 54.1 | 57.7 | 60.5 | 45.9 | 58.5 | 64.1 | 65.8 | 65.6 | 68.7 | 70.1 |
| Samoa | 862 | .2 | .2 | .2 | .2 | .2 | .2 | .3 | .3 | .3 | .3 | .... | .... |
| Solomon Islands | 813 | .1 | .2 | .2 | .3 | .3 | .3 | .4 | .5 | .5 | .5 | .5 | .5 |
| Sri Lanka | 524 | 8.0 | 8.8 | 10.3 | 11.3 | 14.0 | 10.0 | 13.5 | 20.3 | 19.1 | 18.0 | 19.7 | 19.1 |
| Thailand | 578 | 94.4 | 118.1 | 130.6 | 141.3 | 179.2 | 134.7 | 185.1 | 229.1 | 250.6 | 249.7 | 228.0 | 201.9 |
| Tonga | 866 | .1 | .1 | .1 | .1 | .2 | .1 | .2 | .2 | .2 | .2 | .2 | .2 |
| Vanuatu | 846 | .1 | .1 | .2 | .2 | .3 | .3 | .3 | .3 | .3 | .3 | .3 | .4 |
| Vietnam | 582 | 31.5 | 36.4 | 44.4 | 60.7 | 80.7 | 69.9 | 83.8 | 104.0 | 115.1 | 131.3 | 148.8 | 162.8 |
| Europe | 170 | 567.6 | 676.5 | 843.3 | 1,094.8 | 1,364.3 | 930.6 | 1,127.6 | 1,414.3 | 1,410.6 | 1,454.8 | 1,407.0 | 1,110.5 |
| Emerging & Dev. Europe | 903 | 344.3 | 400.1 | 487.4 | 615.6 | 744.0 | 525.5 | 619.7 | 758.1 | 724.9 | 759.5 | 785.1 | 681.1 |
| Albania | 914 | 2.3 | 2.6 | 3.1 | 4.2 | 5.3 | 4.5 | 4.6 | 5.4 | 4.9 | 4.9 | 5.2 | 4.3 |
| Bulgaria | 918 | 14.5 | 18.2 | 23.3 | 30.1 | 37.0 | 23.6 | 25.5 | 32.6 | 32.7 | 34.3 | 34.7 | 28.8 |
| Croatia | 960 | 16.6 | 18.6 | 21.5 | 25.8 | 30.7 | 21.2 | 20.1 | 22.7 | 20.8 | 21.0 | 22.5 | 20.6 |
| Hungary | 944 | 59.6 | 65.8 | 77.2 | 94.4 | 106.4 | 78.0 | 87.6 | 101.0 | 94.3 | 99.1 | 103.9 | 91.4 |
| Macedonia, FYR | 962 | 2.9 | 3.2 | 3.8 | 5.2 | 6.8 | 5.0 | 5.5 | 7.0 | 6.5 | 6.6 | 7.3 | 6.4 |
| Montenegro | 943 | 1.1 | 1.3 | 1.8 | 2.9 | 3.7 | 2.3 | 2.2 | 2.5 | 2.3 | 2.4 | 2.4 | 2.0 |
| Poland | 964 | 87.9 | 100.9 | 124.6 | 159.5 | 206.1 | 149.6 | 178.1 | 208.3 | 195.4 | 204.3 | 222.2 | 195.2 |
| Romania | 968 | 32.7 | 40.5 | 51.1 | 69.6 | 83.0 | 54.3 | 61.9 | 76.3 | 70.3 | 73.5 | 77.9 | 69.9 |
| Turkey | 186 | 97.5 | 116.8 | 139.6 | 170.1 | 202.0 | 140.9 | 185.5 | 240.8 | 236.5 | 251.7 | 242.2 | 207.2 |
| CIS | 901 | 177.0 | 222.0 | 288.3 | 390.7 | 511.0 | 327.5 | 415.3 | 542.4 | 572.3 | 580.2 | 511.8 | 342.4 |
| Armenia | 911 | 1.4 | 1.8 | 2.2 | 3.3 | 4.4 | 3.3 | 3.8 | 4.2 | 4.3 | 4.4 | 4.4 | 3.3 |
| Azerbaijan, Republic of | 912 | 3.5 | 4.2 | 5.3 | 5.7 | 7.2 | 6.1 | 6.6 | 9.8 | 9.7 | 10.7 | 9.2 | 9.4 |
| Belarus | 913 | 16.5 | 16.7 | 22.4 | 28.7 | 39.4 | 28.6 | 34.9 | 45.8 | 46.4 | 43.0 | 40.5 | 30.3 |
| Georgia | 915 | 1.8 | 2.5 | 3.7 | 5.2 | 6.3 | 4.5 | 5.3 | 7.0 | 8.0 | 8.0 | 8.6 | 7.7 |
| Kazakhstan | 916 | 13.8 | 18.0 | 24.1 | 33.3 | 38.5 | 28.4 | 24.0 | 30.0 | 35.3 | 46.0 | 41.2 | 30.2 |

# Imports, c.i.f.

| | | 2004 | 2005 | 2006 | 2007 | 2008 | 2009 | 2010 | 2011 | 2012 | 2013 | 2014 | 2015 |
|---|---|---|---|---|---|---|---|---|---|---|---|---|---|
| | | | | | | | *Billions of US Dollars* | | | | | | |
| **CIS(Cont.)** | | | | | | | | | | | | | |
| Kyrgyz Republic | 917 | .9 | 1.1 | 1.7 | 2.4 | 4.1 | 3.0 | 3.2 | 4.3 | 5.6 | 6.1 | 5.7 | 4.1 |
| Moldova | 921 | 1.8 | 2.3 | 2.7 | 3.7 | 4.9 | 3.3 | 3.9 | 5.2 | 5.2 | 5.5 | 5.3 | 4.0 |
| Russia | 922 | 107.1 | 138.0 | 179.5 | 245.4 | 317.5 | 202.3 | 270.2 | 350.4 | 369.3 | 375.5 | 338.8 | 213.5 |
| Ukraine | 926 | 29.0 | 36.1 | 45.0 | 60.6 | 85.5 | 45.4 | 60.7 | 82.6 | 84.7 | 77.0 | 54.4 | 37.5 |
| **Middle East,N.Africa & Pakistan** | 440 | 328.3 | 404.2 | 454.1 | 568.5 | 752.7 | 651.9 | 733.5 | 841.8 | 916.0 | 967.4 | 993.6 | 906.3 |
| Algeria | 612 | 18.0 | 19.9 | 21.0 | 27.4 | 39.5 | 39.3 | 40.2 | 47.3 | 50.4 | 54.9 | 58.3 | 51.6 |
| Bahrain, Kingdom of | 419 | 7.4 | 9.4 | 10.5 | 11.5 | 10.8 | 7.3 | 9.8 | 12.7 | 14.9 | 13.0 | 13.9 | 9.7 |
| Djibouti | 611 | .3 | .3 | .3 | .5 | .6 | .5 | .4 | .5 | .6 | .6 | .8 | .9 |
| Egypt | 469 | 12.8 | 19.8 | 20.7 | 27.1 | 48.8 | 44.9 | 52.9 | 58.9 | 65.8 | 59.7 | 61.0 | 65.0 |
| Iran, I.R. of | 429 | 32.0 | 40.0 | 40.8 | 45.0 | 57.4 | 50.8 | 65.4 | 61.8 | 53.5 | 49.7 | 53.6 | 42.5 |
| Jordan | 439 | 8.1 | 10.5 | 11.4 | 13.5 | 16.8 | 14.5 | 15.1 | 18.5 | 20.7 | 21.7 | 23.0 | 20.0 |
| Kuwait | 443 | 12.6 | 15.8 | 17.2 | 21.4 | 24.8 | 19.9 | 22.7 | 25.1 | 27.3 | 29.3 | 31.0 | 31.9 |
| Lebanon | 446 | 9.6 | 9.6 | 9.6 | 12.3 | 16.8 | 16.6 | 18.5 | 20.2 | 21.3 | 21.2 | 21.1 | 18.4 |
| Libya | 672 | 6.3 | 6.1 | 6.0 | 6.7 | 9.1 | 10.0 | 10.5 | 8.0 | 23.0 | 27.0 | 19.0 | 13.0 |
| Morocco | 686 | 17.8 | 20.8 | 24.0 | 32.0 | 42.4 | 32.9 | 35.4 | 44.3 | 44.9 | 45.6 | 45.9 | 37.5 |
| Oman | 449 | 8.9 | 8.8 | 10.9 | 16.0 | 22.9 | 17.9 | 19.8 | 23.6 | 29.4 | 34.3 | 29.4 | 29.0 |
| Pakistan | 564 | 17.9 | 25.4 | 29.8 | 32.6 | 42.3 | 31.6 | 37.8 | 44.0 | 44.1 | 44.6 | 47.4 | 43.8 |
| Qatar | 453 | 6.0 | 10.1 | 16.4 | 23.4 | 27.9 | 24.9 | 23.2 | 22.3 | 25.2 | 27.0 | 30.5 | 32.6 |
| Saudi Arabia | 456 | 44.7 | 59.5 | 69.8 | 90.2 | 115.1 | 95.5 | 106.9 | 131.6 | 155.6 | 168.2 | 173.8 | 174.7 |
| Sudan | 732 | 4.1 | 6.8 | 8.1 | 8.5 | 9.4 | 9.7 | 10.0 | 9.2 | 9.2 | 9.9 | 9.2 | 8.6 |
| Syrian Arab Rep | 463 | 8.4 | 10.9 | 11.5 | 14.7 | 18.1 | 15.3 | 17.0 | 16.9 | 7.8 | 5.8 | .... | .... |
| Tunisia | 744 | 12.8 | 13.2 | 15.0 | 19.1 | 24.6 | 19.2 | 22.2 | 24.0 | 24.4 | 24.3 | 24.8 | 20.2 |
| United Arab Emirates | 466 | 72.1 | 84.7 | 100.1 | 132.5 | 177.0 | 150.0 | 165.0 | 205.0 | 220.0 | 245.0 | 262.0 | 230.0 |
| Yemen, Republic of | 474 | 4.0 | 5.4 | 6.1 | 8.5 | 10.5 | 9.2 | 9.7 | 10.0 | 12.0 | 12.5 | .... | .... |
| **Sub-Saharan Africa** | 603 | 120.6 | 146.9 | 179.3 | 216.7 | 261.1 | 212.6 | 258.4 | 330.4 | 318.8 | 321.4 | 331.4 | 294.8 |
| Benin | 638 | .9 | 1.0 | 1.2 | 2.0 | 2.3 | 1.6 | 1.5 | 2.7 | 2.2 | 2.2 | .... | 2.4 |
| Botswana | 616 | 3.2 | 3.2 | 3.1 | 4.1 | 5.2 | 4.7 | 5.7 | 7.3 | 8.1 | 8.4 | 8.1 | 6.3 |
| Burkina Faso | 748 | 1.3 | 1.3 | 1.3 | 1.7 | 2.0 | 2.1 | 2.2 | 2.6 | 3.4 | 4.2 | 3.4 | .... |
| Burundi | 618 | .2 | .3 | .4 | .3 | .4 | .4 | .5 | .8 | .8 | .8 | .8 | .7 |
| Cameroon | 622 | 2.6 | 2.9 | 3.2 | 4.7 | 5.7 | 4.4 | 5.1 | 6.8 | 6.5 | 6.6 | 7.6 | 6.7 |
| Cabo Verde | 624 | .4 | .4 | .5 | .7 | .8 | .7 | .7 | .9 | .8 | .7 | .7 | .6 |
| Central African Rep | 626 | .2 | .2 | .2 | .3 | .3 | .3 | .2 | .3 | .3 | .3 | .... | .... |
| Chad | 628 | 1.0 | 1.0 | 1.4 | 1.8 | 1.9 | 2.3 | 2.5 | 2.7 | 2.6 | 3.0 | 3.5 | 2.2 |
| Congo, Rep. of | 634 | 1.0 | 1.3 | 2.1 | 2.6 | 3.1 | 3.0 | 3.0 | 5.2 | 5.2 | 5.5 | 6.2 | 7.7 |
| Côte d'Ivoire | 662 | 4.7 | 5.9 | 5.8 | 6.7 | 7.9 | 7.0 | 7.9 | 6.7 | 9.8 | 12.6 | 10.7 | 9.9 |
| Equatorial Guinea | 642 | 1.1 | 1.3 | 2.0 | 2.4 | 3.9 | 5.2 | 5.7 | 6.0 | 6.0 | 7.0 | 6.5 | .... |
| Ethiopia | 644 | 2.9 | 4.1 | 5.3 | 5.8 | 8.3 | 7.7 | 8.6 | 8.9 | 11.9 | 12.0 | 19.0 | 19.1 |
| Gabon | 646 | 1.3 | 1.5 | 1.7 | 2.2 | 2.6 | 2.5 | 3.0 | 3.7 | 3.6 | 3.9 | 3.1 | 3.0 |
| Gambia, The | 648 | .2 | .3 | .3 | .3 | .3 | .3 | .3 | .3 | .4 | .3 | .... | .... |
| Ghana | 652 | 4.1 | 5.3 | 6.8 | 8.1 | 10.3 | 8.1 | 11.0 | 12.6 | 13.6 | 12.8 | 14.7 | 13.3 |
| Guinea | 656 | .7 | .8 | .9 | 1.2 | 1.4 | 1.1 | 1.4 | 2.1 | 2.3 | 2.2 | 2.1 | .... |
| Guinea-Bissau | 654 | .1 | .1 | .1 | .1 | .2 | .2 | .2 | .3 | .3 | .2 | .... | .... |
| Kenya | 664 | 4.6 | 6.1 | 7.3 | 9.0 | 11.1 | 10.2 | 12.1 | 14.8 | 16.3 | 16.4 | 18.4 | 16.1 |
| Lesotho | 666 | 1.5 | 1.4 | 1.5 | 1.7 | 2.0 | 2.0 | 2.2 | 1.5 | 1.6 | 2.3 | 2.2 | 2.0 |
| Madagascar | 674 | 1.7 | 1.7 | 1.7 | 2.4 | 3.8 | 3.2 | 2.5 | 2.6 | 2.5 | 3.2 | 3.3 | 3.2 |
| Malawi | 676 | .9 | 1.2 | 1.2 | 1.4 | 2.2 | 2.0 | 2.2 | 2.4 | 2.3 | 2.8 | 2.8 | 2.9 |
| Mali | 678 | 1.4 | 1.5 | 1.8 | 2.2 | 3.3 | 2.5 | 3.4 | 3.4 | 2.9 | 3.7 | 4.0 | 3.2 |
| Mauritius | 684 | 2.8 | 3.2 | 3.6 | 3.9 | 4.7 | 3.7 | 4.4 | 5.1 | 5.4 | 5.4 | 5.6 | 4.8 |
| Mozambique | 688 | 2.0 | 2.4 | 2.9 | 3.0 | 4.0 | 3.8 | 3.9 | 6.3 | 8.7 | 10.1 | 11.6 | 8.3 |
| Namibia | 728 | 2.5 | 2.7 | 3.2 | 4.5 | 5.3 | 6.5 | 6.5 | 6.6 | 7.3 | 7.6 | .... | .... |
| Niger | 692 | .8 | .9 | .9 | 1.1 | 1.7 | 1.5 | 2.2 | 1.8 | 1.8 | 1.9 | 2.3 | 2.0 |
| Nigeria | 694 | 14.2 | 21.3 | 26.8 | 37.6 | 42.4 | 33.9 | 44.2 | 64.4 | 35.7 | 44.6 | .... | .... |
| Rwanda | 714 | .3 | .4 | .5 | .7 | 1.1 | 1.2 | 1.4 | 1.8 | 1.7 | 1.7 | 1.7 | .... |
| Senegal | 722 | 2.9 | 3.2 | 3.4 | 4.3 | 5.7 | 4.6 | 4.4 | 5.4 | 5.9 | 6.1 | 6.0 | 5.2 |
| Seychelles | 718 | .5 | .7 | .8 | .9 | 1.1 | .8 | 1.0 | 1.0 | 1.1 | 1.1 | 1.1 | 1.0 |
| Sierra Leone | 724 | .2 | .3 | .4 | .4 | .5 | .5 | .8 | 1.7 | 1.6 | 1.6 | 1.6 | 1.5 |
| South Africa | 199 | 53.8 | 62.2 | 78.0 | 88.6 | 101.6 | 74.1 | 94.2 | 121.5 | 124.3 | 106.9 | 104.8 | 90.4 |
| South Sudan, Republic of | 733 | .... | .... | .... | .... | .... | .... | .... | .... | .... | .... | .... | .... |
| Swaziland | 734 | 1.9 | 1.9 | 1.9 | 1.8 | 1.7 | 1.6 | 1.7 | 2.0 | 2.0 | 1.5 | .... | .... |
| Tanzania | 738 | 2.7 | 3.3 | 4.2 | 5.3 | 7.1 | 6.3 | 7.7 | 10.7 | 11.3 | 12.3 | 12.0 | 10.3 |
| Togo | 742 | .9 | 1.1 | 1.1 | 1.2 | 1.5 | 2.0 | 1.0 | 1.8 | 1.8 | 2.1 | .... | .... |
| Uganda | 746 | 1.7 | 2.0 | 2.6 | 3.5 | 4.5 | 4.3 | 4.7 | 4.6 | 5.2 | 4.9 | 5.1 | 4.8 |
| Zambia | 754 | 2.2 | 2.6 | 3.1 | 4.0 | 5.0 | 3.8 | 5.3 | 7.3 | 8.8 | 10.2 | 9.5 | 8.4 |
| Zimbabwe | 698 | 2.2 | 2.4 | 2.3 | 2.6 | 3.0 | 2.9 | 3.8 | 4.4 | 4.4 | 4.3 | 4.2 | 4.0 |
| **Western Hemisphere** | 205 | 450.5 | 531.5 | 633.7 | 756.8 | 919.5 | 688.7 | 881.8 | 1,082.2 | 1,113.2 | 1,154.7 | 1,159.3 | 1,040.0 |
| Anguilla | 312 | .1 | .1 | .1 | .2 | .3 | .2 | .2 | .1 | .1 | .1 | .2 | .2 |
| Argentina | 213 | 22.4 | 28.7 | 34.2 | 44.7 | 57.4 | 39.1 | 48.0 | 74.3 | 68.5 | 74.0 | 65.3 | 59.8 |
| Aruba | 314 | .9 | 1.0 | 1.0 | 1.1 | 1.1 | 1.1 | 1.1 | 1.3 | 1.3 | 1.3 | 1.3 | 1.2 |
| Bahamas, The | 313 | 1.9 | 2.2 | 2.4 | 2.4 | 2.4 | 2.7 | 2.9 | 3.4 | 3.7 | 3.4 | 3.8 | .... |
| Barbados | 316 | 1.4 | 1.6 | 1.6 | 1.7 | 1.9 | 1.5 | 1.6 | 1.8 | 1.8 | 1.8 | 1.7 | 1.6 |
| Belize | 339 | .5 | .6 | .7 | .7 | .8 | .7 | .7 | .8 | .9 | .9 | 1.0 | .... |
| Bolivia | 218 | 1.8 | 2.3 | 2.8 | 3.5 | 5.1 | 4.5 | 5.6 | 7.9 | 8.6 | 9.3 | 10.4 | 9.5 |
| Brazil | 223 | 66.4 | 77.6 | 95.8 | 126.6 | 182.4 | 133.7 | 191.5 | 236.9 | 228.4 | 244.7 | 239.2 | 178.8 |
| Chile | 228 | 24.8 | 32.7 | 38.4 | 47.2 | 61.9 | 41.4 | 57.9 | 73.5 | 79.1 | 80.4 | 72.4 | 62.8 |
| Colombia | 233 | 16.7 | 21.2 | 26.0 | 33.2 | 39.3 | 32.9 | 40.7 | 54.7 | 58.6 | 59.4 | 64.1 | 54.1 |
| Costa Rica | 238 | 8.3 | 9.8 | 11.5 | 13.0 | 15.4 | 11.5 | 13.6 | 16.2 | 17.5 | 17.9 | 17.2 | 15.4 |
| Dominica | 321 | .1 | .2 | .2 | .2 | .2 | .2 | .2 | .2 | .2 | .2 | .2 | .2 |
| Dominican Republic | 243 | 6.2 | 8.3 | 10.1 | 13.0 | 16.1 | 11.6 | 14.8 | 17.4 | 17.5 | 16.5 | .... | 19.0 |
| Ecuador | 248 | 8.2 | 10.3 | 12.1 | 13.6 | 18.9 | 15.1 | 20.6 | 24.3 | 25.3 | 27.0 | 27.7 | 21.5 |
| El Salvador | 253 | 6.3 | 6.8 | 7.6 | 8.7 | 9.8 | 7.3 | 8.5 | 10.1 | 10.3 | 10.8 | 10.5 | 10.4 |
| Grenada | 328 | .3 | .3 | .3 | .4 | .4 | .3 | .3 | .3 | .3 | .4 | .3 | .4 |
| Guatemala | 258 | 7.8 | 8.8 | 10.2 | 11.9 | 12.8 | 10.1 | 12.1 | 14.5 | 14.9 | 14.4 | 14.9 | 15.0 |

# Imports, c.i.f.

|  | | 2004 | 2005 | 2006 | 2007 | 2008 | 2009 | 2010 | 2011 | 2012 | 2013 | 2014 | 2015 |
|---|---|---|---|---|---|---|---|---|---|---|---|---|---|
| | | | | | | | *Billions of US Dollars* | | | | | | |
| **Western Hemisphere(Cont.)** | | | | | | | | | | | | | |
| Guyana......................................... | 336 | .7 | .8 | .9 | 1.1 | 1.3 | 1.2 | 1.4 | 1.8 | 2.0 | 1.8 | 1.8 | 1.6 |
| Haiti............................................. | 263 | 1.3 | 1.5 | 1.9 | 1.7 | 2.3 | 2.1 | 3.1 | 3.0 | 3.2 | 3.4 | 3.7 | .... |
| Honduras...................................... | 268 | 4.2 | 4.9 | 5.7 | 6.8 | 8.8 | 6.1 | 7.1 | 9.0 | 9.5 | 9.2 | 9.3 | 9.4 |
| Jamaica........................................ | 343 | 3.8 | 4.5 | 5.3 | 6.4 | 7.7 | 4.9 | 5.2 | 6.5 | 6.5 | 6.2 | 5.8 | 5.1 |
| Mexico......................................... | 273 | 206.6 | 231.8 | 268.2 | 296.6 | 325.2 | 246.1 | 316.6 | 368.4 | 389.3 | 400.3 | 420.0 | 415.0 |
| Netherlands Antilles..................... | 353 | 1.7 | 2.0 | 2.2 | 2.5 | 3.1 | 2.6 | 2.7 | .... | .... | .... | .... | .... |
| Nicaragua..................................... | 278 | 2.2 | 2.6 | 3.0 | 3.6 | 4.3 | 3.4 | 4.2 | 5.2 | 5.8 | 5.6 | 5.9 | 5.9 |
| Panama........................................ | 283 | 3.6 | 4.2 | 4.8 | 6.9 | 9.1 | 7.8 | 9.1 | 11.3 | 12.5 | 13.0 | .... | .... |
| Paraguay...................................... | 288 | 3.1 | 3.8 | 6.1 | 5.9 | 9.0 | 6.9 | 10.0 | 12.3 | 11.5 | 12.1 | 12.2 | 10.2 |
| Peru............................................. | 293 | 11.8 | 14.5 | 17.9 | 23.5 | 29.9 | 20.9 | 30.1 | 37.6 | 41.1 | 41.5 | 42.7 | .... |
| St. Lucia....................................... | 362 | .4 | .5 | .6 | .6 | .7 | .5 | .6 | .7 | .7 | .6 | .6 | .6 |
| St. Vincent & Grens...................... | 364 | .2 | .2 | .3 | .3 | .4 | .3 | .3 | .3 | .4 | .4 | .4 | .3 |
| Suriname...................................... | 366 | .6 | .8 | .9 | 1.1 | 1.5 | 1.4 | 1.4 | 1.7 | 2.0 | 2.1 | 2.0 | 2.0 |
| Trinidad and Tobago.................... | 369 | 4.9 | 5.7 | 6.8 | 7.7 | 9.6 | 7.0 | 6.5 | 9.5 | 9.1 | 8.9 | 8.8 | 6.5 |
| Uruguay....................................... | 298 | 3.1 | 3.9 | 4.8 | 5.7 | 8.9 | 6.2 | 8.6 | 10.6 | 10.6 | 11.0 | 10.9 | 9.1 |
| Venezuela, Rep. Bol...................... | 299 | 16.7 | 24.0 | 33.6 | 46.1 | 49.6 | 40.6 | 33.8 | 38.3 | 43.5 | 46.4 | 44.5 | 40.1 |

2016, International Monetary Fund : *International Financial Statistics Yearbook*

# Export Unit Values/Export Prices

| | | 2004 | 2005 | 2006 | 2007 | 2008 | 2009 | 2010 | 2011 | 2012 | 2013 | 2014 | 2015 |
|---|---|---|---|---|---|---|---|---|---|---|---|---|---|
| | | *Indices of Unit Values (Prices) In Terms of US Dollars: 2010=100* | | | | | | | | | | | |
| World........................................ | 001 | **82.0** | **85.8** | **89.6** | **97.0** | **106.3** | **95.3** | **100.0** | **111.1** | **108.7** | **108.3** | **106.6** | **91.7** |
| Advanced Economies................ | 110 | **84.7** | **87.5** | **90.3** | **97.6** | **106.3** | **96.8** | **100.0** | **110.1** | **107.3** | **107.1** | **106.0** | **92.2** |
| Euro Area | | | | | | | | | | | | | |
| Belgium........................... | 124 | 78.2 | 82.2 | 86.4 | 98.3 | 109.1 | 97.3 | 100.0 | 113.0 | 107.0 | 110.5 | 110.3 | 92.7 |
| Finland............................. | 172 | 94.3 | 95.4 | 98.2 | 107.8 | 115.8 | 100.5 | 100.0 | 110.1 | 102.2 | 103.9 | 102.7 | 84.7 |
| France.............................. | 132 | 100.6 | 100.0 | 100.4 | 109.6 | 115.4 | .... | 100.0 | .... | .... | .... | .... | .... |
| Germany........................... | 134 | 93.2 | 93.8 | 95.4 | 106.4 | 114.6 | 107.1 | 100.0 | 108.2 | 103.9 | 106.4 | 107.8 | 92.3 |
| Greece.............................. | 174 | 76.9 | 79.9 | 84.5 | 95.0 | 108.1 | 96.4 | 100.0 | 114.2 | 109.9 | 111.6 | 108.5 | 80.4 |
| Ireland.............................. | 178 | 96.5 | 97.1 | 97.8 | 104.0 | 107.7 | 102.6 | 100.0 | 104.5 | 101.8 | 103.8 | 103.1 | .... |
| Italy.................................. | 136 | 73.9 | 77.4 | 82.1 | 94.1 | 106.3 | 98.9 | 100.0 | 112.4 | 108.8 | 113.7 | 115.0 | 97.7 |
| Latvia............................... | 941 | 68.2 | 71.9 | 79.5 | 98.2 | 113.0 | 96.9 | 100.0 | 118.7 | 112.8 | 118.7 | .... | .... |
| Netherlands...................... | 138 | 84.4 | 87.7 | 91.4 | 101.2 | 113.3 | 98.4 | 100.0 | 110.4 | 104.2 | 106.9 | 104.4 | 83.8 |
| Spain................................ | 184 | 86.8 | 91.0 | 96.0 | 107.4 | 116.9 | 103.3 | 100.0 | 110.0 | 103.8 | 107.1 | 105.9 | 89.0 |
| Australia............................... | 193 | 49.9 | 59.1 | 67.4 | 75.3 | 94.4 | 81.8 | 100.0 | 126.7 | 117.2 | 108.7 | 97.7 | 73.9 |
| Canada................................. | 156 | 73.6 | 81.9 | 87.9 | 94.6 | 106.9 | 87.1 | 100.0 | 110.6 | 107.7 | 106.5 | 104.3 | 85.9 |
| China, P.R.: Hong Kong.............. | 532 | 86.8 | 88.0 | 88.9 | 90.6 | 94.2 | 95.7 | 100.0 | 107.8 | 111.8 | 113.2 | 115.6 | 115.7 |
| Denmark............................... | 128 | 85.9 | 90.3 | 93.0 | 100.9 | 111.4 | 100.2 | 100.0 | 108.9 | 104.4 | 105.6 | 102.4 | 84.5 |
| Iceland................................. | 176 | 85.4 | 91.4 | 103.1 | 115.8 | 115.2 | 86.7 | 100.0 | .... | .... | .... | .... | .... |
| Israel.................................... | 436 | 74.8 | 80.8 | 84.4 | 89.6 | 103.6 | 96.3 | 100.0 | † 106.5 | 110.7 | 113.0 | 112.0 | 106.0 |
| Japan................................... | 158 | 92.1 | 92.2 | 90.1 | 90.9 | 97.3 | 96.2 | 100.0 | 107.6 | 105.4 | 96.2 | 91.5 | 81.0 |
| Korea................................... | 542 | 97.5 | 98.8 | 99.4 | 102.6 | 107.1 | 89.4 | 100.0 | 108.5 | 105.5 | .... | .... | .... |
| New Zealand........................ | 196 | 73.2 | 78.5 | 78.9 | 92.0 | 103.4 | 77.5 | 100.0 | 113.7 | 106.1 | 116.6 | 112.1 | 91.2 |
| Norway................................ | 142 | 58.9 | 74.7 | 89.8 | 98.4 | 122.4 | 86.7 | 100.0 | 127.3 | 126.3 | 127.5 | 115.4 | 81.5 |
| Singapore............................ | 576 | 85.6 | 88.7 | 94.8 | 96.3 | 103.9 | 92.5 | 100.0 | 111.0 | 110.5 | 107.4 | 103.6 | 88.9 |
| Sweden................................ | 144 | 83.7 | 85.7 | 90.3 | 102.3 | 107.8 | 95.3 | 100.0 | 111.2 | 105.4 | 104.4 | 102.0 | 84.1 |
| Switzerland.......................... | 146 | 72.3 | 73.5 | 75.4 | 82.0 | 93.9 | 96.0 | 100.0 | 110.9 | 106.0 | 107.2 | 110.5 | 103.4 |
| United Kingdom.................... | 112 | 91.6 | 94.3 | 96.9 | 104.8 | 109.7 | 94.3 | 100.0 | 111.9 | 110.2 | 110.3 | 109.7 | 94.5 |
| United States....................... | 111 | 84.1 | 86.8 | 89.9 | 94.3 | 100.0 | 95.4 | 100.0 | 108.1 | 108.4 | 108.0 | 107.4 | 100.6 |
| Emerging & Dev. Economies..... | 200 | **66.4** | **75.3** | **84.3** | **92.8** | **106.4** | **85.9** | **100.0** | **117.0** | **117.4** | **115.6** | **110.7** | **89.2** |
| Emerging & Developing Asia..... | 505 | **75.7** | **84.6** | **92.4** | **83.2** | **93.5** | **85.9** | **100.0** | **113.7** | **114.2** | **113.4** | **109.8** | **101.0** |
| India................................... | 534 | 60.6 | 67.9 | 71.5 | 82.3 | 91.4 | 83.0 | 100.0 | 117.7 | 109.0 | 109.2 | 100.8 | .... |
| Indonesia............................. | 536 | 147.9 | 100.0 | .... | .... | .... | .... | 100.0 | .... | .... | .... | .... | .... |
| Papua New Guinea................ | 853 | 43.3 | 53.8 | 85.1 | 93.3 | 113.0 | 76.3 | 100.0 | 130.6 | 128.4 | 118.2 | 105.3 | 79.4 |
| Philippines........................... | 566 | 89.4 | 100.0 | 104.5 | .... | .... | .... | .... | .... | .... | .... | .... | .... |
| Sri Lanka.............................. | 524 | 76.4 | 78.7 | 82.4 | 85.7 | 90.6 | 89.5 | 100.0 | .... | .... | .... | .... | .... |
| Thailand.............................. | 578 | 70.8 | 75.2 | 80.0 | 84.3 | 95.0 | 92.5 | 100.0 | 110.1 | 111.9 | 109.5 | 107.6 | 95.9 |
| Europe................................... | 170 | **82.9** | **87.6** | **90.9** | **102.7** | **115.7** | **98.8** | **100.0** | **109.4** | **103.7** | **104.0** | **102.0** | **....** |
| Emerging & Dev. Europe......... | 903 | **82.9** | **87.6** | **90.9** | **102.7** | **115.7** | **98.8** | **100.0** | **109.4** | **103.7** | **104.0** | **102.0** | **....** |
| Hungary............................... | 944 | 96.8 | 97.6 | 98.5 | 107.8 | 115.4 | 101.1 | 100.0 | 106.8 | 98.2 | 98.8 | 96.0 | 79.7 |
| Poland................................. | 964 | 92.2 | 100.0 | 106.5 | 123.0 | 139.0 | 121.8 | .... | .... | .... | .... | .... | .... |
| Turkey................................. | 186 | 80.7 | 85.6 | 88.6 | 99.8 | 115.3 | 96.7 | 100.0 | 111.5 | 108.4 | 108.5 | 107.0 | .... |
| Middle East,N.Africa & Pakistan | 440 | **48.8** | **62.6** | **74.6** | **84.1** | **116.7** | **77.4** | **100.0** | **121.0** | **129.1** | **126.2** | **120.2** | **66.9** |
| Jordan.................................. | 439 | 54.9 | 63.2 | 69.2 | 82.0 | 126.0 | 114.4 | 100.0 | 112.4 | 121.4 | 111.1 | 111.1 | 109.7 |
| Morocco............................... | 686 | 99.3 | 100.0 | 105.1 | 116.6 | .... | .... | .... | .... | 145.0 | .... | .... | .... |
| Pakistan............................... | 564 | 78.5 | 78.8 | 80.8 | 83.5 | 94.1 | 88.1 | 100.0 | 118.3 | 118.8 | 116.1 | 119.7 | 113.9 |
| Saudi Arabia......................... | 456 | 43.2 | 62.1 | 74.8 | 85.6 | 120.0 | 76.1 | 100.0 | 138.9 | 132.2 | 134.3 | 124.3 | 63.4 |
| Sub-Saharan Africa.................. | 603 | **....** | **....** | **....** | **....** | **....** | **....** | **....** | **....** | **....** | **....** | **....** | **....** |
| Kenya.................................. | 664 | .... | .... | .... | .... | .... | .... | .... | .... | .... | .... | .... | .... |
| Mauritius............................. | 684 | 101.5 | 100.0 | 99.0 | 105.6 | .... | .... | .... | .... | .... | .... | .... | .... |
| South Africa......................... | 199 | 93.9 | 100.0 | .... | .... | .... | .... | .... | .... | .... | .... | .... | .... |
| Western Hemisphere................ | 205 | **62.6** | **71.2** | **82.1** | **89.2** | **107.0** | **86.3** | **100.0** | **122.0** | **118.3** | **115.0** | **107.6** | **81.8** |
| Argentina............................. | 213 | 63.0 | 66.0 | 72.7 | 82.5 | 104.3 | 92.9 | 100.0 | 119.2 | 121.9 | 119.7 | 116.9 | .... |
| Bolivia................................. | 218 | 38.7 | 50.7 | 86.4 | 97.0 | 107.9 | 86.8 | 100.0 | 144.9 | 152.9 | 142.6 | 136.5 | 113.5 |
| Brazil.................................. | 223 | 67.7 | 77.1 | 84.9 | 90.1 | 110.4 | 87.1 | 100.0 | 121.5 | 115.7 | 112.5 | 101.5 | 78.0 |
| Colombia.............................. | 233 | 86.8 | 100.0 | 107.5 | 117.1 | 142.6 | 135.8 | .... | .... | .... | .... | .... | .... |
| Ecuador............................... | 248 | 44.3 | 56.9 | 69.0 | 79.4 | 108.3 | 75.9 | 100.0 | 138.4 | 129.8 | 128.2 | 115.6 | 68.7 |
| Honduras.............................. | 268 | 47.9 | 68.5 | 70.1 | 74.0 | 88.6 | 83.3 | 100.0 | 143.7 | 122.8 | 95.0 | 100.4 | 100.7 |
| Peru..................................... | 293 | 39.9 | 52.0 | 85.4 | 94.0 | 88.4 | 68.6 | 100.0 | 120.2 | 109.5 | 105.1 | 96.6 | .... |

| | | 2004 | 2005 | 2006 | 2007 | 2008 | 2009 | 2010 | 2011 | 2012 | 2013 | 2014 | 2015 |
|---|---|---|---|---|---|---|---|---|---|---|---|---|---|
| | | *Indices of Unit Values (Prices) In Terms of US Dollars: 2010=100* | | | | | | | | | | | |
| World | 001 | 80.4 | 84.9 | 89.5 | 96.6 | 108.4 | 94.7 | 100.0 | 114.3 | 113.3 | 111.9 | 110.2 | 95.7 |
| Advanced Economies | 110 | 81.3 | 85.8 | 90.4 | 97.3 | 108.8 | 95.1 | 100.0 | 112.6 | 111.0 | 110.0 | 108.2 | 92.6 |
| Euro Area | | | | | | | | | | | | | |
| Belgium | 124 | 78.7 | 83.8 | 88.7 | 98.9 | 110.9 | 95.7 | 100.0 | 113.7 | 109.4 | 112.4 | 109.6 | 92.0 |
| Finland | 172 | 81.8 | 86.4 | 92.9 | 103.3 | 114.2 | 99.0 | 100.0 | 113.7 | 108.0 | 109.1 | 106.7 | 83.9 |
| France | 132 | 100.5 | 100.0 | 102.0 | 112.3 | 120.1 | .... | .... | .... | .... | .... | .... | .... |
| Germany | 134 | 88.5 | 90.7 | 94.9 | 105.3 | 116.4 | 103.4 | 100.0 | 112.1 | 108.6 | 110.0 | 108.6 | 91.5 |
| Ireland | 178 | 89.3 | 90.1 | 93.5 | 101.7 | 111.0 | 100.2 | 100.0 | 111.3 | 108.8 | 111.2 | 111.6 | .... |
| Italy | 136 | 71.2 | 76.8 | 84.9 | 95.4 | 111.3 | 94.9 | 100.0 | 116.3 | 112.2 | 113.8 | 110.7 | 89.1 |
| Netherlands | 138 | 83.7 | 86.5 | 90.5 | 100.3 | 112.7 | 97.8 | 100.0 | 110.2 | 104.6 | 106.4 | 103.0 | 81.7 |
| Spain | 184 | 88.6 | 93.3 | 97.8 | 107.6 | 120.0 | 100.3 | 100.0 | 113.9 | 110.1 | 108.9 | 106.3 | 86.6 |
| Australia | 193 | 76.9 | 80.7 | 82.8 | 88.4 | 96.7 | 89.8 | 100.0 | 113.1 | 115.2 | 109.9 | 105.9 | 89.2 |
| Canada | 156 | 78.4 | 84.3 | 90.3 | 94.2 | 101.4 | 94.3 | 100.0 | 108.1 | 108.0 | 105.0 | 102.4 | 92.5 |
| China, P.R.: Hong Kong | 532 | 83.8 | 86.2 | 88.2 | 89.8 | 93.9 | 94.2 | 100.0 | 107.9 | 111.9 | 112.8 | 115.0 | 114.6 |
| Denmark | 128 | 88.2 | 91.7 | 95.0 | 106.4 | 114.7 | 102.6 | 100.0 | 108.5 | 101.5 | 102.2 | 102.0 | 83.6 |
| Iceland | 176 | 83.0 | 89.1 | 94.2 | 106.0 | 112.3 | 95.1 | 100.0 | .... | .... | .... | .... | .... |
| Israel | 436 | 77.7 | 83.3 | 88.3 | 95.9 | 109.4 | 93.0 | 100.0 | † 114.5 | 111.3 | 110.2 | 108.3 | 93.1 |
| Japan | 158 | 67.5 | 74.9 | 80.9 | 85.9 | 106.2 | 87.6 | 100.0 | 118.2 | 118.0 | 110.4 | 106.0 | 82.4 |
| Korea | 542 | 77.7 | 85.0 | 91.5 | 96.9 | 117.3 | 89.1 | 100.0 | 118.4 | 116.0 | .... | .... | .... |
| New Zealand | 196 | 84.0 | 90.8 | 89.6 | 96.9 | 106.0 | 86.9 | 100.0 | 111.1 | 111.6 | 107.4 | 103.2 | 86.3 |
| Norway | 142 | 80.5 | 84.3 | 88.4 | 100.6 | 108.9 | 96.9 | 100.0 | 112.1 | 108.5 | 109.8 | 108.0 | 89.3 |
| Singapore | 576 | 79.6 | 85.0 | 91.6 | 94.7 | 104.0 | 93.0 | 100.0 | 113.6 | 114.0 | 110.7 | 106.3 | 85.5 |
| Sweden | 144 | 80.2 | 84.7 | 90.7 | 101.2 | 110.3 | 94.2 | 100.0 | 112.9 | 107.1 | 107.1 | 103.1 | 82.8 |
| Switzerland | 146 | 75.8 | 79.6 | 83.2 | 90.4 | 100.4 | 95.7 | 100.0 | 114.1 | 109.2 | 112.1 | 114.8 | 101.9 |
| United Kingdom | 112 | 89.4 | 92.6 | 96.5 | 104.9 | 110.1 | 95.4 | 100.0 | 112.5 | 111.1 | 110.4 | 110.3 | 96.5 |
| United States | 111 | 80.7 | 86.7 | 91.0 | 94.8 | 105.7 | 93.6 | 100.0 | 110.9 | 111.2 | 110.0 | 108.8 | 97.7 |
| **Emerging & Dev. Economies** | 200 | 73.2 | 77.8 | 82.4 | 91.0 | 105.6 | 91.4 | 100.0 | 126.5 | 129.8 | 125.5 | 124.5 | 118.5 |
| **Emerging & Developing Asia** | 505 | 84.7 | 85.7 | 88.3 | 96.8 | 104.1 | 88.6 | 100.0 | 143.4 | 152.9 | 145.4 | 146.3 | 138.1 |
| India | 534 | 93.3 | 85.6 | 85.6 | 95.6 | 103.4 | 83.6 | 100.0 | 171.4 | 161.6 | 166.3 | 159.7 | .... |
| Philippines | 566 | 86.1 | 100.0 | 120.6 | .... | .... | .... | .... | .... | .... | .... | .... | .... |
| Thailand | 578 | 69.3 | 74.4 | 78.2 | 82.7 | 91.4 | 91.6 | 100.0 | 105.6 | 106.3 | 105.8 | 104.8 | 102.3 |
| **Europe** | 170 | 79.3 | 84.7 | 90.0 | 99.7 | 115.8 | 95.2 | 100.0 | 112.9 | 108.4 | 107.2 | 103.9 | .... |
| **Emerging & Dev. Europe** | 903 | 79.3 | 84.7 | 90.0 | 99.7 | 115.8 | 95.2 | 100.0 | 112.9 | 108.4 | 107.2 | 103.9 | .... |
| Hungary | 944 | 93.4 | 96.2 | 98.5 | 107.9 | 117.5 | 101.1 | 100.0 | 108.6 | 101.2 | 101.2 | 97.4 | 80.2 |
| Poland | 964 | 92.4 | 100.0 | 106.7 | 120.8 | 138.7 | 121.4 | .... | .... | .... | .... | .... | .... |
| Turkey | 186 | 75.0 | 80.2 | 87.1 | 95.5 | 114.7 | 92.3 | 100.0 | 114.9 | 111.9 | 110.1 | 107.0 | .... |
| **Middle East,N.Africa & Pakistan** | 440 | 57.6 | 63.0 | 67.6 | 75.7 | 92.1 | 86.9 | 100.0 | 119.9 | 106.5 | 108.0 | 107.5 | 98.7 |
| Jordan | 439 | 53.7 | 61.0 | 66.8 | 75.8 | 91.2 | 81.1 | 100.0 | 125.5 | 123.9 | 125.1 | 132.5 | 117.0 |
| Morocco | 686 | 94.3 | 100.0 | 104.1 | 117.8 | .... | .... | .... | .... | 127.0 | .... | .... | .... |
| Pakistan | 564 | 60.0 | 67.8 | 74.6 | 82.4 | 105.6 | 87.9 | 100.0 | 123.8 | 129.5 | 132.5 | 131.7 | 122.3 |
| **Sub-Saharan Africa** | 603 | .... | .... | .... | .... | .... | .... | .... | .... | .... | .... | .... | .... |
| Kenya | 664 | .... | .... | .... | .... | .... | .... | .... | .... | .... | .... | .... | .... |
| Mauritius | 684 | 92.5 | 100.0 | 104.8 | 112.3 | .... | .... | .... | .... | .... | .... | .... | .... |
| South Africa | 199 | 94.3 | 100.0 | .... | .... | .... | .... | .... | .... | .... | .... | .... | .... |
| **Western Hemisphere** | 205 | 57.7 | 67.3 | 73.7 | 81.3 | 102.6 | 94.6 | 100.0 | 108.7 | 112.8 | 109.5 | 106.7 | 113.7 |
| Argentina | 213 | 78.8 | 85.0 | 89.7 | 96.1 | 108.2 | 95.5 | 100.0 | 107.1 | 105.3 | 111.0 | 111.2 | .... |
| Brazil | 223 | 46.5 | 59.8 | 68.6 | 77.0 | 105.7 | 93.8 | 100.0 | 115.5 | 120.4 | 114.5 | 107.6 | 89.2 |
| Colombia | 233 | 91.1 | 100.0 | 100.3 | 103.2 | 108.6 | 101.7 | .... | .... | .... | .... | .... | .... |
| Venezuela, Rep. Bol. | 299 | 52.2 | 53.2 | 56.0 | 63.8 | 75.9 | 96.2 | 100.0 | 72.4 | 78.6 | 77.3 | 102.9 | 254.7 |

# Terms of Trade

| | | 2004 | 2005 | 2006 | 2007 | 2008 | 2009 | 2010 | 2011 | 2012 | 2013 | 2014 | 2015 |
|---|---|---|---|---|---|---|---|---|---|---|---|---|---|
| | | | | | *Percent Change over Previous Year; Calculated from Indices* | | | | | | | | |
| World................. | 001 | −.5 | −.9 | −.9 | .4 | −2.4 | 2.7 | −.7 | −2.9 | −1.2 | .9 | — | −1.0 |
| Advanced Economies................ | 110 | −.4 | −2.2 | −2.0 | .4 | −2.6 | 4.2 | −1.8 | −2.2 | −1.1 | .7 | .6 | 1.6 |
| Euro Area........................ | 163 | −2.7 | −4.6 | −4.0 | 1.1 | −5.2 | 7.6 | −5.4 | −4.7 | −1.0 | 2.0 | 2.8 | 4.9 |
| Belgium......................... | 124 | .2 | −1.4 | −.6 | 2.1 | −1.0 | 3.3 | −1.7 | −.6 | −1.6 | .6 | 2.3 | .1 |
| Finland.......................... | 172 | −2.9 | −4.2 | −4.3 | −1.2 | −2.9 | .1 | −1.5 | −3.2 | −2.3 | .6 | 1.1 | 5.0 |
| France........................... | 132 | .6 | −.1 | −1.6 | −.8 | −1.6 | .... | .... | .... | .... | .... | .... | .... |
| Germany......................... | 134 | — | −1.8 | −2.8 | .5 | −2.5 | 5.2 | −3.5 | −3.4 | −.9 | 1.0 | 2.7 | 1.6 |
| Greece........................... | 174 | 1.9 | −4.7 | .6 | .4 | −.7 | −4.3 | 2.1 | 1.1 | −.4 | 1.0 | 1.1 | −.9 |
| Ireland.......................... | 178 | −1.4 | −.4 | −2.9 | −2.2 | −5.2 | 5.6 | −2.4 | −6.1 | −.3 | −.4 | −1.0 | .... |
| Italy............................. | 136 | −1.1 | −2.9 | −4.0 | 2.0 | −3.2 | 9.1 | −4.0 | −3.3 | .3 | 3.0 | 4.0 | 5.6 |
| Malta............................ | 181 | −7.5 | .... | .... | .... | .... | .... | .... | .... | .... | .... | .... | .... |
| Netherlands..................... | 138 | −.5 | .6 | −.4 | −.1 | −.3 | .1 | −.6 | .2 | −.5 | .8 | .9 | 1.3 |
| Portugal......................... | 182 | — | — | 1.9 | 1.4 | −3.9 | 8.4 | −5.3 | .... | .... | .... | .... | .... |
| Spain............................ | 184 | −1.4 | −.3 | .6 | 1.7 | −2.5 | 5.8 | −2.9 | −3.4 | −2.4 | 4.3 | 1.3 | 3.2 |
| Australia........................ | 193 | 9.7 | 12.8 | 11.0 | 4.7 | 14.6 | −6.7 | 9.8 | 12.0 | −9.2 | −2.7 | −6.7 | −10.2 |
| Canada.......................... | 156 | 3.7 | 3.6 | .1 | 3.1 | 5.1 | −12.4 | 8.3 | 2.3 | −2.5 | 1.7 | .4 | −8.8 |
| China, P.R.: Hong Kong........ | 532 | −1.7 | −1.4 | −1.2 | .1 | −.6 | 1.2 | −1.5 | −.2 | .1 | .4 | .1 | .5 |
| Denmark......................... | 128 | .5 | 1.2 | −.6 | −3.2 | 2.4 | .6 | 2.3 | .4 | 2.6 | .4 | −2.8 | .6 |
| Iceland.......................... | 176 | −2.2 | −.4 | 6.9 | −.3 | −6.1 | −11.1 | 9.6 | .... | .... | .... | .... | .... |
| Israel............................ | 436 | −2.0 | .7 | −1.5 | −2.2 | 1.4 | 9.3 | −3.4 | −7.0 | 7.0 | 3.0 | .8 | 10.2 |
| Japan............................ | 158 | −5.3 | −9.9 | −9.5 | −4.9 | −13.5 | 19.9 | −9.0 | −9.0 | −1.8 | −2.5 | −1.0 | 14.0 |
| Korea............................ | 542 | −4.1 | −7.4 | −6.6 | −2.5 | −13.8 | 9.9 | −.3 | −8.3 | −.7 | .... | .... | .... |
| New Zealand..................... | 196 | 5.8 | −.8 | 1.9 | 7.8 | 2.8 | −8.5 | 12.1 | 2.4 | −7.1 | 14.2 | — | −2.7 |
| Norway.......................... | 142 | 11.2 | 21.2 | 14.5 | −3.7 | 14.9 | −20.3 | 11.7 | 13.5 | 2.5 | −.3 | −7.9 | −14.6 |
| Singapore....................... | 576 | −1.4 | −2.9 | −.8 | −1.8 | −1.7 | −.5 | .6 | −2.3 | −.8 | .1 | .4 | 6.7 |
| Sweden.......................... | 144 | −2.5 | −2.9 | −1.7 | 1.5 | −3.3 | 3.5 | −1.1 | −1.5 | −.1 | −.8 | 1.4 | 2.7 |
| Switzerland...................... | 146 | −.3 | −3.3 | −1.8 | — | 3.0 | 7.3 | −.3 | −2.8 | −.1 | −1.5 | .7 | 5.4 |
| United Kingdom................. | 112 | 1.1 | −.7 | −1.3 | −.5 | −.3 | −.7 | 1.1 | −.5 | −.3 | .7 | −.3 | −1.6 |
| United States.................... | 111 | −1.7 | −4.0 | −1.2 | .6 | −4.9 | 7.8 | −1.9 | −2.6 | .1 | .7 | .6 | 4.3 |
| | | | | | | | | | | | | | |
| Emerging & Dev. Economies..... | 200 | −2.3 | 6.8 | 5.7 | −.4 | −1.1 | −6.7 | 6.4 | −7.5 | −2.2 | 1.9 | −3.5 | −15.4 |
| Emerging & Developing Asia..... | 505 | −9.7 | 10.5 | 6.0 | −17.9 | 4.5 | 8.0 | 3.1 | −20.7 | −5.8 | 4.5 | −3.7 | −2.5 |
| India............................ | 534 | −10.5 | 22.1 | 5.3 | 3.1 | 2.7 | 12.3 | .7 | −31.3 | −1.9 | −2.7 | −3.8 | .... |
| Philippines...................... | 566 | −3.2 | −3.7 | −13.3 | .... | .... | .... | .... | .... | .... | .... | .... | .... |
| Sri Lanka........................ | 524 | 13.3 | 12.1 | −34.9 | 120.8 | 17.2 | −15.4 | .... | .... | .... | .... | .... | .... |
| Thailand......................... | 578 | −1.8 | −.9 | 1.1 | −.3 | 2.0 | −2.9 | −1.0 | 4.3 | 1.0 | −1.6 | −.8 | −8.8 |
| Europe........................... | 170 | 1.6 | −1.2 | −2.3 | 2.0 | −3.0 | 4.0 | −3.7 | −3.1 | −1.3 | 1.4 | 1.2 | .... |
| Emerging & Dev. Europe......... | 903 | 1.6 | −1.2 | −2.3 | 2.0 | −3.0 | 4.0 | −3.7 | −3.1 | −1.3 | 1.4 | 1.2 | .... |
| Hungary......................... | 944 | −.7 | −2.1 | −1.4 | −.1 | −1.7 | 1.8 | −.1 | −1.7 | −1.3 | .6 | 1.0 | .9 |
| Poland........................... | 964 | 4.8 | .2 | −.2 | 2.0 | −1.6 | .2 | .... | .... | .... | .... | .... | .... |
| Turkey........................... | 186 | .6 | −.9 | −4.7 | 2.8 | −3.8 | 4.2 | −4.6 | −3.0 | −.1 | 1.7 | 1.5 | .... |
| Middle East,N.Africa & Pakistan | 440 | 11.1 | 17.4 | 10.9 | .6 | 14.1 | −29.7 | 12.3 | .9 | 20.1 | −3.7 | −4.3 | −39.4 |
| Jordan........................... | 439 | −1.2 | 1.3 | — | 4.4 | 27.7 | 2.0 | −29.0 | −10.4 | 9.4 | −9.3 | −5.6 | 11.8 |
| Morocco......................... | 686 | −.7 | −5.0 | .9 | −2.0 | −2.0 | −2.0 | −2.0 | −2.0 | 24.9 | .... | .... | .... |
| Oman............................ | 449 | −4.5 | 38.8 | .... | .... | .... | .... | .... | .... | .... | .... | .... | .... |
| Pakistan......................... | 564 | −4.6 | −11.1 | −6.9 | −6.4 | −12.1 | 12.5 | −.2 | −4.5 | −4.0 | −4.5 | 3.8 | 2.4 |
| Sub-Saharan Africa.................. | 603 | .... | .... | .... | .... | .... | .... | .... | .... | .... | .... | .... | .... |
| WAEMU | | | | | | | | | | | | | |
| Togo............................. | 742 | 21.2 | −27.5 | .... | .... | .... | .... | .... | .... | .... | .... | .... | .... |
| Kenya............................ | 664 | .... | .... | .... | .... | .... | .... | .... | .... | .... | .... | .... | .... |
| Mauritius........................ | 684 | −3.4 | −8.8 | −5.5 | −.5 | .... | .... | .... | .... | .... | .... | .... | .... |
| South Africa..................... | 199 | 1.1 | .4 | .... | .... | .... | .... | .... | .... | .... | .... | .... | .... |
| Western Hemisphere................ | 205 | −3.7 | −2.5 | 5.3 | −1.4 | −5.0 | −12.5 | 9.6 | 12.3 | −6.6 | .2 | −3.9 | −28.7 |
| Argentina........................ | 213 | 1.6 | −3.0 | 4.4 | 6.1 | 12.2 | .9 | 2.8 | 11.3 | 4.0 | −6.8 | −2.5 | .... |
| Brazil............................ | 223 | −4.6 | −11.3 | −4.1 | −5.4 | −10.8 | −11.1 | 7.8 | 5.2 | −8.6 | 2.2 | −4.1 | −7.3 |
| Colombia......................... | 233 | 1.0 | 5.0 | 7.2 | 5.9 | 15.7 | 1.7 | .... | .... | .... | .... | .... | .... |

# Indices

| | | 2004 | 2005 | 2006 | 2007 | 2008 | 2009 | 2010 | 2011 | 2012 | 2013 | 2014 | 2015 |
|---|---|---|---|---|---|---|---|---|---|---|---|---|---|
| | | | | | *Index Numbers: 2010=100* | | | | | | | | |
| World................. | 001 | 102.0 | 101.0 | 100.1 | 100.5 | 98.1 | 100.7 | 100.0 | 97.1 | 96.0 | 96.8 | 96.8 | 95.8 |
| Industrial Countries................ | 110 | 104.2 | 101.9 | 99.9 | 100.3 | 97.7 | 101.8 | 100.0 | 97.8 | 96.7 | 97.4 | 97.9 | 99.5 |
| Developing Countries.............. | 200 | 90.7 | 96.9 | 102.4 | 101.9 | 100.8 | 94.0 | 100.0 | 92.5 | 90.5 | 92.2 | 89.0 | 75.3 |
| Africa............................ | 605 | .... | .... | .... | .... | 104.1 | 102.0 | 100.0 | 98.0 | 122.4 | .... | .... | .... |
| Asia.............................. | 505 | 89.4 | 98.7 | 104.7 | 85.9 | 89.8 | 97.0 | 100.0 | 79.3 | 74.7 | 78.0 | 75.1 | 73.2 |
| Europe........................... | 170 | 104.6 | 103.4 | 101.1 | 103.0 | 99.9 | 103.9 | 100.0 | 96.9 | 95.7 | 97.0 | 98.2 | .... |
| Middle East...................... | 405 | .... | .... | .... | .... | 131.7 | 93.2 | 100.0 | 96.7 | 106.4 | 103.5 | 93.5 | 55.5 |
| Middle East,N.Africa & Pakist | 440 | 84.7 | 99.5 | 110.3 | 111.0 | 126.7 | 89.1 | 100.0 | 100.9 | 121.2 | 116.8 | 111.8 | 67.8 |
| Sub-Saharan Africa............... | 603 | .... | .... | .... | .... | .... | .... | .... | .... | .... | .... | .... | .... |
| Western Hemisphere............ | 205 | 108.5 | 105.8 | 111.3 | 109.8 | 104.3 | 91.2 | 100.0 | 112.3 | 104.8 | 105.0 | 100.9 | 71.9 |

# GDP Volume Measures

| | | 2004 | 2005 | 2006 | 2007 | 2008 | 2009 | 2010 | 2011 | 2012 | 2013 | 2014 | 2015 |
|---|---|---|---|---|---|---|---|---|---|---|---|---|---|
| | | *Percent Change over Previous Year; Calculated from Indices* | | | | | | | | | | | |
| World........................... | 001 | **5.1** | **4.5** | **5.0** | **4.9** | **2.2** | **−.4** | **6.5** | **3.8** | **3.0** | **2.8** | **3.0** | **2.8** |
| Advanced Economies............... | 110 | **3.2** | **2.7** | **3.0** | **2.6** | **—** | **−3.5** | **2.9** | **1.6** | **1.2** | **1.1** | **1.8** | **1.9** |
| Euro Area...................... | 163 | 2.0 | 1.7 | 3.3 | 3.4 | .6 | −3.8 | 2.0 | 1.8 | −.7 | −.4 | 1.0 | 1.9 |
| Austria....................... | 122 | 2.7 | 2.1 | 3.4 | 3.6 | 1.5 | −3.8 | 1.9 | 3.1 | .9 | .2 | .3 | .8 |
| Belgium....................... | 124 | 3.4 | 1.9 | 2.6 | 3.0 | 1.0 | −2.6 | 2.5 | 1.6 | .1 | .3 | 1.1 | 2.5 |
| Cyprus........................ | 423 | 4.2 | 4.0 | 4.0 | 4.4 | 3.0 | −2.0 | 1.4 | .4 | −2.4 | −5.9 | −2.5 | 1.6 |
| Finland....................... | 172 | 3.9 | 2.8 | 4.1 | 5.2 | .7 | −8.3 | 3.0 | 2.6 | −1.4 | −1.3 | −.1 | .2 |
| France........................ | 132 | 2.6 | 1.6 | 2.6 | 2.3 | .1 | −2.9 | 1.9 | 2.1 | .4 | .4 | .4 | 1.1 |
| Germany....................... | 134 | .7 | .9 | 3.9 | 3.4 | .8 | −5.6 | 3.9 | 3.7 | .6 | .4 | 1.6 | 1.4 |
| Greece........................ | 174 | 5.0 | .9 | 5.8 | 3.3 | −.3 | −4.3 | −5.5 | −9.1 | −7.3 | −3.2 | .7 | −.2 |
| Ireland....................... | 178 | 4.4 | 6.3 | 6.3 | 5.5 | −2.2 | −5.6 | .4 | 2.6 | .2 | 1.4 | 5.2 | 7.8 |
| Italy......................... | 136 | 1.4 | 1.2 | 2.1 | 1.3 | −1.1 | −5.5 | 1.7 | .7 | −2.3 | −1.9 | −.6 | .5 |
| Latvia........................ | 941 | 8.9 | 10.2 | 11.6 | 9.8 | −3.2 | −14.2 | −2.9 | 5.0 | 4.8 | 4.2 | .2 | 2.7 |
| Lithuania..................... | 946 | 6.6 | 7.7 | 7.4 | 11.1 | 2.6 | −14.8 | 1.6 | 6.0 | 3.8 | 3.5 | 3.0 | 1.6 |
| Luxembourg.................... | 137 | 4.9 | 4.1 | 4.9 | 6.5 | .5 | −5.3 | 5.1 | 2.6 | −.2 | 2.0 | 7.9 | 3.3 |
| Malta......................... | 181 | .6 | 3.2 | 3.4 | 4.0 | 3.3 | −2.5 | 3.5 | 2.1 | 2.5 | 2.3 | 3.5 | 8.1 |
| Netherlands................... | 138 | 2.0 | 2.2 | 3.5 | 3.7 | 1.7 | −3.8 | 1.4 | 1.7 | −1.1 | −.5 | 1.0 | 2.0 |
| Portugal...................... | 182 | 1.8 | .8 | 1.6 | 2.5 | .2 | −3.0 | 1.9 | −1.8 | −4.0 | −1.1 | .9 | 1.5 |
| Slovak Republic............... | 936 | 5.0 | 6.7 | 8.5 | 10.6 | 6.2 | −5.1 | 5.1 | 2.8 | 1.5 | 1.4 | 2.5 | 3.6 |
| Slovenia...................... | 961 | 4.4 | 4.0 | 5.8 | 7.0 | 3.3 | −7.8 | 1.2 | .6 | −2.7 | −1.1 | 3.0 | 2.9 |
| Spain......................... | 184 | 3.2 | 3.7 | 4.2 | 3.8 | 1.1 | −3.6 | — | −.6 | −2.1 | −1.2 | 1.4 | 1.7 |
| Australia..................... | 193 | 4.1 | 3.2 | 2.7 | 4.5 | 2.6 | 1.8 | 2.3 | 2.7 | 3.5 | 2.0 | 2.7 | 2.5 |
| Canada........................ | 156 | 3.1 | 3.2 | 2.6 | 2.1 | 1.0 | −2.9 | 3.1 | 3.1 | 1.7 | 2.2 | 2.5 | 1.1 |
| China, P.R.: Hong Kong........ | 532 | 8.7 | 7.4 | 7.0 | 6.5 | 2.1 | −2.5 | 6.8 | 4.8 | 1.7 | 3.1 | 2.7 | 2.4 |
| Czech Republic................ | 935 | 4.9 | 6.4 | 6.9 | 5.5 | 2.7 | −4.8 | 2.3 | 2.0 | −.9 | −.5 | 2.0 | 4.2 |
| Denmark....................... | 128 | 2.6 | 2.4 | 3.8 | .8 | −.7 | −5.1 | 1.6 | 1.2 | −.7 | −.5 | 1.1 | 2.1 |
| Iceland....................... | 176 | 8.2 | 6.0 | 4.2 | 9.5 | 1.5 | −4.7 | −3.6 | 2.0 | 1.2 | 3.9 | 1.8 | 4.2 |
| Israel........................ | 436 | 5.1 | 4.4 | 5.8 | 6.1 | 3.1 | 1.3 | 5.5 | 5.0 | 2.9 | 3.3 | 2.6 | — |
| Japan......................... | 158 | 2.3 | 1.3 | 1.7 | 2.2 | −1.1 | −5.5 | 4.7 | −.4 | 1.7 | 1.4 | −.1 | .6 |
| Korea......................... | 542 | 4.9 | 3.9 | 5.2 | 5.5 | 2.8 | .7 | 6.5 | 3.7 | 2.3 | 2.9 | 3.3 | 2.6 |
| New Zealand................... | 196 | 3.2 | 3.3 | 2.6 | 3.7 | −1.5 | 1.9 | 1.0 | 2.7 | 2.7 | 1.6 | 3.2 | 3.1 |
| Norway........................ | 142 | 4.0 | 2.6 | 2.4 | 2.9 | .4 | −1.6 | .6 | 1.0 | 2.7 | .7 | 2.2 | 4.4 |
| Singapore..................... | 576 | 9.5 | 7.5 | 8.9 | 9.1 | 1.8 | −.6 | 15.2 | 6.2 | 3.4 | 4.4 | 2.9 | .... |
| Sweden........................ | 144 | 4.3 | 2.8 | 4.7 | 3.4 | −.6 | −5.2 | 6.0 | 2.7 | −.3 | 1.2 | 2.3 | 4.2 |
| Switzerland................... | 146 | 2.7 | 3.1 | 4.1 | 4.1 | 2.2 | −2.1 | 2.9 | 1.9 | 1.1 | 1.9 | 2.0 | .... |
| United Kingdom................ | 112 | 2.5 | 3.0 | 2.7 | 2.6 | −.5 | −4.2 | 1.5 | 2.0 | 1.2 | 2.2 | 2.9 | 2.3 |
| United States................. | 111 | 3.8 | 3.3 | 2.7 | 1.8 | −.3 | −2.8 | 2.5 | 1.6 | 2.2 | 1.5 | 2.4 | 2.4 |
| Emerging & Dev. Economies...... | 200 | **7.8** | **7.0** | **8.0** | **8.3** | **5.4** | **3.3** | **10.7** | **6.3** | **5.2** | **4.9** | **4.6** | **4.3** |
| Emerging & Developing Asia..... | 505 | **8.7** | **9.1** | **10.3** | **11.1** | **8.1** | **7.8** | **16.2** | **7.8** | **7.0** | **6.7** | **6.7** | **6.4** |
| Bangladesh.................... | 513 | 6.3 | 6.0 | 6.6 | 7.1 | 6.0 | 5.0 | 5.6 | 6.5 | 6.5 | 6.0 | 6.1 | 6.6 |
| Brunei Darussalam............. | 516 | .5 | .4 | 4.4 | .2 | −1.9 | −1.8 | 2.6 | 2.2 | 2.2 | −1.8 | −2.3 | .... |
| Cambodia...................... | 522 | 10.3 | 13.3 | 10.8 | 10.2 | 6.7 | .1 | 6.0 | 7.1 | 7.3 | 7.4 | 7.1 | .... |
| China, P.R.: Mainland......... | 924 | 10.1 | 11.3 | 12.7 | 14.2 | 9.6 | 9.2 | 10.3 | 9.4 | 7.8 | .... | .... | .... |
| China, P.R.: Macao............ | 546 | 30.8 | 8.1 | 13.3 | 14.4 | 3.4 | 1.3 | 25.3 | 21.7 | 9.2 | 11.2 | −.9 | −20.3 |
| Fiji.......................... | 819 | 5.4 | .7 | 1.9 | −.9 | 1.0 | −1.4 | 3.0 | 2.7 | 1.4 | 4.7 | 5.3 | .... |
| India......................... | 534 | 7.0 | 9.5 | 9.6 | 9.3 | 6.7 | 8.6 | 9.3 | 6.3 | 5.4 | 6.3 | 7.1 | .... |
| Indonesia..................... | 536 | 5.0 | 5.7 | 5.5 | 6.3 | 6.0 | 4.6 | 6.2 | 6.2 | 6.0 | 5.6 | 5.0 | 4.8 |
| Lao People's Dem. Rep......... | 544 | 7.0 | 6.8 | 8.7 | 6.8 | 8.8 | 7.5 | 8.1 | 8.0 | 7.9 | 8.0 | .... | .... |
| Malaysia...................... | 548 | 6.8 | 5.3 | 5.6 | 6.3 | 4.8 | −1.5 | 7.4 | 5.3 | 5.5 | 4.7 | 6.0 | 5.0 |
| Maldives...................... | 556 | 13.2 | −8.1 | 19.9 | 10.2 | 12.7 | −5.3 | 7.2 | 8.7 | 2.5 | .... | 6.5 | .... |
| Mongolia...................... | 948 | 10.6 | 7.3 | 8.6 | 10.2 | 8.9 | −1.3 | 6.4 | 17.5 | 12.3 | 11.9 | .... | .... |
| Myanmar....................... | 518 | .... | .... | .... | .... | .... | .... | .... | .... | .... | .... | .... | .... |
| Nepal......................... | 558 | 4.7 | 3.5 | 3.4 | 3.4 | 6.1 | 4.5 | 4.8 | 3.4 | 4.8 | 4.1 | 5.4 | .... |
| Papua New Guinea.............. | 853 | 2.9 | 3.0 | .... | .... | .... | .... | .... | .... | .... | .... | .... | .... |
| Philippines................... | 566 | 6.7 | 4.8 | 5.2 | 6.6 | 4.2 | 1.1 | 7.6 | 3.7 | 6.7 | 7.1 | 6.2 | 5.9 |
| Samoa......................... | 862 | 3.2 | .... | .... | .... | .... | .... | .... | .... | .... | .... | .... | .... |
| Solomon Islands............... | 813 | .... | .... | .... | .... | .... | .... | .... | .... | .... | .... | .... | .... |
| Sri Lanka..................... | 524 | 5.4 | 6.2 | 7.7 | 6.8 | 6.0 | 3.5 | 8.0 | 8.2 | 6.3 | 7.2 | 7.4 | .... |
| Thailand...................... | 578 | 6.2 | 4.5 | 5.6 | 4.9 | 2.5 | −2.3 | 7.8 | .1 | 6.5 | 2.7 | .8 | 2.8 |
| Tonga......................... | 866 | .8 | 1.6 | −1.1 | −4.5 | 1.9 | 3.2 | 3.3 | 2.9 | .8 | .... | .... | .... |
| Vanuatu....................... | 846 | 4.0 | 5.3 | 8.5 | 5.2 | 6.5 | 3.3 | 1.6 | 1.2 | 1.8 | 2.0 | .... | .... |
| Vietnam....................... | 582 | 7.8 | 8.4 | 7.0 | 7.1 | 5.7 | 5.4 | 6.4 | 6.2 | 5.2 | 5.4 | 6.0 | .... |
| Europe........................ | 170 | **7.6** | **6.0** | **6.8** | **6.6** | **3.9** | **−5.7** | **4.3** | **4.6** | **2.3** | **1.9** | **1.5** | **....** |
| Emerging & Dev. Europe........ | 903 | **7.0** | **5.7** | **5.1** | **4.7** | **2.6** | **−3.0** | **4.0** | **4.8** | **1.5** | **2.6** | **2.6** | **3.5** |
| Albania....................... | 914 | .... | .... | .... | .... | .... | .... | .... | .... | .... | .... | .... | .... |
| Bulgaria...................... | 918 | 6.6 | 7.2 | 6.8 | 7.7 | 5.6 | −4.2 | .1 | 1.6 | .2 | 1.3 | 1.5 | 3.0 |
| Croatia....................... | 960 | 4.1 | 4.2 | 4.8 | 5.2 | 2.1 | −7.4 | −1.7 | −.3 | −2.2 | −1.1 | −.4 | 1.6 |
| Estonia....................... | 939 | 7.2 | 9.4 | 10.1 | 7.5 | −3.7 | −14.3 | 2.3 | 9.5 | 4.7 | 1.6 | 2.1 | 1.9 |
| Hungary....................... | 944 | 4.9 | 4.4 | 3.8 | .4 | .8 | −6.6 | .7 | 1.8 | −1.7 | 1.9 | 3.7 | 2.9 |
| Macedonia, FYR................ | 962 | .5 | 4.4 | 5.0 | 6.1 | 5.0 | −.9 | 2.9 | 2.8 | −.4 | 3.1 | 9.6 | 3.7 |
| Poland........................ | 964 | 5.3 | 3.6 | 6.2 | 6.8 | 5.1 | 1.6 | 3.9 | 5.0 | 1.8 | 1.7 | 3.4 | .... |
| Romania....................... | 968 | 8.3 | 4.2 | 8.1 | 6.8 | 8.6 | −7.1 | −.8 | 1.1 | .6 | 3.4 | 2.8 | 4.1 |
| Turkey........................ | 186 | 9.4 | 8.4 | 6.9 | 4.7 | .7 | −4.8 | 9.2 | 8.8 | 2.2 | 4.1 | 2.9 | 4.1 |
| CIS........................... | 901 | **8.0** | **6.2** | **8.3** | **8.5** | **5.0** | **−8.2** | **4.6** | **4.5** | **3.0** | **1.2** | **.8** | **....** |
| Belarus....................... | 913 | 11.4 | 9.4 | 10.0 | 8.6 | 10.2 | .2 | 7.7 | 5.5 | 1.5 | 1.2 | 1.7 | −3.9 |
| Georgia....................... | 915 | 5.9 | 9.6 | 9.4 | 12.6 | 2.6 | −3.7 | 6.2 | 7.2 | 6.4 | 3.3 | 4.8 | .... |
| Kazakhstan.................... | 916 | 9.6 | 9.7 | 10.7 | 8.9 | 3.3 | 1.2 | .... | .... | .... | .... | .... | .... |
| Kyrgyz Republic............... | 917 | 7.0 | −.2 | 3.1 | 8.5 | 8.4 | 2.9 | −.5 | 6.0 | .6 | 10.8 | 4.3 | 3.5 |
| Russia........................ | 922 | 7.2 | 6.4 | 8.2 | 8.5 | 5.2 | −7.8 | 4.5 | 4.3 | 3.4 | 1.3 | .6 | .... |
| Ukraine....................... | 926 | 12.1 | 3.0 | 7.4 | 7.6 | 2.3 | −14.8 | 4.1 | 5.2 | .3 | — | .... | .... |

# GDP Volume Measures

| | | 2004 | 2005 | 2006 | 2007 | 2008 | 2009 | 2010 | 2011 | 2012 | 2013 | 2014 | 2015 |
|---|---|---|---|---|---|---|---|---|---|---|---|---|---|
| | | *Percent Change over Previous Year; Calculated from Indices* | | | | | | | | | | | |
| **Middle East,N.Africa & Pakistan** | 440 | **9.0** | **5.8** | **6.8** | **6.4** | **4.4** | **3.8** | **5.4** | **4.8** | **4.2** | **3.1** | .... | .... |
| Bahrain, Kingdom of...................... | 419 | 7.0 | 6.8 | 6.5 | 8.3 | 6.2 | 2.5 | 4.3 | 2.1 | 3.2 | 5.7 | 4.5 | .... |
| Egypt........................................... | 469 | 4.1 | 4.5 | 6.8 | 7.0 | 7.2 | 4.6 | 5.2 | 1.8 | 3.7 | 1.5 | .... | .... |
| Iran, I.R. of.................................. | 429 | 6.1 | 4.7 | 6.2 | 6.4 | .6 | 4.0 | 5.9 | .... | .... | .... | .... | .... |
| Jordan.......................................... | 439 | 8.6 | 8.1 | 8.1 | 8.8 | 7.7 | 1.8 | 3.1 | 4.4 | .... | .... | .... | .... |
| Kuwait......................................... | 443 | 10.2 | 10.6 | 7.5 | 6.0 | 2.5 | −7.1 | −2.4 | 9.6 | 6.6 | 1.1 | −1.6 | .... |
| Morocco....................................... | 686 | 4.8 | 3.3 | 7.6 | 3.5 | 5.9 | 4.2 | 3.8 | 5.2 | 3.0 | 4.7 | 2.4 | .... |
| Oman............................................ | 449 | 3.4 | 4.0 | 5.5 | 4.5 | 8.2 | 6.1 | 4.8 | −1.1 | 7.1 | 3.9 | 2.9 | .... |
| Pakistan....................................... | 564 | 7.4 | 7.7 | 6.2 | 4.8 | 1.7 | 2.8 | 1.6 | 2.7 | 3.5 | 4.4 | 4.7 | 5.5 |
| Saudi Arabia................................ | 456 | 9.3 | 7.3 | 5.6 | 6.0 | 8.4 | 1.8 | 7.4 | 10.0 | 5.4 | 2.7 | 3.6 | 3.5 |
| Syrian Arab Republic.................... | 463 | 6.9 | 6.2 | 5.0 | 5.7 | 4.5 | 6.0 | 3.2 | .... | .... | .... | .... | .... |
| Tunisia......................................... | 744 | 6.2 | 3.5 | 5.2 | 6.7 | 4.2 | 3.0 | 3.5 | −1.9 | 4.1 | 2.9 | 2.7 | .... |
| Yemen, Republic of...................... | 474 | 4.6 | 5.1 | 4.6 | 3.5 | 4.0 | 4.1 | 5.7 | −12.8 | 2.0 | .... | .... | .... |
| **Sub-Saharan Africa**................... | 603 | **5.7** | **5.5** | **5.2** | **5.8** | **−2.6** | **2.7** | **5.4** | **3.8** | **4.1** | **4.6** | .... | .... |
| CEMAC | | | | | | | | | | | | | |
| Cameroon.................................. | 622 | 3.7 | 2.3 | 3.2 | 3.3 | 2.9 | 1.9 | 3.3 | 4.1 | 4.6 | 5.6 | | |
| Congo. Rep. of.......................... | 634 | .... | .... | .... | .... | .... | .... | .... | .... | .... | .... | | |
| Equatorial Guinea..................... | 642 | 20.7 | 6.0 | .... | .... | .... | .... | .... | .... | .... | .... | | |
| WAEMU | | | | | | | | | | | | | |
| Benin........................................ | 638 | 3.1 | 2.9 | 3.8 | 4.6 | 5.0 | 2.7 | 2.6 | 3.3 | 5.4 | 5.6 | 5.7 | .... |
| Burkina Faso............................. | 748 | 3.9 | 7.1 | 5.5 | 3.6 | 35.1 | 3.0 | 8.4 | 6.6 | 6.5 | 6.6 | 4.0 | .... |
| Guinea Bissau........................... | 654 | 2.8 | 4.3 | 2.1 | 3.2 | 5.8 | 3.3 | 4.4 | 9.0 | −2.2 | .9 | 2.9 | .... |
| Niger........................................ | 692 | −.8 | 7.4 | 5.8 | 3.1 | 9.6 | −.7 | 8.4 | 2.3 | 11.8 | 4.6 | 6.9 | .... |
| Senegal..................................... | 722 | 5.8 | 5.7 | 2.5 | 4.9 | 4.0 | 2.4 | 4.2 | 1.8 | 4.4 | 3.6 | 4.7 | .... |
| Togo......................................... | 742 | 2.5 | 1.2 | 3.9 | 2.1 | 7.0 | 5.5 | −18.5 | 4.8 | 5.8 | 5.4 | 5.9 | .... |
| Angola........................................... | 614 | 11.1 | 15.7 | .... | .... | .... | .... | .... | .... | .... | .... | .... | .... |
| Botswana....................................... | 616 | 6.0 | 1.7 | 8.4 | 8.3 | 3.9 | −7.8 | 8.6 | 6.2 | 4.3 | 5.9 | .... | .... |
| Burundi......................................... | 618 | 4.4 | .9 | 5.4 | 3.5 | 4.9 | 3.8 | 4.8 | 4.2 | 4.2 | 4.8 | .... | .... |
| Cabo Verde.................................... | 624 | 4.3 | .... | .... | .... | .... | .... | .... | .... | .... | .... | .... | .... |
| Congo, Dem. Rep. of...................... | 636 | .... | .... | .... | .... | .... | .... | .... | .... | .... | .... | .... | .... |
| Gambia, The.................................. | 648 | .... | −.9 | 1.1 | 3.6 | 5.7 | 6.4 | 6.5 | −4.3 | 5.9 | 4.8 | .... | .... |
| Kenya............................................ | 664 | 5.1 | 5.9 | 6.3 | 7.0 | 1.5 | 2.7 | 5.8 | 4.4 | 4.6 | .... | .... | .... |
| Lesotho......................................... | 666 | 2.3 | 2.7 | 4.3 | 4.7 | 5.7 | 3.4 | 7.9 | 4.0 | 5.0 | 4.5 | 3.6 | .... |
| Madagascar.................................... | 674 | 5.3 | 4.6 | 5.0 | 6.2 | 7.1 | −4.1 | .4 | 1.4 | 3.0 | 2.3 | 3.3 | 3.0 |
| Malawi.......................................... | 676 | 5.4 | 3.3 | 4.7 | 9.6 | 7.6 | 8.3 | 6.9 | 2.9 | 1.9 | 5.4 | .... | .... |
| Mauritius...................................... | 684 | 4.3 | 1.5 | 4.5 | 6.6 | 5.5 | 3.1 | 4.1 | 3.9 | 3.2 | 3.1 | 3.6 | 3.5 |
| Mozambique.................................. | 688 | 7.9 | 8.4 | 8.7 | 7.3 | 6.9 | 6.4 | 6.7 | 7.1 | 7.2 | 7.1 | 7.4 | .... |
| Namibia......................................... | 728 | 12.3 | 2.5 | 7.1 | 61.5 | 2.6 | .3 | 6.0 | 5.1 | 5.2 | 5.1 | .... | .... |
| Nigeria.......................................... | 694 | .... | .... | .... | .... | .... | 6.9 | 7.8 | 4.9 | 4.3 | 5.4 | .... | .... |
| Rwanda......................................... | 714 | 7.5 | 9.6 | 9.0 | 7.6 | 11.2 | 6.2 | 7.2 | 8.2 | 8.0 | .... | .... | .... |
| Seychelles..................................... | 718 | .... | .... | .... | .... | .... | .... | .... | .... | .... | .... | .... | .... |
| Sierra Leone.................................. | 724 | 2.7 | 1.7 | 1.8 | 7.6 | 9.3 | 7.0 | 1.7 | 6.0 | 15.2 | 20.1 | 6.6 | .... |
| South Africa.................................. | 199 | 4.6 | 5.3 | 5.6 | 5.6 | 3.6 | −1.7 | 2.8 | 2.5 | 2.5 | 2.8 | 1.7 | 1.2 |
| South Sudan, Republic of.............. | 733 | .... | .... | .... | .... | .... | 5.0 | 5.5 | −4.6 | −46.1 | 26.7 | 16.1 | 2.0 |
| Swaziland...................................... | 734 | 2.5 | 2.2 | 2.8 | .... | .... | .... | .... | .... | .... | .... | .... | .... |
| Uganda.......................................... | 746 | 6.8 | 6.3 | 10.8 | 8.4 | 8.7 | 7.3 | 5.9 | 6.7 | 3.9 | 5.2 | .... | .... |
| Zambia.......................................... | 754 | 5.4 | 5.3 | 6.2 | 6.2 | 5.7 | 6.4 | 7.6 | 6.8 | 7.3 | 6.5 | .... | .... |
| Zimbabwe..................................... | 698 | −4.1 | .... | .... | .... | .... | .... | .... | .... | .... | .... | .... | .... |
| **Western Hemisphere**................. | 205 | **6.2** | **4.5** | **5.6** | **5.6** | **3.6** | **−1.2** | **6.1** | **4.9** | **3.1** | **3.0** | **1.2** | **−.2** |
| ECCU | | | | | | | | | | | | | |
| Anguilla.................................... | 312 | 14.1 | 13.1 | 20.3 | 13.3 | −1.5 | −18.4 | −4.3 | 5.0 | −6.7 | .... | | .... |
| Antigua and Barbuda................. | 311 | 5.4 | 5.0 | 12.9 | 6.5 | 1.8 | −8.9 | −6.3 | .... | .... | .... | | .... |
| Dominica................................... | 321 | 6.3 | 3.4 | 6.3 | 4.9 | 3.5 | −.8 | −.5 | .... | .... | .... | | .... |
| Montserrat................................ | 351 | 6.8 | .4 | −5.9 | 1.5 | 6.7 | 3.6 | .... | .... | .... | .... | | .... |
| St. Kitts and Nevis.................... | 361 | 3.8 | 9.2 | 3.5 | 5.0 | 4.0 | −5.6 | −2.7 | .... | .... | .... | | .... |
| St. Lucia................................... | 362 | 6.0 | −2.6 | 7.4 | 1.5 | 5.8 | −1.3 | 4.4 | .... | .... | .... | | .... |
| St. Vincent & Grenadines........... | 364 | 4.2 | 2.5 | 7.7 | 3.6 | 1.7 | −1.2 | −1.3 | .... | .... | .... | | .... |
| Argentina....................................... | 213 | 9.0 | 9.2 | 8.4 | 8.0 | 3.1 | .1 | 9.1 | 8.6 | .9 | 2.9 | .4 | .... |
| Aruba............................................ | 314 | 7.9 | 1.2 | 1.1 | 2.0 | .1 | −11.3 | −3.3 | 3.5 | −1.3 | 3.9 | | .... |
| Barbados....................................... | 316 | 1.4 | 4.0 | 5.7 | 1.7 | .3 | −4.1 | .3 | .8 | — | .... | | .... |
| Belize............................................ | 339 | 4.6 | 2.6 | 4.6 | 1.1 | 3.2 | .8 | 3.3 | 2.1 | 3.7 | 1.3 | 4.1 | 1.0 |
| Bolivia........................................... | 218 | 4.2 | 4.4 | 4.8 | 4.6 | 6.1 | 3.4 | 4.1 | 5.2 | 5.1 | 6.8 | 5.5 | 4.8 |
| Brazil............................................ | 223 | 5.7 | 3.2 | 4.0 | 6.1 | 5.2 | −.3 | 7.5 | 2.7 | .... | .... | | |
| Chile............................................. | 228 | 7.0 | 6.2 | 5.7 | 5.2 | 3.3 | −1.0 | 5.8 | 5.8 | 5.5 | 4.0 | 1.9 | 2.1 |
| Colombia....................................... | 233 | 5.3 | 4.7 | 6.7 | 6.9 | 3.5 | 1.5 | 4.3 | .... | .... | .... | | |
| Costa Rica..................................... | 238 | 4.3 | 5.9 | 8.8 | 7.9 | 2.7 | −1.0 | 5.0 | 4.4 | 5.1 | 3.6 | 3.5 | .... |
| Dominican Republic....................... | 243 | 1.3 | 9.3 | 10.7 | 8.5 | 3.1 | .9 | 8.3 | 2.8 | 2.6 | 4.8 | 7.3 | 7.0 |
| Ecuador......................................... | 248 | 8.2 | 5.3 | 4.4 | 2.2 | 6.4 | .6 | 3.5 | 7.9 | 5.6 | 4.6 | 3.7 | .3 |
| El Salvador.................................... | 253 | 1.9 | 3.6 | 3.9 | 3.8 | 1.3 | −3.1 | 1.4 | 2.2 | 1.9 | 1.8 | 1.4 | 2.5 |
| Guatemala..................................... | 258 | 3.2 | 3.3 | 5.4 | 6.3 | 3.3 | .5 | 2.9 | 4.2 | 3.0 | 3.7 | 4.3 | 4.1 |
| Guyana.......................................... | 336 | 2.5 | .... | .... | .... | .... | .... | .... | .... | .... | .... | | |
| Haiti.............................................. | 263 | −3.5 | 1.8 | 2.3 | 3.3 | .8 | 3.1 | −5.5 | 5.5 | 2.9 | .... | | |
| Honduras....................................... | 268 | 6.2 | 6.1 | 6.6 | 6.2 | 4.2 | −2.4 | 3.7 | 3.8 | 4.1 | 2.8 | 3.1 | 3.6 |
| Jamaica......................................... | 343 | 1.3 | .9 | 2.9 | 1.4 | −.8 | −3.4 | −1.5 | 1.4 | −.5 | .2 | .5 | .9 |
| Mexico........................................... | 273 | 4.2 | 3.1 | 5.0 | 3.2 | 1.4 | −4.7 | 5.2 | 3.9 | 4.0 | 1.4 | 2.2 | 2.6 |
| Nicaragua...................................... | 278 | 5.3 | 4.3 | 4.2 | 5.0 | 4.0 | −2.2 | 3.6 | 5.4 | 5.2 | .... | | |
| Panama.......................................... | 283 | 7.5 | 7.2 | 8.5 | 12.1 | 8.6 | 1.6 | 5.8 | 11.8 | 9.2 | 6.6 | 6.1 | .... |
| Paraguay....................................... | 288 | 4.1 | 2.1 | 4.8 | 5.4 | 6.4 | −4.0 | 13.1 | 4.3 | −1.2 | 14.3 | 4.2 | .... |
| Peru.............................................. | 293 | 5.6 | 6.3 | 7.5 | 8.5 | 9.1 | 1.0 | 8.5 | 6.5 | 6.0 | 5.8 | 2.3 | .... |
| Suriname....................................... | 366 | 8.5 | 4.5 | 3.8 | 5.1 | 4.1 | 3.0 | 5.2 | 5.3 | 3.1 | 2.8 | 1.8 | .2 |

# GDP Volume Measures

| | | 2004 | 2005 | 2006 | 2007 | 2008 | 2009 | 2010 | 2011 | 2012 | 2013 | 2014 | 2015 |
|---|---|---|---|---|---|---|---|---|---|---|---|---|---|
| | | | | | *Percent Change over Previous Year; Calculated from Indices* | | | | | | | | |
| **Western Hemisphere(Cont.)** | | | | | | | | | | | | | |
| Trinidad and Tobago..................... | **369** | 8.0 | 5.4 | 14.1 | 4.8 | 2.4 | −3.4 | .2 | −1.6 | 1.5 | 2.8 | .... | .... |
| Uruguay....................................... | **298** | 5.0 | 7.5 | 4.1 | 6.5 | 7.2 | 4.2 | 7.8 | 5.2 | 3.5 | 4.6 | 3.2 | 1.0 |
| Venezuela, Rep. Bol...................... | **299** | 18.3 | 10.3 | 9.9 | 8.8 | 5.3 | −3.2 | −1.5 | 4.2 | 5.6 | 1.3 | −3.9 | .... |

# GDP Deflators

| | | 2004 | 2005 | 2006 | 2007 | 2008 | 2009 | 2010 | 2011 | 2012 | 2013 | 2014 | 2015 |
|---|---|---|---|---|---|---|---|---|---|---|---|---|---|
| | | *Percent Change over Previous Year; Calculated from Indices* | | | | | | | | | | | |
| **World** | 001 | **5.0** | **4.9** | **4.5** | **4.9** | **4.7** | **1.5** | **4.9** | **5.1** | **2.7** | **2.7** | **1.5** | **1.1** |
| **Advanced Economies** | 110 | **2.1** | **2.2** | **2.1** | **2.3** | **1.9** | **.7** | **1.0** | **1.4** | **1.2** | **1.2** | **1.3** | **1.1** |
| Euro Area | 163 | 1.9 | 1.9 | 1.8 | 2.3 | 1.8 | 1.1 | .7 | 1.2 | 1.4 | 1.5 | 4.2 | 1.1 |
| Austria | 122 | 1.8 | 2.6 | 1.9 | 2.3 | 1.8 | 1.1 | .9 | 1.8 | 1.9 | 1.5 | 1.6 | 1.7 |
| Belgium | 124 | 2.2 | 2.3 | 2.5 | 2.3 | 1.9 | 1.1 | 2.0 | 2.2 | 2.1 | 1.5 | .6 | -.6 |
| Cyprus | 423 | 3.2 | 2.3 | 3.1 | 3.5 | 17.1 | .2 | 2.0 | 1.8 | 2.1 | -1.3 | -1.2 | -1.4 |
| Finland | 172 | .6 | .9 | .9 | 2.8 | 3.1 | 1.9 | .4 | 2.6 | 3.0 | 3.1 | 1.1 | .9 |
| France | 132 | 1.7 | 1.9 | 2.1 | 2.6 | 2.4 | .1 | 1.1 | 1.0 | 1.0 | 1.0 | .8 | .7 |
| Germany | 134 | 1.6 | .5 | .1 | 1.6 | 1.1 | 1.7 | .9 | 1.0 | 1.3 | 1.8 | 1.7 | 2.6 |
| Greece | 174 | 3.4 | 1.9 | 3.3 | 3.4 | 4.3 | 2.6 | .7 | .8 | -.4 | -2.5 | -2.2 | -.6 |
| Ireland | 178 | 2.6 | 2.4 | 2.3 | 1.0 | -2.7 | -4.3 | -2.3 | 2.0 | .4 | 1.2 | .1 | 5.3 |
| Italy | 136 | 2.8 | 1.7 | 1.8 | 2.6 | 2.5 | 2.0 | .4 | 1.3 | .9 | 1.6 | 1.1 | .6 |
| Latvia | 941 | 6.8 | 11.2 | 12.5 | 20.2 | 11.8 | -9.8 | -1.0 | 6.4 | 3.6 | 1.1 | 1.4 | .6 |
| Lithuania | 946 | 3.3 | 6.9 | 6.7 | 8.6 | 9.7 | -3.3 | 2.3 | 5.2 | 2.7 | 1.3 | .8 | .9 |
| Luxembourg | 137 | 1.9 | 3.8 | 6.7 | 1.4 | 3.9 | 1.6 | 3.7 | 5.0 | 3.5 | 1.4 | -1.5 | 5.5 |
| Malta | 181 | 2.2 | 3.1 | 8.5 | 2.8 | 3.0 | 3.0 | 2.7 | 3.8 | 2.3 | 2.0 | 1.9 | 1.8 |
| Netherlands | 138 | 1.4 | 1.9 | 2.6 | 2.1 | 2.5 | .4 | .8 | .1 | 1.4 | 1.4 | .8 | .3 |
| Portugal | 182 | 2.4 | 3.3 | 3.2 | 3.0 | 1.7 | 1.1 | .6 | -.3 | -.4 | 2.3 | 1.0 | 1.9 |
| Slovak Republic | 936 | 6.0 | 2.3 | 2.7 | 1.2 | 2.1 | -1.4 | .5 | 1.6 | 1.3 | .5 | -.2 | -.3 |
| Slovenia | 961 | 3.3 | 1.5 | 2.0 | 4.2 | 4.5 | 3.4 | -1.0 | 1.1 | .3 | .8 | .8 | .4 |
| Spain | 184 | 3.9 | 4.1 | 4.0 | 3.3 | 2.1 | .3 | .2 | .1 | .2 | .7 | -.5 | .4 |
| Australia | 193 | 3.5 | 4.5 | 5.1 | 4.4 | 6.4 | .2 | 5.4 | 4.4 | -.2 | 1.2 | .2 | -.7 |
| Canada | 156 | 3.0 | 2.8 | 2.5 | 4.3 | 3.6 | -1.8 | 3.0 | 2.8 | 3.9 | 1.2 | 2.6 | -.6 |
| China, P.R.: Hong Kong | 532 | -3.6 | -.2 | -.5 | 3.1 | 1.3 | -.4 | .3 | 3.9 | 3.5 | 1.8 | 2.9 | 3.6 |
| Czech Republic | 935 | 4.0 | .1 | .7 | 3.5 | 2.0 | 2.6 | -1.5 | -.2 | 1.4 | 1.4 | 2.5 | .7 |
| Denmark | 128 | 2.1 | 2.9 | 2.2 | 2.5 | 4.1 | .5 | 3.2 | .8 | 2.5 | 1.5 | .6 | 1.3 |
| Iceland | 176 | 2.6 | 3.6 | 8.9 | 4.5 | 11.0 | 7.5 | 6.0 | 3.0 | 3.3 | 1.7 | 4.1 | 5.6 |
| Israel | 436 | — | 1.2 | 1.5 | 1.0 | 2.3 | 3.9 | 1.5 | 1.8 | 3.9 | 2.2 | 1.0 | 5.2 |
| Japan | 158 | -1.3 | -1.3 | -1.1 | -.9 | -1.2 | -.5 | -2.2 | -1.9 | -.9 | .2 | 1.6 | .... |
| Korea | 542 | 3.0 | 1.0 | -.1 | 2.4 | 3.0 | 3.5 | 3.2 | 1.6 | 1.0 | .9 | .6 | 2.2 |
| New Zealand | 196 | 3.6 | 2.0 | 3.0 | 4.7 | 3.1 | .5 | 3.7 | 2.1 | -.5 | 4.4 | .5 | .7 |
| Norway | 142 | 5.9 | 8.9 | 8.7 | 2.8 | 10.6 | -5.4 | 6.2 | 7.1 | 2.9 | 2.5 | 2.6 | -4.5 |
| Singapore | 576 | 4.2 | 2.2 | 1.7 | 5.9 | -1.5 | 3.5 | — | 1.2 | 1.2 | -.1 | .2 | .... |
| Sweden | 144 | .4 | .8 | 1.8 | 2.9 | 3.3 | 2.4 | 1.0 | 1.2 | 1.1 | 1.1 | 1.6 | 1.9 |
| Switzerland | 146 | .3 | .7 | 1.9 | 2.3 | 1.8 | .5 | .2 | .2 | -.2 | -.1 | — | .... |
| United Kingdom | 112 | 2.9 | 2.6 | 3.1 | 2.8 | 3.0 | 1.9 | 3.5 | 1.8 | 1.1 | 1.3 | 1.7 | 1.7 |
| United States | 111 | 2.7 | 3.2 | 3.1 | 2.7 | 2.0 | .8 | 1.2 | 2.1 | 1.8 | 1.6 | 1.6 | 1.0 |
| **Emerging & Dev. Economies** | 200 | **9.4** | **8.9** | **8.0** | **8.9** | **9.0** | **2.5** | **9.5** | **9.7** | **4.5** | **4.4** | **1.7** | **1.2** |
| **Emerging & Developing Asia** | 505 | **6.1** | **5.9** | **5.5** | **8.2** | **8.8** | **1.9** | **7.8** | **7.8** | **2.4** | **3.3** | **-2.3** | **—** |
| Bangladesh | 513 | 4.2 | 5.1 | 22.0 | 6.5 | 7.9 | 6.8 | 7.1 | 7.0 | 9.0 | 7.2 | 5.7 | 5.9 |
| Bhutan | 514 | -.1 | -2.3 | 16.9 | -6.0 | 10.9 | 1.5 | 7.1 | 13.8 | 12.3 | 12.0 | -4.3 | .... |
| Brunei Darussalam | 516 | 15.9 | 18.8 | 10.0 | 1.1 | 12.7 | -22.1 | 5.3 | 19.4 | .8 | -3.2 | 10.1 | .... |
| Cambodia | 522 | 4.8 | 6.1 | 4.6 | 6.5 | 12.3 | 2.5 | 3.1 | 3.4 | 1.4 | .8 | 3.1 | .... |
| China, P.R.: Mainland | 924 | 6.9 | 4.6 | 4.2 | 7.2 | 7.4 | -.3 | 7.0 | 7.4 | .7 | 2.0 | -6.3 | -.5 |
| China, P.R.: Macao | 546 | 2.1 | 5.6 | 7.8 | 8.8 | 10.1 | .9 | 4.8 | 7.5 | 6.9 | 7.7 | 8.6 | 4.4 |
| Fiji | 819 | 2.3 | 7.7 | 3.1 | 3.2 | 4.3 | .5 | 4.3 | 7.1 | 3.3 | 2.3 | 5.1 | .... |
| India | 534 | 5.9 | 4.2 | 6.4 | 6.0 | 8.5 | 6.1 | 8.5 | 5.2 | 7.8 | 6.0 | 3.2 | .... |
| Indonesia | 536 | 8.6 | 14.3 | 14.1 | 11.3 | 18.1 | 8.3 | 15.3 | 7.5 | 3.8 | 5.0 | 5.4 | 4.2 |
| Lao People's Dem. Rep. | 544 | 22.3 | 7.8 | 6.5 | 3.9 | 6.6 | -4.5 | 10.1 | 7.6 | 4.1 | 5.4 | .... | .... |
| Malaysia | 548 | 6.0 | 8.9 | 4.0 | 4.9 | 10.4 | -6.0 | 7.3 | 5.4 | 1.0 | .2 | 2.5 | -.4 |
| Maldives | 556 | 1.8 | 1.4 | 9.8 | 7.5 | 7.3 | 7.6 | .9 | 10.6 | 5.5 | .... | 3.0 | .... |
| Mongolia | 948 | 16.4 | 19.2 | 23.0 | 12.6 | 20.9 | .2 | 21.1 | 12.3 | 16.6 | 18.2 | .... | .... |
| Myanmar | 518 | .... | .... | .... | .... | .... | .... | .... | .... | .... | .... | .... | .... |
| Nepal | 558 | 4.2 | 6.1 | 7.4 | 7.6 | 5.6 | 15.9 | 15.1 | 10.8 | 6.6 | 6.4 | 8.1 | .... |
| Papua New Guinea | 853 | 4.0 | .... | .... | .... | .... | .... | .... | .... | .... | .... | .... | .... |
| Philippines | 566 | 5.5 | 5.8 | 4.9 | 3.1 | 7.5 | 2.8 | 4.2 | 4.0 | 2.0 | 2.0 | 3.2 | -.6 |
| Samoa | 862 | 3.7 | .... | .... | .... | .... | .... | .... | .... | .... | .... | .... | .... |
| Solomon Islands | 813 | .... | .... | .... | .... | .... | .... | .... | .... | .... | .... | .... | .... |
| Sri Lanka | 524 | 8.8 | 10.4 | 11.3 | 14.0 | 16.3 | 5.9 | 7.3 | 7.9 | 8.9 | 6.7 | 5.1 | .... |
| Thailand | 578 | 3.3 | 4.6 | 4.7 | 3.6 | 3.8 | 1.9 | 3.7 | 4.2 | 10.0 | 1.7 | 1.0 | .3 |
| Tonga | 866 | 5.6 | 6.7 | 17.2 | 6.3 | 7.3 | -2.4 | 3.7 | 5.8 | 2.3 | .... | .... | .... |
| Vanuatu | 846 | 2.1 | .4 | 3.9 | 5.5 | 7.3 | 2.3 | 2.6 | 3.1 | .4 | 2.7 | .... | .... |
| Vietnam | 582 | 8.2 | 17.8 | 8.6 | 9.6 | 22.7 | 6.2 | 12.1 | 21.3 | 10.9 | 4.8 | 3.7 | .... |
| **Europe** | 170 | **14.6** | **13.4** | **11.6** | **10.5** | **16.2** | **3.8** | **8.9** | **15.1** | **7.9** | **4.8** | **7.6** | **....** |
| **Emerging & Dev. Europe** | 903 | **9.0** | **6.3** | **7.7** | **7.3** | **9.3** | **3.8** | **4.3** | **6.1** | **4.4** | **3.7** | **5.4** | **4.8** |
| Albania | 914 | .... | .... | .... | .... | .... | .... | .... | .... | .... | .... | .... | .... |
| Bulgaria | 918 | 5.6 | 6.5 | 6.7 | 11.1 | 8.2 | 4.0 | 1.2 | 6.9 | 1.6 | -.7 | .4 | .3 |
| Croatia | 960 | 3.7 | 3.4 | 4.0 | 4.1 | 5.7 | 2.8 | .8 | 1.7 | 1.6 | .8 | — | .1 |
| Estonia | 939 | 3.6 | 5.5 | 8.8 | 10.0 | 6.5 | -1.1 | 1.8 | 4.6 | 2.7 | 4.5 | 2.1 | 2.8 |
| Hungary | 944 | 5.0 | 2.4 | 3.5 | 5.4 | 5.0 | 3.9 | 2.3 | 2.2 | 3.5 | 3.1 | 3.2 | 1.8 |
| Macedonia, FYR | 962 | 4.9 | 3.8 | 3.3 | 7.4 | 7.5 | .7 | 2.7 | 3.1 | .1 | .3 | 1.2 | 2.7 |
| Poland | 964 | 4.1 | 2.6 | 1.5 | 4.0 | 3.1 | 3.7 | 1.4 | 2.8 | 2.6 | .6 | 2.2 | .... |
| Romania | 968 | 15.7 | 12.1 | 10.4 | 13.0 | 13.9 | 4.8 | 5.4 | 5.3 | 4.6 | 3.6 | 3.2 | 2.4 |
| Turkey | 186 | 12.4 | 7.1 | 9.3 | 6.2 | 12.0 | 5.3 | 5.7 | 8.6 | 6.8 | 6.3 | 8.3 | 7.4 |
| **CIS** | 901 | **19.4** | **19.9** | **14.9** | **13.4** | **22.3** | **3.7** | **13.0** | **23.6** | **11.0** | **5.7** | **9.1** | **....** |
| Belarus | 913 | 22.7 | 18.9 | 10.8 | 12.8 | 21.2 | 5.7 | 11.1 | 71.2 | 75.8 | 20.9 | 17.8 | 16.3 |
| Georgia | 915 | 8.4 | 7.9 | 8.5 | 9.5 | 9.4 | -2.0 | 8.6 | 9.5 | 1.0 | -.7 | 3.8 | .... |
| Kazakhstan | 916 | 20.0 | 18.9 | 21.1 | 13.1 | 25.5 | -1.0 | .... | .... | .... | .... | .... | .... |

# GDP Deflators

| | | 2004 | 2005 | 2006 | 2007 | 2008 | 2009 | 2010 | 2011 | 2012 | 2013 | 2014 | 2015 |
|---|---|---|---|---|---|---|---|---|---|---|---|---|---|
| **CIS(Cont.)** | | | | | | | | | | | | | |
| Kyrgyz Republic.......... | 917 | 5.1 | 7.2 | 9.4 | 14.9 | 22.2 | 4.0 | 10.1 | 22.5 | 7.9 | 3.2 | 8.1 | 2.1 |
| Russia.......... | 922 | 20.3 | 19.3 | 14.6 | 12.4 | 21.1 | 2.3 | 13.2 | 15.5 | 8.1 | 5.1 | 6.6 | .... |
| Ukraine.......... | 926 | 15.0 | 24.2 | 15.0 | 23.6 | 28.9 | 12.1 | 9.4 | 14.5 | 7.7 | 4.4 | .... | .... |
| **Middle East,N.Africa & Pakistan** | 440 | **11.2** | **15.2** | **10.6** | **10.9** | **17.3** | **−2.7** | **11.5** | **14.5** | **5.4** | **3.7** | | |
| Bahrain, Kingdom of.... | 419 | 11.0 | 13.7 | 8.8 | 8.4 | 11.4 | −13.0 | 7.4 | 10.6 | 1.3 | 2.5 | −1.5 | .... |
| Egypt.......... | 469 | 11.7 | 6.2 | 7.4 | 12.6 | 12.2 | 11.2 | 10.1 | 11.7 | 8.4 | 20.5 | .... | .... |
| Iran, I.R. of.......... | 429 | 21.7 | 19.1 | 14.3 | 20.6 | 16.9 | 2.5 | 14.4 | .... | .... | .... | .... | .... |
| Jordan.......... | 439 | 2.9 | 2.2 | 10.7 | 4.4 | 19.3 | 6.5 | 12.0 | .4 | .... | .... | .... | .... |
| Kuwait.......... | 443 | 11.4 | 21.8 | 16.2 | 4.3 | 18.7 | −17.2 | 11.1 | 17.2 | 7.5 | .2 | −4.2 | .... |
| Morocco.......... | 686 | 1.2 | 1.2 | 1.5 | 3.6 | 4.5 | .1 | 1.0 | −.7 | .4 | 1.5 | .2 | .... |
| Oman.......... | 449 | 10.8 | 20.4 | 14.1 | 8.3 | 33.8 | −25.1 | 15.6 | 17.1 | 4.9 | −1.4 | 1.7 | .... |
| Pakistan.......... | 564 | 7.8 | 7.0 | 10.5 | 8.5 | 16.1 | 25.3 | 10.9 | 19.6 | 6.0 | 7.0 | 6.9 | 3.5 |
| Saudi Arabia.......... | 456 | 10.4 | 18.3 | 8.6 | 4.2 | 15.3 | −18.9 | 14.3 | 15.6 | 4.0 | −1.2 | −2.3 | −17.2 |
| Syrian Arab Republic.... | 463 | 10.3 | 12.0 | 7.7 | 12.0 | 15.9 | −2.8 | 3.3 | .... | .... | .... | .... | .... |
| Tunisia.......... | 744 | 3.8 | 15.8 | 3.8 | 2.1 | 6.3 | 3.4 | 3.5 | 4.3 | 4.8 | 3.8 | 4.7 | .... |
| Yemen, Republic of.... | 474 | 10.9 | 20.2 | 17.8 | 9.6 | 14.5 | −8.7 | 11.2 | 12.2 | 1.4 | .... | .... | .... |
| **Sub-Saharan Africa.......** | 603 | **9.8** | **10.7** | **9.8** | **10.4** | **−29.6** | **5.0** | **27.7** | **8.7** | **7.1** | **5.7** | | |
| Cameroon.......... | 622 | 1.5 | 2.6 | 3.9 | 1.1 | 3.6 | 3.7 | 2.6 | 3.0 | 3.0 | 2.4 | .... | .... |
| Congo, Rep. of.......... | 634 | .... | .... | .... | .... | .... | .... | .... | .... | .... | .... | | |
| Equatorial Guinea.......... | 642 | 30.5 | 42.1 | .... | .... | .... | .... | .... | .... | .... | .... | | |
| WAEMU | | | | | | | | | | | | | |
| Benin.......... | 638 | .4 | 4.4 | 3.2 | 2.5 | 7.2 | 2.0 | 1.9 | 2.5 | 6.2 | .9 | 1.6 | .... |
| Burkina Faso.......... | 748 | .6 | 5.3 | — | 3.0 | −14.5 | 2.4 | 3.8 | 6.7 | 5.8 | −1.5 | −.6 | .... |
| Guinea Bissau.......... | 654 | −1.5 | 5.8 | −2.1 | 4.4 | 9.7 | −2.5 | 3.1 | 13.8 | 7.5 | 3.6 | 1.1 | .... |
| Niger.......... | 692 | −.1 | 8.1 | 1.4 | 4.4 | 7.5 | 6.1 | 2.6 | 4.4 | 4.8 | 2.2 | .7 | .... |
| Senegal.......... | 722 | .6 | 2.4 | 4.0 | 5.4 | 6.6 | −1.5 | 1.6 | 4.1 | 2.6 | −1.9 | .1 | .... |
| Togo.......... | 742 | −5.3 | −.3 | −1.7 | 1.6 | 8.7 | 1.6 | 30.9 | −.4 | 6.1 | −1.5 | 3.5 | .... |
| Angola.......... | 614 | 42.8 | 39.7 | .... | .... | .... | .... | .... | .... | .... | .... | | |
| Botswana.......... | 616 | 11.2 | 5.8 | 7.5 | 4.9 | 8.7 | 3.4 | 18.9 | 5.5 | 1.6 | 5.9 | .... | .... |
| Burundi.......... | 618 | 11.2 | 60.0 | 2.8 | 8.2 | 24.2 | 10.1 | 9.2 | 8.2 | 14.6 | 8.1 | .... | .... |
| Cabo Verde.......... | 624 | −1.0 | .... | .... | .... | .... | .... | .... | .... | .... | .... | | |
| Congo, Dem. Rep. of.......... | 636 | .... | .... | .... | .... | .... | .... | .... | .... | .... | .... | | |
| Ethiopia.......... | 644 | 3.9 | 9.9 | 11.6 | 17.2 | 30.3 | 24.2 | 1.6 | 28.3 | .... | .... | | |
| Kenya.......... | 664 | 7.1 | 4.9 | 7.8 | 5.6 | 13.2 | 9.3 | 2.0 | 14.4 | 7.9 | .... | | |
| Lesotho.......... | 666 | 6.3 | 6.3 | 6.6 | 11.1 | 13.2 | 4.1 | 2.4 | 10.0 | 1.7 | 4.7 | 6.7 | .... |
| Madagascar.......... | 674 | 14.3 | 18.3 | 11.5 | 9.6 | 9.1 | 8.5 | 8.6 | 8.2 | 5.5 | 5.1 | 6.6 | 7.6 |
| Malawi.......... | 676 | 14.8 | 10.7 | 20.0 | 4.1 | 12.0 | 7.9 | 12.1 | 4.0 | 21.3 | 28.5 | .... | .... |
| Mauritius.......... | 684 | 6.9 | 4.3 | 6.7 | 7.2 | 6.6 | −.2 | 1.8 | 3.9 | 3.2 | 3.3 | 2.0 | .7 |
| Mozambique.......... | 688 | 7.5 | 8.8 | 9.3 | 25.2 | 8.0 | 1.1 | 7.6 | 3.3 | 5.9 | 3.9 | 2.6 | .... |
| Namibia.......... | 728 | 1.9 | 5.5 | 9.3 | −29.4 | 10.6 | 7.3 | 3.5 | 3.9 | 12.8 | 11.1 | .... | .... |
| Nigeria.......... | 694 | .... | .... | .... | .... | .... | −4.6 | 107.5 | 9.5 | 9.3 | 5.9 | .... | .... |
| Rwanda.......... | 714 | 13.1 | 8.9 | 21.3 | 11.5 | 13.5 | 3.1 | 4.1 | 8.3 | 5.0 | .... | | |
| Seychelles.......... | 718 | .... | .... | .... | .... | .... | .... | .... | .... | .... | .... | | |
| Sierra Leone.......... | 724 | 16.9 | 19.6 | 15.2 | 7.0 | 5.3 | 4.8 | 23.1 | 17.3 | 12.0 | 7.6 | 4.6 | .... |
| South Africa.......... | 199 | 5.9 | 6.9 | 6.5 | 8.1 | 8.9 | 7.2 | 8.1 | 8.5 | 3.8 | 4.3 | 10.2 | 5.1 |
| South Sudan, Republic of.......... | 733 | .... | .... | .... | .... | .... | −17.3 | 21.6 | 54.1 | 6.7 | 4.0 | 1.0 | 11.4 |
| Swaziland.......... | 734 | 10.7 | 2.8 | 18.1 | .... | .... | .... | .... | .... | .... | .... | | |
| Tanzania.......... | 738 | 7.0 | 6.4 | 5.3 | 39.3 | 14.3 | 11.2 | 6.1 | 10.2 | 12.2 | 10.0 | .... | .... |
| Uganda.......... | 746 | 5.2 | 7.9 | 2.4 | 7.7 | 6.2 | 14.6 | 9.5 | 5.0 | 23.5 | 5.3 | .... | .... |
| Zambia.......... | 754 | 34.8 | 13.7 | 18.8 | −.2 | 5.2 | 20.8 | 21.2 | 12.8 | 7.2 | 16.8 | .... | .... |
| Zimbabwe.......... | 698 | 349.5 | .... | .... | .... | .... | .... | .... | .... | .... | .... | | |
| **Western Hemisphere.......** | 205 | **11.1** | **7.8** | **8.3** | **7.3** | **9.6** | **5.3** | **9.4** | **8.9** | **6.6** | **7.1** | **9.3** | **5.1** |
| ECCU | | | | | | | | | | | | | |
| Anguilla.......... | 312 | 3.8 | .7 | 3.2 | 10.3 | 1.2 | −2.3 | −.7 | 4.8 | 3.3 | .... | | |
| Antigua and Barbuda.......... | 311 | 1.5 | 5.7 | .8 | 6.6 | 2.7 | −1.7 | .5 | .... | .... | .... | | |
| Dominica.......... | 321 | .7 | −4.4 | 1.1 | 2.8 | 5.7 | 7.2 | −.7 | .... | .... | .... | | |
| Montserrat.......... | 351 | — | 10.4 | 12.2 | 3.3 | −.5 | −.1 | .... | .... | .... | .... | | |
| St. Kitts and Nevis.......... | 361 | 4.3 | −.8 | 13.2 | 2.4 | 3.2 | 2.2 | .4 | .... | .... | .... | | |
| St. Lucia.......... | 362 | 3.7 | 8.5 | 5.4 | 6.3 | −3.2 | 1.8 | 1.3 | .... | .... | .... | | |
| St. Vincent & Grenadines.......... | 364 | 4.0 | 3.0 | 3.0 | 8.1 | — | −1.8 | 2.3 | .... | .... | .... | | |
| Argentina.......... | 213 | 9.2 | 8.8 | 13.5 | 14.9 | 23.9 | 10.3 | 15.4 | 17.6 | 16.4 | 49.9 | 32.0 | .... |
| Aruba.......... | 314 | 2.2 | 3.4 | 2.8 | 6.2 | 6.3 | .9 | 2.2 | −.2 | .7 | −1.7 | .... | .... |
| Barbados.......... | 316 | 5.8 | 6.6 | 4.9 | 2.9 | .3 | 5.5 | −3.7 | −2.2 | −3.3 | .... | | |
| Belize.......... | 339 | 2.1 | 2.7 | 4.5 | 4.8 | 2.7 | −3.1 | 1.1 | 4.2 | 2.0 | 1.9 | 1.6 | .... |
| Bolivia.......... | 218 | 8.0 | 5.9 | 13.7 | 7.4 | 10.4 | −2.4 | 8.8 | 14.6 | 7.1 | 6.0 | 2.0 | −4.6 |
| Brazil.......... | 223 | 8.0 | 7.2 | 6.1 | 5.9 | 8.3 | 7.2 | 8.2 | 7.0 | .... | .... | | |
| Chile.......... | 228 | 7.5 | 7.1 | 12.7 | 4.8 | .5 | 3.8 | 8.8 | 3.3 | .9 | 2.3 | 5.6 | 4.3 |
| Colombia.......... | 233 | 7.3 | 5.6 | 5.8 | 5.0 | 7.6 | 3.4 | 3.9 | 6.7 | 3.0 | 2.0 | 2.1 | 2.6 |
| Costa Rica.......... | 238 | 11.8 | 10.6 | 11.0 | 9.4 | 12.4 | 8.4 | 8.0 | 4.1 | 4.0 | 5.5 | 3.9 | .... |
| Dominican Republic.......... | 243 | 45.2 | 2.7 | 5.4 | 12.8 | 10.4 | 3.4 | 5.6 | 9.0 | 4.4 | 2.7 | 1.4 | 1.4 |
| Ecuador.......... | 248 | 4.3 | 7.7 | 8.0 | 6.7 | 13.8 | .7 | 7.5 | 5.7 | 5.0 | 3.1 | 2.7 | −.3 |
| El Salvador.......... | 253 | 3.1 | 4.5 | 4.4 | 4.4 | 5.3 | −.5 | 2.3 | 5.7 | 1.0 | .4 | 1.4 | .7 |
| Guatemala.......... | 258 | 6.1 | 5.6 | 5.0 | 7.1 | 9.4 | 3.5 | 5.1 | 6.9 | 3.3 | 3.4 | 2.9 | 3.3 |
| Guyana.......... | 336 | 5.9 | .... | .... | .... | .... | .... | .... | .... | .... | .... | | |
| Haiti.......... | 263 | 21.5 | 17.6 | 14.8 | 8.0 | 12.9 | 3.7 | 5.5 | 7.5 | 5.3 | .... | | |
| Honduras.......... | 268 | 6.5 | 7.3 | 5.3 | 6.6 | 7.8 | 7.7 | 4.7 | 7.8 | 3.6 | 1.4 | 5.5 | 4.9 |
| Jamaica.......... | 343 | 12.9 | 11.5 | 8.8 | 11.3 | 13.6 | 10.6 | 9.8 | 6.0 | 6.4 | 8.7 | 7.5 | 5.1 |
| Mexico.......... | 273 | 8.4 | 5.2 | 6.3 | 5.0 | 6.1 | 3.4 | 4.5 | 5.4 | 3.2 | 1.6 | 4.7 | 2.7 |
| Nicaragua.......... | 278 | 9.1 | 9.9 | 40.4 | 9.9 | 15.0 | 5.9 | 5.7 | 11.1 | 7.0 | .... | | |
| Panama.......... | 283 | 2.0 | 1.7 | 2.1 | 9.1 | 7.7 | 6.7 | 2.8 | 6.3 | 6.4 | 5.3 | 3.4 | .... |
| Paraguay.......... | 288 | 9.0 | 10.1 | 6.1 | 9.8 | 9.3 | 2.0 | 6.1 | 9.8 | 5.5 | −3.8 | 6.3 | .... |
| Peru.......... | 293 | 2.0 | 2.1 | 8.3 | 2.4 | 1.9 | 1.6 | 6.0 | 5.2 | 2.1 | 1.7 | 2.8 | .... |

# GDP Deflators

| | | 2004 | 2005 | 2006 | 2007 | 2008 | 2009 | 2010 | 2011 | 2012 | 2013 | 2014 | 2015 |
|---|---|---|---|---|---|---|---|---|---|---|---|---|---|
| | | | | | | | *Percent Change over Previous Year; Calculated from Indices* | | | | | | |
| **Western Hemisphere(Cont.)** | | | | | | | | | | | | | |
| Suriname........................... | 366 | 12.9 | 15.5 | 41.7 | 6.4 | 15.5 | 6.9 | 6.3 | .... | .... | .... | .... | .... |
| Trinidad and Tobago.................... | 369 | 9.6 | 13.9 | 1.2 | 12.8 | 25.0 | −28.3 | 8.0 | 16.9 | −2.5 | 2.6 | .... | .... |
| Uruguay............................ | 298 | 10.1 | .7 | 6.5 | 9.4 | 8.0 | 7.7 | 4.9 | 9.0 | 4.4 | 5.0 | 8.5 | 4.6 |
| Venezuela, Rep. Bol...................... | 299 | 34.0 | 29.6 | 17.9 | 15.4 | 30.1 | 7.8 | 45.9 | 28.1 | 14.1 | 35.5 | 40.4 | .... |

# Gross Capital Formation as Percentage of GDP

| | | 2004 | 2005 | 2006 | 2007 | 2008 | 2009 | 2010 | 2011 | 2012 | 2013 | 2014 | 2015 |
|---|---|---|---|---|---|---|---|---|---|---|---|---|---|
| | | | | | | | *Percentages* | | | | | | |
| World | 001 | 24.7 | 24.8 | 25.3 | 25.9 | 26.9 | 25.0 | 26.0 | 26.3 | 26.0 | 25.6 | 25.7 | .... |
| Advanced Economies | 110 | 22.6 | 23.0 | 23.5 | 23.4 | 22.7 | 19.6 | 20.4 | 20.7 | 20.7 | 20.6 | 20.8 | 20.8 |
| Euro Area | 163 | 20.5 | 20.8 | 21.8 | 22.6 | 22.1 | 18.8 | 19.1 | 19.6 | 18.4 | 17.7 | 19.2 | 19.4 |
| Austria | 122 | 24.1 | 23.9 | 23.7 | 24.5 | 24.6 | 22.8 | 22.7 | 24.1 | 24.0 | 23.3 | 22.8 | 22.4 |
| Belgium | 124 | 22.4 | 23.7 | 24.0 | 24.4 | 25.6 | 21.7 | 22.7 | 24.0 | 23.2 | 22.1 | 23.0 | 22.6 |
| Cyprus | 423 | 20.2 | 19.9 | 20.8 | 22.3 | 29.2 | 22.9 | 23.8 | 18.9 | 16.0 | 13.1 | 13.1 | 15.4 |
| Estonia | 939 | 33.1 | 33.8 | 38.7 | 39.6 | 30.0 | 18.5 | 20.3 | 28.9 | 28.7 | 26.8 | 27.8 | 24.4 |
| Finland | 172 | 22.9 | 24.6 | 24.0 | 25.5 | 25.1 | 21.2 | 21.6 | 23.5 | 22.5 | 21.4 | 21.3 | 20.0 |
| France | 132 | 21.8 | 22.4 | 23.2 | 24.2 | 24.1 | 21.3 | 21.8 | 23.2 | 22.7 | 22.4 | 22.5 | 22.4 |
| Germany | 134 | 19.0 | 18.8 | 19.8 | 20.8 | 20.9 | 18.0 | 19.6 | 21.1 | 19.4 | 19.5 | 19.4 | 18.7 |
| Greece | 174 | 25.3 | 22.1 | 26.2 | 27.1 | 24.5 | 18.3 | 17.0 | 15.1 | 12.8 | 11.5 | 12.2 | 9.8 |
| Ireland | 178 | 27.3 | 30.5 | 31.9 | 29.1 | 24.5 | 20.2 | 17.4 | 17.6 | 19.2 | 18.1 | 20.3 | 23.2 |
| Italy | 136 | 21.2 | 21.1 | 21.9 | 22.2 | 21.8 | 19.4 | 20.5 | 20.4 | 17.8 | 17.3 | 16.5 | 16.6 |
| Latvia | 941 | 33.3 | 34.8 | 38.2 | 40.1 | 34.0 | 21.4 | 19.4 | 24.3 | 26.0 | 25.0 | 23.4 | 22.0 |
| Lithuania | 946 | 22.9 | 24.2 | 26.9 | 32.3 | 28.1 | 12.6 | 18.1 | 21.9 | 19.2 | 19.1 | 18.7 | 18.6 |
| Luxembourg | 137 | 22.2 | 22.0 | 19.8 | 20.5 | 22.0 | 17.9 | 18.6 | 20.5 | 20.0 | 18.3 | 19.3 | 17.8 |
| Malta | 181 | 17.2 | 20.9 | 21.3 | 21.0 | 21.7 | 20.8 | 23.6 | 19.4 | 17.5 | 18.2 | 17.7 | 20.0 |
| Netherlands | 138 | 20.7 | 20.9 | 21.5 | 22.3 | 22.4 | 20.9 | 20.4 | 20.5 | 19.2 | 18.0 | 18.1 | 18.9 |
| Portugal | 182 | 24.2 | 23.7 | 23.2 | 23.1 | 23.6 | 20.8 | 21.1 | 18.6 | 15.7 | 14.6 | 15.1 | 15.2 |
| Slovak Republic | 936 | 27.3 | 29.7 | 28.9 | 28.6 | 28.8 | 21.2 | 24.1 | 25.0 | 20.9 | 21.0 | 20.9 | 22.9 |
| Slovenia | 961 | 28.6 | 28.4 | 30.2 | 32.9 | 32.7 | 23.4 | 22.2 | 21.7 | 18.8 | 19.4 | 19.8 | 20.2 |
| Spain | 184 | 28.8 | 30.0 | 31.3 | 31.3 | 29.6 | 24.6 | 23.5 | 21.9 | 20.2 | 19.0 | 19.5 | 20.7 |
| Australia | 193 | 27.2 | 27.9 | 27.3 | 28.7 | 28.9 | 27.7 | 27.1 | 27.5 | 29.1 | 27.6 | 26.8 | 26.1 |
| Canada | 156 | 22.2 | 23.4 | 24.3 | 24.4 | 24.6 | 22.2 | 24.1 | 24.2 | 24.6 | 24.4 | 24.1 | 23.8 |
| China, P.R.: Hong Kong | 532 | 22.4 | 21.1 | 22.3 | 21.4 | 21.0 | 21.8 | 23.9 | 24.1 | 25.2 | 24.0 | 23.8 | 21.7 |
| Czech Republic | 935 | 29.4 | 29.2 | 30.1 | 32.1 | 31.1 | 26.5 | 27.2 | 27.0 | 26.3 | 24.8 | 25.3 | 26.7 |
| Denmark | 128 | 21.8 | 22.2 | 24.5 | 25.4 | 24.1 | 18.9 | 18.4 | 19.5 | 19.7 | 19.4 | 19.9 | 19.5 |
| Iceland | 176 | 24.7 | 29.3 | 36.0 | 29.7 | 25.9 | 15.0 | 13.9 | 15.7 | 16.2 | 15.2 | 16.7 | 19.0 |
| Israel | 436 | 19.5 | 20.4 | 20.3 | 20.9 | 19.7 | 18.0 | 18.2 | 20.2 | 21.0 | 20.2 | 19.9 | 19.4 |
| Japan | 158 | 22.5 | 22.5 | 22.7 | 22.9 | 23.0 | 19.7 | 19.8 | 20.2 | 20.9 | 21.5 | 21.8 | .... |
| Korea | 542 | 32.1 | 32.2 | 32.7 | 32.6 | 33.0 | 28.5 | 32.0 | 33.0 | 31.0 | 29.1 | 29.3 | 28.5 |
| New Zealand | 196 | 25.3 | 25.4 | 23.7 | 24.8 | 22.7 | 19.7 | 20.1 | 20.4 | 21.0 | 21.7 | 22.8 | 23.3 |
| Norway | 142 | 21.6 | 22.6 | 24.1 | 27.2 | 26.2 | 24.8 | 25.3 | 25.8 | 26.5 | 28.3 | 28.6 | 28.6 |
| Singapore | 576 | 23.1 | 21.4 | 22.3 | 23.1 | 30.4 | 27.7 | 27.9 | 27.3 | 30.0 | 29.0 | 27.6 | .... |
| Sweden | 144 | 21.6 | 22.0 | 23.0 | 24.6 | 24.5 | 20.9 | 22.9 | 23.8 | 22.6 | 22.5 | 23.8 | 24.6 |
| Switzerland | 146 | 21.5 | 24.1 | 25.0 | 24.0 | 25.4 | 26.4 | 24.0 | 27.0 | 24.2 | 22.5 | 23.2 | 21.8 |
| United Kingdom | 112 | 18.4 | 18.3 | 18.5 | 19.0 | 18.0 | 15.0 | 16.3 | 16.3 | 16.3 | 17.0 | 17.8 | 17.2 |
| United States | 111 | 22.5 | 23.2 | 23.3 | 22.4 | 20.8 | 17.5 | 18.4 | 18.5 | 19.4 | 19.5 | 19.9 | 20.2 |
| Emerging & Dev. Economies | 200 | 27.6 | 27.3 | 28.0 | 29.4 | 31.4 | 31.0 | 32.1 | 32.4 | 32.0 | 31.2 | 31.1 | .... |
| Emerging & Developing Asia | 505 | 35.6 | 35.4 | 35.4 | 36.3 | 37.6 | 39.2 | 40.6 | 41.2 | 40.5 | 40.0 | 39.5 | .... |
| Bangladesh | 513 | 24.0 | 24.5 | 26.1 | 26.2 | 26.2 | 26.2 | 26.2 | 27.6 | 28.3 | 28.4 | 28.6 | .... |
| Bhutan | 514 | 60.8 | 56.1 | 44.6 | 39.1 | 48.1 | 48.2 | 63.5 | 68.0 | 63.7 | 49.9 | 57.7 | .... |
| Cambodia | 522 | 17.8 | 20.2 | 22.5 | 21.2 | 18.6 | 21.5 | 17.2 | .... | .... | .... | .... | .... |
| China, P.R.: Mainland | 924 | 42.2 | 40.5 | 40.0 | 40.7 | 42.6 | 45.7 | 47.2 | 47.3 | 46.5 | 46.5 | 46.0 | .... |
| China, P.R.: Macao | 546 | 16.2 | 25.7 | 33.7 | 36.7 | 30.6 | 18.6 | 13.3 | 13.8 | 14.7 | 14.1 | 19.7 | 24.2 |
| Fiji | 819 | 19.3 | 21.0 | 18.6 | 15.6 | 23.4 | 19.0 | 18.7 | 21.0 | 16.8 | 27.3 | 18.4 | .... |
| India | 534 | 31.2 | 33.2 | 34.7 | 37.0 | 34.2 | 34.5 | 34.4 | 36.7 | 35.5 | 33.2 | 32.6 | .... |
| Indonesia | 536 | 24.1 | 25.1 | 25.4 | 24.9 | 27.8 | 31.0 | 32.9 | 33.0 | 35.1 | 33.8 | 34.6 | 34.6 |
| Malaysia | 548 | 23.0 | 22.4 | 22.7 | 23.4 | 21.5 | 17.8 | 23.4 | 23.2 | 25.7 | 25.9 | 25.0 | 25.1 |
| Mongolia | 948 | 31.0 | 37.5 | 35.6 | 38.0 | 43.0 | 34.5 | 40.6 | 62.1 | 60.6 | 52.0 | .... | .... |
| Myanmar | 518 | 12.3 | 13.3 | 13.9 | 14.9 | 15.9 | 18.2 | 22.7 | 21.7 | .... | .... | .... | .... |
| Nepal | 558 | 24.5 | 26.5 | 26.9 | 28.7 | 30.3 | 31.7 | 38.3 | 38.0 | 34.5 | 36.9 | 37.6 | .... |
| Papua New Guinea | 853 | 18.3 | .... | .... | .... | .... | .... | .... | .... | .... | .... | .... | .... |
| Philippines | 566 | 21.6 | 21.6 | 18.0 | 17.3 | 19.3 | 16.6 | 20.5 | 20.5 | 18.2 | 20.0 | 20.5 | 20.6 |
| Solomon Islands | 813 | .... | .... | .... | 16.8 | 16.1 | 14.5 | 25.5 | 16.7 | 16.6 | 17.3 | 17.0 | .... |
| Sri Lanka | 524 | 25.3 | 26.8 | 28.0 | 28.0 | 27.6 | 24.4 | 27.6 | 29.9 | 30.6 | 29.5 | 29.7 | .... |
| Thailand | 578 | 27.1 | 31.6 | 28.3 | 26.4 | 28.9 | 21.2 | 25.9 | 26.6 | 28.0 | 27.5 | 24.1 | 24.1 |
| Vanuatu | 846 | 23.2 | 24.1 | 28.4 | 32.3 | 40.6 | 39.9 | 34.7 | 27.5 | 23.0 | 25.9 | .... | .... |
| Vietnam | 582 | 35.5 | 33.8 | 34.5 | 39.6 | 36.5 | 37.2 | 35.7 | 29.8 | 27.2 | 26.7 | 26.8 | .... |
| Europe | 170 | 21.9 | 21.6 | 23.1 | 25.0 | 25.3 | 19.9 | 22.1 | 23.8 | 22.9 | 21.8 | 20.8 | 20.7 |
| Emerging & Dev. Europe | 903 | 21.6 | 21.5 | 23.2 | 23.9 | 24.5 | 19.4 | 20.5 | 22.4 | 20.5 | 20.1 | 20.6 | 20.2 |
| Albania | 914 | 33.4 | 35.8 | 36.2 | 27.8 | 35.8 | 34.6 | 30.3 | 31.4 | 28.3 | 28.1 | 26.8 | .... |
| Bulgaria | 918 | 23.5 | 27.8 | 32.1 | 33.4 | 36.8 | 28.6 | 22.9 | 21.6 | 22.1 | 21.4 | 21.4 | 21.3 |
| Croatia | 960 | 27.5 | 27.9 | 29.8 | 29.7 | 31.4 | 25.0 | 21.4 | 20.6 | 19.3 | 19.1 | 18.2 | 18.3 |
| Hungary | 944 | 27.1 | 25.5 | 25.8 | 24.3 | 24.8 | 20.4 | 20.7 | 20.5 | 19.5 | 20.6 | 22.2 | 22.0 |
| Poland | 964 | 19.5 | 18.5 | 19.6 | 21.4 | 22.1 | 21.0 | 19.7 | 20.1 | 19.1 | 18.3 | 20.3 | 20.4 |
| Romania | 968 | 23.7 | 23.3 | 26.5 | 31.0 | 31.3 | 25.4 | 25.6 | 26.8 | 26.0 | 22.9 | 23.0 | 24.6 |
| Turkey | 186 | 19.4 | 20.0 | 22.1 | 21.1 | 21.8 | 14.9 | 19.5 | 23.6 | 20.1 | 20.6 | 20.2 | 18.5 |
| CIS | 901 | 22.2 | 21.7 | 23.0 | 26.0 | 26.0 | 20.1 | 23.3 | 24.9 | 24.8 | 23.2 | 20.8 | 21.0 |
| Armenia | 911 | 24.9 | 30.5 | 35.9 | 37.8 | 40.9 | 34.7 | 32.9 | 27.3 | 25.4 | 22.3 | 20.9 | 20.4 |
| Azerbaijan, Republic of | 912 | 58.0 | 41.5 | 29.9 | 21.5 | 18.7 | 18.9 | 18.1 | 20.3 | 22.3 | 25.7 | 25.8 | .... |
| Belarus | 913 | 28.7 | 28.5 | 32.2 | 34.1 | 37.6 | 37.3 | 41.2 | 37.6 | 35.4 | 39.3 | 35.6 | 30.0 |
| Georgia | 915 | 31.9 | 33.5 | 30.9 | 32.1 | 26.0 | 13.0 | 21.6 | 26.2 | 28.9 | 24.8 | 29.8 | .... |
| Kazakhstan | 916 | 26.3 | 30.7 | 33.7 | 36.1 | 26.9 | 30.5 | 26.5 | 23.4 | 25.6 | 24.7 | 24.8 | 28.1 |
| Kyrgyz Republic | 917 | 14.5 | 16.4 | 24.2 | 26.6 | 28.9 | 27.3 | 27.4 | 25.5 | 35.0 | 33.9 | 36.8 | 34.7 |
| Moldova | 921 | 26.4 | 30.8 | 32.7 | 38.1 | 39.2 | 23.1 | 23.5 | 24.2 | 23.6 | 24.7 | 26.1 | 22.6 |
| Ukraine | 926 | 21.1 | 22.5 | 24.5 | 27.8 | 27.4 | 17.1 | 20.9 | 22.4 | 21.7 | 18.5 | 13.4 | 15.3 |

# Gross Capital Formation as Percentage of GDP

| | | 2004 | 2005 | 2006 | 2007 | 2008 | 2009 | 2010 | 2011 | 2012 | 2013 | 2014 | 2015 |
|---|---|---|---|---|---|---|---|---|---|---|---|---|---|
| **Middle East,N.Africa & Pakistan** | 440 | **24.5** | **23.7** | **24.4** | **27.6** | **29.6** | **30.8** | **29.6** | **26.1** | **27.1** | **25.4** | **26.5** | .... |
| Algeria.................. | 612 | 33.3 | 31.7 | 30.2 | 34.5 | 37.3 | 46.9 | 41.4 | 38.0 | 39.1 | 43.4 | 45.6 | .... |
| Bahrain, Kingdom of.................. | 419 | 20.5 | 26.7 | 30.4 | 34.7 | 35.2 | 26.1 | 27.3 | 16.4 | 20.3 | 16.7 | .... | .... |
| Egypt.................. | 469 | 16.9 | 18.0 | 18.7 | 20.9 | 22.4 | 19.2 | 19.5 | 17.1 | 16.7 | 13.4 | .... | .... |
| Jordan.................. | 439 | 27.4 | 34.1 | 28.3 | 30.3 | 29.9 | 26.3 | .... | .... | .... | .... | .... | .... |
| Kuwait.................. | 443 | 18.2 | 16.4 | 16.2 | 20.5 | 17.6 | 18.0 | 17.9 | 13.5 | 12.8 | 14.4 | 15.8 | .... |
| Libya.................. | 672 | 8.6 | 7.5 | .... | .... | .... | .... | .... | .... | .... | .... | .... | .... |
| Mauritania.................. | 682 | 47.2 | 61.5 | 30.8 | 31.8 | 36.7 | 20.6 | 18.3 | .... | .... | .... | .... | .... |
| Morocco.................. | 686 | 30.9 | 30.3 | 30.9 | 33.9 | 39.1 | 35.0 | 34.1 | 35.8 | 35.0 | 34.7 | 32.2 | .... |
| Oman.................. | 449 | 27.8 | 21.1 | 25.9 | 31.6 | 30.4 | 33.3 | 27.0 | 24.2 | 27.3 | 28.5 | 28.0 | .... |
| Pakistan.................. | 564 | 16.6 | 19.1 | 22.1 | 22.5 | 22.1 | 17.5 | 15.8 | 14.1 | 15.1 | 15.0 | 15.0 | 15.1 |
| Qatar.................. | 453 | 31.5 | 34.3 | 41.9 | 46.0 | 41.1 | 43.0 | 31.4 | 28.7 | 28.1 | 29.6 | 33.4 | .... |
| Saudi Arabia.................. | 456 | 19.9 | 20.2 | 22.2 | 26.5 | 27.3 | 31.7 | 30.7 | 26.8 | 26.3 | 26.2 | 28.5 | 34.6 |
| Syrian Arab Republic.................. | 463 | 21.7 | 23.0 | 21.8 | 20.4 | 16.7 | 17.9 | .... | .... | .... | .... | .... | .... |
| Tunisia.................. | 744 | 24.6 | 21.7 | 23.4 | 23.7 | 25.4 | 24.7 | 25.6 | 23.1 | 24.4 | 22.7 | 23.2 | .... |
| United Arab Emirates.................. | 466 | 19.3 | 19.2 | 18.4 | 24.4 | 23.7 | 30.2 | 26.1 | 22.6 | 23.1 | 23.2 | 24.3 | .... |
| Yemen, Republic of.................. | 474 | 23.9 | 26.7 | 24.9 | 27.0 | 25.3 | 21.5 | 19.2 | 17.6 | 19.3 | 11.2 | .... | .... |
| **Sub-Saharan Africa.................** | 603 | **18.1** | **16.6** | **18.1** | **19.5** | **19.5** | **18.8** | **20.7** | **21.2** | **21.7** | **21.6** | **22.3** | .... |
| CEMAC | | | | | | | | | | | | | |
| Cameroon.................. | 622 | 26.0 | 26.3 | 25.4 | 26.8 | 18.2 | 18.5 | 19.0 | 20.6 | 19.4 | 19.5 | .... | .... |
| Central African Rep.................. | 626 | 6.3 | 9.6 | 8.8 | 8.1 | 9.8 | 9.7 | .... | .... | .... | .... | .... | .... |
| Congo, Rep. of.................. | 634 | 28.9 | 27.5 | 40.1 | 53.7 | 42.9 | 51.9 | .... | .... | .... | .... | .... | .... |
| Gabon.................. | 646 | 25.0 | 22.3 | 23.0 | 22.6 | 21.6 | 25.3 | .... | .... | .... | .... | .... | .... |
| WAEMU | 759 | 16.4 | 18.4 | 16.8 | 18.4 | 21.0 | 18.5 | 21.3 | 18.8 | 22.3 | 25.7 | 24.7 | .... |
| Benin.................. | 638 | 20.7 | 18.2 | 20.6 | 16.5 | 17.5 | 17.8 | 19.5 | 20.0 | 18.6 | 26.5 | 26.5 | .... |
| Burkina Faso.................. | 748 | 21.7 | 24.1 | 20.9 | 22.2 | 25.4 | 24.9 | 26.9 | 28.0 | 30.8 | 33.0 | 30.5 | .... |
| Côte d'Ivoire.................. | 662 | 8.9 | 11.3 | 7.6 | 9.9 | 12.1 | 8.7 | 13.4 | 4.0 | 15.0 | 19.0 | 17.0 | .... |
| Guinea Bissau.................. | 654 | 7.3 | 6.4 | 6.3 | 7.9 | 6.1 | 6.3 | 6.7 | 6.5 | 5.0 | 4.6 | 5.9 | .... |
| Mali.................. | 678 | 22.0 | 22.0 | 20.4 | 21.6 | 20.2 | 21.2 | 24.5 | 23.9 | 18.5 | 25.7 | 25.4 | .... |
| Niger.................. | 692 | 14.6 | 23.1 | 23.6 | 22.9 | 32.1 | 34.7 | 40.0 | 38.4 | 36.2 | 36.2 | 37.8 | 38.8 |
| Senegal.................. | 722 | 21.6 | 24.5 | 24.7 | 29.3 | 31.3 | 22.4 | 22.9 | 25.6 | 29.1 | 27.9 | 26.7 | .... |
| Togo.................. | 742 | 26.5 | 21.6 | 19.4 | 19.1 | 19.6 | 21.1 | 21.6 | 19.1 | 24.0 | 24.0 | 22.7 | .... |
| Botswana.................. | 616 | 33.2 | 27.2 | 25.9 | 30.8 | 35.6 | 38.4 | 42.8 | 38.7 | 39.2 | 33.9 | 30.7 | .... |
| Burundi.................. | 618 | 11.3 | 13.5 | 16.9 | 16.9 | 15.2 | 16.4 | 20.3 | 22.6 | 22.2 | 23.5 | 26.4 | 6.1 |
| Cabo Verde.................. | 624 | 39.5 | 36.0 | 38.0 | 49.8 | 48.5 | 43.8 | 47.6 | 47.5 | .... | .... | .... | .... |
| Congo, Dem. Rep. of.................. | 636 | 18.3 | 14.8 | 12.4 | 7.9 | 9.8 | 17.5 | 18.1 | .... | .... | .... | .... | .... |
| Ethiopia.................. | 644 | 26.5 | 23.8 | 25.2 | 22.1 | 22.4 | 22.7 | 24.7 | 32.1 | 37.1 | 35.8 | 40.3 | .... |
| Kenya.................. | 664 | 17.1 | 16.9 | 17.9 | 19.0 | 19.2 | 19.9 | 19.8 | 20.5 | 20.1 | .... | .... | .... |
| Lesotho.................. | 666 | 26.6 | 22.0 | 20.7 | 24.2 | 27.6 | 25.5 | 29.1 | 22.4 | 27.2 | 33.1 | .... | .... |
| Madagascar.................. | 674 | 23.4 | 22.2 | 25.3 | 29.3 | 40.3 | 31.7 | 18.8 | 17.5 | 17.6 | 15.9 | 15.6 | 16.6 |
| Malawi.................. | 676 | 16.9 | 19.4 | 20.3 | 11.9 | 24.2 | 13.5 | 16.2 | 9.9 | 19.7 | 23.8 | .... | .... |
| Mauritius.................. | 684 | 24.4 | 22.7 | 26.7 | 26.9 | 27.3 | 21.3 | 23.7 | 26.0 | 24.8 | 22.5 | 22.8 | 21.2 |
| Mozambique.................. | 688 | 18.3 | 17.7 | 17.0 | 15.1 | 17.3 | 14.7 | 18.3 | 25.7 | 47.4 | 54.5 | 46.2 | .... |
| Namibia.................. | 728 | 19.1 | 19.7 | 22.3 | 24.4 | 28.4 | 27.3 | 24.1 | 22.4 | 26.8 | 24.8 | 28.0 | .... |
| Nigeria.................. | 694 | 12.1 | 5.5 | 8.3 | 9.4 | 8.4 | 12.3 | 17.3 | 16.2 | 14.9 | 14.9 | 15.8 | .... |
| Rwanda.................. | 714 | 15.0 | 15.8 | 17.4 | 21.4 | 25.6 | 22.3 | 23.7 | 24.1 | 26.8 | 26.2 | 26.2 | .... |
| Seychelles.................. | 718 | .... | .... | .... | .... | .... | .... | .... | .... | .... | .... | .... | .... |
| Sierra Leone.................. | 724 | 10.4 | 11.4 | 10.4 | 9.6 | 9.3 | 9.9 | 31.1 | 42.1 | 27.9 | 12.7 | 14.5 | .... |
| South Africa.................. | 199 | 17.7 | 18.0 | 19.7 | 21.2 | 22.5 | 19.6 | 19.3 | 19.7 | 19.4 | 19.4 | 20.4 | 20.6 |
| Swaziland.................. | 734 | 15.3 | 15.0 | 12.8 | 12.3 | 11.0 | 10.3 | .... | .... | .... | .... | .... | .... |
| Uganda.................. | 746 | 22.1 | 22.4 | 21.2 | 23.6 | 23.0 | 22.0 | 23.5 | 25.0 | 24.6 | 24.5 | .... | .... |
| Zambia.................. | 754 | 23.0 | 22.5 | 20.0 | 22.5 | 22.9 | 21.1 | 20.9 | 23.1 | 24.1 | .... | .... | .... |
| Zimbabwe.................. | 698 | 10.2 | .... | .... | .... | .... | .... | .... | .... | .... | .... | .... | .... |
| **Western Hemisphere.................** | 205 | **19.6** | **19.6** | **20.8** | **22.0** | **23.6** | **20.7** | **21.8** | **22.3** | **21.8** | **21.1** | **21.7** | **21.1** |
| ECCU | 309 | 28.5 | 32.1 | 35.1 | 34.7 | 34.7 | 30.3 | 26.5 | 23.4 | 22.4 | 23.0 | 21.7 | .... |
| Dominica.................. | 321 | 17.2 | 19.8 | 18.8 | 19.1 | 20.6 | 19.0 | 18.4 | 16.3 | 14.4 | 12.0 | 12.1 | .... |
| Grenada.................. | 328 | 35.1 | 46.3 | 35.6 | 35.4 | 31.1 | 23.9 | 22.0 | 19.9 | 16.3 | 20.1 | 18.2 | .... |
| Montserrat.................. | 351 | 41.1 | 32.2 | 23.3 | 23.3 | 24.3 | 23.2 | 24.1 | 21.4 | 22.3 | 26.2 | 22.4 | .... |
| St. Lucia.................. | 362 | 24.8 | 28.8 | 38.0 | 29.2 | 32.4 | 29.0 | 28.0 | 28.2 | 26.7 | 23.3 | 18.1 | .... |
| St. Vincent & Grenadines.................. | 364 | 26.6 | 25.1 | 28.5 | 27.6 | 29.4 | 24.1 | 25.2 | 24.1 | 23.6 | 24.8 | 21.2 | .... |
| Argentina.................. | 213 | 18.7 | 20.9 | 23.0 | 24.2 | 25.0 | 21.2 | 24.5 | 26.2 | 24.0 | 18.4 | 19.5 | .... |
| Aruba.................. | 314 | 28.8 | 33.6 | 35.2 | 32.4 | 32.7 | 30.3 | 28.1 | 28.5 | 26.7 | 24.0 | 22.3 | .... |
| Bahamas, The.................. | 313 | 21.2 | 25.3 | 30.3 | 28.2 | 26.7 | 25.6 | 25.2 | 27.5 | 28.8 | 27.7 | 31.2 | 27.2 |
| Belize.................. | 339 | 21.5 | 23.3 | 20.1 | 20.4 | 27.4 | 19.0 | 11.2 | 18.7 | 15.9 | 18.5 | 20.9 | .... |
| Bolivia.................. | 218 | 11.0 | 14.3 | 13.9 | 15.2 | 17.6 | 17.0 | 17.0 | 19.8 | 17.7 | 19.0 | 21.0 | 19.2 |
| Brazil.................. | 223 | 17.1 | 16.2 | 16.8 | 18.3 | 20.7 | 17.8 | 20.2 | 19.7 | 17.6 | 18.0 | 20.1 | 17.7 |
| Chile.................. | 228 | 20.3 | 22.0 | 20.7 | 20.6 | 26.0 | 20.3 | 22.3 | 23.7 | 25.5 | 24.4 | 22.2 | 22.5 |
| Colombia.................. | 233 | 19.4 | 20.2 | 22.4 | 23.0 | 23.5 | 22.4 | 22.1 | 23.9 | 23.9 | 24.3 | 26.3 | 27.7 |
| Costa Rica.................. | 238 | 23.1 | 24.3 | 26.4 | 24.7 | 27.6 | 16.3 | 20.6 | 21.6 | 21.2 | 21.3 | 19.3 | .... |
| Dominican Republic.................. | 243 | 14.9 | 16.5 | 18.4 | 28.4 | 30.1 | 23.9 | 26.7 | 25.1 | 23.1 | 21.8 | 21.5 | 21.6 |
| El Salvador.................. | 253 | 15.6 | .... | .... | .... | .... | .... | .... | .... | .... | .... | .... | .... |
| Guatemala.................. | 258 | 20.8 | 19.7 | 20.8 | 20.8 | 16.4 | 13.1 | 13.9 | 15.2 | 15.0 | 14.1 | 13.6 | 13.4 |
| Honduras.................. | 268 | 29.7 | 27.6 | 28.3 | 33.7 | 36.1 | 20.6 | 21.9 | 26.0 | 24.6 | 21.8 | 22.1 | 24.1 |
| Jamaica.................. | 343 | 26.5 | 26.9 | 28.4 | 26.6 | 24.4 | 21.0 | 20.2 | 21.4 | 19.9 | 21.3 | 22.4 | .... |
| Mexico.................. | 273 | 22.7 | 22.3 | 23.5 | 23.4 | 24.4 | 22.9 | 22.1 | 22.3 | 23.1 | 21.7 | 21.6 | 22.7 |
| Nicaragua.................. | 278 | 28.0 | 30.1 | 26.5 | 29.7 | 31.1 | 22.0 | 24.6 | 31.0 | 28.7 | 28.6 | 26.7 | .... |
| Panama.................. | 283 | 18.7 | 18.4 | 19.5 | 36.5 | 41.6 | 30.4 | 37.2 | 43.5 | 44.4 | 45.8 | 47.0 | .... |
| Paraguay.................. | 288 | 16.6 | 17.0 | 17.1 | 15.8 | 16.4 | 13.8 | 16.2 | 16.2 | 14.7 | 15.4 | 16.4 | .... |
| Peru.................. | 293 | 16.9 | 16.2 | 19.2 | 22.3 | 27.5 | 20.9 | 25.2 | 25.7 | 26.7 | 28.3 | 26.6 | .... |
| Suriname.................. | 366 | 3.6 | 2.6 | 40.2 | 46.2 | 44.3 | 50.0 | 36.4 | .... | .... | .... | .... | .... |
| Trinidad and Tobago.................. | 369 | 19.2 | 14.7 | 13.4 | 12.9 | .... | .... | .... | .... | .... | .... | .... | .... |
| Uruguay.................. | 298 | 17.5 | 17.7 | 19.5 | 19.5 | 23.2 | 19.6 | 19.4 | 20.9 | 23.8 | 24.1 | 22.9 | 22.2 |
| Venezuela, Rep. Bol.................. | 299 | 21.8 | 23.0 | 26.9 | 30.3 | 26.8 | 25.8 | 22.0 | 23.1 | 26.6 | 27.3 | 24.8 | .... |

# Final Consumption Expenditure as Percentage of GDP

| | | 2004 | 2005 | 2006 | 2007 | 2008 | 2009 | 2010 | 2011 | 2012 | 2013 | 2014 | 2015 |
|---|---|---|---|---|---|---|---|---|---|---|---|---|---|
| | | | | | | | *Percentages* | | | | | | |
| World | 001 | **74.6** | **74.3** | **73.7** | **73.4** | **72.4** | **74.5** | **73.4** | **73.2** | **73.6** | **74.0** | **73.9** | .... |
| Advanced Economies | 110 | **78.2** | **78.2** | **78.0** | **77.7** | **78.6** | **80.6** | **80.1** | **80.1** | **79.8** | **79.6** | **79.2** | **78.9** |
| Euro Area | 163 | 77.5 | 77.6 | 77.0 | 75.9 | 76.9 | 79.9 | 79.6 | 79.0 | 78.9 | 78.8 | 76.9 | 76.1 |
| Austria | 122 | 72.9 | 73.4 | 72.6 | 71.0 | 71.4 | 74.4 | 74.1 | 73.3 | 73.5 | 73.6 | 73.7 | 73.3 |
| Belgium | 124 | 72.8 | 72.7 | 72.4 | 71.7 | 73.8 | 76.1 | 75.5 | 75.5 | 76.2 | 76.6 | 76.1 | 75.7 |
| Cyprus | 423 | 82.3 | 82.6 | 83.0 | 84.0 | 83.7 | 82.5 | 82.8 | 84.2 | 85.1 | 85.8 | 86.2 | 86.0 |
| Estonia | 939 | 74.0 | 72.7 | 71.5 | 71.4 | 74.1 | 76.5 | 73.2 | 69.4 | 69.8 | 70.6 | 71.4 | 71.9 |
| Finland | 172 | 70.8 | 71.3 | 71.4 | 69.7 | 71.3 | 76.8 | 77.1 | 77.3 | 79.0 | 79.5 | 80.1 | 80.2 |
| France | 132 | 77.6 | 78.1 | 77.7 | 77.1 | 77.7 | 80.1 | 80.0 | 79.3 | 79.5 | 79.6 | 79.5 | 79.0 |
| Germany | 134 | 75.8 | 76.2 | 75.0 | 72.7 | 73.2 | 77.1 | 75.3 | 74.1 | 74.7 | 74.9 | 74.3 | 73.5 |
| Greece | 174 | 86.4 | 87.6 | 86.9 | 87.3 | 90.4 | 93.7 | 94.3 | 96.9 | 91.6 | 91.3 | 90.3 | 90.3 |
| Ireland | 178 | 60.1 | 60.0 | 60.4 | 62.4 | 67.4 | 67.6 | 66.3 | 63.7 | 63.2 | 62.3 | 61.5 | 56.0 |
| Italy | 136 | 78.3 | 79.0 | 79.0 | 78.2 | 79.0 | 81.3 | 81.4 | 81.1 | 81.2 | 80.4 | 80.3 | 80.2 |
| Latvia | 941 | 79.8 | 77.0 | 77.9 | 75.9 | 75.3 | 80.2 | 82.1 | 80.7 | 78.4 | 78.2 | 78.8 | 79.4 |
| Lithuania | 946 | 84.1 | 83.0 | 83.3 | 80.8 | 83.5 | 89.1 | 83.7 | 80.7 | 79.9 | 79.6 | 81.0 | 81.5 |
| Luxembourg | 137 | 54.0 | 53.3 | 49.9 | 47.5 | 48.4 | 52.2 | 49.6 | 48.7 | 49.7 | 48.0 | 48.3 | 46.0 |
| Malta | 181 | 86.7 | 84.4 | 82.1 | 78.5 | 78.6 | 80.7 | 77.3 | 77.9 | 77.4 | 76.4 | 75.9 | 72.3 |
| Netherlands | 138 | 71.4 | 70.4 | 69.8 | 68.9 | 69.0 | 71.7 | 71.2 | 70.9 | 71.2 | 71.0 | 70.5 | 69.7 |
| Portugal | 182 | 84.1 | 85.4 | 85.0 | 84.6 | 86.1 | 86.1 | 86.5 | 85.7 | 84.8 | 84.4 | 84.5 | 84.0 |
| Slovak Republic | 936 | 75.4 | 74.9 | 75.1 | 72.5 | 74.0 | 80.3 | 77.4 | 75.9 | 75.4 | 74.8 | 75.4 | 75.0 |
| Slovenia | 961 | 72.8 | 72.3 | 69.9 | 68.4 | 69.2 | 74.7 | 76.3 | 76.4 | 77.0 | 74.8 | 72.4 | 70.4 |
| Spain | 184 | 75.1 | 75.0 | 74.6 | 74.7 | 75.5 | 76.6 | 77.8 | 78.3 | 78.3 | 77.6 | 78.2 | 76.9 |
| Australia | 193 | 75.7 | 74.2 | 74.1 | 73.9 | 72.0 | 73.4 | 72.4 | 71.5 | 72.6 | 73.0 | 73.8 | 75.8 |
| Canada | 156 | 75.6 | 75.3 | 76.0 | 75.6 | 75.7 | 80.7 | 80.1 | 79.0 | 77.9 | 78.1 | 77.1 | 78.5 |
| China, P.R.: Hong Kong | 532 | 68.9 | 66.7 | 66.6 | 67.9 | 68.8 | 70.3 | 70.2 | 72.0 | 73.6 | 75.4 | 76.0 | 76.0 |
| Czech Republic | 935 | 69.8 | 68.5 | 67.2 | 65.4 | 66.7 | 69.6 | 69.7 | 69.0 | 68.8 | 69.4 | 68.0 | 66.9 |
| Denmark | 128 | 72.7 | 72.3 | 71.6 | 71.8 | 72.6 | 76.8 | 75.5 | 75.0 | 74.9 | 74.5 | 74.0 | 74.1 |
| Iceland | 176 | 80.6 | 82.5 | 81.0 | 79.1 | 76.2 | 76.1 | 75.6 | 76.2 | 77.6 | 76.7 | 76.9 | 74.0 |
| Israel | 436 | 80.3 | 79.5 | 79.3 | 79.8 | 80.7 | 79.1 | 79.6 | 79.1 | 77.7 | 78.0 | 78.4 | 77.7 |
| Japan | 158 | 75.5 | 76.1 | 76.1 | 75.4 | 76.8 | 80.0 | 79.0 | 80.7 | 81.1 | 81.8 | 80.5 | .... |
| Korea | 542 | 64.2 | 65.5 | 66.6 | 66.3 | 67.1 | 66.8 | 64.8 | 65.5 | 66.2 | 65.9 | 65.5 | 64.7 |
| New Zealand | 196 | 74.4 | 76.0 | 76.6 | 75.1 | 77.6 | 78.0 | 77.6 | 78.0 | 78.3 | 76.7 | 76.5 | 76.1 |
| Norway | 142 | 65.1 | 61.4 | 58.9 | 59.4 | 56.9 | 63.9 | 63.5 | 61.3 | 60.6 | 61.5 | 62.8 | 65.7 |
| San Marino | 135 | .... | .... | .... | 42.6 | 43.9 | 49.5 | 51.2 | 54.5 | 59.3 | .... | .... | .... |
| Singapore | 576 | 52.2 | 49.3 | 47.4 | 45.1 | 49.0 | 47.8 | 45.7 | 45.5 | 45.8 | 46.8 | 46.8 | .... |
| Sweden | 144 | 70.8 | 70.8 | 69.4 | 68.4 | 69.2 | 73.3 | 71.6 | 71.5 | 72.5 | 73.0 | 72.6 | 71.2 |
| Switzerland | 146 | 69.5 | 68.7 | 66.5 | 64.6 | 64.0 | 66.0 | 65.2 | 64.6 | 65.4 | 65.3 | 64.7 | 65.8 |
| United Kingdom | 112 | 84.3 | 84.4 | 83.9 | 83.6 | 84.9 | 86.9 | 86.0 | 85.1 | 85.6 | 85.0 | 84.2 | 84.5 |
| United States | 111 | 82.5 | 82.3 | 82.2 | 82.6 | 84.1 | 85.2 | 85.0 | 85.2 | 84.2 | 83.5 | 83.1 | 82.7 |
| | | | | | | | | | | | | | |
| Emerging & Dev. Economies | 200 | **69.4** | **68.7** | **67.5** | **67.2** | **65.5** | **67.7** | **65.9** | **65.6** | **66.7** | **67.8** | **68.1** | .... |
| Emerging & Developing Asia | 505 | **62.9** | **61.9** | **60.5** | **59.4** | **58.3** | **58.6** | **57.3** | **57.9** | **58.4** | **58.7** | **59.0** | .... |
| Bangladesh | 513 | 80.5 | 80.0 | 78.6 | 79.3 | 80.8 | 79.7 | 79.2 | 80.0 | 78.8 | 78.0 | 77.9 | 77.8 |
| Bhutan | 514 | 62.2 | 65.4 | 56.3 | 60.8 | 62.5 | 70.0 | 65.6 | 61.5 | 59.1 | 73.8 | 63.3 | .... |
| Cambodia | 522 | 89.6 | 88.4 | 84.4 | 83.9 | 85.1 | 84.2 | 83.6 | .... | .... | .... | .... | .... |
| China, P.R.: Mainland | 924 | 55.2 | 54.1 | 52.4 | 50.6 | 49.7 | 50.0 | 49.1 | 50.2 | 50.8 | 51.0 | 51.2 | .... |
| China, P.R.: Macao | 546 | 43.0 | 41.7 | 37.8 | 36.0 | 36.5 | 37.7 | 31.6 | 28.2 | 27.3 | 25.7 | 27.0 | 35.2 |
| Fiji | 819 | 65.2 | 92.9 | 94.9 | 89.8 | 97.9 | 92.4 | 87.3 | 84.9 | 85.8 | 84.5 | 83.4 | .... |
| India | 534 | 70.1 | 69.2 | 68.0 | 67.2 | 68.6 | 69.1 | 67.5 | 67.3 | 67.7 | 68.0 | 68.5 | .... |
| Indonesia | 536 | 75.1 | 72.5 | 71.3 | 71.9 | 69.0 | 68.3 | 65.2 | 64.5 | 65.6 | 66.3 | 66.6 | 66.8 |
| Malaysia | 548 | 56.6 | 55.7 | 55.5 | 56.7 | 56.2 | 61.9 | 60.7 | 61.2 | 63.5 | 65.5 | 65.7 | 67.3 |
| Mongolia | 948 | 78.7 | 67.3 | 58.5 | 60.6 | 70.0 | 72.8 | 67.0 | 62.3 | 64.2 | 68.2 | .... | .... |
| Myanmar | 518 | 88.3 | 87.4 | 86.1 | 85.5 | 83.7 | 81.4 | 77.6 | 55.1 | .... | .... | .... | .... |
| Nepal | 558 | 88.3 | 88.4 | 94.0 | 93.4 | 93.3 | 94.3 | 92.0 | 89.3 | 92.6 | 93.2 | 95.2 | .... |
| Papua New Guinea | 853 | 63.7 | .... | .... | .... | .... | .... | .... | .... | .... | .... | .... | .... |
| Philippines | 566 | 83.9 | 84.1 | 83.8 | 82.8 | 83.2 | 84.5 | 81.3 | 83.2 | 85.1 | 84.2 | 83.0 | 84.8 |
| Sri Lanka | 524 | 83.6 | 82.1 | 83.0 | 82.4 | 86.1 | 82.1 | 80.7 | 84.6 | 83.1 | 80.0 | 78.9 | .... |
| Thailand | 578 | 67.8 | 68.7 | 67.6 | 65.6 | 67.5 | 68.7 | 66.7 | 67.7 | 69.2 | 68.8 | 69.7 | 68.8 |
| Vanuatu | 846 | 82.9 | 80.4 | 77.1 | 75.8 | 71.8 | 74.6 | 79.5 | 78.0 | 78.0 | 77.4 | .... | .... |
| Vietnam | 582 | 71.5 | 71.0 | 70.6 | 73.7 | 76.5 | 74.3 | 72.6 | 72.3 | 70.4 | 71.6 | 72.1 | .... |
| | | | | | | | | | | | | | |
| Europe | 170 | **75.3** | **75.1** | **74.4** | **74.4** | **73.5** | **78.2** | **76.1** | **74.1** | **75.2** | **76.9** | **76.8** | **76.1** |
| Emerging & Dev. Europe | 903 | **83.7** | **83.6** | **82.7** | **82.2** | **82.0** | **83.3** | **83.1** | **82.0** | **82.2** | **82.0** | **81.0** | **80.3** |
| Albania | 914 | 89.0 | 88.9 | 87.4 | 90.4 | 93.5 | 92.0 | 89.3 | 89.3 | 88.8 | 91.1 | 93.0 | .... |
| Bulgaria | 918 | 87.7 | 86.9 | 85.0 | 85.3 | 82.9 | 79.7 | 79.9 | 77.4 | 80.7 | 79.2 | 79.4 | 77.2 |
| Croatia | 960 | 78.5 | 78.2 | 76.9 | 77.6 | 76.6 | 78.7 | 79.1 | 79.8 | 80.3 | 80.4 | 79.8 | 79.0 |
| Hungary | 944 | 76.9 | 76.8 | 75.3 | 75.1 | 74.9 | 75.6 | 73.9 | 73.3 | 73.8 | 72.1 | 70.5 | 69.4 |
| Poland | 964 | 82.3 | 81.6 | 81.0 | 78.5 | 80.1 | 79.8 | 80.3 | 79.2 | 79.2 | 78.8 | 78.1 | 76.8 |
| Romania | 968 | 85.3 | 86.9 | 85.6 | 82.9 | 81.8 | 80.7 | 80.2 | 78.5 | 78.7 | 77.6 | 76.9 | .... |
| Turkey | 186 | 83.2 | 83.5 | 82.9 | 84.1 | 82.7 | 86.2 | 86.0 | 85.1 | 85.1 | 85.9 | 84.2 | 84.3 |
| CIS | 901 | **68.3** | **67.8** | **67.4** | **67.8** | **66.5** | **74.2** | **70.4** | **67.6** | **69.4** | **72.6** | **73.5** | **72.6** |
| Armenia | 911 | 92.6 | 86.0 | 82.3 | 81.8 | 81.8 | 93.7 | 95.1 | 96.6 | 101.2 | 99.1 | 97.6 | 91.2 |
| Azerbaijan, Republic of | 912 | 68.7 | 52.5 | 45.6 | 43.1 | 41.9 | 53.9 | 50.2 | 47.4 | 50.0 | 52.2 | 57.2 | .... |
| Belarus | 913 | 74.3 | 72.8 | 70.7 | 70.3 | 68.5 | 72.0 | 71.3 | 61.6 | 60.8 | 63.7 | 65.3 | 65.8 |
| Georgia | 915 | 87.3 | 84.3 | 94.1 | 92.6 | 102.7 | 106.1 | 95.9 | 92.2 | 89.8 | 87.7 | 86.3 | .... |
| Kazakhstan | 916 | 65.1 | 60.6 | 55.6 | 57.1 | 53.5 | 61.3 | 58.6 | 55.5 | 59.4 | 62.9 | 61.3 | 67.9 |
| Kyrgyz Republic | 917 | 94.2 | 102.1 | 113.1 | 104.6 | 110.1 | 96.7 | 102.7 | 101.6 | 115.9 | 115.6 | 113.5 | 105.7 |
| Moldova | 921 | 104.0 | 109.9 | 113.9 | 113.5 | 113.6 | 113.5 | 115.8 | 116.7 | 116.8 | 112.6 | 110.9 | 107.7 |
| Ukraine | 926 | 71.5 | 76.7 | 78.2 | 77.7 | 80.3 | 84.6 | 83.2 | 84.2 | 86.9 | 90.7 | 90.1 | 86.7 |

# Final Consumption Expenditure as Percentage of GDP

|  |  | 2004 | 2005 | 2006 | 2007 | 2008 | 2009 | 2010 | 2011 | 2012 | 2013 | 2014 | 2015 |
|---|---|---|---|---|---|---|---|---|---|---|---|---|---|
|  |  |  |  |  |  |  | *Percentages* |  |  |  |  |  |  |
| **Middle East,N.Africa & Pakistan** | 440 | **66.0** | **63.9** | **63.2** | **62.5** | **61.6** | **66.9** | **64.2** | **63.1** | **65.4** | **66.9** | **69.5** | .... |
| Algeria | 612 | 52.3 | 45.2 | 42.9 | 43.3 | 43.4 | 53.7 | 51.5 | 51.8 | 52.5 | 53.8 | 55.8 | .... |
| Bahrain, Kingdom of | 419 | 63.0 | 53.8 | 47.4 | 43.7 | 45.6 | 54.9 | 54.1 | 52.4 | 52.9 | 55.9 | .... | .... |
| Egypt | 469 | 84.4 | 84.3 | 82.9 | 83.7 | 83.2 | 87.4 | 85.7 | 87.0 | 90.9 | 94.4 | .... | .... |
| Iran, I.R. of | 429 | 57.1 | 56.7 | 56.2 | 52.4 | 54.0 | 55.5 | 51.9 | 54.3 | 59.5 | 60.2 | 61.3 | .... |
| Jordan | 439 | 102.9 | 107.4 | 105.7 | 107.3 | 101.1 | 96.9 | .... | .... | .... | .... | .... | .... |
| Kuwait | 443 | 57.3 | 47.9 | 42.5 | 44.4 | 41.5 | 52.0 | 46.0 | 39.1 | 38.7 | 41.5 | 47.6 | .... |
| Libya | 672 | 43.2 | 37.3 | .... | .... | .... | .... | .... | .... | .... | .... | .... | .... |
| Mauritania | 682 | 93.7 | 90.3 | 74.2 | 81.5 | 87.0 | 99.9 | 95.6 | .... | .... | .... | .... | .... |
| Morocco | 686 | 74.4 | 75.8 | 75.1 | 75.5 | 75.1 | 76.9 | 76.7 | 78.2 | 80.2 | 79.7 | 80.2 | .... |
| Oman | 449 | 59.6 | 51.5 | 48.3 | 49.4 | 42.2 | 55.7 | 50.1 | 46.2 | 48.3 | 51.7 | 55.7 | .... |
| Pakistan | 564 | 82.4 | 84.8 | 85.8 | 84.6 | 89.0 | 89.7 | 90.0 | 90.9 | 92.6 | 91.8 | 91.5 | 91.0 |
| Qatar | 453 | 30.5 | 30.3 | 31.0 | 29.5 | 25.6 | 34.9 | 30.2 | 25.4 | 25.6 | 26.6 | 28.2 | .... |
| Saudi Arabia | 456 | 53.2 | 47.7 | 48.1 | 48.5 | 44.6 | 59.0 | 52.6 | 46.6 | 48.6 | 52.6 | 58.3 | 70.4 |
| Syrian Arab Republic | 463 | 79.6 | 79.6 | 77.3 | 71.4 | 68.1 | 71.9 | .... | .... | .... | .... | .... | .... |
| Tunisia | 744 | 79.0 | 78.7 | 78.4 | 78.2 | 77.5 | 78.2 | 79.5 | 84.4 | 85.0 | 86.8 | 87.8 | .... |
| United Arab Emirates | 466 | 70.2 | 65.1 | 63.8 | 67.7 | 67.1 | 63.9 | 67.3 | 59.3 | 51.5 | 52.3 | 55.3 | .... |
| Yemen, Republic of | 474 | 75.3 | 68.8 | 74.7 | 79.1 | 79.7 | 88.5 | 85.3 | 83.5 | 94.1 | 98.8 | .... | .... |
| **Sub-Saharan Africa** | 603 | **82.3** | **82.2** | **78.9** | **82.9** | **82.7** | **86.1** | **81.9** | **80.8** | **79.8** | **83.5** | **81.8** | .... |
| CEMAC |  |  |  |  |  |  |  |  |  |  |  |  |  |
| Cameroon | 622 | 78.1 | 76.3 | 75.4 | 74.9 | 85.9 | 86.5 | 86.6 | 87.5 | 88.4 | 88.7 | .... | .... |
| Central African Rep. | 626 | 100.1 | 98.0 | 98.5 | 100.6 | 101.9 | 100.9 | .... | .... | .... | .... | .... | .... |
| Congo, Rep. of | 634 | 33.3 | 34.9 | 34.4 | 41.6 | 36.8 | 39.2 | .... | .... | .... | .... | .... | .... |
| Equatorial Guinea | 642 | 13.3 | 10.7 | 10.0 | 9.5 | 8.3 | 12.7 | .... | .... | .... | .... | .... | .... |
| Gabon | 646 | 46.7 | 43.2 | 42.2 | 42.1 | 37.5 | 47.2 | .... | .... | .... | .... | .... | .... |
| WAEMU | 759 | 87.7 | 87.5 | 87.7 | 88.8 | 86.8 | 86.7 | 84.4 | 85.7 | 84.5 | 84.0 | 85.6 | .... |
| Benin | 638 | 87.9 | 88.8 | 88.7 | 90.9 | 90.4 | 93.8 | 90.2 | 88.8 | 90.9 | 84.6 | 83.9 | .... |
| Burkina Faso | 748 | 92.8 | 92.0 | 93.1 | 92.1 | 91.0 | 90.2 | 83.5 | 80.2 | 74.5 | 80.2 | 83.3 | .... |
| Côte d'Ivoire | 662 | 82.9 | 82.8 | 82.7 | 85.1 | 81.0 | 80.4 | 79.3 | 79.8 | 80.8 | 78.0 | 79.7 | .... |
| Guinea Bissau | 654 | 100.9 | 102.6 | 108.4 | 105.9 | 106.9 | 110.1 | 108.5 | 98.7 | 104.4 | 102.2 | 102.7 | .... |
| Mali | 678 | 86.2 | 85.9 | 82.6 | 82.1 | 81.3 | 79.5 | 77.7 | 86.0 | 87.4 | 92.4 | 96.4 | .... |
| Niger | 692 | 97.1 | 90.0 | 88.6 | 90.3 | 85.9 | 91.8 | 86.9 | 88.5 | 81.3 | 80.3 | 80.4 | 83.4 |
| Senegal | 722 | 91.0 | 90.9 | 92.8 | 93.1 | 95.0 | 94.5 | 92.5 | 92.7 | 91.8 | 92.8 | 92.8 | .... |
| Togo | 742 | 88.6 | 94.1 | 96.8 | 98.3 | 96.4 | 93.6 | 93.9 | 102.3 | 89.9 | 96.5 | 101.0 | .... |
| Botswana | 616 | 57.2 | 57.5 | 55.8 | 57.2 | 63.4 | 72.6 | 64.1 | 65.1 | 72.7 | 73.6 | 65.0 | .... |
| Burundi | 618 | 107.2 | 106.9 | 110.9 | 108.7 | 112.2 | 106.2 | 100.7 | 101.1 | 102.1 | 104.9 | 99.2 | 117.9 |
| Congo, Dem. Rep. of | 636 | 89.5 | 54.6 | 48.6 | 55.1 | 51.4 | 37.2 | 42.0 | .... | .... | .... | .... | .... |
| Ethiopia | 644 | 88.1 | 94.1 | 95.4 | 91.3 | 94.8 | 94.3 | 94.8 | 82.8 | 80.8 | 80.8 | 77.5 | .... |
| Kenya | 664 | 93.4 | 92.8 | 92.9 | 93.3 | 91.6 | 94.4 | 94.9 | 93.5 | 94.6 | .... | .... | .... |
| Lesotho | 666 | 146.7 | 146.4 | 143.4 | 141.1 | 139.3 | 142.2 | 140.4 | 134.2 | 136.7 | 129.9 | .... | .... |
| Madagascar | 674 | 94.5 | 95.1 | 90.7 | 92.5 | 84.0 | 91.9 | 95.4 | 94.2 | 92.1 | 92.8 | 88.7 | 87.2 |
| Malawi | 676 | 98.0 | 103.1 | 99.7 | 102.4 | 101.6 | 105.2 | 106.6 | 106.6 | 101.8 | 105.4 | .... | .... |
| Mauritius | 684 | 77.4 | 82.5 | 83.8 | 82.4 | 85.9 | 88.1 | 87.6 | 87.0 | 87.3 | 88.2 | 88.3 | 88.6 |
| Mozambique | 688 | 99.2 | 96.2 | 91.9 | 93.9 | 92.6 | 96.6 | 96.4 | 95.8 | 98.7 | 99.2 | 99.0 | .... |
| Namibia | 728 | 81.1 | 77.2 | 75.6 | 81.0 | 84.1 | 93.5 | 88.8 | 89.6 | 89.8 | 94.1 | 95.5 | .... |
| Nigeria | 694 | 82.6 | 82.9 | 67.7 | 88.5 | 77.7 | 89.0 | 74.8 | 73.9 | 66.6 | 80.0 | 78.2 | .... |
| Rwanda | 714 | 98.6 | 98.0 | 92.8 | 91.4 | 91.6 | 93.9 | 92.5 | 93.0 | 90.1 | 91.1 | 90.4 | .... |
| Seychelles | 718 | 74.4 | 67.4 | .... | .... | .... | .... | .... | .... | .... | .... | .... | .... |
| Sierra Leone | 724 | 102.4 | 100.5 | 97.8 | 99.7 | 103.2 | 104.7 | 86.6 | 97.6 | 91.8 | 88.4 | 75.1 | .... |
| South Africa | 199 | 81.8 | 82.5 | 82.8 | 81.6 | 80.3 | 81.9 | 80.6 | 80.1 | 82.9 | 83.0 | 80.9 | 80.4 |
| Swaziland | 734 | 87.3 | 89.1 | 89.6 | 89.0 | 98.3 | 101.9 | .... | .... | .... | .... | .... | .... |
| Uganda | 746 | 88.9 | 88.3 | 91.9 | 90.2 | 84.7 | 88.2 | 89.5 | 93.5 | 91.1 | 85.8 | .... | .... |
| Zambia | 754 | 79.0 | 79.5 | 72.4 | 75.7 | 79.2 | 76.0 | 68.1 | 70.9 | 74.2 | .... | .... | .... |
| Zimbabwe | 698 | 95.2 | 99.3 | .... | .... | .... | .... | .... | .... | .... | .... | .... | .... |
| **Western Hemisphere** | 205 | **77.5** | **77.6** | **76.7** | **76.8** | **77.0** | **79.5** | **78.1** | **77.7** | **79.7** | **81.7** | **81.6** | **82.7** |
| ECCU (incl. ECCB hqtrs.) | 309 | 82.3 | 77.5 | 77.3 | 82.8 | 89.9 | 99.7 | 88.9 | 91.8 | 94.5 | 92.8 | 90.3 | .... |
| Anguilla | 312 | 93.3 | 89.9 | 113.9 | 98.1 | 96.2 | 100.1 | 97.9 | 98.5 | 97.5 | 93.4 | 89.9 | .... |
| Antigua and Barbuda | 311 | 82.4 | 86.2 | 86.9 | 89.2 | 86.2 | 73.6 | 85.2 | 88.3 | 90.8 | 91.0 | 94.4 | .... |
| Dominica | 321 | 94.4 | 98.3 | 94.9 | 101.5 | 107.2 | 104.4 | 99.9 | 98.2 | 103.0 | 101.2 | 98.3 | .... |
| Grenada | 328 | 85.1 | 89.3 | 98.7 | 94.5 | 98.5 | 98.6 | 103.4 | 105.7 | 107.3 | 105.1 | 101.4 | .... |
| Montserrat | 351 | 129.0 | 139.9 | 129.7 | 127.2 | 143.5 | 125.0 | 130.7 | 130.8 | 134.4 | 152.0 | 151.2 | .... |
| St. Kitts and Nevis | 361 | 67.3 | 67.6 | 71.1 | 71.6 | 86.8 | 86.4 | 88.2 | 88.5 | 85.4 | 80.7 | 81.1 | .... |
| St. Lucia | 362 | 79.3 | 78.6 | 87.1 | 96.2 | 91.8 | 79.9 | 86.3 | 90.7 | 84.7 | 87.9 | 89.5 | .... |
| St. Vincent & Grenadines | 364 | 90.2 | 91.4 | 90.2 | 100.2 | 102.3 | 104.9 | 105.0 | 104.5 | 106.7 | 108.0 | 111.2 | .... |
| Argentina | 213 | 73.9 | 73.2 | 71.4 | 71.5 | 71.1 | 73.5 | 72.2 | 71.6 | 73.7 | 82.0 | 80.1 | .... |
| Aruba | 314 | 74.7 | 75.8 | 77.3 | 78.1 | 76.0 | 82.2 | 85.2 | 87.5 | 90.4 | 90.3 | 86.5 | .... |
| Bahamas, The | 313 | 76.8 | 77.5 | 80.5 | 79.1 | 81.2 | 82.2 | 83.3 | 86.2 | 86.0 | 84.8 | 87.6 | 81.4 |
| Barbados | 316 | 87.7 | 88.6 | 86.1 | 85.9 | 88.8 | 87.1 | 89.4 | 96.3 | 96.4 | .... | .... | .... |
| Belize | 339 | 89.2 | 86.4 | 80.4 | 81.3 | 80.5 | 86.2 | 86.1 | 85.7 | 84.8 | 86.8 | 84.8 | .... |
| Bolivia | 218 | 84.2 | 82.3 | 77.1 | 77.3 | 75.5 | 80.2 | 76.1 | 74.5 | 72.9 | 74.0 | 77.6 | 86.8 |
| Brazil | 223 | 79.0 | 80.2 | 80.3 | 80.2 | 79.1 | 82.3 | 80.8 | 81.0 | 83.8 | 84.6 | 82.7 | 83.6 |
| Chile | 228 | 70.4 | 69.6 | 65.0 | 66.2 | 72.1 | 72.1 | 71.3 | 73.1 | 74.7 | 76.3 | 76.9 | 77.8 |
| Colombia | 233 | 82.9 | 81.7 | 80.5 | 80.2 | 79.0 | 79.8 | 79.7 | 77.3 | 77.9 | 78.2 | 79.1 | 81.8 |
| Costa Rica | 238 | 80.1 | 81.1 | 79.7 | 80.1 | 82.2 | 83.1 | 82.1 | 83.3 | 82.9 | 82.3 | 82.9 | .... |
| Dominican Republic | 243 | 84.3 | 89.0 | 89.6 | 79.9 | 83.4 | 84.4 | 84.3 | 85.0 | 85.6 | 83.9 | 83.3 | 82.7 |
| El Salvador | 253 | 101.5 | .... | .... | .... | .... | .... | .... | .... | .... | .... | .... | .... |
| Guatemala | 258 | 94.3 | 96.2 | 96.1 | 95.9 | 98.3 | 96.1 | 96.6 | 95.5 | 96.3 | 97.0 | 96.6 | 95.3 |
| Guyana | 336 | 78.6 | 100.2 | 153.7 | 167.6 | 180.5 | 159.1 | 101.9 | 106.2 | 103.6 | .... | .... | .... |
| Honduras | 268 | 89.0 | 90.9 | 92.7 | 94.4 | 97.0 | 97.2 | 96.0 | 93.7 | 94.8 | 98.7 | 96.8 | 94.8 |
| Jamaica | 343 | 87.8 | 93.0 | 92.1 | 95.2 | 105.3 | 96.9 | 98.1 | 101.7 | 101.8 | 100.9 | 99.8 | .... |
| Mexico | 273 | 77.9 | 78.5 | 76.8 | 76.8 | 77.8 | 78.8 | 78.8 | 78.0 | 79.2 | 80.9 | 80.4 | 81.6 |
| Nicaragua | 278 | 99.3 | 99.6 | 96.2 | 94.8 | 94.0 | 94.2 | 94.9 | 90.9 | 91.7 | 92.4 | 90.3 | .... |
| Panama | 283 | 77.6 | 75.2 | 73.3 | 70.4 | 70.3 | 69.5 | 72.1 | 67.3 | 64.6 | 62.3 | 60.8 | .... |

# Final Consumption Expenditure as Percentage of GDP

| | | 2004 | 2005 | 2006 | 2007 | 2008 | 2009 | 2010 | 2011 | 2012 | 2013 | 2014 | 2015 |
|---|---|---|---|---|---|---|---|---|---|---|---|---|---|
| | | | | | | | *Percentages* | | | | | | |
| **Western Hemisphere(Cont.)** | | | | | | | | | | | | | |
| Paraguay..................................... | 288 | 70.8 | 71.7 | 73.8 | 74.9 | 79.3 | 79.9 | 80.7 | 83.5 | 84.9 | 77.6 | 80.3 | .... |
| Peru............................................ | 293 | 79.3 | 77.5 | 71.7 | 70.6 | 72.2 | 75.2 | 71.7 | 70.2 | 71.8 | 72.6 | 75.0 | .... |
| Trinidad and Tobago.................... | 369 | 65.8 | 44.2 | 59.6 | 58.4 | 48.7 | .... | .... | .... | .... | .... | .... | .... |
| Uruguay...................................... | 298 | 79.8 | 80.4 | 81.9 | 81.5 | 81.6 | 79.6 | 79.6 | 79.5 | 83.5 | 86.2 | 87.2 | 90.2 |
| Venezuela, Rep. Bol..................... | 299 | 61.2 | 57.8 | 58.7 | 63.6 | 63.4 | 76.6 | 67.1 | 66.7 | 71.5 | 77.5 | 89.9 | .... |

2016, International Monetary Fund : *International Financial Statistics Yearbook*

# Commodity Prices

| | | 2004 | 2005 | 2006 | 2007 | 2008 | 2009 | 2010 | 2011 | 2012 | 2013 | 2014 | 2015 |
|---|---|---|---|---|---|---|---|---|---|---|---|---|---|
| | | *Market Prices unless footnoted [1] as unit values. (For market prices, pricing point in parentheses)* | | | | | | | | | | | |
| **Aluminum (US $/MT)** | | | | | | | | | | | | | |
| All Origins (London) * | 156 | 1,718.5 | 1,900.5 | 2,573.1 | 2,639.9 | 2,577.9 | 1,669.2 | 2,173.0 | 2,400.6 | 2,022.8 | 1,846.7 | 1,867.4 | 1,664.7 |
| **Bananas (US $/MT)** | | | | | | | | | | | | | |
| Latin America (US Ports) * | 248 | 524.8 | 576.8 | 682.9 | 676.9 | 843.6 | 848.0 | 881.4 | 975.9 | 984.3 | 926.4 | 931.9 | 958.7 |
| **Barley (US $/MT)** | | | | | | | | | | | | | |
| Canada (Winnepeg) * | 156 | 99.0 | 95.1 | 116.6 | 172.4 | 200.5 | 128.4 | 158.4 | 207.2 | 238.8 | 206.4 | 146.1 | 127.9 |
| **Beef (US cents/pound)** | | | | | | | | | | | | | |
| Australia-NZ (US Ports) * | 193 | 113.9 | 118.7 | 115.6 | 118.0 | 121.1 | 119.6 | 152.5 | 183.2 | 187.9 | 183.6 | 224.1 | 200.5 |
| Brazil [1] | 223 | 96.3 | 101.1 | 116.0 | 123.0 | 177.7 | 148.0 | 184.1 | 230.6 | 215.6 | 205.2 | 214.0 | 196.1 |
| **Butter (US cents/pound)** | | | | | | | | | | | | | |
| New Zealand [1] | 196 | 88.0 | 93.8 | 78.5 | 130.2 | 157.6 | 102.8 | 188.2 | 201.6 | 150.1 | 195.1 | 180.6 | 151.0 |
| **Coal (US $/MT)** | | | | | | | | | | | | | |
| Australia | 193 | 56.7 | 51.0 | 52.6 | 70.4 | 136.2 | 77.0 | 106.0 | 130.1 | 103.2 | 90.6 | 75.1 | 61.6 |
| Australia [1] | 193 | 43.5 | 71.1 | 73.8 | 69.2 | 152.0 | 112.7 | 130.9 | 172.4 | 135.0 | 107.3 | 88.5 | 73.2 |
| South Africa | 199 | 54.7 | 46.2 | 50.7 | 62.7 | 120.6 | 64.7 | 91.6 | 116.3 | 92.9 | 80.2 | 72.3 | 57.0 |
| **Cocoa Beans (US $/MT)** | | | | | | | | | | | | | |
| New York and London * | 652 | 1,550.7 | 1,544.7 | 1,590.6 | 1,958.1 | 2,572.8 | 2,895.0 | 3,130.6 | 2,978.5 | 2,377.1 | 2,439.1 | 3,062.8 | 3,135.2 |
| Brazil [1] | 223 | 1,686.7 | 1,677.2 | 1,818.8 | 2,379.3 | 3,357.4 | 3,962.7 | 4,334.7 | 4,001.5 | 4,093.2 | 4,040.8 | 4,072.5 | 3,076.9 |
| **Coconut Oil (US $/MT)** | | | | | | | | | | | | | |
| Philippines (New York) * | 566 | 668.3 | 615.6 | 605.8 | 917.7 | 1,222.8 | 723.6 | 1,120.7 | 1,737.0 | 1,109.0 | 939.8 | 1,281.7 | 1,106.0 |
| Philippines [1] | 566 | 602.2 | 571.2 | 542.5 | 810.9 | 1,218.8 | 712.5 | 940.2 | 1,724.2 | 1,176.4 | 1,402.5 | 1,366.0 | 1,360.7 |
| **Coffee (US cents/pound)** | | | | | | | | | | | | | |
| Other Milds (New York) * | 386 | 80.1 | 114.3 | 114.0 | 123.3 | 138.1 | 141.6 | 194.4 | 273.2 | 187.6 | 141.1 | 202.8 | 160.5 |
| Brazil (New York) | 223 | 69.2 | 101.4 | 102.9 | 110.8 | 122.4 | 111.3 | 144.5 | 243.6 | 171.4 | 117.9 | 161.3 | 123.1 |
| Brazil [1] | 223 | 56.3 | 84.4 | 90.0 | 103.0 | 119.6 | 104.1 | 131.2 | 202.6 | 172.6 | 122.3 | 137.9 | 125.7 |
| Uganda (New York) * | 799 | 37.3 | 53.4 | 70.3 | 88.3 | 106.2 | 77.1 | 84.1 | 116.0 | 110.6 | 100.5 | 105.6 | 94.2 |
| **Copper (US $/MT)** | | | | | | | | | | | | | |
| United Kingdom (London) * | 112 | 2,863.5 | 3,676.5 | 6,731.4 | 7,131.6 | 6,963.5 | 5,165.3 | 7,538.4 | 8,823.5 | 7,958.9 | 7,331.5 | 6,863.4 | 5,510.5 |
| **Copra (US $/MT)** | | | | | | | | | | | | | |
| Philippines (Europ. Ports) | 566 | 450.0 | 413.7 | 402.5 | 607.1 | 815.7 | 479.7 | 749.6 | 1,157.3 | 740.6 | 627.0 | 854.3 | 735.3 |
| **Cotton (US cents/pound)** | | | | | | | | | | | | | |
| Liverpool Index * | 111 | 62.0 | 55.2 | 58.1 | 63.3 | 71.4 | 62.8 | 103.5 | 154.6 | 89.2 | 90.4 | 83.1 | 70.4 |
| **DAP (US $/MT)** | | | | | | | | | | | | | |
| US Gulf Coast | 111 | 221.2 | 247.0 | 260.3 | 432.5 | 967.2 | 323.1 | 500.7 | 618.9 | 539.8 | 444.9 | 472.5 | 458.9 |
| **Fish (US $/kilogram)** | | | | | | | | | | | | | |
| Norway * | 142 | 3.3 | 4.1 | 5.1 | 4.5 | 4.8 | 4.9 | 6.1 | 5.9 | 4.8 | 6.8 | 6.6 | 5.3 |
| **Fish Meal (US $/MT)** | | | | | | | | | | | | | |
| Any Origin (Hamburg) * | 293 | 692.9 | 744.2 | 1,074.3 | 1,185.5 | 1,160.2 | 1,255.9 | 1,739.2 | 1,519.3 | 1,624.3 | 1,710.5 | 1,921.5 | 1,759.2 |
| Iceland [1] | 176 | .... | .... | 821.2 | 1,427.5 | .... | .... | .... | .... | .... | .... | .... | .... |
| **Gasoline (US cents/gallon)** | | | | | | | | | | | | | |
| US Gulf Coast | 111 | 117.0 | 158.8 | 182.4 | 203.7 | 246.7 | 163.3 | 205.1 | 274.1 | 281.0 | 269.5 | 248.4 | 155.2 |
| **Gold (US $/troy ounce)** | | | | | | | | | | | | | |
| United Kingdom (London) | 112 | 409.2 | 444.8 | 604.3 | 696.7 | 871.7 | 973.0 | 1,224.7 | 1,569.2 | 1,669.5 | 1,411.5 | 1,265.6 | 1,160.7 |
| **Groundnuts (US $/MT)** | | | | | | | | | | | | | |
| Nigeria (London) * | 694 | 910.0 | 769.1 | 828.9 | 1,177.5 | 1,567.7 | 994.6 | 1,239.4 | 1,724.0 | 1,688.2 | 2,314.5 | 2,148.3 | 1,946.2 |
| **Groundnut Oil (US $/MT)** | | | | | | | | | | | | | |
| Any Origin (Europe) * | 694 | 1,161.0 | 1,060.4 | 970.2 | 1,352.1 | 2,131.1 | 1,183.7 | 1,403.9 | 1,988.2 | 2,435.7 | 1,773.0 | 1,313.0 | 1,336.9 |
| **Hides (US cents/pound)** | | | | | | | | | | | | | |
| United States (Chicago) * | 111 | 67.1 | 65.6 | 68.9 | 72.1 | 64.1 | 44.9 | 72.0 | 82.0 | 83.2 | 94.7 | 110.2 | 87.6 |
| **Iron Ore (US $/MT)** | | | | | | | | | | | | | |
| China (CFR Tianjin Port) | 924 | 16.4 | 28.1 | 33.5 | 36.6 | 61.6 | 80.0 | 146.7 | 167.8 | 128.5 | 135.4 | 96.8 | 55.2 |
| **Jute (US $/MT)** | | | | | | | | | | | | | |
| Bangladesh (Chitta.-Chalna) | 513 | 280.6 | 290.0 | 290.0 | 333.3 | 467.5 | 560.4 | 864.2 | 638.3 | 521.7 | 599.2 | 635.4 | 732.5 |
| **Lamb (US cents/pound)** | | | | | | | | | | | | | |
| New Zealand (London) * | 196 | 165.8 | 160.9 | 153.6 | 161.7 | 170.7 | 146.9 | 145.7 | 149.2 | 100.9 | 106.7 | 130.6 | 107.9 |
| **Lead (US $/MT)** | | | | | | | | | | | | | |
| United Kingdom (London) * | 112 | 881.9 | 974.4 | 1,288.4 | 2,579.1 | 2,093.3 | 1,719.4 | 2,148.2 | 2,400.7 | 2,063.6 | 2,139.7 | 2,095.5 | 1,787.8 |
| **Linseed Oil (US $/MT)** | | | | | | | | | | | | | |
| Any Origin | 001 | 872.8 | 1,101.6 | 671.5 | 1,001.0 | 1,551.2 | 982.3 | 1,163.2 | 1,426.3 | 1,253.7 | 1,213.5 | 1,213.3 | 1,065.4 |
| **Maize (US $/MT)** | | | | | | | | | | | | | |
| United States (US Gulf Pts) * | 111 | 111.8 | 98.4 | 121.6 | 163.3 | 223.2 | 165.5 | 186.0 | 291.8 | 298.4 | 259.0 | 192.9 | 169.8 |
| Thailand | 578 | 148.8 | 300.6 | 211.7 | 287.4 | 334.7 | 230.2 | 314.6 | 448.4 | 691.3 | 355.8 | 369.0 | 862.8 |
| **Natural Gas (US $/MMBTU)** | | | | | | | | | | | | | |
| Russian Federation | 922 | 3.8 | 5.9 | 8.2 | 8.1 | 13.1 | 8.9 | 8.2 | 10.6 | 12.0 | 11.2 | 10.5 | 7.3 |
| Indonesia | 536 | 5.9 | 7.0 | 8.0 | 8.4 | 11.6 | 7.5 | 9.4 | 15.6 | 18.1 | 17.3 | 17.0 | 11.0 |
| United States | 111 | 5.9 | 8.9 | 6.7 | 7.0 | 8.9 | 3.9 | 4.4 | 4.0 | 2.8 | 3.7 | 4.4 | 2.6 |
| **Nickel (US $/MT)** | | | | | | | | | | | | | |
| United Kingdom(N.Europ.Ports)* | 156 | 13,821.0 | 14,777.8 | 24,125.6 | 37,135.8 | 21,141.5 | 14,672.4 | 21,810.0 | 22,909.1 | 17,541.7 | 15,030.0 | 16,893.4 | 11,862.6 |
| **Olive Oil (US $/MT)** | | | | | | | | | | | | | |
| United Kingdom * | 112 | 4,630.9 | 5,519.2 | 5,487.7 | 4,561.0 | 4,167.5 | 3,509.3 | 3,171.3 | 3,070.3 | 3,135.7 | 3,816.7 | 3,911.8 | 4,927.1 |
| **Oranges (US $/MT)** | | | | | | | | | | | | | |
| French Import Price * | 132 | 857.5 | 874.7 | 829.2 | 956.7 | 1,107.3 | 909.0 | 1,033.2 | 891.1 | 868.0 | 967.3 | 782.5 | 675.0 |
| **Palm Kernel Oil(US $/MT)** | | | | | | | | | | | | | |
| Malaysia (Rotterdam) | 548 | 471.3 | 422.1 | 478.4 | 780.3 | 948.5 | 682.8 | 900.8 | 1,125.4 | 999.3 | 856.9 | 821.4 | 622.7 |
| **Palm Oil (US $/MT)** | | | | | | | | | | | | | |
| Malaysia (N.W.Europe)* | 548 | 434.7 | 367.7 | 416.8 | 719.1 | 862.9 | 644.1 | 859.9 | 1,076.5 | 939.8 | 764.2 | 739.4 | 565.1 |
| Malaysia [1] | 548 | 448.7 | 390.8 | 425.5 | 694.7 | 924.9 | 634.1 | 819.5 | 1,068.4 | 960.3 | 743.4 | 744.0 | .... |
| **Pepper (US cents/pound)** | | | | | | | | | | | | | |
| Singapore | 576 | 116.4 | 112.7 | 146.8 | 215.4 | 236.2 | 207.6 | 273.8 | 431.9 | 447.4 | 445.5 | 573.5 | 655.4 |

# Commodity Prices

| | | 2004 | 2005 | 2006 | 2007 | 2008 | 2009 | 2010 | 2011 | 2012 | 2013 | 2014 | 2015 |
|---|---|---|---|---|---|---|---|---|---|---|---|---|---|
| | | *Market Prices unless footnoted [1]  as unit values. (For market prices, pricing point in parentheses)* | | | | | | | | | | | |
| **Petroleum,spot (US$/barrel)** | | | | | | | | | | | | | |
| Average crude price * | 001 | 37.8 | 53.4 | 64.3 | 71.1 | 97.0 | 61.8 | 79.0 | 104.0 | 105.0 | 104.1 | 96.2 | 50.8 |
| Dubai Fateh * | 466 | 33.5 | 49.2 | 61.4 | 68.4 | 93.8 | 61.8 | 78.1 | 106.0 | 108.9 | 105.4 | 96.7 | 51.2 |
| U.K. Brent * | 112 | 38.3 | 54.4 | 65.4 | 72.7 | 97.7 | 61.9 | 79.6 | 111.0 | 112.0 | 108.8 | 98.9 | 52.4 |
| West Texas Intermediate * | 111 | 41.4 | 56.4 | 66.1 | 72.3 | 99.6 | 61.7 | 79.4 | 95.0 | 94.1 | 97.9 | 93.1 | 48.7 |
| **Phosphate Rock (US $/MT)** | | | | | | | | | | | | | |
| Morocco (Casablanca) | 686 | 41.0 | 42.0 | 44.2 | 70.9 | 345.6 | 121.7 | 123.0 | 184.9 | 185.9 | 148.1 | 110.2 | 117.5 |
| **Potash (US $/MT)** | | | | | | | | | | | | | |
| Canada (Vancouver) | 156 | 124.6 | 158.2 | 174.5 | 200.2 | 570.1 | 630.4 | 331.9 | 435.3 | 459.0 | 379.2 | 297.2 | 302.9 |
| **Poultry (US cents/pound)** | | | | | | | | | | | | | |
| United States (Georgia) * | 111 | 75.7 | 73.9 | 69.2 | 78.2 | 84.6 | 85.6 | 85.8 | 87.4 | 94.3 | 103.8 | 110.1 | 114.7 |
| **Plywood (US cents/sheet)** | | | | | | | | | | | | | |
| Philippines (Tokyo) | 566 | 464.8 | 508.6 | 595.6 | 640.7 | 645.5 | 564.6 | 569.1 | 607.5 | 610.3 | 560.2 | 517.3 | 451.2 |
| **Pulp (US $/MT)** | | | | | | | | | | | | | |
| Sweden (North Sea Ports) | 144 | 634.5 | 636.2 | 701.3 | 759.6 | 827.7 | 617.3 | 868.0 | 897.0 | 763.5 | 822.9 | 875.6 | 875.0 |
| **Rice (US $/MT)** | | | | | | | | | | | | | |
| Thailand (Bangkok) * | 578 | 245.8 | 287.8 | 303.5 | 332.4 | 700.2 | 589.4 | 520.6 | 551.7 | 580.2 | 518.8 | .... | .... |
| Thailand [1] | 578 | 270.0 | 308.5 | 345.8 | 375.7 | 597.1 | 582.7 | 593.8 | 593.5 | 683.0 | 658.7 | 490.8 | 464.7 |
| **Rubber (US cents/pound)** | | | | | | | | | | | | | |
| Malaysia (Singapore) * | 548 | 59.2 | 68.1 | 95.6 | 103.9 | 118.6 | 87.2 | 165.7 | 218.5 | 153.2 | 126.8 | 88.8 | 70.7 |
| Malaysia [1] | 548 | 56.1 | 60.2 | 85.7 | 94.9 | 120.5 | 81.6 | 144.0 | 211.2 | 149.8 | 119.6 | 88.0 | .... |
| Thailand [1] | 578 | 51.3 | 56.9 | 80.4 | 86.1 | 107.5 | 70.6 | 130.5 | 190.1 | 131.5 | 107.1 | 79.4 | 61.8 |
| **Shrimp (US $/pound)** | | | | | | | | | | | | | |
| United States(U.S. Gulf Ports)* | 111 | 10.2 | 10.3 | 10.2 | 10.1 | 10.7 | 9.5 | 10.1 | 11.9 | 10.1 | 14.0 | 16.6 | 14.1 |
| **Silver (US cents/troy ounce)** | | | | | | | | | | | | | |
| United States (New York) | 111 | 665.8 | 730.8 | 1,155.9 | 1,339.2 | 1,499.7 | 1,464.4 | 2,015.3 | 3,522.4 | 3,113.7 | 2,385.0 | 1,907.1 | 1,572.1 |
| **Sisal (US $/MT)** | | | | | | | | | | | | | |
| East Africa (Europe) | 639 | 862.1 | 885.0 | 885.0 | 958.3 | 1,076.9 | 770.8 | 1,009.6 | 1,322.5 | 1,486.4 | 1,395.8 | 1,597.9 | 2,009.6 |
| **Sorghum (US $/MT)** | | | | | | | | | | | | | |
| United States (US Gulf Ports) | 111 | 109.8 | 96.2 | 122.9 | 162.7 | 207.8 | 151.1 | 165.4 | 268.7 | 271.9 | 243.3 | 207.2 | 204.7 |
| **Soybeans (US $/MT)** | | | | | | | | | | | | | |
| Brazil [1] | 223 | .... | .... | .... | .... | .... | .... | .... | .... | .... | .... | .... | .... |
| United States (Rotterdam) * | 111 | 276.7 | 223.1 | 217.5 | 317.3 | 453.3 | 378.5 | 384.9 | 484.2 | 537.8 | 517.2 | 457.8 | 347.4 |
| **Soybean Meal (US $/MT)** | | | | | | | | | | | | | |
| United States (Rotterdam) * | 111 | 257.2 | 205.8 | 194.0 | 263.7 | 367.9 | 359.3 | 331.3 | 378.9 | 473.3 | 477.3 | 467.0 | 352.7 |
| **Soybean Oil (US $/MT)** | | | | | | | | | | | | | |
| All Origins (Dutch Ports) * | 111 | 590.5 | 495.7 | 551.5 | 799.7 | 1,133.8 | 787.0 | 924.8 | 1,215.8 | 1,151.8 | 1,011.1 | 812.7 | 672.2 |
| **Sugar (US cents/pound)** | | | | | | | | | | | | | |
| Brazil [1] | 223 | 7.2 | 9.3 | 13.9 | 11.4 | 12.2 | 15.1 | 20.2 | 26.0 | 23.4 | 19.3 | 17.5 | 14.1 |
| EU Import Price * | 112 | 30.5 | 30.3 | 30.6 | 33.3 | 30.8 | 26.0 | 25.7 | 26.7 | 26.4 | 26.0 | 27.4 | 25.4 |
| Free Market * | 001 | 7.5 | 10.1 | 14.8 | 10.0 | 12.5 | 18.2 | 20.9 | 26.2 | 21.4 | 17.7 | 17.1 | 13.2 |
| U.S. Import Price * | 111 | 20.6 | 21.1 | 22.1 | 20.8 | 21.3 | 24.3 | 31.1 | 37.6 | 28.9 | 21.2 | 24.9 | 24.9 |
| Philippines [1] | 566 | 13.1 | 13.3 | 17.6 | 15.0 | 14.3 | 14.3 | 21.9 | 27.5 | 24.4 | 42.4 | 23.5 | 25.5 |
| **Sunflower Oil (US $/MT)** | | | | | | | | | | | | | |
| EU (NW European ports) * | 112 | 734.4 | 1,144.5 | 713.1 | 673.0 | 1,693.6 | 1,041.7 | 1,186.0 | 1,621.8 | 1,489.5 | 1,341.1 | 1,080.3 | 1,022.2 |
| **Superphosphate (US $/MT)** | | | | | | | | | | | | | |
| United States (US Gulf Ports) | 111 | 186.3 | 201.5 | 201.6 | 339.1 | 879.4 | 257.4 | 381.9 | 538.3 | 462.0 | 382.1 | 388.3 | 385.0 |
| **Swine Meat (US cents/pound)** | | | | | | | | | | | | | |
| United States (Iowa) * | 111 | 71.0 | 67.7 | 63.9 | 63.7 | 64.6 | 55.8 | 74.4 | 89.1 | 82.8 | 86.5 | 102.8 | 67.9 |
| **Tea (US cents/kg)** | | | | | | | | | | | | | |
| Average Auction (London) * | 112 | 198.2 | 216.4 | 241.7 | 211.9 | 269.5 | 314.0 | 316.7 | 346.2 | 348.9 | 266.0 | 237.9 | 340.4 |
| Sri Lanka [1] | 524 | 246.4 | 262.4 | 269.4 | 329.4 | 397.3 | 409.0 | 437.3 | .... | .... | .... | .... | .... |
| **Timber (US $/cubic meter)** | | | | | | | | | | | | | |
| Hardwood Logs | | | | | | | | | | | | | |
| Malaysia, Sarawak * | 548 | 197.3 | 203.1 | 239.4 | 268.0 | 292.3 | 287.2 | 278.2 | 390.5 | 360.5 | 305.4 | 282.0 | 246.0 |
| Hardwood Sawnwood | | | | | | | | | | | | | |
| Malaysia * | 548 | 581.3 | 659.4 | 749.3 | 806.3 | 889.1 | 805.5 | 848.3 | 939.4 | 876.3 | 852.8 | 897.9 | 833.2 |
| Softwood Logs | | | | | | | | | | | | | |
| United States * | 111 | 173.7 | 181.5 | 187.0 | 151.3 | 147.3 | 136.7 | 141.5 | 150.0 | 148.0 | 164.5 | 174.3 | 162.0 |
| Softwood Sawnwood | | | | | | | | | | | | | |
| United States * | 111 | 324.0 | 328.3 | 342.4 | 325.9 | 313.1 | 291.0 | 281.8 | 280.9 | 284.7 | 301.4 | 307.3 | 308.7 |
| **Tin (US $/MT)** | | | | | | | | | | | | | |
| Any Origin (London) * | 112 | 8,480.9 | 7,385.2 | 8,754.9 | 14,495.4 | 18,466.6 | 13,602.7 | 20,367.2 | 26,051.4 | 21,109.4 | 22,281.6 | 21,898.9 | 16,066.6 |
| Malaysia [1] | 548 | 8,342.0 | 7,347.9 | 8,203.9 | 13,738.4 | 18,465.6 | 12,986.6 | 19,195.8 | 24,980.4 | 20,967.3 | 22,040.2 | 21,906.0 | .... |
| Bolivia [1] | 218 | 5,574.2 | 5,100.2 | 6,131.1 | 11,484.8 | 13,171.7 | 11,038.7 | 17,091.5 | 25,186.6 | 20,602.1 | 15,214.8 | 14,908.8 | 14,850.0 |
| Thailand [1] | 578 | 8,648.4 | 7,748.6 | 8,669.3 | 14,280.5 | 18,161.5 | 12,990.9 | 19,986.9 | 26,575.7 | 21,234.3 | 21,928.4 | 22,365.6 | 16,619.1 |
| **Tobacco (US $/MT)** | | | | | | | | | | | | | |
| United States (All Markets) | 111 | 2,740.5 | 2,789.8 | 2,969.3 | 3,315.1 | 3,569.7 | 4,235.3 | 4,313.4 | 4,475.1 | 4,302.3 | 4,573.5 | 4,990.8 | 4,908.3 |
| **Uranium (US $/pound)** | | | | | | | | | | | | | |
| Restricted * | 001 | 18.0 | 27.9 | 47.7 | 99.2 | 64.2 | 46.7 | 46.0 | 56.2 | 48.9 | 38.6 | 33.5 | 36.8 |
| **Urea (US $/MT)** | | | | | | | | | | | | | |
| Ukraine | 926 | 175.3 | 219.0 | 223.0 | 309.4 | 492.7 | 249.6 | 288.6 | 421.0 | 405.4 | 340.1 | 316.2 | 272.9 |
| **Wheat (US $/MT)** | | | | | | | | | | | | | |
| Australia [1] | 193 | 167.1 | 163.4 | 169.4 | 243.4 | 383.3 | 247.0 | 241.8 | 317.4 | 287.2 | 326.2 | 291.9 | 256.2 |
| United States (Kansas City) * | 111 | 133.5 | 129.9 | 168.6 | 226.9 | 287.0 | 190.1 | 194.5 | 280.0 | 276.1 | 265.8 | 242.5 | 185.6 |
| Argentina [1] | 213 | 139.5 | 121.4 | 153.3 | 209.6 | 289.4 | 200.2 | 233.5 | 304.8 | 248.5 | 314.0 | 324.0 | .... |
| **Wool (US cents/kilogram)** | | | | | | | | | | | | | |
| Australia-NZ(UK) 48's * | 112 | 553.2 | 530.6 | 540.6 | 764.9 | 709.2 | 611.4 | 820.1 | 1,209.2 | 1,212.6 | 1,128.1 | 1,030.4 | 922.8 |
| Australia-NZ(UK) 64's * | 112 | 713.3 | 677.7 | 715.9 | 972.9 | 968.2 | 778.5 | 1,023.2 | 1,638.2 | 1,345.3 | 1,197.7 | 1,074.4 | 1,005.8 |
| Australia (greasy wool) [1] | 193 | 397.1 | 377.4 | 380.1 | 517.9 | 472.2 | 403.9 | 554.4 | 824.6 | 759.0 | 713.6 | 649.8 | 622.6 |

# Commodity Prices

| | | 2004 | 2005 | 2006 | 2007 | 2008 | 2009 | 2010 | 2011 | 2012 | 2013 | 2014 | 2015 |
|---|---|---|---|---|---|---|---|---|---|---|---|---|---|
| | | *Market Prices unless footnoted [1] as unit values. (For market prices, pricing point in parentheses)* | | | | | | | | | | | |
| **Zinc (US $/MT)** | | | | | | | | | | | | | |
| United Kingdom (London) *........... | 112 | 1,048.0 | 1,380.5 | 3,266.2 | 3,249.7 | 1,884.8 | 1,658.4 | 2,160.4 | 2,195.5 | 1,950.0 | 1,910.2 | 2,161.0 | 1,931.7 |
| Bolivia [1]........................................ | 218 | 614.9 | 788.1 | 1,823.2 | 1,950.6 | 1,134.6 | 953.2 | 708.3 | 1,316.3 | 1,147.8 | 1,133.4 | 1,279.2 | 1,775.0 |

(1) Unit values
(*) Included in the All-Non Fuel Commodities

# Commodity Prices

| | | 2004 | 2005 | 2006 | 2007 | 2008 | 2009 | 2010 | 2011 | 2012 | 2013 | 2014 | 2015 |
|---|---|---|---|---|---|---|---|---|---|---|---|---|---|
| All Primary Commodities........... | 001 | 52.7 | 65.6 | 79.3 | 88.6 | 113.2 | 79.2 | 100.0 | 126.4 | 122.3 | 120.3 | 112.8 | 73.0 |
| Non-Fuel Primary Commodities | 001 | 58.3 | 62.0 | 76.4 | 87.1 | 94.0 | 79.0 | 100.0 | 118.0 | 106.1 | 104.7 | 100.5 | 83.0 |
| Food....................................... | 001 | 66.9 | 66.5 | 73.5 | 84.6 | 105.1 | 89.2 | 100.0 | 120.2 | 117.2 | 118.1 | 113.2 | 93.8 |
| Beverages............................ | 001 | 48.1 | 56.7 | 61.5 | 70.0 | 86.3 | 87.6 | 100.0 | 116.6 | 95.0 | 83.7 | 101.0 | 97.9 |
| Agricultural Raw Materials.... | 001 | 79.4 | 79.9 | 86.9 | 91.3 | 90.6 | 75.1 | 100.0 | 122.7 | 107.1 | 108.9 | 110.9 | 95.9 |
| Metals................................. | 001 | 40.4 | 49.4 | 77.2 | 90.6 | 83.5 | 67.5 | 100.0 | 113.5 | 94.4 | 90.4 | 81.1 | 62.4 |
| Energy..................................... | 001 | 49.1 | 68.0 | 81.2 | 89.7 | 125.6 | 79.4 | 100.0 | 131.8 | 132.7 | 130.4 | 120.6 | 66.6 |
| World Bank LMICs.................... | 200 | 49.4 | 55.3 | 71.3 | 83.5 | 101.1 | 80.1 | 100.0 | 118.8 | 105.9 | 97.8 | 93.0 | 79.1 |
| **Aluminum (US $/MT)** | | | | | | | | | | | | | |
| All Origins (London) *................... | 156 | 79.1 | 87.5 | 118.4 | 121.5 | 118.6 | 76.8 | 100.0 | 110.5 | 93.1 | 85.0 | 85.9 | 76.6 |
| **Bananas (US $/MT)** | | | | | | | | | | | | | |
| Latin America (US Ports) *............ | 248 | 59.5 | 65.4 | 77.5 | 76.8 | 95.7 | 96.2 | 100.0 | 110.7 | 111.7 | 105.1 | 105.7 | 108.8 |
| **Barley (US $/MT)** | | | | | | | | | | | | | |
| Canada (Winnepeg) *.................... | 156 | 62.5 | 60.0 | 73.6 | 108.8 | 126.6 | 81.1 | 100.0 | 130.8 | 150.8 | 130.3 | 92.2 | 80.7 |
| **Beef (US cents/pound)** | | | | | | | | | | | | | |
| Australia-NZ (US Ports) *.......... | 193 | 74.7 | 77.9 | 75.8 | 77.4 | 79.4 | 78.5 | 100.0 | 120.1 | 123.3 | 120.4 | 146.9 | 131.5 |
| Brazil [1] | 223 | 52.3 | 54.9 | 63.0 | 66.8 | 96.5 | 80.4 | 100.0 | 125.2 | 117.1 | 111.5 | 116.2 | 106.5 |
| **Butter (US cents/pound)** | | | | | | | | | | | | | |
| New Zealand [1]............................. | 196 | 46.7 | 49.8 | 41.7 | 69.1 | 83.7 | 54.6 | 100.0 | 107.1 | 79.7 | 103.7 | 96.0 | 80.2 |
| **Coal (US $/MT)** | | | | | | | | | | | | | |
| Australia........................... | 193 | 53.5 | 48.1 | 49.6 | 66.4 | 128.4 | 72.6 | 100.0 | 122.7 | 97.4 | 85.4 | 70.9 | 58.1 |
| Australia [1] | 193 | 33.2 | 54.3 | 56.4 | 52.9 | 116.2 | 86.1 | 100.0 | 131.7 | 103.1 | 82.0 | 67.6 | 55.9 |
| South Africa..................... | 199 | 59.7 | 50.4 | 55.3 | 68.4 | 131.6 | 70.6 | 100.0 | 126.9 | 101.4 | 87.6 | 79.0 | 62.3 |
| **Cocoa Beans (US $/MT)** | | | | | | | | | | | | | |
| Brazil [1] | 223 | 38.9 | 38.7 | 42.0 | 54.9 | 77.5 | 91.4 | 100.0 | 92.3 | 94.4 | 93.2 | 94.0 | 71.0 |
| New York and London *................ | 652 | 49.5 | 49.3 | 50.8 | 62.5 | 82.2 | 92.5 | 100.0 | 95.1 | 75.9 | 77.9 | 97.8 | 100.1 |
| **Coconut Oil (US $/MT)** | | | | | | | | | | | | | |
| Philippines (New York) *............... | 566 | 59.6 | 54.9 | 54.1 | 81.9 | 109.1 | 64.6 | 100.0 | 155.0 | 99.0 | 83.9 | 114.4 | 98.7 |
| Philippines [1] | 566 | 64.1 | 60.8 | 57.7 | 86.2 | 129.6 | 75.8 | 100.0 | 183.4 | 125.1 | 149.2 | 145.3 | 144.7 |
| **Coffee (US cents/pound)** | | | | | | | | | | | | | |
| Other Milds (New York) *............. | 386 | 41.2 | 58.8 | 58.6 | 63.4 | 71.1 | 72.9 | 100.0 | 140.6 | 96.5 | 72.6 | 104.4 | 82.6 |
| Brazil (New York).......................... | 223 | 47.9 | 70.2 | 71.2 | 76.7 | 84.7 | 77.1 | 100.0 | 168.6 | 118.6 | 81.6 | 111.6 | 85.2 |
| Brazil [1] | 223 | 42.9 | 64.3 | 68.6 | 78.5 | 91.1 | 79.3 | 100.0 | 154.4 | 131.5 | 93.2 | 105.1 | 95.8 |
| Uganda (New York) *.................... | 799 | 44.3 | 63.5 | 83.6 | 105.0 | 126.3 | 91.7 | 100.0 | 137.9 | 131.6 | 119.5 | 125.6 | 112.0 |
| **Copper (US $/MT)** | | | | | | | | | | | | | |
| United Kingdom (London) *......... | 112 | 38.0 | 48.8 | 89.3 | 94.6 | 92.4 | 68.5 | 100.0 | 117.0 | 105.6 | 97.3 | 91.0 | 73.1 |
| **Copra (US $/MT)** | | | | | | | | | | | | | |
| Philippines (Europ. Ports)............. | 566 | 60.0 | 55.2 | 53.7 | 81.0 | 108.8 | 64.0 | 100.0 | 154.4 | 98.8 | 83.6 | 114.0 | 98.1 |
| **Cotton (US cents/pound)** | | | | | | | | | | | | | |
| Liverpool Index *......................... | 111 | 59.9 | 53.3 | 56.1 | 61.1 | 69.0 | 60.6 | 100.0 | 149.3 | 86.2 | 87.3 | 80.3 | 68.0 |
| **DAP (US $/MT)** | | | | | | | | | | | | | |
| US Gulf Coast................................ | 111 | 44.2 | 49.3 | 52.0 | 86.4 | 193.2 | 64.5 | 100.0 | 123.6 | 107.8 | 88.9 | 94.4 | 91.7 |
| **Fish (US $/kilogram)** | | | | | | | | | | | | | |
| Norway *...................................... | 142 | 54.4 | 66.1 | 82.3 | 73.9 | 78.9 | 80.1 | 100.0 | 96.1 | 77.6 | 109.9 | 107.4 | 86.3 |
| **Fish Meal (US $/MT)** | | | | | | | | | | | | | |
| Any Origin (Hamburg) *................ | 293 | 39.8 | 42.8 | 61.8 | 68.2 | 66.7 | 72.2 | 100.0 | 87.4 | 93.4 | 98.3 | 110.5 | 101.1 |
| Iceland [1]....................................... | 176 | .... | .... | 175.2 | 304.5 | .... | .... | .... | .... | .... | .... | .... | .... |
| **Gasoline (US cents/gallon)** | | | | | | | | | | | | | |
| US Gulf Coast.................... | 111 | 57.1 | 77.4 | 88.9 | 99.3 | 120.3 | 79.6 | 100.0 | 133.6 | 137.0 | 131.4 | 121.1 | 75.7 |
| **Gold (US $/troy ounce)** | | | | | | | | | | | | | |
| United Kingdom (London)............. | 112 | 33.4 | 36.3 | 49.3 | 56.9 | 71.2 | 79.4 | 100.0 | 128.1 | 136.3 | 115.3 | 103.3 | 94.8 |
| **Groundnuts (US $/MT)** | | | | | | | | | | | | | |
| Nigeria (London) *....................... | 694 | 73.4 | 62.1 | 66.9 | 95.0 | 126.5 | 80.3 | 100.0 | 139.1 | 136.2 | 186.7 | 173.3 | 157.0 |
| **Groundnut Oil (US $/MT)** | | | | | | | | | | | | | |
| Any Origin (Europe) *.................. | 694 | 82.7 | 75.5 | 69.1 | 96.3 | 151.8 | 84.3 | 100.0 | 141.6 | 173.5 | 126.3 | 93.5 | 95.2 |
| **Hides (US cents/pound)** | | | | | | | | | | | | | |
| United States (Chicago) *............. | 111 | 93.3 | 91.2 | 95.8 | 100.3 | 89.1 | 62.4 | 100.0 | 114.0 | 115.6 | 131.6 | 153.2 | 121.7 |
| **Iron Ore (US $/MT)** | | | | | | | | | | | | | |
| China (CFR Tianjin Port)................ | 924 | 11.2 | 19.2 | 22.8 | 25.0 | 42.0 | 54.5 | 100.0 | 114.4 | 87.6 | 92.3 | 66.0 | 37.6 |
| **Jute (US $/MT)** | | | | | | | | | | | | | |
| Bangladesh (Chitta.-Chalna).......... | 513 | 32.5 | 33.6 | 33.6 | 38.6 | 54.1 | 64.9 | 100.0 | 73.9 | 60.4 | 69.3 | 73.5 | 84.8 |
| **Lamb (US cents/pound)** | | | | | | | | | | | | | |
| New Zealand (London) *............... | 196 | 113.8 | 110.5 | 105.4 | 111.0 | 117.2 | 100.9 | 100.0 | 102.4 | 69.3 | 73.2 | 89.6 | 74.0 |
| **Lead (US $/MT)** | | | | | | | | | | | | | |
| United Kingdom (London) *.......... | 112 | 41.1 | 45.4 | 60.0 | 120.1 | 97.4 | 80.0 | 100.0 | 111.8 | 96.1 | 99.6 | 97.5 | 83.2 |
| **Linseed Oil (US $/MT)** | | | | | | | | | | | | | |
| Any Origin.................................... | 001 | 75.0 | 94.7 | 57.7 | 86.1 | 133.4 | 84.5 | 100.0 | 122.6 | 107.8 | 104.3 | 104.3 | 91.6 |
| **Maize (US $/MT)** | | | | | | | | | | | | | |
| United States (US Gulf Pts) *.......... | 111 | 60.1 | 52.9 | 65.4 | 87.8 | 120.0 | 89.0 | 100.0 | 156.9 | 160.4 | 139.2 | 103.7 | 91.3 |
| Thailand [1]..................................... | 578 | 47.3 | 95.5 | 67.3 | 91.3 | 106.4 | 73.2 | 100.0 | 142.5 | 219.7 | 113.1 | 117.3 | 274.2 |
| **Natural Gas (US $/MMBTU)** | | | | | | | | | | | | | |
| Russian Federation....................... | 922 | 45.7 | 71.9 | 99.9 | 99.0 | 159.8 | 107.7 | 100.0 | 128.9 | 145.7 | 136.1 | 127.3 | 88.8 |
| Indonesia...................................... | 536 | 62.8 | 75.0 | 85.8 | 89.7 | 123.6 | 79.9 | 100.0 | 165.8 | 193.4 | 184.8 | 181.2 | 116.8 |
| United States................................ | 111 | 134.6 | 201.9 | 153.6 | 158.9 | 201.8 | 89.9 | 100.0 | 91.1 | 62.8 | 84.9 | 99.6 | 59.5 |
| **Nickel (US $/MT)** | | | | | | | | | | | | | |
| United Kingdom(N.Europ.Ports)*... | 156 | 63.4 | 67.8 | 110.6 | 170.3 | 96.9 | 67.3 | 100.0 | 105.0 | 80.4 | 68.9 | 77.5 | 54.4 |
| **Olive Oil (US $/MT)** | | | | | | | | | | | | | |
| United Kingdom *......................... | 112 | 146.0 | 174.0 | 173.0 | 143.8 | 131.4 | 110.7 | 100.0 | 96.8 | 98.9 | 120.4 | 123.4 | 155.4 |
| **Oranges (US $/MT)** | | | | | | | | | | | | | |
| French Import Price *.................... | 132 | 83.0 | 84.7 | 80.3 | 92.6 | 107.2 | 88.0 | 100.0 | 86.2 | 84.0 | 93.6 | 75.7 | 65.3 |

# Commodity Prices

Indices of Market Prices unless footnoted [1] otherwise as indices of unit values.
2010=100

| | | 2004 | 2005 | 2006 | 2007 | 2008 | 2009 | 2010 | 2011 | 2012 | 2013 | 2014 | 2015 |
|---|---|---|---|---|---|---|---|---|---|---|---|---|---|
| **Palm Kernel Oil(US $/MT)** | | | | | | | | | | | | | |
| Malaysia (Rotterdam).................. | 548 | 52.3 | 46.9 | 53.1 | 86.6 | 105.3 | 75.8 | 100.0 | 124.9 | 110.9 | 95.1 | 91.2 | 69.1 |
| **Palm Oil (US $/MT)** | | | | | | | | | | | | | |
| Malaysia (N.W.Europe)*............. | 548 | 50.6 | 42.8 | 48.5 | 83.6 | 100.3 | 74.9 | 100.0 | 125.2 | 109.3 | 88.9 | 86.0 | 65.7 |
| Malaysia [1]............................... | 548 | 54.8 | 47.7 | 51.9 | 84.8 | 112.9 | 77.4 | 100.0 | 130.4 | 117.2 | 90.7 | 90.8 | . . . . |
| **Pepper (US cents/pound)** | | | | | | | | | | | | | |
| Malaysia (New York)..................... | 548 | 42.5 | 41.2 | 53.6 | 78.7 | 86.3 | 75.8 | 100.0 | 157.8 | 163.4 | 162.7 | 209.5 | 239.4 |
| Singapore........................................ | 576 | 42.5 | 41.2 | 53.6 | 78.7 | 86.3 | 75.8 | 100.0 | 157.8 | 163.4 | 162.7 | 209.5 | 239.4 |
| **Petroleum,spot (US$/barrel)** | | | | | | | | | | | | | |
| Average crude price *.................. | 001 | 47.8 | 67.5 | 81.3 | 90.0 | 122.8 | 78.2 | 100.0 | 131.6 | 132.9 | 131.7 | 121.8 | 64.3 |
| Dubai Fateh *.............................. | 466 | 42.9 | 63.0 | 78.7 | 87.6 | 120.1 | 79.1 | 100.0 | 135.8 | 139.5 | 135.1 | 123.8 | 65.6 |
| U.K. Brent *................................. | 112 | 48.1 | 68.4 | 82.1 | 91.3 | 122.6 | 77.7 | 100.0 | 139.3 | 140.6 | 136.7 | 124.3 | 65.8 |
| West Texas Intermediate *........... | 111 | 52.2 | 71.1 | 83.2 | 91.0 | 125.4 | 77.7 | 100.0 | 119.7 | 118.6 | 123.3 | 117.3 | 61.4 |
| **Phosphate Rock (US $/MT)** | | | | | | | | | | | | | |
| Morocco (Casablanca)................... | 686 | 33.3 | 34.1 | 35.9 | 57.7 | 280.9 | 98.9 | 100.0 | 150.3 | 151.1 | 120.4 | 89.6 | 95.5 |
| **Potash (US $/MT)** | | | | | | | | | | | | | |
| Canada (Vancouver)...................... | 156 | 37.5 | 47.7 | 52.6 | 60.3 | 171.8 | 190.0 | 100.0 | 131.2 | 138.3 | 114.2 | 89.5 | 91.3 |
| **Poultry (US cents/pound)** | | | | | | | | | | | | | |
| United States (Georgia) *.............. | 111 | 88.2 | 86.1 | 80.6 | 91.1 | 98.6 | 99.7 | 100.0 | 101.8 | 109.8 | 121.0 | 128.3 | 133.6 |
| **Plywood (US cents/sheet)** | | | | | | | | | | | | | |
| Philippines (Tokyo)....................... | 566 | 81.7 | 89.4 | 104.7 | 112.6 | 113.4 | 99.2 | 100.0 | 106.8 | 107.2 | 98.4 | 90.9 | 79.3 |
| **Pulp (US $/MT)** | | | | | | | | | | | | | |
| Sweden (North Sea Ports)............. | 144 | 73.1 | 73.3 | 80.8 | 87.5 | 95.3 | 71.1 | 100.0 | 103.3 | 88.0 | 94.8 | 100.9 | 100.8 |
| **Rice (US $/MT)** | | | | | | | | | | | | | |
| Thailand (Bangkok) *.................... | 578 | 47.2 | 55.3 | 58.3 | 63.9 | 134.5 | 113.2 | 100.0 | 106.0 | 111.5 | 99.7 | 81.9 | 73.0 |
| Thailand [1]................................. | 578 | 45.5 | 51.9 | 58.2 | ·63.3 | 100.6 | 98.1 | 100.0 | 100.0 | 115.0 | 110.9 | 82.7 | 78.3 |
| **Rubber (US cents/pound)** | | | | | | | | | | | | | |
| Malaysia (Singapore) *................. | 548 | 35.7 | 41.1 | 57.7 | 62.7 | 71.5 | 52.6 | 100.0 | 131.9 | 92.4 | 76.5 | 53.6 | 42.7 |
| Malaysia [1]................................. | 548 | 38.9 | 41.8 | 59.5 | 65.9 | 83.7 | 56.7 | 100.0 | 146.7 | 104.0 | 83.0 | 61.1 | . . . . |
| Thailand [1]................................. | 578 | 39.3 | 43.6 | 61.6 | 66.0 | 82.4 | 54.1 | 100.0 | 145.6 | 100.7 | 82.0 | 60.8 | 47.3 |
| **Shrimp (US $/pound)** | | | | | | | | | | | | | |
| United States(U.S. Gulf Ports) *..... | 111 | 101.1 | 102.2 | 101.2 | 99.8 | 105.7 | 93.4 | 100.0 | 118.0 | 99.5 | 138.7 | 163.9 | 139.2 |
| **Silver (US cents/troy ounce)** | | | | | | | | | | | | | |
| United States (New York)............... | 111 | 33.0 | 36.3 | 57.4 | 66.5 | 74.4 | 72.7 | 100.0 | 174.8 | 154.5 | 118.3 | 94.6 | 78.0 |
| **Sisal (US $/MT)** | | | | | | | | | | | | | |
| East Africa (Europe)...................... | 639 | 85.4 | 87.7 | 87.7 | 94.9 | 106.7 | 76.4 | 100.0 | 131.0 | 147.2 | 138.3 | 158.3 | 199.1 |
| **Sorghum (US $/MT)** | | | | | | | | | | | | | |
| United States (US Gulf Ports)......... | 111 | 66.4 | 58.2 | 74.3 | 98.4 | 125.7 | 91.3 | 100.0 | 162.5 | 164.4 | 147.1 | 125.3 | 123.8 |
| **Soybeans (US $/MT)** | | | | | | | | | | | | | |
| United States (Rotterdam) *........... | 111 | 71.9 | 58.0 | 56.5 | 82.4 | 117.8 | 98.3 | 100.0 | 125.8 | 139.7 | 134.4 | 118.9 | 90.2 |
| **Soybean Meal (US $/MT)** | | | | | | | | | | | | | |
| United States (Rotterdam) *........... | 111 | 77.6 | 62.1 | 58.5 | 79.6 | 111.1 | 108.4 | 100.0 | 114.4 | 142.8 | 144.1 | 140.9 | 106.5 |
| **Soybean Oil (US $/MT)** | | | | | | | | | | | | | |
| All Origins (Dutch Ports) *............. | 111 | 63.8 | 53.6 | 59.6 | 86.5 | 122.6 | 85.1 | 100.0 | 131.5 | 124.5 | 109.3 | 87.9 | 72.7 |
| **Sugar (US cents/pound)** | | | | | | | | | | | | | |
| Brazil [1] | 223 | 35.5 | 46.3 | 69.1 | 56.6 | 60.3 | 75.0 | 100.0 | 128.9 | 115.9 | 95.8 | 87.0 | 70.1 |
| EU Import Price *.......................... | 112 | 118.5 | 117.7 | 119.2 | 129.4 | 119.8 | 101.2 | 100.0 | 103.7 | 102.5 | 101.2 | 106.5 | 98.9 |
| Free Market *................................ | 001 | 36.1 | 48.2 | 70.8 | 47.7 | 59.6 | 86.9 | 100.0 | 125.6 | 102.3 | 84.8 | 82.0 | 63.4 |
| U.S. Import Price *........................ | 111 | 66.2 | 67.9 | 71.2 | 66.9 | 68.7 | 78.4 | 100.0 | 121.0 | 93.1 | 68.3 | 80.1 | 80.0 |
| Philippines [1] | 566 | 59.8 | 60.6 | 80.2 | 68.3 | 65.2 | 65.4 | 100.0 | 125.5 | 111.4 | 193.2 | 107.1 | 116.1 |
| **Sunflower Oil (US $/MT)** | | | | | | | | | | | | | |
| EU (NW European ports) *............. | 112 | 61.9 | 96.5 | 60.1 | 56.7 | 142.8 | 87.8 | 100.0 | 136.7 | 125.6 | 113.1 | 91.1 | 86.2 |
| **Superphosphate (US $/MT)** | | | | | | | | | | | | | |
| United States (US Gulf Ports)......... | 111 | 48.8 | 52.8 | 52.8 | 88.8 | 230.3 | 67.4 | 100.0 | 140.9 | 121.0 | 100.0 | 101.7 | 100.8 |
| **Swine Meat (US cents/pound)** | | | | | | | | | | | | | |
| United States (Iowa) *.................. | 111 | 95.4 | 90.9 | 85.8 | 85.5 | 86.8 | 74.9 | 100.0 | 119.6 | 111.2 | 116.3 | 138.1 | 91.2 |
| **Tea (US cents/kg)** | | | | | | | | | | | | | |
| Average Auction (London) *.......... | 112 | 62.6 | 68.3 | 76.3 | 66.9 | 85.1 | 99.1 | 100.0 | 109.3 | 110.2 | 84.0 | 75.1 | 107.5 |
| Sri Lanka [1]................................. | 524 | 56.3 | 60.0 | 61.6 | 75.3 | 90.9 | 93.5 | 100.0 | . . . . | . . . . | . . . . | . . . . | . . . . |
| **Timber (US $/cubic meter)** | | | | | | | | | | | | | |
| Hardwood Logs | | | | | | | | | | | | | |
| Malaysia, Sarawak *..................... | 548 | 70.9 | 73.0 | 86.1 | 96.3 | 105.1 | 103.2 | 100.0 | 140.4 | 129.6 | 109.8 | 101.4 | 88.4 |
| Hardwood Sawnwood | | | | | | | | | | | | | |
| Malaysia *................................... | 548 | 68.5 | 77.7 | 88.3 | 95.1 | 104.8 | 95.0 | 100.0 | 110.7 | 103.3 | 100.5 | 105.9 | 98.2 |
| Softwood Logs | | | | | | | | | | | | | |
| United States *............................. | 111 | 122.8 | 128.3 | 132.2 | 106.9 | 104.1 | 96.6 | 100.0 | 106.0 | 104.6 | 116.3 | 123.2 | 114.5 |
| Softwood Sawnwood | | | | | | | | | | | | | |
| United States *............................. | 111 | 115.0 | 116.5 | 121.5 | 115.7 | 111.1 | 103.3 | 100.0 | 99.7 | 101.1 | 107.0 | 109.1 | 109.6 |
| **Tin (US $/MT)** | | | | | | | | | | | | | |
| Any Origin (London) *................... | 112 | 41.6 | 36.3 | 43.0 | 71.2 | 90.7 | 66.8 | 100.0 | 127.9 | 103.6 | 109.4 | 107.5 | 78.9 |
| Malaysia [1]................................. | 548 | 43.5 | 38.3 | 42.7 | 71.6 | 96.2 | 67.7 | 100.0 | 130.1 | 109.2 | 114.8 | 114.1 | . . . . |
| Bolivia [1]................................... | 218 | 32.6 | 29.8 | 35.9 | 67.2 | 77.1 | 64.6 | 100.0 | 147.4 | 120.5 | 89.0 | 87.2 | 86.9 |
| Thailand [1]................................. | 578 | 43.3 | 38.8 | 43.4 | 71.4 | 90.9 | 65.0 | 100.0 | 133.0 | 106.2 | 109.7 | 111.9 | 83.2 |
| **Tobacco (US $/MT)** | | | | | | | | | | | | | |
| United States (All Markets)........... | 111 | 63.5 | 64.7 | 68.8 | 76.9 | 82.8 | 98.2 | 100.0 | 103.7 | 99.7 | 106.0 | 115.7 | 113.8 |
| **Uranium (US $/pound)** | | | | | | | | | | | | | |
| Restricted *................................. | 001 | 39.3 | 60.8 | 103.8 | 215.9 | 139.6 | 101.5 | 100.0 | 122.4 | 106.4 | 83.9 | 72.9 | 80.0 |
| **Urea (US $/MT)** | | | | | | | | | | | | | |
| Ukraine................................. | 926 | 60.7 | 75.9 | 77.3 | 107.2 | 170.7 | 86.5 | 100.0 | 145.9 | 140.5 | 117.9 | 109.6 | 94.6 |

# Commodity Prices

| | | 2004 | 2005 | 2006 | 2007 | 2008 | 2009 | 2010 | 2011 | 2012 | 2013 | 2014 | 2015 |
|---|---|---|---|---|---|---|---|---|---|---|---|---|---|
| | | *Indices of Market Prices unless footnoted [1] otherwise as indices of unit values.* | | | | | | | | | | | |
| | | | | | | *2010=100* | | | | | | | |
| **Wheat (US $/MT)** | | | | | | | | | | | | | |
| Australia [1] | 193 | 69.1 | 67.6 | 70.0 | 100.7 | 158.5 | 102.1 | 100.0 | 131.3 | 118.8 | 134.9 | 120.7 | 106.0 |
| United States (Kansas City) * | 111 | 68.6 | 66.8 | 86.7 | 116.6 | 147.5 | 97.7 | 100.0 | 144.0 | 142.0 | 136.6 | 124.7 | 95.4 |
| Argentina [1] | 213 | 59.7 | 52.0 | 65.7 | 89.8 | 123.9 | 85.7 | 100.0 | 130.5 | 106.4 | 134.5 | 138.8 | . . . . |
| **Wool (US cents/kilogram)** | | | | | | | | | | | | | |
| Australia-NZ(UK) 48's * | 112 | 67.5 | 64.7 | 65.9 | 93.3 | 86.5 | 74.5 | 100.0 | 147.4 | 147.9 | 137.6 | 125.6 | 112.5 |
| Australia-NZ(UK) 64's * | 112 | 69.7 | 66.2 | 70.0 | 95.1 | 94.6 | 76.1 | 100.0 | 160.1 | 131.5 | 117.1 | 105.0 | 98.3 |
| Australia (greasy wool) [1] | 193 | 71.6 | 68.1 | 68.6 | 93.4 | 85.2 | 72.9 | 100.0 | 148.8 | 136.9 | 128.7 | 117.2 | 112.3 |
| **Zinc (US $/MT)** | | | | | | | | | | | | | |
| United Kingdom (London) * | 112 | 48.5 | 63.9 | 151.2 | 150.4 | 87.2 | 76.8 | 100.0 | 101.6 | 90.3 | 88.4 | 100.0 | 89.4 |
| Bolivia [1] | 218 | 86.8 | 111.3 | 257.4 | 275.4 | 160.2 | 134.6 | 100.0 | 185.8 | 162.0 | 160.0 | 180.6 | 250.6 |

(1) Unit values
(*) Included in the All-Non Fuel Commodities

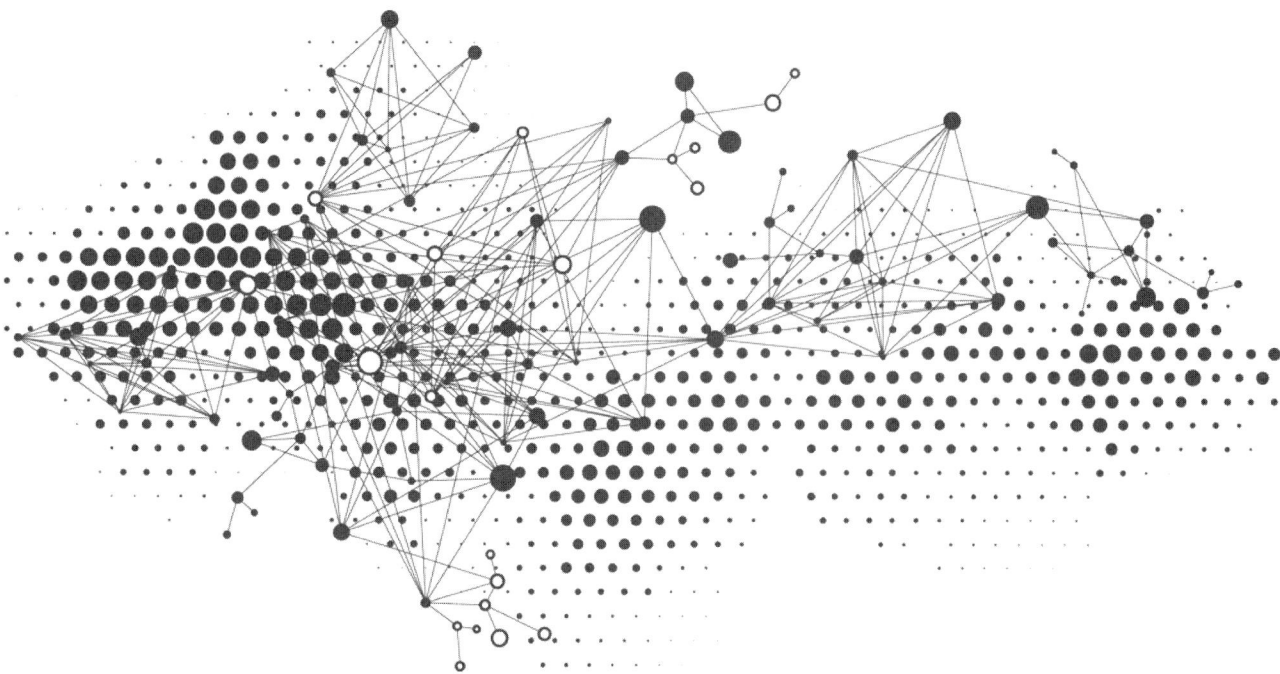

# Country Tables

# Afghanistan, Islamic Republic of   512

|  |  | 2004 | 2005 | 2006 | 2007 | 2008 | 2009 | 2010 | 2011 | 2012 | 2013 | 2014 | 2015 |
|---|---|---|---|---|---|---|---|---|---|---|---|---|---|
| **Exchange Rates** |  | | | | | | | | | | | | |
| | | | | | | *Afghanis per SDR: End of Period* | | | | | | | |
| Market Rate | aa | 74.89 | 72.05 | 74.99 | 78.57 | 80.31 | 76.41 | 69.72 | 75.29 | 80.14 | 87.23 | 83.77 | 94.30 |
| | | | | | | *Afghanis per US Dollar: End of Period (ae) Period Average (rf)* | | | | | | | |
| Market Rate | ae | 48.22 | 50.41 | 49.85 | 49.72 | 52.14 | 48.74 | 45.27 | 49.04 | 52.14 | 56.64 | 57.82 | 68.05 |
| Market Rate | rf | 47.85 | 49.49 | 49.93 | 49.96 | 50.25 | 50.33 | 46.45 | 46.75 | 50.92 | 55.38 | 57.25 | 61.14 |
| **Fund Position** |  | | | | | *Millions of SDRs: End of Period* | | | | | | | |
| Quota | 2f.s | 161.90 | 161.90 | 161.90 | 161.90 | 161.90 | 161.90 | 161.90 | 161.90 | 161.90 | 161.90 | 161.90 | 161.90 |
| SDR Holdings | 1b.s | .04 | .03 | .03 | .12 | .02 | 128.47 | 128.39 | 128.27 | 126.26 | 117.94 | 105.09 | 90.56 |
| Reserve Position in the Fund | 1c.s | — | — | — | — | — | — | — | — | — | — | — | .19 |
| Total Fund Cred.&Loans Outstg. | 2tl | — | — | — | 35.80 | 58.40 | 69.70 | 75.35 | 87.35 | 96.90 | 88.61 | 75.80 | 61.30 |
| SDR Allocations | 1bd | 26.70 | 26.70 | 26.70 | 26.70 | 26.70 | 155.31 | 155.31 | 155.31 | 155.31 | 155.31 | 155.31 | 155.31 |
| **International Liquidity** |  | | | | | *Millions of US Dollars Unless Otherwise Indicated: End of Period* | | | | | | | |
| Total Reserves minus Gold | 1l.d | .... | .... | .... | .... | 2,430.8 | 3,501.4 | 4,174.4 | 5,268.3 | 5,982.5 | 6,441.9 | 6,680.7 | 6,231.8 |
| SDR Holdings | 1b.d | .06 | .04 | .05 | .19 | .04 | 201.40 | 197.72 | 196.93 | 194.05 | 181.63 | 152.26 | 125.49 |
| Reserve Position in the Fund | 1c.d | | | | | | | | | | | | .27 |
| Foreign Exchange | 1d.d | .... | .... | .... | .... | 2,431 | 3,300 | 3,977 | 5,071 | 5,788 | 6,260 | 6,528 | 6,106 |
| Gold (Million Fine Troy Ounces) | 1ad | .... | .... | .... | .... | .7 | .7 | .7 | .7 | .7 | .7 | .7 | .7 |
| Gold (National Valuation) | 1and | .... | .... | .... | .... | † 587.5 | 777.2 | 972.3 | 1,130.4 | 1,160.3 | 840.3 | 840.4 | 758.4 |
| Central Bank: Other Assets | 3..d | .... | .... | .... | .... | | | | | | | | 7.48 |
| Central Bank: Other Liabs | 4..d | .... | .... | 22.5 | 16.8 | .3 | .3 | 1.1 | .8 | .8 | .7 | .7 | .7 |
| Other Depository Corps.: Assets | 7a.d | .... | .... | 183.8 | 465.3 | 591.5 | 870.0 | 1,154.5 | 1,369.1 | 1,592.2 | 1,681.1 | 1,500.1 | 1,412.4 |
| Other Depository Corps.: Liabs. | 7b.d | .... | .... | 50.2 | 72.5 | 248.1 | 316.5 | 329.4 | 293.5 | 191.6 | 154.9 | 140.8 | 157.9 |
| **Central Bank** |  | | | | | *Millions of Afghanis: End of Period* | | | | | | | |
| Net Foreign Assets | 11n | .... | .... | 97,162.1 | 127,555.2 | 154,882.1 | 187,851.6 | 210,749.2 | 285,380.4 | 352,403.0 | 400,493.9 | 407,865.3 | 447,137.8 |
| Claims on Nonresidents | 11 | .... | .... | 100,285.8 | 133,299.1 | 161,734.4 | 205,060.9 | 226,880.9 | 303,688.8 | 372,658.5 | 421,809.7 | 427,349.2 | 467,612.3 |
| Liabilities to Nonresidents | 16c | .... | .... | 3,123.7 | 5,743.9 | 6,852.3 | 17,209.2 | 16,131.8 | 18,308.4 | 20,255.5 | 21,315.8 | 19,483.8 | 20,474.5 |
| Claims on Other Depository Corps. | 12e | .... | .... | — | — | — | — | 18,108.3 | 16,002.7 | 30,414.9 | 29,139.9 | 27,158.6 | — |
| Net Claims on Central Government | 12an | .... | .... | −40,204.1 | −33,895.1 | −25,291.2 | −39,505.7 | −51,958.5 | −66,849.8 | −85,139.6 | −89,915.5 | −70,118.3 | −38,696.6 |
| Claims on Central Government | 12a | .... | .... | 2,003.9 | 16,706.6 | 19,227.0 | 30,857.0 | 29,637.4 | 30,286.5 | 32,826.2 | 33,708.8 | 32,899.3 | 61,205.8 |
| Liabilities to Central Government | 16d | .... | .... | 42,208.0 | 50,601.7 | 44,518.2 | 70,362.7 | 81,595.9 | 97,136.3 | 117,965.8 | 123,624.3 | 103,017.6 | 99,902.4 |
| Claims on Other Sectors | 12s | .... | .... | — | — | — | — | 500.0 | 500.0 | 500.0 | 500.0 | 742.9 | 500.0 |
| Claims on Other Financial Corps. | 12g | .... | .... | — | — | — | — | 500.0 | 500.0 | 500.0 | 500.0 | 742.9 | 500.0 |
| Claims on State & Local Govts. | 12b | .... | .... | — | — | — | — | — | — | — | — | — | — |
| Claims on Public Nonfin. Corps. | 12c | .... | .... | — | — | — | — | — | — | — | — | — | — |
| Claims on Private Sector | 12d | .... | .... | — | — | — | — | — | — | — | — | — | — |
| Monetary Base | 14 | .... | .... | 53,789.4 | 67,761.1 | 92,641.1 | 117,359.4 | 159,294.1 | 200,263.5 | 207,458.8 | 238,279.1 | 270,580.0 | 277,662.1 |
| Currency in Circulation | 14a | .... | .... | 47,418.1 | 58,546.9 | 72,825.5 | 89,843.8 | 122,866.0 | 148,380.9 | 150,008.5 | 168,796.7 | 196,980.2 | 202,169.3 |
| Liabs. to Other Depository Corps. | 14c | .... | .... | 3,798.0 | 6,623.8 | 18,188.1 | 24,801.8 | 32,928.8 | 43,160.3 | 48,314.1 | 58,644.1 | 63,996.9 | 67,175.5 |
| Liabilities to Other Sectors | 14d | .... | .... | 2,573.3 | 2,590.3 | 1,627.5 | 2,713.8 | 3,499.4 | 8,722.3 | 9,136.2 | 10,838.3 | 9,602.9 | 8,317.3 |
| Other Liabs. to Other Dep. Corps. | 14n | .... | .... | 902.3 | 1,756.5 | 8,377.3 | 11,678.3 | 10,900.7 | 25,709.8 | 34,857.6 | 29,572.6 | 35,887.3 | 30,936.1 |
| Dep. & Sec. Excl. f/Monetary Base | 14o | .... | .... | — | — | — | — | — | — | — | — | — | — |
| Deposits Included in Broad Money | 15 | .... | .... | — | — | — | — | — | — | — | — | — | — |
| Sec.Ot.th.Shares Incl.in Brd. Money | 16a | .... | .... | — | — | — | — | — | — | — | — | — | — |
| Deposits Excl. from Broad Money | 16b | .... | .... | — | — | — | — | — | — | — | — | — | — |
| Sec.Ot.th.Shares Excl.f/Brd.Money | 16s | .... | .... | — | — | — | — | — | — | — | — | — | — |
| Loans | 16l | .... | .... | — | — | — | — | — | — | — | — | — | — |
| Financial Derivatives | 16m | .... | .... | — | — | — | — | — | — | — | — | — | — |
| Shares and Other Equity | 17a | .... | .... | 13,793.4 | 23,535.5 | 23,459.3 | 28,184.5 | 17,009.6 | 20,833.7 | 66,878.7 | 84,414.1 | 71,089.3 | 114,488.2 |
| Other Items (Net) | 17r | .... | .... | −11,527.1 | 607.1 | 5,113.1 | −8,876.2 | −9,805.5 | −11,773.7 | −11,016.7 | −12,047.4 | −11,908.1 | −14,145.1 |
| Memo Item: |  | | | | | | | | | | | | |
| Total Assets | 10ra | .... | .... | 124,333.9 | 174,803.7 | 202,629.4 | 265,678.3 | 305,517.7 | 383,609.1 | 469,636.6 | 520,360.5 | 521,685.6 | 565,188.5 |
| **Other Depository Corporations** |  | | | | | *Millions of Afghanis: End of Period* | | | | | | | |
| Net Foreign Assets | 21n | .... | .... | 6,664.5 | 19,524.3 | 17,901.7 | 26,977.3 | 37,349.6 | 52,745.9 | 73,028.1 | 83,392.5 | 78,931.3 | 85,364.6 |
| Claims on Nonresidents | 21 | .... | .... | 9,165.5 | 23,130.8 | 30,838.9 | 42,405.1 | 52,262.3 | 67,141.4 | 83,017.5 | 91,855.6 | 87,108.8 | 96,111.2 |
| Liabilities to Nonresidents | 26c | .... | .... | 2,501.1 | 3,606.5 | 12,937.2 | 15,427.8 | 14,912.6 | 14,395.5 | 9,989.4 | 8,463.1 | 8,177.5 | 10,746.6 |
| Claims on Central Bank | 20 | .... | .... | 6,163.9 | 10,342.6 | 28,496.0 | 40,231.4 | 47,250.9 | 73,771.8 | 82,843.0 | 83,352.1 | 96,772.8 | 100,765.5 |
| Currency | 20a | .... | .... | 603.0 | 1,327.6 | 2,683.0 | 3,922.1 | 5,913.1 | 7,135.6 | 7,247.4 | 6,852.2 | 8,529.2 | 6,035.7 |
| Reserve Deposits and Securities | 20b | .... | .... | 5,461.5 | 7,553.2 | 14,487.0 | 25,828.2 | 30,559.3 | 47,209.5 | 45,444.8 | 49,990.9 | 57,155.3 | 66,164.8 |
| Other Claims | 20n | .... | .... | 99.4 | 1,461.8 | 11,326.0 | 10,481.0 | 10,778.6 | 19,426.8 | 30,150.9 | 26,509.0 | 31,088.3 | 28,565.0 |
| Net Claims on Central Government | 22an | .... | .... | −222.2 | −1,128.8 | −3,319.8 | −2,239.6 | −2,020.3 | −1,376.1 | −1,127.0 | −995.7 | −958.7 | −4,527.2 |
| Claims on Central Government | 22a | .... | .... | — | — | — | 1.9 | 6.3 | 5.5 | 4.6 | 17.8 | 22.4 | 25.6 |
| Liabilities to Central Government | 26d | .... | .... | 222.2 | 1,128.8 | 3,319.8 | 2,241.4 | 2,026.6 | 1,381.6 | 1,131.6 | 1,013.5 | 981.1 | 4,552.8 |
| Claims on Other Sectors | 22s | .... | .... | 23,430.6 | 37,648.4 | 54,182.8 | 66,278.4 | 84,069.7 | 42,215.3 | 43,032.2 | 46,922.3 | 44,085.4 | 46,861.5 |
| Claims on Other Financial Corps. | 22g | .... | .... | 5,824.0 | 1,764.3 | 1,105.3 | 1,528.1 | — | — | — | 100.6 | 50.3 | 120.9 |
| Claims on State & Local Govts. | 22b | .... | .... | — | — | — | — | — | — | — | — | — | — |
| Claims on Public Nonfin. Corps. | 22c | .... | .... | 751.2 | 2,681.5 | 4,723.2 | 8.0 | 8.1 | 8.1 | 8.1 | 8.1 | 91.7 | 94.3 |
| Claims on Private Sector | 22d | .... | .... | 16,855.5 | 33,202.6 | 48,354.3 | 64,742.3 | 84,061.6 | 42,207.2 | 43,024.0 | 46,813.5 | 43,943.4 | 46,646.3 |
| Liabilities to Central Bank | 26g | .... | .... | — | — | — | — | 18,108.3 | — | 599.9 | — | — | 500.0 |
| Transf.Dep.Included in Broad Money | 24 | .... | .... | 30,692.0 | 51,967.7 | 75,679.2 | 103,541.4 | 120,329.3 | 141,607.2 | 167,891.3 | 177,915.6 | 186,206.4 | 185,474.6 |
| Other Dep.Included in Broad Money | 25 | .... | .... | 1,167.5 | 3,915.8 | 4,552.9 | 10,054.5 | 15,945.2 | 19,858.2 | 19,051.1 | 19,985.2 | 17,322.3 | 24,894.0 |
| Sec.Ot.th.Shares Incl.in Brd. Money | 26a | .... | .... | — | — | — | — | — | — | — | — | — | — |
| Deposits Excl. from Broad Money | 26b | .... | .... | — | — | — | — | — | — | — | — | — | — |
| Sec.Ot.th.Shares Excl.f/Brd.Money | 26s | .... | .... | — | — | — | — | — | — | — | — | — | — |
| Loans | 26l | .... | .... | 25.0 | 186.5 | 250.0 | — | — | 950.0 | 1,450.0 | 1,950.0 | 1,950.0 | 2,099.2 |
| Financial Derivatives | 26m | .... | .... | — | — | — | — | — | — | — | — | — | — |
| Insurance Technical Reserves | 26r | .... | .... | — | — | — | — | — | — | — | — | — | — |
| Shares and Other Equity | 27a | .... | .... | 10,245.3 | 12,531.6 | 17,866.2 | 21,582.7 | −16,529.1 | 15,966.7 | 16,807.7 | 26,069.8 | 29,131.1 | 36,631.7 |
| Other Items (Net) | 27r | .... | .... | −6,093.0 | −2,215.0 | −1,087.4 | −3,931.1 | 28,796.3 | −11,025.2 | −8,023.7 | −13,249.3 | −15,779.1 | −21,135.2 |
| Memo Item: |  | | | | | | | | | | | | |
| Total Assets | 20ra | .... | .... | 46,736.5 | 75,759.0 | 120,311.4 | 164,245.9 | 237,944.2 | 202,747.6 | 230,919.7 | 251,164.6 | 263,701.8 | 293,280.4 |

# Afghanistan, Islamic Republic of   512

| | | 2004 | 2005 | 2006 | 2007 | 2008 | 2009 | 2010 | 2011 | 2012 | 2013 | 2014 | 2015 |
|---|---|---|---|---|---|---|---|---|---|---|---|---|---|
| **Depository Corporations** | | | | *Millions of Afghanis: End of Period* | | | | | | | | | |
| Net Foreign Assets............................ | 31n | .... | .... | 103,826.6 | 147,079.5 | 172,783.9 | 214,828.9 | 248,098.8 | 338,126.3 | 425,431.1 | 483,886.4 | 486,796.6 | 532,502.4 |
| Claims on Nonresidents................ | 31 | .... | .... | 109,451.4 | 156,429.9 | 192,573.4 | 247,466.0 | 279,143.2 | 370,830.2 | 455,676.0 | 513,665.3 | 514,457.9 | 563,723.5 |
| Liabilities to Nonresidents............. | 36c | .... | .... | 5,624.8 | 9,350.4 | 19,789.5 | 32,637.0 | 31,044.4 | 32,703.9 | 30,244.9 | 29,778.9 | 27,661.3 | 31,221.1 |
| Domestic Claims................................ | 32 | .... | .... | −16,995.7 | 2,624.5 | 25,571.8 | 24,533.1 | 30,590.9 | −25,510.5 | −42,734.4 | −43,489.0 | −26,248.7 | 4,137.7 |
| Net Claims on Central Government | 32an | .... | .... | −40,426.3 | −35,023.8 | −28,611.0 | −41,745.3 | −53,978.8 | −68,225.8 | −86,266.6 | −90,911.2 | −71,077.0 | −43,223.8 |
| Claims on Central Government.... | 32a | .... | .... | 2,003.9 | 16,706.6 | 19,227.0 | 30,858.8 | 29,643.7 | 30,292.0 | 32,830.8 | 33,726.6 | 32,921.7 | 61,231.4 |
| Liabilities to Central Government. | 36d | .... | .... | 42,430.2 | 51,730.5 | 47,838.0 | 72,604.1 | 83,622.5 | 98,517.9 | 119,097.4 | 124,637.8 | 103,998.7 | 104,455.2 |
| Claims on Other Sectors................ | 32s | .... | .... | 23,430.6 | 37,648.4 | 54,182.8 | 66,278.4 | 84,569.7 | 42,715.3 | 43,532.2 | 47,422.3 | 44,828.3 | 47,361.5 |
| Claims on Other Financial Corps.. | 32g | .... | .... | 5,824.0 | 1,764.3 | 1,105.3 | 1,528.1 | 500.0 | 500.0 | 500.0 | 600.6 | 793.2 | 620.9 |
| Claims on State & Local Govts..... | 32b | .... | .... | — | — | — | — | — | — | — | — | — | — |
| Claims on Public Nonfin. Corps.... | 32c | .... | .... | 751.2 | 2,681.5 | 4,723.2 | 8.0 | 8.1 | 8.1 | 8.1 | 8.1 | 91.7 | 94.3 |
| Claims on Private Sector.............. | 32d | .... | .... | 16,855.5 | 33,202.6 | 48,354.3 | 64,742.3 | 84,061.6 | 42,207.2 | 43,024.0 | 46,813.5 | 43,943.4 | 46,646.3 |
| Broad Money Liabilities.................... | 35l | .... | .... | 81,247.9 | 115,693.1 | 152,002.1 | 202,231.3 | 256,726.8 | 311,433.1 | 338,839.6 | 370,683.5 | 401,582.6 | 414,819.5 |
| Currency Outside Depository Corps | 34a | .... | .... | 46,815.1 | 57,219.3 | 70,142.5 | 85,921.6 | 116,952.9 | 141,245.3 | 142,761.1 | 161,944.5 | 188,451.0 | 196,133.6 |
| Transferable Deposits.................... | 34 | .... | .... | 32,690.7 | 54,558.0 | 77,306.7 | 106,255.2 | 123,304.3 | 149,476.6 | 176,403.0 | 188,751.4 | 195,700.9 | 193,782.3 |
| Other Deposits............................. | 35 | .... | .... | 1,742.1 | 3,915.8 | 4,552.9 | 10,054.5 | 16,469.5 | 20,711.2 | 19,675.5 | 19,987.7 | 17,430.6 | 24,903.6 |
| Securities Other than Shares.......... | 36a | .... | .... | — | — | — | — | — | — | — | — | — | — |
| Deposits Excl. from Broad Money..... | 36b | .... | .... | | | | | | | | | | |
| Sec.Ot.th.Shares Excl.f/Brd.Money.... | 36s | .... | .... | — | — | — | — | — | — | — | — | — | — |
| Loans................................................. | 36l | .... | .... | 25.0 | 186.5 | 250.0 | — | — | 950.0 | 1,450.0 | 1,950.0 | 1,950.0 | 2,099.2 |
| Financial Derivatives........................ | 36m | .... | .... | — | — | — | — | — | — | — | — | — | — |
| Insurance Technical Reserves........... | 36r | .... | .... | — | — | — | — | — | — | — | — | — | — |
| Shares and Other Equity.................. | 37a | .... | .... | 24,038.7 | 36,067.1 | 41,325.5 | 49,767.2 | 480.5 | 36,800.4 | 83,686.5 | 110,483.8 | 100,220.5 | 151,119.9 |
| Other Items (Net)............................. | 37r | .... | .... | −18,480.7 | −2,242.6 | 4,778.1 | −12,636.4 | 21,482.5 | −36,567.8 | −41,279.4 | −42,719.9 | −43,205.1 | −31,398.5 |
| Broad Money Liabs., Seasonally Adj. | 35l.b | .... | .... | 80,156.2 | 114,282.0 | 150,322.1 | 200,164.8 | 253,933.3 | 307,218.3 | 332,572.9 | 361,961.0 | 390,666.2 | 402,824.1 |
| **Monetary Aggregates** | | | | *Millions of Afghanis: End of Period* | | | | | | | | | |
| Broad Money.................................... | 59m | .... | .... | 81,247.9 | 115,693.1 | 152,002.1 | 202,231.3 | 256,726.8 | 311,433.1 | 338,839.6 | 370,683.5 | 401,582.6 | 414,819.5 |
| o/w:Currency Issued by Cent.Govt | 59m.a | .... | .... | | | | | | | | | | |
| o/w: Dep.in Nonfin. Corporations. | 59m.b | .... | .... | — | — | — | — | — | — | — | — | — | — |
| o/w:Secs. Issued by Central Govt.. | 59m.c | .... | .... | | | | | | | | | | |
| Money (National Definitions) | | | | | | | | | | | | | |
| M1.................................................. | 59ma | .... | .... | 79,505.8 | 111,777.3 | 147,449.2 | 192,176.8 | 240,257.2 | 290,722.0 | 319,164.1 | 350,695.8 | 384,152.0 | 389,915.9 |
| M2.................................................. | 59mb | .... | .... | 81,247.9 | 115,693.1 | 152,002.1 | 202,231.3 | 256,726.8 | 311,433.1 | 338,839.6 | 370,683.5 | 401,582.6 | 414,819.5 |
| **Interest Rates** | | | | *Percent Per Annum* | | | | | | | | | |
| Money Market Rate........................ | 60b | .... | .... | 2.50 | 5.65 | .... | .... | 2.01 | .20 | .... | .... | .... | .... |
| Money Market Rate (Fgn. Currency). | 60b.f | .... | .... | 5.23 | 4.53 | 2.23 | .10 | .20 | .12 | .90 | 1.14 | 1.34 | .... |
| Savings Rate..................................... | 60k | .... | .... | 5.02 | 5.37 | 7.50 | 7.08 | 5.39 | 4.67 | 3.78 | 2.87 | 3.41 | 2.71 |
| Savings Rate (Fgn. Currency)........... | 60k.f | .... | .... | 3.49 | 4.33 | 5.25 | 4.28 | 3.49 | 4.13 | 3.33 | 2.40 | 1.86 | 1.94 |
| Deposit Rate (Fgn. Currency)........... | 60l.f | .... | .... | 2.91 | 4.15 | 5.02 | 4.06 | 3.04 | 2.95 | 2.01 | 1.70 | .... | 3.56 |
| Lending Rate.................................... | 60p | .... | .... | 17.97 | 18.14 | 14.92 | 15.00 | 15.69 | 15.15 | 15.00 | 15.08 | 15.00 | 15.00 |
| Lending Rate (Fgn. Currency).......... | 60p.f | .... | .... | 17.48 | 13.45 | 13.25 | 14.00 | 11.66 | 10.92 | 7.24 | 7.37 | 15.92 | .... |
| **Prices** | | | | *Index Numbers (2010=100): Period Averages* | | | | | | | | | |
| Consumer Prices............................. | 64 | 63.1 | 71.1 | 76.3 | 82.8 | 108.1 | 99.1 | 100.0 | † 110.2 | 118.2 | 127.2 | 133.1 | 131.0 |

# Afghanistan, Islamic Republic of   512

| | | 2004 | 2005 | 2006 | 2007 | 2008 | 2009 | 2010 | 2011 | 2012 | 2013 | 2014 | 2015 |
|---|---|---|---|---|---|---|---|---|---|---|---|---|---|
| **Balance of Payments** | | | | | | *Millions of US Dollars* | | | | | | | |
| A. Current Account* | 109bx | .... | .... | .... | .... | −2,162.1 | −2,383.9 | −3,710.7 | −4,757.7 | −8,308.8 | −8,113.1 | −6,854.6 | .... |
| Goods, credit (exports) | 1a9cx | .... | .... | .... | .... | 563.4 | 423.1 | 389.1 | 430.8 | 519.7 | 524.5 | 608.3 | .... |
| Goods, debit (imports) | 1a9dx | .... | .... | .... | .... | 3,215.9 | 3,627.5 | 4,679.7 | 5,736.1 | 7,929.1 | 7,433.6 | 6,743.2 | .... |
| Balance on goods | 1a9bx | .... | .... | .... | .... | −2,652.6 | −3,204.4 | −4,290.6 | −5,305.4 | −7,409.3 | −6,909.1 | −6,135.0 | .... |
| Services, credit (exports) | 1b9cx | .... | .... | .... | .... | 1,184.6 | 1,814.8 | 2,125.4 | 2,765.1 | 1,468.7 | 1,013.1 | 1,253.2 | .... |
| Services, debit (imports) | 1b9dx | .... | .... | .... | .... | 629.0 | 714.1 | 1,380.3 | 2,023.1 | 2,311.1 | 2,055.0 | 1,850.3 | .... |
| Balance on goods & services | 1z9bx | .... | .... | .... | .... | −2,097.0 | −2,103.7 | −3,545.5 | −4,563.3 | −8,251.8 | −7,950.9 | −6,732.1 | .... |
| Primary income: credit | 1c9cx | .... | .... | .... | .... | 139.7 | 102.3 | 167.3 | 143.5 | 172.9 | 205.8 | 244.7 | .... |
| Primary income: debit | 1c9dx | .... | .... | .... | .... | 141.8 | 140.1 | 138.2 | 167.1 | 119.0 | 142.8 | 182.1 | .... |
| Balance on gds, serv. & prim. inc. | 1y9bx | .... | .... | .... | .... | −2,099.1 | −2,141.5 | −3,516.3 | −4,586.9 | −8,197.9 | −7,888.0 | −6,669.5 | .... |
| Secondary income: credit | 1d9ca | .... | .... | .... | .... | 33.8 | 77.0 | 190.9 | 78.5 | 130.5 | 144.8 | 87.1 | .... |
| Secondary income: debit | 1d9da | .... | .... | .... | .... | 96.8 | 319.4 | 385.2 | 249.4 | 241.4 | 369.9 | 272.2 | .... |
| B. Capital Account* | 209ba | .... | .... | .... | .... | 1,752.9 | 2,595.7 | 2,668.0 | 2,305.6 | 2,382.2 | 2,791.1 | 2,052.6 | .... |
| Capital account: credit | 209ca | .... | .... | .... | .... | 1,762.3 | 2,616.9 | 2,689.3 | 2,323.0 | 2,407.5 | 2,805.4 | 2,085.4 | .... |
| Capital account: debit | 209da | .... | .... | .... | .... | 9.4 | 21.2 | 21.4 | 17.4 | 25.3 | 14.4 | 32.8 | .... |
| Balance on current & capital acct. | 129ba | .... | .... | .... | .... | −409.2 | 211.8 | −1,042.7 | −2,452.1 | −5,926.6 | −5,322.0 | −4,802.0 | .... |
| C. Financial Account* | 309na | .... | .... | .... | .... | −424.5 | −10.7 | 272.4 | 35.2 | 340.2 | 96.8 | −87.8 | .... |
| Direct investment: assets | 3a9aa | .... | .... | .... | .... | — | — | — | — | — | — | — | .... |
| Equity & investment fund shares | 3aaaa | .... | .... | .... | .... | — | — | — | — | — | — | — | .... |
| Debt instruments | 3abaa | .... | .... | .... | .... | — | — | — | — | — | — | — | .... |
| Direct investment: liabilities | 3a9la | .... | .... | .... | .... | 46.0 | 197.5 | 54.2 | 57.6 | 61.5 | 39.7 | 48.8 | .... |
| Equity & investment fund shares | 3aala | .... | .... | .... | .... | 46.0 | 197.5 | 54.2 | 57.6 | 61.5 | 39.7 | 48.8 | .... |
| Debt instruments | 3abla | .... | .... | .... | .... | — | — | — | — | — | — | — | .... |
| Portfolio investment: assets | 3b9aa | .... | .... | .... | .... | 15.3 | .3 | 9.4 | 79.9 | 42.8 | 29.2 | −27.0 | .... |
| Equity & investment fund shares | 3baaa | .... | .... | .... | .... | −1.9 | .3 | −.5 | 1.2 | −9.2 | −21.3 | −75.4 | .... |
| Debt securities | 3bbaa | .... | .... | .... | .... | 17.2 | — | 9.9 | 78.7 | 52.0 | 50.6 | 48.4 | .... |
| Portfolio investment: liabilities | 3b9la | .... | .... | .... | .... | — | — | — | — | — | — | — | .... |
| Equity & investment fund shares | 3bala | .... | .... | .... | .... | — | — | — | — | — | — | — | .... |
| Debt securities | 3bbla | .... | .... | .... | .... | — | — | — | — | — | — | — | .... |
| Fin. der.& empl.stk.ops.(ESOs): net. | 3c9na | .... | .... | .... | .... | — | — | — | .2 | −.2 | — | −.5 | .... |
| Fin. der. & ESOs.: assets | 3c9aa | .... | .... | .... | .... | — | — | — | 46.7 | −42.9 | — | — | .... |
| Fin. der. & ESOs.: liabilities | 3c9la | .... | .... | .... | .... | — | — | — | 46.4 | −42.7 | — | .5 | .... |
| Other investment: assets | 3d9aa | .... | .... | .... | .... | 225.8 | 275.7 | 19.0 | 169.7 | 276.8 | 122.7 | −112.6 | .... |
| Other equity | 3daaa | .... | .... | .... | .... | | | | | | | | .... |
| Debt instruments | 3dzaa | .... | .... | .... | .... | 225.8 | 275.7 | 19.0 | 169.7 | 276.8 | 122.7 | −112.6 | .... |
| Other investment: liabilities | 3d9la | .... | .... | .... | .... | 619.5 | 89.2 | −298.1 | 157.1 | −82.4 | 15.6 | −101.0 | .... |
| Other equity | 3dala | .... | .... | .... | .... | | | | | | | | .... |
| Debt instruments | 3dzla | .... | .... | .... | .... | 619.5 | 89.2 | −298.1 | 157.1 | −82.4 | 15.6 | −101.0 | .... |
| Curr.+ cap.− finan. acct. balance | 4y9na | .... | .... | .... | .... | 15.3 | 222.5 | −1,315.1 | −2,487.2 | −6,266.8 | −5,418.8 | −4,714.2 | .... |
| D. Net Errors and Omissions | 409na | .... | .... | .... | .... | −92.9 | −1,333.3 | 1,163.1 | 2,145.9 | 4,348.7 | 2,962.3 | 2,900.7 | .... |
| E. Reserves and Related Items | 4z9na | .... | .... | .... | .... | −77.6 | −1,110.8 | −152.0 | −341.4 | −1,918.1 | −2,456.5 | −1,813.5 | .... |
| Reserve assets | 3e9aa | .... | .... | .... | .... | 1,144.3 | 502.3 | 2,185.2 | 1,703.4 | 741.9 | 623.0 | 1,055.4 | .... |
| Credit and loans from the IMF | 3dcla | .... | .... | .... | .... | 18.4 | 25.7 | — | 18.8 | 8.9 | −16.1 | −18.9 | .... |
| Exceptional financing | 409la | .... | .... | .... | .... | 1,203.5 | 1,587.4 | 2,337.2 | 2,026.0 | 2,651.1 | 3,095.6 | 2,887.8 | .... |

*Excludes components in group E

| | | 2004 | 2005 | 2006 | 2007 | 2008 | 2009 | 2010 | 2011 | 2012 | 2013 | 2014 | 2015 |
|---|---|---|---|---|---|---|---|---|---|---|---|---|---|
| **International Investment Position** | | | | | | *Millions of US Dollars* | | | | | | | |
| Assets | 809aa | .... | .... | .... | .... | .... | 5,325.3 | 6,404.4 | 8,251.9 | 10,114.9 | 9,562.9 | 8,955.3 | .... |
| Direct investment | 8a9aa | .... | .... | .... | .... | .... | 98.0 | 166.0 | 231.0 | 68.0 | 292.0 | .... | .... |
| Equity & investment fund shares | 8aaaa | .... | .... | .... | .... | .... | 98.0 | 166.0 | 231.0 | 68.0 | 292.0 | .... | .... |
| Debt instruments | 8abaa | .... | .... | .... | .... | .... | .... | .... | .... | .... | .... | .... | .... |
| Portfolio investment | 8b9aa | .... | .... | .... | .... | .... | 16.4 | 16.1 | 462.3 | 1,257.9 | 169.5 | 206.2 | .... |
| Equity & investment fund shares | 8baaa | .... | .... | .... | .... | .... | 16.4 | 16.1 | 16.0 | 6.6 | 6.7 | 6.5 | .... |
| Debt securities | 8bbaa | .... | .... | .... | .... | .... | .... | .... | 446.3 | 1,251.2 | 162.8 | 199.7 | .... |
| Fin. der.(oth.than reserves) & ESOs | 8c9aa | .... | .... | .... | .... | .... | .... | .... | .... | .... | .... | .... | .... |
| Other investment | 8d9aa | .... | .... | .... | .... | .... | 990.6 | 1,267.1 | 1,407.3 | 1,644.1 | 1,585.6 | 1,408.0 | .... |
| Other equity | 8daaa | .... | .... | .... | .... | .... | | | | | | | .... |
| Debt instruments | 8dzaa | .... | .... | .... | .... | .... | 990.6 | 1,267.1 | 1,407.3 | 1,644.1 | 1,585.6 | 1,408.0 | .... |
| Reserve assets | 8e9aa | .... | .... | .... | .... | .... | 4,220.3 | 4,955.2 | 6,151.3 | 7,144.8 | 7,515.9 | 7,341.1 | .... |
| Liabilities | 809la | .... | .... | .... | .... | .... | 3,972.0 | 4,330.7 | 4,247.8 | 4,330.1 | 4,226.1 | 4,152.3 | .... |
| Direct investment | 8a9la | .... | .... | .... | .... | .... | 1,167.9 | 1,359.6 | 1,422.5 | 1,485.0 | 1,496.4 | 1,539.6 | .... |
| Equity & investment fund shares | 8aala | .... | .... | .... | .... | .... | 1,167.9 | 1,359.6 | 1,422.5 | 1,485.0 | 1,496.4 | 1,539.6 | .... |
| Debt instruments | 8abla | .... | .... | .... | .... | .... | | | | | | | .... |
| Portfolio investment | 8b9la | .... | .... | .... | .... | .... | .... | 7.0 | 6.0 | 7.0 | 12.0 | .1 | .... |
| Equity & investment fund shares | 8bala | .... | .... | .... | .... | .... | .... | 7.0 | 6.0 | 7.0 | 12.0 | .1 | .... |
| Debt securities | 8bbla | .... | .... | .... | .... | .... | | | | | | | .... |
| Fin. der.(oth.than reserves) & ESOs | 8c9la | .... | .... | .... | .... | .... | .... | .... | .... | .... | .... | .... | .... |
| Other investment | 8d9la | .... | .... | .... | .... | .... | 2,804.1 | 2,964.2 | 2,819.2 | 2,838.1 | 2,717.7 | 2,612.5 | .... |
| Other equity | 8dala | .... | .... | .... | .... | .... | .... | .... | .... | .... | .... | .... | .... |
| Debt instruments | 8dzla | .... | .... | .... | .... | .... | 2,804.1 | 2,964.2 | 2,819.2 | 2,838.1 | 2,717.7 | 2,612.5 | .... |

# Afghanistan, Islamic Republic of   512

| | | 2004 | 2005 | 2006 | 2007 | 2008 | 2009 | 2010 | 2011 | 2012 | 2013 | 2014 | 2015 |
|---|---|---|---|---|---|---|---|---|---|---|---|---|---|
| **Government Finance** | | | | | | | | | | | | | |
| **Cash Flow Statement** | | | | | | | | | | | | | |
| **Budgetary Central Government** | | | | | *Millions of Afghanis: Fiscal Year Begins March* | | | | | | | | |
| Cash Receipts:Operating Activities... | c1 | 43,385.8 | 55,170.0 | 68,615.2 | 87,596.3 | 96,243.7 | 131,387.9 | 161,172.0 | 191,282.8 | 239,624.8 | 299,001.3 | 293,284.2 | 298,792.8 |
| Taxes............................................ | c11 | 9,721.9 | 14,035.2 | 24,250.6 | 25,514.4 | 31,285.1 | 50,111.2 | 65,662.8 | 71,572.5 | 77,986.4 | 82,458.7 | 80,610.5 | 86,521.4 |
| Social Contributions..................... | c12 | 314.0 | 199.5 | 357.4 | 398.5 | 752.0 | 956.7 | 1,587.6 | 2,550.4 | 3,112.7 | 3,661.3 | 3,792.0 | 3,480.9 |
| Grants........................................... | c13 | 30,606.6 | 32,534.4 | 37,600.5 | 53,888.5 | 55,026.2 | 68,024.5 | 81,135.3 | 97,424.0 | 138,635.1 | 191,598.4 | 193,792.0 | 171,799.2 |
| Other Receipts............................. | c14 | 2,743.3 | 8,400.9 | 6,406.7 | 7,795.0 | 9,180.3 | 12,295.5 | 12,786.3 | 19,735.9 | 19,890.6 | 21,282.9 | 15,089.7 | 36,991.3 |
| Cash Payments:Operating Activities. | c2 | 39,911.3 | 43,350.3 | 57,144.0 | 65,300.7 | 82,658.5 | 101,172.9 | 125,091.1 | 167,510.7 | 190,276.2 | 236,456.5 | 253,926.1 | 269,448.1 |
| Compensation of Employees.......... | c21 | 15,260.3 | 20,502.8 | 26,262.7 | 33,137.8 | 47,381.3 | 63,463.8 | 85,940.1 | 110,937.9 | 126,335.2 | 141,316.4 | 147,747.0 | 151,190.9 |
| Purchases of Goods & Services....... | c22 | 22,221.9 | 19,707.5 | 24,779.5 | 28,379.4 | 30,298.7 | 31,112.3 | 31,957.9 | 45,650.7 | 51,218.7 | 75,333.0 | 83,799.6 | 92,820.6 |
| Interest........................................ | c24 | 97.9 | 149.9 | 169.4 | 106.7 | 103.1 | 103.9 | 79.5 | 92.0 | 140.5 | 282.4 | 388.5 | 658.4 |
| Subsidies..................................... | c25 | 47.7 | 8.6 | 8.0 | .7 | 4.5 | 19.8 | 18.0 | 1,099.6 | 1,000.0 | 1,150.0 | 296.7 | 1,100.0 |
| Grants........................................... | c26 | 343.9 | 63.2 | 3,185.6 | 413.3 | 385.1 | 352.2 | 580.2 | 319.4 | 319.4 | 540.2 | 1,032.2 | 1,673.1 |
| Social Benefits............................. | c27 | 1,365.6 | 1,935.2 | 2,677.0 | 3,243.8 | 3,812.3 | 5,546.4 | 5,948.9 | 8,549.1 | 9,859.6 | 12,442.9 | 18,153.8 | 21,355.5 |
| Other Payments............................ | c28 | 573.9 | 983.0 | 61.9 | 18.9 | 673.6 | 574.5 | 566.6 | 862.0 | 1,402.8 | 5,391.7 | 2,508.4 | 649.6 |
| Net Cash Inflow:Operating Act.[1-2] | ccio | 3,474.6 | 11,819.7 | 11,471.2 | 22,295.7 | 13,585.2 | 30,215.0 | 36,080.9 | 23,772.1 | 49,348.6 | 62,544.8 | 39,358.1 | 29,344.7 |
| Net Cash Outflow:Invest. in NFA...... | c31 | 5,325.6 | 8,651.4 | 20,744.7 | 33,287.7 | 27,109.2 | 29,869.3 | 28,714.1 | 28,413.8 | 37,209.4 | 50,619.6 | 38,520.9 | 50,143.8 |
| Purchases of Nonfinancial Assets... | c31.1 | 5,357.4 | 9,630.1 | 20,876.2 | 33,441.1 | 31,318.3 | 30,237.0 | 28,885.9 | 28,786.1 | 37,979.5 | 51,095.5 | 39,071.4 | 50,621.2 |
| Sales of Nonfinancial Assets.......... | c31.2 | 31.8 | 978.8 | 131.5 | 153.4 | 4,209.1 | 367.7 | 171.7 | 372.3 | 770.1 | 475.9 | 550.5 | 477.4 |
| Cash Surplus/Deficit [1-2-31=1-2M] | ccsd | −1,851.1 | 3,168.3 | −9,273.5 | −10,992.0 | −13,524.0 | 345.7 | 7,366.8 | −4,641.6 | 12,139.2 | 11,925.1 | 837.3 | −20,799.1 |
| Net Acq. Fin. Assets, excl. Cash....... | c32x | 268.1 | 1,055.3 | −33.1 | −25.0 | 165.4 | 258.6 | 979.8 | 1,402.1 | 14,007.7 | 2,227.6 | −1,570.3 | −17,398.5 |
| Domestic...................................... | c321x | 268.1 | 1,055.3 | −33.1 | −25.0 | 165.4 | 258.6 | 979.8 | 1,402.1 | 14,007.7 | 2,227.6 | −1,570.3 | −17,398.5 |
| Foreign......................................... | c322x | — | — | — | — | — | — | — | — | — | — | — | — |
| Net Incurrence of Liabilities.............. | c33 | 9,969.2 | 5,672.7 | 9,728.0 | 11,301.3 | 16,180.6 | 6,886.9 | 10,278.7 | 7,019.7 | 13,228.2 | 7,485.7 | 262.1 | −8,757.7 |
| Domestic...................................... | c331 | 724.4 | 479.6 | 1,125.8 | — | 6,322.0 | −82.6 | 4,008.8 | −1,107.2 | 18,598.4 | 6,817.1 | −2,030.8 | −12,900.9 |
| Foreign......................................... | c332 | 9,244.8 | 5,193.1 | 8,602.2 | 11,301.3 | 9,858.6 | 6,969.5 | 6,269.9 | 8,126.8 | −5,370.2 | 668.7 | 2,292.9 | 4,143.3 |
| Net Cash Inflow, Fin.Act.[-32x+33].. | cnfb | 9,701.1 | 4,617.4 | 9,761.1 | 11,326.2 | 16,015.3 | 6,628.3 | 9,298.9 | 5,617.5 | −779.5 | 5,258.2 | 1,832.4 | 8,640.8 |
| Net Change in Stock of Cash........... | cncb | 7,850.1 | 7,785.7 | 487.6 | 334.2 | 2,491.3 | 7,862.9 | 16,665.7 | 975.9 | 11,359.8 | 17,183.3 | 2,669.7 | −12,158.3 |
| Stat. Discrep. [32X-33+NCB-CSD].... | ccsdz | — | — | — | — | — | 888.9 | — | — | — | — | | |
| Memo Item:Cash Expenditure[2+31] | c2m | 45,236.9 | 52,001.7 | 77,888.7 | 98,588.4 | 109,767.7 | 131,042.2 | 153,805.2 | 195,924.4 | 227,485.6 | 287,076.2 | 292,447.0 | 319,591.9 |
| Memo Item: Gross Debt.................. | c63 | 29,930.1 | 34,062.4 | 38,954.5 | .... | .... | .... | .... | .... | .... | .... | .... | .... |
| **Population...............................** | 99z | 23.50 | 24.40 | 25.18 | 25.88 | 26.53 | 27.21 | 27.96 | 28.81 | 29.73 | 30.68 | 31.63 | 32.53 |

# Albania 914

| | | 2004 | 2005 | 2006 | 2007 | 2008 | 2009 | 2010 | 2011 | 2012 | 2013 | 2014 | 2015 |
|---|---|---|---|---|---|---|---|---|---|---|---|---|---|
| **Exchange Rates** | | | | | | *Leks per SDR: End of Period* | | | | | | | |
| Market Rate | aa | 143.87 | 148.04 | 141.62 | 130.99 | 135.41 | 150.20 | 160.16 | 165.10 | 162.68 | 156.86 | 166.95 | 174.31 |
| | | | | | *Leks per US Dollar: End of Period (ae) Period Average (rf)* | | | | | | | | |
| Market Rate | ae | 92.64 | 103.58 | 94.14 | 82.89 | 87.91 | 95.81 | 104.00 | 107.54 | 105.85 | 101.86 | 115.23 | 125.79 |
| Market Rate | rf | 102.78 | 99.87 | 98.10 | 90.43 | 83.89 | 94.98 | 103.94 | 100.89 | 108.18 | 105.67 | 105.48 | 125.96 |
| **Fund Position** | | | | | | *Millions of SDRs: End of Period* | | | | | | | |
| Quota | 2f.s | 48.70 | 48.70 | 48.70 | 48.70 | 48.70 | 48.70 | 48.70 | 48.70 | 60.00 | 60.00 | 60.00 | 60.00 |
| SDR Holdings | 1b.s | 64.90 | 8.75 | 5.99 | 1.22 | 4.70 | 50.40 | 50.71 | 49.97 | 54.02 | 66.98 | 73.73 | 136.51 |
| Reserve Position in the Fund | 1c.s | 3.35 | 3.35 | 3.35 | 3.35 | 3.35 | 3.35 | 3.35 | 3.35 | 6.18 | 6.18 | 6.18 | 6.18 |
| Total Fund Cred.&Loans Outstg | 2tl | 62.43 | 64.27 | 61.54 | 57.00 | 52.25 | 45.60 | 37.56 | 29.91 | 23.19 | 16.38 | 57.67 | 129.33 |
| SDR Allocations | 1bd | — | — | — | — | — | 46.45 | 46.45 | 46.45 | 46.45 | 46.45 | 46.45 | 46.45 |
| **International Liquidity** | | | | | *Millions of US Dollars Unless Otherwise Indicated: End of Period* | | | | | | | | |
| Total Reserves minus Gold | 1l.d | 1,357.60 | 1,404.09 | 1,768.80 | 2,104.22 | 2,319.78 | 2,313.91 | 2,469.55 | 2,393.92 | 2,515.65 | 2,712.32 | 2,604.18 | 3,084.87 |
| SDR Holdings | 1b.d | 100.79 | 12.50 | 9.00 | 1.93 | 7.24 | 79.02 | 78.10 | 76.72 | 83.03 | 103.14 | 106.82 | 189.16 |
| Reserve Position in the Fund | 1c.d | 5.21 | 4.80 | 5.05 | 5.30 | 5.17 | 5.26 | 5.17 | 5.15 | 9.50 | 9.52 | 8.95 | 8.56 |
| Foreign Exchange | 1d.d | 1,251.60 | 1,386.79 | 1,754.75 | 2,096.99 | 2,307.37 | 2,229.63 | 2,386.28 | 2,312.06 | 2,423.13 | 2,599.66 | 2,488.41 | 2,887.15 |
| Gold (Million Fine Troy Ounces) | 1ad | .07 | .07 | .07 | .07 | .05 | .05 | .05 | .05 | .05 | .05 | .05 | .05 |
| Gold (National Valuation) | 1and | 30.25 | 35.49 | 43.91 | 57.93 | 43.93 | 55.83 | 71.37 | 79.54 | 84.23 | 60.79 | 60.71 | 53.74 |
| Central Bank: Other Assets | 3..d | 14.09 | 14.80 | 19.44 | 24.66 | 21.95 | 26.11 | 31.55 | 34.49 | 37.41 | 27.74 | 28.99 | 1.64 |
| Central Bank: Other Liabs | 4..d | 16.76 | 13.00 | 15.50 | 17.72 | 16.71 | 13.61 | 12.34 | 11.79 | 13.29 | 12.56 | 13.12 | 12.22 |
| Other Depository Corps.: Assets | 7a.d | 911.85 | 855.05 | 1,167.59 | 1,269.63 | 984.96 | 904.80 | 1,191.79 | 1,671.42 | 2,203.23 | 2,605.40 | 2,491.16 | 2,367.09 |
| Other Depository Corps.: Liabs | 7b.d | 153.90 | 160.04 | 402.52 | 528.77 | 922.67 | 591.93 | 359.28 | 430.72 | 459.19 | 596.13 | 470.00 | 368.58 |
| **Central Bank** | | | | | | *Billions of Leks: End of Period* | | | | | | | |
| Net Foreign Assets | 11n | 118.59 | 138.80 | 161.21 | 171.04 | 201.17 | 214.43 | 252.80 | 255.58 | 266.55 | 274.23 | 291.59 | 363.37 |
| Claims on Nonresidents | 11 | 129.13 | 149.66 | 171.39 | 179.97 | 209.71 | 229.56 | 267.54 | 269.45 | 279.29 | 285.37 | 310.49 | 395.55 |
| Liabilities to Nonresidents | 16c | 10.53 | 10.86 | 10.17 | 8.94 | 8.54 | 15.13 | 14.74 | 13.88 | 12.74 | 11.14 | 18.89 | 32.18 |
| Claims on Other Depository Corps | 12e | .28 | .21 | 9.04 | 1.60 | 20.14 | 32.37 | 12.54 | 25.49 | 21.80 | 21.50 | 25.55 | 12.99 |
| Net Claims on Central Government | 12an | 62.10 | 62.90 | 51.36 | 57.46 | 64.07 | 71.37 | 57.94 | 57.10 | 55.15 | 44.50 | 55.20 | 48.75 |
| Claims on Central Government | 12a | 70.53 | 73.18 | 72.48 | 78.27 | 83.43 | 82.29 | 66.93 | 67.59 | 68.06 | 66.77 | 71.83 | 75.14 |
| Liabilities to Central Government | 16d | 8.43 | 10.28 | 21.12 | 20.81 | 19.35 | 10.92 | 8.99 | 10.49 | 12.91 | 22.27 | 16.63 | 26.39 |
| Claims on Other Sectors | 12s | .67 | .72 | .88 | 1.05 | 1.18 | 1.52 | 1.77 | 1.91 | 1.91 | 1.84 | 1.78 | 1.66 |
| Claims on Other Financial Corps | 12g | | | | | | | | | | | | |
| Claims on State & Local Govts | 12b | — | — | — | — | — | — | — | — | — | — | — | — |
| Claims on Public Nonfin. Corps. | 12c | — | — | — | — | — | — | — | — | — | — | — | — |
| Claims on Private Sector | 12d | .67 | .72 | .88 | 1.05 | 1.18 | 1.52 | 1.77 | 1.91 | 1.91 | 1.84 | 1.78 | 1.66 |
| Monetary Base | 14 | 178.60 | 198.25 | 217.62 | 228.23 | 271.73 | 284.84 | 283.45 | 289.81 | 297.72 | 308.07 | 332.90 | 383.97 |
| Currency in Circulation | 14a | 141.64 | 153.57 | 168.25 | 161.18 | 203.73 | 216.77 | 202.39 | 202.91 | 200.90 | 207.79 | 226.43 | 239.22 |
| Liabs. to Other Depository Corps. | 14c | 36.95 | 44.67 | 49.37 | 67.04 | 67.79 | 68.07 | 80.81 | 86.80 | 96.64 | 100.03 | 106.31 | 142.97 |
| Liabilities to Other Sectors | 14d | .01 | .01 | — | .01 | .20 | — | .26 | .10 | .19 | .25 | .15 | 1.79 |
| Other Liabs. to Other Dep. Corps. | 14n | 2.37 | .51 | 4.20 | — | — | — | — | 1.77 | .42 | — | — | — |
| Dep. & Sec. Excl. f/Monetary Base | 14o | .27 | .48 | .64 | .59 | .90 | .71 | .63 | .66 | .71 | .79 | 1.09 | .45 |
| Deposits Included in Broad Money | 15 | — | — | — | — | — | — | — | — | — | — | — | — |
| Sec.Ot.th.Shares Incl.in Brd. Money | 16a | — | — | — | — | — | — | — | — | — | — | — | — |
| Deposits Excl. from Broad Money | 16b | .27 | .48 | .64 | .59 | .90 | .71 | .63 | .66 | .71 | .79 | 1.09 | .45 |
| Sec.Ot.th.Shares Excl.f/Brd.Money | 16s | — | — | — | — | — | — | — | — | — | — | — | — |
| Loans | 16l | — | — | — | — | — | — | — | — | — | — | — | — |
| Financial Derivatives | 16m | — | — | — | — | — | — | — | — | — | — | — | — |
| Shares and Other Equity | 17a | 3.39 | 6.75 | 3.43 | 6.78 | 19.46 | 40.00 | 52.25 | 59.99 | 59.95 | 45.97 | 55.79 | 63.39 |
| Other Items (Net) | 17r | −2.99 | −3.36 | −3.40 | −4.46 | −5.53 | −5.85 | −11.28 | −12.16 | −13.38 | −12.76 | −15.66 | −21.05 |
| Memo Item: | | | | | | | | | | | | | |
| Total Assets | 10ra | 213.95 | 237.68 | 267.89 | 275.96 | 330.32 | 363.79 | 372.69 | 389.60 | 400.08 | 404.20 | 440.06 | 522.70 |
| **Other Depository Corporations** | | | | | | *Billions of Leks: End of Period* | | | | | | | |
| Net Foreign Assets | 21n | 70.22 | 71.99 | 72.02 | 61.41 | 5.48 | 29.98 | 86.58 | 133.42 | 184.61 | 204.66 | 232.90 | 251.39 |
| Claims on Nonresidents | 21 | 84.47 | 88.57 | 109.92 | 105.24 | 86.59 | 86.69 | 123.95 | 179.74 | 233.21 | 265.39 | 287.06 | 297.76 |
| Liabilities to Nonresidents | 26c | 14.26 | 16.58 | 37.89 | 43.83 | 81.11 | 56.71 | 37.37 | 46.32 | 48.61 | 60.72 | 54.16 | 46.36 |
| Claims on Central Bank | 20 | 42.89 | 50.47 | 64.50 | 72.66 | 76.56 | 75.73 | 88.27 | 97.11 | 105.50 | 112.83 | 115.40 | 152.84 |
| Currency | 20a | 3.55 | 3.90 | 4.99 | 6.23 | 7.92 | 7.72 | 7.33 | 7.98 | 8.19 | 8.90 | 8.77 | 8.62 |
| Reserve Deposits and Securities | 20b | 37.08 | 46.07 | 55.31 | 66.43 | 68.65 | 68.01 | 80.94 | 89.12 | 97.30 | 103.93 | 106.63 | 144.22 |
| Other Claims | 20n | 2.26 | .51 | 4.20 | — | — | — | — | — | — | — | — | — |
| Net Claims on Central Government | 22an | 213.71 | 218.42 | 241.04 | 249.02 | 257.99 | 269.92 | 285.46 | 304.56 | 298.88 | 320.36 | 330.84 | 305.28 |
| Claims on Central Government | 22a | 215.08 | 219.84 | 241.76 | 254.73 | 260.90 | 273.06 | 291.44 | 309.95 | 305.87 | 325.82 | 338.20 | 314.53 |
| Liabilities to Central Government | 26d | 1.37 | 1.42 | .72 | 5.71 | 2.91 | 3.13 | 5.98 | 5.39 | 6.99 | 5.46 | 7.36 | 9.25 |
| Claims on Other Sectors | 22s | 71.72 | 124.45 | 195.07 | 293.17 | 395.53 | 439.44 | 481.98 | 540.59 | 553.42 | 546.80 | 560.63 | 547.44 |
| Claims on Other Financial Corps. | 22g | .55 | .73 | .15 | .35 | .82 | 6.59 | 9.33 | 10.44 | 10.75 | 10.28 | 10.65 | 11.68 |
| Claims on State & Local Govts | 22b | — | — | — | — | — | — | .08 | .15 | .19 | .26 | .78 | .89 |
| Claims on Public Nonfin. Corps. | 22c | .12 | .07 | .18 | 3.92 | 12.90 | 12.06 | 9.37 | 18.68 | 23.78 | 24.96 | 27.33 | 27.42 |
| Claims on Private Sector | 22d | 71.05 | 123.65 | 194.74 | 288.90 | 381.81 | 420.80 | 463.20 | 511.33 | 518.69 | 511.30 | 521.87 | 507.44 |
| Liabilities to Central Bank | 26g | .84 | .76 | 10.18 | 1.68 | 20.65 | 32.49 | 13.01 | 26.38 | 22.11 | 25.78 | 26.56 | 14.88 |
| Transf.Dep.Included in Broad Money | 24 | 45.68 | 65.45 | 88.49 | 116.15 | 116.70 | 115.88 | 129.78 | 130.17 | 137.94 | 157.31 | 219.47 | 283.95 |
| Other Dep.Included in Broad Money | 25 | 319.45 | 359.19 | 414.71 | 486.49 | 502.98 | 546.54 | 655.19 | 744.95 | 792.57 | 792.53 | 757.79 | 701.78 |
| Sec.Ot.th.Shares Incl.in Brd. Money | 26a | — | — | — | — | — | — | — | — | — | — | — | — |
| Deposits Excl. from Broad Money | 26b | 7.52 | 8.83 | 16.02 | 18.71 | 18.13 | 17.23 | 20.73 | 25.44 | 28.05 | 38.91 | 54.31 | 73.17 |
| Sec.Ot.th.Shares Excl.f/Brd.Money | 26s | — | — | — | — | — | — | — | — | — | — | — | — |
| Loans | 26l | .10 | 1.34 | 2.17 | 2.73 | 2.70 | 2.55 | 2.57 | 3.31 | 3.68 | 3.55 | 5.51 | 7.43 |
| Financial Derivatives | 26m | — | — | — | — | — | — | — | — | — | — | — | — |
| Insurance Technical Reserves | 26r | — | — | — | — | — | — | — | — | — | — | — | — |
| Shares and Other Equity | 27a | 27.16 | 35.40 | 45.24 | 60.78 | 69.82 | 84.24 | 92.06 | 95.36 | 101.58 | 103.35 | 109.65 | 126.35 |
| Other Items (Net) | 27r | −2.20 | −5.64 | −4.18 | −2.46 | 4.58 | 16.13 | 28.95 | 50.06 | 56.46 | 63.23 | 66.46 | 49.39 |
| Memo Item: | | | | | | | | | | | | | |
| Total Assets | 20ra | 427.43 | 497.68 | 627.68 | 744.27 | 841.39 | 903.70 | 1,017.31 | 1,159.96 | 1,241.34 | 1,306.24 | 1,361.39 | 1,372.35 |

# Albania 914

| | | 2004 | 2005 | 2006 | 2007 | 2008 | 2009 | 2010 | 2011 | 2012 | 2013 | 2014 | 2015 |
|---|---|---|---|---|---|---|---|---|---|---|---|---|---|
| **Depository Corporations** | | | | | | *Billions of Leks: End of Period* | | | | | | | |
| Net Foreign Assets............................ | 31n | 188.81 | 210.79 | 233.24 | 232.45 | 206.64 | 244.41 | 339.38 | 389.00 | 451.16 | 478.90 | 524.49 | 614.76 |
| Claims on Nonresidents................ | 31 | 213.60 | 238.23 | 281.31 | 285.21 | 296.30 | 316.25 | 391.48 | 449.20 | 512.50 | 550.75 | 597.55 | 693.30 |
| Liabilities to Nonresidents............. | 36c | 24.79 | 27.44 | 48.07 | 52.77 | 89.66 | 71.84 | 52.10 | 60.20 | 61.34 | 71.86 | 73.05 | 78.54 |
| Domestic Claims............................. | 32 | 348.20 | 406.49 | 488.34 | 600.70 | 718.78 | 782.25 | 827.15 | 904.16 | 909.35 | 913.49 | 948.44 | 903.12 |
| Net Claims on Central Government | 32an | 275.81 | 281.32 | 292.40 | 306.48 | 322.07 | 341.29 | 343.40 | 361.66 | 354.02 | 364.86 | 386.04 | 354.03 |
| Claims on Central Government.... | 32a | 285.61 | 293.02 | 314.24 | 333.00 | 344.33 | 355.34 | 358.37 | 377.54 | 373.93 | 392.58 | 410.03 | 389.67 |
| Liabilities to Central Government. | 36d | 9.80 | 11.70 | 21.84 | 26.52 | 22.27 | 14.05 | 14.97 | 15.88 | 19.90 | 27.72 | 23.99 | 35.64 |
| Claims on Other Sectors................ | 32s | 72.39 | 125.17 | 195.94 | 294.22 | 396.71 | 440.96 | 483.75 | 542.50 | 555.33 | 548.63 | 562.40 | 549.09 |
| Claims on Other Financial Corps.. | 32g | .55 | .73 | .15 | .35 | .82 | 6.59 | 9.33 | 10.44 | 10.75 | 10.28 | 10.65 | 11.68 |
| Claims on State & Local Govts..... | 32b | — | — | — | — | — | — | .08 | .15 | .19 | .26 | .78 | .89 |
| Claims on Public Nonfin. Corps.... | 32c | .12 | .07 | .18 | 3.92 | 12.90 | 12.06 | 9.37 | 18.68 | 23.78 | 24.96 | 27.33 | 27.42 |
| Claims on Private Sector............. | 32d | 71.72 | 124.37 | 195.61 | 289.95 | 382.99 | 422.32 | 464.97 | 513.24 | 520.60 | 513.14 | 523.65 | 509.10 |
| Broad Money Liabilities................... | 35l | 503.23 | 574.31 | 666.47 | 757.61 | 815.70 | 871.47 | 980.28 | 1,070.15 | 1,123.41 | 1,148.98 | 1,195.09 | 1,218.12 |
| Currency Outside Depository Corps | 34a | 138.09 | 149.67 | 163.26 | 154.95 | 195.82 | 209.04 | 195.06 | 194.92 | 192.71 | 198.89 | 217.67 | 230.60 |
| Transferable Deposits................... | 34 | 45.69 | 65.46 | 88.49 | 116.16 | 116.70 | 115.89 | 130.03 | 130.27 | 138.02 | 157.35 | 219.58 | 283.99 |
| Other Deposits............................. | 35 | 319.45 | 359.19 | 414.71 | 486.49 | 503.19 | 546.54 | 655.20 | 744.96 | 792.68 | 792.74 | 757.84 | 703.53 |
| Securities Other than Shares.......... | 36a | — | — | — | — | — | — | — | — | — | — | — | — |
| Deposits Excl. from Broad Money..... | 36b | 7.79 | 9.31 | 16.66 | 19.30 | 19.03 | 17.94 | 21.36 | 26.11 | 28.75 | 39.69 | 55.40 | 73.62 |
| Sec.Ot.th.Shares Excl.f/Brd.Money.... | 36s | — | — | — | — | — | — | — | — | — | — | — | — |
| Loans.................................... | 36l | .10 | 1.34 | 2.17 | 2.73 | 2.70 | 2.55 | 2.57 | 3.31 | 3.68 | 3.55 | 5.51 | 7.43 |
| Financial Derivatives....................... | 36m | — | — | — | — | — | — | — | — | — | — | — | — |
| Insurance Technical Reserves........... | 36r | — | — | — | — | — | — | — | — | — | — | — | — |
| Shares and Other Equity.................. | 37a | 30.55 | 42.15 | 48.67 | 67.56 | 89.28 | 124.24 | 144.31 | 155.35 | 161.53 | 149.32 | 165.44 | 189.74 |
| Other Items (Net)............................ | 37r | −4.66 | −9.84 | −12.39 | −6.24 | −1.30 | 10.46 | 18.01 | 38.24 | 43.14 | 50.85 | 51.50 | 28.98 |
| Broad Money Liabs., Seasonally Adj. | 35l.b | 498.80 | 568.72 | 659.47 | 749.18 | 806.67 | 862.29 | 970.99 | 1,060.80 | 1,114.12 | 1,139.60 | 1,185.35 | 1,208.00 |
| **Monetary Aggregates** | | | | | | *Billions of Leks: End of Period* | | | | | | | |
| Broad Money............................... | 59m | 503.23 | 574.31 | 666.47 | 757.61 | 815.70 | 871.47 | 980.28 | 1,070.15 | 1,123.41 | 1,148.98 | 1,195.09 | 1,218.12 |
| o/w:Currency Issued by Cent.Govt | 59m.a | — | — | — | — | — | — | — | — | — | — | — | — |
| o/w: Dep.in Nonfin. Corporations. | 59m.b | — | — | — | — | — | — | — | — | — | — | — | — |
| o/w:Secs. Issued by Central Govt.. | 59m.c | — | — | — | — | — | — | — | — | — | — | — | — |
| Money (National Definitions) | | | | | | | | | | | | | |
| M1................................................ | 59ma | 170.08 | 223.66 | 242.39 | 242.68 | 282.86 | 284.51 | 275.43 | 276.90 | 281.25 | 295.88 | 353.32 | 384.11 |
| M2................................................ | 59mb | 393.28 | 427.01 | 477.37 | 506.14 | 555.00 | 578.18 | 604.52 | 647.00 | 669.58 | 693.17 | 722.36 | 724.00 |
| M3................................................ | 59mc | 503.26 | 574.38 | 666.47 | 757.61 | 815.70 | 871.47 | 980.28 | 1,070.15 | 1,123.41 | 1,148.98 | 1,195.09 | 1,218.12 |
| **Interest Rates** | | | | | | *Percent Per Annum* | | | | | | | |
| Central Bank Policy Rate (EOP)........ | 60 | 5.25 | 5.00 | 5.50 | 6.25 | 6.25 | 5.25 | 5.00 | 4.75 | 4.00 | 3.00 | 2.25 | 1.75 |
| Treasury Bill Rate............................ | 60c | 6.79 | 5.52 | 5.49 | 5.93 | 6.24 | 6.27 | 5.83 | 5.46 | 5.15 | 4.21 | 3.11 | 2.40 |
| Deposit Rate................................... | 60l | 6.61 | 5.09 | 5.23 | 5.66 | 6.80 | 6.77 | 6.42 | 5.86 | 5.42 | 4.16 | 1.91 | 1.39 |
| Lending Rate................................... | 60p | 11.76 | 13.08 | 12.94 | 14.10 | 13.02 | 12.66 | 12.82 | 12.43 | 10.88 | 9.83 | 8.66 | 8.70 |
| **Prices and Labor** | | | | | | *Index Numbers (2010=100): Period Averages* | | | | | | | |
| Producer Prices............................... | 63 | 87.0 | † 91.3 | 92.0 | 95.2 | 101.4 | 99.7 | 100.0 | 102.6 | . . . . | 102.5 | . . . . | . . . . |
| Consumer Prices............................. | 64 | 84.7 | 86.7 | 88.7 | † 91.3 | 94.4 | 96.6 | 100.0 | 103.5 | 105.6 | 107.6 | 109.4 | † 111.4 |
| Wages:Average Monthly Earnings.... | 65 | 55.9 | 61.5 | 66.2 | 79.6 | 83.8 | 93.7 | 100.0 | 107.0 | 114.8 | . . . . | . . . . | . . . . |
| | | | | | | *Number in Thousands: Period Averages* | | | | | | | |
| Labor Force..................................... | 67d | 1,082 | 1,086 | 1,083 | 1,080 | 1,103 | 1,047 | 1,048 | 1,068 | 1,098 | 1,069 | 1,067 | . . . . |
| Employment.................................... | 67e | 923 | 931 | 933 | 935 | 962 | 905 | 904 | 925 | 955 | 926 | 925 | . . . . |
| Unemployment................................ | 67c | 159 | 155 | 150 | 144 | 141 | 142 | 144 | 142 | 143 | 143 | 142 | . . . . |
| Unemployment Rate (%)................. | 67r | 14.8 | 14.3 | 13.9 | 13.4 | 12.8 | 13.6 | 13.7 | 13.4 | 13.0 | 13.0 | 13.3 | . . . . |
| **Intl. Transactions & Positions** | | | | | | *Millions of Leks* | | | | | | | |
| Exports........................................... | 70 | 62,121 | 65,818 | 77,405 | 97,171 | 112,572 | 104,515 | 161,548 | 196,897 | 213,030 | 246,397 | 255,758 | 243,181 |
| Imports, c.i.f................................... | 71 | 236,072 | 262,191 | 299,147 | 376,194 | 439,894 | 428,839 | 477,768 | 544,004 | 528,490 | 517,376 | 552,278 | 544,588 |

# Albania   914

| Balance of Payments | | 2004 | 2005 | 2006 | 2007 | 2008 | 2009 | 2010 | 2011 | 2012 | 2013 | 2014 | 2015 |
|---|---|---|---|---|---|---|---|---|---|---|---|---|---|
| | | | | | | *Millions of US Dollars* | | | | | | | |
| A. Current Account* | 109bx | −357.9 | −571.5 | −670.9 | −1,150.8 | −2,018.4 | −1,851.3 | −1,352.8 | −1,668.8 | −1,258.0 | † −1,395.2 | −1,702.8 | −1,277.2 |
| Goods, credit (exports) | 1a9cx | 149.0 | 194.1 | 223.6 | 359.8 | 546.1 | 403.6 | 736.9 | 962.1 | 1,124.3 | † 1,394.8 | 1,240.6 | 854.7 |
| Goods, debit (imports) | 1a9dx | 1,837.9 | 2,117.5 | 2,499.8 | 3,419.7 | 4,358.7 | 3,795.8 | 3,775.1 | 4,460.7 | 3,983.8 | † 4,028.2 | 4,170.4 | 3,401.5 |
| Balance on goods | 1a9bx | −1,688.9 | −1,923.3 | −2,276.1 | −3,059.9 | −3,812.5 | −3,392.2 | −3,038.1 | −3,498.7 | −2,859.4 | † −2,633.3 | −2,929.8 | −2,546.8 |
| Services, credit (exports) | 1b9cx | 1,100.8 | 1,266.7 | 1,645.9 | 2,104.6 | 2,732.1 | 2,657.8 | 2,587.2 | 2,814.4 | 2,433.3 | † 2,281.8 | 2,492.7 | 2,250.6 |
| Services, debit (imports) | 1b9dx | 1,054.8 | 1,382.9 | 1,573.4 | 1,924.4 | 2,372.2 | 2,232.6 | 2,006.7 | 2,248.4 | 1,871.2 | † 1,979.9 | 2,068.7 | 1,667.3 |
| Balance on Goods & Services | 1z9bx | −1,642.9 | −2,039.6 | −2,203.5 | −2,879.7 | −3,452.6 | −2,966.9 | −2,457.7 | −2,932.6 | −2,297.4 | † −2,331.4 | −2,505.7 | −1,963.4 |
| Primary income: credit | 1c9cx | 203.7 | 226.7 | 332.1 | 382.4 | 472.9 | 377.4 | 380.0 | 301.8 | 242.1 | † 182.8 | 167.1 | 126.8 |
| Primary income: debit | 1c9dx | 28.3 | 52.6 | 69.1 | 85.1 | 418.1 | 569.7 | 497.8 | 300.9 | 333.9 | † 150.1 | 323.2 | 292.8 |
| Balance on gds, serv. & prim. inc. | 1y9bx | −1,467.5 | −1,865.5 | −1,940.5 | −2,582.4 | −3,397.8 | −3,159.2 | −2,575.6 | −2,931.6 | −2,389.2 | † −2,298.6 | −2,661.9 | −2,129.4 |
| Secondary income: credit | 1d9ca | 1,200.2 | 1,519.2 | 1,426.3 | 1,673.6 | 1,643.1 | 1,529.3 | 1,427.3 | 1,409.3 | 1,320.0 | † 1,076.6 | 1,127.2 | 1,021.9 |
| Secondary income: debit | 1d9da | 90.6 | 225.1 | 156.7 | 242.0 | 263.7 | 221.4 | 204.5 | 146.5 | 188.8 | † 173.2 | 168.1 | 169.7 |
| B. Capital Account* | 209ba | 132.4 | 122.9 | 179.8 | 123.6 | 115.3 | 118.8 | 112.3 | 118.3 | 104.0 | † 63.7 | 115.2 | 139.5 |
| Capital account: credit | 209ca | 132.4 | 122.9 | 179.8 | 123.6 | 195.4 | 213.8 | 210.3 | 215.9 | 202.4 | † 188.7 | 241.5 | 251.9 |
| Capital account: debit | 209da | .... | .... | .... | — | 80.1 | 95.0 | 98.0 | 97.7 | 98.4 | † 125.0 | 126.3 | 112.4 |
| Balance on current & capital acct. | 129ba | −225.5 | −448.6 | −491.1 | −1,027.2 | −1,903.1 | −1,732.5 | −1,240.5 | −1,550.6 | −1,154.0 | † −1,331.5 | −1,587.6 | −1,137.7 |
| C. Financial Account* | 309na | −396.3 | −392.6 | −523.4 | −857.8 | −2,205.5 | −1,289.9 | −722.6 | −1,215.3 | −908.2 | † −1,224.2 | −1,305.6 | −1,421.2 |
| Direct investment: assets | 3a9aa | 13.6 | 4.1 | 10.5 | 4.9 | 366.7 | 391.6 | 46.0 | 201.9 | 84.4 | † 28.2 | 75.7 | 12.4 |
| Equity & investment fund shares | 3aaaa | 13.6 | 4.1 | 10.5 | 4.9 | 94.0 | 38.3 | 17.3 | 15.1 | 31.0 | † 78.3 | 32.8 | 35.8 |
| Debt instruments | 3abaa | .... | .... | .... | — | 272.7 | 353.3 | 28.7 | 186.8 | 53.4 | † −50.2 | 42.8 | −23.4 |
| Direct investment: liabilities | 3a9la | 341.3 | 262.5 | 325.1 | 652.3 | 1,241.0 | 1,343.1 | 1,089.4 | 1,049.4 | 920.1 | † 1,253.8 | 1,149.4 | 981.5 |
| Equity & investment fund shares | 3aala | 341.3 | 262.5 | 75.7 | 460.3 | 881.4 | 1,038.0 | 1,051.5 | 813.4 | 714.3 | † 846.2 | 932.3 | 863.4 |
| Debt instruments | 3abla | .... | .... | 249.5 | 191.9 | 359.6 | 305.1 | 37.9 | 236.0 | 205.8 | † 407.6 | 217.1 | 118.1 |
| Portfolio investment: assets | 3b9aa | 3.6 | 5.7 | −34.2 | −25.8 | 83.5 | −18.7 | 110.5 | 126.8 | 113.0 | † 167.2 | 162.3 | −197.7 |
| Equity & investment fund shares | 3baaa | .... | .... | .... | .... | — | −.6 | — | 26.0 | 3.4 | † 14.2 | −3.3 | .... |
| Debt securities | 3bbaa | 3.6 | 5.7 | −34.2 | −25.8 | 83.5 | −18.1 | 110.5 | 100.8 | 109.6 | † 153.1 | 165.7 | −197.7 |
| Portfolio investment: liabilities | 3b9la | .... | .... | .... | .... | 57.4 | −3.6 | 430.7 | 220.2 | 70.1 | † 15.8 | 11.3 | 155.7 |
| Equity & investment fund shares | 3bala | .... | .... | .... | .... | 23.3 | −4.1 | 6.9 | 23.5 | 18.0 | † 1.7 | 33.9 | 63.3 |
| Debt securities | 3bbla | .... | .... | .... | .... | 34.1 | .4 | 423.9 | 196.7 | 52.1 | † 14.1 | −22.6 | 92.4 |
| Fin. der.& empl.stk.ops.(ESOs): net. | 3c9na | .... | .... | .... | .... | — | — | — | −2.5 | −4.7 | † 1.2 | .... | .... |
| Fin. der. & ESOs.: assets | 3c9aa | .... | .... | .... | .... | — | — | — | −2.5 | — | † −1.9 | .... | .... |
| Fin. der. & ESOs.: liabilities | 3c9la | .... | .... | .... | .... | — | — | — | — | 4.7 | † −3.1 | .... | .... |
| Other investment: assets | 3d9aa | 113.8 | −6.6 | 210.7 | 88.1 | −287.0 | −62.1 | 244.9 | 413.4 | 369.9 | † 283.1 | −30.4 | 237.1 |
| Other equity | 3daaa | .... | .... | .... | .... | .... | .... | .... | .... | .... | .... | .... | −2.0 |
| Debt instruments | 3dzaa | 113.8 | −6.6 | 210.7 | 88.1 | −287.0 | −62.1 | 244.9 | 413.4 | 369.9 | † 283.1 | −30.4 | 239.0 |
| Other investment: liabilities | 3d9la | 186.1 | 133.2 | 385.2 | 272.8 | 1,070.3 | 261.2 | −396.1 | 685.2 | 480.7 | † 434.3 | 352.5 | 335.7 |
| Other equity | 3dala | .... | .... | .... | .... | .... | .... | .... | .... | .... | .... | .... | .... |
| Debt instruments | 3dzla | 186.1 | 133.2 | 385.2 | 272.8 | 1,070.3 | 261.2 | −396.1 | 685.2 | 480.7 | † 434.3 | 352.5 | 335.7 |
| Curr.+ cap.− finan. acct. balance | 4y9na | 170.8 | −56.0 | 32.2 | −169.3 | 302.4 | −442.6 | −517.9 | −335.2 | −245.8 | † −107.3 | −282.0 | 283.5 |
| D. Net Errors and Omissions | 409na | 115.3 | 203.8 | 237.0 | 189.0 | −33.2 | 417.6 | 442.3 | 307.3 | 346.2 | † 257.8 | 350.0 | 292.6 |
| E. Reserves and Related Items | 4z9na | 286.1 | 147.8 | 269.2 | 19.7 | 269.1 | −25.0 | −75.6 | −27.9 | 100.4 | † 150.5 | 68.0 | 576.0 |
| Reserve assets | 3e9aa | 288.4 | 150.7 | 265.1 | 202.3 | 261.9 | −34.9 | 236.5 | −37.7 | 96.0 | † 136.2 | 131.7 | 677.0 |
| Credit and loans from the IMF | 3dcla | 2.4 | 3.0 | −4.1 | −7.0 | −7.4 | −10.3 | −12.3 | −12.0 | −10.3 | † −10.4 | 63.8 | 101.0 |
| Exceptional financing | 409la | .... | .... | — | 189.7 | .2 | .3 | 324.4 | 2.3 | 5.9 | † −3.9 | .... | .... |

*Excludes components in group E

| International Investment Position | | 2004 | 2005 | 2006 | 2007 | 2008 | 2009 | 2010 | 2011 | 2012 | 2013 | 2014 | 2015 |
|---|---|---|---|---|---|---|---|---|---|---|---|---|---|
| | | | | | | *Millions of US Dollars* | | | | | | | |
| Assets | 809aa | .... | .... | .... | 3,611.0 | † 3,992.9 | 4,250.3 | 4,683.9 | 5,145.2 | 5,890.6 | 7,587.6 | 6,847.3 | .... |
| Direct investment | 8a9aa | .... | .... | .... | 198.2 | † 648.5 | 968.6 | 941.9 | 1,023.1 | 1,026.7 | 1,978.2 | 1,495.5 | .... |
| Equity & investment fund shares | 8aaaa | .... | .... | .... | 77.0 | † 164.5 | 181.2 | 180.6 | 180.8 | 211.2 | 203.5 | 210.0 | .... |
| Debt instruments | 8abaa | .... | .... | .... | 121.1 | † 484.0 | 787.4 | 761.3 | 842.3 | 815.6 | 1,774.8 | 1,285.5 | .... |
| Portfolio investment | 8b9aa | .... | .... | .... | 89.9 | † 154.6 | 149.0 | 241.5 | 329.2 | 513.2 | 682.9 | 786.5 | .... |
| Equity & investment fund shares | 8baaa | .... | .... | .... | — | † 1.0 | .4 | .6 | 11.8 | 30.4 | 33.4 | 28.5 | .... |
| Debt securities | 8bbaa | .... | .... | .... | 89.9 | † 153.6 | 148.6 | 240.9 | 317.4 | 482.8 | 649.5 | 758.0 | .... |
| Fin. der.(oth.than reserves) & ESOs | 8c9aa | .... | .... | .... | .... | .... | .... | .... | .... | .... | .... | .... | .... |
| Other investment | 8d9aa | .... | .... | .... | 1,178.3 | † 830.5 | 762.0 | 958.9 | 1,321.9 | 1,749.5 | 2,152.7 | 1,899.7 | .... |
| Other equity | 8daaa | .... | .... | .... | .... | † 5.8 | 5.5 | 5.2 | 5.1 | 5.1 | 5.3 | 4.9 | .... |
| Debt instruments | 8dzaa | .... | .... | .... | 1,178.3 | † 824.7 | 756.5 | 953.7 | 1,316.8 | 1,744.4 | 2,147.4 | 1,894.8 | .... |
| Reserve assets | 8e9aa | .... | .... | .... | 2,144.7 | † 2,359.4 | 2,370.7 | 2,541.6 | 2,471.0 | 2,601.2 | 2,773.8 | 2,665.5 | .... |
| Liabilities | 809la | .... | .... | .... | 5,782.1 | † 7,366.9 | 8,382.2 | 8,659.4 | 10,623.4 | 11,206.7 | 12,301.8 | 12,266.6 | .... |
| Direct investment | 8a9la | .... | .... | .... | 2,811.7 | † 3,403.7 | 4,058.3 | 4,038.6 | 5,243.4 | 5,133.8 | 5,661.7 | 5,537.8 | .... |
| Equity & investment fund shares | 8aala | .... | .... | .... | 2,391.8 | † 2,571.5 | 3,111.9 | 3,090.4 | 4,105.0 | 3,799.9 | 3,395.4 | 3,559.0 | .... |
| Debt instruments | 8abla | .... | .... | .... | 419.9 | † 832.2 | 946.4 | 948.2 | 1,138.4 | 1,333.9 | 2,266.3 | 1,978.7 | .... |
| Portfolio investment | 8b9la | .... | .... | .... | 158.2 | † 202.2 | 201.9 | 588.5 | 769.7 | 857.5 | 904.6 | 974.4 | .... |
| Equity & investment fund shares | 8bala | .... | .... | .... | 85.2 | † 99.7 | 97.1 | 98.4 | 112.5 | 133.7 | 141.3 | 282.6 | .... |
| Debt securities | 8bbla | .... | .... | .... | 73.0 | † 102.5 | 104.8 | 490.1 | 657.2 | 723.8 | 763.3 | 691.9 | .... |
| Fin. der.(oth.than reserves) & ESOs | 8c9la | .... | .... | .... | .... | .... | .... | .... | .... | 3.2 | .... | .... | .... |
| Other investment | 8d9la | .... | .... | .... | 2,812.2 | † 3,761.0 | 4,122.0 | 4,032.3 | 4,610.3 | 5,212.2 | 5,735.5 | 5,754.4 | .... |
| Other equity | 8dala | .... | .... | .... | .... | .... | .... | .... | .... | .... | .... | .... | .... |
| Debt instruments | 8dzla | .... | .... | .... | 2,812.2 | † 3,761.0 | 4,122.0 | 4,032.3 | 4,610.3 | 5,212.2 | 5,735.5 | 5,754.4 | .... |

# Albania 914

| | | 2004 | 2005 | 2006 | 2007 | 2008 | 2009 | 2010 | 2011 | 2012 | 2013 | 2014 | 2015 |
|---|---|---|---|---|---|---|---|---|---|---|---|---|---|
| **Government Finance** | | | | | | | | | | | | | |
| **Cash Flow Statement** | | | | | | | | | | | | | |
| **General Government** | | | | | | *Millions of Leks: Fiscal Year Ends December 31* | | | | | | | |
| Cash Receipts:Operating Activities... | c1 | .... | 203,445 | 228,972 | 251,317 | 291,191 | 299,605 | 324,723 | 330,450 | 330,386 | 321,274 | 397,156 | 492,601 |
| Taxes.............................. | c11 | .... | 144,939 | 163,348 | 184,029 | 214,577 | 221,023 | 234,915 | 247,300 | 243,452 | 241,376 | 265,860 | 272,161 |
| Social Contributions..................... | c12 | .... | 35,891 | 39,027 | 41,393 | 47,253 | 49,812 | 53,648 | 56,627 | 57,411 | 60,035 | 70,008 | 73,407 |
| Grants.............................. | c13 | .... | 6,168 | 8,025 | .... | 4,228 | 4,430 | 4,605 | 3,791 | 5,559 | 4,303 | 40,621 | 121,459 |
| Other Receipts............................. | c14 | .... | 16,448 | 18,572 | .... | 25,133 | 24,340 | 31,555 | 22,732 | 23,964 | 15,560 | 20,667 | 25,574 |
| Cash Payments:Operating Activities. | c2 | .... | 186,823 | 198,866 | 222,061 | 248,273 | 281,900 | 300,879 | 305,621 | 314,584 | 328,236 | 341,081 | 351,218 |
| Compensation of Employees.......... | c21 | .... | 61,018 | 64,475 | 67,510 | 76,667 | 62,360 | 65,762 | 67,446 | 69,443 | 70,714 | 71,373 | 72,489 |
| Purchases of Goods & Services....... | c22 | .... | 26,576 | 25,969 | 29,098 | 32,900 | 31,798 | 34,319 | 32,995 | 31,471 | 32,426 | 33,134 | 42,409 |
| Interest.............................. | c24 | .... | 26,029 | 25,006 | 25,594 | 31,340 | 36,302 | 41,603 | 41,121 | 41,498 | 43,335 | 40,075 | 38,643 |
| Subsidies.............................. | c25 | .... | 3,739 | 3,929 | 3,631 | 2,638 | 2,004 | 3,534 | 3,301 | 1,884 | 1,574 | 1,599 | 1,735 |
| Grants.............................. | c26 | .... | 127 | 146 | — | — | — | — | — | — | — | — | — |
| Social Benefits....................... | c27 | .... | 10,218 | 13,775 | 14,360 | 16,750 | 115,855 | 124,896 | 132,639 | 140,955 | 150,803 | 161,933 | 162,093 |
| Other Payments........................... | c28 | .... | 59,115 | 65,567 | .... | .... | 33,581 | 30,765 | 28,119 | 29,333 | 29,384 | 32,967 | 33,849 |
| Net Cash Inflow:Operating Act.[1-2] | ccio | .... | 16,623 | 30,106 | 29,256 | 42,918 | 17,705 | 23,844 | 24,829 | 15,806 | −6,962 | 56,075 | 141,383 |
| Net Cash Outflow:Invest. in NFA...... | c31 | .... | 45,239 | 59,800 | 63,533 | 103,172 | 97,619 | 67,490 | 70,562 | 61,655 | 62,907 | 60,611 | 61,622 |
| Purchases of Nonfinancial Assets.. | c31.1 | .... | 45,516 | 59,949 | 63,613 | 103,219 | 97,619 | 67,490 | 70,562 | 61,655 | 62,907 | 60,611 | 61,622 |
| Sales of Nonfinancial Assets.......... | c31.2 | .... | 277 | 149 | 80 | 47 | — | — | — | — | — | — | — |
| Cash Surplus/Deficit [1-2-31=1-2M] | ccsd | .... | −28,616 | −29,695 | −34,278 | −60,254 | −79,914 | −43,646 | −45,733 | −45,847 | −69,869 | −4,536 | 79,761 |
| Net Acq. Fin. Assets, excl. Cash...... | c32x | .... | −772 | −204 | −658 | −4,796 | −27,565 | −6,028 | −438 | −1,221 | −13,168 | −35 | −877 |
| Domestic.............................. | c321x | .... | −772 | −204 | −379 | −4,505 | −27,565 | −6,028 | −438 | −1,221 | −13,168 | −35 | −877 |
| Foreign.............................. | c322x | .... | — | — | −279 | −292 | — | — | — | — | — | — | — |
| Net Incurrence of Liabilities............. | c33 | .... | 28,310 | 31,019 | 35,817 | 59,435 | 55,498 | 33,548 | 47,837 | 44,359 | 51,706 | 3,852 | −87,384 |
| Domestic.............................. | c331 | .... | 22,453 | 25,673 | 30,807 | 23,889 | 45,317 | 23,336 | 28,175 | 24,783 | 42,825 | 2,701 | −40,864 |
| Foreign.............................. | c332 | .... | 5,857 | 5,346 | 5,010 | 35,546 | 10,181 | 10,212 | 19,662 | 19,576 | 8,881 | 1,151 | −46,520 |
| Net Cash Inflow, Fin.Act.[-32x+33].. | cnfb | .... | 29,082 | 31,223 | 36,475 | 64,231 | 83,063 | 39,576 | 48,275 | 45,580 | 64,874 | 3,887 | −86,507 |
| Net Change in Stock of Cash........... | cncb | .... | 466 | 1,528 | 2,197 | 3,977 | 3,149 | −4,070 | 2,542 | −267 | −4,995 | −649 | −6,746 |
| Stat. Discrep. [32X-33+NCB-CSD].... | ccsdz | .... | — | — | — | — | — | — | — | 1 | — | .... | .... |
| Memo Item:Cash Expenditure[2+31] | c2m | .... | 232,061 | 258,667 | 285,594 | 351,445 | 379,519 | 368,369 | 376,183 | 376,239 | 391,143 | 401,692 | 412,840 |
| Memo Item: Gross Debt.................. | c63 | .... | .... | .... | .... | .... | .... | .... | .... | .... | .... | .... | .... |
| **National Accounts** | | | | | | | *Millions of Leks* | | | | | | |
| Househ.Cons.Expend.,incl.NPISHs.... | 96f | 585,703 | 635,663 | 681,694 | 776,585 | 897,974 | 925,018 | 968,278 | 1,018,381 | 1,039,151 | 1,080,439 | 1,137,497 | .... |
| Government Consumption Expend... | 91f | 82,484 | 88,508 | 89,411 | 98,352 | 112,163 | 127,085 | 138,312 | 142,733 | 144,541 | 148,850 | 159,788 | .... |
| Gross Fixed Capital Formation......... | 93e | 279,378 | 301,354 | 343,882 | 374,058 | 366,882 | 374,169 | 352,412 | 381,944 | 353,044 | 352,088 | 342,844 | .... |
| Changes in Inventories................... | 93i | −28,376 | −9,904 | −24,712 | −105,379 | 19,767 | 21,151 | 23,308 | 26,628 | 24,522 | 26,636 | 31,154 | .... |
| Exports of Goods and Services......... | 90c | 165,097 | 185,970 | 219,970 | 271,763 | 319,735 | 338,800 | 401,947 | 442,390 | 444,514 | 387,975 | 393,657 | .... |
| Imports of Goods and Services (-)..... | 98c | 333,265 | 386,794 | 428,057 | 530,169 | 609,836 | 615,484 | 656,966 | 738,093 | 692,887 | 633,950 | 658,512 | .... |
| Gross Domestic Product (GDP)......... | 99b | 751,022 | 814,797 | 882,209 | 967,670 | 1,080,676 | 1,143,936 | 1,239,645 | 1,300,624 | 1,332,811 | 1,350,053 | 1,394,419 | .... |
| GDP Volume 2005 Ref., Chained..... | 99b.p | .... | 714,128 | 750,544 | 790,350 | 850,205 | 880,556 | 909,218 | 936,952 | 944,187 | .... | .... | .... |
| | | | | | | | *Milliions: Midyear Estimates* | | | | | | |
| Population................................ | 99z | 3.10 | 3.08 | 3.05 | 3.01 | 2.97 | 2.93 | 2.90 | 2.89 | 2.88 | 2.88 | 2.89 | 2.90 |

| | | 2004 | 2005 | 2006 | 2007 | 2008 | 2009 | 2010 | 2011 | 2012 | 2013 | 2014 | 2015 |
|---|---|---|---|---|---|---|---|---|---|---|---|---|---|
| **Exchange Rates** | | | | | | *Dinars per SDR: End of Period* | | | | | | | | |
| Official Rate.................................... | aa | 112.770 | 104.880 | 107.050 | 105.608 | 109.640 | 114.020 | 115.416 | 116.767 | 120.037 | 120.355 | 127.356 | 148.456 |
| | | | | | *Dinars per US Dollar: End of Period (ae) Period Average (rf)* | | | | | | | | | |
| Official Rate.................................... | ae | 72.614 | 73.380 | 71.158 | 66.830 | 71.183 | 72.731 | 74.944 | 76.056 | 78.103 | 78.152 | 87.904 | 107.132 |
| Official Rate.................................... | rf | 72.061 | 73.276 | 72.647 | 69.292 | 64.583 | 72.647 | 74.386 | 72.938 | 77.536 | 79.368 | 80.579 | 100.691 |
| | | | | | *Index Numbers (2010=100): Period Averages* | | | | | | | | | |
| Nominal Effective Exchange Rate..... | nec | 109.15 | 105.79 | 105.90 | 104.13 | 106.63 | 100.91 | 100.00 | 98.25 | 97.67 | 95.00 | 96.01 | 89.59 |
| CPI-Based Real Effect. Ex. Rate........ | rec | 102.19 | 97.80 | 97.64 | 96.40 | 100.66 | 99.53 | 100.00 | 99.42 | 104.82 | 103.29 | 105.39 | 100.86 |
| **Fund Position** | | | | | | *Millions of SDRs: End of Period* | | | | | | | | |
| Quota....................................... | 2f.s | 1,254.70 | 1,254.70 | 1,254.70 | 1,254.70 | 1,254.70 | 1,254.70 | 1,254.70 | 1,254.70 | 1,254.70 | 1,254.70 | 1,254.70 | 1,254.70 |
| SDR Holdings........................... | 1b.s | .80 | 2.44 | 3.15 | 1.99 | 6.46 | 1,075.61 | 1,073.34 | 1,074.05 | 1,074.33 | 1,074.51 | 1,074.77 | 1,074.86 |
| Reserve Position in the Fund........... | 1c.s | 85.08 | 85.08 | 85.08 | 85.08 | 85.08 | 85.08 | 255.68 | 390.18 | 413.78 | 454.78 | 468.78 | 392.78 |
| Total Fund Cred.&Loans Outstg....... | 2tl | 413.98 | — | — | — | — | — | — | — | — | — | — | — |
| SDR Allocations........................... | 1bd | 128.64 | 128.64 | 128.64 | 128.64 | 128.64 | 1,198.18 | 1,198.18 | 1,198.18 | 1,198.18 | 1,198.18 | 1,198.18 | 1,198.18 |
| **International Liquidity** | | | | | *Millions of US Dollars Unless Otherwise Indicated: End of Period* | | | | | | | | | |
| Total Reserves minus Gold............... | 1l.d | 43,246 | 56,303 | 77,914 | 110,318 | 143,243 | 149,041 | 162,614 | 182,822 | 191,297 | 194,712 | 179,618 | 144,677 |
| SDR Holdings.............................. | 1b.d | 1 | 3 | 5 | 3 | 10 | 1,686 | 1,653 | 1,649 | 1,651 | 1,655 | 1,557 | 1,489 |
| Reserve Position in the Fund.......... | 1c.d | 132 | 122 | 128 | 134 | 131 | 133 | 394 | 599 | 636 | 700 | 679 | 544 |
| Foreign Exchange........................ | 1d.d | 43,113 | 56,178 | 77,781 | 110,180 | 143,102 | 147,221 | 160,568 | 180,574 | 189,010 | 192,357 | 177,381 | 142,644 |
| Gold (Million Fine Troy Ounces)........ | 1ad | 5.58 | 5.58 | 5.58 | 5.58 | 5.58 | 5.58 | 5.58 | 5.58 | 5.58 | 5.58 | 5.58 | 5.58 |
| Gold (National Valuation)............... | 1and | 303 | 279 | 294 | 309 | 301 | 306 | 301 | 300 | 300 | 301 | 283 | 271 |
| Central Bank:Other Assets............... | 3..d | 276 | 363 | 288 | 337 | 536 | 412 | 241 | 240 | 241 | 284 | 271 | 264 |
| Central Bank: Other Liabs............... | 4..d | 244 | 281 | 624 | 573 | 467 | 420 | 520 | 684 | 682 | 25 | 23 | 25 |
| Other Depository Corps.: Assets....... | 7a.d | 542 | 628 | 582 | 783 | 999 | 798 | 388 | 1,007 | 1,017 | 616 | 508 | 536 |
| Other Depository Corps.: Liabs......... | 7b.d | 1,043 | 583 | 962 | 592 | 763 | 638 | 594 | 526 | 972 | 1,200 | 1,574 | 1,945 |
| Other Financial Corps.: Assets.......... | 7e.d | — | — | — | — | — | — | — | — | — | — | — | — |
| Other Financial Corps.: Liabs............ | 7f.d | 74 | 86 | 72 | 55 | 52 | 51 | 9 | 4 | 1 | — | — | — |
| **Central Bank** | | | | | | *Billions of Dinars: End of Period* | | | | | | | | |
| Net Foreign Assets......................... | 11n | 3,109.44 | 4,153.82 | 5,528.61 | 7,385.04 | 10,230.00 | 10,746.45 | 11,886.65 | 13,758.63 | 14,807.36 | 15,144.81 | 15,695.44 | 15,372.64 |
| Claims on Nonresidents................ | 11 | 3,188.38 | 4,187.96 | 5,586.77 | 7,436.95 | 10,277.33 | 10,913.58 | 12,061.53 | 13,950.55 | 15,004.41 | 15,291.03 | 15,850.04 | 15,553.15 |
| Liabilities to Nonresidents.............. | 16c | 78.94 | 34.14 | 58.16 | 51.91 | 47.33 | 167.13 | 174.87 | 191.92 | 197.05 | 146.23 | 154.61 | 180.51 |
| Claims on Other Depository Corps.... | 12e | | | | | | | | | | | | |
| Net Claims on Central Government.. | 12an | −920.98 | −1,990.58 | −2,515.20 | −3,299.32 | −4,368.98 | −4,404.88 | −4,919.40 | −5,458.60 | −5,712.67 | −5,646.78 | −4,488.00 | −2,156.48 |
| Claims on Central Government...... | 12a | 122.11 | 118.13 | 733.65 | 5.10 | 3.82 | 5.01 | 6.72 | 6.84 | 7.86 | 3.97 | 2.80 | 1.46 |
| Liabilities to Central Government... | 16d | 1,043.09 | 2,108.71 | 3,248.84 | 3,304.42 | 4,372.80 | 4,409.88 | 4,926.11 | 5,465.45 | 5,720.53 | 5,650.75 | 4,490.80 | 2,157.95 |
| Claims on Other Sectors.................. | 12s | 1.89 | 6.98 | 2.17 | 2.46 | 2.56 | 2.53 | 2.56 | 3.05 | 3.17 | 2.83 | 4.69 | 5.47 |
| Claims on Other Financial Corps.... | 12g | — | — | — | — | — | — | — | — | — | — | — | — |
| Claims on State & Local Govts....... | 12b | — | — | — | — | — | — | — | — | — | — | — | — |
| Claims on Public Nonfin. Corps...... | 12c | .36 | .77 | .47 | .47 | .47 | .47 | .47 | .47 | .49 | .50 | .50 | .50 |
| Claims on Private Sector................ | 12d | 1.53 | 6.21 | 1.71 | 2.00 | 2.09 | 2.06 | 2.09 | 2.58 | 2.68 | 2.33 | 4.19 | 4.97 |
| Monetary Base............................. | 14 | 1,160.53 | 1,178.69 | 1,342.52 | 1,729.00 | 1,925.52 | 2,214.17 | 2,616.88 | 3,137.92 | 3,709.15 | 4,137.80 | 4,673.00 | 5,220.47 |
| Currency in Circulation.................. | 14a | 882.46 | 930.26 | 1,092.10 | 1,301.32 | 1,561.73 | 1,849.91 | 2,132.19 | 2,610.47 | 2,997.20 | 3,247.65 | 3,734.64 | 4,183.78 |
| Liabs. to Other Depository Corps.... | 14c | 273.05 | 232.29 | 240.22 | 418.07 | 345.55 | 325.24 | 433.03 | 487.05 | 688.18 | 863.09 | 912.28 | 1,019.90 |
| Liabilities to Other Sectors............ | 14d | 5.02 | 16.14 | 10.20 | 9.62 | 18.24 | 39.01 | 51.65 | 40.40 | 23.77 | 27.07 | 26.08 | 16.80 |
| Other Liabs. to Other Dep. Corps..... | 14n | 683.17 | 777.72 | 1,210.06 | 1,880.23 | 2,815.60 | 2,409.96 | 2,434.45 | 2,689.95 | 2,558.49 | 2,232.87 | 2,266.12 | 1,356.99 |
| Dep. & Sec. Excl. f/Monetary Base.... | 14o | — | — | 12.61 | 16.90 | 17.76 | 14.60 | 13.95 | 23.80 | 89.37 | 10.97 | 14.28 | 20.36 |
| Deposits Included in Broad Money. | 15 | — | — | — | — | — | — | — | — | — | — | — | — |
| Sec.Ot.th.Shares Incl.in Brd. Money | 16a | — | — | — | — | — | — | — | — | — | — | — | — |
| Deposits Excl. from Broad Money... | 16b | — | — | 12.61 | 16.90 | 17.76 | 14.60 | 13.95 | 23.80 | 89.37 | 10.97 | 14.28 | 20.36 |
| Sec.Ot.th.Shares Excl.f/Brd.Money.. | 16s | — | — | — | — | — | — | — | — | — | — | — | — |
| Loans...................................... | 16l | — | — | — | — | — | — | — | — | — | — | — | — |
| Financial Derivatives...................... | 16m | — | — | — | — | — | — | — | — | — | — | — | — |
| Shares and Other Equity.................. | 17a | 123.13 | 189.73 | 176.39 | 168.95 | 217.62 | 350.52 | 435.11 | 471.18 | 842.66 | 934.98 | 960.22 | 994.31 |
| Other Items (Net)........................... | 17r | 223.53 | 24.07 | 274.00 | 293.10 | 887.07 | 1,354.86 | 1,469.44 | 1,980.22 | 1,898.19 | 2,184.23 | 3,298.51 | 5,629.49 |
| Memo Item: | | | | | | | | | | | | | |
| Total Assets.................................. | 10ra | 3,534.39 | 4,520.73 | 6,556.56 | 7,711.46 | 10,560.41 | 11,248.29 | 12,380.58 | 14,266.91 | 15,326.35 | 15,581.98 | 16,056.85 | 15,772.97 |

# Algeria 612

| | | 2004 | 2005 | 2006 | 2007 | 2008 | 2009 | 2010 | 2011 | 2012 | 2013 | 2014 | 2015 |
|---|---|---|---|---|---|---|---|---|---|---|---|---|---|
| **Other Depository Corporations** | | *Billions of Dinars: End of Period* | | | | | | | | | | | |
| Net Foreign Assets | 21n | −36.39 | 3.30 | −27.04 | 12.76 | 16.83 | 11.59 | −15.23 | 36.59 | 3.55 | −45.68 | −93.64 | −150.88 |
| Claims on Nonresidents | 21 | 39.36 | 46.07 | 41.40 | 52.33 | 71.14 | 58.02 | 28.70 | 76.61 | 79.45 | 48.12 | 44.68 | 57.46 |
| Liabilities to Nonresidents | 26c | 75.75 | 42.77 | 68.44 | 39.57 | 54.32 | 46.43 | 43.92 | 40.02 | 75.90 | 93.80 | 138.32 | 208.34 |
| Claims on Central Bank | 20 | 964.64 | 974.39 | 1,480.39 | 2,309.71 | 3,191.52 | 2,755.13 | 2,903.39 | 3,228.29 | 3,286.74 | 3,134.86 | 3,275.08 | 2,463.30 |
| Currency | 20a | 8.12 | 9.30 | 10.75 | 16.82 | 21.75 | 20.56 | 33.56 | 38.99 | 44.86 | 43.65 | 75.72 | 75.72 |
| Reserve Deposits and Securities | 20b | 956.52 | 965.09 | 1,469.64 | 2,292.89 | 3,169.77 | 2,734.57 | 2,869.83 | 3,189.30 | 3,241.89 | 3,091.21 | 3,199.36 | 2,387.57 |
| Other Claims | 20n | — | — | — | — | — | — | — | — | — | — | — | — |
| Net Claims on Central Government | 22an | 687.82 | 735.27 | 841.55 | 697.59 | 277.21 | 325.39 | 776.39 | 1,000.46 | 1,004.78 | 904.85 | 985.24 | 1,123.81 |
| Claims on Central Government | 22a | 821.29 | 898.19 | 1,038.03 | 962.01 | 713.66 | 841.13 | 1,150.07 | 1,420.33 | 1,502.19 | 1,432.51 | 1,570.14 | 1,685.97 |
| Liabilities to Central Government | 26d | 133.47 | 162.92 | 196.48 | 264.42 | 436.45 | 515.74 | 373.67 | 419.87 | 497.41 | 527.66 | 584.90 | 562.16 |
| Claims on Other Sectors | 22s | 1,562.68 | 1,803.23 | 1,981.63 | 2,259.19 | 2,686.86 | 3,184.47 | 3,345.80 | 3,796.53 | 4,362.45 | 5,239.12 | 6,599.66 | 7,643.70 |
| Claims on Other Financial Corps | 22g | 4.27 | 2.34 | 2.66 | 24.61 | 41.79 | 58.09 | 44.11 | 34.02 | 31.38 | 40.49 | 196.34 | 201.74 |
| Claims on State & Local Govts | 22b | .26 | .10 | .29 | .36 | .33 | .78 | .77 | .69 | .44 | .36 | .58 | .71 |
| Claims on Public Nonfin. Corps | 22c | 883.42 | 904.91 | 950.24 | 1,021.27 | 1,233.70 | 1,506.29 | 1,479.31 | 1,763.46 | 2,059.87 | 2,454.05 | 3,245.14 | 3,815.53 |
| Claims on Private Sector | 22d | 674.73 | 895.87 | 1,028.44 | 1,212.95 | 1,411.04 | 1,619.32 | 1,821.61 | 1,998.37 | 2,270.77 | 2,744.22 | 3,157.60 | 3,625.73 |
| Liabilities to Central Bank | 26g | — | — | — | — | — | — | — | — | — | — | — | — |
| Transf.Dep.Included in Broad Money | 24 | 971.33 | 1,095.20 | 1,633.41 | 2,395.00 | 2,777.19 | 2,621.43 | 2,870.72 | 3,550.79 | 3,495.40 | 3,613.77 | 4,495.12 | 3,967.22 |
| Other Dep.Included in Broad Money | 25 | 1,635.28 | 1,762.08 | 1,809.27 | 1,926.84 | 2,160.77 | 2,229.06 | 2,524.28 | 2,732.49 | 3,194.64 | 3,615.40 | 4,023.38 | 4,366.41 |
| Sec.Ot.Shares Incl.in Brd. Money | 26a | — | — | — | — | — | — | — | — | — | — | — | — |
| Deposits Excl. from Broad Money | 26b | 102.29 | 104.39 | 116.48 | 197.88 | 226.43 | 320.07 | 319.22 | 342.81 | 358.09 | 408.86 | 429.30 | 673.95 |
| Sec.Ot.Shares Excl.f/Brd.Money | 26s | 2.07 | .01 | .01 | .01 | .01 | — | — | — | — | — | — | — |
| Loans | 26l | — | 16.07 | 2.81 | — | 2.20 | — | — | — | — | — | — | — |
| Financial Derivatives | 26m | — | — | — | — | — | — | — | — | — | — | — | — |
| Insurance Technical Reserves | 26r | — | — | — | — | — | — | — | — | — | — | — | — |
| Shares and Other Equity | 27a | 228.43 | 240.24 | 268.10 | 283.79 | 459.69 | 600.64 | 664.74 | 752.92 | 860.90 | 893.76 | 935.57 | 1,133.17 |
| Other Items (Net) | 27r | 239.36 | 298.20 | 446.45 | 475.74 | 546.13 | 505.40 | 631.40 | 682.85 | 748.50 | 701.37 | 882.97 | 939.17 |
| Memo Item: | | | | | | | | | | | | | |
| Total Assets | 20ra | 3,810.24 | 4,117.23 | 5,110.70 | 6,354.80 | 7,096.25 | 7,327.34 | 7,989.13 | 8,960.87 | 9,654.44 | 10,320.04 | 11,976.39 | 12,486.26 |
| **Depository Corporations** | | *Billions of Dinars: End of Period* | | | | | | | | | | | |
| Net Foreign Assets | 31n | 3,073.05 | 4,157.12 | 5,501.57 | 7,397.80 | 10,246.82 | 10,758.04 | 11,871.43 | 13,795.22 | 14,810.91 | 15,099.13 | 15,601.80 | 15,221.76 |
| Claims on Nonresidents | 31 | 3,227.74 | 4,234.03 | 5,628.17 | 7,489.28 | 10,348.47 | 10,971.60 | 12,090.22 | 14,027.15 | 15,083.86 | 15,339.15 | 15,894.73 | 15,610.61 |
| Liabilities to Nonresidents | 36c | 154.69 | 76.91 | 126.60 | 91.48 | 101.65 | 213.56 | 218.80 | 231.94 | 272.95 | 240.03 | 292.93 | 388.85 |
| Domestic Claims | 32 | 1,331.42 | 554.89 | 310.16 | −340.07 | −1,402.36 | −892.48 | −794.64 | −658.56 | −342.27 | 500.03 | 3,101.59 | 6,616.49 |
| Net Claims on Central Government | 32an | −233.16 | −1,255.31 | −1,673.65 | −2,601.73 | −4,091.78 | −4,079.48 | −4,143.00 | −4,458.15 | −4,707.89 | −4,741.93 | −3,502.76 | −1,032.68 |
| Claims on Central Government | 32a | 943.40 | 1,016.32 | 1,771.68 | 967.10 | 717.47 | 846.14 | 1,156.78 | 1,427.17 | 1,510.05 | 1,436.48 | 1,572.94 | 1,687.44 |
| Liabilities to Central Government | 36d | 1,176.55 | 2,271.63 | 3,445.33 | 3,568.83 | 4,809.25 | 4,925.62 | 5,299.79 | 5,885.32 | 6,217.94 | 6,178.40 | 5,075.70 | 2,720.11 |
| Claims on Other Sectors | 32s | 1,564.57 | 1,810.20 | 1,983.81 | 2,261.65 | 2,689.42 | 3,187.01 | 3,348.36 | 3,799.58 | 4,365.62 | 5,241.96 | 6,604.35 | 7,649.16 |
| Claims on Other Financial Corps | 32g | 4.27 | 2.34 | 2.66 | 24.61 | 41.79 | 58.09 | 44.11 | 34.02 | 31.38 | 40.49 | 196.34 | 201.74 |
| Claims on State & Local Govts | 32b | .26 | .10 | .29 | .36 | .33 | .78 | .77 | .69 | .44 | .36 | .58 | .71 |
| Claims on Public Nonfin. Corps | 32c | 883.78 | 905.68 | 950.70 | 1,021.73 | 1,234.17 | 1,506.76 | 1,479.78 | 1,763.93 | 2,060.36 | 2,454.55 | 3,245.64 | 3,816.03 |
| Claims on Private Sector | 32d | 676.27 | 902.08 | 1,030.15 | 1,214.95 | 1,413.13 | 1,621.38 | 1,823.71 | 2,000.95 | 2,273.45 | 2,746.56 | 3,161.79 | 3,630.69 |
| Broad Money Liabilities | 35l | 3,485.98 | 3,794.39 | 4,534.22 | 5,615.95 | 6,496.18 | 6,718.84 | 7,545.28 | 8,895.16 | 9,666.15 | 10,460.23 | 12,203.49 | 12,458.48 |
| Currency Outside Depository Corps | 34a | 874.35 | 920.96 | 1,081.35 | 1,284.49 | 1,539.97 | 1,829.35 | 2,098.63 | 2,571.48 | 2,952.34 | 3,203.99 | 3,658.92 | 4,108.05 |
| Transferable Deposits | 34 | 976.35 | 1,111.34 | 1,643.61 | 2,404.62 | 2,795.43 | 2,660.44 | 2,922.37 | 3,591.19 | 3,519.17 | 3,640.84 | 4,521.19 | 3,984.02 |
| Other Deposits | 35 | 1,635.28 | 1,762.09 | 1,809.27 | 1,926.84 | 2,160.77 | 2,229.06 | 2,524.28 | 2,732.49 | 3,194.64 | 3,615.40 | 4,023.38 | 4,366.41 |
| Securities Other than Shares | 36a | — | — | — | — | — | — | — | — | — | — | — | — |
| Deposits Excl. from Broad Money | 36b | 102.29 | 104.39 | 129.09 | 214.78 | 244.19 | 334.67 | 333.17 | 366.61 | 447.45 | 419.83 | 443.58 | 694.31 |
| Sec.Ot.th.Shares Excl.f/Brd.Money | 36s | 2.07 | .01 | .01 | .01 | .01 | — | — | — | — | — | — | — |
| Loans | 36l | — | 16.07 | 2.81 | — | 2.20 | — | — | — | — | — | — | — |
| Financial Derivatives | 36m | — | — | — | — | — | — | — | — | — | — | — | — |
| Insurance Technical Reserves | 36r | — | — | — | — | — | — | — | — | — | — | — | — |
| Shares and Other Equity | 37a | 351.55 | 429.98 | 444.50 | 452.74 | 677.32 | 951.15 | 1,099.85 | 1,224.11 | 1,703.56 | 1,828.74 | 1,895.79 | 2,127.48 |
| Other Items (Net) | 37r | 462.58 | 367.18 | 701.09 | 774.25 | 1,424.57 | 1,860.89 | 2,098.49 | 2,650.78 | 2,651.47 | 2,890.36 | 4,160.52 | 6,557.97 |
| Broad Money Liabs., Seasonally Adj. | 35l.b | 3,518.71 | 3,814.18 | 4,538.64 | 5,600.19 | 6,463.85 | 6,685.64 | 7,521.92 | 8,884.60 | 9,670.65 | 10,474.76 | 12,222.42 | 12,476.71 |
| **Other Financial Corporations** | | *Billions of Dinars: End of Period* | | | | | | | | | | | |
| Net Foreign Assets | 41n | −5.34 | −6.32 | −5.11 | −3.68 | −3.68 | −3.68 | −.67 | −.33 | −.10 | — | — | — |
| Claims on Nonresidents | 41 | — | — | — | — | — | — | — | — | — | — | — | — |
| Liabilities to Nonresidents | 46c | 5.34 | 6.32 | 5.11 | 3.68 | 3.68 | 3.68 | .67 | .33 | .10 | — | — | — |
| Claims on Depository Corporations | 40 | 16.44 | 14.06 | 10.30 | 4.91 | 7.31 | 7.19 | 13.99 | 13.60 | 14.68 | 15.81 | 11.92 | 15.00 |
| Net Claims on Central Government | 42an | −.35 | .73 | 3.83 | 5.58 | 5.31 | 5.35 | 3.19 | 4.16 | 2.26 | .93 | .01 | .09 |
| Claims on Central Government | 42a | .78 | .78 | 4.06 | 6.36 | 5.63 | 5.52 | 4.24 | 5.07 | 3.00 | 1.68 | .89 | .78 |
| Liabilities to Central Government | 46d | 1.13 | .05 | .22 | .78 | .32 | .17 | 1.05 | .91 | .75 | .75 | .88 | .70 |
| Claims on Other Sectors | 42s | 10.39 | 8.94 | 23.58 | 45.22 | 44.88 | 37.81 | 59.46 | 41.30 | 36.40 | 42.05 | 40.46 | 58.40 |
| Claims on State & Local Govts | 42b | — | — | — | — | — | — | — | — | — | — | — | — |
| Claims on Public Nonfin. Corps | 42c | 3.14 | 2.72 | 3.62 | 3.26 | 4.04 | 3.26 | 8.52 | 8.12 | 5.74 | 3.74 | 4.74 | 1.96 |
| Claims on Private Sector | 42d | 7.25 | 6.22 | 19.96 | 41.95 | 40.83 | 34.54 | 50.94 | 33.18 | 30.66 | 38.30 | 35.72 | 56.44 |
| Deposits | 46b | 3.45 | — | 4.05 | 2.66 | 3.50 | .02 | 22.20 | 13.32 | 4.46 | 5.17 | 6.08 | 5.00 |
| Securities Other than Shares | 46s | 2.48 | 2.48 | 4.80 | 8.09 | 8.09 | 8.09 | 6.93 | 4.54 | 2.98 | 9.95 | 5.42 | 15.82 |
| Loans | 46l | — | — | 3.74 | 17.43 | 17.09 | 17.09 | 1.15 | — | — | .70 | .50 | .50 |
| Financial Derivatives | 46m | — | — | — | — | — | — | — | — | — | — | — | — |
| Insurance Technical Reserves | 46r | — | — | — | — | — | — | — | — | — | — | — | — |
| Shares and Other Equity | 47a | 13.44 | 10.79 | 14.95 | 17.17 | 17.47 | 15.44 | 29.67 | 33.42 | 40.63 | 41.37 | 36.22 | 42.52 |
| Other Items (Net) | 47r | 1.77 | 4.14 | 5.07 | 6.67 | 7.66 | 6.03 | 16.01 | 7.46 | 5.17 | 1.59 | 4.17 | 9.65 |
| Memo Item: | | | | | | | | | | | | | |
| Total Assets | 40ra | 32.50 | 25.66 | 41.03 | 60.68 | 60.84 | 52.88 | 87.58 | 70.44 | 63.82 | 69.44 | 62.54 | 83.10 |
| **Monetary Aggregates** | | *Billions of Dinars: End of Period* | | | | | | | | | | | |
| Broad Money | 59m | 3,644.29 | 4,070.44 | 4,870.07 | 5,994.61 | 6,955.97 | 7,292.69 | 8,280.74 | 9,929.19 | 11,015.13 | 11,941.51 | 13,663.91 | 13,703.07 |
| o/w:Currency Issued by Cent.Govt | 59m.a | 37.98 | 131.22 | 132.01 | 167.37 | 194.20 | 265.37 | 322.63 | 518.70 | 758.69 | 860.19 | 765.93 | 707.39 |
| o/w: Dep.in Nonfin. Corporations | 59m.b | 120.33 | 144.83 | 203.84 | 211.29 | 265.59 | 308.48 | 412.83 | 515.32 | 590.29 | 621.09 | 694.50 | 537.20 |
| o/w:Secs. Issued by Central Govt | 59m.c | — | — | — | — | — | — | — | — | — | — | — | — |
| Money (National Definitions) | | | | | | | | | | | | | |
| M1 | 59ma | 2,160.58 | 2,421.42 | 3,210.90 | 4,233.57 | 4,964.93 | 5,021.63 | 5,756.46 | 7,141.70 | 7,681.49 | 8,249.81 | 9,580.18 | 9,259.07 |
| M2 | 59mb | 3,738.04 | 4,157.59 | 4,975.34 | † 5,994.61 | 6,955.97 | 7,292.69 | 8,280.74 | 9,929.19 | 11,015.13 | 11,941.51 | 13,663.91 | 13,703.07 |

# Algeria 612

| | | 2004 | 2005 | 2006 | 2007 | 2008 | 2009 | 2010 | 2011 | 2012 | 2013 | 2014 | 2015 |
|---|---|---|---|---|---|---|---|---|---|---|---|---|---|
| **Interest Rates** | | | | | | *Percent Per Annum* | | | | | | | |
| Discount Rate (End of Period).......... | 60.a | 4.00 | 4.00 | 4.00 | 4.00 | 4.00 | 4.00 | 4.00 | 4.00 | 4.00 | 4.00 | 4.00 | 4.00 |
| Money Market Rate....................... | 60b | 1.64 | 1.43 | 2.05 | 3.13 | 3.27 | 3.68 | 3.22 | 2.14 | .47 | 1.57 | 2.24 | .91 |
| Treasury Bill Rate......................... | 60c | .87 | .75 | 2.14 | .96 | .33 | .67 | .31 | .21 | .49 | .25 | .29 | .50 |
| Deposit Rate............................... | 60l | 3.65 | 1.94 | 1.75 | 1.75 | 1.75 | 1.75 | 1.75 | 1.75 | 1.75 | 1.75 | 1.75 | 1.75 |
| Lending Rate.............................. | 60p | 8.00 | 8.00 | 8.00 | 8.00 | 8.00 | 8.00 | 8.00 | 8.00 | 8.00 | 8.00 | 8.00 | 8.00 |
| **Prices, Production, Labor** | | | | | | *Index Numbers (2010=100): Period Averages* | | | | | | | |
| Producer Prices............................. | 63 | 78.6 | 81.3 | 83.3 | 85.8 | 93.8 | 97.0 | 100.0 | 102.1 | 104.8 | 105.0 | 106.1 | 108.5 |
| Consumer Prices.......................... | 64 | 80.7 | 81.8 | 83.7 | 86.8 | 91.0 | 96.2 | 100.0 | 104.5 | 113.8 | 117.5 | 120.9 | 126.7 |
| Industrial Production..................... | 66 | 97.2 | 98.7 | 98.4 | 100.4 | 102.2 | 102.6 | 100.0 | 100.4 | 102.1 | 103.0 | 107.5 | 109.0 |
| Crude Petroleum Production........... | 66aa | 103.7 | 112.9 | 113.6 | 113.2 | 115.8 | 101.7 | 100.0 | 97.5 | 98.8 | 98.4 | 96.9 | 93.6 |
| | | | | | | *Number in Thousands: Period Averages* | | | | | | | |
| Labor Force.................................. | 67d | 9,470 | 9,656 | 10,110 | 9,969 | 10,315 | 10,544 | 10,812 | 10,661 | 11,423 | 11,964 | 11,453 | 11,932 |
| Employment................................ | 67e | 7,798 | 8,182 | 8,869 | 8,594 | 9,146 | 9,472 | 9,735 | 9,599 | 10,170 | 10,788 | 10,239 | 10,594 |
| Unemployment............................ | 67c | 1,672 | 1,475 | 1,241 | 1,375 | 1,169 | 1,072 | 1,076 | 1,062 | 1,253 | 1,175 | 1,214 | 1,337 |
| Unemployment Rate (%)................. | 67r | 17.7 | 15.3 | 12.3 | 13.8 | 11.3 | 10.2 | 10.0 | 10.0 | 11.0 | 9.8 | 10.6 | 11.2 |
| **Intl. Transactions & Positions** | | | | | | *Millions of Dinars* | | | | | | | |
| Exports........................................ | 70 | 2,337,448 | 3,421,548 | 3,837,340 | 4,128,641 | 5,108,652 | 3,286,505 | 4,297,730 | 5,371,285 | 5,631,784 | 5,198,496 | 4,920,259 | 3,530,108 |
| Imports, c.i.f................................ | 71 | 1,314,400 | 1,493,645 | 1,525,942 | 1,903,392 | 2,549,096 | 2,857,894 | 2,991,938 | 3,446,053 | 3,906,677 | 4,358,250 | 4,699,100 | 5,188,569 |
| Volume of Exports | | | | | | *2010=100* | | | | | | | |
| Petroleum (2000=100).................. | 72a | .... | .... | .... | .... | .... | .... | .... | .... | .... | .... | .... | .... |
| Crude Petroleum....................... | 72aa | 124.1 | 136.4 | 133.3 | 131.2 | 118.8 | 105.4 | 100.0 | 98.3 | 96.7 | 86.1 | 71.4 | 73.3 |
| Refined Petroleum..................... | 72ab | 70.8 | 67.8 | 68.3 | 69.9 | 73.7 | 76.5 | 100.0 | 95.5 | 87.5 | 90.8 | 118.2 | 115.4 |
| Export Prices | | | | | | *2010=100: Index of Prices in US Dollars* | | | | | | | |
| Crude Petroleum........................... | 76aad | 48.1 | 68.1 | 81.9 | 93.3 | 124.7 | 77.6 | 100.0 | 141.0 | 138.1 | 136.9 | 125.0 | 66.2 |
| **Balance of Payments** | | | | | | *Millions of US Dollars* | | | | | | | |
| A. Current Account*....................... | 109bx | .... | 21,180.0 | 28,923.0 | 30,353.6 | 33,954.3 | 431.7 | 12,220.3 | 17,673.9 | 12,211.6 | 1,039.2 | −9,681.6 | .... |
| Goods, credit (exports).................. | 1a9cx | .... | 46,334.0 | 54,740.0 | 60,490.1 | 78,062.6 | 45,174.6 | 57,098.4 | 72,779.5 | 71,558.2 | 64,669.7 | 59,674.9 | .... |
| Goods, debit (imports)................... | 1a9dx | .... | 19,817.0 | 20,520.0 | 26,408.2 | 37,980.0 | 37,384.7 | 38,797.1 | 46,801.0 | 51,508.9 | 54,871.8 | 59,443.5 | .... |
| Balance on goods...................... | 1a9bx | .... | 26,517.0 | 34,220.0 | 34,081.9 | 40,082.6 | 7,789.9 | 18,301.3 | 25,978.6 | 20,049.3 | 9,797.9 | 231.3 | .... |
| Services, credit (exports)............... | 1b9cx | .... | 2,507.0 | 2,564.0 | 2,839.2 | 3,481.9 | 2,934.8 | 3,489.2 | 3,607.8 | 3,748.9 | 3,772.8 | 3,537.0 | .... |
| Services, debit (imports)................ | 1b9dx | .... | 4,823.0 | 4,837.0 | 6,795.5 | 11,088.1 | 11,634.4 | 11,847.4 | 12,586.3 | 10,873.4 | 10,794.6 | 11,804.0 | .... |
| Balance on Goods & Services....... | 1z9bx | .... | 24,201.0 | 31,947.0 | 30,125.6 | 32,476.3 | −909.8 | 9,943.1 | 17,000.0 | 12,924.8 | 2,776.0 | −8,035.6 | .... |
| Primary income: credit.................. | 1c9cx | .... | 1,427.0 | 2,417.0 | 3,798.2 | 5,110.4 | 4,751.5 | 4,580.4 | 4,443.3 | 3,906.7 | 3,545.3 | 3,173.6 | .... |
| Primary income: debit................... | 1c9dx | .... | 6,515.0 | 7,052.0 | 5,775.4 | 6,341.1 | 6,064.2 | 4,967.8 | 6,556.9 | 7,778.8 | 8,073.3 | 8,101.8 | .... |
| Balance on gds, serv. & prim. inc. | 1y9bx | .... | 19,113.0 | 27,312.0 | 28,148.5 | 31,245.7 | −2,222.5 | 9,555.7 | 14,886.4 | 9,052.7 | −1,752.0 | −12,963.9 | .... |
| Secondary income: credit.............. | 1d9ca | .... | 2,347.0 | 2,058.0 | 2,627.8 | 2,985.3 | 2,954.1 | 2,990.8 | 3,312.2 | 3,613.7 | 3,438.7 | 3,907.8 | .... |
| Secondary income: debit............... | 1d9da | .... | 280.0 | 447.0 | 422.7 | 276.7 | 300.0 | 326.3 | 524.7 | 454.8 | 647.5 | 625.5 | .... |
| B. Capital Account*........................ | 209ba | .... | −3.0 | −5.0 | −.2 | −.2 | −.1 | 3.8 | −1.3 | −8.9 | .2 | −3.1 | .... |
| Capital account: credit................. | 209ca | .... | — | — | 1.8 | .4 | — | 10.2 | .1 | .4 | .3 | .2 | .... |
| Capital account: debit.................. | 209da | .... | 3.0 | 5.0 | 2.0 | .6 | .1 | 6.3 | 1.4 | 9.3 | — | 3.3 | .... |
| Balance on current & capital acct. | 129ba | .... | 21,177.0 | 28,918.0 | 30,353.4 | 33,954.1 | 431.6 | 12,224.1 | 17,672.6 | 12,202.8 | 1,039.4 | −9,684.7 | .... |
| C. Financial Account* ................. | 309na | .... | 4,084.0 | 9,221.0 | −402.6 | −6,276.3 | −5,554.6 | −4,286.3 | −2,600.8 | −2,345.8 | 111.9 | −3,781.2 | .... |
| Direct investment: assets.............. | 3a9aa | .... | 55.0 | 79.0 | 147.0 | 317.9 | 214.4 | 219.2 | 533.9 | −41.4 | −271.7 | −18.4 | .... |
| Equity & investment fund shares.. | 3aaaa | .... | 55.0 | 74.0 | 141.6 | 64.9 | 124.2 | 189.2 | 558.4 | 1.3 | −216.1 | 19.9 | .... |
| Debt instruments........................ | 3abaa | .... | — | 5.0 | 5.4 | 253.0 | 90.2 | 30.0 | −24.5 | −42.7 | −55.6 | −38.4 | .... |
| Direct investment: liabilities .......... | 3a9la | .... | 1,156.0 | 1,841.0 | 1,686.7 | 2,638.6 | 2,746.9 | 2,300.4 | 2,571.2 | 1,500.4 | 1,691.9 | 1,504.7 | .... |
| Equity & investment fund shares . | 3aala | .... | 1,156.0 | 1,735.0 | 1,686.7 | 2,519.6 | 2,833.0 | 2,315.4 | 2,628.4 | 1,565.4 | 1,719.8 | 1,468.3 | .... |
| Debt instruments........................ | 3abla | .... | — | 106.0 | — | 119.0 | −86.0 | −15.0 | −57.2 | −64.9 | −27.9 | 36.4 | .... |
| Portfolio investment: assets .......... | 3b9aa | .... | — | — | .2 | — | — | −1,429.8 | −8.3 | — | — | — | .... |
| Equity & investment fund shares | 3baaa | .... | — | — | — | — | — | — | — | — | — | — | .... |
| Debt securities ............................ | 3bbaa | .... | — | — | .2 | — | — | −1,429.8 | −8.3 | — | — | — | .... |
| Portfolio investment: liabilities....... | 3b9la | .... | — | — | — | — | — | — | — | — | — | — | .... |
| Equity & investment fund shares . | 3bala | .... | — | — | — | — | — | — | — | — | — | — | .... |
| Debt securities............................ | 3bbla | .... | — | — | — | — | — | — | — | — | — | — | .... |
| Fin. der.& empl.stk.ops.(ESOs): net. | 3c9na | .... | — | — | — | — | — | — | — | — | — | — | .... |
| Fin. der. & ESOs.: assets................ | 3c9aa | .... | — | — | — | — | — | — | — | — | — | — | .... |
| Fin. der. & ESOs.: liabilities.......... | 3c9la | .... | — | — | — | — | — | — | — | — | — | — | .... |
| Other investment: assets............... | 3d9aa | .... | 1,720.0 | 231.0 | 1,381.2 | −3,024.3 | 136.6 | 495.6 | −509.7 | −29.8 | 2,135.2 | −1,783.3 | .... |
| Other equity.............................. | 3daaa | .... | .... | .... | .... | .... | .... | .... | .... | .... | .... | .... | .... |
| Debt instruments........................ | 3dzaa | .... | 1,720.0 | 231.0 | 1,381.2 | −3,024.3 | 136.6 | 495.6 | −509.7 | −29.8 | 2,135.2 | −1,783.3 | .... |
| Other investment: liabilities........... | 3d9la | .... | −3,465.0 | −10,752.0 | 244.2 | 931.2 | 3,158.7 | 1,271.1 | 45.6 | 774.1 | 59.7 | 474.7 | .... |
| Other equity.............................. | 3dala | .... | .... | .... | .... | .... | .... | .... | .... | .... | .... | .... | .... |
| Debt instruments........................ | 3dzla | .... | −3,465.0 | −10,752.0 | 244.2 | 931.2 | 3,158.7 | 1,271.1 | 45.6 | 774.1 | 59.7 | 474.7 | .... |
| Curr.+ cap.− finan. acct. balance... | 4y9na | .... | 17,093.0 | 19,697.0 | 30,756.0 | 40,230.4 | 5,986.2 | 16,510.4 | 20,273.4 | 14,548.5 | 927.6 | −5,903.5 | .... |
| D. Net Errors and Omissions........... | 409na | .... | −189.2 | −1,960.9 | −1,302.4 | −3,371.0 | −2,129.6 | −1,303.2 | −79.5 | −2,508.5 | −820.3 | −37.5 | .... |
| E. Reserves and Related Items.......... | 4z9na | .... | 16,903.8 | 17,736.1 | 29,453.6 | 36,859.5 | 3,856.6 | 15,207.3 | 20,193.9 | 12,040.0 | 107.3 | −5,941.0 | .... |
| Reserve assets............................ | 3e9aa | .... | 16,303.7 | 17,736.1 | 29,453.6 | 36,859.5 | 3,856.6 | 15,207.3 | 20,193.9 | 12,040.0 | 107.3 | −5,941.0 | .... |
| Credit and loans from the IMF........ | 3dcla | .... | −600.1 | — | — | — | — | — | — | — | — | — | .... |
| Exceptional financing.................... | 409la | .... | — | — | — | — | — | — | — | — | — | — | .... |

*Excludes components in group E

# Algeria 612

| | | 2004 | 2005 | 2006 | 2007 | 2008 | 2009 | 2010 | 2011 | 2012 | 2013 | 2014 | 2015 |
|---|---|---|---|---|---|---|---|---|---|---|---|---|---|
| **Government Finance** | | | | | | | | | | | | | |
| **Cash Flow Statement** | | | | | | | | | | | | | |
| **Budgetary Central Government** | | | | | | *Billions of Dinars: Fiscal Year Ends December 31* | | | | | | | |
| Cash Receipts:Operating Activities... | c1 | 2,252.5 | 3,112.7 | 3,651.3 | 3,715.7 | 5,211.5 | 3,740.5 | 4,443.3 | 5,897.5 | .... | .... | .... | .... |
| Taxes............................... | c11 | 1,648.2 | 2,326.5 | 3,464.5 | 3,500.9 | 4,997.6 | 3,503.1 | 4,125.4 | 5,424.9 | .... | .... | .... | .... |
| Social Contributions...................... | c12 | — | — | — | — | — | — | — | — | .... | .... | .... | .... |
| Grants............................. | c13 | — | — | .1 | .1 | — | — | — | — | .... | .... | .... | .... |
| Other Receipts.............................. | c14 | 604.3 | 786.2 | 186.8 | 214.7 | 213.9 | 237.5 | 317.9 | 472.6 | .... | .... | .... | .... |
| Cash Payments:Operating Activities. | c2 | 1,285.3 | 1,292.9 | 1,631.5 | 1,965.3 | 2,566.5 | 2,556.9 | 2,934.4 | 4,308.2 | .... | .... | .... | .... |
| Compensation of Employees.......... | c21 | 378.5 | 385.4 | 454.0 | 620.4 | 797.4 | 860.5 | 1,113.3 | 1,733.4 | .... | .... | .... | .... |
| Purchases of Goods & Services....... | c22 | 71.7 | 76.0 | 133.5 | 204.0 | 300.4 | 288.3 | 355.7 | 396.7 | .... | .... | .... | .... |
| Interest............................. | c24 | 143.5 | 101.2 | 97.4 | 77.7 | 63.9 | 35.9 | 30.2 | 37.7 | .... | .... | .... | .... |
| Subsidies............................. | c25 | .9 | .8 | 84.7 | 111.5 | 273.7 | 154.9 | 179.3 | 345.7 | .... | .... | .... | .... |
| Grants............................. | c26 | 176.5 | 187.5 | 385.8 | 338.0 | 430.5 | 449.5 | 449.9 | 718.7 | .... | .... | .... | .... |
| Social Benefits............................. | c27 | 212.2 | 225.5 | 353.5 | 450.3 | 542.9 | 555.6 | 677.1 | 870.2 | .... | .... | .... | .... |
| Other Payments............................. | c28 | 302.0 | 316.4 | 122.6 | 163.4 | 157.8 | 212.2 | 128.9 | 205.7 | .... | .... | .... | .... |
| Net Cash Inflow:Operating Act.[1-2] | ccio | 967.2 | 1,819.8 | 2,061.7 | 1,781.0 | 2,698.2 | 1,155.9 | 1,508.9 | 1,589.3 | .... | .... | .... | .... |
| Net Cash Outflow:Invest. in NFA...... | c31 | 640.7 | 806.9 | 899.3 | 1,285.1 | 1,620.2 | 1,631.4 | 1,460.1 | 1,630.6 | .... | .... | .... | .... |
| Purchases of Nonfinancial Assets... | c31.1 | 640.7 | 806.9 | 899.0 | 1,214.6 | 1,678.0 | 1,636.7 | .... | .... | .... | .... | .... | .... |
| Sales of Nonfinancial Assets.......... | c31.2 | — | — | 9.9 | 11.0 | 13.7 | — | .... | .... | .... | .... | .... | .... |
| Cash Surplus/Deficit [1-2-31=1-2M] | ccsd | 326.5 | 1,012.9 | 1,172.6 | 577.4 | 1,033.9 | −480.8 | 48.8 | −41.3 | .... | .... | .... | .... |
| Net Acq. Fin. Assets, excl. Cash....... | c32x | 11.8 | 5.2 | 31.1 | 110.5 | 146.3 | 231.4 | .... | .... | .... | .... | .... | .... |
| Domestic....................... | c321x | 11.8 | 5.2 | 31.1 | 110.5 | 146.3 | 231.4 | .... | .... | .... | .... | .... | .... |
| Foreign........................... | c322x | — | — | — | — | — | — | .... | .... | .... | .... | .... | .... |
| Net Incurrence of Liabilities.............. | c33 | 116.1 | 32.6 | 41.1 | −587.8 | 119.3 | 601.9 | 602.5 | 493.8 | .... | .... | .... | .... |
| Domestic....................... | c331 | 169.3 | 148.3 | 199.8 | −477.1 | 123.6 | 603.1 | 602.5 | 494.6 | .... | .... | .... | .... |
| Foreign........................... | c332 | −53.2 | −115.7 | −158.7 | −110.7 | −4.3 | −1.2 | — | −.8 | .... | .... | .... | .... |
| Net Cash Inflow, Fin.Act.[-32x+33].. | cnfb | 104.3 | 27.5 | 49.1 | −593.9 | −28.5 | 407.4 | −48.8 | 41.2 | .... | .... | .... | .... |
| Net Change in Stock of Cash........... | cncb | 430.8 | 1,040.4 | 1,221.7 | −16.5 | 1,005.4 | −73.4 | 424.0 | 277.4 | .... | .... | .... | .... |
| Stat. Discrep. [32X-33+NCB-CSD].... | ccsdz | — | — | — | — | — | — | .... | .... | .... | .... | .... | .... |
| Memo Item:Cash Expenditure[2+31] | c2m | 1,926.0 | 2,099.8 | 2,530.8 | 3,250.4 | 4,186.7 | 4,188.2 | 4,394.5 | 5,938.8 | .... | .... | .... | .... |
| Memo Item: Gross Debt.................. | c63 | .... | .... | .... | .... | .... | .... | .... | .... | .... | .... | .... | .... |
| **National Accounts** | | | | | | *Billions of Dinars* | | | | | | | |
| Househ.Cons.Expend.,incl.NPISHs.... | 96f | 2,371.0 | 2,553.0 | 2,695.6 | 2,963.8 | 3,333.3 | 3,743.9 | 4,115.6 | 4,548.2 | 5,211.0 | 5,769.8 | 6,264.7 | .... |
| Government Consumption Expend... | 91f | 846.9 | 865.9 | 954.9 | 1,089.0 | 1,458.5 | 1,609.4 | 2,065.8 | 3,015.2 | 3,293.5 | 3,185.7 | 3,343.5 | .... |
| Gross Fixed Capital Formation.......... | 93e | 1,476.9 | 1,691.6 | 1,969.5 | 2,462.1 | 3,228.3 | 3,811.4 | 4,350.9 | 4,620.3 | 4,992.4 | 5,690.9 | 6,311.8 | .... |
| Changes in Inventories.................... | 93i | 568.5 | 702.2 | 595.5 | 761.8 | 896.3 | 861.2 | 617.6 | 919.1 | 1,344.1 | 1,529.8 | 1,534.9 | .... |
| Exports of Goods and Services......... | 90c | 2,462.9 | 3,569.6 | 4,149.7 | 4,402.2 | 5,298.0 | 3,525.9 | 4,610.1 | 5,658.6 | 5,979.8 | 5,528.8 | 5,252.6 | .... |
| Imports of Goods and Services (-)..... | 98c | 1,577.1 | 1,820.4 | 1,863.5 | 2,326.1 | 3,170.8 | 3,583.8 | 3,768.0 | 4,172.9 | 4,612.1 | 5,061.1 | 5,502.4 | .... |
| Gross Domestic Product (GDP)......... | 99b | 6,149.1 | 7,562.0 | 8,501.6 | 9,352.9 | 11,043.7 | 9,968.0 | 11,991.6 | 14,588.5 | 16,208.7 | 16,643.8 | 17,205.1 | .... |
| | | | | | | *Millions: Midyear Estimates* | | | | | | | |
| Population................................ | 99z | 32.82 | 33.27 | 33.75 | 34.26 | 34.81 | 35.40 | 36.04 | 36.72 | 37.44 | 38.19 | 38.93 | 39.67 |

# Angola   614

| | | 2004 | 2005 | 2006 | 2007 | 2008 | 2009 | 2010 | 2011 | 2012 | 2013 | 2014 | 2015 |
|---|---|---|---|---|---|---|---|---|---|---|---|---|---|
| **Exchange Rates** | | | | | | *Kwanzas per SDR: End of Period* | | | | | | | |
| Market Rate | aa | 133.54 | 115.46 | 120.75 | 118.56 | 115.78 | 140.15 | 142.67 | 146.27 | 147.28 | 150.25 | 149.03 | 187.51 |
| | | | | | | *Kwanzas per US Dollar: End of Period (ae) Period Average (rf)* | | | | | | | |
| Market Rate | ae | 85.988 | 80.780 | 80.264 | 75.023 | 75.169 | 89.398 | 92.643 | 95.272 | 95.826 | 97.562 | 102.863 | 135.315 |
| Market Rate | rf | 83.541 | 87.159 | 80.368 | 76.706 | 75.033 | 79.328 | 91.906 | 93.935 | 95.468 | 96.518 | 98.302 | 120.061 |
| **Fund Position** | | | | | | *Millions of SDRs: End of Period* | | | | | | | |
| Quota | 2f.s | 286.30 | 286.30 | 286.30 | 286.30 | 286.30 | 286.30 | 286.30 | 286.30 | 286.30 | 286.30 | 286.30 | 286.30 |
| SDR Holdings | 1b.s | .15 | .15 | .16 | .16 | .17 | 271.52 | 266.31 | 256.05 | 247.23 | 238.19 | 231.69 | 228.73 |
| Reserve Position in the Fund | 1c.s | — | — | — | — | — | — | — | — | — | — | — | — |
| Total Fund Cred.&Loans Outstg | 2tl | — | — | — | — | — | — | 572.60 | 773.01 | 858.90 | 687.12 | 357.88 | 110.94 |
| SDR Allocations | 1bd | — | — | — | — | — | 273.01 | 273.01 | 273.01 | 273.01 | 273.01 | 273.01 | 273.01 |
| **International Liquidity** | | | | | | *Millions of US Dollars Unless Otherwise Indicated: End of Period* | | | | | | | |
| Total Reserves minus Gold | 1l.d | 1,374.05 | 3,196.85 | 8,598.58 | 11,196.80 | 17,869.41 | 13,664.10 | 19,749.47 | 28,786.21 | 33,414.77 | 32,780.38 | 28,130.31 | 24,074.98 |
| SDR Holdings | 1b.d | .23 | .21 | .23 | .26 | .26 | 425.65 | 410.13 | 393.11 | 379.97 | 366.81 | 335.67 | 316.96 |
| Reserve Position in the Fund | 1c.d | — | — | — | — | — | — | — | — | — | — | — | — |
| Foreign Exchange | 1d.d | 1,373.82 | 3,196.64 | 8,598.35 | 11,196.54 | 17,869.15 | 13,238.45 | 19,339.35 | † 28,393.10 | 33,034.81 | 32,413.56 | 27,794.64 | 23,758.02 |
| Central Bank: Other Assets | 3..d | 5.2 | 5.4 | 4.4 | 4.4 | 4.4 | 4.5 | 4.5 | † 1,269.1 | 1,080.9 | 989.1 | † 1,355.3 | 1,249.1 |
| Central Bank: Other Liabs | 4..d | 27.2 | 31.2 | 27.4 | 27.6 | 27.5 | 62.5 | 28.5 | † 9.6 | 9.9 | — | † — | 318.2 |
| Other Depository Corps.: Assets | 7a.d | 1,364.5 | 1,758.2 | 3,132.7 | 3,146.3 | 5,987.6 | 4,575.0 | † 4,758.4 | 8,790.2 | 6,491.8 | 6,024.7 | 5,362.2 | 4,649.1 |
| Other Depository Corps.: Liabs | 7b.d | 109.2 | 138.8 | 198.4 | 726.3 | 3,764.8 | 4,551.0 | † 4,425.9 | 5,234.1 | 4,942.4 | 5,834.0 | 3,485.6 | 3,101.6 |
| **Central Bank** | | | | | | *Millions of Kwanzas: End of Period* | | | | | | | |
| Net Foreign Assets | 11n | 43,469 | 255,973 | 655,775 | 841,187 | 1,342,053 | 1,179,430 | 1,700,218 | † 2,588,615 | 3,017,255 | 3,096,754 | † 2,904,432 | 3,396,777 |
| Claims on Nonresidents | 11 | 45,809 | 258,489 | 657,977 | 843,258 | 1,344,122 | 1,223,283 | 1,823,503 | † 2,742,546 | 3,184,908 | 3,241,092 | † 2,998,452 | 3,511,828 |
| Liabilities to Nonresidents | 16c | 2,341 | 2,517 | 2,202 | 2,071 | 2,070 | 43,853 | 123,285 | † 153,931 | 167,653 | 144,339 | † 94,020 | 115,050 |
| Claims on Other Depository Corps | 12e | 1,421 | 994 | 2,173 | 23,014 | 5,348 | 88,694 | 56,631 | † 86,169 | 54,852 | 1,484 | † 108,286 | 239,095 |
| Net Claims on Central Government | 12an | 5,350 | −121,978 | −419,822 | −458,261 | −934,609 | −282,473 | −624,942 | † −982,385 | −1,339,417 | −1,203,925 | † −964,409 | −1,105,607 |
| Claims on Central Government | 12a | 22,747 | 24,089 | 32,405 | 31,120 | 31,156 | 68,929 | 68,241 | † 371,153 | 326,138 | 261,273 | † 239,466 | 244,049 |
| Liabilities to Central Government | 16d | 17,397 | 146,068 | 452,227 | 489,381 | 965,765 | 351,402 | 693,183 | † 1,353,539 | 1,665,555 | 1,465,198 | † 1,203,875 | 1,349,655 |
| Claims on Other Sectors | 12s | 3,219 | 3,033 | 3,222 | 3,206 | 3,212 | 3,253 | 26,591 | † 1,189 | 6,375 | 3,749 | † 3,492 | 4,754 |
| Claims on Other Financial Corps | 12g | 75 | 89 | 16 | 43 | 60 | 106 | 217 | † 235 | 430 | — | † — | — |
| Claims on State & Local Govts | 12b | — | — | — | — | — | — | — | † — | — | — | † — | — |
| Claims on Public Nonfin. Corps | 12c | — | — | — | — | — | — | — | † — | — | — | † — | — |
| Claims on Private Sector | 12d | 3,144 | 2,944 | 3,206 | 3,162 | 3,147 | 3,147 | 26,374 | † 954 | 5,944 | 3,749 | † 3,492 | 4,754 |
| Monetary Base | 14 | 91,406 | 152,099 | 153,593 | 246,574 | 400,014 | 702,136 | 802,811 | † 989,393 | 1,006,830 | 1,160,258 | † 1,237,686 | 1,631,402 |
| Currency in Circulation | 14a | 56,346 | 78,543 | 93,503 | 113,508 | 168,373 | 213,937 | 229,840 | † 287,546 | 335,505 | 410,182 | † 477,970 | 519,588 |
| Liabs. to Other Depository Corps | 14c | 35,059 | 73,556 | 60,090 | 133,066 | 231,641 | 488,198 | 572,970 | † 701,847 | 671,325 | 750,077 | † 759,715 | 1,111,814 |
| Liabilities to Other Sectors | 14d | — | — | — | — | — | — | — | † — | — | — | † — | — |
| Other Liabs. to Other Dep. Corps | 14n | 11,353 | 28,898 | 109,766 | 212,546 | 93,776 | 145,818 | 281,460 | † 285,726 | 316,753 | 277,628 | † 349,949 | 44,337 |
| Dep. & Sec. Excl. f/Monetary Base | 14o | — | — | — | — | — | — | — | † — | — | — | † — | — |
| Deposits Included in Broad Money | 15 | — | — | — | — | — | — | — | † — | — | — | † — | — |
| Sec.Ot.th.Shares Incl.in Brd. Money | 16a | — | — | — | — | — | — | — | † — | — | — | † — | — |
| Deposits Excl. from Broad Money | 16b | — | — | — | — | — | — | — | † — | — | — | † — | — |
| Sec.Ot.th.Shares Excl.f/Brd.Money | 16s | — | — | — | — | — | — | — | † — | — | — | † — | — |
| Loans | 16l | — | — | — | — | — | — | — | † — | — | — | † — | — |
| Financial Derivatives | 16m | — | — | — | — | — | — | — | † — | — | — | † — | — |
| Shares and Other Equity | 17a | 1,923 | −25,752 | −13,624 | −36,486 | −86,404 | 95,973 | 102,649 | † 408,848 | 389,571 | 337,291 | † 308,522 | 749,022 |
| Other Items (Net) | 17r | −51,223 | −17,223 | −8,387 | −13,488 | 8,618 | 44,978 | −28,421 | † 9,620 | 25,911 | 122,885 | † 155,644 | 110,259 |
| Memo Item: | | | | | | | | | | | | | |
| Total Assets | 10ra | 167,792 | 341,123 | 751,628 | 956,498 | 1,443,052 | 1,449,640 | 2,049,526 | † 3,293,191 | 3,676,242 | 3,597,057 | † 3,436,676 | 4,087,282 |
| **Other Depository Corporations** | | | | | | *Millions of Kwanzas: End of Period* | | | | | | | |
| Net Foreign Assets | 21n | 107,944 | 130,812 | 235,516 | 181,551 | 167,088 | 2,143 | † 30,808 | 338,826 | 148,467 | 18,616 | 193,033 | 209,391 |
| Claims on Nonresidents | 21 | 117,332 | 142,028 | 251,442 | 236,043 | 450,081 | 408,996 | † 440,834 | 837,544 | 622,079 | 588,124 | 551,575 | 629,091 |
| Liabilities to Nonresidents | 26c | 9,388 | 11,216 | 15,926 | 54,492 | 282,993 | 406,853 | † 410,025 | 498,718 | 473,612 | 569,509 | 358,543 | 419,700 |
| Claims on Central Bank | 20 | 60,479 | 120,786 | 196,288 | 357,749 | 486,013 | 657,686 | † 1,018,260 | 1,120,709 | 1,075,524 | 1,124,909 | 1,231,778 | 1,403,447 |
| Currency | 20a | 10,918 | 19,918 | 23,873 | 28,747 | 43,970 | 46,487 | † 58,013 | 79,148 | 90,874 | 133,822 | 138,302 | 138,886 |
| Reserve Deposits and Securities | 20b | 38,488 | 77,690 | 62,976 | 126,015 | 348,267 | 464,241 | † 464,844 | 636,069 | 674,429 | 766,740 | 772,425 | 1,150,953 |
| Other Claims | 20n | 11,073 | 23,178 | 109,439 | 202,986 | 93,776 | 146,958 | † 495,403 | 405,492 | 310,220 | 224,346 | 321,050 | 113,607 |
| Net Claims on Central Government | 22an | 6,545 | 32,515 | −38,612 | 28,991 | 667,099 | 679,706 | † 402,429 | 536,006 | 397,126 | 538,376 | 1,033,575 | 1,489,528 |
| Claims on Central Government | 22a | 46,977 | 93,996 | 52,543 | 180,657 | 798,827 | 901,398 | † 646,485 | 834,110 | 860,002 | 1,180,526 | 1,762,319 | 2,338,123 |
| Liabilities to Central Government | 26d | 40,432 | 61,481 | 91,155 | 151,666 | 131,728 | 221,692 | † 244,056 | 298,104 | 462,876 | 642,150 | 728,744 | 848,596 |
| Claims on Other Sectors | 22s | 95,401 | 146,985 | 286,999 | 512,940 | 861,156 | 1,347,281 | † 1,656,245 | 2,072,587 | 2,641,020 | 2,923,342 | 2,943,211 | 3,464,600 |
| Claims on Other Financial Corps | 22g | — | — | — | — | — | — | † 69,975 | 11,188 | 110,365 | 33,767 | 33,078 | 33,048 |
| Claims on State & Local Govts | 22b | 1,362 | 235 | 510 | 154 | 1,341 | 546 | † 9,964 | 1,416 | 1,381 | 1,904 | — | — |
| Claims on Public Nonfin. Corps | 22c | 7,484 | 11,296 | 15,987 | 23,429 | 61,918 | 64,180 | † 70,408 | 87,370 | 83,834 | 71,704 | 61,581 | 81,979 |
| Claims on Private Sector | 22d | 86,555 | 135,453 | 270,502 | 489,357 | 797,896 | 1,282,555 | † 1,505,899 | 1,972,613 | 2,445,440 | 2,815,968 | 2,848,551 | 3,349,573 |
| Liabilities to Central Bank | 26g | — | — | — | 6,020 | 1 | 56,559 | † 114,054 | 89,113 | 56,364 | 3,385 | 35,556 | 135,788 |
| Transf.Dep.Included in Broad Money | 24 | 141,319 | 252,289 | 401,341 | 620,431 | 1,106,897 | 1,463,617 | † 1,491,813 | 1,947,401 | 1,983,536 | 2,310,733 | 2,757,194 | 3,039,120 |
| Other Dep.Included in Broad Money | 25 | 68,056 | 109,712 | 174,542 | 263,641 | 590,200 | 736,250 | † 964,612 | 1,409,778 | 1,620,181 | 1,809,217 | 2,006,708 | 2,284,003 |
| Sec.Ot.th.Shares Incl.in Brd. Money | 26a | 11,874 | 7,942 | 39,555 | 54,806 | 272,519 | 176,406 | † 49,978 | 107,535 | 4,679 | 1,789 | 6,546 | 8,075 |
| Deposits Excl. from Broad Money | 26b | — | — | — | — | — | — | † — | — | — | — | — | — |
| Sec.Ot.th.Shares Excl.f/Brd.Money | 26s | — | — | — | — | — | — | † — | — | — | — | — | — |
| Loans | 26l | — | — | — | — | — | — | † 154,692 | 84,737 | 153,171 | 196,594 | 26,872 | 115,700 |
| Financial Derivatives | 26m | — | — | — | — | — | — | † — | — | — | 166 | 284 | 3,840 |
| Insurance Technical Reserves | 26r | — | — | — | — | — | — | † — | — | — | — | — | — |
| Shares and Other Equity | 27a | 37,591 | 50,959 | 79,489 | 151,980 | 199,741 | 335,843 | † 441,892 | 565,396 | 623,751 | 731,586 | 722,476 | 880,709 |
| Other Items (Net) | 27r | 11,528 | 10,197 | −14,736 | −15,648 | 11,998 | −81,859 | † −109,299 | −135,832 | −179,545 | −448,227 | −154,040 | 99,731 |
| Memo Item: | | | | | | | | | | | | | |
| Total Assets | 20ra | 332,112 | 520,005 | 838,212 | 1,360,355 | 2,684,362 | 3,495,836 | † 4,354,162 | 5,595,207 | 6,215,452 | 6,961,878 | 7,537,873 | 8,955,042 |

# Angola  614

| | Code | 2004 | 2005 | 2006 | 2007 | 2008 | 2009 | 2010 | 2011 | 2012 | 2013 | 2014 | 2015 |
|---|---|---|---|---|---|---|---|---|---|---|---|---|---|
| **Depository Corporations** | | | | | | | *Millions of Kwanzas: End of Period* | | | | | | |
| Net Foreign Assets | 31n | 151,413 | 386,785 | 891,291 | 1,022,738 | 1,509,141 | 1,181,572 | †1,731,026 | †2,927,440 | 3,165,722 | 3,115,369 | †3,097,464 | 3,606,169 |
| Claims on Nonresidents | 31 | 163,142 | 400,518 | 909,419 | 1,079,301 | 1,794,204 | 1,632,279 | †2,264,337 | †3,580,089 | 3,806,987 | 3,829,217 | †3,550,027 | 4,140,919 |
| Liabilities to Nonresidents | 36c | 11,728 | 13,732 | 18,129 | 56,563 | 285,063 | 450,707 | †533,310 | †652,649 | 641,265 | 713,847 | †452,563 | 534,750 |
| Domestic Claims | 32 | 110,515 | 60,554 | −168,213 | 86,875 | 596,858 | 1,747,767 | †1,460,323 | †1,627,397 | 1,705,104 | 2,261,543 | †3,015,869 | 3,853,274 |
| Net Claims on Central Government | 32an | 11,895 | −89,463 | −458,434 | −429,270 | −267,510 | 397,233 | †−222,513 | †−446,380 | −942,291 | −665,549 | †69,166 | 383,921 |
| Claims on Central Government | 32a | 69,724 | 118,085 | 84,948 | 211,777 | 829,983 | 970,327 | †714,726 | †1,205,263 | 1,186,140 | 1,441,799 | †2,001,785 | 2,582,172 |
| Liabilities to Central Government | 36d | 57,829 | 207,548 | 543,382 | 641,047 | 1,097,493 | 573,094 | †937,239 | †1,651,643 | 2,128,431 | 2,107,348 | †1,932,619 | 2,198,251 |
| Claims on Other Sectors | 32s | 98,620 | 150,017 | 290,221 | 516,145 | 864,368 | 1,350,534 | †1,682,836 | †2,073,776 | 2,647,395 | 2,927,092 | †2,946,703 | 3,469,354 |
| Claims on Other Financial Corps. | 32g | 75 | 89 | 16 | 43 | 60 | 106 | †70,193 | †11,423 | 110,795 | 33,767 | †33,078 | 33,048 |
| Claims on State & Local Govts. | 32b | 1,362 | 235 | 510 | 154 | 1,341 | 546 | †9,964 | †1,416 | 1,381 | 1,904 | †— | — |
| Claims on Public Nonfin. Corps. | 32c | 7,484 | 11,297 | 15,987 | 23,429 | 61,919 | 64,180 | †70,408 | †87,370 | 83,834 | 71,704 | †61,581 | 81,979 |
| Claims on Private Sector | 32d | 89,699 | 138,397 | 273,708 | 492,519 | 801,048 | 1,285,702 | †1,532,272 | †1,973,568 | 2,451,384 | 2,819,717 | †2,852,043 | 3,354,327 |
| Broad Money Liabilities | 35l | 266,678 | 428,567 | 685,068 | 1,023,639 | 2,094,011 | 2,543,723 | †2,678,230 | †3,673,111 | 3,853,027 | 4,398,099 | †5,110,116 | 5,711,899 |
| Currency Outside Depository Corps | 34a | 45,429 | 58,625 | 69,630 | 84,761 | 124,402 | 167,450 | †171,827 | †208,398 | 244,630 | 276,360 | †339,668 | 380,702 |
| Transferable Deposits | 34 | 141,319 | 252,289 | 401,341 | 620,431 | 1,106,897 | 1,463,617 | †1,491,813 | †1,947,401 | 1,983,536 | 2,310,733 | †2,757,194 | 3,039,120 |
| Other Deposits | 35 | 68,056 | 109,712 | 174,542 | 263,641 | 590,200 | 736,250 | †964,612 | †1,409,778 | 1,620,181 | 1,809,217 | †2,006,708 | 2,284,003 |
| Securities other than Shares | 36a | 11,874 | 7,942 | 39,555 | 54,806 | 272,519 | 176,406 | †49,978 | †107,535 | 4,679 | 1,789 | †6,546 | 8,075 |
| Deposits Excl. from Broad Money | 36b | — | — | — | — | — | — | †— | †— | — | — | †— | — |
| Sec.Ot.th.Shares Excl.f/Brd.Money. | 36s | — | — | — | — | — | — | †— | †— | — | — | †— | — |
| Loans | 36l | — | — | — | — | — | — | †154,692 | †84,737 | 153,171 | 196,594 | †26,872 | 115,700 |
| Financial Derivatives | 36m | — | — | — | — | — | — | †— | †— | — | 166 | †284 | 3,840 |
| Insurance Technical Reserves | 36r | — | — | — | — | — | — | †— | †— | — | — | †— | — |
| Shares and Other Equity | 37a | 39,515 | 25,206 | 65,865 | 115,494 | 113,337 | 431,816 | †544,540 | †974,244 | 1,013,323 | 1,068,877 | †1,030,998 | 1,629,731 |
| Other Items (Net) | 37r | −44,264 | −6,434 | −27,855 | −29,520 | −101,357 | −46,199 | †−186,113 | †−177,255 | −148,694 | −286,824 | †−54,937 | −1,728 |
| Broad Money Liabs., Seasonally Adj. | 35l.b | 254,493 | 410,179 | 656,469 | 980,604 | 2,003,618 | 2,432,269 | †2,527,960 | †3,478,500 | 3,660,286 | 4,180,327 | †4,904,324 | .... |
| **Monetary Aggregates** | | | | | | | *Millions of Kwanzas: End of Period* | | | | | | |
| Broad Money | 59m | .... | .... | .... | .... | .... | .... | 2,678,230 | 3,673,111 | 3,853,027 | 4,398,099 | 5,110,116 | 5,711,899 |
| o/w:Currency Issued by Cent.Govt | 59m.a | .... | .... | .... | .... | .... | .... | — | — | — | — | — | — |
| o/w: Dep.in Nonfin. Corporations. | 59m.b | .... | .... | .... | .... | .... | — | — | — | — | — | — | — |
| o/w:Secs. Issued by Central Govt. | 59m.c | .... | .... | .... | .... | .... | — | — | — | — | — | — | — |
| Money (National Definitions) | | | | | | | | | | | | | |
| Base Money | 19ma | 91,406 | 152,099 | 153,593 | 246,574 | 400,014 | 702,136 | 802,811 | 989,393 | 1,006,830 | 1,160,258 | 1,237,686 | 1,631,402 |
| Reserve Money | 19mb | 102,759 | 180,996 | 263,359 | 459,120 | 493,789 | 847,953 | 1,084,271 | 1,275,119 | 1,323,583 | 1,392,045 | 1,580,641 | 1,675,316 |
| M1 | 59ma | 186,747 | 310,914 | 470,971 | 705,192 | 1,231,299 | 1,631,067 | 1,663,640 | 2,155,799 | 2,228,167 | 2,587,093 | 3,096,862 | 3,419,821 |
| M2 | 59mb | 243,716 | 391,256 | 615,581 | 852,901 | 1,417,145 | 2,303,840 | †2,589,839 | 3,527,163 | 3,817,589 | 4,396,121 | 5,103,483 | 5,703,745 |
| M3 | 59mc | 269,257 | 431,321 | 688,212 | 1,027,446 | 2,097,451 | 2,547,956 | †2,678,230 | 3,673,111 | 3,853,027 | 4,398,099 | 5,110,116 | 5,711,899 |
| **Interest Rates** | | | | | | | *Percent Per Annum* | | | | | | |
| Discount Rate (End of Period) | 60.a | 104.17 | 57.92 | 17.88 | 17.88 | 19.57 | 25.35 | 29.17 | 21.67 | 20.00 | 19.19 | 9.92 | 11.00 |
| Overnight Lending Rate | 60.d | .... | .... | .... | .... | .... | .... | .... | 12.50 | 11.79 | 11.04 | 9.92 | 11.00 |
| Overnight Deposit Rate | 60.r | .... | .... | .... | .... | .... | .... | .... | 2.00 | 1.67 | 1.00 | 1.58 | .73 |
| Money Market Rate | 60b | .... | 19.06 | 6.13 | 8.79 | 13.59 | 14.79 | 22.10 | 11.27 | 5.86 | 5.77 | 3.87 | 9.56 |
| Treasury Bill Rate | 60c | 57.21 | 31.63 | .... | .... | .... | .... | 10.82 | 6.93 | 3.45 | 3.06 | 4.28 | 7.20 |
| Deposit Rate | 60l | 15.44 | 13.40 | 4.50 | 6.76 | 6.54 | 7.59 | 12.76 | 6.31 | 3.60 | 3.15 | 3.53 | 3.31 |
| Lending Rate | 60p | 82.33 | 67.72 | 19.51 | 17.70 | 12.53 | 15.68 | 22.54 | 18.76 | 16.66 | 15.81 | 16.38 | 16.88 |
| Government Bond Yield | 61 | .... | .... | .... | .... | .... | .... | .... | .... | .... | 8.25 | 8.17 | 7.77 |
| **Prices** | | | | | | | *Index Numbers (2010=100): Period Averages* | | | | | | |
| Consumer Prices | 64 | 43.7 | 53.7 | 60.8 | 68.3 | 76.8 | †87.4 | 100.0 | 113.5 | 125.1 | †136.1 | †146.0 | 161.1 |
| **Intl. Transactions & Positions** | | | | | | | *Millions of US Dollars* | | | | | | |
| Exports, f.o.b. | 70..d | 13,475.0 | 24,109.4 | 31,862.2 | 44,396.2 | 63,913.9 | 40,827.9 | 50,594.9 | 67,310.3 | 71,093.3 | 68,246.5 | 59,169.9 | 33,164.5 |
| Imports, f.o.b. | 71.vd | 5,831.8 | 8,353.2 | 8,777.6 | 13,661.5 | 20,982.2 | 22,659.9 | 16,666.9 | 22,937.6 | 23,716.9 | 26,344.0 | 28,586.8 | 20,094.9 |

# Angola   614

| Balance of Payments | | 2004 | 2005 | 2006 | 2007 | 2008 | 2009 | 2010 | 2011 | 2012 | 2013 | 2014 | 2015 |
|---|---|---|---|---|---|---|---|---|---|---|---|---|---|
| | | | | | | | *Millions of US Dollars* | | | | | | |
| A. Current Account* | 109bx | 681.2 | 5,137.9 | 10,689.8 | 10,581.3 | 7,194.2 | † −7,571.7 | 7,506.0 | 13,084.6 | 13,853.3 | 8,348.4 | −3,722.4 | .... |
| Goods, credit (exports) | 1a9cx | 13,475.0 | 24,109.4 | 31,862.2 | 44,396.2 | 63,913.9 | † 40,827.9 | 50,594.9 | 67,310.3 | 71,093.3 | 68,246.5 | 59,169.9 | .... |
| Goods, debit (imports) | 1a9dx | 5,831.8 | 8,353.2 | 8,777.6 | 13,661.5 | 20,982.2 | † 22,659.9 | 16,666.9 | 20,228.4 | 23,716.9 | 26,344.0 | 28,586.8 | .... |
| Balance on goods | 1a9bx | 7,643.2 | 15,756.2 | 23,084.6 | 30,734.7 | 42,931.8 | † 18,168.0 | 33,928.0 | 47,081.8 | 47,376.3 | 41,902.6 | 30,583.1 | .... |
| Services, credit (exports) | 1b9cx | 322.8 | 176.8 | 1,484.2 | 310.7 | 329.5 | † 623.2 | 856.9 | 732.3 | 780.0 | 1,315.7 | 1,681.3 | .... |
| Services, debit (imports) | 1b9dx | 4,802.7 | 6,791.0 | 7,511.2 | 12,643.2 | 22,139.3 | † 19,169.4 | 18,754.4 | 23,669.9 | 22,119.2 | 22,846.4 | 24,927.7 | .... |
| Balance on Goods & Services | 1z9bx | 3,163.3 | 9,142.0 | 17,057.7 | 18,402.2 | 21,121.9 | † −378.2 | 16,030.5 | 24,144.2 | 26,037.2 | 20,371.8 | 7,336.8 | .... |
| Primary income: credit | 1c9cx | 33.0 | 25.8 | 145.0 | 622.6 | 422.3 | † 131.3 | 134.0 | 209.8 | 259.8 | 818.3 | 645.6 | .... |
| Primary income: debit | 1c9dx | 2,521.6 | 4,056.6 | 6,322.9 | 8,221.6 | 14,139.8 | † 6,954.5 | 8,220.9 | 9,907.1 | 10,681.6 | 10,718.3 | 9,495.5 | .... |
| Balance on gds, serv. & prim. inc. | 1y9bx | 674.7 | 5,111.1 | 10,879.8 | 10,803.2 | 7,404.3 | † −7,201.3 | 7,943.6 | 14,446.9 | 15,615.4 | 10,471.8 | −1,513.1 | .... |
| Secondary income: credit | 1d9ca | 124.4 | 172.5 | 59.5 | 45.7 | 154.5 | † 56.8 | 58.4 | 115.6 | 66.9 | 68.2 | 55.0 | .... |
| Secondary income: debit | 1d9da | 117.9 | 145.8 | 249.5 | 267.6 | 364.5 | † 427.1 | 496.1 | 1,477.8 | 1,829.0 | 2,191.6 | 2,264.3 | .... |
| B. Capital Account* | 209ba | — | — | — | 6.9 | 6.5 | † 4.1 | .9 | 2.3 | .2 | .... | .... | .... |
| Capital account: credit | 209ca | — | — | — | 6.9 | 6.5 | † 4.1 | .9 | 2.3 | .2 | .... | .... | .... |
| Capital account: debit | 209da | — | — | — | — | — | .... | .... | .... | .... | .... | .... | .... |
| Balance on current & capital acct. | 129ba | 681.2 | 5,137.9 | 10,689.8 | 10,588.1 | 7,200.8 | † −7,567.5 | 7,506.9 | 13,086.9 | 13,853.5 | 8,348.4 | −3,722.4 | .... |
| C. Financial Account* | 309na | −993.2 | 3,126.0 | 3,982.9 | 5,842.2 | −1,218.7 | † −2,152.8 | 1,661.4 | 4,292.6 | 9,016.3 | 7,948.1 | 462.5 | .... |
| Direct investment: assets | 3a9aa | 783.2 | 219.4 | 190.6 | 911.8 | 2,569.6 | † 6.8 | 1,340.4 | 2,092.6 | 2,740.8 | 6,044.2 | 4,253.1 | .... |
| Equity & investment fund shares | 3aaaa | 748.0 | 17.9 | — | 80.5 | 593.8 | † .1 | 85.0 | 516.2 | .... | 34.0 | .... | .... |
| Debt instruments | 3abaa | 35.2 | 201.5 | 190.6 | 831.3 | 1,975.8 | † 6.7 | 1,255.4 | 1,576.4 | 2,740.8 | 6,010.1 | 4,253.1 | .... |
| Direct investment: liabilities | 3a9la | 2,197.2 | −1,303.8 | −37.7 | −893.3 | 1,679.0 | † 2,205.3 | −3,227.2 | −3,023.8 | −6,898.0 | −7,120.0 | 1,921.7 | .... |
| Equity & investment fund shares | 3aala | 1,057.9 | 1,139.7 | 2,915.8 | 3,242.7 | 5,266.0 | † 2,743.2 | 3,325.6 | 4,070.2 | 4,356.9 | 4,183.7 | 3,523.5 | .... |
| Debt instruments | 3abla | 1,139.4 | −2,443.6 | −2,953.5 | −4,136.1 | −3,587.0 | † −537.9 | −6,552.8 | −7,094.0 | −11,254.8 | −11,303.7 | −1,601.8 | .... |
| Portfolio investment: assets | 3b9aa | 2.7 | 1,267.0 | 1,439.5 | 2,015.4 | 1,757.5 | † 558.1 | 273.5 | 52.2 | 200.0 | 100.0 | 8.7 | .... |
| Equity & investment fund shares | 3baaa | 3.3 | 1,264.0 | 1,491.0 | 1,965.9 | 1,757.5 | † 558.1 | 273.5 | 52.2 | 200.0 | 100.0 | .1 | .... |
| Debt securities | 3bbaa | −.6 | 3.0 | −51.5 | 49.5 | — | .... | .... | .... | .... | .... | 8.6 | .... |
| Portfolio investment: liabilities | 3b9la | — | — | — | — | — | † 68.0 | 3.0 | .... | .... | .... | .... | .... |
| Equity & investment fund shares | 3bala | — | — | — | — | — | .... | .... | .... | .... | .... | .... | .... |
| Debt securities | 3bbla | — | — | — | — | — | † 68.0 | 3.0 | .... | .... | .... | .... | .... |
| Fin. der.& empl.stk.ops.(ESOs): net | 3c9na | — | — | — | — | — | .... | .... | .... | .... | .... | .... | .... |
| Fin. der. & ESOs.: assets | 3c9aa | .... | .... | .... | .... | .... | .... | .... | .... | .... | .... | .... | .... |
| Fin. der. & ESOs.: liabilities | 3c9la | .... | .... | .... | .... | .... | .... | .... | .... | .... | .... | .... | .... |
| Other investment: assets | 3d9aa | 1,951.5 | 1,850.1 | 1,633.1 | 4,854.9 | 2,709.2 | † 1,369.0 | 158.6 | 2,543.4 | 2,123.8 | 3,408.4 | 1,581.5 | .... |
| Other equity | 3daaa | .... | .... | .... | .... | .... | .... | .... | .... | .... | .... | .... | .... |
| Debt instruments | 3dzaa | 1,951.5 | 1,850.1 | 1,633.1 | 4,854.9 | 2,709.2 | † 1,369.0 | 158.6 | 2,543.4 | 2,123.8 | 3,408.4 | 1,581.5 | .... |
| Other investment: liabilities | 3d9la | 1,533.4 | 1,514.3 | −682.1 | 2,833.3 | 6,576.1 | † 1,813.4 | 3,335.4 | 3,419.4 | 2,946.1 | 8,724.4 | 3,459.1 | .... |
| Other equity | 3dala | .... | .... | .... | .... | .... | .... | .... | .... | .... | .... | .... | .... |
| Debt instruments | 3dzla | 1,533.4 | 1,514.3 | −682.1 | 2,833.3 | 6,576.1 | † 1,813.4 | 3,335.4 | 3,419.4 | 2,946.1 | 8,724.4 | 3,459.1 | .... |
| Curr.+ cap.− finan. acct. balance | 4y9na | 1,674.5 | 2,011.9 | 6,706.9 | 4,746.0 | 8,419.4 | † −5,414.7 | 5,845.5 | 8,794.3 | 4,837.1 | 400.3 | −4,184.9 | .... |
| D. Net Errors and Omissions | 409na | 282.2 | −574.2 | 266.5 | −1,641.0 | −1,235.9 | † 454.7 | −645.9 | −345.4 | −472.3 | 192.4 | 288.2 | .... |
| E. Reserves and Related Items | 4z9na | 1,956.7 | 1,437.7 | 6,973.4 | 3,105.0 | 7,183.5 | † −4,959.9 | 5,199.7 | 8,448.9 | 4,364.9 | 592.6 | −3,896.7 | .... |
| Reserve assets | 3e9aa | 780.3 | 1,817.3 | 5,401.7 | 3,019.1 | 6,672.6 | † −5,003.8 | 5,569.1 | 8,723.6 | 4,495.2 | 338.0 | −4,396.7 | .... |
| Credit and loans from the IMF | 3dcla | — | — | — | — | — | † — | 877.6 | 311.7 | 132.3 | −260.9 | −499.3 | .... |
| Exceptional financing | 409la | −1,176.4 | 379.6 | −1,571.7 | −85.9 | −510.9 | † −43.9 | −508.2 | −37.0 | −2.1 | 6.3 | −.7 | .... |

*Excludes components in group E

| International Investment Position | | 2004 | 2005 | 2006 | 2007 | 2008 | 2009 | 2010 | 2011 | 2012 | 2013 | 2014 | 2015 |
|---|---|---|---|---|---|---|---|---|---|---|---|---|---|
| | | | | | | | *Millions of US Dollars* | | | | | | |
| Assets | 809aa | 5,845.6 | 11,194.3 | 19,438.3 | 30,226.2 | 43,824.3 | † 41,131.9 | 48,484.7 | 61,895.1 | 71,455.2 | 81,346.2 | 83,887.9 | .... |
| Direct investment | 8a9aa | 23.9 | 24.4 | 215.0 | 1,126.8 | 3,696.4 | † 3,703.2 | 5,043.6 | 7,136.2 | 9,877.0 | 15,921.1 | 20,174.2 | .... |
| Equity & investment fund shares | 8aaaa | .... | .... | .... | .... | .... | .... | .... | .... | .... | .... | .... | .... |
| Debt instruments | 8abaa | .... | .... | .... | .... | .... | .... | .... | .... | .... | .... | .... | .... |
| Portfolio investment | 8b9aa | 49.8 | 1,316.8 | 2,756.3 | 4,771.7 | 6,529.2 | † 7,087.4 | 7,360.9 | 7,413.1 | 7,613.1 | 7,713.1 | 7,721.7 | .... |
| Equity & investment fund shares | 8baaa | .... | 1,316.8 | 2,756.3 | 4,771.7 | 6,529.2 | † 7,087.4 | 7,360.9 | 7,413.1 | 7,613.1 | 7,713.1 | 7,721.7 | .... |
| Debt securities | 8bbaa | .... | .... | .... | .... | .... | .... | .... | .... | .... | .... | .... | .... |
| Fin. der.(oth.than reserves) & ESOs | 8c9aa | .... | .... | .... | .... | .... | .... | .... | .... | .... | .... | .... | .... |
| Other investment | 8d9aa | 4,392.3 | 6,656.2 | 8,289.3 | 13,130.9 | 16,092.9 | † 17,462.0 | 17,639.4 | 20,182.2 | 22,306.0 | 25,714.3 | 28,197.3 | .... |
| Other equity | 8daaa | .... | .... | .... | .... | .... | .... | .... | .... | .... | .... | .... | .... |
| Debt instruments | 8dzaa | 4,392.3 | 6,656.2 | 8,289.3 | 13,130.9 | 16,092.9 | † 17,462.0 | 17,639.4 | 20,182.2 | 22,306.0 | 25,714.3 | 28,197.3 | .... |
| Reserve assets | 8e9aa | 1,379.6 | 3,196.9 | 8,177.7 | 11,196.8 | 17,505.7 | † 12,879.4 | 18,440.9 | 27,163.6 | 31,659.2 | 31,997.7 | 27,794.6 | .... |
| Liabilities | 809la | 22,547.2 | 22,487.4 | 20,202.6 | 21,951.0 | 30,583.7 | † 64,583.8 | 66,555.0 | 67,412.0 | 63,703.5 | 64,971.3 | 73,613.1 | .... |
| Direct investment | 8a9la | 13,436.7 | 12,132.9 | 12,095.1 | 11,201.8 | 12,880.8 | † 44,247.0 | 41,019.8 | 37,996.0 | 31,098.1 | 23,978.0 | 25,899.7 | .... |
| Equity & investment fund shares | 8aala | .... | .... | .... | .... | .... | .... | .... | .... | .... | .... | .... | .... |
| Debt instruments | 8abla | .... | .... | .... | .... | .... | .... | .... | .... | .... | .... | .... | .... |
| Portfolio investment | 8b9la | .... | .... | .... | .... | .... | † 68.0 | 71.0 | 71.0 | 71.0 | 71.0 | 71.0 | .... |
| Equity & investment fund shares | 8bala | .... | .... | .... | .... | .... | .... | .... | .... | .... | .... | .... | .... |
| Debt securities | 8bbla | .... | .... | .... | .... | .... | † 68.0 | 71.0 | 71.0 | 71.0 | 71.0 | 71.0 | .... |
| Fin. der.(oth.than reserves) & ESOs | 8c9la | .... | .... | .... | .... | .... | .... | .... | .... | .... | .... | .... | .... |
| Other investment | 8d9la | 9,110.5 | 10,354.6 | 8,107.4 | 10,749.2 | 17,703.0 | † 20,268.8 | 25,464.2 | 29,345.0 | 32,534.4 | 40,922.3 | 47,642.4 | .... |
| Other equity | 8dala | .... | .... | .... | .... | .... | .... | .... | .... | .... | .... | .... | .... |
| Debt instruments | 8dzla | 9,110.5 | 10,354.6 | 8,107.4 | 10,749.2 | 17,703.0 | † 20,268.8 | 25,464.2 | 29,345.0 | 32,534.4 | 40,922.3 | 47,642.4 | .... |

# Angola 614

| | | 2004 | 2005 | 2006 | 2007 | 2008 | 2009 | 2010 | 2011 | 2012 | 2013 | 2014 | 2015 |
|---|---|---|---|---|---|---|---|---|---|---|---|---|---|
| **Government Finance** | | | | | | | | | | | | | |
| **Cash Flow Statement** | | | | | | | | | | | | | |
| **Budgetary Central Government** | | | | | | *Millions of Kwanzas: Fiscal Year Ends December 31* | | | | | | | |
| Cash Receipts:Operating Activities... | c1 | 544,974 | 787,060 | 1,940,820 | 2,252,180 | 2,834,560 | 1,241,000 | 2,695,150 | 4,682,610 | 4,428,540 | 4,711,390 | 4,423,859 | .... |
| Taxes......................................... | c11 | 355,630 | 551,316 | 984,460 | 1,076,320 | 1,704,030 | 1,024,060 | 1,278,470 | 1,691,010 | 1,812,070 | 1,871,680 | 1,939,827 | .... |
| Social Contributions...................... | c12 | — | 25 | 63,666 | 48,195 | 93,398 | 16,078 | 75,611 | 89,776 | 106,582 | 120,720 | 86,856 | .... |
| Grants...................................... | c13 | 7,467 | — | — | — | — | — | — | — | — | — | — | .... |
| Other Receipts............................. | c14 | 181,877 | 235,719 | 892,690 | 1,127,660 | 1,037,130 | 200,856 | 1,341,080 | 2,901,820 | 2,509,880 | 2,718,990 | 2,397,176 | .... |
| Cash Payments:Operating Activities. | c2 | 317,673 | 671,073 | 801,229 | 1,042,470 | 1,487,150 | 1,422,250 | 1,975,410 | 2,800,740 | 2,866,730 | 3,722,210 | 4,006,005 | .... |
| Compensation of Employees.......... | c21 | 167,407 | 244,916 | 310,041 | 364,410 | 542,953 | 664,862 | 713,857 | 877,330 | 1,030,280 | 1,154,830 | 1,318,902 | .... |
| Purchases of Goods & Services....... | c22 | 84,726 | 237,649 | 277,730 | 342,749 | 499,019 | 358,456 | 521,502 | 914,656 | 1,016,570 | 1,510,290 | 1,371,320 | .... |
| Interest...................................... | c24 | 17,751 | 18,069 | 10,664 | 23,460 | 135,479 | 104,791 | 115,831 | 81,456 | 102,804 | 99,105 | 147,161 | .... |
| Subsidies................................... | c25 | 15,481 | 115,726 | 127,142 | 219,868 | 167,931 | 172,739 | 506,620 | 767,965 | 513,024 | 710,179 | 735,497 | .... |
| Grants....................................... | c26 | 4,380 | 1,459 | 3,521 | 2,579 | 29,622 | 16,618 | 10,209 | 2,210 | 2,916 | 3,207 | 99,611 | .... |
| Social Benefits............................. | c27 | 19,289 | 29,712 | 47,468 | 64,777 | 87,316 | 88,371 | 85,486 | 127,025 | 154,384 | 210,245 | 233,305 | .... |
| Other Payments........................... | c28 | 8,640 | 23,541 | 24,661 | 24,624 | 24,830 | 16,411 | 21,905 | 30,098 | 46,755 | 34,354 | 100,209 | .... |
| Net Cash Inflow:Operating Act.[1-2] | ccio | 227,301 | 115,987 | 1,139,591 | 1,209,710 | 1,347,410 | −181,250 | 719,740 | 1,881,870 | 1,561,810 | 989,180 | 417,854 | .... |
| Net Cash Outflow:Invest. in NFA...... | c31 | 35,484 | 93,856 | 322,979 | 530,290 | 891,634 | 476,029 | 654,581 | 762,719 | 828,285 | 1,532,680 | 1,905,956 | .... |
| Purchases of Nonfinancial Assets... | c31.1 | 35,845 | 94,403 | 323,645 | 531,343 | 892,632 | 477,042 | 655,265 | 763,490 | 829,083 | .... | .... | .... |
| Sales of Nonfinancial Assets.......... | c31.2 | 361 | 547 | 665 | 1,053 | 998 | 1,013 | 684 | 771 | 798 | .... | .... | .... |
| Cash Surplus/Deficit [1-2-31=1-2M] | ccsd | 191,817 | 22,131 | 816,612 | 679,420 | 455,776 | −657,279 | 65,159 | 1,119,151 | 733,525 | −543,500 | −1,488,102 | .... |
| Net Acq. Fin. Assets, excl. Cash....... | c32x | −108 | 3,121 | 3,029 | 22,807 | 28,877 | 4,544 | 25,116 | 45,620 | 66,117 | .... | .... | .... |
| Domestic.................................... | c321x | −108 | 3,121 | 3,029 | 22,807 | 28,877 | 4,544 | 25,116 | 45,620 | 66,117 | .... | .... | .... |
| Foreign...................................... | c322x | — | — | — | — | — | — | — | — | — | .... | .... | .... |
| Net Incurrence of Liabilities............. | c33 | −4,488 | 2,883 | −42,184 | 129,640 | 79,440 | 106,046 | −196,356 | −175,316 | −172,170 | 364,325 | 762,193 | .... |
| Domestic.................................... | c331 | 49,581 | 71,568 | −8,796 | 92,795 | −62,838 | 121,564 | −161,396 | −220,748 | −394,945 | 24,867 | 279,116 | .... |
| Foreign...................................... | c332 | −54,069 | −68,685 | −33,388 | 36,845 | 142,278 | −15,518 | −34,959 | 45,432 | 222,775 | 339,458 | 483,077 | .... |
| Net Cash Inflow, Fin.Act.[-32x+33].. | cnfb | −4,380 | −238 | −45,212 | 106,833 | 50,562 | 101,501 | −221,472 | −220,936 | −238,287 | 68,807 | 1,232,608 | .... |
| Net Change in Stock of Cash........... | cncb | 187,437 | 21,893 | 771,396 | 786,253 | 506,337 | −555,779 | −156,310 | 898,214 | 495,234 | −474,702 | −690,611 | .... |
| Stat. Discrep. [32X-33+NCB-CSD].... | ccsdz | — | — | −4 | — | −1 | −1 | 3 | −1 | −4 | −9 | −514,700 | .... |
| Memo Item:Cash Expenditure[2+31] | c2m | 353,157 | 764,929 | 1,124,208 | 1,572,760 | 2,378,784 | 1,898,279 | 2,629,991 | 3,563,459 | 3,695,015 | 5,254,890 | 5,911,961 | .... |
| Memo Item: Gross Debt.................. | c63 | .... | .... | .... | .... | .... | .... | .... | .... | .... | .... | .... | .... |
| **National Accounts** | | | | | | *Millions of Kwanzas* | | | | | | | |
| Gross Domestic Product (GDP)........ | 99b | 1,652,049 | 2,669,889 | 3,629,684 | 4,545,860 | 6,373,700 | .... | .... | .... | .... | .... | .... | .... |
| GDP Volume 1992 Prices................. | 99b.p | 5.6 | 6.5 | .... | .... | .... | .... | .... | .... | .... | .... | .... | .... |
| GDP Deflator (2005=100).............. | 99bip | 71.6 | 100.0 | .... | .... | .... | .... | .... | .... | .... | .... | .... | .... |
| GDP Volume (2005=100)................ | 99bvp | 86.4 | 100.0 | .... | .... | .... | .... | .... | .... | .... | .... | .... | .... |
| | | | | | | *Millions: Midyear Estimates* | | | | | | | |
| Population.............................. | 99z | 17.30 | 17.91 | 18.54 | 19.18 | 19.84 | 20.52 | 21.22 | 21.94 | 22.69 | 23.45 | 24.23 | 25.02 |

# Anguilla 312

| | | 2004 | 2005 | 2006 | 2007 | 2008 | 2009 | 2010 | 2011 | 2012 | 2013 | 2014 | 2015 |
|---|---|---|---|---|---|---|---|---|---|---|---|---|---|
| **Exchange Rates** | | | | | | *E. Caribbean Dollars per SDR: End of Period* | | | | | | | |
| Official Rate........................ | aa | 4.1931 | 3.8590 | 4.0619 | 4.2667 | 4.1587 | 4.2328 | 4.1581 | 4.1452 | 4.1497 | 4.1580 | 3.9118 | 3.7415 |
| | | | | | *E. Caribbean Dollars per US Dollar: End of Period (ae) Period Average (rf)* | | | | | | | | |
| Official Rate........................ | ae | 2.7000 | 2.7000 | 2.7000 | 2.7000 | 2.7000 | 2.7000 | 2.7000 | 2.7000 | 2.7000 | 2.7000 | 2.7000 | 2.7000 |
| Official Rate........................ | rf | 2.7000 | 2.7000 | 2.7000 | 2.7000 | 2.7000 | 2.7000 | 2.7000 | 2.7000 | 2.7000 | 2.7000 | 2.7000 | 2.7000 |
| **International Liquidity** | | | | | *Millions of US Dollars Unless Otherwise Indicated: End of Period* | | | | | | | | |
| Total Reserves minus Gold.............. | 1l.d | 34.25 | 39.70 | 41.82 | 44.87 | 41.00 | 37.46 | 39.89 | 37.53 | 40.01 | 41.04 | 47.28 | 48.14 |
| Foreign Exchange....................... | 1d.d | 34.25 | 39.70 | 41.82 | 44.87 | 41.00 | 37.46 | 39.89 | 37.53 | 40.01 | 41.04 | 47.28 | 48.14 |
| Central Bank: Other Assets........... | 3..d | — | — | — | — | — | — | — | — | — | — | — | — |
| Central Bank: Other Liabs............ | 4..d | — | — | — | — | — | — | — | — | — | — | — | — |
| Other Depository Corps.: Assets....... | 7a.d | 205.60 | 247.57 | 251.59 | 236.29 | 176.50 | 161.64 | 170.97 | 155.76 | 147.47 | 125.22 | 126.02 | 147.83 |
| Other Depository Corps.: Liabs....... | 7b.d | 116.00 | 95.49 | 97.73 | 134.39 | 158.19 | 185.21 | 138.11 | 124.14 | 118.50 | 79.67 | 75.73 | 75.35 |
| **Central Bank** | | | | | *Millions of E. Caribbean Dollars: End of Period* | | | | | | | | |
| Net Foreign Assets..................... | 11n | 90.20 | 107.58 | 113.01 | 121.48 | 110.91 | 101.37 | 108.09 | 101.76 | 108.04 | 110.82 | 127.66 | 129.98 |
| Claims on Nonresidents................ | 11 | 90.20 | 107.58 | 113.01 | 121.48 | 110.91 | 101.37 | 108.09 | 101.76 | 108.04 | 110.82 | 127.66 | 129.98 |
| Liabilities to Nonresidents............. | 16c | — | — | — | — | — | — | — | — | — | — | — | — |
| Claims on Other Depository Corps.... | 12e | 2.35 | .01 | 3.02 | 10.10 | — | .02 | .02 | .01 | .01 | .03 | .04 | .04 |
| Net Claims on Central Government.. | 12an | −.05 | −.38 | −.24 | −.61 | 6.92 | 20.57 | 6.67 | 3.55 | 9.26 | 9.40 | 9.36 | 9.42 |
| Claims on Central Government...... | 12a | — | — | — | — | 6.97 | 21.06 | 6.83 | 3.83 | 9.59 | 9.81 | 9.69 | 9.65 |
| Liabilities to Central Government... | 16d | .05 | .38 | .24 | .61 | .05 | .48 | .15 | .28 | .33 | .40 | .33 | .23 |
| Claims on Other Sectors............. | 12s | — | — | — | — | — | — | — | — | — | — | — | — |
| Claims on Other Financial Corps.... | 12g | — | — | — | — | — | — | — | — | — | — | — | — |
| Claims on State & Local Govts....... | 12b | — | — | — | — | — | — | — | — | — | — | — | — |
| Claims on Public Nonfin. Corps...... | 12c | — | — | — | — | — | — | — | — | — | — | — | — |
| Claims on Private Sector.............. | 12d | — | — | — | — | — | — | — | — | — | — | — | — |
| Monetary Base.......................... | 14 | 92.48 | 107.19 | 115.77 | 130.83 | 117.67 | 121.73 | 114.40 | 104.89 | 116.72 | 119.45 | 133.07 | 135.44 |
| Currency in Circulation................. | 14a | 14.20 | 14.41 | 18.41 | 18.95 | 24.09 | 22.85 | 18.66 | 17.88 | 16.93 | 16.71 | 16.42 | 22.25 |
| Liabs. to Other Depository Corps.... | 14c | 78.28 | 92.78 | 97.36 | 111.88 | 93.58 | 98.88 | 95.74 | 87.01 | 99.79 | 102.75 | 116.65 | 113.19 |
| Liabilities to Other Sectors............ | 14d | — | — | — | — | — | — | — | — | — | — | — | — |
| Other Liabs. to Other Dep. Corps..... | 14n | .02 | .02 | .02 | .14 | .16 | .23 | .38 | .43 | .58 | .80 | 3.99 | 4.00 |
| Dep. & Sec. Excl. f/Monetary Base.... | 14o | — | — | — | — | — | — | — | — | — | — | — | — |
| Deposits Included in Broad Money. | 15 | — | — | — | — | — | — | — | — | — | — | — | — |
| Sec.Ot.th.Shares Incl.in Brd. Money | 16a | — | — | — | — | — | — | — | — | — | — | — | — |
| Deposits Excl. from Broad Money... | 16b | — | — | — | — | — | — | — | — | — | — | — | — |
| Sec.Ot.th.Shares Excl.f/Brd.Money.. | 16s | — | — | — | — | — | — | — | — | — | — | — | — |
| Loans................................... | 16l | — | — | — | — | — | — | — | — | — | — | — | — |
| Financial Derivatives.................... | 16m | — | — | — | — | — | — | — | — | — | — | — | — |
| Shares and Other Equity................ | 17a | — | — | — | — | — | — | — | — | — | — | — | — |
| Other Items (Net).......................... | 17r | — | — | — | — | — | — | — | — | — | — | — | — |
| Memo Item: | | | | | | | | | | | | | |
| Total Assets................................ | 10ra | 92.56 | 107.59 | 116.03 | 131.58 | 117.88 | 122.45 | 114.94 | 105.60 | 117.63 | 120.65 | 137.40 | 139.67 |
| **Other Depository Corporations** | | | | | *Millions of E. Caribbean Dollars: End of Period* | | | | | | | | |
| Net Foreign Assets..................... | 21n | 241.92 | 410.61 | 415.43 | 275.13 | 49.44 | −63.63 | 88.71 | 85.36 | 78.24 | 123.01 | 135.80 | 195.70 |
| Claims on Nonresidents................ | 21 | 555.11 | 668.44 | 679.30 | 638.00 | 476.54 | 436.44 | 461.61 | 420.55 | 398.18 | 338.11 | 340.27 | 399.15 |
| Liabilities to Nonresidents............. | 26c | 313.19 | 257.83 | 263.87 | 362.86 | 427.11 | 500.07 | 372.89 | 335.19 | 319.94 | 215.10 | 204.47 | 203.45 |
| Claims on Central Bank................. | 20 | 82.95 | 97.41 | 104.50 | 113.55 | 94.70 | 105.12 | 104.15 | 91.99 | 100.61 | 102.70 | 118.72 | 125.27 |
| Currency.............................. | 20a | 4.69 | 4.83 | 4.88 | 6.51 | 8.71 | 6.45 | 7.04 | 6.66 | 5.74 | 4.50 | 4.12 | 4.87 |
| Reserve Deposits and Securities..... | 20b | 78.26 | 92.58 | 99.62 | 107.05 | 85.99 | 98.67 | 97.11 | 85.34 | 94.84 | 98.20 | 114.60 | 120.40 |
| Other Claims............................ | 20n | — | — | — | — | — | — | — | — | .03 | — | — | — |
| Net Claims on Central Government.. | 22an | 36.76 | 53.45 | 23.13 | 44.88 | 64.80 | 108.73 | −53.54 | −57.87 | −67.08 | −75.35 | −83.88 | −74.37 |
| Claims on Central Government...... | 22a | 53.53 | 76.41 | 81.77 | 92.79 | 113.46 | 138.26 | — | — | 5.08 | 10.85 | 10.06 | 12.13 |
| Liabilities to Central Government... | 26d | 16.77 | 22.96 | 58.64 | 47.91 | 48.66 | 29.54 | 53.54 | 57.87 | 72.15 | 86.20 | 93.93 | 86.49 |
| Claims on Other Sectors................. | 22s | 600.46 | 719.65 | 852.90 | 1,164.42 | 1,358.11 | 1,393.37 | 1,415.04 | 1,414.54 | 1,362.59 | 1,308.99 | 1,250.61 | 1,205.66 |
| Claims on Other Financial Corps.... | 22g | 6.95 | 4.91 | 7.75 | 8.96 | 7.33 | 6.49 | 5.69 | 6.96 | 5.67 | 5.30 | 4.13 | 3.88 |
| Claims on State & Local Govts....... | 22b | — | — | — | — | — | — | — | — | — | — | — | — |
| Claims on Public Nonfin. Corps...... | 22c | 3.62 | 3.62 | 2.53 | 2.16 | 3.21 | 2.05 | 18.58 | 19.40 | 14.55 | 12.49 | .37 | .33 |
| Claims on Private Sector............... | 22d | 589.89 | 711.12 | 842.62 | 1,153.30 | 1,347.57 | 1,384.84 | 1,390.77 | 1,388.18 | 1,342.37 | 1,291.21 | 1,246.11 | 1,201.46 |
| Liabilities to Central Bank............... | 26g | 2.36 | .02 | 3.02 | 10.01 | 1.73 | 3.27 | 4.60 | 5.43 | 1.02 | .03 | .04 | .04 |
| Transf.Dep.Included in Broad Money | 24 | 630.75 | 838.09 | 926.79 | 1,063.33 | 1,016.05 | 947.04 | 912.75 | 865.36 | 854.14 | 877.07 | 876.41 | 913.92 |
| Other Dep.Included in Broad Money. | 25 | 162.21 | 197.17 | 221.49 | 257.04 | 239.16 | 275.67 | 290.29 | 318.15 | 341.16 | 352.75 | 362.23 | 367.01 |
| Sec.Ot.th.Shares Incl.in Brd. Money.. | 26a | — | — | — | — | — | — | — | — | — | — | — | — |
| Deposits Excl. from Broad Money..... | 26b | — | — | — | — | — | — | — | — | — | — | — | — |
| Sec.Ot.th.Shares Excl.f/Brd.Money.... | 26s | — | — | — | — | — | — | — | — | — | — | — | — |
| Loans................................... | 26l | — | — | — | — | — | — | — | — | — | — | — | — |
| Financial Derivatives.................... | 26m | — | — | — | — | — | — | — | — | — | — | — | — |
| Insurance Technical Reserves.......... | 26r | — | — | — | — | — | — | — | — | — | — | — | — |
| Shares and Other Equity................ | 27a | 131.63 | 153.02 | 198.33 | 219.51 | 216.20 | 262.07 | 241.65 | 193.72 | 144.56 | 29.18 | −83.92 | −66.83 |
| Other Items (Net).......................... | 27r | 35.14 | 92.82 | 46.33 | 48.09 | 93.90 | 55.54 | 105.08 | 151.37 | 133.48 | 200.32 | 266.49 | 238.12 |
| Memo Item: | | | | | | | | | | | | | |
| Total Assets................................ | 20ra | 1,373.08 | 1,655.87 | 1,818.34 | 2,122.24 | 2,168.79 | 2,265.64 | 2,127.39 | 2,129.47 | 2,088.42 | 1,991.14 | 2,003.76 | 2,043.05 |

# Anguilla 312

|  |  | 2004 | 2005 | 2006 | 2007 | 2008 | 2009 | 2010 | 2011 | 2012 | 2013 | 2014 | 2015 |
|---|---|---|---|---|---|---|---|---|---|---|---|---|---|
| **Depository Corporations** |  | *Millions of E. Caribbean Dollars: End of Period* | | | | | | | | | | | |
| Net Foreign Assets | 31n | 332.12 | 518.18 | 528.44 | 396.61 | 160.34 | 37.74 | 196.81 | 187.12 | 186.28 | 233.83 | 263.46 | 325.68 |
| Claims on Nonresidents | 31 | 645.31 | 776.01 | 792.31 | 759.48 | 587.45 | 537.81 | 569.70 | 522.31 | 506.21 | 448.92 | 467.93 | 529.14 |
| Liabilities to Nonresidents | 36c | 313.19 | 257.83 | 263.87 | 362.86 | 427.11 | 500.07 | 372.89 | 335.19 | 319.94 | 215.10 | 204.47 | 203.45 |
| Domestic Claims | 32 | 637.17 | 772.72 | 875.79 | 1,208.68 | 1,429.82 | 1,522.67 | 1,368.17 | 1,360.22 | 1,304.78 | 1,243.04 | 1,176.10 | 1,140.71 |
| Net Claims on Central Government | 32an | 36.71 | 53.07 | 22.89 | 44.26 | 71.71 | 129.30 | −46.87 | −54.32 | −57.81 | −65.95 | −74.52 | −64.95 |
| Claims on Central Government | 32a | 53.53 | 76.41 | 81.77 | 92.79 | 120.43 | 159.32 | 6.83 | 3.84 | 14.67 | 20.66 | 19.75 | 21.77 |
| Liabilities to Central Government | 36d | 16.82 | 23.34 | 58.88 | 48.52 | 48.72 | 30.02 | 53.70 | 58.15 | 72.48 | 86.60 | 94.27 | 86.72 |
| Claims on Other Sectors | 32s | 600.46 | 719.65 | 852.90 | 1,164.42 | 1,358.11 | 1,393.37 | 1,415.04 | 1,414.54 | 1,362.59 | 1,308.99 | 1,250.61 | 1,205.66 |
| Claims on Other Financial Corps | 32g | 6.95 | 4.91 | 7.75 | 8.96 | 7.33 | 6.49 | 5.69 | 6.96 | 5.67 | 5.30 | 4.13 | 3.88 |
| Claims on State & Local Govts | 32b | — | — | — | — | — | — | — | — | — | — | — | — |
| Claims on Public Nonfin. Corps | 32c | 3.62 | 3.62 | 2.53 | 2.16 | 3.21 | 2.05 | 18.58 | 19.40 | 14.55 | 12.49 | .37 | .33 |
| Claims on Private Sector | 32d | 589.89 | 711.12 | 842.62 | 1,153.30 | 1,347.57 | 1,384.84 | 1,390.77 | 1,388.18 | 1,342.37 | 1,291.21 | 1,246.11 | 1,201.46 |
| Broad Money Liabilities | 35l | 802.47 | 1,044.83 | 1,161.81 | 1,332.81 | 1,270.60 | 1,239.11 | 1,214.66 | 1,194.73 | 1,206.49 | 1,242.03 | 1,250.94 | 1,298.31 |
| Currency Outside Depository Corps | 34a | 9.51 | 9.58 | 13.52 | 12.44 | 15.39 | 16.40 | 11.62 | 11.22 | 11.19 | 12.21 | 12.31 | 17.38 |
| Transferable Deposits | 34 | 630.75 | 838.09 | 926.80 | 1,063.33 | 1,016.05 | 947.04 | 912.75 | 865.36 | 854.14 | 877.07 | 876.41 | 913.92 |
| Other Deposits | 35 | 162.21 | 197.17 | 221.49 | 257.04 | 239.16 | 275.67 | 290.29 | 318.15 | 341.16 | 352.75 | 362.23 | 367.01 |
| Securities Other than Shares | 36a | — | — | — | — | — | — | — | — | — | — | — | — |
| Deposits Excl. from Broad Money | 36b | — | — | — | — | — | — | — | — | — | — | — | — |
| Sec.Ot.th.Shares Excl.f/Brd.Money | 36s | — | — | — | — | — | — | — | — | — | — | — | — |
| Loans | 36l | — | — | — | — | — | — | — | — | — | — | — | — |
| Financial Derivatives | 36m | — | — | — | — | — | — | — | — | — | — | — | — |
| Insurance Technical Reserves | 36r | — | — | — | — | — | — | — | — | — | — | — | — |
| Shares and Other Equity | 37a | 131.63 | 153.02 | 198.33 | 219.51 | 216.20 | 262.07 | 241.65 | 193.72 | 144.56 | 29.18 | −83.92 | −66.83 |
| Other Items (Net) | 37r | 35.19 | 93.04 | 44.09 | 52.98 | 103.37 | 59.23 | 108.67 | 158.89 | 140.00 | 205.66 | 272.53 | 234.91 |
| Broad Money Liabs., Seasonally Adj. | 35l.b | 808.30 | 1,051.61 | 1,166.85 | 1,336.96 | 1,273.58 | 1,243.58 | 1,221.06 | 1,203.78 | 1,217.85 | 1,255.53 | 1,264.96 | 1,312.58 |
| **Monetary Aggregates** |  | *Millions of E. Caribbean Dollars: End of Period* | | | | | | | | | | | |
| Broad Money | 59m | 802.47 | 1,044.83 | 1,161.81 | 1,332.81 | 1,270.60 | 1,239.11 | 1,214.66 | 1,194.73 | 1,206.49 | 1,242.03 | 1,250.94 | 1,298.31 |
| o/w:Currency Issued by Cent.Govt | 59m.a | — | — | — | — | — | — | — | — | — | — | — | — |
| o/w: Dep.in Nonfin. Corporations | 59m.b | — | — | — | — | — | — | — | — | — | — | — | — |
| o/w:Secs. Issued by Central Govt | 59m.c | — | — | — | — | — | — | — | — | — | — | — | — |
| Money (National Definitions) |  |  |  |  |  |  |  |  |  |  |  |  |  |
| M1 | 59ma | 26.06 | 29.82 | 44.75 | 52.36 | 52.85 | 51.38 | 46.05 | 45.43 | 42.62 | 43.06 | 51.51 | 70.14 |
| M2 | 59mb | 697.72 | 912.77 | 1,028.42 | 1,161.75 | 1,125.17 | 1,074.55 | 1,062.36 | 1,014.55 | 1,007.59 | 1,030.90 | 1,040.34 | 1,073.94 |
| **Interest Rates** |  | *Percent Per Annum* | | | | | | | | | | | |
| Discount Rate (End of Period) | 60.a | 6.50 | 6.50 | 6.50 | 6.50 | 6.50 | 6.50 | 6.50 | 6.50 | 6.50 | 6.50 | 6.50 | 6.50 |
| Money Market Rate | 60b | 4.67 | 4.01 | 4.76 | 5.24 | 4.92 | 6.03 | 6.36 | 5.68 | 5.19 | 6.28 | 6.19 | 6.44 |
| Savings Rate | 60k | 3.81 | 3.63 | 3.86 | 3.61 | 3.76 | 3.41 | 3.06 | 3.05 | 3.06 | 3.04 | 3.04 | 2.76 |
| Savings Rate (Fgn. Currency) | 60k.f | 2.80 | 2.83 | 2.54 | 2.54 | 2.53 | 2.15 | 1.62 | 2.02 | 2.52 | 2.65 | 2.53 | 2.39 |
| Deposit Rate | 60l | 4.83 | 4.81 | 4.87 | 4.69 | 4.74 | 4.72 | 3.89 | 3.57 | 4.07 | 3.87 | 3.73 | 3.47 |
| Deposit Rate (Fgn. Currency) | 60l.f | 3.21 | 3.19 | 3.22 | 3.31 | 3.62 | 3.31 | 2.48 | 2.94 | 3.12 | 3.16 | 2.66 | 2.39 |
| Lending Rate | 60p | 10.99 | 10.38 | 10.04 | 9.76 | 9.51 | 9.27 | 11.38 | 9.30 | 9.38 | 9.08 | 9.09 | 9.05 |
| Lending Rate (Fgn. Currency) | 60p.f | 10.24 | 9.74 | 9.91 | 9.66 | 9.50 | 10.10 | 8.42 | 10.30 | 9.36 | 9.18 | 9.31 | 9.14 |
| **Prices, Tourism, Labor** |  | *Index Numbers (2010=100): Period Averages* | | | | | | | | | | | |
| Consumer Prices | 64 | 78.3 | 81.9 | 88.8 | 93.3 | 99.7 | 99.0 | † 100.0 | 104.7 | 106.2 | 106.4 | 106.1 | 105.0 |
| Number of Tourists | 66t | 101.7 | 120.6 | 140.9 | 138.2 | 32.3 | 43.7 | 100.0 | 104.1 | 109.0 | 127.4 | .... | .... |
|  |  | *Number in Thousands: Period Averages* | | | | | | | | | | | |
| Employment | 67e | .... | .... | .... | .... | .... | .... | .... | .... | .... | .... | .... | .... |
| **Intl. Transactions & Positions** |  | *Millions of E. Caribbean Dollars* | | | | | | | | | | | |
| Exports | 70 | 15.5 | 19.6 | 35.9 | 24.8 | 31.0 | 62.3 | 33.6 | 44.3 | 22.4 | 9.8 | 10.8 | 4.2 |
| Imports, c.i.f. | 71 | 284.8 | 359.6 | 385.7 | 669.3 | 733.7 | 456.2 | 425.0 | 414.2 | 404.7 | 391.1 | 409.4 | 427.3 |

| | | 2004 | 2005 | 2006 | 2007 | 2008 | 2009 | 2010 | 2011 | 2012 | 2013 | 2014 | 2015 |
|---|---|---|---|---|---|---|---|---|---|---|---|---|---|
| **Balance of Payments** | | | | | | *Millions of US Dollars* | | | | | | | |
| A. Current Account* | 109bx | −47.4 | −52.1 | −144.6 | −183.6 | −220.0 | −95.6 | −50.6 | −37.1 | −55.5 | −47.9 | .... | .... |
| Goods, credit (exports) | 1a9cx | 6.0 | 15.0 | 12.3 | 9.2 | 11.5 | 23.2 | 12.4 | 7.2 | 7.5 | 4.3 | .... | .... |
| Goods, debit (imports) | 1a9dx | 90.2 | 114.3 | 197.1 | 218.2 | 239.2 | 148.7 | 131.9 | 129.0 | 129.3 | 127.7 | .... | .... |
| Balance on goods | 1a9bx | −84.2 | −99.3 | −184.8 | −209.0 | −227.7 | −125.5 | −119.4 | −121.8 | −121.8 | −123.4 | .... | .... |
| Services, credit (exports) | 1b9cx | 77.9 | 98.6 | 123.9 | 134.3 | 124.4 | 111.2 | 115.1 | 129.9 | 129.4 | 138.6 | .... | .... |
| Services, debit (imports) | 1b9dx | 46.6 | 56.3 | 91.5 | 102.9 | 102.4 | 69.9 | 54.8 | 55.2 | 55.6 | 56.2 | .... | .... |
| Balance on Goods & Services | 1z9bx | −52.8 | −57.0 | −152.5 | −177.6 | −205.7 | −84.2 | −59.1 | −47.0 | −48.0 | −41.0 | .... | .... |
| Primary income: credit | 1c9cx | 7.7 | 11.7 | 15.0 | 12.6 | 6.8 | 6.5 | 6.0 | 5.5 | 2.2 | 2.2 | .... | .... |
| Primary income: debit | 1c9dx | 6.9 | 7.7 | 7.2 | 11.0 | 15.1 | 12.9 | 3.3 | 5.8 | 4.4 | 4.4 | .... | .... |
| Balance on gds, serv. & prim. inc. | 1y9bx | −52.0 | −53.0 | −144.7 | −175.9 | −214.0 | −90.7 | −56.4 | −47.4 | −50.1 | −43.2 | .... | .... |
| Secondary income: credit | 1d9ca | 14.4 | 10.7 | 14.3 | 10.8 | 9.1 | 7.9 | 16.9 | 25.3 | 11.5 | 11.6 | .... | .... |
| Secondary income: debit | 1d9da | 9.7 | 9.8 | 14.2 | 18.4 | 15.1 | 12.8 | 11.1 | 15.1 | 16.8 | 16.3 | .... | .... |
| B. Capital Account* | 209ba | .6 | 1.6 | 5.5 | — | 3.4 | — | 4.3 | — | 4.6 | 5.8 | .... | .... |
| Capital account: credit | 209ca | .6 | 1.6 | 5.5 | — | 3.4 | — | 4.3 | — | 4.6 | 5.8 | .... | .... |
| Capital account: debit | 209da | — | — | — | — | — | — | — | — | — | — | .... | .... |
| Balance on current & capital acct. | 129ba | −46.8 | −50.4 | −139.1 | −183.6 | −216.6 | −95.6 | −46.4 | −37.1 | −50.8 | −42.1 | .... | .... |
| C. Financial Account* | 309na | −42.2 | −47.2 | −132.7 | −173.4 | −181.7 | −74.9 | −37.5 | −28.1 | −56.7 | −36.1 | .... | .... |
| Direct investment: assets | 3a9aa | — | — | — | — | — | — | — | — | — | — | .... | .... |
| Equity & investment fund shares | 3aaaa | .... | .... | .... | .... | .... | .... | .... | .... | .... | .... | .... | .... |
| Debt instruments | 3abaa | .... | .... | .... | .... | .... | .... | .... | .... | .... | .... | .... | .... |
| Direct investment: liabilities | 3a9la | 86.7 | 117.3 | 142.0 | 118.9 | 98.7 | 43.6 | 11.4 | 38.9 | 43.5 | 56.5 | .... | .... |
| Equity & investment fund shares | 3aala | 24.1 | 91.5 | 75.8 | 81.2 | 48.1 | 27.1 | .6 | 6.9 | 16.5 | 30.3 | .... | .... |
| Debt instruments | 3abla | 62.6 | 25.8 | 66.2 | 37.7 | 50.6 | 16.5 | 10.8 | 32.0 | 27.1 | 26.2 | .... | .... |
| Portfolio investment: assets | 3b9aa | — | — | .2 | .1 | — | 5.6 | — | — | −.1 | — | .... | .... |
| Equity & investment fund shares | 3baaa | .... | .... | .... | .... | .... | .... | .... | .... | .... | .... | .... | .... |
| Debt securities | 3bbaa | .... | .... | .... | .... | .... | .... | .... | .... | .... | .... | .... | .... |
| Portfolio investment: liabilities | 3b9la | 1.2 | .6 | 3.7 | −.2 | 5.4 | 2.1 | −1.5 | −1.3 | .1 | .1 | .... | .... |
| Equity & investment fund shares | 3bala | .... | .... | .... | .... | .... | .... | .... | .... | .... | .... | .... | .... |
| Debt securities | 3bbla | .... | .... | .... | .... | .... | .... | .... | .... | .... | .... | .... | .... |
| Fin. der.& empl.stk.ops.(ESOs): net | 3c9na | .... | .... | .... | .... | .... | .... | .... | .... | .... | .... | .... | .... |
| Fin. der. & ESOs.: assets | 3c9aa | .... | .... | .... | .... | .... | .... | .... | .... | .... | .... | .... | .... |
| Fin. der. & ESOs.: liabilities | 3c9la | .... | .... | .... | .... | .... | .... | .... | .... | .... | .... | .... | .... |
| Other investment: assets | 3d9aa | 63.2 | 72.8 | 15.6 | 24.6 | 30.1 | 17.4 | 66.9 | 10.5 | 2.9 | 19.5 | .... | .... |
| Other equity | 3daaa | .... | .... | .... | .... | .... | .... | .... | .... | .... | .... | .... | .... |
| Debt instruments | 3dzaa | 63.2 | 72.8 | 15.6 | 24.6 | 30.1 | 17.4 | 66.9 | 10.5 | 2.9 | 19.5 | .... | .... |
| Other investment: liabilities | 3d9la | 17.5 | 2.1 | 2.8 | 79.4 | 107.6 | 52.2 | 94.5 | .9 | 15.9 | −1.0 | .... | .... |
| Other equity | 3dala | .... | .... | .... | .... | .... | .... | .... | .... | .... | .... | .... | .... |
| Debt instruments | 3dzla | 17.5 | 2.1 | 2.8 | 79.4 | 107.6 | 52.2 | 94.5 | .9 | 15.9 | −1.0 | .... | .... |
| Curr.+ cap.− finan. acct. balance | 4y9na | −4.6 | −3.2 | −6.4 | −10.2 | −34.9 | −20.7 | −8.9 | −9.0 | 5.9 | −6.0 | .... | .... |
| D. Net Errors and Omissions | 409na | 5.6 | 8.6 | 8.5 | 13.2 | 31.0 | 17.2 | 11.4 | 6.7 | −3.6 | 7.0 | .... | .... |
| E. Reserves and Related Items | 4z9na | 1.0 | 5.4 | 2.1 | 3.1 | −3.9 | −3.5 | 2.5 | −2.3 | 2.3 | 1.0 | .... | .... |
| Reserve assets | 3e9aa | 1.0 | 5.4 | 2.1 | 3.1 | −3.9 | −3.5 | 2.5 | −2.3 | 2.3 | 1.0 | .... | .... |
| Credit and loans from the IMF | 3dcla | .... | .... | .... | .... | .... | .... | .... | .... | .... | .... | .... | .... |
| Exceptional financing | 409la | .... | .... | .... | .... | .... | .... | .... | .... | .... | .... | .... | .... |
| *Excludes components in group E | | | | | | | | | | | | | |

**Government Finance**
**Cash Flow Statement**
**Budgetary Central Government**

| | | 2004 | 2005 | 2006 | 2007 | 2008 | 2009 | 2010 | 2011 | 2012 | 2013 | 2014 | 2015 |
|---|---|---|---|---|---|---|---|---|---|---|---|---|---|
| | | | | | | *Millions of E. Caribbean Dollars: Fiscal Year Ends December 31* | | | | | | | |
| Cash Receipts:Operating Activities | c1 | 117.43 | 126.83 | 181.33 | 210.37 | 213.57 | 148.32 | 191.49 | 205.04 | 179.89 | 189.13 | 202.85 | .... |
| Taxes | c11 | 96.90 | 102.42 | 153.83 | 164.28 | 155.26 | 111.59 | 114.01 | 180.71 | 155.13 | 147.47 | 156.31 | .... |
| Social Contributions | c12 | — | — | — | — | — | — | — | — | — | — | — | .... |
| Grants | c13 | — | — | — | — | 9.19 | — | 38.65 | — | — | 15.72 | 14.82 | .... |
| Other Receipts | c14 | 20.53 | 24.40 | 27.50 | 46.09 | 49.13 | 36.73 | 38.83 | 24.33 | 24.75 | 25.94 | 31.72 | .... |
| Cash Payments:Operating Activities | c2 | 93.92 | 105.87 | 145.23 | 170.35 | 206.74 | 202.39 | 188.22 | 173.83 | 170.43 | 175.78 | 178.16 | .... |
| Compensation of Employees | c21 | 36.33 | 40.82 | 49.12 | 68.51 | 83.89 | 90.74 | 88.29 | 80.46 | 79.91 | 80.32 | 81.15 | .... |
| Purchases of Goods & Services | c22 | 34.55 | 35.28 | 52.22 | 53.75 | 59.83 | 48.41 | 39.91 | 38.74 | 38.33 | 40.45 | 42.20 | .... |
| Interest | c24 | 3.24 | 4.69 | 6.31 | 7.11 | 8.02 | 8.27 | 12.64 | 9.12 | 8.35 | 9.11 | 9.39 | .... |
| Subsidies | c25 | 17.98 | 23.05 | 34.99 | 36.11 | 48.60 | 47.61 | 38.40 | 37.40 | 36.07 | 37.70 | 37.46 | .... |
| Grants | c26 | — | — | — | — | — | — | — | — | — | — | — | .... |
| Social Benefits | c27 | 1.81 | 2.04 | 2.60 | 4.88 | 6.40 | 7.36 | 8.98 | 8.11 | 7.77 | 8.21 | 7.96 | .... |
| Other Payments | c28 | — | — | — | — | — | — | — | — | — | — | — | .... |
| Net Cash Inflow:Operating Act.[1-2] | ccio | 23.51 | 20.95 | 36.10 | 40.02 | 6.83 | −54.07 | 3.27 | 31.21 | 9.46 | 13.35 | 24.69 | .... |
| Net Cash Outflow:Invest. in NFA | c31 | 41.72 | 41.02 | 43.08 | 55.64 | 27.11 | 10.58 | 3.13 | 9.55 | 9.51 | 8.27 | 3.44 | .... |
| Purchases of Nonfinancial Assets | c31.1 | 41.72 | 41.03 | 43.16 | 59.03 | 36.94 | 10.58 | 3.13 | 9.55 | 9.51 | 8.27 | 3.44 | .... |
| Sales of Nonfinancial Assets | c31.2 | — | .01 | .08 | 3.39 | 9.83 | — | — | — | — | — | — | .... |
| Cash Surplus/Deficit [1-2-31=1-2M] | ccsd | −18.21 | −20.07 | −6.98 | −15.62 | −20.28 | −64.65 | .14 | 21.65 | −.05 | 5.08 | 21.25 | .... |
| Net Acq. Fin. Assets, excl. Cash | c32x | — | — | — | — | — | — | — | — | — | — | — | .... |
| Domestic | c321x | — | — | — | — | — | — | — | — | — | — | — | .... |
| Foreign | c322x | — | — | — | — | — | — | — | — | — | — | — | .... |
| Net Incurrence of Liabilities | c33 | 25.23 | 16.00 | −30.58 | 34.35 | 29.74 | 59.52 | −48.69 | −9.33 | −10.05 | −8.21 | −9.59 | .... |
| Domestic | c331 | 24.34 | 16.39 | −30.18 | 35.37 | 13.45 | 57.58 | −176.17 | −6.61 | −8.96 | −7.15 | −8.46 | .... |
| Foreign | c332 | .89 | −.39 | −.40 | −1.03 | 16.29 | 1.94 | 127.48 | −2.72 | −1.09 | −1.06 | −1.13 | .... |
| Net Cash Inflow, Fin.Act.[-32x+33] | cnfb | 25.23 | 16.00 | −30.58 | 34.35 | 29.74 | 59.52 | −48.69 | −9.33 | −10.05 | −8.21 | −9.59 | .... |
| Net Change in Stock of Cash | cncb | 8.54 | .35 | −22.77 | 18.72 | 9.46 | −5.13 | −48.55 | 12.32 | −10.10 | −3.13 | 11.66 | .... |
| Stat. Discrep. [32X-33+NCB-CSD] | ccsdz | 1.52 | 4.42 | 14.79 | — | — | — | −.23 | .01 | −11.64 | 17.14 | .... | .... |
| Memo Item:Cash Expenditure[2+31] | c2m | 135.64 | 146.89 | 188.31 | 225.99 | 233.85 | 212.97 | 191.35 | 183.39 | 179.94 | 184.05 | 181.60 | .... |
| Memo Item: Gross Debt | c63 | .... | .... | .... | .... | .... | .... | .... | .... | .... | .... | .... | .... |

# Anguilla   312

| National Accounts | | 2004 | 2005 | 2006 | 2007 | 2008 | 2009 | 2010 | 2011 | 2012 | 2013 | 2014 | 2015 |
|---|---|---|---|---|---|---|---|---|---|---|---|---|---|
| | | | | | | *Millions of E. Caribbean Dollars* | | | | | | | |
| House.Cons.Expend.,incl.NPISHs...... | 96f | 450.17 | 480.82 | 788.06 | 837.50 | 805.50 | 640.83 | 580.53 | 659.98 | 627.07 | 608.30 | 620.25 | .... |
| Government Consumption Expend... | 91f | 56.82 | 75.07 | 85.96 | 103.05 | 114.64 | 122.46 | 129.11 | 125.69 | 122.56 | 122.37 | 122.98 | .... |
| Gross Fixed Capital Formation......... | 93e | 178.80 | 216.61 | 305.36 | 498.26 | 549.60 | 226.88 | 174.57 | 138.54 | 145.89 | 158.22 | 167.84 | .... |
| Exports of Goods and Services......... | 90c | 226.58 | 306.65 | 367.53 | 387.50 | 366.92 | 362.99 | 344.32 | 370.33 | 372.30 | 397.16 | 412.17 | .... |
| Imports of Goods and Services (-)..... | 98c | 369.20 | 460.54 | 779.40 | 867.06 | 879.98 | 590.39 | 503.92 | 497.30 | 499.08 | 503.80 | 496.56 | .... |
| Gross Domestic Product (GDP)......... | 99b | 543.2 | 618.6 | 767.5 | 959.3 | 956.7 | 762.8 | 724.6 | 797.2 | 768.7 | 782.3 | 826.7 | .... |
| Net Primary Income from Abroad..... | 98.n | 2.09 | 10.73 | 21.07 | 4.53 | −22.44 | −17.48 | 7.28 | −.90 | −5.87 | −11.42 | −11.96 | .... |
| Gross National Income (GNI)............ | 99a | 545.26 | 629.34 | 788.58 | 963.78 | 934.23 | 745.28 | 731.88 | 796.33 | 762.87 | 770.83 | 814.72 | .... |
| Net Current Transf.from Abroad....... | 98t | 12.56 | 2.62 | .41 | −20.58 | −16.16 | −13.24 | 15.60 | 27.62 | −14.37 | −12.89 | −13.07 | .... |
| Gross Nat'l Disposable Inc.(GNDI).... | 99i | 557.82 | 631.95 | 789.00 | 943.21 | 918.08 | 732.04 | 747.47 | 823.95 | 748.50 | 757.94 | 801.65 | .... |
| Gross Saving................................ | 99s | 50.83 | 76.07 | −85.02 | 2.66 | −2.06 | −31.24 | 37.84 | 38.28 | −1.13 | 27.27 | 58.42 | .... |
| GDP Volume 1990 Prices................. | 99b.p | 221.4 | 245.2 | 294.6 | 366.6 | 383.0 | 289.6 | .... | .... | .... | .... | .... | .... |
| GDP Volume 2006 Prices................. | 99b.p | 564.03 | 638.11 | 767.51 | 869.88 | 857.23 | 699.44 | 669.11 | 702.27 | 655.48 | .... | .... | .... |
| GDP Volume (2010=100)................ | 99bvp | 84.3 | 95.4 | 114.7 | 130.0 | 128.1 | 104.5 | 100.0 | 105.0 | 98.0 | .... | .... | .... |
| GDP Deflator (2010=100).............. | 99bip | 88.9 | 89.5 | 92.3 | 101.8 | 103.1 | 100.7 | 100.0 | 104.8 | 108.3 | .... | .... | .... |
| | | | | | | *Millions: Midyear Estimates* | | | | | | | |
| Population................................ | 99z | .012 | .013 | .013 | .013 | .013 | .014 | .014 | .014 | .014 | .014 | .014 | .015 |

| | | 2004 | 2005 | 2006 | 2007 | 2008 | 2009 | 2010 | 2011 | 2012 | 2013 | 2014 | 2015 |
|---|---|---|---|---|---|---|---|---|---|---|---|---|---|
| **Exchange Rates** | | | | | | | *E. Caribbean Dollars per SDR: End of Period* | | | | | | |
| Official Rate | aa | 4.1931 | 3.8590 | 4.0619 | 4.2667 | 4.1587 | 4.2328 | 4.1581 | 4.1452 | 4.1497 | 4.1580 | 3.9118 | 3.7415 |
| | | | | | | *E. Caribbean Dollars per US Dollar: End of Period (ae) Period Average (rf)* | | | | | | | |
| Official Rate | ae | 2.7000 | 2.7000 | 2.7000 | 2.7000 | 2.7000 | 2.7000 | 2.7000 | 2.7000 | 2.7000 | 2.7000 | 2.7000 | 2.7000 |
| Official Rate | rf | 2.7000 | 2.7000 | 2.7000 | 2.7000 | 2.7000 | 2.7000 | 2.7000 | 2.7000 | 2.7000 | 2.7000 | 2.7000 | 2.7000 |
| | | | | | | *Index Numbers (2010=100): Period Averages* | | | | | | | |
| Official Rate | ahx | 100.0 | 100.0 | 100.0 | 100.0 | 100.0 | 100.0 | 100.0 | 100.0 | 100.0 | 100.0 | 100.0 | 100.0 |
| Nominal Effective Exchange Rate | nec | 100.1 | 104.0 | 103.1 | 95.8 | 90.2 | 96.5 | 100.0 | 99.4 | 105.4 | 105.9 | 106.1 | 122.0 |
| CPI-Based Real Effect. Ex. Rate | rec | 107.1 | 110.3 | 108.2 | 98.4 | 92.7 | 96.6 | 100.0 | 104.1 | 102.1 | 99.5 | 109.9 | |
| **Fund Position** | | | | | | | *Millions of SDRs: End of Period* | | | | | | |
| Quota | 2f.s | 13.50 | 13.50 | 13.50 | 13.50 | 13.50 | 13.50 | 13.50 | 13.50 | 13.50 | 13.50 | 13.50 | 13.50 |
| SDR Holdings | 1b.s | .01 | .01 | .01 | .01 | .01 | 12.51 | .31 | .44 | .46 | .01 | .09 | .11 |
| Reserve Position in the Fund | 1c.s | .01 | .01 | .01 | .01 | .01 | .01 | .03 | .05 | .05 | .05 | .05 | .05 |
| Total Fund Cred.&Loans Outstg | 2tl | — | — | — | — | — | — | 20.25 | 27.00 | 43.88 | 63.28 | 51.47 | 37.97 |
| SDR Allocations | 1bd | — | — | — | — | — | 12.50 | 12.50 | 12.50 | 12.50 | 12.50 | 12.50 | 12.50 |
| **International Liquidity** | | | | | | | *Millions of US Dollars: End of Period* | | | | | | |
| Total Reserves minus Gold | 1l.d | 120.14 | 127.32 | 142.63 | 143.85 | 138.02 | 127.86 | 136.60 | 147.87 | 162.05 | 202.58 | 297.05 | 355.73 |
| SDR Holdings | 1b.d | .01 | .01 | .01 | .01 | .01 | 19.61 | .47 | .68 | .71 | .01 | .13 | .16 |
| Reserve Position in the Fund | 1c.d | .01 | .01 | .01 | .01 | .01 | .01 | .05 | .08 | .08 | .08 | .07 | .07 |
| Foreign Exchange | 1d.d | 120.12 | 127.30 | 142.61 | 143.83 | 138.00 | 108.24 | 136.08 | 147.11 | 161.25 | 202.49 | 296.84 | 355.50 |
| Central Bank: Other Assets | 3..d | — | — | — | — | — | — | — | — | — | — | — | — |
| Central Bank: Other Liabs | 4..d | — | — | — | — | — | — | — | — | — | — | — | — |
| Other Depository Corps.: Assets | 7a.d | 342.80 | 568.03 | 655.26 | 813.06 | 724.06 | 744.46 | 545.18 | 933.67 | 843.12 | 736.29 | 725.51 | 930.88 |
| Other Depository Corps.: Liabs | 7b.d | 225.21 | 432.17 | 454.87 | 629.94 | 658.11 | 712.05 | 526.47 | 950.07 | 831.99 | 731.71 | 695.29 | 721.69 |
| **Central Bank** | | | | | | | *Millions of E. Caribbean Dollars: End of Period* | | | | | | |
| Net Foreign Assets | 11n | 327.43 | 347.26 | 389.18 | 392.66 | 378.16 | 298.00 | 233.68 | 234.83 | 203.81 | 232.09 | 552.02 | 771.87 |
| Claims on Nonresidents | 11 | 327.43 | 347.26 | 389.18 | 392.66 | 378.16 | 351.00 | 369.85 | 398.56 | 437.75 | 547.19 | 802.25 | 960.69 |
| Liabilities to Nonresidents | 16c | | | | | | 52.91 | 136.18 | 163.73 | 233.94 | 315.10 | 250.23 | 188.83 |
| Claims on Other Depository Corps | 12e | .26 | .02 | .05 | 20.04 | .03 | 3.66 | 2.74 | 13.43 | 11.14 | 9.60 | 9.64 | 9.68 |
| Net Claims on Central Government | 12an | 20.94 | 22.16 | 20.31 | 4.93 | 19.20 | 96.77 | 69.84 | 110.11 | 108.66 | 90.87 | 91.62 | 3.56 |
| Claims on Central Government | 12a | 22.23 | 22.17 | 20.64 | 6.12 | 19.28 | 99.45 | 117.03 | 120.20 | 111.51 | 95.27 | 97.06 | 89.64 |
| Liabilities to Central Government | 16d | 1.28 | .01 | .32 | 1.18 | .07 | 2.68 | 47.19 | 10.09 | 2.85 | 4.39 | 5.45 | 86.08 |
| Claims on Other Sectors | 12s | — | — | — | — | — | — | — | — | — | — | — | — |
| Claims on Other Financial Corps | 12g | — | — | — | — | — | — | — | — | — | — | — | — |
| Claims on State & Local Govts | 12b | — | — | — | — | — | — | — | — | — | — | — | — |
| Claims on Public Nonfin. Corps | 12c | — | — | — | — | — | — | — | — | — | — | — | — |
| Claims on Private Sector | 12d | — | — | — | — | — | — | — | — | — | — | — | — |
| Monetary Base | 14 | 345.19 | 365.56 | 405.28 | 413.25 | 391.70 | 392.54 | 434.85 | 513.07 | 546.11 | 637.64 | 869.75 | 916.19 |
| Currency in Circulation | 14a | 154.46 | 169.83 | 183.84 | 194.19 | 201.38 | 182.60 | 172.23 | 169.95 | 164.17 | 180.25 | 192.31 | 202.22 |
| Liabs. to Other Depository Corps | 14c | 190.72 | 195.71 | 221.45 | 219.07 | 190.32 | 209.78 | 262.61 | 343.12 | 381.94 | 457.39 | 677.42 | 713.92 |
| Liabilities to Other Sectors | 14d | — | .01 | — | — | — | .16 | — | — | — | .01 | .01 | .05 |
| Other Liabs. to Other Dep. Corps | 14n | 3.23 | 3.66 | 4.05 | 4.16 | 5.47 | 5.75 | 6.03 | 6.76 | 9.08 | 9.55 | 32.98 | 56.92 |
| Dep. & Sec. Excl. f/Monetary Base | 14o | — | — | — | — | — | — | — | — | — | — | — | — |
| Deposits Included in Broad Money | 15 | — | — | — | — | — | — | — | — | — | — | — | — |
| Sec.Ot.th.Shares Incl.in Brd. Money | 16a | — | — | — | — | — | — | — | — | — | — | — | — |
| Deposits Excl. from Broad Money | 16b | — | — | — | — | — | — | — | — | — | — | — | — |
| Sec.Ot.th.Shares Excl.f/Brd.Money | 16s | — | — | — | — | — | — | — | — | — | — | — | — |
| Loans | 16l | — | — | — | — | — | — | — | — | — | — | — | — |
| Financial Derivatives | 16m | — | — | — | — | — | — | — | — | — | — | — | — |
| Shares and Other Equity | 17a | — | — | — | — | — | — | — | — | — | — | — | — |
| Other Items (Net) | 17r | .21 | .21 | .21 | .22 | .23 | .23 | −134.62 | −161.47 | −231.57 | −314.63 | −249.45 | −188.00 |
| Memo Item: | | | | | | | | | | | | | |
| Total Assets | 10ra | 349.86 | 369.40 | 409.81 | 418.75 | 397.41 | 401.15 | 488.22 | 530.14 | 558.25 | 651.81 | 908.39 | 1,059.40 |
| **Other Depository Corporations** | | | | | | | *Millions of E. Caribbean Dollars: End of Period* | | | | | | |
| Net Foreign Assets | 21n | 317.51 | 366.82 | 541.07 | 494.42 | 178.06 | 87.51 | 50.52 | −44.28 | 30.07 | 12.37 | 81.59 | 564.82 |
| Claims on Nonresidents | 21 | 925.57 | 1,533.69 | 1,769.21 | 2,195.26 | 1,954.95 | 2,010.05 | 1,471.98 | 2,520.91 | 2,276.43 | 1,987.98 | 1,958.88 | 2,513.38 |
| Liabilities to Nonresidents | 26c | 608.06 | 1,166.87 | 1,228.14 | 1,700.84 | 1,776.90 | 1,922.54 | 1,421.46 | 2,565.19 | 2,246.37 | 1,975.61 | 1,877.29 | 1,948.55 |
| Claims on Central Bank | 20 | 244.86 | 248.81 | 313.19 | 293.49 | 276.02 | 253.84 | 304.34 | 429.42 | 478.15 | 542.47 | 700.22 | 807.98 |
| Currency | 20a | 41.12 | 47.69 | 40.12 | 60.31 | 58.49 | 36.46 | 34.49 | 39.89 | 42.44 | 43.67 | 43.08 | 42.62 |
| Reserve Deposits and Securities | 20b | 203.74 | 194.54 | 267.02 | 227.70 | 212.67 | 213.21 | 266.43 | 359.05 | 405.98 | 470.11 | 629.99 | 765.36 |
| Other Claims | 20n | — | 6.58 | 6.06 | 5.48 | 4.85 | 4.17 | 3.41 | 30.49 | 29.73 | 28.69 | 27.15 | — |
| Net Claims on Central Government | 22an | 246.90 | 239.89 | 176.67 | 259.42 | 444.92 | 494.94 | 395.09 | 433.35 | 443.08 | 432.81 | 423.60 | 331.35 |
| Claims on Central Government | 22a | 290.74 | 282.32 | 349.32 | 403.98 | 567.66 | 570.13 | 461.94 | 496.48 | 503.27 | 496.75 | 500.70 | 461.50 |
| Liabilities to Central Government | 26d | 43.84 | 42.43 | 172.65 | 144.56 | 122.74 | 75.19 | 66.85 | 63.13 | 60.19 | 63.94 | 77.10 | 130.16 |
| Claims on Other Sectors | 22s | 1,651.67 | 1,822.07 | 2,118.38 | 2,440.43 | 2,585.75 | 2,619.99 | 2,623.73 | 2,519.66 | 2,449.45 | 2,394.29 | 2,272.26 | 2,047.86 |
| Claims on Other Financial Corps | 22g | 54.72 | 60.38 | 35.82 | 45.06 | 31.21 | 16.11 | 19.24 | 20.55 | 29.58 | 30.64 | 21.78 | 14.95 |
| Claims on State & Local Govts | 22b | .21 | .45 | .47 | .52 | .37 | .47 | .54 | .39 | .89 | .48 | .48 | .49 |
| Claims on Public Nonfin. Corps | 22c | 88.64 | 95.59 | 76.64 | 111.11 | 87.33 | 140.42 | 151.23 | 145.01 | 138.92 | 170.11 | 164.15 | 145.56 |
| Claims on Private Sector | 22d | 1,508.11 | 1,665.65 | 2,005.46 | 2,283.74 | 2,466.84 | 2,462.99 | 2,452.73 | 2,353.72 | 2,280.07 | 2,193.05 | 2,085.85 | 1,886.86 |
| Liabilities to Central Bank | 26g | 9.71 | .02 | .06 | 20.02 | .05 | 92.64 | 7.46 | 14.96 | 11.12 | 9.59 | 9.62 | 9.63 |
| Transf.Dep.Included in Broad Money | 24 | 721.15 | 838.51 | 1,010.59 | 1,167.54 | 1,095.22 | 820.66 | 840.24 | 819.76 | 842.96 | 868.92 | 868.09 | 984.54 |
| Other Dep.Included in Broad Money | 25 | 1,554.34 | 1,639.50 | 1,747.23 | 1,929.91 | 2,099.95 | 2,044.21 | 2,040.58 | 2,112.97 | 2,177.32 | 2,178.72 | 2,211.21 | 2,091.89 |
| Sec.Ot.th.Shares Incl.in Brd. Money | 26a | — | — | — | — | — | — | — | — | — | — | — | — |
| Deposits Excl. from Broad Money | 26b | — | — | — | — | — | 191.66 | 192.10 | 192.39 | 191.81 | 192.21 | 192.42 | 180.25 |
| Sec.Ot.th.Shares Excl.f/Brd.Money | 26s | — | — | — | — | — | — | — | — | — | — | — | — |
| Loans | 26l | — | — | — | — | — | — | — | — | — | — | — | — |
| Financial Derivatives | 26m | — | — | — | — | — | — | — | — | — | — | — | — |
| Insurance Technical Reserves | 26r | — | — | — | — | — | — | — | — | — | — | — | — |
| Shares and Other Equity | 27a | 231.51 | 288.75 | 372.60 | 433.93 | 471.03 | 470.22 | 371.80 | 147.14 | 122.83 | −28.13 | −36.89 | 323.05 |
| Other Items (Net) | 27r | −55.75 | −89.18 | 18.84 | −63.66 | −181.50 | −163.11 | −78.51 | 50.93 | 54.71 | 160.64 | 233.24 | 162.65 |
| Memo Item: | | | | | | | | | | | | | |
| Total Assets | 20ra | 3,393.50 | 4,281.01 | 4,870.83 | 5,785.77 | 5,952.67 | 5,932.96 | 5,258.04 | 6,285.73 | 6,106.19 | 5,800.38 | 5,826.73 | 6,155.57 |

| | | 2004 | 2005 | 2006 | 2007 | 2008 | 2009 | 2010 | 2011 | 2012 | 2013 | 2014 | 2015 |
|---|---|---|---|---|---|---|---|---|---|---|---|---|---|
| **Depository Corporations** | | \multicolumn{12}{c}{*Millions of E. Caribbean Dollars: End of Period*} | | | | | | | | | | | |
| Net Foreign Assets.......................... | 31n | 644.94 | 714.08 | 930.25 | 887.08 | 556.22 | 385.60 | 284.20 | 190.55 | 233.87 | 244.47 | 633.61 | 1,336.69 |
| Claims on Nonresidents................ | 31 | 1,253.00 | 1,880.95 | 2,158.39 | 2,587.91 | 2,333.12 | 2,361.05 | 1,841.83 | 2,919.47 | 2,714.18 | 2,535.17 | 2,761.13 | 3,474.07 |
| Liabilities to Nonresidents............. | 36c | 608.06 | 1,166.87 | 1,228.14 | 1,700.84 | 1,776.90 | 1,975.45 | 1,557.64 | 2,728.93 | 2,480.30 | 2,290.70 | 2,127.52 | 2,137.38 |
| Domestic Claims............................. | 32 | 1,919.52 | 2,084.11 | 2,315.37 | 2,704.79 | 3,049.88 | 3,211.69 | 3,088.66 | 3,063.12 | 3,001.19 | 2,917.97 | 2,787.47 | 2,382.77 |
| Net Claims on Central Government | 32an | 267.84 | 262.04 | 196.98 | 264.36 | 464.12 | 591.71 | 464.93 | 543.46 | 551.74 | 523.68 | 515.02 | 334.91 |
| Claims on Central Government.... | 32a | 312.96 | 304.49 | 369.96 | 410.10 | 586.93 | 669.58 | 578.97 | 616.67 | 614.78 | 592.02 | 597.77 | 551.14 |
| Liabilities to Central Government. | 36d | 45.12 | 42.44 | 172.97 | 145.74 | 122.81 | 77.87 | 114.04 | 73.21 | 63.03 | 68.34 | 82.55 | 216.24 |
| Claims on Other Sectors................ | 32s | 1,651.67 | 1,822.07 | 2,118.38 | 2,440.43 | 2,585.75 | 2,619.99 | 2,623.73 | 2,519.66 | 2,449.45 | 2,394.29 | 2,272.26 | 2,047.86 |
| Claims on Other Financial Corps.. | 32g | 54.72 | 60.38 | 35.82 | 45.06 | 31.21 | 16.11 | 19.24 | 20.55 | 29.58 | 30.64 | 21.78 | 14.95 |
| Claims on State & Local Govts..... | 32b | .21 | .45 | .47 | .52 | .37 | .47 | .54 | .39 | .89 | .48 | .48 | .49 |
| Claims on Public Nonfin. Corps.... | 32c | 88.64 | 95.59 | 76.64 | 111.11 | 87.33 | 140.42 | 151.23 | 145.01 | 138.92 | 170.11 | 164.15 | 145.56 |
| Claims on Private Sector.............. | 32d | 1,508.11 | 1,665.65 | 2,005.46 | 2,283.74 | 2,466.84 | 2,462.99 | 2,452.73 | 2,353.72 | 2,280.07 | 2,193.05 | 2,085.85 | 1,886.86 |
| Broad Money Liabilities.................. | 35l | 2,388.83 | 2,600.16 | 2,901.54 | 3,231.33 | 3,338.06 | 3,011.16 | 3,018.56 | 3,062.80 | 3,142.02 | 3,184.23 | 3,228.53 | 3,236.08 |
| Currency Outside Depository Corps | 34a | 113.34 | 122.14 | 143.71 | 133.88 | 142.89 | 146.13 | 137.74 | 130.06 | 121.73 | 136.59 | 149.23 | 159.59 |
| Transferable Deposits.................... | 34 | 721.15 | 838.52 | 1,010.59 | 1,167.54 | 1,095.22 | 820.82 | 840.24 | 819.77 | 842.97 | 868.92 | 868.10 | 984.59 |
| Other Deposits.............................. | 35 | 1,554.34 | 1,639.50 | 1,747.23 | 1,929.91 | 2,099.95 | 2,044.21 | 2,040.58 | 2,112.97 | 2,177.32 | 2,178.72 | 2,211.21 | 2,091.89 |
| Securities other than Shares.......... | 36a | — | — | — | — | — | — | — | — | — | — | — | — |
| Deposits Excl. from Broad Money..... | 36b | — | — | — | — | — | 191.66 | 192.10 | 192.39 | 191.81 | 192.21 | 192.42 | 180.25 |
| Sec.Ot.th.Shares Excl.f/Brd.Money.... | 36s | — | — | — | — | — | — | — | — | — | — | — | — |
| Loans............................................. | 36l | — | — | — | — | — | — | — | — | — | — | — | — |
| Financial Derivatives...................... | 36m | — | — | — | — | — | — | — | — | — | — | — | — |
| Insurance Technical Reserves.......... | 36r | — | — | — | — | — | — | — | — | — | — | — | — |
| Shares and Other Equity................. | 37a | 231.51 | 288.75 | 372.60 | 433.93 | 471.03 | 470.22 | 371.80 | 147.14 | 122.83 | −28.13 | −36.89 | 323.05 |
| Other Items (Net)............................ | 37r | −55.89 | −90.72 | −28.52 | −73.41 | −202.99 | −75.75 | −209.61 | −148.66 | −221.58 | −185.87 | 37.03 | −19.91 |
| Broad Money Liabs., Seasonally Adj. | 35l.b | 2,412.77 | 2,624.02 | 2,926.12 | 3,258.01 | 3,364.30 | 3,032.90 | 3,039.64 | 3,085.22 | 3,168.11 | 3,214.56 | 3,263.01 | 3,272.88 |
| **Monetary Aggregates** | | \multicolumn{12}{c}{*Millions of E. Caribbean Dollars: End of Period*} | | | | | | | | | | | |
| Broad Money.................................. | 59m | 2,388.83 | 2,600.16 | 2,901.54 | 3,231.33 | 3,338.06 | 3,011.16 | 3,018.56 | 3,062.80 | 3,142.02 | 3,184.23 | 3,228.53 | 3,236.08 |
| o/w:Currency Issued by Cent.Govt | 59m.a | — | — | — | — | — | — | — | — | — | — | — | — |
| o/w: Dep.in Nonfin. Corporations. | 59m.b | — | — | — | — | — | — | — | — | — | — | — | — |
| o/w:Secs. Issued by Central Govt.. | 59m.c | — | — | — | — | — | — | — | — | — | — | — | — |
| Money (National Definitions) | | | | | | | | | | | | | |
| M1.................................................. | 59ma | 444.54 | 525.35 | 641.75 | 671.78 | 720.00 | 630.02 | 618.89 | 603.09 | 554.01 | 597.23 | 632.21 | 694.15 |
| M2.................................................. | 59mb | 2,042.92 | 2,184.05 | 2,475.56 | 2,752.39 | 2,981.20 | 2,996.88 | 3,006.40 | 2,800.15 | 2,790.11 | 2,908.44 | 3,011.78 | 3,100.51 |
| **Interest Rates** | | \multicolumn{12}{c}{*Percent Per Annum*} | | | | | | | | | | | |
| Discount Rate (End of Period).......... | 60.a | 6.50 | 6.50 | 6.50 | 6.50 | 6.50 | 6.50 | 6.50 | 6.50 | 6.50 | 6.50 | 6.50 | 6.50 |
| Money Market Rate........................ | 60b | 4.67 | 4.01 | 4.76 | 5.24 | 4.92 | 6.03 | 6.36 | 5.68 | 5.04 | 6.28 | 6.19 | 6.44 |
| Treasury Bill Rate............................ | 60c | 7.00 | 7.00 | 6.52 | 6.33 | 6.02 | 6.38 | 6.25 | 6.50 | 5.88 | 5.00 | 5.00 | . . . . |
| Savings Rate.................................. | 60k | 3.43 | 3.35 | 3.28 | 3.35 | 3.32 | 3.24 | 3.24 | 3.27 | 3.15 | 3.22 | 3.20 | 2.75 |
| Savings Rate (Fgn. Currency)............ | 60k.f | 4.77 | 5.14 | 4.45 | 3.89 | 4.07 | 4.55 | 4.95 | 4.30 | 4.61 | 3.72 | 3.56 | 2.91 |
| Deposit Rate.................................. | 60l | 4.12 | 3.86 | 3.83 | 3.52 | 3.54 | 3.48 | 3.37 | 3.38 | 3.16 | 3.04 | 2.89 | 2.47 |
| Deposit Rate (Fgn. Currency)........... | 60l.f | 2.36 | 2.95 | 3.60 | 2.78 | 1.79 | 2.19 | 2.27 | 1.99 | 2.59 | 2.60 | 2.56 | 2.11 |
| Lending Rate.................................. | 60p | 11.96 | 11.39 | 10.89 | 10.44 | 10.43 | 10.07 | 11.00 | 10.91 | 10.16 | 9.95 | 10.07 | 9.83 |
| Lending Rate (Fgn. Currency).......... | 60p.f | 6.54 | 7.90 | 8.88 | 9.15 | 7.63 | 6.14 | 5.85 | 5.62 | 5.04 | 6.49 | 6.95 | 5.49 |
| **Prices** | | \multicolumn{12}{c}{*Index Numbers (2010=100): Period Averages*} | | | | | | | | | | | |
| Consumer Prices............................. | 64 | 87.6 | 89.5 | 91.1 | 92.3 | 97.3 | 96.7 | 100.0 | 103.5 | 107.0 | 108.1 | 109.3 | 110.3 |
| **Intl. Transactions & Positions** | | \multicolumn{12}{c}{*Millions of US Dollars*} | | | | | | | | | | | |
| Exports.......................................... | 70..d | . . . . | 120.6 | 163.5 | 174.0 | 92.4 | 205.7 | 34.8 | 29.0 | 29.0 | 32.3 | 25.1 | 26.3 |
| Imports, c.i.f.................................... | 71..d | . . . . | 525.6 | 670.7 | 727.0 | 805.6 | 699.0 | 501.2 | 471.1 | 534.8 | 514.9 | 552.6 | 488.4 |

| | | 2004 | 2005 | 2006 | 2007 | 2008 | 2009 | 2010 | 2011 | 2012 | 2013 | 2014 | 2015 |
|---|---|---|---|---|---|---|---|---|---|---|---|---|---|
| **Balance of Payments** | | | | | | *Millions of US Dollars* | | | | | | | |
| A. Current Account* | 109bx | −95.1 | −171.5 | −291.8 | −385.5 | −359.2 | −169.0 | −167.1 | −117.7 | −166.8 | −204.4 | .... | .... |
| Goods, credit (exports) | 1a9cx | 57.1 | 82.7 | 74.0 | 59.3 | 65.4 | 50.7 | 45.7 | 56.2 | 59.0 | 64.2 | .... | .... |
| Goods, debit (imports) | 1a9dx | 402.4 | 455.4 | 559.7 | 648.9 | 669.9 | 478.9 | 453.9 | 430.7 | 483.5 | 494.4 | .... | .... |
| Balance on goods | 1a9gx | −345.3 | −372.7 | −485.7 | −589.6 | −604.5 | −428.2 | −408.2 | −374.6 | −424.5 | −430.2 | .... | .... |
| Services, credit (exports) | 1b9cx | 476.9 | 462.6 | 474.2 | 522.0 | 560.0 | 510.9 | 478.1 | 481.6 | 482.5 | 465.0 | .... | .... |
| Services, debit (imports) | 1b9dx | 190.0 | 227.4 | 258.7 | 283.5 | 282.3 | 227.6 | 225.0 | 210.9 | 204.1 | 219.5 | .... | .... |
| Balance on Goods & Services | 1z9bx | −58.4 | −137.5 | −270.2 | −351.1 | −326.8 | −144.9 | −155.1 | −103.9 | −146.1 | −184.7 | .... | .... |
| Primary income: credit | 1c9cx | 11.5 | 18.0 | 26.7 | 25.8 | 16.1 | 13.1 | 11.1 | 10.2 | 10.5 | 10.6 | .... | .... |
| Primary income: debit | 1c9dx | 56.6 | 60.0 | 73.5 | 78.5 | 77.2 | 63.9 | 42.6 | 49.7 | 61.6 | 60.8 | .... | .... |
| Balance on gds, serv. & prim. inc. | 1y9bx | −103.5 | −179.5 | −317.0 | −403.8 | −387.9 | −195.7 | −186.6 | −143.4 | −197.2 | −234.8 | .... | .... |
| Secondary income: credit | 1d9ca | 25.1 | 26.2 | 44.4 | 47.4 | 47.8 | 40.5 | 38.5 | 42.5 | 47.6 | 48.2 | .... | .... |
| Secondary income: debit | 1d9da | 16.8 | 18.2 | 19.2 | 29.2 | 19.0 | 13.8 | 19.1 | 16.8 | 17.2 | 17.7 | .... | .... |
| B. Capital Account* | 209ba | 18.0 | 210.6 | 27.9 | 7.4 | 11.1 | .5 | 16.6 | 8.5 | 2.5 | 11.9 | .... | .... |
| Capital account: credit | 209ca | 18.0 | 210.6 | 27.9 | 7.4 | 11.1 | .5 | 16.6 | 8.5 | 2.5 | 11.9 | .... | .... |
| Capital account: debit | 209da | — | — | — | — | — | — | — | — | — | — | .... | .... |
| Balance on current & capital acct. | 129bx | −77.1 | 39.1 | −263.9 | −378.1 | −348.1 | −168.6 | −150.5 | −109.2 | −164.3 | −192.5 | .... | .... |
| C. Financial Account* | 309na | −99.5 | 24.5 | −286.2 | −382.5 | −331.8 | −179.2 | −138.0 | −132.8 | −144.0 | −200.9 | .... | .... |
| Direct investment: assets | 3a9aa | — | — | — | — | — | — | — | — | — | — | .... | .... |
| Equity & investment fund shares | 3aaaa | .... | .... | .... | .... | .... | .... | .... | .... | .... | .... | .... | .... |
| Debt instruments | 3abaa | .... | .... | .... | .... | .... | .... | .... | .... | .... | .... | .... | .... |
| Direct investment: liabilities | 3a9la | 80.4 | 221.0 | 358.8 | 338.2 | 158.8 | 80.6 | 96.7 | 65.2 | 129.4 | 134.3 | .... | .... |
| Equity & investment fund shares | 3aala | 25.6 | 191.1 | 281.0 | 266.7 | 102.5 | 43.1 | 34.8 | 29.6 | 73.2 | 89.3 | .... | .... |
| Debt instruments | 3abla | 54.7 | 29.9 | 77.9 | 71.5 | 56.3 | 37.6 | 61.9 | 35.5 | 56.2 | 45.0 | .... | .... |
| Portfolio investment: assets | 3b9aa | 1.4 | −.5 | — | — | — | — | 7.5 | −.2 | −.1 | −3.3 | .... | .... |
| Equity & investment fund shares | 3baaa | .... | .... | .... | .... | .... | .... | .... | .... | .... | .... | .... | .... |
| Debt securities | 3bbaa | .... | .... | .... | .... | .... | .... | .... | .... | .... | .... | .... | .... |
| Portfolio investment: liabilities | 3b9la | 13.5 | 10.1 | 24.8 | −1.2 | 10.8 | −7.1 | — | 10.0 | 6.6 | 2.0 | .... | .... |
| Equity & investment fund shares | 3bala | .... | .... | .... | .... | .... | .... | .... | .... | .... | .... | .... | .... |
| Debt securities | 3bbla | .... | .... | .... | .... | .... | .... | .... | .... | .... | .... | .... | .... |
| Fin. der.& empl.stk.ops.(ESOs): net. | 3c9na | .... | .... | .... | .... | .... | .... | .... | .... | .... | .... | .... | .... |
| Fin. der. & ESOs.: assets | 3c9aa | .... | .... | .... | .... | .... | .... | .... | .... | .... | .... | .... | .... |
| Fin. der. & ESOs.: liabilities | 3c9la | .... | .... | .... | .... | .... | .... | .... | .... | .... | .... | .... | .... |
| Other investment: assets | 3d9aa | 37.9 | 143.2 | 149.8 | 82.0 | 80.1 | 70.7 | 121.7 | 28.4 | 53.2 | 83.8 | .... | .... |
| Other equity | 3daaa | .... | .... | .... | .... | .... | .... | .... | .... | .... | .... | .... | .... |
| Debt instruments | 3dzaa | 37.9 | 143.2 | 149.8 | 82.0 | 80.1 | 70.7 | 121.7 | 28.4 | 53.2 | 83.8 | .... | .... |
| Other investment: liabilities | 3d9la | 44.9 | −112.8 | 52.4 | 127.5 | 242.3 | 176.4 | 170.5 | 85.9 | 61.2 | 145.1 | .... | .... |
| Other equity | 3dala | .... | .... | .... | .... | .... | .... | .... | .... | .... | .... | .... | .... |
| Debt instruments | 3dzla | 44.9 | −112.8 | 52.4 | 127.5 | 242.3 | 176.4 | 170.5 | 85.9 | 61.2 | 145.1 | .... | .... |
| Curr.+ cap.− finan. acct. balance | 4y9na | 22.3 | 14.6 | 22.3 | 4.4 | −16.2 | 10.7 | −12.5 | 23.6 | −20.3 | 8.4 | .... | .... |
| D. Net Errors and Omissions | 409na | −15.9 | −7.4 | −7.0 | −4.0 | 10.4 | −20.8 | −7.4 | −23.6 | 5.9 | 4.1 | .... | .... |
| E. Reserves and Related Items | 4z9na | 6.4 | 7.2 | 15.4 | .4 | −5.8 | −10.1 | −19.9 | — | −14.4 | 12.5 | .... | .... |
| Reserve assets | 3e9aa | 6.4 | 7.2 | 15.4 | .4 | −5.8 | −10.1 | 10.1 | 10.7 | 11.2 | 41.7 | .... | .... |
| Credit and loans from the IMF | 3dcla | — | — | — | — | — | — | 30.0 | 10.8 | 25.6 | 29.3 | .... | .... |
| Exceptional financing | 409la | .... | .... | .... | .... | .... | .... | .... | .... | .... | .... | .... | .... |
| *Excludes components in group E | | | | | | | | | | | | | |

**Government Finance**
**Cash Flow Statement**

| **Budgetary Central Government** | | | | | | *Millions of E. Caribbean Dollars: Fiscal Year Ends December 31* | | | | | | | |
|---|---|---|---|---|---|---|---|---|---|---|---|---|---|
| Cash Receipts:Operating Activities | c1 | 520.80 | 1,062.40 | 677.90 | 744.70 | 766.00 | 593.88 | 671.47 | 604.06 | 646.64 | 597.82 | 674.71 | .... |
| Taxes | c11 | 427.20 | 455.00 | 567.60 | 690.90 | 692.40 | 571.55 | 576.46 | 546.75 | 604.21 | 555.24 | 571.14 | .... |
| Social Contributions | c12 | — | — | — | — | — | — | — | — | — | — | — | .... |
| Grants | c13 | 48.50 | 568.70 | 75.30 | 20.00 | 30.00 | — | 31.88 | 15.80 | — | — | 13.79 | .... |
| Other Receipts | c14 | 45.10 | 38.60 | 35.10 | 33.80 | 43.60 | 22.33 | 63.13 | 41.51 | 42.43 | 42.58 | 89.78 | .... |
| Cash Payments:Operating Activities. | c2 | 553.00 | 563.30 | 684.10 | 749.60 | 766.30 | 909.30 | 673.94 | 706.66 | 671.49 | 700.66 | 722.37 | .... |
| Compensation of Employees | c21 | 251.10 | 252.80 | 268.20 | 309.00 | 300.40 | 291.85 | 272.58 | 264.68 | 273.81 | 276.88 | 300.58 | .... |
| Purchases of Goods & Services | c22 | 109.90 | 111.00 | 126.20 | 147.60 | 185.00 | 161.57 | 125.49 | 126.65 | 113.75 | 147.65 | 122.71 | .... |
| Interest | c24 | 109.10 | 89.30 | 98.10 | 104.50 | 102.60 | 231.05 | 74.82 | 76.80 | 80.02 | 66.27 | 103.00 | .... |
| Subsidies | c25 | 50.20 | 72.00 | 148.70 | 109.00 | 120.40 | 157.04 | 132.20 | 173.73 | 133.25 | 134.22 | 135.49 | .... |
| Grants | c26 | — | — | — | — | — | — | — | — | — | — | — | .... |
| Social Benefits | c27 | 32.70 | 38.20 | 42.90 | 79.50 | 58.00 | 67.79 | 68.85 | 64.81 | 70.66 | 75.63 | 60.59 | .... |
| Other Payments | c28 | — | — | — | — | — | — | — | — | — | — | — | .... |
| Net Cash Inflow:Operating Act.[1-2] | ccio | −32.20 | 499.10 | −6.20 | −4.90 | −.30 | −315.42 | −2.47 | −102.60 | −24.85 | −102.84 | −47.66 | .... |
| Net Cash Outflow:Invest. in NFA | c31 | 33.10 | 76.20 | 208.60 | 195.40 | 220.70 | 212.98 | 36.52 | 57.24 | 18.68 | 41.78 | 47.45 | .... |
| Purchases of Nonfinancial Assets | c31.1 | 55.20 | 94.20 | 213.60 | 200.50 | 225.00 | 215.49 | 39.49 | 60.22 | 20.89 | 43.08 | 48.84 | .... |
| Sales of Nonfinancial Assets | c31.2 | 22.10 | 18.00 | 5.00 | 5.10 | 4.30 | 2.51 | 2.97 | 2.98 | 2.21 | 1.30 | 1.39 | .... |
| Cash Surplus/Deficit [1-2-31=1-2M] | ccsd | −65.30 | 422.90 | −214.70 | −200.30 | −220.90 | −528.40 | −38.99 | −159.84 | −43.53 | −144.61 | −95.11 | .... |
| Net Acq. Fin. Assets, excl. Cash | c32x | — | — | — | — | — | — | 2.33 | — | — | — | — | .... |
| Domestic | c321x | — | — | — | — | — | — | 2.33 | — | — | — | — | .... |
| Foreign | c322x | — | — | — | — | — | — | — | — | — | — | — | .... |
| Net Incurrence of Liabilities | c33 | 51.30 | −472.70 | 8.60 | 123.10 | 292.40 | 386.56 | −1,203.02 | 68.64 | 18.68 | 9.86 | −50.11 | .... |
| Domestic | c331 | −17.10 | 7.30 | −58.20 | 54.00 | 225.90 | 137.85 | −1,076.32 | 23.57 | −8.90 | −81.23 | −8.32 | .... |
| Foreign | c332 | 68.40 | −480.00 | 66.70 | 69.10 | 66.50 | 248.71 | −126.70 | 45.07 | 27.58 | 91.09 | −41.79 | .... |
| Net Cash Inflow, Fin.Act.[-32x+33].. | cnfb | 51.30 | −472.70 | 8.60 | 123.10 | 292.40 | 386.56 | −1,205.35 | 68.64 | 18.68 | 9.86 | −50.11 | .... |
| Net Change in Stock of Cash | cncb | −14.00 | −49.90 | −206.20 | −77.20 | 71.50 | −141.84 | −1,244.34 | −91.20 | −24.85 | −134.75 | −145.22 | .... |
| Stat. Discrep. [32X-33+NCB-CSD] | ccsdz | — | −.10 | — | — | .10 | — | — | — | — | — | — | .... |
| Memo Item:Cash Expenditure[2+31] | c2m | 586.10 | 639.50 | 892.70 | 945.00 | 987.00 | 1,122.28 | 710.46 | 763.90 | 690.17 | 742.43 | 769.82 | .... |
| Memo Item: Gross Debt | c63 | .... | .... | .... | .... | .... | .... | .... | .... | .... | 2,509.83 | 2,855.46 | .... |

# Antigua and Barbuda   311

| National Accounts | | 2004 | 2005 | 2006 | 2007 | 2008 | 2009 | 2010 | 2011 | 2012 | 2013 | 2014 | 2015 |
|---|---|---|---|---|---|---|---|---|---|---|---|---|---|
| | | *Millions of E. Caribbean Dollars* | | | | | | | | | | | |
| Househ.Cons.Expend.,incl.NPISHs.... | 96f | 1,544.4 | 1,866.1 | 2,194.2 | 2,562.6 | 2,478.8 | 1,750.7 | 2,058.7 | 2,154.6 | 2,387.3 | 2,351.7 | 2,510.9 | .... |
| Government Consumption Expend... | 91f | 455.0 | 454.7 | 469.4 | 542.8 | 657.1 | 647.7 | 554.0 | 538.9 | 566.9 | 598.9 | 602.5 | .... |
| Gross Fixed Capital Formation......... | 93e | 583.8 | 743.2 | 1,131.0 | 1,323.5 | 1,384.4 | 1,250.0 | 872.1 | 637.1 | 716.5 | 752.6 | 825.7 | .... |
| Exports of Goods and Services.......... | 90c | 1,441.7 | 1,472.2 | 1,480.1 | 1,569.5 | 1,688.5 | 1,516.4 | 1,414.4 | 1,451.9 | 1,477.4 | 1,484.5 | 1,499.7 | .... |
| Imports of Goods and Services (-)..... | 98c | 1,599.3 | 1,843.4 | 2,209.7 | 2,517.4 | 2,571.0 | 1,907.5 | 1,833.1 | 1,731.7 | 1,895.4 | 1,946.1 | 2,012.0 | .... |
| Gross Domestic Product (GDP)........ | 99b | 2,425.6 | 2,692.9 | 3,064.9 | 3,481.0 | 3,637.8 | 3,257.3 | 3,066.0 | 3,050.8 | 3,252.7 | 3,241.6 | 3,296.6 | .... |
| Net Primary Income from Abroad..... | 98.n | −121.7 | −113.5 | −126.2 | −142.2 | −164.9 | −137.2 | −85.0 | −106.6 | −137.9 | −83.5 | −106.2 | .... |
| Gross National Income (GNI)............ | 99a | 2,303.8 | 2,579.4 | 2,938.7 | 3,338.8 | 3,472.9 | 3,120.1 | 2,980.9 | 2,944.2 | 3,114.8 | 3,158.1 | 3,320.4 | .... |
| Net Current Transf.from Abroad....... | 98t | 22.5 | 21.6 | 68.1 | 49.2 | 77.6 | 72.0 | 52.6 | 69.3 | 81.9 | 70.7 | 77.1 | .... |
| Gross Nat'l Disposable Inc.(GNDI).... | 99i | 2,326.4 | 2,601.0 | 3,006.8 | 3,388.0 | 3,550.6 | 3,192.1 | 3,033.5 | 3,013.5 | 3,196.7 | 3,228.8 | 3,397.5 | .... |
| Gross Saving................................... | 99s | 327.0 | 280.1 | 343.2 | 282.7 | 414.6 | 793.7 | 420.9 | 320.0 | 242.5 | 278.2 | 284.2 | .... |
| GDP Volume 1990 Prices................ | 99b.p | 1,423.0 | 1,494.4 | 1,686.9 | 1,796.5 | 1,827.9 | 1,665.4 | 1,559.9 | .... | .... | .... | .... | .... |
| GDP Volume (2010=100)................ | 99bvp | 91.2 | 95.8 | 108.1 | 115.2 | 117.2 | 106.8 | 100.0 | .... | .... | .... | .... | .... |
| GDP Deflator (2010=100)............... | 99bip | 86.7 | 91.7 | 92.4 | 98.6 | 101.3 | 99.5 | 100.0 | .... | .... | .... | .... | .... |
| | | *Millions: Midyear Estimates* | | | | | | | | | | | |
| Population................................. | 99z | .08 | .08 | .08 | .08 | .09 | .09 | .09 | .09 | .09 | .09 | .09 | .09 |

| | | 2004 | 2005 | 2006 | 2007 | 2008 | 2009 | 2010 | 2011 | 2012 | 2013 | 2014 | 2015 |
|---|---|---|---|---|---|---|---|---|---|---|---|---|---|
| **Exchange Rates** | | | | | | *Pesos per SDR: End of Period* | | | | | | | |
| Market Rate | aa | 4.5954 | 4.3050 | 4.5764 | 4.9446 | 5.2877 | 5.9259 | 6.0924 | 6.5771 | 7.5278 | 10.0115 | 12.3294 | 18.1531 |
| | | | | | | *Pesos per US Dollar: End of Period (ae) Period Average (rf)* | | | | | | | |
| Market Rate | ae | 2.9590 | 3.0120 | 3.0420 | 3.1290 | 3.4330 | 3.7800 | 3.9560 | 4.2840 | 4.8980 | 6.5010 | 8.5100 | 13.1000 |
| Market Rate | rf | 2.9233 | 2.9037 | 3.0543 | 3.0956 | 3.1442 | 3.7101 | 3.8963 | 4.1101 | 4.5369 | 5.4594 | 8.0753 | 9.2332 |
| **Fund Position** | | | | | | *Millions of SDRs: End of Period* | | | | | | | |
| Quota | 2f.s | 2,117.10 | 2,117.10 | 2,117.10 | 2,117.10 | 2,117.10 | 2,117.10 | 2,117.10 | 2,117.10 | 2,117.10 | 2,117.10 | 2,117.10 | 2,117.10 |
| SDR Holdings | 1b.s | 564.49 | 3,104.08 | 320.55 | 320.62 | 320.67 | 2,022.33 | 2,022.18 | 2,053.04 | 2,053.07 | 2,053.08 | 2,053.10 | 2,053.08 |
| Reserve Position in the Fund | 1c.s | .16 | .20 | .20 | .20 | .20 | .20 | .20 | .20 | .20 | .20 | .20 | .20 |
| Total Fund Cred.&Loans Outstg | 2tl | 9,073.05 | 6,655.73 | — | — | — | — | — | — | — | — | — | — |
| SDR Allocations | 1bd | 318.37 | 318.37 | 318.37 | 318.37 | 318.37 | 2,020.04 | 2,020.04 | 2,020.04 | 2,020.04 | 2,020.04 | 2,020.04 | 2,020.04 |
| **International Liquidity** | | | | | | *Millions of US Dollars Unless Otherwise Indicated: End of Period* | | | | | | | |
| Total Reserves minus Gold | 1l.d | 18,884 | 27,179 | 30,903 | 44,682 | 44,855 | 46,093 | 49,734 | 43,227 | 39,920 | 28,143 | 29,017 | 23,417 |
| SDR Holdings | 1b.d | 877 | 4,437 | 482 | 507 | 494 | 3,170 | 3,114 | 3,152 | 3,155 | 3,162 | 2,975 | 2,845 |
| Reserve Position in the Fund | 1c.d | — | — | — | — | — | — | — | — | — | — | — | — |
| Foreign Exchange | 1d.d | 18,007 | 22,742 | 30,421 | 44,175 | 44,360 | 42,922 | 46,619 | 40,075 | 36,765 | 24,981 | 26,042 | 20,571 |
| Gold (Million Fine Troy Ounces) | 1ad | 1.770 | 1.760 | 1.760 | 1.760 | 1.760 | 1.760 | 1.760 | 1.985 | 1.985 | 1.985 | 1.985 | 1.985 |
| Gold (National Valuation) | 1and | 769 | 908 | 1,123 | 1,434 | 1,514 | 1,932 | 2,497 | 3,127 | 3,326 | 2,389 | 2,387 | 2,107 |
| Monetary Authorities:Other Assets | 3..d | — | — | 24 | 73 | 55 | — | — | — | — | — | — | — |
| Monetary Authorities: Other Liabs | 4..d | 4 | 10 | — | — | — | 71 | 75 | 127 | 185 | 169 | 191 | 174 |
| Deposit Money Banks: Assets | 7a.d | 2,878 | 2,877 | 3,396 | 4,989 | 4,845 | 3,183 | 2,998 | 2,793 | 3,502 | 2,283 | 2,491 | 3,135 |
| Deposit Money Banks: Liabs | 7b.d | 7,290 | 5,513 | 5,536 | 6,126 | 5,235 | 3,542 | 3,077 | 3,861 | 2,917 | 2,444 | 2,547 | 3,261 |
| Other Banking Insts.: Assets | 7e.d | 8 | 10 | 9 | 11 | 13 | 48 | 11 | 14 | 7 | 5 | 5 | 7 |
| Other Banking Insts.: Liabs | 7f.d | 28 | 13 | 23 | 3 | 60 | 32 | 5 | 4 | 4 | 1 | 2 | 2 |
| **Monetary Authorities** | | | | | | *Millions of Pesos: End of Period* | | | | | | | |
| Foreign Assets | 11 | 58,444 | 85,145 | 98,327 | 145,386 | 160,200 | 182,371 | 207,781 | 199,561 | 212,869 | 199,450 | 268,902 | 332,549 |
| Claims on Central Government | 12a | 65,538 | 55,537 | 55,015 | 58,211 | 69,983 | 97,263 | 141,385 | 206,051 | 331,326 | 500,029 | 741,728 | 1,208,915 |
| Claims on Deposit Money Banks | 12e | 24,897 | 16,579 | 7,410 | 3,965 | 3,247 | 1,845 | 2,106 | 2,690 | 4,366 | 5,601 | 5,302 | 3,967 |
| Claims on Other Banking Insts | 12f | 116 | 14 | 14 | 14 | 18 | 17 | 8 | 8 | 8 | — | — | — |
| Reserve Money | 14 | 60,525 | 61,256 | 87,445 | 107,655 | 126,645 | 150,186 | 199,567 | 247,558 | 348,984 | 448,530 | 534,862 | 769,062 |
| of which: Currency Outside DMBs | 14a | 33,872 | 43,764 | 53,812 | 67,067 | 74,099 | 86,073 | 113,554 | 151,282 | 209,979 | 257,805 | 315,903 | 425,718 |
| Liabs. of Central Bank: Securities | 16ac | 21,817 | 35,268 | 42,066 | 57,182 | 53,110 | 54,397 | 88,576 | 84,182 | 99,855 | 110,547 | 282,135 | 416,892 |
| Foreign Liabilities | 16c | 43,385 | 30,247 | 1,470 | 1,585 | 1,694 | 12,295 | 12,667 | 13,893 | 16,175 | 21,376 | 26,659 | 38,661 |
| Central Government Deposits | 16d | 161 | 1,899 | 4,697 | 5,565 | 6,414 | 2,266 | 10,545 | 2,842 | 6,683 | 12,166 | 35,316 | 5,078 |
| Capital Accounts | 17a | 5,736 | 6,872 | 7,727 | 9,963 | 8,802 | 13,084 | 9,714 | 8,683 | 12,470 | 16,456 | 12,698 | 13,637 |
| Other Items (Net) | 17r | 17,370 | 21,733 | 17,362 | 25,625 | 36,782 | 49,268 | 30,211 | 51,153 | 64,401 | 96,006 | 124,262 | 302,101 |
| Memo Item: | | | | | | | | | | | | | |
| Total Assets | 10ra | 108,617 | 130,004 | 162,442 | 204,610 | 229,234 | 270,286 | 342,925 | 394,927 | 538,224 | 692,584 | 1,010,669 | 1,541,647 |
| **Deposit Money Banks** | | | | | | *Millions of Pesos: End of Period* | | | | | | | |
| Reserves | 20 | 26,439 | 17,122 | 33,365 | 39,845 | 51,558 | 63,125 | 85,553 | 95,930 | 138,153 | 187,749 | 214,627 | 334,908 |
| Foreign Assets | 21 | 8,559 | 8,722 | 10,423 | 15,719 | 16,733 | 12,085 | 11,921 | 12,020 | 17,219 | 14,884 | 21,299 | 40,768 |
| Claims on Central Government | 22a | 101,363 | 99,199 | 86,784 | 80,134 | 83,801 | 106,551 | 143,341 | 141,952 | 159,713 | 184,170 | 333,796 | 447,846 |
| Claims on State and Local Govts | 22b | 1,902 | 1,481 | 1,808 | 2,857 | 3,472 | 7,042 | 9,742 | 17,128 | 30,708 | 39,257 | 56,037 | 66,462 |
| Claims on Official Entities | 22bx | 591 | 317 | 358 | 371 | 294 | 299 | 581 | 474 | 377 | 354 | 171 | 5,006 |
| Claims on Private Sector | 22d | 46,092 | 60,683 | 82,561 | 113,129 | 135,920 | 149,743 | 204,430 | 295,047 | 387,489 | 508,479 | 616,661 | 838,470 |
| Demand Deposits | 24 | 22,055 | 27,478 | 24,569 | 39,148 | 37,604 | 44,996 | 59,247 | 64,001 | 111,504 | 148,674 | 219,195 | 259,405 |
| Time, Savings,& Fgn.Currency Dep | 25 | 81,485 | 95,733 | 122,427 | 143,723 | 158,391 | 184,941 | 247,833 | 314,849 | 393,249 | 501,655 | 644,127 | 960,745 |
| Foreign Liabilities | 26c | 21,679 | 16,712 | 16,992 | 19,304 | 18,079 | 13,446 | 12,235 | 16,613 | 14,345 | 15,931 | 21,784 | 42,409 |
| Central Government Deposits | 26d | 13,491 | 13,324 | 23,045 | 21,924 | 40,318 | 43,579 | 74,822 | 91,641 | 109,952 | 127,358 | 153,549 | 174,358 |
| Credit from Monetary Authorities | 26g | 29,239 | 17,415 | 7,833 | 2,479 | 2,000 | 380 | 307 | 1,961 | 3,581 | 4,734 | 4,259 | 3,000 |
| Capital Accounts | 27a | 23,045 | 26,099 | 31,947 | 35,423 | 39,297 | 46,077 | 55,165 | 67,336 | 87,494 | 117,724 | 163,336 | 221,115 |
| Other Items (Net) | 27r | −6,049 | −9,238 | −11,514 | −9,945 | −3,911 | 5,424 | 5,959 | 6,151 | 13,534 | 18,816 | 36,341 | 72,430 |
| Memo Item: | | | | | | | | | | | | | |
| Total Assets | 20ra | 219,757 | 224,849 | 254,743 | 293,635 | 342,163 | 388,144 | 511,506 | 626,795 | 800,691 | 1,012,652 | 1,366,446 | 1,877,776 |
| **Monetary Survey** | | | | | | *Millions of Pesos: End of Period* | | | | | | | |
| Foreign Assets (Net) | 31n | 1,939 | 46,907 | 90,288 | 140,216 | 157,160 | 168,715 | 194,800 | 181,075 | 199,568 | 177,027 | 241,758 | 292,248 |
| Domestic Credit | 32 | 201,950 | 202,007 | 198,799 | 227,226 | 246,756 | 315,069 | 414,121 | 566,177 | 792,986 | 1,092,765 | 1,559,528 | 2,387,264 |
| Claims on Central Govt. (Net) | 32an | 153,249 | 139,512 | 114,058 | 110,856 | 107,052 | 157,968 | 199,360 | 253,520 | 374,404 | 544,675 | 886,659 | 1,477,325 |
| Claims on State & Local Govts | 32b | 1,902 | 1,481 | 1,808 | 2,857 | 3,472 | 7,042 | 9,742 | 17,128 | 30,708 | 39,257 | 56,037 | 66,462 |
| Claims on Official Entities | 32bx | 591 | 317 | 358 | 371 | 294 | 299 | 581 | 474 | 377 | 354 | 171 | 5,006 |
| Claims on Private Sector | 32d | 46,092 | 60,683 | 82,561 | 113,129 | 135,920 | 149,743 | 204,430 | 295,047 | 387,489 | 508,479 | 616,661 | 838,470 |
| Claims on Other Banking Insts | 32f | 116 | 14 | 14 | 14 | 18 | 17 | 8 | 8 | 8 | — | — | — |
| Money | 34 | 55,927 | 71,242 | 78,381 | 106,215 | 111,703 | 131,069 | 172,801 | 215,282 | 321,483 | 406,478 | 535,098 | 685,123 |
| Quasi-Money | 35 | 81,485 | 95,733 | 122,427 | 143,723 | 158,391 | 184,941 | 247,833 | 314,849 | 393,249 | 501,655 | 644,127 | 960,745 |
| Capital Accounts | 37a | 28,781 | 32,971 | 39,673 | 45,386 | 48,099 | 59,161 | 64,879 | 76,019 | 99,964 | 134,180 | 176,034 | 234,752 |
| Other Items (Net) | 37r | 37,695 | 48,968 | 48,606 | 72,119 | 85,722 | 108,613 | 123,408 | 141,102 | 177,857 | 227,478 | 446,027 | 798,892 |
| Money plus Quasi-Money | 35l | 137,412 | 166,975 | 200,808 | 249,937 | 270,094 | 316,010 | 420,633 | 530,131 | 714,732 | 908,133 | 1,179,225 | 1,645,868 |

|  |  | 2004 | 2005 | 2006 | 2007 | 2008 | 2009 | 2010 | 2011 | 2012 | 2013 | 2014 | 2015 |
|---|---|---|---|---|---|---|---|---|---|---|---|---|---|
| **Other Banking Institutions** | | | | | | *Millions of Pesos: End of Period* | | | | | | | |
| Reserves................................... | 40 | 79 | 126 | 150 | 254 | 314 | 283 | 262 | 380 | 531 | 650 | 708 | 1,066 |
| Foreign Assets........................... | 41 | 25 | 31 | 26 | 35 | 46 | 181 | 45 | 59 | 36 | 32 | 39 | 88 |
| Claims on Central Government....... | 42a | 525 | 173 | 170 | 138 | 145 | 121 | 399 | 324 | 442 | 114 | 802 | 169 |
| Claims on State & Local Govts........ | 42b | — | — | — | — | — | — | — | — | — | — | — | — |
| Claims on Official Entities.............. | 42bx | — | — | — | — | — | — | — | — | — | — | — | — |
| Claims on Private Sector................ | 42d | 879 | 1,378 | 2,705 | 4,362 | 5,647 | 5,203 | 6,444 | 10,206 | 13,812 | 18,180 | 16,341 | 19,827 |
| Claims on Deposit Money Banks...... | 42e | 128 | 90 | 115 | 207 | 170 | 199 | 211 | 272 | 427 | 479 | 590 | 499 |
| Time, Savings,& Fgn.Currency Dep... | 45 | 203 | 286 | 461 | 719 | 623 | 1,016 | 1,198 | 1,444 | 2,207 | 2,408 | 3,283 | 3,159 |
| Foreign Liabilities........................ | 46c | 82 | 39 | 72 | 10 | 209 | 122 | 18 | 18 | 19 | 7 | 20 | 20 |
| Central Government Deposits.......... | 46d | — | — | — | — | 50 | 109 | 3 | — | — | — | — | — |
| Credit from Monetary Authorities..... | 46g | 116 | 14 | 14 | 14 | 18 | 17 | 8 | 8 | 8 | — | — | — |
| Capital Accounts......................... | 47a | 834 | 819 | 1,068 | 1,335 | 2,083 | 2,257 | 2,387 | 2,781 | 3,326 | 3,965 | 4,877 | 5,748 |
| Other Items (Net).......................... | 47r | 401 | 641 | 1,552 | 2,918 | 3,339 | 2,466 | 3,745 | 6,990 | 9,688 | 13,075 | 10,301 | 12,723 |
| Memo Item: | | | | | | | | | | | | | |
| Total Assets................................ | 40ra | 1,727 | 1,948 | 3,484 | 5,440 | 7,197 | 6,564 | 8,026 | 12,250 | 16,384 | 20,738 | 19,567 | 23,319 |
| **Banking Survey** | | | | | | *Millions of Pesos: End of Period* | | | | | | | |
| Foreign Assets (Net)...................... | 51n | 1,881 | 46,900 | 90,243 | 140,242 | 156,997 | 168,774 | 181,115 | 199,585 | 177,052 | 241,778 | 292,316 |
| Domestic Credit........................... | 52 | 203,239 | 203,543 | 201,660 | 231,713 | 252,480 | 320,266 | 420,952 | 576,700 | 807,232 | 1,111,058 | 1,576,671 | 2,407,260 |
| Claims on Central Govt. (Net)........ | 52an | 153,774 | 139,685 | 114,228 | 110,994 | 107,147 | 157,980 | 199,756 | 253,845 | 374,846 | 544,789 | 887,461 | 1,477,495 |
| Claims on State & Local Govts....... | 52b | 1,902 | 1,481 | 1,808 | 2,857 | 3,472 | 7,042 | 9,742 | 17,128 | 30,708 | 39,257 | 56,037 | 66,462 |
| Claims on Official Entities.............. | 52bx | 591 | 317 | 358 | 471 | 294 | 299 | 581 | 474 | 377 | 354 | 171 | 5,006 |
| Claims on Private Sector................ | 52d | 46,971 | 62,061 | 85,266 | 117,491 | 141,567 | 154,945 | 210,874 | 305,253 | 401,301 | 526,659 | 633,002 | 858,297 |
| Liquid Liabilities.......................... | 55l | 137,536 | 167,134 | 201,119 | 250,403 | 270,404 | 316,742 | 421,570 | 531,195 | 716,408 | 909,891 | 1,181,800 | 1,647,961 |
| Capital Accounts......................... | 57a | 29,615 | 33,790 | 40,741 | 46,720 | 50,182 | 61,418 | 67,267 | 78,800 | 103,290 | 138,145 | 180,911 | 240,500 |
| Other Items (Net).......................... | 57r | 37,968 | 49,519 | 50,043 | 74,831 | 88,891 | 110,880 | 126,942 | 147,820 | 187,118 | 240,074 | 455,738 | 811,116 |
| **Money (National Definitions)** | | | | | | *Millions of Pesos: End of Period* | | | | | | | |
| Base Money................................ | 19ma | 52,477 | 54,710 | 80,066 | 99,279 | 109,449 | 122,350 | 160,408 | 222,922 | 307,352 | 377,197 | 462,564 | 623,890 |
| M1............................................ | 59ma | 64,468 | 82,064 | 98,458 | 123,931 | 144,856 | 164,193 | 223,007 | 288,767 | 397,842 | 496,728 | 640,870 | 804,666 |
| M2............................................ | 59mb | 91,931 | 112,200 | 133,680 | 168,529 | 196,265 | 229,041 | 317,628 | 392,388 | 530,022 | 662,411 | 859,921 | 1,133,787 |
| M3............................................ | 59mc | 147,498 | 177,180 | 220,553 | 267,815 | 305,422 | 352,479 | 485,229 | 605,084 | 796,440 | 999,888 | 1,283,153 | 1,761,355 |
| M3 Total.................................... | 59mca | 147,793 | 177,765 | 222,057 | 269,932 | 307,192 | 353,896 | 486,243 | 607,164 | 798,788 | 1,001,333 | 1,284,545 | 1,763,508 |
| **Interest Rates** | | | | | | *Percent Per Annum* | | | | | | | |
| Money Market Rate........................ | 60b | 1.96 | 4.11 | 7.20 | 8.67 | 10.07 | 10.23 | 9.09 | 9.98 | 9.79 | 13.10 | 17.90 | 22.01 |
| Money Market Rate (Fgn. Cur.)....... | 60b.f | 2.03 | 2.86 | 3.32 | 4.55 | 3.37 | 1.93 | 2.33 | .83 | 1.91 | . . . . | . . . . | 2.75 |
| Savings Rate................................ | 60k | .73 | .77 | .82 | .62 | .57 | .54 | .35 | .28 | .26 | .24 | .21 | .19 |
| Savings Rate (Fgn. Cur.)................. | 60k.f | .13 | .13 | .13 | .12 | .11 | .12 | .06 | .05 | .06 | .06 | .04 | .03 |
| Deposit Rate............................... | 60l | 2.61 | 3.76 | 6.42 | 7.97 | 11.05 | 11.60 | 9.17 | 10.68 | 12.02 | 14.85 | 20.42 | 21.17 |
| Deposit Rate (Fgn. Currency)........... | 60l.f | .38 | .43 | .78 | 1.12 | 1.34 | .95 | .31 | .29 | .47 | .48 | .87 | 1.59 |
| Lending Rate............................... | 60p | 6.78 | 6.16 | 8.63 | 11.05 | 19.47 | † 15.66 | 10.56 | 14.09 | 14.06 | 17.15 | 24.01 | 24.92 |
| Lending Rate (Fgn. Currency).......... | 60p.f | 6.54 | 5.13 | 4.98 | 5.59 | 5.80 | 6.01 | 3.30 | 2.72 | 4.97 | 4.94 | 5.12 | 5.44 |
| **Prices, Production, Labor** | | | | | | *Index Numbers (2010=100): Period Averages* | | | | | | | |
| Share Prices............................... | 62 | 43.4 | 58.6 | 68.8 | 84.8 | 69.5 | 63.9 | 100.0 | 122.1 | 98.0 | 156.4 | 316.3 | 435.4 |
| Producer Prices............................ | 63 | 53.1 | 57.6 | 63.9 | 71.4 | 81.8 | 86.9 | 100.0 | 113.8 | 127.6 | 148.5 | 187.8 | . . . . |
| CPI (IPCNu) (09/13 - 10/14=100).... | 64 | . . . . | . . . . | . . . . | . . . . | . . . . | . . . . | . . . . | . . . . | . . . . | . . . . | † 105.5 | . . . . |
| Consumer Prices (CPI-GBA)............ | 64a | 59.1 | 64.8 | 71.9 | † 78.2 | † 84.9 | † 90.3 | † 100.0 | † 109.5 | † 120.4 | † 133.2 | . . . . | . . . . |
| Manuf. Prod.,Seas.Adj.(2005=100).. | 66eyc | 89.5 | 100.0 | 108.2 | 116.2 | 124.1 | . . . . | . . . . | . . . . | . . . . | . . . . | . . . . | . . . . |
| Crude Petroleum Prod.(2005=100).. | 66aa | 104.8 | 100.0 | 98.6 | 96.2 | 86.3 | . . . . | . . . . | . . . . | . . . . | . . . . | . . . . | . . . . |
| | | | | | | *Number in Thousands: Period Averages* | | | | | | | |
| Labor Force................................ | 67d | 10,702 | 10,764 | 11,038 | 11,142 | 11,154 | 11,386 | 11,412 | 11,598 | 11,687 | 11,779 | 11,918 | . . . . |
| Employment................................ | 67e | 9,255 | 9,526 | 9,926 | 10,206 | 10,280 | 10,402 | 10,532 | 10,766 | 10,844 | 10,943 | 11,052 | . . . . |
| Unemployment............................. | 67c | 1,447 | 1,239 | 1,112 | 936 | 874 | 984 | 880 | 833 | 843 | 836 | 866 | . . . . |
| Unemployment Rate (%)................. | 67r | 13.5 | 11.5 | 10.1 | 8.4 | 7.8 | 8.6 | 7.7 | 7.2 | 7.2 | 7.1 | 7.3 | . . . . |
| **Intl. Transactions & Positions** | | | | | | *Millions of US Dollars* | | | | | | | |
| Exports..................................... | 70..d | 34,576 | 40,351 | 46,568 | 55,779 | 70,588 | 56,065 | 64,722 | 84,269 | 75,218 | 83,026 | 71,936 | 59,706 |
| Wheat..................................... | 70d.d | 1,367 | 1,280 | 1,478 | 2,015 | 2,570 | 1,039 | 905 | 2,498 | 2,951 | . . . . | 649 | . . . . |
| Imports, c.i.f............................... | 71..d | 22,445 | 28,693 | 34,158 | 44,707 | 57,413 | 39,105 | 48,048 | 74,319 | 68,505 | 74,002 | 65,323 | 59,789 |
| Imports, f.o.b............................... | 71.vd | 21,311 | 27,301 | 32,592 | 42,524 | 54,152 | 37,461 | 50,183 | 71,125 | 65,555 | 70,870 | 62,520 | . . . . |
| | | | | | | *2010=100* | | | | | | | |
| Volume of Exports......................... | 72 | 80.5 | 89.8 | 93.9 | 99.4 | 98.5 | 87.9 | 100.0 | 103.4 | 96.5 | 100.0 | 90.0 | . . . . |
| Wheat (2000=100)..................... | 72d | 90.6 | . . . . | . . . . | . . . . | . . . . | . . . . | 100.0 | 122.1 | . . . . | . . . . | . . . . | . . . . |
| Volume of Imports......................... | 73 | 50.2 | 59.4 | 67.0 | 82.0 | 93.5 | 71.5 | 100.0 | 122.1 | 113.7 | 116.7 | 103.1 | . . . . |
| | | | | | | *2010=100: Indices of Unit Values in US Dollars* | | | | | | | |
| Unit Value of Exports/Export Prices.. | 74..d | 63.0 | 66.0 | 72.7 | 82.5 | 104.3 | 92.9 | 100.0 | 119.2 | 121.9 | 119.7 | 116.9 | . . . . |
| Wheat..................................... | 74d.d | 59.7 | 52.0 | 65.7 | 89.8 | 123.9 | 85.7 | 100.0 | 130.5 | 106.4 | 134.5 | 138.8 | . . . . |
| Unit Value of Imports/Import Prices.. | 75..d | 78.8 | 85.0 | 89.7 | 96.1 | 108.2 | 95.5 | 100.0 | 107.1 | 105.3 | 111.0 | 111.2 | . . . . |

# Argentina 213

| Balance of Payments | | 2004 | 2005 | 2006 | 2007 | 2008 | 2009 | 2010 | 2011 | 2012 | 2013 | 2014 | 2015 |
|---|---|---|---|---|---|---|---|---|---|---|---|---|---|
| | | | | | | | *Millions of US Dollars* | | | | | | |
| A. Current Account* | 109bx | 3,211.8 | 5,273.8 | 7,767.0 | 7,354.4 | 6,755.9 | 8,206.6 | −1,516.5 | −4,471.2 | −1,439.8 | −12,142.8 | −8,074.7 | −15,934.2 |
| Goods, credit (exports) | 1a9cx | 34,588.8 | 40,434.2 | 46,593.8 | 56,032.4 | 70,148.6 | 55,790.8 | 68,195.3 | 82,926.0 | 79,976.3 | 75,974.8 | 68,331.0 | 56,719.6 |
| Goods, debit (imports) | 1a9dx | 21,311.1 | 27,300.1 | 32,587.9 | 42,524.5 | 54,596.2 | 37,146.1 | 54,158.8 | 70,768.8 | 65,042.7 | 71,293.0 | 62,428.3 | 57,205.3 |
| Balance on goods | 1a9bx | 13,277.7 | 13,134.1 | 14,005.9 | 13,507.9 | 15,552.4 | 18,644.7 | 14,036.6 | 12,157.2 | 14,933.5 | 4,681.8 | 5,902.8 | −485.7 |
| Services, credit (exports) | 1b9cx | 5,168.5 | 6,458.1 | 7,837.4 | 10,136.9 | 11,840.0 | 10,677.4 | 13,358.5 | 15,289.5 | 15,012.6 | 14,561.4 | 13,694.8 | 13,860.7 |
| Services, debit (imports) | 1b9dx | 6,512.5 | 7,496.9 | 8,385.7 | 10,701.7 | 13,254.0 | 12,081.4 | 14,614.2 | 17,469.2 | 17,991.1 | 18,281.7 | 16,765.3 | 17,818.1 |
| Balance on Goods & Services | 1z9bx | 11,933.6 | 12,095.2 | 13,457.7 | 12,943.1 | 14,138.4 | 17,240.6 | 12,780.9 | 9,977.5 | 11,955.1 | 961.5 | 2,832.2 | −4,443.0 |
| Primary income: credit | 1c9cx | 3,720.8 | 4,311.8 | 5,685.3 | 6,624.6 | 5,620.4 | 3,523.2 | 2,765.2 | 3,235.9 | 2,254.4 | 2,425.5 | 2,625.3 | 2,367.0 |
| Primary income: debit | 1c9dx | 13,003.6 | 11,617.2 | 11,835.3 | 12,566.8 | 13,172.7 | 12,604.9 | 16,654.8 | 17,118.3 | 15,108.7 | 14,704.1 | 13,357.6 | 13,446.5 |
| Balance on gds, serv. & prim. inc. | 1y9bx | 2,650.8 | 4,789.9 | 7,307.6 | 7,000.9 | 6,586.2 | 8,158.9 | −1,108.7 | −3,904.9 | −899.2 | −11,317.1 | −7,900.0 | −15,522.5 |
| Secondary income: credit | 1d9ca | 1,109.7 | 1,225.2 | 1,409.3 | 1,627.5 | 1,867.3 | 1,878.9 | 1,964.8 | 2,256.4 | 2,118.4 | 2,248.2 | 2,010.0 | 1,857.5 |
| Secondary income: debit | 1d9da | 548.7 | 741.3 | 949.8 | 1,274.1 | 1,697.6 | 1,831.3 | 2,372.6 | 2,822.7 | 2,658.9 | 3,073.8 | 2,184.7 | 2,269.2 |
| B. Capital Account* | 209ba | 196.3 | 88.9 | 97.1 | 121.1 | 180.9 | 74.0 | 89.0 | 62.3 | 47.8 | 33.3 | 54.7 | 48.1 |
| Capital account: credit | 209ca | 200.6 | 92.7 | 106.5 | 140.8 | 202.2 | 82.1 | 103.3 | 71.3 | 72.2 | 55.3 | 71.1 | 77.7 |
| Capital account: debit | 209da | 4.3 | 3.8 | 9.4 | 19.7 | 21.2 | 8.1 | 14.2 | 9.0 | 24.3 | 22.0 | 16.3 | 29.6 |
| Balance on current & capital acct. | 129dx | 3,408.1 | 5,362.7 | 7,864.1 | 7,475.5 | 6,936.8 | 8,280.6 | −1,427.5 | −4,408.9 | −1,391.9 | −12,109.5 | −8,020.0 | −15,886.0 |
| C. Financial Account* | 309na | 10,892.4 | −1,954.9 | −5,178.1 | −4,054.6 | 11,298.5 | 8,520.4 | −13,383.3 | 6,740.0 | 1,719.3 | −1,553.9 | −7,178.9 | −11,442.6 |
| Direct investment: assets | 3a9aa | 676.0 | 1,311.1 | 2,438.7 | 1,504.2 | 1,390.9 | 711.5 | 964.8 | 1,488.0 | 1,054.9 | 890.0 | 1,920.5 | 1,138.8 |
| Equity & investment fund shares | 3aaaa | 686.9 | 1,311.1 | 2,438.7 | 1,504.2 | 1,390.9 | 711.5 | 964.8 | 1,488.0 | 1,054.9 | 890.0 | 1,920.5 | 1,138.8 |
| Debt instruments | 3abaa | −10.9 | | | | | | | | | | | |
| Direct investment: liabilities | 3a9la | 4,124.7 | 5,265.3 | 5,537.3 | 6,473.2 | 9,725.6 | 4,017.2 | 11,332.7 | 10,839.9 | 15,323.9 | 9,821.7 | 5,065.3 | 11,654.9 |
| Equity & investment fund shares | 3aala | 3,096.0 | 5,746.5 | 5,274.3 | 4,627.5 | 4,948.9 | 5,027.0 | 7,826.0 | 8,240.4 | 12,203.8 | 10,604.7 | 6,009.9 | 9,438.6 |
| Debt instruments | 3abla | 1,028.7 | −481.3 | 263.0 | 1,845.6 | 4,776.6 | −1,009.8 | 3,506.7 | 2,599.6 | 3,120.1 | −783.0 | −944.5 | 2,216.3 |
| Portfolio investment: assets | 3b9aa | 76.8 | −1,368.3 | 1.0 | 1.6 | 11.6 | 1.5 | −1,261.4 | 9.4 | 14.9 | 19.1 | 9.5 | 29.0 |
| Equity & investment fund shares | 3baaa | 72.2 | 4.4 | −6.2 | −12.7 | −.6 | | | | | | −2.9 | 15.3 |
| Debt securities | 3bbaa | 4.6 | −1,372.7 | 7.3 | 14.2 | 12.2 | 1.5 | −1,261.4 | 9.4 | 14.9 | 19.1 | 12.5 | 13.7 |
| Portfolio investment: liabilities | 3b9la | −9,338.8 | −1,730.8 | 7,921.4 | 7,097.7 | −7,062.1 | −3,156.5 | 8,868.5 | −1,576.0 | −1,166.5 | −338.8 | 6,214.8 | 231.9 |
| Equity & investment fund shares | 3aala | −86.2 | −48.1 | 706.7 | 1,784.9 | −530.6 | −211.9 | −71.0 | −208.2 | −134.9 | 341.9 | 217.9 | 239.1 |
| Debt securities | 3bbla | −9,252.7 | −1,682.7 | 7,214.7 | 5,312.8 | −6,531.5 | −2,944.6 | 8,939.6 | −1,367.8 | −1,031.6 | −680.7 | 5,997.0 | −7.3 |
| Fin. der.& empl.stk.ops.(ESOs): net. | 3c9na | — | — | 126.6 | 564.6 | 934.7 | 1,248.3 | −712.3 | 2,356.2 | 2,908.2 | −32.4 | −168.2 | −25.0 |
| Fin. der. & ESOs.: assets | 3c9aa | . . . . | . . . . | . . . . | . . . . | . . . . | . . . . | . . . . | . . . . | . . . . | . . . . | . . . . | . . . . |
| Fin. der. & ESOs.: liabilities | 3c9la | — | — | −126.6 | −564.6 | −934.7 | −1,248.3 | 712.3 | −2,356.2 | −2,908.2 | 32.4 | 168.2 | 25.0 |
| Other investment: assets | 3d9aa | 2,346.7 | −2,004.6 | 4,500.6 | 11,728.7 | 14,384.5 | 6,823.3 | 9,392.0 | 18,612.4 | 9,972.1 | 4,370.1 | 1,639.8 | 8,653.7 |
| Other equity | 3daaa | | | | | | | | | | | | |
| Debt instruments | 3dzaa | 2,346.7 | −2,004.6 | 4,500.6 | 11,728.7 | 14,384.5 | 6,823.3 | 9,392.0 | 18,612.4 | 9,972.1 | 4,370.1 | 1,639.8 | 8,653.7 |
| Other investment: liabilities | 3d9la | −2,578.8 | −3,641.4 | −1,213.7 | 4,282.8 | 2,759.7 | −596.3 | 1,565.1 | 6,462.1 | −1,926.7 | −2,682.2 | −699.6 | 9,352.3 |
| Other equity | 3dala | . . . . | | | | | | | | | | | |
| Debt instruments | 3dzla | −2,578.8 | −3,641.4 | −1,213.7 | 4,282.8 | 2,759.7 | −596.3 | 1,565.1 | 6,462.1 | −1,926.7 | −2,682.2 | −699.6 | 9,352.3 |
| Curr.+ cap.− finan. acct. balance | 4y9na | −7,484.3 | 7,317.6 | 13,042.3 | 11,530.1 | −4,361.7 | −239.7 | 11,955.8 | −11,148.9 | −3,111.2 | −10,555.6 | −841.1 | −4,443.4 |
| D. Net Errors and Omissions | 409na | 490.9 | 336.3 | 1,192.2 | 39.4 | 1,076.9 | −352.4 | −1,675.1 | 343.5 | −518.4 | −3,180.3 | −8.7 | −3,111.4 |
| E. Reserves and Related Items | 4z9na | −6,993.4 | 7,653.9 | 14,234.5 | 11,569.5 | −3,284.8 | −592.1 | 10,280.8 | −10,805.4 | −3,629.7 | −13,735.9 | −849.8 | −7,554.8 |
| Reserve assets | 3e9aa | 5,282.6 | 9,088.3 | 3,458.3 | 13,074.6 | 23.7 | 1,326.7 | 4,212.3 | −6,095.4 | −3,307.5 | −11,830.3 | 1,382.7 | −4,741.5 |
| Credit and loans from the IMF | 3dcla | −2,038.0 | −3,581.8 | −9,630.4 | — | — | — | — | — | — | — | — | — |
| Exceptional financing | 409la | 14,314.1 | 5,016.3 | −1,145.7 | 1,505.1 | 3,308.6 | 1,918.8 | −6,068.4 | 4,709.9 | 322.1 | 1,905.6 | 2,232.5 | 2,813.3 |

*Excludes components in group E

| International Investment Position | | 2004 | 2005 | 2006 | 2007 | 2008 | 2009 | 2010 | 2011 | 2012 | 2013 | 2014 | 2015 |
|---|---|---|---|---|---|---|---|---|---|---|---|---|---|
| | | | | | | | *Millions of US Dollars* | | | | | | |
| Assets | 809aa | 154,672.9 | 165,854.9 | 177,994.4 | 206,097.2 | 210,708.0 | 223,776.1 | 236,549.1 | 249,129.6 | 256,770.3 | 261,839.5 | 271,956.3 | . . . . |
| Direct investment | 8a9aa | 21,803.8 | 23,339.9 | 25,896.6 | 27,543.4 | 28,788.8 | 29,535.6 | 30,328.3 | 31,891.3 | 32,916.2 | 34,517.2 | 36,149.5 | . . . . |
| Equity & investment fund shares | 8aaaa | 21,803.8 | 23,339.9 | 25,896.6 | 27,543.4 | 28,788.8 | 29,535.6 | 30,328.3 | 31,891.3 | 32,916.2 | 34,517.2 | 36,149.5 | . . . . |
| Debt instruments | 8abaa | . . . . | | | | | | | | | | | . . . . |
| Portfolio investment | 8b9aa | 1,016.5 | 191.6 | 191.8 | 194.9 | 1,430.7 | 1,684.1 | 420.2 | 226.0 | 238.5 | 258.0 | 262.4 | . . . . |
| Equity & investment fund shares | 8baaa | 73.0 | 76.5 | 70.0 | 58.0 | 57.0 | 57.0 | 64.0 | 62.0 | 69.9 | 82.2 | 79.2 | . . . . |
| Debt securities | 8bbaa | 943.5 | 115.1 | 121.8 | 136.9 | 1,373.7 | 1,627.1 | 356.2 | 164.0 | 168.5 | 175.9 | 183.2 | . . . . |
| Fin. der.(oth.than reserves) & ESOs | 8c9aa | . . . . | . . . . | . . . . | | | | | | | | | . . . . |
| Other investment | 8d9aa | 111,329.7 | 109,810.6 | 119,386.6 | 132,185.8 | 134,103.5 | 144,590.3 | 153,612.8 | 170,637.3 | 180,325.8 | 196,464.4 | 204,137.0 | . . . . |
| Other equity | 8daaa | . . . . | | | | | | | | | | | . . . . |
| Debt instruments | 8dzaa | 111,329.7 | 109,810.6 | 119,386.6 | 132,185.8 | 134,103.5 | 144,590.3 | 153,612.8 | 170,637.3 | 180,325.8 | 196,464.4 | 204,137.0 | . . . . |
| Reserve assets | 8e9aa | 20,522.9 | 32,512.9 | 32,519.5 | 46,173.1 | 46,385.0 | 47,966.2 | 52,187.8 | 46,375.0 | 43,289.8 | 30,599.9 | 31,407.3 | . . . . |
| Liabilities | 809la | 152,035.9 | 145,021.6 | 156,583.3 | 172,156.2 | 153,399.3 | 168,055.2 | 194,521.5 | 200,119.9 | 202,175.6 | 200,504.2 | 198,061.9 | . . . . |
| Direct investment | 8a9la | 52,507.3 | 55,138.8 | 60,253.3 | 67,573.6 | 77,066.3 | 79,871.3 | 88,455.5 | 93,198.8 | 100,438.2 | 93,691.5 | 82,215.7 | . . . . |
| Equity & investment fund shares | 8aala | 36,897.0 | 40,694.0 | 46,276.3 | 50,921.9 | 55,585.8 | 60,461.3 | 66,385.8 | 67,663.5 | 70,998.1 | 63,034.0 | 53,905.5 | . . . . |
| Debt instruments | 8abla | 15,610.3 | 14,444.8 | 13,977.0 | 16,651.7 | 21,480.5 | 19,410.0 | 22,069.7 | 25,535.3 | 29,440.2 | 30,657.4 | 28,310.3 | . . . . |
| Portfolio investment | 8b9la | 36,121.7 | 33,794.0 | 46,351.9 | 48,971.5 | 17,983.5 | 29,154.8 | 41,728.5 | 32,982.4 | 32,359.4 | 37,960.4 | 46,244.5 | . . . . |
| Equity & investment fund shares | 8aala | 2,371.0 | 2,496.5 | 4,843.2 | 6,785.9 | 2,510.2 | 3,493.8 | 5,375.5 | 3,376.9 | 4,161.3 | 6,210.6 | 7,795.0 | . . . . |
| Debt securities | 8bbla | 33,750.7 | 31,297.4 | 41,508.8 | 42,185.6 | 15,473.3 | 25,661.0 | 36,353.0 | 29,605.5 | 28,198.1 | 31,749.8 | 38,449.5 | . . . . |
| Fin. der.(oth.than reserves) & ESOs | 8c9la | . . . . | 1,832.1 | 5,322.6 | 4,641.4 | 1,177.6 | 2,282.9 | 6,669.1 | 4,805.5 | 2,687.2 | 3,588.5 | 2,760.1 | . . . . |
| Other investment | 8d9la | 63,407.0 | 54,256.7 | 44,655.4 | 50,969.7 | 57,171.8 | 56,746.2 | 57,668.4 | 69,133.1 | 66,690.8 | 65,263.8 | 66,841.6 | . . . . |
| Other equity | 8dala | . . . . | . . . . | . . . . | . . . . | . . . . | . . . . | . . . . | . . . . | . . . . | . . . . | . . . . | . . . . |
| Debt instruments | 8dzla | 63,407.0 | 54,256.7 | 44,655.4 | 50,969.7 | 57,171.8 | 56,746.2 | 57,668.4 | 69,133.1 | 66,690.8 | 65,263.8 | 66,841.6 | . . . . |

# Argentina 213

|  |  | 2004 | 2005 | 2006 | 2007 | 2008 | 2009 | 2010 | 2011 | 2012 | 2013 | 2014 | 2015 |
|---|---|---|---|---|---|---|---|---|---|---|---|---|---|
| **National Accounts** |  |  |  |  |  | *Millions of Pesos* |  |  |  |  |  |  |  |
| Househ.Cons.Expend.,incl.NPISHs.... | 96fa | 281,189 | 326,276 | 386,305 | 475,876 | 598,839 | 667,375 | 826,794 | 1,039,072 | 1,235,401 | 2,220,192 | 2,847,938 | .... |
| Government Consumption Expend... | 91fa | 49,826 | 63,359 | 81,248 | 105,013 | 139,336 | 174,002 | 215,278 | 278,961 | 359,628 | 517,847 | 698,823 | .... |
| Gross Fixed Capital Formation......... | 93ea | 85,800 | 114,132 | 152,838 | 196,622 | 240,621 | 239,637 | 317,417 | 415,837 | 471,364 | 568,491 | 757,233 | .... |
| Changes in Inventories.................... | 93ia | −2,014 | −3,102 | −2,124 | 94 | 18,582 | 3,176 | 35,469 | 65,934 | 47,852 | 45,243 | 107,696 | .... |
| Exports of Goods and Services.......... | 90ca | 115,075 | 133,346 | 162,035 | 200,080 | 251,367 | 244,569 | 313,150 | 401,992 | 426,670 | 484,709 | 654,371 | .... |
| Imports of Goods and Services (-)..... | 98ca | 82,233 | 102,072 | 125,863 | 165,230 | 210,557 | 183,301 | 265,452 | 359,774 | 376,670 | 495,419 | 641,365 | .... |
| Gross Domestic Product (GDP)......... | 99b.a | 447,643 | 531,939 | 654,439 | 812,456 | † 1,038,188 | † 1,145,458 | † 1,442,656 | † 1,842,022 | † 2,164,246 | † 3,339,630 | † 4,425,695 | .... |
| Net Primary Income from Abroad..... | 98na | −26,087 | −18,029 | −15,843 | −16,384 | −11,411 | 35,225 | 39,582 | 44,689 | 45,995 | 57,910 | .... | .... |
| Gross National Income (GNI)............ | 99aa | 421,556 | 513,910 | 638,596 | 796,072 | 1,010,096 | 1,110,234 | 1,403,073 | 1,797,333 | 2,118,251 | 3,281,720 | .... | .... |
| GDP Volume 1993 Prices................ | 99bup | 279,141 | 304,764 | 330,565 | 359,189 | † 384,201 | † 386,704 | † 422,130 | † 459,571 | † 468,301 | .... | .... | .... |
| GDP Volume 2004 Prices................ | 99bup | 535,828 | 585,116 | 634,055 | 684,798 | † 706,041 | † 706,398 | † 770,936 | † 836,889 | † 844,807 | † 869,520 | † 872,816 | .... |
| GDP Volume (2010=100)............... | 99bvp | † 69.5 | 75.9 | 82.2 | † 88.8 | † 91.6 | † 91.6 | † 100.0 | † 108.6 | † 109.6 | † 112.8 | † 113.2 | .... |
| GDP Deflator (2010=100).............. | 99bip | 44.6 | 48.6 | 55.2 | 63.4 | 78.6 | 86.7 | 100.0 | 117.6 | 136.9 | 205.2 | 271.0 | .... |
|  |  |  |  |  |  | *Millions: Midyear Estimates* |  |  |  |  |  |  |  |
| **Population**................................ | 99z | 38.73 | 39.15 | 39.56 | 39.97 | 40.38 | 40.80 | 41.22 | 41.66 | 42.10 | 42.54 | 42.98 | 43.42 |

| | | 2004 | 2005 | 2006 | 2007 | 2008 | 2009 | 2010 | 2011 | 2012 | 2013 | 2014 | 2015 |
|---|---|---|---|---|---|---|---|---|---|---|---|---|---|
| **Exchange Rates** | | | | | | *Drams per SDR: End of Period* | | | | | | | |
| Official Rate.................... | aa | 754.51 | 643.44 | 546.85 | 480.74 | 472.45 | 592.41 | 559.71 | 592.26 | 620.27 | 624.69 | 688.14 | 670.35 |
| | | | | | | *Drams per US Dollar: End of Period (ae) Period Average (rf)* | | | | | | | |
| Official Rate.................... | ae | 485.84 | 450.19 | 363.50 | 304.22 | 306.73 | 377.89 | 363.44 | 385.77 | 403.58 | 405.64 | 474.97 | 483.75 |
| Official Rate.................... | rf | 533.45 | 457.69 | 416.04 | 342.08 | 305.97 | 363.28 | 373.66 | 372.50 | 401.76 | 409.63 | 415.92 | 477.92 |
| | | | | | | *Index Numbers (2010=100): Period Averages* | | | | | | | |
| Nominal Effective Exchange Rate..... | nec | 72.40 | 84.01 | 92.26 | 105.36 | 112.01 | 102.62 | 100.00 | 97.15 | 94.86 | 93.99 | 97.66 | 100.45 |
| CPI-Based Real Effect. Ex. Rate........ | rec | 70.48 | 78.67 | 85.42 | 97.51 | 105.86 | 97.92 | 100.00 | 100.09 | 96.82 | 97.97 | 101.79 | 104.88 |
| **Fund Position** | | | | | | *Millions of SDRs: End of Period* | | | | | | | |
| Quota.................................... | 2f.s | 92.00 | 92.00 | 92.00 | 92.00 | 92.00 | 92.00 | 92.00 | 92.00 | 92.00 | 92.00 | 92.00 | 92.00 |
| SDR Holdings........................... | 1b.s | 7.70 | 7.12 | 9.28 | 6.08 | 1.89 | 79.50 | 21.74 | 37.15 | 20.64 | 1.23 | 4.31 | 2.06 |
| Reserve Position in the Fund........... | 1c.s | — | — | — | — | — | — | — | — | — | — | — | — |
| Total Fund Cred.&Loans Outstg. | 2tl | 140.13 | 123.42 | 108.80 | 99.92 | 87.50 | 374.25 | 481.01 | 538.97 | 504.97 | 379.75 | 305.14 | 299.00 |
| SDR Allocations.......................... | 1bd | — | — | — | — | — | 87.99 | 87.99 | 87.99 | 87.99 | 87.99 | 87.99 | 87.99 |
| **International Liquidity** | | | | | | *Millions of US Dollars Unless Otherwise Indicated: End of Period* | | | | | | | |
| Total Reserves minus Gold.............. | 1l.d | 547.76 | 669.48 | 1,071.92 | 1,659.09 | 1,406.80 | 2,003.62 | 1,865.82 | 1,932.47 | 1,799.37 | 2,251.61 | 1,489.44 | 1,775.29 |
| SDR Holdings.......................... | 1b.d | 11.96 | 10.18 | 13.96 | 9.60 | 2.91 | 124.64 | 33.48 | 57.03 | 31.72 | 1.90 | 6.24 | 2.86 |
| Reserve Position in the Fund.......... | 1c.d | | | | | | | | | | | | |
| Foreign Exchange........................ | 1d.d | 535.80 | 659.30 | 1,057.96 | 1,649.49 | 1,403.89 | 1,878.98 | 1,832.34 | 1,875.44 | 1,767.65 | 2,249.71 | 1,483.20 | 1,772.43 |
| Gold (Million Fine Troy Ounces)........ | 1ad | — | — | — | — | — | — | — | — | — | — | — | — |
| Gold (National Valuation)............... | 1and | — | — | — | — | — | — | — | — | — | — | — | — |
| Central Bank: Other Assets............. | 3..d | 4.85 | 8.00 | .47 | .71 | .08 | 12.43 | 13.85 | 41.78 | 12.02 | .60 | .36 | .40 |
| Central Bank: Other Liabs.............. | 4..d | 22.96 | 20.82 | 22.90 | 35.37 | 41.21 | 75.66 | 76.48 | 101.47 | 131.98 | 144.20 | 150.73 | 204.55 |
| Other Depository Corps.: Assets....... | 7a.d | 252.21 | 211.34 | 225.96 | 249.18 | 329.41 | 513.59 | 512.22 | 525.34 | 532.25 | 609.97 | 593.72 | 736.38 |
| Other Depository Corps.: Liabs......... | 7b.d | 128.88 | 158.46 | 185.19 | 485.03 | 904.14 | 913.21 | 1,163.08 | 1,674.23 | 1,963.00 | 2,446.96 | 2,376.43 | 2,189.40 |
| Other Financial Corps.: Assets......... | 7e.d | .... | .... | .... | .... | .... | 2.92 | 2.25 | 2.67 | 4.66 | 8.37 | 7.83 | 6.89 |
| Other Financial Corps.: Liabs........... | 7f.d | .... | .... | .... | .... | .... | 4.52 | 5.62 | 3.43 | 4.50 | 10.84 | 6.49 | 4.74 |
| **Central Bank** | | | | | | *Millions of Drams: End of Period* | | | | | | | |
| Net Foreign Assets......................... | 11n | 165,191 | 254,725 | 321,991 | 446,141 | 377,542 | 520,278 | 429,255 | 471,203 | 436,396 | 652,196 | 437,640 | 568,770 |
| Claims on Nonresidents............. | 11 | 282,080 | 343,511 | 389,812 | 504,937 | 431,518 | 761,884 | 683,169 | 761,796 | 731,080 | 913,516 | 707,566 | 858,896 |
| Liabilities to Nonresidents............. | 16c | 116,890 | 88,786 | 67,820 | 58,796 | 53,976 | 241,606 | 253,914 | 290,593 | 294,685 | 261,320 | 269,926 | 290,126 |
| Claims on Other Depository Corps.... | 12e | 12,857 | 11,700 | 15,277 | 24,596 | 80,627 | 69,941 | 69,528 | 137,020 | 177,952 | 198,516 | 318,322 | 225,417 |
| Net Claims on Central Government.. | 12an | −36,830 | −17,366 | −57,716 | −89,770 | −96,457 | −152,451 | −95,609 | −66,735 | −93,342 | −175,865 | −102,138 | −120,216 |
| Claims on Central Government...... | 12a | 5,904 | 5,573 | 4,024 | 4,541 | 8,393 | 25,937 | 12,124 | 12,953 | 15,940 | 15,259 | 14,634 | 13,822 |
| Liabilities to Central Government... | 16d | 42,735 | 22,939 | 61,740 | 94,311 | 104,849 | 178,388 | 107,733 | 79,687 | 109,283 | 191,124 | 116,772 | 134,038 |
| Claims on Other Sectors.................. | 12s | 2,492 | 2,470 | 2,689 | 3,105 | 3,987 | 17,987 | 24,836 | 37,496 | 42,833 | 48,239 | 73,185 | 95,531 |
| Claims on Other Financial Corps.... | 12g | — | — | — | — | — | — | — | — | — | — | — | — |
| Claims on State & Local Govts...... | 12b | — | — | — | — | — | — | — | — | — | — | — | — |
| Claims on Public Nonfin. Corps...... | 12c | — | — | — | — | — | — | — | — | — | — | — | — |
| Claims on Private Sector............... | 12d | 2,492 | 2,470 | 2,689 | 3,105 | 3,987 | 17,987 | 24,836 | 37,496 | 42,833 | 48,239 | 73,185 | 95,531 |
| Monetary Base............................. | 14 | 134,050 | 208,273 | 290,397 | 427,118 | 449,731 | 511,678 | 519,655 | 671,271 | 708,855 | 912,562 | 886,765 | 921,725 |
| Currency in Circulation.................. | 14a | 105,534 | 155,275 | 226,841 | 350,274 | 344,503 | 320,670 | 348,165 | 398,777 | 440,117 | 446,833 | 412,345 | 413,614 |
| Liabs. to Other Depository Corps.... | 14c | 27,800 | 52,236 | 62,351 | 75,866 | 104,432 | 189,123 | 157,855 | 265,690 | 265,567 | 462,321 | 470,498 | 505,914 |
| Liabilities to Other Sectors............. | 14d | 716 | 762 | 1,206 | 979 | 795 | 1,885 | 13,635 | 6,803 | 3,171 | 3,408 | 3,922 | 2,198 |
| Other Liabs. to Other Dep. Corps...... | 14n | 641 | 21,216 | 38,988 | 49,408 | 3,083 | 11,361 | 10,302 | 12 | 55 | 334 | 5,962 | 3,288 |
| Dep. & Sec. Excl. f/Monetary Base.... | 14o | 616 | 2,406 | 2,026 | 1,591 | 1,562 | 1,911 | 1,939 | 1,755 | 2,008 | 2,206 | 2,036 | 1,970 |
| Deposits Included in Broad Money. | 15 | — | — | — | — | — | — | — | — | — | — | — | — |
| Sec.Ot.th.Shares Incl.in Brd. Money. | 16a | — | — | — | — | — | — | — | — | — | — | — | — |
| Deposits Excl. from Broad Money... | 16b | 616 | 2,406 | 2,026 | 1,591 | 1,562 | 1,911 | 1,939 | 1,755 | 2,008 | 2,206 | 2,036 | 1,970 |
| Sec.Ot.th.Shares Excl.f/Brd.Money.. | 16s | — | — | — | — | — | — | — | — | — | — | — | — |
| Loans.................................... | 16l | — | — | — | — | — | — | — | — | — | — | — | — |
| Financial Derivatives...................... | 16m | — | — | — | — | — | — | — | — | — | — | — | — |
| Shares and Other Equity................. | 17a | −2,980 | −14,763 | −39,256 | −49,382 | 5,285 | 44,997 | −28,446 | −1,908 | −14,046 | −10,202 | 27,594 | 3,139 |
| Other Items (Net)........................... | 17r | 11,382 | 34,398 | −9,913 | −44,664 | −93,961 | −114,192 | −75,439 | −92,145 | −133,032 | −181,813 | −195,350 | −160,621 |
| Memo Item: | | | | | | | | | | | | | |
| Total Assets.................................. | 10ra | 384,232 | 434,002 | 487,771 | 637,843 | 671,217 | 1,042,998 | 931,046 | 1,127,953 | 1,175,368 | 1,424,472 | 1,375,693 | 1,434,326 |

# Armenia, Republic of   911

|  |  | 2004 | 2005 | 2006 | 2007 | 2008 | 2009 | 2010 | 2011 | 2012 | 2013 | 2014 | 2015 |
|---|---|---|---|---|---|---|---|---|---|---|---|---|---|
| **Other Depository Corporations** | | *Milliions of Drams: End of Period* | | | | | | | | | | | |
| Net Foreign Assets.................. | 21n | 59,918 | 23,808 | 14,821 | −71,751 | −176,287 | −151,011 | −236,547 | −443,208 | −577,423 | −745,156 | −846,733 | −702,898 |
| Claims on Nonresidents............... | 21 | 122,534 | 95,145 | 82,138 | 75,805 | 101,041 | 194,080 | 186,162 | 202,660 | 214,806 | 247,427 | 282,000 | 356,223 |
| Liabilities to Nonresidents............ | 26c | 62,616 | 71,338 | 67,317 | 147,556 | 277,328 | 345,091 | 422,709 | 645,868 | 792,229 | 992,583 | 1,128,732 | 1,059,121 |
| Claims on Central Bank................ | 20 | 34,083 | 83,187 | 115,312 | 144,486 | 133,727 | 230,986 | 201,672 | 314,961 | 323,159 | 526,882 | 535,718 | 575,572 |
| Currency................................ | 20a | 6,965 | 10,964 | 15,372 | 24,257 | 28,555 | 38,229 | 43,841 | 49,370 | 56,052 | 62,366 | 63,986 | 68,107 |
| Reserve Deposits and Securities..... | 20b | 27,118 | 51,008 | 61,798 | 75,027 | 104,000 | 189,001 | 157,831 | 265,591 | 267,107 | 464,516 | 471,732 | 507,465 |
| Other Claims............................. | 20n | — | 21,215 | 38,142 | 45,202 | 1,172 | 3,757 | — | — | — | — | — | — |
| Net Claims on Central Government.. | 22an | 17,952 | 21,254 | 24,653 | 33,819 | 58,239 | 26,364 | 39,950 | 59,265 | 102,918 | 154,382 | 166,741 | 194,677 |
| Claims on Central Government...... | 22a | 33,504 | 39,828 | 45,047 | 56,732 | 75,851 | 97,801 | 126,920 | 149,231 | 181,588 | 229,997 | 239,886 | 258,212 |
| Liabilities to Central Government... | 26d | 15,552 | 18,574 | 20,394 | 22,913 | 17,612 | 71,437 | 86,970 | 89,966 | 78,670 | 75,615 | 73,145 | 63,535 |
| Claims on Other Sectors.................. | 22s | 143,917 | 190,768 | 244,570 | 434,989 | 697,680 | 781,332 | 989,911 | 1,338,775 | 1,705,069 | 1,931,166 | 2,334,535 | 2,259,444 |
| Claims on Other Financial Corps..... | 22g | 6,348 | 6,826 | 9,751 | 8,806 | 3,602 | 11,389 | 16,885 | 18,521 | 25,268 | 34,487 | 32,270 | 33,782 |
| Claims on State & Local Govts....... | 22b | — | — | — | — | — | — | — | — | — | — | — | — |
| Claims on Public Nonfin. Corps...... | 22c | 6,684 | 5,905 | 2,768 | 1,680 | 6,302 | 9,131 | 16,051 | 24,706 | 21,963 | 25,234 | 21,905 | 26,532 |
| Claims on Private Sector............... | 22d | 130,886 | 178,038 | 232,050 | 424,503 | 687,776 | 760,813 | 956,975 | 1,295,548 | 1,657,838 | 1,871,445 | 2,280,359 | 2,199,130 |
| Liabilities to Central Bank............... | 26g | 13,094 | 11,899 | 15,275 | 24,139 | 83,891 | 77,966 | 69,135 | 131,668 | 168,741 | 205,478 | 323,563 | 230,183 |
| Transf.Dep.Included in Broad Money | 24 | 107,736 | 115,339 | 142,655 | 191,054 | 166,137 | 216,460 | 229,320 | 280,491 | 307,071 | 338,129 | 385,589 | 446,713 |
| Other Dep.Included in Broad Money | 25 | 78,923 | 105,142 | 130,408 | 173,295 | 224,907 | 314,204 | 364,107 | 490,277 | 652,057 | 819,368 | 936,325 | 1,061,259 |
| Sec.Ot.th.Shares Incl.in Brd. Money.. | 26a | | | | | | | | | | | | |
| Deposits Excl. from Broad Money..... | 26b | 738 | 839 | 945 | 2,443 | 1,934 | 2,485 | 599 | 485 | 23 | 23 | 23 | 1,176 |
| Sec.Ot.th.Shares Excl.f/Brd.Money... | 26s | 3,406 | 519 | 3,925 | 614 | 4,514 | 7,089 | 9,323 | 5,535 | — | — | — | — |
| Loans.......................................... | 26l | 162 | 113 | 88 | 56 | — | 1,915 | 9,197 | — | — | 5 | — | — |
| Financial Derivatives...................... | 26m | — | 1 | — | — | 20 | 5 | 47 | 769 | 51 | 9 | 432 | 65 |
| Insurance Technical Reserves........... | 26r | | | | | | | | | | | | |
| Shares and Other Equity................. | 27a | 65,036 | 95,087 | 120,664 | 172,765 | 254,742 | 305,763 | 356,586 | 404,826 | 460,869 | 539,884 | 579,554 | 640,234 |
| Other Items (Net)......................... | 27r | −13,225 | −9,922 | −14,603 | −22,823 | −22,786 | −38,215 | −43,328 | −44,258 | −35,089 | −35,623 | −35,227 | −52,836 |
| Memo Item: | | | | | | | | | | | | | |
| Total Assets.................................... | 20ra | 379,535 | 460,446 | 554,405 | 806,875 | 1,130,999 | 1,491,785 | 1,754,978 | 2,319,438 | 2,729,381 | 3,263,430 | 3,819,929 | 3,923,128 |
| **Depository Corporations** | | *Millions of Drams: End of Period* | | | | | | | | | | | |
| Net Foreign Assets....................... | 31n | 225,108 | 278,533 | 336,812 | 374,390 | 201,255 | 369,267 | 192,708 | 27,995 | −141,027 | −92,960 | −409,093 | −134,128 |
| Claims on Nonresidents................ | 31 | 404,614 | 438,656 | 471,949 | 580,742 | 532,559 | 955,964 | 869,331 | 964,456 | 945,886 | 1,160,943 | 989,566 | 1,215,118 |
| Liabilities to Nonresidents.............. | 36c | 179,506 | 160,123 | 135,137 | 206,352 | 331,304 | 586,697 | 676,623 | 936,460 | 1,086,914 | 1,253,904 | 1,398,659 | 1,349,247 |
| Domestic Claims............................. | 32 | 127,531 | 197,126 | 214,196 | 382,143 | 663,450 | 673,232 | 959,088 | 1,368,802 | 1,757,478 | 1,957,923 | 2,472,322 | 2,429,435 |
| Net Claims on Central Government.. | 32an | −18,878 | 3,888 | −33,063 | −55,951 | −38,217 | −126,087 | −55,659 | −7,470 | 9,576 | −21,482 | 64,603 | 74,460 |
| Claims on Central Government..... | 32a | 39,409 | 45,401 | 49,071 | 61,273 | 84,244 | 123,738 | 139,044 | 162,184 | 197,528 | 245,257 | 254,520 | 272,034 |
| Liabilities to Central Government. | 36d | 58,287 | 41,513 | 82,133 | 117,224 | 122,461 | 249,825 | 194,703 | 169,653 | 187,953 | 266,739 | 189,917 | 197,573 |
| Claims on Other Sectors................ | 32s | 146,409 | 193,238 | 247,259 | 438,094 | 701,668 | 799,319 | 1,014,747 | 1,376,271 | 1,747,903 | 1,979,405 | 2,407,719 | 2,354,975 |
| Claims on Other Financial Corps.... | 32g | 6,348 | 6,826 | 9,751 | 8,806 | 3,602 | 11,389 | 16,885 | 18,521 | 25,268 | 34,487 | 32,270 | 33,782 |
| Claims on State & Local Govts..... | 32b | — | — | — | — | — | — | — | — | — | — | — | — |
| Claims on Public Nonfin. Corps.... | 32c | 6,684 | 5,905 | 2,768 | 1,680 | 6,302 | 9,131 | 16,051 | 24,706 | 21,963 | 25,234 | 21,905 | 26,532 |
| Claims on Private Sector.............. | 32d | 133,378 | 180,508 | 234,740 | 427,608 | 691,763 | 778,800 | 981,811 | 1,333,045 | 1,700,672 | 1,919,684 | 2,353,544 | 2,294,661 |
| Broad Money Liabilities............... | 35l | 285,943 | 365,554 | 485,737 | 691,343 | 707,788 | 814,990 | 911,386 | 1,126,978 | 1,346,365 | 1,545,372 | 1,674,196 | 1,855,676 |
| Currency Outside Depository Corps | 34a | 98,569 | 144,311 | 211,469 | 326,016 | 315,949 | 282,441 | 304,324 | 349,407 | 384,065 | 384,467 | 348,359 | 345,507 |
| Transferable Deposits.................... | 34 | 108,452 | 116,101 | 143,860 | 192,032 | 166,933 | 218,345 | 242,955 | 287,294 | 310,242 | 341,537 | 389,511 | 448,911 |
| Other Deposits.............................. | 35 | 78,923 | 105,142 | 130,408 | 173,295 | 224,907 | 314,204 | 364,107 | 490,277 | 652,057 | 819,368 | 936,325 | 1,061,259 |
| Securities Other than Shares.......... | 36a | — | — | — | — | — | — | — | — | — | — | — | — |
| Deposits Excl. from Broad Money..... | 36b | 1,354 | 3,245 | 2,971 | 4,035 | 3,496 | 4,396 | 2,538 | 2,240 | 2,031 | 2,229 | 2,059 | 3,145 |
| Sec.Ot.Shares Excl.f/Brd.Money.... | 36s | 3,406 | 519 | 3,925 | 614 | 4,514 | 7,089 | 9,323 | 5,535 | — | — | — | — |
| Loans......................................... | 36l | 162 | 113 | 88 | 56 | — | 1,915 | 9,197 | — | — | 5 | — | — |
| Financial Derivatives...................... | 36m | — | 1 | — | — | 20 | 5 | 47 | 769 | 51 | 9 | 432 | 65 |
| Insurance Technical Reserves........... | 36r | | | | | | | | | | | | |
| Shares and Other Equity................... | 37a | 62,056 | 80,324 | 81,407 | 123,383 | 260,027 | 350,760 | 328,140 | 402,917 | 446,823 | 529,682 | 607,149 | 643,374 |
| Other Items (Net)............................ | 37r | −283 | 25,904 | −23,119 | −62,898 | −111,140 | −136,656 | −108,835 | −141,643 | −178,819 | −212,335 | −220,607 | −206,954 |
| Broad Money Liabs., Seasonally Adj. | 35l.b | 265,373 | 340,350 | 454,750 | 650,557 | 669,810 | 776,102 | 873,374 | 1,084,703 | 1,299,962 | 1,496,432 | 1,624,085 | 1,800,641 |
| **Other Financial Corporations** | | *Milliions of Drams: End of Period* | | | | | | | | | | | |
| Net Foreign Assets....................... | 41n | .... | .... | .... | .... | .... | −602 | −1,224 | −295 | 63 | −1,004 | 638 | 1,040 |
| Claims on Nonresidents................ | 41 | .... | .... | .... | .... | .... | 1,105 | 818 | 1,030 | 1,880 | 3,395 | 3,718 | 3,335 |
| Liabilities to Nonresidents.............. | 46c | .... | .... | .... | .... | .... | 1,707 | 2,042 | 1,325 | 1,817 | 4,399 | 3,080 | 2,295 |
| Claims on Depository Corporations.. | 40 | .... | .... | .... | .... | .... | 14,197 | 18,849 | 17,663 | 17,173 | 18,170 | 17,702 | 18,442 |
| Net Claims on Central Government.. | 42an | .... | .... | .... | .... | .... | 12,496 | 17,827 | 21,056 | 25,137 | 31,303 | 28,599 | 31,615 |
| Claims on Central Government..... | 42a | .... | .... | .... | .... | .... | 12,525 | 17,865 | 21,140 | 25,142 | 31,311 | 28,601 | 31,624 |
| Liabilities to Central Government... | 46d | .... | .... | .... | .... | .... | 30 | 38 | 84 | 5 | 8 | 2 | 9 |
| Claims on Other Sectors.................. | 42s | .... | .... | .... | .... | .... | 2,055 | 2,450 | 3,135 | 8,475 | 11,007 | 8,484 | 6,788 |
| Claims on State & Local Govts....... | 42b | .... | .... | .... | .... | .... | — | — | — | — | — | — | — |
| Claims on Public Nonfin. Corps...... | 42c | .... | .... | .... | .... | .... | — | — | — | — | — | — | — |
| Claims on Private Sector.............. | 42d | .... | .... | .... | .... | .... | 2,055 | 2,450 | 3,135 | 8,475 | 11,007 | 8,484 | 6,788 |
| Deposits........................................ | 46b | .... | .... | .... | .... | .... | — | — | — | 78 | 78 | — | — |
| Securities Other than Shares............ | 46s | .... | .... | .... | .... | .... | | | | | | | |
| Loans............................................ | 46l | .... | .... | .... | .... | .... | 12,304 | 16,176 | 20,839 | 5,528 | 10,605 | 14,364 | 13,176 |
| Financial Derivatives...................... | 46m | .... | .... | .... | .... | .... | — | 3 | 134 | 6 | — | — | 1 |
| Insurance Technical Reserves........... | 46r | .... | .... | .... | .... | .... | 2,766 | 8,280 | 9,406 | 17,580 | 18,114 | 16,299 | 17,490 |
| Shares and Other Equity.................. | 47a | .... | .... | .... | .... | .... | 15,230 | 15,823 | 17,439 | 31,726 | 35,773 | 28,559 | 31,644 |
| Other Items (Net)............................ | 47r | .... | .... | .... | .... | .... | −2,155 | −2,380 | −6,259 | −4,070 | −5,094 | −3,799 | −4,425 |
| Memo Item: | | | | | | | | | | | | | |
| Total Assets.................................... | 40ra | .... | .... | .... | .... | .... | 32,853 | 44,440 | 52,965 | 61,621 | 76,557 | 69,117 | 70,656 |

# Armenia, Republic of   911

| | | 2004 | 2005 | 2006 | 2007 | 2008 | 2009 | 2010 | 2011 | 2012 | 2013 | 2014 | 2015 |
|---|---|---|---|---|---|---|---|---|---|---|---|---|---|
| **Financial Corporations** | | | | | | | *Milliions of Drams: End of Period* | | | | | | |
| Net Foreign Assets | 51n | .... | .... | .... | .... | .... | 368,665 | 191,484 | 27,700 | −140,964 | −93,964 | −408,454 | −133,088 |
| Claims on Nonresidents | 51 | .... | .... | .... | .... | .... | 957,068 | 870,149 | 965,486 | 947,766 | 1,164,339 | 993,285 | 1,218,454 |
| Liabilities to Nonresidents | 56c | .... | .... | .... | .... | .... | 588,404 | 678,665 | 937,786 | 1,088,730 | 1,258,303 | 1,401,739 | 1,351,542 |
| Domestic Claims | 52 | .... | .... | .... | .... | .... | 676,394 | 962,480 | 1,374,471 | 1,765,822 | 1,965,745 | 2,477,135 | 2,434,056 |
| Net Claims on Central Government | 52an | .... | .... | .... | .... | .... | −113,592 | −37,832 | 13,586 | 34,713 | 9,820 | 93,202 | 106,075 |
| Claims on Central Government | 52a | .... | .... | .... | .... | .... | 136,263 | 156,909 | 183,324 | 222,670 | 276,567 | 283,121 | 303,657 |
| Liabilities to Central Government | 56d | .... | .... | .... | .... | .... | 249,855 | 194,741 | 169,738 | 187,957 | 266,747 | 189,919 | 197,582 |
| Claims on Other Sectors | 52s | .... | .... | .... | .... | .... | 789,985 | 1,000,312 | 1,360,885 | 1,731,110 | 1,955,925 | 2,383,933 | 2,327,981 |
| Claims on State & Local Govts | 52b | .... | .... | .... | .... | .... | | | | | | | |
| Claims on Public Nonfin. Corps | 52c | .... | .... | .... | .... | .... | 9,131 | 16,051 | 24,706 | 21,963 | 25,234 | 21,905 | 26,532 |
| Claims on Private Sector | 52d | .... | .... | .... | .... | .... | 780,855 | 984,260 | 1,336,180 | 1,709,146 | 1,930,690 | 2,362,027 | 2,301,449 |
| Currency Outside Financial Corps | 54a | .... | .... | .... | .... | .... | 282,319 | 304,038 | 349,250 | 383,867 | 384,246 | 348,245 | 345,466 |
| Deposits | 55l | .... | .... | .... | .... | .... | 524,438 | 593,385 | 762,150 | 946,231 | 1,141,211 | 1,301,675 | 1,483,232 |
| Securities Other than Shares | 56a | .... | .... | .... | .... | .... | 7,089 | 9,323 | 5,535 | — | — | — | — |
| Loans | 56l | .... | .... | .... | .... | .... | 293 | 149 | 59 | 343 | 90 | 72 | 74 |
| Financial Derivatives | 56m | .... | .... | .... | .... | .... | 5 | 47 | 769 | 3 | 5 | 35 | 4 |
| Insurance Technical Reserves | 56r | .... | .... | .... | .... | .... | 2,766 | 8,280 | 9,406 | 17,580 | 18,114 | 16,299 | 17,490 |
| Shares and Other Equity | 57a | .... | .... | .... | .... | .... | 365,989 | 343,963 | 420,356 | 478,549 | 565,455 | 635,708 | 675,018 |
| Other Items (Net) | 57r | .... | .... | .... | .... | .... | −137,841 | −105,222 | −145,353 | −201,714 | −237,340 | −233,353 | −220,314 |
| **Monetary Aggregates** | | | | | | | *Millions of Drams: End of Period* | | | | | | |
| Broad Money | 59m | 285,943 | 365,554 | 485,737 | 691,343 | 707,788 | 814,990 | 911,386 | 1,126,978 | 1,346,365 | 1,545,372 | 1,674,196 | 1,855,676 |
| o/w:Currency Issued by Cent.Govt | 59m.a | — | — | — | — | — | — | — | — | — | — | — | — |
| o/w: Dep.in Nonfin. Corporations | 59m.b | — | — | — | — | — | — | — | — | — | — | — | — |
| o/w:Secs. Issued by Central Govt | 59m.c | — | — | — | — | — | — | — | — | — | — | — | — |
| Money (National Definitions) | | | | | | | | | | | | | |
| Reserve Money | 19mb | 133,895 | 208,273 | 290,397 | 427,118 | 449,731 | 515,435 | 519,655 | 671,271 | 708,855 | 912,562 | 892,579 | 921,725 |
| M1 | 59ma | 132,414 | 202,056 | 295,328 | 458,558 | 415,641 | 386,795 | 432,689 | 513,792 | 545,793 | 583,369 | 531,245 | 555,621 |
| M2 | 59mb | 145,718 | 224,797 | 342,326 | 561,024 | 537,958 | 450,878 | 521,633 | 659,437 | 737,983 | 848,046 | 818,277 | 860,477 |
| M2X | 59mba | 285,943 | 365,554 | 485,737 | 691,343 | 707,788 | 814,990 | 911,386 | 1,126,978 | 1,346,365 | 1,545,372 | 1,674,196 | 1,855,676 |
| **Interest Rates** | | | | | | | *Percent Per Annum* | | | | | | |
| Central Bank Policy Rate (EOP) | 60 | 3.75 | 3.50 | 4.75 | 5.75 | 7.25 | 5.00 | 7.25 | 8.00 | 8.00 | 7.75 | 8.50 | 8.75 |
| Money Market Rate | 60b | 4.18 | 3.17 | 4.34 | 4.47 | 6.75 | 6.25 | 6.58 | 7.69 | 8.68 | 8.23 | 8.15 | 13.80 |
| Treasury Bill Rate | 60c | 5.27 | 4.05 | 4.87 | 6.09 | 7.69 | 9.42 | 10.59 | 9.53 | 9.80 | 9.30 | 7.80 | 12.90 |
| Deposit Rate | 60l | 4.90 | 5.81 | 5.84 | 6.25 | 6.63 | 8.65 | 8.95 | 9.25 | 9.57 | 10.16 | 10.43 | 14.15 |
| Lending Rate | 60p | 18.63 | 17.98 | 16.53 | 17.52 | 17.05 | 18.76 | 19.20 | 17.75 | 17.23 | 15.99 | 16.41 | 17.59 |
| Government Bond Yield | 61 | 8.21 | 5.18 | 5.86 | 6.56 | 8.32 | 11.86 | 13.88 | 13.80 | 14.30 | 13.20 | 9.82 | 14.41 |
| **Prices, Production, Labor** | | | | | | | *Index Numbers (2010=100): Period Averages* | | | | | | |
| Producer Prices | 63 | 68.2 | 73.4 | 74.1 | 74.6 | † 76.2 | 81.6 | 100.0 | † 107.7 | 115.3 | 120.7 | 130.9 | 129.9 |
| Consumer Prices | 64 | 75.9 | † 76.4 | 78.6 | 82.0 | 89.4 | 92.4 | † 100.0 | 107.7 | 110.4 | 116.8 | † 120.3 | 124.8 |
| Wages:Avg. Month.Earn | 65 | 40.9 | 50.9 | 62.6 | 75.6 | 90.3 | 99.9 | 100.0 | 112.5 | 118.1 | 154.2 | 166.9 | 180.0 |
| Industrial Production | 66 | 64.6 | 78.2 | 78.4 | 86.6 | 91.8 | 81.1 | 100.0 | 123.1 | 138.3 | 153.9 | 159.8 | 164.6 |
| | | | | | | | *Number in Thousands: Period Averages* | | | | | | |
| Employment | 67e | 1,081.7 | 1,097.8 | 1,092.4 | 1,101.5 | 1,183.1 | 1,152.8 | 1,185.2 | 1,175.1 | 1,172.8 | 1,163.8 | 1,156.1 | .... |
| Unemployment | 67c | 114.4 | 97.2 | 88.7 | 82.4 | † 74.9 | 78.8 | 84.3 | 76.2 | 64.7 | 58.3 | 62.0 | 73.7 |
| Unemployment Rate (%) | 67r | 9.6 | 8.2 | 7.5 | 7.0 | † 16.4 | 18.7 | 19.0 | 18.4 | 17.3 | 16.2 | 17.6 | .... |
| **Intl. Transactions & Positions** | | | | | | | *Millions of US Dollars* | | | | | | |
| Exports | 70..d | 715.03 | 950.40 | 1,004.00 | 1,219.09 | 1,057.15 | 697.74 | 1,011.43 | 1,315.56 | 1,428.14 | 1,478.75 | 1,519.30 | 1,486.89 |
| Imports, c.i.f | 71..d | 1,350.98 | 1,767.90 | 2,194.40 | 3,281.85 | 4,427.36 | 3,303.17 | 3,782.88 | 4,196.30 | 4,266.81 | 4,385.87 | 4,401.61 | 3,253.97 |
| Imports, f.o.b | 71.vd | 1,199.67 | 1,545.20 | 1,917.90 | 2,861.91 | 3,719.69 | 2,785.89 | 3,204.59 | 3,526.41 | 3,495.62 | 3,710.44 | 3,723.75 | 2,752.85 |

# Armenia, Republic of   911

| | | 2004 | 2005 | 2006 | 2007 | 2008 | 2009 | 2010 | 2011 | 2012 | 2013 | 2014 | 2015 |
|---|---|---|---|---|---|---|---|---|---|---|---|---|---|
| **Balance of Payments** | | | | | | | *Millions of US Dollars* | | | | | | |
| A. Current Account* | 109bx | −78.8 | −123.9 | −152.9 | −677.3 | −1,658.9 | −1,425.5 | −1,261.4 | −1,058.9 | −1,057.9 | −844.7 | −849.1 | −279.3 |
| Goods, credit (exports) | 1a9cx | 770.4 | 1,028.7 | 1,053.0 | 1,204.2 | 1,106.3 | 773.6 | 1,197.5 | 1,431.6 | 1,515.7 | 1,635.9 | 1,698.1 | 1,626.4 |
| Goods, debit (imports) | 1a9dx | 1,261.0 | 1,663.4 | 1,999.9 | 2,921.1 | 3,922.6 | 2,863.6 | 3,263.2 | 3,541.4 | 3,627.6 | 3,728.1 | 3,753.6 | 2,780.3 |
| Balance on goods | 1a9bx | −490.7 | −634.7 | −947.0 | −1,716.9 | −2,816.3 | −2,090.0 | −2,065.7 | −2,109.8 | −2,111.9 | −2,092.3 | −2,055.4 | −1,153.9 |
| Services, credit (exports) | 1b9cx | 347.0 | 430.1 | 593.7 | 764.2 | 837.3 | 785.7 | 1,013.2 | 1,310.6 | 1,402.2 | 1,520.0 | 1,620.7 | 1,513.3 |
| Services, debit (imports) | 1b9dx | 501.5 | 578.1 | 682.0 | 954.2 | 1,148.5 | 1,062.0 | 1,274.0 | 1,376.4 | 1,503.8 | 1,636.9 | 1,714.2 | 1,577.2 |
| Balance on Goods & Services | 1z9bx | −645.2 | −782.6 | −1,035.3 | −1,906.8 | −3,127.5 | −2,366.3 | −2,326.5 | −2,175.6 | −2,213.5 | −2,209.1 | −2,148.8 | −1,217.7 |
| Primary income: credit | 1c9cx | 394.4 | 484.9 | 656.0 | 956.5 | 1,133.3 | 875.8 | 1,049.1 | 1,065.5 | 1,115.2 | 1,259.1 | 1,212.9 | 885.9 |
| Primary income: debit | 1c9dx | 246.0 | 278.8 | 353.9 | 459.0 | 442.0 | 517.0 | 590.8 | 705.5 | 692.2 | 719.7 | 657.0 | 471.9 |
| Balance on gds, serv. & prim. inc. | 1y9bx | −496.8 | −576.6 | −733.2 | −1,409.4 | −2,436.2 | −2,007.5 | −1,868.2 | −1,815.6 | −1,790.4 | −1,669.7 | −1,592.9 | −803.7 |
| Secondary income: credit | 1d9ca | 552.9 | 608.3 | 733.1 | 939.1 | 988.5 | 750.3 | 813.5 | 997.9 | 990.3 | 1,118.3 | 1,056.1 | 788.6 |
| Secondary income: debit | 1d9da | 135.0 | 155.6 | 152.8 | 207.0 | 211.2 | 168.3 | 206.7 | 241.2 | 257.7 | 293.4 | 312.2 | 264.2 |
| B. Capital Account* | 209ba | 64.3 | 84.0 | 92.8 | 124.8 | 171.4 | 87.9 | 98.9 | 94.6 | 108.4 | 84.1 | 70.4 | 39.5 |
| Capital account: credit | 209ca | 65.1 | 85.0 | 112.9 | 146.8 | 192.5 | 103.0 | 111.0 | 113.5 | 129.2 | 102.8 | 85.9 | 52.4 |
| Capital account: debit | 209da | .7 | 1.0 | 20.1 | 22.0 | 21.0 | 15.1 | 12.1 | 18.9 | 20.8 | 18.7 | 15.4 | 13.0 |
| Balance on current & capital acct. | 129ba | −14.5 | −39.9 | −60.1 | −552.4 | −1,487.4 | −1,337.6 | −1,162.6 | −964.3 | −949.4 | −760.6 | −778.7 | −239.8 |
| C. Financial Account* | 309na | −258.5 | −442.0 | −489.9 | −1,085.0 | −1,317.2 | −1,604.8 | −1,027.2 | −1,042.9 | −763.1 | −1,724.1 | −299.4 | −853.5 |
| Direct investment: assets | 3a9aa | −.4 | 4.9 | 21.9 | 13.8 | 18.7 | 50.4 | 7.9 | 215.9 | 15.8 | 26.6 | 16.0 | 10.7 |
| Equity & investment fund shares | 3aaaa | −.4 | 4.9 | 21.9 | 13.8 | 18.7 | 50.4 | 7.9 | 77.9 | 15.8 | 18.7 | 19.8 | 10.8 |
| Debt instruments | 3abaa | — | — | — | — | — | — | — | 138.0 | — | 7.9 | −3.8 | −.1 |
| Direct investment: liabilities | 3a9la | 247.1 | 292.1 | 466.5 | 667.7 | 943.7 | 760.0 | 529.3 | 653.2 | 496.6 | 379.9 | 404.3 | 180.5 |
| Equity & investment fund shares | 3aala | 224.5 | 278.5 | 424.0 | 427.1 | 1,036.2 | 718.1 | 360.7 | 385.9 | 589.0 | 363.2 | 335.3 | 150.8 |
| Debt instruments | 3abla | 22.6 | 13.6 | 42.6 | 240.5 | −92.5 | 41.9 | 168.6 | 267.3 | −92.4 | 16.6 | 69.1 | 29.7 |
| Portfolio investment: assets | 3b9aa | .4 | 2.7 | .2 | −.5 | −2.6 | 11.3 | .9 | — | 1.1 | 5.4 | 3.1 | 3.1 |
| Equity & investment fund shares | 3baaa | .1 | .2 | −.4 | .1 | — | 1.3 | −.5 | −.3 | .4 | .9 | 1.1 | .9 |
| Debt securities | 3bbaa | .2 | 2.5 | .6 | −.7 | −2.6 | 10.0 | 1.4 | .3 | .7 | 4.5 | 2.0 | 2.1 |
| Portfolio investment: liabilities | 3b9la | −2.4 | −.1 | 9.5 | −8.6 | 9.4 | 7.2 | 19.2 | −8.4 | 2.0 | 694.8 | −40.1 | 261.6 |
| Equity & investment fund shares | 3bala | 1.4 | .1 | −.5 | 1.4 | 2.9 | 1.0 | 7.4 | 2.6 | 2.3 | −1.8 | .7 | 4.0 |
| Debt securities | 3bbla | −3.8 | −.2 | 10.0 | −9.9 | 6.5 | 6.2 | 11.8 | −11.0 | −.3 | 696.7 | −40.8 | 257.5 |
| Fin. der.& empl.stk.ops.(ESOs): net | 3c9na | — | — | — | — | — | — | — | — | — | −.6 | 1.2 | −1.7 |
| Fin. der. & ESOs.: assets | 3c9aa | .... | .... | .... | .... | .... | .... | .... | .... | .... | .... | .... | .... |
| Fin. der. & ESOs.: liabilities | 3c9la | .... | .... | .... | .... | .... | .... | .... | .... | .... | .... | .... | .... |
| Other investment: assets | 3d9aa | 71.6 | −59.9 | 109.3 | 130.4 | 273.9 | 281.3 | 133.2 | 120.8 | 151.9 | −73.5 | 407.9 | −44.5 |
| Other equity | 3daaa | — | 2.6 | 2.1 | 2.3 | 1.6 | .3 | 1.9 | 2.4 | 2.7 | 3.1 | 2.2 | 1.7 |
| Debt instruments | 3dzaa | 71.6 | −62.5 | 107.2 | 128.0 | 272.3 | 281.0 | 131.3 | 118.5 | 149.1 | −76.6 | 405.7 | −46.2 |
| Other investment: liabilities | 3d9la | 85.3 | 97.8 | 145.3 | 569.5 | 654.1 | 1,180.6 | 620.7 | 734.7 | 433.3 | 607.3 | 363.5 | 379.0 |
| Other equity | 3dala | — | — | — | — | — | — | — | — | — | — | — | — |
| Debt instruments | 3dzla | 85.3 | 97.8 | 145.3 | 569.5 | 654.1 | 1,180.6 | 620.7 | 734.7 | 433.3 | 607.3 | 363.5 | 379.0 |
| Curr.+ cap.− finan. acct. balance | 4y9na | 244.0 | 402.1 | 429.8 | 532.6 | −170.2 | 267.2 | −135.4 | 78.6 | −186.3 | 963.6 | −479.2 | 613.6 |
| D. Net Errors and Omissions | 409na | −187.8 | −163.5 | −128.1 | 28.3 | −41.3 | −101.7 | −155.4 | −36.6 | 190.6 | −302.0 | −65.9 | −276.3 |
| E. Reserves and Related Items | 4z9na | 56.2 | 238.7 | 301.7 | 560.9 | −211.6 | 165.5 | −290.7 | 42.0 | 4.2 | 661.6 | −545.1 | 337.4 |
| Reserve assets | 3e9aa | 49.8 | 213.9 | 280.3 | 547.4 | −231.0 | 600.2 | −128.7 | 132.9 | −48.3 | 470.6 | −659.6 | 328.7 |
| Credit and loans from the IMF | 3dcla | −6.4 | −24.7 | −21.4 | −13.5 | −19.4 | 435.0 | 161.9 | 90.9 | −52.5 | −191.0 | −114.5 | −8.6 |
| Exceptional financing | 409la | .... | .... | .... | .... | .... | −.3 | .1 | .... | .... | .... | .... | .... |

*Excludes components in group E

| | | 2004 | 2005 | 2006 | 2007 | 2008 | 2009 | 2010 | 2011 | 2012 | 2013 | 2014 | 2015 |
|---|---|---|---|---|---|---|---|---|---|---|---|---|---|
| **International Investment Position** | | | | | | | *Millions of US Dollars* | | | | | | |
| Assets | 809aa | 957.4 | 1,130.1 | 1,546.6 | 2,286.3 | 2,282.3 | 3,201.0 | 3,193.3 | 3,874.6 | 3,997.2 | 4,345.6 | 4,005.1 | 4,208.9 |
| Direct investment | 8a9aa | .4 | 7.3 | 31.0 | 45.7 | 64.4 | 113.5 | 121.6 | 337.2 | 352.7 | 292.7 | 310.8 | 321.5 |
| Equity & investment fund shares | 8aaaa | .4 | 7.3 | 31.0 | 45.7 | 64.4 | 113.5 | 121.6 | 199.2 | 214.7 | 145.5 | 165.3 | 176.2 |
| Debt instruments | 8abaa | .... | .... | .... | .... | .... | — | .... | 138.0 | 138.0 | 147.2 | 145.4 | 145.3 |
| Portfolio investment | 8b9aa | 4.6 | 5.9 | 3.4 | 3.1 | .5 | 12.5 | 13.8 | 12.9 | 14.0 | 19.4 | 19.2 | 21.8 |
| Equity & investment fund shares | 8baaa | 4.5 | 3.3 | .2 | .5 | .4 | 2.2 | 1.8 | 1.4 | 2.4 | 3.3 | 3.9 | 4.7 |
| Debt securities | 8bbaa | .1 | 2.7 | 3.2 | 2.6 | .1 | 10.3 | 12.0 | 11.4 | 11.7 | 16.0 | 15.3 | 17.1 |
| Fin. der.(oth.than reserves) & ESOs | 8c9aa | .... | .... | .... | .... | .... | .... | .... | .... | .... | .5 | 4.2 | 1.5 |
| Other investment | 8d9aa | 374.3 | 354.7 | 440.2 | 580.6 | 810.6 | 1,071.3 | 1,192.0 | 1,592.1 | 1,831.2 | 1,781.4 | 2,181.5 | 2,092.9 |
| Other equity | 8daaa | — | 2.6 | 4.8 | 7.1 | 8.6 | 9.0 | 10.9 | 13.3 | 15.6 | 17.7 | 19.8 | 21.5 |
| Debt instruments | 8dzaa | 374.3 | 352.1 | 435.5 | 573.5 | 802.0 | 1,062.4 | 1,181.1 | 1,578.9 | 1,815.7 | 1,763.7 | 2,161.7 | 2,071.4 |
| Reserve assets | 8e9aa | 578.1 | 762.2 | 1,071.9 | 1,656.8 | 1,406.8 | 2,003.6 | 1,865.8 | 1,932.4 | 1,799.3 | 2,251.6 | 1,489.4 | 1,771.2 |
| Liabilities | 809la | 2,719.1 | 2,995.1 | 3,660.1 | 5,032.5 | 6,720.5 | 8,420.8 | 10,094.5 | 11,776.4 | 12,015.9 | 13,274.5 | 11,786.0 | 12,273.1 |
| Direct investment | 8a9la | 1,039.2 | 1,382.8 | 1,879.8 | 2,586.3 | 3,642.8 | 3,734.4 | 4,404.7 | 5,241.2 | 5,287.2 | 5,524.4 | 4,211.3 | 4,269.2 |
| Equity & investment fund shares | 8aala | 831.7 | 1,151.1 | 1,605.5 | 2,084.6 | 3,248.3 | 3,375.8 | 3,771.0 | 4,340.8 | 4,322.9 | 4,529.5 | 3,231.6 | 3,324.8 |
| Debt instruments | 8abla | 207.5 | 231.7 | 274.4 | 501.7 | 394.5 | 358.6 | 633.8 | 900.4 | 964.3 | 995.0 | 979.7 | 944.4 |
| Portfolio investment | 8b9la | 5.0 | 4.3 | 14.5 | 8.4 | 16.8 | 22.1 | 42.6 | 26.6 | 34.4 | 725.9 | 691.4 | 935.8 |
| Equity & investment fund shares | 8bala | 4.8 | 4.3 | 4.5 | 8.3 | 10.2 | 9.5 | 18.2 | 20.0 | 21.3 | 13.4 | 13.8 | 18.7 |
| Debt securities | 8bbla | .2 | — | 10.0 | .1 | 6.6 | 12.6 | 24.5 | 6.7 | 13.1 | 712.5 | 677.6 | 917.1 |
| Fin. der.(oth.than reserves) & ESOs | 8c9la | .... | .... | .... | .... | .... | .... | .... | .... | .... | .6 | 3.3 | 2.2 |
| Other investment | 8d9la | 1,674.9 | 1,608.0 | 1,765.8 | 2,437.7 | 3,060.9 | 4,664.3 | 5,647.1 | 6,508.6 | 6,694.2 | 7,023.5 | 6,880.0 | 7,066.0 |
| Other equity | 8dala | .... | .... | .... | .... | .... | .... | .... | .... | .... | 1.4 | 1.2 | 1.2 |
| Debt instruments | 8dzla | 1,674.9 | 1,608.0 | 1,765.8 | 2,437.7 | 3,060.9 | 4,664.3 | 5,647.1 | 6,508.6 | 6,694.2 | 7,022.1 | 6,878.8 | 7,064.8 |

|  |  | 2004 | 2005 | 2006 | 2007 | 2008 | 2009 | 2010 | 2011 | 2012 | 2013 | 2014 | 2015 |
|---|---|---|---|---|---|---|---|---|---|---|---|---|---|
| **Government Finance** | | | | | | | | | | | | | |
| **Cash Flow Statement** | | | | | | | | | | | | | |
| **Central Government** | | | | | | *Millions of Drams: Fiscal Year Ends December 31* | | | | | | | |
| Cash Receipts:Operating Activities... | c1 | 293,155 | 432,636 | 514,858 | 667,884 | 803,450 | 704,505 | 797,088 | 903,825 | 986,758 | 1,112,468 | 1,206,523 | 1,197,757 |
| Taxes.............................. | c11 | 267,044 | 321,532 | 385,131 | 502,590 | 618,080 | 518,557 | 590,658 | 650,540 | 746,274 | 979,192 | 1,047,735 | 1,053,516 |
| Social Contributions...................... | c12 | .... | 50,117 | 62,575 | 68,740 | 88,269 | 84,940 | 87,373 | 104,912 | 129,059 | 17,632 | 12,214 | 10,876 |
| Grants............................... | c13 | 13,717 | 15,204 | 16,080 | 25,248 | 15,557 | 23,348 | 33,073 | 63,772 | 22,632 | 18,015 | 22,807 | 33,058 |
| Other Receipts............................ | c14 | 12,394 | 45,783 | 51,072 | 71,306 | 81,544 | 77,660 | 85,983 | 84,602 | 88,794 | 97,629 | 123,767 | 100,308 |
| Cash Payments:Operating Activities. | c2 | 262,812 | 391,505 | 429,316 | 506,314 | 726,497 | 731,696 | 777,792 | 834,070 | 911,898 | 1,055,270 | 1,195,017 | 1,264,841 |
| Compensation of Employees.......... | c21 | 24,241 | 83,260 | 97,007 | 115,331 | 141,757 | 167,947 | 169,798 | 182,271 | 203,244 | 224,212 | 250,143 | 265,502 |
| Purchases of Goods & Services....... | c22 | 160,517 | 162,057 | 158,389 | 190,399 | 89,639 | 95,349 | 106,239 | 121,052 | 149,261 | 161,950 | 198,160 | 201,320 |
| Interest..................................... | c24 | 9,835 | 9,933 | 9,025 | 9,957 | 11,054 | 16,282 | 30,436 | 35,532 | 40,667 | 46,746 | 61,644 | 74,084 |
| Subsidies.................................. | c25 | 18,074 | 9,866 | 11,334 | 11,166 | 76,641 | 7,303 | 6,075 | 7,019 | 8,218 | 11,327 | 12,139 | 14,438 |
| Grants...................................... | c26 | 24,823 | 11,618 | 14,010 | 20,065 | 70,326 | 63,923 | 77,317 | 81,419 | 92,472 | 100,685 | 112,528 | 124,706 |
| Social Benefits............................ | c27 | 19,112 | 99,807 | 115,071 | 131,777 | 207,937 | 241,970 | 245,913 | 258,348 | 290,402 | 296,820 | 349,626 | 392,745 |
| Other Payments........................... | c28 | 6,211 | 14,965 | 24,481 | 27,620 | 129,144 | 138,921 | 142,016 | 148,428 | 127,636 | 213,530 | 210,777 | 192,046 |
| Net Cash Inflow:Operating Act.[1-2] | ccio | 30,343 | 41,130 | 85,542 | 161,570 | 76,952 | −27,190 | 19,295 | 69,756 | 74,859 | 57,198 | 11,506 | −67,084 |
| Net Cash Outflow:Invest. in NFA...... | c31 | 51,525 | 63,656 | 93,522 | 179,510 | 96,319 | 211,601 | 190,497 | 174,194 | 130,510 | 127,514 | 133,747 | 171,366 |
| Purchases of Nonfinancial Assets... | c31.1 | 60,618 | 76,176 | 109,529 | 198,663 | 184,949 | 222,810 | 192,060 | 177,714 | 133,190 | 129,076 | 136,680 | 172,207 |
| Sales of Nonfinancial Assets.......... | c31.2 | 9,094 | 12,520 | 16,007 | 19,153 | 88,630 | 11,209 | 1,563 | 3,520 | 2,680 | 1,563 | 2,933 | 841 |
| Cash Surplus/Deficit [1-2-31=1-2M] | ccsd | −21,182 | −22,526 | −7,980 | −17,940 | −19,367 | −238,791 | −171,202 | −104,438 | −55,651 | −70,315 | −122,241 | −238,450 |
| Net Acq. Fin. Assets, excl. Cash....... | c32x | 10,539 | 13,109 | 17,914 | 23,265 | 19,113 | 130,176 | 21,213 | 39,745 | 33,649 | 8,585 | 55,966 | −42,215 |
| Domestic....................................... | c321x | .... | .... | .... | .... | .... | 159,135 | −80,794 | −37,403 | 24,202 | 127,983 | −60,784 | 198,716 |
| Foreign......................................... | c322x | .... | .... | .... | .... | .... | 33,078 | 33,092 | 35,052 | 35,225 | .... | 42,384 | −43,459 |
| Net Incurrence of Liabilities............. | c33 | 40,425 | 19,585 | 33,090 | 64,711 | 68,760 | 431,534 | 124,712 | 106,778 | 119,791 | −136,665 | 83,765 | 181,138 |
| Domestic....................................... | c331 | 5,564 | 6,325 | 6,983 | 8,269 | 24,349 | 42,203 | 26,652 | 28,636 | 30,507 | 18,575 | 14,999 | 13,910 |
| Foreign......................................... | c332 | 34,860 | 13,260 | 26,107 | 56,442 | 44,411 | 389,332 | 98,059 | 78,142 | 89,284 | −155,240 | 68,766 | 167,228 |
| Net Cash Inflow, Fin.Act.[-32x+33].. | cnfb | 29,886 | 6,476 | 15,176 | 41,446 | 49,647 | 301,358 | 103,498 | 67,033 | 86,142 | −145,251 | 27,799 | 223,353 |
| Net Change in Stock of Cash........... | cncb | 8,704 | −16,049 | 7,196 | 23,506 | 30,281 | 62,567 | −67,703 | −37,405 | 30,491 | −215,566 | −94,442 | −15,097 |
| Stat. Discrep. [32X-33+NCB-CSD].... | ccsdz | — | — | — | — | 1 | — | — | — | — | — | — | — |
| Memo Item:Cash Expenditure[2+31] | c2m | 314,337 | 455,161 | 522,838 | 685,824 | 822,816 | 943,296 | 968,289 | 1,008,264 | 1,042,409 | 1,182,783 | 1,328,764 | 1,436,207 |
| Memo Item: Gross Debt.................. | c63 | .... | .... | .... | .... | .... | .... | .... | .... | .... | .... | .... | .... |
| **National Accounts** | | | | | | *Millions of Drams* | | | | | | | |
| Househ.Cons.Expend.,incl.NPISHs.... | 96f | 1,573,592 | 1,693,330 | 1,919,112 | 2,255,863 | 2,553,780 | 2,524,986 | 2,837,267 | 3,160,969 | 3,538,368 | 3,971,175 | 4,130,754 | 3,929,598 |
| Government Consumption Expend... | 91f | 194,095 | 236,646 | 268,017 | 320,382 | 365,001 | 418,990 | 452,281 | 488,400 | 509,529 | 543,718 | 583,581 | 660,102 |
| Gross Fixed Capital Formation......... | 93e | 455,305 | 668,268 | 943,780 | 1,163,203 | 1,418,785 | 1,143,829 | 1,156,732 | 985,877 | 942,721 | 966,365 | 965,487 | 1,027,796 |
| Changes in Inventories.................... | 93i | 19,361 | 15,055 | 9,955 | 26,677 | 39,590 | −54,628 | −19,389 | 44,771 | 73,770 | 47,881 | 42,338 | 896 |
| Exports of Goods and Services......... | 90c | 522,485 | 646,157 | 620,459 | 604,210 | 536,915 | 486,154 | 720,764 | 897,521 | 983,174 | 1,291,939 | 1,379,304 | 1,500,789 |
| Imports of Goods and Services (-)..... | 98c | 803,769 | 969,591 | 1,042,560 | 1,232,970 | 1,450,690 | 1,351,048 | 1,568,067 | 1,789,009 | 1,974,185 | 2,195,684 | 2,271,702 | 2,082,767 |
| Gross Domestic Product (GDP)......... | 99b | 1,907,945 | 2,242,881 | 2,656,190 | 3,149,283 | 3,568,228 | 3,141,651 | 3,460,203 | 3,777,946 | 4,000,722 | 4,555,638 | 4,828,626 | 5,032,089 |
| Statistical Discrepancy..................... | 99bs | −53,123 | −46,984 | −62,573 | 11,918 | 104,846 | −26,632 | −119,384 | −10,583 | −72,655 | −69,756 | −1,135 | −4,324 |
| | | | | | | *Millions: Midyear Estimates* | | | | | | | |
| Population............................... | 99z | 3.03 | 3.01 | 3.00 | 2.99 | 2.98 | 2.97 | 2.96 | 2.97 | 2.98 | 2.99 | 3.01 | 3.02 |

| | | 2004 | 2005 | 2006 | 2007 | 2008 | 2009 | 2010 | 2011 | 2012 | 2013 | 2014 | 2015 |
|---|---|---|---|---|---|---|---|---|---|---|---|---|---|
| **Exchange Rates** | | | | | | *Aruban Florins per SDR: End of Period* | | | | | | | |
| Official Rate | aa | 2.7799 | 2.5584 | 2.6929 | 2.8286 | 2.7571 | 2.8062 | 2.7567 | 2.7481 | 2.7511 | 2.7566 | 2.5934 | 2.4805 |
| | | | | | *Aruban Florins per US Dollar: End of Period (ae) Period Average (rf)* | | | | | | | | |
| Official Rate | ae | 1.7900 | 1.7900 | 1.7900 | 1.7900 | 1.7900 | 1.7900 | 1.7900 | 1.7900 | 1.7900 | 1.7900 | 1.7900 | 1.7900 |
| Official Rate | rf | 1.7900 | 1.7900 | 1.7900 | 1.7900 | 1.7900 | 1.7900 | 1.7900 | 1.7900 | 1.7900 | 1.7900 | 1.7900 | 1.7900 |
| **International Liquidity** | | | | | | *Millions of US Dollars: End of Period* | | | | | | | |
| Total Reserves minus Gold | 1l.d | 295.42 | 273.51 | 337.82 | 372.08 | 604.90 | 578.22 | 568.16 | 536.68 | 602.22 | 532.72 | 559.75 | 709.80 |
| Foreign Exchange | 1d.d | 295.42 | 273.51 | 337.82 | 372.08 | 604.90 | 578.22 | 568.16 | 536.68 | 602.22 | 532.72 | 559.75 | 709.80 |
| Gold (Million Fine Troy Ounces) | 1ad | .100 | .100 | .100 | .100 | .100 | .100 | .100 | .100 | .100 | .100 | .100 | .100 |
| Gold (National Valuation) | 1and | 48.663 | 56.996 | 70.628 | 92.937 | 96.104 | 122.869 | 156.953 | 175.232 | 185.193 | 133.720 | 133.469 | 118.222 |
| Monetary Authorities: Other Liabs | 4..d | .84 | 1.66 | 9.59 | 2.46 | 4.20 | 1.75 | .66 | .46 | 2.08 | .03 | .62 | 1.24 |
| Deposit Money Banks: Assets | 7a.d | 329.04 | 324.76 | 330.72 | 376.70 | 427.22 | 484.19 | 397.00 | 402.73 | 382.81 | 370.87 | 366.35 | 373.37 |
| Deposit Money Banks: Liabs | 7b.d | 268.50 | 276.20 | 306.65 | 359.38 | 325.63 | 302.59 | 298.16 | 279.87 | 294.93 | 357.93 | 338.48 | 300.15 |
| **Monetary Authorities** | | | | | | *Millions of Aruban Florins: End of Period* | | | | | | | |
| Foreign Assets | 11 | 615.92 | 591.61 | 731.12 | 832.39 | 1,254.80 | 1,254.95 | 1,296.78 | 1,274.32 | 1,409.47 | 1,192.93 | 1,240.87 | 1,482.16 |
| Claims on Central Government | 12a | — | — | — | — | — | — | — | — | — | — | — | — |
| Claims on Nonfin.Pub.Enterprises | 12c | — | — | — | — | — | — | — | — | — | — | — | — |
| Claims on Private Sector | 12d | — | — | — | — | — | — | — | — | — | — | — | — |
| Claims on Deposit Money Banks | 12e | — | — | — | — | — | — | — | — | — | — | — | — |
| Reserve Money | 14 | 444.57 | 450.08 | 524.71 | 560.34 | 846.87 | 895.37 | 988.16 | 798.80 | 1,077.21 | 980.53 | 1,029.23 | 1,235.15 |
| of which: Currency Outside DMBs | 14a | 130.66 | 144.12 | 157.36 | 174.79 | 181.19 | 174.61 | 175.25 | 182.76 | 199.91 | 213.60 | 227.18 | 240.01 |
| Time, Savings,& Fgn.Currency Dep | 15 | .69 | .78 | .79 | .79 | .79 | .79 | .79 | .79 | .79 | .79 | .79 | .79 |
| Foreign Liabilities | 16c | 1.51 | 2.97 | 17.17 | 4.41 | 7.52 | 3.13 | 1.19 | .83 | 3.73 | .06 | 1.11 | 2.21 |
| Central Government Deposits | 16d | 48.28 | 6.91 | 26.96 | 62.15 | 183.53 | 201.16 | 84.17 | 216.34 | 58.78 | 82.45 | 57.15 | 107.86 |
| Capital Accounts | 17a | 143.41 | 157.37 | 184.09 | 220.76 | 232.53 | 184.82 | 247.49 | 293.71 | 307.27 | 173.25 | 204.16 | 184.96 |
| Other Items (Net) | 17r | −22.54 | −26.50 | −22.60 | −16.06 | −16.43 | −30.33 | −25.02 | −36.14 | −38.30 | −44.15 | −51.58 | −48.82 |
| **Deposit Money Banks** | | | | | | *Millions of Aruban Florins: End of Period* | | | | | | | |
| Reserves | 20 | 306.59 | 302.13 | 364.29 | 375.91 | 666.07 | 708.33 | 812.85 | 615.66 | 879.17 | 767.33 | 787.73 | 996.12 |
| Foreign Assets | 21 | 588.99 | 581.31 | 591.98 | 674.30 | 764.73 | 866.71 | 710.63 | 720.89 | 685.23 | 663.85 | 655.76 | 668.33 |
| Claims on Central Government | 22a | 84.89 | 125.30 | 119.37 | 129.05 | 83.21 | 123.39 | 241.71 | 276.99 | 313.26 | 318.15 | 314.99 | 336.02 |
| Claims on Private Sector | 22d | 2,090.13 | 2,283.76 | 2,382.17 | 2,479.28 | 2,578.02 | 2,555.03 | 2,582.49 | 2,656.02 | 2,747.22 | 2,888.87 | 3,009.39 | 3,002.39 |
| Demand Deposits | 24 | 826.72 | 808.37 | 883.59 | 971.55 | 1,213.27 | 1,366.09 | 1,197.52 | 1,371.60 | 1,629.61 | 1,499.84 | 1,545.23 | 1,819.77 |
| Time and Savings Deposits | 25 | 1,313.76 | 1,455.89 | 1,436.07 | 1,418.50 | 1,592.77 | 1,621.39 | 1,780.83 | 1,603.07 | 1,588.15 | 1,575.82 | 1,703.07 | 1,744.34 |
| Bonds | 26ab | 5.00 | 5.00 | 5.00 | 5.00 | — | — | — | — | — | 12.51 | 12.51 | 47.51 |
| Foreign Liabilities | 26c | 480.62 | 494.40 | 548.91 | 643.28 | 582.88 | 541.64 | 533.71 | 500.97 | 527.92 | 640.70 | 605.88 | 537.26 |
| Central Government Deposits | 26d | 65.18 | 142.36 | 160.80 | 133.31 | 113.36 | 96.98 | 198.92 | 124.88 | 147.56 | 161.09 | 127.65 | 65.69 |
| Credit from Monetary Authorities | 26g | — | — | — | — | — | — | — | — | — | — | — | — |
| Capital Accounts | 27a | 233.36 | 243.86 | 269.30 | 325.91 | 422.53 | 460.23 | 454.62 | 475.14 | 512.99 | 542.18 | 592.73 | 640.96 |
| Other Items (Net) | 27r | 145.96 | 142.62 | 154.14 | 160.98 | 167.21 | 167.13 | 182.09 | 193.90 | 218.64 | 206.08 | 180.82 | 147.34 |
| **Monetary Survey** | | | | | | *Millions of Aruban Florins: End of Period* | | | | | | | |
| Foreign Assets (Net) | 31n | 722.78 | 675.56 | 757.02 | 858.99 | 1,429.12 | 1,576.89 | 1,472.52 | 1,493.41 | 1,563.05 | 1,216.03 | 1,289.64 | 1,611.02 |
| Domestic Credit | 32 | 2,061.56 | 2,259.79 | 2,313.77 | 2,412.87 | 2,364.34 | 2,380.28 | 2,541.11 | 2,591.80 | 2,854.14 | 2,963.49 | 3,139.58 | 3,164.85 |
| Claims on Central Govt. (Net) | 32an | −28.56 | −23.96 | −68.40 | −66.40 | −213.68 | −174.75 | −41.38 | −64.22 | 106.92 | 74.62 | 130.19 | 162.47 |
| Claims on Nonfin.Pub.Enterprises | 32c | — | — | — | — | — | — | — | — | — | — | — | — |
| Claims on Private Sector | 32d | 2,090.13 | 2,283.76 | 2,382.17 | 2,479.28 | 2,578.02 | 2,555.03 | 2,582.49 | 2,656.02 | 2,747.22 | 2,888.87 | 3,009.39 | 3,002.39 |
| Money | 34 | 960.83 | 964.99 | 1,055.45 | 1,147.13 | 1,397.94 | 1,541.33 | 1,373.10 | 1,554.73 | 1,829.94 | 1,713.44 | 1,772.41 | 2,059.77 |
| Quasi-Money | 35 | 1,314.45 | 1,456.67 | 1,436.86 | 1,419.29 | 1,593.56 | 1,622.18 | 1,781.62 | 1,603.86 | 1,588.94 | 1,576.61 | 1,703.86 | 1,745.13 |
| Bonds | 36ab | 5.00 | 5.00 | 5.00 | 5.00 | — | — | — | — | — | 12.51 | 12.51 | 47.51 |
| Capital Accounts | 37a | 376.77 | 401.24 | 453.39 | 546.67 | 655.06 | 645.04 | 702.11 | 768.85 | 820.25 | 715.43 | 796.88 | 825.92 |
| Other Items (Net) | 37r | 127.29 | 107.46 | 120.09 | 153.78 | 146.90 | 148.61 | 156.80 | 157.76 | 178.05 | 161.53 | 143.56 | 97.53 |
| Money plus Quasi-Money | 35l | 2,275.29 | 2,421.66 | 2,492.31 | 2,566.41 | 2,991.51 | 3,163.51 | 3,154.72 | 3,158.59 | 3,418.88 | 3,290.05 | 3,476.27 | 3,804.91 |
| **Money (National Definitions)** | | | | | | *Millions of Aruban Florins: End of Period* | | | | | | | |
| Narrow Money | 59mak | 960.80 | 965.00 | 1,047.40 | 1,147.10 | 1,397.10 | 1,541.30 | 1,373.00 | 1,554.70 | 1,830.20 | 1,713.40 | 1,773.20 | 2,008.40 |
| Quasi-Money | 59mal | 1,324.50 | 1,461.90 | 1,437.00 | 1,419.30 | 1,593.60 | 1,622.20 | 1,781.60 | 1,603.90 | 1,588.90 | 1,578.60 | 1,703.10 | 1,744.30 |
| Broad Money | 59mea | 2,285.30 | 2,426.80 | 2,484.40 | 2,566.40 | 2,991.50 | 3,163.50 | 3,154.60 | 3,158.60 | 3,419.20 | 3,292.00 | 3,476.30 | 3,804.90 |
| **Interest Rates** | | | | | | *Percent Per Annum* | | | | | | | |
| Discount Rate (End of Period) | 60.a | 5.00 | 5.00 | 5.00 | 5.00 | 5.00 | 3.00 | 1.00 | 1.00 | 1.00 | 1.00 | 1.00 | 1.00 |
| Money Market Rate | 60b | .11 | .51 | 2.27 | 2.53 | .45 | .05 | .05 | .05 | .05 | .05 | .05 | .05 |
| Deposit Rate | 60l | 4.26 | 3.94 | 3.89 | 4.03 | 3.62 | 3.35 | 2.58 | 1.68 | 1.54 | 1.63 | 2.18 | 1.95 |
| Lending Rate | 60p | 11.58 | 11.53 | 11.33 | 11.01 | 11.23 | 10.77 | 10.65 | 9.66 | 9.18 | 8.73 | 8.23 | 8.25 |
| **Prices and Tourism** | | | | | | *Index Numbers (2010=100): Period Averages* | | | | | | | |
| Consumer Prices | 64 | 81.4 | 84.1 | 87.2 | 91.9 | 100.1 | 98.0 | 100.0 | 104.4 | 105.0 | 102.5 | 102.9 | 103.4 |
| Number of Tourists | 66ta | 88.3 | 88.9 | 84.2 | 93.7 | 100.3 | 98.6 | 100.0 | 105.4 | 109.7 | 118.8 | 130.1 | . . . . |
| Number of Tourist Nights | 66tb | 87.2 | 88.1 | 84.6 | 91.1 | 96.9 | 95.4 | 100.0 | 103.4 | 106.8 | 110.2 | 119.0 | 128.8 |
| **Intl. Transactions & Positions** | | | | | | *Millions of US Dollars* | | | | | | | |
| Exports | 70..d | 79.6 | 101.8 | 109.0 | 97.9 | 99.9 | 135.7 | 124.5 | 151.3 | 172.7 | 167.2 | 111.1 | 80.6 |
| Imports, c.i.f | 71..d | 875.2 | 1,028.4 | 1,041.3 | 1,113.9 | 1,134.3 | 1,147.3 | 1,069.0 | 1,282.7 | 1,257.5 | 1,303.0 | 1,261.7 | 1,167.2 |

# Aruba   314

|  |  | 2004 | 2005 | 2006 | 2007 | 2008 | 2009 | 2010 | 2011 | 2012 | 2013 | 2014 | 2015 |
|---|---|---|---|---|---|---|---|---|---|---|---|---|---|
| **Balance of Payments** |  | | | | | *Millions of US Dollars* | | | | | | | |
| A. Current Account* | 109bx | 270.9 | 105.0 | 310.6 | 258.3 | .1 | 171.7 | −460.1 | −260.6 | 90.8 | −331.2 | −136.7 | 95.9 |
| Goods, credit (exports) | 1a9cx | 3,434.6 | 4,416.2 | 4,717.0 | 5,206.6 | 5,456.6 | 1,951.8 | 264.5 | 5,180.2 | 1,388.9 | 279.1 | 259.0 | 334.1 |
| Goods, debit (imports) | 1a9dx | 3,589.0 | 4,296.2 | 4,724.3 | 5,126.0 | 6,018.0 | 2,453.2 | 1,394.2 | 5,916.8 | 2,044.9 | 1,376.6 | 1,350.9 | 1,253.6 |
| Balance on goods | 1a9bx | −154.5 | 120.0 | −7.3 | 80.6 | −561.4 | −501.3 | −1,129.7 | −736.6 | −656.0 | −1,097.6 | −1,092.0 | −919.6 |
| Services, credit (exports) | 1b9cx | 1,253.3 | 1,307.8 | 1,309.2 | 1,471.2 | 1,603.1 | 1,538.3 | 1,560.1 | 1,680.9 | 1,762.1 | 1,882.8 | 2,040.1 | 2,087.1 |
| Services, debit (imports) | 1b9dx | 645.3 | 711.7 | 755.2 | 785.4 | 793.9 | 692.6 | 679.3 | 843.4 | 824.5 | 892.4 | 911.4 | 880.4 |
| Balance on Goods & Services | 1z9bx | 453.5 | 716.1 | 546.7 | 766.4 | 247.8 | 344.4 | −248.9 | 101.0 | 281.6 | −107.2 | 36.8 | 287.1 |
| Primary income: credit | 1c9cx | 35.7 | 42.4 | 62.2 | 90.8 | 71.8 | 59.1 | 45.9 | 40.4 | 36.2 | 37.7 | 45.0 | 48.7 |
| Primary income: debit | 1c9dx | 109.9 | 520.9 | 168.1 | 475.4 | 188.5 | 148.2 | 186.1 | 286.1 | 151.3 | 202.3 | 148.1 | 173.4 |
| Balance on gds, serv. & prim. inc. | 1y9bx | 379.3 | 237.6 | 440.8 | 381.8 | 131.0 | 255.3 | −389.2 | −144.6 | 166.5 | −271.8 | −66.4 | 162.4 |
| Secondary income: credit | 1d9ca | 44.7 | 51.0 | 53.2 | 56.8 | 66.6 | 67.9 | 69.9 | 74.2 | 79.4 | 103.2 | 93.1 | 96.6 |
| Secondary income: debit | 1d9da | 153.1 | 183.6 | 183.5 | 180.4 | 197.5 | 151.5 | 140.9 | 190.1 | 155.1 | 162.5 | 163.4 | 163.1 |
| B. Capital Account* | 209ba | 17.3 | 16.0 | 18.5 | 19.4 | 159.1 | 28.2 | 3.5 | — | — | — | — | — |
| Capital account: credit | 209ca | 17.3 | 16.0 | 18.5 | 19.4 | 159.1 | 28.2 | 3.5 | — | — | — | — | — |
| Capital account: debit | 209da | — | — | — | — | — | — | — | — | — | — | — | — |
| Balance on current & capital acct. | 129ba | 288.2 | 120.9 | 329.1 | 277.7 | 159.2 | 199.9 | −456.6 | −260.6 | 90.8 | −331.2 | −136.7 | 95.9 |
| C. Financial Account* | 309na | 291.4 | 169.8 | 277.4 | 238.9 | −74.7 | 46.7 | −435.1 | −225.4 | 36.9 | −340.1 | −181.5 | −35.1 |
| Direct investment: assets | 3a9aa | −8.2 | −8.9 | −12.8 | 39.6 | 2.8 | 1.5 | 2.7 | 3.1 | 2.8 | 8.1 | 8.9 | 10.6 |
| Equity & investment fund shares | 3aaaa | .1 | .4 | −1.0 | −1.5 | 3.8 | .4 | 3.2 | 4.5 | 2.7 | 3.5 | 8.3 | 10.6 |
| Debt instruments | 3abaa | −8.3 | −9.3 | −11.9 | 41.0 | −1.0 | 1.1 | −.4 | −1.4 | .1 | 4.6 | .6 | .1 |
| Direct investment: liabilities | 3a9la | −105.7 | −207.8 | 220.3 | −471.0 | 18.9 | −10.6 | 186.8 | 488.2 | −314.7 | 229.9 | 246.8 | −22.7 |
| Equity & investment fund shares | 3aala | 115.2 | 109.6 | 266.4 | 32.7 | 219.4 | 191.7 | 36.2 | 75.0 | 105.1 | 60.2 | 224.9 | 102.6 |
| Debt instruments | 3abla | −220.9 | −317.4 | −46.1 | −503.7 | −200.5 | −202.3 | 150.6 | 413.1 | −419.8 | 169.7 | 21.9 | −125.3 |
| Portfolio investment: assets | 3b9aa | 44.8 | 18.5 | 83.9 | 26.1 | 2.6 | 16.4 | 3.2 | 9.7 | 21.7 | 7.8 | 35.2 | 47.1 |
| Equity & investment fund shares | 3baaa | 36.8 | 3.3 | 75.3 | 39.1 | 12.3 | −9.1 | .8 | 3.3 | −178.2 | 50.3 | 14.7 | 8.5 |
| Debt securities | 3bbaa | 8.1 | 15.2 | 8.6 | −13.0 | −9.7 | 25.5 | 2.3 | 6.4 | 199.9 | −42.5 | 20.5 | 38.5 |
| Portfolio investment: liabilities | 3b9la | 61.8 | 40.9 | 36.0 | 87.0 | 45.2 | 14.5 | 12.1 | 22.3 | 164.9 | 138.5 | 144.1 | 108.0 |
| Equity & investment fund shares | 3bala | — | — | — | — | — | — | — | — | — | — | — | — |
| Debt securities | 3bbla | 61.8 | 40.9 | 36.0 | 87.0 | 45.2 | 14.5 | 12.1 | 22.3 | 164.9 | 138.5 | 144.1 | 108.0 |
| Fin. der.& empl.stk.ops.(ESOs): net | 3c9na | 1.4 | −1.5 | 2.7 | −1.1 | 10.3 | .9 | — | — | −1.7 | −.2 | 3.7 | 40.5 |
| Fin. der. & ESOs: assets | 3c9aa | −.2 | −2.6 | −1.2 | −2.8 | −.1 | −.6 | — | — | −1.7 | −.7 | −1.1 | — |
| Fin. der. & ESOs: liabilities | 3c9la | −1.6 | −1.0 | −3.9 | −1.8 | −10.4 | −1.6 | — | — | — | −.6 | −4.8 | −40.5 |
| Other investment: assets | 3d9aa | 104.0 | −52.4 | 423.0 | −209.9 | −83.4 | −9.6 | −243.2 | 223.3 | −209.7 | 4.5 | 122.3 | −71.0 |
| Other equity | 3daaa | .... | .... | .... | .... | .... | .... | .... | .... | .... | .... | .... | .... |
| Debt instruments | 3dzaa | 104.0 | −52.4 | 423.0 | −209.9 | −83.4 | −9.6 | −243.2 | 223.3 | −209.7 | 4.5 | 122.3 | −71.0 |
| Other investment: liabilities | 3d9la | −105.4 | −47.2 | −37.0 | −.2 | −57.0 | −41.3 | −1.1 | −48.9 | −74.1 | −8.1 | −39.3 | −23.0 |
| Other equity | 3dala | .... | .... | .... | .... | .... | .... | .... | .... | .... | .... | .... | .... |
| Debt instruments | 3dzla | −105.4 | −47.2 | −37.0 | −.2 | −57.0 | −41.3 | −1.1 | −48.9 | −74.1 | −8.1 | −39.3 | −23.0 |
| Curr.+ cap.− finan. acct. balance | 4y9na | −3.2 | −48.9 | 51.6 | 38.7 | 233.9 | 153.2 | −21.5 | −35.1 | 53.9 | 8.9 | 44.7 | 131.0 |
| D. Net Errors and Omissions | 409na | 4.8 | 26.7 | 3.5 | 4.5 | −8.6 | −119.0 | 10.9 | −1.1 | 12.4 | −52.0 | −35.5 | 14.6 |
| E. Reserves and Related Items | 4z9na | 1.6 | −22.2 | 55.1 | 43.2 | 225.3 | 34.2 | −10.6 | −36.3 | 66.3 | −43.1 | 9.2 | 145.6 |
| Reserve assets | 3e9aa | 1.6 | −22.2 | 55.1 | 43.2 | 225.3 | 34.2 | −10.6 | −36.3 | 66.3 | −43.1 | 9.2 | 145.6 |
| Credit and loans from the IMF | 3dcla | .... | .... | .... | .... | .... | .... | .... | .... | .... | .... | .... | .... |
| Exceptional financing | 409la | .... | .... | .... | .... | .... | .... | .... | .... | .... | .... | .... | .... |

*Excludes components in group E

| **International Investment Position** |  | | | | | *Millions of US Dollars* | | | | | | | |
|---|---|---|---|---|---|---|---|---|---|---|---|---|---|
| Assets | 809aa | 1,893.3 | 1,841.2 | 2,427.9 | 2,291.6 | 2,326.5 | 2,549.3 | 2,402.8 | 2,595.4 | 2,487.2 | 2,353.0 | 2,550.9 | 2,691.0 |
| Direct investment | 8a9aa | 646.8 | 636.7 | 623.0 | 609.7 | 612.3 | 613.9 | 616.7 | 619.8 | 622.6 | 627.0 | 635.6 | 646.1 |
| Equity & investment fund shares | 8aaaa | .... | .... | .... | .... | .... | .... | .... | .... | .... | .... | .... | .... |
| Debt instruments | 8abaa | .... | .... | .... | .... | .... | .... | .... | .... | .... | .... | .... | .... |
| Portfolio investment | 8b9aa | 382.5 | 409.6 | 507.0 | 513.6 | 397.2 | 480.7 | 561.9 | 521.1 | 569.3 | 554.0 | 621.1 | 627.2 |
| Equity & investment fund shares | 8baaa | 261.0 | 279.1 | 342.8 | 407.6 | 275.2 | 326.7 | 402.9 | 398.1 | 199.9 | 254.0 | 280.0 | 260.8 |
| Debt securities | 8bbaa | 121.5 | 130.6 | 164.2 | 106.0 | 122.0 | 154.0 | 159.0 | 123.0 | 369.4 | 300.0 | 341.1 | 366.3 |
| Fin. der.(oth.than reserves) & ESOs | 8c9aa | .... | .... | .... | .... | .... | .... | .... | .... | 3.5 | 3.2 | .... | .... |
| Other investment | 8d9aa | 519.9 | 464.4 | 889.5 | 703.3 | 615.9 | 753.6 | 499.8 | 742.6 | 504.4 | 502.3 | 601.0 | 589.7 |
| Other equity | 8daaa | .... | .... | .... | .... | .... | .... | .... | .... | .... | .... | .... | .... |
| Debt instruments | 8dzaa | 519.9 | 464.4 | 889.5 | 703.3 | 615.9 | 753.6 | 499.8 | 742.6 | 504.4 | 502.3 | 601.0 | 589.7 |
| Reserve assets | 8e9aa | 344.1 | 330.5 | 408.4 | 465.0 | 701.0 | 701.1 | 724.5 | 711.9 | 787.4 | 666.4 | 693.2 | 828.0 |
| Liabilities | 809la | 3,273.0 | 3,779.3 | 4,933.0 | 5,515.9 | 5,935.3 | 5,818.0 | 5,845.8 | 6,362.9 | 4,966.8 | 5,283.1 | 5,714.6 | 5,790.0 |
| Direct investment | 8a9la | 1,880.0 | 2,383.0 | 3,743.0 | 4,178.0 | 4,527.0 | 4,440.0 | 4,567.0 | 5,065.3 | 3,511.0 | 3,737.0 | 3,975.0 | 3,952.5 |
| Equity & investment fund shares | 8aala | .... | .... | .... | .... | .... | .... | .... | .... | .... | .... | .... | .... |
| Debt instruments | 8abla | .... | .... | .... | .... | .... | .... | .... | .... | .... | .... | .... | .... |
| Portfolio investment | 8b9la | 460.7 | 514.4 | 381.8 | 518.9 | 599.9 | 616.2 | 575.7 | 597.5 | 761.5 | 840.4 | 978.8 | 1,095.9 |
| Equity & investment fund shares | 8bala | .... | .... | .... | .... | .... | .... | .... | .... | .... | .... | .... | .... |
| Debt securities | 8bbla | 460.7 | 514.4 | 381.8 | 518.9 | 599.9 | 616.2 | 575.7 | 597.5 | 761.5 | 840.4 | 978.8 | 1,095.9 |
| Fin. der.(oth.than reserves) & ESOs | 8c9la | .... | .... | .... | .... | .... | .... | .... | .... | .... | .1 | 86.9 | 90.7 |
| Other investment | 8d9la | 932.3 | 881.9 | 808.2 | 819.0 | 808.4 | 761.9 | 703.1 | 700.1 | 694.3 | 705.6 | 673.9 | 651.0 |
| Other equity | 8dala | .... | .... | .... | .... | .... | .... | .... | .... | .... | .... | .... | .... |
| Debt instruments | 8dzla | 932.3 | 881.9 | 808.2 | 819.0 | 808.4 | 761.9 | 703.1 | 700.1 | 694.3 | 705.6 | 673.9 | 651.0 |

| **National Accounts** |  | | | | | *Millions of Aruban Florins* | | | | | | | |
|---|---|---|---|---|---|---|---|---|---|---|---|---|---|
| Exports of Goods and Services | 90c | 2,595.8 | 2,860.2 | 2,838.7 | 3,095.6 | 3,311.5 | 2,853.2 | 2,716.7 | 3,096.0 | 2,960.0 | 3,170.0 | 3,346.0 | .... |
| Government Consumption Expend | 91f | 923.7 | 964.7 | 986.9 | 1,026.4 | 1,081.3 | 1,135.2 | 1,162.3 | 1,186.0 | 1,268.0 | 1,303.0 | 1,250.0 | .... |
| Gross Capital Formation | 93 | 1,148.3 | 1,400.8 | 1,526.1 | 1,521.6 | 1,633.7 | 1,355.0 | 1,242.2 | 1,301.0 | 1,209.0 | 1,112.0 | 1,064.0 | .... |
| Househ.Cons.Expend.,incl.NPISHs | 96f | 2,055.8 | 2,198.6 | 2,362.5 | 2,643.4 | 2,715.6 | 2,541.6 | 2,600.8 | 2,806.0 | 2,833.0 | 2,876.0 | 2,874.0 | .... |
| Imports of Goods and Services (-) | 98c | 2,735.1 | 3,251.8 | 3,379.7 | 3,590.5 | 3,744.5 | 3,411.9 | 3,304.8 | 3,824.0 | 3,735.0 | 3,831.0 | 3,766.0 | .... |
| Gross Domestic Product (GDP) | 99b | 3,988.6 | 4,172.5 | 4,334.4 | 4,696.5 | 4,997.6 | 4,473.1 | 4,417.2 | 4,564.0 | 4,534.0 | 4,629.0 | 4,768.0 | .... |
| GDP at 2000 Prices | 99b.p | 3,464.0 | 3,506.0 | 3,543.0 | 3,615.0 | 3,620.0 | 3,210.0 | 3,103.0 | 3,211.0 | 3,169.0 | 3,293.0 | .... | .... |
| GDP Volume (2010=100) | 99bvp | 111.6 | 113.0 | 114.2 | 116.5 | 116.7 | 103.4 | 100.0 | 103.5 | 102.1 | 106.1 | .... | .... |
| GDP Deflator (2010=100) | 99bip | 80.9 | 83.6 | 85.9 | 91.3 | 97.0 | 97.9 | 100.0 | 99.8 | 100.5 | 98.7 | .... | .... |

| | | | | | | *Millions: Midyear Estimates* | | | | | | | |
|---|---|---|---|---|---|---|---|---|---|---|---|---|---|
| **Population** | 99z | .10 | .10 | .10 | .10 | .10 | .10 | .10 | .10 | .10 | .10 | .10 | .10 |

# Australia   193

|  |  | 2004 | 2005 | 2006 | 2007 | 2008 | 2009 | 2010 | 2011 | 2012 | 2013 | 2014 | 2015 |
|---|---|---|---|---|---|---|---|---|---|---|---|---|---|
| **Exchange Rates** | | | | | | *Australian Dollars per SDR: End of Period* | | | | | | | |
| Market Rate..................................... | aa | 1.9936 | 1.9480 | 1.9012 | 1.7925 | 2.2233 | 1.7479 | 1.5153 | 1.5117 | 1.4771 | 1.7372 | 1.7664 | 1.8967 |
| | | | | | *Australian Dollars per US Dollar: End of Period (ae) Period Average (rf)* | | | | | | | | |
| Market Rate..................................... | ae | 1.2837 | 1.3630 | 1.2637 | 1.1343 | 1.4434 | 1.1150 | .9840 | .9846 | .9611 | 1.1280 | 1.2192 | 1.3687 |
| Market Rate..................................... | rf | 1.3598 | 1.3095 | 1.3280 | 1.1951 | 1.1922 | 1.2822 | 1.0902 | .9695 | .9658 | 1.0358 | 1.1094 | 1.3311 |
| | | | | | *Index Numbers (2010=100): Period Averages* | | | | | | | | |
| Market Rate..................................... | ahx | 80.1 | 83.1 | 81.9 | 91.2 | 93.0 | 86.1 | 100.0 | 112.3 | 112.6 | 105.3 | 98.2 | 81.9 |
| Nominal Effective Exchange Rate..... | nec | 87.5 | 89.9 | 88.1 | 93.5 | 91.8 | 87.9 | 100.0 | 107.1 | 110.3 | 105.1 | 99.4 | 91.7 |
| CPI-Based Real Effect. Ex. Rate........ | rec | 84.5 | 87.1 | 86.3 | 91.3 | 89.8 | 87.3 | 100.0 | 107.1 | 109.8 | 105.2 | 100.1 | 92.9 |
| ULC-Based Real Effect. Ex. Rate....... | rel | 71.2 | 76.7 | 79.3 | 88.1 | 87.0 | 80.8 | 100.0 | 111.6 | 118.1 | 114.0 | 109.0 | 103.9 |
| **Fund Position** | | | | | | *Millions of SDRs: End of Period* | | | | | | | |
| Quota............................................. | 2f.s | 3,236.40 | 3,236.40 | 3,236.40 | 3,236.40 | 3,236.40 | 3,236.40 | 3,236.40 | 3,236.40 | 3,236.40 | 3,236.40 | 3,236.40 | 3,236.40 |
| SDR Holdings................................. | 1b.s | 125.50 | 135.11 | 132.68 | 121.91 | 113.02 | 3,097.75 | 3,093.65 | 3,017.98 | 2,951.20 | 3,107.26 | 2,946.46 | 3,016.57 |
| Reserve Position in the Fund............ | 1c.s | 1,098.71 | 543.00 | 284.28 | 214.46 | 421.66 | 696.66 | 715.68 | 1,398.68 | 1,616.86 | 1,575.83 | 1,287.48 | 1,000.70 |
| Total Fund Cred.&Loans Outstg....... | 2tl | — | — | — | — | — | — | — | — | — | — | — | — |
| SDR Allocations............................. | 1bd | 470.55 | 470.55 | 470.55 | 470.55 | 470.55 | 3,083.17 | 3,083.17 | 3,083.17 | 3,083.17 | 3,083.17 | 3,083.17 | 3,083.17 |
| **International Liquidity** | | | | | | *Millions of US Dollars Unless Otherwise Indicated: End of Period* | | | | | | | |
| Total Reserves minus Gold.............. | 1l.d | 35,803 | 41,941 | 53,448 | 24,768 | 30,691 | 38,950 | 38,659 | 42,783 | 44,866 | 49,745 | 50,814 | 46,540 |
| SDR Holdings................................. | 1b.d | 195 | 193 | 200 | 193 | 174 | 4,856 | 4,764 | 4,633 | 4,536 | 4,785 | 4,269 | 4,180 |
| Reserve Position in the Fund......... | 1c.d | 1,706 | 776 | 428 | 339 | 649 | 1,092 | 1,102 | 2,147 | 2,485 | 2,427 | 1,865 | 1,387 |
| Foreign Exchange....................... | 1d.d | 33,901 | 40,972 | 52,821 | 24,237 | 29,867 | 33,002 | 32,793 | 36,003 | 37,845 | 42,533 | 44,680 | 40,973 |
| Gold (Million Fine Troy Ounces)........ | 1ad | 2.56 | 2.57 | 2.57 | 2.57 | 2.57 | 2.57 | 2.57 | 2.57 | 2.57 | 2.57 | 2.57 | 2.57 |
| Gold (National Valuation)................ | 1and | 1,123 | 1,316 | 1,631 | 2,140 | 2,233 | 2,792 | 3,608 | 4,042 | 4,281 | 3,056 | 3,079 | 2,727 |
| Central Bank: Other Assets............. | 3..d | — | — | — | † 224 | 1,068 | 264 | 292 | 311 | 337 | 349 | 307 | 303 |
| Central Bank: Other Liabs............... | 4..d | 390 | 457 | 1,239 | † 10,688 | 5,427 | 1,130 | 3,564 | 1,908 | 908 | 1,655 | 2,464 | 2,416 |
| Other Depository Corps.: Assets....... | 7a.d | 56,564 | 54,121 | 76,764 | † 144,584 | 200,598 | 171,644 | 227,162 | 269,572 | 313,774 | 324,661 | 394,783 | 427,597 |
| Other Depository Corps.: Liabs......... | 7b.d | 203,281 | 221,737 | 305,869 | † 457,086 | 464,283 | 555,389 | 612,521 | 640,090 | 708,797 | 678,486 | 722,816 | 715,187 |
| Other Financial Corps.: Assets.......... | 7e.d | .... | .... | .... | 21,444 | 21,590 | 12,590 | 12,556 | 10,459 | 11,873 | 8,624 | 27,927 | 26,412 |
| Other Financial Corps.: Liabs............ | 7f.d | .... | .... | .... | 42,060 | 36,436 | 20,687 | 23,474 | 24,026 | 29,272 | 26,715 | 42,322 | 40,058 |
| **Central Bank** | | | | | | *Millions of Australian Dollars: End of Period* | | | | | | | |
| Net Foreign Assets........................... | 11n | 50,374 | 50,916 | 60,914 | † 30,854 | 49,054 | 48,547 | 41,896 | 47,712 | 49,053 | 61,286 | 67,082 | 68,370 |
| Claims on Nonresidents................ | 11 | 50,875 | 51,539 | 62,480 | † 42,977 | 56,888 | 49,807 | 45,403 | 49,591 | 49,927 | 63,136 | 70,086 | 71,677 |
| Liabilities to Nonresidents............ | 16c | 501 | 623 | 1,566 | † 12,123 | 7,833 | 1,260 | 3,507 | 1,879 | 874 | 1,850 | 3,004 | 3,307 |
| Claims on Other Depository Corps.... | 12e | 11,409 | 16,117 | 21,397 | † 44,263 | 96,438 | 32,210 | 24,336 | 30,554 | 31,119 | 59,066 | 73,755 | 73,435 |
| Net Claims on Central Government.. | 12an | −7,725 | −9,917 | −23,964 | † −13,171 | −11,004 | −15,712 | −8,237 | −16,167 | −14,310 | −18,861 | −25,028 | −16,314 |
| Claims on Central Government...... | 12a | — | — | — | † 1,702 | 129 | 298 | 1,540 | 1,987 | 7,019 | 5,641 | 4,294 | 7,886 |
| Liabilities to Central Government... | 16d | 7,725 | 9,917 | 23,964 | † 14,873 | 11,133 | 16,010 | 9,777 | 18,154 | 21,329 | 24,502 | 29,322 | 24,200 |
| Claims on Other Sectors.................. | 12s | — | — | — | † 3,004 | 5,002 | 3,887 | 3,928 | 6,941 | 5,877 | 2,933 | 2,840 | 2,419 |
| Claims on Other Financial Corps.... | 12g | — | — | — | † — | — | — | — | — | — | — | — | — |
| Claims on State & Local Govts....... | 12b | — | — | — | † 3,004 | 5,002 | 3,887 | 3,928 | 6,941 | 5,877 | 2,933 | 2,840 | 2,419 |
| Claims on Public Nonfin. Corps...... | 12c | — | — | — | † — | — | — | — | — | — | — | — | — |
| Claims on Private Sector................ | 12d | — | — | — | † — | — | — | — | — | — | — | — | — |
| Monetary Base................................. | 14 | 34,927 | 37,042 | 38,962 | † 44,961 | 52,147 | 51,635 | 53,139 | 55,856 | 59,083 | 63,200 | 67,063 | 72,187 |
| Currency in Circulation.................. | 14a | 34,861 | 37,001 | 38,946 | † 44,939 | 51,709 | 51,615 | 53,082 | 55,817 | 58,982 | 63,018 | 66,854 | 71,924 |
| Liabs. to Other Depository Corps. | 14c | — | — | — | † — | — | — | — | — | — | — | — | — |
| Liabilities to Other Sectors............. | 14d | 66 | 41 | 16 | † 22 | 438 | 20 | 57 | 39 | 101 | 182 | 209 | 263 |
| Other Liabs. to Other Dep. Corps..... | 14n | 768 | 769 | 795 | † 8,022 | 26,758 | 5,684 | 2,529 | 4,247 | 3,453 | 25,070 | 24,418 | 26,459 |
| Dep. & Sec. Excl. f/Monetary Base.... | 14o | 7 | 2 | 4 | † — | — | — | — | — | — | — | — | — |
| Deposits Included in Broad Money. | 15 | — | — | — | † — | — | — | — | — | — | — | — | — |
| Sec.Ot.th.Shares Incl.in Brd. Money | 16a | — | — | — | † — | — | — | — | — | — | — | — | — |
| Deposits Excl. from Broad Money.. | 16b | 7 | 2 | 4 | † — | — | — | — | — | — | — | — | — |
| Sec.Ot.th.Shares Excl.f/Brd.Money.. | 16s | — | — | — | † — | — | — | — | — | — | — | — | — |
| Loans............................................. | 16l | — | — | — | † — | — | — | — | — | — | — | — | — |
| Financial Derivatives....................... | 16m | — | — | — | † — | — | — | — | — | — | — | — | — |
| Shares and Other Equity.................. | 17a | 6,325 | 6,325 | 6,325 | † 6,326 | 6,326 | 6,903 | 6,223 | 6,067 | 6,533 | 11,952 | 21,597 | 24,039 |
| Other Items (Net)............................ | 17r | 12,031 | 12,978 | 12,261 | † 5,640 | 54,259 | 4,710 | 32 | 2,870 | 2,670 | 4,202 | 5,571 | 5,225 |
| Memo Item: | | | | | | | | | | | | | |
| Total Assets..................................... | 10ra | 62,234 | 67,320 | 84,248 | † 93,232 | 158,843 | 86,147 | 74,946 | 87,703 | 92,948 | 128,943 | 149,562 | 154,421 |

# Australia 193

| | | 2004 | 2005 | 2006 | 2007 | 2008 | 2009 | 2010 | 2011 | 2012 | 2013 | 2014 | 2015 |
|---|---|---|---|---|---|---|---|---|---|---|---|---|---|
| **Other Depository Corporations** | | | | | *Millions of Australian Dollars: End of Period* | | | | | | | | |
| Net Foreign Assets.......................... | 21n | −188,340 | −228,452 | −289,530 | † −354,472 | −380,607 | −427,857 | −379,193 | −364,812 | −380,415 | −395,424 | −399,938 | −393,625 |
| Claims on Nonresidents................. | 21 | 72,612 | 73,765 | 97,010 | † 164,001 | 289,547 | 191,375 | 223,528 | 265,421 | 302,170 | 362,830 | 481,319 | 585,252 |
| Liabilities to Nonresidents............... | 26c | 260,952 | 302,217 | 386,540 | † 518,473 | 670,154 | 619,232 | 602,720 | 630,233 | 682,585 | 758,254 | 881,257 | 978,877 |
| Claims on Central Bank.................... | 20 | 7,375 | 8,573 | 7,934 | † 16,303 | 33,488 | 14,381 | 11,298 | 11,819 | 11,847 | 33,288 | 32,745 | 34,188 |
| Currency................................... | 20a | 7,375 | 8,573 | 7,934 | † 8,085 | 10,000 | 9,122 | 8,851 | 8,686 | 9,060 | 9,177 | 8,864 | 8,471 |
| Reserve Deposits and Securities..... | 20b | — | — | — | † — | — | — | — | — | — | — | — | — |
| Other Claims.............................. | 20n | — | — | — | † 8,217 | 23,488 | 5,259 | 2,446 | 3,133 | 2,787 | 24,112 | 23,881 | 25,718 |
| Net Claims on Central Government.. | 22an | −465 | −5,319 | −3,910 | † −3,109 | −7,491 | 8,863 | 14,690 | 14,593 | 17,334 | 20,598 | 36,779 | 41,408 |
| Claims on Central Government... | 22a | 354 | −4,383 | −2,824 | † 5,331 | 8,979 | 28,530 | 28,122 | 26,368 | 32,756 | 37,314 | 54,059 | 55,897 |
| Liabilities to Central Government... | 26d | 820 | 936 | 1,086 | † 8,440 | 16,471 | 19,667 | 13,432 | 11,775 | 15,422 | 16,716 | 17,280 | 14,489 |
| Claims on Other Sectors................ | 22s | 939,093 | 1,060,462 | 1,206,334 | † 1,604,127 | 1,890,340 | 1,903,153 | 1,990,759 | 2,136,016 | 2,238,663 | 2,381,024 | 2,613,826 | 2,771,756 |
| Claims on Other Financial Corps.... | 22g | 46,922 | 51,898 | 64,510 | † 286,266 | 437,134 | 339,796 | 338,470 | 391,538 | 404,670 | 447,057 | 541,302 | 537,338 |
| Claims on State & Local Govts....... | 22b | 4,906 | 4,200 | 4,814 | † 2,993 | 11,073 | 11,976 | 12,922 | 4,971 | 6,842 | 9,574 | 11,749 | 11,811 |
| Claims on Public Nonfin. Corps...... | 22c | 610 | 880 | 1,466 | † 2,466 | 6,366 | 6,022 | 6,404 | 6,484 | 8,552 | 7,354 | 6,555 | 6,125 |
| Claims on Private Sector................ | 22d | 886,655 | 1,003,485 | 1,135,544 | † 1,312,401 | 1,435,767 | 1,545,359 | 1,632,963 | 1,733,022 | 1,818,599 | 1,917,040 | 2,054,220 | 2,216,482 |
| Liabilities to Central Government | 26g | — | — | — | † 44,725 | 96,447 | 32,211 | 24,344 | 30,704 | 31,119 | 59,066 | 73,956 | 73,593 |
| Transf.Dep.Included in Broad Money | 24 | 211,060 | 233,923 | 260,762 | † 310,469 | 352,196 | 367,711 | 398,902 | 405,012 | 450,779 | 523,551 | 591,207 | 676,008 |
| Other Dep.Included in Broad Money. | 25 | 428,873 | 461,836 | 541,530 | † 421,202 | 546,322 | 602,092 | 694,005 | 782,226 | 842,245 | 872,995 | 889,057 | 900,344 |
| Sec.Ot.th.Shares Incl.in Brd. Money.. | 26a | — | — | — | † 216,712 | 212,134 | 177,461 | 173,115 | 180,305 | 175,617 | 170,560 | 196,680 | 201,807 |
| Deposits Excl. from Broad Money..... | 26b | — | — | — | † 33,764 | 42,603 | 41,744 | 59,305 | 70,544 | 75,799 | 88,632 | 106,094 | 118,377 |
| Sec.Ot.th.Shares Excl.f/Brd.Money.... | 26s | — | — | — | † 113,060 | 113,024 | 113,799 | 102,069 | 107,903 | 96,153 | 79,214 | 85,417 | 98,776 |
| Loans....................................... | 26l | — | — | — | † 7,859 | 5,860 | 6,947 | 6,597 | 6,458 | 3,740 | 4,775 | 7,041 | 17,654 |
| Financial Derivatives....................... | 26m | — | — | — | † 89,686 | 182,702 | 89,734 | 106,271 | 110,856 | 80,147 | 72,346 | 103,413 | 92,716 |
| Insurance Technical Reserves.......... | 26r | — | — | — | † — | | | | | | | | |
| Shares and Other Equity.................. | 27a | 86,204 | 91,620 | 99,953 | † 127,160 | 159,544 | 184,115 | 189,784 | 193,471 | 201,659 | 211,872 | 224,265 | 253,456 |
| Other Items (Net)............................ | 27r | 31,525 | 47,886 | 18,583 | † −101,788 | −175,102 | −117,274 | −116,837 | −89,861 | −69,829 | −43,525 | 6,282 | 20,996 |
| Memo Item: | | | | | | | | | | | | | |
| Total Assets................................... | 20ra | 1,237,815 | 1,384,816 | 1,656,321 | † 2,229,843 | 2,750,861 | 2,669,037 | 2,762,907 | 2,913,246 | 3,090,857 | 3,339,512 | 3,718,909 | 3,974,336 |
| **Depository Corporations** | | | | | *Millions of Australian Dollars: End of Period* | | | | | | | | |
| Net Foreign Assets.......................... | 31n | −137,967 | −177,536 | −228,616 | † −323,618 | −331,553 | −379,311 | −337,297 | −317,100 | −331,362 | −334,138 | −332,856 | −325,255 |
| Claims on Nonresidents................. | 31 | 123,486 | 125,304 | 159,489 | † 206,978 | 346,435 | 241,181 | 268,930 | 315,012 | 352,097 | 425,966 | 551,405 | 656,929 |
| Liabilities to Nonresidents............... | 36c | 261,453 | 302,840 | 388,106 | † 530,596 | 677,988 | 620,492 | 606,227 | 632,112 | 683,459 | 760,104 | 884,261 | 982,184 |
| Domestic Claims............................ | 32 | 930,903 | 1,045,227 | 1,178,460 | † 1,590,851 | 1,876,846 | 1,900,191 | 2,001,140 | 2,141,383 | 2,247,564 | 2,385,694 | 2,628,417 | 2,799,269 |
| Net Claims on Central Government | 32an | −8,190 | −15,236 | −27,874 | † −16,280 | −18,495 | −6,849 | 6,453 | −1,574 | 3,024 | 1,737 | 11,751 | 25,094 |
| Claims on Central Government..... | 32a | 354 | −4,383 | −2,824 | † 7,033 | 9,108 | 28,828 | 29,662 | 28,355 | 39,775 | 42,955 | 58,353 | 63,783 |
| Liabilities to Central Government. | 36d | 8,545 | 10,853 | 25,050 | † 23,313 | 27,604 | 35,677 | 23,209 | 29,929 | 36,751 | 41,218 | 46,602 | 38,689 |
| Claims on Other Sectors................ | 32s | 939,093 | 1,060,462 | 1,206,334 | † 1,607,131 | 1,895,342 | 1,907,040 | 1,994,687 | 2,142,957 | 2,244,540 | 2,383,957 | 2,616,666 | 2,774,175 |
| Claims on Other Financial Corps.... | 32g | 46,922 | 51,898 | 64,510 | † 286,266 | 437,134 | 339,796 | 338,470 | 391,538 | 404,670 | 447,057 | 541,302 | 537,338 |
| Claims on State & Local Govts..... | 32b | 4,906 | 4,200 | 4,814 | † 5,997 | 16,075 | 15,863 | 16,850 | 11,912 | 12,719 | 12,507 | 14,589 | 14,230 |
| Claims on Public Nonfin. Corps..... | 32c | 610 | 880 | 1,466 | † 2,466 | 6,366 | 6,022 | 6,404 | 6,484 | 8,552 | 7,354 | 6,555 | 6,125 |
| Claims on Private Sector.............. | 32d | 886,655 | 1,003,485 | 1,135,544 | † 1,312,401 | 1,435,767 | 1,545,359 | 1,632,963 | 1,733,022 | 1,818,599 | 1,917,040 | 2,054,220 | 2,216,482 |
| Broad Money Liabilities.................. | 35l | 667,486 | 724,228 | 833,320 | † 985,259 | 1,152,800 | 1,189,776 | 1,310,309 | 1,414,712 | 1,518,664 | 1,621,130 | 1,735,142 | 1,841,875 |
| Currency Outside Depository Corps | 34a | 27,486 | 28,428 | 31,012 | † 36,854 | 41,709 | 42,493 | 44,231 | 47,131 | 49,922 | 53,841 | 57,990 | 63,453 |
| Transferable Deposits.................... | 34 | 211,126 | 233,964 | 260,778 | † 310,491 | 352,634 | 367,731 | 398,959 | 405,051 | 450,880 | 523,733 | 591,416 | 676,271 |
| Other Deposits.............................. | 35 | 428,873 | 461,836 | 541,530 | † 421,202 | 546,322 | 602,092 | 694,005 | 782,226 | 842,245 | 872,995 | 889,057 | 900,344 |
| Securities Other than Shares........... | 36a | — | — | — | † 216,712 | 212,134 | 177,461 | 173,115 | 180,305 | 175,617 | 170,560 | 196,680 | 201,807 |
| Deposits Excl. from Broad Money..... | 36b | 7 | 2 | 4 | † 33,764 | 42,603 | 41,744 | 59,305 | 70,544 | 75,799 | 88,632 | 106,094 | 118,377 |
| Sec.Ot.th.Shares Excl.f/Brd.Money.... | 36s | — | — | — | † 113,060 | 113,024 | 113,799 | 102,069 | 107,903 | 96,153 | 79,214 | 85,417 | 98,776 |
| Loans....................................... | 36l | — | — | — | † 7,859 | 5,860 | 6,947 | 6,597 | 6,458 | 3,740 | 4,775 | 7,041 | 17,654 |
| Financial Derivatives....................... | 36m | — | — | — | † 89,686 | 182,702 | 89,734 | 106,271 | 110,856 | 80,147 | 72,346 | 103,413 | 92,716 |
| Insurance Technical Reserves.......... | 36r | — | — | — | † — | | | | | | | | |
| Shares and Other Equity.................. | 37a | 92,529 | 97,945 | 106,278 | † 133,486 | 165,870 | 191,018 | 196,007 | 199,538 | 208,192 | 223,824 | 245,862 | 277,495 |
| Other Items (Net)............................ | 37r | 32,914 | 45,516 | 10,242 | † −95,881 | −117,564 | −112,138 | −116,715 | −85,727 | −66,493 | −38,364 | 12,591 | 27,121 |
| Broad Money Liabs., Seasonally Adj. | 35l.b | 661,313 | 717,531 | 825,694 | † 973,668 | 1,140,393 | 1,179,303 | 1,300,944 | 1,406,476 | 1,510,584 | 1,613,472 | 1,727,888 | 1,834,882 |
| **Other Financial Corporations** | | | | | *Millions of Australian Dollars: End of Period* | | | | | | | | |
| Net Foreign Assets.......................... | 41n | .... | .... | .... | −23,384 | −21,428 | −9,029 | −10,743 | −13,358 | −16,756 | −20,218 | −17,550 | −18,676 |
| Claims on Nonresidents................. | 41 | .... | .... | .... | 24,324 | 31,164 | 14,037 | 12,355 | 10,298 | 11,433 | 9,638 | 34,049 | 36,150 |
| Liabilities to Nonresidents.............. | 46c | .... | .... | .... | 47,708 | 52,592 | 23,065 | 23,098 | 23,656 | 28,190 | 29,856 | 51,598 | 54,827 |
| Claims on Depository Corporations.. | 40 | .... | .... | .... | 30,595 | 34,574 | 26,623 | 27,523 | 26,279 | 16,137 | 17,402 | 18,202 | 25,184 |
| Net Claims on Central Government.. | 42an | .... | .... | .... | 855 | 1,677 | 2,321 | 1,868 | 1,789 | 934 | 543 | 339 | 332 |
| Claims on Central Government...... | 42a | .... | .... | .... | 1,839 | 2,693 | 3,338 | 2,531 | 2,560 | 1,783 | 1,395 | 1,485 | 1,566 |
| Liabilities to Central Government... | 46d | .... | .... | .... | 984 | 1,016 | 1,017 | 663 | 771 | 849 | 852 | 1,146 | 1,235 |
| Claims on Other Sectors................ | 42s | .... | .... | .... | 146,160 | 144,806 | 117,777 | 116,832 | 112,443 | 108,343 | 106,349 | 105,763 | 104,848 |
| Claims on State & Local Govts....... | 42b | .... | .... | .... | — | — | — | — | — | — | — | — | — |
| Claims on Public Nonfin. Corps...... | 42c | .... | .... | .... | 2,959 | 3,552 | 2,727 | 1,515 | 1,563 | 1,746 | 1,570 | 1,008 | 836 |
| Claims on Private Sector............... | 42d | .... | .... | .... | 143,201 | 141,255 | 115,050 | 115,317 | 110,880 | 106,597 | 104,778 | 104,755 | 104,012 |
| Deposits.................................... | 46b | .... | .... | .... | 41,161 | 46,868 | 33,999 | 40,701 | 39,024 | 27,331 | 22,192 | 23,103 | 20,164 |
| Securities Other than Shares........... | 46s | .... | .... | .... | 24,503 | 16,569 | 10,823 | 13,587 | 16,438 | 17,933 | 17,595 | 18,204 | 20,966 |
| Loans....................................... | 46l | .... | .... | .... | 29,335 | 33,679 | 34,425 | 33,548 | 31,706 | 30,156 | 35,815 | 40,206 | 43,235 |
| Financial Derivatives....................... | 46m | .... | .... | .... | — | — | — | — | — | — | — | — | — |
| Insurance Technical Reserves.......... | 46r | .... | .... | .... | — | — | — | — | — | — | — | — | — |
| Shares and Other Equity.................. | 47a | .... | .... | .... | 14,583 | 14,360 | 13,864 | 12,896 | 13,333 | 16,250 | 14,455 | 15,617 | 16,039 |
| Other Items (Net)............................ | 47r | .... | .... | .... | 44,644 | 48,152 | 44,582 | 34,747 | 26,652 | 16,987 | 14,018 | 9,625 | 11,283 |
| Memo Item: | | | | | | | | | | | | | |
| Total Assets................................... | 40ra | .... | .... | .... | 224,841 | 245,898 | 176,197 | 172,141 | 163,753 | 149,587 | 145,294 | 170,265 | 178,784 |

| | | 2004 | 2005 | 2006 | 2007 | 2008 | 2009 | 2010 | 2011 | 2012 | 2013 | 2014 | 2015 |
|---|---|---|---|---|---|---|---|---|---|---|---|---|---|
| **Monetary Aggregates** | | *Millions of Australian Dollars: End of Period* | | | | | | | | | | | |
| Broad Money.................. | 59m | 667,486 | 724,228 | 833,320 | 985,259 | 1,152,800 | 1,189,776 | 1,310,309 | 1,414,712 | 1,518,664 | 1,621,130 | 1,735,142 | 1,841,875 |
| o/w:Currency Issued by Cent.Govt | 59m.a | — | — | — | — | — | — | — | — | — | — | — | — |
| o/w: Dep.in Nonfin. Corporations. | 59m.b | — | — | — | — | — | — | — | — | — | — | — | — |
| o/w:Secs. Issued by Central Govt.. | 59m.c | — | — | — | — | — | — | — | — | — | — | — | — |
| Money (National Definitions) | | | | | | | | | | | | | |
| Money Base.................... | 19ma | 40,108 | 43,022 | 45,462 | 51,823 | 73,596 | 57,096 | 58,116 | 60,560 | 63,533 | 88,513 | 92,311 | 100,595 |
| Currency........................ | 19mca | 32,803 | 34,901 | 37,792 | 39,988 | 45,063 | 46,056 | 47,902 | 50,805 | 53,743 | 57,637 | 61,894 | 67,461 |
| Currency, Seasonally Adjusted......... | 19mcd | 32,251 | 34,258 | 37,030 | 39,123 | 44,064 | 45,045 | 46,908 | 49,807 | 52,740 | 56,609 | 60,814 | 66,311 |
| M1............................. | 59ma | 168,856 | 182,770 | 206,796 | 231,373 | 232,135 | 242,016 | 262,648 | 263,163 | 271,558 | 298,110 | 290,967 | 322,394 |
| M1, Seasonally Adjusted............... | 59mac | 165,061 | 178,654 | 202,064 | 225,976 | 226,536 | 235,922 | 255,650 | 255,765 | 263,547 | 288,960 | 281,914 | 314,445 |
| M3............................. | 59mc | 655,708 | 710,109 | 802,492 | 984,506 | 1,145,670 | 1,191,375 | 1,313,271 | 1,416,981 | 1,516,301 | 1,620,778 | 1,738,348 | 1,844,139 |
| M3, Seasonally Adjusted............... | 59mcc | 647,976 | 701,033 | 792,179 | 972,708 | 1,133,759 | 1,180,763 | 1,303,781 | 1,408,855 | 1,508,879 | 1,612,869 | 1,730,435 | 1,837,325 |
| Broad Money.................... | 59mea | 722,584 | 789,077 | 887,228 | 1,063,351 | 1,211,135 | 1,235,673 | 1,340,893 | 1,440,614 | 1,533,570 | 1,625,952 | 1,743,430 | 1,852,178 |
| Broad Money, Seasonally Adjusted... | 59mef | 729,265 | 795,702 | 893,250 | 1,057,755 | 1,204,482 | 1,230,899 | 1,334,750 | 1,435,025 | 1,527,684 | 1,618,390 | 1,735,230 | 1,845,592 |
| **Interest Rates** | | *Percent Per Annum* | | | | | | | | | | | |
| Central Bank Policy Rate (EOP)........ | 60 | 5.25 | 5.50 | 6.25 | 6.75 | 4.35 | 3.74 | 4.75 | 4.30 | 3.03 | 2.50 | 2.50 | 2.00 |
| Money Market Rate...................... | 60b | 5.25 | 5.46 | 5.81 | 6.39 | 6.67 | 3.28 | 4.35 | 4.69 | 3.70 | 2.74 | 2.50 | 2.11 |
| Savings Rate............................ | 60k | 3.00 | 3.40 | 4.03 | 4.60 | 5.00 | 2.39 | 3.94 | 5.11 | 5.03 | 4.37 | 3.79 | 2.89 |
| Deposit Rate........................... | 60l | 3.85 | 3.89 | 4.06 | 4.53 | 4.73 | 3.08 | 4.21 | 4.34 | 3.92 | 3.25 | 2.90 | 2.30 |
| Lending Rate........................... | 60p | 8.85 | 9.06 | 9.41 | † 8.20 | 8.91 | 6.02 | 7.28 | 7.74 | 6.98 | 6.18 | 5.95 | 5.58 |
| Govt. Bond Yield: Short-Term........... | 61a | 5.27 | 5.28 | 5.68 | 6.30 | 5.73 | 4.22 | 4.89 | 4.37 | 2.83 | 2.81 | 2.75 | 1.95 |
| Govt. Bond Yield: Long-Term........... | 61 | 5.59 | 5.34 | 5.59 | 5.99 | 5.82 | 5.04 | 5.37 | 4.88 | 3.38 | 3.70 | 3.66 | 2.71 |
| **Prices, Production, Labor** | | *Index Numbers (2010=100): Period Averages* | | | | | | | | | | | |
| Share Prices (End of Month)............ | 62.ep | 85.36 | 100.38 | 119.49 | 133.60 | 78.44 | 102.64 | 100.00 | 85.50 | 97.97 | 112.79 | 114.03 | 111.61 |
| Prices: Manufacturing Output.......... | 63 | 81.86 | 86.74 | 93.62 | 95.82 | 103.76 | 98.12 | † 100.00 | 103.39 | 102.89 | 104.01 | 107.24 | 107.52 |
| Consumer Prices........................ | 64 | 84.13 | 86.37 | 89.43 | 91.51 | 95.50 | 97.23 | † 100.00 | 103.30 | 105.12 | 107.70 | 110.38 | 112.04 |
| Wages, Weekly Earnings................. | 65 | 75.65 | 79.84 | 82.85 | 86.69 | 90.22 | 95.52 | 100.00 | 104.83 | 109.57 | 113.74 | 117.44 | 119.25 |
| Industrial Production.................... | 66 | 95.63 | 96.66 | 97.17 | † 98.54 | † 100.34 | † 98.72 | 100.00 | 101.20 | 104.53 | 106.69 | 111.47 | 113.24 |
| Mfg. Employment, Seas. Adj........... | 67eyc | 106.23 | 104.37 | 103.15 | 105.02 | 106.76 | 102.00 | 100.00 | 96.79 | 96.85 | 94.09 | 94.13 | 90.47 |
| | | *Number in Thousands: Period Averages* | | | | | | | | | | | |
| Labor Force.............................. | 67d | 10,103.41 | 10,404.22 | 10,632.72 | 10,911.88 | 11,205.63 | 11,441.82 | 11,628.23 | 11,815.20 | 11,972.51 | 12,137.21 | 12,277.75 | 12,504.12 |
| Employment............................. | 67e | 9,558.36 | 9,880.63 | 10,124.23 | 10,434.27 | 10,731.17 | 10,805.58 | 11,022.24 | 11,214.89 | 11,347.44 | 11,450.76 | 11,532.18 | 11,746.47 |
| Unemployment.......................... | 67c | 545.05 | 523.59 | 508.49 | 477.61 | 474.46 | 636.24 | 605.98 | 600.32 | 625.07 | 686.46 | 745.57 | 757.65 |
| Unemployment Rate (%)................. | 67r | 5.39 | 5.03 | 4.78 | 4.38 | 4.23 | 5.56 | 5.21 | 5.08 | 5.22 | 5.66 | 6.07 | 6.06 |
| **Intl. Transactions & Positions** | | *Millions of Australian Dollars* | | | | | | | | | | | |
| Exports................................. | 70 | 117,577 | 138,716 | 163,551 | 168,067 | 222,364 | 196,091 | 230,820 | 263,000 | 248,002 | 262,308 | 267,323 | 250,586 |
| Wheat................................ | 70d | 4,192 | 2,978 | 3,362 | 1,967 | 3,795 | 4,752 | 4,182 | 6,076 | 6,530 | 6,088 | 5,920 | 5,815 |
| Coal.................................. | 70vr | 13,302 | 21,814 | 23,272 | 20,764 | 46,439 | 39,183 | 42,967 | 47,012 | 41,274 | 39,811 | 38,065 | 37,800 |
| Greasy Wool.......................... | 70ha | 1,973 | 1,864 | 1,975 | 2,353 | 1,948 | 1,594 | 1,984 | 2,567 | 2,311 | 2,385 | 2,152 | 2,633 |
| Imports, c.i.f........................... | 71 | 148,744 | 164,137 | 184,750 | 196,756 | 236,528 | 208,834 | 219,177 | 236,109 | 251,966 | 251,101 | 262,646 | 277,514 |
| Imports, f.o.b........................... | 71.v | 140,956 | 155,626 | 175,786 | 187,611 | 225,666 | 200,393 | 209,892 | 227,028 | 241,985 | 241,005 | 252,298 | 266,514 |
| | | *2010=100* | | | | | | | | | | | |
| Volume of Exports........................ | 72 | 50.9 | 60.4 | 71.2 | 73.3 | 96.0 | 85.4 | 100.0 | 113.4 | 107.5 | 113.4 | 115.1 | 108.0 |
| Wheat................................ | 72d | 116.3 | 87.7 | 94.2 | 42.6 | 52.4 | 94.6 | 100.0 | 124.5 | 148.4 | 113.6 | 115.2 | 107.5 |
| Coal.................................. | 72vr | 74.6 | 77.6 | 78.7 | 83.3 | 86.5 | 91.1 | 100.0 | 93.2 | 104.9 | 119.1 | 128.6 | 128.8 |
| Greasy Wool.......................... | 72ha | 111.2 | 114.7 | 119.0 | 115.8 | 107.3 | 94.9 | 100.0 | 97.7 | 95.9 | 98.4 | 90.9 | 96.8 |
| Volume of Imports........................ | 73 | 65.1 | 72.3 | 82.6 | 88.5 | 105.2 | 93.2 | 100.0 | 109.8 | 117.9 | 117.7 | 121.0 | 125.8 |
| Export Prices........................... | 76 | 62.3 | 71.0 | 82.1 | 82.5 | † 103.2 | 96.3 | 100.0 | 112.6 | 103.8 | 103.3 | 99.5 | 90.3 |
| Coal (Unit Value)......................... | 74vr | 41.5 | 65.4 | 68.8 | 58.0 | 124.9 | 100.1 | 100.0 | 117.4 | 91.5 | 77.8 | 68.9 | 68.3 |
| Greasy Wool (Unit Value)............... | 74ha | 89.4 | 82.0 | 83.7 | 102.4 | 91.6 | 84.7 | 100.0 | 132.5 | 121.5 | 122.2 | 119.4 | 137.2 |
| Import Prices........................... | 76.x | 95.9 | 96.9 | 100.9 | 96.9 | † 105.7 | 105.7 | 100.0 | 100.5 | 102.0 | 104.4 | 107.8 | 108.9 |

| | | 2004 | 2005 | 2006 | 2007 | 2008 | 2009 | 2010 | 2011 | 2012 | 2013 | 2014 | 2015 |
|---|---|---|---|---|---|---|---|---|---|---|---|---|---|
| **Balance of Payments** | | | | | | | *Millions of US Dollars* | | | | | | |
| A. Current Account* | 109bx | −41,287.0 | −43,342.2 | −45,318.6 | −64,160.5 | −52,121.0 | −48,897.5 | −44,714.2 | −44,457.7 | −66,345.7 | −51,156.0 | −44,058.5 | −58,434.3 |
| Goods, credit (exports) | 1a9cx | 87,128.0 | 106,941.6 | 124,640.9 | 142,512.5 | 188,946.6 | 154,778.0 | 213,809.7 | 271,921.7 | 258,382.4 | 254,180.0 | 240,704.1 | 188,345.2 |
| Goods, debit (imports) | 1a9dx | 105,747.0 | 121,207.0 | 136,761.5 | 163,676.2 | 196,733.8 | 162,253.0 | 202,474.2 | 249,204.5 | 268,575.1 | 249,699.8 | 240,251.5 | 207,657.9 |
| Balance on goods | 1a9bx | −18,619.0 | −14,265.4 | −12,120.6 | −21,163.7 | −7,787.2 | −7,474.9 | 11,335.5 | 22,717.3 | −10,192.7 | 4,480.2 | 452.6 | −19,312.7 |
| Services, credit (exports) | 1b9cx | 27,773.8 | 30,507.3 | 33,108.0 | 40,481.6 | 43,733.8 | 40,326.9 | 46,439.8 | 52,214.6 | 53,961.0 | 53,549.8 | 54,240.2 | 49,715.9 |
| Services, debit (imports) | 1b9dx | 28,343.5 | 31,054.9 | 33,268.6 | 42,155.0 | 49,691.8 | 42,887.6 | 51,589.6 | 62,395.2 | 66,749.5 | 67,976.5 | 63,548.9 | 57,269.1 |
| Balance on Goods & Services | 1z9bx | −19,188.7 | −14,813.0 | −12,281.1 | −22,837.1 | −13,745.2 | −10,035.7 | 6,185.6 | 12,536.7 | −22,981.2 | −9,946.5 | −8,856.1 | −26,865.9 |
| Primary income: credit | 1c9cx | 16,683.0 | 19,828.3 | 26,298.1 | 37,975.6 | 44,713.0 | 31,066.2 | 40,050.2 | 47,973.7 | 47,639.5 | 46,315.9 | 46,637.2 | 38,105.4 |
| Primary income: debit | 1c9dx | 38,696.8 | 47,925.9 | 58,847.1 | 79,125.0 | 82,705.8 | 69,099.1 | 89,343.2 | 102,753.5 | 88,624.7 | 85,288.7 | 79,805.2 | 67,841.8 |
| Balance on gds, serv. & prim. inc. | 1y9bx | −41,202.5 | −42,910.6 | −44,830.1 | −63,986.6 | −51,738.0 | −48,068.6 | −43,107.4 | −42,243.0 | −63,966.5 | −48,919.3 | −42,024.1 | −56,602.3 |
| Secondary income: credit | 1d9ca | 3,909.8 | 4,078.4 | 4,558.3 | 5,553.3 | 5,861.7 | 5,038.2 | 5,863.5 | 7,524.3 | 7,263.8 | 7,108.9 | 6,962.1 | 5,852.8 |
| Secondary income: debit | 1d9da | 3,994.2 | 4,510.0 | 5,046.7 | 5,727.3 | 6,244.7 | 5,867.2 | 7,470.4 | 9,738.9 | 9,643.0 | 9,345.5 | 8,996.5 | 7,684.9 |
| B. Capital Account* | 209ba | −169.9 | −121.2 | 248.0 | −202.4 | −382.5 | −347.9 | −286.8 | −360.4 | −408.6 | −460.6 | −357.8 | −403.0 |
| Capital account: credit | 209ca | .... | .... | 355.1 | 26.2 | 6.1 | 20.7 | 66.1 | 1.0 | — | — | 64.2 | 4.4 |
| Capital account: debit | 209da | .... | .... | 107.0 | 228.7 | 388.7 | 368.5 | 352.9 | 361.5 | 408.6 | 460.6 | 422.0 | 407.4 |
| Balance on current & capital acct. | 129ba | −41,456.8 | −43,463.4 | −45,070.5 | −64,363.0 | −52,503.5 | −49,245.4 | −45,001.1 | −44,818.1 | −66,754.4 | −51,616.6 | −44,416.3 | −58,837.3 |
| C. Financial Account* | 309na | −41,789.8 | −49,428.4 | −53,437.7 | −27,787.1 | −54,849.6 | −56,802.3 | −44,535.0 | −47,097.6 | −75,380.0 | −63,899.5 | −45,231.5 | −54,589.0 |
| Direct investment: assets | 3a9aa | 9,785.0 | −32,713.4 | 24,082.5 | 14,420.8 | 31,887.7 | 11,463.8 | 18,068.6 | 8,250.6 | 5,247.6 | −734.3 | 5,795.4 | −4,094.7 |
| Equity & investment fund shares.. | 3aaaa | 7,320.4 | −33,811.9 | 14,947.5 | 9,539.5 | 27,083.3 | 4,071.2 | 14,928.6 | 1,664.2 | 2,508.7 | 5,811.5 | 1,987.1 | 10,456.7 |
| Debt instruments | 3abaa | 2,464.6 | 1,098.5 | 9,133.6 | 4,880.5 | 4,803.8 | 7,393.5 | 3,139.9 | 6,586.5 | 2,738.9 | −6,545.9 | 3,808.3 | −14,550.7 |
| Direct investment: liabilities | 3a9la | 42,907.7 | −25,093.1 | 30,551.1 | 44,440.1 | 45,160.0 | 28,683.3 | 35,210.7 | 65,554.9 | 57,616.9 | 54,554.0 | 45,913.0 | 36,852.3 |
| Equity & investment fund shares . | 3aala | 35,348.6 | −31,642.5 | 14,468.1 | 29,461.1 | 27,012.8 | 30,376.3 | 35,084.6 | 47,722.9 | 33,215.1 | 26,385.4 | 33,738.8 | 22,348.8 |
| Debt instruments | 3abla | 7,559.0 | 6,549.3 | 16,083.0 | 14,979.0 | 18,147.3 | −1,693.1 | 127.0 | 17,834.0 | 24,400.7 | 28,168.6 | 12,174.2 | 14,505.0 |
| Portfolio investment: assets | 3b9aa | 25,361.3 | 29,809.8 | 53,052.4 | 84,892.5 | −3,894.9 | 71,398.7 | 48,894.7 | 55,730.6 | 45,893.1 | 25,667.9 | 48,702.9 | 22,609.4 |
| Equity & investment fund shares | 3baaa | 11,050.0 | 14,879.0 | 25,393.9 | 51,470.7 | −4,096.3 | 38,516.0 | 20,108.3 | 33,090.0 | 17,531.9 | 13,873.7 | 22,299.5 | −2,610.2 |
| Debt securities | 3bbaa | 14,310.6 | 14,930.0 | 27,658.5 | 33,422.7 | 202.9 | 32,884.1 | 28,787.2 | 22,639.6 | 28,361.2 | 11,794.2 | 26,404.4 | 25,220.4 |
| Portfolio investment: liabilities | 3b9la | 41,305.1 | 62,528.9 | 105,345.9 | 61,439.4 | 28,970.7 | 147,220.2 | 117,680.1 | 84,474.2 | 60,713.7 | 82,376.4 | 72,037.6 | 77,484.6 |
| Equity & investment fund shares . | 3bala | −24,586.0 | 9,668.3 | 14,032.3 | 14,096.7 | 19,794.7 | 34,461.1 | 13,149.5 | 1,307.7 | 14,323.8 | 15,626.2 | 10,894.3 | 13,966.6 |
| Debt securities | 3bbla | 65,891.1 | 52,860.6 | 91,314.3 | 47,343.6 | 9,176.9 | 112,759.0 | 104,529.5 | 83,165.4 | 46,391.0 | 66,749.2 | 61,143.3 | 63,518.0 |
| Fin. der.& empl.stk.ops.(ESOs): net. | 3c9na | 792.9 | 794.9 | −2,783.5 | 8,450.5 | −2,866.0 | 6,569.2 | −1,742.0 | 25,015.8 | 8,321.2 | 17,520.6 | 4,774.2 | 5,478.1 |
| Fin. der. & ESOs: assets | 3c9aa | −18,364.7 | −14,564.1 | −12,297.1 | −996.2 | −4,492.5 | −39,016.5 | −29,684.6 | −27,956.3 | −37,987.1 | −44,807.5 | −51,678.6 | −73,305.4 |
| Fin. der. & ESOs: liabilities | 3c9la | −19,157.6 | −15,357.4 | −9,514.3 | −9,447.6 | −1,627.4 | −45,585.7 | −27,942.5 | −52,972.0 | −46,308.4 | −62,330.0 | −56,453.7 | −78,783.5 |
| Other investment: assets | 3d9aa | 5,324.9 | 3,203.7 | 16,200.5 | 2,226.8 | 41,302.0 | 11,360.2 | 14,432.1 | 29,507.7 | 19,735.6 | 49,441.6 | 20,666.3 | 80,908.1 |
| Other equity | 3daaa | .... | .... | .... | .... | .... | .... | 273.3 | −176.3 | −30.4 | 33.9 | −20.8 | −62.4 |
| Debt instruments | 3dzaa | 5,324.9 | 3,203.7 | 16,200.5 | 2,226.8 | 41,302.0 | 11,359.2 | 14,158.8 | 29,684.1 | 19,766.1 | 49,407.8 | 20,687.1 | 80,970.5 |
| Other investment: liabilities | 3d9la | −1,159.0 | 13,086.7 | 8,090.4 | 31,894.8 | 47,146.9 | −18,309.4 | −28,701.4 | 15,573.3 | 36,243.8 | 18,866.6 | 7,219.6 | 45,155.4 |
| Other equity | 3dala | | | | | | | 92.2 | −102.5 | | — | — | — |
| Debt instruments | 3dzla | −1,159.0 | 13,086.7 | 8,090.4 | 31,894.8 | 47,146.9 | −18,320.8 | −28,793.6 | 15,675.8 | 36,243.8 | 18,866.6 | 7,219.6 | 45,155.4 |
| Curr.+ cap.− finan. acct. balance... | 4y9na | 332.9 | 5,965.1 | 8,367.1 | −36,575.9 | 2,346.0 | 7,557.0 | −466.0 | 2,279.4 | 8,625.6 | 12,282.9 | 815.1 | −4,248.4 |
| D. Net Errors and Omissions | 409na | 834.5 | 1,290.7 | 1,355.6 | 1,431.1 | 1,345.9 | 993.3 | 895.9 | 2,266.7 | −6,091.2 | −6,776.5 | 2,829.4 | 1,902.6 |
| E. Reserves and Related Items | 4z9na | 1,165.9 | 7,254.2 | 9,722.7 | −35,146.5 | 3,691.2 | 8,549.2 | 430.0 | 4,546.2 | 2,535.5 | 5,507.4 | 3,644.5 | −2,345.8 |
| Reserve assets | 3e9aa | 1,165.9 | 7,254.2 | 9,722.7 | −35,146.5 | 3,691.2 | 8,549.2 | 430.0 | 4,546.2 | 2,535.5 | 5,507.4 | 3,644.5 | −2,345.8 |
| Credit and loans from the IMF | 3dcla | — | — | — | — | — | — | — | — | — | — | — | — |
| Exceptional financing | 409la | .... | .... | .... | .... | .... | .... | .... | .... | .... | .... | .... | .... |
| *Excludes components in group E | | | | | | | | | | | | | |

| | | 2004 | 2005 | 2006 | 2007 | 2008 | 2009 | 2010 | 2011 | 2012 | 2013 | 2014 | 2015 |
|---|---|---|---|---|---|---|---|---|---|---|---|---|---|
| **International Investment Position** | | | | | | | *Millions of US Dollars* | | | | | | |
| Assets | 809aa | 546,059.2 | 552,086.5 | 740,155.7 | 948,756.7 | 747,536.6 | 1,015,485.7 | 1,334,546.6 | 1,358,642.9 | 1,531,485.4 | 1,534,713.5 | 1,613,321.8 | 1,564,532.1 |
| Direct investment | 8a9aa | 229,203.6 | 208,900.5 | 266,963.3 | 339,741.3 | 241,224.0 | 344,033.8 | 483,198.8 | 458,559.6 | 515,723.8 | 490,513.7 | 483,092.1 | 437,762.4 |
| Equity & investment fund shares.. | 8aaaa | 205,136.4 | 184,709.7 | 231,173.5 | 294,997.5 | 200,208.1 | 289,676.3 | 421,656.8 | 390,844.5 | 442,856.6 | 429,867.4 | 423,035.4 | 396,560.2 |
| Debt instruments | 8abaa | 24,067.2 | 24,190.8 | 35,789.7 | 44,744.7 | 41,015.8 | 54,357.5 | 61,542.0 | 67,716.1 | 72,868.3 | 60,646.4 | 60,055.9 | 41,202.2 |
| Portfolio investment | 8b9aa | 168,007.7 | 198,465.9 | 278,809.8 | 395,682.4 | 255,949.4 | 386,875.1 | 479,658.0 | 497,712.0 | 581,446.0 | 589,725.5 | 623,747.3 | 595,002.8 |
| Equity & investment fund shares.. | 8baaa | 114,631.4 | 135,364.0 | 185,432.5 | 263,549.0 | 157,329.3 | 238,844.5 | 289,469.7 | 298,958.1 | 351,098.0 | 380,556.7 | 403,289.9 | 374,280.5 |
| Debt securities | 8bbaa | 53,376.3 | 63,101.9 | 93,377.4 | 132,133.3 | 98,619.4 | 148,030.7 | 190,188.3 | 198,752.9 | 230,346.9 | 209,168.8 | 220,457.5 | 220,721.6 |
| Fin. der.(oth.than reserves) & ESOs | 8c9aa | 38,255.9 | 25,595.9 | 38,954.9 | 70,857.7 | 86,949.2 | 80,771.2 | 101,935.9 | 101,365.0 | 106,093.5 | 103,966.9 | 146,932.3 | 120,723.6 |
| Other investment | 8d9aa | 73,663.8 | 75,867.5 | 100,347.9 | 115,567.2 | 130,491.7 | 162,063.6 | 227,486.6 | 254,181.3 | 278,999.7 | 297,707.1 | 305,657.4 | 361,776.3 |
| Other equity | 8daaa | .... | .... | .... | .... | .... | 84.3 | 312.0 | 152.3 | 258.0 | 328.0 | 325.6 | 143.9 |
| Debt instruments | 8dzaa | 73,663.8 | 75,867.5 | 100,347.9 | 115,567.2 | 130,491.7 | 161,979.2 | 227,174.6 | 254,029.0 | 278,741.6 | 297,379.1 | 305,331.8 | 361,632.4 |
| Reserve assets | 8e9aa | 36,926.6 | 43,256.7 | 55,079.8 | 26,908.1 | 32,922.4 | 41,742.8 | 42,268.3 | 46,824.9 | 49,222.4 | 52,801.1 | 53,892.8 | 49,267.0 |
| Liabilities | 809la | 919,543.3 | 934,282.3 | 1,200,958.1 | 1,510,296.7 | 1,233,899.1 | 1,696,286.4 | 2,088,912.2 | 2,172,826.2 | 2,396,092.7 | 2,288,561.8 | 2,339,149.8 | 2,266,251.7 |
| Direct investment | 8a9la | 284,952.0 | 242,166.5 | 296,565.0 | 386,251.9 | 305,870.5 | 425,645.4 | 560,522.0 | 594,671.4 | 653,842.9 | 601,611.7 | 599,510.4 | 582,556.3 |
| Equity & investment fund shares.. | 8aala | 227,203.9 | 181,398.5 | 215,271.6 | 279,453.1 | 197,794.4 | 296,191.4 | 416,945.2 | 434,077.6 | 465,624.8 | 405,676.6 | 404,362.7 | 392,856.8 |
| Debt instruments | 8abla | 57,748.0 | 60,768.0 | 81,294.2 | 106,798.8 | 108,076.8 | 129,454.1 | 143,576.8 | 160,593.8 | 188,218.1 | 195,935.1 | 195,147.7 | 189,699.6 |
| Portfolio investment | 8b9la | 483,249.5 | 541,070.0 | 723,297.3 | 872,843.9 | 645,909.2 | 988,038.5 | 1,186,049.5 | 1,215,019.2 | 1,322,640.9 | 1,260,855.7 | 1,256,145.3 | 1,194,817.4 |
| Equity & investment fund shares.. | 8bala | 146,733.2 | 178,806.4 | 248,052.0 | 320,833.6 | 169,192.8 | 331,114.9 | 402,396.9 | 341,020.2 | 398,185.8 | 387,173.6 | 374,650.1 | 336,274.0 |
| Debt securities | 8bbla | 336,516.3 | 362,263.6 | 475,245.3 | 552,009.4 | 476,716.4 | 656,922.7 | 783,652.7 | 873,999.0 | 924,455.1 | 873,682.1 | 881,496.0 | 858,542.7 |
| Fin. der.(oth.than reserves) & ESOs | 8c9la | 37,307.9 | 26,235.6 | 41,697.6 | 66,999.8 | 80,797.8 | 70,772.6 | 102,038.6 | 94,521.9 | 99,502.0 | 103,535.2 | 158,265.0 | 133,574.1 |
| Other investment | 8d9la | 114,034.0 | 124,810.9 | 139,398.2 | 184,201.0 | 201,321.5 | 211,830.8 | 240,302.1 | 268,613.8 | 320,106.9 | 322,559.2 | 325,228.3 | 355,304.6 |
| Other equity | 8dala | .... | .... | .... | .... | .... | 122.9 | 103.7 | .... | .... | .... | — | — |
| Debt instruments | 8dzla | 114,034.0 | 124,810.9 | 139,398.2 | 184,201.0 | 201,321.5 | 211,707.9 | 240,198.5 | 268,613.8 | 320,106.9 | 322,559.2 | 325,228.3 | 355,304.6 |

# Australia   193

| | | 2004 | 2005 | 2006 | 2007 | 2008 | 2009 | 2010 | 2011 | 2012 | 2013 | 2014 | 2015 |
|---|---|---|---|---|---|---|---|---|---|---|---|---|---|

**Government Finance Operations Statement**
**General Government**

*Millions of Australian Dollars: Fiscal Year Ends June 30*

| | | 2004 | 2005 | 2006 | 2007 | 2008 | 2009 | 2010 | 2011 | 2012 | 2013 | 2014 | 2015 |
|---|---|---|---|---|---|---|---|---|---|---|---|---|---|
| Revenue | a1 | 310,510 | 336,269 | 363,669 | 387,818 | 418,636 | 417,908 | 406,611 | 443,708 | 483,887 | 513,887 | 536,711 | 552,570 |
| Taxes | a11 | 257,255 | 278,685 | 297,941 | 319,509 | 347,899 | 340,054 | 326,779 | 358,296 | 392,166 | 415,958 | 434,295 | 443,326 |
| Social Contributions | a12 | — | — | — | — | — | — | — | — | — | — | — | — |
| Grants | a13 | 7 | 9 | 10 | 13 | 13 | 10 | 16 | 17 | 30 | 2 | 1 | −1 |
| Other Revenue | a14 | 53,248 | 57,575 | 65,716 | 68,299 | 70,722 | 77,844 | 79,816 | 85,395 | 91,691 | 97,927 | 102,414 | 109,246 |
| Expense | a2 | 295,052 | 316,051 | 334,587 | 358,001 | 388,968 | 436,487 | 443,503 | 496,223 | 516,336 | 534,152 | 557,883 | 578,153 |
| Compensation of Employees | a21 | 80,836 | 86,257 | 93,284 | 99,001 | 108,571 | 117,202 | 120,663 | 142,933 | 142,598 | 148,118 | 150,925 | 156,157 |
| Use of Goods & Services | a22 | 55,698 | 59,914 | 64,219 | 69,775 | 76,251 | 83,018 | 80,791 | 95,245 | 97,056 | 99,045 | 101,467 | 107,466 |
| Consumption of Fixed Capital | a23 | 12,123 | 13,087 | 13,728 | 14,594 | 15,584 | 17,142 | 15,720 | 19,612 | 21,062 | 22,965 | 23,920 | 24,915 |
| Interest | a24 | 14,968 | 14,912 | 15,127 | 15,597 | 15,822 | 17,691 | 21,854 | 26,894 | 30,396 | 31,168 | 35,038 | 37,440 |
| Subsidies | a25 | 11,740 | 12,882 | 13,234 | 14,013 | 16,310 | 17,366 | 17,296 | 17,445 | 19,065 | 23,032 | 24,578 | 22,128 |
| Grants | a26 | 1,444 | 2,334 | 1,870 | 1,889 | 1,955 | 2,859 | 2,897 | 3,260 | 3,614 | 3,720 | 4,841 | 4,729 |
| Social Benefits | a27 | 94,529 | 99,114 | 102,946 | 109,793 | 117,089 | 146,561 | 137,105 | 148,805 | 158,220 | 163,792 | 173,228 | 179,818 |
| Other Expense | a28 | 23,714 | 27,247 | 30,178 | 33,339 | 37,385 | 34,650 | 47,179 | 42,026 | 44,326 | 42,311 | 43,887 | 45,501 |
| Gross Operating Balance [1-2+23] | agob | 27,580 | 33,307 | 42,809 | 44,411 | 45,252 | −1,438 | −21,173 | −32,904 | −11,388 | 2,700 | 2,748 | −667 |
| Net Operating Balance [1-2] | anob | 15,457 | 20,220 | 29,082 | 29,816 | 29,667 | −18,580 | −36,892 | −52,515 | −32,449 | −20,265 | −21,171 | −25,582 |
| Net Acq. of Nonfinancial Assets | a31 | 5,005 | 5,832 | 9,278 | 11,580 | 15,198 | 22,791 | 29,053 | 27,950 | 26,826 | 16,367 | 21,757 | 21,702 |
| Aquisition of Nonfin. Assets | a31.1 | .... | .... | .... | .... | .... | .... | .... | .... | .... | .... | .... | .... |
| Disposal of Nonfin. Assets | a31.2 | .... | .... | .... | .... | .... | .... | .... | .... | .... | .... | .... | .... |
| Net Lending/Borrowing [1-2-31] | anlb | 10,452 | 14,388 | 19,805 | 18,237 | 14,470 | −41,372 | −65,945 | −80,466 | −59,276 | −36,632 | −42,927 | −47,284 |
| Net Acq. of Financial Assets | a32 | 9,324 | 20,298 | 26,078 | 11,164 | .... | .... | .... | .... | .... | .... | .... | .... |
| By instrument | | | | | | | | | | | | | |
| Monetary Gold & SDRs | a3201 | .... | .... | .... | .... | .... | .... | .... | .... | .... | .... | .... | .... |
| Currency & Deposits | a3202 | .... | .... | .... | .... | .... | .... | .... | .... | .... | .... | .... | .... |
| Securities other than Shares | a3203 | .... | .... | .... | .... | .... | .... | .... | .... | .... | .... | .... | .... |
| Loans | a3204 | .... | .... | .... | .... | .... | .... | .... | .... | .... | .... | .... | .... |
| Shares & Other Equity | a3205 | .... | .... | .... | .... | .... | .... | .... | .... | .... | .... | .... | .... |
| Insurance Technical Reserves | a3206 | .... | .... | .... | .... | .... | .... | .... | .... | .... | .... | .... | .... |
| Financial Derivatives | a3207 | .... | .... | .... | .... | .... | .... | .... | .... | .... | .... | .... | .... |
| Other Accounts Receivable | a3208 | .... | .... | .... | .... | .... | .... | .... | .... | .... | .... | .... | .... |
| By debtor | | | | | | | | | | | | | |
| Domestic | a321 | .... | .... | .... | .... | .... | .... | .... | .... | .... | .... | .... | .... |
| Foreign | a322 | .... | .... | .... | .... | .... | .... | .... | .... | .... | .... | .... | .... |
| Net Incurrence of Liabilities | a33 | .... | .... | .... | .... | .... | .... | .... | .... | .... | .... | .... | .... |
| By instrument | | | | | | | | | | | | | |
| Special Drawing Rights (SDRs) | a3301 | .... | .... | .... | .... | .... | .... | .... | .... | .... | .... | .... | .... |
| Currency & Deposits | a3302 | .... | .... | .... | .... | .... | .... | .... | .... | .... | .... | .... | .... |
| Securities other than Shares | a3303 | .... | .... | .... | .... | .... | .... | .... | .... | .... | .... | .... | .... |
| Loans | a3304 | .... | .... | .... | .... | .... | .... | .... | .... | .... | .... | .... | .... |
| Shares & Other Equity | a3305 | .... | .... | .... | .... | .... | .... | .... | .... | .... | .... | .... | .... |
| Insurance Technical Reserves | a3306 | .... | .... | .... | .... | .... | .... | .... | .... | .... | .... | .... | .... |
| Financial Derivatives | a3307 | .... | .... | .... | .... | .... | .... | .... | .... | .... | .... | .... | .... |
| Other Accounts Payable | a3308 | .... | .... | .... | .... | .... | .... | .... | .... | .... | .... | .... | .... |
| By creditor | | | | | | | | | | | | | |
| Domestic | a331 | .... | .... | .... | .... | .... | .... | .... | .... | .... | .... | .... | .... |
| Foreign | a332 | .... | .... | .... | .... | .... | .... | .... | .... | .... | .... | .... | .... |
| Stat. Discrepancy [32-33-NLB] | anlbz | .... | .... | .... | .... | .... | .... | .... | .... | .... | .... | .... | .... |
| Memo Item: Expenditure [2+31] | a2m | 300,057 | 321,883 | 343,865 | 369,581 | 404,166 | 459,278 | 472,556 | 524,173 | 543,162 | 550,519 | 579,640 | 599,855 |

**Balance Sheet**

| | | 2004 | 2005 | 2006 | 2007 | 2008 | 2009 | 2010 | 2011 | 2012 | 2013 | 2014 | 2015 |
|---|---|---|---|---|---|---|---|---|---|---|---|---|---|
| Net Worth | a6 | 509,017 | 600,495 | 681,993 | 753,930 | 895,629 | 937,226 | 930,941 | 908,855 | 726,055 | 836,896 | 833,404 | .... |
| Nonfinancial Assets | a61 | 480,887 | 547,944 | 590,884 | 643,994 | 758,825 | 867,915 | 942,440 | 963,895 | 1,010,529 | 1,054,171 | 1,088,954 | .... |
| Financial Assets | a62 | 350,650 | 391,136 | 456,854 | 477,020 | 519,741 | 580,882 | 603,537 | 637,287 | 637,342 | 693,708 | 767,416 | .... |
| By instrument | | | | | | | | | | | | | |
| Monetary Gold & SDRs | a6201 | — | — | — | — | — | — | — | — | — | — | — | .... |
| Currency & Deposits | a6202 | 15,342 | 16,320 | 18,666 | 18,653 | 23,630 | 26,686 | 25,995 | 32,044 | 30,927 | 32,432 | 35,535 | .... |
| Securities other than Shares | a6203 | 63,148 | 78,597 | 102,595 | 124,450 | 140,877 | 157,410 | 158,883 | 160,724 | 163,247 | 179,981 | 190,947 | .... |
| Loans | a6204 | 26,529 | 32,317 | 34,138 | 39,283 | 36,587 | 35,680 | 32,268 | 39,809 | 43,437 | 49,293 | 59,627 | .... |
| Shares and Other Equity | a6205 | 208,153 | 221,272 | 248,003 | 230,443 | 255,518 | 291,872 | 308,758 | 326,588 | 317,482 | 339,527 | 385,066 | .... |
| Insurance Technical Reserves | a6206 | — | — | — | — | — | — | — | — | — | — | — | .... |
| Financial Derivatives | a6207 | — | — | — | — | — | — | — | — | — | — | — | .... |
| Other Accounts Receivable | a6208 | 37,478 | 42,630 | 53,452 | 64,193 | 63,129 | 69,233 | 77,633 | 78,123 | 82,248 | 92,475 | 96,241 | .... |
| By debtor | | | | | | | | | | | | | |
| Domestic | a621 | .... | .... | .... | .... | .... | .... | .... | .... | .... | .... | .... | .... |
| Foreign | a622 | .... | .... | .... | .... | .... | .... | .... | .... | .... | .... | .... | .... |
| Liabilities | a63 | 322,520 | 338,585 | 365,745 | 367,085 | 382,937 | 511,571 | 615,036 | 689,068 | 930,151 | 916,020 | 1,028,026 | .... |
| By instrument | | | | | | | | | | | | | |
| Special Drawing Rights (SDRs) | a6301 | 1,001 | 897 | 936 | 846 | 798 | 900 | 5,350 | 4,595 | 4,591 | 5,038 | 5,060 | .... |
| Currency & Deposits | a6302 | 4,323 | 5,002 | 5,436 | 5,618 | 7,760 | 6,563 | 7,011 | 7,943 | 8,573 | 8,386 | 7,919 | .... |
| Securities other than Shares | a6303 | 61,179 | 63,102 | 59,695 | 58,040 | 60,773 | 109,486 | 165,669 | 207,672 | 277,211 | 297,729 | 359,560 | .... |
| Loans | a6304 | 36,665 | 37,869 | 36,436 | 40,520 | 46,310 | 59,213 | 73,939 | 94,171 | 109,508 | 135,530 | 149,430 | .... |
| Shares and Other Equity | a6305 | — | — | — | — | — | — | — | — | — | — | — | .... |
| Insurance Technical Reserves | a6306 | 147,325 | 152,632 | 174,236 | 170,615 | 177,244 | 229,847 | 254,649 | 259,836 | .... | 327,819 | 364,055 | .... |
| Financial Derivatives | a6307 | — | — | — | — | — | — | — | — | — | — | — | .... |
| Other Accounts Payable | a6308 | 72,027 | 79,083 | 89,006 | 92,293 | 90,850 | 106,462 | 113,769 | 122,705 | 132,697 | 141,518 | 142,002 | .... |
| By creditor | | | | | | | | | | | | | |
| Domestic | a631 | .... | .... | .... | .... | .... | .... | .... | .... | .... | .... | .... | .... |
| Foreign | a632 | .... | .... | .... | .... | .... | .... | .... | .... | .... | .... | .... | .... |
| Net Financial Worth [62-63] | a6m2 | 28,130 | 52,551 | 91,109 | 109,935 | 136,804 | 69,311 | −11,499 | −55,039 | −284,474 | −217,274 | −260,610 | .... |
| Memo Item: Debt at Market Value | a6m3 | 322,520 | 338,585 | 365,745 | 367,086 | 382,937 | 511,571 | 615,037 | 692,327 | 921,816 | 910,982 | 1,028,026 | .... |
| Memo Item: Debt at Face Value | a6m35 | .... | .... | .... | .... | .... | .... | .... | .... | .... | .... | .... | .... |
| Memo Item: Debt at Nominal Value | a6m4 | .... | .... | .... | .... | .... | .... | .... | .... | .... | .... | .... | .... |

| National Accounts | | 2004 | 2005 | 2006 | 2007 | 2008 | 2009 | 2010 | 2011 | 2012 | 2013 | 2014 | 2015 |
|---|---|---|---|---|---|---|---|---|---|---|---|---|---|
| | | *Billions of Australian Dollars* | | | | | | | | | | | |
| Househ.Cons.Expend.,incl.NPISHs.... | 96f.c | 519.60 | 547.83 | 588.98 | 642.19 | 676.34 | 700.16 | 739.36 | 782.44 | 820.56 | 855.41 | 897.68 | 937.06 |
| Government Consumption Expend... | 91f.c | 155.04 | 165.43 | 179.75 | 193.72 | 212.54 | 224.24 | 243.56 | 258.62 | 272.66 | 280.24 | 283.82 | 297.86 |
| Gross Fixed Capital Formation.......... | 93e.c | 238.19 | 266.36 | 286.70 | 319.88 | 355.86 | 352.42 | 367.97 | 393.77 | 431.98 | 429.73 | 429.24 | 423.79 |
| Changes in Inventories.................... | 93i.c | 4.12 | 1.89 | −3.63 | 4.55 | .89 | −3.93 | −.05 | 6.70 | 5.64 | −.87 | .27 | .55 |
| Exports of Goods and Services......... | 90c.c | 155.80 | 180.07 | 209.23 | 218.23 | 274.07 | 249.34 | 282.84 | 314.19 | 301.40 | 318.63 | 327.39 | 316.81 |
| Imports of Goods and Services (-)..... | 98c.c | 181.64 | 199.69 | 225.70 | 244.63 | 289.48 | 259.02 | 275.93 | 301.91 | 323.56 | 329.02 | 336.53 | 352.68 |
| Gross Domestic Product (GDP)........ | 99b.c | 891.62 | 961.11 | 1,036.91 | 1,130.99 | 1,235.15 | 1,259.60 | 1,358.31 | 1,456.71 | 1,505.41 | 1,554.86 | 1,600.37 | 1,628.89 |
| Net Primary Income from Abroad..... | 98.nc | −29.99 | −36.91 | −43.26 | −49.36 | −44.67 | −47.64 | −53.73 | −53.39 | −39.88 | −40.86 | −37.22 | −40.08 |
| Gross National Income (GNI)............ | 99a.c | 861.63 | 924.19 | 993.65 | 1,081.63 | 1,190.48 | 1,211.96 | 1,304.58 | 1,403.32 | 1,465.53 | 1,514.00 | 1,563.16 | 1,588.81 |
| Net Current Transf.from Abroad....... | 98t.c | .68 | −.85 | −1.32 | −.09 | −1.59 | 1.18 | −1.26 | −1.00 | −3.57 | −2.58 | −2.55 | 4.80 |
| Gross Nat'l Disposable Inc.(GNDI).... | 99i.c | 862.32 | 923.35 | 992.33 | 1,081.54 | 1,188.89 | 1,213.14 | 1,303.31 | 1,402.31 | 1,461.96 | 1,511.42 | 1,560.60 | 1,593.61 |
| Gross Saving.................................. | 99s.c | 187.68 | 210.09 | 223.59 | 245.63 | 300.02 | 288.74 | 320.40 | 361.25 | 368.75 | 375.77 | 379.10 | 358.69 |
| Consumption of Fixed Capital.......... | 99cfc | 140.85 | 152.49 | 166.00 | 180.21 | 194.13 | 205.57 | 214.69 | 224.01 | 234.73 | 249.38 | 265.14 | 280.97 |
| GDP Volume 2011/12 Ref.,Chained. | 99b.r | 1,217.55 | 1,256.37 | 1,290.22 | 1,348.12 | 1,383.53 | 1,407.89 | 1,440.23 | 1,478.80 | 1,531.29 | 1,562.33 | 1,604.11 | 1,643.96 |
| GDP Volume (2010=100)............... | 99bvr | 84.5 | 87.2 | 89.6 | 93.6 | 96.1 | 97.8 | 100.0 | 102.7 | 106.3 | 108.5 | 111.4 | 114.1 |
| GDP Deflator (2010=100)............... | 99bir | 77.6 | 81.1 | 85.2 | 89.0 | 94.7 | 94.9 | 100.0 | 104.4 | 104.2 | 105.5 | 105.8 | 105.1 |
| | | *Millions: Midyear Estimates* | | | | | | | | | | | |
| Population................................ | 99z | 19.99 | 20.27 | 20.61 | 20.98 | 21.37 | 21.77 | 22.16 | 22.54 | 22.91 | 23.27 | 23.62 | 23.97 |

# Austria 122

| | | 2004 | 2005 | 2006 | 2007 | 2008 | 2009 | 2010 | 2011 | 2012 | 2013 | 2014 | 2015 |
|---|---|---|---|---|---|---|---|---|---|---|---|---|---|
| **Exchange Rates** | | | | | *Euros per SDR: End of Period* | | | | | | | | |
| Market Rate.................... | aa | 1.1402 | 1.2116 | 1.1423 | 1.0735 | 1.1068 | 1.0882 | 1.1525 | 1.1865 | 1.1649 | 1.1167 | 1.1933 | 1.2728 |
| | | | | *Euros per US Dollar: End of Period (ae) Period Average (rf)* | | | | | | | | | |
| Market Rate.................... | ae | .7342 | .8477 | .7593 | .6793 | .7185 | .6942 | .7484 | .7729 | .7579 | .7251 | .8237 | .9185 |
| Market Rate.................... | rf | .8054 | .8041 | .7971 | .7306 | .6827 | .7198 | .7550 | .7194 | .7783 | .7532 | .7537 | .9017 |
| | | | | *Index Numbers (2010=100): Period Averages* | | | | | | | | | |
| Nominal Effective Exchange Rate..... | nec | 100.1 | 99.4 | 99.4 | 100.7 | 101.8 | 102.7 | 100.0 | 100.0 | 98.2 | 100.0 | 100.8 | 97.8 |
| CPI-Based Real Effect. Ex. Rate........ | rec | 101.8 | 101.3 | 100.5 | 101.3 | 102.0 | 102.8 | 100.0 | 100.5 | 98.8 | 101.0 | 102.3 | 99.6 |
| ULC-Based Real Effect. Ex. Rate....... | rel | 105.9 | 106.5 | 104.6 | 104.1 | 100.6 | 99.4 | 100.0 | 100.0 | 99.2 | 100.9 | 101.2 | 97.9 |
| **Fund Position** | | | | | *Millions of SDRs: End of Period* | | | | | | | | |
| Quota............................. | 2f.s | 1,872.30 | 1,872.30 | 1,872.30 | 1,872.30 | 1,872.30 | 1,872.30 | 1,872.30 | 2,113.90 | 2,113.90 | 2,113.90 | 2,113.90 | 2,113.90 |
| SDR Holdings..................... | 1b.s | 103.10 | 102.59 | 126.30 | 147.40 | 198.37 | 1,750.53 | 1,747.54 | 1,689.71 | 1,671.89 | 1,780.71 | 1,594.09 | 1,624.31 |
| Reserve Position in the Fund............ | 1c.s | 602.32 | 275.67 | 164.08 | 123.44 | 235.02 | 375.48 | 469.77 | 860.84 | 1,100.07 | 1,032.05 | 826.62 | 597.58 |
| Total Fund Cred. & Loans Outstg...... | 2tl | — | — | — | — | — | — | — | — | — | — | — | — |
| SDR Allocations.............................. | 1bd | 179.05 | 179.05 | 179.05 | 179.05 | 179.05 | 1,736.31 | 1,736.31 | 1,736.31 | 1,736.31 | 1,736.31 | 1,736.31 | 1,736.31 |
| **International Liquidity** | | | | *Millions of US Dollars Unless Otherwise Indicated: End of Period* | | | | | | | | | |
| Total Res.Min.Gold (Eurosys.Def)..... | 1l.d | 7,858 | 6,839 | 7,010 | 10,689 | 8,912 | 8,114 | 9,589 | 10,987 | 12,232 | 12,474 | 14,145 | 12,698 |
| SDR Holdings..................... | 1b.d | 160 | 147 | 190 | 233 | 306 | 2,744 | 2,691 | 2,594 | 2,570 | 2,742 | 2,310 | 2,251 |
| Reserve Position in the Fund......... | 1c.d | 935 | 394 | 247 | 195 | 362 | 589 | 723 | 1,322 | 1,691 | 1,589 | 1,198 | 828 |
| Foreign Exchange..................... | 1d.d | 6,763 | 6,298 | 6,573 | 10,261 | 8,244 | 4,781 | 6,175 | 7,071 | 7,972 | 8,142 | 10,638 | 9,619 |
| o/w:Fin.Deriv.Rel.to Reserves....... | 1ddd | — | — | 5.27 | 2.94 | 2.78 | 1.44 | 1.34 | — | 19.79 | 56.54 | −15.78 | −21.77 |
| Other Reserve Assets.................... | 1e.d | — | — | — | — | — | — | — | — | — | — | — | — |
| Gold (Million Fine Troy Ounces)....... | 1ad | 9.89 | 9.73 | 9.28 | 9.00 | 9.00 | 9.00 | 9.00 | 9.00 | 9.00 | 9.00 | 9.00 | 9.00 |
| Gold (Eurosystem Valuation).......... | 1and | 4,330 | 4,989 | 5,901 | 7,530 | 7,787 | 9,938 | 12,695 | 14,174 | 14,979 | 10,816 | 10,796 | 9,538 |
| Memo:Euro Cl. on Non-EA Res........ | 1dgd | . . . . | . . . . | . . . . | . . . . | . . . . | . . . . | . . . . | . . . . | . . . . | . . . . | . . . . | . . . . |
| Non-Euro Cl. on EA Res.............. | 1dhd | 3,742 | 3,165 | 3,057 | 2,631 | 19,549 | 252 | 115 | 5,722 | 1,385 | 985 | 1,003 | 1,323 |
| Central Bank: Other Assets............. | 3..d | 15,080 | 13,253 | 13,713 | 17,779 | 16,901 | 22,138 | 29,883 | 30,232 | 29,437 | 32,432 | 28,476 | 24,491 |
| Central Bank: Other Liabs.............. | 4..d | 286 | 265 | 288 | 305 | 280 | 2,731 | 2,681 | 2,673 | 2,702 | 3,015 | 3,075 | 3,208 |
| Other Depository Corps.: Assets....... | 7a.d | 157,545 | 161,095 | 220,512 | 286,343 | 292,747 | 256,797 | 235,479 | 226,685 | 217,503 | 211,213 | 177,710 | 149,678 |
| Other Depository Corps.: Liabs......... | 7b.d | 86,973 | 89,682 | 116,261 | 132,149 | 119,429 | 112,602 | 93,535 | 108,484 | 90,506 | 82,473 | 67,074 | 57,310 |
| **Central Bank** | | | | | *Millions of Euros: End of Period* | | | | | | | | |
| Euro Area Wide Residency Criterion | | | | | | | | | | | | | |
| Net Foreign Assets...................... | 11n.u | 11,350 | 11,641 | 10,280 | 13,247 | 14,001 | 12,498 | 17,603 | 19,788 | 20,972 | 17,400 | 20,984 | 19,883 |
| Claims on Nonresidents................ | 11..u | 11,560 | 11,867 | 10,992 | 14,130 | 14,203 | 14,394 | 19,610 | 21,854 | 23,040 | 19,586 | 23,517 | 22,830 |
| Liabilities to Nonresidents.............. | 16c.u | 210 | 226 | 712 | 883 | 201 | 1,895 | 2,006 | 2,066 | 2,068 | 2,186 | 2,533 | 2,947 |
| Claims on Other Depository Corps.... | 12e.u | 11,114 | 15,234 | 15,960 | 17,588 | 43,290 | 24,630 | 13,709 | 20,066 | 21,411 | 11,856 | 17,949 | 21,504 |
| Net Claims on Central Government.. | 12anu | 4,291 | 4,202 | 2,902 | 3,581 | 3,767 | 7,807 | 12,697 | 13,646 | 11,836 | 12,417 | 7,953 | 15,627 |
| Claims on Central Govt................. | 12a.u | 4,298 | 4,206 | 2,907 | 3,592 | 3,776 | 7,869 | 12,765 | 13,654 | 12,039 | 12,633 | 10,493 | 20,741 |
| Liabs. to Central Govt.................. | 16d.u | 7 | 4 | 5 | 11 | 9 | 62 | 68 | 8 | 203 | 216 | 2,540 | 5,114 |
| Claims on Other Sectors.............. | 12s.u | 2,865 | 3,369 | 5,007 | 4,903 | 5,061 | 4,965 | 5,666 | 6,874 | 8,396 | 9,163 | 10,440 | 11,502 |
| Claims on Other Financial Corps.... | 12g.u | 1,822 | 1,982 | 3,469 | 3,330 | 3,541 | 3,688 | 4,203 | 5,171 | 6,198 | 6,941 | 8,230 | 8,737 |
| Claims on State & Local Govts....... | 12b.u | 186 | 179 | 194 | 296 | 289 | 237 | 272 | 325 | 741 | 880 | 929 | 1,208 |
| Claims on Public Nonfin. Corps...... | 12c.u | — | — | — | — | — | — | — | — | — | — | — | — |
| Claims on Private Sector.............. | 12d.u | 857 | 1,208 | 1,344 | 1,277 | 1,231 | 1,040 | 1,191 | 1,378 | 1,457 | 1,342 | 1,281 | 1,557 |
| Monetary Base....................... | 14..u | 18,107 | 20,884 | 22,126 | 25,533 | 37,117 | 37,328 | 34,461 | 44,882 | 48,066 | 41,082 | 40,654 | 52,520 |
| Currency in Circulation.................. | 14a.u | 14,106 | 15,904 | 17,651 | 18,979 | 21,352 | 21,810 | 22,760 | 24,044 | 24,754 | 26,049 | 27,868 | 29,500 |
| Liabs. to Other Depository Corps.... | 14c.u | 4,000 | 4,976 | 4,474 | 6,548 | 15,693 | 15,517 | 11,700 | 20,837 | 23,235 | 14,945 | 12,642 | 22,866 |
| Liabs. to Other Sectors................. | 14d.u | 1 | 4 | 1 | 6 | 72 | 1 | 1 | 1 | 77 | 88 | 144 | 154 |
| Other Liabs. to Other Dep. Corps..... | 14n.u | — | — | — | — | — | — | — | — | — | — | — | — |
| Dep. & Sec. Excl. f/Monetary Base.... | 14o.u | — | — | — | — | — | — | — | — | — | — | — | — |
| Deposits Included in Broad Money... | 15..u | — | — | — | — | — | — | — | — | — | — | — | — |
| Sec.Ot.th.Shares Inc.in.Brd.Money.. | 16a.u | — | — | — | — | — | — | — | — | — | — | — | — |
| Deposits Excl. from Broad Money... | 16b.u | — | — | — | — | — | — | — | — | — | — | — | — |
| Sec.Oh.th.Shares Excl. f/Brd.Money | 16s.u | — | — | — | — | — | — | — | — | — | — | — | — |
| Loans......................................... | 16l.u | — | — | — | — | — | — | — | — | — | — | — | — |
| Financial Derivatives...................... | 16m.u | — | — | — | — | — | — | — | — | — | — | — | — |
| Shares and Other Equity................. | 17a.u | 6,325 | 7,494 | 7,419 | 7,981 | 8,683 | 10,110 | 12,855 | 13,601 | 15,890 | 11,717 | 12,828 | 12,744 |
| Other Items (Net)........................ | 17r.u | 5,189 | 6,068 | 4,604 | 5,806 | 20,319 | 2,462 | 2,359 | 1,891 | −1,341 | −1,963 | 3,844 | 3,252 |
| Memorandum Items | | | | | | | | | | | | | |
| National Residency Criterion | | | | | | | | | | | | | |
| Net Foreign Assets...................... | 11n | 10,815 | 5,332 | −1,663 | −1,840 | −11,759 | 6,372 | 9,568 | 6,153 | 865 | −1,018 | 11,265 | 10,706 |
| Claims on Nonresidents................ | 11 | 20,019 | 21,260 | 20,216 | 24,453 | 24,143 | 27,899 | 39,042 | 42,810 | 42,935 | 40,405 | 43,997 | 42,920 |
| Liabilities to Nonresidents.............. | 16c | 9,204 | 15,928 | 21,879 | 26,293 | 35,901 | 21,526 | 29,473 | 36,657 | 42,070 | 41,423 | 32,732 | 32,214 |
| Claims on Other Depository Corps.... | 12e | 9,380 | 12,931 | 12,569 | 13,866 | 40,286 | 21,266 | 9,716 | 16,238 | 17,988 | 8,626 | 14,497 | 18,604 |
| Net Claims on Central Government.. | 12an | 562 | 565 | 614 | 641 | 619 | 1,232 | 1,489 | 1,951 | 2,152 | 2,237 | −332 | 7,978 |
| Claims on Central Government...... | 12a | 569 | 569 | 619 | 652 | 628 | 1,294 | 1,557 | 1,959 | 2,355 | 2,453 | 2,208 | 13,092 |
| Liabilities to Central Government... | 16d | 7 | 4 | 5 | 11 | 9 | 62 | 68 | 8 | 203 | 216 | 2,540 | 5,114 |
| Claims on Other Sectors.............. | 12s | 1,026 | 1,073 | 2,619 | 2,403 | 2,434 | 2,518 | 2,554 | 2,560 | 2,727 | 2,877 | 2,835 | 3,099 |
| Claims on Other Fin. Corps........... | 12g | 211 | 229 | 1,740 | 1,502 | 1,513 | 1,546 | 1,551 | 1,507 | 1,577 | 1,580 | 1,578 | 1,576 |
| Claims on State & Local Govts....... | 12b | — | — | — | — | — | — | — | — | — | — | — | — |
| Claims on Private Sector.............. | 12d | 815 | 844 | 879 | 901 | 921 | 972 | 1,003 | 1,053 | 1,150 | 1,297 | 1,257 | 1,523 |
| Liabs.to ODCs, Inc.in Mon.Base....... | 14c | 4,000 | 4,976 | 4,473 | 6,548 | 15,692 | 15,516 | 11,700 | 20,837 | 23,235 | 14,944 | 12,642 | 22,866 |
| Liabs.to Ot.Sectors, Inc.in Mon.Base | 14d | 1 | 4 | 1 | 6 | 72 | 1 | 1 | 1 | 1 | 2 | 32 | 42 |
| Liabs.to ODCs,Excl.f/Mon.Base........ | 14n | — | — | — | — | — | — | — | — | — | — | — | — |
| Net Claims on Eurosystem.............. | 12e.s | −7,721 | −14,429 | −19,893 | −24,132 | −34,421 | −18,399 | −26,204 | −33,295 | −38,598 | −37,815 | −28,727 | −27,795 |

| | | 2004 | 2005 | 2006 | 2007 | 2008 | 2009 | 2010 | 2011 | 2012 | 2013 | 2014 | 2015 |
|---|---|---|---|---|---|---|---|---|---|---|---|---|---|
| **Other Depository Corporations** | | *Millions of Euros: End of Period* | | | | | | | | | | | |
| Euro Area Wide Residency Criterion | | | | | | | | | | | | | |
| Net Foreign Assets.......................... | 21n.u | 51,811 | 60,535 | 79,158 | 104,744 | 124,537 | 100,094 | 106,229 | 91,352 | 96,254 | 93,351 | 91,126 | 84,842 |
| Claims on Nonresidents................ | 21..u | 115,663 | 136,556 | 167,435 | 194,513 | 210,352 | 178,257 | 176,230 | 175,195 | 164,850 | 153,153 | 146,372 | 137,483 |
| Liabilities to Nonresidents............. | 26c.u | 63,852 | 76,021 | 88,277 | 89,769 | 85,815 | 78,163 | 70,001 | 83,843 | 68,596 | 59,802 | 55,246 | 52,641 |
| Claims on Eurosystem.................... | 20..u | 5,939 | 7,073 | 7,525 | 10,728 | 17,392 | 18,168 | 16,087 | 21,548 | 24,623 | 16,796 | 15,412 | 24,180 |
| Currency............................... | 20a.u | 2,120 | 2,439 | 2,650 | 2,637 | 2,586 | 2,461 | 2,389 | 2,706 | 2,809 | 2,837 | 2,832 | 2,774 |
| Reserve Deposits and Securities..... | 20b.u | 3,819 | 4,634 | 4,875 | 8,091 | 14,806 | 15,707 | 13,698 | 18,842 | 21,814 | 13,959 | 12,580 | 21,406 |
| Other Claims.............................. | 20n.u | — | — | — | — | — | — | — | — | — | — | — | — |
| Net Claims on Central Government.. | 22anu | 26,784 | 27,404 | 25,842 | 21,239 | 18,101 | 25,945 | 26,746 | 24,613 | 28,989 | 32,966 | 41,331 | 39,846 |
| Claims on Central Government...... | 22a.u | 30,914 | 31,130 | 28,976 | 24,825 | 23,164 | 28,484 | 30,142 | 27,665 | 32,670 | 36,838 | 48,325 | 47,631 |
| Liabilities to Central Government... | 26d.u | 4,130 | 3,726 | 3,134 | 3,586 | 5,063 | 2,539 | 3,396 | 3,052 | 3,681 | 3,872 | 6,994 | 7,785 |
| Claims on Other Sectors................. | 22s.u | 292,305 | 332,293 | 354,805 | 381,907 | 412,059 | 423,206 | 433,386 | 443,612 | 459,420 | 445,231 | 436,558 | 433,458 |
| Claims on Other Financial Corps.... | 22g.u | 43,822 | 54,123 | 60,407 | 69,581 | 77,121 | 86,064 | 81,460 | 80,027 | 96,284 | 86,150 | 83,344 | 77,302 |
| Claims on State & Local Govts....... | 22b.u | 23,506 | 23,952 | 24,272 | 24,828 | 25,069 | 25,852 | 28,054 | 31,292 | 30,540 | 28,752 | 32,351 | 31,980 |
| Claims on Public Nonfin. Corps...... | 22c.u | — | — | — | — | — | — | — | — | — | — | — | — |
| Claims on Private Sector.............. | 22d.u | 224,977 | 254,218 | 270,126 | 287,498 | 309,869 | 311,290 | 323,872 | 332,293 | 332,596 | 330,329 | 320,863 | 324,176 |
| Liabilities to Eurosystem................. | 26g.u | 12,058 | 15,440 | 15,993 | 19,627 | 41,097 | 24,802 | 18,168 | 19,832 | 21,616 | 12,577 | 18,456 | 21,921 |
| Transf.Dep.Included in Broad Money | 24..u | 68,888 | 77,118 | 81,980 | 88,207 | 94,495 | 111,204 | 115,309 | 119,043 | 136,675 | 148,332 | 157,791 | 177,956 |
| Other.Dep.Included in Broad Money. | 25..u | 89,999 | 101,176 | 111,503 | 140,574 | 160,116 | 136,774 | 128,920 | 135,976 | 125,650 | 120,263 | 122,049 | 113,377 |
| Sec.Ot.th.Shares Inc.in.Brd. Money... | 26a.u | 3,072 | 4,439 | 7,407 | 9,309 | 10,568 | 5,450 | 6,727 | 4,968 | 5,145 | 4,436 | 4,735 | 5,647 |
| Deposits Excl. from Broad Money..... | 26b.u | 52,921 | 55,597 | 54,444 | 48,523 | 45,690 | 57,456 | 60,684 | 62,078 | 59,342 | 59,717 | 54,981 | 50,074 |
| Sec.Ot.th.Shares Excl.f/Brd. Money... | 26s.u | 108,190 | 117,444 | 129,857 | 142,591 | 156,474 | 158,272 | 157,868 | 155,828 | 146,602 | 139,977 | 122,278 | 114,007 |
| Loans....................................... | 26l.u | — | — | — | — | — | — | — | — | — | — | — | — |
| Financial Derivatives...................... | 26m.u | 498 | 1,003 | 1,132 | 1,007 | 978 | 1,959 | 6,196 | 2,026 | 16,733 | 9,318 | 14,920 | 13,136 |
| Insurance Technical Reserves.......... | 26r.u | — | — | — | — | — | — | — | — | — | — | — | — |
| Shares and Other Equity................ | 27a.u | 38,185 | 43,753 | 50,032 | 63,134 | 62,556 | 74,836 | 74,750 | 74,825 | 84,024 | 81,339 | 68,219 | 67,664 |
| Other Items (Net)........................... | 27r.u | 3,027 | 11,331 | 14,981 | 5,649 | 120 | −3,343 | 13,822 | 6,544 | 13,502 | 12,387 | 20,883 | 18,523 |
| Memorandum Items | | | | | | | | | | | | | |
| Total Assets................................. | 20ra | 635,348 | 719,265 | 787,509 | 884,734 | 1,060,156 | 1,030,169 | 978,759 | 1,010,103 | 974,900 | 913,618 | 876,033 | 854,243 |
| National Residency Criterion | | | | | | | | | | | | | |
| Net Foreign Assets.......................... | 21n | 86,810 | 101,081 | 125,105 | 171,137 | 200,529 | 182,957 | 170,035 | 153,913 | 148,236 | 145,479 | 144,471 | 133,450 |
| Claims on Nonresidents................ | 21 | 194,375 | 233,097 | 276,213 | 333,730 | 363,746 | 330,811 | 309,737 | 309,886 | 286,506 | 267,005 | 260,379 | 243,010 |
| Liabilities to Nonresidents............. | 26c | 107,565 | 132,016 | 151,108 | 162,593 | 163,217 | 147,854 | 139,702 | 155,973 | 138,270 | 121,526 | 115,908 | 109,560 |
| Net Claims on Central Government.. | 22an | 16,369 | 14,105 | 12,521 | 9,162 | 7,380 | 15,244 | 16,762 | 16,746 | 21,051 | 22,668 | 27,134 | 24,981 |
| Claims on Central Government...... | 22a | 20,444 | 17,295 | 15,484 | 11,705 | 11,220 | 17,387 | 19,519 | 19,334 | 24,243 | 25,926 | 33,216 | 32,350 |
| Liabilities to Central Government... | 26d | 4,075 | 3,190 | 2,963 | 2,543 | 3,840 | 2,143 | 2,757 | 2,588 | 3,192 | 3,258 | 6,082 | 7,369 |
| Claims on Other Sectors................. | 22s | 269,370 | 304,340 | 320,795 | 336,231 | 360,589 | 370,131 | 378,829 | 388,384 | 405,060 | 394,680 | 388,130 | 389,191 |
| Claims on Other Fin. Corps............ | 22g | 36,140 | 44,285 | 47,556 | 51,650 | 58,200 | 66,977 | 63,335 | 63,369 | 78,289 | 70,212 | 68,175 | 65,746 |
| Claims on State & Local Govts....... | 22b | 21,346 | 21,245 | 21,191 | 21,610 | 21,848 | 22,593 | 24,955 | 28,155 | 27,674 | 25,961 | 29,524 | 29,232 |
| Claims on Private Sector.............. | 22d | 211,884 | 238,810 | 252,048 | 262,971 | 280,541 | 280,561 | 290,539 | 296,860 | 299,097 | 298,507 | 290,431 | 294,213 |
| Transf.Dep.Included in Broad Money | 24 | 66,081 | 73,049 | 77,303 | 83,665 | 88,355 | 104,866 | 109,500 | 112,379 | 128,772 | 140,557 | 150,216 | 169,504 |
| Other.Dep.Included in Broad Money. | 25 | 85,726 | 96,423 | 106,485 | 132,548 | 150,642 | 128,216 | 122,243 | 127,980 | 118,095 | 113,572 | 113,511 | 107,983 |
| Sec.Ot.th.Shares Inc.in.Brd. Money... | 26a | 1,087 | 2,214 | 5,799 | 9,078 | 9,683 | 6,040 | 6,280 | 2,941 | 2,017 | 2,490 | 3,153 | 2,173 |
| Deposits Excl. from Broad Money..... | 26b | 47,013 | 49,040 | 45,892 | 38,636 | 34,795 | 45,378 | 47,290 | 46,366 | 44,771 | 44,064 | 42,376 | 40,001 |
| Sec.Ot.th.Shares Excl.f/Brd. Money... | 26s | 129,345 | 140,029 | 154,614 | 170,181 | 185,845 | 186,257 | 185,022 | 180,066 | 167,312 | 159,366 | 141,378 | 128,940 |

| | | 2004 | 2005 | 2006 | 2007 | 2008 | 2009 | 2010 | 2011 | 2012 | 2013 | 2014 | 2015 |
|---|---|---|---|---|---|---|---|---|---|---|---|---|---|
| **Depository Corporations** | | | | | | | *Millions of Euros: End of Period* | | | | | | |
| Euro Area Wide Residency Criterion | | | | | | | | | | | | | |
| Net Foreign Assets | 31n.u | 63,161 | 72,176 | 89,438 | 117,991 | 138,538 | 112,592 | 123,832 | 111,140 | 117,226 | 110,751 | 112,110 | 104,725 |
| Claims on Nonresidents | 31..u | 127,223 | 148,423 | 178,427 | 208,643 | 224,555 | 192,651 | 195,840 | 197,049 | 187,890 | 172,739 | 169,889 | 160,313 |
| Liabilities to Nonresidents | 36c.u | 64,062 | 76,247 | 88,989 | 90,652 | 86,016 | 80,058 | 72,007 | 85,909 | 70,664 | 61,988 | 57,779 | 55,588 |
| Domestic Claims | 32..u | 326,245 | 367,268 | 388,556 | 411,630 | 438,988 | 461,923 | 478,495 | 488,745 | 508,641 | 499,777 | 496,282 | 500,433 |
| Net Claims on Central Government | 32anu | 31,075 | 31,606 | 28,744 | 24,820 | 21,868 | 33,752 | 39,443 | 38,259 | 40,825 | 45,383 | 49,284 | 55,473 |
| Claims on Central Government | 32a.u | 35,212 | 35,336 | 31,883 | 28,417 | 26,940 | 36,353 | 42,907 | 41,319 | 44,709 | 49,471 | 58,818 | 68,372 |
| Liabilities to Central Government | 36d.u | 4,137 | 3,730 | 3,139 | 3,597 | 5,072 | 2,601 | 3,464 | 3,060 | 3,884 | 4,088 | 9,534 | 12,899 |
| Claims on Other Sectors | 32s.u | 295,170 | 335,662 | 359,812 | 386,810 | 417,120 | 428,171 | 439,052 | 450,486 | 467,816 | 454,394 | 446,998 | 444,960 |
| Claims on Other Financial Corps | 32g.u | 45,644 | 56,105 | 63,876 | 72,911 | 80,662 | 89,752 | 85,663 | 85,198 | 102,482 | 93,091 | 91,574 | 86,039 |
| Claims on State & Local Govts | 32b.u | 23,692 | 24,131 | 24,466 | 25,124 | 25,358 | 26,089 | 28,326 | 31,617 | 31,281 | 29,632 | 33,280 | 33,188 |
| Claims on Public Nonfin. Corps | 32c.u | — | — | — | — | — | — | — | — | — | — | — | — |
| Claims on Private Sector | 32d.u | 225,834 | 255,426 | 271,470 | 288,775 | 311,100 | 312,330 | 325,063 | 333,671 | 334,053 | 331,671 | 322,144 | 325,733 |
| Broad Money Liabilities | 35l.u | 173,946 | 196,202 | 215,892 | 254,438 | 284,017 | 272,778 | 271,328 | 281,326 | 289,492 | 296,331 | 309,755 | 323,860 |
| Currency Outside Depository Corps | 34a.u | 11,986 | 13,465 | 15,001 | 16,342 | 18,766 | 19,349 | 20,371 | 21,338 | 21,945 | 23,212 | 25,036 | 26,726 |
| Transferable Deposits | 34..u | 68,889 | 77,122 | 81,981 | 88,213 | 94,567 | 111,205 | 115,310 | 119,044 | 136,752 | 148,420 | 157,935 | 178,110 |
| Other Deposits | 35..u | 89,999 | 101,176 | 111,503 | 140,574 | 160,116 | 136,774 | 128,920 | 135,976 | 125,650 | 120,263 | 122,049 | 113,377 |
| Securities Other than Shares | 36a.u | 3,072 | 4,439 | 7,407 | 9,309 | 10,568 | 5,450 | 6,727 | 4,968 | 5,145 | 4,436 | 4,735 | 5,647 |
| Deposits Excl. from Broad Money | 36b.u | 52,921 | 55,597 | 54,444 | 48,523 | 45,690 | 57,456 | 60,684 | 62,078 | 59,342 | 59,717 | 54,981 | 50,074 |
| Sec.Oth.th.Shares Excl.f/Brd. Money | 36s.u | 108,190 | 117,444 | 129,857 | 142,591 | 156,474 | 158,272 | 157,868 | 155,828 | 146,602 | 139,977 | 122,278 | 114,007 |
| Loans | 36l.u | — | — | — | — | — | — | — | — | — | — | — | — |
| Financial Derivatives | 36m.u | 498 | 1,003 | 1,132 | 1,007 | 978 | 1,959 | 6,196 | 2,026 | 16,733 | 9,318 | 14,920 | 13,136 |
| Insurance Technical Reserves | 36r.u | — | — | — | — | — | — | — | — | — | — | — | — |
| Shares and Other Equity | 37a.u | 44,510 | 51,247 | 57,451 | 71,115 | 71,239 | 84,946 | 87,605 | 88,426 | 99,914 | 93,056 | 81,047 | 80,408 |
| Other Items (Net) | 37r.u | 9,341 | 17,947 | 19,217 | 11,951 | 19,133 | −899 | 18,642 | 10,196 | 13,787 | 12,131 | 25,296 | 23,652 |
| Broad Money Liabs., Seasonally Adj. | 35lub | 173,328 | 195,293 | 214,594 | 252,859 | 282,408 | 271,621 | 270,612 | 280,979 | 289,210 | 295,834 | 308,922 | 322,879 |
| Memorandum Items | | | | | | | | | | | | | |
| National Residency Criterion | | | | | | | | | | | | | |
| Net Foreign Assets | 31n | 97,625 | 106,413 | 123,442 | 169,297 | 188,770 | 189,329 | 179,603 | 160,066 | 149,101 | 144,461 | 155,736 | 144,156 |
| Claims on Nonresidents | 31 | 214,394 | 254,357 | 296,429 | 358,183 | 387,889 | 358,710 | 348,779 | 352,696 | 329,441 | 307,410 | 304,376 | 285,930 |
| Liabilities to Nonresidents | 36c | 116,769 | 147,944 | 172,987 | 188,886 | 199,118 | 169,380 | 169,175 | 192,630 | 180,340 | 162,949 | 148,640 | 141,774 |
| Domestic Claims | 32 | 287,327 | 320,083 | 336,549 | 348,437 | 371,022 | 389,125 | 399,634 | 409,641 | 430,990 | 422,462 | 417,767 | 425,249 |
| Net Claims on Central Government | 32an | 16,931 | 14,670 | 13,135 | 9,803 | 7,999 | 16,476 | 18,251 | 18,697 | 23,203 | 24,905 | 26,802 | 32,959 |
| Claims on Central Government | 32a | 21,013 | 17,864 | 16,103 | 12,357 | 11,848 | 18,681 | 21,076 | 21,293 | 26,598 | 28,379 | 35,424 | 45,442 |
| Liabilities to Central Government | 36d | 4,082 | 3,194 | 2,968 | 2,554 | 3,849 | 2,205 | 2,825 | 2,596 | 3,395 | 3,474 | 8,622 | 12,483 |
| Claims on Other Sectors | 32s | 270,396 | 305,413 | 323,414 | 338,634 | 363,023 | 372,649 | 381,383 | 390,944 | 407,787 | 397,557 | 390,965 | 392,290 |
| Claims on Other Financial Corps | 32g | 36,351 | 44,514 | 49,296 | 53,152 | 59,713 | 68,523 | 64,886 | 64,876 | 79,866 | 71,792 | 69,753 | 67,322 |
| Claims on State & Local Govts | 32b | 21,346 | 21,245 | 21,191 | 21,610 | 21,848 | 22,593 | 24,955 | 28,155 | 27,674 | 25,961 | 29,524 | 29,232 |
| Claims on Private Sector | 32d | 212,699 | 239,654 | 252,927 | 263,872 | 281,462 | 281,533 | 291,542 | 297,913 | 300,247 | 299,804 | 291,688 | 295,736 |
| Transf.Dep.Included in Broad Money | 34 | 66,082 | 73,053 | 77,304 | 83,671 | 88,427 | 104,867 | 109,501 | 112,380 | 128,773 | 140,559 | 150,248 | 169,546 |
| Other Dep.Included in Broad Money | 35 | 85,726 | 96,423 | 106,485 | 132,548 | 150,642 | 128,216 | 122,243 | 127,980 | 118,095 | 113,572 | 113,511 | 107,983 |
| Sec.Ot.th.Shares Inc.in.Brd. Money | 36a | 1,087 | 2,214 | 5,799 | 9,078 | 9,683 | 6,040 | 6,280 | 2,941 | 2,017 | 2,490 | 3,153 | 2,173 |
| Deposits Excl. from Broad Money | 36b | 47,013 | 49,040 | 45,892 | 38,636 | 34,795 | 45,378 | 47,290 | 46,366 | 44,771 | 44,064 | 42,376 | 40,001 |
| Sec.Ot.th.Shares Excl./f.Brd. Money | 36s | 129,345 | 140,029 | 154,614 | 170,181 | 185,845 | 186,257 | 185,022 | 180,066 | 167,312 | 159,366 | 141,378 | 128,940 |
| **Interest Rates** | | | | | | | *Percent Per Annum* | | | | | | |
| Deposit Rate | | | | | | | | | | | | | |
| Households: Stocks, up to 2 years | 60lhs | 1.71 | 1.70 | 2.15 | 3.16 | 3.88 | 2.43 | 1.24 | 1.39 | 1.43 | .88 | .64 | .44 |
| New Business, up to 1 year | 60lhn | 1.91 | 1.96 | 2.73 | 3.86 | 4.27 | 1.56 | 1.08 | 1.65 | 1.25 | .73 | .58 | .38 |
| Corporations: Stocks, up to 2 years | 60lcs | 1.91 | 1.99 | 2.66 | 3.83 | 4.35 | 1.85 | 1.05 | 1.55 | 1.38 | .76 | .65 | .48 |
| New Business, up to 1 year | 60lcn | 1.97 | 2.05 | 2.85 | 4.02 | 4.30 | 1.17 | .86 | 1.43 | .81 | .42 | .43 | .30 |
| Lending Rate | | | | | | | | | | | | | |
| Households: Stocks, up to 1 year | 60phs | 7.53 | 7.11 | 7.36 | 7.82 | 8.17 | 6.97 | 6.02 | 5.98 | 5.70 | 5.26 | 5.32 | 5.15 |
| New Bus., Floating & up to 1 year | 60pns | 5.28 | 5.00 | 5.51 | 6.30 | 6.82 | 5.04 | 4.74 | 5.01 | 4.80 | 4.76 | 4.96 | 4.87 |
| House Purch., Stocks,Over 5 years | 60phm | 4.59 | 4.38 | 4.43 | 5.20 | 5.71 | 4.50 | 3.29 | 3.31 | 2.97 | 2.43 | 2.38 | 2.13 |
| House Purch., New Bus., 5-10 yrs | 60phn | 4.92 | 4.60 | 4.85 | 5.12 | 5.30 | 4.94 | 4.84 | 4.58 | 3.67 | 3.39 | 3.05 | 2.51 |
| Corporations: Stocks, up to 1 year | 60pcs | 3.86 | 3.68 | 4.16 | 5.10 | 5.56 | 3.10 | 2.56 | 2.95 | 2.50 | 2.21 | 2.15 | 2.00 |
| New Bus., Over € 1 mil.,up to 1 yr | 60pcn | 2.88 | 2.89 | 3.62 | 4.69 | 5.04 | 2.28 | 1.89 | 2.49 | 1.92 | 1.70 | 1.67 | 1.54 |
| Government Bond Yield | 61 | 4.13 | 3.39 | 3.80 | 4.30 | 4.36 | 3.94 | 3.23 | 3.32 | 2.37 | 2.01 | 1.49 | .75 |
| **Prices, Production, Labor** | | | | | | | *Index Numbers (2010=100): Period Averages* | | | | | | |
| Share Prices (End of Month) | 62.ep | 78.8 | 119.8 | 156.6 | 182.3 | 130.0 | 84.6 | 100.0 | 97.1 | 83.3 | 96.3 | 94.0 | 95.4 |
| Wholesale Prices | 63 | 88.4 | 90.2 | 92.9 | 96.6 | 102.9 | 95.3 | † 100.0 | 108.1 | 110.9 | 109.7 | 107.6 | † 103.6 |
| Consumer Prices | 64 | 89.3 | 91.3 | 92.7 | 94.7 | 97.7 | 98.2 | 100.0 | 103.3 | 105.8 | 108.0 | † 109.7 | 110.7 |
| Harmonized CPI | 64h | 89.4 | 91.3 | 92.8 | 94.9 | 97.9 | 98.3 | 100.0 | 103.6 | 106.2 | 108.5 | 110.0 | 110.9 |
| Wages: Monthly Earnings (1995=10 | 65 | 85.9 | 87.8 | 90.2 | 92.4 | 95.3 | 98.5 | 100.0 | 102.0 | 103.5 | 108.0 | 110.6 | 113.0 |
| Industrial Production | 66 | 86.7 | 90.4 | 97.4 | 102.9 | 104.9 | 93.2 | 100.0 | 106.1 | 107.5 | 107.7 | 108.1 | 109.9 |
| Employment | 67 | 93.6 | 94.1 | 95.9 | 98.0 | 99.6 | 99.1 | 100.0 | 101.0 | 101.8 | 102.2 | 102.3 | 103.1 |
| | | | | | | | *Number in Thousands: Period Averages* | | | | | | |
| Labor Force | 67d | 3,890 | 3,934 | 3,994 | 4,064 | 4,101 | 4,132 | 4,147 | 4,176 | 4,222 | 4,261 | 4,279 | 4,319 |
| Employment | 67e | 3,693 | 3,712 | 3,783 | 3,864 | 3,929 | 3,910 | 3,944 | 3,983 | 4,014 | 4,030 | 4,034 | 4,068 |
| Unemployment | 67c | 213 | 223 | 212 | 200 | 172 | 223 | 203 | 194 | 209 | 231 | 245 | 252 |
| Unemployment Rate (%) | 67r | 5.5 | 5.6 | 5.3 | 4.9 | 4.1 | 5.3 | 4.8 | 4.6 | 4.9 | 5.4 | 5.6 | 5.7 |
| **Intl. Transactions & Positions** | | | | | | | *Billions of Euros* | | | | | | |
| Exports | 70 | 89.85 | 94.71 | 103.74 | 114.68 | 117.53 | 93.74 | 109.37 | 121.77 | 123.54 | 125.41 | 127.36 | 131.55 |
| Imports, c.i.f. | 71 | 91.09 | 96.50 | 104.20 | 114.25 | 119.57 | 97.57 | 113.65 | 131.01 | 131.98 | 129.96 | 128.96 | 132.93 |
| | | | | | | | *2010=100* | | | | | | |
| Volume of Exports | 72 | 76.8 | 77.0 | 78.5 | 84.6 | 89.0 | 92.7 | 100.0 | 104.3 | 110.4 | 96.7 | 113.5 | 115.3 |
| Volume of Imports | 73 | 77.5 | 78.3 | 81.2 | 86.6 | 91.0 | 93.8 | 100.0 | 104.9 | 107.0 | 99.3 | 110.4 | 113.0 |
| Export Prices | 76 | 91.7 | 93.6 | 96.1 | 97.7 | 100.0 | 96.9 | 100.0 | 104.0 | 104.9 | 103.9 | 102.7 | 103.1 |
| Import Prices | 76.x | 88.8 | 91.4 | 94.8 | 96.3 | 100.8 | 94.9 | 100.0 | 106.5 | 108.3 | 107.1 | 105.2 | 103.6 |

# Austria   122

|  |  | 2004 | 2005 | 2006 | 2007 | 2008 | 2009 | 2010 | 2011 | 2012 | 2013 | 2014 | 2015 |
|---|---|---|---|---|---|---|---|---|---|---|---|---|---|
| **Balance of Payments** | | | | | | | *Millions of US Dollars* | | | | | | |
| A. Current Account* | 109bx | .... | 6,245.0 | † 10,993.0 | 14,750.9 | 19,304.6 | 10,299.1 | 11,479.8 | 6,795.9 | 6,142.1 | 8,375.0 | 8,290.5 | 9,618.4 |
| Goods, credit (exports) | 1a9cx | .... | 114,099.1 | † 129,452.9 | 156,840.5 | 172,799.1 | 131,710.3 | 145,062.8 | 170,157.6 | 160,238.6 | 164,304.5 | 166,009.6 | 142,877.6 |
| Goods, debit (imports) | 1a9dx | .... | 113,144.0 | † 126,220.9 | 151,506.3 | 170,239.7 | 132,386.2 | 146,904.5 | 175,200.1 | 164,302.6 | 165,647.9 | 163,993.9 | 139,945.9 |
| Balance on goods | 1a9bx | .... | 955.1 | † 3,233.2 | 5,334.2 | 2,559.4 | −675.9 | −1,841.6 | −5,042.5 | −4,062.8 | −1,344.8 | 2,017.1 | 2,931.7 |
| Services, credit (exports) | 1b9cx | .... | 44,959.9 | † 45,575.1 | 54,472.7 | 63,077.2 | 53,927.2 | 52,739.0 | 59,165.6 | 57,932.9 | 64,579.1 | 67,311.4 | 58,551.9 |
| Services, debit (imports) | 1b9dx | .... | 35,805.6 | † 35,215.6 | 41,046.3 | 45,269.9 | 39,041.9 | 38,757.0 | 44,493.8 | 44,124.2 | 51,040.9 | 53,330.3 | 45,603.1 |
| Balance on Goods & Services | 1z9bx | .... | 10,109.4 | † 13,591.5 | 18,760.6 | 20,366.7 | 14,209.5 | 12,140.3 | 9,629.3 | 9,744.6 | 12,194.7 | 15,996.8 | 15,880.4 |
| Primary income: credit | 1c9cx | .... | 25,914.0 | † 35,204.8 | 46,842.6 | 47,589.7 | 37,171.1 | 39,894.0 | 49,242.8 | 43,093.4 | 27,865.6 | 38,581.0 | 31,125.0 |
| Primary income: debit | 1c9dx | .... | 27,957.0 | † 34,359.5 | 47,157.6 | 44,177.8 | 37,265.0 | 36,563.2 | 47,906.3 | 42,578.8 | 26,491.4 | 41,871.6 | 33,556.3 |
| Balance on gds, serv. & prim. inc. | 1y9bx | .... | 8,066.4 | † 14,436.9 | 18,445.6 | 23,778.6 | 14,115.6 | 15,471.1 | 10,965.8 | 10,259.2 | 13,568.9 | 12,706.2 | 13,449.1 |
| Secondary income: credit | 1d9ca | .... | 3,948.9 | † 2,247.7 | 2,455.3 | 2,903.2 | 2,968.6 | 2,914.1 | 3,370.5 | 3,273.8 | 3,495.3 | 3,688.5 | 2,899.0 |
| Secondary income: debit | 1d9da | .... | 5,770.3 | † 5,691.6 | 6,150.0 | 7,377.2 | 6,785.1 | 6,905.4 | 7,540.4 | 7,390.9 | 8,689.2 | 8,104.1 | 6,729.7 |
| B. Capital Account* | 209ba | .... | −83.5 | † −1,140.8 | 40.5 | −245.6 | −151.7 | 269.8 | −459.3 | −576.8 | −649.3 | −608.8 | −2,142.4 |
| Capital account: credit | 209ca | .... | 445.1 | † 75.3 | 593.5 | 235.2 | 576.7 | 878.5 | 187.3 | 95.4 | 110.2 | 81.1 | 338.5 |
| Capital account: debit | 209da | .... | 528.7 | † 1,216.1 | 553.1 | 480.8 | 728.5 | 608.7 | 646.6 | 672.2 | 759.6 | 689.9 | 2,480.9 |
| Balance on current & capital acct. | 129ba | .... | 6,161.5 | † 9,852.2 | 14,791.4 | 19,059.0 | 10,147.3 | 11,749.6 | 6,336.6 | 5,565.3 | 7,725.7 | 7,681.7 | 7,476.0 |
| C. Financial Account* | 309na | .... | 917.3 | † 15,509.3 | 14,323.4 | 15,842.8 | 13,748.9 | 3,312.9 | 5,095.7 | 5,409.0 | 13,902.1 | −952.7 | 6,497.3 |
| Direct investment: assets | 3a9aa | .... | 81,481.7 | † 16,078.7 | 79,062.5 | 27,908.9 | 15,557.7 | −14,324.7 | 38,119.7 | 18,449.7 | 11,029.8 | 6,598.6 | 14,777.5 |
| Equity & investment fund shares.. | 3aaaa | .... | 80,789.9 | † 12,295.6 | 73,513.3 | 23,823.7 | 12,742.5 | −16,473.7 | 30,204.8 | 15,826.6 | 1,133.5 | −872.4 | 12,319.7 |
| Debt instruments | 3abaa | .... | 691.9 | † 3,783.1 | 5,549.1 | 4,082.3 | 2,816.8 | 2,147.7 | 7,917.7 | 2,621.8 | 9,896.3 | 7,471.0 | 2,457.8 |
| Direct investment: liabilities | 3a9la | .... | 81,287.9 | † 10,497.4 | 68,885.4 | 6,310.8 | 14,293.2 | −22,005.6 | 22,974.4 | 5,219.6 | 451.3 | 11,293.2 | 5,746.8 |
| Equity & investment fund shares . | 3aala | .... | 83,446.0 | † 351.6 | 44,470.0 | 6,066.5 | 6,104.8 | −24,543.2 | 24,857.9 | 8,913.9 | −4,397.1 | 10,325.4 | 9,276.6 |
| Debt instruments | 3abla | .... | −2,158.1 | † 10,145.8 | 24,415.4 | 244.5 | 8,188.4 | 2,537.6 | −1,886.3 | −3,694.2 | 4,847.1 | 967.8 | −3,528.8 |
| Portfolio investment: assets | 3b9aa | .... | 44,004.1 | † 33,467.3 | 16,452.6 | −11,303.3 | 4,983.1 | 8,640.2 | −11,413.8 | −14,516.5 | 2,906.2 | 9,642.3 | 850.4 |
| Equity & investment fund shares | 3baaa | .... | 5,690.2 | † 8,711.9 | 977.2 | −7,462.5 | 6,325.2 | 9,664.5 | −1,786.2 | 4,400.9 | 4,121.4 | 4,731.6 | 5,650.8 |
| Debt securities | 3bbaa | .... | 38,313.9 | † 24,758.0 | 15,475.4 | −3,842.4 | −1,342.1 | −1,024.3 | −9,627.6 | −18,916.2 | −1,217.8 | 4,910.6 | −4,800.4 |
| Portfolio investment: liabilities | 3b9la | .... | 30,525.0 | † 47,930.2 | 46,608.8 | 24,536.9 | −6,048.0 | −1,301.3 | 10,861.6 | −7,055.6 | 5,674.4 | −7,160.0 | −15,329.8 |
| Equity & investment fund shares . | 3bala | .... | 5,998.8 | † 10,357.8 | 3,941.3 | −6,655.8 | 149.9 | −539.0 | −225.8 | 730.3 | 1,767.8 | 1,141.5 | 1,390.3 |
| Debt instruments | 3bbla | .... | 24,526.2 | † 37,572.4 | 42,667.5 | 31,192.8 | −6,196.5 | −762.3 | 11,087.4 | −7,784.6 | 3,906.7 | −8,304.2 | −16,720.1 |
| Fin. der.& empl.stk.ops.(ESOs): net. | 3c9na | .... | −153.4 | † 1,225.4 | 916.6 | −829.7 | −789.8 | 199.9 | −1,036.3 | −1,370.3 | −5,067.1 | −1,776.8 | −535.8 |
| Fin. der. & ESOs.: assets | 3c9aa | .... | .... | .... | .... | .... | .... | .... | .... | .... | .... | .... | .... | .... |
| Fin. der. & ESOs.: liabilities | 3c9la | .... | .... | .... | .... | .... | .... | .... | .... | .... | .... | .... | .... | .... |
| Other investment: assets | 3d9aa | .... | 30,098.5 | † 73,283.9 | 50,146.6 | 53,163.8 | −31,103.6 | −20,922.6 | 33,370.4 | −1,603.3 | −5,087.6 | −23,049.5 | −21,648.3 |
| Other equity | 3daaa | .... | .... | † — | 1.3 | | −6.5 | 43.5 | 55.6 | 1,227.0 | 1,591.0 | 662.1 | −16.1 |
| Debt instruments | 3dzaa | .... | 30,098.5 | † 73,283.9 | 50,145.3 | 53,163.8 | −31,097.1 | −20,966.1 | 33,314.8 | −2,830.3 | −6,678.6 | −23,711.5 | −21,632.2 |
| Other investment: liabilities | 3d9la | .... | 42,700.7 | † 50,119.7 | 16,757.9 | 22,246.1 | −33,350.8 | −6,408.0 | 20,109.6 | −2,616.1 | −16,249.3 | −11,763.4 | −3,468.1 |
| Other equity | 3dala | .... | .... | † — | — | — | — | — | — | — | — | — | — |
| Debt instruments | 3dzla | .... | 42,700.7 | † 50,119.7 | 16,757.9 | 22,246.1 | −33,350.8 | −6,408.0 | 20,109.6 | −2,616.1 | −16,249.3 | −11,763.4 | −3,468.1 |
| Curr.+ cap.− finan. acct. balance... | 4y9na | .... | 5,244.2 | † −5,657.0 | 468.0 | 3,216.1 | −3,601.5 | 8,436.8 | 1,240.9 | 156.3 | −6,176.5 | 8,634.4 | 978.8 |
| D. Net Errors and Omissions | 409na | .... | −5,994.0 | † 4,781.2 | 2,054.5 | −4,055.9 | 2,554.0 | −6,990.1 | −247.6 | 1,087.5 | 6,698.1 | −5,745.5 | −1,343.4 |
| E. Reserves and Related Items | 4z9na | .... | −749.8 | † −874.5 | 2,526.5 | −836.7 | −1,050.4 | 1,445.2 | 991.7 | 1,243.8 | 525.7 | 2,890.3 | −363.5 |
| Reserve assets | 3e9aa | .... | −749.8 | † −874.5 | 2,526.5 | −836.7 | −1,050.4 | 1,445.2 | 991.7 | 1,243.8 | 525.7 | 2,890.3 | −363.5 |
| Credit and loans from the IMF | 3dcla | .... | — | † — | — | — | — | — | — | — | — | — | — |
| Exceptional financing | 409la | .... | .... | .... | .... | .... | .... | .... | .... | .... | .... | .... | .... |
| *Excludes components in group E | | | | | | | | | | | | | |

| **International Investment Position** | | | | | | | | *Millions of US Dollars* | | | | | | |
|---|---|---|---|---|---|---|---|---|---|---|---|---|---|---|
| Assets | 809aa | .... | 651,030.0 | † 893,428.7 | 1,136,275.3 | 1,090,808.4 | 1,147,722.5 | 1,078,515.9 | 1,087,914.2 | 1,138,594.6 | 1,186,032.8 | 1,080,099.4 | 978,447.5 |
| Direct investment | 8a9aa | .... | 146,925.0 | † 212,268.8 | 305,613.8 | 304,465.0 | 339,098.5 | 318,054.3 | 337,370.2 | 366,199.5 | 393,221.4 | 367,210.6 | 355,687.0 |
| Equity & investment fund shares.. | 8aaaa | .... | 139,699.4 | † 181,536.6 | 263,497.1 | 262,104.4 | 291,133.7 | 267,970.9 | 281,366.3 | 307,050.8 | 323,637.5 | 296,888.7 | 289,151.1 |
| Debt instruments | 8abaa | .... | 7,225.6 | † 30,730.9 | 42,118.3 | 42,360.6 | 47,964.8 | 50,083.4 | 56,003.9 | 59,148.7 | 69,582.5 | 70,321.9 | 66,534.8 |
| Portfolio investment | 8b9aa | .... | 284,228.5 | † 352,957.3 | 405,598.9 | 322,423.5 | 360,462.6 | 355,828.7 | 320,022.9 | 334,252.8 | 354,722.4 | 339,308.2 | 306,261.1 |
| Equity & investment fund shares.. | 8bbaa | .... | 63,610.8 | † 88,108.6 | 100,796.2 | 54,860.8 | 75,206.5 | 87,505.1 | 74,039.5 | 86,708.3 | 101,631.4 | 99,761.4 | 97,599.8 |
| Debt securities | 8bbaa | .... | 220,617.7 | † 264,848.7 | 304,802.7 | 267,562.7 | 285,257.5 | 268,323.7 | 245,983.3 | 247,544.5 | 253,091.1 | 239,546.8 | 208,661.3 |
| Fin. der.(oth.than reserves) & ESOs | 8c9aa | .... | .... | † 4,637.2 | 9,972.0 | 20,207.5 | 16,343.6 | 14,540.5 | 15,940.8 | 16,478.0 | 12,392.6 | 11,419.8 | 7,507.7 |
| Other investment | 8d9aa | .... | 208,044.2 | † 310,664.5 | 396,881.1 | 427,025.1 | 413,776.3 | 367,809.1 | 389,419.9 | 394,451.8 | 402,406.2 | 337,218.7 | 286,756.0 |
| Other equity | 8daaa | .... | .... | † 152.8 | 172.2 | 162.8 | 161.3 | 192.4 | 240.7 | 1,502.8 | 2,932.0 | 3,195.5 | 2,874.2 |
| Debt instruments | 8dzaa | .... | 208,044.2 | † 310,511.7 | 396,708.9 | 426,862.2 | 413,615.0 | 367,616.7 | 389,179.2 | 392,949.0 | 399,474.2 | 334,023.2 | 283,881.8 |
| Reserve assets | 8e9aa | .... | 11,832.2 | † 12,900.9 | 18,209.5 | 16,688.8 | 18,040.0 | 22,283.2 | 25,160.3 | 27,212.6 | 23,290.1 | 24,940.9 | 22,235.7 |
| Liabilities | 809la | .... | 714,114.5 | † 938,797.8 | 1,176,925.1 | 1,131,683.3 | 1,168,616.9 | 1,098,947.2 | 1,095,595.9 | 1,151,992.6 | 1,180,257.1 | 1,071,576.8 | 966,741.7 |
| Direct investment | 8a9la | .... | 154,666.4 | † 216,233.0 | 313,267.3 | 297,278.3 | 336,457.9 | 295,848.0 | 292,228.6 | 313,889.2 | 335,957.0 | 321,029.9 | 305,267.1 |
| Equity & investment fund shares.. | 8aala | .... | 148,295.0 | † 181,211.3 | 241,851.3 | 229,181.0 | 257,481.3 | 218,940.4 | 237,530.3 | 262,077.7 | 277,382.5 | 267,981.0 | 260,316.9 |
| Debt instruments | 8abla | .... | 6,371.3 | † 35,020.3 | 71,417.5 | 68,097.3 | 78,976.6 | 76,906.3 | 54,698.3 | 51,811.5 | 58,575.9 | 53,050.1 | 44,950.2 |
| Portfolio investment | 8b9la | .... | 350,605.2 | † 447,307.2 | 535,237.9 | 496,746.4 | 519,035.2 | 505,199.8 | 490,292.4 | 521,255.4 | 534,780.5 | 484,690.6 | 423,454.2 |
| Equity & investment fund shares.. | 8bala | .... | 59,235.7 | † 92,955.2 | 105,124.1 | 46,804.3 | 60,307.8 | 62,709.2 | 47,413.7 | 57,855.7 | 65,576.2 | 54,764.4 | 54,654.9 |
| Debt securities | 8bbla | .... | 291,369.5 | † 354,350.7 | 430,113.8 | 449,940.8 | 458,725.9 | 442,490.6 | 442,878.7 | 463,398.3 | 469,204.3 | 429,926.2 | 368,799.3 |
| Fin. der.(oth.than reserves) & ESOs | 8c9la | .... | .... | † 4,649.0 | 11,111.4 | 15,162.6 | 10,398.3 | 10,966.2 | 12,279.1 | 11,800.7 | 10,656.3 | 10,064.9 | 7,802.2 |
| Other investment | 8d9la | .... | 208,843.0 | † 270,609.9 | 317,308.5 | 322,496.1 | 302,727.0 | 286,933.2 | 300,795.8 | 305,047.3 | 298,863.2 | 255,791.4 | 230,211.1 |
| Other equity | 8dala | .... | .... | † — | — | — | — | — | — | — | — | — | 1.1 |
| Debt instruments | 8dzla | .... | 208,843.0 | † 270,609.9 | 317,308.5 | 322,496.1 | 302,727.0 | 286,933.2 | 300,795.8 | 305,047.3 | 298,863.2 | 255,791.4 | 230,210.0 |

## Government Finance Operations Statement
### General Government

*Millions of Euros: Fiscal Year Ends December 31; Data Reported through Eurostat*

| | | 2004 | 2005 | 2006 | 2007 | 2008 | 2009 | 2010 | 2011 | 2012 | 2013 | 2014 | 2015 |
|---|---|---|---|---|---|---|---|---|---|---|---|---|---|
| Revenue | a1 | 117,515 | 122,629 | 127,165 | 134,982 | 141,145 | 139,659 | 142,305 | 148,938 | 155,196 | 159,827 | 164,220 | 170,437 |
| Taxes | a11 | 67,069 | 68,270 | 70,704 | 75,914 | 80,604 | 76,592 | 78,817 | 83,049 | 87,034 | 90,181 | 92,940 | 97,321 |
| Social Contributions | a12 | 36,876 | 37,888 | 39,372 | 40,972 | 42,687 | 43,155 | 43,960 | 45,854 | 47,332 | 49,179 | 50,593 | 52,373 |
| Grants | a13 | .... | .... | .... | .... | .... | .... | .... | .... | .... | .... | .... | .... |
| Other Revenue | a14 | .... | .... | .... | .... | .... | .... | .... | .... | .... | .... | .... | .... |
| Expense | a2 | 128,661 | 127,843 | 133,030 | 136,830 | 142,941 | 152,825 | 153,628 | 155,706 | 161,294 | 164,911 | 172,180 | 173,187 |
| Compensation of Employees | a21 | 25,767 | 27,499 | 28,582 | 29,418 | 30,816 | 32,065 | 32,637 | 33,017 | 33,802 | 34,194 | 34,904 | 35,958 |
| Use of Goods & Services | a22 | 13,125 | 15,747 | 16,580 | 16,664 | 18,019 | 19,049 | 19,456 | 19,692 | 20,120 | 20,550 | 20,798 | 21,404 |
| Consumption of Fixed Capital | a23 | 5,380 | 6,383 | 6,621 | 6,918 | 7,300 | 7,594 | 7,899 | 8,118 | 8,353 | 8,495 | 8,667 | 8,809 |
| Interest | a24 | 7,283 | 8,181 | 8,390 | 8,892 | 8,643 | 9,039 | 8,547 | 8,615 | 8,622 | 8,398 | 8,128 | 7,933 |
| Subsidies | a25 | 4,720 | 4,102 | 4,273 | 4,234 | 4,626 | 4,706 | 4,747 | 4,693 | 4,739 | 4,416 | 4,663 | 4,852 |
| Grants | a26 | .... | .... | .... | .... | .... | .... | .... | .... | .... | .... | .... | .... |
| Social Benefits | a27 | 53,421 | 54,936 | 57,142 | 59,141 | 62,034 | 65,629 | 67,923 | 68,968 | 71,505 | 74,188 | 76,756 | 79,350 |
| Other Expense | a28 | .... | .... | .... | .... | .... | .... | .... | .... | .... | .... | .... | .... |
| Gross Operating Balance [1-2+23] | agob | −5,766 | 1,169 | 757 | 5,070 | 5,504 | −5,572 | −3,424 | 1,351 | 2,255 | 3,411 | 707 | 6,058 |
| Net Operating Balance [1-2] | anob | −11,146 | −5,214 | −5,865 | −1,848 | −1,797 | −13,166 | −11,323 | −6,768 | −6,098 | −5,084 | −7,960 | −2,751 |
| Net Acq. of Nonfinancial Assets | a31 | 388 | 1,137 | 794 | 1,870 | 2,432 | 2,052 | 1,781 | 1,125 | 781 | −849 | 940 | 1,134 |
| Aquisition of Nonfin. Assets | a31.1 | .... | .... | .... | .... | .... | .... | .... | .... | .... | .... | .... | .... |
| Disposal of Nonfin. Assets | a31.2 | .... | .... | .... | .... | .... | .... | .... | .... | .... | .... | .... | .... |
| Net Lending/Borrowing [1-2-31] | anlb | −11,535 | −6,351 | −6,658 | −3,717 | −4,229 | −15,218 | −13,104 | −7,893 | −6,879 | −4,236 | −8,900 | −3,885 |
| Net Acq. of Financial Assets | a32 | −5,199 | 1,373 | −242 | 4,661 | 12,780 | −5,294 | 82 | 1,760 | −3,442 | −834 | −2,142 | 348 |
| By instrument | | | | | | | | | | | | | |
| Monetary Gold & SDRs | a3201 | — | — | — | — | — | — | — | — | — | — | — | — |
| Currency & Deposits | a3202 | −946 | 756 | −336 | 1,826 | 9,232 | −7,868 | −83 | 3,246 | −1,992 | 702 | −954 | 3,190 |
| Securities other than Shares | a3203 | −6 | 219 | −230 | 771 | 534 | 273 | −2,113 | −1,192 | −1,474 | −2,247 | −2,616 | −687 |
| Loans | a3204 | −5,107 | 205 | 262 | −2,017 | 1,291 | −2,077 | −683 | 1,314 | 3,412 | 945 | 681 | −3,296 |
| Shares & Other Equity | a3205 | −189 | 527 | −213 | 1,437 | 337 | 3,824 | 1,524 | −884 | −1,212 | −1,030 | 459 | 2,836 |
| Insurance Technical Reserves | a3206 | — | — | — | — | — | — | — | — | — | — | — | — |
| Financial Derivatives | a3207 | — | — | 191 | 1,887 | 531 | −61 | −429 | −511 | −844 | −234 | −239 | −569 |
| Other Accounts Receivable | a3208 | 1,050 | −333 | 83 | 757 | 856 | 616 | 1,865 | −213 | −1,333 | 1,028 | 526 | −1,126 |
| By debtor | | | | | | | | | | | | | |
| Domestic | a321 | .... | .... | .... | .... | .... | .... | .... | .... | .... | .... | .... | .... |
| Foreign | a322 | .... | .... | .... | .... | .... | .... | .... | .... | .... | .... | .... | .... |
| Net Incurrence of Liabilities | a33 | 5,998 | 8,984 | 8,025 | 8,838 | 16,945 | 11,379 | 12,932 | 10,103 | 6,149 | 4,760 | 7,115 | 5,676 |
| By instrument | | | | | | | | | | | | | |
| Special Drawing Rights (SDRs) | a3301 | — | — | — | — | — | — | — | — | — | — | — | — |
| Currency & Deposits | a3302 | — | — | — | — | — | — | −3,162 | −636 | −2,518 | −1,333 | 1,010 | −2,303 |
| Securities other than Shares | a3303 | 3,633 | 5,009 | 7,792 | 7,505 | 15,373 | 10,930 | 12,868 | 7,923 | 7,940 | 4,723 | 1,724 | 7,145 |
| Loans | a3304 | 1,837 | 2,876 | −456 | −1,087 | −1,949 | 2,526 | 3,184 | 3,889 | 2,023 | 363 | 968 | −427 |
| Shares & Other Equity | a3305 | −26 | 257 | 5 | −57 | 11 | 258 | — | 7 | −1 | −4 | 2 | 17 |
| Insurance Technical Reserves | a3306 | — | — | — | — | — | — | — | — | −1 | — | — | −2 |
| Financial Derivatives | a3307 | 734 | 1,046 | 547 | 1,577 | 2,429 | −1,088 | −501 | −1,124 | −1,066 | −827 | −571 | −106 |
| Other Accounts Payable | a3308 | −179 | −204 | 138 | 899 | 1,082 | −1,247 | 543 | 43 | −229 | 1,838 | 3,982 | 1,352 |
| By creditor | | | | | | | | | | | | | |
| Domestic | a331 | .... | .... | .... | .... | .... | .... | .... | .... | .... | .... | .... | .... |
| Foreign | a332 | .... | .... | .... | .... | .... | .... | .... | .... | .... | .... | .... | .... |
| Stat. Discrepancy [32-33-NLB] | anlbz | 338 | −1,260 | −1,609 | −460 | 63 | −1,456 | 255 | −450 | −2,713 | −1,358 | −357 | −1,444 |
| Memo Item: Expenditure [2+31] | a2m | 129,049 | 128,980 | 133,824 | 138,699 | 145,373 | 154,877 | 155,410 | 156,831 | 162,075 | 164,062 | 173,120 | 174,321 |

## Balance Sheet

| | | 2004 | 2005 | 2006 | 2007 | 2008 | 2009 | 2010 | 2011 | 2012 | 2013 | 2014 | 2015 |
|---|---|---|---|---|---|---|---|---|---|---|---|---|---|
| Net Worth | a6 | .... | .... | .... | .... | .... | .... | .... | .... | .... | .... | .... | .... |
| Nonfinancial Assets | a61 | .... | .... | .... | .... | .... | .... | .... | .... | .... | .... | .... | .... |
| Financial Assets | a62 | 84,367 | 90,262 | 94,527 | 99,186 | 105,489 | 121,492 | 131,404 | 135,007 | 159,030 | 153,323 | 172,004 | 186,325 |
| By instrument | | | | | | | | | | | | | |
| Monetary Gold & SDRs | a6201 | — | — | — | — | — | — | — | — | — | — | — | — |
| Currency & Deposits | a6202 | 10,290 | 11,203 | 10,249 | 12,559 | 21,822 | 21,744 | 18,242 | 21,471 | 19,513 | 20,341 | 26,397 | 32,690 |
| Securities other than Shares | a6203 | 2,236 | 2,436 | 2,981 | 2,954 | 3,851 | 12,807 | 14,041 | 12,548 | 11,954 | 9,507 | 8,772 | 10,248 |
| Loans | a6204 | 32,016 | 32,084 | 32,482 | 29,011 | 29,910 | 30,408 | 31,497 | 32,752 | 35,760 | 36,519 | 46,283 | 48,569 |
| Shares and Other Equity | a6205 | 34,165 | 37,447 | 41,466 | 44,056 | 40,807 | 46,176 | 55,286 | 55,538 | 56,441 | 51,626 | 54,006 | 58,821 |
| Insurance Technical Reserves | a6206 | — | — | — | — | — | — | — | — | 4 | 4 | 4 | 4 |
| Financial Derivatives | a6207 | — | — | 4 | 2,605 | 495 | 1,319 | 1,404 | 1,286 | 1,539 | 668 | 1,104 | 939 |
| Other Accounts Receivable | a6208 | 5,660 | 7,091 | 7,345 | 8,001 | 8,605 | 9,037 | 10,934 | 11,412 | 33,820 | 34,658 | 35,438 | 35,055 |
| By debtor | | | | | | | | | | | | | |
| Domestic | a621 | .... | .... | .... | .... | .... | .... | .... | .... | .... | .... | .... | .... |
| Foreign | a622 | .... | .... | .... | .... | .... | .... | .... | .... | .... | .... | .... | .... |
| Liabilities | a63 | 175,732 | 203,274 | 207,585 | 210,856 | 233,180 | 264,413 | 282,924 | 298,404 | 338,221 | 333,227 | 367,005 | 376,182 |
| By instrument | | | | | | | | | | | | | |
| Special Drawing Rights (SDRs) | a6301 | — | — | — | — | — | — | — | — | — | — | — | — |
| Currency & Deposits | a6302 | — | — | — | — | — | 8,417 | 6,474 | 5,838 | 3,320 | 1,987 | 2,997 | 3,973 |
| Securities other than Shares | a6303 | 141,336 | 152,076 | 152,497 | 153,731 | 176,496 | 197,106 | 214,242 | 226,332 | 248,095 | 242,696 | 269,826 | 275,226 |
| Loans | a6304 | 26,320 | 34,352 | 33,571 | 32,449 | 30,611 | 33,584 | 36,965 | 41,006 | 42,027 | 42,366 | 48,004 | 49,205 |
| Shares and Other Equity | a6305 | 3,635 | 11,379 | 13,788 | 13,924 | 13,586 | 14,117 | 14,152 | 14,058 | 14,336 | 14,507 | 14,567 | 14,714 |
| Insurance Technical Reserves | a6306 | — | — | — | — | — | — | — | — | 2 | 2 | 2 | — |
| Financial Derivatives | a6307 | — | — | 937 | 2,893 | 3,458 | 3,454 | 2,703 | 2,477 | 1,628 | 1,212 | 1,027 | 915 |
| Other Accounts Payable | a6308 | 4,441 | 5,467 | 6,792 | 7,859 | 9,028 | 7,735 | 8,387 | 8,693 | 28,813 | 30,458 | 30,581 | 32,149 |
| By creditor | | | | | | | | | | | | | |
| Domestic | a631 | .... | .... | .... | .... | .... | .... | .... | .... | .... | .... | .... | .... |
| Foreign | a632 | .... | .... | .... | .... | .... | .... | .... | .... | .... | .... | .... | .... |
| Net Financial Worth [62-63] | a6m2 | −91,365 | −113,011 | −113,057 | −111,670 | −127,690 | −142,921 | −151,520 | −163,397 | −179,191 | −179,904 | −195,001 | −189,857 |
| Memo Item: Debt at Market Value | a6m3 | 172,097 | 191,895 | 192,860 | 194,039 | 216,135 | 246,842 | 266,069 | 281,869 | 322,258 | 317,509 | 351,410 | 360,553 |
| Memo Item: Debt at Face Value | a6m35 | 160,942 | 178,308 | 185,450 | 190,843 | 209,053 | 235,900 | 251,130 | 262,366 | 287,608 | 291,340 | 308,025 | 322,865 |
| Memo Item: Maastricht Debt | a6m36 | 156,501 | 172,842 | 178,658 | 182,984 | 200,024 | 228,166 | 242,743 | 253,673 | 258,795 | 260,882 | 277,444 | 290,716 |
| Memo Item: Debt at Nominal Value | a6m4 | .... | .... | .... | .... | .... | .... | .... | .... | .... | .... | .... | .... |

# Austria  122

| National Accounts | | 2004 | 2005 | 2006 | 2007 | 2008 | 2009 | 2010 | 2011 | 2012 | 2013 | 2014 | 2015 |
|---|---|---|---|---|---|---|---|---|---|---|---|---|---|
| | | | | | | | *Billions of Euros* | | | | | | |
| Househ.Cons.Expend.,incl.NPISHs..... | 96f | 130.7 | 136.9 | 142.7 | 147.8 | 152.3 | 153.9 | 158.9 | 165.3 | 170.3 | 173.8 | 177.1 | 179.8 |
| Government Consumption Expend... | 91f | 45.3 | 48.6 | 51.0 | 52.7 | 56.0 | 58.9 | 60.0 | 61.1 | 62.8 | 64.0 | 65.4 | 67.4 |
| Gross Fixed Capital Formation......... | 93e | 57.1 | 58.5 | 60.4 | 64.9 | 68.2 | 64.3 | 63.5 | 69.7 | 71.5 | 71.6 | 72.8 | 74.6 |
| Changes in Inventories................... | 93i | 1.1 | 2.0 | 2.7 | 4.6 | 3.4 | 1.0 | 2.9 | 5.2 | 4.7 | 2.1 | 1.4 | .6 |
| Exports of Goods and Services......... | 90c | 113.3 | 123.0 | 135.5 | 148.2 | 155.2 | 128.5 | 149.1 | 165.6 | 170.0 | 172.5 | 176.4 | 180.1 |
| Imports of Goods and Services (-)..... | 98c | 106.3 | 115.2 | 126.3 | 136.5 | 143.0 | 119.9 | 139.9 | 157.9 | 162.0 | 161.0 | 164.2 | 165.0 |
| Gross Domestic Product (GDP)......... | 99b | 241.5 | 253.0 | 266.5 | 282.3 | 291.9 | 286.2 | 294.2 | 308.7 | 317.2 | 322.6 | 328.9 | 337.2 |
| Net Primary Income from Abroad..... | 98.n | −8.5 | −10.1 | −10.2 | −11.6 | −9.8 | −12.6 | −8.8 | −11.5 | −12.1 | −11.9 | .... | .... |
| Gross National Income (GNI)............ | 99a | 233.0 | 242.9 | 256.2 | 270.7 | 282.1 | 273.6 | 285.4 | 297.2 | 305.1 | 310.7 | .... | .... |
| Net Current Transf.from Abroad....... | 98t | −1.9 | −2.1 | −2.0 | −1.5 | −1.9 | −2.3 | −2.4 | −2.4 | −2.5 | −3.5 | .... | .... |
| Gross Nat'l Disposable Inc.(GNDI).... | 99i | 231.0 | 240.8 | 254.3 | 269.2 | 280.2 | 271.3 | 283.0 | 294.8 | 302.6 | 307.2 | .... | .... |
| Gross Saving................................ | 99s | 59.1 | 60.8 | 66.6 | 74.8 | 78.2 | 65.5 | 70.5 | 74.2 | 75.2 | 75.9 | .... | .... |
| GDP Volume 2010 Ref., Chained..... | 99b.p | 270.2 | 276.0 | 285.3 | 295.6 | 300.2 | 288.8 | 294.2 | 303.2 | 305.9 | 306.6 | 307.5 | 309.9 |
| GDP Volume (2010=100)............... | 99bvp | 91.9 | 93.8 | 97.0 | 100.5 | 102.0 | 98.2 | 100.0 | 103.1 | 104.0 | 104.2 | 104.5 | 105.3 |
| GDP Deflator (2010=100)............... | 99bip | 89.4 | 91.7 | 93.4 | 95.5 | 97.3 | 99.1 | 100.0 | 101.8 | 103.7 | 105.2 | 106.9 | 108.8 |
| | | | | | | | *Millions: Midyear Estimates* | | | | | | |
| Population................................. | 99z | 8.20 | 8.23 | 8.27 | 8.30 | 8.33 | 8.36 | 8.39 | 8.42 | 8.46 | 8.49 | 8.52 | 8.54 |

# Azerbaijan, Republic of  912

| | | 2004 | 2005 | 2006 | 2007 | 2008 | 2009 | 2010 | 2011 | 2012 | 2013 | 2014 | 2015 |
|---|---|---|---|---|---|---|---|---|---|---|---|---|---|
| **Exchange Rates** | | | | | | *Manat per SDR: End of Period* | | | | | | | |
| Official Rate | aa | 1.5229 | 1.3129 | 1.3109 | 1.3358 | 1.2338 | 1.2590 | 1.2288 | 1.2075 | 1.2065 | 1.2081 | 1.1364 | 2.1609 |
| | | | | | | *Manat per US Dollar: End of Period (ae) Period Average (rf)* | | | | | | | |
| Official Rate | ae | .9806 | .9186 | .8714 | .8453 | .8010 | .8031 | .7979 | .7865 | .7850 | .7845 | .7844 | 1.5594 |
| Official Rate | rf | .9827 | .9454 | .8934 | .8581 | .8216 | .8038 | .8027 | .7897 | .7856 | .7845 | .7843 | 1.0246 |
| **Fund Position** | | | | | | *Millions of SDRs: End of Period* | | | | | | | |
| Quota | 2f.s | 160.90 | 160.90 | 160.90 | 160.90 | 160.90 | 160.90 | 160.90 | 160.90 | 160.90 | 160.90 | 160.90 | 160.90 |
| SDR Holdings | 1b.s | 9.36 | 9.74 | 10.26 | 6.41 | 1.05 | 151.71 | 153.63 | 153.67 | 154.22 | 154.16 | 153.59 | 153.57 |
| Reserve Position in the Fund | 1c.s | .01 | .01 | .01 | .05 | .08 | .13 | .13 | .13 | .13 | .13 | .13 | .13 |
| Total Fund Cred.&Loans Outstg | 2tl | 134.18 | 114.48 | 89.23 | 65.17 | 51.45 | 39.42 | 29.77 | 18.82 | 10.30 | 3.86 | 1.29 | — |
| SDR Allocations | 1bd | — | — | — | — | — | 153.58 | 153.58 | 153.58 | 153.58 | 153.58 | 153.58 | 153.58 |
| **International Liquidity** | | | | | *Millions of US Dollars Unless Otherwise Indicated: End of Period* | | | | | | | | |
| Total Reserves minus Gold | 1l.d | 1,075.08 | 1,177.74 | 2,500.37 | 4,273.11 | 6,467.24 | 5,363.78 | 6,408.97 | 10,273.83 | 11,277.24 | 14,400.55 | 14,646.56 | 6,291.17 |
| SDR Holdings | 1b.d | 14.53 | 13.91 | 15.43 | 10.13 | 1.61 | 237.84 | 236.59 | 235.92 | 237.02 | 237.41 | 222.52 | 212.81 |
| Reserve Position in the Fund | 1c.d | .02 | .01 | .02 | .08 | .12 | .21 | .21 | .21 | .21 | .21 | .19 | .19 |
| Foreign Exchange | 1d.d | 1,060.53 | 1,163.82 | 2,484.93 | 4,262.91 | 6,465.51 | 5,125.73 | 6,172.17 | 10,037.70 | 11,040.01 | 14,162.93 | 14,423.85 | 6,078.17 |
| Gold (Million Fine Troy Ounces) | 1ad | — | — | — | — | — | — | — | — | — | .64 | .97 | .97 |
| Gold (National Valuation) | 1and | — | — | — | — | — | .06 | .07 | .08 | .08 | 613.13 | 902.03 | 1,618.70 |
| Central Bank: Other Assets | 3..d | 20.66 | 13.11 | 93.26 | 69.05 | 86.84 | 130.80 | 132.68 | 128.06 | 126.19 | 135.60 | 535.17 | 183.10 |
| Central Bank: Other Liabs | 4..d | 6.05 | 7.74 | 8.04 | 6.53 | 9.49 | 255.04 | 260.33 | 278.16 | 266.37 | 259.29 | 266.99 | 163.03 |
| Other Depository Corps.: Assets | 7a.d | 204.20 | 291.32 | 351.55 | 601.39 | 1,480.01 | 1,592.57 | 2,138.44 | 2,325.65 | 2,614.56 | 2,955.38 | 4,079.54 | 4,376.48 |
| Other Depository Corps.: Liabs | 7b.d | 90.79 | 176.27 | 481.56 | 1,377.28 | 2,824.04 | 2,498.85 | 3,203.82 | 3,215.68 | 4,051.17 | 5,220.70 | 6,171.33 | 4,735.49 |
| **Central Bank** | | | | | | *Millions of Manat: End of Period* | | | | | | | |
| Net Foreign Assets | 11n | 839.84 | 922.44 | 2,057.21 | 3,512.49 | 5,108.70 | 3,859.97 | 4,463.86 | 7,948.64 | 9,018.39 | 10,716.27 | 8,766.45 | 10,807.83 |
| Claims on Nonresidents | 11 | 1,050.11 | 1,079.85 | 2,181.20 | 3,605.06 | 5,179.77 | 4,307.78 | 4,896.87 | 8,375.58 | 9,425.20 | 11,109.89 | 9,151.87 | 11,393.92 |
| Liabilities to Nonresidents | 16c | 210.27 | 157.41 | 123.98 | 92.57 | 71.07 | 447.81 | 433.01 | 426.94 | 406.81 | 393.62 | 385.42 | 586.09 |
| Claims on Other Depository Corps | 12e | 67.74 | 75.57 | 101.69 | 106.89 | 234.05 | 1,481.94 | 1,573.53 | 636.72 | 1,348.75 | 2,012.34 | 2,080.48 | 7,528.00 |
| Net Claims on Central Government | 12an | 22.04 | −49.27 | 27.23 | 94.04 | −475.75* | −591.14 | −199.43 | −1,886.56 | −1,935.23 | −2,508.65 | −992.09 | −5,635.31 |
| Claims on Central Government | 12a | 138.30 | 135.90 | 134.39 | 132.26 | 129.84 | 385.24 | 1,054.80 | 616.69 | 413.08 | 1,160.29 | 3,576.79 | 334.13 |
| Liabilities to Central Government | 16d | 116.26 | 185.17 | 107.16 | 38.23 | 605.59 | 976.38 | 1,254.23 | 2,503.24 | 2,348.31 | 3,668.93 | 4,568.89 | 5,969.43 |
| Claims on Other Sectors | 12s | .65 | 6.75 | 15.08 | 49.61 | 26.28 | 45.70 | 476.70 | 1,536.29 | 2,134.03 | 1,630.71 | 1,682.96 | 1,702.39 |
| Claims on Other Financial Corps | 12g | — | — | — | — | — | — | — | — | — | — | — | — |
| Claims on State & Local Govts | 12b | — | — | — | — | — | — | — | — | — | — | — | — |
| Claims on Public Nonfin. Corps | 12c | — | — | — | — | — | — | 397.60 | 1,488.28 | 2,091.85 | 1,575.26 | 1,645.76 | 1,645.76 |
| Claims on Private Sector | 12d | .65 | 6.75 | 15.08 | 49.61 | 26.28 | 45.70 | 79.10 | 48.01 | 42.18 | 55.45 | 37.19 | 56.62 |
| Monetary Base | 14 | 833.70 | 886.03 | 2,044.78 | 3,441.49 | 4,963.89 | 4,907.72 | 6,520.91 | 8,489.40 | 10,660.29 | 11,793.51 | 11,867.21 | 7,560.97 |
| Currency in Circulation | 14a | 526.21 | 594.11 | 1,449.29 | 2,911.16 | 4,425.82 | 4,512.71 | 5,793.22 | 7,658.49 | 9,777.52 | 11,033.73 | 10,846.21 | 5,417.05 |
| Liabs. to Other Depository Corps | 14c | 307.48 | 291.92 | 595.10 | 529.98 | 537.52 | 392.01 | 725.54 | 826.42 | 868.60 | 749.17 | 1,013.14 | 2,137.25 |
| Liabilities to Other Sectors | 14d | .01 | — | .39 | .35 | .54 | 3.00 | 2.16 | 4.50 | 14.17 | 10.61 | 7.86 | 6.68 |
| Other Liabs. to Other Dep. Corps | 14n | 19.89 | 31.69 | 113.54 | 252.16 | 179.76 | 9.10 | 40.19 | 91.26 | 120.01 | 19.99 | 58.49 | .22 |
| Dep. & Sec. Excl. f/Monetary Base | 14o | .01 | — | .01 | .01 | .74 | 1.66 | 1.84 | .53 | .85 | .01 | .02 | 1,198.87 |
| Deposits Included in Broad Money | 15 | .01 | — | .01 | .01 | .03 | — | — | — | — | — | — | — |
| Sec.Ot.th.Shares Incl.in Brd. Money | 16a | — | — | — | — | — | — | — | — | — | — | — | — |
| Deposits Excl. from Broad Money | 16b | — | — | — | — | .72 | 1.66 | 1.84 | .53 | .85 | .01 | .02 | 1,198.87 |
| Sec.Ot.th.Shares Excl.f/Brd.Money | 16s | — | — | — | — | — | — | — | — | — | — | — | — |
| Loans | 16l | — | — | — | — | — | — | — | — | — | — | — | — |
| Financial Derivatives | 16m | — | — | — | — | — | — | — | — | — | — | — | — |
| Shares and Other Equity | 17a | 96.15 | 60.73 | 61.24 | 89.65 | −232.75 | 32.34 | −79.39 | −170.93 | −35.91 | 219.29 | −80.44 | 5,435.53 |
| Other Items (Net) | 17r | −19.50 | −22.97 | −18.35 | −20.29 | −18.35 | −154.36 | −168.90 | −175.16 | −179.31 | −182.14 | −307.47 | 207.32 |
| Memo Item: | | | | | | | | | | | | | |
| Total Assets | 10ra | 1,600.61 | 1,633.88 | 2,735.01 | 4,196.04 | 5,881.48 | 6,505.85 | 8,306.89 | 11,495.59 | 13,703.90 | 16,270.99 | 16,983.79 | 21,542.62 |
| **Other Depository Corporations** | | | | | | *Millions of Manat: End of Period* | | | | | | | |
| Net Foreign Assets | 21n | 111.20 | 105.69 | −113.29 | −655.86 | −1,076.57 | −727.83 | −850.07 | −700.01 | −1,127.74 | −1,777.14 | −1,640.80 | −559.84 |
| Claims on Nonresidents | 21 | 200.24 | 267.61 | 306.34 | 508.36 | 1,185.49 | 1,279.00 | 1,706.26 | 1,829.12 | 2,052.43 | 2,318.50 | 3,199.99 | 6,824.68 |
| Liabilities to Nonresidents | 26c | 89.03 | 161.92 | 419.63 | 1,164.21 | 2,262.05 | 2,006.83 | 2,556.33 | 2,529.13 | 3,180.17 | 4,095.64 | 4,840.79 | 7,384.52 |
| Claims on Central Bank | 20 | 368.47 | 363.13 | 844.84 | 903.59 | 997.76 | 748.54 | 1,098.26 | 1,418.74 | 1,482.09 | 1,363.22 | 1,769.83 | 2,843.97 |
| Currency | 20a | 48.41 | 46.67 | 137.94 | 197.65 | 280.15 | 337.94 | 337.44 | 500.33 | 520.89 | 574.68 | 693.50 | 640.82 |
| Reserve Deposits and Securities | 20b | 301.66 | 286.21 | 594.30 | 502.30 | 527.30 | 390.90 | 723.85 | 824.32 | 841.34 | 739.27 | 1,020.01 | 2,198.14 |
| Other Claims | 20n | 18.39 | 30.26 | 112.60 | 203.63 | 190.32 | 19.70 | 36.98 | 94.09 | 119.86 | 49.26 | 56.32 | 5.01 |
| Net Claims on Central Government | 22an | −48.39 | −20.77 | 2.32 | 30.05 | −288.10 | 193.00 | 494.55 | 419.17 | 464.67 | 282.04 | 258.82 | 781.67 |
| Claims on Central Government | 22a | 17.71 | 25.33 | 41.59 | 197.50 | 108.73 | 361.53 | 522.93 | 472.69 | 514.44 | 551.07 | 492.64 | 1,030.48 |
| Liabilities to Central Government | 26d | 66.10 | 46.10 | 39.27 | 167.45 | 396.83 | 168.53 | 28.38 | 53.52 | 49.77 | 269.03 | 233.82 | 248.80 |
| Claims on Other Sectors | 22s | 957.87 | 1,461.57 | 2,407.94 | 4,693.72 | 7,245.85 | 8,347.70 | 9,007.48 | 9,936.85 | 12,682.54 | 15,307.58 | 18,957.35 | 22,365.29 |
| Claims on Other Financial Corps | 22g | .13 | .34 | 1.46 | 10.86 | 19.14 | 11.21 | 23.06 | 41.57 | 41.15 | 79.04 | 121.93 | 138.00 |
| Claims on State & Local Govts | 22b | — | .02 | .01 | .01 | .05 | .01 | .31 | .06 | .15 | .52 | .37 | .32 |
| Claims on Public Nonfin. Corps | 22c | 163.20 | 274.60 | 225.29 | 639.09 | 994.19 | 1,594.32 | 1,468.44 | 942.74 | 1,837.96 | 592.09 | 751.86 | 1,384.82 |
| Claims on Private Sector | 22d | 794.55 | 1,186.61 | 2,181.18 | 4,043.75 | 6,232.47 | 6,742.16 | 7,515.67 | 8,952.48 | 10,803.28 | 14,635.92 | 18,083.19 | 20,842.15 |
| Liabilities to Central Bank | 26g | 62.80 | 67.23 | 93.49 | 101.70 | 235.09 | 1,474.91 | 1,550.57 | 699.84 | 1,570.40 | 1,282.27 | 1,276.11 | 2,383.23 |
| Transf.Dep.Included in Broad Money | 24 | 466.55 | 540.28 | 1,080.26 | 1,335.24 | 1,551.61 | 1,489.60 | 1,823.39 | 2,441.98 | 2,654.00 | 3,006.70 | 3,771.80 | 7,154.50 |
| Other Dep.Included in Broad Money | 25 | 516.48 | 711.74 | 971.59 | 1,776.87 | 2,707.18 | 2,764.27 | 3,227.28 | 4,246.36 | 4,776.21 | 5,579.22 | 6,928.05 | 9,297.38 |
| Sec.Ot.th.Shares Incl.in Brd. Money | 26a | 45.04 | 39.26 | 71.37 | 71.28 | 89.20 | 37.55 | 18.92 | 52.19 | 74.24 | 234.26 | 706.20 | 84.10 |
| Deposits Excl. from Broad Money | 26b | 25.55 | 90.93 | 131.32 | 226.22 | 390.74 | 487.11 | 717.70 | 832.50 | 829.15 | 698.34 | 790.86 | 1,253.72 |
| Sec.Ot.th.Shares Excl.f/Brd.Money | 26s | — | — | — | — | — | — | — | — | — | — | — | — |
| Loans | 26l | 44.69 | 86.76 | 241.31 | 482.82 | 485.46 | 597.45 | 670.35 | 766.78 | 840.04 | 998.41 | 1,209.97 | 1,426.77 |
| Financial Derivatives | 26m | — | — | — | — | — | — | — | — | — | — | — | — |
| Insurance Technical Reserves | 26r | — | — | — | — | — | — | — | — | — | — | — | — |
| Shares and Other Equity | 27a | 248.93 | 339.45 | 533.14 | 940.35 | 1,380.00 | 1,652.03 | 1,817.06 | 2,032.08 | 2,157.47 | 2,935.76 | 3,825.34 | 3,223.91 |
| Other Items (Net) | 27r | −20.90 | 33.97 | 19.33 | 37.00 | 39.66 | 58.49 | −74.99 | 3.01 | 599.99 | 440.74 | 836.87 | 607.48 |
| Memo Item: | | | | | | | | | | | | | |
| Total Assets | 20ra | 2,240.09 | 3,026.19 | 4,991.96 | 8,806.74 | 13,598.66 | 16,297.61 | 18,263.19 | 19,634.94 | 25,958.41 | 29,355.38 | 35,750.76 | 49,242.69 |

|  |  | 2004 | 2005 | 2006 | 2007 | 2008 | 2009 | 2010 | 2011 | 2012 | 2013 | 2014 | 2015 |
|---|---|---|---|---|---|---|---|---|---|---|---|---|---|
| **Depository Corporations** |  | | | | | *Millions of Manat: End of Period* | | | | | | | |
| Net Foreign Assets | 31n | 951.04 | 1,028.12 | 1,943.92 | 2,856.63 | 4,032.13 | 3,132.14 | 3,613.80 | 7,248.63 | 7,890.65 | 8,939.13 | 7,125.65 | 10,247.99 |
| Claims on Nonresidents | 31 | 1,250.34 | 1,347.46 | 2,487.54 | 4,113.42 | 6,365.26 | 5,586.77 | 6,603.14 | 10,204.71 | 11,477.63 | 13,428.38 | 12,351.86 | 18,218.61 |
| Liabilities to Nonresidents | 36c | 299.30 | 319.33 | 543.61 | 1,256.79 | 2,333.12 | 2,454.63 | 2,989.34 | 2,956.07 | 3,586.97 | 4,489.26 | 5,226.21 | 7,970.62 |
| Domestic Claims | 32 | 932.16 | 1,398.28 | 2,452.57 | 4,867.41 | 6,508.28 | 7,995.26 | 9,779.31 | 10,005.75 | 13,346.00 | 14,711.69 | 19,907.03 | 19,214.04 |
| Net Claims on Central Government | 32an | −26.35 | −70.05 | 29.55 | 124.08 | −763.85 | −398.14 | 295.12 | −1,467.39 | −1,470.56 | −2,226.61 | −733.27 | −4,853.63 |
| Claims on Central Government | 32a | 156.01 | 161.23 | 175.98 | 329.76 | 238.57 | 746.77 | 1,577.73 | 1,089.38 | 927.52 | 1,711.36 | 4,069.44 | 1,364.60 |
| Liabilities to Central Government | 36d | 182.36 | 231.27 | 146.43 | 205.68 | 1,002.42 | 1,144.91 | 1,282.61 | 2,556.77 | 2,398.08 | 3,937.97 | 4,802.71 | 6,218.24 |
| Claims on Other Sectors | 32s | 958.52 | 1,468.32 | 2,423.02 | 4,743.32 | 7,272.13 | 8,393.40 | 9,484.19 | 11,473.14 | 14,816.56 | 16,938.29 | 20,640.30 | 24,067.68 |
| Claims on Other Financial Corps | 32g | .13 | .34 | 1.46 | 10.86 | 19.14 | 11.21 | 23.06 | 41.57 | 41.15 | 79.04 | 121.93 | 138.00 |
| Claims on State & Local Govts | 32b | — | .02 | .01 | .01 | .05 | .01 | .31 | .06 | .15 | .52 | .37 | .32 |
| Claims on Public Nonfin. Corps | 32c | 163.20 | 274.60 | 225.29 | 639.09 | 994.19 | 1,594.32 | 1,866.03 | 2,431.02 | 3,929.81 | 2,167.36 | 2,397.62 | 3,030.58 |
| Claims on Private Sector | 32d | 795.19 | 1,193.36 | 2,196.26 | 4,093.36 | 6,258.75 | 6,787.86 | 7,594.78 | 9,000.49 | 10,845.45 | 14,691.37 | 18,120.38 | 20,898.78 |
| Broad Money Liabilities | 35l | 1,505.88 | 1,838.72 | 3,434.97 | 5,897.26 | 8,494.23 | 8,469.18 | 10,527.49 | 13,903.18 | 16,775.30 | 19,289.83 | 21,566.62 | 21,318.89 |
| Currency Outside Depository Corps | 34a | 477.79 | 547.44 | 1,311.35 | 2,713.51 | 4,145.67 | 4,174.77 | 5,455.78 | 7,158.16 | 9,256.64 | 10,459.05 | 10,152.71 | 4,776.23 |
| Transferable Deposits | 34 | 466.57 | 540.29 | 1,080.66 | 1,335.60 | 1,552.17 | 1,492.60 | 1,825.50 | 2,446.48 | 2,668.21 | 3,017.19 | 3,778.68 | 7,159.89 |
| Other Deposits | 35 | 516.48 | 711.74 | 971.59 | 1,776.87 | 2,707.18 | 2,764.27 | 3,227.28 | 4,246.36 | 4,776.21 | 5,579.33 | 6,929.04 | 9,298.67 |
| Securities Other than Shares | 36a | 45.04 | 39.26 | 71.37 | 71.28 | 89.20 | 37.55 | 18.92 | 52.19 | 74.24 | 234.26 | 706.20 | 84.10 |
| Deposits Excl. from Broad Money | 36b | 25.55 | 90.93 | 131.32 | 226.23 | 391.46 | 488.77 | 719.54 | 833.03 | 829.99 | 698.35 | 790.88 | 2,452.59 |
| Sec.Ot.th.Shares Excl.f/Brd.Money | 36s | — | — | — | — | — | — | — | — | — | — | — | — |
| Loans | 36l | 44.69 | 86.76 | 241.31 | 482.82 | 485.46 | 597.45 | 670.35 | 766.78 | 840.04 | 998.41 | 1,209.97 | 1,426.77 |
| Financial Derivatives | 36m | — | — | — | — | — | — | — | — | — | — | — | — |
| Insurance Technical Reserves | 36r | — | — | — | — | — | — | — | — | — | — | — | — |
| Shares and Other Equity | 37a | 345.08 | 400.18 | 594.37 | 1,030.00 | 1,147.25 | 1,684.37 | 1,737.67 | 1,861.15 | 2,121.56 | 3,155.06 | 3,744.89 | 8,659.44 |
| Other Items (Net) | 37r | −38.01 | 9.81 | −5.47 | 87.73 | 22.02 | −112.38 | −261.95 | −109.75 | 669.75 | −490.84 | −279.68 | −4,395.65 |
| Broad Money Liabs., Seasonally Adj. | 35l.b | 1,444.73 | 1,755.19 | 3,261.81 | 5,574.85 | 8,018.78 | 8,007.08 | 10,008.77 | 13,297.37 | 16,124.03 | 18,589.66 | 20,807.52 | 20,574.69 |
| **Monetary Aggregates** |  | | | | | *Millions of Manat: End of Period* | | | | | | | |
| Broad Money | 59m | 1,505.88 | 1,838.72 | 3,434.97 | 5,897.26 | 8,494.23 | 8,469.18 | 10,527.49 | 13,903.18 | 16,775.30 | 19,289.83 | 21,566.62 | 21,318.89 |
| o/w:Currency Issued by Cent.Govt | 59m.a | — | — | — | — | — | — | — | — | — | — | — | — |
| o/w: Dep.in Nonfin. Corporations | 59m.b | — | — | — | — | — | — | — | — | — | — | — | — |
| o/w:Secs. Issued by Central Govt | 59m.c | — | — | — | — | — | — | — | — | — | — | — | — |
| Money (National Definitions) |  | | | | | | | | | | | | |
| Reserve Money | 19mb | 833.70 | 886.00 | 1,547.21 | 3,441.49 | 4,963.90 | 4,907.72 | 6,520.91 | 8,489.40 | 10,660.09 | 11,793.11 | 11,866.94 | 7,560.67 |
| M1 | 59ma | 657.26 | 747.84 | 1,605.20 | 3,652.70 | 5,145.00 | 5,239.80 | 6,718.90 | 8,824.80 | 11,122.31 | 12,736.89 | 12,830.42 | 6,896.81 |
| M2 | 59mb | 685.67 | 796.70 | 1,820.39 | 4,401.61 | 6,081.00 | 6,169.23 | 8,297.47 | 10,997.16 | 13,820.75 | 16,434.78 | 17,435.83 | 8,613.11 |
| M3 | 59mc | 1,505.88 | 1,838.70 | 3,040.66 | 5,897.26 | 8,494.23 | 8,469.18 | 10,527.49 | 13,903.18 | 16,789.67 | 19,289.44 | 21,566.36 | 21,318.59 |
| **Interest Rates** |  | | | | | *Percent Per Annum* | | | | | | | |
| Central Bank Policy Rate (EOP) | 60 | 7.00 | 9.00 | 9.50 | 13.00 | 8.00 | 2.00 | 3.00 | 5.25 | 5.00 | 4.75 | 3.50 | 3.00 |
| Treasury Bill Rate | 60c | 4.62 | 7.52 | 10.04 | 10.64 | 10.48 | 3.31 | 1.83 | 2.28 | 2.43 | 1.89 | 1.89 | .... |
| Deposit Rate | 60l | 9.18 | 8.52 | 10.58 | 11.56 | 12.22 | 12.20 | 11.64 | 10.87 | 10.22 | 9.89 | 9.17 | 9.00 |
| Deposit Rate (Fgn. Currency) | 60l.f | 9.09 | 9.32 | 10.88 | 11.85 | 12.32 | 12.39 | 11.21 | 10.81 | 9.87 | 9.37 | 8.60 | 8.38 |
| Lending Rate | 60p | 15.72 | 17.03 | 17.86 | 19.13 | 19.76 | 20.03 | 20.70 | 18.99 | 18.35 | 18.21 | 17.86 | 17.53 |
| Lending Rate (Fgn. Currency) | 60p.f | 19.68 | 19.14 | 19.55 | 19.88 | 20.62 | 20.97 | 20.15 | 17.80 | 17.45 | 16.76 | 14.10 | 11.37 |
| **Prices and Labor** |  | | | | | *Percent Change over Previous Period* | | | | | | | |
| Consumer Prices | 64.xx | 6.7 | 9.7 | 8.4 | 16.6 | 20.8 | 1.4 | 5.7 | 7.9 | 1.0 | 2.4 | 1.4 | 4.2 |
|  |  | | | | | *Number in Thousands: Period Averages* | | | | | | | |
| Employment | 67e | 3,809.1 | 3,932.5 | .... | .... | 4,198.5 | 4,244.2 | 4,321.1 | 4,347.4 | 4,402.8 | 4,491.3 | 4,568.0 | .... |
| Unemployment | 67c | 56.0 | 56.3 | 53.9 | .... | 254.4 | 259.1 | 260.7 | 270.7 | 245.2 | 239.4 | 237.3 | .... |
| Unemployment Rate (%) | 67r | 1.4 | .... | .... | .... | 5.7 | 5.8 | 5.7 | 5.9 | 5.3 | 5.1 | 4.9 | .... |
| **Intl. Transactions & Positions** |  | | | | | *Millions of US Dollars* | | | | | | | |
| Exports | 70..d | 3,615.4 | 4,347.2 | 13,014.6 | 21,268.6 | 30,586.3 | 21,096.8 | 26,476.0 | 34,494.9 | 32,634.0 | 31,702.9 | 30,274.4 | 14,500.0 |
| Imports, cif | 71.vd | 1,025.342 | 1,008.022 | 1,590.324 | 1,885.833 | 2,078.844 | 1,792.300 | 2,083.102 | 2,938.762 | 3,120.490 | 2,519.775 | .... | .... |

# Azerbaijan, Republic of   912

| | | 2004 | 2005 | 2006 | 2007 | 2008 | 2009 | 2010 | 2011 | 2012 | 2013 | 2014 | 2015 |
|---|---|---|---|---|---|---|---|---|---|---|---|---|---|
| **Balance of Payments** | | | | | | | *Millions of US Dollars* | | | | | | |
| A. Current Account* | 109bx | −2,589.2 | 167.3 | 3,707.6 | 9,018.9 | 16,452.8 | 10,174.9 | 15,040.4 | 17,144.9 | 14,976.0 | † 12,231.7 | 10,208.8 | −222.5 |
| Goods, credit (exports) | 1a9cx | 3,586.9 | 7,398.1 | 12,749.1 | 20,899.8 | 30,220.6 | 20,658.4 | 25,741.1 | 33,996.3 | 31,877.1 | † 31,781.1 | 28,259.7 | 15,586.1 |
| Goods, debit (imports) | 1a9dx | 3,464.4 | 4,151.6 | 4,953.9 | 5,876.8 | 7,305.0 | 6,113.5 | 6,306.9 | 9,867.9 | 9,963.5 | † 11,172.9 | 9,332.0 | 9,773.6 |
| Balance on goods | 1a9bx | 122.5 | 3,246.4 | 7,795.2 | 15,023.0 | 22,915.5 | 14,544.9 | 19,434.2 | 24,128.4 | 21,913.6 | † 20,608.2 | 18,927.7 | 5,812.4 |
| Services, credit (exports) | 1b9cx | 536.4 | 741.5 | 965.3 | 1,455.4 | 1,668.6 | 2,100.9 | 2,493.6 | 3,042.5 | 4,808.7 | † 4,130.9 | 4,297.2 | 4,444.0 |
| Services, debit (imports) | 1b9dx | 2,736.0 | 2,658.8 | 2,938.6 | 3,385.2 | 3,915.7 | 3,673.5 | 3,929.5 | 5,839.5 | 7,429.6 | † 8,319.9 | 10,386.7 | 8,672.9 |
| Balance on goods & services | 1z9bx | −2,077.1 | 1,329.1 | 5,821.9 | 13,093.3 | 20,668.4 | 12,972.3 | 17,998.4 | 21,331.4 | 19,292.8 | † 16,419.2 | 12,838.1 | 1,583.6 |
| Primary income: credit | 1c9cx | 65.3 | 201.8 | 280.0 | 327.8 | 595.1 | 551.4 | 675.5 | 1,018.7 | 1,151.6 | † 1,029.4 | 1,673.9 | 1,258.2 |
| Primary income: debit | 1c9dx | 765.9 | 1,847.4 | 2,960.6 | 5,407.2 | 5,861.2 | 4,070.6 | 4,142.6 | 5,878.6 | 5,418.4 | † 5,157.0 | 4,255.6 | 3,286.0 |
| Balance on gds, serv. & prim. inc. | 1y9bx | −2,777.7 | −316.6 | 3,141.3 | 8,013.9 | 15,402.4 | 9,453.2 | 14,531.3 | 16,471.6 | 15,026.0 | † 12,291.7 | 10,256.4 | −444.2 |
| Secondary income: credit | 1d9ca | 262.6 | 626.2 | 748.2 | 1,313.4 | 1,500.1 | 1,292.4 | 1,420.4 | 1,882.3 | 1,953.1 | † 1,681.8 | 1,799.7 | 1,227.0 |
| Secondary income: debit | 1d9da | 74.1 | 142.3 | 182.0 | 308.4 | 449.7 | 570.7 | 911.3 | 1,209.0 | 2,003.1 | † 1,741.7 | 1,847.3 | 1,005.3 |
| B. Capital Account* | 209ba | −.1 | −.1 | .3 | 8.5 | — | — | — | .9 | −7.0 | † −12.9 | −6.9 | −43.9 |
| Capital account: credit | 209ca | — | — | 2.7 | 8.5 | — | — | — | 14.3 | .... | .... | .1 | .... |
| Capital account: debit | 209da | .1 | .1 | 2.4 | — | — | — | — | 13.4 | 7.0 | † 12.9 | 7.1 | 43.9 |
| Balance on current & capital acct. | 129ba | −2,589.4 | 167.2 | 3,707.9 | 9,027.4 | 16,452.8 | 10,174.9 | 15,040.4 | 17,145.8 | 14,969.0 | † 12,218.8 | 10,201.9 | −266.4 |
| C. Financial Account* | 309na | −2,960.2 | −78.0 | 2,105.3 | 6,874.1 | 13,158.9 | 9,682.0 | 12,695.0 | 13,547.1 | 11,943.8 | † 8,106.3 | 7,182.0 | 6,076.5 |
| Direct investment: assets | 3a9aa | 2,367.8 | 4,017.2 | 5,775.4 | 9,628.8 | 4,527.6 | 2,752.8 | 3,021.8 | 3,552.5 | 4,480.8 | † 1,477.9 | 1,987.1 | 3,209.4 |
| Equity & investment fund shares.. | 3aaaa | 2,367.8 | 4,017.2 | 5,774.9 | 9,622.0 | 4,352.0 | 2,748.6 | 3,021.8 | 3,552.5 | 4,480.8 | † 1,477.9 | 1,987.1 | 3,209.4 |
| Debt instruments | 3abaa | — | — | .6 | 6.8 | 175.7 | 4.2 | — | — | — | .... | .... | .... |
| Direct investment: liabilities | 3a9la | 4,719.1 | 4,476.4 | 4,486.0 | 4,594.2 | 3,986.8 | 2,900.0 | 3,353.0 | 4,485.1 | 5,293.3 | † 2,619.4 | 4,430.5 | 4,047.6 |
| Equity & investment fund shares . | 3aala | 4,719.1 | 4,476.4 | 4,303.4 | 4,079.1 | 3,520.8 | 2,524.7 | 3,353.0 | 4,485.1 | 5,293.3 | † 2,619.4 | 4,430.5 | 4,047.6 |
| Debt instruments | 3abla | — | — | 182.5 | 515.1 | 466.0 | 375.4 | — | — | — | .... | .... | .... |
| Portfolio investment: assets | 3b9aa | 18.1 | 47.8 | 34.4 | 110.9 | 320.8 | 84.3 | 163.3 | 344.8 | 253.1 | † 322.8 | 429.5 | −308.1 |
| Equity & investment fund shares.. | 3baaa | −1.9 | — | 3.1 | 11.9 | 21.4 | 3.5 | −9.8 | 1.2 | — | † 5.7 | — | 5.6 |
| Debt securities | 3bbaa | 20.0 | 47.8 | 31.3 | 99.0 | 299.5 | 80.8 | 173.1 | 343.6 | 253.1 | † 317.1 | 429.5 | −313.7 |
| Portfolio investment: liabilities | 3b9la | — | 78.3 | 22.3 | 84.5 | −26.6 | −54.5 | 24.5 | 27.9 | 521.3 | † 1,041.3 | 1,750.9 | 772.6 |
| Equity & investment fund shares . | 3bala | .... | — | .8 | 2.0 | — | — | .6 | .1 | — | † 29.8 | 10.4 | 24.5 |
| Debt securities | 3bbla | .... | 78.3 | 21.6 | 82.5 | −26.6 | −54.5 | 23.9 | 27.9 | 521.2 | † 1,011.5 | 1,740.5 | 748.2 |
| Fin. der.& empl.stk.ops.(ESOs): net. | 3c9na | .... | — | — | — | — | — | — | — | — | .... | .... | .... |
| Fin. der. & ESOs.: assets | 3c9aa | .... | — | — | — | — | — | — | — | — | .... | .... | .... |
| Fin. der. & ESOs.: liabilities | 3c9la | .... | — | — | — | — | — | — | — | — | .... | .... | .... |
| Other investment: assets | 3d9aa | 360.4 | 1,365.3 | 1,416.7 | 2,687.8 | 13,197.5 | 9,326.4 | 14,698.0 | 15,487.8 | 14,282.6 | † 11,576.1 | 13,038.6 | 7,870.8 |
| Other equity | 3daaa | .... | .... | .... | .... | .... | .... | .... | .... | .... | .... | .... | .... |
| Debt instruments | 3dzaa | 360.4 | 1,365.3 | 1,416.7 | 2,687.8 | 13,197.5 | 9,326.4 | 14,698.0 | 15,487.8 | 14,282.6 | † 11,576.1 | 13,038.6 | 7,870.8 |
| Other investment: liabilities | 3d9la | 987.4 | 953.7 | 612.9 | 874.6 | 926.9 | −364.0 | 1,810.6 | 1,325.0 | 1,258.3 | † 1,609.8 | 2,091.7 | −124.7 |
| Other equity | 3dala | .... | .... | .... | .... | .... | .... | .... | .... | .... | .... | .... | .... |
| Debt instruments | 3dzla | 987.4 | 953.7 | 612.9 | 874.6 | 926.9 | −364.0 | 1,810.6 | 1,325.0 | 1,258.3 | † 1,609.8 | 2,091.7 | −124.7 |
| Curr.+ cap.− finan. acct. balance... | 4y9na | 370.9 | 245.2 | 1,602.6 | 2,153.3 | 3,293.9 | 492.9 | 2,345.4 | 3,598.7 | 3,025.2 | † 4,112.5 | 3,019.8 | −6,342.9 |
| D. Net Errors and Omissions | 409na | −53.9 | −84.7 | −260.0 | −371.9 | −834.4 | −1,455.8 | −975.4 | 586.8 | −1,919.4 | † −1,879.8 | −2,806.3 | −2,086.0 |
| E. Reserves and Related Items | 4z9na | 317.0 | 160.5 | 1,342.6 | 1,781.3 | 2,459.5 | −963.0 | 1,370.0 | 4,185.5 | 1,105.8 | † 2,232.7 | 213.5 | −8,428.8 |
| Reserve assets | 3e9aa | 257.2 | 132.0 | 1,305.5 | 1,744.8 | 2,437.7 | −981.5 | 1,355.4 | 4,168.3 | 1,092.8 | † 2,222.9 | 209.6 | −8,430.7 |
| Credit and loans from the IMF | 3dcla | −59.8 | −28.5 | −37.1 | −36.5 | −21.8 | −18.5 | −14.6 | −17.2 | −13.0 | † −9.8 | −4.0 | −1.8 |
| Exceptional financing | 409la | — | — | — | — | — | — | — | — | — | .... | .... | .... |

*Excludes components in group E

| | | 2004 | 2005 | 2006 | 2007 | 2008 | 2009 | 2010 | 2011 | 2012 | 2013 | 2014 | 2015 |
|---|---|---|---|---|---|---|---|---|---|---|---|---|---|
| **International Investment Position** | | | | | | | *Millions of US Dollars* | | | | | | |
| Assets | 809aa | 9,096.1 | 14,816.5 | 23,437.5 | 36,786.8 | 55,119.5 | .... | .... | .... | .... | .... | .... | .... |
| Direct investment | 8a9aa | 6,623.3 | 11,045.4 | 17,647.8 | 27,275.8 | 31,802.9 | .... | .... | .... | .... | .... | .... | .... |
| Equity & investment fund shares.. | 8aaaa | 6,623.3 | 11,045.4 | 17,647.8 | 27,275.8 | 31,802.9 | .... | .... | .... | .... | .... | .... | .... |
| Debt instruments | 8abaa | .... | .... | .... | .... | .... | .... | .... | .... | .... | .... | .... | .... |
| Portfolio investment | 8b9aa | 20.4 | 84.6 | 119.0 | 229.9 | 550.7 | .... | .... | .... | .... | .... | .... | .... |
| Equity & investment fund shares.. | 8baaa | .... | .... | .... | .... | .... | .... | .... | .... | .... | .... | .... | .... |
| Debt securities | 8bbaa | 20.4 | 84.6 | 119.0 | 229.9 | 550.7 | .... | .... | .... | .... | .... | .... | .... |
| Fin. der.(oth.than reserves) & ESOs | 8c9aa | .... | .... | .... | .... | .... | .... | .... | .... | .... | .... | .... | .... |
| Other investment | 8d9aa | 1,376.4 | 2,508.8 | 3,170.4 | 5,008.0 | 16,298.6 | .... | .... | .... | .... | .... | .... | .... |
| Other equity | 8daaa | .... | .... | .... | .... | .... | .... | .... | .... | .... | .... | .... | .... |
| Debt instruments | 8dzaa | 1,376.4 | 2,508.8 | 3,170.4 | 5,008.0 | 16,298.6 | .... | .... | .... | .... | .... | .... | .... |
| Reserve assets | 8e9aa | 1,076.0 | 1,177.7 | 2,500.3 | 4,273.1 | 6,467.3 | .... | .... | .... | .... | .... | .... | .... |
| Liabilities | 809la | 18,554.2 | 24,165.2 | 30,504.0 | 36,155.0 | 42,516.5 | .... | .... | .... | .... | .... | .... | .... |
| Direct investment | 8a9la | 15,641.2 | 20,117.6 | 24,603.5 | 29,197.0 | 33,182.6 | .... | .... | .... | .... | .... | .... | .... |
| Equity & investment fund shares.. | 8aala | 15,641.2 | 20,117.6 | 24,603.5 | 28,962.9 | 32,948.8 | .... | .... | .... | .... | .... | .... | .... |
| Debt instruments | 8abla | .... | .... | .... | 234.1 | 233.8 | .... | .... | .... | .... | .... | .... | .... |
| Portfolio investment | 8b9la | .... | 97.1 | 119.4 | 203.9 | 177.3 | .... | .... | .... | .... | .... | .... | .... |
| Equity & investment fund shares.. | 8bala | .... | .... | .... | .... | .... | .... | .... | .... | .... | .... | .... | .... |
| Debt securities | 8bbla | .... | 97.1 | 119.4 | 203.9 | 177.3 | .... | .... | .... | .... | .... | .... | .... |
| Fin. der.(oth.than reserves) & ESOs | 8c9la | .... | .... | .... | .... | .... | .... | .... | .... | .... | .... | .... | .... |
| Other investment | 8d9la | 2,913.0 | 3,950.5 | 5,781.1 | 6,754.1 | 9,156.6 | .... | .... | .... | .... | .... | .... | .... |
| Other equity | 8dala | .... | .... | .... | .... | .... | .... | .... | .... | .... | .... | .... | .... |
| Debt instruments | 8dzla | 2,913.0 | 3,950.5 | 5,781.1 | 6,754.1 | 9,156.6 | .... | .... | .... | .... | .... | .... | .... |

| | | 2004 | 2005 | 2006 | 2007 | 2008 | 2009 | 2010 | 2011 | 2012 | 2013 | 2014 | 2015 |
|---|---|---|---|---|---|---|---|---|---|---|---|---|---|
| **Government Finance** | | | | | | | | | | | | | |
| **Cash Flow Statement** | | | | | | | | | | | | | |
| **Budgetary Central Government** | | | | | | *Millions of Manat: Fiscal Year Ends December 31* | | | | | | | |
| Cash Receipts:Operating Activities... | c1 | .... | .... | .... | .... | 10,757.8 | 10,320.7 | 11,512.2 | 15,831.7 | 17,406.6 | 19,664.1 | 18,395.7 | .... |
| Taxes.................................. | c11 | .... | .... | .... | .... | 6,591.0 | 5,022.2 | 5,162.8 | 6,366.9 | 6,995.5 | 7,789.6 | 8,387.4 | .... |
| Social Contributions...................... | c12 | — | — | — | — | — | — | — | — | — | — | — | .... |
| Grants.................................. | c13 | .... | .... | .... | .... | 3,800.0 | 4,915.0 | 5,918.1 | 9,006.7 | 9,917.0 | 11,350.0 | 9,337.0 | .... |
| Other Receipts.......................... | c14 | .... | .... | .... | .... | 366.8 | 383.5 | 431.3 | 458.1 | 494.1 | 524.5 | 671.3 | .... |
| Cash Payments:Operating Activities. | c2 | .... | .... | .... | .... | 5,987.8 | 6,727.2 | 7,195.3 | 7,827.1 | 10,081.5 | 9,751.3 | 10,535.5 | .... |
| Compensation of Employees.......... | c21 | .... | .... | .... | .... | 1,343.6 | 1,538.1 | 1,568.0 | 1,750.3 | 1,688.7 | 1,707.6 | 1,925.7 | .... |
| Purchases of Goods & Services....... | c22 | .... | .... | .... | .... | 667.5 | 776.3 | 848.8 | 916.2 | 1,290.6 | 1,450.3 | 1,631.6 | .... |
| Interest.................................. | c24 | .... | .... | .... | .... | 32.7 | 78.7 | 39.5 | 169.6 | 90.2 | 154.5 | 84.2 | .... |
| Subsidies................................ | c25 | .... | .... | .... | .... | 190.6 | 289.2 | 238.7 | 210.4 | 295.2 | 333.9 | 682.9 | .... |
| Grants.................................. | c26 | .... | .... | .... | .... | 642.1 | 822.3 | 810.8 | 1,150.7 | 1,316.7 | 1,372.6 | 1,443.7 | .... |
| Social Benefits........................... | c27 | .... | .... | .... | .... | 304.9 | 407.8 | 462.5 | 506.7 | 622.0 | 565.6 | 635.3 | .... |
| Other Payments.......................... | c28 | .... | .... | .... | .... | 2,806.4 | 2,814.8 | 3,227.0 | 3,123.8 | 4,778.1 | 4,166.8 | 4,132.1 | .... |
| Net Cash Inflow:Operating Act.[1-2] | ccio | .... | .... | .... | .... | 4,770.0 | 3,593.5 | 4,316.9 | 8,004.0 | 7,325.1 | 9,912.8 | 7,860.2 | .... |
| Net Cash Outflow:Invest. in NFA... | c31 | .... | .... | .... | .... | 4,496.4 | 3,638.2 | 4,455.9 | 7,325.0 | 7,168.3 | 8,454.5 | 7,773.3 | .... |
| Purchases of Nonfinancial Assets... | c31.1 | .... | .... | .... | .... | 4,610.1 | 3,702.0 | 4,518.0 | 7,386.3 | 7,208.2 | .... | .... | .... |
| Sales of Nonfinancial Assets.......... | c31.2 | .... | .... | .... | .... | 113.7 | 63.8 | 62.1 | 61.3 | 39.9 | .... | .... | .... |
| Cash Surplus/Deficit [1-2-31=1-2M] | ccsd | .... | .... | .... | .... | 273.6 | −44.7 | −139.0 | 679.0 | 156.8 | 1,458.3 | 86.9 | .... |
| Net Acq. Fin. Assets, excl. Cash....... | c32x | .... | .... | .... | .... | 2.7 | — | .2 | .1 | .1 | .... | .... | .... |
| Domestic................................ | c321x | .... | .... | .... | .... | 2.7 | — | .2 | .1 | .1 | .... | .... | .... |
| Foreign.................................. | c322x | .... | .... | .... | .... | — | — | — | — | — | .... | .... | .... |
| Net Incurrence of Liabilities.............. | c33 | .... | .... | .... | .... | −6.3 | −126.0 | 53.2 | −282.6 | −76.3 | −940.7 | 705.5 | .... |
| Domestic................................ | c331 | .... | .... | .... | .... | 73.8 | −52.3 | 105.5 | −109.2 | 45.3 | −470.0 | 987.2 | .... |
| Foreign.................................. | c332 | .... | .... | .... | .... | −80.1 | −73.7 | −52.3 | −173.4 | −121.6 | −470.7 | −281.7 | .... |
| Net Cash Inflow, Fin.Act.[-32x+33].. | cnfb | .... | .... | .... | .... | −9.0 | −126.0 | 53.0 | −282.7 | −76.4 | −940.8 | 644.8 | .... |
| Net Change in Stock of Cash........... | cncb | .... | .... | .... | .... | 264.6 | −170.7 | −86.0 | 396.3 | 80.4 | 517.5 | 731.7 | .... |
| Stat. Discrep. [32X-33+NCB-CSD].... | ccsdz | .... | .... | .... | .... | — | — | — | — | — | — | — | .... |
| Memo Item:Cash Expenditure[2+31] | c2m | .... | .... | .... | .... | 10,484.2 | 10,365.4 | 11,651.2 | 15,152.7 | 17,249.8 | 18,205.8 | 18,308.8 | .... |
| Memo Item: Gross Debt.................. | c63 | .... | .... | .... | .... | 1,836.6 | 2,240.5 | 2,711.3 | .... | .... | .... | .... | .... |
| **National Accounts** | | | | | | *Millions of Manat* | | | | | | | |
| Househ.Cons.Expend.,incl.NPISHs.... | 96f | 4,761 | 5,275 | 6,955 | 9,473 | 13,420 | 15,222 | 16,715 | 19,405 | 21,608 | 24,380 | 27,302 | .... |
| Government Consumption Expend... | 91f | 1,100 | 1,305 | 1,601 | 2,740 | 3,410 | 3,960 | 4,621 | 5,275 | 5,762 | 5,983 | 6,414 | .... |
| Gross Fixed Capital Formation.......... | 93e | 4,923 | 5,173 | 5,568 | 6,069 | 7,457 | 6,700 | 7,715 | 10,509 | 12,293 | 15,007 | 15,238 | .... |
| Changes in Inventories.................... | 93i | 24 | 28 | 30 | 36 | 46 | 46 | −46 | 47 | −76 | −79 | −46 | .... |
| Exports of Goods and Services.......... | 90c | 4,162 | 7,882 | 12,467 | 19,322 | 26,401 | 18,383 | 23,061 | 29,388 | 29,000 | 28,169 | 25,538 | .... |
| Imports of Goods and Services (-)..... | 98c | 6,203 | 6,625 | 7,266 | 8,086 | 9,419 | 8,227 | 8,782 | 12,542 | 13,844 | 15,279 | 15,467 | .... |
| Gross Domestic Product (GDP)........ | 99b | 8,530 | 12,523 | 18,746 | 28,361 | 40,137 | 35,602 | 42,465 | 52,082 | 54,744 | 58,182 | 58,978 | .... |
| Statistical Discrepancy.................... | 99bs | −237 | −516 | −609 | −1,192 | −1,178 | −483 | −818 | — | — | — | — | .... |
| **Population..............................** | 99z | 8.47 | 8.56 | 8.66 | 8.76 | 8.87 | 8.98 | 9.10 | 9.23 | 9.36 | 9.50 | 9.63 | 9.75 |

| | | 2004 | 2005 | 2006 | 2007 | 2008 | 2009 | 2010 | 2011 | 2012 | 2013 | 2014 | 2015 |
|---|---|---|---|---|---|---|---|---|---|---|---|---|---|
| **Exchange Rates** | | *Bahamian Dollars per SDR: End of Period* | | | | | | | | | | | |
| Principal Rate..................aa=......... | wa | 1.5530 | 1.4293 | 1.5044 | 1.5803 | 1.5403 | 1.5677 | 1.5400 | 1.5353 | 1.5369 | 1.5400 | 1.4488 | 1.3857 |
| | | *Bahamian Dollars per US Dollar: End of Period (we and xe) Period Average (xf)* | | | | | | | | | | | |
| Principal Rate..................ae=......... | we | 1.0000 | 1.0000 | 1.0000 | 1.0000 | 1.0000 | 1.0000 | 1.0000 | 1.0000 | 1.0000 | 1.0000 | 1.0000 | 1.0000 |
| Secondary Rate................................ | xe | 1.2250 | 1.2250 | 1.2250 | 1.2250 | 1.2250 | 1.2250 | 1.2250 | 1.2250 | 1.2250 | 1.2250 | 1.2250 | 1.2250 |
| Secondary Rate................................ | xf | 1.2250 | 1.2250 | 1.2250 | 1.2250 | 1.2250 | 1.2250 | 1.2250 | 1.2250 | 1.2250 | 1.2250 | 1.2250 | 1.2250 |
| | | *Index Numbers (2010=100): Period Averages* | | | | | | | | | | | |
| Principal Rate.................................. | ahx | 100.0 | 100.0 | 100.0 | 100.0 | 100.0 | 100.0 | 100.0 | 100.0 | 100.0 | 100.0 | 100.0 | 100.0 |
| Nominal Effective Exchange Rate..... | nec | 103.6 | 102.3 | 100.8 | 96.8 | 95.9 | 101.3 | 100.0 | 96.5 | 99.5 | 99.3 | 99.2 | 108.5 |
| CPI-Based Real Effect. Ex. Rate........ | rec | 102.9 | 100.7 | 99.1 | 95.2 | 95.0 | 101.9 | 100.0 | 96.6 | 99.6 | 98.4 | 98.6 | 110.1 |
| **Fund Position** | | *Millions of SDRs: End of Period* | | | | | | | | | | | |
| Quota............................................... | 2f.s | 130.30 | 130.30 | 130.30 | 130.30 | 130.30 | 130.30 | 130.30 | 130.30 | 130.30 | 130.30 | 130.30 | 130.30 |
| SDR Holdings.................................... | 1b.s | .02 | .01 | .01 | .06 | .04 | 114.19 | 114.16 | 114.12 | 18.49 | 38.03 | 54.16 | 54.12 |
| Reserve Position in the Fund............ | 1c.s | 6.26 | 6.26 | 6.26 | 6.26 | 6.26 | 6.26 | 6.26 | 6.26 | 6.26 | 6.26 | 6.26 | 6.26 |
| Total Fund Cred.&Loans Outstg........ | 2tl | — | — | — | — | — | — | — | — | — | — | — | — |
| SDR Allocations............................... | 1bd | 10.23 | 10.23 | 10.23 | 10.23 | 10.23 | 124.41 | 124.41 | 124.41 | 124.41 | 124.41 | 124.41 | 124.41 |
| **International Liquidity** | | *Millions of US Dollars Unless Otherwise Indicated: End of Period* | | | | | | | | | | | |
| Total Reserves minus Gold............... | 1l.d | 674.4 | 586.3 | 461.3 | 464.5 | 567.9 | 1,009.8 | 1,044.2 | 1,070.2 | 846.9 | 807.4 | 874.3 | 895.5 |
| SDR Holdings................................. | 1b.d | — | — | — | .1 | .1 | 179.0 | 175.8 | 175.2 | 28.4 | 58.6 | 78.5 | 75.0 |
| Reserve Position in the Fund.......... | 1c.d | 9.7 | 8.9 | 9.4 | 9.9 | 9.6 | 9.8 | 9.6 | 9.6 | 9.6 | 9.6 | 9.1 | 8.7 |
| Foreign Exchange............................ | 1d.d | 664.7 | 577.3 | 451.9 | 454.5 | 558.2 | 821.0 | 858.7 | 885.4 | 808.9 | 739.2 | 786.8 | 811.8 |
| Central Bank: Other Liabs................ | 4..d | .8 | .8 | .5 | .4 | .4 | .2 | .3 | .3 | .4 | .4 | .6 | .3 |
| Deposit Money Banks: Assets........... | 7a.d | 70,339 | 81,465 | 90,090 | 105,523 | 110,756 | 85,921 | 80,716 | 90,200 | 87,064 | 63,327 | 30,073 | 16,664 |
| Deposit Money Banks: Liabs............ | 7b.d | 70,878 | 81,960 | 90,741 | 106,084 | 111,631 | 86,582 | 81,456 | 93,921 | 87,681 | 63,975 | 30,590 | 17,193 |
| Other Banking Insts.: Assets............ | 7e.d | 2,398 | 2,553 | 2,953 | 3,304 | 2,912 | 2,389 | 2,631 | 3,212 | 3,078 | 3,343 | 3,031 | 2,432 |
| Other Banking Insts.: Liabs.............. | 7f.d | 1,825 | 2,047 | 2,493 | 2,835 | 2,422 | 1,842 | 2,029 | 2,626 | 2,669 | 2,917 | 2,638 | 2,036 |
| **Monetary Authorities** | | *Millions of Bahamian Dollars: End of Period* | | | | | | | | | | | |
| Foreign Assets.................................. | 11 | 668 | 579 | 500 | 454 | 563 | 816 | 859 | 885 | 810 | 742 | 786 | 812 |
| Claims on Central Government........ | 12a | 150 | 150 | 191 | 348 | 203 | 202 | 274 | 301 | 405 | 542 | 567 | 519 |
| Claims on Nonfin.Pub.Enterprises.... | 12c | — | — | — | — | 1 | 1 | 1 | 1 | 1 | 1 | 1 | 1 |
| Claims on Deposit Money Banks...... | 12e | — | — | — | — | — | — | — | — | — | — | — | — |
| Claims on Other Banking Insts......... | 12f | — | — | — | — | 4 | 4 | 4 | 4 | 4 | 4 | 4 | 4 |
| Claims on Nonbank Financial Insts... | 12g | 9 | 8 | 8 | 8 | 7 | 7 | 6 | 6 | 6 | 6 | 5 | 4 |
| Reserve Money................................. | 14 | 643 | 591 | 582 | 677 | 651 | 699 | 835 | 886 | 907 | 873 | 996 | 992 |
| of which: Currency Outside DMBs.. | 14a | 177 | 195 | 202 | 224 | 206 | 208 | 195 | 197 | 217 | 215 | 233 | 247 |
| Foreign Liabilities............................. | 16c | 17 | 15 | 16 | 17 | 16 | 195 | 192 | 191 | 192 | 192 | 181 | 173 |
| Central Government Deposits........... | 16d | 91 | 51 | 14 | 22 | 9 | 32 | 20 | 14 | 17 | 56 | 57 | 35 |
| Capital Accounts.............................. | 17a | 96 | 104 | 111 | 119 | 126 | 121 | 131 | 136 | 139 | 134 | 147 | 150 |
| Other Items (Net)............................. | 17r | −21 | −25 | −25 | −26 | −23 | −18 | −33 | −31 | −30 | 39 | −19 | −9 |
| **Deposit Money Banks** | | *Millions of Bahamian Dollars: End of Period* | | | | | | | | | | | |
| Reserves........................................... | 20 | 457 | 384 | 361 | 450 | 438 | 486 | 630 | 685 | 688 | 648 | 746 | 726 |
| Foreign Assets.................................. | 21 | 70,339 | 81,465 | 90,090 | 105,523 | 110,756 | 85,921 | 80,716 | 90,200 | 87,064 | 63,327 | 30,073 | 16,664 |
| Claims on Central Government........ | 22a | 494 | 613 | 598 | 637 | 857 | 980 | 1,265 | 1,259 | 1,320 | 1,599 | 1,703 | 1,964 |
| Claims on Official Entities................ | 22bx | 314 | 266 | 268 | 244 | 344 | 306 | 336 | 327 | 339 | 369 | 251 | 238 |
| Claims on Private Sector.................. | 22d | 4,200 | 4,807 | 5,607 | 6,189 | 6,513 | 6,572 | 6,556 | 6,630 | 6,613 | 6,496 | 6,445 | 6,373 |
| Claims on Other Banking Insts......... | 22f | 105 | 107 | 89 | 98 | 98 | 107 | 166 | 117 | 119 | 119 | 119 | 124 |
| Demand Deposits.............................. | 24 | 860 | 1,002 | 1,018 | 1,045 | 1,041 | 1,038 | 1,105 | 1,204 | 1,311 | 1,385 | 1,696 | 1,761 |
| Time, Savings,& Fgn.Currency Dep... | 25 | 3,193 | 3,493 | 3,826 | 4,324 | 4,637 | 4,738 | 4,840 | 4,858 | 4,707 | 4,688 | 4,381 | 4,292 |
| Bonds............................................... | 26ab | 1 | — | — | 27 | 28 | 25 | 99 | 99 | 80 | 32 | 32 | 44 |
| Foreign Liabilities............................. | 26c | 70,878 | 81,960 | 90,741 | 106,084 | 111,631 | 86,582 | 81,456 | 93,921 | 87,681 | 63,975 | 30,590 | 17,193 |
| Central Government Deposits........... | 26d | 93 | 88 | 109 | 105 | 134 | 152 | 121 | 119 | 135 | 155 | 213 | 271 |
| Credit from Monetary Authorities..... | 26g | 1 | 1 | 1 | 1 | 1 | 1 | 1 | 1 | 1 | 1 | 1 | 1 |
| Liabilities to Other Banking Insts...... | 26i | 38 | 49 | 39 | 37 | 47 | 46 | 51 | 66 | 56 | 85 | 85 | 124 |
| Capital Accounts.............................. | 27a | 1,047 | 1,221 | 1,409 | 1,605 | 1,488 | 1,759 | 1,931 | −1,113 | 2,100 | 2,089 | 1,841 | 1,963 |
| Other Items (Net)............................. | 27r | −205 | −172 | −128 | −88 | −3 | 29 | 65 | 62 | 71 | 152 | 499 | 441 |
| **Monetary Survey** | | *Millions of Bahamian Dollars: End of Period* | | | | | | | | | | | |
| Foreign Assets (Net)......................... | 31n | 112 | 69 | −167 | −124 | −328 | −41 | −72 | −3,028 | 1 | −98 | 88 | 110 |
| Domestic Credit................................ | 32 | 5,086 | 5,811 | 6,639 | 7,395 | 7,883 | 7,993 | 8,466 | 8,511 | 8,653 | 8,926 | 8,825 | 8,922 |
| Claims on Central Govt. (Net)........ | 32an | 460 | 624 | 666 | 857 | 917 | 997 | 1,398 | 1,427 | 1,573 | 1,931 | 2,000 | 2,177 |
| Claims on Official Entities.............. | 32bx | 314 | 266 | 268 | 244 | 344 | 306 | 336 | 327 | 339 | 369 | 251 | 238 |
| Claims on Nonfin.Pub.Enterprises... | 32c | — | — | — | — | 1 | 1 | 1 | 1 | 1 | 1 | 1 | 1 |
| Claims on Private Sector................ | 32d | 4,200 | 4,807 | 5,607 | 6,189 | 6,513 | 6,572 | 6,556 | 6,630 | 6,613 | 6,496 | 6,445 | 6,373 |
| Claims on Other Banking Insts........ | 32f | 105 | 107 | 89 | 98 | 102 | 111 | 170 | 121 | 123 | 123 | 123 | 128 |
| Claims on Nonbank Financial Insts. | 32g | 9 | 8 | 8 | 8 | 7 | 7 | 6 | 6 | 6 | 6 | 5 | 4 |
| Money.............................................. | 34 | 1,047 | 1,207 | 1,239 | 1,274 | 1,255 | 1,252 | 1,310 | 1,408 | 1,537 | 1,611 | 1,948 | 2,022 |
| Quasi-Money.................................... | 35 | 3,193 | 3,493 | 3,826 | 4,324 | 4,637 | 4,738 | 4,840 | 4,858 | 4,707 | 4,688 | 4,381 | 4,292 |
| Bonds............................................... | 36ab | 1 | — | — | 27 | 28 | 25 | 99 | 99 | 80 | 32 | 32 | 44 |
| Liabilities to Other Banking Insts...... | 36i | 38 | 49 | 39 | 37 | 47 | 46 | 51 | 66 | 56 | 85 | 85 | 124 |
| Capital Accounts.............................. | 37a | 1,143 | 1,325 | 1,520 | 1,725 | 1,614 | 1,880 | 2,062 | −977 | 2,239 | 2,223 | 1,988 | 2,112 |
| Other Items (Net)............................. | 37r | −225 | −194 | −152 | −115 | −26 | 11 | 32 | 29 | 34 | 190 | 479 | 437 |
| Money plus Quasi-Money................. | 35l | 4,241 | 4,700 | 5,065 | 5,598 | 5,893 | 5,991 | 6,150 | 6,266 | 6,244 | 6,298 | 6,329 | 6,314 |

| | | 2004 | 2005 | 2006 | 2007 | 2008 | 2009 | 2010 | 2011 | 2012 | 2013 | 2014 | 2015 |
|---|---|---|---|---|---|---|---|---|---|---|---|---|---|
| **Other Banking Institutions** | | *Millions of Bahamian Dollars End of Period* | | | | | | | | | | | |
| Reserves............................................. | 40 | 6 | 6 | 6 | 2 | 2 | 2 | 2 | 2 | 3 | 3 | 3 | 4 |
| Foreign Assets.................................. | 41 | 2,398 | 2,553 | 2,953 | 3,304 | 2,912 | 2,389 | 2,631 | 3,212 | 3,078 | 3,343 | 3,031 | 2,432 |
| Claims on Central Government........ | 42a | 4 | 5 | 5 | 3 | 3 | 16 | 10 | 9 | 12 | 9 | 11 | 11 |
| Claims on Private Sector.................. | 42d | 140 | 147 | 149 | 30 | 23 | 24 | 21 | 18 | 17 | 18 | 23 | 29 |
| Claims on Deposit Money Banks...... | 42e | 54 | 55 | 57 | 44 | 47 | 54 | 54 | 60 | 72 | 133 | 110 | 161 |
| Demand Deposits............................ | 44 | 10 | 25 | 13 | 21 | 17 | 22 | 18 | 27 | 33 | 30 | 41 | 46 |
| Time, Savings,& Fgn.Currency Dep... | 45 | 94 | 89 | 68 | 13 | 12 | 10 | 19 | 17 | 22 | 21 | 13 | 11 |
| Foreign Liabilities............................ | 46c | 1,825 | 2,047 | 2,493 | 2,835 | 2,422 | 1,842 | 2,029 | 2,626 | 2,669 | 2,917 | 2,638 | 2,036 |
| Central Government Deposits........... | 46d | — | — | — | — | — | — | — | — | — | — | — | — |
| Credit from Monetary Authorities..... | 46g | — | — | — | — | — | — | — | — | — | — | — | — |
| Credit from Deposit Money Banks.... | 46h | 86 | 86 | 56 | — | — | — | 51 | — | — | — | — | — |
| Capital Accounts............................. | 47a | 613 | 545 | 544 | 547 | 563 | 632 | 609 | 639 | 471 | 488 | 548 | 526 |
| Other Items (Net)............................ | 47r | −27 | −27 | −4 | −33 | −26 | −23 | −8 | −6 | −12 | 51 | −62 | 17 |
| **Banking Survey** | | *Millions of Bahamian Dollars: End of Period* | | | | | | | | | | | |
| Foreign Assets (Net)........................ | 51n | 684 | 574 | 293 | 346 | 162 | 505 | 529 | −2,441 | 411 | 329 | 481 | 506 |
| Domestic Credit................................ | 52 | 5,126 | 5,856 | 6,703 | 7,330 | 7,808 | 7,922 | 8,328 | 8,418 | 8,559 | 8,830 | 8,735 | 8,834 |
| Claims on Central Govt. (Net)........ | 52an | 464 | 628 | 672 | 860 | 920 | 1,012 | 1,408 | 1,437 | 1,585 | 1,940 | 2,011 | 2,188 |
| Claims on Official Entities.............. | 52bx | 314 | 266 | 268 | 244 | 344 | 306 | 336 | 327 | 339 | 369 | 251 | 238 |
| Claims on Private Sector.............. | 52d | 4,339 | 4,954 | 5,756 | 6,218 | 6,537 | 6,596 | 6,577 | 6,648 | 6,630 | 6,515 | 6,468 | 6,402 |
| Claims on Nonfin.Pub.Enterprises... | 52c | — | — | — | — | 1 | 1 | 1 | 1 | 1 | 1 | 1 | 1 |
| Claims on Nonbank Financial Insts. | 52g | 9 | 8 | 8 | 8 | 7 | 7 | 6 | 6 | 6 | 6 | 5 | 4 |
| Liquid Liabilities............................. | 55l | 4,339 | 4,808 | 5,140 | 5,631 | 5,920 | 6,021 | 6,184 | 6,308 | 6,297 | 6,347 | 6,379 | 6,368 |
| Bonds............................................. | 56ab | 1 | — | — | 27 | 28 | 25 | 99 | 99 | 80 | 32 | 32 | 44 |
| Capital Accounts............................ | 57a | 1,756 | 1,870 | 2,064 | 2,271 | 2,177 | 2,513 | 2,671 | −338 | 2,710 | 2,711 | 2,536 | 2,639 |
| Other Items (Net)............................ | 57r | −286 | −247 | −208 | −253 | −154 | −131 | −97 | −92 | −116 | 69 | 269 | 289 |
| **Money (National Definitions)** | | *Millions of Bahamian Dollars: End of Period* | | | | | | | | | | | |
| Base Money.................................... | 19ma | 639 | 587 | 570 | 673 | 645 | 695 | 826 | 881 | 899 | 865 | 981 | 980 |
| M1.................................................. | 59ma | 1,134 | 1,248 | 1,251 | 1,300 | 1,275 | 1,284 | 1,335 | 1,435 | 1,575 | 1,641 | 1,996 | .... |
| M2.................................................. | 59mb | 4,325 | 4,686 | 4,983 | 5,437 | 5,723 | 5,800 | 5,966 | 6,104 | 6,088 | 6,076 | 6,164 | .... |
| M3.................................................. | 59mc | 4,422 | 4,830 | 5,142 | 5,637 | 5,924 | 6,032 | 6,191 | 6,310 | 6,304 | 6,350 | 6,389 | 6,471 |
| **Interest Rates** | | *Percent Per Annum* | | | | | | | | | | | |
| Central Bank Policy Rate (EOP)........ | 60 | 5.75 | 5.25 | 5.25 | 5.25 | 5.25 | 5.25 | 5.25 | 4.50 | 4.50 | 4.50 | 4.50 | 4.50 |
| Treasury Bill Rate............................ | 60c | .56 | .14 | .87 | 2.66 | 2.73 | 2.62 | 2.28 | 1.75 | .24 | .30 | .53 | .68 |
| Savings Rate................................... | 60k | 2.58 | 2.27 | 2.17 | 2.06 | 2.20 | 2.15 | 1.94 | 1.74 | 1.53 | .97 | .87 | .83 |
| Deposit Rate................................... | 60l | 3.83 | 3.22 | 3.36 | 3.69 | 3.92 | 3.78 | 3.44 | 2.63 | 2.01 | 1.68 | 1.42 | 1.41 |
| Lending Rate.................................. | 60p | 6.00 | 5.54 | 5.50 | 5.50 | 5.50 | 5.50 | 5.50 | 5.06 | 4.75 | 4.75 | 4.75 | 4.75 |
| **Prices and Labor** | | *Index Numbers (2010=100): Period Averages* | | | | | | | | | | | |
| Consumer Prices............................. | 64 | 86.8 | 88.2 | 90.3 | 92.5 | 96.7 | † 98.7 | 100.0 | 103.2 | 105.2 | † 105.6 | 107.2 | 109.2 |
| Tourist Arrivals............................... | 66t | 95.4 | 96.4 | 90.2 | 87.6 | 83.6 | 88.5 | 100.0 | 106.4 | 113.2 | 117.2 | 120.5 | .... |
| | | *Number in Thousands: Period Averages* | | | | | | | | | | | |
| Labor Force..................................... | 67d | 176 | 179 | 180 | 186 | 192 | 184 | .... | 190 | 192 | .... | .... | .... |
| Employment.................................... | 67e | 158 | 161 | 167 | 171 | 175 | 158 | .... | 160 | 165 | .... | .... | .... |
| Unemployment................................ | 67c | 18 | 18 | 14 | 15 | 17 | 26 | .... | 30 | 27 | .... | .... | .... |
| Unemployment Rate (%)................... | 67r | 10.2 | 10.2 | 7.6 | 7.9 | 8.7 | 14.2 | .... | 15.9 | 14.0 | .... | .... | .... |
| **Intl. Transactions & Positions** | | *Millions of Bahamian Dollars* | | | | | | | | | | | |
| Exports........................................... | 70 | 477 | 562 | 674 | 485 | 560 | 585 | 621 | 927 | 829 | 812 | 689 | .... |
| Imports, c.i.f................................... | 71 | 1,905 | 2,230 | 2,401 | 2,449 | 2,354 | 2,699 | 2,887 | 3,411 | 3,658 | 3,366 | 3,791 | .... |

# Bahamas, The 313

| | | 2004 | 2005 | 2006 | 2007 | 2008 | 2009 | 2010 | 2011 | 2012 | 2013 | 2014 | 2015 |
|---|---|---|---|---|---|---|---|---|---|---|---|---|---|
| **Balance of Payments** | | | | | | | *Millions of US Dollars* | | | | | | | |
| A. Current Account* | 109bx | −307.1 | −700.6 | −1,403.7 | −1,315.1 | −1,222.1 | −809.0 | −814.0 | −1,203.1 | −1,504.8 | −1,493.9 | −1,897.5 | .... |
| Goods, credit (exports) | 1a9cx | 477.5 | 549.1 | 703.5 | 801.9 | 955.8 | 710.7 | 702.4 | 833.5 | 984.0 | 954.9 | 859.0 | .... |
| Goods, debit (imports) | 1a9dx | 1,906.8 | 2,377.4 | 2,766.5 | 2,956.9 | 3,199.0 | 2,535.8 | 2,591.5 | 2,965.7 | 3,385.5 | 3,165.9 | 3,309.1 | .... |
| Balance on goods | 1a9bx | −1,429.4 | −1,828.3 | −2,063.0 | −2,155.0 | −2,243.2 | −1,825.1 | −1,889.1 | −2,132.1 | −2,401.4 | −2,211.0 | −2,450.1 | .... |
| Services, credit (exports) | 1b9cx | 2,244.1 | 2,510.9 | 2,436.1 | 2,599.3 | 2,533.9 | 2,350.9 | 2,493.6 | 2,493.6 | 2,691.4 | 2,671.2 | 2,716.4 | .... |
| Services, debit (imports) | 1b9dx | 1,231.3 | 1,286.4 | 1,610.9 | 1,579.6 | 1,402.9 | 1,196.1 | 1,181.1 | 1,292.4 | 1,537.7 | 1,628.3 | 1,725.0 | .... |
| Balance on Goods & Services | 1z9bx | −416.6 | −603.8 | −1,237.8 | −1,135.3 | −1,112.2 | −670.3 | −576.6 | −930.9 | −1,247.7 | −1,168.1 | −1,458.6 | .... |
| Primary income: credit | 1c9cx | 79.7 | 97.0 | 119.4 | 121.3 | 113.4 | 57.7 | 38.8 | 55.4 | 49.7 | 48.0 | 55.1 | .... |
| Primary income: debit | 1c9dx | 221.1 | 279.1 | 337.4 | 352.9 | 198.6 | 209.9 | 273.6 | 291.4 | 317.3 | 377.1 | 493.2 | .... |
| Balance on gds, serv. & prim. inc. | 1y9bx | −557.9 | −785.9 | −1,455.8 | −1,366.9 | −1,197.5 | −822.5 | −811.5 | −1,167.0 | −1,515.3 | −1,497.1 | −1,896.8 | .... |
| Secondary income: credit | 1d9ca | 264.7 | 103.3 | 66.4 | 71.0 | 75.9 | 96.6 | 99.3 | 124.0 | 131.3 | 138.2 | 145.9 | .... |
| Secondary income: debit | 1d9da | 13.9 | 18.1 | 14.3 | 19.2 | 100.5 | 83.1 | 101.9 | 160.2 | 120.8 | 135.0 | 146.6 | .... |
| B. Capital Account* | 209ba | — | — | — | — | — | — | — | — | — | — | — | .... |
| Capital account: credit | 209ca | — | .... | .... | .... | .... | — | .... | — | — | — | — | .... |
| Capital account: debit | 209da | — | — | — | — | — | — | — | — | — | — | — | .... |
| Balance on current & capital acct. | 129ba | −307.1 | −700.6 | −1,403.7 | −1,315.1 | −1,222.1 | −809.0 | −814.0 | −1,203.1 | −1,504.8 | −1,493.9 | −1,897.5 | .... |
| C. Financial Account* | 309na | −358.5 | −822.1 | −1,280.2 | −1,030.6 | −1,223.4 | −1,120.2 | −1,144.9 | −992.0 | −1,313.6 | −980.9 | −1,509.4 | .... |
| Direct investment: assets | 3a9aa | — | — | — | — | — | — | — | — | — | — | — | .... |
| Equity & investment fund shares.. | 3aaaa | .... | — | — | — | — | — | — | — | — | — | — | .... |
| Debt instruments | 3abaa | .... | — | — | — | — | — | — | — | — | — | — | .... |
| Direct investment: liabilities | 3a9la | 273.6 | 563.4 | 706.4 | 713.4 | 860.2 | 664.0 | 872.0 | 666.6 | 526.2 | 382.3 | 251.3 | .... |
| Equity & investment fund shares . | 3aala | 90.2 | 219.8 | 233.9 | 356.0 | 285.8 | 201.4 | 148.3 | 23.2 | 13.4 | 78.1 | 3.0 | .... |
| Debt instruments | 3abla | 183.4 | 343.6 | 472.5 | 357.4 | 574.4 | 462.5 | 723.7 | 643.4 | 512.7 | 304.1 | 248.3 | .... |
| Portfolio investment: assets | 3b9aa | .... | .... | 18.8 | 7.2 | 21.9 | 16.7 | 25.4 | 44.2 | 37.0 | 52.8 | 26.9 | .... |
| Equity & investment fund shares | 3baaa | .... | .... | .... | 4.1 | 12.5 | 4.2 | 13.0 | 22.3 | 12.0 | 15.3 | 26.9 | .... |
| Debt securities | 3bbaa | .... | .... | 18.8 | 3.1 | 9.4 | 12.5 | 12.4 | 21.9 | 25.0 | 37.5 | — | .... |
| Portfolio investment: liabilities | 3b9la | .... | .... | .... | .... | .... | .... | .... | .... | .... | .... | .... | .... |
| Equity & investment fund shares . | 3bala | .... | .... | .... | .... | .... | .... | .... | .... | .... | .... | .... | .... |
| Debt securities | 3bbla | .... | .... | .... | .... | .... | .... | .... | .... | .... | .... | .... | .... |
| Fin. der.& empl.stk.ops.(ESOs): net | 3c9na | .... | .... | .... | .... | .... | .... | .... | .... | .... | .... | .... | .... |
| Fin. der. & ESOs.: assets | 3c9aa | .... | .... | .... | .... | .... | .... | .... | .... | .... | .... | .... | .... |
| Fin. der. & ESOs.: liabilities | 3c9la | .... | .... | .... | .... | .... | .... | .... | .... | .... | .... | .... | .... |
| Other investment: assets | 3d9aa | −19,293.4 | 11,064.2 | 9,016.7 | 15,801.8 | 4,830.6 | −25,373.1 | −4,969.8 | 10,061.3 | −3,255.9 | −23,476.1 | −33,490.3 | .... |
| Other equity | 3daaa | .... | .... | .... | .... | .... | .... | .... | .... | .... | .... | .... | .... |
| Debt instruments | 3dzaa | −19,293.4 | 11,064.2 | 9,016.7 | 15,801.8 | 4,830.6 | −25,373.1 | −4,969.8 | 10,061.3 | −3,255.9 | −23,476.1 | −33,490.3 | .... |
| Other investment: liabilities | 3d9la | −19,208.5 | 11,322.9 | 9,609.3 | 16,126.3 | 5,215.8 | −24,900.1 | −4,671.5 | 10,430.9 | −2,431.5 | −22,824.7 | −32,205.3 | .... |
| Other equity | 3dala | .... | .... | .... | .... | .... | .... | .... | .... | .... | .... | .... | .... |
| Debt instruments | 3dzla | −19,208.5 | 11,322.9 | 9,609.3 | 16,126.3 | 5,215.8 | −24,900.1 | −4,671.5 | 10,430.9 | −2,431.5 | −22,824.7 | −32,205.3 | .... |
| Curr.+ cap.– finan. acct. balance... | 4y9na | 51.3 | 121.5 | −123.5 | −284.5 | 1.4 | 311.2 | 330.9 | −211.2 | −191.2 | −513.0 | −388.1 | .... |
| D. Net Errors and Omissions | 409na | 131.9 | −209.7 | 44.0 | 238.2 | 107.8 | −58.9 | −283.1 | 236.2 | 116.1 | 444.4 | 439.6 | .... |
| E. Reserves and Related Items | 4z9na | 183.3 | −88.1 | −79.5 | −46.3 | 109.2 | 252.3 | 47.8 | 25.1 | −75.0 | −68.6 | 51.5 | .... |
| Reserve assets | 3e9aa | 183.3 | −88.1 | −79.5 | −46.3 | 109.2 | 252.3 | 47.8 | 25.1 | −75.0 | −68.6 | 51.5 | .... |
| Credit and loans from the IMF | 3dcla | — | — | — | — | — | — | — | — | — | — | — | .... |
| Exceptional financing | 409la | — | .... | .... | .... | .... | .... | .... | .... | .... | .... | .... | .... |

*Excludes components in group E

| | | 2004 | 2005 | 2006 | 2007 | 2008 | 2009 | 2010 | 2011 | 2012 | 2013 | 2014 | 2015 |
|---|---|---|---|---|---|---|---|---|---|---|---|---|---|
| **Government Finance** | | | | | | | | | | | | | | |
| **Cash Flow Statement** | | | | | | | | | | | | | | |
| **Budgetary Central Government** | | | | | *Millions of Bahamian Dollars: Fiscal Year Ends June 30* | | | | | | | | | |
| Cash Receipts:Operating Activities... | c1 | 943.7 | † 1,027.1 | 1,199.7 | 1,336.1 | 1,428.7 | 1,323.8 | 1,302.1 | 1,432.2 | 1,426.1 | 1,352.9 | 1,448.6 | 1,697.8 |
| Taxes | c11 | .... | † 925.1 | 1,074.4 | 1,206.1 | 1,275.9 | 1,130.5 | 1,109.0 | 1,296.9 | 1,276.6 | 1,215.5 | 1,247.7 | 1,500.5 |
| Social Contributions | c12 | .... | † — | | | | | | | | | | |
| Grants | c13 | .... | † — | | | | | | .1 | .2 | .1 | .4 | .4 |
| Other Receipts | c14 | .... | † 102.0 | 124.3 | 130.0 | 152.8 | 193.3 | 193.1 | 135.2 | 149.3 | 137.2 | 200.6 | 196.9 |
| Cash Payments:Operating Activities. | c2 | 1,110.1 | † 1,055.6 | 1,149.9 | 1,260.1 | 1,345.0 | 1,423.9 | 1,399.5 | 1,527.3 | 1,553.3 | 1,563.5 | 1,505.2 | 1,714.4 |
| Compensation of Employees | c21 | .... | † 452.3 | 494.0 | 536.7 | 552.0 | 573.1 | 580.2 | 581.8 | 608.2 | 594.0 | 565.1 | 640.2 |
| Purchases of Goods & Services | c22 | .... | † 210.4 | 230.7 | 263.6 | 284.6 | 321.2 | 264.6 | 313.3 | 356.6 | 353.6 | 288.3 | 329.6 |
| Interest | c24 | .... | † 117.4 | 117.1 | 127.2 | 143.1 | 154.2 | 178.8 | 210.8 | 186.1 | 197.1 | 211.8 | 233.4 |
| Subsidies | c25 | .... | † 147.7 | 150.1 | 169.8 | 194.3 | 206.7 | 224.7 | 226.5 | 243.5 | 242.1 | 267.5 | 328.1 |
| Grants | c26 | .... | † 16.5 | 8.4 | — | — | 5.6 | 9.0 | 12.1 | 10.4 | 10.4 | 27.8 | 13.9 |
| Social Benefits | c27 | .... | † 105.0 | 109.2 | 79.2 | 91.0 | 92.7 | 98.0 | 125.2 | 101.6 | 105.0 | 108.8 | 120.7 |
| Other Payments | c28 | .... | † 6.2 | 40.4 | 83.6 | 79.9 | 70.5 | 44.2 | 57.7 | 46.8 | 61.3 | 35.8 | 48.5 |
| Net Cash Inflow:Operating Act.[1-2] | ccio | .... | † −28.5 | 49.8 | 76.0 | 83.7 | −100.1 | −97.4 | −95.2 | −127.2 | −210.7 | −56.5 | −16.6 |
| Net Cash Outflow:Invest. in NFA..... | c31 | .... | † 75.6 | 121.0 | 156.3 | 170.9 | 137.5 | 152.3 | 194.0 | 211.0 | 230.9 | 221.6 | 273.4 |
| Purchases of Nonfinancial Assets... | c31.1 | .... | † 87.9 | 122.8 | 156.7 | 174.8 | 138.5 | 152.7 | 194.9 | 231.6 | 232.6 | 223.0 | 277.2 |
| Sales of Nonfinancial Assets | c31.2 | .... | † 12.2 | 1.8 | .4 | 3.9 | 1.0 | .4 | .8 | 20.6 | 1.7 | 1.4 | 3.8 |
| Cash Surplus/Deficit [1-2-31=1-2M] | ccsd | −166.4 | † −104.1 | −71.1 | −80.3 | −87.2 | −237.6 | −249.7 | −289.2 | −338.1 | −441.5 | −278.1 | −290.0 |
| Net Acq. Fin. Assets, excl. Cash | c32x | .... | † 71.4 | 54.9 | 69.0 | 55.1 | 123.1 | 89.4 | −122.2 | 112.8 | 103.3 | 80.5 | 92.0 |
| Domestic | c321x | .... | † 71.4 | 54.9 | 69.0 | 55.1 | 123.1 | 89.4 | −122.2 | 112.8 | 103.3 | 80.5 | 92.0 |
| Foreign | c322x | | | | | | | | | | | | |
| Net Incurrence of Liabilities | c33 | 191.5 | † 221.4 | 115.5 | 273.4 | 260.0 | 405.2 | 312.7 | 140.6 | 457.5 | 572.3 | 409.4 | 458.8 |
| Domestic | c331 | −5.9 | † 224.2 | 113.4 | 273.4 | 160.0 | 367.2 | 26.8 | 91.7 | 384.7 | 354.1 | −16.9 | 335.1 |
| Foreign | c332 | 197.4 | † −2.9 | 2.1 | — | 100.0 | 38.0 | 285.9 | 48.9 | 72.8 | 218.2 | 426.3 | 123.7 |
| Net Cash Inflow, Fin.Act.[-32x+33].. | cnfb | .... | † 149.9 | 60.6 | 204.4 | 204.9 | 282.1 | 223.3 | 262.9 | 344.6 | 469.1 | 328.9 | 366.8 |
| Net Change in Stock of Cash | cncb | 24.9 | † 45.8 | −10.5 | 124.0 | 117.7 | 44.5 | −26.4 | −26.4 | 6.5 | 27.6 | 50.8 | 76.8 |
| Stat. Discrep. [32X-33+NCB-CSD]... | ccsdz | | † — | | | | | | | | | | |
| Memo Item:Cash Expenditure[2+31] | c2m | .... | † 1,131.2 | 1,270.9 | 1,416.5 | 1,515.9 | 1,561.4 | 1,551.8 | 1,721.4 | 1,764.3 | 1,794.4 | 1,726.8 | 1,987.8 |
| Memo Item: Gross Debt | c63 | 1,941.1 | 2,235.2 | 2,316.3 | 2,438.7 | 2,766.6 | 3,084.8 | 3,400.9 | 3,552.9 | 3,905.7 | 4,690.4 | 5,158.4 | 5,628.8 |

| National Accounts | | 2004 | 2005 | 2006 | 2007 | 2008 | 2009 | 2010 | 2011 | 2012 | 2013 | 2014 | 2015 |
|---|---|---|---|---|---|---|---|---|---|---|---|---|---|
| | | *Millions of Bahamian Dollars* | | | | | | | | | | | |
| Househ.Cons.Expend.,incl.NPISHs.... | 96f | 4,623.1 | 5,103.0 | 5,461.4 | 5,600.2 | 5,628.5 | 5,279.9 | 5,436.3 | 5,535.7 | 5,949.0 | 5,875.6 | 6,227.6 | 5,789.1 |
| Government Consumption Expend... | 91f | 826.3 | 873.2 | 947.6 | 976.1 | 1,071.7 | 1,151.5 | 1,150.4 | 1,261.3 | 1,277.2 | 1,353.3 | 1,320.0 | 1,414.2 |
| Gross Fixed Capital Formation......... | 93e | 1,426.8 | 1,863.9 | 2,330.6 | 2,257.7 | 2,113.0 | 1,908.1 | 1,900.7 | 2,040.4 | 2,337.5 | 2,291.5 | 2,599.1 | 2,319.5 |
| Changes in Inventories.................... | 93i | 76.4 | 84.2 | 85.6 | 86.2 | 88.4 | 91.7 | 93.7 | 131.4 | 79.5 | 67.1 | 91.4 | 90.6 |
| Exports of Goods and Services......... | 90c | 3,160.7 | 3,482.1 | 3,557.6 | 3,888.2 | 3,796.9 | 3,117.2 | 3,223.1 | 3,443.3 | 3,733.3 | 3,728.5 | 3,662.1 | 3,418.9 |
| Imports of Goods and Services (-)..... | 98c | 3,018.9 | 3,700.2 | 4,417.2 | 4,489.4 | 4,451.8 | 3,728.0 | 3,894.5 | 4,522.4 | 4,977.4 | 4,794.0 | 5,282.4 | 4,178.8 |
| Statistical Discrepancy..................... | 99bs | — | — | — | — | — | — | — | — | — | — | — | — |
| Gross Domestic Product (GDP)......... | 99b | 7,094.4 | 7,706.2 | 7,965.6 | 8,319.0 | 8,246.7 | 7,820.4 | 7,909.6 | 7,889.8 | 8,399.0 | 8,522.0 | 8,617.7 | 8,853.5 |
| Net Primary Income from Abroad..... | 98.n | −78.0 | −130.0 | −125.1 | −146.7 | −59.3 | −140.3 | −207.5 | −188.1 | −222.5 | −293.3 | −370.8 | −432.9 |
| Gross National Income (GNI)............ | 99a | 7,016.4 | 7,576.2 | 7,840.5 | 8,172.3 | 8,187.4 | 7,680.1 | 7,702.0 | 7,701.6 | 8,176.6 | 8,228.7 | 8,246.9 | 8,420.7 |
| Net Current Transf.from Abroad....... | 98t | 256.8 | 90.4 | 56.0 | 54.8 | 16.1 | 36.5 | 27.9 | 42.2 | 27.3 | 24.7 | 32.3 | 41.5 |
| Gross Nat'l Disposable Inc.(GNDI).... | 99i | 7,273.2 | 7,666.6 | 7,896.5 | 8,227.1 | 8,203.4 | 7,716.6 | 7,730.0 | 7,688.4 | 8,158.8 | 8,217.6 | 8,214.8 | 8,400.1 |
| Gross Saving............................... | 99s | 1,823.8 | 1,690.4 | 1,487.4 | 1,650.8 | 1,503.1 | 1,285.2 | 1,143.4 | 946.8 | 977.7 | 1,024.6 | 731.7 | 1,258.8 |
| GDP Volume 2006 Prices................. | 99b.p | 7,514.9 | 7,770.0 | 7,965.6 | 8,080.8 | 7,893.1 | 7,563.5 | 7,679.9 | 7,726.9 | 7,965.4 | 7,966.2 | 7,924.5 | 7,792.6 |
| GDP Volume (2010=100).............. | 99bvp | 97.9 | 101.2 | 103.7 | 105.2 | 102.8 | 98.5 | 100.0 | 100.6 | 103.7 | 103.7 | 103.2 | 101.5 |
| GDP Deflator (2010=100).............. | 99bip | 91.7 | 96.3 | 97.1 | 100.0 | 101.4 | 100.4 | 100.0 | 99.1 | 102.4 | 103.9 | 105.6 | 110.3 |
| | | *Millions: Midyear Estimates* | | | | | | | | | | | |
| Population............................... | 99z | .32 | .33 | .34 | .34 | .35 | .35 | .36 | .37 | .37 | .38 | .38 | .39 |

# Bahrain, Kingdom of   419

|  |  | 2004 | 2005 | 2006 | 2007 | 2008 | 2009 | 2010 | 2011 | 2012 | 2013 | 2014 | 2015 |
|---|---|---|---|---|---|---|---|---|---|---|---|---|---|
| **Exchange Rates** | | | | | | | *SDRs per Dinar: End of Period* | | | | | | |
| Official Rate | ac | 1.7125 | 1.8608 | 1.7679 | 1.6830 | 1.7267 | 1.6965 | 1.7270 | 1.7323 | 1.7305 | 1.7270 | 1.8357 | 1.9193 |
| | | | | | *US Dollars per Dinar: End of Period (ag) Period Average (rh)* | | | | | | | | |
| Official Rate | ag | 2.6596 | 2.6596 | 2.6596 | 2.6596 | 2.6596 | 2.6596 | 2.6596 | 2.6596 | 2.6596 | 2.6596 | 2.6596 | 2.6596 |
| Official Rate | rh | 2.6596 | 2.6596 | 2.6596 | 2.6596 | 2.6596 | 2.6596 | 2.6596 | 2.6596 | 2.6596 | 2.6596 | 2.6596 | 2.6596 |
| | | | | | *Index Numbers (2010=100): Period Averages* | | | | | | | | |
| Official Rate | ahx | 100.0 | 100.0 | 100.0 | 100.0 | 100.0 | 100.0 | 100.0 | 100.0 | 100.0 | 100.0 | 100.0 | 100.0 |
| Nominal Effective Exchange Rate | nec | 107.8 | 106.3 | 105.9 | 101.5 | 98.4 | 101.5 | 100.0 | 96.8 | 100.5 | 104.8 | 108.1 | 119.8 |
| CPI-Based Real Effect. Ex. Rate | rec | 118.1 | 111.3 | 113.8 | 106.4 | 98.0 | 102.4 | 100.0 | 93.3 | 95.9 | 98.4 | 100.7 | 111.5 |
| **Fund Position** | | | | | | | *Millions of SDRs: End of Period* | | | | | | |
| Quota | 2f.s | 135.00 | 135.00 | 135.00 | 135.00 | 135.00 | 135.00 | 135.00 | 135.00 | 135.00 | 135.00 | 135.00 | 135.00 |
| SDR Holdings | 1b.s | .58 | 1.68 | 3.77 | 6.43 | 9.07 | 127.60 | 127.79 | 128.10 | 128.58 | 129.63 | 129.69 | 129.72 |
| Reserve Position in the Fund | 1c.s | 70.84 | 71.20 | 71.20 | 71.20 | 71.20 | 71.20 | 71.20 | 71.20 | 71.20 | 71.20 | 71.20 | 71.20 |
| Total Fund Cred. & Loans Outstg. | 2tl | — | — | — | — | — | — | — | — | — | — | — | — |
| SDR Allocations | 1bd | 6.20 | 6.20 | 6.20 | 6.20 | 6.20 | 124.35 | 124.35 | 124.35 | 124.35 | 124.35 | 124.35 | 124.35 |
| **International Liquidity** | | | | | *Millions of US Dollars Unless Otherwise Indicated: End of Period* | | | | | | | | |
| Total Reserves minus Gold | 1l.d | 1,940.5 | 1,975.0 | 2,800.3 | 4,217.1 | 3,920.5 | 3,845.2 | 5,088.6 | 4,544.5 | 5,204.7 | 5,347.0 | 6,048.5 | .... |
| SDR Holdings | 1b.d | .9 | 2.4 | 5.7 | 10.2 | 14.0 | 200.0 | 196.8 | 196.7 | 197.6 | 199.6 | 187.9 | 179.8 |
| Reserve Position in the Fund | 1c.d | 110.0 | 101.8 | 107.1 | 112.5 | 109.7 | 111.6 | 109.7 | 109.3 | 109.4 | 109.7 | 103.2 | 98.7 |
| Foreign Exchange | 1d.d | 1,829.6 | 1,870.8 | 2,687.5 | 4,094.4 | 3,796.8 | 3,533.5 | 4,782.2 | 4,238.6 | 4,897.6 | 5,037.8 | 5,757.4 | .... |
| Central Bank | 1dad | 1,579.6 | 1,870.8 | 2,687.5 | 4,094.4 | 3,796.8 | 3,533.5 | 4,782.2 | 4,238.6 | 4,897.6 | 5,037.8 | 5,757.4 | .... |
| Government | 1dbd | 250.0 | .... | .... | .... | .... | .... | .... | .... | .... | .... | .... | .... |
| Gold (Million Fine Troy Ounces) | 1ad | .150 | .150 | .150 | .150 | .150 | .150 | .150 | .150 | .150 | .150 | .150 | .150 |
| Gold (National Valuation) | 1and | 6.6 | 6.6 | 6.6 | 6.6 | 6.6 | 6.6 | 6.6 | 6.6 | 6.6 | 6.6 | 6.6 | 6.6 |
| Monetary Authorities: Other Liabs. | 4..d | — | — | — | — | — | — | — | — | — | — | — | — |
| Deposit Money Banks: Assets | 7a.d | 4,238.6 | 4,655.3 | 8,538.0 | 28,104.2 | 33,878.9 | 30,718.9 | 30,593.4 | 29,995.2 | 31,338.8 | 34,080.3 | 38,578.5 | 38,241.2 |
| Deposit Money Banks: Liabs. | 7b.d | 2,856.7 | 2,810.4 | 5,305.0 | 22,539.3 | 30,540.4 | 28,705.9 | 30,013.0 | 29,990.2 | 31,822.6 | 35,023.4 | 38,252.9 | 39,229.3 |
| Other Banking Insts.: Assets | 7e.d | 96,443.4 | 114,366.8 | 157,547.6 | 187,083.6 | 182,797.3 | 162,180.1 | 158,751.0 | 131,718.3 | 119,469.3 | 119,011.3 | 111,934.3 | 109,786.1 |
| Other Banking Insts.: Liabs. | 7f.d | 93,835.5 | 110,338.9 | 153,339.5 | 185,020.2 | 179,350.2 | 157,020.0 | 153,159.3 | 128,785.1 | 115,151.3 | 115,513.2 | 108,166.8 | 107,920.2 |
| **Monetary Authorities** | | | | | | | *Millions of Dinars: End of Period* | | | | | | |
| Foreign Assets | 11 | 734.0 | 841.3 | 1,058.1 | 1,592.2 | 1,480.4 | 1,448.3 | 1,915.8 | 1,711.2 | 1,959.5 | 2,013.0 | 2,276.7 | 1,772.8 |
| Claims on Central Government | 12a | 127.4 | 131.9 | — | — | — | — | 102.4 | — | — | — | — | — |
| Claims on Deposit Money Banks | 12e | 175.3 | 223.2 | 242.0 | 418.0 | 513.8 | 545.9 | 477.9 | 621.4 | 586.4 | 569.9 | 532.5 | 380.2 |
| Reserve Money | 14 | 485.6 | 609.1 | 663.7 | 1,373.2 | 1,334.7 | 1,439.3 | 1,726.4 | 1,546.6 | 1,862.0 | 1,837.4 | 2,156.7 | 1,917.7 |
| of which: Currency Outside DMBs | 14a | 173.7 | 190.8 | 227.7 | 256.2 | 304.2 | 323.0 | 349.6 | 402.2 | 421.4 | 461.1 | 493.2 | 525.2 |
| Time and Savings Deposits | 15 | 44.4 | 53.3 | 67.0 | 83.5 | 92.8 | 44.9 | 80.7 | 104.0 | 63.2 | — | — | — |
| Foreign Liabilities | 16c | 3.6 | 3.3 | 3.5 | 3.7 | 3.6 | 73.3 | 72.0 | 71.8 | 71.9 | 72.0 | 67.7 | 64.8 |
| Central Government Deposits | 16d | 133.5 | 137.0 | 144.1 | 99.6 | 80.8 | 43.9 | 43.2 | 43.3 | 43.6 | 44.3 | 41.7 | 39.9 |
| Capital Accounts | 17a | 363.9 | 391.4 | 418.6 | 450.3 | 474.7 | 485.0 | 491.0 | 498.5 | 505.1 | 436.4 | 444.8 | 459.7 |
| Other Items (Net) | 17r | 5.7 | 2.2 | 3.2 | −.1 | 7.6 | 10.2 | −19.6 | 68.5 | .1 | 192.8 | 98.3 | −329.1 |
| **Deposit Money Banks** | | | | | | | *Millions of Dinars: End of Period* | | | | | | |
| Reserves | 20 | 296.0 | 386.8 | 405.6 | 1,102.7 | 998.3 | 1,062.8 | 1,352.0 | 1,112.2 | 1,400.9 | 1,385.4 | 1,693.1 | 1,308.6 |
| Foreign Assets | 21 | 1,593.7 | 1,750.4 | 3,210.3 | 10,567.2 | 12,738.5 | 11,550.3 | 11,503.1 | 11,278.2 | 11,783.4 | 12,814.2 | 14,505.5 | 14,378.7 |
| Claims on Central Government | 22a | 518.0 | 543.7 | 577.6 | 598.6 | 691.0 | 1,208.5 | 1,615.2 | 2,114.2 | 2,360.8 | 3,189.5 | 3,465.8 | 3,901.9 |
| Claims on Other Resident Sectors | 22d | 2,172.7 | 2,622.9 | 3,122.5 | 4,340.0 | 6,207.7 | 6,161.3 | 6,545.1 | 7,525.6 | 7,994.2 | 8,519.2 | 8,019.2 | 8,627.4 |
| Demand Deposits | 24 | 687.4 | 871.7 | 1,058.1 | 1,328.1 | 1,594.5 | 1,835.3 | 1,954.3 | 2,234.7 | 2,189.7 | 2,334.7 | 2,601.9 | 2,769.2 |
| Time and Savings Deposits | 25 | 1,974.1 | 2,397.0 | 2,683.1 | 3,954.2 | 4,736.9 | 4,916.1 | 5,482.9 | 5,394.2 | 5,790.5 | 6,363.3 | 6,660.4 | 6,748.5 |
| Foreign Liabilities | 26c | 1,074.1 | 1,056.7 | 1,994.7 | 8,474.8 | 11,483.2 | 10,793.4 | 11,284.9 | 11,276.3 | 11,965.3 | 13,168.6 | 14,383.1 | 14,750.2 |
| Central Government Deposits | 26d | 665.1 | 649.7 | 752.3 | 917.3 | 1,278.2 | 1,286.1 | 1,627.8 | 1,782.8 | 1,968.0 | 1,975.2 | 1,879.1 | 1,851.7 |
| Capital Accounts | 27a | 463.5 | 565.4 | 797.5 | 1,424.6 | 1,420.7 | 1,662.5 | 1,763.4 | 1,923.4 | 2,033.0 | 2,216.4 | 2,447.7 | 2,588.0 |
| Other Items (Net) | 27r | −283.7 | −236.7 | 30.3 | 509.5 | 122.0 | −510.5 | −1,097.9 | −581.2 | −407.2 | −150.1 | −288.6 | −491.0 |
| **Monetary Survey** | | | | | | | *Millions of Dinars: End of Period* | | | | | | |
| Foreign Assets (Net) | 31n | 1,250.0 | 1,531.6 | 2,270.2 | 3,680.9 | 2,732.1 | 2,131.9 | 2,062.0 | 1,641.4 | 1,705.7 | 1,586.4 | 2,331.4 | 1,336.5 |
| Domestic Credit | 32 | 2,019.5 | 2,511.8 | 2,803.7 | 3,921.7 | 5,539.7 | 6,142.2 | 6,489.3 | 7,813.7 | 8,343.4 | 9,689.2 | 9,564.2 | 10,637.7 |
| Claims on Central Govt. (Net) | 32an | −153.2 | −111.1 | −318.8 | −418.3 | −668.0 | −19.1 | −55.8 | 288.1 | 349.2 | 1,170.0 | 1,545.0 | 2,010.3 |
| Claims on Other Resident Sectors | 32d | 2,172.7 | 2,622.9 | 3,122.5 | 4,340.0 | 6,207.7 | 6,161.3 | 6,545.1 | 7,525.6 | 7,994.2 | 8,519.2 | 8,019.2 | 8,627.4 |
| Money | 34 | 861.0 | 1,062.5 | 1,285.8 | 1,584.3 | 1,898.7 | 2,158.3 | 2,303.9 | 2,636.9 | 2,611.0 | 2,795.8 | 3,095.1 | 3,294.4 |
| Quasi-Money | 35 | 2,018.5 | 2,450.3 | 2,750.1 | 4,037.7 | 4,829.7 | 4,961.0 | 5,563.6 | 5,498.2 | 5,853.7 | 6,363.3 | 6,660.4 | 6,748.5 |
| Capital Accounts | 37a | 827.4 | 956.8 | 1,216.1 | 1,874.9 | 1,895.4 | 2,147.5 | 2,254.4 | 2,421.9 | 2,538.1 | 2,652.8 | 2,892.5 | 3,047.7 |
| Other Items (Net) | 37r | −437.4 | −426.2 | −178.1 | 105.7 | −352.0 | −992.7 | −1,570.6 | −1,101.9 | −953.8 | −536.3 | −752.4 | −1,116.4 |
| Money plus Quasi-Money | 35l | 2,879.5 | 3,512.7 | 4,035.9 | 5,622.0 | 6,728.4 | 7,119.3 | 7,867.5 | 8,135.1 | 8,464.8 | 9,159.1 | 9,755.5 | 10,042.9 |
| **Other Banking Institutions** | | | | | | | *Millions of Dinars: End of Period* | | | | | | |
| Reserves | 40 | .... | .... | .... | .... | .... | .... | .... | .... | .... | .... | .... | .... |
| Claims on Mon.Author.:Securities | 40c | .... | .... | .... | .... | .... | .... | .... | .... | .... | .... | .... | .... |
| Foreign Assets | 41 | 36,262.8 | 43,002.0 | 59,238.0 | 70,343.6 | 68,731.9 | 60,979.7 | 59,690.4 | 49,526.1 | 44,920.5 | 44,748.2 | 42,087.3 | 41,279.6 |
| Claims on Central Government | 42a | 153.8 | 160.2 | 161.5 | 218.3 | 323.2 | 250.1 | 211.3 | 300.0 | 327.8 | 334.0 | 397.8 | 735.5 |
| Claims on Other Resident Sectors | 42d | 471.6 | 536.8 | 1,541.5 | 2,497.3 | 3,611.1 | 3,762.6 | 3,508.5 | 3,351.6 | 3,247.1 | 3,606.1 | 3,672.4 | 4,090.5 |
| Other Claims on Dep.Money Banks | 42e | .... | .... | .... | .... | .... | .... | .... | .... | .... | .... | .... | .... |
| Liquid Liabilities | 45l | 267.0 | 461.9 | 1,251.4 | 1,911.5 | 2,507.1 | 2,534.1 | 2,723.5 | 2,757.9 | 3,021.7 | 3,348.1 | 3,604.5 | 3,599.0 |
| Foreign Liabilities | 46c | 35,282.4 | 41,487.5 | 57,655.7 | 69,567.7 | 67,435.8 | 59,039.5 | 57,587.9 | 48,423.2 | 43,296.9 | 43,433.0 | 40,670.7 | 40,578.0 |
| Central Government Deposits | 46d | 332.7 | 355.5 | 463.6 | 373.8 | 454.6 | 265.4 | 395.5 | 336.2 | 408.0 | 471.9 | 472.3 | 455.9 |
| Credit from Monetary Authorities | 46g | .... | .... | .... | .... | .... | .... | .... | .... | .... | .... | .... | .... |
| Credit from Deposit Money Banks | 46h | .... | .... | .... | .... | .... | .... | .... | .... | .... | .... | .... | .... |
| Capital Accounts | 47a | .... | .... | .... | .... | .... | .... | .... | .... | .... | .... | .... | .... |
| Other Items (Net) | 47r | .... | .... | .... | .... | .... | .... | .... | .... | .... | .... | .... | .... |
| **Money (National Definitions)** | | | | | | | *Millions of Dinars: End of Period* | | | | | | |
| M1 | 59ma | 861.1 | 1,062.5 | 1,285.8 | 1,584.3 | 1,898.7 | 2,158.3 | 2,303.9 | 2,636.9 | 2,611.0 | 2,795.8 | 3,095.1 | 3,294.4 |
| M2 | 59mb | 2,879.6 | 3,512.8 | 4,035.2 | 5,622.0 | 6,728.4 | 7,119.3 | 7,867.5 | 8,135.1 | 8,464.8 | 9,159.1 | 9,755.5 | 10,042.9 |
| M3 | 59mc | 3,545.8 | 4,169.4 | 4,892.6 | 6,596.5 | 7,981.8 | 8,404.2 | 9,495.7 | 9,994.0 | 10,435.1 | 11,219.7 | 11,635.2 | 11,895.2 |

# Bahrain, Kingdom of   419

| | | 2004 | 2005 | 2006 | 2007 | 2008 | 2009 | 2010 | 2011 | 2012 | 2013 | 2014 | 2015 |
|---|---|---|---|---|---|---|---|---|---|---|---|---|---|
| **Interest Rates** | | | | | *Percent Per Annum* | | | | | | | | |
| Central Bank Policy Rate (EOP)........ | 60 | .... | .... | .... | 4.00 | .75 | .50 | .50 | .50 | .50 | .50 | .50 | .75 |
| Repurchase Agreement Rate (EOP)... | 60.q | .... | .... | .... | 5.25 | 2.75 | 2.25 | 2.25 | 2.25 | 2.25 | 2.25 | 2.25 | .... |
| Money Market Rate........................ | 60b | 1.74 | 3.63 | 5.25 | 5.12 | 3.09 | 1.82 | .38 | .60 | .... | .... | .... | .... |
| Treasury Bill Rate............................ | 60c | 1.56 | 3.57 | 5.04 | 4.86 | 2.53 | 1.06 | .83 | .96 | 1.21 | .85 | .79 | .... |
| Savings Rate................................... | 60k | 1.57 | 3.45 | 5.25 | 5.12 | 3.09 | 1.82 | .24 | .24 | .23 | .23 | .25 | .25 |
| Deposit Rate................................... | 60l | 1.54 | 3.14 | 4.37 | 4.49 | 1.65 | 1.58 | 1.23 | 1.02 | 1.08 | 1.06 | .98 | .99 |
| Lending Rate................................... | 60p | 7.90 | 7.82 | 7.98 | 8.27 | 8.22 | † 7.94 | 7.25 | 6.79 | 6.04 | 5.94 | 5.87 | 5.16 |
| **Prices, Production, Labor** | | | | | *Index Numbers (2010=100): Period Averages* | | | | | | | | |
| Share Prices (End of Month)............ | 62.ep | 121.1 | 144.5 | 148.2 | 164.7 | 176.2 | 106.0 | 100.0 | 88.5 | 75.7 | 79.6 | 97.1 | 91.5 |
| Consumer Prices............................. | 64 | 85.3 | 87.5 | † 89.3 | 92.2 | 95.4 | 98.1 | 100.0 | 99.6 | 102.4 | 105.8 | 108.6 | 110.6 |
| Refined Petroleum Prod.(2005=100) | 66ab | 94.8 | 100.0 | 98.5 | 100.2 | 98.6 | .... | .... | .... | .... | .... | .... | .... |
| | | | | | | *Number in Thousands: Period Averages* | | | | | | | |
| Labor Force.................................... | 67d | 373 | 418 | 460 | 504 | 578 | .... | .... | .... | .... | .... | .... | .... |
| Employment.................................. | 67e | .... | .... | .... | .... | .... | .... | .... | .... | .... | .... | 673 | .... |
| Unemployment............................. | 67c | .... | .... | .... | .... | .... | 6 | .... | .... | .... | .... | .... | .... |
| Unemployment Rate (%)................. | 67r | .... | .... | .... | .... | .... | 3.8 | .... | 4.0 | .... | .... | .... | .... |
| **Intl. Transactions & Positions** | | | | | *Millions of Dinars* | | | | | | | | |
| Exports........................................... | 70 | 2,841.8 | 3,851.0 | 4,587.2 | 5,126.4 | 6,510.8 | 4,464.5 | 5,790.4 | .... | .... | .... | .... | .... |
| Imports, c.i.f.................................. | 71 | 2,776.6 | 3,531.8 | 3,953.7 | 4,319.5 | 4,060.8 | 2,744.8 | 3,684.8 | .... | .... | .... | .... | .... |
| **Balance of Payments** | | | | | *Millions of US Dollars* | | | | | | | | |
| A. Current Account*....................... | 109bx | 471.6 | 1,474.2 | 2,187.4 | 2,906.6 | 2,256.9 | 560.0 | 770.1 | 3,247.3 | 2,222.1 | 2,560.1 | 1,123.7 | .... |
| Goods, credit (exports)................. | 1a9cx | 7,558.2 | 10,242.0 | 12,200.0 | 13,633.5 | 17,315.7 | 11,873.7 | 13,647.1 | 19,650.3 | 19,768.1 | 20,926.6 | 20,753.5 | .... |
| Goods, debit (imports).................. | 1a9dx | 6,922.6 | 8,870.7 | 9,953.8 | 10,925.4 | 14,246.3 | 9,613.0 | 11,190.4 | 12,105.9 | 13,239.4 | 13,656.4 | 13,317.8 | .... |
| Balance on goods..................... | 1a9bx | 635.6 | 1,371.3 | 2,246.2 | 2,708.1 | 3,069.4 | 2,260.6 | 2,456.6 | 7,544.4 | 6,528.7 | 7,270.2 | 7,435.6 | .... |
| Services, credit (exports)............. | 1b9cx | 2,778.5 | 3,154.9 | 3,462.3 | 3,680.9 | 3,915.7 | 3,831.1 | 4,233.2 | 3,295.7 | 3,085.1 | 3,301.6 | 3,335.1 | .... |
| Services, debit (imports).............. | 1b9dx | 1,247.8 | 1,416.2 | 1,605.2 | 1,700.9 | 2,030.1 | 1,741.0 | 1,905.1 | 1,778.5 | 1,480.1 | 1,560.4 | 1,618.4 | .... |
| Balance on Goods & Services....... | 1z9bx | 2,166.3 | 3,110.0 | 4,103.2 | 4,688.0 | 4,955.1 | 4,350.8 | 4,784.8 | 9,061.7 | 8,133.8 | 9,011.4 | 9,152.4 | .... |
| Primary income: credit................. | 1c9cx | 2,544.3 | 5,015.8 | 7,633.7 | 10,373.6 | 7,088.0 | 1,680.1 | 1,467.6 | 6,821.8 | 2,997.6 | 3,327.4 | 1,952.7 | .... |
| Primary income: debit.................. | 1c9dx | 3,119.1 | 5,428.1 | 8,018.6 | 10,672.3 | 8,011.7 | 4,080.0 | 3,840.6 | 10,586.2 | 6,834.8 | 7,612.8 | 7,617.0 | .... |
| Balance on gds, serv. & prim. inc. | 1y9bx | 1,591.5 | 2,697.6 | 3,718.3 | 4,389.3 | 4,031.4 | 1,950.9 | 2,411.8 | 5,297.3 | 4,296.5 | 4,726.1 | 3,488.0 | .... |
| Secondary income: credit.............. | 1d9ca | — | — | — | — | — | — | — | — | — | — | — | .... |
| Secondary income: debit............... | 1d9da | 1,119.9 | 1,223.4 | 1,530.9 | 1,482.8 | 1,774.5 | 1,391.0 | 1,641.8 | 2,050.0 | 2,074.5 | 2,166.0 | 2,364.4 | .... |
| B. Capital Account*........................ | 209ba | 50.0 | 50.0 | 75.0 | 50.0 | 50.0 | 50.0 | 50.0 | 76.1 | 100.0 | 100.0 | 100.0 | .... |
| Capital account: credit.................. | 209ca | 50.0 | 50.0 | 75.0 | 50.0 | 50.0 | 50.0 | 50.0 | 76.1 | 100.0 | 100.0 | 100.0 | .... |
| Capital account: debit................... | 209da | — | — | — | — | — | — | — | — | — | — | — | .... |
| Balance on current & capital acct. | 129ba | 521.6 | 1,524.2 | 2,262.4 | 2,956.6 | 2,306.9 | 610.0 | 820.1 | 3,323.4 | 2,322.1 | 2,660.1 | 1,223.7 | .... |
| C. Financial Account* | 309na | 390.8 | 1,380.0 | 1,451.4 | 1,552.2 | 2,570.8 | 478.4 | −352.4 | 3,982.2 | 1,766.8 | 2,363.3 | −3,707.2 | .... |
| Direct investment: assets.............. | 3a9aa | 1,035.6 | 1,135.4 | 980.1 | 1,669.1 | 1,620.5 | −1,791.5 | 334.0 | 893.6 | 922.3 | 1,052.4 | −79.5 | .... |
| Equity & investment fund shares.. | 3aaaa | 1,035.6 | 1,135.4 | 980.1 | 1,669.1 | 1,620.5 | −1,791.5 | 334.0 | 893.6 | 922.3 | 1,052.4 | −79.5 | .... |
| Debt instruments...................... | 3abaa | | | | | | | | .... | .... | .... | .... | .... |
| Direct investment: liabilities .......... | 3a9la | 865.3 | 1,048.6 | 2,914.7 | 1,756.3 | 1,794.0 | 257.1 | 155.8 | 780.9 | 891.2 | 988.8 | 957.7 | .... |
| Equity & investment fund shares . | 3aala | 865.3 | 1,048.6 | 2,914.7 | 1,756.3 | 1,794.0 | 257.1 | 155.8 | 780.9 | 891.2 | 988.8 | 957.7 | .... |
| Debt instruments....................... | 3abla | .... | .... | .... | .... | .... | .... | .... | .... | .... | .... | .... | .... |
| Portfolio investment: assets .......... | 3b9aa | 3,892.6 | 7,036.2 | 10,527.3 | 9,890.1 | −6,286.8 | −6,710.1 | −2,051.6 | −5,164.1 | −2,741.2 | −2,447.6 | 22,482.4 | .... |
| Equity & investment fund shares | 3baaa | 1,999.0 | 2,219.7 | 2,200.7 | 3,368.1 | 793.2 | −1,641.6 | −253.1 | −4,740.4 | −4,898.7 | −4,883.5 | 23,414.9 | .... |
| Debt securities ........................... | 3bbaa | 1,893.6 | 4,816.5 | 8,326.7 | 6,522.0 | −7,079.9 | −5,068.5 | −1,798.5 | −423.7 | 2,157.4 | 2,435.9 | −932.4 | .... |
| Portfolio investment: liabilities....... | 3b9la | 387.7 | 2,421.9 | 1,696.1 | 1,330.2 | 2,990.1 | 1,565.5 | 2,704.2 | 419.1 | 1,101.6 | 1,052.1 | −7,126.1 | .... |
| Equity & investment fund shares . | 3bala | 20.9 | 1,801.1 | 133.8 | 138.8 | 156.4 | −487.2 | 1,652.7 | 981.9 | 1,383.0 | 1,385.6 | −7,688.8 | .... |
| Debt securities........................... | 3bbla | 366.8 | 620.8 | 1,562.3 | 1,191.5 | 2,833.7 | 2,052.8 | 1,051.5 | −562.8 | −281.4 | −333.5 | 562.8 | .... |
| Fin. der.& empl.stk.ops.(ESOs): net. | 3c9na | .... | .... | .... | .... | .... | .... | .... | .... | .... | .... | .... | .... |
| Fin. der. & ESOs.: assets.............. | 3c9aa | .... | .... | .... | .... | .... | .... | .... | .... | .... | .... | .... | .... |
| Fin. der. & ESOs.: liabilities.......... | 3c9la | .... | .... | .... | .... | .... | .... | .... | .... | .... | .... | .... | .... |
| Other investment: assets................ | 3d9aa | 9,779.9 | 11,562.4 | 30,234.9 | 38,504.7 | 3,264.6 | −18,123.8 | −2,739.7 | −17,327.4 | −2,809.6 | 7,527.7 | −23,140.2 | .... |
| Other equity.............................. | 3daaa | .... | .... | .... | .... | .... | .... | .... | .... | .... | .... | .... | .... |
| Debt instruments....................... | 3dzaa | 9,779.9 | 11,562.4 | 30,234.9 | 38,504.7 | 3,264.6 | −18,123.8 | −2,739.7 | −17,327.4 | −2,809.6 | 7,527.7 | −23,140.2 | .... |
| Other investment: liabilities............ | 3d9la | 13,064.3 | 14,883.6 | 35,680.1 | 45,425.2 | −8,756.6 | −28,926.4 | −6,964.8 | −26,780.1 | −8,388.0 | 1,728.2 | 9,138.3 | .... |
| Other equity.............................. | 3dala | .... | .... | .... | .... | .... | .... | .... | .... | .... | .... | .... | .... |
| Debt instruments....................... | 3dzla | 13,064.3 | 14,883.6 | 35,680.1 | 45,425.2 | −8,756.6 | −28,926.4 | −6,964.8 | −26,780.1 | −8,388.0 | 1,728.2 | 9,138.3 | .... |
| Curr.+ cap.– finan. acct. balance... | 4y9na | 130.7 | 144.2 | 811.1 | 1,404.4 | −263.9 | 131.5 | 1,172.4 | −658.8 | 555.3 | 296.8 | 4,930.9 | .... |
| D. Net Errors and Omissions............ | 409na | 27.2 | 149.9 | 10.9 | 10.3 | −30.3 | −250.0 | 107.1 | 71.5 | 117.5 | −124.2 | −4,374.4 | .... |
| E. Reserves and Related Items.......... | 4z9na | 157.9 | 294.2 | 822.0 | 1,414.7 | −294.2 | −118.5 | 1,279.5 | −587.3 | 672.8 | 172.6 | 556.5 | .... |
| Reserve assets............................... | 3e9aa | 157.9 | 294.2 | 822.0 | 1,414.7 | −294.2 | −118.5 | 1,279.5 | −587.3 | 672.8 | 172.6 | 556.5 | .... |
| Credit and loans from the IMF........ | 3dcla | — | — | — | — | — | — | — | — | — | — | — | .... |
| Exceptional financing.................... | 409la | .... | .... | .... | .... | .... | .... | .... | .... | .... | .... | .... | .... |

*Excludes components in group E

# Bahrain, Kingdom of   419

| | | 2004 | 2005 | 2006 | 2007 | 2008 | 2009 | 2010 | 2011 | 2012 | 2013 | 2014 | 2015 |
|---|---|---|---|---|---|---|---|---|---|---|---|---|---|
| **International Investment Position** | | | | | | | *Millions of US Dollars* | | | | | | |
| Assets.................................. | 809aa | 104,666.0 | 124,680.7 | 167,239.0 | 218,712.8 | 217,015.2 | 190,238.9 | 187,046.4 | 164,838.7 | 160,883.4 | 167,189.3 | 171,386.8 | .... |
| Direct investment........................... | 8a9aa | 3,935.1 | 5,070.5 | 6,050.5 | 7,719.7 | 9,340.1 | 7,548.7 | 7,882.7 | 8,776.3 | 9,698.7 | 10,751.1 | 10,671.5 | .... |
| Equity & investment fund shares.. | 8aaaa | 3,935.1 | 5,070.5 | 6,050.5 | 7,719.7 | 9,340.1 | 7,548.7 | 7,882.7 | 8,776.3 | 9,698.7 | 10,751.1 | 10,671.5 | .... |
| Debt instruments...................... | 8abaa | .... | .... | .... | .... | .... | .... | .... | .... | .... | .... | .... | .... |
| Portfolio investment..................... | 8b9aa | 26,295.5 | 33,331.7 | 43,859.0 | 53,749.1 | 47,463.4 | 40,754.4 | 38,702.8 | 33,538.8 | 30,797.6 | 28,350.0 | 50,832.7 | .... |
| Equity & investment fund shares.. | 8baaa | 5,860.7 | 8,080.4 | 10,281.1 | 13,649.2 | 14,442.4 | 12,800.8 | 12,547.6 | 7,807.2 | 2,908.5 | −1,975.0 | 21,440.2 | .... |
| Debt securities......................... | 8bbaa | 20,434.8 | 25,251.2 | 33,577.9 | 40,099.9 | 33,021.0 | 27,953.7 | 26,155.2 | 25,731.6 | 27,889.1 | 30,325.0 | 29,392.6 | .... |
| Fin. der.(oth.than reserves) & ESOs | 8c9aa | .... | .... | .... | .... | .... | .... | .... | .... | .... | .... | .... | .... |
| Other investment......................... | 8d9aa | 72,734.1 | 84,291.9 | 114,515.3 | 153,009.4 | 156,274.5 | 138,114.3 | 135,365.3 | 118,016.2 | 115,206.9 | 122,734.6 | 103,827.4 | .... |
| Other equity............................ | 8daaa | .... | .... | .... | .... | .... | .... | .... | .... | .... | .... | .... | .... |
| Debt instruments...................... | 8dzaa | 72,734.1 | 84,291.9 | 114,515.3 | 153,009.4 | 156,274.5 | 138,114.3 | 135,365.3 | 118,016.2 | 115,206.9 | 122,734.6 | 103,827.4 | .... |
| Reserve assets............................. | 8e9aa | 1,701.4 | 1,986.6 | 2,814.1 | 4,234.6 | 3,937.2 | 3,821.5 | 5,095.6 | 4,507.3 | 5,180.5 | 5,353.7 | 6,055.2 | .... |
| Liabilities................................ | 809la | 98,680.2 | 116,854.3 | 157,077.1 | 205,555.1 | 201,569.7 | 174,386.1 | 170,277.3 | 144,603.4 | 138,458.4 | 142,227.7 | 145,186.3 | .... |
| Direct investment........................... | 8a9la | 7,354.0 | 8,276.1 | 11,190.7 | 12,947.0 | 14,741.0 | 14,998.2 | 15,154.0 | 15,934.8 | 16,826.1 | 17,814.9 | 18,772.6 | .... |
| Equity & investment fund shares.. | 8aala | 7,354.0 | 8,276.1 | 11,190.7 | 12,947.0 | 14,741.0 | 14,998.2 | 15,154.0 | 15,934.8 | 16,826.1 | 17,814.9 | 18,772.6 | .... |
| Debt instruments...................... | 8abla | .... | .... | .... | .... | .... | .... | .... | .... | .... | .... | .... | .... |
| Portfolio investment..................... | 8b9la | 2,576.6 | 4,998.4 | 6,694.6 | 8,024.8 | 11,014.9 | 12,580.4 | 15,284.6 | 15,703.7 | 17,055.3 | 18,107.4 | 10,981.4 | .... |
| Equity & investment fund shares.. | 8bala | 652.4 | 2,453.5 | 2,587.3 | 2,726.1 | 2,882.4 | 2,395.2 | 4,047.9 | 4,920.2 | 6,303.2 | 7,688.8 | .... | .... |
| Debt securities......................... | 8bbla | 1,924.2 | 2,545.0 | 4,107.3 | 5,298.7 | 8,132.4 | 10,185.2 | 11,236.7 | 10,783.5 | 10,752.1 | 10,418.6 | 10,981.4 | .... |
| Fin. der.(oth.than reserves) & ESOs | 8c9la | .... | .... | .... | .... | .... | .... | .... | .... | .... | .... | .... | .... |
| Other investment......................... | 8d9la | 88,749.6 | 103,579.8 | 139,191.8 | 184,583.2 | 175,813.8 | 146,807.5 | 139,838.8 | 112,964.8 | 104,577.0 | 106,305.3 | 115,432.3 | .... |
| Other equity............................ | 8dala | .... | .... | .... | .... | .... | .... | .... | .... | .... | .... | .... | .... |
| Debt instruments...................... | 8dzla | 88,749.6 | 103,579.8 | 139,191.8 | 184,583.2 | 175,813.8 | 146,807.5 | 139,838.8 | 112,964.8 | 104,577.0 | 106,305.3 | 115,432.3 | .... |
| **Government Finance** | | | | | | | | | | | | | |
| **Cash Flow Statement** | | | | | | | | | | | | | |
| **Budgetary Central Government** | | | | | | | *Millions of Dinars: Fiscal Year Ends December 31* | | | | | | |
| Cash Receipts:Operating Activities... | c1 | 1,284.1 | 1,671.4 | 1,839.5 | 2,036.7 | 2,677.7 | 1,708.0 | 2,175.6 | 2,819.1 | .... | 2,941.5 | .... | .... |
| Taxes................................. | c11 | 208.5 | 69.8 | 81.1 | 93.6 | 119.5 | 117.6 | 113.7 | 120.6 | .... | 130.9 | .... | .... |
| Social Contributions...................... | c12 | | | | | | | | | .... | | .... | .... |
| Grants................................ | c13 | 22.0 | 39.7 | 28.2 | 35.9 | 29.5 | 28.4 | 28.6 | 100.0 | .... | | .... | .... |
| Other Receipts....................... | c14 | 1,053.6 | 1,561.9 | 1,730.2 | 1,907.2 | 2,528.7 | 1,562.0 | 2,033.3 | 2,598.6 | .... | 2,810.6 | .... | .... |
| Cash Payments:Operating Activities. | c2 | 957.7 | 1,039.6 | 1,133.4 | 1,307.7 | 1,567.8 | 1,704.5 | 1,882.2 | 2,434.8 | .... | 2,857.5 | .... | .... |
| Compensation of Employees.......... | c21 | 537.8 | 564.9 | 602.4 | 710.2 | 788.6 | 799.8 | 832.4 | 1,004.9 | .... | 1,300.4 | .... | .... |
| Purchases of Goods & Services....... | c22 | 145.7 | 263.0 | 293.6 | 339.4 | 396.5 | 317.5 | 330.2 | 318.1 | .... | 405.9 | .... | .... |
| Interest................................ | c24 | 45.9 | 62.1 | 73.7 | 65.9 | 53.6 | 50.1 | 90.6 | 114.5 | .... | 192.3 | .... | .... |
| Subsidies................................ | c25 | 17.1 | 9.6 | 10.7 | 16.8 | 34.1 | 33.7 | 43.0 | 86.4 | .... | 52.5 | .... | .... |
| Grants................................ | c26 | 74.1 | 103.4 | 119.4 | 95.6 | 130.2 | 342.3 | 390.2 | 635.1 | .... | 695.0 | .... | .... |
| Social Benefits......................... | c27 | | 5.9 | 18.7 | 20.2 | 146.0 | 134.4 | 170.8 | 217.6 | .... | 197.3 | .... | .... |
| Other Payments....................... | c28 | 137.1 | 30.6 | 15.0 | 59.7 | 19.0 | 26.7 | 25.0 | 27.6 | .... | −2.7 | .... | .... |
| Net Cash Inflow:Operating Act.[1-2] | ccio | 326.4 | 631.9 | 709.5 | 746.6 | 1,127.4 | 46.1 | 267.2 | 576.5 | .... | 231.0 | .... | .... |
| Net Cash Outflow:Invest. in NFA...... | c31 | 103.0 | 238.7 | 428.6 | 454.2 | 579.8 | 381.0 | 755.6 | 442.7 | .... | 511.4 | .... | .... |
| Purchases of Nonfinancial Assets.... | c31.1 | 103.5 | 238.7 | 405.3 | 525.3 | 572.5 | 554.4 | 674.1 | 453.1 | .... | .... | .... | .... |
| Sales of Nonfinancial Assets.......... | c31.2 | .5 | | .7 | 2.7 | .8 | .9 | .4 | .3 | .... | .... | .... | .... |
| Cash Surplus/Deficit [1-2-31=1-2M] | ccsd | 223.4 | 393.2 | 304.9 | 224.0 | 555.5 | −507.4 | −406.5 | 123.7 | .... | −336.4 | .... | .... |
| Net Acq. Fin. Assets, excl. Cash...... | c32x | | | | | | | | | .... | .... | .... | .... |
| Domestic................................ | c321x | | | | | | | | | .... | .... | .... | .... |
| Foreign................................ | c322x | | | | | | | | | .... | .... | .... | .... |
| Net Incurrence of Liabilities.............. | c33 | −191.9 | −.3 | 43.6 | 134.9 | 166.5 | 664.1 | 1,021.1 | 820.8 | .... | 1,293.3 | .... | .... |
| Domestic................................ | c331 | −203.3 | −11.1 | 56.9 | 152.3 | 1.0 | 355.4 | 572.7 | 548.7 | .... | 769.7 | .... | .... |
| Foreign................................ | c332 | 11.4 | 10.8 | −13.4 | −17.4 | 165.4 | 308.7 | 448.4 | 272.1 | .... | 523.7 | .... | .... |
| Net Cash Inflow, Fin.Act.[-32x+33].. | cnfb | −191.9 | −.3 | 43.6 | 89.1 | 117.7 | 627.7 | 1,027.8 | 670.5 | .... | 1,192.6 | .... | .... |
| Net Change in Stock of Cash.......... | cncb | −92.7 | 431.0 | 348.5 | 313.0 | 673.4 | 120.2 | 621.3 | 794.1 | .... | 856.2 | .... | .... |
| Stat. Discrep. [32X-33+NCB-CSD].... | ccsdz | −124.0 | 38.1 | | | | −.1 | | | .... | | .... | .... |
| Memo Item:Cash Expenditure[2+31] | c2m | 1,060.7 | 1,278.2 | 1,562.0 | 1,761.9 | 2,147.6 | 2,085.5 | 2,637.7 | 2,877.5 | .... | 3,368.8 | .... | .... |
| Memo Item: Gross Debt.................. | c63 | 1,453.6 | 1,452.4 | 1,409.2 | 616.5 | 705.0 | 1,348.0 | 2,930.1 | 3,888.3 | .... | 5,375.7 | .... | .... |
| **National Accounts** | | | | | | | *Millions of Dinars* | | | | | | |
| Househ.Cons.Expend.,incl.NPISHs.... | 96f | 2,352.0 | 2,385.7 | 2,416.2 | 2,582.9 | 3,333.9 | 3,528.4 | 3,981.7 | 4,226.4 | 4,372.2 | 4,988.2 | | |
| Government Consumption Expend... | 91f | 763.3 | 844.0 | 884.4 | 988.6 | 1,070.1 | 1,205.6 | 1,249.9 | 1,501.1 | 1,667.0 | 1,928.7 | .... | |
| Gross Fixed Capital Formation......... | 93e | 1,113.2 | 1,542.3 | 2,052.5 | 2,741.3 | 3,337.4 | 2,178.6 | 2,518.1 | 1,706.4 | 2,225.9 | 1,925.7 | .... | |
| Changes in Inventories................... | 93i | −98.6 | 63.0 | 61.8 | 94.9 | 62.7 | 76.2 | 120.0 | 79.7 | 92.7 | 138.7 | .... | |
| Exports of Goods and Services......... | 90c | 3,886.6 | 5,037.2 | 5,889.0 | 6,510.2 | 7,983.0 | 5,905.0 | 6,723.0 | 8,627.5 | 8,592.8 | 9,109.8 | .... | |
| Imports of Goods and Services (-)..... | 98c | 3,072.1 | 3,867.9 | 4,346.2 | 4,747.5 | 6,119.9 | 4,269.1 | 4,924.5 | 5,220.5 | 5,534.5 | 5,721.5 | .... | |
| Gross Domestic Product (GDP)........ | 99b | 4,944.5 | 6,004.2 | 6,957.8 | 8,170.5 | 9,667.3 | 8,624.8 | 9,668.2 | 10,920.6 | 11,416.1 | 12,369.5 | 12,734.7 | |
| Net Primary Income from Abroad..... | 98.n | −216.2 | −155.4 | −145.1 | −112.3 | −347.3 | −902.3 | −892.3 | −1,415.5 | −1,442.8 | −1,611.6 | .... | |
| Gross National Income (GNI)........... | 99a | 4,728.3 | 5,848.8 | 6,812.7 | 8,058.2 | 9,320.0 | 7,722.5 | 8,775.9 | 9,505.1 | 9,973.3 | 10,758.0 | .... | |
| Consumption of Fixed Capital.......... | 99cf | 373.5 | 384.5 | 425.9 | 477.2 | 481.5 | 487.7 | 541.9 | 617.8 | 628.7 | 625.5 | .... | |
| Net National Income...................... | 99e | 4,354.7 | 5,464.4 | 6,386.8 | 7,580.9 | 8,838.5 | 7,234.8 | 8,234.0 | 8,887.2 | 9,344.6 | 10,019.1 | .... | |
| GDP 2010 Prices........................ | 99b.p | 6,909.6 | 7,377.3 | 7,854.4 | 8,505.8 | 9,036.3 | 9,266.3 | 9,668.2 | 9,871.2 | 10,186.5 | 10,771.3 | 11,256.7 | |
| GDP Volume (2010=100)............... | 99bvp | 71.5 | 76.3 | 81.2 | 88.0 | 93.5 | 95.8 | 100.0 | 102.1 | 105.4 | 111.4 | 116.4 | |
| GDP Deflator (2010=100)............... | 99bip | 71.6 | 81.4 | 88.6 | 96.1 | 107.0 | 93.1 | 100.0 | 110.6 | 112.1 | 114.8 | 113.1 | |
| | | | | | | | *Millions: Midyear Estimates* | | | | | | |
| Population.................................. | 99z | .81 | .87 | .94 | 1.03 | 1.12 | 1.20 | 1.26 | 1.31 | 1.33 | 1.35 | 1.36 | 1.38 |

# Bangladesh   513

| | | 2004 | 2005 | 2006 | 2007 | 2008 | 2009 | 2010 | 2011 | 2012 | 2013 | 2014 | 2015 |
|---|---|---|---|---|---|---|---|---|---|---|---|---|---|
| **Exchange Rates** | | | | | | *Taka per SDR: End of Period* | | | | | | | |
| Official Rate............aa=......... | wa | 94.333 | 94.632 | 103.902 | 108.367 | 106.155 | 108.589 | 108.957 | 125.666 | 122.723 | 119.735 | 112.934 | 108.780 |
| | | | | | | *Taka per US Dollar: End of Period (we) Period Average (wf)* | | | | | | | |
| Official Rate............ae=......... | we | 60.742 | 66.210 | 69.065 | 68.576 | 68.920 | 69.267 | 70.750 | 81.853 | 79.850 | 77.750 | 77.949 | 78.500 |
| Official Rate............rf=......... | wf | 59.513 | 64.327 | 68.933 | 68.875 | 68.598 | 69.039 | 69.649 | 74.152 | 81.863 | 78.103 | 77.641 | 77.947 |
| **Fund Position** | | | | | | *Millions of SDRs: End of Period* | | | | | | | |
| Quota.............................. | 2f.s | 533.30 | 533.30 | 533.30 | 533.30 | 533.30 | 533.30 | 533.30 | 533.30 | 533.30 | 533.30 | 533.30 | 533.30 |
| SDR Holdings.................... | 1b.s | .80 | .65 | .88 | .49 | 1.37 | 458.33 | 428.30 | 477.99 | 414.56 | 638.99 | 682.03 | 881.30 |
| Reserve Position in the Fund... | 1c.s | .21 | .23 | .25 | .28 | .30 | .31 | .41 | .41 | .49 | .49 | .57 | .57 |
| Total Fund Cred.&Loans Outstg....... | 2tl | 148.50 | 215.78 | 316.73 | 316.73 | 445.11 | 430.26 | 400.56 | 317.34 | 278.75 | 461.30 | 504.22 | 653.42 |
| SDR Allocations................ | 1bd | 47.12 | 47.12 | 47.12 | 47.12 | 47.12 | 510.40 | 510.40 | 510.40 | 510.40 | 510.40 | 510.40 | 510.40 |
| **International Liquidity** | | | | | | *Millions of US Dollars Unless Otherwise Indicated: End of Period* | | | | | | | |
| Total Reserves minus Gold.............. | 1l.d | 3,172.4 | 2,767.2 | 3,805.6 | 5,183.4 | 5,689.3 | 10,218.9 | 10,564.3 | 8,509.5 | 12,031.2 | 17,564.4 | 21,785.4 | 27,023.4 |
| SDR Holdings.................... | 1b.d | 1.2 | .9 | 1.3 | .8 | 2.1 | 718.5 | 659.6 | 733.8 | 637.2 | 984.0 | 988.1 | 1,221.2 |
| Reserve Position in the Fund.......... | 1c.d | .3 | .3 | .4 | .4 | .5 | .5 | .6 | .6 | .8 | .8 | .8 | .8 |
| Foreign Exchange................ | 1d.d | 3,170.9 | 2,766.0 | 3,803.9 | 5,182.2 | 5,686.7 | 9,499.9 | 9,904.1 | 7,775.1 | 11,393.3 | 16,579.6 | 20,796.4 | 25,801.3 |
| Gold (Million Fine Troy Ounces)....... | 1ad | .113 | .113 | .113 | .113 | .113 | .113 | .434 | .435 | .435 | .434 | .443 | .443 |
| Gold (National Valuation).............. | 1and | 49.9 | 58.1 | 71.4 | 94.6 | 99.3 | 124.4 | 613.2 | 682.5 | 719.9 | 527.7 | 525.3 | 469.7 |
| Central Bank: Other Assets............. | 3..d | 5.9 | 6.1 | 6.1 | 7.0 | 7.1 | 10.3 | 20.5 | 18.9 | 19.0 | 55.0 | 71.4 | 101.2 |
| Central Bank: Other Liabs............. | 4..d | 307.5 | 265.2 | 328.4 | 449.9 | 467.5 | 485.4 | 910.4 | 747.8 | 590.7 | 769.7 | 904.3 | 948.3 |
| Other Depository Corps.: Assets......... | 7a.d | 827.3 | 912.2 | 1,117.8 | 1,093.6 | 1,105.5 | 1,088.0 | 1,731.7 | 1,733.5 | 2,257.8 | 2,342.0 | 3,951.0 | 4,144.9 |
| Other Depository Corps.: Liabs......... | 7b.d | 732.2 | 865.2 | 1,056.6 | 1,080.6 | 1,316.0 | 1,355.0 | 1,539.9 | 1,575.0 | 1,615.0 | 1,855.4 | 3,995.1 | 4,379.9 |
| **Central Bank** | | | | | | *Millions of Taka: End of Period* | | | | | | | |
| Net Foreign Assets.......................... | 11n | 158,957 | 145,032 | 207,697 | 292,146 | 314,971 | 581,342 | 628,632 | 588,721 | 875,677 | 1,234,742 | 1,559,593 | 1,965,113 |
| Claims on Nonresidents................ | 11 | 196,090 | 187,468 | 268,185 | 362,428 | 399,443 | 717,107 | 792,299 | 753,951 | 1,019,691 | 1,410,934 | 1,744,670 | 2,166,157 |
| Liabilities to Nonresidents.......... | 16c | 37,133 | 42,436 | 60,488 | 70,281 | 84,472 | 135,765 | 163,667 | 165,230 | 144,014 | 176,192 | 185,077 | 201,044 |
| Claims on Other Depository Corps.... | 12e | 59,970 | 66,840 | 66,043 | 89,176 | 111,205 | 89,598 | 140,925 | 180,406 | 178,370 | 88,135 | 105,397 | 74,317 |
| Net Claims on Central Government.. | 12an | 77,881 | 163,443 | 253,094 | 228,193 | 226,611 | 108,811 | 177,036 | 392,107 | 309,958 | 135,132 | −119,231 | −82,636 |
| Claims on Central Government...... | 12a | 87,480 | 174,132 | 267,974 | 251,130 | 251,334 | 236,742 | 220,671 | 412,271 | 345,890 | 239,646 | 99,287 | 96,512 |
| Liabilities to Central Government... | 16d | 9,599 | 10,689 | 14,880 | 22,937 | 24,723 | 127,931 | 43,635 | 20,164 | 35,932 | 104,514 | 218,518 | 179,148 |
| Claims on Other Sectors.................. | 12s | 24,690 | 23,462 | 23,515 | 23,132 | 22,670 | 22,351 | 24,083 | 27,872 | 36,321 | 42,835 | 54,922 | 55,148 |
| Claims on Other Financial Corps..... | 12g | 10,338 | 9,573 | 9,084 | 8,586 | 8,088 | 7,349 | 8,159 | 8,025 | 12,338 | 16,760 | 12,937 | 12,406 |
| Claims on State & Local Govts....... | 12b | | | | | | | | | | | | |
| Claims on Public Nonfin. Corps...... | 12c | 649 | 500 | 500 | 500 | 500 | 500 | 500 | 500 | 500 | 500 | 12,000 | 12,000 |
| Claims on Private Sector............... | 12d | 13,703 | 13,389 | 13,931 | 14,046 | 14,082 | 14,502 | 15,424 | 19,347 | 23,483 | 25,575 | 29,985 | 30,742 |
| Monetary Base.............................. | 14 | 262,394 | 328,942 | 453,614 | 505,225 | 594,710 | 700,689 | 853,401 | 987,028 | 1,155,239 | 1,204,540 | 1,383,487 | 1,594,172 |
| Currency in Circulation.................. | 14a | 182,820 | 219,784 | 314,356 | 349,972 | 403,675 | 444,593 | 573,182 | 631,812 | 717,332 | 819,032 | 897,426 | 1,005,131 |
| Liabs. to Other Depository Corps.... | 14c | 79,485 | 109,040 | 139,074 | 155,225 | 190,993 | 256,043 | 280,070 | 354,722 | 437,862 | 385,482 | 485,793 | 588,901 |
| Liabilities to Other Sectors.......... | 14d | 89 | 118 | 184 | 28 | 42 | 53 | 149 | 494 | 45 | 26 | 268 | 140 |
| Other Liabs. to Other Dep. Corps..... | 14n | 2,903 | 9,855 | 10,260 | 3,678 | 1,223 | 13,167 | 978 | 504 | 25,052 | 147,109 | 91,318 | 297,583 |
| Dep. & Sec. Excl. f/Monetary Base..... | 14o | 876 | 1,932 | 2,794 | 18,041 | 3,390 | 7,500 | 16,197 | 4,690 | 12,633 | 1,302 | 5,863 | 10,978 |
| Deposits Included in Broad Money. | 15 | — | — | — | — | — | — | — | — | — | — | — | — |
| Sec.Ot.th.Shares Incl.in Brd. Money. | 16a | — | — | — | — | — | — | — | — | — | — | — | — |
| Deposits Excl. from Broad Money... | 16b | 876 | 852 | 1,200 | 1,437 | 2,720 | 1,945 | 15,121 | 3,527 | 3,791 | 1,302 | 5,863 | 10,926 |
| Sec.Ot.th.Shares Excl.f/Brd.Money... | 16s | — | 1,080 | 1,594 | 16,604 | 670 | 5,555 | 1,076 | 1,163 | 8,842 | — | — | 52 |
| Loans............................... | 16l | — | — | — | — | — | — | — | — | — | — | — | — |
| Financial Derivatives................. | 16m | — | — | — | — | — | — | — | — | — | — | — | — |
| Shares and Other Equity................. | 17a | 42,115 | 58,288 | 83,956 | 108,620 | 85,495 | 109,888 | 129,320 | 227,018 | 236,744 | 178,924 | 166,234 | 152,728 |
| Other Items (Net)........................... | 17r | 13,210 | −240 | −275 | −2,917 | −9,361 | −29,142 | −29,220 | −30,134 | −29,342 | −31,031 | −46,221 | −43,519 |
| Memo Item: | | | | | | | | | | | | | |
| Total Assets.................................. | 10ra | 420,938 | 511,763 | 693,199 | 794,147 | 854,746 | 1,147,805 | 1,261,304 | 1,470,286 | 1,679,719 | 1,877,645 | 2,116,238 | 2,498,011 |
| **Other Depository Corporations** | | | | | | *Millions of Taka: End of Period* | | | | | | | |
| Net Foreign Assets.......................... | 21n | 5,775 | 3,112 | 4,227 | 895 | −14,510 | −18,498 | 13,571 | 12,972 | 51,326 | 37,830 | −3,435 | −18,449 |
| Claims on Nonresidents................ | 21 | 50,250 | 60,394 | 77,200 | 74,995 | 76,190 | 75,361 | 122,519 | 141,891 | 180,285 | 182,091 | 307,979 | 325,372 |
| Liabilities to Nonresidents.............. | 26c | 44,475 | 57,282 | 72,973 | 74,100 | 90,700 | 93,859 | 108,948 | 128,919 | 128,959 | 144,261 | 311,414 | 343,821 |
| Claims on Central Bank.................. | 20 | 112,662 | 147,329 | 177,058 | 199,813 | 231,529 | 307,746 | 347,093 | 462,085 | 556,010 | 642,770 | 674,578 | 991,912 |
| Currency................................. | 20a | 16,375 | 18,369 | 18,938 | 31,232 | 32,855 | 35,430 | 49,654 | 57,112 | 75,348 | 97,926 | 85,925 | 87,688 |
| Reserve Deposits and Securities..... | 20b | 88,287 | 122,515 | 148,898 | 165,902 | 198,674 | 259,841 | 297,439 | 404,973 | 457,711 | 467,700 | 575,783 | 673,656 |
| Other Claims............................. | 20n | 8,000 | 6,445 | 9,222 | 2,679 | — | 12,475 | — | — | 22,951 | 77,144 | 12,870 | 230,568 |
| Net Claims on Central Government.. | 22an | 475,040 | 457,890 | 498,393 | 629,809 | 730,835 | 891,647 | 928,143 | 1,106,699 | 1,233,390 | 1,620,749 | 2,058,875 | 2,224,607 |
| Claims on Central Government...... | 22a | 562,619 | 569,219 | 619,474 | 777,130 | 905,918 | 1,083,710 | 1,172,941 | 1,399,071 | 1,594,061 | 2,079,921 | 2,575,706 | 2,798,683 |
| Liabilities to Central Government... | 26d | 87,579 | 111,329 | 121,081 | 147,321 | 175,083 | 192,063 | 244,798 | 292,372 | 360,671 | 459,172 | 516,831 | 574,076 |
| Claims on Other Sectors.................. | 22s | 1,149,134 | 1,390,754 | 1,641,726 | 1,869,222 | 2,260,858 | 2,689,287 | 3,449,251 | 4,085,909 | 4,753,737 | 5,145,729 | 6,037,936 | 6,850,788 |
| Claims on Other Financial Corps..... | 22g | 24,702 | 24,594 | 20,875 | 36,542 | 28,813 | 42,050 | 49,003 | 74,176 | 98,997 | 82,211 | 108,647 | 131,237 |
| Claims on State & Local Govts....... | 22b | 581 | 435 | 289 | 202 | 174 | 137 | 105 | 72 | 39 | 9 | — | — |
| Claims on Public Nonfin. Corps...... | 22c | 67,650 | 125,915 | 131,256 | 84,810 | 105,781 | 109,874 | 148,743 | 141,461 | 140,736 | 78,214 | 116,912 | 91,387 |
| Claims on Private Sector............... | 22d | 1,056,201 | 1,239,810 | 1,489,306 | 1,747,668 | 2,126,090 | 2,537,226 | 3,251,400 | 3,870,200 | 4,513,965 | 4,985,295 | 5,812,377 | 6,628,164 |
| Liabilities to Central Bank............... | 26g | 54,805 | 65,102 | 62,508 | 80,623 | 103,672 | 82,037 | 133,161 | 173,490 | 168,097 | 81,715 | 101,025 | 68,092 |
| Transf.Dep.Included in Broad Money | 24 | 151,439 | 173,896 | 200,237 | 260,326 | 269,689 | 336,851 | 466,526 | 493,958 | 531,510 | 550,955 | 670,041 | 763,476 |
| Other Dep.Included in Broad Money. | 25 | 1,099,625 | 1,299,922 | 1,556,865 | 1,774,322 | 2,143,456 | 2,621,652 | 3,115,319 | 3,826,757 | 4,652,947 | 5,462,290 | 6,195,295 | 6,984,151 |
| Sec.Ot.th.Shares Incl.in Brd. Money.. | 26a | 327,563 | 346,057 | 377,865 | 406,513 | 429,396 | 496,861 | 574,059 | 575,111 | 575,771 | 619,324 | 825,657 | 1,105,101 |
| Deposits Excl. from Broad Money... | 26b | 252 | 237 | 155 | 302 | 633 | 303 | 318 | 270 | 272 | 295 | 1,510 | 552 |
| Sec.Ot.th.Shares Excl.f/Brd.Money..... | 26s | 329 | 364 | 559 | 341 | 570 | 340 | 5,207 | 9,277 | 9,747 | 11,279 | 14,913 | 14,278 |
| Loans................................... | 26l | 1,273 | 5,514 | 6,025 | 8,815 | 12,946 | 13,372 | 22,447 | 29,714 | 38,454 | 225 | 1,902 | 793 |
| Financial Derivatives...................... | 26m | — | — | — | — | — | — | — | — | — | — | — | — |
| Insurance Technical Reserves........... | 26r | — | — | — | — | — | — | — | — | — | — | — | — |
| Shares and Other Equity.................. | 27a | 104,005 | 124,515 | 156,837 | 230,359 | 296,961 | 409,687 | 541,196 | 691,073 | 762,886 | 868,127 | 983,465 | 1,083,058 |
| Other Items (Net)........................... | 27r | 3,320 | −16,522 | −39,647 | −61,862 | −48,611 | −90,921 | −120,175 | −131,985 | −145,221 | −147,132 | −25,854 | 29,357 |
| Memo Item: | | | | | | | | | | | | | |
| Total Assets................................... | 20ra | 2,199,259 | 2,539,667 | 2,944,238 | 3,437,922 | 4,112,397 | 4,901,206 | 6,012,541 | 7,205,236 | 8,299,302 | 9,543,404 | 11,342,585 | 12,769,895 |

# Bangladesh 513

| | | 2004 | 2005 | 2006 | 2007 | 2008 | 2009 | 2010 | 2011 | 2012 | 2013 | 2014 | 2015 |
|---|---|---|---|---|---|---|---|---|---|---|---|---|---|
| **Depository Corporations** | | | | | | | *Millions of Taka: End of Period* | | | | | | |
| Net Foreign Assets.......................... | 31n | 164,732 | 148,144 | 211,924 | 293,041 | 300,461 | 562,844 | 642,203 | 601,693 | 927,003 | 1,272,572 | 1,556,158 | 1,946,664 |
| Claims on Nonresidents................. | 31 | 246,340 | 247,862 | 345,385 | 437,423 | 475,633 | 792,468 | 914,818 | 895,842 | 1,199,976 | 1,593,025 | 2,052,649 | 2,491,529 |
| Liabilities to Nonresidents............. | 36c | 81,608 | 99,718 | 133,461 | 144,381 | 175,172 | 229,624 | 272,615 | 294,149 | 272,973 | 320,453 | 496,491 | 544,865 |
| Domestic Claims............................ | 32 | 1,726,745 | 2,035,549 | 2,416,728 | 2,750,356 | 3,240,974 | 3,712,096 | 4,578,513 | 5,612,587 | 6,333,406 | 6,944,445 | 8,032,502 | 9,047,907 |
| Net Claims on Central Government | 32an | 552,921 | 621,333 | 751,487 | 858,002 | 957,446 | 1,000,458 | 1,105,179 | 1,498,806 | 1,543,348 | 1,755,881 | 1,939,644 | 2,141,971 |
| Claims on Central Government.... | 32a | 650,099 | 743,351 | 887,448 | 1,028,260 | 1,157,252 | 1,320,452 | 1,393,612 | 1,811,342 | 1,939,951 | 2,319,567 | 2,674,993 | 2,895,195 |
| Liabilities to Central Government. | 36d | 97,178 | 122,018 | 135,961 | 170,258 | 199,806 | 319,994 | 288,433 | 312,536 | 396,603 | 563,686 | 735,349 | 753,224 |
| Claims on Other Sectors.............. | 32s | 1,173,824 | 1,414,216 | 1,665,241 | 1,892,354 | 2,283,528 | 2,711,638 | 3,473,334 | 4,113,781 | 4,790,058 | 5,188,564 | 6,092,858 | 6,905,936 |
| Claims on Other Financial Corps.. | 32g | 35,040 | 34,167 | 29,959 | 45,128 | 36,901 | 49,399 | 57,162 | 82,201 | 111,335 | 98,971 | 121,584 | 143,643 |
| Claims on State & Local Govts..... | 32b | 581 | 435 | 289 | 202 | 174 | 137 | 105 | 72 | 39 | 9 | — | — |
| Claims on Public Nonfin. Corps.... | 32c | 68,299 | 126,415 | 131,756 | 85,310 | 106,281 | 110,374 | 149,243 | 141,961 | 141,236 | 78,714 | 128,912 | 103,387 |
| Claims on Private Sector.............. | 32d | 1,069,904 | 1,253,199 | 1,503,237 | 1,761,714 | 2,140,172 | 2,551,728 | 3,266,824 | 3,889,547 | 4,537,448 | 5,010,870 | 5,842,362 | 6,658,906 |
| Broad Money Liabilities.................... | 35l | 1,745,161 | 2,021,408 | 2,430,569 | 2,759,929 | 3,213,403 | 3,864,580 | 4,679,581 | 5,471,020 | 6,402,257 | 7,353,701 | 8,502,762 | 9,770,311 |
| Currency Outside Depository Corps | 34a | 166,445 | 201,415 | 295,418 | 318,740 | 370,820 | 409,163 | 523,528 | 574,700 | 641,984 | 721,106 | 811,501 | 917,443 |
| Transferable Deposits................... | 34 | 151,439 | 173,896 | 200,237 | 260,326 | 269,689 | 336,851 | 466,526 | 493,958 | 531,510 | 550,955 | 670,041 | 763,476 |
| Other Deposits............................. | 35 | 1,099,714 | 1,300,040 | 1,557,049 | 1,774,350 | 2,143,498 | 2,621,705 | 3,115,468 | 3,827,251 | 4,652,992 | 5,462,316 | 6,195,563 | 6,984,291 |
| Securities Other than Shares.......... | 36a | 327,563 | 346,057 | 377,865 | 406,513 | 429,396 | 496,861 | 574,059 | 575,111 | 575,771 | 619,324 | 825,657 | 1,105,101 |
| Deposits Excl. from Broad Money..... | 36b | 1,128 | 1,089 | 1,355 | 1,739 | 3,353 | 2,248 | 15,439 | 3,797 | 4,063 | 1,597 | 7,373 | 11,478 |
| Sec.Ot.th.Shares Excl.f/Brd.Money.... | 36s | 329 | 1,444 | 2,153 | 16,945 | 1,240 | 5,895 | 6,283 | 10,440 | 18,589 | 11,279 | 14,913 | 14,330 |
| Loans........................................... | 36l | 1,273 | 5,514 | 6,025 | 8,815 | 12,946 | 13,372 | 22,447 | 29,714 | 38,454 | 225 | 1,902 | 793 |
| Financial Derivatives...................... | 36m | — | — | — | — | — | — | — | — | — | — | — | — |
| Insurance Technical Reserves.......... | 36r | — | — | — | — | — | — | — | — | — | — | — | — |
| Shares and Other Equity................. | 37a | 146,120 | 182,803 | 240,793 | 338,979 | 382,456 | 519,575 | 670,516 | 918,091 | 999,630 | 1,047,051 | 1,149,699 | 1,235,786 |
| Other Items (Net)........................... | 37r | −2,534 | −28,565 | −52,243 | −83,010 | −71,963 | −130,730 | −173,550 | −218,782 | −202,584 | −196,836 | −87,989 | −38,127 |
| Broad Money Liabs., Seasonally Adj. | 35l.b | 1,723,844 | 1,998,597 | 2,405,112 | 2,733,356 | 3,184,785 | 3,831,963 | 4,641,426 | 5,427,517 | 6,352,052 | 7,296,338 | 8,438,261 | 9,699,343 |
| **Monetary Aggregates** | | | | | | | *Millions of Taka: End of Period* | | | | | | |
| Broad Money................................. | 59m | 1,748,702 | 2,025,231 | 2,434,644 | 2,764,498 | 3,218,075 | 3,869,555 | 4,685,213 | 5,477,734 | 6,409,569 | 7,361,378 | 8,510,719 | 9,778,287 |
| o/w:Currency Issued by Cent.Govt | 59m.a | 3,541 | 3,823 | 4,075 | 4,569 | 4,672 | 4,975 | 5,632 | 6,714 | 7,312 | 7,677 | 7,957 | 7,976 |
| o/w: Dep.in Nonfin. Corporations. | 59m.b | — | — | — | — | — | — | — | — | — | — | — | — |
| o/w:Secs. Issued by Central Govt.. | 59m.c | — | — | — | — | — | — | — | — | — | — | — | — |
| Money (National Definitions) | | | | | | | | | | | | | |
| Reserve Money............................ | 19mb | 265,935 | 332,765 | 457,688 | 509,794 | 599,382 | 705,664 | 859,033 | 993,742 | 1,069,945 | 1,212,217 | 1,391,176 | 1,602,008 |
| M1............................................. | 59ma | 322,376 | 380,170 | 501,274 | 585,526 | 647,125 | 753,601 | 999,189 | 1,079,563 | 1,186,091 | 1,286,351 | 1,480,327 | 1,683,193 |
| M2............................................. | 59mb | 1,405,905 | 1,645,940 | 2,010,965 | 2,307,211 | 2,719,789 | 3,281,923 | 3,992,790 | 4,754,969 | 5,659,060 | 6,539,666 | 7,412,483 | 8,381,142 |
| M3............................................. | 59mc | 1,748,702 | 2,025,237 | 2,434,641 | 2,764,499 | 3,218,073 | 3,869,555 | 4,685,213 | 5,477,734 | 6,409,569 | 7,361,378 | 8,510,719 | 9,778,287 |
| **Interest Rates** | | | | | | | *Percent Per Annum* | | | | | | |
| Central Bank Policy Rate (EOP)........ | 60 | 5.00 | 5.00 | 5.00 | 5.00 | 5.00 | 5.00 | 5.00 | 5.00 | 5.00 | 5.00 | 5.00 | 5.00 |
| Reverse Repurchase Agmt.Rate(EOP) | 60.c | .... | 4.49 | 6.10 | 6.50 | 6.54 | 5.54 | 2.92 | 4.56 | 5.75 | 5.29 | 5.25 | 5.25 |
| Repurchase Agreement Rate (EOP)... | 60.q | .... | 8.11 | 8.33 | 9.00 | 8.58 | 7.88 | 4.92 | 6.56 | 7.75 | 7.29 | 7.25 | 7.25 |
| Central Bank Bill Rate..................... | 60ae | .... | .... | 7.34 | 7.37 | .... | 1.51 | 2.89 | .... | 9.21 | 7.62 | 5.99 | 5.02 |
| Money Market Rate........................ | 60b | 5.91 | 9.46 | 11.26 | 7.37 | 10.24 | 4.39 | 8.06 | 11.15 | 12.82 | 7.78 | 7.14 | 6.20 |
| Treasury Bill Rate........................... | 60c | .... | .... | 7.52 | 7.61 | 6.01 | 6.29 | 4.50 | 3.88 | 10.77 | 8.67 | 7.18 | 5.76 |
| Savings Rate.................................. | 60k | 5.49 | 5.48 | 5.82 | 5.79 | 5.76 | 5.24 | 5.66 | 5.63 | 5.79 | 5.92 | 5.56 | 5.05 |
| Deposit Rate.................................. | 60l | 5.80 | 5.53 | 5.99 | 6.99 | 7.55 | 7.81 | 7.21 | 8.84 | 10.22 | 11.72 | 9.80 | 8.24 |
| Lending Rate.................................. | 60p | 10.40 | 10.62 | 11.66 | 12.64 | 12.89 | 13.33 | 12.22 | 13.32 | 13.94 | 13.59 | 12.95 | 11.71 |
| Government Bond Yield.................. | 61 | .... | .... | .... | .... | .... | 10.14 | 8.86 | 9.49 | 11.60 | 12.13 | 11.49 | 9.44 |
| **Prices, Production, Labor** | | | | | | | *Index Numbers (2010=100): Period Averages* | | | | | | |
| Share Prices (End of Month)............. | 62.ep | 20.8 | 25.7 | 22.4 | 34.6 | 43.6 | 46.6 | 100.0 | 89.6 | 68.4 | 61.7 | 71.0 | 69.8 |
| Consumer Prices............................ | 64 | 64.6 | 69.2 | 73.8 | 80.6 | 87.7 | 92.5 | 100.0 | † 110.7 | 117.6 | 126.4 | 135.3 | 143.7 |
| Industrial Production...................... | 66 | 60.6 | 68.6 | 74.4 | 78.5 | 85.8 | 91.2 | † 100.0 | 115.0 | 127.6 | 139.7 | .... | .... |
| | | | | | | | *Number in Thousands: Period Averages* | | | | | | |
| Labor Force................................... | 67d | .... | .... | 49,500 | .... | .... | .... | .... | .... | .... | .... | .... | .... |
| Employment.................................. | 67e | .... | .... | 47,357 | .... | .... | .... | .... | .... | .... | .... | .... | .... |
| Unemployment.............................. | 67c | .... | .... | 2,100 | .... | .... | .... | .... | .... | .... | .... | .... | .... |
| Unemployment Rate....................... | 67r | .... | .... | 4.2 | .... | .... | .... | .... | .... | .... | .... | .... | .... |
| **Intl. Transactions & Positions** | | | | | | | *Millions of Taka* | | | | | | |
| Exports........................................ | 70 | 393,862 | 465,466 | 627,999 | 704,728 | 807,824 | 859,045 | 989,345 | 1,468,337 | 2,268,000 | 1,749,090 | .... | .... |
| Imports, c.i.f................................. | 71 | 750,513 | 828,667 | 1,032,514 | 1,188,832 | 1,541,411 | 1,424,359 | 1,817,435 | 2,519,295 | 3,144,270 | 2,379,400 | .... | .... |
| Imports, f.o.b................................. | 71.v | 676,138 | 746,547 | 930,193 | 1,071,020 | 1,388,659 | 1,283,206 | 1,637,329 | 2,269,635 | .... | .... | .... | .... |

## Balance of Payments

| | | 2004 | 2005 | 2006 | 2007 | 2008 | 2009 | 2010 | 2011 | 2012 | 2013 | 2014 | 2015 |
|---|---|---|---|---|---|---|---|---|---|---|---|---|---|
| | | | | | | | *Millions of US Dollars* | | | | | | |
| A. Current Account* | 109bx | −278.7 | †507.7 | 1,196.1 | 856.8 | 926.2 | 3,556.1 | 2,108.5 | −161.8 | 2,575.5 | 2,058.5 | 755.8 | 2,686.9 |
| Goods, credit (exports) | 1a9cx | 7,977.8 | †9,732.4 | 11,233.8 | 12,137.7 | 15,298.3 | 15,051.7 | 19,209.4 | 24,537.2 | 24,904.2 | 28,638.2 | 29,924.5 | 31,735.7 |
| Goods, debit (imports) | 1a9dx | 11,021.3 | †12,758.1 | 14,245.7 | 16,469.8 | 21,411.1 | 19,677.7 | 25,081.6 | 32,607.4 | 32,170.7 | 35,000.6 | 37,406.4 | 37,626.8 |
| Balance on goods | 1a9bx | −3,043.4 | †−3,025.7 | −3,011.9 | −4,332.1 | −6,112.7 | −4,626.0 | −5,872.2 | −8,070.2 | −7,266.5 | −6,362.4 | −7,481.9 | −5,891.1 |
| Services, credit (exports) | 1b9cx | 1,139.6 | †1,454.7 | 1,653.7 | 1,952.6 | 2,196.7 | 1,995.7 | 2,445.1 | 2,452.9 | 2,686.9 | 2,997.0 | 3,132.7 | 3,116.6 |
| Services, debit (imports) | 1b9dx | 1,951.0 | †2,297.3 | 2,538.2 | 3,083.4 | 3,756.7 | 3,395.0 | 4,389.2 | 5,270.7 | 5,578.3 | 6,567.8 | 7,770.2 | 7,699.5 |
| Balance on Goods & Services | 1z9bx | −3,854.9 | †−3,868.3 | −3,896.3 | −5,462.9 | −7,672.6 | −6,025.3 | −7,816.3 | −10,888.0 | −10,157.9 | −9,933.2 | −12,119.4 | −10,474.0 |
| Primary income: credit | 1c9cx | 102.6 | †135.2 | 177.4 | 244.1 | 192.3 | 35.2 | 109.6 | 157.8 | 177.0 | 132.3 | 81.0 | 76.9 |
| Primary income: debit | 1c9dx | 473.9 | †914.2 | 1,018.1 | 1,212.0 | 1,211.2 | 1,434.6 | 1,564.1 | 1,674.6 | 1,991.5 | 2,640.0 | 2,808.4 | 2,786.8 |
| Balance on gds, serv. & prim. inc. | 1y9bx | −4,226.2 | †−4,647.4 | −4,737.0 | −6,430.9 | −8,691.6 | −7,424.6 | −9,270.8 | −12,404.8 | −11,972.4 | −12,440.9 | −14,846.8 | −13,183.9 |
| Secondary income: credit | 1d9ca | 3,960.4 | †5,166.1 | 5,941.3 | 7,297.4 | 9,768.0 | 11,246.7 | 11,740.6 | 12,727.2 | 14,791.5 | 14,552.0 | 15,680.0 | 15,958.3 |
| Secondary income: debit | 1d9da | 12.9 | †11.0 | 8.2 | 9.8 | 150.3 | 265.9 | 361.3 | 484.3 | 243.6 | 52.6 | 77.4 | 87.5 |
| B. Capital Account* | 209ba | 142.1 | †263.3 | 152.5 | 715.4 | 490.5 | 474.9 | 603.4 | 512.4 | 500.3 | 725.5 | 496.6 | 418.3 |
| Capital account: credit | 209ca | 142.1 | †263.3 | 152.5 | 715.4 | 490.5 | 474.9 | 603.4 | 512.4 | 500.3 | 725.5 | 496.6 | 418.3 |
| Capital account: debit | 209da | — | .... | .... | .... | .... | .... | .... | .... | .... | .... | .... | .... |
| Balance on current & capital acct. | 129bx | −136.6 | †771.1 | 1,348.6 | 1,572.2 | 1,416.6 | 4,031.1 | 2,711.9 | 350.6 | 3,075.8 | 2,783.9 | 1,252.4 | 3,105.2 |
| C. Financial Account* | 309na | −665.0 | †206.2 | −1,322.4 | −1,295.5 | −3,131.5 | −2,540.6 | −2,764.5 | −368.3 | −2,698.6 | −4,324.7 | −4,413.1 | −3,231.1 |
| Direct investment: assets | 3a9aa | 4.1 | †2.0 | 3.6 | 134.3 | 190.7 | 180.8 | 66.4 | 297.4 | 289.1 | 546.9 | 41.8 | 49.8 |
| Equity & investment fund shares | 3aaaa | 4.1 | †2.0 | 3.6 | 21.0 | 8.7 | 13.0 | 14.0 | 12.9 | 43.1 | 26.7 | 41.5 | 28.3 |
| Debt instruments | 3abaa | — | .... | .... | 113.3 | 182.0 | 167.8 | 52.4 | 284.6 | 246.0 | 520.2 | .3 | 21.5 |
| Direct investment: liabilities | 3a9la | 448.9 | †760.5 | 456.5 | 651.0 | 1,328.4 | 901.3 | 1,232.3 | 1,264.7 | 1,584.4 | 2,603.0 | 2,539.2 | 3,380.3 |
| Equity & investment fund shares | 3aala | 352.2 | †625.6 | 424.7 | 449.6 | 1,054.9 | 583.5 | 884.6 | 921.5 | 1,084.9 | 1,935.4 | 2,257.0 | 2,986.3 |
| Debt instruments | 3abla | 96.7 | †134.9 | 31.8 | 201.4 | 273.6 | 317.8 | 347.7 | 343.2 | 499.5 | 667.6 | 282.2 | 394.0 |
| Portfolio investment: assets | 3b9aa | — | †.1 | 116.1 | −38.4 | 18.3 | −93.4 | 419.8 | 1,147.3 | 169.2 | 304.7 | −93.1 | 85.5 |
| Equity & investment fund shares | 3baaa | — | †.1 | .... | .... | 4.3 | .... | .... | .... | .... | 12.8 | 34.4 | −22.4 |
| Debt securities | 3bbaa | — | .... | 116.1 | −38.4 | 14.0 | −93.4 | 419.8 | 1,147.3 | 169.2 | 291.9 | −127.5 | 107.9 |
| Portfolio investment: liabilities | 3b9la | 4.3 | †20.0 | −399.5 | 92.3 | 92.2 | 127.0 | 18.6 | −32.4 | 168.6 | 431.2 | 874.8 | 385.9 |
| Equity & investment fund shares | 3bala | 4.3 | †20.0 | .... | .... | .... | .... | −53.9 | 50.2 | 133.6 | 261.9 | 357.7 | −117.6 |
| Debt securities | 3bbla | — | .... | −399.5 | 92.3 | 92.2 | 127.0 | 72.6 | −82.6 | 35.0 | 169.4 | 517.0 | 503.5 |
| Fin. der.& empl.stk.ops.(ESOs): net. | 3c9na | .... | .... | .... | .... | .... | .... | .... | .... | .... | .... | .... | .... |
| Fin. der. & ESOs.: assets | 3c9aa | .... | .... | .... | .... | .... | .... | .... | .... | .... | .... | .... | .... |
| Fin. der. & ESOs.: liabilities | 3c9la | .... | .... | .... | .... | .... | .... | .... | .... | .... | .... | .... | .... |
| Other investment: assets | 3d9aa | 495.1 | †1,072.2 | 88.1 | 15.8 | −5.9 | 95.6 | 424.9 | 266.6 | 486.6 | 287.3 | 213.0 | 790.3 |
| Other equity | 3daaa | .... | .... | .... | .... | .... | .... | .... | .... | .... | .... | .... | .... |
| Debt instruments | 3dzaa | 495.1 | †1,072.2 | 88.1 | 15.8 | −5.9 | 95.6 | 424.9 | 266.6 | 486.6 | 287.3 | 213.0 | 790.3 |
| Other investment: liabilities | 3d9la | 711.0 | †87.5 | 1,473.2 | 663.8 | 1,914.0 | 1,695.3 | 2,424.7 | 847.3 | 1,890.5 | 2,429.4 | 1,160.7 | 390.6 |
| Other equity | 3dala | .... | .... | .... | .... | .... | .... | .... | .... | .... | .... | .... | .... |
| Debt instruments | 3dzla | 711.0 | †87.5 | 1,473.2 | 663.8 | 1,914.0 | 1,695.3 | 2,424.7 | 847.3 | 1,890.5 | 2,429.4 | 1,160.7 | 390.6 |
| Curr.+ cap.– finan. acct. balance | 4y9na | 528.5 | †564.8 | 2,671.0 | 2,867.7 | 4,548.1 | 6,571.6 | 5,476.4 | 718.9 | 5,774.3 | 7,108.6 | 5,665.5 | 6,336.3 |
| D. Net Errors and Omissions | 409na | −25.0 | †−668.5 | −1,805.7 | −1,494.9 | −3,529.4 | −2,237.0 | −4,456.7 | −2,532.8 | −2,230.9 | −1,831.9 | −1,094.4 | −919.5 |
| E. Reserves and Related Items | 4z9na | 503.4 | †−103.6 | 865.3 | 1,372.8 | 1,018.8 | 4,334.6 | 1,019.7 | −1,813.9 | 3,543.4 | 5,276.8 | 4,571.0 | 5,416.8 |
| Reserve assets | 3e9aa | 649.8 | †−6.1 | 1,012.0 | 1,372.8 | 1,229.4 | 4,311.5 | 974.5 | −1,945.4 | 3,485.6 | 5,553.8 | 4,637.3 | 5,626.6 |
| Credit and loans from the IMF | 3dcla | 146.3 | †97.5 | 146.7 | — | 210.6 | −23.2 | −45.2 | −131.5 | −57.7 | 277.1 | 66.3 | 209.8 |
| Exceptional financing | 409la | — | .... | .... | .... | .... | .... | .... | .... | .... | .... | .... | .... |

*Excludes components in group E

## International Investment Position

| | | 2004 | 2005 | 2006 | 2007 | 2008 | 2009 | 2010 | 2011 | 2012 | 2013 | 2014 | 2015 |
|---|---|---|---|---|---|---|---|---|---|---|---|---|---|
| | | | | | | | *Millions of US Dollars* | | | | | | |
| Assets | 809aa | 4,142.5 | .... | 5,035.5 | 6,544.3 | 7,507.2 | 12,195.6 | 13,759.4 | 13,177.7 | 17,298.4 | 23,154.2 | 27,601.3 | 33,361.0 |
| Direct investment | 8a9aa | 136.5 | .... | 61.0 | 192.7 | 169.5 | 326.0 | 239.7 | 266.5 | 121.6 | 173.5 | 525.3 | 748.3 |
| Equity & investment fund shares | 8aaaa | 61.3 | .... | 61.0 | 65.3 | 60.3 | 74.0 | 80.5 | 88.3 | 91.0 | 113.9 | 137.8 | 149.0 |
| Debt instruments | 8abaa | 75.2 | .... | .... | 127.4 | 109.2 | 252.0 | 159.1 | 178.3 | 30.5 | 59.7 | 387.6 | 599.4 |
| Portfolio investment | 8b9aa | 26.9 | .... | 573.6 | 534.5 | 549.3 | 455.7 | 875.5 | 2,023.7 | 2,238.2 | 2,497.9 | 2,397.8 | 2,451.8 |
| Equity & investment fund shares | 8baaa | 26.9 | .... | .... | .... | .... | .... | .... | .... | .... | 12.8 | 42.6 | 20.0 |
| Debt securities | 8bbaa | .... | .... | 573.6 | 534.5 | 549.3 | 455.7 | 875.5 | 2,023.7 | 2,238.2 | 2,485.0 | 2,355.2 | 2,431.8 |
| Fin. der.(oth.than reserves) & ESOs | 8c9aa | .... | .... | .... | .... | .... | .... | .... | .... | .... | .... | .... | .... |
| Other investment | 8d9aa | 806.6 | .... | 524.0 | 539.1 | 999.7 | 1,071.3 | 1,466.0 | 1,695.3 | 2,187.5 | 2,390.8 | 2,367.5 | 2,667.7 |
| Other equity | 8daaa | .... | .... | .... | .... | .... | .... | .... | .... | .... | .... | .... | .... |
| Debt instruments | 8dzaa | 806.6 | .... | 524.0 | 539.1 | 999.7 | 1,071.3 | 1,466.0 | 1,695.3 | 2,187.5 | 2,390.8 | 2,367.5 | 2,667.7 |
| Reserve assets | 8e9aa | 3,172.4 | .... | 3,877.0 | 5,278.0 | 5,788.6 | 10,342.6 | 11,178.2 | 9,192.1 | 12,751.1 | 18,092.0 | 22,310.7 | 27,493.1 |
| Liabilities | 809la | 22,666.5 | .... | 24,740.9 | 26,058.5 | 29,275.8 | 31,112.4 | 35,745.3 | 36,480.4 | 38,555.3 | 42,370.6 | 47,315.3 | 51,009.1 |
| Direct investment | 8a9la | 2,871.9 | .... | 4,155.9 | 4,538.5 | 5,001.0 | 5,577.1 | 6,635.4 | 6,716.8 | 8,376.7 | 9,185.3 | 9,962.5 | 12,891.5 |
| Equity & investment fund shares | 8aala | 2,573.0 | .... | 3,957.8 | 4,177.3 | 4,566.4 | 4,900.3 | 5,729.5 | 5,613.7 | 7,065.6 | 7,315.5 | 7,859.8 | 10,584.0 |
| Debt instruments | 8abla | 299.0 | .... | 198.2 | 361.3 | 434.7 | 676.8 | 905.9 | 1,103.1 | 1,311.1 | 1,869.8 | 2,102.7 | 2,307.5 |
| Portfolio investment | 8b9la | 87.2 | .... | 459.1 | 550.7 | 643.8 | 770.6 | 1,838.5 | 1,513.8 | 1,839.7 | 2,319.7 | 3,923.9 | 3,992.2 |
| Equity & investment fund shares | 8bala | 85.3 | .... | .... | .... | .... | .... | 995.4 | 753.3 | 1,027.8 | 1,354.8 | 2,485.9 | 2,582.3 |
| Debt securities | 8bbla | 1.9 | .... | 459.1 | 550.7 | 643.8 | 770.6 | 843.1 | 760.5 | 811.9 | 964.9 | 1,437.9 | 1,409.9 |
| Fin. der.(oth.than reserves) & ESOs | 8c9la | .... | .... | .... | .... | .... | .... | .... | .... | .... | .... | .... | .... |
| Other investment | 8d9la | 19,707.4 | .... | 20,125.8 | 20,969.2 | 23,631.0 | 24,764.7 | 27,271.5 | 28,249.8 | 28,338.9 | 30,865.6 | 33,428.9 | 34,125.4 |
| Other equity | 8dala | .... | .... | .... | .... | .... | .... | .... | .... | .... | .... | .... | .... |
| Debt instruments | 8dzla | 19,707.4 | .... | 20,125.8 | 20,969.2 | 23,631.0 | 24,764.7 | 27,271.5 | 28,249.8 | 28,338.9 | 30,865.6 | 33,428.9 | 34,125.4 |

# Bangladesh 513

|  |  | 2004 | 2005 | 2006 | 2007 | 2008 | 2009 | 2010 | 2011 | 2012 | 2013 | 2014 | 2015 |
|---|---|---|---|---|---|---|---|---|---|---|---|---|---|
| **Government Finance** | | | | | | | | | | | | | |
| **Cash Flow Statement** | | | | | | | | | | | | | |
| **Central Government** | | | | | | *Billions of Taka: Fiscal Year Ends June 30* | | | | | | | |
| Cash Receipts:Operating Activities... | c1 | 347.30 | 399.99 | 438.78 | 500.20 | 622.51 | 697.38 | 809.38 | 982.69 | 1,211.97 | 1,399.63 | .... | .... |
| Taxes.............................. | c11 | 270.09 | 304.75 | 339.72 | 380.31 | 481.32 | 528.67 | 624.85 | 795.48 | 952.28 | 1,074.52 | .... | .... |
| Social Contributions..................... | c12 | — | — | — | — | — | — | — | — | — | — | .... | .... |
| Grants............................ | c13 | 15.49 | 17.81 | 15.37 | 15.78 | 24.45 | 17.48 | 32.27 | 24.50 | 35.92 | 68.79 | .... | .... |
| Other Receipts........................ | c14 | 61.72 | 77.44 | 83.69 | 104.10 | 116.74 | 151.23 | 152.26 | 162.71 | 223.78 | 256.32 | .... | .... |
| Cash Payments:Operating Activities. | c2 | 291.49 | 347.75 | 402.02 | 476.28 | 592.77 | 696.02 | 739.02 | 901.49 | 992.16 | 1,124.40 | .... | .... |
| Compensation of Employees.......... | c21 | 74.31 | 80.73 | 95.70 | 118.30 | 122.16 | 131.68 | 157.14 | 196.28 | 207.22 | 218.81 | .... | .... |
| Purchases of Goods & Services....... | c22 | 49.30 | 58.66 | 58.49 | 61.69 | 73.65 | 86.55 | 99.59 | 116.39 | 102.39 | 151.39 | .... | .... |
| Interest............................ | c24 | 56.86 | 67.58 | 83.74 | 103.52 | 135.77 | 151.53 | 148.16 | 155.88 | 202.94 | 239.16 | .... | .... |
| Subsidies.......................... | c25 | 8.88 | 15.33 | 12.28 | 24.61 | 52.01 | 67.32 | 65.21 | 76.18 | 98.95 | 144.17 | .... | .... |
| Grants............................ | c26 | 48.83 | 58.55 | 61.86 | 68.22 | 74.97 | 92.09 | 119.80 | 158.70 | 169.50 | 173.46 | .... | .... |
| Social Benefits...................... | c27 | 28.14 | 32.58 | 42.63 | 46.81 | 59.57 | 83.30 | 80.87 | 75.21 | 93.52 | 99.79 | .... | .... |
| Other Payments.................... | c28 | 25.16 | 34.34 | 47.32 | 53.13 | 74.64 | 83.54 | 68.24 | 122.86 | 117.66 | 97.63 | .... | .... |
| Net Cash Inflow:Operating Act.[1-2] | ccio | 55.81 | 52.24 | 36.76 | 23.92 | 29.74 | 1.37 | 70.36 | 81.20 | 219.81 | 275.23 | .... | .... |
| Net Cash Outflow:Invest. in NFA...... | c31 | 80.00 | 93.70 | 96.61 | 86.88 | 81.90 | 103.12 | 135.25 | 155.00 | 189.03 | 266.12 | .... | .... |
| Purchases of Nonfinancial Assets... | c31.1 | 80.33 | 94.32 | 97.11 | 87.59 | 82.15 | 103.10 | 135.20 | 155.00 | .... | .... | .... | .... |
| Sales of Nonfinancial Assets.......... | c31.2 | .33 | .62 | .50 | .71 | .25 | — | — | — | .... | .... | .... | .... |
| Cash Surplus/Deficit [1-2-31=1-2M] | ccsd | −24.19 | −41.46 | −59.85 | −62.96 | −52.17 | −101.80 | −64.90 | −73.80 | 30.78 | 9.11 | .... | .... |
| Net Acq. Fin. Assets, excl. Cash....... | c32x | 31.98 | 22.13 | 25.66 | 22.20 | 173.36 | 53.17 | 80.66 | 180.76 | .... | .... | .... | .... |
| Domestic............................ | c321x | 31.98 | 22.13 | 25.66 | 22.20 | 173.36 | 53.17 | 80.66 | 180.76 | .... | .... | .... | .... |
| Foreign............................ | c322x | | | | | | | | | .... | .... | .... | .... |
| Net Incurrence of Liabilities............. | c33 | 105.98 | 127.56 | 154.11 | 138.86 | 288.00 | 215.05 | 223.87 | 328.36 | 341.85 | 390.04 | .... | .... |
| Domestic............................ | c331 | 76.92 | 93.52 | 115.76 | 115.11 | 225.87 | 192.68 | 163.51 | 302.05 | 305.60 | 331.93 | .... | .... |
| Foreign............................ | c332 | 29.06 | 34.04 | 38.35 | 23.75 | 62.13 | 22.37 | 60.36 | 26.31 | 36.25 | 58.12 | .... | .... |
| Net Cash Inflow, Fin.Act.[-32x+33].. | cnfb | 74.00 | 105.43 | 128.44 | 116.66 | 114.64 | 161.89 | 143.21 | 147.60 | 83.58 | 65.25 | .... | .... |
| Net Change in Stock of Cash.......... | cncb | 49.81 | 63.97 | 68.60 | 53.70 | 62.48 | 63.07 | 78.31 | 73.80 | 114.36 | 74.37 | .... | .... |
| Stat. Discrep. [32X-33+NCB-CSD].... | ccsdz | — | — | — | — | — | .05 | — | — | — | — | .... | .... |
| Memo Item:Cash Expenditure[2+31] | c2m | 371.49 | 441.45 | 498.63 | 563.16 | 674.67 | 799.14 | 874.27 | 1,056.49 | 1,181.19 | 1,390.52 | .... | .... |
| Memo Item: Gross Debt.................. | c63 | .... | .... | .... | .... | .... | .... | .... | .... | .... | .... | .... | .... |
| **National Accounts** | | | | | | *Billions of Taka: Fiscal Year Ends June 30* | | | | | | | |
| Househ.Cons.Expend.,incl.NPISHs.... | 96f | 2,495.2 | 2,759.8 | 3,527.0 | 4,062.6 | 4,754.9 | 5,258.0 | 5,910.9 | 6,802.8 | 7,780.7 | 8,733.9 | 9,751.4 | 10,980.1 |
| Government Consumption Expend... | 91f | 184.1 | 205.3 | 262.4 | 294.7 | 325.5 | 359.1 | 404.8 | 466.8 | 531.8 | 613.4 | 717.2 | 819.2 |
| Gross Fixed Capital Formation......... | 93e | 799.9 | 909.2 | 1,261.0 | 1,439.3 | 1,647.3 | 1,847.7 | 2,093.3 | 2,511.3 | 2,982.3 | 3,403.7 | 3,839.9 | 4,378.7 |
| Changes in Inventories................... | 93i | | | | | | | | | | | | |
| Exports of Goods and Services......... | 90c | 514.9 | 614.7 | 788.8 | 934.4 | 1,110.2 | 1,194.4 | 1,278.0 | 1,824.5 | 2,127.5 | 2,342.4 | 2,551.6 | 2,627.9 |
| Imports of Goods and Services (-)..... | 98c | 693.0 | 854.3 | 1,049.5 | 1,261.6 | 1,569.3 | 1,632.4 | 1,736.9 | 2,518.4 | 2,949.2 | 3,208.1 | 3,429.7 | 3,751.5 |
| Gross Domestic Product (GDP)........ | 99b | 3,329.7 | 3,707.1 | 4,823.4 | 5,498.0 | 6,286.8 | 7,050.7 | 7,975.4 | 9,087.1 | 10,552.0 | 11,989.2 | 13,436.7 | 15,158.0 |
| Net Primary Income from Abroad..... | 98.n | 175.5 | 189.3 | 272.1 | 352.8 | 483.9 | 559.0 | 646.0 | 725.1 | 893.0 | 964.3 | 895.5 | 984.0 |
| Gross National Income (GNI)........... | 99a | 3,505.3 | 3,896.4 | 5,095.4 | 5,850.8 | 6,770.7 | 7,609.7 | 8,621.4 | 9,883.4 | 11,445.1 | 12,953.5 | 14,332.2 | 16,142.0 |
| Consumption of Fixed Capital.......... | 99cf | 262.6 | 290.8 | 420.9 | 479.1 | 546.6 | 615.7 | 692.7 | 789.2 | 905.7 | 1,036.7 | .... | .... |
| GDP Volume 1995/96 Prices............ | 99b.p | 2,519.7 | 2,669.7 | 2,846.7 | 3,029.7 | 3,217.3 | 3,402.0 | 3,608.4 | 3,850.5 | 4,090.5 | 4,337.2 | .... | .... |
| GDP Volume 2005/2006 Prices........ | 99b.p | .... | .... | 4,823.4 | 5,163.8 | 5,474.4 | 5,750.6 | 6,071.0 | 6,463.4 | 6,884.9 | 7,299.0 | 7,741.4 | 8,248.6 |
| GDP Volume (2010=100)............... | 99bvp | 70.3 | 74.5 | † 79.4 | 85.1 | 90.2 | 94.7 | 100.0 | 106.5 | 113.4 | 120.2 | 127.5 | 135.9 |
| GDP Deflator (2010=100)............... | 99bip | 59.4 | 62.4 | 76.1 | 81.0 | 87.4 | 93.3 | 100.0 | 107.0 | 116.7 | 125.0 | 132.1 | 139.9 |
| | | | | | | *Millions: Midyear Estimates* | | | | | | | |
| Population................................ | 99z | 140.84 | 142.93 | 144.84 | 146.59 | 148.25 | 149.91 | 151.62 | 153.41 | 155.26 | 157.16 | 159.08 | 161.00 |

# Barbados 316

| | | 2004 | 2005 | 2006 | 2007 | 2008 | 2009 | 2010 | 2011 | 2012 | 2013 | 2014 | 2015 |
|---|---|---|---|---|---|---|---|---|---|---|---|---|---|
| **Exchange Rates** | | | | | | *Barbados Dollars per SDR: End of Period* | | | | | | | |
| Official Rate.................................... | aa | 3.106 | 2.859 | 3.009 | 3.161 | 3.081 | 3.135 | 3.080 | 3.071 | 3.074 | 3.080 | 2.898 | 2.771 |
| | | | | | | *Barbados Dollars per US Dollar: End of Period (ae) Period Average (rf)* | | | | | | | |
| Official Rate.................................... | ae | 2.00 | 2.00 | 2.00 | 2.00 | 2.00 | 2.00 | 2.00 | 2.00 | 2.00 | 2.00 | 2.00 | 2.00 |
| Official Rate.................................... | rf | 2.00 | 2.00 | 2.00 | 2.00 | 2.00 | 2.00 | 2.00 | 2.00 | 2.00 | 2.00 | 2.00 | 2.00 |
| **Fund Position** | | | | | | *Millions of SDRs: End of Period* | | | | | | | |
| Quota.............................................. | 2f.s | 67.50 | 67.50 | 67.50 | 67.50 | 67.50 | 67.50 | 67.50 | 67.50 | 67.50 | 67.50 | 67.50 | 67.50 |
| SDR Holdings................................... | 1b.s | .04 | .01 | .02 | .07 | .04 | 56.35 | 56.33 | 56.31 | 56.50 | 56.49 | 56.49 | 56.48 |
| Reserve Position in the Fund........... | 1c.s | 5.15 | 5.30 | 5.45 | 5.58 | 5.64 | 5.74 | 5.81 | 5.81 | 5.81 | 5.81 | 5.81 | 5.81 |
| Total Fund Cred.&Loans Outstg....... | 2tl | — | — | — | — | — | — | — | — | — | — | — | — |
| SDR Allocations............................... | 1bd | 8.04 | 8.04 | 8.04 | 8.04 | 8.04 | 64.37 | 64.37 | 64.37 | 64.37 | 64.37 | 64.37 | 64.37 |
| **International Liquidity** | | | | | | *Millions of US Dollars Unless Otherwise Indicated: End of Period* | | | | | | | |
| Total Reserves minus Gold.............. | 1l.d | 579.86 | 603.47 | 636.09 | 839.43 | 738.53 | 871.15 | 833.54 | 812.60 | 839.72 | 680.96 | 632.26 | .... |
| SDR Holdings................................ | 1b.d | .06 | .02 | .03 | .11 | .07 | 88.33 | 86.75 | 86.44 | 86.83 | 87.00 | 81.84 | 78.27 |
| Reserve Position in the Fund.......... | 1c.d | 8.00 | 7.57 | 8.20 | 8.82 | 8.69 | 9.00 | 8.94 | 8.91 | 8.92 | 8.94 | 8.41 | 8.04 |
| Foreign Exchange........................ | 1d.d | 571.80 | 595.87 | 627.86 | 830.50 | 729.77 | 773.81 | 737.85 | 717.24 | 743.97 | 585.02 | 542.01 | .... |
| Monetary Authorities................... | 1dad | 387.02 | 416.72 | 446.66 | 622.46 | 522.59 | 563.03 | 584.40 | 585.59 | 630.30 | 515.88 | 467.25 | .... |
| Government................................ | 1dbd | 184.78 | 179.15 | 181.20 | 208.04 | 207.18 | 210.79 | 153.45 | 131.65 | 113.67 | 69.14 | 74.76 | .... |
| Gold (Million Fine Troy Ounces)........ | 1ad | — | — | — | — | — | — | — | — | — | — | — | — |
| Gold (National Valuation)............... | 1and | — | — | — | — | — | — | — | — | — | — | — | — |
| Central Bank: Other Assets........... | 3..d | 7.54 | 8.03 | † 14.97 | 8.74 | 9.40 | 8.83 | 9.01 | 9.65 | .... | .... | .... | .... |
| Central Bank: Other Liabs.............. | 4..d | .57 | .37 | † .31 | .62 | .51 | .09 | .13 | .11 | .... | .... | .... | .... |
| Other Depository Corps.: Assets....... | 7a.d | 649.11 | 796.39 | † 863.00 | 1,471.80 | 1,329.31 | 896.63 | .... | .... | .... | .... | .... | .... |
| Other Depository Corps.: Liabs......... | 7b.d | 176.92 | 255.60 | † 398.97 | 545.51 | 880.96 | 475.46 | .... | .... | .... | .... | .... | .... |
| **Central Bank** | | | | | | *Millions of Barbados Dollars: End of Period* | | | | | | | |
| Net Foreign Assets......................... | 11n | 764.0 | 824.7 | † 893.6 | 1,235.9 | 1,036.8 | 948.5 | 971.4 | 982.9 | .... | .... | .... | .... |
| Claims on Nonresidents................. | 11 | 790.1 | 848.4 | † 918.4 | 1,262.6 | 1,062.5 | 1,150.5 | 1,169.9 | 1,180.8 | .... | .... | .... | .... |
| Liabilities to Nonresidents.............. | 16c | 26.1 | 23.7 | † 24.8 | 26.6 | 25.8 | 202.0 | 198.5 | 197.9 | .... | .... | .... | .... |
| Claims on Other Depository Corps.... | 12e | — | — | † 4.5 | 3.7 | 7.2 | 5.3 | 3.0 | 2.1 | .... | .... | .... | .... |
| Net Claims on Central Government.. | 12an | −21.9 | −99.0 | † −10.5 | 10.6 | 245.7 | 276.1 | −11.0 | 159.9 | .... | .... | .... | .... |
| Claims on Central Government....... | 12a | 52.7 | 199.2 | † 134.0 | 123.0 | 312.3 | 375.4 | 324.3 | 500.0 | .... | .... | .... | .... |
| Liabilities to Central Government... | 16d | 74.6 | 298.2 | † 144.5 | 112.4 | 66.6 | 99.2 | 335.4 | 340.2 | .... | .... | .... | .... |
| Claims on Other Sectors................. | 12s | 37.2 | 34.3 | † 30.0 | 27.2 | 33.1 | 39.3 | 37.2 | 32.7 | .... | .... | .... | .... |
| Claims on Other Financial Corps.... | 12g | 9.0 | 9.0 | † 9.0 | 9.0 | 9.0 | 16.7 | 14.2 | 9.0 | .... | .... | .... | .... |
| Claims on State & Local Govts....... | 12b | — | — | † — | — | — | — | — | — | .... | .... | .... | ····×$؟ |
| Claims on Public Nonfin. Corps...... | 12c | — | — | † — | — | — | — | — | — | .... | .... | .... | .... |
| Claims on Private Sector............... | 12d | 28.2 | 25.3 | † 21.0 | 18.2 | 24.1 | 22.6 | 22.9 | 23.7 | .... | .... | .... | .... |
| Monetary Base............................. | 14 | 773.8 | 779.3 | † 932.6 | 1,273.8 | 1,293.6 | 1,220.3 | 1,031.9 | 1,200.0 | .... | .... | .... | .... |
| Currency in Circulation................. | 14a | 513.3 | 575.9 | † 596.1 | 635.2 | 622.4 | 629.0 | 648.8 | 650.2 | .... | .... | .... | .... |
| Liabs. to Other Depository Corps.... | 14c | 258.3 | 198.8 | † 336.3 | 633.3 | 663.1 | 591.3 | 382.8 | 549.6 | .... | .... | .... | .... |
| Liabilities to Other Sectors.............. | 14d | 2.2 | 4.6 | † .3 | 5.3 | 8.1 | — | .3 | .2 | .... | .... | .... | .... |
| Other Liabs. to Other Dep. Corps.... | 14n | — | — | † 13.3 | 15.2 | 16.4 | 18.5 | 20.4 | 22.6 | .... | .... | .... | .... |
| Dep. & Sec. Excl. f/Monetary Base... | 14o | — | — | † — | — | — | — | — | — | .... | .... | .... | .... |
| Deposits Included in Broad Money. | 15 | — | — | † — | — | — | — | — | — | .... | .... | .... | .... |
| Sec.Ot.th.Shares Incl.in Brd. Money | 16a | — | — | † — | — | — | — | — | — | .... | .... | .... | .... |
| Deposits Excl. from Broad Money... | 16b | — | — | † — | — | — | — | — | — | .... | .... | .... | .... |
| Sec.Ot.th.Shares Excl.f/Brd.Money.. | 16s | — | — | † — | — | — | — | — | — | .... | .... | .... | .... |
| Loans............................................ | 16l | — | — | † — | — | — | — | — | — | .... | .... | .... | .... |
| Financial Derivatives........................ | 16m | — | — | † — | — | — | — | — | — | .... | .... | .... | .... |
| Shares and Other Equity............... | 17a | 23.5 | 9.0 | † 14.4 | 25.5 | 23.7 | 11.9 | 23.5 | 29.5 | .... | .... | .... | .... |
| Other Items (Net)............................ | 17r | −18.0 | −28.3 | † −42.7 | −37.0 | −10.9 | 18.6 | −75.3 | −74.6 | .... | .... | .... | .... |
| Memo Item: | | | | | | | | | | | | | |
| Total Assets.................................... | 10ra | 956.6 | 1,157.0 | † 1,158.0 | 1,484.8 | 1,486.4 | 1,637.6 | 1,608.2 | 1,803.6 | .... | .... | .... | .... |
| **Other Depository Corporations** | | | | | | *Millions of Barbados Dollars: End of Period* | | | | | | | |
| Net Foreign Assets......................... | 21n | 944.4 | 1,081.6 | † 928.1 | 1,852.6 | 896.7 | 842.3 | .... | .... | .... | .... | .... | .... |
| Claims on Nonresidents................. | 21 | 1,298.2 | 1,592.8 | † 1,726.0 | 2,943.6 | 2,658.6 | 1,793.3 | .... | .... | .... | .... | .... | .... |
| Liabilities to Nonresidents.............. | 26c | 353.8 | 511.2 | † 797.9 | 1,091.0 | 1,761.9 | 950.9 | .... | .... | .... | .... | .... | .... |
| Claims on Central Bank.................. | 20 | 371.0 | 303.9 | † 455.5 | 765.5 | 701.3 | 720.0 | .... | .... | .... | .... | .... | .... |
| Currency..................................... | 20a | 114.3 | 126.8 | † 130.2 | 142.6 | 141.4 | 135.0 | .... | .... | .... | .... | .... | .... |
| Reserve Deposits and Securities..... | 20b | 256.7 | 177.1 | † 325.2 | 622.9 | 560.0 | 585.0 | .... | .... | .... | .... | .... | .... |
| Other Claims............................... | 20n | — | — | † — | — | — | — | .... | .... | .... | .... | .... | .... |
| Net Claims on Central Government.. | 22an | 1,126.8 | 1,042.5 | † 829.2 | 930.0 | 942.0 | 1,098.3 | .... | .... | .... | .... | .... | .... |
| Claims on Central Government...... | 22a | 1,312.3 | 1,199.0 | † 948.0 | 1,112.8 | 1,151.1 | 1,270.1 | .... | .... | .... | .... | .... | .... |
| Liabilities to Central Government... | 26d | 185.5 | 156.5 | † 118.7 | 182.8 | 209.2 | 171.9 | .... | .... | .... | .... | .... | .... |
| Claims on Other Sectors................. | 22s | 5,139.7 | 6,210.1 | † 6,956.9 | 7,477.5 | 8,159.7 | 8,390.0 | .... | .... | .... | .... | .... | .... |
| Claims on Other Financial Corps.... | 22g | 112.1 | 151.4 | † 161.2 | 227.3 | 294.6 | 403.7 | .... | .... | .... | .... | .... | .... |
| Claims on State & Local Govts....... | 22b | — | — | † — | — | — | — | .... | .... | .... | .... | .... | .... |
| Claims on Public Nonfin. Corps...... | 22c | 421.7 | 525.6 | † 601.8 | 599.9 | 644.8 | 608.2 | .... | .... | .... | .... | .... | .... |
| Claims on Private Sector............... | 22d | 4,605.9 | 5,533.2 | † 6,193.9 | 6,650.4 | 7,220.3 | 7,378.1 | .... | .... | .... | .... | .... | .... |
| Liabilities to Central Bank............... | 26g | 26.5 | 26.2 | † 29.6 | 74.0 | 37.3 | 44.6 | .... | .... | .... | .... | .... | .... |
| Transf.Dep.Included in Broad Money | 24 | 2,363.2 | 2,622.8 | † 2,604.6 | 3,220.6 | 3,015.9 | 3,098.2 | .... | .... | .... | .... | .... | .... |
| Other Dep.Included in Broad Money. | 25 | 4,463.5 | 5,371.9 | † 5,829.3 | 7,042.7 | 7,380.4 | 7,355.6 | .... | .... | .... | .... | .... | .... |
| Sec.Ot.th.Shares Incl.in Brd. Money.. | 26a | — | — | † — | — | — | — | .... | .... | .... | .... | .... | .... |
| Deposits Excl. from Broad Money..... | 26b | — | — | † — | — | — | — | .... | .... | .... | .... | .... | .... |
| Sec.Ot.th.Shares Excl.f/Brd.Money.... | 26s | — | — | † — | — | — | — | .... | .... | .... | .... | .... | .... |
| Loans............................................ | 26l | — | — | † — | — | — | — | .... | .... | .... | .... | .... | .... |
| Financial Derivatives........................ | 26m | — | — | † — | — | — | — | .... | .... | .... | .... | .... | .... |
| Insurance Technical Reserves.......... | 26r | — | — | † — | — | — | — | .... | .... | .... | .... | .... | .... |
| Shares and Other Equity.................. | 27a | 1,249.7 | 1,352.7 | † 1,464.9 | 1,572.5 | 1,352.6 | 1,426.8 | .... | .... | .... | .... | .... | .... |
| Other Items (Net)............................ | 27r | −521.1 | −735.6 | † −758.8 | −884.2 | −1,086.4 | −874.5 | .... | .... | .... | .... | .... | .... |
| Memo Item: | | | | | | | | | | | | | |
| Total Assets.................................... | 20ra | 9,005.0 | 10,437.3 | † 11,321.1 | 13,964.4 | 14,374.2 | 13,858.9 | .... | .... | .... | .... | .... | .... |

| | | 2004 | 2005 | 2006 | 2007 | 2008 | 2009 | 2010 | 2011 | 2012 | 2013 | 2014 | 2015 |
|---|---|---|---|---|---|---|---|---|---|---|---|---|---|
| **Depository Corporations** | | | | | | *Millions of Barbados Dollars: End of Period* | | | | | | | |
| Net Foreign Assets | 31n | 1,708.4 | 1,906.3 | † 1,821.6 | 3,088.5 | 1,933.5 | 1,790.9 | .... | .... | .... | .... | .... | .... |
| Claims on Nonresidents | 31 | 2,088.4 | 2,441.2 | † 2,644.4 | 4,206.2 | 3,721.2 | 2,943.8 | .... | .... | .... | .... | .... | .... |
| Liabilities to Nonresidents | 36c | 379.9 | 534.9 | † 822.7 | 1,117.7 | 1,787.7 | 1,152.9 | .... | .... | .... | .... | .... | .... |
| Domestic Claims | 32 | 6,281.7 | 7,187.9 | † 7,805.6 | 8,445.4 | 9,380.6 | 9,803.7 | .... | .... | .... | .... | .... | .... |
| Net Claims on Central Government | 32an | 1,104.9 | 943.5 | † 818.8 | 940.6 | 1,187.7 | 1,374.4 | .... | .... | .... | .... | .... | .... |
| Claims on Central Government | 32a | 1,365.0 | 1,398.2 | † 1,082.0 | 1,235.8 | 1,463.4 | 1,645.5 | .... | .... | .... | .... | .... | .... |
| Liabilities to Central Government | 36d | 260.1 | 454.7 | † 263.2 | 295.2 | 275.7 | 271.1 | .... | .... | .... | .... | .... | .... |
| Claims on Other Sectors | 32s | 5,176.9 | 6,244.4 | † 6,986.9 | 7,504.8 | 8,192.8 | 8,429.3 | .... | .... | .... | .... | .... | .... |
| Claims on Other Financial Corps. | 32g | 121.1 | 160.4 | † 170.2 | 236.3 | 303.6 | 420.4 | .... | .... | .... | .... | .... | .... |
| Claims on State & Local Govts. | 32b | — | — | † — | — | — | — | .... | .... | .... | .... | .... | .... |
| Claims on Public Nonfin. Corps. | 32c | 421.7 | 525.6 | † 601.8 | 599.9 | 644.8 | 608.2 | .... | .... | .... | .... | .... | .... |
| Claims on Private Sector | 32d | 4,634.1 | 5,558.5 | † 6,214.9 | 6,668.6 | 7,244.4 | 7,400.7 | .... | .... | .... | .... | .... | .... |
| Broad Money Liabilities | 35l | 7,228.0 | 8,448.4 | † 8,900.0 | 10,761.2 | 10,885.4 | 10,947.8 | .... | .... | .... | .... | .... | .... |
| Currency Outside Depository Corps | 34a | 399.1 | 449.1 | † 465.8 | 492.6 | 481.0 | 494.0 | .... | .... | .... | .... | .... | .... |
| Transferable Deposits | 34 | 2,363.2 | 2,622.8 | † 2,604.6 | 3,220.6 | 3,015.9 | 3,098.2 | .... | .... | .... | .... | .... | .... |
| Other Deposits | 35 | 4,465.7 | 5,376.5 | † 5,829.6 | 7,048.0 | 7,388.5 | 7,355.6 | .... | .... | .... | .... | .... | .... |
| Securities Other than Shares | 36a | — | — | † — | — | — | — | .... | .... | .... | .... | .... | .... |
| Deposits Excl. from Broad Money | 36b | — | — | † — | — | — | — | .... | .... | .... | .... | .... | .... |
| Sec.Ot.th.Shares Excl.f/Brd.Money | 36s | — | — | † — | — | — | — | .... | .... | .... | .... | .... | .... |
| Loans | 36l | — | — | † — | — | — | — | .... | .... | .... | .... | .... | .... |
| Financial Derivatives | 36m | — | — | † — | — | — | — | .... | .... | .... | .... | .... | .... |
| Insurance Technical Reserves | 36r | — | — | † — | — | — | — | .... | .... | .... | .... | .... | .... |
| Shares and Other Equity | 37a | 1,273.2 | 1,361.7 | † 1,479.3 | 1,598.0 | 1,376.2 | 1,438.7 | .... | .... | .... | .... | .... | .... |
| Other Items (Net) | 37r | −511.0 | −716.0 | † −752.0 | −825.3 | −947.6 | −791.9 | .... | .... | .... | .... | .... | .... |
| Broad Money Liabs., Seasonally Adj. | 35l.b | 7,195.2 | 8,428.5 | † 8,945.1 | 10,815.7 | 10,940.5 | 11,003.2 | .... | .... | .... | .... | .... | .... |
| **Monetary Aggregates** | | | | | | *Millions of Barbados Dollars: End of Period* | | | | | | | |
| Broad Money | 59m | .... | .... | 8,900.0 | 10,761.2 | 10,885.4 | 10,947.8 | .... | .... | .... | .... | .... | .... |
| o/w:Currency Issued by Cent.Govt | 59m.a | .... | .... | — | — | — | — | .... | .... | .... | .... | .... | .... |
| o/w: Dep.in Nonfin. Corporations. | 59m.b | .... | .... | — | — | — | — | .... | .... | .... | .... | .... | .... |
| o/w: Secs. Issued by Central Govt. | 59m.c | .... | .... | — | — | — | — | .... | .... | .... | .... | .... | .... |
| Money (National Definitions) | | | | | | | | | | | | | |
| Money | 59maj | 2,863.2 | 3,187.5 | 3,157.0 | 3,802.9 | 3,672.6 | 3,739.0 | 3,559.5 | 3,136.9 | .... | .... | .... | .... |
| Quasi-Money | 59mal | 3,663.2 | 4,299.6 | 4,662.4 | 5,751.0 | 5,796.0 | 5,566.3 | 5,604.9 | 5,585.7 | .... | .... | .... | .... |
| Total Monetary Liabilities | 59met | 5,923.0 | 6,500.6 | 7,100.9 | 8,187.6 | 8,417.1 | 8,414.1 | 8,453.3 | 8,423.8 | .... | .... | .... | .... |
| **Interest Rates** | | | | | | *Percent Per Annum* | | | | | | | |
| Discount Rate (End of Period) | 60.a | 7.50 | 10.00 | 12.00 | 12.00 | 10.00 | 7.00 | 7.00 | 7.00 | 7.00 | 7.00 | 7.00 | 7.00 |
| Treasury Bill Rate | 60c | 1.20 | 4.62 | 5.96 | 5.65 | 4.20 | 3.76 | 3.30 | 3.41 | 3.50 | 3.40 | 3.20 | 2.82 |
| Savings Rate | 60k | 3.63 | 4.08 | 5.29 | 5.75 | 5.44 | 3.88 | 3.50 | 3.50 | 3.50 | 3.50 | 3.50 | 3.50 |
| Deposit Rate | 60l | 2.54 | 3.18 | 4.60 | 5.13 | 4.46 | 2.87 | 2.67 | 2.68 | 2.56 | 2.51 | 2.51 | 1.32 |
| Lending Rate | 60p | 8.33 | 9.17 | 10.29 | 10.76 | 10.03 | 9.20 | 8.70 | 8.70 | 8.70 | 8.70 | 8.38 | 8.06 |
| **Prices, Production, Labor** | | | | | | *Index Numbers (2010=100): Period Averages* | | | | | | | |
| Consumer Prices | 64 | 71.2 | 75.5 | 81.1 | 84.3 | 91.2 | 94.5 | 100.0 | 109.4 | 114.4 | 116.5 | 118.7 | 117.4 |
| Industrial Production | 66 | † 111.5 | 113.3 | 115.0 | 114.7 | 113.0 | 101.9 | 100.0 | 95.8 | 91.1 | 89.1 | .... | .... |
| | | | | | | *Number in Thousands: Period Averages* | | | | | | | |
| Labor Force | 67d | 146 | 147 | 143 | 144 | 144 | 143 | 142 | 145 | 142 | 143 | 142 | .... |
| Employment | 67e | 132 | 133 | 131 | 133 | 132 | 129 | 127 | 128 | 125 | 126 | 125 | .... |
| Unemployment | 67c | 14 | 13 | 13 | 11 | 12 | 14 | 15 | 16 | 16 | 17 | 17 | .... |
| Unemployment Rate (%) | 67r | 9.6 | 9.1 | 8.7 | 7.4 | 8.1 | 10.0 | 10.8 | 11.2 | 11.6 | 11.7 | 12.3 | .... |
| **Intl. Transactions & Positions** | | | | | | *Millions of Barbados Dollars* | | | | | | | |
| Exports | 70 | 556.5 | 718.9 | 770.0 | 837.3 | 890.9 | 737.4 | 858.0 | 929.5 | 1,139.9 | 925.5 | 948.8 | 965.8 |
| Imports, c.i.f. | 71 | 2,825.9 | 3,208.9 | 3,172.1 | 3,418.9 | 3,757.1 | 2,941.0 | 3,123.7 | 3,609.8 | 3,611.4 | 3,517.9 | 3,478.3 | 3,236.2 |

# Barbados 316

| Balance of Payments | | 2004 | 2005 | 2006 | 2007 | 2008 | 2009 | 2010 | 2011 | 2012 | 2013 | 2014 | 2015 |
|---|---|---|---|---|---|---|---|---|---|---|---|---|---|
| | | | | | | *Millions of US Dollars* | | | | | | | |
| A. Current Account* | 109bx | −413.6 | −466.6 | −358.2 | −282.3 | −482.3 | −261.1 | −236.4 | † −254.2 | −411.0 | −248.2 | .... | .... |
| Goods, credit (exports) | 1a9cx | 278.4 | 361.5 | 510.1 | 525.5 | 489.4 | 380.2 | 430.6 | † 861.9 | 851.0 | 885.4 | .... | .... |
| Goods, debit (imports) | 1a9dx | 1,260.1 | 1,515.6 | 1,602.4 | 1,699.6 | 1,811.0 | 1,366.1 | 1,506.6 | † 1,738.1 | 1,697.1 | 1,687.1 | .... | .... |
| Balance on goods | 1a9bx | −981.7 | −1,154.1 | −1,092.4 | −1,174.1 | −1,321.6 | −985.9 | −1,076.0 | † −876.1 | −846.1 | −801.7 | .... | .... |
| Services, credit (exports) | 1b9cx | 1,137.3 | 1,453.6 | 1,603.4 | 1,700.7 | 1,822.6 | 1,503.7 | 1,638.2 | † 1,292.7 | 1,252.4 | 1,434.7 | .... | .... |
| Services, debit (imports) | 1b9dx | 550.9 | 655.8 | 692.0 | 668.6 | 757.5 | 710.9 | 733.8 | † 519.6 | 505.3 | 700.6 | .... | .... |
| Balance on Goods & Services | 1z9bx | −395.3 | −356.3 | −180.9 | −142.1 | −256.5 | −193.1 | −171.5 | † −103.0 | −99.0 | −67.6 | .... | .... |
| Primary income: credit | 1c9cx | 98.2 | 119.9 | 111.1 | 198.2 | 178.5 | 376.7 | 235.0 | † 446.9 | 202.3 | 262.2 | .... | .... |
| Primary income: debit | 1c9dx | 202.1 | 294.9 | 367.4 | 388.0 | 424.5 | 463.5 | 348.1 | † 538.6 | 502.5 | 391.9 | .... | .... |
| Balance on gds, serv. & prim. inc. | 1y9bx | −499.2 | −531.3 | −437.3 | −331.8 | −502.5 | −279.9 | −284.6 | † −194.7 | −399.3 | −197.3 | .... | .... |
| Secondary income: credit | 1d9ca | 123.8 | 131.8 | 138.1 | 159.2 | 113.9 | 92.1 | 120.5 | † 128.8 | 101.6 | 91.2 | .... | .... |
| Secondary income: debit | 1d9da | 38.2 | 67.2 | 59.0 | 109.7 | 93.7 | 73.3 | 72.3 | † 188.4 | 113.3 | 142.1 | .... | .... |
| B. Capital Account* | 209ba | — | — | — | — | — | — | — | † −8.9 | −6.8 | −7.0 | .... | .... |
| Capital account: credit | 209ca | — | — | — | — | — | — | — | † — | | .2 | .... | .... |
| Capital account: debit | 209da | — | — | — | — | — | — | — | † 9.0 | 6.8 | 7.2 | .... | .... |
| Balance on current & capital acct. | 129ba | −413.6 | −466.6 | −358.2 | −282.3 | −482.3 | −261.1 | −236.4 | † −263.2 | −417.7 | −255.2 | .... | .... |
| C. Financial Account* | 309na | −221.3 | −417.9 | −202.3 | −376.8 | −386.8 | −356.6 | −256.6 | † −274.0 | −479.4 | −46.5 | .... | .... |
| Direct investment: assets | 3a9aa | 3.9 | 9.1 | 44.4 | 82.2 | −6.2 | 105.8 | 339.8 | † 304.3 | −128.0 | 54.0 | .... | .... |
| Equity & investment fund shares | 3aaaa | 2.0 | 11.2 | 10.4 | 24.8 | −13.8 | 126.5 | 389.8 | † 208.0 | 116.2 | 103.0 | .... | .... |
| Debt instruments | 3abaa | 1.9 | −2.1 | 34.0 | 57.5 | 7.5 | −20.7 | −50.0 | † 96.4 | −244.1 | −49.0 | .... | .... |
| Direct investment: liabilities | 3a9la | −12.1 | 238.3 | 342.2 | 451.7 | 462.0 | 458.2 | 668.8 | † 387.6 | 437.2 | −8.1 | .... | .... |
| Equity & investment fund shares | 3aala | −12.1 | 212.1 | 293.6 | 427.4 | 345.9 | 328.4 | 628.1 | † 206.1 | 383.0 | 60.4 | .... | .... |
| Debt instruments | 3abla | — | 26.1 | 48.6 | 24.3 | 116.1 | 129.8 | 40.8 | † 181.6 | 54.2 | −68.5 | .... | .... |
| Portfolio investment: assets | 3b9aa | 29.9 | 76.4 | −4.1 | 85.4 | 125.5 | −28.6 | −.9 | † −327.1 | 284.7 | 85.2 | .... | .... |
| Equity & investment fund shares | 3baaa | 44.7 | 53.2 | 14.9 | 34.7 | 8.1 | 36.9 | 22.3 | † 14.0 | 17.0 | 55.8 | .... | .... |
| Debt securities | 3bbaa | −14.8 | 23.2 | −19.0 | 50.6 | 117.4 | −65.5 | −23.2 | † −341.1 | 267.7 | 29.4 | .... | .... |
| Portfolio investment: liabilities | 3b9la | −12.5 | 108.9 | 51.3 | 33.8 | 2.8 | 98.3 | 97.6 | † 108.7 | −15.1 | 106.1 | .... | .... |
| Equity & investment fund shares | 3bala | — | −4.8 | 1.6 | 52.5 | 20.1 | −8.7 | −4.1 | † .8 | −2.2 | −1.0 | .... | .... |
| Debt securities | 3bbla | −12.5 | 113.7 | 49.7 | −18.7 | −17.3 | 107.0 | 101.7 | † 107.9 | −13.0 | 107.1 | .... | .... |
| Fin. der.& empl.stk.ops.(ESOs): net. | 3c9na | .... | 3.4 | — | .1 | .6 | −.5 | −4.9 | † — | | −.5 | .... | .... |
| Fin. der. & ESOs: assets | 3c9aa | .... | −1.6 | — | — | — | −.5 | −4.9 | † — | −.2 | −.6 | .... | .... |
| Fin. der. & ESOs: liabilities | 3c9la | .... | −5.0 | — | −.1 | −.6 | — | — | † — | −.1 | −.1 | .... | .... |
| Other investment: assets | 3d9aa | −31.3 | 297.5 | 492.1 | 962.8 | 261.4 | −271.8 | 8.6 | † 44.4 | −71.0 | 31.9 | .... | .... |
| Other equity | 3daaa | .... | .... | .... | .... | .... | .... | .... | | .... | .... | .... | .... |
| Debt instruments | 3dzaa | −31.3 | 297.5 | 492.1 | 962.8 | 261.4 | −271.8 | 8.6 | † 44.4 | −71.0 | 31.9 | .... | .... |
| Other investment: liabilities | 3d9la | 248.4 | 457.1 | 341.2 | 1,021.7 | 303.1 | −395.1 | −167.2 | † −200.7 | 143.1 | 119.1 | .... | .... |
| Other equity | 3dala | .... | .... | .... | .... | .... | .... | .... | | .... | .... | .... | .... |
| Debt instruments | 3dzla | 248.4 | 457.1 | 341.2 | 1,021.7 | 303.1 | −395.1 | −167.2 | † −200.7 | 143.1 | 119.1 | .... | .... |
| Curr.+ cap.− finan. acct. balance | 4y9na | −192.3 | −48.7 | −156.0 | 94.5 | −95.5 | 95.5 | 20.2 | † 10.8 | 61.6 | −208.7 | .... | .... |
| D. Net Errors and Omissions | 409na | 26.2 | 70.6 | 131.1 | 75.2 | −7.2 | −28.9 | −65.5 | † −23.5 | −33.6 | 52.6 | .... | .... |
| E. Reserves and Related Items | 4z9na | −166.1 | 21.9 | −24.8 | 169.7 | −102.7 | 66.5 | −45.3 | † −12.7 | 28.0 | −156.1 | .... | .... |
| Reserve assets | 3e9aa | −165.6 | 22.7 | −21.0 | 176.3 | −96.0 | 68.0 | −27.3 | † −12.7 | 28.0 | −156.1 | .... | .... |
| Credit and loans from the IMF | 3dcla | — | — | — | — | — | — | — | † — | — | — | .... | .... |
| Exceptional financing | 409la | .6 | .8 | 3.8 | 6.6 | 6.6 | 1.5 | 18.0 | † — | — | — | .... | .... |

*Excludes components in group E

| International Investment Position | | | | | | | | | | | | | |
|---|---|---|---|---|---|---|---|---|---|---|---|---|---|
| | | | | | | *Millions of US Dollars* | | | | | | | |
| Assets | 809aa | .... | .... | .... | .... | 32,742.0 | 31,088.7 | † 6,154.7 | 6,150.3 | 6,231.1 | 6,233.4 | .... | .... |
| Direct investment | 8a9aa | .... | .... | .... | .... | 3,784.6 | 4,018.9 | † 3,764.3 | 4,026.0 | 3,884.2 | 3,927.2 | .... | .... |
| Equity & investment fund shares | 8aaaa | .... | .... | .... | .... | 3,633.0 | 3,812.3 | † 2,229.1 | 2,396.6 | 2,510.4 | 2,612.0 | .... | .... |
| Debt instruments | 8abaa | .... | .... | .... | .... | 151.6 | 206.7 | † 1,535.2 | 1,629.4 | 1,373.8 | 1,315.3 | .... | .... |
| Portfolio investment | 8b9aa | .... | .... | .... | .... | 19,873.7 | 18,368.5 | † 989.4 | 662.7 | 958.1 | 1,041.2 | .... | .... |
| Equity & investment fund shares | 8baaa | .... | .... | .... | .... | 1,910.9 | 2,792.2 | † 344.8 | 363.2 | 389.2 | 449.8 | .... | .... |
| Debt securities | 8bbaa | .... | .... | .... | .... | 17,962.8 | 15,576.3 | † 644.6 | 299.5 | 568.9 | 591.3 | .... | .... |
| Fin. der.(oth.than reserves) & ESOs | 8c9aa | .... | .... | .... | .... | 165.5 | 140.4 | † .7 | .7 | .... | .6 | .... | .... |
| Other investment | 8d9aa | .... | .... | .... | .... | 8,042.9 | 7,642.3 | † 656.7 | 735.8 | 635.1 | 666.6 | .... | .... |
| Other equity | 8daaa | .... | .... | .... | .... | .... | .... | † 54.8 | 54.8 | 54.7 | 54.7 | .... | .... |
| Debt instruments | 8dzaa | .... | .... | .... | .... | 8,042.9 | 7,642.3 | † 602.0 | 681.0 | 580.4 | 611.9 | .... | .... |
| Reserve assets | 8e9aa | .... | .... | .... | .... | 875.3 | 918.5 | † 743.6 | 725.2 | 753.6 | 597.7 | .... | .... |
| Liabilities | 809la | .... | .... | .... | .... | 22,159.0 | 21,257.6 | † 7,362.5 | 7,675.5 | 8,423.9 | 8,513.0 | .... | .... |
| Direct investment | 8a9la | .... | .... | .... | .... | 2,872.4 | 2,952.1 | † 4,339.8 | 4,740.6 | 5,350.8 | 5,206.5 | .... | .... |
| Equity & investment fund shares | 8aala | .... | .... | .... | .... | 1,144.6 | 1,321.6 | † 3,595.8 | 3,815.9 | 4,368.7 | 4,291.2 | .... | .... |
| Debt instruments | 8abla | .... | .... | .... | .... | 1,727.7 | 1,630.5 | † 744.1 | 924.7 | 982.1 | 915.3 | .... | .... |
| Portfolio investment | 8b9la | .... | .... | .... | .... | 741.9 | 847.6 | † 1,250.0 | 1,358.6 | 1,344.6 | 1,455.7 | .... | .... |
| Equity & investment fund shares | 8bala | .... | .... | .... | .... | 68.0 | 60.4 | † 449.1 | 450.2 | 448.0 | 452.0 | .... | .... |
| Debt securities | 8bbla | .... | .... | .... | .... | 673.9 | 787.2 | † 801.0 | 908.4 | 896.6 | 1,003.7 | .... | .... |
| Fin. der.(oth.than reserves) & ESOs | 8c9la | .... | .... | .... | .... | .1 | .... | .... | .1 | — | .1 | .... | .... |
| Other investment | 8d9la | .... | .... | .... | .... | 18,544.6 | 17,457.9 | † 1,772.7 | 1,576.2 | 1,728.5 | 1,850.7 | .... | .... |
| Other equity | 8dala | .... | .... | .... | .... | .... | .... | .... | .... | .... | .... | .... | .... |
| Debt instruments | 8dzla | .... | .... | .... | .... | 18,544.6 | 17,457.9 | † 1,772.7 | 1,576.2 | 1,728.5 | 1,850.7 | .... | .... |

# Barbados 316

| | | 2004 | 2005 | 2006 | 2007 | 2008 | 2009 | 2010 | 2011 | 2012 | 2013 | 2014 | 2015 |
|---|---|---|---|---|---|---|---|---|---|---|---|---|---|
| **Government Finance** | | | | | | | | | | | | | |
| **Operations Statement** | | | | | | | | | | | | | |
| **Budgetary Central Government** | | | | | *Millions of Barbados Dollars: Fiscal Year Ends March 31* | | | | | | | | |
| Revenue | a1 | .... | .... | .... | 2,533.4 | 2,622.5 | 2,531.8 | 2,410.4 | 2,596.9 | 2,425.6 | 2,312.3 | .... | .... |
| Taxes | a11 | .... | .... | .... | 2,426.7 | 2,433.5 | 2,207.3 | 2,239.0 | 2,416.3 | 2,255.0 | 2,157.0 | .... | .... |
| Social Contributions | a12 | .... | .... | .... | 1.0 | .9 | .8 | .8 | .5 | .5 | .4 | .... | .... |
| Grants | a13 | .... | .... | .... | 4.0 | 7.5 | 35.6 | 2.8 | 15.9 | 33.5 | .1 | .... | .... |
| Other Revenue | a14 | .... | .... | .... | 101.6 | 180.5 | 288.2 | 167.8 | 164.2 | 136.6 | 154.8 | .... | .... |
| Expense | a2 | .... | .... | .... | 2,735.0 | 2,957.0 | 3,035.6 | 3,112.3 | 3,006.2 | 3,274.7 | 3,322.4 | .... | .... |
| Compensation of Employees | a21 | .... | .... | .... | 809.1 | 832.7 | 882.3 | 885.1 | 893.3 | 906.1 | 895.6 | .... | .... |
| Use of Goods & Services | a22 | .... | .... | .... | 367.0 | 434.5 | 444.3 | 435.3 | 459.0 | 469.3 | 438.8 | .... | .... |
| Consumption of Fixed Capital | a23 | .... | .... | .... | 26.1 | 45.5 | 50.7 | 52.7 | 52.5 | 51.8 | 52.7 | .... | .... |
| Interest | a24 | .... | .... | .... | 389.0 | 394.8 | 430.3 | 488.5 | 527.2 | 565.0 | 597.9 | .... | .... |
| Subsidies | a25 | .... | .... | .... | 825.4 | 926.3 | 856.7 | 871.9 | 709.2 | 881.8 | 927.3 | .... | .... |
| Grants | a26 | .... | .... | .... | 24.9 | 25.0 | 36.1 | 30.7 | 25.5 | 22.7 | 23.1 | .... | .... |
| Social Benefits | a27 | .... | .... | .... | 293.4 | 298.2 | 335.1 | 348.2 | 339.4 | 378.0 | 386.9 | .... | .... |
| Other Expense | a28 | .... | .... | .... | | | | | | | | .... | .... |
| Gross Operating Balance [1-2+23] | agob | .... | .... | .... | −175.5 | −289.1 | −453.1 | −649.2 | −356.7 | −797.4 | −957.4 | .... | .... |
| Net Operating Balance [1-2] | anob | .... | .... | .... | −201.6 | −334.5 | −503.8 | −701.9 | −409.3 | −849.1 | −1,010.1 | .... | .... |
| Net Acq. of Nonfinancial Assets | a31 | .... | .... | .... | 507.8 | 77.3 | 22.7 | 5.8 | −9.4 | 5.7 | 38.0 | .... | .... |
| Aquisition of Nonfin. Assets | a31.1 | .... | .... | .... | .... | .... | .... | .... | .... | .... | .... | .... | .... |
| Disposal of Nonfin. Assets | a31.2 | .... | .... | .... | .... | .... | .... | .... | .... | .... | .... | .... | .... |
| Net Lending/Borrowing [1-2-31] | anlb | .... | .... | .... | −709.4 | −411.8 | −526.4 | −707.7 | −399.8 | −854.9 | −1,048.1 | .... | .... |
| Net Acq. of Financial Assets | a32 | .... | .... | .... | 325.2 | 310.1 | 277.0 | 149.4 | 398.4 | 319.1 | 540.5 | .... | .... |
| By instrument | | | | | | | | | | | | | |
| Monetary Gold & SDRs | a3201 | .... | .... | .... | — | — | — | — | — | — | — | .... | .... |
| Currency & Deposits | a3202 | .... | .... | .... | 143.3 | 267.7 | 24.4 | 147.5 | 327.0 | −27.3 | 185.1 | .... | .... |
| Securities other than Shares | a3203 | .... | .... | .... | | | | | | | | .... | .... |
| Loans | a3204 | .... | .... | .... | 48.6 | 25.7 | 8.5 | −117.1 | .6 | 109.2 | −6.1 | .... | .... |
| Shares & Other Equity | a3205 | .... | .... | .... | 64.1 | 28.3 | −3.8 | .2 | 5.4 | 61.2 | 20.7 | .... | .... |
| Insurance Technical Reserves | a3206 | .... | .... | .... | — | — | — | — | — | — | — | .... | .... |
| Financial Derivatives | a3207 | .... | .... | .... | | | | | | | | .... | .... |
| Other Accounts Receivable | a3208 | .... | .... | .... | 69.2 | −11.6 | 247.9 | 118.8 | 65.5 | 176.1 | 340.7 | .... | .... |
| By debtor | | | | | | | | | | | | | |
| Domestic | a321 | .... | .... | .... | 325.2 | 310.1 | 277.0 | 149.4 | 398.4 | 319.1 | 540.5 | .... | .... |
| Foreign | a322 | .... | .... | .... | | | | | | | | .... | .... |
| Net Incurrence of Liabilities | a33 | .... | .... | .... | 986.4 | 654.8 | 955.0 | 917.5 | 671.9 | 1,064.6 | 876.0 | .... | .... |
| By instrument | | | | | | | | | | | | | |
| Special Drawing Rights (SDRs) | a3301 | .... | .... | .... | — | — | — | — | — | — | — | .... | .... |
| Currency & Deposits | a3302 | .... | .... | .... | 115.8 | −181.6 | −13.3 | 66.7 | 24.5 | 63.5 | 122.8 | .... | .... |
| Securities other than Shares | a3303 | .... | .... | .... | 472.7 | 528.5 | 668.8 | 510.0 | 460.7 | 1,063.5 | 756.4 | .... | .... |
| Loans | a3304 | .... | .... | .... | 393.5 | 229.5 | 330.3 | 298.0 | 224.5 | −119.0 | −.7 | .... | .... |
| Shares & Other Equity | a3305 | .... | .... | .... | — | — | — | — | — | — | — | .... | .... |
| Insurance Technical Reserves | a3306 | .... | .... | .... | — | — | — | — | — | — | — | .... | .... |
| Financial Derivatives | a3307 | .... | .... | .... | — | — | — | — | — | — | — | .... | .... |
| Other Accounts Payable | a3308 | .... | .... | .... | 4.4 | 78.5 | −30.8 | 42.7 | −37.8 | 56.7 | −2.5 | .... | .... |
| By creditor | | | | | | | | | | | | | |
| Domestic | a331 | .... | .... | .... | 667.1 | 670.3 | 580.3 | 670.4 | 480.1 | 1,183.2 | 879.2 | .... | .... |
| Foreign | a332 | .... | .... | .... | 319.3 | −15.5 | 374.8 | 247.1 | 191.8 | −118.6 | −3.2 | .... | .... |
| Stat. Discrepancy [32-33-NLB] | anlbz | .... | .... | .... | 48.2 | 67.1 | −151.6 | −60.4 | 126.4 | 109.3 | 712.5 | .... | .... |
| Memo Item: Expenditure [2+31] | a2m | .... | .... | .... | 3,242.8 | 3,034.3 | 3,058.2 | 3,118.1 | 2,996.7 | 3,280.5 | 3,360.4 | .... | .... |
| **Balance Sheet** | | | | | | | | | | | | | |
| Net Worth | a6 | .... | .... | .... | −2,134.7 | −2,129.4 | −2,778.7 | −3,373.8 | −3,732.5 | −4,553.3 | −5,061.7 | .... | .... |
| Nonfinancial Assets | a61 | .... | .... | .... | 2,275.3 | 2,711.2 | 2,769.7 | 2,942.8 | 2,942.5 | 2,953.5 | 2,996.7 | .... | .... |
| Financial Assets | a62 | .... | .... | .... | 1,837.0 | 1,965.9 | 2,210.8 | 2,356.1 | 2,663.3 | 2,891.2 | 3,211.9 | .... | .... |
| By instrument | | | | | | | | | | | | | |
| Monetary Gold & SDRs | a6201 | .... | .... | .... | | | | | | | | .... | .... |
| Currency & Deposits | a6202 | .... | .... | .... | 770.7 | 857.3 | 849.4 | 992.9 | 1,228.6 | 1,110.1 | 1,251.3 | .... | .... |
| Securities other than Shares | a6203 | .... | .... | .... | — | — | — | — | — | — | — | .... | .... |
| Loans | a6204 | .... | .... | .... | 382.7 | 408.4 | 416.9 | 299.8 | 300.4 | 409.6 | 403.5 | .... | .... |
| Shares and Other Equity | a6205 | .... | .... | .... | 200.1 | 228.4 | 224.6 | 224.7 | 230.1 | 291.3 | 312.0 | .... | .... |
| Insurance Technical Reserves | a6206 | .... | .... | .... | — | — | — | — | — | — | — | .... | .... |
| Financial Derivatives | a6207 | .... | .... | .... | — | — | — | — | — | — | — | .... | .... |
| Other Accounts Receivable | a6208 | .... | .... | .... | 483.5 | 471.9 | 719.9 | 838.7 | 904.2 | 1,080.2 | 1,245.1 | .... | .... |
| By debtor | | | | | | | | | | | | | |
| Domestic | a621 | .... | .... | .... | 1,837.0 | 1,965.9 | 2,210.8 | 2,356.1 | 2,663.3 | 2,891.2 | 3,211.9 | .... | .... |
| Foreign | a622 | .... | .... | .... | — | — | — | — | — | — | — | .... | .... |
| Liabilities | a63 | .... | .... | .... | 6,247.0 | 6,806.6 | 7,759.2 | 8,672.7 | 9,338.3 | 10,397.9 | 11,270.3 | .... | .... |
| By instrument | | | | | | | | | | | | | |
| Special Drawing Rights (SDRs) | a6301 | .... | .... | .... | | | | | | | | .... | .... |
| Currency & Deposits | a6302 | .... | .... | .... | 246.2 | 64.6 | 51.3 | 118.0 | 142.5 | 206.0 | 328.9 | .... | .... |
| Securities other than Shares | a6303 | .... | .... | .... | 3,614.4 | 4,142.9 | 4,811.7 | 5,321.7 | 5,782.4 | 6,845.9 | 7,603.5 | .... | .... |
| Loans | a6304 | .... | .... | .... | 2,377.6 | 2,511.8 | 2,839.7 | 3,133.7 | 3,351.4 | 3,227.3 | 3,221.8 | .... | .... |
| Shares and Other Equity | a6305 | .... | .... | .... | — | — | — | — | — | — | — | .... | .... |
| Insurance Technical Reserves | a6306 | .... | .... | .... | — | — | — | — | — | — | — | .... | .... |
| Financial Derivatives | a6307 | .... | .... | .... | — | — | — | — | — | — | — | .... | .... |
| Other Accounts Payable | a6308 | .... | .... | .... | 8.9 | 87.3 | 56.5 | 99.2 | 62.0 | 118.7 | 116.2 | .... | .... |
| By creditor | | | | | | | | | | | | | |
| Domestic | a631 | .... | .... | .... | 4,226.8 | 4,801.8 | 5,379.7 | 6,046.1 | 6,519.9 | 7,698.1 | 8,573.6 | .... | .... |
| Foreign | a632 | .... | .... | .... | 2,020.2 | 2,004.7 | 2,379.5 | 2,626.6 | 2,818.4 | 2,699.8 | 2,696.6 | .... | .... |
| Net Financial Worth [62-63] | a6m2 | .... | .... | .... | −4,409.9 | −4,840.6 | −5,548.5 | −6,316.6 | −6,675.0 | −7,506.8 | −8,058.4 | .... | .... |
| Memo Item: Debt at Market Value | a6m3 | .... | .... | .... | .... | .... | .... | .... | .... | .... | .... | .... | .... |
| Memo Item: Debt at Face Value | a6m35 | .... | .... | .... | .... | .... | .... | .... | .... | .... | .... | .... | .... |
| Memo Item: Debt at Nominal Value | a6m4 | .... | .... | .... | .... | .... | .... | .... | .... | .... | .... | .... | .... |

# Barbados 316

| National Accounts | | 2004 | 2005 | 2006 | 2007 | 2008 | 2009 | 2010 | 2011 | 2012 | 2013 | 2014 | 2015 |
|---|---|---|---|---|---|---|---|---|---|---|---|---|---|
| | | | | | | *Millions of Barbados Dollars* | | | | | | | |
| Househ.Cons.Expend.,incl.NPISHs.... | 96f | 4,941 | 5,617 | 6,208 | 6,236 | 6,380 | 6,207 | 6,257 | 6,655 | 6,780 | .... | .... | .... |
| Government Consumption Expend... | 91f | 1,217 | 1,276 | 1,224 | 1,518 | 1,689 | 1,791 | 1,669 | 1,763 | 1,364 | .... | .... | .... |
| Gross Fixed Capital Formation.......... | 93e | 1,325 | 1,445 | 1,616 | 1,667 | 1,673 | 1,382 | 1,206 | 1,296 | 1,204 | .... | .... | .... |
| Exports of Goods and Services......... | 90c | 2,872 | 3,423 | 3,877 | 4,088 | 4,181 | 3,810 | 4,109 | 3,438 | 3,590 | .... | .... | .... |
| Imports of Goods and Services (-)..... | 98c | 3,469 | 4,034 | 4,264 | 4,432 | 4,867 | 4,091 | 4,480 | 4,692 | 4,591 | .... | .... | .... |
| Gross Domestic Product (GDP)......... | 99b | 7,019 | 7,783 | 8,628 | 9,027 | 9,083 | 9,185 | 8,867 | 8,738 | 8,450 | .... | .... | .... |
| Statistical Discrepancy.................... | 99bs | 44.500 | 83.900 | 27.300 | 98.200 | −17.200 | −20.500 | −18.300 | .... | .... | .... | .... | .... |
| GDP Volume 1974 Prices................. | 99b.p | 990.8 | 1,030.4 | 1,089.2 | 1,107.4 | 1,111.2 | 1,065.2 | 1,067.9 | 1,076.0 | 1,076.1 | .... | .... | .... |
| GDP Volume (2010=100)............... | 99bvp | 92.8 | 96.5 | 102.0 | 103.7 | 104.1 | 99.7 | 100.0 | 100.8 | 100.8 | .... | .... | .... |
| GDP Deflator (2010=100)............... | 99bip | 85.3 | 91.0 | 95.4 | 98.2 | 98.4 | 103.8 | 100.0 | 97.8 | 94.6 | .... | .... | .... |
| | | | | | | *Millions: Midyear Estimates* | | | | | | | |
| Population................................ | 99z | .27 | .27 | .28 | .28 | .28 | .28 | .28 | .28 | .28 | .28 | .28 | .28 |

Belarus 913

| | | 2004 | 2005 | 2006 | 2007 | 2008 | 2009 | 2010 | 2011 | 2012 | 2013 | 2014 | 2015 |
|---|---|---|---|---|---|---|---|---|---|---|---|---|---|
| **Exchange Rates** | | | | | | | *Rubels per SDR: End of Period* | | | | | | |
| Official Rate | aa | 3,370.0 | 3,075.8 | 3,219.4 | 3,397.5 | 3,388.6 | 4,488.3 | 4,620.1 | 12,819.5 | 13,171.4 | 14,645.4 | 17,168.4 | 25,731.6 |
| | | | | | | | *Rubels per US Dollar: End of Period (ae) Period Average (rf)* | | | | | | |
| Official Rate | ae | 2,170.0 | 2,152.0 | 2,140.0 | 2,150.0 | 2,200.0 | 2,863.0 | 3,000.0 | 8,350.0 | 8,570.0 | 9,510.0 | 11,850.0 | 18,569.0 |
| Official Rate | rf | 2,160.3 | 2,153.8 | 2,144.6 | 2,146.1 | 2,136.4 | 2,793.0 | 2,978.5 | 4,974.6 | 8,336.9 | 8,880.1 | 10,224.1 | 15,926.0 |
| **Fund Position** | | | | | | | *Millions of SDRs: End of Period* | | | | | | |
| Quota | 2f.s | 386.40 | 386.40 | 386.40 | 386.40 | 386.40 | 386.40 | 386.40 | 386.40 | 386.40 | 386.40 | 386.40 | 386.40 |
| SDR Holdings | 1b.s | .01 | .02 | .03 | .03 | .63 | 368.95 | 368.65 | 372.84 | 369.28 | 371.20 | 371.80 | 371.80 |
| Reserve Position in the Fund | 1c.s | .02 | .02 | .02 | .02 | .02 | .02 | .02 | .02 | .02 | .02 | .02 | .02 |
| Total Fund Cred.&Loans Outstg | 2tl | 5.84 | — | — | — | — | 1,831.59 | 2,269.52 | 2,269.52 | 1,965.86 | 885.84 | 54.74 | — |
| SDR Allocations | 1bd | — | — | — | — | — | 368.64 | 368.64 | 368.64 | 368.64 | 368.64 | 368.64 | 368.64 |
| **International Liquidity** | | | | | | | *Millions of US Dollars Unless Otherwise Indicated: End of Period* | | | | | | |
| Total Reserves minus Gold | 1l.d | 749.37 | 1,136.62 | 1,068.56 | 3,952.13 | 2,686.99 | 4,831.38 | 3,431.04 | 6,011.24 | 5,808.99 | 4,937.83 | 3,422.01 | 2,743.60 |
| SDR Holdings | 1b.d | .01 | .03 | .04 | .04 | .97 | 578.40 | 567.73 | 572.40 | 567.55 | 571.65 | 538.66 | 515.22 |
| Reserve Position in the Fund | 1c.d | .03 | .03 | .03 | .03 | .03 | .03 | .03 | .03 | .03 | .03 | .03 | .03 |
| Foreign Exchange | 1d.d | 749.33 | 1,136.56 | 1,068.49 | 3,952.06 | 2,685.99 | 4,252.95 | 2,863.27 | 5,438.80 | 5,241.41 | 4,366.14 | 2,883.32 | 2,228.36 |
| Gold (Million Fine Troy Ounces) | 1ad | .2000 | .4000 | .5000 | .2716 | .4325 | .7438 | 1.1344 | 1.2097 | 1.3738 | 1.4257 | 1.3646 | 1.3483 |
| Gold (National Valuation) | 1and | .... | .... | .... | 230.00 | 374.14 | 821.10 | 1,599.78 | 1,904.71 | 2,286.04 | 1,713.90 | 1,637.07 | 1,432.24 |
| Central Bank: Other Assets | 3..d | † 38.47 | 15.91 | 257.26 | 658.33 | 601.37 | 294.88 | 1,011.23 | 2,152.36 | 1,087.98 | 580.53 | 558.85 | 533.46 |
| Central Bank: Other Liabs | 4..d | † 84.91 | 14.66 | 12.84 | 607.00 | 436.69 | 428.51 | 1,880.48 | 1,577.69 | 441.26 | 1,300.87 | 2,203.28 | 1,743.68 |
| Other Depository Corps.: Assets | 7a.d | † 455.29 | 690.59 | 429.11 | 1,240.58 | 985.27 | 1,434.94 | 1,485.76 | 2,282.62 | 1,563.92 | 1,469.10 | 1,193.79 | 1,772.85 |
| Other Depository Corps.: Liabs | 7b.d | † 616.11 | 845.59 | 1,377.40 | 2,481.58 | 2,363.04 | 3,547.19 | 5,733.36 | 5,985.93 | 6,117.48 | 8,183.75 | 7,356.66 | 6,430.16 |
| Other Financial Corps.: Assets | 7e.d | .... | .... | .... | .25 | 1.40 | 8.02 | 13.81 | 5.55 | 10.22 | 24.22 | 84.21 | 361.03 |
| Other Financial Corps.: Liabs | 7f.d | .... | .... | .... | 4.22 | 5.48 | 4.17 | 7.81 | 1.79 | 3.96 | 17.53 | 239.24 | 912.33 |
| **Central Bank** | | | | | | | *Billions of Rubels: End of Period* | | | | | | |
| Net Foreign Assets | 11n | † 1,852.6 | 2,977.9 | 3,452.8 | 9,055.7 | 7,043.5 | 14,049.3 | 10,654.0 | 65,715.8 | 69,617.6 | 50,613.9 | 33,646.7 | 44,899.2 |
| Claims on Nonresidents | 11 | † 2,056.5 | 3,009.4 | 3,480.3 | 10,360.7 | 8,004.2 | 15,276.1 | 16,295.5 | 78,889.5 | 73,399.2 | 62,985.2 | 59,755.5 | 77,277.7 |
| Liabilities to Nonresidents | 16c | † 203.9 | 31.6 | 27.5 | 1,305.1 | 960.7 | 1,226.8 | 5,641.4 | 13,173.7 | 3,781.6 | 12,371.3 | 26,108.9 | 32,378.5 |
| Claims on Other Depository Corps | 12e | † 645.2 | 818.7 | 1,650.8 | 1,804.2 | 3,358.7 | 8,568.8 | 27,962.8 | 19,141.9 | 12,033.1 | 13,075.5 | 16,297.5 | 16,908.8 |
| Net Claims on Central Government | 12an | † 198.9 | 271.0 | −203.6 | −4,189.0 | −3,964.7 | −15,542.1 | −15,687.2 | −63,957.3 | −56,481.5 | −48,058.8 | −33,182.3 | −47,246.3 |
| Claims on Central Government | 12a | † 951.0 | 1,035.2 | 1,214.4 | 1,652.5 | 1,710.2 | 1,017.1 | 1,017.1 | 991.3 | 971.9 | 950.1 | 4,829.8 | 4,771.5 |
| Liabilities to Central Government | 16d | † 752.1 | 764.2 | 1,418.0 | 5,841.5 | 5,674.9 | 16,559.2 | 16,704.3 | 64,948.6 | 57,453.4 | 49,008.9 | 38,012.1 | 52,017.8 |
| Claims on Other Sectors | 12s | † 91.9 | 330.4 | 652.7 | 1,137.0 | 1,838.7 | 2,295.7 | 4,475.7 | 15,290.2 | 14,590.8 | 14,848.1 | 14,921.4 | 14,723.6 |
| Claims on Other Financial Corps | 12g | † 10.7 | 9.8 | 6.5 | 8.2 | 10.2 | 112.3 | 112.9 | 13,866.4 | 13,630.5 | 13,637.7 | 13,638.6 | 13,658.4 |
| Claims on State & Local Govts | 12b | † — | — | — | — | .1 | .3 | 1,116.4 | 1,046.6 | 498.5 | 407.4 | 390.6 | 169.2 |
| Claims on Public Nonfin. Corps | 12c | † 33.6 | 39.4 | 83.9 | 21.7 | .5 | .3 | 261.6 | 60.2 | 249.9 | 630.3 | 654.2 | 691.7 |
| Claims on Private Sector | 12d | † 47.6 | 281.2 | 562.3 | 1,107.1 | 1,827.8 | 2,182.8 | 2,984.8 | 317.0 | 211.9 | 172.6 | 237.9 | 204.4 |
| Monetary Base | 14 | † 2,394.0 | 4,159.1 | 4,983.9 | 6,896.3 | 7,702.7 | 6,813.2 | 10,187.6 | 18,757.5 | 30,318.4 | 34,388.4 | 39,139.1 | 44,962.5 |
| Currency in Circulation | 14a | † 1,553.4 | 2,368.3 | 3,365.3 | 4,007.4 | 4,941.8 | 4,924.5 | 6,207.9 | 9,449.9 | 16,136.6 | 17,892.9 | 20,446.9 | 21,146.3 |
| Liabs. to Other Depository Corps | 14c | † 840.1 | 1,789.9 | 1,617.1 | 2,165.4 | 2,759.6 | 1,887.3 | 3,977.2 | 9,285.1 | 14,181.1 | 16,494.6 | 18,202.9 | 23,816.2 |
| Liabilities to Other Sectors | 14d | † .6 | .9 | 1.4 | 723.5 | 1.2 | 1.4 | 2.5 | 22.4 | .7 | .9 | 489.3 | — |
| Other Liabs. to Other Dep. Corps | 14n | † 99.5 | 77.3 | 117.3 | 153.0 | 361.8 | 1,139.6 | 14,902.5 | 48,630.0 | 38,298.5 | 33,606.5 | 37,206.1 | 52,218.5 |
| Dep. & Sec. Excl. f/Monetary Base | 14o | † .2 | .1 | — | — | — | 427.6 | 641.2 | 1,755.7 | 2,757.6 | 4,370.5 | 5,698.2 | 11,012.5 |
| Deposits Included in Broad Money | 15 | † — | — | — | — | — | — | — | — | — | — | — | — |
| Sec.Ot.th.Shares Incl.in Brd. Money | 16a | † — | — | — | — | — | — | — | — | — | — | — | 557.1 |
| Deposits Excl. from Broad Money | 16b | † .2 | .1 | — | — | — | 123.7 | 385.2 | 1,438.5 | 2,323.2 | 3,820.1 | 5,527.1 | 10,455.5 |
| Sec.Ot.th.Shares Excl.f/Brd.Money | 16s | † — | — | — | — | — | 304.0 | 255.9 | 317.2 | 434.3 | 550.4 | 171.2 | — |
| Loans | 16l | † — | — | — | — | — | — | — | — | — | — | — | — |
| Financial Derivatives | 16m | † — | — | — | — | — | — | — | — | — | — | — | — |
| Shares and Other Equity | 17a | † 761.7 | 807.4 | 968.4 | 1,394.5 | 1,260.1 | 2,346.6 | 4,176.1 | −24,989.5 | −22,430.8 | −32,602.8 | −40,835.2 | −69,120.8 |
| Other Items (Net) | 17r | † −466.9 | −646.0 | −516.9 | −636.0 | −1,048.4 | −1,355.5 | −2,502.0 | −7,963.0 | −9,183.8 | −9,283.9 | −9,525.0 | −9,787.5 |
| Memo Item: | | | | | | | | | | | | | |
| Total Assets | 10ra | † 6,908.4 | 9,320.5 | 13,898.4 | 19,713.3 | 22,308.2 | 38,151.2 | 62,290.0 | 147,821.6 | 136,821.0 | 129,315.5 | 155,152.1 | 206,758.6 |
| **Other Depository Corporations** | | | | | | | *Billions of Rubels: End of Period* | | | | | | |
| Net Foreign Assets | 21n | † −349.0 | −333.6 | −2,029.3 | −2,668.1 | −3,944.6 | −6,047.4 | −12,742.8 | −30,922.6 | −39,024.0 | −63,856.4 | −73,030.0 | −86,481.6 |
| Claims on Nonresidents | 21 | † 988.0 | 1,486.1 | 918.3 | 2,667.3 | 2,820.8 | 4,108.2 | 4,457.3 | 19,059.9 | 13,402.8 | 13,971.1 | 14,146.4 | 32,920.1 |
| Liabilities to Nonresidents | 26c | † 1,337.0 | 1,819.7 | 2,947.6 | 5,335.4 | 6,765.4 | 10,155.6 | 17,200.1 | 49,982.5 | 52,426.8 | 77,827.5 | 87,176.4 | 119,401.7 |
| Claims on Central Bank | 20 | † 1,136.1 | 2,104.7 | 2,350.0 | 2,846.6 | 3,516.9 | 3,481.5 | 18,897.6 | 57,537.8 | 56,506.4 | 54,424.6 | 62,367.2 | 83,685.1 |
| Currency | 20a | † 213.9 | 351.9 | 547.0 | 684.2 | 1,105.5 | 1,277.3 | 1,714.0 | 2,738.2 | 4,829.3 | 5,590.9 | 6,523.0 | 6,910.2 |
| Reserve Deposits and Securities | 20b | † 920.6 | 1,458.3 | 1,802.3 | 1,726.5 | 2,411.4 | 1,917.5 | 16,851.9 | 45,336.7 | 41,915.5 | 36,876.1 | 42,701.8 | 35,279.5 |
| Other Claims | 20n | † 1.6 | 294.5 | .8 | 435.9 | — | 286.7 | 331.6 | 9,463.0 | 9,761.6 | 11,957.6 | 13,142.4 | 41,495.4 |
| Net Claims on Central Government | 22an | † 265.3 | 8.8 | −279.9 | −1,975.7 | −3,254.4 | −7,075.5 | −8,734.0 | −2,129.0 | −9,063.0 | −5,017.9 | −11,493.3 | 21,520.7 |
| Claims on Central Government | 22a | † 1,063.6 | 1,766.2 | 2,649.3 | 2,710.5 | 5,328.7 | 2,681.3 | 2,394.5 | 9,900.8 | 10,574.7 | 19,853.6 | 27,238.6 | 58,064.5 |
| Liabilities to Central Government | 26d | † 798.4 | 1,757.4 | 2,929.2 | 4,686.2 | 8,583.1 | 9,756.7 | 11,128.5 | 12,029.8 | 19,637.7 | 24,871.5 | 38,731.9 | 36,543.8 |
| Claims on Other Sectors | 22s | † 10,047.0 | 13,550.3 | 21,384.9 | 31,176.3 | 48,075.3 | 67,706.4 | 95,697.6 | 161,794.2 | 225,576.9 | 288,466.7 | 353,257.5 | 423,841.8 |
| Claims on Other Financial Corps | 22g | † 49.6 | 63.9 | 83.0 | 135.3 | 370.2 | 829.5 | 1,687.1 | 3,159.7 | 8,401.2 | 7,661.0 | 7,657.7 | 11,679.0 |
| Claims on State & Local Govts | 22b | † 83.8 | 296.3 | 527.6 | 675.4 | 966.0 | 1,323.3 | 2,822.9 | 4,385.6 | 5,084.4 | 5,079.3 | 6,332.5 | 7,519.9 |
| Claims on Public Nonfin. Corps | 22c | † 2,985.7 | 3,126.3 | 5,336.5 | 7,377.2 | 11,407.9 | 16,981.4 | 21,559.2 | 39,744.0 | 98,486.2 | 131,846.4 | 161,083.5 | 189,153.0 |
| Claims on Private Sector | 22d | † 6,928.0 | 10,063.7 | 15,437.8 | 22,988.5 | 35,331.2 | 48,572.1 | 69,628.5 | 114,504.9 | 113,605.1 | 143,880.1 | 178,183.8 | 215,489.8 |
| Liabilities to Central Bank | 26g | † 512.3 | 735.9 | 1,579.7 | 1,693.3 | 3,238.0 | 8,465.7 | 27,934.2 | 19,003.4 | 11,843.1 | 12,725.8 | 15,393.6 | 16,018.4 |
| Transf.Dep.Included in Broad Money | 24 | † 3,296.2 | 4,788.7 | 6,488.4 | 8,289.3 | 10,283.1 | 11,237.0 | 14,218.4 | 28,431.4 | 38,753.5 | 43,837.8 | 50,746.5 | 63,975.7 |
| Other Dep.Included in Broad Money | 25 | † 4,081.4 | 5,615.4 | 8,068.0 | 11,794.3 | 15,923.6 | 21,527.0 | 28,822.1 | 70,145.4 | 104,125.4 | 129,143.2 | 163,226.6 | 230,425.6 |
| Sec.Ot.th.Shares Incl.in Brd. Money | 26a | † 121.4 | 149.2 | 129.7 | 375.7 | 917.0 | 1,694.4 | 2,723.2 | 5,884.3 | 7,106.9 | 8,022.9 | 11,056.5 | 17,744.3 |
| Deposits Excl. from Broad Money | 26b | † 277.7 | 292.4 | 152.6 | 336.3 | 3,539.2 | 2,314.9 | 3,158.9 | 6,099.8 | 12,209.0 | 13,820.5 | 16,010.1 | 17,001.4 |
| Sec.Ot.th.Shares Excl.f/Brd.Money | 26s | † — | — | — | — | — | — | — | 13,466.1 | 12,103.8 | 10,488.0 | 9,659.6 | 8,957.8 |
| Loans | 26l | † — | — | .9 | 1.0 | 1.8 | 32.7 | 30.1 | 90.9 | 88.6 | 150.5 | 148.6 | 100.8 |
| Financial Derivatives | 26m | † — | — | — | — | — | 2.7 | 2.9 | 35.6 | .3 | 3.3 | 19.1 | 2.8 |
| Insurance Technical Reserves | 26r | † — | — | — | — | — | — | — | — | — | — | — | — |
| Shares and Other Equity | 27a | † 3,016.2 | 4,122.8 | 5,314.8 | 6,904.5 | 11,776.5 | 13,855.2 | 17,528.3 | 36,487.4 | 46,655.3 | 55,895.4 | 64,920.2 | 79,899.1 |
| Other Items (Net) | 27r | † −205.7 | −374.2 | −308.5 | −15.3 | −1,285.8 | −1,064.5 | −1,299.7 | 6,635.9 | 1,110.4 | −70.4 | −79.4 | 8,440.1 |
| Memo Item: | | | | | | | | | | | | | |
| Total Assets | 20ra | † 15,018.9 | 21,141.2 | 29,910.0 | 42,956.7 | 66,816.6 | 86,509.0 | 130,847.1 | 264,547.5 | 329,781.3 | 407,440.9 | 495,353.7 | 649,323.6 |

# Belarus 913

| | | 2004 | 2005 | 2006 | 2007 | 2008 | 2009 | 2010 | 2011 | 2012 | 2013 | 2014 | 2015 |
|---|---|---|---|---|---|---|---|---|---|---|---|---|---|
| **Depository Corporations** | | | | | | *Billions of Rubels: End of Period* | | | | | | | |
| Net Foreign Assets | 31n | † 1,503.6 | 2,644.3 | 1,423.5 | 6,387.5 | 3,098.9 | 8,001.9 | −2,088.8 | 34,793.2 | 30,593.6 | −13,242.5 | −39,383.4 | −41,582.4 |
| Claims on Nonresidents | 31 | † 3,044.5 | 4,495.5 | 4,398.6 | 13,028.0 | 10,825.0 | 19,384.3 | 20,752.7 | 97,949.3 | 86,802.0 | 76,956.3 | 73,901.9 | 110,197.8 |
| Liabilities to Nonresidents | 36c | † 1,540.9 | 1,851.3 | 2,975.1 | 6,640.4 | 7,726.1 | 11,382.4 | 22,841.5 | 63,156.2 | 56,208.4 | 90,198.8 | 113,285.3 | 151,780.1 |
| Domestic Claims | 32 | † 10,603.1 | 14,160.4 | 21,554.1 | 26,148.6 | 42,694.9 | 47,384.5 | 75,752.1 | 110,998.1 | 174,623.2 | 250,238.1 | 323,503.2 | 412,839.8 |
| Net Claims on Central Government | 32an | † 464.2 | 279.8 | −483.6 | −6,164.7 | −7,219.1 | −22,617.6 | −24,421.2 | −66,086.3 | −65,544.5 | −53,076.7 | −44,675.6 | −25,725.7 |
| Claims on Central Government | 32a | † 2,014.7 | 2,801.4 | 3,863.7 | 4,363.0 | 7,039.0 | 3,698.4 | 3,411.6 | 10,892.1 | 11,546.6 | 20,803.8 | 32,068.4 | 62,836.0 |
| Liabilities to Central Government | 36d | † 1,550.5 | 2,521.6 | 4,347.2 | 10,527.7 | 14,258.0 | 26,316.0 | 27,832.8 | 76,978.4 | 77,091.1 | 73,880.5 | 76,744.0 | 88,561.6 |
| Claims on Other Sectors | 32s | † 10,138.9 | 13,880.7 | 22,037.7 | 32,313.3 | 49,914.0 | 70,002.1 | 100,173.3 | 177,084.4 | 240,167.7 | 303,314.8 | 368,178.8 | 438,565.5 |
| Claims on Other Financial Corps. | 32g | † 60.3 | 73.8 | 89.6 | 143.5 | 380.5 | 941.8 | 1,800.0 | 17,026.1 | 22,031.7 | 21,298.7 | 21,296.3 | 25,337.3 |
| Claims on State & Local Govts | 32b | † 83.8 | 296.3 | 527.6 | 675.4 | 966.1 | 1,323.7 | 3,939.3 | 5,432.2 | 5,582.9 | 5,486.7 | 6,723.1 | 7,689.1 |
| Claims on Public Nonfin. Corps. | 32c | † 3,019.2 | 3,165.7 | 5,420.4 | 7,398.9 | 11,408.4 | 16,981.7 | 21,820.8 | 39,804.2 | 98,736.1 | 132,476.7 | 161,737.7 | 189,844.7 |
| Claims on Private Sector | 32d | † 6,975.6 | 10,344.9 | 16,000.1 | 24,095.6 | 37,159.0 | 50,754.9 | 72,613.3 | 114,821.9 | 113,817.0 | 144,052.8 | 178,421.7 | 215,694.3 |
| Broad Money Liabilities | 35l | † 8,839.0 | 12,570.6 | 17,505.9 | 24,506.0 | 30,961.1 | 38,107.1 | 50,260.2 | 111,195.3 | 161,293.8 | 193,306.8 | 239,442.7 | 326,938.8 |
| Currency Outside Depository Corps | 34a | † 1,339.4 | 2,016.4 | 2,818.3 | 3,323.2 | 3,836.2 | 3,647.2 | 4,493.9 | 6,711.8 | 11,307.3 | 12,302.0 | 13,923.8 | 14,236.1 |
| Transferable Deposits | 34 | † 3,296.8 | 4,789.6 | 6,489.8 | 8,290.9 | 10,284.3 | 11,238.4 | 14,220.9 | 28,453.9 | 38,754.2 | 43,838.7 | 51,235.8 | 63,975.8 |
| Other Deposits | 35 | † 4,081.4 | 5,615.4 | 8,068.0 | 11,794.3 | 15,923.6 | 21,527.0 | 28,822.1 | 70,145.4 | 104,125.4 | 129,143.2 | 163,226.6 | 230,425.6 |
| Securities Other than Shares | 36a | † 121.4 | 149.2 | 129.7 | 1,097.7 | 917.0 | 1,694.4 | 2,723.2 | 5,884.3 | 7,106.9 | 8,022.9 | 11,056.5 | 18,301.3 |
| Deposits Excl. from Broad Money | 36b | † 277.9 | 292.5 | 152.6 | 336.4 | 3,539.2 | 2,438.5 | 3,544.1 | 7,538.3 | 14,532.3 | 17,640.6 | 21,537.1 | 27,456.9 |
| Sec.Ot.th.Shares Excl.f/Brd.Money | 36s | † — | — | — | — | — | 304.0 | 255.9 | 13,783.2 | 12,538.2 | 11,038.4 | 9,830.8 | 8,957.8 |
| Loans | 36l | † — | — | .9 | 1.0 | 1.8 | 32.7 | 30.1 | 90.9 | 88.6 | 150.5 | 148.6 | 100.8 |
| Financial Derivatives | 36m | † — | — | — | — | — | 2.7 | 2.9 | 35.6 | .3 | 3.3 | 19.1 | 2.8 |
| Insurance Technical Reserves | 36r | † — | — | — | — | — | — | — | — | — | — | — | — |
| Shares and Other Equity | 37a | † 3,777.8 | 4,930.2 | 6,283.2 | 8,299.0 | 13,036.6 | 16,201.8 | 21,704.4 | 11,497.9 | 24,224.6 | 23,292.5 | 24,085.0 | 10,778.4 |
| Other Items (Net) | 37r | † −788.0 | −988.6 | −965.0 | −606.1 | −1,744.9 | −1,700.5 | −2,134.2 | 1,649.9 | −7,460.9 | −8,436.5 | −10,943.5 | −2,977.9 |
| Broad Money Liabs., Seasonally Adj. | 35l.b | † 8,467.1 | 12,045.5 | 16,767.9 | 23,478.0 | 29,655.7 | 36,594.0 | 48,418.9 | 107,684.8 | 157,193.6 | 189,818.3 | 236,483.1 | 323,764.9 |
| **Other Financial Corporations** | | | | | | *Billions of Rubels: End of Period* | | | | | | | |
| Net Foreign Assets | 41n | .... | .... | .... | −8.5 | −9.0 | 11.0 | 18.0 | 31.4 | 53.6 | 63.6 | −1,837.1 | −6,532.8 |
| Claims on Nonresidents | 41 | .... | .... | .... | .5 | 3.1 | 23.0 | 41.4 | 46.3 | 87.6 | 230.3 | 997.9 | 4,278.3 |
| Liabilities to Nonresidents | 46c | .... | .... | .... | 9.1 | 12.0 | 11.9 | 23.4 | 14.9 | 34.0 | 166.7 | 2,835.0 | 10,811.1 |
| Claims on Depository Corporations | 40 | .... | .... | .... | 537.2 | 1,750.0 | 2,178.5 | 2,170.8 | 18,968.5 | 22,949.1 | 22,055.4 | 25,031.2 | 35,689.6 |
| Net Claims on Central Government | 42an | .... | .... | .... | −4.4 | −2.9 | −4.0 | 202.2 | −1,920.5 | 9,135.7 | 8,610.9 | 9,125.5 | 12,853.6 |
| Claims on Central Government | 42a | .... | .... | .... | — | — | — | 204.6 | 263.5 | 9,804.6 | 11,524.8 | 13,352.3 | 18,586.8 |
| Liabilities to Central Government | 46d | .... | .... | .... | 4.4 | 2.9 | 4.0 | 2.4 | 2,184.1 | 668.8 | 2,913.9 | 4,226.8 | 5,733.2 |
| Claims on Other Sectors | 42s | .... | .... | .... | 75.9 | 96.3 | 378.3 | 372.5 | 2,425.5 | 8,192.1 | 16,800.1 | 21,500.1 | 47,242.2 |
| Claims on State & Local Govts | 42b | .... | .... | .... | 70.8 | 90.8 | 71.8 | 7.0 | 5.0 | 7.0 | 454.9 | 1,443.4 | 1,738.0 |
| Claims on Public Nonfin. Corps. | 42c | .... | .... | .... | — | — | — | — | 616.5 | 2,744.6 | 6,634.5 | 8,048.2 | 10,504.5 |
| Claims on Private Sector | 42d | .... | .... | .... | 5.2 | 5.6 | 306.5 | 365.5 | 1,804.0 | 5,440.6 | 9,710.6 | 12,008.6 | 34,999.6 |
| Deposits | 46b | .... | .... | .... | — | — | — | — | — | .1 | 222.4 | 691.6 | 1,271.1 |
| Securities Other than Shares | 46s | .... | .... | .... | — | — | — | — | 13,716.7 | 18,269.3 | 17,408.4 | 17,452.9 | 19,314.4 |
| Loans | 46l | .... | .... | .... | 7.2 | 3.7 | 26.7 | 22.8 | 45.1 | 90.9 | 259.7 | 229.3 | 8,465.5 |
| Financial Derivatives | 46m | .... | .... | .... | — | — | — | — | — | — | — | 4.2 | .8 |
| Insurance Technical Reserves | 46r | .... | .... | .... | 454.1 | 656.2 | 875.1 | 1,060.7 | 1,854.6 | 2,896.7 | 5,543.9 | 8,157.6 | 9,717.7 |
| Shares and Other Equity | 47a | .... | .... | .... | 333.9 | 1,422.1 | 1,941.5 | 2,051.3 | 4,764.7 | 18,500.2 | 26,296.1 | 30,522.8 | 45,840.5 |
| Other Items (Net) | 47r | .... | .... | .... | −195.0 | −247.5 | −279.5 | −371.4 | −876.2 | 573.4 | −2,200.5 | −3,238.6 | 4,642.7 |
| Memo Item: | | | | | | | | | | | | | |
| Total Assets | 40ra | .... | .... | .... | 836.9 | 2,129.2 | 2,895.3 | 3,215.6 | 22,925.3 | 43,155.1 | 57,054.9 | 70,052.7 | 121,508.4 |
| **Financial Corporations** | | | | | | *Billions of Rubels: End of Period* | | | | | | | |
| Net Foreign Assets | 51n | .... | .... | .... | 6,379.0 | 3,089.9 | 8,012.9 | −2,070.8 | 34,824.5 | 30,647.2 | −13,178.9 | −41,220.5 | −48,115.2 |
| Claims on Nonresidents | 51 | .... | .... | .... | 13,028.5 | 10,828.1 | 19,407.3 | 20,794.2 | 97,995.7 | 86,889.6 | 77,186.6 | 74,899.8 | 114,476.0 |
| Liabilities to Nonresidents | 56c | .... | .... | .... | 6,649.5 | 7,738.2 | 11,394.4 | 22,865.0 | 63,171.1 | 56,242.4 | 90,365.5 | 116,120.2 | 162,591.2 |
| Domestic Claims | 52 | .... | .... | .... | 26,076.7 | 42,407.9 | 46,817.0 | 74,526.8 | 94,477.0 | 169,919.3 | 254,350.4 | 332,832.6 | 447,598.3 |
| Net Claims on Central Government | 52an | .... | .... | .... | −6,169.1 | −7,222.0 | −22,621.6 | −24,219.1 | −68,006.9 | −56,408.8 | −44,465.8 | −35,550.1 | −12,872.1 |
| Claims on Central Government | 52a | .... | .... | .... | 4,363.0 | 7,039.0 | 3,698.4 | 3,616.2 | 11,155.6 | 21,351.2 | 32,328.5 | 45,420.7 | 81,422.8 |
| Liabilities to Central Government | 56d | .... | .... | .... | 10,532.1 | 14,260.9 | 26,320.0 | 27,835.2 | 79,162.5 | 77,760.0 | 76,794.4 | 80,970.8 | 94,294.8 |
| Claims on Other Sectors | 52s | .... | .... | .... | 32,245.8 | 49,629.8 | 69,438.6 | 98,745.8 | 162,483.9 | 226,328.1 | 298,816.2 | 368,382.7 | 460,470.3 |
| Claims on State & Local Govts | 52b | .... | .... | .... | 746.2 | 1,056.9 | 1,395.5 | 3,946.3 | 5,437.2 | 5,589.9 | 5,941.6 | 8,166.5 | 9,427.1 |
| Claims on Public Nonfin. Corps. | 52c | .... | .... | .... | 7,398.9 | 11,408.4 | 16,981.7 | 21,820.8 | 40,420.7 | 101,480.7 | 139,111.2 | 169,785.9 | 200,349.3 |
| Claims on Private Sector | 52d | .... | .... | .... | 24,100.8 | 37,164.5 | 51,061.4 | 72,978.8 | 116,626.0 | 119,257.5 | 153,763.4 | 190,430.3 | 250,693.9 |
| Currency Outside Financial Corps. | 54a | .... | .... | .... | 3,322.9 | 3,836.1 | 3,647.0 | 4,493.7 | 6,711.1 | 11,306.4 | 12,301.3 | 13,920.7 | 14,234.4 |
| Deposits | 55l | .... | .... | .... | 20,079.1 | 29,255.3 | 34,206.2 | 44,511.7 | 100,937.3 | 147,833.0 | 180,878.3 | 223,615.7 | 303,052.5 |
| Securities Other than Shares | 56a | .... | .... | .... | 905.2 | 649.1 | 1,450.9 | 2,662.2 | 5,477.4 | 6,568.3 | 7,117.0 | 10,419.2 | 17,862.2 |
| Loans | 56l | .... | .... | .... | — | .8 | 31.4 | 31.3 | 90.9 | 88.6 | 97.1 | 134.9 | 212.1 |
| Financial Derivatives | 56m | .... | .... | .... | — | — | 2.7 | 2.9 | 35.6 | .3 | 3.3 | 19.1 | 2.8 |
| Insurance Technical Reserves | 56r | .... | .... | .... | 454.1 | 656.2 | 875.1 | 1,060.7 | 1,854.6 | 2,896.7 | 5,543.9 | 8,157.6 | 9,717.7 |
| Shares and Other Equity | 57a | .... | .... | .... | 8,632.9 | 14,458.7 | 18,143.3 | 23,755.6 | 16,262.6 | 42,724.8 | 49,588.6 | 54,607.8 | 56,618.9 |
| Other Items (Net) | 57r | .... | .... | .... | −938.5 | −3,358.4 | −3,526.8 | −4,062.2 | −2,068.0 | −10,851.6 | −14,357.9 | −19,262.9 | −2,217.4 |
| **Monetary Aggregates** | | | | | | *Billions of Rubels: End of Period* | | | | | | | |
| Broad Money | 59m | 8,839.0 | 12,570.6 | 17,505.9 | 24,506.0 | 30,961.1 | 38,107.1 | 50,260.2 | 111,195.3 | 161,293.8 | 193,306.8 | 239,442.7 | 326,938.8 |
| o/w:Currency Issued by Cent.Govt | 59m.a | — | — | — | — | — | — | — | — | — | — | — | — |
| o/w: Dep.in Nonfin. Corporations. | 59m.b | — | — | — | — | — | — | — | — | — | — | — | — |
| o/w:Secs. Issued by Central Govt. | 59m.c | — | — | — | — | — | — | — | — | — | — | — | — |
| Money (National Definitions) | | | | | | | | | | | | | |
| Base Money | 19ma | 2,394.0 | 4,159.1 | 4,983.9 | 6,896.3 | 7,702.7 | 6,813.2 | 10,187.6 | 18,757.5 | 30,318.4 | 34,388.4 | 39,139.1 | 44,962.5 |
| M1 | 59ma | 3,111.4 | 4,945.8 | 7,023.2 | 8,739.9 | 10,718.5 | 11,342.0 | 13,662.9 | 20,340.3 | 34,438.2 | 37,099.1 | 41,764.6 | 42,733.3 |
| M2 | 59mb | 5,288.3 | 8,465.8 | 12,321.3 | 15,732.5 | 19,836.3 | 20,191.6 | 25,399.3 | 41,165.5 | 65,601.8 | 77,482.2 | 90,151.3 | 89,135.6 |
| M2* | 59mba | 5,388.3 | 8,594.9 | 12,415.6 | 16,764.6 | 20,541.7 | 20,737.0 | 26,425.0 | 43,354.6 | 68,669.5 | 79,331.2 | 90,844.5 | 90,496.3 |
| M3 | 59mc | 8,839.0 | 12,570.6 | 17,505.9 | 24,506.0 | 30,961.1 | 38,107.1 | 50,260.2 | 111,195.3 | 160,761.4 | 193,306.8 | 239,442.7 | 326,938.8 |
| **Interest Rates** | | | | | | *Percent Per Annum* | | | | | | | |
| Central Bank Policy Rate (EOP) | 60 | 17.00 | 11.00 | 10.00 | 10.00 | 12.00 | 13.50 | 10.50 | 45.00 | 30.00 | 23.50 | 20.00 | 25.00 |
| Deposit Rate | 60l | 12.72 | 9.23 | 7.68 | 8.31 | 8.53 | 10.68 | 9.09 | 13.31 | 22.30 | 20.26 | 18.58 | .... |
| Lending Rate | 60p | 16.91 | 11.36 | 8.84 | 8.58 | 8.55 | 11.68 | 9.22 | 13.58 | 19.49 | 19.13 | 18.74 | .... |

# Belarus 913

| | | 2004 | 2005 | 2006 | 2007 | 2008 | 2009 | 2010 | 2011 | 2012 | 2013 | 2014 | 2015 |
|---|---|---|---|---|---|---|---|---|---|---|---|---|---|
| **Prices and Labor** | | | | | | *Percent Change over Previous Period* | | | | | | | |
| Producer Prices | 63.xx | 24.1 | 12.1 | 8.3 | 16.3 | 14.7 | 14.5 | 13.4 | 71.4 | 76.1 | 13.6 | 12.8 | 16.8 |
| Consumer Prices | 64.xx | 18.1 | 10.3 | 7.0 | 8.4 | 14.8 | 12.9 | 7.7 | 53.2 | 59.2 | 18.3 | 18.1 | 13.5 |
| Wages | 65.xx | 3.2 | 33.4 | 25.5 | 19.2 | 25.1 | 13.1 | 24.0 | 56.1 | 93.5 | 37.7 | 19.6 | 10.9 |
| | | | | | | *Number in Thousands: Period Averages* | | | | | | | |
| Employment | 67e | 4,320 | 4,332 | 4,391 | 4,530 | 4,541 | 4,609 | 4,703 | 4,691 | 4,612 | 4,578 | 4,551 | 4,494 |
| Unemployment | 67c | 112 | 77 | 64 | 49 | 44 | 42 | 39 | 32 | 28 | 23 | 22 | 41 |
| Unemployment Rate (%) | 67r | 2.5 | 1.7 | 1.4 | 1.1 | 1.0 | .9 | .8 | .7 | .6 | .5 | .5 | .9 |
| **Intl. Transactions & Positions** | | | | | | *Millions of US Dollars* | | | | | | | |
| Exports | 70..d | 13,774 | 15,979 | 19,734 | 24,275 | 32,571 | 21,304 | 25,284 | 41,419 | 46,060 | 37,232 | 36,081 | 26,686 |
| Imports, c.i.f. | 71..d | 16,491 | 16,708 | 22,351 | 28,693 | 39,381 | 28,569 | 34,884 | 45,771 | 46,404 | 42,999 | 40,502 | 30,312 |
| **Balance of Payments** | | | | | | *Millions of US Dollars* | | | | | | | |
| A. Current Account* | 109bx | −1,191.9 | 458.6 | −1,387.9 | −3,012.5 | −4,958.7 | −6,132.6 | −8,280.1 | −5,052.5 | −1,862.2 | −7,567.3 | −5,221.6 | −2,073.7 |
| Goods, credit (exports) | 1a9cx | 13,014.6 | 15,194.0 | 18,895.8 | 23,309.6 | 31,627.4 | 20,595.4 | 24,506.1 | 40,927.6 | 45,574.3 | 36,540.1 | 35,423.3 | 26,189.7 |
| Goods, debit (imports) | 1a9dx | 15,470.6 | 16,053.7 | 21,350.3 | 27,584.4 | 38,121.5 | 27,700.3 | 33,794.8 | 44,394.4 | 45,008.9 | 41,133.5 | 38,058.7 | 28,327.3 |
| Balance on goods | 1a9bx | −2,456.0 | −859.7 | −2,454.5 | −4,274.8 | −6,494.1 | −7,104.9 | −9,288.7 | −3,466.8 | 565.4 | −4,593.4 | −2,635.4 | −2,137.6 |
| Services, credit (exports) | 1b9cx | 1,962.3 | 2,342.3 | 2,673.5 | 3,541.8 | 4,589.8 | 3,714.9 | 4,795.6 | 5,609.5 | 6,311.7 | 7,506.0 | 7,888.6 | 6,647.7 |
| Services, debit (imports) | 1b9dx | 1,000.2 | 1,141.0 | 1,711.1 | 2,084.8 | 2,748.0 | 2,218.0 | 3,007.0 | 3,351.6 | 4,043.1 | 5,253.5 | 5,736.0 | 4,335.8 |
| Balance on Goods & Services | 1z9bx | −1,493.9 | 341.6 | −1,492.1 | −2,817.8 | −4,652.3 | −5,608.0 | −7,500.1 | −1,208.9 | 2,834.0 | −2,340.9 | −482.8 | 174.3 |
| Primary income: credit | 1c9cx | 157.6 | 168.4 | 246.6 | 297.1 | 660.3 | 507.4 | 503.3 | 705.0 | 916.7 | 858.6 | 900.4 | 518.8 |
| Primary income: debit | 1c9dx | 158.5 | 216.1 | 346.3 | 662.2 | 1,137.5 | 1,306.1 | 1,599.9 | 2,066.4 | 2,389.9 | 3,543.4 | 3,314.7 | 3,065.1 |
| Balance on gds, serv. & prim. inc. | 1y9bx | −1,494.8 | 293.9 | −1,591.8 | −3,182.9 | −5,129.5 | −6,406.7 | −8,596.7 | −2,570.3 | 1,360.8 | −5,025.7 | −2,897.1 | −2,372.0 |
| Secondary income: credit | 1d9ca | 390.6 | 266.8 | 316.6 | 330.2 | 400.6 | 505.5 | 885.0 | 1,870.9 | 2,090.2 | 1,902.8 | 1,193.7 | |
| Secondary income: debit | 1d9da | 87.7 | 102.1 | 112.7 | 159.8 | 229.8 | 231.4 | 568.4 | 4,353.1 | 5,197.0 | 4,631.8 | 4,227.3 | 895.4 |
| B. Capital Account* | 209ba | — | .... | .1 | .1 | .5 | .... | .... | 4.1 | 3.7 | 10.3 | 7.7 | 4.6 |
| Capital account: credit | 209ca | — | .... | .1 | .1 | .5 | .... | .... | 4.6 | 6.6 | 11.7 | 10.0 | 6.1 |
| Capital account: debit | 209da | — | .... | | | | .... | .... | .5 | 2.9 | 1.4 | 2.3 | 1.5 |
| Balance on current & capital acct. | 129ba | −1,191.9 | 458.6 | −1,387.8 | −3,012.4 | −4,958.2 | −6,132.6 | −8,280.1 | −5,048.4 | −1,858.5 | −7,557.0 | −5,213.9 | −2,069.1 |
| C. Financial Account* | 309na | −1,110.9 | 37.1 | −1,672.9 | −5,261.1 | −4,149.7 | −5,303.5 | −6,101.1 | −5,564.6 | −1,068.1 | −8,401.8 | −3,523.7 | −754.1 |
| Direct investment: assets | 3a9aa | 1.3 | 2.5 | 3.0 | 15.2 | 30.6 | 102.3 | 50.6 | 125.5 | 155.5 | 262.2 | 73.4 | 102.6 |
| Equity & investment fund shares | 3aaaa | 1.3 | 2.9 | 2.4 | 13.6 | 27.3 | 68.7 | 57.7 | 63.6 | 129.7 | 175.5 | 77.1 | 90.6 |
| Debt instruments | 3abaa | — | −.4 | .6 | 1.6 | 3.3 | 33.6 | −7.1 | 61.9 | 25.8 | 86.7 | −3.7 | 12.0 |
| Direct investment: liabilities | 3a9la | 163.8 | 306.6 | 357.1 | 1,807.3 | 2,187.9 | 1,876.5 | 1,393.4 | 4,002.4 | 1,463.6 | 2,246.1 | 1,862.0 | 1,568.3 |
| Equity & investment fund shares | 3aala | 143.9 | 313.7 | 363.3 | 1,643.7 | 2,016.1 | 1,822.6 | 1,347.5 | 3,773.2 | 1,250.8 | 1,772.4 | 1,545.9 | 1,424.7 |
| Debt instruments | 3abla | 19.9 | −7.1 | −6.2 | 163.6 | 171.8 | 53.9 | 45.9 | 229.2 | 212.8 | 473.7 | 316.1 | 143.6 |
| Portfolio investment: assets | 3b9aa | −3.2 | 2.9 | 1.7 | 41.2 | −4.8 | −16.5 | 59.4 | 10.8 | −27.9 | 17.7 | 23.1 | 25.0 |
| Equity & investment fund shares | 3baaa | −.6 | — | 5.6 | 5.8 | −.9 | 1.8 | .2 | −1.7 | −8.5 | .8 | — | .5 |
| Debt securities | 3bbaa | −2.6 | 2.9 | −3.9 | 35.4 | −3.9 | −18.3 | 59.2 | 12.5 | −19.4 | 16.9 | 23.1 | 24.5 |
| Portfolio investment: liabilities | 3b9la | 59.6 | −38.6 | −24.7 | 2.4 | .5 | 2.3 | 1,245.0 | 864.9 | −218.9 | −41.4 | 3.5 | −943.2 |
| Equity & investment fund shares | 3bala | .5 | .6 | −1.2 | 4.5 | .7 | 1.2 | .7 | −.1 | −3.5 | 2.0 | 5.3 | 4.5 |
| Debt securities | 3bbla | 59.1 | −39.2 | −23.5 | −2.1 | −.2 | 1.1 | 1,244.3 | 865.0 | −215.4 | −43.4 | −1.8 | −947.7 |
| Fin. der.& empl.stk.ops.(ESOs): net | 3c9na | — | .2 | 12.9 | .... | .... | .... | .... | 594.6 | −51.2 | −.8 | 29.6 | 25.1 |
| Fin. der. & ESOs.: assets | 3c9aa | — | −1.6 | −.1 | .... | .... | .... | .... | 1.7 | −51.0 | −2.1 | 2.0 | .9 |
| Fin. der. & ESOs.: liabilities | 3c9la | — | −1.8 | −13.0 | .... | .... | .... | .... | −592.9 | .2 | −1.3 | −27.6 | −24.2 |
| Other investment: assets | 3d9aa | 187.3 | 492.2 | 166.1 | 1,931.7 | 477.0 | 507.6 | 1,178.2 | 2,672.9 | −452.4 | −332.0 | −218.0 | 442.4 |
| Other equity | 3daaa | .... | .... | .... | .... | .... | .... | .... | .... | .... | .... | .... | .... |
| Debt instruments | 3dzaa | 187.3 | 492.2 | 166.1 | 1,931.7 | 477.0 | 507.6 | 1,178.2 | 2,672.9 | −452.4 | −332.0 | −218.0 | 442.4 |
| Other investment: liabilities | 3d9la | 1,072.9 | 192.7 | 1,524.2 | 5,439.5 | 2,464.1 | 4,018.1 | 4,750.9 | 4,101.1 | −552.6 | 6,144.2 | 1,566.3 | 724.1 |
| Other equity | 3dala | .... | .... | .... | .... | .... | .... | .... | .... | .... | .... | .... | .... |
| Debt instruments | 3dzla | 1,072.9 | 192.7 | 1,524.2 | 5,439.5 | 2,464.1 | 4,018.1 | 4,750.9 | 4,101.1 | −552.6 | 6,144.2 | 1,566.3 | 724.1 |
| Curr.+ cap.− finan. acct. balance | 4y9na | −81.0 | 421.5 | 285.1 | 2,248.7 | −808.5 | −829.1 | −2,179.0 | 516.2 | −790.4 | 844.8 | −1,690.2 | −1,315.0 |
| D. Net Errors and Omissions | 409na | 318.2 | 126.6 | −286.5 | 529.4 | −193.2 | 414.7 | 701.6 | 1,034.3 | 897.0 | −939.2 | −455.7 | 770.7 |
| E. Reserves and Related Items | 4z9na | 237.2 | 548.1 | −1.4 | 2,778.1 | −1,001.7 | −414.4 | −1,477.4 | 1,550.5 | 106.6 | −94.4 | −2,145.9 | −544.3 |
| Reserve assets | 3e9aa | 219.9 | 539.2 | −1.4 | 2,778.1 | −1,001.7 | 2,441.5 | −808.4 | 2,790.5 | 81.0 | −857.4 | −1,410.3 | −620.1 |
| Credit and loans from the IMF | 3dcla | −17.3 | −8.9 | — | — | — | 2,855.9 | 668.9 | — | −465.6 | −1,643.0 | −1,264.4 | −75.8 |
| Exceptional financing | 409la | — | .... | .... | .... | .... | .... | .... | 1,240.0 | 440.0 | 880.0 | 2,000.0 | — |
| *Excludes components in group E | | | | | | | | | | | | | |
| **International Investment Position** | | | | | | *Millions of US Dollars* | | | | | | | |
| Assets | 809aa | 2,240.2 | 3,288.9 | 3,583.4 | 8,592.3 | 7,771.3 | 11,001.9 | 11,681.8 | 17,375.6 | 17,287.3 | 15,642.5 | 14,323.4 | 13,556.8 |
| Direct investment | 8a9aa | 8.2 | 13.9 | 18.5 | 46.3 | 72.4 | 144.6 | 204.8 | 305.1 | 470.7 | 730.2 | 668.6 | 710.2 |
| Equity & investment fund shares | 8aaaa | 7.1 | 12.4 | 16.6 | 36.6 | 66.4 | 137.7 | 193.1 | 234.0 | 372.9 | 552.0 | 558.5 | 615.8 |
| Debt instruments | 8abaa | 1.1 | 1.5 | 1.9 | 9.7 | 6.0 | 6.9 | 11.7 | 71.1 | 97.8 | 178.2 | 110.1 | 94.4 |
| Portfolio investment | 8b9aa | 9.1 | 21.3 | 23.0 | 65.8 | 61.5 | 43.4 | 101.7 | 111.2 | 76.2 | 94.5 | 113.2 | 133.3 |
| Equity & investment fund shares | 8baaa | .3 | .3 | 5.9 | 13.1 | 12.9 | 13.1 | 12.8 | 10.7 | 2.5 | 2.7 | 1.8 | 1.6 |
| Debt securities | 8bbaa | 8.8 | 21.0 | 17.1 | 52.7 | 48.6 | 30.3 | 88.9 | 100.5 | 73.7 | 91.8 | 111.4 | 131.7 |
| Fin. der.(oth.than reserves) & ESOs | 8c9aa | 2.0 | | | | | | | .2 | 6.1 | .2 | 15.9 | 1.8 |
| Other investment | 8d9aa | 1,450.8 | 1,957.1 | 2,158.9 | 4,297.9 | 4,576.3 | 5,161.4 | 6,344.5 | 9,043.2 | 8,639.2 | 8,166.7 | 8,466.6 | 8,535.7 |
| Other equity | 8daaa | .... | .... | .... | .... | .... | — | | | | | | |
| Debt instruments | 8dzaa | 1,450.8 | 1,957.1 | 2,158.9 | 4,297.9 | 4,576.3 | 5,161.4 | 6,344.5 | 9,043.2 | 8,639.2 | 8,166.7 | 8,466.6 | 8,535.7 |
| Reserve assets | 8e9aa | 770.1 | 1,296.6 | 1,383.0 | 4,182.3 | 3,061.1 | 5,652.5 | 5,030.8 | 7,915.9 | 8,095.1 | 6,650.9 | 5,059.1 | 4,175.8 |
| Liabilities | 809la | 6,674.6 | 7,184.7 | 9,200.6 | 16,501.2 | 21,160.4 | 29,846.8 | 37,527.1 | 46,094.8 | 47,204.4 | 54,748.1 | 56,156.3 | 54,530.1 |
| Direct investment | 8a9la | 2,057.0 | 2,382.8 | 2,734.3 | 4,483.0 | 6,682.7 | 8,536.7 | 9,904.2 | 13,008.2 | 14,586.2 | 16,675.0 | 17,773.0 | 17,911.2 |
| Equity & investment fund shares | 8aala | 1,718.8 | 2,030.9 | 2,337.9 | 3,981.2 | 5,977.2 | 7,751.6 | 9,081.7 | 12,001.0 | 13,408.9 | 15,091.6 | 16,070.9 | 16,243.0 |
| Debt instruments | 8abla | 338.2 | 351.9 | 396.4 | 501.8 | 705.5 | 785.1 | 822.5 | 1,007.2 | 1,177.3 | 1,583.4 | 1,702.1 | 1,668.2 |
| Portfolio investment | 8b9la | 87.7 | 52.4 | 32.1 | 37.2 | 50.3 | 46.6 | 1,281.3 | 2,133.4 | 1,926.4 | 1,890.3 | 1,888.8 | 933.6 |
| Equity & investment fund shares | 8bala | 16.9 | 18.7 | 18.6 | 23.2 | 29.2 | 24.4 | 24.7 | 24.4 | 25.7 | 33.4 | 34.8 | 28.4 |
| Debt securities | 8bbla | 70.8 | 33.7 | 13.5 | 14.0 | 21.1 | 22.2 | 1,256.6 | 2,109.0 | 1,900.7 | 1,856.9 | 1,854.0 | 905.2 |
| Fin. der.(oth.than reserves) & ESOs | 8c9la | 3.7 | 7.1 | — | — | — | — | 18.2 | 46.3 | 3.9 | 2.0 | 26.8 | 2.5 |
| Other investment | 8d9la | 4,526.2 | 4,742.4 | 6,434.2 | 11,981.0 | 14,427.4 | 21,263.5 | 26,323.4 | 30,906.9 | 30,687.9 | 36,180.8 | 36,467.7 | 35,682.8 |
| Other equity | 8dala | .... | .... | .... | .... | .... | .... | | | | | | |
| Debt instruments | 8dzla | 4,526.2 | 4,742.4 | 6,434.2 | 11,981.0 | 14,427.4 | 21,263.5 | 26,323.4 | 30,906.9 | 30,687.9 | 36,180.8 | 36,467.7 | 35,682.8 |

# Belarus 913

| | | 2004 | 2005 | 2006 | 2007 | 2008 | 2009 | 2010 | 2011 | 2012 | 2013 | 2014 | 2015 |
|---|---|---|---|---|---|---|---|---|---|---|---|---|---|
| **Government Finance** | | | | | | | | | | | | | |
| **Cash Flow Statement** | | | | | | | | | | | | | |
| **General Government** | | | | | | *Billions of Rubels: Fiscal Year Ends December 31* | | | | | | |
| Cash Receipts:Operating Activities... | c1 | 23,766 | 31,749 | 39,472 | 49,344 | 67,495 | 64,924 | 70,682 | 118,263 | 222,826 | 277,471 | 323,280 | 376,717 |
| Taxes...................................... | c11 | 16,773 | 22,327 | 26,929 | 34,236 | 48,882 | 41,305 | 44,875 | 73,446 | 138,014 | 164,922 | 189,017 | 222,767 |
| Social Contributions...................... | c12 | 5,374 | 7,345 | 9,288 | 11,257 | 14,497 | 15,799 | 19,249 | 28,802 | 55,436 | 76,298 | 90,909 | 97,152 |
| Grants......................................... | c13 | — | — | — | — | — | — | — | — | — | — | 937 | 756 |
| Other Receipts.......................... | c14 | 1,619 | 2,077 | 3,255 | 3,851 | 4,117 | 7,820 | 6,557 | 16,015 | 29,376 | 36,251 | 42,417 | 56,042 |
| Cash Payments:Operating Activities. | c2 | 20,514 | 27,031 | 33,471 | 42,126 | 55,423 | 58,723 | 66,212 | 100,578 | 196,390 | 246,551 | 288,744 | 329,762 |
| Compensation of Employees.......... | c21 | 5,152 | 7,085 | 8,731 | 10,030 | 11,628 | 12,444 | 15,479 | 24,906 | 47,294 | 59,918 | 70,395 | 82,666 |
| Purchases of Goods & Services....... | c22 | 5,245 | 5,333 | 7,761 | 9,526 | 11,935 | 10,711 | 12,183 | 18,945 | 38,217 | 48,567 | 58,391 | 59,865 |
| Interest...................................... | c24 | 243 | 229 | 293 | 387 | 742 | 1,069 | 1,110 | 3,296 | 7,532 | 6,614 | 8,341 | 15,049 |
| Subsidies................................... | c25 | 2,493 | 3,816 | 4,532 | 7,784 | 12,279 | 12,167 | 8,845 | 13,801 | 26,848 | 31,711 | 35,249 | 37,572 |
| Grants....................................... | c26 | 124 | 155 | 107 | 125 | 138 | 179 | 203 | 418 | 630 | 657 | 658 | 715 |
| Social Benefits............................. | c27 | 6,431 | 8,522 | 10,252 | 12,212 | 14,953 | 17,861 | 22,350 | 33,764 | 67,141 | 91,358 | 108,719 | 127,680 |
| Other Payments........................... | c28 | 825 | 1,890 | 1,795 | 2,063 | 3,748 | 4,292 | 6,042 | 5,448 | 8,727 | 7,726 | 6,989 | 6,215 |
| Net Cash Inflow:Operating Act.[1-2] | ccio | 3,252 | 4,719 | 6,000 | 7,218 | 12,072 | 6,201 | 4,470 | 17,684 | 26,436 | 30,920 | 34,536 | 46,955 |
| Net Cash Outflow:Invest. in NFA...... | c31 | 2,944 | 4,566 | 4,572 | 6,070 | 7,485 | 6,637 | 7,441 | 8,611 | 22,118 | 32,295 | 27,920 | 23,384 |
| Purchases of Nonfinancial Assets... | c31.1 | 3,076 | 4,706 | 4,824 | 6,378 | 7,799 | 6,922 | 7,820 | 9,569 | 23,307 | 34,098 | 30,993 | 26,819 |
| Sales of Nonfinancial Assets.......... | c31.2 | 132 | 140 | 252 | 308 | 314 | 284 | 379 | 958 | 1,188 | 1,803 | 3,073 | 3,435 |
| Cash Surplus/Deficit [1-2-31=1-2M] | ccsd | 308 | 153 | 1,428 | 1,148 | 4,587 | −436 | −2,971 | 9,073 | 4,318 | −1,374 | 6,617 | 23,571 |
| Net Acq. Fin. Assets, excl. Cash...... | c32x | 214 | 422 | 1,190 | −1,265 | 3,781 | −1,426 | 1,895 | −3,084 | 11,502 | 6,193 | 8,252 | 27,889 |
| Domestic................................... | c321x | 214 | 422 | 1,190 | −1,265 | 3,781 | −1,426 | 1,895 | −3,084 | 11,502 | 6,193 | 8,252 | 27,889 |
| Foreign...................................... | c322x | — | — | — | — | — | — | — | — | — | — | — | — |
| Net Incurrence of Liabilities.............. | c33 | 480 | 1,166 | 1,120 | 3,543 | 6,576 | 6,677 | 5,929 | 26,482 | 3,663 | 1,977 | 3,673 | −4,768 |
| Domestic................................... | c331 | 243 | 968 | 1,104 | 452 | 3,564 | −4,806 | 1,301 | 17,366 | 7,410 | 7,972 | 9,469 | 13,739 |
| Foreign...................................... | c332 | 236 | 198 | 16 | 3,091 | 3,012 | 11,483 | 4,628 | 9,117 | −3,747 | −5,996 | −5,796 | −18,507 |
| Net Cash Inflow, Fin.Act.[-32x+33].. | cnfb | 265 | 744 | −71 | 4,808 | 2,795 | 8,103 | 4,034 | 29,565 | −7,839 | −4,217 | −4,579 | −32,657 |
| Net Change in Stock of Cash.......... | cncb | 574 | 897 | 1,357 | 5,956 | 7,382 | 7,667 | 1,063 | 38,639 | −3,522 | −5,591 | 2,039 | −9,087 |
| Stat. Discrep. [32X-33+NCB-CSD].. | ccsdz | — | — | — | — | −1 | — | — | — | — | −1 | 1 | — |
| Memo Item:Cash Expenditure[2+31] | c2m | 23,458 | 31,597 | 38,044 | 48,196 | 62,908 | 65,360 | 73,653 | 109,190 | 218,508 | 278,845 | 316,663 | 353,146 |
| Memo Item: Gross Debt.................. | c63 | .... | 4,729 | 6,231 | 9,735 | 16,650 | 26,976 | 35,682 | .... | .... | .... | .... | .... |
| **National Accounts** | | | | | | *Billions of Rubels* | | | | | | |
| Househ.Cons.Expend.,incl.NPISHs.... | 96f | 26,858.8 | 33,827.0 | 40,803.1 | 50,342.4 | 67,435.7 | 75,926.7 | 89,576.9 | 141,646.8 | 248,009.6 | 322,398.1 | 396,971.3 | 442,285.7 |
| Government Consumption Expend... | 91f | 10,299.9 | 13,524.4 | 15,225.1 | 17,998.1 | 21,447.9 | 23,001.3 | 27,638.1 | 41,387.3 | 74,705.1 | 90,886.7 | 111,297.0 | 129,965.9 |
| Gross Fixed Capital Formation......... | 93e | 12,656.6 | 17,253.6 | 23,511.2 | 30,486.9 | 43,225.2 | 49,345.6 | 64,698.4 | 113,230.1 | 178,454.5 | 244,295.8 | 263,693.0 | 248,349.9 |
| Changes in Inventories.................... | 93i | 1,674.7 | 1,264.8 | 2,000.2 | 2,638.6 | 5,630.2 | 1,885.0 | 3,118.3 | −1,438.8 | 9,189.9 | 10,806.0 | 13,027.0 | 12,583.7 |
| Exports of Goods and Services......... | 90c | 33,937.6 | 38,908.7 | 47,608.8 | 59,215.5 | 79,091.6 | 69,449.2 | 89,270.9 | 241,080.9 | 431,395.5 | 391,236.6 | 442,710.6 | 520,324.9 |
| Imports of Goods and Services (-)..... | 98c | 37,119.0 | 38,445.9 | 50,916.2 | 65,305.6 | 89,116.6 | 84,912.6 | 111,657.7 | 244,287.1 | 406,925.0 | 412,355.3 | 448,910.5 | 520,324.9 |
| Statistical Discrepancy..................... | 99bs | 1,683.2 | −1,265.5 | 1,034.8 | 1,789.4 | 2,076.8 | 2,747.0 | 1,831.2 | 5,538.5 | −4,474.1 | 1,842.8 | −693.7 | 34,827.0 |
| Gross Domestic Product (GDP)......... | 99b | 49,991.8 | 65,067.1 | 79,267.0 | 97,165.3 | 129,790.8 | 137,442.2 | 164,476.1 | 297,157.7 | 530,355.5 | 649,110.7 | 778,094.7 | 869,701.7 |
| Net Primary Income from Abroad..... | 98.n | −40.2 | 119.5 | −246.1 | −882.0 | −1,683.2 | −3,110.6 | −3,462.9 | −3,395.2 | −12,258.4 | −23,551.9 | −24,173.3 | −39,404.9 |
| Gross National Income (GNI)........... | 99a | 49,951.6 | 65,186.6 | 79,020.9 | 96,283.3 | 128,107.6 | 134,331.6 | 161,013.2 | 293,762.5 | 518,097.1 | 625,558.8 | 753,921.4 | 830,296.8 |
| Net Current Transf.from Abroad....... | 98t | 616.3 | 359.8 | 440.8 | 407.3 | 412.7 | 679.9 | 910.8 | −14,745.4 | −26,843.3 | −22,441.4 | −23,559.3 | 4,822.7 |
| Gross Nat'l Disposable Inc.(GNDI).... | 99i | 50,567.9 | 65,546.4 | 79,461.7 | 96,690.6 | 128,520.3 | 135,011.5 | 161,924.0 | 279,017.1 | 491,253.8 | 603,117.4 | 730,362.1 | 835,119.5 |
| Gross Saving................................ | 99s | 13,409.2 | 18,195.0 | 23,433.5 | 28,350.1 | 39,636.7 | 36,083.5 | 44,709.0 | 95,983.0 | 168,539.1 | 189,832.6 | 222,093.8 | 262,867.9 |
| GDP Volume 2009 Prices................. | 99b.p | .... | .... | .... | .... | .... | 137,442.2 | 148,081.3 | 156,290.5 | 158,701.3 | 160,624.6 | 163,392.3 | 157,040.1 |
| GDP Volume (2010=100).............. | 99bvp | 64.3 | † 70.3 | 77.4 | 84.1 | 92.7 | † 92.8 | 100.0 | 105.5 | 107.2 | 108.5 | 110.3 | 106.0 |
| GDP Deflator (2010=100).............. | 99bip | 47.3 | 56.3 | 62.3 | 70.3 | 85.2 | 90.0 | 100.0 | 171.2 | 300.9 | 363.8 | 428.7 | 498.6 |
| | | | | | | *Millions: Midyear Estimates* | | | | | | | |
| Population............................... | 99z | 9.70 | 9.64 | 9.59 | 9.56 | 9.53 | 9.51 | 9.49 | 9.49 | 9.49 | 9.50 | 9.50 | 9.50 |

# Belgium   124

| | | 2004 | 2005 | 2006 | 2007 | 2008 | 2009 | 2010 | 2011 | 2012 | 2013 | 2014 | 2015 |
|---|---|---|---|---|---|---|---|---|---|---|---|---|---|
| **Exchange Rates** | | | | | | | *Euros per SDR: End of Period* | | | | | | |
| Market Rate...................... | aa | 1.1402 | 1.2116 | 1.1423 | 1.0735 | 1.1068 | 1.0882 | 1.1525 | 1.1865 | 1.1649 | 1.1167 | 1.1933 | 1.2728 |
| | | | | | *Euros per US Dollar: End of Period (ae) Period Average (rf)* | | | | | | | | |
| Market Rate...................... | ae | .7342 | .8477 | .7593 | .6793 | .7185 | .6942 | .7484 | .7729 | .7579 | .7251 | .8237 | .9185 |
| Market Rate...................... | rf | .8054 | .8041 | .7971 | .7306 | .6827 | .7198 | .7550 | .7194 | .7783 | .7532 | .7537 | .9017 |
| | | | | | *Index Numbers (2010=100): Period Averages* | | | | | | | | |
| Nominal Effective Exchange Rate..... | nec | 98.3 | 97.9 | 98.1 | 99.8 | 102.4 | 103.3 | 100.0 | 100.6 | 98.1 | 100.4 | 100.8 | 96.4 |
| CPI-Based Real Effect. Ex. Rate....... | rec | 99.0 | 99.3 | 98.9 | 99.7 | 103.1 | 103.3 | 100.0 | 101.0 | 98.8 | 100.4 | 99.7 | 95.1 |
| ULC-Based Real Effect. Ex. Rate....... | rel | 97.0 | 97.5 | 100.1 | 102.3 | 103.8 | 103.5 | 100.0 | 100.0 | 99.1 | 102.0 | 103.2 | 100.0 |
| **Fund Position** | | | | | | | *Millions of SDRs: End of Period* | | | | | | |
| Quota............................... | 2f.s | 4,605.20 | 4,605.20 | 4,605.20 | 4,605.20 | 4,605.20 | 4,605.20 | 4,605.20 | 4,605.20 | 4,605.20 | 4,605.20 | 4,605.20 | 4,605.20 |
| SDR Holdings...................... | 1b.s | 225.28 | 219.90 | 361.98 | 385.23 | 369.81 | 4,405.78 | 4,408.38 | 4,233.87 | 4,243.62 | 4,137.13 | 4,038.75 | 4,067.29 |
| Reserve Position in the Fund........... | 1c.s | 1,478.63 | 777.89 | 412.09 | 302.10 | 637.39 | 764.73 | 1,188.68 | 2,231.22 | 2,360.07 | 2,226.16 | 1,797.25 | 1,281.36 |
| Total Fund Cred. & Loans Outstg...... | 2tl | — | — | — | — | — | — | — | — | — | — | — | — |
| SDR Allocations...................... | 1bd | 485.25 | 485.25 | 485.25 | 485.25 | 485.25 | 4,323.34 | 4,323.34 | 4,323.34 | 4,323.34 | 4,323.34 | 4,323.34 | 4,323.34 |
| **International Liquidity** | | | | | | *Millions of US Dollars Unless Otherwise Indicated: End of Period* | | | | | | | |
| Total Res.Min.Gold (Eurosys.Def)..... | 1l.d | 10,361 | 8,241 | 8,783 | 10,384 | 9,318 | 15,907 | 16,499 | 17,918 | 18,600 | 18,139 | 16,626 | 16,352 |
| SDR Holdings.......................... | 1b.d | 350 | 314 | 545 | 609 | 570 | 6,907 | 6,789 | 6,500 | 6,522 | 6,371 | 5,851 | 5,636 |
| Reserve Position in the Fund.......... | 1c.d | 2,296 | 1,112 | 620 | 477 | 982 | 1,199 | 1,831 | 3,426 | 3,627 | 3,428 | 2,604 | 1,776 |
| Foreign Exchange..................... | 1d.d | 7,715 | 6,815 | 7,619 | 9,298 | 7,767 | 7,801 | 7,880 | 7,992 | 8,451 | 8,339 | 7,836 | 8,453 |
| o/w:Fin.Deriv.Rel.to Reserves....... | 1ddd | 120 | −55 | 63 | 84 | 42 | −52 | −47 | −101 | 107 | 74 | −168 | −33 |
| Other Reserve Assets................. | 1e.d | — | — | — | — | — | — | — | — | — | — | 335 | 488 |
| Gold (Million Fine Troy Ounces)........ | 1ad | 8.29 | 7.32 | 7.32 | 7.32 | 7.32 | 7.32 | 7.31 | 7.31 | 7.31 | 7.31 | 7.31 | 7.31 |
| Gold (Eurosystem Valuation)............ | 1and | 3,630 | 3,755 | 4,653 | 6,122 | 6,327 | 8,076 | 10,315 | 11,514 | 12,169 | 8,785 | 8,769 | 7,746 |
| Memo:Euro Cl. on Non-EA Res........ | 1dgd | .... | .... | .... | .... | .... | .... | .... | .... | .... | .... | .... | .... |
| Non-Euro Cl. on EA Res........ | 1dhd | 569 | 556 | 354 | 1,169 | 52,172 | 326 | 544 | 9,918 | 334 | 405 | 484 | 355 |
| Central Bank: Other Assets.............. | 3..d | 8,288 | 7,447 | 8,574 | 22,192 | 21,775 | 22,629 | 25,928 | 30,039 | 27,851 | 26,192 | 23,734 | 22,135 |
| Central Bank: Other Liabs............... | 4..d | 1,330 | 1,072 | 1,417 | 1,375 | 1,129 | 7,149 | 7,018 | 7,077 | 7,079 | 7,265 | 6,457 | 7,121 |
| Other Depository Corps.: Assets....... | 7a.d | 236,399 | 274,516 | 314,101 | 399,425 | 331,543 | 285,768 | 252,412 | 222,661 | 231,878 | 251,879 | 242,067 | 208,611 |
| Other Depository Corps.: Liabs......... | 7b.d | 276,832 | 328,567 | 351,098 | 478,084 | 336,889 | 310,014 | 295,749 | 233,480 | 204,924 | 202,354 | 192,496 | 176,687 |
| **Central Bank** | | | | | | | *Millions of Euros: End of Period* | | | | | | |
| Euro Area Wide Residency Criterion | | | | | | | | | | | | | |
| Net Foreign Assets.......................... | 11n.u | 8,540 | 9,400 | 8,988 | 9,389 | 8,449 | 10,209 | 13,960 | 16,576 | 17,625 | 14,968 | 16,353 | 15,784 |
| Claims on Nonresidents............... | 11..u | 10,531 | 10,687 | 10,770 | 11,887 | 11,791 | 17,379 | 20,869 | 23,786 | 24,097 | 20,236 | 21,671 | 22,467 |
| Liabilities to Nonresidents............ | 16c.u | 1,990 | 1,287 | 1,782 | 2,498 | 3,342 | 7,170 | 6,909 | 7,210 | 6,472 | 5,268 | 5,318 | 6,683 |
| Claims on Other Depository Corps.... | 12e.u | 24,395 | 31,018 | 42,314 | 61,778 | 101,421 | 48,718 | 15,252 | 62,751 | 46,505 | 19,959 | 16,463 | 15,265 |
| Net Claims on Central Government.. | 12anu | 3,298 | 3,197 | 3,057 | 9,707 | 10,390 | 10,195 | 13,502 | 17,844 | 17,647 | 17,304 | 16,784 | 30,880 |
| Claims on Central Govt................. | 12a.u | 3,433 | 3,234 | 3,103 | 9,753 | 10,451 | 10,303 | 13,584 | 17,909 | 17,943 | 17,430 | 16,833 | 30,918 |
| Liabs. to Central Govt................ | 16d.u | 135 | 37 | 46 | 46 | 61 | 108 | 82 | 65 | 296 | 126 | 49 | 38 |
| Claims on Other Sectors................. | 12s.u | 37 | 38 | 214 | 331 | 388 | 338 | 370 | 512 | 468 | 502 | 609 | 579 |
| Claims on Other Financial Corps.... | 12g.u | — | — | — | — | — | 1 | — | 34 | 150 | 242 | 317 | 267 |
| Claims on State & Local Govts....... | 12b.u | 15 | 33 | 180 | 276 | 328 | 278 | 300 | 382 | 233 | 194 | 224 | 240 |
| Claims on Public Nonfin. Corps...... | 12c.u | — | — | — | — | — | — | — | — | — | — | — | — |
| Claims on Private Sector............... | 12d.u | 22 | 5 | 34 | 55 | 60 | 59 | 70 | 96 | 85 | 66 | 68 | 72 |
| Monetary Base................................ | 14..u | 22,724 | 26,437 | 29,559 | 41,038 | 37,009 | 42,069 | 41,975 | 54,119 | 50,685 | 45,900 | 45,452 | 62,060 |
| Currency in Circulation................ | 14a.u | 17,223 | 19,434 | 21,618 | 23,238 | 26,047 | 27,059 | 28,229 | 29,809 | 30,544 | 31,960 | 34,452 | 36,457 |
| Liabs. to Other Depository Corps.... | 14c.u | 5,495 | 6,997 | 7,931 | 17,793 | 10,936 | 15,004 | 13,699 | 23,836 | 19,871 | 13,799 | 10,764 | 25,398 |
| Liabs. to Other Sectors................ | 14d.u | 6 | 6 | 10 | 7 | 26 | 6 | 47 | 474 | 270 | 141 | 236 | 205 |
| Other Liabs. to Other Dep. Corps..... | 14n.u | — | — | — | — | — | — | — | — | — | — | — | — |
| Dep. & Sec. Excl. f/Monetary Base.... | 14o.u | — | — | — | — | — | — | — | — | — | — | — | — |
| Deposits Included in Broad Money. | 15..u | — | — | — | — | — | — | — | — | — | — | — | — |
| Sec.Ot.th.Shares Inc.in.Brd.Money. | 16a.u | — | — | — | — | — | — | — | — | — | — | — | — |
| Deposits Excl. from Broad Money... | 16b.u | — | — | — | — | — | — | — | — | — | — | — | — |
| Sec.Oh.th.Shares Excl. f/Brd.Money | 16s.u | — | — | — | — | — | — | — | — | — | — | — | — |
| Loans....................................... | 16l.u | — | — | — | — | — | — | — | — | — | — | — | — |
| Financial Derivatives....................... | 16m.u | — | — | — | — | — | — | — | — | — | — | — | — |
| Shares and Other Equity.................. | 17a.u | 3,685 | 4,640 | 4,927 | 5,768 | 6,679 | 7,845 | 11,227 | 12,759 | 13,403 | 10,614 | 11,951 | 12,324 |
| Other Items (Net)........................... | 17r.u | 9,862 | 12,575 | 20,088 | 34,398 | 76,961 | 19,543 | −10,119 | 30,803 | 18,156 | −3,780 | −7,196 | −11,875 |
| *Memorandum Items* | | | | | | | | | | | | | |
| National Residency Criterion | | | | | | | | | | | | | |
| Net Foreign Assets.......................... | 11n | −15,699 | −20,590 | −30,343 | −37,879 | −80,819 | −17,561 | 18,004 | −15,380 | −503 | 17,751 | 22,774 | 27,862 |
| Claims on Nonresidents............... | 11 | 16,357 | 16,482 | 16,712 | 26,287 | 26,889 | 32,356 | 39,472 | 45,963 | 44,429 | 38,515 | 40,466 | 42,467 |
| Liabilities to Nonresidents............ | 16c | 32,055 | 37,072 | 47,055 | 64,166 | 107,708 | 49,917 | 21,468 | 61,343 | 44,932 | 20,764 | 17,692 | 14,605 |
| Claims on Other Depository Corps.... | 12e | 22,775 | 29,061 | 40,302 | 56,786 | 95,971 | 43,212 | 8,565 | 55,958 | 40,824 | 16,036 | 11,917 | 9,201 |
| Net Claims on Central Government.. | 12an | 546 | 814 | 758 | 2,051 | 2,551 | 2,457 | 3,351 | 4,367 | 4,858 | 4,845 | 4,577 | 18,956 |
| Claims on Central Government...... | 12a | 681 | 851 | 804 | 2,097 | 2,612 | 2,565 | 3,433 | 4,432 | 5,154 | 4,971 | 4,626 | 18,994 |
| Liabilities to Central Government.... | 16d | 135 | 37 | 46 | 46 | 61 | 108 | 82 | 65 | 296 | 126 | 49 | 38 |
| Claims on Other Sectors................. | 12s | 2 | 2 | 2 | 2 | 2 | 2 | 2 | 2 | 3 | 6 | 3 | 3 |
| Claims on Other Fin. Corps............ | 12g | — | — | — | — | — | — | — | — | — | — | 2 | 2 |
| Claims on State & Local Govts....... | 12b | — | — | — | — | — | — | — | — | — | — | — | — |
| Claims on Private Sector............... | 12d | 2 | 2 | 2 | 2 | 2 | 2 | 2 | 2 | 3 | 6 | 1 | 1 |
| Liabs.to ODCs, Inc.in Mon.Base....... | 14c | 5,416 | 6,786 | 7,928 | 17,789 | 10,804 | 14,777 | 12,996 | 22,570 | 19,572 | 13,798 | 10,763 | 25,224 |
| Liabs.to Ot.Sectors, Inc.in Mon.Base | 14d | 5 | 5 | 9 | 6 | 25 | 6 | 47 | 474 | 270 | 141 | 236 | 205 |
| Liabs.to ODCs,Excl.f/Mon.Base........ | 14n | — | — | — | — | — | — | — | — | — | — | — | — |
| Net Claims on Eurosystem.............. | 12e.s | −28,423 | −34,011 | −43,707 | −60,096 | −102,666 | −40,983 | −12,279 | −51,249 | −36,503 | −13,830 | −10,650 | −6,025 |

# Belgium   124

| | | 2004 | 2005 | 2006 | 2007 | 2008 | 2009 | 2010 | 2011 | 2012 | 2013 | 2014 | 2015 |
|---|---|---|---|---|---|---|---|---|---|---|---|---|---|
| **Other Depository Corporations** | | | | | | *Millions of Euros: End of Period* | | | | | | | |
| Euro Area Wide Residency Criterion | | | | | | | | | | | | | |
| Net Foreign Assets......................... | 21n.u | −29,684 | −45,817 | −28,092 | −53,433 | −3,841 | −16,831 | −32,433 | −8,362 | 20,429 | 35,911 | 40,830 | 29,323 |
| Claims on Nonresidents................. | 21..u | 173,555 | 232,700 | 238,497 | 271,330 | 238,229 | 198,367 | 188,903 | 172,085 | 175,745 | 182,640 | 199,380 | 191,615 |
| Liabilities to Nonresidents.............. | 26c.u | 203,239 | 278,517 | 266,589 | 324,763 | 242,070 | 215,198 | 221,336 | 180,447 | 155,316 | 146,729 | 158,550 | 162,292 |
| Claims on Eurosystem...................... | 20..u | 7,062 | 8,329 | 9,511 | 21,194 | 12,711 | 17,258 | 16,073 | 26,148 | 23,432 | 18,072 | 15,337 | 29,901 |
| Currency............................................ | 20a.u | 1,611 | 1,538 | 1,577 | 1,700 | 1,907 | 1,888 | 1,766 | 1,893 | 2,010 | 2,124 | 2,174 | 2,041 |
| Reserve Deposits and Securities..... | 20b.u | 5,451 | 6,791 | 7,934 | 19,494 | 10,804 | 15,370 | 14,307 | 24,255 | 21,422 | 15,948 | 13,163 | 27,860 |
| Other Claims................................... | 20n.u | — | — | — | — | — | — | — | — | — | — | — | — |
| Net Claims on Central Government.. | 22anu | 152,778 | 154,328 | 138,098 | 98,810 | 106,001 | 111,807 | 101,444 | 103,923 | 86,805 | 80,350 | 79,047 | 78,033 |
| Claims on Central Government...... | 22a.u | 154,213 | 157,562 | 140,847 | 103,491 | 117,825 | 116,097 | 104,541 | 107,075 | 88,663 | 81,986 | 80,543 | 79,686 |
| Liabilities to Central Government... | 26d.u | 1,435 | 3,234 | 2,749 | 4,681 | 11,824 | 4,290 | 3,097 | 3,152 | 1,858 | 1,636 | 1,496 | 1,653 |
| Claims on Other Sectors.................. | 22s.u | 275,078 | 301,967 | 346,748 | 412,653 | 434,366 | 433,798 | 428,550 | 432,063 | 425,975 | 431,671 | 617,636 | 597,614 |
| Claims on Other Financial Corps.... | 22g.u | 47,112 | 53,068 | 77,111 | 121,220 | 159,767 | 189,296 | 178,550 | 178,791 | 169,578 | 162,315 | 322,036 | 280,747 |
| Claims on State & Local Govts....... | 22b.u | 24,377 | 25,438 | 25,103 | 24,143 | 23,795 | 18,954 | 21,568 | 22,689 | 24,950 | 27,724 | 40,301 | 40,238 |
| Claims on Public Nonfin. Corps...... | 22c.u | — | — | — | — | — | — | — | — | — | — | — | — |
| Claims on Private Sector................. | 22d.u | 203,589 | 223,461 | 244,534 | 267,290 | 250,804 | 225,548 | 228,432 | 230,583 | 231,447 | 241,632 | 255,299 | 276,629 |
| Liabilities to Eurosystem.................. | 26g.u | 25,748 | 33,735 | 45,414 | 68,301 | 102,756 | 50,221 | 24,824 | 63,260 | 45,899 | 20,881 | 17,612 | 15,262 |
| Transf.Dep.Included in Broad Money | 24..u | 78,155 | 90,395 | 92,387 | 99,521 | 100,070 | 112,980 | 113,924 | 109,970 | 122,916 | 130,248 | 147,208 | 162,060 |
| Other.Dep.Included in Broad Money. | 25..u | 223,059 | 234,766 | 250,030 | 270,007 | 273,810 | 258,041 | 272,727 | 280,254 | 292,434 | 303,621 | 313,150 | 331,390 |
| Sec.Ot.th.Shares Inc.in.Brd. Money... | 26a.u | 5,458 | 3,671 | 1,953 | 4,817 | 11,110 | 22,154 | 15,072 | −6,389 | 13,022 | −1,612 | 4,651 | 15,333 |
| Deposits Excl. from Broad Money..... | 26b.u | 30,296 | 35,033 | 45,227 | 56,106 | 74,712 | 85,366 | 80,886 | 86,695 | 81,670 | 71,859 | 64,578 | 54,776 |
| Sec.Ot.th.Shares Excl.f/Brd. Money... | 26s.u | 30,846 | 23,631 | 24,693 | 23,401 | 27,080 | 38,979 | 32,571 | 43,772 | 18,535 | 34,343 | 31,492 | 30,828 |
| Loans............................................... | 26l.u | — | — | — | — | — | — | — | — | — | — | — | — |
| Financial Derivatives........................ | 26m.u | — | — | — | — | — | — | — | — | — | — | 156,854 | 120,834 |
| Insurance Technical Reserves........... | 26r.u | — | — | — | — | — | — | — | — | — | — | — | — |
| Shares and Other Equity.................. | 27a.u | 32,343 | 33,259 | 40,511 | 63,145 | 53,013 | 49,993 | 52,649 | 53,562 | 54,439 | 58,117 | 60,088 | 58,137 |
| Other Items (Net)............................. | 27r.u | −20,675 | −35,684 | −33,951 | −106,068 | −93,319 | −71,705 | −79,023 | −77,347 | −72,273 | −51,457 | −42,615 | −53,705 |
| Memorandum Items | | | | | | | | | | | | | |
| Total Assets..................................... | 20ra | 916,484 | 1,057,749 | 1,124,527 | 1,301,894 | 1,276,321 | 1,157,429 | 1,134,735 | 1,200,781 | 1,085,302 | 1,021,570 | 1,101,830 | 1,073,452 |
| National Residency Criterion | | | | | | | | | | | | | |
| Net Foreign Assets..................... | 21n | 105,212 | 103,505 | 109,487 | 140,701 | 184,727 | 127,809 | 92,532 | 122,884 | 106,686 | 110,133 | 113,959 | 111,475 |
| Claims on Nonresidents.................. | 21 | 486,112 | 594,586 | 637,416 | 748,279 | 646,690 | 548,112 | 514,497 | 493,381 | 417,326 | 396,662 | 410,896 | 406,549 |
| Liabilities to Nonresidents.............. | 26c | 380,900 | 491,081 | 527,929 | 607,578 | 461,963 | 420,303 | 421,965 | 370,497 | 310,640 | 286,529 | 296,937 | 295,074 |
| Net Claims on Central Government.. | 22an | 65,515 | 64,127 | 59,562 | 44,574 | 40,857 | 51,953 | 55,376 | 62,938 | 62,353 | 55,471 | 51,723 | 48,076 |
| Claims on Central Government...... | 22a | 66,393 | 65,051 | 60,371 | 45,771 | 47,198 | 53,595 | 57,247 | 64,914 | 63,949 | 56,763 | 53,007 | 49,326 |
| Liabilities to Central Government... | 26d | 878 | 924 | 809 | 1,197 | 6,341 | 1,642 | 1,871 | 1,976 | 1,596 | 1,292 | 1,284 | 1,250 |
| Claims on Other Sectors.................. | 22s | 231,527 | 248,884 | 285,941 | 328,374 | 348,192 | 350,361 | 356,314 | 364,877 | 371,570 | 379,345 | 561,898 | 539,919 |
| Claims on Other Fin. Corps............ | 22g | 23,805 | 26,633 | 47,473 | 70,039 | 104,509 | 128,809 | 129,934 | 134,136 | 135,379 | 131,728 | 291,092 | 250,308 |
| Claims on State & Local Govts....... | 22b | 24,163 | 25,076 | 24,411 | 23,151 | 22,937 | 18,248 | 20,113 | 22,378 | 24,807 | 26,007 | 37,507 | 37,055 |
| Claims on Private Sector................. | 22d | 183,559 | 197,175 | 214,057 | 235,184 | 220,746 | 203,304 | 206,267 | 208,363 | 211,384 | 221,610 | 233,299 | 252,556 |
| Transf.Dep.Included in Broad Money | 24 | 72,711 | 81,171 | 83,670 | 85,464 | 86,833 | 101,218 | 102,610 | 101,386 | 110,920 | 119,633 | 135,564 | 149,986 |
| Other.Dep.Included in Broad Money. | 25 | 198,117 | 210,197 | 224,585 | 232,565 | 240,467 | 235,582 | 254,911 | 266,866 | 276,919 | 285,873 | 293,955 | 308,657 |
| Sec.Ot.th.Shares Inc.in.Brd. Money... | 26a | 6,506 | 6,477 | 7,068 | 10,494 | 13,644 | 15,459 | 8,730 | 3,857 | 5,499 | 9,268 | 9,306 | 10,830 |
| Deposits Excl. from Broad Money..... | 26b | 11,799 | 12,804 | 13,797 | 18,201 | 23,328 | 22,634 | 24,809 | 27,228 | 28,501 | 28,506 | 27,479 | 24,312 |
| Sec.Ot.th.Shares Excl.f/Brd. Money... | 26s | 49,343 | 42,398 | 40,429 | 50,834 | 48,554 | 60,584 | 53,914 | 61,135 | 45,403 | 46,562 | 43,986 | 43,916 |

# Belgium 124

| | | 2004 | 2005 | 2006 | 2007 | 2008 | 2009 | 2010 | 2011 | 2012 | 2013 | 2014 | 2015 |
|---|---|---|---|---|---|---|---|---|---|---|---|---|---|
| **Depository Corporations** | | | | | | Millions of Euros: End of Period | | | | | | | |
| Euro Area Wide Residency Criterion | | | | | | | | | | | | | |
| Net Foreign Assets............ | 31n.u | −21,144 | −36,417 | −19,104 | −44,044 | 4,608 | −6,622 | −18,473 | 8,214 | 38,054 | 50,879 | 57,183 | 45,107 |
| Claims on Nonresidents............. | 31..u | 184,086 | 243,387 | 249,267 | 283,217 | 250,020 | 215,746 | 209,772 | 195,871 | 199,842 | 202,876 | 221,051 | 214,082 |
| Liabilities to Nonresidents............ | 36c.u | 205,229 | 279,804 | 268,371 | 327,261 | 245,412 | 222,368 | 228,245 | 187,657 | 161,788 | 151,997 | 163,868 | 168,975 |
| Domestic Claims............. | 32..u | 431,191 | 459,530 | 488,117 | 521,501 | 551,145 | 556,138 | 543,866 | 554,342 | 530,895 | 529,827 | 714,076 | 707,106 |
| Net Claims on Central Government | 32anu | 156,076 | 157,525 | 141,155 | 108,517 | 116,391 | 122,002 | 114,946 | 121,767 | 104,452 | 97,654 | 95,831 | 108,913 |
| Claims on Central Government...... | 32a.u | 157,646 | 160,796 | 143,950 | 113,244 | 128,276 | 126,400 | 118,125 | 124,984 | 106,606 | 99,416 | 97,376 | 110,604 |
| Liabilities to Central Government... | 36d.u | 1,570 | 3,271 | 2,795 | 4,727 | 11,885 | 4,398 | 3,179 | 3,217 | 2,154 | 1,762 | 1,545 | 1,691 |
| Claims on Other Sectors............. | 32s.u | 275,115 | 302,005 | 346,962 | 412,984 | 434,754 | 434,136 | 428,920 | 432,575 | 426,443 | 432,173 | 618,245 | 598,193 |
| Claims on Other Financial Corps.... | 32g.u | 47,112 | 53,068 | 77,111 | 121,220 | 159,767 | 189,297 | 178,550 | 178,825 | 169,728 | 162,557 | 322,353 | 281,014 |
| Claims on State & Local Govts....... | 32b.u | 24,392 | 25,471 | 25,283 | 24,419 | 24,123 | 19,232 | 21,868 | 23,071 | 25,183 | 27,918 | 40,525 | 40,478 |
| Claims on Public Nonfin. Corps...... | 32c.u | — | — | — | — | — | — | — | — | — | — | — | — |
| Claims on Private Sector................ | 32d.u | 203,611 | 223,466 | 244,568 | 267,345 | 250,864 | 225,607 | 228,502 | 230,679 | 231,532 | 241,698 | 255,367 | 276,701 |
| Broad Money Liabilities............ | 35l.u | 322,290 | 346,734 | 364,421 | 395,890 | 409,156 | 418,352 | 428,233 | 412,225 | 457,176 | 462,234 | 497,523 | 543,404 |
| Currency Outside Depository Corps | 34a.u | 15,612 | 17,896 | 20,041 | 21,538 | 24,140 | 25,171 | 26,463 | 27,916 | 28,534 | 29,836 | 32,278 | 34,416 |
| Transferable Deposits................... | 34..u | 78,161 | 90,401 | 92,397 | 99,528 | 100,096 | 112,986 | 113,971 | 110,444 | 123,186 | 130,389 | 147,444 | 162,265 |
| Other Deposits..................... | 35..u | 223,059 | 234,766 | 250,030 | 270,007 | 273,810 | 258,041 | 272,727 | 280,254 | 292,434 | 303,621 | 313,150 | 331,390 |
| Securities Other than Shares......... | 36a.u | 5,458 | 3,671 | 1,953 | 4,817 | 11,110 | 22,154 | 15,072 | −6,389 | 13,022 | −1,612 | 4,651 | 15,333 |
| Deposits Excl. from Broad Money..... | 36b.u | 30,296 | 35,033 | 45,227 | 56,106 | 74,712 | 85,366 | 80,886 | 86,695 | 81,670 | 71,859 | 64,578 | 54,776 |
| Sec.Oth.th.Shares Excl.f/Brd. Money. | 36s.u | 30,846 | 23,631 | 24,693 | 23,401 | 27,080 | 38,979 | 32,571 | 43,772 | 18,535 | 34,343 | 31,492 | 30,828 |
| Loans................. | 36l.u | — | — | — | — | — | — | — | — | — | — | — | — |
| Financial Derivatives.................. | 36m.u | — | — | — | — | — | — | — | — | — | — | 156,854 | 120,834 |
| Insurance Technical Reserves........... | 36r.u | — | — | — | — | — | — | — | — | — | — | — | — |
| Shares and Other Equity................ | 37a.u | 36,028 | 37,899 | 45,438 | 68,913 | 59,692 | 57,838 | 63,876 | 66,321 | 67,842 | 68,731 | 72,039 | 70,461 |
| Other Items (Net)..................... | 37r.u | −9,416 | −20,186 | −10,766 | −66,848 | −14,891 | −51,025 | −80,178 | −46,454 | −56,274 | −56,464 | −51,061 | −68,045 |
| Broad Money Liabs., Seasonally Adj. | 35lub | 320,324 | 345,530 | 364,275 | 396,925 | 411,131 | 420,868 | 430,892 | 414,864 | 460,612 | 466,244 | 502,325 | 548,864 |
| Memorandum Items | | | | | | | | | | | | | |
| National Residency Criterion | | | | | | | | | | | | | |
| Net Foreign Assets........................ | 31n | 89,513 | 82,915 | 79,144 | 102,822 | 103,908 | 110,248 | 110,536 | 107,504 | 106,183 | 127,884 | 136,733 | 139,337 |
| Claims on Nonresidents................. | 31 | 502,469 | 611,068 | 654,128 | 774,566 | 673,579 | 580,468 | 553,969 | 539,344 | 461,755 | 435,177 | 451,362 | 449,016 |
| Liabilities to Nonresidents............. | 36c | 412,955 | 528,153 | 574,984 | 671,744 | 569,671 | 470,220 | 443,433 | 431,840 | 355,572 | 307,293 | 314,629 | 309,679 |
| Domestic Claims............... | 32 | 297,590 | 313,827 | 346,263 | 375,001 | 391,602 | 404,773 | 415,043 | 432,184 | 438,784 | 439,667 | 618,201 | 606,954 |
| Net Claims on Central Government | 32an | 66,061 | 64,941 | 60,320 | 46,625 | 43,408 | 54,410 | 58,727 | 67,305 | 67,211 | 60,316 | 56,300 | 67,032 |
| Claims on Central Government.... | 32a | 67,074 | 65,902 | 61,175 | 47,868 | 49,810 | 56,160 | 60,680 | 69,346 | 69,103 | 61,734 | 57,633 | 68,320 |
| Liabilities to Central Government. | 36d | 1,013 | 961 | 855 | 1,243 | 6,402 | 1,750 | 1,953 | 2,041 | 1,892 | 1,418 | 1,333 | 1,288 |
| Claims on Other Sectors................ | 32s | 231,529 | 248,886 | 285,943 | 328,376 | 348,194 | 350,363 | 356,316 | 364,879 | 371,573 | 379,351 | 561,901 | 539,922 |
| Claims on Other Financial Corps.. | 32g | 23,805 | 26,633 | 47,473 | 70,039 | 104,509 | 128,809 | 129,934 | 134,136 | 135,379 | 131,728 | 291,094 | 250,310 |
| Claims on State & Local Govts..... | 32b | 24,163 | 25,076 | 24,411 | 23,151 | 22,937 | 18,248 | 20,113 | 22,378 | 24,807 | 26,007 | 37,507 | 37,055 |
| Claims on Private Sector............. | 32d | 183,561 | 197,177 | 214,059 | 235,186 | 220,748 | 203,306 | 206,269 | 208,365 | 211,387 | 221,616 | 233,300 | 252,557 |
| Transf.Dep.Included in Broad Money | 34 | 72,716 | 81,176 | 83,679 | 85,470 | 86,858 | 101,224 | 102,657 | 101,860 | 111,190 | 119,774 | 135,800 | 150,191 |
| Other Dep.Included in Broad Money. | 35 | 198,117 | 210,197 | 224,585 | 232,565 | 240,467 | 235,582 | 254,911 | 266,866 | 276,919 | 285,873 | 293,955 | 308,657 |
| Sec.Ot.th.Shares Inc.in.Brd. Money... | 36a | 6,506 | 6,477 | 7,068 | 10,494 | 13,644 | 15,459 | 8,730 | 3,857 | 5,499 | 9,268 | 9,306 | 10,830 |
| Deposits Excl. from Broad Money..... | 36b | 11,799 | 12,804 | 13,797 | 18,201 | 23,328 | 22,634 | 24,809 | 27,228 | 28,501 | 28,506 | 27,479 | 24,312 |
| Sec.Ot.th.Shares Excl./f.Brd. Money.. | 36s | 49,343 | 42,398 | 40,429 | 50,834 | 48,554 | 60,584 | 53,914 | 61,135 | 45,403 | 46,562 | 43,986 | 43,916 |
| **Interest Rates** | | | | | | Percent Per Annum | | | | | | | |
| Treasury Bill Rate.................... | 60c | 1.97 | 2.02 | 2.73 | 3.80 | 3.63 | .58 | .32 | .78 | .07 | .02 | .02 | −.24 |
| Households: Stocks, up to 2 years.. | 60lhs | 2.39 | 2.48 | 2.87 | 3.87 | 4.28 | 3.32 | 2.61 | 2.42 | 2.35 | 1.90 | 1.47 | 1.38 |
| New Business, up to 1 year.......... | 60lhn | 1.83 | 1.95 | 2.66 | 3.84 | 4.13 | 1.18 | .77 | 1.18 | .64 | .84 | 1.00 | 1.01 |
| Corporations: Stocks, up to 2 years | 60lcs | 2.12 | 2.10 | 2.69 | 3.80 | 4.18 | 1.53 | .93 | 1.50 | 1.20 | .91 | .69 | .40 |
| New Business, up to 1 year.......... | 60lcn | 2.01 | 2.03 | 2.73 | 3.81 | 3.87 | .64 | .39 | .89 | .39 | .26 | .30 | .12 |
| Lending Rate........................ | 60p | 6.70 | 6.72 | 7.49 | 8.57 | 9.21 | 9.50 | .... | .... | .... | .... | .... | .... |
| Households: Stocks, up to 1 year.... | 60phs | 8.33 | 7.69 | 7.73 | 8.25 | 8.89 | 7.95 | 6.83 | 6.78 | 6.68 | 6.03 | 5.95 | 5.46 |
| New Bus., Floating & up to 1 year | 60pns | 6.48 | 6.32 | 6.56 | 6.98 | 7.03 | 6.15 | 5.78 | 5.98 | 6.21 | 5.96 | 4.81 | 3.93 |
| House Purch., Stocks,Over 5 years | 60phv | 5.19 | 4.67 | 4.40 | 4.53 | 4.63 | 4.47 | 4.09 | 4.03 | 3.94 | 3.66 | 3.48 | 2.99 |
| House Purch., New Bus., 5-10 yrs | 60phn | 4.41 | 3.97 | 4.13 | 4.80 | 5.19 | 4.58 | 4.22 | 3.93 | 3.62 | 3.49 | 3.23 | 2.46 |
| Corporations: Stocks, up to 1 year. | 60pcs | 4.11 | 3.82 | 4.20 | 5.28 | 5.67 | 3.17 | 2.75 | 3.13 | 2.75 | 2.49 | 2.49 | 2.24 |
| New Bus., Over € 1 mil.,up to 1 yr | 60pcn | 2.80 | 2.77 | 3.48 | 4.73 | 5.04 | 2.05 | 1.70 | 2.22 | 1.74 | 1.76 | 1.77 | 1.60 |
| Government Bond Yield................ | 61 | 4.15 | 3.43 | 3.82 | 4.33 | 4.42 | 3.90 | 3.46 | 4.23 | 3.00 | 2.41 | 1.71 | .84 |
| **Prices, Production, Labor** | | | | | | Index Numbers (2010=100): Period Averages | | | | | | | |
| Industrial Share Prices.................... | 62 | 100.0 | 124.9 | 152.7 | 172.6 | 122.4 | 83.6 | 100.0 | 94.7 | 89.6 | 105.3 | 121.8 | 141.4 |
| Producer Prices | | | | | | | | | | | | | |
| Home and Import Goods............... | 63 | 83.2 | 87.6 | 92.9 | 95.4 | 101.3 | 92.7 | † 100.0 | 108.9 | 113.0 | 112.4 | 108.5 | 103.1 |
| Industrial Production Prices........... | 63b | 81.9 | 86.6 | 91.6 | 93.5 | 102.2 | 94.9 | † 100.0 | 108.1 | 111.9 | 112.5 | 107.4 | 102.9 |
| Consumer Prices..................... | 64 | 88.0 | † 90.4 | † 92.0 | 93.7 | 97.9 | 97.9 | 100.0 | 103.5 | 106.5 | 107.7 | 108.0 | 108.6 |
| Harmonized CPI..................... | 64h | 87.5 | 89.8 | 91.9 | 93.5 | 97.7 | 97.7 | 100.0 | 103.4 | 106.1 | 107.4 | 107.9 | 108.6 |
| Wages............................. | 65 | 84.2 | 86.3 | 88.4 | 90.2 | 93.2 | 96.6 | † 100.0 | 104.0 | 106.6 | 106.7 | † 106.1 | 106.2 |
| Industrial Production.................. | 66 | 82.4 | 85.4 | 90.6 | 96.7 | 100.1 | 90.1 | 100.0 | 104.0 | 101.8 | 102.8 | 103.7 | 103.4 |
| | | | | | | Number in Thousands: Period Averages | | | | | | | |
| Labor Force.......................... | 67d | 4,473 | 4,589 | 4,616 | 4,701 | 4,747 | 4,769 | 4,856 | 4,817 | 4,848 | 4,901 | 4,920 | 4,921 |
| Employment......................... | 67e | 4,144 | 4,199 | 4,233 | 4,348 | 4,414 | 4,390 | 4,451 | 4,471 | 4,479 | 4,485 | 4,498 | 4,499 |
| Unemployment....................... | 67c | 379 | 390 | 383 | 353 | 334 | 380 | 406 | 347 | 369 | 417 | 423 | 422 |
| Unemployment Rate (%)................ | 67r | 8.4 | 8.5 | 8.3 | 7.5 | 7.0 | 7.9 | 8.3 | 7.2 | 7.6 | 8.4 | 8.5 | 8.5 |
| **Intl. Transactions & Positions** | | | | | | Billions of Euros | | | | | | | |
| Exports........................... | 70 | 247.47 | 269.74 | 292.09 | 315.00 | 319.75 | 266.24 | 306.99 | 341.94 | 347.33 | 352.35 | 356.71 | 361.70 |
| Imports, c.i.f........................ | 71 | 230.33 | 256.44 | 281.17 | 301.12 | 316.33 | 254.37 | 295.08 | 335.46 | 341.76 | 340.33 | 342.69 | 342.82 |
| | | | | | | 2010=100 | | | | | | | |
| Volume of Exports.................... | 72 | 96.6 | 100.3 | 104.2 | 107.8 | 105.5 | 93.5 | 100.0 | 103.5 | 102.6 | 104.1 | 105.5 | 106.5 |
| Volume of Imports.................... | 73 | 93.0 | 97.3 | 101.8 | 106.7 | 107.0 | 94.5 | 100.0 | 105.0 | 102.8 | 103.0 | 106.2 | 105.8 |
| Unit Value of Exports.................. | 74 | 83.4 | 87.5 | 91.3 | 95.2 | 98.7 | 92.8 | 100.0 | 107.7 | 110.3 | 110.3 | 110.1 | 110.7 |
| Unit Value of Imports.................. | 75 | 84.0 | 89.3 | 93.7 | 95.7 | 100.3 | 91.2 | 100.0 | 108.4 | 112.8 | 112.1 | 109.4 | 109.9 |

## Balance of Payments

*Millions of US Dollars*

| | | 2004 | 2005 | 2006 | 2007 | 2008 | 2009 | 2010 | 2011 | 2012 | 2013 | 2014 | 2015 |
|---|---|---|---|---|---|---|---|---|---|---|---|---|---|
| A. Current Account* | 109bx | 11,425.5 | 7,702.6 | 7,545.1 | 7,041.3 | † −4,282.3 | −5,244.1 | 7,973.4 | −5,486.7 | −229.5 | −1,100.0 | −1,186.5 | −249.5 |
| Goods, credit (exports) | 1a9cx | 207,194.5 | 228,048.6 | 246,875.8 | 287,771.1 | † 315,429.5 | 241,527.9 | 271,479.4 | 323,727.7 | 300,948.4 | 315,882.7 | 320,184.0 | 259,933.1 |
| Goods, debit (imports) | 1a9dx | 198,517.9 | 224,172.5 | 244,013.6 | 285,411.8 | † 329,773.2 | 246,103.3 | 276,219.2 | 337,190.7 | 313,373.3 | 324,459.1 | 325,242.2 | 259,570.5 |
| Balance on goods | 1a9bx | 8,676.6 | 3,876.1 | 2,862.2 | 2,359.3 | † −14,340.8 | −4,573.9 | −4,738.4 | −13,463.0 | −12,424.9 | −8,575.1 | −5,058.9 | 361.5 |
| Services, credit (exports) | 1b9cx | 54,093.6 | 57,271.8 | 60,542.3 | 74,000.4 | † 97,005.2 | 92,305.5 | 98,494.1 | 105,239.8 | 106,401.7 | 112,683.9 | 123,864.3 | 111,091.1 |
| Services, debit (imports) | 1b9dx | 50,491.1 | 52,499.8 | 54,269.0 | 69,971.3 | † 89,304.8 | 82,406.3 | 87,676.9 | 95,236.5 | 97,937.7 | 104,151.1 | 116,930.8 | 105,626.7 |
| Balance on Goods & Services | 1z9bx | 12,279.0 | 8,648.1 | 9,135.5 | 6,388.3 | † −6,643.2 | 5,323.9 | 6,077.4 | −3,459.7 | −3,960.8 | −43.6 | 1,873.3 | 5,827.0 |
| Primary income: credit | 1c9cx | 48,893.1 | 59,027.8 | 74,277.4 | 100,085.7 | † 109,053.8 | 75,433.3 | 70,607.0 | 69,178.6 | 72,144.2 | 65,867.7 | 67,347.5 | 54,609.1 |
| Primary income: debit | 1c9dx | 43,269.0 | 53,604.2 | 69,325.5 | 93,074.8 | † 98,341.4 | 78,112.9 | 61,953.1 | 63,291.0 | 60,683.8 | 57,745.1 | 61,890.2 | 53,484.8 |
| Balance on gds, serv. & prim. inc. | 1y9bx | 17,903.1 | 14,071.8 | 14,087.4 | 13,399.2 | † 4,069.2 | 2,644.2 | 14,731.3 | 2,427.9 | 7,499.6 | 8,079.0 | 7,330.6 | 6,951.2 |
| Secondary income: credit | 1d9ca | 7,948.9 | 9,356.0 | 8,810.4 | 9,884.8 | † 8,149.8 | 9,067.1 | 9,902.5 | 10,149.7 | 10,206.4 | 9,800.7 | 9,658.8 | 8,462.2 |
| Secondary income: debit | 1d9da | 14,426.5 | 15,725.1 | 15,352.7 | 16,242.7 | † 16,501.2 | 16,955.5 | 16,660.5 | 18,064.3 | 17,935.5 | 18,979.7 | 18,175.9 | 15,662.9 |
| B. Capital Account* | 209ba | −528.8 | −921.6 | −491.4 | −1,882.1 | † −2,739.6 | −911.5 | −1,142.0 | −573.3 | 3,017.8 | −551.7 | −1,351.0 | −319.6 |
| Capital account: credit | 209ca | 91.2 | 44.3 | 761.8 | 284.0 | † 610.2 | 599.8 | 319.3 | 1,375.8 | 4,382.8 | 656.9 | 376.6 | 649.1 |
| Capital account: debit | 209da | 620.0 | 965.8 | 1,253.2 | 2,166.1 | † 3,349.8 | 1,511.2 | 1,461.3 | 1,949.1 | 1,364.9 | 1,208.5 | 1,727.5 | 968.8 |
| Balance on current & capital acct. | 129ba | 10,896.7 | 6,781.1 | 7,053.8 | 5,159.2 | † −7,021.9 | −6,155.6 | 6,831.4 | −6,060.0 | 2,788.3 | −1,651.6 | −2,537.5 | −569.1 |
| C. Financial Account* | 309na | 10,660.1 | 11,396.8 | 7,514.5 | 6,254.9 | † −8,334.3 | −24,561.4 | 5,746.8 | −10,832.4 | 1,650.9 | 588.8 | −1,632.9 | 1,854.2 |
| Direct investment: assets | 3a9aa | 34,682.0 | 32,544.6 | 50,139.6 | 83,492.3 | † 223,390.5 | 24,741.6 | 58,046.3 | 126,119.8 | 33,854.9 | −30,741.2 | −1,826.7 | −13,304.6 |
| Equity & investment fund shares | 3aaaa | 21,242.8 | 25,660.5 | 25,354.6 | 54,305.7 | † 25,635.5 | 22,352.5 | 11,626.6 | 72,617.2 | 25,954.3 | 4,410.7 | 11,798.4 | 46,658.1 |
| Debt instruments | 3abaa | 13,439.2 | 6,884.1 | 24,785.0 | 29,186.6 | † 197,756.3 | 2,391.9 | 46,421.0 | 53,502.6 | 7,900.6 | −35,151.9 | −13,625.5 | −59,961.5 |
| Direct investment: liabilities | 3a9la | 44,415.2 | 33,683.8 | 58,827.7 | 96,587.9 | † 190,542.7 | 86,528.0 | 111,490.2 | 158,028.6 | 6,683.3 | −35,815.1 | −16,408.3 | −20,716.2 |
| Equity & investment fund shares | 3aala | 36,301.1 | 35,435.3 | 65,038.7 | 79,875.1 | † 134,762.4 | 61,841.9 | 86,515.6 | 49,905.2 | −16,319.2 | −42,152.2 | −780.2 | −15,554.7 |
| Debt instruments | 3abla | 8,114.1 | −1,751.4 | −6,211.0 | 16,712.9 | † 55,780.1 | 24,688.8 | 24,974.6 | 108,124.8 | 23,005.1 | 6,337.1 | −15,629.4 | −5,161.5 |
| Portfolio investment: assets | 3b9aa | 35,557.7 | 43,491.3 | 26,528.6 | 80,503.3 | † 295.2 | −18,622.7 | 2,331.8 | −5,458.6 | −41,503.3 | 92.4 | 32,231.0 | 6,756.5 |
| Equity & investment fund shares | 3baaa | 8,037.3 | 20,448.8 | 19,980.4 | 20,401.3 | † −31,861.0 | −3,153.9 | 6,653.4 | −8,706.2 | 13,670.8 | 24,973.5 | 28,200.6 | 11,057.4 |
| Debt securities | 3bbaa | 27,520.4 | 23,042.6 | 6,548.2 | 60,102.0 | † 32,156.2 | −15,471.6 | −4,320.3 | 3,246.2 | −55,174.1 | −24,882.5 | 4,030.4 | −4,302.1 |
| Portfolio investment: liabilities | 3b9la | 5,069.9 | −1,215.1 | 17,348.0 | 37,480.6 | † 48,102.3 | 21,627.9 | −25,026.4 | −28,601.4 | 21,683.7 | 38,350.7 | 45,721.0 | 26,386.8 |
| Equity & investment fund shares | 3bala | 4,092.2 | 5,711.6 | 4,588.1 | 3,360.0 | † 8,817.7 | −3,240.3 | −3,866.5 | −4,893.4 | 3,687.1 | 7,678.9 | 3,232.1 | 6,610.1 |
| Debt securities | 3bbla | 977.7 | −6,926.7 | 12,759.9 | 34,120.7 | † 39,284.7 | 24,866.6 | −21,159.9 | −23,709.4 | 17,995.3 | 30,673.2 | 42,488.9 | 19,779.0 |
| Fin. der.& empl.stk.ops.(ESOs): net. | 3c9na | 5,585.9 | 5,448.1 | −3,372.4 | −1,424.4 | † −5,904.2 | −740.7 | −1,877.8 | 2,748.5 | −2,711.1 | −2,750.8 | −3,282.1 | −5,256.6 |
| Fin. der. & ESOs: assets | 3c9aa | 8,648.5 | 9,647.5 | 1,497.5 | .... | .... | .... | .... | .... | .... | .... | .... | .... |
| Fin. der. & ESOs: liabilities | 3c9la | 3,062.6 | 4,199.4 | 4,869.9 | .... | .... | .... | .... | .... | .... | .... | .... | .... |
| Other investment: assets | 3d9aa | 64,684.6 | 87,398.7 | 91,914.9 | 158,360.5 | † −75,672.5 | −118,057.0 | −13,710.8 | 31,403.9 | −44,856.0 | 17,341.8 | 4,058.5 | −8,073.3 |
| Other equity | 3daaa | .... | .... | .... | .... | † — | −1.3 | 54.3 | 53.9 | 1,495.7 | 2,078.5 | 804.2 | 11.1 |
| Debt instruments | 3dzaa | 64,684.6 | 87,398.7 | 91,914.9 | 158,360.5 | † −75,672.5 | −118,055.7 | −13,765.2 | 31,350.0 | −46,351.7 | 15,263.3 | 3,254.3 | −8,084.4 |
| Other investment: liabilities | 3d9la | 80,365.1 | 125,017.2 | 81,520.4 | 180,608.2 | † −88,204.8 | −196,272.0 | −47,421.1 | 36,221.6 | −85,237.2 | −19,182.1 | 3,503.5 | −27,405.1 |
| Other equity | 3dala | .... | .... | .... | .... | † — | — | | | | | | |
| Debt instruments | 3dzla | 80,365.1 | 125,017.2 | 81,520.4 | 180,608.2 | † −88,204.8 | −196,272.0 | −47,421.1 | 36,221.6 | −85,237.2 | −19,182.1 | 3,503.5 | −27,405.1 |
| Curr.+ cap.− finan. acct. balance | 4y9na | 236.7 | −4,615.7 | −460.7 | −1,095.7 | † 1,312.5 | 18,405.8 | 1,084.7 | 4,772.4 | 1,137.4 | −2,240.5 | −904.5 | −2,423.3 |
| D. Net Errors and Omissions | 409na | −960.0 | 2,440.2 | 616.4 | 2,321.6 | † −2,627.4 | −11,449.1 | −267.9 | −3,275.9 | −465.1 | 1,764.7 | −454.0 | 1,345.1 |
| E. Reserves and Related Items | 4z9na | −723.3 | −2,175.5 | 155.7 | 1,225.9 | † −1,318.1 | 6,970.8 | 820.4 | 1,498.0 | 668.4 | −471.7 | −1,355.9 | −1,074.8 |
| Reserve assets | 3e9aa | −723.3 | −2,175.5 | 155.7 | 1,225.9 | † −1,318.1 | 6,970.8 | 820.4 | 1,498.0 | 668.4 | −471.7 | −1,355.9 | −1,074.8 |
| Credit and loans from the IMF | 3dcla | — | — | — | — | † — | — | — | — | — | — | — | — |
| Exceptional financing | 409la | .... | .... | .... | .... | .... | .... | .... | .... | .... | .... | .... | .... |

*Excludes components in group E

## International Investment Position

*Millions of US Dollars*

| | | 2004 | 2005 | 2006 | 2007 | 2008 | 2009 | 2010 | 2011 | 2012 | 2013 | 2014 | 2015 |
|---|---|---|---|---|---|---|---|---|---|---|---|---|---|
| Assets | 809aa | 1,500,461.7 | 1,557,568.4 | 1,892,377.8 | 2,452,421.2 | † 2,577,251.3 | 2,637,324.7 | 2,552,216.6 | 2,581,082.2 | 2,588,479.9 | 2,528,189.1 | 2,348,552.9 | 2,147,414.9 |
| Direct investment | 8a9aa | 369,229.9 | 378,157.6 | 481,355.6 | 621,095.2 | † 919,209.5 | 1,003,029.3 | 1,037,608.7 | 1,118,935.0 | 1,136,590.5 | 1,130,189.0 | 1,023,517.9 | 927,791.2 |
| Equity & investment fund shares | 8aaaa | 203,559.0 | 225,814.6 | 290,647.4 | 374,309.4 | † 318,711.8 | 355,900.2 | 343,109.4 | 378,681.8 | 391,960.8 | 412,584.0 | 400,912.8 | 404,489.1 |
| Debt instruments | 8abaa | 165,670.9 | 152,342.9 | 190,708.2 | 246,785.8 | † 600,496.3 | 647,129.0 | 694,500.6 | 740,253.1 | 744,629.8 | 717,605.0 | 622,605.0 | 523,303.3 |
| Portfolio investment | 8b9aa | 534,074.0 | 554,645.4 | 643,193.8 | 837,345.2 | † 735,530.2 | 769,234.3 | 723,596.4 | 659,015.6 | 675,852.1 | 716,579.0 | 699,857.0 | 640,457.2 |
| Equity & investment fund shares | 8baaa | 172,164.0 | 204,560.0 | 248,209.7 | 313,728.1 | † 209,830.8 | 230,637.2 | 233,971.3 | 197,108.8 | 232,545.6 | 284,279.4 | 293,803.7 | 284,103.9 |
| Debt securities | 8bbaa | 361,910.0 | 350,085.4 | 394,984.1 | 523,617.1 | † 525,699.4 | 538,597.1 | 489,625.1 | 461,906.8 | 443,307.8 | 432,299.6 | 406,053.3 | 356,352.2 |
| Fin. der.(oth.than reserves) & ESOs | 8c9aa | 1,667.2 | 3,634.7 | 10,561.0 | 21,738.5 | † 26,029.0 | 20,985.2 | 10,975.5 | 8,218.9 | 17,160.1 | 14,328.8 | 13,040.6 | 22,589.4 |
| Other investment | 8d9aa | 581,502.3 | 609,134.6 | 743,831.1 | 955,737.4 | † 880,837.5 | 820,091.8 | 753,219.9 | 765,479.0 | 728,109.6 | 640,168.6 | 586,741.7 | 532,478.8 |
| Other equity | 8daaa | .... | .... | .... | .... | † 1,326.3 | 1,367.1 | 1,524.6 | 1,564.3 | 3,134.9 | 5,453.0 | 5,629.8 | 5,178.9 |
| Debt instruments | 8dzaa | 581,502.3 | 609,134.6 | 743,831.1 | 955,737.4 | † 879,511.3 | 818,724.7 | 751,695.3 | 763,914.7 | 724,974.7 | 634,715.6 | 581,112.0 | 527,299.9 |
| Reserve assets | 8e9aa | 13,988.4 | 11,996.2 | 13,436.3 | 16,504.9 | † 15,646.5 | 23,982.6 | 26,814.7 | 29,432.5 | 30,768.9 | 26,923.7 | 25,394.4 | 24,098.3 |
| Liabilities | 809la | 1,388,725.3 | 1,438,250.0 | 1,772,794.3 | 2,310,288.6 | † 2,321,835.8 | 2,348,409.6 | 2,234,181.0 | 2,282,360.5 | 2,323,871.2 | 2,247,134.2 | 2,069,266.1 | 1,871,683.1 |
| Direct investment | 8a9la | 471,071.4 | 478,183.1 | 618,531.7 | 784,576.3 | † 946,326.8 | 1,045,988.0 | 1,089,079.2 | 1,158,747.0 | 1,207,536.0 | 1,192,182.3 | 1,054,988.6 | 930,195.1 |
| Equity & investment fund shares | 8aala | 387,166.0 | 406,455.0 | 549,246.9 | 674,480.9 | † 658,943.5 | 753,059.2 | 783,666.6 | 799,810.1 | 809,418.9 | 784,963.0 | 703,401.0 | 612,668.1 |
| Debt instruments | 8abla | 83,905.4 | 71,728.1 | 69,284.7 | 110,095.4 | † 287,383.3 | 292,927.3 | 305,412.6 | 358,938.2 | 398,115.8 | 407,217.9 | 351,586.4 | 317,527.0 |
| Portfolio investment | 8b9la | 259,902.3 | 244,760.6 | 285,067.3 | 396,669.1 | † 400,916.8 | 496,203.1 | 439,229.0 | 394,194.4 | 466,219.2 | 531,069.3 | 539,747.6 | 519,031.2 |
| Equity & investment fund shares | 8bala | 44,250.5 | 43,015.4 | 57,745.2 | 72,899.9 | † 47,647.6 | 85,335.4 | 80,723.9 | 70,900.5 | 94,929.5 | 120,264.4 | 112,998.7 | 124,347.0 |
| Debt securities | 8bbla | 215,651.8 | 201,745.2 | 227,322.1 | 323,769.3 | † 353,269.1 | 410,867.8 | 358,505.1 | 323,292.6 | 371,291.0 | 410,804.9 | 426,748.9 | 394,684.2 |
| Fin. der.(oth.than reserves) & ESOs | 8c9la | 16.3 | 3,381.0 | 9,776.1 | 22,704.2 | † 22,283.9 | 17,813.0 | 7,887.6 | 9,419.6 | 12,100.2 | 16,905.0 | 14,808.4 | 9,804.8 |
| Other investment | 8d9la | 657,735.3 | 711,925.2 | 859,419.3 | 1,106,338.9 | † 952,308.4 | 788,405.4 | 697,985.2 | 719,998.2 | 638,015.8 | 506,978.9 | 459,722.8 | 412,652.0 |
| Other equity | 8dala | .... | .... | .... | .... | .... | .... | .... | .... | .... | .... | .... | .... |
| Debt instruments | 8dzla | 657,735.3 | 711,925.2 | 859,419.3 | 1,106,338.9 | † 952,308.4 | 788,405.4 | 697,985.2 | 719,998.2 | 638,015.8 | 506,978.9 | 459,722.8 | 412,652.0 |

# Belgium 124

| | | 2004 | 2005 | 2006 | 2007 | 2008 | 2009 | 2010 | 2011 | 2012 | 2013 | 2014 | 2015 |
|---|---|---|---|---|---|---|---|---|---|---|---|---|---|
| **Government Finance Operations Statement General Government** | | | | | *Millions of Euros: Fiscal Year Ends December 31; Data Reported through Eurostat* | | | | | | | | |
| Revenue | a1 | 145,695 | 152,188 | 158,934 | 166,492 | 174,067 | 170,036 | 180,054 | 190,709 | 199,950 | 206,396 | 208,236 | 210,329 |
| Taxes | a11 | 88,508 | 92,508 | 96,623 | 100,670 | 103,739 | 97,896 | 104,934 | 110,732 | 116,541 | 120,799 | 122,845 | 124,376 |
| Social Contributions | a12 | 46,320 | 47,550 | 49,775 | 52,851 | 55,913 | 57,321 | 58,715 | 61,776 | 64,287 | 65,996 | 66,721 | 67,873 |
| Grants | a13 | .... | .... | .... | .... | .... | .... | .... | .... | .... | .... | .... | .... |
| Other Revenue | a14 | .... | .... | .... | .... | .... | .... | .... | .... | .... | .... | .... | .... |
| Expense | a2 | 146,123 | 160,911 | 159,424 | 166,767 | 178,115 | 187,982 | 194,143 | 205,121 | 214,937 | 217,980 | 220,077 | 221,070 |
| Compensation of Employees | a21 | 34,612 | 36,418 | 38,012 | 39,632 | 41,897 | 43,748 | 44,909 | 46,771 | 48,604 | 50,028 | 50,862 | 51,314 |
| Use of Goods & Services | a22 | 12,138 | 12,486 | 12,862 | 12,918 | 14,009 | 15,009 | 15,166 | 15,870 | 16,472 | 16,670 | 17,136 | 17,211 |
| Consumption of Fixed Capital | a23 | 6,111 | 6,617 | 7,120 | 7,471 | 7,827 | 7,695 | 8,074 | 8,585 | 8,883 | 8,965 | 9,030 | 9,285 |
| Interest | a24 | 14,353 | 13,575 | 13,372 | 13,722 | 14,032 | 13,338 | 13,171 | 13,638 | 13,967 | 13,200 | 12,731 | 11,886 |
| Subsidies | a25 | 5,098 | 6,735 | 7,969 | 9,272 | 10,292 | 10,695 | 12,372 | 13,375 | 13,308 | 13,672 | 13,786 | 13,896 |
| Grants | a26 | .... | .... | .... | .... | .... | .... | .... | .... | .... | .... | .... | .... |
| Social Benefits | a27 | 65,081 | 67,709 | 69,774 | 73,447 | 79,046 | 84,887 | 87,447 | 91,583 | 96,121 | 99,412 | 101,295 | 103,944 |
| Other Expense | a28 | .... | .... | .... | .... | .... | .... | .... | .... | .... | .... | .... | .... |
| Gross Operating Balance [1-2+23] | agob | 5,683 | −2,106 | 6,630 | 7,195 | 3,779 | −10,251 | −6,015 | −5,827 | −6,104 | −2,619 | −2,812 | −1,456 |
| Net Operating Balance [1-2] | anob | −428 | −8,723 | −490 | −275 | −4,048 | −17,946 | −14,089 | −14,412 | −14,987 | −11,584 | −11,841 | −10,741 |
| Net Acq. of Nonfinancial Assets | a31 | 45 | −711 | −1,187 | −487 | −122 | 851 | 411 | 1,166 | 1,318 | 314 | 483 | −82 |
| Aquisition of Nonfin. Assets | a31.1 | .... | .... | .... | .... | .... | .... | .... | .... | .... | .... | .... | .... |
| Disposal of Nonfin. Assets | a31.2 | .... | .... | .... | .... | .... | .... | .... | .... | .... | .... | .... | .... |
| Net Lending/Borrowing [1-2-31] | anlb | −473 | −8,012 | 697 | 211 | −3,927 | −18,796 | −14,500 | −15,579 | −16,305 | −11,897 | −12,325 | −10,659 |
| Net Acq. of Financial Assets | a32 | 596 | 435 | 2,389 | 2,673 | 23,270 | 2,175 | 1,033 | 7,676 | 2,143 | −2,716 | 1,827 | −2,360 |
| By instrument | | | | | | | | | | | | | |
| Monetary Gold & SDRs | a3201 | — | — | — | — | — | — | — | — | — | — | — | — |
| Currency & Deposits | a3202 | 902 | 766 | −368 | 1,388 | 7,327 | −3,220 | 1,729 | 892 | −525 | −330 | −1,091 | 724 |
| Securities other than Shares | a3203 | 276 | −111 | −173 | 70 | 897 | −95 | −690 | −140 | −145 | −219 | −391 | −63 |
| Loans | a3204 | −348 | 512 | 608 | 862 | 1,182 | 1,935 | 1,578 | 2,860 | 5,640 | 2,712 | 1,739 | 561 |
| Shares & Other Equity | a3205 | −711 | −113 | 198 | 768 | 13,817 | 3,955 | 456 | 3,373 | −2,802 | −4,328 | 846 | −3,307 |
| Insurance Technical Reserves | a3206 | — | — | — | — | — | — | — | — | — | — | — | — |
| Financial Derivatives | a3207 | −294 | −330 | −252 | −96 | −19 | −278 | −2,545 | −358 | −108 | −769 | 9 | −734 |
| Other Accounts Receivable | a3208 | 768 | −290 | 2,375 | −318 | 66 | −122 | 506 | 1,051 | 84 | 220 | 715 | 462 |
| By debtor | | | | | | | | | | | | | |
| Domestic | a321 | .... | .... | .... | .... | .... | .... | .... | .... | .... | .... | .... | .... |
| Foreign | a322 | .... | .... | .... | .... | .... | .... | .... | .... | .... | .... | .... | .... |
| Net Incurrence of Liabilities | a33 | 1,459 | 7,506 | 1,731 | 2,887 | 25,960 | 20,319 | 16,770 | 23,930 | 18,457 | 9,574 | 14,847 | 9,936 |
| By instrument | | | | | | | | | | | | | |
| Special Drawing Rights (SDRs) | a3301 | — | — | — | — | — | — | — | — | — | — | — | — |
| Currency & Deposits | a3302 | 98 | 109 | 116 | 107 | 60 | 103 | 114 | 83 | −29 | −54 | −47 | 32 |
| Securities other than Shares | a3303 | 2,228 | 3,746 | 498 | 1,638 | 25,322 | 16,607 | 12,630 | 16,698 | 13,446 | 6,150 | 11,301 | 10,725 |
| Loans | a3304 | −176 | 4,217 | 1,473 | 27 | 1,844 | 2,657 | 4,429 | 6,330 | 4,815 | 4,425 | 4,710 | −1,116 |
| Shares & Other Equity | a3305 | — | — | — | — | — | — | — | — | — | — | — | — |
| Insurance Technical Reserves | a3306 | 36 | 54 | 29 | −14 | — | 42 | 37 | 33 | 92 | 51 | 23 | 27 |
| Financial Derivatives | a3307 | — | — | — | — | — | — | — | — | — | −144 | — | — |
| Other Accounts Payable | a3308 | −724 | −621 | −385 | 1,130 | −1,267 | 912 | −440 | 783 | 134 | −855 | −1,143 | 265 |
| By creditor | | | | | | | | | | | | | |
| Domestic | a331 | .... | .... | .... | .... | .... | .... | .... | .... | .... | .... | .... | .... |
| Foreign | a332 | .... | .... | .... | .... | .... | .... | .... | .... | .... | .... | .... | .... |
| Stat. Discrepancy [32-33-NLB] | anlbz | −390 | 941 | −39 | −425 | 1,237 | 652 | −1,238 | −675 | −9 | −393 | −696 | −1,637 |
| Memo Item: Expenditure [2+31] | a2m | 146,168 | 160,200 | 158,237 | 166,281 | 177,994 | 188,833 | 194,553 | 206,287 | 216,255 | 218,294 | 220,561 | 220,988 |
| **Balance Sheet** | | | | | | *Millions of Euros: Fiscal Year Ends December 31; Data Reported through Eurostat* | | | | | | | |
| Net Worth | a6 | .... | .... | .... | .... | .... | .... | .... | .... | .... | .... | .... | .... |
| Nonfinancial Assets | a61 | .... | .... | .... | .... | .... | .... | .... | .... | .... | .... | .... | .... |
| Financial Assets | a62 | 57,670 | 59,205 | 63,732 | 67,608 | 86,552 | 92,340 | 95,202 | 101,884 | 109,272 | 109,921 | 117,245 | 117,059 |
| By instrument | | | | | | | | | | | | | |
| Monetary Gold & SDRs | a6201 | — | — | — | — | — | — | — | — | — | — | — | — |
| Currency & Deposits | a6202 | 7,687 | 8,453 | 8,086 | 9,473 | 16,345 | 15,389 | 17,142 | 18,034 | 17,508 | 17,178 | 16,849 | 17,572 |
| Securities other than Shares | a6203 | 2,152 | 2,042 | 1,868 | 1,937 | 2,835 | 2,740 | 2,050 | 1,910 | 1,765 | 1,546 | 1,198 | 1,131 |
| Loans | a6204 | 15,765 | 16,310 | 16,970 | 17,785 | 18,890 | 20,654 | 21,817 | 24,280 | 29,718 | 31,816 | 33,883 | 33,653 |
| Shares and Other Equity | a6205 | 17,386 | 18,010 | 20,042 | 21,964 | 31,967 | 36,552 | 36,683 | 38,399 | 40,935 | 39,180 | 44,261 | 43,206 |
| Insurance Technical Reserves | a6206 | — | — | — | — | — | — | — | — | — | — | — | — |
| Financial Derivatives | a6207 | — | — | — | — | — | — | — | — | — | — | — | — |
| Other Accounts Receivable | a6208 | 14,680 | 14,390 | 16,766 | 16,449 | 16,516 | 17,005 | 17,511 | 19,261 | 19,346 | 20,201 | 21,054 | 21,496 |
| By debtor | | | | | | | | | | | | | |
| Domestic | a621 | .... | .... | .... | .... | .... | .... | .... | .... | .... | .... | .... | .... |
| Foreign | a622 | .... | .... | .... | .... | .... | .... | .... | .... | .... | .... | .... | .... |
| Liabilities | a63 | 329,248 | 335,815 | 326,445 | 323,048 | 357,706 | 381,627 | 393,095 | 417,214 | 465,412 | 463,437 | 518,909 | 519,515 |
| By instrument | | | | | | | | | | | | | |
| Special Drawing Rights (SDRs) | a6301 | — | — | — | — | — | — | — | — | — | — | — | — |
| Currency & Deposits | a6302 | 784 | 894 | 1,009 | 1,116 | 1,176 | 1,279 | 1,393 | 1,477 | 1,447 | 1,395 | 1,348 | 1,380 |
| Securities other than Shares | a6303 | 274,766 | 278,614 | 268,011 | 263,365 | 297,384 | 316,010 | 323,233 | 340,127 | 382,343 | 376,798 | 422,250 | 423,139 |
| Loans | a6304 | 40,858 | 44,035 | 45,508 | 45,535 | 47,379 | 50,662 | 55,159 | 61,484 | 66,298 | 70,725 | 80,883 | 79,878 |
| Shares and Other Equity | a6305 | — | — | — | — | — | — | — | — | — | — | 412 | 758 |
| Insurance Technical Reserves | a6306 | 429 | 482 | 512 | 498 | 498 | 539 | 614 | 647 | 739 | 789 | 820 | 849 |
| Financial Derivatives | a6307 | — | — | — | — | — | — | — | — | — | — | — | — |
| Other Accounts Payable | a6308 | 12,411 | 11,790 | 11,405 | 12,535 | 11,268 | 13,137 | 12,696 | 13,479 | 14,584 | 13,729 | 13,196 | 13,511 |
| By creditor | | | | | | | | | | | | | |
| Domestic | a631 | .... | .... | .... | .... | .... | .... | .... | .... | .... | .... | .... | .... |
| Foreign | a632 | .... | .... | .... | .... | .... | .... | .... | .... | .... | .... | .... | .... |
| Net Financial Worth [62-63] | a6m2 | −271,578 | −276,610 | −262,713 | −255,440 | −271,154 | −289,287 | −297,893 | −315,330 | −356,140 | −353,516 | −401,664 | −402,456 |
| Memo Item: Debt at Market Value | a6m3 | 329,248 | 335,815 | 326,445 | 323,049 | 357,705 | 381,627 | 393,095 | 417,214 | 465,411 | 463,436 | 518,497 | 518,757 |
| Memo Item: Debt at Face Value | a6m35 | 300,736 | 306,535 | 308,792 | 312,508 | 338,880 | 360,396 | 376,739 | 401,445 | 417,976 | 426,769 | 439,903 | 447,697 |
| Memo Item: Maastricht Debt | a6m36 | 288,325 | 294,745 | 297,387 | 299,973 | 327,612 | 347,259 | 364,043 | 387,966 | 403,392 | 413,040 | 426,707 | 434,186 |
| Memo Item: Debt at Nominal Value | a6m4 | .... | .... | .... | .... | .... | .... | .... | .... | .... | .... | .... | .... |

# Belgium 124

| | | 2004 | 2005 | 2006 | 2007 | 2008 | 2009 | 2010 | 2011 | 2012 | 2013 | 2014 | 2015 |
|---|---|---|---|---|---|---|---|---|---|---|---|---|---|
| **National Accounts** | | | | | | | *Billions of Euros* | | | | | | |
| Househ.Cons.Expend.,incl.NPISHs.... | 96f | 150.5 | 156.6 | 163.8 | 171.8 | 180.4 | 179.9 | 188.1 | 195.1 | 200.9 | 204.0 | 207.3 | 210.7 |
| Government Consumption Expend... | 91f | 66.0 | 69.1 | 72.1 | 74.9 | 80.5 | 84.4 | 86.4 | 90.4 | 94.3 | 96.6 | 98.8 | 99.1 |
| Gross Fixed Capital Formation......... | 93e | 64.0 | 69.2 | 74.1 | 80.9 | 86.2 | 80.0 | 81.5 | 87.4 | 89.2 | 88.2 | 92.8 | 95.2 |
| Changes in Inventories.................... | 93i | 3.4 | 4.5 | 5.0 | 4.2 | 6.1 | −3.2 | 3.2 | 4.6 | 1.9 | 1.1 | −4.5 | −1.8 |
| Exports of Goods and Services......... | 90c | 210.9 | 229.5 | 247.7 | 267.5 | 282.3 | 242.2 | 278.8 | 309.3 | 319.3 | 327.1 | 328.5 | 337.5 |
| Imports of Goods and Services (-)..... | 98c | 196.4 | 217.7 | 235.4 | 254.2 | 280.5 | 233.6 | 272.4 | 307.0 | 317.5 | 321.8 | 336.1 | 337.8 |
| Gross Domestic Product (GDP)......... | 99b | 298.4 | 311.2 | 327.4 | 345.1 | 355.1 | 349.7 | 365.7 | 379.9 | 388.2 | 395.2 | 402.0 | 409.8 |
| Net Primary Income from Abroad..... | 98.n | −3.9 | −5.7 | −5.8 | −5.9 | −3.7 | −11.2 | −3.8 | −7.2 | −11.3 | −13.1 | 2.0 | 2.8 |
| Gross National Income (GNI)............ | 99a | 294.5 | 305.4 | 321.6 | 339.2 | 351.3 | 338.5 | 361.9 | 372.7 | 376.9 | 382.1 | 404.0 | 412.6 |
| Net Current Transf.from Abroad....... | 98t | −4.4 | −4.2 | −4.1 | −3.1 | −4.2 | −4.6 | −4.3 | −4.8 | −6.0 | −7.2 | −7.0 | . . . . |
| Gross Nat'l Disposable Inc.(GNDI).... | 99i | 290.2 | 301.2 | 317.4 | 336.1 | 347.1 | 334.0 | 358.8 | 369.1 | . . . . | . . . . | . . . . | . . . . |
| Gross Saving.................................. | 99s | 74.0 | 76.3 | 82.3 | 90.4 | 86.9 | 70.0 | 84.0 | 84.4 | . . . . | . . . . | . . . . | . . . . |
| Consumption of Fixed Capital.......... | 99cf | 45.1 | 47.6 | 51.0 | 54.0 | 57.2 | 59.0 | 61.3 | 64.2 | . . . . | . . . . | . . . . | . . . . |
| GDP Volume 2011 Ref., Chained..... | 99b.p | 351.6 | 358.3 | 367.7 | 378.7 | 382.3 | 372.3 | 381.6 | 387.9 | 388.3 | 389.3 | 393.5 | 403.4 |
| GDP Volume (2010=100)................ | 99bvp | 92.1 | 93.9 | 96.3 | 99.2 | 100.2 | 97.6 | 100.0 | 101.6 | 101.7 | 102.0 | 103.1 | 105.7 |
| GDP Deflator (2010=100).............. | 99bip | 88.5 | 90.6 | 92.9 | 95.1 | 96.9 | 98.0 | 100.0 | 102.2 | 104.3 | 105.9 | 106.6 | 106.0 |
| | | | | | | | *Millions: Midyear Estimates* | | | | | | |
| Population................................ | 99z | 10.49 | 10.56 | 10.63 | 10.70 | 10.78 | 10.85 | 10.93 | 11.01 | 11.08 | 11.15 | 11.23 | 11.30 |

# Belize 339

|  |  | 2004 | 2005 | 2006 | 2007 | 2008 | 2009 | 2010 | 2011 | 2012 | 2013 | 2014 | 2015 |
|---|---|---|---|---|---|---|---|---|---|---|---|---|---|
| **Exchange Rates** | | | | | *Belize Dollars per SDR: End of Period* | | | | | | | | |
| Official Rate | aa | 3.11 | 2.86 | 3.01 | 3.16 | 3.08 | 3.14 | 3.08 | 3.07 | 3.07 | 3.08 | 2.90 | 2.77 |
| | | | | | *Belize Dollars per US Dollar: End of Period (ae) Period Average (rf)* | | | | | | | | |
| Official Rate | ae | 2.00 | 2.00 | 2.00 | 2.00 | 2.00 | 2.00 | 2.00 | 2.00 | 2.00 | 2.00 | 2.00 | 2.00 |
| Official Rate | rf | 2.00 | 2.00 | 2.00 | 2.00 | 2.00 | 2.00 | 2.00 | 2.00 | 2.00 | 2.00 | 2.00 | 2.00 |
| | | | | | *Index Numbers (2010=100): Period Averages* | | | | | | | | |
| Official Rate | ahx | 100.0 | 100.0 | 100.0 | 100.0 | 100.0 | 100.0 | 100.0 | 100.0 | 100.0 | 100.0 | 100.0 | 100.0 |
| Nominal Effective Exchange Rate | nec | 103.2 | 102.2 | 101.1 | 97.1 | 95.1 | 101.3 | 100.0 | 97.0 | 100.1 | 100.8 | 102.4 | 113.7 |
| CPI-Based Real Effect. Ex. Rate | rec | 100.5 | 99.7 | 99.9 | 94.9 | 94.5 | 98.6 | 100.0 | 90.0 | 91.7 | 90.6 | 91.2 | 99.0 |
| **Fund Position** | | | | | *Millions of SDRs: End of Period* | | | | | | | | |
| Quota | 2f.s | 18.80 | 18.80 | 18.80 | 18.80 | 18.80 | 18.80 | 18.80 | 18.80 | 18.80 | 18.80 | 18.80 | 18.80 |
| SDR Holdings | 1b.s | 1.64 | 1.76 | 1.93 | 2.15 | 2.31 | 20.17 | 20.12 | 20.08 | 20.04 | 20.02 | 20.02 | 20.02 |
| Reserve Position in the Fund | 1c.s | 4.24 | 4.24 | 4.24 | 4.24 | 4.24 | 4.24 | 4.24 | 4.24 | 4.24 | 4.24 | 4.24 | 4.24 |
| Total Fund Cred.&Loans Outstg. | 2tl | — | — | — | — | — | 4.70 | 4.70 | 4.70 | 2.94 | .59 | — | — |
| SDR Allocations | 1bd | — | — | — | — | — | 17.89 | 17.89 | 17.89 | 17.89 | 17.89 | 17.89 | 17.89 |
| **International Liquidity** | | | | | *Millions of US Dollars Unless Otherwise Indicated: End of Period* | | | | | | | | |
| Total Reserves minus Gold | 1l.d | 48.25 | 71.36 | 113.72 | 108.51 | 166.16 | 213.68 | 218.00 | 237.11 | 288.92 | 402.75 | 486.88 | 437.15 |
| SDR Holdings | 1b.d | 2.55 | 2.52 | 2.91 | 3.40 | 3.56 | 31.62 | 30.99 | 30.83 | 30.80 | 30.83 | 29.01 | 27.75 |
| Reserve Position in the Fund | 1c.d | 6.58 | 6.06 | 6.38 | 6.70 | 6.53 | 6.64 | 6.53 | 6.51 | 6.51 | 6.53 | 6.14 | 5.87 |
| Foreign Exchange | 1d.d | 39.12 | 62.78 | 104.44 | 98.42 | 156.07 | 175.42 | 180.48 | 199.78 | 251.61 | 365.40 | 451.73 | 403.53 |
| Central Bank: Other Assets | 3..d | — | — | † .62 | .38 | .85 | 4.34 | 11.65 | 13.25 | 8.59 | 8.23 | 6.34 | 4.39 |
| Central Bank: Other Liabs. | 4..d | 1.40 | 1.37 | † 4.47 | 6.39 | 7.52 | 3.89 | 5.19 | 1.89 | 2.21 | 2.42 | 2.21 | 9.01 |
| Other Depository Corps.: Assets | 7a.d | 67.05 | 73.82 | † 77.05 | 91.87 | 110.87 | 97.19 | 113.71 | 129.78 | 160.42 | 139.61 | 139.35 | 120.82 |
| Other Depository Corps.: Liabs. | 7b.d | 17.98 | 18.06 | † 39.93 | 13.38 | 25.75 | 19.05 | 12.78 | 4.28 | 3.08 | 5.35 | 6.90 | 6.82 |
| **Central Bank** | | | | | *Millions of Belize Dollars: End of Period* | | | | | | | | |
| Net Foreign Assets | 11n | 93.62 | 139.88 | † 199.98 | 204.78 | 318.21 | 357.16 | 368.66 | 427.10 | 526.16 | 759.64 | 926.73 | 814.92 |
| Claims on Nonresidents | 11 | 96.41 | 142.61 | † 208.93 | 217.57 | 333.25 | 435.78 | 448.64 | 500.26 | 594.61 | 821.40 | 983.00 | 882.53 |
| Liabilities to Nonresidents | 16c | 2.79 | 2.74 | † 8.95 | 12.78 | 15.03 | 78.62 | 79.98 | 73.16 | 68.45 | 61.76 | 56.27 | 67.61 |
| Claims on Other Depository Corps. | 12e | — | — | † .07 | — | .06 | .04 | .06 | .06 | .03 | .03 | .03 | .09 |
| Net Claims on Central Government | 12an | 114.56 | 81.62 | † 131.04 | 146.36 | 100.17 | 79.98 | 56.57 | 36.72 | 37.13 | −104.95 | −114.18 | 196.64 |
| Claims on Central Government | 12a | 165.29 | 181.83 | † 230.92 | 231.51 | 214.15 | 173.22 | 157.73 | 169.36 | 158.41 | 157.74 | 148.42 | 250.99 |
| Liabilities to Central Government | 16d | 50.73 | 100.21 | † 99.89 | 85.16 | 113.98 | 93.24 | 101.16 | 132.64 | 121.28 | 262.69 | 262.60 | 54.35 |
| Claims on Other Sectors | 12s | 32.52 | 27.52 | † 1.19 | 4.06 | 2.21 | 3.47 | 3.65 | 26.42 | 24.65 | 24.82 | 26.57 | 24.77 |
| Claims on Other Financial Corps. | 12g | 32.52 | 27.52 | † — | — | — | — | — | — | — | — | — | — |
| Claims on State & Local Govts | 12b | — | — | † — | — | — | — | — | — | — | — | — | — |
| Claims on Public Nonfin. Corps. | 12c | — | — | † — | — | — | — | — | 20.00 | 20.00 | 20.00 | 20.00 | 20.00 |
| Claims on Private Sector | 12d | — | — | † 1.19 | 4.06 | 2.21 | 3.47 | 3.65 | 6.42 | 4.65 | 4.82 | 6.57 | 4.77 |
| Monetary Base | 14 | 230.01 | 255.42 | † 321.46 | 336.25 | 382.89 | 428.63 | 416.88 | 476.19 | 567.62 | 658.35 | 817.99 | 1,017.42 |
| Currency in Circulation | 14a | 141.95 | 143.09 | † 169.35 | 185.77 | 193.20 | 191.97 | 191.60 | 210.58 | 238.14 | 262.47 | 286.03 | 345.08 |
| Liabs. to Other Depository Corps. | 14c | 88.06 | 112.33 | † 152.10 | 150.47 | 189.69 | 236.66 | 225.28 | 265.61 | 329.48 | 395.88 | 531.95 | 672.34 |
| Liabilities to Other Sectors | 14d | — | — | † — | — | — | — | — | — | — | — | — | — |
| Other Liabs. to Other Dep. Corps. | 14n | — | — | † — | — | — | — | .03 | — | .02 | .09 | — | .83 |
| Dep. & Sec. Excl. f/Monetary Base | 14o | — | — | † 1.17 | 9.96 | 32.67 | 3.65 | 7.59 | 3.92 | 8.58 | 5.91 | 3.52 | 3.14 |
| Deposits Included in Broad Money | 15 | — | — | † — | — | — | — | — | — | — | — | — | — |
| Sec.Ot.th.Shares Incl.in Brd.Money | 16a | — | — | † — | — | — | — | — | — | — | — | — | — |
| Deposits Excl. from Broad Money | 16b | — | — | † 1.17 | 9.96 | 32.67 | 3.65 | 7.59 | 3.92 | 8.58 | 5.91 | 3.52 | 3.14 |
| Sec.Ot.th.Shares Excl.f/Brd.Money | 16s | — | — | † — | — | — | — | — | — | — | — | — | — |
| Loans | 16l | — | — | † — | — | — | — | — | — | — | — | — | — |
| Financial Derivatives | 16m | — | — | † — | — | — | — | — | — | — | — | — | — |
| Shares and Other Equity | 17a | 19.35 | 23.44 | † 40.22 | 39.25 | 39.46 | 40.20 | 34.72 | 39.32 | 38.31 | 42.75 | 43.93 | 44.89 |
| Other Items (Net) | 17r | −8.65 | −29.84 | † −30.58 | −30.25 | −34.37 | −31.83 | −30.28 | −29.13 | −26.57 | −27.56 | −26.29 | −29.87 |
| Memo Item: | | | | | | | | | | | | | |
| Total Assets | 10ra | 331.63 | 390.51 | † 483.25 | 498.16 | 595.29 | 657.18 | 655.75 | 739.65 | 825.31 | 1,050.36 | 1,204.02 | 1,208.27 |
| **Other Depository Corporations** | | | | | *Millions of Belize Dollars: End of Period* | | | | | | | | |
| Net Foreign Assets | 21n | 98.13 | 111.52 | † 74.23 | 156.98 | 170.24 | 156.29 | 201.86 | 251.00 | 314.68 | 268.52 | 264.89 | 228.01 |
| Claims on Nonresidents | 21 | 134.10 | 147.64 | † 154.10 | 183.73 | 221.74 | 194.39 | 227.43 | 259.56 | 320.84 | 279.22 | 278.69 | 241.65 |
| Liabilities to Nonresidents | 26c | 35.97 | 36.11 | † 79.87 | 26.76 | 51.50 | 38.10 | 25.57 | 8.56 | 6.16 | 10.70 | 13.80 | 13.64 |
| Claims on Central Bank | 20 | 114.69 | 137.81 | † 187.58 | 182.87 | 229.00 | 274.12 | 259.11 | 304.93 | 374.56 | 446.63 | 580.63 | 725.92 |
| Currency | 20a | 26.65 | 25.57 | † 32.47 | 32.40 | 39.31 | 37.46 | 33.84 | 39.32 | 45.08 | 50.75 | 48.68 | 53.89 |
| Reserve Deposits and Securities | 20b | 88.05 | 112.24 | † 155.10 | 150.47 | 189.69 | 236.66 | 225.27 | 265.61 | 329.48 | 395.88 | 531.95 | 672.03 |
| Other Claims | 20n | — | — | † — | — | — | — | — | — | — | — | — | — |
| Net Claims on Central Government | 22an | 68.30 | 45.99 | † 22.77 | 46.58 | 87.55 | 91.57 | 136.12 | 129.82 | 139.96 | 133.80 | 124.90 | 107.12 |
| Claims on Central Government | 22a | 81.55 | 67.33 | † 42.75 | 64.79 | 94.96 | 108.42 | 165.24 | 164.73 | 179.29 | 173.58 | 166.38 | 152.60 |
| Liabilities to Central Government | 26d | 13.24 | 21.33 | † 19.98 | 18.21 | 7.41 | 16.86 | 29.12 | 34.91 | 39.33 | 39.78 | 41.48 | 45.48 |
| Claims on Other Sectors | 22s | 1,137.80 | 1,216.34 | † 1,371.35 | 1,567.13 | 1,729.75 | 1,793.82 | 1,747.62 | 1,743.22 | 1,788.80 | 1,841.03 | 1,922.22 | 2,019.24 |
| Claims on Other Financial Corps. | 22g | — | — | † 1.80 | .99 | 1.23 | 2.01 | 1.93 | .10 | .06 | .07 | 3.41 | 2.44 |
| Claims on State & Local Govts | 22b | 5.43 | 4.38 | † 5.81 | 8.17 | 7.74 | 6.20 | 3.31 | 3.15 | 1.26 | .94 | .99 | .76 |
| Claims on Public Nonfin. Corps. | 22c | 7.45 | 29.38 | † 21.80 | 7.69 | 5.17 | 3.99 | 2.83 | 1.92 | 10.00 | 18.44 | 13.04 | 7.93 |
| Claims on Private Sector | 22d | 1,124.92 | 1,182.58 | † 1,341.94 | 1,550.28 | 1,715.61 | 1,781.62 | 1,739.55 | 1,738.04 | 1,777.47 | 1,821.58 | 1,904.79 | 2,008.11 |
| Liabilities to Central Bank | 26g | — | — | † — | — | — | — | — | — | — | — | — | — |
| Transf.Dep.Included in Broad Money | 24 | 389.69 | 417.36 | † 480.86 | 551.03 | 552.35 | 558.77 | 550.14 | 668.04 | 909.81 | 910.21 | 1,076.47 | 1,237.30 |
| Other Dep.Included in Broad Money | 25 | 707.27 | 757.07 | † 887.05 | 1,031.70 | 1,260.40 | 1,379.89 | 1,382.87 | 1,361.89 | 1,340.65 | 1,354.65 | 1,358.23 | 1,345.61 |
| Sec.Ot.th.Shares Incl.in Brd. Money | 26a | — | — | † — | — | — | — | — | — | — | — | — | — |
| Deposits Excl. from Broad Money | 26b | — | — | † — | — | — | — | — | — | — | — | — | — |
| Sec.Ot.th.Shares Excl.f/Brd.Money | 26s | — | — | † — | — | — | — | — | — | — | — | — | — |
| Loans | 26l | — | — | † 3.00 | 9.00 | 22.00 | — | — | — | — | — | — | — |
| Financial Derivatives | 26m | — | — | † — | — | — | — | — | — | — | — | — | — |
| Insurance Technical Reserves | 26r | — | — | † — | — | — | — | — | — | — | — | — | — |
| Shares and Other Equity | 27a | 192.03 | 227.62 | † 320.96 | 381.72 | 364.16 | 399.70 | 401.49 | 374.82 | 360.21 | 346.18 | 368.47 | 409.01 |
| Other Items (Net) | 27r | 129.94 | 109.62 | † −35.95 | −19.89 | 17.63 | −22.56 | 10.20 | 24.22 | 7.33 | 78.94 | 89.46 | 88.37 |
| Memo Item: | | | | | | | | | | | | | |
| Total Assets | 20ra | 1,564.47 | 1,702.58 | † 1,857.85 | 2,105.35 | 2,427.60 | 2,517.87 | 2,518.12 | 2,592.04 | 2,792.82 | 2,844.90 | 3,071.91 | 3,245.93 |

# Belize 339

|  |  | 2004 | 2005 | 2006 | 2007 | 2008 | 2009 | 2010 | 2011 | 2012 | 2013 | 2014 | 2015 |
|---|---|---|---|---|---|---|---|---|---|---|---|---|---|
| **Depository Corporations** | | \*Millions of Belize Dollars: End of Period\* | | | | | | | | | | | |
| Net Foreign Assets | 31n | 191.75 | 251.40 | † 274.21 | 361.76 | 488.46 | 513.45 | 570.52 | 678.10 | 840.84 | 1,028.16 | 1,191.63 | 1,042.93 |
| Claims on Nonresidents | 31 | 230.51 | 290.25 | † 363.03 | 401.30 | 554.99 | 630.17 | 676.07 | 759.82 | 915.45 | 1,100.62 | 1,261.70 | 1,124.18 |
| Liabilities to Nonresidents | 36c | 38.76 | 38.85 | † 88.82 | 39.54 | 66.53 | 116.72 | 105.55 | 81.72 | 74.61 | 72.46 | 70.07 | 81.25 |
| Domestic Claims | 32 | 1,353.19 | 1,371.48 | † 1,526.34 | 1,764.13 | 1,919.68 | 1,968.84 | 1,943.96 | 1,936.18 | 1,990.54 | 1,894.69 | 1,959.49 | 2,347.77 |
| Net Claims on Central Government | 32an | 182.86 | 127.61 | † 153.81 | 192.93 | 187.72 | 171.55 | 192.69 | 166.54 | 177.09 | 28.85 | 10.71 | 303.76 |
| Claims on Central Government | 32a | 246.84 | 249.16 | † 273.67 | 296.30 | 309.12 | 281.64 | 322.97 | 334.09 | 337.70 | 331.32 | 314.79 | 403.59 |
| Liabilities to Central Government | 36d | 63.98 | 121.54 | † 119.86 | 103.37 | 121.39 | 110.10 | 130.28 | 167.55 | 160.61 | 302.47 | 304.08 | 99.83 |
| Claims on Other Sectors | 32s | 1,170.33 | 1,243.86 | † 1,372.53 | 1,571.19 | 1,731.96 | 1,797.29 | 1,751.27 | 1,769.64 | 1,813.44 | 1,865.85 | 1,948.78 | 2,044.01 |
| Claims on Other Financial Corps.. | 32g | 32.52 | 27.52 | † 1.80 | .99 | 1.23 | 2.01 | 1.93 | .10 | .06 | .07 | 3.41 | 2.44 |
| Claims on State & Local Govts..... | 32b | 5.43 | 4.38 | † 5.81 | 8.17 | 7.74 | 6.20 | 3.31 | 3.15 | 1.26 | .94 | .99 | .76 |
| Claims on Public Nonfin. Corps.... | 32c | 7.45 | 29.38 | † 21.80 | 7.69 | 5.17 | 3.99 | 2.83 | 21.92 | 30.00 | 38.44 | 33.04 | 27.93 |
| Claims on Private Sector | 32d | 1,124.92 | 1,182.58 | † 1,343.13 | 1,554.34 | 1,717.82 | 1,785.09 | 1,743.20 | 1,744.46 | 1,782.12 | 1,826.39 | 1,911.35 | 2,012.88 |
| Broad Money Liabilities | 35l | 1,212.26 | 1,291.95 | † 1,504.80 | 1,736.10 | 1,966.63 | 2,093.17 | 2,090.78 | 2,201.19 | 2,443.51 | 2,476.57 | 2,672.06 | 2,874.10 |
| Currency Outside Depository Corps | 34a | 115.31 | 117.52 | † 136.88 | 153.38 | 153.88 | 154.52 | 157.76 | 171.26 | 193.06 | 211.72 | 237.35 | 291.19 |
| Transferable Deposits | 34 | 389.69 | 417.36 | † 480.86 | 551.03 | 552.35 | 558.77 | 550.14 | 668.04 | 909.81 | 910.21 | 1,076.47 | 1,237.30 |
| Other Deposits | 35 | 707.27 | 757.07 | † 887.05 | 1,031.70 | 1,260.40 | 1,379.89 | 1,382.87 | 1,361.89 | 1,340.65 | 1,354.65 | 1,358.23 | 1,345.61 |
| Securities Other than Shares | 36a | — | — | † — | — | — | — | — | — | — | — | — | — |
| Deposits Excl. from Broad Money | 36b | — | — | † 1.17 | 9.96 | 32.67 | 3.65 | 7.59 | 3.92 | 8.58 | 5.91 | 3.52 | 3.14 |
| Sec.Ot.th.Shares Excl.f/Brd.Money.... | 36s | — | — | † — | — | — | — | — | — | — | — | — | — |
| Loans | 36l | — | — | † 3.00 | 9.00 | 22.00 | — | — | — | — | — | — | — |
| Financial Derivatives | 36m | — | — | † — | — | — | — | — | — | — | — | — | — |
| Insurance Technical Reserves | 36r | — | — | † — | — | — | — | — | — | — | — | — | — |
| Shares and Other Equity | 37a | 211.38 | 251.06 | † 361.18 | 420.97 | 403.62 | 439.90 | 436.22 | 414.14 | 398.52 | 388.94 | 412.40 | 453.90 |
| Other Items (Net) | 37r | 121.30 | 79.87 | † −69.61 | −50.14 | −16.79 | −54.44 | −20.10 | −4.97 | −19.24 | 51.44 | 63.14 | 59.55 |
| Broad Money Liabs., Seasonally Adj. | 35l.b | 1,225.72 | 1,306.29 | † 1,512.61 | 1,745.03 | 1,976.17 | 2,101.93 | 2,098.57 | 2,208.53 | 2,450.93 | 2,482.60 | 2,677.65 | 2,880.12 |
| **Monetary Aggregates** | | \*Millions of Belize Dollars: End of Period\* | | | | | | | | | | | |
| Broad Money | 59m | .... | .... | 1,504.80 | 1,736.10 | 1,966.63 | 2,093.17 | 2,090.78 | 2,201.19 | 2,443.51 | 2,476.57 | 2,672.06 | 2,874.10 |
| o/w:Currency Issued by Cent.Govt | 59m.a | .... | .... | — | — | — | — | — | — | — | — | — | — |
| o/w: Dep.in Nonfin. Corporations. | 59m.b | .... | .... | — | — | — | — | — | — | — | — | — | — |
| o/w: Secs. Issued by Central Govt. | 59m.c | .... | .... | — | — | — | — | — | — | — | — | — | — |
| Money (National Definitions) | | | | | | | | | | | | | |
| M1 | 59ma | 406.71 | 423.16 | 617.75 | 704.41 | 706.24 | 713.28 | 707.90 | 839.29 | 1,102.87 | 1,121.92 | 1,313.82 | 1,528.49 |
| M2 | 59mb | 1,248.23 | 1,329.95 | 1,504.80 | 1,736.10 | 1,966.63 | 2,093.17 | 2,090.78 | 2,201.19 | 2,443.51 | 2,476.57 | 2,672.06 | 2,874.10 |
| **Interest Rates** | | \*Percent Per Annum\* | | | | | | | | | | | |
| Central Bank Policy Rate (EOP) | 60 | 12.00 | 12.00 | 12.00 | 12.00 | 12.00 | 12.00 | 18.00 | 11.00 | 11.00 | 11.00 | 11.00 | 11.00 |
| Treasury Bill Rate | 60c | 3.22 | 3.22 | 3.22 | 3.22 | 3.22 | 3.22 | 3.04 | 2.42 | 2.09 | 1.49 | .47 | .11 |
| Savings Rate | 60k | 5.08 | 5.09 | 5.21 | 5.24 | 5.27 | 5.27 | 5.13 | 4.44 | 2.89 | 2.69 | 2.35 | 2.37 |
| Deposit Rate | 60l | 7.42 | 7.71 | 8.16 | 8.32 | 8.46 | 8.37 | 7.76 | 6.44 | 4.41 | 3.59 | 2.90 | 2.60 |
| Lending Rate | 60p | 13.94 | 14.26 | 14.21 | 14.33 | 14.14 | 14.08 | 13.88 | 13.36 | 12.44 | 11.57 | 10.82 | 10.32 |
| **Prices and Labor** | | \*Index Numbers (2010=100): Period Averages\* | | | | | | | | | | | |
| Consumer Prices | 64 | 81.4 | 84.4 | 88.0 | 90.0 | 95.8 | 94.7 | † 100.0 | † 96.4 | 97.6 | 98.1 | 99.3 | 98.4 |
| | | \*Number in Thousands: Period Averages\* | | | | | | | | | | | |
| Labor Force | 67d | 108 | 111 | 113 | 122 | 125 | .... | .... | .... | 151 | 149 | .... | .... |
| Employment | 67e | 96 | 99 | 102 | 112 | 115 | 121 | 101 | .... | 127 | 131 | .... | .... |
| Unemployment | 67c | 13 | 12 | 11 | 10 | 10 | .... | .... | .... | 24 | 17 | .... | .... |
| Unemployment Rate (%) | 67r | 11.6 | 11.0 | 9.4 | 8.5 | 8.2 | 13.1 | 23.3 | .... | 16.1 | 11.7 | .... | .... |
| **Intl. Transactions & Positions** | | \*Millions of US Dollars\* | | | | | | | | | | | |
| Exports | 70..d | 213.00 | 208.00 | 266.24 | 253.94 | 290.05 | 224.00 | 279.78 | 340.45 | 340.44 | 314.58 | 303.32 | .... |
| Imports, c.i.f. | 71..d | 519.69 | 592.94 | 675.95 | 684.36 | 837.12 | 668.64 | 709.28 | 831.23 | 881.87 | 930.20 | 1,004.50 | .... |

## Balance of Payments

| | | 2004 | 2005 | 2006 | 2007 | 2008 | 2009 | 2010 | 2011 | 2012 | 2013 | 2014 | 2015 |
|---|---|---|---|---|---|---|---|---|---|---|---|---|---|
| | | *Millions of US Dollars* | | | | | | | | | | | |
| A. Current Account* | 109bx | −154.9 | −151.2 | −25.4 | −52.1 | −144.9 | −82.8 | −45.7 | † −19.9 | −33.1 | −72.6 | −135.9 | −174.7 |
| Goods, credit (exports) | 1a9cx | 289.9 | 308.0 | 408.9 | 416.3 | 480.0 | 384.0 | 475.7 | † 603.6 | 627.9 | 608.1 | 588.7 | 537.9 |
| Goods, debit (imports) | 1a9dx | 465.1 | 544.2 | 597.9 | 634.7 | 788.2 | 620.5 | 647.2 | † 778.2 | 837.0 | 875.9 | 925.5 | 961.3 |
| Balance on goods | 1a9bx | −175.1 | −236.2 | −188.9 | −218.5 | −308.3 | −236.6 | −171.5 | † −174.6 | −209.1 | −267.8 | −336.8 | −423.4 |
| Services, credit (exports) | 1b9cx | 238.1 | 307.0 | 367.0 | 400.1 | 386.6 | 344.3 | 353.8 | † 340.2 | 406.6 | 448.1 | 494.3 | 495.7 |
| Services, debit (imports) | 1b9dx | 147.1 | 158.8 | 152.2 | 168.2 | 169.6 | 161.7 | 162.4 | † 171.1 | 188.1 | 207.8 | 224.6 | 221.4 |
| Balance on Goods & Services | 1z9bx | −84.1 | −88.0 | 25.9 | 13.5 | −91.2 | −54.0 | 20.0 | † −5.5 | 9.4 | −27.6 | −67.1 | −149.0 |
| Primary income: credit | 1c9cx | 4.3 | 6.8 | 10.1 | 7.0 | 5.9 | 4.5 | 4.6 | † 4.8 | 5.1 | 6.1 | 8.4 | 7.3 |
| Primary income: debit | 1c9dx | 121.1 | 121.2 | 135.4 | 165.9 | 171.1 | 112.7 | 162.1 | † 103.0 | 123.4 | 124.0 | 151.1 | 102.7 |
| Balance on gds, serv. & prim. inc. | 1y9bx | −200.8 | −202.4 | −99.4 | −145.5 | −256.4 | −162.2 | −137.6 | † −103.7 | −108.9 | −145.6 | −209.8 | −244.4 |
| Secondary income: credit | 1d9ca | 60.8 | 68.4 | 92.2 | 136.6 | 141.1 | 101.9 | 114.8 | † 107.4 | 103.1 | 104.4 | 106.6 | 109.9 |
| Secondary income: debit | 1d9da | 14.9 | 17.1 | 18.2 | 43.2 | 29.5 | 22.5 | 22.9 | † 23.7 | 27.4 | 31.4 | 32.6 | 40.1 |
| B. Capital Account* | 209ba | 9.3 | 2.6 | 8.6 | 3.4 | 8.7 | 17.1 | 5.3 | † 25.8 | 22.5 | 37.7 | 34.2 | 8.6 |
| Capital account: credit | 209ca | 9.3 | 2.6 | 8.6 | 3.4 | 8.7 | 17.1 | 5.3 | † 26.4 | 22.5 | 37.7 | 34.2 | 8.6 |
| Capital account: debit | 209da | — | — | — | — | — | — | — | † .6 | — | — | — | — |
| Balance on current & capital acct. | 129ba | −145.6 | −148.6 | −16.8 | −48.6 | −136.2 | −65.7 | −40.4 | † 5.9 | −10.6 | −34.9 | −101.6 | −166.1 |
| C. Financial Account* | 309na | −117.4 | −144.3 | −74.1 | −109.7 | −205.5 | −145.0 | −27.0 | † −18.9 | −67.4 | −136.4 | −164.0 | −44.8 |
| Direct investment: assets | 3a9aa | .1 | 1.0 | .6 | 1.0 | 2.8 | .5 | 1.1 | † .6 | .9 | .7 | 2.7 | .5 |
| Equity & investment fund shares | 3aaaa | .1 | 1.0 | .6 | 1.0 | 2.8 | .5 | 1.1 | † .6 | .9 | .7 | 2.7 | .5 |
| Debt instruments | 3abaa | | | | | | | | | .... | .... | | |
| Direct investment: liabilities | 3a9la | 111.5 | 126.9 | 108.8 | 140.4 | 169.7 | 108.8 | 96.4 | † 95.3 | 194.2 | 92.2 | 141.1 | 59.1 |
| Equity & investment fund shares | 3aala | 98.0 | 106.3 | 123.5 | 127.3 | 162.0 | 102.4 | 94.3 | † 94.5 | 194.2 | 92.2 | 141.1 | 59.1 |
| Debt instruments | 3abla | 13.5 | 20.7 | −14.7 | 13.1 | 7.6 | 6.4 | 2.1 | † .9 | .... | .... | .... | .... |
| Portfolio investment: assets | 3b9aa | .2 | .2 | .3 | .4 | −2.9 | 4.5 | 2.2 | † .6 | .2 | — | — | — |
| Equity & investment fund shares | 3baaa | .2 | .2 | .3 | .4 | −2.9 | .5 | .1 | † .1 | .2 | — | — | — |
| Debt securities | 3bbaa | — | — | — | — | — | 4.0 | 2.1 | † 7.0 | .... | .... | .... | .... |
| Portfolio investment: liabilities | 3b9la | 76.9 | 18.1 | −21.4 | 79.1 | −2.7 | −5.1 | −5.6 | † −6.1 | −3.3 | −15.9 | | |
| Equity & investment fund shares | 3bala | — | — | 4.0 | — | 2.0 | — | — | | | | | |
| Debt securities | 3bbla | 76.9 | 18.1 | −25.4 | 79.1 | −4.7 | −5.1 | −5.6 | † −6.1 | −3.3 | −15.9 | | |
| Fin. der.& empl.stk.ops.(ESOs): net | 3c9na | −.5 | 5.3 | — | — | — | — | — | | | | | |
| Fin. der. & ESOs.: assets | 3c9aa | −.5 | −.3 | — | — | — | — | — | | | | | |
| Fin. der. & ESOs.: liabilities | 3c9la | — | −5.6 | — | — | — | — | — | | | | | |
| Other investment: assets | 3d9aa | 4.4 | 39.1 | 13.6 | −4.7 | 13.8 | −13.5 | 13.1 | † 23.6 | 43.2 | −22.8 | −8.7 | 13.4 |
| Other equity | 3daaa | .... | .... | .... | .... | | | | | | | | |
| Debt instruments | 3dzaa | 4.4 | 39.1 | 13.6 | −4.7 | 13.8 | −13.5 | 13.1 | † 23.6 | 43.2 | −22.8 | −8.7 | 13.4 |
| Other investment: liabilities | 3d9la | −66.8 | 45.0 | 1.1 | −113.1 | 52.2 | 32.8 | −47.4 | † −39.1 | −79.3 | 37.9 | 16.9 | −.5 |
| Other equity | 3dala | .... | .... | .... | | | | | | | | | .... |
| Debt instruments | 3dzla | −66.8 | 45.0 | 1.1 | −113.1 | 52.2 | 32.8 | −47.4 | † −39.1 | −79.3 | 37.9 | 16.9 | −.5 |
| Curr.+ cap.– finan. acct. balance | 4y9na | −28.2 | −4.3 | 57.3 | 61.1 | 69.3 | 79.3 | −13.4 | † 24.8 | 56.8 | 101.5 | 62.4 | −121.4 |
| D. Net Errors and Omissions | 409na | −3.2 | −7.2 | −7.9 | −38.7 | −11.1 | −39.3 | 18.4 | † −6.6 | −1.3 | 15.9 | 22.5 | 17.7 |
| E. Reserves and Related Items | 4z9na | −31.4 | −11.5 | 49.3 | 22.4 | 58.2 | 40.0 | 5.0 | † 18.2 | 55.5 | 117.3 | 84.9 | −103.7 |
| Reserve assets | 3e9aa | −31.4 | −11.5 | 49.3 | 22.4 | 58.2 | 47.0 | 5.0 | † 18.2 | 52.8 | 113.8 | 84.0 | −103.7 |
| Credit and loans from the IMF | 3dcla | — | — | — | — | — | 7.0 | — | † — | −2.7 | −3.6 | −.9 | — |
| Exceptional financing | 409la | — | — | — | — | — | — | — | .... | .... | .... | .... | .... |

*Excludes components in group E

## Government Finance
## Cash Flow Statement
**Budgetary Central Government**

| | | 2004 | 2005 | 2006 | 2007 | 2008 | 2009 | 2010 | 2011 | 2012 | 2013 | 2014 | 2015 |
|---|---|---|---|---|---|---|---|---|---|---|---|---|---|
| | | *Thousands of Belize Dollars: Fiscal Year Begins April 1* | | | | | | | | | | | |
| Cash Receipts:Operating Activities | c1 | 470,293 | 551,642 | 620,701 | 731,276 | 752,438 | 707,149 | 774,417 | 827,135 | 807,657 | 937,862 | 945,902 | .... |
| Taxes | c11 | 416,017 | 474,746 | 530,429 | 591,664 | 593,959 | 601,126 | 659,344 | 671,122 | 706,803 | 752,494 | 798,316 | .... |
| Social Contributions | c12 | — | — | — | — | — | — | — | — | — | — | — | .... |
| Grants | c13 | 14,863 | 27,638 | 36,815 | 65,263 | 67,046 | 33,663 | 12,130 | 42,536 | 21,342 | 71,957 | 39,167 | .... |
| Other Receipts | c14 | 39,413 | 49,258 | 53,457 | 74,349 | 91,433 | 72,360 | 102,943 | 113,477 | 79,512 | 113,411 | 108,419 | .... |
| Cash Payments:Operating Activities | c2 | 537,994 | 548,723 | 620,744 | 612,281 | 633,841 | 669,019 | 689,824 | 729,103 | 707,634 | 777,387 | 827,974 | .... |
| Compensation of Employees | c21 | 212,643 | 222,884 | 219,464 | 233,920 | 250,104 | 274,032 | 279,053 | 296,421 | 296,976 | 303,081 | 338,098 | .... |
| Purchases of Goods & Services | c22 | 78,526 | 95,048 | 138,699 | 134,186 | 148,721 | 158,027 | 164,844 | 174,117 | 179,276 | 199,750 | 187,264 | .... |
| Interest | c24 | 175,868 | 153,740 | 170,217 | 111,188 | 102,344 | 95,790 | 103,376 | 102,342 | 58,942 | 84,060 | 87,404 | .... |
| Subsidies | c25 | 33,677 | 36,949 | 52,372 | 75,688 | 85,144 | 93,046 | 97,205 | 104,589 | 118,755 | 136,992 | 150,797 | .... |
| Grants | c26 | | | | | | | | | | | | .... |
| Social Benefits | c27 | 32,280 | 40,102 | 39,992 | 42,299 | 47,528 | 48,124 | 45,346 | 51,634 | 53,685 | 53,504 | 64,411 | .... |
| Other Payments | c28 | 5,000 | — | — | 15,000 | — | — | — | — | — | — | — | .... |
| Net Cash Inflow:Operating Act.[1-2] | ccio | −67,701 | 2,919 | −43 | 118,995 | 118,597 | 38,130 | 84,593 | 98,032 | 100,023 | 160,475 | 117,928 | .... |
| Net Cash Outflow:Invest. in NFA | c31 | 134,613 | 75,087 | 99,558 | 96,550 | 126,049 | 75,261 | 106,029 | 147,507 | 136,615 | 213,815 | 242,016 | .... |
| Purchases of Nonfinancial Assets | c31.1 | 146,018 | 82,237 | 110,885 | 126,674 | 130,432 | 94,234 | 110,718 | 155,346 | 144,438 | .... | .... | .... |
| Sales of Nonfinancial Assets | c31.2 | 11,405 | 7,150 | 11,327 | 30,124 | 4,383 | 18,973 | 4,689 | 7,839 | 4,619 | | | .... |
| Cash Surplus/Deficit [1-2-31=1-2M] | ccsd | −202,314 | −72,168 | −99,601 | 22,445 | −7,452 | −37,131 | −21,436 | −49,475 | −36,592 | −53,340 | −124,088 | .... |
| Net Acq. Fin. Assets, excl. Cash | c32x | .... | .... | .... | .... | .... | — | — | — | — | .... | .... | .... |
| Domestic | c321x | .... | .... | .... | .... | .... | — | — | — | — | .... | .... | .... |
| Foreign | c322x | .... | .... | .... | .... | .... | — | — | — | — | .... | .... | .... |
| Net Incurrence of Liabilities | c33 | 363,923 | −185,318 | 56,649 | 39,695 | −15,352 | 19,875 | 102,289 | 63,644 | 52,948 | 171,691 | 129,991 | .... |
| Domestic | c331 | −115,372 | 23,456 | 32,493 | −10,779 | −29,193 | 4,257 | 99,554 | 38,426 | 6,074 | −4,365 | 32,932 | .... |
| Foreign | c332 | 479,295 | −208,774 | 24,156 | 50,474 | 13,841 | 15,618 | 2,735 | 25,218 | 46,874 | 176,056 | 97,059 | .... |
| Net Cash Inflow, Fin.Act.[-32x+33] | cnfb | 393,716 | −173,474 | 55,637 | 1,244 | 2,463 | 24,525 | 89,601 | 70,081 | 77,731 | 169,723 | 128,308 | .... |
| Net Change in Stock of Cash | cncb | 191,400 | −245,641 | −43,966 | 23,689 | −4,987 | −12,605 | 68,166 | 20,608 | 41,139 | 116,383 | 4,220 | .... |
| Stat. Discrep. [32X-33+NCB-CSD] | ccsdz | −2 | 1 | −2 | — | 2 | 1 | 1 | 2 | — | — | — | .... |
| Memo Item:Cash Expenditure[2+31] | c2m | 672,607 | 623,810 | 720,302 | 708,831 | 759,890 | 744,280 | 795,853 | 876,610 | 844,249 | 991,202 | 1,069,990 | .... |
| Memo Item: Gross Debt | c63 | 2,200,126 | 2,054,694 | 2,134,440 | 2,187,249 | 2,156,840 | 2,192,727 | 2,240,073 | 2,286,248 | 2,344,154 | 2,488,400 | 2,609,974 | .... |

| | | 2004 | 2005 | 2006 | 2007 | 2008 | 2009 | 2010 | 2011 | 2012 | 2013 | 2014 | 2015 |
|---|---|---|---|---|---|---|---|---|---|---|---|---|---|
| **National Accounts** | | | | | | *Millions of Belize Dollars* | | | | | | | |
| Househ.Cons.Expend.,incl.NPISHs.... | 96f | 1,591.7 | 1,603.6 | 1,613.5 | 1,710.8 | 1,783.8 | 1,880.9 | 1,961.2 | 2,090.1 | 2,198.1 | 2,327.8 | 2,399.1 | .... |
| Government Consumption Expend... | 91f | 295.3 | 322.0 | 345.2 | 388.1 | 420.9 | 425.3 | 445.6 | 458.8 | 471.6 | 491.7 | 514.6 | .... |
| Gross Fixed Capital Formation.......... | 93e | 413.7 | 466.2 | 470.1 | 506.1 | 700.5 | 510.1 | 369.5 | 506.1 | 503.7 | 589.8 | 676.2 | .... |
| Changes in Inventories.................... | 93i | 40.4 | 53.5 | 19.5 | 20.8 | 48.5 | −1.7 | −57.8 | 49.6 | −1.9 | 9.9 | 42.0 | .... |
| Exports of Goods and Services......... | 90c | 1,069.7 | 1,218.1 | 1,488.5 | 1,576.9 | 1,707.3 | 1,380.4 | 1,626.6 | 1,787.2 | 1,965.9 | 1,976.9 | 2,063.9 | .... |
| Imports of Goods and Services (-)..... | 98c | 1,238.0 | 1,397.1 | 1,501.2 | 1,580.1 | 1,906.6 | 1,503.4 | 1,605.9 | 1,876.7 | 1,980.6 | 2,154.5 | 2,251.4 | .... |
| Gross Domestic Product (GDP)......... | 99b | 2,115.7 | 2,228.4 | 2,434.9 | 2,581.1 | 2,737.3 | 2,673.9 | 2,794.2 | 2,974.0 | 3,147.7 | 3,248.6 | 3,435.7 | .... |
| Net Primary Income from Abroad..... | 98.n | −248.5 | −245.4 | −264.0 | −30.4 | −27.5 | −28.1 | −29.1 | −35.4 | −281.8 | −281.9 | −321.9 | .... |
| Gross National Income (GNI)............ | 99a | 1,867.2 | 1,983.0 | 2,170.9 | 2,550.7 | 2,709.7 | 2,645.8 | 2,765.1 | 2,938.6 | 2,865.9 | 2,966.7 | 3,113.9 | .... |
| GDP Volume 2000 Prices................. | 99b.p | 2,101.8 | 2,156.0 | 2,254.8 | 2,279.7 | 2,353.3 | 2,372.1 | 2,450.9 | 2,502.4 | 2,596.0 | 2,630.1 | 2,737.5 | 2,763.9 |
| GDP Volume (2010=100)................ | 99bvp | 85.8 | 88.0 | 92.0 | 93.0 | 96.0 | 96.8 | 100.0 | 102.1 | 105.9 | 107.3 | 111.7 | 112.8 |
| GDP Deflator (2010=100)............... | 99bip | 88.3 | 90.7 | 94.7 | 99.3 | 102.0 | 98.9 | 100.0 | 104.2 | 106.4 | 108.3 | 110.1 | .... |
| | | | | | | *Millions: Midyear Estimates* | | | | | | | |
| Population................................ | 99z | .28 | .28 | .29 | .30 | .31 | .31 | .32 | .33 | .34 | .34 | .35 | .36 |

# Benin 638

| | | 2004 | 2005 | 2006 | 2007 | 2008 | 2009 | 2010 | 2011 | 2012 | 2013 | 2014 | 2015 |
|---|---|---|---|---|---|---|---|---|---|---|---|---|---|
| **Exchange Rates** | | | | | | *CFA Francs per SDR: End of Period* | | | | | | | |
| Official Rate............................. | aa | 747.90 | 794.73 | 749.30 | 704.15 | 725.98 | 713.83 | 756.02 | 778.32 | 764.10 | 732.49 | 782.77 | 834.92 |
| | | | | | | *CFA Francs per US Dollar: End of Period (ae) Period Average (rf)* | | | | | | | |
| Official Rate............................. | ae | 481.58 | 556.04 | 498.07 | 445.59 | 471.34 | 455.34 | 490.91 | 506.96 | 497.16 | 475.64 | 540.28 | 602.51 |
| Official Rate............................. | rf | 528.28 | 527.47 | 522.89 | 479.27 | 447.81 | 472.19 | 495.28 | 471.87 | 510.53 | 494.04 | 494.41 | 591.45 |
| **Fund Position** | | | | | | *Millions of SDRs: End of Period* | | | | | | | |
| Quota.................................... | 2f.s | 61.90 | 61.90 | 61.90 | 61.90 | 61.90 | 61.90 | 61.90 | 61.90 | 61.90 | 61.90 | 61.90 | 61.90 |
| SDR Holdings........................... | 1b.s | .02 | .12 | .03 | .07 | .05 | 49.70 | 49.75 | 49.71 | 49.70 | 49.69 | 49.68 | 43.83 |
| Reserve Position in the Fund........... | 1c.s | 2.19 | 2.19 | 2.19 | 2.19 | 2.19 | 2.19 | 2.19 | 2.24 | 2.30 | 2.35 | 2.38 | 2.40 |
| Total Fund Cred.&Loans Outstg........ | 2tl | 42.04 | 36.94 | 1.76 | 2.64 | 14.57 | 24.77 | 35.39 | 56.43 | 77.21 | 87.21 | 92.87 | 86.85 |
| SDR Allocations......................... | 1bd | 9.41 | 9.41 | 9.41 | 9.41 | 9.41 | 59.17 | 59.17 | 59.17 | 59.17 | 59.17 | 59.17 | 59.17 |
| **International Liquidity** | | | | | | *Millions of US Dollars Unless Otherwise Indicated: End of Period* | | | | | | | |
| Total Reserves minus Gold.............. | 1l.d | 634.9 | 654.5 | 912.2 | 1,209.2 | 1,263.4 | 1,229.8 | 1,200.1 | 887.4 | 712.8 | 694.9 | 726.0 | 731.6 |
| SDR Holdings........................ | 1b.d | — | .2 | .1 | .1 | .1 | 77.9 | 76.6 | 76.3 | 76.4 | 76.5 | 72.0 | 60.7 |
| Reserve Position in the Fund......... | 1c.d | 3.4 | 3.1 | 3.3 | 3.5 | 3.4 | 3.4 | 3.4 | 3.4 | 3.5 | 3.6 | 3.4 | 3.3 |
| Foreign Exchange..................... | 1d.d | 631.5 | 651.2 | 908.9 | 1,205.6 | 1,259.9 | 1,148.5 | 1,120.1 | 807.7 | 632.9 | 614.8 | 650.6 | 667.5 |
| Gold (Million Fine Troy Ounces)........ | 1ad | — | — | — | — | — | — | — | — | — | — | — | — |
| Gold (National Valuation)................ | 1and | — | — | — | — | — | — | — | — | — | — | — | . . . . |
| Monetary Authorities: Other Liabs..... | 4..d | 26.6 | 14.8 | 16.2 | 16.2 | 20.6 | 31.7 | 24.7 | 21.8 | 8.9 | 15.3 | 28.0 | 28.9 |
| Deposit Money Banks: Assets.......... | 7a.d | 332.6 | 283.7 | 380.4 | 528.7 | 520.7 | 669.4 | 772.2 | 1,041.6 | 1,544.4 | 1,974.3 | 2,110.9 | 2,287.7 |
| Deposit Money Banks: Liabs........... | 7b.d | 172.7 | 184.4 | 212.8 | 224.6 | 264.4 | 313.9 | 319.5 | 323.0 | 457.3 | 564.7 | 632.1 | 891.1 |
| **Monetary Authorities** | | | | | | *Billions of CFA Francs: End of Period* | | | | | | | |
| Foreign Assets.......................... | 11 | 305.8 | 364.0 | 454.4 | 538.8 | 595.5 | 560.0 | 589.1 | 449.9 | 354.4 | 330.5 | 392.3 | 440.8 |
| Claims on Central Government........ | 12a | 36.2 | 32.1 | 1.3 | 2.0 | 10.1 | 50.2 | 58.6 | 77.1 | 92.1 | 95.4 | 95.1 | 85.9 |
| Claims on Deposit Money Banks...... | 12e | — | — | — | 15.3 | 75.4 | 124.1 | 99.2 | 230.0 | 312.1 | 378.6 | 515.5 | 510.3 |
| Reserve Money......................... | 14 | 221.5 | 295.2 | 333.0 | 357.6 | 527.4 | 504.8 | 506.6 | 512.7 | 513.4 | 607.0 | 776.3 | 769.9 |
| of which: Currency Outside DMBs.. | 14a | 129.9 | 195.2 | 253.0 | 238.9 | 361.6 | 339.7 | 347.6 | 376.8 | 398.5 | 504.0 | 626.0 | 605.9 |
| Foreign Liabilities...................... | 16c | 51.3 | 45.1 | 16.4 | 15.7 | 27.1 | 74.3 | 83.6 | 101.0 | 108.6 | 114.5 | 134.1 | 139.3 |
| Central Government Deposits.......... | 16d | 66.1 | 57.4 | 100.7 | 180.9 | 126.9 | 153.5 | 157.1 | 146.8 | 135.8 | 81.4 | 95.4 | 128.7 |
| Other Items (Net)....................... | 17r | 3.0 | −1.6 | 5.6 | 1.8 | −.4 | 1.6 | −.4 | −3.5 | .8 | 1.7 | −2.9 | −1.0 |
| **Deposit Money Banks** | | | | | | *Billions of CFA Francs: End of Period* | | | | | | | |
| Reserves................................ | 20 | 112.3 | 88.5 | 74.8 | 120.1 | 162.8 | 158.2 | 184.2 | 137.2 | 161.3 | 204.9 | 236.3 | 241.1 |
| Foreign Assets.......................... | 21 | 160.2 | 157.8 | 189.5 | 235.6 | 245.4 | 304.8 | 379.1 | 528.1 | 767.8 | 939.1 | 1,140.5 | 1,378.4 |
| Claims on Central Government........ | 22a | 20.0 | 29.6 | 24.9 | 49.8 | 146.6 | 170.9 | 173.2 | 220.7 | 178.7 | 225.9 | 279.7 | 413.1 |
| Claims on Private Sector............... | 22d | 312.1 | 375.1 | 415.8 | 519.9 | 624.4 | 698.5 | 757.8 | 845.0 | 924.4 | 1,022.6 | 1,084.3 | 1,064.5 |
| Claims on Other Financial Insts........ | 22f | — | — | — | — | — | — | — | — | — | — | — | — |
| Demand Deposits....................... | 24 | 198.6 | 225.3 | 239.5 | 337.7 | 378.1 | 415.2 | 449.0 | 483.4 | 468.5 | 565.5 | 627.2 | 691.0 |
| Time Deposits........................... | 25 | 165.4 | 185.3 | 223.6 | 279.5 | 350.1 | 424.3 | 466.7 | 507.5 | 590.6 | 638.2 | 761.6 | 863.8 |
| Foreign Liabilities...................... | 26c | 81.2 | 99.1 | 101.9 | 86.8 | 113.4 | 132.6 | 149.5 | 157.6 | 221.6 | 244.6 | 328.6 | 512.8 |
| Long-Term Foreign Liabilities.......... | 26cl | 2.0 | 3.5 | 4.1 | 13.3 | 11.2 | 10.3 | 7.4 | 6.2 | 5.8 | 24.0 | 13.0 | 24.1 |
| Central Government Deposits.......... | 26d | 97.0 | 108.1 | 95.4 | 171.4 | 220.8 | 175.8 | 247.9 | 256.5 | 304.0 | 390.7 | 404.1 | 462.5 |
| Credit from Monetary Authorities..... | 26g | — | — | — | 15.3 | 75.4 | 124.1 | 99.2 | 230.0 | 312.1 | 378.6 | 515.5 | 510.3 |
| Capital Accounts........................ | 27a | 67.7 | ·72.6 | 85.9 | 100.7 | 110.6 | 143.5 | 177.1 | 196.5 | 217.6 | 232.1 | 242.7 | 269.4 |
| Other Items (Net)....................... | 27r | −7.4 | −42.9 | −45.5 | −79.2 | −80.5 | −93.4 | −102.4 | −106.8 | −87.9 | −81.2 | −151.8 | −236.9 |
| Treasury Claims: Private Sector....... | 22d.i | — | — | — | — | — | — | — | — | — | — | — | — |
| Post Office: Checking Deposits....... | 24..i | 8.1 | 8.2 | 9.2 | 12.6 | 8.9 | 8.9 | 9.2 | 8.3 | 4.9 | 8.6 | 8.5 | 10.5 |
| **Monetary Survey** | | | | | | *Billions of CFA Francs: End of Period* | | | | | | | |
| Foreign Assets (Net)..................... | 31n | 333.5 | 377.6 | 525.5 | 671.9 | 700.3 | 657.8 | 735.2 | 719.4 | 792.0 | 910.5 | 1,070.1 | 1,167.0 |
| Domestic Credit......................... | 32 | 213.2 | 279.5 | 255.1 | 232.0 | 442.3 | 599.3 | 593.7 | 747.7 | 760.4 | 880.4 | 968.1 | 982.7 |
| Claims on Central Govt. (Net)........ | 32an | −98.8 | −95.6 | −160.8 | −287.9 | −182.1 | −99.2 | −164.1 | −97.2 | −164.0 | −142.1 | −116.2 | −81.8 |
| Claims on Private Sector............... | 32d | 312.1 | 375.1 | 415.8 | 519.9 | 624.4 | 698.5 | 757.8 | 845.0 | 924.4 | 1,022.6 | 1,084.3 | 1,064.5 |
| Claims on Other Financial Insts...... | 32f | — | — | — | — | — | — | — | — | — | — | — | — |
| Money.................................. | 34 | 337.2 | 429.7 | 502.3 | 589.9 | 750.2 | 764.3 | 806.2 | 869.5 | 872.4 | 1,078.7 | 1,262.2 | 1,308.7 |
| Quasi-Money........................... | 35 | 165.4 | 185.3 | 223.6 | 279.5 | 350.1 | 424.3 | 466.7 | 507.5 | 590.6 | 638.2 | 761.6 | 863.8 |
| Long-Term Foreign Liabilities.......... | 36cl | 2.0 | 3.5 | 4.1 | 13.3 | 11.2 | 10.3 | 7.4 | 6.2 | 5.8 | 24.0 | 13.0 | 24.1 |
| Other Items (Net)....................... | 37r | 42.0 | 38.7 | 50.5 | 21.3 | 31.1 | 58.3 | 48.6 | 83.9 | 83.7 | 50.1 | 1.4 | −46.8 |
| Money plus Quasi-Money................ | 35l | 502.6 | 614.9 | 726.0 | 869.3 | 1,100.3 | 1,188.6 | 1,272.9 | 1,377.1 | 1,463.0 | 1,716.9 | 2,023.8 | 2,172.5 |
| **Interest Rates** | | | | | | *Percent Per Annum* | | | | | | | |
| Repurchase Agreement Rate........... | 60.q | 4.00 | 4.00 | 4.25 | 4.25 | 4.75 | 4.25 | 4.25 | 4.25 | 4.00 | 3.50 | 3.50 | 3.50 |
| Deposit Rate............................ | 60l | 3.50 | 3.50 | 3.50 | 3.50 | 3.50 | 3.50 | 3.50 | 3.50 | 3.50 | 3.50 | 3.50 | 3.50 |
| **Prices and Labor** | | | | | | *Index Numbers (2010=100): Period Averages* | | | | | | | |
| Consumer Prices........................ | 64 | 80.0 | 84.3 | 87.5 | 88.6 | 95.7 | †97.7 | 100.0 | 102.7 | 109.6 | 110.7 | 109.5 | 109.9 |
| **Intl. Transactions & Positions** | | | | | | *Billions of CFA Francs* | | | | | | | |
| Exports................................. | 70 | 300.37 | 305.00 | 384.85 | 501.72 | 574.20 | 199.30 | 216.90 | . . . . | . . . . | . . . . | . . . . | 369.17 |
| Imports, c.i.f............................ | 71 | 472.17 | 536.96 | 642.11 | 976.27 | 1,025.19 | 729.90 | 739.00 | . . . . | . . . . | . . . . | . . . . | 1,401.13 |

# Benin 638

| | | 2004 | 2005 | 2006 | 2007 | 2008 | 2009 | 2010 | 2011 | 2012 | 2013 | 2014 | 2015 |
|---|---|---|---|---|---|---|---|---|---|---|---|---|---|
| **Balance of Payments** | | | | | | | *Millions of US Dollars* | | | | | | |
| A. Current Account* | 109bx | −316.5 | −270.3 | −327.3 | −652.1 | −618.6 | −755.8 | −617.8 | † −551.5 | −577.0 | −673.2 | −884.9 | .... |
| Goods, credit (exports) | 1a9cx | 568.5 | 578.1 | 735.5 | 1,046.8 | 1,282.2 | 1,224.6 | 1,281.5 | † 1,250.8 | 1,442.6 | 1,981.9 | 2,562.2 | .... |
| Goods, debit (imports) | 1a9dx | 839.7 | 863.4 | 1,042.0 | 1,601.6 | 1,889.7 | 1,737.8 | 1,775.2 | † 1,800.4 | 2,002.1 | 2,593.7 | 3,272.7 | .... |
| Balance on goods | 1a9bx | −271.2 | −285.3 | −306.5 | −554.8 | −607.5 | −513.2 | −493.6 | † −549.5 | −559.5 | −611.8 | −710.5 | .... |
| Services, credit (exports) | 1b9cx | 215.6 | 193.8 | 217.1 | 301.5 | 348.0 | 220.9 | 376.5 | † 411.2 | 433.9 | 514.4 | 478.6 | .... |
| Services, debit (imports) | 1b9dx | 289.4 | 281.2 | 356.0 | 500.7 | 510.0 | 495.9 | 514.7 | † 503.9 | 585.2 | 761.0 | 885.4 | .... |
| Balance on Goods & Services | 1z9bx | −345.0 | −372.7 | −445.4 | −754.0 | −769.5 | −788.2 | −631.9 | † −642.3 | −710.7 | −858.4 | −1,117.2 | .... |
| Primary income: credit | 1c9cx | 22.9 | 25.4 | 23.8 | 37.6 | 44.9 | 43.1 | 49.4 | † 103.5 | 92.2 | 154.3 | 156.6 | .... |
| Primary income: debit | 1c9dx | 59.9 | 43.2 | 54.0 | 86.1 | 56.2 | 76.1 | 102.9 | † 119.0 | 158.9 | 223.3 | 217.8 | .... |
| Balance on gds, serv. & prim. inc. | 1y9bx | −382.0 | −390.5 | −475.6 | −802.5 | −780.8 | −821.2 | −685.4 | † −657.8 | −777.4 | −927.4 | −1,178.4 | .... |
| Secondary income: credit | 1d9ca | 73.4 | 152.8 | 205.5 | 258.8 | 235.1 | 137.8 | 134.6 | † 166.0 | 282.0 | 357.6 | 437.0 | .... |
| Secondary income: debit | 1d9da | 7.9 | 32.6 | 57.2 | 108.4 | 72.9 | 72.5 | 67.0 | † 59.8 | 81.5 | 103.3 | 143.6 | .... |
| B. Capital Account* | 209ba | 52.1 | 79.5 | 60.4 | 129.5 | 66.2 | 134.9 | 114.9 | † 265.4 | 156.5 | 185.9 | 253.2 | .... |
| Capital account: credit | 209ca | 52.2 | 79.5 | 60.4 | 129.7 | 66.3 | 135.0 | 115.0 | † 269.1 | 164.9 | 195.9 | 263.2 | .... |
| Capital account: debit | 209da | — | — | — | .1 | .1 | .1 | .1 | † 3.7 | 8.4 | 9.9 | 10.0 | .... |
| Balance on current & capital acct. | 129ba | −264.4 | −190.8 | −266.9 | −522.5 | −552.4 | −620.9 | −502.9 | † −286.2 | −420.4 | −487.3 | −631.7 | .... |
| C. Financial Account* | 309na | 23.7 | −110.9 | 899.6 | −239.2 | −372.3 | −186.1 | −175.7 | † 258.8 | .5 | −415.3 | −732.1 | .... |
| Direct investment: assets | 3a9aa | −105.9 | −62.2 | −67.3 | −122.3 | −125.8 | −121.8 | −141.3 | † 59.6 | 40.3 | 58.6 | 17.3 | .... |
| Equity & investment fund shares | 3aaaa | −94.2 | −62.4 | −70.1 | −122.1 | −129.2 | −127.9 | −136.0 | † 64.7 | 40.1 | 58.8 | 16.8 | .... |
| Debt instruments | 3abaa | −11.7 | .2 | 2.8 | −.1 | 3.3 | 6.1 | −5.3 | † −5.0 | .2 | −.2 | .5 | .... |
| Direct investment: liabilities | 3a9la | −40.7 | −8.8 | −12.4 | 139.0 | 48.0 | −18.7 | 53.5 | † 161.1 | 281.6 | 360.2 | 405.2 | .... |
| Equity & investment fund shares | 3aala | −17.2 | −30.5 | −51.3 | 6.6 | −48.7 | −32.1 | −25.7 | † 149.0 | 197.6 | 178.2 | 176.3 | .... |
| Debt instruments | 3abla | −23.5 | 21.8 | 39.0 | 132.4 | 96.7 | 13.3 | 79.1 | † 12.1 | 84.0 | 182.0 | 228.9 | .... |
| Portfolio investment: assets | 3b9aa | −2.5 | −14.7 | −6.0 | 57.7 | 10.7 | 27.6 | 203.0 | † 262.2 | 231.8 | 179.1 | 118.6 | .... |
| Equity & investment fund shares | 3baaa | −.5 | −1.4 | −.3 | 5.7 | −1.3 | 2.8 | 5.4 | † −.1 | 2.9 | .1 | −.8 | .... |
| Debt securities | 3bbaa | −2.0 | −13.3 | −5.7 | 52.0 | 12.0 | 24.8 | 197.6 | † 262.3 | 228.9 | 179.0 | 119.4 | .... |
| Portfolio investment: liabilities | 3b9la | −2.9 | 2.3 | .3 | 4.9 | 15.0 | 106.2 | 4.9 | † 1.3 | −15.8 | 26.8 | 39.5 | .... |
| Equity & investment fund shares | 3bala | −2.9 | 2.3 | .3 | 4.9 | −1.8 | 9.0 | 4.9 | † 1.3 | 1.3 | 3.8 | 5.8 | .... |
| Debt securities | 3bbla | — | — | — | — | 16.7 | 97.2 | — | † — | −17.1 | 23.0 | 33.7 | .... |
| Fin. der.& empl.stk.ops.(ESOs): net. | 3c9na | .5 | .3 | — | .1 | .7 | −.4 | .4 | .... | .... | .... | .... | .... |
| Fin. der. & ESOs.: assets | 3c9aa | .5 | .3 | — | .1 | .7 | −.4 | .4 | .... | .... | .... | .... | .... |
| Fin. der. & ESOs.: liabilities | 3c9la | — | .... | .... | .... | .... | .... | .... | .... | .... | .... | .... | .... |
| Other investment: assets | 3d9aa | 19.3 | −6.7 | 51.4 | 97.6 | 43.6 | 245.6 | −131.0 | † 153.2 | 158.8 | 235.5 | 302.7 | .... |
| Other equity | 3daaa | .... | .... | .... | .... | .... | .... | .... | .... | .... | .... | .... | .... |
| Debt instruments | 3dzaa | 19.3 | −6.7 | 51.4 | 97.6 | 43.6 | 245.6 | −131.0 | † 153.2 | 158.8 | 235.5 | 302.7 | .... |
| Other investment: liabilities | 3d9la | −68.6 | 34.1 | −909.4 | 128.4 | 238.6 | 249.8 | 48.4 | † 53.9 | 164.7 | 501.3 | 726.0 | .... |
| Other equity | 3dala | .... | .... | .... | .... | .... | .... | .... | † .1 | .1 | — | .1 | .... |
| Debt instruments | 3dzla | −68.6 | 34.1 | −909.4 | 128.4 | 238.6 | 249.8 | 48.4 | † 53.8 | 164.5 | 501.4 | 725.9 | .... |
| Curr.+ cap.− finan. acct. balance | 4y9na | −288.0 | −80.0 | −1,166.5 | −283.3 | −180.0 | −434.8 | −327.2 | † −544.9 | −421.0 | −72.0 | 100.4 | .... |
| D. Net Errors and Omissions | 409na | −10.7 | 28.3 | 50.4 | 106.0 | 31.7 | 13.5 | 33.1 | † 13.8 | 26.1 | 19.2 | 5.5 | .... |
| E. Reserves and Related Items | 4z9na | −298.7 | −51.6 | −1,116.0 | −177.3 | −148.4 | −421.3 | −294.2 | † −531.2 | −394.9 | −52.7 | 106.0 | .... |
| Reserve assets | 3e9aa | −126.9 | 111.7 | 171.5 | 176.4 | 126.4 | −72.1 | 54.4 | † −297.5 | −185.6 | −37.5 | 114.8 | .... |
| Credit and loans from the IMF | 3dcla | −10.6 | −7.6 | −50.8 | 1.3 | 19.3 | 15.8 | 15.6 | † 33.2 | 31.9 | 15.2 | 8.9 | .... |
| Exceptional financing | 409la | 182.5 | 170.9 | 1,338.4 | 352.4 | 255.5 | 333.5 | 333.0 | † 200.5 | 177.4 | .... | .... | .... |
| *Excludes components in group E | | | | | | | | | | | | | |
| | | | | | | | | | | | | | |
| **International Investment Position** | | | | | | | *Millions of US Dollars* | | | | | | |
| Assets | 809aa | 1,155.9 | 1,093.8 | 1,514.1 | 2,053.2 | 2,070.2 | 2,357.9 | 2,310.9 | † 2,320.8 | 2,618.0 | 3,325.4 | .... | .... |
| Direct investment | 8a9aa | 18.1 | 19.6 | 15.7 | 29.7 | 24.3 | 57.5 | 44.4 | † 72.1 | 115.2 | 178.8 | .... | .... |
| Equity & investment fund shares | 8aaaa | 18.1 | 16.2 | 15.7 | 20.1 | 20.4 | 48.3 | 44.4 | † 58.1 | 100.7 | 163.6 | .... | .... |
| Debt instruments | 8abaa | — | 3.4 | — | 9.6 | 3.9 | 9.2 | .... | † 14.0 | 14.5 | 15.2 | .... | .... |
| Portfolio investment | 8b9aa | 114.6 | 99.5 | 102.1 | 189.7 | 134.5 | 206.3 | 396.7 | † 636.4 | 886.9 | 1,203.6 | .... | .... |
| Equity & investment fund shares | 8baaa | 4.5 | 1.6 | .8 | 7.2 | 4.6 | 6.9 | 11.8 | † 21.7 | 25.1 | 9.9 | .... | .... |
| Debt securities | 8bbaa | 110.1 | 98.0 | 101.3 | 182.5 | 129.9 | 199.4 | 384.8 | † 614.7 | 861.8 | 1,193.7 | .... | .... |
| Fin. der.(oth.than reserves) & ESOs | 8c9aa | 1.1 | 1.1 | .1 | .2 | .8 | .2 | .5 | .... | .... | .... | .... | .... |
| Other investment | 8d9aa | 387.2 | 317.5 | 484.1 | 624.4 | 647.3 | 864.1 | 669.3 | † 724.9 | 903.1 | 1,248.1 | .... | .... |
| Other equity | 8daaa | .... | .... | .... | .... | .... | .... | .... | .... | .... | .... | .... | .... |
| Debt instruments | 8dzaa | 387.2 | 317.5 | 484.1 | 624.4 | 647.3 | 864.1 | 669.3 | † 724.9 | 903.1 | 1,248.1 | .... | .... |
| Reserve assets | 8e9aa | 634.9 | 656.0 | 912.2 | 1,209.2 | 1,263.4 | 1,229.8 | 1,200.1 | † 887.4 | 712.8 | 694.9 | .... | .... |
| Liabilities | 809la | 2,646.1 | 2,473.7 | 2,179.7 | 2,021.8 | 2,469.8 | 3,188.5 | 3,592.2 | † 3,049.6 | 3,714.0 | 4,163.8 | .... | .... |
| Direct investment | 8a9la | 277.7 | 284.3 | 385.8 | 556.3 | 602.4 | 762.8 | 895.6 | † 674.8 | 977.2 | 603.1 | .... | .... |
| Equity & investment fund shares | 8aala | 194.6 | 182.4 | 210.1 | 280.7 | 300.8 | 437.9 | 517.6 | † 575.8 | 790.0 | 364.0 | .... | .... |
| Debt instruments | 8abla | 83.2 | 102.0 | 175.6 | 275.6 | 301.6 | 324.9 | 378.0 | † 99.0 | 187.2 | 239.1 | .... | .... |
| Portfolio investment | 8b9la | 13.6 | 14.0 | 33.8 | 25.3 | 36.6 | 202.5 | 268.1 | † 346.1 | 414.0 | 592.6 | .... | .... |
| Equity & investment fund shares | 8bala | 8.8 | 12.3 | 12.9 | 17.5 | 9.2 | 18.5 | 22.1 | † 10.7 | 12.2 | 6.5 | .... | .... |
| Debt securities | 8bbla | 4.8 | 1.7 | 20.9 | 7.8 | 27.4 | 184.0 | 246.0 | † 335.4 | 401.7 | 586.1 | .... | .... |
| Fin. der.(oth.than reserves) & ESOs | 8c9la | .... | .... | .... | .... | — | .... | .... | .... | .... | .... | .... | .... |
| Other investment | 8d9la | 2,354.8 | 2,175.4 | 1,760.2 | 1,440.2 | 1,830.8 | 2,223.2 | 2,428.5 | † 2,028.8 | 2,322.8 | 2,968.1 | .... | .... |
| Other equity | 8dala | .... | .... | .... | .... | .... | .... | .... | † 1.3 | 1.4 | 1.5 | .... | .... |
| Debt instruments | 8dzla | 2,354.8 | 2,175.4 | 1,760.2 | 1,440.2 | 1,830.8 | 2,223.2 | 2,428.5 | † 2,027.5 | 2,321.4 | 2,966.7 | .... | .... |

# Benin 638

| | | 2004 | 2005 | 2006 | 2007 | 2008 | 2009 | 2010 | 2011 | 2012 | 2013 | 2014 | 2015 |
|---|---|---|---|---|---|---|---|---|---|---|---|---|---|
| **Government Finance** | | | | | | | | | | | | | |
| **Operations Statement** | | | | | | | | | | | | | |
| **Budgetary Central Government** | | | | | | *Billions of CFA Francs: Fiscal Year Ends December 31* | | | | | | | |
| Revenue............................ | a1 | 424.35 | 422.63 | 459.87 | 623.75 | 609.09 | 631.96 | 648.38 | 676.75 | 701.46 | 803.05 | .... | .... |
| Taxes............................. | a11 | 349.59 | 349.90 | 382.18 | 449.02 | 514.75 | 502.48 | 536.25 | 546.56 | 599.90 | 695.97 | .... | .... |
| Social Contributions.................... | a12 | — | — | 12.71 | 12.96 | 14.78 | 16.21 | 16.37 | 18.60 | 20.72 | 22.80 | .... | .... |
| Grants............................. | a13 | 55.71 | 51.63 | 47.02 | 80.64 | 55.61 | 81.70 | 52.31 | 80.54 | 46.59 | 45.89 | .... | .... |
| Other Revenue......................... | a14 | 19.05 | 21.10 | 17.96 | 81.13 | 23.94 | 31.57 | 43.45 | 31.04 | 34.24 | 38.39 | .... | .... |
| Expense............................. | a2 | 269.96 | 306.34 | 335.74 | 345.18 | 419.13 | 442.62 | 459.01 | 457.66 | 534.67 | 577.48 | .... | .... |
| Compensation of Employees......... | a21 | 123.48 | 130.28 | 128.47 | 133.19 | 179.70 | 222.91 | 235.60 | 242.12 | 267.90 | 296.25 | .... | .... |
| Use of Goods & Services............... | a22 | 73.26 | 85.94 | 98.61 | 95.34 | 94.96 | 73.92 | 71.20 | 68.70 | 94.44 | 106.11 | .... | .... |
| Consumption of Fixed Capital....... | a23 | .... | .... | .... | .... | .... | .... | .... | .... | .... | .... | .... | .... |
| Interest............................ | a24 | 6.97 | 6.89 | 10.15 | 5.13 | 10.35 | 15.60 | 17.73 | 14.97 | 23.14 | 19.85 | .... | .... |
| Subsidies.......................... | a25 | — | — | 21.22 | 21.59 | 10.30 | 11.87 | 20.53 | 33.55 | 55.09 | 49.53 | .... | .... |
| Grants............................. | a26 | 3.55 | 3.96 | 69.47 | 80.97 | 114.57 | 107.72 | 101.79 | 86.98 | 80.50 | 91.12 | .... | .... |
| Social Benefits......................... | a27 | — | — | .66 | .71 | .66 | .81 | .78 | .99 | .78 | .91 | .... | .... |
| Other Expense....................... | a28 | 62.69 | 79.28 | 7.16 | 8.26 | 8.59 | 9.79 | 11.38 | 10.35 | 12.81 | 13.70 | .... | .... |
| Gross Operating Balance [1-2+23]... | agob | 154.39 | 116.29 | 124.13 | 278.57 | 189.96 | 189.33 | 189.36 | 219.09 | 166.79 | 225.57 | .... | .... |
| Net Operating Balance [1-2]........... | anob | .... | .... | .... | .... | .... | .... | .... | .... | .... | .... | .... | .... |
| Net Acq. of Nonfinancial Assets....... | a31 | 134.72 | 130.48 | 64.28 | 41.29 | 114.00 | 221.61 | 122.28 | 124.86 | 101.18 | 102.32 | .... | .... |
| Aquisition of Nonfin. Assets........... | a31.1 | .... | .... | .... | .... | .... | .... | .... | .... | .... | .... | .... | .... |
| Disposal of Nonfin. Assets............. | a31.2 | .... | .... | .... | .... | .... | .... | .... | .... | .... | .... | .... | .... |
| Net Lending/Borrowing [1-2-31]...... | anlb | 19.67 | −14.19 | 59.85 | 237.27 | 75.96 | −32.28 | 67.08 | 94.23 | 65.60 | 123.25 | .... | .... |
| Net Acq. of Financial Assets............ | a32 | 8.15 | .... | −1.35 | −2.61 | 240.21 | −27.38 | 22.44 | −.91 | −16.75 | −5.70 | .... | .... |
| By instrument | | | | | | | | | | | | | |
| Monetary Gold & SDRs................. | a3201 | — | .... | — | — | — | — | — | — | — | — | .... | .... |
| Currency & Deposits.................... | a3202 | 9.05 | .... | — | — | 197.79 | −21.13 | 14.53 | −11.42 | −20.02 | −34.02 | .... | .... |
| Securities other than Shares........... | a3203 | .... | .... | — | — | — | — | — | — | — | — | .... | .... |
| Loans.............................. | a3204 | .... | .... | −1.35 | −2.61 | 42.42 | 11.61 | 25.40 | 10.51 | 3.27 | 28.33 | .... | .... |
| Shares & Other Equity.................... | a3205 | .... | .... | — | — | — | −17.86 | −17.50 | — | — | — | .... | .... |
| Insurance Technical Reserves......... | a3206 | .... | .... | — | — | — | — | — | — | — | — | .... | .... |
| Financial Derivatives...................... | a3207 | .... | .... | — | — | — | — | — | — | — | — | .... | .... |
| Other Accounts Receivable............. | a3208 | .... | .... | — | — | — | — | — | — | — | — | .... | .... |
| By debtor | | | | | | | | | | | | | |
| Domestic............................... | a321 | 8.15 | .... | −1.35 | −2.61 | 240.21 | −27.38 | 22.44 | −.91 | −16.75 | −5.70 | .... | .... |
| Foreign................................. | a322 | — | .... | — | — | — | — | — | — | — | — | .... | .... |
| Net Incurrence of Liabilities.............. | a33 | −11.52 | .... | 35.46 | 77.38 | 195.51 | 189.98 | 90.19 | 133.51 | 80.83 | 161.04 | .... | .... |
| By instrument | | | | | | | | | | | | | |
| Special Drawing Rights (SDRs)....... | a3301 | — | — | — | — | — | — | — | — | — | — | .... | .... |
| Currency & Deposits...................... | a3302 | .10 | .... | — | — | — | — | — | — | — | — | .... | .... |
| Securities other than Shares........... | a3303 | — | .... | — | — | 130.96 | 99.32 | 52.53 | 112.59 | 38.85 | 1.49 | .... | .... |
| Loans.............................. | a3304 | 18.00 | .... | 35.46 | 77.38 | 80.92 | 131.88 | 94.57 | 68.13 | 57.82 | 187.86 | .... | .... |
| Shares & Other Equity.................... | a3305 | — | .... | — | — | — | — | — | — | — | — | .... | .... |
| Insurance Technical Reserves......... | a3306 | −20.54 | .... | — | — | — | — | — | — | — | — | .... | .... |
| Financial Derivatives...................... | a3307 | — | .... | — | — | — | — | — | — | — | — | .... | .... |
| Other Accounts Payable................. | a3308 | −9.00 | .... | — | — | −16.37 | −41.22 | −56.91 | −47.21 | −15.84 | −28.31 | .... | .... |
| By creditor | | | | | | | | | | | | | |
| Domestic............................... | a331 | −50.64 | .... | −2.14 | −1.54 | 129.91 | 115.35 | 10.05 | 91.26 | 36.54 | −2.39 | .... | .... |
| Foreign................................. | a332 | 39.12 | .... | 37.60 | 78.92 | 65.61 | 74.63 | 80.14 | 42.25 | 44.29 | 163.42 | .... | .... |
| Stat. Discrepancy [32-33-NLB]........ | anlbz | — | .... | −96.66 | −317.27 | −31.27 | −185.08 | −134.83 | −228.64 | −163.18 | −289.99 | .... | .... |
| Memo Item: Expenditure [2+31]...... | a2m | 404.68 | 436.82 | 400.02 | 386.47 | 533.12 | 664.23 | 581.30 | 582.52 | 635.85 | 679.80 | .... | .... |
| **National Accounts** | | | | | | *Billions of CFA Francs* | | | | | | | |
| Househ.Cons.Expend.,incl.NPISHs.... | 96f | 1,622.9 | 1,765.8 | 1,884.5 | 2,123.3 | 2,386.6 | 2,594.0 | 2,578.3 | 2,679.0 | 3,116.5 | 3,028.2 | 3,262.4 | .... |
| Government Consumption Expend... | 91f | 258.7 | 275.8 | 297.9 | 275.8 | 297.9 | 323.7 | 351.9 | 374.5 | 385.4 | 442.4 | 434.8 | .... |
| Gross Fixed Capital Formation.......... | 93e | 415.5 | 445.0 | 481.1 | 417.4 | 505.7 | 545.0 | 615.6 | 659.7 | 683.5 | 1,047.5 | 1,170.0 | .... |
| Changes in Inventories.................... | 93i | 27.0 | −27.6 | 24.6 | 19.0 | 13.1 | 8.1 | 17.0 | 29.5 | 33.3 | 40.8 | — | .... |
| Exports of Goods and Services......... | 90c | 428.7 | 495.9 | 454.5 | 407.2 | 498.1 | 646.2 | 821.2 | 784.2 | 944.9 | 1,147.8 | 1,224.6 | .... |
| Imports of Goods and Services (-)..... | 98c | 612.7 | 656.2 | 682.4 | 603.8 | 731.0 | 1,007.6 | 1,134.1 | 1,087.3 | 1,312.7 | 1,602.4 | 1,684.5 | .... |
| Gross Domestic Product (GDP)......... | 99b | 2,140.0 | 2,298.7 | 2,460.2 | 2,638.9 | 2,970.4 | 3,109.4 | 3,249.8 | 3,439.7 | 3,850.9 | 4,104.2 | 4,407.3 | .... |
| GDP Volume 2008 Prices................. | 99b.p | 2,532.9 | 2,605.5 | 2,703.3 | 2,828.6 | 2,970.4 | 3,049.4 | 3,129.1 | 3,231.2 | 3,405.3 | 3,597.6 | 3,803.2 | .... |
| GDP Volume (2010=100)................ | 99bvp | 80.9 | 83.3 | 86.4 | 90.4 | 94.9 | 97.5 | 100.0 | 103.3 | 108.8 | 115.0 | 121.5 | .... |
| GDP Deflator (2010=100)................ | 99bip | 81.3 | 84.9 | 87.6 | 89.8 | 96.3 | 98.2 | 100.0 | 102.5 | 108.9 | 109.8 | 111.6 | .... |
| | | | | | | *Millions: Midyear Estimates* | | | | | | | |
| Population................................ | 99z | 7.92 | 8.18 | 8.44 | 8.71 | 8.97 | 9.24 | 9.51 | 9.78 | 10.05 | 10.32 | 10.60 | 10.88 |

# Bhutan 514

| | | 2004 | 2005 | 2006 | 2007 | 2008 | 2009 | 2010 | 2011 | 2012 | 2013 | 2014 | 2015 |
|---|---|---|---|---|---|---|---|---|---|---|---|---|---|
| **Exchange Rates** | | | | | | *Ngultrum per SDR: End of Period* | | | | | | | |
| Official Rate............................. | aa | 67.688 | 64.410 | 66.562 | 62.286 | 74.634 | 73.180 | 69.009 | 81.768 | 84.188 | 95.321 | 91.755 | 91.910 |
| | | | | | | *Ngultrum per US Dollar: End of Period (ae) Period Average (rf)* | | | | | | | |
| Official Rate............................. | ae | 43.585 | 45.065 | 44.245 | 39.415 | 48.455 | 46.680 | 44.810 | 53.260 | 54.777 | 61.897 | 63.332 | 66.326 |
| Official Rate............................. | rf | 45.316 | 44.100 | 45.307 | 41.349 | 43.505 | 48.405 | 45.726 | 46.670 | 53.437 | 58.598 | 61.030 | 64.152 |
| **Fund Position** | | | | | | *Millions of SDRs: End of Period* | | | | | | | |
| Quota............................. | 2f.s | 6.30 | 6.30 | 6.30 | 6.30 | 6.30 | 6.30 | 6.30 | 6.30 | 6.30 | 6.30 | 6.30 | 6.30 |
| SDR Holdings............................. | 1b.s | .27 | .30 | .33 | .38 | .42 | 6.42 | 6.42 | 6.43 | 6.43 | 6.43 | 6.43 | 6.43 |
| Reserve Position in the Fund............ | 1c.s | 1.02 | 1.02 | 1.02 | 1.02 | 1.02 | 1.02 | 1.02 | 1.02 | 1.02 | 1.02 | 1.02 | 1.02 |
| Total Fund Cred.&Loans Outstg....... | 2tl | — | — | — | — | — | — | — | — | — | — | — | — |
| SDR Allocations............................. | 1bd | — | — | — | — | — | 5.99 | 5.99 | 5.99 | 5.99 | 5.99 | 5.99 | 5.99 |
| **International Liquidity** | | | | | | *Millions of US Dollars Unless Otherwise Indicated: End of Period* | | | | | | | |
| Total Reserves minus Gold............... | 1l.d | 398.62 | 467.43 | 545.32 | 699.05 | 764.80 | 890.89 | 1,002.14 | 789.64 | 954.68 | 991.31 | 1,245.09 | 1,103.18 |
| SDR Holdings............................. | 1b.d | .42 | .42 | .50 | .60 | .65 | 10.06 | 9.89 | 9.87 | 9.88 | 9.90 | 9.32 | 8.91 |
| Reserve Position in the Fund.......... | 1c.d | 1.58 | 1.46 | 1.54 | 1.61 | 1.57 | 1.60 | 1.57 | 1.57 | 1.57 | 1.57 | 1.48 | 1.41 |
| Foreign Exchange......................... | 1d.d | 396.62 | 465.55 | 543.29 | 696.84 | 762.58 | 879.23 | 990.68 | 778.21 | 943.23 | 979.83 | 1,234.29 | 1,092.85 |
| of which: Convertible Currency..... | 1dxd | 271.65 | 359.49 | 457.72 | 594.73 | 681.37 | 760.70 | 855.24 | 757.60 | 916.75 | 875.40 | 902.16 | 876.89 |
| Central Bank: Other Assets............... | 3..d | 50.36 | 2.83 | 4.38 | 4.65 | 7.51 | 60.17 | 60.09 | 60.06 | 60.22 | 60.11 | 60.29 | 59.89 |
| Central Bank: Other Liabs............... | 4..d | .47 | .47 | 2.21 | 60.51 | 59.76 | 125.05 | 127.05 | 117.94 | 360.28 | 223.84 | 218.52 | 165.65 |
| Other Depository Corps.: Assets....... | 7a.d | 99.27 | 89.15 | 136.23 | 81.91 | 50.31 | 59.91 | 51.76 | 42.59 | 85.31 | 57.32 | 56.52 | 67.77 |
| Other Depository Corps.: Liabs......... | 7b.d | — | — | — | — | — | — | 7.88 | 7.13 | 7.94 | — | — | — |
| Other Financial Corps.: Assets......... | 7e.d | .08 | .21 | .24 | .19 | .64 | .64 | .04 | .03 | .04 | .42 | .58 | .21 |
| Other Financial Corps.: Liabs............ | 7f.d | — | — | — | — | — | — | — | — | — | — | — | — |
| **Central Bank** | | | | | | *Millions of Ngultrum: End of Period* | | | | | | | |
| Net Foreign Assets........................... | 11n | 12,944 | 16,938 | 17,912 | 21,917 | 30,352 | 32,599 | 36,531 | 33,379 | 27,691 | 43,545 | 61,039 | 57,244 |
| Claims on Nonresidents................. | 11 | 12,965 | 16,959 | 18,009 | 24,302 | 33,248 | 38,868 | 42,685 | 40,075 | 47,883 | 57,983 | 75,428 | 68,781 |
| Liabilities to Nonresidents............... | 16c | 21 | 21 | 98 | 2,385 | 2,896 | 6,269 | 6,154 | 6,696 | 20,192 | 14,438 | 14,389 | 11,537 |
| Claims on Other Depository Corps.... | 12e | 895 | 768 | 103 | 157 | 115 | 169 | 232 | 716 | 3,458 | 1,104 | 166 | 745 |
| Net Claims on Central Government.. | 12an | −1,052 | −737 | −1,496 | −3,005 | −7,662 | −158 | −299 | −284 | −316 | −456 | −651 | −268 |
| Claims on Central Government...... | 12a | 37 | 100 | — | — | — | — | — | — | 1,900 | — | — | — |
| Liabilities to Central Government... | 16d | 1,089 | 837 | 1,496 | 3,005 | 7,662 | 158 | 299 | 284 | 2,216 | 456 | 651 | 268 |
| Claims on Other Sectors.................. | 12s | 1 | — | 10 | 11 | 17 | 17 | 22 | 21 | 18 | 17 | 21 | 41 |
| Claims on Other Financial Corps.... | 12g | — | — | — | — | — | — | — | — | — | 3 | 3 | — |
| Claims on State & Local Govts....... | 12b | — | — | — | — | — | — | — | — | — | — | — | — |
| Claims on Public Nonfin. Corps...... | 12c | — | — | — | — | — | — | — | — | — | — | — | — |
| Claims on Private Sector................ | 12d | 1 | — | 10 | 11 | 17 | 17 | 22 | 21 | 18 | 14 | 18 | 41 |
| Monetary Base................................ | 14 | 9,222 | 12,733 | 12,285 | 14,518 | 15,785 | 22,318 | 27,249 | 21,173 | 19,148 | 21,953 | 34,746 | 25,801 |
| Currency in Circulation.................. | 14a | 2,143 | 2,519 | 2,908 | 4,070 | 4,816 | 5,219 | 6,189 | 7,576 | 6,730 | 7,318 | 8,315 | 9,407 |
| Liabs. to Other Depository Corps.... | 14c | 7,080 | 10,214 | 9,376 | 10,446 | 10,969 | 17,099 | 21,059 | 13,597 | 12,419 | 14,635 | 26,431 | 16,395 |
| Liabilities to Other Sectors............. | 14d | — | — | — | 2 | — | — | — | — | — | — | — | — |
| Other Liabs. to Other Dep. Corps..... | 14n | 200 | 100 | 100 | 2,000 | 1,000 | 4,504 | 4,812 | 2,499 | 107 | 4,823 | 7,400 | 11,361 |
| Dep. & Sec. Excl. f/Monetary Base..... | 14o | — | — | — | — | — | — | — | — | — | — | 1 | — |
| Deposits Included in Broad Money.... | 15 | — | — | — | — | — | — | — | — | — | — | — | — |
| Sec.Ot.th.Shares Incl.in Brd. Money | 16a | — | — | — | — | — | — | — | — | — | — | — | — |
| Deposits Excl. from Broad Money... | 16b | — | — | — | — | — | — | — | — | — | — | 1 | — |
| Sec.Ot.th.Shares Excl.f/Brd.Money.. | 16s | — | — | — | — | — | — | — | — | — | — | — | — |
| Loans........................................ | 16l | — | — | — | — | — | — | — | — | — | — | — | — |
| Financial Derivatives....................... | 16m | — | — | — | — | — | — | — | — | — | — | — | — |
| Shares and Other Equity.................. | 17a | 3,531 | 4,352 | 4,387 | 4,122 | 6,778 | 6,096 | 4,676 | 10,543 | 11,948 | 17,855 | 18,915 | 20,985 |
| Other Items (Net)............................. | 17r | −165 | −215 | −242 | −1,560 | −742 | −292 | −251 | −383 | −352 | −422 | −487 | −385 |
| Memo Item: | | | | | | | | | | | | | |
| Total Assets................................... | 10ra | 14,064 | 18,393 | 18,716 | 26,361 | 34,466 | 39,832 | 43,630 | 41,661 | 54,327 | 60,102 | 76,835 | 70,646 |
| **Other Depository Corporations** | | | | | | *Millions of Ngultrum: End of Period* | | | | | | | |
| Net Foreign Assets........................... | 21n | 4,327 | 4,017 | 6,028 | 3,229 | 2,438 | 2,793 | 1,966 | 1,868 | 4,228 | 3,551 | 3,580 | 4,495 |
| Claims on Nonresidents................. | 21 | 4,327 | 4,017 | 6,028 | 3,229 | 2,438 | 2,793 | 2,319 | 2,243 | 4,662 | 3,551 | 3,580 | 4,495 |
| Liabilities to Nonresidents............... | 26c | — | — | — | — | — | — | 353 | 376 | 434 | — | — | — |
| Claims on Central Bank.................. | 20 | 6,410 | 9,325 | 9,792 | 11,500 | 14,632 | 19,152 | 23,066 | 14,492 | 12,497 | 15,771 | 27,940 | 18,299 |
| Currency........................................ | 20a | 71 | 114 | 145 | 841 | 719 | 238 | 580 | 663 | 1,474 | 1,910 | 2,644 | 2,819 |
| Reserve Deposits and Securities...... | 20b | 6,339 | 9,210 | 9,647 | 10,659 | 13,912 | 18,915 | 22,486 | 13,829 | 11,023 | 13,861 | 25,297 | 15,479 |
| Other Claims................................. | 20n | — | — | — | — | — | — | — | — | — | — | — | — |
| Net Claims on Central Government.. | 22an | 2,192 | 469 | 116 | 285 | 59 | 3,041 | 2,050 | 1,584 | 4,590 | 2,310 | 722 | 3,242 |
| Claims on Central Government...... | 22a | 2,192 | 469 | 116 | 285 | 59 | 3,041 | 2,050 | 1,584 | 4,590 | 2,891 | 2,997 | 5,465 |
| Liabilities to Central Government... | 26d | — | — | — | — | — | — | — | — | — | 581 | 2,275 | 2,224 |
| Claims on Other Sectors.................. | 22s | 6,677 | 8,132 | 10,598 | 13,662 | 18,360 | 20,599 | 31,264 | 41,557 | 46,915 | 50,555 | 56,506 | 65,389 |
| Claims on Other Financial Corps.... | 22g | 196 | 269 | 488 | 518 | 555 | 587 | 820 | 565 | 734 | 830 | 958 | 875 |
| Claims on State & Local Govts....... | 22b | — | — | — | — | — | — | — | — | — | — | — | — |
| Claims on Public Nonfin. Corps...... | 22c | 1,445 | 1,338 | 1,412 | 1,572 | 1,420 | 180 | 414 | 1,247 | 1,645 | 1,646 | 3,184 | 4,865 |
| Claims on Private Sector................ | 22d | 5,036 | 6,525 | 8,698 | 11,572 | 16,385 | 19,832 | 30,029 | 39,745 | 44,535 | 48,078 | 52,364 | 59,650 |
| Liabilities to Central Bank................ | 26g | — | — | — | — | — | — | — | — | — | — | — | — |
| Transf.Dep.Included in Broad Money | 24 | 6,828 | 7,837 | 9,799 | 14,255 | 12,407 | 17,653 | 23,465 | 26,303 | 28,042 | 28,672 | 37,625 | 37,842 |
| Other Dep.Included in Broad Money. | 25 | 9,821 | 10,911 | 12,539 | 10,570 | 18,895 | 21,914 | 22,888 | 21,027 | 24,086 | 25,453 | 31,665 | 33,447 |
| Sec.Ot.th.Shares Incl.in Brd. Money.. | 26a | — | — | — | — | — | — | — | — | — | — | — | — |
| Deposits Excl. from Broad Money... | 26b | — | — | — | — | — | — | — | — | — | — | — | — |
| Sec.Ot.th.Shares Excl.f/Brd.Money.... | 26s | — | — | — | — | — | — | — | — | — | — | — | — |
| Loans........................................ | 26l | — | — | — | — | — | — | 568 | 494 | 1,048 | 1,007 | 922 | 809 |
| Financial Derivatives....................... | 26m | — | — | — | — | — | — | — | — | — | — | — | — |
| Insurance Technical Reserves.......... | 26r | — | — | — | — | — | — | — | — | — | — | — | — |
| Shares and Other Equity.................. | 27a | 1,824 | 2,029 | 2,273 | 2,581 | 3,040 | 3,783 | 6,150 | 8,957 | 11,948 | 12,963 | 13,967 | 16,532 |
| Other Items (Net)............................. | 27r | 1,133 | 1,165 | 1,923 | 1,269 | 1,147 | 2,236 | 5,276 | 2,720 | 3,106 | 4,091 | 4,568 | 2,795 |
| Memo Item: | | | | | | | | | | | | | |
| Total Assets................................... | 20ra | 20,317 | 22,520 | 27,328 | 30,441 | 38,052 | 50,546 | 68,038 | 67,023 | 75,871 | 80,123 | 100,799 | 106,120 |

# Bhutan 514

| | | 2004 | 2005 | 2006 | 2007 | 2008 | 2009 | 2010 | 2011 | 2012 | 2013 | 2014 | 2015 |
|---|---|---|---|---|---|---|---|---|---|---|---|---|---|
| **Depository Corporations** | | | | | | *Millions of Ngultrum: End of Period* | | | | | | | |
| Net Foreign Assets | 31n | 17,271 | 20,955 | 23,939 | 25,145 | 32,790 | 35,393 | 38,497 | 35,247 | 31,919 | 47,096 | 64,618 | 61,739 |
| Claims on Nonresidents | 31 | 17,291 | 20,976 | 24,037 | 27,530 | 35,686 | 41,662 | 45,004 | 42,318 | 52,545 | 61,534 | 79,007 | 73,276 |
| Liabilities to Nonresidents | 36c | 21 | 21 | 98 | 2,385 | 2,896 | 6,269 | 6,507 | 7,071 | 20,625 | 14,438 | 14,389 | 11,537 |
| Domestic Claims | 32 | 7,818 | 7,865 | 9,228 | 10,953 | 10,774 | 23,499 | 33,038 | 42,878 | 51,207 | 52,426 | 56,598 | 68,404 |
| Net Claims on Central Government | 32an | 1,140 | −267 | −1,380 | −2,721 | −7,603 | 2,883 | 1,751 | 1,300 | 4,274 | 1,854 | 71 | 2,974 |
| Claims on Central Government | 32a | 2,229 | 569 | 116 | 285 | 59 | 3,041 | 2,051 | 1,584 | 6,490 | 2,891 | 2,997 | 5,465 |
| Liabilities to Central Government | 36d | 1,089 | 837 | 1,496 | 3,005 | 7,662 | 158 | 299 | 284 | 2,216 | 1,037 | 2,926 | 2,492 |
| Claims on Other Sectors | 32s | 6,677 | 8,132 | 10,608 | 13,673 | 18,377 | 20,616 | 31,287 | 41,578 | 46,933 | 50,571 | 56,527 | 65,431 |
| Claims on Other Financial Corps. | 32g | 196 | 269 | 488 | 518 | 555 | 587 | 820 | 565 | 734 | 833 | 961 | 875 |
| Claims on State & Local Govts. | 32b | — | — | — | — | — | — | — | — | — | — | — | — |
| Claims on Public Nonfin. Corps. | 32c | 1,445 | 1,338 | 1,412 | 1,572 | 1,420 | 180 | 414 | 1,247 | 1,645 | 1,646 | 3,184 | 4,865 |
| Claims on Private Sector | 32d | 5,036 | 6,525 | 8,708 | 11,583 | 16,402 | 19,849 | 30,052 | 39,767 | 44,554 | 48,092 | 52,382 | 59,691 |
| Broad Money Liabilities | 35l | 18,721 | 21,153 | 25,101 | 28,057 | 35,399 | 44,548 | 51,962 | 54,243 | 57,384 | 59,534 | 74,962 | 77,876 |
| Currency Outside Depository Corps | 34a | 2,072 | 2,404 | 2,763 | 3,229 | 4,097 | 4,981 | 5,609 | 6,913 | 5,256 | 5,408 | 5,672 | 6,587 |
| Transferable Deposits | 34 | 6,828 | 7,837 | 9,799 | 14,257 | 12,407 | 17,653 | 23,465 | 26,303 | 28,042 | 28,672 | 37,625 | 37,842 |
| Other Deposits | 35 | 9,821 | 10,911 | 12,539 | 10,570 | 18,895 | 21,914 | 22,888 | 21,027 | 24,086 | 25,453 | 31,665 | 33,447 |
| Securities Other than Shares | 36a | — | — | — | — | — | — | — | — | — | — | — | — |
| Deposits Excl. from Broad Money | 36b | — | — | — | — | — | — | — | — | — | — | 1 | — |
| Sec.Ot.th.Shares Excl.f/Brd.Money | 36s | — | — | — | — | — | — | — | — | — | — | — | — |
| Loans | 36l | — | — | — | — | — | — | 568 | 494 | 1,048 | 1,007 | 922 | 809 |
| Financial Derivatives | 36m | — | — | — | — | — | — | — | — | — | — | — | — |
| Insurance Technical Reserves | 36r | — | — | — | — | — | — | — | — | — | — | — | — |
| Shares and Other Equity | 37a | 5,355 | 6,382 | 6,659 | 6,703 | 9,818 | 9,880 | 10,826 | 19,500 | 23,896 | 30,818 | 32,882 | 37,517 |
| Other Items (Net) | 37r | 1,013 | 1,285 | 1,407 | 1,338 | −1,653 | 4,464 | 8,179 | 3,888 | 799 | 8,163 | 12,450 | 13,941 |
| Broad Money Liabs., Seasonally Adj. | 35l.b | 18,472 | 20,743 | 24,430 | 27,057 | 34,019 | 42,754 | 49,995 | 52,396 | 55,745 | 57,921 | 72,980 | 75,826 |
| **Other Financial Corporations** | | | | | | *Millions of Ngultrum: End of Period* | | | | | | | |
| Net Foreign Assets | 41n | 4 | 10 | 11 | 8 | 31 | 30 | 2 | 1 | 2 | 26 | 37 | 14 |
| Claims on Nonresidents | 41 | 4 | 10 | 11 | 8 | 31 | 30 | 2 | 1 | 2 | 26 | 37 | 14 |
| Liabilities to Nonresidents | 46c | — | — | — | — | — | — | — | — | — | — | — | — |
| Claims on Depository Corporations | 40 | 56 | 55 | 129 | 107 | 378 | 440 | 846 | 1,085 | 1,603 | 1,703 | 2,695 | 2,008 |
| Net Claims on Central Government | 42an | — | — | — | — | — | — | 62 | — | — | — | — | — |
| Claims on Central Government | 42a | — | — | — | — | — | — | 62 | — | — | — | — | — |
| Liabilities to Central Government | 46d | — | — | — | — | — | — | — | — | — | — | — | — |
| Claims on Other Sectors | 42s | 1,366 | 1,590 | 1,630 | 1,914 | 2,223 | 2,973 | 4,901 | 5,724 | 6,053 | 6,971 | 8,735 | 12,760 |
| Claims on State & Local Govts. | 42b | — | — | — | — | — | — | — | — | — | — | — | — |
| Claims on Pub. Nonfin. Corps. | 42c | 21 | 15 | 18 | 37 | 46 | 44 | 69 | 14 | 14 | 13 | 39 | 101 |
| Claims on Private Sector | 42d | 1,345 | 1,575 | 1,612 | 1,876 | 2,177 | 2,929 | 4,832 | 5,710 | 6,039 | 6,957 | 8,696 | 12,659 |
| Deposits | 46b | — | — | — | — | — | — | — | — | — | — | — | — |
| Securities Other than Shares | 46s | — | — | — | — | — | — | — | 1,600 | 1,600 | 1,600 | 2,000 | 2,000 |
| Loans | 46l | 95 | 170 | 172 | — | — | — | 350 | 586 | 686 | 777 | 647 | 1,255 |
| Financial Derivatives | 46m | — | — | — | — | — | — | — | — | — | — | — | — |
| Insurance Technical Reserves | 46r | 372 | 444 | 525 | 732 | 914 | 1,132 | 1,456 | 1,833 | 2,293 | 2,805 | 4,640 | 6,249 |
| Shares and Other Equity | 47a | 306 | 373 | 445 | 532 | 646 | 915 | 1,084 | 1,350 | 1,757 | 2,038 | 2,408 | 2,973 |
| Other Items (Net) | 47r | 653 | 667 | 627 | 764 | 1,073 | 1,397 | 2,921 | 1,443 | 1,322 | 1,481 | 1,772 | 2,304 |
| Memo Item: | | | | | | | | | | | | | |
| Total Assets | 40ra | 1,645 | 1,869 | 1,997 | 2,297 | 2,980 | 3,985 | 6,375 | 7,485 | 8,503 | 9,857 | 12,944 | 16,396 |
| **Monetary Aggregates** | | | | | | *Millions of Ngultrum: End of Period* | | | | | | | |
| Broad Money | 59m | 18,721 | 21,153 | 25,101 | 28,057 | 35,399 | 44,548 | 51,962 | 54,243 | 57,384 | 59,534 | 74,962 | 77,876 |
| o/w:Currency Issued by Cent.Govt | 59m.a | — | — | — | — | — | — | — | — | — | — | — | — |
| o/w: Dep.in Nonfin. Corporations. | 59m.b | — | — | — | — | — | — | — | — | — | — | — | — |
| o/w:Secs. Issued by Central Govt. | 59m.c | — | — | — | — | — | — | — | — | — | — | — | — |
| Money (National Definitions) | | | | | | | | | | | | | |
| M1 | 59ma | 8,900 | 10,241 | 12,561 | 17,484 | 16,505 | 22,634 | 29,074 | 33,216 | 33,298 | 34,080 | 43,296 | 44,429 |
| M2 | 59mb | 18,721 | 21,153 | 25,101 | 28,057 | 35,399 | 44,548 | 51,962 | 54,243 | 57,384 | 59,534 | 74,962 | 77,876 |
| **Interest Rates** | | | | | | *Percent Per Annum* | | | | | | | |
| Deposit Rate | 60l | 4.50 | 4.50 | 4.50 | 4.50 | 2.00 | 2.00 | 2.00 | 4.50 | 5.50 | 6.00 | 4.00 | 4.00 |
| Lending Rate | 60p | 15.00 | 14.00 | 14.00 | 14.00 | 13.75 | 13.75 | 14.00 | 14.00 | 14.00 | 14.00 | 14.15 | 13.75 |
| **Prices and Tourism** | | | | | | *Index Numbers (2010=100): Period Averages* | | | | | | | |
| Consumer Prices | 64 | 71.1 | 74.8 | 78.6 | 82.6 | 89.5 | 93.4 | 100.0 | 108.8 | † 120.7 | 129.2 | 139.8 | 146.1 |
| Tourist Arrivals | 66ta | 22.6 | 33.2 | 42.3 | 51.4 | 67.4 | 57.3 | 100.0 | 91.4 | 191.7 | 283.5 | . . . . | . . . . |
| **Intl. Transactions & Positions** | | | | | | *Millions of Ngultrum: Fiscal Year Ends June 30* | | | | | | | |
| Exports | 70 | 10,053.2 | 11,386.2 | 18,771.9 | 27,859.1 | 22,590.6 | 23,973.9 | 29,324.4 | 31,485.9 | 28,600.1 | 31,853.0 | . . . . | . . . . |
| Imports, c.i.f. | 71 | 18,407.0 | 17,035.1 | 19,012.0 | 21,745.4 | 23,495.1 | 25,650.2 | 39,084.1 | 48,697.6 | 53,089.6 | 53,273.0 | . . . . | . . . . |

# Bhutan 514

| | | 2004 | 2005 | 2006 | 2007 | 2008 | 2009 | 2010 | 2011 | 2012 | 2013 | 2014 | 2015 |
|---|---|---|---|---|---|---|---|---|---|---|---|---|---|
| **Balance of Payments** | | | | | *Millions of US Dollars* | | | | | | | | |
| A. Current Account*........................ | 109bx | .... | .... | † −37.9 | 84.9 | −112.5 | −65.9 | −323.1 | −526.2 | −378.5 | −472.4 | −483.6 | −578.8 |
| Goods, credit (exports)................... | 1a9cx | .... | .... | † 312.0 | 576.5 | 598.9 | 518.0 | 521.6 | 663.7 | 626.9 | 544.5 | 534.7 | 580.3 |
| Goods, debit (imports)................... | 1a9dx | .... | .... | † 434.9 | 496.9 | 644.9 | 583.4 | 795.0 | 1,128.0 | 1,012.4 | 923.5 | 928.8 | 997.0 |
| Balance on goods........................ | 1a9bx | .... | .... | † −122.9 | 79.7 | −46.1 | −65.5 | −273.4 | −464.3 | −385.5 | −379.0 | −394.1 | −416.7 |
| Services, credit (exports)................ | 1b9cx | .... | .... | † 51.7 | 60.2 | 54.8 | 56.3 | 68.8 | 81.9 | 102.2 | 123.3 | 124.5 | 123.8 |
| Services, debit (imports)................ | 1b9dx | .... | .... | † 64.5 | 89.4 | 120.7 | 98.7 | 140.2 | 176.6 | 196.9 | 177.6 | 189.5 | 183.8 |
| Balance on Goods & Services....... | 1z9bx | .... | .... | † −135.7 | 50.4 | −112.0 | −107.9 | −344.8 | −559.0 | −480.3 | −433.2 | −459.2 | −476.8 |
| Primary income: credit.................. | 1c9cx | .... | .... | † 18.2 | 26.4 | 34.7 | 21.1 | 16.4 | 16.6 | 17.4 | 17.6 | 19.4 | 22.8 |
| Primary income: debit.................. | 1c9dx | .... | .... | † 25.2 | 26.7 | 69.7 | 52.7 | 88.5 | 120.8 | 130.9 | 183.3 | 140.9 | 205.3 |
| Balance on gds, serv. & prim. inc. | 1y9bx | .... | .... | † −142.7 | 50.1 | −147.0 | −139.6 | −416.8 | −663.2 | −593.7 | −598.9 | −580.6 | −659.3 |
| Secondary income: credit.............. | 1d9ca | .... | .... | † 163.5 | 86.9 | 85.3 | 109.4 | 138.3 | 189.0 | 257.8 | 157.3 | 120.1 | 111.0 |
| Secondary income: debit.............. | 1d9da | .... | .... | † 58.7 | 52.1 | 50.9 | 35.8 | 44.5 | 52.0 | 42.5 | 30.7 | 23.1 | 30.5 |
| B. Capital Account*........................ | 209ba | .... | .... | † 39.1 | 73.1 | 83.3 | 68.0 | 149.6 | 167.5 | 94.7 | 262.6 | 276.3 | 226.3 |
| Capital account: credit.................. | 209ca | .... | .... | † 39.1 | 73.1 | 83.3 | 68.0 | 149.6 | 167.5 | 94.7 | 262.6 | 276.3 | 226.3 |
| Capital account: debit.................. | 209da | .... | .... | † — | .... | .... | .... | .... | .... | .... | .... | .... | .... |
| Balance on current & capital acct. | 129bx | .... | .... | † 1.2 | 158.1 | −29.2 | 2.0 | −173.5 | −358.7 | −283.8 | −209.8 | −207.3 | −352.5 |
| C. Financial Account*...................... | 309na | .... | .... | † −91.5 | −64.9 | −24.0 | −90.3 | −195.1 | −416.7 | −297.1 | −356.5 | −228.4 | −387.2 |
| Direct investment: assets.............. | 3a9aa | .... | .... | † — | .... | .... | .... | .... | .... | .... | .... | .... | .... |
| Equity & investment fund shares.. | 3aaaa | .... | .... | † — | .... | .... | .... | .... | .... | .... | .... | .... | .... |
| Debt instruments....................... | 3abaa | .... | .... | † — | .... | .... | .... | .... | .... | .... | .... | .... | .... |
| Direct investment: liabilities .......... | 3a9la | .... | .... | † 6.1 | 73.9 | 3.1 | 18.3 | 75.3 | 31.1 | 24.4 | 49.8 | 8.4 | 33.6 |
| Equity & investment fund shares . | 3aala | .... | .... | † 2.8 | 1.9 | 2.4 | 6.2 | 20.2 | 20.1 | 11.3 | 48.8 | 10.0 | 32.9 |
| Debt instruments....................... | 3abla | .... | .... | † 3.3 | 72.0 | .7 | 12.1 | 55.0 | 11.1 | 13.1 | 1.0 | −1.7 | .7 |
| Portfolio investment: assets .......... | 3b9aa | .... | .... | † — | .... | .... | .... | .... | .... | .... | .... | .... | .... |
| Equity & investment fund shares | 3baaa | .... | .... | † — | .... | .... | .... | .... | .... | .... | .... | .... | .... |
| Debt securities ........................... | 3bbaa | .... | .... | † — | .... | .... | .... | .... | .... | .... | .... | .... | .... |
| Portfolio investment: liabilities....... | 3b9la | .... | .... | † — | .... | .... | .... | .... | .... | .... | .... | .... | .... |
| Equity & investment fund shares . | 3bala | .... | .... | † — | .... | .... | .... | .... | .... | .... | .... | .... | .... |
| Debt securities........................... | 3bbla | .... | .... | † — | .... | .... | .... | .... | .... | .... | .... | .... | .... |
| Fin. der.& empl.stk.ops.(ESOs): net. | 3c9na | .... | .... | † — | .... | .... | .... | .... | .... | .... | .... | .... | .... |
| Fin. der. & ESOs.: assets.............. | 3c9aa | .... | .... | † — | .... | .... | .... | .... | .... | .... | .... | .... | .... |
| Fin. der. & ESOs.: liabilities.......... | 3c9la | .... | .... | † — | .... | .... | .... | .... | .... | .... | .... | .... | .... |
| Other investment: assets................ | 3d9aa | .... | .... | † — | 20.1 | 10.6 | −6.7 | .8 | −3.9 | 4.1 | 15.6 | −2.6 | −13.7 |
| Other equity............................... | 3daaa | .... | .... | .... | .... | .... | .... | .... | .... | .... | .... | .... | .... |
| Debt instruments....................... | 3dzaa | .... | .... | † — | 20.1 | 10.6 | −6.7 | .8 | −3.9 | 4.1 | 15.6 | −2.6 | −13.7 |
| Other investment: liabilities............ | 3d9la | .... | .... | † 85.4 | 11.1 | 31.5 | 65.3 | 120.6 | 381.7 | 276.8 | 322.3 | 217.4 | 339.8 |
| Other equity............................... | 3dala | .... | .... | .... | .... | .... | .... | .... | .... | .... | .... | .... | .... |
| Debt instruments....................... | 3dzla | .... | .... | † 85.4 | 11.1 | 31.5 | 65.3 | 120.6 | 381.7 | 276.8 | 322.3 | 217.4 | 339.8 |
| Curr.+ cap.− finan. acct. balance... | 4y9na | .... | .... | † 92.8 | 223.0 | −5.2 | 92.3 | 21.6 | 58.0 | 13.3 | 146.8 | 21.1 | 34.7 |
| D. Net Errors and Omissions............ | 409na | .... | .... | † 23.7 | −100.7 | 23.5 | 49.7 | 68.3 | −43.9 | −172.7 | 21.2 | 49.4 | −39.2 |
| E. Reserves and Related Items......... | 4z9na | .... | .... | † 116.5 | 122.3 | 18.4 | 142.0 | 89.9 | 14.1 | −159.4 | 167.9 | 70.5 | −4.5 |
| Reserve assets............................. | 3e9aa | .... | .... | † 116.5 | 122.3 | 18.4 | 142.0 | 89.9 | 14.1 | −159.4 | 167.9 | 70.5 | −4.5 |
| Credit and loans from the IMF....... | 3dcla | .... | .... | † — | — | — | | | | | | | |
| Exceptional financing..................... | 409la | .... | .... | † — | .... | .... | .... | .... | .... | .... | .... | .... | .... |
| *Excludes components in group E | | | | | | | | | | | | | |

| | | 2004 | 2005 | 2006 | 2007 | 2008 | 2009 | 2010 | 2011 | 2012 | 2013 | 2014 | 2015 |
|---|---|---|---|---|---|---|---|---|---|---|---|---|---|
| **International Investment Position** | | | | | *Millions of US Dollars* | | | | | | | | |
| Assets...................................... | 809aa | .... | .... | .... | † 638.8 | 699.0 | 807.1 | 871.5 | 993.0 | 861.7 | 1,029.7 | 1,106.6 | 1,055.1 |
| Direct investment....................... | 8a9aa | .... | .... | .... | .... | .... | .... | .... | .... | .... | .... | .... | .... |
| Equity & investment fund shares.. | 8aaaa | .... | .... | .... | .... | .... | .... | .... | .... | .... | .... | .... | .... |
| Debt instruments....................... | 8abaa | .... | .... | .... | .... | .... | .... | .... | .... | .... | .... | .... | .... |
| Portfolio investment.................... | 8b9aa | .... | .... | .... | .... | .... | .... | .... | .... | .... | .... | .... | .... |
| Equity & investment fund shares.. | 8baaa | .... | .... | .... | .... | .... | .... | .... | .... | .... | .... | .... | .... |
| Debt securities........................... | 8bbaa | .... | .... | .... | .... | .... | .... | .... | .... | .... | .... | .... | .... |
| Fin. der.(oth.than reserves) & ESOs | 8c9aa | .... | .... | .... | .... | .... | .... | .... | .... | .... | .... | .... | .... |
| Other investment....................... | 8d9aa | .... | .... | .... | † 102.9 | 150.3 | 122.7 | 114.6 | 216.4 | 189.3 | 111.8 | 108.9 | 96.5 |
| Other equity............................... | 8daaa | .... | .... | .... | .... | .... | .... | .... | .... | .... | .... | .... | .... |
| Debt instruments....................... | 8dzaa | .... | .... | .... | † 102.9 | 150.3 | 122.7 | 114.6 | 216.4 | 189.3 | 111.8 | 108.9 | 96.5 |
| Reserve assets............................. | 8e9aa | .... | .... | .... | † 535.9 | 548.7 | 684.4 | 756.9 | 776.6 | 672.4 | 917.9 | 997.7 | 958.6 |
| Liabilities................................. | 809la | .... | .... | .... | † 889.8 | 873.6 | 908.6 | 1,030.6 | 1,484.1 | 1,563.8 | 1,952.1 | 2,195.9 | 2,444.5 |
| Direct investment....................... | 8a9la | .... | .... | .... | † 17.9 | 20.6 | 26.7 | 52.6 | 66.7 | 83.0 | 128.8 | 145.4 | 210.6 |
| Equity & investment fund shares.. | 8aala | .... | .... | .... | † 15.8 | 18.0 | 24.3 | 50.2 | 53.0 | 58.1 | 103.3 | 106.3 | 153.4 |
| Debt instruments....................... | 8abla | .... | .... | .... | † 2.1 | 2.6 | 2.4 | 2.4 | 13.7 | 24.9 | 25.5 | 39.1 | 57.2 |
| Portfolio investment.................... | 8b9la | .... | .... | .... | .... | .... | .... | .... | .... | .... | .... | .... | .... |
| Equity & investment fund shares.. | 8bala | .... | .... | .... | .... | .... | .... | .... | .... | .... | .... | .... | .... |
| Debt securities........................... | 8bbla | .... | .... | .... | .... | .... | .... | .... | .... | .... | .... | .... | .... |
| Fin. der.(oth.than reserves) & ESOs | 8c9la | .... | .... | .... | .... | .... | .... | .... | .... | .... | .... | .... | .... |
| Other investment....................... | 8d9la | .... | .... | .... | † 871.9 | 852.9 | 881.9 | 978.0 | 1,417.5 | 1,480.8 | 1,823.4 | 2,050.4 | 2,234.0 |
| Other equity............................... | 8dala | .... | .... | .... | .... | .... | .... | .... | .... | .... | .... | .... | .... |
| Debt instruments....................... | 8dzla | .... | .... | .... | † 871.9 | 852.9 | 881.9 | 978.0 | 1,417.5 | 1,480.8 | 1,823.4 | 2,050.4 | 2,234.0 |

| | | 2004 | 2005 | 2006 | 2007 | 2008 | 2009 | 2010 | 2011 | 2012 | 2013 | 2014 | 2015 |
|---|---|---|---|---|---|---|---|---|---|---|---|---|---|
| **Government Finance** | | | | | | | | | | | | | |
| **Cash Flow Statement** | | | | | | | | | | | | | |
| **Budgetary Central Government** | | | | | | | *Millions of Ngultrum: Fiscal Year Ends June 30* | | | | | | |
| Cash Receipts:Operating Activities... | c1 | 10,371.5 | 10,439.2 | 13,454.3 | 16,083.1 | 18,277.9 | 20,624.1 | 26,691.4 | 27,880.3 | 32,795.6 | 30,613.0 | 37,425.4 | .... |
| Taxes............................................ | c11 | 2,446.6 | 3,014.1 | 3,673.2 | 3,718.9 | 4,607.2 | 5,654.1 | 9,528.5 | 11,474.7 | 14,329.6 | 15,151.2 | 15,943.7 | .... |
| Social Contributions...................... | c12 | — | 36.0 | 44.1 | 49.4 | 58.2 | 71.3 | 22.8 | 23.3 | 23.3 | 22.6 | 24.1 | .... |
| Grants............................................ | c13 | 5,367.4 | 4,373.1 | 6,551.4 | 6,000.9 | 5,931.9 | 6,575.1 | 11,118.9 | 10,497.7 | 12,501.5 | 9,562.6 | 14,236.4 | .... |
| Other Receipts.............................. | c14 | 2,557.5 | 3,016.0 | 3,185.6 | 6,313.9 | 7,680.6 | 8,323.7 | 6,021.2 | 5,884.5 | 5,941.1 | 5,876.6 | 7,221.3 | .... |
| Cash Payments:Operating Activities. | c2 | 5,409.2 | 7,134.2 | 7,849.2 | 9,092.2 | 12,352.5 | 14,257.0 | 15,734.9 | 18,569.3 | 19,915.4 | 21,225.5 | 21,715.4 | .... |
| Compensation of Employees.......... | c21 | 2,086.8 | 2,652.3 | 3,092.8 | 3,595.0 | 3,903.2 | 4,991.4 | 5,991.1 | 7,040.2 | 7,576.6 | 7,953.7 | 8,271.3 | .... |
| Purchases of Goods & Services....... | c22 | 2,386.6 | 3,179.7 | 3,487.9 | 3,972.5 | 4,350.5 | 4,657.0 | 5,824.7 | 7,298.3 | 7,102.9 | 6,998.6 | 6,905.1 | .... |
| Interest.......................................... | c24 | 220.3 | 405.4 | 382.1 | 443.3 | 1,719.2 | 1,733.8 | 1,743.2 | 1,794.0 | 1,886.0 | 2,642.5 | 2,090.5 | .... |
| Subsidies........................................ | c25 | 114.3 | 209.8 | 208.1 | 224.2 | 244.9 | 249.7 | 244.1 | 301.8 | 283.4 | 323.1 | 199.8 | .... |
| Grants............................................ | c26 | 61.7 | — | .9 | .1 | — | — | 41.2 | 55.5 | 66.3 | 94.8 | 119.0 | .... |
| Social Benefits.............................. | c27 | 279.6 | 68.4 | 61.6 | 80.3 | 115.2 | 92.0 | 390.9 | 527.6 | 631.7 | 750.5 | 719.6 | .... |
| Other Payments............................ | c28 | 260.0 | 618.5 | 615.9 | 776.7 | 2,019.5 | 2,533.1 | 1,499.8 | 1,551.9 | 2,368.4 | 2,462.4 | 3,410.2 | .... |
| Net Cash Inflow:Operating Act.[1-2] | ccio | 4,962.2 | 3,305.0 | 5,605.2 | 6,990.9 | 5,925.4 | 6,367.1 | 10,956.5 | 9,310.9 | 12,880.2 | 9,387.5 | 15,710.1 | .... |
| Net Cash Outflow:Invest. in NFA... | c31 | 4,319.5 | 3,661.4 | 5,067.3 | 5,773.2 | 6,684.0 | 6,060.7 | 9,542.4 | 10,639.2 | 14,550.5 | 14,741.0 | 10,499.2 | .... |
| Purchases of Nonfinancial Assets... | c31.1 | 4,393.0 | 3,661.4 | 5,067.3 | 5,773.2 | 6,684.0 | 6,060.7 | .... | .... | .... | .... | .... | .... |
| Sales of Nonfinancial Assets.......... | c31.2 | 73.5 | — | — | — | — | — | .... | .... | .... | .... | .... | .... |
| Cash Surplus/Deficit [1-2-31=1-2M] | ccsd | 642.7 | −356.4 | 537.9 | 1,217.7 | −758.7 | 306.4 | 1,414.2 | −1,328.3 | −1,670.2 | −5,353.4 | 5,210.9 | .... |
| Net Acq. Fin. Assets, excl. Cash...... | c32x | 62.9 | 1,902.3 | 729.8 | 387.5 | −1,149.0 | −1,007.4 | .... | .... | .... | .... | .... | .... |
| Domestic...................................... | c321x | 62.9 | 2,260.9 | 1,030.7 | 387.5 | −1,149.0 | 665.7 | .... | .... | .... | .... | .... | .... |
| Foreign........................................ | c322x | — | −358.6 | −300.9 | — | — | −1,673.1 | .... | .... | .... | .... | .... | .... |
| Net Incurrence of Liabilities.............. | c33 | −556.3 | 2,492.4 | 215.5 | 354.8 | −1,319.2 | −1,218.7 | 192.5 | 509.2 | −1,216.8 | 484.1 | −704.2 | .... |
| Domestic...................................... | c331 | −1,488.4 | 1,753.0 | −500.0 | −175.3 | −175.3 | −175.3 | −64.7 | 39.9 | 6.4 | −183.5 | 162.9 | .... |
| Foreign........................................ | c332 | 932.1 | 739.4 | 715.5 | 530.1 | −1,143.9 | −1,043.4 | 257.3 | 469.3 | −1,223.2 | 667.6 | −867.0 | .... |
| Net Cash Inflow, Fin.Act.[-32x+33].. | cnfb | −619.2 | 590.2 | −514.3 | −32.6 | −170.2 | −211.3 | 439.0 | −48.4 | −378.6 | 1,601.0 | −1,956.9 | .... |
| Net Change in Stock of Cash........... | cncb | 23.5 | 99.8 | −103.3 | 642.6 | −915.7 | −126.2 | 1,853.1 | −1,376.7 | −2,048.8 | −3,752.4 | 3,254.0 | .... |
| Stat. Discrep. [32X-33+NCB-CSD].... | ccsdz | — | −134.0 | −126.8 | −542.5 | 13.2 | −221.4 | — | — | — | — | — | .... |
| Memo Item:Cash Expenditure[2+31] | c2m | 9,802.3 | 10,795.6 | 12,916.5 | 14,865.3 | 19,036.6 | 20,317.7 | 25,277.2 | 29,208.5 | 34,465.8 | 35,966.5 | 32,214.5 | .... |
| Memo Item: Gross Debt.................. | c63 | 23,959.3 | 28,721.4 | 30,457.7 | 31,056.4 | 33,071.0 | 34,759.0 | 39,788.5 | 53,119.2 | 70,668.7 | 101,310.0 | 108,370.0 | .... |
| **National Accounts** | | | | | | | *Millions of Ngultrum: Calendar Year* | | | | | | |
| Househ.Cons.Expend.,incl.NPISHs.... | 96f | 13,807 | 14,586 | 15,554 | 19,522 | 21,762 | 27,202 | 31,752 | 34,927 | 42,690 | 53,363 | 55,486 | .... |
| Government Consumption Expend... | 91f | 6,650 | 7,912 | 8,644 | 9,455 | 10,373 | 13,082 | 14,488 | 17,048 | 18,691 | 18,274 | 20,194 | .... |
| Gross Fixed Capital Formation.......... | 93e | 20,078 | 19,294 | 19,108 | 20,004 | 24,145 | 28,001 | 44,360 | 57,785 | 66,253 | 48,979 | 69,909 | .... |
| Changes in Inventories.................... | 93i | −88 | −5 | 54 | −1,359 | 615 | −269 | 372 | −316 | −72 | −546 | −875 | .... |
| Exports of Goods and Services......... | 90c | 9,881 | 13,813 | 22,134 | 27,186 | 26,868 | 27,367 | 30,777 | 35,004 | 37,739 | 42,636 | 43,377 | .... |
| Imports of Goods and Services (-)..... | 98c | 17,450 | 21,192 | 22,512 | 27,156 | 31,723 | 38,082 | 51,278 | 59,878 | 61,433 | 65,625 | 68,545 | .... |
| Gross Domestic Product (GDP)........ | 99b | 32,877 | 34,408 | 42,983 | 47,652 | 51,424 | 57,569 | 70,471 | 84,570 | 103,868 | 97,081 | 119,546 | .... |
| Net Primary Income from Abroad..... | 98.n | −724 | −510 | −161 | −660 | −1,415 | −2,143 | −4,023 | −5,316 | −7,594 | −6,793 | −8,238 | .... |
| Gross National Income (GNI)........... | 99a | 32,153 | 33,898 | 42,822 | 46,993 | 53,329 | 59,077 | 68,474 | 79,634 | 89,859 | 98,586 | 111,307 | .... |
| GDP Volume 2000 Prices................ | 99b.p | 26,959 | 28,879 | 30,857 | 36,389 | 35,405 | 39,063 | 44,637 | 47,090 | 51,496 | 42,983 | 55,324 | .... |
| GDP Volume (2010=100)................ | 99bvp | 60.4 | 64.7 | 69.1 | 81.5 | 79.3 | 87.5 | 100.0 | 105.5 | 115.4 | 96.3 | 123.9 | .... |
| GDP Deflator (2010=100).............. | 99bip | 77.2 | 75.5 | 88.2 | 82.9 | 92.0 | 93.4 | 100.0 | 113.8 | 127.8 | 143.1 | 136.9 | .... |
| | | | | | | | *Millions: Midyear Estimates* | | | | | | |
| Population................................ | 99z | .63 | .65 | .67 | .68 | .69 | .71 | .72 | .73 | .74 | .75 | .77 | .77 |

# Bolivia 218

| | | 2004 | 2005 | 2006 | 2007 | 2008 | 2009 | 2010 | 2011 | 2012 | 2013 | 2014 | 2015 |
|---|---|---|---|---|---|---|---|---|---|---|---|---|---|
| **Exchange Rates** | | | | | | *Bolivianos per SDR: End of Period* | | | | | | | |
| Market Rate................................... | aa | 12.502 | 11.491 | 12.005 | 12.042 | 10.813 | 11.005 | 10.765 | 10.609 | 10.620 | 10.641 | 10.011 | 9.575 |
| | | | | | | *Bolivianos per US Dollar: End of Period (ae) Period Average (rf)* | | | | | | | |
| Market Rate................................... | ae | 8.050 | 8.040 | 7.980 | 7.620 | 7.020 | 7.020 | 6.990 | 6.910 | 6.910 | 6.910 | 6.910 | 6.910 |
| Market Rate................................... | rf | 7.936 | 8.066 | 8.012 | 7.851 | 7.238 | 7.020 | 7.017 | 6.937 | 6.910 | 6.910 | 6.910 | 6.910 |
| | | | | | | *Index Numbers (2010=100): Period Averages* | | | | | | | |
| Market Rate................................... | ahx | 88.42 | 86.99 | 87.59 | 89.39 | 97.02 | 99.95 | 100.00 | 101.15 | 101.54 | 101.54 | 101.54 | 101.54 |
| Nominal Effective Exchange Rate..... | nec | 100.20 | 94.56 | 93.40 | 90.67 | 95.21 | 103.59 | 100.00 | 97.81 | 102.92 | 107.17 | 114.18 | 131.93 |
| CPI-Based Real Effect. Ex. Rate....... | rec | 88.99 | 84.97 | 84.16 | 85.09 | 96.21 | 105.17 | 100.00 | 101.87 | 107.16 | 113.14 | 122.11 | 141.75 |
| **Fund Position** | | | | | | *Millions of SDRs: End of Period* | | | | | | | |
| Quota.......................................... | 2f.s | 171.50 | 171.50 | 171.50 | 171.50 | 171.50 | 171.50 | 171.50 | 171.50 | 171.50 | 171.50 | 171.50 | 171.50 |
| SDR Holdings................................. | 1b.s | 26.56 | 26.75 | 26.75 | 26.80 | 27.48 | 164.91 | 164.91 | 164.91 | 165.42 | 166.68 | 166.68 | 166.70 |
| Reserve Position in the Fund............ | 1c.s | 8.87 | 8.87 | 8.87 | 8.87 | 8.87 | 8.87 | 8.87 | 8.87 | 8.87 | 8.87 | 8.87 | 8.87 |
| Total Fund Cred.&Loans Outstg........ | 2tl | 197.67 | 170.59 | 9.66 | — | — | — | — | — | — | — | — | — |
| SDR Allocations............................. | 1bd | 26.70 | 26.70 | 26.70 | 26.70 | 26.70 | 164.13 | 164.13 | 164.13 | 164.13 | 164.13 | 164.13 | 164.13 |
| **International Liquidity** | | | | | | *Millions of US Dollars Unless Otherwise Indicated: End of Period* | | | | | | | |
| Total Reserves minus Gold.............. | 1l.d | 872.4 | 1,327.6 | 2,614.8 | 4,554.0 | 6,927.4 | 7,583.8 | 8,133.9 | 9,910.7 | 11,659.3 | 12,782.7 | 13,480.9 | 11,600.8 |
| SDR Holdings............................. | 1b.d | 41.2 | 38.2 | 40.2 | 42.3 | 42.3 | 258.5 | 254.0 | 253.2 | 254.2 | 256.7 | 241.5 | 231.0 |
| Reserve Position in the Fund......... | 1c.d | 13.8 | 12.7 | 13.4 | 14.0 | 13.7 | 13.9 | 13.7 | 13.6 | 13.6 | 13.7 | 12.9 | 12.3 |
| Foreign Exchange........................ | 1d.d | 817.3 | 1,276.7 | 2,561.2 | 4,497.7 | 6,871.4 | 7,311.3 | 7,866.2 | 9,643.9 | 11,391.4 | 12,512.4 | 13,226.5 | 11,357.5 |
| Gold (Million Fine Troy Ounces)....... | 1ad | .911 | .911 | .911 | .911 | .911 | .911 | 1.136 | 1.361 | 1.361 | 1.367 | 1.367 | 1.367 |
| Gold (National Valuation)............... | 1and | 399.4 | 470.6 | 577.6 | 764.3 | 794.5 | 997.6 | 1,596.2 | 2,109.1 | 2,267.3 | 1,647.4 | 1,642.3 | 1,455.1 |
| Central Bank: Other Assets............. | 3..d | 315.8 | 321.2 | 320.7 | 332.0 | 341.7 | 353.9 | 412.1 | 397.4 | 518.7 | 486.4 | 493.3 | 490.8 |
| Central Bank: Other Liabs............... | 4..d | 59.7 | 61.7 | 63.8 | 67.0 | 70.0 | 73.1 | 102.6 | 104.1 | 85.8 | 77.0 | 61.8 | 53.9 |
| Other Depository Corps.: Assets....... | 7a.d | 607.1 | 846.0 | 915.2 | 785.7 | 938.6 | 1,518.4 | 1,456.4 | 1,193.0 | 1,408.2 | 1,687.2 | 2,229.6 | 2,709.7 |
| Other Depository Corps.: Liabs......... | 7b.d | 182.1 | 225.4 | 236.4 | 237.2 | 391.0 | 442.5 | 315.3 | 213.5 | 185.4 | 197.8 | 214.6 | 499.1 |
| Other Financial Corps.: Assets......... | 7e.d | .... | 83.7 | 83.4 | 84.2 | 19.4 | 26.1 | 33.5 | 32.6 | 162.1 | 363.5 | 450.6 | 643.7 |
| Other Financial Corps.: Liabs........... | 7f.d | .... | 47.5 | 36.1 | 109.5 | 109.6 | 120.3 | 125.3 | 131.4 | 144.8 | 157.9 | 196.9 | 106.8 |
| **Central Bank** | | | | | | *Millions of Bolivianos: End of Period* | | | | | | | |
| Net Foreign Assets........................ | 11n | 9,552 | 14,284 | 27,006 | 42,045 | 55,528 | 60,057 | 68,005 | 82,825 | 96,868 | 100,145 | 105,132 | 91,060 |
| Claims on Nonresidents................. | 11 | 12,837 | 17,047 | 27,952 | 42,877 | 56,308 | 62,360 | 70,472 | 85,268 | 99,187 | 102,406 | 107,187 | 92,990 |
| Liabilities to Nonresidents............. | 16c | 3,286 | 2,764 | 946 | 832 | 780 | 2,303 | 2,466 | 2,443 | 2,319 | 2,262 | 2,055 | 1,930 |
| Claims on Other Depository Corps.... | 12e | 4,795 | 2,280 | 2,239 | 2,433 | 2,044 | 1,785 | 1,675 | 1,455 | 1,459 | 1,457 | 1,498 | 1,401 |
| Net Claims on Central Government.. | 12an | 3,515 | 3,922 | −115 | −1,716 | −2,369 | −5,740 | −10,484 | −13,408 | −19,849 | −24,117 | −22,827 | −16,085 |
| Claims on Central Government...... | 12a | 7,869 | 8,044 | 6,220 | 6,511 | 8,910 | 9,530 | 10,216 | 10,234 | 10,146 | 10,059 | 9,972 | 10,387 |
| Liabilities to Central Government... | 16d | 4,354 | 4,122 | 6,335 | 8,227 | 11,280 | 15,269 | 20,700 | 23,642 | 29,995 | 34,177 | 32,799 | 26,472 |
| Claims on Other Sectors................. | 12s | 161 | 153 | 5 | 3 | 31 | 4 | 29 | 3,247 | 8,008 | 16,621 | 20,505 | 25,254 |
| Claims on Other Financial Corps.... | 12g | 5 | 5 | 2 | — | — | — | — | — | — | 4,116 | 4,116 | 4,276 |
| Claims on State & Local Govts....... | 12b | — | — | — | — | 28 | — | 22 | — | — | — | — | — |
| Claims on Public Nonfin. Corps...... | 12c | — | — | — | — | — | — | — | 3,241 | 8,005 | 12,496 | 16,383 | 20,974 |
| Claims on Private Sector............... | 12d | 156 | 148 | 3 | 3 | 3 | 4 | 8 | 6 | 4 | 9 | 7 | 4 |
| Monetary Base.............................. | 14 | 9,438 | 11,019 | 16,024 | 23,533 | 28,695 | 35,110 | 40,581 | 53,670 | 63,884 | 70,221 | 74,705 | 82,980 |
| Currency in Circulation................. | 14a | 4,283 | 6,180 | 8,774 | 14,103 | 17,043 | 18,892 | 24,586 | 28,585 | 32,665 | 37,001 | 41,372 | 42,923 |
| Liabs. to Other Depository Corps... | 14c | 3,744 | 1,867 | 2,451 | 3,354 | 5,228 | 10,653 | 7,991 | 13,182 | 16,004 | 16,486 | 19,884 | 28,643 |
| Liabilities to Other Sectors............. | 14d | 1,411 | 2,973 | 4,799 | 6,076 | 6,424 | 5,564 | 8,004 | 11,903 | 15,215 | 16,734 | 13,449 | 11,415 |
| Other Liabs. to Other Dep. Corps..... | 14n | 709 | 711 | 1,925 | 7,583 | 15,298 | 10,901 | 8,036 | 9,602 | 8,847 | 10,811 | 11,491 | 8,807 |
| Dep. & Sec. Excl. f/Monetary Base..... | 14o | 545 | 474 | 1,482 | 685 | 3,660 | 1,225 | 950 | 1,769 | 2,658 | 9,820 | 16,801 | 11,109 |
| Deposits Included in Broad Money. | 15 | 524 | 451 | 1,456 | 592 | 3,468 | 1,123 | 891 | 1,485 | 2,484 | 5,711 | 9,666 | 9,756 |
| Sec.Ot.th.Shares Incl.in Brd. Money | 16a | — | — | — | — | — | — | — | — | — | — | — | — |
| Deposits Excl. from Broad Money... | 16b | — | — | — | — | — | 29 | — | 2 | 2 | 17 | 13 | 43 |
| Sec.Ot.th.Shares Excl.f/Brd.Money.. | 16s | 21 | 23 | 25 | 93 | 191 | 73 | 59 | 282 | 172 | 4,093 | 7,122 | 1,310 |
| Loans........................................... | 16l | — | — | — | — | — | — | — | — | — | — | — | — |
| Financial Derivatives...................... | 16m | — | — | — | — | — | — | — | — | — | — | — | — |
| Shares and Other Equity................. | 17a | 6,385 | 7,569 | 8,953 | 10,082 | 6,833 | 8,474 | 9,271 | 8,705 | 10,742 | 2,759 | 866 | −1,029 |
| Other Items (Net)........................... | 17r | 945 | 865 | 750 | 881 | 747 | 397 | 389 | 374 | 356 | 494 | 446 | −236 |
| Memo Item: | | | | | | | | | | | | | |
| Total Assets................................... | 10ra | 26,546 | 28,390 | 37,424 | 52,818 | 68,190 | 74,637 | 83,340 | 101,134 | 119,724 | 131,369 | 139,997 | 131,612 |

# Bolivia 218

| | | 2004 | 2005 | 2006 | 2007 | 2008 | 2009 | 2010 | 2011 | 2012 | 2013 | 2014 | 2015 |
|---|---|---|---|---|---|---|---|---|---|---|---|---|---|
| **Other Depository Corporations** | | *Millions of Bolivianos: End of Period* | | | | | | | | | | | |
| Net Foreign Assets | 21n | 3,422 | 4,990 | 5,417 | 4,179 | 3,844 | 7,499 | 7,919 | 6,719 | 8,389 | 10,218 | 13,823 | 15,165 |
| Claims on Nonresidents | 21 | 4,887 | 6,802 | 7,303 | 5,987 | 6,589 | 10,583 | 10,107 | 8,184 | 9,660 | 11,574 | 15,295 | 18,589 |
| Liabilities to Nonresidents | 26c | 1,466 | 1,812 | 1,886 | 1,808 | 2,745 | 3,084 | 2,188 | 1,465 | 1,272 | 1,357 | 1,472 | 3,424 |
| Claims on Central Bank | 20 | 2,164 | 2,632 | 4,829 | 9,806 | 16,224 | 18,118 | 14,771 | 21,501 | 26,079 | 28,138 | 32,519 | 37,833 |
| Currency | 20a | 418 | 585 | 762 | 985 | 1,236 | 1,813 | 2,101 | 2,771 | 3,360 | 4,285 | 4,701 | 5,742 |
| Reserve Deposits and Securities | 20b | 1,478 | 1,537 | 1,876 | 2,274 | 3,213 | 9,122 | 6,354 | 11,035 | 13,576 | 13,446 | 13,951 | 24,285 |
| Other Claims | 20n | 269 | 510 | 2,191 | 6,546 | 11,775 | 7,183 | 6,317 | 7,694 | 9,143 | 10,408 | 13,867 | 7,805 |
| Net Claims on Central Government | 22an | 2,872 | 2,402 | 2,108 | 1,572 | 957 | 2,128 | 1,615 | 184 | 20 | 527 | 521 | 374 |
| Claims on Central Government | 22a | 3,064 | 2,618 | 2,315 | 1,801 | 1,233 | 2,342 | 1,855 | 683 | 814 | 1,323 | 1,464 | 1,361 |
| Liabilities to Central Government | 26d | 192 | 216 | 207 | 230 | 275 | 213 | 241 | 499 | 794 | 796 | 943 | 987 |
| Claims on Other Sectors | 22s | 30,320 | 31,215 | 33,213 | 36,402 | 39,524 | 43,875 | 51,612 | 63,104 | 74,770 | 89,247 | 102,356 | 121,029 |
| Claims on Other Financial Corps. | 22g | 445 | 466 | 736 | 781 | 1,292 | 2,164 | 1,621 | 1,714 | 1,455 | 2,126 | 2,140 | 3,143 |
| Claims on State & Local Govts. | 22b | 195 | 151 | 134 | 158 | 143 | 192 | 200 | 279 | 339 | 390 | 436 | 504 |
| Claims on Public Nonfin. Corps. | 22c | 141 | 94 | 70 | 86 | 79 | 110 | 124 | 21 | 54 | 25 | 36 | 67 |
| Claims on Private Sector | 22d | 29,540 | 30,504 | 32,272 | 35,377 | 38,010 | 41,409 | 49,668 | 61,090 | 72,922 | 86,706 | 99,744 | 117,315 |
| Liabilities to Central Bank | 26g | 3,122 | 2,985 | 2,869 | 3,006 | 2,542 | 1,999 | 1,863 | 1,693 | 1,629 | 1,600 | 1,609 | 1,507 |
| Transf.Dep.Included in Broad Money | 24 | 5,469 | 5,744 | 6,727 | 8,020 | 9,482 | 12,140 | 14,030 | 17,651 | 21,424 | 24,965 | 28,879 | 33,090 |
| Other Dep.Included in Broad Money. | 25 | 21,001 | 23,038 | 25,887 | 31,336 | 37,387 | 45,230 | 47,612 | 56,555 | 68,272 | 80,108 | 94,437 | 115,486 |
| Sec.Ot.th.Shares Incl.in Brd. Money.. | 26a | — | — | — | — | — | — | 140 | 758 | 1,211 | 1,867 | 1,957 | 1,532 |
| Deposits Excl. from Broad Money | 26b | 1,759 | 2,189 | 2,501 | 2,219 | 2,750 | 2,765 | 3,084 | 3,745 | 4,229 | 5,307 | 6,912 | 7,430 |
| Sec.Ot.th.Shares Excl.f/Brd.Money | 26s | — | — | — | — | — | — | — | — | — | — | — | — |
| Loans | 26l | 2,915 | 2,497 | 2,317 | 1,645 | 1,451 | 1,484 | 1,113 | 1,027 | 1,008 | 1,424 | 1,609 | 1,966 |
| Financial Derivatives | 26m | — | — | — | — | — | — | — | — | — | — | — | — |
| Insurance Technical Reserves | 26r | — | — | — | — | — | — | — | — | — | — | — | — |
| Shares and Other Equity | 27a | 1,698 | 2,092 | 2,259 | 2,887 | 4,185 | 4,972 | 5,337 | 6,769 | 8,414 | 9,553 | 11,388 | 13,307 |
| Other Items (Net) | 27r | 2,813 | 2,694 | 3,007 | 2,847 | 2,752 | 3,030 | 2,740 | 3,311 | 3,070 | 3,305 | 2,428 | 82 |
| Memo Item: | | | | | | | | | | | | | |
| Total Assets | 20ra | 45,832 | 48,565 | 52,979 | 59,428 | 68,957 | 80,552 | 84,158 | 99,499 | 117,878 | 137,882 | 160,552 | 191,257 |
| **Depository Corporations** | | *Millions of Bolivianos: End of Period* | | | | | | | | | | | |
| Net Foreign Assets | 31n | 12,973 | 19,274 | 32,423 | 46,224 | 59,372 | 67,556 | 75,925 | 89,544 | 105,257 | 110,362 | 118,955 | 106,225 |
| Claims on Nonresidents | 31 | 17,725 | 23,849 | 35,255 | 48,864 | 62,897 | 72,943 | 80,579 | 93,452 | 108,848 | 113,981 | 122,482 | 111,579 |
| Liabilities to Nonresidents | 36c | 4,751 | 4,575 | 2,832 | 2,640 | 3,525 | 5,387 | 4,654 | 3,908 | 3,591 | 3,618 | 3,527 | 5,354 |
| Domestic Claims | 32 | 36,869 | 37,691 | 35,211 | 36,261 | 38,143 | 40,267 | 42,773 | 53,127 | 62,949 | 82,277 | 100,556 | 130,572 |
| Net Claims on Central Government | 32an | 6,387 | 6,324 | 1,993 | -144 | -1,412 | -3,611 | -8,869 | -13,224 | -19,829 | -23,591 | -22,306 | -15,711 |
| Claims on Central Government | 32a | 10,932 | 10,662 | 8,536 | 8,313 | 10,143 | 11,872 | 12,071 | 10,917 | 10,961 | 11,383 | 11,436 | 11,749 |
| Liabilities to Central Government | 36d | 4,545 | 4,339 | 6,543 | 8,457 | 11,555 | 15,483 | 20,940 | 24,141 | 30,789 | 34,973 | 33,742 | 27,459 |
| Claims on Other Sectors | 32s | 30,481 | 31,367 | 33,218 | 36,405 | 39,554 | 43,879 | 51,642 | 66,351 | 82,778 | 105,868 | 122,862 | 146,283 |
| Claims on Other Financial Corps. | 32g | 450 | 471 | 738 | 781 | 1,292 | 2,164 | 1,621 | 1,714 | 1,455 | 6,242 | 6,256 | 7,418 |
| Claims on State & Local Govts. | 32b | 195 | 151 | 134 | 158 | 171 | 192 | 221 | 279 | 339 | 390 | 436 | 504 |
| Claims on Public Nonfin. Corps. | 32c | 141 | 94 | 70 | 86 | 79 | 110 | 124 | 3,262 | 8,059 | 12,521 | 16,418 | 21,041 |
| Claims on Private Sector | 32d | 29,696 | 30,652 | 32,275 | 35,380 | 38,012 | 41,413 | 49,675 | 61,096 | 72,926 | 86,715 | 99,751 | 117,320 |
| Broad Money Liabilities | 35l | 32,271 | 37,799 | 46,882 | 59,142 | 72,569 | 81,137 | 93,162 | 114,165 | 137,911 | 162,101 | 185,059 | 208,460 |
| Currency Outside Depository Corps | 34a | 3,865 | 5,594 | 8,012 | 13,117 | 15,807 | 17,080 | 22,485 | 25,814 | 29,305 | 32,716 | 36,671 | 37,181 |
| Transferable Deposits | 34 | 7,367 | 9,065 | 12,918 | 14,528 | 19,279 | 18,723 | 22,763 | 30,956 | 39,073 | 47,365 | 51,964 | 53,895 |
| Other Deposits | 35 | 21,039 | 23,140 | 25,952 | 31,497 | 37,483 | 45,334 | 47,774 | 56,638 | 68,322 | 80,152 | 94,468 | 115,852 |
| Securities Other than Shares | 36a | — | — | — | — | — | — | 140 | 758 | 1,211 | 1,867 | 1,957 | 1,532 |
| Deposits Excl. from Broad Money | 36b | 1,759 | 2,189 | 2,501 | 2,219 | 2,750 | 2,794 | 3,084 | 3,746 | 4,231 | 5,323 | 6,925 | 7,473 |
| Sec.Ot.th.Shares Excl.f/Brd.Money | 36s | 21 | 23 | 25 | 93 | 191 | 73 | 59 | 282 | 172 | 4,093 | 7,122 | 1,310 |
| Loans | 36l | 2,915 | 2,497 | 2,317 | 1,645 | 1,451 | 1,484 | 1,113 | 1,027 | 1,008 | 1,424 | 1,609 | 1,966 |
| Financial Derivatives | 36m | — | — | — | — | — | — | — | — | — | — | — | — |
| Insurance Technical Reserves | 36r | — | — | — | — | — | — | — | — | — | — | — | — |
| Shares and Other Equity | 37a | 8,083 | 9,661 | 11,213 | 12,969 | 11,018 | 13,446 | 14,608 | 15,474 | 19,156 | 12,312 | 12,254 | 12,278 |
| Other Items (Net) | 37r | 4,792 | 4,795 | 4,696 | 6,417 | 9,535 | 8,890 | 6,673 | 7,978 | 5,729 | 7,386 | 6,541 | 5,311 |
| Broad Money Liabs., Seasonally Adj. | 35l.b | 31,131 | 36,793 | 45,931 | 58,156 | 71,268 | 79,356 | 90,542 | 110,396 | 132,954 | 156,136 | 178,279 | 200,850 |
| **Other Financial Corporations** | | *Millions of Bolivianos: End of Period* | | | | | | | | | | | |
| Net Foreign Assets | 41n | .... | 292 | 377 | -192 | -633 | -657 | -637 | -678 | 118 | 1,410 | 1,740 | 3,683 |
| Claims on Nonresidents | 41 | .... | 673 | 665 | 642 | 136 | 182 | 232 | 224 | 1,112 | 2,494 | 3,091 | 4,416 |
| Liabilities to Nonresidents | 46c | .... | 382 | 288 | 834 | 769 | 839 | 869 | 902 | 994 | 1,083 | 1,351 | 733 |
| Claims on Depository Corporations | 40 | .... | 3,510 | 4,640 | 6,629 | 10,720 | 15,432 | 16,417 | 22,507 | 30,111 | 35,146 | 41,790 | 49,202 |
| Net Claims on Central Government | 42an | .... | 13,641 | 15,843 | 16,933 | 17,585 | 18,447 | 20,887 | 22,361 | 19,789 | 17,717 | 16,476 | 14,834 |
| Claims on Central Government | 42a | .... | 13,715 | 15,911 | 16,973 | 17,636 | 18,514 | 20,945 | 22,436 | 19,888 | 17,847 | 16,632 | 14,955 |
| Liabilities to Central Government | 46d | .... | 74 | 68 | 39 | 51 | 67 | 58 | 75 | 99 | 130 | 156 | 121 |
| Claims on Other Sectors | 42s | .... | 4,036 | 2,409 | 2,704 | 3,931 | 3,718 | 6,032 | 6,800 | 9,775 | 12,317 | 15,112 | 15,127 |
| Claims on State & Local Govts | 42b | .... | — | — | — | 67 | 69 | 81 | 80 | 78 | 75 | 48 | 24 |
| Claims on Pub. Nonfin. Corps. | 42c | .... | 7 | 3 | 4 | 4 | 2 | 4 | 5 | 19 | 64 | 78 | 53 |
| Claims on Private Sector | 42d | .... | 4,029 | 2,406 | 2,701 | 3,860 | 3,648 | 5,947 | 6,715 | 9,678 | 12,179 | 14,986 | 15,050 |
| Deposits | 46b | .... | — | — | — | — | — | — | — | — | — | — | — |
| Securities Other than Shares | 46s | .... | 554 | 359 | 5 | 2 | 4 | 6 | 450 | 459 | 956 | 810 | 6 |
| Loans | 46l | .... | 877 | 853 | — | — | — | 45 | 34 | 316 | 87 | 74 | — |
| Financial Derivatives | 46m | .... | — | — | — | — | — | — | — | — | — | — | — |
| Insurance Technical Reserves | 46r | .... | 19,213 | 21,150 | 25,032 | 30,336 | 35,570 | 41,306 | 49,308 | 57,556 | 67,594 | 77,300 | 88,431 |
| Shares and Other Equity | 47a | .... | 1,037 | 1,088 | 1,123 | 1,360 | 1,452 | 1,445 | 1,485 | 1,609 | 1,778 | 1,953 | 1,591 |
| Other Items (Net) | 47r | .... | -203 | -179 | -85 | -96 | -86 | -103 | -286 | -147 | -3,825 | -5,019 | -7,182 |
| Memo Item: | | | | | | | | | | | | | |
| Total Assets | 40ra | .... | 22,402 | 24,092 | 27,499 | 33,187 | 38,691 | 44,481 | 52,951 | 61,778 | 72,425 | 82,513 | 91,792 |

# Bolivia 218

| | | 2004 | 2005 | 2006 | 2007 | 2008 | 2009 | 2010 | 2011 | 2012 | 2013 | 2014 | 2015 |
|---|---|---|---|---|---|---|---|---|---|---|---|---|---|
| **Financial Corporations** | | | | | | *Millions of Bolivianos: End of Period* | | | | | | | |
| Net Foreign Assets.......... | 51n | .... | 19,565 | 32,800 | 46,031 | 58,739 | 66,900 | 75,288 | 88,867 | 105,375 | 111,773 | 120,695 | 109,908 |
| Claims on Nonresidents......... | 51 | .... | 24,522 | 35,920 | 49,505 | 63,033 | 73,125 | 80,811 | 93,676 | 109,960 | 116,475 | 125,573 | 115,995 |
| Liabilities to Nonresidents......... | 56c | .... | 4,957 | 3,120 | 3,474 | 4,294 | 6,226 | 5,524 | 4,809 | 4,584 | 4,702 | 4,878 | 6,087 |
| Domestic Claims.......... | 52 | .... | 54,898 | 52,725 | 55,118 | 58,367 | 60,269 | 68,071 | 80,575 | 91,059 | 106,070 | 125,888 | 153,115 |
| Net Claims on Central Government | 52an | .... | 19,965 | 17,837 | 16,789 | 16,173 | 14,836 | 12,018 | 9,137 | −39 | −5,873 | −5,830 | −876 |
| Claims on Central Government.... | 52a | .... | 24,378 | 24,447 | 25,286 | 27,778 | 30,386 | 33,016 | 33,353 | 30,849 | 29,230 | 28,068 | 26,704 |
| Liabilities to Central Government. | 56d | .... | 4,413 | 6,611 | 8,496 | 11,606 | 15,550 | 20,998 | 24,216 | 30,888 | 35,103 | 33,898 | 27,580 |
| Claims on Other Sectors.... | 52s | .... | 34,933 | 34,889 | 38,329 | 42,194 | 45,433 | 56,053 | 71,437 | 91,098 | 111,944 | 131,718 | 153,991 |
| Claims on State & Local Govts..... | 52b | .... | 151 | 134 | 158 | 239 | 261 | 303 | 359 | 417 | 465 | 485 | 528 |
| Claims on Pub. Nonfin. Corps...... | 52c | .... | 102 | 73 | 90 | 83 | 112 | 128 | 3,268 | 8,078 | 12,585 | 16,496 | 21,094 |
| Claims on Private Sector.......... | 52d | .... | 34,680 | 34,681 | 38,081 | 41,872 | 45,061 | 55,622 | 67,811 | 82,604 | 98,894 | 114,737 | 132,370 |
| Currency Outside Fin. Corporations.. | 54a | .... | 5,590 | 8,006 | 13,108 | 15,795 | 17,060 | 22,477 | 25,808 | 29,299 | 32,708 | 36,663 | 37,170 |
| Deposits.......... | 55l | .... | 31,668 | 37,414 | 44,722 | 55,234 | 60,937 | 69,066 | 85,504 | 106,613 | 128,016 | 148,121 | 170,172 |
| Securities Other than Shares.......... | 56a | .... | 578 | 384 | 98 | 193 | 77 | 204 | 1,489 | 1,842 | 3,188 | 3,950 | 2,848 |
| Loans.......... | 56l | .... | 7 | 27 | 16 | 2 | 294 | 360 | 346 | 376 | 657 | 912 | 1,172 |
| Financial Derivatives.......... | 56m | .... | — | — | — | — | — | — | — | — | — | — | — |
| Insurance Technical Reserves.......... | 56r | .... | 19,213 | 21,150 | 25,032 | 30,336 | 35,570 | 41,306 | 49,308 | 57,556 | 67,594 | 77,300 | 88,431 |
| Shares and Other Equity.......... | 57a | .... | 10,698 | 12,300 | 14,092 | 12,378 | 14,898 | 16,053 | 16,959 | 20,765 | 14,090 | 14,207 | 13,868 |
| Other Items (Net).......... | 57r | .... | 6,709 | 6,244 | 4,081 | 3,167 | −1,668 | −6,107 | −9,972 | −20,016 | −28,412 | −34,569 | −50,638 |
| **Monetary Aggregates** | | | | | | *Millions of Bolivianos: End of Period* | | | | | | | |
| Broad Money.......... | 59m | 34,862 | 39,688 | 48,959 | 62,149 | 77,494 | 85,343 | 96,125 | 118,201 | 141,095 | 166,646 | 192,716 | 218,039 |
| o/w:Currency Issued by Cent.Govt | 59m.a | — | — | — | — | — | — | — | — | — | — | — | — |
| o/w: Dep.in Nonfin. Corporations. | 59m.b | — | — | — | — | — | — | — | — | — | — | — | — |
| o/w:Secs. Issued by Central Govt.. | 59m.c | 2,591 | 1,889 | 2,077 | 3,007 | 4,925 | 4,206 | 2,963 | 4,037 | 3,184 | 4,545 | 7,657 | 9,579 |
| Money (National Definitions) | | | | | | | | | | | | | |
| Base Money.......... | 19ma | 5,769 | 7,883 | 11,227 | 17,458 | 22,293 | 29,568 | 32,577 | 41,768 | 48,671 | 51,606 | 61,257 | 71,567 |
| M1.......... | 59ma | 5,258 | 7,486 | 10,752 | 17,098 | 21,719 | 24,918 | 31,890 | 37,092 | 44,297 | 50,527 | 57,946 | 61,815 |
| M'1.......... | 59maa | 9,372 | 11,542 | 14,891 | 21,326 | 25,646 | 30,295 | 37,244 | 42,821 | 50,998 | 57,981 | 65,694 | 70,425 |
| M2.......... | 59mb | 6,392 | 9,414 | 14,161 | 24,062 | 32,673 | 36,649 | 45,856 | 55,354 | 66,554 | 78,367 | 91,780 | 106,772 |
| M'2.......... | 59mba | 16,279 | 19,636 | 25,237 | 35,605 | 44,350 | 52,335 | 59,796 | 70,470 | 82,646 | 95,836 | 109,988 | 126,573 |
| M3.......... | 59mc | 6,764 | 10,263 | 15,783 | 27,364 | 37,751 | 44,811 | 57,454 | 73,286 | 94,909 | 114,827 | 136,582 | 161,323 |
| M'3.......... | 59mca | 30,194 | 34,371 | 40,519 | 52,240 | 62,633 | 74,985 | 84,382 | 99,315 | 119,367 | 138,661 | 160,279 | 186,305 |
| M4.......... | 59md | 6,824 | 10,351 | 17,099 | 30,075 | 42,618 | 48,994 | 60,415 | 77,322 | 98,093 | 119,372 | 144,239 | 170,902 |
| M'4.......... | 59mda | 32,785 | 36,308 | 42,596 | 55,247 | 67,640 | 79,191 | 87,346 | 103,352 | 122,551 | 143,206 | 167,936 | 195,884 |
| **Interest Rates** | | | | | | *Percent Per Annum* | | | | | | | |
| Discount Rate (End of Period).......... | 60.a | 6.000 | 5.250 | 5.250 | 6.500 | 13.000 | 3.000 | 3.000 | 4.000 | 4.000 | 4.500 | 3.300 | 2.500 |
| Discount Rate (Fgn.Cur.)(End per).... | 60.f | 7.458 | 7.250 | 7.250 | 7.250 | 8.292 | 8.750 | 8.750 | 8.750 | 5.583 | 4.000 | 4.000 | 4.000 |
| Money Market Rate.......... | 60b | 4.051 | 3.526 | 3.795 | 4.269 | 7.678 | 3.551 | .899 | 1.871 | .674 | 1.592 | 4.209 | 1.578 |
| Money Market Rate (Fgn. Cur.)........ | 60b.f | 3.021 | 3.369 | 4.617 | 4.593 | 6.362 | 1.630 | 1.044 | 1.134 | .849 | 1.101 | 2.213 | 1.202 |
| Treasury Bill Rate.......... | 60c | 7.411 | 4.964 | 4.558 | 6.036 | 8.309 | 2.857 | .070 | .461 | .523 | 1.092 | 1.978 | .574 |
| Treasury Bill Rate (Fgn.Currency)...... | 60c.f | 3.336 | 2.853 | 3.680 | 4.308 | 4.866 | .651 | .077 | .122 | .004 | .004 | .... | .... |
| Savings Rate.......... | 60k | 4.507 | 3.592 | 2.485 | 2.184 | 2.747 | 1.494 | .475 | .784 | .828 | .988 | .900 | .663 |
| Savings Rate (Fgn. Currency).......... | 60k.f | .568 | .550 | 1.164 | 1.310 | 2.782 | 1.369 | .202 | .129 | .096 | .070 | .041 | .012 |
| Deposit Rate.......... | 60l | 7.420 | 4.934 | 4.027 | 3.546 | 4.656 | 3.439 | 1.047 | 1.403 | 1.626 | 1.739 | 2.950 | 1.414 |
| Deposit Rate (Fgn. Currency).......... | 60l.f | 1.978 | 1.870 | 2.494 | 2.442 | 3.524 | 1.883 | .362 | .338 | .243 | .185 | .228 | .130 |
| Lending Rate.......... | 60p | 14.470 | 16.615 | 11.891 | 12.861 | 13.873 | 12.360 | 9.910 | 10.915 | 11.135 | 11.051 | 9.694 | 8.073 |
| Lending Rate (Fgn. Currency).......... | 60p.f | 10.003 | 11.327 | 11.647 | 10.509 | 11.457 | 11.236 | 8.287 | 8.163 | 7.933 | 7.746 | 7.628 | 7.572 |
| **Prices, Production, Labor** | | | | | | *Index Numbers (2010=100): Period Averages* | | | | | | | |
| Consumer Prices.......... | 64 | 69.3 | 73.0 | 76.2 | 82.8 | 94.4 | 97.6 | 100.0 | 109.8 | 114.8 | 121.4 | 128.4 | 133.7 |
| Crude Petroleum Production.......... | 66aa | 134.8 | 146.9 | 141.2 | 142.6 | 138.2 | 97.8 | 100.0 | 102.8 | 119.7 | 137.5 | 147.8 | 142.0 |
| | | | | | | *Number in Thousands: Period Averages* | | | | | | | |
| Labor Force.......... | 67d | .... | .... | .... | .... | .... | 2,214 | 2,284 | .... | .... | .... | .... | .... |
| Employment.......... | 67e | .... | .... | .... | .... | .... | 2,039 | 2,148 | .... | .... | .... | .... | .... |
| Unemployment.......... | 67c | .... | .... | .... | .... | .... | 175 | 137 | .... | .... | .... | .... | .... |
| Unemployment Rate (%).......... | 67r | .... | .... | .... | .... | .... | 7.9 | 6.0 | .... | .... | .... | .... | .... |
| **Intl. Transactions & Positions** | | | | | | *Millions of US Dollars* | | | | | | | |
| Exports.......... | 70..d | 2,146.1 | 2,791.1 | 3,874.5 | 4,458.3 | 7,058.0 | 4,917.5 | 6,179.3 | 8,106.5 | 10,311.5 | 11,188.5 | 12,265.8 | 8,260.7 |
| Tin.......... | 70q.d | 131.7 | 113.9 | 132.9 | 199.1 | 257.4 | 220.8 | 335.2 | 434.2 | 331.6 | 347.2 | 347.3 | 264.1 |
| Zinc.......... | 70t.d | 90.0 | 118.8 | 325.6 | 411.3 | 439.8 | 409.4 | 618.6 | 555.5 | 435.0 | 442.9 | 582.3 | 775.2 |
| Imports, c.i.f.......... | 71..d | 1,844.2 | 2,341.4 | 2,814.3 | 3,457.0 | 5,081.4 | 4,544.9 | 5,590.2 | 7,927.3 | 8,578.3 | 9,337.7 | 10,420.9 | 9,479.9 |
| Imports, f.o.b.......... | 71.vd | 1,724.9 | 2,191.5 | 2,638.4 | 3,242.3 | 4,764.1 | 4,248.3 | 5,208.4 | 7,381.1 | 7,997.5 | 8,729.2 | 9,794.4 | 8,842.8 |
| | | | | | | *2010=100* | | | | | | | |
| Volume of Exports.......... | 72 | 60.3 | 70.4 | 76.2 | 79.9 | 90.8 | 82.5 | 100.0 | 94.8 | 105.3 | 119.2 | 124.4 | 122.4 |
| Tin.......... | 72q | 99.3 | 93.6 | 96.1 | 82.3 | 85.6 | 98.5 | 100.0 | 96.1 | 92.7 | 93.2 | 93.6 | 92.7 |
| Zinc.......... | 72t | 16.8 | 17.3 | 20.4 | 24.1 | 44.4 | 49.2 | 100.0 | 48.3 | 43.4 | 44.7 | 52.1 | 50.0 |
| | | | | | | *2010=100: Indices of Unit Values in US Dollars* | | | | | | | |
| Unit Value of Exports/Export Prices... | 74..d | 38.7 | 50.7 | 86.4 | 97.0 | 107.9 | 86.8 | 100.0 | 144.9 | 152.9 | 142.6 | 136.5 | 113.5 |
| Tin.......... | 74q.d | 32.6 | 29.8 | 35.9 | 67.2 | 77.1 | 64.6 | 100.0 | 147.4 | 120.5 | 89.0 | 87.2 | 86.9 |
| Zinc.......... | 74t.d | 86.8 | 111.3 | 257.4 | 275.4 | 160.2 | 134.6 | 100.0 | 185.8 | 162.0 | 160.0 | 180.6 | 250.6 |

# Bolivia 218

|  |  | 2004 | 2005 | 2006 | 2007 | 2008 | 2009 | 2010 | 2011 | 2012 | 2013 | 2014 | 2015 |
|---|---|---|---|---|---|---|---|---|---|---|---|---|---|
| **Balance of Payments** |  |  |  |  |  | *Millions of US Dollars* |  |  |  |  |  |  |  |
| A. Current Account* | 109bx | 337.5 | 622.4 | 1,317.5 | 1,591.2 | 1,992.7 | 813.5 | 873.7 | 537.2 | 1,970.0 | 1,054.0 | −16.4 | .... |
| Goods, credit (exports) | 1a9cx | 2,044.3 | 2,622.2 | 3,662.0 | 4,262.8 | 6,271.4 | 4,709.8 | 6,129.3 | 8,174.8 | 11,132.8 | 11,538.7 | 12,147.4 | .... |
| Goods, debit (imports) | 1a9dx | 1,724.7 | 2,182.6 | 2,632.1 | 3,243.5 | 4,764.1 | 4,143.6 | 5,006.8 | 7,126.4 | 7,997.5 | 8,729.2 | 9,935.0 | .... |
| Balance on goods | 1a9bx | 319.5 | 439.6 | 1,029.9 | 1,019.4 | 1,507.4 | 566.3 | 1,122.5 | 1,048.5 | 3,135.3 | 2,809.5 | 2,212.4 | .... |
| Services, credit (exports) | 1b9cx | 517.8 | 657.2 | 687.4 | 691.9 | 751.6 | 720.1 | 707.7 | 948.0 | 1,125.2 | 1,214.0 | 1,346.8 | .... |
| Services, debit (imports) | 1b9dx | 606.2 | 682.0 | 824.8 | 896.7 | 1,014.0 | 1,012.2 | 1,148.8 | 1,650.7 | 1,921.4 | 2,331.5 | 3,052.8 | .... |
| Balance on Goods & Services | 1z9bx | 231.1 | 414.8 | 892.5 | 814.5 | 1,245.0 | 274.2 | 681.4 | 345.8 | 2,339.1 | 1,692.0 | 506.4 | .... |
| Primary income: credit | 1c9cx | 76.0 | 121.2 | 235.4 | 369.8 | 346.4 | 232.7 | 81.7 | 136.8 | 141.4 | 170.7 | 168.9 | .... |
| Primary income: debit | 1c9dx | 460.6 | 497.6 | 632.7 | 859.3 | 882.8 | 906.4 | 970.6 | 1,122.5 | 1,770.7 | 2,078.5 | 1,875.8 | .... |
| Balance on gds, serv. & prim. inc. | 1y9bx | −153.6 | 38.4 | 495.2 | 325.1 | 708.6 | −399.6 | −207.5 | −640.0 | 709.8 | −215.8 | −1,200.5 | .... |
| Secondary income: credit | 1d9ca | 542.6 | 648.7 | 895.1 | 1,344.9 | 1,391.0 | 1,315.4 | 1,187.6 | 1,299.3 | 1,411.3 | 1,441.6 | 1,368.9 | .... |
| Secondary income: debit | 1d9da | 51.5 | 64.7 | 72.9 | 78.7 | 106.9 | 102.3 | 106.3 | 122.2 | 151.0 | 171.8 | 184.8 | .... |
| B. Capital Account* | 209ba | — | — | 1,804.3 | 1,171.0 | — | 99.8 | — | — | — | — | — | .... |
| Capital account: credit | 209ca | — | — | 1,804.3 | 1,171.0 | — | 99.8 | — | — | — | — | — | .... |
| Capital account: debit | 209da | — | — | — | — | — | — | — | — | — | — | — | .... |
| Balance on current & capital acct. | 129ba | 337.5 | 622.4 | 3,121.8 | 2,762.2 | 1,992.7 | 913.3 | 873.7 | 537.2 | 1,970.0 | 1,054.0 | −16.4 | .... |
| C. Financial Account* | 309na | −360.5 | −180.6 | 1,588.6 | 794.6 | −370.3 | −69.7 | −860.1 | −1,522.8 | −536.2 | −2,021.8 | 923.6 | .... |
| Direct investment: assets | 3a9aa | 2.8 | 3.0 | 3.0 | 3.0 | 3.0 | 3.0 | −28.8 | .3 | — | — | — | .... |
| Equity & investment fund shares.. | 3aaaa | 2.8 | 3.0 | 3.0 | 3.0 | 3.0 | 3.0 | −28.8 | .3 | — | — | — | .... |
| Debt instruments | 3abaa | — | — | — | — | — | — | — | — | — | — | — | .... |
| Direct investment: liabilities | 3a9la | 65.4 | −238.6 | 280.8 | 366.3 | 512.3 | 423.0 | 622.0 | 858.9 | 1,060.0 | 1,749.6 | 72.6 | .... |
| Equity & investment fund shares . | 3aala | 76.4 | −91.3 | 225.3 | 151.6 | 280.1 | 504.8 | 773.6 | 901.6 | 1,223.6 | 1,699.3 | 648.4 | .... |
| Debt instruments | 3abla | −11.0 | −147.3 | 55.5 | 214.7 | 232.2 | −81.7 | −151.7 | −42.7 | −163.6 | 50.3 | −575.8 | .... |
| Portfolio investment: assets | 3b9aa | 35.4 | 153.4 | −25.1 | 29.9 | 208.1 | 153.6 | −90.1 | −156.0 | 360.3 | 428.7 | 560.5 | .... |
| Equity & investment fund shares | 3baaa | −1.2 | — | — | — | — | — | — | — | — | — | — | .... |
| Debt securities | 3bbaa | 36.6 | 153.4 | −25.1 | 29.9 | 208.1 | 153.6 | −90.1 | −156.0 | 360.3 | 428.7 | 560.5 | .... |
| Portfolio investment: liabilities | 3b9la | — | — | — | — | — | — | — | — | — | — | — | .... |
| Equity & investment fund shares . | 3bala | — | — | — | — | — | — | — | — | — | — | — | .... |
| Debt securities | 3bbla | — | — | — | — | — | — | — | — | — | — | — | .... |
| Fin. der.& empl.stk.ops.(ESOs): net. | 3c9na | — | — | — | — | — | — | — | — | — | — | — | .... |
| Fin. der. & ESOs.: assets | 3c9aa | .... | .... | .... | .... | .... | .... | .... | .... | .... | .... | .... | .... |
| Fin. der. & ESOs.: liabilities | 3c9la | .... | .... | .... | .... | .... | .... | .... | .... | .... | .... | .... | .... |
| Other investment: assets | 3d9aa | −94.3 | −123.8 | 262.4 | −100.8 | 222.8 | 425.8 | 32.3 | 127.8 | 2,334.5 | 2,432.2 | 1,009.8 | .... |
| Other equity | 3daaa | | | | | | | | | | | | |
| Debt instruments | 3dzaa | −94.3 | −123.8 | 262.4 | −100.8 | 222.8 | 425.8 | 32.3 | 127.8 | 2,334.5 | 2,432.2 | 1,009.8 | .... |
| Other investment: liabilities | 3d9la | 239.0 | 451.8 | −1,629.1 | −1,228.8 | 291.9 | 229.1 | 151.4 | 636.0 | 2,171.1 | 3,133.0 | 574.1 | .... |
| Other equity | 3dala | .... | | | | | | | | | | | |
| Debt instruments | 3dzla | 239.0 | 451.8 | −1,629.1 | −1,228.8 | 291.9 | 229.1 | 151.4 | 636.0 | 2,171.1 | 3,133.0 | 574.1 | .... |
| Curr.+ cap.– finan. acct. balance.. | 4y9na | 698.0 | 803.0 | 1,533.2 | 1,967.6 | 2,363.0 | 983.1 | 1,733.8 | 2,060.1 | 2,506.3 | 3,075.8 | −940.0 | .... |
| D. Net Errors and Omissions | 409na | −625.4 | −365.8 | −94.4 | −102.6 | 11.2 | −442.8 | −809.5 | 100.7 | −794.6 | −1,952.1 | 1,911.7 | .... |
| E. Reserves and Related Items | 4z9na | 72.6 | 437.2 | 1,438.8 | 1,865.1 | 2,374.2 | 540.2 | 924.3 | 2,160.8 | 1,711.7 | 1,123.7 | 971.7 | .... |
| Reserve assets | 3e9aa | 157.2 | 463.4 | 1,286.3 | 1,937.7 | 2,374.2 | 540.2 | 924.3 | 2,160.8 | 1,711.7 | 1,123.7 | 971.7 | .... |
| Credit and loans from the IMF | 3dcla | 14.3 | −39.2 | −232.9 | −14.6 | — | — | — | — | — | — | — | .... |
| Exceptional financing | 409la | 70.3 | 65.3 | 80.4 | 87.3 | — | — | — | — | — | — | — | .... |
| *Excludes components in group E |  |  |  |  |  |  |  |  |  |  |  |  |  |
| **International Investment Position** |  |  |  |  |  | *Millions of US Dollars* |  |  |  |  |  |  |  |
| Assets | 809aa | 3,316.3 | 4,200.1 | 6,196.9 | 8,459.7 | 12,029.7 | 13,407.1 | 14,170.4 | 16,509.4 | 19,011.3 | 21,364.5 | 22,915.2 | .... |
| Direct investment | 8a9aa | 290.0 | 296.9 | 90.2 | 94.2 | 63.8 | 49.5 | 7.7 | .... | .... | .... | .... | |
| Equity & investment fund shares.. | 8aaaa | 26.1 | 29.1 | 32.1 | 36.1 | 43.1 | 28.8 | .... | .... | .... | .... | .... | |
| Debt instruments | 8abaa | 264.0 | 267.8 | 58.1 | 58.1 | 20.7 | 20.7 | 7.7 | .... | .... | .... | .... | |
| Portfolio investment | 8b9aa | 433.8 | 587.2 | 562.2 | 484.8 | 583.8 | 885.6 | 761.4 | 550.1 | 868.7 | 1,674.2 | 2,225.5 | .... |
| Equity & investment fund shares.. | 8baaa | .... | .... | .... | .... | .... | .... | .... | 4.7 | 4.0 | | 13.6 | |
| Debt securities | 8bbaa | 433.8 | 587.2 | 562.2 | 484.8 | 583.8 | 885.6 | 761.4 | 545.3 | 864.6 | 1,674.2 | 2,211.9 | |
| Fin. der.(oth. than reserves) & ESOs | 8c9aa | .... | .... | .... | .... | .... | .... | .... | .... | .... | .... | .... | |
| Other investment | 8d9aa | 1,160.6 | 1,356.6 | 2,352.2 | 2,561.7 | 3,660.2 | 3,890.6 | 3,671.2 | 3,939.6 | 4,216.0 | 5,260.3 | 5,566.5 | |
| Other equity | 8daaa | | | | | | | | | | | | |
| Debt instruments | 8dzaa | 1,160.6 | 1,356.6 | 2,352.2 | 2,561.7 | 3,660.2 | 3,890.6 | 3,671.2 | 3,939.6 | 4,216.0 | 5,260.3 | 5,566.5 | |
| Reserve assets | 8e9aa | 1,431.9 | 1,959.3 | 3,192.4 | 5,319.0 | 7,721.8 | 8,581.4 | 9,730.0 | 12,019.8 | 13,926.7 | 14,430.1 | 15,123.2 | |
| Liabilities | 809la | 11,152.9 | 11,457.0 | 9,860.9 | 9,190.9 | 9,916.4 | 10,374.1 | 11,039.2 | 12,543.5 | 14,099.2 | 16,962.7 | 18,337.8 | |
| Direct investment | 8a9la | 5,022.4 | 5,114.2 | 5,118.9 | 5,485.0 | 5,998.0 | 6,421.1 | 6,890.0 | 7,748.9 | 8,808.9 | 10,558.5 | 11,206.3 | |
| Equity & investment fund shares.. | 8aala | 3,360.4 | 3,506.4 | 3,635.2 | 3,580.4 | 3,859.9 | 4,263.2 | 5,056.0 | 5,957.6 | 7,181.2 | 8,880.4 | 9,497.3 | |
| Debt instruments | 8abla | 1,662.1 | 1,607.8 | 1,483.7 | 1,904.6 | 2,138.1 | 2,157.8 | 1,834.0 | 1,791.3 | 1,627.7 | 1,678.1 | 1,709.1 | |
| Portfolio investment | 8b9la | 41.8 | 41.8 | 41.8 | 127.3 | 37.5 | 32.6 | 30.0 | 35.6 | 33.6 | 40.3 | 46.6 | |
| Equity & investment fund shares.. | 8bala | 40.9 | 40.9 | 40.9 | 126.5 | 36.6 | 32.6 | 30.0 | 35.6 | 33.6 | 40.3 | 46.6 | |
| Debt securities | 8bbla | .9 | .9 | .9 | .9 | .9 | .... | .... | .... | .... | .... | .... | |
| Fin. der.(oth.than reserves) & ESOs | 8c9la | .... | .... | .... | .... | .... | .... | .... | .... | .... | .... | .... | |
| Other investment | 8d9la | 6,088.7 | 6,301.0 | 4,700.2 | 3,578.6 | 3,881.0 | 3,920.4 | 4,119.2 | 4,758.9 | 5,256.7 | 6,363.9 | 7,084.8 | |
| Other equity | 8dala | .... | .... | .... | .... | .... | .... | .... | .... | .... | .... | .... | |
| Debt instruments | 8dzla | 6,088.7 | 6,301.0 | 4,700.2 | 3,578.6 | 3,881.0 | 3,920.4 | 4,119.2 | 4,758.9 | 5,256.7 | 6,363.9 | 7,084.8 | |
| **National Accounts** |  |  |  |  |  | *Millions of Bolivianos* |  |  |  |  |  |  |  |
| Househ.Cons.Expend.,incl.NPISHs.... | 96f | 47,281 | 51,080 | 57,595 | 65,128 | 75,100 | 79,733 | 85,894 | 100,910 | 111,364 | 127,509 | 143,500 | 158,079 |
| Government Consumption Expend... | 91f | 11,320 | 12,304 | 13,170 | 14,482 | 16,025 | 17,905 | 19,070 | 22,902 | 25,153 | 29,324 | 33,533 | 39,895 |
| Gross Fixed Capital Formation | 93e | 8,137 | 10,006 | 13,117 | 16,625 | 20,818 | 20,060 | 22,849 | 31,527 | 34,367 | 40,380 | 47,840 | 48,567 |
| Changes in Inventories | 93i | −463 | 973 | −396 | −982 | 367 | 599 | 599 | 1,413 | −1,291 | −90 | 118 | −4,704 |
| Exports of Goods and Services | 90c | 21,680 | 27,381 | 38,325 | 43,053 | 54,194 | 43,484 | 56,787 | 73,294 | 88,273 | 93,413 | 98,710 | 70,389 |
| Imports of Goods and Services (-).... | 98c | 18,330 | 24,720 | 30,062 | 35,297 | 45,816 | 40,054 | 47,325 | 63,814 | 70,712 | 78,680 | 95,696 | 84,211 |
| Gross Domestic Product (GDP) | 99b | 69,626 | 77,024 | 91,748 | 103,009 | 120,694 | 121,727 | 137,876 | 166,232 | 187,154 | 211,856 | 228,004 | 228,014 |
| GDP Volume 1990 Prices | 99b.p | 24,928 | 26,030 | 27,279 | 28,524 | 30,278 | 31,294 | 32,586 | 34,281 | 36,037 | 38,487 | 40,588 | 42,556 |
| GDP Volume (2010=100) | 99bvp | 76.5 | 79.9 | 83.7 | 87.5 | 92.9 | 96.0 | 100.0 | 105.2 | 110.6 | 118.1 | 124.6 | 130.6 |
| GDP Deflator (2010=100) | 99bip | 66.0 | 69.9 | 79.5 | 85.4 | 94.2 | 91.9 | 100.0 | 114.6 | 122.7 | 130.1 | 132.8 | 126.6 |
| |  |  |  |  |  | *Millions: Midyear Estimates* |  |  |  |  |  |  |  |
| **Population** | 99z | 8.97 | 9.13 | 9.28 | 9.44 | 9.60 | 9.76 | 9.92 | 10.08 | 10.24 | 10.40 | 10.56 | 10.72 |

# Bosnia and Herzegovina   963

| | | 2004 | 2005 | 2006 | 2007 | 2008 | 2009 | 2010 | 2011 | 2012 | 2013 | 2014 | 2015 |
|---|---|---|---|---|---|---|---|---|---|---|---|---|---|
| **Exchange Rates** | | | | | *Convertible Marka per SDR: End of Period* | | | | | | | | |
| Official Rate | aa | 2.2300 | 2.3696 | 2.2341 | 2.0995 | 2.1646 | 2.1284 | 2.2542 | 2.3207 | 2.2783 | 2.1840 | 2.3339 | 2.4894 |
| | | | | *Convertible Marka per US Dollar: End of Period (ae) Period Average (rf)* | | | | | | | | | |
| Official Rate | ae | 1.4359 | 1.6579 | 1.4851 | 1.3286 | 1.4054 | 1.3576 | 1.4637 | 1.5116 | 1.4824 | 1.4182 | 1.6109 | 1.7965 |
| Official Rate | rf | 1.5752 | 1.5727 | 1.5591 | 1.4290 | 1.3352 | 1.4079 | 1.4767 | 1.4069 | 1.5222 | 1.4731 | 1.4742 | 1.7635 |
| **Fund Position** | | | | | *Millions of SDRs: End of Period* | | | | | | | | |
| Quota | 2f.s | 169.10 | 169.10 | 169.10 | 169.10 | 169.10 | 169.10 | 169.10 | 169.10 | 169.10 | 169.10 | 169.10 | 169.10 |
| SDR Holdings | 1b.s | .32 | .23 | .25 | .17 | .18 | 2.69 | .01 | .48 | 1.98 | 1.25 | 2.23 | 1.52 |
| Reserve Position in the Fund | 1c.s | — | — | — | — | — | .05 | .05 | .05 | .05 | .05 | .05 | .05 |
| Total Fund Cred.&Loans Outstg | 2tl | 70.02 | 43.35 | 13.50 | 1.50 | — | 182.63 | 338.20 | 338.20 | 416.83 | 389.78 | 454.88 | 416.41 |
| SDR Allocations | 1bd | 20.48 | 20.48 | 20.48 | 20.48 | 20.48 | 160.89 | 160.89 | 160.89 | 160.89 | 160.89 | 160.89 | 160.89 |
| **International Liquidity** | | | | *Millions of US Dollars Unless Otherwise Indicated: End of Period* | | | | | | | | | |
| Total Reserves minus Gold | 1l.d | 2,427.27 | 2,547.61 | 3,671.01 | 5,041.78 | 4,479.83 | 4,529.04 | 4,366.19 | 4,149.56 | 4,283.49 | 4,868.37 | 4,744.43 | 4,689.22 |
| SDR Holdings | 1b.d | .50 | .33 | .38 | .27 | .28 | 4.21 | .02 | .74 | 3.05 | 1.92 | 3.23 | 2.10 |
| Reserve Position in the Fund | 1c.d | — | — | — | — | — | .07 | .07 | .07 | .07 | .07 | .07 | .06 |
| Foreign Exchange | 1d.d | 2,426.76 | 2,547.29 | 3,670.63 | 5,041.51 | 4,479.55 | 4,524.75 | 4,366.10 | 4,148.75 | 4,280.37 | 4,866.38 | 4,741.14 | 4,687.06 |
| Gold (Million Fine Troy Ounces) | 1ad | — | — | — | — | — | .042 | .032 | .064 | .064 | .096 | .096 | .096 |
| Gold (National Valuation) | 1and | — | — | — | — | — | 46.64 | 45.70 | 100.08 | 107.25 | 115.74 | 113.44 | 101.48 |
| Central Bank: Other Assets | 3..d | — | — | † 19.29 | 21.00 | 19.80 | 20.51 | 19.77 | 19.64 | 18.80 | 19.75 | 17.31 | 15.47 |
| Central Bank: Other Liabs | 4..d | — | — | † .45 | .30 | .59 | .29 | .67 | .19 | .29 | .39 | .37 | .47 |
| Other Depository Corps: Assets | 7a.d | 1,318.73 | 1,259.60 | † 1,586.56 | 2,678.48 | 2,210.18 | 2,349.84 | 1,922.63 | 1,802.41 | 1,691.71 | 1,858.57 | 1,631.23 | 1,374.13 |
| Other Depository Corps: Liabs | 7b.d | 1,846.30 | 2,146.86 | † 2,488.38 | 3,626.04 | 4,268.71 | 3,967.20 | 3,003.07 | 2,499.77 | 2,400.56 | 2,346.63 | 1,838.54 | 1,451.84 |
| **Central Bank** | | | | | *Millions of Convertible Marka:  End of Period* | | | | | | | | |
| Net Foreign Assets | 11n | 3,507 | 4,252 | † 5,480 | 6,726 | 6,323 | 6,240 | 6,486 | 6,453 | 6,536 | 7,096 | 7,853 | 8,633 |
| Claims on Nonresidents | 11 | 3,507 | 4,252 | † 5,480 | 6,726 | 6,324 | 6,240 | 6,487 | 6,453 | 6,537 | 7,096 | 7,854 | 8,634 |
| Liabilities to Nonresidents | 16c | — | — | † 1 | — | 1 | — | 1 | — | — | 1 | 1 | 1 |
| Claims on Other Depository Corps | 12e | — | — | † 1 | 1 | 1 | 1 | 1 | 1 | 1 | 1 | 1 | 1 |
| Net Claims on Central Government | 12an | −45 | −38 | † −126 | −75 | −23 | −57 | −70 | −66 | −185 | −258 | −293 | −450 |
| Claims on Central Government | 12a | — | — | † — | — | — | — | — | — | — | — | — | — |
| Liabilities to Central Government | 16d | 45 | 38 | † 126 | 75 | 23 | 57 | 70 | 66 | 185 | 258 | 293 | 450 |
| Claims on Other Sectors | 12s | 1 | 2 | † 2 | 2 | 2 | 1 | 1 | 1 | 1 | 2 | 1 | 1 |
| Claims on Other Financial Corps | 12g | — | — | † — | — | — | — | — | — | — | — | — | — |
| Claims on State & Local Govts | 12b | — | — | † — | — | — | — | — | — | — | — | — | — |
| Claims on Public Nonfin. Corps | 12c | — | — | † — | — | — | — | — | — | — | — | — | — |
| Claims on Private Sector | 12d | 1 | 2 | † 2 | 2 | 2 | 1 | 1 | 1 | 1 | 2 | 1 | 1 |
| Monetary Base | 14 | 3,241 | 3,972 | † 5,057 | 6,229 | 5,704 | 5,649 | 5,900 | 5,849 | 5,802 | 6,401 | 7,000 | 7,615 |
| Currency in Circulation | 14a | 1,817 | 1,907 | † 2,154 | 2,440 | 2,552 | 2,268 | 2,498 | 2,645 | 2,748 | 2,910 | 3,211 | 3,499 |
| Liabs. to Other Depository Corps | 14c | 1,421 | 2,062 | † 2,892 | 3,777 | 3,144 | 3,375 | 3,394 | 3,193 | 3,041 | 3,475 | 3,751 | 4,064 |
| Liabilities to Other Sectors | 14d | 2 | 3 | † 10 | 12 | 7 | 6 | 9 | 11 | 14 | 16 | 38 | 52 |
| Other Liabs. to Other Dep. Corps | 14n | — | — | † — | — | — | — | — | — | — | — | — | — |
| Dep. & Sec. Excl. f/Monetary Base | 14o | — | — | † — | — | — | — | — | — | — | — | — | — |
| Deposits Included in Broad Money | 15 | — | — | † — | — | — | — | — | — | — | — | — | — |
| Sec.Ot.th.Shares Incl.in Brd. Money | 16a | — | — | † — | — | — | — | — | — | — | — | — | — |
| Deposits Excl. from Broad Money | 16b | — | — | † — | — | — | — | — | — | — | — | — | — |
| Sec.Ot.th.Shares Excl.f/Brd.Money | 16s | — | — | † — | — | — | — | — | — | — | — | — | — |
| Loans | 16l | — | — | † — | — | — | — | — | — | — | — | — | — |
| Financial Derivatives | 16m | — | — | † — | — | — | — | — | — | — | — | — | — |
| Shares and Other Equity | 17a | 227 | 245 | † 301 | 386 | 499 | 502 | 534 | 548 | 576 | 466 | 585 | 594 |
| Other Items (Net) | 17r | −3 | −1 | † −2 | 38 | 98 | 34 | −16 | −8 | −25 | −27 | −23 | −23 |
| Memo Item: | | | | | | | | | | | | | |
| Total Assets | 10ra | 3,538 | 4,281 | † 5,531 | 6,780 | 6,379 | 6,297 | 6,557 | 6,526 | 6,621 | 7,184 | 7,943 | 8,722 |
| **Other Depository Corporations** | | | | | *Millions of Convertible Marka:  End of Period* | | | | | | | | |
| Net Foreign Assets | 21n | −758 | −1,471 | † −1,339 | −1,259 | −2,893 | −2,196 | −1,581 | −1,054 | −1,051 | −693 | −334 | −140 |
| Claims on Nonresidents | 21 | 1,894 | 2,088 | † 2,356 | 3,559 | 3,106 | 3,190 | 2,814 | 2,724 | 2,508 | 2,637 | 2,626 | 2,473 |
| Liabilities to Nonresidents | 26c | 2,651 | 3,559 | † 3,695 | 4,818 | 5,999 | 5,386 | 4,396 | 3,779 | 3,559 | 3,330 | 2,960 | 2,613 |
| Claims on Central Bank | 20 | 1,567 | 2,234 | † 3,064 | 4,023 | 3,393 | 3,632 | 3,680 | 3,470 | 3,370 | 3,844 | 4,115 | 4,513 |
| Currency | 20a | 147 | 178 | † 176 | 254 | 250 | 258 | 287 | 279 | 333 | 368 | 397 | 446 |
| Reserve Deposits and Securities | 20b | 1,420 | 2,056 | † 2,888 | 3,768 | 3,143 | 3,373 | 3,393 | 3,191 | 3,034 | 3,476 | 3,718 | 4,067 |
| Other Claims | 20n | — | — | † — | 1 | 1 | — | — | — | 3 | — | — | — |
| Net Claims on Central Government | 22an | −506 | −617 | † −846 | −2,304 | −1,632 | −1,238 | −927 | −374 | 3 | 239 | 364 | 583 |
| Claims on Central Government | 22a | 21 | 19 | † 7 | 31 | 117 | 160 | 195 | 582 | 850 | 957 | 1,345 | 1,597 |
| Liabilities to Central Government | 26d | 527 | 635 | † 853 | 2,335 | 1,750 | 1,398 | 1,122 | 956 | 847 | 718 | 981 | 1,014 |
| Claims on Other Sectors | 22s | 5,906 | 7,526 | † 8,935 | 11,634 | 14,128 | 13,659 | 14,091 | 14,713 | 15,197 | 15,630 | 15,968 | 16,367 |
| Claims on Other Financial Corps | 22g | 60 | 68 | † 89 | 160 | 169 | 103 | 80 | 94 | 74 | 67 | 61 | 75 |
| Claims on State & Local Govts | 22b | 25 | 31 | † 62 | 96 | 148 | 196 | 271 | 323 | 386 | 422 | 509 | 536 |
| Claims on Public Nonfin. Corps | 22c | — | — | † 248 | 271 | 256 | 268 | 351 | 360 | 391 | 452 | 444 | 400 |
| Claims on Private Sector | 22d | 5,821 | 7,426 | † 8,535 | 11,107 | 13,554 | 13,092 | 13,388 | 13,936 | 14,346 | 14,688 | 14,954 | 15,357 |
| Liabilities to Central Bank | 26g | — | — | † 1 | — | — | — | — | — | — | — | — | 2 |
| Transf.Dep.Included in Broad Money | 24 | 2,175 | 2,773 | † 3,442 | 4,368 | 4,489 | 4,608 | 4,890 | 4,908 | 4,768 | 5,327 | 5,759 | 6,436 |
| Other Dep.Included in Broad Money | 25 | 2,877 | 3,468 | † 4,471 | 5,388 | 5,641 | 6,085 | 6,517 | 7,132 | 7,714 | 8,209 | 8,657 | 9,108 |
| Sec.Ot.th.Shares Incl.in Brd. Money | 26a | — | — | † — | — | — | — | — | — | — | — | — | — |
| Deposits Excl. from Broad Money | 26b | — | — | † — | — | — | — | — | — | — | — | — | — |
| Sec.Ot.th.Shares Excl.f/Brd.Money | 26s | — | — | † — | 5 | 18 | 14 | 9 | — | — | — | — | 8 |
| Loans | 26l | — | — | † 114 | 106 | 264 | 447 | 595 | 675 | 712 | 708 | 681 | 599 |
| Financial Derivatives | 26m | — | — | † — | — | — | — | — | — | — | — | — | — |
| Insurance Technical Reserves | 26r | — | — | † — | — | — | — | — | — | — | — | — | — |
| Shares and Other Equity | 27a | 1,472 | 1,712 | † 1,596 | 1,969 | 2,272 | 2,319 | 2,508 | 3,045 | 3,191 | 3,349 | 3,408 | 3,718 |
| Other Items (Net) | 27r | −314 | −282 | † 189 | 259 | 313 | 384 | 742 | 994 | 1,134 | 1,428 | 1,607 | 1,453 |
| Memo Item: | | | | | | | | | | | | | |
| Total Assets | 20ra | 9,912 | 12,415 | † 15,328 | 20,333 | 21,956 | 21,950 | 22,182 | 23,055 | 23,473 | 24,641 | 25,690 | 26,599 |

# Bosnia and Herzegovina   963

| | | 2004 | 2005 | 2006 | 2007 | 2008 | 2009 | 2010 | 2011 | 2012 | 2013 | 2014 | 2015 |
|---|---|---|---|---|---|---|---|---|---|---|---|---|---|
| **Depository Corporations** | | | | | *Millions of Convertible Marka: End of Period* | | | | | | | | |
| Net Foreign Assets............... | 31n | 2,749 | 2,781 | † 4,140 | 5,467 | 3,430 | 4,044 | 4,904 | 5,399 | 5,485 | 6,403 | 7,519 | 8,494 |
| Claims on Nonresidents............... | 31 | 5,400 | 6,341 | † 7,836 | 10,285 | 9,430 | 9,430 | 9,301 | 9,178 | 9,044 | 9,734 | 10,480 | 11,108 |
| Liabilities to Nonresidents............. | 36c | 2,651 | 3,559 | † 3,696 | 4,818 | 6,000 | 5,386 | 4,397 | 3,779 | 3,559 | 3,330 | 2,961 | 2,614 |
| Domestic Claims......................... | 32 | 5,357 | 6,873 | † 7,965 | 9,258 | 12,474 | 12,366 | 13,095 | 14,274 | 15,016 | 15,612 | 16,039 | 16,502 |
| Net Claims on Central Government | 32an | −550 | −654 | † −972 | −2,378 | −1,656 | −1,295 | −997 | −440 | −183 | −19 | 71 | 133 |
| Claims on Central Government.... | 32a | 21 | 19 | † 7 | 31 | 117 | 160 | 195 | 582 | 850 | 957 | 1,345 | 1,597 |
| Liabilities to Central Government. | 36d | 571 | 673 | † 979 | 2,410 | 1,773 | 1,455 | 1,192 | 1,022 | 1,033 | 976 | 1,274 | 1,464 |
| Claims on Other Sectors............... | 32s | 5,908 | 7,527 | † 8,937 | 11,636 | 14,130 | 13,660 | 14,092 | 14,714 | 15,198 | 15,632 | 15,968 | 16,368 |
| Claims on Other Financial Corps.. | 32g | 60 | 68 | † 89 | 160 | 169 | 103 | 80 | 94 | 74 | 67 | 61 | 75 |
| Claims on State & Local Govts..... | 32b | 25 | 31 | † 62 | 96 | 148 | 196 | 271 | 323 | 386 | 422 | 509 | 536 |
| Claims on Public Nonfin. Corps.... | 32c | — | — | † 248 | 271 | 256 | 268 | 351 | 360 | 391 | 452 | 444 | 400 |
| Claims on Private Sector............. | 32d | 5,823 | 7,428 | † 8,537 | 11,109 | 13,556 | 13,094 | 13,390 | 13,937 | 14,347 | 14,690 | 14,954 | 15,358 |
| Broad Money Liabilities.................... | 35l | 6,724 | 7,973 | † 9,902 | 11,953 | 12,439 | 12,709 | 13,627 | 14,417 | 14,910 | 16,094 | 17,269 | 18,650 |
| Currency Outside Depository Corps | 34a | 1,671 | 1,729 | † 1,978 | 2,185 | 2,302 | 2,009 | 2,211 | 2,366 | 2,414 | 2,542 | 2,814 | 3,054 |
| Transferable Deposits.................... | 34 | 2,177 | 2,776 | † 3,453 | 4,380 | 4,496 | 4,614 | 4,899 | 4,919 | 4,781 | 5,343 | 5,798 | 6,488 |
| Other Deposits............................. | 35 | 2,877 | 3,468 | † 4,471 | 5,388 | 5,641 | 6,085 | 6,517 | 7,132 | 7,714 | 8,209 | 8,657 | 9,108 |
| Securities Other than Shares.......... | 36a | — | — | † — | — | — | — | — | — | — | — | — | — |
| Deposits Excl. from Broad Money... | 36b | — | — | † — | — | — | — | — | — | — | — | — | — |
| Sec.Ot.th.Shares Excl.f/Brd.Money.... | 36s | — | — | † — | 5 | 18 | 14 | 9 | — | — | — | — | 8 |
| Loans............................................. | 36l | — | — | † 114 | 106 | 264 | 447 | 595 | 675 | 712 | 708 | 681 | 599 |
| Financial Derivatives...................... | 36m | — | — | † — | — | — | — | — | — | — | — | — | — |
| Insurance Technical Reserves.......... | 36r | — | — | † — | — | — | — | — | — | — | — | — | — |
| Shares and Other Equity.................. | 37a | 1,699 | 1,957 | † 1,897 | 2,355 | 2,771 | 2,822 | 3,042 | 3,593 | 3,767 | 3,815 | 3,994 | 4,311 |
| Other Items (Net)............................ | 37r | −316 | −277 | † 192 | 305 | 412 | 418 | 726 | 987 | 1,112 | 1,399 | 1,615 | 1,427 |
| Broad Money Liabs., Seasonally Adj. | 35l.b | 6,686 | 7,924 | † 9,839 | 11,878 | 12,359 | 12,627 | 13,536 | 14,322 | 14,811 | 15,986 | 17,145 | 18,518 |
| **Monetary Aggregates** | | | | | *Millions of Convertible Marka: End of Period* | | | | | | | | |
| Broad Money.............................. | 59m | .... | .... | 9,902 | 11,953 | 12,439 | 12,709 | 13,627 | 14,417 | 14,910 | 16,094 | 17,269 | 18,650 |
| o/w:Currency Issued by Cent.Govt | 59m.a | .... | .... | — | — | — | — | — | — | — | — | — | — |
| o/w: Dep.in Nonfin. Corporations. | 59m.b | .... | .... | — | — | — | — | — | — | — | — | — | — |
| o/w:Secs. Issued by Central Govt.. | 59m.c | .... | .... | — | — | — | — | — | — | — | — | — | — |
| Money (National Definitions) | | | | | | | | | | | | | |
| Reserve Money............................ | 19mb | 3,241 | 3,972 | 5,057 | 6,229 | 5,704 | 5,649 | 5,900 | 5,849 | 5,802 | 6,401 | 7,000 | 7,615 |
| M1.................................................. | 59ma | 3,535 | 4,103 | 4,740 | 5,732 | 5,691 | 5,546 | 5,900 | 6,185 | 6,143 | 6,696 | 7,310 | 8,181 |
| M2.................................................. | 59mb | 6,832 | 8,075 | 9,902 | 11,953 | 12,439 | 12,709 | 13,627 | 14,417 | 14,910 | 16,094 | 17,269 | 18,650 |
| **Interest Rates** | | | | | *Percent Per Annum* | | | | | | | | |
| Deposit Rate.................................. | 60l | 3.72 | 3.56 | 3.69 | 3.56 | 3.49 | 3.60 | 3.16 | 2.80 | 3.18 | 3.01 | 2.66 | 2.06 |
| Lending Rate.................................. | 60p | 10.28 | 9.61 | 8.01 | 7.17 | 6.98 | 7.93 | 7.89 | 7.43 | 7.33 | 7.04 | 6.64 | 5.79 |
| **Prices and Labor** | | | | | *Index Numbers (2010=100): Period Averages* | | | | | | | | |
| Share Prices (End of Month)............. | 62.ep | 215.9 | 266.0 | 338.9 | 430.3 | 140.5 | 120.9 | 100.0 | 101.4 | 105.2 | 104.7 | 97.3 | 94.9 |
| Share Prices FIRS (End of Month)..... | 62bep | 113.1 | 143.5 | 369.7 | 405.4 | 96.9 | 96.9 | 100.0 | 111.6 | 115.6 | 119.0 | 108.9 | .... |
| Consumer Prices............................. | 64 | .... | 84.9 | 90.1 | † 91.5 | 98.2 | 97.9 | 100.0 | 103.7 | 105.8 | 105.7 | 104.7 | 103.9 |
| | | | | | *Number in Thousands: Period Averages* | | | | | | | | |
| Labor Force.................................... | 67d | .... | .... | .... | .... | 1,229.9 | 1,198.9 | 1,207.1 | 1,223.0 | 1,231.5 | 1,133.0 | 1,120.0 | .... |
| Employment.................................. | 67e | .... | .... | .... | .... | 736.5 | 701.3 | 690.1 | 693.3 | 688.3 | 822.0 | 812.0 | .... |
| Unemployment.............................. | 67c | 315.9 | 337.5 | 355.2 | 526.2 | 493.4 | 497.6 | 517.0 | 529.7 | 543.2 | 552.5 | 549.6 | 541.8 |
| Unemployment Rate (%).................. | 67r | .... | .... | .... | .... | 40.1 | 41.5 | 42.9 | 43.3 | 44.1 | .... | .... | .... |
| **Intl. Transactions & Positions** | | | | | *Millions of Convertible Marka* | | | | | | | | |
| Exports............................................ | 70 | 3,013 | 3,783 | 5,164 | 5,937 | 6,714 | 5,510 | 7,097 | 8,218 | 7,858 | 8,380 | 8,684 | 8,987 |
| Imports, f.o.b.................................... | 71 | 9,423 | 11,181 | 11,389 | 13,898 | 16,287 | 12,324 | 13,611 | 15,514 | 15,253 | 15,170 | 16,199 | 15,852 |

## Balance of Payments

| | | 2004 | 2005 | 2006 | 2007 | 2008 | 2009 | 2010 | 2011 | 2012 | 2013 | 2014 | 2015 |
|---|---|---|---|---|---|---|---|---|---|---|---|---|---|
| | | | | | | *Millions of US Dollars* | | | | | | | |
| A. Current Account* | 109bx | −1,639.3 | −1,844.4 | −998.1 | † −1,450.1 | −2,643.8 | −1,135.3 | −1,030.7 | −1,767.4 | −1,485.7 | −963.3 | −1,384.2 | −898.8 |
| Goods, credit (exports) | 1a9cx | 2,086.7 | 2,555.3 | 3,381.4 | † 2,299.1 | 2,926.6 | 2,546.1 | 3,230.8 | 4,109.9 | 3,837.3 | 4,363.3 | 4,488.8 | 3,949.9 |
| Goods, debit (imports) | 1a9dx | 6,656.4 | 7,454.2 | 7,679.4 | † 8,454.3 | 10,803.2 | 7,984.4 | 8,253.2 | 9,858.4 | 9,088.6 | 9,337.2 | 9,981.8 | 8,173.4 |
| Balance on goods | 1a9bx | −4,569.7 | −4,898.9 | −4,298.0 | † −6,155.2 | −7,876.6 | −5,438.4 | −5,022.4 | −5,748.6 | −5,251.3 | −4,973.9 | −5,493.0 | −4,223.5 |
| Services, credit (exports) | 1b9cx | 863.5 | 989.0 | 1,139.7 | † 1,988.5 | 2,241.6 | 1,884.5 | 1,863.7 | 1,870.8 | 1,728.0 | 1,770.1 | 1,834.7 | 1,641.9 |
| Services, debit (imports) | 1b9dx | 432.2 | 435.6 | 466.7 | † 495.3 | 595.0 | 640.4 | 540.9 | 557.2 | 513.2 | 505.8 | 532.8 | 488.9 |
| Balance on Goods & Services | 1z9bx | −4,138.4 | −4,345.5 | −3,624.9 | † −4,662.0 | −6,229.9 | −4,194.3 | −3,699.6 | −4,435.0 | −4,036.5 | −3,709.6 | −4,191.0 | −3,070.4 |
| Primary income: credit | 1c9cx | 674.6 | 682.3 | 732.6 | † 1,091.9 | 1,244.1 | 897.8 | 596.7 | 665.3 | 572.0 | 573.7 | 627.9 | 503.1 |
| Primary income: debit | 1c9dx | 170.1 | 212.8 | 340.1 | † 623.2 | 534.2 | 218.2 | 317.1 | 515.7 | 437.6 | 337.6 | 511.3 | 348.7 |
| Balance on gds, serv. & prim. inc. | 1y9bx | −3,633.9 | −3,876.0 | −3,232.5 | † −4,193.3 | −5,519.9 | −3,514.7 | −3,420.1 | −4,285.4 | −3,902.1 | −3,473.5 | −4,074.4 | −2,916.0 |
| Secondary income: credit | 1d9ca | 2,204.2 | 2,171.9 | 2,399.1 | † 2,883.2 | 3,032.8 | 2,549.4 | 2,563.8 | 2,716.1 | 2,598.6 | 2,699.7 | 2,892.2 | 2,209.4 |
| Secondary income: debit | 1d9da | 209.6 | 140.3 | 164.7 | † 140.0 | 156.8 | 169.9 | 174.4 | 198.1 | 182.3 | 189.5 | 202.0 | 192.2 |
| B. Capital Account* | 209ba | 282.0 | 276.4 | 286.2 | † 291.9 | 288.8 | 249.2 | 263.7 | 253.7 | 220.3 | 229.5 | 299.1 | 210.0 |
| Capital account: credit | 209ca | 282.0 | 276.4 | 286.2 | † 291.9 | 288.8 | 249.2 | 263.7 | 253.7 | 220.3 | 229.5 | 299.1 | 210.0 |
| Capital account: debit | 209da | — | .... | .... | .... | .... | .... | .... | .... | .... | .... | .... | .... |
| Balance on current & capital acct. | 129bx | −1,357.4 | −1,568.0 | −711.9 | † −1,158.3 | −2,355.0 | −886.0 | −767.0 | −1,513.7 | −1,265.4 | −733.8 | −1,085.0 | −688.8 |
| C. Financial Account* | 309na | −1,388.9 | −1,827.9 | −1,299.5 | † −2,137.9 | −2,174.9 | −449.8 | −586.3 | −1,424.3 | −1,100.6 | −1,137.5 | −1,303.7 | −1,131.9 |
| Direct investment: assets | 3a9aa | 181.3 | 16.4 | 81.8 | † 64.6 | 39.4 | −93.5 | 81.2 | −4.8 | 59.6 | 81.7 | 6.2 | 40.2 |
| Equity & investment fund shares | 3aaaa | 99.1 | −.7 | 2.8 | † 22.1 | 11.6 | −2.1 | 46.3 | 13.8 | 9.1 | −12.6 | 3.7 | 13.1 |
| Debt instruments | 3abaa | 82.2 | 17.2 | 79.0 | † 42.5 | 27.8 | −91.4 | 34.8 | −18.7 | 50.5 | 94.3 | 2.5 | 27.1 |
| Direct investment: liabilities | 3a9la | 889.6 | 623.8 | 846.0 | † 1,842.0 | 1,004.9 | 138.5 | 443.8 | 471.6 | 392.0 | 336.8 | 496.8 | 267.3 |
| Equity & investment fund shares . | 3aala | 559.8 | 314.1 | 539.5 | † 1,698.5 | 588.5 | −202.0 | 148.8 | 343.5 | 162.2 | 248.7 | 232.0 | 193.9 |
| Debt instruments | 3abla | 329.8 | 309.8 | 306.4 | † 143.5 | 416.4 | 340.5 | 295.1 | 128.1 | 229.8 | 88.1 | 264.8 | 73.4 |
| Portfolio investment: assets | 3b9aa | 2.8 | −2.6 | .4 | † −4.8 | 13.0 | 192.8 | 86.0 | −5.8 | −30.8 | 50.5 | 20.1 | 15.4 |
| Equity & investment fund shares | 3baaa | .... | .... | .... | † −.9 | 1.2 | −1.4 | −1.2 | .2 | .4 | −1.2 | −.1 | .1 |
| Debt securities | 3bbaa | 2.8 | −2.6 | .4 | † −3.9 | 11.8 | 194.2 | 87.2 | −6.0 | −31.2 | 51.6 | 20.2 | 15.3 |
| Portfolio investment: liabilities | 3b9la | — | .... | .... | † −7.5 | −7.7 | −11.4 | −35.0 | −40.8 | −41.3 | −42.7 | −41.9 | −35.3 |
| Equity & investment fund shares . | 3bala | .... | .... | .... | .... | .... | .... | .... | .... | .... | .... | .... | .... |
| Debt securities | 3bbla | .... | .... | .... | † −7.5 | −7.7 | −11.4 | −35.0 | −40.8 | −41.3 | −42.7 | −41.9 | −35.3 |
| Fin. der.& empl.stk.ops.(ESOs): net. | 3c9na | — | .... | .... | .... | .... | .... | .... | .... | .... | .... | .... | −.2 |
| Fin. der. & ESOs.: assets | 3c9aa | — | .... | .... | .... | .... | .... | .... | .... | .... | .... | .... | −.2 |
| Fin. der. & ESOs.: liabilities | 3c9la | .... | .... | .... | .... | .... | .... | .... | .... | .... | .... | .... | .... |
| Other investment: assets | 3d9aa | −296.4 | −305.1 | −21.1 | † 1,077.7 | 490.5 | 120.3 | −509.4 | −399.8 | −237.2 | −128.7 | −381.0 | −366.4 |
| Other equity | 3daaa | .... | .... | .... | .... | .... | .... | .... | .... | .... | .... | .... | .... |
| Debt instruments | 3dzaa | −296.4 | −305.1 | −21.1 | † 1,077.7 | 490.5 | 120.3 | −509.4 | −399.8 | −237.2 | −128.7 | −381.0 | −366.4 |
| Other investment: liabilities | 3d9la | 387.0 | 912.9 | 514.7 | † 1,441.0 | 1,720.7 | 542.3 | −164.8 | 583.0 | 541.4 | 846.8 | 494.1 | 588.9 |
| Other equity | 3dala | .... | .... | .... | † −12.4 | 4.1 | .6 | 2.6 | −7.3 | 1.2 | .5 | −9.1 | −4.0 |
| Debt instruments | 3dzla | 387.0 | 912.9 | 514.7 | † 1,453.4 | 1,716.6 | 541.7 | −167.4 | 590.3 | 540.3 | 846.3 | 503.2 | 593.0 |
| Curr.+ cap.− finan. acct. balance | 4y9na | 31.6 | 259.9 | 587.6 | † 979.7 | −180.2 | −436.2 | −180.7 | −89.3 | −164.9 | 403.6 | 218.6 | 443.1 |
| D. Net Errors and Omissions | 409na | 427.6 | 231.5 | 173.1 | † −87.3 | −120.2 | 99.1 | 120.4 | 65.2 | 82.5 | 120.8 | 158.4 | 106.7 |
| E. Reserves and Related Items | 4z9na | 459.2 | 491.4 | 760.8 | † 892.4 | −300.4 | −337.1 | −60.3 | −24.1 | −82.3 | 524.4 | 377.0 | 549.8 |
| Reserve assets | 3e9aa | 433.0 | 461.4 | 789.6 | † 874.1 | −302.8 | −53.7 | 178.7 | −24.1 | 38.6 | 482.9 | 479.2 | 496.3 |
| Credit and loans from the IMF | 3dcla | −29.7 | −39.4 | −44.1 | † −18.3 | −2.4 | 283.4 | 239.1 | — | 120.9 | −41.5 | 102.2 | −53.6 |
| Exceptional financing | 409la | 3.5 | 9.3 | 72.9 | .... | .... | .... | .... | .... | .... | .... | .... | .... |

*Excludes components in group E

## International Investment Position

| | | 2004 | 2005 | 2006 | 2007 | 2008 | 2009 | 2010 | 2011 | 2012 | 2013 | 2014 | 2015 |
|---|---|---|---|---|---|---|---|---|---|---|---|---|---|
| | | | | | | *Millions of US Dollars* | | | | | | | |
| Assets | 809aa | 4,509.8 | † 4,666.8 | 6,487.8 | 9,397.7 | 8,827.0 | 8,928.3 | 8,132.3 | 7,716.5 | 7,912.0 | 9,057.5 | 8,341.7 | .... |
| Direct investment | 8a9aa | 60.9 | † 69.0 | 165.3 | 256.4 | 283.8 | 196.0 | 292.8 | 275.9 | 353.8 | 448.9 | 400.3 | .... |
| Equity & investment fund shares.. | 8aaaa | 53.1 | † 45.2 | 53.4 | 83.2 | 89.6 | 91.4 | 159.6 | 165.8 | 177.4 | 167.0 | 150.2 | .... |
| Debt instruments | 8abaa | 7.8 | † 23.8 | 111.9 | 173.2 | 194.2 | 104.7 | 133.2 | 110.2 | 176.3 | 281.8 | 250.1 | .... |
| Portfolio investment | 8b9aa | 11.2 | † 9.2 | 19.4 | 12.2 | 29.0 | 232.1 | 308.1 | 286.8 | 315.4 | 375.8 | 362.1 | .... |
| Equity & investment fund shares.. | 8baaa | 2.5 | † .9 | 3.7 | 3.5 | 9.3 | 10.0 | 10.6 | 13.0 | 15.0 | 16.1 | 17.7 | .... |
| Debt securities | 8bbaa | 8.7 | † 8.3 | 15.7 | 8.7 | 19.7 | 222.1 | 297.5 | 273.8 | 300.5 | 359.8 | 344.4 | .... |
| Fin. der.(oth.than reserves) & ESOs | 8c9aa | .... | .... | .... | .... | .... | .... | .... | .... | .... | .... | .... | .... |
| Other investment | 8d9aa | 1,973.6 | † 2,023.8 | 2,613.3 | 4,066.3 | 4,014.6 | 3,904.0 | 3,100.6 | 2,885.8 | 2,833.3 | 3,229.1 | 2,704.1 | .... |
| Other equity | 8daaa | .... | † .9 | 2.7 | 3.0 | 3.3 | 2.4 | 2.3 | 2.8 | .8 | 13.9 | 13.1 | .... |
| Debt instruments | 8dzaa | 1,973.6 | † 2,022.9 | 2,610.6 | 4,063.2 | 4,011.3 | 3,901.6 | 3,098.2 | 2,883.0 | 2,832.5 | 3,215.2 | 2,691.0 | .... |
| Reserve assets | 8e9aa | 2,464.2 | † 2,564.9 | 3,689.7 | 5,062.7 | 4,499.6 | 4,596.2 | 4,430.9 | 4,268.0 | 4,409.5 | 5,003.7 | 4,875.1 | .... |
| Liabilities | 809la | 7,991.1 | † 8,183.2 | 10,336.9 | 15,151.4 | 17,096.2 | 19,037.3 | 17,929.2 | 17,899.6 | 18,713.9 | 19,979.9 | 18,105.0 | .... |
| Direct investment | 8a9la | 2,289.2 | † 2,319.8 | 3,307.0 | 5,555.0 | 6,274.0 | 7,006.7 | 6,806.7 | 7,200.2 | 7,647.3 | 8,344.3 | 7,323.1 | .... |
| Equity & investment fund shares.. | 8aala | 1,976.7 | † 1,988.2 | 2,839.9 | 4,880.7 | 5,187.2 | 5,500.3 | 5,105.7 | 5,216.8 | 5,411.5 | 5,972.5 | 4,988.5 | .... |
| Debt instruments | 8abla | 312.5 | † 331.6 | 467.1 | 674.3 | 1,086.8 | 1,506.4 | 1,701.0 | 1,983.4 | 2,235.8 | 2,371.8 | 2,334.6 | .... |
| Portfolio investment | 8b9la | 41.1 | † 154.8 | 169.4 | 183.8 | 235.8 | 553.8 | 478.1 | 424.9 | 391.1 | 294.1 | 220.6 | .... |
| Equity & investment fund shares.. | 8bala | 41.1 | .... | — | 2.1 | .... | .... | .... | .... | .... | .... | .... | .... |
| Debt securities | 8bbla | — | † 154.8 | 169.3 | 181.7 | 235.8 | 553.8 | 478.1 | 424.9 | 391.1 | 294.1 | 220.6 | .... |
| Fin. der.(oth.than reserves) & ESOs | 8c9la | .... | .... | .... | .... | .... | .... | .... | .... | .... | .... | .... | .... |
| Other investment | 8d9la | 5,660.7 | † 5,708.5 | 6,860.5 | 9,412.5 | 10,586.4 | 11,476.8 | 10,644.4 | 10,274.5 | 10,675.6 | 11,341.4 | 10,561.3 | .... |
| Other equity | 8dala | .... | † 47.9 | 73.2 | 92.7 | 98.8 | 105.9 | 98.8 | 88.2 | 84.7 | 84.6 | 69.5 | .... |
| Debt instruments | 8dzla | 5,660.7 | † 5,660.6 | 6,787.3 | 9,319.8 | 10,487.6 | 11,370.9 | 10,545.6 | 10,186.3 | 10,590.9 | 11,256.7 | 10,491.7 | .... |

| | | 2004 | 2005 | 2006 | 2007 | 2008 | 2009 | 2010 | 2011 | 2012 | 2013 | 2014 | 2015 |
|---|---|---|---|---|---|---|---|---|---|---|---|---|---|
| **Government Finance Operations Statement Central Government** | | *Millions of Convertible Marka: Fiscal Year Ends December 31* | | | | | | | | | | | |
| Revenue........................... | a1 | 5,667.9 | 6,168.8 | 7,632.5 | † 8,525.4 | 9,459.5 | 9,177.2 | 9,551.7 | 9,944.2 | 10,085.7 | 10,048.6 | 10,595.9 | . . . . |
| Taxes........................... | a11 | 3,004.2 | 3,407.6 | 4,282.7 | † 4,732.9 | 5,073.8 | 4,610.3 | 4,898.7 | 5,147.2 | 5,209.4 | 5,127.2 | 5,255.1 | . . . . |
| Social Contributions...................... | a12 | 2,002.3 | 2,099.8 | 2,536.5 | † 2,908.6 | 3,568.5 | 3,638.4 | 3,812.9 | 4,036.4 | 4,046.6 | 4,105.2 | 4,234.8 | . . . . |
| Grants........................... | a13 | 39.3 | 51.4 | 28.3 | † 32.0 | 29.4 | 84.3 | 41.4 | 58.2 | 45.9 | 55.6 | 70.3 | . . . . |
| Other Revenue........................... | a14 | 622.0 | 610.0 | 784.9 | † 852.0 | 787.7 | 844.3 | 798.8 | 702.5 | 783.7 | 760.6 | 1,035.6 | . . . . |
| Expense........................... | a2 | 5,285.7 | 5,656.1 | 6,827.5 | † 8,021.3 | 9,518.9 | 9,807.9 | 9,776.0 | 9,889.3 | 10,086.9 | 9,884.4 | 10,277.7 | . . . . |
| Compensation of Employees........... | a21 | 1,572.6 | 1,605.0 | 1,962.3 | † 2,234.4 | 2,575.7 | 2,781.1 | 2,712.9 | 2,831.2 | 2,836.2 | 2,780.0 | 2,851.4 | . . . . |
| Use of Goods & Services................ | a22 | 1,223.5 | 1,312.0 | 1,733.8 | † 1,877.8 | 2,024.0 | 2,197.9 | 2,198.8 | 1,709.6 | 1,715.7 | 1,726.4 | 1,727.8 | . . . . |
| Consumption of Fixed Capital........ | a23 | . . . . | . . . . | . . . . | . . . . | . . . . | . . . . | . . . . | . . . . | . . . . | . . . . | . . . . | . . . . |
| Interest........................... | a24 | 82.8 | 92.6 | 104.7 | † 105.1 | 113.9 | 110.9 | 105.5 | 140.9 | 174.8 | 169.6 | 201.1 | . . . . |
| Subsidies........................... | a25 | 168.3 | 196.8 | 287.5 | † 345.8 | 387.9 | 379.2 | 436.1 | 361.9 | 368.6 | 343.6 | 320.7 | . . . . |
| Grants........................... | a26 | 100.9 | 30.8 | 117.1 | † 243.3 | 247.4 | 230.0 | 185.6 | 1,257.0 | 211.2 | 203.6 | 147.5 | . . . . |
| Social Benefits........................... | a27 | 1,888.5 | 2,200.1 | 2,363.7 | † 2,928.9 | 3,773.3 | 3,818.1 | 3,641.2 | 3,208.4 | 4,306.2 | 4,316.1 | 4,528.6 | . . . . |
| Other Expense........................... | a28 | 249.1 | 218.9 | 258.3 | † 285.9 | 396.7 | 337.7 | 496.0 | 380.3 | 474.1 | 345.1 | 500.6 | . . . . |
| Gross Operating Balance [1-2+23]... | agob | 382.2 | 512.7 | 805.0 | † 504.2 | −59.4 | −630.8 | −316.1 | 55.0 | −1.2 | 164.1 | 318.2 | . . . . |
| Net Operating Balance [1-2]........... | anob | . . . . | . . . . | . . . . | . . . . | . . . . | . . . . | . . . . | . . . . | . . . . | . . . . | . . . . | . . . . |
| Net Acq. of Nonfinancial Assets....... | a31 | 138.0 | 160.3 | 251.6 | † 294.0 | 378.1 | 310.4 | 308.7 | 225.7 | 189.9 | 194.2 | 362.7 | . . . . |
| Aquisition of Nonfin. Assets........... | a31.1 | . . . . | . . . . | . . . . | † 340.7 | 383.3 | 292.1 | 328.7 | 227.3 | 199.7 | 198.2 | 372.1 | . . . . |
| Disposal of Nonfin. Assets............. | a31.2 | . . . . | . . . . | . . . . | † 46.7 | 5.2 | 14.9 | 20.0 | 1.6 | 9.8 | 3.9 | 9.4 | . . . . |
| Net Lending/Borrowing [1-2-31]...... | anlb | 244.2 | 352.4 | 553.4 | † 210.1 | −437.5 | −941.2 | −533.0 | −170.7 | −191.1 | −30.1 | −44.4 | . . . . |
| Net Acq. of Financial Assets............ | a32 | 395.5 | 434.7 | 478.6 | . . . . | . . . . | . . . . | . . . . | . . . . | . . . . | . . . . | . . . . | . . . . |
| Domestic........................... | a321 | 395.5 | 425.2 | 478.6 | . . . . | . . . . | . . . . | . . . . | . . . . | . . . . | . . . . | . . . . | . . . . |
| Foreign........................... | a322 | — | 9.4 | — | . . . . | . . . . | . . . . | . . . . | . . . . | . . . . | . . . . | . . . . | . . . . |
| Net Incurrence of Liabilities.............. | a33 | 151.3 | 82.3 | −74.8 | . . . . | . . . . | . . . . | . . . . | . . . . | . . . . | . . . . | . . . . | . . . . |
| Domestic........................... | a331 | 15.0 | −11.9 | −87.0 | . . . . | . . . . | . . . . | . . . . | . . . . | . . . . | . . . . | . . . . | . . . . |
| Foreign........................... | a332 | 136.3 | 94.2 | 12.3 | . . . . | . . . . | . . . . | . . . . | . . . . | . . . . | . . . . | . . . . | . . . . |
| Stat. Discrepancy [32-33-NLB]........ | anlbz | — | — | — | . . . . | . . . . | . . . . | . . . . | . . . . | . . . . | . . . . | . . . . | . . . . |
| Memo Item: Expenditure [2+31]....... | a2m | 7,240.5 | 7,773.8 | 9,594.8 | † 8,315.3 | 9,897.0 | 10,118.3 | 10,084.7 | 10,115.0 | 10,276.8 | 10,078.7 | 10,640.4 | . . . . |
| **National Accounts** | | *Millions of Convertible Marka* | | | | | | | | | | | |
| Househ.Cons.Expend.,incl.NPISHs.... | 96f | 15,139 | 16,684 | 18,241 | 19,322 | 21,752 | 20,927 | 21,294 | 21,927 | 22,337 | 22,515 | 22,886 | . . . . |
| Government Consumption Expend... | 91f | 3,535 | 3,814 | 4,188 | 4,697 | 5,570 | 5,734 | 5,780 | 5,975 | 6,016 | 5,978 | 6,078 | . . . . |
| Gross Fixed Capital Formation.......... | 93e | 4,044 | 4,789 | 4,532 | 5,035 | 6,052 | 4,810 | 4,299 | 4,750 | 4,783 | 4,714 | 5,159 | . . . . |
| Changes in Inventories.................... | 93i | 476 | 13 | −193 | 684 | 746 | −15 | −267 | 58 | 149 | 56 | −140 | . . . . |
| Exports of Goods and Services......... | 90c | 4,641 | 5,583 | 7,024 | 6,111 | 6,851 | 6,202 | 7,532 | 8,403 | 8,434 | 8,991 | 9,257 | . . . . |
| Imports of Goods and Services (-).... | 98c | 11,156 | 12,644 | 12,640 | 12,728 | 15,137 | 12,086 | 13,005 | 14,637 | 14,635 | 14,501 | 15,536 | . . . . |
| Gross Domestic Product (GDP)......... | 99b | 16,680 | 18,240 | 21,152 | 23,483 | 26,256 | 26,005 | 26,075 | 26,931 | 27,564 | 28,189 | 28,198 | . . . . |
| | | *Millions: Midyear Estimates* | | | | | | | | | | | |
| **Population................................** | 99z | 3.83 | 3.83 | 3.84 | 3.84 | 3.84 | 3.84 | 3.84 | 3.83 | 3.83 | 3.82 | 3.82 | 3.81 |

# Botswana 616

| | | 2004 | 2005 | 2006 | 2007 | 2008 | 2009 | 2010 | 2011 | 2012 | 2013 | 2014 | 2015 |
|---|---|---|---|---|---|---|---|---|---|---|---|---|---|
| **Exchange Rates** | | | | | | *Pula per SDR: End of Period* | | | | | | | |
| Official Rate | aa | 6.648 | 7.879 | 9.074 | 9.491 | 11.581 | 10.461 | 9.920 | 11.554 | 11.949 | 13.431 | 13.785 | 15.569 |
| | | | | | | *Pula per US Dollar: End of Period (ae) Period Average (rf)* | | | | | | | |
| Official Rate | ae | 4.2808 | 5.5127 | 6.0314 | 6.0060 | 7.5191 | 6.6730 | 6.4412 | 7.5260 | 7.7747 | 8.7212 | 9.5146 | 11.2351 |
| Official Rate | rf | 4.6929 | 5.1104 | 5.8366 | 6.1388 | 6.8269 | 7.1551 | 6.7936 | 6.8382 | 7.6191 | 8.3989 | 8.9761 | 10.1263 |
| **Fund Position** | | | | | | *Millions of SDRs: End of Period* | | | | | | | |
| Quota | 2f.s | 63.00 | 63.00 | 63.00 | 63.00 | 63.00 | 63.00 | 63.00 | 87.80 | 87.80 | 87.80 | 87.80 | 87.80 |
| SDR Holdings | 1b.s | 34.42 | 35.58 | 36.91 | 38.44 | 39.56 | 92.86 | 92.98 | 87.00 | 85.58 | 85.68 | 85.74 | 85.76 |
| Reserve Position in the Fund | 1c.s | 20.50 | 7.41 | 6.25 | 4.43 | 8.48 | 11.35 | 13.55 | 27.28 | 28.08 | 31.28 | 31.28 | 27.28 |
| Total Fund Cred.&Loans Outstg | 2tl | — | — | — | — | — | — | — | — | — | — | — | — |
| SDR Allocations | 1bd | 4.36 | 4.36 | 4.36 | 4.36 | 4.36 | 57.43 | 57.43 | 57.43 | 57.43 | 57.43 | 57.43 | 57.43 |
| **International Liquidity** | | | | | | *Millions of US Dollars Unless Otherwise Indicated: End of Period* | | | | | | | |
| Total Reserves minus Gold | 1l.d | 5,661.43 | 6,309.06 | 7,992.39 | 9,789.74 | 9,118.64 | 8,703.96 | 7,885.21 | 8,081.89 | 7,627.97 | 7,726.05 | 8,322.78 | 7,546.14 |
| SDR Holdings | 1b.d | 53.46 | 50.85 | 55.53 | 60.74 | 60.93 | 145.57 | 143.19 | 133.57 | 131.52 | 131.95 | 124.21 | 118.84 |
| Reserve Position in the Fund | 1c.d | 31.84 | 10.59 | 9.40 | 6.99 | 13.06 | 17.79 | 20.86 | 41.88 | 43.15 | 48.16 | 45.31 | 37.80 |
| Foreign Exchange | 1d.d | 5,576.13 | 6,247.62 | 7,927.47 | 9,722.01 | 9,044.66 | 8,540.60 | 7,721.16 | 7,906.44 | 7,453.30 | 7,545.94 | 8,153.25 | 7,389.50 |
| Central Bank: Other Assets | 3..d | .71 | .56 | 2.30 | 3.40 | .47 | — | — | — | — | — | — | — |
| Central Bank: Other Liabs. | 4..d | 25.21 | 22.18 | 22.00 | 21.56 | 17.28 | 70.08 | 96.49 | 163.21 | 83.94 | 75.02 | 68.46 | 54.32 |
| Other Depository Corps.: Assets | 7a.d | 415.56 | 542.92 | 474.71 | 624.59 | 805.79 | 578.57 | 906.39 | 733.95 | 915.19 | 779.46 | 824.65 | 878.91 |
| Other Depository Corps.: Liabs. | 7b.d | 119.39 | 265.15 | 293.56 | 262.08 | 218.43 | 204.96 | 446.04 | 108.06 | 169.36 | 134.56 | 235.70 | 194.55 |
| **Central Bank** | | | | | | *Millions of Pula: End of Period* | | | | | | | |
| Net Foreign Assets | 11n | 23,972 | 34,338 | 47,680 | 58,368 | 68,364 | 56,781 | 49,585 | 58,899 | 57,884 | 66,317 | 77,651 | 83,353 |
| Claims on Nonresidents | 11 | 24,109 | 34,494 | 47,852 | 58,538 | 68,544 | 57,847 | 50,776 | 60,791 | 59,223 | 67,743 | 79,094 | 84,858 |
| Liabilities to Nonresidents | 16c | 137 | 157 | 172 | 171 | 180 | 1,067 | 1,191 | 1,892 | 1,339 | 1,426 | 1,442 | 1,504 |
| Claims on Other Depository Corps. | 12e | 12 | — | — | — | — | 3 | — | 36 | — | 302 | — | — |
| Net Claims on Central Government | 12an | −9,541 | −13,223 | −21,236 | −27,871 | −31,768 | −23,252 | −14,882 | −24,075 | −22,279 | −28,531 | −38,927 | −37,130 |
| Claims on Central Government | 12a | 108 | 88 | 88 | 89 | 41 | 45 | 44 | 24 | 24 | 25 | 24 | 24 |
| Liabilities to Central Government | 16d | 9,649 | 13,312 | 21,325 | 27,960 | 31,809 | 23,297 | 14,926 | 24,099 | 22,303 | 28,556 | 38,951 | 37,154 |
| Claims on Other Sectors | 12s | 39 | 45 | 57 | 63 | 73 | 80 | 79 | 71 | 63 | 53 | 50 | 53 |
| Claims on Other Financial Corps. | 12g | — | — | — | — | — | — | — | — | — | — | — | — |
| Claims on State & Local Govts. | 12b | — | — | — | — | — | — | — | — | — | — | — | — |
| Claims on Public Nonfin. Corps. | 12c | — | — | — | — | — | — | — | — | — | — | — | — |
| Claims on Private Sector | 12d | 39 | 45 | 57 | 63 | 73 | 80 | 79 | 71 | 63 | 53 | 50 | 53 |
| Monetary Base | 14 | 5,070 | 6,104 | 16,131 | 19,140 | 20,827 | 20,751 | 23,293 | 16,015 | 15,257 | 12,900 | 11,801 | 13,996 |
| Currency in Circulation | 14a | 911 | 935 | 1,070 | 1,361 | 1,594 | 1,659 | 1,916 | 2,089 | 2,275 | 2,382 | 2,599 | 2,708 |
| Liabs. to Other Depository Corps. | 14c | 3,555 | 5,003 | 15,045 | 17,685 | 19,038 | 18,694 | 19,983 | 13,717 | 12,832 | 9,858 | 8,662 | 11,209 |
| Liabilities to Other Sectors | 14d | 603 | 166 | 17 | 94 | 194 | 398 | 1,394 | 209 | 150 | 660 | 540 | 79 |
| Other Liabs. to Other Dep. Corps. | 14n | — | — | — | — | — | — | — | 1,497 | 999 | — | 304 | 1,673 |
| Dep. & Sec. Excl. f/Monetary Base | 14o | 6,447 | 7,873 | — | — | — | — | — | — | — | — | — | — |
| Deposits Included in Broad Money | 15 | — | — | — | — | — | — | — | — | — | — | — | — |
| Sec.Ot.th.Shares Incl.in Brd. Money | 16a | 6,447 | 7,873 | — | — | — | — | — | — | — | — | — | — |
| Deposits Excl. from Broad Money | 16b | — | — | — | — | — | — | — | — | — | — | — | — |
| Sec.Ot.th.Shares Excl.f/Brd.Money | 16s | — | — | — | — | — | — | — | — | — | — | — | — |
| Loans | 16l | — | — | — | — | — | — | — | — | — | — | — | — |
| Financial Derivatives | 16m | — | — | — | — | — | — | — | — | — | — | — | — |
| Shares and Other Equity | 17a | 3,026 | 7,168 | 10,317 | 11,128 | 15,629 | 12,615 | 11,358 | 17,450 | 19,521 | 25,244 | 26,569 | 30,504 |
| Other Items (Net) | 17r | −61 | 13 | 52 | 291 | 214 | 245 | 131 | −30 | −109 | −3 | 99 | 102 |
| Memo Item: | | | | | | | | | | | | | |
| Total Assets | 10ra | 24,493 | 34,879 | 48,282 | 58,844 | 68,892 | 58,213 | 51,206 | 61,287 | 59,839 | 68,599 | 79,690 | 85,431 |
| **Other Depository Corporations** | | | | | | *Millions of Pula: End of Period* | | | | | | | |
| Net Foreign Assets | 21n | 1,268 | 1,531 | 1,093 | 2,177 | 4,416 | 2,489 | 2,965 | 4,710 | 5,799 | 5,624 | 5,601 | 7,692 |
| Claims on Nonresidents | 21 | 1,779 | 2,993 | 2,863 | 3,751 | 6,059 | 3,855 | 5,838 | 5,524 | 7,115 | 6,798 | 7,842 | 9,879 |
| Liabilities to Nonresidents | 26c | 511 | 1,462 | 1,771 | 1,574 | 1,642 | 1,365 | 2,873 | 813 | 1,317 | 1,174 | 2,241 | 2,187 |
| Claims on Central Bank | 20 | 3,964 | 5,723 | 15,560 | 18,510 | 17,910 | 18,748 | 20,254 | 14,687 | 13,503 | 10,873 | 9,737 | 13,956 |
| Currency | 20a | 278 | 310 | 317 | 453 | 491 | 514 | 674 | 659 | 717 | 797 | 916 | 1,020 |
| Reserve Deposits and Securities | 20b | 542 | 445 | 1,027 | 1,256 | 1,462 | 1,772 | 2,578 | 3,985 | 4,130 | 4,377 | 4,421 | 2,983 |
| Other Claims | 20n | 3,144 | 4,968 | 14,216 | 16,801 | 15,957 | 16,462 | 17,002 | 10,043 | 8,656 | 5,699 | 4,400 | 9,953 |
| Net Claims on Central Government | 22an | 31 | 62 | 12 | 38 | 2,038 | 848 | 302 | 1,349 | 1,208 | 1,644 | 1,765 | 1,578 |
| Claims on Central Government | 22a | 464 | 228 | 196 | 183 | 2,568 | 1,245 | 614 | 1,596 | 1,342 | 1,819 | 1,959 | 1,889 |
| Liabilities to Central Government | 26d | 433 | 165 | 184 | 145 | 530 | 397 | 312 | 247 | 134 | 175 | 194 | 311 |
| Claims on Other Sectors | 22s | 9,624 | 10,339 | 12,350 | 15,387 | 19,423 | 21,506 | 23,941 | 31,036 | 37,495 | 43,027 | 49,214 | 53,633 |
| Claims on Other Financial Corps. | 22g | 70 | 91 | 39 | 61 | 126 | 29 | 11 | 1,306 | 1,338 | 1,726 | 2,274 | 3,091 |
| Claims on State & Local Govts. | 22b | — | — | — | 1 | 9 | 20 | 8 | 24 | 13 | 10 | 12 | 8 |
| Claims on Public Nonfin. Corps. | 22c | 372 | 262 | 261 | 167 | 93 | 283 | 378 | 997 | 1,237 | 1,554 | 1,731 | 1,255 |
| Claims on Private Sector | 22d | 9,182 | 9,986 | 12,051 | 15,157 | 19,195 | 21,174 | 23,543 | 28,710 | 34,908 | 39,737 | 45,196 | 49,279 |
| Liabilities to Central Bank | 26g | 4 | 105 | 50 | 126 | 21 | 49 | — | — | 20 | 142 | 12 | 2 |
| Transf.Dep.Included in Broad Money | 24 | 2,989 | 3,206 | 4,387 | 5,236 | 6,471 | 5,564 | 6,629 | 7,035 | 8,847 | 10,268 | 10,984 | 11,970 |
| Other Dep.Included in Broad Money | 25 | 9,037 | 10,676 | 19,411 | 26,058 | 31,459 | 31,609 | 33,596 | 36,088 | 38,682 | 40,876 | 42,635 | 53,204 |
| Sec.Ot.th.Shares Incl.in Brd. Money | 26a | — | — | — | — | — | — | — | — | — | — | — | — |
| Deposits Excl. from Broad Money | 26b | — | — | — | — | — | — | — | — | — | — | — | — |
| Sec.Ot.th.Shares Excl.f/Brd.Money | 26s | — | — | — | — | — | — | — | 1,603 | 2,000 | 2,191 | 2,488 | 2,936 |
| Loans | 26l | 605 | 633 | 1,061 | 1,273 | 1,488 | 1,467 | 1,484 | 204 | 781 | 657 | 661 | 1,163 |
| Financial Derivatives | 26m | — | — | — | — | — | — | — | 51 | 45 | 75 | 79 | 236 |
| Insurance Technical Reserves | 26r | — | — | — | — | — | — | — | — | — | — | — | — |
| Shares and Other Equity | 27a | 1,922 | 2,137 | 2,651 | 3,300 | 4,126 | 4,912 | 5,948 | 6,481 | 7,603 | 8,453 | 9,388 | 9,588 |
| Other Items (Net) | 27r | 330 | 897 | 1,456 | 118 | 222 | −10 | −195 | 319 | 27 | −1,495 | 69 | −2,240 |
| Memo Item: | | | | | | | | | | | | | |
| Total Assets | 20ra | 16,784 | 20,067 | 32,152 | 39,445 | 48,029 | 47,164 | 52,833 | 55,636 | 63,407 | 68,338 | 76,069 | 88,587 |

# Botswana 616

| | | 2004 | 2005 | 2006 | 2007 | 2008 | 2009 | 2010 | 2011 | 2012 | 2013 | 2014 | 2015 |
|---|---|---|---|---|---|---|---|---|---|---|---|---|---|
| **Depository Corporations** | | | | | | *Millions of Pula: End of Period* | | | | | | | |
| Net Foreign Assets.......................... | 31n | 25,240 | 35,869 | 48,773 | 60,545 | 72,780 | 59,270 | 52,550 | 63,610 | 63,682 | 71,941 | 83,252 | 91,045 |
| Claims on Nonresidents................ | 31 | 25,888 | 37,487 | 50,715 | 62,290 | 74,603 | 61,702 | 56,615 | 66,315 | 66,338 | 74,540 | 86,936 | 94,737 |
| Liabilities to Nonresidents............. | 36c | 648 | 1,618 | 1,943 | 1,745 | 1,823 | 2,432 | 4,064 | 2,705 | 2,656 | 2,599 | 3,684 | 3,691 |
| Domestic Claims........................... | 32 | 152 | −2,777 | −8,817 | −12,383 | −10,233 | −818 | 9,440 | 8,381 | 16,488 | 16,192 | 12,101 | 18,133 |
| Net Claims on Central Government | 32an | −9,510 | −13,161 | −21,224 | −27,833 | −29,730 | −22,404 | −14,580 | −22,726 | −21,071 | −26,887 | −37,162 | −35,552 |
| Claims on Central Government..... | 32a | 572 | 316 | 284 | 272 | 2,609 | 1,290 | 658 | 1,620 | 1,366 | 1,844 | 1,983 | 1,913 |
| Liabilities to Central Government. | 36d | 10,082 | 13,477 | 21,508 | 28,105 | 32,338 | 23,694 | 15,238 | 24,346 | 22,437 | 28,731 | 39,145 | 37,465 |
| Claims on Other Sectors................. | 32s | 9,662 | 10,384 | 12,407 | 15,449 | 19,496 | 21,585 | 24,020 | 31,107 | 37,558 | 43,079 | 49,263 | 53,685 |
| Claims on Other Financial Corps.. | 32g | 70 | 91 | 39 | 61 | 126 | 29 | 11 | 1,306 | 1,338 | 1,726 | 2,274 | 3,091 |
| Claims on State & Local Govts..... | 32b | — | — | — | 1 | 9 | 20 | 8 | 24 | 13 | 10 | 12 | 8 |
| Claims on Public Nonfin. Corps.... | 32c | 372 | 262 | 261 | 167 | 93 | 283 | 378 | 997 | 1,237 | 1,554 | 1,731 | 1,255 |
| Claims on Private Sector............. | 32d | 9,221 | 10,030 | 12,108 | 15,220 | 19,268 | 21,254 | 23,622 | 28,781 | 34,971 | 39,789 | 45,246 | 49,331 |
| Broad Money Liabilities.................. | 35l | 19,708 | 22,547 | 24,568 | 32,297 | 39,228 | 38,717 | 42,860 | 44,763 | 49,237 | 53,390 | 55,842 | 66,941 |
| Currency Outside Depository Corps | 34a | 632 | 625 | 753 | 908 | 1,103 | 1,145 | 1,241 | 1,431 | 1,558 | 1,585 | 1,682 | 1,688 |
| Transferable Deposits................... | 34 | 3,592 | 3,372 | 4,404 | 5,331 | 6,666 | 5,963 | 8,023 | 7,244 | 8,997 | 10,929 | 11,525 | 12,049 |
| Other Deposits........................... | 35 | 9,037 | 10,676 | 19,411 | 26,058 | 31,459 | 31,609 | 33,596 | 36,088 | 38,682 | 40,876 | 42,635 | 53,204 |
| Securities Other than Shares.......... | 36a | 6,447 | 7,873 | — | — | — | — | — | — | — | — | — | — |
| Deposits Excl. from Broad Money..... | 36b | — | — | — | — | — | — | — | — | — | — | — | — |
| Sec.Ot.th.Shares Excl.f/Brd.Money.... | 36s | — | — | — | — | — | — | — | 1,603 | 2,000 | 2,191 | 2,488 | 2,936 |
| Loans......................................... | 36l | 605 | 633 | 1,061 | 1,273 | 1,488 | 1,467 | 1,484 | 204 | 781 | 657 | 661 | 1,163 |
| Financial Derivatives..................... | 36m | — | — | — | — | — | — | — | 51 | 45 | 75 | 79 | 236 |
| Insurance Technical Reserves.......... | 36r | — | — | — | — | — | — | — | — | — | — | — | — |
| Shares and Other Equity................. | 37a | 4,948 | 9,306 | 12,968 | 14,429 | 19,755 | 17,527 | 17,306 | 23,930 | 27,124 | 33,697 | 35,957 | 40,092 |
| Other Items (Net).......................... | 37r | 131 | 606 | 1,359 | 163 | 2,077 | 741 | 341 | 1,438 | 983 | −1,876 | 326 | −2,189 |
| Broad Money Liabs., Seasonally Adj. | 35l.b | 20,323 | 23,127 | 25,033 | 32,691 | 39,518 | 38,914 | 43,051 | 45,067 | 49,797 | 54,285 | 56,988 | 68,401 |
| **Monetary Aggregates** | | | | | | *Millions of Pula: End of Period* | | | | | | | |
| Broad Money............................... | 59m | 19,708 | 22,547 | 24,568 | 32,297 | 39,228 | 38,717 | 42,860 | 44,763 | 49,237 | 53,390 | 55,842 | 66,941 |
| o/w:Currency Issued by Cent.Govt | 59m.a | — | — | — | — | — | — | — | — | — | — | — | — |
| o/w: Dep.in Nonfin. Corporations. | 59m.b | — | — | — | — | — | — | — | — | — | — | — | — |
| o/w:Secs. Issued by Central Govt.. | 59m.c | — | — | — | — | — | — | — | — | — | — | — | — |
| Money (National Definitions) | | | | | | | | | | | | | |
| M1.............................................. | 59ma | 4,225 | 3,998 | 5,157 | 6,238 | 7,768 | 7,108 | 9,264 | 8,675 | 10,555 | 12,513 | 13,207 | 13,737 |
| M2.............................................. | 59mb | 13,262 | 14,674 | 24,568 | 32,297 | 39,228 | 38,717 | 42,860 | 44,763 | 49,237 | 53,390 | 55,842 | 66,941 |
| M3.............................................. | 59mc | 19,708 | 22,547 | 24,568 | 32,297 | 39,228 | 38,717 | 42,860 | 44,763 | 49,237 | 53,390 | 55,842 | 66,941 |
| **Interest Rates** | | | | | | *Percent Per Annum* | | | | | | | |
| Discount Rate (End of Period).......... | 60.a | 14.25 | 14.50 | 15.00 | 14.50 | 15.00 | 10.00 | 9.50 | 9.50 | 9.50 | 7.50 | 7.50 | 6.00 |
| Savings Rate................................. | 60k | 7.66 | 8.05 | 6.48 | 7.08 | 7.37 | 5.68 | 3.96 | 3.45 | 3.07 | 2.86 | 2.58 | 2.53 |
| Deposit Rate................................. | 60l | 9.85 | 9.25 | 8.87 | 8.62 | 8.67 | 7.47 | 5.60 | 5.15 | 3.61 | 3.11 | 2.53 | 2.50 |
| Deposit Rate (Fgn. Currency)............ | 60l.f | 1.36 | 2.17 | 3.87 | 5.57 | 3.37 | 1.68 | 1.10 | 1.19 | .80 | .80 | 1.07 | 1.25 |
| Lending Rate................................. | 60p | 15.75 | 15.74 | 16.46 | 16.22 | 16.54 | 13.76 | 11.46 | 11.00 | 11.00 | 10.19 | 9.00 | 7.95 |
| Government Bond Yield.................. | 61 | 10.07 | 9.49 | 11.60 | 10.73 | 10.19 | 8.63 | 7.69 | 7.44 | 5.67 | 5.01 | 4.21 | 3.67 |
| **Prices and Labor** | | | | | | *Index Numbers (2010=100): Period Averages* | | | | | | | |
| Share Prices (End of Month)............ | 62.ep | 38.2 | 44.6 | 65.5 | 118.2 | 105.5 | 91.2 | 100.0 | 95.8 | 99.2 | 116.6 | 126.8 | 141.6 |
| Consumer Prices............................ | 64 | † 59.2 | 64.3 | 71.7 | 76.8 | 86.6 | 93.5 | 100.0 | 108.5 | 116.6 | 123.5 | 128.9 | 132.9 |
| | | | | | | *Number in Thousands: Period Averages* | | | | | | | |
| Employment.................................. | 67e | 297 | 289 | 299 | 306 | 316 | . . . . | . . . . | . . . . | . . . . | . . . . | . . . . | . . . . |
| **Intl. Transactions & Positions** | | | | | | *Millions of Pula* | | | | | | | |
| Exports........................................ | 70 | 16,486.5 | 22,615.1 | 26,434.0 | 31,765.0 | 33,798.9 | 24,726.1 | 31,884.1 | 39,981.3 | 45,598.9 | 65,250.5 | 76,193.6 | . . . . |
| Imports, c.i.f................................. | 71 | 15,165.0 | 16,153.8 | 18,010.5 | 24,965.3 | 35,575.4 | 33,829.7 | 38,430.2 | 49,819.3 | 61,967.8 | 58,761.1 | 72,391.5 | . . . . |

# Botswana 616

| | | 2004 | 2005 | 2006 | 2007 | 2008 | 2009 | 2010 | 2011 | 2012 | 2013 | 2014 | 2015 |
|---|---|---|---|---|---|---|---|---|---|---|---|---|---|
| **Balance of Payments** | | | | | | | *Millions of US Dollars* | | | | | | |
| A. Current Account* | 109bx | 350.8 | 1,633.9 | 1,957.1 | 1,651.8 | −120.5 | −648.2 | −356.3 | 475.3 | −167.3 | 1,384.1 | 2,477.7 | 1,117.3 |
| Goods, credit (exports) | 1a9cx | 3,692.6 | 4,443.9 | 4,520.7 | 5,163.0 | 4,798.3 | 3,335.5 | 4,598.0 | 6,440.7 | 5,822.3 | 7,924.9 | 8,513.5 | 6,273.5 |
| Goods, debit (imports) | 1a9dx | 3,043.3 | 2,854.1 | 2,780.2 | 4,007.4 | 5,175.3 | 4,646.0 | 5,598.7 | 7,139.6 | 8,016.0 | 8,205.0 | 7,990.6 | 7,089.6 |
| Balance on goods | 1a9bx | 649.3 | 1,589.8 | 1,740.5 | 1,155.7 | −377.0 | −1,310.5 | −1,000.7 | −698.9 | −2,193.7 | −280.1 | 522.9 | −816.1 |
| Services, credit (exports) | 1b9cx | 748.2 | 833.3 | 770.6 | 848.8 | 200.8 | 842.5 | 981.4 | 1,227.7 | 1,079.8 | 1,242.1 | 1,352.2 | 1,253.7 |
| Services, debit (imports) | 1b9dx | 562.1 | 585.0 | 571.8 | 727.1 | 411.5 | 794.8 | 956.4 | 1,088.4 | 838.8 | 888.6 | 774.4 | 628.4 |
| Balance on Goods & Services | 1z9bx | 835.4 | 1,838.0 | 1,939.3 | 1,277.3 | −587.7 | −1,262.8 | −975.7 | −559.6 | −1,952.8 | 73.9 | 1,100.6 | −190.8 |
| Primary income: credit | 1c9cx | 256.7 | 462.0 | 528.5 | 524.0 | 474.7 | 296.8 | 255.6 | 249.6 | 212.7 | 208.3 | 230.9 | 216.5 |
| Primary income: debit | 1c9dx | 1,216.3 | 1,297.5 | 1,301.5 | 1,262.1 | 1,223.6 | 534.8 | 805.1 | 361.9 | 169.2 | 583.6 | 576.5 | 514.0 |
| Balance on gds, serv. & prim. inc. | 1y9bx | −124.2 | 1,002.5 | 1,166.4 | 539.2 | −1,336.5 | −1,500.8 | −1,525.3 | −672.0 | −1,909.3 | −301.3 | 755.0 | −488.4 |
| Secondary income: credit | 1d9ca | 691.8 | 845.0 | 992.8 | 1,376.8 | 1,317.6 | 933.4 | 1,295.5 | 1,435.6 | 1,944.1 | 1,859.1 | 1,834.5 | 1,740.3 |
| Secondary income: debit | 1d9da | 216.8 | 213.6 | 202.0 | 264.1 | 101.6 | 80.8 | 126.5 | 288.3 | 202.1 | 173.7 | 111.9 | 134.6 |
| B. Capital Account* | 209ba | — | — | — | — | — | — | — | — | — | — | — | — |
| Capital account: credit | 209ca | — | — | — | — | — | — | — | — | — | — | — | — |
| Capital account: debit | 209da | — | — | — | — | — | — | — | — | — | — | — | — |
| Balance on current & capital acct. | 129ba | 350.8 | 1,633.9 | 1,957.1 | 1,651.8 | −120.5 | −648.2 | −356.3 | 475.3 | −167.3 | 1,384.1 | 2,477.7 | 1,117.3 |
| C. Financial Account* | 309na | −13.1 | 384.5 | 127.1 | 34.6 | −727.8 | −428.8 | 362.7 | −1,024.9 | −568.2 | 482.1 | −296.2 | 848.2 |
| Direct investment: assets | 3a9aa | −38.7 | 55.9 | 49.8 | 31.6 | −91.4 | 7.8 | .9 | −9.7 | 8.0 | 84.6 | 111.4 | 84.5 |
| Equity & investment fund shares | 3aaaa | −49.7 | 52.2 | 28.8 | 29.3 | −102.7 | 4.0 | −.7 | 1.3 | 1.4 | 80.9 | 30.9 | 47.2 |
| Debt instruments | 3abaa | 11.0 | 3.7 | 21.0 | 2.4 | 11.3 | 3.8 | 1.6 | −11.0 | 6.6 | 3.8 | 80.5 | 37.2 |
| Direct investment: liabilities | 3a9la | 391.1 | 278.6 | 486.6 | 494.7 | 520.9 | 208.7 | 218.4 | 1,371.1 | 855.5 | 880.9 | 515.2 | 393.6 |
| Equity & investment fund shares | 3aala | 414.6 | 210.8 | 490.9 | 499.2 | 513.6 | 212.6 | 222.1 | 1,412.6 | 671.3 | 639.7 | 415.7 | 449.5 |
| Debt instruments | 3abla | −23.5 | 67.8 | −4.3 | −4.5 | 7.3 | −3.9 | −3.7 | −41.5 | 184.1 | 241.2 | 99.5 | −56.0 |
| Portfolio investment: assets | 3b9aa | 437.9 | 404.5 | 729.0 | 340.2 | −564.0 | 347.8 | 413.1 | 193.1 | 166.6 | 1,245.1 | 79.1 | 877.9 |
| Equity & investment fund shares | 3baaa | 415.1 | 289.4 | 729.0 | 410.7 | −567.7 | 456.5 | 405.0 | −113.9 | 262.5 | 1,175.2 | −219.0 | 907.1 |
| Debt securities | 3bbaa | 22.9 | 115.0 | — | −70.5 | 3.7 | −108.7 | 8.1 | 307.0 | −96.0 | 69.9 | 298.0 | −29.3 |
| Portfolio investment: liabilities | 3b9la | −29.2 | −18.2 | 36.2 | 13.7 | −29.5 | 17.7 | 11.0 | −20.2 | −8.6 | 1.9 | .1 | .1 |
| Equity & investment fund shares | 3bala | .6 | 27.2 | 36.0 | 9.4 | −36.7 | 17.7 | 11.2 | −17.4 | −8.6 | 1.8 | .1 | .1 |
| Debt securities | 3bbla | −29.8 | −45.4 | .2 | 4.3 | 7.2 | .1 | −.2 | −2.8 | — | .1 | −.1 | −.1 |
| Fin. der.& empl.stk.ops.(ESOs): net | 3c9na | — | — | — | — | — | — | — | — | — | — | — | — |
| Fin. der. & ESOs.: assets | 3c9aa | — | — | — | — | — | — | — | — | — | — | — | — |
| Fin. der. & ESOs.: liabilities | 3c9la | — | — | — | — | — | — | — | — | — | — | — | — |
| Other investment: assets | 3d9aa | −130.0 | 353.1 | 107.3 | 167.2 | 353.0 | 602.8 | 402.8 | 647.7 | 274.3 | −31.0 | 113.3 | 200.8 |
| Other equity | 3daaa | . . . . | . . . . | . . . . | . . . . | . . . . | . . . . | . . . . | . . . . | . . . . | . . . . | . . . . | . . . . |
| Debt instruments | 3dzaa | −130.0 | 353.1 | 107.3 | 167.2 | 353.0 | 602.8 | 402.8 | 647.7 | 274.3 | −31.0 | 113.3 | 200.8 |
| Other investment: liabilities | 3d9la | −79.6 | 168.6 | 236.1 | −3.9 | −65.9 | 1,160.7 | 224.7 | 505.2 | 170.2 | −66.1 | 84.7 | −78.7 |
| Other equity | 3dala | . . . . | . . . . | . . . . | . . . . | . . . . | . . . . | . . . . | . . . . | . . . . | . . . . | . . . . | . . . . |
| Debt instruments | 3dzla | −79.6 | 168.6 | 236.1 | −3.9 | −65.9 | 1,160.7 | 224.7 | 505.2 | 170.2 | −66.1 | 84.7 | −78.7 |
| Curr.+ cap.− finan. acct. balance | 4y9na | 363.9 | 1,249.4 | 1,830.0 | 1,617.2 | 607.3 | −219.4 | −719.0 | 1,500.2 | 400.9 | 902.0 | 2,773.8 | 269.1 |
| D. Net Errors and Omissions | 409na | −265.4 | 783.6 | 451.2 | 97.3 | 857.2 | −1,262.7 | −313.9 | −145.9 | −533.3 | 83.6 | −1,513.8 | 280.3 |
| E. Reserves and Related Items | 4z9na | 98.5 | 2,033.1 | 2,281.2 | 1,714.5 | 1,464.5 | −1,482.1 | −1,032.9 | 1,354.3 | −132.4 | 985.6 | 1,260.1 | 549.4 |
| Reserve assets | 3e9aa | 108.0 | 2,033.2 | 2,281.2 | 1,714.5 | 1,464.5 | −1,482.1 | −1,032.9 | 1,354.3 | −132.4 | 985.6 | 1,260.1 | 549.4 |
| Credit and loans from the IMF | 3dcla | — | — | — | — | — | — | — | — | — | — | — | — |
| Exceptional financing | 409la | 9.5 | .1 | — | — | — | — | — | — | — | — | — | — |

*Excludes components in group E

| | | 2004 | 2005 | 2006 | 2007 | 2008 | 2009 | 2010 | 2011 | 2012 | 2013 | 2014 | 2015 |
|---|---|---|---|---|---|---|---|---|---|---|---|---|---|
| **International Investment Position** | | | | | | | *Millions of US Dollars* | | | | | | |
| Assets | 809aa | 9,875.9 | 10,706.1 | 13,263.7 | 15,427.2 | 13,449.4 | 13,535.7 | 13,630.3 | 13,049.1 | 12,892.9 | 13,711.0 | 14,043.5 | 13,431.8 |
| Direct investment | 8a9aa | 1,457.1 | 1,183.3 | 1,129.7 | 1,171.9 | 853.1 | 968.6 | 1,007.0 | 852.1 | 832.6 | 822.0 | 854.6 | 801.5 |
| Equity & investment fund shares | 8aaaa | 1,444.4 | 1,170.0 | 1,097.3 | 1,136.9 | 814.9 | 921.4 | 956.5 | 818.9 | 794.1 | 784.0 | 743.9 | 674.2 |
| Debt instruments | 8abaa | 12.7 | 13.3 | 32.4 | 35.0 | 38.2 | 47.1 | 50.5 | 33.2 | 38.6 | 38.0 | 110.8 | 127.3 |
| Portfolio investment | 8b9aa | 2,254.0 | 2,607.3 | 3,149.7 | 3,408.0 | 2,271.1 | 2,928.2 | 3,311.2 | 3,009.3 | 3,076.3 | 3,941.5 | 3,687.4 | 3,888.2 |
| Equity & investment fund shares | 8baaa | 1,494.5 | 1,819.5 | 2,399.1 | 2,726.2 | 1,723.1 | 2,427.3 | 2,783.7 | 2,279.0 | 2,463.4 | 3,327.8 | 2,843.7 | 3,200.1 |
| Debt securities | 8bbaa | 759.6 | 787.8 | 750.6 | 681.8 | 548.0 | 500.9 | 527.5 | 730.3 | 612.9 | 613.7 | 843.7 | 688.1 |
| Fin. der.(oth.than reserves) & ESOs | 8c9aa | . . . . | . . . . | . . . . | . . . . | . . . . | . . . . | . . . . | . . . . | . . . . | . . . . | . . . . | . . . . |
| Other investment | 8d9aa | 510.5 | 637.4 | 1,029.9 | 1,104.1 | 1,200.1 | 960.1 | 1,419.5 | 1,178.1 | 1,357.1 | 1,180.0 | 1,188.5 | 1,189.1 |
| Other equity | 8daaa | . . . . | . . . . | . . . . | . . . . | . . . . | . . . . | . . . . | . . . . | . . . . | . . . . | . . . . | . . . . |
| Debt instruments | 8dzaa | 510.5 | 637.4 | 1,029.9 | 1,104.1 | 1,200.1 | 960.1 | 1,419.5 | 1,178.1 | 1,357.1 | 1,180.0 | 1,188.5 | 1,189.1 |
| Reserve assets | 8e9aa | 5,654.3 | 6,278.2 | 7,954.3 | 9,743.2 | 9,125.1 | 8,678.8 | 7,892.7 | 8,009.5 | 7,626.9 | 7,767.6 | 8,313.0 | 7,552.9 |
| Liabilities | 809la | 3,582.9 | 3,499.5 | 3,497.6 | 4,338.9 | 3,758.4 | 5,678.2 | 6,387.7 | 7,177.6 | 8,154.1 | 8,215.8 | 8,233.8 | 7,442.4 |
| Direct investment | 8a9la | 910.7 | 806.3 | 1,871.0 | 2,505.7 | 2,474.4 | 3,011.9 | 3,350.6 | 4,113.5 | 4,820.2 | 5,145.4 | 5,202.4 | 4,760.4 |
| Equity & investment fund shares | 8aala | 845.9 | 691.0 | 1,771.7 | 2,410.6 | 2,391.8 | 2,923.0 | 3,262.5 | 4,075.8 | 4,603.3 | 4,719.7 | 4,718.3 | 4,401.0 |
| Debt instruments | 8abla | 64.8 | 115.2 | 99.3 | 95.1 | 82.6 | 88.9 | 88.2 | 37.7 | 217.0 | 425.7 | 484.0 | 359.5 |
| Portfolio investment | 8b9la | 1,239.3 | 959.6 | 457.2 | 496.3 | 369.6 | 435.5 | 462.8 | 377.7 | 357.1 | 320.2 | 293.5 | 248.7 |
| Equity & investment fund shares | 8bala | 590.3 | 433.2 | 99.2 | 132.4 | 72.4 | 100.6 | 115.9 | 83.4 | 72.4 | 66.2 | 60.8 | 51.6 |
| Debt securities | 8bbla | 649.0 | 526.4 | 358.0 | 363.9 | 297.2 | 334.9 | 346.8 | 294.2 | 284.8 | 254.0 | 232.7 | 197.0 |
| Fin. der.(oth.than reserves) & ESOs | 8c9la | . . . . | . . . . | . . . . | . . . . | . . . . | . . . . | . . . . | . . . . | . . . . | . . . . | . . . . | . . . . |
| Other investment | 8d9la | 1,432.9 | 1,733.6 | 1,169.5 | 1,336.9 | 914.3 | 2,230.8 | 2,574.3 | 2,686.5 | 2,976.7 | 2,750.2 | 2,737.9 | 2,433.3 |
| Other equity | 8dala | . . . . | . . . . | . . . . | . . . . | . . . . | . . . . | . . . . | . . . . | . . . . | . . . . | . . . . | . . . . |
| Debt instruments | 8dzla | 1,432.9 | 1,733.6 | 1,169.5 | 1,336.9 | 914.3 | 2,230.8 | 2,574.3 | 2,686.5 | 2,976.7 | 2,750.2 | 2,737.9 | 2,433.3 |

# Botswana 616

| | | 2004 | 2005 | 2006 | 2007 | 2008 | 2009 | 2010 | 2011 | 2012 | 2013 | 2014 | 2015 |
|---|---|---|---|---|---|---|---|---|---|---|---|---|---|
| **Government Finance** | | | | | | | | | | | | | |
| **Cash Flow Statement** | | | | | | | | | | | | | |
| **Budgetary Central Government** | | | | | | *Millions of Pula: Fiscal Year Ends March 31* | | | | | | | |
| Cash Receipts:Operating Activities... | c1 | 17,965.8 | 22,266.6 | 27,364.8 | 28,534.6 | 30,348.2 | 29,798.5 | 31,838.6 | 38,379.5 | 41,591.2 | 48,980.8 | 52,335.6 | . . . . |
| Taxes.............................. | c11 | . . . . | . . . . | 15,919.0 | 17,266.8 | 20,454.3 | 20,045.0 | 20,504.6 | 24,846.1 | 29,791.8 | 32,151.6 | 35,862.3 | . . . . |
| Social Contributions...................... | c12 | . . . . | . . . . | — | — | — | — | — | — | — | — | — | . . . . |
| Grants............................. | c13 | . . . . | . . . . | 448.4 | 577.4 | 623.2 | 647.9 | 329.4 | 532.4 | 506.8 | 325.7 | 377.4 | . . . . |
| Other Receipts.............................. | c14 | . . . . | . . . . | 10,997.4 | 10,690.4 | 9,270.7 | 9,105.6 | 11,004.7 | 13,001.0 | 11,292.6 | 16,503.5 | 16,095.9 | . . . . |
| Cash Payments:Operating Activities. | c2 | 17,392.6 | 17,631.9 | 16,964.1 | 20,206.6 | 26,190.6 | 28,362.4 | 28,774.1 | 30,778.7 | 33,493.3 | 35,341.5 | 41,039.0 | . . . . |
| Compensation of Employees.......... | c21 | . . . . | . . . . | 6,777.4 | 7,990.3 | 10,066.0 | 10,682.7 | 11,899.0 | 12,940.7 | 14,547.7 | 15,338.3 | 16,589.3 | . . . . |
| Purchases of Goods & Services....... | c22 | . . . . | . . . . | 5,519.6 | 6,733.4 | 8,639.7 | 8,801.9 | 7,940.7 | 8,840.1 | 10,182.9 | 10,854.3 | 13,603.7 | . . . . |
| Interest........................................ | c24 | . . . . | . . . . | 235.5 | 248.4 | 282.1 | 369.8 | 523.5 | 586.6 | 672.0 | 687.2 | 701.7 | . . . . |
| Subsidies........................................ | c25 | . . . . | . . . . | . . . . | . . . . | . . . . | . . . . | . . . . | . . . . | . . . . | . . . . | . . . . | . . . . |
| Grants........................................ | c26 | . . . . | . . . . | . . . . | . . . . | . . . . | . . . . | . . . . | . . . . | . . . . | . . . . | . . . . | . . . . |
| Social Benefits............................ | c27 | . . . . | . . . . | . . . . | . . . . | . . . . | . . . . | . . . . | . . . . | . . . . | . . . . | . . . . | . . . . |
| Other Payments.......................... | c28 | . . . . | . . . . | 4,431.6 | 5,234.5 | 7,202.8 | 8,508.0 | 8,411.0 | 8,411.4 | 8,090.8 | 8,461.8 | 10,144.4 | . . . . |
| Net Cash Inflow:Operating Act.[1-2] | ccio | . . . . | . . . . | 10,400.7 | 8,328.0 | 4,157.6 | 1,436.1 | 3,064.5 | 7,600.8 | 8,097.9 | 13,639.3 | 11,296.6 | . . . . |
| Net Cash Outflow:Invest. in NFA...... | c31 | . . . . | . . . . | 3,012.0 | 4,825.2 | 9,050.1 | 10,464.0 | 9,616.3 | 8,028.7 | 6,828.1 | 6,736.5 | 10,141.3 | . . . . |
| Purchases of Nonfinancial Assets... | c31.1 | . . . . | . . . . | 3,045.0 | 4,920.0 | 9,157.1 | 10,567.6 | 9,686.8 | 8,134.8 | 6,894.7 | 6,805.7 | 10,201.5 | . . . . |
| Sales of Nonfinancial Assets.......... | c31.2 | . . . . | . . . . | 33.0 | 94.8 | 107.0 | 103.5 | 70.6 | 106.1 | 66.6 | 69.2 | 60.2 | . . . . |
| Cash Surplus/Deficit [1-2-31=1-2M] | ccsd | 573.2 | 4,634.8 | 7,388.7 | 3,502.8 | −4,892.5 | −9,027.9 | −6,551.8 | −427.9 | 1,269.8 | 6,902.8 | 1,155.3 | . . . . |
| Net Acq. Fin. Assets, excl. Cash....... | c32x | . . . . | . . . . | −272.2 | −304.6 | −196.9 | 751.7 | −43.8 | −124.4 | 350.5 | −398.8 | −91.0 | . . . . |
| Domestic.................................... | c321x | . . . . | . . . . | −272.2 | −304.6 | −196.9 | 751.7 | −43.8 | −124.4 | 350.5 | −398.8 | −91.0 | . . . . |
| Foreign....................................... | c322x | . . . . | . . . . | — | — | — | — | — | — | — | — | — | . . . . |
| Net Incurrence of Liabilities.............. | c33 | −1,747.4 | −1,284.4 | −578.7 | 211.4 | 88.5 | 5,189.6 | 4,462.3 | 387.1 | −2,902.7 | 1,419.9 | 5,099.4 | . . . . |
| Domestic.................................... | c331 | . . . . | . . . . | −333.4 | 304.8 | 262.5 | −1,252.7 | 848.4 | 299.6 | −1,889.1 | 1,486.4 | 5,732.4 | . . . . |
| Foreign....................................... | c332 | . . . . | . . . . | −245.3 | −93.4 | −174.0 | 6,442.3 | 3,613.9 | 87.5 | −1,013.6 | −66.4 | −633.0 | . . . . |
| Net Cash Inflow, Fin.Act.[-32x+33].. | cnfb | . . . . | . . . . | −306.5 | 516.0 | 285.4 | 4,438.0 | 4,506.1 | 511.5 | −3,253.2 | 1,818.7 | 5,190.4 | . . . . |
| Net Change in Stock of Cash........... | cncb | −1,174.2 | 3,350.4 | 7,081.6 | 4,019.0 | −4,607.1 | −4,398.2 | −2,045.9 | 84.0 | −1,983.4 | 8,721.5 | 6,345.7 | . . . . |
| Stat. Discrep. [32X-33+NCB-CSD].... | ccsdz | . . . . | . . . . | .6 | −.2 | — | −191.8 | .2 | −.3 | — | — | — | . . . . |
| Memo Item:Cash Expenditure[2+31] | c2m | . . . . | . . . . | 19,976.1 | 25,031.8 | 35,240.7 | 38,826.5 | 38,390.4 | 38,807.4 | 40,321.4 | 42,078.0 | 51,180.3 | . . . . |
| Memo Item: Gross Debt.................. | c63 | . . . . | . . . . | . . . . | . . . . | 5,863.6 | 13,938.1 | 18,790.0 | 21,609.6 | 21,571.0 | 22,501.8 | 22,971.9 | . . . . |
| **National Accounts** | | | | | | *Millions of Pula* | | | | | | | |
| Househ.Cons.Expend.,incl.NPISHs.... | 96f | 17,022.0 | 19,340.0 | 22,892.7 | 26,622.2 | 32,929.1 | 37,023.5 | 42,692.1 | 48,629.1 | 59,302.3 | 66,900.2 | 68,844.2 | . . . . |
| Government Consumption Expend... | 91f | 9,970.5 | 9,846.3 | 10,070.5 | 11,815.4 | 15,206.6 | 15,492.9 | 17,162.0 | 19,407.3 | 21,195.6 | 24,466.8 | 23,387.6 | . . . . |
| Gross Fixed Capital Formation.......... | 93e | 11,703.7 | 12,860.5 | 15,486.6 | 19,061.5 | 22,851.6 | 25,645.5 | 29,201.5 | 33,640.6 | 40,487.8 | 42,130.4 | 42,136.0 | . . . . |
| Changes in Inventories.................... | 93i | 3,929.3 | 918.9 | −175.2 | 1,616.4 | 4,187.7 | 2,153.6 | 10,815.1 | 6,855.8 | 2,925.4 | −63.3 | 1,494.6 | . . . . |
| Exports of Goods and Services........ | 90c | 20,855.9 | 26,859.8 | 30,886.0 | 36,609.0 | 34,128.0 | 25,565.6 | 33,377.0 | 47,621.0 | 48,158.9 | 68,454.5 | 88,574.0 | . . . . |
| Imports of Goods and Services (-)..... | 98c | 17,396.4 | 18,058.5 | 20,143.7 | 27,256.3 | 38,139.0 | 38,116.0 | 43,188.0 | 55,061.0 | 65,822.0 | 74,387.0 | 78,663.0 | . . . . |
| Gross Domestic Product (GDP)........ | 99b | 47,157.3 | 50,752.1 | 59,106.9 | 67,152.7 | 75,867.1 | 72,315.8 | 93,390.0 | 104,573.2 | 110,763.2 | 124,223.2 | 141,942.3 | . . . . |
| GDP Volume 2006 Prices................. | 99b.p | . . . . | 54,544.8 | 59,106.9 | 63,999.1 | 66,496.0 | 61,282.0 | 66,548.7 | 70,663.3 | 73,671.3 | 78,015.9 | . . . . | . . . . |
| GDP Volume (2010=100)................ | 99bvp | 80.6 | † 82.0 | 88.8 | 96.2 | 99.9 | 92.1 | 100.0 | 106.2 | 110.7 | 117.2 | . . . . | . . . . |
| GDP Deflator (2010=100)............... | 99bip | 62.7 | 66.3 | 71.3 | 74.8 | 81.3 | 84.1 | 100.0 | 105.5 | 107.1 | 113.5 | . . . . | . . . . |
| | | | | | | *Millions: Midyear Estimates* | | | | | | | |
| **Population..............................** | 99z | 1.84 | 1.86 | 1.90 | 1.93 | 1.97 | 2.01 | 2.05 | 2.09 | 2.13 | 2.18 | 2.22 | 2.26 |

# Brazil 223

|  |  | 2004 | 2005 | 2006 | 2007 | 2008 | 2009 | 2010 | 2011 | 2012 | 2013 | 2014 | 2015 |
|---|---|---|---|---|---|---|---|---|---|---|---|---|---|
| **Exchange Rates** |  | *Reais per SDR: End of Period* | | | | | | | | | | | |
| Principal Rate............................ | aa | 4.1211 | 3.3443 | 3.2152 | 2.7978 | 3.5984 | 2.7284 | 2.5962 | 2.8538 | 3.1481 | 3.6249 | 3.8483 | 5.4102 |
|  |  | *Reais per US Dollar: End of Period (ae) Period Average (rf)* | | | | | | | | | | | |
| Principal Rate............................ | ae | 2.6536 | 2.3399 | 2.1372 | 1.7705 | 2.3362 | 1.7404 | 1.6858 | 1.8588 | 2.0483 | 2.3538 | 2.6562 | 3.9042 |
| Principal Rate............................ | rf | 2.9251 | 2.4344 | 2.1753 | 1.9471 | 1.8338 | 1.9994 | 1.7592 | 1.6728 | 1.9531 | 2.1561 | 2.3530 | 3.3283 |
| Nominal Effective Exchange Rate..... | nec | 62.62 | 74.06 | 82.22 | 88.80 | 92.61 | 89.32 | 100.00 | 101.94 | 90.67 | 83.44 | 80.50 | 63.66 |
| CPI-Based Real Effect. Ex. Rate........ | rec | 58.15 | 70.99 | 79.20 | 85.07 | 88.83 | 88.16 | 100.00 | 103.49 | 93.12 | 87.86 | 87.00 | 73.29 |
| **Fund Position** |  | *Millions of SDRs: End of Period* | | | | | | | | | | | |
| Quota............................................ | 2f.s | 3,036.10 | 3,036.10 | 3,036.10 | 3,036.10 | 3,036.10 | 3,036.10 | 3,036.10 | 4,250.50 | 4,250.50 | 4,250.50 | 4,250.50 | 4,250.50 |
| SDR Holdings.............................. | 1b.s | 2.67 | 20.19 | 5.56 | 1.32 | .72 | 2,887.42 | 2,889.30 | 2,591.45 | 2,593.47 | 2,594.75 | 2,596.22 | 2,596.68 |
| Reserve Position in the Fund............ | 1c.s | — | — | — | — | .14 | 605.83 | 1,322.42 | 1,949.68 | 2,266.26 | 2,071.43 | 1,653.94 | 1,237.75 |
| Total Fund Cred.&Loans Outstg........ | 2tl | 16,116.68 | — | — | — | — | — | — | — | — | — | — | — |
| SDR Allocations................................ | 1bd | 358.67 | 358.67 | 358.67 | 358.67 | 358.67 | 2,887.08 | 2,887.08 | 2,887.08 | 2,887.08 | 2,887.08 | 2,887.08 | 2,887.08 |
| **International Liquidity** |  | *Millions of US Dollars Unless Otherwise Indicated: End of Period* | | | | | | | | | | | |
| Total Reserves minus Gold.............. | 1l.d | 52,462 | 53,245 | 85,156 | 179,433 | 192,844 | 237,364 | 287,056 | 350,356 | 369,566 | 356,214 | 360,965 | 354,175 |
| SDR Holdings........................... | 1b.d | 4 | 29 | 8 | 2 | 1 | 4,527 | 4,450 | 3,979 | 3,986 | 3,996 | 3,761 | 3,598 |
| Reserve Position in the Fund.......... | 1c.d | — | — | — | — | — | 950 | 2,037 | 2,993 | 3,483 | 3,190 | 2,396 | 1,715 |
| Foreign Exchange......................... | 1d.d | 52,458 | 53,216 | 85,148 | 179,431 | 192,842 | 231,888 | 280,570 | 343,384 | 362,097 | 349,028 | 354,807 | 348,861 |
| Other Liquid Foreign Assets............. | 1e.d | — | — | — | — | — | — | — | — | — | — | — | — |
| Gold (Million Fine Troy Ounces)........ | 1ad | 1.08 | 1.08 | 1.08 | 1.08 | 1.08 | 1.08 | 1.08 | 1.08 | 2.16 | 2.16 | 2.16 | 2.16 |
| Gold (National Valuation)................ | 1and | 473 | 554 | 683 | 901 | 940 | 1,175 | 1,519 | 1,654 | 3,581 | 2,592 | 2,586 | 2,289 |
| Central Bank: Other Assets.............. | 3..d | 4,309 | 562 | 3,096 | † 16,528 | 6,388 | 3,716 | 5,361 | 3,752 | 494 | 3,301 | 442 | 1,195 |
| Central Bank: Other Liabs............... | 4..d | 4,854 | 2,656 | 3,815 | † 1,002 | 973 | 5,040 | 5,465 | 8,060 | 4,816 | 7,715 | 4,571 | 5,129 |
| Other Depository Corps.: Assets........ | 7a.d | † 21,657 | 27,246 | 33,878 | 46,497 | 42,414 | 50,274 | 65,684 | 69,492 | 77,995 | 83,642 | 91,521 | 90,772 |
| Other Depository Corps.: Liabs......... | 7b.d | † 44,362 | 44,394 | 55,994 | 93,064 | 88,573 | 83,308 | 123,760 | 157,633 | 177,061 | 153,308 | 175,948 | 165,591 |
| Other Financial Corps.: Assets.......... | 7e.d | 11 | 27 | † 105 | 85 | 166 | 204 | 685 | 903 | 1,062 | 1,297 | 1,787 | 1,371 |
| Other Financial Corps.: Liabs............ | 7f.d | 419 | 384 | † 386 | 389 | 379 | 452 | 540 | 912 | 841 | 546 | 446 | 316 |
| **Central Bank** |  | *Millions of Reais: End of Period* | | | | | | | | | | | |
| Net Foreign Assets............................ | 11n | 67,674 | 118,828 | 179,497 | † 317,733 | 450,928 | 407,096 | 473,003 | 651,604 | 753,687 | 830,369 | 954,884 | 1,376,878 |
| Claims on Nonresidents................. | 11 | 147,076 | 125,176 | 187,835 | † 347,115 | 467,462 | 421,849 | 489,639 | 667,108 | 764,137 | 849,150 | 967,880 | 1,398,128 |
| Liabilities to Nonresidents............. | 16c | 79,402 | 6,348 | 8,337 | † 29,382 | 16,534 | 14,753 | 16,636 | 15,505 | 10,450 | 18,780 | 12,996 | 21,251 |
| Claims on Other Depository Corps.... | 12e | 22,379 | 45,136 | 20,423 | † 27,673 | 65,553 | 29,864 | 39,276 | 48,472 | 111,550 | 77,948 | 58,265 | 83,021 |
| Net Claims on Central Government..... | 12an | 152,381 | 72,858 | 79,791 | † 84,886 | 61,769 | 228,157 | 292,685 | 176,386 | 276,715 | 266,016 | 415,367 | 242,625 |
| Claims on Central Government....... | 12a | 311,198 | 283,534 | 306,248 | † 361,201 | 499,168 | 640,217 | 703,176 | 754,546 | 910,223 | 953,069 | 1,113,236 | 1,279,202 |
| Liabilities to Central Government... | 16d | 158,817 | 210,676 | 226,457 | † 276,315 | 437,399 | 412,060 | 410,491 | 578,160 | 633,508 | 687,053 | 697,869 | 1,036,577 |
| Claims on Other Sectors................... | 12s | 1,146 | 86 | — | † 4 | — | 1 | 1 | — | — | — | — | — |
| Claims on Other Financial Corps... | 12g | — | — | — | † — | — | — | — | — | — | — | — | — |
| Claims on State & Local Govts....... | 12b | 1,146 | 86 | — | † 4 | — | 1 | 1 | — | — | — | — | — |
| Claims on Public Nonfin. Corps...... | 12c | — | — | — | † — | — | — | — | — | — | — | — | — |
| Claims on Private Sector............... | 12d | — | — | — | † — | — | — | — | — | — | — | — | — |
| Monetary Base.............................. | 14 | 168,345 | 181,385 | 204,249 | † 248,840 | 205,623 | 228,924 | 530,561 | 587,671 | 508,030 | 574,550 | 548,461 | 594,427 |
| Currency in Circulation.................. | 14a | 61,936 | 70,033 | 85,825 | † 102,885 | 115,591 | 131,861 | 151,145 | 162,770 | 187,435 | 204,052 | 220,854 | 225,485 |
| Liabs. to Other Depository Corps.... | 14c | 106,366 | 111,322 | 118,424 | † 145,955 | 90,032 | 97,063 | 379,416 | 424,901 | 320,025 | 369,043 | 325,746 | 368,386 |
| Liabilities to Other Sectors............. | 14d | 43 | 30 | — | † — | — | — | — | — | 570 | 1,455 | 1,861 | 556 |
| Other Liabs. to Other Dep. Corps..... | 14n | 64,180 | 63,123 | 77,833 | † 180,668 | 336,801 | 441,370 | 266,673 | 337,115 | 585,673 | 556,998 | 822,553 | 965,884 |
| Dep. & Sec. Excl. f/Monetary Base..... | 14o | 164 | 159 | 194 | † 10,295 | 11,971 | 13,616 | 22,559 | 14,145 | 11,119 | 12,064 | 12,876 | 14,229 |
| Deposits Included in Broad Money. | 15 | 154 | 153 | 187 | † 10,283 | 11,956 | 13,602 | 22,550 | 14,133 | 11,099 | 12,031 | 12,856 | 14,196 |
| Sec.Ot.th.Shares Incl.in Brd. Money | 16a | — | — | — | † — | — | — | — | — | — | — | — | — |
| Deposits Excl. from Broad Money... | 16b | 10 | 6 | 7 | † 12 | 15 | 14 | 9 | 12 | 20 | 33 | 20 | 33 |
| Sec.Ot.th.Shares Excl.f/Brd.Money.. | 16s | — | — | — | † — | — | — | — | — | — | — | — | — |
| Loans............................................ | 16l | — | — | — | † — | — | — | — | — | — | — | — | — |
| Financial Derivatives........................ | 16m | — | — | — | † — | — | — | — | — | — | — | — | — |
| Shares and Other Equity................... | 17a | 12,169 | –3,085 | –1,077 | † –17,263 | 16,802 | –33,638 | –32,789 | –78,951 | 12,239 | 9,538 | 20,147 | 108,312 |
| Other Items (Net)............................ | 17r | –1,278 | –4,675 | –1,488 | † 7,756 | 7,053 | 14,846 | 17,961 | 16,482 | 24,891 | 21,183 | 24,479 | 19,671 |
| Memo Item: |  |  |  |  |  |  |  |  |  |  |  |  |  |
| Total Assets..................................... | 10ra | 497,429 | 470,850 | 528,562 | † 749,086 | 1,047,155 | 1,103,651 | 1,241,762 | 1,482,534 | 1,799,654 | 1,897,429 | 2,157,903 | 2,785,098 |

| | | 2004 | 2005 | 2006 | 2007 | 2008 | 2009 | 2010 | 2011 | 2012 | 2013 | 2014 | 2015 |
|---|---|---|---|---|---|---|---|---|---|---|---|---|---|
| **Other Depository Corporations** | | | | | | | *Millions of Reais: End of Period* | | | | | | | |
| Net Foreign Assets............................ | 21n | † −60,260 | −40,133 | −47,277 | −82,465 | −107,855 | −57,505 | −96,620 | −165,304 | −202,411 | −163,178 | −224,231 | −292,131 |
| Claims on Nonresidents................. | 21 | † 57,477 | 63,763 | 72,417 | 82,342 | 99,104 | 87,517 | 109,279 | 130,329 | 159,360 | 195,916 | 243,070 | 354,419 |
| Liabilities to Nonresidents.............. | 26c | † 117,736 | 103,896 | 119,694 | 164,807 | 206,959 | 145,023 | 205,899 | 295,633 | 361,771 | 359,093 | 467,301 | 646,550 |
| Claims on Central Bank................... | 20 | † 169,616 | 173,471 | 198,602 | 342,060 | 422,299 | 560,486 | 672,941 | 778,978 | 916,758 | 907,079 | 1,148,630 | 1,291,109 |
| Currency......................................... | 20a | † 9,996 | 11,859 | 17,019 | 20,875 | 23,419 | 26,296 | 29,450 | 31,407 | 37,808 | 40,189 | 42,595 | 40,199 |
| Reserve Deposits and Securities..... | 20b | † 93,896 | 104,555 | 118,396 | 145,895 | 87,481 | 97,288 | 378,386 | 424,903 | 319,953 | 366,564 | 325,774 | 368,571 |
| Other Claims.............................. | 20n | † 65,724 | 57,057 | 63,187 | 175,289 | 311,399 | 436,903 | 265,105 | 322,668 | 558,997 | 500,326 | 780,262 | 882,338 |
| Net Claims on Central Government.. | 22an | † 650,565 | 807,317 | 914,780 | 960,865 | 912,944 | 919,732 | 932,999 | 1,033,755 | 1,091,456 | 1,079,615 | 1,073,407 | 1,385,461 |
| Claims on Central Government....... | 22a | † 713,085 | 868,644 | 972,978 | 1,034,738 | 1,049,025 | 1,173,669 | 1,336,420 | 1,525,311 | 1,688,739 | 1,713,641 | 1,775,787 | 2,142,024 |
| Liabilities to Central Government.... | 26d | † 62,520 | 61,326 | 58,198 | 73,873 | 136,081 | 253,937 | 403,421 | 491,556 | 597,282 | 634,027 | 702,380 | 756,563 |
| Claims on Other Sectors.................. | 22s | † 623,281 | 774,488 | 1,003,106 | 1,329,451 | 1,696,880 | 1,867,675 | 2,403,257 | 2,954,225 | 3,497,820 | 3,988,438 | 4,489,006 | 4,791,194 |
| Claims on Other Financial Corps..... | 22g | † 29,748 | 64,450 | 132,559 | 204,947 | 247,626 | 231,984 | 294,184 | 342,711 | 383,676 | 431,635 | 496,098 | 526,038 |
| Claims on State & Local Govts...... | 22b | † 9,045 | 9,160 | 9,696 | 10,723 | 12,048 | 17,271 | 23,860 | 30,409 | 42,999 | 65,496 | 92,467 | 120,285 |
| Claims on Public Nonfin. Corps...... | 22c | † 9,442 | 9,769 | 7,299 | 6,881 | 13,468 | 35,417 | 34,860 | 39,368 | 60,990 | 66,777 | 84,685 | 137,904 |
| Claims on Private Sector............... | 22d | † 575,046 | 691,109 | 853,552 | 1,106,901 | 1,423,738 | 1,583,003 | 2,050,354 | 2,541,737 | 3,010,154 | 3,424,529 | 3,815,757 | 4,006,967 |
| Liabilities to Central Bank............... | 26g | † 4,737 | 31,216 | 726 | 4,193 | 3,702 | 496 | 6 | 13,221 | 61,850 | 5 | — | — |
| Transf.Dep.Included in Broad Money | 24 | † 77,333 | 88,002 | 107,344 | 153,626 | 133,917 | 147,823 | 165,171 | 159,835 | 182,279 | 189,793 | 183,891 | 160,875 |
| Other Dep.Included in Broad Money. | 25 | † 730,029 | 861,336 | 1,024,520 | 1,201,027 | 1,282,466 | 1,570,605 | 1,788,024 | 2,036,187 | 2,401,806 | 2,614,772 | 2,980,347 | 3,255,918 |
| Sec.Ot.th.Shares Incl.in Brd. Money.. | 26a | † 124,304 | 157,781 | 174,126 | 184,862 | 401,353 | 397,580 | 491,251 | 726,338 | 810,407 | 890,770 | 1,039,492 | 1,206,331 |
| Deposits Excl. from Broad Money..... | 26b | † 222,559 | 281,929 | 348,260 | 445,911 | 403,995 | 409,372 | 510,518 | 581,159 | 518,246 | 575,185 | 568,436 | 650,252 |
| Sec.Ot.th.Shares Excl.f/Brd.Money.... | 26s | † — | — | — | — | — | — | — | — | — | — | — | — |
| Loans.............................................. | 26l | † 942 | 2,660 | 4,745 | 20,468 | 3,807 | 8,144 | 15,235 | 23,257 | 28,684 | 25,585 | 15,739 | 14,057 |
| Financial Derivatives........................ | 26m | † 352 | 237 | 345 | 705 | 1,697 | 670 | 1,003 | 1,312 | 1,125 | 1,677 | 2,668 | 3,444 |
| Insurance Technical Reserves........... | 26r | † — | — | — | — | — | — | — | — | — | — | — | — |
| Shares and Other Equity................... | 27a | † 190,508 | 219,516 | 275,011 | 353,036 | 497,551 | 523,746 | 645,969 | 710,137 | 802,458 | 808,134 | 837,722 | 746,965 |
| Other Items (Net)............................ | 27r | † 32,438 | 72,466 | 134,136 | 186,083 | 195,782 | 231,954 | 295,402 | 350,209 | 496,769 | 706,032 | 858,518 | 1,137,791 |
| Memo Item: | | | | | | | | | | | | | |
| Total Assets..................................... | 20ra | † 2,150,290 | 2,578,020 | 3,103,439 | 3,920,124 | 4,737,513 | 5,294,713 | 6,403,557 | 7,530,440 | 8,664,792 | 9,386,667 | 10,510,433 | 11,312,789 |
| **Depository Corporations** | | | | | | | *Millions of Reais: End of Period* | | | | | | | |
| Net Foreign Assets........................... | 31n | † 7,414 | 78,694 | 132,221 | † 235,268 | 343,074 | 349,591 | 376,383 | 486,300 | 551,275 | 667,192 | 730,653 | 1,084,747 |
| Claims on Nonresidents................. | 31 | † 204,553 | 188,938 | 260,252 | † 429,457 | 566,566 | 509,367 | 598,918 | 797,438 | 923,497 | 1,045,065 | 1,210,950 | 1,752,548 |
| Liabilities to Nonresidents.............. | 36c | † 197,138 | 110,244 | 128,031 | † 194,189 | 223,493 | 159,776 | 222,535 | 311,138 | 372,222 | 377,873 | 480,297 | 667,801 |
| Domestic Claims.............................. | 32 | † 1,427,372 | 1,654,749 | 1,997,677 | † 2,375,207 | 2,671,594 | 3,015,566 | 3,628,942 | 4,164,366 | 4,865,991 | 5,334,068 | 5,977,780 | 6,419,280 |
| Net Claims on Central Government | 32an | † 802,946 | 880,175 | 994,571 | † 1,045,751 | 974,713 | 1,147,889 | 1,225,684 | 1,210,141 | 1,368,171 | 1,345,631 | 1,488,774 | 1,628,086 |
| Claims on Central Government.... | 32a | † 1,024,283 | 1,152,178 | 1,279,226 | † 1,395,939 | 1,548,193 | 1,813,886 | 2,039,596 | 2,279,857 | 2,598,962 | 2,666,710 | 2,889,023 | 3,421,226 |
| Liabilities to Central Government. | 36d | † 221,337 | 272,002 | 284,655 | † 350,188 | 573,480 | 665,997 | 813,912 | 1,069,716 | 1,230,790 | 1,321,080 | 1,400,249 | 1,793,140 |
| Claims on Other Sectors................ | 32s | † 624,427 | 774,574 | 1,003,106 | † 1,329,455 | 1,696,880 | 1,867,676 | 2,403,258 | 2,954,225 | 3,497,820 | 3,988,438 | 4,489,006 | 4,791,194 |
| Claims on Other Financial Corps..... | 32g | † 29,748 | 64,450 | 132,559 | † 204,947 | 247,626 | 231,984 | 294,184 | 342,711 | 383,676 | 431,635 | 496,098 | 526,038 |
| Claims on State & Local Govts...... | 32b | † 10,191 | 9,246 | 9,696 | † 10,727 | 12,048 | 17,272 | 23,861 | 30,409 | 42,999 | 65,496 | 92,467 | 120,285 |
| Claims on Public Nonfin. Corps...... | 32c | † 9,442 | 9,769 | 7,299 | † 6,881 | 13,468 | 35,417 | 34,860 | 39,368 | 60,990 | 66,777 | 84,685 | 137,904 |
| Claims on Private Sector.............. | 32d | † 575,046 | 691,109 | 853,552 | † 1,106,901 | 1,423,738 | 1,583,003 | 2,050,354 | 2,541,737 | 3,010,154 | 3,424,529 | 3,815,757 | 4,006,967 |
| Broad Money Liabilities................... | 35l | † 983,802 | 1,165,477 | 1,374,982 | † 1,631,808 | 1,921,865 | 2,235,175 | 2,588,689 | 3,067,856 | 3,555,787 | 3,872,684 | 4,396,706 | 4,823,162 |
| Currency Outside Depository Corps | 34a | † 51,940 | 58,174 | 68,806 | † 82,010 | 92,172 | 105,565 | 121,695 | 131,363 | 149,627 | 163,863 | 178,259 | 185,286 |
| Transferable Deposits.................... | 34 | † 77,333 | 88,002 | 107,344 | † 153,626 | 133,917 | 147,823 | 165,171 | 159,835 | 182,279 | 189,793 | 183,891 | 160,875 |
| Other Deposits............................. | 35 | † 730,183 | 861,489 | 1,024,707 | † 1,211,310 | 1,294,423 | 1,584,207 | 1,810,573 | 2,050,320 | 2,413,474 | 2,628,259 | 2,995,064 | 3,270,671 |
| Securities Other than Shares......... | 36a | † 124,347 | 157,811 | 174,126 | † 184,862 | 401,353 | 397,580 | 491,251 | 726,338 | 810,407 | 890,770 | 1,039,492 | 1,206,331 |
| Deposits Excl. from Broad Money..... | 36b | † 222,569 | 281,935 | 348,267 | † 445,923 | 404,010 | 409,386 | 510,527 | 581,171 | 518,266 | 575,218 | 568,456 | 650,285 |
| Sec.Ot.th.Shares Excl.f/Brd.Money..... | 36s | † — | — | — | † — | — | — | — | — | — | — | — | — |
| Loans.............................................. | 36l | † 942 | 2,660 | 4,745 | † 20,468 | 3,807 | 8,144 | 15,235 | 23,257 | 28,684 | 25,585 | 15,739 | 14,057 |
| Financial Derivatives........................ | 36m | † 352 | 237 | 345 | † 705 | 1,697 | 670 | 1,003 | 1,312 | 1,125 | 1,677 | 2,668 | 3,444 |
| Insurance Technical Reserves........... | 36r | † — | — | — | † — | — | — | — | — | — | — | — | — |
| Shares and Other Equity................... | 37a | † 202,677 | 216,431 | 273,934 | † 335,773 | 514,353 | 490,108 | 613,180 | 631,186 | 814,697 | 817,672 | 857,869 | 855,277 |
| Other Items (Net)............................ | 37r | † 24,445 | 66,704 | 127,625 | † 175,797 | 168,936 | 221,675 | 276,691 | 345,884 | 498,707 | 708,425 | 866,996 | 1,157,802 |
| Broad Money Liabs., Seasonally Adj. | 35l.b | † 974,361 | 1,154,293 | 1,361,787 | † 1,607,532 | 1,895,041 | 2,207,229 | 2,560,990 | 3,040,259 | 3,528,640 | 3,845,631 | 4,366,232 | 4,788,608 |
| **Other Financial Corporations** | | | | | | | *Millions of Reais: End of Period* | | | | | | | |
| Net Foreign Assets........................... | 41n | −1,083 | −836 | † −602 | −538 | −498 | −432 | 241 | −17 | 451 | 1,758 | 3,562 | 4,120 |
| Claims on Nonresidents................. | 41 | 29 | 63 | † 223 | 150 | 388 | 356 | 1,140 | 1,694 | 2,169 | 3,037 | 4,746 | 5,353 |
| Liabilities to Nonresidents.............. | 46c | 1,112 | 899 | † 825 | 688 | 887 | 787 | 898 | 1,711 | 1,718 | 1,279 | 1,183 | 1,233 |
| Claims on Depository Corporations.. | 40 | 23,972 | 69,951 | † 241,870 | 321,414 | 329,664 | 388,899 | 557,839 | 639,098 | 665,355 | 728,014 | 791,891 | 855,729 |
| Net Claims on Central Government.. | 42an | 3,093 | 3,726 | † 51,399 | 73,241 | 90,105 | 98,611 | 107,035 | 104,238 | 117,776 | 83,556 | 96,473 | 121,198 |
| Claims on Central Government....... | 42a | 3,094 | 3,726 | † 52,173 | 73,832 | 90,571 | 99,108 | 107,831 | 104,814 | 118,312 | 84,025 | 97,128 | 121,730 |
| Liabilities to Central Government.... | 46d | 1 | 1 | † 775 | 591 | 466 | 497 | 797 | 576 | 536 | 469 | 655 | 531 |
| Claims on Other Sectors.................. | 42s | 15,991 | 22,236 | † 207,357 | 293,918 | 255,401 | 339,435 | 334,584 | 309,439 | 314,048 | 318,561 | 283,745 | 233,429 |
| Claims on State & Local Govts....... | 42b | 399 | 466 | † 593 | 775 | 980 | 933 | 1,209 | 1,371 | 1,845 | 1,886 | 2,065 | 1,954 |
| Claims on Public Nonfin. Corps...... | 42c | 34 | 22 | † 1,117 | 29 | 21 | 22 | 29 | 159 | 216 | 178 | 129 | 235 |
| Claims on Private Sector............... | 42d | 15,558 | 21,748 | † 205,648 | 293,114 | 254,400 | 338,480 | 333,345 | 307,909 | 311,987 | 316,497 | 281,550 | 231,239 |
| Deposits........................................... | 46b | 37 | 59 | † 2,983 | 3,490 | 7,157 | 6,723 | 2,746 | 2,303 | 1,720 | 1,306 | 1,292 | 788 |
| Securities Other than Shares........... | 46s | 16,734 | 52,341 | † 106,236 | 153,653 | 176,049 | 184,032 | 224,945 | 259,087 | 276,624 | 316,981 | 376,781 | 410,881 |
| Loans.............................................. | 46l | 2,401 | 2,420 | † 4,514 | 10,963 | 7,120 | 10,168 | 10,859 | 9,107 | 9,832 | 11,741 | 11,718 | 10,933 |
| Financial Derivatives........................ | 46m | — | — | † 1,902 | 2,641 | 2,694 | 2,621 | 1,527 | 817 | 1,354 | 453 | 431 | 760 |
| Insurance Technical Reserves........... | 46r | — | — | † 290,725 | 331,825 | 361,059 | 397,943 | 444,238 | 486,176 | 548,752 | 585,803 | 626,397 | 702,457 |
| Shares and Other Equity................... | 47a | 21,429 | 39,101 | † 179,030 | 281,608 | 207,837 | 332,557 | 379,508 | 370,667 | 344,856 | 313,828 | 249,879 | 152,941 |
| Other Items (Net)............................ | 47r | 1,372 | 1,156 | † −85,366 | −96,146 | −87,244 | −107,531 | −64,123 | −75,398 | −85,507 | −98,223 | −90,827 | −64,284 |
| Memo Item: | | | | | | | | | | | | | |
| Total Assets..................................... | 40ra | 43,645 | 96,749 | † 633,530 | 846,885 | 825,626 | 1,005,780 | 1,141,012 | 1,208,024 | 1,265,698 | 1,312,428 | 1,350,328 | 1,364,835 |

| | | 2004 | 2005 | 2006 | 2007 | 2008 | 2009 | 2010 | 2011 | 2012 | 2013 | 2014 | 2015 |
|---|---|---|---|---|---|---|---|---|---|---|---|---|---|
| **Monetary Aggregates** | | | | | | *Millions of Reais: End of Period* | | | | | | | |
| Broad Money.......................... | 59m | 1,104,699 | 1,311,374 | 1,555,885 | 1,899,037 | 2,255,804 | 2,633,693 | 3,079,445 | 3,587,829 | 4,140,457 | 4,453,209 | 5,070,355 | 5,618,183 |
| o/w:Currency Issued by Cent.Govt | 59m.a | — | — | — | — | — | — | — | — | — | — | — | — |
| o/w: Dep.in Nonfin. Corporations. | 59m.b | — | — | — | — | — | — | — | — | — | — | — | — |
| o/w:Secs. Issued by Central Govt.. | 59m.c | 120,897 | 145,897 | 180,903 | 267,229 | 333,939 | 398,518 | 490,756 | 519,973 | 584,670 | 580,525 | 673,649 | 795,021 |
| Money (National Definitions) | | | | | | | | | | | | | |
| Base Money.............................. | 19ma | 88,733 | 101,247 | 121,102 | 146,617 | 147,550 | 166,073 | 206,853 | 214,235 | 233,371 | 249,510 | 263,529 | 255,289 |
| Base Money (B1)....................... | 19maa | 94,694 | 108,117 | 129,554 | 157,679 | 152,845 | 172,408 | 223,196 | 233,226 | 250,231 | 267,447 | .... | .... |
| Base Money (BA)....................... | 19mab | 979,233 | 1,154,051 | 1,336,845 | 1,616,618 | 1,768,289 | 2,051,351 | 2,394,948 | 2,682,798 | 2,894,997 | 3,114,577 | 3,525,418 | 4,180,456 |
| Base Money (B2)....................... | 19mac | 980,140 | 1,154,806 | 1,336,980 | 1,616,769 | .... | .... | .... | .... | .... | .... | .... | .... |
| M1.......................................... | 59ma | 127,946 | 144,778 | 174,345 | 231,430 | 223,440 | 248,097 | 281,876 | 285,377 | 325,045 | 344,508 | 351,603 | 334,417 |
| M2.......................................... | 59mb | 493,497 | 582,464 | 661,500 | 781,280 | 1,072,986 | 1,164,855 | 1,362,389 | 1,617,480 | 1,764,611 | 1,956,838 | 2,150,684 | 2,285,721 |
| M3.......................................... | 59mc | 988,622 | 1,166,502 | 1,377,704 | 1,617,618 | 1,908,187 | 2,203,750 | 2,549,739 | 3,030,280 | 3,519,063 | 3,821,960 | 4,319,484 | 4,759,312 |
| M4.......................................... | 59md | 1,109,519 | 1,312,399 | 1,558,607 | 1,884,847 | 2,242,126 | 2,602,269 | 3,040,495 | 3,550,253 | 4,103,727 | 4,402,485 | 4,993,133 | 5,554,333 |
| **Interest Rates** | | | | | | *Percent Per Annum* | | | | | | | |
| Central Bank Policy Rate (EOP)........ | 60 | 17.75 | 18.00 | 13.25 | 11.25 | 13.75 | 8.75 | 10.75 | 11.00 | 7.25 | 10.00 | 11.75 | 14.25 |
| Discount Rate (End of Period).......... | 60.a | 24.55 | 25.34 | 19.98 | 17.85 | 20.48 | 15.17 | 17.30 | 17.55 | 13.59 | 16.49 | 18.27 | 21.00 |
| Money Market Rate...................... | 60b | 16.24 | 19.12 | 15.28 | 11.98 | 12.36 | 10.06 | 9.80 | 11.66 | 8.48 | 8.18 | 10.86 | 13.37 |
| Treasury Bill Rate...................... | 60c | 17.14 | 18.76 | 14.38 | 11.50 | 13.68 | 9.70 | 10.93 | 11.66 | 8.07 | 8.99 | 11.54 | 14.16 |
| Savings Rate............................... | 60k | 8.09 | 9.21 | 8.32 | 7.70 | 7.77 | 6.94 | 6.96 | 7.51 | 6.52 | 6.37 | 7.06 | 8.17 |
| Deposit Rate............................... | 60l | 15.42 | 17.63 | 13.93 | 10.58 | 11.66 | 9.28 | 8.87 | 10.99 | 7.91 | 7.81 | 10.02 | 12.62 |
| Lending Rate............................... | 60p | 54.93 | 55.38 | 50.81 | 43.72 | 47.25 | 44.65 | 39.99 | 43.88 | 36.64 | 27.39 | 32.01 | 43.96 |
| **Prices and Labor** | | | | | | *Index Numbers (2010=100): Period Averages* | | | | | | | |
| Share Prices............................... | 62 | 33.2 | 41.0 | 56.7 | 79.1 | 82.2 | 78.5 | 100.0 | 91.1 | 88.6 | 79.8 | 78.2 | 74.0 |
| Share Prices (End of Month)............ | 62.ep | 33.5 | 41.7 | 57.7 | 81.1 | 82.8 | 79.7 | 100.0 | 91.5 | 88.6 | 79.6 | 78.6 | 73.2 |
| Wholesale Prices............................ | 63 | 74.2 | 78.3 | 79.0 | 83.4 | 94.8 | 94.6 | 100.0 | 109.4 | 115.9 | 122.7 | 128.4 | 136.1 |
| Consumer Prices............................ | 64 | 74.4 | 79.6 | 82.9 | 85.9 | 90.8 | 95.2 | 100.0 | 106.6 | 112.4 | 119.4 | 126.9 | 138.4 |
| | | | | | | *Number in Thousands: Period Averages* | | | | | | | |
| Labor Force.................................... | 67d | 21,753 | 21,990 | 22,526 | 22,535 | 22,934 | 23,148 | 23,611 | 23,898 | 24,295 | 24,433 | 24,263 | 24,386 |
| Employment.................................... | 67e | 19,259 | 19,830 | 20,281 | 20,435 | 21,122 | 21,276 | 22,019 | 22,428 | 22,956 | 23,116 | 23,087 | 22,712 |
| Unemployment.............................. | 67c | 2,493 | 2,160 | 2,245 | 2,100 | 1,813 | 1,872 | 1,591 | 1,426 | 1,338 | 1,318 | 1,176 | 1,673 |
| Unemployment Rate (%)................. | 67r | 11.5 | 9.8 | 10.0 | 9.3 | 7.9 | 8.1 | 6.7 | 6.0 | 5.5 | 5.4 | 4.9 | 6.8 |
| **Intl. Transactions & Positions** | | | | | | *Millions of US Dollars* | | | | | | | |
| Exports............................................ | 70..d | 96,678 | 118,529 | 137,807 | 160,649 | 197,942 | 152,995 | 201,915 | 256,040 | 242,580 | 242,179 | 225,101 | 191,134 |
| Beef....................................... | 70m.d | 1,963.1 | 2,419.1 | 3,134.5 | 3,485.7 | 4,006.2 | 3,022.6 | 3,861.1 | 4,169.3 | 4,494.9 | 5,358.7 | 5,794.3 | 4,664.1 |
| Cocoa Beans.............................. | 70r.d | 1.87 | 1.79 | .83 | 1.71 | 1.58 | .94 | 1.05 | 2.90 | 1.98 | 1.37 | 2.04 | 21.02 |
| Coffee........................................... | 70e.d | 1,749.8 | 2,516.1 | 2,928.2 | 3,378.0 | 4,131.5 | 3,761.3 | 5,181.6 | 8,000.0 | 5,721.7 | 4,582.2 | 6,041.1 | 5,555.4 |
| Soybeans................................... | 70s.d | 5,394.9 | 5,345.0 | 5,663.4 | 6,709.4 | 10,952.2 | 11,424.3 | 11,043.0 | 16,327.3 | 17,455.2 | 22,812.3 | 23,277.4 | 20,983.6 |
| Sugar....................................... | 70i.d | 1,511.0 | 2,382.1 | 3,935.8 | 3,129.8 | 3,649.6 | 5,978.6 | 9,306.9 | 11,548.8 | 10,030.1 | 9,163.7 | 7,450.1 | 5,901.1 |
| Imports, c.i.f.................................... | 71..d | 66,433 | 77,628 | 95,838 | 126,645 | 182,377 | 133,673 | 191,537 | 236,946 | 228,377 | 244,677 | 239,156 | 178,832 |
| Imports, f.o.b.................................... | 71.vd | 62,836 | 73,600 | 91,351 | 120,617 | 172,985 | 127,705 | 181,768 | 226,247 | 223,164 | 239,628 | 229,145 | 171,461 |
| | | | | | | *2010=100* | | | | | | | |
| Volume of Exports........................ | 72 | 72.3 | 76.3 | 81.6 | 88.8 | 90.2 | 87.6 | 100.0 | 104.6 | 105.0 | 107.4 | 110.9 | 122.6 |
| Beef....................................... | 72m | 97.2 | 114.1 | 128.8 | 135.2 | 107.5 | 97.4 | 100.0 | 86.2 | 99.4 | 124.5 | 129.1 | 113.4 |
| Cocoa Beans.............................. | 72r | 458.1 | 439.3 | 188.0 | 296.0 | 194.0 | 97.4 | 100.0 | 298.3 | 199.0 | 139.3 | 206.3 | 2,814.9 |
| Coffee.......................................... | 72e | 78.8 | 75.5 | 82.4 | 83.1 | 87.5 | 91.5 | 100.0 | 100.0 | 84.0 | 94.9 | 110.9 | 112.0 |
| Soybeans.................................... | 72s | 66.2 | 77.2 | 85.8 | 81.6 | 84.3 | 98.2 | 100.0 | 113.5 | 113.2 | 147.2 | 157.2 | 186.9 |
| Sugar....................................... | 72i | 45.7 | 55.3 | 61.2 | 59.4 | 65.1 | 85.6 | 100.0 | 96.2 | 93.0 | 102.8 | 92.0 | 90.4 |
| Volume of Imports........................ | 73 | 74.4 | 67.7 | 74.0 | 86.1 | 90.1 | 75.2 | 100.0 | 107.6 | 102.6 | 115.5 | 119.6 | 106.0 |
| | | | | | | *2010=100: Indices of Unit Values in US Dollars* | | | | | | | |
| Unit Value of Exports/Export Prices... | 74..d | 67.7 | 77.1 | 84.9 | 90.1 | 110.4 | 87.1 | 100.0 | 121.5 | 115.7 | 112.5 | 101.5 | 78.0 |
| Beef....................................... | 74m.d | 52.3 | 54.9 | 63.0 | 66.8 | 96.5 | 80.4 | 100.0 | 125.2 | 117.1 | 111.5 | 116.2 | 106.5 |
| Cocoa Beans (Unit Value)........... | 74r.d | 38.9 | 38.7 | 42.0 | 54.9 | 77.5 | 91.4 | 100.0 | 92.3 | 94.4 | 93.2 | 94.0 | 71.0 |
| Coffee (Unit Value)...................... | 74e.d | 42.9 | 64.3 | 68.6 | 78.5 | 91.1 | 79.3 | 100.0 | 154.4 | 131.5 | 93.2 | 105.1 | 95.8 |
| Coffee (Wholesale Price).............. | 76ebd | 47.9 | 70.2 | 71.2 | 76.7 | 84.7 | 77.1 | 100.0 | 168.6 | 118.6 | 81.6 | 111.6 | 85.2 |
| Soybeans (Unit Value)................. | 74jfd | 73.8 | 62.7 | 59.7 | 74.4 | 117.7 | 105.3 | 100.0 | 130.3 | 139.6 | 140.3 | .... | .... |
| Sugar (Unit Value)...................... | 74i.d | 35.5 | 46.3 | 69.1 | 56.6 | 60.3 | 75.0 | 100.0 | 128.9 | 115.9 | 95.8 | 87.0 | 70.1 |
| Unit Value of Imports/Import Prices... | 75..d | 46.5 | 59.8 | 68.6 | 77.0 | 105.7 | 93.8 | 100.0 | 115.5 | 120.4 | 114.5 | 107.6 | 89.2 |

|  |  | 2004 | 2005 | 2006 | 2007 | 2008 | 2009 | 2010 | 2011 | 2012 | 2013 | 2014 | 2015 |
|---|---|---|---|---|---|---|---|---|---|---|---|---|---|
| **Balance of Payments** |  | | | | | | *Millions of US Dollars* | | | | | | |
| A. Current Account* | 109bx | 11,737.6 | 13,984.3 | 13,619.7 | 1,550.8 | −28,192.0 | −24,305.6 | † −75,759.7 | −76,970.4 | −74,058.6 | −74,769.1 | −104,181.3 | −58,882.2 |
| Goods, credit (exports) | 1a9cx | 96,240.6 | 118,029.3 | 137,808.2 | 160,649.1 | 197,942.4 | 152,994.7 | † 201,259.6 | 255,444.1 | 242,123.5 | 241,507.4 | 224,097.8 | 190,092.1 |
| Goods, debit (imports) | 1a9dx | 62,348.1 | 73,139.8 | 91,349.6 | 120,617.4 | 173,106.7 | 127,723.3 | † 182,833.1 | 227,880.8 | 224,863.6 | 241,188.7 | 230,727.0 | 172,422.2 |
| Balance on goods | 1a9bx | 33,892.5 | 44,889.6 | 46,458.6 | 40,031.6 | 24,835.8 | 25,271.4 | † 18,426.5 | 27,563.4 | 17,259.9 | 318.7 | −6,629.2 | 17,669.9 |
| Services, credit (exports) | 1b9cx | 11,744.1 | 14,975.9 | 18,495.0 | 23,954.3 | 30,450.5 | 27,728.3 | † 30,800.4 | 37,105.5 | 39,135.8 | 38,150.3 | 39,965.3 | 33,777.5 |
| Services, debit (imports) | 1b9dx | 16,647.1 | 23,471.1 | 28,149.4 | 37,172.9 | 47,140.4 | 46,974.1 | † 60,827.8 | 74,148.5 | 78,984.4 | 84,382.7 | 88,072.1 | 70,696.2 |
| Balance on Goods & Services | 1z9bx | 28,989.5 | 36,394.3 | 36,804.2 | 26,813.0 | 8,145.9 | 6,025.6 | † −11,600.8 | −9,479.7 | −22,588.7 | −45,913.7 | −54,736.0 | −19,248.8 |
| Primary income: credit | 1c9cx | 3,198.9 | 3,194.3 | 6,438.1 | 11,492.7 | 12,510.8 | 8,841.3 | † 17,696.4 | 22,881.8 | 8,618.2 | 12,129.9 | 12,849.3 | 11,930.7 |
| Primary income: debit | 1c9dx | 23,719.1 | 29,161.7 | 33,927.1 | 40,783.9 | 53,072.6 | 42,510.0 | † 84,751.3 | 93,356.9 | 62,925.7 | 44,668.3 | 65,019.6 | 54,287.9 |
| Balance on gds, serv. & prim. inc. | 1y9bx | 8,469.4 | 10,426.9 | 9,315.3 | −2,478.2 | −32,415.9 | −27,643.1 | † −78,655.6 | −79,954.7 | −76,896.3 | −78,452.2 | −106,906.3 | −61,606.0 |
| Secondary income: credit | 1d9ca | 3,582.5 | 4,050.4 | 4,845.5 | 4,971.8 | 5,316.6 | 4,735.7 | † 4,765.7 | 4,909.3 | 4,615.9 | 5,793.6 | 4,930.4 | 4,712.5 |
| Secondary income: debit | 1d9da | 314.3 | 493.0 | 541.0 | 942.8 | 1,092.8 | 1,398.2 | † 1,869.8 | 1,925.0 | 1,778.2 | 2,110.5 | 2,205.4 | 1,988.7 |
| B. Capital Account* | 209ba | −362.0 | 51.7 | 65.0 | 12.2 | −13.4 | 55.6 | † 242.1 | 255.8 | 207.9 | 322.3 | 231.5 | 440.2 |
| Capital account: credit | 209ca | 1.8 | 170.8 | 118.1 | 12.2 | 59.4 | 83.7 | † 346.9 | 376.4 | 321.8 | 426.2 | 376.3 | 549.0 |
| Capital account: debit | 209da | 363.8 | 119.1 | 53.1 | — | 72.8 | 28.1 | † 104.8 | 120.6 | 113.9 | 103.9 | 144.8 | 108.8 |
| Balance on current & capital acct. | 129ba | 11,375.6 | 14,036.0 | 13,684.7 | 1,563.0 | −28,205.4 | −24,250.1 | † −75,517.6 | −76,714.6 | −73,850.7 | −74,446.8 | −103,949.8 | −58,442.0 |
| C. Financial Account* | 309na | 3,333.0 | −13,144.1 | −15,113.1 | −88,329.7 | −28,296.5 | −70,162.8 | † −125,000.1 | −137,614.1 | −92,826.6 | −66,409.9 | −111,431.2 | −56,302.7 |
| Direct investment: assets | 3a9aa | 9,486.3 | 2,910.4 | 28,798.4 | 17,061.3 | 26,115.3 | −4,551.9 | † 26,763.0 | 16,067.1 | 5,207.6 | 14,941.8 | 26,039.7 | 13,498.4 |
| Equity & investment fund shares | 3aaaa | 6,640.2 | 2,694.6 | 23,413.5 | 10,091.3 | 13,859.1 | 4,545.3 | † 36,537.2 | 31,087.5 | 4,742.7 | 16,300.3 | 25,328.0 | 14,337.4 |
| Debt instruments | 3abaa | 2,846.1 | 215.8 | 5,384.9 | 6,969.9 | 12,256.2 | −9,097.1 | † −9,774.2 | −15,020.4 | 464.9 | −1,358.5 | 711.6 | −839.1 |
| Direct investment: liabilities | 3a9la | 18,181.2 | 15,460.0 | 19,378.1 | 44,579.5 | 50,716.4 | 31,480.9 | † 88,452.1 | 101,157.8 | 86,606.5 | 69,181.4 | 96,895.0 | 75,074.6 |
| Equity & investment fund shares | 3aala | 18,570.3 | 15,044.9 | 15,373.3 | 26,074.4 | 30,064.0 | 19,906.4 | † 74,981.8 | 84,707.1 | 64,065.6 | 30,835.3 | 57,918.2 | 56,421.2 |
| Debt instruments | 3abla | −389.1 | 415.1 | 4,004.8 | 18,505.1 | 20,652.4 | 11,574.6 | † 13,470.3 | 16,450.7 | 22,540.9 | 38,346.1 | 38,976.7 | 18,653.4 |
| Portfolio investment: assets | 3b9aa | 754.6 | 1,770.8 | −522.6 | −286.1 | −1,900.0 | −4,124.5 | † 4,735.2 | −16,855.5 | 7,402.7 | 8,981.3 | 2,819.7 | −3,547.9 |
| Equity & investment fund shares | 3baaa | 121.4 | 830.8 | 915.2 | 1,413.4 | −257.1 | −2,582.2 | † −4,264.4 | −7,656.5 | 6,941.8 | 6,219.2 | 2,144.3 | −98.0 |
| Debt securities | 3bbaa | 633.2 | 940.0 | −1,437.9 | −1,699.5 | −1,643.0 | −1,542.3 | † 8,999.6 | −9,199.0 | 460.8 | 2,761.9 | 675.4 | −3,450.0 |
| Portfolio investment: liabilities | 3b9la | −3,995.6 | 6,655.3 | 9,050.6 | 48,104.3 | −766.9 | 46,158.5 | † 71,648.1 | 24,392.2 | 23,228.5 | 41,767.6 | 41,527.3 | 18,499.5 |
| Equity & investment fund shares | 3bala | 2,080.9 | 6,451.3 | 7,715.8 | 26,217.3 | −7,565.4 | 37,071.2 | † 37,671.3 | 7,173.9 | 5,601.8 | 11,636.3 | 11,773.0 | 10,030.4 |
| Debt securities | 3bbla | −6,076.5 | 204.1 | 1,334.8 | 21,886.9 | 6,798.4 | 9,087.3 | † 33,976.8 | 17,218.3 | 17,626.7 | 30,131.3 | 29,754.3 | 8,469.2 |
| Fin. der.& empl.stk.ops.(ESOs): net | 3c9na | 677.4 | 40.0 | −383.2 | 710.3 | 312.4 | −156.2 | † 112.1 | −2.8 | −24.6 | −110.3 | 1,568.2 | 3,449.7 |
| Fin. der. & ESOs.: assets | 3c9aa | −467.2 | −508.0 | −482.1 | −88.4 | −298.1 | −322.2 | † −356.2 | −386.9 | −301.1 | −497.2 | −7,614.1 | −20,659.1 |
| Fin. der. & ESOs.: liabilities | 3c9la | −1,144.6 | −548.0 | −98.9 | −798.7 | −610.5 | −166.0 | † −468.3 | −384.1 | −276.4 | −386.8 | −9,182.2 | −24,108.7 |
| Other investment: assets | 3d9aa | 2,195.9 | 5,034.9 | 8,913.7 | 18,551.5 | 5,268.8 | 30,303.2 | † 40,454.7 | 36,054.9 | 23,867.2 | 39,772.6 | 50,666.5 | 44,000.8 |
| Other equity | 3daaa | . . . . | . . . . | . . . . | . . . . | . . . . | . . . . | † 84.5 | 132.6 | 34.9 | .2 | 94.9 | 171.5 |
| Debt instruments | 3dzaa | 2,195.9 | 5,034.9 | 8,913.7 | 18,551.5 | 5,268.8 | 30,303.2 | † 40,370.2 | 35,922.3 | 23,832.3 | 39,772.4 | 50,571.6 | 43,829.2 |
| Other investment: liabilities | 3d9la | −4,404.4 | 784.9 | 23,490.7 | 31,682.9 | 8,143.4 | 13,993.9 | † 36,964.9 | 47,327.7 | 19,444.4 | 19,045.9 | 54,102.9 | 20,129.5 |
| Other equity | 3dala | . . . . | . . . . | . . . . | . . . . | . . . . | . . . . | † — | | | | | |
| Debt instruments | 3dzla | −4,404.4 | 784.9 | 23,490.7 | 31,682.9 | 8,143.4 | 13,993.9 | † 36,964.9 | 47,327.7 | 19,444.4 | 19,045.9 | 54,102.9 | 20,129.5 |
| Curr.+ cap.– finan. acct. balance | 4y9na | 8,042.6 | 27,180.1 | 28,797.8 | 89,892.7 | 91.1 | 45,912.7 | † 49,482.5 | 60,899.5 | 18,975.8 | −8,036.9 | 7,481.3 | −2,139.3 |
| D. Net Errors and Omissions | 409na | −1,443.5 | 386.4 | 1,771.5 | −2,408.5 | 2,878.2 | 1,664.9 | † −402.5 | −2,264.7 | −76.7 | 2,113.1 | 3,351.6 | 3,707.9 |
| E. Reserves and Related Items | 4z9na | 6,599.1 | 27,566.4 | 30,569.3 | 87,484.2 | 2,969.3 | 47,577.6 | † 49,080.0 | 58,634.9 | 18,899.1 | −5,923.8 | 10,832.9 | 1,568.7 |
| Reserve assets | 3e9aa | 2,237.6 | 4,324.3 | 30,571.0 | 87,484.2 | 2,969.3 | 47,577.6 | † 49,080.0 | 58,634.9 | 18,899.1 | −5,923.8 | 10,832.9 | 1,568.7 |
| Credit and loans from the IMF | 3dcla | −4,361.5 | −23,242.5 | — | — | — | — | † — | — | — | — | — | — |
| Exceptional financing | 409la | — | .4 | 1.7 | — | — | — | † — | — | — | — | . . . . | . . . . |

*Excludes components in group E

**International Investment Position**   *Millions of US Dollars*

|  |  | 2004 | 2005 | 2006 | 2007 | 2008 | 2009 | 2010 | 2011 | 2012 | 2013 | 2014 | 2015 |
|---|---|---|---|---|---|---|---|---|---|---|---|---|---|
| Assets | 809aa | 161,367.9 | 182,027.5 | 253,511.7 | 394,262.8 | 421,526.7 | 475,710.7 | 578,948.1 | 650,066.4 | 738,173.3 | 758,982.5 | 765,471.1 | 775,995.1 |
| Direct investment | 8a9aa | 69,196.2 | 79,259.3 | 113,925.1 | 141,880.0 | 157,795.9 | 167,147.8 | 191,349.2 | 206,187.2 | 270,864.0 | 300,791.4 | 299,748.3 | 310,424.6 |
| Equity & investment fund shares | 8aaaa | 54,027.0 | 65,417.5 | 97,464.7 | 113,183.2 | 115,609.0 | 135,038.1 | 171,777.6 | 196,533.6 | 251,783.9 | 278,330.5 | 275,531.9 | 286,543.8 |
| Debt instruments | 8abaa | 15,169.3 | 13,841.8 | 16,460.5 | 28,696.9 | 42,186.9 | 32,109.6 | 19,571.6 | 9,653.6 | 19,080.1 | 22,460.8 | 24,216.4 | 23,880.7 |
| Portfolio investment | 8b9aa | 9,353.0 | 10,834.3 | 14,429.0 | 19,269.4 | 14,636.8 | 16,518.6 | 38,202.8 | 28,484.6 | 22,124.4 | 25,436.7 | 28,240.6 | 25,222.3 |
| Equity & investment fund shares | 8baaa | 2,352.0 | 2,808.5 | 3,753.6 | 6,548.2 | 4,828.0 | 8,641.3 | 14,730.5 | 16,903.2 | 13,367.1 | 16,929.9 | 18,622.3 | 18,217.4 |
| Debt securities | 8bbaa | 7,001.0 | 8,025.8 | 10,675.4 | 12,721.2 | 9,808.7 | 7,877.3 | 23,472.3 | 11,581.5 | 8,757.3 | 8,506.8 | 9,618.3 | 7,004.9 |
| Fin. der.(oth.than reserves) & ESOs | 8c9aa | 108.9 | 118.9 | 113.4 | 142.5 | 608.9 | 426.3 | 797.1 | 667.7 | 554.6 | 646.6 | 609.4 | 756.0 |
| Other investment | 8d9aa | 29,774.9 | 38,015.7 | 39,205.3 | 52,637.2 | 54,701.8 | 53,078.6 | 60,024.4 | 62,716.7 | 71,483.2 | 73,301.4 | 73,322.4 | 83,128.8 |
| Other equity | 8daaa | 970.7 | 1,102.0 | 1,072.1 | 1,087.9 | 1,325.9 | 1,327.5 | 1,414.5 | 1,568.8 | 1,609.2 | 1,715.0 | 1,802.9 | 1,974.4 |
| Debt instruments | 8dzaa | 28,804.2 | 36,913.7 | 38,133.2 | 51,549.4 | 53,375.9 | 51,751.2 | 58,609.9 | 61,147.9 | 69,874.0 | 71,586.4 | 71,519.5 | 81,154.4 |
| Reserve assets | 8e9aa | 52,934.9 | 53,799.3 | 85,838.9 | 180,333.6 | 193,783.4 | 238,539.5 | 288,574.6 | 352,010.2 | 373,146.9 | 358,806.5 | 363,550.4 | 356,463.5 |
| Liabilities | 809la | 443,508.3 | 481,765.0 | 603,953.5 | 890,347.2 | 665,235.2 | 1,034,856.2 | 1,485,340.2 | 1,471,969.5 | 1,547,311.5 | 1,506,670.4 | 1,564,742.1 | 1,248,329.2 |
| Direct investment | 8a9la | 161,258.9 | 181,344.3 | 220,620.9 | 309,668.0 | 287,696.9 | 400,807.7 | 682,345.9 | 696,408.3 | 743,963.6 | 747,891.2 | 762,049.9 | 630,518.2 |
| Equity & investment fund shares | 8aala | 142,450.8 | 162,807.3 | 193,837.6 | 262,391.5 | 223,127.1 | 321,436.2 | 587,208.9 | 590,495.3 | 616,258.4 | 573,745.4 | 554,293.9 | 424,807.6 |
| Debt instruments | 8abla | 18,808.0 | 18,537.1 | 26,783.3 | 47,276.5 | 64,569.8 | 79,371.6 | 95,137.1 | 105,912.9 | 127,705.1 | 174,145.7 | 207,756.0 | 205,710.7 |
| Portfolio investment | 8b9la | 184,162.8 | 231,891.1 | 304,241.8 | 482,796.5 | 264,694.0 | 522,704.0 | 646,495.1 | 584,919.4 | 604,635.6 | 554,249.0 | 526,356.1 | 368,614.8 |
| Equity & investment fund shares | 8bala | 77,260.7 | 125,531.7 | 191,513.3 | 363,998.6 | 149,607.9 | 376,462.9 | 441,617.8 | 360,782.9 | 357,233.5 | 305,234.9 | 259,855.7 | 146,215.6 |
| Debt securities | 8bbla | 106,902.1 | 106,359.5 | 112,728.5 | 118,797.9 | 115,086.1 | 146,241.1 | 204,877.3 | 224,136.5 | 247,402.1 | 249,014.1 | 266,500.5 | 222,399.2 |
| Fin. der.(oth.than reserves) & ESOs | 8c9la | 319.7 | 219.1 | 444.6 | 1,771.3 | 2,450.1 | 3,412.7 | 3,781.0 | 4,678.0 | 3,027.9 | 6,295.6 | 37,984.0 | 12,219.2 |
| Other investment | 8d9la | 97,766.9 | 68,310.4 | 78,646.2 | 96,111.5 | 110,394.1 | 107,931.9 | 152,718.1 | 185,963.8 | 195,684.4 | 198,234.7 | 238,352.0 | 236,977.0 |
| Other equity | 8dala | . . . . | . . . . | . . . . | . . . . | . . . . | . . . . | . . . . | . . . . | . . . . | . . . . | . . . . | . . . . |
| Debt instruments | 8dzla | 97,766.9 | 68,310.4 | 78,646.2 | 96,111.5 | 110,394.1 | 107,931.9 | 152,718.1 | 185,963.8 | 195,684.4 | 198,234.7 | 238,352.0 | 236,977.0 |

|  |  | 2004 | 2005 | 2006 | 2007 | 2008 | 2009 | 2010 | 2011 | 2012 | 2013 | 2014 | 2015 |
|---|---|---|---|---|---|---|---|---|---|---|---|---|---|
| **Government Finance Operations Statement Central Government** | | | | | | *Millions of Reais: Fiscal Year Ends December 31* | | | | | | | |
| Revenue | a1 | 418,241 | 486,746 | 619,100 | 701,070 | 840,406 | 799,299 | 1,048,724 | 1,118,211 | 1,227,434 | 1,326,527 | 1,372,869 | 1,519,154 |
| Taxes | a11 | 288,870 | 335,809 | 370,605 | 429,136 | 481,796 | 480,542 | 553,164 | 653,557 ` | 678,161 | 752,678 | 774,362 | 803,110 |
| Social Contributions | a12 | 93,765 | 108,434 | 130,895 | 148,767 | 172,992 | 192,908 | 224,206 | 259,193 | 289,474 | 321,889 | 353,371 | 367,710 |
| Grants | a13 | — | — | 166 | 582 | 473 | 184 | 292 | 472 | 635 | 414 | 507 | 438 |
| Other Revenue | a14 | 35,606 | 42,503 | 117,435 | 122,585 | 185,145 | 125,665 | 271,063 | 204,988 | 259,163 | 251,546 | 244,629 | 347,895 |
| Expense | a2 | 454,438 | 564,155 | 670,663 | 729,295 | 849,146 | 877,825 | 1,067,039 | 1,172,716 | 1,254,713 | 1,403,020 | 1,586,501 | 2,007,158 |
| Compensation of Employees | a21 | 83,656 | 92,231 | 105,496 | 116,372 | 130,829 | 151,653 | 166,486 | 179,277 | 186,097 | 202,744 | 219,834 | 235,764 |
| Use of Goods & Services | a22 | 68,142 | 79,635 | 43,008 | 51,869 | 49,857 | 55,320 | 67,300 | 74,951 | 87,012 | 118,254 | 148,035 | 187,450 |
| Consumption of Fixed Capital | a23 | .... | .... | .... | .... | .... | .... | .... | .... | .... | .... | .... | .... |
| Interest | a24 | 85,694 | 130,159 | 194,758 | 191,925 | 234,464 | 214,837 | 273,807 | 332,233 | 331,573 | 366,256 | 426,152 | 700,467 |
| Subsidies | a25 | 5,564 | 10,333 | 8,099 | 9,522 | 5,355 | 4,625 | 7,521 | 9,981 | 10,605 | 9,459 | 8,985 | 58,929 |
| Grants | a26 | 67,557 | 83,937 | 124,457 | 140,455 | 176,106 | 178,390 | 199,565 | 232,267 | 250,979 | 259,940 | 284,581 | 294,292 |
| Social Benefits | a27 | 143,203 | 167,307 | 192,667 | 218,133 | 236,625 | 271,255 | 307,672 | 341,334 | 385,463 | 435,635 | 487,140 | 526,602 |
| Other Expense | a28 | 622 | 553 | 2,178 | 1,019 | 15,911 | 1,745 | 44,688 | 2,673 | 2,984 | 10,733 | 11,774 | 3,655 |
| Gross Operating Balance [1-2+23] | agob | −36,197 | −77,409 | −51,563 | −28,225 | −8,741 | −78,526 | −18,315 | −54,505 | −27,279 | −76,494 | −213,631 | −488,005 |
| Net Operating Balance [1-2] | anob | .... | .... | .... | .... | .... | .... | .... | .... | .... | .... | .... | .... |
| Net Acq. of Nonfinancial Assets | a31 | −138 | −235 | 16,801 | 21,563 | 27,910 | 33,880 | 44,595 | 52,477 | 59,424 | 63,061 | 77,332 | 55,355 |
| Aquisition of Nonfin. Assets | a31.1 | — | — | 17,112 | 21,889 | 28,106 | 34,008 | 44,741 | 52,631 | 59,449 | 63,224 | 77,536 | 55,532 |
| Disposal of Nonfin. Assets | a31.2 | 138 | 235 | 311 | 326 | 196 | 128 | 146 | 154 | 25 | 164 | 203 | 177 |
| Net Lending/Borrowing [1-2-31] | anlb | −36,059 | −77,174 | −68,364 | −49,787 | −36,650 | −112,406 | −62,910 | −106,982 | −86,703 | −139,555 | −290,964 | −543,360 |
| Net Acq. of Financial Assets | a32 | 77,358 | 85,372 | 34,128 | 77,172 | 88,000 | 146,880 | 190,753 | 91,964 | 183,749 | 12,982 | 19,425 | −789 |
| By instrument | | | | | | | | | | | | | |
| Monetary Gold & SDRs | a3201 | — | — | — | — | — | — | — | — | — | — | — | — |
| Currency & Deposits | a3202 | 42,287 | 80,540 | 27,934 | 59,295 | 20,298 | 59,102 | 42,077 | 18,581 | 77,495 | −58,529 | −70,564 | −60,619 |
| Securities other than Shares | a3203 | — | — | — | — | — | — | — | — | — | — | — | — |
| Loans | a3204 | 35,071 | 4,832 | 6,194 | 17,877 | 67,702 | 87,779 | 148,675 | 73,383 | 106,254 | 71,510 | 89,989 | 59,830 |
| Shares & Other Equity | a3205 | — | — | — | — | — | — | — | — | — | — | — | — |
| Insurance Technical Reserves | a3206 | — | — | — | — | — | — | — | — | — | — | — | — |
| Financial Derivatives | a3207 | — | — | — | — | — | — | — | — | — | — | — | — |
| Other Accounts Receivable | a3208 | — | — | — | — | — | — | — | — | — | — | — | — |
| By debtor | | | | | | | | | | | | | |
| Domestic | a321 | 76,997 | 85,051 | 37,408 | 77,172 | 88,000 | 146,880 | 190,397 | 91,788 | 183,389 | 13,535 | 19,622 | −368 |
| Foreign | a322 | 361 | 321 | −3,280 | — | — | — | 356 | 176 | 360 | −553 | −197 | −421 |
| Net Incurrence of Liabilities | a33 | 110,334 | 159,478 | 99,887 | 125,171 | 124,780 | 256,279 | 253,713 | 199,434 | 272,629 | 154,239 | 313,642 | 543,395 |
| By instrument | | | | | | | | | | | | | |
| Special Drawing Rights (SDRs) | a3301 | — | — | — | — | — | — | — | — | — | — | — | — |
| Currency & Deposits | a3302 | — | — | — | — | — | — | — | — | — | — | — | — |
| Securities other than Shares | a3303 | 118,150 | 158,490 | 102,730 | 126,148 | 120,766 | 267,293 | 252,664 | 213,569 | 273,923 | 162,445 | 314,545 | 539,583 |
| Loans | a3304 | −7,816 | 988 | −2,843 | −978 | 4,015 | −11,014 | 1,049 | −14,135 | −1,294 | −8,206 | −904 | 3,812 |
| Shares & Other Equity | a3305 | — | — | — | — | — | — | — | — | — | — | — | — |
| Insurance Technical Reserves | a3306 | — | — | — | — | — | — | — | — | — | — | — | — |
| Financial Derivatives | a3307 | — | — | — | — | — | — | — | — | — | — | — | — |
| Other Accounts Payable | a3308 | — | — | — | — | — | — | — | — | — | — | — | — |
| By creditor | | | | | | | | | | | | | |
| Domestic | a331 | 118,714 | 158,042 | 130,215 | 137,329 | 125,207 | 247,772 | 236,581 | 195,482 | 266,700 | 145,215 | 281,273 | 481,851 |
| Foreign | a332 | −8,380 | 1,435 | −30,328 | −12,158 | −426 | 8,508 | 17,132 | 3,952 | 5,929 | 9,024 | 32,368 | 61,544 |
| Stat. Discrepancy [32-33-NLB] | anlbz | 3,082 | 3,068 | 2,604 | 1,788 | −130 | 3,007 | −50 | −488 | −2,177 | −1,703 | −3,253 | −824 |
| Memo Item: Expenditure [2+31] | a2m | 454,300 | 563,920 | 687,464 | 750,857 | 877,056 | 911,705 | 1,111,634 | 1,225,193 | 1,314,137 | 1,466,081 | 1,663,833 | 2,062,514 |
| **Balance Sheet** | | | | | | | | | | | | | |
| Net Worth | a6 | .... | .... | .... | .... | .... | .... | .... | .... | .... | .... | .... | .... |
| Nonfinancial Assets | a61 | .... | .... | .... | .... | .... | .... | .... | .... | .... | .... | .... | .... |
| Financial Assets | a62 | 703,044 | 778,094 | † 813,583 | 890,755 | 1,126,034 | 1,155,011 | 1,338,236 | 1,535,209 | 1,819,751 | 1,960,807 | 2,105,511 | 2,548,825 |
| By instrument | | | | | | | | | | | | | |
| Monetary Gold & SDRs | a6201 | — | — | — | — | — | — | — | — | — | — | — | — |
| Currency & Deposits | a6202 | 334,288 | 405,283 | † 410,891 | 470,186 | 636,496 | 577,694 | 614,484 | 733,957 | 908,145 | 972,587 | 1,025,499 | 1,394,968 |
| Securities other than Shares | a6203 | — | — | — | — | — | — | — | — | — | — | — | — |
| Loans | a6204 | 368,756 | 372,810 | 402,692 | 420,569 | 489,538 | 577,317 | 723,752 | 801,252 | 911,607 | 988,220 | 1,080,011 | 1,153,857 |
| Shares and Other Equity | a6205 | — | — | — | — | — | — | — | — | — | — | — | — |
| Insurance Technical Reserves | a6206 | — | — | — | — | — | — | — | — | — | — | — | — |
| Financial Derivatives | a6207 | — | — | — | — | — | — | — | — | — | — | — | — |
| Other Accounts Receivable | a6208 | — | — | — | — | — | — | — | — | — | — | — | — |
| By debtor | | | | | | | | | | | | | |
| Domestic | a621 | 699,361 | 774,563 | † 813,583 | 890,755 | 1,126,034 | 1,155,011 | 1,337,929 | 1,534,666 | 1,818,795 | 1,960,299 | 2,105,133 | 2,548,720 |
| Foreign | a622 | 3,683 | 3,531 | — | — | — | — | 307 | 543 | 957 | 508 | 377 | 106 |
| Liabilities | a63 | 1,313,122 | 1,438,279 | † 1,540,901 | 1,698,850 | 1,886,283 | 2,126,735 | 2,382,754 | 2,597,018 | 2,881,609 | 3,051,201 | 3,378,218 | 4,049,408 |
| By instrument | | | | | | | | | | | | | |
| Special Drawing Rights (SDRs) | a6301 | — | — | — | — | — | — | — | — | — | — | — | — |
| Currency & Deposits | a6302 | — | — | † — | — | — | — | — | — | — | — | — | — |
| Securities other than Shares | a6303 | 1,081,301 | 1,235,721 | 1,488,112 | 1,651,532 | 1,828,615 | 2,087,640 | 2,343,504 | 2,570,777 | 2,855,666 | 3,032,287 | 3,359,358 | 4,023,673 |
| Loans | a6304 | 231,821 | 202,558 | 52,790 | 47,318 | 57,668 | 39,096 | 39,250 | 26,241 | 25,943 | 18,913 | 18,860 | 25,735 |
| Shares and Other Equity | a6305 | — | — | — | — | — | — | — | — | — | — | — | — |
| Insurance Technical Reserves | a6306 | — | — | — | — | — | — | — | — | — | — | — | — |
| Financial Derivatives | a6307 | — | — | — | — | — | — | — | — | — | — | — | — |
| Other Accounts Payable | a6308 | — | — | — | — | — | — | — | — | — | — | — | — |
| By creditor | | | | | | | | | | | | | |
| Domestic | a631 | 1,111,241 | 1,262,716 | † 1,404,794 | 1,557,131 | 1,697,933 | 1,934,417 | 2,128,479 | 2,331,163 | 2,564,373 | 2,652,581 | 2,879,520 | 3,442,516 |
| Foreign | a632 | 201,881 | 175,563 | 136,108 | 141,719 | 188,349 | 192,318 | 254,275 | 265,854 | 317,237 | 398,619 | 498,699 | 606,892 |
| Net Financial Worth [62-63] | a6m2 | −610,078 | −660,186 | −727,319 | −808,095 | −760,249 | −971,724 | −1,044,518 | −1,061,809 | −1,061,858 | −1,090,393 | −1,272,707 | −1,500,582 |
| Memo Item: Debt at Market Value | a6m3 | .... | .... | .... | .... | .... | .... | .... | .... | .... | .... | .... | .... |
| Memo Item: Debt at Face Value | a6m35 | .... | .... | .... | .... | .... | .... | .... | .... | .... | .... | .... | .... |
| Memo Item: Debt at Nominal Value | a6m4 | 1,313,122 | 1,438,279 | † 1,540,901 | 1,698,850 | 1,886,283 | 2,126,735 | 2,382,754 | 2,597,018 | 2,881,609 | 3,051,201 | 3,378,218 | 4,049,408 |

# Brazil 223

| National Accounts | | 2004 | 2005 | 2006 | 2007 | 2008 | 2009 | 2010 | 2011 | 2012 | 2013 | 2014 | 2015 |
|---|---|---|---|---|---|---|---|---|---|---|---|---|---|
| | | | | | | | *Millions of Reais* | | | | | | |
| Househ.Cons.Expend.,incl.NPISHs.... | 96f | 1,160,611 | 1,294,230 | 1,428,906 | 1,594,067 | 1,786,840 | 1,979,751 | 2,248,624 | 2,499,489 | 2,744,452 | 3,033,694 | 3,449,807 | 3,741,855 |
| Government Consumption Expend... | 91f | 373,284 | 427,553 | 474,773 | 539,061 | 612,105 | 687,001 | 797,332 | 856,647 | 944,543 | 1,064,528 | 1,114,901 | 1,192,401 |
| Gross Fixed Capital Formation......... | 93e | 312,516 | 342,237 | 389,328 | 464,137 | 579,531 | 585,317 | 733,712 | 798,720 | 798,695 | 886,981 | 1,090,116 | 1,072,458 |
| Changes in Inventories.................... | 93i | 19,817 | 5,739 | 7,699 | 23,624 | 47,966 | −7,471 | 29,300 | 18,540 | −22,230 | −14,024 | 18,650 | −26,687 |
| Exports of Goods and Services.......... | 90c | 318,892 | 324,842 | 340,457 | 355,672 | 414,295 | 355,653 | 409,868 | 492,570 | 552,843 | 608,210 | 635,910 | 770,084 |
| Imports of Goods and Services (-)..... | 98c | 243,622 | 247,362 | 271,679 | 315,217 | 408,534 | 360,847 | 448,752 | 522,953 | 615,765 | 728,528 | 788,127 | 845,779 |
| Gross Domestic Product (GDP)......... | 99b | 1,941,498 | 2,147,239 | 2,369,484 | 2,661,344 | 3,032,203 | 3,239,404 | 3,770,085 | 4,143,013 | 4,402,537 | 4,844,815 | 5,521,256 | 5,904,331 |
| Net Primary Income from Abroad..... | 98.n | −59,009 | −62,118 | −58,975 | −55,684 | −72,815 | −65,295 | −68,907 | −79,076 | −69,818 | −124,488 | −86,470 | −128,920 |
| Gross National Income (GNI)............ | 99a | 1,882,489 | 2,085,121 | 2,310,509 | 2,605,660 | 2,959,388 | 3,174,109 | 3,701,178 | 4,063,937 | 4,332,719 | 4,760,090 | 5,434,786 | 5,775,412 |
| GDP Volume 2000 Prices............... | 99b.p | 1,311,677 | 1,353,126 | 1,406,710 | 1,492,378 | 1,569,534 | 1,564,355 | 1,682,151 | 1,728,073 | .... | .... | .... | .... |
| GDP Volume (2010=100)............... | 99bvp | 78.0 | 80.4 | 83.6 | 88.7 | 93.3 | 93.0 | 100.0 | 102.7 | .... | .... | .... | .... |
| GDP Deflator (2010=100)............... | 99bip | 66.0 | 70.8 | 75.2 | 79.6 | 86.2 | 92.4 | 100.0 | 107.0 | .... | .... | .... | .... |
| | | | | | | | *Millions: Midyear Estimates* | | | | | | |
| Population................................ | 99z | 186.12 | 188.48 | 190.70 | 192.78 | 194.77 | 196.70 | 198.61 | 200.52 | 202.40 | 204.26 | 206.08 | 207.85 |

# Brunei Darussalam  516

| | | 2004 | 2005 | 2006 | 2007 | 2008 | 2009 | 2010 | 2011 | 2012 | 2013 | 2014 | 2015 |
|---|---|---|---|---|---|---|---|---|---|---|---|---|---|
| **Exchange Rates** | | | | | | *Brunei Dollars per SDR: End of Period* | | | | | | | |
| Official Rate.................. | aa | 2.5377 | 2.3789 | 2.3075 | 2.2778 | 2.2171 | 2.2001 | 1.9897 | 1.9969 | 1.8804 | 1.9547 | 1.9143 | 1.9593 |
| | | | | | *Brunei Dollars per US Dollar: End of Period (ae) Period Average (rf)* | | | | | | | | |
| Official Rate.................. | ae | 1.6340 | 1.6644 | 1.5338 | 1.4414 | 1.4394 | 1.4034 | 1.2920 | 1.3007 | 1.2235 | 1.2693 | 1.3213 | 1.4139 |
| Official Rate.................. | rf | 1.6902 | 1.6644 | 1.5889 | 1.5071 | 1.4172 | 1.4546 | 1.3635 | 1.2579 | 1.2496 | 1.2512 | 1.2670 | 1.3749 |
| **Fund Position** | | | | | | *Millions of SDRs: End of Period* | | | | | | | |
| Quota................................ | 2f.s | 215.20 | 215.20 | 215.20 | 215.20 | 215.20 | 215.20 | 215.20 | 215.20 | 215.20 | 215.20 | 215.20 | 215.20 |
| SDR Holdings................... | 1b.s | 8.81 | 10.17 | 11.20 | 12.04 | 12.73 | 216.33 | 216.38 | 216.46 | 216.48 | 216.49 | 216.51 | 216.51 |
| Reserve Position in the Fund............ | 1c.s | 58.29 | 32.27 | 24.58 | 14.56 | 13.67 | 13.67 | 13.67 | 13.67 | 13.67 | 13.67 | 13.67 | 13.67 |
| Total Fund Cred.&Loans Outstg....... | 2tl | — | — | — | — | — | — | — | — | — | — | — | — |
| SDR Allocations.................... | 1bd | — | — | — | — | — | 203.50 | 203.50 | 203.50 | 203.50 | 203.50 | 203.50 | 203.50 |
| **International Liquidity** | | | | | | *Millions of US Dollars Unless Otherwise Indicated: End of Period* | | | | | | | |
| Total Reserves minus Gold.............. | 1l.d | 488.89 | 491.89 | 513.57 | 667.49 | 751.16 | 1,357.27 | 1,563.16 | 2,486.78 | 3,285.31 | 3,398.52 | 3,471.23 | 3,211.36 |
| SDR Holdings................... | 1b.d | 13.69 | 14.54 | 16.84 | 19.03 | 19.61 | 339.14 | 333.23 | 332.32 | 332.71 | 333.39 | 313.68 | 300.03 |
| Reserve Position in the Fund......... | 1c.d | 90.52 | 46.12 | 36.97 | 23.00 | 21.06 | 21.44 | 21.06 | 20.99 | 21.01 | 21.06 | 19.81 | 18.95 |
| Foreign Exchange............. | 1d.d | 384.68 | 431.23 | 459.75 | 625.46 | 710.49 | 996.69 | 1,208.87 | 2,133.47 | 2,931.59 | 3,044.07 | 3,137.74 | 2,892.38 |
| Gold (Million Fine Troy Ounces)........ | 1ad | | | | | | | | .06 | .10 | .15 | .15 | .15 |
| Gold (National Valuation)............... | 1and | | | | | | | | 104.57 | 163.21 | 176.76 | 176.60 | 155.30 |
| Central Bank: Other Assets........ | 3..d | 14.0 | 21.5 | 21.1 | 24.8 | 23.5 | 23.7 | † 22.8 | 15.8 | 16.2 | 15.6 | 15.2 | 14.2 |
| Central Bank: Other Liabs......... | 4..d | 17.2 | 14.6 | 49.5 | 24.1 | 24.5 | 28.9 | † 23.7 | 16.3 | 16.6 | 16.2 | 196.9 | 14.6 |
| Other Depository Corps.: Assets....... | 7a.d | 4,433.9 | 4,982.0 | 4,837.1 | 5,336.7 | 6,842.1 | 5,374.0 | † 7,616.3 | 10,070.0 | 9,351.6 | 8,155.7 | 7,028.2 | 5,191.4 |
| Other Depository Corps.: Liabs......... | 7b.d | 90.5 | 299.1 | 346.9 | 355.5 | 263.5 | 295.0 | † 330.8 | 154.4 | 164.6 | 116.4 | 130.6 | 190.5 |
| Other Financial Corps.: Assets.......... | 7e.d | .... | .... | 477.8 | 552.9 | 582.2 | 561.0 | 682.0 | † 779.6 | 852.1 | 8,044.2 | 4,367.7 | 4,518.1 |
| Other Financial Corps.: Liabs.......... | 7f.d | .... | .... | 7.4 | 19.1 | 81.7 | 8.3 | 113.9 | † 204.7 | 228.2 | 181.0 | 212.9 | 137.2 |
| **Central Bank** | | | | | | *Millions of Brunei Dollars: End of Period* | | | | | | | |
| Net Foreign Assets.......................... | 11n | 793.6 | 830.1 | 744.1 | 963.0 | 1,079.6 | 1,449.7 | † 1,552.0 | 2,695.7 | 3,632.3 | 3,875.4 | 3,956.8 | 4,141.3 |
| Claims on Nonresidents................ | 11 | 821.6 | 854.4 | 820.0 | 997.7 | 1,114.9 | 1,938.0 | † 1,986.0 | 3,108.2 | 4,034.7 | 4,292.4 | 4,606.6 | 4,560.6 |
| Liabilities to Nonresidents......... | 16c | 28.1 | 24.3 | 75.9 | 34.7 | 35.3 | 488.4 | † 434.0 | 412.5 | 402.5 | 417.0 | 649.7 | 419.4 |
| Claims on Other Depository Corps.... | 12e | 836.6 | 888.3 | 944.0 | 800.6 | 941.8 | 536.9 | † 570.6 | 850.2 | 423.5 | 193.7 | 180.0 | 142.2 |
| Net Claims on Central Government.. | 12an | −303.6 | −305.7 | −293.0 | −306.5 | −270.6 | −268.4 | † −269.6 | 138.2 | −69.5 | −57.0 | −56.3 | −55.7 |
| Claims on Central Government...... | 12a | .3 | .3 | .6 | .5 | .6 | .9 | † .8 | 300.8 | .8 | 1.1 | 1.3 | 1.3 |
| Liabilities to Central Government... | 16d | 303.9 | 306.1 | 293.6 | 307.0 | 271.2 | 269.3 | † 270.5 | 162.6 | 70.3 | 58.1 | 57.5 | 57.0 |
| Claims on Other Sectors................. | 12s | — | — | — | — | — | — | † — | — | — | — | — | — |
| Claims on Other Financial Corps.... | 12g | — | — | — | — | — | — | † — | — | — | — | — | — |
| Claims on State & Local Govts....... | 12b | — | — | — | — | — | — | † — | — | — | — | — | — |
| Claims on Public Nonfin. Corps...... | 12c | — | — | — | — | — | — | † — | — | — | — | — | — |
| Claims on Private Sector............... | 12d | — | — | — | — | — | — | † — | — | — | — | — | — |
| Monetary Base................................ | 14 | 1,262.9 | 1,376.9 | 1,394.6 | 1,458.9 | 1,691.3 | 1,624.3 | † 1,744.1 | 2,665.5 | 2,887.0 | 2,970.9 | 3,005.2 | 3,161.8 |
| Currency in Circulation.................. | 14a | 667.1 | 704.7 | 739.9 | 848.8 | 921.8 | 954.5 | † 1,023.7 | 1,690.0 | 1,627.1 | 1,219.7 | 1,271.7 | 1,322.0 |
| Liabs. to Other Depository Corps.... | 14c | 595.9 | 672.2 | 654.7 | 610.1 | 769.5 | 669.8 | † 720.4 | 975.5 | 1,260.0 | 1,751.2 | 1,733.5 | 1,839.8 |
| Liabilities to Other Sectors............ | 14d | — | — | — | — | — | — | † — | — | — | — | — | — |
| Other Liabs. to Other Dep. Corps.... | 14n | — | — | — | — | — | — | † — | — | 1.1 | 1.3 | 1.1 | 3.2 |
| Dep. & Sec. Excl. f/Monetary Base.... | 14o | — | — | — | — | — | — | † — | — | — | — | — | — |
| Deposits Included in Broad Money. | 15 | — | — | — | — | — | — | † — | — | — | — | — | — |
| Sec.Ot.th.Shares Incl.in Brd. Money | 16a | — | — | — | — | — | — | † — | — | — | — | — | — |
| Deposits Excl. from Broad Money.. | 16b | — | — | — | — | — | — | † — | — | — | — | — | — |
| Sec.Ot.th.Shares Excl.f/Brd.Money.. | 16s | — | — | — | — | — | — | † — | — | — | — | — | — |
| Loans............................................. | 16l | — | — | — | — | — | — | † — | — | — | — | — | — |
| Financial Derivatives..................... | 16m | — | — | — | — | — | — | † — | — | — | — | — | — |
| Shares and Other Equity................. | 17a | 86.2 | 122.4 | 68.7 | 88.0 | 79.2 | 114.2 | † 126.7 | 1,045.4 | 1,159.5 | 1,070.3 | 1,103.3 | 1,091.2 |
| Other Items (Net)........................... | 17r | −22.5 | −86.6 | −68.1 | −89.8 | −19.6 | −20.4 | † −17.8 | −26.9 | −61.4 | −30.3 | −29.0 | −28.4 |
| Memo Item: | | | | | | | | | | | | | |
| Total Assets...................... | 10ra | 2,096.9 | 2,237.1 | 2,277.3 | 2,334.4 | 2,545.6 | 2,970.2 | † 3,003.5 | 4,730.6 | 4,931.1 | 4,947.4 | 5,240.6 | 5,168.8 |
| **Other Depository Corporations** | | | | | | *Millions of Brunei Dollars: End of Period* | | | | | | | |
| Net Foreign Assets.......................... | 21n | 7,096.3 | 7,793.3 | 6,886.1 | 7,178.9 | 9,468.0 | 7,127.8 | † 9,380.2 | 12,897.3 | 11,227.4 | 10,172.1 | 9,113.8 | 7,070.7 |
| Claims on Nonresidents................ | 21 | 7,244.1 | 8,291.1 | 7,418.1 | 7,691.2 | 9,847.1 | 7,541.9 | † 9,806.0 | 13,098.1 | 11,428.6 | 10,319.4 | 9,286.3 | 7,340.1 |
| Liabilities to Nonresidents............. | 26c | 147.8 | 497.8 | 532.0 | 512.3 | 379.2 | 414.1 | † 425.9 | 200.8 | 201.2 | 147.3 | 172.5 | 269.4 |
| Claims on Central Bank................. | 20 | 684.8 | 774.1 | 793.6 | 761.3 | 954.9 | 841.6 | † 922.5 | 1,833.6 | 1,960.9 | 1,991.8 | 1,847.7 | 2,034.9 |
| Currency............................... | 20a | 91.5 | 103.9 | 98.5 | 151.4 | 182.6 | 170.9 | † 199.3 | 858.9 | 701.0 | 242.2 | 250.7 | 249.1 |
| Reserve Deposits and Securities..... | 20b | 593.3 | 670.2 | 695.1 | 609.9 | 772.3 | 670.7 | † 723.2 | 974.7 | 1,259.8 | 1,749.5 | 1,597.0 | 1,785.8 |
| Other Claims........................ | 20n | | | | | | | † — | | | | | |
| Net Claims on Central Government.. | 22an | −3,226.0 | −4,509.8 | −3,124.8 | −3,270.2 | −5,105.2 | −1,713.0 | † −2,479.6 | −5,120.4 | −3,917.5 | −3,101.5 | −1,811.9 | −629.8 |
| Claims on Central Government...... | 22a | 53.8 | 50.1 | 180.2 | 129.2 | 202.8 | 288.2 | † 208.6 | 495.7 | 499.7 | 499.6 | 699.0 | 523.7 |
| Liabilities to Central Government... | 26d | 3,279.8 | 4,559.9 | 3,304.9 | 3,399.4 | 5,308.0 | 2,001.2 | † 2,688.2 | 5,616.1 | 4,417.2 | 3,601.1 | 2,511.0 | 1,153.4 |
| Claims on Other Sectors................. | 22s | 6,260.6 | 6,462.6 | 6,394.8 | 7,005.0 | 7,228.9 | 6,983.7 | † 6,943.0 | 6,712.0 | 6,864.0 | 7,540.7 | 7,783.3 | 8,211.7 |
| Claims on Other Financial Corps... | 22g | — | — | — | — | .1 | .1 | † 19.9 | 108.7 | 60.0 | 220.4 | 385.6 | 440.8 |
| Claims on State & Local Govts....... | 22b | — | — | — | — | — | — | † — | — | — | — | — | — |
| Claims on Public Nonfin. Corps...... | 22c | 81.9 | 70.7 | 59.8 | 122.7 | 92.0 | 63.3 | † 84.7 | 107.9 | 194.1 | 320.2 | 268.6 | 457.0 |
| Claims on Private Sector............... | 22d | 6,178.7 | 6,392.0 | 6,335.0 | 6,882.3 | 7,136.8 | 6,920.2 | † 6,838.5 | 6,495.3 | 6,610.0 | 7,000.0 | 7,129.1 | 7,313.9 |
| Liabilities to Central Bank.............. | 26g | 836.4 | 857.8 | 936.4 | 770.5 | 920.2 | 484.0 | † 533.2 | 700.2 | 322.9 | 425.8 | 467.9 | 601.1 |
| Transf.Dep.Included in Broad Money | 24 | 2,955.3 | 2,974.8 | 3,321.2 | 3,153.8 | 3,646.9 | 4,607.0 | † 2,992.6 | 3,402.4 | 3,367.4 | 3,487.1 | 3,375.1 | 3,606.7 |
| Other Dep.Included in Broad Money. | 25 | 6,060.1 | 5,583.6 | 5,392.1 | 6,131.9 | 6,552.8 | 6,604.7 | † 8,755.9 | 9,603.7 | 9,668.2 | 9,701.7 | 10,226.5 | 9,685.8 |
| Sec.Ot.th.Shares Incl.in Brd. Money.. | 26a | 2.8 | 3.1 | 1.6 | .5 | 1.1 | 1.1 | † — | — | — | — | — | — |
| Deposits Excl. from Broad Money..... | 26b | — | — | — | — | — | — | † — | — | — | — | — | — |
| Sec.Ot.th.Shares Excl.f/Brd.Money.... | 26s | — | — | — | — | — | — | † — | — | — | — | — | — |
| Loans............................................. | 26l | — | — | — | — | — | — | † — | — | — | — | — | 8.7 |
| Financial Derivatives...................... | 26m | — | — | — | — | — | — | † — | — | — | — | — | — |
| Insurance Technical Reserves......... | 26r | — | — | — | — | — | — | † — | — | — | — | — | — |
| Shares and Other Equity................. | 27a | 881.7 | 973.6 | 1,150.7 | 1,572.2 | 1,705.2 | 1,904.4 | † 1,932.4 | 2,073.3 | 2,184.2 | 2,349.0 | 2,420.7 | 2,546.3 |
| Other Items (Net)........................... | 27r | 79.4 | 127.2 | 147.9 | 45.9 | −279.7 | −361.0 | † 552.0 | 542.9 | 592.1 | 639.5 | 442.6 | 238.9 |
| Memo Item: | | | | | | | | | | | | | |
| Total Assets...................... | 20ra | 17,250.1 | 18,222.7 | 16,977.3 | 17,759.3 | 21,110.8 | 18,313.5 | † 19,510.3 | 23,716.2 | 22,372.7 | 22,237.6 | 21,396.9 | 19,656.1 |

# Brunei Darussalam  516

| | | 2004 | 2005 | 2006 | 2007 | 2008 | 2009 | 2010 | 2011 | 2012 | 2013 | 2014 | 2015 |
|---|---|---|---|---|---|---|---|---|---|---|---|---|---|
| **Depository Corporations** | | *Millions of Brunei Dollars: End of Period* | | | | | | | | | | | |
| Net Foreign Assets | 31n | 7,889.9 | 8,623.4 | 7,630.2 | 8,141.9 | 10,547.6 | 8,577.4 | † 10,932.2 | 15,593.0 | 14,859.7 | 14,047.5 | 13,070.6 | 11,211.9 |
| Claims on Nonresidents | 31 | 8,065.7 | 9,145.5 | 8,238.2 | 8,688.9 | 10,962.0 | 9,479.9 | † 11,792.0 | 16,206.3 | 15,463.3 | 14,611.8 | 13,892.8 | 11,900.7 |
| Liabilities to Nonresidents | 36c | 175.9 | 522.1 | 608.0 | 547.0 | 414.5 | 902.4 | † 859.8 | 613.3 | 603.6 | 564.3 | 822.2 | 688.8 |
| Domestic Claims | 32 | 2,731.0 | 1,647.1 | 2,977.1 | 3,428.3 | 1,853.1 | 5,002.3 | † 4,193.8 | 1,729.7 | 2,877.0 | 4,382.2 | 5,915.1 | 7,526.3 |
| Net Claims on Central Government | 32an | –3,529.5 | –4,815.5 | –3,417.7 | –3,576.6 | –5,375.8 | –1,981.4 | † –2,749.2 | –4,982.2 | –3,987.0 | –3,158.4 | –1,868.2 | –685.4 |
| Claims on Central Government | 32a | 54.1 | 50.5 | 180.8 | 129.7 | 203.5 | 289.1 | 209.5 | 796.4 | 500.5 | 500.7 | 700.3 | 525.0 |
| Liabilities to Central Government | 36d | 3,583.7 | 4,866.0 | 3,598.5 | 3,706.3 | 5,579.3 | 2,270.5 | † 2,958.7 | 5,778.7 | 4,487.5 | 3,659.1 | 2,568.5 | 1,210.4 |
| Claims on Other Sectors | 32s | 6,260.6 | 6,462.6 | 6,394.8 | 7,005.0 | 7,228.9 | 6,983.7 | † 6,943.0 | 6,712.0 | 6,864.0 | 7,540.7 | 7,783.3 | 8,211.7 |
| Claims on Other Financial Corps | 32g | — | — | — | — | .1 | .1 | † 19.9 | 108.7 | 60.0 | 220.4 | 385.6 | 440.8 |
| Claims on State & Local Govts | 32b | — | — | — | — | — | — | † — | — | — | — | — | — |
| Claims on Public Nonfin. Corps | 32c | 81.9 | 70.7 | 59.8 | 122.7 | 92.0 | 63.3 | † 84.7 | 107.9 | 194.1 | 320.2 | 268.6 | 457.0 |
| Claims on Private Sector | 32d | 6,178.7 | 6,392.0 | 6,335.0 | 6,882.3 | 7,136.8 | 6,920.2 | † 6,838.5 | 6,495.3 | 6,610.0 | 7,000.0 | 7,129.1 | 7,313.9 |
| Broad Money Liabilities | 35l | 9,593.8 | 9,162.3 | 9,356.2 | 9,983.7 | 10,940.0 | 11,996.3 | † 12,573.0 | 13,837.2 | 13,961.6 | 14,166.3 | 14,622.6 | 14,365.4 |
| Currency Outside Depository Corps | 34a | 575.6 | 600.8 | 641.4 | 697.4 | 739.2 | 783.6 | † 824.5 | 831.1 | 926.0 | 977.5 | 1,021.0 | 1,072.9 |
| Transferable Deposits | 34 | 2,955.3 | 2,974.8 | 3,321.2 | 3,153.8 | 3,646.9 | 4,607.0 | † 2,992.6 | 3,402.4 | 3,367.4 | 3,487.1 | 3,375.1 | 3,606.7 |
| Other Deposits | 35 | 6,060.1 | 5,583.6 | 5,392.1 | 6,131.9 | 6,552.8 | 6,604.7 | † 8,755.9 | 9,603.7 | 9,668.2 | 9,701.7 | 10,226.5 | 9,685.8 |
| Securities Other than Shares | 36a | 2.8 | 3.1 | 1.6 | .5 | 1.1 | 1.1 | † — | — | — | — | — | — |
| Deposits Excl. from Broad Money | 36b | — | — | — | — | — | — | † — | — | — | — | — | — |
| Sec.Ot.th.Shares Excl.f/Brd.Money | 36s | — | — | — | — | — | — | † — | — | — | — | — | — |
| Loans | 36l | — | — | — | — | — | — | † — | — | — | — | — | 8.7 |
| Financial Derivatives | 36m | — | — | — | — | — | — | † — | — | — | — | — | — |
| Insurance Technical Reserves | 36r | — | — | — | — | — | — | † — | — | — | — | — | — |
| Shares and Other Equity | 37a | 967.9 | 1,096.1 | 1,219.3 | 1,660.3 | 1,784.4 | 2,018.6 | † 2,059.0 | 3,118.7 | 3,343.7 | 3,419.2 | 3,524.1 | 3,637.5 |
| Other Items (Net) | 37r | 59.2 | 12.2 | 31.7 | –73.7 | –323.7 | –435.2 | † 494.0 | 366.9 | 431.4 | 844.2 | 839.1 | 726.7 |
| Broad Money Liabs., Seasonally Adj. | 35l.b | 9,650.0 | 9,227.5 | 9,434.6 | 10,051.2 | 11,006.0 | 12,055.0 | † 12,732.1 | 14,022.4 | 14,159.6 | 14,372.0 | 14,807.4 | 14,543.5 |
| **Other Financial Corporations** | | *Millions of Brunei Dollars: End of Period* | | | | | | | | | | | |
| Net Foreign Assets | 41n | .... | .... | 721.4 | 769.4 | 720.4 | 775.7 | 731.5 | † 747.7 | 762.5 | 9,949.3 | 5,489.8 | 6,194.2 |
| Claims on Nonresidents | 41 | .... | .... | 732.8 | 796.9 | 838.0 | 787.4 | 878.1 | † 1,014.1 | 1,041.4 | 10,178.3 | 5,771.1 | 6,388.2 |
| Liabilities to Nonresidents | 46c | .... | .... | 11.4 | 27.5 | 117.5 | 11.7 | 146.6 | † 266.3 | 278.8 | 229.0 | 281.3 | 194.0 |
| Claims on Depository Corporations | 40 | .... | .... | 184.2 | 202.0 | 183.5 | 208.9 | 269.2 | † 265.2 | 304.4 | 1,117.7 | 1,186.9 | 1,043.1 |
| Net Claims on Central Government | 42an | .... | .... | –1.2 | 1.1 | .4 | –3.2 | –1.5 | † –10.6 | –10.9 | –66.0 | –68.5 | –41.2 |
| Claims on Central Government | 42a | .... | .... | — | 2.1 | 1.6 | 1.1 | 1.6 | † 10.9 | 12.3 | 17.5 | 5.9 | 5.6 |
| Liabilities to Central Government | 46d | .... | .... | 1.2 | 1.0 | 1.2 | 4.3 | 3.2 | † 21.5 | 23.2 | 83.5 | 74.4 | 46.9 |
| Claims on Other Sectors | 42s | .... | .... | 35.0 | 42.3 | 36.5 | 30.6 | 63.7 | † 58.4 | 55.0 | 62.9 | 67.1 | 63.1 |
| Claims on State & Local Govts | 42b | .... | .... | — | — | — | — | — | † — | — | — | — | — |
| Claims on Public Nonfin. Corps | 42c | .... | .... | .2 | 1.2 | 3.0 | 1.9 | 4.0 | † .9 | 2.2 | 1.4 | 2.1 | 5.7 |
| Claims on Private Sector | 42d | .... | .... | 34.9 | 41.0 | 33.5 | 28.7 | 59.6 | † 57.6 | 52.8 | 61.5 | 65.0 | 57.4 |
| Deposits | 46b | .... | .... | 15.0 | 7.1 | 6.5 | 6.5 | 8.6 | † — | — | — | — | — |
| Securities Other than Shares | 46s | .... | .... | — | — | — | — | — | † — | — | — | — | — |
| Loans | 46l | .... | .... | 72.4 | 72.4 | 72.4 | 72.4 | 72.4 | † 73.1 | 76.1 | 81.2 | 76.6 | 2.0 |
| Financial Derivatives | 46m | .... | .... | — | — | — | — | — | † — | — | — | — | .1 |
| Insurance Technical Reserves | 46r | .... | .... | 510.9 | 527.4 | 584.5 | 594.4 | 614.1 | † 558.9 | 598.7 | 3,221.1 | 3,689.0 | 4,025.9 |
| Shares and Other Equity | 47a | .... | .... | 375.8 | 418.2 | 273.2 | 319.9 | 347.3 | † 403.9 | 422.2 | 7,742.1 | 2,902.4 | 3,197.5 |
| Other Items (Net) | 47r | .... | .... | –34.7 | –10.4 | 4.2 | 18.9 | 20.5 | † 24.8 | 14.1 | 19.6 | 7.1 | 33.6 |
| Memo Item: | | | | | | | | | | | | | |
| Total Assets | 40ra | .... | .... | 1,044.6 | 1,132.7 | 1,139.3 | 1,116.0 | 1,307.5 | † 1,459.6 | 1,528.6 | 11,504.7 | 7,163.2 | 7,562.1 |
| **Financial Corporations** | | *Millions of Brunei Dollars: End of Period* | | | | | | | | | | | |
| Net Foreign Assets | 51n | .... | .... | 8,351.6 | 8,911.3 | 11,268.0 | 9,353.1 | † 11,663.7 | † 16,340.7 | 15,622.2 | 23,996.9 | 18,560.4 | 17,406.1 |
| Claims on Nonresidents | 51 | .... | .... | 8,971.0 | 9,485.8 | 11,800.0 | 10,267.2 | † 12,670.1 | † 17,220.3 | 16,504.7 | 24,790.1 | 19,663.9 | 18,288.9 |
| Liabilities to Nonresidents | 56c | .... | .... | 619.3 | 574.5 | 532.0 | 914.1 | † 1,006.4 | † 879.6 | 882.5 | 793.3 | 1,103.5 | 882.8 |
| Domestic Claims | 52 | .... | .... | 3,010.8 | 3,471.7 | 1,889.9 | 5,029.5 | † 4,236.1 | † 1,668.8 | 2,861.1 | 4,158.7 | 5,528.0 | 7,107.3 |
| Net Claims on Central Government | 52an | .... | .... | –3,419.0 | –3,575.5 | –5,375.4 | –1,984.6 | † –2,750.7 | † –4,992.9 | –3,997.9 | –3,224.4 | –1,936.7 | –726.7 |
| Claims on Central Government | 52a | .... | .... | 180.8 | 131.8 | 205.0 | 290.2 | † 211.1 | † 807.3 | 512.7 | 518.2 | 706.2 | 530.6 |
| Liabilities to Central Government | 56d | .... | .... | 3,599.8 | 3,707.3 | 5,580.5 | 2,274.8 | † 2,961.8 | † 5,800.2 | 4,510.7 | 3,742.6 | 2,642.9 | 1,257.3 |
| Claims on Other Sectors | 52s | .... | .... | 6,429.8 | 7,047.2 | 7,265.3 | 7,014.1 | † 6,986.8 | † 6,661.7 | 6,859.0 | 7,383.1 | 7,464.8 | 7,834.0 |
| Claims on State & Local Govts | 52b | .... | .... | — | — | — | — | † — | † — | — | — | — | — |
| Claims on Public Nonfin. Corps | 52c | .... | .... | 59.9 | 123.9 | 95.0 | 65.2 | † 88.7 | † 108.8 | 196.2 | 321.6 | 270.7 | 462.7 |
| Claims on Private Sector | 52d | .... | .... | 6,369.9 | 6,923.3 | 7,170.3 | 6,948.9 | † 6,898.1 | † 6,552.9 | 6,662.8 | 7,061.6 | 7,194.0 | 7,371.3 |
| Currency Outside Financial Corps | 54a | .... | .... | 620.7 | 682.7 | 709.9 | 750.7 | † 789.7 | † 828.9 | 919.6 | 797.4 | 906.7 | 1,025.5 |
| Deposits | 55l | .... | .... | 8,564.7 | 9,105.6 | 10,052.1 | 11,042.1 | † 11,605.9 | † 12,826.3 | 12,858.1 | 12,965.7 | 13,324.1 | 12,909.0 |
| Securities Other than Shares | 56a | .... | .... | 1.6 | .5 | 1.1 | 1.1 | † — | † — | — | — | — | — |
| Loans | 56l | .... | .... | 72.4 | 72.4 | 72.4 | 72.4 | † 72.4 | † 72.4 | 75.6 | 81.2 | 75.6 | 8.7 |
| Financial Derivatives | 56m | .... | .... | — | — | — | — | † — | † — | — | — | — | — |
| Insurance Technical Reserves | 56r | .... | .... | 510.9 | 527.4 | 584.5 | 594.4 | † 614.1 | † 558.8 | 598.5 | 3,220.8 | 3,688.7 | 4,025.3 |
| Shares and Other Equity | 57a | .... | .... | 1,595.2 | 2,078.5 | 2,057.5 | 2,338.5 | † 2,406.3 | † 3,522.6 | 3,765.9 | 11,161.3 | 6,426.5 | 6,835.0 |
| Other Items (Net) | 57r | .... | .... | –3.0 | –84.1 | –319.5 | –416.5 | † 411.4 | † 200.6 | 265.7 | –70.9 | –333.1 | –290.1 |
| **Monetary Aggregates** | | *Millions of Brunei Dollars: End of Period* | | | | | | | | | | | |
| Broad Money | 59m | 9,593.8 | 9,162.3 | 9,356.2 | 9,983.7 | 10,940.0 | 11,996.3 | 12,573.0 | 13,837.2 | 13,961.6 | 14,166.3 | 14,622.6 | 14,365.4 |
| o/w:Currency Issued by Cent.Govt | 59m.a | — | — | — | — | — | — | — | — | — | — | — | — |
| o/w: Dep.in Nonfin. Corporations. | 59m.b | — | — | — | — | — | — | — | — | — | — | — | — |
| o/w:Secs. Issued by Central Govt.. | 59m.c | — | — | — | — | — | — | — | — | — | — | — | — |
| Money (National Definitions) | | | | | | | | | | | | | |
| M0 | 19mc | 667.1 | 704.7 | 739.9 | 848.8 | 921.8 | 954.5 | 1,023.7 | 1,690.0 | 1,627.1 | 1,219.7 | 1,271.7 | 1,322.0 |
| Money | 59maj | 3,530.8 | 3,575.6 | 3,962.6 | 3,851.2 | 4,386.1 | 5,390.5 | † 3,817.1 | 4,233.5 | 4,293.4 | 4,464.6 | 4,396.1 | 4,679.6 |
| Quasi-Money | 59mal | 6,062.9 | 5,586.7 | 5,393.7 | 6,132.4 | 6,553.9 | 6,605.8 | † 8,755.9 | 9,603.7 | 9,668.2 | 9,701.7 | 10,226.5 | 9,685.8 |
| Broad Money | 59mea | 9,593.8 | 9,162.3 | 9,356.2 | 9,983.7 | 10,940.0 | 11,996.3 | 12,573.0 | 13,837.2 | 13,961.6 | 14,166.3 | 14,622.6 | 14,365.4 |
| **Interest Rates** | | *Percent Per Annum* | | | | | | | | | | | |
| Deposit Rate | 60l | 1.044 | 1.006 | 1.042 | 1.173 | .876 | .700 | .471 | .396 | .232 | .284 | .300 | .336 |
| Lending Rate | 60p | 5.500 | † 5.500 | 5.500 | 5.500 | 5.500 | 5.500 | 5.500 | 5.500 | 5.500 | 5.500 | 5.500 | 5.500 |

# Brunei Darussalam  516

| | | 2004 | 2005 | 2006 | 2007 | 2008 | 2009 | 2010 | 2011 | 2012 | 2013 | 2014 | 2015 |
|---|---|---|---|---|---|---|---|---|---|---|---|---|---|
| **Prices and Labor** | | *Index Numbers (2010=100): Period Averages* | | | | | | | | | | | |
| Consumer Prices.............................. | 64 | 94.4 | † 95.5 | 95.7 | 96.6 | 98.6 | 99.6 | 100.0 | 102.0 | † 102.5 | 102.9 | 102.7 | 102.2 |
| | | *Number in Thousands: Period Averages* | | | | | | | | | | | |
| Labor Force.................................... | 67d | 167.2 | 174.5 | 181.7 | 184.8 | 188.8 | 194.8 | 198.8 | .... | .... | .... | 203.7 | .... |
| Employment................................... | 67e | 161.4 | 167.3 | 174.4 | 178.5 | 181.8 | 188.0 | 193.5 | .... | .... | .... | 189.6 | .... |
| Unemployment............................... | 67c | 5.8 | 7.2 | 7.3 | 6.3 | 6.4 | 4.7 | 5.0 | .... | 2.1 | .... | 14.1 | 13.0 |
| Unemployment Rate (%)................. | 67r | 3.5 | 4.1 | 4.0 | 3.4 | 3.7 | 3.5 | 2.7 | .... | .... | .... | 6.9 | .... |
| **Intl. Transactions & Positions** | | *Millions of Brunei Dollars* | | | | | | | | | | | |
| Exports........................................... | 70 | 8,547.5 | .... | 12,133.3 | 11,556.4 | 14,592.6 | 10,477.3 | 12,477.4 | .... | 16,220.7 | .... | .... | .... |
| Imports, c.i.f................................... | 71 | 2,403.5 | .... | 2,663.3 | 3,166.0 | 3,647.3 | 3,569.5 | 4,581.8 | .... | 4,455.2 | .... | .... | .... |
| **Balance of Payments** | | *Millions of US Dollars* | | | | | | | | | | | |
| A. Current Account*....................... | 109bx | 2,882.2 | 4,032.6 | 5,229.4 | 4,828.4 | 6,938.9 | 3,977.4 | † 5,016.2 | 6,430.1 | 5,683.7 | 3,778.2 | 4,749.6 | .... |
| Goods, credit (exports).................... | 1a9cx | 5,068.8 | 6,241.0 | 7,626.9 | 7,691.6 | 10,697.7 | 7,171.9 | † 8,799.6 | 12,376.2 | 12,881.8 | 11,835.5 | 11,111.4 | .... |
| Goods, debit (imports).................... | 1a9dx | 1,337.6 | 1,411.8 | 1,588.3 | 1,991.8 | 2,857.7 | 2,282.4 | † 2,568.0 | 3,756.6 | 4,116.2 | 4,911.7 | 3,667.9 | .... |
| Balance on goods...................... | 1a9bx | 3,731.3 | 4,829.2 | 6,038.6 | 5,699.8 | 7,840.0 | 4,889.5 | † 6,231.6 | 8,619.6 | 8,765.6 | 6,923.8 | 7,443.5 | .... |
| Services, credit (exports)............... | 1b9cx | 544.2 | 616.1 | 744.5 | 813.3 | 867.3 | 914.9 | † 462.1 | 501.7 | 482.9 | 492.6 | 556.8 | .... |
| Services, debit (imports)................ | 1b9dx | 1,075.7 | 1,110.1 | 1,213.6 | 1,316.8 | 1,402.5 | 1,434.2 | † 1,269.2 | 1,818.1 | 2,639.3 | 2,859.2 | 2,186.8 | .... |
| Balance on Goods & Services...... | 1z9bx | 3,199.8 | 4,335.1 | 5,569.6 | 5,196.3 | 7,304.8 | 4,370.2 | † 5,424.4 | 7,303.2 | 6,609.2 | 4,557.1 | 5,813.5 | .... |
| Primary income: credit.................. | 1c9cx | 236.3 | 263.2 | 247.9 | 268.3 | 303.6 | 316.3 | † 937.0 | 959.9 | 974.1 | 996.5 | 1,011.3 | .... |
| Primary income: debit.................... | 1c9dx | 200.1 | 190.1 | 182.7 | 205.9 | 249.1 | 264.2 | † 1,036.5 | 1,458.1 | 1,424.0 | 1,198.7 | 1,031.0 | .... |
| Balance on gds, serv. & prim. inc. | 1y9bx | 3,236.0 | 4,408.2 | 5,634.9 | 5,258.7 | 7,359.3 | 4,422.2 | † 5,324.9 | 6,805.0 | 6,159.3 | 4,354.8 | 5,793.8 | .... |
| Secondary income: credit............. | 1d9ca | .... | .... | .... | .... | .... | .... | † 12.1 | 20.0 | 33.1 | 34.3 | 39.5 | .... |
| Secondary income: debit.............. | 1d9da | 353.8 | 375.6 | 405.5 | 430.3 | 420.4 | 444.8 | † 320.8 | 394.9 | 508.7 | 610.9 | 1,083.7 | .... |
| B. Capital Account*........................ | 209ba | −11.3 | −8.2 | −7.1 | −7.4 | −7.9 | −10.9 | .... | .... | .... | .... | .... | .... |
| Capital account: credit................... | 209ca | .... | .... | .... | .... | .... | .... | .... | .... | .... | .... | .... | .... |
| Capital account: debit................... | 209da | 11.3 | 8.2 | 7.1 | 7.4 | 7.9 | 10.9 | .... | .... | .... | .... | .... | .... |
| Balance on current & capital acct. | 129ba | 2,870.9 | 4,024.5 | 5,222.4 | 4,820.9 | 6,931.0 | 3,966.4 | † 5,016.2 | 6,430.1 | 5,683.7 | 3,778.2 | 4,749.6 | .... |
| C. Financial Account* ................. | 309na | 1,651.5 | 82.2 | −602.7 | −1,166.8 | −1,346.4 | −1,607.3 | † 4,842.5 | 3,872.3 | 2,761.2 | 2,698.2 | 4,372.2 | .... |
| Direct investment: assets............ | 3a9aa | 41.6 | .... | 17.5 | .... | .... | .... | .... | .... | .... | .... | .... | .... |
| Equity & investment fund shares.. | 3aaaa | .... | .... | .... | .... | .... | .... | .... | .... | .... | .... | .... | .... |
| Debt instruments......................... | 3abaa | .... | .... | .... | .... | .... | .... | .... | .... | .... | .... | .... | .... |
| Direct investment: liabilities .......... | 3a9la | 113.2 | 175.1 | 87.8 | 257.6 | 222.2 | 325.6 | .... | .... | .... | .... | .... | .... |
| Equity & investment fund shares . | 3aala | 111.4 | 153.4 | 84.7 | 240.1 | — | — | .... | .... | .... | .... | .... | .... |
| Debt instruments......................... | 3abla | 1.8 | 21.7 | 3.2 | 17.6 | 222.2 | 325.6 | .... | .... | .... | .... | .... | .... |
| Portfolio investment: assets .......... | 3b9aa | 44.8 | −21.6 | 90.2 | −357.9 | −87.8 | −139.3 | † 865.5 | 165.9 | 565.2 | 458.4 | 770.0 | .... |
| Equity & investment fund shares | 3baaa | 55.6 | −12.6 | 90.2 | −357.9 | −87.8 | −139.3 | † −10.9 | 18.5 | 271.8 | 169.2 | 254.7 | .... |
| Debt securities.......................... | 3bbaa | −10.9 | −9.0 | — | — | — | — | † 876.4 | 147.4 | 293.4 | 289.2 | 515.3 | .... |
| Portfolio investment: liabilities....... | 3b9la | .... | .... | .... | .... | .... | .... | .... | .... | .... | .... | .... | .... |
| Equity & investment fund shares . | 3bala | .... | .... | .... | .... | .... | .... | .... | .... | .... | .... | .... | .... |
| Debt securities.......................... | 3bbla | .... | .... | .... | .... | .... | .... | .... | .... | .... | .... | .... | .... |
| Fin. der.& empl.stk.ops.(ESOs): net. | 3c9na | .... | .... | .... | .... | .... | .... | .... | .... | .... | .... | .... | .... |
| Fin. der. & ESOs.: assets.......... | 3c9aa | .... | .... | .... | .... | .... | .... | .... | .... | .... | .... | .... | .... |
| Fin. der. & ESOs.: liabilities.......... | 3c9la | .... | .... | .... | .... | .... | .... | .... | .... | .... | .... | .... | .... |
| Other investment: assets............... | 3d9aa | 1,568.8 | 493.2 | −355.8 | −1,008.9 | −749.5 | −644.4 | † 4,635.0 | 4,386.2 | 2,935.9 | 2,615.8 | 4,410.7 | .... |
| Other equity............................. | 3daaa | .... | .... | .... | .... | .... | .... | .... | .... | .... | .... | .... | .... |
| Debt instruments......................... | 3dzaa | 1,568.8 | 493.2 | −355.8 | −1,008.9 | −749.5 | −644.4 | † 4,635.0 | 4,386.2 | 2,935.9 | 2,615.8 | 4,410.7 | .... |
| Other investment: liabilities........... | 3d9la | −109.6 | 214.3 | 266.7 | −457.6 | 286.9 | 498.1 | † 178.5 | −24.0 | −119.2 | −402.5 | 234.6 | .... |
| Other equity............................. | 3dala | .... | .... | .... | .... | .... | .... | .... | .... | .... | .... | .... | .... |
| Debt instruments......................... | 3dzla | −109.6 | 214.3 | 266.7 | −457.6 | 286.9 | 498.1 | † 178.5 | −24.0 | −119.2 | −402.5 | 234.6 | .... |
| Curr.+ cap.− finan. acct. balance... | 4y9na | 1,219.4 | 3,942.3 | 5,825.0 | 5,987.8 | 8,277.4 | 5,573.7 | † 173.7 | 2,557.7 | 2,922.6 | 1,080.0 | 377.4 | .... |
| D. Net Errors and Omissions........... | 409na | −1,190.4 | −4,005.7 | −5,795.8 | −5,845.8 | −8,232.7 | −5,420.0 | † −98.2 | −1,777.0 | −2,219.9 | −901.7 | −131.3 | .... |
| E. Reserves and Related Items......... | 4z9na | 29.0 | −63.4 | 29.2 | 142.0 | 44.7 | 153.7 | † 75.5 | 780.8 | 702.7 | 178.3 | 246.1 | .... |
| Reserve assets............................ | 3e9aa | 29.0 | −63.4 | 29.2 | 142.0 | 44.7 | 153.7 | † 75.5 | 780.8 | 702.7 | 178.3 | 246.1 | .... |
| Credit and loans from the IMF....... | 3dcla | — | — | — | — | — | — | † — | — | — | — | — | .... |
| Exceptional financing.................... | 409la | .... | .... | .... | .... | .... | .... | .... | .... | .... | .... | .... | .... |
| *Excludes components in group E | | | | | | | | | | | | | |
| **National Accounts** | | *Millions of Brunei Dollars* | | | | | | | | | | | |
| Househ.Cons.Expend.,incl.NPISHs.... | 96f | 3,534.4 | 3,563.2 | 3,610.4 | 3,722.0 | 3,608.0 | 3,803.0 | 3,908.6 | 4,088.9 | 4,333.2 | 4,492.2 | 3,379.9 | .... |
| Government Consumption Expend... | 91f | 2,934.3 | 2,920.4 | 3,291.9 | 4,175.4 | 3,496.4 | 3,635.5 | 3,780.7 | 3,566.6 | 3,659.4 | 3,691.8 | 4,685.7 | .... |
| Gross Fixed Capital Formation......... | 93e | 1,787.2 | 1,801.3 | 1,907.4 | 2,398.5 | 2,788.9 | 2,739.6 | 2,678.3 | 2,750.4 | 2,880.6 | 3,087.1 | 5,909.5 | .... |
| Changes in Inventories................... | 93i | 7.3 | 1.9 | −5.1 | −1.7 | −.9 | 1.2 | .7 | .7 | .6 | .4 | 35.5 | .... |
| Exports of Goods and Services......... | 90c | 9,154.3 | 11,131.6 | 13,072.4 | 12,524.6 | 15,971.4 | 11,362.4 | 13,736.6 | 16,346.9 | 17,237.3 | 15,351.4 | 15,382.7 | .... |
| Imports of Goods and Services (-)..... | 98c | 4,230.0 | 4,329.2 | 4,595.9 | 5,149.5 | 5,632.8 | 5,587.2 | 5,544.7 | 5,994.5 | 6,616.0 | 6,519.8 | 7,728.4 | .... |
| Statistical Discrepancy................... | 99bs | 118.4 | 774.8 | 944.7 | 789.2 | 166.8 | −343.4 | −1,692.1 | −558.4 | −309.2 | 55.1 | 7.0 | .... |
| Gross Domestic Product (GDP)......... | 99b | 13,305.8 | 15,864.1 | 18,225.8 | 18,458.4 | 20,397.9 | 15,611.4 | 16,867.3 | 20,579.4 | 21,185.1 | 20,157.7 | 21,671.6 | .... |
| GDP Volume 2000 Prices................. | 99b.p | 11,419.4 | 11,463.7 | 11,967.8 | 11,986.2 | 11,753.9 | 11,546.4 | 11,846.5 | 12,108.1 | 12,368.9 | 12,152.4 | .... | .... |
| GDP Volume 2010 Prices................. | 99b.p | .... | .... | .... | .... | .... | .... | .... | .... | .... | 19,151.0 | 18,702.1 | .... |
| GDP Volume (2010=100)................. | 99bvp | 96.4 | 96.8 | 101.0 | 101.2 | 99.2 | 97.5 | 100.0 | 102.2 | 104.4 | † 102.6 | 100.2 | .... |
| GDP Deflator (2010=100)............... | 99bip | 81.8 | 97.2 | 107.0 | 108.2 | 121.9 | 95.0 | 100.0 | 119.4 | 120.3 | 116.5 | 128.3 | .... |
| | | *Millions: Midyear Estimates* | | | | | | | | | | | |
| Population.................................. | 99z | .36 | .36 | .37 | .37 | .38 | .39 | .39 | .40 | .41 | .41 | .42 | .42 |

# Bulgaria   918

| | | 2004 | 2005 | 2006 | 2007 | 2008 | 2009 | 2010 | 2011 | 2012 | 2013 | 2014 | 2015 |
|---|---|---|---|---|---|---|---|---|---|---|---|---|---|
| **Exchange Rates** | | | | | | | *Leva per SDR: End of Period* | | | | | | |
| Official Rate | aa | 2.2300 | 2.3696 | 2.2342 | 2.1036 | 2.1368 | 2.1385 | 2.2682 | 2.3207 | 2.2802 | 2.1853 | 2.3303 | 2.4806 |
| | | | | | | *Leva per US Dollar: End of Period (ae) Period Average (rf)* | | | | | | | |
| Official Rate | ae | 1.4359 | 1.6579 | 1.4851 | 1.3312 | 1.3873 | 1.3641 | 1.4728 | 1.5116 | 1.4836 | 1.4190 | 1.6084 | 1.7901 |
| Official Rate | rf | 1.5751 | 1.5741 | 1.5593 | 1.4291 | 1.3371 | 1.4067 | 1.4774 | 1.4065 | 1.5221 | 1.4736 | 1.4742 | 1.7644 |
| | | | | | | *Index Numbers (2010=100): Period Averages* | | | | | | | |
| Nominal Effective Exchange Rate | nec | 97.78 | 96.40 | 97.00 | 98.08 | 100.17 | 103.34 | 100.00 | 102.09 | 100.23 | 102.73 | 105.67 | 104.37 |
| CPI-Based Real Effect. Ex. Rate | rec | 82.47 | 82.60 | 86.27 | 91.28 | 99.76 | 104.06 | 100.00 | 102.71 | 100.72 | 101.98 | 101.43 | 98.20 |
| **Fund Position** | | | | | | | *Millions of SDRs: End of Period* | | | | | | |
| Quota | 2f.s | 640.20 | 640.20 | 640.20 | 640.20 | 640.20 | 640.20 | 640.20 | 640.20 | 640.20 | 640.20 | 640.20 | 640.20 |
| SDR Holdings | 1b.s | 8.45 | .70 | .71 | .66 | 4.20 | 610.88 | 610.89 | 610.92 | 611.11 | 611.59 | 611.59 | 611.58 |
| Reserve Position in the Fund | 1c.s | 32.85 | 33.00 | 33.14 | 33.32 | 33.53 | 33.71 | 33.92 | 34.10 | 34.10 | 34.10 | 34.10 | 34.10 |
| Total Fund Cred.&Loans Outstg | 2tl | 761.95 | 461.83 | 226.63 | — | — | — | 610.88 | 610.88 | 610.88 | 610.88 | 610.88 | 610.88 |
| SDR Allocations | 1bd | — | — | — | — | — | 610.88 | 610.88 | 610.88 | 610.88 | 610.88 | 610.88 | 610.88 |
| **International Liquidity** | | | | | | *Millions of US Dollars Unless Otherwise Indicated: End of Period* | | | | | | | |
| Total Reserves minus Gold | 1l.d | 8,776.25 | 8,040.54 | 10,943.01 | 16,477.94 | 16,815.53 | 17,127.29 | 15,420.51 | 15,251.92 | 18,371.02 | 18,334.73 | 18,576.13 | 20,783.32 |
| SDR Holdings | 1b.d | 13.12 | 1.00 | 1.07 | 1.04 | 6.47 | 957.66 | 940.80 | 937.93 | 939.23 | 941.84 | 886.08 | 847.49 |
| Reserve Position in the Fund | 1c.d | 51.02 | 47.17 | 49.86 | 52.66 | 51.64 | 52.85 | 52.23 | 52.35 | 52.41 | 52.52 | 49.41 | 47.26 |
| Foreign Exchange | 1d.d | 8,712.10 | 7,992.37 | 10,892.07 | 16,424.24 | 16,757.42 | 16,116.78 | 14,427.48 | 14,261.64 | 17,379.38 | 17,340.37 | 17,640.65 | 19,888.57 |
| Gold (Million Fine Troy Ounces) | 1ad | 1.281 | 1.280 | 1.279 | 1.279 | 1.282 | 1.283 | 1.283 | 1.283 | 1.284 | 1.286 | 1.288 | 1.292 |
| Gold (National Valuation) | 1and | 445.90 | † 654.22 | 813.13 | 1,059.45 | 1,107.18 | 1,399.45 | 1,812.53 | 2,019.99 | 2,131.84 | 1,548.39 | 1,529.70 | 1,379.79 |
| Central Bank: Other Assets | 3..d | † 1,989.2 | 2,057.4 | 2,856.3 | 2,588.3 | 1,866.9 | 2,000.9 | 2,865.4 | 3,471.7 | 5,358.4 | 3,517.1 | 3,018.2 | 5,126.5 |
| Central Bank: Other Liabs | 4..d | † 1,179.4 | 660.1 | 340.9 | 24.7 | 70.2 | 86.3 | 47.6 | 86.3 | 54.4 | 59.4 | 95.7 | 54.7 |
| Other Depository Corps.: Assets | 7a.d | † 3,126.2 | 3,271.6 | 5,567.0 | 5,915.6 | 5,511.0 | 5,874.9 | 5,412.5 | 6,001.6 | 6,760.7 | 9,594.5 | 9,503.1 | 5,943.3 |
| Other Depository Corps.: Liabs | 7b.d | † 3,381.0 | 3,219.8 | 4,248.4 | 8,872.7 | 13,273.3 | 12,536.4 | 10,023.5 | 8,259.7 | 9,107.9 | 8,320.1 | 6,721.5 | 4,356.7 |
| **Central Bank** | | | | | | | *Millions of Leva: End of Period* | | | | | | |
| Net Foreign Assets | 11n | † 9,686.7 | 12,081.7 | 16,318.6 | 23,225.0 | 24,388.1 | 23,711.7 | 23,860.1 | 24,499.6 | 28,922.9 | 26,817.9 | 30,739.8 | 38,073.3 |
| Claims on Nonresidents | 11 | † 13,079.2 | 14,270.4 | 17,331.2 | 23,257.9 | 24,485.5 | 25,135.8 | 25,315.8 | 26,047.7 | 30,396.5 | 28,237.1 | 32,317.2 | 39,686.7 |
| Liabilities to Nonresidents | 16c | † 3,392.6 | 2,188.7 | 1,012.7 | 32.9 | 97.4 | 1,424.1 | 1,455.7 | 1,548.2 | 1,473.6 | 1,419.2 | 1,577.4 | 1,613.3 |
| Claims on Other Depository Corps | 12e | † 6.8 | 5.0 | — | — | — | — | — | — | — | — | — | — |
| Net Claims on Central Government | 12an | † −1,836.5 | −2,218.8 | −3,961.9 | −5,944.1 | −6,712.5 | −6,147.1 | −5,281.5 | −4,235.6 | −5,663.6 | −4,299.6 | −6,665.4 | −6,012.0 |
| Claims on Central Government | 12a | † 1,693.5 | 1,094.4 | 506.3 | — | — | — | — | — | — | — | — | — |
| Liabilities to Central Government | 16d | † 3,530.0 | 3,313.2 | 4,468.3 | 5,944.1 | 6,712.5 | 6,147.1 | 5,281.5 | 4,235.6 | 5,663.6 | 4,299.6 | 6,665.4 | 6,012.0 |
| Claims on Other Sectors | 12s | † 74.2 | 75.3 | 75.3 | 79.2 | 79.2 | 79.2 | 76.6 | 76.5 | 76.5 | 76.5 | 76.5 | 77.0 |
| Claims on Other Financial Corps | 12g | † 2.5 | 3.5 | 3.5 | 6.9 | 6.9 | 6.9 | 6.4 | 6.4 | 6.3 | 6.3 | 6.3 | 6.8 |
| Claims on State & Local Govts | 12b | † — | — | — | — | — | — | — | — | — | — | — | — |
| Claims on Public Nonfin. Corps | 12c | † — | — | — | — | — | — | — | — | — | — | — | — |
| Claims on Private Sector | 12d | † 71.7 | 71.7 | 71.7 | 72.2 | 72.2 | 72.2 | 70.2 | 70.2 | 70.2 | 70.2 | 70.2 | 70.2 |
| Monetary Base | 14 | † 8,435.0 | 9,333.4 | 11,114.5 | 15,000.0 | 14,956.6 | 14,217.1 | 14,666.1 | 15,905.0 | 18,683.6 | 18,923.3 | 20,074.1 | 28,148.9 |
| Currency in Circulation | 14a | † 5,020.2 | 5,867.2 | 6,888.6 | 8,410.9 | 9,179.4 | 8,049.1 | 8,302.4 | 8,728.8 | 9,549.9 | 10,253.7 | 11,586.9 | 12,725.0 |
| Liabs. to Other Depository Corps | 14c | † 2,038.2 | 2,483.9 | 3,593.5 | 5,783.3 | 5,006.4 | 4,897.2 | 5,812.0 | 6,177.7 | 7,843.1 | 7,063.3 | 7,647.2 | 14,777.0 |
| Liabilities to Other Sectors | 14d | † 1,376.5 | 982.2 | 632.4 | 805.8 | 770.8 | 1,270.7 | 551.7 | 998.6 | 1,290.6 | 1,606.2 | 840.0 | 646.9 |
| Other Liabs. to Other Dep. Corps | 14n | † — | — | — | — | — | — | — | — | — | — | — | — |
| Dep. & Sec. Excl. f/Monetary Base | 14o | † — | — | — | — | — | — | — | — | — | — | — | — |
| Deposits Included in Broad Money | 15 | † — | — | — | — | — | — | — | — | — | — | — | — |
| Sec.Ot.th.Shares Incl.in Brd. Money | 16a | † — | — | — | — | — | — | — | — | — | — | — | — |
| Deposits Excl. from Broad Money | 16b | † — | — | — | — | — | — | — | — | — | — | — | — |
| Sec.Ot.th.Shares Excl.f/Brd.Money | 16s | † — | — | — | — | — | — | — | — | — | — | — | — |
| Loans | 16l | † — | — | — | — | — | — | — | — | — | — | — | — |
| Financial Derivatives | 16m | † — | — | — | — | — | — | — | — | — | — | — | — |
| Shares and Other Equity | 17a | † 1,487.9 | 1,985.5 | 2,096.8 | 2,611.8 | 3,366.0 | 3,822.7 | 4,303.3 | 4,724.1 | 4,912.0 | 3,820.9 | 4,286.6 | 4,154.0 |
| Other Items (Net) | 17r | † −1,991.7 | −1,375.7 | −779.4 | −251.7 | −567.7 | −396.0 | −314.2 | −288.6 | −259.8 | −149.3 | −209.8 | −165.1 |
| **Other Depository Corporations** | | | | | | | *Millions of Leva: End of Period* | | | | | | |
| Net Foreign Assets | 21n | † −366.0 | 85.9 | 1,958.2 | −3,936.5 | −10,767.3 | −9,087.0 | −6,791.1 | −3,413.3 | −3,482.4 | 1,808.4 | 4,473.9 | 2,840.2 |
| Claims on Nonresidents | 21 | † 4,488.9 | 5,423.9 | 8,267.5 | 7,874.9 | 7,645.4 | 8,013.9 | 7,971.6 | 9,072.1 | 10,030.1 | 13,614.6 | 15,284.8 | 10,639.1 |
| Liabilities to Nonresidents | 26c | † 4,854.8 | 5,338.0 | 6,309.4 | 11,811.4 | 18,412.7 | 17,101.0 | 14,762.6 | 12,485.4 | 13,512.5 | 11,806.2 | 10,810.9 | 7,798.9 |
| Claims on Central Bank | 20 | † 2,428.4 | 2,954.4 | 4,244.3 | 6,732.7 | 6,135.6 | 5,830.3 | 6,817.4 | 7,117.8 | 8,860.1 | 8,241.9 | 9,070.5 | 16,117.0 |
| Currency | 20a | † 392.4 | 471.7 | 657.9 | 977.5 | 1,150.3 | 934.2 | 945.8 | 935.4 | 1,050.7 | 1,178.6 | 1,418.8 | 1,347.0 |
| Reserve Deposits and Securities | 20b | † 2,036.1 | 2,482.7 | 3,586.4 | 5,755.2 | 4,985.3 | 4,896.2 | 5,871.7 | 6,182.4 | 7,809.4 | 7,063.3 | 7,651.7 | 14,770.0 |
| Other Claims | 20n | † — | — | — | — | — | — | — | — | — | — | — | — |
| Net Claims on Central Government | 22an | † 1,446.7 | 1,790.6 | 1,677.0 | 1,442.3 | 1,308.9 | 1,879.4 | 2,728.7 | 3,367.8 | 4,655.8 | 5,162.1 | 6,843.8 | 8,150.4 |
| Claims on Central Government | 22a | † 2,189.2 | 2,673.9 | 2,786.7 | 3,085.2 | 2,949.5 | 2,812.0 | 3,598.1 | 4,261.7 | 5,277.9 | 5,818.4 | 8,286.4 | 9,194.4 |
| Liabilities to Central Government | 26d | † 742.5 | 883.3 | 1,109.7 | 1,642.9 | 1,640.6 | 932.6 | 869.4 | 893.9 | 622.1 | 656.4 | 1,442.6 | 1,044.0 |
| Claims on Other Sectors | 22s | † 14,123.8 | 18,673.5 | 23,335.0 | 37,938.2 | 49,964.2 | 51,851.8 | 52,589.8 | 54,678.9 | 56,177.0 | 56,231.8 | 51,973.8 | 51,184.2 |
| Claims on Other Financial Corps | 22g | † 488.9 | 313.3 | 529.4 | 687.7 | 1,058.5 | 1,202.4 | 1,291.3 | 1,461.4 | 1,553.2 | 1,572.0 | 1,946.7 | 1,880.5 |
| Claims on State & Local Govts | 22b | † 50.6 | 65.4 | 120.4 | 204.9 | 228.4 | 256.8 | 294.2 | 329.3 | 328.9 | 289.0 | 259.5 | 293.6 |
| Claims on Public Nonfin. Corps | 22c | † — | — | — | — | — | — | — | — | — | — | — | — |
| Claims on Private Sector | 22d | † 13,584.3 | 18,294.8 | 22,685.3 | 37,045.7 | 48,677.2 | 50,392.7 | 51,004.4 | 52,888.2 | 54,295.0 | 54,370.8 | 49,767.6 | 49,010.1 |
| Liabilities to Central Bank | 26g | † .3 | .3 | .3 | .3 | .3 | .3 | .3 | .3 | .3 | — | — | — |
| Transf.Dep.Included in Broad Money | 24 | † 5,163.9 | 6,898.3 | 9,718.5 | 13,185.4 | 11,680.5 | 10,426.7 | 10,972.5 | 13,095.1 | 14,279.7 | 17,438.8 | 20,143.5 | 23,967.0 |
| Other Dep.Included in Broad Money | 25 | † 9,226.2 | 11,983.6 | 15,479.8 | 20,636.7 | 25,296.8 | 28,877.3 | 31,860.2 | 35,034.8 | 37,652.2 | 39,116.8 | 36,854.6 | 37,975.4 |
| Sec.Ot.th.Shares Incl.in Brd. Money | 26a | † −1.0 | — | — | 30.9 | 42.8 | 42.1 | — | — | — | — | — | — |
| Deposits Excl. from Broad Money | 26b | † 394.1 | 616.5 | 967.2 | 1,329.8 | 1,465.4 | 1,117.8 | 1,167.5 | 1,464.3 | 1,750.6 | 1,902.6 | 2,253.3 | 2,676.0 |
| Sec.Ot.th.Shares Excl.f/Brd.Money | 26s | † 188.9 | 398.0 | 439.6 | 356.4 | 164.4 | 116.2 | 189.6 | 202.0 | 244.9 | 400.1 | 396.5 | 333.0 |
| Loans | 26l | † — | — | — | — | — | — | — | — | — | — | — | — |
| Financial Derivatives | 26m | † 60.9 | 15.2 | 21.2 | 26.6 | 127.1 | 98.1 | 140.6 | 143.6 | 179.6 | 96.5 | 184.0 | 208.0 |
| Insurance Technical Reserves | 26r | † — | — | — | — | — | — | — | — | — | — | — | — |
| Shares and Other Equity | 27a | † 2,708.2 | 3,403.6 | 4,373.8 | 6,214.3 | 7,972.2 | 9,428.7 | 10,003.0 | 10,396.9 | 10,778.4 | 11,106.2 | 10,784.5 | 17,189.0 |
| Other Items (Net) | 27r | † −108.3 | 189.1 | 214.2 | 396.4 | −108.2 | 367.3 | 1,011.3 | 1,414.3 | 1,324.9 | 1,383.1 | 1,745.6 | −4,058.9 |
| Memo Item: | | | | | | | | | | | | | |
| Total Assets | 20ra | 25,864.5 | 34,131.5 | 43,618.1 | 61,095.8 | 72,022.9 | 74,222.8 | 78,408.9 | 82,468.1 | 88,807.3 | 92,725.4 | 92,645.5 | 95,022.7 |

# Bulgaria   918

|  |  | 2004 | 2005 | 2006 | 2007 | 2008 | 2009 | 2010 | 2011 | 2012 | 2013 | 2014 | 2015 |
|---|---|---|---|---|---|---|---|---|---|---|---|---|---|
| **Depository Corporations** | | | | | | *Millions of Leva: End of Period* | | | | | | | |
| Net Foreign Assets | 31n | † 9,320.7 | 12,167.5 | 18,276.7 | 19,288.5 | 13,620.8 | 14,624.7 | 17,069.0 | 21,086.2 | 25,440.5 | 28,626.3 | 35,213.7 | 40,913.5 |
| Claims on Nonresidents | 31 | † 17,568.1 | 19,694.3 | 25,598.8 | 31,132.8 | 32,130.9 | 33,149.7 | 33,287.4 | 35,119.8 | 40,426.6 | 41,851.8 | 47,602.0 | 50,325.7 |
| Liabilities to Nonresidents | 36c | † 8,247.4 | 7,526.7 | 7,322.0 | 11,844.3 | 18,510.1 | 18,525.1 | 16,218.3 | 14,033.5 | 14,986.1 | 13,225.5 | 12,388.3 | 9,412.2 |
| Domestic Claims | 32 | † 13,808.2 | 18,320.6 | 21,125.4 | 33,515.7 | 44,639.8 | 47,663.2 | 50,113.5 | 53,887.7 | 55,245.8 | 57,170.8 | 52,228.8 | 53,399.6 |
| Net Claims on Central Government | 32an | † −389.8 | −428.2 | −2,284.9 | −4,501.7 | −5,403.6 | −4,267.8 | −2,552.8 | −867.8 | −1,007.7 | 862.5 | 178.4 | 2,138.4 |
| Claims on Central Government | 32a | † 3,882.7 | 3,768.3 | 3,293.1 | 3,085.2 | 2,949.5 | 2,812.0 | 3,598.1 | 4,261.7 | 5,277.9 | 5,818.4 | 8,286.4 | 9,194.4 |
| Liabilities to Central Government | 36d | † 4,272.5 | 4,196.5 | 5,578.0 | 7,587.0 | 8,353.0 | 7,079.8 | 6,150.9 | 5,129.5 | 6,285.7 | 4,955.9 | 8,108.0 | 7,056.0 |
| Claims on Other Sectors | 32s | † 14,198.0 | 18,748.8 | 23,410.3 | 38,017.4 | 50,043.4 | 51,931.0 | 52,666.4 | 54,755.5 | 56,253.5 | 56,308.3 | 52,050.3 | 51,261.2 |
| Claims on Other Financial Corps | 32g | † 491.4 | 316.8 | 532.9 | 694.6 | 1,065.5 | 1,209.4 | 1,297.6 | 1,467.8 | 1,559.5 | 1,578.3 | 1,953.1 | 1,887.3 |
| Claims on State & Local Govts | 32b | † 50.6 | 65.4 | 120.4 | 204.9 | 228.4 | 256.8 | 294.2 | 329.3 | 328.9 | 289.0 | 259.5 | 293.6 |
| Claims on Public Nonfin. Corps | 32c | † — | — | — | — | — | — | — | — | — | — | — | — |
| Claims on Private Sector | 32d | † 13,656.0 | 18,366.6 | 22,757.0 | 37,117.9 | 48,749.5 | 50,464.9 | 51,074.6 | 52,958.4 | 54,365.2 | 54,441.0 | 49,837.8 | 49,080.3 |
| Broad Money Liabilities | 35l | † 20,393.4 | 25,259.7 | 32,061.4 | 42,092.1 | 45,820.0 | 47,731.7 | 50,741.0 | 56,921.9 | 61,721.7 | 67,237.0 | 68,006.2 | 73,967.3 |
| Currency Outside Depository Corps | 34a | † 4,627.9 | 5,395.5 | 6,230.7 | 7,433.4 | 8,029.2 | 7,114.9 | 7,356.7 | 7,793.4 | 8,499.2 | 9,075.2 | 10,168.1 | 11,378.0 |
| Transferable Deposits | 34 | † 5,670.0 | 7,047.5 | 9,847.8 | 13,293.3 | 11,837.5 | 11,010.1 | 11,030.4 | 13,233.5 | 14,515.0 | 17,964.0 | 20,942.9 | 24,590.0 |
| Other Deposits | 35 | † 10,096.5 | 12,816.6 | 15,983.0 | 21,334.6 | 25,910.7 | 29,564.6 | 32,353.9 | 35,895.0 | 38,707.5 | 40,197.8 | 36,895.2 | 37,999.3 |
| Securities Other than Shares | 36a | † −1.0 | — | — | 30.9 | 42.8 | 42.1 | — | — | — | — | — | — |
| Deposits Excl. from Broad Money | 36b | † 394.1 | 616.5 | 967.2 | 1,329.8 | 1,465.4 | 1,117.8 | 1,167.5 | 1,464.3 | 1,750.6 | 1,902.6 | 2,253.3 | 2,676.0 |
| Sec.Ot.th.Shares Excl.f/Brd.Money | 36s | † 188.9 | 398.0 | 439.6 | 356.4 | 164.4 | 116.2 | 189.6 | 202.0 | 244.9 | 400.1 | 396.5 | 333.0 |
| Loans | 36l | † — | — | — | — | — | — | — | — | — | — | — | — |
| Financial Derivatives | 36m | † 60.9 | 15.2 | 21.2 | 26.6 | 127.1 | 98.1 | 140.6 | 143.6 | 179.6 | 96.5 | 184.0 | 208.0 |
| Insurance Technical Reserves | 36r | † — | — | — | — | — | — | — | — | — | — | — | — |
| Shares and Other Equity | 37a | † 4,196.1 | 5,389.1 | 6,470.6 | 8,826.2 | 11,338.1 | 13,251.4 | 14,306.3 | 15,121.0 | 15,690.4 | 14,927.2 | 15,071.1 | 21,343.0 |
| Other Items (Net) | 37r | † −2,104.4 | −1,190.1 | −557.8 | 173.1 | −654.6 | −27.4 | 637.6 | 1,121.1 | 1,099.1 | 1,233.8 | 1,531.3 | −4,217.0 |
| Broad Money Liabs., Seasonally Adj. | 35l.b | † 19,922 | 24,681 | 31,354 | 41,245 | 45,027 | 47,058 | 50,178 | 56,434 | 61,307 | 66,862 | 67,677 | 73,646 |
| **Monetary Aggregates** | | | | | | *Millions of Leva: End of Period* | | | | | | | |
| Broad Money | 59m | .... | 25,259.7 | 32,061.4 | 42,092.1 | 45,820.0 | 47,731.7 | 50,741.0 | 56,921.9 | 61,721.7 | 67,237.0 | 68,006.2 | 73,967.3 |
| o/w:Currency Issued by Cent.Govt | 59m.a | .... | — | — | — | — | — | — | — | — | — | — | — |
| o/w: Dep.in Nonfin. Corporations | 59m.b | .... | — | — | — | — | — | — | — | — | — | — | — |
| o/w:Secs. Issued by Central Govt | 59m.c | .... | — | — | — | — | — | — | — | — | — | — | — |
| Money (National Definitions) | | | | | | | | | | | | | |
| M1 | 59ma | 10,298 | 12,443 | 16,078 | 20,727 | 19,867 | 18,127 | 18,387 | 21,027 | 23,014 | 27,039 | 31,111 | 35,970 |
| M2 | 59mb | 20,302 | 25,237 | 32,021 | 42,042 | 45,688 | 47,699 | 50,669 | 56,837 | 61,631 | 67,163 | 67,937 | 73,891 |
| M3 | 59mc | 20,394 | 25,260 | 32,061 | 42,062 | 45,778 | 47,756 | 50,741 | 56,956 | 61,744 | 67,236 | 68,006 | 73,961 |
| **Interest Rates** | | | | | | *Percent Per Annum* | | | | | | | |
| Central Bank Policy Rate (EOP) | 60 | 2.37 | † 2.05 | 3.26 | 4.58 | 5.77 | .55 | .18 | .22 | .03 | .02 | .02 | .01 |
| Money Market Rate | 60b | 1.95 | † 2.02 | 2.79 | 4.03 | 5.16 | 2.01 | .18 | .20 | .10 | .02 | .03 | .01 |
| Treasury Bill Rate | 60c | 2.64 | 2.23 | † 2.58 | 3.79 | 4.06 | 4.67 | 2.56 | 1.25 | .... | .40 | 1.21 | .... |
| Deposit Rate | 60l | 3.05 | 3.08 | 3.17 | 3.68 | 4.44 | 6.18 | 4.08 | 3.37 | 3.08 | 2.41 | 1.66 | .61 |
| Lending Rate | 60p | 8.87 | 8.66 | 8.89 | 10.00 | 10.86 | 11.34 | 11.14 | 10.63 | 9.71 | 9.05 | 8.28 | 7.48 |
| Government Bond Yield | 61 | 5.36 | 3.87 | 4.18 | 4.54 | 5.38 | 7.22 | 6.00 | 5.36 | 4.50 | 3.47 | 3.35 | 2.49 |
| **Prices, Production, Labor** | | | | | | *Index Numbers (2010=100): Period Averages* | | | | | | | |
| Share Prices (End of Month) | 62.ep | 137.2 | 208.8 | 248.1 | 394.6 | 250.2 | 97.4 | 100.0 | 100.5 | 81.3 | 111.7 | 143.1 | 121.8 |
| Producer Prices | 63 | 68.8 | † 73.6 | 82.6 | 89.0 | 98.4 | 92.0 | 100.0 | 109.4 | 114.1 | 112.3 | 111.0 | 108.8 |
| Consumer Prices | 64 | 69.2 | 72.7 | 78.0 | 84.6 | 95.0 | 97.6 | 100.0 | 104.2 | 107.3 | 108.3 | 106.7 | 106.6 |
| Harmonized CPI | 64h | 69.0 | 73.2 | 78.6 | 84.6 | 94.7 | 97.1 | 100.0 | 103.4 | 105.9 | 106.3 | 104.6 | 103.4 |
| Industrial Production | 66 | 95.9 | 102.5 | 108.7 | 119.1 | 119.9 | 98.0 | 100.0 | 105.8 | 105.4 | 105.3 | 107.3 | 110.3 |
| | | | | | | *Number in Thousands: Period Averages* | | | | | | | |
| Labor Force | 67d | 3,376 | 3,281 | 3,376 | 3,448 | 3,505 | 3,441 | 3,387 | 3,302 | 3,304 | 3,323 | 3,309 | 3,276 |
| Employment | 67e | 2,970 | 2,947 | 3,072 | 3,209 | 3,306 | 3,205 | 3,037 | 2,928 | 2,895 | 2,889 | 2,927 | 2,974 |
| Unemployment | 67c | 400 | 334 | 308 | 243 | 201 | 239 | 352 | 376 | 410 | 436 | 385 | 305 |
| Unemployment Rate (%) | 67r | 12.1 | 10.1 | 9.0 | 6.9 | 5.6 | 6.9 | 10.3 | 11.3 | 12.3 | 13.0 | 11.4 | 9.2 |
| **Intl. Transactions & Positions** | | | | | | *Millions of Leva* | | | | | | | |
| Exports | 70 | 15,617.1 | 18,514.6 | 23,493.2 | 26,426.9 | 29,736.1 | 22,881.8 | 30,435.0 | 39,633.6 | 40,622.9 | 43,446.9 | 45,527.0 | 45,448.9 |
| Imports, c.i.f | 71 | 22,725.8 | 28,687.6 | 36,142.4 | 42,756.9 | 49,078.7 | 33,006.0 | 37,639.5 | 45,778.5 | 49,793.7 | 50,593.6 | 51,206.2 | 50,785.9 |

# Bulgaria   918

| | | 2004 | 2005 | 2006 | 2007 | 2008 | 2009 | 2010 | 2011 | 2012 | 2013 | 2014 | 2015 |
|---|---|---|---|---|---|---|---|---|---|---|---|---|---|
| **Balance of Payments** | | | | | | | *Millions of US Dollars* | | | | | | |
| A. Current Account* | 109bx | −1,671.1 | −3,347.0 | −5,863.2 | −11,437.0 | −11,875.3 | −4,256.3 | † 504.4 | 606.4 | −210.2 | 983.5 | 692.9 | .... |
| Goods, credit (exports) | 1a9cx | 9,921.4 | 11,790.9 | 15,154.0 | 19,533.5 | 22,503.6 | 16,380.0 | † 24,625.5 | 26,542.5 | 25,254.3 | 28,158.5 | 27,877.1 | .... |
| Goods, debit (imports) | 1a9dx | 13,619.1 | 17,204.4 | 22,129.5 | 30,041.0 | 35,108.7 | 22,153.3 | † 28,409.2 | 30,208.1 | 30,340.7 | 32,001.3 | 31,514.2 | .... |
| Balance on goods | 1a9bx | −3,697.8 | −5,413.4 | −6,975.5 | −10,507.5 | −12,605.1 | −5,773.3 | † −3,783.7 | −3,665.6 | −5,086.4 | −3,842.7 | −3,637.1 | .... |
| Services, credit (exports) | 1b9cx | 4,019.9 | 4,367.3 | 5,236.7 | 6,764.6 | 7,942.6 | 6,884.9 | † 8,939.3 | 9,063.9 | 8,721.7 | 9,097.4 | 8,965.2 | .... |
| Services, debit (imports) | 1b9dx | 3,219.1 | 3,403.8 | 4,105.6 | 5,202.3 | 5,957.7 | 5,034.4 | † 4,885.8 | 4,974.3 | 5,282.5 | 5,476.1 | 5,592.6 | .... |
| Balance on Goods & Services | 1z9bx | −2,896.9 | −4,450.0 | −5,844.4 | −8,945.2 | −10,620.2 | −3,922.8 | † 269.7 | 424.0 | −1,647.2 | −221.4 | −264.5 | .... |
| Primary income: credit | 1c9cx | 1,539.3 | 1,515.6 | 1,581.7 | 1,189.4 | 1,450.9 | 1,119.6 | † 895.2 | 870.2 | 928.8 | 1,159.3 | 1,178.7 | .... |
| Primary income: debit | 1c9dx | 1,235.9 | 1,426.0 | 2,444.8 | 4,665.4 | 4,029.4 | 2,778.0 | † 3,047.7 | 3,019.6 | 2,201.3 | 3,113.1 | 2,392.7 | .... |
| Balance on gds, serv. & prim. inc. | 1y9bx | −2,593.5 | −4,360.4 | −6,707.5 | −12,421.2 | −13,198.7 | −5,581.3 | † −1,882.8 | −1,725.3 | −2,919.8 | −2,175.2 | −1,478.5 | .... |
| Secondary income: credit | 1d9ca | 1,121.0 | 1,238.0 | 1,065.7 | 1,813.1 | 2,421.1 | 2,164.8 | † 3,057.4 | 3,072.1 | 3,497.6 | 4,023.4 | 3,037.6 | .... |
| Secondary income: debit | 1d9da | 198.6 | 224.7 | 221.5 | 828.9 | 1,097.7 | 839.8 | † 670.2 | 740.4 | 788.0 | 864.8 | 866.2 | .... |
| B. Capital Account* | 209ba | 204.0 | 289.7 | 228.5 | −852.6 | 419.6 | 654.8 | † 397.9 | 685.1 | 698.9 | 624.0 | 1,254.0 | .... |
| Capital account: credit | 209ca | 204.1 | 293.6 | 228.5 | 563.2 | 419.7 | 657.4 | † 405.4 | 702.6 | 906.6 | 1,082.8 | 1,572.2 | .... |
| Capital account: debit | 209da | .1 | 3.9 | — | 1,415.8 | — | 2.6 | † 7.5 | 17.5 | 207.7 | 458.8 | 318.2 | .... |
| Balance on current & capital acct. | 129ba | −1,467.1 | −3,057.3 | −5,634.7 | −12,289.6 | −11,455.7 | −3,601.6 | † 902.4 | 1,291.5 | 488.8 | 1,607.5 | 1,946.9 | .... |
| C. Financial Account* | 309na | −2,839.6 | −4,985.4 | −8,879.0 | −19,769.1 | −17,153.4 | −2,653.0 | † 2,594.1 | 1,705.1 | −1,470.8 | 1,915.5 | −2,078.7 | .... |
| Direct investment: assets | 3a9na | 193.4 | 93.3 | 291.7 | 972.2 | 1,117.5 | 361.2 | † 823.9 | 493.2 | 410.0 | 351.5 | 879.9 | .... |
| Equity & investment fund shares.. | 3aaaa | 32.1 | 72.4 | 98.8 | 294.5 | 865.3 | −181.2 | † 176.8 | 143.9 | 276.7 | 143.5 | 251.3 | .... |
| Debt instruments | 3abaa | 161.3 | 20.9 | 192.9 | 677.7 | 252.2 | 542.5 | † 647.1 | 349.3 | 133.3 | 208.1 | 628.6 | .... |
| Direct investment: liabilities | 3a9la | 3,072.6 | 4,098.1 | 7,874.5 | 13,875.3 | 10,296.7 | 3,896.7 | † 1,241.9 | 2,099.8 | 1,788.0 | 1,989.0 | 1,971.2 | .... |
| Equity & investment fund shares . | 3aala | 2,102.6 | 2,017.3 | 5,282.6 | 7,120.2 | 5,821.3 | 2,249.0 | † 1,291.5 | 1,299.6 | 928.4 | 1,805.3 | 978.3 | .... |
| Debt instruments | 3abla | 969.9 | 2,080.8 | 2,591.9 | 6,755.1 | 4,475.5 | 1,647.7 | † −49.6 | 800.2 | 859.6 | 183.7 | 992.8 | .... |
| Portfolio investment: assets | 3b9aa | −9.6 | −29.1 | 364.7 | 242.2 | 396.3 | 842.6 | † 152.2 | 60.8 | 1,877.2 | 858.6 | 414.6 | .... |
| Equity & investment fund shares | 3baaa | 7.2 | 6.0 | 129.2 | 204.4 | 20.5 | 228.6 | † −85.7 | −117.6 | 40.6 | 175.3 | 469.5 | .... |
| Debt securities | 3bbaa | −16.7 | −35.1 | 235.6 | 37.8 | 375.8 | 614.1 | † 237.9 | 178.5 | 1,836.5 | 683.3 | −54.9 | .... |
| Portfolio investment: liabilities | 3b9la | −530.6 | −1,333.2 | 728.2 | −594.4 | −680.5 | 20.8 | † −221.4 | −427.6 | 684.3 | 698.8 | 2,027.6 | .... |
| Equity & investment fund shares . | 3bala | 21.5 | 449.0 | 147.6 | 88.6 | −105.5 | 7.6 | † −27.4 | −46.1 | 4.5 | −19.1 | −77.0 | .... |
| Debt securities | 3bbla | −552.1 | −1,782.2 | 580.6 | −682.9 | −575.0 | 13.2 | † −194.0 | −381.5 | 679.8 | 717.9 | 2,104.6 | .... |
| Fin. der.& empl.stk.ops.(ESOs): net. | 3c9na | 85.9 | 112.0 | 143.0 | 98.6 | 75.6 | 27.8 | † 106.3 | 126.9 | −4.0 | 138.2 | 56.2 | .... |
| Fin. der. & ESOs.: assets | 3c9aa | 85.9 | 112.5 | 168.0 | 146.1 | 132.5 | 55.2 | .... | .... | .... | .... | 56.2 | .... |
| Fin. der. & ESOs.: liabilities | 3c9la | — | .5 | 25.1 | 47.5 | 56.9 | 27.5 | .... | .... | .... | .... | — | .... |
| Other investment: assets | 3d9aa | 1,784.5 | −15.7 | 2,968.9 | −590.3 | −157.8 | 909.7 | † 2,763.4 | 1,054.1 | −867.9 | 2,083.4 | 1,606.9 | .... |
| Other equity | 3daaa | .... | .... | .... | .... | .... | .... | † — | | | | | |
| Debt instruments | 3dzaa | 1,784.5 | −15.7 | 2,968.9 | −590.3 | −157.8 | 909.7 | † 2,763.4 | 1,054.1 | −867.9 | 2,083.4 | 1,606.9 | .... |
| Other investment: liabilities | 3d9la | 2,351.9 | 2,381.0 | 4,044.7 | 7,210.7 | 8,968.8 | 876.9 | † 231.2 | −1,642.2 | 413.9 | −1,171.5 | 1,037.5 | .... |
| Other equity | 3dala | .... | .... | .... | .... | .... | .... | † — | | | | | |
| Debt instruments | 3dzla | 2,351.9 | 2,381.0 | 4,044.7 | 7,210.7 | 8,968.8 | 876.9 | † 231.2 | −1,642.2 | 413.9 | −1,171.5 | 1,037.5 | .... |
| Curr.+ cap.− finan. acct. balance... | 4y9na | 1,372.5 | 1,928.1 | 3,244.3 | 7,479.5 | 5,697.7 | −948.5 | † −1,691.7 | −413.6 | 1,959.6 | −308.0 | 4,025.6 | .... |
| D. Net Errors and Omissions | 409na | 370.8 | −1,219.4 | −985.7 | −3,045.2 | −4,228.6 | 1,118.0 | † 2,215.7 | 680.1 | 719.3 | −447.2 | −1,700.8 | .... |
| E. Reserves and Related Items | 4z9na | 1,743.3 | 708.8 | 2,258.6 | 4,434.3 | 1,469.1 | 169.5 | † 523.9 | 266.5 | 2,678.9 | −755.3 | 2,324.8 | .... |
| Reserve assets | 3e9aa | 1,846.4 | 415.0 | 1,924.2 | 4,099.1 | 1,469.1 | 169.5 | † 523.9 | 266.5 | 2,678.9 | −755.3 | 2,324.8 | .... |
| Credit and loans from the IMF | 3dcla | −55.2 | −436.2 | −341.4 | −344.2 | — | — | † — | — | — | — | — | .... |
| Exceptional financing | 409la | 158.4 | 142.5 | 7.0 | 9.0 | — | — | † — | — | — | — | — | .... |

*Excludes components in group E

| **International Investment Position** | | | | | | | *Millions of US Dollars* | | | | | | |
|---|---|---|---|---|---|---|---|---|---|---|---|---|---|
| Assets | 809aa | 17,195.5 | 16,014.0 | 23,452.9 | 30,162.2 | 30,880.0 | 33,546.5 | † 33,359.7 | 34,664.5 | 40,125.6 | 43,168.5 | 42,731.7 | .... |
| Direct investment | 8a9aa | 473.4 | 479.5 | 877.3 | 1,888.4 | 2,736.5 | 2,919.7 | † 3,713.8 | 4,081.1 | 4,488.3 | 4,930.9 | 4,268.3 | .... |
| Equity & investment fund shares.. | 8aaaa | 85.0 | 120.8 | 371.8 | 683.8 | 1,402.9 | 1,265.6 | † 1,308.3 | 1,381.0 | 1,633.9 | 1,865.1 | 986.8 | .... |
| Debt instruments | 8abaa | 388.3 | 358.8 | 505.5 | 1,204.7 | 1,333.6 | 1,654.1 | † 2,405.5 | 2,700.1 | 2,854.3 | 3,065.8 | 3,281.5 | .... |
| Portfolio investment | 8b9aa | 904.5 | 790.5 | 1,250.3 | 1,538.6 | 1,551.0 | 2,609.8 | † 3,460.2 | 3,469.0 | 6,031.0 | 6,905.5 | 6,808.9 | .... |
| Equity & investment fund shares.. | 8baaa | 19.4 | 23.2 | 166.8 | 409.9 | 161.4 | 495.5 | † 843.3 | 599.8 | 699.7 | 970.0 | 1,376.9 | .... |
| Debt securities | 8bbaa | 885.2 | 767.4 | 1,083.5 | 1,128.7 | 1,389.6 | 2,114.3 | † 2,616.9 | 2,869.2 | 5,331.2 | 5,935.4 | 5,432.0 | .... |
| Fin. der.(oth.than reserves) & ESOs | 8c9aa | 97.6 | 28.6 | 265.9 | 151.7 | 129.4 | 39.4 | † 33.8 | 93.6 | 68.0 | 72.3 | 4.8 | .... |
| Other investment | 8d9aa | 6,383.6 | 6,020.5 | 9,303.3 | 9,046.1 | 8,540.4 | 9,450.9 | † 8,919.5 | 9,749.2 | 9,035.6 | 11,376.8 | 11,543.9 | .... |
| Other equity | 8daaa | .... | .... | .... | .... | .... | .... | .... | .... | .... | .... | .... | .... |
| Debt instruments | 8dzaa | 6,383.6 | 6,020.5 | 9,303.3 | 9,046.1 | 8,540.4 | 9,450.9 | † 8,919.5 | 9,749.2 | 9,035.6 | 11,376.8 | 11,543.9 | .... |
| Reserve assets | 8e9aa | 9,336.4 | 8,694.8 | 11,756.1 | 17,537.4 | 17,922.7 | 18,526.7 | † 17,232.5 | 17,271.6 | 20,502.8 | 19,883.1 | 20,105.8 | .... |
| Liabilities | 809la | 25,542.1 | 28,115.1 | 43,668.5 | 66,841.5 | 80,054.0 | 85,498.1 | † 80,039.1 | 78,876.3 | 83,005.7 | 85,343.5 | 80,323.2 | .... |
| Direct investment | 8a9la | 10,757.0 | 14,225.2 | 23,906.7 | 38,937.7 | 45,905.6 | 50,519.9 | † 45,840.6 | 46,885.8 | 49,849.5 | 51,686.1 | 47,343.2 | .... |
| Equity & investment fund shares.. | 8aala | 7,924.8 | 9,342.7 | 15,659.3 | 23,141.4 | 26,763.1 | 29,641.9 | † 29,112.0 | 29,572.6 | 31,318.4 | 32,196.7 | 29,467.7 | .... |
| Debt instruments | 8abla | 2,832.3 | 4,882.6 | 8,247.4 | 15,796.3 | 19,142.5 | 20,878.0 | † 16,728.6 | 17,313.3 | 18,531.1 | 19,489.3 | 17,875.5 | .... |
| Portfolio investment | 8b9la | 4,193.6 | 2,646.7 | 3,620.9 | 3,499.0 | 2,536.6 | 2,472.1 | † 2,319.9 | 1,991.3 | 2,551.5 | 3,292.6 | 4,801.0 | .... |
| Equity & investment fund shares.. | 8bala | 290.6 | 439.7 | 675.0 | 1,018.4 | 702.6 | 632.5 | † 514.4 | 634.7 | 353.5 | 333.8 | 223.0 | .... |
| Debt securities | 8bbla | 3,903.1 | 2,207.0 | 2,945.9 | 2,480.6 | 1,834.0 | 1,839.6 | † 1,805.5 | 1,356.6 | 2,197.9 | 2,958.8 | 4,578.0 | .... |
| Fin. der.(oth.than reserves) & ESOs | 8c9la | 216.2 | 38.6 | 84.2 | 49.9 | 78.0 | 44.6 | † 180.8 | 150.4 | 110.7 | 14.0 | 200.6 | .... |
| Other investment | 8d9la | 10,375.3 | 11,204.7 | 16,056.7 | 24,354.8 | 31,533.8 | 32,461.4 | † 31,697.8 | 29,848.9 | 30,494.1 | 30,350.9 | 27,978.4 | .... |
| Other equity | 8dala | .... | .... | .... | .... | .... | .... | .... | .... | .... | .... | .... | .... |
| Debt instruments | 8dzla | 10,375.3 | 11,204.7 | 16,056.7 | 24,354.8 | 31,533.8 | 32,461.4 | † 31,697.8 | 29,848.9 | 30,494.1 | 30,350.9 | 27,978.4 | .... |

# Bulgaria 918

| | | 2004 | 2005 | 2006 | 2007 | 2008 | 2009 | 2010 | 2011 | 2012 | 2013 | 2014 | 2015 |
|---|---|---|---|---|---|---|---|---|---|---|---|---|---|
| **Government Finance Operations Statement General Government** | | *Millions of Leva: Fiscal Year Ends December 31; Data Reported through Eurostat* | | | | | | | | | | | |
| Revenue | a1 | 16,323 | 17,751 | 19,015 | 24,632 | 28,163 | 25,780 | 24,717 | 25,729 | 28,023 | 30,530 | 30,623 | 32,970 |
| Taxes | a11 | 8,877 | 9,799 | 11,609 | 15,046 | 16,794 | 14,443 | 14,352 | 14,942 | 16,211 | 16,974 | 17,079 | 18,393 |
| Social Contributions | a12 | 4,080 | 4,420 | 4,297 | 4,890 | 5,393 | 5,273 | 4,970 | 5,417 | 5,596 | 6,116 | 6,575 | 6,966 |
| Grants | a13 | .... | .... | .... | .... | .... | .... | .... | .... | .... | .... | .... | .... |
| Other Revenue | a14 | .... | .... | .... | .... | .... | .... | .... | .... | .... | .... | .... | .... |
| Expense | a2 | 15,770 | 17,345 | 17,804 | 22,856 | 25,153 | 26,943 | 25,032 | 26,066 | 27,139 | 29,350 | 32,826 | 31,039 |
| Compensation of Employees | a21 | 4,028 | 4,327 | 4,571 | 5,366 | 6,414 | 6,842 | 6,765 | 6,977 | 7,103 | 7,776 | 7,956 | 8,033 |
| Use of Goods & Services | a22 | 3,275 | 3,838 | 3,802 | 4,538 | 5,008 | 4,249 | 4,240 | 4,413 | 4,410 | 4,668 | 4,584 | 5,015 |
| Consumption of Fixed Capital | a23 | 1,523 | 1,633 | 1,798 | 1,964 | 1,981 | 1,714 | 1,411 | 1,489 | 1,594 | 1,656 | 1,790 | 1,356 |
| Interest | a24 | 760 | 732 | 691 | 709 | 611 | 531 | 521 | 582 | 658 | 614 | 723 | 823 |
| Subsidies | a25 | 389 | 348 | 374 | 500 | 797 | 807 | 849 | 726 | 730 | 1,066 | 1,119 | 1,079 |
| Grants | a26 | .... | .... | .... | .... | .... | .... | .... | .... | .... | .... | .... | .... |
| Social Benefits | a27 | 5,013 | 5,347 | 5,871 | 6,524 | 8,120 | 9,426 | 10,080 | 10,391 | 10,609 | 11,358 | 12,117 | 12,320 |
| Other Expense | a28 | .... | .... | .... | .... | .... | .... | .... | .... | .... | .... | .... | .... |
| Gross Operating Balance [1-2+23] | agob | 2,076 | 2,039 | 3,009 | 3,741 | 4,991 | 551 | 1,095 | 1,151 | 2,478 | 2,836 | -412 | 3,288 |
| Net Operating Balance [1-2] | anob | 553 | 406 | 1,210 | 1,777 | 3,010 | -1,162 | -315 | -338 | 884 | 1,180 | -2,202 | 1,931 |
| Net Acq. of Nonfinancial Assets | a31 | -187 | -68 | 241 | 1,078 | 1,853 | 1,798 | 2,013 | 1,252 | 1,136 | 1,507 | 2,351 | 3,706 |
| Aquisition of Nonfin. Assets | a31.1 | .... | .... | .... | .... | .... | .... | .... | .... | .... | .... | .... | .... |
| Disposal of Nonfin. Assets | a31.2 | .... | .... | .... | .... | .... | .... | .... | .... | .... | .... | .... | .... |
| Net Lending/Borrowing [1-2-31] | anlb | 740 | 474 | 970 | 699 | 1,157 | -2,961 | -2,328 | -1,590 | -253 | -328 | -4,553 | -1,774 |
| Net Acq. of Financial Assets | a32 | -179 | -2,161 | 2,141 | 715 | 748 | -1,372 | -2,126 | -848 | 2,063 | 211 | 4,126 | -1,890 |
| By instrument | | | | | | | | | | | | | |
| Monetary Gold & SDRs | a3201 | — | — | — | — | — | — | — | — | — | — | — | — |
| Currency & Deposits | a3202 | 987 | -610 | 1,978 | 2,276 | 770 | -1,290 | -1,773 | -748 | 1,842 | -1,108 | 1,373 | -1,782 |
| Securities other than Shares | a3203 | -425 | — | — | — | — | — | — | — | — | 1 | — | — |
| Loans | a3204 | -128 | 302 | 105 | -1,789 | -463 | 11 | -192 | -64 | -46 | -50 | 816 | -423 |
| Shares & Other Equity | a3205 | -2,157 | -697 | -674 | -622 | -84 | 512 | 26 | -322 | -265 | -228 | 872 | -30 |
| Insurance Technical Reserves | a3206 | -5 | -6 | 3 | 5 | 10 | 3 | 1 | — | 2 | -2 | 4 | 9 |
| Financial Derivatives | a3207 | — | — | — | — | — | — | — | — | — | — | — | — |
| Other Accounts Receivable | a3208 | 1,548 | -1,149 | 731 | 845 | 515 | -607 | -188 | 286 | 530 | 1,598 | 1,061 | 336 |
| By debtor | | | | | | | | | | | | | |
| Domestic | a321 | .... | .... | .... | .... | .... | .... | .... | .... | .... | .... | .... | .... |
| Foreign | a322 | .... | .... | .... | .... | .... | .... | .... | .... | .... | .... | .... | .... |
| Net Incurrence of Liabilities | a33 | -718 | -2,694 | 1,495 | 21 | -428 | 1,625 | 215 | 704 | 2,328 | 602 | 8,488 | -164 |
| By instrument | | | | | | | | | | | | | |
| Special Drawing Rights (SDRs) | a3301 | — | — | — | — | — | — | — | — | — | — | — | — |
| Currency & Deposits | a3302 | — | — | — | — | — | — | — | — | — | — | — | — |
| Securities other than Shares | a3303 | -844 | -2,248 | 71 | -331 | -496 | -103 | 810 | 498 | 2,425 | -426 | 5,020 | 3,408 |
| Loans | a3304 | 87 | -605 | -1,082 | -356 | -549 | 512 | 403 | 296 | -51 | 868 | 3,328 | -3,057 |
| Shares & Other Equity | a3305 | -1 | — | -1 | 1 | — | — | — | — | — | — | — | — |
| Insurance Technical Reserves | a3306 | — | — | — | — | — | — | — | — | — | — | — | — |
| Financial Derivatives | a3307 | 52 | -320 | -3 | -2 | -4 | -8 | -2 | -2 | -3 | -23 | — | 10 |
| Other Accounts Payable | a3308 | -12 | 480 | 2,508 | 708 | 620 | 1,224 | -995 | -88 | -43 | 183 | 140 | -526 |
| By creditor | | | | | | | | | | | | | |
| Domestic | a331 | .... | .... | .... | .... | .... | .... | .... | .... | .... | .... | .... | .... |
| Foreign | a332 | .... | .... | .... | .... | .... | .... | .... | .... | .... | .... | .... | .... |
| Stat. Discrepancy [32-33-NLB] | anlbz | -202 | 59 | -323 | -5 | 19 | -36 | -14 | 37 | -13 | -63 | 192 | 49 |
| Memo Item: Expenditure [2+31] | a2m | 15,583 | 17,277 | 18,045 | 23,934 | 27,006 | 28,741 | 27,045 | 27,319 | 28,275 | 30,858 | 35,176 | 34,744 |
| **Balance Sheet** | | | | | | | | | | | | | |
| Net Worth | a6 | .... | .... | .... | .... | .... | .... | .... | .... | .... | .... | .... | .... |
| Nonfinancial Assets | a61 | .... | .... | .... | .... | .... | .... | .... | .... | .... | .... | .... | .... |
| Financial Assets | a62 | 18,905 | 17,884 | 19,943 | 20,934 | 22,243 | 21,439 | 20,024 | 19,532 | 22,311 | 21,559 | 26,207 | 24,185 |
| By instrument | | | | | | | | | | | | | |
| Monetary Gold & SDRs | a6201 | — | — | — | — | — | — | — | — | — | — | — | — |
| Currency & Deposits | a6202 | 5,619 | 5,104 | 7,073 | 9,342 | 10,183 | 8,997 | 7,305 | 6,557 | 8,969 | 7,862 | 9,268 | 7,486 |
| Securities other than Shares | a6203 | — | — | — | — | — | — | — | — | — | 1 | 1 | 1 |
| Loans | a6204 | 3,276 | 4,016 | 3,820 | 1,777 | 1,300 | 1,254 | 1,095 | 1,041 | 965 | 888 | 1,728 | 1,329 |
| Shares and Other Equity | a6205 | 7,069 | 6,978 | 6,428 | 6,344 | 6,762 | 7,784 | 8,377 | 8,402 | 8,312 | 7,148 | 8,486 | 8,299 |
| Insurance Technical Reserves | a6206 | 13 | 7 | 10 | 14 | 24 | 27 | 28 | 28 | 30 | 28 | 32 | 41 |
| Financial Derivatives | a6207 | — | — | — | — | — | — | — | — | — | — | — | — |
| Other Accounts Receivable | a6208 | 2,928 | 1,779 | 2,612 | 3,458 | 3,972 | 3,378 | 3,218 | 3,504 | 4,034 | 5,632 | 6,691 | 7,028 |
| By debtor | | | | | | | | | | | | | |
| Domestic | a621 | .... | .... | .... | .... | .... | .... | .... | .... | .... | .... | .... | .... |
| Foreign | a622 | .... | .... | .... | .... | .... | .... | .... | .... | .... | .... | .... | .... |
| Liabilities | a63 | 17,127 | 15,386 | 16,253 | 15,877 | 15,199 | 17,256 | 17,794 | 18,439 | 19,959 | 20,282 | 28,891 | 28,779 |
| By instrument | | | | | | | | | | | | | |
| Special Drawing Rights (SDRs) | a6301 | — | — | — | — | — | — | — | — | — | — | — | — |
| Currency & Deposits | a6302 | — | — | — | — | — | — | — | — | — | — | — | — |
| Securities other than Shares | a6303 | 9,636 | 7,755 | 7,423 | 6,790 | 6,003 | 6,260 | 7,254 | 7,670 | 9,310 | 8,688 | 13,855 | 17,252 |
| Loans | a6304 | 5,864 | 5,463 | 4,268 | 3,946 | 3,482 | 4,135 | 4,615 | 4,906 | 4,750 | 5,526 | 8,834 | 5,833 |
| Shares and Other Equity | a6305 | 3 | 3 | 2 | 3 | 3 | 3 | 3 | — | — | — | — | — |
| Insurance Technical Reserves | a6306 | — | — | — | — | — | — | — | — | — | — | — | — |
| Financial Derivatives | a6307 | 455 | 515 | 369 | 239 | 192 | 99 | 95 | 125 | 204 | 190 | 208 | 225 |
| Other Accounts Payable | a6308 | 1,170 | 1,650 | 4,190 | 4,898 | 5,518 | 6,759 | 5,826 | 5,738 | 5,695 | 5,878 | 5,994 | 5,469 |
| By creditor | | | | | | | | | | | | | |
| Domestic | a631 | .... | .... | .... | .... | .... | .... | .... | .... | .... | .... | .... | .... |
| Foreign | a632 | .... | .... | .... | .... | .... | .... | .... | .... | .... | .... | .... | .... |
| Net Financial Worth [62-63] | a6m2 | 1,778 | 2,498 | 3,691 | 5,057 | 7,044 | 4,183 | 2,230 | 1,093 | 2,352 | 1,278 | -2,684 | -4,593 |
| Memo Item: Debt at Market Value | a6m3 | 16,669 | 14,868 | 15,881 | 15,635 | 15,003 | 17,154 | 17,695 | 18,314 | 19,755 | 20,091 | 28,683 | 28,554 |
| Memo Item: Debt at Face Value | a6m35 | 15,890 | 14,148 | 15,380 | 15,258 | 14,999 | 16,751 | 17,279 | 18,029 | 19,395 | 19,855 | 28,554 | 28,497 |
| Memo Item: Maastricht Debt | a6m36 | 14,720 | 12,498 | 11,189 | 10,360 | 9,481 | 9,992 | 11,453 | 12,291 | 13,700 | 13,977 | 22,560 | 23,027 |
| Memo Item: Debt at Nominal Value | a6m4 | .... | .... | .... | .... | .... | .... | .... | .... | .... | .... | .... | .... |

# Bulgaria   918

| National Accounts | | 2004 | 2005 | 2006 | 2007 | 2008 | 2009 | 2010 | 2011 | 2012 | 2013 | 2014 | 2015 |
|---|---|---|---|---|---|---|---|---|---|---|---|---|---|
| | | | | | | | *Millions of Leva* | | | | | | |
| Househ.Cons.Expend.,incl.NPISHs.... | 96f | 27,835 | 31,962 | 35,451 | 43,489 | 47,760 | 45,953 | 47,211 | 49,866 | 53,343 | 51,256 | 52,635 | 52,627 |
| Government Consumption Expend... | 91f | 8,209 | 8,838 | 10,006 | 11,091 | 12,809 | 12,081 | 11,706 | 12,130 | 12,479 | 13,646 | 13,778 | 14,060 |
| Gross Fixed Capital Formation......... | 93e | 8,632 | 12,067 | 14,709 | 17,962 | 24,025 | 20,331 | 16,606 | 16,896 | 17,443 | 17,365 | 17,653 | 18,296 |
| Changes in Inventories.................... | 93i | 1,019 | 965 | 2,488 | 3,380 | 2,876 | 520 | 266 | 443 | 558 | 169 | 275 | 138 |
| Exports of Goods and Services......... | 90c | 16,875 | 19,996 | 25,184 | 33,243 | 38,228 | 30,896 | 39,648 | 49,914 | 51,710 | 54,907 | 54,441 | 57,408 |
| Imports of Goods and Services (-)..... | 98c | 21,469 | 26,887 | 34,347 | 45,194 | 52,604 | 36,937 | 41,657 | 49,149 | 53,990 | 55,372 | 55,170 | 56,156 |
| Gross Domestic Product (GDP)......... | 99b | 41,102 | 46,942 | 53,491 | 63,970 | 73,095 | 72,844 | 73,780 | 80,100 | 81,544 | 81,971 | 83,612 | 86,373 |
| Statistical Discrepancy..................... | 99bs | — | — | — | — | — | — | — | — | — | — | — | — |
| Net Primary Income from Abroad..... | 98.n | 538 | −46 | −1,316 | −4,204 | −3,104 | −1,368 | −1,854 | −3,043 | −1,731 | −1,491 | 62 | −150 |
| Gross National Income (GNI)............ | 99a | 41,639 | 46,896 | 52,174 | 59,766 | 69,991 | 71,476 | 71,926 | 77,057 | 79,813 | 80,480 | 83,674 | 86,223 |
| Net Current Transf.from Abroad....... | 98t | 1,456 | 1,600 | 1,310 | 1,069 | 1,365 | 1,445 | 2,327 | 2,593 | 2,928 | 3,105 | 1,503 | 1,532 |
| Gross Nat'l Disposable Inc.(GNDI).... | 99i | 43,095 | 48,496 | 53,485 | 60,835 | 71,356 | 72,921 | 74,253 | 79,650 | 82,741 | 83,585 | 85,177 | 87,755 |
| Gross Saving................................. | 99s | 7,050 | 7,695 | 8,028 | 6,256 | 10,786 | 14,887 | 15,336 | 17,654 | 16,919 | 18,683 | 18,764 | 21,067 |
| GDP Volume 2005 Prices................. | 99b.p | 42,765 | 45,484 | 48,445 | 51,569 | 54,761 | 51,762 | 51,966 | 52,922 | 53,233 | 53,691 | .... | .... |
| GDP Volume 2010 Prices................. | 99b.p | 59,120 | 63,398 | 67,679 | 72,873 | 76,989 | 73,740 | 73,780 | 74,949 | 75,126 | 76,090 | 77,268 | 79,562 |
| GDP Volume (2010=100)................ | 99bvp | 80.1 | 85.9 | 91.7 | 98.8 | 104.3 | 99.9 | 100.0 | 101.6 | 101.8 | 103.1 | 104.7 | 107.8 |
| GDP Deflator (2010=100)............... | 99bip | 69.5 | 74.0 | 79.0 | 87.8 | 94.9 | 98.8 | 100.0 | 106.9 | 108.5 | 107.7 | 108.2 | 108.6 |
| | | | | | | | *Millions: Midyear Estimates* | | | | | | |
| Population............................... | 99z | 7.74 | 7.68 | 7.62 | 7.57 | 7.51 | 7.46 | 7.41 | 7.36 | 7.30 | 7.25 | 7.20 | 7.15 |

| | | 2004 | 2005 | 2006 | 2007 | 2008 | 2009 | 2010 | 2011 | 2012 | 2013 | 2014 | 2015 |
|---|---|---|---|---|---|---|---|---|---|---|---|---|---|
| **Exchange Rates** | | | | | | *CFA Francs per SDR: End of Period* | | | | | | | |
| Official Rate............................ | aa | 747.90 | 794.73 | 749.30 | 704.15 | 725.98 | 713.83 | 756.02 | 778.32 | 764.10 | 732.49 | 782.77 | 834.92 |
| | | | | | | *CFA Francs per US Dollar: End of Period (ae) Period Average (rf)* | | | | | | | |
| Official Rate............................ | ae | 481.58 | 556.04 | 498.07 | 445.59 | 471.34 | 455.34 | 490.91 | 506.96 | 497.16 | 475.64 | 540.28 | 602.51 |
| Official Rate............................ | rf | 528.28 | 527.47 | 522.89 | 479.27 | 447.81 | 472.19 | 495.28 | 471.87 | 510.53 | 494.04 | 494.41 | 591.45 |
| **Fund Position** | | | | | | *Millions of SDRs: End of Period* | | | | | | | |
| Quota....................................... | 2f.s | 60.20 | 60.20 | 60.20 | 60.20 | 60.20 | 60.20 | 60.20 | 60.20 | 60.20 | 60.20 | 60.20 | 60.20 |
| SDR Holdings........................... | 1b.s | .11 | .14 | .02 | .08 | .05 | 48.09 | 48.17 | 48.15 | 48.14 | 48.14 | 48.13 | 37.07 |
| Reserve Position in the Fund........... | 1c.s | 7.31 | 7.33 | 7.37 | 7.39 | 7.42 | 7.44 | 7.47 | 7.52 | 7.54 | 7.58 | 7.64 | 7.70 |
| Total Fund Cred.&Loans Outstg........ | 2tl | 73.85 | 72.44 | 23.22 | 23.72 | 35.26 | 70.38 | 83.59 | 94.08 | 138.41 | 139.77 | 137.71 | 146.61 |
| SDR Allocations........................ | 1bd | 9.41 | 9.41 | 9.41 | 9.41 | 9.41 | 57.58 | 57.58 | 57.58 | 57.58 | 57.58 | 57.58 | 57.58 |
| **International Liquidity** | | | | | | *Millions of US Dollars Unless Otherwise Indicated: End of Period* | | | | | | | |
| Total Reserves minus Gold............... | 1l.d | 659.8 | 438.4 | 554.9 | 1,029.2 | 927.6 | 1,295.8 | 1,068.2 | 957.0 | 1,024.5 | 628.5 | 297.1 | 259.6 |
| SDR Holdings........................ | 1b.d | .2 | .2 | — | .1 | .1 | 75.4 | 74.2 | 73.9 | 74.0 | 74.1 | 69.7 | 51.4 |
| Reserve Position in the Fund........ | 1c.d | 11.3 | 10.5 | 11.1 | 11.7 | 11.4 | 11.7 | 11.5 | 11.6 | 11.6 | 11.7 | 11.1 | 10.7 |
| Foreign Exchange................... | 1d.d | 648.2 | 427.7 | 543.7 | 1,017.4 | 916.1 | 1,208.8 | 982.5 | 871.5 | 938.9 | 542.7 | 216.3 | 197.6 |
| Gold (Million Fine Troy Ounces)........ | 1ad | — | — | — | — | — | — | — | — | — | — | — | — |
| Gold (National Valuation)............... | 1and | — | — | — | — | — | — | — | — | — | — | — | .... |
| Monetary Authorities: Other Liabs.... | 4..d | 41.2 | 28.2 | 96.1 | 176.6 | 193.7 | 244.9 | 239.1 | 187.6 | 252.1 | 226.8 | 214.2 | 217.2 |
| Deposit Money Banks: Assets........... | 7a.d | 274.0 | 206.2 | 260.5 | 395.4 | 388.8 | 633.3 | 932.1 | 1,095.5 | 1,319.5 | 1,563.6 | 1,540.3 | 1,873.3 |
| Deposit Money Banks: Liabs........... | 7b.d | 186.2 | 195.8 | 224.3 | 273.5 | 274.4 | 242.9 | 225.7 | 294.2 | 424.5 | 533.9 | 605.7 | 551.9 |
| **Monetary Authorities** | | | | | | *Billions of CFA Francs: End of Period* | | | | | | | |
| Foreign Assets............................... | 11 | 317.7 | 243.7 | 276.4 | 458.6 | 437.2 | 590.0 | 524.4 | 485.2 | 509.4 | 298.9 | 160.5 | 156.4 |
| Claims on Central Government........ | 12a | 92.5 | 88.0 | 40.6 | 37.6 | 42.3 | 95.7 | 102.2 | 108.8 | 138.6 | 134.3 | 128.3 | 132.1 |
| Claims on Deposit Money Banks...... | 12e | — | — | — | 5.4 | 44.6 | 71.5 | 102.3 | 153.2 | 219.6 | 314.4 | 519.6 | 656.8 |
| Claims on Other Financial Insts....... | 12f | 1.2 | 1.1 | 1.0 | 1.0 | 1.0 | 1.0 | 1.2 | 1.1 | 1.1 | .8 | — | — |
| Reserve Money............................... | 14 | 241.8 | 202.4 | 203.9 | 291.3 | 334.7 | 392.4 | 356.1 | 349.8 | 369.8 | 354.1 | 404.3 | 499.0 |
| of which: Currency Outside DMBs.. | 14a | 175.0 | 153.8 | 142.0 | 202.4 | 213.6 | 251.8 | 215.1 | 189.6 | 230.3 | 203.2 | 250.2 | 299.1 |
| Foreign Liabilities........................ | 16c | 82.1 | 80.7 | 72.3 | 102.0 | 123.7 | 202.9 | 224.1 | 213.1 | 275.1 | 252.4 | 268.6 | 301.4 |
| Central Government Deposits........... | 16d | 83.3 | 50.9 | 40.2 | 107.8 | 65.4 | 137.2 | 150.0 | 188.0 | 220.4 | 140.4 | 138.1 | 145.9 |
| Other Items (Net)........................ | 17r | 4.2 | −1.1 | 1.5 | 1.5 | 1.3 | 25.7 | — | −2.8 | 3.3 | 1.6 | −2.6 | −.9 |
| **Deposit Money Banks** | | | | | | *Billions of CFA Francs: End of Period* | | | | | | | |
| Reserves..................................... | 20 | 65.8 | 45.4 | 60.1 | 87.5 | 115.3 | 134.9 | 128.3 | 155.6 | 147.1 | 147.3 | 157.1 | 186.3 |
| Foreign Assets............................... | 21 | 131.9 | 114.6 | 129.8 | 176.2 | 183.3 | 288.4 | 457.6 | 555.4 | 656.0 | 743.7 | 832.2 | 1,128.7 |
| Claims on Central Government........ | 22a | 36.0 | 18.1 | 23.3 | 46.4 | 53.1 | 71.4 | 99.2 | 116.8 | 112.6 | 169.6 | 260.1 | 273.3 |
| Claims on Private Sector.................. | 22d | 380.3 | 473.9 | 540.9 | 545.3 | 662.1 | 671.0 | 769.4 | 950.1 | 1,179.5 | 1,491.3 | 1,738.4 | 1,897.2 |
| Claims on Other Financial Insts........ | 22f | — | — | — | — | — | — | — | — | — | — | — | — |
| Demand Deposits........................... | 24 | 193.9 | 196.6 | 220.9 | 260.2 | 282.9 | 356.0 | 437.9 | 593.5 | 678.4 | 778.9 | 800.5 | 973.0 |
| Time Deposits............................... | 25 | 205.5 | 204.6 | 248.5 | 295.4 | 354.1 | 433.0 | 591.3 | 630.9 | 744.7 | 849.3 | 971.4 | 1,130.1 |
| Foreign Liabilities.......................... | 26c | 79.9 | 96.9 | 97.6 | 109.3 | 114.6 | 100.8 | 100.1 | 145.5 | 210.2 | 242.5 | 310.5 | 279.0 |
| Long-Term Foreign Liabilities........... | 26cl | 9.8 | 12.0 | 14.1 | 12.6 | 14.8 | 9.8 | 10.7 | 3.7 | .8 | 11.4 | 16.8 | 53.6 |
| Central Government Deposits........... | 26d | 86.4 | 91.0 | 102.2 | 122.6 | 146.3 | 123.7 | 107.7 | 129.9 | 161.3 | 209.4 | 209.1 | 239.5 |
| Credit from Monetary Authorities..... | 26g | — | — | — | 5.4 | 40.6 | 71.5 | 111.7 | 153.2 | 219.6 | 314.4 | 519.0 | 654.2 |
| Capital Accounts........................... | 27a | 59.7 | 72.7 | 81.5 | 98.9 | 137.0 | 158.0 | 169.2 | 190.3 | 199.8 | 222.1 | 240.5 | 264.9 |
| Other Items (Net)........................... | 27r | −21.2 | −21.9 | −10.8 | −49.0 | −76.5 | −87.2 | −74.2 | −69.1 | −119.5 | −76.1 | −79.9 | −108.7 |
| Treasury Claims: Private Sector....... | 22d.i | .4 | .3 | .5 | .4 | .3 | .1 | — | .4 | .6 | .2 | .1 | .3 |
| Post Office: Checking Deposits....... | 24..i | 4.5 | 2.7 | 3.7 | 3.5 | 4.8 | 5.5 | 3.9 | 5.5 | 5.5 | 8.1 | 4.5 | 6.0 |
| **Monetary Survey** | | | | | | *Billions of CFA Francs: End of Period* | | | | | | | |
| Foreign Assets (Net)........................ | 31n | 287.6 | 180.7 | 236.2 | 423.5 | 382.2 | 574.7 | 657.7 | 682.0 | 680.0 | 547.7 | 413.6 | 704.8 |
| Domestic Credit.............................. | 32 | 344.8 | 442.0 | 467.0 | 403.3 | 551.6 | 583.6 | 718.3 | 864.4 | 1,055.6 | 1,454.4 | 1,784.1 | 1,923.2 |
| Claims on Central Govt. (Net)........ | 32an | −37.2 | −33.3 | −75.4 | −143.3 | −111.8 | −88.5 | −52.3 | −87.2 | −125.6 | −38.0 | 45.6 | 25.6 |
| Claims on Private Sector............... | 32d | 380.7 | 474.2 | 541.4 | 545.6 | 662.4 | 671.1 | 769.4 | 950.5 | 1,180.1 | 1,491.5 | 1,738.4 | 1,897.5 |
| Claims on Other Financial Insts...... | 32f | 1.2 | 1.1 | 1.0 | 1.0 | 1.0 | 1.0 | 1.2 | 1.1 | 1.1 | .8 | — | — |
| Money....................................... | 34 | 378.2 | 354.0 | 367.9 | 468.2 | 503.2 | 615.1 | 659.2 | 790.7 | 917.2 | 993.1 | 1,063.9 | 1,279.8 |
| Quasi-Money.............................. | 35 | 205.5 | 204.6 | 248.5 | 295.4 | 354.1 | 433.0 | 591.3 | 630.9 | 744.7 | 849.3 | 971.4 | 1,130.1 |
| Long-Term Foreign Liabilities........... | 36cl | 9.8 | 12.0 | 14.1 | 12.6 | 14.8 | 9.8 | 10.7 | 3.7 | .8 | 11.4 | 16.8 | 53.6 |
| Other Items (Net)........................... | 37r | 38.9 | 52.1 | 72.7 | 50.6 | 61.7 | 100.4 | 114.9 | 121.0 | 72.8 | 148.2 | 145.7 | 164.5 |
| Money plus Quasi-Money............... | 35l | 583.7 | 558.7 | 616.4 | 763.6 | 857.3 | 1,048.1 | 1,250.5 | 1,421.6 | 1,662.0 | 1,842.4 | 2,035.3 | 2,409.9 |
| **Interest Rates** | | | | | | *Percent Per Annum* | | | | | | | |
| Repurchase Agreement Rate............ | 60.q | 4.00 | 4.00 | 4.25 | 4.25 | 4.75 | 4.25 | 4.25 | 4.25 | 4.00 | 3.50 | 3.50 | 3.50 |
| Deposit Rate................................. | 60l | 3.50 | 3.50 | 3.50 | 3.50 | 3.50 | 3.50 | 3.50 | 3.50 | 3.50 | 3.50 | 3.50 | 3.50 |
| **Prices and Labor** | | | | | | *Index Numbers (2010=100): Period Averages* | | | | | | | |
| Consumer Prices............................ | 64 | 81.7 | 86.9 | 89.0 | 88.7 | 98.2 | † 100.8 | 100.0 | 102.8 | 106.7 | 107.3 | 107.0 | 108.0 |
| **Intl. Transactions & Positions** | | | | | | *Billions of CFA Francs* | | | | | | | |
| Exports....................................... | 70 | 253.2 | 246.9 | 307.5 | 298.6 | 310.4 | 411.5 | 650.2 | 1,110.4 | 1,111.5 | 1,162.6 | 1,226.1 | .... |
| Imports, c.i.f................................. | 71 | 670.9 | 664.6 | 689.7 | 804.3 | 903.6 | 977.0 | 1,067.2 | 1,214.1 | 1,747.1 | 2,057.0 | 1,654.2 | .... |

# Burkina Faso   748

## Balance of Payments

*Millions of US Dollars*

| | | 2004 | 2005 | 2006 | 2007 | 2008 | 2009 | 2010 | 2011 | 2012 | 2013 | 2014 | 2015 |
|---|---|---|---|---|---|---|---|---|---|---|---|---|---|
| A. Current Account* | 109bx | .... | −818.6 | −720.6 | −851.2 | −1,248.0 | −766.4 | −548.7 | † −160.2 | −162.3 | −1,345.2 | −997.6 | .... |
| Goods, credit (exports) | 1a9cx | .... | 480.9 | 607.2 | 654.8 | 857.6 | 900.2 | 1,591.0 | † 2,398.9 | 2,868.3 | 2,662.4 | 2,755.4 | .... |
| Goods, debit (imports) | 1a9dx | .... | 1,034.4 | 1,089.8 | 1,254.4 | 1,746.0 | 1,381.0 | 1,723.4 | † 2,368.9 | 2,655.8 | 3,328.0 | 3,015.5 | .... |
| Balance on goods | 1a9bx | .... | −553.6 | −482.7 | −599.7 | −888.4 | −480.9 | −132.4 | † 30.0 | 212.5 | −665.6 | −260.2 | .... |
| Services, credit (exports) | 1b9cx | .... | 64.3 | 60.5 | 85.8 | 126.2 | 152.9 | 298.1 | † 415.6 | 420.8 | 496.6 | 452.6 | .... |
| Services, debit (imports) | 1b9dx | .... | 359.2 | 360.7 | 447.0 | 606.6 | 560.8 | 833.3 | † 1,142.7 | 1,219.1 | 1,426.4 | 1,308.5 | .... |
| Balance on Goods & Services | 1z9bx | .... | −848.5 | −782.8 | −960.9 | −1,368.8 | −888.8 | −667.6 | † −697.0 | −585.8 | −1,595.5 | −1,116.1 | .... |
| Primary income: credit | 1c9cx | .... | 38.0 | 60.5 | 63.4 | 85.3 | 87.4 | 91.7 | † 98.6 | 104.2 | 121.5 | 158.5 | .... |
| Primary income: debit | 1c9dx | .... | 58.6 | 60.9 | 65.7 | 89.0 | 92.9 | 98.1 | † 106.5 | 180.7 | 310.3 | 517.6 | .... |
| Balance on gds, serv. & prim. inc. | 1y9bx | .... | −869.0 | −783.2 | −963.2 | −1,372.4 | −894.3 | −674.1 | † −704.9 | −662.3 | −1,784.2 | −1,475.1 | .... |
| Secondary income: credit | 1d9ca | .... | 124.1 | 140.5 | 196.7 | 216.1 | 219.8 | 235.7 | † 682.1 | 617.5 | 629.5 | 674.9 | .... |
| Secondary income: debit | 1d9da | .... | 73.7 | 77.9 | 84.6 | 91.7 | 91.9 | 110.3 | † 137.4 | 117.5 | 190.4 | 197.4 | .... |
| B. Capital Account* | 209ba | .... | 209.0 | 1,565.8 | 292.5 | 190.9 | 281.5 | 199.7 | † 193.0 | 269.9 | 482.6 | 404.9 | .... |
| Capital account: credit | 209ca | .... | 209.1 | 1,565.8 | 292.5 | 191.8 | 281.5 | 199.7 | † 193.4 | 272.4 | 483.5 | 405.4 | .... |
| Capital account: debit | 209da | .... | .1 | .1 | — | 1.0 | — | — | † .4 | 2.5 | .9 | .5 | .... |
| Balance on current & capital acct. | 129ba | .... | −609.6 | 845.2 | −558.7 | −1,057.1 | −485.0 | −349.0 | † 32.8 | 107.6 | −862.6 | −592.7 | .... |
| C. Financial Account* | 309na | .... | −149.4 | 905.5 | −422.7 | −504.3 | −172.1 | 382.3 | † 124.9 | 136.1 | −443.6 | −325.3 | .... |
| Direct investment: assets | 3a9aa | .... | 17.8 | 49.3 | −315.2 | −70.8 | −14.7 | .7 | † 102.2 | 73.0 | 58.3 | 69.5 | .... |
| Equity & investment fund shares | 3aaaa | .... | 18.2 | 46.9 | −316.4 | −70.7 | −15.9 | −.4 | † 108.9 | 84.1 | 69.2 | 50.9 | .... |
| Debt instruments | 3abaa | .... | −.4 | 2.4 | 1.1 | −.1 | 1.2 | 1.1 | † −6.7 | −11.2 | −10.9 | 18.5 | .... |
| Direct investment: liabilities | 3a9la | .... | 32.3 | 83.8 | 21.7 | 33.1 | 56.4 | 38.8 | † 143.7 | 329.3 | 490.3 | 356.8 | .... |
| Equity & investment fund shares | 3aala | .... | 1.5 | 79.9 | 2.3 | 27.7 | 9.1 | −32.4 | † 132.3 | 118.1 | 266.4 | 241.0 | .... |
| Debt instruments | 3abla | .... | 30.8 | 3.9 | 19.4 | 5.4 | 47.4 | 71.3 | † 11.4 | 211.2 | 223.9 | 115.8 | .... |
| Portfolio investment: assets | 3b9aa | .... | 8.7 | 11.5 | 47.3 | 63.2 | 42.4 | 123.5 | † 201.6 | −122.4 | 11.0 | 157.4 | .... |
| Equity & investment fund shares | 3baaa | .... | .6 | | −.7 | −6.0 | −1.0 | — | † −135.7 | 20.5 | −171.3 | .4 | .... |
| Debt securities | 3bbaa | .... | 8.1 | 11.5 | 48.0 | 69.2 | 43.4 | 123.5 | † 337.3 | −143.0 | 182.3 | 157.0 | .... |
| Portfolio investment: liabilities | 3b9la | .... | −4.3 | 1.4 | −.9 | −2.3 | — | 17.2 | † 105.2 | −89.8 | 25.0 | 84.6 | .... |
| Equity & investment fund shares | 3bala | .... | −4.3 | 1.4 | −.9 | −2.3 | — | 2.6 | † −3.9 | −188.3 | −193.6 | 65.6 | .... |
| Debt securities | 3bbla | .... | — | — | — | — | — | 14.6 | † 109.1 | 98.5 | 218.6 | 19.0 | .... |
| Fin. der.& empl.stk.ops.(ESOs): net | 3c9na | .... | — | — | .... | .... | .... | .... | .... | .... | .... | .... | .... |
| Fin. der. & ESOs.: assets | 3c9aa | .... | — | — | .... | .... | .... | .... | .... | .... | .... | .... | .... |
| Fin. der. & ESOs.: liabilities | 3c9la | .... | — | — | .... | .... | .... | .... | .... | .... | .... | .... | .... |
| Other investment: assets | 3d9aa | .... | 73.8 | 148.7 | 200.5 | −385.7 | −91.8 | 372.1 | † 1,958.8 | 2,762.3 | 1,547.5 | 3,685.7 | .... |
| Other equity | 3daaa | .... | .... | .... | .... | .... | .... | .... | .... | .... | .... | .... | .... |
| Debt instruments | 3dzaa | .... | 73.8 | 148.7 | 200.5 | −385.7 | −91.8 | 372.1 | † 1,958.8 | 2,762.3 | 1,547.5 | 3,685.7 | .... |
| Other investment: liabilities | 3d9la | .... | 221.7 | −781.1 | 334.5 | 80.3 | 51.7 | 57.9 | † 1,888.9 | 2,337.2 | 1,545.2 | 3,796.4 | .... |
| Other equity | 3dala | .... | .... | .... | .... | .... | .... | .... | .... | .... | .... | .... | .... |
| Debt instruments | 3dzla | .... | 221.7 | −781.1 | 334.5 | 80.3 | 51.7 | 57.9 | † 1,888.9 | 2,337.2 | 1,545.2 | 3,796.4 | .... |
| Curr.+ cap.− finan. acct. balance | 4y9na | .... | −460.2 | −60.3 | −136.0 | −552.9 | −312.9 | −731.3 | † −92.0 | −28.6 | −418.9 | −267.4 | .... |
| D. Net Errors and Omissions | 409na | .... | −5.4 | −7.9 | 5.5 | −2.8 | −48.4 | −2.1 | † −10.2 | 10.0 | −5.5 | −15.1 | .... |
| E. Reserves and Related Items | 4z9na | .... | −465.5 | −68.2 | −130.5 | −555.7 | −361.3 | −733.5 | † −102.2 | −18.6 | −424.5 | −282.6 | .... |
| Reserve assets | 3e9aa | .... | −146.2 | 65.7 | 383.7 | −48.1 | 326.3 | −137.3 | † −85.8 | 48.9 | −422.4 | −285.6 | .... |
| Credit and loans from the IMF | 3dcla | .... | −1.8 | −70.9 | .8 | 18.2 | 55.5 | 19.8 | † 16.5 | 67.5 | 2.1 | −3.1 | .... |
| Exceptional financing | 409la | .... | 321.2 | 204.9 | 513.5 | 489.3 | 632.0 | 576.4 | .... | .... | .... | .... | .... |

*Excludes components in group E

## International Investment Position

*Millions of US Dollars*

| | | 2004 | 2005 | 2006 | 2007 | 2008 | 2009 | 2010 | 2011 | 2012 | 2013 | 2014 | 2015 |
|---|---|---|---|---|---|---|---|---|---|---|---|---|---|
| Assets | 809aa | .... | 801.4 | 856.1 | 1,614.8 | 1,380.8 | 1,912.2 | 2,244.4 | † 6,964.5 | 8,779.4 | 10,434.1 | 12,522.7 | .... |
| Direct investment | 8a9aa | .... | 15.4 | 17.5 | 20.7 | 12.6 | 10.6 | 47.0 | † 415.6 | 498.7 | 1,282.9 | 1,205.7 | .... |
| Equity & investment fund shares | 8aaaa | .... | 15.4 | 17.5 | 20.7 | 12.6 | 10.6 | 47.0 | † 307.8 | 400.2 | 281.4 | 307.1 | .... |
| Debt instruments | 8abaa | .... | — | — | .... | .... | .... | .... | † 107.8 | 98.4 | 1,001.5 | 898.7 | .... |
| Portfolio investment | 8b9aa | .... | 47.5 | 16.7 | 100.1 | 164.0 | 216.7 | 571.2 | † 2,358.2 | 1,128.6 | 2,251.2 | 3,155.9 | .... |
| Equity & investment fund shares | 8baaa | .... | 6.8 | 6.8 | 10.2 | 4.7 | 5.4 | 5.0 | † 201.5 | 70.7 | 517.7 | 456.1 | .... |
| Debt securities | 8bbaa | .... | 40.7 | 9.9 | 89.9 | 159.3 | 211.3 | 566.2 | † 2,156.7 | 1,057.9 | 1,733.5 | 2,699.8 | .... |
| Fin. der.(oth.than reserves) & ESOs | 8c9aa | .... | — | .... | .9 | 5.7 | .... | .... | † 4.8 | .... | .... | .... | .... |
| Other investment | 8d9aa | .... | 305.0 | 269.7 | 463.9 | 271.0 | 389.1 | 557.9 | † 3,228.9 | 6,127.6 | 6,271.5 | 7,864.0 | .... |
| Other equity | 8daaa | .... | .... | .... | .... | .... | .... | .... | .... | .... | .... | .... | .... |
| Debt instruments | 8dzaa | .... | 305.0 | 269.7 | 463.9 | 271.0 | 389.1 | 557.9 | † 3,228.9 | 6,127.6 | 6,271.5 | 7,864.0 | .... |
| Reserve assets | 8e9aa | .... | 433.4 | 552.2 | 1,029.2 | 927.6 | 1,295.8 | 1,068.2 | † 957.0 | 1,024.5 | 628.5 | 297.1 | .... |
| Liabilities | 809la | .... | 2,545.9 | 1,969.0 | 3,232.9 | 2,977.5 | 3,310.6 | 3,370.1 | † 7,426.1 | 9,191.9 | 14,484.7 | 15,295.9 | .... |
| Direct investment | 8a9la | .... | 83.4 | 178.7 | 570.3 | 334.2 | 570.1 | 393.3 | † 636.3 | 1,003.9 | 2,230.5 | 1,975.5 | .... |
| Equity & investment fund shares | 8aala | .... | 45.8 | 136.0 | 440.6 | 206.5 | 146.2 | 150.9 | † 527.3 | 658.9 | 648.3 | 476.6 | .... |
| Debt instruments | 8abla | .... | 37.6 | 42.6 | 129.7 | 127.7 | 423.9 | 242.4 | † 109.1 | 345.0 | 1,582.2 | 1,498.9 | .... |
| Portfolio investment | 8b9la | .... | 1.9 | 2.9 | 54.6 | 9.5 | 15.1 | 12.5 | † 1,617.5 | 579.8 | 3,118.0 | 2,822.4 | .... |
| Equity & investment fund shares | 8bala | .... | 1.8 | 2.9 | 10.0 | 7.2 | 6.8 | 8.9 | † 649.2 | 161.4 | 1,045.4 | 980.3 | .... |
| Debt securities | 8bbla | .... | .1 | .... | 44.7 | 2.3 | 8.3 | 3.7 | † 968.3 | 418.4 | 2,072.6 | 1,842.1 | .... |
| Fin. der.(oth.than reserves) & ESOs | 8c9la | .... | .... | .... | .... | .... | .... | .... | .... | .... | .... | .... | .... |
| Other investment | 8d9la | .... | 2,460.6 | 1,787.4 | 2,607.9 | 2,633.7 | 2,725.4 | 2,964.2 | † 5,172.2 | 7,608.2 | 9,136.2 | 10,498.0 | .... |
| Other equity | 8dala | .... | .... | .... | .... | .... | .... | .... | .... | .... | .... | .... | .... |
| Debt instruments | 8dzla | .... | 2,460.6 | 1,787.4 | 2,607.9 | 2,633.7 | 2,725.4 | 2,964.2 | † 5,172.2 | 7,608.2 | 9,136.2 | 10,498.0 | .... |

# Burkina Faso   748

| | | 2004 | 2005 | 2006 | 2007 | 2008 | 2009 | 2010 | 2011 | 2012 | 2013 | 2014 | 2015 |
|---|---|---|---|---|---|---|---|---|---|---|---|---|---|
| **Government Finance Operations Statement Budgetary Central Government** | | *Billions of CFA Francs: Fiscal Year Ends December 31* | | | | | | | | | | | |
| Revenue | a1 | 462.1 | 496.3 | 561.3 | 650.4 | 630.7 | 771.5 | 880.2 | 1,047.3 | 1,276.3 | 1,441.6 | 1,321.1 | .... |
| Taxes | a11 | 318.6 | 336.8 | 362.3 | 405.2 | 444.7 | 494.6 | 565.7 | 695.6 | 890.8 | 992.6 | 940.7 | .... |
| Social Contributions | a12 | — | — | — | — | — | — | — | — | — | — | — | .... |
| Grants | a13 | 117.3 | 131.5 | 170.0 | 210.3 | 146.9 | 232.4 | 198.9 | 253.7 | 277.5 | 324.4 | 256.4 | .... |
| Other Revenue | a14 | 26.2 | 28.0 | 29.0 | 34.9 | 39.2 | 44.5 | 115.5 | 98.0 | 108.0 | 124.7 | 124.0 | .... |
| Expense | a2 | 237.6 | 332.2 | 387.3 | 450.3 | 350.3 | 499.1 | 530.0 | 628.3 | 828.7 | 819.0 | 886.6 | .... |
| Compensation of Employees | a21 | 123.5 | 141.3 | 159.9 | 187.6 | 198.8 | 228.4 | 245.8 | 281.4 | 332.3 | 355.5 | 437.3 | .... |
| Use of Goods & Services | a22 | 67.3 | 75.1 | 82.2 | 94.8 | 95.3 | 95.1 | 90.8 | 97.1 | 120.6 | 118.6 | 102.4 | .... |
| Consumption of Fixed Capital | a23 | .... | .... | .... | .... | .... | .... | .... | .... | .... | .... | .... | .... |
| Interest | a24 | 19.1 | 18.2 | 17.3 | 13.1 | 12.7 | 16.9 | 21.4 | 28.3 | 41.8 | 34.8 | 44.0 | .... |
| Subsidies | a25 | 13.3 | 17.9 | 20.6 | 18.1 | 18.3 | 24.8 | 18.1 | 31.7 | 13.2 | 11.0 | 23.6 | .... |
| Grants | a26 | 13.5 | 15.2 | 21.8 | 25.5 | 25.1 | 30.7 | 44.7 | 36.7 | 61.1 | 57.3 | 89.5 | .... |
| Social Benefits | a27 | — | — | — | — | — | — | — | — | — | — | — | .... |
| Other Expense | a28 | .8 | 64.5 | 85.3 | 111.2 | — | 103.1 | 109.3 | 153.0 | 259.6 | 241.8 | 189.9 | .... |
| Gross Operating Balance [1-2+23] | agob | 217.7 | 164.2 | 174.0 | 200.1 | 280.5 | 272.4 | 350.3 | 419.0 | 447.6 | 622.7 | 434.5 | .... |
| Net Operating Balance [1-2] | anob | .... | .... | .... | .... | .... | .... | .... | .... | .... | .... | .... | .... |
| Net Acq. of Nonfinancial Assets | a31 | 370.2 | 322.6 | 362.3 | 383.2 | 325.1 | 457.4 | 552.4 | 535.1 | 625.1 | 858.4 | 554.1 | .... |
| Aquisition of Nonfin. Assets | a31.1 | .... | .... | .... | .... | .... | .... | 552.4 | 535.1 | 625.1 | 858.4 | 554.1 | .... |
| Disposal of Nonfin. Assets | a31.2 | .... | .... | .... | .... | .... | .... | .... | .... | .... | .... | .... | .... |
| Net Lending/Borrowing [1-2-31] | anlb | −73.4 | −158.5 | −188.3 | −183.0 | −44.6 | −184.9 | −202.1 | −116.1 | −177.4 | −235.8 | −119.6 | .... |
| Net Acq. of Financial Assets | a32 | −18.1 | −51.2 | −16.7 | −76.8 | −32.3 | 72.7 | 16.5 | 1.1 | 82.9 | −67.6 | 68.3 | .... |
| By instrument | | | | | | | | | | | | | |
| Monetary Gold & SDRs | a3201 | — | — | — | — | — | — | — | — | — | — | — | .... |
| Currency & Deposits | a3202 | .... | .... | .... | .... | .... | .... | 29.6 | −1.5 | 83.8 | −42.8 | 74.5 | .... |
| Securities other than Shares | a3203 | .... | .... | .... | .... | .... | .... | — | — | — | — | — | .... |
| Loans | a3204 | .... | .... | .... | .... | .... | .... | −6.2 | 2.7 | −.9 | −24.8 | −6.1 | .... |
| Shares & Other Equity | a3205 | .... | .... | .... | .... | .... | .... | −6.9 | — | — | — | — | .... |
| Insurance Technical Reserves | a3206 | .... | .... | .... | .... | .... | .... | — | — | — | — | — | .... |
| Financial Derivatives | a3207 | .... | .... | .... | .... | .... | .... | — | — | — | — | — | .... |
| Other Accounts Receivable | a3208 | .... | .... | .... | .... | .... | .... | — | — | — | — | — | .... |
| By debtor | | | | | | | | | | | | | |
| Domestic | a321 | −18.1 | −51.2 | −16.7 | −76.8 | −32.3 | 72.7 | 16.5 | 1.1 | 82.9 | −67.6 | 68.3 | .... |
| Foreign | a322 | — | — | — | — | — | — | — | — | — | — | — | .... |
| Net Incurrence of Liabilities | a33 | 139.7 | 107.3 | 171.6 | 102.2 | 247.7 | 268.4 | 219.5 | 117.2 | 260.2 | 168.1 | 187.9 | .... |
| By instrument | | | | | | | | | | | | | |
| Special Drawing Rights (SDRs) | a3301 | .... | .... | .... | .... | .... | .... | — | — | — | — | — | .... |
| Currency & Deposits | a3302 | .... | .... | .... | .... | .... | .... | −.2 | .2 | −.1 | .1 | .1 | .... |
| Securities other than Shares | a3303 | .... | .... | .... | .... | .... | .... | 35.9 | −9.1 | 65.2 | 91.7 | 74.7 | .... |
| Loans | a3304 | .... | .... | .... | .... | .... | .... | 223.3 | 145.2 | 168.8 | 97.1 | 99.1 | .... |
| Shares & Other Equity | a3305 | .... | .... | .... | .... | .... | .... | — | — | — | — | — | .... |
| Insurance Technical Reserves | a3306 | .... | .... | .... | .... | .... | .... | — | — | — | — | — | .... |
| Financial Derivatives | a3307 | .... | .... | .... | .... | .... | .... | — | — | — | — | — | .... |
| Other Accounts Payable | a3308 | .... | .... | .... | .... | .... | .... | −39.6 | −19.0 | 26.3 | −20.8 | 14.0 | .... |
| By creditor | | | | | | | | | | | | | |
| Domestic | a331 | 14.9 | −26.9 | 37.6 | 5.0 | 79.4 | 158.9 | 68.8 | 8.4 | 174.7 | 133.6 | 136.5 | .... |
| Foreign | a332 | 124.8 | 134.2 | 134.1 | 97.3 | 168.3 | 109.6 | 150.7 | 108.8 | 85.5 | 34.4 | 51.4 | .... |
| Stat. Discrepancy [32-33-NLB] | anlbz | −84.4 | — | — | 4.0 | — | — | — | — | — | — | — | .... |
| Memo Item: Expenditure [2+31] | a2m | 607.8 | 654.8 | 749.6 | 833.4 | 675.3 | 956.4 | 1,082.3 | 1,163.4 | 1,453.7 | 1,677.4 | 1,440.8 | .... |
| **National Accounts** | | *Billions of CFA Francs* | | | | | | | | | | | |
| Househ.Cons.Expend.,incl.NPISHs | 96f | 1,841.3 | 2,079.9 | 2,172.2 | 2,214.1 | 2,608.6 | 2,707.7 | 2,795.0 | 3,016.7 | 3,056.5 | 3,558.4 | 3,860.6 | .... |
| Government Consumption Expend | 91f | 531.0 | 569.6 | 659.3 | 774.1 | 800.7 | 854.9 | 918.0 | 1,040.7 | 1,188.2 | 1,243.4 | 1,294.8 | .... |
| Gross Fixed Capital Formation | 93e | 496.9 | 567.3 | 584.4 | 700.3 | 784.4 | 905.6 | 1,089.7 | 1,336.6 | 1,672.0 | 1,906.2 | 1,929.4 | .... |
| Changes in Inventories | 93i | 56.8 | 127.0 | 50.5 | 21.7 | 168.0 | 77.3 | 108.0 | 78.6 | 82.9 | 66.9 | −41.2 | .... |
| Exports of Goods and Services | 90c | 289.6 | 280.8 | 346.8 | 342.4 | 373.6 | 501.9 | 855.1 | 1,265.3 | 1,679.2 | 1,530.7 | 1,609.5 | .... |
| Imports of Goods and Services (-) | 98c | 659.5 | 743.2 | 772.0 | 807.2 | 987.3 | 1,095.5 | 1,318.3 | 1,677.5 | 1,978.2 | 2,318.9 | 2,461.7 | .... |
| Gross Domestic Product (GDP) | 99b | 2,556.1 | 2,881.4 | 3,041.3 | 3,245.2 | 3,748.0 | 3,951.8 | 4,447.6 | 5,060.3 | 5,700.6 | 5,986.6 | 6,191.4 | .... |
| Net Primary Income from Abroad | 98.n | −16.2 | −22.6 | −1.2 | −1.1 | −1.4 | −35.6 | −116.5 | −186.5 | −112.1 | .... | .... | .... |
| Gross National Income (GNI) | 99a | 2,539.9 | 2,858.8 | 3,040.1 | 3,244.1 | 3,746.6 | 3,916.3 | 4,331.0 | 4,873.8 | 5,588.5 | .... | .... | .... |
| GDP Volume 2008 Prices | 99b.p | 2,369.6 | 2,537.9 | 2,677.4 | 2,774.2 | 3,748.0 | 3,859.0 | 4,184.9 | 4,462.3 | 4,750.2 | 5,062.2 | 5,267.1 | .... |
| GDP Volume (2010=100) | 99bvp | 56.6 | 60.6 | 64.0 | 66.3 | 89.6 | 92.2 | 100.0 | 106.6 | 113.5 | 121.0 | 125.9 | .... |
| GDP Deflator (2010=100) | 99bip | 101.5 | 106.8 | 106.9 | 110.1 | 94.1 | 96.4 | 100.0 | 106.7 | 112.9 | 111.3 | 110.6 | .... |
| | | *Millions: Midyear Estimates* | | | | | | | | | | | |
| **Population** | 99z | 13.03 | 13.42 | 13.83 | 14.26 | 14.71 | 15.17 | 15.63 | 16.11 | 16.59 | 17.08 | 17.59 | 18.11 |

# Burundi 618

| | | 2004 | 2005 | 2006 | 2007 | 2008 | 2009 | 2010 | 2011 | 2012 | 2013 | 2014 | 2015 |
|---|---|---|---|---|---|---|---|---|---|---|---|---|---|
| **Exchange Rates** | | *Francs per SDR: End of Period* | | | | | | | | | | | |
| Official Rate.................... | aa | 1,717.4 | 1,425.9 | 1,506.9 | 1,767.2 | 1,911.5 | 1,922.0 | 1,898.7 | 2,083.6 | 2,376.2 | 2,382.4 | 2,249.4 | 2,243.4 |
| | | *Francs per US Dollar: End of Period (ae) Period Average (rf)* | | | | | | | | | | | |
| Official Rate.................... | ae | 1,109.5 | 997.8 | 1,002.5 | 1,119.5 | 1,235.0 | 1,230.5 | 1,232.5 | 1,361.5 | 1,546.1 | 1,542.0 | 1,553.1 | 1,617.1 |
| Official Rate.................... | rf | 1,100.9 | 1,081.6 | 1,028.7 | 1,081.9 | 1,185.7 | 1,230.2 | 1,230.7 | 1,261.1 | 1,442.5 | 1,555.1 | 1,546.7 | 1,571.9 |
| | | *Index Numbers (2010=100): Period Averages* | | | | | | | | | | | |
| Official Rate.................... | ahx | 111.8 | 114.0 | 119.7 | 113.9 | 103.8 | 100.0 | 100.0 | 97.7 | 85.4 | 79.2 | 79.6 | 78.3 |
| Nominal Effective Exchange Rate..... | nec | 110.5 | 111.3 | 117.1 | 106.8 | 96.0 | 99.2 | 100.0 | 96.1 | 87.8 | 84.3 | 87.0 | 96.6 |
| CPI-Based Real Effect. Ex. Rate........ | rec | 79.4 | 87.4 | 90.7 | 85.7 | 88.5 | 97.4 | 100.0 | 99.3 | 102.2 | 102.2 | 106.4 | 121.4 |
| **Fund Position** | | *Millions of SDRs: End of Period* | | | | | | | | | | | |
| Quota............................. | 2f.s | 77.00 | 77.00 | 77.00 | 77.00 | 77.00 | 77.00 | 77.00 | 77.00 | 77.00 | 77.00 | 77.00 | 77.00 |
| SDR Holdings..................... | 1b.s | .23 | .19 | .22 | .24 | .10 | 66.65 | 73.22 | 79.01 | 84.04 | 82.32 | 81.76 | 39.28 |
| Reserve Position in the Fund........... | 1c.s | .36 | .36 | .36 | .36 | .36 | .36 | .36 | .36 | .36 | .36 | .36 | .36 |
| Total Fund Cred.&Loans Outstg....... | 2tl | 26.40 | 40.70 | 55.00 | 62.15 | 75.90 | 57.99 | 71.19 | 82.96 | 87.96 | 91.23 | 90.67 | 83.18 |
| SDR Allocations.................... | 1bd | 13.70 | 13.70 | 13.70 | 13.70 | 13.70 | 73.85 | 73.85 | 73.85 | 73.85 | 73.85 | 73.85 | 73.85 |
| **International Liquidity** | | *Millions of US Dollars Unless Otherwise Indicated: End of Period* | | | | | | | | | | | |
| Total Reserves minus Gold.............. | 1l.d | 65.75 | 100.08 | 130.53 | 176.33 | 265.70 | 322.04 | 330.73 | 293.98 | 307.16 | 328.15 | 315.98 | 135.12 |
| SDR Holdings..................... | 1b.d | .35 | .27 | .33 | .38 | .15 | 104.48 | 112.77 | 121.31 | 129.17 | 126.77 | 118.46 | 54.43 |
| Reserve Position in the Fund......... | 1c.d | .56 | .51 | .54 | .57 | .55 | .56 | .55 | .55 | .55 | .55 | .52 | .50 |
| Foreign Exchange......................... | 1d.d | 64.84 | 99.30 | 129.66 | 175.38 | 265.00 | 217.00 | 217.41 | 172.12 | 177.44 | 200.83 | 197.00 | 80.19 |
| Gold (Million Fine Troy Ounces)........ | 1ad | .001 | .001 | .001 | .001 | .001 | .001 | .001 | .001 | .001 | .001 | .001 | .001 |
| Gold (National Valuation)............... | 1and | .42 | .49 | .61 | .81 | .84 | 1.06 | 1.36 | 1.50 | 1.61 | 1.26 | 1.16 | 1.03 |
| Central Bank: Other Assets............. | 3..d | 4.67 | 4.06 | 3.54 | 3.90 | 4.45 | 2.81 | 7.11 | 7.43 | 4.87 | 3.87 | 5.46 | .80 |
| Central Bank: Other Liabs............. | 4..d | 12.27 | 9.86 | 6.80 | 7.12 | 3.35 | 2.10 | 1.03 | 2.73 | 21.39 | 1.91 | 1.55 | 1.53 |
| Other Depository Corps.: Assets....... | 7a.d | 48.87 | 59.17 | 74.28 | 87.80 | 101.84 | 126.59 | 132.15 | 128.50 | 124.82 | 130.62 | 128.52 | 127.92 |
| Other Depository Corps.: Liabs......... | 7b.d | 12.54 | 14.18 | 18.24 | 25.77 | 24.30 | 29.45 | 40.63 | 38.38 | 40.50 | 58.23 | 95.14 | 92.78 |
| Other Financial Corps.: Assets......... | 7e.d | — | — | — | — | — | — | — | — | — | — | .04 | — |
| Other Financial Corps.: Liabs............ | 7f.d | 8.17 | 2.76 | 3.05 | 3.36 | 1.68 | 1.43 | 1.10 | .80 | .53 | .21 | .21 | .20 |
| **Central Bank** | | *Millions of Francs: End of Period* | | | | | | | | | | | |
| Net Foreign Assets.......................... | 11n | −2,882 | 28,986 | 24,625 | 61,120 | 160,300 | 144,511 | 141,611 | 81,781 | 67,464 | 118,995 | 128,694 | −132,635 |
| Claims on Nonresidents................. | 11 | 79,823 | 116,396 | 135,046 | 203,277 | 334,864 | 401,421 | 418,270 | 413,270 | 485,029 | 513,943 | 501,269 | 221,732 |
| Liabilities to Nonresidents............. | 16c | 82,705 | 87,411 | 110,422 | 142,158 | 174,563 | 256,910 | 276,659 | 331,490 | 417,565 | 394,947 | 372,576 | 354,367 |
| Claims on Other Depository Corps.... | 12e | 4,336 | 1,032 | 1,032 | 2,024 | 1,024 | 1,014 | 906 | 26,189 | 888 | 888 | 888 | 20,688 |
| Net Claims on Central Government.. | 12an | 109,020 | 114,440 | 163,152 | 123,443 | 76,725 | 167,661 | 149,140 | 211,567 | 263,353 | 227,215 | 263,564 | 452,514 |
| Claims on Central Government...... | 12a | 129,775 | 154,371 | 208,516 | 181,741 | 170,799 | 250,334 | 253,190 | 322,019 | 410,025 | 396,574 | 448,064 | 641,725 |
| Liabilities to Central Government... | 16d | 20,755 | 39,931 | 45,364 | 58,298 | 94,074 | 82,673 | 104,050 | 110,452 | 146,672 | 169,359 | 184,500 | 189,211 |
| Claims on Other Sectors.................. | 12s | 3,316 | 2,775 | 2,855 | 3,547 | 4,309 | 4,757 | 5,085 | 6,600 | 8,172 | 10,172 | 14,145 | 17,002 |
| Claims on Other Financial Corps.... | 12g | 1,474 | 519 | 466 | 397 | 392 | 394 | 393 | 395 | 26 | 33 | 2,021 | 2,048 |
| Claims on State & Local Govts....... | 12b | — | — | — | — | — | — | — | — | — | — | — | — |
| Claims on Public Nonfin. Corps...... | 12c | 25 | 25 | 25 | 25 | 25 | 20 | 20 | 20 | 20 | 20 | 20 | 20 |
| Claims on Private Sector................ | 12d | 1,817 | 2,231 | 2,364 | 3,126 | 3,892 | 4,343 | 4,672 | 6,184 | 8,126 | 10,119 | 12,103 | 14,934 |
| Monetary Base............................ | 14 | 76,336 | 101,221 | 108,144 | 125,491 | 156,439 | 198,044 | 209,860 | 211,229 | 245,341 | 303,348 | 355,001 | 324,508 |
| Currency in Circulation.................. | 14a | 61,610 | 73,204 | 76,883 | 92,976 | 124,231 | 136,206 | 155,835 | 170,106 | 198,247 | 211,684 | 227,341 | 230,724 |
| Liabs. to Other Depository Corps.... | 14c | 12,943 | 25,564 | 28,175 | 24,934 | 24,966 | 53,862 | 45,700 | 34,907 | 39,880 | 82,711 | 120,095 | 84,351 |
| Liabilities to Other Sectors........... | 14d | 1,783 | 2,454 | 3,086 | 7,581 | 7,242 | 7,976 | 8,324 | 6,216 | 7,215 | 8,954 | 7,565 | 9,434 |
| Other Liabs. to Other Dep. Corps.... | 14n | — | 12,000 | 10,500 | 6,000 | 18,283 | 16,330 | 13,530 | 6,825 | 7,747 | 1,248 | 1,064 | 1,188 |
| Dep. & Sec. Excl. f/Monetary Base.... | 14o | 7,406 | 3,669 | 7,743 | 2,376 | 5,505 | 3,636 | 10,533 | 12,322 | 15,938 | 8,685 | 9,223 | 5,645 |
| Deposits Included in Broad Money. | 15 | 156 | 254 | 6,307 | 1 | 5 | 8 | 17 | 20 | 280 | 1,152 | — | — |
| Sec.Ot.th.Shares Incl.in Brd. Money | 16a | — | — | — | — | — | — | — | — | — | — | — | — |
| Deposits Excl. from Broad Money... | 16b | 7,249 | 3,415 | 1,436 | 2,375 | 5,500 | 3,628 | 10,516 | 12,302 | 15,658 | 7,533 | 9,223 | 5,645 |
| Sec.Ot.th.Shares Excl.f/Brd.Money.. | 16s | — | — | — | — | — | — | — | — | — | — | — | — |
| Loans............................................. | 16l | — | — | — | — | — | — | — | — | — | — | — | — |
| Financial Derivatives.................... | 16m | — | — | — | — | — | — | — | — | — | — | — | — |
| Shares and Other Equity.................. | 17a | 30,599 | 25,421 | 28,605 | 27,067 | 29,353 | 37,163 | 40,915 | 51,331 | 59,860 | 49,130 | 90,278 | 89,110 |
| Other Items (Net)......................... | 17r | −550 | 4,922 | 36,672 | 29,200 | 32,778 | 62,770 | 21,904 | 44,430 | 10,990 | −5,141 | −48,275 | −62,882 |
| Memo Item: | | | | | | | | | | | | | |
| Total Assets..................................... | 10ra | 229,504 | 286,906 | 357,991 | 397,540 | 513,971 | 659,975 | 680,429 | 772,035 | 911,954 | 923,747 | 1,028,667 | 970,787 |

# Burundi  618

| | | 2004 | 2005 | 2006 | 2007 | 2008 | 2009 | 2010 | 2011 | 2012 | 2013 | 2014 | 2015 |
|---|---|---|---|---|---|---|---|---|---|---|---|---|---|
| **Other Depository Corporations** | | | | | | | *Millions of Francs: End of Period* | | | | | | | |
| Net Foreign Assets | 21n | 40,306 | 44,888 | 56,175 | 69,449 | 95,760 | 119,531 | 112,836 | 122,696 | 130,360 | 111,622 | 51,853 | 56,836 |
| Claims on Nonresidents | 21 | 54,220 | 59,039 | 74,465 | 98,301 | 125,769 | 155,769 | 162,923 | 174,949 | 192,979 | 201,411 | 199,604 | 206,870 |
| Liabilities to Nonresidents | 26c | 13,915 | 14,151 | 18,290 | 28,852 | 30,009 | 36,238 | 50,087 | 52,253 | 62,619 | 89,789 | 147,752 | 150,034 |
| Claims on Central Bank | 20 | 17,406 | 42,922 | 47,119 | 39,245 | 56,258 | 84,592 | 76,325 | 48,442 | 76,259 | 107,188 | 146,491 | 109,484 |
| Currency | 20a | 4,452 | 5,348 | 8,447 | 8,823 | 11,607 | 15,291 | 16,732 | 16,892 | 24,375 | 24,197 | 27,525 | 23,417 |
| Reserve Deposits and Securities | 20b | 12,954 | 37,575 | 38,672 | 30,422 | 44,651 | 69,301 | 59,594 | 31,550 | 51,884 | 82,991 | 118,966 | 86,067 |
| Other Claims | 20n | — | — | — | — | — | — | — | — | — | — | — | — |
| Net Claims on Central Government | 22an | −34,166 | −13,843 | −6,805 | 760 | 17,237 | 283 | 46,829 | 6,563 | −21,666 | 27,346 | 106,514 | 221,338 |
| Claims on Central Government | 22a | 10,874 | 14,247 | 8,172 | 35,537 | 60,268 | 66,118 | 109,383 | 85,168 | 52,730 | 109,548 | 182,336 | 289,096 |
| Liabilities to Central Government | 26d | 45,040 | 28,089 | 14,977 | 34,776 | 43,031 | 65,836 | 62,554 | 78,604 | 74,396 | 82,202 | 75,822 | 67,758 |
| Claims on Other Sectors | 22s | 180,055 | 178,911 | 215,119 | 221,692 | 279,479 | 325,414 | 425,309 | 559,899 | 634,858 | 687,392 | 736,996 | 685,872 |
| Claims on Other Financial Corps. | 22g | 6 | — | — | 126 | 231 | 216 | 221 | 225 | 227 | 234 | 218 | 144 |
| Claims on State & Local Govts. | 22b | 142 | 225 | 70 | 80 | 121 | 497 | 599 | 1,022 | 998 | 2,409 | 3,361 | 26 |
| Claims on Public Nonfin. Corps. | 22c | 6,895 | 5,195 | 10,044 | 7,836 | 21,902 | 8,421 | 8,291 | 3,801 | 6,581 | 8,185 | 10,553 | 6,511 |
| Claims on Private Sector | 22d | 173,012 | 173,492 | 205,005 | 213,651 | 257,225 | 316,281 | 416,197 | 554,852 | 627,052 | 676,564 | 722,865 | 679,192 |
| Liabilities to Central Bank | 26g | 3,682 | — | — | 1,000 | — | — | — | 23,888 | — | — | — | 19,805 |
| Transf.Dep.Included in Broad Money | 24 | 112,298 | 134,012 | 173,874 | 175,643 | 251,488 | 307,539 | 379,994 | 366,999 | 441,709 | 491,050 | 574,090 | 523,014 |
| Other Dep.Included in Broad Money. | 25 | 51,647 | 72,820 | 89,835 | 89,709 | 103,537 | 118,264 | 145,692 | 183,918 | 196,551 | 229,915 | 249,338 | 307,180 |
| Sec.Ot.th.Shares Incl.in Brd. Money. | 26a | — | — | — | — | — | — | — | — | — | — | — | — |
| Deposits Excl. from Broad Money | 26b | — | — | — | — | — | — | — | — | — | — | — | — |
| Sec.Ot.th.Shares Excl.f/Brd.Money. | 26s | — | — | — | — | — | — | — | — | — | — | — | — |
| Loans | 26l | — | — | — | — | — | — | — | — | — | — | — | — |
| Financial Derivatives | 26m | — | — | — | — | — | — | — | — | — | — | — | — |
| Insurance Technical Reserves | 26r | — | — | — | — | — | — | — | — | — | — | — | — |
| Shares and Other Equity | 27a | 23,299 | 28,411 | 29,377 | 42,905 | 60,252 | 88,493 | 117,700 | 146,544 | 180,688 | 202,229 | 221,077 | 231,543 |
| Other Items (Net) | 27r | 12,676 | 17,636 | 18,522 | 21,889 | 33,457 | 15,524 | 17,913 | 16,251 | 863 | 10,355 | −2,652 | −8,012 |
| Memo Item: | | | | | | | | | | | | | |
| Total Assets | 20ra | 291,627 | 324,518 | 382,249 | 431,439 | 562,075 | 687,067 | 839,467 | 940,787 | 1,050,407 | 1,212,993 | 1,404,652 | 1,453,349 |
| **Depository Corporations** | | | | | | | *Millions of Francs: End of Period* | | | | | | | |
| Net Foreign Assets | 31n | 37,423 | 73,874 | 80,800 | 130,568 | 256,060 | 264,043 | 254,447 | 204,477 | 197,824 | 230,618 | 180,547 | −75,800 |
| Claims on Nonresidents | 31 | 134,043 | 175,436 | 209,511 | 301,578 | 460,633 | 557,190 | 581,193 | 588,219 | 678,009 | 715,354 | 700,874 | 428,602 |
| Liabilities to Nonresidents | 36c | 96,620 | 101,562 | 128,711 | 171,010 | 204,573 | 293,147 | 326,746 | 383,742 | 480,185 | 484,736 | 520,327 | 504,401 |
| Domestic Claims | 32 | 258,225 | 282,284 | 374,320 | 349,443 | 377,751 | 498,115 | 626,362 | 784,629 | 884,717 | 952,125 | 1,121,218 | 1,376,727 |
| Net Claims on Central Government | 32an | 74,854 | 100,597 | 156,347 | 124,203 | 93,962 | 167,944 | 195,969 | 218,131 | 241,687 | 254,561 | 370,078 | 673,852 |
| Claims on Central Government | 32a | 140,649 | 168,617 | 216,688 | 217,277 | 231,067 | 316,453 | 362,573 | 407,186 | 462,755 | 506,122 | 630,400 | 930,821 |
| Liabilities to Central Government. | 36d | 65,795 | 68,020 | 60,341 | 93,074 | 137,105 | 148,508 | 166,604 | 189,056 | 221,068 | 251,562 | 260,322 | 256,968 |
| Claims on Other Sectors | 32s | 183,371 | 181,687 | 217,973 | 225,240 | 283,788 | 330,171 | 430,393 | 566,499 | 643,030 | 697,564 | 751,140 | 702,874 |
| Claims on Other Financial Corps. | 32g | 1,480 | 519 | 466 | 523 | 623 | 610 | 614 | 620 | 253 | 268 | 2,239 | 2,192 |
| Claims on State & Local Govts. | 32b | 142 | 225 | 70 | 80 | 121 | 497 | 599 | 1,022 | 998 | 2,409 | 3,361 | 26 |
| Claims on Public Nonfin. Corps. | 32c | 6,920 | 5,220 | 10,069 | 7,861 | 21,927 | 8,441 | 8,311 | 3,821 | 6,601 | 8,205 | 10,573 | 6,531 |
| Claims on Private Sector | 32d | 174,829 | 175,723 | 207,369 | 216,776 | 261,117 | 320,624 | 420,869 | 561,036 | 635,177 | 686,682 | 734,968 | 694,125 |
| Broad Money Liabilities | 35l | 223,042 | 277,395 | 341,538 | 357,088 | 474,895 | 554,702 | 673,131 | 710,367 | 819,626 | 918,557 | 1,030,809 | 1,046,934 |
| Currency Outside Depository Corps | 34a | 57,158 | 67,856 | 68,437 | 84,153 | 112,624 | 120,916 | 139,103 | 153,214 | 173,872 | 187,487 | 199,816 | 207,307 |
| Transferable Deposits | 34 | 114,237 | 136,719 | 183,267 | 183,225 | 258,734 | 315,523 | 388,335 | 373,235 | 449,204 | 501,155 | 581,654 | 532,447 |
| Other Deposits | 35 | 51,647 | 72,820 | 89,835 | 89,709 | 103,537 | 118,264 | 145,692 | 183,918 | 196,551 | 229,915 | 249,338 | 307,180 |
| Securities Other than Shares | 36a | — | — | — | — | — | — | — | — | — | — | — | — |
| Deposits Excl. from Broad Money | 36b | 7,249 | 3,415 | 1,436 | 2,375 | 5,500 | 3,628 | 10,516 | 12,302 | 15,658 | 7,533 | 9,223 | 5,645 |
| Sec.Ot.th.Shares Excl.f/Brd.Money. | 36s | — | — | — | — | — | — | — | — | — | — | — | — |
| Loans | 36l | — | — | — | — | — | — | — | — | — | — | — | — |
| Financial Derivatives | 36m | — | — | — | — | — | — | — | — | — | — | — | — |
| Insurance Technical Reserves | 36r | — | — | — | — | — | — | — | — | — | — | — | — |
| Shares and Other Equity | 37a | 53,897 | 53,832 | 57,982 | 69,972 | 89,605 | 125,657 | 158,615 | 197,875 | 240,549 | 251,359 | 311,355 | 320,653 |
| Other Items (Net) | 37r | 11,460 | 21,515 | 54,164 | 50,578 | 63,810 | 78,171 | 38,547 | 68,562 | 6,708 | 5,294 | −49,622 | −72,305 |
| Broad Money Liabs., Seasonally Adj. | 35l.b | 218,537 | 271,206 | 332,832 | 346,491 | 459,749 | 537,197 | 653,818 | 692,239 | 802,734 | 903,061 | 1,015,500 | 1,031,417 |
| **Other Financial Corporations** | | | | | | | *Millions of Francs: End of Period* | | | | | | | |
| Net Foreign Assets | 41n | −9,061 | −2,755 | −3,056 | −3,760 | −2,074 | −1,765 | −1,350 | −1,088 | −813 | −331 | −264 | −331 |
| Claims on Nonresidents | 41 | — | — | — | — | — | — | — | — | — | — | 67 | — |
| Liabilities to Nonresidents | 46c | 9,061 | 2,755 | 3,056 | 3,760 | 2,074 | 1,765 | 1,350 | 1,088 | 813 | 331 | 331 | 331 |
| Claims on Depository Corporations | 40 | 257 | 2,880 | 1,405 | 1,646 | 1,861 | 2,470 | 2,803 | 1,069 | 4,185 | 1,736 | 4,224 | 15,774 |
| Net Claims on Central Government | 42an | 6,005 | −1,611 | −2,264 | −3,614 | −5,046 | −8,489 | −15,193 | −12,218 | −14,039 | −15,486 | −18,489 | −12,504 |
| Claims on Central Government | 42a | 8,084 | 1,672 | 1,783 | 2,780 | 2,874 | 2,734 | 1,840 | 1,730 | 1,933 | 610 | — | 23 |
| Liabilities to Central Government | 46d | 2,078 | 3,283 | 4,047 | 6,394 | 7,920 | 11,223 | 17,033 | 13,948 | 15,972 | 16,095 | 18,489 | 12,528 |
| Claims on Other Sectors | 42s | 18,627 | 16,726 | 21,286 | 26,307 | 29,492 | 34,519 | 47,507 | 57,419 | 60,089 | 74,044 | 88,066 | 87,170 |
| Claims on State & Local Govts. | 42b | 83 | 54 | 16 | 1 | — | — | — | — | — | — | — | — |
| Claims on Public Nonfin. Corps. | 42c | 443 | 714 | 424 | 973 | 354 | 764 | 921 | 968 | 839 | 605 | 598 | 529 |
| Claims on Private Sector | 42d | 18,102 | 15,958 | 20,846 | 25,332 | 29,138 | 33,755 | 46,586 | 56,451 | 59,250 | 73,439 | 87,469 | 86,641 |
| Deposits | 46b | 2,247 | 1,868 | 3,727 | 5,627 | 7,625 | 9,576 | 13,968 | 20,934 | 22,928 | 28,691 | 36,172 | 48,126 |
| Securities Other than Shares | 46s | — | — | — | — | — | — | — | — | — | — | — | — |
| Loans | 46l | 837 | — | — | — | — | — | — | — | — | — | 2,000 | 2,023 |
| Financial Derivatives | 46m | — | — | — | — | — | — | — | — | — | — | — | — |
| Insurance Technical Reserves | 46r | — | — | — | — | — | — | — | — | — | — | — | — |
| Shares and Other Equity | 47a | 8,926 | 10,076 | 10,779 | 11,866 | 13,715 | 15,016 | 15,569 | 19,472 | 21,758 | 24,689 | 25,974 | 30,646 |
| Other Items (Net) | 47r | 3,819 | 3,296 | 2,865 | 3,085 | 2,893 | 2,143 | 4,230 | 4,776 | 4,737 | 6,582 | 9,391 | 9,314 |
| Memo Item: | | | | | | | | | | | | | |
| Total Assets | 40ra | 28,660 | 23,304 | 26,915 | 33,155 | 37,178 | 43,531 | 56,327 | 64,830 | 72,232 | 83,109 | 101,933 | 119,462 |

# Burundi  618

| | | 2004 | 2005 | 2006 | 2007 | 2008 | 2009 | 2010 | 2011 | 2012 | 2013 | 2014 | 2015 |
|---|---|---|---|---|---|---|---|---|---|---|---|---|---|
| **Monetary Aggregates** | | | | | | | *Millions of Francs: End of Period* | | | | | | |
| Broad Money............................ | 59m | 224,954 | 280,589 | 344,175 | 361,227 | 482,732 | 565,200 | 687,030 | 724,410 | 834,891 | 936,480 | 1,045,337 | 1,061,261 |
| o/w:Currency Issued by Cent.Govt | 59m.a | — | — | — | — | — | — | — | — | — | — | — | — |
| o/w: Dep.in Nonfin. Corporations. | 59m.b | 1,912 | 3,193 | 2,637 | 4,139 | 7,837 | 10,498 | 13,899 | 14,043 | 15,264 | 17,923 | 14,528 | 14,328 |
| o/w:Secs. Issued by Central Govt.. | 59m.c | — | — | — | — | — | — | — | — | — | — | | |
| Money (National Definitions) | | | | | | | | | | | | | |
| M1............................................ | 59ma | 159,862 | 195,119 | 225,885 | 230,715 | 319,692 | 367,127 | 453,249 | 457,048 | 513,994 | 578,604 | 640,425 | 643,151 |
| M2............................................ | 59mb | 205,572 | 260,413 | 305,247 | 318,269 | 419,880 | 484,415 | 598,112 | 635,961 | 708,632 | 804,348 | 883,060 | 923,742 |
| M3............................................ | 59mc | 224,954 | 280,589 | 344,175 | 361,227 | 482,732 | 565,200 | 687,030 | 724,410 | 834,891 | 936,480 | 1,045,337 | 1,061,261 |
| **Interest Rates** | | | | | | | *Percent Per Annum* | | | | | | |
| Discount Rate (End of Period).......... | 60.a | 14.50 | 14.50 | 11.07 | 10.12 | 10.08 | 10.00 | 11.25 | 14.34 | 13.77 | 12.50 | 8.00 | .... |
| Treasury Bill Rate............................ | 60c | 14.95 | 7.92 | 8.84 | .... | .... | .... | .... | .... | .... | .... | | |
| Lending Rate.................................. | 60p | 18.25 | 18.45 | 17.07 | 16.84 | 16.52 | 14.08 | 12.42 | 13.23 | 14.32 | 15.15 | 15.67 | 15.33 |
| **Prices** | | | | | | | *Index Numbers (2010=100): Period Averages* | | | | | | |
| Consumer Prices............................ | 64 | 54.0 | 61.3 | 63.0 | 68.2 | 84.7 | 94.0 | 100.0 | 109.7 | 129.5 | † 139.8 | 145.9 | 154.0 |
| **Intl. Transactions & Positions** | | | | | | | *Millions of Francs* | | | | | | |
| Exports........................................ | 70 | 51,706 | 104,300 | 60,536 | 67,364 | 64,301 | 76,330 | 123,698 | 154,405 | 192,156 | 153,896 | 191,411 | 178,544 |
| Imports, c.i.f................................. | 71 | 194,054 | 286,959 | 442,512 | 346,099 | 477,345 | 494,828 | 626,742 | 952,852 | 1,084,054 | 1,261,189 | 1,188,986 | 1,135,870 |
| **Balance of Payments** | | | | | | | *Millions of US Dollars* | | | | | | |
| A. Current Account*....................... | 109bx | −165.5 | † −222.0 | −324.0 | −111.3 | −259.4 | −161.2 | −301.0 | −283.6 | −255.1 | −253.3 | .... | .... |
| Goods, credit (exports)................. | 1a9cx | 48.5 | † 60.8 | 58.7 | 58.8 | 69.6 | 68.4 | 101.2 | 124.0 | 134.7 | 90.9 | .... | .... |
| Goods, debit (imports).................. | 1a9dx | 145.4 | † 188.9 | 244.7 | 254.1 | 335.5 | 343.0 | 438.4 | 552.5 | 711.0 | 675.6 | .... | .... |
| Balance on goods...................... | 1a9bx | −96.9 | † −128.1 | −186.0 | −195.3 | −265.8 | −274.6 | −337.2 | −428.5 | −576.3 | −584.7 | .... | .... |
| Services, credit (exports)............... | 1b9cx | 15.8 | † 34.8 | 34.5 | 30.8 | 83.3 | 49.9 | 79.5 | 111.7 | 92.8 | 131.2 | .... | .... |
| Services, debit (imports)................ | 1b9dx | 86.6 | † 134.1 | 202.2 | 182.1 | 258.8 | 176.6 | 168.3 | 212.9 | 211.6 | 234.1 | .... | .... |
| Balance on Goods & Services....... | 1z9bx | −167.8 | † −227.4 | −353.8 | −346.6 | −441.3 | −401.3 | −426.0 | −529.7 | −695.1 | −687.6 | .... | .... |
| Primary income: credit.................. | 1c9cx | 1.3 | † 3.2 | 4.6 | 8.7 | 10.9 | 1.4 | 1.1 | 7.5 | 11.4 | 14.0 | .... | .... |
| Primary income: debit................... | 1c9dx | 20.5 | † 20.9 | 13.4 | 14.6 | 15.2 | 18.4 | 12.0 | 25.0 | 17.9 | 12.2 | .... | .... |
| Balance on gds, serv. & prim. inc. | 1y9bx | −187.0 | † −245.2 | −362.6 | −352.5 | −445.6 | −418.3 | −436.9 | −547.1 | −701.6 | −685.8 | .... | .... |
| Secondary income: credit.............. | 1d9ca | 24.3 | † 26.5 | 41.3 | 241.7 | 188.2 | 260.4 | 149.5 | 277.1 | 456.4 | 448.4 | .... | .... |
| Secondary income: debit............... | 1d9da | 2.8 | † 3.3 | 2.7 | .5 | 2.0 | 3.2 | 13.6 | 13.5 | 9.9 | 15.9 | .... | .... |
| B. Capital Account*....................... | 209ba | 18.6 | † 24.4 | 46.3 | 128.0 | 140.7 | 1,025.3 | 77.9 | 96.5 | 153.7 | 103.9 | .... | .... |
| Capital account: credit.................. | 209ca | 18.9 | † 25.3 | 47.4 | 129.3 | 146.2 | 1,028.7 | 86.5 | 112.7 | 164.2 | 114.5 | .... | .... |
| Capital account: debit................... | 209da | .3 | † .9 | 1.1 | 1.3 | 5.5 | 3.3 | 8.6 | 16.2 | 10.6 | 10.6 | .... | .... |
| Balance on current & capital acct. | 129bx | −146.9 | † −197.6 | −277.7 | 16.7 | −118.7 | 864.2 | −223.1 | −187.1 | −101.4 | −149.4 | .... | .... |
| C. Financial Account* ................... | 309na | 23.3 | † 10.9 | 15.5 | −58.4 | −149.4 | 672.7 | −216.7 | −147.4 | −122.9 | −166.8 | .... | .... |
| Direct investment: assets............. | 3a9aa | — | † — | — | — | .6 | .... | .... | .... | .... | .2 | .... | .... |
| Equity & investment fund shares.. | 3aaaa | .... | .... | .... | — | .6 | .... | .... | .... | .... | .2 | .... | .... |
| Debt instruments....................... | 3abaa | .... | .... | .... | .... | .... | .... | .... | .... | .... | .... | .... | .... |
| Direct investment: liabilities .......... | 3a9la | — | † .6 | — | .5 | 3.8 | .3 | .8 | 3.4 | .6 | 6.9 | .... | .... |
| Equity & investment fund shares . | 3aala | — | † .6 | — | .5 | 3.8 | .3 | .8 | 3.4 | .6 | 6.9 | .... | .... |
| Debt instruments....................... | 3abla | .... | .... | .... | .... | .... | .... | .... | .... | .... | .... | .... | .... |
| Portfolio investment: assets .......... | 3b9aa | .... | .... | .... | .... | .... | .... | .... | .... | .... | .... | .... | .... |
| Equity & investment fund shares | 3baaa | .... | .... | .... | .... | .... | .... | .... | .... | .... | .... | .... | .... |
| Debt securities ........................... | 3bbaa | .... | .... | .... | .... | .... | .... | .... | .... | .... | .... | .... | .... |
| Portfolio investment: liabilities....... | 3b9la | .... | .... | .... | .... | .... | .... | .... | .... | .... | .... | .... | .... |
| Equity & investment fund shares . | 3bala | .... | .... | .... | .... | .... | .... | .... | .... | .... | .... | .... | .... |
| Debt securities........................... | 3bbla | .... | .... | .... | .... | .... | .... | .... | .... | .... | .... | .... | .... |
| Fin. der.& empl.stk.ops.(ESOs): net. | 3c9na | .... | .... | .... | .... | .... | .... | .... | .... | .... | .... | .... | .... |
| Fin. der. & ESOs.: assets.............. | 3c9aa | .... | .... | .... | .... | .... | .... | .... | .... | .... | .... | .... | .... |
| Fin. der. & ESOs.: liabilities.......... | 3c9la | .... | .... | .... | .... | .... | .... | .... | .... | .... | .... | .... | .... |
| Other investment: assets............... | 3d9aa | 22.0 | † 7.8 | 30.2 | 34.2 | 30.8 | 28.9 | 43.6 | 33.3 | 50.0 | 56.2 | .... | .... |
| Other equity............................... | 3daaa | .... | .... | .... | .... | .... | .... | .... | .... | .... | .... | .... | .... |
| Debt instruments....................... | 3dzaa | 22.0 | † 7.8 | 30.2 | 34.2 | 30.8 | 28.9 | 43.6 | 33.3 | 50.0 | 56.2 | .... | .... |
| Other investment: liabilities........... | 3d9la | −1.4 | † −3.6 | 14.7 | 92.2 | 177.0 | −644.1 | 259.5 | 177.4 | 172.4 | 216.3 | .... | .... |
| Other equity............................... | 3dala | .... | .... | .... | .... | .... | .... | .... | .... | .... | .... | .... | .... |
| Debt instruments....................... | 3dzla | −1.4 | † −3.6 | 14.7 | 92.2 | 177.0 | −644.1 | 259.5 | 177.4 | 172.4 | 216.3 | .... | .... |
| Curr.+ cap.− finan. acct. balance... | 4y9na | −170.2 | † −208.5 | −293.2 | 75.1 | 30.8 | 191.5 | −6.3 | −39.7 | 21.5 | 17.3 | .... | .... |
| D. Net Errors and Omissions............ | 409na | −20.1 | † −84.3 | 3.8 | −24.1 | 57.3 | −109.9 | −3.0 | 4.5 | 6.1 | −2.6 | .... | .... |
| E. Reserves and Related Items.......... | 4z9na | −190.3 | † −292.7 | −289.3 | 51.0 | 88.1 | 81.6 | −9.3 | −35.2 | 27.6 | 14.8 | .... | .... |
| Reserve assets............................ | 3e9aa | 2.0 | † 33.9 | 18.2 | 61.8 | 110.1 | 55.4 | 10.8 | −16.5 | 35.3 | 19.8 | .... | .... |
| Credit and loans from the IMF........ | 3dcla | 10.7 | † 21.3 | 21.3 | 10.8 | 22.1 | −26.2 | 20.2 | 18.7 | 7.6 | 5.0 | .... | .... |
| Exceptional financing.................... | 409la | 181.7 | † 305.3 | 286.3 | .... | .... | .... | .... | .... | .... | .... | .... | .... |

*Excludes components in group E

# Burundi 618

| | | 2004 | 2005 | 2006 | 2007 | 2008 | 2009 | 2010 | 2011 | 2012 | 2013 | 2014 | 2015 |
|---|---|---|---|---|---|---|---|---|---|---|---|---|---|
| **International Investment Position** | | | | | | *Millions of US Dollars* | | | | | | | |
| Assets............................................ | 809aa | 129.8 | † 248.2 | 298.2 | 362.3 | 462.8 | 549.3 | 601.2 | 570.4 | 597.1 | 672.3 | .... | .... |
| Direct investment......................... | 8a9aa | .7 | † 1.3 | 2.3 | 2.1 | 2.5 | 2.5 | 2.5 | 2.2 | 2.0 | 2.2 | .... | .... |
| Equity & investment fund shares.. | 8aaaa | .7 | † 1.3 | 2.3 | 2.1 | 2.5 | 2.5 | 2.5 | 2.2 | 2.0 | 2.2 | .... | .... |
| Debt instruments......................... | 8abaa | .... | .... | .... | .... | .... | .... | .... | .... | .... | .... | .... | .... |
| Portfolio investment...................... | 8b9aa | .... | .... | .... | .... | .... | .... | .... | .... | .... | .... | .... | .... |
| Equity & investment fund shares.. | 8baaa | .... | .... | .... | .... | .... | .... | .... | .... | .... | .... | .... | .... |
| Debt securities............................. | 8bbaa | .... | .... | .... | .... | .... | .... | .... | .... | .... | .... | .... | .... |
| Fin. der.(oth.than reserves) & ESOs | 8c9aa | .... | .... | .... | .... | .... | .... | .... | .... | .... | .... | .... | .... |
| Other investment........................... | 8d9aa | 60.6 | † 133.0 | 163.4 | 181.2 | 193.8 | 223.4 | 266.5 | 272.2 | 286.4 | 340.7 | .... | .... |
| Other equity............................... | 8daaa | .... | .... | .... | .... | .... | .... | .... | .... | .... | .... | .... | .... |
| Debt instruments......................... | 8dzaa | 60.6 | † 133.0 | 163.4 | 181.2 | 193.8 | 223.4 | 266.5 | 272.2 | 286.4 | 340.7 | .... | .... |
| Reserve assets............................... | 8e9aa | 68.5 | † 113.9 | 132.5 | 179.0 | 266.5 | 323.4 | 332.2 | 295.9 | 308.8 | 329.4 | .... | .... |
| Liabilities....................................... | 809la | 1,428.1 | † 1,414.5 | 1,539.6 | 1,608.9 | 1,573.5 | 960.5 | 1,035.3 | 1,090.1 | 1,204.8 | 1,438.8 | .... | .... |
| Direct investment......................... | 8a9la | — | † 9.3 | 9.9 | 9.4 | 12.2 | 12.6 | 13.3 | 15.2 | 13.9 | 20.9 | .... | .... |
| Equity & investment fund shares.. | 8aala | — | † 9.3 | 9.9 | 9.4 | 12.2 | 12.6 | 13.3 | 15.2 | 13.9 | 20.9 | .... | .... |
| Debt instruments......................... | 8abla | .... | .... | .... | .... | .... | .... | .... | .... | .... | .... | .... | .... |
| Portfolio investment...................... | 8b9la | .... | .... | .... | .... | .... | .... | .... | .... | .... | .... | .... | .... |
| Equity & investment fund shares.. | 8bala | .... | .... | .... | .... | .... | .... | .... | .... | .... | .... | .... | .... |
| Debt securities............................. | 8bbla | .... | .... | .... | .... | .... | .... | .... | .... | .... | .... | .... | .... |
| Fin. der.(oth.than reserves) & ESOs | 8c9la | .... | .... | .... | .... | .... | .... | .... | .... | .... | .... | .... | .... |
| Other investment........................... | 8d9la | 1,428.1 | † 1,405.2 | 1,529.7 | 1,599.5 | 1,561.3 | 947.9 | 1,021.9 | 1,074.9 | 1,190.9 | 1,417.9 | .... | .... |
| Other equity............................... | 8dala | .... | .... | .... | .... | .... | .... | .... | .... | .... | .... | .... | .... |
| Debt instruments......................... | 8dzla | 1,428.1 | † 1,405.2 | 1,529.7 | 1,599.5 | 1,561.3 | 947.9 | 1,021.9 | 1,074.9 | 1,190.9 | 1,417.9 | .... | .... |
| **Government Finance** | | | | | | | | | | | | | |
| **Operations Statement** | | | | | | | | | | | | | |
| **Budgetary Central Government** | | | | | | *Millions of Francs: Fiscal Year Ends December 31* | | | | | | | |
| Revenue........................................ | a1 | .... | .... | .... | .... | .... | .... | 687,893 | 761,328 | 1,047,062 | 1,074,496 | .... | .... |
| Taxes............................................ | a11 | .... | .... | .... | .... | .... | .... | 364,334 | 480,245 | 594,266 | 580,455 | .... | .... |
| Social Contributions..................... | a12 | .... | .... | .... | .... | .... | .... | — | — | — | — | .... | .... |
| Grants.......................................... | a13 | .... | .... | .... | .... | .... | .... | 290,453 | 247,310 | 395,168 | 451,742 | .... | .... |
| Other Revenue.............................. | a14 | .... | .... | .... | .... | .... | .... | 33,107 | 33,773 | 57,628 | 42,299 | .... | .... |
| Expense......................................... | a2 | .... | .... | .... | .... | .... | .... | 538,554 | 601,127 | 711,405 | 713,524 | .... | .... |
| Compensation of Employees.......... | a21 | .... | .... | .... | .... | .... | .... | 228,745 | 259,327 | 281,000 | 293,317 | .... | .... |
| Use of Goods & Services................ | a22 | .... | .... | .... | .... | .... | .... | 103,036 | 99,581 | 105,356 | 120,494 | .... | .... |
| Consumption of Fixed Capital....... | a23 | .... | .... | .... | .... | .... | .... | .... | .... | .... | .... | .... | .... |
| Interest......................................... | a24 | .... | .... | .... | .... | .... | .... | 33,002 | 32,668 | 33,452 | 30,041 | .... | .... |
| Subsidies...................................... | a25 | .... | .... | .... | .... | .... | .... | 6,297 | — | — | — | .... | .... |
| Grants.......................................... | a26 | .... | .... | .... | .... | .... | .... | 158,524 | 190,946 | 278,399 | 241,615 | .... | .... |
| Social Benefits.............................. | a27 | .... | .... | .... | .... | .... | .... | 4,583 | 15,479 | 4,048 | 3,608 | .... | .... |
| Other Expense.............................. | a28 | .... | .... | .... | .... | .... | .... | 4,368 | 3,126 | 9,150 | 24,448 | .... | .... |
| Gross Operating Balance [1-2+23]... | agob | .... | .... | .... | .... | .... | .... | 149,339 | 160,201 | 335,657 | 360,972 | .... | .... |
| Net Operating Balance [1-2].......... | anob | .... | .... | .... | .... | .... | .... | .... | .... | .... | .... | .... | .... |
| Net Acq. of Nonfinancial Assets...... | a31 | .... | .... | .... | .... | .... | .... | 155,915 | 208,153 | 420,966 | 437,212 | .... | .... |
| Aquisition of Nonfin. Assets.......... | a31.1 | .... | .... | .... | .... | .... | .... | .... | .... | .... | .... | .... | .... |
| Disposal of Nonfin. Assets............. | a31.2 | .... | .... | .... | .... | .... | .... | .... | .... | .... | .... | .... | .... |
| Net Lending/Borrowing [1-2-31]...... | anlb | .... | .... | .... | .... | .... | .... | −6,576 | −47,952 | −85,309 | −76,240 | .... | .... |
| Net Acq. of Financial Assets............ | a32 | .... | .... | .... | .... | .... | .... | 227,405 | −73,702 | −76,533 | 170,468 | .... | .... |
| By instrument | | | | | | | | | | | | | |
| Monetary Gold & SDRs.................. | a3201 | .... | .... | .... | .... | .... | .... | — | — | — | — | .... | .... |
| Currency & Deposits...................... | a3202 | .... | .... | .... | .... | .... | .... | 224,992 | −74,545 | −71,651 | 168,331 | .... | .... |
| Securities other than Shares........... | a3203 | .... | .... | .... | .... | .... | .... | — | — | — | — | .... | .... |
| Loans........................................... | a3204 | .... | .... | .... | .... | .... | .... | −3,976 | — | −2,490 | — | .... | .... |
| Shares & Other Equity.................... | a3205 | .... | .... | .... | .... | .... | .... | 1,404 | 4,188 | 2,051 | 2,137 | .... | .... |
| Insurance Technical Reserves......... | a3206 | .... | .... | .... | .... | .... | .... | — | — | — | — | .... | .... |
| Financial Derivatives..................... | a3207 | .... | .... | .... | .... | .... | .... | — | — | — | — | .... | .... |
| Other Accounts Receivable............. | a3208 | .... | .... | .... | .... | .... | .... | 4,986 | −3,345 | −4,443 | — | .... | .... |
| By debtor | | | | | | | | | | | | | |
| Domestic...................................... | a321 | .... | .... | .... | .... | .... | .... | 227,405 | −73,702 | −76,533 | 170,468 | .... | .... |
| Foreign......................................... | a322 | .... | .... | .... | .... | .... | .... | — | — | — | — | .... | .... |
| Net Incurrence of Liabilities.............. | a33 | .... | .... | .... | .... | .... | .... | 245,145 | −28,875 | 11,260 | 244,416 | .... | .... |
| By instrument | | | | | | | | | | | | | |
| Special Drawing Rights (SDRs)....... | a3301 | .... | .... | .... | .... | .... | .... | — | — | — | — | .... | .... |
| Currency & Deposits...................... | a3302 | .... | .... | .... | .... | .... | .... | — | — | — | — | .... | .... |
| Securities other than Shares........... | a3303 | .... | .... | .... | .... | .... | .... | 55,651 | −6,042 | −17,613 | 57,682 | .... | .... |
| Loans........................................... | a3304 | .... | .... | .... | .... | .... | .... | 164,954 | −18,007 | 45,528 | 148,002 | .... | .... |
| Shares & Other Equity.................... | a3305 | .... | .... | .... | .... | .... | .... | — | — | — | — | .... | .... |
| Insurance Technical Reserves......... | a3306 | .... | .... | .... | .... | .... | .... | — | — | — | — | .... | .... |
| Financial Derivatives..................... | a3307 | .... | .... | .... | .... | .... | .... | — | — | — | — | .... | .... |
| Other Accounts Payable................. | a3308 | .... | .... | .... | .... | .... | .... | 24,540 | −4,827 | −16,655 | 38,732 | .... | .... |
| By creditor | | | | | | | | | | | | | |
| Domestic...................................... | a331 | .... | .... | .... | .... | .... | .... | 245,651 | −14,566 | −15,253 | 238,215 | .... | .... |
| Foreign......................................... | a332 | .... | .... | .... | .... | .... | .... | −506 | −14,309 | 26,513 | 6,201 | .... | .... |
| Stat. Discrepancy [32-33-NLB]........ | anlbz | .... | .... | .... | .... | .... | .... | −11,164 | 3,126 | −2,484 | 2,292 | .... | .... |
| Memo Item: Expenditure [2+31]...... | a2m | .... | .... | .... | .... | .... | .... | 694,469 | 809,280 | 1,132,372 | 1,150,736 | .... | .... |

# Burundi 618

|  |  | 2004 | 2005 | 2006 | 2007 | 2008 | 2009 | 2010 | 2011 | 2012 | 2013 | 2014 | 2015 |
|---|---|---|---|---|---|---|---|---|---|---|---|---|---|
| **National Accounts** |  |  |  |  |  | *Millions of Francs:* |  |  |  |  |  |  |  |
| Househ.Cons.Expend.,incl.NPISHs.... | 96f | 638,547 | 1,091,032 | 1,231,200 | 1,333,300 | 1,786,500 | 1,903,000 | 2,038,000 | 2,327,500 | 2,866,500 | 3,373,700 | 3,698,300 | 4,526,600 |
| Government Consumption Expend... | 91f | 163,470 | 200,550 | 221,501 | 261,210 | 357,600 | 415,700 | 479,300 | 521,800 | 568,600 | 627,100 | 674,300 | 724,700 |
| Gross Fixed Capital Formation......... | 93e | 84,139 | 282,516 | 276,299 | 271,922 | 274,207 | 267,312 | 478,400 | 602,300 | 822,300 | 1,064,600 | 1,130,600 | 708,400 |
| Changes in Inventories.................... | 93i | 176 | −119,902 | −55,190 | −24,203 | 16,042 | 91,851 | 29,700 | 36,000 | −76,700 | −167,700 | 35,200 | −436,300 |
| Exports of Goods and Services.......... | 90c | 60,201 | 103,390 | 95,840 | 96,970 | 181,380 | 145,590 | 222,400 | 297,200 | 356,100 | 345,400 | 325,100 | 292,600 |
| Imports of Goods and Services (-)..... | 98c | 198,047 | 349,342 | 459,750 | 471,968 | 704,590 | 639,276 | 746,700 | 965,100 | 1,171,000 | 1,430,500 | 1,455,100 | 1,360,500 |
| Gross Domestic Product (GDP)......... | 99b | 748,486 | 1,208,244 | 1,309,900 | 1,467,231 | 1,911,139 | 2,184,177 | 2,501,000 | 2,819,500 | 3,365,800 | 3,812,500 | 4,408,400 | 4,455,500 |
| Net Primary Income from Abroad..... | 98.n | −34,286 | −26,053 | −9,078 | −6,369 | −5,104 | −20,888 | −13,376 | −22,055 | −9,384 | 2,775 | −10,489 | −3,707 |
| Gross National Income (GNI)............ | 99a | 714,200 | 1,182,191 | 1,300,822 | 1,460,862 | 1,906,035 | 2,163,289 | 2,487,624 | 2,797,445 | 3,356,416 | 3,815,275 | 4,397,911 | 4,451,793 |
| GDP Volume 1980 Prices................. | 99b.p | 119,037 | 120,108 | 126,611 | 131,012 | 137,391 | 142,636 | 149,526 | 155,768 | 162,310 | 170,101 | . . . . | . . . . |
| GDP Volume (2010=100)............... | 99bvp | 79.6 | 80.3 | 84.7 | 87.6 | 91.9 | 95.4 | 100.0 | 104.2 | 108.5 | 113.8 | . . . . | . . . . |
| GDP Deflator (2010=100)............... | 99bip | 37.6 | 60.1 | 61.9 | 67.0 | 83.2 | 91.6 | 100.0 | 108.2 | 124.0 | 134.0 | . . . . | . . . . |
|  |  |  |  |  |  | *Millions: Midyear Estimates* |  |  |  |  |  |  |  |
| Population................................ | 99z | 7.66 | 7.93 | 8.22 | 8.51 | 8.82 | 9.14 | 9.46 | 9.79 | 10.12 | 10.47 | 10.82 | 11.18 |

# Cabo Verde   624

| | | 2004 | 2005 | 2006 | 2007 | 2008 | 2009 | 2010 | 2011 | 2012 | 2013 | 2014 | 2015 |
|---|---|---|---|---|---|---|---|---|---|---|---|---|---|
| **Exchange Rates** | | | | | | *Escudos per SDR: End of Period* | | | | | | | |
| Official Rate.................................... | aa | 125.725 | 133.598 | 125.961 | 118.371 | 122.042 | 119.998 | 127.091 | 130.840 | 128.449 | 123.135 | 131.587 | 140.355 |
| | | | | | | *Escudos per US Dollar: End of Period (ae) Period Average (rf)* | | | | | | | |
| Official Rate.................................... | ae | 80.956 | 93.473 | 83.728 | 74.907 | 79.234 | 76.544 | 82.525 | 85.223 | 83.576 | 79.958 | 90.824 | 101.286 |
| Official Rate.................................... | rf | 88.808 | 88.670 | 87.901 | 80.567 | 75.279 | 79.377 | 83.259 | 79.323 | 85.822 | 83.051 | 83.114 | 99.426 |
| **Fund Position** | | | | | | *Millions of SDRs: End of Period* | | | | | | | |
| Quota........................................... | 2f.s | 9.60 | 9.60 | 9.60 | 9.60 | 9.60 | 9.60 | 9.60 | 9.60 | 9.60 | 11.20 | 11.20 | 11.20 |
| SDR Holdings................................. | 1b.s | .02 | .02 | — | .07 | .15 | 8.22 | 6.73 | 4.99 | 3.38 | 1.82 | 1.07 | .82 |
| Reserve Position in the Fund........... | 1c.s | — | .02 | .02 | .02 | .02 | .02 | .02 | .02 | .02 | .42 | .42 | .42 |
| Total Fund Cred.&Loans Outstg........ | 2tl | 6.15 | 8.64 | 8.64 | 8.52 | 8.03 | 7.04 | 5.56 | 3.83 | 2.23 | .99 | .25 | — |
| SDR Allocations............................. | 1bd | .62 | .62 | .62 | .62 | .62 | 9.17 | 9.17 | 9.17 | 9.17 | 9.17 | 9.17 | 9.17 |
| **International Liquidity** | | | | | | *Millions of US Dollars Unless Otherwise Indicated: End of Period* | | | | | | | |
| Total Reserves minus Gold.............. | 1l.d | 139.53 | 173.97 | 254.46 | 364.46 | 361.47 | 397.88 | 382.19 | 338.62 | 375.84 | 475.33 | 510.93 | 494.50 |
| SDR Holdings............................. | 1b.d | .04 | .02 | — | .12 | .24 | 12.88 | 10.37 | 7.67 | 5.20 | 2.81 | 1.55 | 1.14 |
| Reserve Position in the Fund.......... | 1c.d | .01 | .02 | .02 | .03 | .02 | .03 | .02 | .02 | .02 | .64 | .60 | .58 |
| Foreign Exchange........................ | 1d.d | 139.49 | 173.92 | 254.43 | 364.32 | 361.21 | 384.97 | 371.80 | 330.93 | 370.62 | 471.88 | 508.77 | 492.78 |
| Central Bank: Other Assets............. | 3..d | 1.85 | 1.82 | 1.77 | 1.77 | 1.77 | 1.71 | — | — | — | — | — | — |
| Central Bank: Other Liabs............... | 4..d | .76 | .76 | .80 | .83 | 2.52 | 7.42 | 8.99 | 7.98 | 3.57 | 3.01 | 1.52 | .79 |
| Other Depository Corps.: Assets....... | 7a.d | 66.49 | 118.40 | 116.83 | 134.07 | 91.21 | 89.28 | 77.46 | 133.63 | 237.24 | 368.21 | 249.67 | 256.65 |
| Other Depository Corps.: Liabs......... | 7b.d | 28.34 | 47.67 | 59.75 | 88.98 | 101.29 | 96.17 | 94.26 | 211.45 | 307.59 | 409.19 | 274.86 | 258.15 |
| **Central Bank** | | | | | | *Millions of Escudos: End of Period* | | | | | | | |
| Net Foreign Assets....................... | 11n | 10,623.7 | 15,269.2 | 20,410.6 | 27,614.3 | 29,779.8 | 27,924.0 | 29,877.2 | 26,643.7 | 31,223.1 | 36,819.2 | 44,901.4 | 48,614.3 |
| Claims on Nonresidents................. | 11 | 11,537.0 | 16,574.6 | 21,643.7 | 28,760.5 | 31,018.6 | 30,537.4 | 32,507.1 | 29,034.4 | 32,976.1 | 38,311.6 | 46,276.5 | 49,978.9 |
| Liabilities to Nonresidents.............. | 16c | 913.4 | 1,305.4 | 1,233.1 | 1,146.2 | 1,238.8 | 2,613.4 | 2,629.9 | 2,390.7 | 1,753.0 | 1,492.4 | 1,375.2 | 1,364.7 |
| Claims on Other Depository Corps.... | 12e | 45.0 | 27.8 | 9.6 | — | 1.4 | — | — | .6 | .6 | 1.5 | 2.5 | 12.9 |
| Net Claims on Central Government.. | 12an | 9,520.2 | 7,683.1 | 7,492.0 | 5,064.3 | 5,941.6 | 4,176.2 | 1,829.4 | 2,228.3 | 5,560.7 | 4,914.8 | 5,361.0 | 3,743.1 |
| Claims on Central Government...... | 12a | 10,705.3 | 10,579.7 | 9,482.6 | 9,409.9 | 9,502.8 | 9,248.1 | 8,979.5 | 8,999.1 | 8,828.0 | 8,693.1 | 8,541.3 | 8,277.4 |
| Liabilities to Central Government.... | 16d | 1,185.1 | 2,896.6 | 1,990.6 | 4,345.6 | 3,561.3 | 5,071.9 | 7,150.1 | 6,770.8 | 3,267.2 | 3,778.3 | 3,180.3 | 4,534.2 |
| Claims on Other Sectors................. | 12s | 1,265.1 | 1,239.3 | 1,225.5 | 1,167.8 | 1,105.9 | 1,110.8 | 1,307.6 | 686.2 | 718.9 | 780.3 | 777.2 | 704.6 |
| Claims on Other Financial Corps.... | 12g | 29.5 | 15.2 | 9.4 | 3.3 | — | — | — | — | — | — | — | — |
| Claims on State & Local Govts....... | 12b | — | — | — | — | — | — | — | — | — | — | — | — |
| Claims on Public Nonfin. Corps...... | 12c | .1 | .1 | .1 | .1 | .1 | .1 | .1 | — | — | — | — | — |
| Claims on Private Sector............... | 12d | 1,235.5 | 1,223.9 | 1,215.9 | 1,164.4 | 1,105.8 | 1,110.7 | 1,307.5 | 686.2 | 718.9 | 780.3 | 777.2 | 704.6 |
| Monetary Base............................. | 14 | 18,463.4 | 21,113.5 | 21,861.1 | 24,040.7 | 25,958.9 | 26,829.1 | 25,916.2 | 24,438.9 | 32,579.8 | 38,427.1 | 45,780.9 | 46,748.9 |
| Currency in Circulation................. | 14a | 7,837.3 | 8,691.5 | 9,188.0 | 9,982.8 | 10,349.8 | 9,850.6 | 10,190.3 | 9,846.2 | 9,828.6 | 10,096.4 | 10,762.0 | 11,062.0 |
| Liabs. to Other Depository Corps.... | 14c | 10,626.1 | 12,422.0 | 12,673.2 | 14,057.9 | 15,609.2 | 16,978.5 | 15,726.0 | 14,592.8 | 22,751.2 | 28,330.7 | 35,019.0 | 35,687.0 |
| Liabilities to Other Sectors.............. | 14d | — | — | — | — | — | — | — | — | — | — | — | — |
| Other Liabs. to Other Dep. Corps..... | 14n | 3.8 | 20.5 | 4,009.1 | 6,486.3 | 6,922.8 | 2,939.8 | 3,364.2 | 1,742.1 | 1,991.1 | 1,999.8 | 2,498.0 | 2,502.0 |
| Dep. & Sec. Excl. f/Monetary Base... | 14o | 21.4 | 1.6 | 2.6 | 8.5 | .6 | 3.3 | 3.8 | 5.0 | 12.5 | 6.3 | 46.3 | 9.5 |
| Deposits Included in Broad Money. | 15 | 21.4 | 1.6 | 2.6 | 8.5 | .6 | 3.3 | 3.8 | 5.0 | 12.5 | 6.3 | 46.3 | 9.5 |
| Sec.Ot.th.Shares Incl.in Brd. Money | 16a | — | — | — | — | — | — | — | — | — | — | — | — |
| Deposits Excl. from Broad Money... | 16b | — | — | — | — | — | — | — | — | — | — | — | — |
| Sec.Ot.th.Shares Excl.f/Brd.Money.. | 16s | — | — | — | — | — | — | — | — | — | — | — | — |
| Loans.......................................... | 16l | — | — | — | — | — | — | — | — | — | — | — | — |
| Financial Derivatives...................... | 16m | — | — | — | — | — | — | — | — | — | — | — | — |
| Shares and Other Equity.................. | 17a | 439.5 | 529.4 | 620.2 | 716.4 | 944.0 | 362.4 | 95.3 | −1,379.3 | −2,391.5 | −2,408.6 | −508.6 | 452.2 |
| Other Items (Net)........................... | 17r | 2,525.9 | 2,554.3 | 2,644.5 | 2,594.6 | 3,002.4 | 3,076.5 | 3,634.8 | 4,752.0 | 5,311.3 | 4,491.3 | 3,225.5 | 3,362.2 |
| Memo Item: | | | | | | | | | | | | | |
| Total Assets................................... | 10ra | 24,739.8 | 29,566.7 | 33,474.8 | 40,448.9 | 42,798.2 | 41,834.1 | 43,880.8 | 40,277.6 | 43,721.6 | 48,932.7 | 57,461.3 | 60,654.7 |
| **Other Depository Corporations** | | | | | | *Millions of Escudos: End of Period* | | | | | | | |
| Net Foreign Assets.......................... | 21n | 3,092.1 | 6,594.8 | 4,778.1 | 3,383.9 | −788.8 | −548.0 | −1,394.8 | −6,658.2 | −5,847.6 | −3,278.3 | −2,284.7 | −150.9 |
| Claims on Nonresidents................. | 21 | 5,389.0 | 11,040.3 | 9,779.7 | 10,062.1 | 7,133.5 | 7,107.0 | 6,431.6 | 11,431.7 | 19,719.6 | 29,457.2 | 22,639.7 | 25,901.4 |
| Liabilities to Nonresidents.............. | 26c | 2,296.9 | 4,445.5 | 5,001.6 | 6,678.2 | 7,922.3 | 7,655.0 | 7,826.4 | 18,089.9 | 25,567.2 | 32,735.4 | 24,924.3 | 26,052.3 |
| Claims on Central Bank................... | 20 | 11,695.1 | 13,546.7 | 18,242.0 | 21,922.6 | 23,427.9 | 20,506.7 | 20,340.3 | 16,687.1 | 25,733.4 | 32,736.2 | 39,356.5 | 39,656.6 |
| Currency................................... | 20a | 1,072.3 | 1,057.9 | 1,456.8 | 1,595.3 | 1,637.1 | 1,488.9 | 1,902.5 | 1,469.9 | 1,934.1 | 2,091.4 | 2,055.2 | 2,094.8 |
| Reserve Deposits and Securities...... | 20b | 10,622.8 | 12,488.8 | 12,735.2 | 13,687.3 | 15,430.8 | 17,267.8 | 16,687.8 | 14,597.1 | 23,458.3 | 29,867.9 | 34,500.2 | 34,651.7 |
| Other Claims............................... | 20n | — | — | 4,050.0 | 6,640.0 | 6,360.0 | 1,750.0 | 1,750.0 | 620.0 | 341.0 | 777.0 | 2,801.0 | 2,910.0 |
| Net Claims on Central Government.. | 22an | 17,673.0 | 19,638.3 | 20,053.3 | 16,293.8 | 13,588.8 | 14,373.3 | 15,366.9 | 18,227.7 | 19,367.3 | 21,941.5 | 24,113.9 | 25,324.5 |
| Claims on Central Government...... | 22a | 19,268.4 | 21,999.5 | 22,517.8 | 19,528.3 | 17,170.7 | 18,016.3 | 19,232.4 | 22,114.0 | 23,407.1 | 26,594.9 | 31,642.7 | 33,240.1 |
| Liabilities to Central Government.... | 26d | 1,595.4 | 2,361.2 | 2,464.5 | 3,234.6 | 3,581.9 | 3,643.0 | 3,865.5 | 3,886.3 | 4,039.8 | 4,653.4 | 7,528.8 | 7,915.5 |
| Claims on Other Sectors................. | 22s | 30,820.9 | 33,783.7 | 44,212.5 | 56,029.2 | 70,744.7 | 79,532.1 | 86,985.5 | 100,372.0 | 99,371.6 | 101,572.4 | 101,326.5 | 104,368.9 |
| Claims on Other Financial Corps.... | 22g | 14.2 | 10.5 | 6.3 | 2.5 | .2 | — | — | — | — | — | — | — |
| Claims on State & Local Govts....... | 22b | 277.0 | 275.7 | 241.4 | 295.5 | 771.6 | 1,408.7 | 1,956.5 | 2,704.7 | 1,819.7 | 2,282.3 | 3,053.7 | 3,379.5 |
| Claims on Public Nonfin. Corps...... | 22c | 704.0 | 1,022.2 | 1,498.0 | 1,336.8 | 636.0 | 473.1 | 521.9 | 1,105.7 | 1,558.3 | 1,402.6 | 1,302.7 | 3,588.9 |
| Claims on Private Sector............... | 22d | 29,825.6 | 32,475.3 | 42,466.8 | 54,394.4 | 69,336.9 | 77,650.2 | 84,507.1 | 96,561.7 | 95,993.6 | 97,887.5 | 96,970.0 | 97,400.5 |
| Liabilities to Central Bank............... | 26g | 45.0 | 28.3 | 9.4 | — | — | 250.0 | — | — | — | — | — | — |
| Transf.Dep.Included in Broad Money | 24 | 20,519.0 | 24,302.4 | 32,828.5 | 37,177.4 | 37,398.8 | 36,173.5 | 39,831.0 | 36,951.0 | 39,837.8 | 46,957.0 | 52,295.1 | 55,318.0 |
| Other Dep.Included in Broad Money. | 25 | 35,218.0 | 40,451.9 | 44,878.6 | 49,043.3 | 55,671.4 | 60,768.4 | 62,876.7 | 70,755.9 | 75,662.0 | 82,522.6 | 86,668.2 | 92,634.7 |
| Sec.Ot.th.Shares Incl.in Brd. Money.. | 26a | — | — | — | — | — | — | — | — | — | — | — | — |
| Deposits Excl. from Broad Money..... | 26b | 134.2 | 255.5 | 582.2 | 605.4 | 369.0 | 357.2 | 414.7 | 302.7 | 154.8 | 157.2 | 248.8 | 361.6 |
| Sec.Ot.th.Shares Excl.f/Brd.Money.... | 26s | — | — | — | — | 500.0 | 500.0 | 500.0 | 1,500.0 | 1,998.5 | 1,898.8 | 1,246.7 | 1,147.9 |
| Loans.......................................... | 26l | 120.0 | 108.3 | 96.7 | 85.0 | 573.3 | 61.7 | 572.4 | 889.7 | 326.7 | 295.0 | 365.8 | 341.7 |
| Financial Derivatives...................... | 26m | — | — | — | — | — | — | — | — | — | — | — | — |
| Insurance Technical Reserves.......... | 26r | — | — | — | — | — | — | — | — | — | — | — | — |
| Shares and Other Equity.................. | 27a | 5,025.6 | 5,239.0 | 5,819.2 | 7,785.9 | 9,275.6 | 10,773.8 | 11,915.9 | 13,538.3 | 14,065.9 | 15,107.5 | 15,503.7 | 15,685.1 |
| Other Items (Net)........................... | 27r | 2,219.2 | 3,178.2 | 3,071.2 | 2,932.3 | 3,184.5 | 4,979.5 | 5,187.2 | 4,691.2 | 6,579.1 | 6,033.7 | 6,183.8 | 3,710.2 |
| Memo Item: | | | | | | | | | | | | | |
| Total Assets................................... | 20ra | 73,047.4 | 86,047.5 | 100,915.7 | 114,110.0 | 126,763.2 | 133,870.9 | 142,706.2 | 164,511.7 | 181,309.4 | 206,692.8 | 211,610.8 | 223,853.5 |

# Cabo Verde   624

| | | 2004 | 2005 | 2006 | 2007 | 2008 | 2009 | 2010 | 2011 | 2012 | 2013 | 2014 | 2015 |
|---|---|---|---|---|---|---|---|---|---|---|---|---|---|
| **Depository Corporations** | | | | | | *Millions of Escudos: End of Period* | | | | | | | |
| Net Foreign Assets.......................... | 31n | 13,715.8 | 21,864.1 | 25,188.7 | 30,998.2 | 28,991.0 | 27,376.0 | 28,482.5 | 19,985.5 | 25,375.5 | 33,541.0 | 42,616.7 | 48,463.4 |
| Claims on Nonresidents................ | 31 | 16,926.0 | 27,614.9 | 31,423.4 | 38,822.6 | 38,152.1 | 37,644.4 | 38,938.7 | 40,466.1 | 52,695.7 | 67,768.8 | 68,916.2 | 75,880.4 |
| Liabilities to Nonresidents............ | 36c | 3,210.3 | 5,750.8 | 6,234.7 | 7,824.4 | 9,161.2 | 10,268.4 | 10,456.3 | 20,480.6 | 27,320.2 | 34,227.9 | 26,299.5 | 27,417.0 |
| Domestic Claims.............................. | 32 | 59,279.1 | 62,344.4 | 72,983.3 | 78,555.0 | 91,381.0 | 99,192.4 | 105,489.4 | 121,514.2 | 125,018.5 | 129,209.0 | 131,578.5 | 134,141.2 |
| Net Claims on Central Government | 32an | 27,193.2 | 27,321.4 | 27,545.3 | 21,358.0 | 19,530.4 | 18,549.5 | 17,196.3 | 20,456.0 | 24,928.0 | 26,856.3 | 29,474.8 | 29,067.7 |
| Claims on Central Government.... | 32a | 29,973.7 | 32,579.2 | 32,000.4 | 28,938.2 | 26,673.5 | 27,264.0 | 28,212.0 | 31,113.1 | 32,235.1 | 35,288.0 | 40,184.0 | 41,517.5 |
| Liabilities to Central Government. | 36d | 2,780.5 | 5,257.8 | 4,455.1 | 7,580.2 | 7,143.1 | 8,714.8 | 11,015.6 | 10,657.1 | 7,307.0 | 8,431.7 | 10,709.2 | 12,449.8 |
| Claims on Other Sectors................ | 32s | 32,086.0 | 35,023.0 | 45,438.0 | 57,197.0 | 71,850.7 | 80,642.9 | 88,293.1 | 101,058.2 | 100,090.4 | 102,352.7 | 102,103.6 | 105,073.5 |
| Claims on Other Financial Corps.. | 32g | 43.7 | 25.7 | 15.7 | 5.8 | .3 | | | | | | | |
| Claims on State & Local Govts..... | 32b | 277.0 | 275.7 | 241.4 | 295.5 | 771.6 | 1,408.7 | 1,956.5 | 2,704.7 | 1,819.7 | 2,282.3 | 3,053.7 | 3,379.5 |
| Claims on Public Nonfin. Corps.... | 32c | 704.1 | 1,022.3 | 1,498.1 | 1,336.9 | 636.1 | 473.2 | 522.0 | 1,105.7 | 1,558.3 | 1,402.6 | 1,302.7 | 3,588.9 |
| Claims on Private Sector.............. | 32d | 31,061.1 | 33,699.2 | 43,682.7 | 55,558.8 | 70,442.7 | 78,760.9 | 85,814.6 | 97,247.9 | 96,712.4 | 98,667.8 | 97,747.2 | 98,105.1 |
| Broad Money Liabilities................... | 35l | 62,523.4 | 72,389.5 | 85,440.9 | 94,616.7 | 101,783.5 | 105,306.9 | 110,999.2 | 116,088.0 | 123,406.8 | 137,490.8 | 147,716.2 | 156,929.4 |
| Currency Outside Depository Corps | 34a | 6,765.0 | 7,633.6 | 7,731.2 | 8,387.5 | 8,712.7 | 8,361.7 | 8,287.5 | 8,376.2 | 7,894.5 | 8,005.0 | 8,706.7 | 8,967.1 |
| Transferable Deposits.................... | 34 | 20,540.4 | 24,304.0 | 32,831.1 | 37,185.9 | 37,399.4 | 36,176.8 | 39,834.7 | 36,955.9 | 39,850.3 | 46,963.3 | 52,341.4 | 55,327.5 |
| Other Deposits.............................. | 35 | 35,218.0 | 40,451.9 | 44,878.6 | 49,043.3 | 55,671.4 | 60,768.4 | 62,876.7 | 70,755.9 | 75,662.0 | 82,522.6 | 86,668.2 | 92,634.7 |
| Securities Other than Shares.......... | 36a | — | — | — | — | | | | | | | | |
| Deposits Excl. from Broad Money..... | 36b | 134.2 | 255.5 | 582.2 | 605.4 | 369.0 | 357.2 | 414.7 | 302.7 | 154.8 | 157.2 | 248.8 | 361.6 |
| Sec.Ot.th.Shares Excl.f/Brd.Money.... | 36s | — | — | — | — | 500.0 | 500.0 | 500.0 | 1,500.0 | 1,998.5 | 1,898.8 | 1,246.7 | 1,147.9 |
| Loans................................................ | 36l | 120.0 | 108.3 | 96.7 | 85.0 | 573.3 | 61.7 | 572.4 | 889.7 | 326.7 | 295.0 | 365.8 | 341.7 |
| Financial Derivatives...................... | 36m | — | — | — | — | — | — | — | — | — | — | — | — |
| Insurance Technical Reserves........... | 36r | — | — | — | — | — | — | — | — | — | — | — | — |
| Shares and Other Equity.................. | 37a | 5,465.1 | 5,768.4 | 6,439.5 | 8,502.3 | 10,219.6 | 11,136.2 | 12,011.2 | 12,158.9 | 11,674.5 | 12,699.0 | 14,995.1 | 16,137.3 |
| Other Items (Net)............................ | 37r | 4,752.2 | 5,686.7 | 5,612.6 | 5,743.8 | 6,926.6 | 9,206.5 | 9,474.3 | 10,560.4 | 12,832.8 | 10,209.0 | 9,622.5 | 7,686.7 |
| Broad Money Liabs., Seasonally Adj. | 35l.b | 62,377.6 | 72,222.9 | 85,263.7 | 94,391.8 | 101,478.3 | 104,812.3 | 110,276.4 | 115,088.8 | 122,137.5 | 135,835.9 | 145,783.6 | 154,779.1 |
| **Monetary Aggregates** | | | | | | *Millions of Escudos: End of Period* | | | | | | | |
| Broad Money..................................... | 59m | 62,523.4 | 72,389.5 | 85,440.9 | 94,616.7 | 101,783.5 | 105,306.9 | 110,999.2 | 116,088.0 | 123,406.8 | 137,490.9 | 147,716.2 | 156,929.4 |
| o/w:Currency Issued by Cent.Govt | 59m.a | — | — | — | — | — | — | — | — | — | — | — | — |
| o/w: Dep.in Nonfin. Corporations. | 59m.b | — | — | — | — | — | — | — | — | — | — | — | — |
| o/w:Secs. Issued by Central Govt.. | 59m.c | — | — | — | — | — | — | — | — | — | — | — | — |
| Money (National Definitions) | | | | | | | | | | | | | |
| Base Money.................................... | 19ma | 18,467.2 | 21,134.1 | 25,834.1 | 23,948.4 | 25,951.8 | 26,830.3 | 25,914.6 | 24,438.6 | 32,573.6 | 38,427.4 | 45,778.5 | 46,749.5 |
| M1...................................................... | 59ma | 24,404.8 | 28,716.4 | 35,853.9 | 40,339.5 | 42,170.4 | 39,866.6 | 42,811.6 | 39,131.6 | 40,993.8 | 47,782.3 | 54,274.5 | 56,469.9 |
| M2...................................................... | 59mb | 62,848.3 | 72,641.3 | 86,215.8 | 94,607.9 | 102,088.9 | 105,451.7 | 110,383.7 | 115,321.1 | 122,141.8 | 136,080.4 | 146,004.8 | 154,586.4 |
| **Interest Rates** | | | | | | *Percent Per Annum* | | | | | | | |
| Rediscount Rate (End of Period)....... | 60.a | 8.50 | 8.50 | 8.50 | 8.50 | 7.50 | 7.50 | 7.50 | 7.25 | 8.75 | 8.75 | 6.75 | 6.50 |
| Treasury Bill Rate............................ | 60c | 6.42 | 4.07 | 2.70 | 3.41 | 3.41 | 3.52 | 3.89 | 3.96 | 4.18 | 3.39 | 1.51 | 1.15 |
| Deposit Rate.................................... | 60l | 3.46 | 3.38 | † 4.43 | 3.29 | 3.81 | 2.88 | 3.11 | 3.35 | 3.79 | 4.17 | 3.48 | 2.87 |
| Lending Rate.................................... | 60p | 12.69 | 12.29 | † 9.86 | 10.55 | 9.99 | 10.98 | 11.04 | 9.81 | 9.90 | 10.52 | 10.89 | 10.41 |
| **Prices** | | | | | | *Index Numbers (2010=100): Period Averages* | | | | | | | |
| Consumer Prices............................. | 64 | 82.2 | 82.6 | † 87.0 | 90.8 | 97.0 | 98.0 | 100.0 | 104.5 | 107.1 | 108.8 | 108.5 | 108.6 |
| **Intl. Transactions & Positions** | | | | | | *Millions of Escudos* | | | | | | | |
| Exports............................................. | 70 | 1,340.5 | 1,562.0 | 1,815.2 | 1,548.4 | 2,407.6 | 2,796.1 | 3,707.8 | .... | .... | .... | .... | .... |
| Imports, c.i.f..................................... | 71 | 38,304.2 | 38,855.8 | 47,654.4 | 60,415.7 | 62,127.6 | 56,295.6 | 61,809.6 | .... | .... | .... | .... | .... |

# Cabo Verde  624

| | | 2004 | 2005 | 2006 | 2007 | 2008 | 2009 | 2010 | 2011 | 2012 | 2013 | 2014 | 2015 |
|---|---|---|---|---|---|---|---|---|---|---|---|---|---|
| **Balance of Payments** | | | | | | | *Millions of US Dollars* | | | | | | |
| A. Current Account* | 109bx | −130.0 | −40.7 | −82.7 | −198.3 | −205.5 | −246.8 | −222.8 | −304.4 | −244.9 | −107.4 | −168.5 | −68.8 |
| Goods, credit (exports) | 1a9cx | 42.9 | 77.1 | 85.8 | 69.7 | 102.9 | 80.5 | 122.7 | 196.5 | 173.1 | 184.2 | 253.3 | 149.3 |
| Goods, debit (imports) | 1a9dx | 421.9 | 427.2 | 544.7 | 731.9 | 816.4 | 756.7 | 805.8 | 1,039.7 | 830.5 | 805.5 | 857.4 | 630.6 |
| Balance on goods | 1a9bx | −379.0 | −350.0 | −458.9 | −662.2 | −713.5 | −676.2 | −683.1 | −843.2 | −657.4 | −621.3 | −604.1 | −481.4 |
| Services, credit (exports) | 1b9cx | 242.6 | 276.6 | 386.5 | 496.3 | 607.6 | 486.9 | 507.0 | 585.3 | 598.4 | 651.3 | 632.5 | 517.9 |
| Services, debit (imports) | 1b9dx | 209.4 | 214.6 | 259.1 | 301.6 | 366.7 | 326.0 | 307.9 | 333.7 | 370.2 | 347.4 | 368.8 | 305.8 |
| Balance on Goods & Services | 129bx | −345.8 | −288.0 | −331.5 | −467.4 | −472.6 | −515.3 | −484.0 | −591.5 | −429.3 | −317.4 | −340.4 | −269.3 |
| Primary income: credit | 1c9cx | 17.8 | 19.2 | 19.1 | 26.7 | 27.7 | 22.9 | 13.9 | 14.3 | 12.6 | 13.9 | 13.9 | 12.4 |
| Primary income: debit | 1c9dx | 36.2 | 52.7 | 59.4 | 58.9 | 75.7 | 66.3 | 93.1 | 86.0 | 87.8 | 78.6 | 106.3 | 70.1 |
| Balance on gds, serv. & prim. inc. | 1y9bx | −364.3 | −321.5 | −371.8 | −499.6 | −520.6 | −558.7 | −563.1 | −663.2 | −504.5 | −382.2 | −432.8 | −327.0 |
| Secondary income: credit | 1d9ca | 277.6 | 312.0 | 334.0 | 405.5 | 422.3 | 390.3 | 409.7 | 450.9 | 306.0 | 324.3 | 298.6 | 284.4 |
| Secondary income: debit | 1d9da | 43.3 | 31.2 | 44.9 | 104.2 | 107.1 | 78.4 | 69.4 | 92.1 | 46.4 | 49.6 | 34.3 | 26.1 |
| B. Capital Account* | 209ba | 23.6 | 20.7 | 17.5 | 27.0 | 26.7 | 44.5 | 38.3 | 11.0 | 12.3 | 5.5 | 6.8 | 17.6 |
| Capital account: credit | 209ca | 23.6 | 21.1 | 17.5 | 27.0 | 26.7 | 44.5 | 38.3 | 11.0 | 12.3 | 5.5 | 6.8 | 17.6 |
| Capital account: debit | 209da | — | .4 | — | — | — | — | — | — | — | — | — | — |
| Balance on current & capital acct. | 129ba | −106.4 | −20.0 | −65.3 | −171.2 | −178.7 | −202.3 | −184.6 | −293.4 | −232.6 | −101.9 | −161.7 | −51.2 |
| C. Financial Account* | 309na | −124.5 | −83.1 | −151.2 | −278.5 | −315.5 | −231.9 | −297.9 | −278.3 | −308.1 | −173.5 | −221.8 | −92.5 |
| Direct investment: assets | 3a9aa | — | — | −.2 | .4 | −2.8 | 1.9 | — | 1.4 | 11.1 | 32.8 | 12.9 | −16.5 |
| Equity & investment fund shares | 3aaaa | — | — | — | .4 | — | 1.9 | — | 1.4 | 7.7 | 13.9 | 8.7 | 3.2 |
| Debt instruments | 3abaa | — | — | −.2 | — | −2.9 | — | — | — | 3.5 | 18.9 | 4.2 | −19.8 |
| Direct investment: liabilities | 3a9la | 67.6 | 80.4 | 131.6 | 191.9 | 211.0 | 127.1 | 116.2 | 102.2 | 129.0 | 89.3 | 135.4 | 75.3 |
| Equity & investment fund shares | 3aala | 54.4 | 63.4 | 148.8 | 192.8 | 210.4 | 123.9 | 95.3 | 91.0 | 164.2 | 121.1 | 127.9 | 79.4 |
| Debt instruments | 3abla | 13.2 | 17.0 | −17.3 | −.9 | .6 | 3.2 | 20.9 | 11.2 | −35.2 | −31.7 | 7.5 | −4.1 |
| Portfolio investment: assets | 3b9aa | .... | — | .1 | .4 | — | — | — | — | 18.0 | 27.7 | 17.7 | 21.1 |
| Equity & investment fund shares | 3baaa | .... | — | .1 | .4 | — | — | — | — | — | — | — | — |
| Debt securities | 3bbaa | .... | .... | .... | .... | .... | — | — | — | 18.0 | 27.7 | 17.7 | 21.1 |
| Portfolio investment: liabilities | 3b9la | .... | — | .3 | 4.1 | .1 | 5.6 | 5.4 | — | −1.7 | .2 | −6.2 | — |
| Equity & investment fund shares | 3bala | .... | — | .3 | 2.2 | — | 1.8 | — | — | — | — | — | — |
| Debt securities | 3bbla | .... | — | — | 1.9 | .1 | 3.8 | 5.4 | — | −1.7 | .2 | −6.2 | — |
| Fin. der.& empl.stk.ops.(ESOs): net. | 3c9na | .... | .... | .... | .... | .... | — | — | — | — | — | — | — |
| Fin. der. & ESOs: assets | 3c9aa | .... | .... | .... | .... | .... | — | — | — | — | — | — | — |
| Fin. der. & ESOs: liabilities | 3c9la | .... | .... | .... | .... | .... | — | — | — | — | — | — | — |
| Other investment: assets | 3d9aa | 7.5 | 76.3 | −14.6 | 9.2 | −40.9 | −16.4 | 8.6 | 80.5 | 93.8 | 152.2 | −88.7 | 54.8 |
| Other equity | 3daaa | .... | .... | .... | .... | .... | .... | .... | .... | .... | .... | .... | .... |
| Debt instruments | 3dzaa | 7.5 | 76.3 | −14.6 | 9.2 | −40.9 | −16.4 | 8.6 | 80.5 | 93.8 | 152.2 | −88.7 | 54.8 |
| Other investment: liabilities | 3d9la | 64.4 | 79.0 | 4.7 | 92.4 | 60.7 | 84.7 | 185.0 | 258.0 | 303.8 | 296.6 | 34.5 | 76.5 |
| Other equity | 3dala | .... | .... | .... | .... | .... | .... | .... | .... | .... | .... | .... | .... |
| Debt instruments | 3dzla | 64.4 | 79.0 | 4.7 | 92.4 | 60.7 | 84.7 | 185.0 | 258.0 | 303.8 | 296.6 | 34.5 | 76.5 |
| Curr.+ cap.− finan. acct. balance | 4y9na | 18.0 | 63.2 | 85.9 | 107.2 | 136.8 | 29.6 | 113.4 | −15.1 | 75.5 | 71.6 | 60.1 | 41.4 |
| D. Net Errors and Omissions | 409na | 9.7 | 1.7 | −10.0 | −.1 | −107.8 | −33.7 | −85.1 | −33.3 | −26.0 | −1.3 | 30.6 | −4.5 |
| E. Reserves and Related Items | 4z9na | 27.8 | 64.9 | 76.0 | 107.1 | 29.1 | −4.1 | 28.3 | −48.4 | 49.5 | 70.3 | 90.7 | 36.8 |
| Reserve assets | 3e9aa | 37.4 | 56.1 | 58.0 | 86.9 | 28.1 | −5.6 | 26.0 | −51.1 | 47.1 | 68.4 | 89.6 | 36.5 |
| Credit and loans from the IMF | 3dcla | 1.8 | 3.7 | — | −.2 | −.8 | −1.5 | −2.3 | −2.7 | −2.5 | −1.9 | −1.1 | −.4 |
| Exceptional financing | 409la | 7.8 | −12.6 | −18.0 | −20.1 | −.2 | — | — | — | — | — | — | — |
| *Excludes components in group E | | | | | | | | | | | | | |
| | | | | | | | | | | | | | |
| **International Investment Position** | | | | | | | *Millions of US Dollars* | | | | | | |
| Assets | 809aa | 391.6 | 482.5 | 600.1 | 789.0 | 724.1 | 746.8 | 712.8 | 710.7 | 897.2 | 1,224.0 | 1,126.4 | 1,111.0 |
| Direct investment | 8a9aa | — | — | — | .4 | .4 | 2.3 | 2.1 | 3.4 | 15.2 | 49.7 | 54.0 | 32.4 |
| Equity & investment fund shares | 8aaaa | .... | .... | .... | .4 | .4 | 2.3 | 2.1 | 3.4 | 11.3 | 26.2 | 31.0 | 31.0 |
| Debt instruments | 8abaa | — | — | — | — | — | — | — | — | 3.8 | 23.5 | 22.9 | 1.4 |
| Portfolio investment | 8b9aa | .... | .... | .1 | .6 | .6 | .6 | .5 | .5 | 19.0 | 48.7 | 59.0 | 73.6 |
| Equity & investment fund shares | 8baaa | .... | .... | .1 | .6 | .6 | .6 | .5 | .5 | .5 | .5 | .5 | .4 |
| Debt securities | 8bbaa | .... | .... | .... | .... | .... | .... | .... | .... | 18.5 | 48.1 | 58.5 | 73.1 |
| Fin. der.(oth.than reserves) & ESOs | 8c9aa | .... | .... | .... | .... | .... | .... | .... | .... | .... | .... | .... | .... |
| Other investment | 8d9aa | 252.1 | 308.5 | 345.5 | 408.5 | 335.9 | 348.9 | 317.3 | 370.9 | 472.0 | 647.8 | 505.1 | 511.7 |
| Other equity | 8daaa | .... | .... | .... | .... | .... | .... | .... | .... | .... | .... | .... | .... |
| Debt instruments | 8dzaa | 252.1 | 308.5 | 345.5 | 408.5 | 335.9 | 348.9 | 317.3 | 370.9 | 472.0 | 647.8 | 505.1 | 511.7 |
| Reserve assets | 8e9aa | 139.5 | 174.0 | 254.5 | 379.5 | 387.3 | 395.0 | 392.9 | 335.8 | 391.0 | 477.8 | 508.3 | 493.3 |
| Liabilities | 809la | 1,067.9 | 1,067.1 | 1,289.6 | 1,727.0 | 1,949.9 | 2,306.2 | 2,486.4 | 2,762.4 | 3,366.3 | 3,916.3 | 3,611.5 | 3,437.1 |
| Direct investment | 8a9la | 326.7 | 360.3 | 539.2 | 807.4 | 1,012.3 | 1,229.9 | 1,300.5 | 1,401.9 | 1,584.8 | 1,747.9 | 1,663.3 | 1,565.3 |
| Equity & investment fund shares | 8aala | 314.4 | 333.2 | 526.3 | 794.0 | 1,005.6 | 1,221.6 | 1,275.6 | 1,354.2 | 1,546.6 | 1,741.1 | 1,650.8 | 1,558.2 |
| Debt instruments | 8abla | 12.3 | 27.1 | 12.9 | 13.4 | 6.7 | 8.3 | 24.9 | 47.7 | 38.2 | 6.8 | 12.5 | 7.1 |
| Portfolio investment | 8b9la | .1 | .1 | .4 | 4.7 | 4.5 | 10.5 | 15.3 | 14.9 | 16.6 | 17.6 | 9.6 | 8.7 |
| Equity & investment fund shares | 8bala | .1 | .1 | .4 | 2.7 | 2.5 | 4.7 | 4.3 | 4.2 | 4.3 | 4.5 | 3.9 | 3.5 |
| Debt securities | 8bbla | .... | .... | .... | 2.0 | 1.9 | 5.8 | 11.0 | 10.7 | 12.4 | 13.2 | 5.7 | 5.2 |
| Fin. der.(oth.than reserves) & ESOs | 8c9la | .... | .... | .... | .... | .... | .... | .... | .... | .... | .... | .... | .... |
| Other investment | 8d9la | 741.1 | 706.7 | 750.1 | 914.8 | 933.2 | 1,065.8 | 1,170.6 | 1,345.6 | 1,764.9 | 2,150.8 | 1,938.6 | 1,863.1 |
| Other equity | 8dala | .... | .... | .... | .... | .... | .... | .... | .... | .... | .... | .... | .... |
| Debt instruments | 8dzla | 741.1 | 706.7 | 750.1 | 914.8 | 933.2 | 1,065.8 | 1,170.6 | 1,345.6 | 1,764.9 | 2,150.8 | 1,938.6 | 1,863.1 |

# Cabo Verde  624

| | | 2004 | 2005 | 2006 | 2007 | 2008 | 2009 | 2010 | 2011 | 2012 | 2013 | 2014 | 2015 |
|---|---|---|---|---|---|---|---|---|---|---|---|---|---|
| **Government Finance** | | | | | | | | | | | | | |
| **Cash Flow Statement** | | | | | | | | | | | | | |
| **Budgetary Central Government** | | | | | | *Millions of Escudos: Fiscal Year Ends December 31* | | | | | | | |
| Cash Receipts:Operating Activities... | c1 | .... | 26,762 | 30,406 | 32,908 | 37,190 | 36,764 | 38,833 | 37,290 | 34,138 | 36,718 | .... | .... |
| Taxes...................................... | c11 | .... | 18,165 | 22,147 | 25,501 | 28,669 | 25,030 | 25,561 | 29,197 | 26,828 | 27,411 | .... | .... |
| Social Contributions....................... | c12 | .... | 533 | 497 | 87 | 50 | 46 | 42 | 37 | 13 | 38 | .... | .... |
| Grants........................................ | c13 | .... | 6,611 | 6,400 | 5,364 | 5,865 | 7,533 | 9,486 | 4,342 | 2,768 | 3,779 | .... | .... |
| Other Receipts............................. | c14 | .... | 1,454 | 1,362 | 1,956 | 2,607 | 4,156 | 3,745 | 3,714 | 4,529 | 5,491 | .... | .... |
| Cash Payments:Operating Activities. | c2 | .... | 23,876 | 26,217 | 27,427 | 28,128 | 31,384 | 32,138 | 33,919 | 33,149 | 34,714 | .... | .... |
| Compensation of Employees.......... | c21 | .... | 8,903 | 9,384 | 9,587 | 9,877 | 14,304 | 14,892 | 15,861 | 15,753 | 17,046 | .... | .... |
| Purchases of Goods & Services....... | c22 | .... | 4,916 | 4,792 | 5,418 | 4,306 | 5,292 | 5,264 | 5,343 | 4,571 | 4,963 | .... | .... |
| Interest...................................... | c24 | .... | 1,927 | 1,920 | 1,885 | 1,845 | 1,818 | 2,159 | 2,276 | 2,866 | 3,367 | .... | .... |
| Subsidies.................................... | c25 | .... | 596 | 1,752 | 200 | 610 | 443 | 699 | 509 | 274 | 101 | .... | .... |
| Grants........................................ | c26 | .... | 4,276 | 5,243 | 6,171 | 6,885 | 3,456 | 4,713 | 4,075 | 4,054 | 3,735 | .... | .... |
| Social Benefits............................. | c27 | .... | 1,885 | 2,079 | 2,289 | 2,591 | 2,877 | 2,886 | 3,710 | 3,916 | 4,136 | .... | .... |
| Other Payments........................... | c28 | .... | 1,373 | 1,047 | 1,877 | 2,013 | 3,194 | 1,526 | 2,144 | 1,715 | 1,366 | .... | .... |
| Net Cash Inflow:Operating Act.[1-2] | ccio | .... | 2,886 | 4,189 | 5,480 | 9,063 | 5,380 | 6,695 | 3,371 | 989 | 2,004 | .... | .... |
| Net Cash Outflow:Invest. in NFA...... | c31 | .... | 6,991 | 8,416 | 6,278 | 11,373 | 13,243 | 21,214 | 18,352 | 16,188 | 15,663 | .... | .... |
| Purchases of Nonfinancial Assets... | c31.1 | .... | 7,285 | 8,929 | 8,510 | 12,362 | 13,262 | 21,214 | 18,415 | 16,234 | 15,677 | .... | .... |
| Sales of Nonfinancial Assets.......... | c31.2 | .... | 294 | 513 | 2,232 | 988 | 18 | — | 62 | 47 | 14 | .... | .... |
| Cash Surplus/Deficit [1-2-31=1-2M] | ccsd | .... | −4,105 | −4,227 | −797 | −2,310 | −7,863 | −14,519 | −14,982 | −15,199 | −13,659 | .... | .... |
| Net Acq. Fin. Assets, excl. Cash....... | c32x | .... | 670 | 361 | 2,434 | 131 | 836 | 1,445 | 4,243 | 6,427 | 7,171 | .... | .... |
| Domestic..................................... | c321x | .... | 670 | 361 | 2,434 | 131 | 836 | 1,445 | 4,243 | 6,427 | 7,171 | .... | .... |
| Foreign....................................... | c322x | .... | — | — | — | — | — | — | — | — | — | .... | .... |
| Net Incurrence of Liabilities............. | c33 | .... | 5,755 | 3,310 | 1,580 | 1,115 | 8,857 | 17,069 | 19,211 | 19,741 | 22,364 | .... | .... |
| Domestic..................................... | c331 | .... | 3,179 | 1,012 | −1,197 | −2,131 | 2,557 | 2,545 | 2,601 | 2,516 | 2,642 | .... | .... |
| Foreign....................................... | c332 | .... | 2,576 | 2,298 | 2,777 | 3,246 | 6,301 | 14,524 | 16,610 | 17,225 | 19,722 | .... | .... |
| Net Cash Inflow, Fin.Act.[-32x+33].. | cnfb | .... | 5,086 | 2,949 | −854 | 984 | 8,022 | 15,623 | 14,968 | 13,314 | 15,193 | .... | .... |
| Net Change in Stock of Cash........... | cncb | .... | −1,541 | −120 | −3,117 | 580 | 159 | 1,104 | −1,751 | −1,885 | 815 | .... | .... |
| Stat. Discrep. [32X-33+NCB-CSD].... | ccsdz | .... | −2,521 | 1,158 | −1,465 | 1,907 | — | — | −1,737 | — | −719 | .... | .... |
| Memo Item:Cash Expenditure[2+31] | c2m | .... | 30,868 | 34,634 | 33,705 | 39,501 | 44,627 | 53,352 | 52,272 | 49,336 | 50,377 | .... | .... |
| Memo Item: Gross Debt................... | c63 | .... | .... | .... | .... | .... | .... | .... | .... | .... | .... | .... | .... |
| **National Accounts** | | | | | | *Millions of Escudos* | | | | | | | |
| Gross Domestic Product (GDP)......... | 99b | 82,086 | 86,185 | 97,384 | 121,974 | 134,698 | 135,879 | 138,569 | 147,924 | .... | .... | .... | .... |
| GDP Volume 1980 Prices................. | 99b.p | 22,375 | .... | .... | .... | .... | .... | .... | .... | .... | .... | .... | .... |
| GDP Volume (2000=100)............... | 99bvp | 122.0 | .... | .... | .... | .... | .... | .... | .... | .... | .... | .... | .... |
| GDP Deflator (2000=100)............... | 99bip | 104.3 | .... | .... | .... | .... | .... | .... | .... | .... | .... | .... | .... |
| | | | | | | *Millions: Midyear Estimates* | | | | | | | |
| Population.................................. | 99z | .47 | .47 | .48 | .48 | .48 | .49 | .49 | .50 | .50 | .51 | .51 | .52 |

# Cambodia 522

| | | 2004 | 2005 | 2006 | 2007 | 2008 | 2009 | 2010 | 2011 | 2012 | 2013 | 2014 | 2015 |
|---|---|---|---|---|---|---|---|---|---|---|---|---|---|
| **Exchange Rates** | | | | | | *Riels per SDR: End of Period* | | | | | | | |
| Official Rate................... | aa | 6,254.0 | 5,877.2 | 6,103.4 | 6,319.4 | 6,279.7 | 6,529.4 | 6,238.7 | 6,201.0 | 6,140.0 | 6,152.3 | 5,903.9 | 5,614.3 |
| | | | | | | *Riels per US Dollar: End of Period (ae) Period Average (rf)* | | | | | | | |
| Official Rate................... | ae | 4,027.0 | 4,112.0 | 4,057.0 | 3,999.0 | 4,077.0 | 4,165.0 | 4,051.0 | 4,039.0 | 3,995.0 | 3,995.0 | 4,075.0 | 4,051.5 |
| Official Rate................... | rf | 4,016.3 | 4,092.5 | 4,103.3 | 4,056.2 | 4,054.2 | 4,139.3 | 4,184.9 | 4,058.5 | 4,033.0 | 4,027.3 | 4,037.5 | 4,067.8 |
| **Fund Position** | | | | | | *Millions of SDRs: End of Period* | | | | | | | |
| Quota................... | 2f.s | 87.50 | 87.50 | 87.50 | 87.50 | 87.50 | 87.50 | 87.50 | 87.50 | 87.50 | 87.50 | 87.50 | 87.50 |
| SDR Holdings................... | 1b.s | .05 | .17 | .12 | .14 | .07 | 68.50 | 68.46 | 68.39 | 68.37 | 68.36 | 68.35 | 88.34 |
| Reserve Position in the Fund........... | 1c.s | — | — | — | — | — | — | — | — | — | — | — | — |
| Total Fund Cred.&Loans Outstg....... | 2tl | 62.70 | 56.83 | — | — | — | — | — | — | — | — | — | — |
| SDR Allocations................... | 1bd | 15.42 | 15.42 | 15.42 | 15.42 | 15.42 | 83.92 | 83.92 | 83.92 | 83.92 | 83.92 | 83.92 | 83.92 |
| **International Liquidity** | | | | | | *Millions of US Dollars Unless Otherwise Indicated: End of Period* | | | | | | | |
| Total Reserves minus Gold.............. | 1l.d | 943.21 | 952.98 | 1,157.25 | 1,806.91 | 2,291.55 | 2,851.13 | 3,255.11 | 3,449.69 | 4,267.33 | 4,516.27 | 5,626.01 | 6,882.94 |
| SDR Holdings................... | 1b.d | .08 | .24 | .19 | .22 | .11 | 107.39 | 105.43 | 105.00 | 105.09 | 105.28 | 99.02 | 122.41 |
| Reserve Position in the Fund.......... | 1c.d | — | — | — | — | — | — | — | — | — | — | — | — |
| Foreign Exchange................... | 1d.d | 943.13 | 952.74 | 1,157.07 | 1,806.69 | 2,291.44 | 2,743.74 | 3,149.68 | 3,344.69 | 4,162.24 | 4,410.99 | 5,526.99 | 6,760.53 |
| Gold (Million Fine Troy Ounces).... | 1ad | .3998 | .3998 | .3998 | .3998 | .3998 | .3998 | .3998 | .3998 | .3998 | .3998 | .3998 | .3998 |
| Gold (National Valuation)........... | 1and | 175.00 | 205.60 | 253.41 | 336.26 | 349.01 | 437.32 | 547.01 | 619.32 | 670.66 | 479.11 | 479.62 | 493.40 |
| Central Bank: Other Assets............. | 3..d | † — | — | — | — | — | .07 | — | — | — | — | — | — |
| Central Bank: Other Liabs............... | 4..d | † .53 | .17 | .08 | .07 | .08 | .07 | .12 | .12 | .13 | .13 | .14 | .16 |
| Other Depository Corps.: Assets......... | 7a.d | † 242.81 | 334.24 | 487.32 | 799.49 | 491.09 | 639.99 | 929.67 | 1,019.11 | 2,066.25 | 1,966.50 | 2,117.90 | 2,124.03 |
| Other Depository Corps.: Liabs......... | 7b.d | † 66.67 | 77.21 | 97.63 | 284.91 | 624.03 | 355.67 | 436.41 | 635.59 | 1,519.92 | 1,712.64 | 2,034.78 | 3,256.93 |
| **Central Bank** | | | | | | *Billions of Riels: End of Period* | | | | | | | |
| Net Foreign Assets................... | 11n | † 4,015.27 | 4,342.40 | 5,634.31 | 8,481.31 | 10,678.99 | 13,160.77 | 14,885.83 | 15,913.98 | 18,487.57 | 19,439.79 | 24,384.49 | 29,402.66 |
| Claims on Nonresidents................. | 11 | † 4,506.44 | 4,767.72 | 5,728.72 | 8,579.12 | 10,776.23 | 13,709.55 | 15,410.11 | 16,434.84 | 19,003.34 | 19,956.63 | 24,880.52 | 29,874.26 |
| Liabilities to Nonresidents.......... | 16c | † 491.17 | 425.32 | 94.41 | 97.81 | 97.24 | 548.78 | 524.29 | 520.86 | 515.77 | 516.84 | 496.03 | 471.60 |
| Claims on Other Depository Corps.... | 12e | † 16.67 | 10.52 | 43.52 | 71.80 | 88.12 | 39.02 | 30.67 | 18.61 | 2.60 | 10.40 | — | — |
| Net Claims on Central Government.. | 12an | † −238.11 | −404.79 | −803.10 | −1,625.03 | −2,686.48 | −1,968.81 | −1,782.61 | −1,777.63 | −2,123.10 | −2,340.42 | −3,892.64 | −5,802.31 |
| Claims on Central Government...... | 12a | † 269.78 | 270.41 | 286.45 | 296.76 | 270.25 | 270.24 | 270.24 | 270.24 | 270.24 | 270.24 | 270.24 | 270.24 |
| Liabilities to Central Government... | 16d | † 507.89 | 675.20 | 1,089.55 | 1,921.79 | 2,956.73 | 2,239.06 | 2,052.85 | 2,047.87 | 2,393.34 | 2,610.66 | 4,162.88 | 6,072.55 |
| Claims on Other Sectors............. | 12s | † 21.45 | 15.71 | 11.53 | 10.26 | 8.51 | 11.70 | 13.12 | 9.37 | 15.88 | 9.92 | 186.28 | 106.03 |
| Claims on Other Financial Corps.... | 12g | † — | — | — | — | — | — | — | — | — | — | — | — |
| Claims on State & Local Govts....... | 12b | † — | — | — | — | — | — | — | — | — | — | — | — |
| Claims on Public Nonfin. Corps...... | 12c | † — | — | — | — | — | — | — | — | — | — | — | — |
| Claims on Private Sector............... | 12d | † 21.45 | 15.71 | 11.53 | 10.26 | 8.51 | 11.70 | 13.12 | 9.37 | 15.88 | 9.92 | 186.28 | 106.03 |
| Monetary Base................... | 14 | † 2,681.06 | 2,639.44 | 3,387.28 | 5,025.84 | 6,109.75 | 8,752.35 | 10,270.12 | 11,072.81 | 13,080.95 | 14,776.98 | 18,298.60 | 20,437.11 |
| Currency in Circulation................. | 14a | † 1,158.50 | 1,310.96 | 1,633.10 | 2,043.89 | 2,393.76 | 3,094.68 | 3,240.99 | 3,953.45 | 3,986.47 | 4,794.55 | 5,984.86 | 6,303.83 |
| Liabs. to Other Depository Corps.... | 14c | † 1,516.77 | 1,321.51 | 1,736.09 | 2,968.37 | 3,687.67 | 5,621.18 | 6,978.13 | 7,032.24 | 8,982.05 | 9,814.99 | 11,966.80 | 13,822.80 |
| Liabilities to Other Sectors............. | 14d | † 5.79 | 6.97 | 18.09 | 13.58 | 28.33 | 36.49 | 50.99 | 87.12 | 112.43 | 167.44 | 346.94 | 310.48 |
| Other Liabs. to Other Dep. Corps..... | 14n | † 90.49 | 96.03 | 111.10 | 150.54 | 246.76 | 320.06 | 438.99 | 552.90 | 613.15 | 727.68 | 934.18 | 2,639.19 |
| Dep. & Sec. Excl. f/Monetary Base.... | 14o | † — | — | — | — | — | — | — | — | 1.12 | 1.04 | .96 | 45.56 |
| Deposits Included in Broad Money... | 15 | † — | — | — | — | — | — | — | — | — | — | — | — |
| Sec.Ot.th.Shares Incl.in Brd. Money | 16a | † — | — | — | — | — | — | — | — | — | — | — | — |
| Deposits Excl. from Broad Money... | 16b | † — | — | — | — | — | — | — | — | 1.12 | 1.04 | .96 | .80 |
| Sec.Ot.th.Shares Excl.f/Brd.Money.. | 16s | † — | — | — | — | — | — | — | — | — | — | — | 44.76 |
| Loans................... | 16l | † — | — | — | — | — | — | — | — | — | — | — | — |
| Financial Derivatives................... | 16m | † — | — | — | — | — | — | — | — | — | — | — | — |
| Shares and Other Equity................... | 17a | † 1,157.62 | 1,405.22 | 1,649.89 | 1,987.07 | 2,056.23 | 2,605.36 | 2,879.14 | 3,036.97 | 3,207.84 | 2,174.10 | 2,112.94 | 1,548.88 |
| Other Items (Net)................... | 17r | † −113.90 | −176.84 | −262.02 | −225.10 | −323.60 | −435.09 | −441.23 | −498.34 | −520.11 | −560.10 | −668.56 | −964.35 |
| Memo Item: | | | | | | | | | | | | | |
| Total Assets................... | 10ra | † 5,519.57 | 5,873.07 | 7,011.07 | 9,994.17 | 12,325.69 | 15,294.08 | 17,029.54 | 18,134.85 | 20,700.42 | 21,693.60 | 26,918.34 | 32,105.88 |
| **Other Depository Corporations** | | | | | | *Billions of Riels: End of Period* | | | | | | | |
| Net Foreign Assets................... | 21n | † 709.99 | 1,056.94 | 1,580.95 | 2,059.87 | −542.56 | 1,185.34 | 1,999.18 | 1,549.07 | 2,182.60 | 1,014.15 | 338.70 | −4,588.23 |
| Claims on Nonresidents................. | 21 | † 978.75 | 1,374.41 | 1,977.04 | 3,200.36 | 2,004.13 | 2,668.11 | 3,767.95 | 4,116.20 | 8,254.67 | 7,856.15 | 8,630.44 | 8,602.32 |
| Liabilities to Nonresidents.......... | 26c | † 268.75 | 317.47 | 396.09 | 1,140.49 | 2,546.68 | 1,482.78 | 1,768.77 | 2,567.13 | 6,072.07 | 6,842.01 | 8,291.73 | 13,190.55 |
| Claims on Central Bank................... | 20 | † 1,557.07 | 1,413.44 | 1,847.00 | 3,112.54 | 4,036.15 | 6,070.12 | 7,385.72 | 6,612.63 | 9,531.27 | 10,697.50 | 12,437.86 | 16,141.53 |
| Currency................... | 20a | † 26.05 | 27.17 | 29.99 | 46.72 | 88.76 | 86.11 | 137.44 | 171.18 | 208.84 | 306.61 | 339.41 | 361.98 |
| Reserve Deposits and Securities..... | 20b | † 1,531.02 | 1,386.27 | 1,817.01 | 3,065.78 | 3,947.27 | 5,983.52 | 7,247.69 | 6,441.32 | 9,321.80 | 10,388.63 | 12,098.05 | 15,779.28 |
| Other Claims................... | 20n | † — | — | — | .04 | .12 | .49 | .59 | .12 | .64 | 2.26 | .40 | .27 |
| Net Claims on Central Government.. | 22an | † 1.41 | −69.25 | −155.66 | −249.98 | −374.76 | −409.48 | −531.09 | −475.97 | −687.37 | −880.21 | −969.01 | −1,234.45 |
| Claims on Central Government...... | 22a | † 104.92 | 70.86 | 18.95 | 10.43 | 7.12 | 8.49 | 5.81 | 8.02 | 12.93 | 11.48 | 17.44 | 24.97 |
| Liabilities to Central Government... | 26d | † 103.52 | 140.11 | 174.62 | 260.41 | 381.87 | 417.97 | 536.90 | 483.99 | 700.30 | 891.69 | 986.45 | 1,259.42 |
| Claims on Other Sectors................... | 22s | † 1,925.86 | 2,318.72 | 3,593.13 | 6,385.93 | 9,863.13 | 10,609.52 | 12,997.05 | 14,823.69 | 21,974.34 | 27,914.85 | 36,631.53 | 46,539.11 |
| Claims on Other Financial Corps.... | 22g | † 12.44 | 22.68 | 22.93 | 15.06 | 26.00 | 31.98 | 42.98 | 121.98 | 26.23 | 85.48 | 166.02 | 309.68 |
| Claims on State & Local Govts....... | 22b | † .08 | — | — | — | — | — | — | — | — | — | — | .01 |
| Claims on Public Nonfin. Corps...... | 22c | † — | — | 2.09 | 1.18 | .18 | — | 1.77 | — | 5.57 | 14.70 | 11.16 | 4.47 |
| Claims on Private Sector............... | 22d | † 1,913.34 | 2,296.05 | 3,568.11 | 6,369.70 | 9,836.95 | 10,577.54 | 12,952.30 | 14,701.71 | 21,942.54 | 27,814.67 | 36,454.34 | 46,224.96 |
| Liabilities to Central Bank................... | 26g | † — | — | — | 40.00 | — | — | — | — | — | — | — | — |
| Transf.Dep.Included in Broad Money | 24 | † 1,516.17 | 1,627.25 | 2,403.91 | 2,142.27 | 2,214.18 | 2,540.43 | 3,002.48 | 2,910.44 | 5,028.97 | 7,075.35 | 8,301.62 | 8,846.00 |
| Other Dep.Included in Broad Money. | 25 | † 1,630.41 | 2,044.54 | 2,949.54 | 7,134.51 | 7,354.75 | 10,551.92 | 13,417.64 | 13,565.68 | 19,444.70 | 21,170.13 | 28,358.59 | 33,998.74 |
| Sec.Ot.th.Shares Incl.in Brd. Money.. | 26a | † — | — | — | — | — | — | — | — | — | — | — | — |
| Deposits Excl. from Broad Money..... | 26b | † 15.89 | 27.25 | 19.52 | 35.09 | 23.08 | 28.22 | 44.83 | 336.54 | 366.12 | 118.82 | 179.58 | 217.44 |
| Sec.Ot.th.Shares Excl.f/Brd.Money.... | 26s | † 2.65 | — | — | .48 | 7.05 | 1.33 | 1.85 | 1.55 | 7.73 | .88 | — | — |
| Loans................... | 26l | † — | — | .37 | 6.64 | 13.27 | 3.54 | — | 22.43 | 18.10 | 17.98 | 29.62 | 47.50 |
| Financial Derivatives................... | 26m | † — | — | — | — | — | — | — | — | — | — | — | — |
| Insurance Technical Reserves........... | 26r | † — | — | — | — | — | — | — | — | — | — | — | — |
| Shares and Other Equity................... | 27a | † 923.54 | 1,164.07 | 1,490.35 | 2,241.95 | 3,728.10 | 4,639.03 | 5,612.87 | 5,954.88 | 8,522.58 | 10,285.49 | 12,132.07 | 14,497.33 |
| Other Items (Net)................... | 27r | † 105.66 | −143.25 | 1.72 | −292.59 | −358.45 | −308.99 | −228.81 | −282.09 | −387.36 | 77.64 | −562.41 | −749.05 |
| Memo Item: | | | | | | | | | | | | | |
| Total Assets................... | 20ra | † 4,823.36 | 5,703.54 | 7,962.97 | 13,514.92 | 17,241.43 | 21,343.57 | 26,214.34 | 28,702.06 | 44,371.27 | 51,959.07 | 66,320.10 | 80,961.96 |

# Cambodia 522

| | | 2004 | 2005 | 2006 | 2007 | 2008 | 2009 | 2010 | 2011 | 2012 | 2013 | 2014 | 2015 |
|---|---|---|---|---|---|---|---|---|---|---|---|---|---|
| **Depository Corporations** | | *Billions of Riels: End of Period* | | | | | | | | | | | |
| Net Foreign Assets.......................... | 31n | † 4,725.26 | 5,399.34 | 7,215.26 | 10,541.18 | 10,136.44 | 14,346.11 | 16,885.01 | 17,463.05 | 20,670.17 | 20,453.94 | 24,723.19 | 24,814.43 |
| Claims on Nonresidents................ | 31 | † 5,485.19 | 6,142.13 | 7,705.76 | 11,779.48 | 12,780.36 | 16,377.66 | 19,178.06 | 20,551.04 | 27,258.00 | 27,812.78 | 33,510.96 | 38,476.58 |
| Liabilities to Nonresidents............. | 36c | † 759.93 | 742.79 | 490.50 | 1,238.30 | 2,643.92 | 2,031.55 | 2,293.06 | 3,087.99 | 6,587.84 | 7,358.84 | 8,787.77 | 13,662.15 |
| Domestic Claims............................. | 32 | † 1,710.60 | 1,860.40 | 2,645.89 | 4,521.18 | 6,810.41 | 8,242.94 | 10,696.48 | 12,579.47 | 19,179.75 | 24,704.14 | 31,956.15 | 39,608.38 |
| Net Claims on Central Government | 32an | † −236.71 | −474.04 | −958.77 | −1,875.01 | −3,061.23 | −2,378.29 | −2,313.69 | −2,253.60 | −2,810.47 | −3,220.63 | −4,861.65 | −7,036.76 |
| Claims on Central Government.... | 32a | † 374.70 | 341.27 | 305.40 | 307.19 | 277.37 | 278.74 | 276.05 | 278.26 | 283.17 | 281.72 | 287.69 | 295.21 |
| Liabilities to Central Government. | 36d | † 611.41 | 815.31 | 1,264.16 | 2,182.20 | 3,338.60 | 2,657.02 | 2,589.75 | 2,531.86 | 3,093.64 | 3,502.35 | 5,149.33 | 7,331.97 |
| Claims on Other Sectors................. | 32s | † 1,947.31 | 2,334.44 | 3,604.65 | 6,396.19 | 9,871.64 | 10,621.23 | 13,010.17 | 14,833.07 | 21,990.22 | 27,924.77 | 36,817.80 | 46,645.14 |
| Claims on Other Financial Corps.. | 32g | † 12.44 | 22.68 | 22.93 | 15.06 | 26.00 | 31.98 | 42.98 | 121.98 | 26.23 | 85.48 | 166.02 | 309.68 |
| Claims on State & Local Govts..... | 32b | † .08 | — | — | — | — | — | — | — | — | — | — | .01 |
| Claims on Public Nonfin. Corps.... | 32c | † — | — | 2.09 | 1.18 | .18 | — | 1.77 | — | 5.57 | 14.70 | 11.16 | 4.47 |
| Claims on Private Sector.............. | 32d | † 1,934.79 | 2,311.76 | 3,579.64 | 6,379.96 | 9,845.45 | 10,589.24 | 12,965.42 | 14,711.08 | 21,958.42 | 27,824.59 | 36,640.62 | 46,330.99 |
| Broad Money Liabilities................... | 35l | † 4,284.83 | 4,962.54 | 6,974.65 | 11,287.53 | 11,902.26 | 16,137.41 | 19,574.66 | 20,345.51 | 28,363.73 | 32,900.87 | 42,652.60 | 49,097.07 |
| Currency Outside Depository Corps | 34a | † 1,132.45 | 1,283.79 | 1,603.11 | 1,997.17 | 2,305.00 | 3,008.57 | 3,103.56 | 3,782.27 | 3,777.63 | 4,487.94 | 5,645.45 | 5,941.85 |
| Transferable Deposits.................... | 34 | † 1,521.18 | 1,633.42 | 2,421.05 | 2,155.05 | 2,241.74 | 2,572.67 | 3,030.17 | 2,963.72 | 5,119.95 | 7,226.00 | 8,633.46 | 9,141.33 |
| Other Deposits.............................. | 35 | † 1,631.21 | 2,045.34 | 2,950.49 | 7,135.32 | 7,355.51 | 10,556.17 | 13,440.93 | 13,599.53 | 19,466.16 | 21,186.93 | 28,373.69 | 34,013.89 |
| Securities Other than Shares.......... | 36a | † — | | | | | | | | | | | |
| Deposits Excl. from Broad Money..... | 36b | † 15.89 | 27.25 | 19.52 | 35.09 | 23.08 | 28.22 | 44.83 | 336.54 | 367.24 | 119.86 | 180.54 | 218.24 |
| Sec.Ot.th.Shares Excl.f/Brd.Money.... | 36s | † 2.65 | — | — | .48 | 7.05 | 1.33 | 1.85 | 1.55 | 7.73 | .88 | — | 44.76 |
| Loans..................................... | 36l | † — | — | .37 | 6.64 | 13.27 | 3.54 | — | 22.43 | 18.10 | 17.98 | 29.62 | 47.50 |
| Financial Derivatives...................... | 36m | † — | — | — | — | — | — | — | — | — | — | — | — |
| Insurance Technical Reserves.......... | 36r | † — | | | | | | | | | | | |
| Shares and Other Equity.................. | 37a | † 2,081.16 | 2,569.29 | 3,140.25 | 4,229.02 | 5,784.33 | 7,244.39 | 8,492.00 | 8,991.86 | 11,730.42 | 12,459.59 | 14,245.01 | 16,046.21 |
| Other Items (Net)............................ | 37r | † 51.33 | −299.34 | −273.64 | −496.40 | −783.14 | −825.86 | −531.87 | 344.64 | −637.31 | −341.09 | −428.43 | −1,030.96 |
| Broad Money Liabs., Seasonally Adj. | 35l.b | † 4,329.05 | 5,011.44 | 7,045.07 | 11,403.76 | 12,038.69 | 16,334.83 | 19,823.40 | 20,582.21 | 28,620.82 | 33,093.77 | 42,780.19 | 49,164.37 |
| **Monetary Aggregates** | | *Billions of Riels: End of Period* | | | | | | | | | | | |
| Broad Money................................. | 59m | 4,284.83 | 4,962.54 | 6,974.65 | 11,287.53 | 11,902.26 | 16,137.41 | 19,574.66 | 20,345.51 | 28,363.73 | 32,900.87 | 42,652.60 | 49,097.07 |
| o/w:Currency Issued by Cent.Govt | 59m.a | — | — | — | — | — | — | — | — | — | — | — | — |
| o/w: Dep.in Nonfin. Corporations. | 59m.b | — | — | — | — | — | — | — | — | — | — | — | — |
| o/w:Secs. Issued by Central Govt.. | 59m.c | — | — | — | — | — | — | — | — | — | — | — | — |
| Money (National Definitions) | | | | | | | | | | | | | |
| M1.................................................. | 59ma | 1,153.39 | 1,308.41 | 1,653.47 | 2,043.22 | 2,387.87 | 3,093.07 | 3,199.79 | 3,900.85 | 3,975.26 | 4,768.94 | 6,038.22 | 6,488.57 |
| M2.................................................. | 59mb | 4,284.83 | 4,962.54 | 6,974.65 | 11,287.53 | 11,902.26 | 16,137.41 | 19,574.66 | 20,345.51 | 28,363.73 | 32,900.87 | 42,652.60 | 49,097.07 |
| **Interest Rates** | | *Percent Per Annum* | | | | | | | | | | | |
| Deposit Rate.................................... | 60l | 1.79 | 1.92 | 1.84 | 1.90 | 1.91 | 1.66 | 1.26 | 1.34 | 1.33 | 1.34 | 1.42 | 1.42 |
| Lending Rate (Fgn. Currency)........... | 60p.f | 17.62 | 17.33 | 16.40 | 16.18 | 16.01 | 15.81 | 15.63 | 15.22 | 12.97 | 12.80 | 12.31 | 11.71 |
| **Prices and Labor** | | *Index Numbers (2010=100): Period Averages* | | | | | | | | | | | |
| Consumer Prices.............................. | 64 | 63.7 | 67.8 | 71.9 | 77.4 | 96.8 | 96.2 | 100.0 | 105.5 | 108.6 | 111.8 | 116.1 | 117.5 |
| | | *Number in Thousands: Period Averages* | | | | | | | | | | | |
| Labor Force..................................... | 67d | . . . . | . . . . | . . . . | . . . . | . . . . | . . . . | . . . . | . . . . | . . . . | . . . . | . . . . | . . . . |
| **Intl. Transactions & Positions** | | *Millions of US Dollars* | | | | | | | | | | | |
| Exports............................................ | 70..d | 2,798 | 3,200 | 3,800 | 4,400 | 4,708 | 4,196 | 5,143 | 6,950 | 8,200 | 9,100 | 10,800 | 11,960 |
| Imports, c.i.f.................................... | 71..d | 3,193 | 3,927 | 4,749 | 5,300 | 6,508 | 5,830 | 6,791 | 9,300 | 11,000 | 13,000 | 13,500 | 14,400 |

# Cambodia  522

| | | 2004 | 2005 | 2006 | 2007 | 2008 | 2009 | 2010 | 2011 | 2012 | 2013 | 2014 | 2015 |
|---|---|---|---|---|---|---|---|---|---|---|---|---|---|
| **Balance of Payments** | | | | | | ***Millions of US Dollars*** | | | | | | | |
| A. Current Account* | 109bx | −182.9 | † −321.2 | −239.9 | −425.7 | −819.9 | −397.8 | −410.1 | −475.4 | −1,037.9 | −1,607.4 | −1,656.7 | .... |
| Goods, credit (exports) | 1a9cx | 2,588.9 | † 2,908.0 | 3,692.4 | 3,247.8 | 3,493.1 | 3,147.9 | 3,938.5 | 5,034.6 | 5,632.8 | 6,530.2 | 7,445.2 | .... |
| Goods, debit (imports) | 1a9dx | 3,269.5 | † 3,932.4 | 4,777.4 | 4,518.4 | 5,076.7 | 4,624.8 | 5,502.2 | 6,937.3 | 8,088.5 | 9,488.6 | 10,669.2 | .... |
| Balance on goods | 1a9bx | −680.6 | † −1,024.5 | −1,085.0 | −1,270.6 | −1,583.6 | −1,476.9 | −1,563.6 | −1,902.7 | −2,455.7 | −2,958.4 | −3,223.9 | .... |
| Services, credit (exports) | 1b9cx | 804.9 | † 1,118.0 | 1,324.6 | 1,432.9 | 1,527.4 | 1,811.9 | 2,028.5 | 2,730.1 | 3,192.1 | 3,486.0 | 3,810.9 | .... |
| Services, debit (imports) | 1b9dx | 514.4 | † 641.7 | 803.9 | 816.8 | 900.1 | 830.2 | 969.9 | 1,314.2 | 1,535.2 | 1,757.0 | 1,881.5 | .... |
| Balance on Goods & Services | 1z9bx | −390.1 | † −548.2 | −564.2 | −654.5 | −956.3 | −495.3 | −505.1 | −486.8 | −798.7 | −1,229.4 | −1,294.5 | .... |
| Primary income: credit | 1c9cx | 48.6 | † 67.7 | 90.0 | 112.2 | 108.2 | 55.5 | 58.7 | 61.3 | 67.6 | 70.8 | 132.2 | .... |
| Primary income: debit | 1c9dx | 269.6 | † 361.1 | 396.1 | 476.2 | 583.0 | 526.1 | 602.9 | 630.0 | 719.1 | 829.2 | 1,087.4 | .... |
| Balance on gds, serv. & prim. inc. | 1y9bx | −611.1 | † −841.6 | −870.4 | −1,018.4 | −1,431.1 | −965.8 | −1,049.3 | −1,055.5 | −1,450.3 | −1,987.8 | −2,249.7 | .... |
| Secondary income: credit | 1d9ca | 443.7 | † 541.1 | 655.0 | 618.5 | 639.1 | 592.8 | 663.9 | 605.9 | 499.5 | 502.6 | 734.4 | .... |
| Secondary income: debit | 1d9da | 15.5 | † 20.7 | 24.5 | 25.8 | 27.9 | 24.7 | 24.7 | 25.8 | 87.2 | 122.2 | 141.5 | .... |
| B. Capital Account* | 209ba | 111.3 | † 82.6 | 295.0 | 258.3 | 232.7 | 311.6 | 331.0 | 222.1 | 276.5 | 342.0 | 277.6 | .... |
| Capital account: credit | 209ca | 111.3 | † 138.1 | 348.1 | 325.6 | 292.5 | 367.8 | 418.4 | 305.3 | 366.3 | 342.0 | 277.6 | .... |
| Capital account: debit | 209da | — | † 55.5 | 53.2 | 67.2 | 59.8 | 56.2 | 87.4 | 83.2 | 89.8 | — | — | .... |
| Balance on current & capital acct. | 129ba | −71.6 | † −238.6 | 55.0 | −167.4 | −587.1 | −86.2 | −79.1 | −253.3 | −761.4 | −1,265.4 | −1,379.1 | .... |
| C. Financial Account* | 309na | −219.1 | † −310.8 | −213.5 | −632.8 | −1,154.2 | −211.7 | −256.0 | −609.5 | −1,179.8 | −1,665.6 | −2,165.0 | .... |
| Direct investment: assets | 3a9aa | 10.2 | † 4.3 | 8.4 | 1.1 | 20.5 | 18.9 | 20.6 | 29.2 | 36.2 | 46.3 | 31.9 | .... |
| Equity & investment fund shares | 3aaaa | 10.2 | † 6.3 | 8.4 | 1.1 | 20.5 | 18.9 | 20.6 | 29.2 | 36.2 | 46.3 | 31.9 | .... |
| Debt instruments | 3abaa | — | † −2.0 | | | | | | | | | | |
| Direct investment: liabilities | 3a9la | 131.4 | † 377.2 | 483.2 | 867.3 | 815.2 | 511.1 | 735.2 | 795.5 | 1,441.0 | 1,345.0 | 1,730.4 | .... |
| Equity & investment fund shares | 3aala | 131.4 | † 379.2 | 483.2 | 867.3 | 815.2 | 511.1 | 735.2 | 795.5 | 1,441.0 | 1,345.0 | 1,730.4 | .... |
| Debt instruments | 3abla | — | † −2.0 | .... | .... | .... | .... | .... | .... | .... | .... | .... | .... |
| Portfolio investment: assets | 3b9aa | 8.0 | † 4.9 | 7.6 | 6.3 | 11.6 | 7.6 | 36.7 | 6.1 | 34.2 | 18.8 | 19.7 | .... |
| Equity & investment fund shares | 3baaa | 8.0 | † 7.2 | 8.2 | 6.5 | 11.6 | 7.6 | 9.4 | 11.7 | 13.7 | 16.5 | 13.2 | .... |
| Debt securities | 3bbaa | — | † −2.3 | −.6 | −.1 | — | — | 27.2 | −5.6 | 20.5 | 2.3 | 6.5 | .... |
| Portfolio investment: liabilities | 3b9la | — | .... | .... | .... | .... | .... | .... | .... | .... | .... | .... | .... |
| Equity & investment fund shares | 3bala | — | .... | .... | .... | .... | .... | .... | .... | .... | .... | .... | .... |
| Debt securities | 3bbla | — | .... | .... | .... | .... | .... | .... | .... | .... | .... | .... | .... |
| Fin. der.& empl.stk.ops.(ESOs): net. | 3c9na | — | .... | .... | .... | .... | .... | .... | .... | .... | .... | .... | .... |
| Fin. der. & ESOs.: assets | 3c9aa | — | .... | .... | .... | .... | .... | .... | .... | .... | .... | .... | .... |
| Fin. der. & ESOs.: liabilities | 3c9la | — | .... | .... | .... | .... | .... | .... | .... | .... | .... | .... | .... |
| Other investment: assets | 3d9aa | 91.3 | † 327.2 | 539.6 | 733.1 | 126.8 | 516.5 | 897.6 | 918.3 | 2,150.8 | 963.4 | 873.9 | .... |
| Other equity | 3daaa | .... | .... | .... | .... | .... | .... | .... | .... | .... | .... | .... | .... |
| Debt instruments | 3dzaa | 91.3 | † 327.2 | 539.6 | 733.1 | 126.8 | 516.5 | 897.6 | 918.3 | 2,150.8 | 963.4 | 873.9 | .... |
| Other investment: liabilities | 3d9la | 197.2 | † 270.0 | 285.8 | 506.0 | 497.9 | 243.6 | 475.6 | 767.6 | 1,959.9 | 1,349.1 | 1,360.1 | .... |
| Other equity | 3dala | .... | .... | .... | .... | .... | .... | .... | .... | .... | .... | .... | .... |
| Debt instruments | 3dzla | 197.2 | † 270.0 | 285.8 | 506.0 | 497.9 | 243.6 | 475.6 | 767.6 | 1,959.9 | 1,349.1 | 1,360.1 | .... |
| Curr.+ cap.− finan. acct. balance | 4y9na | 147.4 | † 72.2 | 268.5 | 465.4 | 567.1 | 125.5 | 176.9 | 356.2 | 418.3 | 400.2 | 785.9 | .... |
| D. Net Errors and Omissions | 409na | −89.0 | † 2.2 | −65.4 | −42.2 | −44.7 | −23.3 | −26.6 | −47.4 | −42.9 | −48.4 | −31.5 | .... |
| E. Reserves and Related Items | 4z9na | 58.5 | † 74.5 | 203.1 | 423.2 | 522.4 | 102.2 | 150.3 | 308.7 | 375.4 | 351.8 | 754.4 | .... |
| Reserve assets | 3e9aa | 61.0 | † 78.4 | 133.7 | 436.0 | 535.2 | 115.0 | 163.0 | 321.5 | 388.2 | 362.6 | 754.7 | .... |
| Credit and loans from the IMF. | 3dcla | −10.3 | † −8.8 | −82.2 | — | — | — | — | 1 | — | — | — | .... |
| Exceptional financing | 409la | 12.8 | † 12.8 | 12.8 | 12.8 | 12.8 | 12.8 | 12.8 | 12.8 | 12.8 | 10.8 | .3 | .... |
| *Excludes components in group E | | | | | | | | | | | | | |
| | | | | | | | | | | | | | |
| **International Investment Position** | | | | | | ***Millions of US Dollars*** | | | | | | | |
| Assets | 809aa | 3,558.4 | 4,033.4 | † 4,518.2 | 5,813.8 | 6,530.4 | 7,358.6 | 8,591.7 | 9,883.0 | 12,581.1 | 13,710.4 | 17,294.2 | .... |
| Direct investment | 8a9aa | 255.6 | 267.0 | † 279.0 | 283.8 | 308.0 | 325.6 | 349.9 | 382.8 | 422.7 | 472.7 | 519.8 | .... |
| Equity & investment fund shares.. | 8aaaa | 255.6 | 267.0 | † 279.0 | 283.8 | 308.0 | 325.6 | 349.9 | 382.8 | 422.7 | 472.7 | 519.8 | .... |
| Debt instruments | 8abaa | .... | .... | .... | .... | .... | .... | .... | .... | .... | .... | .... | .... |
| Portfolio investment | 8b9aa | 270.3 | 286.4 | † 313.0 | 332.4 | 345.6 | 355.2 | 395.5 | 406.1 | 446.0 | 470.5 | 496.8 | .... |
| Equity & investment fund shares.. | 8baaa | 243.3 | 257.8 | † 281.6 | 299.1 | 311.1 | 319.7 | 331.4 | 346.0 | 363.5 | 383.5 | 401.2 | .... |
| Debt securities | 8bbaa | 27.0 | 28.6 | † 31.4 | 33.3 | 34.6 | 35.5 | 64.1 | 60.1 | 82.5 | 87.0 | 95.5 | .... |
| Fin. der.(oth.than reserves) & ESOs | 8c9aa | .... | .... | .... | .... | .... | .... | .... | .... | .... | .... | .... | .... |
| Other investment | 8d9aa | 2,096.8 | 2,438.2 | † 2,829.4 | 3,582.1 | 3,713.2 | 4,310.6 | 5,193.1 | 6,062.5 | 8,249.4 | 9,124.7 | 11,886.2 | .... |
| Other equity | 8daaa | .... | .... | .... | .... | .... | .... | .... | .... | .... | .... | .... | .... |
| Debt instruments | 8dzaa | 2,096.8 | 2,438.2 | † 2,829.4 | 3,582.1 | 3,713.2 | 4,310.6 | 5,193.1 | 6,062.5 | 8,249.4 | 9,124.7 | 11,886.2 | .... |
| Reserve assets | 8e9aa | 935.7 | 1,041.7 | † 1,096.7 | 1,615.6 | 2,163.5 | 2,367.3 | 2,653.2 | 3,031.6 | 3,463.0 | 3,642.5 | 4,391.5 | .... |
| Liabilities | 809la | 4,481.7 | 5,127.6 | † 5,997.5 | 7,131.8 | 8,457.0 | 9,290.9 | 10,521.1 | 12,060.3 | 15,445.0 | 17,984.0 | 22,935.8 | .... |
| Direct investment | 8a9la | 2,089.8 | 2,471.0 | † 2,954.2 | 3,821.5 | 4,636.7 | 5,130.4 | 5,865.6 | 6,661.1 | 8,102.1 | 9,447.1 | 12,936.6 | .... |
| Equity & investment fund shares.. | 8aala | 1,414.1 | 1,793.3 | † 2,276.5 | 3,143.8 | 3,959.0 | 4,452.7 | 5,187.9 | 5,983.4 | 7,424.3 | 8,769.4 | 12,510.3 | .... |
| Debt instruments | 8abla | 675.7 | 677.7 | † 677.7 | 677.7 | 677.7 | 677.7 | 677.7 | 677.7 | 677.7 | 677.7 | 426.2 | .... |
| Portfolio investment | 8b9la | .... | .... | .... | .... | .... | .... | .... | .... | .... | .... | .... | .... |
| Equity & investment fund shares.. | 8bala | .... | .... | .... | .... | .... | .... | .... | .... | .... | .... | .... | .... |
| Debt securities | 8bbla | .... | .... | .... | .... | .... | .... | .... | .... | .... | .... | .... | .... |
| Fin. der.(oth.than reserves) & ESOs | 8c9la | .... | .... | .... | .... | .... | .... | .... | .... | .... | .... | .... | .... |
| Other investment | 8d9la | 2,391.9 | 2,656.6 | † 3,043.3 | 3,310.3 | 3,820.3 | 4,160.4 | 4,655.5 | 5,399.2 | 7,343.0 | 8,536.9 | 9,999.3 | .... |
| Other equity | 8dala | .... | .... | .... | .... | .... | .... | .... | .... | .... | .... | .... | .... |
| Debt instruments | 8dzla | 2,391.9 | 2,656.6 | † 3,043.3 | 3,310.3 | 3,820.3 | 4,160.4 | 4,655.5 | 5,399.2 | 7,343.0 | 8,536.9 | 9,999.3 | .... |

# Cambodia 522

2016, International Monetary Fund : *International Financial Statistics Yearbook*

| | | 2004 | 2005 | 2006 | 2007 | 2008 | 2009 | 2010 | 2011 | 2012 | 2013 | 2014 | 2015 |
|---|---|---|---|---|---|---|---|---|---|---|---|---|---|
| **Government Finance Operations Statement** | | | | | | | | | | | | | |
| **Central Government** | | | | | | *Billions of Riels: Fiscal Year Ends December 31* | | | | | | | |
| Revenue | a1 | 2,497.4 | 3,134.5 | 3,398.5 | 4,674.3 | 6,199.8 | 6,532.4 | 7,770.5 | 7,873.9 | 8,699.1 | 10,703.2 | 12,908.6 | 13,208.2 |
| Taxes | a11 | 1,740.2 | 2,032.8 | 2,441.3 | 3,398.0 | 4,429.8 | 4,154.0 | 4,706.2 | 5,287.4 | 6,571.1 | 7,407.6 | 9,863.7 | 10,402.7 |
| Social Contributions | a12 | — | — | — | — | — | — | — | — | — | — | — | — |
| Grants | a13 | 392.4 | 646.5 | 474.7 | 753.8 | 945.5 | 1,860.8 | 2,373.8 | 1,858.9 | 1,240.3 | 2,273.9 | 1,728.3 | 1,507.5 |
| Other Revenue | a14 | 364.9 | 455.1 | 482.5 | 522.4 | 824.4 | 517.5 | 690.5 | 727.6 | 887.6 | 1,021.6 | 1,316.6 | 1,297.9 |
| Expense | a2 | 1,753.7 | 1,955.0 | 2,563.2 | 2,873.9 | 3,592.5 | 4,721.5 | 5,002.5 | 5,754.3 | 6,637.4 | 7,246.5 | 8,397.7 | 8,514.8 |
| Compensation of Employees | a21 | 639.7 | 711.0 | 846.6 | 1,058.2 | 1,396.9 | 1,788.3 | 1,788.3 | 1,922.2 | 2,215.8 | 2,636.3 | 3,313.2 | 3,720.8 |
| Use of Goods & Services | a22 | 717.1 | 782.9 | 1,046.9 | 1,129.4 | 1,166.9 | 1,510.9 | 1,558.9 | 1,673.2 | 1,943.9 | 2,075.3 | 2,118.7 | 2,025.2 |
| Consumption of Fixed Capital | a23 | .... | .... | .... | .... | .... | .... | .... | .... | .... | .... | .... | .... |
| Interest | a24 | 48.6 | 55.2 | 50.0 | 69.7 | 76.1 | 86.3 | 109.3 | 139.2 | 168.6 | 204.3 | 228.3 | 217.4 |
| Subsidies | a25 | 63.8 | 85.4 | 137.3 | 41.6 | 204.3 | 28.6 | 112.8 | 163.0 | 240.5 | 130.1 | 323.8 | 20.7 |
| Grants | a26 | 114.0 | 127.4 | 166.1 | 200.5 | 229.4 | 306.3 | 472.7 | 588.0 | 677.2 | 682.3 | 727.2 | 977.0 |
| Social Benefits | a27 | 141.2 | 151.6 | 187.4 | 280.6 | 451.2 | 526.8 | 624.8 | 675.3 | 843.6 | 878.7 | 917.5 | 986.5 |
| Other Expense | a28 | 29.3 | 41.3 | 128.9 | 93.9 | 67.8 | 474.3 | 335.8 | 593.5 | 547.8 | 639.5 | 769.1 | 567.1 |
| Gross Operating Balance [1-2+23] | agob | 743.8 | 1,179.5 | 835.4 | 1,800.4 | 2,607.2 | 1,810.9 | 2,768.0 | 2,119.6 | 2,061.7 | 3,456.7 | 4,510.9 | 4,693.3 |
| Net Operating Balance [1-2] | anob | .... | .... | .... | .... | .... | .... | .... | .... | .... | .... | .... | .... |
| Net Acq. of Nonfinancial Assets | a31 | 1,206.3 | 1,169.1 | 1,346.8 | 2,082.3 | 2,736.5 | 3,764.7 | 4,427.5 | 4,496.0 | 4,541.0 | 5,373.5 | 5,404.5 | 5,260.1 |
| Aquisition of Nonfin. Assets | a31.1 | .... | .... | .... | 464.0 | 2,617.2 | 3,786.7 | 4,520.7 | 4,553.1 | 4,590.5 | 5,474.9 | 5,478.8 | 5,260.1 |
| Disposal of Nonfin. Assets | a31.2 | .... | .... | .... | 87.1 | — | 22.1 | 93.2 | 57.1 | 49.4 | 101.2 | 74.3 | — |
| Net Lending/Borrowing [1-2-31] | anlb | −462.5 | 10.4 | −511.4 | −281.9 | −129.3 | −1,953.8 | −1,659.5 | −2,376.4 | −2,479.4 | −1,916.8 | −893.6 | −566.8 |
| Net Acq. of Financial Assets | a32 | −37.6 | 162.6 | −263.3 | 1,296.9 | 1,045.7 | −870.1 | −147.9 | −315.1 | −340.2 | 112.7 | 1,568.2 | 1,968.5 |
| By instrument | | | | | | | | | | | | | |
| Monetary Gold & SDRs | a3201 | — | — | — | — | — | — | — | — | — | — | — | — |
| Currency & Deposits | a3202 | −37.6 | 162.6 | 74.0 | 1,297.9 | 1,071.7 | −698.4 | −51.7 | −350.0 | −111.2 | −83.2 | 1,679.3 | 2,059.3 |
| Securities other than Shares | a3203 | — | — | — | — | — | — | — | — | — | — | — | — |
| Loans | a3204 | — | — | — | — | — | −29.3 | 75.1 | 121.9 | −143.5 | 17.7 | −111.1 | −90.7 |
| Shares & Other Equity | a3205 | — | — | — | −1.0 | −26.0 | −142.4 | −171.3 | −86.9 | −85.4 | −.3 | — | — |
| Insurance Technical Reserves | a3206 | — | — | — | — | — | — | — | — | — | — | — | — |
| Financial Derivatives | a3207 | — | — | — | — | — | — | — | — | — | — | — | — |
| Other Accounts Receivable | a3208 | — | — | −337.3 | — | — | — | — | — | — | — | — | — |
| By debtor | | | | | | | | | | | | | |
| Domestic | a321 | −37.6 | 162.6 | −263.3 | 1,296.9 | 1,045.7 | −870.1 | −147.9 | −315.1 | −340.2 | 112.7 | 1,568.2 | 1,968.5 |
| Foreign | a322 | — | — | — | — | — | — | — | — | — | — | — | — |
| Net Incurrence of Liabilities | a33 | 451.7 | 137.3 | 541.2 | 1,578.3 | 1,176.9 | 1,083.7 | 1,511.6 | 2,061.3 | 2,139.2 | 2,029.5 | 2,461.9 | 2,535.3 |
| By instrument | | | | | | | | | | | | | |
| Special Drawing Rights (SDRs) | a3301 | — | — | — | — | — | — | — | — | — | — | — | — |
| Currency & Deposits | a3302 | −129.5 | −83.2 | −22.6 | 346.1 | 119.6 | — | — | — | — | — | — | — |
| Securities other than Shares | a3303 | — | −34.0 | −15.9 | — | — | — | — | — | — | — | — | — |
| Loans | a3304 | 521.4 | 414.7 | 514.6 | 1,061.1 | 1,411.5 | 1,012.0 | 1,039.7 | 1,783.9 | 2,409.9 | 1,910.8 | 2,306.0 | 2,250.5 |
| Shares & Other Equity | a3305 | — | — | 109.2 | — | — | — | — | — | — | — | — | — |
| Insurance Technical Reserves | a3306 | — | — | — | — | — | — | — | — | — | — | — | — |
| Financial Derivatives | a3307 | — | — | — | — | — | — | — | — | — | — | — | — |
| Other Accounts Payable | a3308 | 59.8 | −160.1 | −44.2 | 171.2 | −354.3 | 71.6 | 471.9 | 277.4 | −270.7 | −177.2 | 155.9 | 284.8 |
| By creditor | | | | | | | | | | | | | |
| Domestic | a331 | −69.7 | −277.3 | −79.7 | 521.3 | −233.0 | 71.7 | 471.9 | 277.3 | −270.7 | −159.6 | 155.9 | 284.8 |
| Foreign | a332 | 521.4 | 414.7 | 620.9 | 1,057.0 | 1,409.9 | 1,012.0 | 1,039.7 | 1,784.0 | 2,409.9 | 2,189.1 | 2,306.0 | 2,250.5 |
| Stat. Discrepancy [32-33-NLB] | anlbz | −26.8 | 14.9 | −293.1 | .5 | −1.9 | | | | | | | |
| Memo Item: Expenditure [2+31] | a2m | 2,960.0 | 3,124.1 | 3,910.0 | 4,956.2 | 6,329.0 | 8,486.1 | 9,430.0 | 10,250.3 | 11,178.4 | 12,620.0 | 13,802.2 | 13,774.9 |
| **National Accounts** | | | | | | *Billions of Riels* | | | | | | | |
| Househ.Cons.Expend.,incl.NPISHs | 96f | 18,251 | 21,709 | 24,167 | 27,385 | 33,341 | 32,792 | 35,384 | .... | .... | .... | .... | .... |
| Government Consumption Expend | 91f | 961 | 1,048 | 1,033 | 2,008 | 2,365 | 3,447 | 3,929 | .... | .... | .... | .... | .... |
| Gross Fixed Capital Formation | 93e | 3,932 | 4,864 | 5,775 | 6,928 | 7,247 | 8,670 | 7,531 | .... | .... | .... | .... | .... |
| Changes in Inventories | 93i | −110 | 347 | 947 | 500 | 566 | 566 | 566 | .... | .... | .... | .... | .... |
| Exports of Goods and Services | 90c | 13,636 | 16,505 | 20,475 | 22,892 | 27,507 | 25,805 | 31,084 | .... | .... | .... | .... | .... |
| Imports of Goods and Services (-) | 98c | 15,201 | 18,736 | 22,692 | 25,561 | 28,445 | 27,122 | 31,684 | .... | .... | .... | .... | .... |
| Statistical Discrepancy | 99bs | −30 | 16 | 146 | 890 | −613 | −1,092 | −868 | .... | .... | .... | .... | .... |
| Gross Domestic Product (GDP) | 99b | 21,438 | 25,754 | 29,849 | 35,042 | 41,968 | 43,057 | 47,048 | 52,069 | 56,682 | 61,327 | 67,740 | .... |
| GDP Volume 2000 Prices | 99b.p | 19,434 | 22,009 | 24,380 | 26,870 | 28,668 | 28,692 | 30,406 | 32,553 | 34,933 | 37,503 | 40,182 | .... |
| GDP Volume (2010=100) | 99bvp | 63.9 | 72.4 | 80.2 | 88.4 | 94.3 | 94.4 | 100.0 | 107.1 | 114.9 | 123.3 | 132.2 | .... |
| GDP Deflator (2010=100) | 99bip | 71.3 | 75.6 | 79.1 | 84.3 | 94.6 | 97.0 | 100.0 | 103.4 | 104.9 | 105.7 | 109.0 | .... |
| | | | | | | *Millions: Midyear Estimates* | | | | | | | |
| **Population** | 99z | 13.11 | 13.32 | 13.53 | 13.73 | 13.93 | 14.14 | 14.36 | 14.59 | 14.83 | 15.08 | 15.33 | 15.58 |

# Cameroon 622

| | | 2004 | 2005 | 2006 | 2007 | 2008 | 2009 | 2010 | 2011 | 2012 | 2013 | 2014 | 2015 |
|---|---|---|---|---|---|---|---|---|---|---|---|---|---|
| **Exchange Rates** | | *CFA Francs per SDR: End of Period* | | | | | | | | | | | |
| Official Rate.................................. | aa | 747.90 | 794.73 | 749.30 | 704.15 | 725.98 | 713.83 | 756.02 | 778.32 | 764.10 | 732.49 | 782.77 | 834.92 |
| | | *CFA Francs per US Dollar: End of Period (ae) Period Average (rf)* | | | | | | | | | | | |
| Official Rate.................................. | ae | 481.58 | 556.04 | 498.07 | 445.59 | 471.34 | 455.34 | 490.91 | 506.96 | 497.16 | 475.64 | 540.28 | 602.51 |
| Official Rate.................................. | rf | 528.28 | 527.47 | 522.89 | 479.27 | 447.81 | 472.19 | 495.28 | 471.87 | 510.53 | 494.04 | 494.41 | 591.45 |
| | | *Index Numbers (2010=100): Period Averages* | | | | | | | | | | | |
| Official Rate.................................. | ahx | 93.7 | 93.9 | 94.6 | 103.3 | 110.9 | 105.0 | 100.0 | 104.9 | 96.9 | 100.1 | 100.1 | 83.6 |
| Nominal Effective Exchange Rate..... | nec | 100.3 | 98.6 | 98.1 | 101.1 | 103.7 | 104.6 | 100.0 | 101.2 | 98.1 | 101.7 | 103.3 | 99.5 |
| CPI-Based Real Effect. Ex. Rate........ | rec | 101.5 | 98.9 | 100.3 | 101.3 | 104.4 | 106.7 | 100.0 | 100.2 | 96.7 | 99.5 | 100.8 | 97.8 |
| **Fund Position** | | *Millions of SDRs: End of Period* | | | | | | | | | | | |
| Quota........................................... | 2f.s | 185.70 | 185.70 | 185.70 | 185.70 | 185.70 | 185.70 | 185.70 | 185.70 | 185.70 | 185.70 | 185.70 | 185.70 |
| SDR Holdings................................ | 1b.s | .43 | 1.49 | 3.08 | 3.03 | 2.96 | 155.46 | 17.62 | 16.23 | 15.26 | 15.16 | 15.16 | 15.15 |
| Reserve Position in the Fund........... | 1c.s | .65 | .70 | .72 | .79 | .82 | .84 | .87 | .90 | .93 | .96 | .99 | 1.01 |
| Total Fund Cred.&Loans Outstg....... | 2tl | 214.69 | 190.32 | 5.30 | 10.60 | 15.90 | 111.42 | 111.42 | 110.63 | 109.04 | 106.65 | 103.20 | 80.92 |
| SDR Allocations............................. | 1bd | 24.46 | 24.46 | 24.46 | 24.46 | 24.46 | 177.27 | 177.27 | 177.27 | 177.27 | 177.27 | 177.27 | 177.27 |
| **International Liquidity** | | *Millions of US Dollars Unless Otherwise Indicated: End of Period* | | | | | | | | | | | |
| Total Reserves minus Gold.............. | 1l.d | 829.31 | 949.38 | 1,716.22 | 2,906.77 | 3,086.81 | 3,675.52 | 3,642.64 | 3,198.72 | 3,380.70 | 3,472.00 | 3,168.22 | 3,536.26 |
| SDR Holdings............................ | 1b.d | .67 | 2.13 | 4.63 | 4.79 | 4.56 | 243.71 | 27.13 | 24.92 | 23.45 | 23.34 | 21.96 | 21.00 |
| Reserve Position in the Fund......... | 1c.d | 1.01 | 1.00 | 1.08 | 1.24 | 1.26 | 1.32 | 1.34 | 1.38 | 1.42 | 1.49 | 1.44 | 1.39 |
| Foreign Exchange....................... | 1d.d | 827.63 | 946.25 | 1,710.51 | 2,900.73 | 3,080.99 | 3,430.49 | 3,614.17 | 3,172.42 | 3,355.83 | 3,447.17 | 3,144.82 | 3,513.86 |
| Gold (Million Fine Troy Ounces)........ | 1ad | .030 | .030 | .030 | .030 | .030 | .... | .... | .... | .... | .... | .... | .... |
| Gold (National Valuation)................ | 1and | 13.14 | 15.37 | 19.00 | 25.21 | 4.35 | — | 22.69 | 45.78 | 50.43 | .... | .... | .... |
| Central Bank: Other Assets.............. | 3..d | — | — | — | — | — | — | — | — | — | — | — | — |
| Central Bank: Other Liabs................ | 4..d | 7.84 | 6.61 | 7.93 | 7.70 | −.39 | 8.73 | 4.65 | 5.05 | 49.91 | 89.05 | 119.59 | 6.92 |
| Other Depository Corps.: Assets....... | 7a.d | 397.87 | 420.74 | 560.07 | 802.04 | 900.24 | 968.82 | 834.30 | 871.06 | 581.82 | 946.56 | 921.86 | 946.31 |
| Other Depository Corps.: Liabs......... | 7b.d | 155.55 | 209.94 | 203.46 | 296.74 | 244.30 | 272.35 | 283.05 | 453.98 | 422.65 | 663.41 | 509.66 | 506.93 |
| **Central Bank** | | *Billions of CFA Francs: End of Period* | | | | | | | | | | | |
| Net Foreign Assets........................... | 11n | 223.07 | 362.07 | 838.01 | 1,278.35 | 1,427.13 | 1,463.67 | 1,578.82 | 1,418.20 | 1,462.26 | 1,418.30 | 1,447.10 | 1,930.08 |
| Claims on Nonresidents................ | 11 | 405.71 | 536.44 | 864.26 | 1,306.47 | 1,456.25 | 1,673.72 | 1,799.36 | 1,644.84 | 1,705.83 | 1,668.62 | 1,731.26 | 2,149.82 |
| Liabilities to Nonresidents.......... | 16c | 182.64 | 174.37 | 26.25 | 28.12 | 29.12 | 210.05 | 220.53 | 226.63 | 243.58 | 250.32 | 284.16 | 219.73 |
| Claims on Other Depository Corps.... | 12e | | | | | | | | | 4.90 | 4.90 | 27.83 | 93.56 |
| Net Claims on Central Government.. | 12an | 319.90 | 202.57 | −87.50 | −264.74 | −441.45 | −363.52 | −302.31 | −191.54 | −115.50 | −159.52 | −72.49 | −419.19 |
| Claims on Central Government...... | 12a | 442.91 | 333.12 | 171.82 | 88.83 | 12.03 | 79.83 | 189.64 | 193.41 | 188.94 | 179.26 | 188.76 | 320.86 |
| Liabilities to Central Government... | 16d | 123.01 | 130.55 | 259.32 | 353.57 | 453.47 | 443.35 | 491.94 | 384.95 | 304.44 | 338.78 | 261.25 | 740.06 |
| Claims on Other Sectors................. | 12s | .17 | .23 | .36 | .32 | 2.23 | 2.65 | 3.28 | 6.05 | 6.62 | 6.77 | 6.78 | 7.61 |
| Claims on Other Financial Corps.... | 12g | .17 | .23 | .36 | .32 | .37 | .68 | .59 | .50 | .38 | .49 | .39 | .44 |
| Claims on State & Local Govts....... | 12b | — | — | — | — | — | — | — | — | — | — | — | — |
| Claims on Public Nonfin. Corps...... | 12c | — | — | — | — | — | — | — | — | — | — | — | — |
| Claims on Private Sector................ | 12d | — | — | — | — | 1.87 | 1.97 | 2.69 | 5.55 | 6.24 | 6.29 | 6.39 | 7.17 |
| Monetary Base............................... | 14 | 675.89 | 675.10 | 860.35 | 1,121.64 | 1,126.17 | 1,219.17 | 1,384.56 | 1,343.74 | 1,458.34 | 1,349.75 | 1,466.11 | 1,638.58 |
| Currency in Circulation.................. | 14a | 391.86 | 363.81 | 392.26 | 491.97 | 557.07 | 582.13 | 639.16 | 662.00 | 705.34 | 707.07 | 760.94 | 961.76 |
| Liabs. to Other Depository Corps.... | 14c | 282.41 | 309.11 | 446.43 | 609.53 | 557.37 | 633.38 | 741.03 | 678.90 | 750.72 | 640.97 | 703.24 | 673.19 |
| Liabilities to Other Sectors............. | 14d | 1.62 | 2.18 | 21.66 | 20.14 | 11.73 | 3.65 | 4.37 | 2.85 | 2.29 | 1.71 | 1.92 | 3.64 |
| Other Liabs. to Other Dep. Corps..... | 14n | — | — | — | — | — | — | — | — | — | — | — | — |
| Dep. & Sec. Excl. f/Monetary Base.... | 14o | — | — | — | — | — | — | — | — | — | — | — | — |
| Deposits Included in Broad Money. | 15 | — | — | — | — | — | — | — | — | — | — | — | — |
| Sec.Ot.th.Shares Incl.in Brd. Money | 16a | — | — | — | — | — | — | — | — | — | — | — | — |
| Deposits Excl. from Broad Money... | 16b | — | — | — | — | — | — | — | — | — | — | — | — |
| Sec.Ot.th.Shares Excl.f/Brd.Money.. | 16s | — | — | — | — | — | — | — | — | — | — | — | — |
| Loans........................................... | 16l | — | — | — | — | — | — | — | — | — | — | — | — |
| Financial Derivatives....................... | 16m | — | — | — | — | — | — | — | — | — | — | — | — |
| Shares and Other Equity................. | 17a | −135.05 | −112.10 | −109.11 | −111.19 | −132.39 | −125.03 | −125.96 | −125.55 | −121.72 | −119.92 | −121.99 | −115.32 |
| Other Items (Net).......................... | 17r | 2.30 | 1.87 | −.38 | 3.48 | −5.86 | 8.67 | 21.20 | 14.53 | 21.65 | 40.63 | 65.11 | 88.81 |
| Memo Item: | | | | | | | | | | | | | |
| Total Assets.................................... | 10ra | 890.15 | 911.53 | 1,077.94 | 1,440.36 | 1,511.78 | 1,795.49 | 2,034.20 | 1,886.16 | 1,946.27 | 1,896.60 | 1,994.96 | 2,617.10 |

# Cameroon   622

| | | 2004 | 2005 | 2006 | 2007 | 2008 | 2009 | 2010 | 2011 | 2012 | 2013 | 2014 | 2015 |
|---|---|---|---|---|---|---|---|---|---|---|---|---|---|
| **Other Depository Corporations** | | *Billions of CFA Francs: End of Period* | | | | | | | | | | | |
| Net Foreign Assets | 21n | 116.70 | 117.21 | 177.62 | 225.16 | 309.17 | 317.13 | 270.62 | 211.45 | 79.13 | 134.68 | 222.70 | 264.73 |
| Claims on Nonresidents | 21 | 191.60 | 233.95 | 278.95 | 357.38 | 424.32 | 441.14 | 409.57 | 441.60 | 289.26 | 450.22 | 498.06 | 570.16 |
| Liabilities to Nonresidents | 26c | 74.91 | 116.74 | 101.34 | 132.22 | 115.15 | 124.01 | 138.95 | 230.15 | 210.13 | 315.55 | 275.36 | 305.43 |
| Claims on Central Bank | 20 | 305.39 | 349.48 | 497.68 | 646.12 | 615.18 | 715.42 | 849.89 | 791.84 | 870.77 | 798.11 | 878.65 | 821.83 |
| Currency | 20a | 53.28 | 65.53 | 94.00 | 85.90 | 106.04 | 107.58 | 100.29 | 114.50 | 127.45 | 128.08 | 105.59 | 139.00 |
| Reserve Deposits and Securities | 20b | 252.12 | 283.95 | 403.68 | 560.22 | 509.14 | 607.84 | 749.60 | 677.34 | 743.32 | 670.03 | 773.06 | 682.83 |
| Other Claims | 20n | — | — | — | — | — | — | — | — | — | — | — | — |
| Net Claims on Central Government | 22an | 17.28 | 19.80 | −27.34 | −116.91 | −144.43 | −194.71 | −193.86 | −182.31 | −46.59 | 4.42 | −6.93 | −49.73 |
| Claims on Central Government | 22a | 154.37 | 150.28 | 155.99 | 134.85 | 118.07 | 123.91 | 139.43 | 168.08 | 311.69 | 401.25 | 421.44 | 451.76 |
| Liabilities to Central Government | 26d | 137.09 | 130.49 | 183.33 | 251.76 | 262.50 | 318.62 | 333.30 | 350.39 | 358.28 | 396.83 | 428.37 | 501.49 |
| Claims on Other Sectors | 22s | 884.70 | 982.59 | 989.24 | 1,064.06 | 1,283.11 | 1,421.76 | 1,695.30 | 2,038.48 | 2,095.47 | 2,410.00 | 2,649.09 | 3,010.91 |
| Claims on Other Financial Corps. | 22g | 8.76 | 19.25 | 9.12 | 7.86 | 7.23 | 18.49 | 113.89 | 140.73 | 75.89 | 110.76 | 60.96 | 67.81 |
| Claims on State & Local Govts. | 22b | — | — | — | — | — | — | — | — | — | — | — | — |
| Claims on Public Nonfin. Corps. | 22c | 102.03 | 98.97 | 92.69 | 107.33 | 135.63 | 138.35 | 117.15 | 124.03 | 114.87 | 146.39 | 128.18 | 196.37 |
| Claims on Private Sector | 22d | 773.91 | 864.37 | 887.43 | 948.88 | 1,140.25 | 1,264.92 | 1,464.26 | 1,773.72 | 1,904.71 | 2,152.85 | 2,459.96 | 2,746.74 |
| Liabilities to Central Bank | 26g | 2.50 | .59 | .01 | .02 | .55 | .75 | .19 | 1.72 | 4.90 | 5.07 | 27.83 | 97.58 |
| Transf.Dep.Included in Broad Money | 24 | 405.49 | 454.97 | 501.61 | 605.01 | 739.07 | 828.84 | 910.94 | 1,089.99 | 1,015.69 | 1,219.21 | 1,465.43 | 1,475.45 |
| Other Dep.Included in Broad Money. | 25 | 607.58 | 674.36 | 724.47 | 744.69 | 821.85 | 883.22 | 1,038.49 | 1,104.88 | 1,147.74 | 1,257.69 | 1,339.83 | 1,465.49 |
| Sec.Ot.th.Shares Incl.in Brd. Money. | 26a | — | — | — | — | — | — | — | — | — | — | — | — |
| Deposits Excl. from Broad Money | 26b | 29.45 | 22.44 | 22.36 | 19.49 | 16.97 | 15.62 | 23.50 | 16.41 | 19.72 | 24.37 | 15.35 | 22.61 |
| Sec.Ot.th.Shares Excl.f/Brd.Money. | 26s | — | — | — | — | — | — | — | — | — | — | — | — |
| Loans | 26l | — | — | — | — | — | — | — | — | — | — | — | 6.90 |
| Financial Derivatives | 26m | — | — | — | — | — | — | — | — | — | — | — | — |
| Insurance Technical Reserves | 26r | — | — | — | — | — | — | — | — | — | — | — | — |
| Shares and Other Equity | 27a | 200.87 | 211.33 | 229.33 | 237.35 | 259.92 | 251.08 | 298.41 | 264.92 | 307.44 | 394.67 | 444.35 | 479.40 |
| Other Items (Net) | 27r | 78.18 | 105.39 | 159.41 | 211.87 | 224.67 | 280.10 | 350.41 | 381.54 | 503.30 | 446.19 | 450.74 | 500.33 |
| Memo Item: | | | | | | | | | | | | | |
| Total Assets | 20ra | 1,702.17 | 1,885.14 | 2,088.54 | 2,377.58 | 2,623.31 | 2,882.18 | 3,362.78 | 3,721.40 | 3,818.62 | 4,371.53 | 4,771.77 | 5,224.86 |
| **Depository Corporations** | | *Billions of CFA Francs: End of Period* | | | | | | | | | | | |
| Net Foreign Assets | 31n | 339.77 | 479.28 | 1,015.62 | 1,503.51 | 1,736.30 | 1,780.80 | 1,849.44 | 1,629.65 | 1,541.39 | 1,552.98 | 1,669.81 | 2,194.82 |
| Claims on Nonresidents | 31 | 597.31 | 770.39 | 1,143.21 | 1,663.85 | 1,880.56 | 2,114.85 | 2,208.93 | 2,086.43 | 1,995.09 | 2,118.84 | 2,229.32 | 2,719.98 |
| Liabilities to Nonresidents | 36c | 257.55 | 291.11 | 127.59 | 160.35 | 144.27 | 334.05 | 359.49 | 456.78 | 453.70 | 565.87 | 559.52 | 525.16 |
| Domestic Claims | 32 | 1,222.05 | 1,205.19 | 874.75 | 682.73 | 699.47 | 866.19 | 1,202.41 | 1,670.68 | 1,940.00 | 2,261.67 | 2,576.45 | 2,549.61 |
| Net Claims on Central Government | 32an | 337.18 | 222.37 | −114.84 | −381.65 | −585.87 | −558.23 | −496.17 | −373.85 | −162.09 | −155.10 | −79.42 | −468.92 |
| Claims on Central Government | 32a | 597.28 | 483.41 | 327.81 | 223.68 | 130.10 | 203.74 | 329.07 | 361.49 | 500.63 | 580.51 | 610.20 | 772.63 |
| Liabilities to Central Government | 36d | 260.10 | 261.04 | 442.65 | 605.33 | 715.97 | 761.97 | 825.24 | 735.34 | 662.72 | 735.61 | 689.62 | 1,241.55 |
| Claims on Other Sectors | 32s | 884.87 | 982.82 | 989.60 | 1,064.38 | 1,285.34 | 1,424.42 | 1,698.58 | 2,044.53 | 2,102.09 | 2,416.77 | 2,655.87 | 3,018.53 |
| Claims on Other Financial Corps. | 32g | 8.93 | 19.48 | 9.48 | 8.18 | 7.60 | 19.18 | 114.48 | 141.23 | 76.27 | 111.25 | 61.35 | 68.25 |
| Claims on State & Local Govts. | 32b | — | — | — | — | — | — | — | — | — | — | — | — |
| Claims on Public Nonfin. Corps. | 32c | 102.03 | 98.97 | 92.69 | 107.33 | 135.63 | 138.35 | 117.15 | 124.03 | 114.87 | 146.39 | 128.18 | 196.37 |
| Claims on Private Sector | 32d | 773.91 | 864.37 | 887.43 | 948.88 | 1,142.12 | 1,266.89 | 1,466.95 | 1,779.27 | 1,910.94 | 2,159.14 | 2,466.35 | 2,753.91 |
| Broad Money Liabilities | 35l | 1,353.27 | 1,429.79 | 1,546.00 | 1,775.91 | 2,023.68 | 2,190.27 | 2,492.67 | 2,745.21 | 2,743.60 | 3,057.60 | 3,462.53 | 3,767.33 |
| Currency Outside Depository Corps | 34a | 338.59 | 298.29 | 298.26 | 406.07 | 451.03 | 474.56 | 538.87 | 547.50 | 577.89 | 578.99 | 655.35 | 822.76 |
| Transferable Deposits | 34 | 407.11 | 457.15 | 523.28 | 625.16 | 750.80 | 832.49 | 915.31 | 1,092.83 | 1,017.98 | 1,220.92 | 1,467.35 | 1,479.08 |
| Other Deposits | 35 | 607.58 | 674.36 | 724.47 | 744.69 | 821.85 | 883.22 | 1,038.49 | 1,104.88 | 1,147.74 | 1,257.69 | 1,339.83 | 1,465.49 |
| Securities Other than Shares | 36a | — | — | — | — | — | — | — | — | — | — | — | — |
| Deposits Excl. from Broad Money | 36b | 29.45 | 22.44 | 22.36 | 19.49 | 16.97 | 15.62 | 23.50 | 16.41 | 19.72 | 24.37 | 15.35 | 22.61 |
| Sec.Ot.th.Shares Excl.f/Brd.Money. | 36s | — | — | — | — | — | — | — | — | — | — | — | — |
| Loans | 36l | — | — | — | — | — | — | — | — | — | — | — | 6.90 |
| Financial Derivatives | 36m | — | — | — | — | — | — | — | — | — | — | — | — |
| Insurance Technical Reserves | 36r | — | — | — | — | — | — | — | — | — | — | — | — |
| Shares and Other Equity | 37a | 65.82 | 99.23 | 120.22 | 126.16 | 127.52 | 126.05 | 172.46 | 139.37 | 185.72 | 274.75 | 322.36 | 364.07 |
| Other Items (Net) | 37r | 113.27 | 133.01 | 201.80 | 264.68 | 267.58 | 315.06 | 363.22 | 399.34 | 532.34 | 457.93 | 446.03 | 583.51 |
| Broad Money Liabs., Seasonally Adj. | 35l.b | 1,305.61 | 1,381.55 | 1,496.17 | 1,720.26 | 1,961.87 | 2,125.20 | 2,421.60 | 2,669.54 | 2,669.61 | 2,975.74 | 3,369.71 | 3,665.50 |
| **Monetary Aggregates** | | *Billions of CFA Francs: End of Period* | | | | | | | | | | | |
| Broad Money | 59m | 1,353.27 | 1,429.79 | 1,546.00 | 1,775.91 | 2,023.68 | 2,190.27 | 2,492.67 | 2,745.21 | 2,743.60 | 3,057.60 | 3,462.53 | 3,767.33 |
| o/w:Currency Issued by Cent.Govt | 59m.a | — | — | — | — | — | — | — | — | — | — | — | — |
| o/w: Dep.in Nonfin. Corporations. | 59m.b | — | — | — | — | — | — | — | — | — | — | — | — |
| o/w:Secs. Issued by Central Govt. | 59m.c | — | — | — | — | — | — | — | — | — | — | — | — |
| Money (National Definitions) | | | | | | | | | | | | | |
| M1 | 59ma | 741.13 | 731.54 | 790.36 | 979.26 | 1,180.24 | 1,280.05 | 1,415.84 | 1,601.99 | 1,572.74 | 1,780.12 | 2,094.65 | 2,277.67 |
| M2 | 59mb | 1,348.35 | 1,382.17 | 1,484.27 | 1,674.68 | 1,983.17 | 2,136.27 | 2,415.99 | 2,706.87 | 2,720.48 | 3,037.81 | 3,434.47 | 3,743.15 |
| **Interest Rates** | | *Percent Per Annum* | | | | | | | | | | | |
| Discount Rate (End of Period) | 60.a | 6.00 | 5.50 | 5.25 | 5.25 | 4.75 | 4.25 | 4.00 | 4.00 | 4.00 | 3.25 | 2.95 | 2.45 |
| Deposit Rate | 60l | 5.00 | 4.92 | 4.33 | 4.25 | 3.75 | 3.25 | 3.25 | 3.25 | 3.25 | 3.21 | 2.60 | 2.45 |
| **Prices and Production** | | *Index Numbers (2010=100): Period Averages* | | | | | | | | | | | |
| Consumer Prices | 64 | 84.1 | 85.7 | 90.1 | 91.0 | 95.8 | 98.7 | 100.0 | 102.9 | † 106.0 | 108.0 | 110.1 | 113.1 |
| Industrial Production | 66 | 96.0 | 98.2 | † 100.2 | 101.5 | 104.8 | 100.9 | 100.0 | 102.3 | 105.0 | 118.4 | 125.2 | .... |
| **Intl. Transactions & Positions** | | *Billions of CFA Francs* | | | | | | | | | | | |
| Exports | 70 | 1,256.79 | 1,509.22 | 1,868.45 | 2,017.27 | 2,358.59 | 1,667.12 | 1,924.21 | 2,133.61 | 2,340.78 | 2,230.68 | 2,557.86 | .... |
| Imports, c.i.f. | 71 | 1,364.25 | 1,524.46 | 1,648.11 | 2,229.29 | 2,563.72 | 2,086.75 | 2,502.96 | 3,209.78 | 3,325.17 | 3,285.08 | 3,747.28 | .... |

# Cameroon 622

| | | 2004 | 2005 | 2006 | 2007 | 2008 | 2009 | 2010 | 2011 | 2012 | 2013 | 2014 | 2015 |
|---|---|---|---|---|---|---|---|---|---|---|---|---|---|
| **Balance of Payments** | | | | | | | *Millions of US Dollars* | | | | | | |
| A. Current Account* | 109bx | −415.4 | −495.4 | 193.3 | 285.7 | −449.7 | −1,118.7 | −856.3 | −748.2 | −956.0 | −1,127.8 | .... | .... |
| Goods, credit (exports) | 1a9cx | 2,708.2 | 3,265.2 | 3,848.6 | 4,956.0 | 5,841.6 | 4,064.2 | 4,313.3 | 5,652.9 | 5,757.1 | 6,079.8 | .... | .... |
| Goods, debit (imports) | 1a9dx | 2,472.5 | 2,883.6 | 3,168.2 | 4,221.3 | 5,357.9 | 4,272.0 | 4,625.9 | 6,232.5 | 6,031.2 | 6,174.4 | .... | .... |
| Balance on goods | 1a9bx | 235.6 | 381.7 | 680.5 | 734.8 | 483.7 | −207.8 | −312.6 | −579.6 | −274.1 | −94.6 | .... | .... |
| Services, credit (exports) | 1b9cx | 1,108.8 | 969.9 | 1,016.5 | 1,370.0 | 1,483.7 | 1,248.9 | 1,294.5 | 1,858.1 | 1,628.2 | 1,978.6 | .... | .... |
| Services, debit (imports) | 1b9dx | 1,492.1 | 1,463.0 | 1,485.3 | 1,764.3 | 2,686.0 | 1,961.3 | 1,745.6 | 1,981.6 | 2,128.6 | 2,701.1 | .... | .... |
| Balance on Goods & Services | 1z9bx | −147.7 | −111.4 | 211.7 | 340.4 | −718.6 | −920.2 | −763.7 | −703.1 | −774.5 | −817.2 | .... | .... |
| Primary income: credit | 1c9cx | 105.1 | 44.9 | 46.3 | 66.9 | 65.8 | 131.4 | 93.1 | 163.2 | 205.7 | 167.7 | .... | .... |
| Primary income: debit | 1c9dx | 548.5 | 665.3 | 377.5 | 566.0 | 394.5 | 608.5 | 331.7 | 465.9 | 650.5 | 782.8 | .... | .... |
| Balance on gds, serv. & prim. inc. | 1y9bx | −591.2 | −731.8 | −119.5 | −158.7 | −1,047.3 | −1,397.2 | −1,002.3 | −1,005.9 | −1,219.3 | −1,432.2 | .... | .... |
| Secondary income: credit | 1d9ca | 225.1 | 331.7 | 526.8 | 619.8 | 774.6 | 532.0 | 334.3 | 542.4 | 506.2 | 553.9 | .... | .... |
| Secondary income: debit | 1d9da | 49.4 | 95.3 | 214.0 | 175.4 | 177.0 | 253.5 | 188.3 | 284.7 | 242.9 | 249.4 | .... | .... |
| B. Capital Account* | 209ba | 42.3 | 203.7 | 1,585.5 | 197.2 | 146.9 | 183.5 | 147.0 | 130.4 | 117.1 | 97.4 | .... | .... |
| Capital account: credit | 209ca | 42.8 | 203.8 | 1,586.0 | 197.7 | 147.6 | 184.1 | 148.3 | 131.2 | 117.7 | 3.7 | .... | .... |
| Capital account: debit | 209da | .5 | .1 | .5 | .5 | .7 | .5 | 1.3 | .7 | .7 | −93.7 | .... | .... |
| Balance on current & capital acct. | 129ba | −373.1 | −291.7 | 1,778.9 | 482.9 | −302.9 | −935.1 | −709.3 | −617.8 | −838.9 | −1,030.4 | .... | .... |
| C. Financial Account* | 309na | 115.2 | 77.6 | 332.2 | −156.6 | −365.2 | −1,004.7 | −527.4 | −385.4 | −1,092.1 | −1,089.2 | .... | .... |
| Direct investment: assets | 3a9aa | −8.7 | −13.7 | −5.3 | −7.7 | −2.2 | −65.8 | 500.5 | 186.8 | −282.3 | −157.5 | .... | .... |
| Equity & investment fund shares | 3aaaa | 32.5 | 4.7 | .9 | 14.3 | 57.3 | −22.5 | 684.9 | −8.8 | 46.2 | 8.2 | .... | .... |
| Debt instruments | 3abaa | −41.3 | −18.4 | −6.2 | −22.0 | −59.5 | −43.3 | −184.4 | 195.6 | −328.6 | −165.7 | .... | .... |
| Direct investment: liabilities | 3a9la | 67.9 | 243.5 | 59.1 | 189.3 | 20.9 | 743.3 | 535.7 | 652.4 | 527.4 | 547.2 | .... | .... |
| Equity & investment fund shares | 3aala | 128.7 | 120.2 | −67.2 | 221.5 | 56.1 | 813.9 | 525.4 | 137.9 | 277.4 | 143.4 | .... | .... |
| Debt instruments | 3abla | −60.9 | 123.3 | 126.3 | −32.1 | −35.2 | −70.6 | 10.3 | 514.5 | 250.0 | 403.8 | .... | .... |
| Portfolio investment: assets | 3b9aa | −38.9 | 9.8 | .8 | 3.4 | 39.3 | 97.2 | 10.8 | 55.7 | −19.2 | 49.2 | .... | .... |
| Equity & investment fund shares | 3baaa | .1 | 10.2 | .8 | 2.8 | −5.1 | −6.5 | 4.4 | 24.4 | −19.0 | 36.3 | .... | .... |
| Debt securities | 3bbaa | −38.9 | −.4 | — | .7 | 44.4 | 103.7 | 6.4 | 31.3 | −.2 | 12.9 | .... | .... |
| Portfolio investment: liabilities | 3b9la | −8.2 | −3.1 | −3.8 | −14.5 | −1.4 | −.7 | 85.2 | −1.2 | −20.7 | −20.6 | .... | .... |
| Equity & investment fund shares | 3bala | −8.2 | −4.2 | −5.6 | −14.5 | −1.2 | −.3 | — | −.1 | −.1 | — | .... | .... |
| Debt securities | 3bbla | .1 | 1.1 | 1.8 | — | −.2 | −.5 | 85.1 | −1.1 | −20.6 | −20.6 | .... | .... |
| Fin. der.& empl.stk.ops.(ESOs): net. | 3c9na | .... | .... | .... | .... | .... | .... | .... | .... | .... | .... | .... | .... |
| Fin. der. & ESOs.: assets | 3c9aa | .... | .... | .... | .... | .... | .... | .... | .... | .... | .... | .... | .... |
| Fin. der. & ESOs.: liabilities | 3c9la | .... | .... | .... | .... | .... | .... | .... | .... | .... | .... | .... | .... |
| Other investment: assets | 3d9aa | −72.1 | −67.0 | 319.5 | 2.1 | 66.4 | 100.9 | −550.6 | 34.6 | −105.3 | 214.7 | .... | .... |
| Other equity | 3daaa | .... | .... | .... | .... | .... | .... | .... | .... | .... | .... | .... | .... |
| Debt instruments | 3dzaa | −72.1 | −67.0 | 319.5 | 2.1 | 66.4 | 100.9 | −550.6 | 34.6 | −105.3 | 214.7 | .... | .... |
| Other investment: liabilities | 3d9la | −294.6 | −388.9 | −72.6 | −20.4 | 449.2 | 394.4 | −132.8 | 11.3 | 178.7 | 668.9 | .... | .... |
| Other equity | 3dala | .... | .... | .... | .... | .... | .... | .... | .... | .... | .... | .... | .... |
| Debt instruments | 3dzla | −294.6 | −388.9 | −72.6 | −20.4 | 449.2 | 394.4 | −132.8 | 11.3 | 178.7 | 668.9 | .... | .... |
| Curr.+ cap.− finan. acct. balance | 4y9na | −488.3 | −369.3 | 1,446.6 | 639.4 | 62.3 | 69.6 | −181.9 | −232.4 | 253.2 | 58.8 | .... | .... |
| D. Net Errors and Omissions | 409na | 54.0 | −27.4 | 170.0 | 179.9 | 204.7 | 160.2 | 188.8 | −93.3 | −157.1 | −143.0 | .... | .... |
| E. Reserves and Related Items | 4z9na | −434.3 | −396.7 | 1,616.6 | 819.4 | 267.0 | 229.8 | 6.8 | −325.7 | 96.2 | −84.2 | .... | .... |
| Reserve assets | 3e9aa | 127.2 | 243.4 | 627.0 | 919.3 | 354.8 | 472.4 | 226.1 | −328.3 | 93.7 | −87.8 | .... | .... |
| Credit and loans from the IMF | 3dcla | −27.9 | −36.2 | −268.3 | 8.0 | 8.5 | 148.2 | — | −1.3 | −2.4 | −3.6 | .... | .... |
| Exceptional financing | 409la | 589.3 | 676.3 | −721.2 | 92.0 | 79.3 | 94.5 | 219.3 | −1.3 | — | — | .... | .... |

*Excludes components in group E

| | | 2004 | 2005 | 2006 | 2007 | 2008 | 2009 | 2010 | 2011 | 2012 | 2013 | 2014 | 2015 |
|---|---|---|---|---|---|---|---|---|---|---|---|---|---|
| **National Accounts** | | | | | | | *Billions of CFA Francs* | | | | | | |
| Househ.Cons.Expend.,incl.NPISHs | 96f | 5,831.5 | 5,965.9 | 6,284.7 | 6,483.8 | 7,840.1 | 8,303.7 | 8,776.3 | 9,519.1 | 10,403.6 | 11,273.2 | .... | .... |
| Government Consumption Expend | 91f | 679.7 | 709.4 | 796.2 | 860.6 | 1,127.4 | 1,243.3 | 1,358.4 | 1,457.2 | 1,548.2 | 1,690.6 | .... | .... |
| Gross Fixed Capital Formation | 93e | 2,167.3 | 2,297.8 | 2,385.9 | 2,620.4 | 1,842.3 | 1,964.9 | 2,219.9 | 2,582.6 | 2,600.1 | 2,834.1 | .... | .... |
| Changes in Inventories | 93i | 3.0 | 3.0 | 3.0 | 4.0 | 60.3 | 79.5 | 8.0 | 1.0 | 18.7 | 15.1 | .... | .... |
| Exports of Goods and Services | 90c | 1,836.2 | 2,030.4 | 2,333.4 | 2,394.3 | 2,520.1 | 1,770.5 | 2,029.6 | 2,306.8 | 2,540.1 | 3,017.5 | .... | .... |
| Imports of Goods and Services (-) | 98c | 2,183.7 | 2,256.8 | 2,416.0 | 2,560.7 | 2,946.4 | 2,321.6 | 2,692.5 | 3,321.1 | 3,595.9 | 4,222.9 | .... | .... |
| Gross Domestic Product (GDP) | 99b | 8,333.9 | 8,749.6 | 9,387.2 | 9,802.5 | 10,443.8 | 11,040.3 | 11,699.7 | 12,545.7 | 13,514.7 | 14,607.5 | .... | .... |
| GDP Volume 2000 Prices | 99b.p | 7,754.5 | 7,932.6 | 8,188.4 | 8,454.9 | 8,698.8 | 8,866.8 | 9,156.7 | 9,535.8 | 9,973.4 | 10,528.1 | .... | .... |
| GDP Volume (2010=100) | 99bvp | 84.7 | 86.6 | 89.4 | 92.3 | 95.0 | 96.8 | 100.0 | 104.1 | 108.9 | 115.0 | .... | .... |
| GDP Deflator (2010=100) | 99bip | 84.1 | 86.3 | 89.7 | 90.7 | 94.0 | 97.4 | 100.0 | 103.0 | 106.1 | 108.6 | .... | .... |
| | | | | | | | *Millions: Midyear Estimates* | | | | | | |
| **Population** | 99z | 17.67 | 18.13 | 18.60 | 19.08 | 19.57 | 20.07 | 20.59 | 21.12 | 21.66 | 22.21 | 22.77 | 23.34 |

# Canada 156

| | | 2004 | 2005 | 2006 | 2007 | 2008 | 2009 | 2010 | 2011 | 2012 | 2013 | 2014 | 2015 |
|---|---|---|---|---|---|---|---|---|---|---|---|---|---|
| **Exchange Rates** | | | | | | *Canadian Dollars per SDR: End of Period* | | | | | | | |
| Market Rate.................................. | aa | 1.8692 | 1.6644 | 1.7531 | 1.5614 | 1.8862 | 1.6407 | 1.5414 | 1.5675 | 1.5295 | 1.6386 | 1.6805 | 1.9179 |
| | | | | | | *Canadian Dollars per US Dollar: End of Period (ae) Period Average (rf)* | | | | | | | |
| Market Rate.................................. | ae | 1.2036 | 1.1645 | 1.1653 | .9881 | 1.2246 | 1.0466 | 1.0009 | 1.0210 | .9952 | 1.0640 | 1.1599 | 1.3840 |
| Market Rate.................................. | rf | 1.3010 | 1.2118 | 1.1344 | 1.0741 | 1.0670 | 1.1431 | 1.0302 | .9895 | .9992 | 1.0298 | 1.1061 | 1.2791 |
| | | | | | | *Index Numbers (2010=100): Period Averages* | | | | | | | |
| Market Rate.................................. | ahx | 79.3 | 85.1 | 90.8 | 96.3 | 97.1 | 90.5 | 100.0 | 104.1 | 103.1 | 100.0 | 93.1 | 80.6 |
| Nominal Effective Exchange Rate..... | nec | 81.4 | 87.3 | 92.9 | 96.6 | 95.6 | 90.7 | 100.0 | 102.2 | 102.6 | 100.0 | 93.4 | 84.6 |
| CPI-Based Real Effect. Ex. Rate........ | rec | 84.0 | 89.5 | 94.5 | 97.7 | 95.3 | 90.7 | 100.0 | 102.0 | 101.7 | 98.4 | 92.1 | 84.0 |
| ULC-Based Real Effect. Ex. Rate....... | rel | 78.0 | 85.1 | 92.7 | 98.9 | 96.8 | 89.3 | 100.0 | 102.5 | 101.3 | 98.5 | 92.7 | 85.0 |
| **Fund Position** | | | | | | *Millions of SDRs: End of Period* | | | | | | | |
| Quota...................................... | 2f.s | 6,369.20 | 6,369.20 | 6,369.20 | 6,369.20 | 6,369.20 | 6,369.20 | 6,369.20 | 6,369.20 | 6,369.20 | 6,369.20 | 6,369.20 | 6,369.20 |
| SDR Holdings.............................. | 1b.s | 595.19 | 627.61 | 640.25 | 642.88 | 643.56 | 5,875.85 | 5,879.16 | 5,840.11 | 5,695.99 | 5,633.06 | 5,634.89 | 5,700.44 |
| Reserve Position in the Fund............ | 1c.s | 2,149.58 | 980.30 | 553.45 | 418.49 | 811.07 | 1,546.40 | 1,984.28 | 2,523.98 | 2,841.84 | 3,062.69 | 2,529.21 | 1,962.26 |
| Total Fund Cred. & Loans Outstg...... | 2tl | — | — | — | — | — | — | — | — | — | — | — | — |
| SDR Allocations........................... | 1bd | 779.29 | 779.29 | 779.29 | 779.29 | 779.29 | 5,988.08 | 5,988.08 | 5,988.08 | 5,988.08 | 5,988.08 | 5,988.08 | 5,988.08 |
| **International Liquidity** | | | | | | *Millions of US Dollars Unless Otherwise Indicated: End of Period* | | | | | | | |
| Total Reserves minus Gold.............. | 1l.d | 34,429 | 32,962 | 34,994 | 40,991 | 43,778 | 54,238 | 56,998 | 65,652 | 68,365 | 71,821 | 74,584 | 79,695 |
| SDR Holdings.............................. | 1b.d | 924 | 897 | 963 | 1,016 | 991 | 9,212 | 9,054 | 8,966 | 8,754 | 8,675 | 8,164 | 7,899 |
| Reserve Position in the Fund.......... | 1c.d | 3,338 | 1,401 | 833 | 661 | 1,249 | 2,424 | 3,056 | 3,875 | 4,368 | 4,717 | 3,664 | 2,719 |
| Foreign Exchange....................... | 1d.d | 30,166 | 30,664 | 33,198 | 39,314 | 41,537 | 42,602 | 44,888 | 52,811 | 55,243 | 58,430 | 62,756 | 69,077 |
| of which: US Dollars................. | 1dxd | 14,427 | 16,842 | 15,608 | 19,257 | 22,804 | 23,879 | 26,677 | 32,826 | 35,622 | 39,514 | 43,756 | 48,229 |
| Gold (Million Fine Troy Ounces)....... | 1ad | .11 | .11 | .11 | .11 | .11 | .11 | .11 | .11 | .11 | .10 | .10 | .05 |
| Gold (National Valuation)............... | 1and | 48 | 56 | 69 | 91 | 95 | 119 | 153 | 167 | 181 | 115 | 116 | 58 |
| Central Bank: Other Assets............. | 3..d | 428 | 108 | 35 | 42 | 129 | 56 | 43 | 331 | 351 | 322 | 313 | 301 |
| Central Bank: Other Liabs............... | 4..d | 426 | 122 | 121 | — | — | — | — | — | — | — | — | — |
| Other Depository Corps.: Assets....... | 7a.d | 4,229 | 5,655 | 8,863 | 8,319 | 9,060 | .... | .... | .... | .... | .... | .... | .... |
| Other Depository Corps.: Liabs......... | 7b.d | — | — | — | — | — | .... | .... | .... | .... | .... | .... | .... |
| Other Financial Corps.: Assets.......... | 7e.d | — | — | — | .... | .... | .... | .... | .... | .... | .... | .... | .... |
| Other Financial Corps.: Liabs............ | 7f.d | — | — | — | .... | .... | .... | .... | .... | .... | .... | .... | .... |
| **Central Bank** | | | | | | *Billions of Canadian Dollars: End of Period* | | | | | | | |
| Net Foreign Assets.......................... | 11n | 3.68 | 1.36 | .63 | .48 | 1.43 | 2.41 | 2.92 | 4.05 | 4.25 | 4.78 | 4.02 | 3.63 |
| Claims on Nonresidents................ | 11 | 5.65 | 2.81 | 2.13 | 1.70 | 2.90 | 12.24 | 12.09 | 13.40 | 13.40 | 14.59 | 14.09 | 15.11 |
| Liabilities to Nonresidents............. | 16c | 1.97 | 1.44 | 1.51 | 1.22 | 1.47 | 9.82 | 9.17 | 9.35 | 9.16 | 9.81 | 10.06 | 11.48 |
| Claims on Other Depository Corps.... | 12e | — | — | .01 | 3.96 | 37.23 | 25.37 | 2.08 | 1.53 | 1.90 | 2.21 | 2.76 | 6.09 |
| Net Claims on Central Government.. | 12an | 42.13 | 45.50 | 46.04 | 47.71 | 17.39 | 33.82 | 56.59 | 60.59 | 63.57 | 65.92 | 68.95 | 71.49 |
| Claims on Central Government...... | 12a | 43.19 | 46.41 | 48.27 | 49.68 | 40.99 | 45.67 | 58.46 | 62.10 | 75.27 | 88.25 | 90.47 | 94.11 |
| Liabilities to Central Government... | 16d | 1.06 | .91 | 2.23 | 1.97 | 23.60 | 11.85 | 1.87 | 1.51 | 11.70 | 22.33 | 21.53 | 22.62 |
| Claims on Other Sectors.................. | 12s | — | — | — | — | — | — | — | — | — | — | — | — |
| Claims on Other Financial Corps.... | 12g | — | — | — | — | — | — | — | — | — | — | — | — |
| Claims on State & Local Govts....... | 12b | — | — | — | — | — | — | — | — | — | — | — | — |
| Claims on Public Nonfin. Corps...... | 12c | — | — | — | — | — | — | — | — | — | — | — | — |
| Claims on Private Sector............... | 12d | — | — | — | — | — | — | — | — | — | — | — | — |
| Monetary Base.............................. | 14 | 44.74 | 46.13 | 48.77 | 51.07 | 53.76 | 58.47 | 57.92 | 61.14 | 63.89 | 66.80 | 70.17 | 76.00 |
| Currency in Circulation.................. | 14a | 44.24 | 46.08 | 48.76 | 50.57 | 53.73 | 55.47 | 57.87 | 61.03 | 63.70 | 66.62 | 70.02 | 75.50 |
| Liabs. to Other Depository Corps.... | 14c | .50 | .05 | .01 | .50 | .03 | 3.00 | .05 | .11 | .19 | .19 | .15 | .50 |
| Liabilities to Other Sectors............. | 14d | — | — | — | — | — | — | — | — | — | — | — | — |
| Other Liabs. to Other Dep. Corps..... | 14n | — | — | — | — | — | — | — | — | — | — | — | — |
| Dep. & Sec. Excl. f/Monetary Base.... | 14o | .25 | .28 | .30 | .51 | .78 | .70 | .64 | .86 | 1.40 | 1.31 | 1.52 | 1.48 |
| Deposits Included in Broad Money. | 15 | — | — | — | — | — | — | — | — | — | — | — | — |
| Sec.Ot.th.Shares Incl.in Brd. Money | 16a | — | — | — | — | — | — | — | — | — | — | — | — |
| Deposits Excl. from Broad Money... | 16b | .25 | .28 | .30 | .51 | .78 | .70 | .64 | .86 | 1.40 | 1.31 | 1.52 | 1.48 |
| Sec.Ot.th.Shares Excl.f/Brd.Money. | 16s | — | — | — | — | — | — | — | — | — | — | — | — |
| Loans........................................ | 16l | — | — | — | — | — | — | — | — | — | — | — | — |
| Financial Derivatives...................... | 16m | — | — | — | — | — | — | — | — | — | — | — | — |
| Shares and Other Equity.................. | 17a | .03 | .03 | .03 | .15 | .21 | .14 | .13 | .42 | .44 | .44 | .45 | .50 |
| Other Items (Net)........................... | 17r | .78 | .43 | −2.43 | .42 | 1.29 | 2.30 | 2.90 | 3.74 | 3.99 | 4.36 | 3.59 | 3.24 |
| Memo Item: | | | | | | | | | | | | | |
| Total Assets................................... | 10ra | 46.73 | 48.32 | 51.63 | 53.90 | 78.58 | 71.35 | 60.88 | 64.25 | 77.81 | 91.31 | 94.11 | 101.15 |

# Canada   156

| | | 2004 | 2005 | 2006 | 2007 | 2008 | 2009 | 2010 | 2011 | 2012 | 2013 | 2014 | 2015 |
|---|---|---|---|---|---|---|---|---|---|---|---|---|---|
| **Other Depository Corporations** | | *Billions of Canadian Dollars: End of Period* | | | | | | | | | | | |
| Net Foreign Assets | 21n | 5.09 | 6.59 | 10.33 | 8.22 | 11.09 | .... | .... | .... | .... | .... | .... | .... |
| Claims on Nonresidents | 21 | 5.09 | 6.59 | 10.33 | 8.22 | 11.09 | .... | .... | .... | .... | .... | .... | .... |
| Liabilities to Nonresidents | 26c | — | — | — | — | — | .... | .... | .... | .... | .... | .... | .... |
| Claims on Central Bank | 20 | 5.41 | 5.44 | 6.22 | 6.72 | 5.98 | .... | .... | .... | .... | .... | .... | .... |
| Currency | 20a | 4.91 | 4.86 | 4.90 | 5.82 | 5.12 | .... | .... | .... | .... | .... | .... | .... |
| Reserve Deposits and Securities | 20b | .51 | .59 | 1.33 | .89 | .86 | .... | .... | .... | .... | .... | .... | .... |
| Other Claims | 20n | — | — | — | — | — | .... | .... | .... | .... | .... | .... | .... |
| Net Claims on Central Government | 22an | 107.50 | 114.24 | 141.28 | 125.91 | 237.93 | .... | .... | .... | .... | .... | .... | .... |
| Claims on Central Government | 22a | 109.95 | 116.81 | 143.04 | 128.11 | 243.33 | .... | .... | .... | .... | .... | .... | .... |
| Liabilities to Central Government | 26d | 2.45 | 2.57 | 1.77 | 2.19 | 5.40 | .... | .... | .... | .... | .... | .... | .... |
| Claims on Other Sectors | 22s | 1,745.21 | 1,919.78 | 2,201.66 | 2,184.86 | 2,593.12 | .... | .... | .... | .... | .... | .... | .... |
| Claims on Other Financial Corps | 22g | 174.68 | 156.33 | 162.86 | 200.74 | 495.59 | .... | .... | .... | .... | .... | .... | .... |
| Claims on State & Local Govts | 22b | 28.53 | 33.95 | 31.59 | 35.18 | 41.18 | .... | .... | .... | .... | .... | .... | .... |
| Claims on Public Nonfin. Corps | 22c | — | — | — | — | — | .... | .... | .... | .... | .... | .... | .... |
| Claims on Private Sector | 22d | 1,542.00 | 1,729.50 | 2,007.22 | 1,948.94 | 2,056.35 | .... | .... | .... | .... | .... | .... | .... |
| Liabilities to Central Bank | 26g | .02 | .01 | .03 | .03 | .25 | .... | .... | .... | .... | .... | .... | .... |
| Transf.Dep.Included in Broad Money | 24 | 439.99 | 463.94 | 515.47 | 452.82 | 566.41 | .... | .... | .... | .... | .... | .... | .... |
| Other Dep.Included in Broad Money | 25 | 1,422.22 | 1,582.15 | 1,791.51 | 1,257.50 | 1,404.76 | .... | .... | .... | .... | .... | .... | .... |
| Sec.Ot.th.Shares Incl.in Brd. Money | 26a | — | — | — | — | — | .... | .... | .... | .... | .... | .... | .... |
| Deposits Excl. from Broad Money | 26b | — | — | — | — | — | .... | .... | .... | .... | .... | .... | .... |
| Sec.Ot.th.Shares Excl.f/Brd.Money | 26s | — | — | — | — | — | .... | .... | .... | .... | .... | .... | .... |
| Loans | 26l | — | — | — | — | — | .... | .... | .... | .... | .... | .... | .... |
| Financial Derivatives | 26m | 159.20 | 150.98 | 156.50 | 192.94 | 457.56 | .... | .... | .... | .... | .... | .... | .... |
| Insurance Technical Reserves | 26r | — | — | — | — | — | .... | .... | .... | .... | .... | .... | .... |
| Shares and Other Equity | 27a | 97.78 | 106.02 | 124.55 | 110.60 | 142.11 | .... | .... | .... | .... | .... | .... | .... |
| Other Items (Net) | 27r | −255.98 | −257.04 | −228.55 | 311.82 | 277.04 | .... | .... | .... | .... | .... | .... | .... |
| Memo Item: | | | | | | | | | | | | | |
| Total Assets | 20ra | 2,561.26 | 2,772.04 | 3,167.59 | 2,595.45 | 3,182.61 | .... | .... | .... | .... | .... | .... | .... |
| **Depository Corporations** | | *Billions of Canadian Dollars: End of Period* | | | | | | | | | | | |
| Net Foreign Assets | 31n | 8.77 | 7.96 | 10.95 | 8.70 | 12.53 | .... | .... | .... | .... | .... | .... | .... |
| Claims on Nonresidents | 31 | 10.74 | 9.40 | 12.46 | 9.92 | 14.00 | .... | .... | .... | .... | .... | .... | .... |
| Liabilities to Nonresidents | 36c | 1.97 | 1.44 | 1.51 | 1.22 | 1.47 | .... | .... | .... | .... | .... | .... | .... |
| Domestic Claims | 32 | 1,894.84 | 2,079.52 | 2,388.98 | 2,358.48 | 2,848.44 | .... | .... | .... | .... | .... | .... | .... |
| Net Claims on Central Government | 32an | 149.63 | 159.74 | 187.32 | 173.62 | 255.32 | .... | .... | .... | .... | .... | .... | .... |
| Claims on Central Government | 32a | 153.14 | 163.22 | 191.31 | 177.78 | 284.32 | .... | .... | .... | .... | .... | .... | .... |
| Liabilities to Central Government | 36d | 3.51 | 3.49 | 3.99 | 4.16 | 29.00 | .... | .... | .... | .... | .... | .... | .... |
| Claims on Other Sectors | 32s | 1,745.21 | 1,919.78 | 2,201.66 | 2,184.86 | 2,593.12 | .... | .... | .... | .... | .... | .... | .... |
| Claims on Other Financial Corps | 32g | 174.68 | 156.33 | 162.86 | 200.74 | 495.59 | .... | .... | .... | .... | .... | .... | .... |
| Claims on State & Local Govts | 32b | 28.53 | 33.95 | 31.59 | 35.18 | 41.18 | .... | .... | .... | .... | .... | .... | .... |
| Claims on Public Nonfin. Corps | 32c | — | — | — | — | — | .... | .... | .... | .... | .... | .... | .... |
| Claims on Private Sector | 32d | 1,542.00 | 1,729.50 | 2,007.22 | 1,948.94 | 2,056.35 | .... | .... | .... | .... | .... | .... | .... |
| Broad Money Liabilities | 35l | 1,901.54 | 2,087.30 | 2,350.84 | 1,755.05 | 2,019.77 | .... | .... | .... | .... | .... | .... | .... |
| Currency Outside Depository Corps | 34a | 39.34 | 41.22 | 43.87 | 44.74 | 48.61 | .... | .... | .... | .... | .... | .... | .... |
| Transferable Deposits | 34 | 439.99 | 463.94 | 515.47 | 452.82 | 566.41 | .... | .... | .... | .... | .... | .... | .... |
| Other Deposits | 35 | 1,422.22 | 1,582.15 | 1,791.51 | 1,257.50 | 1,404.76 | .... | .... | .... | .... | .... | .... | .... |
| Securities Other than Shares | 36a | — | — | — | — | — | .... | .... | .... | .... | .... | .... | .... |
| Deposits Excl. from Broad Money | 36b | .25 | .28 | .30 | .51 | .78 | .... | .... | .... | .... | .... | .... | .... |
| Sec.Ot.th.Shares Excl.f/Brd.Money | 36s | — | — | — | — | — | .... | .... | .... | .... | .... | .... | .... |
| Loans | 36l | — | — | — | — | — | .... | .... | .... | .... | .... | .... | .... |
| Financial Derivatives | 36m | 159.20 | 150.98 | 156.50 | 192.94 | 457.56 | .... | .... | .... | .... | .... | .... | .... |
| Insurance Technical Reserves | 36r | — | — | — | — | — | .... | .... | .... | .... | .... | .... | .... |
| Shares and Other Equity | 37a | 97.81 | 106.05 | 124.58 | 110.76 | 142.32 | .... | .... | .... | .... | .... | .... | .... |
| Other Items (Net) | 37r | −255.19 | −257.14 | −232.28 | 307.92 | 240.53 | .... | .... | .... | .... | .... | .... | .... |
| Broad Money Liabs., Seasonally Adj. | 35l.b | 1,899.32 | 2,075.50 | 2,324.72 | 1,730.37 | 1,989.34 | .... | .... | .... | .... | .... | .... | .... |
| **Other Financial Corporations** | | *Billions of Canadian Dollars: End of Period* | | | | | | | | | | | |
| Net Foreign Assets | 41n | — | — | — | .... | .... | .... | .... | .... | .... | .... | .... | .... |
| Claims on Nonresidents | 41 | — | — | — | .... | .... | .... | .... | .... | .... | .... | .... | .... |
| Liabilities to Nonresidents | 46c | — | — | — | .... | .... | .... | .... | .... | .... | .... | .... | .... |
| Claims on Depository Corporations | 40 | 17.79 | 20.31 | 19.77 | .... | .... | .... | .... | .... | .... | .... | .... | .... |
| Net Claims on Central Government | 42an | 77.27 | 80.14 | 82.79 | .... | .... | .... | .... | .... | .... | .... | .... | .... |
| Claims on Central Government | 42a | 77.27 | 80.14 | 82.79 | .... | .... | .... | .... | .... | .... | .... | .... | .... |
| Liabilities to Central Government | 46d | — | — | — | .... | .... | .... | .... | .... | .... | .... | .... | .... |
| Claims on Other Sectors | 42s | 712.50 | 781.39 | 876.45 | .... | .... | .... | .... | .... | .... | .... | .... | .... |
| Claims on State & Local Govts | 42b | 59.74 | 63.03 | 67.07 | .... | .... | .... | .... | .... | .... | .... | .... | .... |
| Claims on Public Nonfin. Corps | 42c | — | — | — | .... | .... | .... | .... | .... | .... | .... | .... | .... |
| Claims on Private Sector | 42d | 652.76 | 718.36 | 809.38 | .... | .... | .... | .... | .... | .... | .... | .... | .... |
| Deposits | 46b | — | — | — | .... | .... | .... | .... | .... | .... | .... | .... | .... |
| Securities Other than Shares | 46s | 65.98 | 76.29 | 80.61 | .... | .... | .... | .... | .... | .... | .... | .... | .... |
| Loans | 46l | — | — | — | .... | .... | .... | .... | .... | .... | .... | .... | .... |
| Financial Derivatives | 46m | — | — | — | .... | .... | .... | .... | .... | .... | .... | .... | .... |
| Insurance Technical Reserves | 46r | 148.37 | 153.26 | 159.50 | .... | .... | .... | .... | .... | .... | .... | .... | .... |
| Shares and Other Equity | 47a | 622.79 | 686.41 | 782.99 | .... | .... | .... | .... | .... | .... | .... | .... | .... |
| Other Items (Net) | 47r | −29.57 | −34.10 | −44.09 | .... | .... | .... | .... | .... | .... | .... | .... | .... |

|  |  | 2004 | 2005 | 2006 | 2007 | 2008 | 2009 | 2010 | 2011 | 2012 | 2013 | 2014 | 2015 |
|---|---|---|---|---|---|---|---|---|---|---|---|---|---|
| **Financial Corporations** | | | *Billions of Canadian Dollars: End of Period* | | | | | | | | | | |
| Net Foreign Assets | 51n | 8.77 | 7.96 | 10.95 | .... | .... | .... | .... | .... | .... | .... | .... | .... |
| Claims on Nonresidents | 51 | 10.74 | 9.40 | 12.46 | .... | .... | .... | .... | .... | .... | .... | .... | .... |
| Liabilities to Nonresidents | 56c | 1.97 | 1.44 | 1.51 | .... | .... | .... | .... | .... | .... | .... | .... | ... |
| Domestic Claims | 52 | 2,509.93 | 2,784.72 | 3,185.36 | .... | .... | .... | .... | .... | .... | .... | .... | .... |
| Net Claims on Central Government | 52an | 226.90 | 239.88 | 270.10 | .... | .... | .... | .... | .... | .... | .... | .... | .... |
| Claims on Central Government | 52a | 230.41 | 243.36 | 274.10 | .... | .... | .... | .... | .... | .... | .... | .... | .... |
| Liabilities to Central Government | 56d | 3.51 | 3.49 | 3.99 | .... | .... | .... | .... | .... | .... | .... | .... | .... |
| Claims on Other Sectors | 52s | 2,283.03 | 2,544.84 | 2,915.26 | .... | .... | .... | .... | .... | .... | .... | .... | .... |
| Claims on State & Local Govts | 52b | 88.27 | 96.98 | 98.67 | .... | .... | .... | .... | .... | .... | .... | .... | .... |
| Claims on Public Nonfin. Corps | 52c | — | — | — | .... | .... | .... | .... | .... | .... | .... | .... | .... |
| Claims on Private Sector | 52d | 2,194.77 | 2,447.86 | 2,816.60 | .... | .... | .... | .... | .... | .... | .... | .... | .... |
| Currency Outside Financial Corps | 54a | 37.03 | 37.36 | 39.43 | .... | .... | .... | .... | .... | .... | .... | .... | .... |
| Deposits | 55l | 1,592.95 | 1,728.65 | 1,948.27 | .... | .... | .... | .... | .... | .... | .... | .... | .... |
| Securities Other than Shares | 56a | 65.98 | 76.29 | 80.61 | .... | .... | .... | .... | .... | .... | .... | .... | .... |
| Loans | 56l | — | — | — | .... | .... | .... | .... | .... | .... | .... | .... | .... |
| Financial Derivatives | 56m | — | — | — | .... | .... | .... | .... | .... | .... | .... | .... | .... |
| Insurance Technical Reserves | 56r | 148.37 | 153.26 | 159.50 | .... | .... | .... | .... | .... | .... | .... | .... | .... |
| Shares and Other Equity | 57a | 720.60 | 792.46 | 907.57 | .... | .... | .... | .... | .... | .... | .... | .... | .... |
| Other Items (Net) | 57r | −46.23 | 4.67 | 60.94 | .... | .... | .... | .... | .... | .... | .... | .... | .... |
| **Monetary Aggregates** | | | *Billions of Canadian Dollars: End of Period* | | | | | | | | | | |
| Broad Money | 59m | 1,925.98 | 2,111.74 | 2,375.28 | 1,768.38 | 2,032.25 | .... | .... | .... | .... | .... | .... | .... |
| o/w:Currency Issued by Cent.Govt | 59m.a | — | — | — | — | — | .... | .... | .... | .... | .... | .... | .... |
| o/w: Dep.in Nonfin. Corporations | 59m.b | — | — | — | — | — | .... | .... | .... | .... | .... | .... | .... |
| o/w:Secs. Issued by Central Govt | 59m.c | 24.44 | 24.44 | 24.44 | 13.32 | 12.48 | 12.15 | 10.76 | 9.43 | 8.08 | 6.94 | 6.19 | 5.61 |
| Money (National Definitions) | | | | | | | | | | | | | |
| M1+ Gross | 59mab | 329.21 | 348.95 | 386.90 | 414.54 | 468.64 | 529.34 | 577.51 | 633.08 | 679.50 | 720.45 | 768.90 | 831.76 |
| M1+ Gross,Seasonally Adjusted | 59mag | 322.48 | 341.45 | 378.00 | 404.38 | 456.91 | 516.18 | 563.63 | 618.32 | 664.07 | 705.21 | 753.59 | 815.12 |
| M1++ Gross | 59mad | 441.63 | 474.02 | 516.46 | 556.78 | 630.50 | 747.33 | 815.20 | 896.49 | 964.83 | 1,054.24 | 1,121.62 | 1,214.02 |
| M1++ Gross,Seasonally Adjusted | 59mah | 435.23 | 467.06 | 508.62 | 547.99 | 620.40 | 735.25 | 801.97 | 881.66 | 948.66 | 1,038.72 | 1,105.24 | 1,196.35 |
| M2 Gross | 59mbd | 642.03 | 680.08 | 742.94 | 793.52 | 903.15 | 987.48 | 1,041.05 | 1,108.13 | 1,173.41 | 1,253.79 | 1,312.59 | 1,391.71 |
| M2 Gross,Seasonally Adjusted | 59mbi | 634.79 | 672.12 | 733.84 | 783.45 | 891.64 | 974.95 | 1,027.98 | 1,094.17 | 1,158.61 | 1,238.94 | 1,297.12 | 1,375.43 |
| M2+ Gross | 59mbe | 893.16 | 939.47 | 1,018.12 | 1,097.21 | 1,241.42 | 1,328.54 | 1,378.06 | 1,455.43 | 1,525.53 | 1,616.11 | 1,683.64 | 1,771.99 |
| M2+ Gross,Seasonally Adjusted | 59mbk | 886.00 | 931.50 | 1,009.02 | 1,087.15 | 1,229.91 | 1,316.00 | 1,364.99 | 1,441.47 | 1,510.72 | 1,601.27 | 1,668.17 | 1,755.72 |
| M2++ Gross | 59mbj | 1,293.21 | 1,377.76 | 1,496.33 | 1,628.93 | 1,772.04 | 1,888.49 | 1,976.98 | 2,095.31 | 2,221.01 | 2,380.40 | 2,550.44 | 2,744.26 |
| M2++ Gross,Seasonally Adjusted | 59mbl | 1,287.95 | 1,371.75 | 1,489.14 | 1,620.62 | 1,761.98 | 1,877.17 | 1,965.01 | 2,082.43 | 2,207.44 | 2,367.34 | 2,535.46 | 2,728.04 |
| M3 Gross | 59mca | 904.68 | 973.55 | 1,069.23 | 1,198.69 | 1,315.91 | 1,326.93 | 1,418.15 | 1,537.99 | 1,628.74 | 1,779.72 | 1,911.79 | 2,086.47 |
| M3 Gross,Seasonally Adjusted | 59mcf | 893.49 | 961.47 | 1,056.03 | 1,184.17 | 1,301.07 | 1,313.28 | 1,405.11 | 1,524.98 | 1,615.60 | 1,761.80 | 1,894.26 | 2,066.96 |
| **Interest Rates** | | | *Percent Per Annum* | | | | | | | | | | |
| Central Bank Policy Rate (EOP) | 60 | 2.50 | 3.25 | 4.25 | 4.25 | 1.50 | .25 | 1.00 | 1.00 | 1.25 | 1.25 | 1.25 | .75 |
| Borrowing Facility Rate (EOP) | 60.g | 2.75 | 3.50 | 4.50 | 4.50 | 1.75 | .50 | 1.25 | 1.25 | 1.25 | 1.25 | 1.25 | .75 |
| Money Market Rate | 60b | 2.25 | 2.66 | 4.02 | 4.34 | 2.96 | .39 | .60 | 1.00 | 1.00 | 1.00 | 1.00 | .63 |
| Corporate Paper Rate | 60bc | 2.31 | 2.84 | 4.21 | 4.63 | 3.23 | .65 | .79 | 1.17 | 1.16 | 1.17 | 1.18 | .80 |
| Treasury Bill Rate | 60c | 2.22 | 2.73 | 4.03 | 4.15 | 2.39 | .35 | .60 | .92 | .97 | .97 | .91 | .50 |
| Savings Rate | 60k | .05 | .05 | .05 | .08 | .10 | .05 | .05 | .05 | .05 | .05 | .05 | .03 |
| Deposit Rate | 60l | .78 | .79 | 1.83 | 2.08 | 1.50 | .10 | .20 | .48 | .48 | .55 | .55 | .08 |
| Lending Rate | 60p | 4.00 | 4.42 | 5.81 | 6.10 | 4.73 | 2.40 | 2.60 | 3.00 | 3.00 | 3.00 | 3.00 | 2.78 |
| Govt. Bond Yield: Med.-Term | 61a | 3.67 | 3.50 | 4.10 | 4.21 | 2.96 | 2.15 | 2.21 | 1.85 | 1.30 | 1.48 | 1.38 | .66 |
| Govt. Bond Yield: Long-Term | 61 | 5.08 | 4.39 | 4.30 | 4.34 | 4.04 | 3.89 | 3.66 | 3.21 | 2.33 | 2.72 | 2.60 | 2.02 |
| **Prices, Production, Labor** | | | *Index Numbers (2010=100): Period Averages* | | | | | | | | | | |
| Share Prices | 62 | 71.2 | 83.7 | 99.2 | 112.8 | 103.4 | 84.2 | 100.0 | 107.4 | 100.2 | 105.6 | 121.2 | 118.7 |
| Share Prices (End of Month) | 62.ep | 71.5 | 84.0 | 99.9 | 113.3 | 103.6 | 84.6 | 100.0 | 107.9 | 100.6 | 106.0 | 121.7 | 118.0 |
| Prices: Industry Selling | 63 | 92.7 | 94.2 | 96.4 | 97.8 | † 102.1 | 98.5 | 100.0 | 106.9 | 108.1 | 108.6 | 111.3 | 110.3 |
| Consumer Prices | 64 | 89.9 | 91.9 | 93.7 | 95.7 | 98.0 | 98.3 | 100.0 | 102.9 | 104.5 | 105.5 | 107.5 | 108.7 |
| Wages: Hourly Earnings(Mfg) | 65ey | 91.4 | 93.8 | 93.6 | 98.6 | 100.4 | 95.3 | 100.0 | 103.2 | 106.1 | 106.1 | 107.0 | 111.8 |
| Industrial Production | 66 | 109.5 | 111.7 | 111.0 | 110.1 | 106.9 | 95.3 | 100.0 | 103.7 | 104.8 | 106.1 | 111.0 | 109.4 |
| Manufacturing Employment | 67ey | 126.6 | 124.5 | 123.3 | 119.1 | 113.7 | 101.0 | 100.0 | 101.5 | 102.2 | 101.7 | 101.0 | 101.4 |
| | | | *Number in Thousands: Period Averages* | | | | | | | | | | |
| Labor Force | 67d | 17,147 | 17,292 | 17,502 | 17,847 | 18,122 | 18,250 | 18,451 | 18,620 | 18,810 | 19,038 | 19,125 | 19,278 |
| Employment | 67e | 15,915 | 16,124 | 16,396 | 16,769 | 17,010 | 16,728 | 16,964 | 17,221 | 17,438 | 17,691 | 17,802 | 17,947 |
| Unemployment | 67c | 1,232 | 1,169 | 1,106 | 1,077 | 1,112 | 1,523 | 1,486 | 1,399 | 1,372 | 1,347 | 1,322 | 1,331 |
| Unemployment Rate (%) | 67r | 7.2 | 6.8 | 6.3 | 6.0 | 6.1 | 8.3 | 8.1 | 7.5 | 7.3 | 7.1 | 6.9 | 6.9 |
| **Intl. Transactions & Positions** | | | *Millions of Canadian Dollars* | | | | | | | | | | |
| Exports | 70 | 395,897 | 436,351 | 440,365 | 450,321 | 483,488 | 357,373 | 398,857 | 447,502 | 454,416 | 472,025 | 519,735 | 522,837 |
| Imports, f.o.b | 71.v | 354,859 | 380,858 | 397,044 | 407,301 | 433,999 | 365,359 | 403,701 | 446,442 | 462,026 | 475,686 | 515,316 | 541,353 |
| | | | *2010=100* | | | | | | | | | | |
| Volume of Exports | 72 | 109.5 | 112.0 | 112.9 | † 114.5 | 109.4 | 93.3 | 100.0 | 105.4 | 109.2 | 111.1 | 117.6 | 123.2 |
| Volume of Imports | 73 | 85.1 | 91.7 | 97.2 | † 102.8 | 102.5 | 86.6 | 100.0 | 106.5 | 109.3 | 112.3 | 115.3 | 115.6 |
| Unit Value of Exports | 74 | 93.0 | 96.4 | 96.8 | † 98.6 | 110.8 | 96.7 | 100.0 | 106.3 | 104.5 | 106.5 | 112.0 | 106.7 |
| Unit Value of Imports | 75 | 99.0 | 99.1 | 99.4 | † 98.3 | 105.0 | 104.7 | 100.0 | 103.8 | 104.7 | 105.0 | 110.0 | 114.8 |

# Canada 156

| Balance of Payments | | 2004 | 2005 | 2006 | 2007 | 2008 | 2009 | 2010 | 2011 | 2012 | 2013 | 2014 | 2015 |
|---|---|---|---|---|---|---|---|---|---|---|---|---|---|
| | | | | | | | *Millions of US Dollars* | | | | | | |
| A. Current Account* | 109bx | 23,240.5 | 21,931.4 | 17,990.2 | 11,050.5 | 3,179.5 | −40,737.0 | −58,160.3 | −49,728.6 | −65,697.7 | −58,038.7 | −40,562.3 | −51,712.7 |
| Goods, credit (exports) | 1a9cx | 328,648.2 | 370,464.7 | 398,504.0 | 430,471.9 | 460,255.6 | 322,670.0 | 392,338.1 | 461,316.8 | 461,876.0 | 466,381.5 | 478,252.1 | 409,681.4 |
| Goods, debit (imports) | 1a9dx | 279,301.2 | 319,892.6 | 356,735.9 | 388,423.9 | 417,674.0 | 328,828.1 | 401,704.7 | 460,913.4 | 475,168.2 | 472,709.6 | 473,883.9 | 428,281.7 |
| Balance on goods | 1a9bx | 49,347.0 | 50,572.0 | 41,768.1 | 42,048.0 | 42,581.7 | −6,158.1 | −9,366.6 | 403.4 | −13,292.2 | −6,328.1 | 4,368.2 | −18,600.4 |
| Services, credit (exports) | 1b9cx | 53,177.5 | 60,271.9 | 66,375.4 | 71,138.9 | 75,495.1 | 69,035.5 | 76,925.3 | 85,307.7 | 89,303.6 | 90,095.5 | 86,614.1 | 77,587.3 |
| Services, debit (imports) | 1b9dx | 57,670.9 | 65,175.7 | 72,941.4 | 82,575.1 | 89,929.4 | 83,150.2 | 98,432.6 | 107,381.6 | 111,923.5 | 112,682.6 | 107,795.8 | 96,330.5 |
| Balance on Goods & Services | 1z9bx | 44,853.6 | 45,668.2 | 35,202.1 | 30,611.7 | 28,147.4 | −20,272.8 | −30,873.8 | −21,670.5 | −35,912.1 | −28,915.2 | −16,813.5 | −37,343.5 |
| Primary income: credit | 1c9cx | 29,571.6 | 40,822.5 | 58,891.8 | 72,578.3 | 66,271.0 | 49,392.2 | 61,074.7 | 70,210.7 | 72,865.2 | 72,291.2 | 77,386.3 | 72,199.6 |
| Primary income: debit | 1c9dx | 50,683.5 | 63,119.7 | 74,447.6 | 90,008.1 | 89,644.8 | 66,828.0 | 84,522.5 | 94,586.0 | 98,458.4 | 97,589.1 | 98,764.5 | 83,987.9 |
| Balance on gds, serv. & prim. inc. | 1y9bx | 23,741.7 | 23,370.9 | 19,646.3 | 13,181.9 | 4,773.6 | −37,708.7 | −54,321.6 | −46,045.8 | −61,505.2 | −54,213.1 | −38,191.8 | −49,131.8 |
| Secondary income: credit | 1d9ca | 5,775.6 | 7,124.5 | 8,436.4 | 8,910.3 | 9,627.0 | 7,902.4 | 8,751.2 | 9,503.6 | 8,929.9 | 9,526.0 | 9,988.8 | 8,609.8 |
| Secondary income: debit | 1d9da | 6,276.8 | 8,564.0 | 10,092.4 | 11,041.8 | 11,221.0 | 10,930.8 | 12,589.9 | 13,186.4 | 13,122.3 | 13,351.6 | 12,359.3 | 11,190.7 |
| B. Capital Account* | 209ba | −149.6 | −190.7 | −206.7 | −268.5 | −246.9 | −732.3 | −121.3 | 4,665.3 | −273.1 | −103.1 | 361.1 | −85.5 |
| Capital account: credit | 209ca | 148.7 | 167.5 | 187.8 | 209.1 | 221.4 | 216.6 | 251.4 | 5,002.6 | 285.7 | 291.1 | 796.1 | 258.6 |
| Capital account: debit | 209da | 298.3 | 358.2 | 394.5 | 477.6 | 468.2 | 948.9 | 372.7 | 337.2 | 558.7 | 394.1 | 434.9 | 344.1 |
| Balance on current & capital acct. | 129ba | 23,090.9 | 21,740.7 | 17,783.6 | 10,782.0 | 2,932.7 | −41,469.3 | −58,281.6 | −45,063.3 | −65,970.7 | −58,141.8 | −40,201.2 | −51,798.2 |
| C. Financial Account* | 309na | 27,682.3 | 19,069.7 | 19,127.5 | 9,469.3 | −3,073.9 | −52,531.4 | −62,113.9 | −57,377.8 | −64,481.3 | −59,355.0 | −44,277.3 | −52,171.1 |
| Direct investment: assets | 3a9aa | 44,821.8 | 27,270.4 | 50,360.6 | 65,136.6 | 88,684.3 | 37,706.8 | 36,336.2 | 50,092.7 | 62,259.2 | 51,967.1 | 62,203.4 | 82,284.3 |
| Equity & investment fund shares | 3aaaa | 44,821.8 | 27,270.4 | 50,360.6 | 65,136.6 | 88,684.3 | 37,706.8 | 36,336.2 | 50,092.7 | 56,271.2 | 47,389.1 | 57,710.0 | 63,591.8 |
| Debt instruments | 3abaa | .... | .... | .... | .... | .... | .... | .... | .... | 5,988.1 | 4,578.0 | 4,493.4 | 18,692.5 |
| Direct investment: liabilities | 3a9la | 1,441.9 | 25,545.3 | 64,302.2 | 120,423.1 | 70,116.9 | 20,931.4 | 29,712.9 | 38,318.1 | 49,377.8 | 69,427.6 | 65,440.7 | 63,170.8 |
| Equity & investment fund shares | 3aala | 1,441.9 | 25,545.3 | 64,302.2 | 120,423.1 | 70,116.9 | 20,931.4 | 29,712.9 | 38,318.1 | 47,380.2 | 53,382.5 | 61,440.3 | 63,238.1 |
| Debt instruments | 3abla | .... | .... | .... | .... | .... | .... | .... | .... | 1,997.6 | 16,045.1 | 4,000.5 | −67.3 |
| Portfolio investment: assets | 3b9aa | 19,503.7 | 44,993.7 | 69,392.4 | 42,785.2 | −8,386.2 | 6,287.6 | 13,935.8 | 18,375.0 | 35,309.0 | 28,350.2 | 50,921.5 | 46,597.6 |
| Equity & investment fund shares | 3baaa | 6,197.0 | 18,104.0 | 24,775.6 | 28,902.5 | 8,602.5 | 13,030.2 | 12,856.8 | 26,718.6 | 23,248.5 | 6,155.3 | 32,448.9 | 19,792.4 |
| Debt securities | 3bbaa | 13,306.7 | 26,889.7 | 44,616.8 | 13,882.7 | −16,988.7 | −6,742.6 | 1,079.0 | −8,343.6 | 12,060.5 | 22,194.9 | 18,472.6 | 26,805.2 |
| Portfolio investment: liabilities | 3b9la | 43,139.2 | 11,231.4 | 27,486.1 | −27,711.7 | 39,444.9 | 98,902.4 | 124,073.0 | 122,615.5 | 98,852.4 | 49,603.2 | 68,842.1 | 76,036.5 |
| Equity & investment fund shares | 3bala | 27,145.0 | 7,564.7 | 9,500.7 | −42,041.3 | 3,109.1 | 23,349.4 | 17,791.2 | 21,313.1 | 948.8 | 17,901.9 | 23,127.0 | 11,490.2 |
| Debt securities | 3bbla | 15,994.2 | 3,666.6 | 17,985.4 | 14,329.6 | 36,335.8 | 75,553.0 | 106,281.8 | 101,302.4 | 97,903.5 | 31,701.3 | 45,715.1 | 64,546.3 |
| Fin. der.& empl.stk.ops.(ESOs): net. | 3c9na | .... | .... | .... | .... | .... | .... | .... | .... | .... | .... | .... | .... |
| Fin. der. & ESOs.: assets | 3c9aa | .... | .... | .... | .... | .... | .... | .... | .... | .... | .... | .... | .... |
| Fin. der. & ESOs.: liabilities | 3c9la | .... | .... | .... | .... | .... | .... | .... | .... | .... | .... | .... | .... |
| Other investment: assets | 3d9aa | 3,695.9 | 12,750.7 | 26,767.0 | 53,371.6 | 32,501.0 | 31,945.9 | 42,415.4 | 36,396.8 | 31,539.1 | −8,736.7 | 14,774.7 | 25,359.4 |
| Other equity | 3daaa | .... | .... | .... | .... | .... | .... | .... | .... | .... | .... | .... | .... |
| Debt instruments | 3dzaa | 3,695.9 | 12,750.7 | 26,767.0 | 53,371.6 | 32,501.0 | 31,945.9 | 42,415.4 | 36,396.8 | 31,539.1 | −8,736.7 | 14,774.7 | 25,359.4 |
| Other investment: liabilities | 3d9la | −4,242.1 | 29,168.4 | 35,604.2 | 59,112.8 | 6,311.1 | 8,637.8 | 1,015.5 | 1,308.7 | 45,358.6 | 11,904.7 | 37,894.1 | 67,205.0 |
| Other equity | 3dala | .... | .... | .... | .... | .... | .... | .... | .... | .... | .... | .... | .... |
| Debt instruments | 3dzla | −4,242.1 | 29,168.4 | 35,604.2 | 59,112.8 | 6,311.1 | 8,637.8 | 1,015.5 | 1,308.7 | 45,358.6 | 11,904.7 | 37,894.1 | 67,205.0 |
| Curr.+ cap.− finan. acct. balance | 4y9na | −4,591.4 | 2,671.0 | −1,343.9 | 1,312.7 | 6,006.6 | 11,062.0 | 3,832.3 | 12,314.5 | −1,489.4 | 1,213.2 | 4,076.1 | 372.9 |
| D. Net Errors and Omissions | 409na | 1,755.8 | −1,335.5 | 2,170.1 | 2,593.5 | −4,237.2 | −592.2 | −17.6 | −4,398.2 | 3,218.2 | 3,537.9 | 1,168.9 | 8,083.1 |
| E. Reserves and Related Items | 4z9na | −2,835.6 | 1,335.5 | 826.2 | 3,906.1 | 1,769.4 | 10,469.8 | 3,814.7 | 7,916.3 | 1,728.8 | 4,751.0 | 5,245.0 | 8,456.0 |
| Reserve assets | 3e9aa | −2,835.6 | 1,335.5 | 826.2 | 3,906.1 | 1,769.4 | 10,469.8 | 3,814.7 | 7,916.3 | 1,728.8 | 4,751.0 | 5,245.0 | 8,456.0 |
| Credit and loans from the IMF | 3dcla | — | — | — | — | — | — | — | — | — | — | — | — |
| Exceptional financing | 409la | .... | .... | .... | .... | .... | .... | .... | .... | .... | .... | .... | .... |

*Excludes components in group E

| International Investment Position | | 2004 | 2005 | 2006 | 2007 | 2008 | 2009 | 2010 | 2011 | 2012 | 2013 | 2014 | 2015 |
|---|---|---|---|---|---|---|---|---|---|---|---|---|---|
| | | | | | | | *Millions of US Dollars* | | | | | | |
| Assets | 809aa | 1,241,424.3 | 1,409,242.7 | 1,703,288.2 | 2,090,869.3 | 1,514,373.7 | 1,975,005.2 | 2,239,869.5 | 2,176,017.4 | 2,459,569.3 | 2,754,682.4 | 2,918,888.5 | 2,929,277.2 |
| Direct investment | 8a9aa | 660,122.1 | 721,912.4 | 815,592.8 | 989,408.8 | 684,062.4 | 935,801.0 | 1,045,237.6 | 928,268.7 | 1,021,930.2 | 1,154,180.1 | 1,175,803.6 | 1,140,632.9 |
| Equity & investment fund shares | 8aaaa | .... | .... | .... | .... | .... | .... | .... | 852,365.9 | 939,976.2 | 1,061,175.5 | 1,083,514.6 | 1,039,624.3 |
| Debt instruments | 8abaa | .... | .... | .... | .... | .... | .... | .... | 75,902.9 | 81,954.1 | 93,004.6 | 92,289.0 | 101,008.5 |
| Portfolio investment | 8b9aa | 381,108.6 | 469,616.3 | 631,565.7 | 773,380.0 | 476,236.6 | 616,541.4 | 738,877.2 | 744,960.6 | 903,465.2 | 1,073,990.7 | 1,185,959.6 | 1,215,043.0 |
| Equity & investment fund shares | 8baaa | 319,415.0 | 382,107.5 | 499,649.0 | 610,427.8 | 357,081.8 | 480,126.6 | 576,709.9 | 581,858.7 | 702,517.5 | 856,692.9 | 941,972.6 | 946,292.6 |
| Debt securities | 8bbaa | 61,693.6 | 87,508.8 | 131,916.6 | 162,952.2 | 119,154.8 | 136,414.7 | 162,167.3 | 163,102.9 | 200,947.7 | 217,297.7 | 243,987.1 | 268,750.4 |
| Fin. der.(oth.than reserves) & ESOs | 8c9aa | .... | .... | .... | .... | .... | .... | .... | .... | .... | .... | .... | .... |
| Other investment | 8d9aa | 165,756.2 | 184,735.5 | 221,064.1 | 286,870.6 | 310,426.6 | 368,126.4 | 398,887.3 | 437,175.4 | 465,644.6 | 454,597.3 | 482,414.2 | 493,847.9 |
| Other equity | 8daaa | .... | .... | .... | .... | .... | .... | .... | .... | .... | .... | .... | .... |
| Debt instruments | 8dzaa | 165,756.2 | 184,735.5 | 221,064.1 | 286,870.6 | 310,426.6 | 368,126.4 | 398,887.3 | 437,175.4 | 465,644.6 | 454,597.3 | 482,414.2 | 493,847.9 |
| Reserve assets | 8e9aa | 34,437.5 | 32,978.6 | 35,065.7 | 41,209.8 | 43,648.1 | 54,536.4 | 56,867.4 | 65,611.6 | 68,529.3 | 71,914.5 | 74,711.1 | 79,753.4 |
| Liabilities | 809la | 1,376,821.5 | 1,563,646.4 | 1,756,890.0 | 2,276,662.4 | 1,635,009.0 | 2,186,444.0 | 2,540,905.3 | 2,472,503.4 | 2,787,991.4 | 2,766,718.0 | 2,828,330.1 | 2,578,852.4 |
| Direct investment | 8a9la | 573,335.8 | 668,275.6 | 740,541.1 | 1,071,080.2 | 659,430.2 | 910,930.1 | 1,030,660.7 | 899,347.9 | 1,003,391.3 | 1,013,882.8 | 1,009,816.2 | 814,865.2 |
| Equity & investment fund shares | 8aala | .... | .... | .... | .... | .... | .... | .... | 746,471.0 | 832,549.0 | 838,436.3 | 845,708.3 | 677,416.0 |
| Debt instruments | 8abla | .... | .... | .... | .... | .... | .... | .... | 152,876.9 | 170,842.2 | 175,446.5 | 164,107.9 | 137,449.2 |
| Portfolio investment | 8b9la | 603,508.0 | 655,737.3 | 739,818.7 | 849,400.0 | 631,385.0 | 898,747.4 | 1,130,134.6 | 1,186,615.1 | 1,344,239.1 | 1,311,100.6 | 1,336,349.0 | 1,205,749.6 |
| Equity & investment fund shares | 8bala | 225,899.2 | 280,843.4 | 346,101.1 | 418,081.0 | 209,170.9 | 353,642.9 | 462,355.4 | 408,241.3 | 441,961.1 | 436,887.2 | 452,034.4 | 346,025.1 |
| Debt securities | 8bbla | 377,608.8 | 374,893.9 | 393,717.6 | 431,319.0 | 422,214.1 | 545,104.5 | 667,779.2 | 778,373.8 | 902,278.0 | 874,213.4 | 884,314.6 | 859,724.5 |
| Fin. der.(oth.than reserves) & ESOs | 8c9la | .... | .... | .... | .... | .... | .... | .... | .... | .... | .... | .... | .... |
| Other investment | 8d9la | 199,977.7 | 239,633.5 | 276,530.2 | 356,182.1 | 344,193.8 | 376,766.5 | 380,110.0 | 386,540.4 | 440,361.0 | 441,734.7 | 482,164.8 | 558,237.6 |
| Other equity | 8dala | .... | .... | .... | .... | .... | .... | .... | .... | .... | .... | .... | .... |
| Debt instruments | 8dzla | 199,977.7 | 239,633.5 | 276,530.2 | 356,182.1 | 344,193.8 | 376,766.5 | 380,110.0 | 386,540.4 | 440,361.0 | 441,734.7 | 482,164.8 | 558,237.6 |

# Canada 156

Millions of Canadian Dollars: Fiscal Year Begins April 1

## Government Finance
## Operations Statement
### General Government

| | | 2004 | 2005 | 2006 | 2007 | 2008 | 2009 | 2010 | 2011 | 2012 | 2013 | 2014 | 2015 |
|---|---|---|---|---|---|---|---|---|---|---|---|---|---|
| Revenue | a1 | 542,035 | 579,717 | 613,278 | 646,922 | 638,328 | 624,253 | 646,350 | 687,975 | 705,087 | 740,634 | 760,357 | .... |
| Taxes | a11 | 380,920 | 404,710 | 428,532 | 450,406 | 441,147 | 434,439 | 447,626 | 474,563 | 490,965 | 513,595 | 529,844 | .... |
| Social Contributions | a12 | 63,185 | 66,215 | 69,578 | 76,431 | 74,360 | 74,448 | 76,002 | 80,954 | 86,046 | 90,151 | 93,585 | .... |
| Grants | a13 | — | — | — | −1 | — | — | — | — | — | — | — | .... |
| Other Revenue | a14 | 97,930 | 108,792 | 115,168 | 120,086 | 122,821 | 115,366 | 122,722 | 132,458 | 128,076 | 136,888 | 136,928 | .... |
| Expense | a2 | 516,456 | 543,348 | 568,523 | 602,838 | 634,145 | 667,775 | 696,678 | 720,684 | 734,577 | 753,043 | 769,647 | .... |
| Compensation of Employees | a21 | 150,878 | 158,176 | 169,134 | 178,934 | 191,218 | 201,285 | 208,416 | 217,074 | 224,534 | 230,823 | 236,075 | |
| Use of Goods & Services | a22 | 109,144 | 115,743 | 123,122 | 130,284 | 139,678 | 146,168 | 150,548 | 157,086 | 158,373 | 162,958 | 166,447 | |
| Consumption of Fixed Capital | a23 | 34,177 | 36,446 | 39,363 | 43,086 | 47,195 | 49,801 | 52,817 | 56,620 | 59,886 | 62,918 | 65,311 | |
| Interest | a24 | 64,111 | 63,566 | 63,527 | 62,964 | 61,082 | 58,438 | 62,105 | 64,077 | 63,846 | 63,997 | 63,746 | |
| Subsidies | a25 | 17,308 | 17,612 | 16,334 | 15,396 | 14,991 | 17,117 | 19,601 | 19,545 | 19,126 | 17,760 | 17,464 | |
| Grants | a26 | 4,471 | 4,394 | 4,447 | 4,712 | 4,619 | 4,991 | 5,111 | 4,999 | 5,023 | 4,789 | 5,252 | |
| Social Benefits | a27 | 113,757 | 118,824 | 125,787 | 138,237 | 143,816 | 157,606 | 160,790 | 165,927 | 170,231 | 175,735 | 181,583 | |
| Other Expense | a28 | 22,610 | 28,587 | 26,809 | 29,225 | 31,546 | 32,369 | 37,290 | 35,356 | 33,558 | 34,063 | 33,769 | |
| Gross Operating Balance [1-2+23] | agob | 59,756 | 72,815 | 84,118 | 87,170 | 51,378 | 6,279 | 2,489 | 23,911 | 30,396 | 50,509 | 56,021 | |
| Net Operating Balance [1-2] | anob | 25,579 | 36,369 | 44,755 | 44,084 | 4,183 | −43,522 | −50,328 | −32,709 | −29,490 | −12,409 | −9,290 | |
| Net Acq. of Nonfinancial Assets | a31 | 10,413 | 13,995 | 14,968 | 17,394 | 15,171 | 24,902 | 28,800 | 18,989 | 16,751 | 9,417 | 5,585 | |
| Aquisition of Nonfin. Assets | a31.1 | .... | .... | .... | .... | .... | .... | .... | .... | .... | .... | .... | |
| Disposal of Nonfin. Assets | a31.2 | .... | .... | .... | .... | .... | .... | .... | .... | .... | .... | .... | |
| Net Lending/Borrowing [1-2-31] | anlb | 15,166 | 22,374 | 29,787 | 26,690 | −10,988 | −68,424 | −79,128 | −51,698 | −46,241 | −21,826 | −14,875 | |
| Net Acq. of Financial Assets | a32 | 44,656 | 49,924 | 53,509 | 44,906 | 161,334 | 37,434 | 34,439 | 39,370 | 54,870 | −976 | 93,497 | |
| By instrument | | | | | | | | | | | | | |
| Monetary Gold & SDRs | a3201 | — | — | — | — | — | — | — | — | — | — | — | |
| Currency & Deposits | a3202 | 5,422 | −709 | 3,458 | 6,045 | 56,339 | −22,973 | −13,160 | 3,272 | 14,058 | 6,825 | 7,956 | |
| Securities other than Shares | a3203 | 31,113 | 17,384 | 24,093 | 9,100 | −21,114 | −7,912 | 1,939 | −5,294 | −812 | 13,235 | 18,344 | |
| Loans | a3204 | 1,279 | 4,450 | 5,831 | 11,769 | 46,198 | 59,955 | 16,821 | 8,889 | 11,517 | −8,654 | −6,161 | |
| Shares & Other Equity | a3205 | 10,234 | 9,270 | 14,275 | 12,022 | 31,204 | 17,925 | 13,999 | 19,149 | 24,296 | 1,938 | 25,482 | |
| Insurance Technical Reserves | a3206 | — | — | — | — | — | — | — | — | — | — | — | |
| Financial Derivatives | a3207 | — | — | — | — | — | — | — | — | — | — | — | |
| Other Accounts Receivable | a3208 | −3,392 | 19,529 | 5,852 | 5,970 | 48,707 | −9,561 | 14,840 | 13,354 | 5,811 | −14,320 | 47,876 | |
| By debtor | | | | | | | | | | | | | |
| Domestic | a321 | .... | .... | .... | .... | .... | .... | .... | .... | .... | .... | .... | |
| Foreign | a322 | .... | .... | .... | .... | .... | .... | .... | .... | .... | .... | .... | |
| Net Incurrence of Liabilities | a33 | 28,376 | 27,495 | 24,252 | 18,040 | 171,586 | 105,636 | 113,325 | 92,225 | 100,868 | 20,325 | 108,527 | |
| By instrument | | | | | | | | | | | | | |
| Special Drawing Rights (SDRs) | a3301 | — | — | — | — | — | — | — | — | — | — | — | |
| Currency & Deposits | a3302 | 116 | 224 | 217 | 175 | 173 | 105 | 129 | 106 | 120 | 85 | 82 | |
| Securities other than Shares | a3303 | 9,941 | −3,291 | 5,194 | −9,911 | 134,515 | 94,818 | 79,412 | 77,104 | 85,145 | 15,762 | 33,047 | |
| Loans | a3304 | 2,082 | −1,888 | 77 | 473 | 7,320 | 680 | 2,773 | 178 | 1,935 | 4,114 | 1,030 | |
| Shares & Other Equity | a3305 | — | — | — | — | — | — | — | — | — | — | — | |
| Insurance Technical Reserves | a3306 | 13,413 | 13,374 | 11,291 | 14,271 | 14,025 | 12,460 | 13,718 | 13,345 | 9,302 | 9,510 | 12,803 | |
| Financial Derivatives | a3307 | — | — | — | — | — | — | — | — | — | — | — | |
| Other Accounts Payable | a3308 | 2,824 | 19,076 | 7,473 | 13,032 | 15,553 | −2,427 | 17,293 | 1,492 | 4,366 | −9,146 | 61,565 | |
| By creditor | | | | | | | | | | | | | |
| Domestic | a331 | .... | .... | .... | .... | .... | .... | .... | .... | .... | .... | .... | |
| Foreign | a332 | .... | .... | .... | .... | .... | .... | .... | .... | .... | .... | .... | |
| Stat. Discrepancy [32-33-NLB] | anlbz | 664 | −466 | −878 | 175 | 736 | 222 | 242 | −1,157 | 243 | 525 | −155 | |
| Memo Item: Expenditure [2+31] | a2m | 526,869 | 557,343 | 583,491 | 620,232 | 649,316 | 692,677 | 725,478 | 739,673 | 751,328 | 762,460 | 775,232 | |

### Balance Sheet

| | | 2004 | 2005 | 2006 | 2007 | 2008 | 2009 | 2010 | 2011 | 2012 | 2013 | 2014 | 2015 |
|---|---|---|---|---|---|---|---|---|---|---|---|---|---|
| Net Worth | a6 | −188,418 | −64,819 | −6,846 | 98,937 | −102,013 | 34,673 | 24,675 | −91,926 | −87,504 | 24,966 | −117,053 | .... |
| Nonfinancial Assets | a61 | 530,720 | 617,668 | 640,013 | 748,476 | 613,773 | 797,193 | 851,739 | 844,445 | 870,844 | 945,683 | 871,023 | |
| Financial Assets | a62 | 586,102 | 660,648 | 733,392 | 759,773 | 833,938 | 887,076 | 943,116 | 999,233 | 1,087,276 | 1,135,235 | 1,238,373 | |
| By instrument | | | | | | | | | | | | | |
| Monetary Gold & SDRs | a6201 | — | — | — | — | — | — | — | — | — | — | — | |
| Currency & Deposits | a6202 | 31,016 | 30,295 | 33,776 | 39,758 | 96,149 | 73,146 | 59,964 | 63,248 | 77,303 | 84,156 | 92,129 | |
| Securities other than Shares | a6203 | 108,510 | 125,540 | 150,206 | 155,004 | 120,894 | 114,784 | 116,609 | 113,738 | 114,755 | 126,468 | 149,414 | |
| Loans | a6204 | 112,429 | 117,740 | 124,442 | 137,947 | 138,918 | 196,227 | 212,368 | 219,303 | 227,971 | 218,028 | 210,409 | |
| Shares and Other Equity | a6205 | 230,216 | 262,955 | 291,031 | 296,986 | 273,674 | 310,131 | 350,858 | 385,579 | 426,440 | 479,038 | 545,877 | |
| Insurance Technical Reserves | a6206 | — | — | — | — | — | — | — | — | — | — | — | |
| Financial Derivatives | a6207 | — | — | — | — | — | — | — | — | — | — | — | |
| Other Accounts Receivable | a6208 | 103,931 | 124,118 | 133,937 | 130,078 | 204,303 | 192,788 | 203,317 | 217,365 | 240,807 | 227,545 | 240,544 | |
| By debtor | | | | | | | | | | | | | |
| Domestic | a621 | .... | .... | .... | .... | .... | .... | .... | .... | .... | .... | .... | |
| Foreign | a622 | .... | .... | .... | .... | .... | .... | .... | .... | .... | .... | .... | |
| Liabilities | a63 | 1,305,240 | 1,343,135 | 1,380,251 | 1,409,312 | 1,549,724 | 1,649,596 | 1,770,180 | 1,935,604 | 2,045,624 | 2,055,952 | 2,226,449 | |
| By instrument | | | | | | | | | | | | | |
| Special Drawing Rights (SDRs) | a6301 | — | — | — | — | — | — | — | — | — | — | — | |
| Currency & Deposits | a6302 | 4,309 | 4,533 | 4,750 | 4,925 | 5,098 | 5,203 | 5,332 | 5,438 | 5,558 | 5,643 | 5,725 | |
| Securities other than Shares | a6303 | 783,649 | 778,891 | 791,726 | 786,817 | 942,821 | 1,035,648 | 1,120,107 | 1,259,868 | 1,336,484 | 1,328,134 | 1,445,402 | |
| Loans | a6304 | 58,908 | 55,267 | 54,663 | 54,910 | 48,366 | 49,032 | 51,084 | 53,785 | 55,524 | 58,993 | 59,425 | |
| Shares and Other Equity | a6305 | — | — | — | — | — | — | — | — | — | — | — | |
| Insurance Technical Reserves | a6306 | 259,909 | 261,354 | 259,182 | 286,411 | 324,035 | 315,558 | 339,883 | 354,494 | 365,701 | 331,920 | 356,145 | |
| Financial Derivatives | a6307 | — | — | — | — | — | — | — | — | — | — | — | |
| Other Accounts Payable | a6308 | 198,465 | 243,090 | 269,930 | 276,249 | 229,404 | 244,155 | 253,774 | 262,019 | 282,357 | 331,262 | 359,752 | |
| By creditor | | | | | | | | | | | | | |
| Domestic | a631 | .... | .... | .... | .... | .... | .... | .... | .... | .... | .... | .... | |
| Foreign | a632 | .... | .... | .... | .... | .... | .... | .... | .... | .... | .... | .... | |
| Net Financial Worth [62-63] | a6m2 | −719,138 | −682,487 | −646,859 | −649,539 | −715,786 | −762,520 | −827,064 | −936,371 | −958,348 | −920,717 | −988,076 | |
| Memo Item: Debt at Market Value | a6m3 | .... | .... | .... | .... | .... | .... | .... | .... | .... | .... | .... | |
| Memo Item: Debt at Face Value | a6m35 | 1,251,872 | 1,287,496 | 1,317,640 | 1,338,091 | 1,488,169 | 1,583,030 | 1,698,880 | 1,803,828 | 1,920,737 | 1,958,920 | 2,046,240 | |
| Memo Item: Debt at Nominal Value | a6m4 | .... | .... | .... | .... | .... | .... | .... | .... | .... | .... | .... | |

# Canada 156

| National Accounts | | 2004 | 2005 | 2006 | 2007 | 2008 | 2009 | 2010 | 2011 | 2012 | 2013 | 2014 | 2015 |
|---|---|---|---|---|---|---|---|---|---|---|---|---|---|
| | | | | | | *Billions of Canadian dollars* | | | | | | | |
| Househ.Cons.Expend.,incl.NPISHs.... | 96fac | 727.43 | 768.65 | 811.24 | 860.35 | 899.14 | 901.17 | 946.35 | 988.58 | 1,020.60 | 1,059.40 | 1,106.70 | 1,139.93 |
| Government Consumption Expend... | 91fac | 248.53 | 262.37 | 282.67 | 298.07 | 314.04 | 331.81 | 352.70 | 368.58 | 394.68 | 407.92 | 417.67 | 419.20 |
| Gross Fixed Capital Formation......... | 93eac | 278.82 | 310.60 | 342.71 | 366.11 | 386.53 | 348.30 | 387.98 | 412.04 | 439.27 | 446.19 | 467.56 | 466.21 |
| Changes in Inventories.................... | 93iac | 7.22 | 9.47 | 7.22 | 7.15 | 6.95 | −9.00 | 2.05 | 4.03 | 7.98 | 11.50 | 8.10 | 6.17 |
| Exports of Goods and Services......... | 90cac | 492.58 | 518.26 | 525.61 | 534.67 | 559.76 | 438.16 | 476.51 | 534.56 | 545.83 | 565.74 | 623.76 | 622.83 |
| Imports of Goods and Services (-)..... | 98cac | 438.35 | 464.03 | 487.38 | 503.45 | 534.10 | 464.02 | 507.32 | 556.43 | 582.27 | 597.62 | 641.62 | 670.23 |
| Gross Domestic Product (GDP)......... | 99bac | 1,290.19 | 1,368.73 | 1,439.29 | 1,531.43 | 1,602.47 | 1,527.67 | 1,621.53 | 1,718.69 | 1,817.60 | 1,879.48 | 1,976.23 | 1,985.65 |
| Net Primary Income from Abroad..... | 98nac | −22.48 | −24.52 | −17.10 | −19.78 | −14.74 | −19.69 | −27.56 | −30.20 | −30.78 | −24.86 | −28.82 | −26.53 |
| Gross National Income (GNI)............ | 99aac | 1,270.81 | 1,344.21 | 1,422.19 | 1,511.65 | 1,587.73 | 1,507.99 | 1,593.97 | 1,688.49 | 1,784.85 | 1,852.47 | 1,945.33 | 1,957.43 |
| Gross Nat'l Disposable Inc.(GNDI).... | 99iac | 1,270.04 | 1,343.99 | 1,422.35 | 1,511.33 | 1,587.36 | 1,505.81 | 1,591.53 | 1,684.47 | .... | .... | .... | .... |
| Gross Saving................................. | 99sac | 262.69 | 291.48 | 317.16 | 347.47 | 370.94 | 327.78 | 357.29 | 389.70 | .... | .... | .... | .... |
| Consumption of Fixed Capital......... | 99cac | 174.22 | 181.43 | 185.51 | 193.81 | 206.68 | 217.33 | 229.06 | 241.26 | .... | .... | .... | .... |
| GDP Volume 2007 Ref., Chained..... | 99bar | 1,455.72 | 1,502.32 | 1,541.73 | 1,573.53 | 1,589.27 | 1,542.40 | 1,589.96 | 1,639.90 | 1,668.52 | 1,705.53 | 1,747.71 | 1,766.55 |
| GDP Volume (2010=100)............... | 99bvr | 91.6 | 94.5 | 97.0 | 99.0 | 100.0 | 97.0 | 100.0 | 103.1 | 104.9 | 107.3 | 109.9 | 111.1 |
| GDP Deflator (2010=100)............... | 99bir | 86.9 | 89.3 | 91.5 | 95.4 | 98.9 | 97.1 | 100.0 | 102.8 | 106.8 | 108.1 | 110.9 | 110.2 |
| | | | | | | *Millions: Midyear Estimates* | | | | | | | |
| Population............................... | 99z | 31.92 | 32.26 | 32.61 | 32.98 | 33.36 | 33.75 | 34.13 | 34.50 | 34.87 | 35.23 | 35.59 | 35.94 |

|  |  | 2004 | 2005 | 2006 | 2007 | 2008 | 2009 | 2010 | 2011 | 2012 | 2013 | 2014 | 2015 |
|---|---|---|---|---|---|---|---|---|---|---|---|---|---|
| **Exchange Rates** |  | *CFA Francs per SDR: End of Period* | | | | | | | | | | | |
| Official Rate | aa | 747.90 | 794.73 | 749.30 | 704.15 | 725.98 | 713.83 | 756.02 | 778.32 | 764.10 | 732.49 | 782.77 | 834.92 |
|  |  | *CFA Francs per US Dollar: End of Period (ae) Period Average (rf)* | | | | | | | | | | | |
| Official Rate | ae | 481.58 | 556.04 | 498.07 | 445.59 | 471.34 | 455.34 | 490.91 | 506.96 | 497.16 | 475.64 | 540.28 | 602.51 |
| Official Rate | rf | 528.28 | 527.47 | 522.89 | 479.27 | 447.81 | 472.19 | 495.28 | 471.87 | 510.53 | 494.04 | 494.41 | 591.45 |
| **Fund Position** |  | *Millions of SDRs: End of Period* | | | | | | | | | | | |
| Quota | 2f.s | 568.90 | 568.90 | 568.90 | 568.90 | 568.90 | 568.90 | 568.90 | 599.20 | 599.20 | 599.20 | 599.20 | 599.20 |
| SDR Holdings | 1b.s | 16.35 | 3.88 | 15.23 | 4.96 | 4.94 | 473.67 | 466.15 | 452.35 | 244.12 | 243.41 | 241.66 | 239.61 |
| Reserve Position in the Fund | 1c.s | 1.81 | 1.90 | 1.94 | 2.15 | 2.28 | 2.41 | 2.50 | 10.20 | 10.28 | 10.34 | 10.59 | 10.89 |
| Total Fund Cred.&Loans Outstg. | 2tl | 387.94 | 337.11 | 139.64 | 116.31 | 109.75 | 206.83 | 198.48 | 196.23 | 197.28 | 188.38 | 198.72 | 208.16 |
| SDR Allocations | 1bd | 72.82 | 72.82 | 72.82 | 72.82 | 72.82 | 541.96 | 541.96 | 541.96 | 541.96 | 541.96 | 541.96 | 541.96 |
| **International Liquidity** |  | *Millions of US Dollars Unless Otherwise Indicated: End of Period* | | | | | | | | | | | |
| Total Reserves minus Gold | 1l.d | 3,110.41 | 5,143.90 | 8,888.57 | 11,936.85 | 15,662.09 | 14,353.62 | 13,657.98 | 15,717.29 | 17,530.69 | 18,221.64 | 15,309.34 | 10,139.30 |
| SDR Holdings | 1b.d | 25.39 | 5.55 | 22.91 | 7.84 | 7.60 | 742.57 | 717.89 | 694.48 | 375.19 | 374.85 | 350.11 | 332.04 |
| Reserve Position in the Fund | 1c.d | 2.81 | 2.71 | 2.92 | 3.40 | 3.52 | 3.78 | 3.85 | 15.66 | 15.80 | 15.93 | 15.35 | 15.10 |
| Foreign Exchange | 1d.d | 3,082.21 | 5,135.64 | 8,862.74 | 11,925.62 | 15,650.97 | 13,607.26 | 12,936.25 | 15,007.15 | 17,139.70 | 17,830.86 | 14,943.88 | 9,792.17 |
| Gold (Million Fine Troy Ounces) | 1ad | .229 | .229 | .229 | .229 | .229 | .... | .... | .... | .... | .... | .... | .... |
| Gold (National Valuation) | 1and | 78.32 | 91.61 | 143.55 | 150.15 | 25.92 | — | 68.32 | 272.68 | 300.37 | 215.30 | 215.25 | 214.45 |
| Monetary Authorities: Other Liabs. | 4..d | .63 | .51 | .23 | .25 | .26 | .42 | .37 | .43 | .46 | .54 | .51 | .40 |
| Deposit Money Banks: Assets | 7a.d | .91 | .92 | 1.26 | 2.92 | 1.57 | 2.10 | 1.79 | 1.79 | 1.97 | 2.31 | 1.25 | 1.22 |
| Deposit Money Banks: Liabs. | 7b.d | .31 | .23 | .30 | .52 | .48 | .60 | .58 | .81 | .91 | 1.05 | .89 | .88 |
| **Monetary Authorities** |  | *Billions of CFA Francs: End of Period* | | | | | | | | | | | |
| Foreign Assets | 11 | 1,535.59 | 2,911.10 | 4,498.62 | 5,385.88 | 7,394.30 | 6,535.76 | 6,748.21 | 8,112.51 | 8,870.59 | 8,777.48 | 8,387.47 | 6,238.28 |
| Claims on Central Government | 12a | 1,002.31 | 886.11 | 559.42 | 525.77 | 192.87 | 529.24 | 695.87 | 707.10 | 711.79 | 699.20 | 1,433.30 | 2,387.88 |
| Claims on Nonfin.Pub.Enterprises | 12c |  |  |  |  |  |  |  |  |  |  |  |  |
| Claims on Deposit Money Banks | 12e | 12.27 | 15.00 | 8.60 | 5.91 | 6.00 | 5.00 | — | 2.45 | 4.90 | 7.40 | 80.03 | 276.62 |
| Claims on Other Banking Insts. | 12f | — | — | — | — | — | — | — | — | — | — | — | — |
| Claims on Nonbank Financial Insts. | 12g | .17 | .23 | .36 | .32 | .37 | 8.03 | .59 | .50 | .38 | .49 | 29.50 | 35.26 |
| Reserve Money | 14 | 1,516.18 | 1,926.01 | 2,368.49 | 2,788.29 | 3,271.84 | 3,457.07 | 4,328.32 | 4,614.12 | 5,815.91 | 5,324.31 | 6,320.14 | 5,477.93 |
| of which: Currency Outside DMBs | 14a | 855.81 | 980.37 | 1,122.31 | 1,200.28 | 1,458.49 | 1,525.39 | 1,728.06 | 1,974.90 | 2,150.18 | 2,325.10 | 2,548.43 | 2,556.27 |
| Foreign Liabilities | 16c | 647.30 | 611.09 | 275.65 | 243.19 | 253.08 | 725.40 | 743.63 | 794.23 | 793.27 | 792.03 | 852.69 | 864.31 |
| Central Government Deposits | 16d | 584.89 | 1,407.86 | 2,362.18 | 2,763.97 | 3,944.09 | 2,850.23 | 2,679.01 | 3,488.52 | 3,084.18 | 3,498.75 | 2,879.05 | 2,471.98 |
| Capital Accounts | 17a | 228.63 | 225.52 | 248.39 | 315.84 | 357.76 | 423.81 | 381.73 | 403.58 | 440.13 | 397.87 | 424.77 | 506.38 |
| Other Items (Net) | 17r | −426.66 | −358.03 | −187.72 | −193.47 | −233.25 | −378.48 | −688.03 | −477.90 | −545.83 | −528.40 | −545.95 | −382.54 |
| **Deposit Money Banks** |  | *Billions of CFA Francs: End of Period* | | | | | | | | | | | |
| Reserves | 20 | 633.62 | 903.29 | 1,165.31 | 1,497.22 | 1,714.74 | 1,844.51 | 2,492.97 | 2,575.65 | 3,583.97 | 2,940.10 | 3,716.32 | 2,845.59 |
| Foreign Assets | 21 | 437.39 | 511.32 | 629.66 | 1,300.23 | 738.96 | 956.66 | 880.10 | 905.98 | 981.48 | 1,097.30 | 672.88 | 735.24 |
| Claims on Central Government | 22a | 290.49 | 272.96 | 299.43 | 290.95 | 259.34 | 269.38 | 444.53 | 557.86 | 655.81 | 720.17 | 901.58 | 975.14 |
| Claims on Nonfin.Pub.Enterprises | 22c | 133.97 | 141.05 | 146.54 | 134.07 | 199.91 | 194.67 | 188.36 | 193.24 | 190.69 | 273.61 | 242.07 | 372.86 |
| Claims on Private Sector | 22d | 1,369.97 | 1,565.74 | 1,713.94 | 1,950.72 | 2,476.87 | 2,663.17 | 3,112.23 | 4,074.06 | 4,555.09 | 5,634.70 | 6,275.63 | 6,850.73 |
| Claims on Other Banking Insts. | 22f | .62 | .63 | .89 | .61 | .66 | .09 | .18 | 1.58 | 7.76 | 11.63 | 14.06 | 15.19 |
| Claims on Nonbank Financial Insts. | 22g | 41.07 | 36.03 | 46.48 | 80.52 | 89.73 | 67.99 | 105.11 | 130.60 | 111.40 | 165.41 | 121.17 | 96.59 |
| Demand Deposits | 24 | 1,059.25 | 1,317.62 | 1,665.33 | 2,037.88 | 2,516.07 | 2,688.28 | 3,587.34 | 4,484.23 | 5,315.42 | 5,630.89 | 5,944.21 | 5,640.44 |
| Time and Savings Deposits | 25 | 1,007.06 | 1,135.75 | 1,277.32 | 1,329.71 | 1,442.48 | 1,555.89 | 1,830.22 | 2,052.87 | 2,431.82 | 2,600.55 | 2,744.77 | 2,873.00 |
| Bonds | 26ab | 1.53 | 5.14 | 4.49 | 4.49 | 44.50 | 41.65 | 4.58 | 11.60 | 12.25 | — | 13.75 | 19.34 |
| Foreign Liabilities | 26c | 136.84 | 107.98 | 140.37 | 212.59 | 215.07 | 262.09 | 268.26 | 368.79 | 379.66 | 432.44 | 418.05 | 394.53 |
| Long-Term Foreign Liabilities | 26cl | 10.65 | 20.30 | 11.10 | 18.81 | 11.74 | 12.84 | 16.38 | 39.87 | 75.22 | 65.85 | 62.08 | 138.52 |
| Central Government Deposits | 26d | 287.39 | 455.68 | 451.06 | 1,037.17 | 695.64 | 665.26 | 711.95 | 818.99 | 876.25 | 1,078.02 | 1,415.54 | 1,400.88 |
| Credit from Monetary Authorities | 26g | 12.27 | 15.00 | 8.60 | 5.91 | 6.00 | 5.00 | — | 2.45 | 4.90 | 7.40 | 80.03 | 276.62 |
| Capital Accounts | 27a | 474.74 | 510.71 | 551.38 | 594.56 | 708.07 | 809.30 | 869.05 | 1,007.47 | 1,125.87 | 1,342.51 | 1,539.76 | 1,775.67 |
| Other Items (Net) | 27r | −82.57 | −137.16 | −107.40 | 13.11 | −159.35 | −43.84 | −64.30 | −347.31 | −135.19 | −314.74 | −274.48 | −627.64 |
| **Monetary Survey** |  | *Billions of CFA Francs: End of Period* | | | | | | | | | | | |
| Foreign Assets (Net) | 31n | 1,178.20 | 2,683.05 | 4,701.15 | 6,211.53 | 7,653.37 | 6,492.09 | 6,600.04 | 7,815.58 | 8,603.91 | 8,584.45 | 7,727.53 | 5,576.16 |
| Domestic Credit | 32 | 1,966.33 | 1,039.21 | −46.18 | −818.19 | −1,419.99 | 217.08 | 1,155.91 | 1,357.43 | 2,272.49 | 2,928.44 | 4,722.73 | 6,860.81 |
| Claims on Central Govt. (Net) | 32an | 420.52 | −704.46 | −1,954.38 | −2,984.42 | −4,187.52 | −2,716.87 | −2,250.56 | −3,042.55 | −2,592.83 | −3,157.40 | −1,959.71 | −509.83 |
| Claims on Nonfin.Pub.Enterprises | 32c | 133.97 | 141.05 | 146.54 | 134.07 | 199.91 | 194.67 | 188.36 | 193.24 | 190.69 | 273.61 | 242.07 | 372.86 |
| Claims on Private Sector | 32d | 1,369.97 | 1,565.74 | 1,713.94 | 1,950.72 | 2,476.87 | 2,663.17 | 3,112.23 | 4,074.06 | 4,555.09 | 5,634.70 | 6,275.63 | 6,850.73 |
| Claims on Other Banking Insts. | 32f | .62 | .63 | .89 | .61 | .66 | .09 | .18 | 1.58 | 7.76 | 11.63 | 14.06 | 15.19 |
| Claims on Nonbank Financial Insts. | 32g | 41.24 | 36.26 | 46.84 | 80.83 | 90.10 | 76.02 | 105.71 | 131.10 | 111.78 | 165.89 | 150.67 | 131.86 |
| Money | 34 | 1,941.80 | 2,340.34 | 2,868.51 | 3,328.95 | 4,073.16 | 4,300.84 | 5,422.69 | 6,522.69 | 7,547.36 | 8,015.10 | 8,548.02 | 8,272.77 |
| Quasi-Money | 35 | 1,007.06 | 1,135.75 | 1,277.32 | 1,329.71 | 1,442.48 | 1,555.89 | 1,830.22 | 2,052.87 | 2,431.82 | 2,600.55 | 2,744.77 | 2,873.00 |
| Bonds | 36ab | 1.53 | 5.14 | 4.49 | 4.49 | 44.50 | 41.65 | 4.58 | 11.60 | 12.25 | — | 13.75 | 19.34 |
| Capital Accounts | 37a | 703.38 | 736.23 | 799.77 | 910.40 | 1,065.83 | 1,233.10 | 1,250.78 | 1,411.05 | 1,566.00 | 1,740.38 | 1,964.53 | 2,282.05 |
| Other Items (Net) | 37r | −509.23 | −495.19 | −295.12 | −180.36 | −392.59 | −422.32 | −752.33 | −825.21 | −681.02 | −843.13 | −820.43 | −1,010.19 |
| Money plus Quasi-Money | 35l | 2,948.86 | 3,476.09 | 4,145.83 | 4,658.66 | 5,515.64 | 5,856.73 | 7,252.91 | 8,575.57 | 9,979.18 | 10,615.65 | 11,292.80 | 11,145.77 |
| **Interest Rates** |  | *Percent Per Annum* | | | | | | | | | | | |
| Discount Rate (End of Period) | 60.a | 6.00 | 5.50 | 5.25 | 5.25 | 4.75 | 4.25 | 4.00 | 4.00 | 4.00 | 3.25 | 2.95 | 2.45 |
| Deposit Rate | 60l | 5.00 | 4.92 | 4.33 | 4.25 | 3.75 | 3.25 | 3.25 | 3.25 | 3.25 | 3.21 | 2.60 | 2.45 |

# Central African Republic 626

| | | 2004 | 2005 | 2006 | 2007 | 2008 | 2009 | 2010 | 2011 | 2012 | 2013 | 2014 | 2015 |
|---|---|---|---|---|---|---|---|---|---|---|---|---|---|
| **Exchange Rates** | | | | | | *CFA Francs per SDR: End of Period* | | | | | | | |
| Official Rate.................................... | aa | 747.90 | 794.73 | 749.30 | 704.15 | 725.98 | 713.83 | 756.02 | 778.32 | 764.10 | 732.49 | 782.77 | 834.92 |
| | | | | | *CFA Francs per US Dollar: End of Period (ae) Period Average (rf)* | | | | | | | | |
| Official Rate.................................... | ae | 481.58 | 556.04 | 498.07 | 445.59 | 471.34 | 455.34 | 490.91 | 506.96 | 497.16 | 475.64 | 540.28 | 602.51 |
| Official Rate.................................... | rf | 528.28 | 527.47 | 522.89 | 479.27 | 447.81 | 472.19 | 495.28 | 471.87 | 510.53 | 494.04 | 494.41 | 591.45 |
| | | | | | *Index Numbers (2010=100): Period Averages* | | | | | | | | |
| Official Rate.................................... | ahx | 93.7 | 93.9 | 94.6 | 103.3 | 110.9 | 105.0 | 100.0 | 104.9 | 96.9 | 100.1 | 100.1 | 83.6 |
| Nominal Effective Exchange Rate..... | nec | 101.1 | 99.7 | 99.6 | 102.6 | 105.2 | 104.3 | 100.0 | 100.8 | 97.8 | 101.3 | 103.0 | 98.7 |
| CPI-Based Real Effect. Ex. Rate........ | rec | 91.3 | 90.7 | 94.2 | 95.4 | 102.8 | 104.9 | 100.0 | 99.0 | 99.2 | 102.3 | 128.0 | 168.5 |
| **Fund Position** | | | | | | *Millions of SDRs: End of Period* | | | | | | | |
| Quota............................................. | 2f.s | 55.70 | 55.70 | 55.70 | 55.70 | 55.70 | 55.70 | 55.70 | 55.70 | 55.70 | 55.70 | 55.70 | 55.70 |
| SDR Holdings................................. | 1b.s | 1.58 | .08 | .47 | .48 | .02 | 2.76 | 2.78 | 2.76 | 2.76 | 2.75 | .98 | .39 |
| Reserve Position in the Fund............ | 1c.s | .16 | .16 | .16 | .16 | .16 | .20 | .23 | .26 | .26 | .26 | .29 | .36 |
| Total Fund Cred.&Loans Outstg....... | 2tl | 28.40 | 25.11 | 27.97 | 31.24 | 40.90 | 50.01 | 58.68 | 58.68 | 65.64 | 64.15 | 68.98 | 72.86 |
| SDR Allocations.............................. | 1bd | 9.33 | 9.33 | 9.33 | 9.33 | 9.33 | 53.37 | 53.37 | 53.37 | 53.37 | 53.37 | 53.37 | 53.37 |
| **International Liquidity** | | | | | *Millions of US Dollars Unless Otherwise Indicated: End of Period* | | | | | | | | |
| Total Reserves minus Gold.............. | 1l.d | 148.32 | 139.22 | 125.35 | 82.59 | 121.79 | 210.59 | 181.18 | 154.51 | 157.90 | 193.66 | 259.57 | 213.80 |
| SDR Holdings............................. | 1b.d | 2.46 | .12 | .71 | .76 | .03 | 4.33 | 4.28 | 4.23 | 4.24 | 4.24 | 1.41 | .54 |
| Reserve Position in the Fund......... | 1c.d | .25 | .23 | .24 | .25 | .24 | .32 | .36 | .40 | .40 | .40 | .42 | .49 |
| Foreign Exchange........................ | 1d.d | 145.62 | 138.87 | 124.40 | 81.58 | 121.51 | 205.94 | 176.54 | 149.88 | 153.27 | 189.02 | 257.73 | 212.76 |
| Gold (Million Fine Troy Ounces)........ | 1ad | .011 | .011 | .011 | .011 | .011 | .... | .... | .... | .... | .... | .... | .... |
| Gold (National Valuation)................ | 1and | 4.88 | 5.71 | 7.06 | 9.37 | 1.62 | — | 4.78 | 17.01 | 18.73 | .... | .... | .... |
| Central Bank: Other Assets............. | 3..d | — | — | — | — | — | — | — | — | — | — | — | — |
| Central Bank: Other Liabs............... | 4..d | 2.48 | 1.68 | 2.87 | 2.92 | 2.41 | 1.59 | 13.28 | 9.04 | 8.24 | 8.44 | 7.60 | 5.94 |
| Other Depository Corps.: Assets....... | 7a.d | 12.95 | 8.80 | 19.84 | 53.22 | 37.89 | 47.64 | 55.32 | 74.73 | 49.24 | 39.80 | 42.86 | 42.90 |
| Other Depository Corps.: Liabs........ | 7b.d | 14.06 | 12.70 | 18.29 | 20.38 | 29.51 | 31.63 | 33.92 | 38.90 | 57.67 | 39.35 | 35.26 | 17.59 |
| **Central Bank** | | | | | | *Billions of CFA Francs: End of Period* | | | | | | | |
| Net Foreign Assets......................... | 11n | 44.37 | 52.29 | 36.57 | 11.11 | 20.45 | 21.37 | .06 | −4.84 | −7.22 | 8.40 | 47.62 | 26.97 |
| Claims on Nonresidents................. | 11 | 73.78 | 80.58 | 65.95 | 40.98 | 58.05 | 95.89 | 91.29 | 86.95 | 87.82 | 98.50 | 147.50 | 135.94 |
| Liabilities to Nonresidents.............. | 16c | 29.41 | 28.30 | 29.38 | 29.87 | 37.60 | 74.52 | 91.23 | 91.79 | 95.03 | 90.10 | 99.88 | 108.96 |
| Claims on Other Depository Corps.... | 12e | 4.07 | — | — | — | — | — | — | — | — | — | — | — |
| Net Claims on Central Government.. | 12an | 60.15 | 67.82 | 75.20 | 78.12 | 82.72 | 108.69 | 129.24 | 143.90 | 145.99 | 150.47 | 143.82 | 161.06 |
| Claims on Central Government...... | 12a | 60.86 | 69.22 | 75.57 | 79.25 | 89.27 | 130.02 | 143.09 | 147.02 | 153.39 | 151.14 | 162.76 | 173.04 |
| Liabilities to Central Government... | 16d | .72 | 1.39 | .37 | 1.13 | 6.55 | 21.32 | 13.85 | 3.13 | 7.40 | .67 | 18.94 | 11.99 |
| Claims on Other Sectors................. | 12s | — | — | — | — | .68 | .60 | .72 | 1.32 | 1.66 | 1.71 | 1.88 | 2.14 |
| Claims on Other Financial Corps.... | 12g | — | — | — | — | — | — | — | — | — | — | — | — |
| Claims on State & Local Govts....... | 12b | — | — | — | — | — | — | — | — | — | — | — | — |
| Claims on Public Nonfin. Corps..... | 12c | — | — | — | — | — | — | — | — | — | — | — | — |
| Claims on Private Sector................ | 12d | — | — | — | — | .68 | .60 | .72 | 1.32 | 1.66 | 1.71 | 1.88 | 2.14 |
| Monetary Base.............................. | 14 | 83.85 | 98.38 | 83.84 | 68.30 | 82.77 | 105.93 | 108.36 | 117.20 | 114.42 | 133.13 | 164.60 | 161.61 |
| Currency in Circulation................. | 14a | 83.33 | 92.25 | 82.67 | 62.42 | 76.49 | 86.43 | 98.78 | 110.80 | 110.79 | 124.19 | 143.26 | 143.09 |
| Liabs. to Other Depository Corps.... | 14c | .52 | 6.13 | 1.17 | 5.88 | 5.48 | 19.50 | 9.58 | 6.40 | 3.63 | 8.94 | 21.32 | 18.46 |
| Liabilities to Other Sectors............. | 14d | — | — | — | — | .81 | — | — | — | — | — | .02 | .05 |
| Other Liabs. to Other Dep. Corps..... | 14n | — | — | — | — | — | — | — | — | — | — | — | — |
| Dep. & Sec. Excl. f/Monetary Base.... | 14o | — | — | — | — | — | — | — | — | — | — | — | — |
| Deposits Included in Broad Money. | 15 | — | — | — | — | — | — | — | — | — | — | — | — |
| Sec.Ot.th.Shares Incl.in Brd. Money | 16a | — | — | — | — | — | — | — | — | — | — | — | — |
| Deposits Excl. from Broad Money... | 16b | — | — | — | — | — | — | — | — | — | — | — | — |
| Sec.Ot.th.Shares Excl.f/Brd.Money.. | 16s | — | — | — | — | — | — | — | — | — | — | — | — |
| Loans............................................. | 16l | — | — | — | — | — | — | — | — | — | — | — | — |
| Financial Derivatives...................... | 16m | — | — | — | — | — | — | — | — | — | — | — | — |
| Shares and Other Equity................. | 17a | 27.66 | 23.96 | 24.91 | 24.25 | 21.16 | 26.28 | 19.84 | 19.49 | 20.53 | 20.91 | 19.92 | 20.43 |
| Other Items (Net)............................ | 17r | −2.92 | −2.23 | 3.01 | −3.33 | −.08 | −1.54 | 1.82 | 3.70 | 5.48 | 6.54 | 8.80 | 8.13 |
| Memo Item: | | | | | | | | | | | | | |
| Total Assets.................................... | 10ra | 152.15 | 162.90 | 155.28 | 135.42 | 161.04 | 238.81 | 247.87 | 248.20 | 255.13 | 263.02 | 324.45 | 325.08 |

2016, International Monetary Fund : *International Financial Statistics Yearbook*

# Central African Republic 626

| | | 2004 | 2005 | 2006 | 2007 | 2008 | 2009 | 2010 | 2011 | 2012 | 2013 | 2014 | 2015 |
|---|---|---|---|---|---|---|---|---|---|---|---|---|---|
| **Other Depository Corporations** | | | | | | *Billions of CFA Francs: End of Period* | | | | | | | |
| Net Foreign Assets.................... | 21n | −.53 | −2.17 | .77 | 14.64 | 3.95 | 7.29 | 10.51 | 18.17 | −4.19 | .21 | 4.10 | 15.25 |
| Claims on Nonresidents................ | 21 | 6.24 | 4.89 | 9.88 | 23.72 | 17.86 | 21.69 | 27.16 | 37.89 | 24.48 | 18.93 | 23.15 | 25.85 |
| Liabilities to Nonresidents.............. | 26c | 6.77 | 7.06 | 9.11 | 9.08 | 13.91 | 14.40 | 16.65 | 19.72 | 28.67 | 18.72 | 19.05 | 10.60 |
| Claims on Central Bank................ | 20 | 2.08 | 7.41 | 2.85 | 9.87 | 10.28 | 28.67 | 23.94 | 12.21 | 13.05 | 16.21 | 23.58 | 26.78 |
| Currency............................... | 20a | 1.84 | 2.25 | 1.60 | 3.41 | 3.39 | 7.03 | 4.34 | 5.25 | 5.66 | 4.01 | 5.02 | 8.36 |
| Reserve Deposits and Securities..... | 20b | .24 | 5.16 | 1.25 | 6.46 | 6.89 | 21.63 | 19.59 | 6.95 | 7.39 | 12.20 | 18.55 | 18.42 |
| Other Claims........................... | 20n | — | — | — | — | — | — | — | — | — | — | — | — |
| Net Claims on Central Government.. | 22an | .04 | 2.93 | 7.70 | 7.10 | 13.24 | 7.84 | 3.02 | 10.73 | 5.07 | 9.38 | 19.33 | 24.96 |
| Claims on Central Government...... | 22a | 5.45 | 7.82 | 12.90 | 15.50 | 20.93 | 16.75 | 16.24 | 24.17 | 19.24 | 17.01 | 31.22 | 39.77 |
| Liabilities to Central Government... | 26d | 5.41 | 4.89 | 5.20 | 8.40 | 7.69 | 8.91 | 13.22 | 13.43 | 14.17 | 7.63 | 11.88 | 14.80 |
| Claims on Other Sectors................ | 22s | 55.01 | 54.31 | 56.39 | 60.55 | 65.04 | 70.00 | 89.88 | 107.60 | 140.12 | 116.90 | 121.48 | 120.97 |
| Claims on Other Financial Corps.... | 22g | .22 | — | — | 1.16 | 1.16 | 1.13 | .87 | .62 | .61 | 1.75 | .80 | 2.42 |
| Claims on State & Local Govts....... | 22b | — | — | — | — | — | — | — | — | — | — | — | — |
| Claims on Public Nonfin. Corps...... | 22c | 6.74 | 5.65 | 5.18 | 4.19 | 2.14 | 1.78 | 1.64 | 2.83 | 3.13 | 3.44 | 2.90 | 3.23 |
| Claims on Private Sector................ | 22d | 48.05 | 48.67 | 51.21 | 55.20 | 61.74 | 67.09 | 87.37 | 104.15 | 136.39 | 111.72 | 117.79 | 115.32 |
| Liabilities to Central Bank............... | 26g | 5.13 | .01 | .01 | .03 | — | — | — | .05 | 2.81 | — | — | — |
| Transf.Dep.Included in Broad Money | 24 | 13.77 | 22.80 | 23.19 | 35.58 | 36.67 | 46.09 | 49.94 | 53.52 | 57.65 | 49.45 | 58.85 | 64.81 |
| Other Dep.Included in Broad Money. | 25 | 12.51 | 14.66 | 17.35 | 19.35 | 24.36 | 25.25 | 30.67 | 40.13 | 39.51 | 44.02 | 47.69 | 58.18 |
| Sec.Ot.th.Shares Incl.in Brd. Money.. | 26a | — | — | — | — | — | — | — | — | — | — | — | — |
| Deposits Excl. from Broad Money..... | 26b | .80 | 1.81 | .40 | .57 | .52 | .35 | .39 | 1.02 | .05 | .18 | .20 | .05 |
| Sec.Ot.th.Shares Excl.f/Brd.Money.... | 26s | — | — | — | — | — | — | — | — | — | — | — | — |
| Loans................................... | 26l | — | — | — | — | — | — | — | — | — | — | — | — |
| Financial Derivatives........................ | 26m | — | — | — | — | — | — | — | — | — | — | — | — |
| Insurance Technical Reserves........... | 26r | — | — | — | — | — | — | — | — | — | — | — | — |
| Shares and Other Equity.................. | 27a | 9.02 | 9.28 | 11.44 | 15.53 | 18.06 | 24.70 | 24.92 | 38.76 | 43.98 | 42.17 | 40.36 | 39.60 |
| Other Items (Net)............................ | 27r | 15.38 | 13.92 | 15.32 | 21.11 | 12.88 | 17.40 | 21.43 | 15.24 | 10.06 | 6.88 | 21.39 | 25.32 |
| Memo Item: | | | | | | | | | | | | | |
| Total Assets................................. | 20ra | 74.62 | 81.62 | 88.25 | 116.17 | 128.83 | 148.04 | 170.02 | 197.71 | 213.07 | 193.17 | 213.86 | 230.55 |
| **Depository Corporations** | | | | | | *Billions of CFA Francs: End of Period* | | | | | | | |
| Net Foreign Assets.................... | 31n | 43.84 | 50.12 | 37.34 | 25.74 | 24.40 | 28.66 | 10.57 | 13.33 | −11.41 | 8.61 | 51.72 | 42.22 |
| Claims on Nonresidents................ | 31 | 80.02 | 85.48 | 75.83 | 64.69 | 75.91 | 117.58 | 118.45 | 124.84 | 112.30 | 117.43 | 170.65 | 161.78 |
| Liabilities to Nonresidents.............. | 36c | 36.18 | 35.36 | 38.49 | 38.95 | 51.51 | 88.92 | 107.88 | 111.51 | 123.70 | 108.82 | 118.93 | 119.56 |
| Domestic Claims............................ | 32 | 115.20 | 125.06 | 139.29 | 145.77 | 161.67 | 187.13 | 222.85 | 263.55 | 292.85 | 278.46 | 286.52 | 309.13 |
| Net Claims on Central Government | 32an | 60.19 | 70.75 | 82.89 | 85.22 | 95.96 | 116.53 | 132.26 | 154.63 | 151.06 | 159.85 | 163.16 | 186.02 |
| Claims on Central Government.... | 32a | 66.32 | 77.04 | 88.46 | 94.75 | 110.20 | 146.77 | 159.33 | 171.19 | 172.63 | 168.15 | 193.98 | 212.81 |
| Liabilities to Central Government. | 36d | 6.13 | 6.29 | 5.57 | 9.53 | 14.24 | 30.24 | 27.08 | 16.56 | 21.57 | 8.30 | 30.82 | 26.79 |
| Claims on Other Sectors................ | 32s | 55.01 | 54.31 | 56.39 | 60.55 | 65.71 | 70.60 | 90.60 | 108.92 | 141.78 | 118.61 | 123.37 | 123.11 |
| Claims on Other Financial Corps.. | 32g | .22 | — | — | 1.16 | 1.16 | 1.13 | .87 | .62 | .61 | 1.75 | .80 | 2.42 |
| Claims on State & Local Govts...... | 32b | — | — | — | — | — | — | — | — | — | — | — | — |
| Claims on Public Nonfin. Corps.... | 32c | 6.74 | 5.65 | 5.18 | 4.19 | 2.14 | 1.78 | 1.64 | 2.83 | 3.13 | 3.44 | 2.90 | 3.23 |
| Claims on Private Sector.............. | 32d | 48.05 | 48.67 | 51.21 | 55.20 | 62.41 | 67.70 | 88.09 | 105.47 | 138.05 | 113.43 | 119.67 | 117.46 |
| Broad Money Liabilities.................. | 35l | 107.76 | 127.46 | 121.61 | 113.94 | 134.93 | 150.73 | 175.05 | 199.19 | 202.29 | 213.65 | 244.80 | 257.78 |
| Currency Outside Depository Corps | 34a | 81.49 | 90.00 | 81.08 | 59.01 | 73.09 | 79.39 | 94.44 | 105.55 | 105.13 | 120.18 | 138.24 | 134.74 |
| Transferable Deposits.................... | 34 | 13.77 | 22.80 | 23.19 | 35.58 | 37.48 | 46.09 | 49.94 | 53.52 | 57.65 | 49.45 | 58.87 | 64.86 |
| Other Deposits............................. | 35 | 12.51 | 14.66 | 17.35 | 19.35 | 24.36 | 25.25 | 30.67 | 40.13 | 39.51 | 44.02 | 47.69 | 58.18 |
| Securities Other than Shares......... | 36a | — | — | — | — | — | — | — | — | — | — | — | — |
| Deposits Excl. from Broad Money..... | 36b | .80 | 1.81 | .40 | .57 | .52 | .35 | .39 | 1.02 | .05 | .18 | .20 | .05 |
| Sec.Ot.th.Shares Excl.f/Brd.Money.... | 36s | — | — | — | — | — | — | — | — | — | — | — | — |
| Loans................................... | 36l | — | — | — | — | — | — | — | — | — | — | — | — |
| Financial Derivatives........................ | 36m | — | — | — | — | — | — | — | — | — | — | — | — |
| Insurance Technical Reserves........... | 36r | — | — | — | — | — | — | — | — | — | — | — | — |
| Shares and Other Equity.................. | 37a | 36.68 | 33.24 | 36.35 | 39.78 | 39.22 | 50.98 | 44.76 | 58.24 | 64.51 | 63.08 | 60.28 | 60.04 |
| Other Items (Net)............................ | 37r | 13.80 | 12.67 | 18.27 | 17.23 | 11.40 | 13.74 | 13.23 | 18.43 | 14.59 | 10.16 | 32.97 | 33.49 |
| Broad Money Liabs., Seasonally Adj. | 35l.b | 107.58 | 127.25 | 121.69 | 114.41 | 135.94 | 152.14 | 176.23 | 199.94 | 201.95 | 212.52 | 242.39 | 254.72 |
| **Monetary Aggregates** | | | | | | *Billions of CFA Francs: End of Period* | | | | | | | |
| Broad Money............................... | 59m | 107.76 | 127.46 | 121.61 | 113.94 | 134.93 | 150.73 | 175.05 | 199.19 | 202.29 | 213.65 | 244.80 | 257.78 |
| o/w:Currency Issued by Cent.Govt | 59m.a | — | — | — | — | — | — | — | — | — | — | — | — |
| o/w: Dep.in Nonfin. Corporations. | 59m.b | — | — | — | — | — | — | — | — | — | — | — | — |
| o/w: Secs. Issued by Central Govt. | 59m.c | — | — | — | — | — | — | — | — | — | — | — | — |
| Money (National Definitions) | | | | | | | | | | | | | |
| M1.................................... | 59ma | 95.11 | 112.65 | 104.11 | 94.58 | 110.39 | 124.29 | 144.34 | 158.95 | 162.33 | 169.49 | 196.98 | 199.47 |
| M2.................................... | 59mb | 107.61 | 127.32 | 121.46 | 113.92 | 134.75 | 149.54 | 175.02 | 199.07 | 201.84 | 213.52 | 244.67 | 257.65 |
| **Interest Rates** | | | | | | *Percent Per Annum* | | | | | | | |
| Discount Rate (End of Period).......... | 60.a | 6.00 | 5.50 | 5.25 | 5.25 | 4.75 | 4.25 | 4.00 | 4.00 | 4.00 | 3.25 | 2.95 | 2.45 |
| Deposit Rate................................. | 60l | 5.00 | 4.92 | 4.33 | 4.25 | 3.75 | 3.25 | 3.25 | 3.25 | 3.25 | 3.21 | 2.60 | 2.45 |
| **Prices** | | | | | | *Index Numbers (2010=100): Period Averages* | | | | | | | |
| Wholesale Prices (2005=100).......... | 63 | 97.8 | 100.0 | .... | .... | .... | .... | .... | .... | .... | .... | .... | .... |
| Consumer Prices............................ | 64 | 78.6 | 80.9 | 86.3 | 87.1 | 95.2 | 98.5 | 100.0 | 101.3 | 107.1 | 108.8 | 136.3 | 186.9 |
| **Intl. Transactions & Positions** | | | | | | *Millions of CFA Francs* | | | | | | | |
| Exports.................................... | 70 | 70,700 | 67,516 | 82,400 | 86,268 | 67,171 | 38,100 | 45,000 | 54,600 | 57,300 | .... | .... | .... |
| Imports, c.i.f................................. | 71 | 79,900 | 92,307 | 105,900 | 119,817 | 134,342 | 128,100 | 120,800 | 130,500 | 140,800 | .... | .... | .... |

# Central African Republic  626

| | | 2004 | 2005 | 2006 | 2007 | 2008 | 2009 | 2010 | 2011 | 2012 | 2013 | 2014 | 2015 |
|---|---|---|---|---|---|---|---|---|---|---|---|---|---|
| **Government Finance Operations Statement** | | | | | | | | | | | | | |
| **Budgetary Central Government** | | | | | | *Millions of CFA Francs: Fiscal Year Ends December 31* | | | | | | | |
| Revenue................................. | a1 | .... | .... | .... | .... | 125,741 | 138,081 | 159,856 | 125,400 | 201,430 | .... | .... | .... |
| Taxes.................................. | a11 | .... | .... | .... | .... | 73,653 | 76,892 | 89,136 | 86,631 | 104,734 | .... | .... | .... |
| Social Contributions................ | a12 | .... | .... | .... | .... | 2,001 | 2,365 | 1,825 | 1,987 | 2,197 | .... | .... | .... |
| Grants................................ | a13 | .... | .... | .... | .... | 42,222 | 49,502 | 62,245 | 26,305 | 78,989 | .... | .... | .... |
| Other Revenue........................ | a14 | .... | .... | .... | .... | 7,865 | 9,321 | 6,651 | 10,477 | 15,510 | .... | .... | .... |
| Expense................................ | a2 | .... | .... | .... | .... | 97,851 | 154,244 | 173,192 | 154,688 | 104,889 | .... | .... | .... |
| Compensation of Employees.......... | a21 | .... | .... | .... | .... | 38,626 | 42,243 | 42,810 | 45,991 | 51,213 | .... | .... | .... |
| Use of Goods & Services.............. | a22 | .... | .... | .... | .... | 19,125 | 66,462 | 100,288 | 75,433 | 24,993 | .... | .... | .... |
| Consumption of Fixed Capital........ | a23 | .... | .... | .... | .... | .... | .... | .... | .... | .... | .... | .... | .... |
| Interest................................ | a24 | .... | .... | .... | .... | 10,622 | 10,833 | 9,512 | 6,983 | 5,924 | .... | .... | .... |
| Subsidies............................. | a25 | .... | .... | .... | .... | 19,355 | 16,397 | 20,182 | 23,281 | 22,759 | .... | .... | .... |
| Grants................................ | a26 | .... | .... | .... | .... | — | — | — | — | — | .... | .... | .... |
| Social Benefits....................... | a27 | .... | .... | .... | .... | — | — | — | — | — | .... | .... | .... |
| Other Expense........................ | a28 | .... | .... | .... | .... | 10,122 | 18,309 | 400 | 3,000 | — | .... | .... | .... |
| Gross Operating Balance [1-2+23]... | agob | .... | .... | .... | .... | 27,890 | −16,163 | −13,335 | −29,288 | 96,541 | .... | .... | .... |
| Net Operating Balance [1-2].......... | anob | .... | .... | .... | .... | .... | .... | .... | .... | .... | .... | .... | .... |
| Net Acq. of Nonfinancial Assets...... | a31 | .... | .... | .... | .... | 36,494 | 41,255 | 75,406 | 39,304 | 89,208 | .... | .... | .... |
| Aquisition of Nonfin. Assets.......... | a31.1 | .... | .... | .... | .... | .... | .... | .... | .... | .... | .... | .... | .... |
| Disposal of Nonfin. Assets............ | a31.2 | .... | .... | .... | .... | .... | .... | .... | .... | .... | .... | .... | .... |
| Net Lending/Borrowing [1-2-31]...... | anlb | .... | .... | .... | .... | −8,604 | −57,418 | −88,742 | −68,592 | 7,333 | .... | .... | .... |
| Net Acq. of Financial Assets.......... | a32 | .... | .... | .... | .... | 2,247 | .... | .... | .... | .... | .... | .... | .... |
| Domestic............................. | a321 | .... | .... | .... | .... | 2,247 | .... | .... | .... | .... | .... | .... | .... |
| Foreign............................... | a322 | .... | .... | .... | .... | — | .... | .... | .... | .... | .... | .... | .... |
| Net Incurrence of Liabilities.......... | a33 | .... | .... | .... | .... | 10,819 | .... | .... | .... | .... | .... | .... | .... |
| Domestic............................. | a331 | .... | .... | .... | .... | 15,219 | .... | .... | .... | .... | .... | .... | .... |
| Foreign............................... | a332 | .... | .... | .... | .... | −4,400 | .... | .... | .... | .... | .... | .... | .... |
| Stat. Discrepancy [32-33-NLB]........ | anlbz | .... | .... | .... | .... | 32 | .... | .... | .... | .... | .... | .... | .... |
| Memo Item: Expenditure [2+31]...... | a2m | .... | .... | .... | .... | 134,344 | 195,499 | 248,598 | 193,993 | 194,097 | .... | .... | .... |
| **National Accounts** | | | | | | *Billions of CFA Francs* | | | | | | | |
| Househ.Cons.Expend.,incl.NPISHs..... | 96f | 632.3 | 673.8 | 751.8 | 815.0 | 905.3 | 938.8 | .... | .... | .... | .... | .... | .... |
| Government Consumption Expend... | 91f | 56.7 | 61.4 | 52.4 | 50.7 | 58.9 | 62.3 | .... | .... | .... | .... | .... | .... |
| Gross Fixed Capital Formation.......... | 93e | 42.9 | 71.0 | 70.9 | 68.9 | 91.3 | 95.7 | .... | .... | .... | .... | .... | .... |
| Changes in Inventories.................... | 93i | .4 | 1.0 | 1.0 | 1.0 | 1.0 | 1.0 | .... | .... | .... | .... | .... | .... |
| Exports of Goods and Services.......... | 90c | 92.2 | 90.7 | 109.4 | 114.9 | 97.7 | 86.5 | .... | .... | .... | .... | .... | .... |
| Imports of Goods and Services (-)..... | 98c | 135.9 | 147.8 | 168.8 | 190.2 | 208.3 | 192.3 | .... | .... | .... | .... | .... | .... |
| Gross Domestic Product (GDP)........ | 99b | 688.6 | 750.0 | 816.8 | 860.2 | 945.9 | 991.9 | .... | .... | .... | .... | .... | .... |
| Net Primary Income from Abroad..... | 98.n | −3.3 | .... | .... | .... | .... | .... | .... | .... | .... | .... | .... | .... |
| Gross National Income (GNI)........... | 99a | 677.4 | .... | .... | .... | .... | .... | .... | .... | .... | .... | .... | .... |
| GDP Volume 1985 Prices................ | 99b.p | 466.5 | 476.0 | .... | .... | .... | .... | .... | .... | .... | .... | .... | .... |
| GDP Volume (2005=100)............... | 99bvp | 98.0 | 100.0 | .... | .... | .... | .... | .... | .... | .... | .... | .... | .... |
| GDP Deflator (2005=100)................ | 99bip | 93.7 | 100.0 | .... | .... | .... | .... | .... | .... | .... | .... | .... | .... |
| | | | | | | *Millions: Midyear Estimates* | | | | | | | |
| **Population................................** | 99z | 3.99 | 4.06 | 4.13 | 4.20 | 4.28 | 4.36 | 4.44 | 4.53 | 4.62 | 4.71 | 4.80 | 4.90 |

# Chad  628

| | | 2004 | 2005 | 2006 | 2007 | 2008 | 2009 | 2010 | 2011 | 2012 | 2013 | 2014 | 2015 |
|---|---|---|---|---|---|---|---|---|---|---|---|---|---|
| **Exchange Rates** | | | | | | | *CFA Francs per SDR: End of Period* | | | | | | |
| Official Rate.............................. | aa | 747.90 | 794.73 | 749.30 | 704.15 | 725.98 | 713.83 | 756.02 | 778.32 | 764.10 | 732.49 | 782.77 | 834.92 |
| | | | | | | *CFA Francs per US Dollar: End of Period (ae) Period Average (rf)* | | | | | | | |
| Official Rate.............................. | ae | 481.58 | 556.04 | 498.07 | 445.59 | 471.34 | 455.34 | 490.91 | 506.96 | 497.16 | 475.64 | 540.28 | 602.51 |
| Official Rate.............................. | rf | 528.28 | 527.47 | 522.89 | 479.27 | 447.81 | 472.19 | 495.28 | 471.87 | 510.53 | 494.04 | 494.41 | 591.45 |
| **Fund Position** | | | | | | | *Millions of SDRs: End of Period* | | | | | | |
| Quota...................................... | 2f.s | 56.00 | 56.00 | 56.00 | 56.00 | 56.00 | 56.00 | 56.00 | 66.60 | 66.60 | 66.60 | 66.60 | 66.60 |
| SDR Holdings............................ | 1b.s | .04 | .05 | .06 | .06 | .06 | 2.71 | 2.73 | .06 | .05 | .05 | .05 | .05 |
| Reserve Position in the Fund........... | 1c.s | .28 | .28 | .28 | .28 | .28 | .28 | .28 | 2.93 | 2.93 | 2.93 | 2.93 | 3.01 |
| Total Fund Cred.&Loans Outstg....... | 2tl | 61.78 | 55.55 | 44.95 | 35.26 | 26.43 | 18.20 | 10.90 | 5.82 | 3.14 | 1.26 | 13.73 | 45.44 |
| SDR Allocations.......................... | 1bd | 9.41 | 9.41 | 9.41 | 9.41 | 9.41 | 53.62 | 53.62 | 53.62 | 53.62 | 53.62 | 53.62 | 53.62 |
| **International Liquidity** | | | | | | *Millions of US Dollars Unless Otherwise Indicated: End of Period* | | | | | | | |
| Total Reserves minus Gold.............. | 1l.d | 221.73 | 225.58 | 625.09 | 955.06 | 1,345.47 | 616.70 | 632.41 | 951.10 | 1,155.66 | 1,183.03 | 1,075.90 | 368.92 |
| SDR Holdings........................ | 1b.d | .07 | .07 | .10 | .10 | .09 | 4.25 | 4.20 | .09 | .08 | .08 | .08 | .07 |
| Reserve Position in the Fund......... | 1c.d | .44 | .40 | .42 | .44 | .43 | .44 | .43 | 4.50 | 4.51 | 4.51 | 4.25 | 4.17 |
| Foreign Exchange...................... | 1d.d | 221.23 | 225.10 | 624.57 | 954.52 | 1,344.94 | 612.01 | 627.77 | 946.51 | 1,151.07 | 1,178.44 | 1,071.58 | 364.67 |
| Gold (Million Fine Troy Ounces)....... | 1ad | .011 | .011 | .011 | .011 | .011 | . . . . | . . . . | . . . . | . . . . | . . . . | . . . . | . . . . |
| Gold (National Valuation).............. | 1and | 4.88 | 5.71 | 7.06 | 9.36 | 1.62 | — | 6.19 | 17.01 | 18.73 | . . . . | . . . . | . . . . |
| Central Bank: Other Assets............. | 3..d | — | — | — | — | — | — | — | — | — | — | — | — |
| Central Bank: Other Liabs.............. | 4..d | 1.25 | .92 | 1.70 | 1.66 | 3.96 | 4.66 | 5.56 | 27.64 | 3.72 | 2.00 | 2.36 | 2.15 |
| Other Depository Corps.: Assets....... | 7a.d | 39.56 | 50.57 | 76.26 | 149.18 | 143.54 | 141.63 | 164.50 | 115.08 | 125.07 | 153.33 | 157.73 | 70.14 |
| Other Depository Corps.: Liabs....... | 7b.d | 53.27 | 58.27 | 103.85 | 128.41 | 121.55 | 116.52 | 80.73 | 64.77 | 86.03 | 132.82 | 179.68 | 164.42 |
| **Central Bank** | | | | | | | *Billions of CFA Francs: End of Period* | | | | | | |
| Net Foreign Assets...................... | 11n | 55.29 | 76.47 | 273.27 | 397.54 | 606.82 | 227.42 | 261.98 | 430.51 | 538.65 | 527.94 | 534.55 | 145.40 |
| Claims on Nonresidents................. | 11 | 109.13 | 128.60 | 314.85 | 429.74 | 634.70 | 280.81 | 313.49 | 490.79 | 583.86 | 569.09 | 588.55 | 229.40 |
| Liabilities to Nonresidents........... | 16c | 53.84 | 52.14 | 41.58 | 32.20 | 27.88 | 53.39 | 51.51 | 60.28 | 45.22 | 41.15 | 54.00 | 84.00 |
| Claims on Other Depository Corps.... | 12e | 7.81 | 15.00 | 8.60 | 3.11 | 6.00 | 5.00 | — | 2.45 | — | 2.50 | 10.70 | 54.50 |
| Net Claims on Central Government.. | 12an | 96.45 | 112.07 | 29.46 | −73.28 | −209.72 | 145.17 | 202.23 | 86.68 | 28.63 | 96.85 | 228.78 | 492.21 |
| Claims on Central Government...... | 12a | 105.73 | 121.80 | 73.02 | 76.78 | 73.22 | 217.37 | 289.81 | 278.91 | 279.84 | 260.34 | 268.26 | 529.96 |
| Liabilities to Central Government... | 16d | 9.28 | 9.73 | 43.56 | 150.06 | 282.94 | 72.20 | 87.58 | 192.22 | 251.21 | 163.48 | 39.48 | 37.74 |
| Claims on Other Sectors................. | 12s | — | — | — | — | .51 | .53 | .86 | 1.63 | 2.42 | 2.89 | 3.10 | 3.69 |
| Claims on Other Financial Corps.... | 12g | — | — | — | — | — | — | — | — | — | — | — | — |
| Claims on State & Local Govts....... | 12b | — | — | — | — | — | — | — | — | — | — | — | — |
| Claims on Public Nonfin. Corps...... | 12c | — | — | — | — | — | — | — | — | — | — | — | — |
| Claims on Private Sector.............. | 12d | — | — | — | — | .51 | .53 | .86 | 1.63 | 2.42 | 2.89 | 3.10 | 3.69 |
| Monetary Base............................. | 14 | 148.63 | 194.44 | 302.02 | 324.92 | 399.35 | 367.51 | 448.44 | 509.89 | 555.89 | 615.32 | 746.73 | 682.65 |
| Currency in Circulation.................. | 14a | 128.52 | 171.68 | 235.18 | 262.35 | 343.94 | 310.00 | 368.40 | 400.33 | 428.39 | 480.16 | 572.28 | 513.98 |
| Liabs. to Other Depository Corps.... | 14c | 20.09 | 22.74 | 66.82 | 62.46 | 54.97 | 57.29 | 79.98 | 109.37 | 127.35 | 134.96 | 174.34 | 168.58 |
| Liabilities to Other Sectors............. | 14d | .01 | .02 | .01 | .12 | .45 | .22 | .06 | .19 | .16 | .20 | .11 | .09 |
| Other Liabs. to Other Dep. Corps..... | 14n | — | — | — | — | — | — | — | — | — | — | — | — |
| Dep. & Sec. Excl. f/Monetary Base..... | 14o | — | — | — | — | — | — | — | — | — | — | — | — |
| Deposits Included in Broad Money. | 15 | — | — | — | — | — | — | — | — | — | — | — | — |
| Sec.Ot.th.Shares Incl.in Brd. Money | 16a | — | — | — | — | — | — | — | — | — | — | — | — |
| Deposits Excl. from Broad Money... | 16b | — | — | — | — | — | — | — | — | — | — | — | — |
| Sec.Ot.th.Shares Excl.f/Brd.Money.. | 16s | — | — | — | — | — | — | — | — | — | — | — | — |
| Loans...................................... | 16l | — | — | — | — | — | — | — | — | — | — | — | — |
| Financial Derivatives.................... | 16m | — | — | — | — | — | — | — | — | — | — | — | — |
| Shares and Other Equity................. | 17a | 9.70 | 10.03 | 11.06 | 9.76 | 7.19 | 9.73 | 12.79 | 15.35 | 11.03 | 13.24 | 13.51 | 11.60 |
| Other Items (Net)......................... | 17r | 1.22 | −.92 | −1.75 | −7.30 | −2.93 | .88 | 3.85 | −3.97 | 2.78 | 1.62 | 16.90 | 1.55 |
| Memo Item: | | | | | | | | | | | | | |
| Total Assets................................ | 10ra | 236.54 | 278.52 | 409.60 | 531.35 | 727.85 | 515.79 | 617.36 | 787.88 | 878.98 | 846.49 | 883.28 | 831.97 |
| **Other Depository Corporations** | | | | | | | *Billions of CFA Francs: End of Period* | | | | | | |
| Net Foreign Assets........................ | 21n | −6.60 | −4.28 | −13.74 | 9.26 | 10.37 | 11.43 | 41.13 | 25.50 | 19.41 | 9.75 | −11.86 | −56.81 |
| Claims on Nonresidents................ | 21 | 19.05 | 28.12 | 37.99 | 66.48 | 67.66 | 64.49 | 80.76 | 58.34 | 62.18 | 72.93 | 85.22 | 42.26 |
| Liabilities to Nonresidents............. | 26c | 25.65 | 32.40 | 51.73 | 57.22 | 57.29 | 53.06 | 39.63 | 32.84 | 42.77 | 63.18 | 97.08 | 99.07 |
| Claims on Central Bank.................. | 20 | 28.36 | 30.77 | 76.89 | 73.30 | 71.24 | 70.91 | 90.47 | 129.47 | 150.44 | 138.41 | 189.09 | 192.37 |
| Currency............................... | 20a | 9.87 | 8.59 | 9.70 | 13.77 | 17.13 | 18.14 | 22.70 | 26.79 | 27.65 | 31.83 | 33.05 | 31.63 |
| Reserve Deposits and Securities..... | 20b | 16.04 | 18.79 | 64.13 | 59.53 | 54.11 | 52.78 | 67.77 | 102.68 | 122.79 | 106.58 | 142.50 | 160.74 |
| Other Claims........................... | 20n | 2.45 | 3.40 | 3.06 | — | — | — | — | — | — | — | 13.54 | — |
| Net Claims on Central Government.. | 22an | −4.92 | −18.40 | 1.42 | −21.30 | −29.07 | −40.34 | −52.78 | −47.07 | −69.51 | −61.15 | −63.17 | −74.90 |
| Claims on Central Government...... | 22a | 22.79 | 16.97 | 28.46 | 17.80 | 20.01 | 26.97 | 61.47 | 54.47 | 50.15 | 66.59 | 86.15 | 74.16 |
| Liabilities to Central Government... | 26d | 27.71 | 35.37 | 27.05 | 39.10 | 49.08 | 67.31 | 114.25 | 101.55 | 119.66 | 127.74 | 149.32 | 149.06 |
| Claims on Other Sectors................. | 22s | 92.88 | 131.11 | 138.07 | 128.56 | 179.38 | 208.57 | 253.29 | 308.35 | 386.04 | 426.77 | 591.72 | 722.61 |
| Claims on Other Financial Corps... | 22g | .89 | 1.19 | .70 | .71 | .45 | .82 | 3.95 | 9.10 | 8.63 | 25.37 | 19.21 | 22.85 |
| Claims on State & Local Govts....... | 22b | — | — | — | — | — | — | — | — | — | — | — | — |
| Claims on Public Nonfin. Corps...... | 22c | 18.90 | 40.81 | 51.39 | 28.59 | 37.49 | 36.52 | 26.57 | 22.76 | 12.50 | 14.73 | 38.60 | 59.80 |
| Claims on Private Sector............... | 22d | 73.09 | 89.11 | 85.98 | 99.27 | 141.44 | 171.23 | 222.77 | 276.49 | 364.90 | 386.67 | 533.91 | 639.96 |
| Liabilities to Central Bank.............. | 26g | 7.85 | 15.13 | 12.60 | 3.70 | 6.27 | 5.01 | .77 | 2.45 | — | 2.50 | 11.85 | 54.50 |
| Transf.Dep.Included in Broad Money | 24 | 57.86 | 73.17 | 133.14 | 126.41 | 147.16 | 157.80 | 222.95 | 258.70 | 325.84 | 336.07 | 460.37 | 453.80 |
| Other Dep.Included in Broad Money. | 25 | 13.84 | 16.79 | 20.64 | 25.66 | 31.98 | 33.00 | 36.56 | 58.90 | 57.55 | 67.51 | 78.01 | 90.81 |
| Sec.Ot.th.Shares Incl.in Brd. Money.. | 26a | — | — | — | — | — | — | — | — | — | — | — | — |
| Deposits Excl. from Broad Money..... | 26b | .86 | .35 | .48 | .98 | .76 | .35 | 2.18 | 1.54 | .88 | 1.24 | .67 | 1.10 |
| Sec.Ot.th.Shares Excl.f/Brd.Money.... | 26s | — | — | — | — | — | — | — | — | — | — | — | — |
| Loans...................................... | 26l | — | — | — | — | — | — | — | — | — | — | — | — |
| Financial Derivatives...................... | 26m | — | — | — | — | — | — | — | — | — | — | — | — |
| Insurance Technical Reserves........... | 26r | — | — | — | — | — | — | — | — | — | — | — | — |
| Shares and Other Equity................. | 27a | 22.75 | 25.23 | 28.21 | 31.96 | 45.45 | 53.20 | 52.05 | 74.54 | 93.69 | 100.68 | 89.38 | 107.31 |
| Other Items (Net)......................... | 27r | 6.57 | 8.54 | 7.56 | 1.12 | .30 | 1.21 | 17.58 | 20.12 | 8.42 | 5.78 | 65.52 | 75.76 |
| Memo Item: | | | | | | | | | | | | | |
| Total Assets................................ | 20ra | 182.69 | 227.37 | 303.02 | 310.28 | 363.89 | 410.13 | 530.24 | 594.23 | 698.34 | 751.66 | 1,011.63 | 1,102.09 |

| | | 2004 | 2005 | 2006 | 2007 | 2008 | 2009 | 2010 | 2011 | 2012 | 2013 | 2014 | 2015 |
|---|---|---|---|---|---|---|---|---|---|---|---|---|---|
| **Depository Corporations** | | | | | | *Billions of CFA Francs: End of Period* | | | | | | | |
| Net Foreign Assets............... | 31n | 48.69 | 72.18 | 259.53 | 406.80 | 617.18 | 238.85 | 303.11 | 456.02 | 558.06 | 537.69 | 522.69 | 88.59 |
| Claims on Nonresidents............ | 31 | 128.18 | 156.72 | 352.84 | 496.22 | 702.35 | 345.30 | 394.25 | 549.13 | 646.05 | 642.02 | 673.76 | 271.66 |
| Liabilities to Nonresidents........ | 36c | 79.49 | 84.54 | 93.31 | 89.41 | 85.17 | 106.45 | 91.14 | 93.12 | 87.99 | 104.33 | 151.07 | 183.07 |
| Domestic Claims.................... | 32 | 184.42 | 224.78 | 168.94 | 33.98 | −58.89 | 313.93 | 403.60 | 349.59 | 347.58 | 465.36 | 760.43 | 1,143.60 |
| Net Claims on Central Government | 32an | 91.54 | 93.67 | 30.87 | −94.58 | −238.79 | 104.83 | 149.45 | 39.61 | −40.88 | 35.70 | 165.61 | 417.31 |
| Claims on Central Government.... | 32a | 128.52 | 138.77 | 101.48 | 94.58 | 93.23 | 244.34 | 351.28 | 333.38 | 329.99 | 326.92 | 354.41 | 604.11 |
| Liabilities to Central Government. | 36d | 36.99 | 45.10 | 70.61 | 189.16 | 332.01 | 139.51 | 201.83 | 293.77 | 370.87 | 291.22 | 188.79 | 186.81 |
| Claims on Other Sectors......... | 32s | 92.88 | 131.11 | 138.07 | 128.56 | 179.90 | 209.10 | 254.15 | 309.98 | 388.46 | 429.66 | 594.82 | 726.30 |
| Claims on Other Financial Corps.. | 32g | .89 | 1.19 | .70 | .71 | .45 | .82 | 3.95 | 9.10 | 8.63 | 25.37 | 19.21 | 22.85 |
| Claims on State & Local Govts..... | 32b | — | — | — | — | — | — | — | — | — | — | — | — |
| Claims on Public Nonfin. Corps.... | 32c | 18.90 | 40.81 | 51.39 | 28.59 | 37.49 | 36.52 | 26.57 | 22.76 | 12.50 | 14.73 | 38.60 | 59.80 |
| Claims on Private Sector............ | 32d | 73.09 | 89.11 | 85.98 | 99.27 | 141.95 | 171.76 | 223.64 | 278.12 | 367.32 | 389.56 | 537.01 | 643.65 |
| Broad Money Liabilities................ | 35l | 190.37 | 253.06 | 379.27 | 400.76 | 506.40 | 482.88 | 605.28 | 691.33 | 784.28 | 852.11 | 1,077.71 | 1,027.05 |
| Currency Outside Depository Corps | 34a | 118.65 | 163.09 | 225.48 | 248.58 | 326.81 | 291.86 | 345.70 | 373.54 | 400.74 | 448.33 | 539.23 | 482.36 |
| Transferable Deposits.................. | 34 | 57.88 | 73.19 | 133.15 | 126.53 | 147.61 | 158.02 | 223.01 | 258.89 | 326.00 | 336.27 | 460.47 | 453.88 |
| Other Deposits.......................... | 35 | 13.84 | 16.79 | 20.64 | 25.66 | 31.98 | 33.00 | 36.56 | 58.90 | 57.55 | 67.51 | 78.01 | 90.81 |
| Securities Other than Shares......... | 36a | — | — | — | — | — | — | — | — | — | — | — | — |
| Deposits Excl. from Broad Money..... | 36b | .86 | .35 | .48 | .98 | .76 | .35 | 2.18 | 1.54 | .88 | 1.24 | .67 | 1.10 |
| Sec.Ot.th.Shares Excl.f/Brd.Money.... | 36s | — | — | — | — | — | — | — | — | — | — | — | — |
| Loans....................................... | 36l | — | — | — | — | — | — | — | — | — | — | — | — |
| Financial Derivatives.................... | 36m | — | — | — | — | — | — | — | — | — | — | — | — |
| Insurance Technical Reserves.......... | 36r | — | — | — | — | — | — | — | — | — | — | — | — |
| Shares and Other Equity................ | 37a | 32.45 | 35.26 | 39.27 | 41.71 | 52.64 | 62.93 | 64.84 | 89.89 | 104.71 | 113.92 | 102.88 | 118.91 |
| Other Items (Net)......................... | 37r | 9.43 | 8.30 | 9.45 | −2.67 | −1.50 | 6.61 | 34.40 | 22.85 | 15.76 | 35.78 | 101.87 | 85.15 |
| Broad Money Liabs., Seasonally Adj. | 35l.b | 194.16 | 255.74 | 379.74 | 398.09 | 499.82 | 475.54 | 595.86 | 680.40 | 769.12 | 832.69 | 1,049.10 | 998.00 |
| **Monetary Aggregates** | | | | | | *Billions of CFA Francs: End of Period* | | | | | | | |
| Broad Money.............................. | 59m | 190.37 | 253.06 | 379.27 | 400.76 | 506.40 | 482.88 | 605.28 | 691.33 | 784.28 | 852.11 | 1,077.71 | 1,027.05 |
| o/w:Currency Issued by Cent.Govt | 59m.a | — | — | — | — | — | — | — | — | — | — | — | — |
| o/w: Dep.in Nonfin. Corporations. | 59m.b | — | — | — | — | — | — | — | — | — | — | — | — |
| o/w: Secs. Issued by Central Govt. | 59m.c | — | — | — | — | — | — | — | — | — | — | — | — |
| Money (National Definitions) | | | | | | | | | | | | | |
| M1.......................................... | 59ma | 168.00 | 228.01 | 350.37 | 355.52 | 464.08 | 438.12 | 556.95 | 615.10 | 705.61 | 736.17 | 938.03 | 877.57 |
| M2.......................................... | 59mb | 181.84 | 244.79 | 371.01 | 381.17 | 496.06 | 471.12 | 593.52 | 674.00 | 763.16 | 803.68 | 1,016.03 | 968.38 |
| **Interest Rates** | | | | | | *Percent Per Annum* | | | | | | | |
| Discount Rate (End of Period)........... | 60.a | 6.00 | 5.50 | 5.25 | 5.25 | 4.75 | 4.25 | 4.00 | 4.00 | 4.00 | 3.25 | 2.95 | 2.45 |
| Deposit Rate................................ | 60l | 5.00 | 4.92 | 4.33 | 4.25 | 3.75 | 3.25 | 3.25 | 3.25 | 3.25 | 3.21 | 2.60 | 2.45 |
| **Prices** | | | | | | *Index Numbers (2010=100): Period Averages* | | | | | | | |
| Consumer Prices............................ | 64 | 79.4 | 85.6 | 92.5 | 84.2 | †92.9 | 102.1 | 100.0 | 96.3 | 109.8 | 110.0 | 111.8 | 115.9 |
| **Intl. Transactions & Positions** | | | | | | *Millions of CFA Francs* | | | | | | | |
| Exports.................................... | 70 | 1,157,472 | 1,625,100 | 1,752,700 | 1,757,099 | 1,938,997 | 1,251,294 | 1,683,942 | .... | .... | .... | .... | .... |
| Imports, c.i.f............................... | 71 | 503,455 | 501,095 | 705,902 | 862,680 | 850,830 | 1,086,028 | 1,238,193 | .... | .... | .... | .... | .... |
| **National Accounts** | | | | | | *Billions of CFA Francs* | | | | | | | |
| Gross Domestic Product (GDP)......... | 99b | 2,356.9 | 3,125.6 | 3,323.1 | 3,381.9 | 3,876.0 | 3,310.3 | .... | .... | .... | .... | .... | .... |
| | | | | | | *Millions: Midyear Estimates* | | | | | | | |
| Population.............................. | 99z | 9.71 | 10.07 | 10.42 | 10.78 | 11.14 | 11.51 | 11.90 | 12.30 | 12.72 | 13.15 | 13.59 | 14.04 |

| | | 2004 | 2005 | 2006 | 2007 | 2008 | 2009 | 2010 | 2011 | 2012 | 2013 | 2014 | 2015 |
|---|---|---|---|---|---|---|---|---|---|---|---|---|---|
| **Exchange Rates** | | | | | | *Pesos per SDR: End of Period* | | | | | | | |
| Market Rate..................................... | aa | 869.42 | 734.94 | 804.00 | 783.52 | 969.00 | 793.93 | 721.30 | 800.58 | 735.57 | 806.59 | 879.98 | 980.18 |
| | | | | | | *Pesos per US Dollar: End of Period (ae) Period Average (rf)* | | | | | | | |
| Market Rate..................................... | ae | 559.83 | 514.21 | 534.43 | 495.82 | 629.11 | 506.43 | 468.37 | 521.46 | 478.60 | 523.76 | 607.38 | 707.34 |
| Market Rate..................................... | rf | 609.53 | 559.77 | 530.28 | 522.46 | 522.46 | 560.86 | 510.25 | 483.67 | 486.47 | 495.27 | 570.35 | 654.12 |
| | | | | | | *Index Numbers (2010=100): Period Averages* | | | | | | | |
| Market Rate..................................... | ahx | 83.0 | 91.1 | 96.1 | 97.6 | 99.2 | 91.2 | 100.0 | 105.5 | 104.7 | 103.0 | 89.4 | 78.1 |
| Nominal Effective Exchange Rate..... | nec | 90.6 | 97.2 | 101.1 | 97.7 | 95.8 | 93.3 | 100.0 | 101.3 | 104.8 | 105.4 | 94.8 | 94.2 |
| CPI-Based Real Effect. Ex. Rate........ | rec | 87.9 | 94.2 | 98.4 | 95.9 | 97.3 | 94.9 | 100.0 | 100.4 | 103.6 | 102.9 | 93.9 | 95.2 |
| **Fund Position** | | | | | | *Millions of SDRs: End of Period* | | | | | | | |
| Quota........................................... | 2f.s | 856.10 | 856.10 | 856.10 | 856.10 | 856.10 | 856.10 | 856.10 | 856.10 | 856.10 | 856.10 | 856.10 | 856.10 |
| SDR Holdings................................... | 1b.s | 33.88 | 36.63 | 36.06 | 33.64 | 36.86 | 731.72 | 789.95 | 790.78 | 788.21 | 744.75 | 745.01 | 763.09 |
| Reserve Position in the Fund........... | 1c.s | 287.04 | 131.39 | 74.99 | 55.91 | 108.41 | 183.11 | 183.11 | 391.53 | 450.06 | 415.98 | 338.05 | 261.77 |
| Total Fund Cred.&Loans Outstg....... | 2tl | — | — | — | — | — | — | — | — | — | — | — | — |
| SDR Allocations.............................. | 1bd | 121.92 | 121.92 | 121.92 | 121.92 | 121.92 | 816.89 | 816.89 | 816.89 | 816.89 | 816.89 | 816.89 | 816.89 |
| **International Liquidity** | | | | | | *Millions of US Dollars Unless Otherwise Indicated: End of Period* | | | | | | | |
| Total Reserves minus Gold.............. | 1l.d | 15,993.8 | 16,929.2 | 19,392.0 | 16,836.8 | 23,072.4 | 25,283.5 | 27,816.3 | 41,931.8 | 41,636.1 | 41,083.7 | 40,437.9 | 38,632.8 |
| SDR Holdings.............................. | 1b.d | 52.6 | 52.3 | 54.2 | 53.2 | 56.8 | 1,147.1 | 1,216.6 | 1,214.1 | 1,211.4 | 1,146.9 | 1,079.4 | 1,057.4 |
| Reserve Position in the Fund......... | 1c.d | 445.8 | 187.8 | 112.8 | 88.4 | 167.0 | 287.1 | 282.0 | 601.1 | 691.7 | 640.6 | 489.8 | 362.7 |
| Foreign Exchange........................ | 1d.d | 15,495.4 | 16,689.1 | 19,224.9 | 16,695.3 | 22,848.6 | 23,849.3 | 26,317.8 | 40,116.6 | 39,733.0 | 39,296.2 | 38,868.7 | 37,212.6 |
| Gold (Million Fine Troy Ounces)........ | 1ad | .008 | .008 | .008 | .008 | .008 | .008 | .008 | .008 | .008 | .008 | .008 | .008 |
| Gold (National Valuation)............... | 1and | 3.0 | 3.3 | 4.3 | 5.4 | 5.7 | 8.8 | 11.2 | 12.2 | 13.1 | 9.6 | 9.4 | 8.5 |
| Central Bank: Other Assets.............. | 3..d | 19.4 | 32.9 | 31.9 | 67.6 | 83.6 | † 250.4 | 249.5 | 250.9 | 249.0 | 255.6 | 249.8 | 246.0 |
| Central Bank: Other Liabs............... | 4..d | 269.0 | 318.8 | 283.2 | 299.6 | 290.5 | † 148.1 | 148.1 | 110.6 | 116.0 | 97.5 | 96.2 | 82.0 |
| Other Depository Corps.: Assets....... | 7a.d | 2,478.1 | 3,368.3 | 4,920.5 | 9,737.9 | † 6,225.0 | 7,496.0 | 7,281.0 | 8,627.0 | 8,594.7 | 9,099.7 | 10,438.2 | 9,467.8 |
| Other Depository Corps.: Liabs....... | 7b.d | 5,423.4 | 6,725.0 | 6,745.1 | 9,619.0 | † 11,672.8 | 14,853.4 | 16,790.3 | 20,970.0 | 20,017.7 | 18,965.4 | 17,776.2 | 17,520.5 |
| Other Financial Corps.: Assets.......... | 7e.d | 16,484.5 | 22,656.9 | 28,526.1 | 39,582.3 | 24,328.2 | 58,333.9 | 76,490.0 | 56,217.8 | 70,430.3 | 78,620.6 | 84,271.3 | 79,971.4 |
| Other Financial Corps.: Liabs............ | 7f.d | — | .7 | 5.7 | 5.1 | 348.7 | 370.9 | 520.6 | 608.7 | 682.2 | 721.5 | 769.7 | 678.3 |
| **Central Bank** | | | | | | *Billions of Pesos: End of Period* | | | | | | | |
| Net Foreign Assets.......................... | 11n | 8,891.0 | 8,664.9 | 10,327.1 | 8,328.1 | 14,510.8 | † 12,255.0 | 12,508.4 | 21,309.5 | 19,396.1 | 20,947.0 | 23,941.3 | 26,647.8 |
| Claims on Nonresidents................. | 11 | 9,147.6 | 8,918.4 | 10,576.5 | 8,572.1 | 14,811.7 | † 12,978.6 | 13,167.0 | 22,021.1 | 20,052.5 | 21,657.0 | 24,718.6 | 27,506.5 |
| Liabilities to Nonresidents............. | 16c | 256.6 | 253.6 | 249.4 | 244.1 | 300.9 | † 723.6 | 658.6 | 711.6 | 656.4 | 710.0 | 777.3 | 858.7 |
| Claims on Other Depository Corps.... | 12e | 145.4 | 62.1 | 50.8 | 54.6 | 94.4 | † 3,736.9 | 1.9 | 956.3 | 1,111.3 | .6 | 8.2 | .5 |
| Net Claims on Central Government.. | 12an | 3,118.7 | 1,976.3 | 308.1 | 634.3 | 737.6 | † 636.2 | 619.7 | 208.7 | 435.9 | 809.9 | −1,026.4 | −124.0 |
| Claims on Central Government...... | 12a | 3,324.1 | 2,234.4 | 1,376.1 | 840.9 | 873.3 | † 939.1 | 998.1 | 1,074.4 | 1,140.8 | 1,207.3 | 284.4 | 296.0 |
| Liabilities to Central Government... | 16d | 205.4 | 258.1 | 1,068.0 | 206.6 | 135.8 | † 303.0 | 378.4 | 865.7 | 705.0 | 397.4 | 1,310.8 | 420.0 |
| Claims on Other Sectors.................. | 12s | 934.7 | 947.0 | 933.3 | 957.0 | 957.8 | † 914.6 | 876.8 | 821.4 | 754.8 | 651.3 | 566.9 | 466.4 |
| Claims on Other Financial Corps.... | 12g | — | — | — | — | — | † — | — | — | — | — | — | — |
| Claims on State & Local Govts...... | 12b | — | — | — | — | — | † — | — | — | — | — | — | — |
| Claims on Public Nonfin. Corps...... | 12c | — | — | — | — | — | † — | — | — | — | — | — | — |
| Claims on Private Sector................ | 12d | 934.7 | 947.0 | 933.3 | 957.0 | 957.8 | † 914.6 | 876.8 | 821.4 | 754.8 | 651.3 | 566.9 | 466.4 |
| Monetary Base................................ | 14 | 8,275.5 | 2,928.2 | 3,405.6 | 3,672.2 | 4,229.8 | † 4,582.2 | 5,525.9 | 6,855.6 | 7,890.4 | 8,754.5 | 8,183.1 | 9,151.6 |
| Currency in Circulation................. | 14a | 2,143.4 | 2,466.3 | 2,823.1 | 3,315.8 | 3,685.8 | † 4,189.6 | 4,748.5 | 5,265.7 | 6,195.1 | 6,917.6 | 7,578.1 | 8,417.7 |
| Liabs. to Other Depository Corps.... | 14c | 6,132.0 | 461.9 | 582.5 | 356.3 | 544.0 | † 392.6 | 777.4 | 1,589.9 | 1,695.2 | 1,836.9 | 605.0 | 733.9 |
| Liabilities to Other Sectors............. | 14d | .1 | — | — | — | — | † — | — | — | — | — | — | — |
| Other Liabs. to Other Dep. Corps..... | 14n | — | 5,300.1 | 6,075.8 | 5,437.3 | 6,778.3 | † 10,584.3 | 8,194.1 | 10,945.2 | 9,936.7 | 8,099.7 | 10,922.9 | 11,526.8 |
| Dep. & Sec. Excl. f/Monetary Base.... | 14o | 6,464.1 | 6,731.1 | 4,843.6 | 3,353.6 | 4,268.1 | † 4,359.4 | 3,747.5 | 7,851.3 | 8,346.2 | 9,372.1 | 7,915.7 | 8,271.4 |
| Deposits Included in Broad Money. | 15 | 19.0 | 8.7 | 9.8 | 10.7 | 1.2 | † — | — | — | — | — | — | — |
| Sec.Ot.th.Shares Incl.in Brd. Money | 16a | 6,445.2 | 6,722.4 | 4,833.8 | 3,342.9 | 4,266.9 | † 4,359.4 | 3,747.5 | 7,851.3 | 8,346.1 | 9,372.1 | 7,915.6 | 8,271.4 |
| Deposits Excl. from Broad Money... | 16b | — | — | — | — | — | † — | — | — | — | — | — | — |
| Sec.Ot.th.Shares Excl.f/Brd.Money... | 16s | — | — | — | — | — | † — | — | — | — | — | — | — |
| Loans.......................................... | 16l | — | — | — | — | — | † — | — | — | — | — | — | — |
| Financial Derivatives...................... | 16m | — | — | — | — | — | † — | — | — | — | — | — | — |
| Shares and Other Equity................. | 17a | −1,633.7 | −2,841.6 | −2,143.7 | −2,177.3 | 617.7 | † −1,960.2 | −3,449.1 | −2,353.9 | −4,479.2 | −3,820.2 | −3,544.5 | −1,975.8 |
| Other Items (Net)............................ | 17r | −15.9 | −467.4 | −562.1 | −311.7 | 406.7 | † −22.9 | −11.6 | −2.4 | 4.1 | 2.6 | 12.8 | 16.6 |
| Memo Item: | | | | | | | | | | | | | |
| Total Assets..................................... | 10ra | 23,133.8 | 19,777.0 | 21,228.4 | 18,708.3 | 31,468.2 | † 18,612.1 | 15,090.9 | 24,911.9 | 23,099.8 | 23,561.7 | 25,626.3 | 28,325.2 |

|  |  | 2004 | 2005 | 2006 | 2007 | 2008 | 2009 | 2010 | 2011 | 2012 | 2013 | 2014 | 2015 |
|---|---|---|---|---|---|---|---|---|---|---|---|---|---|
| **Other Depository Corporations** |  | *Billions of Pesos: End of Period* | | | | | | | | | | | |
| Net Foreign Assets............................ | 21n | −1,648.9 | −1,726.1 | −975.1 | 58.9 | † −3,427.3 | −3,726.0 | −4,453.9 | −6,436.4 | −5,467.0 | −5,167.5 | −4,457.0 | −5,696.0 |
| Claims on Nonresidents................ | 21 | 1,387.3 | 1,732.0 | 2,629.7 | 4,828.2 | † 3,916.2 | 3,796.2 | 3,410.2 | 4,498.6 | 4,113.4 | 4,766.2 | 6,340.0 | 6,697.0 |
| Liabilities to Nonresidents............. | 26c | 3,036.2 | 3,458.1 | 3,604.8 | 4,769.3 | † 7,343.5 | 7,522.2 | 7,864.1 | 10,935.0 | 9,580.5 | 9,933.7 | 10,796.9 | 12,392.9 |
| Claims on Central Bank.................. | 20 | 6,645.5 | 6,485.2 | 6,763.2 | 6,324.0 | † 8,335.9 | 11,014.9 | 10,294.9 | 13,893.3 | 13,357.1 | 12,054.5 | 13,004.4 | 14,883.9 |
| Currency............................... | 20a | 516.8 | 589.5 | 673.7 | 886.7 | † 1,009.6 | 1,254.2 | 1,325.3 | 1,373.5 | 1,715.1 | 1,932.1 | 2,207.2 | 2,560.2 |
| Reserve Deposits and Securities..... | 20b | 1,403.6 | 2,093.6 | 2,964.3 | 1,569.2 | † 1,904.0 | 2,540.9 | 3,801.3 | 7,134.2 | 7,082.4 | 6,218.6 | 5,886.6 | 6,773.0 |
| Other Claims.......................... | 20n | 4,725.2 | 3,802.1 | 3,125.2 | 3,868.1 | † 5,422.4 | 7,219.8 | 5,168.3 | 5,385.6 | 4,559.6 | 3,903.7 | 4,910.6 | 5,550.7 |
| Net Claims on Central Government.. | 22an | −1,062.6 | −2,235.7 | −2,157.8 | −1,821.2 | † −4,340.3 | −3,741.0 | −4,048.7 | −3,338.6 | −3,010.4 | −2,273.3 | −1,557.5 | −3,165.1 |
| Claims on Central Government...... | 22a | 398.8 | 443.6 | 389.0 | 705.2 | † 1,486.7 | 2,131.9 | 2,171.8 | 2,523.9 | 3,111.6 | 3,469.6 | 4,831.6 | 4,269.4 |
| Liabilities to Central Government... | 26d | 1,461.3 | 2,679.3 | 2,546.8 | 2,526.4 | † 5,827.0 | 5,873.0 | 6,220.4 | 5,862.5 | 6,122.0 | 5,742.9 | 6,389.1 | 7,434.6 |
| Claims on Other Sectors................. | 22s | 38,599.3 | 44,933.5 | 52,132.3 | 63,264.1 | † 70,911.5 | 69,531.2 | 75,430.4 | 87,892.4 | 98,759.0 | 108,831.2 | 121,744.3 | 136,073.2 |
| Claims on Other Financial Corps... | 22g | 391.7 | 416.0 | 497.1 | 609.4 | † 2,179.6 | 1,978.4 | 2,167.0 | 2,883.6 | 3,699.0 | 3,552.5 | 4,651.1 | 7,049.0 |
| Claims on State & Local Govts...... | 22b | .6 | .9 | 1.2 | 2.3 | † — | | | | — | — | — | — |
| Claims on Public Nonfin. Corps..... | 22c | 161.6 | 229.7 | 186.6 | 210.9 | † 320.5 | 294.2 | 324.1 | 252.9 | 209.2 | 233.1 | 271.1 | 310.1 |
| Claims on Private Sector............... | 22d | 38,045.4 | 44,286.8 | 51,447.4 | 62,441.5 | † 68,411.4 | 67,258.6 | 72,939.2 | 84,755.9 | 94,850.8 | 105,045.6 | 116,822.1 | 128,714.0 |
| Liabilities to Central Bank.............. | 26g | 1,062.5 | 419.7 | 658.9 | 569.6 | † 990.6 | 3,493.9 | 24.3 | 953.0 | 1,104.9 | 23.7 | 37.8 | 18.1 |
| Transf.Dep.Included in Broad Money | 24 | 4,512.4 | 5,081.3 | 5,894.0 | 6,327.4 | † 10,834.5 | 13,453.4 | 15,965.2 | 17,536.5 | 19,954.8 | 22,086.1 | 25,392.7 | 29,497.3 |
| Other Dep.Included in Broad Money. | 25 | 23,239.4 | 28,109.6 | 32,659.4 | 39,338.6 | † 28,837.8 | 26,001.2 | 27,454.2 | 34,704.2 | 39,738.9 | 46,226.3 | 50,929.0 | 58,212.1 |
| Sec.Ot.th.Shares Incl.in Brd. Money.. | 26a | 10,126.1 | 9,314.4 | 15,373.7 | 20,896.7 | † 25,899.9 | 22,360.4 | 23,851.0 | 27,486.5 | 28,373.2 | 30,070.9 | 32,989.0 | 31,978.3 |
| Deposits Excl. from Broad Money..... | 26b | — | — | — | — | † 402.7 | 525.3 | 626.3 | 758.6 | 1,004.6 | 1,153.6 | 1,337.8 | 1,336.6 |
| Sec.Ot.th.Shares Excl.f/Brd.Money.... | 26s | — | — | — | — | † — | | — | — | — | — | — | — |
| Loans............................................. | 26l | 1,615.4 | 1,676.0 | 1,651.6 | 1,724.6 | † 1,136.5 | 718.0 | 759.9 | 1,008.8 | 903.4 | 874.2 | 1,060.4 | 995.6 |
| Financial Derivatives....................... | 26m | — | — | — | — | † — | | — | — | — | — | — | — |
| Insurance Technical Reserves........... | 26r | — | — | — | — | † — | | — | — | — | — | — | — |
| Shares and Other Equity.................. | 27a | 4,797.8 | 5,279.7 | 5,900.2 | 7,365.8 | † 7,658.4 | 8,003.5 | 8,484.4 | 9,774.7 | 11,165.3 | 12,562.5 | 14,054.7 | 15,009.1 |
| Other Items (Net)............................ | 27r | −2,820.2 | −2,423.9 | −6,375.1 | −8,396.7 | † −4,280.7 | −1,476.7 | 57.4 | −211.5 | 1,393.6 | 447.7 | 2,932.7 | 5,048.8 |
| Memo Item: |  |  |  |  |  |  |  |  |  |  |  |  |  |
| Total Assets................................... | 20ra | 116,225.8 | 138,058.9 | 77,223.6 | 94,206.5 | † 102,899.3 | 101,420.8 | 107,423.5 | 125,424.2 | 137,054.9 | 149,758.2 | 171,483.8 | 189,399.9 |
| **Depository Corporations** |  | *Billions of Pesos: End of Period* | | | | | | | | | | | |
| Net Foreign Assets........................... | 31n | 7,242.1 | 6,938.8 | 9,352.0 | 8,387.0 | † 11,083.5 | † 8,529.0 | 8,054.5 | 14,873.1 | 13,929.1 | 15,779.5 | 19,484.3 | 20,951.9 |
| Claims on Nonresidents................ | 31 | 10,534.9 | 10,650.5 | 13,206.1 | 13,400.4 | † 18,727.9 | † 16,774.8 | 16,577.2 | 26,519.8 | 24,165.9 | 26,423.2 | 31,058.5 | 34,203.5 |
| Liabilities to Nonresidents............. | 36c | 3,292.8 | 3,711.6 | 3,854.1 | 5,013.4 | † 7,644.4 | † 8,245.8 | 8,522.7 | 11,646.7 | 10,236.9 | 10,643.7 | 11,574.2 | 13,251.6 |
| Domestic Claims.............................. | 32 | 41,590.3 | 45,621.0 | 51,215.9 | 63,034.3 | † 68,266.6 | † 67,341.0 | 72,878.2 | 85,583.9 | 96,939.3 | 108,019.1 | 119,727.3 | 133,250.4 |
| Net Claims on Central Government | 32an | 2,056.2 | −259.4 | −1,849.7 | −1,186.9 | † −3,602.7 | † −3,104.9 | −3,429.0 | −3,130.0 | −2,574.5 | −1,463.4 | −2,583.8 | −3,289.2 |
| Claims on Central Government..... | 32a | 3,722.9 | 2,678.0 | 1,765.1 | 1,546.1 | † 2,360.0 | † 3,071.1 | 3,169.8 | 3,598.3 | 4,252.4 | 4,676.9 | 5,116.0 | 4,565.4 |
| Liabilities to Central Government. | 36d | 1,666.7 | 2,937.4 | 3,614.8 | 2,733.0 | † 5,962.7 | † 6,175.9 | 6,598.8 | 6,728.2 | 6,826.9 | 6,140.3 | 7,699.9 | 7,854.6 |
| Claims on Other Sectors................. | 32s | 39,534.1 | 45,880.5 | 53,065.6 | 64,221.2 | † 71,869.3 | † 70,445.8 | 76,307.2 | 88,713.8 | 99,513.8 | 109,482.5 | 122,311.2 | 136,539.5 |
| Claims on Other Financial Corps... | 32g | 391.7 | 416.0 | 497.1 | 609.4 | † 2,179.6 | † 1,978.4 | 2,167.0 | 2,883.6 | 3,699.0 | 3,552.5 | 4,651.1 | 7,049.0 |
| Claims on State & Local Govts..... | 32b | .6 | .9 | 1.2 | 2.3 | † — | † — | | — | — | — | — | — |
| Claims on Public Nonfin. Corps..... | 32c | 161.6 | 229.7 | 186.6 | 210.9 | † 320.5 | † 294.2 | 324.1 | 252.9 | 209.2 | 233.1 | 271.1 | 310.1 |
| Claims on Private Sector............. | 32d | 38,980.2 | 45,233.8 | 52,380.6 | 63,398.5 | † 69,369.2 | † 68,173.2 | 73,816.0 | 85,577.3 | 95,605.6 | 105,696.9 | 117,389.0 | 129,180.3 |
| Broad Money Liabilities................... | 35l | 45,968.7 | 51,113.3 | 60,920.1 | 72,345.4 | † 72,516.5 | † 69,109.7 | 74,441.2 | 91,470.8 | 100,893.0 | 112,740.8 | 122,597.2 | 133,816.7 |
| Currency Outside Depository Corps | 34a | 1,626.6 | 1,876.9 | 2,149.4 | 2,429.1 | † 2,676.2 | † 2,935.4 | 3,423.2 | 3,892.3 | 4,480.0 | 4,985.5 | 5,370.9 | 5,857.5 |
| Transferable Deposits.................... | 34 | 4,512.4 | 5,081.3 | 5,894.0 | 6,327.4 | † 10,834.5 | † 13,453.4 | 15,965.2 | 17,536.5 | 19,954.8 | 22,086.1 | 25,392.7 | 29,497.3 |
| Other Deposits.............................. | 35 | 23,258.4 | 28,118.3 | 32,669.1 | 39,349.2 | † 28,839.0 | † 26,001.2 | 27,454.2 | 34,704.2 | 39,738.9 | 46,226.3 | 50,929.0 | 58,212.1 |
| Securities Other than Shares......... | 36a | 16,571.3 | 16,036.8 | 20,207.5 | 24,239.7 | † 30,166.9 | † 26,719.8 | 27,598.5 | 35,337.8 | 36,719.4 | 39,443.0 | 40,904.6 | 40,249.7 |
| Deposits Excl. from Broad Money..... | 36b | — | — | — | — | † 402.7 | † 525.3 | 626.3 | 758.6 | 1,004.6 | 1,153.6 | 1,337.9 | 1,336.6 |
| Sec.Ot.th.Shares Excl.f/Brd.Money.... | 36s | — | — | — | — | † — | † — | | — | — | — | — | — |
| Loans............................................. | 36l | 1,615.4 | 1,676.0 | 1,651.6 | 1,724.6 | † 1,136.5 | † 718.0 | 759.9 | 1,008.8 | 903.4 | 874.2 | 1,060.4 | 995.6 |
| Financial Derivatives....................... | 36m | — | — | — | — | † — | † — | | — | — | — | — | — |
| Insurance Technical Reserves........... | 36r | — | — | — | — | † — | † — | | — | — | — | — | — |
| Shares and Other Equity.................. | 37a | 3,164.1 | 2,438.1 | 3,756.5 | 5,188.4 | † 8,276.1 | † 6,043.3 | 5,035.2 | 7,420.8 | 6,686.0 | 8,742.4 | 10,510.3 | 13,033.3 |
| Other Items (Net)............................ | 37r | −1,915.8 | −2,667.5 | −5,760.3 | −7,837.1 | † −2,981.7 | † −526.4 | 70.1 | −202.0 | 1,381.3 | 287.6 | 3,706.0 | 5,020.0 |
| Broad Money Liabs., Seasonally Adj. | 35l.b | 46,258.2 | 51,290.3 | 60,967.5 | 72,258.4 | † 72,371.8 | † 69,299.1 | 74,589.5 | 91,536.6 | 100,803.9 | 112,473.7 | 122,176.5 | 133,291.9 |
| **Other Financial Corporations** |  | *Billions of Pesos: End of Period* | | | | | | | | | | | |
| Net Foreign Assets........................... | 41n | 9,228.5 | 11,650.0 | 15,242.2 | 19,623.2 | 15,085.7 | 29,354.2 | 35,581.8 | 28,997.9 | 33,381.5 | 40,802.0 | 50,717.2 | 56,087.2 |
| Claims on Nonresidents................ | 41 | 9,228.5 | 11,650.4 | 15,245.2 | 19,625.7 | 15,305.1 | 29,542.0 | 35,825.6 | 29,315.3 | 33,707.9 | 41,179.9 | 51,184.7 | 56,567.0 |
| Liabilities to Nonresidents............. | 46c | — | .4 | 3.0 | 2.5 | 219.4 | 187.8 | 243.8 | 317.4 | 326.5 | 377.9 | 467.5 | 479.8 |
| Claims on Depository Corporations.. | 40 | 13,842.8 | 15,139.2 | 16,523.3 | 18,600.0 | 33,019.6 | 30,835.6 | 29,365.5 | 35,934.5 | 39,273.7 | 43,379.7 | 52,436.1 | 57,491.2 |
| Net Claims on Central Government.. | 42an | 2,073.8 | 2,229.5 | 2,504.0 | 2,274.8 | 4,782.9 | 5,119.8 | 8,138.8 | 11,040.8 | 12,035.3 | 13,347.0 | 17,089.1 | 21,056.5 |
| Claims on Central Government...... | 42a | 2,073.8 | 2,229.5 | 2,504.0 | 2,274.8 | 4,800.0 | 5,138.1 | 8,162.0 | 11,064.7 | 12,117.6 | 13,393.9 | 17,138.0 | 21,123.6 |
| Liabilities to Central Government... | 46d | — | — | — | — | 17.1 | 18.3 | 23.2 | 23.8 | 82.3 | 46.9 | 48.9 | 67.1 |
| Claims on Other Sectors................. | 42s | 7,370.5 | 7,920.9 | 11,342.3 | 12,403.3 | 25,521.0 | 31,491.9 | 37,449.7 | 38,793.3 | 40,678.6 | 40,645.6 | 44,873.5 | 46,893.9 |
| Claims on State & Local Govts....... | 42b | — | — | — | — | | | | | | | | |
| Claims on Public Nonfin. Corps...... | 42c | — | — | — | — | 910.8 | 933.5 | 1,082.6 | 1,089.2 | 1,041.5 | 1,053.3 | 1,170.9 | 1,307.7 |
| Claims on Private Sector............... | 42d | 7,370.5 | 7,920.9 | 11,342.3 | 12,403.3 | 24,610.3 | 30,558.4 | 36,367.2 | 37,704.1 | 39,637.1 | 39,592.3 | 43,702.6 | 45,586.2 |
| Deposits.......................................... | 46b | — | — | — | — | | | | | | | | |
| Securities Other than Shares............ | 46s | — | — | — | — | 252.9 | 254.3 | 458.0 | 529.8 | 649.6 | 1,058.3 | 624.7 | 706.3 |
| Loans............................................. | 46l | — | — | — | — | 686.8 | 655.4 | 571.3 | 844.0 | 1,033.4 | 998.5 | 1,908.5 | 2,177.4 |
| Financial Derivatives....................... | 46m | — | — | — | — | | | | | | | | |
| Insurance Technical Reserves........... | 46r | 33,271.7 | 37,806.2 | 46,542.3 | 54,371.2 | 61,229.4 | 74,926.9 | 86,748.0 | 89,201.3 | 97,892.0 | 107,601.8 | 126,893.5 | 138,206.4 |
| Shares and Other Equity.................. | 47a | 239.3 | 90.8 | 136.6 | 227.8 | 15,980.3 | 23,062.8 | 25,424.7 | 25,123.4 | 27,057.2 | 29,620.3 | 36,914.7 | 39,636.3 |
| Other Items (Net)............................ | 47r | −995.5 | −957.3 | −1,067.1 | −1,697.8 | 259.9 | −2,097.9 | −2,666.2 | −931.7 | −1,263.0 | −1,104.6 | −1,225.4 | 802.3 |
| Memo Item: |  |  |  |  |  |  |  |  |  |  |  |  |  |
| Total Assets................................... | 40ra | 33,889.1 | 38,313.1 | 47,189.7 | 55,175.7 | 82,136.1 | 101,478.5 | 116,246.7 | 119,628.1 | 130,554.9 | 143,235.0 | 171,126.0 | 188,406.0 |

# Chile   228

| | | 2004 | 2005 | 2006 | 2007 | 2008 | 2009 | 2010 | 2011 | 2012 | 2013 | 2014 | 2015 |
|---|---|---|---|---|---|---|---|---|---|---|---|---|---|
| **Financial Corporations** | | *Billions of Pesos: End of Period* | | | | | | | | | | | |
| Net Foreign Assets...................... | 51n | 16,470.6 | 18,588.8 | 24,594.2 | 28,010.1 | † 26,169.3 | † 37,883.2 | 43,636.3 | 43,871.0 | 47,310.5 | 56,581.5 | 70,201.6 | 77,039.1 |
| Claims on Nonresidents................. | 51 | 19,763.4 | 22,300.8 | 28,451.4 | 33,026.1 | † 34,033.0 | † 46,316.8 | 52,402.8 | 55,835.1 | 57,873.9 | 67,603.1 | 82,243.2 | 90,770.5 |
| Liabilities to Nonresidents.............. | 56c | 3,292.8 | 3,712.0 | 3,857.2 | 5,015.9 | † 7,863.8 | † 8,433.6 | 8,766.5 | 11,964.1 | 10,563.3 | 11,021.6 | 12,041.7 | 13,731.4 |
| Domestic Claims........................... | 52 | 50,642.9 | 55,355.5 | 64,565.0 | 77,103.0 | † 96,390.9 | † 101,974.3 | 116,299.7 | 132,534.4 | 145,954.2 | 158,459.2 | 177,038.9 | 194,151.7 |
| Net Claims on Central Government | 52an | 4,130.0 | 1,970.1 | 654.3 | 1,087.9 | † 1,180.2 | † 2,015.0 | 4,709.8 | 7,910.8 | 9,460.8 | 11,883.6 | 14,505.3 | 17,767.4 |
| Claims on Central Government..... | 52a | 5,796.7 | 4,907.6 | 4,269.1 | 3,820.9 | † 7,160.1 | † 8,209.2 | 11,331.8 | 14,662.9 | 16,370.0 | 18,070.8 | 22,254.0 | 25,689.0 |
| Liabilities to Central Government. | 56d | 1,666.7 | 2,937.4 | 3,614.8 | 2,733.0 | † 5,979.8 | † 6,194.2 | 6,622.0 | 6,752.1 | 6,909.2 | 6,187.2 | 7,748.8 | 7,921.7 |
| Claims on Other Sectors................. | 52s | 46,512.9 | 53,385.4 | 63,910.7 | 76,015.1 | † 95,210.7 | † 99,959.3 | 111,589.9 | 124,623.6 | 136,493.4 | 146,575.6 | 162,533.6 | 176,384.4 |
| Claims on State & Local Govts..... | 52b | .6 | .9 | 1.2 | 2.3 | † — | † — | | | | | | |
| Claims on Public Nonfin. Corps.... | 52c | 161.6 | 229.7 | 186.6 | 210.9 | † 1,231.3 | † 1,227.7 | 1,406.7 | 1,342.2 | 1,250.6 | 1,286.4 | 1,442.0 | 1,617.8 |
| Claims on Private Sector.............. | 52d | 46,350.7 | 53,154.8 | 63,722.9 | 75,801.8 | † 93,979.4 | † 98,731.6 | 110,183.2 | 123,281.4 | 135,242.8 | 145,289.2 | 161,091.6 | 174,766.5 |
| Currency Outside Financial Corps..... | 54a | 1,626.6 | 1,876.9 | 2,149.4 | 2,429.1 | † 2,660.2 | † 2,925.5 | 3,412.8 | 3,876.1 | 4,463.0 | 4,965.7 | 5,347.9 | 5,834.8 |
| Deposits....................................... | 55l | 19,227.2 | 21,846.9 | 25,936.7 | 28,834.9 | † 38,865.7 | † 38,460.8 | 42,415.5 | 51,343.6 | 58,998.6 | 67,547.0 | 75,222.0 | 85,765.0 |
| Securities Other than Shares............ | 56a | 4,018.3 | 2,900.0 | 6,601.9 | 8,797.4 | † 7,488.9 | † 6,831.6 | 7,225.5 | 7,438.5 | 7,355.3 | 7,815.1 | 7,534.5 | 7,643.5 |
| Loans.......................................... | 56l | 1,180.1 | 1,149.8 | 1,170.3 | 1,297.3 | † — | † — | | | | | | |
| Financial Derivatives...................... | 56m | — | — | — | — | † — | † — | | | | | | |
| Insurance Technical Reserves........... | 56r | 33,271.7 | 37,806.2 | 46,542.3 | 54,371.2 | † 61,229.4 | † 74,926.9 | 86,748.0 | 89,201.3 | 97,892.0 | 107,601.8 | 126,893.5 | 138,206.4 |
| Shares and Other Equity.................. | 57a | 3,403.4 | 2,528.9 | 3,893.1 | 5,416.2 | † 24,256.4 | † 29,106.1 | 30,459.9 | 32,544.1 | 33,743.2 | 38,362.7 | 47,425.0 | 52,669.7 |
| Other Items (Net).......................... | 57r | 4,386.1 | 5,835.6 | 2,865.6 | 3,967.0 | † −11,940.5 | † −12,393.3 | −10,325.7 | −7,998.2 | −9,187.3 | −11,251.7 | −15,182.5 | −18,928.5 |
| **Monetary Aggregates** | | *Billions of Pesos: End of Period* | | | | | | | | | | | |
| Broad Money................................ | 59m | 45,968.7 | 51,113.3 | 60,920.1 | 72,345.4 | 72,516.5 | 69,109.7 | 74,441.2 | 91,470.8 | 100,893.0 | 112,740.8 | 122,597.2 | 133,816.7 |
| o/w:Currency Issued by Cent.Govt | 59m.a | — | — | — | — | — | — | — | — | — | — | — | — |
| o/w: Dep.in Nonfin. Corporations. | 59m.b | — | — | — | — | — | — | — | — | — | — | — | — |
| o/w:Secs. Issued by Central Govt.. | 59m.c | — | — | — | — | — | — | — | — | — | — | — | — |
| Money (National Definitions) | | | | | | | | | | | | | |
| Base Money................................ | 19ma | 2,329.2 | 2,928.1 | 3,405.6 | 3,672.2 | 4,229.8 | 4,582.2 | 4,814.8 | 6,851.1 | 7,890.6 | 8,754.5 | 8,183.1 | 9,151.6 |
| M1............................................. | 59ma | 7,148.6 | 7,913.7 | 9,221.0 | 10,797.2 | 11,093.2 | 14,204.6 | 15,881.8 | 18,838.8 | 20,560.5 | 22,693.8 | 26,348.0 | 29,419.4 |
| M2............................................. | 59mb | 26,826.6 | 32,547.6 | 38,427.1 | 46,687.9 | 53,505.3 | 52,561.1 | 55,137.2 | 68,450.4 | 73,958.1 | 83,565.3 | 91,952.4 | 101,451.6 |
| M3............................................. | 59mc | 51,577.5 | 57,553.7 | 64,670.8 | 74,514.2 | 86,882.7 | 86,585.3 | 95,176.6 | 116,120.0 | 123,371.6 | 138,819.5 | 154,979.5 | 173,070.1 |
| **Interest Rates** | | *Percent Per Annum* | | | | | | | | | | | |
| Central Bank Policy Rate (EOP)........ | 60 | 2.25 | 4.50 | 5.25 | 6.00 | 8.25 | .50 | 3.12 | 5.25 | 5.00 | 4.50 | 3.00 | 3.35 |
| Discount Rate (End of Period).......... | 60.a | 2.25 | 4.50 | 5.25 | 6.00 | 8.25 | .50 | 3.12 | 5.25 | 5.00 | 4.50 | 3.00 | 3.35 |
| Money Market Rate........................ | 60b | 1.88 | 3.48 | .5.02 | 5.36 | 7.11 | 1.95 | 1.40 | 4.67 | 5.01 | 4.93 | 3.76 | 3.06 |
| Savings Rate................................. | 60k | .22 | .20 | .20 | .20 | .19 | .20 | .19 | .19 | .20 | .20 | .20 | .20 |
| Deposit Rate................................. | 60l | 1.94 | 3.93 | 5.11 | 5.61 | 7.49 | 2.05 | 1.75 | 5.29 | 5.79 | 5.17 | 3.92 | 3.61 |
| Deposit Rate (Fgn. Currency)........... | 60l.f | 1.63 | 2.94 | 4.38 | 4.90 | 3.45 | 1.09 | .82 | .84 | .72 | .32 | .35 | .30 |
| Lending Rate................................. | 60p | 5.13 | 6.68 | 8.00 | 8.67 | 13.26 | 7.25 | 4.75 | 9.03 | 10.06 | 9.26 | 8.10 | 5.51 |
| Lending Rate (Fgn. Currency).......... | 60p.f | 2.95 | 4.44 | 5.77 | 5.85 | 4.97 | 3.30 | 1.80 | 1.64 | 1.84 | 1.42 | 1.36 | 1.43 |
| **Prices, Production, Labor** | | *Index Numbers (2010=100): Period Averages* | | | | | | | | | | | |
| Share Prices................................. | 62 | 36.68 | 46.99 | 52.34 | 74.02 | 64.97 | 70.77 | 100.00 | 104.48 | 101.69 | 95.40 | 89.74 | 90.51 |
| Producer Prices (2012=100)............ | 63 | .... | .... | .... | .... | .... | .... | .... | .... | 100.0 | 96.1 | 96.3 | 89.6 |
| Wholesale Prices............................ | 63a | 72.6 | † 76.5 | 81.8 | 87.3 | 101.8 | 102.1 | 100.0 | 105.9 | .... | .... | .... | .... |
| Consumer Prices (National).............. | 64 | .... | .... | .... | .... | .... | 98.6 | 100.0 | 103.3 | 106.4 | † 108.4 | 113.1 | 118.0 |
| Cons. Pr.(Capital City)(2005=100)... | 64a | 97.0 | 100.0 | 103.4 | 107.9 | 117.4 | 119.1 | .... | .... | .... | .... | .... | .... |
| Wages, Hourly............................... | 65a | 70.4 | 73.9 | 77.9 | 83.6 | 90.7 | † 96.5 | 100.0 | 105.9 | .... | .... | .... | .... |
| Industrial Production........................ | 66 | 93.9 | 99.0 | 102.2 | 106.4 | 106.7 | 99.5 | 100.0 | 105.4 | 113.5 | 113.6 | 112.5 | 111.5 |
| Manufacturing Production............... | 66ey | 91.5 | 96.4 | 99.6 | 103.7 | † 103.9 | 96.9 | 100.0 | 108.0 | 110.4 | 109.9 | .... | .... |
| Mining Production........................... | 66zx | 100.1 | 99.3 | 100.0 | 103.9 | † 98.5 | 98.9 | 100.0 | 99.9 | 103.8 | 109.6 | .... | .... |
| Copper Production (2005=100)..... | 66c | 101.7 | 100.0 | .... | .... | .... | .... | .... | .... | .... | .... | .... | .... |
| Employment (2005=100)................ | 67 | 96.7 | 100.0 | .... | .... | .... | .... | .... | .... | .... | .... | .... | .... |
| | | *Number in Thousands: Period Averages* | | | | | | | | | | | |
| Labor Force.................................. | 67d | 6,608 | 6,798 | 6,803 | 6,944 | 7,203 | 7,300 | 7,763 | 8,061 | 8,150 | 8,231 | 8,443 | 8,560 |
| Employment.................................. | 67e | 5,946 | 6,170 | 6,272 | 6,449 | 6,642 | 6,593 | 7,131 | 7,487 | 7,626 | 7,735 | 7,903 | 8,028 |
| Unemployment.............................. | 67c | 661 | 628 | 531 | 496 | 562 | 707 | 632 | 574 | 524 | 496 | 540 | 532 |
| Unemployment Rate (%)................. | 67r | 10.0 | 9.2 | 7.8 | 7.1 | 7.8 | 9.7 | 8.1 | 7.1 | 6.4 | 6.0 | 6.4 | 6.2 |
| **Intl. Transactions & Positions** | | *Millions of US Dollars* | | | | | | | | | | | |
| Exports....................................... | 70..d | 32,520 | 41,267 | 58,680 | 67,666 | 66,455 | 51,963 | 68,996 | 80,027 | 79,712 | 77,877 | 74,547 | 64,087 |
| Imports, c.i.f................................. | 71..d | 24,793 | 32,735 | 38,406 | 47,164 | 61,903 | 41,364 | 57,928 | 73,545 | 79,080 | 80,443 | 72,433 | 62,797 |
| Imports, f.o.b................................ | 71.vd | 22,935 | 30,492 | 35,900 | 44,031 | 57,610 | 39,906 | 54,201 | 67,883 | 73,148 | 75,800 | 65,861 | 58,770 |

# Chile   228

| | | 2004 | 2005 | 2006 | 2007 | 2008 | 2009 | 2010 | 2011 | 2012 | 2013 | 2014 | 2015 |
|---|---|---|---|---|---|---|---|---|---|---|---|---|---|
| **Balance of Payments** | | | | | | | *Millions of US Dollars* | | | | | | |
| A. Current Account* | 109bx | 2,074.5 | 1,448.8 | 7,154.3 | 7,458.2 | −3,307.2 | † 3,517.8 | 3,581.2 | −3,069.9 | −9,624.4 | −10,311.4 | −3,316.4 | −4,761.5 |
| Goods, credit (exports) | 1a9cx | 32,519.7 | 41,266.1 | 58,678.3 | 67,971.0 | 66,258.4 | † 55,462.7 | 71,108.5 | 81,437.8 | 77,790.6 | 76,386.3 | 74,923.9 | 62,232.1 |
| Goods, debit (imports) | 1a9dx | 22,869.3 | 30,429.2 | 35,862.9 | 43,967.7 | 57,662.9 | † 40,102.6 | 55,372.1 | 70,398.2 | 75,457.7 | 74,678.2 | 68,580.2 | 58,737.8 |
| Balance on goods | 1a9bx | 9,650.4 | 10,837.0 | 22,815.4 | 24,003.3 | 8,595.6 | † 15,360.0 | 15,736.5 | 11,039.6 | 2,332.9 | 1,708.1 | 6,343.6 | 3,494.3 |
| Services, credit (exports) | 1b9cx | 6,034.3 | 7,134.9 | 7,832.2 | 8,962.9 | 10,823.9 | † 8,492.8 | 11,148.7 | 13,105.3 | 12,386.9 | 12,355.3 | 11,010.8 | 9,777.1 |
| Services, debit (imports) | 1b9dx | 6,845.4 | 7,818.8 | 8,498.7 | 10,012.7 | 11,854.5 | † 10,503.3 | 13,028.6 | 16,158.3 | 15,130.7 | 16,085.0 | 14,828.5 | 13,588.8 |
| Balance on Goods & Services | 1z9bx | 8,839.3 | 10,153.0 | 22,148.9 | 22,953.5 | 7,564.9 | † 13,349.6 | 13,856.6 | 7,986.6 | −410.9 | −2,021.6 | 2,525.9 | −317.4 |
| Primary income: credit | 1c9cx | 1,983.1 | 2,452.1 | 3,374.4 | 6,325.0 | 5,928.1 | † 6,570.8 | 6,797.1 | 7,007.1 | 8,179.7 | 8,421.1 | 8,458.5 | 7,361.0 |
| Primary income: debit | 1c9dx | 9,819.8 | 12,939.2 | 21,775.4 | 24,949.7 | 19,730.0 | † 17,965.8 | 21,482.8 | 20,928.4 | 19,453.3 | 18,825.8 | 16,150.1 | 13,555.4 |
| Balance on gds, serv. & prim. inc. | 1y9bx | 1,002.6 | −334.1 | 3,747.9 | 4,328.8 | −6,236.9 | † 1,954.6 | −829.2 | −5,934.8 | −11,684.5 | −12,426.3 | −5,165.6 | −6,511.8 |
| Secondary income: credit | 1d9ca | 1,411.0 | 2,199.2 | 4,002.9 | 3,857.3 | 3,875.2 | † 2,512.2 | 5,656.7 | 4,350.6 | 3,890.2 | 4,159.8 | 3,846.8 | 3,691.0 |
| Secondary income: debit | 1d9da | 339.1 | 416.3 | 596.5 | 727.9 | 945.5 | † 949.1 | 1,246.3 | 1,485.7 | 1,830.1 | 2,045.0 | 1,997.5 | 1,940.6 |
| B. Capital Account* | 209ba | 5.1 | 41.2 | 13.3 | 15.7 | 3.1 | † 14.5 | 6,240.5 | 11.9 | 11.7 | 11.4 | 10.2 | 584.8 |
| Capital account: credit | 209ca | 5.1 | 41.2 | 13.3 | 15.7 | 3.1 | † 14.5 | 6,240.5 | 11.9 | 11.7 | 11.4 | 10.2 | 584.8 |
| Capital account: debit | 209da | — | | | | | .... | .... | .... | .... | .... | .... | .... |
| Balance on current & capital acct. | 129ba | 2,079.6 | 1,490.0 | 7,167.6 | 7,473.9 | −3,304.1 | † 3,532.3 | 9,821.7 | −3,058.0 | −9,612.7 | −10,300.0 | −3,306.1 | −4,176.7 |
| C. Financial Account* | 309na | 2,000.8 | −1,549.6 | 3,644.0 | 10,238.2 | −8,598.5 | † 2,528.8 | 5,942.9 | −17,828.1 | −8,954.5 | −12,231.7 | −4,900.7 | −4,952.1 |
| Direct investment: assets | 3a9aa | 1,563.1 | 2,182.7 | 2,171.5 | 2,572.8 | 8,041.2 | † 7,232.9 | 9,460.7 | 20,251.9 | 20,555.4 | 9,871.8 | 12,914.5 | 15,793.9 |
| Equity & investment fund shares | 3aaaa | 1,330.8 | 1,708.2 | 1,894.1 | 1,932.0 | 7,408.2 | † 7,406.5 | 7,572.3 | 10,900.7 | 12,722.5 | 13,208.3 | 11,300.2 | 5,172.7 |
| Debt instruments | 3abaa | 232.3 | 474.5 | 277.4 | 640.9 | 633.0 | † −173.6 | 1,888.4 | 9,351.3 | 7,832.8 | −3,336.5 | 1,614.3 | 10,621.2 |
| Direct investment: liabilities | 3a9la | 7,172.7 | 6,983.8 | 7,298.4 | 12,533.6 | 15,149.8 | † 12,887.5 | 15,725.2 | 23,443.9 | 28,457.0 | 19,362.5 | 22,342.2 | 20,457.2 |
| Equity & investment fund shares | 3aala | 7,194.5 | 7,320.3 | 9,122.8 | 12,803.2 | 14,372.2 | † 12,424.5 | 12,525.0 | 20,147.4 | 17,616.5 | 10,778.6 | 13,919.3 | 10,412.0 |
| Debt instruments | 3abla | −21.8 | −336.5 | −1,824.4 | −269.6 | 777.6 | † 463.0 | 3,200.3 | 3,296.5 | 10,840.5 | 8,583.9 | 8,422.9 | 10,045.2 |
| Portfolio investment: assets | 3b9aa | 4,430.2 | 4,227.2 | 10,084.7 | 15,953.2 | 10,252.4 | † 14,268.6 | 15,709.6 | −798.4 | 15,043.0 | 10,667.7 | 8,710.3 | 436.5 |
| Equity & investment fund shares | 3baaa | 3,204.9 | 4,024.5 | 2,264.5 | 10,150.3 | 5,162.1 | † 20,890.7 | 12,189.6 | −6,964.1 | 11,416.8 | 8,630.4 | 6,088.0 | −768.1 |
| Debt securities | 3bbaa | 1,225.3 | 202.7 | 7,820.2 | 5,802.9 | 5,090.3 | † −6,622.1 | 3,520.0 | 6,165.7 | 3,626.2 | 2,037.4 | 2,622.3 | 1,204.7 |
| Portfolio investment: liabilities | 3b9la | 1,121.8 | 1,394.3 | 846.2 | −508.0 | 2,632.9 | † 1,870.0 | 9,289.0 | 10,685.3 | 11,071.9 | 15,390.0 | 12,754.8 | 2,990.4 |
| Equity & investment fund shares | 3bala | 7.6 | 1,570.6 | −124.1 | 388.3 | 1,948.3 | † 328.0 | 1,764.3 | 4,650.5 | 5,632.9 | 5,883.5 | 2,184.7 | −6.2 |
| Debt securities | 3bbla | 1,114.2 | −176.4 | 970.2 | −896.3 | 684.6 | † 1,542.1 | 7,524.7 | 6,034.8 | 5,438.9 | 9,506.5 | 10,570.0 | 2,996.6 |
| Fin. der.& empl.stk.ops.(ESOs): net. | 3c9na | 84.0 | 62.5 | −300.8 | −453.6 | 952.1 | † 1,048.6 | 933.7 | 2,418.2 | −10.4 | 1,005.3 | 1,611.7 | 933.3 |
| Fin. der. & ESOs.: assets | 3c9aa | −638.9 | −1,244.4 | −1,551.7 | −2,608.1 | −11,708.2 | † −8,252.2 | −8,668.1 | −12,270.2 | −9,674.4 | −7,344.9 | −7,294.1 | −9,412.7 |
| Fin. der. & ESOs.: liabilities | 3c9la | −722.9 | −1,307.0 | −1,251.0 | −2,154.5 | −12,660.4 | † −9,300.8 | −9,601.7 | −14,688.4 | −9,663.9 | −8,350.2 | −8,905.8 | −10,346.0 |
| Other investment: assets | 3d9aa | 3,388.6 | 2,384.2 | 3,927.5 | 11,097.8 | −3,715.4 | † 611.8 | 6,383.7 | −662.0 | −2,334.2 | −1,093.1 | 3,813.9 | −1,916.2 |
| Other equity | 3daaa | .... | | .... | | .... | .... | .... | .... | .... | .... | .... | .... |
| Debt instruments | 3dzaa | 3,388.6 | 2,384.2 | 3,927.5 | 11,097.8 | −3,715.4 | † 611.8 | 6,383.7 | −662.0 | −2,334.2 | −1,093.1 | 3,813.9 | −1,916.2 |
| Other investment: liabilities | 3d9la | −829.3 | 2,028.2 | 4,094.2 | 6,906.3 | 6,346.2 | † 5,875.6 | 1,530.7 | 4,908.6 | 2,679.3 | −2,069.0 | −3,145.9 | −3,248.0 |
| Other equity | 3dala | .... | | .... | | .... | .... | .... | .... | .... | .... | .... | .... |
| Debt instruments | 3dzla | −829.3 | 2,028.2 | 4,094.2 | 6,906.3 | 6,346.2 | † 5,875.6 | 1,530.7 | 4,908.6 | 2,679.3 | −2,069.0 | −3,145.9 | −3,248.0 |
| Curr.+ cap.− finan. acct. balance. | 4y9na | 78.8 | 3,039.6 | 3,523.5 | −2,764.3 | 5,294.3 | † 1,003.5 | 3,878.9 | 14,770.1 | −658.2 | 1,931.7 | 1,594.5 | 775.4 |
| D. Net Errors and Omissions | 409na | −270.2 | −1,328.8 | −1,525.2 | −449.4 | 1,166.9 | † 644.3 | −855.8 | −578.3 | 292.3 | −1,619.6 | −537.7 | −549.5 |
| E. Reserves and Related Items | 4z9na | −191.5 | 1,710.8 | 1,998.3 | −3,213.7 | 6,461.2 | † 1,647.8 | 3,023.1 | 14,191.8 | −365.9 | 312.0 | 1,056.8 | 225.9 |
| Reserve assets | 3e9aa | −191.5 | 1,710.8 | 1,998.3 | −3,213.7 | 6,461.2 | † 1,647.8 | 3,023.1 | 14,191.8 | −365.9 | 312.0 | 1,056.8 | 225.9 |
| Credit and loans from the IMF. | 3dcla | — | — | — | — | — | † — | | | | | | |
| Exceptional financing | 409la | — | — | — | — | — | .... | .... | .... | .... | .... | .... | .... |
| *Excludes components in group E | | | | | | | | | | | | | |
| | | | | | | | | | | | | | |
| **International Investment Position** | | | | | | | *Millions of US Dollars* | | | | | | |
| Assets | 809aa | 75,975.3 | 91,898.4 | 120,957.1 | 164,585.4 | 142,710.8 | † 191,961.1 | 235,083.3 | 254,512.3 | 291,529.8 | 306,144.4 | 324,390.4 | 314,232.0 |
| Direct investment | 8a9aa | 17,412.7 | 21,358.9 | 26,024.9 | 31,688.4 | 31,820.2 | † 51,426.3 | 60,386.1 | 78,180.9 | 97,727.0 | 100,698.4 | 107,077.2 | 108,817.4 |
| Equity & investment fund shares.. | 8aaaa | 15,289.8 | 18,761.4 | 23,150.1 | 28,172.7 | 27,671.5 | † 43,386.1 | 50,457.4 | 58,901.0 | 70,614.2 | 76,922.0 | 81,686.6 | 72,805.5 |
| Debt instruments | 8abaa | 2,122.9 | 2,597.5 | 2,874.8 | 3,515.7 | 4,148.7 | † 8,040.2 | 9,928.6 | 19,279.9 | 27,112.8 | 23,776.3 | 25,390.6 | 36,011.8 |
| Portfolio investment | 8b9aa | 28,550.6 | 37,041.1 | 55,328.6 | 83,449.2 | 57,299.0 | † 89,902.3 | 116,606.1 | 103,838.6 | 125,115.2 | 136,475.1 | 144,367.1 | 137,103.7 |
| Equity & investment fund shares.. | 8baaa | 24,321.3 | 32,741.3 | 43,020.8 | 64,176.4 | 33,250.4 | † 71,077.9 | 93,782.9 | 75,891.3 | 91,172.3 | 101,611.6 | 107,331.4 | 100,399.4 |
| Debt securities | 8bbaa | 4,229.3 | 4,299.8 | 12,307.9 | 19,272.8 | 24,048.6 | † 18,824.3 | 22,823.2 | 27,947.4 | 33,942.9 | 34,863.6 | 37,035.7 | 36,704.3 |
| Fin. der.(oth.than reserves) & ESOs | 8c9aa | 995.0 | 1,023.2 | 827.0 | 1,718.1 | 3,026.7 | † 4,306.8 | 3,587.7 | 3,840.3 | 3,291.5 | 5,239.8 | 6,303.1 | 5,619.8 |
| Other investment | 8d9aa | 13,000.8 | 15,513.0 | 19,348.4 | 30,819.9 | 27,403.9 | † 20,948.5 | 26,640.7 | 26,673.6 | 23,746.8 | 22,637.6 | 26,195.7 | 24,049.9 |
| Other equity | 8daaa | .... | .... | .... | .... | .... | .... | .... | .... | .... | .... | .... | .... |
| Debt instruments | 8dzaa | 13,000.8 | 15,513.0 | 19,348.4 | 30,819.9 | 27,403.9 | † 20,948.5 | 26,640.7 | 26,673.6 | 23,746.8 | 22,637.6 | 26,195.7 | 24,049.9 |
| Reserve assets | 8e9aa | 16,016.2 | 16,962.1 | 19,428.2 | 16,909.8 | 23,161.0 | † 25,377.2 | 27,862.9 | 41,978.8 | 41,649.3 | 41,093.4 | 40,447.3 | 38,641.3 |
| Liabilities | 809la | 106,358.4 | 124,738.2 | 136,868.3 | 163,858.5 | 172,544.4 | † 214,557.4 | 264,716.0 | 286,223.3 | 333,685.0 | 344,197.2 | 360,709.0 | 359,338.3 |
| Direct investment | 8a9la | 60,540.5 | 74,196.4 | 80,296.7 | 99,413.3 | 99,359.0 | † 127,940.1 | 160,612.0 | 172,699.2 | 205,999.3 | 213,128.8 | 223,112.6 | 229,228.7 |
| Equity & investment fund shares.. | 8aala | 56,319.5 | 69,932.4 | 77,906.8 | 96,597.3 | 95,954.7 | † 122,389.9 | 151,712.3 | 160,533.2 | 179,730.7 | 177,926.6 | 179,951.1 | 176,757.2 |
| Debt instruments | 8abla | 4,221.0 | 4,264.0 | 2,390.0 | 2,816.0 | 3,404.3 | † 5,550.2 | 8,899.7 | 12,166.0 | 26,268.6 | 35,202.2 | 43,161.6 | 52,471.6 |
| Portfolio investment | 8b9la | 16,192.5 | 17,985.0 | 19,822.1 | 19,961.9 | 20,014.1 | † 27,593.9 | 42,670.4 | 48,302.5 | 61,960.4 | 67,938.3 | 76,945.6 | 72,283.3 |
| Equity & investment fund shares.. | 8bala | 4,622.0 | 6,832.0 | 8,050.7 | 9,190.7 | 8,959.2 | † 14,115.3 | 21,713.4 | 21,182.4 | 28,217.4 | 26,732.0 | 25,061.5 | 20,272.9 |
| Debt securities | 8bbla | 11,570.5 | 11,153.0 | 11,771.4 | 10,771.2 | 11,054.9 | † 13,478.7 | 20,957.0 | 27,120.1 | 33,743.0 | 41,206.4 | 51,884.2 | 52,010.4 |
| Fin. der.(oth.than reserves) & ESOs | 8c9la | 695.2 | 954.0 | 931.5 | 2,129.4 | 4,088.4 | † 5,432.1 | 6,304.4 | 5,200.6 | 5,190.6 | 4,989.2 | 6,044.1 | 6,653.0 |
| Other investment | 8d9la | 28,930.2 | 31,602.8 | 35,818.0 | 42,353.9 | 49,082.9 | † 53,591.3 | 55,129.2 | 60,020.0 | 60,534.6 | 58,141.0 | 54,606.6 | 51,173.2 |
| Other equity | 8dala | .... | .... | .... | .... | .... | .... | .... | .... | .... | .... | .... | .... |
| Debt instruments | 8dzla | 28,930.2 | 31,602.8 | 35,818.0 | 42,353.9 | 49,082.9 | † 53,591.3 | 55,129.2 | 60,020.0 | 60,534.6 | 58,141.0 | 54,606.6 | 51,173.2 |

| | | 2004 | 2005 | 2006 | 2007 | 2008 | 2009 | 2010 | 2011 | 2012 | 2013 | 2014 | 2015 |
|---|---|---|---|---|---|---|---|---|---|---|---|---|---|
| **Government Finance Operations Statement** | | | | | | | | | | | | | |
| **Budgetary Central Government** | | | | | | ***Billions of Pesos: Fiscal Year Ends December 31*** | | | | | | | |
| Revenue | a1 | 12,489.5 | 15,305.0 | 19,382.0 | 22,784.1 | 22,353.1 | 17,709.9 | 23,352.4 | 26,941.6 | 28,099.9 | 28,244.2 | 30,169.2 | 33,196.4 |
| Taxes | a11 | 9,918.2 | 12,407.0 | 15,999.0 | 18,373.0 | 17,536.9 | 13,972.5 | 18,843.5 | 22,431.0 | 24,066.1 | 23,399.3 | 24,832.9 | 27,823.7 |
| Social Contributions | a12 | 827.6 | 932.0 | 1,050.0 | 1,148.7 | 1,289.2 | 1,371.6 | 1,493.9 | 1,623.8 | 1,802.5 | 1,969.0 | 2,110.1 | 2,252.5 |
| Grants | a13 | 3.2 | 3.0 | — | — | — | 1.9 | 145.8 | 55.8 | 5.5 | 10.0 | 56.4 | 59.6 |
| Other Revenue | a14 | 1,740.5 | 1,963.0 | 2,333.0 | 3,262.4 | 3,527.0 | 2,363.8 | 2,869.4 | 2,831.0 | 2,225.8 | 2,866.0 | 3,169.8 | 3,060.6 |
| Expense | a2 | 10,490.2 | 11,481.0 | 12,673.0 | 13,582.9 | 16,382.8 | 19,507.7 | 21,310.5 | 22,558.2 | 24,756.9 | 26,481.6 | 29,310.5 | 32,977.9 |
| Compensation of Employees | a21 | 2,301.6 | 2,518.0 | 2,760.0 | 3,107.9 | 3,544.9 | 4,210.6 | 4,659.9 | 4,946.9 | 5,409.7 | 5,894.2 | 6,511.0 | 7,208.8 |
| Use of Goods & Services | a22 | 803.4 | 989.0 | 1,129.0 | 1,328.9 | 1,561.1 | 1,845.6 | 1,902.7 | 2,016.8 | 2,211.1 | 2,419.3 | 2,735.9 | 3,073.2 |
| Consumption of Fixed Capital | a23 | 439.1 | . . . . | . . . . | . . . . | . . . . | . . . . | . . . . | . . . . | . . . . | . . . . | . . . . | . . . . |
| Interest | a24 | 253.2 | 253.0 | 252.0 | 234.8 | 190.6 | 261.3 | 255.5 | 444.5 | 589.8 | 637.2 | 656.2 | 914.1 |
| Subsidies | a25 | 2,451.6 | 2,729.0 | 3,098.0 | 4,319.9 | 5,454.7 | 4,463.0 | 4,953.1 | 5,032.3 | 3,653.1 | 3,978.6 | 4,343.1 | 4,754.2 |
| Grants | a26 | 547.9 | 570.0 | 592.0 | — | — | 2,005.6 | 2,497.9 | 2,568.9 | 1,866.5 | 2,117.9 | 4,679.1 | 5,195.0 |
| Social Benefits | a27 | 2,848.7 | 3,076.0 | 3,347.0 | 3,590.2 | 4,084.1 | 4,591.5 | 4,975.4 | 5,150.8 | 6,184.7 | 6,520.6 | 7,004.8 | 7,617.6 |
| Other Expense | a28 | 844.8 | 877.0 | 986.0 | 1,001.3 | 1,547.4 | 2,130.5 | 2,066.3 | 2,398.0 | 4,842.1 | 4,913.9 | 3,380.4 | 4,215.0 |
| Gross Operating Balance [1-2+23] | agob | 2,438.4 | 4,293.0 | 7,218.0 | 9,201.1 | 5,970.3 | −1,797.8 | 2,041.6 | 4,383.3 | 3,343.0 | 1,762.7 | 858.7 | 218.5 |
| Net Operating Balance [1-2] | anob | 1,999.3 | . . . . | . . . . | . . . . | . . . . | . . . . | . . . . | . . . . | . . . . | . . . . | . . . . | . . . . |
| Net Acq. of Nonfinancial Assets | a31 | 591.5 | 713.0 | 847.0 | 1,776.3 | 1,991.8 | 2,424.6 | 2,317.6 | 2,583.1 | 2,641.2 | 2,679.3 | 2,946.4 | 3,616.1 |
| Aquisition of Nonfin. Assets | a31.1 | . . . . | 1,208.9 | 1,374.7 | 1,789.3 | 2,015.9 | 2,477.0 | 2,345.5 | 2,604.5 | 2,675.3 | 2,724.9 | 2,979.6 | 3,658.4 |
| Disposal of Nonfin. Assets | a31.2 | . . . . | 26.6 | 18.6 | 13.0 | 24.1 | 52.3 | 27.8 | 21.4 | 34.1 | 45.6 | 33.1 | 42.3 |
| Net Lending/Borrowing [1-2-31] | anlb | 1,407.7 | 3,110.0 | 5,862.0 | 7,424.9 | 3,978.5 | −4,222.6 | −275.8 | 1,800.2 | 701.8 | −916.7 | −2,087.7 | −3,397.6 |
| Net Acq. of Financial Assets | a32 | 622.0 | 1,143.0 | 4,067.0 | 5,940.4 | 3,152.8 | −4,121.9 | 2,209.2 | 3,761.9 | 1,088.5 | −895.8 | 318.2 | −494.2 |
| By instrument | | | | | | | | | | | | | |
| Monetary Gold & SDRs | a3201 | — | — | — | — | — | — | — | — | — | — | — | — |
| Currency & Deposits | a3202 | 55.7 | 444.0 | 808.0 | −1,215.4 | 577.4 | −270.0 | −242.3 | −233.9 | 153.4 | −896.3 | −1,208.4 | 46.2 |
| Securities other than Shares | a3203 | 551.7 | 750.0 | 3,407.0 | 6,982.5 | 2,283.0 | −3,922.2 | 2,422.9 | 4,084.8 | 981.2 | 190.1 | 1,610.7 | −586.7 |
| Loans | a3204 | 14.7 | −51.0 | −147.0 | 173.3 | 292.4 | 70.3 | 28.8 | −88.9 | −46.1 | −189.5 | −84.1 | 46.2 |
| Shares & Other Equity | a3205 | — | — | — | — | — | — | — | — | — | — | — | — |
| Insurance Technical Reserves | a3206 | — | — | — | — | — | — | — | — | — | — | — | — |
| Financial Derivatives | a3207 | — | — | — | — | — | — | — | — | — | — | — | — |
| Other Accounts Receivable | a3208 | — | — | — | — | — | — | — | — | — | — | — | — |
| By debtor | | | | | | | | | | | | | |
| Domestic | a321 | 622.0 | 1,143.0 | 4,067.0 | 5,940.4 | 2,800.9 | −4,862.0 | 2,057.9 | 3,611.1 | 926.8 | −1,074.4 | 102.6 | −730.2 |
| Foreign | a322 | — | — | — | — | 351.9 | 740.0 | 151.5 | 150.8 | 161.7 | 178.7 | 215.5 | 235.9 |
| Net Incurrence of Liabilities | a33 | −785.7 | −1,968.0 | −1,795.0 | −1,484.5 | −825.6 | 100.5 | 2,485.3 | 1,961.7 | 386.7 | 20.9 | 2,405.9 | 2,903.4 |
| By instrument | | | | | | | | | | | | | |
| Special Drawing Rights (SDRs) | a3301 | — | — | — | — | — | — | — | — | — | — | — | — |
| Currency & Deposits | a3302 | — | — | — | — | — | — | — | — | — | — | — | — |
| Securities other than Shares | a3303 | −649.0 | −718.0 | −803.0 | −864.0 | −841.4 | −992.0 | 2,947.2 | −1,023.3 | −1,025.5 | −1,010.5 | −940.9 | −874.1 |
| Loans | a3304 | −136.7 | −1,250.0 | −992.0 | −620.5 | 15.8 | 1,092.5 | −461.1 | 2,984.9 | 1,412.2 | 1,031.4 | 3,346.8 | 3,777.4 |
| Shares & Other Equity | a3305 | — | — | — | — | — | — | — | — | — | — | — | — |
| Insurance Technical Reserves | a3306 | — | — | — | — | — | — | — | — | — | — | — | — |
| Financial Derivatives | a3307 | — | — | — | — | — | — | — | — | — | — | — | — |
| Other Accounts Payable | a3308 | — | — | — | — | — | — | — | — | — | — | — | — |
| By creditor | | | | | | | | | | | | | |
| Domestic | a331 | −851.4 | −1,605.0 | −1,750.0 | −1,208.2 | −495.9 | 468.9 | 1,698.7 | 1,360.3 | 75.8 | 475.4 | 1,538.4 | 2,066.0 |
| Foreign | a332 | 65.7 | −363.0 | −45.0 | −276.3 | −329.8 | −368.3 | 786.7 | 601.4 | 310.9 | −454.5 | 867.5 | 837.4 |
| Stat. Discrepancy [32-33-NLB] | anlbz | | | | | | | −.3 | | | | | |
| Memo Item: Expenditure [2+31] | a2m | 11,081.7 | 12,194.0 | 13,520.0 | 15,359.2 | 18,374.6 | 21,932.4 | 23,628.4 | 25,141.3 | 27,398.1 | 29,160.9 | 32,256.9 | 36,594.0 |
| **National Accounts** | | | | | | ***Billions of Pesos*** | | | | | | | |
| Househ.Cons.Expend.,incl.NPISHs | 96f | 35,954.4 | 40,599.4 | 45,145.9 | 50,470.1 | 57,081.9 | 57,357.8 | 65,522.8 | 74,017.8 | 80,664.7 | 87,538.9 | 94,356.0 | 101,141.5 |
| Government Consumption Expend | 91f | 6,655.4 | 7,317.5 | 8,200.5 | 9,371.7 | 10,553.3 | 12,219.9 | 13,645.2 | 14,690.6 | 15,674.3 | 17,220.3 | 19,196.9 | 21,103.8 |
| Gross Fixed Capital Formation | 93e | 11,971.7 | 14,839.3 | 15,841.2 | 18,145.4 | 23,178.5 | 21,026.6 | 23,296.1 | 27,132.0 | 31,044.5 | 32,683.9 | 33,964.2 | 35,707.9 |
| Changes in Inventories | 93i | 313.0 | 309.2 | 1,118.4 | 447.5 | 1,183.5 | −1,464.6 | 1,441.3 | 1,652.6 | 1,900.1 | 855.5 | −1,262.6 | −391.9 |
| Exports of Goods and Services | 90c | 24,092.7 | 27,738.7 | 36,012.1 | 40,885.4 | 38,953.2 | 35,849.0 | 42,246.0 | 46,162.8 | 44,265.7 | 44,319.1 | 49,312.9 | 47,221.9 |
| Imports of Goods and Services (-) | 98c | 18,440.8 | 21,921.2 | 24,299.8 | 28,891.3 | 37,102.5 | 28,545.0 | 35,152.7 | 42,336.3 | 44,521.7 | 45,388.0 | 47,999.3 | 47,652.3 |
| Gross Domestic Product (GDP) | 99b | 60,546.5 | 68,882.8 | 82,018.2 | 90,428.8 | 93,847.9 | 96,443.8 | 110,998.7 | 121,319.5 | 129,027.6 | 137,229.6 | 147,568.1 | 157,130.9 |
| Net Primary Income from Abroad | 98.n | −4,781.6 | −5,756.3 | −9,735.3 | −9,853.6 | −6,745.9 | −6,241.3 | −7,465.8 | −6,728.9 | −5,487.4 | −5,170.7 | −4,368.8 | −4,057.7 |
| Gross National Income (GNI) | 99a | 55,764.9 | 63,126.5 | 72,282.9 | 80,575.2 | 87,102.1 | 90,202.5 | 103,533.0 | 114,590.6 | 123,540.1 | 132,058.9 | 143,199.3 | 153,073.2 |
| Net Current Transf.from Abroad | 98t | 681.7 | 1,015.4 | 1,833.5 | 1,662.2 | 1,523.4 | 911.1 | 2,310.0 | 1,425.1 | 1,058.0 | 1,119.8 | 1,126.7 | 1,220.9 |
| Gross Nat'l Disposable Inc.(GNDI) | 99i | 56,446.6 | 64,141.9 | 74,116.4 | 82,237.3 | 88,625.5 | 91,113.6 | 105,843.0 | 116,015.6 | 124,598.1 | 133,178.7 | 144,326.0 | 154,294.1 |
| Gross Saving | 99s | 13,836.8 | 16,225.0 | 20,770.1 | 22,395.6 | 20,990.3 | 21,535.9 | 26,674.9 | 27,307.3 | 28,259.1 | 28,419.6 | 30,773.1 | 32,048.8 |
| Consumption of Fixed Capital | 99cf | 7,028.3 | 7,477.3 | 8,299.1 | 9,084.7 | — | — | — | — | — | — | — | — |
| GDP Volume 2008 Prices | 99b.p | 76,987.7 | 81,743.0 | 86,397.7 | 90,856.5 | 93,847.9 | 92,875.3 | 98,219.0 | 103,954.7 | 109,627.6 | 113,987.1 | 116,125.9 | 118,525.2 |
| GDP Volume (2010=100) | 99bvp | 78.4 | 83.2 | 88.0 | 92.5 | 95.5 | 94.6 | 100.0 | 105.8 | 111.6 | 116.1 | 118.2 | 120.7 |
| GDP Deflator (2010=100) | 99bip | 69.6 | 74.6 | 84.0 | 88.1 | 88.5 | 91.9 | 100.0 | 103.3 | 104.1 | 106.5 | 112.4 | 117.3 |
| | | | | | | ***Millions: Midyear Estimates*** | | | | | | | |
| **Population** | 99z | 15.91 | 16.10 | 16.28 | 16.46 | 16.65 | 16.83 | 17.02 | 17.20 | 17.39 | 17.58 | 17.76 | 17.95 |

# China, P.R.: Mainland 924

| | | 2004 | 2005 | 2006 | 2007 | 2008 | 2009 | 2010 | 2011 | 2012 | 2013 | 2014 | 2015 |
|---|---|---|---|---|---|---|---|---|---|---|---|---|---|
| **Exchange Rates** | | *Yuan per SDR: End of Period* | | | | | | | | | | | |
| Market Rate....................aa=........ | wa | 12.853 | 11.534 | 11.747 | 11.543 | 10.527 | 10.705 | 10.199 | 9.674 | 9.667 | 9.398 | 8.865 | 8.995 |
| | | *Yuan per US Dollar: End of Period (we) Period Average (wf)* | | | | | | | | | | | |
| Market Rate....................ae=........ | we | 8.2765 | 8.0702 | 7.8087 | 7.3046 | 6.8346 | 6.8282 | 6.6229 | 6.3009 | 6.2896 | 6.1024 | 6.1190 | 6.4915 |
| Market Rate....................rf=.......... | wf | 8.2768 | 8.1943 | 7.9734 | 7.6075 | 6.9487 | 6.8314 | 6.7703 | 6.4615 | 6.3123 | 6.1958 | 6.1434 | 6.2275 |
| | | *Index Numbers (2010=100): Period Averages* | | | | | | | | | | | |
| Nominal Effective Exchange Rate..... | nec | 88.01 | 87.85 | 89.87 | 91.14 | 97.16 | 101.99 | 100.00 | 100.13 | 105.12 | 110.68 | 114.10 | 124.96 |
| CPI-Based Real Effect. Ex. Rate........ | rec | 84.73 | 84.25 | 85.57 | 88.93 | 97.11 | 100.41 | 100.00 | 102.69 | 108.44 | 115.29 | 118.98 | 131.63 |
| **Fund Position** | | *Millions of SDRs: End of Period* | | | | | | | | | | | |
| Quota............................................ | 2f.s | 6,369.20 | 6,369.20 | 8,090.10 | 8,090.10 | 8,090.10 | 8,090.10 | 8,090.10 | 9,525.90 | 9,525.90 | 9,525.90 | 9,525.90 | 9,525.90 |
| SDR Holdings.................................. | 1b.s | 803.01 | 875.38 | 710.00 | 754.39 | 778.59 | 7,979.64 | 8,015.75 | 7,722.15 | 7,388.76 | 7,255.35 | 7,215.95 | 7,421.57 |
| Reserve Position in the Fund........... | 1c.s | 2,138.08 | 973.02 | 718.50 | 531.81 | 1,318.41 | 2,795.06 | 4,153.59 | 6,373.44 | 5,318.99 | 4,584.11 | 3,931.18 | 3,281.64 |
| Total Fund Cred.&Loans Outstg........ | 2tl | — | — | — | — | — | — | — | — | — | — | — | — |
| SDR Allocations.............................. | 1bd | 236.80 | 236.80 | 236.80 | 236.80 | 236.80 | 6,989.67 | 6,989.67 | 6,989.67 | 6,989.67 | 6,989.67 | 6,989.67 | 6,989.67 |
| **International Liquidity** | | *Millions of US Dollars Unless Otherwise Indicated: End of Period* | | | | | | | | | | | |
| Total Reserves Minus Gold.............. | 1l.d | 614,500 | 821,514 | 1,068,493 | 1,530,282 | 1,949,260 | 2,416,044 | 2,866,079 | 3,202,789 | 3,331,120 | 3,839,548 | 3,859,168 | 3,345,194 |
| SDR Holdings................................ | 1b.d | 1,247 | 1,251 | 1,068 | 1,192 | 1,199 | 12,510 | 12,344 | 11,856 | 11,356 | 11,173 | 10,455 | 10,284 |
| Reserve Position in the Fund.......... | 1c.d | 3,320 | 1,391 | 1,081 | 840 | 2,031 | 4,382 | 6,397 | 9,785 | 8,175 | 7,060 | 5,696 | 4,547 |
| Foreign Exchange......................... | 1d.d | 609,932 | 818,872 | 1,066,344 | 1,528,249 | 1,946,030 | 2,399,152 | 2,847,338 | 3,181,148 | 3,311,589 | 3,821,315 | 3,843,018 | 3,330,362 |
| Gold (Million Fine Troy Ounces)........ | 1ad | 19.3 | 19.3 | 19.3 | 19.3 | 19.3 | 33.9 | 33.9 | 33.9 | 33.9 | 33.9 | 33.9 | 56.7 |
| Gold (National Valuation)................ | 1and | 4,074 | 4,074 | 4,074 | 4,074 | 4,074 | 9,815 | 9,815 | 9,815 | 9,815 | 9,815 | 9,815 | † 60,191 |
| Monetary Authorities:Other Assets... | 3..d | 8,251 | 11,929 | 13,761 | 127,580 | 184,093 | 139,254 | 120,537 | 76,806 | 64,823 | 119,521 | 118,838 | 45,653 |
| Monetary Authorities: Other Liabs... | 4..d | 6,794 | 7,950 | 11,863 | 12,968 | 10,719 | 11,156 | 10,873 | 42,842 | 23,280 | 34,220 | 29,969 | 27,841 |
| Banking Institutions: Assets............ | 7a.d | 172,751 | 222,694 | 273,227 | 272,598 | 326,326 | 260,790 | 279,708 | 384,258 | 457,875 | 472,176 | 599,591 | 640,753 |
| Banking Institutions: Liabs.............. | 7b.d | 64,588 | 62,868 | 68,094 | 82,676 | 75,255 | 88,146 | 108,402 | 123,251 | 157,407 | 294,524 | 409,995 | 199,929 |
| **Monetary Authorities** | | *Billions of Yuan: End of Period* | | | | | | | | | | | |
| Foreign Assets................................ | 11 | 4,696.01 | 6,343.99 | 8,577.26 | 12,482.52 | 16,254.35 | 18,533.30 | 21,541.96 | 23,789.81 | 24,141.69 | 27,223.35 | 27,862.29 | 25,383.07 |
| Claims on General Government........ | 12a | 296.96 | 289.24 | 285.64 | 1,631.77 | 1,619.60 | 1,566.20 | 1,542.11 | 1,539.97 | 1,531.37 | 1,531.27 | 1,531.27 | 1,531.27 |
| Claims on Other Sectors.................. | 12d | 13.63 | 6.67 | 6.63 | 6.36 | 4.41 | 4.40 | 2.50 | 2.50 | 2.50 | 2.50 | 1.16 | 7.17 |
| Claims on Deposit Money Banks...... | 12e | 937.64 | 781.77 | 651.67 | 786.28 | 843.25 | 716.19 | 948.57 | 1,024.75 | 1,670.11 | 1,314.79 | 2,498.53 | 2,662.64 |
| Claims on Other Banking Insts......... | 12f | 104.79 | 487.43 | — | — | — | — | — | — | — | — | — | — |
| Claims on Nonbank Financial Insts... | 12g | 886.51 | 1,322.61 | 2,194.98 | 1,297.23 | 1,185.27 | 1,153.01 | 1,132.58 | 1,064.40 | 1,003.86 | 890.74 | 784.88 | 665.66 |
| Reserve Money............................... | 14 | 5,885.63 | 6,434.43 | 7,775.78 | 10,154.54 | 12,922.23 | 14,398.50 | 18,531.11 | 22,464.18 | 25,234.52 | 27,102.31 | 29,409.30 | 27,637.75 |
| of which: Currency Outside Bls....... | 14a | 2,131.29 | 2,365.61 | 2,707.26 | 3,037.52 | 3,421.90 | 3,824.70 | 4,462.82 | 5,074.85 | 5,465.98 | 5,857.45 | 6,025.96 | 6,321.66 |
| Bonds............................................. | 16ab | 1,107.90 | 2,029.60 | 2,974.06 | 3,446.91 | 4,577.98 | 4,206.42 | 4,049.72 | 2,333.67 | 1,388.00 | 776.20 | 652.20 | 657.20 |
| Restricted Deposits......................... | 16b | — | — | — | — | 59.12 | 62.48 | 65.72 | 90.84 | 134.88 | 133.03 | 155.84 | 282.64 |
| Foreign Liabilities............................ | 16c | 59.27 | 66.89 | 95.41 | 97.46 | 75.75 | 150.99 | 143.30 | 337.56 | 213.99 | 274.51 | 245.35 | 243.60 |
| General Government Deposits.......... | 16d | 583.22 | 752.72 | 1,021.07 | 1,712.11 | 1,696.38 | 2,122.64 | 2,427.73 | 2,273.37 | 2,075.33 | 2,861.06 | 3,127.53 | 2,717.90 |
| Capital Accounts............................. | 17a | 21.98 | 21.98 | 21.98 | 21.98 | 21.98 | 21.98 | 21.98 | 21.98 | 21.98 | 21.98 | 21.98 | 21.98 |
| Other Items (Net)............................ | 17r | −722.45 | −73.78 | −172.11 | 771.16 | 553.43 | 1,010.10 | −71.83 | −100.15 | −719.17 | −206.43 | −934.06 | −1,311.26 |
| Memo Item: | | | | | | | | | | | | | |
| Total Assets.................................... | 10ra | 7,865.53 | 10,367.60 | 12,857.47 | 16,913.98 | 20,709.60 | 22,753.05 | 25,927.49 | 28,097.76 | 29,453.72 | 31,727.86 | 33,824.88 | 31,783.70 |
| **Banking Institutions** | | *Billions of Yuan: End of Period* | | | | | | | | | | | |
| Reserves.......................................... | 20 | 3,739.81 | 4,028.35 | 5,023.09 | 7,050.35 | 9,391.53 | 10,457.55 | 13,683.50 | 17,300.41 | 19,713.25 | 21,177.56 | 23,348.87 | 21,933.01 |
| Foreign Assets................................ | 21 | 1,429.77 | 1,797.19 | 2,133.55 | 1,991.22 | 2,230.31 | 1,780.72 | 1,852.48 | 2,421.17 | 2,879.85 | 2,881.41 | 3,668.90 | 4,159.45 |
| Claims on General Government........ | 22a | 1,849.78 | 1,983.21 | 2,270.46 | 2,901.12 | 3,020.24 | 3,805.28 | 4,346.05 | 4,969.78 | 5,612.33 | 6,234.15 | 7,100.96 | 11,016.33 |
| Claims on Other Sectors.................. | 22d | 19,186.46 | 20,943.62 | 23,946.92 | 28,566.04 | 32,559.68 | 43,354.00 | 52,163.35 | 60,060.95 | 69,432.65 | 79,643.88 | 90,250.12 | 105,108.80 |
| Claims on Nonbank Financial Insts... | 22g | 791.80 | 1,044.08 | 1,190.22 | 1,275.52 | 1,245.05 | 1,697.77 | 1,973.55 | 3,432.92 | 5,051.99 | 7,259.23 | 11,155.35 | 17,657.94 |
| Demand Deposits............................ | 24 | 7,442.32 | 8,314.92 | 9,880.26 | 12,202.69 | 13,199.82 | 18,319.88 | 22,199.34 | 23,909.92 | 25,400.45 | 27,871.66 | 28,779.69 | 33,773.69 |
| Savings Deposits............................. | 25aa | 11,955.54 | 14,105.10 | 16,158.73 | 17,261.61 | 21,780.14 | 26,023.67 | 30,309.30 | 35,279.75 | 41,136.26 | 46,703.11 | 50,887.81 | 55,207.35 |
| Time Deposits................................. | 25ab | 2,538.22 | 3,310.00 | 5,276.71 | 6,411.73 | 8,233.99 | 11,343.07 | 14,323.21 | 16,661.60 | 19,594.01 | 23,269.66 | 26,405.57 | 28,824.07 |
| Foreign Currency Deposits.............. | 25b | 1,212.86 | 1,235.86 | 1,174.32 | 1,047.79 | 1,121.09 | 1,178.95 | 1,356.61 | 1,680.91 | 2,445.41 | 2,594.03 | 3,113.58 | 3,643.99 |
| Bonds............................................. | 26ab | 1,520.35 | 2,037.88 | 2,587.26 | 3,356.46 | 4,233.53 | 5,192.45 | 5,910.52 | 7,540.97 | 9,231.83 | 10,367.21 | 12,311.94 | 16,000.36 |
| Restricted Deposits......................... | 26b | 1,062.62 | 1,536.78 | 48.79 | 366.69 | 390.32 | 240.68 | 297.32 | 472.21 | 566.66 | 839.42 | 1,033.60 | 3,525.19 |
| Foreign Liabilities............................ | 26c | 534.57 | 507.36 | 531.72 | 603.92 | 514.34 | 601.88 | 717.94 | 776.59 | 990.03 | 1,797.30 | 2,508.76 | 1,297.84 |
| Credit from Monetary Authorities..... | 26g | 980.29 | 784.48 | 620.20 | 715.96 | 461.00 | 558.45 | 562.90 | 676.39 | 1,390.31 | 1,166.32 | 2,661.67 | 3,363.81 |
| Liabs. to Nonbank Financial Insts..... | 26j | 951.54 | 1,012.70 | 1,875.98 | 3,705.42 | 3,202.98 | 4,216.16 | 4,425.52 | 5,221.09 | 6,299.92 | 7,480.47 | 11,240.08 | 15,591.49 |
| Capital Accounts............................. | 27a | 1,179.14 | 1,403.24 | 1,310.12 | 1,842.48 | 2,175.11 | 2,313.08 | 2,650.68 | 2,864.20 | 3,072.53 | 3,254.58 | 3,641.04 | 4,299.47 |
| Other Items (Net)............................ | 27r | −2,379.83 | −4,451.87 | −4,899.85 | −5,730.52 | −6,865.49 | −8,892.94 | −8,734.41 | −6,898.38 | −7,437.34 | −8,147.55 | −7,059.55 | −5,651.71 |
| Memo Item: | | | | | | | | | | | | | |
| Total Assets.................................... | 20ra | 29,959.68 | 35,528.24 | 44,130.26 | 54,120.30 | 64,150.17 | 80,981.80 | 96,160.86 | 113,786.71 | 133,686.28 | 152,475.15 | 172,202.99 | 199,155.65 |
| **Banking Survey** | | *Billions of Yuan: End of Period* | | | | | | | | | | | |
| Foreign Assets (Net)........................ | 31n | 5,531.95 | 7,566.93 | 10,083.67 | 13,772.36 | 17,894.57 | 19,561.15 | 22,533.20 | 25,096.83 | 25,817.52 | 28,032.95 | 28,777.07 | 28,001.07 |
| Domestic Credit.............................. | 32 | 22,441.91 | 24,836.71 | 28,873.78 | 33,965.92 | 37,937.87 | 49,458.03 | 58,732.40 | 68,797.15 | 80,559.37 | 92,700.70 | 107,696.22 | 133,269.28 |
| Claims on General Govt. (Net)....... | 32an | 1,563.52 | 1,519.73 | 1,535.03 | 2,820.78 | 2,943.46 | 3,248.84 | 3,460.43 | 4,236.39 | 5,068.37 | 4,904.36 | 5,504.70 | 9,829.70 |
| Claims on Other Sectors................ | 32d | 19,200.09 | 20,950.29 | 23,953.55 | 28,572.39 | 32,564.09 | 43,358.40 | 52,165.85 | 60,063.45 | 69,435.15 | 79,646.38 | 90,251.29 | 105,115.98 |
| Claims on Nonbank Financial Insts. | 32g | 1,678.30 | 2,366.69 | 3,385.20 | 2,572.75 | 2,430.32 | 2,850.79 | 3,106.13 | 4,497.32 | 6,055.85 | 8,149.96 | 11,940.23 | 18,323.60 |
| Money............................................ | 34 | 9,581.54 | 10,690.32 | 12,603.51 | 15,256.01 | 16,621.71 | 22,144.58 | 26,662.15 | 28,984.77 | 30,866.43 | 33,729.11 | 34,805.64 | 40,095.35 |
| Quasi-Money.................................. | 35 | 14,661.07 | 17,610.91 | 21,956.85 | 25,088.21 | 30,894.95 | 38,877.87 | 45,923.02 | 56,174.32 | 66,548.46 | 76,923.39 | 88,031.84 | 99,132.47 |
| Foreign Currency Deposits.............. | 35b | 1,212.86 | 1,235.86 | 1,174.32 | 1,047.79 | 1,121.09 | 1,178.95 | 1,356.61 | 1,680.91 | 2,445.41 | 2,594.03 | 3,113.58 | 3,643.99 |
| Bonds............................................. | 36ab | 1,678.71 | 2,388.23 | 2,386.38 | 2,940.04 | 4,543.22 | 3,935.64 | 5,932.83 | 7,642.24 | 9,348.93 | 10,113.27 | 12,307.74 | 16,034.64 |
| Restricted Deposits......................... | 36b | 1,062.62 | 1,536.78 | 48.79 | 366.69 | 449.44 | 303.16 | 363.04 | 563.05 | 701.54 | 972.45 | 1,189.43 | 3,807.83 |
| Capital Accounts............................. | 37a | 1,201.11 | 1,425.21 | 1,332.10 | 1,864.45 | 2,197.08 | 2,335.06 | 2,672.65 | 2,886.18 | 3,094.51 | 3,276.56 | 3,663.02 | 4,321.44 |
| Other Items (Net)............................ | 37r | −1,424.06 | −2,483.67 | −544.49 | 1,175.09 | 4.95 | 243.92 | −1,644.70 | −4,037.45 | −6,628.38 | −6,875.15 | −6,637.98 | −5,765.36 |
| Money plus Quasi-Money................ | 35l | 24,242.61 | 28,301.23 | 34,560.36 | 40,344.22 | 47,516.66 | 61,022.45 | 72,585.18 | 85,159.09 | 97,414.89 | 110,652.50 | 122,837.48 | 139,227.81 |
| **Money (National Definitions)** | | *Billions of Yuan: End of Period* | | | | | | | | | | | |
| M0................................................. | 19mc | 2,146.83 | 2,403.17 | 2,707.26 | 3,033.43 | 3,421.90 | 3,824.60 | 4,462.82 | 5,074.85 | 5,465.98 | 5,857.44 | 6,025.95 | 6,321.66 |
| M1................................................. | 59ma | 9,597.08 | 10,727.86 | 12,602.81 | 15,251.92 | 16,621.71 | 22,000.15 | 26,662.15 | 28,984.77 | 30,866.42 | 33,729.11 | 34,805.64 | 40,095.34 |
| M2................................................. | 59mb | 25,320.77 | 29,875.55 | 34,557.79 | 40,340.13 | 47,516.66 | 60,622.50 | 72,585.18 | 85,159.09 | 97,414.88 | 110,652.50 | 122,837.48 | 139,227.81 |

# China, P.R.: Mainland   924

|  |  | 2004 | 2005 | 2006 | 2007 | 2008 | 2009 | 2010 | 2011 | 2012 | 2013 | 2014 | 2015 |
|---|---|---|---|---|---|---|---|---|---|---|---|---|---|
| **Interest Rates** | | | | | | *Percent per Annum: End of Period* | | | | | | | |
| Discount Rate (End of Period).......... | 60.a | 3.33 | 3.33 | 3.33 | 3.33 | 2.79 | 2.79 | 3.25 | 3.25 | 3.25 | 3.25 | 3.25 | † 2.90 |
| Deposit Rate (End of Period)............ | 60l | 2.25 | 2.25 | 2.52 | 4.14 | 2.25 | 2.25 | 2.75 | 3.50 | 3.00 | 3.00 | 2.75 | 1.50 |
| Lending Rate (End of Period)........... | 60p | 5.58 | 5.58 | 6.12 | 7.47 | 5.31 | 5.31 | 5.81 | 6.56 | 6.00 | 6.00 | 5.60 | 4.35 |
| **Prices, Production, Labor** | | | | | | *Index Numbers (2010=100): Period Averages* | | | | | | | |
| Share Prices................................... | 62 | 51.81 | 40.34 | 57.04 | 148.91 | 107.64 | 96.71 | 100.00 | 94.27 | 78.39 | 77.57 | 78.77 | 130.72 |
| | | | | | | *Percent Change over Corresponding Period of Previous Year* | | | | | | | |
| Producer Prices.............................. | 63 | .... | .... | .... | .... | .... | .... | 105.1 | 103.1 | 101.7 | 98.3 | 92.5 |
| Consumer Prices............................. | 64 | .... | .... | .... | .... | .... | .... | 100.0 | 105.4 | 108.2 | 111.0 | 113.2 | 114.9 |
| Industrial Production....................... | 66 | .... | .... | .... | .... | .... | .... | .... | 113.7 | 125.0 | 137.2 | 148.5 | 157.5 |
| Producer Prices.............................. | 63..x | 7.1 | 3.2 | 3.1 | 3.1 | 6.9 | −5.4 | 5.5 | 6.0 | −1.9 | −1.4 | −3.3 | −5.9 |
| Consumer Prices............................. | 64..x | 3.9 | 1.8 | 1.5 | 4.8 | 5.9 | −.7 | 3.3 | 5.4 | 2.6 | 2.6 | 2.0 | 1.4 |
| Industrial Production....................... | 66..x | .... | .... | .... | .... | .... | .... | .... | 10.0 | 9.7 | 8.3 | 6.1 |
| | | | | | | *Number in Thousands: Period Averages* | | | | | | | |
| Employment................................... | 67e | 742,640 | 746,470 | 749,780 | 753,210 | 755,640 | 758,280 | 761,050 | 764,200 | 767,040 | 769,770 | 772,530 | .... |
| Unemployment............................... | 67c | 8,270 | 8,390 | 8,470 | 8,300 | 8,860 | 9,210 | 9,080 | 9,220 | 9,170 | 9,260 | 9,520 | .... |
| Unemployment Rate (%)................. | 67r | 4.3 | 4.2 | 4.2 | 4.1 | 4.1 | 4.3 | 4.1 | 4.1 | 4.1 | 4.1 | 4.1 | 4.0 |
| **Intl. Transactions & Positions** | | | | | | *Millions of US Dollars* | | | | | | | |
| Exports........................................... | 70..d | 593,326 | 761,953 | 969,380 | 1,217,795 | 1,428,657 | 1,201,786 | 1,578,269 | 1,899,182 | 2,048,940 | 2,210,249 | 2,343,186 | 2,284,478 |
| Imports, c.i.f.................................... | 71..d | 561,229 | 660,206 | 791,797 | 956,233 | 1,131,619 | 1,004,175 | 1,396,195 | 1,742,851 | 1,818,174 | 1,949,300 | 1,963,105 | 1,680,786 |
| **Balance of Payments** | | | | | | *Millions of US Dollars* | | | | | | | |
| A. Current Account*........................ | 109bx | 68,941.0 | † 132,378.5 | 231,843.0 | 353,182.7 | 420,568.5 | 243,256.6 | 237,810.4 | 136,096.8 | 215,391.7 | 148,203.9 | 277,433.9 | 330,602.2 |
| Goods, credit (exports)................. | 1a9cx | 525,615.3 | † 694,870.3 | 897,660.4 | 1,131,606.1 | 1,349,973.7 | 1,127,160.0 | 1,486,412.0 | 1,807,805.4 | 1,973,516.4 | 2,148,588.9 | 2,243,761.3 | 2,142,753.5 |
| Goods, debit (imports)................. | 1a9dx | 480,719.7 | † 564,741.5 | 681,974.3 | 819,890.8 | 990,087.6 | 883,614.0 | 1,239,986.3 | 1,579,104.7 | 1,661,946.7 | 1,789,607.6 | 1,808,719.7 | 1,575,755.6 |
| Balance on goods...................... | 1a9bx | 44,895.6 | † 130,128.7 | 215,686.1 | 311,715.2 | 359,886.1 | 243,546.1 | 246,425.7 | 228,700.8 | 311,569.8 | 358,981.3 | 435,041.6 | 566,997.9 |
| Services, credit (exports).............. | 1b9cx | 79,159.4 | † 78,468.7 | 94,071.0 | 125,446.6 | 145,343.3 | 122,563.5 | 117,532.1 | 201,047.0 | 201,575.6 | 207,005.8 | 280,477.1 | 286,539.7 |
| Services, debit (imports)............... | 1b9dx | 72,880.6 | † 83,970.7 | 100,838.2 | 129,125.8 | 156,396.9 | 145,979.2 | 140,934.0 | 247,844.0 | 281,300.5 | 330,607.5 | 452,832.1 | 468,895.9 |
| Balance on Goods & Services....... | 1z9bx | 51,174.4 | † 124,626.8 | 208,918.9 | 308,036.0 | 348,832.5 | 220,130.4 | 223,023.9 | 181,903.7 | 231,844.9 | 235,379.6 | 262,686.6 | 384,641.7 |
| Primary income: credit................. | 1c9cx | 20,557.5 | † 39,272.8 | 54,563.2 | 83,476.2 | 111,787.2 | 108,250.9 | 142,424.5 | 144,267.6 | 167,037.0 | 183,973.2 | 239,372.3 | 227,804.8 |
| Primary income: debit.................. | 1c9dx | 25,689.1 | † 55,386.6 | 59,706.6 | 75,431.8 | 83,207.2 | 116,783.5 | 168,323.8 | 214,585.2 | 186,923.9 | 262,415.3 | 226,071.1 | 273,167.4 |
| Balance on gds, serv. & prim. inc. | 1y9bx | 46,042.8 | † 108,513.0 | 203,775.5 | 316,080.4 | 377,412.6 | 211,597.8 | 197,124.5 | 111,586.2 | 211,958.0 | 156,937.4 | 275,987.8 | 339,279.1 |
| Secondary income: credit.............. | 1d9ca | 24,326.3 | † 27,734.9 | 31,577.6 | 42,645.7 | 52,565.2 | 42,645.2 | 49,520.7 | 55,570.1 | 51,167.1 | 53,161.6 | 41,126.7 | 35,938.4 |
| Secondary income: debit.............. | 1d9da | 1,428.1 | † 3,869.4 | 3,510.1 | 5,543.4 | 9,409.2 | 10,986.5 | 8,834.9 | 31,059.5 | 47,733.4 | 61,895.1 | 39,680.6 | 44,615.2 |
| B. Capital Account*........................ | 209ba | −69.3 | † 4,101.8 | 4,020.1 | 3,099.1 | 3,051.4 | 3,939.3 | 4,630.5 | 5,446.3 | 4,272.3 | 3,052.0 | −32.7 | 316.1 |
| Capital account: credit.................. | 209ca | — | † 4,155.1 | 4,102.5 | 3,314.7 | 3,319.9 | 4,204.3 | 4,815.4 | 5,620.5 | 4,549.8 | 4,452.2 | 1,939.5 | 512.3 |
| Capital account: debit.................. | 209da | 69.3 | † 53.4 | 82.4 | 215.6 | 268.4 | 265.0 | 184.9 | 174.2 | 277.5 | 1,400.2 | 1,972.2 | 196.2 |
| Balance on current & capital acct. | 129ba | 68,871.6 | † 136,480.3 | 235,863.2 | 356,281.8 | 423,620.0 | 247,195.9 | 242,440.8 | 141,543.0 | 219,664.0 | 151,256.0 | 277,401.2 | 330,918.3 |
| C. Financial Account*  .................. | 309na | −108,221.5 | † −91,247.3 | −45,285.3 | −91,132.5 | −37,074.8 | −194,493.7 | −282,234.2 | −260,024.1 | 36,038.1 | −343,048.3 | 51,361.0 | 485,614.0 |
| Direct investment: assets.............. | 3a9aa | 7,972.6 | † 13,729.6 | 23,932.2 | 17,154.8 | 56,742.3 | 43,890.0 | 57,953.6 | 48,420.6 | 64,963.4 | 72,970.9 | 123,129.6 | 187,800.6 |
| Equity & investment fund shares.. | 3aaaa | 3,982.0 | † 9,171.6 | 15,055.7 | 12,980.5 | 36,371.5 | 28,590.7 | 62,223.1 | 57,667.8 | 72,766.0 | 88,235.6 | 142,329.6 | 145,187.0 |
| Debt instruments..................... | 3abaa | 3,990.6 | † 4,557.9 | 8,876.5 | 4,174.3 | 20,370.8 | 15,299.3 | −4,269.5 | −9,247.2 | −7,802.6 | −15,264.7 | −19,200.0 | 42,613.6 |
| Direct investment: liabilities ......... | 3a9la | 68,117.3 | † 104,108.7 | 124,082.0 | 156,249.3 | 171,534.7 | 131,057.1 | 243,703.4 | 280,072.2 | 241,213.9 | 290,928.4 | 268,097.2 | 249,858.9 |
| Equity & investment fund shares . | 3aala | 58,773.0 | † 91,655.7 | 111,637.1 | 139,127.5 | 144,085.7 | 126,955.5 | 225,593.2 | 250,767.9 | 214,522.6 | 265,407.9 | 210,897.2 | 219,626.5 |
| Debt instruments..................... | 3abla | 9,344.3 | † 12,453.0 | 12,445.0 | 17,121.8 | 27,448.9 | 4,101.5 | 18,110.3 | 29,304.3 | 26,691.3 | 25,520.6 | 57,200.0 | 30,232.4 |
| Portfolio investment: assets.......... | 3b9aa | −6,540.2 | † 26,156.9 | 111,277.7 | 4,521.5 | −25,198.4 | 2,525.7 | 7,642.5 | −6,247.7 | 6,390.7 | 5,353.0 | 10,814.7 | 73,209.0 |
| Equity & investment fund shares | 3baaa | — | | 1,454.0 | 15,188.6 | 2,181.3 | 40,646.9 | 8,429.1 | −1,104.1 | −2,029.2 | 2,531.1 | 1,401.5 | 39,678.8 |
| Debt securities .......................... | 3bbaa | −6,540.2 | † 26,156.9 | 109,823.7 | −10,667.1 | −27,379.3 | −38,121.2 | −786.6 | −5,143.6 | 8,419.9 | 2,821.9 | 9,413.2 | 33,530.2 |
| Portfolio investment: liabilities....... | 3b9la | 13,203.4 | † 21,447.1 | 42,861.2 | 20,964.5 | 9,654.4 | 29,613.1 | 31,680.9 | 13,391.5 | 54,169.9 | 58,244.1 | 93,244.2 | 6,738.9 |
| Equity & investment fund shares . | 3bala | 10,923.2 | † 20,569.0 | 42,861.2 | 18,478.1 | 8,464.0 | 29,116.7 | 31,357.1 | 5,308.4 | 29,902.7 | 32,595.0 | 51,915.8 | 14,964.5 |
| Debt securities......................... | 3bbla | 2,280.2 | † 878.1 | .... | 2,486.4 | 1,190.4 | 496.4 | 323.9 | 8,083.0 | 24,267.2 | 25,649.1 | 41,328.4 | −8,225.6 |
| Fin. der.& empl.stk.ops.(ESOs): net. | 3c9na | .... | .... | .... | .... | .... | .... | .... | .... | .... | .... | .... | 2,087.1 |
| Fin. der. & ESOs.: assets.............. | 3c9aa | .... | .... | .... | .... | .... | .... | .... | .... | .... | .... | .... | 3,420.0 |
| Fin. der. & ESOs.: liabilities......... | 3c9la | .... | .... | .... | .... | .... | .... | .... | .... | .... | .... | .... | 1,332.9 |
| Other investment: assets............... | 3d9aa | 6,137.9 | † 44,659.6 | 31,940.0 | 154,769.2 | 97,577.6 | −18,414.4 | 116,262.0 | 183,604.1 | 231,680.3 | 141,962.3 | 328,909.5 | 127,576.8 |
| Other equity............................. | 3daaa | .... | .... | .... | .... | .... | .... | .... | .... | .... | .... | .... | 12.3 |
| Debt instruments..................... | 3dzaa | 6,137.9 | † 44,659.6 | 31,940.0 | 154,769.2 | 97,577.6 | −18,414.4 | 116,262.0 | 183,604.1 | 231,680.3 | 141,962.3 | 328,909.5 | 127,564.6 |
| Other investment: liabilities........... | 3d9la | 34,471.1 | † 50,237.6 | 45,492.0 | 90,364.1 | −14,992.5 | 61,824.8 | 188,707.9 | 192,337.5 | −28,387.6 | 214,161.9 | 50,151.4 | −351,538.3 |
| Other equity............................. | 3dala | .... | .... | .... | .... | .... | .... | .... | .... | .... | .... | .... | .... |
| Debt instruments..................... | 3dzla | 34,471.1 | † 50,237.6 | 45,492.0 | 90,364.1 | −14,992.5 | 61,824.8 | 188,707.9 | 192,337.5 | −28,387.6 | 214,161.9 | 50,151.4 | −351,538.3 |
| Curr.+ cap.− finan. acct. balance... | 4y9na | 177,093.1 | † 227,727.5 | 281,148.4 | 447,414.2 | 460,694.7 | 441,689.5 | 524,675.0 | 401,567.2 | 183,625.9 | 494,304.2 | 226,040.1 | −154,695.7 |
| D. Net Errors and Omissions......... | 409na | 12,756.0 | † 23,247.0 | 3,502.3 | 13,236.8 | 18,858.6 | −41,181.1 | −53,016.4 | −13,768.0 | −87,071.1 | −62,923.3 | −108,256.6 | −188,245.3 |
| E. Reserves and Related Items.......... | 4z9na | 189,849.1 | † 250,974.5 | 284,650.7 | 460,651.0 | 479,553.3 | 400,508.4 | 471,658.6 | 387,799.2 | 96,554.8 | 431,381.9 | 117,783.6 | −342,941.0 |
| Reserve assets.............................. | 3e9aa | 189,849.1 | † 250,974.5 | 284,650.7 | 460,651.0 | 479,553.3 | 400,508.4 | 471,658.6 | 387,799.2 | 96,554.8 | 431,381.9 | 117,783.6 | −342,941.0 |
| Credit and loans from the IMF....... | 3dcla | — | † — | — | — | — | — | — | — | — | — | — | — |
| Exceptional financing.................... | 409la | .... | .... | .... | .... | .... | .... | .... | .... | .... | .... | .... | .... |

*Excludes components in group E

# China, P.R.: Mainland 924

| | | 2004 | 2005 | 2006 | 2007 | 2008 | 2009 | 2010 | 2011 | 2012 | 2013 | 2014 | 2015 |
|---|---|---|---|---|---|---|---|---|---|---|---|---|---|
| **International Investment Position** | | | | | | | *Millions of US Dollars* | | | | | | | |
| Assets............................................ | 809aa | 933,438.9 | 1,229,107.1 | 1,690,429.6 | 2,416,204.3 | 2,956,691.1 | 3,436,900.7 | 4,118,858.8 | † 4,734,500.2 | 5,213,130.8 | 5,986,120.2 | 6,438,302.8 | 6,218,905.4 |
| Direct investment........................... | 8a9aa | 52,704.1 | 64,492.9 | 90,630.0 | 115,960.2 | 185,693.9 | 245,750.0 | 317,210.0 | † 424,780.0 | 531,900.0 | 660,480.0 | 882,640.0 | 1,129,345.7 |
| Equity & investment fund shares.. | 8aaaa | .... | .... | .... | .... | .... | .... | .... | .... | .... | .... | — | 939,250.6 |
| Debt instruments........................ | 8abaa | .... | .... | .... | .... | .... | .... | .... | .... | .... | .... | — | 190,095.0 |
| Portfolio investment....................... | 8b9aa | 92,028.0 | 116,739.4 | 265,178.6 | 284,620.2 | 252,509.3 | 242,774.2 | 257,112.0 | † 204,414.4 | 240,600.0 | 258,526.6 | 262,536.0 | 261,293.6 |
| Equity & investment fund shares.. | 8baaa | | | 1,454.0 | 19,642.6 | 21,389.2 | 54,575.2 | 63,004.3 | † 86,430.3 | 129,800.0 | 153,035.5 | 161,312.4 | 161,985.2 |
| Debt securities............................. | 8bbaa | 92,028.0 | 116,739.4 | 263,724.6 | 264,977.6 | 231,120.2 | 188,199.0 | 194,107.7 | † 117,984.1 | 110,800.0 | 105,491.1 | 101,223.6 | 99,308.4 |
| Fin. der.(oth.than reserves) & ESOs | 8c9aa | .... | .... | .... | .... | .... | .... | .... | .... | .... | .... | — | 3,640.1 |
| Other investment............................ | 8d9aa | 165,756.4 | 216,384.0 | 253,853.8 | 468,305.5 | 552,287.4 | 495,199.8 | 630,352.5 | † 849,520.1 | 1,052,800.0 | 1,186,730.2 | 1,393,834.7 | 1,418,514.4 |
| Other equity................................ | 8daaa | .... | .... | .... | .... | .... | .... | .... | .... | .... | .... | .... | 52.6 |
| Debt instruments........................ | 8dzaa | 165,756.4 | 216,384.0 | 253,853.8 | 468,305.5 | 552,287.4 | 495,199.8 | 630,352.5 | † 849,520.1 | 1,052,800.0 | 1,186,730.2 | 1,393,834.7 | 1,418,461.8 |
| Reserve assets................................ | 8e9aa | 622,950.5 | 831,490.7 | 1,080,767.3 | 1,547,318.4 | 1,966,200.4 | 2,453,176.7 | 2,914,184.3 | † 3,255,785.7 | 3,387,830.8 | 3,880,383.4 | 3,899,292.1 | 3,406,111.8 |
| Liabilities..................................... | 809la | 653,044.3 | 815,971.3 | 1,050,621.8 | 1,228,463.0 | 1,463,239.6 | 1,946,385.2 | 2,430,826.9 | † 3,046,084.4 | 3,346,742.6 | 3,990,113.0 | 4,835,551.5 | 4,622,452.4 |
| Direct investment........................... | 8a9la | 368,970.1 | 471,549.2 | 614,383.5 | 703,667.2 | 915,524.4 | 1,314,770.7 | 1,569,603.7 | † 1,906,908.2 | 2,068,000.0 | 2,331,237.7 | 2,599,102.0 | 2,842,298.1 |
| Equity & investment fund shares.. | 8aala | .... | .... | .... | .... | .... | .... | .... | .... | .... | .... | .... | .... |
| Debt instruments........................ | 8abla | .... | .... | .... | .... | .... | .... | .... | .... | .... | .... | .... | .... |
| Portfolio investment....................... | 8b9la | 56,622.5 | 76,617.3 | 120,714.8 | 146,648.0 | 167,749.5 | 189,984.8 | 223,879.1 | † 248,501.1 | 336,100.0 | 386,512.0 | 796,249.6 | 810,510.1 |
| Equity & investment fund shares.. | 8bala | 43,290.2 | 63,636.2 | 106,497.4 | 129,012.6 | 150,530.0 | 174,765.4 | 206,122.5 | † 211,431.0 | 261,900.0 | 297,651.3 | 651,323.0 | 590,552.6 |
| Debt securities............................. | 8bbla | 13,332.3 | 12,981.1 | 14,217.4 | 17,635.3 | 17,219.5 | 15,219.4 | 17,756.5 | † 37,070.1 | 74,200.0 | 88,860.7 | 144,926.6 | 219,957.5 |
| Fin. der.(oth.than reserves) & ESOs | 8c9la | .... | .... | .... | .... | .... | .... | .... | .... | .... | .... | — | 5,335.6 |
| Other investment............................ | 8d9la | 227,451.6 | 267,804.8 | 315,523.5 | 378,147.8 | 379,965.7 | 441,629.6 | 637,344.1 | † 890,675.1 | 942,642.6 | 1,272,363.3 | 1,440,199.9 | 964,308.6 |
| Other equity................................ | 8dala | .... | .... | .... | .... | .... | .... | .... | .... | .... | .... | .... | — |
| Debt instruments........................ | 8dzla | 227,451.6 | 267,804.8 | 315,523.5 | 378,147.8 | 379,965.7 | 441,629.6 | 637,344.1 | † 890,675.1 | 942,642.6 | 1,272,363.3 | 1,440,199.9 | 964,308.6 |
| **Government Finance** | | | | | | | | | | | | | |
| **Cash Flow Statement** | | | | | | | | | | | | | |
| **Budgetary Central Government** | | | | | | | *Billions of Yuan: Fiscal Year Ends December 31* | | | | | | | |
| Cash Receipts:Operating Activities... | c1 | 1,574.52 | 1,833.85 | 2,253.88 | 4,553.11 | 3,652.70 | 4,065.32 | 4,628.54 | 5,483.83 | 5,999.22 | 6,496.65 | .... | .... |
| Taxes.......................................... | c11 | 1,416.61 | 1,605.18 | 1,987.51 | 2,639.18 | 3,224.82 | 3,593.02 | 4,208.58 | 5,032.03 | 5,524.09 | 5,874.92 | .... | .... |
| Social Contributions...................... | c12 | — | — | — | | | | | | | | .... | .... |
| Grants......................................... | c13 | 60.72 | 71.20 | 78.73 | 86.28 | 165.78 | .66 | — | — | — | — | .... | .... |
| Other Receipts.............................. | c14 | 97.19 | 157.47 | 187.64 | 1,827.65 | 262.09 | 471.64 | 419.96 | 451.80 | 475.14 | 621.72 | .... | .... |
| Cash Payments:Operating Activities. | c2 | 1,778.43 | 1,994.37 | 2,410.08 | .... | .... | .... | .... | .... | .... | .... | .... | .... |
| Compensation of Employees.......... | c21 | .... | 20.92 | 117.17 | .... | .... | .... | .... | .... | .... | .... | .... | .... |
| Purchases of Goods & Services....... | c22 | .... | 556.79 | 650.42 | .... | .... | .... | .... | .... | .... | .... | .... | .... |
| Interest........................................ | c24 | 74.14 | 81.50 | 97.54 | .... | 127.00 | 84.62 | 150.89 | 183.00 | 206.04 | 231.54 | .... | .... |
| Subsidies...................................... | c25 | 47.11 | 63.52 | 58.69 | .... | .... | .... | .... | .... | .... | .... | .... | .... |
| Grants......................................... | c26 | 1,075.75 | 1,167.10 | 1,384.29 | .... | .... | .... | .... | .... | .... | .... | .... | .... |
| Social Benefits.............................. | c27 | 12.57 | 13.18 | 12.38 | .... | .... | .... | .... | .... | .... | .... | .... | .... |
| Other Payments............................ | c28 | 67.96 | 91.36 | 89.59 | .... | .... | .... | .... | .... | .... | .... | .... | .... |
| Net Cash Inflow:Operating Act.[1-2] | ccio | −203.91 | −160.52 | −156.20 | .... | .... | .... | .... | .... | .... | .... | .... | .... |
| Net Cash Outflow:Invest. in NFA..... | c31 | 134.38 | 136.56 | 148.35 | .... | .... | .... | .... | .... | .... | 36.50 | .... | .... |
| Purchases of Nonfinancial Assets... | c31.1 | 134.38 | 136.56 | 148.35 | .... | .... | .... | .... | .... | .... | .... | .... | .... |
| Sales of Nonfinancial Assets.......... | c31.2 | — | — | — | .... | .... | .... | .... | .... | .... | .... | .... | .... |
| Cash Surplus/Deficit [1-2-31=1-2M] | ccsd | −338.29 | −297.08 | −304.55 | −98.20 | −288.46 | −700.10 | −477.43 | | | | .... | .... |
| Net Acq. Fin. Assets, excl. Cash....... | c32x | .... | .... | .... | .... | .... | .... | .... | .... | .... | .... | .... | .... |
| Domestic...................................... | c321x | .... | .... | .... | .... | .... | .... | .... | .... | .... | .... | .... | .... |
| Foreign........................................ | c322x | .... | .... | .... | .... | .... | .... | .... | .... | .... | .... | .... | .... |
| Net Incurrence of Liabilities............. | c33 | 319.20 | 299.95 | 240.10 | 1,705.90 | 119.70 | 696.61 | 731.04 | 449.64 | 552.10 | 918.12 | .... | .... |
| Domestic...................................... | c331 | 319.20 | 304.44 | 253.20 | 1,708.70 | 133.20 | 693.76 | 725.10 | 442.28 | 533.70 | 908.81 | .... | .... |
| Foreign........................................ | c332 | — | −4.49 | −13.10 | −2.80 | −13.50 | 2.85 | 5.94 | 7.36 | 18.40 | 9.31 | .... | .... |
| Net Cash Inflow, Fin.Act.[-32x+33].. | cnfb | .... | .... | .... | .... | .... | .... | .... | .... | .... | .... | .... | .... |
| Net Change in Stock of Cash........... | cncb | .... | .... | .... | .... | .... | .... | .... | .... | .... | .... | .... | .... |
| Stat. Discrep. [32X-33+NCB-CSD].... | ccsdz | .... | .... | .... | .... | .... | .... | .... | .... | .... | .... | .... | .... |
| Memo Item:Cash Expenditure[2+31] | c2m | 1,912.81 | 2,520.59 | 2,558.43 | 4,651.31 | 3,941.16 | 4,765.42 | 5,105.97 | | | | .... | .... |
| Memo Item: Gross Debt.................. | c63 | .... | .... | .... | .... | .... | .... | .... | .... | .... | .... | .... | .... |
| **National Accounts** | | | | | | | *Billions of Yuan* | | | | | | | |
| Househ.Cons.Expend.,incl.NPISHs.... | 96f | 6,658.7 | 7,523.2 | 8,411.9 | 9,979.3 | 11,533.8 | 12,666.1 | 14,605.8 | 17,653.2 | 19,853.7 | 21,976.3 | 24,154.1 | .... |
| Government Consumption Expend... | 91f | 2,263.8 | 2,637.2 | 3,077.6 | 3,664.5 | 4,240.8 | 4,643.2 | 5,345.1 | 6,504.7 | 7,318.2 | 8,124.6 | 8,677.1 | .... |
| Gross Fixed Capital Formation.......... | 93e | 6,440.5 | 7,423.0 | 8,527.5 | 10,263.0 | 12,495.8 | 15,291.8 | 18,119.0 | 21,393.7 | 23,775.1 | 26,302.8 | 28,301.8 | .... |
| Changes in Inventories.................... | 93i | 375.1 | 172.4 | 260.0 | 699.5 | 1,024.1 | 538.3 | 1,082.6 | 1,365.6 | 1,063.9 | 1,114.9 | 1,200.5 | .... |
| Exports of Goods and Services......... | 90c | 5,428 | 6,856 | 8,464 | 10,206 | 10,985 | 9,108 | 11,864 | 13,446 | 14,192 | .... | .... | .... |
| Imports of Goods and Services (-).... | 98c | 5,020 | 5,833 | 6,798 | 7,868 | 8,562 | 7,604 | 10,293 | 12,226 | 12,729 | .... | .... | .... |
| Gross Domestic Product (GDP)......... | 99b | 16,161.6 | 18,776.7 | 21,942.5 | 26,948.6 | 31,717.2 | 34,643.1 | 40,658.1 | 48,086.1 | 53,474.5 | 58,973.7 | 64,079.6 | .... |
| Net Primary Income from Abroad..... | 98.n | −132.7 | −319.1 | −217.8 | −85.5 | 156.5 | −138.5 | 55.7 | −128.5 | −187.3 | −654.1 | −642.9 | .... |
| Gross National Income (GNI)............ | 99a | 16,029.0 | 18,457.6 | 21,724.7 | 26,863.1 | 31,873.7 | 34,504.6 | 40,713.8 | 47,957.6 | 53,287.2 | 58,319.7 | 63,436.7 | .... |
| GDP Volume 2000 Prices.................. | 99b.p | 21,418.2 | 23,849.7 | 26,875.8 | 30,690.8 | 33,644.3 | 36,750.8 | 40,658.1 | 44,514.3 | 47,964.3 | 51,649.8 | 55,404.0 | .... |
| GDP Volume (2010=100).................. | 99bvp | 52.6 | 58.2 | 65.4 | 75.1 | 82.6 | 90.4 | 100.0 | 110.3 | 120.8 | 130.4 | 150.7 | 161.0 |
| GDP Deflator (2010=100)................. | 99bip | 74.7 | 78.1 | 81.4 | 87.3 | 93.8 | 93.5 | 100.0 | 107.4 | 108.1 | 110.2 | 103.3 | 102.8 |
| | | | | | | | *Millions: Midyear Estimates* | | | | | | | |
| **Population**............................... | 99z | 1,298.6 | 1,305.6 | 1,312.6 | 1,319.6 | 1,326.7 | 1,333.8 | 1,341.0 | 1,348.2 | 1,355.4 | 1,362.5 | 1,369.4 | 1,376.0 |

# China, P.R.: Hong Kong   532

| | | 2004 | 2005 | 2006 | 2007 | 2008 | 2009 | 2010 | 2011 | 2012 | 2013 | 2014 | 2015 |
|---|---|---|---|---|---|---|---|---|---|---|---|---|---|
| **Exchange Rates** | | \multicolumn{12}{c}{*Hong Kong Dollars per SDR: End of Period*} | | | | | | | | | | | |
| Market Rate | aa | 12.072 | 11.080 | 11.696 | 12.328 | 11.938 | 12.158 | 11.973 | 11.922 | 11.912 | 11.940 | 11.236 | 10.740 |
| | | \multicolumn{12}{c}{*Hong Kong Dollars per US Dollar: End of Period (ae) Period Average (rf)*} | | | | | | | | | | | |
| Market Rate | ae | 7.774 | 7.753 | 7.775 | 7.802 | 7.751 | 7.756 | 7.775 | 7.766 | 7.751 | 7.754 | 7.756 | 7.751 |
| Market Rate | rf | 7.788 | 7.777 | 7.768 | 7.801 | 7.787 | 7.752 | 7.769 | 7.784 | 7.756 | 7.756 | 7.754 | 7.752 |
| | | \multicolumn{12}{c}{*Index Numbers (2010=100) Period Averages*} | | | | | | | | | | | |
| ULC-Based Real Effect. Ex. Rate | rel | 116.77 | 112.34 | 109.68 | 105.37 | 100.95 | 101.95 | 100.00 | 98.81 | 105.31 | 107.68 | 109.41 | 119.55 |
| **International Liquidity** | | \multicolumn{12}{c}{*Millions of US Dollars Unless Otherwise Indicated: End of Period*} | | | | | | | | | | | |
| Total Reserves minus Gold | 1l.d | 123,540 | 124,244 | 133,168 | 152,637 | 182,469 | 255,768 | 268,649 | 285,296 | †317,251 | 311,129 | 328,436 | 358,702 |
| Reserve Position in the Fund | 1c.d | — | — | — | — | — | — | — | 36 | 62 | 68 | 59 | 46 |
| Foreign Exchange | 1d.d | 123,540 | 124,244 | 133,168 | 152,637 | 182,469 | 255,768 | 268,649 | 285,260 | †317,189 | 311,061 | 328,377 | 358,656 |
| Gold (Million Fine Troy Ounces) | 1ad | .067 | .067 | .067 | .067 | .067 | .067 | .067 | .067 | .067 | .067 | .067 | .067 |
| Gold (National Valuation) | 1and | 29 | 34 | 42 | 56 | 58 | 74 | 94 | 105 | 111 | 80 | 80 | 71 |
| Monetary Authorities: Other Liabs | 4..d | 13 | 153 | 25 | 43 | 57 | 51 | 37 | 26 | 25 | 41 | 51 | 38 |
| Banking Institutions: Assets | 7a.d | 508,073 | 512,640 | 621,337 | 798,274 | 788,521 | 747,786 | 829,768 | 919,451 | 984,571 | 1,132,883 | 1,220,678 | 1,254,747 |
| Banking Institutions: Liabs | 7b.d | 308,545 | 305,686 | 352,789 | 476,488 | 504,374 | 497,991 | 604,804 | 688,033 | 724,516 | 838,240 | 927,741 | 1,004,463 |
| **Monetary Authorities** | | \multicolumn{12}{c}{*Billions of Hong Kong Dollars: End of Period*} | | | | | | | | | | | |
| Foreign Assets | 11 | 904.91 | 884.91 | 985.00 | 1,087.86 | 1,272.53 | 1,907.19 | 2,035.78 | 2,177.96 | 2,431.65 | 2,581.83 | 2,792.77 | 3,051.73 |
| Reserve Money | 14 | 294.87 | 283.98 | 297.95 | 320.24 | 506.58 | 1,010.70 | 1,039.53 | 1,075.98 | 1,217.30 | 1,255.87 | 1,345.43 | 1,591.72 |
| of which: Currency Outside Banks | 14a | 140.55 | 142.05 | 149.98 | 157.76 | 170.23 | 194.07 | 218.55 | 248.05 | 281.61 | 313.63 | 329.83 | 349.09 |
| Foreign Liabilities | 16c | .10 | 1.19 | .20 | .34 | .44 | .40 | .29 | .20 | .19 | .32 | .39 | .29 |
| Government Deposits | 16d | 280.09 | 297.09 | 324.53 | 464.59 | 531.37 | 504.12 | 592.28 | 663.51 | 717.54 | 773.86 | 788.68 | 833.55 |
| Capital Accounts | 17a | 423.59 | 443.15 | 507.71 | 616.98 | 480.49 | 553.46 | 591.50 | 567.91 | 623.88 | 637.51 | 635.45 | 544.86 |
| Other Items (Net) | 17r | −93.75 | −140.48 | −145.39 | −314.28 | −246.35 | −161.48 | −187.83 | −129.65 | −127.26 | −85.73 | 22.82 | 81.31 |
| **Banking Institutions** | | \multicolumn{12}{c}{*Billions of Hong Kong Dollars: End of Period*} | | | | | | | | | | | |
| Reserves | 20 | 28.36 | 15.51 | 16.30 | 23.86 | 173.35 | 279.16 | 165.78 | 170.38 | 275.91 | 190.43 | 262.61 | 413.83 |
| Foreign Assets | 21 | 3,949.50 | 3,974.24 | 4,830.59 | 6,227.73 | 6,111.43 | 5,799.45 | 6,451.03 | 7,140.00 | 7,630.92 | 8,783.81 | 9,466.97 | 9,724.91 |
| Claims on Government | 22a | 272.53 | 255.26 | 257.59 | 239.62 | 232.84 | 651.84 | 768.95 | 762.79 | 775.24 | 876.09 | 858.09 | 935.20 |
| Claims on Other Sectors | 22d | 1,906.44 | 2,021.14 | 2,056.59 | 2,256.25 | 2,395.36 | 2,578.90 | 3,296.55 | 3,913.21 | 4,044.20 | 4,664.93 | 5,270.58 | 4,986.41 |
| Demand Deposits | 24 | 231.83 | 173.65 | 197.19 | 242.00 | 265.07 | 391.14 | 420.37 | 444.26 | 510.47 | 544.77 | 619.69 | 711.59 |
| Time, Savings,& Fgn.Currency Dep | 25 | 3,060.47 | 3,238.82 | 3,784.07 | 4,508.91 | 4,680.41 | 4,798.00 | 5,141.65 | 5,657.13 | 6,053.80 | 6,637.83 | 7,216.80 | 7,642.19 |
| Money Market Instruments | 26aa | 190.98 | 207.60 | 205.80 | 174.63 | 116.17 | 60.79 | 95.77 | 229.88 | 369.47 | 547.36 | 626.94 | 381.71 |
| Foreign Liabilities | 26c | 2,398.47 | 2,369.83 | 2,742.76 | 3,717.32 | 3,909.15 | 3,862.17 | 4,702.05 | 5,342.92 | 5,615.36 | 6,499.29 | 7,195.09 | 7,785.09 |
| Government Deposits | 26d | 4.16 | 5.61 | 5.24 | 5.81 | 7.84 | 4.51 | 3.01 | 5.51 | 5.27 | 7.35 | 6.52 | 6.50 |
| Capital Accounts | 27a | 214.60 | 234.59 | 249.23 | 262.47 | 224.60 | 274.36 | 323.01 | 350.92 | 410.06 | 484.08 | 520.40 | 386.55 |
| Other Items (Net) | 27r | 56.33 | 36.06 | −23.22 | −163.67 | −290.25 | −81.61 | −3.55 | −44.24 | −238.16 | −205.42 | −327.19 | −853.27 |
| **Banking Survey** | | \multicolumn{12}{c}{*Billions of Hong Kong Dollars: End of Period*} | | | | | | | | | | | |
| Foreign Assets (Net) | 31n | 2,455.84 | 2,488.14 | 3,072.63 | 3,597.94 | 3,474.37 | 3,844.07 | 3,784.47 | 3,974.83 | 4,447.01 | 4,866.03 | 5,064.25 | 4,991.27 |
| Domestic Credit | 32 | 1,894.73 | 1,973.71 | 1,984.41 | 2,025.47 | 2,089.00 | 2,722.11 | 3,470.21 | 4,006.98 | 4,096.63 | 4,759.81 | 5,333.47 | 5,081.57 |
| Claims on Government (net) | 32an | −11.71 | −47.44 | −72.18 | −230.78 | −306.37 | 143.21 | 173.66 | 93.77 | 52.43 | 94.87 | 62.89 | 95.15 |
| Claims on Other Sectors | 32d | 1,906.44 | 2,021.14 | 2,056.59 | 2,256.25 | 2,395.36 | 2,578.90 | 3,296.55 | 3,913.21 | 4,044.20 | 4,664.93 | 5,270.58 | 4,986.41 |
| Money | 34 | 372.38 | 315.70 | 347.17 | 399.76 | 435.30 | 585.21 | 638.92 | 692.31 | 792.08 | 858.39 | 949.53 | 1,060.68 |
| Quasi-Money | 35 | 3,060.47 | 3,238.82 | 3,784.07 | 4,508.91 | 4,680.41 | 4,798.00 | 5,141.65 | 5,657.13 | 6,053.80 | 6,637.83 | 7,216.80 | 7,642.19 |
| Money Market Instruments | 36aa | 190.98 | 207.60 | 205.80 | 174.63 | 116.17 | 60.79 | 95.77 | 229.88 | 369.47 | 547.36 | 626.94 | 381.71 |
| Capital Accounts | 37a | 638.19 | 677.74 | 756.94 | 879.45 | 705.08 | 827.81 | 914.52 | 918.83 | 1,033.95 | 1,121.59 | 1,155.85 | 931.40 |
| Other Items (Net) | 37r | 88.54 | 21.98 | −36.94 | −339.33 | −373.60 | 294.37 | 463.82 | 483.66 | 294.35 | 460.67 | 448.61 | 56.86 |
| Money plus Quasi-Money | 35l | 3,432.85 | 3,554.52 | 4,131.24 | 4,908.67 | 5,115.71 | 5,383.21 | 5,780.57 | 6,349.43 | 6,845.88 | 7,496.22 | 8,166.32 | 8,702.86 |
| **Money (National Definitions)** | | \multicolumn{12}{c}{*Billions of Hong Kong Dollars: End of Period*} | | | | | | | | | | | |
| Base Money | 19ma | 295.43 | 284.23 | 296.25 | 320.56 | 507.46 | 1,010.96 | 1,039.81 | 1,073.30 | 1,219.14 | 1,255.77 | 1,346.06 | 1,592.78 |
| M1 | 59ma | 484.49 | 434.68 | 491.66 | 616.71 | 645.83 | 901.82 | 1,017.23 | 1,127.32 | 1,377.36 | 1,510.90 | 1,708.72 | 1,971.16 |
| M2 | 59mb | 4,166.71 | 4,379.06 | 5,054.48 | 6,106.35 | 6,268.06 | 6,602.31 | 7,136.27 | 8,057.53 | 8,950.00 | 10,056.44 | 11,011.37 | 11,618.46 |
| M3 | 59mc | 4,189.54 | 4,407.19 | 5,089.88 | 6,139.76 | 6,300.75 | 6,626.84 | 7,156.26 | 8,081.08 | 8,970.40 | 10,085.24 | 11,048.94 | 11,655.04 |
| **Interest Rates** | | \multicolumn{12}{c}{*Percent Per Annum:*} | | | | | | | | | | | |
| Discount Rate (End of Period) | 60.a | 3.75 | 5.75 | 6.75 | 5.75 | .50 | .50 | .50 | .50 | .50 | .50 | .50 | .75 |
| Money Market Rate (End of Period) | 60b | .13 | 4.25 | 3.94 | 1.88 | .23 | .13 | .13 | .13 | .06 | .06 | .13 | .08 |
| Treasury Bill Rate (End of Period) | 60c | .07 | 3.65 | 3.29 | 1.96 | .05 | .07 | .28 | .22 | .05 | .11 | .04 | .04 |
| Deposit Rate | 60l | .03 | 1.26 | 2.70 | 2.42 | .45 | .01 | .01 | .01 | .01 | .01 | .01 | .01 |
| Lending Rate (End of Period) | 60p | 5.00 | 7.75 | 7.75 | 6.75 | 5.00 | 5.00 | 5.00 | 5.00 | 5.00 | 5.00 | 5.00 | 5.00 |
| **Prices, Production, Labor** | | \multicolumn{12}{c}{*Index Numbers (2010=100): Period Averages*} | | | | | | | | | | | |
| Share Prices | 62 | 60.1 | 66.7 | 78.6 | 107.9 | 97.3 | 83.9 | 100.0 | 99.7 | 95.3 | 105.2 | 108.1 | 113.3 |
| Producer Prices | 63 | 93.7 | †86.3 | 88.2 | 90.9 | 96.0 | 94.3 | 100.0 | 108.3 | 108.4 | 105.1 | 103.3 | 100.5 |
| Consumer Prices | 64 | 88.8 | 89.5 | 91.3 | 93.2 | 97.2 | 97.8 | 100.0 | 105.3 | 109.5 | 114.3 | 119.4 | 123.0 |
| Wages: Avg. Earnings | 65 | 90.8 | 90.8 | 93.8 | 96.4 | 101.0 | 98.9 | 100.0 | 104.9 | 114.0 | 117.5 | 123.9 | 129.6 |
| Wage Rates (Manufacturing) | 65a | 93.8 | 93.2 | 95.7 | 99.1 | 102.3 | 100.3 | 100.0 | 107.3 | 111.9 | 117.5 | 122.9 | 128.3 |
| Manufacturing Production | 66ey | 84.8 | †112.0 | 114.4 | 112.8 | 105.3 | 96.5 | 100.0 | 100.7 | 99.9 | 100.0 | 99.6 | 98.1 |
| | | \multicolumn{12}{c}{*Number in Thousands: Period Averages*} | | | | | | | | | | | |
| Labor Force | 67d | 3,516 | 3,538 | 3,582 | 3,625 | 3,637 | 3,661 | 3,635 | 3,705 | 3,781 | 3,859 | 3,885 | 3,926 |
| Employment | 67e | 3,276 | 3,340 | 3,411 | 3,478 | 3,508 | 3,471 | 3,478 | 3,580 | 3,668 | 3,741 | 3,764 | 3,798 |
| Unemployment | 67c | 239 | 198 | 171 | 145 | 128 | 193 | 157 | 127 | 125 | 131 | 125 | 129 |
| Unemployment Rate (%) | 67r | 6.8 | 5.6 | 4.8 | 4.0 | 3.5 | 5.3 | 4.3 | 3.4 | 3.3 | 3.4 | 3.2 | 3.3 |
| **Intl. Transactions & Positions** | | \multicolumn{12}{c}{*Billions of US Dollars*} | | | | | | | | | | | |
| Exports | 70..d | 259.26 | 289.34 | 316.82 | 344.51 | 362.68 | 318.51 | 390.14 | 428.73 | 442.80 | 458.96 | 473.66 | 465.08 |
| Imports, c.i.f | 71..d | 271.07 | 299.53 | 334.68 | 367.65 | 388.51 | 347.31 | 433.11 | 483.63 | 504.41 | 523.56 | 544.11 | 521.98 |
| | | \multicolumn{12}{c}{*2010=100*} | | | | | | | | | | | |
| Volume of Exports | 72 | 75.1 | 83.0 | 90.4 | 96.5 | 98.1 | 85.0 | 100.0 | 102.3 | 102.2 | 105.0 | 106.6 | 104.8 |
| Volume of Imports | 73 | 71.7 | 77.6 | 85.1 | 92.5 | 94.1 | 84.7 | 100.0 | 104.0 | 105.1 | 108.8 | 111.4 | 107.8 |
| Unit Value of Exports | 74 | 87.0 | 88.1 | 88.9 | 91.0 | 94.5 | 95.5 | 100.0 | 108.0 | 111.6 | 113.0 | 115.3 | 115.5 |
| Unit Value of Imports | 75 | 84.0 | 86.3 | 88.2 | 90.1 | 94.1 | 94.0 | 100.0 | 108.2 | 111.7 | 112.6 | 114.8 | 114.4 |

# China, P.R.: Hong Kong   532

| | | 2004 | 2005 | 2006 | 2007 | 2008 | 2009 | 2010 | 2011 | 2012 | 2013 | 2014 | 2015 |
|---|---|---|---|---|---|---|---|---|---|---|---|---|---|
| **Balance of Payments** | | | | | | | *Millions of US Dollars* | | | | | | |
| A. Current Account* | 109bx | 16,822.0 | 21,574.6 | 24,555.4 | 27,554.8 | 32,872.2 | 21,155.9 | 16,012.3 | 13,808.5 | 4,147.2 | 4,152.8 | 3,787.7 | 9,632.3 |
| Goods, credit (exports) | 1a9cx | 242,916.6 | 274,879.4 | 303,914.0 | 330,035.5 | 354,231.1 | 316,630.8 | 388,900.9 | 437,661.3 | 468,397.8 | 506,204.2 | 515,741.2 | 505,739.5 |
| Goods, debit (imports) | 1a9dx | 218,688.7 | 243,811.8 | 273,057.1 | 303,174.5 | 329,202.1 | 303,342.5 | 385,608.7 | 445,143.3 | 487,310.5 | 534,125.1 | 548,111.6 | 528,558.6 |
| Balance on goods | 1a9bx | 24,228.0 | 31,067.6 | 30,857.0 | 26,861.0 | 25,029.0 | 13,288.3 | 3,292.1 | −7,482.0 | −18,912.7 | −27,920.9 | −32,370.5 | −22,819.1 |
| Services, credit (exports) | 1b9cx | 40,782.7 | 47,380.1 | 54,441.2 | 64,453.7 | 69,906.2 | 64,669.9 | 80,541.1 | 91,303.6 | 98,504.1 | 104,738.7 | 106,652.2 | 104,231.8 |
| Services, debit (imports) | 1b9dx | 50,280.7 | 56,253.4 | 63,704.5 | 68,719.3 | 72,609.2 | 61,107.9 | 70,398.4 | 74,258.8 | 76,618.1 | 75,197.2 | 73,952.6 | 74,182.5 |
| Balance on Goods & Services | 1z9bx | 14,730.0 | 22,194.4 | 21,593.6 | 22,595.3 | 22,326.0 | 16,850.3 | 13,434.8 | 9,562.8 | 2,973.4 | 1,620.7 | 329.1 | 7,230.2 |
| Primary income: credit | 1c9cx | 52,674.2 | 65,627.4 | 84,952.7 | 115,792.2 | 120,810.8 | 101,555.1 | 119,667.8 | 136,104.2 | 140,686.8 | 152,594.7 | 161,821.4 | 164,076.7 |
| Primary income: debit | 1c9dx | 49,082.4 | 64,678.2 | 80,381.8 | 109,026.0 | 107,900.7 | 95,136.0 | 114,827.7 | 129,316.3 | 136,890.9 | 147,371.2 | 155,811.1 | 158,981.5 |
| Balance on gds, serv. & prim. inc. | 1y9bx | 18,321.8 | 23,143.6 | 26,164.5 | 29,361.5 | 35,236.1 | 23,269.5 | 18,275.0 | 16,350.7 | 6,769.2 | 6,844.2 | 6,339.3 | 12,325.5 |
| Secondary income: credit | 1d9ca | 625.5 | 942.9 | 959.9 | 937.8 | 611.4 | 469.2 | 572.7 | 881.2 | 905.1 | 1,042.9 | 1,135.1 | 1,188.3 |
| Secondary income: debit | 1d9da | 2,125.3 | 2,511.9 | 2,569.0 | 2,744.6 | 2,975.4 | 2,582.8 | 2,835.4 | 3,423.5 | 3,527.1 | 3,734.4 | 3,686.7 | 3,881.4 |
| B. Capital Account* | 209ba | −73.1 | −74.5 | −98.5 | −87.4 | −251.5 | −389.6 | −570.5 | −259.9 | −184.7 | −207.6 | −96.5 | −9.5 |
| Capital account: credit | 209ca | 1.3 | 51.9 | .6 | 3.6 | 2.6 | 31.7 | 14.0 | 2.4 | .1 | .5 | .3 | 33.0 |
| Capital account: debit | 209da | 74.4 | 126.4 | 99.2 | 91.0 | 254.1 | 421.3 | 584.6 | 262.3 | 184.8 | 208.1 | 96.7 | 42.6 |
| Balance on current & capital acct. | 129ba | 16,748.9 | 21,500.2 | 24,456.8 | 27,467.4 | 32,620.7 | 20,766.3 | 15,441.8 | 13,548.6 | 3,962.5 | 3,945.2 | 3,691.3 | 9,622.8 |
| C. Financial Account* | 309na | 19,298.7 | 21,142.6 | 18,549.3 | 25,046.3 | 3,710.9 | −60,762.7 | 3,251.3 | 3,130.2 | −15,816.8 | 3,459.6 | −8,516.0 | −19,419.2 |
| Direct investment: assets | 3a9aa | 36,671.0 | 33,916.4 | 47,577.5 | 67,897.9 | 57,078.5 | 57,943.4 | 98,430.8 | 95,905.8 | 88,122.7 | 83,328.5 | 140,892.1 | 61,096.1 |
| Equity & investment fund shares | 3aaaa | 23,554.1 | 31,022.4 | 34,986.4 | 49,432.7 | 46,617.8 | 61,951.8 | 83,733.0 | 81,736.7 | 69,209.0 | 82,370.2 | 122,145.8 | 63,873.2 |
| Debt instruments | 3abaa | 13,117.0 | 2,893.9 | 12,591.1 | 18,465.4 | 10,460.9 | −4,008.3 | 14,697.7 | 14,169.0 | 18,913.8 | 958.0 | 18,746.0 | −2,777.1 |
| Direct investment: liabilities | 3a9la | 22,194.2 | 40,963.1 | 44,901.8 | 62,121.0 | 67,035.2 | 54,275.7 | 82,709.1 | 96,135.1 | 74,887.1 | 76,857.5 | 129,847.5 | 180,844.3 |
| Equity & investment fund shares | 3aala | 26,168.7 | 29,478.2 | 37,857.7 | 57,877.0 | 57,723.3 | 54,408.1 | 58,998.8 | 88,627.6 | 67,340.8 | 78,101.8 | 114,019.9 | 176,142.1 |
| Debt instruments | 3abla | −3,974.6 | 11,485.1 | 7,044.1 | 4,243.9 | 9,311.7 | −132.2 | 23,710.3 | 7,507.4 | 7,546.4 | −1,244.2 | 15,827.6 | 4,702.2 |
| Portfolio investment: assets | 3b9aa | 42,958.9 | 40,503.1 | 41,459.9 | 77,090.4 | 24,516.5 | 50,787.8 | 80,686.5 | 19,996.9 | 40,122.0 | 66,366.4 | 35,614.4 | 99,228.5 |
| Equity & investment fund shares | 3baaa | 30,523.3 | 27,990.2 | 15,681.1 | 69,448.7 | 18,455.4 | 25,784.7 | 46,998.5 | 30,465.4 | 20,592.4 | 23,125.0 | 41,034.4 | 52,614.2 |
| Debt securities | 3bbaa | 12,435.5 | 12,512.9 | 25,778.8 | 7,641.8 | 6,061.0 | 25,003.1 | 33,687.8 | −10,468.6 | 19,529.7 | 43,241.3 | −5,420.1 | 46,614.4 |
| Portfolio investment: liabilities | 3b9la | 4,054.3 | 9,463.0 | 15,281.1 | 75,707.1 | −11,832.7 | 10,779.5 | 23,716.8 | 18,603.7 | 36,024.5 | 16,580.9 | 27,320.2 | −42,014.1 |
| Equity & investment fund shares | 3bala | 1,988.0 | 9,968.7 | 14,467.9 | 43,594.1 | 17,385.2 | 9,448.7 | 18,480.4 | 6,049.4 | 28,949.6 | 8,714.2 | 17,647.9 | −48,452.1 |
| Debt securities | 3bbla | 2,066.3 | −505.8 | 813.3 | 32,113.1 | −29,217.8 | 1,330.8 | 5,236.5 | 12,554.2 | 7,074.9 | 7,866.7 | 9,672.6 | 6,437.9 |
| Fin. der.& empl.stk.ops.(ESOs): net | 3c9na | −5,693.0 | −3,920.6 | −3,337.9 | −5,573.9 | −8,126.5 | −3,168.5 | −2,403.2 | −2,684.1 | −1,960.4 | −7,047.8 | −15,263.1 | −15,185.5 |
| Fin. der. & ESOs.: assets | 3c9aa | −20,604.6 | −20,797.5 | −19,437.1 | −29,817.6 | −68,600.9 | −48,541.6 | −35,903.8 | −46,215.0 | −39,731.2 | −54,784.4 | −57,914.8 | −73,450.1 |
| Fin. der.: ESOs.: liabilities | 3c9la | −14,911.7 | −16,876.8 | −16,099.5 | −24,243.7 | −60,474.4 | −45,373.1 | −33,500.4 | −43,531.0 | −37,770.7 | −47,736.3 | −42,651.6 | −58,264.6 |
| Other investment: assets | 3d9aa | 35,491.5 | 17,347.4 | 64,360.7 | 179,861.2 | −51,848.0 | −83,063.8 | 69,542.6 | 100,290.1 | 17,042.9 | 82,431.0 | 119,290.3 | −26,582.3 |
| Other equity | 3daaa | .... | .... | .... | .... | .... | .... | .... | .... | .... | .... | .... | .... |
| Debt instruments | 3dzaa | 35,491.5 | 17,347.4 | 64,360.7 | 179,861.2 | −51,848.0 | −83,063.8 | 69,542.6 | 100,290.1 | 17,042.9 | 82,431.0 | 119,290.3 | −26,582.3 |
| Other investment: liabilities | 3d9la | 63,881.2 | 16,277.6 | 71,328.3 | 156,401.3 | −37,292.6 | 18,206.1 | 136,579.3 | 95,639.8 | 48,232.6 | 128,179.9 | 131,882.0 | −854.5 |
| Other equity | 3dala | .... | .... | .... | .... | .... | .... | .... | .... | .... | .... | .... | .... |
| Debt instruments | 3dzla | 63,881.2 | 16,277.6 | 71,328.3 | 156,401.3 | −37,292.6 | 18,206.1 | 136,579.3 | 95,639.8 | 48,232.6 | 128,179.9 | 131,882.0 | −854.5 |
| Curr.+ cap.− finan. acct. balance | 4y9na | −2,549.8 | 357.6 | 5,907.5 | 2,421.1 | 28,909.7 | 81,529.0 | 12,190.5 | 10,418.4 | 19,779.3 | 485.6 | 12,207.3 | 29,042.0 |
| D. Net Errors and Omissions | 409na | 5,257.3 | −2,131.1 | 3,801.3 | 5,825.5 | −142.8 | −2,511.5 | −4,574.4 | 734.4 | 4,580.7 | 6,978.1 | 5,731.9 | 7,339.2 |
| E. Reserves and Related Items | 4z9na | 2,707.5 | −1,773.5 | 9,708.6 | 8,246.7 | 28,766.8 | 79,017.0 | 7,615.9 | 11,152.7 | 24,360.1 | 7,463.8 | 17,939.1 | 36,381.1 |
| Reserve assets | 3e9aa | 2,707.5 | −1,773.5 | 9,708.6 | 8,246.7 | 28,766.8 | 79,017.0 | 7,615.9 | 11,152.7 | 24,360.1 | 7,463.8 | 17,939.1 | 36,381.1 |
| Credit and loans from the IMF | 3dcla | .... | .... | .... | .... | .... | .... | .... | .... | .... | .... | .... | .... |
| Exceptional financing | 409la | .... | .... | .... | .... | .... | .... | .... | .... | .... | .... | .... | .... |
| *Excludes components in group E | | | | | | | | | | | | | |
| **International Investment Position** | | | | | | | *Millions of US Dollars* | | | | | | |
| Assets | 809aa | 1,430,950.5 | 1,560,007.5 | 2,003,264.5 | 2,807,795.9 | 2,347,309.1 | 2,666,455.7 | 2,987,975.4 | 3,098,571.8 | 3,465,325.4 | 3,756,341.0 | 4,176,578.7 | 4,314,096.2 |
| Direct investment | 8a9aa | 472,816.4 | 551,008.7 | 759,802.2 | 1,107,964.6 | 858,421.3 | 928,946.3 | 1,039,043.2 | 1,129,058.8 | 1,273,797.2 | 1,352,096.0 | 1,593,516.2 | 1,657,205.2 |
| Equity & investment fund shares | 8aaaa | 340,021.6 | 411,005.5 | 604,291.6 | 941,210.0 | 675,517.7 | 749,282.7 | 849,567.3 | 912,865.1 | 1,023,557.3 | 1,095,353.8 | 1,297,144.5 | 1,321,342.2 |
| Debt instruments | 8abaa | 132,794.9 | 140,003.2 | 155,510.6 | 166,754.2 | 182,903.6 | 179,663.7 | 189,475.7 | 216,193.7 | 250,240.0 | 256,742.1 | 296,371.9 | 335,862.8 |
| Portfolio investment | 8b9aa | 400,889.2 | 436,598.6 | 580,551.5 | 778,579.9 | 557,156.4 | 811,482.0 | 929,450.9 | 825,764.1 | 987,223.3 | 1,121,244.2 | 1,170,486.2 | 1,256,928.7 |
| Equity & investment fund shares | 8baaa | 199,684.3 | 227,848.8 | 338,899.2 | 514,544.0 | 275,177.6 | 498,739.6 | 581,741.6 | 478,924.0 | 605,503.9 | 693,798.2 | 738,401.5 | 789,089.5 |
| Debt securities | 8bbaa | 201,204.9 | 208,749.8 | 241,652.5 | 264,035.9 | 281,979.0 | 312,742.4 | 347,709.2 | 346,840.1 | 381,719.2 | 427,446.1 | 432,084.8 | 467,839.2 |
| Fin. der.(oth.than reserves) & ESOs | 8c9aa | 22,441.6 | 17,192.9 | 22,535.7 | 47,890.7 | 87,131.3 | 48,897.4 | 58,768.9 | 69,441.0 | 85,354.5 | 73,259.6 | 80,396.0 | 83,882.7 |
| Other investment | 8d9aa | 418,394.8 | 441,059.8 | 513,673.0 | 733,908.7 | 680,400.9 | 631,665.7 | 703,805.3 | 803,815.3 | 818,264.6 | 898,546.7 | 1,003,697.4 | 957,272.4 |
| Other equity | 8daaa | .... | .... | .... | .... | .... | .... | .... | .... | .... | .... | .... | .... |
| Debt instruments | 8dzaa | 418,394.8 | 441,059.8 | 513,673.0 | 733,908.7 | 680,400.9 | 631,665.7 | 703,805.3 | 803,815.3 | 818,264.6 | 898,546.7 | 1,003,697.4 | 957,272.4 |
| Reserve assets | 8e9aa | 116,408.7 | 114,147.4 | 126,702.0 | 139,452.4 | 164,199.1 | 245,464.3 | 256,907.2 | 270,492.3 | 300,686.0 | 311,194.5 | 328,482.9 | 358,807.0 |
| Liabilities | 809la | 1,005,161.3 | 1,111,681.8 | 1,474,767.4 | 2,315,919.1 | 1,715,093.0 | 1,931,208.4 | 2,322,837.1 | 2,387,361.7 | 2,743,852.4 | 2,998,362.3 | 3,306,387.3 | 3,335,088.6 |
| Direct investment | 8a9la | 491,665.0 | 568,710.6 | 783,064.6 | 1,226,806.0 | 873,281.6 | 994,020.8 | 1,162,625.2 | 1,184,511.4 | 1,355,913.7 | 1,463,425.2 | 1,639,420.0 | 1,744,147.6 |
| Equity & investment fund shares | 8aala | 392,610.8 | 456,724.4 | 662,087.7 | 1,098,117.7 | 736,821.0 | 852,568.6 | 998,272.2 | 1,010,873.1 | 1,180,813.0 | 1,283,600.2 | 1,445,574.0 | 1,537,229.6 |
| Debt instruments | 8abla | 99,054.2 | 111,986.3 | 120,977.0 | 128,688.3 | 136,460.5 | 141,452.1 | 164,353.1 | 173,638.3 | 175,100.7 | 179,824.9 | 193,846.0 | 206,918.0 |
| Portfolio investment | 8b9la | 155,262.8 | 178,438.4 | 259,663.5 | 477,603.7 | 229,908.3 | 340,813.5 | 413,978.1 | 359,637.0 | 482,998.0 | 521,808.9 | 526,822.4 | 459,119.2 |
| Equity & investment fund shares | 8bala | 143,405.4 | 167,568.3 | 247,870.3 | 433,622.5 | 214,489.4 | 326,143.9 | 395,398.9 | 329,975.9 | 450,042.8 | 487,980.7 | 488,878.6 | 420,094.7 |
| Debt securities | 8bbla | 11,857.3 | 10,870.2 | 11,793.2 | 43,981.0 | 15,418.9 | 14,669.6 | 18,579.2 | 29,661.1 | 32,955.2 | 33,828.2 | 37,943.8 | 39,024.5 |
| Fin. der.(oth.than reserves) & ESOs | 8c9la | 21,136.2 | 17,100.9 | 20,366.3 | 32,536.8 | 73,885.2 | 40,033.3 | 50,131.8 | 61,470.7 | 82,413.1 | 66,043.3 | 70,953.4 | 73,929.8 |
| Other investment | 8d9la | 337,097.3 | 347,431.8 | 411,672.9 | 578,972.6 | 538,017.8 | 556,340.8 | 696,101.9 | 781,742.7 | 822,527.6 | 947,084.9 | 1,069,191.5 | 1,057,841.9 |
| Other equity | 8dala | .... | .... | .... | .... | .... | .... | .... | .... | .... | .... | .... | .... |
| Debt instruments | 8dzla | 337,097.3 | 347,431.8 | 411,672.9 | 578,972.6 | 538,017.8 | 556,340.8 | 696,101.9 | 781,742.7 | 822,527.6 | 947,084.9 | 1,069,191.5 | 1,057,841.9 |

# China, P.R.: Hong Kong   532

| | | 2004 | 2005 | 2006 | 2007 | 2008 | 2009 | 2010 | 2011 | 2012 | 2013 | 2014 | 2015 |
|---|---|---|---|---|---|---|---|---|---|---|---|---|---|
| **Government Finance Operations Statement** | | | | | | | | | | | | | |
| **General Government** | | *Millions of Hong Kong Dollars: Fiscal Year Begins April 1* | | | | | | | | | | | |
| Revenue | a1 | 243,746 | 260,580 | 302,026 | 373,362 | 335,500 | 327,977 | 393,620 | 452,025 | 459,602 | 473,332 | 498,109 | .... |
| Taxes | a11 | 155,611 | 175,069 | 187,699 | 230,137 | 217,201 | 207,400 | 240,496 | 271,696 | 278,644 | 285,474 | 351,725 | .... |
| Social Contributions | a12 | 20 | 18 | 17 | 17 | 16 | 14 | 13 | 13 | 10 | 9 | 8 | .... |
| Grants | a13 | — | — | — | — | — | — | — | — | — | — | — | .... |
| Other Revenue | a14 | 88,115 | 85,493 | 114,310 | 143,208 | 118,283 | 120,563 | 153,111 | 180,316 | 180,948 | 187,849 | 146,376 | .... |
| Expense | a2 | 225,008 | 209,597 | 204,679 | 216,081 | 268,099 | 266,177 | 261,965 | 313,147 | 332,195 | 364,075 | 350,222 | .... |
| Compensation of Employees | a21 | 64,051 | 53,095 | 52,503 | 54,743 | 57,473 | 58,373 | 58,954 | 59,165 | 63,382 | 64,974 | 67,172 | .... |
| Use of Goods & Services | a22 | 48,747 | 47,542 | 69,015 | 73,459 | 78,608 | 85,566 | 99,713 | 96,826 | 123,472 | 119,791 | 143,881 | .... |
| Consumption of Fixed Capital | a23 | 9,844 | 10,110 | 9,396 | 9,336 | 9,928 | 10,583 | 9,971 | 10,723 | 11,134 | 11,680 | | .... |
| Interest | a24 | 586 | 1,054 | 1,023 | 998 | 894 | 733 | 913 | 1,375 | 1,833 | 2,469 | 2,709 | .... |
| Subsidies | a25 | 333 | 313 | 216 | 182 | 277 | 451 | 365 | 322 | 327 | 342 | 3,295 | .... |
| Grants | a26 | 73 | 59 | 61 | 314 | 2,352 | 7,036 | 489 | 162 | 102 | 543 | −27 | .... |
| Social Benefits | a27 | 61,214 | 87,406 | 33,883 | 35,859 | 40,702 | 42,561 | 43,118 | 52,318 | 47,871 | 75,122 | .... | .... |
| Other Expense | a28 | | | | | | | | | 101 | 147 | | |
| Gross Operating Balance [1-2+23] | agob | 2,720 | 9,702 | 68,961 | 114,504 | 23,924 | 34,219 | 96,702 | 101,437 | 100,798 | 44,545 | | .... |
| Net Operating Balance [1-2] | anob | −7,124 | −408 | 59,565 | 105,168 | 13,996 | 23,636 | 86,731 | 90,714 | 89,664 | 32,865 | .... | .... |
| Net Acq. of Nonfinancial Assets | a31 | 5,755 | −19,809 | 2,394 | −2,362 | 3,302 | 5,501 | 13,180 | 17,596 | 17,773 | 18,453 | 22,340 | .... |
| Aquisition of Nonfin. Assets | a31.1 | .... | .... | .... | .... | .... | .... | .... | .... | .... | .... | .... | .... |
| Disposal of Nonfin. Assets | a31.2 | .... | .... | .... | .... | .... | .... | .... | .... | .... | .... | .... | .... |
| Net Lending/Borrowing [1-2-31] | anlb | −12,879 | 19,401 | 57,171 | 107,530 | 10,694 | 18,135 | 73,551 | 73,118 | 71,891 | 14,412 | .... | .... |
| Net Acq. of Financial Assets | a32 | 25,205 | 59,557 | 72,333 | 124,151 | 26,027 | 49,370 | 105,070 | 108,531 | 112,828 | 58,095 | 118,153 | .... |
| **By instrument** | | | | | | | | | | | | | |
| Monetary Gold & SDRs | a3201 | — | — | — | — | — | — | — | — | — | — | — | .... |
| Currency & Deposits | a3202 | 3,584 | 32,441 | −17,954 | −13,074 | 11,869 | −3,643 | 2,471 | −7,507 | 878 | 475 | −4,338 | .... |
| Securities other than Shares | a3203 | — | — | — | — | — | — | — | — | — | — | — | .... |
| Loans | a3204 | 2,248 | 2,074 | 755 | 1,588 | 1,285 | −3,034 | −931 | −769 | 1,034 | 1,813 | 1,723 | .... |
| Shares & Other Equity | a3205 | 18,318 | 25,406 | 86,705 | 138,002 | 12,866 | 56,055 | 104,221 | 111,661 | 93,783 | 72,938 | 91,346 | .... |
| Insurance Technical Reserves | a3206 | — | — | — | — | — | — | — | — | — | — | — | .... |
| Financial Derivatives | a3207 | — | 15 | — | — | — | 6 | — | — | — | — | 2 | .... |
| Other Accounts Receivable | a3208 | 1,055 | −379 | 2,827 | −2,365 | 7 | −14 | −691 | 5,146 | 17,133 | −17,131 | 29,420 | .... |
| **By debtor** | | | | | | | | | | | | | |
| Domestic | a321 | 25,205 | 59,557 | 72,333 | 124,151 | 26,027 | 49,370 | 105,070 | 108,531 | 112,828 | 58,095 | 118,153 | .... |
| Foreign | a322 | | | | | | | | | | | | |
| Net Incurrence of Liabilities | a33 | 38,084 | 40,156 | 15,162 | 16,621 | 15,333 | 31,235 | 31,519 | 35,413 | 40,937 | 43,683 | 22,196 | .... |
| **By instrument** | | | | | | | | | | | | | |
| Special Drawing Rights (SDRs) | a3301 | — | — | — | — | — | — | — | — | — | — | — | .... |
| Currency & Deposits | a3302 | | | | | | | | | | | | |
| Securities other than Shares | a3303 | 25,621 | −1,033 | −3,032 | −1,656 | −3,469 | 7,064 | 16,025 | 21,188 | 20,996 | 23,493 | 8,458 | .... |
| Loans | a3304 | — | — | — | — | — | — | — | — | — | — | — | .... |
| Shares & Other Equity | a3305 | — | — | — | — | — | — | — | — | — | — | — | .... |
| Insurance Technical Reserves | a3306 | — | — | 15,999 | 16,529 | 17,444 | 16,997 | 16,228 | 16,237 | 19,669 | 18,170 | 16,671 | .... |
| Financial Derivatives | a3307 | — | — | — | — | — | — | — | — | — | — | — | .... |
| Other Accounts Payable | a3308 | 12,463 | 41,189 | 2,195 | 1,748 | 1,358 | 7,174 | −734 | −2,012 | 272 | 2,020 | −2,933 | .... |
| **By creditor** | | | | | | | | | | | | | |
| Foreign | a332 | 12,261 | 587 | 174 | 570 | −1,054 | −1,770 | 174 | −214 | −114 | 402 | 158 | .... |
| Stat. Discrepancy [32-33-NLB] | anlbz | | | | | | | | | | | | |
| Memo Item: Expenditure [2+31] | a2m | 259,416 | 257,707 | 248,181 | 260,712 | 319,595 | 317,658 | 322,328 | 386,819 | 407,828 | 444,458 | 436,332 | .... |
| **Balance Sheet** | | *Millions of Hong Kong Dollars: Fiscal Year Begins April 1* | | | | | | | | | | | |
| Net Worth | a6 | 374,937 | 380,806 | 435,832 | 531,017 | 551,584 | 568,345 | 644,505 | 644,079 | 686,243 | 705,856 | 772,019 | .... |
| Nonfinancial Assets | a61 | 305,558 | 285,937 | 291,922 | 289,781 | 297,621 | 305,254 | 317,955 | 335,798 | 353,871 | 373,313 | 396,070 | .... |
| Financial Assets | a62 | 475,128 | 540,774 | 614,177 | 738,305 | 764,337 | 814,325 | 958,341 | 1,066,790 | 1,185,520 | 1,243,620 | 1,361,221 | .... |
| **By instrument** | | | | | | | | | | | | | |
| Monetary Gold & SDRs | a6201 | — | — | — | — | — | — | — | — | — | — | — | .... |
| Currency & Deposits | a6202 | 13,987 | 43,750 | 25,796 | 14,670 | 26,539 | 22,896 | 25,400 | 17,893 | 18,777 | 19,252 | 14,914 | .... |
| Securities other than Shares | a6203 | — | — | — | — | — | — | — | — | — | — | — | .... |
| Loans | a6204 | 20,119 | 22,193 | 22,948 | 24,536 | 25,821 | 22,788 | 21,857 | 21,088 | 21,916 | 23,729 | 25,453 | .... |
| Shares and Other Equity | a6205 | 434,679 | 468,834 | 556,628 | 692,682 | 705,549 | 762,220 | 867,088 | 978,665 | 1,078,550 | 1,151,490 | 1,242,289 | .... |
| Insurance Technical Reserves | a6206 | — | — | — | — | — | — | — | — | — | — | — | .... |
| Financial Derivatives | a6207 | — | 32 | 13 | −10 | −6 | 1 | — | — | — | — | 2 | .... |
| Other Accounts Receivable | a6208 | 6,343 | 5,965 | 8,792 | 6,427 | 6,434 | 6,420 | 43,996 | 49,141 | 66,274 | 49,143 | 78,563 | .... |
| **By debtor** | | | | | | | | | | | | | |
| Domestic | a621 | 473,966 | 539,612 | 613,015 | 737,143 | 763,175 | 813,163 | 957,179 | 1,065,630 | 1,184,360 | 1,242,450 | 1,360,059 | .... |
| Foreign | a622 | 1,162 | 1,162 | 1,162 | 1,162 | 1,162 | 1,162 | 1,162 | 1,162 | 1,162 | 1,162 | 1,162 | .... |
| Liabilities | a63 | 405,749 | 445,905 | 470,267 | 497,069 | 510,374 | 551,234 | 631,791 | 758,506 | 853,147 | 911,072 | 985,272 | .... |
| **By instrument** | | | | | | | | | | | | | |
| Special Drawing Rights (SDRs) | a6301 | — | — | — | — | — | — | — | — | — | — | — | .... |
| Currency & Deposits | a6302 | — | — | — | — | — | — | — | — | — | — | — | .... |
| Securities other than Shares | a6303 | 25,621 | 24,588 | 21,556 | 19,900 | 16,431 | 23,495 | 39,520 | 60,708 | 81,704 | 105,197 | 113,655 | .... |
| Loans | a6304 | — | — | — | — | — | — | — | — | — | — | — | .... |
| Shares and Other Equity | a6305 | — | — | — | — | — | — | — | — | — | — | — | .... |
| Insurance Technical Reserves | a6306 | — | — | 400,892 | 427,602 | 443,018 | 469,640 | 533,832 | 641,371 | 714,744 | 747,157 | 815,832 | .... |
| Financial Derivatives | a6307 | — | — | — | — | — | — | — | — | — | — | — | .... |
| Other Accounts Payable | a6308 | 380,128 | 421,317 | 47,819 | 49,567 | 50,925 | 58,099 | 58,439 | 56,427 | 56,699 | 58,718 | 55,785 | .... |
| **By creditor** | | | | | | | | | | | | | |
| Domestic | a631 | 393,488 | 433,057 | 457,245 | 483,477 | 497,836 | 540,466 | 620,849 | 747,778 | 842,533 | 900,056 | 974,098 | .... |
| Foreign | a632 | 12,261 | 12,848 | 13,022 | 13,592 | 12,538 | 10,768 | 10,942 | 10,728 | 10,614 | 11,016 | 11,174 | .... |
| Net Financial Worth [62-63] | a6m2 | 69,379 | 94,869 | 143,910 | 241,236 | 253,963 | 263,091 | 326,550 | 308,281 | 332,372 | 332,543 | 375,949 | .... |
| Memo Item: Debt at Market Value | a6m3 | 405,749 | 445,905 | 470,267 | 497,069 | 510,374 | 551,234 | 631,791 | 758,506 | 853,147 | .... | .... | |
| Memo Item: Debt at Face Value | a6m35 | .... | .... | .... | .... | .... | .... | .... | .... | .... | .... | .... | |
| Memo Item: Debt at Nominal Value | a6m4 | .... | .... | .... | .... | .... | .... | .... | .... | .... | .... | .... | |

# China, P.R.: Hong Kong  532

| National Accounts | | 2004 | 2005 | 2006 | 2007 | 2008 | 2009 | 2010 | 2011 | 2012 | 2013 | 2014 | 2015 |
|---|---|---|---|---|---|---|---|---|---|---|---|---|---|
| | | | | | | *Billions of Hong Kong Dollars* | | | | | | | |
| Househ.Cons.Expend.,incl.NPISHs.... | 96f | 771 | 812 | 869 | 982 | 1,026 | 1,014 | 1,090 | 1,224 | 1,315 | 1,413 | 1,503 | 1,589 |
| Government Consumption Expend... | 91f | 136 | 131 | 132 | 139 | 148 | 153 | 157 | 169 | 185 | 199 | 214 | 231 |
| Gross Fixed Capital Formation......... | 93e | 287 | 302 | 337 | 340 | 351 | 340 | 387 | 455 | 517 | 516 | 531 | 544 |
| Changes in Inventories................... | 93i | 7 | −5 | −2 | 13 | 8 | 23 | 38 | 12 | −4 | −2 | 7 | −23 |
| Exports of Goods and Services......... | 90c | 2,458 | 2,749 | 3,034 | 3,363 | 3,565 | 3,173 | 3,897 | 4,361 | 4,595 | 4,875 | 4,955 | 4,833 |
| Imports of Goods and Services (-)..... | 98c | 2,343 | 2,576 | 2,866 | 3,187 | 3,391 | 3,042 | 3,793 | 4,287 | 4,572 | 4,862 | 4,953 | 4,777 |
| Gross Domestic Product (GDP)......... | 99b | 1,317 | 1,412 | 1,503 | 1,651 | 1,707 | 1,659 | 1,776 | 1,934 | 2,037 | 2,138 | 2,258 | 2,397 |
| Net Primary Income from Abroad..... | 98.n | 28 | 7 | 36 | 53 | 101 | 50 | 38 | 53 | 29 | 41 | 47 | 39 |
| Gross National Income (GNI)........... | 99a | 1,345 | 1,420 | 1,539 | 1,704 | 1,808 | 1,709 | 1,814 | 1,987 | 2,067 | 2,179 | 2,305 | 2,437 |
| Net Current Transf.from Abroad....... | 98t | −12 | −12 | −13 | −14 | −18 | −16 | −18 | −20 | −20 | −21 | −20 | −21 |
| Gross Nat'l Disposable Inc.(GNDI).... | 99i | 1,333 | 1,407 | 1,526 | 1,689 | 1,790 | 1,693 | 1,796 | 1,967 | 2,046 | 2,158 | 2,285 | 2,416 |
| Gross Saving................................. | 99s | 425 | 465 | 526 | 568 | 615 | 526 | 549 | 575 | 546 | 546 | 568 | 595 |
| GDP Volume 2014 Ref., Chained..... | 99b.p | 1,538 | 1,651 | 1,767 | 1,882 | 1,922 | 1,874 | 2,001 | 2,098 | 2,133 | 2,199 | 2,258 | 2,313 |
| GDP Volume (2010=100)............... | 99bvp | 76.8 | 82.5 | 88.3 | 94.0 | 96.0 | 93.7 | 100.0 | 104.8 | 106.6 | 109.9 | 112.8 | 115.6 |
| GDP Deflator (2010=100)............... | 99bip | 96.5 | 96.3 | 95.8 | 98.8 | 100.1 | 99.7 | 100.0 | 103.9 | 107.6 | 109.5 | 112.7 | 116.8 |
| | | | | | | *Millions: Midyear Estimates* | | | | | | | |
| Population................................. | 99z | 6.84 | 6.84 | 6.86 | 6.88 | 6.91 | 6.95 | 6.99 | 7.04 | 7.10 | 7.16 | 7.23 | 7.29 |

2016, International Monetary Fund : *International Financial Statistics Yearbook*

# China, P.R.: Macao  546

| | | 2004 | 2005 | 2006 | 2007 | 2008 | 2009 | 2010 | 2011 | 2012 | 2013 | 2014 | 2015 |
|---|---|---|---|---|---|---|---|---|---|---|---|---|---|
| **Exchange Rates** | | | | | | *Patacas Per SDR: End of Period* | | | | | | | |
| Market Rate.................................. | aa | 12.439 | 11.416 | 12.044 | 12.696 | 12.295 | 12.522 | 12.345 | 12.289 | 12.271 | 12.300 | 11.576 | 11.063 |
| | | | | | | *Patacas per US Dollar: End of Period (ae) Period Average (rf)* | | | | | | | |
| Market Rate.................................. | ae | 8.010 | 7.987 | 8.006 | 8.034 | 7.982 | 7.988 | 8.016 | 8.005 | 7.984 | 7.987 | 7.990 | 7.983 |
| Market Rate.................................. | rf | 8.022 | 8.011 | 8.001 | 8.036 | 8.020 | 7.984 | 8.002 | 8.018 | 7.990 | 7.989 | 7.987 | 7.985 |
| **International Liquidity** | | | | | | *Millions of US Dollars Unless Otherwise Indicated: End of Period* | | | | | | | |
| Total Reserves minus Gold............... | 1l.d | 5,436 | 6,689 | 9,132 | 13,230 | 15,930 | 18,350 | 23,726 | 34,026 | 16,600 | 16,146 | 16,444 | 18,891 |
| Foreign Exchange.......................... | 1d.d | 5,436 | 6,689 | 9,132 | 13,230 | 15,930 | 18,350 | 23,726 | 34,026 | 16,600 | 16,146 | 16,444 | 18,891 |
| Gold (Million Fine Troy Ounces)....... | 1ad | — | — | — | — | — | — | — | — | — | — | — | — |
| Gold (National Valuation)............... | 1and | — | — | — | — | — | — | — | — | — | — | — | — |
| Central Bank: Other Assets............. | 3..d | 1,092 | 1,267 | 1,423 | 1,522 | 1,532 | 1,557 | 1,299 | 1,213 | 18,102 | 21,903 | 24,182 | 15,700 |
| Central Bank: Other Liabs............... | 4..d | — | — | — | — | — | — | — | — | — | — | — | — |
| Other Depository Corps.: Assets....... | 7a.d | 12,884 | 17,510 | 22,674 | 25,183 | 27,631 | 35,356 | 45,126 | 52,816 | 64,793 | 81,791 | 93,847 | 105,418 |
| Other Depository Corps.: Liabs......... | 7b.d | 3,096 | 6,794 | 9,236 | 12,992 | 15,871 | 20,814 | 28,504 | 34,925 | 39,038 | 49,536 | 61,891 | 76,753 |
| **Central Bank** | | | | | | *Millions of Patacas: End of Period* | | | | | | | |
| Net Foreign Assets.......................... | 11n | 52,282.2 | 63,547.4 | 84,505.5 | 118,519.9 | 139,390.0 | 159,014.1 | 200,597.3 | 282,076.6 | 277,065.4 | 303,886.3 | 324,604.3 | 276,149.5 |
| Claims on Nonresidents................ | 11 | 52,284.2 | 63,547.4 | 84,506.1 | 118,519.9 | 139,390.3 | 159,014.1 | 200,597.3 | 282,077.2 | 277,065.5 | 303,886.3 | 324,604.3 | 276,150.5 |
| Liabilities to Nonresidents............ | 16c | 1.9 | — | .6 | — | .2 | — | — | .6 | .1 | — | — | 1.0 |
| Claims on Other Depository Corps.... | 12e | 2,212.2 | 1,000.2 | 402.7 | 239.9 | 273.6 | 549.9 | 2,773.8 | 3,774.8 | 520.4 | 384.0 | 272.9 | 339.6 |
| Net Claims on Central Government.. | 12an | −27,890.0 | −35,346.1 | −46,098.8 | −68,540.6 | −93,850.4 | −112,962.1 | −155,758.5 | −220,408.4 | −198,407.0 | −227,973.5 | −245,572.6 | −177,658.8 |
| Claims on Central Government...... | 12a | — | — | — | — | — | — | — | — | — | — | — | — |
| Liabilities to Central Government... | 16d | 27,890.0 | 35,346.1 | 46,098.8 | 68,540.6 | 93,850.4 | 112,962.1 | 155,758.5 | 220,408.4 | 198,407.0 | 227,973.5 | 245,572.6 | 177,658.8 |
| Claims on Other Sectors................. | 12s | — | — | — | — | — | — | — | — | — | — | — | — |
| Claims on Other Financial Corps.... | 12g | — | — | — | — | — | — | — | — | — | — | — | — |
| Claims on State & Local Govts....... | 12b | — | — | — | — | — | — | — | — | — | — | — | — |
| Claims on Public Nonfin. Corps...... | 12c | — | — | — | — | — | — | — | — | — | — | — | — |
| Claims on Private Sector............... | 12d | — | — | — | — | — | — | — | — | — | — | — | — |
| Monetary Base................................ | 14 | 5,370.8 | 5,775.3 | 6,943.7 | 8,233.6 | 9,238.9 | 17,123.2 | 19,736.7 | 23,697.0 | 31,571.2 | 25,547.0 | 33,179.7 | 38,392.9 |
| Currency in Circulation.................. | 14a | 2,933.7 | 3,250.0 | 3,806.9 | 4,458.1 | 5,016.6 | 5,572.8 | 6,054.4 | 7,067.2 | 8,806.8 | 10,742.9 | 12,703.6 | 14,141.3 |
| Liabs. to Other Depository Corps.... | 14c | 2,437.1 | 2,525.3 | 3,136.9 | 3,775.5 | 4,222.3 | 11,550.4 | 13,682.3 | 16,629.8 | 22,764.4 | 14,804.1 | 20,476.1 | 24,251.6 |
| Liabilities to Other Sectors............ | 14d | — | — | — | — | — | — | — | — | — | — | — | — |
| Other Liabs. to Other Dep. Corps.... | 14n | 18,157.0 | 20,326.5 | 26,640.0 | 33,705.0 | 25,265.0 | 15,091.0 | 11,356.0 | 24,181.5 | 27,621.5 | 26,626.5 | 20,050.0 | 34,459.0 |
| Dep. & Sec. Excl. f/Monetary Base.... | 14o | — | — | — | — | — | — | — | — | — | — | — | — |
| Deposits Included in Broad Money. | 15 | — | — | — | — | — | — | — | — | — | — | — | — |
| Sec.Ot.th.Shares Incl.in Brd. Money | 16a | — | — | — | — | — | — | — | — | — | — | — | — |
| Deposits Excl. from Broad Money.... | 16b | — | — | — | — | — | — | — | — | — | — | — | — |
| Sec.Ot.th.Shares Excl.f/Brd.Money.. | 16s | — | — | — | — | — | — | — | — | — | — | — | — |
| Loans............................................ | 16l | — | — | — | — | — | — | — | — | — | — | — | — |
| Financial Derivatives...................... | 16m | — | — | — | — | — | — | — | — | — | — | — | — |
| Shares and Other Equity.................. | 17a | 3,836.4 | 4,418.9 | 6,501.0 | 9,897.3 | 12,199.9 | 15,249.3 | 17,569.0 | 18,930.4 | 20,971.0 | 25,177.5 | 27,233.8 | 26,505.6 |
| Other Items (Net)............................ | 17r | −759.7 | −1,319.2 | −1,275.4 | −1,616.8 | −890.5 | −861.6 | −1,049.1 | −1,366.0 | −984.9 | −1,054.1 | −1,158.8 | −527.3 |
| Memo Item: | | | | | | | | | | | | | |
| Total Assets.................................... | 10ra | 55,312.5 | 65,916.6 | 86,246.6 | 120,551.6 | 141,115.7 | 160,563.8 | 204,618.3 | 287,271.9 | 278,632.7 | 305,554.2 | 326,343.5 | 277,386.9 |
| **Other Depository Corporations** | | | | | | *Millions of Patacas: End of Period* | | | | | | | |
| Net Foreign Assets.......................... | 21n | 78,392.7 | 85,595.0 | 107,583.2 | 97,945.6 | 93,866.5 | 116,157.6 | 133,240.2 | 143,213.9 | 205,628.4 | 257,609.1 | 255,325.9 | 228,841.8 |
| Claims on Nonresidents................ | 21 | 103,190.6 | 139,855.5 | 181,522.8 | 202,321.8 | 220,559.2 | 282,414.1 | 361,721.1 | 422,779.1 | 517,307.6 | 653,247.1 | 749,827.0 | 841,591.7 |
| Liabilities to Nonresidents............. | 26c | 24,797.9 | 54,260.5 | 73,939.6 | 104,376.2 | 126,692.6 | 166,256.5 | 228,480.9 | 279,565.3 | 311,679.1 | 395,637.9 | 494,501.1 | 612,749.8 |
| Claims on Central Bank................. | 20 | 20,975.8 | 23,368.2 | 30,445.2 | 38,299.1 | 30,421.2 | 27,636.9 | 26,016.6 | 42,162.9 | 52,126.3 | 43,624.7 | 42,843.1 | 61,317.8 |
| Currency............................ | 20a | 381.7 | 516.4 | 668.3 | 818.6 | 933.9 | 995.5 | 977.2 | 1,349.7 | 1,738.2 | 2,191.9 | 2,315.4 | 2,607.2 |
| Reserve Deposits and Securities..... | 20b | 2,437.1 | 2,525.3 | 3,136.9 | 3,775.5 | 4,222.3 | 11,550.4 | 13,682.3 | 16,629.8 | 22,764.4 | 14,804.1 | 20,476.1 | 24,251.6 |
| Other Claims............................ | 20n | 18,157.0 | 20,326.5 | 26,640.0 | 33,705.0 | 25,265.0 | 15,091.0 | 11,357.1 | 24,183.4 | 27,623.7 | 26,628.7 | 20,051.6 | 34,459.0 |
| Net Claims on Central Government.. | 22an | −5,477.1 | −7,074.2 | −8,010.1 | −10,315.0 | −11,650.2 | −16,306.6 | −22,942.4 | −29,581.7 | −51,524.7 | −82,064.7 | −112,013.4 | −156,949.3 |
| Claims on Central Government...... | 22a | — | — | — | — | — | — | — | — | — | — | — | — |
| Liabilities to Central Government... | 26d | 5,477.1 | 7,074.2 | 8,010.1 | 10,315.0 | 11,650.2 | 16,306.6 | 22,942.4 | 29,581.7 | 51,524.7 | 82,064.7 | 112,013.4 | 156,949.3 |
| Claims on Other Sectors.................. | 22s | 36,715.4 | 44,714.1 | 50,670.5 | 72,053.9 | 91,801.6 | 101,125.2 | 130,676.9 | 167,855.8 | 198,701.9 | 257,512.1 | 339,352.0 | 389,406.8 |
| Claims on Other Financial Corps.... | 22g | — | — | — | — | — | — | — | — | — | — | — | — |
| Claims on State & Local Govts....... | 22b | — | — | — | — | — | — | — | — | — | — | — | — |
| Claims on Public Nonfin. Corps...... | 22c | 1,947.2 | 1,947.2 | 1,975.7 | 1,947.2 | 1,947.2 | 2,084.6 | 2,150.6 | 2,026.8 | 19.4 | .6 | .6 | .6 |
| Claims on Private Sector............... | 22d | 34,768.2 | 42,766.8 | 48,694.8 | 70,106.7 | 89,854.3 | 99,040.6 | 128,526.3 | 165,829.0 | 198,682.5 | 257,511.5 | 339,351.5 | 389,406.3 |
| Liabilities to Central Bank............... | 26g | 2,212.2 | 1,000.2 | 402.6 | 239.8 | 273.6 | 549.9 | 2,979.7 | 3,978.6 | 520.1 | 383.8 | 272.7 | 338.9 |
| Transf.Dep.Included in Broad Money | 24 | 10,668.0 | 9,814.6 | 14,851.5 | 18,681.4 | 20,329.0 | 25,700.9 | 29,315.2 | 30,162.7 | 40,157.4 | 49,955.9 | 51,002.3 | 49,618.5 |
| Other Dep.Included in Broad Money. | 25 | 107,506.3 | 122,870.9 | 150,656.7 | 162,934.0 | 165,060.8 | 181,626.5 | 208,324.1 | 261,432.4 | 327,104.3 | 382,473.1 | 425,608.5 | 411,167.7 |
| Sec.Ot.th.Shares Incl.in Brd. Money.. | 26a | — | — | — | — | — | — | — | 288.2 | 204.9 | — | — | — |
| Deposits Excl. from Broad Money..... | 26b | — | — | — | — | — | — | — | — | — | — | — | — |
| Sec.Ot.th.Shares Excl.f/Brd.Money... | 26s | — | — | — | — | — | — | — | — | — | — | — | — |
| Loans............................................ | 26l | — | — | — | — | — | — | — | — | — | — | — | — |
| Financial Derivatives...................... | 26m | — | — | — | — | — | — | — | — | — | — | — | — |
| Insurance Technical Reserves.......... | 26r | — | — | — | — | — | — | — | — | — | — | — | — |
| Shares and Other Equity.................. | 27a | 9,511.1 | 11,879.5 | 14,113.2 | 16,399.9 | 17,293.1 | 18,767.9 | 22,632.1 | 26,022.2 | 31,262.0 | 36,083.8 | 42,334.8 | 56,825.4 |
| Other Items (Net)............................ | 27r | 709.1 | 1,037.9 | 664.8 | −271.5 | 1,482.6 | 1,967.9 | 3,740.2 | 1,766.7 | 5,683.2 | 7,784.5 | 6,289.2 | 4,666.6 |
| Memo Item: | | | | | | | | | | | | | |
| Total Assets.................................... | 20ra | 168,196.9 | 213,215.9 | 269,834.3 | 323,442.7 | 354,561.5 | 421,620.2 | 533,864.6 | 651,478.6 | 787,847.6 | 979,877.0 | 1,162,002.0 | 1,326,852.8 |

| | | 2004 | 2005 | 2006 | 2007 | 2008 | 2009 | 2010 | 2011 | 2012 | 2013 | 2014 | 2015 |
|---|---|---|---|---|---|---|---|---|---|---|---|---|---|
| **Depository Corporations** | | | | | | *Millions of Patacas: End of Period* | | | | | | | |
| Net Foreign Assets.................... | 31n | 130,675.0 | 149,142.3 | 192,088.7 | 216,465.6 | 233,256.6 | 275,171.7 | 333,837.5 | 425,290.4 | 482,693.8 | 561,495.4 | 579,930.2 | 504,991.3 |
| Claims on Nonresidents............... | 31 | 155,474.8 | 203,402.9 | 266,028.9 | 320,841.7 | 359,949.4 | 441,428.2 | 562,318.4 | 704,856.3 | 794,373.0 | 957,133.3 | 1,074,431.3 | 1,117,742.2 |
| Liabilities to Nonresidents............. | 36c | 24,799.8 | 54,260.5 | 73,940.1 | 104,376.2 | 126,692.9 | 166,256.5 | 228,480.9 | 279,565.9 | 311,679.2 | 395,637.9 | 494,501.1 | 612,750.8 |
| Domestic Claims........................... | 32 | 3,348.4 | 2,293.8 | −3,438.4 | −6,801.8 | −13,699.0 | −28,143.5 | −48,023.9 | −82,134.3 | −51,229.9 | −52,526.2 | −18,234.0 | 54,798.7 |
| Net Claims on Central Government | 32an | −33,367.0 | −42,420.3 | −54,108.9 | −78,855.7 | −105,500.6 | −129,268.7 | −178,700.9 | −249,990.1 | −249,931.8 | −310,038.2 | −357,586.0 | −334,608.1 |
| Claims on Central Government.... | 32a | — | — | — | — | — | — | — | — | — | — | — | — |
| Liabilities to Central Government. | 36d | 33,367.0 | 42,420.3 | 54,108.9 | 78,855.7 | 105,500.6 | 129,268.7 | 178,700.9 | 249,990.1 | 249,931.8 | 310,038.2 | 357,586.0 | 334,608.1 |
| Claims on Other Sectors................. | 32s | 36,715.4 | 44,714.1 | 50,670.5 | 72,053.9 | 91,801.6 | 101,125.2 | 130,676.9 | 167,855.8 | 198,701.9 | 257,512.1 | 339,352.0 | 389,406.8 |
| Claims on Other Financial Corps.. | 32g | — | — | — | — | — | — | — | — | — | — | — | — |
| Claims on State & Local Govts..... | 32b | — | — | — | — | — | — | — | — | — | — | — | — |
| Claims on Public Nonfin. Corps.... | 32c | 1,947.2 | 1,947.2 | 1,975.7 | 1,947.2 | 1,947.2 | 2,084.6 | 2,150.6 | 2,026.8 | 19.4 | .6 | .6 | .6 |
| Claims on Private Sector.............. | 32d | 34,768.2 | 42,766.8 | 48,694.8 | 70,106.7 | 89,854.3 | 99,040.6 | 128,526.3 | 165,829.0 | 198,682.5 | 257,511.5 | 339,351.5 | 389,406.3 |
| Broad Money Liabilities.................. | 35l | 120,726.4 | 135,419.1 | 168,646.8 | 185,254.9 | 189,472.4 | 211,904.7 | 242,716.6 | 297,600.8 | 374,535.2 | 440,980.0 | 486,999.1 | 472,320.4 |
| Currency Outside Depository Corps | 34a | 2,552.0 | 2,733.6 | 3,138.6 | 3,639.5 | 4,082.7 | 4,577.3 | 5,077.2 | 5,717.5 | 7,068.6 | 8,551.0 | 10,388.3 | 11,534.2 |
| Transferable Deposits................... | 34 | 10,668.0 | 9,814.6 | 14,851.5 | 18,681.4 | 20,329.0 | 25,700.9 | 29,315.2 | 30,162.7 | 40,157.4 | 49,955.9 | 51,002.3 | 49,618.5 |
| Other Deposits............................. | 35 | 107,506.3 | 122,870.9 | 150,656.7 | 162,934.0 | 165,060.8 | 181,626.5 | 208,324.1 | 261,432.4 | 327,104.3 | 382,473.1 | 425,608.5 | 411,167.7 |
| Securities Other than Shares......... | 36a | — | — | — | — | — | — | 288.2 | 204.9 | — | — | — | — |
| Deposits Excl. from Broad Money..... | 36b | — | — | — | — | — | — | — | — | — | — | — | — |
| Sec.Ot.th.Shares Excl.f/Brd.Money.... | 36s | — | — | — | — | — | — | — | — | — | — | — | — |
| Loans.......................................... | 36l | — | — | — | — | — | — | — | — | — | — | — | — |
| Financial Derivatives.................... | 36m | — | — | — | — | — | — | — | — | — | — | — | — |
| Insurance Technical Reserves.......... | 36r | — | — | — | — | — | — | — | — | — | — | — | — |
| Shares and Other Equity.................. | 37a | 13,347.5 | 16,298.4 | 20,614.2 | 26,297.2 | 29,493.1 | 34,017.2 | 40,201.2 | 44,952.6 | 52,232.9 | 61,261.3 | 69,568.6 | 83,331.0 |
| Other Items (Net)........................... | 37r | −50.5 | −281.3 | −610.7 | −1,888.4 | 592.1 | 1,106.3 | 2,895.8 | 602.6 | 4,695.8 | 6,728.0 | 5,128.6 | 4,138.7 |
| Broad Money Liabs., Seasonally Adj. | 35l.b | 119,907.9 | 134,641.2 | 167,918.3 | 184,757.0 | 189,383.8 | 212,223.6 | 243,563.9 | 298,869.5 | 375,989.3 | 442,117.2 | 487,761.2 | 472,996.8 |
| **Monetary Aggregates** | | | | | | *Millions of Patacas: End of Period* | | | | | | | |
| Broad Money.............................. | 59m | 120,947.0 | 135,659.8 | 168,911.9 | 185,540.6 | 189,790.3 | 212,233.3 | 243,053.8 | 297,963.9 | 374,931.0 | 441,410.5 | 487,471.8 | 472,826.4 |
| o/w:Currency Issued by Cent.Govt | 59m.a | 220.7 | 240.7 | 265.1 | 285.6 | 317.9 | 328.6 | 337.3 | 363.1 | 395.8 | 430.6 | 472.7 | 506.0 |
| o/w: Dep.in Nonfin. Corporations. | 59m.b | — | — | — | — | — | — | — | — | — | — | — | — |
| o/w:Secs. Issued by Central Govt.. | 59m.c | — | — | — | — | — | — | — | — | — | — | — | — |
| Money (National Definitions) | | | | | | | | | | | | | |
| M1.............................................. | 59ma | 13,440.7 | 12,788.9 | 18,255.2 | 22,606.6 | 24,729.6 | 30,606.8 | 34,729.7 | 36,243.3 | 47,621.8 | 58,937.4 | 61,863.3 | 61,661.3 |
| M2.............................................. | 59mb | 120,947.0 | 135,659.8 | 168,911.9 | 185,540.6 | 189,790.3 | 212,233.3 | 243,053.8 | 297,963.9 | 374,931.0 | 441,410.5 | 487,471.8 | 472,829.0 |
| **Interest Rates** | | | | | | *Percent Per Annum* | | | | | | | |
| Money Market Rate........................ | 60b | .27 | 4.09 | 3.91 | 3.27 | .30 | .11 | .25 | .38 | .31 | .24 | .26 | .24 |
| Deposit Rate................................... | 60l | .08 | 1.58 | 2.85 | 2.85 | 1.10 | .03 | .02 | .05 | .06 | .04 | .05 | .04 |
| Lending Rate................................. | 60p | 6.01 | 7.05 | 8.76 | 7.81 | 5.43 | 5.25 | 5.25 | 5.25 | 5.25 | 5.25 | 5.25 | 5.25 |
| **Prices and Labor** | | | | | | *Index Numbers (2010=100): Period Averages* | | | | | | | |
| Consumer Prices............................ | 64 | 76.4 | 79.7 | 83.9 | 88.5 | 96.1 | 97.3 | 100.0 | 105.8 | 112.3 | 118.4 | 125.6 | 131.3 |
| | | | | | | *Number in Thousands: Period Averages* | | | | | | | |
| Labor Force.................................... | 67d | 230 | 248 | 275 | 303 | 327 | 323 | 324 | 336 | 350 | 368 | 395 | 404 |
| Employment................................... | 67e | 219 | 238 | 264 | 293 | 317 | 312 | 315 | 328 | 343 | 361 | 388 | 397 |
| Unemployment............................... | 67c | 11 | 10 | 10 | 10 | 10 | 11 | 9 | 9 | 7 | 7 | 7 | 7 |
| Unemployment Rate (%)................. | 67r | 4.9 | 4.1 | 3.8 | 3.2 | 3.0 | 3.5 | 2.8 | 2.6 | 2.0 | 1.8 | 1.7 | 1.8 |
| **Intl. Transactions & Positions** | | | | | | *Millions of US Dollars* | | | | | | | |
| Exports........................................... | 70..d | 2,811.8 | 2,475.9 | 2,557.3 | 2,542.7 | 1,997.4 | 961.0 | 869.8 | 869.4 | 1,021.3 | 1,138.3 | 1,241.4 | 1,339.0 |
| Imports, c.i.f................................... | 71..d | 3,477.9 | 3,913.4 | 4,564.8 | 5,365.6 | 5,365.4 | 4,621.9 | 5,513.3 | 7,768.5 | 8,877.4 | 10,140.6 | 11,262.1 | 10,602.8 |

| | | 2004 | 2005 | 2006 | 2007 | 2008 | 2009 | 2010 | 2011 | 2012 | 2013 | 2014 | 2015 |
|---|---|---|---|---|---|---|---|---|---|---|---|---|---|
| **Balance of Payments** | | | | | | | *Millions of US Dollars* | | | | | | |
| A. Current Account* | 109bx | 3,561.5 | 2,965.0 | 2,490.0 | 4,368.2 | 3,998.9 | 6,663.8 | 12,092.5 | 15,836.2 | 17,956.2 | 21,937.6 | 21,081.8 | .... |
| Goods, credit (exports) | 1a9cx | 2,812.3 | 2,474.5 | 2,557.2 | 2,542.4 | 2,093.0 | 1,086.2 | 1,040.2 | 1,125.6 | 1,481.8 | 1,589.0 | 1,902.7 | .... |
| Goods, debit (imports) | 1a9dx | 4,507.5 | 4,800.7 | 5,768.1 | 7,180.3 | 7,146.8 | 5,426.5 | 6,502.0 | 8,919.2 | 10,323.1 | 12,283.3 | 14,196.3 | .... |
| Balance on goods | 1a9bx | −1,695.1 | −2,326.2 | −3,210.9 | −4,637.8 | −5,053.8 | −4,340.3 | −5,461.8 | −7,793.7 | −8,841.3 | −10,694.4 | −12,293.6 | .... |
| Services, credit (exports) | 1b9cx | 8,175.5 | 8,679.3 | 10,563.8 | 14,336.9 | 18,023.8 | 18,977.3 | 29,006.7 | 39,844.3 | 45,363.9 | 53,619.2 | 53,134.3 | .... |
| Services, debit (imports) | 1b9dx | 2,325.7 | 2,546.6 | 3,154.4 | 4,712.4 | 5,969.1 | 5,143.7 | 7,628.8 | 10,657.8 | 11,465.4 | 11,885.6 | 10,641.1 | .... |
| Balance on Goods & Services | 1z9bx | 4,154.6 | 3,806.5 | 4,198.6 | 4,986.7 | 7,000.9 | 9,493.3 | 15,916.1 | 21,392.8 | 25,057.1 | 31,039.2 | 30,199.7 | .... |
| Primary income: credit | 1c9cx | 450.2 | 908.2 | 1,552.0 | 2,138.7 | 1,720.5 | 1,142.8 | 1,079.4 | 1,633.7 | 2,321.9 | 2,857.8 | 4,389.1 | .... |
| Primary income: debit | 1c9dx | 997.2 | 1,657.0 | 3,024.3 | 2,181.9 | 3,892.2 | 3,128.1 | 4,122.6 | 6,620.4 | 8,725.4 | 10,977.1 | 12,285.6 | .... |
| Balance on gds, serv. & prim. inc. | 1y9bx | 3,607.6 | 3,057.7 | 2,726.3 | 4,943.4 | 4,829.3 | 7,508.0 | 12,872.8 | 16,406.1 | 18,653.6 | 22,919.9 | 22,303.2 | .... |
| Secondary income: credit | 1d9ca | 79.2 | 83.1 | 108.1 | 94.9 | 79.8 | 87.4 | 75.0 | 73.9 | 71.1 | 82.9 | 84.1 | .... |
| Secondary income: debit | 1d9da | 125.3 | 175.9 | 344.4 | 670.1 | 910.1 | 931.5 | 855.4 | 643.9 | 768.5 | 1,065.2 | 1,305.4 | .... |
| B. Capital Account* | 209ba | 274.0 | 514.5 | 438.5 | 318.6 | 393.5 | 604.2 | 19.6 | 1,328.8 | −.3 | −.6 | −1.6 | .... |
| Capital account: credit | 209ca | 301.8 | 534.4 | 456.0 | 338.6 | 444.3 | 660.1 | 45.8 | 1,486.2 | .... | .... | .... | .... |
| Capital account: debit | 209da | 27.8 | 19.8 | 17.5 | 20.0 | 50.8 | 55.9 | 26.2 | 157.4 | .3 | .6 | 1.6 | .... |
| Balance on current & capital acct. | 129ba | 3,835.5 | 3,479.5 | 2,928.4 | 4,686.8 | 4,392.4 | 7,268.0 | 12,112.1 | 17,165.0 | 17,955.9 | 21,937.0 | 21,080.2 | .... |
| C. Financial Account* | 309na | 1,888.8 | 319.9 | 1,297.0 | −6,290.2 | −3,409.7 | 3,280.4 | 1,629.3 | 2,305.9 | 15,069.9 | 18,022.6 | 11,944.4 | .... |
| Direct investment: assets | 3a9aa | −77.0 | 65.3 | 658.7 | 302.2 | 844.7 | −593.4 | −301.9 | 322.5 | 971.2 | 2,187.3 | 1,363.8 | .... |
| Equity & investment fund shares | 3aaaa | −101.0 | 31.6 | −66.3 | 65.0 | −31.6 | 110.4 | 73.7 | 153.3 | 25.5 | 11.1 | 553.1 | .... |
| Debt instruments | 3abaa | 24.0 | 33.7 | 725.0 | 237.1 | 876.2 | −703.7 | −375.6 | 169.2 | 945.7 | 2,176.2 | 810.7 | .... |
| Direct investment: liabilities | 3a9la | 771.5 | 1,775.0 | 2,916.9 | 5,357.7 | 3,982.6 | −412.6 | 3,629.3 | 1,759.4 | 3,566.3 | 3,714.7 | 2,308.1 | .... |
| Equity & investment fund shares . | 3aala | 286.8 | 826.3 | 1,837.3 | 1,219.8 | 2,117.1 | 936.3 | 2,501.7 | 821.6 | 3,461.1 | 3,459.8 | 1,988.0 | .... |
| Debt instruments | 3abla | 484.7 | 948.7 | 1,079.6 | 4,138.0 | 1,865.6 | −1,348.9 | 1,127.6 | 937.8 | 105.2 | 254.9 | 320.1 | .... |
| Portfolio investment: assets | 3b9aa | 2,180.9 | 617.4 | 1,434.5 | 1,251.5 | 1,391.2 | 1,674.0 | 1,006.9 | 2,092.6 | 3,299.3 | 12,269.1 | 6,805.9 | .... |
| Equity & investment fund shares | 3baaa | 487.1 | 356.5 | 213.3 | 1,476.1 | 795.7 | 1,036.0 | 659.9 | 1,456.2 | −308.0 | 466.6 | 3,195.3 | .... |
| Debt securities | 3bbaa | 1,693.8 | 261.0 | 1,221.2 | −224.6 | 595.5 | 637.9 | 347.1 | 636.5 | 3,607.2 | 11,802.5 | 3,610.6 | .... |
| Portfolio investment: liabilities | 3b9la | −.3 | — | −.1 | .... | .... | −.9 | 163.1 | 213.3 | 419.5 | −175.2 | 1,141.9 | .... |
| Equity & investment fund shares . | 3bala | −.3 | — | −.1 | .... | .... | −.9 | | | | | | |
| Debt securities | 3bbla | .... | .... | .... | .... | .... | .... | 163.1 | 213.3 | 419.5 | −175.2 | 1,141.9 | .... |
| Fin. der.& empl.stk.ops.(ESOs): net | 3c9na | 583.6 | 522.5 | 211.8 | −48.0 | 29.3 | 15.2 | 8.1 | 43.7 | −124.0 | −629.4 | −540.9 | .... |
| Fin. der. & ESOs.: assets | 3c9aa | 583.6 | 522.5 | 211.8 | −48.0 | 29.3 | 15.2 | 8.1 | 43.7 | −124.0 | −629.4 | −540.9 | .... |
| Fin. der. & ESOs.: liabilities | 3c9la | .... | .... | .... | .... | .... | .... | .... | .... | .... | .... | .... | .... |
| Other investment: assets | 3d9aa | 510.2 | 4,495.6 | 6,008.7 | 3,972.6 | 2,693.4 | 7,981.5 | 9,982.4 | 8,277.0 | 19,094.2 | 18,457.9 | 17,562.5 | .... |
| Other equity | 3daaa | .... | .... | .... | .... | .... | .... | .... | .... | 2.7 | 292.0 | 645.5 | .... |
| Debt instruments | 3dzaa | 510.2 | 4,495.6 | 6,008.7 | 3,972.6 | 2,693.4 | 7,981.5 | 9,982.4 | 8,277.0 | 19,091.5 | 18,165.9 | 16,917.0 | .... |
| Other investment: liabilities | 3d9la | 537.6 | 3,605.9 | 4,099.9 | 6,410.8 | 4,385.7 | 6,210.5 | 5,273.8 | 6,457.4 | 4,185.0 | 10,722.9 | 9,796.9 | .... |
| Other equity | 3dala | .... | .... | .... | .3 | 2.9 | .4 | 1.3 | — | — | .1 | −.5 | .... |
| Debt instruments | 3dzla | 537.6 | 3,605.9 | 4,099.9 | 6,410.5 | 4,382.8 | 6,210.0 | 5,272.5 | 6,457.3 | 4,185.0 | 10,722.8 | 9,797.5 | .... |
| Curr.+ cap.− finan. acct. balance | 4y9na | 1,946.7 | 3,159.6 | 1,631.5 | 10,977.1 | 7,802.1 | 3,987.6 | 10,482.8 | 14,859.2 | 2,886.0 | 3,914.4 | 9,135.8 | .... |
| D. Net Errors and Omissions | 409na | −922.3 | −2,033.8 | 426.7 | −7,470.1 | −5,527.7 | −1,872.9 | −5,325.0 | −4,680.4 | 884.7 | −4,486.0 | −9,058.5 | .... |
| E. Reserves and Related Items | 4z9na | 1,024.3 | 1,125.8 | 2,058.2 | 3,507.0 | 2,274.4 | 2,114.7 | 5,157.8 | 10,178.8 | 3,770.7 | −571.6 | 77.3 | .... |
| Reserve assets | 3e9aa | 1,024.3 | 1,125.8 | 2,058.2 | 3,507.0 | 2,274.4 | 2,114.7 | 5,157.8 | 10,178.8 | 3,770.7 | −571.6 | 77.3 | .... |
| Credit and loans from the IMF | 3dcla | .... | .... | .... | .... | .... | .... | .... | .... | .... | .... | .... | .... |
| Exceptional financing | 409la | .... | .... | .... | .... | .... | .... | .... | .... | .... | .... | .... | .... |

*Excludes components in group E

**Government Finance**
**Cash Flow Statement**
**General Government**

| | | 2004 | 2005 | 2006 | 2007 | 2008 | 2009 | 2010 | 2011 | 2012 | 2013 | 2014 | 2015 |
|---|---|---|---|---|---|---|---|---|---|---|---|---|---|
| | | | | | | *Millions of Patacas: Fiscal Year Ends December 31* | | | | | | | |
| Cash Receipts:Operating Activities | c1 | 25,054.2 | 23,817.2 | 29,073.6 | 42,231.8 | 55,930.9 | 56,673.5 | 82,564.0 | 117,739.2 | 134,335.3 | 157,531.4 | 163,391.9 | .... |
| Taxes | c11 | 22,412.4 | 20,438.2 | 25,153.4 | 37,035.5 | 50,989.5 | 50,514.2 | 77,716.8 | 110,565.5 | 126,998.9 | 149,823.7 | 153,863.8 | .... |
| Social Contributions | c12 | 131.6 | 118.4 | 137.1 | 142.0 | 164.5 | 172.2 | 157.2 | 304.6 | 180.7 | 180.6 | 184.7 | .... |
| Grants | c13 | — | — | — | — | — | — | — | — | — | — | — | .... |
| Other Receipts | c14 | 2,510.3 | 3,260.6 | 3,783.1 | 5,054.4 | 4,776.8 | 5,987.2 | 4,690.0 | 6,869.1 | 7,155.7 | 7,527.2 | 9,343.4 | .... |
| Cash Payments:Operating Activities. | c2 | 12,238.6 | 11,262.2 | 12,931.8 | 14,953.6 | 23,078.1 | 29,395.4 | 33,231.3 | 35,451.5 | 37,629.5 | 43,112.8 | 49,857.7 | .... |
| Compensation of Employees | c21 | 6,089.1 | 5,544.6 | 5,861.5 | 6,475.4 | 7,847.5 | 8,401.7 | 9,150.3 | 10,718.2 | 11,943.9 | 13,204.0 | 14,921.8 | .... |
| Purchases of Goods & Services | c22 | 2,376.1 | 2,493.1 | 2,849.3 | 3,096.4 | 3,837.6 | 4,766.4 | 5,006.1 | 5,829.8 | 6,940.6 | 7,555.6 | 8,769.1 | .... |
| Interest | c24 | — | — | — | — | — | — | — | — | — | — | — | .... |
| Subsidies | c25 | 485.9 | 465.1 | 690.0 | 997.3 | 2,307.2 | 2,489.7 | 2,610.7 | 2,706.7 | 2,708.2 | 2,288.2 | 2,407.0 | .... |
| Grants | c26 | 6.8 | 7.9 | 5.8 | 44.6 | 758.1 | 2,746.6 | 2,465.1 | 1,019.2 | 118.3 | 156.9 | 166.9 | .... |
| Social Benefits | c27 | 1,284.8 | 729.8 | 852.1 | 700.8 | 1,072.2 | 1,350.6 | 2,135.0 | 9,061.3 | 10,137.3 | 12,014.9 | 13,797.5 | .... |
| Other Payments | c28 | 1,995.8 | 2,021.7 | 2,673.1 | 3,639.1 | 7,255.4 | 9,640.3 | 11,864.1 | 6,116.2 | 5,781.2 | 7,893.2 | 9,795.5 | .... |
| Net Cash Inflow:Operating Act.[1-2] | ccio | 12,815.7 | 12,555.0 | 16,141.8 | 27,278.2 | 32,852.8 | 27,278.1 | 49,332.6 | 82,287.7 | 96,705.8 | 114,418.6 | 113,534.2 | .... |
| Net Cash Outflow:Invest. in NFA | c31 | 3,541.8 | 4,454.8 | 4,549.5 | 3,736.9 | 3,376.1 | 4,241.0 | 5,477.2 | 9,400.9 | 13,951.2 | 3,306.2 | 7,587.0 | .... |
| Purchases of Nonfinancial Assets | c31.1 | 3,590.8 | 4,500.4 | 4,597.3 | 3,773.5 | 3,413.4 | 4,244.8 | 5,586.8 | 9,642.3 | 14,732.4 | 7,987.5 | 8,085.1 | .... |
| Sales of Nonfinancial Assets | c31.2 | 49.0 | 45.7 | 47.8 | 36.6 | 37.4 | 3.8 | 109.6 | 241.4 | 781.2 | 4,681.4 | 498.0 | .... |
| Cash Surplus/Deficit [1-2-31=1-2M] | ccsd | 9,273.8 | 8,100.2 | 11,592.3 | 23,541.3 | 29,476.8 | 23,037.1 | 43,855.4 | 72,886.8 | 82,754.6 | 111,112.4 | 105,947.2 | .... |
| Net Acq. Fin. Assets, excl. Cash | c32x | 364.3 | 145.2 | 197.1 | 951.6 | 910.9 | 754.0 | −902.2 | 1,521.6 | 2,374.1 | 1,157.4 | 770.7 | .... |
| Domestic | c321x | 364.3 | 145.2 | 197.1 | 951.6 | 910.9 | 754.0 | −902.2 | 1,521.6 | 2,374.1 | 1,157.4 | 770.7 | .... |
| Foreign | c322x | — | — | — | — | — | — | — | — | — | — | — | .... |
| Net Incurrence of Liabilities | c33 | — | — | — | — | — | — | — | — | — | — | — | .... |
| Domestic | c331 | — | — | — | — | — | — | — | — | — | — | — | .... |
| Foreign | c332 | — | — | — | — | — | — | — | — | — | — | — | .... |
| Net Cash Inflow, Fin.Act.[-32x+33] | cnfb | −364.3 | −145.2 | −197.1 | −951.6 | −910.9 | −754.0 | 902.2 | −1,521.6 | −2,374.1 | −1,157.4 | −770.7 | .... |
| Net Change in Stock of Cash | cncb | 8,909.5 | 7,955.0 | 11,395.2 | 22,589.7 | 28,565.9 | 22,283.1 | 44,757.6 | 71,365.2 | 80,380.5 | 109,955.1 | 105,176.4 | .... |
| Stat. Discrep. [32X-33+NCB-CSD] | ccsdz | — | — | — | — | — | — | — | — | — | — | — | .... |
| Memo Item:Cash Expenditure[2+31] | c2m | 15,780.4 | 15,716.9 | 17,481.3 | 18,690.6 | 26,454.1 | 33,636.3 | 38,708.5 | 44,852.4 | 51,580.7 | 46,419.0 | 57,444.7 | .... |
| Memo Item: Gross Debt | c63 | .... | .... | .... | .... | .... | .... | .... | .... | .... | .... | .... | .... |

# China, P.R.: Macao   546

| | | 2004 | 2005 | 2006 | 2007 | 2008 | 2009 | 2010 | 2011 | 2012 | 2013 | 2014 | 2015 |
|---|---|---|---|---|---|---|---|---|---|---|---|---|---|
| National Accounts | | | | | | | *Millions of Patacas* | | | | | | | |
| Househ.Cons.Expend.,incl.NPISHs.... | 96f | 28,289.0 | 30,905.0 | 34,384.0 | 40,134.0 | 46,496.0 | 48,041.0 | 52,614.0 | 61,974.0 | 70,017.0 | 79,116.0 | 88,406.0 | 94,766.0 |
| Government Consumption Expend... | 91f | 8,213.0 | 9,527.0 | 10,374.0 | 12,943.0 | 14,706.0 | 16,612.0 | 18,414.0 | 20,950.0 | 23,691.0 | 26,766.0 | 31,132.0 | 34,947.0 |
| Gross Fixed Capital Formation.......... | 93e | 13,087.0 | 24,230.0 | 38,854.0 | 53,265.0 | 49,965.0 | 31,676.0 | 28,200.0 | 36,409.0 | 46,647.0 | 54,928.0 | 83,227.0 | 85,290.0 |
| Changes in Inventories.................... | 93i | 634.0 | 648.0 | 1,040.0 | 892.0 | 1,309.0 | 220.0 | 1,738.0 | 4,282.0 | 3,897.0 | 2,967.0 | 4,060.0 | 3,818.0 |
| Exports of Goods and Services.......... | 90c | 80,917.0 | 82,205.0 | 93,479.0 | 116,889.0 | 134,397.0 | 135,322.0 | 197,573.0 | 266,895.0 | 313,215.0 | 373,281.0 | 375,477.0 | 286,824.0 |
| Imports of Goods and Services (-)..... | 98c | 46,219.0 | 50,642.0 | 59,793.0 | 76,739.0 | 79,113.0 | 60,404.0 | 73,488.0 | 69,164.0 | 113,671.0 | 125,219.0 | 138,835.0 | 136,917.0 |
| Gross Domestic Product (GDP).......... | 99b | 84,920.0 | 96,872.0 | 118,338.0 | 147,382.0 | 167,760.0 | 171,467.0 | 225,051.0 | 294,347.0 | 343,795.0 | 411,839.0 | 443,468.0 | 368,728.0 |
| GDP Volume 2002 Prices................. | 99b.p | 79,681.7 | 85,193.5 | 99,244.7 | 125,034.6 | 141,993.4 | 143,240.7 | 198,346.4 | .... | .... | | | |
| GDP Volume 2010 Ref., Chained..... | 99b.p | .... | .... | .... | .... | .... | .... | 238,949.2 | 276,449.0 | 303,951.0 | | | |
| GDP Volume 2011 Ref., Chained..... | 99b.p | .... | .... | .... | .... | .... | .... | .... | 293,745.0 | 320,591.0 | 358,704.0 | .... | .... |
| GDP Volume 2013 Ref., Chained..... | 99b.p | 151,535.0 | 163,748.0 | 185,550.0 | 212,357.0 | 219,564.0 | 222,465.0 | 278,668.0 | 339,063.0 | 370,357.0 | 411,839.0 | 408,330.0 | 325,240.0 |
| GDP Volume (2010=100)............... | 99bvp | 54.4 | 58.8 | 66.6 | 76.2 | 78.8 | 79.8 | 100.0 | 121.7 | 132.9 | 147.8 | 146.5 | 116.7 |
| GDP Deflator (2010=100)............... | 99bip | 69.4 | 73.3 | 79.0 | 85.9 | 94.6 | 95.4 | 100.0 | 107.5 | 114.9 | 123.8 | 134.5 | 140.4 |
| | | | | | | | *Millions: Midyear Estimates* | | | | | | | |
| Population................................ | 99z | .46 | .47 | .48 | .49 | .51 | .52 | .53 | .55 | .56 | .57 | .58 | .59 |

# Colombia 233

| | | 2004 | 2005 | 2006 | 2007 | 2008 | 2009 | 2010 | 2011 | 2012 | 2013 | 2014 | 2015 |
|---|---|---|---|---|---|---|---|---|---|---|---|---|---|
| **Exchange Rates** | | | | | | | *Pesos per SDR: End of Period* | | | | | | | |
| Principal Rate............................ | aa | 3,746.0 | 3,264.8 | 3,348.0 | 3,141.2 | 3,385.7 | 3,204.7 | 3,064.5 | 2,982.6 | 2,722.7 | 2,960.7 | 3,466.2 | 4,364.3 |
| | | | | | *Pesos per US Dollar: End of Period (ae) Period Average (rf)* | | | | | | | | |
| Principal Rate............................ | ae | 2,412.1 | 2,284.2 | 2,225.4 | 1,987.8 | 2,198.1 | 2,044.2 | 1,989.9 | 1,942.7 | 1,771.5 | 1,922.6 | 2,392.5 | 3,149.5 |
| Principal Rate............................ | rf | 2,628.6 | 2,320.8 | 2,361.1 | 2,078.3 | 1,967.7 | 2,158.3 | 1,898.6 | 1,848.1 | 1,796.9 | 1,868.8 | 2,001.8 | 2,741.9 |
| | | | | | *Index Numbers (2010=100): Period Averages* | | | | | | | | |
| Principal Rate............................ | ahx | 72.2 | 81.7 | 80.5 | 91.5 | 97.4 | 88.6 | 100.0 | 102.7 | 105.6 | 101.6 | 95.1 | 69.9 |
| Nominal Effective Exchange Rate..... | nec | 74.7 | 83.7 | 81.8 | 90.0 | 93.4 | 88.7 | 100.0 | 104.1 | 110.3 | 110.3 | 105.9 | 85.0 |
| CPI-Based Real Effect. Ex. Rate........ | rec | 74.1 | 83.6 | 82.0 | 91.2 | 94.9 | 90.7 | 100.0 | 102.1 | 106.8 | 103.7 | 96.4 | 75.6 |
| **Fund Position** | | | | | | | *Millions of SDRs: End of Period* | | | | | | | |
| Quota............................................ | 2f.s | 774.00 | 774.00 | 774.00 | 774.00 | 774.00 | 774.00 | 774.00 | 774.00 | 774.00 | 774.00 | 774.00 | 774.00 |
| SDR Holdings.............................. | 1b.s | 116.51 | 120.71 | 128.47 | 138.98 | 148.42 | 755.35 | 751.39 | 742.83 | 736.06 | 732.62 | 723.54 | 714.50 |
| Reserve Position in the Fund........... | 1c.s | 285.80 | 285.80 | 285.80 | 285.80 | 285.80 | 258.67 | 168.68 | 240.73 | 255.28 | 281.34 | 287.39 | 242.44 |
| Total Fund Cred.&Loans Outstg....... | 2tl | — | — | — | — | — | — | — | — | — | — | — | — |
| SDR Allocations............................. | 1bd | 114.27 | 114.27 | 114.27 | 114.27 | 114.27 | 738.32 | 738.32 | 738.32 | 738.32 | 738.32 | 738.32 | 738.32 |
| **International Liquidity** | | | | | | *Millions of US Dollars Unless Otherwise Indicated: End of Period* | | | | | | | | |
| Total Reserves minus Gold.............. | 1l.d | 13,394 | 14,787 | 15,296 | 20,767 | 23,479 | 24,748 | 27,766 | 31,386 | 36,444 | 42,758 | 46,408 | 46,104 |
| SDR Holdings.............................. | 1b.d | 181 | 173 | 193 | 220 | 229 | 1,184 | 1,157 | 1,140 | 1,131 | 1,128 | 1,048 | 990 |
| Reserve Position in the Fund......... | 1c.d | 444 | 408 | 430 | 452 | 440 | 406 | 260 | 370 | 392 | 433 | 416 | 336 |
| Foreign Exchange........................ | 1d.d | 12,769 | 14,206 | 14,673 | 20,096 | 22,810 | 23,158 | 26,349 | 29,876 | 34,920 | 41,196 | 44,943 | 44,778 |
| Gold (Million Fine Troy Ounces)....... | 1ad | .327 | .327 | .222 | .221 | .221 | .221 | .221 | .333 | .333 | .333 | .333 | .112 |
| Gold (National Valuation)............... | 1and | 143 | 168 | 141 | 185 | 191 | 243 | 311 | 524 | 554 | 400 | 399 | 119 |
| Central Bank: Other Assets.............. | 3..d | 525 | 537 | 565 | 576 | 939 | 957 | 974 | 1,090 | 1,186 | 1,193 | 1,175 | 1,161 |
| Central Bank: Other Liabs............... | 4..d | 190 | 260 | 219 | 223 | 343 | 349 | 526 | 891 | 315 | 3,084 | 102 | 107 |
| Other Depository Corps.: Assets....... | 7a.d | 1,375 | 1,778 | 1,906 | 1,514 | 1,875 | 1,814 | 2,683 | 3,261 | 4,768 | 6,684 | 7,197 | 10,384 |
| Other Depository Corps.: Liabs....... | 7b.d | 5,311 | 4,133 | 2,137 | 3,991 | 4,100 | 2,919 | 7,320 | 10,653 | 11,674 | 14,607 | 15,263 | 14,848 |
| Other Financial Corps.: Assets.......... | 7e.d | 2,774.91 | 4,576.57 | 7,458.88 | 8,096.31 | 7,159.88 | 9,937.22 | 11,155.44 | 12,142.49 | 16,439.10 | 18,400.00 | 22,454.51 | .... |
| Other Financial Corps.: Liabilities..... | 7f.d | 528.46 | 593.81 | 624.99 | 777.81 | 722.97 | 828.65 | 1,118.97 | 1,358.92 | 1,620.59 | 1,571.28 | 1,381.12 | .... |
| **Central Bank** | | | | | | | *Billions of Pesos: End of Period* | | | | | | | |
| Net Foreign Assets........................... | 11n | 33,014.1 | 34,818.6 | 35,264.9 | 42,880.8 | 54,660.9 | 50,526.1 | 53,265.2 | 61,750.0 | 65,356.0 | 83,091.8 | 112,111.1 | 145,823.2 |
| Claims on Nonresidents................. | 11 | 33,901.5 | 35,784.8 | 36,134.7 | 43,693.0 | 55,826.1 | 53,605.3 | 56,448.2 | 65,683.4 | 67,920.3 | 91,225.9 | 114,913.3 | 149,383.2 |
| Liabilities to Nonresidents.............. | 16c | 887.4 | 966.2 | 869.8 | 812.2 | 1,165.2 | 3,079.1 | 3,183.0 | 3,933.4 | 2,564.3 | 8,134.0 | 2,802.2 | 3,559.9 |
| Claims on Other Depository Corps.... | 12e | 2,439.3 | 3,871.3 | 6,526.2 | 5,331.6 | 1,548.4 | 462.6 | 2,511.6 | 3,618.3 | 2,451.1 | 3,991.4 | 6,866.6 | 6,906.2 |
| Net Claims on Central Government.. | 12an | −201.8 | −1,541.2 | −283.6 | −3,629.5 | −1,792.2 | 621.6 | −2,097.6 | −4,623.5 | −8,007.9 | −14,526.1 | −21,024.3 | −9,268.0 |
| Claims on Central Government....... | 12a | 991.1 | 2,613.2 | 2,461.3 | 1,352.3 | 897.1 | 3,600.7 | 1,336.4 | 1,169.6 | 912.7 | 144.7 | 19.0 | 136.4 |
| Liabilities to Central Government.... | 16d | 1,192.9 | 4,154.4 | 2,744.9 | 4,981.8 | 2,689.3 | 2,979.1 | 3,434.0 | 5,793.1 | 8,920.6 | 14,670.8 | 21,043.4 | 9,404.4 |
| Claims on Other Sectors................. | 12s | 272.2 | 365.8 | 304.4 | 246.5 | 162.3 | 158.1 | 192.0 | 316.6 | 251.6 | 309.2 | 231.9 | 175.2 |
| Claims on Other Financial Corps.... | 12g | 106.0 | 200.9 | 140.0 | 99.6 | 13.5 | 6.0 | 35.9 | 139.8 | 89.1 | 106.0 | 30.7 | 12.3 |
| Claims on State & Local Govts....... | 12b | — | — | — | — | — | — | — | — | — | — | — | — |
| Claims on Public Nonfin. Corps...... | 12c | — | — | — | — | — | — | — | — | — | — | — | — |
| Claims on Private Sector............... | 12d | 166.3 | 164.9 | 164.4 | 146.9 | 148.9 | 152.1 | 156.1 | 176.8 | 162.5 | 203.3 | 201.2 | 163.0 |
| Monetary Base............................... | 14 | 19,261.6 | 22,804.6 | 27,032.2 | 32,415.3 | 36,194.9 | 39,546.6 | 44,877.6 | 51,341.9 | 56,464.4 | 65,098.8 | 69,682.4 | 82,522.0 |
| Currency in Circulation.................. | 14a | 16,688.1 | 19,639.1 | 24,462.9 | 27,461.3 | 30,541.3 | 32,304.7 | 36,707.4 | 41,188.2 | 43,864.7 | 49,095.5 | 56,393.8 | 66,739.5 |
| Liabs. to Other Depository Corps.... | 14c | 2,537.8 | 3,149.8 | 2,552.9 | 4,930.5 | 5,642.0 | 7,231.7 | 8,123.4 | 10,124.3 | 12,572.6 | 15,909.2 | 13,205.2 | 15,711.5 |
| Liabilities to Other Sectors............. | 14d | 35.7 | 15.8 | 16.4 | 23.5 | 11.7 | 10.2 | 46.8 | 29.4 | 27.1 | 94.1 | 83.4 | 70.9 |
| Other Liabs. to Other Dep. Corps..... | 14n | 27.2 | 95.5 | 26.8 | 310.5 | 1,344.4 | 750.4 | 492.2 | 611.3 | 624.4 | 176.4 | 25.8 | 342.5 |
| Dep. & Sec. Excl. f/Monetary Base.... | 14o | 6.9 | 23.7 | 41.8 | 974.0 | 406.4 | 138.2 | 539.9 | 70.6 | 84.5 | 192.6 | 104.2 | 49.9 |
| Deposits Included in Broad Money. | 15 | — | — | — | — | — | — | — | — | — | — | — | — |
| Sec.Ot.th.Shares Incl.in Brd. Money | 16a | — | — | — | — | — | — | — | — | — | — | — | — |
| Deposits Excl. from Broad Money... | 16b | 6.8 | 23.6 | 41.8 | 973.9 | 406.4 | 138.2 | 539.9 | 70.6 | 84.5 | 192.6 | 104.2 | 49.9 |
| Sec.Ot.th.Shares Excl.f/Brd.Money.. | 16s | — | — | — | — | — | — | — | — | — | — | — | — |
| Loans............................................. | 16l | — | — | — | — | — | — | — | — | — | — | — | — |
| Financial Derivatives........................ | 16m | — | — | — | — | — | — | — | — | — | — | — | — |
| Shares and Other Equity................... | 17a | 18,022.3 | 16,419.2 | 16,646.6 | 13,217.1 | 19,045.1 | 13,841.5 | 10,614.1 | 11,585.2 | 5,714.5 | 10,475.9 | 31,981.2 | 63,076.2 |
| Other Items (Net)............................. | 17r | −1,794.2 | −1,828.6 | −1,935.4 | −2,087.7 | −2,411.2 | −2,508.2 | −2,652.7 | −2,547.7 | −2,836.9 | −3,077.4 | −3,608.3 | −2,353.9 |
| Memo Item: | | | | | | | | | | | | | |
| Total Assets...................................... | 10ra | 42,812.2 | 47,769.4 | 50,757.5 | 56,038.2 | 64,157.7 | 64,041.1 | 66,843.6 | 76,750.3 | 77,742.9 | 102,051.7 | 128,988.8 | 162,186.1 |

# Colombia 233

| | | 2004 | 2005 | 2006 | 2007 | 2008 | 2009 | 2010 | 2011 | 2012 | 2013 | 2014 | 2015 |
|---|---|---|---|---|---|---|---|---|---|---|---|---|---|
| **Other Depository Corporations** | | *Billions of Pesos: End of Period* | | | | | | | | | | | |
| Net Foreign Assets | 21n | −9,494.2 | −5,379.8 | −514.3 | −4,990.4 | −4,991.1 | −2,259.2 | −8,873.5 | −14,360.7 | −12,211.3 | −15,265.6 | −19,296.3 | −14,060.3 |
| Claims on Nonresidents | 21 | 3,315.7 | 4,061.4 | 4,242.2 | 3,051.1 | 4,206.5 | 3,707.9 | 5,136.1 | 6,335.3 | 8,431.4 | 12,878.7 | 17,218.9 | 32,703.9 |
| Liabilities to Nonresidents | 26c | 12,809.9 | 9,441.2 | 4,756.4 | 8,041.5 | 9,197.7 | 5,967.1 | 14,009.6 | 20,695.9 | 20,642.7 | 28,144.3 | 36,515.2 | 46,764.2 |
| Claims on Central Bank | 20 | 5,476.2 | 6,403.6 | 6,902.5 | 10,257.7 | 15,070.9 | 17,785.4 | 15,625.6 | 18,496.9 | 21,929.5 | 25,253.7 | 24,126.1 | 28,866.7 |
| Currency | 20a | 2,903.6 | 3,262.4 | 4,343.2 | 5,044.1 | 6,189.7 | 6,633.5 | 7,033.3 | 7,821.3 | 8,801.4 | 9,344.5 | 10,965.2 | 12,874.7 |
| Reserve Deposits and Securities | 20b | 2,572.1 | 3,140.7 | 2,558.8 | 5,212.9 | 6,955.4 | 7,971.9 | 8,592.2 | 10,675.6 | 13,128.1 | 15,909.2 | 13,160.9 | 15,992.0 |
| Other Claims | 20n | .4 | .5 | .5 | .6 | 1,925.8 | 3,180.0 | | | | | | |
| Net Claims on Central Government | 22an | 16,889.6 | 24,174.0 | 15,379.6 | 10,244.4 | 12,083.5 | 22,078.2 | 23,564.3 | 24,666.3 | 31,014.1 | 34,527.6 | 36,708.1 | 24,705.3 |
| Claims on Central Government | 22a | 24,849.1 | 31,203.8 | 22,667.3 | 20,848.2 | 22,108.9 | 31,350.9 | 33,981.0 | 36,813.2 | 43,028.9 | 47,605.5 | 49,988.6 | 43,001.0 |
| Liabilities to Central Government | 26d | 7,959.5 | 7,029.8 | 7,287.7 | 10,603.8 | 10,025.4 | 9,272.8 | 10,416.7 | 12,146.9 | 12,014.8 | 13,077.9 | 13,280.4 | 18,295.7 |
| Claims on Other Sectors | 22s | 78,271.2 | 85,359.5 | 114,658.3 | 143,154.9 | 160,564.1 | 165,121.9 | 195,132.6 | 234,396.0 | 269,319.5 | 300,408.7 | 344,488.1 | 405,652.4 |
| Claims on Other Financial Corps | 22g | 3,717.6 | 3,236.5 | 5,147.4 | 6,542.6 | 5,205.3 | 4,654.5 | 6,935.6 | 5,699.2 | 6,054.8 | 5,445.3 | 5,981.6 | 11,370.4 |
| Claims on State & Local Govts | 22b | 2,891.2 | 3,047.1 | 2,894.1 | 3,169.9 | 2,789.1 | 3,428.8 | 4,256.1 | 5,318.8 | 4,853.1 | 5,316.0 | 5,666.0 | 7,138.4 |
| Claims on Public Nonfin. Corps | 22c | 3,508.2 | 2,346.2 | 2,491.4 | 2,609.8 | 3,352.8 | 6,424.8 | 8,077.5 | 7,144.4 | 7,002.0 | 7,900.3 | 9,688.2 | 9,862.6 |
| Claims on Private Sector | 22d | 68,154.2 | 76,729.7 | 104,125.4 | 130,832.7 | 149,216.9 | 150,613.7 | 175,863.4 | 216,233.5 | 251,409.6 | 281,747.0 | 323,152.2 | 377,281.0 |
| Liabilities to Central Bank | 26g | 2,381.2 | 3,850.6 | 6,500.9 | 5,309.7 | 3,344.1 | 4,599.6 | 2,507.9 | 3,635.3 | 2,470.8 | 4,006.3 | 6,879.1 | 10,030.5 |
| Transf.Dep.Included in Broad Money | 24 | 13,781.7 | 16,363.8 | 18,748.2 | 20,920.1 | 23,064.2 | 24,786.1 | 29,743.7 | 33,147.5 | 36,667.6 | 43,820.4 | 46,410.3 | 47,242.9 |
| Other Dep.Included in Broad Money | 25 | 32,038.8 | 39,820.4 | 48,317.5 | 54,175.5 | 58,409.5 | 66,134.6 | 78,180.1 | 95,573.2 | 109,695.5 | 128,805.0 | 137,612.3 | 155,717.2 |
| Sec.Ot.th.Shares Incl.in Brd.Money | 26a | 29,164.0 | 31,886.5 | 36,017.6 | 47,106.4 | 65,538.9 | 68,579.6 | 68,754.7 | 83,340.9 | 103,453.4 | 111,567.9 | 124,285.7 | 137,334.4 |
| Deposits Excl. from Broad Money | 26b | 651.9 | 680.4 | 751.9 | 855.9 | 940.7 | 1,038.3 | 1,067.6 | 1,176.3 | 1,439.5 | 1,342.7 | 1,776.1 | 860.7 |
| Sec.Ot.th.Shares Excl.f/Brd.Money | 26s | 153.6 | 40.1 | 32.1 | 95.3 | 104.5 | 71.2 | 2,352.1 | 68.4 | 183.0 | 139.6 | 437.9 | 3,491.6 |
| Loans | 26l | 3,447.7 | 4,126.5 | 3,973.3 | 5,030.7 | 5,434.8 | 6,587.3 | 6,509.7 | 6,873.6 | 8,505.4 | 7,610.3 | 7,716.0 | 10,208.5 |
| Financial Derivatives | 26m | 2,997.8 | 3,359.0 | 8,344.9 | 1,879.2 | 1,290.6 | 4,411.5 | 756.3 | 706.2 | 974.7 | 609.8 | 3,571.6 | 3,989.3 |
| Insurance Technical Reserves | 26r | — | — | — | — | — | — | — | — | — | — | — | — |
| Shares and Other Equity | 27a | 16,119.8 | 19,366.4 | 21,219.4 | 25,039.5 | 28,829.6 | 35,267.7 | 40,301.9 | 48,310.9 | 56,936.3 | 65,710.1 | 74,841.2 | 79,071.0 |
| Other Items (Net) | 27r | −9,593.8 | −8,936.4 | −7,479.7 | −1,746.0 | −4,229.7 | −8,749.8 | −4,725.0 | −9,633.7 | −10,274.6 | −18,687.7 | −17,504.2 | −2,781.9 |
| Memo Item: | | | | | | | | | | | | | |
| Total Assets | 20ra | 138,330.3 | 152,856.4 | 175,033.4 | 207,151.8 | 236,749.9 | 257,768.1 | 288,986.0 | 346,154.3 | 395,142.6 | 450,602.5 | 504,209.2 | 564,232.5 |
| **Depository Corporations** | | *Billions of Pesos: End of Period* | | | | | | | | | | | |
| Net Foreign Assets | 31n | 23,519.8 | 29,438.9 | 34,750.6 | 37,890.4 | 49,669.8 | 48,267.0 | 44,391.7 | 47,389.4 | 53,144.8 | 67,826.3 | 92,814.8 | 131,762.9 |
| Claims on Nonresidents | 31 | 37,217.2 | 39,846.2 | 40,376.8 | 46,744.2 | 60,032.6 | 57,313.2 | 61,584.3 | 72,018.7 | 76,351.7 | 104,104.6 | 132,132.2 | 182,087.1 |
| Liabilities to Nonresidents | 36c | 13,697.4 | 10,407.3 | 5,626.2 | 8,853.8 | 10,362.8 | 9,046.2 | 17,192.6 | 24,629.3 | 23,206.9 | 36,278.3 | 39,317.4 | 50,324.2 |
| Domestic Claims | 32 | 95,231.2 | 108,358.1 | 130,058.7 | 150,016.3 | 171,017.8 | 187,979.8 | 216,791.2 | 254,755.3 | 292,577.3 | 320,719.3 | 360,403.8 | 421,265.0 |
| Net Claims on Central Government | 32an | 16,687.8 | 22,632.8 | 15,096.0 | 6,614.9 | 10,291.4 | 22,699.8 | 21,466.7 | 20,042.8 | 23,006.2 | 20,001.4 | 15,683.8 | 15,437.3 |
| Claims on Central Government | 32a | 25,840.3 | 33,817.0 | 25,128.6 | 22,200.5 | 23,006.0 | 34,951.7 | 35,317.4 | 37,982.8 | 43,941.7 | 47,750.2 | 50,007.6 | 43,137.5 |
| Liabilities to Central Government | 36d | 9,152.5 | 11,184.2 | 10,032.6 | 15,585.6 | 12,714.7 | 12,251.9 | 13,850.7 | 17,940.1 | 20,935.5 | 27,748.7 | 34,323.8 | 27,700.1 |
| Claims on Other Sectors | 32s | 78,543.4 | 85,725.3 | 114,962.7 | 143,401.4 | 160,726.4 | 165,280.0 | 195,324.5 | 234,712.6 | 269,571.1 | 300,717.9 | 344,720.0 | 405,827.6 |
| Claims on Other Financial Corps | 32g | 3,823.5 | 3,437.3 | 5,287.4 | 6,642.1 | 5,218.8 | 4,660.5 | 6,971.4 | 5,839.1 | 6,143.9 | 5,551.3 | 6,012.3 | 11,382.7 |
| Claims on State & Local Govts | 32b | 2,891.2 | 3,047.1 | 2,894.1 | 3,169.9 | 2,789.1 | 3,428.8 | 4,256.1 | 5,318.8 | 4,853.1 | 5,316.0 | 5,666.0 | 7,138.4 |
| Claims on Public Nonfin. Corps | 32c | 3,508.2 | 2,346.2 | 2,491.4 | 2,609.8 | 3,352.8 | 6,424.8 | 8,077.5 | 7,144.4 | 7,002.0 | 7,900.3 | 9,688.2 | 9,862.6 |
| Claims on Private Sector | 32d | 68,320.5 | 76,894.6 | 104,289.8 | 130,979.6 | 149,365.8 | 150,765.9 | 176,019.5 | 216,410.3 | 251,572.1 | 281,950.3 | 323,353.4 | 377,443.9 |
| Broad Money Liabilities | 35l | 88,804.8 | 104,463.1 | 123,219.3 | 144,643.0 | 171,375.9 | 185,181.8 | 206,399.3 | 245,457.9 | 284,907.0 | 324,038.3 | 353,820.4 | 394,230.2 |
| Currency Outside Depository Corps | 34a | 13,784.5 | 16,376.6 | 20,119.7 | 22,417.2 | 24,351.6 | 25,671.2 | 29,674.1 | 33,366.9 | 35,063.3 | 39,751.0 | 45,428.6 | 53,864.8 |
| Transferable Deposits | 34 | 13,817.4 | 16,379.5 | 18,764.6 | 20,943.6 | 23,075.9 | 24,796.3 | 29,790.5 | 33,177.0 | 36,694.8 | 43,914.5 | 46,493.7 | 47,313.8 |
| Other Deposits | 35 | 32,038.8 | 39,820.4 | 48,317.5 | 54,175.5 | 58,409.5 | 66,134.6 | 78,180.1 | 95,573.2 | 109,695.5 | 128,805.0 | 137,612.3 | 155,717.2 |
| Securities Other than Shares | 36a | 29,164.0 | 31,886.5 | 36,017.6 | 47,106.4 | 65,538.9 | 68,579.6 | 68,754.7 | 83,340.9 | 103,453.4 | 111,567.9 | 124,285.7 | 137,334.4 |
| Deposits Excl. from Broad Money | 36b | 658.7 | 704.0 | 793.7 | 1,829.8 | 1,347.0 | 1,176.6 | 1,607.6 | 1,247.0 | 1,524.0 | 1,535.3 | 1,880.3 | 910.7 |
| Sec.Ot.th.Shares Excl.f/Brd.Money | 36s | 153.6 | 40.2 | 32.2 | 95.3 | 104.5 | 71.2 | 2,352.1 | 68.4 | 183.0 | 139.6 | 437.9 | 3,491.6 |
| Loans | 36l | 3,447.7 | 4,126.5 | 3,973.3 | 5,030.7 | 5,434.8 | 6,587.3 | 6,509.7 | 6,873.6 | 8,505.4 | 7,610.3 | 7,716.0 | 10,208.5 |
| Financial Derivatives | 36m | 2,997.8 | 3,359.0 | 8,344.9 | 1,879.2 | 1,290.6 | 4,411.5 | 756.3 | 706.2 | 974.7 | 609.8 | 3,571.6 | 3,989.3 |
| Insurance Technical Reserves | 36r | — | — | — | — | — | — | — | — | — | — | — | — |
| Shares and Other Equity | 37a | 34,142.1 | 35,785.6 | 37,866.0 | 38,256.7 | 47,874.7 | 49,109.2 | 50,916.0 | 59,896.1 | 62,650.8 | 76,186.0 | 106,822.4 | 142,147.2 |
| Other Items (Net) | 37r | −11,453.7 | −10,681.6 | −9,420.0 | −3,828.0 | −6,740.2 | −10,290.8 | −7,358.0 | −12,104.5 | −13,023.0 | −21,573.7 | −21,030.0 | −1,949.5 |
| Broad Money Liabs., Seasonally Adj. | 35l.b | 85,713.3 | 100,841.6 | 119,039.5 | 139,836.2 | 165,837.9 | 179,155.3 | 199,767.2 | 237,785.7 | 276,538.7 | 315,152.0 | 344,851.2 | 384,711.8 |
| **Other Financial Corporations** | | *Billions of Pesos: End of Period* | | | | | | | | | | | |
| Net Foreign Assets | 41n | 5,418.7 | 9,097.5 | 15,208.4 | 14,745.0 | 14,441.8 | 18,620.0 | 19,209.6 | 20,949.2 | 26,202.5 | 32,426.1 | 50,417.3 | .... |
| Claims on Nonresidents | 41 | 6,693.4 | 10,453.9 | 16,599.3 | 16,312.1 | 16,063.8 | 20,314.0 | 21,351.3 | 23,589.2 | 29,068.1 | 35,453.7 | 53,721.5 | .... |
| Liabilities to Nonresidents | 46c | 1,274.7 | 1,356.4 | 1,390.9 | 1,567.1 | 1,622.1 | 1,694.0 | 2,141.7 | 2,640.0 | 2,865.6 | 3,027.6 | 3,304.3 | .... |
| Claims on Depository Corporations | 40 | 19,978.6 | 26,016.2 | 28,177.6 | 35,740.1 | 45,703.9 | 54,307.3 | 58,777.7 | 67,970.2 | 86,254.7 | 90,199.0 | 99,549.0 | .... |
| Net Claims on Central Government | 42an | 30,066.7 | 38,659.5 | 47,474.1 | 49,613.9 | 66,261.4 | 73,411.5 | 81,220.6 | 86,508.4 | 95,242.4 | 99,442.0 | 99,001.6 | .... |
| Claims on Central Government | 42a | 30,920.5 | 40,174.0 | 49,686.4 | 52,525.8 | 70,015.7 | 78,809.5 | 88,309.1 | 94,287.7 | 105,572.0 | 110,285.1 | 112,075.3 | .... |
| Liabilities to Central Government | 46d | 853.8 | 1,514.5 | 2,212.3 | 2,911.9 | 3,754.3 | 5,398.0 | 7,088.5 | 7,779.3 | 10,329.6 | 10,843.1 | 13,073.8 | .... |
| Claims on Other Sectors | 42s | 17,739.4 | 24,807.0 | 26,166.7 | 33,624.6 | 34,275.2 | 56,186.9 | 68,547.1 | 68,397.1 | 80,467.2 | 81,450.6 | 83,921.1 | .... |
| Claims on State & Local Govts | 42b | 2,101.6 | 2,140.4 | 2,375.0 | 2,347.5 | 2,543.3 | 5,258.5 | 6,393.6 | 7,579.3 | 7,051.7 | 8,154.4 | 8,545.5 | .... |
| Claims on Public Nonfin. Corps | 42c | 9.7 | 7.3 | 3.9 | 6.2 | 2.2 | 15.2 | 24.8 | 20.6 | 20.1 | 32.3 | 30.7 | .... |
| Claims on Private Sector | 42d | 15,628.1 | 22,659.2 | 23,787.7 | 31,271.0 | 31,729.6 | 50,913.1 | 62,128.7 | 60,797.3 | 73,395.4 | 73,263.9 | 75,345.0 | .... |
| Deposits | 46b | 4,408.1 | 5,281.1 | 7,172.7 | 8,512.4 | 9,172.0 | 10,804.1 | 12,162.6 | 12,670.0 | 13,861.6 | 16,232.7 | 17,693.3 | .... |
| Securities Other than Shares | 46s | 6,503.3 | 6,553.2 | 6,036.9 | 5,448.0 | 5,443.8 | 5,549.2 | 5,200.2 | 5,630.9 | 5,839.8 | 7,885.4 | 7,227.7 | .... |
| Loans | 46l | 275.8 | 367.9 | 333.1 | 365.8 | 509.2 | 552.0 | 796.8 | 1,480.1 | 759.1 | 1,670.8 | 1,952.3 | .... |
| Financial Derivatives | 46m | 332.7 | 171.3 | 210.0 | 284.7 | 634.4 | 306.9 | 261.8 | 253.8 | 142.6 | 153.9 | 1,360.4 | .... |
| Insurance Technical Reserves | 46r | 45,834.8 | 62,042.1 | 78,005.9 | 91,031.4 | 110,696.5 | 141,876.5 | 166,557.9 | 178,283.4 | 213,741.1 | 222,972.1 | 245,382.2 | .... |
| Shares and Other Equity | 47a | 17,195.3 | 26,656.5 | 25,766.0 | 28,118.6 | 33,001.1 | 42,282.5 | 46,380.3 | 51,511.0 | 60,916.8 | 64,936.5 | 74,296.6 | .... |
| Other Items (Net) | 47r | −1,346.6 | −2,491.9 | −497.8 | −37.2 | 1,225.3 | 1,154.4 | −3,604.5 | −6,004.2 | −7,094.1 | −10,333.8 | −15,023.6 | .... |
| Memo Item: | | | | | | | | | | | | | |
| Total Assets | 40ra | 82,529.1 | 109,125.7 | 127,439.5 | 145,538.8 | 175,417.8 | 221,161.7 | 254,340.3 | 274,961.7 | 325,185.9 | 344,689.1 | 381,859.7 | .... |

# Colombia   233

| | | 2004 | 2005 | 2006 | 2007 | 2008 | 2009 | 2010 | 2011 | 2012 | 2013 | 2014 | 2015 |
|---|---|---|---|---|---|---|---|---|---|---|---|---|---|
| **Financial Corporations** | | | | | | *Billions of Pesos: End of Period* | | | | | | | |
| Net Foreign Assets................. | 51n | 28,938.5 | 38,536.4 | 49,959.0 | 52,635.4 | 64,111.6 | 66,887.0 | 63,601.3 | 68,338.6 | 79,347.3 | 100,252.3 | 143,232.0 | .... |
| Claims on Nonresidents............... | 51 | 43,910.6 | 50,300.1 | 56,976.1 | 63,056.3 | 76,096.4 | 77,627.2 | 82,935.6 | 95,607.9 | 105,419.8 | 139,558.3 | 185,853.7 | .... |
| Liabilities to Nonresidents............. | 56c | 14,972.1 | 11,763.7 | 7,017.1 | 10,420.9 | 11,984.9 | 10,740.2 | 19,334.3 | 27,269.3 | 26,072.5 | 39,305.9 | 42,621.7 | .... |
| Domestic Claims................. | 52 | 139,213.8 | 168,387.3 | 198,412.0 | 226,612.7 | 266,335.6 | 312,917.7 | 359,587.5 | 403,821.7 | 462,143.0 | 496,060.6 | 537,314.2 | .... |
| Net Claims on Central Government | 52an | 46,754.5 | 61,292.3 | 62,570.1 | 56,228.8 | 76,552.8 | 96,111.2 | 102,687.3 | 106,551.1 | 118,248.6 | 119,443.4 | 114,685.4 | .... |
| Claims on Central Government.... | 52a | 56,760.8 | 73,991.0 | 74,815.0 | 74,726.3 | 93,021.7 | 113,761.2 | 123,626.5 | 132,270.5 | 149,513.6 | 158,035.2 | 162,083.0 | .... |
| Liabilities to Central Government. | 56d | 10,006.2 | 12,698.7 | 12,244.9 | 18,497.5 | 16,469.0 | 17,649.9 | 20,939.2 | 25,719.4 | 31,265.1 | 38,591.8 | 47,397.6 | .... |
| Claims on Other Sectors................. | 52s | 92,459.3 | 107,094.9 | 135,841.9 | 170,383.9 | 189,782.8 | 216,806.5 | 256,900.2 | 297,270.6 | 343,894.5 | 376,617.2 | 422,628.8 | .... |
| Claims on State & Local Govts..... | 52b | 4,992.8 | 5,187.6 | 5,269.2 | 5,517.4 | 5,332.4 | 8,687.3 | 10,649.7 | 12,898.1 | 11,904.8 | 13,470.5 | 14,211.5 | .... |
| Claims on Public Nonfin. Corps.... | 52c | 3,517.9 | 2,353.5 | 2,495.3 | 2,616.0 | 3,355.0 | 6,440.1 | 8,102.3 | 7,164.9 | 7,022.2 | 7,932.6 | 9,718.9 | .... |
| Claims on Private Sector............. | 52d | 83,948.6 | 99,553.9 | 128,077.5 | 162,250.5 | 181,095.4 | 201,679.0 | 238,148.2 | 277,207.6 | 324,967.4 | 355,214.1 | 398,698.4 | .... |
| Currency Outside Financial Corps..... | 54c | 13,756.6 | 16,345.0 | 20,080.6 | 22,381.0 | 24,294.2 | 25,632.7 | 29,641.6 | 33,331.0 | 35,031.9 | 39,718.0 | 45,392.1 | .... |
| Deposits................. | 55l | 48,477.5 | 58,862.4 | 70,844.1 | 79,010.9 | 83,905.2 | 92,941.9 | 107,982.4 | 129,041.5 | 145,021.1 | 171,849.8 | 183,794.8 | .... |
| Securities Other than Shares............ | 56a | 24,351.3 | 25,825.8 | 30,267.2 | 38,231.2 | 52,985.6 | 56,269.0 | 34,396.7 | 46,266.5 | 45,908.8 | 53,224.0 | 60,536.2 | .... |
| Loans................. | 56l | 468.8 | 411.4 | 415.7 | 206.5 | 636.7 | 750.3 | 197.8 | 205.4 | 232.1 | 255.3 | 381.6 | .... |
| Financial Derivatives................. | 56m | 2,851.7 | 1,594.9 | 4,674.4 | 1,881.9 | 1,173.6 | 2,465.4 | 634.6 | 608.7 | 554.4 | 382.4 | 3,121.7 | .... |
| Insurance Technical Reserves........... | 56r | 45,834.8 | 62,042.1 | 78,005.9 | 91,031.4 | 110,696.5 | 141,876.5 | 166,557.9 | 178,283.4 | 213,741.1 | 222,972.1 | 245,382.2 | .... |
| Shares and Other Equity................. | 57a | 51,337.4 | 62,442.1 | 63,632.0 | 66,375.3 | 80,875.8 | 91,391.7 | 97,296.3 | 111,407.1 | 123,567.7 | 141,122.6 | 181,119.0 | .... |
| Other Items (Net)................. | 57r | −18,925.8 | −20,600.0 | −19,548.9 | −19,870.1 | −24,120.4 | −31,522.8 | −13,518.7 | −26,983.4 | −22,566.7 | −33,211.2 | −39,181.4 | .... |
| **Monetary Aggregates** | | | | | | *Billions of Pesos: End of Period* | | | | | | | |
| Broad Money................. | 59m | 88,804.8 | 104,463.1 | 123,219.3 | 144,643.0 | 171,375.9 | 185,181.8 | 206,399.3 | 245,457.9 | 284,907.0 | 324,038.3 | 353,820.4 | 394,230.2 |
| o/w:Currency Issued by Cent.Govt | 59m.a | — | — | — | — | — | — | — | — | — | — | — | — |
| o/w: Dep.in Nonfin. Corporations. | 59m.b | — | — | — | — | — | — | — | — | — | — | — | — |
| o/w:Secs. Issued by Central Govt.. | 59m.c | — | — | — | — | — | — | — | — | — | — | — | — |
| Money (National Definitions) | | | | | | | | | | | | | |
| Reserve Money............................. | 19mb | 19,260.2 | 22,804.0 | 27,031.8 | 32,415.1 | 36,193.8 | 39,544.7 | 44,872.7 | 51,336.4 | 56,459.1 | 65,090.9 | 69,668.4 | 82,518.9 |
| M1................................. | 59ma | 29,124.1 | 34,381.5 | 40,738.0 | 45,518.9 | 49,281.9 | 52,672.3 | 62,053.9 | 68,860.2 | 73,727.4 | 85,838.2 | 93,947.9 | 103,214.3 |
| M2................................. | 59mb | 88,455.6 | 104,109.8 | 122,246.8 | 143,855.1 | 167,991.1 | 177,753.9 | 195,850.9 | 232,818.0 | 270,767.0 | 311,488.4 | 337,992.8 | 382,783.2 |
| M3................................. | 59mc | 97,839.1 | 113,448.4 | 132,721.1 | 156,821.5 | 183,460.6 | 197,492.2 | 219,829.4 | 259,929.7 | 300,208.6 | 341,304.2 | 371,418.5 | 416,937.3 |
| **Interest Rates** | | | | | | *Percent Per Annum* | | | | | | | |
| Central Bank Policy Rate (EOP)........ | 60 | 6.50 | 6.00 | 7.50 | 9.50 | 9.50 | 3.50 | 3.00 | 4.75 | 4.25 | 3.25 | 4.50 | 5.75 |
| Discount Rate (End of Period).......... | 60.a | 11.25 | 10.75 | 9.50 | 11.50 | 11.50 | 5.50 | 5.00 | 6.75 | 6.50 | 5.25 | 6.50 | 7.75 |
| Money Market Rate........................ | 60b | 7.01 | 6.18 | 6.49 | 8.66 | 9.72 | 5.65 | 3.15 | 4.03 | 5.01 | 3.41 | 3.85 | 4.69 |
| Deposit Rate.................................. | 60l | 7.80 | 7.01 | 6.28 | 8.01 | 9.74 | 6.15 | 3.66 | 4.26 | 5.36 | 4.17 | 4.09 | 4.58 |
| Lending Rate................................. | 60p | 15.08 | 14.56 | 12.89 | 15.38 | 17.18 | 13.01 | 9.38 | 11.22 | 12.59 | 10.99 | 10.87 | 11.45 |
| **Prices, Production, Labor** | | | | | | *Index Numbers (2010=100): Period Averages* | | | | | | | |
| Share Prices (End of Month)............ | 62.ep | 24.78 | 46.44 | 74.85 | 79.45 | 65.96 | 72.55 | 100.00 | 101.51 | 107.07 | 102.54 | 98.69 | 72.87 |
| Producer Prices............................... | 63 | 82.9 | 85.5 | 89.1 | 90.0 | 96.5 | 98.3 | 100.0 | 105.5 | 105.8 | 104.2 | 107.6 | 114.7 |
| Consumer Prices............................. | 64 | 75.8 | 79.7 | 83.1 | 87.7 | 93.8 | 97.8 | 100.0 | 103.4 | 106.7 | 108.9 | 112.0 | 117.6 |
| Manufacturing Prod. (2000=100).... | 66ey | 111.1 | .... | .... | .... | .... | .... | .... | .... | .... | .... | .... | .... |
| Crude Petroleum Production............ | 66aa | 65.8 | 67.4 | 68.1 | 67.1 | 73.6 | 86.4 | 100.0 | 117.3 | 121.3 | 128.7 | 126.1 | 128.4 |
| **Intl. Transactions & Positions** | | | | | | *Number in Thousands: Period Averages* | | | | | | | |
| Labor Force.................................... | 67d | 19,286 | 19,329 | 19,209 | 19,280 | 19,664 | 20,941 | 21,776 | 22,446 | 23,091 | 23,292 | 23,662 | 24,130 |
| Employment.................................... | 67e | 16,655 | 17,049 | 16,898 | 17,125 | 17,448 | 18,427 | 19,215 | 20,020 | 20,696 | 21,048 | 21,512 | 21,973 |
| Unemployment.................................. | 67c | 2,632 | 2,279 | 2,311 | 2,155 | 2,216 | 2,514 | 2,561 | 2,426 | 2,394 | 2,243 | 2,150 | 2,157 |
| Unemployment Rate (%).................. | 67r | 13.6 | 11.8 | 12.1 | 11.2 | 11.3 | 12.0 | 11.8 | 10.8 | 10.4 | 9.6 | 9.1 | 9.0 |
| **Intl. Transactions & Positions** | | | | | | *Millions of US Dollars* | | | | | | | |
| Exports............................................ | 70..d | 16,223.5 | 21,145.7 | 24,387.7 | 29,785.9 | 38,265.2 | 32,783.9 | 39,709.9 | 56,507.3 | 59,573.3 | 58,657.1 | 54,788.0 | 35,606.3 |
| Coffee......................................... | 70e.d | 949.9 | 1,470.6 | 1,461.3 | 1,714.3 | 1,883.2 | 1,534.5 | 1,882.1 | 2,591.5 | 1,909.6 | 1,883.9 | 2,473.4 | .... |
| Imports, c.i.f................................. | 71..d | 16,745.7 | 21,204.4 | 26,046.1 | 33,164.1 | 39,320.2 | 32,897.5 | 40,682.8 | 54,675.0 | 58,632.5 | 59,396.9 | 64,060.2 | 54,057.6 |
| Imports, f.o.b................................. | 71.vd | 15,629.2 | 19,798.8 | 24,534.0 | 30,815.6 | 37,155.3 | 31,187.7 | 38,350.6 | 51,997.9 | 55,574.0 | 56,622.0 | 61,117.3 | 51,598.0 |
| Volume of Exports | | | | | | *2010=100* | | | | | | | |
| Coffee......................................... | 72e | 134.6 | 139.0 | 139.7 | 150.8 | 141.7 | 100.9 | 100.0 | 98.8 | 91.7 | 123.7 | 140.2 | .... |
| Export Prices in Pesos (2005=100)... | 76 | 98.3 | 100.0 | 109.3 | 104.9 | 120.9 | 126.3 | .... | .... | .... | .... | .... | .... |
| Import Prices in Pesos (2005=100).. | 76.x | 103.2 | 100.0 | 102.0 | 92.4 | 92.1 | 94.5 | .... | .... | .... | .... | .... | .... |
| Export Prices | | | | | | *2010=100: Indices of Prices in US Dollars* | | | | | | | |
| Coffee......................................... | 76e.d | 36.6 | 52.3 | 52.9 | 56.6 | 65.2 | 80.8 | 100.0 | 126.8 | 91.1 | 66.3 | 88.4 | .... |

# Colombia 233

| | | 2004 | 2005 | 2006 | 2007 | 2008 | 2009 | 2010 | 2011 | 2012 | 2013 | 2014 | 2015 |
|---|---|---|---|---|---|---|---|---|---|---|---|---|---|
| **Balance of Payments** | | | | | | | *Millions of US Dollars* | | | | | | |
| A. Current Account* | 109bx | −782.0 | −1,892.4 | −2,911.2 | −6,008.9 | −6,460.9 | −4,647.8 | −8,662.5 | −9,710.0 | −11,132.0 | −12,325.5 | −19,593.1 | −18,925.0 |
| Goods, credit (exports) | 1a9cx | 17,194.9 | 21,708.4 | 25,165.5 | 30,555.9 | 38,475.8 | 33,977.3 | 40,762.0 | 58,262.4 | 61,604.1 | 60,281.4 | 56,922.9 | 38,124.9 |
| Goods, debit (imports) | 1a9dx | 15,838.5 | 20,094.4 | 24,810.0 | 31,116.3 | 37,511.4 | 31,428.1 | 38,405.8 | 52,125.5 | 56,648.3 | 57,100.9 | 61,553.0 | 52,150.6 |
| Balance on goods | 1a9bx | 1,356.4 | 1,614.0 | 355.5 | −560.4 | 964.4 | 2,549.3 | 2,356.2 | 6,136.9 | 4,955.8 | 3,180.5 | −4,630.0 | −14,025.7 |
| Services, credit (exports) | 1b9cx | 2,452.9 | 2,995.3 | 3,751.2 | 3,975.6 | 4,575.9 | 4,581.8 | 5,112.9 | 5,635.9 | 6,430.2 | 6,859.3 | 6,875.7 | 7,265.3 |
| Services, debit (imports) | 1b9dx | 4,251.4 | 5,318.5 | 6,041.1 | 6,824.7 | 7,902.0 | 7,981.5 | 9,362.5 | 10,837.7 | 12,246.5 | 12,802.2 | 13,558.2 | 11,246.6 |
| Balance on Goods & Services | 1z9bx | −442.0 | −709.1 | −1,934.4 | −3,409.4 | −2,361.8 | −850.5 | −1,893.4 | 935.1 | −860.5 | −2,762.5 | −11,312.5 | −18,007.0 |
| Primary income: credit | 1c9cx | 660.9 | 1,083.5 | 1,575.1 | 1,931.3 | 1,957.4 | 1,605.8 | 1,674.0 | 2,780.2 | 3,854.5 | 3,626.8 | 3,999.2 | 4,438.5 |
| Primary income: debit | 1c9dx | 4,725.2 | 6,348.6 | 7,266.1 | 9,683.7 | 11,511.1 | 9,961.3 | 12,890.7 | 18,259.5 | 18,705.3 | 17,783.4 | 16,637.4 | 10,427.2 |
| Balance on gds, serv. & prim. inc. | 1y9bx | −4,506.3 | −5,974.3 | −7,625.4 | −11,161.8 | −11,915.5 | −9,206.0 | −13,110.1 | −14,544.3 | −15,711.3 | −16,919.1 | −23,950.7 | −23,995.7 |
| Secondary income: credit | 1d9ca | 3,993.8 | 4,342.2 | 5,008.1 | 5,578.7 | 5,840.7 | 5,197.8 | 5,315.5 | 5,569.6 | 5,394.4 | 5,473.4 | 5,305.6 | 5,847.9 |
| Secondary income: debit | 1d9da | 269.5 | 260.3 | 293.9 | 425.8 | 386.1 | 639.5 | 867.9 | 735.4 | 815.1 | 879.9 | 948.0 | 777.2 |
| B. Capital Account* | 209ba | .... | .... | .... | .... | .... | .... | .... | .... | .... | .... | .... | .... |
| Capital account: credit | 209ca | .... | .... | .... | .... | .... | .... | .... | .... | .... | .... | .... | .... |
| Capital account: debit | 209da | .... | .... | .... | .... | .... | .... | .... | .... | .... | .... | .... | .... |
| Balance on current & capital acct. | 129ba | −782.0 | −1,892.4 | −2,911.2 | −6,008.9 | −6,460.9 | −4,647.8 | −8,662.5 | −9,710.0 | −11,132.0 | −12,325.5 | −19,593.1 | −18,925.0 |
| C. Financial Account* | 309na | −3,177.4 | −3,230.8 | −2,887.3 | −10,326.3 | −9,463.8 | −6,438.4 | −12,405.1 | −12,661.7 | −17,074.8 | −18,786.5 | −24,271.7 | −19,615.1 |
| Direct investment: assets | 3a9aa | 192.4 | 4,795.5 | 1,267.8 | 1,278.8 | 3,085.1 | 3,504.7 | 5,482.7 | 8,419.8 | −606.2 | 7,652.1 | 3,899.0 | 4,217.7 |
| Equity & investment fund shares | 3aaaa | 142.4 | 4,661.9 | 1,098.3 | 912.8 | 2,486.0 | 2,807.1 | 6,892.8 | 7,254.4 | −557.1 | 7,468.2 | 2,935.5 | 5,282.6 |
| Debt instruments | 3abaa | 50.0 | 133.6 | 169.5 | 366.0 | 599.1 | 697.5 | −1,410.2 | 1,165.4 | −49.1 | 183.9 | 963.5 | −1,064.9 |
| Direct investment: liabilities | 3a9la | 3,115.6 | 10,235.4 | 6,750.6 | 8,885.8 | 10,564.7 | 8,034.6 | 6,429.9 | 14,647.8 | 15,039.4 | 16,208.7 | 16,324.5 | 12,107.6 |
| Equity & investment fund shares | 3aala | 3,083.8 | 10,266.5 | 6,687.3 | 9,006.9 | 10,518.1 | 7,303.2 | 7,065.3 | 12,776.0 | 13,800.4 | 13,840.4 | 13,831.9 | 10,101.4 |
| Debt instruments | 3abla | 31.8 | −31.1 | 63.3 | −121.1 | 46.6 | 731.4 | −635.3 | 1,871.8 | 1,238.9 | 2,368.3 | 2,492.6 | 2,006.2 |
| Portfolio investment: assets | 3b9aa | 1,564.1 | 1,694.7 | 3,656.6 | 564.1 | −67.4 | 2,906.2 | 2,290.0 | 2,111.3 | 1,666.1 | 4,095.5 | 7,006.6 | 121.5 |
| Equity & investment fund shares | 3baaa | .... | .... | .... | .... | .... | .... | .... | .... | .... | .... | .... | .... |
| Debt securities | 3bbaa | 1,564.1 | 1,694.7 | 3,656.6 | 564.1 | −67.4 | 2,906.2 | 2,290.0 | 2,111.3 | 1,666.1 | 4,095.5 | 7,006.6 | 121.5 |
| Portfolio investment: liabilities | 3b9la | 1,305.7 | −52.5 | 902.0 | 1,883.9 | −1,195.2 | 4,668.2 | 3,262.6 | 8,201.7 | 7,355.7 | 11,073.1 | 18,660.8 | 9,807.3 |
| Equity & investment fund shares | 3bala | 129.7 | 85.8 | −30.1 | 790.1 | −86.3 | 67.4 | 1,318.2 | 2,287.9 | 3,179.9 | 1,926.1 | 3,882.7 | 1,759.8 |
| Debt securities | 3bbla | 1,176.0 | −138.3 | 932.1 | 1,093.8 | −1,108.9 | 4,600.8 | 1,944.4 | 5,913.8 | 4,175.8 | 9,147.0 | 14,778.1 | 8,047.5 |
| Fin. der.& empl.stk.ops.(ESOs): net. | 3c9na | 190.0 | 62.0 | 8.6 | .... | −97.2 | −477.7 | −354.2 | −81.7 | −714.4 | −32.5 | 268.4 | 1,525.6 |
| Fin. der. & ESOs: assets | 3c9aa | .... | .... | .... | .... | −650.9 | −643.5 | −354.2 | −201.8 | −780.3 | −156.3 | −411.1 | −287.3 |
| Fin. der. & ESOs: liabilities | 3c9la | −190.0 | −62.0 | −8.6 | .... | −553.7 | −165.7 | .... | −120.1 | −65.9 | −123.8 | −679.5 | −1,813.0 |
| Other investment: assets | 3d9aa | −424.5 | 44.9 | 243.2 | 2,295.0 | −776.7 | 1,694.7 | 222.8 | 3,422.4 | 2,741.1 | 1,831.0 | 1,820.9 | −489.1 |
| Other equity | 3daaa | .... | .... | .... | .... | .... | .... | .... | .... | .... | .... | .... | .... |
| Debt instruments | 3dzaa | −424.5 | 44.9 | 243.2 | 2,295.0 | −776.7 | 1,694.7 | 222.8 | 3,422.4 | 2,741.1 | 1,831.0 | 1,820.9 | −489.1 |
| Other investment: liabilities | 3d9la | 278.0 | −354.9 | 411.0 | 3,694.5 | 2,238.1 | 1,363.5 | 10,353.9 | 3,684.0 | −2,233.6 | 5,050.8 | 2,281.3 | 3,076.0 |
| Other equity | 3dala | .... | .... | .... | .... | .... | .... | .... | .... | .... | .... | .... | .... |
| Debt instruments | 3dzla | 278.0 | −354.9 | 411.0 | 3,694.5 | 2,238.1 | 1,363.5 | 10,353.9 | 3,684.0 | −2,233.6 | 5,050.8 | 2,281.3 | 3,076.0 |
| Curr.+ cap.− finan. acct. balance | 4y9na | 2,395.4 | 1,338.4 | −23.9 | 4,317.4 | 3,002.9 | 1,790.6 | 3,742.5 | 2,951.6 | 5,942.8 | 6,460.9 | 4,678.6 | 690.1 |
| D. Net Errors and Omissions | 409na | 67.2 | 385.2 | 46.5 | 370.4 | −431.5 | −349.5 | −625.3 | 785.0 | −621.4 | 479.8 | −243.0 | −273.4 |
| E. Reserves and Related Items | 4z9na | 2,462.6 | 1,723.6 | 22.6 | 4,687.8 | 2,571.4 | 1,441.1 | 3,117.2 | 3,736.6 | 5,321.4 | 6,940.8 | 4,435.6 | 416.7 |
| Reserve assets | 3e9aa | 2,462.6 | 1,723.6 | 22.6 | 4,687.8 | 2,571.4 | 1,441.1 | 3,117.2 | 3,736.6 | 5,321.4 | 6,940.8 | 4,435.6 | 416.7 |
| Credit and loans from the IMF | 3dcla | — | — | — | — | — | — | — | — | — | — | — | — |
| Exceptional financing | 409la | .... | .... | .... | .... | .... | .... | .... | .... | .... | .... | .... | .... |
| *Excludes components in group E | | | | | | | | | | | | | |
| **International Investment Position** | | | | | | | *Millions of US Dollars* | | | | | | |
| Assets | 809aa | 33,493.1 | 41,343.9 | 47,052.3 | 56,695.2 | 62,064.3 | 71,495.9 | 82,543.4 | 100,621.7 | 109,369.3 | 128,979.1 | 145,702.6 | 148,825.3 |
| Direct investment | 8a9aa | 4,407.2 | 9,098.3 | 10,366.1 | 11,644.9 | 14,730.0 | 18,234.7 | 23,717.3 | 32,137.1 | 31,530.9 | 39,183.0 | 43,082.1 | 47,299.8 |
| Equity & investment fund shares | 8aaaa | 4,357.2 | 8,914.7 | 10,013.0 | 10,925.8 | 13,412.0 | 16,219.1 | 23,112.0 | 30,366.3 | 29,809.2 | 37,277.4 | 40,212.8 | 45,495.5 |
| Debt instruments | 8abaa | 50.0 | 183.6 | 353.0 | 719.1 | 1,318.0 | 2,015.5 | 605.4 | 1,770.8 | 1,721.7 | 1,905.6 | 2,869.2 | 1,804.3 |
| Portfolio investment | 8b9aa | 10,196.8 | 11,891.5 | 15,548.2 | 16,112.3 | 16,044.9 | 18,951.1 | 21,241.1 | 23,352.4 | 25,018.5 | 29,114.0 | 36,120.7 | 36,242.2 |
| Equity & investment fund shares | 8baaa | .... | .... | .... | .... | .... | .... | .... | .... | .... | .... | .... | .... |
| Debt securities | 8bbaa | 10,196.8 | 11,891.5 | 15,548.2 | 16,112.3 | 16,044.9 | 18,951.1 | 21,241.1 | 23,352.4 | 25,018.5 | 29,114.0 | 36,120.7 | 36,242.2 |
| Fin. der.(oth.than reserves) & ESOs | 8c9aa | .... | .... | .... | .... | 114.2 | .... | .... | 280.2 | 142.8 | 24.4 | 325.2 | 182.0 |
| Other investment | 8d9aa | 5,748.4 | 5,801.7 | 6,102.1 | 8,412.3 | 7,630.3 | 9,340.0 | 9,522.4 | 12,957.8 | 15,714.9 | 17,546.6 | 19,367.4 | 18,878.0 |
| Other equity | 8daaa | .... | .... | .... | .... | .... | .... | .... | .... | .... | .... | .... | .... |
| Debt instruments | 8dzaa | 5,748.4 | 5,801.7 | 6,102.1 | 8,412.3 | 7,630.3 | 9,340.0 | 9,522.4 | 12,957.8 | 15,714.9 | 17,546.6 | 19,367.4 | 18,878.0 |
| Reserve assets | 8e9aa | 13,140.7 | 14,552.3 | 15,036.0 | 20,525.8 | 23,544.9 | 24,970.1 | 28,062.6 | 31,894.1 | 36,962.1 | 43,111.0 | 46,807.3 | 46,223.3 |
| Liabilities | 809la | 65,702.5 | 77,156.9 | 87,434.6 | 104,767.1 | 115,852.4 | 131,378.5 | 152,312.9 | 178,535.8 | 200,185.4 | 230,769.5 | 261,705.7 | 277,373.7 |
| Direct investment | 8a9la | 24,883.3 | 36,986.6 | 45,405.7 | 56,463.5 | 67,266.7 | 75,974.3 | 82,976.9 | 97,364.4 | 112,926.0 | 128,191.2 | 141,942.1 | 149,692.0 |
| Equity & investment fund shares | 8aala | 24,711.6 | 36,846.0 | 45,201.9 | 56,380.8 | 67,137.5 | 75,113.6 | 82,751.5 | 95,267.3 | 109,589.9 | 122,486.7 | 133,745.1 | 139,488.4 |
| Debt instruments | 8abla | 171.7 | 140.5 | 203.8 | 82.7 | 129.3 | 860.7 | 225.4 | 2,097.2 | 3,336.1 | 5,704.4 | 8,197.0 | 10,203.5 |
| Portfolio investment | 8b9la | 14,750.2 | 14,719.4 | 16,068.5 | 18,585.4 | 16,716.0 | 21,773.8 | 25,317.2 | 33,565.2 | 41,824.8 | 51,986.7 | 66,914.0 | 71,825.9 |
| Equity & investment fund shares | 8bala | 719.0 | 898.6 | 873.8 | 1,800.8 | 1,639.7 | 1,814.1 | 3,207.2 | 5,415.1 | 8,763.7 | 10,504.3 | 14,028.6 | 15,110.3 |
| Debt securities | 8bbla | 14,031.2 | 13,820.8 | 15,194.8 | 16,784.5 | 15,076.3 | 19,959.7 | 22,110.0 | 28,150.1 | 33,061.1 | 41,482.4 | 52,885.4 | 56,715.6 |
| Fin. der.(oth.than reserves) & ESOs | 8c9la | .... | .... | .... | .... | 152.2 | 87.1 | .... | 1.0 | 3.3 | 162.5 | 188.7 |
| Other investment | 8d9la | 26,069.0 | 25,451.0 | 25,960.4 | 29,718.3 | 31,869.6 | 33,478.1 | 43,931.7 | 47,606.2 | 45,433.6 | 50,588.3 | 52,687.2 | 55,667.2 |
| Other equity | 8dala | .... | .... | .... | .... | .... | .... | .... | .... | .... | .... | .... | .... |
| Debt instruments | 8dzla | 26,069.0 | 25,451.0 | 25,960.4 | 29,718.3 | 31,869.6 | 33,478.1 | 43,931.7 | 47,606.2 | 45,433.6 | 50,588.3 | 52,687.2 | 55,667.2 |

| | | 2004 | 2005 | 2006 | 2007 | 2008 | 2009 | 2010 | 2011 | 2012 | 2013 | 2014 | 2015 |
|---|---|---|---|---|---|---|---|---|---|---|---|---|---|
| **Government Finance** | | | | | | | | | | | | | |
| **Operations Statement** | | | | | | | | | | | | | |
| **Budgetary Central Government** | | *Billions of Pesos: Fiscal Year Ends December 31* | | | | | | | | | | | |
| Revenue........................... | a1 | 60,747 | 63,286 | 83,585 | 103,986 | 74,158 | 79,016 | 82,319 | 106,031 | 148,185 | 149,541 | 138,291 | .... |
| Taxes............................ | a11 | 32,414 | 43,584 | 45,423 | 58,644 | 58,592 | 59,587 | 61,730 | 85,397 | 87,257 | 93,619 | 107,049 | .... |
| Social Contributions.......... | a12 | 3,380 | 3,054 | 3,366 | 4,273 | 639 | 428 | 405 | 439 | 12,932 | 20,614 | 805 | .... |
| Grants........................... | a13 | 153 | 239 | 93 | 170 | 287 | 1,453 | 185 | 214 | –274 | 107 | 616 | .... |
| Other Revenue................. | a14 | 24,800 | 16,409 | 34,702 | 40,899 | 14,639 | 17,548 | 19,999 | 19,980 | 48,270 | 35,200 | 29,821 | .... |
| Expense.......................... | a2 | 68,571 | 90,930 | 92,238 | 110,014 | 87,937 | 92,050 | 97,497 | 103,500 | 145,542 | 178,106 | 173,822 | .... |
| Compensation of Employees.......... | a21 | 14,477 | 17,344 | 17,322 | 20,468 | 5,919 | 6,677 | 7,113 | 7,609 | 16,165 | 32,075 | 17,669 | .... |
| Use of Goods & Services.............. | a22 | 3,472 | 4,026 | 4,528 | 5,645 | 6,045 | 5,990 | 6,871 | 6,923 | 17,478 | 21,116 | 23,530 | .... |
| Consumption of Fixed Capital....... | a23 | 391 | 293 | 511 | 914 | 393 | 750 | 832 | 998 | 1,088 | 1,296 | 1,433 | .... |
| Interest......................... | a24 | 19,894 | 19,067 | 29,644 | 27,562 | 14,846 | 16,205 | 15,189 | 16,106 | 16,088 | 17,459 | 19,310 | .... |
| Subsidies....................... | a25 | 331 | 178 | 289 | 273 | 1,060 | 1,741 | 1,836 | 1,660 | 1,902 | 1,059 | 1,317 | .... |
| Grants........................... | a26 | 26,013 | 29,439 | 34,296 | 41,689 | 27,360 | 30,017 | 31,737 | 38,331 | 52,825 | 66,261 | 63,032 | .... |
| Social Benefits................. | a27 | 2,760 | 2,981 | 3,077 | 6,221 | 17,801 | 17,860 | 23,533 | 15,112 | 17,816 | 11,244 | 10,626 | .... |
| Other Expense................. | a28 | 1,234 | 17,602 | 2,571 | 7,240 | 14,513 | 12,808 | 10,385 | 16,761 | 22,180 | 27,597 | 36,905 | .... |
| Gross Operating Balance [1-2+23]... | agob | –7,433 | –27,352 | –8,142 | –5,114 | –13,386 | –12,283 | –14,346 | 3,529 | 3,731 | –27,270 | –34,098 | .... |
| Net Operating Balance [1-2]........... | anob | –7,825 | –27,645 | –8,654 | –6,028 | –13,779 | –13,033 | –15,178 | 2,531 | 2,644 | –28,565 | –35,531 | .... |
| Net Acq. of Nonfinancial Assets....... | a31 | 17,490 | –21,087 | 3,780 | 1,694 | 18,417 | 8,567 | 7,348 | 625 | –16,003 | 9,051 | 10,149 | .... |
| Aquisition of Nonfin. Assets.......... | a31.1 | .... | .... | .... | .... | .... | .... | .... | .... | .... | .... | .... | .... |
| Disposal of Nonfin. Assets............. | a31.2 | .... | .... | .... | .... | .... | .... | .... | .... | .... | .... | .... | .... |
| Net Lending/Borrowing [1-2-31]...... | anlb | –25,315 | –6,558 | –12,433 | –7,722 | –32,196 | –21,600 | –22,526 | 1,906 | 18,646 | –37,616 | –45,680 | .... |
| Net Acq. of Financial Assets............. | a32 | –13,164 | 6,678 | 23,531 | –5,610 | –14,478 | –14,568 | 18,614 | –9,127 | 42,975 | –3,167 | 1,745 | .... |
| By instrument | | | | | | | | | | | | | |
| Monetary Gold & SDRs................. | a3201 | — | — | — | — | — | — | — | — | — | — | — | .... |
| Currency & Deposits.................... | a3202 | 900 | 2,362 | –2,241 | 6,659 | –7,305 | 1,652 | 23,441 | –21,821 | 3,590 | 7,863 | 6,662 | .... |
| Securities other than Shares........... | a3203 | 1,153 | 225 | 1,350 | –982 | 634 | –1,641 | –4,107 | –1,622 | –4,803 | –2,358 | –3,600 | .... |
| Loans............................ | a3204 | –1,288 | 82 | 979 | –54 | –2,025 | 78 | –1,902 | –1,735 | 1,390 | 934 | –5,782 | .... |
| Shares & Other Equity................. | a3205 | 547 | 3,654 | 6,107 | –2,527 | 8,894 | –3,138 | 5,373 | 11,686 | 13,873 | –8,484 | –3,050 | .... |
| Insurance Technical Reserves......... | a3206 | — | — | — | — | — | — | — | — | — | — | — | .... |
| Financial Derivatives.................... | a3207 | — | — | — | — | –56 | –97 | –1 | –14 | 332 | –336 | — | .... |
| Other Accounts Receivable............. | a3208 | –14,477 | 356 | 17,336 | –8,706 | –14,620 | –11,422 | –4,190 | 4,380 | 28,593 | –787 | 7,515 | .... |
| By debtor | | | | | | | | | | | | | |
| Domestic....................... | a321 | –14,102 | 6,091 | 22,137 | –1,243 | –4,044 | –1,600 | 28,707 | –1,295 | 52,767 | –5,553 | 779 | .... |
| Foreign.......................... | a322 | 938 | 587 | 1,395 | –4,368 | –10,433 | –12,968 | –10,093 | –7,831 | –9,792 | 2,386 | 965 | .... |
| Net Incurence of Liabilities.............. | a33 | 12,151 | 13,236 | 35,965 | 2,112 | 12,839 | 20,188 | 37,113 | –24,631 | 19,926 | 33,598 | 63,097 | .... |
| By instrument | | | | | | | | | | | | | |
| Special Drawing Rights (SDRs)....... | a3301 | — | — | — | — | — | — | — | — | — | — | — | .... |
| Currency & Deposits.................... | a3302 | — | — | — | — | –5,461 | 1,018 | 20,939 | –26,492 | –68 | — | — | .... |
| Securities other than Shares........... | a3303 | 6,994 | 17,546 | 10,483 | –3,254 | 9,835 | 16,235 | 15,497 | 16,925 | 7,728 | 27,738 | 34,159 | .... |
| Loans............................ | a3304 | –1,280 | –4,596 | 1,156 | 7,339 | –12,358 | –10,253 | –4,137 | –8,526 | –6,726 | –5,487 | 4,048 | .... |
| Shares & Other Equity.................. | a3305 | — | — | — | — | — | –2 | –3 | –2 | — | — | — | .... |
| Insurance Technical Reserves......... | a3306 | — | — | — | — | — | — | — | — | — | — | — | .... |
| Financial Derivatives.................... | a3307 | — | — | — | — | — | –205 | –69 | –50 | — | 363 | –441 | .... |
| Other Accounts Payable................ | a3308 | 6,437 | 286 | 24,325 | –1,974 | 20,822 | 13,394 | 4,886 | –6,486 | 18,993 | 10,983 | 25,332 | .... |
| By creditor | | | | | | | | | | | | | |
| Foreign.......................... | a332 | –4,292 | –5,785 | 4,836 | –4,279 | –8,195 | –6,021 | –4,623 | –4,525 | –9,076 | 1,820 | 21,866 | .... |
| Stat. Discrepancy [32-33-NLB]........ | anlbz | — | — | — | — | 4,880 | –13,156 | 4,027 | 13,598 | 4,402 | 852 | –15,672 | .... |
| Memo Item: Expenditure [2+31]...... | a2m | 86,062 | 69,843 | 96,018 | 111,708 | 106,354 | 100,616 | 104,844 | 104,124 | 129,539 | 187,157 | 183,972 | .... |
| **National Accounts** | | *Billions of Pesos: Quarterly Data Seasonally Adjusted* | | | | | | | | | | | |
| Househ.Cons.Expend.,incl.NPISHs... | 96f.c | 206,814 | 224,580 | 249,954 | 279,673 | 306,137 | 319,769 | 343,666 | 381,263 | 408,677 | 432,164 | 465,630 | 511,061 |
| Government Consumption Expend... | 91f.c | 48,262 | 53,373 | 59,068 | 66,152 | 73,064 | 82,830 | 90,653 | 98,041 | 108,939 | 123,769 | 133,803 | 143,917 |
| Gross Fixed Capital Formation......... | 93e.c | 57,957 | 66,894 | 82,943 | 96,822 | 110,786 | 114,532 | 119,091 | 146,318 | 157,340 | 172,337 | 195,176 | 213,851 |
| Changes in Inventories.................... | 93i.c | 1,875 | 1,889 | 3,062 | 2,441 | 1,973 | –1,289 | 1,480 | 1,690 | 1,098 | 374 | 3,720 | 8,272 |
| Exports of Goods and Services......... | 90c.c | 51,614 | 57,316 | 67,710 | 71,296 | 85,405 | 80,899 | 86,839 | 116,144 | 121,282 | 124,848 | 120,923 | 117,842 |
| Imports of Goods and Services (-).... | 98c.c | 58,760 | 63,896 | 78,839 | 85,312 | 97,278 | 92,094 | 96,805 | 123,562 | 133,096 | 142,995 | 161,746 | 194,094 |
| Gross Domestic Product (GDP)........ | 99b.c | 307,762 | 340,156 | 383,898 | 431,072 | 480,087 | 504,647 | 544,924 | 619,894 | 664,240 | 710,497 | 757,506 | 800,849 |
| Net Primary Income from Abroad.... | 98.n | –13,434 | –12,320 | –10,789 | –12,557 | .... | .... | .... | .... | .... | .... | .... | .... |
| Gross National Income (GNI).......... | 99a | 294,325 | 327,840 | 373,103 | 418,519 | .... | .... | .... | .... | .... | .... | .... | .... |
| Net Current Transf.from Abroad....... | 98t | 14,625 | 16,373 | 18,459 | 19,081 | .... | .... | .... | .... | .... | .... | .... | .... |
| Gross Nat'l Disposable Inc.(GNDI).... | 99i | 314,383 | 344,555 | 387,122 | 432,756 | 477,712 | 500,228 | 535,776 | 605,351 | 647,778 | 695,335 | 744,228 | .... |
| Gross Saving............................. | 99s | 59,307 | 66,602 | 78,100 | 86,931 | 98,511 | 97,629 | 101,457 | 126,047 | 130,162 | 139,402 | 144,795 | .... |
| GDP Volume 2005 Prices............... | 99b.r | 324,866 | 340,156 | 362,938 | 387,983 | 401,744 | 408,379 | 424,599 | 452,578 | 470,880 | 493,831 | 515,489 | 531,383 |
| GDP Volume (2010=100)............... | 99bvr | 76.5 | 80.1 | 85.5 | 91.4 | 94.6 | 96.2 | 100.0 | 106.6 | 110.9 | 116.3 | 121.4 | 125.1 |
| GDP Deflator (2010=100)............... | 99bir | 73.8 | 77.9 | 82.4 | 86.6 | 93.1 | 96.3 | 100.0 | 106.7 | 109.9 | 112.1 | 114.5 | 117.4 |
| | | *Millions: Midyear Estimates* | | | | | | | | | | | |
| Population............................... | 99z | 42.72 | 43.29 | 43.84 | 44.37 | 44.90 | 45.42 | 45.92 | 46.41 | 46.88 | 47.34 | 47.79 | 48.23 |

# Comoros 632

| | | 2004 | 2005 | 2006 | 2007 | 2008 | 2009 | 2010 | 2011 | 2012 | 2013 | 2014 | 2015 |
|---|---|---|---|---|---|---|---|---|---|---|---|---|---|
| **Exchange Rates** | | | | | | *Francs per SDR: End of Period (aa)* | | | | | | | |
| Official Rate | aa | 560.92 | 596.05 | 561.97 | 528.11 | 544.49 | 535.37 | 567.02 | 583.74 | 573.08 | 549.37 | 587.08 | 626.19 |
| | | | | | | *Francs per US Dollar: End of Period (ae) Period Average (rf)* | | | | | | | |
| Official Rate | ae | 361.18 | 417.03 | 373.55 | 334.19 | 353.50 | 341.50 | 368.18 | 380.22 | 372.87 | 356.73 | 405.21 | 451.89 |
| Official Rate | rf | 396.21 | 395.60 | 392.17 | 359.45 | 335.85 | 354.14 | 371.46 | 353.90 | 382.90 | 370.53 | 370.81 | 443.59 |
| **Fund Position** | | | | | | *Millions of SDRs: End of Period* | | | | | | | |
| Quota | 2f.s | 8.90 | 8.90 | 8.90 | 8.90 | 8.90 | 8.90 | 8.90 | 8.90 | 8.90 | 8.90 | 8.90 | 8.90 |
| SDR Holdings | 1b.s | — | — | — | .01 | — | 6.67 | 8.22 | 9.79 | 11.35 | 14.46 | 11.47 | 11.21 |
| Reserve Position in the Fund | 1c.s | .54 | .54 | .54 | .54 | .54 | .54 | .54 | .54 | .58 | .58 | .58 | .58 |
| Total Fund Cred.&Loans Outstg. | 2tl | — | — | — | — | — | 3.34 | 6.45 | 8.01 | 9.57 | 9.71 | 12.83 | 12.57 |
| SDR Allocations | 1bd | .72 | .72 | .72 | .72 | .72 | 8.50 | 8.50 | 8.50 | 8.50 | 8.50 | 8.50 | 8.50 |
| **International Liquidity** | | | | | | *Millions of US Dollars Unless Otherwise Indicated: End of Period* | | | | | | | |
| Total Reserves minus Gold | 1l.d | 103.74 | 85.80 | 93.52 | 117.16 | 112.16 | 150.27 | 145.26 | 155.18 | 194.06 | 173.37 | 170.46 | 199.95 |
| SDR Holdings | 1b.d | — | — | — | .01 | — | 10.46 | 12.67 | 15.03 | 17.44 | 22.27 | 16.62 | 15.54 |
| Reserve Position in the Fund | 1c.d | .84 | .78 | .82 | .86 | .84 | .85 | .84 | .83 | .89 | .89 | .84 | .80 |
| Foreign Exchange | 1d.d | 102.89 | 85.02 | 92.70 | 116.29 | 111.32 | 138.96 | 131.76 | 139.32 | 175.73 | 150.21 | 153.01 | 183.61 |
| Gold (Million Fine Troy Ounces) | 1ad | .001 | .001 | .001 | .001 | .001 | .001 | .001 | .001 | .001 | .001 | .001 | .001 |
| Gold (National Valuation) | 1and | .25 | .29 | .33 | .47 | .49 | .64 | .82 | .92 | 1.06 | .76 | .76 | .67 |
| Central Bank: Other Assets | 3..d | .04 | .05 | .03 | .06 | .10 | .19 | .06 | .05 | .02 | .04 | .61 | .50 |
| Central Bank: Other Liabs. | 4..d | .45 | .44 | .28 | .61 | .49 | .30 | .30 | .48 | .40 | .49 | .27 | .38 |
| Other Depository Corps.: Assets | 7a.d | 2.84 | 7.07 | 17.35 | 15.15 | 10.22 | 6.12 | 13.64 | 22.72 | 14.74 | 30.24 | 12.15 | 13.07 |
| Other Depository Corps.: Liabs. | 7b.d | .07 | 1.18 | 2.22 | 3.55 | 2.52 | 4.30 | 9.19 | 10.27 | 13.30 | 12.51 | 10.74 | 9.00 |
| Other Financial Corps.: Assets | 7e.d | — | — | — | — | .01 | — | .31 | .... | .... | .... | .... | .... |
| Other Financial Corps.: Liabs. | 7f.d | 1.16 | .86 | .88 | .90 | 1.45 | 2.20 | 4.87 | .... | .... | .... | .... | .... |
| **Central Bank** | | | | | | *Millions of Francs: End of Period* | | | | | | | |
| Net Foreign Assets | 11n | 37,011 | 35,342 | 34,511 | 39,280 | 37,481 | 43,493 | 44,335 | 49,127 | 62,172 | 50,242 | 56,996 | 77,522 |
| Claims on Nonresidents | 11 | 37,575 | 35,952 | 35,017 | 39,864 | 39,861 | 51,601 | 53,810 | 59,859 | 72,761 | 62,136 | 69,628 | 90,889 |
| Liabilities to Nonresidents | 16c | 564 | 610 | 506 | 584 | 2,379 | 8,108 | 9,475 | 10,732 | 10,589 | 11,894 | 12,632 | 13,367 |
| Claims on Other Depository Corps. | 12e | | | | | | | | 50 | 50 | 50 | — | — |
| Net Claims on Central Government | 12an | 1,209 | 2,787 | 2,748 | 2,534 | 4,204 | 6,683 | 4,991 | 6,759 | 1,937 | 5,712 | 8,856 | −3,372 |
| Claims on Central Government | 12a | 3,029 | 4,556 | 5,877 | 5,982 | 7,757 | 9,212 | 11,462 | 13,214 | 13,114 | 14,980 | 15,293 | 11,056 |
| Liabilities to Central Government | 16d | 1,820 | 1,770 | 3,130 | 3,449 | 3,553 | 2,528 | 6,471 | 6,455 | 11,178 | 9,267 | 6,437 | 14,429 |
| Claims on Other Sectors | 12s | 194 | 138 | 154 | 160 | 205 | 751 | 454 | 400 | 901 | 955 | 726 | 823 |
| Claims on Other Financial Corps. | 12g | 50 | 50 | 50 | 50 | 50 | 553 | 110 | — | — | — | — | — |
| Claims on State & Local Govts. | 12b | — | — | — | — | — | — | — | — | — | — | — | — |
| Claims on Public Nonfin. Corps. | 12c | — | — | — | — | — | — | — | — | — | — | — | — |
| Claims on Private Sector | 12d | 144 | 88 | 104 | 110 | 155 | 198 | 344 | 400 | 901 | 955 | 726 | 823 |
| Monetary Base | 14 | 27,551 | 27,175 | 26,899 | 28,567 | 31,633 | 37,043 | 39,193 | 45,099 | 53,589 | 45,614 | 54,051 | 63,353 |
| Currency in Circulation | 14a | 11,895 | 11,599 | 12,926 | 13,698 | 13,972 | 16,050 | 19,616 | 22,136 | 24,456 | 23,912 | 27,217 | 33,204 |
| Liabs. to Other Depository Corps. | 14c | 14,031 | 13,819 | 12,911 | 12,871 | 16,380 | 20,504 | 19,071 | 22,599 | 28,624 | 21,230 | 25,826 | 28,110 |
| Liabilities to Other Sectors | 14d | 1,624 | 1,757 | 1,062 | 1,998 | 1,281 | 489 | 506 | 364 | 509 | 473 | 1,008 | 2,039 |
| Other Liabs. to Other Dep. Corps. | 14n | 4 | — | — | — | — | — | — | — | — | — | — | — |
| Dep. & Sec. Excl. f/Monetary Base | 14o | — | 40 | 70 | 2,498 | 154 | 3,775 | 105 | 106 | 328 | 359 | 202 | 285 |
| Deposits Included in Broad Money | 15 | — | — | — | — | — | — | — | — | — | — | — | — |
| Sec.Ot.th.Shares Incl.in Brd. Money | 16a | — | — | — | — | — | — | — | — | — | — | — | — |
| Deposits Excl. from Broad Money | 16b | — | 40 | 70 | 2,498 | 154 | 3,775 | 105 | 106 | 328 | 359 | 202 | 285 |
| Sec.Ot.th.Shares Excl.f/Brd.Money | 16s | — | — | — | — | — | — | — | — | — | — | — | — |
| Loans | 16l | — | — | — | — | — | — | — | — | — | — | — | — |
| Financial Derivatives | 16m | — | — | — | — | — | — | — | — | — | — | — | — |
| Shares and Other Equity | 17a | 11,744 | 11,674 | 11,737 | 12,138 | 13,144 | 12,965 | 13,223 | 13,253 | 13,549 | 13,522 | 14,211 | 14,413 |
| Other Items (Net) | 17r | −885 | −622 | −1,292 | −1,229 | −3,041 | −2,855 | −2,742 | −2,121 | −2,407 | −2,536 | −1,886 | −3,079 |
| Memo Item: | | | | | | | | | | | | | |
| Total Assets | 10ra | 42,286 | 46,247 | 47,377 | 52,360 | 55,520 | 69,465 | 73,836 | 81,318 | 94,368 | 85,527 | 93,489 | 111,441 |
| **Other Depository Corporations** | | | | | | *Millions of Francs: End of Period* | | | | | | | |
| Net Foreign Assets | 21n | 1,000 | 2,456 | 5,654 | 3,875 | 2,722 | 621 | 1,640 | 4,733 | 537 | 6,325 | 570 | 1,837 |
| Claims on Nonresidents | 21 | 1,024 | 2,950 | 6,482 | 5,062 | 3,612 | 2,089 | 5,023 | 8,638 | 5,496 | 10,787 | 4,923 | 5,904 |
| Liabilities to Nonresidents | 26c | 24 | 494 | 828 | 1,187 | 890 | 1,468 | 3,384 | 3,905 | 4,959 | 4,463 | 4,353 | 4,067 |
| Claims on Central Bank | 20 | 14,247 | 13,481 | 11,917 | 13,557 | 14,175 | 19,026 | 20,549 | 24,927 | 31,314 | 23,223 | 28,950 | 30,351 |
| Currency | 20a | 120 | 411 | 881 | 975 | 1,638 | 1,759 | 1,501 | 2,151 | 2,701 | 2,172 | 2,525 | 2,817 |
| Reserve Deposits and Securities | 20b | 14,127 | 13,071 | 11,036 | 12,582 | 12,538 | 17,267 | 19,048 | 22,776 | 28,613 | 21,051 | 26,426 | 27,533 |
| Other Claims | 20n | — | — | — | — | — | — | — | — | — | — | — | — |
| Net Claims on Central Government | 22an | −318 | −828 | 123 | 405 | 1,043 | 582 | 753 | −743 | −333 | −201 | −398 | −891 |
| Claims on Central Government | 22a | 481 | 1 | 504 | 771 | 1,466 | 1,240 | 1,292 | 577 | 664 | 808 | 910 | 1,006 |
| Liabilities to Central Government | 26d | 798 | 829 | 381 | 366 | 423 | 658 | 539 | 1,320 | 997 | 1,009 | 1,309 | 1,897 |
| Claims on Other Sectors | 22s | 10,309 | 13,900 | 14,342 | 16,315 | 22,052 | 29,156 | 37,506 | 39,429 | 46,861 | 53,228 | 58,342 | 67,778 |
| Claims on Other Financial Corps. | 22g | 18 | 10 | 38 | 103 | 3 | 2 | — | — | — | 97 | 21 | — |
| Claims on State & Local Govts. | 22b | — | 300 | — | — | — | — | 315 | 220 | 188 | 154 | 166 | 110 |
| Claims on Public Nonfin. Corps. | 22c | 180 | 297 | 959 | 1,040 | 2,744 | 1,303 | 2,232 | 1,178 | 512 | 986 | 861 | 797 |
| Claims on Private Sector | 22d | 10,111 | 13,293 | 13,345 | 15,172 | 19,305 | 27,850 | 34,960 | 38,032 | 46,161 | 51,991 | 57,294 | 66,870 |
| Liabilities to Central Bank | 26g | — | — | — | — | — | — | — | 2 | 2 | — | — | — |
| Transf.Dep.Included in Broad Money | 24 | 9,636 | 8,652 | 15,277 | 17,450 | 21,154 | 20,975 | 24,028 | 28,471 | 34,261 | 34,665 | 36,552 | 43,953 |
| Other Dep.Included in Broad Money | 25 | 11,476 | 15,351 | 13,184 | 13,371 | 16,024 | 21,817 | 26,097 | 26,506 | 30,871 | 32,985 | 34,886 | 37,380 |
| Sec.Ot.th.Shares Incl.in Brd. Money | 26a | — | — | — | — | — | — | — | — | — | — | — | — |
| Deposits Excl. from Broad Money | 26b | — | — | — | — | — | — | — | — | — | — | — | — |
| Sec.Ot.th.Shares Excl.f/Brd.Money | 26s | — | — | — | — | — | — | — | — | — | — | — | — |
| Loans | 26l | — | — | — | — | — | 116 | 85 | 1,623 | 1,675 | 1,649 | 1,652 | 1,554 |
| Financial Derivatives | 26m | — | — | — | — | — | — | — | — | — | — | — | — |
| Insurance Technical Reserves | 26r | — | — | — | — | — | — | — | — | — | — | — | — |
| Shares and Other Equity | 27a | 2,449 | 1,911 | 3,213 | 5,262 | 5,806 | 11,395 | 11,942 | 14,730 | 11,819 | 12,469 | 13,954 | 15,087 |
| Other Items (Net) | 27r | 1,677 | 3,097 | 362 | −1,930 | −2,992 | −4,918 | −1,705 | −2,987 | −249 | 806 | 419 | 1,101 |
| Memo Item: | | | | | | | | | | | | | |
| Total Assets | 20ra | 28,303 | 36,256 | 40,853 | 45,424 | 52,133 | 65,160 | 75,971 | 89,650 | 101,652 | 103,531 | 109,159 | 123,865 |

# Comoros 632

| | | 2004 | 2005 | 2006 | 2007 | 2008 | 2009 | 2010 | 2011 | 2012 | 2013 | 2014 | 2015 |
|---|---|---|---|---|---|---|---|---|---|---|---|---|---|
| **Depository Corporations** | | | | | | *Millions of Francs: End of Period* | | | | | | | |
| Net Foreign Assets........................ | 31n | 38,011 | 37,799 | 40,166 | 43,156 | 40,203 | 44,114 | 45,974 | 53,860 | 62,709 | 56,567 | 57,566 | 79,360 |
| Claims on Nonresidents................ | 31 | 38,599 | 38,902 | 41,500 | 44,926 | 43,472 | 53,690 | 58,833 | 68,497 | 78,256 | 72,923 | 74,551 | 96,794 |
| Liabilities to Nonresidents............. | 36c | 588 | 1,103 | 1,334 | 1,771 | 3,269 | 9,576 | 12,858 | 14,637 | 15,548 | 16,357 | 16,985 | 17,434 |
| Domestic Claims............................ | 32 | 11,394 | 15,997 | 17,367 | 19,413 | 27,503 | 37,172 | 43,704 | 45,845 | 49,366 | 59,694 | 67,525 | 64,337 |
| Net Claims on Central Government | 32an | 891 | 1,959 | 2,871 | 2,938 | 5,246 | 7,266 | 5,743 | 6,016 | 1,604 | 5,511 | 8,457 | −4,264 |
| Claims on Central Government.... | 32a | 3,510 | 4,557 | 6,382 | 6,753 | 9,223 | 10,452 | 12,753 | 13,791 | 13,779 | 15,787 | 16,203 | 12,062 |
| Liabilities to Central Government. | 36d | 2,619 | 2,599 | 3,511 | 3,815 | 3,977 | 3,186 | 7,010 | 7,775 | 12,175 | 10,276 | 7,746 | 16,325 |
| Claims on Other Sectors................ | 32s | 10,503 | 14,038 | 14,496 | 16,475 | 22,257 | 29,906 | 37,961 | 39,829 | 47,762 | 54,183 | 59,068 | 68,600 |
| Claims on Other Financial Corps.. | 32g | 68 | 60 | 88 | 153 | 53 | 555 | 110 | — | — | 97 | 21 | — |
| Claims on State & Local Govts..... | 32b | — | 300 | — | — | — | — | 315 | 220 | 188 | 154 | 166 | 110 |
| Claims on Public Nonfin. Corps.... | 32c | 180 | 297 | 959 | 1,040 | 2,744 | 1,303 | 2,232 | 1,178 | 512 | 986 | 861 | 797 |
| Claims on Private Sector............. | 32d | 10,255 | 13,381 | 13,449 | 15,282 | 19,460 | 28,048 | 35,304 | 38,431 | 47,062 | 52,946 | 58,020 | 67,693 |
| Broad Money Liabilities.................... | 35l | 34,512 | 36,948 | 41,568 | 45,541 | 50,793 | 57,571 | 68,747 | 75,327 | 87,396 | 89,862 | 97,139 | 113,759 |
| Currency Outside Depository Corps | 34a | 11,775 | 11,188 | 12,045 | 12,723 | 12,335 | 14,291 | 18,115 | 19,985 | 21,755 | 21,740 | 24,693 | 30,387 |
| Transferable Deposits................... | 34 | 11,260 | 10,409 | 16,339 | 19,418 | 22,435 | 21,464 | 24,534 | 28,835 | 34,770 | 35,138 | 37,560 | 45,992 |
| Other Deposits.............................. | 35 | 11,476 | 15,351 | 13,184 | 13,400 | 16,024 | 21,817 | 26,097 | 26,506 | 30,871 | 32,985 | 34,886 | 37,380 |
| Securities Other than Shares......... | 36a | — | — | — | — | — | — | — | — | — | — | — | — |
| Deposits Excl. from Broad Money..... | 36b | — | 40 | 70 | 2,498 | 154 | 3,775 | 105 | 106 | 328 | 359 | 202 | 285 |
| Sec.Ot.th.Shares Excl.f/Brd.Money.... | 36s | — | — | — | — | — | — | — | — | — | — | — | — |
| Loans........................................... | 36l | — | — | — | — | — | 116 | 85 | 1,623 | 1,675 | 1,649 | 1,652 | 1,554 |
| Financial Derivatives...................... | 36m | — | — | — | — | — | — | — | — | — | — | — | — |
| Insurance Technical Reserves......... | 36r | — | — | — | — | — | — | — | — | — | — | — | — |
| Shares and Other Equity................. | 37a | 14,193 | 13,585 | 14,951 | 17,400 | 18,950 | 24,360 | 25,165 | 27,983 | 25,368 | 25,991 | 28,166 | 29,500 |
| Other Items (Net)........................... | 37r | 700 | 3,223 | 945 | −2,870 | −2,191 | −4,536 | −4,423 | −5,333 | −2,693 | −1,602 | −2,067 | −1,401 |
| Broad Money Liabs., Seasonally Adj. | 35l.b | 33,819 | 36,143 | 40,725 | 44,673 | 49,886 | 56,568 | 67,543 | 73,854 | 85,479 | 87,783 | 94,843 | 110,994 |
| **Other Financial Corporations** | | | | | | *Millions of Francs: End of Period* | | | | | | | |
| Net Foreign Assets........................ | 41n | −419 | −358 | −328 | −300 | −509 | −753 | −1,677 | .... | .... | .... | .... | .... |
| Claims on Nonresidents................ | 41 | — | — | 1 | — | 3 | — | 116 | .... | .... | .... | .... | .... |
| Liabilities to Nonresidents............. | 46c | 419 | 358 | 329 | 300 | 512 | 753 | 1,793 | .... | .... | .... | .... | .... |
| Claims on Depository Corporations.. | 40 | 699 | 505 | 403 | 531 | 801 | 494 | 425 | .... | .... | .... | .... | .... |
| Net Claims on Central Government.. | 42an | — | — | — | — | — | — | — | .... | .... | .... | .... | .... |
| Claims on Central Government...... | 42a | — | — | — | — | — | — | — | .... | .... | .... | .... | .... |
| Liabilities to Central Government... | 46d | — | — | — | — | — | — | — | .... | .... | .... | .... | .... |
| Claims on Other Sectors................ | 42s | 1,279 | 1,199 | 1,237 | 984 | 994 | 2,193 | 3,136 | .... | .... | .... | .... | .... |
| Claims on State & Local Govts....... | 42b | — | — | — | — | — | — | — | .... | .... | .... | .... | .... |
| Claims on Public Nonfin. Corps...... | 42c | 9 | 7 | — | — | — | — | — | .... | .... | .... | .... | .... |
| Claims on Private Sector............... | 42d | 1,269 | 1,192 | 1,237 | 984 | 994 | 2,193 | 3,136 | .... | .... | .... | .... | .... |
| Deposits........................................ | 46b | — | — | — | — | 68 | 375 | 800 | .... | .... | .... | .... | .... |
| Securities Other than Shares............ | 46s | — | — | — | — | — | — | — | .... | .... | .... | .... | .... |
| Loans............................................. | 46l | — | — | — | — | — | 500 | 63 | .... | .... | .... | .... | .... |
| Financial Derivatives........................ | 46m | — | — | — | — | — | — | — | .... | .... | .... | .... | .... |
| Insurance Technical Reserves........... | 46r | — | — | — | — | — | — | — | .... | .... | .... | .... | .... |
| Shares and Other Equity................... | 47a | 516 | 607 | 569 | 530 | 475 | 1,280 | 1,466 | .... | .... | .... | .... | .... |
| Other Items (Net).......................... | 47r | 1,043 | 738 | 743 | 686 | 743 | −221 | −445 | .... | .... | .... | .... | .... |
| **Monetary Aggregates** | | | | | | *Millions of Francs: End of Period* | | | | | | | |
| Broad Money.............................. | 59m | 34,512 | 36,948 | 41,568 | 45,541 | 50,793 | 57,571 | 68,747 | 75,327 | 87,396 | 89,862 | 97,139 | 113,759 |
| o/w:Currency Issued by Cent.Govt | 59m.a | — | — | — | — | — | — | — | — | — | — | — | — |
| o/w: Dep.in Nonfin. Corporations. | 59m.b | — | — | — | — | — | — | — | — | — | — | — | — |
| o/w: Secs. Issued by Central Govt. | 59m.c | — | — | — | — | — | — | — | — | — | — | — | — |
| Money (National Definitions) | | | | | | | | | | | | | |
| M1.................................... | 59ma | 23,036 | 21,597 | 28,384 | 32,141 | 34,769 | 35,754 | 42,650 | 48,820 | 56,525 | 56,878 | 62,252 | 76,379 |
| M2.................................... | 59mb | 34,512 | 36,948 | 41,568 | 45,541 | 50,793 | 57,571 | 68,747 | 75,327 | 87,396 | 89,862 | 97,139 | 113,759 |
| **Interest Rates** | | | | | | *Percent Per Annum* | | | | | | | |
| Discount Rate............................... | 60.a | 3.55 | 3.59 | 4.34 | 5.36 | 5.36 | 2.21 | 1.93 | 2.37 | 1.73 | 1.59 | 1.60 | 1.40 |
| Deposit Rate.................................. | 60l | 3.50 | 3.00 | 2.50 | 2.50 | 2.50 | 1.88 | 1.75 | 1.75 | 1.75 | 1.75 | 1.75 | 1.75 |
| Lending Rate.................................. | 60p | 11.00 | 11.00 | 10.50 | 10.50 | 10.50 | 10.50 | 10.50 | 10.50 | 10.50 | 10.50 | 10.50 | 10.50 |
| **Prices** | | | | | | *Index Numbers (2010=100): Period Averages* | | | | | | | |
| Consumer Prices............................ | 64 | 81.944 | 84.414 | 87.262 | 91.159 | 92.710 | 96.754 | 100.000 | 101.771 | 103.572 | 105.951 | 106.564 | 97.916 |

# Comoros 632

| Balance of Payments | | 2004 | 2005 | 2006 | 2007 | 2008 | 2009 | 2010 | 2011 | 2012 | 2013 | 2014 | 2015 |
|---|---|---|---|---|---|---|---|---|---|---|---|---|---|
| | | | | | | | *Millions of US Dollars* | | | | | | |
| A. Current Account* | 109bx | −21.1 | −28.5 | −27.3 | −37.5 | −77.2 | −61.1 | −90.5 | −58.2 | −43.7 | .... | .... | .... |
| Goods, credit (exports) | 1a9cx | 20.8 | 14.4 | 13.3 | 16.5 | 9.8 | 18.9 | 22.6 | 25.8 | 19.5 | .... | .... | .... |
| Goods, debit (imports) | 1a9dx | 78.2 | 92.6 | 100.7 | 127.9 | 175.9 | 169.6 | 177.3 | 199.5 | 217.8 | .... | .... | .... |
| Balance on goods | 1a9bx | −57.4 | −78.2 | −87.4 | −111.4 | −166.1 | −150.7 | −154.8 | −173.7 | −198.3 | .... | .... | .... |
| Services, credit (exports) | 1b9cx | 36.1 | 42.7 | 46.8 | 55.0 | 64.3 | 58.8 | 64.9 | 73.8 | 70.0 | .... | .... | .... |
| Services, debit (imports) | 1b9dx | 41.3 | 45.8 | 54.9 | 63.5 | 79.4 | 84.0 | 94.0 | 107.5 | 103.8 | .... | .... | .... |
| Balance on goods & services | 1z9bx | −62.6 | −81.3 | −95.5 | −119.9 | −181.2 | −175.9 | −183.9 | −207.3 | −232.1 | .... | .... | .... |
| Primary income: credit | 1c9cx | 2.8 | 2.4 | 3.4 | 5.3 | 5.5 | 3.2 | 3.2 | 3.8 | 3.8 | .... | .... | .... |
| Primary income: debit | 1c9dx | 6.7 | 5.9 | 5.1 | 3.8 | 7.3 | 4.4 | 4.1 | 4.6 | 5.5 | .... | .... | .... |
| Balance on gds, serv. & prim. inc. | 1y9bx | −66.4 | −84.7 | −97.2 | −118.3 | −183.0 | −177.1 | −184.7 | −208.1 | −233.8 | .... | .... | .... |
| Secondary income: credit | 1d9ca | 61.8 | 77.1 | 91.3 | 105.3 | 140.4 | 147.4 | 135.7 | 200.6 | 240.2 | .... | .... | .... |
| Secondary income: debit | 1d9da | 16.5 | 20.9 | 21.4 | 24.4 | 34.6 | 31.4 | 41.5 | 50.6 | 50.1 | .... | .... | .... |
| B. Capital Account* | 209ba | 9.7 | 14.8 | 18.5 | 30.1 | 48.8 | 29.8 | 29.5 | 42.8 | 49.7 | .... | .... | .... |
| Capital account: credit | 209ca | 9.7 | 14.8 | 18.5 | 30.1 | 49.3 | 30.0 | 29.5 | 42.9 | 49.7 | .... | .... | .... |
| Capital account: debit | 209da | — | — | — | — | .5 | .2 | — | — | — | .... | .... | .... |
| Balance on current & capital acct. | 129ba | −11.4 | −13.7 | −8.8 | −7.4 | −28.4 | −31.3 | −61.0 | −15.3 | 6.0 | .... | .... | .... |
| C. Financial Account* | 309na | −7.6 | −1.1 | — | −14.4 | −28.0 | −29.2 | 31.8 | .6 | −18.4 | .... | .... | .... |
| Direct investment: assets | 3a9aa | — | — | — | — | — | — | — | — | — | .... | .... | .... |
| Equity & investment fund shares | 3aaaa | — | — | — | — | — | — | — | — | — | .... | .... | .... |
| Debt instruments | 3abaa | — | — | — | — | — | — | — | — | — | .... | .... | .... |
| Direct investment: liabilities | 3a9la | .7 | .6 | .8 | 7.7 | 4.6 | 13.8 | 8.3 | 23.1 | 10.4 | .... | .... | .... |
| Equity & investment fund shares | 3aala | .7 | .6 | .8 | 7.7 | 4.6 | 13.8 | 8.3 | 23.1 | 4.9 | .... | .... | .... |
| Debt instruments | 3abla | — | — | — | — | — | — | — | — | 5.5 | .... | .... | .... |
| Portfolio investment: assets | 3b9aa | — | — | — | — | — | — | — | — | — | .... | .... | .... |
| Equity & investment fund shares | 3baaa | — | — | — | — | — | — | — | — | — | .... | .... | .... |
| Debt securities | 3bbaa | — | — | — | — | — | — | — | — | — | .... | .... | .... |
| Portfolio investment: liabilities | 3b9la | — | — | — | — | — | — | — | — | — | .... | .... | .... |
| Equity & investment fund shares | 3bala | — | — | — | — | — | — | — | — | — | .... | .... | .... |
| Debt securities | 3bbla | — | — | — | — | — | — | — | — | — | .... | .... | .... |
| Fin. der.& empl.stk.ops.(ESOs): net. | 3c9na | — | — | — | — | — | — | — | — | — | .... | .... | .... |
| Fin. der. & ESOs.: assets | 3c9aa | .... | .... | .... | .... | .... | .... | .... | .... | .... | .... | .... | .... |
| Fin. der. & ESOs.: liabilities | 3c9la | .... | .... | .... | .... | .... | .... | .... | .... | .... | .... | .... | .... |
| Other investment: assets | 3d9aa | −3.8 | 2.5 | 7.4 | −1.4 | −8.4 | −3.6 | 9.5 | 11.1 | −9.2 | .... | .... | .... |
| Other equity | 3daaa | .... | .... | .... | .... | .... | .... | .... | .... | .... | .... | .... | .... |
| Debt instruments | 3dzaa | −3.8 | 2.5 | 7.4 | −1.4 | −8.4 | −3.6 | 9.5 | 11.1 | −9.2 | .... | .... | .... |
| Other investment: liabilities | 3d9la | 3.1 | 3.1 | 6.7 | 5.3 | 15.0 | 11.9 | −30.7 | −12.6 | −1.2 | .... | .... | .... |
| Other equity | 3dala | .... | .... | .... | .... | .... | .... | .... | .... | .... | .... | .... | .... |
| Debt instruments | 3dzla | 3.1 | 3.1 | 6.7 | 5.3 | 15.0 | 11.9 | −30.7 | −12.6 | −1.2 | .... | .... | .... |
| Curr.+ cap.− finan. acct. balance | 4y9na | −3.8 | −12.6 | −8.9 | 7.0 | −.4 | −2.1 | −92.8 | −15.9 | 24.5 | .... | .... | .... |
| D. Net Errors and Omissions | 409na | 2.9 | 6.7 | 1.7 | .6 | −14.1 | −8.1 | 2.9 | 10.8 | 6.2 | .... | .... | .... |
| E. Reserves and Related Items | 4z9na | −.9 | −5.8 | −7.1 | 7.6 | −14.5 | −10.1 | −89.9 | −5.1 | 30.7 | .... | .... | .... |
| Reserve assets | 3e9aa | −.7 | −4.2 | −2.3 | 13.5 | — | 33.5 | 5.3 | 16.5 | 34.0 | .... | .... | .... |
| Credit and loans from the IMF | 3dcla | −.2 | — | — | — | 5.1 | 4.9 | 2.3 | 2.4 | .2 | .... | .... | .... |
| Exceptional financing | 409la | .4 | 1.7 | 4.8 | 5.9 | 9.3 | 38.7 | 92.9 | 19.2 | 3.1 | .... | .... | .... |

*Excludes components in group E

| National Accounts | | | | | | | | | | | | | |
|---|---|---|---|---|---|---|---|---|---|---|---|---|---|
| | | | | | | | *Billions of Francs* | | | | | | |
| Gross Domestic Product (GDP) | 99b | 145.9 | 150.5 | 159.3 | 166.2 | 174.8 | 184.2 | 194.3 | .... | .... | .... | .... | .... |
| | | | | | | | *Millions: Midyear Estimates* | | | | | | |
| **Population** | 99z | .60 | .62 | .63 | .65 | .67 | .68 | .70 | .72 | .73 | .75 | .77 | .79 |

# Congo, Democratic Republic of   636

|  |  | 2004 | 2005 | 2006 | 2007 | 2008 | 2009 | 2010 | 2011 | 2012 | 2013 | 2014 | 2015 |
|---|---|---|---|---|---|---|---|---|---|---|---|---|---|
| **Exchange Rates** | | | | | | *Congo Francs per SDR: End of Period* | | | | | | | |
| Market Rate................................ | aa | 689.7 | 616.4 | 757.4 | 794.8 | 984.7 | 1,415.1 | 1,409.3 | 1,398.1 | 1,406.6 | 1,425.3 | 1,339.4 | 1,284.2 |
| | | | | | | *Congo Francs per US Dollar: End of Period (ae)  Period Average (rf)* | | | | | | | |
| Market Rate................................ | ae | 444.09 | 431.28 | 503.43 | 502.99 | 639.32 | 902.66 | 915.13 | 910.65 | 915.17 | 925.50 | 924.51 | 926.76 |
| Market Rate................................ | rf | 399.48 | 473.91 | 468.28 | 516.75 | 559.29 | 809.79 | 905.91 | 919.49 | 919.76 | 919.79 | 925.23 | 925.98 |
| | | | | | | *Index Numbers (2010=100):  Period Averages* | | | | | | | |
| Market Rate................................ | ahx | 227.4 | 191.6 | 194.5 | 175.7 | 162.2 | 112.6 | 100.0 | 98.5 | 98.5 | 98.5 | 97.9 | 97.8 |
| Nominal Effective Exchange Rate..... | nec | 241.9 | 200.7 | 201.6 | 172.2 | 153.5 | 113.1 | 100.0 | 94.9 | 100.0 | 100.9 | 102.4 | 117.9 |
| CPI-Based Real Effect. Ex. Rate........ | rec | 138.5 | 135.6 | 149.2 | 144.9 | 144.6 | 827.2 | 100.0 | 105.7 | 118.8 | 119.1 | 120.8 | 139.7 |
| **Fund Position** | | | | | | *Millions of SDRs: End of Period* | | | | | | | |
| Quota........................................ | 2f.s | 533.00 | 533.00 | 533.00 | 533.00 | 533.00 | 533.00 | 533.00 | 533.00 | 533.00 | 533.00 | 533.00 | 533.00 |
| SDR Holdings.............................. | 1b.s | 3.54 | .96 | .17 | 2.08 | 3.88 | 390.76 | 353.20 | 352.51 | 352.31 | 352.19 | 352.03 | 324.49 |
| Reserve Position in the Fund............ | 1c.s | — | — | — | — | — | — | — | — | — | — | — | — |
| Total Fund Cred.&Loans Outstg........ | 2tl | 526.77 | 553.47 | 553.47 | 511.47 | 424.80 | 510.20 | 209.82 | 308.81 | 308.81 | 308.81 | 308.81 | 281.35 |
| SDR Allocations............................ | 1bd | 86.31 | 86.31 | 86.31 | 86.31 | 86.31 | 510.86 | 510.86 | 510.86 | 510.86 | 510.86 | 510.86 | 510.86 |
| **International Liquidity** | | | | | | *Millions of US Dollars Unless Otherwise Indicated: End of Period* | | | | | | | |
| Total Reserves minus Gold.............. | 1l.d | 236.24 | 131.20 | 154.50 | 180.68 | 77.73 | 1,035.38 | 1,299.65 | 1,267.50 | 1,632.55 | 1,678.47 | 1,556.98 | 1,215.93 |
| SDR Holdings............................ | 1b.d | 5.50 | 1.38 | .26 | 3.29 | 5.98 | 612.58 | 543.93 | 541.20 | 541.47 | 542.37 | 510.03 | 449.65 |
| Reserve Position in the Fund.......... | 1c.d | — | — | — | — | — | — | — | — | — | — | — | — |
| Foreign Exchange....................... | 1d.d | 230.74 | 129.82 | 154.24 | 177.39 | 71.75 | 422.80 | 755.72 | 726.30 | 1,091.09 | 1,136.10 | 1,046.95 | 766.28 |
| Gold (Million Fine Troy Ounces)....... | 1ad | — | — | — | — | — | — | — | — | — | — | — | — |
| Central Bank: Other Assets............. | 3..d | 2.81 | 1.75 | .66 | 1.42 | .62 | 1.14 | 2.47 | .39 | 7.71 | 218.84 | 570.26 | 210.96 |
| Central Bank: Other Liabs............... | 4..d | 203.58 | 169.84 | 181.84 | 41.81 | 27.48 | 22.34 | 12.40 | 13.37 | 14.07 | 10.69 | 6.65 | 8.21 |
| Other Depository Corps.: Assets....... | 7a.d | 243.29 | 253.42 | 292.70 | 432.53 | 478.18 | 733.22 | 887.58 | 1,026.66 | 1,331.81 | 1,460.93 | 1,575.29 | 1,644.36 |
| Other Depository Corps.: Liabs......... | 7b.d | 95.11 | 58.86 | 67.21 | 118.26 | 205.82 | 165.87 | 109.63 | 118.40 | 168.62 | 299.11 | 263.51 | 331.34 |
| **Central Bank** | | | | | | *Millions of Congo Francs: End of Period* | | | | | | | |
| Net Foreign Assets........................ | 11n | −408,318 | −411,033 | −498,302 | −405,288 | −471,177 | −560,883 | 168,961 | 22,254 | 339,273 | 379,973 | 353,357 | 167,847 |
| Claims on Nonresidents................. | 11 | 104,913 | 56,584 | 77,782 | 90,878 | 49,697 | 904,164 | 1,195,981 | 1,180,614 | 1,504,708 | 1,558,109 | 1,457,395 | 1,192,834 |
| Liabilities to Nonresidents.............. | 16c | 513,231 | 467,617 | 576,084 | 496,166 | 520,874 | 1,465,047 | 1,027,020 | 1,158,360 | 1,165,434 | 1,178,137 | 1,104,038 | 1,024,988 |
| Claims on Other Depository Corps.... | 12e | 12,628 | 19,985 | 14,801 | 4,457 | 19,725 | 71,183 | 9,342 | 9,042 | 11,605 | 47,768 | 162,483 | 172,824 |
| Net Claims on Central Government.. | 12an | −11,941 | 32,826 | 76,637 | 89,232 | 125,033 | −15,181 | −661,346 | 848,610 | 535,381 | 603,527 | 619,988 | 815,671 |
| Claims on Central Government...... | 12a | 100,288 | 94,243 | 90,509 | 93,323 | 128,573 | 102,114 | — | 1,250,271 | 1,251,251 | 1,251,628 | 1,252,565 | 1,253,260 |
| Liabilities to Central Government... | 16d | 112,228 | 61,416 | 13,871 | 4,091 | 3,540 | 117,295 | 661,346 | 401,661 | 715,869 | 648,101 | 632,577 | 437,588 |
| Claims on Other Sectors................. | 12s | 1,113 | — | 915 | 3,486 | 3,029 | 3,578 | 5,147 | 5,409 | 10,206 | 6,572 | 10,834 | 10,891 |
| Claims on Other Financial Corps.... | 12g | — | — | — | — | — | — | — | 6 | — | — | — | — |
| Claims on State & Local Govts...... | 12b | — | — | — | — | — | — | — | — | — | — | — | — |
| Claims on Public Nonfin. Corps...... | 12c | — | — | 1 | 1 | 1 | 1 | 1 | 1 | 1 | 1 | 1 | 1 |
| Claims on Private Sector............... | 12d | 1,113 | — | 914 | 3,485 | 3,028 | 3,577 | 5,147 | 5,403 | 10,206 | 6,571 | 10,833 | 10,891 |
| Monetary Base.............................. | 14 | 116,680 | 133,640 | 206,000 | 283,235 | 378,372 | 467,683 | 611,029 | 792,239 | 843,832 | 973,695 | 1,092,209 | 1,244,363 |
| Currency in Circulation................. | 14a | 105,889 | 123,794 | 185,334 | 243,785 | 320,274 | 394,659 | 510,071 | 647,487 | 642,560 | 760,458 | 817,423 | 868,056 |
| Liabs. to Other Depository Corps.... | 14c | 5,790 | 5,261 | 18,415 | 38,740 | 56,232 | 69,711 | 99,310 | 142,649 | 198,462 | 210,476 | 272,119 | 371,406 |
| Liabilities to Other Sectors.............. | 14d | 5,001 | 4,586 | 2,252 | 711 | 1,866 | 3,313 | 1,647 | 2,103 | 2,810 | 2,761 | 2,667 | 4,901 |
| Other Liabs. to Other Dep. Corps..... | 14n | 789 | 6,000 | 15,605 | 34,080 | 48,476 | 57,676 | 136,415 | 115,877 | 95,775 | 165,428 | 126,618 | 47,539 |
| Dep. & Sec. Excl. f/Monetary Base.... | 14o | 5,995 | 4,562 | 5,313 | 1,245 | 1,663 | 233 | 4,921 | 1,557 | 1,000 | 1,952 | 1,437 | 2,611 |
| Deposits Included in Broad Money. | 15 | — | 179 | 1,255 | 45 | 115 | 28 | 4,598 | 1,154 | 415 | 1,371 | 624 | 952 |
| Sec.Ot.th.Shares Incl.in Brd. Money | 16a | — | — | — | — | — | — | — | — | — | — | — | — |
| Deposits Excl. from Broad Money... | 16b | 5,995 | 4,383 | 4,058 | 1,200 | 1,547 | 205 | 323 | 403 | 585 | 580 | 813 | 1,659 |
| Sec.Ot.th.Shares Excl.f/Brd.Money.. | 16s | — | — | — | — | — | — | — | — | — | — | — | — |
| Loans........................................ | 16l | — | — | — | — | — | — | — | — | — | — | — | — |
| Financial Derivatives...................... | 16m | — | — | — | — | — | — | — | — | — | — | — | — |
| Shares and Other Equity................. | 17a | −482,880 | −443,856 | −31,986 | −20,996 | −155,038 | −383,851 | −598,346 | 57,825 | 69,713 | 22,246 | −9,054 | −41,709 |
| Other Items (Net)........................... | 17r | −47,100 | −58,568 | −600,881 | −605,677 | −596,863 | −643,046 | −631,915 | −82,183 | −113,855 | −125,481 | −64,549 | −85,570 |
| Memo Item: | | | | | | | | | | | | | |
| Total Assets................................ | 10ra | 633,335 | 565,561 | 1,208,710 | 1,225,014 | 1,340,150 | 2,491,890 | 2,631,814 | 3,348,253 | 3,700,442 | 3,811,311 | 3,775,567 | 2,824,133 |

# Congo, Democratic Republic of   636

|  |  | 2004 | 2005 | 2006 | 2007 | 2008 | 2009 | 2010 | 2011 | 2012 | 2013 | 2014 | 2015 |
|---|---|---|---|---|---|---|---|---|---|---|---|---|---|
| **Other Depository Corporations** | | *Millions of Congo Francs: End of Period* | | | | | | | | | | | |
| Net Foreign Assets | 21n | 65,808 | 83,911 | 113,515 | 158,077 | 174,121 | 512,122 | 711,929 | 827,263 | 1,064,208 | 1,075,262 | 1,212,752 | 1,216,857 |
| Claims on Nonresidents | 21 | 108,043 | 109,294 | 147,353 | 217,559 | 305,708 | 661,850 | 812,255 | 935,102 | 1,218,482 | 1,352,093 | 1,456,368 | 1,523,928 |
| Liabilities to Nonresidents | 26c | 42,235 | 25,383 | 33,838 | 59,482 | 131,587 | 149,728 | 100,326 | 107,839 | 154,274 | 276,831 | 243,616 | 307,071 |
| Claims on Central Bank | 20 | 10,875 | 16,644 | 36,741 | 87,541 | 116,727 | 130,392 | 178,501 | 291,591 | 397,535 | 459,551 | 486,103 | 549,167 |
| Currency | 20a | 4,421 | 3,859 | 3,100 | 10,532 | 15,931 | 13,966 | 20,639 | 33,763 | 49,955 | 69,439 | 77,802 | 98,338 |
| Reserve Deposits and Securities | 20b | 6,434 | 8,471 | 21,250 | 49,244 | 58,861 | 85,227 | 126,401 | 209,703 | 267,032 | 274,497 | 301,249 | 403,829 |
| Other Claims | 20n | 20 | 4,314 | 12,391 | 27,765 | 41,935 | 31,199 | 31,461 | 48,125 | 80,548 | 115,616 | 107,052 | 47,000 |
| Net Claims on Central Government | 22an | −1,780 | −4,512 | −27,701 | −16,074 | −34,190 | −54,988 | 2,922 | −82,664 | −231,064 | −140,997 | −73,124 | −24,976 |
| Claims on Central Government | 22a | 15,490 | 16,725 | 21,441 | 24,348 | 30,812 | 21,928 | 24,032 | 38,473 | 53,087 | 109,873 | 123,148 | 161,901 |
| Liabilities to Central Government | 26d | 17,270 | 21,237 | 49,141 | 40,422 | 65,001 | 76,916 | 21,109 | 121,137 | 284,150 | 250,870 | 196,272 | 186,878 |
| Claims on Other Sectors | 22s | 46,489 | 69,695 | 144,010 | 231,294 | 557,483 | 839,028 | 811,243 | 1,106,723 | 1,445,634 | 1,717,703 | 2,071,546 | 2,357,022 |
| Claims on Other Financial Corps | 22g | 8 | 2 | — | 440 | 3 | 2,939 | 10,642 | 12,886 | 14,484 | 10,934 | 12,489 | 19,277 |
| Claims on State & Local Govts | 22b | — | — | — | — | — | — | 19,125 | 24,598 | 12,426 | 44,235 | 68,157 | 62,056 |
| Claims on Public Nonfin. Corps | 22c | 2,540 | 1,592 | 3,937 | 5,415 | 8,352 | 39,270 | 57,374 | 118,807 | 132,056 | 92,470 | 101,991 | 80,766 |
| Claims on Private Sector | 22d | 43,941 | 68,102 | 140,072 | 225,439 | 549,129 | 796,819 | 724,102 | 950,432 | 1,286,668 | 1,570,064 | 1,888,908 | 2,194,923 |
| Liabilities to Central Bank | 26g | 8,154 | 16,052 | 12,827 | 2,550 | 17,505 | 83,066 | 13,243 | 60,071 | 20,081 | 1,818 | 13,001 | 25,293 |
| Transf.Dep.Included in Broad Money | 24 | 83,105 | 121,993 | 187,507 | 311,754 | 501,896 | 854,253 | 1,221,005 | 1,255,431 | 1,577,320 | 1,825,256 | 1,963,439 | 2,141,816 |
| Other Dep.Included in Broad Money | 25 | 18,690 | 10,181 | 28,838 | 59,725 | 130,589 | 228,265 | 259,707 | 528,839 | 724,454 | 920,218 | 1,238,682 | 1,397,905 |
| Sec.Ot.th.Shares Incl.in Brd. Money | 26a | — | — | — | — | — | — | — | — | — | — | — | — |
| Deposits Excl. from Broad Money | 26b | 2,575 | 7,046 | 9,176 | 16,039 | 44,383 | 41,439 | 21,297 | 25,069 | 22,128 | 26,545 | 16,389 | 16,392 |
| Sec.Ot.th.Shares Excl.f/Brd.Money | 26s | — | — | 4,188 | 3,292 | 8,963 | 2,316 | — | — | — | — | — | — |
| Loans | 26l | — | — | — | — | — | 1,145 | 4,945 | 2,233 | 4,070 | 2,823 | 4,723 | 18,641 |
| Financial Derivatives | 26m | — | — | — | — | — | — | — | — | — | — | — | — |
| Insurance Technical Reserves | 26r | — | — | — | — | — | — | — | 137 | — | — | — | — |
| Shares and Other Equity | 27a | 13,865 | 18,615 | 39,500 | 59,296 | 97,108 | 201,810 | 246,343 | 434,349 | 492,993 | 535,453 | 608,730 | 712,830 |
| Other Items (Net) | 27r | −4,997 | −8,150 | −15,469 | 8,182 | 13,697 | 14,259 | −61,944 | −163,217 | −164,733 | −200,594 | −147,687 | −214,808 |
| Memo Item: | | | | | | | | | | | | | |
| Total Assets | 20ra | 210,715 | 253,538 | 410,062 | 630,809 | 1,105,678 | 1,817,962 | 2,125,233 | 2,750,947 | 3,552,913 | 4,213,242 | 4,747,003 | 5,309,916 |
| **Depository Corporations** | | *Millions of Congo Francs: End of Period* | | | | | | | | | | | |
| Net Foreign Assets | 31n | −342,510 | −327,122 | −384,787 | −247,210 | −297,056 | −48,762 | 880,890 | 849,517 | 1,403,482 | 1,455,234 | 1,566,108 | 1,384,703 |
| Claims on Nonresidents | 31 | 212,956 | 165,878 | 225,135 | 308,437 | 355,405 | 1,566,014 | 2,008,236 | 2,115,716 | 2,723,190 | 2,910,202 | 2,913,763 | 2,716,762 |
| Liabilities to Nonresidents | 36c | 555,466 | 493,000 | 609,921 | 555,648 | 652,461 | 1,614,775 | 1,127,346 | 1,266,199 | 1,319,708 | 1,454,968 | 1,347,654 | 1,332,059 |
| Domestic Claims | 32 | 33,881 | 98,009 | 193,861 | 307,938 | 651,355 | 772,437 | 157,966 | 1,878,078 | 1,760,158 | 2,186,805 | 2,629,243 | 3,158,608 |
| Net Claims on Central Government | 32an | −13,721 | 28,315 | 48,937 | 73,159 | 90,843 | −70,169 | −658,424 | 765,945 | 304,318 | 462,530 | 546,864 | 790,695 |
| Claims on Central Government | 32a | 115,778 | 110,968 | 111,949 | 117,671 | 159,385 | 124,042 | 24,032 | 1,288,744 | 1,304,338 | 1,361,501 | 1,375,712 | 1,415,161 |
| Liabilities to Central Government | 36d | 129,498 | 82,653 | 63,013 | 44,513 | 68,542 | 194,211 | 682,455 | 522,799 | 1,000,020 | 898,971 | 828,849 | 624,466 |
| Claims on Other Sectors | 32s | 47,602 | 69,695 | 144,924 | 234,780 | 560,512 | 842,605 | 816,390 | 1,112,133 | 1,455,840 | 1,724,275 | 2,082,380 | 2,367,913 |
| Claims on Other Financial Corps | 32g | 8 | 2 | — | 440 | 3 | 2,939 | 10,642 | 12,892 | 14,484 | 10,934 | 12,489 | 19,277 |
| Claims on State & Local Govts | 32b | — | — | — | — | — | — | 19,125 | 24,598 | 12,426 | 44,235 | 68,157 | 62,056 |
| Claims on Public Nonfin. Corps | 32c | 2,540 | 1,592 | 3,939 | 5,415 | 8,352 | 39,270 | 57,375 | 118,808 | 132,056 | 92,471 | 101,992 | 80,767 |
| Claims on Private Sector | 32d | 45,054 | 68,101 | 140,985 | 228,924 | 552,157 | 800,396 | 729,249 | 955,836 | 1,296,874 | 1,576,636 | 1,899,741 | 2,205,814 |
| Broad Money Liabilities | 35l | 208,263 | 256,874 | 402,085 | 605,487 | 938,810 | 1,466,553 | 1,976,390 | 2,401,251 | 2,897,604 | 3,440,626 | 3,945,033 | 4,315,292 |
| Currency Outside Depository Corps | 34a | 101,467 | 119,935 | 182,234 | 233,253 | 304,344 | 380,693 | 489,432 | 613,724 | 592,606 | 691,019 | 739,621 | 769,719 |
| Transferable Deposits | 34 | 88,106 | 126,578 | 189,758 | 312,509 | 503,877 | 857,589 | 1,227,220 | 1,258,658 | 1,580,514 | 1,829,357 | 1,966,699 | 2,147,640 |
| Other Deposits | 35 | 18,690 | 10,360 | 30,093 | 59,725 | 130,589 | 228,270 | 259,737 | 528,870 | 724,484 | 920,250 | 1,238,713 | 1,397,933 |
| Securities Other than Shares | 36a | — | — | — | — | — | — | — | — | — | — | — | — |
| Deposits Excl. from Broad Money | 36b | 8,570 | 11,429 | 13,234 | 17,240 | 45,930 | 41,644 | 21,620 | 25,472 | 22,713 | 27,126 | 17,202 | 18,051 |
| Sec.Ot.th.Shares Excl.f/Brd.Money | 36s | — | — | 4,188 | 3,292 | 8,963 | 2,316 | — | — | — | — | — | — |
| Loans | 36l | — | — | — | — | — | 1,145 | 4,945 | 2,233 | 4,070 | 2,823 | 4,723 | 18,641 |
| Financial Derivatives | 36m | — | — | — | — | — | — | — | — | — | — | — | — |
| Insurance Technical Reserves | 36r | — | — | — | — | — | — | — | 137 | — | — | — | — |
| Shares and Other Equity | 37a | −469,015 | −425,241 | 7,514 | 38,300 | −57,930 | −182,041 | −352,003 | 492,174 | 562,706 | 557,699 | 599,676 | 671,121 |
| Other Items (Net) | 37r | −56,447 | −72,174 | −617,946 | −603,591 | −581,474 | −605,942 | −612,096 | −193,673 | −323,454 | −386,234 | −371,282 | −479,794 |
| Broad Money Liabs., Seasonally Adj. | 35l.b | 204,518 | 250,384 | 387,852 | 577,409 | 888,651 | 1,385,351 | 1,869,539 | 2,278,404 | 2,754,722 | 3,274,801 | 3,764,941 | . . . . |
| **Monetary Aggregates** | | *Millions of Congo Francs: End of Period* | | | | | | | | | | | |
| Broad Money | 59m | 208,263 | 256,874 | 402,085 | 605,487 | 938,810 | 1,466,553 | 1,976,390 | 2,401,251 | 2,897,604 | 3,440,626 | 3,945,033 | 4,315,292 |
| o/w:Currency Issued by Cent.Govt | 59m.a | — | — | — | — | — | — | — | — | — | — | — | — |
| o/w: Dep.in Nonfin. Corporations | 59m.b | — | — | — | — | — | — | — | — | — | — | — | — |
| o/w: Secs. Issued by Central Govt | 59m.c | — | — | — | — | — | — | — | — | — | — | — | — |
| Money (National Definitions) | | | | | | | | | | | | | |
| Base Money | 19ma | 116,680 | 133,640 | 206,000 | 283,235 | 378,372 | 467,683 | 611,029 | 792,239 | 845,089 | 973,695 | 1,092,209 | 1,244,363 |
| M1 | 59ma | 116,878 | 135,685 | 207,073 | 294,273 | 384,419 | 470,161 | 645,174 | 747,563 | 833,732 | 978,670 | 1,038,263 | 1,123,956 |
| M2 | 59mb | 208,263 | 256,874 | 402,085 | 605,487 | 938,810 | 1,466,553 | 1,976,390 | 2,401,251 | 2,897,604 | 3,440,626 | 3,945,033 | 4,315,292 |
| **Interest Rates** | | *Percent Per Annum* | | | | | | | | | | | |
| Central Bank Policy Rate (EOP) | 60 | . . . . | . . . . | 40.00 | 22.50 | 40.00 | 70.00 | 22.00 | 20.00 | 4.00 | 2.00 | 2.00 | 2.00 |
| Discount Rate (End of Period) | 60.a | . . . . | . . . . | † 50.00 | 27.50 | 42.50 | 72.50 | 24.50 | 22.50 | 5.25 | 3.00 | 3.00 | 3.00 |
| Money Market Rate (Minimum) | 60ba | . . . . | . . . . | . . . . | 16.50 | 17.00 | 65.00 | 9.00 | 10.00 | 1.00 | 1.00 | 1.00 | 1.70 |
| Money Market Rate (Maximum) | 60bb | . . . . | . . . . | . . . . | 18.30 | 30.00 | 68.00 | 22.00 | 13.00 | 2.00 | 1.75 | 1.75 | 1.75 |
| Deposit Rate (End of Period) | 60l | . . . . | . . . . | . . . . | 14.39 | 7.80 | 16.08 | 16.77 | 13.36 | 7.72 | 4.71 | 4.01 | 3.66 |
| Lending Rate (End of Period) | 60p | . . . . | . . . . | 46.44 | 47.00 | 43.15 | 65.42 | 56.52 | 43.75 | 28.45 | 19.37 | 18.69 | 19.37 |
| Lending Rate in Fgn. Currency (EOP) | 60p.f | . . . . | . . . . | 16.28 | 16.91 | 17.18 | 17.46 | 18.85 | 17.52 | 16.61 | 15.02 | 14.85 | 14.20 |
| **Prices** | | *Index Numbers (2010=100): Period Averages* | | | | | | | | | | | |
| Consumer Prices | 64 | 48.3 | 58.6 | 66.2 | 77.4 | 90.8 | 93.4 | † 100.0 | 115.3 | 126.5 | 128.6 | . . . . | . . . . |
| **Intl. Transactions & Positions** | | *Millions of US Dollars* | | | | | | | | | | | |
| Exports | 70..d | 1,850 | 2,190 | 2,320 | 2,600 | 4,400 | 3,500 | 5,300 | 6,600 | 6,300 | 6,300 | 6,600 | 5,800 |
| Imports, c.i.f. | 71..d | 1,986 | 2,270 | 2,740 | 2,950 | 4,300 | 3,900 | 4,500 | 5,500 | 6,100 | 6,300 | 6,500 | 6,200 |

# Congo, Democratic Republic of   636

| | | 2004 | 2005 | 2006 | 2007 | 2008 | 2009 | 2010 | 2011 | 2012 | 2013 | 2014 | 2015 |
|---|---|---|---|---|---|---|---|---|---|---|---|---|---|
| **Balance of Payments** | | | | | | | *Millions of US Dollars* | | | | | | | |
| A. Current Account* | 109bx | .... | −388.6 | 47.8 | 527.0 | −151.0 | −1,123.1 | −2,173.5 | −1,280.6 | −1,260.5 | −3,108.8 | −1,722.6 | −1,545.6 |
| Goods, credit (exports) | 1a9cx | .... | 2,402.8 | 2,704.7 | 6,147.9 | 6,869.8 | 4,371.0 | 8,477.9 | 9,471.9 | 8,743.4 | 11,613.0 | 12,321.2 | 10,284.8 |
| Goods, debit (imports) | 1a9dx | .... | 2,690.4 | 2,891.6 | 5,257.2 | 6,725.8 | 4,949.0 | 8,042.5 | 8,915.6 | 8,677.2 | 10,808.4 | 12,706.3 | 10,574.6 |
| Balance on goods | 1a9bx | .... | −287.6 | −186.9 | 890.7 | 144.0 | −578.0 | 435.4 | 556.3 | 66.1 | 804.5 | −385.1 | −289.8 |
| Services, credit (exports) | 1b9cx | .... | 343.2 | 432.9 | 392.4 | 828.2 | 649.9 | 388.6 | 739.4 | 287.7 | 296.1 | 314.8 | 173.3 |
| Services, debit (imports) | 1b9dx | .... | 1,169.2 | 905.8 | 1,617.6 | 2,099.6 | 1,817.1 | 2,662.7 | 2,889.3 | 2,331.6 | 2,595.3 | 3,082.2 | 2,025.8 |
| Balance on Goods & Services | 1z9bx | .... | −1,113.6 | −659.8 | −334.5 | −1,127.4 | −1,745.2 | −1,838.7 | −1,593.6 | −1,977.8 | −1,494.7 | −3,152.5 | −2,142.3 |
| Primary income: credit | 1c9cx | .... | 9.5 | 17.7 | 26.0 | 17.8 | 26.0 | 48.3 | 168.2 | 18.3 | 144.8 | 109.4 | 5.3 |
| Primary income: debit | 1c9dx | .... | 32.3 | 31.5 | 26.4 | 37.4 | 805.0 | 1,225.8 | 1,266.1 | 1,065.8 | 3,024.7 | 712.5 | 812.1 |
| Balance on gds, serv. & prim. inc. | 1y9bx | .... | −1,136.4 | −673.6 | −334.9 | −1,147.0 | −2,524.2 | −3,016.2 | −2,691.5 | −3,025.3 | −4,374.5 | −3,755.6 | −2,949.0 |
| Secondary income: credit | 1d9ca | .... | 943.6 | 1,203.1 | 1,484.4 | 1,738.4 | 1,704.3 | 1,688.0 | 2,430.4 | 2,709.6 | 2,369.0 | 2,527.7 | 1,887.0 |
| Secondary income: debit | 1d9da | .... | 195.8 | 481.7 | 622.5 | 742.4 | 303.2 | 845.3 | 1,019.5 | 944.7 | 1,103.3 | 494.8 | 483.6 |
| B. Capital Account* | 209ba | .... | −92.8 | 81.7 | −1.6 | 110.1 | 144.0 | −160.7 | 932.7 | 486.4 | 192.7 | 320.5 | 252.2 |
| Capital account: credit | 209ca | .... | 57.6 | 151.5 | 54.7 | 170.6 | 403.9 | 333.6 | 1,240.5 | 645.1 | 206.6 | 570.9 | 306.5 |
| Capital account: debit | 209da | .... | 150.4 | 69.8 | 56.3 | 60.5 | 259.9 | 494.3 | 307.8 | 158.7 | 13.9 | 250.4 | 54.4 |
| Balance on current & capital acct. | 129ba | .... | −481.4 | 129.5 | 525.4 | −40.9 | −979.1 | −2,334.2 | −347.9 | −774.1 | −2,916.1 | −1,402.1 | −1,293.5 |
| C. Financial Account* | 309na | .... | −333.7 | 299.7 | 481.5 | .8 | −71.9 | 9,464.0 | −272.6 | −1,345.4 | −2,996.0 | −1,531.2 | −1,291.4 |
| Direct investment: assets | 3a9aa | .... | — | — | — | — | 243.2 | −2,611.0 | −1,686.9 | −3,312.1 | −2,098.2 | −1,843.2 | −1,673.5 |
| Equity & investment fund shares.. | 3aaaa | .... | — | — | — | — | 243.2 | −2,604.7 | −1,686.9 | −3,312.1 | −2,098.2 | −1,843.2 | −1,673.5 |
| Debt instruments | 3abaa | .... | — | — | — | — | — | −6.3 | — | — | — | — | — |
| Direct investment: liabilities | 3a9la | .... | 166.6 | 237.7 | 1,793.7 | 1,672.7 | −34.8 | 124.1 | −90.9 | −420.5 | −400.7 | −343.6 | −507.8 |
| Equity & investment fund shares . | 3aala | .... | 180.0 | 256.1 | 1,808.0 | 1,726.8 | — | 131.3 | | | | | |
| Debt instruments | 3abla | .... | −13.4 | −18.4 | −14.3 | −54.1 | −34.8 | −7.2 | −90.9 | −420.5 | −400.7 | −343.6 | −507.8 |
| Portfolio investment: assets | 3b9aa | .... | 13.4 | 413.2 | 1,833.6 | 1,574.9 | 1,189.4 | 3,237.4 | −2.9 | — | — | — | — |
| Equity & investment fund shares | 3baaa | .... | .... | .... | .... | .... | .... | .... | .... | .... | .... | .... | .... |
| Debt securities | 3bbaa | .... | .... | .... | .... | .... | .... | .... | .... | .... | .... | .... | .... |
| Portfolio investment: liabilities | 3b9la | .... | — | — | — | — | — | — | −2,139.8 | −3,532.4 | −3.4 | −13.6 | −94.1 |
| Equity & investment fund shares . | 3bala | .... | | | | | | .... | −2,139.8 | −3,532.4 | −3.4 | −13.6 | −94.1 |
| Debt securities | 3bbla | .... | — | — | — | — | — | — | — | — | — | — | — |
| Fin. der.& empl.stk.ops.(ESOs): net. | 3c9na | .... | — | — | — | — | — | — | — | — | — | — | — |
| Fin. der. & ESOs.: assets | 3c9aa | .... | — | — | — | — | — | — | — | — | — | — | — |
| Fin. der. & ESOs.: liabilities | 3c9la | .... | — | — | — | — | — | — | — | — | — | — | — |
| Other investment: assets | 3d9aa | .... | 40.6 | −88.2 | −101.4 | −113.4 | −401.3 | −216.4 | −1,803.4 | −2,749.2 | −2,134.0 | −984.4 | −1,501.3 |
| Other equity | 3daaa | .... | .... | | | | | | | | | | |
| Debt instruments | 3dzaa | .... | 40.6 | −88.2 | −101.4 | −113.4 | −401.3 | −216.4 | −1,803.4 | −2,749.2 | −2,134.0 | −984.4 | −1,501.3 |
| Other investment: liabilities | 3d9la | .... | 221.1 | −212.5 | −542.9 | −212.0 | 1,138.0 | −9,178.1 | −989.9 | −762.9 | −832.3 | −939.1 | −1,281.4 |
| Other equity | 3dala | .... | .... | | | | | | | | | | |
| Debt instruments | 3dzla | .... | 221.1 | −212.5 | −542.9 | −212.0 | 1,138.0 | −9,178.1 | −989.9 | −762.9 | −832.3 | −939.1 | −1,281.4 |
| Curr.+ cap.− finan. acct. balance... | 4y9na | .... | −147.7 | −170.2 | 44.0 | −41.7 | −907.2 | −11,798.2 | −75.3 | 571.3 | 79.9 | 129.1 | −2.0 |
| D. Net Errors and Omissions | 409na | .... | 104.8 | 169.0 | 25.7 | 180.4 | 1,386.8 | 1,148.4 | −7.0 | 29.4 | −20.6 | −53.1 | −192.9 |
| E. Reserves and Related Items | 4z9na | .... | −42.9 | −1.2 | 69.6 | 138.8 | 479.5 | −10,649.8 | −82.3 | 600.7 | 59.3 | 76.1 | −194.9 |
| Reserve assets | 3e9aa | .... | −3.8 | −1.2 | 3.4 | 2.8 | 603.5 | −429.7 | 74.2 | 600.7 | 59.3 | 76.1 | −233.4 |
| Credit and loans from the IMF | 3dcla | .... | 39.1 | | −66.2 | −135.9 | 124.0 | −450.7 | 156.4 | | | | −38.5 |
| Exceptional financing | 409la | .... | — | — | — | — | — | 10,670.8 | — | — | — | — | — |

*Excludes components in group E

**Government Finance**
**Cash Flow Statement**

| **Central Government** | | | | | | | | | | | | | |
|---|---|---|---|---|---|---|---|---|---|---|---|---|---|
| | | | | | | *Millions of Congo Francs:  Fiscal Year Ends December 31* | | | | | | | |
| Cash Receipts:Operating Activities... | c1 | 536,322 | 1,139,225 | 1,216,224 | 1,523,756 | 2,118,576 | 3,134,562 | 4,034,950 | .... | .... | .... | .... | .... |
| Taxes | c11 | 217,064 | 335,703 | 462,101 | 604,746 | 992,416 | 1,191,812 | 1,631,397 | .... | .... | .... | .... | .... |
| Social Contributions | c12 | — | — | — | — | — | — | — | .... | .... | .... | .... | .... |
| Grants | c13 | 230,297 | 643,962 | 547,057 | 729,966 | 846,898 | 1,029,839 | 1,247,917 | .... | .... | .... | .... | .... |
| Other Receipts | c14 | 88,961 | 159,561 | 207,066 | 189,045 | 279,262 | 912,911 | 1,155,636 | .... | .... | .... | .... | .... |
| Cash Payments:Operating Activities. | c2 | 422,177 | 743,709 | 976,415 | 1,101,599 | 1,367,069 | 1,707,224 | 1,635,171 | .... | .... | .... | .... | .... |
| Compensation of Employees | c21 | 93,223 | 146,776 | 218,898 | 300,984 | 452,220 | 547,562 | 696,667 | .... | .... | .... | .... | .... |
| Purchases of Goods & Services | c22 | 175,514 | 163,506 | 208,684 | 244,485 | 404,119 | 357,694 | 304,658 | .... | .... | .... | .... | .... |
| Interest | c24 | 39,043 | 99,878 | 113,097 | 34,396 | 41,015 | 63,111 | 51,512 | .... | .... | .... | .... | .... |
| Subsidies | c25 | | 78,367 | 146,469 | 231,146 | 205,219 | 601,289 | 539,647 | .... | .... | .... | .... | .... |
| Grants | c26 | | | | | | | | .... | .... | .... | .... | .... |
| Social Benefits | c27 | 3,123 | 3,524 | 5,127 | 9,584 | 8,899 | 8,557 | 24,212 | .... | .... | .... | .... | .... |
| Other Payments | c28 | 111,275 | 251,657 | 284,141 | 281,004 | 255,597 | 129,011 | 18,473 | .... | .... | .... | .... | .... |
| Net Cash Inflow:Operating Act.[1-2] | ccio | 114,145 | 395,517 | 239,809 | 422,157 | 751,507 | 1,427,338 | 2,399,779 | .... | .... | .... | .... | .... |
| Net Cash Outflow:Invest. in NFA | c31 | 140,407 | 429,757 | 298,076 | 477,424 | 758,460 | 1,388,199 | 1,945,974 | .... | .... | .... | .... | .... |
| Purchases of Nonfinancial Assets... | c31.1 | 140,407 | 429,757 | 298,076 | 477,424 | 758,460 | 1,388,199 | 1,945,974 | .... | .... | .... | .... | .... |
| Sales of Nonfinancial Assets | c31.2 | | | | | | | | .... | .... | .... | .... | .... |
| Cash Surplus/Deficit [1-2-31=1-2M] | ccsd | −26,263 | −34,240 | −58,267 | −55,267 | −6,953 | 39,139 | 453,805 | .... | .... | .... | .... | .... |
| Net Acq. Fin. Assets, excl. Cash | c32x | — | — | — | — | — | — | — | .... | .... | .... | .... | .... |
| Domestic | c321x | — | — | — | — | — | — | — | .... | .... | .... | .... | .... |
| Foreign | c322x | — | — | — | — | — | — | — | .... | .... | .... | .... | .... |
| Net Incurrence of Liabilities | c33 | −64,204 | 6,755 | −2,435 | 8,200 | 33,438 | −47,639 | 97,584 | .... | .... | .... | .... | .... |
| Domestic | c331 | −2,370 | 57,356 | 47,521 | 44,124 | 72,687 | −12,262 | −562,890 | .... | .... | .... | .... | .... |
| Foreign | c332 | −61,833 | −50,601 | −49,956 | −35,924 | −39,249 | −35,376 | 660,474 | .... | .... | .... | .... | .... |
| Net Cash Inflow, Fin.Act.[-32x+33].. | cnfb | −64,204 | 6,755 | −2,435 | 8,200 | 33,438 | −47,639 | 97,584 | .... | .... | .... | .... | .... |
| Net Change in Stock of Cash | cncb | −90,467 | −27,485 | −60,701 | −47,067 | 26,486 | −8,500 | 551,389 | .... | .... | .... | .... | .... |
| Stat. Discrep. [32X-33+NCB-CSD].... | ccsdz | — | — | — | — | — | — | — | .... | .... | .... | .... | .... |
| Memo Item:Cash Expenditure[2+31] | c2m | 562,585 | 1,173,465 | 1,274,491 | 1,579,023 | 2,125,529 | 3,095,423 | 3,581,145 | .... | .... | .... | .... | .... |
| Memo Item: Gross Debt | c63 | .... | .... | .... | .... | .... | .... | .... | .... | .... | .... | .... | .... |

| National Accounts | | 2004 | 2005 | 2006 | 2007 | 2008 | 2009 | 2010 | 2011 | 2012 | 2013 | 2014 | 2015 |
|---|---|---|---|---|---|---|---|---|---|---|---|---|---|
| | | | | | | *Millions of Congo Francs* | | | | | | | |
| Househ.Cons.Expend.,incl.NPISHs.... | 96f | 1,908,680 | 2,373,154 | 2,597,466 | 3,702,365 | 4,904,855 | 6,116,851 | 8,110,952 | .... | .... | .... | .... | .... |
| Government Consumption Expend... | 91f | 419,840 | 724,613 | 882,498 | 952,729 | 1,107,709 | 981,256 | 1,405,640 | .... | .... | .... | .... | .... |
| Gross Fixed Capital Formation.......... | 93e | 481,185 | 679,861 | 841,684 | 1,003,507 | 1,362,076 | 1,789,652 | 2,612,195 | .... | .... | .... | .... | .... |
| Changes in Inventories..................... | 93i | −6,056 | 157,958 | 49,809 | −337,604 | −215,960 | 1,546,242 | 1,486,081 | .... | .... | .... | .... | .... |
| Exports of Goods and Services......... | 90c | .... | .... | .... | .... | .... | .... | .... | .... | .... | .... | .... | .... |
| Imports of Goods and Services (-)..... | 98c | .... | .... | .... | .... | .... | .... | .... | .... | .... | .... | .... | .... |
| Gross Domestic Product (GDP)......... | 99b | 2,601,000 | 5,670,100 | 7,167,000 | 8,450,400 | 11,699,000 | 19,106,200 | 22,678,800 | 28,352,700 | 33,481,600 | 36,984,800 | .... | .... |
| Net Primary Income from Abroad..... | 98.n | −150,615 | .... | .... | .... | .... | .... | .... | .... | .... | .... | .... | .... |
| Gross National Income (GNI)............ | 99a | 2,450,385 | 3,212,665 | 3,833,585 | 4,934,433 | 6,030,708 | 9,023,280 | .... | .... | .... | .... | .... | .... |
| | | | | | | *Millions: Midyear Estimates* | | | | | | | |
| Population.................................. | 99z | 54.31 | 56.09 | 57.93 | 59.83 | 61.81 | 63.85 | 65.94 | 68.09 | 70.29 | 72.55 | 74.88 | 77.27 |

# Congo, Republic of  634

| | | 2004 | 2005 | 2006 | 2007 | 2008 | 2009 | 2010 | 2011 | 2012 | 2013 | 2014 | 2015 |
|---|---|---|---|---|---|---|---|---|---|---|---|---|---|
| **Exchange Rates** | | | | | | *CFA Francs per SDR: End of Period* | | | | | | | |
| Official Rate | aa | 747.90 | 794.73 | 749.30 | 704.15 | 725.98 | 713.83 | 756.02 | 778.32 | 764.10 | 732.49 | 782.77 | 834.92 |
| | | | | | | *CFA Francs per US Dollar: End of Period (ae) Period Average (rf)* | | | | | | | |
| Official Rate | ae | 481.58 | 556.04 | 498.07 | 445.59 | 471.34 | 455.34 | 490.91 | 506.96 | 497.16 | 475.64 | 540.28 | 602.51 |
| Official Rate | rf | 528.28 | 527.47 | 522.89 | 479.27 | 447.81 | 472.19 | 495.28 | 471.87 | 510.53 | 494.04 | 494.41 | 591.45 |
| **Fund Position** | | | | | | *Millions of SDRs: End of Period* | | | | | | | |
| Quota | 2f.s | 84.60 | 84.60 | 84.60 | 84.60 | 84.60 | 84.60 | 84.60 | 84.60 | 84.60 | 84.60 | 84.60 | 84.60 |
| SDR Holdings | 1b.s | 4.66 | 1.70 | .13 | .11 | .14 | 70.06 | 70.06 | 70.06 | 70.23 | 70.23 | 69.99 | 69.99 |
| Reserve Position in the Fund | 1c.s | .54 | .54 | .54 | .58 | .58 | .58 | .58 | .58 | .58 | .58 | .58 | .59 |
| Total Fund Cred.&Loans Outstg | 2tl | 18.71 | 18.50 | 23.58 | 23.58 | 24.79 | 27.21 | 17.48 | 21.11 | 19.46 | 16.32 | 12.81 | 8.94 |
| SDR Allocations | 1bd | 9.72 | 9.72 | 9.72 | 9.72 | 9.72 | 79.69 | 79.69 | 79.69 | 79.69 | 79.69 | 79.69 | 79.69 |
| **International Liquidity** | | | | | | *Millions of US Dollars Unless Otherwise Indicated: End of Period* | | | | | | | |
| Total Reserves minus Gold | 1l.d | 119.60 | 731.83 | 1,840.93 | 2,174.29 | 3,871.78 | 3,806.25 | 4,446.85 | 5,641.14 | 5,549.56 | 5,245.01 | 4,926.10 | 2,221.50 |
| SDR Holdings | 1b.d | 7.23 | 2.43 | .19 | .17 | .22 | 109.83 | 107.89 | 107.56 | 107.94 | 108.15 | 101.40 | 96.98 |
| Reserve Position in the Fund | 1c.d | .83 | .77 | .81 | .91 | .89 | .90 | .89 | .88 | .89 | .89 | .83 | .82 |
| Foreign Exchange | 1d.d | 111.54 | 728.63 | 1,839.94 | 2,173.21 | 3,870.68 | 3,695.51 | 4,338.07 | 5,532.70 | 5,440.74 | 5,135.97 | 4,823.87 | 2,123.69 |
| Gold (Million Fine Troy Ounces) | 1ad | .011 | .011 | .011 | .011 | .011 | . . . . | . . . . | . . . . | . . . . | . . . . | . . . . | . . . . |
| Gold (National Valuation) | 1and | 4.88 | 5.71 | 7.06 | 9.37 | 1.62 | — | 17.82 | 17.01 | 18.73 | . . . . | . . . . | . . . . |
| Central Bank: Other Assets | 3..d | — | — | — | — | — | 16.13 | 15.56 | 12.39 | 11.09 | 16.81 | 54.61 | 57.80 |
| Central Bank: Other Liabs | 4..d | 4.66 | 3.87 | 2.78 | 26.34 | 40.66 | 18.59 | 130.19 | 59.81 | 45.29 | 67.98 | 45.67 | 54.62 |
| Other Depository Corps.: Assets | 7a.d | 87.13 | 148.14 | 298.54 | 389.52 | 236.18 | 412.16 | 587.58 | 693.90 | 929.46 | 1,401.00 | 530.33 | 633.42 |
| Other Depository Corps.: Liabs | 7b.d | 57.63 | 16.61 | 15.51 | 20.18 | 52.31 | 27.32 | 51.28 | 116.50 | 83.30 | 120.82 | 192.75 | 158.09 |
| **Central Bank** | | | | | | *Billions of CFA Francs: End of Period* | | | | | | | |
| Net Foreign Assets | 11n | 36.44 | 385.52 | 894.09 | 937.84 | 1,781.13 | 1,655.70 | 2,062.02 | 2,765.97 | 2,675.59 | 2,406.47 | 2,601.16 | 1,273.52 |
| Claims on Nonresidents | 11 | 59.95 | 410.10 | 920.43 | 973.02 | 1,825.35 | 1,740.47 | 2,199.40 | 2,874.74 | 2,773.87 | 2,509.13 | 2,698.24 | 1,380.43 |
| Liabilities to Nonresidents | 16c | 23.50 | 24.58 | 26.34 | 35.19 | 44.22 | 84.77 | 137.38 | 108.77 | 98.28 | 102.66 | 97.08 | 106.91 |
| Claims on Other Depository Corps | 12e | .39 | — | — | 2.80 | — | — | — | — | — | — | — | 6.00 |
| Net Claims on Central Government | 12an | 184.46 | –6.77 | –428.93 | –383.84 | –1,001.29 | –883.74 | –1,250.61 | –1,617.07 | –1,325.96 | –1,258.43 | –938.74 | –111.98 |
| Claims on Central Government | 12a | 194.85 | 187.62 | 149.10 | 170.50 | 18.00 | 61.42 | 55.30 | 16.57 | 15.16 | 12.16 | 360.25 | 579.96 |
| Liabilities to Central Government | 16d | 10.39 | 194.39 | 578.02 | 554.34 | 1,019.29 | 945.16 | 1,305.91 | 1,633.64 | 1,341.13 | 1,270.58 | 1,298.98 | 691.95 |
| Claims on Other Sectors | 12s | — | — | — | — | 1.00 | 1.19 | 1.88 | 2.70 | 3.09 | 3.20 | 3.75 | 4.39 |
| Claims on Other Financial Corps | 12g | — | — | — | — | — | — | — | — | — | — | — | — |
| Claims on State & Local Govts | 12b | — | — | — | — | — | — | — | — | — | — | — | — |
| Claims on Public Nonfin. Corps | 12c | — | — | — | — | — | — | — | — | — | — | — | — |
| Claims on Private Sector | 12d | — | — | — | — | 1.00 | 1.19 | 1.88 | 2.70 | 3.09 | 3.20 | 3.75 | 4.39 |
| Monetary Base | 14 | 221.07 | 374.31 | 457.38 | 557.65 | 803.55 | 723.47 | 841.58 | 1,153.74 | 1,356.50 | 1,157.89 | 1,667.66 | 1,157.23 |
| Currency in Circulation | 14a | 165.41 | 230.79 | 296.07 | 334.32 | 431.56 | 434.65 | 483.51 | 564.03 | 621.56 | 682.33 | 723.36 | 670.54 |
| Liabs. to Other Depository Corps | 14c | 55.47 | 143.49 | 158.77 | 222.51 | 364.74 | 278.90 | 357.62 | 588.97 | 733.60 | 474.07 | 942.30 | 478.16 |
| Liabilities to Other Sectors | 14d | .18 | .02 | 2.54 | .82 | 7.25 | 9.92 | .45 | .73 | 1.34 | 1.49 | 2.00 | 8.52 |
| Other Liabs. to Other Dep. Corps | 14n | — | — | — | — | — | — | — | — | — | — | — | — |
| Dep. & Sec. Excl. f/Monetary Base | 14o | — | — | — | — | — | — | — | — | — | — | — | — |
| Deposits Included in Broad Money | 15 | — | — | — | — | — | — | — | — | — | — | — | — |
| Sec.Ot.th.Shares Incl.in Brd. Money | 16a | — | — | — | — | — | — | — | — | — | — | — | — |
| Deposits Excl. from Broad Money | 16b | — | — | — | — | — | — | — | — | — | — | — | — |
| Sec.Ot.th.Shares Excl.f/Brd.Money | 16s | — | — | — | — | — | — | — | — | — | — | — | — |
| Loans | 16l | — | — | — | — | — | — | — | — | — | — | — | — |
| Financial Derivatives | 16m | — | — | — | — | — | — | — | — | — | — | — | — |
| Shares and Other Equity | 17a | –1.70 | –2.24 | –.83 | –1.79 | –32.94 | –15.46 | –18.01 | –23.54 | –21.55 | –16.31 | –11.17 | 3.64 |
| Other Items (Net) | 17r | 1.92 | 6.69 | 8.62 | .93 | 10.22 | 65.14 | –10.28 | 21.41 | 17.76 | 9.67 | 9.69 | 11.06 |
| Memo Item: | | | | | | | | | | | | | |
| Total Assets | 10ra | 273.90 | 615.33 | 1,087.73 | 1,178.74 | 1,870.46 | 1,824.92 | 2,276.97 | 2,913.24 | 2,810.28 | 2,541.49 | 3,080.35 | 1,990.78 |
| **Other Depository Corporations** | | | | | | *Billions of CFA Francs: End of Period* | | | | | | | |
| Net Foreign Assets | 21n | 14.21 | 73.14 | 140.97 | 164.58 | 86.66 | 175.23 | 263.28 | 292.72 | 420.68 | 608.91 | 182.39 | 286.39 |
| Claims on Nonresidents | 21 | 41.96 | 82.37 | 148.70 | 173.57 | 111.32 | 187.67 | 288.45 | 351.78 | 462.09 | 666.37 | 286.53 | 381.64 |
| Liabilities to Nonresidents | 26c | 27.75 | 9.24 | 7.72 | 8.99 | 24.66 | 12.44 | 25.17 | 59.06 | 41.41 | 57.47 | 104.14 | 95.25 |
| Claims on Central Bank | 20 | 53.42 | 109.41 | 137.56 | 196.72 | 343.39 | 271.56 | 362.65 | 578.76 | 686.82 | 454.20 | 945.54 | 494.87 |
| Currency | 20a | 8.95 | 21.67 | 16.64 | 22.65 | 27.18 | 32.54 | 33.68 | 39.40 | 39.32 | 52.12 | 51.88 | 45.91 |
| Reserve Deposits and Securities | 20b | 44.47 | 87.74 | 119.92 | 115.27 | 316.21 | 239.02 | 328.97 | 539.36 | 647.49 | 402.07 | 893.66 | 448.96 |
| Other Claims | 20n | — | — | 1.00 | 58.79 | — | — | — | — | — | — | — | — |
| Net Claims on Central Government | 22an | 11.11 | –43.83 | –14.42 | –3.29 | –11.63 | –9.36 | –17.36 | –24.80 | 10.02 | –54.55 | –32.84 | –21.69 |
| Claims on Central Government | 22a | 22.39 | 3.50 | 5.43 | 15.30 | 10.96 | 10.31 | 5.20 | 1.38 | 39.46 | 23.16 | 34.47 | 38.75 |
| Liabilities to Central Government | 26d | 11.29 | 47.33 | 19.85 | 18.60 | 22.59 | 19.67 | 22.56 | 26.18 | 29.44 | 77.71 | 67.31 | 60.44 |
| Claims on Other Sectors | 22s | 82.98 | 86.03 | 108.66 | 111.51 | 202.28 | 241.36 | 413.17 | 540.91 | 689.06 | 806.23 | 1,024.92 | 1,218.20 |
| Claims on Other Financial Corps | 22g | .14 | .57 | 14.24 | 10.44 | 13.82 | 3.14 | 11.55 | 4.44 | 11.67 | 12.42 | 18.78 | 44.13 |
| Claims on State & Local Govts | 22b | — | — | — | — | — | — | — | — | — | — | — | — |
| Claims on Public Nonfin. Corps | 22c | 10.82 | 7.96 | 9.63 | 9.85 | 22.50 | 16.61 | 14.47 | 10.25 | 10.88 | 9.49 | 22.49 | 62.68 |
| Claims on Private Sector | 22d | 72.02 | 77.50 | 84.78 | 91.22 | 165.96 | 221.60 | 387.15 | 526.22 | 666.52 | 784.32 | 983.65 | 1,111.39 |
| Liabilities to Central Bank | 26g | .39 | — | — | — | — | — | — | — | — | — | — | 6.00 |
| Transf.Dep.Included in Broad Money | 24 | 100.41 | 150.71 | 255.69 | 319.63 | 423.02 | 459.01 | 715.53 | 1,102.32 | 1,357.81 | 1,259.80 | 1,510.05 | 1,254.46 |
| Other Dep.Included in Broad Money | 25 | 56.82 | 61.91 | 82.66 | 90.94 | 126.80 | 137.61 | 165.15 | 209.74 | 260.48 | 333.60 | 345.43 | 345.24 |
| Sec.Ot.th.Shares Incl.in Brd. Money | 26a | — | — | — | — | — | — | — | — | — | — | — | — |
| Deposits Excl. from Broad Money | 26b | 3.56 | 4.14 | 3.46 | 3.80 | 3.88 | 3.11 | 2.73 | 7.30 | 3.66 | 7.03 | 5.46 | 18.60 |
| Sec.Ot.th.Shares Excl.f/Brd.Money | 26s | — | — | — | — | — | — | — | — | — | — | — | — |
| Loans | 26l | — | — | — | — | — | — | — | — | — | — | — | — |
| Financial Derivatives | 26m | — | — | — | — | — | — | — | — | — | — | — | — |
| Insurance Technical Reserves | 26r | — | — | — | — | — | — | — | — | — | — | — | — |
| Shares and Other Equity | 27a | 15.72 | 25.98 | 32.14 | 42.63 | 57.74 | 61.90 | 84.24 | 106.98 | 140.49 | 180.53 | 213.23 | 278.89 |
| Other Items (Net) | 27r | –15.18 | –18.00 | –1.17 | 12.51 | 9.27 | 17.17 | 54.09 | –38.74 | 44.13 | 33.83 | 45.84 | 74.59 |
| Memo Item: | | | | | | | | | | | | | |
| Total Assets | 20ra | 242.82 | 328.68 | 437.26 | 526.40 | 706.42 | 748.54 | 1,117.38 | 1,612.52 | 1,951.70 | 2,050.39 | 2,376.86 | 2,264.45 |

# Congo, Republic of  634

| Depository Corporations | | 2004 | 2005 | 2006 | 2007 | 2008 | 2009 | 2010 | 2011 | 2012 | 2013 | 2014 | 2015 |
|---|---|---|---|---|---|---|---|---|---|---|---|---|---|
| | | *Billions of CFA Francs: End of Period* | | | | | | | | | | | |
| Net Foreign Assets............................. | 31n | 50.65 | 458.66 | 1,035.06 | 1,102.41 | 1,867.79 | 1,830.93 | 2,325.30 | 3,058.69 | 3,096.26 | 3,015.38 | 2,783.55 | 1,559.91 |
| Claims on Nonresidents................ | 31 | 101.91 | 492.47 | 1,069.12 | 1,146.59 | 1,936.67 | 1,928.14 | 2,487.85 | 3,226.52 | 3,235.96 | 3,175.50 | 2,984.77 | 1,762.07 |
| Liabilities to Nonresidents.............. | 36c | 51.26 | 33.81 | 34.06 | 44.18 | 68.87 | 97.21 | 162.55 | 167.83 | 139.69 | 160.12 | 201.22 | 202.16 |
| Domestic Claims................................ | 32 | 278.54 | 35.44 | −334.69 | −275.63 | −809.64 | −650.55 | −852.93 | −1,098.25 | −623.79 | −503.55 | 57.09 | 1,088.91 |
| Net Claims on Central Government | 32an | 195.57 | −50.59 | −443.35 | −387.13 | −1,012.92 | −893.10 | −1,267.97 | −1,641.87 | −1,315.94 | −1,312.98 | −971.58 | −133.67 |
| Claims on Central Government.... | 32a | 217.24 | 191.13 | 154.53 | 185.80 | 28.96 | 71.73 | 60.50 | 17.95 | 54.63 | 35.32 | 394.71 | 618.71 |
| Liabilities to Central Government. | 36d | 21.67 | 241.72 | 597.87 | 572.94 | 1,041.88 | 964.83 | 1,328.47 | 1,659.82 | 1,370.57 | 1,348.30 | 1,366.29 | 752.38 |
| Claims on Other Sectors............... | 32s | 82.98 | 86.03 | 108.66 | 111.51 | 203.28 | 242.55 | 415.04 | 543.62 | 692.15 | 809.43 | 1,028.67 | 1,222.59 |
| Claims on Other Financial Corps.. | 32g | .14 | .57 | 14.24 | 10.44 | 13.82 | 3.14 | 11.55 | 4.44 | 11.67 | 12.42 | 18.78 | 44.13 |
| Claims on State & Local Govts..... | 32b | — | — | — | — | — | — | — | — | — | — | — | — |
| Claims on Public Nonfin. Corps.... | 32c | 10.82 | 7.96 | 9.63 | 9.85 | 22.50 | 16.61 | 14.47 | 10.25 | 10.88 | 9.49 | 22.49 | 62.68 |
| Claims on Private Sector.............. | 32d | 72.02 | 77.50 | 84.78 | 91.22 | 166.96 | 222.80 | 389.03 | 528.93 | 669.61 | 787.52 | 987.40 | 1,115.78 |
| Broad Money Liabilities.................... | 35l | 313.88 | 421.76 | 620.31 | 723.06 | 961.44 | 1,008.64 | 1,330.96 | 1,837.42 | 2,201.87 | 2,225.10 | 2,528.95 | 2,232.85 |
| Currency Outside Depository Corps | 34a | 156.46 | 209.12 | 279.42 | 311.67 | 404.38 | 402.10 | 449.83 | 524.63 | 582.24 | 630.21 | 671.48 | 624.63 |
| Transferable Deposits.................... | 34 | 100.60 | 150.73 | 258.23 | 320.45 | 430.27 | 468.93 | 715.98 | 1,103.06 | 1,359.15 | 1,261.28 | 1,512.04 | 1,262.99 |
| Other Deposits............................. | 35 | 56.82 | 61.91 | 82.66 | 90.94 | 126.80 | 137.61 | 165.15 | 209.74 | 260.48 | 333.60 | 345.43 | 345.24 |
| Securities Other than Shares.......... | 36a | — | — | — | — | — | — | — | — | — | — | — | — |
| Deposits Excl. from Broad Money..... | 36b | 3.56 | 4.14 | 3.46 | 3.80 | 3.88 | 3.11 | 2.73 | 7.30 | 3.66 | 7.03 | 5.46 | 18.60 |
| Sec.Ot.th.Shares Excl.f/Brd.Money.... | 36s | — | — | — | — | — | — | — | — | — | — | — | — |
| Loans............................................. | 36l | — | — | — | — | — | — | — | — | — | — | — | — |
| Financial Derivatives........................ | 36m | — | — | — | — | — | — | — | — | — | — | — | — |
| Insurance Technical Reserves.......... | 36r | — | — | — | — | — | — | — | — | — | — | — | — |
| Shares and Other Equity................. | 37a | 14.02 | 23.74 | 31.31 | 40.84 | 24.80 | 46.43 | 66.23 | 83.44 | 118.95 | 164.22 | 202.06 | 282.53 |
| Other Items (Net)............................ | 37r | −2.26 | 44.44 | 45.30 | 59.08 | 68.03 | 122.20 | 72.46 | 32.28 | 148.00 | 115.49 | 104.17 | 114.85 |
| Broad Money Liabs., Seasonally Adj. | 35l.b | 303.24 | 409.07 | 606.19 | 712.01 | 955.92 | 1,008.57 | 1,334.84 | 1,845.94 | 2,216.98 | 2,246.02 | 2,556.80 | 2,257.47 |
| **Monetary Aggregates** | | *Billions of CFA Francs: End of Period* | | | | | | | | | | | |
| Broad Money..................... | 59m | 313.88 | 421.76 | 620.31 | 723.06 | 961.44 | 1,008.64 | 1,330.96 | 1,837.42 | 2,201.87 | 2,225.10 | 2,528.95 | 2,232.85 |
| o/w:Currency Issued by Cent.Govt | 59m.a | — | — | — | — | — | — | — | — | — | — | — | — |
| o/w: Dep.in Nonfin. Corporations. | 59m.b | — | — | — | — | — | — | — | — | — | — | — | — |
| o/w: Secs. Issued by Central Govt. | 59m.c | — | — | — | — | — | — | — | — | — | — | — | — |
| Money (National Definitions) | | | | | | | | | | | | | |
| M1............................................. | 59ma | 251.92 | 349.50 | 495.62 | 559.62 | 774.72 | 811.15 | 1,124.52 | 1,591.66 | 1,941.39 | 1,891.49 | 2,180.25 | 1,886.53 |
| M2............................................. | 59mb | 308.74 | 411.41 | 578.28 | 650.57 | 901.52 | 948.76 | 1,289.67 | 1,801.40 | 2,184.45 | 2,219.88 | 2,525.68 | 2,231.77 |
| **Interest Rates** | | *Percent Per Annum* | | | | | | | | | | | |
| Discount Rate (End of Period).......... | 60.a | 6.00 | 5.50 | 5.25 | 5.25 | 4.75 | 4.25 | 4.00 | 4.00 | 4.00 | 3.25 | 2.95 | 2.45 |
| Deposit Rate.................................. | 60l | 5.00 | 4.92 | 4.33 | 4.25 | 3.75 | 3.25 | 3.25 | 3.25 | 3.25 | 3.21 | 2.60 | 2.45 |
| **Prices and Production** | | *Index Numbers (2010=100): Period Averages* | | | | | | | | | | | |
| Consumer Prices............................. | 64 | 74.7 | 77.0 | 82.1 | 84.3 | † 90.4 | 95.2 | 100.0 | 101.3 | 105.3 | 111.6 | 111.6 | 117.3 |
| Crude Petroleum Prod. (2005=100). | 66aa | 92.4 | 100.0 | 223.8 | 209.5 | .... | .... | .... | .... | .... | .... | .... | .... |
| **Intl. Transactions & Positions** | | *Millions of US Dollars* | | | | | | | | | | | |
| Exports........................................... | 70..d | 3.43 | 4.75 | 6.08 | 5.64 | 8.30 | 6.10 | 8.20 | 11.50 | 11.00 | 9.80 | 8.61 | 4.65 |
| Imports, c.i.f................................... | 71..d | 1.00 | 1.34 | 2.07 | 2.61 | 3.14 | 2.99 | 2.99 | 5.20 | 5.20 | 5.50 | 6.20 | 7.75 |

# Congo, Republic of  634

| | | 2004 | 2005 | 2006 | 2007 | 2008 | 2009 | 2010 | 2011 | 2012 | 2013 | 2014 | 2015 |
|---|---|---|---|---|---|---|---|---|---|---|---|---|---|
| **Balance of Payments** | | *Millions of US Dollars* | | | | | | | | | | | |
| A. Current Account* | 109bx | 674.4 | 695.6 | 124.1 | −2,181.0 | .... | .... | .... | .... | .... | .... | .... | .... |
| Goods, credit (exports) | 1a9cx | 3,433.2 | 4,745.3 | 6,065.7 | 5,808.0 | .... | .... | .... | .... | .... | .... | .... | .... |
| Goods, debit (imports) | 1a9dx | 969.0 | 1,305.5 | 2,003.5 | 2,858.1 | .... | .... | .... | .... | .... | .... | .... | .... |
| Balance on goods | 1a9bx | 2,464.2 | 3,439.8 | 4,062.2 | 2,949.9 | .... | .... | .... | .... | .... | .... | .... | .... |
| Services, credit (exports) | 1b9cx | 196.7 | 220.5 | 266.0 | 319.4 | .... | .... | .... | .... | .... | .... | .... | .... |
| Services, debit (imports) | 1b9dx | 1,016.3 | 1,417.1 | 2,425.9 | 3,527.7 | .... | .... | .... | .... | .... | .... | .... | .... |
| Balance on Goods & Services | 1z9bx | 1,644.6 | 2,243.2 | 1,902.3 | −258.3 | .... | .... | .... | .... | .... | .... | .... | .... |
| Primary income: credit | 1c9cx | 13.3 | 17.6 | 20.1 | 23.4 | .... | .... | .... | .... | .... | .... | .... | .... |
| Primary income: debit | 1c9dx | 961.8 | 1,595.5 | 1,772.6 | 1,908.1 | .... | .... | .... | .... | .... | .... | .... | .... |
| Balance on gds, serv. & prim. inc. | 1y9bx | 696.0 | 665.3 | 149.7 | −2,143.1 | .... | .... | .... | .... | .... | .... | .... | .... |
| Secondary income: credit | 1d9ca | 34.5 | 87.2 | 37.9 | 43.0 | .... | .... | .... | .... | .... | .... | .... | .... |
| Secondary income: debit | 1d9da | 56.0 | 56.9 | 63.5 | 81.0 | .... | .... | .... | .... | .... | .... | .... | .... |
| B. Capital Account* | 209ba | 12.7 | 11.2 | 9.6 | 31.7 | .... | .... | .... | .... | .... | .... | .... | .... |
| Capital account: credit | 209ca | 15.1 | 11.2 | 9.6 | 31.7 | .... | .... | .... | .... | .... | .... | .... | .... |
| Capital account: debit | 209da | 2.5 | — | — | — | .... | .... | .... | .... | .... | .... | .... | .... |
| Balance on current & capital acct. | 129ba | 687.1 | 706.8 | 133.7 | −2,149.3 | .... | .... | .... | .... | .... | .... | .... | .... |
| C. Financial Account* | 309na | 775.0 | 226.7 | −425.9 | −2,546.8 | .... | .... | .... | .... | .... | .... | .... | .... |
| Direct investment: assets | 3a9aa | 101.5 | 287.4 | — | — | .... | .... | .... | .... | .... | .... | .... | .... |
| Equity & investment fund shares.. | 3aaaa | .... | .... | .... | .... | .... | .... | .... | .... | .... | .... | .... | .... |
| Debt instruments | 3abaa | 101.5 | 287.4 | — | — | .... | .... | .... | .... | .... | .... | .... | .... |
| Direct investment: liabilities | 3a9la | 88.4 | 801.0 | 1,487.7 | 2,638.4 | .... | .... | .... | .... | .... | .... | .... | .... |
| Equity & investment fund shares . | 3aala | 309.9 | 801.0 | 864.4 | 1,181.2 | .... | .... | .... | .... | .... | .... | .... | .... |
| Debt instruments | 3abla | −221.5 | — | 623.3 | 1,457.2 | .... | .... | .... | .... | .... | .... | .... | .... |
| Portfolio investment: assets | 3b9aa | .... | 1.1 | 1.3 | 1.5 | .... | .... | .... | .... | .... | .... | .... | .... |
| Equity & investment fund shares | 3baaa | .... | 1.1 | 1.3 | 1.5 | .... | .... | .... | .... | .... | .... | .... | .... |
| Debt securities | 3bbaa | .... | .... | .... | .... | .... | .... | .... | .... | .... | .... | .... | .... |
| Portfolio investment: liabilities | 3b9la | 2.1 | — | — | — | .... | .... | .... | .... | .... | .... | .... | .... |
| Equity & investment fund shares . | 3bala | .... | .... | .... | .... | .... | .... | .... | .... | .... | .... | .... | .... |
| Debt securities | 3bbla | 2.1 | — | — | — | .... | .... | .... | .... | .... | .... | .... | .... |
| Fin. der.& empl.stk.ops.(ESOs): net | 3c9na | .... | .... | .... | .... | .... | .... | .... | .... | .... | .... | .... | .... |
| Fin. der. & ESOs.: assets | 3c9aa | .... | .... | .... | .... | .... | .... | .... | .... | .... | .... | .... | .... |
| Fin. der. & ESOs.: liabilities | 3c9la | .... | .... | .... | .... | .... | .... | .... | .... | .... | .... | .... | .... |
| Other investment: assets | 3d9aa | 440.7 | 246.5 | 228.9 | −266.2 | .... | .... | .... | .... | .... | .... | .... | .... |
| Other equity | 3daaa | .... | .... | .... | .... | .... | .... | .... | .... | .... | .... | .... | .... |
| Debt instruments | 3dzaa | 440.7 | 246.5 | 228.9 | −266.2 | .... | .... | .... | .... | .... | .... | .... | .... |
| Other investment: liabilities | 3d9la | −323.3 | −492.7 | −831.5 | −356.4 | .... | .... | .... | .... | .... | .... | .... | .... |
| Other equity | 3dala | .... | .... | .... | .... | .... | .... | .... | .... | .... | .... | .... | .... |
| Debt instruments | 3dzla | −323.3 | −492.7 | −831.5 | −356.4 | .... | .... | .... | .... | .... | .... | .... | .... |
| Curr.+ cap.− finan. acct. balance... | 4y9na | −87.8 | 480.0 | 559.6 | 397.5 | .... | .... | .... | .... | .... | .... | .... | .... |
| D. Net Errors and Omissions | 409na | −92.8 | 30.5 | 142.5 | −201.1 | .... | .... | .... | .... | .... | .... | .... | .... |
| E. Reserves and Related Items | 4z9na | −180.7 | 510.5 | 702.1 | 196.4 | .... | .... | .... | .... | .... | .... | .... | .... |
| Reserve assets | 3e9aa | 75.4 | 659.5 | 975.2 | 88.1 | .... | .... | .... | .... | .... | .... | .... | .... |
| Credit and loans from the IMF | 3dcla | .2 | −.4 | 7.6 | — | .... | .... | .... | .... | .... | .... | .... | .... |
| Exceptional financing | 409la | 255.9 | 149.4 | 265.4 | −108.3 | .... | .... | .... | .... | .... | .... | .... | .... |

*Excludes components in group E

| | | 2004 | 2005 | 2006 | 2007 | 2008 | 2009 | 2010 | 2011 | 2012 | 2013 | 2014 | 2015 |
|---|---|---|---|---|---|---|---|---|---|---|---|---|---|
| **National Accounts** | | *Billions of CFA Francs* | | | | | | | | | | | |
| Househ.Cons.Expend.,incl.NPISHs.... | 96f | 535.9 | 844.2 | 1,023.6 | 1,133.1 | 1,369.7 | 1,282.8 | .... | .... | .... | .... | .... | .... |
| Government Consumption Expend... | 91f | 228.3 | 258.2 | 316.0 | 382.5 | 341.7 | 339.0 | .... | .... | .... | .... | .... | .... |
| Gross Fixed Capital Formation | 93e | 623.2 | 811.0 | 1,508.7 | 1,908.2 | 1,938.5 | 2,082.5 | .... | .... | .... | .... | .... | .... |
| Changes in Inventories | 93i | 40.6 | 55.3 | 50.9 | 50.0 | 55.0 | 67.0 | .... | .... | .... | .... | .... | .... |
| Exports of Goods and Services | 90c | 1,918.0 | 2,617.7 | 3,315.8 | 2,847.1 | 3,909.9 | 3,258.5 | .... | .... | .... | .... | .... | .... |
| Imports of Goods and Services (-) | 98c | 1,049.4 | 1,431.4 | 2,321.2 | 2,675.8 | 2,965.9 | 2,887.4 | .... | .... | .... | .... | .... | .... |
| Gross Domestic Product (GDP) | 99b | 2,296.6 | 3,155.0 | 3,893.8 | 3,645.0 | 4,648.9 | 4,142.4 | .... | .... | .... | .... | .... | .... |
| Net Primary Income from Abroad | 98.n | −588.2 | −832.4 | −916.4 | −835.0 | −1,378.8 | .... | .... | .... | .... | .... | .... | .... |
| Gross National Income (GNI) | 99a | 1,735.7 | 2,328.7 | 2,979.0 | 2,827.3 | 4,231.5 | .... | .... | .... | .... | .... | .... | .... |
| | | *Millions: Midyear Estimates* | | | | | | | | | | | |
| Population | 99z | 3.41 | 3.50 | 3.60 | 3.72 | 3.83 | 3.95 | 4.07 | 4.18 | 4.29 | 4.39 | 4.50 | 4.62 |

| | | 2004 | 2005 | 2006 | 2007 | 2008 | 2009 | 2010 | 2011 | 2012 | 2013 | 2014 | 2015 |
|---|---|---|---|---|---|---|---|---|---|---|---|---|---|
| **Exchange Rates** | | *Colones per SDR: End of Period* | | | | | | | | | | | |
| Market Rate.................................. | aa | 712.23 | 709.89 | 779.12 | 787.12 | 855.57 | 886.12 | 789.99 | 785.81 | 781.06 | 772.16 | 781.52 | 746.08 |
| | | *Colones per US Dollar: End of Period (ae) Period Average (rf)* | | | | | | | | | | | |
| Market Rate.................................. | ae | 458.61 | 496.68 | 517.90 | 498.10 | 555.47 | 565.24 | 512.97 | 511.84 | 508.20 | 501.41 | 539.42 | 538.41 |
| Market Rate.................................. | rf | 437.94 | 477.79 | 511.30 | 516.62 | 526.24 | 573.29 | 525.66 | 502.90 | 499.77 | 538.32 | 534.57 | |
| | | *Index Numbers (2010=100): Period Averages* | | | | | | | | | | | |
| Market Rate.................................. | ahx | 120.0 | 110.0 | 102.7 | 101.7 | 100.0 | 91.6 | 100.0 | 103.9 | 104.5 | 105.1 | 97.6 | 98.3 |
| Nominal Effective Exchange Rate..... | nec | 126.1 | 114.7 | 106.5 | 101.8 | 97.2 | 92.2 | 100.0 | 100.9 | 104.0 | 105.2 | 98.6 | 108.0 |
| CPI-Based Real Effect. Ex. Rate........ | rec | 81.7 | 82.1 | 82.7 | 84.0 | 87.2 | 89.0 | 100.0 | 102.3 | 107.7 | 112.5 | 108.2 | 118.4 |
| **Fund Position** | | *Millions of SDRs: End of Period* | | | | | | | | | | | |
| Quota......................................... | 2f.s | 164.10 | 164.10 | 164.10 | 164.10 | 164.10 | 164.10 | 164.10 | 164.10 | 164.10 | 164.10 | 164.10 | 164.10 |
| SDR Holdings................................ | 1b.s | .09 | .03 | .02 | .07 | .19 | 132.87 | 132.59 | 132.54 | 132.52 | 132.51 | 132.50 | 132.49 |
| Reserve Position in the Fund............ | 1c.s | 20.00 | 20.00 | 20.00 | 20.00 | 20.02 | 20.02 | 20.02 | 20.02 | 20.02 | 20.02 | 20.02 | 20.02 |
| Total Fund Cred.&Loans Outstg........ | 2tl | — | — | — | — | — | — | — | — | — | — | — | — |
| SDR Allocations............................. | 1bd | 23.73 | 23.73 | 23.73 | 23.73 | 23.73 | 156.53 | 156.53 | 156.53 | 156.53 | 156.53 | 156.53 | 156.53 |
| **International Liquidity** | | *Millions of US Dollars Unless Otherwise Indicated: End of Period* | | | | | | | | | | | |
| Total Reserves minus Gold.............. | 1l.d | 1,921.81 | 2,312.65 | 3,114.58 | 4,113.62 | 3,798.66 | 4,066.17 | 4,627.23 | 4,755.81 | 6,856.67 | 7,330.86 | 7,211.41 | 7,833.91 |
| SDR Holdings............................. | 1b.d | .13 | .04 | .04 | .11 | .30 | 208.30 | 204.20 | 203.49 | 203.68 | 204.07 | 191.97 | 183.60 |
| Reserve Position in the Fund......... | 1c.d | 31.06 | 28.59 | 30.09 | 31.61 | 30.83 | 31.38 | 30.83 | 30.73 | 30.77 | 30.83 | 29.00 | 27.74 |
| Foreign Exchange....................... | 1d.d | 1,890.61 | 2,284.02 | 3,084.45 | 4,081.90 | 3,767.53 | 3,826.49 | 4,392.20 | 4,521.58 | 6,622.22 | 7,095.96 | 6,990.43 | 7,622.57 |
| Gold (Million Fine Troy Ounces)........ | 1ad | .002 | .002 | .004 | .002 | .002 | .002 | .002 | .002 | .002 | .002 | .002 | .002 |
| Gold (National Valuation)................. | 1and | .02 | .02 | .02 | . . . . | . . . . | . . . . | . . . . | . . . . | . . . . | . . . . | . . . . | . . . . |
| Central Bank: Other Assets.............. | 3..d | 123.21 | 127.20 | 130.73 | 293.34 | 294.10 | 328.26 | 334.57 | 380.51 | 385.36 | 389.95 | 392.62 | 487.30 |
| Central Bank: Other Liabs.............. | 4..d | 280.48 | 181.66 | 105.95 | 91.70 | 96.38 | 75.24 | 68.74 | 55.89 | 47.72 | 45.51 | 32.65 | 25.31 |
| Other Depository Corps.: Assets........ | 7a.d | 667.19 | 1,316.43 | 1,348.84 | 1,226.58 | 1,729.99 | 1,625.27 | 1,546.09 | 1,288.93 | 1,189.57 | 1,790.26 | 2,118.66 | 1,634.25 |
| Other Depository Corps.: Liabs......... | 7b.d | 1,030.65 | 1,070.60 | 1,214.59 | 1,858.58 | 2,493.06 | 1,660.91 | 1,717.60 | 2,436.35 | 3,217.40 | 4,888.92 | 5,335.64 | 6,287.44 |
| **Central Bank** | | *Billions of Colones: End of Period* | | | | | | | | | | | |
| Net Foreign Assets......................... | 11n | 790.6 | 1,102.5 | 1,601.0 | 2,118.5 | 2,178.2 | 2,275.9 | 2,362.5 | 2,446.0 | 3,491.3 | 3,680.0 | 3,917.0 | 4,297.5 |
| Claims on Nonresidents................ | 11 | 935.8 | 1,209.3 | 1,674.1 | 2,182.5 | 2,251.4 | 2,455.1 | 2,519.9 | 2,595.7 | 3,636.0 | 3,821.9 | 4,055.3 | 4,426.4 |
| Liabilities to Nonresidents.............. | 16c | 145.2 | 106.8 | 73.1 | 64.0 | 73.1 | 179.1 | 157.3 | 149.7 | 144.7 | 141.9 | 138.4 | 128.8 |
| Claims on Other Depository Corps.... | 12e | .8 | .5 | .5 | .5 | .4 | 1.8 | .8 | 82.9 | .2 | 87.4 | .2 | 4.0 |
| Net Claims on Central Government.. | 12an | −36.7 | 39.3 | −46.9 | −63.7 | −20.8 | −49.4 | −288.1 | −86.4 | −561.6 | −200.5 | −64.0 | −121.5 |
| Claims on Central Government...... | 12a | 103.6 | 115.3 | 114.4 | 92.1 | 93.6 | 83.1 | 73.6 | 62.2 | 49.6 | 35.3 | 20.2 | — |
| Liabilities to Central Government... | 16d | 140.3 | 76.0 | 161.2 | 155.8 | 114.4 | 132.5 | 361.8 | 148.6 | 611.2 | 235.8 | 84.2 | 121.5 |
| Claims on Other Sectors................. | 12s | 21.8 | 21.1 | 20.1 | 18.4 | 5.3 | 3.9 | 2.6 | 2.0 | 1.4 | .8 | .3 | — |
| Claims on Other Financial Corps.... | 12g | 3.7 | 3.6 | 3.3 | 2.7 | 2.5 | 2.1 | 1.6 | 1.2 | .8 | .5 | .2 | — |
| Claims on State & Local Govts....... | 12b | — | — | — | — | — | — | — | — | — | — | — | — |
| Claims on Public Nonfin. Corps..... | 12c | 6.0 | 5.4 | 4.6 | 3.5 | 2.8 | 1.8 | 1.0 | .8 | .6 | .3 | .1 | — |
| Claims on Private Sector............... | 12d | 12.2 | 12.2 | 12.2 | 12.2 | — | — | — | — | — | — | — | — |
| Monetary Base.............................. | 14 | 1,603.9 | 2,072.9 | 2,710.3 | 3,245.9 | 3,184.3 | 3,347.4 | 3,410.8 | 3,915.2 | 4,557.9 | 5,414.7 | 5,692.4 | 6,214.2 |
| Currency in Circulation.................. | 14a | 277.7 | 332.2 | 413.2 | 546.3 | 575.0 | 613.0 | 665.0 | 743.1 | 844.8 | 921.5 | 988.5 | 1,050.7 |
| Liabs. to Other Depository Corps.... | 14c | 809.8 | 992.8 | 1,370.5 | 1,463.8 | 1,472.7 | 1,786.1 | 1,767.0 | 1,997.6 | 2,397.4 | 2,934.8 | 3,003.2 | 3,288.7 |
| Liabilities to Other Sectors............. | 14d | 516.3 | 747.9 | 926.6 | 1,235.9 | 1,136.7 | 948.4 | 978.8 | 1,174.5 | 1,315.7 | 1,558.4 | 1,700.7 | 1,874.8 |
| Other Liabs. to Other Dep. Corps..... | 14n | .7 | .7 | .8 | — | — | — | — | .1 | .1 | .1 | .1 | .1 |
| Dep. & Sec. Excl. f/Monetary Base.... | 14o | 7.0 | 6.0 | 7.0 | 3.1 | 7.1 | 11.0 | 14.8 | 11.7 | 9.9 | 13.0 | 19.3 | 27.4 |
| Deposits Included in Broad Money. | 15 | 6.3 | 5.2 | 5.9 | 1.1 | 4.7 | 8.6 | 12.1 | 9.5 | 8.2 | 10.8 | 17.7 | 26.0 |
| Sec.Ot.th.Shares Incl.in Brd. Money. | 16a | — | — | — | — | — | — | — | — | — | — | — | — |
| Deposits Excl. from Broad Money... | 16b | .8 | .9 | 1.1 | 1.9 | 2.3 | 2.3 | 2.7 | 2.3 | 1.7 | 2.2 | 1.6 | 1.4 |
| Sec.Ot.th.Shares Excl.f/Brd.Money.. | 16s | — | — | — | — | — | — | — | — | — | — | — | — |
| Loans........................................ | 16l | — | — | — | — | — | — | — | — | — | — | — | — |
| Financial Derivatives....................... | 16m | — | — | — | — | — | — | — | — | — | — | — | — |
| Shares and Other Equity................. | 17a | −1,015.5 | −1,027.2 | −1,135.9 | −1,181.5 | −1,227.9 | −1,268.4 | −1,356.6 | −1,485.2 | −1,655.2 | −1,887.4 | −1,849.9 | −2,081.2 |
| Other Items (Net)........................... | 17r | 180.4 | 111.1 | −7.5 | 6.1 | 199.8 | 142.2 | 8.7 | 2.6 | 18.6 | 27.4 | −8.6 | 19.5 |
| Memo Item: | | | | | | | | | | | | | |
| Total Assets................................. | 10ra | 1,116.9 | 1,381.0 | 1,848.2 | 2,330.9 | 2,415.4 | 2,628.8 | 2,662.4 | 2,810.3 | 3,745.9 | 4,000.4 | 4,140.0 | 4,493.8 |

# Costa Rica   238

|  |  | 2004 | 2005 | 2006 | 2007 | 2008 | 2009 | 2010 | 2011 | 2012 | 2013 | 2014 | 2015 |
|---|---|---|---|---|---|---|---|---|---|---|---|---|---|
| **Other Depository Corporations** | | | | | | *Billions of Colones: End of Period* | | | | | | | |
| Net Foreign Assets | 21n | −166.3 | 121.8 | 69.3 | −313.0 | −419.8 | −19.9 | −87.1 | −579.8 | −1,018.1 | −1,533.9 | −1,715.6 | −2,475.2 |
| Claims on Nonresidents | 21 | 305.3 | 652.5 | 695.8 | 607.4 | 951.6 | 908.0 | 785.2 | 651.4 | 597.2 | 886.2 | 1,129.9 | 869.3 |
| Liabilities to Nonresidents | 26c | 471.6 | 530.6 | 626.5 | 920.4 | 1,371.4 | 927.9 | 872.3 | 1,231.2 | 1,615.4 | 2,420.1 | 2,845.6 | 3,344.5 |
| Claims on Central Bank | 20 | 863.7 | 1,074.4 | 1,473.1 | 1,612.7 | 1,643.0 | 1,962.5 | 1,884.5 | 2,187.5 | 2,626.1 | 3,159.8 | 3,037.3 | 3,323.7 |
| Currency | 20a | 72.2 | 85.1 | 108.1 | 155.2 | 174.9 | 181.5 | 191.3 | 197.4 | 253.9 | 281.2 | 291.6 | 310.1 |
| Reserve Deposits and Securities | 20b | 348.6 | 540.0 | 851.8 | 860.8 | 1,097.5 | 1,330.9 | 1,297.5 | 1,470.2 | 1,635.5 | 1,812.1 | 2,083.8 | 2,337.8 |
| Other Claims | 20n | 442.9 | 449.3 | 513.2 | 596.8 | 370.6 | 450.1 | 395.8 | 520.0 | 736.8 | 1,066.5 | 661.9 | 675.8 |
| Net Claims on Central Government | 22an | 784.0 | 606.3 | 571.1 | 371.5 | 356.7 | 643.9 | 905.9 | 930.9 | 1,029.0 | 1,124.4 | 1,384.4 | 1,841.4 |
| Claims on Central Government | 22a | 815.2 | 645.5 | 621.2 | 436.6 | 436.6 | 711.0 | 1,024.9 | 1,096.3 | 1,197.7 | 1,369.7 | 1,581.4 | 2,033.0 |
| Liabilities to Central Government | 26d | 31.2 | 39.2 | 50.2 | 65.1 | 80.0 | 67.1 | 119.0 | 165.4 | 168.7 | 245.3 | 197.1 | 191.7 |
| Claims on Other Sectors | 22s | 2,748.3 | 3,531.8 | 4,519.1 | 6,200.4 | 8,169.8 | 8,600.2 | 9,044.0 | 10,168.4 | 11,640.1 | 13,079.2 | 15,496.9 | 17,393.0 |
| Claims on Other Financial Corps. | 22g | 117.6 | 96.1 | 116.6 | 133.0 | 181.9 | 256.5 | 315.2 | 239.0 | 338.0 | 406.0 | 614.9 | 713.6 |
| Claims on State & Local Govts. | 22b | — | — | — | — | — | — | — | — | — | — | — | — |
| Claims on Public Nonfin. Corps. | 22c | 35.4 | 51.5 | 55.0 | 53.9 | 62.7 | 63.0 | 84.1 | 97.5 | 157.3 | 165.7 | 180.8 | 239.6 |
| Claims on Private Sector | 22d | 2,595.2 | 3,384.3 | 4,347.5 | 6,013.5 | 7,925.2 | 8,280.7 | 8,644.7 | 9,831.8 | 11,144.8 | 12,507.5 | 14,701.3 | 16,439.7 |
| Liabilities to Central Bank | 26g | 1.0 | 1.8 | 1.5 | 1.7 | .4 | .3 | .8 | 62.6 | .2 | 39.9 | 1.8 | .6 |
| Transf.Dep.Included in Broad Money | 24 | 1,656.3 | 2,089.6 | 2,698.1 | 3,219.1 | 3,617.0 | 3,807.8 | 4,276.5 | 4,723.6 | 5,005.9 | 5,486.4 | 6,182.6 | 7,014.2 |
| Other Dep.Included in Broad Money | 25 | 57.5 | 34.8 | 54.0 | 61.4 | 61.9 | 53.2 | 76.6 | 77.4 | 82.9 | 99.1 | 57.9 | 38.5 |
| Sec.Oth.Shares Incl.in Brd.Money | 26a | 1,525.0 | 1,940.4 | 2,227.7 | 2,580.9 | 3,576.6 | 4,250.1 | 3,742.8 | 3,668.9 | 4,211.6 | 4,398.6 | 5,245.2 | 4,727.3 |
| Deposits Excl. from Broad Money | 26b | 88.6 | 96.6 | 132.1 | 140.1 | 164.9 | 194.0 | 205.6 | 237.1 | 246.8 | 279.3 | 303.2 | 335.5 |
| Sec.Oth.Shares Excl.f/Brd.Money | 26s | 298.1 | 276.6 | 354.6 | 378.1 | 529.9 | 813.3 | 1,265.8 | 1,481.9 | 1,953.7 | 2,536.2 | 2,988.0 | 4,270.4 |
| Loans | 26l | 24.7 | 24.6 | 31.8 | 53.5 | 65.4 | 79.1 | 86.4 | 87.3 | 94.4 | 103.7 | 124.6 | 130.5 |
| Financial Derivatives | 26m | — | — | — | — | — | — | — | — | — | — | — | — |
| Insurance Technical Reserves | 26r | — | — | — | — | — | — | — | — | — | — | — | — |
| Shares and Other Equity | 27a | 631.3 | 812.8 | 1,037.0 | 1,237.1 | 1,597.1 | 1,829.5 | 2,036.1 | 2,293.9 | 2,602.5 | 2,917.8 | 3,250.7 | 3,627.8 |
| Other Items (Net) | 27r | −52.9 | 57.3 | 95.6 | 199.7 | 136.5 | 159.4 | 56.7 | 74.3 | 79.0 | −31.6 | 48.8 | −62.0 |
| Memo Item: | | | | | | | | | | | | | |
| Total Assets | 20ra | 5,315.8 | 6,665.0 | 8,178.1 | 9,926.6 | 12,500.3 | 13,721.9 | 14,425.1 | 16,062.7 | 18,489.8 | 21,181.4 | 24,236.3 | 27,015.5 |
| **Depository Corporations** | | | | | | *Billions of Colones: End of Period* | | | | | | | |
| Net Foreign Assets | 31n | 624.2 | 1,224.3 | 1,670.3 | 1,805.5 | 1,758.5 | 2,256.0 | 2,275.4 | 1,866.1 | 2,473.2 | 2,146.2 | 2,201.3 | 1,822.3 |
| Claims on Nonresidents | 31 | 1,241.1 | 1,861.8 | 2,369.9 | 2,789.9 | 3,203.0 | 3,363.0 | 3,305.0 | 3,247.0 | 4,233.3 | 4,708.1 | 5,185.2 | 5,295.7 |
| Liabilities to Nonresidents | 36c | 616.8 | 637.5 | 699.6 | 984.4 | 1,444.5 | 1,107.0 | 1,029.6 | 1,380.9 | 1,760.1 | 2,561.9 | 2,983.9 | 3,473.4 |
| Domestic Claims | 32 | 3,517.4 | 4,198.6 | 5,063.3 | 6,526.5 | 8,511.1 | 9,198.6 | 9,664.3 | 11,014.8 | 12,108.9 | 14,003.9 | 16,817.6 | 19,112.8 |
| Net Claims on Central Government | 32an | 747.3 | 645.6 | 524.2 | 307.8 | 335.9 | 594.5 | 617.7 | 844.5 | 923.8 | 1,320.3 | 1,719.8 | |
| Claims on Central Government | 32a | 918.8 | 760.7 | 735.6 | 528.7 | 530.3 | 794.0 | 1,098.5 | 1,158.4 | 1,247.3 | 1,405.0 | 1,601.6 | 2,033.0 |
| Liabilities to Central Government | 36d | 171.5 | 115.1 | 211.4 | 220.9 | 194.4 | 199.5 | 480.8 | 314.0 | 779.9 | 481.1 | 281.2 | 313.2 |
| Claims on Other Sectors | 32s | 2,770.1 | 3,553.0 | 4,539.1 | 6,218.8 | 8,175.2 | 8,604.1 | 9,046.6 | 10,170.3 | 11,641.5 | 13,080.0 | 15,497.2 | 17,393.0 |
| Claims on Other Financial Corps. | 32g | 121.3 | 99.6 | 119.8 | 135.8 | 184.5 | 258.7 | 316.7 | 240.2 | 338.8 | 406.5 | 615.1 | 713.6 |
| Claims on State & Local Govts. | 32b | — | — | — | — | — | — | — | — | — | — | — | — |
| Claims on Public Nonfin. Corps. | 32c | 41.4 | 56.8 | 59.6 | 57.3 | 65.5 | 64.7 | 85.1 | 98.3 | 157.9 | 166.0 | 180.9 | 239.6 |
| Claims on Private Sector | 32d | 2,607.4 | 3,396.5 | 4,359.7 | 6,025.7 | 7,925.2 | 8,280.7 | 8,644.7 | 9,831.8 | 11,144.8 | 12,507.5 | 14,701.3 | 16,439.7 |
| Broad Money Liabilities | 35l | 3,967.0 | 5,064.9 | 6,217.4 | 7,489.6 | 8,797.0 | 9,499.6 | 9,560.5 | 10,199.5 | 11,215.2 | 12,193.6 | 13,901.1 | 14,421.4 |
| Currency Outside Depository Corps | 34a | 205.6 | 247.1 | 305.1 | 391.1 | 400.1 | 431.5 | 473.7 | 545.7 | 590.9 | 640.2 | 696.9 | 740.6 |
| Transferable Deposits | 34 | 1,660.5 | 2,091.9 | 2,699.2 | 3,220.0 | 3,619.2 | 3,813.1 | 4,286.8 | 4,731.5 | 5,013.6 | 5,496.3 | 6,195.5 | 7,026.9 |
| Other Deposits | 35 | 99.6 | 121.8 | 107.9 | 138.1 | 138.5 | 119.2 | 101.3 | 102.2 | 98.6 | 114.6 | 70.2 | 59.3 |
| Securities Other than Shares | 36a | 2,001.3 | 2,604.1 | 3,105.2 | 3,740.4 | 4,639.1 | 5,135.8 | 4,698.8 | 4,820.1 | 5,512.1 | 5,942.4 | 6,937.4 | 6,594.6 |
| Deposits Excl. from Broad Money | 36b | 89.4 | 97.4 | 133.2 | 142.0 | 167.3 | 196.4 | 208.2 | 239.4 | 248.6 | 281.5 | 304.8 | 336.9 |
| Sec.Oth.Shares Excl.f/Brd.Money | 36s | 298.1 | 276.6 | 354.6 | 378.1 | 529.9 | 813.3 | 1,265.8 | 1,481.9 | 1,953.7 | 2,536.2 | 2,988.0 | 4,270.4 |
| Loans | 36l | 24.7 | 24.6 | 31.8 | 53.5 | 65.4 | 79.1 | 86.4 | 87.3 | 94.4 | 103.7 | 124.6 | 130.5 |
| Financial Derivatives | 36m | — | — | — | — | — | — | — | — | — | — | — | — |
| Insurance Technical Reserves | 36r | — | — | — | — | — | — | — | — | — | — | — | — |
| Shares and Other Equity | 37a | −384.2 | −214.5 | −98.9 | 55.6 | 369.2 | 561.1 | 679.5 | 808.7 | 947.3 | 1,030.4 | 1,400.8 | 1,546.7 |
| Other Items (Net) | 37r | 146.7 | 173.8 | 95.5 | 213.3 | 340.8 | 305.1 | 139.2 | 64.1 | 122.9 | 4.7 | 299.5 | 229.2 |
| Broad Money Liabs., Seasonally Adj. | 35l.b | 3,994.3 | 5,104.5 | 6,265.5 | 7,543.4 | 8,842.7 | 9,519.6 | 9,546.6 | 10,154.6 | 11,144.4 | 12,100.9 | 13,790.6 | 14,308.4 |
| **Monetary Aggregates** | | | | | | *Billions of Colones: End of Period* | | | | | | | |
| Broad Money | 59m | 3,967.0 | 5,064.9 | 6,217.4 | 7,489.6 | 8,797.0 | 9,499.6 | 9,560.5 | 10,199.5 | 11,215.2 | 12,193.6 | 13,901.1 | 14,421.4 |
| o/w:Currency Issued by Cent.Govt | 59m.a | — | — | — | — | — | — | — | — | — | — | — | — |
| o/w: Dep.in Nonfin. Corporations | 59m.b | — | — | — | — | — | — | — | — | — | — | — | — |
| o/w:Secs. Issued by Central Govt. | 59m.c | — | — | — | — | — | — | — | — | — | — | — | — |
| Money (National Definitions) | | | | | | | | | | | | | |
| Base Money | 19ma | 480.3 | 609.4 | 773.2 | 1,028.4 | 1,151.2 | 1,210.0 | 1,345.0 | 1,500.5 | 1,754.3 | 1,934.0 | 2,135.7 | 2,332.1 |
| M1 | 59ma | 697.1 | 863.7 | 1,191.8 | 1,459.1 | 1,481.8 | 1,478.1 | 1,787.2 | 1,890.1 | 2,132.7 | 2,305.8 | 2,504.3 | 2,839.0 |
| M2 | 59mb | 1,931.8 | 2,429.1 | 3,138.8 | 4,086.6 | 4,609.3 | 5,123.0 | 5,750.7 | 6,430.7 | 7,597.9 | 8,598.1 | 9,709.8 | 11,146.9 |
| M3 | 59mc | 3,737.6 | 4,568.0 | 5,608.0 | 6,620.8 | 8,149.6 | 9,293.4 | 9,803.1 | 10,460.5 | 11,779.3 | 13,087.0 | 15,087.2 | 16,707.1 |
| **Interest Rates** | | | | | | *Percent Per Annum* | | | | | | | |
| Central Bank Policy Rate (EOP) | 60 | .... | .... | 8.97 | 5.52 | 10.00 | 9.00 | 6.50 | 5.00 | 5.00 | 3.75 | 5.25 | 2.25 |
| Deposit Rate | 60l | 9.51 | 10.14 | 9.77 | 6.35 | 4.15 | 6.96 | 5.32 | 4.01 | 4.74 | 3.88 | 3.32 | 2.37 |
| Lending Rate | 60p | 23.43 | 24.66 | 22.19 | 12.80 | 15.83 | 19.72 | 17.09 | 16.15 | 18.21 | 15.19 | 14.90 | 14.23 |
| **Prices and Labor** | | | | | | *Index Numbers (2010=100): Period Averages* | | | | | | | |
| Producer Prices | 63 | 51.8 | 58.8 | 66.5 | 75.6 | 92.6 | 98.3 | 100.0 | 108.4 | 112.5 | 115.4 | † 120.2 | 121.7 |
| Consumer Prices | 64 | 55.8 | † 63.5 | 70.8 | 77.4 | 87.8 | 94.6 | 100.0 | 104.9 | 109.6 | 115.3 | † 120.5 | 121.5 |
| | | | | | | *Number in Thousands: Period Averages* | | | | | | | |
| Labor Force | 67d | 1,769 | 1,903 | 1,946 | 2,018 | 2,060 | 2,151 | 2,052 | 2,031 | 2,197 | 2,212 | 2,290 | .... |
| Employment | 67e | 1,654 | 1,777 | 1,830 | 1,926 | 1,958 | 1,879 | 1,902 | 1,824 | 1,975 | 2,006 | 2,071 | .... |
| Unemployment | 67c | 115 | 126 | 116 | 93 | 102 | 172 | 150 | 207 | 221 | 206 | 220 | .... |
| Unemployment Rate (%) | 67r | 6.5 | 6.6 | 6.0 | 4.6 | 4.9 | 8.4 | 7.3 | 10.2 | 10.1 | 9.3 | 9.6 | .... |
| **Intl. Transactions & Positions** | | | | | | *Millions of US Dollars* | | | | | | | |
| Exports | 70..d | 6,301.5 | 7,026.4 | 8,215.5 | 9,375.7 | 9,574.7 | 8,710.7 | 9,342.9 | 10,237.7 | 11,151.0 | 11,541.9 | 11,217.0 | 9,525.0 |
| Imports, c.i.f. | 71..d | 8,268.0 | 9,812.0 | 11,520.1 | 12,957.4 | 15,366.0 | 11,460.4 | 13,557.2 | 16,217.6 | 17,512.7 | 17,922.9 | 17,228.6 | 15,425.3 |

| Balance of Payments | | 2004 | 2005 | 2006 | 2007 | 2008 | 2009 | 2010 | 2011 | 2012 | 2013 | 2014 | 2015 |
|---|---|---|---|---|---|---|---|---|---|---|---|---|---|
| | | | | | | | *Millions of US Dollars* | | | | | | |
| A. Current Account* | 109bx | −795.8 | −981.0 | −1,022.6 | −1,646.4 | −2,787.3 | † −630.1 | −1,179.2 | −2,340.1 | −2,496.8 | −2,719.3 | −2,580.5 | −2,202.7 |
| Goods, credit (exports) | 1a9cx | 2,807.4 | 3,088.8 | 3,415.8 | 3,860.4 | 4,370.9 | † 6,670.7 | 7,529.6 | 8,301.4 | 8,922.6 | 8,866.3 | 9,270.9 | 9,503.5 |
| Goods, debit (imports) | 1a9dx | 5,379.5 | 6,337.6 | 7,306.5 | 9,000.7 | 11,198.7 | † 9,169.9 | 10,982.2 | 13,328.7 | 14,270.6 | 14,425.1 | 14,838.1 | 14,377.3 |
| Balance on goods | 1a9bx | −2,572.2 | −3,248.8 | −3,890.6 | −5,140.3 | −6,827.8 | † −2,499.2 | −3,452.5 | −5,027.3 | −5,348.0 | −5,558.8 | −5,567.2 | −4,873.8 |
| Services, credit (exports) | 1b9cx | 3,348.6 | 3,639.6 | 4,053.8 | 5,616.0 | 5,795.0 | † 3,938.5 | 4,750.8 | 5,782.1 | 6,208.6 | 6,824.1 | 7,124.3 | 7,595.1 |
| Services, debit (imports) | 1b9dx | 1,340.4 | 1,433.7 | 1,539.2 | 1,727.1 | 1,779.6 | † 1,487.1 | 1,836.8 | 1,949.4 | 2,224.2 | 2,385.5 | 2,383.4 | 2,864.0 |
| Balance on Goods & Services | 1z9bx | −563.9 | −1,042.9 | −1,376.1 | −1,251.4 | −2,812.4 | † −47.8 | −538.6 | −1,194.7 | −1,363.7 | −1,120.2 | −826.3 | −142.7 |
| Primary income: credit | 1c9cx | 144.5 | 806.9 | 1,135.1 | 707.7 | 696.8 | † 159.4 | 145.5 | 286.8 | 303.5 | 213.8 | 281.5 | 268.1 |
| Primary income: debit | 1c9dx | 588.8 | 1,015.4 | 1,130.8 | 1,572.4 | 1,113.9 | † 1,072.2 | 1,123.4 | 1,710.4 | 1,759.2 | 2,082.2 | 2,289.4 | 2,579.9 |
| Balance on gds, serv. & prim. inc. | 1y9bx | −1,008.2 | −1,251.4 | −1,371.8 | −2,116.1 | −3,229.5 | † −960.6 | −1,516.5 | −2,618.2 | −2,819.4 | −2,988.6 | −2,834.2 | −2,454.5 |
| Secondary income: credit | 1d9ca | 371.2 | 470.6 | 586.1 | 734.6 | 706.6 | † 662.1 | 666.7 | 664.7 | 721.8 | 725.6 | 698.3 | 672.0 |
| Secondary income: debit | 1d9da | 158.7 | 200.1 | 237.0 | 264.8 | 264.4 | † 331.6 | 329.5 | 386.5 | 399.2 | 456.4 | 444.6 | 420.2 |
| B. Capital Account* | 209ba | 11.5 | 15.9 | 1.1 | 21.2 | 7.4 | † 58.3 | 53.5 | 21.6 | 46.2 | 7.9 | 6.7 | 31.4 |
| Capital account: credit | 209ca | 11.5 | 15.9 | 1.1 | 21.2 | 7.4 | † 58.3 | 80.5 | 35.2 | 61.0 | 25.5 | 23.9 | 34.6 |
| Capital account: debit | 209da | — | — | — | — | — | † — | 26.9 | 13.6 | 14.8 | 17.6 | 17.3 | 3.2 |
| Balance on current & capital acct. | 129ba | −784.3 | −965.1 | −1,021.5 | −1,625.2 | −2,779.9 | † −571.8 | −1,125.7 | −2,318.5 | −2,450.6 | −2,711.4 | −2,573.8 | −2,171.3 |
| C. Financial Account* | 309na | −471.8 | −877.9 | −1,886.7 | −2,390.0 | −2,521.5 | † −511.5 | −1,875.0 | −3,009.2 | −4,143.8 | −3,931.6 | −3,160.1 | −3,309.2 |
| Direct investment: assets | 3a9aa | 60.6 | −43.0 | 98.1 | 262.4 | 5.9 | † −191.3 | 477.4 | 405.1 | 893.6 | 772.1 | 398.4 | 385.6 |
| Equity & investment fund shares | 3aaaa | 64.6 | −42.3 | 113.5 | 256.1 | 1.5 | † 11.1 | 21.9 | 94.4 | 483.6 | 288.9 | 82.7 | 124.6 |
| Debt instruments | 3abaa | −4.0 | −.7 | −15.4 | 6.3 | 4.4 | † −202.4 | 455.5 | 310.7 | 410.0 | 483.2 | 315.7 | 261.0 |
| Direct investment: liabilities | 3a9la | 793.8 | 861.0 | 1,469.1 | 1,896.1 | 2,078.2 | † 1,031.8 | 1,855.4 | 2,733.3 | 2,696.3 | 3,555.4 | 3,063.8 | 3,094.0 |
| Equity & investment fund shares . | 3aala | 669.8 | 574.6 | 1,444.4 | 1,898.3 | 2,039.6 | † 1,414.4 | 1,258.7 | 1,796.8 | 1,560.2 | 2,841.4 | 2,151.8 | 2,276.6 |
| Debt instruments | 3abla | 124.1 | 286.4 | 24.7 | −2.2 | 38.6 | † −382.6 | 596.7 | 936.4 | 1,136.1 | 714.0 | 912.0 | 817.4 |
| Portfolio investment: assets | 3b9aa | −53.1 | 680.7 | 509.3 | 170.4 | −537.3 | † 321.7 | −218.6 | −98.9 | −177.3 | 377.3 | 330.5 | 171.9 |
| Equity & investment fund shares | 3baaa | 6.6 | 6.1 | −3.9 | 42.2 | 11.5 | † 2.7 | −2.3 | −.4 | −183.4 | 38.2 | 72.5 | 44.5 |
| Debt securities | 3bbaa | −59.8 | 674.6 | 513.2 | 128.2 | −548.8 | † 319.0 | −216.3 | −98.5 | 6.1 | 339.1 | 258.0 | 127.4 |
| Portfolio investment: liabilities | 3b9la | −239.5 | — | — | — | −93.7 | † 35.6 | 154.5 | 138.1 | 1,960.5 | 2,583.4 | 702.2 | 730.9 |
| Equity & investment fund shares . | 3bala | — | — | — | — | | . . . . | . . . . | 8.6 | 8.9 | 13.8 | 14.2 | 14.7 |
| Debt securities | 3bbla | −239.5 | — | — | — | −93.7 | † 35.6 | 154.5 | 129.5 | 1,951.6 | 2,569.6 | 688.0 | 716.2 |
| Fin. der.& empl.stk.ops.(ESOs): net. | 3c9na | — | — | — | — | | . . . . | . . . . | . . . . | −10.4 | −8.7 | −8.9 | −9.2 |
| Fin. der. & ESOs: assets | 3c9aa | . . . . | . . . . | . . . . | . . . . | . . . . | . . . . | . . . . | . . . . | −12.1 | −11.3 | −11.6 | −12.0 |
| Fin. der. & ESOs: liabilities | 3c9la | . . . . | . . . . | . . . . | . . . . | . . . . | . . . . | . . . . | . . . . | −1.7 | −2.6 | −2.7 | −2.8 |
| Other investment: assets | 3d9aa | 308.7 | −154.5 | −654.6 | 155.8 | 684.6 | † −324.3 | 376.5 | 574.0 | 860.6 | 1,670.0 | 956.2 | 1,246.8 |
| Other equity | 3daaa | . . . . | . . . . | . . . . | . . . . | . . . . | † 34.2 | 6.2 | 45.9 | 4.8 | 4.8 | 2.6 | 94.1 |
| Debt instruments | 3dzaa | 308.7 | −154.5 | −654.6 | 155.8 | 684.6 | † −358.5 | 370.3 | 528.1 | 855.8 | 1,665.2 | 953.6 | 1,152.6 |
| Other investment: liabilities | 3d9la | 233.5 | 500.2 | 370.4 | 1,082.4 | 690.2 | † −749.8 | 500.5 | 1,018.1 | 1,053.4 | 603.7 | 1,070.2 | 1,279.3 |
| Other equity | 3dala | . . . . | . . . . | . . . . | . . . . | . . . . | . . . . | . . . . | . . . . | . . . . | . . . . | . . . . | . . . . |
| Debt instruments | 3dzla | 233.5 | 500.2 | 370.4 | 1,082.4 | 690.2 | † −749.8 | 500.5 | 1,018.1 | 1,053.4 | 603.7 | 1,070.2 | 1,279.3 |
| Curr.+ cap.− finan. acct. balance. | 4y9na | −312.6 | −87.2 | 865.1 | 764.8 | −258.3 | † −60.3 | 749.3 | 690.7 | 1,693.2 | 1,220.4 | 586.3 | 1,137.9 |
| D. Net Errors and Omissions | 409na | 63.7 | 144.5 | 149.5 | 213.0 | −47.6 | † 320.2 | −188.2 | −558.3 | 416.4 | −759.5 | −699.5 | −492.5 |
| E. Reserves and Related Items | 4z9na | −248.8 | 57.2 | 1,014.7 | 977.7 | −305.9 | † 259.9 | 561.0 | 132.4 | 2,109.6 | 460.9 | −113.2 | 645.4 |
| Reserve assets | 3e9aa | 80.3 | 393.5 | 1,030.8 | 1,147.7 | −348.0 | † 259.9 | 561.1 | 132.4 | 2,109.6 | 460.9 | −113.2 | 645.4 |
| Credit and loans from the IMF | 3dcla | — | — | — | — | — | † — | — | — | — | — | — | — |
| Exceptional financing | 409la | 329.1 | 336.2 | 16.2 | 170.0 | −42.0 | . . . . | . . . . | . . . . | . . . . | . . . . | . . . . | . . . . |
| *Excludes components in group E | | | | | | | | | | | | | |

| International Investment Position | | | | | | | *Millions of US Dollars* | | | | | | |
|---|---|---|---|---|---|---|---|---|---|---|---|---|---|
| Assets | 809aa | . . . . | 7,863.6 | 9,796.5 | 12,324.2 | 12,371.8 | 12,250.6 † 14,011.6 | 15,062.5 | 18,877.4 | 22,070.7 | 23,744.0 | 25,915.6 | |
| Direct investment | 8a9aa | . . . . | 169.9 | 279.1 | 541.5 | 547.5 | 560.9 † 1,109.6 | 2,017.6 | 2,920.8 | 3,697.5 | 4,086.9 | 4,472.6 | |
| Equity & investment fund shares.. | 8aaaa | . . . . | 163.5 | 276.9 | 533.0 | 534.5 | 542.2 † 565.1 | 859.2 | 1,347.6 | 1,642.7 | 1,732.0 | 1,863.5 | |
| Debt instruments | 8abaa | . . . . | 6.3 | 2.2 | 8.5 | 12.9 | 18.7 † 544.5 | 1,158.4 | 1,573.2 | 2,054.8 | 2,354.9 | 2,609.1 | |
| Portfolio investment | 8b9aa | . . . . | 807.1 | 1,317.9 | 1,488.2 | 950.9 | 1,496.1 † 1,426.9 | 1,383.2 | 1,224.6 | 1,474.0 | 1,885.7 | 1,955.9 | |
| Equity & investment fund shares.. | 8baaa | . . . . | 17.0 | 13.1 | 55.3 | 66.8 | 263.4 † 329.6 | 369.1 | 190.4 | 136.6 | 282.1 | 282.7 | |
| Debt securities | 8bbaa | . . . . | 790.0 | 1,304.7 | 1,432.9 | 884.1 | 1,232.7 † 1,097.2 | 1,014.1 | 1,034.2 | 1,337.4 | 1,603.6 | 1,673.2 | |
| Fin. der.(oth.than reserves) & ESOs | 8c9aa | . . . . | . . . . | . . . . | . . . . | . . . . | . . . . | . . . . | −12.1 | −23.4 | −35.0 | −47.1 | |
| Other investment | 8d9aa | . . . . | 4,574.0 | 5,084.9 | 6,180.8 | 7,074.8 | 6,127.5 † 6,845.4 | 6,903.4 | 7,884.9 | 9,589.2 | 10,592.6 | 11,697.8 | |
| Other equity | 8daaa | . . . . | . . . . | . . . . | . . . . | . . . . | . . . . † 334.6 | 380.5 | 388.4 | 390.1 | 392.4 | 486.6 | |
| Debt instruments | 8dzaa | . . . . | 4,574.0 | 5,084.9 | 6,180.8 | 7,074.8 | 6,127.5 † 6,510.8 | 6,522.9 | 7,496.5 | 9,199.1 | 10,200.2 | 11,211.2 | |
| Reserve assets | 8e9aa | . . . . | 2,312.6 | 3,114.6 | 4,113.6 | 3,798.7 | 4,066.2 † 4,629.7 | 4,758.3 | 6,859.2 | 7,333.4 | 7,213.9 | 7,836.4 | |
| Liabilities | 809la | . . . . | 11,570.1 | 13,305.8 | 16,617.1 | 19,164.0 | 20,002.4 † 22,962.0 | 27,523.3 | 33,537.6 | 40,935.9 | 46,309.3 | 51,784.6 | |
| Direct investment | 8a9la | . . . . | 5,433.1 | 6,796.7 | 8,819.0 | 10,894.1 | 12,402.1 † 14,525.9 | 17,361.3 | 20,310.1 | 24,626.6 | 28,222.9 | 31,854.2 | |
| Equity & investment fund shares.. | 8aala | . . . . | 4,700.4 | 5,991.2 | 8,037.0 | 9,995.2 | 11,691.2 † 13,204.9 | 15,209.2 | 17,023.1 | 20,162.2 | 22,728.1 | 25,447.7 | |
| Debt instruments | 8abla | . . . . | 732.7 | 805.5 | 782.0 | 898.9 | 710.9 † 1,321.0 | 2,152.2 | 3,287.0 | 4,464.4 | 5,494.7 | 6,406.5 | |
| Portfolio investment | 8b9la | . . . . | 961.2 | 1,004.3 | 1,157.2 | 921.7 | 1,010.2 † 1,187.1 | 1,301.5 | 3,222.2 | 5,769.7 | 6,448.4 | 6,980.9 | |
| Equity & investment fund shares.. | 8bala | . . . . | . . . . | . . . . | . . . . | . . . . | . . . . | . . . . | 8.6 | 17.5 | 31.2 | 45.5 | 60.1 | |
| Debt securities | 8bbla | . . . . | 961.2 | 1,004.3 | 1,157.2 | 921.7 | 1,010.2 † 1,187.1 | 1,293.0 | 3,204.8 | 5,738.5 | 6,402.9 | 6,920.2 | |
| Fin. der.(oth.than reserves) & ESOs | 8c9la | . . . . | . . . . | . . . . | . . . . | . . . . | . . . . | . . . . | −1.7 | −4.3 | −7.0 | −9.8 | |
| Other investment | 8d9la | . . . . | 5,175.7 | 5,504.8 | 6,640.8 | 7,348.2 | 6,590.0 † 7,249.0 | 8,859.5 | 10,006.9 | 10,543.9 | 11,645.1 | 12,959.9 | |
| Other equity | 8dala | . . . . | . . . . | . . . . | . . . . | . . . . | . . . . | . . . . | . . . . | . . . . | . . . . | . . . . | |
| Debt instruments | 8dzla | . . . . | 5,175.7 | 5,504.8 | 6,640.8 | 7,348.2 | 6,590.0 † 7,249.0 | 8,859.5 | 10,006.9 | 10,543.9 | 11,645.1 | 12,959.9 | |

# Costa Rica 238

|  |  | 2004 | 2005 | 2006 | 2007 | 2008 | 2009 | 2010 | 2011 | 2012 | 2013 | 2014 | 2015 |
|---|---|---|---|---|---|---|---|---|---|---|---|---|---|
| **Government Finance Operations Statement** | | | | | | | | | | | | | |
| **Budgetary Central Government** | | | | | *Billions of Colones: Fiscal Year Ends December 31* | | | | | | | |
| Revenue | a1 | .... | .... | 1,638.35 | .... | 2,489.59 | 2,362.55 | 2,741.79 | 3,024.13 | 3,274.22 | 3,536.20 | 3,799.20 | .... |
| Taxes | a11 | .... | .... | 1,577.73 | .... | 2,409.22 | 2,262.53 | 2,491.96 | 2,769.59 | 3,007.92 | 3,292.31 | 3,522.44 | .... |
| Social Contributions | a12 | .... | .... | 33.32 | .... | 43.73 | 54.36 | 61.19 | 66.77 | 74.08 | 56.27 | 59.91 | .... |
| Grants | a13 | .... | .... | 16.28 | .... | 24.75 | 32.09 | 157.62 | 164.31 | 168.66 | 165.58 | 189.08 | .... |
| Other Revenue | a14 | .... | .... | 11.02 | .... | 11.88 | 13.57 | 31.02 | 23.46 | 23.55 | 22.04 | 27.77 | .... |
| Expense | a2 | .... | .... | 1,759.41 | .... | 2,339.22 | 2,969.63 | 3,667.43 | 3,807.91 | 4,243.39 | 4,810.43 | 5,281.40 | .... |
| Compensation of Employees | a21 | .... | .... | 635.16 | .... | 855.38 | 1,113.27 | 1,349.43 | 1,513.60 | 1,647.05 | 1,817.38 | 1,968.53 | .... |
| Use of Goods & Services | a22 | .... | .... | 56.31 | .... | 82.21 | 99.04 | 111.42 | 120.31 | 124.96 | 140.94 | 179.58 | .... |
| Consumption of Fixed Capital | a23 | .... | .... | 25.30 | .... | 5.97 | 8.05 | 6.01 | 10.17 | 19.40 | 19.52 | 41.22 | .... |
| Interest | a24 | .... | .... | 436.70 | .... | 340.09 | 360.11 | 401.55 | 449.38 | 471.77 | 631.40 | 696.08 | .... |
| Subsidies | a25 | .... | .... | — | .... | 1.44 | — | — | — | — | — | — | .... |
| Grants | a26 | .... | .... | 289.02 | .... | 501.63 | 631.04 | 971.48 | 933.45 | 1,260.08 | 1,193.44 | 1,410.62 | .... |
| Social Benefits | a27 | .... | .... | 311.53 | .... | 368.52 | 423.62 | 480.61 | 523.33 | 563.95 | 615.32 | 667.24 | .... |
| Other Expense | a28 | .... | .... | 5.38 | .... | 183.99 | 334.71 | 346.92 | 257.67 | 156.19 | 392.43 | 318.14 | .... |
| Gross Operating Balance [1-2+23] | agob | .... | .... | −95.76 | .... | 156.34 | −599.23 | −919.63 | −773.60 | −949.77 | −1,254.71 | −1,440.99 | .... |
| Net Operating Balance [1-2] | anob | .... | .... | −121.06 | .... | 150.36 | −607.28 | −925.63 | −783.77 | −969.17 | −1,274.23 | −1,482.20 | .... |
| Net Acq. of Nonfinancial Assets | a31 | .... | .... | 8.46 | .... | 348.70 | 62.41 | 76.48 | 61.89 | 70.87 | 61.84 | 323.10 | .... |
| Aquisition of Nonfin. Assets | a31.1 | .... | .... | 8.46 | .... | .... | .... | .... | .... | .... | .... | .... | .... |
| Disposal of Nonfin. Assets | a31.2 | .... | .... | .... | .... | .... | .... | .... | .... | .... | .... | .... | .... |
| Net Lending/Borrowing [1-2-31] | anlb | .... | .... | −129.52 | .... | −198.34 | −669.69 | −1,002.11 | −845.66 | −1,040.05 | −1,336.07 | −1,805.30 | .... |
| Net Acq. of Financial Assets | a32 | .... | .... | 84.06 | .... | 45.85 | 21.29 | 240.60 | −156.23 | 458.20 | −316.72 | −152.84 | .... |
| By instrument | | | | | | | | | | | | | |
| Monetary Gold & SDRs | a3201 | .... | .... | .... | .... | — | — | — | — | — | — | — | .... |
| Currency & Deposits | a3202 | .... | .... | 85.32 | .... | −40.15 | 17.79 | 231.39 | −214.22 | 468.16 | −377.14 | −153.21 | .... |
| Securities other than Shares | a3203 | .... | .... | −.01 | .... | — | .18 | −2.72 | 47.88 | −38.81 | — | — | .... |
| Loans | a3204 | .... | .... | −1.26 | .... | −.17 | −.94 | −.23 | −5.96 | −.11 | 1.11 | — | .... |
| Shares & Other Equity | a3205 | .... | .... | — | .... | 65.38 | — | — | — | — | — | — | .... |
| Insurance Technical Reserves | a3206 | .... | .... | — | .... | — | — | — | — | — | — | — | .... |
| Financial Derivatives | a3207 | .... | .... | — | .... | — | — | — | — | — | — | — | .... |
| Other Accounts Receivable | a3208 | .... | .... | — | .... | 20.79 | 4.27 | 12.16 | 16.07 | 28.96 | 59.31 | .37 | .... |
| By debtor | | | | | | | | | | | | | |
| Domestic | a321 | .... | .... | .... | .... | 45.85 | 21.29 | 240.60 | −156.23 | 458.20 | −316.72 | −152.84 | .... |
| Foreign | a322 | .... | .... | .... | .... | — | — | — | — | — | — | — | .... |
| Net Incurrence of Liabilities | a33 | .... | .... | 404.62 | .... | −323.92 | 657.74 | 1,210.49 | 826.27 | 1,479.30 | 1,211.64 | 1,600.05 | .... |
| By instrument | | | | | | | | | | | | | |
| Special Drawing Rights (SDRs) | a3301 | .... | .... | — | .... | — | — | — | — | — | — | — | .... |
| Currency & Deposits | a3302 | .... | .... | — | .... | — | — | — | — | — | — | — | .... |
| Securities other than Shares | a3303 | .... | .... | 379.83 | .... | −642.03 | 619.27 | 724.50 | 809.40 | 1,570.99 | 773.09 | 1,566.87 | .... |
| Loans | a3304 | .... | .... | 24.80 | .... | −52.49 | 38.47 | 233.20 | 16.87 | −23.52 | 141.80 | −21.00 | .... |
| Shares & Other Equity | a3305 | .... | .... | — | .... | — | — | — | — | — | — | — | .... |
| Insurance Technical Reserves | a3306 | .... | .... | — | .... | — | — | — | — | — | — | — | .... |
| Financial Derivatives | a3307 | .... | .... | — | .... | — | — | — | — | — | — | — | .... |
| Other Accounts Payable | a3308 | .... | .... | — | .... | 370.60 | — | 252.79 | — | −68.17 | 296.75 | 54.14 | .... |
| By creditor | | | | | | | | | | | | | |
| Domestic | a331 | .... | .... | .... | .... | −158.37 | 792.51 | 1,039.22 | 939.21 | 1,122.49 | 832.31 | 955.84 | .... |
| Foreign | a332 | .... | .... | .... | .... | −165.55 | −134.77 | 171.26 | −112.94 | 356.81 | 379.33 | 644.17 | .... |
| Stat. Discrepancy [32-33-NLB] | anlbz | .... | .... | .... | .... | 568.12 | 33.30 | 32.20 | −136.84 | 19.00 | −192.29 | 52.41 | .... |
| Memo Item: Expenditure [2+31] | a2m | .... | .... | .... | .... | 2,687.93 | 3,032.25 | 3,743.90 | 3,869.79 | 4,314.27 | 4,872.27 | 5,604.50 | .... |
| **National Accounts** | | | | | *Millions of Colones* | | | | | | | | |
| Househ.Cons.Expend.,incl.NPISHs. | 96f | 5,372,171 | 6,422,404 | 7,624,210 | 9,087,164 | 10,645,097 | 11,176,638 | 12,302,533 | 13,555,428 | 14,758,060 | 15,963,776 | 17,362,470 | .... |
| Government Consumption Expend. | 91f | 1,150,404 | 1,316,361 | 1,559,070 | 1,810,601 | 2,258,176 | 2,825,738 | 3,369,142 | 3,726,859 | 4,057,964 | 4,446,802 | 4,758,010 | .... |
| Gross Fixed Capital Formation | 93e | 1,515,964 | 1,787,195 | 2,293,070 | 2,961,143 | 3,704,619 | 3,714,784 | 3,783,332 | 4,104,918 | 4,584,534 | 5,200,837 | 5,826,500 | .... |
| Changes in Inventories | 93i | 367,626 | 535,209 | 749,616 | 392,900 | 625,785 | −970,749 | 157,986 | 377,020 | 221,824 | 82,713 | −688,370 | .... |
| Exports of Goods and Services | 90c | 3,766,877 | 4,626,409 | 5,658,598 | 6,623,927 | 7,134,126 | 7,122,018 | 7,285,445 | 7,766,578 | 8,545,488 | 8,714,090 | 9,351,460 | .... |
| Imports of Goods and Services (-) | 98c | 4,029,491 | 5,148,601 | 6,366,742 | 7,277,332 | 8,666,042 | 7,023,683 | 7,811,717 | 8,782,848 | 9,483,282 | 9,609,244 | 9,935,080 | .... |
| Gross Domestic Product (GDP) | 99b | 8,143,550 | 9,538,977 | 11,517,822 | 13,598,403 | 15,701,760 | 16,844,745 | 19,086,721 | 20,747,955 | 22,684,587 | 24,798,973 | 26,675,010 | .... |
| Net Primary Income from Abroad | 98.n | −339,153 | −373,196 | −370,036 | −386,258 | −396,443 | −512,336 | −515,790 | −496,519 | −623,962 | −729,809 | −882,200 | .... |
| Gross National Income (GNI) | 99a | 7,804,397 | 9,165,781 | 11,147,786 | 13,212,145 | 15,305,317 | 16,332,409 | 18,570,930 | 20,251,435 | 22,060,625 | 24,069,165 | 25,792,810 | .... |
| Consumption of Fixed Capital | 99cf | 500,986 | 588,390 | 698,038 | 792,999 | 896,870 | 1,022,198 | 1,123,221 | 1,223,606 | 1,337,819 | .... | .... | .... |
| GDP Volume 1991 Prices | 99b.p | 1,642,346 | 1,739,021 | 1,891,701 | 2,041,814 | 2,097,588 | 2,076,283 | 2,179,148 | 2,275,785 | 2,392,510 | 2,478,090 | 2,564,400 | .... |
| GDP Volume (2010=100) | 99bvp | 75.4 | 79.8 | 86.8 | 93.7 | 96.3 | 95.3 | 100.0 | 104.4 | 109.8 | 113.7 | 117.7 | .... |
| GDP Deflator (2010=100) | 99bip | 56.6 | 62.6 | 69.5 | 76.0 | 85.5 | 92.6 | 100.0 | 104.1 | 108.3 | 114.3 | 118.8 | .... |
| | | | | | *Millions: Midyear Estimates* | | | | | | | | |
| **Population** | 99z | 4.19 | 4.25 | 4.31 | 4.37 | 4.43 | 4.49 | 4.55 | 4.60 | 4.65 | 4.71 | 4.76 | 4.81 |

| | | 2004 | 2005 | 2006 | 2007 | 2008 | 2009 | 2010 | 2011 | 2012 | 2013 | 2014 | 2015 |
|---|---|---|---|---|---|---|---|---|---|---|---|---|---|
| **Exchange Rates** | | | | | | *CFA Francs per SDR: End of Period* | | | | | | | |
| Official Rate | aa | 747.90 | 794.73 | 749.30 | 704.15 | 725.98 | 713.83 | 756.02 | 778.32 | 764.10 | 732.49 | 782.77 | 834.92 |
| | | | | | *CFA Francs per US Dollar: End of Period (ae) Period Average (rf)* | | | | | | | | |
| Official Rate | ae | 481.58 | 556.04 | 498.07 | 445.59 | 471.34 | 455.34 | 490.91 | 506.96 | 497.16 | 475.64 | 540.28 | 602.51 |
| Official Rate | rf | 528.28 | 527.47 | 522.89 | 479.27 | 447.81 | 472.19 | 495.28 | 471.87 | 510.53 | 494.04 | 494.41 | 591.45 |
| | | | | | *Index Numbers (2010=100): Period Averages* | | | | | | | | |
| Official Rate | ahx | 93.7 | 93.9 | 94.6 | 103.3 | 110.9 | 105.0 | 100.0 | 104.9 | 96.9 | 100.1 | 100.1 | 83.6 |
| Nominal Effective Exchange Rate | nec | 101.5 | 99.9 | 99.3 | 102.1 | 105.1 | 105.1 | 100.0 | 100.6 | 97.9 | 102.0 | 104.6 | 100.6 |
| CPI-Based Real Effect. Ex. Rate | rec | 101.5 | 100.9 | 100.0 | 101.9 | 106.7 | 106.4 | 100.0 | 102.0 | 97.9 | 102.2 | 103.2 | 98.7 |
| **Fund Position** | | | | | | *Millions of SDRs: End of Period* | | | | | | | |
| Quota | 2f.s | 325.20 | 325.20 | 325.20 | 325.20 | 325.20 | 325.20 | 325.20 | 325.20 | 325.20 | 325.20 | 325.20 | 325.20 |
| SDR Holdings | 1b.s | .13 | .45 | .67 | .36 | .78 | 272.70 | 273.04 | 272.87 | 272.82 | 272.79 | 272.75 | 233.70 |
| Reserve Position in the Fund | 1c.s | .59 | .64 | .69 | .72 | .76 | .80 | .84 | .89 | .94 | 1.00 | 1.00 | 1.07 |
| Total Fund Cred.&Loans Outstg | 2tl | 200.51 | 138.81 | 99.75 | 109.77 | 122.28 | 224.39 | 248.45 | 399.35 | 512.28 | 609.84 | 719.02 | 777.55 |
| SDR Allocations | 1bd | 37.83 | 37.83 | 37.83 | 37.83 | 37.83 | 310.90 | 310.90 | 310.90 | 310.90 | 310.90 | 310.90 | 310.90 |
| **International Liquidity** | | | | | *Millions of US Dollars Unless Otherwise Indicated: End of Period* | | | | | | | | |
| Total Reserves minus Gold | 1l.d | 1,680.0 | 1,366.6 | 1,797.7 | 2,519.0 | 2,252.7 | 3,266.8 | 3,624.4 | 4,316.0 | 3,928.1 | 4,242.7 | 4,478.5 | 4,715.7 |
| SDR Holdings | 1b.d | .2 | .6 | 1.0 | .6 | 1.2 | 427.5 | 420.5 | 418.9 | 419.3 | 420.1 | 395.2 | 323.8 |
| Reserve Position in the Fund | 1c.d | .9 | .9 | 1.0 | 1.1 | 1.2 | 1.3 | 1.3 | 1.4 | 1.5 | 1.5 | 1.4 | 1.5 |
| Foreign Exchange | 1d.d | 1,678.9 | 1,365.0 | 1,795.7 | 2,517.3 | 2,250.3 | 2,838.1 | 3,202.6 | 3,895.6 | 3,507.4 | 3,821.0 | 4,081.9 | 4,390.4 |
| Gold (Million Fine Troy Ounces) | 1ad | — | — | — | — | — | — | — | — | — | — | — | .... |
| Gold (National Valuation) | 1and | — | — | — | — | — | — | — | — | — | — | — | .... |
| Monetary Authorities: Other Liabs | 4..d | 10.8 | 18.7 | 21.2 | 31.6 | 24.7 | 32.7 | 17.2 | 22.8 | 51.1 | 75.0 | 154.3 | 242.0 |
| Deposit Money Banks: Assets | 7a.d | 351.2 | 412.9 | 470.4 | 544.1 | 570.4 | 652.7 | 670.3 | 836.2 | 1,292.9 | 1,359.9 | 1,449.7 | 1,440.7 |
| Deposit Money Banks: Liabs | 7b.d | 301.2 | 257.9 | 378.4 | 449.0 | 419.7 | 506.2 | 601.9 | 503.1 | 769.1 | 815.8 | 1,031.9 | 1,111.6 |
| **Monetary Authorities** | | | | | | *Billions of CFA Francs: End of Period* | | | | | | | |
| Foreign Assets | 11 | 812.9 | 759.9 | 896.2 | 1,123.4 | 1,061.8 | 1,488.0 | 1,779.2 | 2,188.0 | 1,952.9 | 2,018.0 | 2,419.7 | 2,841.3 |
| Claims on Central Government | 12a | 360.3 | 313.7 | 260.8 | 256.1 | 259.7 | 506.1 | 522.6 | 656.2 | 738.3 | 788.2 | 846.5 | 915.2 |
| Claims on Deposit Money Banks | 12e | — | 9.4 | .4 | 52.1 | 95.7 | 57.4 | 56.6 | 50.5 | 109.8 | 290.6 | 410.1 | 767.6 |
| Claims on Other Financial Insts | 12f | — | — | .9 | | | .6 | 3.0 | | 3.5 | 1.6 | 2.9 | 2.1 |
| Reserve Money | 14 | 907.8 | 923.2 | 1,002.3 | 1,254.5 | 1,302.7 | 1,619.9 | 1,933.5 | 2,231.9 | 2,092.5 | 2,296.6 | 2,602.0 | 3,060.5 |
| of which: Currency Outside DMBs | 14a | 671.5 | 754.1 | 815.2 | 1,043.4 | 1,078.7 | 1,343.2 | 1,638.2 | 1,555.3 | 1,590.5 | 1,747.1 | 1,864.5 | 2,137.5 |
| Foreign Liabilities | 16c | 183.4 | 150.8 | 113.7 | 118.0 | 127.9 | 397.0 | 431.3 | 564.3 | 654.4 | 710.1 | 889.5 | 1,054.6 |
| Central Government Deposits | 16d | 75.5 | 27.0 | 46.1 | 62.3 | 23.6 | 54.5 | 35.9 | 159.5 | 107.4 | 143.2 | 255.9 | 421.2 |
| Other Items (Net) | 17r | 6.4 | −18.0 | −3.7 | −3.1 | −37.0 | −19.3 | −39.3 | −61.1 | −49.7 | −51.5 | −68.4 | −10.1 |
| **Deposit Money Banks** | | | | | | *Billions of CFA Francs: End of Period* | | | | | | | |
| Reserves | 20 | 221.1 | 151.4 | 174.2 | 178.6 | 216.5 | 266.4 | 326.3 | 659.3 | 450.9 | 500.8 | 664.3 | 830.4 |
| Foreign Assets | 21 | 169.1 | 229.6 | 234.3 | 242.5 | 268.9 | 297.2 | 329.0 | 423.9 | 642.8 | 646.8 | 783.3 | 868.1 |
| Claims on Central Government | 22a | 277.6 | 283.3 | 309.1 | 423.9 | 329.5 | 319.5 | 540.3 | 635.7 | 785.1 | 924.4 | 1,220.7 | 1,406.4 |
| Claims on Private Sector | 22d | 1,164.1 | 1,175.8 | 1,276.7 | 1,521.6 | 1,693.6 | 1,876.2 | 2,037.4 | 2,047.3 | 2,297.7 | 2,823.0 | 3,434.7 | 4,455.4 |
| Claims on Other Financial Insts | 22f | — | — | | | | | | | | | | — |
| Demand Deposits | 24 | 619.0 | 628.1 | 710.7 | 901.7 | 894.3 | 967.6 | 1,091.1 | 1,555.6 | 1,597.8 | 1,870.9 | 2,279.2 | 2,902.5 |
| Time Deposits | 25 | 632.2 | 683.9 | 743.7 | 853.3 | 997.9 | 1,170.1 | 1,415.6 | 1,453.6 | 1,653.0 | 1,800.2 | 2,141.3 | 2,430.5 |
| Foreign Liabilities | 26c | 131.8 | 136.5 | 178.3 | 187.8 | 194.8 | 230.5 | 270.4 | 252.1 | 377.4 | 352.0 | 498.6 | 635.0 |
| Long-Term Foreign Liabilities | 26cl | 13.3 | 6.9 | 10.2 | 12.2 | 3.1 | — | 25.1 | 3.0 | 5.0 | 36.0 | 58.9 | 34.8 |
| Central Government Deposits | 26d | 214.3 | 185.4 | 178.0 | 193.8 | 173.5 | 163.6 | 231.2 | 304.9 | 277.6 | 259.4 | 311.9 | 446.3 |
| Credit from Monetary Authorities | 26g | — | 9.1 | .4 | 52.1 | 95.7 | 40.5 | 56.6 | 50.5 | 109.8 | 290.6 | 410.4 | 767.6 |
| Capital Accounts | 27a | 220.1 | 226.8 | 237.6 | 252.3 | 306.3 | 331.7 | 400.6 | 466.1 | 523.7 | 577.4 | 573.0 | 636.0 |
| Other Items (Net) | 27r | 1.3 | −36.6 | −64.5 | −86.8 | −157.0 | −144.7 | −257.4 | −319.5 | −367.9 | −291.5 | −170.3 | −292.3 |
| Treasury Claims: Private Sector | 22d.i | 9.8 | 13.6 | 13.3 | 10.1 | 10.4 | 7.7 | 7.6 | 4.8 | 7.1 | 5.9 | 9.2 | 9.2 |
| Post Office: Checking Deposits | 24..i | 5.6 | 8.2 | 12.8 | 16.9 | 17.9 | 22.1 | | | | — | — | — |
| **Monetary Survey** | | | | | | *Billions of CFA Francs: End of Period* | | | | | | | |
| Foreign Assets (Net) | 31n | 666.9 | 702.3 | 838.6 | 1,060.1 | 1,008.0 | 1,157.7 | 1,406.5 | 1,795.6 | 1,563.9 | 1,602.7 | 1,814.8 | 2,019.7 |
| Domestic Credit | 32 | 1,517.7 | 1,568.6 | 1,636.3 | 1,962.5 | 2,103.7 | 2,506.4 | 2,836.3 | 2,874.8 | 3,439.6 | 4,134.6 | 4,937.0 | 5,911.6 |
| Claims on Central Govt. (Net) | 32an | 343.7 | 379.3 | 345.3 | 430.7 | 399.6 | 621.9 | 788.3 | 822.7 | 1,131.3 | 1,304.1 | 1,490.3 | 1,445.0 |
| Claims on Private Sector | 32d | 1,174.0 | 1,189.4 | 1,290.1 | 1,531.7 | 1,704.0 | 1,883.9 | 2,045.0 | 2,052.1 | 2,304.8 | 2,828.9 | 3,443.8 | 4,464.5 |
| Claims on Other Financial Insts | 32f | — | — | .9 | | | .6 | 3.0 | | 3.5 | 1.6 | 2.9 | 2.1 |
| Money | 34 | 1,300.4 | 1,397.1 | 1,551.0 | 1,983.3 | 1,999.5 | 2,341.7 | 2,736.6 | 3,142.0 | 3,257.3 | 3,671.9 | 4,205.9 | 5,130.8 |
| Quasi-Money | 35 | 632.2 | 683.9 | 743.7 | 853.3 | 997.9 | 1,170.1 | 1,415.6 | 1,453.6 | 1,653.0 | 1,800.2 | 2,141.3 | 2,430.5 |
| Long-Term Foreign Liabilities | 36cl | 13.3 | 6.9 | 10.2 | 12.2 | 3.1 | — | 25.1 | 3.0 | 5.0 | 36.0 | 58.9 | 34.8 |
| Other Items (Net) | 37r | 238.7 | 183.0 | 170.0 | 173.7 | 111.2 | 152.4 | 65.5 | 71.8 | 88.2 | 229.2 | 345.6 | 335.3 |
| Money plus Quasi-Money | 35l | 1,932.6 | 2,080.9 | 2,294.8 | 2,836.6 | 2,997.4 | 3,511.8 | 4,152.2 | 4,595.6 | 4,910.4 | 5,472.1 | 6,347.2 | 7,561.3 |
| **Interest Rates** | | | | | | *Percent Per Annum* | | | | | | | |
| Repurchase Agreement Rate | 60.q | 4.00 | 4.00 | 4.25 | 4.25 | 4.75 | 4.25 | 4.25 | 4.25 | 4.00 | 3.50 | 3.50 | 3.50 |
| Deposit Rate | 60l | 3.50 | 3.50 | 3.50 | 3.50 | 3.50 | 3.50 | 3.50 | 3.50 | 3.50 | 3.50 | 3.50 | 3.50 |
| **Prices, Production, Labor** | | | | | | *Index Numbers (2010=100): Period Averages* | | | | | | | |
| Consumer Prices | 64 | 84.8 | 88.1 | 90.3 | 92.0 | 97.8 | 98.8 | 100.0 | 104.9 | 106.3 | 109.0 | 109.5 | 110.9 |
| Industrial Production (2005=100) | 66 | 84.9 | 100.0 | 111.3 | † 107.7 | 141.8 | 160.1 | 125.1 | 107.6 | 94.5 | 85.1 | 68.2 | .... |
| **Intl. Transactions & Positions** | | | | | | *Billions of CFA Francs* | | | | | | | |
| Exports | 70 | 3,655.20 | 4,060.10 | 4,432.54 | 4,154.70 | 4,652.70 | 4,846.70 | 5,063.20 | 5,146.70 | 5,538.30 | 6,754.80 | 6,227.56 | .... |
| Imports, c.i.f | 71 | 2,490.72 | 3,093.58 | 3,043.44 | 3,203.00 | 3,530.35 | 3,279.80 | 3,881.20 | 3,174.00 | 4,987.00 | 6,227.90 | 5,332.91 | .... |

# Côte d'Ivoire   662

| | | 2004 | 2005 | 2006 | 2007 | 2008 | 2009 | 2010 | 2011 | 2012 | 2013 | 2014 | 2015 |
|---|---|---|---|---|---|---|---|---|---|---|---|---|---|
| **Balance of Payments** | | | | | | | *Millions of US Dollars* | | | | | | |
| A. Current Account* | 109bx | .... | 39.7 | 479.0 | −139.0 | 451.6 | 1,617.6 | 464.5 | † 2,662.7 | −320.6 | −632.7 | .... | .... |
| Goods, credit (exports) | 1a9cx | .... | 7,589.0 | 8,362.0 | 8,548.0 | 10,251.4 | 11,168.0 | 11,410.2 | † 12,635.1 | 12,123.5 | 12,049.3 | .... | .... |
| Goods, debit (imports) | 1a9dx | .... | 5,096.8 | 5,209.4 | 5,937.0 | 6,882.2 | 6,911.2 | 7,788.6 | † 6,666.6 | 9,056.7 | 9,055.2 | .... | .... |
| Balance on goods | 1a9bx | .... | 2,492.2 | 3,152.6 | 2,611.0 | 3,369.2 | 4,256.8 | 3,621.6 | † 5,968.5 | 3,066.7 | 2,994.1 | .... | .... |
| Services, credit (exports) | 1b9cx | .... | 934.4 | 953.3 | 1,046.5 | 1,155.2 | 1,171.8 | 1,183.0 | † 1,016.7 | 984.8 | 935.0 | .... | .... |
| Services, debit (imports) | 1b9dx | .... | 2,271.4 | 2,385.4 | 2,643.8 | 2,838.3 | 2,775.1 | 2,986.8 | † 2,801.1 | 2,930.9 | 3,221.4 | .... | .... |
| Balance on Goods & Services | 1z9bx | .... | 1,155.3 | 1,720.5 | 1,013.7 | 1,686.1 | 2,653.4 | 1,817.9 | † 4,184.2 | 1,120.6 | 707.7 | .... | .... |
| Primary income: credit | 1c9cx | .... | 193.9 | 196.2 | 218.1 | 236.6 | 221.9 | 217.3 | † 207.6 | 207.7 | 207.2 | .... | .... |
| Primary income: debit | 1c9dx | .... | 847.1 | 906.4 | 1,027.5 | 1,138.7 | 1,159.0 | 1,131.3 | † 1,195.9 | 1,128.2 | 1,108.2 | .... | .... |
| Balance on gds, serv. & prim. inc. | 1y9bx | .... | 502.0 | 1,010.3 | 204.3 | 784.0 | 1,716.3 | 903.9 | † 3,195.9 | 200.1 | −193.3 | .... | .... |
| Secondary income: credit | 1d9ca | .... | 194.8 | 217.7 | 476.6 | 582.3 | 790.0 | 432.8 | † 356.6 | 305.4 | 420.9 | .... | .... |
| Secondary income: debit | 1d9da | .... | 657.2 | 749.0 | 819.9 | 914.8 | 888.7 | 872.1 | † 889.8 | 826.0 | 860.3 | .... | .... |
| B. Capital Account* | 209bx | .... | 185.2 | 33.0 | 92.9 | 89.3 | 224.9 | 1,178.3 | † 154.6 | 8,111.5 | 191.8 | .... | .... |
| Capital account: credit | 209ca | .... | 185.8 | 33.6 | 93.5 | 89.9 | 226.0 | 1,178.9 | † 155.0 | 8,112.3 | 195.0 | .... | .... |
| Capital account: debit | 209da | .... | .6 | .6 | .6 | .5 | 1.1 | .6 | † .3 | .9 | 3.2 | .... | .... |
| Balance on current & capital acct. | 129ba | .... | 224.9 | 512.0 | −46.2 | 540.9 | 1,842.5 | 1,642.8 | † 2,817.4 | 7,790.9 | −440.9 | .... | .... |
| C. Financial Account* | 309na | .... | 482.5 | 278.5 | −326.9 | 203.9 | 718.8 | 162.4 | † 2,131.6 | 8,382.5 | −124.5 | .... | .... |
| Direct investment: assets | 3a9aa | .... | 37.0 | 31.8 | 16.4 | 20.3 | 9.4 | 44.1 | † 15.3 | 14.3 | −6.4 | .... | .... |
| Equity & investment fund shares.. | 3aaaa | .... | — | — | — | — | −13.7 | 25.5 | † 7.9 | 6.5 | −6.8 | .... | .... |
| Debt instruments | 3abaa | .... | 37.0 | 31.8 | 16.4 | 20.3 | 23.2 | 18.5 | † 7.4 | 7.8 | .4 | .... | .... |
| Direct investment: liabilities | 3a9la | .... | 348.9 | 350.7 | 443.2 | 466.5 | 396.0 | 358.1 | † 301.6 | 330.3 | 407.5 | .... | .... |
| Equity & investment fund shares . | 3aala | .... | 302.3 | 303.7 | 404.3 | 431.3 | 399.7 | 371.0 | † 322.4 | 154.7 | 133.6 | .... | .... |
| Debt instruments | 3abla | .... | 46.6 | 47.0 | 38.9 | 35.2 | −3.6 | −12.9 | † −20.8 | 175.6 | 273.9 | .... | .... |
| Portfolio investment: assets | 3b9aa | .... | 49.9 | 24.2 | 42.9 | 28.6 | 18.6 | 22.1 | † .5 | 7.3 | 3.0 | .... | .... |
| Equity & investment fund shares | 3baaa | .... | −26.9 | 6.0 | 7.7 | 8.3 | 6.9 | 8.3 | † — | 2.1 | .2 | .... | .... |
| Debt securities | 3bbaa | .... | 76.8 | 18.2 | 35.2 | 20.3 | 11.8 | 13.9 | † .5 | 5.2 | 2.8 | .... | .... |
| Portfolio investment: liabilities | 3b9la | .... | 48.1 | 45.3 | 145.6 | 76.6 | −11.8 | 486.5 | † 105.6 | 149.6 | 177.4 | .... | .... |
| Equity & investment fund shares . | 3bala | .... | 13.9 | 1.6 | 1.6 | 1.9 | 2.2 | 2.2 | .... | 30.4 | 1.2 | .... | .... |
| Debt securities | 3bbla | .... | 34.2 | 43.7 | 143.9 | 74.6 | −14.0 | 484.3 | † 105.6 | 119.1 | 176.2 | .... | .... |
| Fin. der.& empl.stk.ops.(ESOs): net. | 3c9na | .... | 4.3 | 6.3 | 7.0 | 6.2 | 7.5 | 7.3 | .... | .... | .... | .... | .... |
| Fin. der. & ESOs.: assets | 3c9aa | .... | 5.2 | 6.3 | 7.0 | 6.2 | 7.5 | 7.3 | .... | .... | .... | .... | .... |
| Fin. der. & ESOs.: liabilities | 3c9la | .... | .9 | — | .... | .... | .... | .... | .... | .... | .... | .... | .... |
| Other investment: assets | 3d9aa | .... | 497.9 | 501.1 | 377.1 | 369.9 | 1,234.5 | 1,383.4 | † 3,425.0 | 1,728.0 | 1,485.4 | .... | .... |
| Other equity | 3daaa | .... | .... | .... | .... | .... | .... | .... | † 2.8 | 16.2 | 15.8 | .... | .... |
| Debt instruments | 3dzaa | .... | 497.9 | 501.1 | 377.1 | 369.9 | 1,234.5 | 1,383.4 | † 3,422.2 | 1,711.8 | 1,469.6 | .... | .... |
| Other investment: liabilities | 3d9la | .... | −290.3 | −111.1 | 181.6 | −322.0 | 167.1 | 449.9 | † 902.0 | −7,112.8 | 1,021.6 | .... | .... |
| Other equity | 3dala | .... | .... | .... | .... | .... | .... | .... | .... | .... | .... | .... | .... |
| Debt instruments | 3dzla | .... | −290.3 | −111.1 | 181.6 | −322.0 | 167.1 | 449.9 | † 902.0 | −7,112.8 | 1,021.6 | .... | .... |
| Curr.+ cap.− finan. acct. balance... | 4y9na | .... | −257.6 | 233.4 | 280.8 | 337.0 | 1,123.7 | 1,480.5 | † 685.7 | −591.6 | −316.4 | .... | .... |
| D. Net Errors and Omissions | 409na | .... | −57.5 | −10.1 | 39.9 | −106.5 | −37.1 | −53.1 | † −70.8 | −34.7 | 299.6 | .... | .... |
| E. Reserves and Related Items | 4z9na | .... | −315.1 | 223.3 | 320.7 | 230.5 | 1,086.6 | 1,427.3 | † 614.9 | −626.4 | −16.6 | .... | .... |
| Reserve assets | 3e9aa | .... | −148.4 | 314.8 | 473.9 | −135.5 | 915.4 | 565.8 | † 853.3 | −452.9 | 132.3 | .... | .... |
| Credit and loans from the IMF | 3dcla | .... | −90.6 | −57.7 | 15.1 | 21.7 | 155.2 | 35.7 | † 238.4 | 173.5 | 148.9 | .... | .... |
| Exceptional financing | 409la | .... | 257.3 | 149.2 | 138.1 | −387.7 | −326.4 | −897.3 | .... | .... | .... | .... | .... |

*Excludes components in group E

| | | 2004 | 2005 | 2006 | 2007 | 2008 | 2009 | 2010 | 2011 | 2012 | 2013 | 2014 | 2015 |
|---|---|---|---|---|---|---|---|---|---|---|---|---|---|
| **International Investment Position** | | | | | | | *Millions of US Dollars* | | | | | | |
| Assets | 809aa | .... | 6,052.7 | 7,645.5 | 9,514.7 | 9,333.5 | 11,893.8 | 13,077.1 | † 16,677.0 | 18,329.4 | 20,817.3 | .... | .... |
| Direct investment | 8a9aa | .... | .... | .... | .... | 80.9 | 73.9 | 93.6 | † 104.9 | 121.7 | 120.5 | .... | .... |
| Equity & investment fund shares.. | 8aaaa | .... | .... | .... | .... | 80.9 | 73.9 | 93.6 | † 104.9 | 121.7 | 120.5 | .... | .... |
| Debt instruments | 8abaa | .... | .... | .... | .... | .... | .... | .... | .... | .... | .... | .... | .... |
| Portfolio investment | 8b9aa | .... | 407.3 | 486.7 | 597.7 | 598.1 | 646.3 | 629.2 | † 609.7 | 629.2 | 660.8 | .... | .... |
| Equity & investment fund shares.. | 8baaa | .... | 13.8 | 21.7 | 32.6 | 38.7 | 47.2 | 52.1 | .... | .... | .... | .... | .... |
| Debt securities | 8bbaa | .... | 393.5 | 465.0 | 565.1 | 559.4 | 599.1 | 577.1 | .... | .... | .... | .... | .... |
| Fin. der.(oth.than reserves) & ESOs | 8c9aa | .... | .... | .... | .... | .... | .... | .... | .... | .... | .... | .... | .... |
| Other investment | 8d9aa | .... | 4,331.0 | 5,361.1 | 6,398.0 | 6,401.8 | 7,906.8 | 8,729.9 | † 11,646.4 | 13,650.4 | 15,810.9 | .... | .... |
| Other equity | 8daaa | .... | .... | .... | .... | .... | .... | .... | .... | 79.2 | 99.2 | .... | .... |
| Debt instruments | 8dzaa | .... | 4,331.0 | 5,361.1 | 6,398.0 | 6,401.8 | 7,906.8 | 8,729.9 | † 11,646.4 | 13,571.2 | 15,711.7 | .... | .... |
| Reserve assets | 8e9aa | .... | 1,314.4 | 1,797.7 | 2,519.0 | 2,252.7 | 3,266.8 | 3,624.4 | † 4,315.9 | 3,928.1 | 4,225.1 | .... | .... |
| Liabilities | 809la | .... | 16,892.3 | 19,322.2 | 22,525.0 | 21,600.5 | 21,202.7 | 21,323.4 | † 22,917.0 | 16,873.5 | 19,517.2 | .... | .... |
| Direct investment | 8a9la | .... | 3,901.3 | 4,690.1 | 5,701.5 | 5,814.0 | 6,409.3 | 6,286.8 | † 6,368.6 | 6,833.2 | 7,565.7 | .... | .... |
| Equity & investment fund shares.. | 8aala | .... | 3,901.3 | 4,690.1 | 5,701.5 | 5,814.0 | 6,409.3 | 6,286.8 | † 6,368.6 | 6,833.2 | 7,565.7 | .... | .... |
| Debt instruments | 8abla | .... | .... | .... | .... | .... | .... | .... | .... | .... | .... | .... | .... |
| Portfolio investment | 8b9la | .... | 471.2 | 573.6 | 797.7 | 826.9 | 843.7 | 1,273.4 | † 1,331.4 | 1,511.2 | 1,763.8 | .... | .... |
| Equity & investment fund shares.. | 8bala | .... | .... | .... | .... | .... | .... | .... | .... | .... | .... | .... | .... |
| Debt securities | 8bbla | .... | 471.2 | 573.6 | 797.7 | 826.9 | 843.7 | 1,273.4 | .... | .... | .... | .... | .... |
| Fin. der.(oth.than reserves) & ESOs | 8c9la | .... | .... | .... | .... | .... | .... | .... | .... | .... | .... | .... | .... |
| Other investment | 8d9la | .... | 12,519.8 | 14,058.6 | 16,025.8 | 14,959.7 | 13,949.7 | 13,763.2 | † 15,217.1 | 8,529.1 | 10,187.7 | .... | .... |
| Other equity | 8dala | .... | .... | .... | .... | .... | .... | .... | .... | .... | .... | .... | .... |
| Debt instruments | 8dzla | .... | 12,519.8 | 14,058.6 | 16,025.8 | 14,959.7 | 13,949.7 | 13,763.2 | † 15,217.1 | 8,529.1 | 10,187.7 | .... | .... |

# Côte d'Ivoire   662

| | | 2004 | 2005 | 2006 | 2007 | 2008 | 2009 | 2010 | 2011 | 2012 | 2013 | 2014 | 2015 |
|---|---|---|---|---|---|---|---|---|---|---|---|---|---|
| **Government Finance** | | | | | | | | | | | | | |
| **Operations Statement** | | | | | | | | | | | | | |
| **Budgetary Central Government** | | | | | | *Billions of CFA Francs: Fiscal Year Ends December 31* | | | | | | | |
| Revenue.......................... | a1 | 1,400.7 | 1,449.2 | 1,493.5 | 1,718.2 | 2,009.9 | 2,157.5 | 2,099.4 | 1,530.4 | 2,325.9 | 2,675.2 | 2,881.4 | .... |
| Taxes............................ | a11 | 1,241.4 | 1,251.2 | 1,364.3 | 1,468.2 | 1,633.0 | 1,673.6 | 1,765.6 | 1,309.2 | 1,968.2 | 2,246.2 | 2,439.9 | .... |
| Social Contributions.................... | a12 | — | — | — | — | — | — | — | — | — | — | — | .... |
| Grants........................... | a13 | 75.9 | 94.6 | 15.1 | 38.4 | 183.3 | 310.9 | 152.8 | 32.9 | 81.2 | 201.5 | 314.4 | .... |
| Other Revenue.............................. | a14 | 83.4 | 103.5 | 114.1 | 211.6 | 193.6 | 173.0 | 181.0 | 188.3 | 276.5 | 227.5 | 127.1 | .... |
| Expense........................... | a2 | 1,253.1 | 1,334.3 | 1,288.1 | 1,467.6 | 1,674.9 | 1,670.0 | 1,836.7 | 1,661.7 | 2,098.4 | 2,097.3 | 2,222.7 | .... |
| Compensation of Employees.......... | a21 | 545.8 | 563.4 | 589.4 | 640.4 | 711.7 | 745.0 | 800.5 | 719.8 | 934.7 | 1,038.9 | 1,183.3 | .... |
| Use of Goods & Services............. | a22 | 436.5 | 423.0 | 433.2 | 467.4 | 585.2 | 355.3 | 371.4 | 299.2 | 388.6 | 377.0 | 475.0 | .... |
| Consumption of Fixed Capital....... | a23 | .... | .... | .... | .... | .... | .... | .... | .... | .... | .... | .... | .... |
| Interest........................... | a24 | 186.1 | 177.1 | 131.9 | 166.2 | 181.9 | 168.4 | 194.3 | 219.3 | 232.9 | 214.8 | 138.5 | .... |
| Subsidies............................ | a25 | 84.7 | 65.0 | 46.4 | 88.0 | 58.1 | 112.4 | 169.7 | 179.6 | 232.2 | 164.1 | 128.0 | .... |
| Grants........................... | a26 | — | — | — | — | — | 27.8 | 25.0 | 66.4 | 84.3 | 83.9 | 93.9 | .... |
| Social Benefits.............................. | a27 | — | 29.3 | 3.4 | 4.7 | 4.0 | — | — | — | — | — | — | .... |
| Other Expense.............................. | a28 | — | 76.5 | 83.8 | 100.9 | 134.0 | 261.1 | 275.7 | 177.5 | 225.7 | 218.7 | 204.0 | .... |
| Gross Operating Balance [1-2+23]... | agob | 147.6 | 114.9 | 205.4 | 250.6 | 335.0 | 487.6 | 262.7 | −131.3 | 227.5 | 577.9 | 658.8 | .... |
| Net Operating Balance [1-2]........... | anob | .... | .... | .... | .... | .... | .... | .... | .... | .... | .... | .... | .... |
| Net Acq. of Nonfinancial Assets...... | a31 | 260.5 | 234.3 | 239.0 | 249.3 | 300.3 | 300.6 | 342.6 | 281.8 | 612.2 | 927.2 | 983.8 | .... |
| Aquisition of Nonfin. Assets.......... | a31.1 | .... | .... | .... | .... | .... | .... | .... | .... | .... | .... | .... | .... |
| Disposal of Nonfin. Assets............. | a31.2 | .... | .... | .... | .... | .... | .... | .... | .... | .... | .... | .... | .... |
| Net Lending/Borrowing [1-2-31]...... | anlb | −112.9 | −119.4 | −33.6 | 1.3 | 34.7 | 187.0 | −79.9 | −413.1 | −384.7 | −349.3 | −325.0 | .... |
| Net Acq. of Financial Assets............ | a32 | −11.2 | 25.1 | .... | 29.4 | 26.7 | 29.8 | 136.3 | 181.9 | −48.3 | 195.4 | 159.9 | .... |
| By instrument | | | | | | | | | | | | | |
| Monetary Gold & SDRs................. | a3201 | .... | — | .... | — | — | — | — | — | — | — | — | .... |
| Currency & Deposits................... | a3202 | −21.8 | .6 | .... | — | 21.7 | 26.9 | 105.9 | 214.7 | −35.8 | 213.2 | 209.1 | .... |
| Securities other than Shares........... | a3203 | .... | 2.1 | .... | 28.8 | — | — | — | — | — | — | — | .... |
| Loans............................... | a3204 | .... | 21.9 | .... | — | — | 12.4 | 33.4 | −.9 | 2.3 | — | −2.4 | .... |
| Shares & Other Equity................. | a3205 | .... | .5 | .... | .6 | 5.0 | −9.5 | −3.0 | −32.0 | −14.7 | −17.9 | −46.8 | .... |
| Insurance Technical Reserves......... | a3206 | .... | — | .... | — | — | — | — | — | — | — | — | .... |
| Financial Derivatives..................... | a3207 | .... | — | .... | — | — | — | — | — | — | — | — | .... |
| Other Accounts Receivable............. | a3208 | .... | — | .... | — | — | — | — | — | — | — | — | .... |
| By debtor | | | | | | | | | | | | | |
| Domestic................................. | a321 | −11.2 | 25.1 | .... | 29.4 | 26.7 | 29.8 | 136.3 | 181.9 | −48.3 | 195.4 | 159.9 | .... |
| Foreign.................................. | a322 | — | — | .... | — | — | — | — | — | — | — | — | .... |
| Net Incurrence of Liabilities.............. | a33 | 126.9 | 143.1 | .... | 85.0 | −.7 | −40.5 | 296.0 | 699.2 | 244.6 | 550.3 | 686.2 | .... |
| By instrument | | | | | | | | | | | | | |
| Special Drawing Rights (SDRs)....... | a3301 | — | — | .... | — | — | — | — | — | — | — | — | .... |
| Currency & Deposits................... | a3302 | — | — | .... | 108.5 | 47.8 | — | — | — | — | — | — | .... |
| Securities other than Shares........... | a3303 | −12.6 | −2.1 | .... | 118.5 | 92.2 | −5.7 | 456.4 | 198.4 | 237.2 | 343.4 | 858.3 | .... |
| Loans............................... | a3304 | 139.5 | 149.4 | .... | 34.0 | −197.4 | 38.1 | −140.7 | 493.5 | −74.7 | 184.3 | 8.0 | .... |
| Shares & Other Equity................. | a3305 | — | — | .... | — | — | — | — | — | — | — | — | .... |
| Insurance Technical Reserves......... | a3306 | — | — | .... | — | — | — | — | — | — | — | — | .... |
| Financial Derivatives..................... | a3307 | — | — | .... | — | — | — | — | — | — | — | — | .... |
| Other Accounts Payable................. | a3308 | — | −4.2 | .... | −176.0 | 56.7 | −72.9 | −19.7 | 7.2 | 82.0 | 22.6 | −180.1 | .... |
| By creditor | | | | | | | | | | | | | |
| Domestic................................. | a331 | 70.2 | −9.9 | .... | −50.4 | 140.0 | 64.3 | −33.6 | 183.8 | 222.4 | 276.4 | 156.9 | .... |
| Foreign.................................. | a332 | 56.7 | 153.0 | .... | 135.4 | −140.7 | −104.8 | 329.6 | 515.4 | 22.2 | 273.9 | 529.3 | .... |
| Stat. Discrepancy [32-33-NLB]........ | anlbz | −25.2 | 1.4 | .... | −56.9 | −7.3 | −116.7 | −79.7 | −104.2 | 91.8 | −5.6 | −201.3 | .... |
| Memo Item: Expenditure [2+31]...... | a2m | 1,513.6 | 1,568.6 | 1,527.1 | 1,716.9 | 1,975.2 | 1,970.5 | 2,179.3 | 1,943.6 | 2,710.6 | 3,024.5 | 3,206.5 | .... |
| **National Accounts** | | | | | | *Billions of CFA Francs* | | | | | | | |
| Househ.Cons.Expend.,incl.NPISHs.... | 96f | 5,943.5 | 6,161.4 | 6,436.7 | 6,994.3 | 7,409.6 | 7,765.2 | 8,267.4 | 8,376.7 | 9,155.0 | 10,041.4 | 11,207.3 | .... |
| Government Consumption Expend... | 91f | 1,302.6 | 1,300.2 | 1,265.1 | 1,300.5 | 1,374.4 | 1,448.5 | 1,500.9 | 1,346.9 | 2,025.4 | 2,037.4 | 2,283.7 | .... |
| Gross Fixed Capital Formation......... | 93e | 817.6 | 826.1 | 911.1 | 1,132.4 | 1,186.6 | 1,246.2 | 1,518.0 | 1,072.1 | 1,671.3 | 2,257.7 | 2,730.3 | .... |
| Changes in Inventories.................... | 93i | −35.7 | 194.7 | −204.6 | −166.1 | 122.6 | −249.2 | 138.1 | −582.8 | 405.1 | 683.3 | 150.6 | .... |
| Exports of Goods and Services......... | 90c | 4,058.3 | 4,496.7 | 4,874.3 | 4,604.6 | 5,111.2 | 5,829.7 | 6,240.3 | 6,449.6 | 6,692.1 | 6,416.2 | 6,644.8 | .... |
| Imports of Goods and Services (-)..... | 98c | 3,340.9 | 3,967.4 | 3,974.7 | 4,115.7 | 4,356.4 | 4,576.8 | 5,339.9 | 4,471.5 | 6,120.0 | 5,960.0 | 6,081.0 | .... |
| Gross Domestic Product (GDP)........ | 99b | 8,745.5 | 9,011.8 | 9,307.9 | 9,750.0 | 10,848.0 | 11,463.5 | 12,324.7 | 12,191.0 | 13,828.9 | 15,476.0 | 16,935.7 | .... |
| GDP Volume 2008 Prices................ | 99b.p | 9,790.0 | 9,958.7 | 10,028.2 | 10,189.3 | 10,848.0 | 11,200.8 | 11,426.8 | 10,925.4 | 12,095.2 | 13,210.2 | 14,337.5 | .... |
| GDP Volume (2010=100)............... | 99bvp | 85.7 | 87.2 | 87.8 | 89.2 | 94.9 | 98.0 | 100.0 | 95.6 | 105.8 | 115.6 | 125.5 | .... |
| GDP Deflator (2010=100)............... | 99bip | 82.8 | 83.9 | 86.1 | 88.7 | 92.7 | 94.9 | 100.0 | 103.5 | 106.0 | 108.6 | 109.5 | .... |
| | | | | | | *Millions: Midyear Estimates* | | | | | | | |
| **Population...........................** | 99z | 17.80 | 18.13 | 18.49 | 18.86 | 19.26 | 19.68 | 20.13 | 20.60 | 21.10 | 21.62 | 22.16 | 22.70 |

# Croatia 960

| | | 2004 | 2005 | 2006 | 2007 | 2008 | 2009 | 2010 | 2011 | 2012 | 2013 | 2014 | 2015 |
|---|---|---|---|---|---|---|---|---|---|---|---|---|---|
| **Exchange Rates** | | | | | | *Kuna per SDR: End of Period* | | | | | | | |
| Official Rate............. | aa | 8.754 | 8.910 | 8.392 | 7.878 | 7.941 | 7.978 | 8.575 | 8.935 | 8.802 | 8.545 | 9.131 | 9.689 |
| | | | | | | *Kuna per US Dollar: End of Period (ae) Period Average (rf)* | | | | | | | |
| Official Rate............. | ae | 5.637 | 6.234 | 5.578 | 4.985 | 5.156 | 5.089 | 5.568 | 5.820 | 5.727 | 5.549 | 6.302 | 6.992 |
| Official Rate............. | rf | 6.034 | 5.949 | 5.838 | 5.365 | 4.935 | 5.284 | 5.498 | 5.344 | 5.850 | 5.705 | 5.748 | 6.858 |
| | | | | | | *Index Numbers (2010=100): Period Averages* | | | | | | | |
| Nominal Effective Exchange Rate..... | nec | 97.19 | 97.71 | 99.02 | 99.58 | 102.11 | 101.58 | 100.00 | 98.50 | 95.93 | 96.72 | 96.86 | 94.86 |
| CPI-Based Real Effect. Ex. Rate........ | rec | 92.91 | 94.37 | 96.33 | 97.03 | 101.46 | 102.64 | 100.00 | 97.90 | 96.07 | 97.41 | 96.34 | 93.45 |
| **Fund Position** | | | | | | *Millions of SDRs: End of Period* | | | | | | | |
| Quota............. | 2f.s | 365.10 | 365.10 | 365.10 | 365.10 | 365.10 | 365.10 | 365.10 | 365.10 | 365.10 | 365.10 | 365.10 | 365.10 |
| SDR Holdings............. | 1b.s | .03 | .18 | .11 | .19 | .15 | 303.14 | 303.16 | 303.20 | 304.22 | 304.99 | 304.95 | 304.92 |
| Reserve Position in the Fund............ | 1c.s | .16 | .16 | .16 | .16 | .16 | .16 | .16 | .16 | .16 | .16 | .17 | .20 |
| Total Fund Cred.&Loans Outstg.... | 2tl | — | — | — | — | — | — | — | — | — | — | | |
| SDR Allocations............. | 1bd | 44.21 | 44.21 | 44.21 | 44.21 | 44.21 | 347.34 | 347.34 | 347.34 | 347.34 | 347.34 | 347.34 | 347.34 |
| **International Liquidity** | | | | | | *Millions of US Dollars Unless Otherwise Indicated: End of Period* | | | | | | | |
| Total Reserves minus Gold............. | 1l.d | 8,758.2 | 8,800.3 | 11,487.8 | 13,674.5 | 12,957.3 | 14,894.5 | 14,132.5 | 14,483.8 | 14,807.1 | 17,766.8 | 15,423.6 | 14,966.9 |
| SDR Holdings............. | 1b.d | .1 | .3 | .2 | .3 | .2 | 475.2 | 466.9 | 465.5 | 467.6 | 469.7 | 441.8 | 422.5 |
| Reserve Position in the Fund........ | 1c.d | .2 | .2 | .2 | .3 | .2 | .2 | .2 | .2 | .2 | .2 | .3 | .3 |
| Foreign Exchange............. | 1d.d | 8,757.9 | 8,799.8 | 11,487.4 | 13,674.0 | 12,956.8 | 14,419.0 | 13,665.4 | 14,018.1 | 14,339.3 | 17,296.8 | 14,981.6 | 14,544.1 |
| Gold (Million Fine Troy Ounces)....... | 1ad | — | — | — | — | — | — | — | — | — | — | — | — |
| Gold (National Valuation)............. | 1and | — | — | — | — | — | — | — | — | — | — | — | — |
| Central Bank: Other Assets....... | 3..d | 4.7 | 7.3 | 7.7 | 8.1 | 7.8 | 8.0 | 7.9 | 7.9 | 7.5 | † 4,577.8 | 3,654.7 | 4,866.8 |
| Central Bank: Other Liabs....... | 4..d | 3.2 | 3.0 | 3.4 | 3.5 | 3.2 | 1.6 | 1.6 | .1 | — | † 682.8 | 629.0 | 1,912.1 |
| Other Depository Corps.: Assets....... | 7a.d | 7,781.5 | 5,770.1 | 7,190.9 | 9,411.4 | 9,804.2 | 9,822.1 | 8,682.2 | 7,013.3 | 6,953.9 | † 6,614.7 | 6,976.2 | 6,877.5 |
| Other Depository Corps.: Liabs......... | 7b.d | 10,986.1 | 10,876.6 | 13,736.2 | 13,209.0 | 14,984.8 | 15,960.0 | 15,135.2 | 16,011.4 | 13,307.0 | † 12,570.2 | 9,900.5 | 6,679.4 |
| **Central Bank** | | | | | | *Millions of Kuna: End of Period* | | | | | | | |
| Net Foreign Assets............. | 11n | 48,994.7 | 54,495.1 | 63,741.3 | 67,852.5 | 66,478.2 | 73,068.0 | 75,754.8 | 81,241.3 | 81,787.7 | † 91,357.4 | 89,638.5 | 87,612.9 |
| Claims on Nonresidents............. | 11 | 49,399.7 | 54,907.9 | 64,131.1 | 68,218.0 | 66,845.8 | 75,847.4 | 78,742.1 | 84,345.2 | 84,844.9 | † 98,114.6 | 96,773.9 | 104,347.2 |
| Liabilities to Nonresidents............. | 16c | 405.1 | 412.8 | 389.9 | 365.5 | 367.7 | 2,779.3 | 2,987.2 | 3,104.0 | 3,057.2 | † 6,757.2 | 7,135.4 | 16,734.3 |
| Claims on Other Depository Corps.... | 12e | 409.5 | 4,222.3 | 3,913.3 | 4,180.4 | 16.2 | 13.5 | 12.9 | 140.5 | 11.8 | † 11.0 | 11.0 | 168.0 |
| Net Claims on Central Government.. | 12an | −267.1 | −343.9 | −240.3 | −223.7 | −258.2 | −4,214.8 | −4,163.5 | −2,066.2 | −1,094.6 | † −13,956.0 | −11,671.0 | −7,877.0 |
| Claims on Central Government...... | 12a | 3.3 | 1.4 | .9 | 1.0 | 1.0 | 2.9 | .3 | 251.8 | — | † — | | |
| Liabilities to Central Government... | 16d | 270.4 | 345.4 | 241.2 | 224.8 | 259.2 | 4,217.6 | 4,163.8 | 2,318.0 | 1,094.6 | † 13,956.0 | 11,671.0 | 7,877.0 |
| Claims on Other Sectors............. | 12s | 117.2 | 112.8 | 104.0 | 100.5 | 94.9 | 29.1 | 29.5 | 29.6 | 27.7 | † 19.0 | 20.0 | 21.0 |
| Claims on Other Financial Corps... | 12g | 87.1 | 77.6 | 68.3 | 69.9 | 64.8 | .7 | .7 | .7 | — | † — | | |
| Claims on State & Local Govts...... | 12b | — | — | — | — | — | — | — | — | — | † — | | |
| Claims on Public Nonfin. Corps.... | 12c | — | — | — | — | — | — | — | — | — | † — | | |
| Claims on Private Sector............. | 12d | 30.0 | 35.1 | 35.7 | 30.6 | 30.1 | 28.5 | 28.8 | 28.9 | 27.7 | † 19.0 | 20.0 | 21.0 |
| Monetary Base............. | 14 | 44,708.7 | 53,898.0 | 62,920.9 | 66,197.6 | 57,765.1 | 61,199.4 | 61,142.8 | 68,098.6 | 66,951.4 | † 67,130.0 | 67,084.0 | 67,871.0 |
| Currency in Circulation............. | 14a | 12,826.6 | 14,374.5 | 17,307.3 | 19,313.2 | 20,479.3 | 18,941.7 | 19,311.5 | 20,943.0 | 21,627.9 | † 21,985.0 | 23,156.0 | 25,318.0 |
| Liabs. to Other Depository Corps..... | 14c | 31,867.0 | 39,523.5 | 45,613.6 | 46,884.4 | 37,285.8 | 42,257.7 | 41,726.6 | 46,975.0 | 44,731.9 | † 45,145.0 | 43,928.0 | 42,246.0 |
| Liabilities to Other Sectors............. | 14d | 15.1 | | | | | | 104.8 | 180.6 | 591.6 | † — | | 307.0 |
| Other Liabs. to Other Dep. Corps..... | 14n | 5.3 | 42.8 | 3.7 | 2.9 | 3.5 | 3.6 | 3.1 | 7.4 | 1.6 | † — | | |
| Dep. & Sec. Excl. f/Monetary Base..... | 14o | — | — | — | — | — | — | 1,145.4 | 153.8 | 2,719.5 | † — | | |
| Deposits Included in Broad Money... | 15 | — | — | — | — | — | — | — | — | — | † — | | |
| Sec.Ot.th.Shares Incl.in Brd. Money | 16a | — | — | — | — | — | — | — | — | — | † — | | |
| Deposits Excl. from Broad Money... | 16b | — | — | — | — | — | — | 1,145.4 | 153.8 | 2,719.5 | † — | | |
| Sec.Ot.th.Shares Excl.f/Brd.Money.. | 16s | — | — | — | — | — | — | — | — | — | † — | | |
| Loans............. | 16l | — | — | — | — | — | — | — | — | — | † — | | |
| Financial Derivatives............. | 16m | — | — | — | — | — | — | — | — | — | † — | | |
| Shares and Other Equity............. | 17a | 4,963.5 | 5,231.7 | 5,290.0 | 6,551.3 | 9,462.2 | 8,664.9 | 10,392.0 | 13,007.2 | 13,000.4 | † 13,419.0 | 15,191.0 | 16,689.0 |
| Other Items (Net)............. | 17r | −423.3 | −686.3 | −696.3 | −842.2 | −899.7 | −972.0 | −1,049.5 | −1,097.5 | −1,131.5 | † −3,116.6 | −4,277.5 | −4,635.1 |
| **Other Depository Corporations** | | | | | | *Millions of Kuna: End of Period* | | | | | | | |
| Net Foreign Assets............. | 21n | −18,064.4 | −31,831.6 | −36,512.1 | −18,933.0 | −26,708.6 | −31,237.3 | −35,931.8 | −52,368.1 | −36,382.8 | † −33,047.0 | −18,429.0 | 1,385.0 |
| Claims on Nonresidents............. | 21 | 43,863.2 | 35,968.9 | 40,113.7 | 46,920.1 | 50,545.4 | 49,987.7 | 48,344.8 | 40,816.6 | 39,823.6 | † 36,705.0 | 43,965.0 | 48,086.0 |
| Liabilities to Nonresidents............. | 26c | 61,927.6 | 67,800.5 | 76,625.8 | 65,853.1 | 77,254.0 | 81,225.0 | 84,276.5 | 93,184.7 | 76,206.4 | † 69,752.0 | 62,394.0 | 46,701.0 |
| Claims on Central Bank............. | 20 | 33,743.4 | 41,789.3 | 48,402.7 | 50,201.5 | 40,721.5 | 45,916.1 | 45,759.7 | 51,114.8 | 49,412.0 | † 49,708.0 | 48,561.0 | 47,416.0 |
| Currency............. | 20a | 1,871.0 | 2,210.7 | 2,698.0 | 3,305.8 | 3,428.3 | 3,659.6 | 4,047.2 | 4,253.6 | 4,680.9 | † 4,565.0 | 4,636.0 | 5,169.0 |
| Reserve Deposits and Securities..... | 20b | 31,872.4 | 39,578.6 | 45,704.7 | 46,895.8 | 37,293.3 | 42,256.5 | 41,712.5 | 46,861.2 | 44,731.1 | † 45,143.0 | 43,925.0 | 42,247.0 |
| Other Claims............. | 20n | — | — | — | — | — | — | — | — | — | † — | | |
| Net Claims on Central Government.. | 22an | 16,218.9 | 21,646.2 | 19,276.7 | 17,883.7 | 24,118.7 | 28,544.2 | 45,878.6 | 31,345.6 | 39,962.1 | † 68,365.0 | 72,701.0 | 75,660.0 |
| Claims on Central Government...... | 22a | 23,134.8 | 30,982.3 | 30,124.7 | 31,465.7 | 40,218.5 | 46,817.0 | 50,027.9 | 57,782.6 | 65,225.2 | † 88,600.0 | 93,549.0 | 95,367.0 |
| Liabilities to Central Government... | 26d | 6,915.9 | 9,336.1 | 10,848.0 | 13,582.1 | 16,099.8 | 18,272.8 | 4,149.3 | 26,437.1 | 25,263.1 | † 20,235.0 | 20,848.0 | 19,707.0 |
| Claims on Other Sectors............. | 22s | 126,490.8 | 148,388.7 | 182,812.4 | 210,298.6 | 232,981.6 | 231,730.3 | 255,910.2 | 266,392.4 | 254,064.0 | † 238,953.0 | 234,543.0 | 228,743.0 |
| Claims on Other Financial Corps... | 22g | 1,534.8 | 1,773.2 | 2,369.7 | 3,466.1 | 1,528.5 | 1,817.7 | 6,248.4 | 4,901.2 | 6,559.3 | † 8,315.0 | 6,955.0 | 9,942.0 |
| Claims on State & Local Govts...... | 22b | 1,819.1 | 1,791.7 | 1,922.8 | 2,188.1 | 2,123.9 | 2,100.7 | 3,387.0 | 3,610.8 | 3,541.7 | † 4,234.0 | 4,717.0 | 4,448.0 |
| Claims on Public Nonfin. Corps...... | 22c | 5,026.6 | 6,468.9 | 8,238.2 | 8,611.8 | 9,283.1 | 9,147.4 | 25,189.2 | 27,793.6 | 22,995.5 | † — | | |
| Claims on Private Sector............. | 22d | 119,929.3 | 140,146.6 | 172,204.5 | 198,220.7 | 222,170.1 | 220,765.1 | 224,472.6 | 233,697.6 | 224,509.2 | † 230,638.0 | 227,588.0 | 218,801.0 |
| Liabilities to Central Bank............. | 26g | 409.0 | 4,217.2 | 3,913.2 | 4,181.9 | 16.2 | 13.6 | 12.9 | 140.2 | 11.8 | † 11.0 | 11.0 | 168.0 |
| Transf.Dep.Included in Broad Money | 24 | 24,254.4 | 27,416.7 | 34,793.8 | 43,121.4 | 38,953.6 | 32,901.4 | 38,418.0 | 41,268.0 | 42,754.3 | † 69,622.0 | 77,463.0 | 89,137.0 |
| Other Dep.Included in Broad Money | 25 | 105,511.2 | 116,030.2 | 134,151.5 | 157,785.1 | 170,411.3 | 176,750.3 | 200,177.0 | 199,085.2 | 204,949.9 | † 140,533.0 | 133,619.0 | 130,785.0 |
| Sec.Ot.th.Shares Incl.in Brd. Money.. | 26a | 172.1 | 166.4 | 346.1 | 635.5 | 611.9 | 768.0 | 241.7 | 923.0 | 1,121.0 | † — | | 1.0 |
| Deposits Excl. from Broad Money..... | 26b | 2,054.6 | 2,036.4 | 2,447.6 | 2,252.3 | 3,038.4 | 2,548.4 | 1,475.4 | 1,786.2 | 1,105.4 | † 37,488.0 | 43,866.0 | 47,898.0 |
| Sec.Ot.th.Shares Excl.f/Brd.Money... | 26s | — | — | — | — | — | — | — | — | — | † 1,184.0 | 1,178.0 | 1,077.0 |
| Loans............. | 26l | — | — | — | — | — | — | — | — | — | † — | | |
| Financial Derivatives............. | 26m | 73.4 | 144.2 | 168.9 | 181.6 | 68.6 | 30.4 | 33.0 | 45.0 | 52.8 | † 1,876.0 | 1,179.0 | 2,339.0 |
| Insurance Technical Reserves.......... | 26r | — | — | — | — | — | — | — | — | — | † — | | |
| Shares and Other Equity............. | 27a | 19,909.0 | 23,833.3 | 31,539.4 | 43,368.0 | 50,124.2 | 53,051.9 | 55,096.1 | 56,306.5 | 58,002.0 | † 56,351.0 | 56,691.0 | 56,537.0 |
| Other Items (Net)............. | 27r | 6,078.2 | 6,292.5 | 6,788.1 | 8,106.6 | 7,957.6 | 8,919.6 | 16,195.5 | 20,118.9 | 23,203.4 | † 22,204.0 | 25,292.0 | 27,604.0 |
| Memo Item: | | | | | | | | | | | | | |
| Total Assets............. | 20ra | 239,056.4 | 269,240.2 | 313,863.4 | 354,584.9 | 380,398.8 | 391,685.3 | 415,226.4 | 433,086.6 | 425,420.3 | † 438,484.0 | 441,828.0 | 442,079.0 |

| | | 2004 | 2005 | 2006 | 2007 | 2008 | 2009 | 2010 | 2011 | 2012 | 2013 | 2014 | 2015 |
|---|---|---|---|---|---|---|---|---|---|---|---|---|---|
| **Depository Corporations** | | *Millions of Kuna: End of Period* | | | | | | | | | | | |
| Net Foreign Assets | 31n | 30,930.3 | 22,663.5 | 27,229.1 | 48,919.6 | 39,769.6 | 41,830.7 | 39,823.1 | 28,873.2 | 45,404.8 | † 58,310.4 | 71,209.5 | 88,997.9 |
| Claims on Nonresidents | 31 | 93,262.9 | 90,876.8 | 104,244.8 | 115,138.1 | 117,391.2 | 125,835.1 | 127,086.8 | 125,161.8 | 124,668.5 | † 134,819.6 | 140,738.9 | 152,433.2 |
| Liabilities to Nonresidents | 36c | 62,332.6 | 68,213.2 | 77,015.7 | 66,218.6 | 77,621.6 | 84,004.4 | 87,263.8 | 96,288.6 | 79,263.6 | † 76,509.2 | 69,529.4 | 63,435.3 |
| Domestic Claims | 32 | 142,559.7 | 169,803.8 | 201,952.8 | 228,059.1 | 256,937.0 | 256,088.8 | 297,654.8 | 295,701.4 | 292,959.3 | † 293,381.0 | 295,593.0 | 296,547.0 |
| Net Claims on Central Government | 32an | 15,951.8 | 21,302.3 | 19,036.4 | 17,659.9 | 23,860.5 | 24,329.4 | 41,715.1 | 29,279.4 | 38,867.5 | † 54,409.0 | 61,030.0 | 67,783.0 |
| Claims on Central Government | 32a | 23,138.1 | 30,983.8 | 30,125.6 | 31,466.8 | 40,219.5 | 46,819.9 | 50,028.2 | 58,034.5 | 65,225.2 | † 88,600.0 | 93,549.0 | 95,367.0 |
| Liabilities to Central Government | 36d | 7,186.3 | 9,681.5 | 11,089.2 | 13,806.8 | 16,359.0 | 22,490.5 | 8,313.1 | 28,755.1 | 26,357.7 | † 34,191.0 | 32,519.0 | 27,584.0 |
| Claims on Other Sectors | 32s | 126,607.9 | 148,501.5 | 182,916.4 | 210,399.1 | 233,076.5 | 231,759.4 | 255,939.7 | 266,422.0 | 254,091.8 | † 238,972.0 | 234,563.0 | 228,764.0 |
| Claims on Other Financial Corps. | 32g | 1,622.0 | 1,850.9 | 2,437.9 | 3,536.0 | 1,593.3 | 1,818.4 | 6,249.1 | 4,901.9 | 6,559.3 | † 8,315.0 | 6,955.0 | 9,942.0 |
| Claims on State & Local Govts. | 32b | 1,819.8 | 1,791.7 | 1,922.8 | 2,188.1 | 2,123.9 | 2,100.7 | 3,387.0 | 3,610.8 | 3,541.7 | † 4,234.0 | 4,717.0 | 4,448.0 |
| Claims on Public Nonfin. Corps. | 32c | 5,026.6 | 6,468.9 | 8,238.2 | 8,611.8 | 9,283.1 | 9,147.4 | 25,189.2 | 27,793.6 | 22,995.5 | † — | — | — |
| Claims on Private Sector | 32d | 119,959.4 | 140,181.7 | 172,240.2 | 198,251.2 | 222,200.1 | 220,793.6 | 224,501.4 | 233,726.5 | 224,536.9 | † 230,657.0 | 227,608.0 | 218,822.0 |
| Broad Money Liabilities | 35l | 140,908.5 | 155,777.2 | 183,900.6 | 217,549.5 | 227,027.8 | 225,701.9 | 254,205.8 | 258,146.3 | 266,363.9 | † 227,575.0 | 229,602.0 | 240,379.0 |
| Currency Outside Depository Corps | 34a | 10,955.6 | 12,163.8 | 14,609.3 | 16,007.5 | 17,051.0 | 15,282.1 | 15,264.2 | 16,689.4 | 16,947.1 | † 17,420.0 | 18,520.0 | 20,149.0 |
| Transferable Deposits | 34 | 24,269.5 | 27,416.7 | 34,793.8 | 43,121.4 | 38,953.6 | 32,901.4 | 38,430.6 | 41,268.4 | 42,818.7 | † 69,622.0 | 77,463.0 | 89,444.0 |
| Other Deposits | 35 | 105,511.2 | 116,030.2 | 134,151.5 | 157,785.1 | 170,411.3 | 176,750.3 | 200,269.2 | 199,265.5 | 205,477.2 | † 140,533.0 | 133,619.0 | 130,785.0 |
| Securities Other than Shares | 36a | 172.1 | 166.4 | 346.1 | 635.5 | 611.9 | 768.0 | 241.7 | 923.0 | 1,121.0 | † — | — | 1.0 |
| Deposits Excl. from Broad Money | 36b | 2,054.6 | 2,036.4 | 2,447.6 | 2,252.3 | 3,038.4 | 2,548.4 | 2,620.8 | 1,940.1 | 3,824.9 | † 37,488.0 | 43,866.0 | 47,898.0 |
| Sec.Ot.th.Shares Excl.f/Brd.Money | 36s | — | — | — | — | — | — | — | — | — | † 1,184.0 | 1,178.0 | 1,077.0 |
| Loans | 36l | — | — | — | — | — | — | — | — | — | † — | — | — |
| Financial Derivatives | 36m | 73.4 | 144.2 | 168.9 | 181.6 | 68.6 | 30.4 | 33.0 | 45.0 | 52.8 | † 1,876.0 | 1,179.0 | 2,339.0 |
| Insurance Technical Reserves | 36r | — | — | — | — | — | — | — | — | — | † — | — | — |
| Shares and Other Equity | 37a | 24,872.6 | 29,065.0 | 36,829.5 | 49,919.3 | 59,586.3 | 61,716.8 | 65,488.1 | 69,313.7 | 71,002.4 | † 69,770.0 | 71,882.0 | 73,226.0 |
| Other Items (Net) | 37r | 5,654.4 | 5,588.7 | 6,004.2 | 7,257.4 | 7,054.0 | 7,952.5 | 15,163.1 | 19,142.3 | 22,074.3 | † 19,089.4 | 21,017.5 | 22,967.9 |
| Broad Money Liabs., Seasonally Adj. | 35l.b | 139,259.7 | 153,932.7 | 181,799.3 | 215,278.4 | 224,934.2 | 223,882.1 | 252,367.3 | 256,515.3 | 264,931.3 | † 226,542.3 | 228,730.1 | 239,561.1 |
| **Monetary Aggregates** | | *Millions of Kuna: End of Period* | | | | | | | | | | | |
| Broad Money | 59m | 140,908.5 | 155,777.2 | 183,900.6 | 217,549.5 | 227,027.8 | 225,701.9 | 254,205.8 | 258,146.3 | 266,363.9 | 227,575.0 | 229,602.0 | 240,379.0 |
| o/w:Currency Issued by Cent.Govt | 59m.a | — | — | — | — | — | — | — | — | — | — | — | — |
| o/w: Dep.in Nonfin. Corporations. | 59m.b | — | — | — | — | — | — | — | — | — | — | — | — |
| o/w:Secs. Issued by Central Govt. | 59m.c | — | — | — | — | — | — | — | — | — | — | — | — |
| Money (National Definitions) | | | | | | | | | | | | | |
| Reserve Money | 19mb | 33,396.7 | 38,796.5 | 46,564.8 | 51,170.4 | 53,900.5 | 54,799.6 | 56,353.8 | 62,559.6 | 61,856.3 | 63,043.9 | 63,380.0 | 63,748.5 |
| M1 | 59ma | 36,200.7 | 40,771.6 | 48,677.0 | 53,193.8 | 47,447.1 | 47,990.1 | 48,859.4 | 48,164.2 | 54,538.3 | 58,532.7 | 63,499.3 | 69,453.9 |
| M4 | 59md | 149,835.5 | 170,206.9 | 204,014.0 | 229,791.5 | 237,569.4 | 242,425.0 | 251,738.5 | 255,730.6 | 263,788.3 | 271,516.1 | 287,563.9 | 285,639.8 |
| **Interest Rates** | | *Percent Per Annum* | | | | | | | | | | | |
| Deposit Rate | | | | | | | | | | | | | |
| Households: Stocks, up to 2 years | 60lhs | .... | .... | .... | .... | .... | .... | .... | 4.17 | 4.26 | 3.87 | 3.47 | 3.17 |
| New Business, 6 months to 1 year | 60lhn | .... | .... | .... | .... | .... | .... | .... | 3.65 | 3.66 | 3.04 | 2.43 | 2.13 |
| Corporations: Stocks, up to 2 years | 60lcs | .... | .... | .... | .... | .... | .... | .... | 3.470 | 3.390 | 2.510 | 2.140 | 1.760 |
| New Business, 6 months to 1 year | 60lcn | .... | .... | .... | .... | .... | .... | .... | 3.11 | 2.65 | 1.53 | 1.39 | 1.21 |
| Repos, Stocks | 60lcr | .... | .... | .... | .... | .... | .... | .... | .... | .52 | .61 | .78 | .48 |
| Lending Rate | | | | | | | | | | | | | |
| Households: Stocks, up to 1 year | 60phs | .... | .... | .... | .... | .... | .... | .... | 10.47 | 10.51 | 10.28 | 9.47 | 9.10 |
| New Bus., Fixed & 3 mo. to 1 yea | 60pns | .... | .... | .... | .... | .... | .... | .... | 6.24 | 6.45 | 5.45 | 5.69 | 6.92 |
| House Purch., Stocks, 5-10 years | 60phm | .... | .... | .... | .... | .... | .... | .... | 6.49 | 6.44 | 6.46 | 6.16 | 5.66 |
| House Purch., New.Bus., 5-10 yrs | 60phn | .... | .... | .... | .... | .... | .... | .... | 6.820 | 7.130 | 5.270 | 5.280 | 5.180 |
| Corporations: Stocks, up to 1 year | 60pcs | .... | .... | .... | .... | .... | .... | .... | 7.67 | 7.66 | 6.70 | 6.28 | 5.83 |
| New Bus., 3 mo.-1 yr | 60pcn | .... | .... | .... | .... | .... | .... | .... | 7.58 | 5.45 | 4.30 | 3.69 | 3.46 |
| **Prices, Production, Labor** | | *Index Numbers (2010=100): Period Averages* | | | | | | | | | | | |
| Share Prices | 62 | 63.3 | 95.1 | 135.6 | 230.2 | 171.3 | 93.3 | 100.0 | 104.6 | 87.1 | 93.1 | 90.0 | 87.0 |
| Producer Prices | 63 | 81.2 | † 83.7 | † 86.0 | 88.9 | 96.3 | 95.9 | 100.0 | 106.4 | 113.8 | 114.3 | 111.2 | 106.9 |
| Consumer Prices | 64 | 83.1 | 85.8 | 88.6 | 91.1 | 96.7 | 99.0 | 100.0 | 102.3 | 105.8 | 108.1 | 107.9 | 107.4 |
| Wages | 65 | 78.1 | 81.9 | 86.1 | 90.6 | 96.9 | 99.4 | 100.0 | 101.8 | 102.5 | 103.2 | 103.6 | 106.9 |
| Industrial Production | 66 | 94.8 | 99.7 | 104.1 | 110.0 | † 111.7 | 101.4 | 100.0 | † 98.8 | 93.3 | 91.6 | 92.7 | 95.2 |
| Total Employment | 67 | 99.4 | 100.1 | 103.5 | 106.9 | 109.6 | 105.6 | .... | .... | .... | .... | .... | .... |
| | | *Number in Thousands: Period Averages* | | | | | | | | | | | |
| Labor Force | 67d | 1,820 | 1,813 | 1,801 | 1,924 | 1,936 | 1,935 | † 1,913 | 1,882 | 1,863 | 1,842 | 1,893 | 1,899 |
| Employment | 67e | 1,563 | 1,573 | 1,586 | 1,734 | 1,771 | 1,757 | † 1,690 | 1,625 | 1,566 | 1,524 | 1,566 | 1,589 |
| Unemployment | 67c | 257 | 240 | 215 | 191 | 165 | 178 | 222 | 257 | 297 | 318 | 327 | 309 |
| Unemployment Rate (%) | 67r | 13.9 | 13.0 | 11.6 | 9.9 | 8.6 | 9.2 | 11.7 | 13.7 | 16.0 | 17.3 | 17.3 | 16.3 |
| **Intl. Transactions & Positions** | | *Millions of US Dollars* | | | | | | | | | | | |
| Exports | 70..d | 8,024.2 | 8,772.6 | 10,376.3 | 12,364.3 | 14,111.7 | 10,473.8 | 11,806.2 | 13,374.8 | 12,347.1 | 11,927.5 | 13,686.4 | 12,843.5 |
| Imports, c.i.f. | 71..d | 16,589.2 | 18,560.4 | 21,488.3 | 25,829.5 | 30,728.4 | 21,202.6 | 20,050.5 | 22,707.6 | 20,761.9 | 20,960.6 | 22,523.3 | 20,580.5 |

# Croatia 960

2016, International Monetary Fund : *International Financial Statistics Yearbook*

| | | 2004 | 2005 | 2006 | 2007 | 2008 | 2009 | 2010 | 2011 | 2012 | 2013 | 2014 | 2015 |
|---|---|---|---|---|---|---|---|---|---|---|---|---|---|
| **Balance of Payments** | | | | | | | *Millions of US Dollars* | | | | | | |
| A. Current Account* | 109bx | −1,800.3 | −2,478.7 | −3,246.2 | −4,351.9 | −6,214.0 | −3,158.0 | −894.4 | −375.7 | −207.9 | 566.9 | 448.1 | 2,528.5 |
| Goods, credit (exports) | 1a9cx | 6,629.8 | 7,525.3 | 8,975.4 | 10,513.0 | 11,711.2 | 9,171.2 | 10,684.1 | 12,181.7 | 11,139.9 | 11,853.7 | 12,949.7 | 11,907.6 |
| Goods, debit (imports) | 1a9dx | 15,196.9 | 17,024.1 | 19,636.5 | 23,667.6 | 27,618.8 | 19,556.8 | 18,522.3 | 21,076.6 | 19,232.5 | 20,571.7 | 21,434.1 | 19,282.9 |
| Balance on goods | 1a9bx | −8,567.0 | −9,498.8 | −10,661.1 | −13,154.6 | −15,907.7 | −10,385.6 | −7,838.1 | −8,895.0 | −8,092.7 | −8,718.0 | −8,484.4 | −7,375.3 |
| Services, credit (exports) | 1b9cx | 9,756.1 | 10,253.4 | 11,170.7 | 13,013.1 | 15,772.9 | 12,626.4 | 11,661.5 | 13,181.4 | 12,254.3 | 13,014.7 | 13,595.4 | 12,491.2 |
| Services, debit (imports) | 1b9dx | 3,722.4 | 3,590.7 | 3,811.2 | 4,224.3 | 5,310.9 | 4,441.7 | 4,208.2 | 4,417.4 | 4,017.7 | 4,067.9 | 3,968.9 | 3,760.3 |
| Balance on Goods & Services | 1z9bx | −2,533.4 | −2,836.1 | −3,301.5 | −4,365.8 | −5,445.7 | −2,200.9 | −384.8 | −130.9 | 143.9 | 228.7 | 1,142.2 | 1,355.6 |
| Primary income: credit | 1c9cx | 911.7 | 919.4 | 1,167.9 | 1,827.4 | 2,034.7 | 1,110.9 | 1,207.8 | 1,330.9 | 1,239.1 | 1,140.2 | 1,102.3 | 1,085.5 |
| Primary income: debit | 1c9dx | 1,659.8 | 2,037.6 | 2,501.0 | 3,242.5 | 4,369.6 | 3,470.2 | 3,120.0 | 3,229.3 | 3,157.2 | 2,312.1 | 2,987.0 | 1,415.9 |
| Balance on gds, serv. & prim. inc. | 1y9bx | −3,281.4 | −3,954.2 | −4,634.6 | −5,780.9 | −7,780.6 | −4,560.3 | −2,297.0 | −2,029.3 | −1,774.3 | −943.2 | −742.5 | 1,025.2 |
| Secondary income: credit | 1d9ca | 1,948.5 | 2,015.9 | 2,032.2 | 2,139.9 | 2,379.6 | 2,168.5 | 2,150.3 | 2,418.5 | 2,318.5 | 2,542.7 | 2,554.9 | 2,592.2 |
| Secondary income: debit | 1d9da | 467.3 | 540.4 | 643.7 | 710.9 | 813.0 | 766.3 | 747.7 | 764.8 | 752.2 | 1,032.6 | 1,364.3 | 1,089.0 |
| B. Capital Account* | 209ba | 39.1 | 63.6 | −159.2 | 38.2 | 23.0 | 86.9 | 77.2 | 53.8 | 63.7 | 78.4 | 102.0 | 194.2 |
| Capital account: credit | 209ca | 48.5 | 70.7 | 54.3 | 72.2 | 76.5 | 126.5 | 109.8 | 75.8 | 86.6 | 112.5 | 133.9 | 220.9 |
| Capital account: debit | 209da | 9.4 | 7.1 | 213.5 | 34.0 | 53.5 | 39.6 | 32.7 | 22.0 | 23.0 | 34.1 | 32.0 | 26.8 |
| Balance on current & capital acct. | 129ba | −1,761.2 | −2,415.1 | −3,405.3 | −4,313.8 | −6,191.0 | −3,071.2 | −817.3 | −321.9 | −144.3 | 645.3 | 550.0 | 2,722.7 |
| C. Financial Account* | 309na | −3,090.3 | −4,767.7 | −6,611.7 | −6,882.9 | −7,741.6 | −6,411.0 | −1,884.8 | −2,419.4 | −678.2 | −2,994.0 | 585.7 | 1,397.7 |
| Direct investment: assets | 3a9aa | 373.3 | 228.2 | 255.9 | 341.9 | 1,315.1 | 1,380.5 | 152.1 | −138.6 | −87.2 | −159.5 | 2,216.7 | −9.8 |
| Equity & investment fund shares.. | 3aaaa | 321.3 | 150.2 | 260.0 | 363.6 | 1,438.0 | 1,291.9 | −363.4 | 350.6 | 100.2 | −88.7 | 1,933.9 | 173.9 |
| Debt instruments | 3abaa | 51.9 | 78.0 | −4.1 | −21.8 | −122.9 | 88.6 | 515.5 | −489.2 | −187.3 | −70.8 | 282.8 | −183.7 |
| Direct investment: liabilities | 3a9la | 1,293.1 | 1,794.3 | 3,299.0 | 4,567.4 | 5,187.8 | 3,198.8 | 1,424.1 | 1,417.6 | 1,465.1 | 937.3 | 3,959.9 | 157.0 |
| Equity & investment fund shares . | 3aala | 745.9 | 1,718.9 | 3,079.7 | 3,727.7 | 3,860.3 | 1,327.6 | 1,227.2 | 3,115.4 | 1,426.0 | 542.3 | 3,428.1 | 1,198.9 |
| Debt instruments | 3abla | 547.2 | 75.4 | 219.4 | 839.7 | 1,327.5 | 1,871.3 | 196.9 | −1,697.8 | 39.1 | 395.0 | 531.7 | −1,041.9 |
| Portfolio investment: assets | 3b9aa | 947.1 | 715.3 | 603.8 | 540.3 | 424.4 | 814.9 | 552.7 | −778.9 | 387.0 | −128.0 | 527.1 | 261.3 |
| Equity & investment fund shares | 3baaa | 47.8 | 237.8 | 403.6 | 1,115.2 | −235.1 | 121.4 | 692.9 | 57.7 | 155.0 | 23.4 | 139.1 | 335.7 |
| Debt securities | 3bbaa | 899.3 | 477.6 | 200.2 | −574.9 | 659.5 | 693.5 | −140.2 | −836.5 | 232.0 | −151.4 | 387.9 | −74.3 |
| Portfolio investment: liabilities | 3b9la | 1,332.0 | −811.3 | 351.2 | 1,061.2 | −615.9 | 1,524.3 | 977.8 | 105.3 | 2,656.4 | 2,455.5 | −420.0 | 340.3 |
| Equity & investment fund shares . | 3bala | 176.7 | 95.0 | 474.0 | 475.3 | −110.0 | 24.9 | 181.9 | 18.1 | −149.0 | −53.2 | −38.0 | 13.6 |
| Debt securities | 3bbla | 1,155.3 | −906.4 | −122.7 | 585.9 | −505.9 | 1,499.3 | 795.9 | 87.3 | 2,805.4 | 2,508.8 | −382.0 | 326.7 |
| Fin. der.& empl.stk.ops.(ESOs): net. | 3c9na | — | 115.9 | — | — | — | — | 333.6 | 112.1 | −49.0 | 55.6 | 44.9 | −16.1 |
| Fin. der. & ESOs: assets | 3c9aa | — | 115.9 | — | — | — | — | −214.1 | .... | .... | .... | .... | .... |
| Fin. der. & ESOs.: liabilities | 3c9la | — | — | — | — | — | — | −547.7 | .... | .... | .... | .... | .... |
| Other investment: assets | 3d9aa | 713.3 | −1,362.6 | 1,010.0 | 2,266.7 | 2,225.8 | −742.9 | −992.3 | −281.5 | −826.6 | −218.9 | 1,384.7 | 27.8 |
| Other equity | 3daaa | — | — | — | — | — | — | — | 3.6 | 8.6 | 41.3 | 32.8 | 29.5 |
| Debt instruments | 3dzaa | 713.3 | −1,362.6 | 1,010.0 | 2,266.7 | 2,225.8 | −742.9 | −992.3 | −285.1 | −835.2 | −260.2 | 1,351.9 | −1.6 |
| Other investment: liabilities | 3d9la | 2,498.9 | 3,481.6 | 4,831.0 | 4,403.2 | 7,134.9 | 3,140.5 | −471.0 | −190.5 | −4,019.1 | −849.5 | 47.8 | −1,631.7 |
| Other equity | 3dala | .... | .... | .... | .... | .... | .... | | | | | | |
| Debt instruments | 3dzla | 2,498.9 | 3,481.6 | 4,831.0 | 4,403.2 | 7,134.9 | 3,140.5 | −471.0 | −190.5 | −4,019.1 | −849.5 | 47.8 | −1,631.7 |
| Curr.+ cap.− finan. acct. balance... | 4y9na | 1,329.1 | 2,352.6 | 3,206.3 | 2,569.1 | 1,550.6 | 3,339.9 | 1,067.6 | 2,097.5 | 533.9 | 3,639.4 | −35.7 | 1,325.0 |
| D. Net Errors and Omissions | 409na | −1,279.6 | −1,334.0 | −1,459.2 | −1,578.6 | −1,907.8 | −1,507.1 | −1,050.0 | −1,554.8 | −455.6 | −1,165.9 | −728.8 | −479.5 |
| E. Reserves and Related Items | 4z9na | 49.4 | 1,018.6 | 1,747.1 | 990.5 | −357.2 | 1,832.7 | 17.5 | 542.7 | 78.3 | 2,473.4 | −764.5 | 845.5 |
| Reserve assets | 3e9aa | 49.4 | 1,018.6 | 1,747.1 | 990.5 | −357.2 | 1,832.7 | 17.5 | 542.7 | 78.3 | 2,473.4 | −764.5 | 845.5 |
| Credit and loans from the IMF | 3dcla | — | — | — | — | — | — | — | — | — | — | — | — |
| Exceptional financing | 409la | .... | .... | .... | .... | .... | .... | .... | .... | .... | .... | .... | .... |

*Excludes components in group E

| | | 2004 | 2005 | 2006 | 2007 | 2008 | 2009 | 2010 | 2011 | 2012 | 2013 | 2014 | 2015 |
|---|---|---|---|---|---|---|---|---|---|---|---|---|---|
| **International Investment Position** | | | | | | | *Millions of US Dollars* | | | | | | |
| Assets | 809aa | 20,536.9 | 18,998.8 | 23,820.6 | 31,631.6 | 31,789.8 | 35,191.7 | 31,594.3 | 30,526.7 | 31,082.3 | 33,917.3 | 34,224.6 | 33,836.6 |
| Direct investment | 8a9aa | 2,103.0 | 2,010.7 | 2,398.4 | 3,829.1 | 5,290.3 | 6,695.7 | 4,859.5 | 5,006.2 | 4,875.6 | 4,786.4 | 5,879.5 | 5,806.8 |
| Equity & investment fund shares.. | 8aaaa | 1,954.1 | 1,823.6 | 2,180.0 | 3,535.9 | 4,943.0 | 6,308.2 | 3,961.6 | 4,110.6 | 4,049.4 | 3,972.8 | 4,899.2 | 4,895.6 |
| Debt instruments | 8abaa | 148.9 | 187.1 | 218.4 | 293.2 | 347.4 | 387.5 | 897.9 | 895.7 | 826.2 | 813.6 | 980.3 | 911.2 |
| Portfolio investment | 8b9aa | 2,049.5 | 2,646.3 | 3,242.8 | 4,671.8 | 3,736.3 | 4,591.6 | 4,853.0 | 3,639.9 | 4,187.3 | 4,519.7 | 4,513.7 | 4,270.1 |
| Equity & investment fund shares.. | 8baaa | 240.7 | 537.0 | 703.0 | 2,459.9 | 910.1 | 1,125.6 | 1,793.0 | 1,465.0 | 1,731.2 | 2,105.9 | 2,017.8 | 2,079.4 |
| Debt securities | 8bbaa | 1,808.8 | 2,109.3 | 2,539.8 | 2,211.8 | 2,826.2 | 3,466.0 | 3,060.0 | 2,174.9 | 2,456.1 | 2,413.8 | 2,495.9 | 2,190.7 |
| Fin. der.(oth.than reserves) & ESOs | 8c9aa | .... | .... | .... | .... | .... | 34.6 | 18.8 | 264.6 | 192.1 | 23.0 | 839.5 | 1,976.7 |
| Other investment | 8d9aa | 7,626.2 | 5,541.4 | 6,691.6 | 9,456.2 | 9,805.8 | 8,975.4 | 7,730.5 | 7,132.0 | 7,020.2 | 6,821.5 | 7,568.3 | 6,816.0 |
| Other equity | 8daaa | | | | | 2.4 | 2.6 | 2.4 | 5.7 | 14.5 | 56.8 | 81.8 | 103.0 |
| Debt instruments | 8dzaa | 7,626.2 | 5,541.4 | 6,691.6 | 9,456.2 | 9,803.3 | 8,972.7 | 7,728.1 | 7,126.3 | 7,005.7 | 6,764.7 | 7,486.5 | 6,713.0 |
| Reserve assets | 8e9aa | 8,758.2 | 8,800.3 | 11,487.8 | 13,674.5 | 12,957.4 | 14,894.5 | 14,132.5 | 14,483.9 | 14,807.1 | 17,766.7 | 15,423.6 | 14,966.9 |
| Liabilities | 809la | 41,627.6 | 43,318.2 | 64,188.4 | 91,189.1 | 82,184.0 | 92,307.4 | 87,986.4 | 83,047.0 | 83,606.8 | 86,996.9 | 80,322.4 | 71,645.3 |
| Direct investment | 8a9la | 11,176.6 | 13,409.9 | 25,997.2 | 43,607.7 | 29,070.8 | 33,673.4 | 32,611.0 | 28,471.5 | 29,881.8 | 30,111.1 | 30,135.4 | 26,797.4 |
| Equity & investment fund shares.. | 8aala | 9,684.7 | 11,737.6 | 23,649.6 | 39,336.5 | 23,577.6 | 25,755.4 | 24,472.2 | 21,979.4 | 22,784.9 | 22,267.6 | 22,379.2 | 20,871.9 |
| Debt instruments | 8abla | 1,491.9 | 1,672.3 | 2,347.7 | 4,271.2 | 5,493.2 | 7,918.0 | 8,138.8 | 6,492.1 | 7,096.9 | 7,843.5 | 7,756.2 | 5,925.6 |
| Portfolio investment | 8b9la | 8,170.3 | 6,833.1 | 7,750.9 | 9,941.2 | 7,859.4 | 9,335.4 | 9,475.3 | 9,364.1 | 12,086.3 | 14,850.5 | 13,929.9 | 13,724.9 |
| Equity & investment fund shares.. | 8bala | 664.2 | 766.1 | 1,333.5 | 2,236.7 | 872.0 | 944.0 | 978.9 | 770.7 | 636.5 | 808.2 | 876.9 | 815.3 |
| Debt securities | 8bbla | 7,506.1 | 6,067.0 | 6,417.4 | 7,704.5 | 6,987.4 | 8,391.4 | 8,496.4 | 8,593.4 | 11,449.8 | 14,042.3 | 13,053.0 | 12,909.6 |
| Fin. der.(oth.than reserves) & ESOs | 8c9la | .... | .... | .... | .... | .... | 74.9 | 258.0 | 195.7 | 430.4 | 594.3 | 273.1 | 173.8 |
| Other investment | 8d9la | 22,280.6 | 23,075.2 | 30,440.3 | 37,640.2 | 45,253.8 | 49,223.7 | 45,642.0 | 45,015.7 | 41,208.4 | 41,441.1 | 35,984.0 | 30,949.2 |
| Other equity | 8dala | .... | .... | .... | .... | .... | .... | .... | — | — | — | — | — |
| Debt instruments | 8dzla | 22,280.6 | 23,075.2 | 30,440.3 | 37,640.2 | 45,253.8 | 49,223.7 | 45,642.0 | 45,015.7 | 41,208.4 | 41,441.1 | 35,984.0 | 30,949.2 |

# Croatia 960

**Government Finance**
**Cash Flow Statement**

| | | 2004 | 2005 | 2006 | 2007 | 2008 | 2009 | 2010 | 2011 | 2012 | 2013 | 2014 | 2015 |
|---|---|---|---|---|---|---|---|---|---|---|---|---|---|
| **Budgetary Central Government** | | | | | | *Millions of Kuna: Fiscal Year Ends December 31* | | | | | | | |
| Cash Receipts:Operating Activities... | c1 | † 80,463.5 | 85,653.0 | 95,235.6 | 108,320.6 | 115,772.7 | 110,257.9 | 107,466.4 | 107,069.7 | 109,558.9 | 108,585.0 | 114,044.5 | 109,110.9 |
| Taxes............................ | c11 | † 47,149.9 | 50,687.6 | 58,469.1 | 64,234.5 | 69,572.7 | 63,678.9 | 62,856.6 | 61,422.2 | 64,693.9 | 63,044.9 | 63,349.9 | 68,280.8 |
| Social Contributions.................... | c12 | † 29,477.6 | 31,301.3 | 33,877.1 | 37,203.5 | 40,703.5 | 39,994.7 | 38,712.4 | 38,605.1 | 37,845.9 | 37,149.3 | 41,701.5 | 22,853.4 |
| Grants............................ | c13 | † 10.1 | 27.5 | 196.0 | 428.0 | 468.6 | 616.3 | 637.1 | 869.0 | 968.4 | 1,737.8 | 2,268.0 | 10,025.6 |
| Other Receipts..................... | c14 | † 3,825.9 | 3,636.6 | 2,693.3 | 6,454.5 | 5,027.8 | 5,968.0 | 5,260.3 | 6,173.4 | 6,050.8 | 6,653.0 | 6,725.1 | 7,951.2 |
| Cash Payments:Operating Activities. | c2 | † 83,131.1 | 87,857.5 | 95,950.0 | 108,007.6 | 115,292.4 | 117,924.0 | 120,323.3 | 119,939.5 | 118,730.0 | 123,505.9 | 125,689.5 | 115,455.8 |
| Compensation of Employees.......... | c21 | † 22,268.3 | 23,182.6 | 24,313.9 | 27,545.1 | 29,948.5 | 31,289.3 | 31,096.5 | 31,737.4 | 31,383.2 | 30,461.8 | 30,032.0 | 25,570.5 |
| Purchases of Goods & Services....... | c22 | † 4,358.7 | 4,951.9 | 6,069.1 | 7,162.4 | 8,113.7 | 7,363.8 | 7,655.7 | 7,943.6 | 7,406.3 | 7,537.4 | 7,186.0 | 10,471.1 |
| Interest......................... | c24 | † 3,972.5 | 4,387.0 | 4,713.6 | 4,535.0 | 4,683.2 | 5,225.2 | 6,236.5 | 7,097.6 | 8,335.7 | 9,259.2 | 9,911.1 | 10,621.3 |
| Subsidies........................ | c25 | † 4,968.1 | 5,248.7 | 5,670.8 | 6,492.0 | 6,859.5 | 6,710.0 | 6,582.2 | 6,555.3 | 5,762.3 | 5,537.8 | 5,174.5 | 6,426.0 |
| Grants........................... | c26 | † 3,420.3 | 3,796.8 | 6,653.0 | 8,363.2 | 5,783.1 | 5,559.6 | 5,778.6 | 5,083.7 | 4,843.8 | 6,511.7 | 8,535.4 | 11,791.0 |
| Social Benefits.................... | c27 | † 39,730.9 | 41,358.5 | 43,444.6 | 48,176.0 | 52,593.2 | 56,148.5 | 56,906.6 | 56,483.0 | 56,169.9 | 58,943.4 | 59,393.1 | 45,136.5 |
| Other Payments.................... | c28 | † 4,412.4 | 4,931.9 | 5,085.0 | 5,733.9 | 7,311.2 | 5,627.6 | 6,067.3 | 5,039.1 | 4,828.9 | 5,254.6 | 5,457.4 | 5,439.4 |
| Net Cash Inflow:Operating Act.[1-2] | ccio | † −2,667.6 | −2,204.5 | −714.4 | 313.0 | 480.2 | −7,666.0 | −12,857.0 | −12,869.8 | −9,171.1 | −14,920.8 | −11,645.0 | −6,344.9 |
| Net Cash Outflow:Invest. in NFA...... | c31 | † 1,419.5 | 1,553.7 | 1,555.8 | 2,545.2 | 2,988.1 | 1,963.4 | 1,232.4 | 1,139.0 | 829.6 | 1,304.5 | 1,167.3 | 2,507.0 |
| Purchases of Nonfinancial Assets... | c31.1 | † 1,663.9 | 1,828.8 | 1,908.5 | 3,043.9 | 3,291.5 | 2,267.4 | 1,550.7 | 1,486.0 | 1,108.0 | 1,564.0 | 1,857.0 | 3,152.0 |
| Sales of Nonfinancial Assets.......... | c31.2 | † 244.4 | 275.1 | 352.7 | 498.7 | 303.4 | 304.0 | 318.3 | 347.0 | 278.4 | 259.5 | 689.7 | 645.0 |
| Cash Surplus/Deficit [1-2-31=1-2M] | ccsd | † −4,087.1 | −3,758.1 | −2,270.2 | −2,232.2 | −2,507.9 | −9,629.4 | −14,089.3 | −14,008.8 | −10,000.7 | −16,225.4 | −12,812.3 | −8,852.0 |
| Net Acq. Fin. Assets, excl. Cash....... | c32x | † 1,336.2 | 1,064.6 | −1,597.5 | −2,013.2 | 262.4 | 2,697.1 | 1,453.2 | 1,580.4 | 747.0 | 9,388.5 | 1,415.4 | −4,030.4 |
| Domestic......................... | c321x | † 1,326.5 | 1,069.5 | −1,614.2 | −2,031.2 | 249.9 | 2,695.4 | 1,452.8 | 1,575.1 | 740.5 | 9,183.3 | 1,209.5 | −4,236.6 |
| Foreign.......................... | c322x | † 9.8 | −4.9 | 16.7 | 18.0 | 12.4 | 2.3 | .4 | 5.3 | 6.5 | 205.2 | 206.0 | 206.2 |
| Net Incurrence of Liabilities.............. | c33 | † 4,309.0 | 5,510.9 | −777.0 | −1,502.6 | 4,210.8 | 16,455.0 | 16,112.0 | 13,390.4 | 9,539.2 | 30,439.8 | 9,346.3 | 5,623.8 |
| Domestic......................... | c331 | † 4,038.7 | 10,591.6 | 3,166.3 | 1,477.6 | 5,656.6 | 9,576.6 | 11,835.1 | 4,793.1 | 1,414.0 | 8,904.9 | 4,822.2 | 1,797.3 |
| Foreign.......................... | c332 | † 270.3 | −5,080.6 | −3,943.2 | −2,980.2 | −1,445.8 | 6,878.4 | 4,277.0 | 8,597.2 | 8,125.2 | 21,534.8 | 4,524.1 | 3,826.5 |
| Net Cash Inflow, Fin.Act.[-32x+33].. | cnfb | † 2,972.8 | 4,446.3 | 820.5 | 510.6 | 3,948.5 | 13,757.2 | 14,658.8 | 11,809.9 | 8,792.1 | 21,051.2 | 7,930.9 | 9,654.2 |
| Net Change in Stock of Cash.......... | cncb | † −1,114.3 | 688.2 | −1,449.7 | −1,721.6 | 1,440.6 | 4,127.8 | 569.5 | −2,198.9 | −1,208.6 | 4,825.9 | −4,881.4 | 802.3 |
| Stat. Discrep. [32X-33+NCB-CSD].... | ccsdz | † — | — | — | — | — | — | — | — | — | — | — | — |
| Memo Item:Cash Expenditure[2+31] | c2m | † 84,550.6 | 89,411.1 | 97,505.7 | 110,552.8 | 118,280.6 | 119,887.4 | 121,555.7 | 121,078.5 | 119,559.6 | 124,810.4 | 126,856.8 | 117,962.8 |
| Memo Item: Gross Debt.................. | c63 | .... | .... | .... | .... | .... | 110,259.5 | .... | .... | .... | .... | .... | .... |
| **National Accounts** | | | | | | *Millions of Kuna:* | | | | | | | |
| Househ.Cons.Expend.,incl.NPISHs.... | 96f | 150,707 | 161,816 | 172,740 | 188,963 | 202,150 | 193,288 | 193,362 | 198,611 | 198,802 | 198,927 | 196,830 | 198,213 |
| Government Consumption Expend... | 91f | 46,184 | 49,469 | 53,775 | 61,035 | 64,197 | 67,104 | 66,028 | 66,908 | 66,414 | 66,151 | 65,148 | 65,759 |
| Gross Fixed Capital Formation......... | 93e | 64,452 | 68,651 | 78,252 | 86,376 | 97,710 | 83,433 | 69,784 | 67,471 | 64,820 | 65,257 | 62,639 | 63,888 |
| Changes in Inventories................... | 93i | 4,623 | 6,836 | 9,513 | 9,360 | 11,583 | −563 | 253 | 1,135 | −1,143 | −2,291 | −2,887 | −2,797 |
| Exports of Goods and Services......... | 90c | 98,980 | 106,173 | 116,783 | 125,702 | 133,780 | 114,260 | 123,794 | 134,383 | 137,385 | 141,814 | 151,985 | 165,032 |
| Imports of Goods and Services (-)..... | 98c | 114,073 | 122,754 | 136,626 | 149,126 | 161,734 | 126,556 | 125,181 | 135,921 | 135,821 | 140,287 | 145,285 | 155,876 |
| Gross Domestic Product (GDP)........ | 99b | 250,873 | 270,191 | 294,437 | 322,310 | 347,685 | 330,966 | 328,041 | 332,587 | 330,456 | 329,571 | 328,431 | 334,219 |
| GDP Volume 2010 Ref., Chained..... | 99b.p | 307,637 | 320,447 | 335,781 | 353,074 | 360,323 | 333,718 | 328,041 | 327,118 | 319,962 | 316,558 | 315,417 | 320,605 |
| GDP Volume (2010=100)............... | 99bvp | 93.8 | 97.7 | 102.4 | 107.6 | 109.8 | 101.7 | 100.0 | 99.7 | 97.5 | 96.5 | 96.2 | 97.7 |
| GDP Deflator (2010=100)............... | 99bip | 81.5 | 84.3 | 87.7 | 91.3 | 96.5 | 99.2 | 100.0 | 101.7 | 103.3 | 104.1 | 104.1 | 104.2 |
| | | | | | | *Millions: Midyear Estimates* | | | | | | | |
| Population................................ | 99z | 4.39 | 4.38 | 4.37 | 4.36 | 4.34 | 4.33 | 4.32 | 4.30 | 4.29 | 4.27 | 4.26 | 4.24 |

# Curaçao  354

| | | 2004 | 2005 | 2006 | 2007 | 2008 | 2009 | 2010 | 2011 | 2012 | 2013 | 2014 | 2015 |
|---|---|---|---|---|---|---|---|---|---|---|---|---|---|
| **Exchange Rates** | | | | | | *Guilders per SDR: End of Period* | | | | | | | |
| Official Rate.................... | aa | 2.780 | 2.558 | 2.693 | 2.829 | 2.757 | 2.806 | 2.757 | 2.748 | 2.751 | 2.757 | 2.593 | 2.480 |
| | | | | | *Guilders per US Dollar: End of Period (ae)  Period Average (rf)* | | | | | | | | |
| Official Rate.................... | ae | 1.790 | 1.790 | 1.790 | 1.790 | 1.790 | 1.790 | 1.790 | 1.790 | 1.790 | 1.790 | 1.790 | 1.790 |
| Official Rate.................... | rf | 1.790 | 1.790 | 1.790 | 1.790 | 1.790 | 1.790 | 1.790 | 1.790 | 1.790 | 1.790 | 1.790 | 1.790 |
| **Prices** | | | | | *Index Numbers (2010=100): Period Averages* | | | | | | | | |
| Consumer Prices........................... | 64 | .... | 84.238 | 86.835 | 89.459 | 95.909 | 97.298 | 100.000 | 102.328 | 105.586 | 107.000 | 108.598 | 108.080 |
| **Balance of Payments** | | | | | | *Millions of US Dollars* | | | | | | | |
| A. Current Account*...................... | 109bx | .... | .... | .... | .... | .... | .... | .... | −830.0 | −875.5 | −662.5 | −376.0 | −481.1 |
| Goods, credit (exports)................... | 1a9cx | .... | .... | .... | .... | .... | .... | .... | 797.6 | 854.5 | 618.5 | 637.4 | 417.9 |
| Goods, debit (imports)................... | 1a9dx | .... | .... | .... | .... | .... | .... | .... | 2,100.2 | 2,237.4 | 1,883.3 | 1,803.7 | 1,499.3 |
| Balance on goods..................... | 1a9bx | .... | .... | .... | .... | .... | .... | .... | −1,302.6 | −1,382.9 | −1,264.8 | −1,166.3 | −1,081.4 |
| Services, credit (exports)................. | 1b9cx | .... | .... | .... | .... | .... | .... | .... | 1,354.6 | 1,509.1 | 1,646.6 | 1,767.6 | 1,555.9 |
| Services, debit (imports)................. | 1b9dx | .... | .... | .... | .... | .... | .... | .... | 823.1 | 890.4 | 909.7 | 889.2 | 911.4 |
| Balance on Goods & Services....... | 1z9bx | .... | .... | .... | .... | .... | .... | .... | −771.1 | −764.3 | −528.0 | −287.9 | −436.9 |
| Primary income: credit.................. | 1c9cx | .... | .... | .... | .... | .... | .... | .... | 117.2 | 104.0 | 108.0 | 133.5 | 155.7 |
| Primary income: debit.................. | 1c9dx | .... | .... | .... | .... | .... | .... | .... | 135.3 | 149.7 | 162.7 | 166.1 | 157.9 |
| Balance on gds, serv. & prim. inc. | 1y9bx | .... | .... | .... | .... | .... | .... | .... | −789.2 | −809.9 | −582.6 | −320.5 | −439.0 |
| Secondary income: credit.............. | 1d9ca | .... | .... | .... | .... | .... | .... | .... | 271.1 | 227.4 | 206.0 | 210.8 | 184.5 |
| Secondary income: debit.............. | 1d9da | .... | .... | .... | .... | .... | .... | .... | 311.9 | 293.0 | 285.8 | 266.3 | 226.5 |
| B. Capital Account*........................ | 209ba | .... | .... | .... | .... | .... | .... | .... | 52.0 | 29.1 | 23.3 | 8.4 | .6 |
| Capital account: credit.................. | 209ca | .... | .... | .... | .... | .... | .... | .... | 52.2 | 29.2 | 23.3 | 8.6 | .7 |
| Capital account: debit.................. | 209da | .... | .... | .... | .... | .... | .... | .... | .2 | — | — | .2 | .1 |
| Balance on current & capital acct. | 129ba | .... | .... | .... | .... | .... | .... | .... | −778.0 | −846.3 | −639.2 | −367.6 | −480.5 |
| C. Financial Account*  ................. | 309na | .... | .... | .... | .... | .... | .... | .... | −769.0 | −706.8 | −595.8 | −517.1 | −458.7 |
| Direct investment: assets.............. | 3a9aa | .... | .... | .... | .... | .... | .... | .... | −30.3 | 11.5 | −16.2 | 43.8 | 49.1 |
| Equity & investment fund shares.. | 3aaaa | .... | .... | .... | .... | .... | .... | .... | 5.5 | 12.1 | 7.5 | 1.1 | 9.6 |
| Debt instruments...................... | 3abaa | .... | .... | .... | .... | .... | .... | .... | −35.8 | −.6 | −23.6 | 42.7 | 39.5 |
| Direct investment: liabilities .......... | 3a9la | .... | .... | .... | .... | .... | .... | .... | 68.9 | 69.7 | 17.5 | 69.3 | 137.1 |
| Equity & investment fund shares . | 3aala | .... | .... | .... | .... | .... | .... | .... | 41.7 | 26.0 | −24.3 | 53.2 | 18.0 |
| Debt instruments........................ | 3abla | .... | .... | .... | .... | .... | .... | .... | 27.2 | 43.7 | 41.8 | 16.1 | 119.1 |
| Portfolio investment: assets .......... | 3b9aa | .... | .... | .... | .... | .... | .... | .... | −145.5 | −361.8 | −203.2 | −210.1 | −182.9 |
| Equity & investment fund shares | 3baaa | .... | .... | .... | .... | .... | .... | .... | 76.7 | 41.2 | −15.7 | −10.1 | .6 |
| Debt securities .... ................ | 3bbaa | .... | .... | .... | .... | .... | .... | .... | −222.2 | −403.0 | −187.5 | −200.0 | −183.4 |
| Portfolio investment: liabilities....... | 3b9la | .... | .... | .... | .... | .... | .... | .... | −8.0 | −1.9 | −20.2 | 127.7 | 152.3 |
| Equity & investment fund shares . | 3bala | .... | .... | .... | .... | .... | .... | .... | .... | .... | .... | .... | .... |
| Debt securities......................... | 3bbla | .... | .... | .... | .... | .... | .... | .... | −8.0 | −1.9 | −20.2 | 127.7 | 152.3 |
| Fin. der.& empl.stk.ops.(ESOs): net | 3c9na | .... | .... | .... | .... | .... | .... | .... | .1 | — | .3 | .8 | .4 |
| Fin. der. & ESOs.: assets.............. | 3c9aa | .... | .... | .... | .... | .... | .... | .... | .1 | — | .3 | .8 | .4 |
| Fin. der. & ESOs.: liabilities.......... | 3c9la | .... | .... | .... | .... | .... | .... | .... | .... | .... | .... | .... | .... |
| Other investment: assets............... | 3d9aa | .... | .... | .... | .... | .... | .... | .... | −549.7 | −359.9 | −136.0 | 62.1 | −97.5 |
| Other equity......................... | 3daaa | .... | .... | .... | .... | .... | .... | .... | .... | .... | .... | .... | .... |
| Debt instruments........................ | 3dzaa | .... | .... | .... | .... | .... | .... | .... | −549.7 | −359.9 | −136.0 | 62.1 | −97.5 |
| Other investment: liabilities........... | 3d9la | .... | .... | .... | .... | .... | .... | .... | −17.2 | −71.2 | 243.4 | 216.9 | −61.5 |
| Other equity........................... | 3dala | .... | .... | .... | .... | .... | .... | .... | .... | .... | .... | .... | .... |
| Debt instruments....................... | 3dzla | .... | .... | .... | .... | .... | .... | .... | −17.2 | −71.2 | 243.4 | 216.9 | −61.5 |
| Curr.+ cap.− finan. acct. balance... | 4y9na | .... | .... | .... | .... | .... | .... | .... | −9.0 | −139.6 | −43.4 | 149.5 | −21.8 |
| D. Net Errors and Omissions............ | 409na | .... | .... | .... | .... | .... | .... | .... | 19.5 | 20.1 | 8.2 | 37.3 | 32.7 |
| E. Reserves and Related Items.......... | 4z9na | .... | .... | .... | .... | .... | .... | .... | 10.4 | −119.4 | −35.2 | 186.8 | 10.9 |
| Reserve assets............................ | 3e9aa | .... | .... | .... | .... | .... | .... | .... | 20.0 | −114.8 | −19.8 | 190.0 | 11.5 |
| Credit and loans from the IMF....... | 3dcla | .... | .... | .... | .... | .... | .... | .... | .... | .... | .... | .... | .... |
| Exceptional financing.................... | 409la | .... | .... | .... | .... | .... | .... | .... | 9.6 | 4.7 | 15.4 | 3.2 | .6 |
| *Excludes components in group E | | | | | | | | | | | | | |
| | | | | | | *Millions: Midyear Estimates* | | | | | | | |
| Population................................ | 99z | .13 | .13 | .13 | .14 | .14 | .14 | .15 | .15 | .15 | .15 | .16 | .16 |

# Curaçao and Sint Maarten   355

| | | 2004 | 2005 | 2006 | 2007 | 2008 | 2009 | 2010 | 2011 | 2012 | 2013 | 2014 | 2015 |
|---|---|---|---|---|---|---|---|---|---|---|---|---|---|
| **Exchange Rates** | | | | | | *Guilders per SDR: End of Period* | | | | | | | |
| Official Rate | aa | 2.780 | 2.558 | 2.693 | 2.829 | 2.757 | 2.806 | 2.757 | 2.748 | 2.751 | 2.757 | 2.593 | 2.480 |
| | | | | | *Guilders per US Dollar: End of Period (ae)  Period Average (rf)* | | | | | | | | |
| Official Rate | ae | 1.790 | 1.790 | 1.790 | 1.790 | 1.790 | 1.790 | 1.790 | 1.790 | 1.790 | 1.790 | 1.790 | 1.790 |
| Official Rate | rf | 1.790 | 1.790 | 1.790 | 1.790 | 1.790 | 1.790 | 1.790 | 1.790 | 1.790 | 1.790 | 1.790 | |
| **International Liquidity** | | | *Millions of US Dollars Unless Otherwise Indicated: End of Period* | | | | | | | | | | |
| Total Reserves minus Gold | 1l.d | .... | .... | .... | .... | .... | .... | 1,263 | 1,290 | 1,135 | 1,108 | 1,408 | 1,345 |
| Foreign Exchange | 1d.d | .... | .... | .... | .... | .... | .... | 1,263 | 1,290 | 1,135 | 1,108 | 1,408 | 1,345 |
| Gold (Million Fine Troy Ounces) | 1ad | .... | .... | .... | .... | .... | .... | .42 | .42 | .42 | .42 | .42 | .42 |
| Gold (National Valuation) | 1and | .... | .... | .... | .... | .... | .... | 591 | 662 | 700 | 505 | 504 | 447 |
| **Balance of Payments** | | | | | | *Millions of US Dollars* | | | | | | | |
| A. Current Account* | 109bx | .... | .... | .... | .... | .... | .... | .... | −821.7 | −783.8 | −647.3 | −409.8 | .... |
| Goods, credit (exports) | 1a9cx | .... | .... | .... | .... | .... | .... | .... | 924.4 | 984.8 | 785.1 | 803.7 | .... |
| Goods, debit (imports) | 1a9dx | .... | .... | .... | .... | .... | .... | .... | 2,833.2 | 3,005.2 | 2,807.7 | 2,765.5 | .... |
| Balance on goods | 1a9bx | .... | .... | .... | .... | .... | .... | .... | −1,908.8 | −2,020.5 | −2,022.6 | −1,961.7 | .... |
| Services, credit (exports) | 1b9cx | .... | .... | .... | .... | .... | .... | .... | 2,275.0 | 2,559.4 | 2,726.6 | 2,901.7 | .... |
| Services, debit (imports) | 1b9dx | .... | .... | .... | .... | .... | .... | .... | 1,067.0 | 1,162.0 | 1,171.2 | 1,204.5 | .... |
| Balance on Goods & Services | 1z9bx | .... | .... | .... | .... | .... | .... | .... | −700.8 | −623.0 | −467.2 | −264.5 | .... |
| Primary income: credit | 1c9cx | .... | .... | .... | .... | .... | .... | .... | 149.1 | 145.7 | 167.2 | 187.8 | .... |
| Primary income: debit | 1c9dx | .... | .... | .... | .... | .... | .... | .... | 187.3 | 200.7 | 218.5 | 237.3 | .... |
| Balance on gds, serv. & prim. inc. | 1y9bx | .... | .... | .... | .... | .... | .... | .... | −739.0 | −678.1 | −518.5 | −314.0 | .... |
| Secondary income: credit | 1d9ca | .... | .... | .... | .... | .... | .... | .... | 339.8 | 299.7 | 281.0 | 288.9 | .... |
| Secondary income: debit | 1d9da | .... | .... | .... | .... | .... | .... | .... | 422.5 | 405.5 | 409.8 | 384.7 | .... |
| B. Capital Account* | 209ba | .... | .... | .... | .... | .... | .... | .... | 67.1 | 41.1 | 30.3 | 12.1 | .... |
| Capital account: credit | 209ca | .... | .... | .... | .... | .... | .... | .... | 67.6 | 41.2 | 30.4 | 12.6 | .... |
| Capital account: debit | 209da | .... | .... | .... | .... | .... | .... | .... | .4 | .1 | .1 | .5 | .... |
| Balance on current & capital acct. | 129ba | .... | .... | .... | .... | .... | .... | .... | −754.5 | −742.7 | −617.0 | −397.7 | .... |
| C. Financial Account* | 309na | .... | .... | .... | .... | .... | .... | .... | −735.1 | −477.8 | −517.4 | −601.3 | .... |
| Direct investment: assets | 3a9aa | .... | .... | .... | .... | .... | .... | .... | −28.8 | 9.7 | −12.7 | 47.6 | .... |
| Equity & investment fund shares | 3aaaa | .... | .... | .... | .... | .... | .... | .... | 7.9 | 13.5 | 9.0 | 2.9 | .... |
| Debt instruments | 3abaa | .... | .... | .... | .... | .... | .... | .... | −37.0 | −4.5 | −21.7 | 44.7 | .... |
| Direct investment: liabilities | 3a9la | .... | .... | .... | .... | .... | .... | .... | 20.4 | 70.4 | 64.8 | 117.0 | .... |
| Equity & investment fund shares | 3aala | .... | .... | .... | .... | .... | .... | .... | −6.6 | 35.1 | −6.9 | 55.4 | .... |
| Debt instruments | 3abla | .... | .... | .... | .... | .... | .... | .... | 26.9 | 35.4 | 71.8 | 61.6 | .... |
| Portfolio investment: assets | 3b9aa | .... | .... | .... | .... | .... | .... | .... | −118.9 | −299.8 | −153.4 | −284.2 | .... |
| Equity & investment fund shares | 3baaa | .... | .... | .... | .... | .... | .... | .... | 98.8 | 104.4 | 19.0 | −8.1 | .... |
| Debt securities | 3bbaa | .... | .... | .... | .... | .... | .... | .... | −217.6 | −404.3 | −172.4 | −276.1 | .... |
| Portfolio investment: liabilities | 3b9la | .... | .... | .... | .... | .... | .... | .... | −35.4 | −21.4 | −32.3 | 149.5 | .... |
| Equity & investment fund shares | 3bala | .... | .... | .... | .... | .... | .... | .... | .... | .... | .... | .... | .... |
| Debt securities | 3bbla | .... | .... | .... | .... | .... | .... | .... | −35.4 | −21.4 | −32.3 | 149.5 | .... |
| Fin. der.& empl.stk.ops.(ESOs): net | 3c9na | .... | .... | .... | .... | .... | .... | .... | .1 | .4 | .3 | 1.4 | .... |
| Fin. der. & ESOs.: assets | 3c9aa | .... | .... | .... | .... | .... | .... | .... | .1 | .4 | .3 | 1.4 | .... |
| Fin. der. & ESOs.: liabilities | 3c9la | .... | .... | .... | .... | .... | .... | .... | | | | | |
| Other investment: assets | 3d9aa | .... | .... | .... | .... | .... | .... | .... | −659.3 | −382.7 | −36.2 | 145.3 | .... |
| Other equity | 3daaa | .... | .... | .... | .... | .... | .... | .... | .... | .... | .... | .... | .... |
| Debt instruments | 3dzaa | .... | .... | .... | .... | .... | .... | .... | −659.3 | −382.7 | −36.2 | 145.3 | .... |
| Other investment: liabilities | 3d9la | .... | .... | .... | .... | .... | .... | .... | −56.8 | −243.6 | 282.9 | 244.9 | .... |
| Other equity | 3dala | .... | .... | .... | .... | .... | .... | .... | .... | .... | .... | .... | .... |
| Debt instruments | 3dzla | .... | .... | .... | .... | .... | .... | .... | −56.8 | −243.6 | 282.9 | 244.9 | .... |
| Curr.+ cap.− finan. acct. balance | 4y9na | .... | .... | .... | .... | .... | .... | .... | −19.5 | −264.9 | −99.6 | 203.7 | .... |
| D. Net Errors and Omissions | 409na | .... | .... | .... | .... | .... | .... | .... | 27.6 | 59.0 | 43.4 | 47.0 | .... |
| E. Reserves and Related Items | 4z9na | .... | .... | .... | .... | .... | .... | .... | 8.1 | −205.9 | −56.3 | 250.6 | .... |
| Reserve assets | 3e9aa | .... | .... | .... | .... | .... | .... | .... | 27.0 | −155.1 | −26.8 | 256.9 | .... |
| Credit and loans from the IMF | 3dcla | .... | .... | .... | .... | .... | .... | .... | .... | .... | .... | .... | .... |
| Exceptional financing | 409la | .... | .... | .... | .... | .... | .... | .... | 19.0 | 50.8 | 29.5 | 6.3 | .... |
| *Excludes components in group E | | | | | | | | | | | | | |
| | | | | | | *Millions: Midyear Estimates* | | | | | | | |
| Population | 99z | .... | .... | .... | .... | .... | .... | .... | .... | .... | .... | .... | .... |

# Cyprus 423

| | | 2004 | 2005 | 2006 | 2007 | 2008 | 2009 | 2010 | 2011 | 2012 | 2013 | 2014 | 2015 |
|---|---|---|---|---|---|---|---|---|---|---|---|---|---|
| **Exchange Rates** | | *SDRs per Pound through 2007; Euros per SDR Thereafter: End of Period* | | | | | | | | | | | |
| Market Rate | ac | 1.5151 | 1.4444 | 1.5138 | 1.5908 | 1.1068 | 1.0882 | 1.1525 | 1.1865 | 1.1649 | 1.1167 | 1.1933 | 1.2728 |
| | | *Pounds per US Dollar through 2007; Euros per US Dollar Thereafter: End of Period (ae) Period Average (rf)* | | | | | | | | | | | |
| Market Rate | ae | .4250 | .4844 | .4391 | .3978 | .7185 | .6942 | .7484 | .7729 | .7579 | .7251 | .8237 | .9185 |
| Market Rate | rf | .4686 | .4641 | .4589 | .4261 | .6827 | .7198 | .7550 | .7194 | .7783 | .7532 | .7537 | .9017 |
| | | *Index Numbers (2010=100): Period Averages* | | | | | | | | | | | |
| Official Rate (2005=100) | ahx | 99.1 | 100.0 | 101.1 | 108.9 | .... | .... | .... | .... | .... | .... | .... | .... |
| Nominal Effective Exchange Rate | nec | 95.8 | 95.9 | 96.0 | 96.3 | 101.2 | 105.2 | 100.0 | 101.0 | 98.0 | 100.6 | 100.9 | 97.2 |
| CPI-Based Real Effect. Ex. Rate | rec | 98.1 | 97.8 | 97.5 | 97.2 | 102.4 | 105.8 | 100.0 | 100.7 | 97.5 | 97.9 | 95.4 | 89.3 |
| **Fund Position** | | *Millions of SDRs: End of Period* | | | | | | | | | | | |
| Quota | 2f.s | 139.60 | 139.60 | 139.60 | 139.60 | 139.60 | 139.60 | 139.60 | 158.20 | 158.20 | 158.20 | 158.20 | 158.20 |
| SDR Holdings | 1b.s | 2.51 | 2.92 | 2.72 | 2.21 | 1.78 | 119.37 | 122.08 | 139.52 | 115.31 | 113.66 | 109.70 | 101.82 |
| Reserve Position in the Fund | 1c.s | 47.28 | 21.73 | 14.07 | 9.50 | 17.47 | 28.35 | 31.85 | 81.92 | 83.22 | 83.22 | 83.24 | 81.10 |
| Total Fund Cred.&Loans Outstg | 2tl | — | — | — | — | — | — | — | — | — | 222.75 | 371.25 | 693.00 |
| SDR Allocations | 1bd | 19.44 | 19.44 | 19.44 | 19.44 | 19.44 | 132.80 | 132.80 | 132.80 | 132.80 | 132.80 | 132.80 | 132.80 |
| **International Liquidity** | | *Millions of US Dollars Unless Otherwise Indicated: End of Period* | | | | | | | | | | | |
| Total Res.Min.Gold (Eurosys.Def) | 1l.d | 3,910.0 | 4,191.1 | 5,646.8 | 6,118.6 | † 616.8 | 796.2 | 514.9 | 504.3 | 448.9 | 379.1 | 354.8 | 334.0 |
| SDR Holdings | 1b.d | 3.9 | 4.2 | 4.1 | 3.5 | 2.7 | 187.1 | 188.0 | 214.2 | 177.2 | 175.0 | 158.9 | 141.1 |
| Reserve Position in the Fund | 1c.d | 73.4 | 31.1 | 21.2 | 15.0 | 26.9 | 44.4 | 49.1 | 125.8 | 127.9 | 128.2 | 120.6 | 112.4 |
| Foreign Exchange | 1d.d | 3,832.7 | 4,155.9 | 5,621.5 | 6,100.1 | † 585.5 | 562.9 | 276.2 | 163.0 | 142.5 | 75.9 | 75.3 | 80.6 |
| o/w:Fin.Deriv.Rel.to Reserves | 1ddd | .... | .... | .... | .... | — | — | — | — | — | — | — | — |
| Other Reserve Assets | 1e.d | .... | .... | .... | .... | 1.7 | 1.7 | 1.6 | 1.3 | 1.3 | — | — | — |
| Gold (Million Fine Troy Ounces) | 1ad | .465 | .465 | .465 | .465 | .446 | .446 | .446 | .446 | .446 | .446 | .447 | .447 |
| Gold (Eurosystem Valuation) | 1and | 204.1 | 238.1 | 295.7 | 388.5 | † 385.8 | 492.4 | 629.0 | 702.2 | 742.1 | 535.9 | 536.1 | 473.6 |
| Memo:Euro Cl. on Non-EA Res | 1dgd | .... | .... | .... | .... | .... | .... | .... | .... | .... | .... | .... | .... |
| Non-Euro Cl. on EA Res | 1dhd | .... | .... | .... | .... | 1,076.6 | 734.1 | 696.3 | 518.9 | 232.2 | 38.6 | 18.2 | 12.0 |
| Central Bank: Other Assets | 3..d | .... | −47 | −53 | −51 | 4,263 | 4,388 | 4,738 | 3,874 | 2,533 | 1,400 | 1,288 | 5,009 |
| Central Bank.: Other Liabs | 4..d | .... | 146 | 71 | 330 | 175 | 370 | 337 | 313 | 238 | 229 | 228 | 204 |
| Other Depository Corps.: Assets | 7a.d | .... | 17,154 | 25,380 | 38,495 | 48,959 | 56,539 | 42,811 | 42,902 | 42,471 | 21,335 | 17,785 | 14,716 |
| Other Depository Corps.: Liabs | 7b.d | .... | 20,960 | 29,777 | 40,249 | 34,841 | 39,755 | 38,683 | 40,671 | 46,356 | 26,600 | 23,765 | 23,591 |
| **Central Bank** | | *Millions of Euros: End of Period* | | | | | | | | | | | |
| Euro Area Wide Residency Criterion | | | | | | | | | | | | | |
| Net Foreign Assets | 11n.u | .... | 1,626 | 1,889 | 1,378 | 670 | 614 | 620 | 694 | 726 | 510 | 644 | 779 |
| Claims on Nonresidents | 11..u | .... | 1,762 | 1,954 | 1,748 | 795 | 915 | 872 | 936 | 906 | 676 | 831 | 966 |
| Liabilities to Nonresidents | 16c.u | .... | 136 | 65 | 370 | 126 | 301 | 252 | 242 | 181 | 166 | 187 | 187 |
| Claims on Other Depository Corps | 12e.u | .... | 867 | 1,306 | 1,030 | 5,170 | 8,011 | 5,663 | 5,785 | 10,022 | 11,395 | 8,837 | 5,196 |
| Net Claims on Central Government | 12anu | .... | 1,221 | 1,663 | 1,458 | 3,673 | 3,555 | 4,193 | 3,190 | 2,781 | 1,218 | 794 | 1,549 |
| Claims on Central Govt | 12a.u | .... | 2,562 | 2,632 | 2,985 | 3,976 | 3,935 | 4,452 | 4,105 | 3,032 | 2,034 | 1,853 | 2,266 |
| Liabs. to Central Govt | 16d.u | .... | 1,341 | 969 | 1,527 | 303 | 380 | 259 | 915 | 251 | 816 | 1,059 | 717 |
| Claims on Other Sectors | 12s.u | .... | 21 | 21 | 21 | 22 | 22 | 24 | 23 | 24 | 21 | 21 | 616 |
| Claims on Other Financial Corps | 12g.u | .... | — | — | — | — | — | — | — | — | — | — | 596 |
| Claims on State & Local Govts | 12b.u | .... | — | — | — | — | — | — | — | — | — | — | — |
| Claims on Public Nonfin. Corps | 12c.u | .... | — | — | — | — | — | — | — | — | — | — | — |
| Claims on Private Sector | 12d.u | .... | 21 | 21 | 21 | 22 | 22 | 24 | 23 | 24 | 21 | 21 | 20 |
| Monetary Base | 14..u | .... | 2,324 | 3,494 | 2,681 | 2,912 | 4,735 | 3,961 | 4,962 | 5,840 | 4,722 | 6,503 | 9,810 |
| Currency in Circulation | 14a.u | .... | 1,076 | 1,178 | 1,071 | 1,452 | 1,537 | 1,607 | 1,696 | 1,739 | 1,787 | 2,127 | 2,252 |
| Liabs. to Other Depository Corps | 14c.u | .... | 1,152 | 2,202 | 1,469 | 1,292 | 3,101 | 2,289 | 3,173 | 3,984 | 2,800 | 4,214 | 7,219 |
| Liabs. to Other Sectors | 14d.u | .... | 96 | 114 | 141 | 168 | 97 | 65 | 93 | 117 | 135 | 162 | 339 |
| Other Liabs. to Other Dep. Corps | 14n.u | .... | — | — | — | — | — | — | — | — | — | — | — |
| Dep. & Sec. Excl. f/Monetary Base | 14o.u | .... | 6 | 7 | 8 | — | — | — | — | — | — | — | — |
| Deposits Included in Broad Money | 15..u | .... | — | — | — | — | — | — | — | — | — | — | — |
| Sec.Ot.th.Shares Inc.in.Brd.Money | 16a.u | — | † — | — | — | — | — | — | — | — | — | — | — |
| Deposits Excl. from Broad Money | 16b.u | .... | 6 | 7 | 8 | — | — | — | — | — | — | — | — |
| Sec.Oh.th.Shares Excl. f/Brd.Money | 16s.u | .... | — | — | — | — | — | — | — | — | — | — | — |
| Loans | 16l.u | .... | — | — | — | — | — | — | — | — | — | — | — |
| Financial Derivatives | 16m.u | .... | — | — | — | — | — | — | — | — | — | — | — |
| Shares and Other Equity | 17a.u | .... | 373 | 372 | 339 | 416 | 557 | 628 | 737 | 949 | 770 | 809 | 798 |
| Other Items (Net) | 17r.u | .... | 1,033 | 1,006 | 857 | 6,186 | 6,911 | 5,910 | 3,995 | 6,764 | 7,655 | 2,987 | −2,469 |
| Memorandum Items | | | | | | | | | | | | | |
| National Residency Criterion | | | | | | | | | | | | | |
| Net Foreign Assets | 11n | 1,701.7 | † 3,578.3 | 4,401.0 | 4,015.7 | −2,883.6 | −3,481.8 | −2,292.6 | −4,221.8 | −4,825.4 | −5,832.4 | −1,072.2 | 5,155.8 |
| Claims on Nonresidents | 11 | 1,773.1 | † 3,713.9 | 4,472.2 | 4,385.6 | 3,784.3 | 3,940.7 | 4,403.4 | 3,927.7 | 2,823.3 | 1,678.9 | 1,794.2 | 5,342.8 |
| Liabilities to Nonresidents | 16c | 71.5 | † 135.6 | 71.2 | 369.9 | 6,667.9 | 7,422.5 | 6,696.1 | 8,149.6 | 7,648.7 | 7,511.3 | 2,866.5 | 187.0 |
| Claims on Other Depository Corps | 12e | — | † — | — | — | 4,675.0 | 7,559.0 | 5,466.0 | 5,521.0 | 9,811.0 | 11,150.0 | 8,516.0 | 4,686.0 |
| Net Claims on Central Government | 12an | 190.3 | † 454.0 | 769.0 | 168.0 | 1,361.0 | 1,216.0 | 1,249.0 | 542.0 | 1,154.0 | 537.0 | 240.0 | 746.0 |
| Claims on Central Government | 12a | 1,048.5 | † 1,795.0 | 1,738.0 | 1,695.0 | 1,664.0 | 1,596.0 | 1,508.0 | 1,457.0 | 1,405.0 | 1,353.0 | 1,299.0 | 1,463.0 |
| Liabilities to Central Government | 16d | 858.2 | † 1,341.0 | 969.0 | 1,527.0 | 303.0 | 380.0 | 259.0 | 915.0 | 251.0 | 816.0 | 1,059.0 | 717.0 |
| Claims on Other Sectors | 12s | — | † 21.0 | 21.0 | 21.0 | 22.0 | 22.0 | 24.0 | 23.0 | 24.0 | 21.0 | 21.0 | 20.0 |
| Claims on Other Fin. Corps | 12g | — | † — | — | — | — | — | — | — | — | — | — | — |
| Claims on State & Local Govts | 12b | — | † — | — | — | — | — | — | — | — | — | — | — |
| Claims on Private Sector | 12d | — | † 21.0 | 21.0 | 21.0 | 22.0 | 22.0 | 24.0 | 23.0 | 24.0 | 21.0 | 21.0 | 20.0 |
| Liabs.to ODCs, Inc.in Mon.Base | 14c | 1,114.0 | † 2,481.0 | 3,525.0 | 2,798.0 | 1,292.0 | 3,101.0 | 2,289.0 | 3,173.0 | 3,984.0 | 2,800.0 | 4,214.0 | 7,219.0 |
| Liabs.to Ot.Sectors, Inc.in Mon.Base | 14d | 11.2 | † 96.0 | 114.0 | 141.0 | 168.0 | 97.0 | 65.0 | 93.0 | 117.0 | 135.0 | 162.0 | 339.0 |
| Liabs.to ODCs,Excl.f/Mon.Base | 14n | — | † — | — | — | — | — | — | — | — | — | — | — |
| Net Claims on Eurosystem | 12e.s | .... | .... | .... | .... | −6,337 | −6,860 | −6,025 | −7,797 | −7,355 | −7,236 | −2,552 | 2,507 |

# Cyprus 423

| | | 2004 | 2005 | 2006 | 2007 | 2008 | 2009 | 2010 | 2011 | 2012 | 2013 | 2014 | 2015 |
|---|---|---|---|---|---|---|---|---|---|---|---|---|---|
| **Other Depository Corporations** | | | | | | *Millions of Euros: End of Period* | | | | | | | |
| Euro Area Wide Residency Criterion | | | | | | | | | | | | | |
| Net Foreign Assets........................ | 21n.u | .... | −3,226 | −3,339 | −1,191 | 10,144 | 11,651 | 3,089 | 1,724 | −2,944 | −3,818 | −4,925 | −8,152 |
| Claims on Nonresidents................ | 21..u | .... | 14,541 | 19,271 | 26,150 | 35,179 | 39,247 | 32,039 | 33,157 | 32,190 | 15,470 | 14,649 | 13,517 |
| Liabilities to Nonresidents............. | 26c.u | .... | 17,767 | 22,610 | 27,341 | 25,035 | 27,596 | 28,950 | 31,433 | 35,134 | 19,288 | 19,574 | 21,669 |
| Claims on Eurosystem.................... | 20..u | .... | 1,204 | 1,234 | 1,605 | 1,626 | 3,379 | 2,650 | 3,462 | 4,164 | 2,975 | 4,533 | 7,549 |
| Currency......................................... | 20a.u | .... | 166 | 196 | 567 | 322 | 329 | 313 | 297 | 307 | 269 | 381 | 362 |
| Reserve Deposits and Securities..... | 20b.u | .... | 1,038 | 1,038 | 1,038 | 1,304 | 3,050 | 2,337 | 3,165 | 3,857 | 2,706 | 4,152 | 7,187 |
| Other Claims.................................. | 20n.u | .... | — | — | — | — | — | — | — | — | — | — | — |
| Net Claims on Central Government.. | 22anu | .... | 4,127 | 4,545 | 4,603 | 5,865 | 12,466 | 16,033 | 9,356 | 6,767 | 5,660 | 4,911 | 3,285 |
| Claims on Central Government...... | 22a.u | .... | 4,372 | 4,662 | 4,742 | 6,023 | 12,623 | 16,161 | 9,528 | 6,978 | 5,787 | 5,109 | 3,461 |
| Liabilities to Central Government... | 26d.u | .... | 245 | 117 | 139 | 158 | 157 | 128 | 172 | 211 | 127 | 198 | 176 |
| Claims on Other Sectors................. | 22s.u | .... | 26,622 | 29,760 | 36,722 | 49,015 | 54,697 | 57,260 | 60,521 | 61,508 | 54,713 | 54,489 | 54,974 |
| Claims on Other Financial Corps..... | 22g.u | .... | 2,375 | 2,261 | 2,954 | 6,228 | 8,474 | 9,295 | 9,677 | 9,452 | 6,269 | 8,660 | 8,372 |
| Claims on State & Local Govts...... | 22b.u | .... | 486 | 514 | 728 | 743 | 733 | 501 | 513 | 510 | 480 | 451 | 433 |
| Claims on Public Nonfin. Corps.... | 22c.u | .... | — | — | — | — | — | — | — | — | — | — | — |
| Claims on Private Sector................ | 22d.u | .... | 23,761 | 26,985 | 33,040 | 42,044 | 45,490 | 47,464 | 50,331 | 51,546 | 47,964 | 45,378 | 46,169 |
| Liabilities to Eurosystem................. | 26g.u | .... | 114 | 158 | 84 | 5,071 | 7,892 | 5,860 | 5,755 | 9,988 | 11,339 | 8,792 | 5,154 |
| Transf.Dep.Included in Broad Money | 24..u | .... | 4,722 | 5,836 | 6,983 | 7,964 | 9,287 | 9,949 | 10,557 | 10,884 | 9,281 | 9,975 | 11,479 |
| Other.Dep.Included in Broad Money. | 25..u | .... | 17,780 | 19,499 | 23,437 | 29,712 | 30,319 | 35,880 | 35,664 | 34,392 | 23,907 | 22,442 | 22,508 |
| Sec.Ot.th.Shares Inc.in.Brd. Money.... | 26a.u | .... | −420 | −200 | −97 | −231 | −342 | −123 | −50 | −41 | 45 | 39 | 61 |
| Deposits Excl. from Broad Money.... | 26b.u | .... | 3,481 | 3,092 | 3,121 | 2,720 | 2,534 | 3,456 | 2,706 | 3,156 | 1,907 | 1,622 | 1,435 |
| Sec.Ot.th.Shares Excl.f/Brd. Money.... | 26s.u | .... | 1,260 | 1,425 | 2,218 | 2,073 | 1,666 | 42 | 1,299 | −557 | 106 | −162 | −164 |
| Loans............................................ | 26l.u | .... | — | — | — | — | — | — | — | — | — | — | — |
| Financial Derivatives...................... | 26m.u | .... | 319 | 330 | 332 | 859 | 747 | 442 | 684 | 316 | 179 | 310 | 67 |
| Insurance Technical Reserves.......... | 26r.u | .... | — | — | — | — | — | — | — | — | — | — | — |
| Shares and Other Equity................. | 27a.u | .... | 4,127 | 7,352 | 7,806 | 7,915 | 8,685 | 10,369 | 8,212 | 10,258 | 7,385 | 8,175 | 7,558 |
| Other Items (Net)........................... | 27r.u | .... | −2,658 | −5,297 | −2,147 | 10,571 | 21,401 | 13,155 | 10,228 | 1,103 | 5,373 | 7,817 | 9,559 |
| Memorandum Items | | | | | | | | | | | | | |
| Total Assets................................... | 20ra | 27,382 | 62,553 | 76,625 | 92,894 | 118,141 | 139,372 | 134,961 | 131,638 | 128,126 | 90,291 | 91,142 | 91,018 |
| National Residency Criterion | | | | | | | | | | | | | |
| Net Foreign Assets......................... | 21n | −589.6 | 1,993.0 | 4,370.0 | 4,915.0 | 10,139.0 | 9,428.0 | 8,094.0 | 4,092.0 | 4,030.0 | 91.0 | 1,246.0 | −4,111.0 |
| Claims on Nonresidents................ | 21 | 10,136.4 | 25,127.0 | 34,406.0 | 43,933.0 | 62,915.0 | 76,391.0 | 68,698.0 | 60,633.0 | 55,315.0 | 24,628.0 | 25,312.0 | 21,504.0 |
| Liabilities to Nonresidents............. | 26c | 10,725.9 | 23,134.0 | 30,036.0 | 39,018.0 | 52,776.0 | 66,963.0 | 60,604.0 | 56,541.0 | 51,285.0 | 24,537.0 | 24,066.0 | 25,615.0 |
| Net Claims on Central Government.. | 22an | 1,635.5 | 3,584.0 | 3,718.0 | 3,789.0 | 2,908.0 | 3,834.0 | 3,864.0 | 4,580.0 | 5,835.0 | 4,796.0 | 3,882.0 | 2,809.0 |
| Claims on Central Government...... | 22a | 1,716.0 | 3,828.0 | 3,834.0 | 3,925.0 | 3,063.0 | 3,989.0 | 3,987.0 | 4,749.0 | 6,042.0 | 4,922.0 | 4,078.0 | 2,983.0 |
| Liabilities to Central Government... | 26d | 80.5 | 244.0 | 116.0 | 136.0 | 155.0 | 155.0 | 123.0 | 169.0 | 207.0 | 126.0 | 196.0 | 174.0 |
| Claims on Other Sectors................. | 22s | 12,120.6 | 25,387.0 | 28,330.0 | 34,594.0 | 44,601.0 | 46,630.0 | 50,152.0 | 53,802.0 | 54,694.0 | 50,175.0 | 49,739.0 | 51,150.0 |
| Claims on Other Fin. Corps........... | 22g | — | 1,888.0 | 1,971.0 | 2,428.0 | 3,702.0 | 3,792.0 | 4,087.0 | 5,148.0 | 5,634.0 | 3,774.0 | 5,282.0 | 7,070.0 |
| Claims on State & Local Govts....... | 22b | 136.3 | 297.0 | 310.0 | 547.0 | 581.0 | 587.0 | 501.0 | 513.0 | 498.0 | 479.0 | 451.0 | 416.0 |
| Claims on Private Sector............... | 22d | 11,948.9 | 23,202.0 | 26,049.0 | 31,619.0 | 40,318.0 | 42,251.0 | 45,564.0 | 48,141.0 | 48,562.0 | 45,922.0 | 44,006.0 | 43,664.0 |
| Transf.Dep.Included in Broad Money | 24 | 910.8 | 4,547.0 | 5,583.0 | 6,618.0 | 7,718.0 | 8,947.0 | 9,295.0 | 9,666.0 | 10,069.0 | 8,648.0 | 9,376.0 | 10,395.0 |
| Other.Dep.Included in Broad Money. | 25 | 11,773.6 | 16,996.0 | 18,621.0 | 22,575.0 | 29,036.0 | 29,432.0 | 32,586.0 | 31,334.0 | 30,043.0 | 22,364.0 | 21,160.0 | 20,941.0 |
| Sec.Ot.th.Shares Inc.in.Brd. Money... | 26a | — | −65.0 | −9.0 | 33.0 | 19.0 | — | — | — | 1.0 | 56.0 | 54.0 | 66.0 |
| Deposits Excl. from Broad Money..... | 26b | — | 3,086.0 | 3,078.0 | 2,963.0 | 2,556.0 | 2,475.0 | 3,376.0 | 2,578.0 | 3,000.0 | 1,834.0 | 1,548.0 | 1,356.0 |
| Sec.Ot.th.Shares Excl.f/Brd. Money... | 26s | — | 2,894.0 | 3,652.0 | 4,642.0 | 4,545.0 | 4,435.0 | 2,425.0 | 2,598.0 | 1,713.0 | 428.0 | 311.0 | 564.0 |

| | | 2004 | 2005 | 2006 | 2007 | 2008 | 2009 | 2010 | 2011 | 2012 | 2013 | 2014 | 2015 |
|---|---|---|---|---|---|---|---|---|---|---|---|---|---|
| **Depository Corporations** | | | | | | *Millions of Euros: End of Period* | | | | | | | |
| Euro Area Wide Residency Criterion | | | | | | | | | | | | | |
| Net Foreign Assets | 31n.u | .... | −1,600 | −1,450 | 187 | 10,814 | 12,265 | 3,709 | 2,418 | −2,218 | −3,308 | −4,281 | −7,373 |
| Claims on Nonresidents | 31.u | .... | 16,303 | 21,225 | 27,898 | 35,974 | 40,162 | 32,911 | 34,093 | 33,096 | 16,146 | 15,480 | 14,483 |
| Liabilities to Nonresidents | 36c.u | .... | 17,903 | 22,675 | 27,711 | 25,161 | 27,897 | 29,202 | 31,675 | 35,315 | 19,454 | 19,761 | 21,856 |
| Domestic Claims | 32..u | .... | 31,991 | 35,989 | 42,804 | 58,575 | 70,740 | 77,510 | 73,090 | 71,080 | 61,612 | 60,215 | 60,424 |
| Net Claims on Central Government | 32anu | .... | 5,348 | 6,208 | 6,061 | 9,538 | 16,021 | 20,226 | 12,546 | 9,548 | 6,878 | 5,705 | 4,834 |
| Claims on Central Government | 32a.u | .... | 6,934 | 7,294 | 7,727 | 9,999 | 16,558 | 20,613 | 13,633 | 10,010 | 7,821 | 6,962 | 5,727 |
| Liabilities to Central Government | 36d.u | .... | 1,586 | 1,086 | 1,666 | 461 | 537 | 387 | 1,087 | 462 | 943 | 1,257 | 893 |
| Claims on Other Sectors | 32s.u | .... | 26,643 | 29,781 | 36,743 | 49,037 | 54,719 | 57,284 | 60,544 | 61,532 | 54,734 | 54,510 | 55,590 |
| Claims on Other Financial Corps. | 32g.u | .... | 2,375 | 2,261 | 2,954 | 6,228 | 8,474 | 9,295 | 9,677 | 9,452 | 6,269 | 8,660 | 8,968 |
| Claims on State & Local Govts. | 32b.u | .... | 486 | 514 | 728 | 743 | 733 | 501 | 513 | 510 | 480 | 451 | 433 |
| Claims on Public Nonfin. Corps. | 32c.u | .... | — | — | — | — | — | — | — | — | — | — | — |
| Claims on Private Sector | 32d.u | .... | 23,782 | 27,006 | 33,061 | 42,066 | 45,512 | 47,488 | 50,354 | 51,570 | 47,985 | 45,399 | 46,189 |
| Broad Money Liabilities | 35l.u | .... | 23,088 | 26,231 | 30,968 | 38,743 | 40,569 | 47,065 | 47,663 | 46,784 | 34,886 | 34,364 | 36,278 |
| Currency Outside Depository Corps | 34a.u | .... | 910 | 982 | 504 | 1,130 | 1,208 | 1,294 | 1,399 | 1,432 | 1,518 | 1,746 | 1,890 |
| Transferable Deposits | 34..u | .... | 4,818 | 5,950 | 7,124 | 8,109 | 9,363 | 9,972 | 10,575 | 10,896 | 9,309 | 9,985 | 11,665 |
| Other Deposits | 35..u | .... | 17,780 | 19,499 | 23,437 | 29,735 | 30,340 | 35,922 | 35,739 | 34,497 | 24,014 | 22,594 | 22,662 |
| Securities Other than Shares | 36a.u | .... | −420 | −200 | −97 | −231 | −342 | −123 | −50 | −41 | 45 | 39 | 61 |
| Deposits Excl. from Broad Money | 36b.u | .... | 3,487 | 3,099 | 3,129 | 2,720 | 2,534 | 3,456 | 2,706 | 3,156 | 1,907 | 1,622 | 1,435 |
| Sec.Oth.th.Shares Excl.f/Brd. Money. | 36s.u | .... | 1,260 | 1,425 | 2,218 | 2,073 | 1,666 | 42 | 1,299 | −557 | 106 | −162 | −164 |
| Loans | 36l.u | .... | — | — | — | — | — | — | — | — | — | — | — |
| Financial Derivatives | 36m.u | .... | 319 | 330 | 332 | 859 | 747 | 442 | 684 | 316 | 179 | 310 | 67 |
| Insurance Technical Reserves | 36r.u | .... | — | — | — | — | — | — | — | — | — | — | — |
| Shares and Other Equity | 37a.u | .... | 4,500 | 7,724 | 8,145 | 8,331 | 9,242 | 10,997 | 8,949 | 11,207 | 8,155 | 8,984 | 8,356 |
| Other Items (Net) | 37r.u | .... | −2,264 | −4,275 | −1,804 | 16,646 | 28,244 | 19,214 | 14,201 | 7,960 | 13,066 | 10,821 | 7,080 |
| Broad Money Liabs., Seasonally Adj. | 35lub | .... | 22,989 | 26,116 | 30,819 | 38,495 | 40,254 | 46,580 | 47,091 | 46,185 | 34,463 | 33,967 | 35,870 |
| Memorandum Items | | | | | | | | | | | | | |
| National Residency Criterion | | | | | | | | | | | | | |
| Net Foreign Assets | 31n | 1,112.1 | † 5,571.3 | 8,771.0 | 8,930.7 | 7,255.4 | 5,946.2 | 5,801.4 | −129.8 | −795.4 | −5,741.4 | 173.8 | 1,044.8 |
| Claims on Nonresidents | 31 | 11,909.5 | † 28,840.9 | 38,878.2 | 48,318.6 | 66,699.3 | 80,331.7 | 73,101.4 | 64,560.7 | 58,138.3 | 26,306.9 | 27,106.2 | 26,846.8 |
| Liabilities to Nonresidents | 36c | 10,797.4 | † 23,269.6 | 30,107.2 | 39,387.9 | 59,443.9 | 74,385.5 | 67,300.1 | 64,690.6 | 58,933.7 | 32,048.3 | 26,932.5 | 25,802.0 |
| Domestic Claims | 32 | 13,946.4 | † 29,446.0 | 32,838.0 | 38,572.0 | 48,892.0 | 51,702.0 | 55,289.0 | 58,947.0 | 61,707.0 | 55,529.0 | 53,882.0 | 54,725.0 |
| Net Claims on Central Government | 32an | 1,825.8 | † 4,038.0 | 4,487.0 | 3,957.0 | 4,269.0 | 5,050.0 | 5,113.0 | 5,122.0 | 6,989.0 | 5,333.0 | 4,122.0 | 3,555.0 |
| Claims on Central Government | 32a | 2,764.5 | † 5,623.0 | 5,572.0 | 5,620.0 | 4,727.0 | 5,585.0 | 5,495.0 | 6,206.0 | 7,447.0 | 6,275.0 | 5,377.0 | 4,446.0 |
| Liabilities to Central Government. | 36d | 938.7 | † 1,585.0 | 1,085.0 | 1,663.0 | 458.0 | 535.0 | 382.0 | 1,084.0 | 458.0 | 942.0 | 1,255.0 | 891.0 |
| Claims on Other Sectors | 32s | 12,120.6 | † 25,408.0 | 28,351.0 | 34,615.0 | 44,623.0 | 46,652.0 | 50,176.0 | 53,825.0 | 54,718.0 | 50,196.0 | 49,760.0 | 51,170.0 |
| Claims on Other Financial Corps. | 32g | — | † 1,888.0 | 1,971.0 | 2,428.0 | 3,702.0 | 3,792.0 | 4,087.0 | 5,148.0 | 5,634.0 | 3,774.0 | 5,282.0 | 7,070.0 |
| Claims on State & Local Govts. | 32b | 136.3 | † 297.0 | 310.0 | 547.0 | 581.0 | 587.0 | 501.0 | 513.0 | 498.0 | 479.0 | 451.0 | 416.0 |
| Claims on Private Sector | 32d | 11,948.9 | † 23,223.0 | 26,070.0 | 31,640.0 | 40,340.0 | 42,273.0 | 45,588.0 | 48,164.0 | 48,586.0 | 45,943.0 | 44,027.0 | 43,684.0 |
| Transf.Dep.Included in Broad Money | 34 | 921.9 | 4,643.0 | 5,697.0 | 6,759.0 | 7,863.0 | 9,023.0 | 9,318.0 | 9,684.0 | 10,081.0 | 8,676.0 | 9,386.0 | 10,580.0 |
| Other Dep.Included in Broad Money. | 35 | 11,773.6 | 16,996.0 | 18,621.0 | 22,575.0 | 29,059.0 | 29,453.0 | 32,628.0 | 31,409.0 | 30,148.0 | 22,471.0 | 21,312.0 | 21,095.0 |
| Sec.Ot.th.Shares Inc.in.Brd. Money. | 36a | — | † −65.0 | −9.0 | 33.0 | 19.0 | — | — | — | 1.0 | 56.0 | 54.0 | 66.0 |
| Deposits Excl. from Broad Money | 36b | — | † 3,091.0 | 3,084.0 | 2,970.0 | 2,556.0 | 2,475.0 | 3,376.0 | 2,578.0 | 3,000.0 | 1,834.0 | 1,548.0 | 1,356.0 |
| Sec.Ot.th.Shares Excl./f.Brd. Money. | 36s | — | † 2,894.0 | 3,652.0 | 4,642.0 | 4,545.0 | 4,435.0 | 2,425.0 | 2,598.0 | 1,713.0 | 428.0 | 311.0 | 564.0 |
| **Money (National Definitions)** | | | | | | *Millions of Pounds: End of Period* | | | | | | | |
| M1 | 59ma | 1,523.5 | 1,804.9 | 2,263.7 | 2,592.6 | .... | .... | .... | .... | .... | .... | .... | .... |
| M2 | 59mb | 8,971.6 | 9,884.9 | 11,352.8 | 13,684.1 | .... | .... | .... | .... | .... | .... | .... | .... |
| **Interest Rates** | | | | | | *Percent Per Annum* | | | | | | | |
| Discount Rate (End of Period) | 60.a | 5.50 | 4.25 | 4.50 | 5.00 | .... | .... | .... | .... | .... | .... | .... | .... |
| Money Market Rate | 60b | 4.01 | 3.27 | 2.90 | 4.01 | .... | .... | .... | .... | .... | .... | .... | .... |
| Treasury Bill Rate | 60c | 4.44 | 4.34 | 2.56 | 3.59 | .... | .... | .... | .... | .... | .... | .... | .... |
| Deposit Rate | 60l | 3.75 | 3.81 | 3.36 | 3.44 | .... | .... | .... | .... | .... | .... | .... | .... |
| Households: Stocks, up to 2 years | 60lhs | .... | .... | .... | .... | 4.74 | 5.05 | 4.02 | 4.03 | 4.30 | 3.67 | 2.79 | 2.24 |
| New Business, up to 1 year | 60lhn | 4.39 | 4.52 | 3.99 | 4.08 | 5.08 | 4.43 | 3.95 | 4.08 | 4.39 | 2.94 | 2.55 | 1.76 |
| Corporations: Stocks, up to 2 years | 60lcs | .... | .... | .... | .... | 4.74 | 4.11 | 3.52 | 3.76 | 4.05 | 3.34 | 2.56 | 2.07 |
| New Business, up to 1 year | 60lcn | 4.31 | 4.44 | 3.92 | 4.01 | 4.62 | 3.06 | 3.15 | 3.47 | 3.94 | 2.68 | 2.42 | 1.70 |
| Lending Rate | 60p | 7.57 | 7.09 | 6.69 | 6.74 | .... | .... | .... | .... | .... | .... | .... | .... |
| Households: Stocks, up to 1 year. | 60phs | .... | .... | .... | .... | 8.03 | 8.29 | 7.88 | 8.00 | 8.05 | 8.10 | 7.63 | 6.60 |
| New Bus., Floating & up to 1 year | 60pns | .... | .... | .... | .... | 7.19 | 7.49 | 6.82 | 6.83 | 7.05 | 6.89 | 5.88 | 4.69 |
| House Purch., Stocks,Over 5 years | 60phm | .... | .... | .... | .... | 5.60 | 5.52 | 4.99 | 5.05 | 5.16 | 5.16 | 4.73 | 3.71 |
| Corporations: Stocks, up to 1 year. | 60pcs | .... | .... | .... | .... | 7.07 | 7.01 | 6.58 | 7.15 | 7.13 | 7.08 | 6.78 | 5.99 |
| New Bus., Over € 1 mil.,up to 1 yr | 60pcn | .... | .... | .... | .... | 6.27 | 5.47 | 5.44 | 6.29 | 6.66 | 5.82 | 5.54 | 4.31 |
| Government Bond Yield | 61 | 5.80 | 5.16 | 4.13 | 4.48 | 4.60 | 4.60 | 4.60 | 5.79 | 7.00 | 6.50 | 6.00 | 4.54 |
| **Prices, Production, Labor** | | | | | | *Index Numbers (2010=100): Period Averages* | | | | | | | |
| Industrial Output Prices | 63 | 77.6 | 81.3 | 85.6 | 88.4 | 98.0 | 96.4 | 100.0 | 105.1 | 112.2 | 109.8 | 106.7 | 101.3 |
| Wholesale Prices: Home Goods | 63a | 80.1 | † 83.7 | 86.9 | 90.4 | 98.1 | 99.3 | 100.0 | 103.2 | 105.5 | .... | .... | .... |
| Consumer Prices | 64 | † 86.4 | 88.6 | 90.8 | 93.0 | 97.3 | 97.7 | 100.0 | 103.3 | 105.8 | 105.3 | 103.9 | † 101.7 |
| Harmonized CPI | 64h | 87.5 | 89.3 | 91.3 | 93.3 | 97.3 | 97.5 | 100.0 | 103.5 | 106.7 | 107.1 | 106.8 | 105.2 |
| Industrial Production | 66 | 101.1 | 101.8 | 102.8 | † 106.0 | 109.4 | † 100.7 | 100.0 | 92.9 | 83.5 | 72.3 | 72.3 | 74.7 |
| Mining Production | 66zx | 96.5 | 97.1 | 99.6 | † 103.2 | 112.0 | 88.9 | 100.0 | 91.7 | 59.6 | 40.2 | 33.5 | 34.8 |
| | | | | | | *Number in Thousands: Period Averages* | | | | | | | |
| Labor Force | 67d | 352 | 358 | 366 | 383 | 386 | 393 | 409 | 420 | 426 | 425 | 424 | 417 |
| Employment | 67e | 337 | 348 | 357 | 378 | 383 | 383 | 395 | 398 | 385 | 365 | 363 | 361 |
| Unemployment | 67c | 16 | 19 | 17 | 16 | 15 | 22 | 26 | 34 | 52 | 69 | 70 | 64 |
| Unemployment Rate (%) | 67r | 4.6 | 5.3 | 4.6 | 3.9 | 3.7 | 5.4 | 6.3 | 7.9 | 11.9 | 15.9 | 16.1 | 15.1 |
| **Intl. Transactions & Positions** | | | | | | *Millions of Pounds through 2007; Millions of Euros Beginning 2008* | | | | | | | |
| Exports | 70 | 505.90 | 1,228.74 | 1,111.76 | 1,082.66 | † 1,190.37 | 970.45 | 1,136.79 | 1,403.98 | 1,422.40 | 1,609.26 | 1,443.17 | 1,736.31 |
| Imports, c.i.f. | 71 | 2,645.64 | 5,069.07 | 5,513.46 | 6,353.44 | † 7,366.65 | 5,691.78 | 6,517.42 | 6,310.51 | 5,742.20 | 4,830.36 | 5,144.64 | 5,111.73 |

## Balance of Payments

*Millions of US Dollars*

| | | 2004 | 2005 | 2006 | 2007 | 2008 | 2009 | 2010 | 2011 | 2012 | 2013 | 2014 | 2015 |
|---|---|---|---|---|---|---|---|---|---|---|---|---|---|
| A. Current Account* | 109bx | −826.8 | −970.9 | −1,279.4 | −1,830.9 | † −4,222.9 | −1,986.5 | −2,728.0 | −1,047.3 | −1,441.0 | −1,074.1 | −1,052.7 | −712.6 |
| Goods, credit (exports) | 1a9cx | 1,572.7 | 2,045.5 | 1,979.1 | 1,986.3 | † 3,354.8 | 3,406.7 | 3,564.1 | 4,206.5 | 3,899.9 | 3,603.9 | 3,751.4 | 2,759.2 |
| Goods, debit (imports) | 1a9dx | 5,216.2 | 5,786.0 | 6,296.6 | 7,947.4 | † 11,790.5 | 9,024.4 | 9,413.3 | 9,746.2 | 8,418.7 | 7,509.4 | 7,472.9 | 6,285.5 |
| Balance on goods | 1a9bx | −3,643.4 | −3,740.5 | −4,317.5 | −5,961.0 | † −8,435.7 | −5,617.7 | −5,849.2 | −5,539.7 | −4,518.8 | −3,905.5 | −3,721.5 | −3,526.2 |
| Services, credit (exports) | 1b9cx | 5,835.8 | 6,001.2 | 6,573.6 | 8,299.6 | † 10,650.5 | 9,295.6 | 9,196.1 | 10,041.1 | 9,324.0 | 10,374.3 | 10,112.3 | 8,824.3 |
| Services, debit (imports) | 1b9dx | 2,650.1 | 2,711.9 | 2,977.0 | 3,773.5 | † 5,788.3 | 5,047.9 | 5,048.2 | 5,331.1 | 5,104.9 | 6,217.0 | 6,224.3 | 5,579.4 |
| Balance on Goods & Services | 1z9bx | −457.8 | −451.2 | −720.9 | −1,434.9 | † −3,573.5 | −1,370.0 | −1,701.4 | −829.6 | −299.7 | 251.8 | 166.5 | −281.3 |
| Primary income: credit | 1c9cx | 1,160.1 | 1,634.8 | 2,139.1 | 4,163.5 | † 10,438.1 | 11,285.5 | 12,498.4 | 12,540.4 | 8,410.6 | 5,848.9 | 6,733.2 | 6,341.1 |
| Primary income: debit | 1c9dx | 1,697.3 | 2,246.6 | 2,903.6 | 4,546.2 | † 11,009.9 | 11,625.4 | 13,268.2 | 12,450.5 | 9,190.1 | 6,676.3 | 7,390.6 | 6,273.8 |
| Balance on gds, serv. & prim. inc. | 1y9bx | −995.0 | −1,063.0 | −1,485.4 | −1,817.6 | † −4,145.3 | −1,709.9 | −2,471.2 | −739.7 | −1,079.2 | −575.5 | −490.9 | −214.0 |
| Secondary income: credit | 1d9ca | 585.1 | 631.2 | 822.3 | 822.3 | † 848.4 | 589.2 | 853.1 | 754.8 | 551.5 | 394.8 | 308.4 | 274.9 |
| Secondary income: debit | 1d9da | 416.9 | 539.1 | 616.2 | 835.6 | † 926.1 | 865.8 | 1,109.6 | 1,062.4 | 913.3 | 893.4 | 870.2 | 773.5 |
| B. Capital Account* | 209ba | 8.3 | 34.9 | 7.9 | 43.8 | † 55.4 | 90.7 | 77.8 | 114.2 | 45.6 | 326.0 | 194.6 | 54.9 |
| Capital account: credit | 209ca | 24.1 | 46.5 | 33.2 | 57.8 | † 55.4 | 90.7 | 77.8 | 132.3 | 45.6 | 341.5 | 196.3 | 54.9 |
| Capital account: debit | 209da | 15.8 | 11.6 | 25.3 | 14.0 | † — | — | — | 18.2 | — | 15.5 | 1.7 | — |
| Balance on current & capital acct. | 129ba | −818.5 | −936.0 | −1,271.5 | −1,787.1 | † −4,167.6 | −1,895.7 | −2,650.1 | −933.1 | −1,395.4 | −748.1 | −858.0 | −657.7 |
| C. Financial Account* | 309na | −912.2 | −1,421.5 | −2,270.2 | −2,335.0 | † −4,120.2 | −2,385.3 | −2,096.4 | −106.9 | −669.2 | 173.7 | −925.7 | 550.0 |
| Direct investment: assets | 3a9aa | 711.7 | 547.6 | 897.8 | 1,263.0 | † 4,629.4 | 760.9 | 34,745.0 | −17,309.3 | 11,105.5 | −11,086.1 | 1,995.0 | 10,346.3 |
| Equity & investment fund shares | 3aaaa | 544.0 | 361.1 | 2,704.2 | 1,207.0 | † 4,333.1 | 1,552.0 | 28,102.7 | −10,712.7 | 12,991.9 | −12,316.9 | 1,717.1 | 10,176.5 |
| Debt instruments | 3abaa | 167.7 | 186.5 | −1,806.5 | 56.0 | † 296.4 | −791.1 | 6,642.4 | −6,596.6 | −1,886.4 | 1,230.8 | 278.6 | 169.8 |
| Direct investment: liabilities | 3a9la | 1,118.8 | 1,162.0 | 1,872.4 | 2,295.5 | † 2,338.0 | 2,830.6 | 35,956.5 | −21,600.1 | 7,643.8 | −12,636.9 | 1,087.7 | 5,243.1 |
| Equity & investment fund shares | 3aala | 868.5 | 1,041.8 | 1,452.8 | 1,925.9 | † 2,041.3 | 3,207.6 | 33,913.3 | −21,714.8 | 7,542.4 | −9,882.6 | −400.0 | 4,585.8 |
| Debt instruments | 3abla | 250.3 | 120.1 | 419.6 | 369.6 | † 296.6 | −377.0 | 2,043.1 | 114.7 | 101.4 | −2,754.3 | 1,487.7 | 657.3 |
| Portfolio investment: assets | 3b9aa | 1,812.6 | 1,620.3 | 3,158.4 | −593.8 | † 14,928.4 | 16,940.1 | 8,621.6 | −18,421.1 | −8,944.0 | −15,379.5 | −2,174.7 | −1,062.5 |
| Equity & investment fund shares | 3baaa | 74.4 | 18.4 | −31.9 | 93.6 | † −3,297.5 | 343.8 | 2,516.2 | 29.2 | 1,669.1 | 950.9 | −242.2 | −411.7 |
| Debt securities | 3bbaa | 1,738.1 | 1,601.9 | 3,190.2 | −687.4 | † 18,225.9 | 16,596.3 | 6,105.3 | −18,450.3 | −10,613.1 | −16,330.4 | −1,932.5 | −650.7 |
| Portfolio investment: liabilities | 3b9la | 2,979.0 | 1,566.5 | 3,010.0 | −1,089.4 | † −1,562.5 | 2,262.6 | 1,358.0 | −13.0 | −865.7 | 1,508.1 | 2,144.6 | 1,356.7 |
| Equity & investment fund shares | 3bala | −13.9 | 13.2 | 45.9 | 1.5 | † 36.9 | 205.0 | 178.3 | 609.8 | 1,250.6 | 516.5 | 1,177.7 | −.5 |
| Debt securities | 3bbla | 2,992.9 | 1,553.3 | 2,964.1 | −1,090.8 | † −1,599.5 | 2,057.6 | 1,179.7 | −622.8 | −2,116.4 | 991.5 | 966.9 | 1,357.3 |
| Fin. der.& empl.stk.ops.(ESOs): net. | 3c9na | 44.7 | 15.2 | 160.4 | −136.8 | † 208.3 | −156.6 | 270.0 | 239.2 | 593.7 | −24.9 | 388.1 | −1,322.1 |
| Fin. der. & ESOs.: assets | 3c9aa | 23.6 | 16.5 | 151.9 | −134.3 | † −182.8 | −436.4 | −202.2 | −532.9 | −57.6 | −325.5 | 11,500.7 | −1,507.1 |
| Fin. der. & ESOs.: liabilities | 3c9la | −21.1 | 1.3 | −8.5 | 2.5 | † −391.1 | −279.8 | −472.2 | −772.1 | −651.3 | −300.6 | 11,112.6 | −185.0 |
| Other investment: assets | 3d9aa | 3,133.5 | 7,154.0 | 3,559.6 | 13,964.1 | † 12,768.3 | 3,694.9 | −19,083.9 | 7,416.9 | 4,285.8 | −5,985.8 | −1,785.6 | 470.6 |
| Other equity | 3daaa | .... | .... | .... | .... | † 38.4 | 4.7 | 8.2 | 11.0 | 86.1 | 89.6 | 56.4 | .6 |
| Debt instruments | 3dzaa | 3,133.5 | 7,154.0 | 3,559.6 | 13,964.1 | † 12,729.9 | 3,690.2 | −19,092.1 | 7,405.9 | 4,199.8 | −6,075.4 | −1,842.1 | 470.0 |
| Other investment: liabilities | 3d9la | 2,516.8 | 8,030.1 | 5,163.9 | 15,625.5 | † 35,879.2 | 18,531.5 | −10,665.4 | −6,354.3 | 932.2 | −21,521.3 | −3,883.2 | 1,282.4 |
| Other equity | 3dala | .... | .... | .... | .... | .... | .... | .... | .... | .... | .... | .... | .... |
| Debt instruments | 3dzla | 2,516.8 | 8,030.1 | 5,163.9 | 15,625.5 | † 35,879.2 | 18,531.5 | −10,665.4 | −6,354.3 | 932.2 | −21,521.3 | −3,883.2 | 1,282.4 |
| Curr.+ cap.– finan. acct. balance. | 4y9na | 93.7 | 485.5 | 998.7 | 547.9 | † −47.4 | 489.5 | −553.7 | −826.2 | −726.2 | −921.8 | 67.7 | −1,207.7 |
| D. Net Errors and Omissions | 409na | 277.7 | 217.2 | 13.5 | −797.7 | † −434.6 | −354.3 | 257.2 | 815.8 | 665.7 | 535.8 | −292.7 | 749.8 |
| E. Reserves and Related Items | 4z9na | 371.4 | 702.7 | 1,012.2 | −249.8 | † −482.0 | 135.2 | −296.5 | −10.4 | −60.5 | −386.0 | −225.0 | −457.9 |
| Reserve assets | 3e9aa | 371.4 | 702.7 | 1,012.2 | −249.8 | † −482.0 | 135.2 | −296.5 | −10.4 | −60.5 | −47.3 | 4.4 | −5.8 |
| Credit and loans from the IMF | 3dcla | — | — | — | — | † — | — | — | — | — | 338.6 | 229.4 | 452.1 |
| Exceptional financing | 409la | — | — | — | — | .... | .... | .... | .... | .... | .... | .... | .... |

*Excludes components in group E

## International Investment Position

*Millions of US Dollars*

| | | 2004 | 2005 | 2006 | 2007 | 2008 | 2009 | 2010 | 2011 | 2012 | 2013 | 2014 | 2015 |
|---|---|---|---|---|---|---|---|---|---|---|---|---|---|
| Assets | 809aa | 40,624.7 | 47,756.8 | 71,366.8 | 91,976.0 | † 308,567.1 | 337,298.1 | 341,234.8 | 294,292.7 | 291,547.7 | 264,865.3 | 238,641.9 | 225,956.7 |
| Direct investment | 8a9aa | 3,166.4 | 3,587.2 | 6,833.9 | 8,930.8 | † 172,797.7 | 176,772.6 | 198,771.9 | 170,365.2 | 171,546.9 | 165,223.4 | 140,805.4 | 135,248.6 |
| Equity & investment fund shares | 8aaaa | 2,431.9 | 2,778.0 | 5,882.2 | 7,807.3 | † 156,951.9 | 161,762.5 | 178,167.0 | 156,531.2 | 159,074.0 | 150,928.0 | 128,217.1 | 124,761.5 |
| Debt instruments | 8abaa | 734.5 | 809.2 | 951.7 | 1,123.5 | † 15,845.8 | 15,010.1 | 20,604.9 | 13,834.0 | 12,473.0 | 14,295.4 | 12,588.4 | 10,487.0 |
| Portfolio investment | 8b9aa | 10,378.8 | 13,378.5 | 26,437.3 | 26,033.1 | † 56,399.5 | 74,865.6 | 66,970.9 | 42,847.6 | 33,858.8 | 19,075.9 | 14,529.6 | 12,750.8 |
| Equity & investment fund shares | 8baaa | 1,909.1 | 2,373.4 | 4,432.4 | 5,012.2 | † 7,209.4 | 6,661.5 | 6,245.4 | 5,962.8 | 6,127.5 | 7,411.3 | 5,634.7 | 4,868.7 |
| Debt securities | 8bbaa | 8,469.7 | 11,005.1 | 22,004.8 | 21,020.9 | † 49,190.1 | 68,204.2 | 60,725.5 | 36,884.8 | 27,731.3 | 11,664.6 | 8,894.9 | 7,882.1 |
| Fin. der.(oth.than reserves) & ESOs | 8c9aa | 42.6 | 51.8 | 506.8 | 331.9 | † 2,496.9 | 2,214.1 | 1,959.3 | 1,965.5 | 2,172.5 | 2,229.7 | 12,905.7 | 10,299.8 |
| Other investment | 8d9aa | 22,962.2 | 26,410.7 | 31,724.4 | 50,168.5 | † 75,869.6 | 82,154.7 | 72,384.9 | 77,900.8 | 82,768.5 | 77,418.2 | 69,511.3 | 66,851.3 |
| Other equity | 8daaa | .... | .... | .... | .... | † 278.4 | 268.4 | 273.0 | 258.8 | 359.9 | 466.3 | 470.0 | 426.4 |
| Debt instruments | 8dzaa | 22,962.2 | 26,410.7 | 31,724.4 | 50,168.5 | † 75,591.2 | 81,886.2 | 72,111.8 | 77,642.1 | 82,408.6 | 76,951.9 | 69,041.2 | 66,424.9 |
| Reserve assets | 8e9aa | 4,074.7 | 4,328.7 | 5,864.6 | 6,511.7 | † 1,003.4 | 1,291.2 | 1,147.8 | 1,213.6 | 1,201.0 | 918.1 | 889.9 | 806.2 |
| Liabilities | 809la | 38,241.7 | 44,573.9 | 64,117.3 | 89,114.4 | † 329,504.9 | 364,318.8 | 370,124.5 | 327,786.3 | 324,552.8 | 298,993.9 | 268,405.7 | 250,512.2 |
| Direct investment | 8a9la | 8,511.0 | 8,482.8 | 13,754.0 | 17,711.4 | † 185,568.1 | 191,474.6 | 213,915.0 | 183,769.2 | 186,000.1 | 178,347.7 | 150,968.6 | 140,377.2 |
| Equity & investment fund shares | 8aala | 5,879.9 | 6,092.1 | 10,654.9 | 13,881.8 | † 167,955.0 | 173,585.8 | 195,041.4 | 165,385.6 | 167,179.1 | 161,708.3 | 134,683.9 | 124,953.4 |
| Debt instruments | 8abla | 2,631.1 | 2,390.8 | 3,099.0 | 3,829.5 | † 17,613.1 | 17,888.8 | 18,873.6 | 18,383.5 | 18,821.0 | 16,639.5 | 16,284.7 | 15,423.8 |
| Portfolio investment | 8b9la | 7,272.5 | 8,692.9 | 13,444.3 | 14,380.7 | † 17,590.3 | 20,465.6 | 15,073.6 | 12,695.4 | 10,189.4 | 12,219.0 | 13,057.2 | 13,034.5 |
| Equity & investment fund shares | 8bala | 176.4 | 313.2 | 1,077.8 | 1,003.9 | † 2,483.4 | 3,638.4 | 3,622.3 | 2,553.8 | 2,373.5 | 2,983.1 | 3,329.2 | 2,830.6 |
| Debt securities | 8bbla | 7,096.1 | 8,379.7 | 12,366.6 | 13,376.7 | † 15,106.9 | 16,827.2 | 11,451.3 | 10,141.6 | 7,815.9 | 9,235.9 | 9,728.0 | 10,204.0 |
| Fin. der.(oth.than reserves) & ESOs | 8c9la | 27.9 | 23.0 | 421.5 | 481.5 | † 2,399.4 | 2,331.5 | 1,752.7 | 1,997.8 | 1,923.3 | 1,951.0 | 12,170.3 | 11,097.4 |
| Other investment | 8d9la | 22,430.2 | 27,375.2 | 36,497.5 | 56,540.9 | † 123,947.1 | 150,047.2 | 139,383.1 | 129,323.9 | 126,440.0 | 106,476.2 | 92,209.6 | 86,003.1 |
| Other equity | 8dala | .... | .... | .... | .... | .... | .... | .... | .... | .... | .... | .... | .... |
| Debt instruments | 8dzla | 22,430.2 | 27,375.2 | 36,497.5 | 56,540.9 | † 123,947.1 | 150,047.2 | 139,383.1 | 129,323.9 | 126,440.0 | 106,476.2 | 92,209.6 | 86,003.1 |

| | | 2004 | 2005 | 2006 | 2007 | 2008 | 2009 | 2010 | 2011 | 2012 | 2013 | 2014 | 2015 |
|---|---|---|---|---|---|---|---|---|---|---|---|---|---|
| **Government Finance** | | | | | | | | | | | | | |
| **Operations Statement** | | | | | | | | | | | | | |
| **General Government** | | | | | | *Millions of Euros: Fiscal Year Ends December 31; Data Reported through Eurostat* | | | | | | | |
| Revenue | a1 | 4,807.5 | 5,471.6 | 5,996.6 | 7,113.7 | 7,429.7 | 6,808.2 | 7,159.7 | 7,187.7 | ·7,018.8 | 6,595.7 | 6,924.2 | 6,801.6 |
| Taxes | a11 | 3,083.5 | 3,493.2 | 3,961.0 | 5,060.5 | 5,212.9 | 4,426.9 | 4,574.6 | 4,686.7 | 4,606.4 | 4,326.8 | 4,366.6 | 4,290.8 |
| Social Contributions | a12 | 972.4 | 1,110.7 | 1,128.4 | 1,194.7 | 1,332.5 | 1,464.2 | 1,552.3 | 1,566.0 | 1,510.4 | 1,362.3 | 1,444.6 | 1,479.9 |
| Grants | a13 | .... | .... | .... | .... | .... | .... | .... | .... | .... | .... | .... | .... |
| Other Revenue | a14 | .... | .... | .... | .... | .... | .... | .... | .... | .... | .... | .... | .... |
| Expense | a2 | 4,996.9 | 5,502.9 | 5,878.9 | 6,297.1 | 6,963.1 | 7,315.9 | 7,525.4 | 7,871.9 | 7,912.8 | 7,566.2 | 8,410.5 | 6,913.2 |
| Compensation of Employees | a21 | 1,886.2 | 2,001.3 | 2,159.2 | 2,311.4 | 2,502.7 | 2,728.5 | 2,763.5 | 2,881.6 | 2,824.6 | 2,572.8 | 2,299.1 | 2,231.6 |
| Use of Goods & Services | a22 | 517.0 | 576.1 | 682.1 | 742.7 | 826.0 | 894.2 | 851.4 | 871.4 | 810.7 | 744.3 | 655.3 | 646.2 |
| Consumption of Fixed Capital | a23 | 198.1 | 211.8 | 232.0 | 244.5 | 276.3 | 233.4 | 259.7 | 289.7 | 277.4 | 264.6 | 251.6 | 253.7 |
| Interest | a24 | 417.4 | 473.1 | 472.0 | 486.8 | 492.0 | 436.1 | 394.8 | 430.2 | 566.4 | 563.4 | 498.2 | 496.0 |
| Subsidies | a25 | 141.8 | 94.5 | 76.7 | 65.4 | 70.0 | 32.0 | 61.5 | 85.2 | 94.9 | 95.1 | 79.6 | 71.5 |
| Grants | a26 | .... | .... | .... | .... | .... | .... | .... | .... | .... | .... | .... | .... |
| Social Benefits | a27 | 1,523.2 | 1,725.5 | 1,785.9 | 1,835.9 | 2,083.8 | 2,257.4 | 2,479.5 | 2,607.7 | 2,579.9 | 2,484.2 | 2,468.9 | 2,468.5 |
| Other Expense | a28 | .... | .... | .... | .... | .... | .... | .... | .... | .... | .... | .... | .... |
| Gross Operating Balance [1-2+23] | agob | 8.7 | 180.5 | 349.7 | 1,061.1 | 742.9 | −274.3 | −106.0 | −394.5 | −616.6 | −705.9 | −1,234.7 | 142.1 |
| Net Operating Balance [1-2] | anob | −189.4 | −31.3 | 117.7 | 816.6 | 466.6 | −507.7 | −365.7 | −684.2 | −894.0 | −970.5 | −1,486.3 | −111.6 |
| Net Acq. of Nonfinancial Assets | a31 | 320.8 | 289.8 | 281.9 | 253.1 | 302.0 | 507.0 | 545.9 | 437.9 | 235.7 | −79.8 | 56.7 | 68.6 |
| Aquisition of Nonfin. Assets | a31.1 | .... | .... | .... | .... | .... | .... | .... | .... | .... | .... | .... | .... |
| Disposal of Nonfin. Assets | a31.2 | .... | .... | .... | .... | .... | .... | .... | .... | .... | .... | .... | .... |
| Net Lending/Borrowing [1-2-31] | anlb | −510.2 | −321.1 | −164.2 | 563.5 | 164.6 | −1,014.7 | −911.6 | −1,122.1 | −1,129.7 | −890.7 | −1,543.0 | −180.2 |
| Net Acq. of Financial Assets | a32 | 215.7 | 109.5 | −120.8 | 485.2 | −748.1 | 455.0 | −91.3 | 960.8 | 1,537.0 | 2,221.4 | −1,070.4 | −179.0 |
| By instrument | | | | | | | | | | | | | |
| Monetary Gold & SDRs | a3201 | — | — | — | — | — | — | — | — | — | — | — | — |
| Currency & Deposits | a3202 | 160.5 | 35.4 | −46.2 | 395.1 | −767.3 | 312.1 | −213.6 | 844.6 | −635.7 | 644.6 | 421.9 | −254.4 |
| Securities other than Shares | a3203 | — | — | — | — | — | — | — | — | — | 1,500.0 | −1,500.0 | — |
| Loans | a3204 | 10.5 | 24.6 | −88.7 | 22.8 | 41.7 | 92.7 | 124.9 | 187.8 | 304.6 | .7 | −70.1 | 9.7 |
| Shares & Other Equity | a3205 | 2.4 | 3.9 | 4.1 | 24.8 | −57.9 | 4.3 | — | — | 1,860.8 | 68.4 | 35.1 | 2.8 |
| Insurance Technical Reserves | a3206 | — | — | — | — | — | — | — | — | — | — | — | — |
| Financial Derivatives | a3207 | — | — | — | — | — | — | — | — | — | — | — | — |
| Other Accounts Receivable | a3208 | 42.4 | 45.6 | 10.1 | 42.5 | 35.4 | 45.9 | −2.6 | −71.6 | 7.3 | 7.6 | 42.7 | 62.9 |
| By debtor | | | | | | | | | | | | | |
| Domestic | a321 | .... | .... | .... | .... | .... | .... | .... | .... | .... | .... | .... | .... |
| Foreign | a322 | .... | .... | .... | .... | .... | .... | .... | .... | .... | .... | .... | .... |
| Net Incurrence of Liabilities | a33 | 731.4 | 446.6 | 99.4 | −64.6 | −866.9 | 1,481.2 | 815.1 | 2,082.9 | 2,666.6 | 3,117.6 | 431.9 | −51.8 |
| By instrument | | | | | | | | | | | | | |
| Special Drawing Rights (SDRs) | a3301 | — | — | — | — | — | — | — | — | — | — | — | — |
| Currency & Deposits | a3302 | — | — | — | — | — | — | — | — | — | — | — | — |
| Securities other than Shares | a3303 | 662.0 | 329.5 | 26.3 | −144.7 | −1,429.1 | 1,547.7 | 827.0 | 1,367.2 | 312.7 | −1,544.0 | −836.2 | −821.8 |
| Loans | a3304 | 81.3 | 89.9 | 68.8 | 87.9 | 552.7 | −62.1 | −12.8 | 719.2 | 2,244.3 | 4,699.2 | 1,175.2 | 881.6 |
| Shares & Other Equity | a3305 | — | — | — | — | — | — | — | — | — | — | — | — |
| Insurance Technical Reserves | a3306 | — | — | — | — | — | — | — | — | — | — | — | — |
| Financial Derivatives | a3307 | — | — | — | — | — | — | — | — | — | — | — | — |
| Other Accounts Payable | a3308 | −12.0 | 27.2 | 4.3 | −7.9 | 9.4 | −4.4 | .9 | −3.4 | 109.6 | −37.6 | 92.9 | −111.5 |
| By creditor | | | | | | | | | | | | | |
| Domestic | a331 | .... | .... | .... | .... | .... | .... | .... | .... | .... | .... | .... | .... |
| Foreign | a332 | .... | .... | .... | .... | .... | .... | .... | .... | .... | .... | .... | .... |
| Stat. Discrepancy [32-33-NLB] | anlbz | −5.5 | −16.0 | −56.0 | −13.6 | −45.8 | −11.5 | 5.2 | — | .1 | −5.5 | 40.7 | 53.0 |
| Memo Item: Expenditure [2+31] | a2m | 5,317.7 | 5,792.7 | 6,160.8 | 6,550.2 | 7,265.1 | 7,822.9 | 8,071.3 | 8,309.8 | 8,148.5 | 7,486.4 | 8,467.2 | 6,981.8 |
| **Balance Sheet** | | | | | | | | | | | | | |
| Net Worth | a6 | .... | .... | .... | .... | .... | .... | .... | .... | .... | .... | .... | .... |
| Nonfinancial Assets | a61 | .... | .... | .... | .... | .... | .... | .... | .... | .... | .... | .... | .... |
| Financial Assets | a62 | 3,728.5 | 3,909.6 | 3,818.5 | 4,417.1 | 3,706.8 | 4,232.6 | 4,218.0 | 5,246.1 | 5,873.6 | 7,421.1 | 7,380.0 | 7,204.5 |
| By instrument | | | | | | | | | | | | | |
| Monetary Gold & SDRs | a6201 | — | — | — | — | — | — | — | — | — | — | — | — |
| Currency & Deposits | a6202 | 1,490.3 | 1,525.6 | 1,479.4 | 1,874.5 | 1,107.2 | 1,419.4 | 1,205.8 | 2,050.4 | 1,414.7 | 2,059.3 | 2,481.2 | 2,226.8 |
| Securities other than Shares | a6203 | — | — | — | — | — | — | — | — | — | 1,500.0 | — | — |
| Loans | a6204 | 375.0 | 399.6 | 310.9 | 333.7 | 375.4 | 468.7 | 595.0 | 782.8 | 1,087.4 | 1,088.1 | 1,018.1 | 1,027.8 |
| Shares and Other Equity | a6205 | 1,620.4 | 1,695.9 | 1,729.8 | 1,867.9 | 1,847.7 | 1,922.8 | 1,998.0 | 2,065.4 | 3,016.6 | 2,411.1 | 3,475.5 | 3,481.9 |
| Insurance Technical Reserves | a6206 | — | — | — | — | — | — | — | — | — | — | — | — |
| Financial Derivatives | a6207 | — | — | — | — | — | — | — | — | — | — | — | — |
| Other Accounts Receivable | a6208 | 242.8 | 288.4 | 298.5 | 341.0 | 376.4 | 421.8 | 419.2 | 347.6 | 354.9 | 362.5 | 405.2 | 468.1 |
| By debtor | | | | | | | | | | | | | |
| Domestic | a621 | .... | .... | .... | .... | .... | .... | .... | .... | .... | .... | .... | .... |
| Foreign | a622 | .... | .... | .... | .... | .... | .... | .... | .... | .... | .... | .... | .... |
| Liabilities | a63 | 8,892.8 | 9,337.4 | 9,436.7 | 9,421.3 | 8,563.4 | 10,042.9 | 10,851.8 | 12,933.5 | 14,750.6 | 18,446.9 | 19,167.3 | 19,397.9 |
| By instrument | | | | | | | | | | | | | |
| Special Drawing Rights (SDRs) | a6301 | — | — | — | — | — | — | — | — | — | — | — | — |
| Currency & Deposits | a6302 | — | — | — | — | — | — | — | .... | .... | .... | .... | .... |
| Securities other than Shares | a6303 | 6,386.7 | 6,716.2 | 6,742.5 | 6,597.8 | 5,168.7 | 6,716.4 | 7,543.5 | 8,910.6 | 8,375.3 | 7,416.3 | 6,843.1 | 6,268.3 |
| Loans | a6304 | 2,480.5 | 2,589.6 | 2,668.3 | 2,805.5 | 3,367.3 | 3,303.6 | 3,284.5 | 4,002.5 | 6,245.3 | 10,938.2 | 12,138.9 | 13,055.8 |
| Shares and Other Equity | a6305 | — | — | — | — | — | — | — | — | — | — | — | — |
| Insurance Technical Reserves | a6306 | — | — | — | — | — | — | — | — | — | — | — | — |
| Financial Derivatives | a6307 | — | — | — | — | — | — | — | — | — | — | — | — |
| Other Accounts Payable | a6308 | 25.6 | 31.6 | 25.8 | 17.9 | 27.3 | 22.9 | 23.8 | 20.4 | 130.0 | 92.4 | 185.3 | 73.8 |
| By creditor | | | | | | | | | | | | | |
| Domestic | a631 | .... | .... | .... | .... | .... | .... | .... | .... | .... | .... | .... | .... |
| Foreign | a632 | .... | .... | .... | .... | .... | .... | .... | .... | .... | .... | .... | .... |
| Net Financial Worth [62-63] | a6m2 | −5,164.3 | −5,427.8 | −5,618.1 | −5,004.1 | −4,856.6 | −5,810.3 | −6,633.7 | −7,687.3 | −8,877.0 | −11,025.8 | −11,787.3 | −12,193.4 |
| Memo Item: Debt at Market Value | a6m3 | 8,892.8 | 9,337.4 | 9,436.7 | 9,421.3 | 8,563.4 | 10,042.9 | 10,851.8 | 12,933.5 | 14,750.6 | 18,446.9 | 19,167.3 | 19,397.9 |
| Memo Item: Debt at Face Value | a6m35 | 8,908.2 | 9,342.8 | 9,415.8 | 9,388.1 | 8,520.3 | 9,987.8 | 10,793.5 | 12,889.7 | 15,560.8 | 18,611.1 | 19,004.2 | 19,039.4 |
| Memo Item: Maastricht Debt | a6m36 | 8,882.6 | 9,311.1 | 9,390.0 | 9,370.1 | 8,493.0 | 9,964.9 | 10,769.7 | 12,869.3 | 15,430.8 | 18,518.7 | 18,818.9 | 18,965.6 |
| Memo Item: Debt at Nominal Value | a6m4 | .... | .... | .... | .... | .... | .... | .... | .... | .... | .... | .... | .... |

# Cyprus   423

|  |  | 2004 | 2005 | 2006 | 2007 | 2008 | 2009 | 2010 | 2011 | 2012 | 2013 | 2014 | 2015 |
|---|---|---|---|---|---|---|---|---|---|---|---|---|---|
| National Accounts |  | *Millions of Pounds through 2007; Millions of Euros Beginning 2008* | | | | | | | | | | | |
| Househ.Cons.Expend.,incl.NPISHs.... | 96f | 4,773.7 | 5,091.2 | 5,441.6 | 6,053.3 | † 12,550.7 | 11,783.3 | 12,381.2 | 12,833.7 | 13,118.0 | 12,335.5 | 12,244.4 | 12,229.6 |
| Government Consumption Expend... | 91f | 1,319.9 | 1,420.5 | 1,570.0 | 1,618.0 | † 3,197.5 | 3,463.2 | 3,452.1 | 3,618.8 | 3,453.6 | 3,160.1 | 2,741.6 | 2,754.9 |
| Gross Fixed Capital Formation.......... | 93e | 1,385.6 | 1,521.3 | 1,741.6 | 1,955.0 | † 5,143.4 | 4,358.7 | 4,181.5 | 3,740.9 | 2,969.2 | 2,511.6 | 2,003.7 | 2,329.1 |
| Changes in Inventories.................... | 93i | 108.2 | 48.3 | 12.1 | 83.6 | † 356.5 | −124.2 | 369.4 | −38.3 | 142.8 | −139.0 | 283.4 | 350.3 |
| Exports of Goods and Services......... | 90c | 3,538.7 | 3,807.1 | 4,055.7 | 4,454.9 | † 9,520.2 | 9,099.1 | 9,644.1 | 10,228.9 | 10,313.7 | 10,521.8 | 10,437.5 | 10,436.8 |
| Imports of Goods and Services (-)..... | 98c | 3,720.6 | 4,009.4 | 4,372.6 | 5,036.8 | † 11,946.5 | 10,097.7 | 10,910.3 | 10,836.8 | 10,528.7 | 10,325.4 | 10,316.9 | 10,680.1 |
| Gross Domestic Product (GDP)......... | 99b | 7,405.6 | 7,879.1 | 8,448.6 | 9,128.1 | † 18,822.0 | 18,482.3 | 19,118.0 | 19,547.3 | 19,468.7 | 18,064.6 | 17,393.6 | 17,420.6 |
| Net Primary Income from Abroad..... | 98.n | −322.0 | −325.8 | −398.1 | −538.7 | −208.7 | −714.3 | −560.8 | 317.4 | −519.1 | −344.7 | . . . . | . . . . |
| Gross National Income (GNI)............ | 99a | 7,083.9 | 7,553.3 | 8,050.5 | 8,755.0 | 16,948.5 | 16,139.3 | 16,845.2 | 18,195.2 | 17,201.1 | 16,159.0 | . . . . | . . . . |
| Consumption of Fixed Capital.......... | 99cf | 740.3 | 803.5 | 864.1 | 928.3 | † 1,748.2 | 1,784.0 | 1,860.3 | 1,930.9 | 1,993.5 | 2,049.3 | . . . . | . . . . |
| GDP Volume 2000 Ref., Chained..... | 99b.p | 6,521.3 | 6,779.1 | 7,052.9 | 7,360.9 | † 12,956.8 | 12,716.6 | 12,861.9 | . . . . | . . . . | . . . . | . . . . | . . . . |
| GDP Volume 2010 Ref., Chained..... | 99b.p | . . . . | . . . . | . . . . | . . . . | † 12,956.8 | 12,716.6 | 12,861.9 | 19,195.1 | 18,725.5 | 17,612.7 | 17,173.1 | 17,445.9 |
| GDP Volume (2010=100)............... | 99bvp | 86.6 | 90.0 | 93.7 | 97.7 | † 100.7 | 98.7 | 100.0 | 100.4 | 97.9 | 92.1 | 89.8 | 91.3 |
| GDP Deflator (2010=100)............... | 99bip | 76.4 | 78.2 | 80.6 | 83.5 | 97.8 | 98.0 | 100.0 | 101.8 | 104.0 | 102.6 | 101.3 | 99.9 |
|  |  | *Millions: Midyear Estimates* | | | | | | | | | | | |
| Population............................... | 99z | 1.02 | 1.03 | 1.05 | 1.06 | 1.08 | 1.09 | 1.10 | 1.12 | 1.13 | 1.14 | 1.15 | 1.17 |

# Czech Republic 935

| | | 2004 | 2005 | 2006 | 2007 | 2008 | 2009 | 2010 | 2011 | 2012 | 2013 | 2014 | 2015 |
|---|---|---|---|---|---|---|---|---|---|---|---|---|---|
| **Exchange Rates** | | | | | | *Koruny per SDR: End of Period* | | | | | | | |
| Official Rate.................. | aa | 34.733 | 35.143 | 31.406 | 28.568 | 29.798 | 28.795 | 28.877 | 30.613 | 29.286 | 30.637 | 33.082 | 34.399 |
| | | | | | | *Koruny per US Dollar: End of Period (ae) Period Average (rf)* | | | | | | | |
| Official Rate.................. | ae | 22.365 | 24.588 | 20.876 | 18.078 | 19.346 | 18.368 | 18.751 | 19.940 | 19.055 | 19.894 | 22.834 | 24.824 |
| Official Rate.................. | rf | 25.700 | 23.957 | 22.596 | 20.294 | 17.072 | 19.063 | 19.098 | 17.696 | 19.578 | 19.571 | 20.758 | 24.599 |
| | | | | | | *Index Numbers (2010=100): Period Averages* | | | | | | | |
| Nominal Effective Exchange Rate..... | nec | 79.39 | 84.27 | 88.62 | 91.12 | 102.47 | 97.96 | 100.00 | 103.14 | 99.21 | 97.50 | 92.46 | 91.26 |
| CPI-Based Real Effect. Ex. Rate........ | rec | 77.16 | 81.66 | 86.19 | 88.86 | 102.57 | 98.40 | 100.00 | 102.16 | 99.09 | 97.12 | 91.37 | 89.90 |
| **Fund Position** | | | | | | *Millions of SDRs: End of Period* | | | | | | | |
| Quota.................................. | 2f.s | 819.30 | 819.30 | 819.30 | 819.30 | 819.30 | 819.30 | 819.30 | 1,002.20 | 1,002.20 | 1,002.20 | 1,002.20 | 1,002.20 |
| SDR Holdings...................... | 1b.s | 3.41 | 8.24 | 11.03 | 12.73 | 13.76 | 794.44 | 794.89 | 750.42 | 750.87 | 751.16 | 751.54 | 751.68 |
| Reserve Position in the Fund........... | 1c.s | 263.97 | 126.56 | 74.08 | 53.33 | 104.98 | 153.98 | 226.83 | 432.55 | 455.15 | 485.75 | 443.23 | 343.90 |
| Total Fund Cred.&Loans Outstg....... | 2tl | — | — | — | — | — | — | — | — | — | — | — | — |
| SDR Allocations........................... | 1bd | — | — | — | — | — | 780.20 | 780.20 | 780.20 | 780.20 | 780.20 | 780.20 | 780.20 |
| **International Liquidity** | | | | | | *Millions of US Dollars Unless Otherwise Indicated: End of Period* | | | | | | | |
| Total Reserves minus Gold.............. | 1l.d | 28,259 | 29,330 | 31,182 | 34,550 | 36,655 | 41,157 | 41,909 | 39,670 | 44,265 | 55,798 | 54,085 | 64,148 |
| SDR Holdings....................... | 1b.d | 5 | 12 | 17 | 20 | 21 | 1,245 | 1,224 | 1,152 | 1,154 | 1,157 | 1,089 | 1,042 |
| Reserve Position in the Fund......... | 1c.d | 410 | 181 | 111 | 84 | 162 | 241 | 349 | 664 | 700 | 748 | 642 | 477 |
| Foreign Exchange....................... | 1d.d | 27,844 | 29,138 | 31,054 | 34,445 | 36,472 | 39,670 | 40,335 | 37,854 | 42,412 | 53,893 | 52,354 | 62,630 |
| Gold (Million Fine Troy Ounces)....... | 1ad | .438 | .435 | .433 | .429 | .422 | .415 | .408 | .400 | .372 | .349 | .340 | .323 |
| Gold (National Valuation)............... | 1and | 190 | 225 | 273 | 356 | 358 | 454 | 584 | 620 | 618 | 419 | 408 | 343 |
| Central Bank: Other Assets....... | 3..d | 2,934.7 | 7,232.9 | 5,919.4 | 3,118.5 | 1,304.8 | 5,088.3 | 5,657.1 | 10,215.3 | 15,576.4 | 11,492.0 | 11,793.2 | 13,304.1 |
| Central Bank: Other Liabs.............. | 4..d | 1,052.8 | 3,537.8 | 3,904.6 | 5,374.8 | 75.4 | 131.4 | 329.6 | 320.4 | 245.8 | 130.7 | 1,171.9 | 1,819.4 |
| Other Depository Corps.: Assets...... | 7a.d | 20,530.2 | 24,100.4 | 27,070.1 | 38,349.7 | 36,000.3 | 32,167.2 | 32,049.7 | 29,275.3 | 33,222.7 | 35,466.6 | 31,923.8 | 29,196.8 |
| Other Depository Corps.: Liabs........ | 7b.d | 10,279.8 | 9,798.5 | 12,052.0 | 19,714.9 | 22,811.3 | 19,464.1 | 20,557.5 | 19,816.5 | 18,110.9 | 25,719.1 | 26,638.1 | 28,970.8 |
| **Central Bank** | | | | | | *Billions of Koruny: End of Period* | | | | | | | |
| Net Foreign Assets...................... | 11n | 633.9 | 724.5 | 658.9 | 633.3 | 719.8 | 747.1 | 776.7 | 780.8 | 836.7 | 1,096.8 | 1,198.1 | 1,535.8 |
| Claims on Nonresidents................ | 11 | 657.4 | 811.5 | 740.5 | 730.5 | 721.2 | 771.9 | 805.4 | 811.1 | 864.2 | 1,123.3 | 1,250.7 | 1,607.8 |
| Liabilities to Nonresidents.............. | 16c | 23.5 | 87.0 | 81.5 | 97.2 | 1.5 | 24.9 | 28.7 | 30.3 | 27.5 | 26.5 | 52.6 | 72.0 |
| Claims on Other Depository Corps.... | 12e | .1 | 29.1 | — | — | 38.0 | — | 1.5 | 3.5 | — | — | — | — |
| Net Claims on Central Government.. | 12an | −79.0 | −174.4 | −156.4 | −179.1 | −176.6 | −105.2 | −120.9 | −73.3 | −125.2 | −25.5 | −3.8 | −112.1 |
| Claims on Central Government...... | 12a | 13.2 | 4.1 | — | — | — | — | — | — | — | — | — | — |
| Liabilities to Central Government... | 16d | 92.2 | 178.5 | 156.4 | 179.1 | 176.6 | 105.2 | 120.9 | 73.3 | 125.2 | 25.5 | 3.8 | 112.1 |
| Claims on Other Sectors............... | 12s | 31.2 | 25.8 | 8.7 | 8.7 | 8.6 | 8.5 | 3.6 | 3.4 | 3.4 | 3.0 | 3.0 | 2.5 |
| Claims on Other Financial Corps..... | 12g | 30.6 | 25.3 | 8.2 | 8.2 | 8.1 | 8.0 | 3.1 | 3.1 | 3.1 | 2.8 | 2.8 | 2.3 |
| Claims on State & Local Govts....... | 12b | — | — | — | — | — | — | — | — | — | — | — | — |
| Claims on Public Nonfin. Corps...... | 12c | — | — | — | — | — | — | — | — | — | — | — | — |
| Claims on Private Sector.............. | 12d | .6 | .5 | .5 | .5 | .5 | .5 | .5 | .4 | .4 | .2 | .2 | .2 |
| Monetary Base......................... | 14 | 692.4 | 689.0 | 655.7 | 635.1 | 709.5 | 771.4 | 789.1 | 804.3 | 807.6 | 1,105.7 | 1,159.3 | 1,391.8 |
| Currency in Circulation.................. | 14a | 261.4 | 287.8 | 321.5 | 353.1 | 398.5 | 386.5 | 390.8 | 410.9 | 421.4 | 440.3 | 467.8 | 508.2 |
| Liabs. to Other Depository Corps.... | 14c | 428.2 | 399.2 | 331.6 | 279.1 | 307.8 | 380.9 | 394.2 | 389.5 | 383.6 | 664.1 | 690.4 | 882.5 |
| Liabilities to Other Sectors.............. | 14d | 2.8 | 2.1 | 2.5 | 3.0 | 3.1 | 4.0 | 4.1 | 3.9 | 2.6 | 1.3 | 1.0 | 1.1 |
| Other Liabs. to Other Dep. Corps.... | 14n | — | — | — | — | — | — | — | — | — | — | — | — |
| Dep. & Sec. Excl. f/Monetary Base.... | 14o | — | — | — | — | — | — | — | — | — | — | — | — |
| Deposits Included in Broad Money. | 15 | — | — | — | — | — | — | — | — | — | — | — | — |
| Sec.Ot.th.Shares Incl.in Brd. Money | 16a | — | — | — | — | — | — | — | — | — | — | — | — |
| Deposits Excl. from Broad Money... | 16b | — | — | — | — | — | — | — | — | — | — | — | — |
| Sec.Ot.th.Shares Excl.f/Brd.Money.. | 16s | — | — | — | — | — | — | — | — | — | — | — | — |
| Loans................................ | 16l | — | — | — | — | — | — | — | — | — | — | — | — |
| Financial Derivatives...................... | 16m | — | — | — | — | — | — | — | — | — | — | — | — |
| Shares and Other Equity................. | 17a | −96.3 | −75.9 | −136.8 | −174.6 | −146.4 | −128.2 | −142.5 | −107.4 | −104.1 | −31.4 | 25.4 | 24.6 |
| Other Items (Net)........................ | 17r | −10.0 | −8.3 | −7.7 | 2.4 | 26.5 | 7.0 | 14.1 | 17.3 | 11.3 | −.1 | 12.5 | 9.7 |
| **Other Depository Corporations** | | | | | | *Billions of Koruny: End of Period* | | | | | | | |
| Net Foreign Assets........................ | 21n | 229.3 | 351.7 | 313.5 | 336.9 | 255.2 | 233.3 | 215.5 | 188.6 | 288.0 | 193.9 | 120.7 | 5.6 |
| Claims on Nonresidents................ | 21 | 459.2 | 592.6 | 565.1 | 693.3 | 696.5 | 590.8 | 601.0 | 583.7 | 633.1 | 705.6 | 728.9 | 724.8 |
| Liabilities to Nonresidents.............. | 26c | 229.9 | 240.9 | 251.6 | 356.4 | 441.3 | 357.5 | 385.5 | 395.1 | 345.1 | 511.7 | 608.3 | 719.2 |
| Claims on Central Bank.................... | 20 | 452.8 | 423.2 | 357.9 | 308.1 | 340.7 | 413.7 | 427.0 | 421.4 | 415.2 | 695.7 | 724.0 | 915.7 |
| Currency............................... | 20a | 24.7 | 24.0 | 26.2 | 29.0 | 33.0 | 32.9 | 33.3 | 33.0 | 32.5 | 34.9 | 35.7 | 41.2 |
| Reserve Deposits and Securities..... | 20b | 428.2 | 399.2 | 331.6 | 279.0 | 307.7 | 380.8 | 393.7 | 388.4 | 382.6 | 660.8 | 688.4 | 874.5 |
| Other Claims........................... | 20n | — | — | — | — | — | — | — | — | — | — | — | — |
| Net Claims on Central Government.. | 22an | 391.4 | 337.5 | 363.3 | 325.2 | 330.9 | 364.7 | 432.0 | 482.2 | 522.3 | 446.4 | 590.1 | 614.5 |
| Claims on Central Government...... | 22a | 438.0 | 403.5 | 420.4 | 430.3 | 457.7 | 532.7 | 585.3 | 661.3 | 760.5 | 726.7 | 769.8 | 666.8 |
| Liabilities to Central Government... | 26d | 46.6 | 66.1 | 57.1 | 105.1 | 126.8 | 168.1 | 153.3 | 179.1 | 238.1 | 280.3 | 179.7 | 52.2 |
| Claims on Other Sectors............... | 22s | 978.9 | 1,168.3 | 1,426.8 | 1,819.6 | 2,182.2 | 2,126.3 | 2,170.6 | 2,340.5 | 2,375.1 | 2,416.6 | 2,540.3 | 2,659.4 |
| Claims on Other Financial Corps..... | 22g | 160.9 | 176.6 | 196.6 | 290.4 | 396.9 | 299.1 | 271.7 | 323.8 | 300.0 | 266.4 | 338.7 | 316.7 |
| Claims on State & Local Govts....... | 22b | 27.9 | 32.1 | 35.8 | 36.9 | 38.2 | 49.1 | 49.5 | 54.1 | 55.2 | 53.8 | 52.6 | 51.4 |
| Claims on Public Nonfin. Corps...... | 22c | — | — | — | — | — | — | — | — | — | — | — | — |
| Claims on Private Sector.............. | 22d | 790.1 | 959.7 | 1,194.4 | 1,492.4 | 1,747.1 | 1,778.0 | 1,849.4 | 1,962.6 | 2,019.9 | 2,096.4 | 2,149.0 | 2,291.3 |
| Liabilities to Central Bank.............. | 26g | .1 | 29.2 | .2 | — | 38.0 | — | 1.5 | 3.5 | — | — | — | — |
| Transf.Dep.Included in Broad Money | 24 | 787.2 | 897.3 | 1,028.4 | 1,200.1 | 1,306.9 | 1,415.1 | 1,660.8 | 1,768.6 | 1,945.4 | 2,108.1 | 2,370.6 | 2,633.5 |
| Other Dep.Included in Broad Money. | 25 | 607.8 | 651.3 | 722.1 | 851.7 | 1,027.0 | 934.8 | 736.5 | 682.9 | 631.9 | 627.6 | 526.9 | 493.8 |
| Sec.Ot.th.Shares Incl.in Brd. Money.. | 26a | .3 | .1 | 1.4 | 1.3 | .8 | 1.7 | 1.0 | 2.7 | 3.1 | 2.1 | — | — |
| Deposits Excl. from Broad Money..... | 26b | 340.2 | 332.6 | 301.9 | 266.0 | 154.7 | 231.8 | 259.8 | 299.1 | 300.1 | 293.5 | 270.3 | 256.7 |
| Sec.Ot.th.Shares Excl.f/Brd.Money.... | 26s | 26.5 | 59.9 | 65.1 | 102.9 | 91.0 | 88.0 | 97.8 | 115.1 | 109.9 | 110.5 | 113.1 | 131.2 |
| Loans................................ | 26l | — | — | — | — | — | — | — | — | — | — | — | — |
| Financial Derivatives...................... | 26m | 57.1 | 49.1 | 64.5 | 85.3 | 196.3 | 123.6 | 107.4 | 150.3 | 124.9 | 104.2 | 124.1 | 94.3 |
| Insurance Technical Reserves........... | 26r | — | — | — | — | — | — | — | — | — | — | — | — |
| Shares and Other Equity.................. | 27a | 198.5 | 227.5 | 243.3 | 275.3 | 282.1 | 315.0 | 337.1 | 355.7 | 399.6 | 444.1 | 478.5 | 495.1 |
| Other Items (Net)........................... | 27r | 34.7 | 33.6 | 34.6 | 7.4 | 12.2 | 28.0 | 43.2 | 54.9 | 85.7 | 62.6 | 91.7 | 90.6 |
| Memo Item: | | | | | | | | | | | | | |
| Total Assets............................. | 20ra | 2,706.1 | 2,990.2 | 3,218.5 | 3,794.5 | 4,221.4 | 4,284.1 | 4,393.8 | 4,651.1 | 4,821.2 | 5,235.1 | 5,421.6 | 5,583.9 |

# Czech Republic 935

| | | 2004 | 2005 | 2006 | 2007 | 2008 | 2009 | 2010 | 2011 | 2012 | 2013 | 2014 | 2015 |
|---|---|---|---|---|---|---|---|---|---|---|---|---|---|
| **Depository Corporations** | | | | | | *Billions of Koruny: End of Period* | | | | | | | |
| Net Foreign Assets.................... | 31n | 863.1 | 1,076.2 | 972.5 | 970.2 | 974.9 | 980.4 | 992.2 | 969.4 | 1,124.7 | 1,290.7 | 1,318.8 | 1,541.4 |
| Claims on Nonresidents................ | 31 | 1,116.6 | 1,404.1 | 1,305.6 | 1,423.8 | 1,417.7 | 1,362.8 | 1,406.4 | 1,394.8 | 1,497.3 | 1,828.9 | 1,979.6 | 2,332.6 |
| Liabilities to Nonresidents............. | 36c | 253.5 | 327.9 | 333.1 | 453.6 | 442.8 | 382.4 | 414.2 | 425.4 | 372.6 | 538.2 | 660.8 | 791.2 |
| Domestic Claims........................ | 32 | 1,322.5 | 1,357.2 | 1,642.4 | 1,974.6 | 2,345.2 | 2,394.3 | 2,485.3 | 2,752.9 | 2,775.7 | 2,840.5 | 3,129.5 | 3,164.3 |
| Net Claims on Central Government | 32an | 312.4 | 163.0 | 206.9 | 146.1 | 154.3 | 259.5 | 311.1 | 408.9 | 397.2 | 420.9 | 586.3 | 502.4 |
| Claims on Central Government.... | 32a | 451.2 | 407.6 | 420.4 | 430.3 | 457.7 | 532.7 | 585.3 | 661.3 | 760.5 | 726.7 | 769.8 | 666.8 |
| Liabilities to Central Government. | 36d | 138.8 | 244.6 | 213.5 | 284.2 | 303.3 | 273.2 | 274.2 | 252.5 | 363.3 | 305.8 | 183.5 | 164.4 |
| Claims on Other Sectors................ | 32s | 1,010.0 | 1,194.2 | 1,435.5 | 1,828.5 | 2,190.8 | 2,134.8 | 2,174.2 | 2,344.0 | 2,378.5 | 2,419.6 | 2,543.2 | 2,661.9 |
| Claims on Other Financial Corps.. | 32g | 191.5 | 201.9 | 204.8 | 298.6 | 405.0 | 307.1 | 274.8 | 326.9 | 303.0 | 269.2 | 341.5 | 319.0 |
| Claims on State & Local Govts..... | 32b | 27.9 | 32.1 | 35.8 | 36.9 | 38.2 | 49.1 | 49.5 | 54.1 | 55.2 | 53.8 | 52.6 | 51.4 |
| Claims on Public Nonfin. Corps.... | 32c | — | — | — | — | — | — | — | — | — | — | — | — |
| Claims on Private Sector............. | 32d | 790.7 | 960.2 | 1,194.9 | 1,492.9 | 1,747.6 | 1,778.5 | 1,849.9 | 1,963.0 | 2,020.3 | 2,096.6 | 2,149.2 | 2,291.5 |
| Broad Money Liabilities............... | 35l | 1,634.9 | 1,814.7 | 2,049.7 | 2,380.0 | 2,703.4 | 2,709.1 | 2,760.0 | 2,836.0 | 2,971.8 | 3,144.5 | 3,330.7 | 3,595.5 |
| Currency Outside Depository Corps | 34a | 236.8 | 263.8 | 295.3 | 324.1 | 365.5 | 353.6 | 357.5 | 377.9 | 388.9 | 405.4 | 432.2 | 467.1 |
| Transferable Deposits................... | 34 | 789.5 | 899.0 | 1,030.4 | 1,202.5 | 1,309.5 | 1,418.3 | 1,664.2 | 1,771.8 | 1,947.4 | 2,108.9 | 2,371.1 | 2,634.1 |
| Other Deposits.......................... | 35 | 608.3 | 651.8 | 722.6 | 852.2 | 1,027.6 | 935.6 | 737.2 | 683.5 | 632.5 | 628.1 | 527.4 | 494.3 |
| Securities Other than Shares.......... | 36a | .3 | .1 | 1.4 | 1.3 | .8 | 1.7 | 1.0 | 2.7 | 3.1 | 2.1 | — | — |
| Deposits Excl. from Broad Money..... | 36b | 340.2 | 332.6 | 301.9 | 266.0 | 154.7 | 231.8 | 259.8 | 299.1 | 300.1 | 293.5 | 270.3 | 256.7 |
| Sec.Ot.th.Shares Excl.f/Brd.Money.... | 36s | 26.5 | 59.9 | 65.1 | 102.9 | 91.0 | 88.0 | 97.8 | 115.1 | 109.9 | 110.5 | 113.1 | 131.2 |
| Loans...................................... | 36l | — | — | — | — | — | — | — | — | — | — | — | — |
| Financial Derivatives................... | 36m | 57.1 | 49.1 | 64.5 | 85.3 | 196.3 | 123.6 | 107.4 | 150.3 | 124.9 | 104.2 | 124.1 | 94.3 |
| Insurance Technical Reserves.......... | 36r | — | — | — | — | — | — | — | — | — | — | — | — |
| Shares and Other Equity................ | 37a | 102.1 | 151.6 | 106.5 | 100.7 | 135.6 | 186.8 | 194.6 | 248.3 | 295.5 | 412.8 | 503.9 | 519.7 |
| Other Items (Net)........................ | 37r | 24.7 | 25.4 | 27.1 | 9.8 | 38.8 | 35.1 | 57.8 | 73.3 | 98.0 | 65.7 | 106.2 | 108.3 |
| Broad Money Liabs., Seasonally Adj. | 35l.b | 1,636.9 | 1,813.8 | 2,043.5 | 2,366.2 | 2,681.9 | 2,684.9 | 2,735.2 | 2,812.6 | 2,949.1 | 3,122.6 | 3,308.5 | 3,568.6 |
| **Monetary Aggregates** | | | | | | *Billions of Koruny: End of Period* | | | | | | | |
| Broad Money.............................. | 59m | 1,634.9 | 1,814.7 | 2,049.7 | 2,380.0 | 2,703.4 | 2,709.1 | 2,760.0 | 2,836.0 | 2,971.8 | 3,144.5 | 3,330.7 | 3,595.5 |
| o/w:Currency Issued by Cent.Govt | 59m.a | — | — | — | — | — | — | — | — | — | — | — | — |
| o/w: Dep.in Nonfin. Corporations. | 59m.b | — | — | — | — | — | — | — | — | — | — | — | — |
| o/w:Secs. Issued by Central Govt.. | 59m.c | — | — | — | — | — | — | — | — | — | — | — | — |
| Money (National Definitions) | | | | | | | | | | | | | |
| M1.......................................... | 59ma | 1,026.30 | 1,162.75 | 1,325.61 | 1,526.50 | 1,674.80 | 1,771.90 | 2,021.73 | 2,149.76 | 2,335.55 | 2,511.83 | 2,803.25 | 3,101.20 |
| M2.......................................... | 59mb | 1,578.89 | 1,746.15 | 1,984.60 | 2,308.60 | 2,633.00 | 2,651.40 | 2,707.99 | 2,818.98 | 2,948.29 | 3,095.43 | 3,301.16 | 3,578.00 |
| M3.......................................... | 59mc | 1,634.87 | 1,814.65 | 2,049.64 | 2,380.00 | 2,705.40 | 2,711.10 | 2,759.97 | 2,836.29 | 2,970.69 | 3,142.00 | 3,330.67 | 3,595.50 |
| **Interest Rates** | | | | | | *Percent Per Annum* | | | | | | | |
| Repurchase Agreement Rate (EOP)... | 60.q | 2.50 | 2.00 | 2.50 | 3.50 | 2.25 | 1.00 | .75 | .75 | .05 | .05 | .05 | .05 |
| Money Market Rate...................... | 60b | 2.39 | 1.99 | 2.32 | 3.17 | 4.04 | 2.13 | 1.30 | 1.19 | .98 | .45 | .36 | .31 |
| Treasury Bill Rate........................ | 60c | 2.26 | 1.95 | 2.14 | 2.84 | 3.62 | 1.29 | .95 | .83 | .62 | . . . . | . . . . | . . . . |
| Deposit Rate.............................. | 60l | 1.28 | 1.17 | 1.19 | 1.32 | 1.61 | 1.27 | 1.08 | 1.04 | 1.02 | .86 | .70 | .53 |
| Lending Rate.............................. | 60p | 6.03 | 5.78 | 5.59 | 5.79 | 6.25 | 5.99 | 5.89 | 5.72 | 5.41 | 4.97 | 4.64 | 4.28 |
| Government Bond Yield................. | 61 | 4.05 | 3.61 | 3.68 | 4.65 | 4.30 | 3.98 | 3.89 | 3.70 | 2.12 | 2.20 | .67 | .49 |
| **Prices, Production, Labor** | | | | | | *Index Numbers (2010=100): Period Averages* | | | | | | | |
| Share Prices.............................. | 62 | 70.6 | 107.0 | 126.2 | 151.5 | 116.0 | 82.1 | 100.0 | 94.8 | 81.0 | 83.1 | 84.5 | 85.1 |
| Producer Prices........................... | 63 | 89.8 | 92.5 | 94.0 | 97.9 | 102.0 | 98.8 | 100.0 | 105.6 | 107.8 | 108.7 | 107.9 | 104.4 |
| Consumer Prices......................... | 64 | 85.4 | 87.0 | 89.2 | 91.8 | 97.6 | 98.6 | 100.0 | 101.9 | 105.3 | 106.8 | 107.2 | 107.5 |
| Harmonized CPI........................... | 64h | 86.6 | 87.9 | 89.8 | 92.4 | 98.2 | 98.8 | 100.0 | 102.2 | 105.8 | 107.2 | 107.7 | 108.0 |
| Wages..................................... | 65 | 73.2 | 76.9 | 81.9 | 87.8 | 94.7 | 97.8 | 100.0 | 102.5 | 105.0 | 104.9 | 108.0 | 110.9 |
| Industrial Production.................... | 66 | 87.2 | 90.6 | 98.1 | 108.6 | 106.6 | 92.1 | 100.0 | 105.9 | 105.0 | 104.9 | 110.1 | 115.2 |
| Industrial Employment.................. | 67 | 104.3 | 104.6 | 106.6 | 107.4 | 104.8 | 93.2 | 100.0 | 108.0 | 104.8 | 103.9 | 106.6 | 108.2 |
| | | | | | | *Number in Thousands: Period Averages* | | | | | | | |
| Labor Force................................ | 67d | 5,101 | 5,118 | 5,140 | 5,132 | 5,163 | 5,209 | 5,192 | 5,146 | 5,175 | 5,214 | 5,206 | 5,201 |
| Employment............................... | 67e | 4,682 | 4,710 | 4,770 | 4,856 | 4,934 | 4,857 | 4,810 | 4,797 | 4,811 | 4,846 | 4,884 | 4,935 |
| Unemployment........................... | 67c | 426 | 410 | 372 | 276 | 230 | 352 | 384 | 351 | 367 | 370 | 324 | 268 |
| Unemployment Rate (%)................. | 67r | 8.3 | 7.9 | 7.1 | 5.3 | 4.4 | 6.7 | 7.3 | 6.7 | 7.0 | 7.0 | 6.1 | 5.1 |
| **Intl. Transactions & Positions** | | | | | | *Millions of Koruny* | | | | | | | |
| Exports.................................... | 70 | 1,722,657 | 1,868,586 | 2,144,573 | 2,479,234 | 2,473,736 | 2,138,623 | 2,532,797 | 2,878,691 | 3,072,598 | 3,174,704 | 3,628,826 | 3,901,698 |
| Imports, c.i.f............................... | 71 | 1,836,550 | 1,829,962 | 2,104,812 | 2,391,319 | 2,406,489 | 1,989,036 | 2,411,556 | 2,687,563 | 2,766,888 | 2,823,485 | 3,199,630 | 3,476,221 |
| Imports, f.o.b.............................. | 71.v | 1,749,095 | 1,804,630 | 2,075,880 | 2,355,055 | 2,366,847 | 1,924,062 | 2,330,064 | 2,601,641 | 2,680,827 | 2,732,197 | 3,096,415 | 3,361,039 |

| | | 2004 | 2005 | 2006 | 2007 | 2008 | 2009 | 2010 | 2011 | 2012 | 2013 | 2014 | 2015 |
|---|---|---|---|---|---|---|---|---|---|---|---|---|---|
| **Balance of Payments** | | | | | | | *Millions of US Dollars* | | | | | | |
| A. Current Account* | 109bx | −5,749.4 | −1,209.6 | −3,130.4 | −7,940.2 † | −4,407.9 | −4,869.8 | −7,351.2 | −5,020.0 | −3,158.5 | −1,105.8 | 438.0 | 1,683.4 |
| Goods, credit (exports) | 1a9cx | 55,929.6 | 64,535.4 | 78,384.9 | 98,787.4 † | 126,345.4 | 101,025.9 | 115,073.3 | 137,892.7 | 134,125.0 | 136,995.4 | 146,624.3 | 131,048.9 |
| Goods, debit (imports) | 1a9dx | 59,243.0 | 63,700.2 | 77,047.3 | 98,004.9 † | 126,415.0 | 97,660.1 | 112,974.3 | 133,616.1 | 127,786.1 | 128,468.6 | 135,923.2 | 122,483.5 |
| Balance on goods | 1a9bx | −3,313.5 | 835.2 | 1,337.6 | 782.5 † | −69.6 | 3,365.7 | 2,099.0 | 4,276.5 | 6,338.8 | 8,526.7 | 10,701.0 | 8,565.4 |
| Services, credit (exports) | 1b9cx | 12,265.1 | 12,989.6 | 15,375.6 | 18,804.9 † | 23,746.0 | 20,607.1 | 21,956.5 | 24,928.7 | 24,235.8 | 23,983.0 | 25,071.9 | 22,714.8 |
| Services, debit (imports) | 1b9dx | 8,845.0 | 10,164.2 | 11,976.0 | 14,429.0 † | 18,456.4 | 16,272.6 | 17,863.2 | 20,310.7 | 20,265.5 | 20,386.0 | 22,356.4 | 19,663.9 |
| Balance on Goods & Services | 1z9bx | 106.6 | 3,660.5 | 4,737.2 | 5,158.4 † | 5,220.0 | 7,700.2 | 6,192.3 | 8,894.6 | 10,309.3 | 12,123.7 | 13,416.5 | 11,616.4 |
| Primary income: credit | 1c9cx | 3,404.5 | 4,874.9 | 6,262.2 | 8,468.3 † | 11,026.6 | 6,435.5 | 6,081.5 | 7,125.4 | 7,821.5 | 6,891.7 | 7,417.8 | 7,303.9 |
| Primary income: debit | 1c9dx | 9,496.6 | 9,948.2 | 13,297.6 | 20,485.8 † | 19,962.1 | 17,952.2 | 19,052.2 | 20,028.1 | 19,890.3 | 19,602.8 | 20,043.1 | 17,204.7 |
| Balance on gds, serv. & prim. inc. | 1y9bx | −5,985.4 | −1,412.7 | −2,298.2 | −6,859.2 † | −3,715.6 | −3,816.6 | −6,778.4 | −4,008.1 | −1,759.6 | −587.3 | 791.2 | 1,715.5 |
| Secondary income: credit | 1d9ca | 2,081.5 | 2,506.9 | 1,684.2 | 2,024.9 † | 2,983.8 | 2,609.3 | 3,127.8 | 3,234.3 | 2,813.2 | 3,841.5 | 3,873.8 | 3,564.8 |
| Secondary income: debit | 1d9da | 1,845.4 | 2,303.8 | 2,516.4 | 3,105.9 † | 3,676.1 | 3,662.5 | 3,700.7 | 4,246.3 | 4,212.1 | 4,360.1 | 4,227.0 | 3,596.9 |
| B. Capital Account* | 209ba | −605.7 | 185.5 | 403.7 | 1,013.5 † | 1,558.6 | 2,726.9 | 1,953.0 | 682.6 | 2,719.4 | 4,215.9 | 1,571.7 | 4,301.7 |
| Capital account: credit | 209ca | 208.8 | 282.3 | 695.7 | 1,101.0 † | 2,352.3 | 2,813.2 | 2,293.3 | 1,003.6 | 3,156.6 | 4,289.8 | 1,586.8 | 4,309.2 |
| Capital account: debit | 209da | 814.5 | 96.7 | 291.9 | 87.4 † | 793.7 | 86.3 | 340.3 | 321.0 | 437.2 | 73.9 | 15.2 | 7.5 |
| Balance on current & capital acct. | 129ba | −6,355.0 | −1,024.1 | −2,726.6 | −6,926.7 † | −2,849.3 | −2,142.8 | −5,398.2 | −4,337.4 | −439.1 | 3,110.1 | 2,009.7 | 5,985.2 |
| C. Financial Account* | 309na | −7,035.7 | −6,588.1 | −4,540.1 | −6,404.4 † | −4,862.2 | −8,522.0 | −8,521.0 | −3,450.6 | −3,516.3 | −6,075.3 | −421.3 | −6,456.7 |
| Direct investment: assets | 3a9aa | 1,037.5 | −26.8 | 1,479.1 | 1,642.3 † | 6,557.8 | 3,320.1 | 5,249.4 | 1,596.2 | 3,252.6 | 7,737.6 | 4,074.2 | 3,564.5 |
| Equity & investment fund shares.. | 3aaaa | 813.0 | 166.6 | 1,513.8 | 1,298.6 † | 4,430.0 | 806.3 | 834.4 | −106.6 | 1,956.1 | 3,297.0 | 2,651.8 | 1,852.2 |
| Debt instruments | 3abaa | 224.5 | −193.4 | −34.7 | 343.7 † | 2,127.8 | 2,513.7 | 4,415.0 | 1,702.8 | 1,296.6 | 4,440.6 | 1,422.5 | 1,712.2 |
| Direct investment: liabilities | 3a9la | 4,977.8 | 11,602.0 | 5,521.8 | 10,606.1 † | 8,815.4 | 5,271.6 | 10,167.8 | 4,188.7 | 9,433.2 | 7,357.6 | 8,088.7 | 2,478.5 |
| Equity & investment fund shares . | 3aala | 4,729.2 | 10,894.0 | 5,804.0 | 9,470.4 † | 3,505.3 | 4,586.1 | 6,323.8 | 1,032.8 | 7,271.0 | 6,165.9 | 3,329.9 | 3,158.3 |
| Debt instruments | 3abla | 248.6 | 707.9 | −282.2 | 1,135.7 † | 5,310.0 | 685.5 | 3,844.0 | 3,155.9 | 2,162.3 | 1,191.7 | 4,758.8 | −679.9 |
| Portfolio investment: assets | 3b9aa | 2,806.4 | 3,466.7 | 3,004.3 | 4,848.5 † | 498.1 | −3,418.8 | −632.0 | 817.9 | 1,382.3 | 97.1 | 3,668.0 | 2,923.5 |
| Equity & investment fund shares | 3baaa | 1,447.6 | 1,472.5 | 1,938.0 | 3,213.4 † | 794.2 | −1,091.0 | 112.8 | −131.9 | 228.5 | 524.2 | 1,594.3 | 1,733.2 |
| Debt securities | 3bbaa | 1,358.9 | 1,994.2 | 1,066.3 | 1,635.1 † | −296.2 | −2,327.8 | −744.9 | 949.8 | 1,153.7 | −427.1 | 2,073.7 | 1,190.2 |
| Portfolio investment: liabilities | 3b9la | 4,794.7 | 78.5 | 1,876.9 | 2,161.4 † | 457.5 | 5,168.9 | 7,098.5 | 1,179.9 | 4,168.5 | 4,820.5 | −735.7 | 9,613.8 |
| Equity & investment fund shares . | 3bala | 737.5 | −1,540.4 | 268.5 | −268.4 † | −1,124.5 | −310.9 | −231.4 | −1.7 | −148.3 | 106.4 | 270.2 | 181.3 |
| Debt securities | 3bbla | 4,057.2 | 1,618.9 | 1,608.5 | 2,429.8 † | 1,582.2 | 5,479.8 | 7,330.1 | 1,181.5 | 4,316.7 | 4,714.2 | −1,006.0 | 9,432.5 |
| Fin. der.& empl.stk.ops.(ESOs): net | 3c9na | 145.7 | −7.9 | −30.3 | −65.9 † | 123.1 | 59.7 | 261.1 | 166.9 | −443.3 | −241.2 | −291.0 | −196.5 |
| Fin. der. & ESOs: assets | 3c9aa | 660.0 | −352.6 | −618.8 | −1,279.5 † | −3,635.7 | −2,663.1 | −3,615.3 | −1,611.6 | −1,876.4 | −1,250.0 | −1,519.6 | −1,655.0 |
| Fin. der. & ESOs.: liabilities | 3c9la | 514.3 | −344.8 | −588.6 | −1,213.6 † | −3,758.8 | −2,722.8 | −3,876.5 | −1,778.5 | −1,433.1 | −1,008.9 | −1,228.6 | −1,458.5 |
| Other investment: assets | 3d9aa | 1,072.4 | 4,727.9 | 1,479.7 | 7,128.7 † | 5,778.8 | −243.2 | 5,084.4 | 2,928.7 | 3,935.3 | 4,344.6 | 2,156.9 | −705.3 |
| Other equity | 3daaa | .... | .... | .... | .... † | .... | .... | .... | .... | .... | — | .8 | 21.2 |
| Debt instruments | 3dzaa | 1,072.4 | 4,727.9 | 1,479.7 | 7,128.7 † | 5,778.8 | −243.2 | 5,084.4 | 2,928.7 | 3,935.3 | 4,344.6 | 2,156.0 | −726.4 |
| Other investment: liabilities | 3d9la | 2,325.3 | 3,067.6 | 3,074.2 | 7,190.6 † | 8,546.8 | −2,200.7 | 1,217.5 | 3,591.6 | −1,958.6 | 5,835.4 | 2,676.3 | −49.5 |
| Other equity | 3dala | | | | | | | | | | | | |
| Debt instruments | 3dzla | 2,325.3 | 3,067.6 | 3,074.2 | 7,190.6 † | 8,546.8 | −2,200.7 | 1,217.5 | 3,591.6 | −1,958.6 | 5,835.4 | 2,676.3 | −49.5 |
| Curr.+ cap.− finan. acct. balance... | 4y9na | 680.7 | 5,564.0 | 1,813.5 | −523.3 † | 2,012.9 | 6,379.1 | 3,122.9 | −886.8 | 3,077.2 | 9,185.4 | 2,430.9 | 12,441.9 |
| D. Net Errors and Omissions | 409na | −418.1 | −1,685.3 | −1,721.4 | 1,393.9 † | 407.1 | −2,094.5 | −1,046.6 | −113.3 | 1,109.2 | 428.4 | 1,109.2 | 1,846.1 |
| E. Reserves and Related Items | 4z9na | 262.6 | 3,878.7 | 92.1 | 871.6 † | 2,420.0 | 4,284.6 | 2,076.2 | −1,000.3 | 4,186.4 | 9,613.6 | 3,540.1 | 14,288.0 |
| Reserve assets | 3e9aa | 262.6 | 3,878.7 | 92.1 | 871.6 † | 2,420.0 | 4,284.6 | 2,076.2 | −1,000.3 | 4,186.4 | 9,613.6 | 3,540.1 | 14,288.0 |
| Credit and loans from the IMF | 3dcla | — | | | | † — | | | | | | — | — |
| Exceptional financing | 409la | — | .... | .... | .... | .... | .... | .... | .... | .... | .... | — | — |

*Excludes components in group E

| | | 2004 | 2005 | 2006 | 2007 | 2008 | 2009 | 2010 | 2011 | 2012 | 2013 | 2014 | 2015 |
|---|---|---|---|---|---|---|---|---|---|---|---|---|---|
| **International Investment Position** | | | | | | | *Millions of US Dollars* | | | | | | |
| Assets | 809aa | 69,276.4 | 76,273.1 | 90,450.8 | 117,194.6 † | 135,699.8 | 143,959.0 | 151,302.7 | 149,213.5 | 167,375.6 | 187,838.1 | 181,874.5 | 184,599.6 |
| Direct investment | 8a9aa | 3,759.8 | 3,610.4 | 5,017.4 | 8,557.4 † | 24,810.5 | 30,637.2 | 34,532.6 | 33,427.6 | 40,011.0 | 46,000.6 | 42,977.5 | 41,476.5 |
| Equity & investment fund shares.. | 8aaaa | 3,159.6 | 3,256.1 | 4,634.5 | 7,757.4 † | 11,851.1 | 13,975.4 | 13,764.8 | 12,340.4 | 16,623.3 | 19,231.1 | 18,227.1 | 18,055.1 |
| Debt instruments | 8abaa | 600.2 | 354.3 | 383.0 | 800.0 † | 12,959.4 | 16,661.9 | 20,767.8 | 21,087.2 | 23,387.7 | 26,769.6 | 24,750.4 | 23,421.4 |
| Portfolio investment | 8b9aa | 16,643.8 | 19,025.9 | 25,491.6 | 34,219.8 † | 26,110.7 | 24,847.0 | 24,179.6 | 22,618.7 | 25,755.3 | 26,307.0 | 27,900.6 | 28,677.0 |
| Equity & investment fund shares.. | 8baaa | 3,403.6 | 5,976.8 | 9,691.6 | 14,204.0 † | 9,805.7 | 10,147.1 | 11,046.1 | 9,491.5 | 10,342.9 | 11,399.9 | 12,350.0 | 13,243.0 |
| Debt securities | 8bbaa | 13,240.2 | 13,049.1 | 15,800.0 | 20,015.8 † | 16,305.0 | 14,699.3 | 13,133.4 | 13,127.1 | 15,412.4 | 14,907.1 | 15,550.6 | 15,434.0 |
| Fin. der.(oth.than reserves) & ESOs | 8c9aa | 1,774.9 | 1,730.8 | 2,558.3 | 3,845.8 † | 7,522.2 | 5,600.3 | 5,068.3 | 6,450.1 | 4,932.8 | 2,797.7 | 4,388.3 | 3,081.3 |
| Other investment | 8d9aa | 18,648.4 | 22,350.9 | 25,929.2 | 35,666.2 † | 40,243.5 | 41,263.4 | 45,029.6 | 46,426.7 | 51,793.3 | 56,515.8 | 52,115.2 | 46,873.9 |
| Other equity | 8daaa | .... | .... | .... | .... | † 164.1 | .... | 174.5 | 194.2 | 203.4 | 221.8 | 685.7 | 589.5 |
| Debt instruments | 8dzaa | 18,648.4 | 22,350.9 | 25,929.2 | 35,666.2 † | 40,079.4 | 41,088.9 | 44,835.4 | 46,223.3 | 51,571.5 | 55,830.1 | 51,513.4 | 46,284.4 |
| Reserve assets | 8e9aa | 28,449.5 | 29,555.2 | 31,454.3 | 34,905.3 † | 37,012.9 | 41,611.0 | 42,492.6 | 40,290.5 | 44,883.3 | 56,216.9 | 54,492.8 | 64,491.0 |
| Liabilities | 809la | 106,162.7 | 110,332.1 | 142,360.9 | 195,627.7 † | 214,984.6 | 237,900.9 | 248,511.8 | 240,625.4 | 265,202.6 | 273,047.1 | 250,989.1 | 240,854.1 |
| Direct investment | 8a9la | 57,258.9 | 60,662.3 | 79,841.0 | 112,408.0 † | 125,452.8 | 141,660.1 | 148,114.1 | 140,782.5 | 159,136.2 | 159,458.6 | 145,999.6 | 136,052.9 |
| Equity & investment fund shares.. | 8aala | 50,160.6 | 53,526.2 | 71,731.5 | 101,914.2 † | 100,821.3 | 113,463.9 | 116,649.7 | 108,309.2 | 122,940.2 | 123,617.1 | 110,485.8 | 104,752.1 |
| Debt instruments | 8abla | 7,098.3 | 7,136.1 | 8,109.5 | 10,493.8 † | 24,631.6 | 28,196.2 | 31,464.4 | 32,473.3 | 36,196.0 | 35,841.6 | 35,513.8 | 31,300.9 |
| Portfolio investment | 8b9la | 17,036.4 | 17,805.7 | 23,375.9 | 30,774.6 † | 26,263.6 | 35,574.7 | 41,641.7 | 40,112.6 | 45,515.9 | 49,217.2 | 43,802.1 | 49,726.7 |
| Equity & investment fund shares.. | 8bala | 9,339.2 | 8,967.6 | 11,572.8 | 14,521.5 † | 9,292.6 | 11,410.7 | 10,627.3 | 9,329.7 | 8,955.4 | 7,770.2 | 7,291.5 | 6,679.9 |
| Debt securities | 8bbla | 7,697.2 | 8,838.1 | 11,803.0 | 16,253.1 † | 16,971.0 | 24,164.0 | 31,014.4 | 30,782.9 | 36,560.5 | 41,447.0 | 36,510.7 | 43,046.8 |
| Fin. der.(oth.than reserves) & ESOs | 8c9la | 1,422.1 | 1,296.1 | 1,747.6 | 2,999.4 † | 8,611.7 | 6,536.3 | 5,803.9 | 7,020.1 | 5,560.6 | 4,284.2 | 4,202.3 | 3,271.3 |
| Other investment | 8d9la | 30,445.3 | 30,568.1 | 37,396.5 | 49,445.8 † | 54,656.6 | 54,129.9 | 52,952.1 | 52,710.2 | 54,989.9 | 60,087.2 | 56,985.1 | 51,803.2 |
| Other equity | 8dala | .... | .... | .... | .... | .... | .... | .... | .... | .... | .... | — | — |
| Debt instruments | 8dzla | 30,445.3 | 30,568.1 | 37,396.5 | 49,445.8 † | 54,656.6 | 54,129.9 | 52,952.1 | 52,710.2 | 54,989.9 | 60,087.2 | 56,985.1 | 51,803.2 |

|  |  | 2004 | 2005 | 2006 | 2007 | 2008 | 2009 | 2010 | 2011 | 2012 | 2013 | 2014 | 2015 |
|---|---|---|---|---|---|---|---|---|---|---|---|---|---|
| **Government Finance Operations Statement General Government** |  | *Millions of Koruny: Fiscal Year Ends December 31; Data Reported through Eurostat* | | | | | | | | | | | |
| Revenue | a1 | 1,205,780 | 1,261,048 | 1,351,743 | 1,504,282 | 1,527,919 | 1,494,421 | 1,524,277 | 1,626,020 | 1,646,284 | 1,694,779 | 1,738,921 | 1,886,314 |
| Taxes | a11 | 601,286 | 626,745 | 657,163 | 735,196 | 722,649 | 695,541 | 702,754 | 763,431 | 784,146 | 815,590 | 826,014 | 886,709 |
| Social Contributions | a12 | 452,801 | 482,132 | 524,783 | 576,714 | 599,173 | 559,659 | 577,806 | 592,514 | 600,265 | 606,639 | 628,548 | 662,912 |
| Grants | a13 | .... | .... | .... | .... | .... | .... | .... | .... | .... | .... | .... | .... |
| Other Revenue | a14 | .... | .... | .... | .... | .... | .... | .... | .... | .... | .... | .... | .... |
| Expense | a2 | 1,298,120 | 1,359,663 | 1,423,183 | 1,534,353 | 1,593,003 | 1,692,422 | 1,705,421 | 1,751,161 | 1,835,654 | 1,793,126 | 1,857,772 | 1,882,015 |
| Compensation of Employees | a21 | 222,237 | 238,039 | 252,520 | 268,688 | 279,780 | 293,042 | 285,830 | 349,916 | 359,397 | 366,707 | 379,553 | 397,949 |
| Use of Goods & Services | a22 | 184,352 | 189,486 | 204,635 | 212,115 | 222,227 | 230,258 | 226,692 | 280,873 | 259,179 | 269,831 | 274,009 | 285,645 |
| Consumption of Fixed Capital | a23 | 149,653 | 154,910 | 160,155 | 169,659 | 178,508 | 185,522 | 185,057 | 195,994 | 196,499 | 197,568 | 201,200 | 206,800 |
| Interest | a24 | 32,798 | 35,232 | 36,423 | 41,163 | 40,229 | 48,794 | 52,596 | 53,023 | 57,831 | 55,017 | 56,136 | 48,372 |
| Subsidies | a25 | 59,371 | 55,066 | 61,431 | 62,421 | 64,153 | 76,255 | 79,046 | 91,141 | 91,121 | 95,779 | 99,399 | 102,121 |
| Grants | a26 | .... | .... | .... | .... | .... | .... | .... | .... | .... | .... | .... | .... |
| Social Benefits | a27 | 522,604 | 544,346 | 580,569 | 643,578 | 673,829 | 727,809 | 739,783 | 651,133 | 663,190 | 677,951 | 695,191 | 712,137 |
| Other Expense | a28 | .... | .... | .... | .... | .... | .... | .... | .... | .... | .... | .... | .... |
| Gross Operating Balance [1-2+23] | agob | 57,313 | 56,295 | 88,715 | 139,588 | 113,424 | −12,479 | 3,913 | 70,853 | 7,129 | 99,221 | 82,349 | 211,099 |
| Net Operating Balance [1-2] | anob | −92,340 | −98,615 | −71,440 | −30,071 | −65,084 | −198,001 | −181,144 | −125,141 | −189,370 | −98,347 | −118,851 | 4,299 |
| Net Acq. of Nonfinancial Assets | a31 | −9,444 | 2,738 | 7,639 | −3,468 | 19,526 | 18,238 | −6,627 | −15,245 | −29,818 | −47,218 | −35,788 | 22,981 |
| Aquisition of Nonfin. Assets | a31.1 | .... | .... | .... | .... | .... | .... | .... | .... | .... | .... | .... | .... |
| Disposal of Nonfin. Assets | a31.2 | .... | .... | .... | .... | .... | .... | .... | .... | .... | .... | .... | .... |
| Net Lending/Borrowing [1-2-31] | anlb | −82,896 | −101,353 | −79,079 | −26,603 | −84,610 | −216,239 | −174,517 | −109,896 | −159,552 | −51,129 | −83,063 | −18,682 |
| Net Acq. of Financial Assets | a32 | 17,148 | −27,343 | 1,154 | 82,011 | 47,499 | 4,794 | −4,251 | 13,869 | 153,351 | −18,823 | −102,873 | 20,087 |
| By instrument |  | | | | | | | | | | | | |
| Monetary Gold & SDRs | a3201 | — | — | — | — | — | — | — | — | — | — | — | — |
| Currency & Deposits | a3202 | 31,122 | 121,252 | −17,092 | 76,966 | 74,252 | −63,015 | −10,217 | −35,749 | 129,986 | −26,105 | −105,892 | 4,132 |
| Securities other than Shares | a3203 | 12,301 | −4,264 | −2,301 | 3,935 | −4,201 | 170 | −5,849 | −558 | −1,774 | −1,478 | −1,784 | 252 |
| Loans | a3204 | −11,171 | −50,026 | −8,120 | −1,038 | 4,728 | 9,462 | 19,461 | 7,040 | 2,595 | 6,862 | 964 | −5,187 |
| Shares & Other Equity | a3205 | −5,275 | −106,950 | −2,163 | −17,337 | −23,350 | −8,825 | 741 | −273 | 1,825 | 1,324 | 964 | −4,160 |
| Insurance Technical Reserves | a3206 | 244 | 151 | 91 | 150 | 99 | 116 | 88 | 56 | 154 | 472 | 543 | 259 |
| Financial Derivatives | a3207 | 876 | 1,808 | 2,710 | 2,361 | 5,326 | 4,047 | 83 | 2,179 | 1,087 | 1,446 | 862 | 507 |
| Other Accounts Receivable | a3208 | −10,949 | 10,686 | 28,029 | 16,974 | −9,355 | 62,839 | −8,558 | 41,174 | 19,478 | −1,344 | 1,470 | 24,284 |
| By debtor |  | | | | | | | | | | | | |
| Domestic | a321 | .... | .... | .... | .... | .... | .... | .... | .... | .... | .... | .... | .... |
| Foreign | a322 | .... | .... | .... | .... | .... | .... | .... | .... | .... | .... | .... | .... |
| Net Incurrence of Liabilities | a33 | 100,044 | 74,010 | 80,233 | 108,614 | 132,109 | 221,033 | 170,266 | 123,765 | 312,903 | 32,306 | −23,214 | 39,481 |
| By instrument |  | | | | | | | | | | | | |
| Special Drawing Rights (SDRs) | a3301 | — | — | — | — | — | — | — | — | — | — | — | — |
| Currency & Deposits | a3302 | 1,372 | −3,014 | −425 | 2,331 | 193 | −934 | 1,264 | −5,256 | 5,189 | −1,701 | 3,102 | −4,645 |
| Securities other than Shares | a3303 | 102,072 | 72,904 | 93,822 | 96,826 | 77,152 | 168,989 | 181,094 | 131,094 | 218,380 | 23,778 | −10,193 | 33,926 |
| Loans | a3304 | −23,777 | −22,319 | −22,969 | −7,536 | 1,918 | 21,781 | 5,844 | 3,111 | −529 | −771 | −8,510 | −3,468 |
| Shares & Other Equity | a3305 | — | — | — | — | — | 300 | — | — | −1,894 | — | — | — |
| Insurance Technical Reserves | a3306 | — | — | — | — | — | — | — | 1,097 | 1,275 | 1,893 | 1,247 | −950 |
| Financial Derivatives | a3307 | 484 | 411 | −261 | 86 | 170 | −1,278 | −3,608 | −452 | −4,982 | −4,689 | −6,459 | −152 |
| Other Accounts Payable | a3308 | 19,893 | 26,028 | 10,066 | 16,908 | 52,676 | 32,175 | −14,328 | −5,829 | 95,464 | 13,796 | −2,401 | 14,770 |
| By creditor |  | | | | | | | | | | | | |
| Domestic | a331 | .... | .... | .... | .... | .... | .... | .... | .... | .... | .... | .... | .... |
| Foreign | a332 | .... | .... | .... | .... | .... | .... | .... | .... | .... | .... | .... | .... |
| Stat. Discrepancy [32-33-NLB] | anlbz | — | — | — | — | — | — | — | — | — | — | 3,404 | −712 |
| Memo Item: Expenditure [2+31] | a2m | 1,288,676 | 1,362,401 | 1,430,822 | 1,530,885 | 1,612,529 | 1,710,660 | 1,698,794 | 1,735,916 | 1,805,836 | 1,745,908 | 1,821,984 | 1,904,996 |
| **Balance Sheet** |  | | | | | | | | | | | | |
| Net Worth | a6 | .... | .... | .... | .... | .... | .... | .... | .... | .... | .... | .... | .... |
| Nonfinancial Assets | a61 | .... | .... | .... | .... | .... | .... | .... | .... | .... | .... | .... | .... |
| Financial Assets | a62 | 1,302,151 | 1,423,683 | 1,533,454 | 1,733,468 | 1,621,651 | 1,680,249 | 1,578,867 | 1,597,266 | 1,695,977 | 1,640,047 | 1,583,470 | 1,554,952 |
| By instrument |  | | | | | | | | | | | | |
| Monetary Gold & SDRs | a6201 | — | — | — | — | — | — | — | — | — | — | — | — |
| Currency & Deposits | a6202 | 225,194 | 343,406 | 324,284 | 400,054 | 477,321 | 414,800 | 329,311 | 400,684 | 529,686 | 507,991 | 402,531 | 403,736 |
| Securities other than Shares | a6203 | 17,439 | 13,288 | 10,969 | 14,661 | 10,368 | 10,502 | 7,047 | 12,973 | 11,996 | 11,228 | 14,033 | 15,061 |
| Loans | a6204 | 142,914 | 90,267 | 78,425 | 75,914 | 73,166 | 81,030 | 97,451 | 113,432 | 113,870 | 128,208 | 133,512 | 128,601 |
| Shares and Other Equity | a6205 | 673,995 | 729,571 | 845,061 | 990,353 | 804,862 | 854,973 | 857,372 | 717,029 | 666,621 | 623,627 | 648,425 | 602,219 |
| Insurance Technical Reserves | a6206 | 527 | 557 | 597 | 994 | 802 | 1,176 | 1,244 | 1,694 | 1,804 | 2,644 | 2,531 | 2,802 |
| Financial Derivatives | a6207 | 2,019 | 4,013 | 6,999 | 9,820 | 14,098 | 17,720 | 2,507 | 2,923 | 3,294 | 364 | 408 | 886 |
| Other Accounts Receivable | a6208 | 240,063 | 242,581 | 267,119 | 241,672 | 241,034 | 300,048 | 283,935 | 348,531 | 368,706 | 365,985 | 382,030 | 401,647 |
| By debtor |  | | | | | | | | | | | | |
| Domestic | a621 | .... | .... | .... | .... | .... | .... | .... | .... | .... | .... | .... | .... |
| Foreign | a622 | .... | .... | .... | .... | .... | .... | .... | .... | .... | .... | .... | .... |
| Liabilities | a63 | 992,040 | 1,049,284 | 1,122,548 | 1,176,316 | 1,388,214 | 1,624,466 | 1,829,867 | 1,968,935 | 2,368,735 | 2,381,479 | 2,452,318 | 2,457,451 |
| By instrument |  | | | | | | | | | | | | |
| Special Drawing Rights (SDRs) | a6301 | — | — | — | — | — | — | — | — | — | — | — | — |
| Currency & Deposits | a6302 | 6,981 | 4,101 | 3,331 | 5,295 | 5,700 | 4,726 | 6,013 | 3,410 | 8,502 | 6,853 | 9,974 | 5,353 |
| Securities other than Shares | a6303 | 643,250 | 714,047 | 801,185 | 893,617 | 997,463 | 1,183,757 | 1,384,586 | 1,498,051 | 1,802,519 | 1,814,838 | 1,881,874 | 1,882,049 |
| Loans | a6304 | 212,129 | 185,660 | 160,114 | 152,076 | 155,427 | 175,360 | 180,545 | 195,408 | 194,921 | 195,070 | 187,971 | 184,032 |
| Shares and Other Equity | a6305 | 500 | 500 | 500 | 500 | 500 | 800 | 800 | 1,578 | — | — | — | — |
| Insurance Technical Reserves | a6306 | — | — | — | — | — | — | — | 7,959 | 9,234 | 11,265 | 7,971 | 8,687 |
| Financial Derivatives | a6307 | 6,270 | 10,460 | 14,515 | 16,646 | 14,367 | 15,182 | 18,649 | 17,146 | 18,899 | 6,218 | 4,681 | 1,845 |
| Other Accounts Payable | a6308 | 122,910 | 134,516 | 142,903 | 108,182 | 214,757 | 244,641 | 239,274 | 245,383 | 334,660 | 347,235 | 359,847 | 375,485 |
| By creditor |  | | | | | | | | | | | | |
| Domestic | a631 | .... | .... | .... | .... | .... | .... | .... | .... | .... | .... | .... | .... |
| Foreign | a632 | .... | .... | .... | .... | .... | .... | .... | .... | .... | .... | .... | .... |
| Net Financial Worth [62-63] | a6m2 | 310,111 | 374,399 | 410,906 | 557,152 | 233,437 | 55,783 | −251,000 | −371,669 | −672,758 | −741,432 | −868,848 | −902,499 |
| Memo Item: Debt at Market Value | a6m3 | 985,270 | 1,038,324 | 1,107,533 | 1,159,170 | 1,373,347 | 1,608,484 | 1,810,418 | 1,950,211 | 2,349,836 | 2,375,261 | 2,447,637 | 2,455,606 |
| Memo Item: Debt at Face Value | a6m35 | 992,944 | 1,047,275 | 1,121,773 | 1,173,691 | 1,365,484 | 1,580,320 | 1,747,792 | 1,851,875 | 2,140,089 | 2,187,647 | 2,178,945 | 2,211,651 |
| Memo Item: Maastricht Debt | a6m36 | 870,034 | 912,759 | 978,870 | 1,065,509 | 1,150,727 | 1,335,679 | 1,508,518 | 1,606,492 | 1,805,429 | 1,840,412 | 1,819,098 | 1,836,166 |
| Memo Item: Debt at Nominal Value | a6m4 | .... | .... | .... | .... | .... | .... | .... | .... | .... | .... | .... | .... |

# Czech Republic   935

| National Accounts | | 2004 | 2005 | 2006 | 2007 | 2008 | 2009 | 2010 | 2011 | 2012 | 2013 | 2014 | 2015 |
|---|---|---|---|---|---|---|---|---|---|---|---|---|---|
| | | *Billions of Koruny* | | | | | | | | | | | |
| Househ.Cons.Expend.,incl.NPISHs.... | 96f | 1,500.1 | 1,566.5 | 1,655.5 | 1,775.2 | 1,913.4 | 1,917.9 | 1,947.1 | 1,984.2 | 1,997.9 | 2,029.8 | 2,070.5 | 2,131.3 |
| Government Consumption Expend... | 91f | 634.1 | 664.5 | 699.7 | 731.6 | 765.5 | 811.7 | 809.7 | 792.1 | 782.7 | 801.5 | 828.2 | 861.3 |
| Gross Fixed Capital Formation......... | 93e | 860.9 | 921.8 | 983.0 | 1,132.4 | 1,165.3 | 1,063.5 | 1,066.0 | 1,069.0 | 1,052.1 | 1,024.8 | 1,065.5 | 1,153.2 |
| Changes in Inventories.................... | 93i | 37.6 | 28.5 | 72.8 | 98.7 | 84.1 | −23.6 | 8.4 | 18.3 | 9.1 | −15.2 | 10.4 | 38.9 |
| Exports of Goods and Services.......... | 90c | 1,756.0 | 2,030.2 | 2,289.9 | 2,550.2 | 2,544.3 | 2,306.5 | 2,616.4 | 2,880.7 | 3,097.2 | 3,150.3 | 3,571.4 | 3,778.5 |
| Imports of Goods and Services (-)..... | 98c | 1,731.1 | 1,953.5 | 2,193.6 | 2,456.3 | 2,457.2 | 2,154.2 | 2,493.9 | 2,721.9 | 2,897.5 | 2,914.1 | 3,285.1 | 3,490.9 |
| Gross Domestic Product (GDP)......... | 99b | 3,057.7 | 3,258.0 | 3,507.1 | 3,831.8 | 4,015.3 | 3,921.8 | 3,953.7 | 4,022.5 | 4,041.6 | 4,077.1 | 4,260.9 | 4,472.3 |
| Net Primary Income from Abroad..... | 98.n | −140.8 | −147.3 | −212.8 | −245.1 | −260.6 | −276.1 | −297.4 | −305.0 | −253.5 | −246.2 | −334.2 | −343.8 |
| Gross National Income (GNI)............ | 99a | 2,916.9 | 3,110.6 | 3,294.3 | 3,586.7 | 3,754.8 | 3,645.7 | 3,656.3 | 3,717.6 | 3,788.2 | 3,830.9 | 3,926.6 | 4,128.5 |
| Net Current Transf.from Abroad....... | 98t | −4.8 | −16.9 | −17.9 | −28.7 | −25.0 | −28.0 | −30.4 | −36.9 | −34.3 | −36.1 | −36.5 | −33.6 |
| Gross Nat'l Disposable Inc.(GNDI).... | 99i | 2,912.0 | 3,093.8 | 3,276.4 | 3,558.0 | 3,729.8 | 3,617.8 | 3,625.9 | 3,680.7 | 3,753.9 | 3,794.8 | 3,890.2 | 4,094.9 |
| Gross Saving.................................. | 99s | 777.8 | 862.8 | 921.2 | 1,051.2 | 1,050.9 | 888.1 | 869.1 | 904.4 | 973.3 | 963.5 | 991.5 | 1,102.3 |
| GDP Volume 2010 Ref., Chained..... | 99b.p | 3,293.9 | 3,506.1 | 3,747.2 | 3,954.4 | 4,061.6 | 3,864.9 | 3,953.7 | 4,031.4 | 3,995.1 | 3,974.0 | 4,052.6 | 4,222.8 |
| GDP Volume (2010=100)............... | 99bvp | 83.3 | 88.7 | 94.8 | 100.0 | 102.7 | 97.8 | 100.0 | 102.0 | 101.0 | 100.5 | 102.5 | 106.8 |
| GDP Deflator (2010=100)............... | 99bip | 92.8 | 92.9 | 93.6 | 96.9 | 98.9 | 101.5 | 100.0 | 99.8 | 101.2 | 102.6 | 105.1 | 105.9 |
| | | *Millions: Midyear Estimates* | | | | | | | | | | | |
| Population................................. | 99z | 10.21 | 10.23 | 10.27 | 10.33 | 10.40 | 10.46 | 10.51 | 10.53 | 10.55 | 10.55 | 10.54 | 10.54 |

| | | 2004 | 2005 | 2006 | 2007 | 2008 | 2009 | 2010 | 2011 | 2012 | 2013 | 2014 | 2015 |
|---|---|---|---|---|---|---|---|---|---|---|---|---|---|
| **Exchange Rates** | | | | | | *Kroner per SDR: End of Period* | | | | | | | |
| Market Rate................................... | aa | 8.491 | 9.039 | 8.517 | 8.020 | 8.140 | 8.136 | 8.645 | 8.821 | 8.698 | 8.336 | 8.869 | 9.465 |
| | | | | *Kroner per US Dollar: End of Period (ae) Period Average (rf)* | | | | | | | | | |
| Market Rate................................... | ae | 5.468 | 6.324 | 5.661 | 5.075 | 5.285 | 5.190 | 5.613 | 5.746 | 5.659 | 5.413 | 6.121 | 6.830 |
| Market Rate................................... | rf | 5.991 | 5.997 | 5.947 | 5.444 | 5.098 | 5.361 | 5.624 | 5.369 | 5.792 | 5.616 | 5.612 | 6.728 |
| | | | | *Kroner per Euro: End of Period (ea) Period Average (eb)* | | | | | | | | | |
| Euro Rate................................... | ea | 7.4334 | 7.4605 | 7.4560 | 7.4566 | 7.4506 | 7.4415 | 7.4544 | 7.4342 | 7.4604 | 7.4603 | 7.4436 | 7.4625 |
| Euro Rate................................... | eb | 7.4399 | 7.4518 | 7.4591 | 7.4508 | 7.4559 | 7.4463 | 7.4472 | 7.4507 | 7.4438 | 7.4579 | 7.4549 | 7.4586 |
| | | | | *Index Numbers (2010=100): Period Averages* | | | | | | | | | |
| Market Rate................................... | ahx | 93.8 | 93.8 | 94.5 | 103.3 | 110.7 | 105.0 | 100.0 | 104.7 | 97.0 | 100.0 | 100.2 | 83.5 |
| Nominal Effective Exchange Rate..... | nec | 98.9 | 98.1 | 98.1 | 99.8 | 102.0 | 103.9 | 100.0 | 99.6 | 97.1 | 98.9 | 100.1 | 96.8 |
| CPI-Based Real Effect. Ex. Rate........ | rec | 99.0 | 98.0 | 97.7 | 98.7 | 100.6 | 103.5 | 100.0 | 99.4 | 97.1 | 98.2 | 98.7 | 95.2 |
| ULC-Based Real Effect. Ex. Rate........ | rel | 102.9 | 104.8 | 104.8 | 108.4 | 106.8 | 106.7 | 100.0 | 96.6 | 96.1 | 99.1 | 101.5 | 99.6 |
| **Fund Position** | | | | | | *Millions of SDRs: End of Period* | | | | | | | |
| Quota......................................... | 2f.s | 1,642.80 | 1,642.80 | 1,642.80 | 1,642.80 | 1,642.80 | 1,642.80 | 1,642.80 | 1,891.40 | 1,891.40 | 1,891.40 | 1,891.40 | 1,891.40 |
| SDR Holdings............................. | 1b.s | 28.77 | 78.13 | 227.07 | 211.86 | 207.84 | 1,520.50 | 1,521.44 | 1,461.57 | 1,467.91 | 1,467.30 | 1,422.98 | 1,451.18 |
| Reserve Position in the Fund............ | 1c.s | 542.81 | 216.00 | 147.61 | 107.98 | 209.48 | 413.48 | 536.18 | 864.08 | 984.75 | 923.71 | 742.90 | 579.97 |
| Total Fund Cred. & Loans Outstg...... | 2tl | — | — | — | — | — | — | — | — | — | — | — | — |
| SDR Allocations........................... | 1bd | 178.86 | 178.86 | 178.86 | 178.86 | 178.86 | 1,531.47 | 1,531.47 | 1,531.47 | 1,531.47 | 1,531.47 | 1,531.47 | 1,531.47 |
| **International Liquidity** | | | | | *Millions of US Dollars Unless Otherwise Indicated: End of Period* | | | | | | | | |
| Total Reserves minus Gold.............. | 1l.d | 39,084 | † 32,930 | 29,724 | 32,534 | 40,466 | 74,291 | 73,503 | 81,680 | 86,138 | 86,099 | 72,812 | 62,917 |
| SDR Holdings............................. | 1b.d | 45 | 112 | 342 | 335 | 320 | 2,384 | 2,343 | 2,244 | 2,256 | 2,260 | 2,062 | 2,011 |
| Reserve Position in the Fund......... | 1c.d | 843 | 309 | 222 | 171 | 323 | 648 | 826 | 1,327 | 1,513 | 1,423 | 1,076 | 804 |
| Foreign Exchange....................... | 1d.d | 38,196 | † 32,510 | 29,160 | 32,029 | 39,823 | 71,259 | 70,334 | 78,109 | 82,368 | 82,417 | 69,674 | 60,102 |
| Gold (Million Fine Troy Ounces)....... | 1ad | 2.140 | 2.140 | 2.140 | 2.140 | 2.140 | 2.140 | 2.140 | 2.140 | 2.140 | 2.140 | 2.140 | 2.140 |
| Gold (National Valuation)............... | 1and | 970 | † 1,098 | 1,360 | 1,790 | 1,851 | 2,362 | 3,017 | 3,368 | 3,560 | 2,568 | 2,565 | 2,269 |
| Central Bank: Other Assets............. | 3..d | 26,925.7 | 25,238.2 | 17,787.8 | 21,529.0 | 26,582.7 | 36,476.4 | 22,410.3 | 24,367.7 | 48,540.6 | 42,099.5 | 24,207.4 | 17,944.9 |
| Central Bank: Other Liabs............... | 4..d | 321.2 | 404.6 | 722.6 | 1,016.5 | 22,865.9 | 966.5 | 819.5 | 822.2 | 797.7 | 904.2 | 796.5 | 601.6 |
| Other Depository Corps.: Assets....... | 7a.d | 128,646.6 | 134,516.1 | 178,610.2 | 253,365.9 | 248,465.1 | 220,614.6 | 210,159.6 | 192,284.2 | 195,236.3 | 225,703.8 | 201,813.1 | 176,431.9 |
| Other Depository Corps.: Liabs........ | 7b.d | 154,401.2 | 157,964.3 | 198,923.9 | 271,996.7 | 273,816.7 | 281,825.4 | 248,082.6 | 224,455.6 | 231,683.3 | 246,574.2 | 186,084.7 | 144,945.2 |
| **Central Bank** | | | | | | *Billions of Kroner: End of Period* | | | | | | | |
| Net Foreign Assets.......................... | 11n | 217.2 | 212.0 | 171.3 | 167.9 | 95.1 | 382.9 | 415.6 | 478.9 | 489.5 | 460.0 | 442.9 | 422.1 |
| Claims on Nonresidents................. | 11 | 220.5 | 216.1 | 176.9 | 174.5 | 217.4 | 400.4 | 433.4 | 497.1 | 507.4 | 477.7 | 461.4 | 440.7 |
| Liabilities to Nonresidents.............. | 16c | 3.3 | 4.2 | 5.6 | 6.6 | 122.3 | 17.5 | 17.8 | 18.2 | 17.8 | 17.7 | 18.5 | 18.6 |
| Claims on Other Depository Corps.... | 12e | 97.6 | 164.7 | 175.0 | 242.9 | 420.3 | 145.6 | 46.0 | 70.2 | 112.9 | 60.5 | 71.6 | 37.0 |
| Net Claims on Central Government.. | 12an | −42.6 | −43.2 | −60.5 | −82.5 | −256.3 | −208.2 | −176.1 | −222.9 | −161.2 | −161.5 | −213.1 | −157.4 |
| Claims on Central Government...... | 12a | 15.4 | 10.3 | 11.0 | 4.6 | 3.4 | 2.7 | 1.2 | .7 | .8 | .4 | .1 | .1 |
| Liabilities to Central Government... | 16d | 58.1 | 53.5 | 71.5 | 87.1 | 259.7 | 210.9 | 177.3 | 223.6 | 162.0 | 162.0 | 213.2 | 157.4 |
| Claims on Other Sectors............. | 12s | .4 | .4 | .4 | .5 | .5 | .6 | .7 | .7 | .6 | .4 | .1 | .1 |
| Claims on Other Financial Corps.... | 12g | .4 | .4 | .4 | .5 | .5 | .6 | .7 | .7 | .6 | .4 | .1 | .1 |
| Claims on State & Local Govts....... | 12b | — | — | — | — | — | — | — | — | — | — | — | — |
| Claims on Public Nonfin. Corps...... | 12c | — | — | — | — | — | — | — | — | — | — | — | — |
| Claims on Private Sector............... | 12d | — | — | — | — | — | — | — | — | — | — | — | — |
| Monetary Base............................... | 14 | 61.5 | 71.0 | 69.6 | 72.3 | 92.6 | 91.6 | 83.5 | 99.5 | 189.2 | 132.4 | 104.4 | 135.4 |
| Currency in Circulation.................. | 14a | 52.0 | 56.2 | 59.8 | 61.6 | 61.3 | 60.8 | 62.5 | 62.4 | 65.8 | 66.5 | 67.3 | 70.2 |
| Liabs. to Other Depository Corps.... | 14c | 9.1 | 14.2 | 9.6 | 10.3 | 30.7 | 28.3 | 14.0 | 30.9 | 111.6 | 58.9 | 29.3 | 50.3 |
| Liabilities to Other Sectors............ | 14d | .4 | .6 | .3 | .4 | .6 | 2.5 | 6.9 | 6.2 | 11.9 | 7.1 | 7.8 | 15.0 |
| Other Liabs. to Other Dep. Corps..... | 14n | 160.4 | 207.6 | 163.2 | 200.5 | 118.5 | 166.2 | 132.5 | 150.0 | 184.1 | 168.0 | 124.8 | 94.1 |
| Dep. & Sec. Excl. f/Monetary Base.... | 14o | — | — | — | — | — | — | — | — | — | — | — | — |
| Deposits Included in Broad Money. | 15 | — | — | — | — | — | — | — | — | — | — | — | — |
| Sec.Ot.th.Shares Incl.in Brd. Money | 16a | — | — | — | — | — | — | — | — | — | — | — | — |
| Deposits Excl. from Broad Money... | 16b | — | — | — | — | — | — | — | — | — | — | — | — |
| Sec.Ot.th.Shares Excl.f/Brd.Money.. | 16s | — | — | — | — | — | — | — | — | — | — | — | — |
| Loans......................................... | 16l | — | — | — | — | — | — | — | — | — | — | — | — |
| Financial Derivatives...................... | 16m | — | — | — | — | — | — | — | — | — | — | — | — |
| Shares and Other Equity.................. | 17a | 52.8 | 57.2 | 55.5 | 58.5 | 62.0 | 63.6 | 70.0 | 72.8 | 74.4 | 64.3 | 69.8 | 72.0 |
| Other Items (Net).......................... | 17r | −3.2 | −1.9 | −2.0 | −2.3 | −13.6 | −.5 | .2 | 4.6 | −5.9 | −5.3 | 2.6 | .3 |

| | | 2004 | 2005 | 2006 | 2007 | 2008 | 2009 | 2010 | 2011 | 2012 | 2013 | 2014 | 2015 |
|---|---|---|---|---|---|---|---|---|---|---|---|---|---|
| **Other Depository Corporations** | | | | | | *Billions of Kroner: End of Period* | | | | | | | |
| Net Foreign Assets | 21n | −140.8 | −148.3 | −115.0 | −94.6 | −134.0 | −317.7 | −212.9 | −184.8 | −206.3 | −113.0 | 96.3 | 215.1 |
| Claims on Nonresidents | 21 | 703.4 | 850.7 | 1,011.2 | 1,285.9 | 1,313.1 | 1,145.0 | 1,179.7 | 1,104.8 | 1,104.9 | 1,221.7 | 1,235.4 | 1,205.0 |
| Liabilities to Nonresidents | 26c | 844.2 | 999.0 | 1,126.2 | 1,380.5 | 1,447.1 | 1,462.7 | 1,392.6 | 1,289.6 | 1,311.1 | 1,334.6 | 1,139.1 | 990.0 |
| Claims on Central Bank | 20 | 188.1 | 233.4 | 185.7 | 218.5 | 163.4 | 207.6 | 153.6 | 186.1 | 302.5 | 238.4 | 164.1 | 151.6 |
| Currency | 20a | 8.3 | 8.9 | 9.0 | 9.7 | 10.9 | 12.2 | 9.9 | 9.9 | 11.2 | 10.7 | 10.8 | 10.4 |
| Reserve Deposits and Securities | 20b | 19.4 | 16.9 | 13.5 | 8.4 | 34.0 | 29.2 | 11.2 | 26.2 | 107.1 | 59.6 | 28.5 | 47.1 |
| Other Claims | 20n | 160.4 | 207.6 | 163.2 | 200.5 | 118.5 | 166.2 | 132.5 | 150.0 | 184.1 | 168.0 | 124.8 | 94.1 |
| Net Claims on Central Government | 22an | 56.5 | 53.2 | 29.1 | 26.0 | 19.8 | 62.5 | 30.4 | 45.9 | 44.1 | 30.7 | 53.0 | 58.2 |
| Claims on Central Government | 22a | 71.5 | 66.8 | 42.2 | 40.8 | 38.9 | 80.4 | 46.8 | 58.1 | 58.1 | 41.3 | 63.4 | 67.6 |
| Liabilities to Central Government | 26d | 15.0 | 13.5 | 13.1 | 14.7 | 19.1 | 17.8 | 16.4 | 12.3 | 14.0 | 10.6 | 10.4 | 9.4 |
| Claims on Other Sectors | 22s | 2,597.5 | 2,922.3 | 3,308.5 | 3,793.5 | 4,543.7 | 4,230.0 | 4,384.3 | 4,567.8 | 4,483.9 | 4,270.6 | 4,481.4 | 4,448.7 |
| Claims on Other Financial Corps. | 22g | 321.0 | 333.8 | 365.0 | 485.9 | 988.6 | 646.7 | 764.6 | 985.7 | 901.7 | 723.8 | 911.9 | 855.1 |
| Claims on State & Local Govts. | 22b | 83.1 | 89.8 | 99.7 | 99.6 | 110.9 | 117.4 | 123.9 | 124.0 | 131.5 | 131.1 | 135.6 | 137.3 |
| Claims on Public Nonfin. Corps. | 22c | — | — | — | — | — | — | — | — | — | — | — | — |
| Claims on Private Sector | 22d | 2,193.4 | 2,498.6 | 2,843.8 | 3,208.0 | 3,444.2 | 3,466.0 | 3,495.8 | 3,458.1 | 3,450.7 | 3,415.8 | 3,433.9 | 3,456.2 |
| Liabilities to Central Bank | 26g | 111.9 | 177.2 | 195.3 | 247.3 | 382.7 | 148.9 | 46.7 | 66.9 | 100.0 | 59.0 | 69.3 | 41.8 |
| Transf.Dep.Included in Broad Money | 24 | 492.5 | 595.8 | 648.5 | 702.8 | 702.2 | 742.2 | 741.1 | 721.1 | 785.1 | 815.2 | 876.4 | 962.7 |
| Other Dep.Included in Broad Money | 25 | 142.2 | 148.6 | 171.6 | 229.3 | 310.2 | 234.0 | 220.7 | 211.2 | 178.6 | 174.4 | 179.8 | 140.9 |
| Sec.Ot.th.Shares Incl.in Brd. Money | 26a | 20.9 | 8.4 | 21.4 | 61.2 | 55.4 | 142.3 | 240.3 | 195.7 | 180.9 | 45.1 | 131.7 | 198.1 |
| Deposits Excl. from Broad Money | 26b | 140.8 | 161.4 | 175.0 | 190.9 | 197.1 | 236.0 | 248.5 | 257.1 | 268.3 | 261.8 | 248.4 | 232.9 |
| Sec.Ot.th.Shares Excl.f/Brd.Money | 26s | 1,340.0 | 1,541.6 | 1,699.5 | 1,822.6 | 1,814.2 | 1,947.7 | 2,007.8 | 2,116.1 | 2,142.6 | 2,250.1 | 2,250.4 | 2,335.6 |
| Loans | 26l | — | — | — | — | — | — | — | — | — | — | — | — |
| Financial Derivatives | 26m | 198.9 | 174.5 | 164.8 | 250.0 | 634.4 | 374.7 | 423.0 | 670.2 | 572.6 | 352.6 | 562.7 | 484.0 |
| Insurance Technical Reserves | 26r | — | — | — | — | — | — | — | — | — | — | — | — |
| Shares and Other Equity | 27a | 236.8 | 271.2 | 353.5 | 452.5 | 445.4 | 440.9 | 449.0 | 422.1 | 445.2 | 434.1 | 437.1 | 494.0 |
| Other Items (Net) | 27r | 17.8 | −16.2 | −21.5 | −15.9 | 50.5 | −87.3 | −24.7 | −47.9 | −48.6 | 34.0 | 38.9 | −16.4 |
| Memo Item: | | | | | | | | | | | | | |
| Total Assets | 20ra | 4,683.0 | 5,562.2 | 6,104.4 | 7,247.7 | 8,129.9 | 8,226.4 | 8,486.8 | 8,514.0 | 8,636.8 | 7,808.9 | 8,058.6 | 7,647.4 |
| **Depository Corporations** | | | | | | *Billions of Kroner: End of Period* | | | | | | | |
| Net Foreign Assets | 31n | 76.4 | 63.7 | 56.3 | 73.4 | −38.9 | 65.3 | 202.7 | 294.0 | 283.3 | 347.1 | 539.2 | 637.1 |
| Claims on Nonresidents | 31 | 923.9 | 1,066.8 | 1,188.1 | 1,460.4 | 1,530.5 | 1,545.4 | 1,613.1 | 1,601.9 | 1,612.2 | 1,699.4 | 1,696.8 | 1,645.7 |
| Liabilities to Nonresidents | 36c | 847.5 | 1,003.2 | 1,131.8 | 1,387.1 | 1,569.4 | 1,480.2 | 1,410.4 | 1,307.9 | 1,329.0 | 1,352.3 | 1,157.6 | 1,008.6 |
| Domestic Claims | 32 | 2,611.8 | 2,932.8 | 3,277.5 | 3,737.5 | 4,307.7 | 4,085.0 | 4,239.3 | 4,391.4 | 4,367.4 | 4,140.2 | 4,321.4 | 4,349.7 |
| Net Claims on Central Government | 32an | 13.9 | 10.1 | −31.4 | −56.4 | −236.5 | −145.7 | −145.8 | −177.0 | −117.1 | −130.9 | −160.1 | −99.1 |
| Claims on Central Government | 32a | 87.0 | 77.1 | 53.2 | 45.4 | 42.3 | 83.1 | 48.0 | 58.8 | 58.9 | 41.7 | 63.5 | 67.7 |
| Liabilities to Central Government | 36d | 73.1 | 67.0 | 84.6 | 101.8 | 278.8 | 228.8 | 193.7 | 235.8 | 176.0 | 172.6 | 223.6 | 166.8 |
| Claims on Other Sectors | 32s | 2,597.9 | 2,922.7 | 3,308.9 | 3,794.0 | 4,544.2 | 4,230.7 | 4,385.0 | 4,568.4 | 4,484.5 | 4,271.1 | 4,481.5 | 4,448.8 |
| Claims on Other Financial Corps. | 32g | 321.4 | 334.3 | 365.5 | 486.3 | 989.1 | 647.4 | 765.3 | 986.4 | 902.3 | 724.2 | 912.0 | 855.2 |
| Claims on State & Local Govts. | 32b | 83.1 | 89.8 | 99.7 | 99.6 | 110.9 | 117.4 | 123.9 | 124.0 | 131.5 | 131.1 | 135.6 | 137.3 |
| Claims on Public Nonfin. Corps. | 32c | — | — | — | — | — | — | — | — | — | — | — | — |
| Claims on Private Sector | 32d | 2,193.5 | 2,498.6 | 2,843.8 | 3,208.0 | 3,444.2 | 3,466.0 | 3,495.8 | 3,458.1 | 3,450.7 | 3,415.8 | 3,433.9 | 3,456.3 |
| Broad Money Liabilities | 35l | 699.7 | 800.5 | 892.4 | 1,045.6 | 1,118.8 | 1,169.5 | 1,261.6 | 1,186.7 | 1,211.0 | 1,097.5 | 1,252.3 | 1,376.4 |
| Currency Outside Depository Corps | 34a | 43.7 | 47.3 | 50.7 | 51.9 | 50.4 | 48.5 | 52.6 | 52.5 | 54.6 | 55.8 | 56.5 | 59.8 |
| Transferable Deposits | 34 | 492.9 | 596.3 | 648.7 | 703.3 | 702.8 | 744.7 | 748.0 | 727.4 | 797.0 | 822.3 | 884.2 | 977.6 |
| Other Deposits | 35 | 142.2 | 148.6 | 171.6 | 229.3 | 310.2 | 234.0 | 220.7 | 211.2 | 178.6 | 174.4 | 179.8 | 140.9 |
| Securities Other than Shares | 36a | 20.9 | 8.4 | 21.4 | 61.2 | 55.4 | 142.3 | 240.3 | 195.7 | 180.9 | 45.1 | 131.7 | 198.1 |
| Deposits Excl. from Broad Money | 36b | 140.8 | 161.4 | 175.0 | 190.9 | 197.1 | 236.0 | 248.5 | 257.1 | 268.3 | 261.8 | 248.4 | 232.9 |
| Sec.Ot.th.Shares Excl.f/Brd.Money | 36s | 1,340.0 | 1,541.6 | 1,699.5 | 1,822.6 | 1,814.2 | 1,947.7 | 2,007.8 | 2,116.1 | 2,142.6 | 2,250.1 | 2,250.4 | 2,335.6 |
| Loans | 36l | — | — | — | — | — | — | — | — | — | — | — | — |
| Financial Derivatives | 36m | 198.9 | 174.5 | 164.8 | 250.0 | 634.4 | 374.7 | 423.0 | 670.2 | 572.6 | 352.6 | 562.7 | 484.0 |
| Insurance Technical Reserves | 36r | — | — | — | — | — | — | — | — | — | — | — | — |
| Shares and Other Equity | 37a | 289.6 | 328.4 | 409.0 | 511.0 | 507.5 | 504.6 | 518.9 | 494.9 | 519.6 | 498.4 | 507.0 | 566.0 |
| Other Items (Net) | 37r | 18.6 | −8.3 | −7.0 | −12.0 | −4.0 | −85.3 | −20.9 | −41.9 | −63.0 | 26.5 | 40.0 | −8.0 |
| Broad Money Liabs., Seasonally Adj. | 35l.b | 722.6 | 823.8 | 914.8 | 1,068.8 | 1,142.6 | 1,195.4 | 1,291.0 | 1,215.7 | 1,240.0 | 1,122.6 | 1,279.1 | 1,405.1 |
| **Monetary Aggregates** | | | | | | *Billions of Kroner: End of Period* | | | | | | | |
| Broad Money | 59m | 699.7 | 800.5 | 892.4 | 1,045.6 | 1,118.8 | 1,169.5 | 1,261.6 | 1,186.7 | 1,211.0 | 1,097.5 | 1,252.3 | 1,376.4 |
| o/w:Currency Issued by Cent.Govt | 59m.a | — | — | — | — | — | — | — | — | — | — | — | — |
| o/w: Dep.in Nonfin. Corporations. | 59m.b | — | — | — | — | — | — | — | — | — | — | — | — |
| o/w:Secs. Issued by Central Govt. | 59m.c | — | — | — | — | — | — | — | — | — | — | — | — |
| Money (National Definitions) | | | | | | | | | | | | | |
| M1 | 59ma | 536.55 | 643.54 | 699.27 | 755.10 | 755.19 | 820.30 | 800.40 | 775.20 | 851.40 | 879.59 | 946.69 | 1,037.46 |
| M2 | 59mb | 676.72 | 775.99 | 860.08 | 972.76 | 1,059.95 | 1,023.10 | 962.30 | 928.20 | 986.20 | 1,024.81 | 1,088.12 | 1,152.90 |
| M3 | 59mc | 698.96 | 798.70 | 889.47 | 1,040.61 | 1,121.09 | 1,177.10 | 1,261.80 | 1,182.50 | 1,211.10 | 1,191.90 | 1,341.02 | 1,500.61 |
| **Interest Rates** | | | | | | *Percent Per Annum* | | | | | | | |
| Central Bank Policy Rate (EOP) | 60 | 2.00 | 2.25 | 3.50 | 4.00 | 3.50 | 1.00 | .75 | .75 | — | — | — | — |
| Money Market Rate | 60b | 2.16 | 2.20 | 3.18 | † 4.33 | 4.88 | 1.81 | .70 | † .89 | .08 | −.02 | .06 | −.13 |
| Government Bond Yield | 61 | 4.31 | 3.40 | 3.81 | 4.29 | 4.28 | 3.59 | 2.93 | 2.73 | 1.40 | 1.75 | 1.33 | .69 |
| Mortgage Bond Yield | 61a | 5.01 | 4.59 | 4.62 | 5.12 | 5.62 | 5.09 | 4.19 | 4.06 | 3.11 | 2.80 | . . . . | . . . . |
| **Prices, Production, Labor** | | | | | | *Index Numbers (2010=100): Period Averages* | | | | | | | |
| Share Prices | 62 | 69.0 | 89.6 | 106.8 | 132.4 | 102.4 | 75.1 | 100.0 | 100.9 | 108.4 | 130.1 | 188.7 | 270.0 |
| Share Prices (End of Month) | 62.ep | 69.0 | 90.1 | 107.3 | 132.8 | 101.2 | 75.4 | 100.0 | 101.2 | 108.6 | 130.6 | 215.5 | 279.5 |
| Prices: Home & Import Goods | 63 | 80.8 | † 84.1 | 90.4 | 92.2 | 103.9 | 93.1 | 100.0 | 108.6 | 111.1 | 112.9 | 111.8 | 107.7 |
| Prices: Home Goods | 63a | 77.8 | † 81.2 | 87.6 | 89.0 | 100.7 | 94.0 | 100.0 | 107.8 | 110.5 | 113.0 | 110.3 | 103.2 |
| Consumer Prices | 64 | 88.4 | 90.0 | 91.7 | 93.3 | 96.5 | 97.8 | 100.0 | 102.8 | 105.2 | 106.1 | 106.7 | 107.1 |
| Harmonized CPI | 64h | 88.7 | 90.3 | 91.9 | 93.4 | 96.8 | 97.8 | 100.0 | 102.7 | 105.1 | 105.6 | 106.0 | 106.2 |
| Wages: Hourly Earnings | 65..c | 82.5 | † 84.9 | 87.5 | 90.9 | 94.9 | 97.8 | 100.0 | 101.8 | 103.4 | 104.7 | 106.1 | 107.6 |
| Industrial Production | 66 | 113.1 | 116.3 | 120.1 | 117.1 | 115.2 | 98.1 | 100.0 | 101.8 | 101.9 | 102.4 | 103.2 | 104.5 |
| | | | | | | *Number in Thousands: Period Averages* | | | | | | | |
| Labor Force | 67d | 2,893 | 2,846 | 2,875 | 2,869 | 2,908 | 2,901 | 2,872 | 2,864 | 2,840 | 2,824 | 2,832 | 2,859 |
| Employment | 67e | 2,742 | 2,706 | 2,762 | 2,759 | 2,807 | 2,724 | 2,654 | 2,643 | 2,621 | 2,622 | 2,640 | 2,678 |
| Unemployment | 67c | 161 | 141 | 109 | † 100 | 71 | 125 | 160 | 159 | 159 | 150 | 131 | 135 |
| Unemployment Rate (%) | 67r | 5.8 | 5.1 | 3.9 | † 3.6 | 2.6 | 4.7 | 6.0 | 6.0 | 6.0 | 5.6 | 4.9 | 4.9 |

Denmark 128

| | | 2004 | 2005 | 2006 | 2007 | 2008 | 2009 | 2010 | 2011 | 2012 | 2013 | 2014 | 2015 |
|---|---|---|---|---|---|---|---|---|---|---|---|---|---|
| **Intl. Transactions & Positions** | | | | | | | *Millions of Kroner* | | | | | | |
| Exports | 70 | 452,400 | 491,479 | 538,296 | 551,637 | 586,893 | 490,066 | 538,321 | 600,069 | 614,674 | 625,217 | 619,090 | 633,887 |
| Imports, c.i.f. | 71 | 400,125 | 435,127 | 499,949 | 528,959 | 553,294 | 429,697 | 467,473 | 517,249 | 534,301 | 552,269 | 555,628 | 568,402 |
| | | | | | | | *2010=100* | | | | | | |
| Volume of Exports | 72 | 91.7 | 96.5 | 102.7 | 109.4 | 107.9 | 95.1 | 100.0 | 106.4 | 106.7 | 109.6 | 113.0 | 117.1 |
| Volume of Imports | 73 | 91.4 | 99.2 | 109.8 | 119.2 | 114.5 | 92.1 | 100.0 | 109.0 | 110.6 | 115.1 | 117.2 | 123.7 |
| Unit Value of Exports | 74 | 91.5 | 96.3 | 98.4 | 97.6 | 101.0 | 95.5 | 100.0 | 103.9 | 107.6 | 105.5 | 102.2 | 101.0 |
| Unit Value of Imports | 75 | 94.0 | 97.8 | 100.5 | 103.0 | 104.0 | 97.8 | 100.0 | 103.6 | 104.5 | 102.1 | 101.8 | 100.0 |
| Import Prices | 76.x | 88.2 | † 91.6 | 94.6 | 96.4 | 100.5 | 95.2 | 100.0 | 105.9 | 108.3 | 106.1 | 104.3 | 105.6 |
| **Balance of Payments** | | | | | | | *Millions of US Dollars* | | | | | | |
| A. Current Account* | 109bx | 5,940.8 | 11,103.9 | 8,218.4 | 4,413.6 | 10,000.3 | 10,767.0 | 18,182.6 | 19,874.6 | 18,749.8 | † 24,248.2 | 21,421.5 | 20,691.3 |
| Goods, credit (exports) | 1a9cx | 75,050.2 | 82,485.5 | 90,732.4 | 100,882.3 | 115,137.0 | 91,108.1 | 95,029.9 | 111,245.3 | 105,449.5 | † 111,671.3 | 111,390.6 | 95,971.2 |
| Goods, debit (imports) | 1a9dx | 65,523.6 | 75,152.6 | 87,683.9 | 100,462.1 | 114,226.8 | 82,126.3 | 85,904.7 | 101,102.1 | 96,947.4 | † 99,785.6 | 101,342.7 | 85,023.5 |
| Balance on goods | 1a9bx | 9,526.6 | 7,333.0 | 3,048.4 | 420.2 | 910.2 | 8,981.8 | 9,125.2 | 10,143.2 | 8,502.1 | † 11,885.8 | 10,047.9 | 10,947.8 |
| Services, credit (exports) | 1b9cx | 36,304.3 | 43,371.5 | 52,307.6 | 61,594.3 | 72,777.9 | 56,243.3 | 61,211.2 | 66,494.4 | 65,999.3 | † 70,686.1 | 72,468.5 | 61,389.5 |
| Services, debit (imports) | 1b9dx | 33,401.0 | 37,002.2 | 45,231.6 | 54,119.7 | 62,583.0 | 52,338.1 | 52,310.2 | 58,643.1 | 58,179.7 | † 63,268.8 | 64,229.8 | 53,772.3 |
| Balance on Goods & Services | 1z9bx | 12,429.9 | 13,702.3 | 10,124.5 | 7,894.7 | 11,105.0 | 12,887.1 | 18,026.3 | 17,994.5 | 16,321.7 | † 19,303.1 | 18,286.5 | 18,564.9 |
| Primary income: credit | 1c9cx | 12,784.1 | 24,928.9 | 27,764.0 | 34,683.0 | 38,522.6 | 25,573.4 | 26,781.6 | 30,918.6 | 27,722.2 | † 32,463.8 | 31,299.1 | 28,599.1 |
| Primary income: debit | 1c9dx | 15,113.8 | 23,331.1 | 24,910.4 | 32,850.5 | 33,957.8 | 22,356.6 | 21,021.9 | 23,124.4 | 19,332.8 | † 20,434.4 | 21,485.0 | 21,038.6 |
| Balance on gds, serv. & prim. inc. | 1y9bx | 10,100.3 | 15,300.1 | 12,978.1 | 9,727.3 | 15,669.8 | 16,103.9 | 23,786.0 | 25,788.8 | 24,711.0 | † 31,332.5 | 28,100.6 | 26,125.4 |
| Secondary income: credit | 1d9ca | 5,119.5 | 3,562.0 | 3,576.7 | 3,936.2 | 4,657.5 | 4,569.0 | 3,871.1 | 4,334.3 | 4,090.3 | † 3,370.3 | 3,321.1 | 2,853.3 |
| Secondary income: debit | 1d9da | 9,279.0 | 7,758.2 | 8,336.4 | 9,249.9 | 10,327.0 | 9,905.9 | 9,474.5 | 10,248.4 | 10,051.6 | † 10,454.5 | 10,000.3 | 8,287.5 |
| B. Capital Account* | 209ba | 13.2 | 518.0 | 6.3 | 49.3 | 72.9 | –49.0 | 82.9 | 1,090.3 | 90.5 | † 10.2 | –55.9 | 98.5 |
| Capital account: credit | 209ca | 511.4 | 1,032.3 | 457.8 | 435.0 | 492.8 | 474.7 | 450.8 | 1,507.6 | 453.7 | † 214.2 | 193.3 | 196.7 |
| Capital account: debit | 209da | 498.2 | 514.3 | 451.5 | 385.7 | 419.9 | 523.7 | 367.9 | 417.3 | 363.2 | † 204.0 | 249.2 | 98.2 |
| Balance on current & capital acct. | 129ba | 5,954.0 | 11,621.8 | 8,224.7 | 4,462.9 | 10,073.2 | 10,718.0 | 18,265.5 | 20,964.9 | 18,840.3 | † 24,258.5 | 21,365.5 | 20,789.8 |
| C. Financial Account* | 309na | 19,023.2 | 10,579.0 | 8,608.8 | 4,124.7 | –10,498.1 | –26,358.6 | –5,326.8 | 7,887.3 | 17,345.5 | † 30,148.7 | 35,340.3 | 24,472.4 |
| Direct investment: assets | 3a9aa | –9,929.9 | 16,206.4 | 8,146.1 | 19,995.3 | 14,324.3 | 5,861.0 | –266.1 | 12,795.1 | 7,964.1 | † 9,763.0 | 8,401.9 | 10,893.2 |
| Equity & investment fund shares | 3aaaa | 2,813.5 | 11,753.5 | 8,167.4 | 14,137.1 | –4,952.2 | 6,734.4 | –2,185.6 | 1,388.2 | 14,526.4 | † 9,344.8 | 7,282.4 | 10,611.0 |
| Debt instruments | 3abaa | –12,743.5 | 4,453.0 | –21.3 | 5,858.1 | 19,276.5 | –873.4 | 1,919.5 | 11,406.8 | –6,562.3 | † 418.4 | 1,119.2 | 282.4 |
| Direct investment: liabilities | 3a9la | –8,804.2 | 12,834.3 | 2,419.9 | 11,809.4 | 2,191.2 | 3,918.2 | –11,766.4 | 13,555.9 | 2,753.9 | † –862.2 | –677.4 | 1,671.1 |
| Equity & investment fund shares | 3aala | –7,149.6 | 10,441.0 | –3,623.8 | 9,875.5 | –1,160.7 | 1,483.7 | –8,999.8 | 10,556.8 | 1,590.4 | † 176.9 | –539.8 | 4,147.6 |
| Debt instruments | 3abla | –1,654.6 | 2,393.3 | 6,043.7 | 1,934.0 | 3,351.9 | 2,434.5 | –2,766.6 | 2,999.2 | 1,163.5 | † –1,038.8 | –137.8 | –2,476.4 |
| Portfolio investment: assets | 3b9aa | 24,767.8 | 33,037.0 | 26,086.5 | 27,521.6 | 8,756.6 | 23,422.6 | 17,324.5 | –988.7 | 26,138.0 | † 7,614.0 | 38,952.4 | –5,458.1 |
| Equity & investment fund shares | 3baaa | 7,298.8 | 14,238.8 | 22,032.0 | 8,850.6 | –9,139.3 | 8,472.0 | 4,648.2 | 5,581.0 | 13,945.5 | † 12,148.0 | 11,904.5 | 5,639.8 |
| Debt securities | 3bbaa | 17,469.0 | 18,798.3 | 4,054.5 | 18,671.0 | 17,895.9 | 14,950.7 | 12,676.4 | –6,569.7 | 12,192.4 | † –4,533.8 | 27,047.9 | –11,097.9 |
| Portfolio investment: liabilities | 3b9la | 10,054.8 | 21,081.1 | 9,240.2 | 20,047.9 | 17,942.5 | 34,907.6 | 15,943.3 | –89.0 | 10,127.9 | † 13,839.7 | 26,672.0 | 9,903.1 |
| Equity & investment fund shares | 3bala | 1,561.6 | –3,005.1 | –5,453.4 | 2,607.3 | 2,786.8 | 7,222.1 | 8,766.1 | –2,251.0 | 4,585.3 | † 6,882.4 | 11,166.6 | –87.2 |
| Debt securities | 3bbla | 8,493.3 | 24,086.2 | 14,693.5 | 17,440.6 | 15,155.8 | 27,685.5 | 7,177.2 | 2,161.9 | 5,542.6 | † 6,957.5 | 15,505.5 | 9,990.2 |
| Fin. der.& empl.stk.ops.(ESOs): net | 3c9na | –3,206.5 | –2,161.3 | –2,636.2 | –136.3 | –5,497.8 | –2,535.5 | –4,854.0 | –989.9 | –7,091.3 | † –6,011.7 | –4,452.2 | 5,127.4 |
| Fin. der. & ESOs.: assets | 3c9aa | –3,206.5 | –2,161.3 | –2,636.2 | –136.3 | –5,497.8 | –2,535.5 | –4,854.0 | –989.9 | –7,091.3 | .... | .... | .... |
| Fin. der. & ESOs.: liabilities | 3c9la | — | — | — | — | — | — | — | — | — | .... | .... | .... |
| Other investment: assets | 3d9aa | 9,020.8 | 19,972.9 | 24,097.8 | 45,483.9 | 22,491.5 | –36,288.6 | 8,152.2 | –8,513.0 | 1,612.7 | † 20,491.4 | –16,858.9 | –7,443.2 |
| Other equity | 3daaa | .... | .... | .... | .... | .... | .... | .... | .... | .... | † — | — | — |
| Debt instruments | 3dzaa | 9,020.8 | 19,972.9 | 24,097.8 | 45,483.9 | 22,491.5 | –36,288.6 | 8,152.2 | –8,513.0 | 1,612.7 | † 20,491.4 | –16,858.9 | –7,443.2 |
| Other investment: liabilities | 3d9la | 378.3 | 22,560.7 | 35,425.4 | 56,882.5 | 30,438.9 | –22,007.7 | 21,506.6 | –19,050.7 | –1,603.8 | † –11,269.4 | –35,291.7 | –32,927.3 |
| Other equity | 3dala | .... | .... | .... | .... | .... | .... | .... | .... | .... | † — | — | — |
| Debt instruments | 3dzla | 378.3 | 22,560.7 | 35,425.4 | 56,882.5 | 30,438.9 | –22,007.7 | 21,506.6 | –19,050.7 | –1,603.8 | † –11,269.4 | –35,291.7 | –32,927.3 |
| Curr.+ cap.– finan. acct. balance | 4y9na | –13,069.2 | 1,042.9 | –384.1 | 338.3 | 20,571.2 | 37,076.6 | 23,592.3 | 13,077.7 | 1,494.8 | † –5,890.2 | –13,974.8 | –3,682.7 |
| D. Net Errors and Omissions | 409na | 11,643.7 | –2,548.6 | –5,603.8 | –548.4 | –13,148.6 | –3,406.0 | –19,312.7 | –2,523.5 | 357.3 | † 5,243.2 | 5,976.1 | 929.7 |
| E. Reserves and Related Items | 4z9na | –1,425.5 | –1,505.8 | –5,988.0 | –210.2 | 7,422.7 | 33,670.7 | 4,279.7 | 10,554.1 | 1,852.1 | † –647.4 | –7,998.7 | –2,753.4 |
| Reserve assets | 3e9aa | –1,425.5 | –1,505.8 | –5,988.0 | –210.2 | 7,422.7 | 33,670.7 | 4,279.7 | 10,554.1 | 1,852.1 | † –647.4 | –7,998.7 | –2,753.4 |
| Credit and loans from the IMF | 3dcla | — | — | — | — | — | — | — | — | — | † — | — | — |
| Exceptional financing | 409la | .... | .... | .... | .... | .... | .... | .... | .... | .... | .... | .... | .... |

*Excludes components in group E

| | | 2004 | 2005 | 2006 | 2007 | 2008 | 2009 | 2010 | 2011 | 2012 | 2013 | 2014 | 2015 |
|---|---|---|---|---|---|---|---|---|---|---|---|---|---|
| **International Investment Position** | | | | | | | *Millions of US Dollars* | | | | | | |
| Assets | 809aa | 488,902.0 | 496,722.9 | 597,554.7 | 739,949.8 | 710,335.1 | 782,546.9 | 822,520.2 | 827,249.5 | 906,568.2 | † 981,459.8 | 942,984.4 | 867,343.5 |
| Direct investment | 8a9aa | 126,216.3 | 129,633.8 | 148,131.6 | 184,869.9 | 194,833.0 | 213,069.5 | 222,244.3 | 231,256.6 | 249,118.9 | † 263,362.8 | 250,024.3 | 239,203.1 |
| Equity & investment fund shares | 8aaaa | 86,162.1 | 89,502.2 | 102,284.6 | 128,156.6 | 123,014.4 | 140,580.3 | 148,499.1 | 147,303.2 | 170,831.2 | † 184,838.3 | 178,770.7 | 173,466.3 |
| Debt instruments | 8abaa | 40,054.1 | 40,131.6 | 45,847.0 | 56,713.3 | 71,818.6 | 72,489.2 | 73,745.2 | 83,953.5 | 78,287.7 | † 78,524.8 | 71,253.6 | 65,736.7 |
| Portfolio investment | 8b9aa | 160,850.8 | 196,731.2 | 251,884.9 | 301,286.8 | 233,540.3 | 296,600.1 | 324,576.6 | 311,304.5 | 367,556.5 | † 402,627.9 | 427,520.3 | 398,134.7 |
| Equity & investment fund shares | 8baaa | 65,428.1 | 88,373.8 | 132,046.8 | 156,797.6 | 85,219.8 | 118,115.5 | 136,087.2 | 129,288.7 | 162,574.8 | † 203,839.7 | 216,343.0 | 214,352.1 |
| Debt securities | 8bbaa | 95,422.7 | 108,357.4 | 119,838.0 | 144,489.2 | 148,320.5 | 178,484.6 | 188,489.5 | 182,015.8 | 204,981.7 | † 198,788.2 | 211,177.5 | 183,782.6 |
| Fin. der.(oth.than reserves) & ESOs | 8c9aa | 36,559.6 | 13,497.1 | 8,350.4 | –7.9 | 15,740.5 | 4,117.5 | 6,583.5 | 20,861.9 | 18,612.0 | † 12,676.3 | 15,230.8 | 8,342.2 |
| Other investment | 8d9aa | 125,173.6 | 122,803.4 | 157,969.8 | 219,408.9 | 223,793.3 | 191,976.5 | 192,407.1 | 178,595.1 | 181,171.7 | † 214,181.5 | 175,381.6 | 157,179.8 |
| Other equity | 8daaa | .... | .... | .... | .... | .... | .... | .... | .... | .... | † — | — | — |
| Debt instruments | 8dzaa | 125,173.6 | 122,803.4 | 157,969.8 | 219,408.9 | 223,793.3 | 191,976.5 | 192,407.1 | 178,595.1 | 181,171.7 | † 214,181.5 | 175,381.6 | 157,179.8 |
| Reserve assets | 8e9aa | 40,101.7 | 34,057.4 | 31,218.1 | 34,392.1 | 42,428.1 | 76,783.5 | 76,708.6 | 85,231.4 | 90,109.1 | † 88,611.1 | 74,827.3 | 64,483.7 |
| Liabilities | 809la | 511,148.8 | 487,386.5 | 598,336.9 | 759,486.2 | 727,501.0 | 770,874.3 | 780,961.8 | 739,981.6 | 787,007.7 | † 847,072.9 | 793,662.1 | 745,394.1 |
| Direct investment | 8a9la | 116,541.1 | 116,123.7 | 132,759.0 | 161,477.5 | 151,946.9 | 154,031.7 | 140,248.5 | 139,982.1 | 145,821.1 | † 146,309.1 | 145,673.5 | 133,248.0 |
| Equity & investment fund shares | 8aala | 78,498.8 | 79,746.5 | 85,056.0 | 106,919.2 | 96,645.5 | 95,670.4 | 88,224.9 | 87,345.4 | 90,701.9 | † 91,806.5 | 92,828.8 | 88,113.5 |
| Debt instruments | 8abla | 38,042.3 | 36,377.2 | 47,703.0 | 54,558.4 | 55,301.3 | 58,361.3 | 52,023.6 | 52,636.6 | 55,119.2 | † 54,502.6 | 52,844.8 | 45,134.6 |
| Portfolio investment | 8b9la | 197,683.5 | 210,158.6 | 251,127.8 | 304,532.9 | 272,439.2 | 329,374.0 | 349,186.8 | 334,167.7 | 374,825.9 | † 424,044.4 | 434,748.8 | 445,273.5 |
| Equity & investment fund shares | 8bala | 44,458.8 | 49,096.6 | 62,886.4 | 83,206.7 | 45,674.1 | 66,976.4 | 92,747.9 | 78,557.9 | 107,380.0 | † 145,416.9 | 166,067.4 | 200,790.6 |
| Debt securities | 8bbla | 153,224.7 | 161,062.0 | 188,241.4 | 221,326.2 | 226,765.1 | 262,397.6 | 256,438.8 | 255,609.9 | 267,445.9 | † 278,627.7 | 268,681.3 | 244,482.9 |
| Fin. der.(oth.than reserves) & ESOs | 8c9la | 32,582.2 | .... | .... | .... | .... | .... | .... | .... | .... | † — | — | — |
| Other investment | 8d9la | 164,342.0 | 161,104.1 | 214,450.0 | 293,475.8 | 303,114.9 | 287,468.6 | 291,526.6 | 265,831.8 | 266,360.7 | † 276,719.5 | 213,239.7 | 166,872.7 |
| Other equity | 8dala | .... | .... | .... | .... | .... | .... | .... | .... | .... | † — | — | — |
| Debt instruments | 8dzla | 164,342.0 | 161,104.1 | 214,450.0 | 293,475.8 | 303,114.9 | 287,468.6 | 291,526.6 | 265,831.8 | 266,360.7 | † 276,719.5 | 213,239.7 | 166,872.7 |

# Denmark   128

|  |  | 2004 | 2005 | 2006 | 2007 | 2008 | 2009 | 2010 | 2011 | 2012 | 2013 | 2014 | 2015 |
|---|---|---|---|---|---|---|---|---|---|---|---|---|---|
| **Government Finance Operations Statement General Government** |  | *Millions of Kroner: Fiscal Year Ends December 31; Data Reported through Eurostat* |  |  |  |  |  |  |  |  |  |  |  |
| Revenue | a1 | 829,362 | 891,269 | 922,161 | 949,616 | 965,311 | 925,447 | 977,230 | 1,004,200 | 1,032,104 | 1,055,917 | 1,115,729 | 1,064,228 |
| Taxes | a11 | 696,659 | 759,232 | 779,492 | 805,049 | 803,971 | 773,363 | 813,594 | 830,584 | 866,096 | 900,125 | 972,500 | 927,996 |
| Social Contributions | a12 | 24,317 | 24,184 | 24,166 | 24,044 | 23,757 | 23,285 | 24,365 | 24,749 | 22,987 | 20,795 | 20,426 | 19,995 |
| Grants | a13 | .... | .... | .... | .... | .... | .... | .... | .... | .... | .... | .... | .... |
| Other Revenue | a14 | .... | .... | .... | .... | .... | .... | .... | .... | .... | .... | .... | .... |
| Expense | a2 | 803,462 | 821,256 | 843,172 | 864,011 | 909,427 | 973,771 | 1,024,102 | 1,038,084 | 1,084,196 | 1,064,784 | 1,071,185 | 1,092,818 |
| Compensation of Employees | a21 | 242,249 | 248,218 | 258,859 | 266,783 | 280,980 | 301,544 | 313,186 | 310,198 | 314,639 | 316,996 | 321,502 | 326,790 |
| Use of Goods & Services | a22 | 120,700 | 128,812 | 135,831 | 139,317 | 154,138 | 166,212 | 170,714 | 170,158 | 178,020 | 178,143 | 179,720 | 182,905 |
| Consumption of Fixed Capital | a23 | 44,596 | 46,335 | 47,675 | 51,072 | 53,548 | 52,694 | 54,634 | 55,211 | 55,927 | 56,944 | 58,317 | 59,176 |
| Interest | a24 | 37,761 | 32,599 | 30,122 | 28,154 | 25,847 | 33,028 | 34,412 | 36,400 | 34,288 | 32,076 | 29,202 | 31,600 |
| Subsidies | a25 | 29,472 | 29,522 | 29,730 | 32,768 | 31,720 | 36,894 | 36,691 | 38,958 | 41,020 | 41,107 | 40,485 | 39,893 |
| Grants | a26 | .... | .... | .... | .... | .... | .... | .... | .... | .... | .... | .... | .... |
| Social Benefits | a27 | 275,240 | 279,968 | 281,258 | 284,612 | 292,377 | 314,775 | 342,642 | 348,423 | 357,951 | 365,254 | 371,554 | 377,063 |
| Other Expense | a28 | .... | .... | .... | .... | .... | .... | .... | .... | .... | .... | .... | .... |
| Gross Operating Balance [1-2+23] | agob | 70,496 | 116,348 | 126,664 | 136,677 | 109,432 | 4,370 | 7,762 | 21,327 | 3,835 | 48,077 | 102,861 | 30,586 |
| Net Operating Balance [1-2] | anob | 25,900 | 70,013 | 78,989 | 85,605 | 55,884 | −48,324 | −46,872 | −33,884 | −52,092 | −8,867 | 44,544 | −28,590 |
| Net Acq. of Nonfinancial Assets | a31 | −5,322 | −8,573 | −4,905 | −1,692 | −1,291 | −135 | 2,208 | 4,082 | 14,052 | 11,490 | 16,051 | 12,486 |
| Aquisition of Nonfin. Assets | a31.1 | .... | .... | .... | .... | .... | .... | .... | .... | .... | .... | .... | .... |
| Disposal of Nonfin. Assets | a31.2 | .... | .... | .... | .... | .... | .... | .... | .... | .... | .... | .... | .... |
| Net Lending/Borrowing [1-2-31] | anlb | 31,222 | 78,586 | 83,894 | 87,297 | 57,175 | −48,189 | −49,080 | −37,966 | −66,144 | −20,357 | 28,493 | −41,076 |
| Net Acq. of Financial Assets | a32 | 7,979 | −6,506 | 68,699 | 10,043 | 188,580 | 54,787 | 42,921 | 42,792 | −60,796 | −13,582 | 50,003 | −118,233 |
| By instrument |  |  |  |  |  |  |  |  |  |  |  |  |  |
| Monetary Gold & SDRs | a3201 | — | — | — | — | — | — | — | — | — | — | — | — |
| Currency & Deposits | a3202 | 24,900 | −1,836 | 62,952 | 23,192 | 147,468 | −78,463 | −14,183 | 61,359 | −62,872 | −1,421 | 51,775 | −51,016 |
| Securities other than Shares | a3203 | −641 | −6,204 | −4,379 | 549 | 2,304 | 79,406 | 19,219 | 4,663 | −19,528 | −12,468 | −35,175 | −694 |
| Loans | a3204 | 4,758 | 10,485 | 7,409 | −3,453 | 28,828 | 33,331 | −916 | 4,724 | 10,611 | 12,450 | 4,525 | 6,598 |
| Shares & Other Equity | a3205 | −12,284 | 9,696 | 5,455 | 14,912 | 2,281 | 2,741 | 4,572 | 3,403 | 6,928 | 3,512 | 2,369 | 7,507 |
| Insurance Technical Reserves | a3206 | 44 | 112 | −24 | 32 | 12 | −76 | −20 | 224 | 12 | 140 | 64 | 64 |
| Financial Derivatives | a3207 | −1,194 | −1,771 | 405 | −1,148 | −223 | 1,475 | −3,344 | −1,795 | −4,398 | −3,519 | −3,385 | −3,125 |
| Other Accounts Receivable | a3208 | −7,605 | −16,989 | −3,118 | −24,039 | 7,912 | 16,371 | 37,594 | −29,789 | 8,451 | −12,277 | 29,836 | −77,565 |
| By debtor |  |  |  |  |  |  |  |  |  |  |  |  |  |
| Domestic | a321 | .... | .... | .... | .... | .... | .... | .... | .... | .... | .... | .... | .... |
| Foreign | a322 | .... | .... | .... | .... | .... | .... | .... | .... | .... | .... | .... | .... |
| Net Incurrence of Liabilities | a33 | −23,244 | −85,093 | −15,197 | −77,255 | 131,403 | 102,974 | 92,001 | 80,757 | 5,348 | 6,775 | 21,511 | −77,156 |
| By instrument |  |  |  |  |  |  |  |  |  |  |  |  |  |
| Special Drawing Rights (SDRs) | a3301 | — | — | — | — | — | — | — | — | — | — | — | — |
| Currency & Deposits | a3302 | 339 | 724 | 771 | 208 | 884 | 323 | 273 | 154 | 173 | −85 | 533 | 414 |
| Securities other than Shares | a3303 | −11,010 | −87,121 | −73,918 | −69,546 | 122,001 | 94,975 | 71,159 | 72,173 | −603 | −11,619 | 15,049 | −81,351 |
| Loans | a3304 | 9,042 | 9,080 | 6,078 | 9,936 | 7,104 | 4,447 | 9,434 | 4,675 | 4,056 | 10,214 | 1,919 | 2,433 |
| Shares & Other Equity | a3305 | — | — | — | — | — | — | — | — | — | — | — | — |
| Insurance Technical Reserves | a3306 | — | — | — | — | — | — | — | — | — | — | — | — |
| Financial Derivatives | a3307 | — | — | — | — | — | — | — | — | — | — | — | — |
| Other Accounts Payable | a3308 | −21,614 | −7,776 | 51,869 | −17,853 | 1,414 | 3,228 | 11,134 | 3,755 | 1,722 | 8,267 | 4,008 | 1,349 |
| By creditor |  |  |  |  |  |  |  |  |  |  |  |  |  |
| Domestic | a331 | .... | .... | .... | .... | .... | .... | .... | .... | .... | .... | .... | .... |
| Foreign | a332 | .... | .... | .... | .... | .... | .... | .... | .... | .... | .... | .... | .... |
| Stat. Discrepancy [32-33-NLB] | anlbz | 1 | 1 | 2 | 1 | 2 | 2 | — | 1 | — | — | −1 | −1 |
| Memo Item: Expenditure [2+31] | a2m | 798,140 | 812,683 | 838,267 | 862,319 | 908,136 | 973,636 | 1,026,310 | 1,042,166 | 1,098,248 | 1,076,274 | 1,087,236 | 1,105,304 |
| **Balance Sheet** |  | *Millions of Kroner: Fiscal Year Ends December 31* |  |  |  |  |  |  |  |  |  |  |  |
| Net Worth | a6 | .... | .... | .... | .... | .... | .... | .... | .... | .... | .... | .... | .... |
| Nonfinancial Assets | a61 | .... | .... | .... | .... | .... | .... | .... | .... | .... | .... | .... | .... |
| Financial Assets | a62 | 574,677 | 565,483 | 662,357 | 681,785 | 875,376 | 949,750 | 1,026,961 | 1,089,467 | 1,024,091 | 1,017,678 | 1,071,912 | 964,669 |
| By instrument |  |  |  |  |  |  |  |  |  |  |  |  |  |
| Monetary Gold & SDRs | a6201 | — | — | — | — | — | — | — | — | — | — | — | — |
| Currency & Deposits | a6202 | 80,855 | 79,019 | 142,926 | 166,154 | 313,622 | 235,392 | 221,210 | 282,569 | 219,697 | 218,277 | 270,051 | 226,474 |
| Securities other than Shares | a6203 | 35,949 | 30,444 | 25,769 | 25,887 | 28,464 | 108,329 | 128,688 | 134,988 | 115,734 | 102,400 | 66,779 | 66,404 |
| Loans | a6204 | 70,058 | 81,195 | 89,982 | 85,872 | 116,775 | 150,365 | 149,108 | 154,087 | 163,991 | 176,070 | 180,302 | 190,017 |
| Shares and Other Equity | a6205 | 293,326 | 306,315 | 325,747 | 354,756 | 361,534 | 378,884 | 404,922 | 411,942 | 415,251 | 415,858 | 425,172 | 427,513 |
| Insurance Technical Reserves | a6206 | 986 | 1,112 | 1,103 | 1,157 | 1,197 | 1,141 | 1,134 | 1,376 | 1,398 | 1,547 | 1,617 | 1,688 |
| Financial Derivatives | a6207 | 5,971 | 7,953 | 3,821 | 534 | −1,009 | 3,028 | 7,897 | 12,082 | 10,829 | 5,500 | 5,407 | 4,836 |
| Other Accounts Receivable | a6208 | 87,532 | 59,445 | 73,009 | 47,425 | 54,794 | 72,611 | 114,002 | 92,422 | 97,190 | 98,026 | 122,584 | 47,737 |
| By debtor |  |  |  |  |  |  |  |  |  |  |  |  |  |
| Domestic | a621 | .... | .... | .... | .... | .... | .... | .... | .... | .... | .... | .... | .... |
| Foreign | a622 | .... | .... | .... | .... | .... | .... | .... | .... | .... | .... | .... | .... |
| Liabilities | a63 | 788,178 | 715,587 | 681,192 | 601,533 | 755,535 | 848,456 | 967,782 | 1,110,166 | 1,148,660 | 1,093,944 | 1,166,166 | 1,072,993 |
| By instrument |  |  |  |  |  |  |  |  |  |  |  |  |  |
| Special Drawing Rights (SDRs) | a6301 | — | — | — | — | — | — | — | — | — | — | — | — |
| Currency & Deposits | a6302 | 11,593 | 12,316 | 13,088 | 13,297 | 14,182 | 14,506 | 14,780 | 14,934 | 15,107 | 15,022 | 15,556 | 15,969 |
| Securities other than Shares | a6303 | 598,492 | 515,332 | 423,351 | 345,305 | 489,537 | 573,620 | 671,653 | 804,955 | 837,134 | 764,463 | 830,608 | 735,741 |
| Loans | a6304 | 93,146 | 102,263 | 107,260 | 121,556 | 128,906 | 134,182 | 144,067 | 149,240 | 153,659 | 163,403 | 164,939 | 167,388 |
| Shares and Other Equity | a6305 | — | — | — | — | — | — | — | — | — | — | — | — |
| Insurance Technical Reserves | a6306 | — | — | — | — | — | — | — | — | — | — | — | — |
| Financial Derivatives | a6307 | — | — | — | — | — | — | — | — | — | — | — | — |
| Other Accounts Payable | a6308 | 84,948 | 85,676 | 137,493 | 121,375 | 122,910 | 126,148 | 137,282 | 141,037 | 142,759 | 151,055 | 155,064 | 153,895 |
| By creditor |  |  |  |  |  |  |  |  |  |  |  |  |  |
| Domestic | a631 | .... | .... | .... | .... | .... | .... | .... | .... | .... | .... | .... | .... |
| Foreign | a632 | .... | .... | .... | .... | .... | .... | .... | .... | .... | .... | .... | .... |
| Net Financial Worth [62-63] | a6m2 | −213,501 | −150,104 | −18,835 | 80,252 | 119,841 | 101,294 | 59,179 | −20,699 | −124,569 | −76,266 | −94,254 | −108,324 |
| Memo Item: Debt at Market Value | a6m3 | 788,179 | 715,587 | 681,192 | 601,533 | 755,535 | 848,456 | 967,782 | 1,110,166 | 1,148,659 | 1,093,943 | 1,166,167 | 1,072,993 |
| Memo Item: Debt at Face Value | a6m35 | 749,937 | 679,028 | 668,236 | 596,879 | 723,037 | 818,136 | 908,517 | 991,899 | 993,505 | 1,000,993 | 1,024,664 | 951,617 |
| Memo Item: Maastricht Debt | a6m36 | 664,989 | 593,352 | 530,743 | 475,504 | 600,127 | 691,988 | 771,235 | 850,862 | 850,746 | 849,938 | 869,600 | 797,722 |
| Memo Item: Debt at Nominal Value | a6m4 | .... | .... | .... | .... | .... | .... | .... | .... | .... | .... | .... | .... |

| National Accounts | | 2004 | 2005 | 2006 | 2007 | 2008 | 2009 | 2010 | 2011 | 2012 | 2013 | 2014 | 2015 |
|---|---|---|---|---|---|---|---|---|---|---|---|---|---|
| | | | | | | | *Billions of Kroner* | | | | | | |
| Househ.Cons.Expend.,incl.NPISHs.... | 96f | 707.2 | 745.1 | 786.6 | 820.4 | 840.0 | 822.0 | 857.6 | 874.5 | 899.8 | 920.3 | 931.7 | 952.8 |
| Government Consumption Expend... | 91f | 375.5 | 388.5 | 407.2 | 423.2 | 452.2 | 481.1 | 495.6 | 490.6 | 502.0 | 504.0 | 513.4 | 521.2 |
| Gross Fixed Capital Formation.......... | 93e | 313.2 | 334.3 | 394.7 | 412.0 | 413.4 | 341.3 | 328.4 | 335.6 | 341.7 | 345.7 | 358.7 | 374.3 |
| Changes in Inventories.................... | 93i | 15.5 | 17.4 | 17.5 | 29.2 | 19.5 | −17.5 | 2.8 | 21.2 | 11.8 | 8.1 | 14.1 | 9.2 |
| Exports of Goods and Services.......... | 90c | 659.3 | 751.9 | 850.4 | 892.9 | 967.9 | 800.8 | 894.3 | 970.7 | 1,007.5 | 1,023.8 | 1,030.2 | 1,058.9 |
| Imports of Goods and Services (-)..... | 98c | 577.0 | 663.6 | 784.4 | 843.6 | 909.1 | 726.1 | 784.3 | 868.9 | 907.5 | 915.5 | 928.9 | 932.7 |
| Gross Domestic Product (GDP)......... | 99b | 1,505.2 | 1,586.5 | 1,682.7 | 1,739.3 | 1,797.5 | 1,714.2 | 1,798.6 | 1,833.4 | 1,866.8 | 1,886.4 | 1,919.2 | 1,983.7 |
| Net Primary Income from Abroad..... | 98.n | −32.3 | −19.7 | −20.6 | −25.8 | −16.7 | −23.1 | 2.0 | 6.9 | 13.9 | 45.4 | 55.4 | .... |
| Gross National Income (GNI)............ | 99a | 1,472.9 | 1,566.8 | 1,662.1 | 1,713.5 | 1,780.9 | 1,691.1 | 1,800.7 | 1,840.3 | 1,880.7 | 1,931.8 | 1,974.6 | .... |
| Net Current Transf.from Abroad....... | 98t | −34.0 | −30.2 | −33.7 | −33.9 | −32.8 | −34.7 | −35.4 | −35.9 | −38.7 | −42.3 | .... | .... |
| Gross Nat'l Disposable Inc.(GNDI).... | 99i | 1,438.9 | 1,536.6 | 1,628.4 | 1,679.6 | 1,748.1 | 1,656.4 | 1,765.3 | 1,804.4 | 1,842.0 | 1,889.5 | 1,936.6 | .... |
| Gross Saving............................. | 99s | 342.7 | 388.9 | 419.2 | 419.2 | 442.6 | 338.4 | 400.3 | 423.8 | 426.9 | 460.4 | 491.4 | .... |
| Consumption of Fixed Capital.......... | 99cf | 239.8 | 245.5 | 257.2 | 272.5 | 298.7 | 298.5 | 298.4 | 297.0 | 302.2 | 297.6 | | |
| GDP Volume 2010 Ref., Chained..... | 99b.p | 1,752.1 | 1,794.7 | 1,862.9 | 1,878.2 | 1,864.8 | 1,769.9 | 1,798.6 | 1,819.4 | 1,807.5 | 1,798.7 | 1,819.1 | 1,856.4 |
| GDP Volume (2010=100)............... | 99bvp | 97.4 | 99.8 | 103.6 | 104.4 | 103.7 | 98.4 | 100.0 | 101.2 | 100.5 | 100.0 | 101.1 | 103.2 |
| GDP Deflator (2010=100)............... | 99bip | 85.9 | 88.4 | 90.3 | 92.6 | 96.4 | 96.9 | 100.0 | 100.8 | 103.3 | 104.9 | 105.5 | 106.9 |
| | | | | | | | *Millions: Midyear Estimates* | | | | | | |
| Population................................ | 99z | 5.40 | 5.42 | 5.44 | 5.47 | 5.50 | 5.52 | 5.55 | 5.58 | 5.60 | 5.62 | 5.65 | 5.67 |

|  |  | 2004 | 2005 | 2006 | 2007 | 2008 | 2009 | 2010 | 2011 | 2012 | 2013 | 2014 | 2015 |
|---|---|---|---|---|---|---|---|---|---|---|---|---|---|
| **Exchange Rates** |  | *Francs per SDR: End of Period (aa)* | | | | | | | | | | | |
| Official Rate | aa | 276.00 | 254.01 | 267.36 | 280.84 | 273.74 | 278.61 | 273.70 | 272.85 | 273.14 | 273.69 | 257.48 | 246.27 |
|  |  | *Francs per US Dollar: End of Period (ae) Period Average (rf)* | | | | | | | | | | | |
| Official Rate | ae | 177.72 | 177.72 | 177.72 | 177.72 | 177.72 | 177.72 | 177.72 | 177.72 | 177.72 | 177.72 | 177.72 | 177.72 |
| Official Rate | rf | 177.72 | 177.72 | 177.72 | 177.72 | 177.72 | 177.72 | 177.72 | 177.72 | 177.72 | 177.72 | 177.72 | 177.72 |
| **Fund Position** |  | *Millions of SDRs: End of Period* | | | | | | | | | | | |
| Quota | 2f.s | 15.90 | 15.90 | 15.90 | 15.90 | 15.90 | 15.90 | 15.90 | 15.90 | 15.90 | 15.90 | 15.90 | 15.90 |
| SDR Holdings | 1b.s | .64 | .02 | .55 | .03 | .06 | 13.05 | 10.87 | 9.21 | 8.30 | 8.29 | 7.37 | 6.29 |
| Reserve Position in the Fund | 1c.s | 1.10 | 1.10 | 1.10 | 1.10 | 1.10 | 1.10 | 1.10 | 1.10 | 1.10 | 1.10 | 1.10 | 1.10 |
| Total Fund Cred.&Loans Outstg | 2tl | 13.63 | 13.08 | 11.99 | 10.18 | 11.32 | 10.07 | 7.88 | 10.68 | 22.26 | 22.26 | 21.34 | 20.27 |
| SDR Allocations | 1bd | 1.18 | 1.18 | 1.18 | 1.18 | 1.18 | 15.16 | 15.16 | 15.16 | 15.16 | 15.16 | 15.16 | 15.16 |
| **International Liquidity** |  | *Millions of US Dollars Unless Otherwise Indicated: End of Period* | | | | | | | | | | | |
| Total Reserves minus Gold | 1l.d | 93.94 | 89.26 | 120.33 | 132.14 | 175.50 | 241.83 | 249.00 | 244.11 | 248.63 | 424.96 | 393.15 | 364.86 |
| SDR Holdings | 1b.d | .99 | .02 | .82 | .05 | .09 | 20.47 | 16.73 | 14.14 | 12.75 | 12.77 | 10.67 | 8.72 |
| Reserve Position in the Fund | 1c.d | 1.71 | 1.57 | 1.65 | 1.74 | 1.69 | 1.72 | 1.69 | 1.69 | 1.69 | 1.69 | 1.59 | 1.52 |
| Foreign Exchange | 1d.d | 91.24 | 87.67 | 117.85 | 130.34 | 173.71 | 219.64 | 230.57 | 228.28 | 234.19 | 410.50 | 380.88 | 354.61 |
| Monetary Authorities: Other Liabs | 4..d | 3.94 | 3.74 | 3.84 | 3.87 | 3.87 | 26.31 | 25.34 | 25.28 | 25.28 | 25.34 | 24.49 | 23.23 |
| Deposit Money Banks: Assets | 7a.d | 372.84 | 430.64 | 483.91 | 507.97 | 575.67 | 670.53 | 744.81 | 692.07 | 774.21 | 834.61 | 903.35 | 1,157.31 |
| Deposit Money Banks: Liabs | 7b.d | 41.92 | 45.97 | 59.75 | 81.26 | 66.97 | 105.71 | 159.11 | 181.61 | 156.12 | 177.78 | 237.92 | 279.85 |
| **Monetary Authorities** |  | *Millions of Francs: End of Period* | | | | | | | | | | | |
| Foreign Assets | 11 | 16,696 | 15,320 | 20,824 | 23,155 | 30,889 | 38,795 | 41,146 | 40,719 | 41,754 | 72,902 | 67,590 | 63,168 |
| Claims on Central Government | 12a | 4,620 | 4,550 | 4,226 | 3,709 | 3,952 | 3,659 | 3,012 | 3,768 | 7,467 | 6,765 | 6,302 | 5,669 |
| Claims on Nonfin.Pub.Enterprises | 12c | — | — | — | — | — | — | — | — | — | — | — | — |
| Claims on Private Sector | 12d | — | — | — | — | — | — | — | — | — | — | — | — |
| Claims on Deposit Money Banks | 12e | — | — | — | — | 998 | 1,284 | 1,282 | 1,285 | 1,294 | 1,301 | 2,716 | 3,826 |
| Reserve Money | 14 | 14,197 | 14,299 | 18,188 | 18,922 | 23,039 | 24,760 | 31,172 | 32,707 | 36,678 | 44,538 | 51,669 | 52,387 |
| of which: Currency Outside DMBs | 14a | 12,358 | 13,272 | 15,235 | 15,500 | 17,624 | 19,629 | 20,085 | 20,350 | 22,029 | 24,752 | 27,296 | 30,817 |
| Foreign Liabilities | 16c | 4,788 | 4,288 | 4,204 | 3,876 | 4,107 | 11,704 | 10,810 | 11,541 | 14,713 | 14,744 | 13,750 | 12,853 |
| Central Government Deposits | 16d | 176 | 184 | 982 | 984 | 2,493 | 3,794 | 2,306 | 1,961 | 77 | 6,906 | 10,051 | 6,781 |
| Capital Accounts | 17a | 2,573 | 2,613 | 2,752 | 2,961 | 2,961 | 2,976 | 2,989 | 2,995 | 2,995 | 2,995 | 2,951 | 2,911 |
| Other Items (Net) | 17r | −418 | −1,514 | −1,076 | 120 | 3,238 | 503 | −1,836 | −3,434 | −3,948 | 11,785 | −1,814 | −2,261 |
| **Deposit Money Banks** |  | *Millions of Francs: End of Period* | | | | | | | | | | | |
| Reserves | 20 | 1,888 | 1,164 | 1,521 | 2,382 | 3,113 | 3,783 | 9,333 | 11,726 | 14,344 | 19,135 | 22,251 | 21,952 |
| Foreign Assets | 21 | 66,261 | 76,533 | 86,000 | 90,276 | 102,309 | 119,168 | 132,369 | 122,995 | 137,593 | 148,327 | 160,543 | 205,677 |
| Claims on Central Government | 22a | 1,069 | 1,333 | 1,410 | 1,927 | 2,161 | 3,374 | 3,630 | 4,378 | 4,751 | 5,390 | 5,641 | 6,243 |
| Claims on Nonfin.Pub.Enterprises | 22c | 1,099 | 1,064 | 951 | 1,744 | 1,519 | 2,625 | 2,646 | 2,339 | 4,685 | 3,262 | 5,400 | 9,364 |
| Claims on Private Sector | 22d | 24,991 | 25,282 | 27,579 | 33,939 | 43,211 | 54,717 | 66,412 | 68,068 | 69,599 | 80,467 | 87,365 | 93,510 |
| Demand Deposits | 24 | 35,085 | 34,456 | 42,036 | 52,041 | 64,612 | 83,049 | 107,207 | 102,746 | 112,841 | 131,116 | 143,928 | 179,167 |
| Time Deposits | 25 | 40,311 | 49,981 | 51,419 | 50,491 | 60,074 | 64,514 | 60,298 | 56,114 | 71,301 | 64,528 | 63,551 | 69,460 |
| Foreign Liabilities | 26c | 7,450 | 8,170 | 10,619 | 14,441 | 11,903 | 18,787 | 28,277 | 32,275 | 27,746 | 31,595 | 42,283 | 49,735 |
| Central Government Deposits | 26d | 54 | 507 | 211 | 410 | 384 | 331 | 1,175 | 837 | 507 | 1,160 | 835 | 1,801 |
| Credit From Monetary Authorities | 26g | — | — | — | — | 1,025 | 1,284 | 1,281 | 1,286 | 1,309 | 1,302 | 3,113 | 3,858 |
| Capital Accounts | 27a | 6,412 | 5,559 | 6,156 | 6,120 | 6,502 | 7,392 | 7,876 | 11,620 | 14,315 | 17,375 | 20,985 | 23,439 |
| Other Items (Net) | 27r | 5,995 | 6,704 | 7,018 | 6,766 | 7,812 | 8,310 | 8,274 | 4,628 | 2,953 | 9,505 | 6,505 | 9,285 |
| **Monetary Survey** |  | *Millions of Francs: End of Period* | | | | | | | | | | | |
| Foreign Assets (Net) | 31n | 70,719 | 79,396 | 92,001 | 95,113 | 117,189 | 127,472 | 134,428 | 119,898 | 136,887 | 174,890 | 172,100 | 206,257 |
| Domestic Credit | 32 | 31,549 | 31,538 | 32,972 | 39,925 | 47,965 | 60,250 | 72,218 | 75,754 | 85,918 | 87,819 | 93,821 | 106,204 |
| Claims on Central Govt. (Net) | 32an | 5,459 | 5,192 | 4,442 | 4,243 | 3,236 | 2,908 | 3,161 | 5,347 | 11,634 | 4,090 | 1,057 | 3,329 |
| Claims on Nonfin.Pub.Enterprises | 32c | 1,099 | 1,064 | 951 | 1,744 | 1,519 | 2,625 | 2,646 | 2,339 | 4,685 | 3,262 | 5,400 | 9,364 |
| Claims on Private Sector | 32d | 24,991 | 25,282 | 27,579 | 33,939 | 43,211 | 54,717 | 66,412 | 68,068 | 69,599 | 80,467 | 87,365 | 93,510 |
| Money | 34 | 47,443 | 47,728 | 57,271 | 67,541 | 82,236 | 102,678 | 127,292 | 123,096 | 134,870 | 155,869 | 171,224 | 209,984 |
| Quasi-Money | 35 | 40,311 | 49,981 | 51,419 | 50,491 | 60,074 | 64,514 | 60,298 | 56,114 | 71,301 | 64,528 | 63,551 | 69,460 |
| Capital Accounts | 37a | 8,985 | 8,172 | 8,908 | 9,081 | 9,464 | 10,367 | 10,865 | 14,615 | 17,310 | 20,370 | 23,937 | 26,350 |
| Other Items (Net) | 37r | 5,528 | 5,053 | 7,375 | 7,926 | 13,379 | 10,161 | 8,191 | 1,827 | −675 | 21,941 | 7,210 | 6,674 |
| Money plus Quasi-Money | 35l | 87,754 | 97,709 | 108,690 | 118,032 | 142,310 | 167,191 | 187,589 | 179,210 | 206,171 | 220,397 | 234,775 | 279,444 |
| **Interest Rates** |  | *Percent Per Annum* | | | | | | | | | | | |
| Deposit Rate | 60l | .88 | .75 | .69 | 4.53 | 2.96 | 1.67 | 1.72 | 1.78 | 2.34 | 2.03 | 1.24 | .... |
| Lending Rate | 60p | 11.36 | 11.36 | 11.63 | 10.94 | 11.38 | 11.45 | 10.44 | 11.49 | 11.99 | 11.94 | 12.69 | .... |
| **Prices** |  | *Index Numbers (2010=100): Period Averages* | | | | | | | | | | | |
| Consumer Prices | 64 | 75.5 | 77.8 | 80.5 | 84.5 | 94.6 | 96.2 | 100.0 | 105.1 | 109.0 | 111.6 | 114.9 | .... |
| **Intl. Transactions & Positions** |  | *Millions of Francs* | | | | | | | | | | | |
| Exports | 70 | 6,750 | 7,020 | 9,805 | 10,320 | 12,218 | 13,750 | 17,772 | .... | .... | .... | .... | .... |
| Imports, c.i.f | 71 | 46,449 | 49,285 | 59,664 | 84,103 | 101,940 | 80,101 | 74,643 | .... | .... | .... | .... | .... |

| | | 2004 | 2005 | 2006 | 2007 | 2008 | 2009 | 2010 | 2011 | 2012 | 2013 | 2014 | 2015 |
|---|---|---|---|---|---|---|---|---|---|---|---|---|---|
| **Balance of Payments** | | | | | | | *Millions of US Dollars* | | | | | | |
| A. Current Account* | 109bx | 3.2 | 20.1 | −16.6 | −171.4 | −225.4 | −71.1 | 50.5 | −171.8 | −148.0 | −308.5 | .... | .... |
| Goods, credit (exports) | 1a9cx | 38.0 | 39.5 | 55.2 | 58.1 | 68.8 | 77.4 | 85.1 | 85.0 | 111.4 | 112.7 | .... | .... |
| Goods, debit (imports) | 1a9dx | 261.4 | 277.3 | 335.7 | 473.2 | 574.1 | 450.7 | 363.8 | 510.6 | 564.4 | 719.4 | .... | .... |
| Balance on goods | 1a9bx | −223.4 | −237.8 | −280.5 | −415.2 | −505.3 | −373.3 | −278.6 | −425.6 | −453.1 | −606.7 | .... | .... |
| Services, credit (exports) | 1b9cx | 212.7 | 248.4 | 251.5 | 248.5 | 296.9 | 322.0 | 335.7 | 318.7 | 330.7 | 357.0 | .... | .... |
| Services, debit (imports) | 1b9dx | 77.2 | 83.8 | 89.3 | 107.7 | 129.5 | 127.6 | 119.1 | 147.8 | 144.6 | 178.1 | .... | .... |
| Balance on Goods & Services | 1z9bx | −87.9 | −73.2 | −118.4 | −274.4 | −337.9 | −178.9 | −62.0 | −254.7 | −267.0 | −427.8 | .... | .... |
| Primary income: credit | 1c9cx | 33.3 | 32.0 | 34.9 | 35.2 | 45.6 | 37.0 | 32.8 | 36.7 | 45.6 | 47.3 | .... | .... |
| Primary income: debit | 1c9dx | 10.7 | 11.2 | 11.8 | 11.3 | 12.9 | 15.3 | 15.4 | 27.9 | 18.0 | 21.0 | .... | .... |
| Balance on gds, serv. & prim. inc. | 1y9bx | −65.3 | −52.4 | −95.3 | −250.6 | −305.2 | −157.2 | −44.7 | −246.0 | −239.4 | −401.5 | .... | .... |
| Secondary income: credit | 1d9ca | 74.1 | 78.3 | 85.5 | 85.9 | 87.2 | 92.2 | 108.7 | 92.1 | 105.3 | 107.2 | .... | .... |
| Secondary income: debit | 1d9da | 5.6 | 5.8 | 6.8 | 6.7 | 7.3 | 6.1 | 13.5 | 17.9 | 13.9 | 14.3 | .... | .... |
| B. Capital Account* | 209ba | 19.7 | 26.8 | 9.3 | 35.3 | 53.7 | 55.1 | 55.3 | 59.7 | 52.4 | 50.5 | .... | .... |
| Capital account: credit | 209ca | 19.7 | 26.8 | 9.3 | 35.3 | 53.7 | 55.1 | 55.3 | 59.7 | 52.4 | 50.5 | .... | .... |
| Capital account: debit | 209da | .... | .... | .... | .... | .... | .... | .... | — | — | — | .... | .... |
| Balance on current & capital acct. | 129ba | 22.8 | 46.9 | −7.3 | −136.1 | −171.6 | −16.0 | 105.8 | −112.2 | −95.6 | −258.1 | .... | .... |
| C. Financial Account* | 309na | 35.7 | 32.8 | −63.7 | −190.4 | −126.6 | −44.1 | −10.8 | −119.4 | 16.7 | −241.0 | .... | .... |
| Direct investment: assets | 3a9aa | .... | .... | .... | .... | .... | .... | .... | — | — | — | .... | .... |
| Equity & investment fund shares | 3aaaa | .... | .... | .... | .... | .... | .... | .... | — | — | — | .... | .... |
| Debt instruments | 3abaa | .... | .... | .... | .... | .... | .... | .... | — | — | — | .... | .... |
| Direct investment: liabilities | 3a9la | 38.5 | 22.2 | 108.3 | 195.4 | 227.7 | 96.9 | 36.5 | 79.0 | 110.0 | 286.0 | .... | .... |
| Equity & investment fund shares | 3aala | 38.5 | 22.2 | 108.3 | 195.4 | 227.7 | 96.9 | 36.5 | 79.0 | 110.0 | 286.0 | .... | .... |
| Debt instruments | 3abla | .... | .... | .... | .... | .... | .... | .... | — | — | — | .... | .... |
| Portfolio investment: assets | 3b9aa | .... | .... | .... | .... | .... | .... | .... | — | — | — | .... | .... |
| Equity & investment fund shares | 3baaa | .... | .... | .... | .... | .... | .... | .... | — | — | — | .... | .... |
| Debt securities | 3bbaa | .... | .... | .... | .... | .... | .... | .... | — | — | — | .... | .... |
| Portfolio investment: liabilities | 3b9la | .... | .... | .... | .... | .... | .... | .... | — | — | — | .... | .... |
| Equity & investment fund shares | 3bala | .... | .... | .... | .... | .... | .... | .... | — | — | — | .... | .... |
| Debt securities | 3bbla | .... | .... | .... | .... | .... | .... | .... | — | — | — | .... | .... |
| Fin. der.& empl.stk.ops.(ESOs): net | 3c9na | .... | .... | .... | .... | .... | .... | .... | — | — | — | .... | .... |
| Fin. der. & ESOs.: assets | 3c9aa | .... | .... | .... | .... | .... | .... | .... | — | — | — | .... | .... |
| Fin. der. & ESOs.: liabilities | 3c9la | .... | .... | .... | .... | .... | .... | .... | — | — | — | .... | .... |
| Other investment: assets | 3d9aa | 84.0 | 65.1 | 62.0 | 31.2 | 74.8 | 101.8 | 81.3 | −11.8 | 89.6 | 68.6 | .... | .... |
| Other equity | 3daaa | .... | .... | .... | .... | .... | .... | .... | .... | .... | .... | .... | .... |
| Debt instruments | 3dzaa | 84.0 | 65.1 | 62.0 | 31.2 | 74.8 | 101.8 | 81.3 | −11.8 | 89.6 | 68.6 | .... | .... |
| Other investment: liabilities | 3d9la | 9.8 | 10.2 | 17.5 | 26.3 | −26.2 | 49.0 | 55.5 | 28.6 | −37.0 | 23.6 | .... | .... |
| Other equity | 3dala | .... | .... | .... | .... | .... | .... | .... | .... | .... | .... | .... | .... |
| Debt instruments | 3dzla | 9.8 | 10.2 | 17.5 | 26.3 | −26.2 | 49.0 | 55.5 | 28.6 | −37.0 | 23.6 | .... | .... |
| Curr.+ cap.– finan. acct. balance | 4y9na | −12.8 | 14.1 | 56.5 | 54.3 | −45.1 | 28.1 | 116.6 | 7.3 | −112.2 | −17.1 | .... | .... |
| D. Net Errors and Omissions | 409na | −15.7 | −45.4 | −51.8 | −80.6 | 35.8 | −33.7 | −123.3 | −48.7 | 75.8 | 161.5 | .... | .... |
| E. Reserves and Related Items | 4z9na | −28.5 | −31.3 | 4.7 | −26.3 | −9.3 | −5.6 | −6.7 | −41.4 | −36.4 | 144.4 | .... | .... |
| Reserve assets | 3e9aa | −5.9 | −7.4 | 30.4 | 12.3 | 43.4 | 64.1 | 9.7 | −4.9 | 4.5 | 176.3 | .... | .... |
| Credit and loans from the IMF | 3dcla | −.2 | −.8 | −1.6 | −2.8 | 1.7 | −1.9 | −3.3 | 4.3 | 17.9 | — | .... | .... |
| Exceptional financing | 409la | 22.8 | 24.7 | 27.3 | 41.4 | 51.0 | 71.6 | 19.8 | 32.2 | 23.1 | 31.9 | .... | .... |
| *Excludes components in group E | | | | | | | | | | | | | |

| | | 2004 | 2005 | 2006 | 2007 | 2008 | 2009 | 2010 | 2011 | 2012 | 2013 | 2014 | 2015 |
|---|---|---|---|---|---|---|---|---|---|---|---|---|---|
| **International Investment Position** | | | | | | | *Millions of US Dollars* | | | | | | |
| Assets | 809aa | 634.7 | 662.3 | 755.3 | 895.9 | 922.3 | 1,066.3 | 1,098.2 | 1,136.5 | 1,184.5 | 1,395.1 | .... | .... |
| Direct investment | 8a9aa | .... | .... | .... | .... | .... | .... | .... | .... | .... | .... | .... | .... |
| Equity & investment fund shares | 8aaaa | .... | .... | .... | .... | .... | .... | .... | .... | .... | .... | .... | .... |
| Debt instruments | 8abaa | .... | .... | .... | .... | .... | .... | .... | .... | .... | .... | .... | .... |
| Portfolio investment | 8b9aa | .... | .... | .... | .... | .... | .... | .... | .... | .... | .... | .... | .... |
| Equity & investment fund shares | 8baaa | .... | .... | .... | .... | .... | .... | .... | .... | .... | .... | .... | .... |
| Debt securities | 8bbaa | .... | .... | .... | .... | .... | .... | .... | .... | .... | .... | .... | .... |
| Fin. der.(oth.than reserves) & ESOs | 8c9aa | .... | .... | .... | .... | .... | .... | .... | .... | .... | .... | .... | .... |
| Other investment | 8d9aa | 540.6 | 576.0 | 638.6 | 765.5 | 748.3 | 847.9 | 866.6 | 907.3 | 949.5 | 984.9 | .... | .... |
| Other equity | 8daaa | .... | .... | .... | .... | .... | .... | .... | .... | .... | .... | .... | .... |
| Debt instruments | 8dzaa | 540.6 | 576.0 | 638.6 | 765.5 | 748.3 | 847.9 | 866.6 | 907.3 | 949.5 | 984.9 | .... | .... |
| Reserve assets | 8e9aa | 94.1 | 86.3 | 116.7 | 130.3 | 174.0 | 218.4 | 231.6 | 229.2 | 235.0 | 410.2 | .... | .... |
| Liabilities | 809la | 526.4 | 537.4 | 588.1 | 685.0 | 879.0 | 1,035.1 | 1,098.1 | 1,245.7 | 1,375.8 | 1,714.7 | .... | .... |
| Direct investment | 8a9la | 85.5 | 104.4 | 130.3 | 180.9 | 235.3 | 295.1 | 331.6 | 408.3 | 513.7 | 799.7 | .... | .... |
| Equity & investment fund shares | 8aala | 85.5 | 104.4 | 130.3 | 180.9 | 235.3 | 295.1 | 331.6 | 408.3 | 513.7 | 799.7 | .... | .... |
| Debt instruments | 8abla | .... | .... | .... | .... | .... | .... | .... | .... | .... | .... | .... | .... |
| Portfolio investment | 8b9la | .... | .... | .... | .... | .... | .... | .... | .... | .... | .... | .... | .... |
| Equity & investment fund shares | 8bala | .... | .... | .... | .... | .... | .... | .... | .... | .... | .... | .... | .... |
| Debt securities | 8bbla | .... | .... | .... | .... | .... | .... | .... | .... | .... | .... | .... | .... |
| Fin. der.(oth.than reserves) & ESOs | 8c9la | .... | .... | .... | .... | .... | .... | .... | .... | .... | .... | .... | .... |
| Other investment | 8d9la | 441.0 | 433.0 | 457.8 | 504.2 | 643.7 | 740.0 | 766.5 | 837.3 | 862.1 | 915.0 | .... | .... |
| Other equity | 8dala | .... | .... | .... | .... | .... | .... | .... | .... | .... | .... | .... | .... |
| Debt instruments | 8dzla | 441.0 | 433.0 | 457.8 | 504.2 | 643.7 | 740.0 | 766.5 | 837.3 | 862.1 | 915.0 | .... | .... |

| | | 2004 | 2005 | 2006 | 2007 | 2008 | 2009 | 2010 | 2011 | 2012 | 2013 | 2014 | 2015 |
|---|---|---|---|---|---|---|---|---|---|---|---|---|---|
| **National Accounts** | | | | | | | *Millions of Francs* | | | | | | |
| Gross Domestic Product (GDP) | 99b | 118,400 | 125,976 | 136,803 | 151,033 | 172,882 | 186,969 | .... | .... | .... | .... | .... | .... |
| | | | | | | | *Millions: Midyear Estimates* | | | | | | |
| Population | 99z | .77 | .78 | .79 | .80 | .81 | .82 | .83 | .84 | .85 | .86 | .88 | .89 |

# Dominica 321

| | | 2004 | 2005 | 2006 | 2007 | 2008 | 2009 | 2010 | 2011 | 2012 | 2013 | 2014 | 2015 |
|---|---|---|---|---|---|---|---|---|---|---|---|---|---|
| **Exchange Rates** | | | | | *E.Caribbean Dollars per SDR: End of Period* | | | | | | | | |
| Official Rate | aa | 4.1931 | 3.8590 | 4.0619 | 4.2667 | 4.1587 | 4.2328 | 4.1581 | 4.1452 | 4.1497 | 4.1580 | 3.9118 | 3.7415 |
| | | | | *E.Caribbean Dollars per US Dollar: End of Period (ae) Period Average (rf)* | | | | | | | | | |
| Official Rate | ae | 2.7000 | 2.7000 | 2.7000 | 2.7000 | 2.7000 | 2.7000 | 2.7000 | 2.7000 | 2.7000 | 2.7000 | 2.7000 | 2.7000 |
| Official Rate | rf | 2.7000 | 2.7000 | 2.7000 | 2.7000 | 2.7000 | 2.7000 | 2.7000 | 2.7000 | 2.7000 | 2.7000 | 2.7000 | 2.7000 |
| | | | | | *Index Numbers (2010=100): Period Averages* | | | | | | | | |
| Nominal Effective Exchange Rate | nec | 98.00 | 97.38 | 96.43 | 94.06 | 95.22 | 101.99 | 100.00 | 97.55 | 99.62 | 102.32 | 103.53 | 111.39 |
| CPI-Based Real Effect. Ex. Rate | rec | 105.78 | 102.12 | 100.16 | 97.03 | 98.07 | 102.96 | 100.00 | 94.40 | 94.63 | 94.09 | 93.37 | 97.88 |
| **Fund Position** | | | | | *Millions of SDRs: End of Period* | | | | | | | | |
| Quota | 2f.s | 8.20 | 8.20 | 8.20 | 8.20 | 8.20 | 8.20 | 8.20 | 8.20 | 8.20 | 8.20 | 8.20 | 8.20 |
| SDR Holdings | 1b.s | .03 | .01 | .01 | .04 | .02 | 7.01 | 6.28 | 4.33 | 1.76 | 1.09 | 1.04 | .57 |
| Reserve Position in the Fund | 1c.s | .01 | .01 | .01 | .01 | .01 | .01 | .01 | .01 | .01 | .01 | .01 | .01 |
| Total Fund Cred.&Loans Outstg | 2tl | 5.95 | 8.08 | 9.30 | 7.69 | 9.74 | 12.52 | 11.80 | 9.96 | 9.44 | 7.65 | 6.61 | 11.29 |
| SDR Allocations | 1bd | .59 | .59 | .59 | .59 | .59 | 7.84 | 7.84 | 7.84 | 7.84 | 7.84 | 7.84 | 7.84 |
| **International Liquidity** | | | | *Millions of US Dollars Unless Otherwise Indicated: End of Period* | | | | | | | | | |
| Total Reserves minus Gold | 1l.d | 42.32 | 49.17 | 63.05 | 60.52 | 55.15 | 75.46 | 76.10 | 81.12 | 94.56 | 87.05 | 101.45 | 126.22 |
| SDR Holdings | 1b.d | .05 | .01 | .01 | .06 | .03 | 10.98 | 9.67 | 6.65 | 2.71 | 1.67 | 1.51 | .78 |
| Reserve Position in the Fund | 1c.d | .01 | .01 | .01 | .01 | .01 | .01 | .01 | .01 | .01 | .01 | .01 | .01 |
| Foreign Exchange | 1d.d | 42.25 | 49.15 | 63.02 | 60.45 | 55.10 | 64.47 | 66.41 | 74.46 | 91.84 | 85.36 | 99.92 | 125.43 |
| Central Bank: Other Assets | 3..d | — | — | — | — | — | — | — | — | — | — | — | — |
| Central Bank: Other Liabs | 4..d | — | — | — | — | — | — | — | — | — | — | — | — |
| Other Depository Corps.: Assets | 7a.d | 152.24 | 149.15 | 178.27 | 214.77 | 235.65 | 244.47 | 227.26 | 207.20 | 217.17 | 217.22 | 246.49 | 287.91 |
| Other Depository Corps.: Liabs | 7b.d | 60.64 | 66.38 | 83.07 | 100.72 | 104.04 | 102.27 | 95.10 | 112.50 | 107.17 | 107.08 | 119.78 | 133.53 |
| **Central Bank** | | | | | *Millions of E.Caribbean Dollars: End of Period* | | | | | | | | |
| Net Foreign Assets | 11n | 87.65 | 100.30 | 131.27 | 129.37 | 94.82 | 102.08 | 115.33 | 139.14 | 183.70 | 170.74 | 217.47 | 269.34 |
| Claims on Nonresidents | 11 | 115.07 | 133.77 | 171.46 | 164.70 | 137.78 | 188.23 | 196.98 | 212.90 | 255.41 | 235.13 | 274.00 | 340.90 |
| Liabilities to Nonresidents | 16c | 27.42 | 33.48 | 40.19 | 35.33 | 42.96 | 86.15 | 81.65 | 73.76 | 71.71 | 64.39 | 56.53 | 71.56 |
| Claims on Other Depository Corps. | 12e | — | .03 | .03 | .01 | .02 | .03 | .01 | .02 | .03 | .06 | .24 | .82 |
| Net Claims on Central Government | 12an | 3.79 | −9.30 | −22.33 | −5.75 | −1.90 | −6.70 | −6.78 | −6.54 | −34.17 | −8.85 | −17.75 | −23.53 |
| Claims on Central Government | 12a | 7.18 | 7.19 | 3.96 | 4.00 | 3.90 | 1.65 | 1.65 | 1.65 | — | — | 1.85 | — |
| Liabilities to Central Government | 16d | 3.39 | 16.48 | 26.29 | 9.75 | 5.80 | 8.35 | 8.43 | 8.19 | 34.17 | 8.85 | 19.60 | 23.53 |
| Claims on Other Sectors | 12s | — | — | — | — | — | — | — | — | — | — | — | — |
| Claims on Other Financial Corps. | 12g | — | — | — | — | — | — | — | — | — | — | — | — |
| Claims on State & Local Govts | 12b | — | — | — | — | — | — | — | — | — | — | — | — |
| Claims on Public Nonfin. Corps. | 12c | — | — | — | — | — | — | — | — | — | — | — | — |
| Claims on Private Sector | 12d | — | — | — | — | — | — | — | — | — | — | — | — |
| Monetary Base | 14 | 117.75 | 123.48 | 147.98 | 157.60 | 134.32 | 150.27 | 161.90 | 185.85 | 211.41 | 218.52 | 242.68 | 302.54 |
| Currency in Circulation | 14a | 52.82 | 57.26 | 62.42 | 67.91 | 63.29 | 70.99 | 67.84 | 67.24 | 63.89 | 62.80 | 75.99 | 68.36 |
| Liabs. to Other Depository Corps. | 14c | 63.97 | 65.13 | 84.52 | 88.18 | 69.53 | 79.22 | 94.04 | 118.60 | 147.50 | 155.70 | 166.65 | 234.12 |
| Liabilities to Other Sectors | 14d | .97 | 1.10 | 1.04 | 1.51 | 1.49 | .05 | .02 | .02 | .02 | .02 | .05 | .05 |
| Other Liabs. to Other Dep. Corps. | 14n | .84 | .87 | 1.02 | 1.08 | 1.37 | 1.50 | 2.05 | 2.44 | 2.42 | 3.17 | 9.59 | 13.41 |
| Dep. & Sec. Excl. f/Monetary Base | 14o | — | — | — | — | — | — | — | — | — | — | — | — |
| Deposits Included in Broad Money | 15 | — | — | — | — | — | — | — | — | — | — | — | — |
| Sec.Ot.th.Shares Incl.in Brd. Money | 16a | — | — | — | — | — | — | — | — | — | — | — | — |
| Deposits Excl. from Broad Money | 16b | — | — | — | — | — | — | — | — | — | — | — | — |
| Sec.Ot.th.Shares Excl.f/Brd.Money | 16s | — | — | — | — | — | — | — | — | — | — | — | — |
| Loans | 16l | — | — | — | — | — | — | — | — | — | — | — | — |
| Financial Derivatives | 16m | — | — | — | — | — | — | — | — | — | — | — | — |
| Shares and Other Equity | 17a | — | — | — | — | — | — | — | — | — | — | — | — |
| Other Items (Net) | 17r | −27.15 | −33.32 | −40.03 | −35.05 | −42.74 | −56.36 | −55.39 | −55.67 | −64.26 | −59.75 | −52.32 | −69.32 |
| Memo Item: | | | | | | | | | | | | | |
| Total Assets | 10ra | 122.08 | 140.92 | 175.38 | 168.51 | 141.57 | 160.21 | 172.48 | 196.58 | 248.09 | 230.64 | 271.97 | 339.56 |
| **Other Depository Corporations** | | | | | *Millions of E.Caribbean Dollars: End of Period* | | | | | | | | |
| Net Foreign Assets | 21n | 247.31 | 223.47 | 257.06 | 307.95 | 355.35 | 383.94 | 356.85 | 255.69 | 297.02 | 297.39 | 342.13 | 416.83 |
| Claims on Nonresidents | 21 | 411.04 | 402.69 | 481.34 | 579.88 | 636.25 | 660.07 | 613.61 | 559.45 | 586.37 | 586.50 | 665.53 | 777.36 |
| Liabilities to Nonresidents | 26c | 163.74 | 179.22 | 224.29 | 271.93 | 280.90 | 276.12 | 256.76 | 303.76 | 289.35 | 289.11 | 323.41 | 360.53 |
| Claims on Central Bank | 20 | 73.79 | 78.36 | 99.58 | 148.74 | 90.85 | 99.04 | 112.60 | 137.90 | 164.72 | 178.11 | 194.28 | 255.03 |
| Currency | 20a | 15.22 | 18.30 | 16.98 | 18.88 | 19.38 | 20.32 | 21.38 | 20.24 | 18.29 | 21.21 | 29.10 | 21.77 |
| Reserve Deposits and Securities | 20b | 58.57 | 60.06 | 82.60 | 129.86 | 71.46 | 78.72 | 91.22 | 117.66 | 146.44 | 156.90 | 165.18 | 233.26 |
| Other Claims | 20n | — | — | — | — | — | — | — | — | — | — | — | — |
| Net Claims on Central Government | 22an | 11.15 | 27.08 | −23.81 | −46.87 | −42.00 | −22.32 | −33.26 | −16.73 | 28.51 | 63.26 | 80.45 | −24.59 |
| Claims on Central Government | 22a | 57.68 | 70.43 | 69.47 | 68.89 | 76.80 | 71.29 | 82.72 | 59.76 | 97.35 | 112.96 | 121.81 | 108.73 |
| Liabilities to Central Government | 26d | 46.53 | 43.34 | 93.27 | 115.76 | 118.80 | 93.62 | 115.98 | 76.49 | 68.84 | 49.71 | 41.36 | 133.31 |
| Claims on Other Sectors | 22s | 474.76 | 500.25 | 550.78 | 573.99 | 620.69 | 660.62 | 721.41 | 780.00 | 813.55 | 808.65 | 787.47 | 797.72 |
| Claims on Other Financial Corps. | 22g | 2.43 | 2.88 | 2.63 | 2.17 | 2.20 | 1.79 | 1.58 | 4.44 | 14.20 | 11.13 | 12.41 | 26.53 |
| Claims on State & Local Govts. | 22b | .05 | .07 | .07 | .08 | .06 | .07 | .11 | .08 | .08 | .04 | .07 | .09 |
| Claims on Public Nonfin. Corps. | 22c | 21.63 | 19.46 | 16.88 | 12.89 | 12.78 | 12.82 | 11.69 | 23.13 | 23.56 | 22.25 | 20.78 | 22.04 |
| Claims on Private Sector | 22d | 450.66 | 477.84 | 531.21 | 558.85 | 605.65 | 645.94 | 708.03 | 752.34 | 775.72 | 775.23 | 754.22 | 749.07 |
| Liabilities to Central Bank | 26g | — | — | — | — | — | — | 1.00 | 2.18 | 1.04 | 4.04 | 1.08 | 1.11 |
| Transf.Dep.Included in Broad Money | 24 | 141.97 | 155.29 | 143.96 | 159.56 | 165.74 | 180.64 | 182.83 | 176.70 | 226.52 | 199.56 | 231.32 | 251.77 |
| Other Dep.Included in Broad Money | 25 | 535.85 | 560.21 | 649.65 | 715.40 | 766.19 | 844.57 | 874.99 | 909.81 | 989.49 | 1,058.86 | 1,086.37 | 1,114.26 |
| Sec.Ot.th.Shares Incl.in Brd. Money | 26a | — | — | — | — | — | — | — | — | — | — | — | — |
| Deposits Excl. from Broad Money | 26b | — | — | — | — | — | — | — | — | — | — | — | — |
| Sec.Ot.th.Shares Excl.f/Brd.Money | 26s | — | — | — | — | — | — | — | — | — | — | — | — |
| Loans | 26l | — | — | — | — | — | — | — | — | — | — | — | — |
| Financial Derivatives | 26m | — | — | — | — | — | — | — | — | — | — | — | — |
| Insurance Technical Reserves | 26r | — | — | — | — | — | — | — | — | — | — | — | — |
| Shares and Other Equity | 27a | 90.45 | 98.71 | 96.70 | 96.31 | 96.66 | 115.00 | 118.54 | 85.68 | 98.35 | 78.91 | 79.83 | 77.37 |
| Other Items (Net) | 27r | 38.74 | 14.96 | −6.69 | 12.52 | −3.70 | −18.92 | −19.76 | −17.51 | −11.59 | 6.03 | 5.72 | .48 |
| Memo Item: | | | | | | | | | | | | | |
| Total Assets | 20ra | 1,090.14 | 1,138.53 | 1,280.78 | 1,494.04 | 1,559.80 | 1,640.56 | 1,687.74 | 1,730.60 | 1,825.65 | 1,853.83 | 1,937.88 | 2,143.52 |

| | | 2004 | 2005 | 2006 | 2007 | 2008 | 2009 | 2010 | 2011 | 2012 | 2013 | 2014 | 2015 |
|---|---|---|---|---|---|---|---|---|---|---|---|---|---|
| **Depository Corporations** | | *Millions of E.Caribbean Dollars: End of Period* | | | | | | | | | | | |
| Net Foreign Assets | 31n | 334.96 | 323.77 | 388.32 | 437.32 | 450.17 | 486.02 | 472.18 | 394.83 | 480.72 | 468.13 | 559.60 | 686.16 |
| Claims on Nonresidents | 31 | 526.11 | 536.46 | 652.80 | 744.58 | 774.03 | 848.29 | 810.58 | 772.35 | 841.78 | 821.63 | 939.54 | 1,118.25 |
| Liabilities to Nonresidents | 36c | 191.16 | 212.70 | 264.48 | 307.26 | 323.86 | 362.27 | 338.40 | 377.51 | 361.06 | 353.50 | 379.94 | 432.09 |
| Domestic Claims | 32 | 489.71 | 518.03 | 504.65 | 521.36 | 576.78 | 631.60 | 681.38 | 756.72 | 807.90 | 863.06 | 850.17 | 749.61 |
| Net Claims on Central Government | 32an | 14.94 | 17.79 | −46.14 | −52.62 | −43.90 | −29.03 | −40.04 | −23.27 | −5.66 | 54.41 | 62.70 | −48.11 |
| Claims on Central Government | 32a | 64.86 | 77.61 | 73.43 | 72.88 | 80.70 | 72.94 | 84.37 | 61.41 | 97.35 | 112.96 | 123.66 | 108.73 |
| Liabilities to Central Government | 36d | 49.92 | 59.83 | 119.56 | 125.51 | 124.60 | 101.97 | 124.41 | 84.68 | 103.01 | 58.56 | 60.96 | 156.84 |
| Claims on Other Sectors | 32s | 474.76 | 500.25 | 550.78 | 573.99 | 620.69 | 660.62 | 721.41 | 780.00 | 813.55 | 808.65 | 787.47 | 797.72 |
| Claims on Other Financial Corps. | 32g | 2.43 | 2.88 | 2.63 | 2.17 | 2.20 | 1.79 | 1.58 | 4.44 | 14.20 | 11.13 | 12.41 | 26.53 |
| Claims on State & Local Govts. | 32b | .05 | .07 | .07 | .08 | .06 | .07 | .11 | .08 | .08 | .04 | .07 | .09 |
| Claims on Public Nonfin. Corps. | 32c | 21.63 | 19.46 | 16.88 | 12.89 | 12.78 | 12.82 | 11.69 | 23.13 | 23.56 | 22.25 | 20.78 | 22.04 |
| Claims on Private Sector | 32d | 450.66 | 477.84 | 531.21 | 558.85 | 605.65 | 645.94 | 708.03 | 752.34 | 775.72 | 775.23 | 754.22 | 749.07 |
| Broad Money Liabilities | 35l | 716.39 | 755.55 | 840.09 | 925.50 | 977.33 | 1,075.93 | 1,104.31 | 1,133.52 | 1,261.63 | 1,300.02 | 1,364.63 | 1,412.68 |
| Currency Outside Depository Corps | 34a | 37.60 | 38.96 | 45.44 | 49.03 | 43.91 | 50.68 | 46.46 | 47.00 | 45.61 | 41.59 | 46.89 | 46.59 |
| Transferable Deposits | 34 | 142.11 | 155.54 | 144.15 | 160.21 | 166.40 | 180.69 | 182.85 | 176.72 | 226.53 | 199.57 | 231.36 | 251.82 |
| Other Deposits | 35 | 536.68 | 561.05 | 650.50 | 716.26 | 767.02 | 844.57 | 874.99 | 909.81 | 989.49 | 1,058.86 | 1,086.37 | 1,114.26 |
| Securities Other than Shares | 36a | — | — | — | — | — | — | — | — | — | — | — | — |
| Deposits Excl. from Broad Money | 36b | — | — | — | — | — | — | — | — | — | — | — | — |
| Sec.Ot.th.Shares Excl.f/Brd.Money | 36s | — | — | — | — | — | — | — | — | — | — | — | — |
| Loans | 36l | — | — | — | — | — | — | — | — | — | — | — | — |
| Financial Derivatives | 36m | — | — | — | — | — | — | — | — | — | — | — | — |
| Insurance Technical Reserves | 36r | — | — | — | — | — | — | — | — | — | — | — | — |
| Shares and Other Equity | 37a | 90.45 | 98.71 | 96.70 | 96.31 | 96.66 | 115.00 | 118.54 | 85.68 | 98.35 | 78.91 | 79.83 | 77.37 |
| Other Items (Net) | 37r | 17.82 | −12.46 | −43.82 | −63.13 | −47.03 | −73.31 | −69.29 | −67.65 | −71.36 | −47.75 | −34.69 | −54.27 |
| Broad Money Liabs., Seasonally Adj. | 35l.b | 716.69 | 757.73 | 844.38 | 931.38 | 984.91 | 1,086.74 | 1,118.46 | 1,151.35 | 1,284.33 | 1,325.57 | 1,391.94 | 1,440.86 |
| **Monetary Aggregates** | | *Millions of E. Caribbean Dollars: End of Period* | | | | | | | | | | | |
| Broad Money | 59m | 716.39 | 755.55 | 840.09 | 925.50 | 977.33 | 1,075.93 | 1,104.31 | 1,133.52 | 1,261.63 | 1,300.02 | 1,364.63 | 1,412.68 |
| o/w:Currency Issued by Cent.Govt | 59m.a | — | — | — | — | — | — | — | — | — | — | — | — |
| o/w: Dep.in Nonfin. Corporations. | 59m.b | — | — | — | — | — | — | — | — | — | — | — | — |
| o/w:Secs. Issued by Central Govt. | 59m.c | — | — | — | — | — | — | — | — | — | — | — | — |
| Money (National Definitions) | | | | | | | | | | | | | |
| M1 | 59ma | 111.20 | 143.04 | 138.31 | 159.12 | 183.44 | 202.06 | 192.70 | 189.77 | 227.83 | 212.86 | 234.69 | 260.78 |
| M2 | 59mb | 587.37 | 626.98 | 687.17 | 749.07 | 881.08 | 973.03 | 1,010.23 | 1,033.96 | 1,138.35 | 1,158.54 | 1,248.94 | 1,298.47 |
| **Interest Rates** | | *Percent Per Annum* | | | | | | | | | | | |
| Discount Rate (End of Period) | 60.a | 6.50 | 6.50 | 6.50 | 6.50 | 6.50 | 6.50 | 6.50 | 6.50 | 6.50 | 6.50 | 6.50 | 6.50 |
| Money Market Rate | 60b | 4.67 | 4.01 | 4.76 | 5.24 | 4.92 | 6.03 | 6.33 | 5.68 | 5.04 | 6.28 | 6.19 | 6.44 |
| Treasury Bill Rate | 60c | 6.40 | 6.40 | 6.40 | 6.40 | 6.40 | 6.40 | 6.40 | 6.40 | 4.35 | 2.81 | 1.82 | .... |
| Savings Rate | 60k | 3.41 | 3.31 | 3.46 | 3.44 | 3.50 | 3.46 | 3.50 | 3.46 | 3.29 | 3.30 | 3.14 | 2.58 |
| Savings Rate (Fgn. Currency) | 60k.f | 1.59 | 1.77 | 1.76 | 2.42 | 2.74 | 1.09 | .82 | .93 | .90 | .90 | .90 | .94 |
| Deposit Rate | 60l | 3.26 | 3.15 | 3.33 | 3.26 | 3.20 | 3.20 | 3.26 | 3.20 | 3.10 | 3.05 | 2.87 | 2.45 |
| Deposit Rate (Fgn. Currency) | 60l.f | .15 | .57 | 2.43 | 2.48 | 2.59 | 1.40 | .44 | .25 | .39 | .48 | .52 | .70 |
| Lending Rate | 60p | 8.94 | 9.92 | 9.50 | 9.17 | 9.06 | 10.02 | 9.46 | 8.84 | 9.04 | 9.07 | 8.94 | 8.67 |
| Lending Rate (Fgn. Currency) | 60p.f | 3.83 | 3.06 | 9.30 | 9.95 | 9.83 | 10.42 | 7.27 | 5.68 | 5.61 | 5.69 | 5.59 | 5.38 |
| **Prices** | | *Index Numbers (2010=100): Period Averages* | | | | | | | | | | | |
| Consumer Prices | 64 | 84.6 | 86.0 | 88.2 | 91.1 | 96.9 | 96.9 | 100.0 | † 102.4 | 103.8 | 103.7 | 104.6 | 103.8 |
| **Intl. Transactions & Positions** | | *Millions of E. Caribbean Dollars* | | | | | | | | | | | |
| Exports | 70 | 111.75 | 111.86 | 114.69 | 102.06 | 107.98 | 91.81 | 99.42 | 82.91 | 91.40 | 95.83 | 97.21 | 81.57 |
| Imports, c.i.f. | 71 | 392.00 | 446.42 | 450.62 | 528.48 | 666.95 | 608.19 | 604.19 | 610.37 | 562.45 | 548.09 | 621.75 | 587.96 |

# Dominica  321

## Balance of Payments

| | | 2004 | 2005 | 2006 | 2007 | 2008 | 2009 | 2010 | 2011 | 2012 | 2013 | 2014 | 2015 |
|---|---|---|---|---|---|---|---|---|---|---|---|---|---|
| | | | | | | *Millions of US Dollars* | | | | | | | |
| A. Current Account* | 109bx | −58.9 | −76.1 | −49.9 | −86.9 | −129.9 | −111.1 | −80.2 | −67.9 | −92.1 | −72.1 | .... | .... |
| Goods, credit (exports) | 1a9cx | 42.9 | 42.9 | 44.3 | 39.0 | 43.9 | 36.8 | 37.2 | 36.2 | 38.6 | 41.0 | .... | .... |
| Goods, debit (imports) | 1a9dx | 127.8 | 145.9 | 146.9 | 172.3 | 217.4 | 198.2 | 196.9 | 198.9 | 183.3 | 178.6 | .... | .... |
| Balance on goods | 1a9bx | −84.8 | −103.0 | −102.6 | −133.3 | −173.5 | −161.4 | −159.7 | −162.8 | −144.7 | −137.6 | .... | .... |
| Services, credit (exports) | 1b9cx | 87.6 | 86.4 | 100.2 | 108.8 | 112.8 | 111.1 | 136.8 | 154.8 | 121.7 | 128.6 | .... | .... |
| Services, debit (imports) | 1b9dx | 46.3 | 50.2 | 52.0 | 64.0 | 69.9 | 66.2 | 67.6 | 65.9 | 67.6 | 70.4 | .... | .... |
| Balance on Goods & Services | 1z9bx | −43.6 | −66.8 | −54.4 | −88.5 | −130.6 | −116.5 | −90.5 | −73.9 | −90.7 | −79.4 | .... | .... |
| Primary income: credit | 1c9cx | 3.8 | 5.9 | 6.2 | 8.5 | 8.4 | 6.6 | 6.1 | 4.9 | 4.8 | 4.6 | .... | .... |
| Primary income: debit | 1c9dx | 37.1 | 34.9 | 21.2 | 28.2 | 26.8 | 20.2 | 15.5 | 15.5 | 23.0 | 18.6 | .... | .... |
| Balance on gds, serv. & prim. inc. | 1y9bx | −77.0 | −95.7 | −69.4 | −108.1 | −148.9 | −130.2 | −99.9 | −84.4 | −108.9 | −93.4 | .... | .... |
| Secondary income: credit | 1d9ca | 24.4 | 28.4 | 25.5 | 28.5 | 26.5 | 25.8 | 27.2 | 25.5 | 27.1 | 31.8 | .... | .... |
| Secondary income: debit | 1d9da | 6.3 | 8.7 | 5.9 | 7.4 | 7.5 | 6.7 | 7.5 | 9.1 | 10.3 | 10.5 | .... | .... |
| B. Capital Account* | 209ba | 20.8 | 15.2 | 24.8 | 54.7 | 54.3 | 40.8 | 30.2 | 15.7 | 8.9 | 4.9 | .... | .... |
| Capital account: credit | 209ca | 20.8 | 15.2 | 24.8 | 54.7 | 54.3 | 40.8 | 30.2 | 15.7 | 8.9 | 4.9 | .... | .... |
| Capital account: debit | 209da | — | — | — | — | — | — | — | — | — | — | .... | .... |
| Balance on current & capital acct. | 129ba | −38.1 | −60.9 | −25.0 | −32.2 | −75.6 | −70.2 | −50.0 | −52.2 | −83.2 | −67.3 | .... | .... |
| C. Financial Account* | 309na | −4.6 | −57.3 | −25.7 | −27.4 | −48.7 | −74.3 | −55.2 | −71.9 | −81.0 | −43.1 | .... | .... |
| Direct investment: assets | 3a9aa | — | — | — | — | — | — | — | — | — | — | .... | .... |
| Equity & investment fund shares | 3aaaa | .... | .... | .... | .... | .... | .... | .... | .... | .... | .... | .... | .... |
| Debt instruments | 3abaa | .... | .... | .... | .... | .... | .... | .... | .... | .... | .... | .... | .... |
| Direct investment: liabilities | 3a9la | 26.2 | 19.2 | 25.9 | 40.5 | 56.5 | 42.4 | 24.3 | 14.2 | 23.2 | 17.9 | .... | .... |
| Equity & investment fund shares | 3aala | 19.9 | 21.7 | 9.8 | 37.6 | 45.1 | 26.3 | 10.0 | 6.8 | 15.7 | 10.0 | .... | .... |
| Debt instruments | 3abla | 6.2 | −2.4 | 16.1 | 2.9 | 11.4 | 16.1 | 14.3 | 7.4 | 7.5 | 7.9 | .... | .... |
| Portfolio investment: assets | 3b9aa | 2.3 | .5 | .7 | −1.1 | 2.6 | .5 | 3.1 | .2 | −.2 | 14.5 | .... | .... |
| Equity & investment fund shares | 3baaa | .... | .... | .... | .... | .... | .... | .... | .... | .... | .... | .... | .... |
| Debt securities | 3bbaa | .... | .... | .... | .... | .... | .... | .... | .... | .... | .... | .... | .... |
| Portfolio investment: liabilities | 3b9la | −.2 | 4.2 | .6 | .6 | −.7 | .8 | −2.5 | −1.8 | .8 | −1.7 | .... | .... |
| Equity & investment fund shares | 3bala | .... | .... | .... | .... | .... | .... | .... | .... | .... | .... | .... | .... |
| Debt securities | 3bbla | .... | .... | .... | .... | .... | .... | .... | .... | .... | .... | .... | .... |
| Fin. der.& empl.stk.ops.(ESOs): net | 3c9na | .... | .... | .... | .... | .... | .... | .... | .... | .... | .... | .... | .... |
| Fin. der. & ESOs.: assets | 3c9aa | .... | .... | .... | .... | .... | .... | .... | .... | .... | .... | .... | .... |
| Fin. der. & ESOs.: liabilities | 3c9la | .... | .... | .... | .... | .... | .... | .... | .... | .... | .... | .... | .... |
| Other investment: assets | 3d9aa | 33.8 | 7.3 | 29.2 | 36.1 | 31.1 | 42.9 | 31.7 | 23.4 | 41.1 | 42.9 | .... | .... |
| Other equity | 3daaa | .... | .... | .... | .... | .... | .... | .... | .... | .... | .... | .... | .... |
| Debt instruments | 3dzaa | 33.8 | 7.3 | 29.2 | 36.1 | 31.1 | 42.9 | 31.7 | 23.4 | 41.1 | 42.9 | .... | .... |
| Other investment: liabilities | 3d9la | 14.6 | 41.6 | 29.0 | 21.3 | 26.5 | 74.5 | 68.1 | 83.1 | 98.0 | 84.4 | .... | .... |
| Other equity | 3dala | | | | | | | | | | | .... | .... |
| Debt instruments | 3dzla | 14.6 | 41.6 | 29.0 | 21.3 | 26.5 | 74.5 | 68.1 | 83.1 | 98.0 | 84.4 | .... | .... |
| Curr.+ cap.− finan. acct. balance | 4y9na | −33.5 | −3.5 | .6 | −4.8 | −26.9 | 4.1 | 5.3 | 19.6 | −2.2 | −24.1 | .... | .... |
| D. Net Errors and Omissions | 409na | 26.8 | 14.7 | 11.0 | 6.0 | 20.3 | 11.3 | −4.0 | −13.2 | 4.9 | 19.3 | .... | .... |
| E. Reserves and Related Items | 4z9na | −6.7 | 11.2 | 11.6 | 1.2 | −6.6 | 15.3 | 1.2 | 6.5 | 2.7 | −4.8 | .... | .... |
| Reserve assets | 3e9aa | −5.8 | 14.4 | 13.4 | −1.3 | −3.4 | 19.6 | .2 | 3.6 | 2.0 | −7.5 | .... | .... |
| Credit and loans from the IMF | 3dcla | .9 | 3.2 | 1.8 | −2.5 | 3.3 | 4.3 | −1.1 | −2.9 | −.8 | −2.7 | .... | .... |
| Exceptional financing | 409la | .... | .... | .... | .... | .... | .... | .... | .... | .... | .... | .... | .... |

*Excludes components in group E

## Government Finance
## Cash Flow Statement
### Budgetary Central Government

| | | 2004 | 2005 | 2006 | 2007 | 2008 | 2009 | 2010 | 2011 | 2012 | 2013 | 2014 | 2015 |
|---|---|---|---|---|---|---|---|---|---|---|---|---|---|
| | | | | | | *Millions of E. Caribbean Dollars: Fiscal Year Ends December 31* | | | | | | | |
| Cash Receipts:Operating Activities | c1 | .... | .... | .... | .... | 430.27 | 411.82 | 390.66 | 389.09 | 351.18 | 395.11 | 438.44 | .... |
| Taxes | c11 | .... | .... | .... | .... | 307.39 | 320.58 | 327.91 | 311.99 | 302.68 | 303.30 | 316.14 | .... |
| Social Contributions | c12 | .... | .... | .... | .... | — | — | — | — | — | — | — | .... |
| Grants | c13 | .... | .... | .... | .... | 92.46 | 61.73 | 38.81 | 31.65 | 1.86 | 12.20 | 60.75 | .... |
| Other Receipts | c14 | .... | .... | .... | .... | 30.42 | 29.51 | 23.94 | 45.45 | 46.64 | 79.61 | 61.55 | .... |
| Cash Payments:Operating Activities | c2 | .... | .... | .... | .... | 299.65 | 288.26 | 316.64 | 325.84 | 336.36 | 358.31 | 350.99 | .... |
| Compensation of Employees | c21 | .... | .... | .... | .... | 120.16 | 125.69 | 127.50 | 138.86 | 134.78 | 149.80 | 148.43 | .... |
| Purchases of Goods & Services | c22 | .... | .... | .... | .... | 86.95 | 84.18 | 99.29 | 96.93 | 92.20 | 113.32 | 107.91 | .... |
| Interest | c24 | .... | .... | .... | .... | 28.88 | 14.06 | 21.01 | 22.66 | 42.68 | 28.06 | 24.85 | .... |
| Subsidies | c25 | .... | .... | .... | .... | 48.53 | 47.21 | 53.76 | 50.82 | 53.18 | 49.72 | 51.67 | .... |
| Grants | c26 | .... | .... | .... | .... | — | — | — | — | — | — | — | .... |
| Social Benefits | c27 | .... | .... | .... | .... | 15.13 | 17.12 | 15.08 | 16.57 | 13.52 | 17.41 | 18.13 | .... |
| Other Payments | c28 | .... | .... | .... | .... | — | — | — | — | — | — | — | .... |
| Net Cash Inflow:Operating Act.[1-2] | ccio | .... | .... | .... | .... | 130.62 | 123.56 | 74.02 | 63.25 | 14.82 | 36.80 | 87.45 | .... |
| Net Cash Outflow:Invest. in NFA | c31 | .... | .... | .... | .... | 153.93 | 151.35 | 159.80 | 190.71 | 149.23 | 160.19 | 121.41 | .... |
| Purchases of Nonfinancial Assets | c31.1 | .... | .... | .... | .... | 154.31 | 151.76 | 161.43 | 192.17 | 150.19 | 160.44 | 121.75 | .... |
| Sales of Nonfinancial Assets | c31.2 | .... | .... | .... | .... | .38 | .41 | 1.63 | 1.46 | .96 | .25 | .34 | .... |
| Cash Surplus/Deficit [1-2-31=1-2M] | ccsd | .... | .... | .... | .... | −23.31 | −27.79 | −85.78 | −127.46 | −134.41 | −123.39 | −33.96 | .... |
| Net Acq. Fin. Assets, excl. Cash | c32x | .... | .... | .... | .... | −1.07 | −1.00 | −1.91 | −.49 | 1.12 | .44 | .04 | .... |
| Domestic | c321x | .... | .... | .... | .... | −1.07 | −1.00 | −1.91 | −.49 | 1.12 | .44 | .04 | .... |
| Foreign | c322x | .... | .... | .... | .... | — | — | — | — | — | — | — | .... |
| Net Incurrence of Liabilities | c33 | .... | .... | .... | .... | −19.62 | 23.84 | 43.50 | 50.59 | 91.61 | 100.17 | 33.91 | .... |
| Domestic | c331 | .... | .... | .... | .... | −10.48 | 6.06 | −5.04 | 22.31 | 18.80 | 65.68 | −.84 | .... |
| Foreign | c332 | .... | .... | .... | .... | −9.14 | 17.78 | 48.54 | 28.28 | 72.81 | 34.49 | 34.75 | .... |
| Net Cash Inflow, Fin.Act.[-32x+33] | cnfb | .... | .... | .... | .... | −18.55 | 24.84 | 45.41 | 51.08 | 90.49 | 99.73 | 33.87 | .... |
| Net Change in Stock of Cash | cncb | .... | .... | .... | .... | −41.86 | −2.95 | −40.37 | −76.38 | −43.92 | −23.66 | −.09 | .... |
| Stat. Discrep. [32X-33+NCB-CSD] | ccsdz | .... | .... | .... | .... | — | — | — | — | — | — | — | .... |
| Memo Item:Cash Expenditure[2+31 | c2m | .... | .... | .... | .... | 453.58 | 439.61 | 476.44 | 516.55 | 485.59 | 518.50 | 472.40 | .... |
| Memo Item: Gross Debt | c63 | .... | .... | .... | .... | .... | .... | .... | .... | 855.37 | 881.07 | 917.22 | .... |

| National Accounts | | 2004 | 2005 | 2006 | 2007 | 2008 | 2009 | 2010 | 2011 | 2012 | 2013 | 2014 | 2015 |
|---|---|---|---|---|---|---|---|---|---|---|---|---|---|
| | | | | | | *Millions of E. Caribbean Dollars* | | | | | | | |
| Househ.Cons.Expend.,incl.NPISHs.... | **96f** | 812.9 | 828.1 | 854.0 | 990.3 | 1,177.2 | 1,178.8 | 1,107.1 | 1,113.0 | 1,190.1 | 1,145.7 | 1,158.8 | .... |
| Government Consumption Expend... | **91f** | 142.4 | 154.7 | 164.9 | 185.0 | 180.9 | 227.0 | 223.1 | 234.9 | 242.0 | 266.3 | 268.9 | .... |
| Gross Fixed Capital Formation.......... | **93e** | 174.4 | 197.6 | 202.1 | 221.2 | 261.0 | 255.9 | 245.1 | 224.4 | 199.6 | 167.6 | 176.0 | .... |
| Exports of Goods and Services......... | **90c** | 352.3 | 349.3 | 390.0 | 399.2 | 423.2 | 399.5 | 470.0 | 515.6 | 432.7 | 473.5 | 497.9 | .... |
| Imports of Goods and Services (-)..... | **98c** | 470.1 | 529.5 | 536.9 | 638.1 | 775.8 | 714.1 | 714.2 | 715.0 | 674.7 | 657.9 | 649.3 | .... |
| Gross Domestic Product (GDP)......... | **99b** | 1,011.9 | 1,000.2 | 1,074.1 | 1,157.5 | 1,266.5 | 1,347.2 | 1,331.0 | 1,372.9 | 1,389.7 | 1,395.2 | 1,452.4 | .... |
| Net Primary Income from Abroad..... | **98.n** | −90.0 | −78.2 | −40.5 | −53.0 | −49.5 | −36.9 | −25.5 | −28.5 | −49.3 | −52.8 | −55.0 | .... |
| Gross National Income (GNI)............. | **99a** | 921.9 | 921.9 | 1,033.6 | 1,104.6 | 1,217.0 | 1,310.3 | 1,305.5 | 1,344.4 | 1,340.4 | 1,342.3 | 1,397.3 | .... |
| Net Current Transf.from Abroad....... | **98t** | 48.9 | 53.1 | 52.9 | 57.1 | 51.4 | 51.6 | 53.2 | 44.5 | 45.4 | 54.8 | 56.4 | .... |
| Gross Nat'l Disposable Inc.(GNDI).... | **99i** | 970.8 | 975.0 | 1,086.4 | 1,161.7 | 1,268.4 | 1,361.8 | 1,358.7 | 1,388.9 | 1,385.8 | 1,397.2 | 1,453.7 | .... |
| Gross Saving.................................. | **99s** | 15.5 | −7.8 | 67.5 | −13.6 | −89.7 | −44.0 | 28.6 | 41.0 | −46.3 | −14.8 | 26.0 | .... |
| GDP Volume 1990 Prices................. | **99b.p** | 539.3 | 557.5 | 592.4 | 621.1 | 643.2 | 638.0 | 634.8 | .... | .... | .... | .... | .... |
| GDP Volume (2010=100)............... | **99bvp** | 88.1 | 86.5 | 89.7 | 93.2 | 100.4 | 99.7 | 100.0 | .... | .... | .... | .... | .... |
| GDP Deflator (2010=100)............... | **99bip** | 89.5 | 85.6 | 86.5 | 88.9 | 93.9 | 100.7 | 100.0 | .... | .... | .... | .... | .... |
| | | | | | | *Millions: Midyear Estimates* | | | | | | | |
| **Population**................................ | **99z** | .07 | .07 | .07 | .07 | .07 | .07 | .07 | .07 | .07 | .07 | .07 | .07 |

| | | 2004 | 2005 | 2006 | 2007 | 2008 | 2009 | 2010 | 2011 | 2012 | 2013 | 2014 | 2015 |
|---|---|---|---|---|---|---|---|---|---|---|---|---|---|
| **Exchange Rates** | | | | | | | *Pesos per SDR: End of Period* | | | | | | |
| Market Rate....................aa=........ | wa | 48.313 | 49.851 | 50.422 | 53.837 | 55.115 | 57.034 | 58.408 | 59.555 | 62.037 | 65.989 | 64.309 | 63.267 |
| | | | | | | *Pesos per US Dollar: End of Period (we) Period Average (wf)* | | | | | | | |
| Market Rate....................ae=........ | we | 31.109 | 34.879 | 33.517 | 34.069 | 35.783 | 36.381 | 37.927 | 38.792 | 40.365 | 42.850 | 44.387 | 45.656 |
| Market Rate....................rf=.......... | wf | 42.099 | 30.511 | 33.254 | 33.312 | 34.866 | 36.114 | 37.307 | 38.232 | 39.336 | 41.808 | 43.556 | 45.052 |
| | | | | | | *Index Numbers (2010=100): Period Averages* | | | | | | | |
| Market Rate.................................. | ahx | 91.6 | 122.8 | 112.2 | 112.0 | 107.0 | 103.3 | 100.0 | 97.6 | 94.8 | 89.2 | 85.6 | 82.8 |
| Nominal Effective Exchange Rate..... | nec | 95.4 | 126.9 | 114.4 | 112.6 | 106.3 | 104.4 | 100.0 | 95.7 | 94.6 | 89.5 | 86.6 | 88.3 |
| CPI-Based Real Effect. Ex. Rate........ | rec | 77.6 | 103.9 | 98.2 | 99.8 | 100.4 | 100.0 | 100.0 | 100.7 | 100.9 | 98.5 | 96.4 | 98.5 |
| **Fund Position** | | | | | | | *Millions of SDRs: End of Period* | | | | | | |
| Quota...................................... | 2f.s | 218.90 | 218.90 | 218.90 | 218.90 | 218.90 | 218.90 | 218.90 | 218.90 | 218.90 | 218.90 | 218.90 | 218.90 |
| SDR Holdings.............................. | 1b.s | 1.02 | .39 | 16.26 | 62.37 | 23.36 | 175.82 | 76.46 | 12.10 | 13.21 | 1.33 | 4.82 | 5.57 |
| Reserve Position in the Fund............ | 1c.s | — | — | — | — | — | — | — | — | — | — | — | — |
| Total Fund Cred.&Loans Outstg........ | 2tl | 131.34 | 280.20 | 305.38 | 346.52 | 319.59 | 488.94 | 739.87 | 848.01 | 775.78 | 646.33 | 345.35 | 82.09 |
| SDR Allocations............................ | 1bd | 31.59 | 31.59 | 31.59 | 31.59 | 31.59 | 208.83 | 208.83 | 208.83 | 208.83 | 208.83 | 208.83 | 208.83 |
| **International Liquidity** | | | | | | *Millions of US Dollars Unless Otherwise Indicated: End of Period* | | | | | | | |
| Total Reserves minus Gold.............. | 1l.d | 818.4 | 1,920.5 | 2,263.8 | 3,029.5 | 2,678.6 | 3,560.3 | 3,848.7 | 4,086.4 | 3,528.2 | 4,678.6 | 4,839.7 | 5,246.6 |
| SDR Holdings.......................... | 1b.d | 1.6 | .6 | 24.5 | 98.6 | 36.0 | 275.6 | 117.7 | 18.6 | 20.3 | 2.1 | 7.0 | 7.7 |
| Reserve Position in the Fund.......... | 1c.d | — | — | — | — | — | — | — | — | — | — | — | — |
| Foreign Exchange........................ | 1d.d | 816.8 | 1,919.9 | 2,239.3 | 2,930.9 | 2,642.6 | 3,284.6 | 3,731.0 | 4,067.8 | 3,507.9 | 4,676.5 | 4,832.7 | 5,238.9 |
| Gold (Million Fine Troy Ounces)........ | 1ad | .018 | .018 | .018 | .018 | .018 | .018 | .018 | .018 | .018 | .018 | .018 | .018 |
| Gold (National Valuation)................ | 1and | 8.0 | 9.4 | 11.6 | 15.3 | 15.9 | 19.9 | 25.7 | 28.0 | 30.3 | 22.0 | 22.1 | 19.4 |
| Central Bank: Other Assets.............. | 3..d | 220.6 | 191.0 | 212.2 | 226.6 | 616.6 | 620.6 | 610.7 | 604.8 | 613.9 | 625.5 | 614.7 | 615.5 |
| Central Bank: Other Liabs.............. | 4..d | 655.7 | 1,162.7 | 1,044.2 | 909.6 | 824.6 | 786.8 | 766.0 | 758.5 | 741.2 | 734.3 | 705.2 | 679.7 |
| Other Depository Corps.: Assets....... | 7a.d | 1,052.7 | 1,101.9 | 1,294.5 | 1,463.7 | 1,119.7 | 1,045.4 | 826.7 | 706.9 | 863.1 | 1,267.6 | 1,557.6 | 918.1 |
| Other Depository Corps.: Liabs........ | 7b.d | 280.5 | 197.5 | 164.0 | 200.4 | 430.6 | 378.8 | 645.7 | 813.8 | 911.0 | 1,433.4 | 1,809.2 | 2,002.8 |
| Other Financial Corps.: Assets......... | 7e.d | .7 | 10.1 | 17.2 | 29.5 | 29.4 | 28.1 | 23.1 | 26.6 | 48.2 | 47.5 | 44.3 | 32.7 |
| Other Financial Corps.: Liabs............ | 7f.d | — | 24.0 | 45.2 | 50.2 | 42.2 | 53.3 | 49.3 | 67.6 | 54.4 | 61.4 | 53.7 | 55.3 |
| **Central Bank** | | | | | | | *Millions of Pesos: End of Period* | | | | | | |
| Net Foreign Assets......................... | 11n | 4,152 | 17,764 | 30,561 | 56,536 | 67,814 | 73,811 | 80,423 | 89,926 | 77,219 | 139,746 | 175,415 | 218,194 |
| Claims on Nonresidents................. | 11 | 31,749 | 73,573 | 82,537 | 107,687 | 115,963 | 141,622 | 163,764 | 182,129 | 167,987 | 227,276 | 242,077 | 267,428 |
| Liabilities to Nonresidents.............. | 16c | 27,597 | 55,809 | 51,977 | 51,150 | 48,149 | 67,811 | 83,341 | 92,203 | 90,768 | 87,530 | 66,662 | 49,234 |
| Claims on Other Depository Corps.... | 12e | 75,877 | 96,749 | 8,345 | 6,840 | 10,590 | 6,735 | 1,758 | 1,880 | 1,120 | 1,332 | 1,323 | 2,176 |
| Net Claims on Central Government... | 12an | 38,717 | 94,276 | 203,298 | 231,313 | 262,317 | 274,060 | 293,258 | 315,145 | 346,278 | 356,446 | 406,726 | 453,686 |
| Claims on Central Government...... | 12a | 39,612 | 95,866 | 204,165 | 232,642 | 262,674 | 278,230 | 300,813 | 317,937 | 350,684 | 376,102 | 410,963 | 457,319 |
| Liabilities to Central Government... | 16d | 894 | 1,590 | 867 | 1,330 | 358 | 4,169 | 7,555 | 2,793 | 4,406 | 19,656 | 4,237 | 3,633 |
| Claims on Other Sectors.................. | 12s | 36,619 | 5,523 | 5,450 | 5,696 | 5,909 | 7,207 | 7,313 | 7,690 | 8,132 | 8,479 | 9,184 | 9,561 |
| Claims on Other Financial Corps... | 12g | — | — | — | — | — | — | — | — | — | — | — | — |
| Claims on State & Local Govts...... | 12b | — | — | — | — | — | — | — | — | — | — | — | — |
| Claims on Public Nonfin. Corps...... | 12c | 950 | 3,288 | 3,231 | 3,223 | 2,943 | 2,952 | 3,063 | 3,170 | 3,296 | 3,493 | 3,618 | 3,722 |
| Claims on Private Sector................ | 12d | 35,670 | 2,234 | 2,220 | 2,473 | 2,966 | 4,255 | 4,250 | 4,520 | 4,836 | 4,986 | 5,566 | 5,839 |
| Monetary Base.............................. | 14 | 97,314 | 156,683 | 154,615 | 176,692 | 181,787 | 187,280 | 209,753 | 225,928 | 229,707 | 254,901 | 294,013 | 307,018 |
| Currency in Circulation................. | 14a | 40,679 | 49,911 | 53,498 | 62,291 | 62,470 | 70,162 | 74,032 | 78,221 | 86,507 | 93,747 | 104,707 | 111,539 |
| Liabs. to Other Depository Corps.... | 14c | 56,346 | 106,773 | 101,117 | 114,401 | 119,317 | 117,118 | 135,721 | 147,708 | 143,200 | 161,154 | 189,305 | 195,479 |
| Liabilities to Other Sectors............. | 14d | 290 | — | — | — | — | — | — | — | — | — | — | — |
| Other Liabs. to Other Dep. Corps.... | 14n | 55,180 | 23,209 | 17,933 | 14,959 | 20,853 | 44,548 | 67,968 | 89,263 | 94,975 | 106,396 | 94,733 | 107,233 |
| Dep. & Sec. Excl. f/Monetary Base.... | 14o | 47,767 | 80,526 | 124,842 | 152,328 | 165,926 | 166,029 | 164,602 | 173,862 | 184,128 | 220,019 | 270,954 | 325,207 |
| Deposits Included in Broad Money. | 15 | — | — | — | — | — | — | — | — | — | — | — | — |
| Sec.Ot.th.Shares Incl.in Brd. Money | 16a | 47,692 | 30,728 | 14,878 | 21,485 | 14,936 | 8,165 | 8,304 | 11,121 | 13,621 | 14,617 | 19,106 | 19,357 |
| Deposits Excl. from Broad Money... | 16b | 75 | 2,894 | 3,042 | 3,049 | 3,055 | 3,114 | 4,559 | 6,543 | 3,791 | 3,821 | 3,676 | 3,975 |
| Sec.Ot.th.Shares Excl.f/Brd.Money.. | 16s | — | 46,904 | 106,921 | 127,794 | 147,936 | 154,751 | 151,738 | 156,197 | 166,715 | 201,581 | 248,172 | 301,875 |
| Loans...................................... | 16l | — | — | — | — | — | — | — | — | — | — | — | — |
| Financial Derivatives...................... | 16m | — | — | — | — | — | — | — | — | — | — | — | — |
| Shares and Other Equity.................. | 17a | −54,008 | −19,674 | −25,787 | −22,627 | −17,192 | −20,179 | −14,780 | −25,571 | −21,308 | −28,369 | −36,492 | −37,073 |
| Other Items (Net)............................ | 17r | 9,112 | −26,432 | −23,950 | −20,967 | −4,745 | −15,867 | −44,791 | −48,841 | −54,753 | −46,944 | −30,560 | −18,767 |
| Memo Item: | | | | | | | | | | | | | |
| Total Assets..................................... | 10ra | 197,950 | 292,812 | 322,184 | 375,929 | 403,185 | 442,283 | 494,748 | 530,862 | 553,118 | 634,412 | 684,877 | 757,057 |

# Dominican Republic   243

| | | 2004 | 2005 | 2006 | 2007 | 2008 | 2009 | 2010 | 2011 | 2012 | 2013 | 2014 | 2015 |
|---|---|---|---|---|---|---|---|---|---|---|---|---|---|
| **Other Depository Corporations** | | *Millions of Pesos: End of Period* | | | | | | | | | | | |
| Net Foreign Assets | 21n | 23,453 | 31,381 | 37,883 | 42,877 | 24,297 | 24,036 | 6,773 | −4,137 | −1,926 | −7,077 | −11,120 | −49,319 |
| Claims on Nonresidents | 21 | 31,971 | 38,235 | 43,379 | 49,678 | 39,482 | 37,694 | 30,939 | 27,375 | 34,751 | 54,090 | 68,851 | 41,747 |
| Liabilities to Nonresidents | 26c | 8,519 | 6,854 | 5,495 | 6,801 | 15,184 | 13,658 | 24,165 | 31,512 | 36,677 | 61,167 | 79,971 | 91,066 |
| Claims on Central Bank | 20 | 112,747 | 132,699 | 127,059 | 137,482 | 144,337 | 168,079 | 207,624 | 240,938 | 242,497 | 269,196 | 276,116 | 296,980 |
| Currency | 20a | 9,042 | 13,052 | 11,033 | 13,230 | 12,145 | 14,954 | 14,665 | 16,992 | 19,894 | 20,249 | 22,162 | 22,167 |
| Reserve Deposits and Securities | 20b | 48,564 | 61,117 | 77,695 | 94,971 | 107,888 | 116,443 | 126,198 | 144,366 | 137,544 | 159,331 | 178,933 | 192,325 |
| Other Claims | 20n | 55,141 | 58,530 | 38,330 | 29,281 | 24,304 | 36,682 | 66,762 | 79,579 | 85,058 | 89,616 | 75,021 | 82,489 |
| Net Claims on Central Government | 22an | 10,383 | 8,539 | 5,466 | 2,522 | 12,379 | 39,914 | 21,239 | 14,120 | 76,205 | 96,632 | 67,157 | 95,200 |
| Claims on Central Government | 22a | 25,531 | 28,078 | 29,428 | 27,083 | 46,041 | 76,440 | 64,636 | 65,031 | 113,354 | 138,101 | 104,755 | 129,650 |
| Liabilities to Central Government | 26d | 15,147 | 19,539 | 23,963 | 24,560 | 33,663 | 36,526 | 43,397 | 50,910 | 37,149 | 41,469 | 37,598 | 34,449 |
| Claims on Other Sectors | 22s | 186,684 | 209,666 | 234,825 | 299,061 | 341,644 | 366,329 | 440,698 | 497,069 | 525,127 | 602,947 | 722,717 | 852,117 |
| Claims on Other Financial Corps | 22g | 1,882 | 1,264 | 2,598 | 1,947 | 1,932 | 2,753 | 3,407 | 6,495 | 8,933 | 9,917 | 13,827 | 21,176 |
| Claims on State & Local Govts | 22b | 413 | 628 | 757 | 903 | 1,348 | 1,472 | 1,396 | 1,343 | 1,421 | 1,349 | 1,233 | 1,185 |
| Claims on Public Nonfin. Corps | 22c | 3,833 | 2,733 | 4,788 | 4,458 | 10,050 | 5,716 | 4,800 | 3,655 | 1,187 | 535 | 659 | 32,933 |
| Claims on Private Sector | 22d | 180,555 | 205,041 | 226,683 | 291,753 | 328,314 | 356,388 | 431,096 | 485,575 | 513,586 | 591,146 | 706,999 | 796,822 |
| Liabilities to Central Bank | 26g | 71,831 | 65,150 | 909 | 828 | 4,576 | 816 | 38 | 180 | 344 | 9 | 1,714 | |
| Transf.Dep.Included in Broad Money | 24 | 38,755 | 48,148 | 68,094 | 90,670 | 78,345 | 97,432 | 107,627 | 114,178 | 126,143 | 149,462 | 161,065 | 183,946 |
| Other Dep.Included in Broad Money | 25 | 125,310 | 154,285 | 167,423 | 200,691 | 217,335 | 243,015 | 291,980 | 342,812 | 377,740 | 426,444 | 444,747 | 504,510 |
| Sec.Ot.th.Shares Incl.in Brd. Money | 26a | 114,982 | 115,321 | 115,456 | 116,380 | 143,231 | 168,573 | 175,736 | 194,510 | 211,931 | 227,117 | 266,435 | 294,292 |
| Deposits Excl. from Broad Money | 26b | 3,239 | 4,955 | 3,734 | 4,772 | 5,560 | 8,423 | 12,221 | 16,141 | 18,836 | 19,276 | 18,760 | 20,160 |
| Sec.Ot.th.Shares Excl.f/Brd.Money | 26s | 1,214 | 2,111 | 2,738 | 3,362 | 4,421 | 4,748 | 10,924 | 12,970 | 16,128 | 17,121 | 29,838 | 32,215 |
| Loans | 26l | 792 | 508 | 848 | 4,895 | 5,276 | 5,356 | 5,412 | 5,328 | 8,785 | 9,668 | 9,397 | 10,333 |
| Financial Derivatives | 26m | — | — | 1 | 33 | 31 | — | — | — | — | — | — | — |
| Insurance Technical Reserves | 26r | | | | | | | | | | | | |
| Shares and Other Equity | 27a | 18,662 | 27,532 | 66,646 | 73,898 | 81,853 | 84,468 | 96,367 | 111,597 | 122,447 | 138,087 | 150,909 | 168,441 |
| Other Items (Net) | 27r | −41,517 | −35,726 | −20,614 | −13,585 | −17,971 | −14,473 | −23,970 | −49,727 | −40,449 | −25,486 | −26,913 | −20,633 |
| Memo Item: | | | | | | | | | | | | | |
| Total Assets | 20ra | 439,544 | 493,030 | 503,161 | 582,249 | 647,357 | 727,502 | 833,219 | 949,382 | 1,036,855 | 1,182,206 | 1,305,667 | 1,462,606 |
| **Depository Corporations** | | *Millions of Pesos: End of Period* | | | | | | | | | | | |
| Net Foreign Assets | 31n | 27,604 | 49,145 | 68,444 | 99,414 | 92,111 | 97,847 | 87,197 | 85,789 | 75,294 | 132,669 | 164,295 | 168,875 |
| Claims on Nonresidents | 31 | 63,720 | 111,808 | 125,916 | 157,365 | 155,444 | 179,316 | 194,703 | 209,504 | 202,739 | 281,367 | 310,928 | 309,175 |
| Liabilities to Nonresidents | 36c | 36,115 | 62,663 | 57,472 | 57,951 | 63,333 | 81,469 | 107,506 | 123,715 | 127,445 | 148,698 | 146,633 | 140,300 |
| Domestic Claims | 32 | 272,404 | 318,004 | 449,039 | 538,593 | 622,248 | 687,510 | 762,508 | 834,024 | 955,743 | 1,064,504 | 1,205,785 | 1,410,564 |
| Net Claims on Central Government | 32an | 49,101 | 102,816 | 208,763 | 233,835 | 274,695 | 313,974 | 314,497 | 329,265 | 422,484 | 453,078 | 473,883 | 548,887 |
| Claims on Central Government | 32a | 65,142 | 123,944 | 233,593 | 259,725 | 308,716 | 354,669 | 365,449 | 382,968 | 464,038 | 514,203 | 515,718 | 586,968 |
| Liabilities to Central Government | 36d | 16,042 | 21,129 | 24,830 | 25,890 | 34,021 | 40,695 | 50,952 | 53,703 | 41,555 | 61,125 | 41,835 | 38,082 |
| Claims on Other Sectors | 32s | 223,303 | 215,189 | 240,276 | 304,758 | 347,553 | 373,536 | 448,011 | 504,759 | 533,259 | 611,426 | 731,901 | 861,678 |
| Claims on Other Financial Corps | 32g | 1,882 | 1,264 | 2,598 | 1,948 | 1,932 | 2,754 | 3,407 | 6,495 | 8,933 | 9,917 | 13,827 | 21,176 |
| Claims on State & Local Govts | 32b | 413 | 628 | 757 | 903 | 1,348 | 1,472 | 1,396 | 1,343 | 1,421 | 1,349 | 1,233 | 1,185 |
| Claims on Public Nonfin. Corps | 32c | 4,783 | 6,021 | 8,018 | 7,681 | 12,993 | 8,667 | 7,863 | 6,825 | 4,483 | 4,028 | 4,277 | 36,655 |
| Claims on Private Sector | 32d | 216,225 | 207,275 | 228,902 | 294,226 | 331,280 | 360,643 | 435,346 | 490,096 | 518,422 | 596,132 | 712,564 | 802,661 |
| Broad Money Liabilities | 35l | 358,665 | 385,341 | 408,316 | 478,287 | 504,171 | 572,393 | 643,014 | 723,849 | 796,048 | 891,138 | 973,898 | 1,091,477 |
| Currency Outside Depository Corps | 34a | 31,636 | 36,858 | 42,465 | 49,061 | 50,326 | 55,209 | 59,367 | 61,228 | 66,613 | 73,498 | 82,545 | 89,372 |
| Transferable Deposits | 34 | 39,045 | 48,148 | 68,094 | 90,670 | 78,345 | 97,432 | 107,627 | 114,178 | 126,143 | 149,462 | 161,065 | 183,946 |
| Other Deposits | 35 | 125,310 | 154,285 | 167,423 | 200,691 | 217,335 | 243,015 | 291,980 | 342,812 | 377,740 | 426,444 | 444,747 | 504,510 |
| Securities Other than Shares | 36a | 162,674 | 146,049 | 130,334 | 137,865 | 158,166 | 176,737 | 184,040 | 205,631 | 225,552 | 241,734 | 285,541 | 313,649 |
| Deposits Excl. from Broad Money | 36b | 3,313 | 7,849 | 6,776 | 7,821 | 8,614 | 11,537 | 16,780 | 22,684 | 22,627 | 23,097 | 22,436 | 24,135 |
| Sec.Ot.th.Shares Excl.f/Brd.Money | 36s | 1,214 | 49,015 | 109,659 | 131,156 | 152,357 | 159,499 | 162,662 | 169,167 | 182,843 | 218,702 | 278,011 | 334,090 |
| Loans | 36l | 792 | 508 | 848 | 4,895 | 5,276 | 5,356 | 5,412 | 5,328 | 8,785 | 9,668 | 9,397 | 10,333 |
| Financial Derivatives | 36m | — | — | 1 | 33 | 31 | — | — | — | — | — | — | — |
| Insurance Technical Reserves | 36r | | | | | | | | | | | | |
| Shares and Other Equity | 37a | −35,345 | 7,858 | 40,859 | 51,271 | 64,661 | 64,289 | 81,588 | 86,027 | 101,139 | 109,718 | 114,418 | 131,368 |
| Other Items (Net) | 37r | −28,630 | −83,422 | −48,976 | −35,457 | −20,751 | −27,717 | −59,752 | −87,242 | −80,405 | −55,151 | −28,079 | −11,964 |
| Broad Money Liabs., Seasonally Adj. | 35l.b | 359,445 | 382,903 | 404,189 | 472,530 | 497,147 | 562,414 | 630,789 | 709,537 | 781,717 | 875,959 | 958,785 | 1,074,836 |
| **Other Financial Corporations** | | *Millions of Pesos: End of Period* | | | | | | | | | | | |
| Net Foreign Assets | 41n | 21 | −484 | −937 | −702 | −449 | −911 | −983 | −1,588 | −249 | −593 | −419 | −1,026 |
| Claims on Nonresidents | 41 | 21 | 351 | 578 | 1,003 | 1,037 | 1,013 | 863 | 1,031 | 1,942 | 2,027 | 1,956 | 1,487 |
| Liabilities to Nonresidents | 46c | — | 834 | 1,515 | 1,705 | 1,486 | 1,923 | 1,846 | 2,620 | 2,191 | 2,620 | 2,375 | 2,512 |
| Claims on Depository Corporations | 40 | 9,571 | 24,369 | 35,362 | 41,580 | 42,389 | 58,904 | 64,756 | 67,604 | 79,420 | 90,130 | 98,709 | 104,839 |
| Net Claims on Central Government | 42an | −260 | 1,830 | 1,377 | 8,457 | 23,176 | 32,465 | 51,674 | 81,691 | 110,053 | 148,659 | 186,865 | 236,842 |
| Claims on Central Government | 42a | 65 | 2,164 | 1,817 | 8,941 | 23,698 | 33,056 | 52,191 | 82,333 | 110,638 | 149,327 | 187,583 | 237,743 |
| Liabilities to Central Government | 46d | 325 | 335 | 440 | 484 | 522 | 590 | 518 | 642 | 585 | 668 | 719 | 902 |
| Claims on Other Sectors | 42s | 5,099 | 5,942 | 8,260 | 9,821 | 13,405 | 13,767 | 15,272 | 16,392 | 18,589 | 16,864 | 25,095 | 30,115 |
| Claims on State & Local Govts | 42b | — | — | — | — | — | — | — | — | — | — | — | — |
| Claims on Public Nonfin. Corps | 42c | 50 | 327 | 1,374 | 2,035 | 282 | 297 | 230 | 233 | 327 | 239 | 179 | 223 |
| Claims on Private Sector | 42d | 5,049 | 5,616 | 6,886 | 7,787 | 13,123 | 13,470 | 15,042 | 16,159 | 18,262 | 16,625 | 24,916 | 29,892 |
| Deposits | 46b | — | — | — | — | — | — | — | — | — | — | — | — |
| Securities Other than Shares | 46s | — | — | — | — | — | — | — | — | — | — | — | — |
| Loans | 46l | 5 | 412 | 520 | 812 | 299 | 622 | 756 | 644 | 474 | 409 | 2,095 | 2,710 |
| Financial Derivatives | 46m | — | — | — | — | — | — | — | — | — | — | — | — |
| Insurance Technical Reserves | 46r | 12,985 | 29,062 | 40,477 | 55,307 | 73,704 | 98,395 | 124,458 | 157,990 | 198,756 | 245,474 | 297,837 | 354,789 |
| Shares and Other Equity | 47a | 3,714 | 4,220 | 5,271 | 5,871 | 7,142 | 8,357 | 8,849 | 9,833 | 10,421 | 11,664 | 12,417 | 14,138 |
| Other Items (Net) | 47r | −2,273 | −2,036 | −2,205 | −2,833 | −2,624 | −3,149 | −3,344 | −4,368 | −1,838 | −2,487 | −2,099 | −869 |
| Memo Item: | | | | | | | | | | | | | |
| Total Assets | 40ra | 22,822 | 38,705 | 52,822 | 69,408 | 89,158 | 116,521 | 144,196 | 180,603 | 223,831 | 273,010 | 329,226 | 390,563 |

2016, International Monetary Fund : *International Financial Statistics Yearbook*

# Dominican Republic   243

| | | 2004 | 2005 | 2006 | 2007 | 2008 | 2009 | 2010 | 2011 | 2012 | 2013 | 2014 | 2015 |
|---|---|---|---|---|---|---|---|---|---|---|---|---|---|
| **Financial Corporations** | | | | | | *Millions of Pesos: End of Period* | | | | | | | |
| Net Foreign Assets............... | 51n | 27,625 | 48,661 | 67,507 | 98,711 | 91,662 | 96,936 | 86,213 | 84,201 | 75,045 | 132,076 | 163,876 | 167,849 |
| Claims on Nonresidents.............. | 51 | 63,741 | 112,158 | 126,494 | 158,367 | 156,481 | 180,328 | 195,566 | 210,535 | 204,681 | 283,393 | 312,884 | 310,661 |
| Liabilities to Nonresidents............ | 56c | 36,115 | 63,497 | 58,987 | 59,656 | 64,819 | 83,393 | 109,352 | 126,334 | 129,636 | 151,317 | 149,008 | 142,812 |
| Domestic Claims......................... | 52 | 275,361 | 324,512 | 456,079 | 554,924 | 656,898 | 730,989 | 826,046 | 925,612 | 1,075,452 | 1,220,110 | 1,403,917 | 1,656,344 |
| Net Claims on Central Government | 52an | 48,841 | 104,645 | 210,141 | 242,293 | 297,871 | 346,439 | 366,171 | 410,956 | 532,537 | 601,737 | 660,748 | 785,728 |
| Claims on Central Government.... | 52a | 65,208 | 126,109 | 235,410 | 268,666 | 332,414 | 387,725 | 417,640 | 465,301 | 574,676 | 663,530 | 703,301 | 824,712 |
| Liabilities to Central Government. | 56d | 16,367 | 21,463 | 25,270 | 26,374 | 34,542 | 41,286 | 51,470 | 54,345 | 42,139 | 61,793 | 42,553 | 38,984 |
| Claims on Other Sectors............... | 52s | 226,520 | 219,867 | 245,938 | 312,632 | 359,026 | 384,549 | 459,876 | 514,655 | 542,915 | 618,373 | 743,169 | 870,616 |
| Claims on State & Local Govts..... | 52b | 413 | 628 | 757 | 903 | 1,348 | 1,472 | 1,396 | 1,343 | 1,421 | 1,349 | 1,233 | 1,185 |
| Claims on Public Nonfin. Corps.... | 52c | 4,833 | 6,348 | 9,392 | 9,716 | 13,275 | 8,964 | 8,092 | 7,058 | 4,810 | 4,267 | 4,456 | 36,878 |
| Claims on Private Sector.............. | 52d | 221,274 | 212,891 | 235,789 | 302,013 | 344,403 | 374,113 | 450,388 | 506,254 | 536,684 | 612,758 | 737,480 | 832,553 |
| Currency Outside Financial Corps..... | 54a | 31,620 | 36,849 | 42,457 | 49,051 | 50,315 | 55,200 | 59,362 | 61,215 | 66,601 | 73,482 | 82,530 | 89,335 |
| Deposits........................................ | 55l | 167,644 | 207,456 | 235,899 | 286,182 | 298,170 | 342,702 | 405,347 | 463,337 | 507,283 | 577,936 | 612,989 | 694,040 |
| Securities Other than Shares............ | 56a | 163,607 | 194,482 | 223,575 | 248,173 | 290,302 | 267,179 | 256,185 | 260,722 | 269,601 | 277,294 | 336,114 | 389,255 |
| Loans............................................ | 56l | 765 | 490 | 848 | 4,895 | 5,276 | 5,356 | 5,412 | 5,328 | 8,785 | 9,668 | 9,397 | 10,333 |
| Financial Derivatives........................ | 56m | — | — | 1 | 33 | 31 | — | — | — | — | — | — | — |
| Insurance Technical Reserves........... | 56r | 12,985 | 29,062 | 40,477 | 55,307 | 73,704 | 98,395 | 124,458 | 157,990 | 198,756 | 245,474 | 297,837 | 354,789 |
| Shares and Other Equity.................. | 57a | −31,631 | 12,078 | 46,130 | 57,142 | 71,803 | 72,647 | 90,436 | 95,859 | 111,560 | 121,382 | 126,835 | 145,506 |
| Other Items (Net)............................ | 57r | −42,003 | −107,243 | −65,802 | −47,148 | −41,041 | −13,554 | −28,941 | −34,640 | −12,089 | 46,951 | 102,092 | 140,935 |
| **Monetary Aggregates** | | | | | | *Millions of Pesos: End of Period* | | | | | | | |
| Broad Money......................... | 59m | 358,665 | 385,341 | 408,316 | 478,287 | 504,171 | 572,393 | 643,014 | 723,849 | 796,048 | 891,138 | 973,898 | 1,091,477 |
| o/w:Currency Issued by Cent.Govt | 59m.a | — | — | — | — | — | — | — | — | — | — | — | — |
| o/w: Dep.in Nonfin. Corporations. | 59m.b | — | — | — | — | — | — | — | — | — | — | — | — |
| o/w:Secs. Issued by Central Govt.. | 59m.c | — | — | — | — | — | — | — | — | — | — | — | — |
| Money (National Definitions) | | | | | | | | | | | | | |
| Base Money (Broad)................... | 19ma | 97,314 | 156,683 | 154,615 | 176,692 | 181,787 | 187,280 | 209,753 | 225,928 | 229,707 | 254,901 | 294,013 | 307,018 |
| Base Money (Narrow)................. | 19maa | 78,755 | 92,631 | 107,516 | 121,954 | 134,190 | 138,393 | 145,234 | 155,125 | 167,850 | 168,109 | 184,140 | 219,717 |
| M1........................................... | 59ma | 70,681 | 85,006 | 110,559 | 139,731 | 128,670 | 152,640 | 166,994 | 175,406 | 192,756 | 222,960 | 243,610 | 273,318 |
| M2........................................... | 59mb | 298,918 | 310,671 | 330,810 | 389,734 | 407,899 | 466,359 | 512,921 | 565,480 | 617,966 | 684,113 | 754,290 | 841,639 |
| M3........................................... | 59mc | 358,665 | 385,341 | 408,316 | 478,287 | 504,171 | 572,393 | 643,014 | 723,849 | 796,048 | 891,138 | 973,898 | 1,091,477 |
| **Interest Rates** | | | | | | *Percent Per Annum* | | | | | | | |
| Central Bank Policy Rate (EOP)........ | 60 | 7.00 | 10.00 | 8.00 | 7.00 | 9.50 | 4.00 | 5.00 | 6.80 | 5.00 | 6.25 | 6.25 | 5.00 |
| Money Market Rate........................ | 60b | 36.76 | 12.57 | 10.60 | 8.24 | 12.24 | 8.08 | 6.25 | 8.29 | 8.07 | 6.07 | 6.45 | 5.90 |
| Savings Rate.................................. | 60k | 4.36 | 4.12 | 3.54 | 3.09 | 3.01 | 2.87 | 2.74 | 2.74 | 2.59 | 2.24 | 2.02 | 1.79 |
| Savings Rate (Fgn. Currency)............ | 60k.f | 2.88 | 2.05 | 1.55 | 1.50 | 1.56 | .63 | .50 | .46 | .40 | .30 | .34 | .51 |
| Deposit Rate.................................. | 60l | 21.12 | 13.86 | 9.83 | 6.96 | 10.35 | 7.81 | 4.86 | 7.87 | 7.49 | 6.02 | 6.73 | 6.56 |
| Deposit Rate (Fgn. Currency)........... | 60l.f | 5.31 | 3.19 | 2.84 | 2.72 | 2.43 | 2.84 | 2.38 | 2.38 | 2.20 | 1.61 | 1.36 | 1.55 |
| Lending Rate.................................. | 60p | 32.63 | 24.11 | 19.48 | 15.83 | 19.95 | 18.14 | 12.14 | 15.55 | 15.48 | 13.59 | 13.90 | 14.88 |
| Lending Rate (Fgn. Currency).......... | 60p.f | 10.79 | 9.41 | 8.35 | 8.05 | 8.18 | 8.49 | 7.51 | 7.30 | 6.86 | 6.62 | 6.52 | 6.36 |
| **Prices and Labor** | | | | | | *Index Numbers (2010=100): Period Averages* | | | | | | | |
| Consumer Prices............................. | 64 | 70.4 | 73.4 | 78.9 | 83.8 | 92.7 | 94.0 | † 100.0 | 108.5 | 112.5 | 117.9 | 121.4 | 122.5 |
| | | | | | | *Number in Thousands: Period Averages* | | | | | | | |
| Labor Force.................................... | 67d | 3,934 | 3,992 | 4,100 | 4,202 | 4,259 | 4,220 | 4,379 | 4,581 | 4,678 | 4,729 | 4,914 | . . . . |
| Employment.................................. | 67e | 3,241 | 3,295 | 3,466 | 3,571 | 3,664 | 3,608 | 3,768 | 3,931 | 3,992 | 4,019 | 4,200 | . . . . |
| Unemployment.............................. | 67c | 796 | 697 | 661 | 656 | 608 | 628 | 625 | 668 | 687 | 710 | 714 | . . . . |
| Unemployment Rate (%)................. | 67r | 18.4 | 17.9 | 16.2 | 15.6 | 14.1 | 14.9 | 14.1 | 14.6 | 14.7 | 15.0 | 14.5 | . . . . |
| **Intl. Transactions & Positions** | | | | | | *Millions of US Dollars* | | | | | | | |
| Exports........................................... | 70..d | 1,250.7 | 1,395.2 | 1,931.2 | 2,635.0 | 2,394.0 | 1,689.8 | 2,711.2 | 3,677.7 | 4,128.6 | 4,474.4 | 4,676.6 | . . . . |
| Imports, f.o.b.................................. | 71.vd | 5,368.1 | 7,206.6 | 8,745.1 | 11,288.7 | 14,019.9 | 10,056.6 | 12,885.2 | 14,522.4 | 14,938.8 | 13,875.7 | 13,838.3 | . . . . |

| | | 2004 | 2005 | 2006 | 2007 | 2008 | 2009 | 2010 | 2011 | 2012 | 2013 | 2014 | 2015 |
|---|---|---|---|---|---|---|---|---|---|---|---|---|---|
| **Balance of Payments** | | | | | | | *Millions of US Dollars* | | | | | | |
| A. Current Account* | 109bx | 1,041.5 | −472.9 | −1,287.4 | −2,166.3 | −4,519.7 | −2,302.9 † −4,006.3 | −4,358.7 | −3,970.6 | −2,536.7 | −2,140.6 | −1,306.7 |
| Goods, credit (exports) | 1a9cx | 1,250.7 | 1,395.1 | 1,931.4 | 2,635.1 | 2,393.4 | 1,689.3 † 6,814.7 | 8,361.6 | 8,935.5 | 9,424.3 | 9,898.9 | 9,523.3 |
| Goods, debit (imports) | 1a9dx | 5,368.1 | 7,366.3 | 9,558.8 | 11,097.3 | 13,564.0 | 9,946.1 † 15,209.9 | 17,301.6 | 17,673.3 | 16,801.2 | 17,273.3 | 16,863.4 |
| Balance on goods | 1a9bx | −4,117.4 | −5,971.2 | −7,627.4 | −8,462.2 | −11,170.6 | −8,256.8 † −8,395.2 | −8,940.0 | −8,737.8 | −7,376.9 | −7,374.4 | −7,340.1 |
| Services, credit (exports) | 1b9cx | 5,669.2 | 6,181.5 | 6,630.9 | 6,850.3 | 6,876.4 | 6,292.8 † 5,530.5 | 5,822.7 | 6,140.0 | 6,449.3 | 7,024.9 | 7,537.4 |
| Services, debit (imports) | 1b9dx | 1,213.2 | 1,478.2 | 1,582.0 | 1,772.4 | 1,989.4 | 1,857.0 † 3,286.8 | 2,899.0 | 2,938.5 | 2,761.2 | 2,835.1 | 3,139.0 |
| Balance on Goods & Services | 1z9bx | 338.6 | −1,267.9 | −2,578.5 | −3,384.3 | −6,283.6 | −3,821.0 † −6,151.5 | −6,016.3 | −5,536.3 | −3,688.8 | −3,184.6 | −2,941.7 |
| Primary income: credit | 1c9cx | 325.0 | 436.6 | 728.7 | 828.6 | 728.7 | 461.4 † 1,180.0 | 704.7 | 678.5 | 665.5 | 552.3 | 554.1 |
| Primary income: debit | 1c9dx | 2,149.6 | 2,338.8 | 2,581.7 | 3,011.8 | 2,477.7 | 2,183.1 † 2,485.8 | 2,880.5 | 3,022.1 | 3,660.0 | 3,816.9 | 3,598.8 |
| Balance on gds, serv. & prim. inc. | 1y9bx | −1,486.0 | −3,170.0 | −4,431.5 | −5,567.5 | −8,032.6 | −5,542.7 † −7,457.4 | −8,192.1 | −7,879.9 | −6,683.3 | −6,449.2 | −5,986.4 |
| Secondary income: credit | 1d9ca | 2,701.4 | 2,907.7 | 3,365.6 | 3,654.8 | 3,789.1 | 3,499.4 † 4,257.3 | 4,644.8 | 4,711.5 | 4,956.0 | 5,191.1 | 5,589.1 |
| Secondary income: debit | 1d9da | 173.9 | 210.6 | 221.5 | 253.6 | 276.2 | 259.6 † 806.2 | 811.4 | 802.2 | 809.4 | 882.5 | 909.4 |
| B. Capital Account* | 209ba | — | — | 223.7 | 165.2 | 73.5 | 54.1 † 38.0 | 30.1 | 40.9 | 40.5 | — | 2,087.1 |
| Capital account: credit | 209ca | — | — | 223.7 | 165.2 | 73.5 | 54.1 † 38.0 | 30.1 | 40.9 | 40.5 | — | 2,087.1 |
| Capital account: debit | 209da | — | — | — | — | — | — | .... | .... | .... | .... | .... | .... |
| Balance on current & capital acct. | 129ba | 1,041.5 | −472.9 | −1,063.7 | −2,001.1 | −4,446.2 | −2,248.8 † −3,968.3 | −4,328.6 | −3,929.7 | −2,496.2 | −2,140.6 | 780.4 |
| C. Financial Account* | 309na | −109.8 | −1,640.9 | −1,365.6 | −2,223.6 | −4,090.6 | −2,814.5 † −5,146.8 | −3,916.2 | −3,595.9 | −4,148.3 | −3,928.5 | −1,669.0 |
| Direct investment: assets | 3a9aa | 25.4 | −4.3 | 444.1 | 585.5 | −141.6 | −470.1 † −203.5 | −79.2 | 273.5 | −390.6 | 176.8 | 22.4 |
| Equity & investment fund shares | 3aaaa | — | — | — | — | — | — † −203.5 | −79.2 | 273.5 | −390.6 | 176.8 | 22.4 |
| Debt instruments | 3abaa | 25.4 | −4.3 | 444.1 | 585.5 | −141.6 | −470.1 | .... | .... | .... | .... | .... | .... |
| Direct investment: liabilities | 3a9la | 934.5 | 1,118.4 | 1,528.7 | 2,252.9 | 2,728.4 | 1,695.3 † 1,418.7 | 2,197.5 | 3,415.9 | 1,599.9 | 2,385.3 | 2,243.9 |
| Equity & investment fund shares | 3aala | 988.2 | 1,171.6 | 1,479.0 | 2,113.7 | 2,592.5 | 1,069.7 † 1,418.7 | 2,197.5 | 3,415.9 | 1,599.9 | 2,374.7 | 2,203.5 |
| Debt instruments | 3abla | −53.7 | −53.2 | 49.7 | 139.2 | 135.9 | 625.6 | .... | — | .... | .... | 10.6 | 40.4 |
| Portfolio investment: assets | 3b9aa | 7.6 | 82.3 | 328.7 | −172.8 | −107.7 | −46.5 † 10.6 | −36.9 | 800.1 | 9.9 | 21.7 | 36.6 |
| Equity & investment fund shares | 3baaa | 2.2 | −.9 | −17.7 | — | 10.3 | −2.3 † 1.0 | −3.7 | 786.3 | .... | .1 | −.6 |
| Debt securities | 3bbaa | 5.4 | 83.2 | 346.4 | −172.8 | −118.0 | −44.2 † 9.6 | −33.2 | 13.8 | 9.9 | 21.6 | 37.2 |
| Portfolio investment: liabilities | 3b9la | −16.7 | 326.4 | 1,102.5 | 776.3 | −457.5 | −379.1 † 770.1 | 709.1 | 353.9 | 1,775.1 | 1,504.1 | 3,413.5 |
| Equity & investment fund shares | 3bala | — | — | — | — | — | — | .... | .... | .... | .... | .... | .... |
| Debt securities | 3bbla | −16.7 | 326.4 | 1,102.5 | 776.3 | −457.5 | −379.1 † 770.1 | 709.1 | 353.9 | 1,775.1 | 1,504.1 | 3,413.5 |
| Fin. der.& empl.stk.ops.(ESOs): net. | 3c9na | — | — | — | — | — | — | .... | .... | .... | .... | .... | .... |
| Fin. der. & ESOs.: assets | 3c9aa | — | — | — | — | — | — | .... | .... | .... | .... | .... | .... |
| Fin. der. & ESOs.: liabilities | 3c9la | — | — | — | — | — | — | .... | .... | .... | .... | .... | .... |
| Other investment: assets | 3d9aa | 436.5 | −67.4 | 1,352.7 | 765.4 | −533.4 | −239.2 † −700.4 | 39.0 | 296.8 | 352.5 | 321.3 | −260.1 |
| Other equity | 3daaa | .... | .... | .... | .... | .... | .... | .... | .... | .... | .... | .... | .... |
| Debt instruments | 3dzaa | 436.5 | −67.4 | 1,352.7 | 765.4 | −533.4 | −239.2 † −700.4 | 39.0 | 296.8 | 352.5 | 321.3 | −260.1 |
| Other investment: liabilities | 3d9la | −338.4 | 206.7 | 860.0 | 372.5 | 1,037.0 | 742.5 † 2,064.7 | 932.5 | 1,196.6 | 745.1 | 558.9 | −4,189.6 |
| Other equity | 3dala | .... | .... | .... | .... | .... | .... | .... | .... | .... | .... | .... | .... |
| Debt instruments | 3dzla | −338.4 | 206.7 | 860.0 | 372.5 | 1,037.0 | 742.5 † 2,064.7 | 932.5 | 1,196.6 | 745.1 | 558.9 | −4,189.6 |
| Curr.+ cap.− finan. acct. balance... | 4y9na | 1,151.3 | 1,167.9 | 301.9 | 222.5 | −355.6 | 565.7 † 1,178.6 | −412.4 | −333.7 | 1,652.1 | 1,787.9 | 2,449.4 |
| D. Net Errors and Omissions | 409na | −946.9 | −420.0 | −134.2 | 403.7 | 30.4 | −159.7 † −1,106.9 | 574.1 | −106.8 | −311.8 | −1,137.2 | −1,675.4 |
| E. Reserves and Related Items | 4z9na | 204.4 | 747.9 | 167.7 | 626.2 | −325.2 | 406.0 † 71.7 | 161.7 | −440.6 | 1,340.3 | 650.7 | 774.1 |
| Reserve assets | 3e9aa | 566.7 | 1,151.6 | 318.1 | 682.2 | −308.5 | 637.1 † 466.5 | 339.6 | −548.2 | 1,145.8 | 195.9 | 407.3 |
| Credit and loans from the IMF | 3dcla | 65.5 | 219.0 | 37.8 | 62.9 | −41.7 | 274.0 † 390.3 | 173.9 | −110.7 | −196.8 | −457.0 | −368.7 |
| Exceptional financing | 409la | 296.9 | 184.7 | 112.6 | −6.8 | 58.3 | −42.9 † 4.5 | 4.0 | 3.1 | 2.3 | 2.2 | 1.9 |

*Excludes components in group E

| **International Investment Position** | | | | | | | *Millions of US Dollars* | | | | | | |
|---|---|---|---|---|---|---|---|---|---|---|---|---|---|
| Assets | 809aa | 4,198.4 | 7,979.5 | 10,496.8 | 12,405.0 | 11,436.1 † 10,959.7 | 10,499.7 | 10,744.6 | 11,844.5 | 12,957.5 | 13,541.7 | 13,678.4 |
| Direct investment | 8a9aa | 180.2 | 528.7 | 972.8 | 1,558.3 | 1,416.7 † 946.9 | 743.4 | 664.2 | 942.7 | 552.1 | 728.9 | 751.3 |
| Equity & investment fund shares | 8aaaa | .... | .... | .... | .... | .... | .... | .... | .... | .... | .... | .... | .... |
| Debt instruments | 8abaa | 180.2 | 528.7 | 972.8 | 1,558.3 | 1,416.7 † 946.9 | 743.4 | 664.2 | 942.7 | 552.1 | 728.9 | 751.3 |
| Portfolio investment | 8b9aa | 122.3 | 204.6 | 533.3 | 360.5 | 252.8 † 206.3 | 216.9 | 180.0 | 980.2 | 990.1 | 1,010.4 | 1,045.5 |
| Equity & investment fund shares | 8baaa | 20.2 | 19.3 | 1.6 | 1.6 | 11.9 † 9.6 | 10.6 | 6.9 | 793.2 | 793.2 | 793.2 | 792.5 |
| Debt securities | 8bbaa | 102.1 | 185.3 | 531.7 | 358.9 | 240.9 † 196.7 | 206.3 | 173.1 | 187.0 | 196.9 | 217.2 | 253.0 |
| Fin. der.(oth.than reserves) & ESOs | 8c9aa | .... | .... | .... | .... | .... | .... | .... | .... | .... | .... | .... | .... |
| Other investment | 8d9aa | 3,072.7 | 5,317.0 | 6,709.7 | 7,506.5 | 7,104.5 † 6,499.4 | 5,773.9 | 5,801.9 | 6,363.0 | 6,714.5 | 6,940.5 | 6,615.7 |
| Other equity | 8daaa | .... | .... | .... | .... | .... | .... | .... | .... | .... | .... | .... | .... |
| Debt instruments | 8dzaa | 3,072.7 | 5,317.0 | 6,709.7 | 7,506.5 | 7,104.5 † 6,499.4 | 5,773.9 | 5,801.9 | 6,363.0 | 6,714.5 | 6,940.5 | 6,615.7 |
| Reserve assets | 8e9aa | 823.2 | 1,929.3 | 2,281.0 | 2,979.8 | 2,662.1 † 3,307.0 | 3,765.5 | 4,098.5 | 3,558.5 | 4,700.8 | 4,861.9 | 5,265.9 |
| Liabilities | 809la | 14,363.3 | 19,238.7 | 23,189.5 | 26,578.2 | 29,193.7 † 31,479.6 | 36,178.0 | 39,949.3 | 45,434.9 | 49,283.2 | 53,236.3 | 53,894.3 |
| Direct investment | 8a9la | 4,515.0 | 9,274.7 | 10,926.0 | 13,183.8 | 15,865.9 † 17,692.9 | 19,536.5 | 21,740.2 | 25,143.0 | 26,660.0 | 29,034.8 | 31,325.9 |
| Equity & investment fund shares | 8aala | 3,943.1 | 8,480.5 | 9,950.2 | 12,068.8 | 14,615.0 † 15,853.5 | 17,314.6 | 19,129.3 | 21,354.8 | 22,791.1 | 25,155.3 | 27,406.0 |
| Debt instruments | 8abla | 571.9 | 794.2 | 975.9 | 1,115.1 | 1,251.0 † 1,839.4 | 2,221.9 | 2,610.9 | 3,788.2 | 3,868.9 | 3,879.5 | 3,919.9 |
| Portfolio investment | 8b9la | 1,600.4 | 2,038.0 | 3,264.6 | 3,937.7 | 2,853.8 † 3,021.5 | 3,883.5 | 4,406.4 | 5,124.3 | 6,739.4 | 8,331.6 | 11,352.4 |
| Equity & investment fund shares | 8bala | .... | .... | .... | .... | .... | .... | .... | .... | .... | .... | .... | .... |
| Debt securities | 8bbla | 1,600.4 | 2,038.0 | 3,264.6 | 3,937.7 | 2,853.8 † 3,021.5 | 3,883.5 | 4,406.4 | 5,124.3 | 6,739.4 | 8,331.6 | 11,352.4 |
| Fin. der.(oth.than reserves) & ESOs | 8c9la | .... | .... | .... | .... | .... | .... | .... | .... | .... | .... | .... | .... |
| Other investment | 8d9la | 8,247.8 | 7,926.0 | 8,998.8 | 9,456.7 | 10,474.0 † 10,437.7 | 12,758.0 | 13,802.7 | 15,167.7 | 15,883.8 | 15,869.9 | 11,216.1 |
| Other equity | 8dala | .... | .... | .... | .... | .... | .... | .... | .... | .... | .... | .... | .... |
| Debt instruments | 8dzla | 8,247.8 | 7,926.0 | 8,998.8 | 9,456.7 | 10,474.0 † 10,437.7 | 12,758.0 | 13,802.7 | 15,167.7 | 15,883.8 | 15,869.9 | 11,216.1 |

| | | 2004 | 2005 | 2006 | 2007 | 2008 | 2009 | 2010 | 2011 | 2012 | 2013 | 2014 | 2015 |
|---|---|---|---|---|---|---|---|---|---|---|---|---|---|
| **Government Finance** | | | | | | | | | | | | | |
| **Operations Statement** | | | | | | | | | | | | | |
| **Budgetary Central Government** | | | | | | | *Millions of Pesos: Fiscal Year Ends December 31* | | | | | | |
| Revenue | a1 | 129,624.0 | 160,874.4 | 192,557.0 | 241,877.8 | 249,823.9 | 229,716.1 | 259,571.3 | 285,784.1 | 323,465.0 | 372,488.6 | .... | .... |
| Taxes | a11 | 117,202.9 | 148,412.0 | 176,529.9 | 217,103.8 | 235,306.1 | 219,364.6 | 242,097.4 | 271,803.8 | 310,814.0 | 353,761.5 | .... | .... |
| Social Contributions | a12 | 95.1 | 37.9 | 1,220.8 | 860.2 | 859.9 | 1,008.7 | 1,845.4 | 1,328.2 | 1,250.2 | 1,552.5 | .... | .... |
| Grants | a13 | 3,427.0 | 3,277.9 | 3,719.0 | 5,866.3 | 2,913.7 | 3,492.6 | 4,500.4 | 5,333.9 | 4,920.4 | 3,076.4 | .... | .... |
| Other Revenue | a14 | 8,898.9 | 9,146.6 | 11,087.3 | 18,047.4 | 10,744.2 | 5,850.2 | 11,128.2 | 7,318.2 | 6,480.7 | 14,098.2 | .... | .... |
| Expense | a2 | 130,756.8 | 150,639.6 | 173,741.9 | 200,292.8 | 254,325.1 | 245,748.2 | 257,346.7 | 285,383.1 | 359,955.0 | 381,779.5 | .... | .... |
| Compensation of Employees | a21 | 29,813.0 | 37,898.5 | 44,269.9 | 48,485.0 | 58,787.5 | 68,495.1 | 72,254.3 | 79,113.7 | 87,846.0 | 105,286.5 | .... | .... |
| Use of Goods & Services | a22 | 15,586.8 | 21,022.4 | 27,354.0 | 33,296.6 | 31,514.6 | 30,010.3 | 33,605.5 | 33,081.0 | 43,822.0 | 38,735.1 | .... | .... |
| Consumption of Fixed Capital | a23 | .... | .... | 13.5 | 15.4 | 23.5 | 41.6 | 563.0 | 603.5 | 1,441.2 | 1,601.1 | .... | .... |
| Interest | a24 | 15,490.5 | 12,535.1 | 16,448.6 | 16,820.3 | 25,229.7 | 31,958.0 | 35,802.8 | 44,830.6 | 56,219.3 | 59,218.9 | .... | .... |
| Subsidies | a25 | 33,159.0 | 27,580.8 | 30,417.9 | 30,441.0 | 53,344.3 | 28,822.7 | 29,085.1 | 34,813.7 | 49,599.0 | 47,288.3 | .... | .... |
| Grants | a26 | 20,006.2 | 33,367.8 | 31,239.9 | 43,350.3 | 56,482.5 | 48,787.5 | 49,743.4 | 52,966.6 | 64,075.3 | 81,087.7 | .... | .... |
| Social Benefits | a27 | 4,524.0 | 8,351.9 | 11,125.1 | 12,573.1 | 17,329.0 | 21,192.0 | 23,243.9 | 24,961.1 | 29,024.0 | 33,118.3 | .... | .... |
| Other Expense | a28 | 12,177.4 | 9,883.1 | 12,873.0 | 15,311.1 | 11,614.2 | 16,441.0 | 13,048.7 | 15,012.7 | 27,928.0 | 15,443.5 | .... | .... |
| Gross Operating Balance [1-2+23] | agob | −1,132.8 | 10,234.8 | 18,828.6 | 41,600.4 | −4,477.7 | −15,990.5 | 2,787.7 | 1,004.5 | −35,048.8 | −7,689.8 | | |
| Net Operating Balance [1-2] | anob | .... | .... | 18,815.1 | 41,585.0 | −4,501.2 | −16,032.1 | 2,224.7 | 401.0 | −36,490.0 | −9,290.9 | | |
| Net Acq. of Nonfinancial Assets | a31 | 19,741.0 | 20,427.5 | 31,392.7 | 39,929.1 | 54,041.9 | 42,918.9 | 54,845.5 | 56,137.2 | 114,440.0 | 68,588.2 | | |
| Aquisition of Nonfin. Assets | a31.1 | .... | .... | .... | .... | .... | .... | .... | .... | .... | .... | | |
| Disposal of Nonfin. Assets | a31.2 | .... | .... | .... | .... | .... | .... | .... | .... | .... | .... | | |
| Net Lending/Borrowing [1-2-31] | anlb | −20,873.9 | −10,192.7 | −12,577.6 | 1,655.9 | −58,543.1 | −58,951.0 | −52,623.9 | −55,736.2 | −150,930.0 | −77,879.1 | | |
| Net Acq. of Financial Assets | a32 | 83.6 | 11,490.4 | 6,848.0 | 1,754.4 | 5,023.2 | 5,091.3 | 12,447.6 | 4,495.6 | −16,663.0 | 13,108.4 | .... | .... |
| By instrument | | | | | | | | | | | | | |
| Monetary Gold & SDRs | a3201 | — | — | — | — | — | — | — | — | — | — | | |
| Currency & Deposits | a3202 | −4,717.4 | 7,147.7 | 1,850.9 | 322.7 | −3,349.0 | 3,046.1 | 14,373.3 | 4,256.5 | −15,244.0 | 8,508.3 | | |
| Securities other than Shares | a3203 | 4,686.6 | — | — | — | — | — | — | — | — | — | | |
| Loans | a3204 | 114.4 | 457.8 | −258.2 | — | 29.4 | 63.4 | 436.3 | 57.7 | 66.1 | 94.1 | | |
| Shares & Other Equity | a3205 | — | 3,885.0 | 537.8 | 530.4 | 4,462.9 | 995.9 | −3,279.6 | −608.9 | 170.2 | 2,247.6 | | |
| Insurance Technical Reserves | a3206 | — | — | — | — | — | — | — | — | — | — | | |
| Financial Derivatives | a3207 | — | — | — | — | — | — | — | — | — | — | | |
| Other Accounts Receivable | a3208 | — | — | 4,717.5 | 901.2 | 3,880.0 | 985.9 | 917.6 | 790.4 | −1,655.3 | 2,258.4 | | |
| By debtor | | | | | | | | | | | | | |
| Domestic | a321 | 83.6 | 11,490.4 | 6,310.2 | 1,224.0 | 4,455.2 | 4,508.3 | 12,447.6 | 4,481.8 | −16,833.2 | 12,860.8 | .... | .... |
| Foreign | a322 | — | — | 537.8 | 530.4 | 568.0 | 583.0 | — | 13.8 | 170.2 | 247.6 | .... | .... |
| Net Incurrence of Liabilities | a33 | 22,451.5 | 20,034.8 | 15,659.1 | 1,224.1 | 60,827.2 | 65,649.2 | 65,508.4 | 64,327.8 | 140,594.0 | 93,072.7 | | |
| By instrument | | | | | | | | | | | | | |
| Special Drawing Rights (SDRs) | a3301 | — | — | — | — | — | — | — | — | — | — | | |
| Currency & Deposits | a3302 | 629.3 | 731.9 | 936.9 | 1,120.1 | 1,382.8 | .... | — | — | — | — | | |
| Securities other than Shares | a3303 | — | 444.8 | 11,124.0 | 1,769.8 | 15,165.9 | .... | 46,426.3 | 44,643.2 | 30,381.2 | 83,675.6 | | |
| Loans | a3304 | 23,331.6 | 11,798.6 | 18,523.9 | 2,062.5 | 37,366.5 | .... | 20,810.6 | 30,383.7 | 83,955.1 | 56,054.0 | | |
| Shares & Other Equity | a3305 | — | — | — | — | — | .... | — | — | — | — | | |
| Insurance Technical Reserves | a3306 | — | — | — | — | — | .... | — | — | — | — | | |
| Financial Derivatives | a3307 | — | — | — | — | — | .... | — | — | — | — | | |
| Other Accounts Payable | a3308 | −1,509.5 | 7,059.5 | −14,925.6 | −3,728.2 | 6,912.0 | .... | −1,728.4 | −10,699.1 | 26,257.7 | −46,657.0 | | |
| By creditor | | | | | | | | | | | | | |
| Domestic | a331 | 2,217.7 | 9,058.2 | −10,500.4 | −6,308.2 | 36,503.6 | 28,861.2 | −73.5 | −1,336.3 | 91,996.0 | 8,001.5 | | |
| Foreign | a332 | 20,233.7 | 10,976.6 | 26,159.5 | 7,532.3 | 24,323.6 | 36,788.0 | 65,581.9 | 65,664.1 | 48,598.0 | 85,071.2 | | |
| Stat. Discrepancy [32-33-NLB] | anlbz | −1,494.0 | 1,648.4 | 3,766.4 | −1,125.6 | 2,739.2 | −1,606.8 | −437.0 | −4,096.0 | −6,327.0 | −2,085.2 | | |
| Memo Item: Expenditure [2+31] | a2m | 150,497.9 | 171,067.2 | 205,134.6 | 240,221.9 | 308,367.1 | 288,667.1 | 312,195.2 | 341,520.3 | 474,395.0 | 450,367.7 | .... | .... |
| **National Accounts** | | | | | | | *Millions of Pesos* | | | | | | |
| Househ.Cons.Expend.,incl.NPISHs | 96f | 710,023 | 839,097 | 980,529 | 1,028,340 | 1,215,394 | 1,276,354 | 1,475,592 | 1,679,234 | 1,786,147 | 1,889,710 | 2,018,228 | 2,145,331 |
| Government Consumption Expend | 91f | 56,428 | 68,338 | 85,284 | 133,840 | 165,907 | 183,187 | 192,926 | 207,221 | 249,223 | 257,391 | 303,027 | 355,905 |
| Gross Fixed Capital Formation | 93e | 134,109 | 166,933 | 217,399 | 394,321 | 466,942 | 402,205 | 495,030 | 516,327 | 545,546 | 532,008 | 572,819 | 645,184 |
| Changes in Inventories | 93i | 1,462 | 1,464 | 1,585 | 19,163 | 31,774 | 11,991 | 32,475 | 39,694 | 2,563 | 26,345 | 27,199 | 6,530 |
| Exports of Goods and Services | 90c | 384,773 | 306,312 | 356,835 | 390,476 | 397,470 | 365,382 | 433,869 | 525,751 | 580,513 | 650,889 | 717,170 | 744,804 |
| Imports of Goods and Services (-) | 98c | 377,758 | 362,143 | 451,830 | 510,886 | 620,524 | 509,650 | 651,041 | 749,798 | 786,488 | 797,757 | 852,213 | 874,638 |
| Gross Domestic Product (GDP) | 99b | 909,037 | 1,020,002 | 1,189,802 | 1,455,253 | 1,656,962 | 1,729,468 | 1,978,852 | 2,218,429 | 2,377,504 | 2,558,586 | 2,786,230 | 3,023,116 |
| Net Primary Income from Abroad | 98.n | −76,024 | −57,390 | −60,573 | −67,080 | .... | .... | .... | .... | .... | .... | .... | .... |
| Gross National Income (GNI) | 99a | 833,013 | 962,612 | 1,129,229 | 1,297,131 | .... | .... | .... | .... | .... | .... | .... | .... |
| Consumption of Fixed Capital | 99cf | 18,464 | 18,399 | .... | .... | .... | .... | .... | .... | .... | .... | .... | .... |
| GDP Volume 2007 Ref., Chained | 99b.p | .... | .... | .... | 1,455,253 | 1,501,002 | 1,515,048 | 1,640,830 | 1,687,116 | 1,731,479 | 1,814,204 | 1,947,383 | 2,082,790 |
| GDP Volume (2010=100) | 99bvp | 67.6 | 73.9 | 81.8 | † 88.7 | 91.5 | 92.3 | 100.0 | 102.8 | 105.5 | 110.6 | 118.7 | 126.9 |
| GDP Deflator (2010=100) | 99bip | 67.9 | 69.8 | 73.5 | 82.9 | 91.5 | 94.7 | 100.0 | 109.0 | 113.9 | 116.9 | 118.6 | 120.4 |
| | | | | | | | *Millions: Midyear Estimates* | | | | | | |
| Population | 99z | 9.10 | 9.24 | 9.37 | 9.50 | 9.64 | 9.77 | 9.90 | 10.03 | 10.16 | 10.28 | 10.41 | 10.53 |

| | | 2004 | 2005 | 2006 | 2007 | 2008 | 2009 | 2010 | 2011 | 2012 | 2013 | 2014 | 2015 |
|---|---|---|---|---|---|---|---|---|---|---|---|---|---|
| **Exchange Rates** | | | | | | *E. Caribbean Dollars per SDR: End of Period* | | | | | | | |
| Official Rate | aa | 4.1931 | 3.8590 | 4.0619 | 4.2667 | 4.1587 | 4.2328 | 4.1581 | 4.1452 | 4.1497 | 4.1580 | 3.9118 | 3.7415 |
| | | | | | *E. Caribbean Dollars per US Dollar: End of Period (ae) Period Average (rf)* | | | | | | | | |
| Official Rate | ae | 2.7000 | 2.7000 | 2.7000 | 2.7000 | 2.7000 | 2.7000 | 2.7000 | 2.7000 | 2.7000 | 2.7000 | 2.7000 | 2.7000 |
| Official Rate | rf | 2.7000 | 2.7000 | 2.7000 | 2.7000 | 2.7000 | 2.7000 | 2.7000 | 2.7000 | 2.7000 | 2.7000 | 2.7000 | 2.7000 |
| **Fund Position** | | | | | | *Millions of SDRs: End of Period* | | | | | | | |
| Quota | 2f.s | 65.90 | 65.90 | 65.90 | 65.90 | 65.90 | 65.90 | 65.90 | 65.90 | 65.90 | 65.90 | 65.90 | 65.90 |
| SDR Holdings | 1b.s | 1.56 | 1.55 | 1.68 | 1.71 | 2.48 | 61.65 | 41.99 | 39.49 | 36.09 | 33.98 | 31.02 | 27.61 |
| Reserve Position in the Fund | 1c.s | .60 | .60 | .60 | .60 | .60 | .60 | .63 | .65 | .65 | .65 | .65 | .65 |
| Total Fund Cred.&Loans Outstg | 2tl | 11.80 | 13.94 | 15.62 | 12.54 | 21.89 | 36.91 | 63.80 | 99.38 | 135.83 | 156.29 | 134.50 | 96.44 |
| SDR Allocations | 1bd | 2.62 | 2.62 | 2.62 | 2.62 | 2.62 | 2.62 | 62.48 | 62.48 | 62.48 | 62.48 | 62.48 | 62.48 |
| **International Liquidity** | | | | | | *Millions of US Dollars: End of Period* | | | | | | | |
| Total Reserves minus Gold | 1l.d | 634.07 | 600.02 | 696.75 | 765.43 | 760.21 | 896.47 | 990.94 | 1,068.26 | 1,179.21 | 1,219.98 | 1,454.95 | 1,596.92 |
| SDR Holdings | 1b.d | 2.42 | 2.22 | 2.53 | 2.71 | 3.82 | 96.65 | 64.67 | 60.62 | 55.47 | 52.33 | 44.94 | 38.25 |
| Reserve Position in the Fund | 1c.d | .94 | .86 | .91 | .96 | .93 | .95 | .97 | 1.00 | 1.00 | 1.00 | .94 | .90 |
| Foreign Exchange | 1d.d | 630.72 | 596.93 | 693.31 | 761.77 | 755.47 | 798.88 | 925.30 | 1,006.65 | 1,122.74 | 1,166.64 | 1,409.07 | 1,557.77 |
| Central Bank: Other Assets | 3..d | .04 | .01 | .71 | .77 | .10 | .02 | — | .13 | .06 | | .44 | |
| Central Bank: Other Liabs | 4..d | 4.52 | 5.33 | 3.56 | 4.48 | 4.29 | 52.48 | 50.06 | 47.70 | 72.28 | 31.63 | 10.66 | 9.24 |
| Other Depository Corps.: Assets | 7a.d | 1,209.93 | 1,364.89 | 1,473.80 | 1,640.33 | 1,452.91 | 2,579.02 | 2,412.01 | 2,796.27 | 1,593.08 | 1,656.87 | 1,914.73 | 2,270.48 |
| Other Depository Corps.: Liabs | 7b.d | 697.18 | 778.26 | 919.90 | 1,220.69 | 1,302.93 | 2,558.39 | 2,338.03 | 2,875.12 | 1,638.22 | 1,434.97 | 1,401.63 | 1,325.13 |
| **Central Bank** | | | | | | *Millions of E. Caribbean Dollars: End of Period* | | | | | | | |
| Net Foreign Assets | 11n | 1,644.00 | 1,552.49 | 1,806.63 | 1,894.05 | 1,948.88 | 1,863.43 | 2,017.45 | 2,087.47 | 2,171.15 | 2,305.55 | 3,136.02 | 3,697.55 |
| Claims on Nonresidents | 11 | 1,716.67 | 1,630.76 | 1,890.32 | 1,970.81 | 2,062.35 | 2,425.83 | 2,677.73 | 2,887.25 | 3,189.25 | 3,300.59 | 3,935.37 | 4,317.12 |
| Liabilities to Nonresidents | 16c | 72.67 | 78.27 | 83.69 | 76.77 | 113.47 | 562.40 | 660.29 | 799.78 | 1,018.10 | 995.03 | 799.35 | 619.57 |
| Claims on Other Depository Corps | 12e | 10.59 | 8.53 | 11.99 | 53.59 | 10.06 | 14.76 | 15.89 | 26.41 | 24.40 | 23.75 | 22.46 | 22.59 |
| Net Claims on Central Government | 12an | −41.13 | −35.15 | −72.67 | −77.71 | −55.14 | −15.80 | −100.52 | −30.18 | −123.27 | −67.37 | −129.49 | −191.59 |
| Claims on Central Government | 12a | 59.31 | 58.25 | 49.68 | 42.09 | 60.64 | 160.26 | 158.93 | 196.81 | 170.19 | 182.25 | 211.29 | 136.22 |
| Liabilities to Central Government | 16d | 100.44 | 93.41 | 122.35 | 119.80 | 115.79 | 176.06 | 259.45 | 226.99 | 293.46 | 249.62 | 340.78 | 327.82 |
| Claims on Other Sectors | 12s | 34.32 | 32.60 | 30.82 | 30.32 | 30.04 | 35.94 | 36.57 | 36.34 | 37.66 | 38.60 | 39.51 | 43.64 |
| Claims on Other Financial Corps | 12g | 23.60 | 23.11 | 23.25 | 23.60 | 23.59 | 27.30 | 31.84 | 31.98 | 33.17 | 34.05 | 36.14 | 40.03 |
| Claims on State & Local Govts | 12b | — | — | — | — | — | — | — | — | — | — | — | — |
| Claims on Public Nonfin. Corps | 12c | — | — | — | — | — | — | — | — | — | — | — | — |
| Claims on Private Sector | 12d | 10.72 | 9.49 | 7.57 | 6.73 | 6.46 | 8.64 | 4.72 | 4.36 | 4.49 | 4.54 | 3.37 | 3.60 |
| Monetary Base | 14 | 1,640.60 | 1,550.66 | 1,743.64 | 1,900.23 | 1,847.50 | 1,909.78 | 2,172.85 | 2,459.87 | 2,622.39 | 2,937.74 | 3,485.66 | 3,778.83 |
| Currency in Circulation | 14a | 662.90 | 732.83 | 783.31 | 842.09 | 878.28 | 835.55 | 833.88 | 875.98 | 895.50 | 925.65 | 991.21 | 1,024.49 |
| Liabs. to Other Depository Corps | 14c | 976.49 | 817.11 | 958.32 | 1,055.19 | 966.78 | 1,070.03 | 1,332.84 | 1,580.22 | 1,721.23 | 2,008.35 | 2,492.97 | 2,739.44 |
| Liabilities to Other Sectors | 14d | 1.21 | .72 | 2.01 | 3.00 | 2.44 | 4.20 | 6.14 | 3.67 | 5.66 | 3.74 | 1.48 | 14.89 |
| Other Liabs. to Other Dep. Corps | 14n | 8.88 | 9.84 | 13.20 | 14.15 | 16.55 | 18.58 | 22.41 | 26.10 | 29.84 | 40.51 | 129.35 | 216.59 |
| Dep. & Sec. Excl. f/Monetary Base | 14o | .82 | .82 | .82 | .82 | .82 | — | — | — | — | — | — | — |
| Deposits Included in Broad Money | 15 | — | — | — | — | — | — | — | — | — | — | — | — |
| Sec.Ot.th.Shares Incl.in Brd. Money | 16a | — | — | — | — | — | — | — | — | — | — | — | — |
| Deposits Excl. from Broad Money | 16b | .82 | .82 | .82 | .82 | .82 | — | — | — | — | — | — | — |
| Sec.Ot.th.Shares Excl.f/Brd.Money | 16s | — | — | — | — | — | — | — | — | — | — | — | — |
| Loans | 16l | — | — | — | — | — | — | — | — | — | — | — | — |
| Financial Derivatives | 16m | — | — | — | — | — | — | — | — | — | — | — | — |
| Shares and Other Equity | 17a | 123.62 | 125.33 | 192.54 | 245.04 | 278.31 | 257.97 | 244.14 | 261.17 | 272.17 | 218.89 | 231.19 | 216.51 |
| Other Items (Net) | 17r | −126.14 | −128.18 | −173.42 | −260.04 | −209.34 | −288.01 | −470.02 | −627.10 | −814.46 | −896.61 | −777.71 | −639.75 |
| Memo Item: | | | | | | | | | | | | | |
| Total Assets | 10ra | 1,941.25 | 1,850.01 | 2,123.27 | 2,233.69 | 2,307.47 | 2,535.96 | 2,870.36 | 3,144.75 | 3,441.43 | 3,571.14 | 4,249.70 | 4,596.72 |
| **Other Depository Corporations** | | | | | | *Millions of E. Caribbean Dollars: End of Period* | | | | | | | |
| Net Foreign Assets | 21n | 1,384.44 | 1,583.89 | 1,495.51 | 1,133.04 | 404.95 | 55.71 | 199.74 | −212.90 | −121.88 | 599.13 | 1,385.38 | 2,552.45 |
| Claims on Nonresidents | 21 | 3,266.82 | 3,685.20 | 3,979.25 | 4,428.90 | 3,922.86 | 6,963.36 | 6,512.42 | 7,549.92 | 4,301.31 | 4,473.54 | 5,169.78 | 6,130.29 |
| Liabilities to Nonresidents | 26c | 1,882.38 | 2,101.31 | 2,483.74 | 3,295.86 | 3,517.90 | 6,907.65 | 6,312.68 | 7,762.82 | 4,423.20 | 3,874.41 | 3,784.40 | 3,577.84 |
| Claims on Central Bank | 20 | 1,185.64 | 1,040.36 | 1,190.15 | 1,314.56 | 1,264.90 | 1,301.34 | 1,549.72 | 1,857.05 | 1,990.39 | 2,280.50 | 2,825.86 | 3,178.74 |
| Currency | 20a | 176.76 | 211.43 | 197.31 | 247.38 | 265.45 | 214.18 | 217.80 | 241.39 | 261.79 | 258.08 | 275.41 | 260.58 |
| Reserve Deposits and Securities | 20b | 1,008.89 | 828.94 | 992.84 | 1,067.18 | 999.45 | 1,083.00 | 1,328.50 | 1,585.17 | 1,728.60 | 2,022.42 | 2,550.45 | 2,918.16 |
| Other Claims | 20n | — | — | — | — | — | 4.17 | 3.41 | 30.49 | — | — | — | — |
| Net Claims on Central Government | 22an | 689.92 | 804.69 | 853.20 | 1,149.63 | 1,268.22 | 1,541.22 | 1,129.84 | 1,098.57 | 1,545.30 | 853.97 | 1,592.90 | 1,291.30 |
| Claims on Central Government | 22a | 1,370.68 | 1,571.91 | 1,774.50 | 2,014.52 | 2,174.47 | 2,317.65 | 2,001.56 | 1,947.01 | 2,388.49 | 1,786.08 | 2,592.78 | 2,525.10 |
| Liabilities to Central Government | 26d | 680.76 | 767.22 | 921.30 | 864.88 | 906.24 | 776.43 | 871.73 | 848.45 | 843.19 | 932.11 | 999.88 | 1,233.80 |
| Claims on Other Sectors | 22s | 7,723.93 | 8,624.84 | 10,018.58 | 11,871.61 | 13,110.74 | 12,795.99 | 13,149.30 | 13,340.55 | 13,916.73 | 13,579.37 | 12,753.81 | 12,202.98 |
| Claims on Other Financial Corps | 22g | 259.11 | 285.31 | 284.12 | 293.61 | 257.28 | 134.37 | 124.87 | 146.53 | 305.15 | 276.71 | 180.67 | 199.12 |
| Claims on State & Local Govts | 22b | 69.53 | 57.07 | 88.57 | 96.19 | 120.58 | 135.20 | 177.44 | 207.01 | 201.47 | 207.89 | 181.41 | 189.80 |
| Claims on Public Nonfin. Corps | 22c | 653.62 | 736.31 | 765.19 | 804.36 | 925.95 | 621.29 | 628.60 | 619.85 | 589.80 | 556.86 | 353.07 | 318.95 |
| Claims on Private Sector | 22d | 6,741.67 | 7,546.17 | 8,880.70 | 10,677.44 | 11,806.94 | 11,905.13 | 12,218.39 | 12,367.17 | 12,820.31 | 12,537.90 | 12,038.66 | 11,495.11 |
| Liabilities to Central Bank | 26g | 20.88 | 11.17 | 9.99 | 48.16 | 18.78 | 110.61 | 15.37 | 32.71 | 27.98 | 37.76 | 24.27 | 22.04 |
| Transf.Dep.Included in Broad Money | 24 | 3,285.62 | 3,680.63 | 4,237.71 | 4,762.01 | 4,536.91 | 3,982.50 | 4,013.84 | 4,047.57 | 4,463.79 | 4,683.82 | 5,298.03 | 5,776.51 |
| Other Dep.Included in Broad Money | 25 | 6,592.46 | 6,938.76 | 7,565.87 | 8,340.90 | 8,999.14 | 9,302.78 | 9,581.14 | 9,964.55 | 10,448.30 | 10,862.05 | 11,089.31 | 11,247.72 |
| Sec.Ot.th.Shares Incl.in Brd. Money | 26a | — | — | — | — | — | — | — | — | — | — | — | — |
| Deposits Excl. from Broad Money | 26b | — | — | — | — | — | 191.66 | 192.10 | 192.39 | 191.81 | 192.21 | 192.42 | 180.25 |
| Sec.Ot.th.Shares Excl.f/Brd.Money | 26s | 1.00 | 1.00 | 1.00 | 1.00 | 1.00 | .91 | .91 | — | — | — | — | — |
| Loans | 26l | — | — | — | — | — | — | — | — | — | — | — | — |
| Financial Derivatives | 26m | — | — | — | — | — | — | — | — | — | — | — | — |
| Insurance Technical Reserves | 26r | — | — | — | — | — | — | — | — | — | — | — | — |
| Shares and Other Equity | 27a | 1,188.67 | 1,433.05 | 1,704.18 | 2,025.52 | 2,258.01 | 2,318.39 | 2,261.94 | 1,781.99 | 1,739.31 | 1,216.15 | 985.27 | 1,339.08 |
| Other Items (Net) | 27r | −104.70 | −10.83 | 38.69 | 291.25 | 234.98 | −212.58 | −36.69 | 64.04 | 459.36 | 320.99 | 968.67 | 659.87 |
| Memo Item: | | | | | | | | | | | | | |
| Total Assets | 20ra | 15,678.62 | 17,807.77 | 20,012.03 | 23,517.38 | 24,526.07 | 25,413.53 | 25,319.39 | 26,997.29 | 27,291.53 | 27,464.59 | 28,403.73 | 29,663.31 |

|  |  | 2004 | 2005 | 2006 | 2007 | 2008 | 2009 | 2010 | 2011 | 2012 | 2013 | 2014 | 2015 |
|---|---|---|---|---|---|---|---|---|---|---|---|---|---|
| **Depository Corporations** |  | *Millions of E. Caribbean Dollars: End of Period* | | | | | | | | | | | |
| Net Foreign Assets............................ | 31n | 3,028.44 | 3,136.38 | 3,302.14 | 3,027.08 | 2,353.83 | 1,919.13 | 2,217.19 | 1,874.57 | 2,049.27 | 2,904.69 | 4,521.40 | 6,249.99 |
| Claims on Nonresidents................ | 31 | 4,983.49 | 5,315.96 | 5,869.57 | 6,399.71 | 5,985.21 | 9,389.19 | 9,190.15 | 10,437.17 | 7,490.56 | 7,774.13 | 9,105.15 | 10,447.40 |
| Liabilities to Nonresidents.............. | 36c | 1,955.05 | 2,179.58 | 2,567.43 | 3,372.63 | 3,631.38 | 7,470.06 | 6,972.96 | 8,562.60 | 5,441.29 | 4,869.44 | 4,583.75 | 4,197.41 |
| Domestic Claims................................ | 32 | 8,407.04 | 9,426.98 | 10,829.93 | 12,973.86 | 14,353.86 | 14,357.35 | 14,215.19 | 14,445.28 | 15,376.42 | 14,404.57 | 14,256.73 | 13,346.32 |
| Net Claims on Central Government | 32an | 648.79 | 769.53 | 780.53 | 1,071.93 | 1,213.08 | 1,525.42 | 1,029.32 | 1,068.38 | 1,422.03 | 786.60 | 1,463.41 | 1,099.71 |
| Claims on Central Government.... | 32a | 1,429.99 | 1,630.16 | 1,824.18 | 2,056.60 | 2,235.11 | 2,477.91 | 2,160.50 | 2,143.82 | 2,558.69 | 1,968.33 | 2,804.06 | 2,661.32 |
| Liabilities to Central Government. | 36d | 781.20 | 860.63 | 1,043.65 | 984.68 | 1,022.03 | 952.49 | 1,131.17 | 1,075.44 | 1,136.66 | 1,181.73 | 1,340.66 | 1,561.61 |
| Claims on Other Sectors................ | 32s | 7,758.25 | 8,657.45 | 10,049.40 | 11,901.93 | 13,140.79 | 12,831.93 | 13,185.87 | 13,376.89 | 13,954.39 | 13,617.97 | 12,793.32 | 12,246.61 |
| Claims on Other Financial Corps.. | 32g | 282.71 | 308.42 | 307.37 | 317.21 | 280.86 | 161.67 | 156.71 | 178.51 | 338.32 | 310.77 | 216.81 | 239.15 |
| Claims on State & Local Govts..... | 32b | 69.53 | 57.07 | 88.57 | 96.19 | 120.58 | 135.20 | 177.44 | 207.01 | 201.47 | 207.89 | 181.41 | 189.80 |
| Claims on Public Nonfin. Corps.... | 32c | 653.62 | 736.31 | 765.19 | 804.36 | 925.95 | 621.29 | 628.60 | 619.85 | 589.80 | 556.86 | 353.07 | 318.95 |
| Claims on Private Sector.............. | 32d | 6,752.40 | 7,555.66 | 8,888.27 | 10,684.17 | 11,813.39 | 11,913.77 | 12,223.12 | 12,371.53 | 12,824.80 | 12,542.45 | 12,042.04 | 11,498.71 |
| Broad Money Liabilities.................... | 35l | 10,365.43 | 11,141.52 | 12,391.59 | 13,700.61 | 14,151.31 | 13,910.84 | 14,217.20 | 14,650.38 | 15,551.45 | 16,217.17 | 17,104.61 | 17,803.04 |
| Currency Outside Depository Corps | 34a | 486.14 | 521.40 | 586.00 | 594.71 | 612.83 | 621.37 | 616.07 | 634.59 | 633.71 | 667.57 | 715.79 | 763.91 |
| Transferable Deposits................... | 34 | 3,286.83 | 3,681.36 | 4,239.72 | 4,765.00 | 4,539.34 | 3,986.69 | 4,019.98 | 4,051.25 | 4,469.44 | 4,687.55 | 5,299.51 | 5,791.41 |
| Other Deposits.............................. | 35 | 6,592.46 | 6,938.76 | 7,565.87 | 8,340.90 | 8,999.14 | 9,302.78 | 9,581.14 | 9,964.55 | 10,448.30 | 10,862.05 | 11,089.31 | 11,247.72 |
| Securities Other than Shares.......... | 36a | — | — | — | — | — | — | — | — | — | — | — | — |
| Deposits Excl. from Broad Money..... | 36b | .82 | .82 | .82 | .82 | .82 | 191.66 | 192.10 | 192.39 | 191.81 | 192.21 | 192.42 | 180.25 |
| Sec.Ot.th.Shares Excl.f/Brd.Money.... | 36s | 1.00 | 1.00 | 1.00 | 1.00 | 1.00 | .91 | .91 | — | — | — | — | — |
| Loans............................................ | 36l | — | — | — | — | — | — | — | — | — | — | — | — |
| Financial Derivatives........................ | 36m | — | — | — | — | — | — | — | — | — | — | — | — |
| Insurance Technical Reserves........... | 36r | — | — | — | — | — | — | — | — | — | — | — | — |
| Shares and Other Equity................. | 37a | 1,312.29 | 1,558.38 | 1,896.71 | 2,270.56 | 2,536.32 | 2,576.36 | 2,506.08 | 2,043.17 | 2,011.48 | 1,435.03 | 1,216.45 | 1,555.59 |
| Other Items (Net).......................... | 37r | −244.06 | −138.36 | −158.06 | 27.95 | 18.25 | −403.29 | −483.90 | −566.10 | −329.04 | −535.16 | 264.64 | 57.43 |
| Broad Money Liabs., Seasonally Adj. | 35l.b | 10,401.47 | 11,185.83 | 12,445.93 | 13,769.28 | 14,229.76 | 13,995.06 | 14,314.45 | 14,763.70 | 15,691.34 | 16,381.21 | 17,296.18 | 18,009.95 |
| **Monetary Aggregates** |  | *Millions of E. Caribbean Dollars: End of Period* | | | | | | | | | | | |
| Broad Money............................... | 59m | 10,365.43 | 11,141.52 | 12,391.59 | 13,700.61 | 14,151.31 | 13,910.84 | 14,217.20 | 14,650.38 | 15,551.45 | 16,217.17 | 17,104.61 | 17,803.04 |
| o/w:Currency Issued by Cent.Govt | 59m.a | — | — | — | — | — | — | — | — | — | — | — | — |
| o/w: Dep.in Nonfin. Corporations. | 59m.b | — | — | — | — | — | — | — | — | — | — | — | — |
| o/w:Secs. Issued by Central Govt.. | 59m.c | — | — | — | — | — | — | — | — | — | — | — | — |
| Money (National Definitions) |  |  |  |  |  |  |  |  |  |  |  |  |  |
| M1.................................................. | 59ma | 1,896.02 | 2,086.69 | 2,258.90 | 2,493.82 | 2,641.16 | 2,586.82 | 2,555.96 | 2,692.94 | 2,810.22 | 2,880.45 | 3,253.35 | 3,525.93 |
| M2.................................................. | 59mb | 8,367.61 | 9,055.64 | 10,105.14 | 11,088.11 | 12,084.70 | 12,635.54 | 12,845.63 | 12,836.17 | 13,350.51 | 13,980.60 | 15,125.74 | 15,722.70 |
| **Interest Rates** |  | *Percent Per Annum* | | | | | | | | | | | |
| Discount Rate (End of Period)......... | 60.a | 6.50 | 6.50 | 6.50 | 6.50 | 6.50 | 6.50 | 6.50 | 6.50 | 6.50 | 6.50 | 6.50 | 6.50 |
| Money Market Rate........................ | 60b | 4.67 | 4.01 | 4.76 | 5.24 | 4.92 | 6.03 | 6.37 | 5.68 | 5.04 | 6.28 | 6.19 | 6.44 |
| Savings Rate................................... | 60k | 3.59 | 3.31 | 3.37 | 3.38 | 3.37 | 3.32 | 3.29 | 3.33 | 3.21 | 3.21 | 3.17 | 2.61 |
| Savings Rate (Fgn. Currency)........... | 60k.f | 2.28 | 2.29 | 2.38 | 2.49 | 2.38 | 2.07 | 1.81 | 1.74 | 2.18 | 2.14 | 1.92 | 1.72 |
| Deposit Rate................................... | 60l | 3.76 | 3.54 | 3.46 | 3.44 | 3.48 | 3.50 | 3.47 | 3.41 | 3.27 | 3.07 | 2.84 | 2.36 |
| Deposit Rate (Fgn. Currency)........... | 60l.f | 2.27 | 2.30 | 2.53 | 2.45 | 2.34 | 2.08 | 1.86 | 1.65 | 2.10 | 2.12 | 1.73 | 1.29 |
| Lending Rate.................................. | 60p | 10.93 | 10.49 | 10.19 | 9.84 | 9.71 | 10.00 | 10.13 | 10.02 | 9.47 | 9.25 | 9.30 | 9.15 |
| Lending Rate (Fgn. Currency).......... | 60p.f | 9.01 | 8.66 | 9.21 | 9.12 | 8.04 | 7.61 | 7.30 | 7.36 | 6.91 | 7.24 | 7.35 | 7.14 |

## Balance of Payments

Millions of US Dollars

| | | 2004 | 2005 | 2006 | 2007 | 2008 | 2009 | 2010 | 2011 | 2012 | 2013 | 2014 | 2015 |
|---|---|---|---|---|---|---|---|---|---|---|---|---|---|
| A. Current Account* | 109bx | −539.8 | −803.9 | −1,234.0 | −1,555.5 | −1,754.2 | −1,099.8 | −1,071.0 | −983.6 | −981.8 | −938.1 | .... | .... |
| Goods, credit (exports) | 1a9cx | 342.7 | 370.1 | 360.6 | 361.4 | 463.8 | 431.4 | 469.3 | 442.6 | 472.8 | 478.9 | .... | .... |
| Goods, debit (imports) | 1a9dx | 1,580.1 | 1,857.5 | 2,205.6 | 2,466.0 | 2,744.2 | 2,132.3 | 2,227.5 | 2,235.6 | 2,238.4 | 2,241.8 | .... | .... |
| Balance on goods | 1a9bx | −1,237.5 | −1,487.4 | −1,845.0 | −2,104.6 | −2,280.3 | −1,700.9 | −1,758.2 | −1,793.0 | −1,765.6 | −1,762.8 | .... | .... |
| Services, credit (exports) | 1b9cx | 1,465.8 | 1,535.8 | 1,534.9 | 1,641.0 | 1,660.9 | 1,525.9 | 1,552.3 | 1,632.1 | 1,637.1 | 1,695.2 | .... | .... |
| Services, debit (imports) | 1b9dx | 706.9 | 806.2 | 899.9 | 1,001.1 | 1,033.7 | 864.1 | 865.5 | 852.8 | 837.5 | 868.7 | .... | .... |
| Balance on Goods & Services | 1z9bx | −478.5 | −757.8 | −1,210.0 | −1,464.8 | −1,653.1 | −1,039.1 | −1,071.4 | −1,013.7 | −966.0 | −936.4 | .... | .... |
| Primary income: credit | 1c9cx | 48.3 | 75.6 | 101.7 | 103.0 | 68.9 | 76.0 | 69.0 | 58.9 | 62.0 | 62.1 | .... | .... |
| Primary income: debit | 1c9dx | 331.0 | 309.8 | 299.0 | 337.3 | 332.7 | 305.7 | 232.0 | 207.1 | 236.0 | 213.3 | .... | .... |
| Balance on gds, serv. & prim. inc. | 1y9bx | −761.2 | −992.0 | −1,407.3 | −1,699.1 | −1,916.9 | −1,268.8 | −1,234.3 | −1,161.8 | −1,140.1 | −1,087.5 | .... | .... |
| Secondary income: credit | 1d9ca | 304.2 | 273.8 | 273.1 | 267.1 | 276.3 | 271.8 | 280.7 | 290.6 | 289.6 | 283.6 | .... | .... |
| Secondary income: debit | 1d9da | 82.8 | 85.7 | 99.8 | 123.6 | 113.5 | 102.8 | 117.3 | 112.4 | 131.3 | 134.1 | .... | .... |
| B. Capital Account* | 209ba | 91.8 | 286.3 | 127.6 | 178.7 | 181.0 | 175.0 | 250.9 | 213.3 | 299.5 | 255.4 | .... | .... |
| Capital account: credit | 209ca | 91.8 | 286.3 | 127.6 | 178.7 | 181.0 | 175.0 | 250.9 | 213.3 | 299.5 | 255.4 | .... | .... |
| Capital account: debit | 209da | — | — | — | — | — | — | — | — | — | — | .... | .... |
| Balance on current & capital acct. | 129ba | −448.0 | −517.6 | −1,106.5 | −1,376.9 | −1,573.2 | −924.8 | −820.1 | −770.2 | −682.2 | −682.6 | .... | .... |
| C. Financial Account* | 309na | −509.0 | −466.5 | −1,161.9 | −1,361.6 | −1,385.0 | −1,145.9 | −929.2 | −766.2 | −636.1 | −643.7 | .... | .... |
| Direct investment: assets | 3a9aa | — | — | — | — | — | — | — | 15.6 | — | — | .... | .... |
| Equity & investment fund shares.. | 3aaaa | .... | .... | .... | .... | .... | .... | .... | .... | .... | .... | .... | .... |
| Debt instruments | 3abaa | .... | .... | .... | .... | .... | .... | .... | .... | .... | .... | .... | .... |
| Direct investment: liabilities | 3a9la | 458.6 | 644.4 | 1,074.0 | 1,186.8 | 959.9 | 659.1 | 531.2 | 455.1 | 513.7 | 606.6 | .... | .... |
| Equity & investment fund shares . | 3aala | 252.8 | 495.0 | 697.3 | 815.0 | 576.5 | 364.3 | 261.6 | 226.0 | 270.9 | 344.0 | .... | .... |
| Debt instruments | 3abla | 205.8 | 149.4 | 376.7 | 371.7 | 383.4 | 294.9 | 269.6 | 229.1 | 242.9 | 262.7 | .... | .... |
| Portfolio investment: assets | 3b9aa | 12.1 | 3.2 | 5.0 | 4.4 | 2.0 | 21.6 | 17.4 | 6.6 | 4.9 | −22.4 | .... | .... |
| Equity & investment fund shares | 3baaa | .... | .... | .... | .... | .... | .... | .... | .... | .... | .... | .... | .... |
| Debt securities | 3bbaa | .... | .... | .... | .... | .... | .... | .... | .... | .... | .... | .... | .... |
| Portfolio investment: liabilities | 3b9la | 84.5 | 34.3 | 26.9 | −22.2 | 12.0 | 3.9 | 18.9 | 39.0 | 77.7 | 89.9 | .... | .... |
| Equity & investment fund shares . | 3bala | .... | .... | .... | .... | .... | .... | .... | .... | .... | .... | .... | .... |
| Debt securities | 3bbla | .... | .... | .... | .... | .... | .... | .... | .... | .... | .... | .... | .... |
| Fin. der.& empl.stk.ops.(ESOs): net. | 3c9na | .... | .... | .... | .... | .... | .... | .... | .... | .... | .... | .... | .... |
| Fin. der. & ESOs.: assets | 3c9aa | .... | .... | .... | .... | .... | .... | .... | .... | .... | .... | .... | .... |
| Fin. der. & ESOs.: liabilities | 3c9la | .... | .... | .... | .... | .... | .... | .... | .... | .... | .... | .... | .... |
| Other investment: assets | 3d9aa | 282.4 | 555.7 | 203.1 | 282.6 | 229.3 | 267.7 | 297.4 | 277.8 | 406.7 | 710.3 | .... | .... |
| Other equity | 3daaa | .... | .... | .... | .... | .... | .... | .... | .... | .... | .... | .... | .... |
| Debt instruments | 3dzaa | 282.4 | 555.7 | 203.1 | 282.6 | 229.3 | 267.7 | 297.4 | 277.8 | 406.7 | 710.3 | .... | .... |
| Other investment: liabilities | 3d9la | 260.3 | 346.7 | 269.1 | 484.0 | 644.5 | 772.2 | 694.0 | 572.2 | 456.2 | 635.1 | .... | .... |
| Other equity | 3dala | .... | .... | .... | .... | .... | .... | .... | .... | .... | .... | .... | .... |
| Debt instruments | 3dzla | 260.3 | 346.7 | 269.1 | 484.0 | 644.5 | 772.2 | 694.0 | 572.2 | 456.2 | 635.1 | .... | .... |
| Curr.+ cap.− finan. acct. balance. | 4y9na | 61.0 | −51.1 | 55.4 | −15.2 | −188.2 | 221.1 | 109.1 | −4.0 | −46.2 | −38.9 | .... | .... |
| D. Net Errors and Omissions | 409na | 35.6 | 30.0 | 34.3 | 66.2 | 154.6 | −93.1 | −49.4 | 16.7 | 90.0 | 63.0 | .... | .... |
| E. Reserves and Related Items | 4z9na | 96.6 | −21.0 | 89.7 | 51.0 | −33.5 | 128.0 | 59.7 | 12.7 | 43.8 | 24.2 | .... | .... |
| Reserve assets | 3e9aa | 101.9 | −17.9 | 92.2 | 46.3 | −18.6 | 151.1 | 100.0 | 69.2 | 99.4 | 54.9 | .... | .... |
| Credit and loans from the IMF | 3dcla | 5.3 | 3.2 | 2.5 | −4.7 | 15.0 | 23.1 | 40.3 | 56.5 | 55.6 | 30.8 | .... | .... |
| Exceptional financing | 409la | .... | .... | .... | .... | .... | .... | .... | .... | .... | .... | .... | .... |

*Excludes components in group E

## Government Finance
## Cash Flow Statement
## Central Government

Millions of E. Caribbean Dollars: Fiscal Year Ends December 31

| | | 2004 | 2005 | 2006 | 2007 | 2008 | 2009 | 2010 | 2011 | 2012 | 2013 | 2014 | 2015 |
|---|---|---|---|---|---|---|---|---|---|---|---|---|---|
| Cash Receipts:Operating Activities... | c1 | 2,669.1 | 2,942.8 | 3,363.8 | 3,582.8 | 3,974.4 | 3,643.0 | 3,746.5 | 3,906.6 | 3,926.2 | 4,003.5 | 4,544.1 | .... |
| Taxes | c11 | 2,107.9 | 2,355.4 | 2,700.6 | 3,016.0 | 3,204.4 | 2,967.8 | 2,926.4 | 3,068.0 | 3,073.3 | 3,113.7 | 3,364.0 | .... |
| Social Contributions | c12 | — | — | — | — | — | — | — | — | — | — | — | .... |
| Grants | c13 | 283.5 | 327.3 | 361.1 | 244.9 | 399.6 | 344.1 | 389.9 | 359.7 | 356.5 | 272.8 | 444.1 | .... |
| Other Receipts | c14 | 277.7 | 260.1 | 302.1 | 321.8 | 370.4 | 331.1 | 430.2 | 479.0 | 496.4 | 617.0 | 735.9 | .... |
| Cash Payments:Operating Activities. | c2 | 2,450.8 | 2,545.1 | 2,862.9 | 3,045.8 | 3,409.1 | 3,592.6 | 3,404.0 | 3,613.3 | 3,585.0 | 3,683.6 | 3,860.4 | .... |
| Compensation of Employees | c21 | 1,101.9 | 1,128.0 | 1,212.3 | 1,308.8 | 1,463.9 | 1,494.6 | 1,512.7 | 1,546.1 | 1,581.2 | 1,653.4 | 1,712.1 | .... |
| Purchases of Goods & Services | c22 | 516.6 | 566.5 | 627.6 | 699.7 | 797.9 | 750.4 | 707.3 | 781.0 | 702.5 | 774.0 | 777.8 | .... |
| Interest | c24 | 397.3 | 349.4 | 400.8 | 422.5 | 442.0 | 552.0 | 418.0 | 420.2 | 483.0 | 430.4 | 477.7 | .... |
| Subsidies | c25 | 282.5 | 336.3 | 442.4 | 381.8 | 521.4 | 588.5 | 561.5 | 612.8 | 530.3 | 535.7 | 596.9 | .... |
| Grants | c26 | — | — | — | — | — | — | — | — | — | — | — | .... |
| Social Benefits | c27 | 152.5 | 164.9 | 179.8 | 233.1 | 183.9 | 207.1 | 204.6 | 253.3 | 288.1 | 290.1 | 296.0 | .... |
| Other Payments | c28 | — | — | — | — | — | — | — | — | — | — | — | .... |
| Net Cash Inflow:Operating Act.[1-2] | ccio | 218.3 | 397.7 | 500.9 | 536.9 | 565.4 | 50.4 | 342.4 | 293.3 | 341.1 | 319.9 | 683.7 | .... |
| Net Cash Outflow:Invest. in NFA | c31 | 559.2 | 736.5 | 1,037.6 | 1,008.1 | 939.1 | 866.5 | 656.5 | 793.7 | 674.4 | 853.3 | 880.5 | .... |
| Purchases of Nonfinancial Assets. | c31.1 | 594.5 | 779.9 | 1,056.2 | 1,053.8 | 1,039.0 | 889.3 | 695.6 | 817.3 | 693.3 | 909.2 | 917.5 | .... |
| Sales of Nonfinancial Assets | c31.2 | 35.3 | 43.4 | 18.6 | 45.7 | 99.9 | 22.9 | 39.1 | 23.6 | 18.9 | 55.9 | 37.0 | .... |
| Cash Surplus/Deficit [1-2-31=1-2M] | ccsd | −340.9 | −338.8 | −536.7 | −471.2 | −373.8 | −816.1 | −314.1 | −500.4 | −333.3 | −533.4 | −196.8 | .... |
| Net Acq. Fin. Assets, excl. Cash | c32x | 27.5 | −7.8 | .6 | 3.4 | 14.3 | 6.6 | 3.8 | 26.4 | 1.2 | 1.5 | .7 | .... |
| Domestic | c321x | 27.5 | −7.8 | .6 | 3.4 | 14.3 | 6.6 | 3.8 | 26.4 | 1.2 | 1.5 | .7 | .... |
| Foreign | c322x | — | — | — | — | — | — | — | — | — | — | — | .... |
| Net Incurrence of Liabilities | c33 | 351.2 | −121.5 | 137.8 | 362.8 | 340.2 | 438.8 | −1,117.0 | 245.7 | 405.5 | −231.9 | 268.5 | .... |
| Domestic | c331 | −34.2 | 158.8 | −12.3 | 253.6 | 175.6 | 220.3 | −1,350.0 | 51.6 | −67.9 | −1,080.2 | −655.8 | .... |
| Foreign | c332 | 385.4 | −280.3 | 150.1 | 109.2 | 164.6 | 218.5 | 232.9 | 194.1 | 473.3 | 848.3 | 924.3 | .... |
| Net Cash Inflow, Fin.Act.[-32x+33].. | cnfb | 323.7 | −113.7 | 137.2 | 359.3 | 325.9 | 432.2 | −1,120.9 | 219.3 | 404.3 | −233.4 | 267.8 | .... |
| Net Change in Stock of Cash | cncb | −17.2 | −452.5 | −399.5 | −111.8 | −47.9 | −383.9 | −1,434.9 | −281.1 | 71.1 | −766.9 | 71.0 | .... |
| Stat. Discrep. [32X-33+NCB-CSD].... | ccsdz | — | — | — | — | — | — | — | — | — | — | — | .... |
| Memo Item:Cash Expenditure[2+31] | c2m | 3,010.0 | 3,281.6 | 3,900.5 | 4,053.9 | 4,348.2 | 4,459.1 | 4,060.6 | 4,407.1 | 4,259.4 | 4,536.9 | 4,740.9 | .... |
| Memo Item: Gross Debt | c63 | 8,556.3 | 8,283.7 | 8,730.5 | 9,230.8 | 9,585.6 | 9,794.2 | 10,008.8 | 10,659.0 | 11,128.7 | 11,070.4 | 11,646.2 | .... |

| | | 2004 | 2005 | 2006 | 2007 | 2008 | 2009 | 2010 | 2011 | 2012 | 2013 | 2014 | 2015 |
|---|---|---|---|---|---|---|---|---|---|---|---|---|---|
| **National Accounts** | | | | | | *Millions of E. Caribbean Dollars* | | | | | | | |
| Househ.Cons.Expend.,incl.NPISHs.... | 96f | 7,232.0 | 7,358.7 | 8,269.2 | 9,903.2 | 11,313.6 | 11,973.2 | 10,417.6 | 11,086.9 | 11,612.0 | 11,665.9 | 11,843.0 | . . . . |
| Government Consumption Expend... | 91f | 1,706.2 | 1,801.4 | 1,916.9 | 2,142.3 | 2,438.7 | 2,506.7 | 2,411.4 | 2,450.7 | 2,604.6 | 2,705.6 | 2,831.9 | . . . . |
| Exports of Goods and Services......... | 90c | 4,882.9 | 5,145.9 | 5,117.8 | 5,406.4 | 5,738.7 | 5,289.6 | 5,469.3 | 5,615.0 | 5,739.7 | 5,948.7 | 6,146.4 | . . . . |
| Imports of Goods and Services (-)..... | 98c | 6,174.9 | 7,191.9 | 8,384.7 | 9,361.3 | 10,157.9 | 8,093.6 | 8,359.9 | 8,371.7 | 8,338.3 | 8,575.3 | 8,507.3 | . . . . |
| Gross Domestic Product (GDP)......... | 99b | 10,864.3 | 11,814.0 | 13,180.1 | 14,546.5 | 15,303.1 | 14,524.1 | 14,437.2 | 14,751.8 | 15,046.1 | 15,490.5 | 16,248.0 | . . . . |
| | | | | | | *Millions: Midyear Estimates* | | | | | | | |
| Population................................. | 99z | .592 | .597 | .602 | .606 | .611 | .616 | .621 | .625 | .629 | .633 | .637 | .641 |

# Ecuador 248

| | | 2004 | 2005 | 2006 | 2007 | 2008 | 2009 | 2010 | 2011 | 2012 | 2013 | 2014 | 2015 |
|---|---|---|---|---|---|---|---|---|---|---|---|---|---|
| **Exchange Rates** | | | | | | *US Dollars per SDR: End of Period* | | | | | | | |
| Market Rate | sa | 1.5530 | 1.4293 | 1.5044 | 1.5803 | 1.5403 | 1.5677 | 1.5400 | 1.5353 | 1.5369 | 1.5400 | 1.4488 | 1.3857 |
| **Fund Position** | | | | | | *Millions of SDRs: End of Period* | | | | | | | |
| Quota | 2f.s | 302.30 | 302.30 | 302.30 | 302.30 | 302.30 | 302.30 | 302.30 | 347.80 | 347.80 | 347.80 | 347.80 | 347.80 |
| SDR Holdings | 1b.s | 36.09 | 15.24 | 5.05 | 15.41 | 17.03 | 16.90 | 16.19 | 15.05 | 15.75 | 18.12 | 17.88 | 17.75 |
| Reserve Position in the Fund | 1c.s | 17.15 | 17.15 | 17.15 | 17.15 | 17.15 | 17.15 | 17.15 | 28.53 | 28.53 | 28.53 | 28.53 | 28.53 |
| Total Fund Cred.&Loans Outstg | 2tl | 186.77 | 54.75 | 15.10 | — | — | — | — | — | — | — | — | — |
| SDR Allocations | 1bd | 32.93 | 32.93 | 32.93 | 32.93 | 32.93 | 288.36 | 288.36 | 288.36 | 288.36 | 288.36 | 288.36 | 288.36 |
| **International Liquidity** | | | | | | *Millions of US Dollars Unless Otherwise Indicated: End of Period* | | | | | | | |
| Total Reserves minus Gold | 1l.d | 1,069.6 | 1,714.2 | 1,489.5 | 2,816.4 | 3,738.2 | 2,873.2 | 1,434.8 | 1,664.3 | 1,080.0 | 3,328.0 | 3,484.1 | 2,085.4 |
| SDR Holdings | 1b.d | 56.1 | 21.8 | 7.6 | 24.3 | 26.2 | 26.5 | 24.9 | 23.1 | 24.2 | 27.9 | 25.9 | 24.6 |
| Reserve Position in the Fund | 1c.d | 26.6 | 24.5 | 25.8 | 27.1 | 26.4 | 26.9 | 26.4 | 43.8 | 43.8 | 43.9 | 41.3 | 39.5 |
| Foreign Exchange | 1d.d | 986.9 | 1,667.9 | 1,456.1 | 2,764.9 | 3,685.5 | 2,819.8 | 1,383.5 | 1,597.4 | 1,011.9 | 3,256.2 | 3,416.9 | 2,021.3 |
| Gold (Million Fine Troy Ounces) | 1ad | .845 | .845 | .845 | .845 | .845 | .845 | .845 | .845 | .845 | .845 | .379 | .379 |
| Gold (National Valuation) | 1and | 368.0 | 433.4 | 533.9 | 704.3 | 734.7 | 918.6 | 1,187.3 | 1,293.3 | 1,402.6 | 1,023.5 | 464.9 | 410.5 |
| Central Bank: Other Assets | 3..d | 602.8 | 721.7 | 1,668.8 | 1,087.2 | 1,414.6 | 1,196.9 | 1,245.5 | 1,630.9 | 2,755.2 | 1,066.5 | 819.8 | 657.5 |
| Central Bank: Other Liabs | 4..d | 39.8 | 14.9 | 10.9 | 13.3 | 41.4 | 71.3 | 92.3 | 59.4 | 126.4 | 59.2 | 77.5 | 82.7 |
| Other Depository Corps.: Assets | 7a.d | 2,606.5 | 3,094.9 | 3,430.7 | 4,315.4 | 4,500.4 | 5,139.7 | 5,840.3 | 5,883.4 | 6,122.8 | 6,345.5 | 6,873.3 | .... |
| Other Depository Corps.: Liabs | 7b.d | 615.3 | 702.1 | 851.9 | 953.3 | 948.7 | 837.1 | 760.2 | 708.4 | 758.9 | 841.3 | 994.0 | .... |
| Other Financial Corps.: Assets | 7e.d | 50.4 | 55.3 | 88.4 | 168.1 | 61.8 | 53.5 | 55.5 | 58.0 | .... | .... | .... | .... |
| Other Financial Corps.: Liabs | 7f.d | 3.3 | 2.7 | 5.3 | 13.7 | 1.6 | 50.6 | 134.2 | 69.5 | .... | .... | .... | .... |
| **Central Bank** | | | | | | *Millions of US Dollars: End of Period* | | | | | | | |
| Net Foreign Assets | 11n | 1,670.5 | 2,729.0 | 3,608.6 | 4,540.4 | 5,821.5 | 4,049.6 | 2,764.5 | 3,440.4 | 4,196.9 | 4,747.8 | 4,092.5 | 2,528.6 |
| Claims on Nonresidents | 11 | 2,051.4 | 2,869.3 | 3,691.7 | 4,605.7 | 5,913.7 | 4,572.9 | 3,300.8 | 3,942.5 | 4,766.5 | 5,251.1 | 4,587.7 | 3,010.9 |
| Liabilities to Nonresidents | 16c | 381.0 | 140.2 | 83.1 | 65.3 | 92.2 | 523.4 | 536.4 | 502.1 | 569.6 | 503.2 | 495.2 | 482.3 |
| Claims on Other Depository Corps | 12e | 151.1 | 115.7 | 115.0 | 109.7 | 105.6 | 128.7 | 153.7 | 527.6 | 204.6 | 233.6 | 190.8 | 129.7 |
| Net Claims on Central Government | 12an | −63.5 | 510.9 | 5.2 | 820.9 | −25.9 | −1,979.2 | −1,187.2 | −1,801.9 | −1,697.0 | −1,417.5 | −481.3 | 61.1 |
| Claims on Central Government | 12a | 1,155.4 | 1,146.9 | 1,168.5 | 1,168.3 | 15.6 | 144.7 | 133.1 | 134.8 | 143.6 | 142.4 | 975.1 | 1,386.0 |
| Liabilities to Central Government | 16d | 1,218.9 | 636.0 | 1,163.3 | 347.4 | 41.5 | 2,123.9 | 1,320.3 | 1,936.6 | 1,840.5 | 1,559.8 | 1,456.4 | 1,324.9 |
| Claims on Other Sectors | 12s | 173.3 | 160.8 | 22.0 | 43.9 | 40.4 | 538.7 | 887.3 | 956.4 | 1,955.5 | 2,541.8 | 2,372.9 | 2,071.4 |
| Claims on Other Financial Corps | 12g | 9.1 | 1.6 | .2 | .2 | .2 | 496.0 | 830.8 | 904.9 | 1,903.9 | 2,501.3 | 2,336.4 | 2,036.5 |
| Claims on State & Local Govts | 12b | 2.6 | 1.9 | 1.5 | 2.8 | 2.6 | 2.4 | 2.3 | 2.1 | 1.9 | 1.7 | 1.5 | 1.2 |
| Claims on Public Nonfin. Corps | 12c | — | — | .4 | — | — | — | — | — | — | — | — | — |
| Claims on Private Sector | 12d | 161.7 | 157.3 | 19.9 | 40.9 | 37.6 | 40.3 | 54.2 | 49.4 | 49.7 | 38.7 | 35.0 | 33.7 |
| Monetary Base | 14 | 723.0 | 1,071.2 | 1,204.5 | 1,620.7 | 2,393.1 | 2,355.2 | 2,205.4 | 2,466.0 | 3,377.0 | 4,853.0 | 4,628.6 | 3,204.4 |
| Currency in Circulation | 14a | 58.1 | 62.8 | 66.0 | 71.4 | 77.3 | 77.4 | 82.4 | 83.2 | 84.5 | 87.3 | 86.6 | 87.0 |
| Liabs. to Other Depository Corps | 14c | 357.1 | 505.8 | 538.6 | 720.2 | 1,191.1 | 1,296.9 | 1,141.3 | 1,242.5 | 1,853.5 | 3,084.4 | 2,335.1 | 1,661.0 |
| Liabilities to Other Sectors | 14d | 307.8 | 502.7 | 599.9 | 829.1 | 1,124.7 | 980.9 | 981.7 | 1,140.3 | 1,439.0 | 1,681.3 | 2,206.9 | 1,456.4 |
| Other Liabs. to Other Dep. Corps | 14n | 13.6 | 5.9 | 3.2 | 2.7 | 2.2 | — | — | — | — | — | — | — |
| Dep. & Sec. Excl. f/Monetary Base | 14o | — | — | — | — | — | 404.5 | 458.5 | 351.3 | 498.9 | 798.0 | 1,053.3 | 1,336.9 |
| Deposits Included in Broad Money | 15 | — | — | — | — | — | — | — | — | — | — | — | — |
| Sec.Ot.th.Shares Incl.in Brd. Money | 16a | — | — | — | — | — | — | — | — | — | — | — | — |
| Deposits Excl. from Broad Money | 16b | — | — | — | — | — | 404.5 | 458.5 | 351.3 | 498.9 | 798.0 | 1,053.3 | 1,336.9 |
| Sec.Ot.th.Shares Excl.f/Brd.Money | 16s | — | — | — | — | — | — | — | — | — | — | — | — |
| Loans | 16l | — | — | — | — | — | — | — | — | — | — | — | — |
| Financial Derivatives | 16m | — | — | — | — | — | — | — | — | — | — | — | — |
| Shares and Other Equity | 17a | 1,532.8 | 1,655.6 | 1,714.5 | 1,918.2 | 938.0 | 753.3 | 758.5 | 1,196.0 | 914.6 | 585.7 | 575.2 | 408.2 |
| Other Items (Net) | 17r | −338.0 | 783.8 | 828.4 | 1,973.2 | 2,608.4 | −775.3 | −804.2 | −890.9 | −130.4 | −130.9 | −82.3 | −158.8 |
| Memo Item: | | | | | | | | | | | | | |
| Total Assets | 10ra | 4,389.1 | 5,115.4 | 5,997.1 | 6,919.8 | 7,103.8 | 6,673.1 | 5,987.5 | 9,197.3 | 9,406.9 | 10,532.0 | 10,455.0 | 8,758.9 |
| **Other Depository Corporations** | | | | | | *Millions of US Dollars: End of Period* | | | | | | | |
| Net Foreign Assets | 21n | 1,991.2 | 2,392.8 | 2,578.8 | 3,362.1 | 3,551.7 | 4,302.6 | 5,080.0 | 5,175.0 | 5,363.9 | 5,504.1 | 5,879.2 | .... |
| Claims on Nonresidents | 21 | 2,606.5 | 3,094.9 | 3,430.7 | 4,315.4 | 4,500.4 | 5,139.7 | 5,840.3 | 5,883.4 | 6,122.8 | 6,345.5 | 6,873.3 | .... |
| Liabilities to Nonresidents | 26c | 615.3 | 702.1 | 851.9 | 953.3 | 948.7 | 837.1 | 760.2 | 708.4 | 758.9 | 841.3 | 994.0 | .... |
| Claims on Central Bank | 20 | 370.6 | 478.3 | 558.4 | 696.1 | 1,218.3 | 1,357.2 | 1,226.6 | 1,331.6 | 1,997.0 | 3,239.8 | 2,531.8 | .... |
| Currency | 20a | — | — | — | — | — | — | — | — | — | — | — | .... |
| Reserve Deposits and Securities | 20b | 340.2 | 450.2 | 531.3 | 686.2 | 1,216.7 | 1,353.3 | 1,225.2 | 1,329.0 | 1,994.0 | 3,237.4 | 2,528.6 | .... |
| Other Claims | 20n | 30.4 | 28.1 | 27.1 | 9.9 | 1.6 | 3.9 | 1.4 | 2.6 | 3.0 | 2.3 | 3.2 | .... |
| Net Claims on Central Government | 22an | −1,394.0 | −1,789.3 | −1,808.9 | −1,867.3 | −2,080.4 | −1,299.7 | −1,193.9 | −466.1 | −126.1 | 175.2 | 748.5 | .... |
| Claims on Central Government | 22a | 280.2 | 279.9 | 208.2 | 167.8 | 149.7 | 145.5 | 179.8 | 402.4 | 904.8 | 1,065.9 | 1,464.4 | .... |
| Liabilities to Central Government | 26d | 1,674.2 | 2,069.2 | 2,017.1 | 2,035.1 | 2,230.1 | 1,445.2 | 1,373.7 | 868.4 | 1,030.9 | 890.7 | 715.9 | .... |
| Claims on Other Sectors | 22s | 7,415.4 | 9,029.1 | 10,655.9 | 11,989.0 | 14,783.8 | 15,128.6 | 18,192.7 | 21,129.7 | 24,416.3 | 26,718.8 | 29,329.1 | .... |
| Claims on Other Financial Corps | 22g | 559.4 | 597.0 | 772.4 | 760.0 | 870.3 | 1,252.1 | 1,155.9 | 1,079.2 | 1,462.6 | 1,468.7 | 1,712.0 | .... |
| Claims on State & Local Govts | 22b | 7.8 | 6.2 | 8.7 | 6.1 | 10.4 | 14.7 | 5.6 | 8.4 | 10.9 | 40.8 | 22.7 | .... |
| Claims on Public Nonfin. Corps | 22c | 1.1 | .7 | 1.3 | 1.6 | 1.8 | .9 | .5 | 2.2 | 4.3 | .7 | .5 | .... |
| Claims on Private Sector | 22d | 6,847.2 | 8,425.2 | 9,873.5 | 11,221.3 | 13,901.4 | 13,860.8 | 17,030.7 | 20,040.0 | 22,938.4 | 25,208.6 | 27,594.0 | .... |
| Liabilities to Central Bank | 26g | 52.6 | 26.2 | 2.4 | 19.6 | 15.1 | 240.1 | 291.9 | 153.2 | 311.6 | 457.1 | 384.8 | .... |
| Transf.Dep.Included in Broad Money | 24 | 2,353.3 | 2,766.8 | 3,288.3 | 3,786.6 | 4,965.0 | 5,201.4 | 6,420.9 | 6,925.9 | 8,390.6 | 9,273.7 | 9,531.1 | .... |
| Other Dep.Included in Broad Money | 25 | 5,003.9 | 5,909.2 | 6,493.3 | 7,681.9 | 9,123.4 | 10,273.2 | 12,145.5 | 14,753.4 | 16,650.4 | 19,168.1 | 21,827.2 | .... |
| Sec.Ot.th.Shares Incl.in Brd. Money | 26a | — | — | — | — | — | — | — | — | — | — | — | .... |
| Deposits Excl. from Broad Money | 26b | 1.6 | 1.3 | 1.4 | 1.7 | 1.9 | 1.8 | 2.6 | — | — | — | — | .... |
| Sec.Ot.th.Shares Excl.f/Brd.Money | 26s | 14.0 | 77.9 | 20.6 | 25.2 | 8.5 | 8.8 | 7.0 | — | — | — | — | .... |
| Loans | 26l | 103.6 | 172.3 | 210.0 | 217.4 | 225.8 | 190.2 | 217.5 | 413.1 | 479.8 | 594.4 | 638.2 | .... |
| Financial Derivatives | 26m | — | — | — | — | — | — | — | — | — | — | — | .... |
| Insurance Technical Reserves | 26r | — | — | — | — | — | — | — | — | — | — | — | .... |
| Shares and Other Equity | 27a | −607.4 | −438.9 | −179.8 | 260.4 | 715.5 | 1,454.2 | 1,793.8 | 3,742.6 | 4,177.0 | 4,404.7 | 4,663.4 | .... |
| Other Items (Net) | 27r | 1,461.7 | 1,596.2 | 2,148.0 | 2,187.1 | 2,418.3 | 2,118.9 | 2,426.1 | 1,182.1 | 1,641.6 | 1,739.8 | 1,443.9 | .... |
| Memo Item: | | | | | | | | | | | | | |
| Total Assets | 20ra | 13,419.2 | 15,631.1 | 17,900.9 | 20,473.1 | 23,914.6 | 25,527.5 | 29,700.8 | 32,028.0 | 37,835.1 | 41,886.5 | 45,360.4 | .... |

# Ecuador 248

|  |  | 2004 | 2005 | 2006 | 2007 | 2008 | 2009 | 2010 | 2011 | 2012 | 2013 | 2014 | 2015 |
|---|---|---|---|---|---|---|---|---|---|---|---|---|---|
| **Depository Corporations** | | | | | | *Millions of US Dollars: End of Period* | | | | | | | |
| Net Foreign Assets | 31n | 3,661.7 | 5,121.8 | 6,187.4 | 7,902.4 | 9,373.2 | 8,352.1 | 7,844.5 | 8,615.4 | 9,560.8 | 10,252.0 | 9,971.8 | .... |
| Claims on Nonresidents | 31 | 4,657.9 | 5,964.2 | 7,122.4 | 8,921.1 | 10,414.1 | 9,712.6 | 9,141.1 | 9,826.0 | 10,889.3 | 11,596.5 | 11,461.0 | .... |
| Liabilities to Nonresidents | 36c | 996.2 | 842.3 | 935.0 | 1,018.6 | 1,040.8 | 1,360.5 | 1,296.6 | 1,210.5 | 1,328.5 | 1,344.6 | 1,489.3 | .... |
| Domestic Claims | 32 | 6,131.3 | 7,911.5 | 8,874.1 | 10,986.5 | 12,718.0 | 12,388.4 | 16,698.9 | 19,818.2 | 24,548.7 | 28,018.2 | 31,969.2 | .... |
| Net Claims on Central Government | 32an | −1,457.4 | −1,278.4 | −1,803.8 | −1,046.4 | −2,106.2 | −3,278.9 | −2,381.0 | −2,268.0 | −1,823.1 | −1,242.3 | 267.2 | .... |
| Claims on Central Government.... | 32a | 1,435.6 | 1,426.8 | 1,376.7 | 1,336.1 | 165.3 | 290.2 | 312.9 | 537.1 | 1,048.4 | 1,208.2 | 2,439.5 | .... |
| Liabilities to Central Government. | 36d | 2,893.1 | 2,705.2 | 3,180.4 | 2,382.5 | 2,271.6 | 3,569.1 | 2,694.0 | 2,805.1 | 2,871.4 | 2,450.5 | 2,172.3 | .... |
| Claims on Other Sectors... | 32s | 7,588.7 | 9,189.9 | 10,677.8 | 12,032.8 | 14,824.2 | 15,667.3 | 19,079.9 | 22,086.1 | 26,371.7 | 29,260.5 | 31,702.1 | .... |
| Claims on Other Financial Corps.. | 32g | 568.5 | 598.6 | 772.6 | 760.2 | 870.5 | 1,748.1 | 1,986.7 | 1,984.1 | 3,366.5 | 3,970.4 | 4,048.4 | .... |
| Claims on State & Local Govts..... | 32b | 10.4 | 8.0 | 10.1 | 8.8 | 13.0 | 17.1 | 7.9 | 10.5 | 12.8 | 42.5 | 24.1 | .... |
| Claims on Public Nonfin. Corps..... | 32c | 1.1 | .7 | 1.7 | 1.6 | 1.8 | .9 | .5 | 2.2 | 4.3 | .7 | .6 | .... |
| Claims on Private Sector | 32d | 7,008.8 | 8,582.6 | 9,893.4 | 11,262.3 | 13,939.0 | 13,901.1 | 17,084.9 | 20,089.3 | 22,988.1 | 25,247.3 | 27,629.0 | .... |
| Broad Money Liabilities | 35l | 7,723.1 | 9,241.3 | 10,447.5 | 12,369.0 | 15,290.4 | 16,532.9 | 19,630.6 | 22,902.8 | 26,564.5 | 30,210.4 | 33,651.9 | .... |
| Currency Outside Depository Corps | 34a | 58.1 | 62.8 | 66.0 | 71.4 | 77.3 | 77.4 | 82.4 | 83.2 | 84.5 | 87.3 | 86.6 | .... |
| Transferable Deposits | 34 | 2,490.2 | 2,978.2 | 3,565.4 | 4,323.4 | 5,829.7 | 5,949.4 | 7,316.3 | 7,931.4 | 9,623.9 | 10,815.0 | 11,528.3 | .... |
| Other Deposits | 35 | 5,174.7 | 6,200.4 | 6,816.1 | 7,974.2 | 9,383.4 | 10,506.1 | 12,231.9 | 14,888.2 | 16,856.1 | 19,308.0 | 22,037.0 | .... |
| Securities Other than Shares | 36a | — | — | — | — | — | — | — | — | — | — | — | .... |
| Deposits Excl. from Broad Money..... | 36b | 1.6 | 1.3 | 1.4 | 1.7 | 1.9 | 406.3 | 461.1 | 351.3 | 498.9 | 798.0 | 1,053.3 | .... |
| Sec.Ot.th.Shares Excl.f/Brd.Money.... | 36s | 14.0 | 77.9 | 20.6 | 25.2 | 8.5 | 8.8 | 7.0 | — | — | — | — | .... |
| Loans | 36l | 103.6 | 172.3 | 210.0 | 217.4 | 225.8 | 190.2 | 217.5 | 413.1 | 479.8 | 594.4 | 638.2 | .... |
| Financial Derivatives | 36m | — | — | — | — | — | — | — | — | — | — | — | .... |
| Insurance Technical Reserves | 36r | — | — | — | — | — | — | — | — | — | — | — | .... |
| Shares and Other Equity | 37a | 925.4 | 1,216.7 | 1,534.8 | 2,178.6 | 1,653.5 | 2,207.4 | 2,552.4 | 4,938.5 | 5,091.6 | 4,990.4 | 5,238.6 | .... |
| Other Items (Net) | 37r | 1,025.3 | 2,323.8 | 2,847.2 | 4,097.1 | 4,911.2 | 1,394.9 | 1,674.8 | −172.2 | 1,474.6 | 1,677.0 | 1,359.0 | .... |
| Broad Money Liabs., Seasonally Adj. | 35l.b | 7,646.3 | 9,128.6 | 10,292.9 | 12,160.0 | 15,016.1 | 16,225.1 | 19,257.2 | 22,452.6 | 26,025.8 | 29,566.5 | 32,911.2 | .... |
| **Other Financial Corporations** | | | | | | *Millions of US Dollars: End of Period* | | | | | | | |
| Net Foreign Assets | 41n | 47.0 | 52.5 | 83.1 | 154.4 | 60.2 | 2.9 | −78.7 | −11.5 | .... | .... | .... | .... |
| Claims on Nonresidents | 41 | 50.4 | 55.3 | 88.4 | 168.1 | 61.8 | 53.5 | 55.5 | 58.0 | .... | .... | .... | .... |
| Liabilities to Nonresidents | 46c | 3.3 | 2.7 | 5.3 | 13.7 | 1.6 | 50.6 | 134.2 | 69.5 | .... | .... | .... | .... |
| Claims on Depository Corporations.. | 40 | 304.4 | 294.4 | 283.8 | 312.7 | 377.1 | 687.2 | 525.9 | 504.9 | .... | .... | .... | .... |
| Net Claims on Central Government.. | 42an | −11.0 | −22.2 | 25.0 | 33.4 | −96.9 | −342.4 | −108.3 | −103.8 | .... | .... | .... | .... |
| Claims on Central Government...... | 42a | 124.9 | 79.2 | 50.2 | 35.5 | 14.1 | 8.1 | 134.6 | 82.3 | .... | .... | .... | .... |
| Liabilities to Central Government... | 46d | 135.9 | 101.4 | 25.2 | 2.1 | 111.0 | 350.5 | 242.8 | 186.2 | .... | .... | .... | .... |
| Claims on Other Sectors | 42s | 28.2 | 39.9 | 62.4 | 104.3 | 320.0 | 592.8 | 821.7 | 1,025.9 | .... | .... | .... | .... |
| Claims on State & Local Govts....... | 42b | — | — | 3.3 | 2.0 | .6 | — | 2.2 | 9.6 | .... | .... | .... | .... |
| Claims on Public Nonfin. Corps...... | 42c | — | — | — | — | — | — | — | — | .... | .... | .... | .... |
| Claims on Private Sector | 42d | 28.2 | 39.9 | 59.0 | 102.3 | 319.4 | 592.7 | 819.5 | 1,016.3 | .... | .... | .... | .... |
| Deposits | 46b | 35.8 | 42.1 | 36.4 | 45.5 | 70.0 | 463.6 | 658.5 | 884.0 | .... | .... | .... | .... |
| Securities Other than Shares | 46s | 10.9 | 3.5 | 1.9 | .5 | .5 | .5 | .8 | .9 | .... | .... | .... | .... |
| Loans | 46l | — | — | 4.6 | 5.1 | 2.6 | 6.2 | 4.7 | 6.0 | .... | .... | .... | .... |
| Financial Derivatives | 46m | — | — | — | — | — | — | — | — | .... | .... | .... | .... |
| Insurance Technical Reserves | 46r | — | — | — | — | — | — | — | — | .... | .... | .... | .... |
| Shares and Other Equity | 47a | 244.0 | 268.0 | 290.3 | 430.5 | 513.8 | 477.4 | 530.1 | 563.7 | .... | .... | .... | .... |
| Other Items (Net) | 47r | 78.0 | 51.1 | 121.1 | 123.2 | 73.5 | −7.2 | −33.4 | −39.1 | .... | .... | .... | .... |
| Memo Item: | | | | | | | | | | | | | |
| Total Assets | 40ra | 634.4 | 596.5 | 603.7 | 741.7 | 912.6 | 1,546.9 | 1,794.3 | 1,963.7 | .... | .... | .... | .... |
| **Monetary Aggregates** | | | | | | *Millions of US Dollars: End of Period* | | | | | | | |
| Broad Money | 59m | 9,978.3 | 11,930.0 | 13,477.5 | 15,648.3 | 19,388.6 | 20,763.0 | 24,176.0 | 28,193.8 | 32,975.2 | 37,577.4 | 43,191.8 | .... |
| o/w:Currency Issued by Cent.Govt | 59m.a | — | — | — | — | — | — | — | — | — | — | — | .... |
| o/w: Dep.in Nonfin. Corporations. | 59m.b | — | — | — | — | — | — | — | — | — | — | — | .... |
| o/w: Secs. Issued by Central Govt. | 59m.c | — | — | — | — | — | — | — | — | — | — | — | .... |
| Money (National Definitions) | | | | | | | | | | | | | |
| Base Money | 19ma | .... | .... | .... | .... | .... | .... | 7,430.9 | 8,391.7 | 10,003.5 | 12,738.6 | 14,731.1 | 16,613.3 |
| M1 | 59ma | .... | .... | .... | .... | .... | .... | 10,776.1 | 12,093.0 | 14,511.6 | 16,272.4 | 18,695.3 | 19,041.5 |
| M2 | 59mb | .... | .... | .... | .... | .... | .... | 22,189.4 | 26,557.0 | 30,905.5 | 35,051.1 | 40,104.4 | 39,637.7 |
| **Interest Rates** | | | | | | *Percent Per Annum* | | | | | | | |
| Discount Rate (End of Period) | 60.a | 10.23 | 9.96 | 9.54 | † 10.72 | 9.14 | 9.19 | 8.68 | 8.17 | 8.17 | 8.17 | 8.19 | 9.12 |
| Savings Rate | 60k | 2.00 | 1.69 | 1.59 | 1.73 | † 1.50 | 1.40 | 1.41 | 1.43 | 1.41 | 1.41 | 1.23 | 1.14 |
| Deposit Rate | 60l | 4.16 | 3.59 | 4.22 | † 5.26 | 4.87 | 4.78 | 3.90 | 3.84 | 3.89 | 3.89 | 4.03 | 4.38 |
| Lending Rate | 60p | 9.95 | 9.62 | 9.81 | .... | .... | .... | .... | .... | .... | .... | .... | .... |
| **Prices, Production, Labor** | | | | | | *Index Numbers (2010=100): Period Averages* | | | | | | | |
| Producer Prices | 63 | 65.9 | 75.5 | 84.5 | 88.9 | 104.9 | 85.4 | 100.0 | 119.4 | 121.7 | 123.1 | 120.6 | 95.5 |
| Consumer Prices | 64 | † 78.5 | 80.4 | 82.8 | 84.7 | 91.8 | 96.6 | 100.0 | 104.5 | 109.8 | 112.8 | † 116.8 | 121.5 |
| Crude Petroleum Production | 66aa | 107.6 | 109.7 | .... | 105.2 | 312.5 | 300.3 | 100.0 | 102.9 | 104.0 | 1,301.0 | 170.7 | 111.9 |
| | | | | | | *Number in Thousands: Period Averages* | | | | | | | |
| Labor Force | 67d | 4,221 | 4,225 | 4,373 | 4,501 | 4,484 | 4,503 | 4,476 | 4,434 | 4,543 | 4,637 | .... | .... |
| Employment | 67e | 3,859 | 3,892 | 4,032 | 4,170 | 4,175 | 4,121 | 4,135 | 4,168 | 4,319 | 4,418 | .... | .... |
| Unemployment | 67c | 362 | 334 | 342 | 331 | 309 | 382 | 341 | 266 | 224 | 219 | .... | .... |
| Unemployment Rate (%) | 67r | 8.6 | 7.9 | 7.8 | 7.4 | 6.9 | 8.5 | 7.6 | 6.0 | 4.9 | 4.7 | .... | .... |
| **Intl. Transactions & Positions** | | | | | | *Millions of US Dollars* | | | | | | | |
| Exports | 70..d | 7,752.9 | 10,100.0 | 12,728.2 | 13,852.4 | 18,818.3 | 13,863.1 | 17,415.2 | 22,345.2 | 23,764.8 | 24,750.9 | 25,724.4 | 18,330.6 |
| Imports, c.i.f. | 71..d | 8,226.3 | 10,286.9 | 12,113.6 | 13,565.3 | 18,851.9 | 15,089.9 | 20,590.9 | 24,286.1 | 25,304.2 | 27,021.3 | 27,726.3 | 21,518.0 |
| Imports, f.o.b. | 71.vd | 7,554.6 | 9,549.4 | 11,266.0 | 12,591.4 | 17,551.9 | 14,071.5 | 19,278.7 | 22,945.8 | 24,018.3 | 25,763.8 | 26,421.5 | 20,446.8 |
| | | | | | | *2010=100* | | | | | | | |
| Volume of Exports | 72 | 100.1 | 87.7 | 107.4 | 104.2 | 105.7 | 102.8 | 100.0 | 103.7 | 105.0 | 110.0 | 118.1 | 119.1 |
| Volume of Imports | 73 | 50.7 | 61.6 | 69.3 | 79.1 | 84.4 | 82.9 | 100.0 | 105.5 | 104.1 | 113.9 | 125.5 | 113.3 |
| Unit Value of Exports/Export Prices.. | 74..d | 44.3 | 56.9 | 69.0 | 79.4 | 108.3 | 75.9 | 100.0 | 138.4 | 129.8 | 128.2 | 115.6 | 68.7 |

# Ecuador 248

| Balance of Payments | | 2004 | 2005 | 2006 | 2007 | 2008 | 2009 | 2010 | 2011 | 2012 | 2013 | 2014 | 2015 |
|---|---|---|---|---|---|---|---|---|---|---|---|---|---|
| | | | | | | | *Millions of US Dollars* | | | | | | |
| A. Current Account* | 109bx | −479.4 | 473.9 | 1,739.9 | 1,886.5 | 1,764.4 | 306.9 | −1,586.2 | −403.8 | −153.7 | −932.1 | −574.0 | −2,200.6 |
| Goods, credit (exports) | 1a9cx | 7,962.2 | 10,461.7 | 13,170.1 | 14,864.2 | 19,454.8 | 14,406.0 | 18,131.1 | 23,076.3 | 24,562.9 | 25,580.8 | 26,590.5 | 19,042.7 |
| Goods, debit (imports) | 1a9dx | 7,673.4 | 9,703.4 | 11,401.7 | 13,041.1 | 17,906.1 | 14,262.4 | 19,635.1 | 23,378.9 | 24,512.9 | 26,109.3 | 26,654.0 | 20,692.5 |
| Balance on goods | 1a9bx | 288.8 | 758.3 | 1,768.4 | 1,823.0 | 1,548.7 | 143.6 | −1,504.0 | −302.6 | 49.9 | −528.6 | −63.5 | −1,649.8 |
| Services, credit (exports) | 1b9cx | 1,019.5 | 1,018.1 | 1,042.5 | 1,206.1 | 1,447.6 | 1,342.5 | 1,478.2 | 1,593.5 | 1,813.2 | 2,044.2 | 2,344.8 | 2,357.0 |
| Services, debit (imports) | 1b9dx | 1,977.9 | 2,148.0 | 2,347.3 | 2,577.6 | 3,019.0 | 2,624.3 | 3,000.7 | 3,156.2 | 3,204.4 | 3,466.9 | 3,561.3 | 3,240.9 |
| Balance on Goods & Services | 1z9bx | −669.6 | −371.5 | 463.7 | 451.6 | −22.7 | −1,138.2 | −3,026.4 | −1,865.3 | −1,341.2 | −1,951.3 | −1,280.0 | −2,533.7 |
| Primary income: credit | 1c9cx | 100.1 | 213.2 | 286.6 | 337.4 | 333.5 | 199.1 | 77.7 | 84.5 | 105.3 | 112.6 | 120.6 | 136.1 |
| Primary income: debit | 1c9dx | 1,940.2 | 2,028.7 | 2,114.2 | 2,305.6 | 1,767.3 | 1,475.6 | 1,118.4 | 1,345.4 | 1,398.0 | 1,492.3 | 1,678.8 | 1,880.8 |
| Balance on gds, serv. & prim. inc. | 1y9bx | −2,509.6 | −2,187.0 | −1,363.9 | −1,516.6 | −1,456.6 | −2,414.7 | −4,067.2 | −3,126.2 | −2,633.9 | −3,330.9 | −2,838.1 | −4,278.4 |
| Secondary income: credit | 1d9ca | 2,048.7 | 2,781.4 | 3,233.8 | 3,552.4 | 3,382.7 | 3,033.1 | 2,927.7 | 2,984.8 | 2,756.6 | 2,702.5 | 2,727.0 | 2,643.6 |
| Secondary income: debit | 1d9da | 18.5 | 120.4 | 129.9 | 149.3 | 161.8 | 311.5 | 446.7 | 262.3 | 276.4 | 303.7 | 462.9 | 565.9 |
| B. Capital Account* | 209ba | 8.1 | 15.9 | 18.6 | 6.8 | 11.8 | 16.2 | 15.1 | 14.1 | 13.7 | 11.8 | 12.9 | −123.6 |
| Capital account: credit | 209ca | 18.1 | 25.9 | 29.0 | 16.8 | 22.2 | 27.4 | 25.8 | 24.5 | 24.5 | 22.6 | 23.7 | 23.9 |
| Capital account: debit | 209da | 10.0 | 10.0 | 10.4 | 10.0 | 10.4 | 11.2 | 10.7 | 10.4 | 10.8 | 10.8 | 10.8 | 147.5 |
| Balance on current & capital acct. | 129ba | −471.3 | 489.8 | 1,758.5 | 1,893.3 | 1,776.2 | 323.2 | −1,571.0 | −389.7 | −140.0 | −920.3 | −561.1 | −2,324.2 |
| C. Financial Account* | 309na | −97.9 | 245.6 | 2,207.2 | 610.3 | 731.2 | 2,384.5 | −393.2 | −373.6 | 635.0 | −2,857.7 | −307.3 | −745.6 |
| Direct investment: assets | 3a9aa | — | — | — | — | — | — | — | — | — | — | — | — |
| Equity & investment fund shares.. | 3aaaa | — | — | — | — | — | — | — | — | — | — | — | — |
| Debt instruments | 3abaa | — | — | — | — | — | — | — | — | — | — | — | — |
| Direct investment: liabilities | 3a9la | 836.9 | 493.4 | 271.4 | 193.9 | 1,056.9 | 308.0 | 165.3 | 643.7 | 567.0 | 726.8 | 772.9 | 1,060.1 |
| Equity & investment fund shares . | 3aala | 567.8 | 519.2 | 531.8 | 562.1 | 527.3 | 533.7 | 477.7 | 579.7 | 527.6 | 733.8 | 1,162.0 | 1,271.5 |
| Debt instruments | 3abla | 269.1 | −25.8 | −260.3 | −368.2 | 529.6 | −225.7 | −312.4 | 64.0 | 39.4 | −7.0 | −389.0 | −211.5 |
| Portfolio investment: assets | 3b9aa | 190.7 | 228.4 | 640.8 | 115.6 | −216.9 | 152.1 | 720.9 | −47.6 | −138.7 | 903.5 | 491.8 | −649.6 |
| Equity & investment fund shares | 3baaa | 24.0 | 22.4 | 60.6 | 40.1 | −5.0 | 110.1 | 534.3 | 141.0 | 460.2 | 482.7 | 409.4 | −1,437.4 |
| Debt securities | 3bbaa | 166.7 | 206.0 | 580.1 | 75.5 | −211.9 | 42.0 | 186.6 | −188.6 | −599.0 | 420.7 | 82.5 | 787.8 |
| Portfolio investment: liabilities | 3b9la | .3 | 594.3 | −743.1 | −2.7 | −3.7 | −2,989.4 | −10.2 | −6.6 | −72.0 | −6.4 | 1,992.2 | 847.5 |
| Equity & investment fund shares . | 3bala | 1.4 | 1.6 | .1 | .5 | 1.4 | 2.4 | .4 | 2.0 | 4.6 | 2.2 | .8 | 1.8 |
| Debt securities | 3bbla | −1.1 | 592.7 | −743.2 | −3.2 | −5.1 | −2,991.9 | −10.6 | −8.6 | −76.6 | −8.6 | 1,991.4 | 845.7 |
| Fin. der.& empl.stk.ops.(ESOs): net. | 3c9na | — | — | — | — | — | — | — | — | — | — | — | — |
| Fin. der. & ESOs.: assets | 3c9aa | — | — | — | — | — | — | — | — | — | — | — | — |
| Fin. der. & ESOs.: liabilities | 3c9la | — | — | — | — | — | — | — | — | — | — | — | — |
| Other investment: assets | 3d9aa | 1,034.5 | 976.1 | 2,182.9 | 1,939.0 | 1,771.6 | 1,449.2 | −247.3 | 2,496.2 | 1,576.2 | 1,131.7 | 5,445.1 | 4,667.2 |
| Other equity | 3daaa | .... | .... | .... | .... | .... | .... | .... | .... | .... | .... | .... | .... |
| Debt instruments | 3dzaa | 1,034.5 | 976.1 | 2,182.9 | 1,939.0 | 1,771.6 | 1,449.2 | −247.3 | 2,496.2 | 1,576.2 | 1,131.7 | 5,445.1 | 4,667.2 |
| Other investment: liabilities | 3d9la | 485.8 | −128.8 | 1,088.1 | 1,253.1 | −229.6 | 1,898.3 | 711.7 | 2,185.1 | 307.4 | 4,172.4 | 3,479.1 | 2,855.6 |
| Other equity | 3dala | .... | .... | .... | .... | .... | .... | .... | .... | .... | .... | .... | .... |
| Debt instruments | 3dzla | 485.8 | −128.8 | 1,088.1 | 1,253.1 | −229.6 | 1,898.3 | 711.7 | 2,185.1 | 307.4 | 4,172.4 | 3,479.1 | 2,855.6 |
| Curr.+ cap.− finan. acct. balance.. | 4y9na | −373.4 | 244.2 | −448.7 | 1,283.0 | 1,045.0 | −2,061.3 | −1,177.8 | −16.1 | −775.0 | 1,937.4 | −253.8 | −1,578.6 |
| D. Net Errors and Omissions | 409na | 765.6 | 621.3 | 374.8 | 78.4 | −178.0 | −779.4 | −104.0 | 220.4 | 85.3 | −145.9 | −220.3 | 37.8 |
| E. Reserves and Related Items | 4z9na | 392.2 | 865.5 | −73.9 | 1,361.4 | 867.0 | −2,840.7 | −1,281.9 | 204.2 | −689.7 | 1,791.5 | −474.1 | −1,540.8 |
| Reserve assets | 3e9aa | 275.5 | 714.0 | −125.3 | 1,495.2 | 953.9 | −686.1 | −1,168.8 | 336.1 | −475.1 | 1,877.9 | −407.2 | −1,450.3 |
| Credit and loans from the IMF | 3dcla | −111.6 | −195.6 | −58.2 | −22.8 | — | — | — | — | — | — | — | — |
| Exceptional financing | 409la | −5.1 | 44.1 | 6.8 | 156.7 | 86.8 | 2,154.6 | 113.0 | 131.9 | 214.6 | 86.4 | 66.9 | 90.5 |

*Excludes components in group E

| International Investment Position | | 2004 | 2005 | 2006 | 2007 | 2008 | 2009 | 2010 | 2011 | 2012 | 2013 | 2014 | 2015 |
|---|---|---|---|---|---|---|---|---|---|---|---|---|---|
| | | | | | | | *Millions of US Dollars* | | | | | | |
| Assets | 809aa | 8,467.9 | 10,287.9 | 12,953.5 | 16,506.4 | 19,040.5 | 20,066.9 | 19,519.8 | 22,303.9 | 23,266.9 | 27,179.6 | 32,705.0 | 35,269.5 |
| Direct investment | 8a9aa | .... | .... | .... | .... | .... | .... | .... | .... | .... | .... | .... | .... |
| Equity & investment fund shares.. | 8aaaa | .... | .... | .... | .... | .... | .... | .... | .... | .... | .... | .... | .... |
| Debt instruments | 8abaa | .... | .... | .... | .... | .... | .... | .... | .... | .... | .... | .... | .... |
| Portfolio investment | 8b9aa | 930.7 | 1,159.1 | 1,799.9 | 1,915.5 | 1,698.7 | 1,850.8 | 2,571.7 | 2,524.1 | 2,385.4 | 3,288.8 | 3,780.6 | 3,131.1 |
| Equity & investment fund shares.. | 8aaaa | .... | .... | .... | .... | .... | .... | .... | .... | .... | .... | .... | .... |
| Debt securities | 8bbaa | 930.7 | 1,159.1 | 1,799.9 | 1,915.5 | 1,698.7 | 1,850.8 | 2,571.7 | 2,524.1 | 2,385.4 | 3,288.8 | 3,780.6 | 3,131.1 |
| Fin. der.(oth.than reserves) & ESOs | 8c9aa | .... | .... | .... | .... | .... | .... | .... | .... | .... | .... | .... | .... |
| Other investment | 8d9aa | 6,099.6 | 6,981.9 | 9,130.2 | 11,070.3 | 12,868.7 | 14,424.4 | 14,326.1 | 16,822.3 | 18,398.4 | 19,530.2 | 24,975.3 | 29,642.4 |
| Other equity | 8daaa | .... | .... | .... | .... | .... | .... | .... | .... | .... | .... | .... | .... |
| Debt instruments | 8dzaa | 6,099.6 | 6,981.9 | 9,130.2 | 11,070.3 | 12,868.7 | 14,424.4 | 14,326.1 | 16,822.3 | 18,398.4 | 19,530.2 | 24,975.3 | 29,642.4 |
| Reserve assets | 8e9aa | 1,437.6 | 2,146.9 | 2,023.4 | 3,520.7 | 4,473.1 | 3,791.8 | 2,622.1 | 2,957.6 | 2,483.1 | 4,360.5 | 3,949.1 | 2,496.0 |
| Liabilities | 809la | 25,189.1 | 26,184.3 | 26,802.5 | 28,314.1 | 29,135.0 | 28,343.4 | 29,223.7 | 32,090.4 | 32,983.6 | 37,890.7 | 44,101.6 | 48,862.0 |
| Direct investment | 8a9la | 9,367.4 | 9,860.8 | 10,132.3 | 10,326.1 | 11,383.9 | 11,691.7 | 11,856.5 | 12,500.3 | 13,067.3 | 13,794.1 | 14,567.1 | 15,627.1 |
| Equity & investment fund shares.. | 8aala | 9,367.4 | 9,860.8 | 10,132.3 | 10,326.1 | 11,383.9 | 11,691.7 | 11,856.5 | 12,500.3 | 13,067.3 | 13,794.1 | 14,567.1 | 15,627.1 |
| Debt instruments | 8abla | .... | .... | .... | .... | .... | .... | .... | .... | .... | .... | .... | .... |
| Portfolio investment | 8b9la | 4,142.8 | 4,791.2 | 4,048.1 | 4,045.4 | 4,041.7 | 1,052.3 | 1,042.1 | 1,035.5 | 963.4 | 957.1 | 2,949.2 | 3,796.8 |
| Equity & investment fund shares.. | 8bala | 66.9 | 68.5 | 68.6 | 69.1 | 70.4 | 72.9 | 73.3 | 75.2 | 79.8 | 82.0 | 82.8 | 84.6 |
| Debt securities | 8bbla | 4,075.9 | 4,722.7 | 3,979.5 | 3,976.3 | 3,971.3 | 979.4 | 968.8 | 960.2 | 883.6 | 875.0 | 2,866.4 | 3,712.2 |
| Fin. der.(oth.than reserves) & ESOs | 8c9la | .... | .... | .... | .... | .... | .... | .... | .... | .... | .... | .... | .... |
| Other investment | 8d9la | 11,678.8 | 11,532.3 | 12,622.1 | 13,942.6 | 13,709.4 | 15,599.4 | 16,325.1 | 18,554.6 | 18,952.9 | 23,139.5 | 26,585.3 | 29,438.0 |
| Other equity | 8dala | .... | .... | .... | .... | .... | .... | .... | .... | .... | .... | .... | .... |
| Debt instruments | 8dzla | 11,678.8 | 11,532.3 | 12,622.1 | 13,942.6 | 13,709.4 | 15,599.4 | 16,325.1 | 18,554.6 | 18,952.9 | 23,139.5 | 26,585.3 | 29,438.0 |

# Ecuador   248

2016, International Monetary Fund : *International Financial Statistics Yearbook*

| | | 2004 | 2005 | 2006 | 2007 | 2008 | 2009 | 2010 | 2011 | 2012 | 2013 | 2014 | 2015 |
|---|---|---|---|---|---|---|---|---|---|---|---|---|---|
| **National Accounts** | | | | | | | *Millions of US Dollars* | | | | | | |
| Househ.Cons.Expend.,incl.NPISHs.... | **96f.d** | 25,787 | 28,436 | 30,881 | 33,201 | 37,991 | 38,913 | 44,012 | 48,657 | 53,008 | 56,421 | 59,460 | 61,512 |
| Government Consumption Expend... | **91f.d** | 3,983 | 4,449 | 4,962 | 5,574 | 7,307 | 8,581 | 9,181 | 10,091 | 11,727 | 13,324 | 14,107 | 14,730 |
| Gross Fixed Capital Formation......... | **93e.d** | 7,209 | 8,477 | 9,760 | 10,594 | 13,819 | 14,258 | 17,128 | 20,471 | 23,708 | 26,374 | 27,819 | 27,214 |
| Changes in Inventories................... | **93i.d** | 182 | 504 | 752 | 987 | 2,479 | 1,772 | 2,374 | 1,840 | 732 | 886 | 1,083 | 427 |
| Exports of Goods and Services......... | **90c.d** | 8,985 | 11,463 | 14,196 | 16,288 | 21,100 | 15,786 | 19,402 | 24,672 | 26,522 | 27,646 | 28,831 | 21,254 |
| Imports of Goods and Services (-)..... | **98c.d** | 9,554 | 11,822 | 13,749 | 15,637 | 20,933 | 16,790 | 22,542 | 26,454 | 27,772 | 29,874 | 30,383 | 24,265 |
| Gross Domestic Product (GDP)......... | **99b.d** | 36,592 | 41,507 | 46,802 | 51,008 | 61,763 | 62,520 | 69,555 | 79,277 | 87,925 | 94,776 | 100,917 | 100,872 |
| GDP Volume 2000 Prices................ | **99bpd** | 19,827 | 20,966 | 21,962 | 22,410 | 24,032 | 24,119 | 24,983 | 26,928 | .... | .... | .... | .... |
| GDP Volume 2007 Prices................ | **99bpd** | 45,407 | 47,809 | 49,915 | 51,008 | 54,250 | 54,558 | 56,481 | 60,925 | 64,362 | 67,293 | 69,766 | 69,969 |
| GDP Volume (2010=100)................ | **99bvp** | 80.4 | 84.6 | 88.4 | 90.3 | 96.1 | 96.6 | 100.0 | 107.9 | 114.0 | 119.1 | 123.5 | 123.9 |
| GDP Deflator (2010=100)............... | **99bip** | 65.4 | 70.5 | 76.1 | 81.2 | 92.4 | 93.1 | 100.0 | 105.7 | 110.9 | 114.4 | 117.5 | 117.1 |
| | | | | | | | *Millions: Midyear Estimates* | | | | | | |
| Population.................................. | **99z** | 13.51 | 13.74 | 13.97 | 14.21 | 14.45 | 14.69 | 14.93 | 15.18 | 15.42 | 15.66 | 15.90 | 16.14 |

| | | 2004 | 2005 | 2006 | 2007 | 2008 | 2009 | 2010 | 2011 | 2012 | 2013 | 2014 | 2015 |
|---|---|---|---|---|---|---|---|---|---|---|---|---|---|
| **Exchange Rates** | | | | | | *Pounds per SDR: End of Period* | | | | | | | |
| Market Rate............aa=........ | wa | 9.5221 | 8.1929 | 8.5805 | 8.6974 | 8.4778 | 8.5837 | 8.9208 | 9.2376 | 9.6914 | 10.6922 | 10.3490 | 10.8198 |
| | | | | | | *Pounds per US Dollar: End of Period* | | | | | | | |
| Market Rate............ae=........ | we | 6.1314 | 5.7322 | 5.7036 | 5.5038 | 5.5041 | 5.4754 | 5.7926 | 6.0169 | 6.3057 | 6.9430 | 7.1431 | 7.8080 |
| **Fund Position** | | | | | | *Millions of SDRs: End of Period* | | | | | | | |
| Quota............................... | 2f.s | 943.70 | 943.70 | 943.70 | 943.70 | 943.70 | 943.70 | 943.70 | 943.70 | 943.70 | 943.70 | 943.70 | 943.70 |
| SDR Holdings...................... | 1b.s | 106.38 | 70.70 | 80.14 | 84.61 | 70.21 | 833.05 | 818.64 | 819.19 | 819.52 | 821.49 | 827.17 | 836.11 |
| Reserve Position in the Fund........... | 1c.s | — | — | — | — | — | — | — | — | — | — | — | — |
| Total Fund Cred.&Loans Outstg....... | 2tl | — | — | — | — | — | — | — | — | — | — | — | — |
| SDR Allocations.................... | 1bd | 135.92 | 135.92 | 135.92 | 135.92 | 135.92 | 898.45 | 898.45 | 898.45 | 898.45 | 898.45 | 898.45 | 898.45 |
| **International Liquidity** | | | | | | *Millions of US Dollars Unless Otherwise Indicated: End of Period* | | | | | | | |
| Total Reserves minus Gold............. | 1l.d | 14,273 | 20,609 | 24,462 | 30,188 | 32,216 | 32,253 | 33,612 | 14,916 | 11,628 | 13,608 | 11,995 | 13,282 |
| SDR Holdings...................... | 1b.d | 165 | 101 | 121 | 134 | 108 | 1,306 | 1,261 | 1,258 | 1,260 | 1,265 | 1,198 | 1,159 |
| Reserve Position in the Fund......... | 1c.d | — | — | — | — | — | — | — | — | — | — | — | — |
| Foreign Exchange..................... | 1d.d | 14,108 | 20,508 | 24,341 | 30,054 | 32,108 | 30,947 | 32,351 | 13,658 | 10,368 | 12,343 | 10,797 | 12,123 |
| Gold (Million Fine Troy Ounces)....... | 1ad | 2.432 | 2.432 | 2.431 | 2.431 | 2.431 | 2.431 | 2.431 | 2.431 | 2.431 | 2.431 | 2.431 | 2.431 |
| Gold (National Valuation)........ | 1and | 717 | 779 | 1,119 | 1,186 | 1,633 | 1,680 | 2,180 | 2,743 | 3,303 | 2,510 | 2,450 | 2,211 |
| Central Bank: Other Assets............. | 3..d | 121 | 105 | 54 | 46 | 69 | 67 | 84 | 92 | 87 | 84 | 76 | 56 |
| Central Bank: Other Liabs.............. | 4..d | † 13,481 | 12,026 | 11,580 | 11,904 | 228 | 169 | 99 | 287 | 5,277 | 9,676 | 9,100 | 16,567 |
| Other Depository Corps.: Assets........ | 7a.d | † 10,826 | 13,752 | 22,332 | 26,942 | 16,908 | 19,260 | 25,568 | 20,555 | 18,204 | 16,372 | 13,112 | 9,868 |
| Other Depository Corps.: Liabs......... | 7b.d | † 3,333 | 3,511 | 3,216 | 4,129 | 5,258 | 4,880 | 7,088 | 5,048 | 4,861 | 4,963 | 5,837 | 10,330 |
| **Central Bank** | | | | | | *Millions of Pounds: End of Period* | | | | | | | |
| Net Foreign Assets...................... | 11n | † 7,595 | 52,881 | 78,966 | 106,025 | 183,366 | 177,115 | 198,164 | 96,858 | 48,504 | 38,431 | 32,455 | −13,640 |
| Claims on Nonresidents................ | 11 | † 91,545 | 122,932 | 146,180 | 172,727 | 185,771 | 185,753 | 206,751 | 106,889 | 89,624 | 114,945 | 106,623 | 123,870 |
| Liabilities to Nonresidents............ | 16c | † 83,950 | 70,051 | 67,214 | 66,702 | 2,405 | 8,638 | 8,587 | 10,031 | 41,120 | 76,514 | 74,168 | 137,511 |
| Claims on Other Depository Corps.... | 12e | 10,480 | 22,663 | 55,149 | 86,539 | 24,509 | 27,445 | 60,877 | 43,688 | 35,941 | 30,533 | 24,823 | 61,974 |
| Net Claims on Central Government.. | 12an | † 140,971 | 124,146 | 131,892 | 132,054 | 85,238 | 103,022 | 99,230 | 163,232 | 222,418 | 393,083 | 522,833 | 679,226 |
| Claims on Central Government...... | 12a | † 248,614 | 191,849 | 185,261 | 185,391 | 141,089 | 158,338 | 157,602 | 225,149 | 286,647 | 405,168 | 539,851 | 693,205 |
| Liabilities to Central Government... | 16d | † 107,643 | 67,702 | 53,369 | 53,337 | 55,851 | 55,316 | 58,373 | 61,917 | 64,229 | 12,086 | 17,018 | 13,979 |
| Claims on Other Sectors............ | 12s | † 2,257 | 5,427 | 14,161 | 24,506 | 17,797 | 18,623 | 18,856 | 8,662 | 11,184 | 13,875 | 17,998 | 18,048 |
| Claims on Other Financial Corps... | 12g | † — | — | — | — | — | — | — | — | — | — | — | — |
| Claims on State & Local Govts....... | 12b | † — | — | — | — | — | — | — | — | — | — | — | — |
| Claims on Public Nonfin. Corps...... | 12c | † 2,257 | 5,427 | 14,161 | 24,506 | 17,797 | 18,623 | 18,856 | 8,662 | 11,184 | 13,875 | 17,998 | 18,048 |
| Claims on Private Sector................ | 12d | † — | — | — | — | — | — | — | — | — | — | — | — |
| Monetary Base........................ | 14 | † 134,577 | 197,386 | 272,403 | 325,345 | 291,060 | 296,302 | 333,296 | 259,872 | 268,322 | 406,069 | 461,348 | 569,918 |
| Currency in Circulation.................. | 14a | † 63,363 | 73,173 | 87,962 | 103,674 | 121,281 | 134,039 | 153,209 | 187,292 | 216,301 | 264,882 | 292,739 | 323,373 |
| Liabs. to Other Depository Corps.... | 14c | † 71,214 | 124,213 | 184,441 | 221,671 | 169,779 | 162,263 | 180,086 | 72,580 | 52,021 | 141,187 | 168,608 | 246,545 |
| Liabilities to Other Sectors............ | 14d | † — | — | — | — | — | — | — | — | — | — | — | — |
| Other Liabs. to Other Dep. Corps.... | 14n | † 45,063 | 24,698 | 17,484 | 18,632 | 20,340 | 20,396 | 21,030 | 23,353 | 25,106 | 33,077 | 38,306 | 78,951 |
| Dep. & Sec. Excl. f/Monetary Base..... | 14o | † 5,473 | 4,329 | 13,306 | 23,572 | 16,869 | 17,634 | 17,812 | 18,644 | 19,409 | 27,256 | 84,768 | 64,176 |
| Deposits Included in Broad Money. | 15 | † — | — | — | — | — | — | — | — | — | — | — | — |
| Sec.Ot.th.Shares Incl.in Brd. Money | 16a | † — | — | — | — | — | — | — | — | — | — | — | — |
| Deposits Excl. from Broad Money... | 16b | † 5,473 | 4,329 | 13,306 | 23,572 | 16,869 | 17,634 | 17,812 | 18,644 | 19,409 | 27,256 | 84,768 | 64,176 |
| Sec.Ot.th.Shares Excl.f/Brd.Money.. | 16s | † — | — | — | — | — | — | — | — | — | — | — | — |
| Loans.................................... | 16l | † — | — | — | — | — | — | — | — | — | — | — | — |
| Financial Derivatives...................... | 16m | † — | — | — | — | — | — | — | — | — | — | — | — |
| Shares and Other Equity.................. | 17a | † 5,001 | 2,870 | 2,782 | 4,345 | 6,872 | 6,072 | 4,679 | 13,685 | 18,476 | 28,489 | 30,812 | 39,406 |
| Other Items (Net)........................ | 17r | † −28,812 | −24,167 | −25,806 | −22,770 | −24,230 | −14,199 | 311 | −3,113 | −13,265 | −18,969 | −17,125 | −6,844 |
| Memo Item: | | | | | | | | | | | | | |
| Total Assets................................ | 10ra | † 396,814 | 377,447 | 436,839 | 504,850 | 411,108 | 416,287 | 461,150 | 406,002 | 455,109 | 594,141 | 722,212 | 929,432 |
| **Other Depository Corporations** | | | | | | *Millions of Pounds: End of Period* | | | | | | | |
| Net Foreign Assets...................... | 21n | † 46,513 | 58,759 | 109,031 | 125,561 | 64,073 | 78,731 | 107,045 | 93,351 | 84,318 | 79,161 | 51,942 | −3,575 |
| Claims on Nonresidents................ | 21 | † 67,202 | 78,907 | 127,371 | 148,285 | 92,994 | 105,446 | 148,104 | 123,741 | 115,034 | 113,596 | 93,619 | 76,280 |
| Liabilities to Nonresidents............ | 26c | † 20,689 | 20,148 | 18,340 | 22,724 | 28,921 | 26,715 | 41,059 | 30,390 | 30,715 | 34,436 | 41,677 | 79,855 |
| Claims on Central Bank............ | 20 | † 125,529 | 140,954 | 169,008 | 248,694 | 197,880 | 190,524 | 211,056 | 106,635 | 89,238 | 187,123 | 221,934 | 343,119 |
| Currency............................. | 20a | † 3,938 | 4,213 | 4,908 | 6,997 | 7,245 | 7,373 | 9,577 | 10,713 | 11,281 | 13,832 | 15,581 | 18,312 |
| Reserve Deposits and Securities..... | 20b | † 86,476 | 112,834 | 126,046 | 241,697 | 190,636 | 183,151 | 201,479 | 95,921 | 77,956 | 173,291 | 206,353 | 324,807 |
| Other Claims.............................. | 20n | † 35,115 | 23,907 | 38,053 | — | — | — | — | — | — | — | — | — |
| Net Claims on Central Government.. | 22an | † 45,382 | 54,889 | 59,165 | 63,972 | 143,764 | 208,913 | 234,020 | 338,652 | 441,433 | 519,554 | 649,314 | 832,828 |
| Claims on Central Government...... | 22a | † 104,620 | 114,741 | 115,866 | 131,357 | 220,236 | 304,781 | 334,583 | 442,239 | 546,628 | 667,980 | 838,900 | 1,075,173 |
| Liabilities to Central Government... | 26d | † 59,238 | 59,851 | 56,700 | 67,386 | 76,472 | 95,867 | 100,563 | 103,586 | 105,195 | 148,426 | 189,587 | 242,345 |
| Claims on Other Sectors.................. | 22s | † 319,679 | 343,383 | 369,038 | 406,190 | 448,991 | 452,285 | 485,540 | 512,435 | 548,442 | 584,819 | 664,143 | 798,128 |
| Claims on Other Financial Corps... | 22g | † 2,181 | 5,412 | 5,472 | 7,693 | 5,196 | 6,140 | 8,676 | 5,623 | 7,013 | 7,751 | 8,934 | 8,106 |
| Claims on State & Local Govts....... | 22b | † 63 | 51 | 23,806 | 31,926 | 31,729 | 34,379 | 45,337 | 40,809 | 38,841 | 45,561 | 51,230 | 69,894 |
| Claims on Public Nonfin. Corps...... | 22c | † 55,165 | 62,394 | 35,290 | 27,574 | 28,814 | 35,608 | 32,478 | 38,838 | 43,914 | 43,665 | 58,557 | 76,981 |
| Claims on Private Sector............... | 22d | † 262,270 | 275,526 | 304,470 | 338,997 | 383,252 | 376,158 | 399,050 | 427,165 | 458,674 | 487,842 | 545,422 | 643,146 |
| Liabilities to Central Bank.............. | 26g | † 9,413 | 17,768 | 46,100 | 77,298 | 10,672 | 13,978 | 44,682 | 35,977 | 25,897 | 20,108 | 15,254 | 53,312 |
| Transf.Dep.Included in Broad Money | 24 | † 43,118 | 51,508 | 59,548 | 82,000 | 86,313 | 99,431 | 113,895 | 119,852 | 133,903 | 179,868 | 229,349 | 284,481 |
| Other Dep.Included in Broad Money. | 25 | † 366,416 | 402,389 | 458,708 | 537,599 | 591,029 | 640,257 | 716,434 | 742,440 | 828,237 | 956,770 | 1,099,997 | 1,315,922 |
| Sec.Ot.th.Shares Incl.in Brd. Money.. | 26a | † — | — | — | — | — | — | — | — | — | — | — | — |
| Deposits Excl. from Broad Money..... | 26b | † 27,957 | 28,332 | 15,399 | 17,902 | 17,882 | 19,338 | 18,682 | 18,250 | 17,369 | 23,806 | 31,557 | 59,002 |
| Sec.Ot.th.Shares Excl.f/Brd.Money.... | 26s | † — | — | — | — | — | — | — | — | — | — | — | — |
| Loans.................................... | 26l | † 1,600 | 4,900 | 5,188 | 5,188 | 7,425 | 5,234 | 1,864 | — | — | — | — | — |
| Financial Derivatives...................... | 26m | † — | — | — | — | — | — | — | — | — | — | — | — |
| Insurance Technical Reserves........... | 26r | † — | — | — | — | — | — | — | — | — | — | — | — |
| Shares and Other Equity.................. | 27a | † 37,542 | 45,522 | 42,324 | 54,608 | 63,651 | 71,007 | 88,125 | 91,050 | 112,904 | 127,357 | 142,323 | 178,986 |
| Other Items (Net)............................ | 27r | † 51,057 | 47,565 | 78,976 | 69,823 | 77,737 | 81,210 | 53,981 | 43,504 | 45,120 | 62,749 | 68,853 | 78,797 |
| Memo Item: | | | | | | | | | | | | | |
| Total Assets................................ | 20ra | † 668,304 | 731,608 | 831,905 | 999,087 | 1,044,144 | 1,149,305 | 1,284,958 | 1,281,434 | 1,408,967 | 1,648,096 | 1,926,153 | 2,431,782 |

| | | 2004 | 2005 | 2006 | 2007 | 2008 | 2009 | 2010 | 2011 | 2012 | 2013 | 2014 | 2015 |
|---|---|---|---|---|---|---|---|---|---|---|---|---|---|
| **Depository Corporations** | | | | | | *Millions of Pounds: End of Period* | | | | | | | |
| Net Foreign Assets.......................... | 31n | † 54,108 | 111,639 | 187,997 | 231,587 | 247,440 | 255,846 | 305,209 | 190,209 | 132,822 | 117,592 | 84,397 | −17,215 |
| Claims on Nonresidents................ | 31 | † 158,748 | 201,838 | 273,551 | 321,012 | 278,765 | 291,199 | 354,855 | 230,630 | 204,658 | 228,541 | 200,242 | 200,151 |
| Liabilities to Nonresidents............. | 36c | † 104,640 | 90,199 | 85,554 | 89,426 | 31,325 | 35,353 | 49,646 | 40,421 | 71,836 | 110,949 | 115,845 | 217,366 |
| Domestic Claims.............................. | 32 | † 508,289 | 527,845 | 574,256 | 626,722 | 695,790 | 782,844 | 837,646 | 1,022,981 | 1,223,477 | 1,511,332 | 1,854,288 | 2,328,230 |
| Net Claims on Central Government | 32an | † 186,352 | 179,036 | 191,057 | 196,026 | 229,002 | 311,935 | 333,250 | 501,884 | 663,851 | 912,637 | 1,172,147 | 1,512,054 |
| Claims on Central Government.... | 32a | † 353,234 | 306,589 | 301,127 | 316,748 | 361,325 | 463,119 | 492,185 | 667,387 | 833,275 | 1,073,149 | 1,378,751 | 1,768,378 |
| Liabilities to Central Government. | 36d | † 166,881 | 127,554 | 110,069 | 120,722 | 132,323 | 151,183 | 158,935 | 165,503 | 169,424 | 160,512 | 206,605 | 256,324 |
| Claims on Other Sectors................ | 32s | † 321,937 | 348,809 | 383,199 | 430,696 | 466,788 | 470,908 | 504,397 | 521,097 | 559,626 | 598,694 | 682,141 | 816,176 |
| Claims on Other Financial Corps.. | 32g | † 2,181 | 5,412 | 5,472 | 7,693 | 5,196 | 6,140 | 8,676 | 5,623 | 7,013 | 7,751 | 8,934 | 8,106 |
| Claims on State & Local Govts..... | 32b | † 63 | 51 | 23,806 | 31,926 | 31,729 | 34,379 | 45,337 | 40,809 | 38,841 | 45,561 | 51,230 | 69,894 |
| Claims on Public Nonfin. Corps.... | 32c | † 57,422 | 67,820 | 49,451 | 52,080 | 46,611 | 54,231 | 51,334 | 47,500 | 55,098 | 57,540 | 76,555 | 95,029 |
| Claims on Private Sector.............. | 32d | † 262,270 | 275,526 | 304,470 | 338,997 | 383,252 | 376,158 | 399,050 | 427,165 | 458,674 | 487,842 | 545,422 | 643,146 |
| Broad Money Liabilities................... | 35l | † 468,959 | 522,857 | 601,309 | 716,275 | 791,378 | 866,354 | 973,962 | 1,038,871 | 1,167,160 | 1,387,688 | 1,606,505 | 1,905,464 |
| Currency Outside Depository Corps | 34a | † 59,425 | 68,960 | 83,053 | 96,677 | 114,036 | 126,666 | 143,632 | 176,578 | 205,020 | 251,050 | 277,159 | 305,061 |
| Transferable Deposits................... | 34 | † 43,118 | 51,508 | 59,548 | 82,000 | 86,313 | 99,431 | 113,895 | 119,852 | 133,903 | 179,868 | 229,349 | 284,481 |
| Other Deposits........................... | 35 | † 366,416 | 402,389 | 458,708 | 537,599 | 591,029 | 640,257 | 716,434 | 742,440 | 828,237 | 956,770 | 1,099,997 | 1,315,922 |
| Securities Other than Shares......... | 36a | † — | — | — | — | — | — | — | — | — | — | — | — |
| Deposits Excl. from Broad Money..... | 36b | † 33,430 | 32,661 | 28,705 | 41,474 | 34,750 | 36,972 | 36,494 | 36,893 | 36,779 | 51,061 | 116,326 | 123,178 |
| Sec.Ot.th.Shares Excl.f/Brd.Money.... | 36s | † — | — | — | — | — | — | — | — | — | — | — | — |
| Loans............................................ | 36l | † 1,600 | 4,900 | 5,188 | 5,188 | 7,425 | 5,234 | 1,864 | — | — | — | — | — |
| Financial Derivatives...................... | 36m | † — | — | — | — | — | — | — | — | — | — | — | — |
| Insurance Technical Reserves.......... | 36r | † — | — | — | — | — | — | — | — | — | — | — | — |
| Shares and Other Equity................. | 37a | † 42,543 | 48,393 | 45,105 | 58,953 | 70,522 | 77,079 | 92,803 | 104,736 | 131,380 | 155,847 | 173,134 | 218,392 |
| Other Items (Net)........................... | 37r | † 15,864 | 30,674 | 81,946 | 36,419 | 39,153 | 53,051 | 37,733 | 32,691 | 20,981 | 34,327 | 42,720 | 63,981 |
| Broad Money Liabs., Seasonally Adj. | 35l.b | † 469,239 | 523,251 | 601,748 | 716,287 | 791,031 | 865,588 | 973,214 | 1,038,327 | 1,167,487 | 1,389,216 | 1,609,083 | 1,908,668 |
| **Monetary Aggregates** | | | | | | *Millions of Pounds: End of Period* | | | | | | | |
| Broad Money.............................. | 59m | 469,181 | 523,087 | 601,561 | 716,545 | 791,660 | 866,651 | 974,276 | 1,039,210 | 1,167,525 | 1,388,079 | 1,606,928 | 1,905,897 |
| o/w:Currency Issued by Cent.Govt | 59m.a | 223 | 230 | 253 | 270 | 282 | 297 | 314 | 339 | 365 | 390 | 424 | 433 |
| o/w: Dep.in Nonfin. Corporations. | 59m.b | — | — | — | — | — | — | — | — | — | — | — | — |
| o/w:Secs. Issued by Central Govt.. | 59m.c | — | — | — | — | — | — | — | — | — | — | — | — |
| Money (National Definitions) | | | | | | | | | | | | | |
| M1................................................ | 59ma | 83,450 | 100,710 | 121,340 | 151,800 | 174,460 | 196,973 | 223,456 | 255,581 | 288,138 | 373,624 | 445,733 | 520,592 |
| M2................................................ | 59mb | 468,260 | 522,300 | 601,310 | 716,280 | 791,378 | 866,354 | 973,962 | 1,038,871 | 1,167,160 | 1,387,688 | 1,606,505 | 1,905,464 |
| **Interest Rates** | | | | | | *Percent Per Annum* | | | | | | | |
| Discount Rate (End of Period).......... | 60.a | 10.00 | 10.00 | 9.00 | 9.00 | 11.50 | 8.50 | 8.50 | 9.50 | 9.50 | 8.75 | 9.75 | 9.75 |
| Treasury Bill Rate........................... | 60c | 9.90 | 8.57 | 9.53 | 6.85 | 11.37 | 9.84 | 9.28 | 13.95 | 12.96 | 11.00 | 11.65 | 11.34 |
| Deposit Rate.................................... | 60l | 7.73 | 7.23 | 6.02 | 6.10 | 6.58 | 6.49 | 6.23 | 6.74 | 7.64 | 7.68 | 6.92 | 6.91 |
| Lending Rate................................... | 60p | 13.38 | 13.14 | 12.60 | 12.51 | 12.33 | 11.98 | 11.01 | 11.03 | 12.00 | 12.29 | 11.71 | 11.63 |
| **Prices and Labor** | | | | | | *Index Numbers (2010=100): Period Averages* | | | | | | | |
| Industrial Share Prices (EOP)........... | 62aep | 66.0 | 102.1 | 131.2 | 142.6 | 150.3 | 99.8 | 100.0 | 77.5 | 64.4 | 55.0 | 76.9 | 65.9 |
| Wholesale Prices............................. | 63 | † 62.7 | 66.0 | 70.7 | † 77.7 | 94.1 | 88.8 | 100.0 | 114.8 | 117.6 | 121.5 | 126.8 | .... |
| Consumer Prices............................. | 64 | 55.1 | 57.8 | 62.2 | † 68.0 | 80.4 | 89.9 | † 100.0 | 110.1 | 117.9 | 129.0 | 142.1 | 156.8 |
| | | | | | | *Number in Thousands: Period Averages* | | | | | | | |
| Labor Force..................................... | 67d | 20,861 | 21,778 | 22,726 | 23,658 | 24,657 | 25,135 | 26,183 | 26,532 | 26,916 | 27,168 | 27,622 | .... |
| Employment..................................... | 67e | 18,620 | 19,372 | 20,303 | 21,528 | 22,512 | 22,776 | 23,833 | 23,352 | 23,502 | 23,576 | 23,986 | .... |
| Unemployment................................. | 67c | 2,242 | 2,406 | 2,424 | 2,130 | 2,145 | 2,360 | 2,350 | 3,180 | 3,414 | 3,592 | 3,637 | .... |
| Unemployment Rate (%)................. | 67r | 10.7 | 11.0 | 10.7 | 9.0 | 8.7 | 9.4 | 9.0 | 12.0 | 12.7 | 13.2 | 12.9 | .... |
| **Intl. Transactions & Positions** | | | | | | *Millions of US Dollars* | | | | | | | |
| Exports in USD................................ | 70..d | 7,682.8 | 10,652.2 | 13,694.4 | 16,200.4 | 26,246.3 | 23,061.9 | 26,437.8 | 30,527.6 | 29,409.2 | 28,493.0 | 24,735.8 | 19,051.3 |
| Imports in USD................................ | 71..d | 12,831.4 | 19,815.6 | 20,722.4 | 27,063.3 | 48,774.6 | 44,946.1 | 52,922.8 | 58,903.1 | 65,774.4 | 59,661.7 | 61,010.4 | 65,043.9 |

| | | 2004 | 2005 | 2006 | 2007 | 2008 | 2009 | 2010 | 2011 | 2012 | 2013 | 2014 | 2015 |
|---|---|---|---|---|---|---|---|---|---|---|---|---|---|
| **Balance of Payments** | | | | | | | *Millions of US Dollars* | | | | | | |
| A. Current Account*....................... | 109bx | 3,921.7 | 2,102.8 | 2,635.4 | 411.6 | −1,414.6 | −3,349.3 | −4,503.8 | −5,483.9 | −6,972.0 | −3,533.7 | −5,972.1 | .... |
| Goods, credit (exports).................. | 1a9cx | 12,319.6 | 16,073.2 | 20,545.6 | 24,454.6 | 29,849.0 | 23,089.3 | 25,024.2 | 27,913.4 | 26,834.5 | 26,533.7 | 25,203.7 | .... |
| Goods, debit (imports)................... | 1a9dx | 18,895.3 | 23,818.2 | 28,983.5 | 39,354.3 | 49,607.9 | 39,906.9 | 45,144.5 | 47,311.5 | 52,350.4 | 48,918.1 | 56,165.4 | .... |
| Balance on goods............... | 1a9bx | −6,575.7 | −7,745.0 | −8,437.9 | −14,899.7 | −19,758.9 | −16,817.6 | −20,120.3 | −19,398.1 | −25,515.9 | −22,384.4 | −30,961.7 | .... |
| Services, credit (exports)............. | 1b9cx | 14,196.6 | 14,642.6 | 16,134.5 | 19,943.4 | 24,911.9 | 21,519.8 | 23,807.0 | 19,139.6 | 21,766.8 | 18,261.5 | 21,897.6 | .... |
| Services, debit (imports)............... | 1b9dx | 8,020.0 | 10,508.1 | 11,569.2 | 14,342.4 | 17,614.9 | 13,935.2 | 14,717.7 | 14,069.6 | 16,450.4 | 16,407.7 | 17,509.5 | .... |
| Balance on Goods & Services....... | 1z9bx | −399.1 | −3,610.5 | −3,872.6 | −9,298.7 | −12,461.9 | −9,233.0 | −11,031.0 | −14,328.1 | −20,199.5 | −20,530.6 | −26,573.6 | .... |
| Primary income: credit.............. | 1c9cx | 572.2 | 1,425.4 | 2,560.4 | 3,309.0 | 3,065.4 | 991.9 | 533.7 | 317.8 | 232.3 | 196.5 | 198.5 | .... |
| Primary income: debit.................. | 1c9dx | 818.1 | 1,460.2 | 1,822.1 | 1,920.8 | 1,776.3 | 3,068.0 | 6,445.5 | 6,694.7 | 6,796.1 | 7,359.9 | 7,254.2 | .... |
| Balance on gds, serv. & prim. inc. | 1y9bx | −645.0 | −3,645.3 | −3,134.3 | −7,910.5 | −11,172.8 | −11,309.1 | −16,942.8 | −20,705.0 | −26,763.3 | −27,694.0 | −33,629.3 | .... |
| Secondary income: credit.............. | 1d9ca | 4,614.6 | 5,830.5 | 5,933.1 | 8,561.8 | 10,072.0 | 8,305.2 | 12,836.0 | 15,565.6 | 20,136.2 | 24,586.2 | 28,075.2 | .... |
| Secondary income: debit.............. | 1d9da | 47.9 | 82.4 | 163.4 | 239.7 | 313.8 | 345.4 | 397.0 | 344.5 | 344.9 | 425.9 | 418.0 | .... |
| B. Capital Account*....................... | 209ba | .... | −40.0 | −35.9 | 1.9 | −.5 | −18.8 | −39.2 | −45.2 | −119.1 | −82.9 | −140.5 | .... |
| Capital account: credit.................. | 209ca | .... | .... | 4.9 | 5.3 | .6 | 1.2 | .4 | 3.1 | 15.3 | 1.9 | 3.7 | .... |
| Capital account: debit.................. | 209da | .... | 40.0 | 40.8 | 3.4 | 1.1 | 20.0 | 39.6 | 48.3 | 134.4 | 84.8 | 144.2 | .... |
| Balance on current & capital acct. | 129ba | 3,921.7 | 2,062.8 | 2,599.5 | 413.5 | −1,415.1 | −3,368.1 | −4,543.0 | −5,529.1 | −7,091.1 | −3,616.6 | −6,112.6 | .... |
| C. Financial Account* ............... | 309na | 4,460.8 | −5,590.5 | 296.7 | −3,022.8 | −5,274.4 | −1,335.5 | −6,469.9 | 11,351.4 | −3,458.4 | −5,836.7 | −1,185.8 | .... |
| Direct investment: assets.............. | 3a9aa | 158.9 | 92.0 | 148.4 | 664.8 | 1,920.2 | 571.2 | 1,175.5 | 625.5 | 211.1 | 301.0 | 252.7 | .... |
| Equity & investment fund shares.. | 3aaaa | .... | .... | .... | .... | .... | .... | — | — | — | — | — | .... |
| Debt instruments.................. | 3abaa | 158.9 | 92.0 | 148.4 | 664.8 | 1,920.2 | 571.2 | 1,175.5 | 625.5 | 211.1 | 301.0 | 252.7 | .... |
| Direct investment: liabilities .......... | 3a9la | 1,253.3 | 5,375.6 | 10,042.8 | 11,578.1 | 9,494.6 | 6,711.6 | 6,385.6 | −482.7 | 2,797.7 | 4,192.2 | 4,783.2 | .... |
| Equity & investment fund shares . | 3aala | .... | .... | 72.0 | 100.5 | 389.5 | 1,007.7 | 1,359.6 | 539.7 | 209.0 | 339.4 | 201.9 | .... |
| Debt instruments.................. | 3abla | 1,253.3 | 5,375.6 | 9,970.8 | 11,477.6 | 9,105.1 | 5,703.9 | 5,026.0 | −1,022.4 | 2,588.7 | 3,852.8 | 4,581.3 | .... |
| Portfolio investment: assets.......... | 3b9aa | −324.0 | 59.9 | 703.2 | 846.4 | 622.7 | 267.4 | 444.8 | 220.4 | −22.6 | −50.2 | 27.9 | .... |
| Equity & investment fund shares | 3baaa | −324.0 | 59.9 | 703.2 | 846.4 | 622.7 | 267.4 | 444.8 | 220.4 | −22.6 | −50.2 | 27.9 | .... |
| Debt securities ...................... | 3bbaa | .... | .... | .... | .... | .... | — | — | — | — | — | — | .... |
| Portfolio investment: liabilities....... | 3b9la | −85.1 | 3,528.1 | 2.8 | −2,727.5 | −7,027.0 | −259.7 | 10,886.7 | −10,431.2 | −1,976.3 | 2,963.1 | −2,083.7 | .... |
| Equity & investment fund shares . | 3bala | 26.1 | 729.4 | 501.9 | −3,198.9 | −673.6 | 393.0 | 1,724.4 | −711.3 | −983.4 | −431.4 | 484.9 | .... |
| Debt securities...................... | 3bbla | −111.2 | 2,798.7 | −499.1 | 471.4 | −6,353.4 | −652.7 | 9,162.3 | −9,719.9 | −992.9 | 3,394.5 | −2,568.6 | .... |
| Fin. der.& empl.stk.ops.(ESOs): net. | 3c9na | .... | .... | .... | .... | .... | .... | — | — | — | — | — | .... |
| Fin. der. & ESOs.: assets.............. | 3c9aa | .... | .... | .... | .... | .... | .... | — | — | — | — | — | .... |
| Fin. der. & ESOs.: liabilities.......... | 3c9la | .... | .... | .... | .... | .... | .... | — | — | — | — | — | .... |
| Other investment: assets............... | 3d9aa | 5,888.1 | 3,245.9 | 9,743.0 | 5,498.1 | −4,632.5 | 5,878.6 | 11,185.0 | −2,875.7 | 591.6 | 2,339.1 | 3,008.9 | .... |
| Other equity...................... | 3daaa | .... | .... | .... | .... | .... | .... | .... | .... | .... | .... | .... | .... |
| Debt instruments.................. | 3dzaa | 5,888.1 | 3,245.9 | 9,743.0 | 5,498.1 | −4,632.5 | 5,878.6 | 11,185.0 | −2,875.7 | 591.6 | 2,339.1 | 3,008.9 | .... |
| Other investment: liabilities........... | 3d9la | 94.0 | 84.6 | 252.3 | 1,181.5 | 717.2 | 1,600.8 | 2,002.9 | −2,467.3 | 3,417.1 | 1,271.3 | 1,775.8 | .... |
| Other equity...................... | 3dala | .... | .... | .... | .... | .... | .... | .... | .... | .... | .... | .... | .... |
| Debt instruments...................... | 3dzla | 94.0 | 84.6 | 252.3 | 1,181.5 | 717.2 | 1,600.8 | 2,002.9 | −2,467.3 | 3,417.1 | 1,271.3 | 1,775.8 | .... |
| Curr.+ cap.− finan. acct. balance.. | 4y9na | −539.1 | 7,653.3 | 2,302.8 | 3,436.3 | 3,859.3 | −2,032.6 | 1,926.9 | −16,880.5 | −3,632.7 | 2,220.1 | −4,926.8 | .... |
| D. Net Errors and Omissions.......... | 409nm | −45.3 | −2,427.2 | 634.0 | 250.6 | −2,927.8 | 398.1 | −2,145.1 | −2,855.1 | −2,159.7 | −1,316.8 | 1,667.3 | .... |
| E. Reserves and Related Items......... | 4z9na | −584.4 | 5,226.1 | 2,936.8 | 3,686.9 | 931.5 | −1,634.5 | −218.2 | −19,735.6 | −5,792.4 | 903.3 | −3,259.5 | .... |
| Reserve assets............................. | 3e9aa | 684.4 | 6,319.2 | 3,607.9 | 5,475.0 | 1,755.0 | −156.2 | 1,276.4 | −18,329.6 | −3,824.6 | 2,787.8 | −1,537.8 | .... |
| Credit and loans from the IMF...... | 3dcla | — | — | — | — | — | — | — | — | — | — | — | .... |
| Exceptional financing.................... | 409la | 1,268.8 | 1,093.1 | 671.1 | 1,788.1 | 823.5 | 1,478.3 | 1,494.6 | 1,406.0 | 1,967.8 | 1,884.5 | 1,721.7 | .... |

*Excludes components in group E

| | | 2004 | 2005 | 2006 | 2007 | 2008 | 2009 | 2010 | 2011 | 2012 | 2013 | 2014 | 2015 |
|---|---|---|---|---|---|---|---|---|---|---|---|---|---|
| **International Investment Position** | | | | | | | *Millions of US Dollars* | | | | | | |
| Assets.......................................... | 809aa | 36,003.2 | 46,722.5 | 61,559.4 | 76,365.1 | 67,350.6 | 72,700.5 | 79,812.3 | 57,779.2 | 50,911.0 | 50,005.0 | 45,771.6 | .... |
| Direct investment......................... | 8a9aa | 875.3 | 967.3 | 1,115.7 | 1,780.5 | 3,700.7 | 4,272.9 | 5,448.4 | 6,073.9 | 6,285.0 | 6,586.0 | 6,838.7 | .... |
| Equity & investment fund shares.. | 8aaaa | .... | .... | .... | .... | .... | .... | .... | .... | .... | .... | .... | .... |
| Debt instruments....................... | 8abaa | .... | .... | .... | .... | .... | .... | .... | .... | .... | .... | .... | .... |
| Portfolio investment..................... | 8b9aa | 1,789.7 | 2,149.8 | 2,434.4 | 2,779.2 | 1,947.1 | 4,120.2 | 9,691.4 | 3,368.6 | 3,334.2 | 2,967.6 | 2,647.3 | .... |
| Equity & investment fund shares.. | 8baaa | 781.9 | 898.2 | 886.4 | 1,098.1 | 910.8 | 965.7 | 961.0 | 796.1 | 717.8 | 736.9 | 802.4 | .... |
| Debt securities............................ | 8bbaa | 1,007.8 | 1,251.6 | 1,548.0 | 1,681.1 | 1,036.3 | 3,154.5 | 8,730.4 | 2,572.5 | 2,616.4 | 2,230.7 | 1,844.9 | .... |
| Fin. der.(oth.than reserves) & ESOs | 8c9aa | .... | .... | .... | .... | .... | .... | .... | .... | .... | .... | .... | .... |
| Other investment........................ | 8d9aa | 18,861.1 | 22,373.9 | 32,854.0 | 40,627.6 | 28,656.2 | 30,839.3 | 28,472.7 | 30,030.0 | 26,444.6 | 23,891.0 | 21,408.6 | .... |
| Other equity............................... | 8daaa | .... | .... | .... | .... | .... | .... | .... | .... | .... | .... | .... | .... |
| Debt instruments....................... | 8dzaa | 18,861.1 | 22,373.9 | 32,854.0 | 40,627.6 | 28,656.2 | 30,839.3 | 28,472.7 | 30,030.0 | 26,444.6 | 23,891.0 | 21,408.6 | .... |
| Reserve assets............................. | 8e9aa | 14,477.1 | 21,231.5 | 25,155.3 | 31,177.8 | 33,046.6 | 33,468.1 | 36,199.8 | 18,306.7 | 14,847.2 | 16,560.4 | 14,877.0 | .... |
| Liabilities.................................... | 809la | 56,763.1 | 62,997.2 | 72,573.8 | 84,943.8 | 94,588.3 | 102,438.6 | 123,261.1 | 110,390.1 | 120,226.1 | 132,292.9 | 131,147.4 | .... |
| Direct investment......................... | 8a9la | 23,506.3 | 28,881.9 | 38,924.7 | 50,502.8 | 59,997.4 | 66,709.0 | 73,094.6 | 72,611.9 | 79,492.6 | 85,045.0 | 87,881.9 | .... |
| Equity & investment fund shares.. | 8aala | .... | .... | .... | .... | .... | .... | .... | .... | .... | .... | .... | .... |
| Debt instruments....................... | 8abla | .... | .... | .... | .... | .... | .... | .... | .... | .... | .... | .... | .... |
| Portfolio investment..................... | 8b9la | 2,530.1 | 6,058.2 | 6,062.7 | 4,032.0 | 4,432.9 | 4,108.2 | 18,241.1 | 6,526.0 | 4,574.0 | 7,611.3 | 5,526.3 | .... |
| Equity & investment fund shares.. | 8bala | 1,946.4 | 2,675.8 | 3,177.7 | | 1,495.0 | 1,756.9 | 3,481.3 | 2,770.1 | 1,786.7 | 1,355.3 | 1,840.2 | .... |
| Debt securities............................ | 8bbla | 583.7 | 3,382.4 | 2,885.0 | 4,032.0 | 2,937.9 | 2,351.3 | 14,759.8 | 3,755.9 | 2,787.3 | 6,256.0 | 3,686.1 | .... |
| Fin. der.(oth.than reserves) & ESOs | 8c9la | .... | .... | .... | .... | .... | .... | .... | .... | .... | .... | .... | .... |
| Other investment........................ | 8d9la | 30,726.7 | 28,057.1 | 27,586.4 | 30,409.0 | 30,158.0 | 31,621.4 | 31,925.4 | 31,252.2 | 36,159.5 | 39,636.6 | 37,739.2 | .... |
| Other equity............................... | 8dala | .... | .... | .... | .... | .... | .... | .... | .... | .... | .... | .... | .... |
| Debt instruments....................... | 8dzla | 30,726.7 | 28,057.1 | 27,586.4 | 30,409.0 | 30,158.0 | 31,621.4 | 31,925.4 | 31,252.2 | 36,159.5 | 39,636.6 | 37,739.2 | .... |

| | | 2004 | 2005 | 2006 | 2007 | 2008 | 2009 | 2010 | 2011 | 2012 | 2013 | 2014 | 2015 |
|---|---|---|---|---|---|---|---|---|---|---|---|---|---|

**Government Finance**
**Cash Flow Statement**
**General Government**

*Millions of Pounds: Fiscal Year Ends June 30*

| | | 2004 | 2005 | 2006 | 2007 | 2008 | 2009 | 2010 | 2011 | 2012 | 2013 | 2014 | 2015 |
|---|---|---|---|---|---|---|---|---|---|---|---|---|---|
| Cash Receipts:Operating Activities... | c1 | 123,963 | .... | 175,929 | 205,654 | 248,835 | 288,545 | 303,361 | 296,341 | 348,865 | 403,637 | 519,449 | 532,352 |
| Taxes............................. | c11 | 67,146 | .... | 97,779 | 114,326 | 142,544 | 163,222 | 170,494 | 191,626 | 207,410 | 251,118 | 260,289 | 305,957 |
| Social Contributions...................... | c12 | — | .... | — | — | — | — | — | — | — | — | — | — |
| Grants.............................. | c13 | 4,383 | .... | 2,379 | 3,886 | 1,463 | 7,984 | 4,332 | 1,723 | 10,103 | 5,208 | 95,856 | 25,437 |
| Other Receipts............................ | c14 | 52,434 | .... | 75,771 | 87,442 | 104,828 | 117,339 | 128,535 | 102,992 | 131,352 | 147,311 | 163,304 | 200,958 |
| Cash Payments:Operating Activities. | c2 | 130,499 | .... | 202,095 | 218,490 | 271,498 | 313,464 | 348,305 | 392,544 | 480,463 | 604,451 | 706,927 | 900,753 |
| Compensation of Employees.......... | c21 | 37,631 | .... | 47,258 | 52,746 | 63,400 | 76,968 | 86,377 | 96,369 | 124,457 | 145,064 | 180,829 | 200,883 |
| Purchases of Goods & Services....... | c22 | 9,409 | .... | 14,493 | 17,121 | 18,775 | 25,203 | 28,244 | 24,283 | 27,079 | 27,155 | 27,556 | 57,171 |
| Interest.......................................... | c24 | 27,517 | .... | 34,812 | 38,368 | 43,850 | 43,755 | 62,277 | 72,366 | 93,401 | 135,331 | 159,330 | 178,364 |
| Subsidies..................................... | c25 | 10,347 | .... | 53,959 | 53,959 | 90,211 | 93,830 | 93,570 | 111,022 | 134,963 | 170,800 | 187,659 | 282,093 |
| Grants........................................... | c26 | — | .... | 2,174 | 2,599 | 3,890 | 4,213 | 4,380 | 5,314 | 5,305 | 5,014 | 5,190 | 6,211 |
| Social Benefits............................... | c27 | 22,964 | .... | 29,495 | 31,854 | 27,174 | 41,936 | 43,868 | 51,173 | 63,628 | 85,445 | 104,624 | 124,561 |
| Other Payments............................ | c28 | 22,631 | .... | 19,904 | 21,843 | 24,198 | 27,559 | 29,589 | 32,017 | 31,630 | 35,642 | 41,739 | 51,470 |
| Net Cash Inflow:Operating Act.[1-2] | ccio | −6,536 | .... | −26,166 | −12,836 | −22,663 | −24,919 | −44,944 | −96,203 | −131,598 | −200,814 | −187,478 | −368,401 |
| Net Cash Outflow:Invest. in NFA...... | c31 | 20,692 | .... | 21,244 | 25,528 | 34,297 | 43,480 | 48,463 | 38,097 | 35,959 | 39,629 | 52,920 | 61,921 |
| Purchases of Nonfinancial Assets... | c31.1 | 20,692 | .... | 21,244 | 25,528 | 34,297 | 43,480 | 48,463 | 38,097 | 35,959 | 39,629 | 52,920 | 61,921 |
| Sales of Nonfinancial Assets.......... | c31.2 | — | .... | — | — | — | — | — | — | — | — | — | — |
| Cash Surplus/Deficit [1-2-31=1-2M] | ccsd | −27,228 | .... | −47,410 | −38,364 | −56,960 | −68,399 | −93,407 | −134,300 | −167,557 | −240,443 | −240,398 | −430,322 |
| Net Acq. Fin. Assets, excl. Cash....... | c32x | 13,581 | .... | 8,816 | 17,677 | 9,930 | 3,797 | 4,713 | −4,284 | −1,819 | 6,398 | 14,002 | 16,764 |
| Domestic...................................... | c321x | 13,481 | .... | 8,816 | 17,677 | 9,930 | 3,797 | 4,713 | −4,284 | −1,819 | 6,398 | 14,002 | 16,764 |
| Foreign.......................................... | c322x | 100 | .... | — | — | — | — | — | — | — | — | — | — |
| Net Incurrence of Liabilities.............. | c33 | 70,243 | .... | 66,813 | 38,288 | 17,987 | 103,003 | 104,873 | 140,584 | 191,390 | 268,069 | 262,421 | 222,709 |
| Domestic....................................... | c331 | 69,739 | .... | 63,172 | 34,707 | 6,548 | 79,660 | 102,415 | 135,560 | 200,452 | 247,799 | 258,399 | 247,828 |
| Foreign.......................................... | c332 | 504 | .... | 3,641 | 3,581 | 11,439 | 23,343 | 2,458 | 5,024 | −9,062 | 20,270 | 4,022 | −25,119 |
| Net Cash Inflow, Fin.Act.[-32x+33].. | cnfb | 56,662 | .... | 57,997 | 20,611 | 8,057 | 99,206 | 100,160 | 144,868 | 193,209 | 261,671 | 248,419 | 205,945 |
| Net Change in Stock of Cash........... | cncb | 27,258 | .... | 10,587 | −17,753 | −48,903 | 30,807 | 6,753 | 10,568 | 25,652 | 21,228 | 8,021 | −224,377 |
| Stat. Discrep. [32X-33+NCB-CSD].... | ccsdz | −2,176 | .... | — | — | — | — | — | — | — | — | — | — |
| Memo Item:Cash Expenditure[2+31] | c2m | 151,191 | .... | 223,339 | 244,018 | 305,795 | 356,944 | 396,768 | 430,641 | 516,422 | 644,080 | 759,847 | 962,674 |
| Memo Item: Gross Debt.................. | c63 | .... | .... | .... | .... | .... | .... | .... | .... | .... | .... | .... | .... |

**National Accounts**

*Millions of Pounds: Fiscal Year Ends June 30*

| | | 2004 | 2005 | 2006 | 2007 | 2008 | 2009 | 2010 | 2011 | 2012 | 2013 | 2014 | 2015 |
|---|---|---|---|---|---|---|---|---|---|---|---|---|---|
| Househ.Cons.Expend.,incl.NPISHs.... | 96f | 347,800 | 385,300 | 436,100 | 539,100 | 647,800 | 793,100 | 899,800 | 1,036,100 | 1,223,200 | 1,559,300 | .... | .... |
| Government Consumption Expend... | 91f | 61,900 | 68,600 | 75,900 | 84,400 | 97,500 | 118,300 | 134,653 | 157,000 | 179,000 | 221,600 | .... | .... |
| Gross Fixed Capital Formation.......... | 93e | 79,600 | 96,500 | 115,700 | 155,300 | 199,500 | 197,100 | 231,827 | 234,500 | 258,100 | 253,800 | .... | .... |
| Changes in Inventories.................... | 93i | 2,600 | 300 | — | — | 900 | 2,900 | 3,641 | — | — | — | .... | .... |
| Exports of Goods and Services......... | 90c | 137,000 | 163,400 | 185,000 | 225,300 | 295,800 | 260,100 | 257,551 | 282,000 | 286,100 | 297,400 | .... | .... |
| Imports of Goods and Services (-)..... | 98c | 143,600 | 175,600 | 195,000 | 259,400 | 346,000 | 329,300 | 320,833 | 338,500 | 404,100 | 445,000 | .... | .... |
| Gross Domestic Product (GDP)......... | 99b | 485,300 | 538,500 | 617,700 | 744,700 | 895,500 | 1,042,200 | 1,206,640 | 1,371,100 | 1,542,300 | 1,887,100 | .... | .... |
| GDP Volume 2011/12...................... | 99b.p | .... | .... | .... | .... | .... | .... | .... | .... | 1,594,400 | 1,618,700 | .... | .... |
| GDP Volume (2010=100)................ | 99bvp | 71.0 | 74.1 | 79.2 | † 84.8 | 90.8 | 95.1 | 100.0 | 101.8 | † 105.6 | 107.2 | .... | .... |
| GDP Deflator (2010=100)............... | 99bip | 56.7 | 60.2 | 64.6 | 72.8 | 81.7 | 90.8 | 100.0 | 111.7 | 121.1 | 145.9 | .... | .... |

*Millions: Midyear Estimates*

| | | 2004 | 2005 | 2006 | 2007 | 2008 | 2009 | 2010 | 2011 | 2012 | 2013 | 2014 | 2015 |
|---|---|---|---|---|---|---|---|---|---|---|---|---|---|
| **Population.............................** | 99z | 73.60 | 74.94 | 76.27 | 77.61 | 78.98 | 80.44 | 82.04 | 83.79 | 85.66 | 87.61 | 89.58 | 91.51 |

# El Salvador   253

| | | 2004 | 2005 | 2006 | 2007 | 2008 | 2009 | 2010 | 2011 | 2012 | 2013 | 2014 | 2015 |
|---|---|---|---|---|---|---|---|---|---|---|---|---|---|
| **Exchange Rates** | | *Colones per SDR: End of Period (aa) Colones per US Dollar: End of Period (ae)* | | | | | | | | | | | |
| Market Rate.................................. | aa | 13.589 | 12.506 | 13.164 | 13.827 | 13.477 | 13.717 | 13.475 | 13.434 | 13.448 | 13.475 | 12.677 | 12.125 |
| Market Rate.................................. | ae | 8.750 | 8.750 | 8.750 | 8.750 | 8.750 | 8.750 | 8.750 | 8.750 | 8.750 | 8.750 | 8.750 | 8.750 |
| **Fund Position** | | *Millions of SDRs: End of Period* | | | | | | | | | | | |
| Quota.......................................... | 2f.s | 171.30 | 171.30 | 171.30 | 171.30 | 171.30 | 171.30 | 171.30 | 171.30 | 171.30 | 171.30 | 171.30 | 171.30 |
| SDR Holdings............................... | 1b.s | 24.98 | 24.98 | 24.98 | 24.98 | 25.01 | 163.83 | 163.81 | 163.80 | 164.30 | 165.56 | 165.56 | 165.56 |
| Reserve Position in the Fund............ | 1c.s | — | — | — | — | — | — | — | — | — | — | — | — |
| Total Fund Cred.&Loans Outstg....... | 2tl | — | — | — | — | — | — | — | — | — | — | — | — |
| SDR Allocations............................ | 1bd | 24.99 | 24.99 | 24.99 | 24.99 | 24.99 | 163.81 | 163.81 | 163.81 | 163.81 | 163.81 | 163.81 | 163.81 |
| **International Liquidity** | | *Millions of US Dollars Unless Otherwise Indicated: End of Period* | | | | | | | | | | | |
| Total Reserves minus Gold.............. | 1l.d | 1,752.4 | 1,721.4 | 1,822.8 | 2,108.5 | 2,441.6 | 2,867.4 | 2,568.2 | 2,151.5 | 2,804.9 | 2,476.2 | 2,430.3 | 2,739.8 |
| SDR Holdings.............................. | 1b.d | 38.8 | 35.7 | 37.6 | 39.5 | 38.5 | 256.8 | 252.3 | 251.5 | 252.5 | 255.0 | 239.9 | 229.4 |
| Reserve Position in the Fund......... | 1c.d | — | — | — | — | — | — | — | — | — | — | — | — |
| Foreign Exchange........................ | 1d.d | 1,713.6 | 1,685.7 | 1,785.2 | 2,069.1 | 2,403.1 | 2,610.5 | 2,315.9 | 1,900.0 | 2,552.4 | 2,221.2 | 2,190.4 | 2,510.4 |
| Gold (Million Fine Troy Ounces)........ | 1ad | .419 | .254 | .233 | .233 | .233 | .233 | .233 | .233 | .233 | .233 | .218 | .044 |
| Gold (National Valuation)............... | 1and | 138.9 | 110.2 | 84.0 | 88.8 | 101.9 | 117.5 | 313.6 | 351.3 | 369.8 | 268.7 | 263.0 | 46.8 |
| Central Bank: Other Assets............. | 3..d | 98.3 | 98.1 | 98.1 | 98.1 | 98.1 | 98.1 | 98.1 | 98.1 | 98.2 | 114.1 | 114.2 | 130.5 |
| Central Bank: Other Liabs............... | 4..d | 226.4 | 221.0 | 124.6 | 89.1 | 354.9 | 231.8 | 177.8 | 172.9 | 190.3 | 316.5 | 294.7 | 297.6 |
| Other Depository Corps.: Assets....... | 7a.d | 1,102.1 | 1,261.6 | 1,142.9 | 1,249.8 | 1,352.3 | 1,163.6 | 1,177.7 | 793.3 | 824.4 | 893.1 | 988.3 | 965.6 |
| Other Depository Corps.: Liabs......... | 7b.d | 1,784.4 | 1,796.9 | 1,558.0 | 1,207.4 | 1,450.7 | 787.2 | 481.1 | 498.0 | 886.0 | 1,310.5 | 1,660.8 | 1,928.8 |
| Other Financial Corps.: Assets....... | 7e.d | 186.8 | 334.0 | 384.7 | 370.5 | 304.0 | 307.7 | 353.0 | 561.0 | 636.3 | 771.7 | 791.4 | 686.1 |
| Other Financial Corps.: Liabs............ | 7f.d | 201.0 | 223.5 | 219.4 | 262.0 | 246.1 | 250.1 | 221.4 | 221.6 | 176.5 | 171.4 | 183.4 | 184.7 |
| **Central Bank** | | *Millions of US Dollars: End of Period* | | | | | | | | | | | |
| Net Foreign Assets........................ | 11n | 1,724.4 | 1,672.9 | 1,842.8 | 2,166.9 | 2,248.2 | 2,594.4 | 2,549.9 | 2,176.5 | 2,830.8 | 2,290.3 | 2,275.4 | 2,392.5 |
| Claims on Nonresidents................ | 11 | 1,989.6 | 1,929.7 | 2,005.0 | 2,295.5 | 2,641.7 | 3,083.0 | 2,979.9 | 2,600.9 | 3,272.9 | 2,859.1 | 2,807.5 | 2,917.1 |
| Liabilities to Nonresidents............ | 16c | 265.2 | 256.8 | 162.1 | 128.6 | 393.4 | 488.6 | 430.0 | 424.4 | 442.1 | 568.8 | 532.0 | 524.6 |
| Claims on Other Depository Corps.... | 12e | | | | | | | | | | | | |
| Net Claims on Central Government.. | 12an | 290.4 | 369.6 | 317.9 | 463.4 | 519.3 | 220.9 | 491.9 | 691.1 | −47.8 | 710.3 | 705.0 | 727.9 |
| Claims on Central Government...... | 12a | 815.4 | 816.7 | 812.7 | 812.1 | 838.8 | 836.1 | 833.2 | 832.7 | 832.2 | 831.7 | 830.9 | 829.5 |
| Liabilities to Central Government... | 16d | 524.9 | 447.1 | 494.7 | 348.7 | 319.5 | 615.2 | 341.3 | 141.6 | 880.0 | 121.4 | 125.9 | 101.6 |
| Claims on Other Sectors............... | 12s | 507.2 | 462.2 | 428.8 | 378.2 | 308.0 | 296.3 | 302.7 | 302.9 | 304.2 | 302.3 | 322.6 | 323.2 |
| Claims on Other Financial Corps.... | 12g | 506.9 | 462.0 | 428.7 | 378.1 | 276.0 | 281.2 | 301.6 | 302.8 | 304.1 | 302.2 | 322.4 | 323.1 |
| Claims on State & Local Govts....... | 12b | .2 | .1 | — | — | — | — | — | — | — | — | — | — |
| Claims on Public Nonfin. Corps...... | 12c | .1 | .1 | .1 | .1 | .1 | .1 | .1 | .1 | .1 | .1 | .1 | .1 |
| Claims on Private Sector................ | 12d | — | — | — | — | 31.9 | 15.0 | 1.0 | | | | | |
| Monetary Base.............................. | 14 | 2,086.6 | 2,063.1 | 2,129.7 | 2,603.2 | 2,670.4 | 2,725.3 | 2,697.8 | 2,524.9 | 2,416.9 | 2,666.6 | 2,684.5 | 2,824.2 |
| Currency in Circulation.................. | 14a | 36.3 | 34.5 | 33.8 | 33.3 | 33.1 | 32.9 | 4.8 | 4.6 | 4.4 | 4.1 | 3.9 | 3.6 |
| Liabs. to Other Depository Corps.... | 14c | 1,606.0 | 1,655.7 | 1,694.3 | 2,043.6 | 2,257.5 | 2,249.6 | 2,349.2 | 2,270.5 | 2,224.2 | 2,476.5 | 2,469.9 | 2,565.2 |
| Liabilities to Other Sectors............ | 14d | 444.3 | 373.0 | 401.6 | 526.2 | 379.9 | 442.8 | 343.9 | 249.8 | 188.4 | 186.0 | 210.7 | 255.4 |
| Other Liabs. to Other Dep. Corps..... | 14n | | | | | | | | | | | | |
| Dep. & Sec. Excl. f/Monetary Base.... | 14o | 164.0 | 170.9 | 165.4 | 164.5 | 140.6 | 87.9 | 82.9 | 82.9 | 82.9 | 82.8 | 82.8 | 82.8 |
| Deposits Included in Broad Money. | 15 | — | — | — | — | — | — | — | — | — | — | — | — |
| Sec.Ot.th.Shares Incl.in Brd. Money. | 16a | 158.0 | 165.0 | 160.0 | 159.1 | 135.2 | 82.6 | 77.6 | 77.6 | 77.6 | 77.6 | 77.6 | 77.6 |
| Deposits Excl. from Broad Money... | 16b | 3.2 | 3.0 | 2.6 | 2.5 | 2.5 | 2.5 | 2.4 | 2.4 | 2.4 | 2.4 | 2.4 | 2.4 |
| Sec.Ot.th.Shares Excl.f/Brd.Money.. | 16s | 2.9 | 2.9 | 2.9 | 2.9 | 2.9 | 2.9 | 2.9 | 2.9 | 2.9 | 2.9 | 2.9 | 2.9 |
| Loans.......................................... | 16l | — | — | — | — | — | — | — | — | — | — | — | — |
| Financial Derivatives...................... | 16m | — | — | — | — | — | — | — | — | — | — | — | — |
| Shares and Other Equity.................. | 17a | 183.2 | 180.1 | 198.5 | 217.7 | 258.3 | 290.9 | 545.2 | 665.4 | 690.7 | 625.8 | 638.5 | 654.9 |
| Other Items (Net)........................... | 17r | 88.3 | 90.6 | 96.0 | 23.2 | 6.3 | 7.5 | 18.7 | −102.6 | −103.2 | −72.4 | −102.8 | −118.3 |
| Memo Item: | | | | | | | | | | | | | |
| Total Assets................................... | 10ra | 3,618.0 | 3,478.3 | 3,528.9 | 3,778.4 | 4,084.3 | 4,511.8 | 4,407.3 | 4,112.7 | 4,786.6 | 4,380.2 | 4,337.3 | 4,438.2 |
| **Other Depository Corporations** | | *Millions of US Dollars: End of Period* | | | | | | | | | | | |
| Net Foreign Assets......................... | 21n | −682.3 | −535.4 | −415.2 | 42.4 | −98.4 | 376.3 | 696.6 | 295.3 | −61.5 | −417.4 | −672.5 | −963.2 |
| Claims on Nonresidents................ | 21 | 1,102.1 | 1,261.6 | 1,142.9 | 1,249.8 | 1,352.3 | 1,163.6 | 1,177.7 | 793.3 | 824.4 | 893.1 | 988.3 | 965.6 |
| Liabilities to Nonresidents............ | 26c | 1,784.4 | 1,796.9 | 1,558.0 | 1,207.4 | 1,450.7 | 787.2 | 481.1 | 498.0 | 886.0 | 1,310.5 | 1,660.8 | 1,928.8 |
| Claims on Central Bank.................. | 20 | 1,931.4 | 1,793.3 | 1,837.4 | 2,317.6 | 2,424.0 | 2,501.3 | 2,596.2 | 2,466.1 | 2,569.4 | 2,670.2 | 2,681.1 | 2,778.6 |
| Currency.................................... | 20a | .9 | .3 | .2 | .1 | .1 | .1 | .1 | .1 | .1 | .1 | .1 | .1 |
| Reserve Deposits and Securities..... | 20b | 1,712.1 | 1,741.1 | 1,812.8 | 2,261.2 | 2,400.8 | 2,382.9 | 2,470.9 | 2,384.1 | 2,485.3 | 2,630.2 | 2,610.4 | 2,683.2 |
| Other Claims............................... | 20n | 218.4 | 51.9 | 24.4 | 56.3 | 23.1 | 118.2 | 125.1 | 81.9 | 83.9 | 39.9 | 70.7 | 95.3 |
| Net Claims on Central Government.. | 22an | 388.2 | 274.7 | 172.8 | 250.6 | 241.3 | 397.0 | 341.4 | 420.3 | 537.0 | 326.4 | 162.3 | 681.5 |
| Claims on Central Government...... | 22a | 527.3 | 431.9 | 305.5 | 394.7 | 352.0 | 570.4 | 515.8 | 629.1 | 714.2 | 617.6 | 442.2 | 927.6 |
| Liabilities to Central Government... | 26d | 139.1 | 157.2 | 132.7 | 144.1 | 110.7 | 173.5 | 174.4 | 208.9 | 177.2 | 291.2 | 279.9 | 246.1 |
| Claims on Other Sectors............... | 22s | 6,917.9 | 7,791.8 | 8,452.1 | 9,132.5 | 9,529.0 | 9,092.0 | 9,044.6 | 9,408.7 | 9,719.3 | 10,517.3 | 11,072.5 | 11,550.5 |
| Claims on Other Financial Corps.... | 22g | 328.4 | 437.5 | 426.1 | 399.8 | 394.7 | 410.4 | 374.3 | 373.2 | 339.2 | 384.7 | 430.1 | 434.3 |
| Claims on State & Local Govts....... | 22b | 60.3 | 86.8 | 72.5 | 73.0 | 76.9 | 77.4 | 92.6 | 37.3 | 38.0 | 49.0 | 99.0 | 85.7 |
| Claims on Public Nonfin. Corps...... | 22c | 27.6 | 56.6 | 46.7 | 42.8 | 40.4 | 32.5 | 18.6 | 14.3 | 9.9 | 5.5 | 4.4 | 2.0 |
| Claims on Private Sector................ | 22d | 6,501.7 | 7,211.0 | 7,906.8 | 8,616.9 | 9,016.9 | 8,571.6 | 8,559.1 | 8,983.8 | 9,332.2 | 10,078.0 | 10,539.0 | 11,028.5 |
| Liabilities to Central Bank............... | 26g | — | — | — | — | — | — | — | — | — | — | — | — |
| Transf.Dep.Included in Broad Money | 24 | 1,283.3 | 1,370.2 | 1,565.9 | 1,833.8 | 1,841.6 | 2,150.1 | 2,537.5 | 2,664.1 | 2,677.0 | 2,754.7 | 2,784.0 | 3,104.7 |
| Other Dep.Included in Broad Money. | 25 | 5,528.3 | 5,646.3 | 6,140.4 | 7,176.9 | 7,113.4 | 7,021.7 | 7,094.8 | 6,878.3 | 7,048.8 | 7,264.1 | 7,197.5 | 7,491.4 |
| Sec.Ot.th.Shares Incl.in Brd. Money.. | 26a | 463.0 | 628.5 | 778.0 | 926.6 | 1,030.0 | 1,034.0 | 721.1 | 657.2 | 644.7 | 585.5 | 620.8 | 679.5 |
| Deposits Excl. from Broad Money..... | 26b | — | — | — | — | — | — | — | — | — | — | — | — |
| Sec.Ot.th.Shares Excl.f/Brd.Money.... | 26s | — | — | — | — | — | .1 | .1 | .1 | .1 | .1 | .1 | — |
| Loans.......................................... | 26l | 161.1 | 190.7 | 163.2 | 265.4 | 237.2 | 199.3 | 180.2 | 179.9 | 209.6 | 223.5 | 234.6 | 244.3 |
| Financial Derivatives....................... | 26m | — | — | — | — | — | — | — | — | — | — | — | — |
| Insurance Technical Reserves........... | 26r | | | | | | | | | | | | |
| Shares and Other Equity.................. | 27a | 1,054.9 | 1,226.2 | 1,471.0 | 1,631.8 | 1,805.4 | 1,827.4 | 1,915.3 | 1,924.8 | 2,009.3 | 2,152.4 | 2,170.5 | 2,303.8 |
| Other Items (Net)........................... | 27r | 64.6 | 262.5 | −71.3 | −91.4 | 68.4 | 133.9 | 229.8 | 285.8 | 174.5 | 116.3 | 236.0 | 223.6 |
| Memo Item: | | | | | | | | | | | | | |
| Total Assets................................... | 20ra | 11,283.6 | 12,099.3 | 12,546.9 | 13,900.6 | 14,451.4 | 14,178.2 | 14,210.2 | 14,169.7 | 14,671.7 | 15,570.5 | 16,105.2 | 17,243.6 |

| | | 2004 | 2005 | 2006 | 2007 | 2008 | 2009 | 2010 | 2011 | 2012 | 2013 | 2014 | 2015 |
|---|---|---|---|---|---|---|---|---|---|---|---|---|---|
| **Depository Corporations** | | | | | | *Millions of US Dollars: End of Period* | | | | | | | |
| Net Foreign Assets | 31n | 1,042.2 | 1,137.6 | 1,427.7 | 2,209.3 | 2,149.8 | 2,970.7 | 3,246.5 | 2,471.8 | 2,769.3 | 1,872.9 | 1,603.0 | 1,429.3 |
| Claims on Nonresidents | 31 | 3,091.7 | 3,191.3 | 3,147.8 | 3,545.3 | 3,993.9 | 4,246.6 | 4,157.6 | 3,394.2 | 4,097.3 | 3,752.2 | 3,795.8 | 3,882.7 |
| Liabilities to Nonresidents | 36c | 2,049.5 | 2,053.7 | 1,720.2 | 1,336.0 | 1,844.1 | 1,275.9 | 911.1 | 922.4 | 1,328.0 | 1,879.3 | 2,192.8 | 2,453.4 |
| Domestic Claims | 32 | 8,103.8 | 8,898.3 | 9,371.6 | 10,224.7 | 10,597.5 | 10,006.1 | 10,180.7 | 10,822.9 | 10,512.6 | 11,856.2 | 12,262.4 | 13,283.1 |
| Net Claims on Central Government | 32an | 678.6 | 644.3 | 490.7 | 714.0 | 760.5 | 617.8 | 833.3 | 1,111.4 | 489.1 | 1,036.6 | 867.3 | 1,409.4 |
| Claims on Central Government | 32a | 1,342.7 | 1,248.6 | 1,118.1 | 1,206.7 | 1,190.8 | 1,406.5 | 1,349.0 | 1,461.9 | 1,546.4 | 1,449.3 | 1,273.1 | 1,757.1 |
| Liabilities to Central Government | 36d | 664.0 | 604.3 | 627.4 | 492.7 | 430.2 | 788.7 | 515.7 | 350.5 | 1,057.3 | 412.6 | 405.8 | 347.7 |
| Claims on Other Sectors | 32s | 7,425.1 | 8,254.0 | 8,881.0 | 9,510.7 | 9,837.0 | 9,388.2 | 9,347.3 | 9,711.5 | 10,023.5 | 10,819.6 | 11,395.0 | 11,873.7 |
| Claims on Other Financial Corps | 32g | 835.3 | 899.5 | 854.8 | 777.8 | 670.7 | 691.6 | 675.9 | 676.0 | 643.3 | 686.8 | 752.6 | 757.4 |
| Claims on State & Local Govts | 32b | 60.5 | 86.9 | 72.5 | 73.0 | 76.9 | 77.4 | 92.6 | 37.3 | 38.0 | 49.0 | 99.0 | 85.7 |
| Claims on Public Nonfin. Corps | 32c | 27.7 | 56.7 | 46.8 | 42.9 | 40.5 | 32.7 | 18.7 | 14.4 | 10.0 | 5.6 | 4.5 | 2.1 |
| Claims on Private Sector | 32d | 6,501.7 | 7,211.0 | 7,906.8 | 8,616.9 | 9,048.8 | 8,586.6 | 8,560.1 | 8,983.8 | 9,332.2 | 10,078.0 | 10,539.0 | 11,028.5 |
| Broad Money Liabilities | 35l | 7,912.4 | 8,217.2 | 9,079.5 | 10,655.9 | 10,532.8 | 10,763.9 | 10,779.5 | 10,531.4 | 10,640.7 | 10,871.9 | 10,894.4 | 11,611.9 |
| Currency Outside Depository Corps | 34a | 35.4 | 34.2 | 33.7 | 33.2 | 33.0 | 32.8 | 4.7 | 4.5 | 4.2 | 4.0 | 3.8 | 3.5 |
| Transferable Deposits | 34 | 1,325.8 | 1,421.1 | 1,622.8 | 1,904.3 | 1,923.1 | 2,279.7 | 2,637.1 | 2,776.5 | 2,792.2 | 2,887.9 | 2,916.4 | 3,249.9 |
| Other Deposits | 35 | 5,530.0 | 5,646.7 | 6,171.6 | 7,242.0 | 7,123.5 | 7,029.4 | 7,102.6 | 6,890.8 | 7,050.8 | 7,264.5 | 7,198.6 | 7,501.8 |
| Securities Other than Shares | 36a | 1,021.1 | 1,115.3 | 1,251.4 | 1,476.3 | 1,453.2 | 1,422.1 | 1,035.2 | 859.7 | 793.5 | 715.4 | 775.6 | 856.8 |
| Deposits Excl. from Broad Money | 36b | 3.2 | 3.0 | 2.6 | 2.5 | 2.5 | 2.5 | 2.4 | 2.4 | 2.4 | 2.4 | 2.4 | 2.4 |
| Sec.Ot.th.Shares Excl.f/Brd.Money | 36s | 2.9 | 2.9 | 2.9 | 2.9 | 2.9 | 3.0 | 3.0 | 3.0 | 2.9 | 2.9 | 2.9 | 2.9 |
| Loans | 36l | 161.1 | 190.7 | 163.2 | 265.4 | 237.2 | 199.3 | 180.2 | 179.9 | 209.6 | 223.5 | 234.6 | 244.3 |
| Financial Derivatives | 36m | — | — | — | — | — | — | — | — | — | — | — | — |
| Insurance Technical Reserves | 36r | — | — | — | — | — | — | — | — | — | — | — | — |
| Shares and Other Equity | 37a | 1,238.0 | 1,406.3 | 1,669.5 | 1,849.4 | 2,063.7 | 2,118.3 | 2,460.5 | 2,590.2 | 2,700.0 | 2,778.2 | 2,809.0 | 2,958.7 |
| Other Items (Net) | 37r | −171.7 | 215.8 | −118.3 | −342.1 | −91.8 | −110.2 | 1.6 | −12.2 | −273.8 | −149.8 | −78.0 | −107.9 |
| Broad Money Liabs., Seasonally Adj. | 35l.b | 7,859.5 | 8,179.8 | 9,058.3 | 10,650.8 | 10,539.2 | 10,780.3 | 10,803.8 | 10,563.8 | 10,682.6 | 10,925.7 | 10,955.8 | 11,679.0 |
| **Other Financial Corporations** | | | | | | *Millions of US Dollars: End of Period* | | | | | | | |
| Net Foreign Assets | 41n | −14.2 | 110.5 | 165.4 | 108.5 | 57.9 | 57.6 | 131.5 | 339.5 | 459.8 | 600.4 | 608.0 | 501.4 |
| Claims on Nonresidents | 41 | 186.8 | 334.0 | 384.7 | 370.5 | 304.0 | 307.7 | 353.0 | 561.0 | 636.3 | 771.7 | 791.4 | 686.1 |
| Liabilities to Nonresidents | 46c | 201.0 | 223.5 | 219.4 | 262.0 | 246.1 | 250.1 | 221.4 | 221.6 | 176.5 | 171.4 | 183.4 | 184.7 |
| Claims on Depository Corporations | 40 | 489.9 | 1,111.0 | 1,352.5 | 1,592.3 | 1,656.2 | 1,729.4 | 1,594.9 | 1,225.7 | 1,099.0 | 1,112.7 | 1,128.5 | 1,274.0 |
| Net Claims on Central Government | 42an | 32.1 | 1,048.3 | 2,038.4 | 2,539.2 | 2,974.5 | 3,559.8 | 4,256.4 | 4,896.1 | 5,584.8 | 5,825.3 | 6,228.9 | 6,695.2 |
| Claims on Central Government | 42a | 32.1 | 1,048.3 | 2,038.4 | 2,539.2 | 2,974.5 | 3,559.8 | 4,256.4 | 4,896.1 | 5,584.8 | 5,825.3 | 6,228.9 | 6,695.2 |
| Liabilities to Central Government | 46d | — | — | — | — | — | — | — | — | — | — | — | — |
| Claims on Other Sectors | 42s | 113.4 | 955.7 | 192.6 | 194.6 | 222.0 | 213.0 | 219.3 | 279.2 | 316.2 | 489.4 | 727.9 | 892.6 |
| Claims on State & Local Govts | 42b | — | — | — | — | — | — | — | 14.1 | 22.2 | 25.1 | 31.6 | 65.7 |
| Claims on Public Nonfin. Corps | 42c | 5.8 | 828.9 | 55.2 | 44.7 | 55.8 | 46.9 | 24.4 | 50.3 | 52.5 | 185.4 | 188.0 | 258.0 |
| Claims on Private Sector | 42d | 107.6 | 126.9 | 137.3 | 150.0 | 166.3 | 166.1 | 194.9 | 214.8 | 241.5 | 278.9 | 508.3 | 568.9 |
| Deposits | 46b | — | — | — | — | — | — | — | — | — | — | — | — |
| Securities Other than Shares | 46s | — | — | — | — | — | — | — | — | — | — | — | — |
| Loans | 46l | 215.7 | 201.1 | 176.5 | 175.3 | 115.4 | 119.5 | 114.6 | 113.1 | 124.2 | 125.1 | 108.4 | 99.2 |
| Financial Derivatives | 46m | — | — | — | — | — | — | — | — | — | — | — | — |
| Insurance Technical Reserves | 46r | 127.7 | 3,094.1 | 3,595.7 | 4,202.0 | 4,710.2 | 5,305.9 | 5,908.0 | 6,435.4 | 7,130.0 | 7,695.7 | 8,380.8 | 8,981.1 |
| Shares and Other Equity | 47a | 320.5 | 307.3 | 312.9 | 344.9 | 426.4 | 478.6 | 528.7 | 503.7 | 532.9 | 554.9 | 582.7 | 600.8 |
| Other Items (Net) | 47r | −42.8 | −377.0 | −336.3 | −287.5 | −341.4 | −344.3 | −349.1 | −311.7 | −327.2 | −348.0 | −378.6 | −318.0 |
| Memo Item: | | | | | | | | | | | | | |
| Total Assets | 40ra | 964.8 | 3,948.6 | 4,458.5 | 5,146.5 | 5,644.9 | 6,305.7 | 6,955.2 | 7,453.6 | 8,111.5 | 8,743.9 | 9,434.3 | 10,134.5 |
| **Financial Corporations** | | | | | | *Millions of US Dollars: End of Period* | | | | | | | |
| Net Foreign Assets | 51n | 1,028.0 | 1,248.0 | 1,593.0 | 2,317.8 | 2,207.7 | 3,028.3 | 3,378.1 | 2,811.3 | 3,229.1 | 2,473.3 | 2,211.0 | 1,930.7 |
| Claims on Nonresidents | 51 | 3,278.5 | 3,525.2 | 3,532.6 | 3,915.8 | 4,298.0 | 4,554.3 | 4,510.6 | 3,955.2 | 4,733.6 | 4,523.9 | 4,587.2 | 4,568.8 |
| Liabilities to Nonresidents | 56c | 2,250.5 | 2,277.2 | 1,939.5 | 1,598.0 | 2,090.3 | 1,526.0 | 1,132.5 | 1,144.0 | 1,504.5 | 2,050.7 | 2,376.2 | 2,638.1 |
| Domestic Claims | 52 | 7,414.0 | 10,002.8 | 10,747.8 | 12,180.7 | 13,123.3 | 13,087.2 | 13,980.4 | 15,322.2 | 15,770.4 | 17,484.1 | 18,466.5 | 20,113.6 |
| Net Claims on Central Government | 52an | 710.7 | 1,692.6 | 2,529.1 | 3,253.2 | 3,735.1 | 4,177.6 | 5,089.7 | 6,007.5 | 6,074.0 | 6,861.9 | 7,096.2 | 8,104.6 |
| Claims on Central Government | 52a | 1,374.8 | 2,296.9 | 3,156.5 | 3,746.0 | 4,165.3 | 4,966.3 | 5,605.3 | 6,358.0 | 7,131.2 | 7,274.6 | 7,502.0 | 8,452.3 |
| Liabilities to Central Government | 56d | 664.0 | 604.3 | 627.4 | 492.7 | 430.2 | 788.7 | 515.7 | 350.5 | 1,057.3 | 412.6 | 405.8 | 347.7 |
| Claims on Other Sectors | 52s | 6,703.3 | 8,310.3 | 8,218.7 | 8,927.5 | 9,388.3 | 8,909.6 | 8,890.8 | 9,314.7 | 9,696.4 | 10,622.2 | 11,370.3 | 12,008.9 |
| Claims on State & Local Govts | 52b | 60.5 | 86.9 | 72.5 | 73.0 | 76.9 | 77.4 | 92.6 | 51.4 | 60.2 | 74.2 | 130.5 | 151.4 |
| Claims on Public Nonfin. Corps | 52c | 33.6 | 885.6 | 102.0 | 87.5 | 96.3 | 79.5 | 43.1 | 64.7 | 62.5 | 191.0 | 192.5 | 260.1 |
| Claims on Private Sector | 52d | 6,609.2 | 7,337.8 | 8,044.2 | 8,766.9 | 9,215.1 | 8,752.7 | 8,755.1 | 9,198.7 | 9,573.7 | 10,357.0 | 11,047.3 | 11,597.4 |
| Currency Outside Financial Corps | 54a | 34.9 | 34.1 | 33.6 | 33.0 | 32.9 | 32.6 | 4.6 | 4.3 | 4.1 | 3.9 | 3.8 | 3.4 |
| Deposits | 55l | 6,642.5 | 6,867.8 | 7,562.1 | 8,869.4 | 8,867.4 | 9,002.6 | 9,442.8 | 9,356.8 | 9,619.2 | 9,872.4 | 9,837.4 | 10,487.9 |
| Securities Other than Shares | 56a | 146.4 | 146.4 | 230.2 | 261.3 | 261.3 | 261.3 | 152.0 | 120.9 | 71.9 | 4.9 | 28.4 | 26.4 |
| Loans | 56l | 4.6 | 15.4 | 16.4 | 13.9 | 13.4 | 31.9 | 26.7 | 23.4 | 26.7 | 35.7 | 37.2 | 38.4 |
| Financial Derivatives | 56m | — | — | — | — | — | — | — | — | — | — | — | — |
| Insurance Technical Reserves | 56r | 127.7 | 3,093.9 | 3,595.6 | 4,201.9 | 4,710.2 | 5,305.8 | 5,907.9 | 6,435.3 | 7,129.9 | 7,695.7 | 8,380.7 | 8,981.1 |
| Shares and Other Equity | 57a | 1,558.6 | 1,713.5 | 1,982.4 | 2,194.3 | 2,490.1 | 2,597.0 | 2,989.2 | 3,094.0 | 3,232.9 | 3,333.1 | 3,391.7 | 3,559.5 |
| Other Items (Net) | 57r | −72.6 | −620.2 | −1,079.3 | −1,075.2 | −1,044.2 | −1,115.5 | −1,164.7 | −901.2 | −1,085.1 | −988.3 | −1,001.7 | −1,052.5 |
| **Monetary Aggregates** | | | | | | *Millions of US Dollars: End of Period* | | | | | | | |
| Broad Money | 59m | 7,912.4 | 8,217.2 | 9,079.5 | 10,655.9 | 10,532.8 | 10,763.9 | 10,779.5 | 10,531.4 | 10,640.7 | 10,871.9 | 10,894.4 | 11,611.9 |
| o/w:Currency Issued by Cent.Govt | 59m.a | — | — | — | — | — | — | — | — | — | — | — | — |
| o/w: Dep.in Nonfin. Corporations | 59m.b | — | — | — | — | — | — | — | — | — | — | — | — |
| o/w:Secs. Issued by Central Govt | 59m.c | — | — | — | — | — | — | — | — | — | — | — | — |
| Money (National Definitions) | | | | | | | | | | | | | |
| Base Money | 19ma | 2,086.6 | 2,063.1 | 2,129.7 | 2,603.2 | 2,670.4 | 2,725.3 | 2,697.8 | 2,524.9 | 2,416.9 | 2,666.6 | 2,684.5 | 2,824.2 |
| M1 | 59ma | 1,202.5 | 1,291.3 | 1,487.4 | 1,732.7 | 1,759.9 | 1,979.0 | 2,392.0 | 2,386.1 | 2,488.4 | 2,566.7 | 2,608.2 | 2,890.4 |
| M2 | 59mb | 6,192.0 | 6,352.8 | 7,093.0 | 8,341.8 | 8,353.2 | 8,455.8 | 8,815.2 | 8,598.7 | 8,870.3 | 9,062.6 | 8,987.1 | 9,548.6 |
| M3 | 59mc | 6,657.3 | 6,982.8 | 7,871.4 | 9,268.4 | 9,382.8 | 9,489.8 | 9,537.4 | 9,257.2 | 9,514.1 | 9,646.6 | 9,608.5 | 10,197.9 |
| Broad Money | 59mea | 7,912.4 | 8,217.2 | 9,079.5 | 10,655.9 | 10,532.8 | 10,763.9 | 10,779.5 | 10,531.4 | 10,640.7 | 10,871.9 | 10,817.9 | 11,513.2 |
| **Interest Rates** | | | | | | *Percent Per Annum* | | | | | | | |
| Money Market Rate | 60b | 4.36 | 5.18 | 6.00 | 5.25 | 4.32 | .... | .... | .... | .... | .... | .... | .... |
| Deposit Rate (Fgn. Currency) | 60l.f | 3.34 | 3.44 | 4.39 | 4.71 | 4.21 | 4.48 | 2.87 | 1.76 | 2.52 | 3.40 | 3.78 | 4.24 |
| Lending Rate (Fgn. Currency) | 60p.f | 6.30 | 6.87 | 7.53 | 7.81 | 7.87 | 9.32 | 7.62 | 5.99 | 5.60 | 5.74 | 5.99 | 6.17 |

| | | 2004 | 2005 | 2006 | 2007 | 2008 | 2009 | 2010 | 2011 | 2012 | 2013 | 2014 | 2015 |
|---|---|---|---|---|---|---|---|---|---|---|---|---|---|
| **Prices, Production, Labor** | | | | | | | *Index Numbers (2010=100): Period Averages* | | | | | | |
| Producer Prices................... | 63 | 77.5 | 84.5 | 88.5 | 92.7 | 108.1 | 95.5 | 100.0 | 111.2 | 114.3 | 114.5 | 112.5 | 103.5 |
| Wholesale Prices.............. | 63a | 81.8 | 88.0 | 92.0 | 96.9 | 105.8 | 95.9 | 100.0 | 114.4 | 112.0 | 108.4 | 110.8 | 111.3 |
| Consumer Prices................ | 64 | 80.7 | 84.5 | 87.9 | 91.9 | 98.1 | 99.1 | † 100.0 | 105.1 | 106.9 | 107.8 | 109.0 | 108.2 |
| Industrial Production (2005=100).... | 66 | 95.0 | 100.0 | 102.6 | 107.0 | 107.6 | 104.3 | .... | .... | .... | .... | .... | .... |
| | | | | | | | *Number in Thousands: Period Averages* | | | | | | | |
| Labor Force................................ | 67d | 2,418 | 2,461 | 2,501 | 2,464 | 2,496 | .... | .... | .... | .... | .... | .... | .... |
| Employment.............................. | 67e | 2,254 | 2,284 | 2,337 | 2,308 | 2,349 | .... | .... | .... | .... | .... | .... | .... |
| Unemployment.......................... | 67c | 164 | 178 | 164 | 156 | 147 | .... | .... | .... | .... | .... | .... | .... |
| Unemployment Rate (%)................ | 67r | 6.8 | 7.2 | 6.6 | 6.3 | 5.9 | 7.3 | .... | .... | .... | .... | .... | .... |
| **Intl. Transactions & Positions** | | | | | | | *Millions of US Dollars* | | | | | | | |
| Including Maquiladoras | | | | | | | | | | | | | |
| Exports................................... | 70..d | 3,304.6 | 3,386.5 | 3,513.3 | 3,976.8 | 4,579.2 | 3,797.3 | 4,471.9 | 4,978.8 | 5,340.2 | 5,491.1 | 5,272.8 | 5,484.9 |
| Imports, c.i.f........................... | 71..d | 6,328.9 | 6,834.3 | 7,627.8 | 8,676.6 | 9,754.4 | 7,254.7 | 8,548.4 | 10,118.2 | 10,269.6 | 10,772.1 | 10,513.1 | 10,415.6 |
| Excluding Maquiladoras | | | | | | | | | | | | | |
| Exports................................... | 70n.d | 1,381.5 | 1,572.1 | 1,903.7 | 2,174.8 | 2,612.4 | 2,310.0 | 2,734.0 | 4,009.8 | 4,156.6 | 4,333.0 | 4,248.9 | 4,372.6 |
| Imports, c.i.f........................... | 71n.d | 4,870.8 | 5,362.5 | 6,365.6 | 7,363.0 | 8,442.7 | 6,415.7 | 7,476.9 | 9,138.5 | 9,493.2 | 10,020.6 | 9,834.7 | 9,740.9 |
| **Balance of Payments** | | | | | | | *Millions of US Dollars* | | | | | | | |
| A. Current Account*.................... | 109bx | −641.9 | −621.6 | −765.6 | −1,216.6 | −1,532.2 | −312.2 | −532.8 | −1,111.8 | −1,279.5 | −1,585.6 | −1,311.9 | −920.0 |
| Goods, credit (exports)............... | 1a9cx | 1,384.5 | 1,864.1 | 2,254.7 | 2,793.7 | 3,275.5 | 2,923.6 | 3,473.2 | 4,242.6 | 4,234.8 | 4,334.2 | 4,255.4 | 4,380.7 |
| Goods, debit (imports)................. | 1a9dx | 4,510.0 | 5,393.5 | 6,338.8 | 7,534.0 | 8,388.8 | 6,430.0 | 7,495.4 | 9,014.8 | 9,161.4 | 9,629.1 | 9,463.1 | 9,320.5 |
| Balance on goods................... | 1a9bx | −3,125.5 | −3,529.4 | −4,084.1 | −4,740.3 | −5,113.3 | −3,506.4 | −4,022.2 | −4,772.2 | −4,926.6 | −5,294.9 | −5,207.7 | −4,939.8 |
| Services, credit (exports)............... | 1b9cx | 1,447.9 | 1,478.0 | 1,516.0 | 1,555.7 | 1,534.3 | 1,292.2 | 1,498.0 | 1,636.0 | 1,866.8 | 2,087.5 | 2,226.3 | 2,329.7 |
| Services, debit (imports)............... | 1b9dx | 1,061.3 | 1,114.7 | 1,231.9 | 1,321.3 | 1,310.7 | 983.9 | 1,099.6 | 1,186.9 | 1,334.8 | 1,469.4 | 1,485.6 | 1,544.4 |
| Balance on Goods & Services....... | 1z9bx | −2,738.9 | −3,166.1 | −3,800.1 | −4,505.9 | −4,889.7 | −3,198.1 | −3,623.9 | −4,323.1 | −4,394.7 | −4,676.8 | −4,467.0 | −4,154.5 |
| Primary income: credit................. | 1c9cx | 143.7 | 174.7 | 234.4 | 308.0 | 179.3 | 77.0 | 56.5 | 61.7 | 68.4 | 70.0 | 68.8 | 80.2 |
| Primary income: debit................. | 1c9dx | 601.6 | 665.0 | 671.9 | 764.3 | 568.3 | 632.9 | 594.7 | 679.9 | 959.7 | 1,062.3 | 1,148.0 | 1,217.4 |
| Balance on gds, serv. & prim. inc. | 1y9bx | −3,196.9 | −3,656.4 | −4,237.6 | −4,962.2 | −5,278.8 | −3,754.0 | −4,162.1 | −4,941.3 | −5,285.9 | −5,669.1 | −5,546.2 | −5,291.6 |
| Secondary income: credit.............. | 1d9ca | 2,615.1 | 3,106.2 | 3,548.8 | 3,841.3 | 3,846.7 | 3,558.9 | 3,700.8 | 3,907.7 | 4,140.1 | 4,150.9 | 4,336.9 | 4,512.7 |
| Secondary income: debit.............. | 1d9da | 60.1 | 71.4 | 76.8 | 95.7 | 100.1 | 117.1 | 71.5 | 78.2 | 133.6 | 67.5 | 102.6 | 141.1 |
| B. Capital Account*.................... | 209ba | 100.3 | 93.6 | 96.8 | 152.8 | 79.8 | 131.2 | 232.0 | 266.4 | 201.2 | 101.1 | 63.6 | 66.0 |
| Capital account: credit............. | 209ca | 100.8 | 94.0 | 97.3 | 153.8 | 80.6 | 132.0 | 233.0 | 267.1 | 201.2 | 101.1 | 63.6 | 66.0 |
| Capital account: debit.................. | 209da | .5 | .4 | .5 | 1.0 | .8 | .8 | 1.0 | .7 | .... | .... | .... | .... |
| Balance on current & capital acct. | 129ba | −541.6 | −528.0 | −668.8 | −1,063.8 | −1,452.4 | −181.0 | −300.8 | −845.4 | −1,078.3 | −1,484.6 | −1,248.4 | −854.1 |
| C. Financial Account*.................... | 309na | −123.0 | −786.7 | −1,199.9 | −559.7 | −1,621.8 | 88.1 | 33.5 | −654.7 | −2,030.7 | −1,020.0 | −702.2 | −1,097.1 |
| Direct investment: assets............... | 3a9aa | −2.8 | 112.9 | −26.3 | 95.2 | 79.4 | 3.0 | 112.4 | −95.9 | −35.9 | 66.1 | 198.2 | 89.7 |
| Equity & investment fund shares.. | 3aaaa | −3.6 | 14.3 | −1.1 | −3.5 | 14.5 | .1 | 7.7 | −1.7 | .9 | .6 | −11.2 | 1.6 |
| Debt instruments...................... | 3abaa | .8 | 98.6 | −25.2 | 98.7 | 65.0 | 2.9 | 104.7 | −94.2 | −36.8 | 65.4 | 209.4 | 88.1 |
| Direct investment: liabilities.......... | 3a9la | 363.3 | 511.1 | 241.1 | 1,550.5 | 903.1 | 368.7 | −113.2 | 122.5 | 447.7 | 242.3 | 509.3 | 518.5 |
| Equity & investment fund shares . | 3aala | 406.9 | 512.1 | 226.9 | 1,447.3 | 538.1 | 241.1 | 281.8 | 169.0 | 533.0 | 148.3 | 374.9 | 321.8 |
| Debt instruments...................... | 3abla | −43.7 | −1.0 | 14.2 | 103.2 | 365.0 | 127.6 | −395.0 | −46.5 | −85.3 | 94.0 | 134.3 | 196.7 |
| Portfolio investment: assets .......... | 3b9aa | 124.8 | −38.7 | −49.7 | 103.4 | −195.7 | −350.2 | 118.2 | −97.6 | −34.3 | −21.3 | 72.1 | −18.2 |
| Equity & investment fund shares | 3baaa | .... | −48.6 | −56.3 | −65.9 | 196.5 | −349.0 | −3.8 | 4.6 | −7.4 | .2 | .1 | 1.5 |
| Debt securities........................ | 3bbaa | 124.8 | 9.9 | 6.6 | 169.3 | −392.2 | −1.2 | 122.0 | −102.2 | −26.9 | −21.5 | 72.0 | −19.7 |
| Portfolio investment: liabilities....... | 3b9la | 181.9 | 86.4 | 715.1 | −63.4 | −65.1 | 396.9 | −3.2 | 1.0 | 836.3 | −7.8 | 861.3 | .9 |
| Equity & investment fund shares . | 3bala | .... | .... | .... | .... | .... | .... | .... | .... | .... | .... | .... | .... |
| Debt securities........................ | 3bbla | 181.9 | 86.4 | 715.1 | −63.4 | −65.1 | 396.9 | −3.2 | 1.0 | 836.3 | −7.8 | 861.3 | .9 |
| Fin. der.& empl.stk.ops.(ESOs): net. | 3c9na | .... | .... | .... | .... | .... | .... | .... | .... | .... | .... | .... | .... |
| Fin. der. & ESOs.: assets.............. | 3c9aa | .... | .... | .... | .... | .... | .... | .... | .... | .... | .... | .... | .... |
| Fin. der. & ESOs.: liabilities.......... | 3c9la | .... | .... | .... | .... | .... | .... | .... | .... | .... | .... | .... | .... |
| Other investment: assets............... | 3d9aa | 159.8 | 246.7 | −72.7 | 472.5 | −25.7 | 646.1 | −106.5 | 98.9 | 91.7 | −86.4 | 139.6 | −248.9 |
| Other equity............................. | 3daaa | .... | .... | .... | .... | .... | .... | .... | .... | .... | .... | .... | .... |
| Debt instruments...................... | 3dzaa | 159.8 | 246.7 | −72.7 | 472.5 | −25.7 | 646.1 | −106.5 | 98.9 | 91.7 | −86.4 | 139.6 | −248.9 |
| Other investment: liabilities............ | 3d9la | −140.4 | 510.0 | 95.0 | −256.4 | 641.8 | −554.8 | 207.0 | 436.6 | 768.3 | 743.8 | −258.5 | 400.4 |
| Other equity............................. | 3dala | .... | .... | .... | .... | .... | .... | .... | .... | .... | .... | .... | .... |
| Debt instruments...................... | 3dzla | −140.4 | 510.0 | 95.0 | −256.4 | 641.8 | −554.8 | 207.0 | 436.6 | 768.3 | 743.8 | −258.5 | 400.4 |
| Curr.+ cap.− finan. acct. balance.... | 4y9na | −418.6 | 258.7 | 531.2 | −504.1 | 169.4 | −269.0 | −334.3 | −190.6 | 952.5 | −464.6 | −546.2 | 243.1 |
| D. Net Errors and Omissions............ | 409na | 366.1 | −449.0 | −484.5 | 783.1 | 164.1 | 693.2 | 36.9 | −223.5 | −301.0 | 137.9 | 513.4 | −130.0 |
| E. Reserves and Related Items.......... | 4z9na | −52.5 | −190.3 | 46.6 | 279.0 | 333.5 | 424.2 | −297.4 | −414.1 | 651.5 | −326.7 | −32.8 | 113.0 |
| Reserve assets........................ | 3e9aa | −52.5 | −190.3 | 46.6 | 279.0 | 333.5 | 424.2 | −297.4 | −414.1 | 651.5 | −326.7 | −32.8 | 113.0 |
| Credit and loans from the IMF........ | 3dcla | — | — | — | — | — | — | — | — | — | — | — | — |
| Exceptional financing................... | 409la | .... | .... | .... | .... | .... | .... | .... | .... | .... | .... | .... | .... |

*Excludes components in group E

| | | 2004 | 2005 | 2006 | 2007 | 2008 | 2009 | 2010 | 2011 | 2012 | 2013 | 2014 | 2015 |
|---|---|---|---|---|---|---|---|---|---|---|---|---|---|
| **International Investment Position** | | | | | | *Millions of US Dollars* | | | | | | | |
| Assets | 809aa | 4,990.5 | 5,425.7 | 5,705.5 | 6,659.2 | 6,780.2 | 7,705.4 | 7,723.3 | 7,303.5 | 8,001.6 | 7,531.7 | 7,883.8 | 8,028.0 |
| Direct investment | 8a9aa | 93.0 | 310.1 | 283.7 | 379.1 | 458.9 | 585.7 | 721.9 | 625.9 | 590.5 | 656.6 | 854.8 | 951.8 |
| Equity & investment fund shares.. | 8aaaa | 19.0 | 33.6 | 32.4 | 29.0 | 43.8 | 15.3 | 23.0 | 21.3 | 22.2 | 22.9 | 11.7 | 13.3 |
| Debt instruments | 8abaa | 73.9 | 276.6 | 251.3 | 350.1 | 415.1 | 570.4 | 698.8 | 604.6 | 568.3 | 633.7 | 843.1 | 938.5 |
| Portfolio investment | 8b9aa | 1,069.2 | 753.5 | 691.2 | 783.7 | 589.8 | 237.3 | 287.8 | 190.2 | 173.9 | 152.6 | 224.7 | 206.6 |
| Equity & investment fund shares.. | 8baaa | 257.9 | 75.9 | 76.3 | 98.3 | 103.6 | 123.8 | 52.2 | 56.8 | 49.8 | 50.1 | 50.1 | 51.7 |
| Debt securities | 8bbaa | 811.3 | 677.6 | 614.9 | 685.5 | 486.3 | 113.5 | 235.5 | 133.3 | 124.1 | 102.6 | 174.6 | 154.9 |
| Fin. der.(oth.than reserves) & ESOs | 8c9aa | .... | .... | .... | .... | .... | .... | .... | .... | .... | .... | .... | .... |
| Other investment | 8d9aa | 1,935.4 | 2,529.0 | 2,822.3 | 3,297.6 | 3,186.5 | 3,896.0 | 3,831.9 | 3,984.7 | 4,062.4 | 3,977.5 | 4,111.0 | 4,083.1 |
| Other equity | 8daaa | .... | .... | .... | .... | .... | .... | .... | .... | .... | .... | .... | .... |
| Debt instruments | 8dzaa | 1,935.4 | 2,529.0 | 2,822.3 | 3,297.6 | 3,186.5 | 3,896.0 | 3,831.9 | 3,984.7 | 4,062.4 | 3,977.5 | 4,111.0 | 4,083.1 |
| Reserve assets | 8e9aa | 1,892.9 | 1,833.0 | 1,908.2 | 2,198.7 | 2,545.0 | 2,986.3 | 2,881.8 | 2,502.7 | 3,174.7 | 2,744.9 | 2,693.3 | 2,786.6 |
| Liabilities | 809la | 11,905.8 | 13,177.5 | 14,461.8 | 15,682.3 | 16,257.8 | 17,807.5 | 18,653.8 | 19,214.9 | 21,756.6 | 22,192.4 | 23,609.4 | 23,933.6 |
| Direct investment | 8a9la | 3,655.5 | 4,166.5 | 4,407.8 | 5,958.4 | 6,862.4 | 8,275.6 | 8,004.5 | 8,119.8 | 8,789.1 | 8,918.4 | 9,392.0 | 10,108.0 |
| Equity & investment fund shares.. | 8aala | 2,996.1 | 3,508.1 | 3,735.0 | 5,182.5 | 5,721.5 | 6,850.9 | 7,036.2 | 7,198.0 | 7,956.3 | 8,103.9 | 8,443.6 | 8,907.2 |
| Debt instruments | 8abla | 659.4 | 658.4 | 672.8 | 775.9 | 1,140.9 | 1,424.7 | 968.3 | 921.8 | 832.8 | 814.5 | 948.4 | 1,200.8 |
| Portfolio investment | 8b9la | 1,569.6 | 1,786.0 | 2,719.3 | 2,618.7 | 1,572.6 | 2,236.6 | 2,850.3 | 2,797.7 | 3,943.4 | 3,550.0 | 4,818.3 | 4,028.5 |
| Equity & investment fund shares.. | 8bala | .... | .... | .... | .... | .... | .... | .... | .... | .... | .... | .... | .... |
| Debt securities | 8bbla | 1,569.6 | 1,786.0 | 2,719.3 | 2,618.7 | 1,572.6 | 2,236.6 | 2,850.3 | 2,797.7 | 3,943.4 | 3,550.0 | 4,818.3 | 4,028.5 |
| Fin. der.(oth.than reserves) & ESOs | 8c9la | .... | .... | .... | .... | .... | .... | .... | .... | .... | .... | .... | .... |
| Other investment | 8d9la | 6,680.7 | 7,225.0 | 7,334.7 | 7,105.2 | 7,822.8 | 7,295.3 | 7,798.9 | 8,297.3 | 9,024.1 | 9,724.0 | 9,399.0 | 9,797.1 |
| Other equity | 8dala | .... | .... | .... | .... | .... | .... | .... | .... | .... | .... | .... | .... |
| Debt instruments | 8dzla | 6,680.7 | 7,225.0 | 7,334.7 | 7,105.2 | 7,822.8 | 7,295.3 | 7,798.9 | 8,297.3 | 9,024.1 | 9,724.0 | 9,399.0 | 9,797.1 |
| **Government Finance** | | | | | | | | | | | | | |
| **Cash Flow Statement** | | | | | | | | | | | | | |
| **Budgetary Central Government** | | | | | | *Millions of US Dollars:  Fiscal Year Ends December 31* | | | | | | | |
| Cash Receipts:Operating Activities... | c1 | 2,095.9 | 2,307.5 | 2,694.6 | 2,972.8 | 3,243.0 | 2,857.4 | 3,213.3 | 3,557.5 | 3,758.0 | 4,001.5 | .... | .... |
| Taxes | c11 | .... | .... | .... | .... | .... | .... | .... | .... | .... | .... | .... | .... |
| Social Contributions | c12 | .... | .... | .... | .... | .... | .... | .... | .... | .... | .... | .... | .... |
| Grants | c13 | .... | .... | 38.6 | 55.6 | 52.2 | 83.5 | 142.8 | 213.9 | 169.7 | 51.7 | .... | .... |
| Other Receipts | c14 | .... | .... | .... | .... | .... | .... | .... | .... | .... | .... | .... | .... |
| Cash Payments:Operating Activities. | c2 | 2,273.1 | 2,484.6 | 2,823.2 | 3,016.0 | 3,375.9 | 3,629.2 | 3,794.3 | 4,081.7 | 4,164.8 | 4,319.3 | .... | .... |
| Compensation of Employees | c21 | .... | .... | .... | .... | .... | .... | .... | .... | .... | .... | .... | .... |
| Purchases of Goods & Services | c22 | .... | .... | .... | .... | .... | .... | .... | .... | .... | .... | .... | .... |
| Interest | c24 | .... | .... | .... | .... | .... | .... | .... | .... | .... | .... | .... | .... |
| Subsidies | c25 | .... | .... | .... | .... | .... | .... | .... | .... | .... | .... | .... | .... |
| Grants | c26 | .... | .... | .... | .... | .... | .... | .... | .... | .... | .... | .... | .... |
| Social Benefits | c27 | .... | .... | .... | .... | .... | .... | .... | .... | .... | .... | .... | .... |
| Other Payments | c28 | .... | .... | .... | .... | .... | .... | .... | .... | .... | .... | .... | .... |
| Net Cash Inflow:Operating Act.[1-2] | ccio | .... | .... | .... | .... | .... | .... | .... | .... | .... | .... | .... | .... |
| Net Cash Outflow:Invest. in NFA | c31 | .... | .... | .... | .... | .... | .... | .... | .... | .... | .... | .... | .... |
| Purchases of Nonfinancial Assets... | c31.1 | .... | .... | .... | .... | .... | .... | .... | .... | .... | .... | .... | .... |
| Sales of Nonfinancial Assets | c31.2 | .... | .... | .... | .... | .... | .... | .... | .... | .... | .... | .... | .... |
| Cash Surplus/Deficit [1-2-31=1-2M] | ccsd | −177.3 | −177.1 | −128.6 | −43.2 | −132.9 | −771.8 | −581.0 | −524.2 | −406.8 | −317.8 | .... | .... |
| Net Acq. Fin. Assets, excl. Cash | c32x | .... | .... | .... | .... | .... | .... | .... | .... | .... | .... | .... | .... |
| Domestic | c321x | .... | .... | .... | .... | .... | .... | .... | .... | .... | .... | .... | .... |
| Foreign | c322x | .... | .... | .... | .... | .... | .... | .... | .... | .... | .... | .... | .... |
| Net Incurrence of Liabilities | c33 | 177.3 | 177.1 | 128.6 | 43.0 | 132.9 | 771.8 | 581.0 | 524.2 | 406.8 | 317.8 | .... | .... |
| Domestic | c331 | −72.4 | −150.8 | −301.4 | 191.1 | 75.3 | 14.8 | 298.9 | 377.4 | −515.1 | 355.7 | .... | .... |
| Foreign | c332 | 249.6 | 327.9 | 430.0 | −148.1 | 57.7 | 757.0 | 282.2 | 146.8 | 921.9 | −37.8 | .... | .... |
| Net Cash Inflow, Fin.Act.[-32x+33].. | cnfb | .... | .... | .... | .... | .... | .... | .... | .... | .... | .... | .... | .... |
| Net Change in Stock of Cash | cncb | .... | .... | .... | .... | .... | .... | .... | .... | .... | .... | .... | .... |
| Stat. Discrep. [32X-33+NCB-CSD] | ccsdz | .... | .... | .... | .... | .... | .... | .... | .... | .... | .... | .... | .... |
| Memo Item:Cash Expenditure[2+31] | c2m | .... | .... | .... | .... | .... | .... | .... | .... | .... | .... | .... | .... |
| Memo Item: Gross Debt | c63 | 6,011.6 | 6,417.1 | 6,993.3 | 7,021.4 | 7,379.7 | 8,867.2 | 9,115.4 | 9,658.9 | 10,879.9 | 10,773.0 | .... | .... |
| **National Accounts** | | | | | | *Millions of US Dollars* | | | | | | | |
| Househ.Cons.Expend.,incl.NPISHs.... | 96f.d | 14,453.1 | 15,870.6 | 17,406.0 | 19,465.3 | 21,096.8 | 18,887.3 | 19,896.9 | 21,580.8 | 22,166.6 | 22,568.9 | 23,219.9 | 23,315.5 |
| Government Consumption Expend... | 91f.d | 1,524.5 | 1,640.2 | 1,822.9 | 1,866.1 | 1,966.3 | 2,196.1 | 2,292.8 | 2,558.2 | 2,673.9 | 2,816.0 | 2,886.9 | 3,074.4 |
| Gross Fixed Capital Formation | 93e.d | 2,473.8 | 2,610.9 | 3,011.9 | 3,279.4 | 3,257.7 | 2,775.6 | 2,852.5 | 3,323.2 | 3,367.8 | 3,642.8 | 3,414.4 | 3,614.7 |
| Changes in Inventories | 93i.d | 85.9 | 138.2 | 110.0 | — | — | — | — | — | — | — | — | — |
| Exports of Goods and Services | 90c.d | 4,259.0 | 4,382.8 | 4,764.2 | 5,203.7 | 5,761.0 | 4,792.7 | 5,552.6 | 6,474.3 | 6,101.6 | 6,421.7 | 6,481.7 | 6,710.4 |
| Imports of Goods and Services (-) | 98c.d | 6,998.1 | 7,548.9 | 8,564.3 | 9,709.6 | 10,650.9 | 7,990.6 | 9,176.5 | 10,797.4 | 10,496.2 | 11,098.6 | 10,948.7 | 10,864.9 |
| Gross Domestic Product (GDP) | 99b.d | 15,798.3 | 17,093.8 | 18,550.7 | 20,104.9 | 21,431.0 | 20,661.0 | 21,418.3 | 23,139.0 | 23,813.6 | 24,350.9 | 25,054.2 | 25,850.2 |
| Net Primary Income from Abroad... | 98.nd | −457.9 | −490.3 | −437.5 | −456.3 | −389.0 | −556.0 | −538.2 | −618.2 | −891.3 | −992.3 | −1,074.0 | −1,137.2 |
| Gross National Income (GNI) | 99a.d | 15,340.4 | 16,603.5 | 18,113.2 | 19,648.6 | 21,042.0 | 20,105.0 | 20,880.1 | 22,520.9 | 22,922.3 | 23,358.7 | 23,980.2 | 24,713.1 |
| GDP Volume 1990 Prices | 99bpd | 8,167.7 | 8,458.7 | 8,789.6 | 9,127.1 | 9,243.4 | 8,953.8 | 9,076.0 | 9,277.2 | 9,451.7 | 9,626.3 | 9,763.5 | 10,003.2 |
| GDP Volume (2010=100) | 99bvp | 90.0 | 93.2 | 96.8 | 100.6 | 101.8 | 98.7 | 100.0 | 102.2 | 104.1 | 106.1 | 107.6 | 110.2 |
| GDP Deflator (2010=100) | 99bip | 82.0 | 85.6 | 89.4 | 93.3 | 98.2 | 97.8 | 100.0 | 105.7 | 106.8 | 107.2 | 108.7 | 109.5 |
| | | | | | | *Millions: Midyear Estimates* | | | | | | | |
| **Population** | 99z | 5.93 | 5.95 | 5.97 | 5.99 | 6.00 | 6.02 | 6.04 | 6.06 | 6.07 | 6.09 | 6.11 | 6.13 |

| | | 2004 | 2005 | 2006 | 2007 | 2008 | 2009 | 2010 | 2011 | 2012 | 2013 | 2014 | 2015 |
|---|---|---|---|---|---|---|---|---|---|---|---|---|---|
| **Exchange Rates** | | \multicolumn{12}{c}{*CFA Francs per SDR: End of Period*} | | | | | | | | | | | |
| Official Rate............................... | aa | 747.90 | 794.73 | 749.30 | 704.15 | 725.98 | 713.83 | 756.02 | 778.32 | 764.10 | 732.49 | 782.77 | 834.92 |
| | | \multicolumn{12}{c}{*CFA Francs per US Dollar: End of Period(ae)Period Average(rf)*} | | | | | | | | | | | |
| Official Rate............................... | ae | 481.58 | 556.04 | 498.07 | 445.59 | 471.34 | 455.34 | 490.91 | 506.96 | 497.16 | 475.64 | 540.28 | 602.51 |
| Official Rate............................... | rf | 528.28 | 527.47 | 522.89 | 479.27 | 447.81 | 472.19 | 495.28 | 471.87 | 510.53 | 494.04 | 494.41 | 591.45 |
| | | \multicolumn{12}{c}{*Index Numbers (2010=100): Period Averages*} | | | | | | | | | | | |
| Nominal Effective Exchange Rate..... | nec | 96.32 | 96.08 | 95.80 | 100.24 | 106.03 | 104.68 | 100.00 | 101.96 | 96.93 | 99.43 | 99.24 | 90.20 |
| CPI-Based Real Effect. Ex. Rate........ | rec | 80.86 | 82.98 | 84.21 | 88.29 | 95.86 | 99.03 | 100.00 | 103.58 | 99.65 | 103.83 | 105.26 | 98.17 |
| **Fund Position** | | \multicolumn{12}{c}{*Millions of SDRs: End of Period*} | | | | | | | | | | | |
| Quota................................... | 2f.s | 32.60 | 32.60 | 32.60 | 32.60 | 32.60 | 32.60 | 32.60 | 52.30 | 52.30 | 52.30 | 52.30 | 52.30 |
| SDR Holdings.............................. | 1b.s | .44 | .44 | .44 | .44 | .46 | 25.94 | 25.94 | 21.01 | 21.16 | 21.16 | 21.15 | 21.15 |
| Reserve Position in the Fund........... | 1c.s | — | — | — | — | — | — | — | 4.93 | 4.93 | 4.93 | 4.93 | 4.93 |
| Total Fund Cred.&Loans Outstg....... | 2tl | — | — | — | — | — | — | — | — | — | — | — | — |
| SDR Allocations........................... | 1bd | 5.81 | 5.81 | 5.81 | 5.81 | 5.81 | 31.29 | 31.29 | 31.29 | 31.29 | 31.29 | 31.29 | 31.29 |
| **International Liquidity** | | \multicolumn{12}{c}{*Millions of US Dollars Unless Otherwise Indicated: End of Period*} | | | | | | | | | | | |
| Total Reserves minus Gold.............. | 1l.d | 944.98 | 2,102.49 | 3,066.74 | 3,845.92 | 4,431.19 | 3,251.94 | 2,346.36 | 3,053.84 | 4,396.98 | 4,566.54 | 2,906.84 | 1,205.15 |
| SDR Holdings........................ | 1b.d | .68 | .63 | .66 | .70 | .71 | 40.66 | 39.95 | 32.25 | 32.52 | 32.58 | 30.65 | 29.31 |
| Reserve Position in the Fund.......... | 1c.d | — | — | — | — | — | — | — | 7.56 | 7.57 | 7.58 | 7.14 | 6.82 |
| Foreign Exchange...................... | 1d.d | 944.30 | 2,101.87 | 3,066.08 | 3,845.22 | 4,430.48 | 3,211.27 | 2,306.41 | 3,014.03 | 4,356.89 | 4,526.37 | 2,869.06 | 1,169.02 |
| Gold (Million Fine Troy Ounces)....... | 1ad | .... | .... | .... | .... | .... | .... | .... | .... | .... | .... | .... | .... |
| Gold (National Valuation).............. | 1and | — | — | — | — | — | — | — | .... | .... | .... | .... | .... |
| Central Bank: Other Assets............. | 3..d | — | — | — | — | — | — | — | — | — | — | — | — |
| Central Bank: Other Liabs............... | 4..d | 1.63 | .99 | .73 | 1.17 | 4.55 | 7.36 | 7.37 | .27 | 20.18 | 34.85 | — | .18 |
| Other Depository Corps.: Assets....... | 7a.d | 109.11 | 154.58 | 139.27 | 311.23 | 421.01 | 359.46 | 202.09 | 260.34 | 384.60 | 669.79 | 330.72 | 318.40 |
| Other Depository Corps.: Liabs......... | 7b.d | 7.82 | 16.52 | 37.07 | 106.47 | 78.63 | 125.69 | 145.68 | 132.84 | 138.79 | 144.86 | 177.00 | 62.46 |
| **Central Bank** | | \multicolumn{12}{c}{*Billions of CFA Francs: End of Period*} | | | | | | | | | | | |
| Net Foreign Assets........................... | 11n | 449.95 | 1,163.90 | 1,522.73 | 1,709.10 | 2,082.09 | 1,455.10 | 1,128.12 | 1,523.69 | 2,152.07 | 2,132.54 | 1,546.02 | 699.89 |
| Claims on Nonresidents................ | 11 | 455.08 | 1,169.07 | 1,527.45 | 1,713.71 | 2,088.45 | 1,480.78 | 1,155.39 | 1,548.18 | 2,186.02 | 2,172.03 | 1,570.52 | 726.12 |
| Liabilities to Nonresidents............ | 16c | 5.13 | 5.17 | 4.72 | 4.61 | 6.37 | 25.69 | 27.27 | 24.49 | 33.94 | 39.50 | 24.49 | 26.23 |
| Claims on Other Depository Corps.... | 12e | — | — | — | — | — | — | — | — | — | — | 30.00 | 90.00 |
| Net Claims on Central Government.. | 12an | −301.98 | −898.79 | −1,242.63 | −1,401.23 | −1,807.37 | −974.52 | −339.79 | −808.64 | −709.82 | −884.50 | −120.10 | 194.05 |
| Claims on Central Government...... | 12a | .79 | .27 | — | — | — | — | — | .14 | .28 | .20 | 369.58 | 517.14 |
| Liabilities to Central Government... | 16d | 302.77 | 899.06 | 1,242.63 | 1,401.23 | 1,807.37 | 974.52 | 339.79 | 808.78 | 710.10 | 884.70 | 489.67 | 323.09 |
| Claims on Other Sectors................ | 12s | — | — | — | — | .45 | .66 | .92 | 1.29 | 1.68 | 2.28 | 2.56 | 2.85 |
| Claims on Other Financial Corps.... | 12g | — | — | — | — | — | — | — | — | — | — | — | — |
| Claims on State & Local Govts....... | 12b | — | — | — | — | — | — | — | — | — | — | — | — |
| Claims on Public Nonfin. Corps...... | 12c | — | — | — | — | — | — | — | — | — | — | — | — |
| Claims on Private Sector................ | 12d | — | — | — | — | .45 | .66 | .92 | 1.29 | 1.68 | 2.28 | 2.56 | 2.85 |
| Monetary Base............................. | 14 | 150.88 | 267.65 | 282.61 | 359.03 | 323.52 | 501.16 | 597.43 | 695.33 | 1,435.78 | 1,254.28 | 1,456.74 | 979.25 |
| Currency in Circulation................. | 14a | 53.05 | 66.85 | 79.25 | 93.99 | 104.70 | 143.65 | 182.94 | 250.57 | 278.79 | 310.15 | 320.07 | 256.37 |
| Liabs. to Other Depository Corps.... | 14c | 97.74 | 200.69 | 202.66 | 264.25 | 218.11 | 356.80 | 413.79 | 444.05 | 1,151.46 | 943.42 | 1,135.96 | 722.17 |
| Liabilities to Other Sectors........... | 14d | .09 | .12 | .70 | .79 | .71 | .71 | .71 | .71 | 5.52 | .71 | .71 | .71 |
| Other Liabs. to Other Dep. Corps..... | 14n | — | — | — | — | — | — | — | — | — | — | — | — |
| Dep. & Sec. Excl. f/Monetary Base.... | 14o | — | — | — | — | — | — | — | — | — | — | — | — |
| Deposits Included in Broad Money. | 15 | — | — | — | — | — | — | — | — | — | — | — | — |
| Sec.Ot.th.Shares Incl.in Brd. Money | 16a | — | — | — | — | — | — | — | — | — | — | — | — |
| Deposits Excl. from Broad Money.. | 16b | — | — | — | — | — | — | — | — | — | — | — | — |
| Sec.Ot.th.Shares Excl.f/Brd.Money.. | 16s | — | — | — | — | — | — | — | — | — | — | — | — |
| Loans...................................... | 16l | — | — | — | — | — | — | — | — | — | — | — | — |
| Financial Derivatives..................... | 16m | — | — | — | — | — | — | — | — | — | — | — | — |
| Shares and Other Equity................. | 17a | −1.16 | −1.21 | −.58 | −1.75 | −49.49 | −22.73 | −3.05 | −5.63 | −3.84 | −3.49 | .59 | 10.05 |
| Other Items (Net).......................... | 17r | −1.75 | −1.34 | −1.94 | −49.41 | 1.15 | 2.81 | 194.85 | 26.64 | 12.00 | −.47 | 1.16 | −2.51 |
| Memo Item: | | | | | | | | | | | | | |
| Total Assets...................................... | 10ra | 462.84 | 1,176.02 | 1,534.18 | 1,761.83 | 2,095.31 | 1,488.70 | 1,167.58 | 1,555.47 | 2,193.79 | 2,182.52 | 1,982.18 | 1,346.19 |

|  |  | 2004 | 2005 | 2006 | 2007 | 2008 | 2009 | 2010 | 2011 | 2012 | 2013 | 2014 | 2015 |
|---|---|---|---|---|---|---|---|---|---|---|---|---|---|
| **Other Depository Corporations** | | *Billions of CFA Francs: End of Period* | | | | | | | | | | | |
| Net Foreign Assets............................ | 21n | 48.78 | 76.77 | 50.90 | 91.24 | 161.38 | 106.45 | 27.69 | 64.64 | 122.21 | 249.68 | 83.05 | 154.21 |
| Claims on Nonresidents................. | 21 | 52.55 | 85.95 | 69.37 | 138.68 | 198.44 | 163.68 | 99.21 | 131.98 | 191.21 | 318.58 | 178.68 | 191.84 |
| Liabilities to Nonresidents............. | 26c | 3.76 | 9.19 | 18.46 | 47.44 | 37.06 | 57.23 | 71.52 | 67.34 | 69.00 | 68.90 | 95.63 | 37.63 |
| Claims on Central Bank................... | 20 | 103.40 | 209.61 | 224.04 | 275.68 | 232.80 | 366.11 | 576.26 | 494.32 | 1,181.66 | 979.14 | 1,094.35 | 733.30 |
| Currency......................................... | 20a | 7.32 | 9.19 | 11.04 | 13.05 | 14.62 | 15.59 | 14.32 | 25.49 | 27.69 | 38.04 | 39.67 | 33.94 |
| Reserve Deposits and Securities..... | 20b | 96.08 | 200.43 | 213.00 | 262.62 | 218.18 | 350.52 | 561.93 | 468.83 | 1,153.97 | 941.10 | 1,054.68 | 699.36 |
| Other Claims.................................. | 20n | — | — | — | — | — | — | — | — | — | — | — | — |
| Net Claims on Central Government.. | 22an | −29.64 | −128.27 | −111.03 | −122.49 | −263.73 | −156.53 | −156.93 | −213.34 | −225.04 | −219.14 | −498.47 | −369.70 |
| Claims on Central Government...... | 22a | 5.78 | 3.53 | 3.73 | 1.74 | 2.50 | 2.12 | 2.68 | 5.72 | 5.24 | 6.06 | 10.02 | 28.52 |
| Liabilities to Central Government... | 26d | 35.42 | 131.80 | 114.76 | 124.23 | 266.22 | 158.65 | 159.60 | 219.06 | 230.27 | 225.20 | 508.49 | 398.22 |
| Claims on Other Sectors................. | 22s | 64.19 | 94.59 | 130.10 | 184.33 | 384.93 | 440.12 | 582.01 | 737.89 | 620.77 | 831.34 | 975.90 | 1,110.61 |
| Claims on Other Financial Corps.... | 22g | — | .02 | — | — | .25 | 6.18 | 19.85 | 7.82 | 3.17 | 2.60 | 1.50 | .97 |
| Claims on State & Local Govts...... | 22b | — | — | — | — | — | — | — | — | — | — | — | — |
| Claims on Public Nonfin. Corps...... | 22c | .76 | 1.44 | 4.95 | 8.75 | 22.16 | 21.66 | 23.96 | 26.51 | 10.28 | 13.29 | 8.65 | 7.70 |
| Claims on Private Sector............... | 22d | 63.43 | 93.13 | 125.15 | 175.58 | 362.52 | 412.28 | 538.20 | 703.56 | 607.32 | 815.44 | 965.74 | 1,101.94 |
| Liabilities to Central Bank............... | 26g | — | — | — | — | — | — | — | — | — | — | 30.00 | 90.00 |
| Transf.Dep.Included in Broad Money | 24 | 119.68 | 174.25 | 185.70 | 278.79 | 418.91 | 539.63 | 722.47 | 735.06 | 1,223.47 | 1,322.33 | 1,050.47 | 914.33 |
| Other Dep.Included in Broad Money. | 25 | 36.75 | 44.92 | 57.63 | 77.78 | 63.06 | 75.79 | 101.78 | 109.03 | 208.52 | 216.84 | 225.42 | 249.37 |
| Sec.Ot.th.Shares Incl.in Brd.Money.. | 26a | — | — | — | — | — | — | — | — | — | — | — | — |
| Deposits Excl. from Broad Money..... | 26b | .54 | 2.36 | 1.82 | 1.44 | 1.38 | 1.11 | 2.04 | 2.66 | 4.97 | 1.10 | 1.40 | .72 |
| Sec.Ot.th.Shares Excl.f/Brd.Money.... | 26s | — | — | — | — | — | — | — | — | — | — | — | — |
| Loans............................................. | 26l | — | — | — | — | — | — | — | — | — | — | — | — |
| Financial Derivatives....................... | 26m | — | — | — | — | — | — | — | — | — | — | — | — |
| Insurance Technical Reserves........... | 26r | — | — | — | — | — | — | — | — | — | — | — | — |
| Shares and Other Equity.................. | 27a | 17.61 | 20.27 | 34.47 | 39.15 | 52.12 | 59.29 | 71.26 | 95.49 | 99.86 | 112.38 | 121.40 | 122.35 |
| Other Items (Net)............................. | 27r | 12.15 | 10.90 | 14.39 | 31.60 | −20.09 | 80.33 | 131.48 | 141.28 | 162.78 | 188.37 | 226.13 | 251.65 |
| Memo Item: | | | | | | | | | | | | | |
| Total Assets...................................... | 20ra | 237.39 | 407.39 | 445.77 | 620.65 | 846.45 | 1,006.52 | 1,303.20 | 1,421.56 | 2,061.48 | 2,192.32 | 2,318.45 | 2,127.05 |
| **Depository Corporations** | | *Billions of CFA Francs: End of Period* | | | | | | | | | | | |
| Net Foreign Assets........................... | 31n | 498.73 | 1,240.66 | 1,573.63 | 1,800.34 | 2,243.46 | 1,561.54 | 1,155.81 | 1,588.33 | 2,274.28 | 2,382.22 | 1,629.07 | 854.10 |
| Claims on Nonresidents................. | 31 | 507.63 | 1,255.02 | 1,596.81 | 1,852.39 | 2,286.89 | 1,644.46 | 1,254.60 | 1,680.16 | 2,377.22 | 2,490.61 | 1,749.20 | 917.96 |
| Liabilities to Nonresidents............. | 36c | 8.90 | 14.36 | 23.18 | 52.06 | 43.42 | 82.92 | 98.79 | 91.84 | 102.95 | 108.40 | 120.12 | 63.86 |
| Domestic Claims............................. | 32 | −267.43 | −932.48 | −1,223.56 | −1,339.39 | −1,685.72 | −690.28 | 86.20 | −282.81 | −312.40 | −270.03 | 359.90 | 937.81 |
| Net Claims on Central Government | 32an | −331.62 | −1,027.07 | −1,353.66 | −1,523.72 | −2,071.10 | −1,131.06 | −496.72 | −1,021.99 | −934.85 | −1,103.65 | −618.56 | −175.65 |
| Claims on Central Government.... | 32a | 6.57 | 3.79 | 3.73 | 1.74 | 2.50 | 2.12 | 2.68 | 5.86 | 5.52 | 6.26 | 379.60 | 545.66 |
| Liabilities to Central Government. | 36d | 338.19 | 1,030.86 | 1,357.39 | 1,525.46 | 2,073.59 | 1,133.17 | 499.39 | 1,027.85 | 940.37 | 1,109.90 | 998.16 | 721.31 |
| Claims on Other Sectors................. | 32s | 64.19 | 94.59 | 130.10 | 184.33 | 385.38 | 440.78 | 582.92 | 739.18 | 622.45 | 833.61 | 978.46 | 1,113.46 |
| Claims on Other Financial Corps.. | 32g | — | .02 | — | — | .25 | 6.18 | 19.85 | 7.82 | 3.17 | 2.60 | 1.50 | .97 |
| Claims on State & Local Govts..... | 32b | — | — | — | — | — | — | — | — | — | — | — | — |
| Claims on Public Nonfin. Corps.... | 32c | .76 | 1.44 | 4.95 | 8.75 | 22.16 | 21.66 | 23.96 | 26.51 | 10.28 | 13.29 | 8.65 | 7.70 |
| Claims on Private Sector............. | 32d | 63.43 | 93.13 | 125.15 | 175.58 | 362.97 | 412.94 | 539.11 | 704.85 | 609.00 | 817.72 | 968.30 | 1,104.79 |
| Broad Money Liabilities................... | 35l | 202.25 | 276.95 | 312.24 | 438.29 | 572.76 | 744.18 | 993.56 | 1,069.87 | 1,688.62 | 1,811.99 | 1,557.01 | 1,386.85 |
| Currency Outside Depository Corps | 34a | 45.73 | 57.66 | 68.21 | 80.93 | 90.08 | 128.06 | 168.61 | 225.08 | 251.11 | 272.11 | 280.40 | 222.43 |
| Transferable Deposits.................... | 34 | 119.77 | 174.37 | 186.40 | 279.58 | 419.62 | 540.33 | 723.17 | 735.77 | 1,228.99 | 1,323.04 | 1,051.18 | 915.04 |
| Other Deposits.............................. | 35 | 36.75 | 44.92 | 57.63 | 77.78 | 63.06 | 75.79 | 101.78 | 109.03 | 208.52 | 216.84 | 225.42 | 249.37 |
| Securities Other than Shares.......... | 36a | — | — | — | — | — | — | — | — | — | — | — | — |
| Deposits Excl. from Broad Money..... | 36b | .54 | 2.36 | 1.82 | 1.44 | 1.38 | 1.11 | 2.04 | 2.66 | 4.97 | 1.10 | 1.40 | .72 |
| Sec.Ot.th.Shares Excl.f/Brd.Money.... | 36s | — | — | — | — | — | — | — | — | — | — | — | — |
| Loans............................................. | 36l | — | — | — | — | — | — | — | — | — | — | — | — |
| Financial Derivatives....................... | 36m | — | — | — | — | — | — | — | — | — | — | — | — |
| Insurance Technical Reserves........... | 36r | — | — | — | — | — | — | — | — | — | — | — | — |
| Shares and Other Equity.................. | 37a | 16.45 | 19.06 | 33.89 | 37.40 | 2.63 | 36.56 | 68.21 | 89.86 | 96.03 | 108.89 | 121.99 | 132.40 |
| Other Items (Net)............................. | 37r | 12.06 | 9.81 | 2.12 | −16.19 | −19.02 | 89.42 | 178.20 | 143.13 | 172.26 | 190.21 | 308.57 | 271.95 |
| Broad Money Liabs., Seasonally Adj. | 35l.b | 194.20 | 266.40 | 303.41 | 434.37 | 571.18 | 740.01 | 965.88 | 1,022.56 | 1,593.07 | 1,709.79 | 1,472.84 | 1,313.48 |
| **Monetary Aggregates** | | *Billions of CFA Francs: End of Period* | | | | | | | | | | | |
| Broad Money.................................... | 59m | 202.25 | 276.95 | 312.24 | 438.29 | 572.76 | 744.18 | 993.56 | 1,069.87 | 1,688.62 | 1,811.99 | 1,557.01 | 1,386.85 |
| o/w:Currency Issued by Cent.Govt | 59m.a | — | — | — | — | — | — | — | — | — | — | — | — |
| o/w: Dep.in Nonfin. Corporations. | 59m.b | — | — | — | — | — | — | — | — | — | — | — | — |
| o/w: Secs. Issued by Central Govt. | 59m.c | — | — | — | — | — | — | — | — | — | — | — | — |
| Money (National Definitions) | | | | | | | | | | | | | |
| M1................................................... | 59ma | 165.50 | 232.03 | 254.62 | 360.52 | 509.70 | 668.40 | 891.79 | 960.84 | 1,480.10 | 1,595.15 | 1,331.59 | 1,137.47 |
| M2................................................... | 59mb | 202.25 | 276.95 | 312.25 | 438.29 | 572.76 | 744.18 | 993.56 | 1,069.87 | 1,688.62 | 1,811.99 | 1,557.01 | 1,386.85 |
| **Interest Rates** | | *Percent Per Annum* | | | | | | | | | | | |
| Discount Rate (End of Period).......... | 60.a | 6.00 | 5.50 | 5.25 | 5.25 | 4.75 | 4.25 | 4.00 | 4.00 | 4.00 | 3.25 | 2.95 | 2.45 |
| Deposit Rate.................................... | 60l | 5.00 | 4.92 | 4.33 | 4.25 | 3.75 | 3.25 | 3.25 | 3.25 | 3.25 | 3.21 | 2.60 | 2.45 |
| **Prices** | | *Index Numbers (2010=100): Period Averages* | | | | | | | | | | | |
| Consumer Prices............................. | 64 | 73.3 | 77.5 | 80.9 | 83.2 | 88.6 | 92.8 | † 100.0 | 102.5 | 103.5 | 104.7 | 109.8 | 122.6 |
| **Intl. Transactions & Positions** | | *Millions of CFA Francs* | | | | | | | | | | | |
| Exports............................................ | 70 | 2,429,499 | 3,726,035 | 4,291,359 | 4,893,314 | 7,120,104 | 4,296,895 | 4,952,770 | .... | .... | .... | .... | .... |
| Imports, c.i.f.................................... | 71 | 576,887 | 690,983 | 1,056,238 | 1,135,862 | 1,750,919 | 2,455,369 | 2,823,079 | .... | .... | .... | .... | .... |

| | | 2004 | 2005 | 2006 | 2007 | 2008 | 2009 | 2010 | 2011 | 2012 | 2013 | 2014 | 2015 |
|---|---|---|---|---|---|---|---|---|---|---|---|---|---|
| **National Accounts** | | | | | | | *Millions of CFA Francs* | | | | | | |
| Househ.Cons.Expend.,incl.NPISHs.... | **96f** | 253,510 | 289,200 | 318,140 | 351,218 | 385,947 | 374,453 | .... | .... | .... | .... | .... | .... |
| Government Consumption Expend... | **91f** | 81,348 | 118,592 | 128,125 | 137,874 | 195,586 | 224,841 | .... | .... | .... | .... | .... | .... |
| Gross Fixed Capital Formation.......... | **93e** | 659,582 | 824,373 | 1,203,670 | 1,593,031 | 2,138,275 | 3,316,536 | .... | .... | .... | .... | .... | .... |
| Exports of Goods and Services......... | **90c** | 2,503,705 | 3,745,182 | 4,312,928 | 4,915,825 | 6,711,217 | 4,198,000 | .... | .... | .... | .... | .... | .... |
| Imports of Goods and Services (-)..... | **98c** | 976,081 | 1,176,874 | 1,505,186 | 1,868,420 | 2,414,863 | 3,407,150 | .... | .... | .... | .... | .... | .... |
| Gross Domestic Product (GDP)........ | **99b** | 2,522,264 | 3,800,674 | 4,457,876 | 5,129,729 | 7,016,363 | 4,706,881 | .... | .... | .... | .... | .... | .... |
| GDP Volume 2000 Prices................ | **99b.p** | 1,716,667 | 1,820,282 | .... | .... | .... | .... | .... | .... | .... | .... | .... | .... |
| GDP Volume (2005=100)............... | **99bvp** | 94.3 | 100.0 | .... | .... | .... | .... | .... | .... | .... | .... | .... | .... |
| GDP Deflator (2005=100)............... | **99bip** | 70.4 | 100.0 | .... | .... | .... | .... | .... | .... | .... | .... | .... | .... |
| | | | | | | | *Millions: Midyear Estimates* | | | | | | |
| **Population................................** | **99z** | .61 | .63 | .65 | .67 | .69 | .71 | .73 | .75 | .77 | .80 | .82 | .85 |

# Eritrea  643

| | | 2004 | 2005 | 2006 | 2007 | 2008 | 2009 | 2010 | 2011 | 2012 | 2013 | 2014 | 2015 |
|---|---|---|---|---|---|---|---|---|---|---|---|---|---|
| **Exchange Rates** | | | | | | *Nakfa per SDR: End of Period* | | | | | | | | |
| Official Rate | aa | 21.412 | 21.975 | 23.130 | 24.296 | 23.682 | 24.103 | 23.678 | 23.605 | 23.630 | 23.678 | 22.275 | .... |
| | | | | | | *Nakfa per US Dollar: End of Period (ae) Period Average (rf)* | | | | | | | | |
| Official Rate | ae | 13.788 | 15.375 | 15.375 | 15.375 | 15.375 | 15.375 | 15.375 | 15.375 | 15.375 | 15.375 | 15.375 | .... |
| Official Rate | rf | 13.788 | 15.368 | 15.375 | 15.375 | 15.375 | 15.375 | 15.375 | 15.375 | 15.375 | 15.375 | 15.375 | .... |
| **Fund Position** | | | | | | *Millions of SDRs: End of Period* | | | | | | | | |
| Quota | 2f.s | 15.90 | 15.90 | 15.90 | 15.90 | 15.90 | 15.90 | 15.90 | 15.90 | 15.90 | 15.90 | 15.90 | 15.90 |
| SDR Holdings | 1b.s | — | — | — | — | — | 3.66 | 3.63 | 3.58 | 3.61 | 3.72 | 3.71 | 3.70 |
| Reserve Position in the Fund | 1c.s | .01 | .01 | .01 | .01 | .01 | .01 | .01 | .01 | .01 | .01 | .01 | .01 |
| Total Fund Cred.&Loans Outstg | 2tl | — | — | — | — | — | — | — | — | — | — | — | — |
| SDR Allocations | 1bd | — | — | — | — | — | 15.16 | 15.16 | 15.16 | 15.16 | 15.16 | 15.16 | 15.16 |
| **International Liquidity** | | | | | | *Millions of US Dollars Unless Otherwise Indicated: End of Period* | | | | | | | | |
| Total Reserves minus Gold | 1l.d | 34.7 | 27.9 | 25.4 | 34.3 | 57.9 | 90.0 | 114.1 | 114.8 | .... | .... | 5.4 | 5.1 |
| SDR Holdings | 1b.d | — | — | — | — | — | 5.7 | 5.6 | 5.5 | 5.5 | 5.7 | 5.4 | 5.1 |
| Reserve Position in the Fund | 1c.d | — | — | — | — | — | — | — | — | — | — | | |
| Foreign Exchange | 1d.d | 34.7 | 27.9 | 25.3 | 34.3 | 57.9 | 84.3 | 108.6 | 109.3 | .... | .... | .... | .... |
| Gold (Million Fine Troy Ounces) | 1ad | — | — | — | — | — | — | — | — | .... | .... | .... | .... |
| Gold (National Valuation) | 1and | — | — | — | — | — | — | — | — | .... | .... | .... | .... |
| Central Bank: Other Assets | 3..d | 56.5 | 51.8 | 47.3 | 26.0 | 27.6 | 25.0 | 25.8 | 26.8 | 25.7 | 25.6 | 25.6 | .... |
| Central Bank: Other Liabs | 4..d | 14.8 | 14.0 | 14.1 | 13.5 | 12.7 | 12.4 | 12.5 | 12.3 | 12.4 | 12.4 | 12.4 | .... |
| Other Depository Corps.: Assets | 7a.d | 247.1 | 165.7 | 146.0 | 136.7 | 119.4 | 191.9 | 270.9 | 352.1 | 415.5 | 409.2 | .... | .... |
| Other Depository Corps.: Liabs | 7b.d | 2.6 | 1.8 | 1.7 | 19.6 | 1.6 | 8.4 | 1.3 | 2.2 | 1.4 | 1.8 | .... | .... |
| **Central Bank** | | | | | | *Millions of Nakfa: End of Period* | | | | | | | | |
| Net Foreign Assets | 11n | 623 | 607 | 529 | 689 | 1,087 | 1,209 | 1,598 | 1,638 | 1,887 | 1,894 | 2,198 | .... |
| Claims on Nonresidents | 11 | 827 | 822 | 745 | 896 | 1,283 | 1,766 | 2,149 | 2,185 | 2,436 | 2,444 | 2,727 | .... |
| Liabilities to Nonresidents | 16c | 204 | 215 | 217 | 207 | 196 | 557 | 551 | 547 | 549 | 550 | 529 | .... |
| Claims on Other Depository Corps | 12e | 181 | 125 | 174 | 302 | 403 | 436 | 158 | 140 | 125 | 159 | 186 | .... |
| Net Claims on Central Government | 12an | 6,323 | 6,963 | 7,463 | 8,968 | 10,987 | 13,415 | 16,343 | 17,771 | 21,090 | 19,843 | 20,222 | .... |
| Claims on Central Government | 12a | 7,716 | 8,822 | 9,013 | 9,970 | 11,745 | 14,587 | 17,688 | 19,145 | 22,956 | 21,719 | 22,004 | .... |
| Liabilities to Central Government | 16d | 1,393 | 1,859 | 1,550 | 1,002 | 758 | 1,172 | 1,345 | 1,374 | 1,867 | 1,877 | 1,782 | .... |
| Claims on Other Sectors | 12s | 281 | 323 | 228 | 160 | 152 | 177 | 485 | 109 | 125 | 8,304 | 13,393 | .... |
| Claims on Other Financial Corps | 12g | 68 | 68 | 64 | 54 | 40 | 23 | 3 | 1 | 1 | 1 | 1 | .... |
| Claims on State & Local Govts | 12b | — | — | — | — | — | — | — | — | — | — | — | .... |
| Claims on Public Nonfin. Corps | 12c | — | — | — | — | — | — | — | — | — | — | — | .... |
| Claims on Private Sector | 12d | 213 | 254 | 165 | 107 | 112 | 154 | 482 | 108 | 125 | 8,303 | 13,392 | .... |
| Monetary Base | 14 | 6,229 | 6,691 | 7,004 | 8,241 | 10,436 | 12,836 | 14,995 | 16,469 | 19,480 | 26,358 | 31,239 | .... |
| Currency in Circulation | 14a | 3,824 | 4,129 | 3,975 | 4,595 | 5,822 | 7,584 | 8,695 | 11,105 | 13,410 | 15,732 | 17,917 | .... |
| Liabs. to Other Depository Corps | 14c | 2,324 | 2,505 | 2,947 | 3,535 | 4,550 | 5,230 | 6,230 | 5,335 | 6,037 | 10,558 | 13,271 | .... |
| Liabilities to Other Sectors | 14d | 81 | 57 | 82 | 111 | 64 | 21 | 70 | 29 | 34 | 68 | 51 | .... |
| Other Liabs. to Other Dep. Corps | 14n | — | — | — | — | — | — | — | — | — | — | — | .... |
| Dep. & Sec. Excl. f/Monetary Base | 14o | 7 | 11 | 4 | 2 | 3 | 11 | 20 | 1 | 10 | 13 | 14 | .... |
| Deposits Included in Broad Money | 15 | — | — | — | — | — | — | — | — | — | — | — | .... |
| Sec.Ot.th.Shares Incl.in Brd.Money | 16a | — | — | — | — | — | — | — | — | — | — | — | .... |
| Deposits Excl. from Broad Money | 16b | 7 | 11 | 4 | 2 | 3 | 11 | 20 | 1 | 10 | 13 | 14 | .... |
| Sec.Ot.th.Shares Excl.f/Brd.Money | 16s | — | — | — | — | — | — | — | — | — | — | — | .... |
| Loans | 16l | — | — | — | — | — | — | — | — | — | — | — | .... |
| Financial Derivatives | 16m | — | — | — | — | — | — | — | — | — | — | — | .... |
| Shares and Other Equity | 17a | 1,803 | 1,909 | 1,986 | 2,203 | 2,506 | 2,965 | 3,489 | 3,731 | 4,221 | 4,326 | 4,957 | .... |
| Other Items (Net) | 17r | −632 | −593 | −600 | −327 | −316 | −574 | 80 | −545 | −485 | −497 | −210 | .... |
| Memo Item: | | | | | | | | | | | | | |
| Total Assets | 10ra | 10,093 | 11,185 | 11,261 | 12,444 | 14,706 | 17,962 | 21,480 | 22,577 | 26,647 | 33,707 | 39,394 | .... |
| **Other Depository Corporations** | | | | | | *Millions of Nakfa: End of Period* | | | | | | | | |
| Net Foreign Assets | 21n | 3,371 | 2,520 | 2,218 | 1,800 | 1,811 | 2,821 | 4,146 | 5,379 | 6,367 | 6,264 | .... | .... |
| Claims on Nonresidents | 21 | 3,407 | 2,547 | 2,245 | 2,101 | 1,836 | 2,951 | 4,165 | 5,413 | 6,388 | 6,292 | .... | .... |
| Liabilities to Nonresidents | 26c | 36 | 28 | 26 | 302 | 25 | 130 | 20 | 34 | 21 | 28 | .... | .... |
| Claims on Central Bank | 20 | 2,906 | 2,984 | 3,402 | 3,950 | 5,181 | 6,222 | 6,920 | 6,428 | 7,017 | 11,140 | .... | .... |
| Currency | 20a | 572 | 474 | 460 | 447 | 669 | 948 | 540 | 1,146 | 1,109 | 946 | .... | .... |
| Reserve Deposits and Securities | 20b | 2,334 | 2,510 | 2,942 | 3,503 | 4,512 | 5,275 | 6,380 | 5,282 | 5,909 | 10,194 | .... | .... |
| Other Claims | 20n | — | — | — | — | — | — | — | — | — | — | .... | .... |
| Net Claims on Central Government | 22an | 7,396 | 8,911 | 10,279 | 10,810 | 12,404 | 13,534 | 14,985 | 17,629 | 18,194 | 20,197 | .... | .... |
| Claims on Central Government | 22a | 7,406 | 8,919 | 10,279 | 11,693 | 13,140 | 14,477 | 16,219 | 19,200 | 19,833 | 21,722 | .... | .... |
| Liabilities to Central Government | 26d | 10 | 8 | — | 883 | 736 | 943 | 1,233 | 1,572 | 1,639 | 1,525 | .... | .... |
| Claims on Other Sectors | 22s | 4,401 | 5,027 | 5,203 | 4,610 | 5,125 | 5,167 | 5,411 | 6,171 | 7,232 | 7,730 | .... | .... |
| Claims on Other Financial Corps | 22g | — | — | — | — | — | — | — | — | — | — | .... | .... |
| Claims on State & Local Govts | 22b | — | — | — | — | — | — | — | — | — | — | .... | .... |
| Claims on Public Nonfin. Corps | 22c | 494 | 628 | 529 | 515 | 556 | 535 | 692 | 702 | 691 | 725 | .... | .... |
| Claims on Private Sector | 22d | 3,907 | 4,399 | 4,675 | 4,095 | 4,569 | 4,633 | 4,718 | 5,469 | 6,541 | 7,004 | .... | .... |
| Liabilities to Central Bank | 26g | 768 | 640 | 702 | 123 | 123 | 123 | 131 | 131 | 131 | 131 | .... | .... |
| Transf.Dep.Included in Broad Money | 24 | 5,772 | 6,570 | 7,266 | 8,451 | 10,102 | 10,633 | 11,484 | 12,338 | 13,799 | 16,105 | .... | .... |
| Other Dep.Included in Broad Money | 25 | 10,608 | 11,535 | 12,211 | 13,159 | 14,656 | 17,397 | 20,388 | 23,635 | 26,444 | 30,279 | .... | .... |
| Sec.Ot.th.Shares Incl.in Brd.Money | 26a | — | — | — | — | — | — | — | — | — | — | .... | .... |
| Deposits Excl. from Broad Money | 26b | 406 | 394 | 410 | 439 | 164 | 483 | 442 | 74 | 54 | 94 | .... | .... |
| Sec.Ot.th.Shares Excl.f/Brd.Money | 26s | — | — | — | — | — | — | — | — | — | — | .... | .... |
| Loans | 26l | — | — | — | — | — | — | — | — | — | — | .... | .... |
| Financial Derivatives | 26m | — | — | — | — | — | — | — | — | — | — | .... | .... |
| Insurance Technical Reserves | 26r | — | — | — | — | — | — | — | — | — | — | .... | .... |
| Shares and Other Equity | 27a | 1,946 | 2,856 | 2,158 | 1,605 | 1,723 | 1,690 | 1,721 | 2,231 | 2,187 | 3,687 | .... | .... |
| Other Items (Net) | 27r | −1,426 | −2,554 | −1,643 | −2,606 | −2,246 | −2,582 | −2,703 | −2,802 | −3,805 | −4,964 | .... | .... |
| Memo Item: | | | | | | | | | | | | | |
| Total Assets | 20ra | 21,790 | 24,420 | 26,068 | 28,665 | 31,784 | 35,979 | 40,581 | 45,392 | 49,671 | 59,439 | .... | .... |

# Eritrea 643

| Depository Corporations | | 2004 | 2005 | 2006 | 2007 | 2008 | 2009 | 2010 | 2011 | 2012 | 2013 | 2014 | 2015 |
|---|---|---|---|---|---|---|---|---|---|---|---|---|---|
| | | | | | | *Millions of Nakfa: End of Period* | | | | | | | |
| Net Foreign Assets | 31n | 3,994 | 3,127 | 2,747 | 2,488 | 2,898 | 4,031 | 5,744 | 7,017 | 8,253 | 8,158 | .... | .... |
| Claims on Nonresidents | 31 | 4,234 | 3,369 | 2,990 | 2,997 | 3,119 | 4,717 | 6,315 | 7,598 | 8,824 | 8,735 | .... | .... |
| Liabilities to Nonresidents | 36c | 240 | 243 | 243 | 509 | 221 | 686 | 571 | 581 | 570 | 578 | .... | .... |
| Domestic Claims | 32 | 18,401 | 21,223 | 23,175 | 24,548 | 28,669 | 32,293 | 37,224 | 41,679 | 46,641 | 56,074 | .... | .... |
| Net Claims on Central Government | 32an | 13,719 | 15,874 | 17,743 | 19,778 | 23,391 | 26,949 | 31,328 | 35,400 | 39,283 | 40,040 | .... | .... |
| Claims on Central Government | 32a | 15,122 | 17,741 | 19,292 | 21,663 | 24,885 | 29,064 | 33,907 | 38,345 | 42,789 | 43,441 | .... | .... |
| Liabilities to Central Government | 36d | 1,403 | 1,867 | 1,550 | 1,886 | 1,494 | 2,115 | 2,579 | 2,946 | 3,506 | 3,401 | .... | .... |
| Claims on Other Sectors | 32s | 4,682 | 5,349 | 5,432 | 4,771 | 5,277 | 5,344 | 5,896 | 6,279 | 7,357 | 16,034 | .... | .... |
| Claims on Other Financial Corps | 32g | 68 | 68 | 64 | 54 | 40 | 23 | 3 | 1 | 1 | 1 | .... | .... |
| Claims on State & Local Govts | 32b | — | — | — | — | — | — | — | — | — | — | .... | .... |
| Claims on Public Nonfin. Corps | 32c | 494 | 628 | 529 | 515 | 556 | 535 | 692 | 702 | 691 | 725 | .... | .... |
| Claims on Private Sector | 32d | 4,120 | 4,653 | 4,839 | 4,202 | 4,681 | 4,787 | 5,201 | 5,577 | 6,665 | 15,307 | .... | .... |
| Broad Money Liabilities | 35l | 19,714 | 21,817 | 23,074 | 25,869 | 29,976 | 34,689 | 40,097 | 45,961 | 52,579 | 61,237 | .... | .... |
| Currency Outside Depository Corps | 34a | 3,253 | 3,654 | 3,515 | 4,148 | 5,153 | 6,637 | 8,155 | 9,959 | 12,301 | 14,785 | .... | .... |
| Transferable Deposits | 34 | 5,853 | 6,628 | 7,348 | 8,562 | 10,166 | 10,655 | 11,554 | 12,367 | 13,833 | 16,173 | .... | .... |
| Other Deposits | 35 | 10,608 | 11,535 | 12,211 | 13,159 | 14,656 | 17,397 | 20,388 | 23,635 | 26,444 | 30,279 | .... | .... |
| Securities Other than Shares | 36a | — | — | — | — | — | — | — | — | — | — | .... | .... |
| Deposits Excl. from Broad Money | 36b | 413 | 405 | 413 | 441 | 167 | 493 | 462 | 75 | 64 | 107 | .... | .... |
| Sec.Ot.th.Shares Excl.f/Brd.Money | 36s | — | — | — | — | — | — | — | — | — | — | .... | .... |
| Loans | 36l | — | — | — | — | — | — | — | — | — | — | .... | .... |
| Financial Derivatives | 36m | — | — | — | — | — | — | — | — | — | — | .... | .... |
| Insurance Technical Reserves | 36r | — | — | — | — | — | — | — | — | — | — | .... | .... |
| Shares and Other Equity | 37a | 3,749 | 4,765 | 4,144 | 3,807 | 4,229 | 4,656 | 5,209 | 5,963 | 6,408 | 8,013 | .... | .... |
| Other Items (Net) | 37r | −1,481 | −2,636 | −1,709 | −3,081 | −2,805 | −3,514 | −2,800 | −3,303 | −4,156 | −5,125 | .... | .... |
| Broad Money Liabs., Seasonally Adj. | 35l.b | 19,423 | 21,521 | 22,781 | 25,550 | 29,632 | 34,331 | 39,762 | 45,644 | 52,291 | 60,932 | .... | .... |
| **Monetary Aggregates** | | | | | | *Millions of Nakfa: End of Period* | | | | | | | |
| Broad Money | 59m | 19,714 | 21,817 | 23,074 | 25,869 | 29,976 | 34,689 | 40,097 | 45,961 | 52,579 | 61,237 | .... | .... |
| o/w: Currency Issued by Cent.Govt | 59m.a | — | — | — | — | — | — | — | — | — | — | .... | .... |
| o/w: Dep.in Nonfin. Corporations | 59m.b | — | — | — | — | — | — | — | — | — | — | .... | .... |
| o/w: Secs. Issued by Central Govt | 59m.c | — | — | — | — | — | — | — | — | — | — | .... | .... |
| Money (National Definitions) | | | | | | | | | | | | | |
| Reserve Money | 19mb | 6,203 | 6,667 | 6,987 | 8,237 | 10,430 | 12,836 | 14,994 | 16,469 | 19,480 | 26,358 | .... | .... |
| M1 | 59ma | 7,799 | 9,102 | 9,636 | 11,521 | 13,783 | 15,858 | 17,976 | 20,433 | 23,552 | 28,331 | .... | .... |
| M2 | 59mb | 16,535 | 18,503 | 19,527 | 22,091 | 25,673 | 30,269 | 35,235 | 40,657 | 46,190 | 54,683 | .... | .... |
| M3 | 59mc | 19,714 | 21,817 | 23,074 | 25,869 | 29,976 | 34,689 | 40,097 | 45,961 | 52,579 | 61,237 | .... | .... |
| **Population** | 99z | 4.06 | 4.19 | 4.30 | 4.41 | 4.50 | 4.59 | 4.69 | 4.79 | 4.89 | 5.00 | 5.11 | 5.23 |

# Estonia 939

| | | 2004 | 2005 | 2006 | 2007 | 2008 | 2009 | 2010 | 2011 | 2012 | 2013 | 2014 | 2015 |
|---|---|---|---|---|---|---|---|---|---|---|---|---|---|
| **Exchange Rates** | | | | | *Krooni per SDR through 2010; Euros per SDR Thereafter: End of Period* | | | | | | | | |
| Official Rate | aa | 17.8147 | 18.8958 | 17.8750 | 16.8110 | 17.1050 | 17.0334 | 18.0348 | 1.1865 | 1.1649 | 1.1167 | 1.1933 | 1.2728 |
| | | | | | *Krooni per US Dollar through 2010; Euros per US Dollar Thereafter: End of Period (ae) Period Average (rf)* | | | | | | | | |
| Official Rate | ae | 11.4711 | 13.2206 | 11.8818 | 10.6382 | 11.1052 | 10.8653 | 11.7107 | .7729 | .7579 | .7251 | .8237 | .9185 |
| Official Rate | rf | 12.5956 | 12.5838 | 12.4655 | 11.4339 | 10.6944 | 11.2574 | 11.8068 | .7194 | .7783 | .7532 | .7537 | .9017 |
| **Fund Position** | | | | | | *Millions of SDRs: End of Period* | | | | | | | |
| Quota | 2f.s | 65.20 | 65.20 | 65.20 | 65.20 | 65.20 | 65.20 | 65.20 | 65.20 | 93.90 | 93.90 | 93.90 | 93.90 |
| SDR Holdings | 1b.s | .05 | .05 | .06 | .06 | .06 | 62.03 | 62.03 | 62.03 | 62.03 | 62.03 | 62.04 | 62.05 |
| Reserve Position in the Fund | 1c.s | .01 | .01 | .01 | .01 | .01 | .01 | .01 | .01 | 8.18 | 13.18 | 14.18 | 14.20 |
| Total Fund Cred.&Loans Outstg. | 2tl | — | — | — | — | — | 61.97 | 61.97 | 61.97 | 61.97 | 61.97 | 61.97 | 61.97 |
| SDR Allocations | 1bd | — | — | — | — | — | | | | | | | |
| **International Liquidity** | | | | | *Millions of US Dollars Unless Otherwise Indicated: End of Period* | | | | | | | | |
| Total Res. Min. Gold (Eurosys.Def) | 1l.d | 1,788.23 | 1,943.21 | 2,781.24 | 3,262.69 | 3,964.88 | 3,971.94 | 2,555.89 | † 194.87 | 287.35 | 304.77 | 427.19 | 406.32 |
| SDR Holdings | 1b.d | .08 | .08 | .09 | .09 | .09 | 97.24 | 95.52 | 95.23 | 95.33 | 95.53 | 89.89 | 85.98 |
| Reserve Position in the Fund | 1c.d | .01 | .01 | .01 | .01 | .01 | .01 | .01 | .01 | 12.58 | 20.30 | 20.55 | 19.68 |
| Foreign Exchange | 1d.d | 1,788.13 | 1,943.12 | 2,781.14 | 3,262.59 | 3,964.77 | 3,874.69 | 2,460.36 | † 99.63 | 179.44 | 188.94 | 316.75 | 300.66 |
| o/w:Fin. Deriv. Rel to Reserves | 1ddd | .... | .... | .... | .... | .... | .... | .... | −1.29 | 2.64 | 1.38 | −2.24 | −.09 |
| Other Reserve Assets | 1e.d | .... | .... | .... | .... | .... | .... | .... | | | | | |
| Gold (Million Fine Troy Ounces) | 1ad | .008 | .008 | .008 | .008 | .008 | .008 | .008 | .008 | .008 | .008 | .008 | .008 |
| Gold (Eurosystem Valuation) | 1and | 3.61 | 4.24 | 5.23 | 6.91 | 7.16 | 9.12 | 11.63 | † 12.60 | 13.31 | 9.61 | 9.59 | 8.48 |
| Memo:Euro Cl. On Non-EA Res. | 1dgd | .... | .... | .... | .... | .... | .... | .... | 35.48 | 35.79 | 34.17 | 26.90 | 39.74 |
| Non-Euro Cl. on EA Res. | 1dhd | .... | .... | .... | .... | .... | .... | .... | 6.47 | 27.71 | 55.16 | 73.54 | 90.75 |
| Central Bank: Other Assets | 3..d | 55 | 48 | 48 | 47 | −241 | −184 | −45 | 1,789 | 3,326 | 3,547 | 4,740 | 4,892 |
| Central Bank: Other Liabs | 4..d | — | — | 1 | 1 | | 97 | 95 | 95 | 95 | 95 | 90 | 86 |
| Other Depository Corps.: Assets | 7a.d | 1,648 | 2,635 | 2,431 | 4,035 | 3,603 | 4,088 | 4,272 | 4,284 | 3,186 | 2,702 | 1,901 | 1,165 |
| Other Depository Corps.: Liabs. | 7b.d | 2,217 | 3,164 | 5,112 | 10,195 | 10,226 | 9,766 | 6,750 | 5,412 | 4,668 | 4,518 | 4,179 | 6,195 |
| **Central Bank** | | | | | | *Millions of Euros: End of Period* | | | | | | | |
| Euro Area Wide Residency Criterion | | | | | | | | | | | | | |
| Net Foreign Assets | 11n.u | 425 | 634 | 684 | 714 | 368 | 456 | 500 | 90 | 137 | 160 | 287 | 308 |
| Claims on Nonresidents | 11..u | 456 | 634 | 708 | 787 | 368 | 531 | 571 | 164 | 228 | 229 | 361 | 396 |
| Liabilities to Nonresidents | 16c.u | 31 | — | 24 | 72 | — | 74 | 71 | 74 | 91 | 69 | 74 | 88 |
| Claims on Other Depository Corps. | 12e.u | 689 | 965 | 872 | 974 | 819 | 384 | 81 | 102 | 134 | 135 | 181 | 190 |
| Net Claims on Central Government | 12anu | — | 10 | 337 | 373 | 1,484 | 1,721 | 1,110 | 527 | 532 | 465 | 414 | 253 |
| Claims on Central Govt | 12a.u | — | 10 | 337 | 374 | 1,484 | 1,721 | 1,110 | 527 | 532 | 465 | 414 | 253 |
| Liabs. to Central Govt | 16d.u | — | — | — | — | — | — | — | — | — | — | — | — |
| Claims on Other Sectors | 12s.u | 214 | 85 | 239 | 121 | 13 | 4 | 5 | 5 | 21 | 42 | 63 | 1,291 |
| Claims on Other Financial Corps. | 12g.u | 72 | — | 191 | 58 | 10 | — | — | — | 15 | 36 | 57 | 1,238 |
| Claims on State & Local Govts | 12b.u | 40 | 15 | 10 | 10 | — | — | — | — | — | — | — | — |
| Claims on Public Nonfin. Corps. | 12c.u | — | — | — | — | — | — | — | — | — | — | — | — |
| Claims on Private Sector | 12d.u | 102 | 70 | 38 | 53 | 3 | 4 | 5 | 5 | 6 | 6 | 6 | 53 |
| Monetary Base | 14..u | 1,065 | 1,416 | 1,850 | 1,875 | 2,379 | 2,303 | 1,489 | 2,592 | 3,718 | 3,716 | 5,424 | 6,115 |
| Currency in Circulation | 14a.u | 569 | 646 | 752 | 749 | 719 | 583 | 357 | 2,118 | 2,180 | 2,287 | 2,615 | 2,772 |
| Liabs. to Other Depository Corps. | 14c.u | 492 | 765 | 1,092 | 1,120 | 1,653 | 1,714 | 1,125 | 466 | 1,528 | 1,417 | 2,800 | 3,331 |
| Liabs. to Other Sectors | 14d.u | 5 | 6 | 6 | 6 | 7 | 6 | 7 | 8 | 10 | 12 | 9 | 12 |
| Other Liabs. to Other Dep. Corps. | 14n.u | — | — | — | — | — | — | — | — | — | — | — | — |
| Dep. & Sec. Excl. f/Monetary Base | 14o.u | — | — | — | — | — | — | — | — | — | — | — | — |
| Deposits Included in Broad Money. | 15..u | — | — | — | — | — | — | — | — | — | — | — | — |
| Sec.Ot.th.Shares Inc.in.Brd.Money | 16a.u | — | — | — | — | — | — | — | — | — | — | — | — |
| Deposits Excl. from Broad Money | 16b.u | — | — | — | — | — | — | — | — | — | — | — | — |
| Sec.Oh.th.Shares Excl. f/Brd.Money | 16s.u | — | — | — | — | — | — | — | — | — | — | — | — |
| Loans | 16l.u | — | — | — | — | — | — | — | — | — | — | — | — |
| Financial Derivatives | 16m.u | — | — | — | — | — | — | — | — | — | — | — | — |
| Shares and Other Equity | 17a.u | 236 | 247 | 257 | 284 | 358 | 355 | 331 | 374 | 406 | 435 | 454 | 485 |
| Other Items (Net) | 17r.u | −48 | −49 | −51 | −47 | −53 | −94 | −125 | −2,239 | −3,298 | −3,349 | −4,932 | −4,545 |
| Memorandum Items | | | | | | | | | | | | | |
| National Residency Criterion | | | | | | | | | | | | | |
| Net Foreign Assets | 11n | 1,325 | 1,691 | 2,129 | 2,180 | 2,681 | 2,561 | 1,817 | 1,470 | 2,658 | 2,731 | 4,190 | 4,787 |
| Claims on Nonresidents | 11 | 1,356 | 1,691 | 2,152 | 2,253 | 2,681 | 2,636 | 1,888 | 1,544 | 2,749 | 2,800 | 4,264 | 4,875 |
| Liabilities to Nonresidents | 16c | 31 | — | 24 | 72 | — | 74 | 71 | 74 | 91 | 69 | 74 | 88 |
| Claims on Other Depository Corps. | 12e | — | — | — | — | — | — | — | — | 14 | 5 | 52 | 75 |
| Net Claims on Central Government | 12an | — | — | — | — | — | — | — | — | — | — | — | — |
| Claims on Central Government | 12a | — | — | — | — | — | — | — | — | — | — | — | — |
| Liabilities to Central Government | 16d | — | — | — | — | — | — | — | — | — | — | — | — |
| Claims on Other Sectors | 12s | 3 | 3 | 3 | 3 | 3 | 4 | 5 | 5 | 6 | 6 | 6 | 53 |
| Claims on Other Fin. Corps. | 12g | — | — | — | — | — | — | — | — | — | — | — | — |
| Claims on State & Local Govts | 12b | — | — | — | — | — | — | — | — | — | — | — | — |
| Claims on Private Sector | 12d | 3 | 3 | 3 | 3 | 3 | 4 | 5 | 5 | 6 | 6 | 6 | 53 |
| Liabs.to ODCs, Inc.in Mon.Base | 14c | 492 | 765 | 1,092 | 1,120 | 1,653 | 1,714 | 1,125 | 466 | 1,528 | 1,417 | 2,800 | 3,331 |
| Liabs.to Ot.Sectors, Inc.in Mon.Base | 14d | 5 | 6 | 6 | 6 | 7 | 6 | 7 | 8 | 10 | 12 | 9 | 12 |
| Liabs.to ODCs,Excl.f/Mon.Base | 14n | — | — | — | — | — | — | — | — | — | — | — | — |
| Net Claims on Eurosystem | 12e.s | .... | .... | .... | .... | .... | .... | .... | 1,512 | 1,456 | 1,413 | 3,392 | 2,962 |

# Estonia 939

| | | 2004 | 2005 | 2006 | 2007 | 2008 | 2009 | 2010 | 2011 | 2012 | 2013 | 2014 | 2015 |
|---|---|---|---|---|---|---|---|---|---|---|---|---|---|
| **Other Depository Corporations** | | | | | | | | | | | | | |
| Euro Area Wide Residency Criterion | | | | | | | | | | | | | |
| Net Foreign Assets | 21n.u | −418 | −449 | −2,036 | −4,184 | −4,759 | −3,941 | −1,855 | −872 | −1,123 | −1,317 | −1,876 | −4,620 |
| Claims on Nonresidents | 21..u | 1,210 | 2,234 | 1,846 | 2,741 | 2,589 | 2,838 | 3,197 | 3,311 | 2,415 | 1,959 | 1,566 | 1,070 |
| Liabilities to Nonresidents | 26c.u | 1,628 | 2,682 | 3,882 | 6,925 | 7,348 | 6,779 | 5,052 | 4,183 | 3,538 | 3,276 | 3,442 | 5,690 |
| Claims on Eurosystem | 20..u | 773 | 786 | 1,213 | 1,259 | 1,767 | 1,814 | 1,234 | 588 | 1,664 | 1,576 | 2,948 | 3,473 |
| Currency | 20a.u | 84 | 97 | 121 | 139 | 122 | 109 | 111 | 122 | 136 | 159 | 148 | 142 |
| Reserve Deposits and Securities | 20b.u | 689 | 689 | 1,092 | 1,120 | 1,645 | 1,705 | 1,123 | 466 | 1,528 | 1,417 | 2,800 | 3,331 |
| Other Claims | 20n.u | — | — | — | — | — | — | — | — | — | — | — | — |
| Net Claims on Central Government | 22anu | −171 | −205 | −150 | −192 | −243 | −55 | 223 | 48 | −295 | −454 | −536 | −590 |
| Claims on Central Government | 22a.u | 66 | 140 | 296 | 204 | 149 | 640 | 678 | 385 | 308 | 543 | 521 | 207 |
| Liabilities to Central Government | 26d.u | 237 | 346 | 446 | 396 | 392 | 695 | 455 | 337 | 603 | 997 | 1,057 | 797 |
| Claims on Other Sectors | 22s.u | 6,119 | 8,048 | 11,394 | 15,074 | 16,118 | 15,305 | 14,575 | 14,005 | 14,003 | 14,658 | 15,284 | 16,582 |
| Claims on Other Financial Corps. | 22g.u | 1,987 | 1,422 | 803 | 1,042 | 835 | 596 | 482 | 583 | 524 | 1,082 | 1,217 | 1,847 |
| Claims on State & Local Govts | 22b.u | 155 | 156 | 151 | 172 | 226 | 269 | 307 | 319 | 327 | 372 | 443 | 407 |
| Claims on Public Nonfin. Corps. | 22c.u | — | — | — | — | — | — | — | — | — | — | — | — |
| Claims on Private Sector | 22d.u | 3,976 | 6,470 | 10,440 | 13,860 | 15,057 | 14,440 | 13,786 | 13,103 | 13,152 | 13,204 | 13,624 | 14,328 |
| Liabilities to Eurosystem | 26g.u | 688 | 939 | 822 | 947 | 555 | 383 | 70 | 15 | 46 | 37 | 83 | 89 |
| Transf.Dep.Included in Broad Money | 24..u | 2,258 | 3,196 | 4,051 | 4,322 | 3,817 | 3,764 | 4,820 | 5,203 | 6,247 | 7,173 | 8,382 | 10,058 |
| Other.Dep.Included in Broad Money. | 25..u | 1,015 | 1,611 | 2,117 | 2,831 | 3,878 | 4,219 | 3,644 | 3,849 | 3,449 | 3,175 | 2,993 | 2,627 |
| Sec.Ot.th.Shares Inc.in.Brd. Money | 26a.u | −461 | −632 | −475 | −478 | −145 | −229 | 8 | −17 | −2 | −1 | −1 | −1 |
| Deposits Excl. from Broad Money | 26b.u | 64 | 66 | 101 | 81 | 83 | 95 | 202 | 280 | 299 | 285 | 285 | 251 |
| Sec.Ot.th.Shares Excl.f/Brd. Money | 26s.u | 1,162 | 1,055 | 737 | 620 | 549 | −68 | −140 | −91 | −182 | −240 | −112 | −76 |
| Loans | 26l.u | — | — | — | — | — | — | — | — | — | — | — | — |
| Financial Derivatives | 26m.u | 21 | 12 | 40 | 64 | 69 | 45 | 50 | 52 | 86 | 57 | 70 | 71 |
| Insurance Technical Reserves | 26r.u | — | — | — | — | — | — | — | — | — | — | — | — |
| Shares and Other Equity | 27..u | 878 | 1,054 | 1,344 | 1,859 | 2,117 | 2,437 | 2,544 | 2,271 | 2,507 | 2,704 | 2,890 | 2,915 |
| Other Items (Net) | 27r.u | 458 | 651 | 1,460 | 1,536 | 1,957 | 2,476 | 2,957 | 2,208 | 1,797 | 1,274 | 1,232 | −1,090 |
| Memorandum Items | | | | | | | | | | | | | |
| Total Assets | 20ra | 8,806 | 12,104 | 15,602 | 20,779 | 22,106 | 21,336 | 20,358 | 19,016 | 19,669 | 19,947 | 21,451 | 23,236 |
| National Residency Criterion | | | | | | | | | | | | | |
| Net Foreign Assets | 21n | −638 | −915 | −2,620 | −4,647 | −5,788 | −5,295 | −3,591 | −2,523 | −2,560 | −1,807 | −2,764 | −3,523 |
| Claims on Nonresidents | 21 | 1,819 | 2,919 | 2,767 | 4,011 | 3,908 | 3,944 | 4,112 | 4,108 | 3,534 | 3,626 | 3,069 | 3,088 |
| Liabilities to Nonresidents | 26c | 2,458 | 3,835 | 5,387 | 8,658 | 9,696 | 9,239 | 7,703 | 6,631 | 6,094 | 5,433 | 5,833 | 6,611 |
| Net Claims on Central Government | 22an | −210 | −315 | −371 | −330 | −243 | −542 | −256 | −149 | −362 | −766 | −834 | −600 |
| Claims on Central Government | 22a | 26 | 29 | 31 | 35 | 118 | 122 | 198 | 187 | 240 | 230 | 223 | 197 |
| Liabilities to Central Government | 26d | 236 | 344 | 402 | 364 | 361 | 664 | 454 | 336 | 602 | 996 | 1,057 | 797 |
| Claims on Other Sectors | 22s | 6,068 | 7,970 | 11,268 | 14,935 | 15,959 | 15,182 | 14,449 | 13,891 | 13,864 | 14,219 | 14,887 | 16,203 |
| Claims on Other Fin. Corps. | 22g | 1,974 | 1,398 | 776 | 1,030 | 834 | 589 | 466 | 564 | 478 | 713 | 1,005 | 1,623 |
| Claims on State & Local Govts | 22b | 157 | 156 | 151 | 172 | 226 | 269 | 307 | 319 | 327 | 372 | 401 | 405 |
| Claims on Private Sector | 22d | 3,938 | 6,416 | 10,342 | 13,734 | 14,899 | 14,324 | 13,676 | 13,008 | 13,059 | 13,134 | 13,481 | 14,175 |
| Transf.Dep.Included in Broad Money | 24 | 2,203 | 3,118 | 3,978 | 4,236 | 3,690 | 3,605 | 4,639 | 5,019 | 6,027 | 6,943 | 8,070 | 9,730 |
| Other.Dep.Included in Broad Money. | 25 | 1,004 | 1,596 | 2,106 | 2,809 | 3,855 | 4,098 | 3,493 | 3,781 | 3,392 | 3,131 | 2,945 | 2,554 |
| Sec.Ot.th.Shares Inc.in.Brd. Money | 26a | 35 | 79 | 102 | 121 | 38 | 16 | 14 | 11 | — | — | — | — |
| Deposits Excl. from Broad Money | 26b | 63 | 66 | 101 | 80 | 81 | 92 | 132 | 143 | 120 | 117 | 131 | 122 |
| Sec.Ot.th.Shares Excl.f/Brd. Money | 26s | 1,339 | 1,316 | 1,020 | 982 | 923 | 72 | 21 | 5 | 2 | 1 | 4 | 9 |

*Millions of Euros: End of Period*

# Estonia 939

|  |  | 2004 | 2005 | 2006 | 2007 | 2008 | 2009 | 2010 | 2011 | 2012 | 2013 | 2014 | 2015 |
|---|---|---|---|---|---|---|---|---|---|---|---|---|---|
| **Depository Corporations** | | | | | | | *Millions of Euros: End of Period* | | | | | | |
| Euro Area Wide Residency Criterion | | | | | | | | | | | | | |
| Net Foreign Assets | 31n.u | 7 | 185 | −1,352 | −3,470 | −4,391 | −3,485 | −1,355 | −782 | −986 | −1,157 | −1,589 | −4,312 |
| Claims on Nonresidents | 31..u | 1,666 | 2,868 | 2,553 | 3,528 | 2,957 | 3,369 | 3,768 | 3,475 | 2,643 | 2,188 | 1,927 | 1,466 |
| Liabilities to Nonresidents | 36c.u | 1,659 | 2,682 | 3,905 | 6,998 | 7,348 | 6,853 | 5,123 | 4,257 | 3,629 | 3,345 | 3,516 | 5,778 |
| Domestic Claims | 32..u | 6,161 | 7,938 | 11,819 | 15,376 | 17,372 | 16,975 | 15,913 | 14,585 | 14,261 | 14,711 | 15,225 | 17,536 |
| Net Claims on Central Government | 32anu | −171 | −196 | 187 | 181 | 1,241 | 1,666 | 1,333 | 575 | 237 | 11 | −122 | −337 |
| Claims on Central Government | 32a.u | 66 | 150 | 633 | 578 | 1,633 | 2,361 | 1,788 | 912 | 840 | 1,008 | 935 | 460 |
| Liabilities to Central Government | 36d.u | 238 | 346 | 446 | 397 | 392 | 695 | 455 | 337 | 603 | 997 | 1,057 | 797 |
| Claims on Other Sectors | 32s.u | 6,333 | 8,133 | 11,632 | 15,195 | 16,131 | 15,309 | 14,580 | 14,010 | 14,024 | 14,700 | 15,347 | 17,873 |
| Claims on Other Financial Corps | 32g.u | 2,060 | 1,422 | 994 | 1,101 | 845 | 596 | 482 | 583 | 539 | 1,118 | 1,274 | 3,085 |
| Claims on State & Local Govts | 32b.u | 195 | 171 | 160 | 182 | 226 | 269 | 307 | 319 | 327 | 372 | 443 | 407 |
| Claims on Public Nonfin. Corps | 32c.u | — | — | — | — | — | — | — | — | — | — | — | — |
| Claims on Private Sector | 32d.u | 4,078 | 6,540 | 10,478 | 13,912 | 15,060 | 14,444 | 13,791 | 13,108 | 13,158 | 13,210 | 13,630 | 14,381 |
| Broad Money Liabilities | 35l.u | 3,302 | 4,730 | 6,330 | 7,291 | 8,154 | 8,234 | 8,725 | 11,039 | 11,748 | 12,487 | 13,850 | 15,326 |
| Currency Outside Depository Corps | 34a.u | 485 | 548 | 631 | 610 | 597 | 474 | 246 | 1,996 | 2,044 | 2,128 | 2,467 | 2,630 |
| Transferable Deposits | 34..u | 2,263 | 3,202 | 4,057 | 4,328 | 3,824 | 3,770 | 4,827 | 5,211 | 6,257 | 7,185 | 8,391 | 10,070 |
| Other Deposits | 35..u | 1,015 | 1,611 | 2,117 | 2,831 | 3,878 | 4,219 | 3,644 | 3,849 | 3,449 | 3,175 | 2,993 | 2,627 |
| Securities Other than Shares | 36a.u | −461 | −632 | −475 | −478 | −145 | −229 | 8 | −17 | −2 | −1 | −1 | −1 |
| Deposits Excl. from Broad Money | 36b.u | 64 | 66 | 101 | 81 | 83 | 95 | 202 | 280 | 299 | 285 | 285 | 251 |
| Sec.Oth.th.Shares Excl.f/Brd. Money | 36s.u | 1,162 | 1,055 | 737 | 620 | 549 | −68 | −140 | −91 | −182 | −240 | −112 | −76 |
| Loans | 36l.u | — | — | — | — | — | — | — | — | — | — | — | — |
| Financial Derivatives | 36m.u | 21 | 12 | 40 | 64 | 69 | 45 | 50 | 52 | 86 | 57 | 70 | 71 |
| Insurance Technical Reserves | 36r.u | — | — | — | — | — | — | — | — | — | — | — | — |
| Shares and Other Equity | 37a.u | 1,114 | 1,301 | 1,601 | 2,143 | 2,475 | 2,792 | 2,875 | 2,645 | 2,913 | 3,139 | 3,344 | 3,400 |
| Other Items (Net) | 37r.u | 212 | 652 | 1,360 | 1,462 | 1,648 | 2,390 | 2,823 | −118 | −1,589 | −2,173 | −3,798 | −5,736 |
| Broad Money Liabs., Seasonally Adj. | 35lub | 3,319 | 4,747 | 6,336 | 7,282 | 8,123 | 8,186 | 8,662 | 10,946 | 11,636 | 12,352 | 13,698 | 15,163 |
| Memorandum Items | | | | | | | | | | | | | |
| National Residency Criterion | | | | | | | | | | | | | |
| Net Foreign Assets | 31n | 686 | 776 | −492 | −2,467 | −3,107 | −2,734 | −1,774 | −1,053 | 98 | 924 | 1,426 | 1,264 |
| Claims on Nonresidents | 31 | 3,175 | 4,611 | 4,920 | 6,264 | 6,589 | 6,580 | 6,000 | 5,652 | 6,283 | 6,426 | 7,333 | 7,963 |
| Liabilities to Nonresidents | 36c | 2,489 | 3,835 | 5,411 | 8,730 | 9,696 | 9,313 | 7,774 | 6,705 | 6,185 | 5,502 | 5,907 | 6,699 |
| Domestic Claims | 32 | 5,862 | 7,657 | 10,900 | 14,608 | 15,719 | 14,644 | 14,198 | 13,747 | 13,508 | 13,459 | 14,059 | 15,656 |
| Net Claims on Central Government | 32an | −210 | −316 | −371 | −330 | −243 | −542 | −256 | −149 | −362 | −766 | −834 | −600 |
| Claims on Central Government | 32a | 26 | 29 | 31 | 35 | 118 | 122 | 198 | 187 | 240 | 230 | 223 | 197 |
| Liabilities to Central Government | 36d | 236 | 345 | 402 | 364 | 361 | 664 | 454 | 336 | 602 | 996 | 1,057 | 797 |
| Claims on Other Sectors | 32s | 6,072 | 7,973 | 11,271 | 14,938 | 15,962 | 15,186 | 14,454 | 13,896 | 13,870 | 14,225 | 14,893 | 16,256 |
| Claims on Other Financial Corps | 32g | 1,974 | 1,398 | 776 | 1,030 | 834 | 589 | 466 | 564 | 478 | 713 | 1,005 | 1,623 |
| Claims on State & Local Govts | 32b | 157 | 156 | 151 | 172 | 226 | 269 | 307 | 319 | 327 | 372 | 401 | 405 |
| Claims on Private Sector | 32d | 3,941 | 6,419 | 10,345 | 13,736 | 14,902 | 14,328 | 13,681 | 13,013 | 13,065 | 13,140 | 13,487 | 14,228 |
| Transf.Dep.Included in Broad Money | 34 | 2,208 | 3,124 | 3,984 | 4,243 | 3,697 | 3,611 | 4,646 | 5,027 | 6,037 | 6,955 | 8,079 | 9,742 |
| Other Dep.Included in Broad Money | 35 | 1,004 | 1,596 | 2,106 | 2,809 | 3,855 | 4,098 | 3,493 | 3,781 | 3,392 | 3,131 | 2,945 | 2,554 |
| Sec.Ot.th.Shares Inc.in.Brd. Money | 36a | 35 | 79 | 102 | 121 | 38 | 16 | 14 | 11 | — | — | — | — |
| Deposits Excl. from Broad Money | 36b | 63 | 66 | 101 | 80 | 81 | 92 | 132 | 143 | 120 | 117 | 131 | 122 |
| Sec.Ot.th.Shares Excl./f.Brd. Money | 36s | 1,339 | 1,316 | 1,020 | 982 | 923 | 72 | 21 | 5 | 2 | 1 | 4 | 9 |
| **Monetary Aggregates** | | | | | | | *Millions of Krooni: End of Period* | | | | | | |
| Money (National Definitions) | | | | | | | | | | | | | |
| M0 | 19mc | 16,676 | 22,175 | 28,979 | 27,390 | 36,109 | 34,227 | 21,181 | .... | .... | .... | .... | .... |
| M1 | 59ma | 42,041 | 57,364 | 72,118 | 75,370 | 67,203 | 65,390 | 77,269 | .... | .... | .... | .... | .... |
| M2 | 59mb | 58,184 | 82,599 | 105,898 | 118,238 | 125,267 | 127,717 | 132,668 | .... | .... | .... | .... | .... |
| **Interest Rates** | | | | | | | *Percent Per Annum* | | | | | | |
| Money Market Rate | 60b | 2.50 | 2.38 | 3.16 | 4.87 | 6.66 | 5.93 | 1.57 | .... | .... | .... | .... | .... |
| Deposit Rate | 60l | 2.16 | 2.13 | 2.84 | 4.37 | 5.72 | 4.82 | 1.11 | 1.27 | .67 | .42 | .51 | .50 |
| Households: Stocks, up to 2 years | 60lhs | .... | .... | .... | .... | .... | .... | .... | 1.70 | 1.01 | .52 | .47 | .40 |
| New Business, up to 1 year | 60lhn | .... | .... | .... | .... | .... | .... | .... | 1.52 | .41 | .36 | .39 | .17 |
| Corporations: Stocks, up to 2 years | 60lcs | .... | .... | .... | .... | .... | .... | .... | 1.69 | .72 | .50 | .53 | .49 |
| New Business, up to 1 year | 60lcn | .... | .... | .... | .... | .... | .... | .... | 1.22 | .31 | .29 | .34 | .03 |
| Lending Rate | 60p | 5.66 | 4.93 | 5.03 | 6.46 | 8.55 | 9.39 | 7.76 | 6.12 | 5.75 | 5.36 | 4.76 | 4.48 |
| Households: Stocks, up to 1 year | 60phs | .... | .... | .... | .... | .... | .... | .... | 13.96 | 14.54 | 15.20 | 15.25 | 12.26 |
| New Bus., Floating & up to 1 year | 60pns | .... | .... | .... | .... | .... | .... | .... | 21.33 | 18.94 | 16.32 | 15.74 | 9.06 |
| House Purch., Stocks,Over 5 years | 60phm | .... | .... | .... | .... | .... | .... | .... | 3.16 | 2.01 | 1.84 | 1.79 | 1.70 |
| House Purch., New Bus., 5-10 yrs | 60phn | .... | .... | .... | .... | .... | .... | .... | 5.01 | 4.95 | 5.08 | 1.79 | 2.74 |
| Corporations: Stocks, up to 1 year | 60pcs | .... | .... | .... | .... | .... | .... | .... | 4.29 | 3.06 | 3.02 | 2.73 | 2.92 |
| New Bus., Over € 1 mil.,up to 1 yr | 60pcn | .... | .... | .... | .... | .... | .... | .... | 3.95 | 3.06 | 3.02 | 2.61 | 2.10 |
| Government Bond Yield | 61 | 4.39 | 3.98 | 4.30 | 5.63 | 8.16 | 7.78 | 5.97 | .... | .... | .... | .... | .... |
| **Prices and Labor** | | | | | | | *Index Numbers (2010=100): Period Averages* | | | | | | |
| Share Prices | 62 | 60.4 | 104.1 | 115.6 | 152.7 | 91.0 | 58.0 | 100.0 | 110.6 | 110.1 | 140.8 | 135.5 | 148.6 |
| Producer Prices | 63 | 78.6 | † 80.3 | 83.9 | 90.8 | 97.3 | 96.8 | 100.0 | 104.4 | 106.9 | 111.3 | 109.5 | 107.3 |
| Consumer Prices | 64 | 76.0 | 79.1 | 82.6 | 88.1 | 97.2 | 97.1 | 100.0 | 105.0 | 109.1 | 112.2 | 112.0 | 111.5 |
| Harmonized CPI | 64h | 75.7 | 78.8 | 82.3 | 87.8 | 97.1 | 97.3 | 100.0 | 105.1 | 109.5 | 113.1 | 113.6 | 113.7 |
| Industrial Production | 66 | 86.5 | 96.0 | 105.5 | 112.3 | 106.6 | 81.0 | 100.0 | 119.9 | 121.2 | 126.2 | 131.1 | 128.2 |
| | | | | | | | *Number in Thousands: Period Averages* | | | | | | |
| Labor Force | 67d | 673 | 647 | 667 | 664 | 670 | 666 | 662 | 666 | 659 | 655 | 648 | 654 |
| Employment | 67e | 604 | 594 | 626 | 632 | 632 | 574 | 548 | 581 | 591 | 597 | 600 | 613 |
| Unemployment | 67c | 68 | 54 | 41 | 32 | 39 | 93 | 114 | 85 | 68 | 59 | 50 | 42 |
| Unemployment Rate (%) | 67r | 10.1 | 8.0 | 5.9 | 4.6 | 5.5 | 13.5 | 16.7 | 12.3 | 10.0 | 8.6 | 7.4 | 6.2 |
| **Intl. Transactions & Positions** | | | | | | | *Millions of Krooni through 2010; Millions of Euros Beginning 2011: End of Period* | | | | | | |
| Exports | 70 | 74,614 | 96,747 | 108,946 | 124,990 | 132,483 | 101,412 | 136,915 | † 12,003.5 | 12,517.9 | 12,269.4 | 11,986.4 | 11,659.3 |
| Imports, c.i.f | 71 | 104,878 | 128,435 | 147,770 | 171,846 | 170,488 | 113,780 | 144,994 | † 12,726.7 | 13,847.7 | 13,664.5 | 13,543.1 | 13,084.9 |

| | | 2004 | 2005 | 2006 | 2007 | 2008 | 2009 | 2010 | 2011 | 2012 | 2013 | 2014 | 2015 |
|---|---|---|---|---|---|---|---|---|---|---|---|---|---|
| **Balance of Payments** | | | | | | | *Millions of US Dollars* | | | | | | |
| A. Current Account* | 109bx | −1,369.2 | −1,386.4 | −2,585.5 | −3,503.2 | −2,216.6 | † 525.5 | 343.7 | 308.8 | −569.8 | −25.5 | 258.6 | 483.8 |
| Goods, credit (exports) | 1a9cx | 5,018.1 | 7,160.2 | 8,308.3 | 9,926.3 | 11,340.9 | † 7,389.4 | 9,912.3 | 14,446.9 | 14,262.9 | 15,435.6 | 15,176.1 | 12,244.6 |
| Goods, debit (imports) | 1a9dx | 7,028.9 | 9,045.9 | 11,133.9 | 13,491.7 | 14,147.1 | † 8,392.4 | 10,447.5 | 14,942.9 | 15,780.4 | 16,627.0 | 16,505.2 | 13,186.5 |
| Balance on goods | 1a9bx | −2,010.8 | −1,885.6 | −2,825.6 | −3,565.4 | −2,806.2 | † −1,003.0 | −535.2 | −496.0 | −1,517.5 | −1,191.4 | −1,329.1 | −942.0 |
| Services, credit (exports) | 1b9cx | 2,906.7 | 3,209.8 | 3,524.9 | 4,456.4 | 5,108.4 | † 4,613.6 | 4,718.2 | 5,627.0 | 5,758.6 | 6,476.4 | 7,059.5 | 5,851.6 |
| Services, debit (imports) | 1b9dx | 1,741.0 | 2,202.4 | 2,482.5 | 3,079.6 | 3,366.9 | † 2,622.1 | 2,951.5 | 3,802.0 | 4,021.5 | 4,724.7 | 4,829.4 | 3,983.0 |
| Balance on Goods & Services | 1z9bx | −845.1 | −878.3 | −1,783.3 | −2,188.6 | −1,064.6 | † 988.5 | 1,231.5 | 1,329.0 | 219.7 | 560.3 | 901.1 | 926.6 |
| Primary income: credit | 1c9cx | 436.2 | 730.7 | 1,091.5 | 1,662.3 | 1,693.2 | † 1,038.5 | 1,117.6 | 1,407.1 | 1,290.3 | 1,522.1 | 1,424.3 | 1,070.4 |
| Primary income: debit | 1c9dx | 1,074.3 | 1,300.3 | 1,956.4 | 3,112.6 | 3,014.6 | † 1,634.8 | 2,147.2 | 2,592.8 | 2,215.7 | 2,121.7 | 2,083.3 | 1,540.6 |
| Balance on gds, serv. & prim. inc. | 1y9bx | −1,483.1 | −1,447.9 | −2,648.2 | −3,638.9 | −2,386.0 | † 392.3 | 202.0 | 143.9 | −705.8 | −39.3 | 242.1 | 456.4 |
| Secondary income: credit | 1d9ca | 416.7 | 465.6 | 528.9 | 652.7 | 621.5 | † 474.5 | 524.6 | 602.7 | 560.0 | 557.4 | 575.4 | 532.9 |
| Secondary income: debit | 1d9da | 302.7 | 404.1 | 466.2 | 517.1 | 452.0 | † 341.2 | 382.9 | 437.7 | 424.0 | 543.6 | 558.9 | 505.5 |
| B. Capital Account* | 209ba | 86.4 | 103.0 | 363.0 | 241.2 | 301.1 | † 691.6 | 680.9 | 938.4 | 783.7 | 696.6 | 286.9 | 467.2 |
| Capital account: credit | 209ca | 93.2 | 109.5 | 383.4 | 297.1 | 322.3 | † 698.2 | 689.7 | 943.7 | 801.0 | 822.5 | 548.3 | 521.0 |
| Capital account: debit | 209da | 6.8 | 6.5 | 20.4 | 55.9 | 21.2 | † 6.6 | 8.8 | 5.3 | 17.3 | 125.9 | 261.4 | 53.8 |
| Balance on current & capital acct. | 129ba | −1,282.8 | −1,283.4 | −2,222.4 | −3,262.1 | −1,915.5 | † 1,217.1 | 1,024.6 | 1,247.2 | 213.9 | 671.1 | 545.5 | 951.0 |
| C. Financial Account* | 309na | −1,717.0 | −1,520.1 | −3,028.6 | −3,321.6 | −2,545.7 | † 1,297.7 | 2,210.1 | 1,380.7 | 565.9 | 608.6 | 222.4 | 1,026.2 |
| Direct investment: assets | 3a9aa | 388.9 | 873.5 | 1,536.6 | 2,451.7 | 1,254.6 | † 1,362.3 | 1,241.7 | −1,369.3 | 1,282.0 | 766.5 | 834.7 | −97.9 |
| Equity & investment fund shares | 3aaaa | 243.6 | 619.7 | 867.4 | 1,347.9 | 426.5 | † 1,253.0 | 361.7 | −1,583.6 | 289.1 | 463.9 | −151.7 | 268.8 |
| Debt instruments | 3abaa | 145.3 | 253.9 | 669.2 | 1,103.8 | 828.1 | † 109.3 | 880.0 | 214.2 | 992.9 | 302.6 | 986.5 | −366.7 |
| Direct investment: liabilities | 3a9la | 1,086.5 | 3,127.3 | 2,212.2 | 3,429.0 | 1,873.3 | † 1,865.6 | 2,592.8 | 1,118.6 | 1,788.0 | 873.6 | 1,571.1 | −174.2 |
| Equity & investment fund shares | 3aala | 1,011.0 | 2,998.4 | 1,436.0 | 2,253.0 | 1,586.6 | † 2,333.1 | 1,775.5 | 912.8 | 1,572.6 | 848.2 | 1,119.4 | −92.1 |
| Debt instruments | 3abla | 75.5 | 128.9 | 776.2 | 1,176.0 | 286.7 | † −467.5 | 817.3 | 205.8 | 215.5 | 25.4 | 451.7 | −82.1 |
| Portfolio investment: assets | 3b9aa | 380.6 | 871.6 | 1,214.6 | 735.5 | −947.0 | † 691.7 | 415.4 | −1,381.9 | 350.8 | 932.0 | 746.3 | 556.1 |
| Equity & investment fund shares | 3baaa | 232.4 | 387.7 | 366.9 | 662.6 | −377.2 | † 79.6 | 415.7 | −110.4 | 229.2 | 419.3 | 179.3 | 237.2 |
| Debt securities | 3bbaa | 148.2 | 483.9 | 847.7 | 72.9 | −569.8 | † 612.1 | −.3 | −1,271.5 | 121.6 | 512.7 | 567.0 | 318.8 |
| Portfolio investment: liabilities | 3b9la | 1,114.3 | −1,382.2 | −68.6 | 240.7 | −247.1 | † −1,374.1 | −130.4 | 252.5 | 228.6 | 246.1 | 100.3 | −45.1 |
| Equity & investment fund shares | 3bala | 176.1 | −1,362.8 | 308.6 | 289.4 | −301.4 | † −100.1 | 98.0 | −28.5 | −122.1 | 53.9 | −57.8 | −42.3 |
| Debt securities | 3bbla | 938.1 | −19.4 | −377.2 | −48.7 | 54.3 | † −1,274.0 | −228.4 | 281.0 | 350.7 | 192.3 | 158.1 | −2.8 |
| Fin. der.& empl.stk.ops.(ESOs): net. | 3c9na | .3 | 7.5 | −5.8 | 71.5 | −72.1 | † −18.7 | −42.3 | 66.3 | −79.4 | −131.4 | −97.3 | −95.4 |
| Fin. der. & ESOs: assets | 3c9aa | 2.9 | −1.3 | 15.4 | 77.5 | −62.6 | . . . . | . . . . | . . . . | . . . . | . . . . | . . . . | . . . . |
| Fin. der. & ESOs: liabilities | 3c9la | 2.6 | −8.8 | 21.2 | 6.0 | 9.5 | . . . . | . . . . | . . . . | . . . . | . . . . | . . . . | . . . . |
| Other investment: assets | 3d9aa | 949.1 | 917.6 | −60.5 | 2,056.8 | 491.3 | † −1,057.6 | 1,075.3 | 2,820.8 | 2,044.1 | −366.0 | 1,621.0 | 508.5 |
| Other equity | 3daaa | . . . . | . . . . | . . . . | . . . . | . . . . | † 7.5 | 4.1 | 109.2 | 81.1 | 90.9 | 51.5 | .3 |
| Debt instruments | 3dzaa | 949.1 | 917.6 | −60.5 | 2,056.8 | 491.3 | † −1,065.1 | 1,071.2 | 2,711.6 | 1,963.0 | −456.9 | 1,569.5 | 508.2 |
| Other investment: liabilities | 3d9la | 1,235.2 | 2,445.3 | 3,569.9 | 4,967.2 | 1,646.4 | † −811.5 | −1,982.5 | −2,616.1 | 1,015.8 | −527.2 | 1,210.9 | 64.3 |
| Other equity | 3dala | . . . . | . . . . | . . . . | . . . . | . . . . | † — | — | — | — | .1 | | |
| Debt instruments | 3dzla | 1,235.2 | 2,445.3 | 3,569.9 | 4,967.2 | 1,646.4 | † −811.5 | −1,982.5 | −2,616.1 | 1,015.8 | −527.3 | 1,210.9 | 64.3 |
| Curr.+ cap.− finan. acct. balance | 4y9na | 434.2 | 236.7 | 806.1 | 59.5 | 630.2 | † −80.6 | −1,185.5 | −133.5 | −352.0 | 62.5 | 323.1 | −75.2 |
| D. Net Errors and Omissions | 409na | −163.0 | 148.8 | −185.4 | 50.7 | 91.3 | † 112.4 | 73.8 | 150.7 | 442.7 | −50.4 | −158.9 | 101.2 |
| E. Reserves and Related Items | 4z9na | 271.2 | 385.5 | 620.7 | 110.3 | 721.6 | † 31.8 | −1,111.8 | 17.1 | 90.8 | 12.0 | 164.2 | 26.0 |
| Reserve assets | 3e9aa | 271.2 | 385.5 | 620.7 | 110.3 | 721.6 | † 31.8 | −1,111.8 | 17.1 | 90.8 | 12.0 | 164.2 | 26.0 |
| Credit and loans from the IMF | 3dcla | — | — | — | — | — | † — | — | — | — | — | — | — |
| Exceptional financing | 409la | . . . . | . . . . | . . . . | . . . . | . . . . | . . . . | . . . . | . . . . | . . . . | . . . . | . . . . | . . . . |

*Excludes components in group E

| **International Investment Position** | | | | | | | *Millions of US Dollars* | | | | | | |
|---|---|---|---|---|---|---|---|---|---|---|---|---|---|
| Assets | 809aa | 9,480.3 | 11,586.5 | 16,877.3 | 25,324.5 | 23,898.8 | † 24,089.6 | 23,757.1 | 26,081.2 | 30,749.7 | 33,546.6 | 33,237.8 | 30,943.6 |
| Direct investment | 8a9aa | 2,064.7 | 2,724.3 | 4,916.1 | 8,426.0 | 8,912.5 | † 8,576.6 | 8,668.1 | 7,846.4 | 9,413.0 | 10,469.7 | 10,317.1 | 9,163.7 |
| Equity & investment fund shares | 8aaaa | 1,057.3 | 1,524.2 | 2,838.2 | 4,898.8 | 4,732.7 | † 4,424.1 | 3,975.3 | 3,216.2 | 3,668.8 | 4,352.4 | 4,091.5 | 4,305.7 |
| Debt instruments | 8abaa | 1,007.4 | 1,200.1 | 2,077.9 | 3,527.2 | 4,179.8 | † 4,152.5 | 4,692.8 | 4,630.2 | 5,744.1 | 6,117.3 | 6,225.6 | 4,858.0 |
| Portfolio investment | 8b9aa | 2,244.0 | 2,962.9 | 4,821.6 | 6,414.0 | 3,761.2 | † 5,005.8 | 5,329.7 | 5,409.7 | 6,173.6 | 7,541.2 | 7,441.0 | 7,245.1 |
| Equity & investment fund shares | 8baaa | 534.9 | 1,014.8 | 1,786.5 | 2,940.7 | 1,123.0 | † 1,589.3 | 2,129.7 | 2,077.4 | 2,533.4 | 3,263.4 | 3,123.2 | 3,067.2 |
| Debt securities | 8bbaa | 1,709.1 | 1,948.1 | 3,035.0 | 3,473.3 | 2,638.2 | † 3,416.5 | 3,199.9 | 3,332.3 | 3,640.2 | 4,277.8 | 4,317.8 | 4,177.8 |
| Fin. der.(oth.than reserves) & ESOs | 8c9aa | 32.1 | 27.2 | 46.0 | 137.9 | 74.4 | † 45.2 | 45.6 | 92.4 | 57.4 | 102.6 | 109.3 | 66.1 |
| Other investment | 8d9aa | 3,343.2 | 3,922.6 | 4,302.9 | 7,051.7 | 7,227.3 | † 6,479.8 | 7,164.2 | 12,525.3 | 14,804.4 | 15,117.6 | 14,933.2 | 14,053.7 |
| Other equity | 8daaa | . . . . | . . . . | . . . . | . . . . | . . . . | † 52.3 | 52.6 | 155.2 | 241.3 | 350.3 | 355.9 | 321.8 |
| Debt instruments | 8dzaa | 3,343.2 | 3,922.6 | 4,302.9 | 7,051.7 | 7,227.3 | † 6,427.5 | 7,111.6 | 12,370.1 | 14,563.1 | 14,767.4 | 14,577.3 | 13,731.9 |
| Reserve assets | 8e9aa | 1,796.2 | 1,949.5 | 2,790.7 | 3,295.0 | 3,923.4 | † 3,982.0 | 2,549.6 | 207.5 | 301.3 | 315.5 | 437.1 | 415.1 |
| Liabilities | 809la | 20,740.1 | 22,699.8 | 29,903.7 | 42,353.6 | 41,233.1 | † 40,405.7 | 37,758.6 | 37,890.2 | 42,848.8 | 45,836.4 | 43,581.5 | 39,961.2 |
| Direct investment | 8a9la | 10,704.5 | 12,074.4 | 14,018.2 | 19,006.5 | 18,669.0 | † 18,155.3 | 18,674.6 | 19,390.8 | 22,284.7 | 24,885.2 | 23,915.0 | 22,016.6 |
| Equity & investment fund shares | 8aala | 8,766.1 | 10,187.8 | 10,940.1 | 14,262.9 | 13,956.4 | † 14,576.7 | 14,407.2 | 15,314.7 | 17,989.6 | 20,502.4 | 19,608.2 | 18,142.0 |
| Debt instruments | 8abla | 1,938.4 | 1,886.6 | 3,078.1 | 4,743.6 | 4,712.6 | † 3,578.6 | 4,267.5 | 4,076.0 | 4,295.0 | 4,382.8 | 4,306.8 | 3,874.6 |
| Portfolio investment | 8b9la | 4,504.7 | 3,380.6 | 3,898.3 | 4,594.5 | 2,904.2 | † 1,872.9 | 1,894.9 | 1,734.0 | 2,392.3 | 2,769.5 | 2,483.3 | 2,175.2 |
| Equity & investment fund shares | 8bala | 1,942.0 | 1,195.7 | 1,884.6 | 2,442.7 | 730.7 | † 878.0 | 1,193.5 | 837.8 | 1,009.3 | 1,139.1 | 888.1 | 792.2 |
| Debt securities | 8bbla | 2,562.7 | 2,184.9 | 2,013.7 | 2,151.8 | 2,173.4 | † 994.9 | 701.4 | 896.2 | 1,382.9 | 1,630.4 | 1,595.1 | 1,383.0 |
| Fin. der.(oth.than reserves) & ESOs | 8c9la | 20.7 | 10.0 | 33.2 | 47.3 | 68.3 | † 70.0 | 122.3 | 102.9 | 157.8 | 122.3 | 135.3 | 114.4 |
| Other investment | 8d9la | 5,510.1 | 7,234.8 | 11,954.0 | 18,705.3 | 19,591.6 | † 20,307.5 | 17,066.9 | 16,662.6 | 18,014.0 | 18,059.3 | 17,047.9 | 15,655.1 |
| Other equity | 8dala | . . . . | . . . . | . . . . | . . . . | . . . . | † — | — | — | — | 1.2 | 1.5 | 1.3 |
| Debt instruments | 8dzla | 5,510.1 | 7,234.8 | 11,954.0 | 18,705.3 | 19,591.6 | † 20,307.5 | 17,066.9 | 16,662.6 | 18,014.0 | 18,058.1 | 17,046.4 | 15,653.8 |

# Estonia  939

| | | 2004 | 2005 | 2006 | 2007 | 2008 | 2009 | 2010 | 2011 | 2012 | 2013 | 2014 | 2015 |
|---|---|---|---|---|---|---|---|---|---|---|---|---|---|
| **Government Finance Operations Statement General Government** | | | | | *Millions of Euros: Fiscal Year Ends December 31; Data Reported through Eurostat* | | | | | | | | |
| Revenue | a1 | 3,564.5 | 3,953.3 | 4,931.6 | 5,979.6 | 6,125.0 | 6,205.7 | 5,989.7 | 6,431.1 | 6,989.7 | 7,247.3 | 7,732.6 | 8,179.6 |
| Taxes | a11 | 2,014.3 | 2,206.2 | 2,750.6 | 3,363.2 | 3,267.8 | 3,100.5 | 2,990.3 | 3,288.4 | 3,649.8 | 3,882.0 | 4,228.8 | 4,534.7 |
| Social Contributions | a12 | 1,014.5 | 1,161.1 | 1,368.1 | 1,703.2 | 1,918.4 | 1,851.4 | 1,909.9 | 1,967.8 | 2,035.8 | 2,115.7 | 2,222.0 | 2,339.0 |
| Grants | a13 | …. | …. | …. | …. | …. | …. | …. | …. | …. | …. | …. | …. |
| Other Revenue | a14 | …. | …. | …. | …. | …. | …. | …. | …. | …. | …. | …. | …. |
| Expense | a2 | 3,124.9 | 3,540.5 | 4,107.2 | 4,882.4 | 5,861.9 | 6,018.0 | 5,879.9 | 6,083.0 | 6,395.2 | 6,822.4 | 7,164.6 | 7,640.9 |
| Compensation of Employees | a21 | 986.0 | 1,107.2 | 1,245.8 | 1,530.8 | 1,835.1 | 1,779.6 | 1,712.7 | 1,775.7 | 1,841.2 | 2,008.5 | 2,162.8 | 2,322.1 |
| Use of Goods & Services | a22 | 650.0 | 736.9 | 830.8 | 938.0 | 1,071.0 | 971.1 | 1,013.5 | 1,095.1 | 1,180.7 | 1,247.4 | 1,324.3 | 1,381.7 |
| Consumption of Fixed Capital | a23 | 179.2 | 204.4 | 248.8 | 308.2 | 364.2 | 394.7 | 416.8 | 430.9 | 477.0 | 535.4 | 596.8 | 621.2 |
| Interest | a24 | 21.3 | 21.4 | 22.5 | 26.9 | 34.1 | 26.8 | 19.4 | 21.5 | 26.1 | 21.2 | 20.8 | 19.5 |
| Subsidies | a25 | 76.6 | 81.4 | 114.6 | 138.3 | 157.7 | 133.6 | 156.4 | 163.5 | 160.4 | 128.4 | 90.6 | 80.9 |
| Grants | a26 | …. | …. | …. | …. | …. | …. | …. | …. | …. | …. | …. | …. |
| Social Benefits | a27 | 1,031.9 | 1,153.5 | 1,335.8 | 1,587.7 | 1,975.9 | 2,217.8 | 2,138.0 | 2,148.8 | 2,235.2 | 2,345.0 | 2,473.2 | 2,723.2 |
| Other Expense | a28 | …. | …. | …. | …. | …. | …. | …. | …. | …. | …. | …. | …. |
| Gross Operating Balance [1-2+23] | agob | 618.8 | 617.2 | 1,073.2 | 1,405.4 | 627.3 | 582.4 | 526.6 | 779.0 | 1,071.5 | 960.3 | 1,164.8 | 1,159.9 |
| Net Operating Balance [1-2] | anob | 439.6 | 412.8 | 824.4 | 1,097.2 | 263.1 | 187.7 | 109.8 | 348.1 | 594.5 | 424.9 | 568.0 | 538.7 |
| Net Acq. of Nonfinancial Assets | a31 | 207.6 | 286.4 | 431.4 | 655.8 | 703.6 | 496.6 | 82.2 | 155.0 | 640.8 | 457.1 | 415.1 | 447.6 |
| Aquisition of Nonfin. Assets | a31.1 | …. | …. | …. | …. | …. | …. | …. | …. | …. | …. | …. | …. |
| Disposal of Nonfin. Assets | a31.2 | …. | …. | …. | …. | …. | …. | …. | …. | …. | …. | …. | …. |
| Net Lending/Borrowing [1-2-31] | anlb | 232.0 | 126.4 | 393.0 | 441.4 | −440.5 | −308.9 | 27.6 | 193.1 | −46.3 | −32.2 | 152.9 | 91.1 |
| Net Acq. of Financial Assets | a32 | 312.2 | 249.7 | 544.7 | 520.7 | −248.5 | 107.6 | 81.2 | −14.6 | 728.1 | 148.2 | 257.1 | −101.1 |
| By instrument | | | | | | | | | | | | | |
| Monetary Gold & SDRs | a3201 | — | — | — | — | — | — | — | — | — | — | — | — |
| Currency & Deposits | a3202 | 102.3 | 145.0 | 92.6 | −29.1 | 43.4 | 396.3 | −207.3 | 97.6 | 123.7 | 175.7 | 6.7 | −313.2 |
| Securities other than Shares | a3203 | 55.5 | 89.2 | 368.2 | 261.6 | −329.5 | −145.0 | 13.9 | −249.1 | 50.9 | −171.3 | 141.1 | −47.5 |
| Loans | a3204 | −17.3 | −15.1 | −.9 | −10.2 | −6.7 | 37.9 | 57.2 | 48.2 | 298.7 | 130.4 | −19.8 | −8.3 |
| Shares & Other Equity | a3205 | 2.9 | −21.0 | 3.3 | 163.2 | 3.4 | −255.4 | 186.3 | 17.0 | 219.3 | 77.8 | 39.4 | 14.7 |
| Insurance Technical Reserves | a3206 | .4 | — | .4 | .4 | — | .5 | — | — | — | — | — | — |
| Financial Derivatives | a3207 | — | — | .6 | .1 | −2.0 | −2.7 | −1.1 | .4 | −1.0 | −3.2 | .8 | .2 |
| Other Accounts Receivable | a3208 | 168.4 | 51.6 | 80.5 | 134.7 | 42.9 | 76.0 | 32.2 | 71.3 | 36.5 | −61.2 | 88.9 | 253.0 |
| By debtor | | | | | | | | | | | | | |
| Domestic | a321 | …. | …. | …. | …. | …. | …. | …. | …. | …. | …. | …. | …. |
| Foreign | a322 | …. | …. | …. | …. | …. | …. | …. | …. | …. | …. | …. | …. |
| Net Incurrence of Liabilities | a33 | 110.1 | 100.4 | 166.3 | 74.5 | 219.4 | 424.9 | 33.3 | −188.9 | 766.2 | 188.4 | 99.4 | −181.7 |
| By instrument | | | | | | | | | | | | | |
| Special Drawing Rights (SDRs) | a3301 | — | — | — | — | — | — | — | — | — | — | — | — |
| Currency & Deposits | a3302 | — | — | — | — | — | — | — | — | — | — | — | — |
| Securities other than Shares | a3303 | 17.1 | 1.7 | 55.7 | −67.6 | 49.3 | 66.3 | 1.4 | 12.8 | −6.7 | 16.0 | −7.8 | −43.0 |
| Loans | a3304 | −18.6 | 5.2 | 29.1 | 65.7 | 97.4 | 185.3 | −32.4 | 9.2 | 735.7 | 137.5 | 126.7 | −35.4 |
| Shares & Other Equity | a3305 | — | — | — | — | — | — | — | — | — | — | — | — |
| Insurance Technical Reserves | a3306 | .7 | .3 | .1 | .3 | 3.1 | 1.8 | 1.0 | −.9 | −.8 | — | −1.1 | −.3 |
| Financial Derivatives | a3307 | .6 | .5 | 2.6 | −2.1 | .1 | .2 | 2.0 | 1.8 | 1.7 | −.5 | −.8 | −2.0 |
| Other Accounts Payable | a3308 | 110.3 | 92.7 | 78.8 | 78.2 | 69.5 | 171.3 | 61.3 | −211.8 | 36.3 | 35.4 | −17.6 | −101.0 |
| By creditor | | | | | | | | | | | | | |
| Domestic | a331 | …. | …. | …. | …. | …. | …. | …. | …. | …. | …. | …. | …. |
| Foreign | a332 | …. | …. | …. | …. | …. | …. | …. | …. | …. | …. | …. | …. |
| Stat. Discrepancy [32-33-NLB] | anlbz | −29.9 | 22.9 | −14.6 | 4.8 | −27.4 | −8.4 | 20.3 | −18.8 | 8.2 | −8.0 | 4.8 | −10.5 |
| Memo Item: Expenditure [2+31] | a2m | 3,332.5 | 3,826.9 | 4,538.6 | 5,538.2 | 6,565.5 | 6,514.6 | 5,962.1 | 6,238.0 | 7,036.0 | 7,279.5 | 7,579.7 | 8,088.5 |
| **Balance Sheet** | | | | | | | | | | | | | |
| Net Worth | a6 | …. | …. | …. | …. | …. | …. | …. | …. | …. | …. | …. | …. |
| Nonfinancial Assets | a61 | …. | …. | …. | …. | …. | …. | …. | …. | …. | …. | …. | …. |
| Financial Assets | a62 | 3,932.4 | 4,526.1 | 5,236.3 | 5,758.7 | 5,573.1 | 5,760.7 | 6,914.8 | 7,138.3 | 7,956.6 | 8,470.7 | 8,819.0 | 8,796.3 |
| By instrument | | | | | | | | | | | | | |
| Monetary Gold & SDRs | a6201 | — | — | — | — | — | — | — | — | — | — | — | — |
| Currency & Deposits | a6202 | 395.5 | 558.8 | 651.4 | 622.4 | 665.9 | 1,062.2 | 854.8 | 952.5 | 1,076.2 | 1,253.5 | 1,262.2 | 948.9 |
| Securities other than Shares | a6203 | 802.9 | 898.8 | 1,273.7 | 1,536.3 | 1,236.4 | 1,107.2 | 1,109.3 | 861.5 | 912.3 | 737.6 | 879.0 | 825.2 |
| Loans | a6204 | 191.9 | 172.9 | 172.0 | 161.8 | 155.2 | 193.1 | 250.3 | 298.5 | 597.3 | 728.0 | 708.2 | 699.9 |
| Shares and Other Equity | a6205 | 2,069.4 | 2,412.6 | 2,573.1 | 2,736.2 | 2,770.4 | 2,579.2 | 3,852.7 | 4,124.3 | 4,433.1 | 4,874.9 | 5,003.2 | 5,103.9 |
| Insurance Technical Reserves | a6206 | 1.6 | 1.7 | 2.9 | 3.3 | 3.3 | 2.9 | 1.4 | 1.4 | 1.4 | 1.4 | 1.4 | .5 |
| Financial Derivatives | a6207 | — | — | 1.4 | 2.2 | 2.4 | .6 | .3 | .2 | — | — | — | — |
| Other Accounts Receivable | a6208 | 471.1 | 481.3 | 561.8 | 696.5 | 739.5 | 815.5 | 846.0 | 899.9 | 936.3 | 875.3 | 965.0 | 1,217.9 |
| By debtor | | | | | | | | | | | | | |
| Domestic | a621 | …. | …. | …. | …. | …. | …. | …. | …. | …. | …. | …. | …. |
| Foreign | a622 | …. | …. | …. | …. | …. | …. | …. | …. | …. | …. | …. | …. |
| Liabilities | a63 | 837.3 | 919.0 | 1,085.3 | 1,178.2 | 1,389.6 | 1,805.3 | 1,758.4 | 1,566.8 | 2,329.7 | 2,545.5 | 2,725.6 | 2,543.8 |
| By instrument | | | | | | | | | | | | | |
| Special Drawing Rights (SDRs) | a6301 | — | — | — | — | — | — | — | — | — | — | — | — |
| Currency & Deposits | a6302 | — | — | — | — | — | — | — | — | — | — | — | — |
| Securities other than Shares | a6303 | 142.4 | 135.6 | 191.3 | 123.8 | 173.1 | 239.4 | 240.8 | 253.6 | 246.8 | 279.0 | 271.2 | 228.2 |
| Loans | a6304 | 354.2 | 381.4 | 410.4 | 476.2 | 573.6 | 758.9 | 726.4 | 735.7 | 1,471.3 | 1,613.2 | 1,801.8 | 1,766.4 |
| Shares and Other Equity | a6305 | — | — | — | — | — | — | — | — | — | — | — | — |
| Insurance Technical Reserves | a6306 | 2.4 | 2.7 | 2.8 | 3.1 | 6.2 | 8.1 | 9.1 | 8.3 | 7.5 | 7.5 | 6.5 | 6.1 |
| Financial Derivatives | a6307 | — | .1 | 2.8 | .7 | 1.0 | 2.8 | 2.3 | 2.1 | 1.8 | 1.2 | 2.7 | .7 |
| Other Accounts Payable | a6308 | 338.3 | 399.2 | 478.0 | 574.4 | 635.7 | 796.1 | 779.8 | 567.1 | 602.3 | 644.6 | 643.4 | 542.4 |
| By creditor | | | | | | | | | | | | | |
| Domestic | a631 | …. | …. | …. | …. | …. | …. | …. | …. | …. | …. | …. | …. |
| Foreign | a632 | …. | …. | …. | …. | …. | …. | …. | …. | …. | …. | …. | …. |
| Net Financial Worth [62-63] | a6m2 | 3,095.1 | 3,607.1 | 4,151.0 | 4,580.5 | 4,183.5 | 3,955.4 | 5,156.4 | 5,571.5 | 5,626.9 | 5,925.2 | 6,093.4 | 6,252.5 |
| Memo Item: Debt at Market Value | a6m3 | 837.3 | 918.9 | 1,082.5 | 1,177.5 | 1,388.6 | 1,802.5 | 1,756.1 | 1,564.7 | 2,327.9 | 2,544.3 | 2,722.9 | 2,543.1 |
| Memo Item: Debt at Face Value | a6m35 | 829.7 | 911.5 | 1,073.5 | 1,169.6 | 1,376.8 | 1,791.7 | 1,743.9 | 1,552.7 | 2,315.7 | 2,533.7 | 2,713.8 | 2,535.1 |
| Memo Item: Maastricht Debt | a6m36 | 491.4 | 512.3 | 595.5 | 595.2 | 741.1 | 995.6 | 964.1 | 985.6 | 1,713.4 | 1,889.1 | 2,070.4 | 1,992.7 |
| Memo Item: Debt at Nominal Value | a6m4 | …. | …. | …. | …. | …. | …. | …. | …. | …. | …. | …. | …. |

# Estonia 939

| National Accounts | | 2004 | 2005 | 2006 | 2007 | 2008 | 2009 | 2010 | 2011 | 2012 | 2013 | 2014 | 2015 |
|---|---|---|---|---|---|---|---|---|---|---|---|---|---|
| | | *Millions of Krooni through 2010; Millions of Euros Beginning 2011: End of Period* | | | | | | | | | | | |
| Househ.Cons.Expend.,incl.NPISHs.... | 96f | 85,383 | 97,130 | 115,974 | 135,391 | 139,207 | 117,099 | 117,372 | † 8,287 | 9,014 | 9,647 | 10,117 | 10,639 |
| Government Consumption Expend... | 91f | 26,740 | 30,088 | 33,933 | 41,359 | 48,946 | 47,519 | 46,748 | † 3,095 | 3,291 | 3,581 | 3,824 | 4,073 |
| Gross Fixed Capital Formation.......... | 93e | 46,805 | 56,153 | 75,405 | 85,349 | 77,026 | 46,150 | 42,779 | † 4,216 | 4,769 | 5,118 | 5,033 | 4,923 |
| Changes in Inventories.................... | 93i | 3,305 | 2,956 | 5,672 | 12,817 | −894 | −6,419 | 2,611 | † 519 | 296 | −88 | 387 | 72 |
| Exports of Goods and Services......... | 90c | 110,738 | 135,972 | 152,322 | 167,344 | 180,479 | 140,077 | 178,001 | † 14,424 | 15,590 | 16,132 | 16,544 | 16,316 |
| Imports of Goods and Services (-)..... | 98c | 121,430 | 147,343 | 173,787 | 193,486 | 190,740 | 127,696 | 162,925 | † 13,469 | 15,414 | 15,862 | 16,032 | 15,491 |
| Statistical Discrepancy..................... | 99bs | — | — | — | −1,128.0 | — | −1,406.3 | −485.1 | † −667 | 90 | 211 | −347 | −77 |
| Gross Domestic Product (GDP)......... | 99b | 151,542 | 174,956 | 209,520 | 247,646 | 254,023 | 215,323 | 224,101 | † 16,404 | 17,637 | 18,739 | 19,525 | 20,454 |
| Net Primary Income from Abroad..... | 98.n | −7,286 | −6,657 | −10,953 | −17,090 | −13,828 | −7,917 | −13,982 | † −855 | −831 | −601 | −477 | −426 |
| Gross National Income (GNI)........... | 99a | 144,256 | 168,300 | 198,567 | 230,556 | 240,195 | 207,406 | 210,119 | † 15,361 | 16,584 | 17,834 | 19,049 | 20,035 |
| Net Current Transf.from Abroad....... | 98t | 818 | 337 | −123 | 1,032 | 2,698 | 2,768 | 3,754 | † 298 | 306 | 128 | 19 | 11 |
| Gross Nat'l Disposable Inc.(GNDI).... | 99i | 145,073 | 168,637 | 198,040 | 231,173 | 242,126 | 210,174 | 213,873 | † 15,659 | 16,891 | 17,963 | 19,068 | 20,045 |
| Gross Saving................................. | 99s | 32,950 | 41,419 | 48,133 | 54,424 | 53,973 | 45,556 | 49,753 | † 4,344 | 4,632 | 4,764 | 5,079 | 5,307 |
| Consumption of Fixed Capital.......... | 99cf | 18,699 | 21,478 | 25,492 | 30,029 | 33,161 | 34,324 | 35,160 | † 2,355 | 2,560 | 2,770 | 3,065 | 3,275 |
| GDP Volume 2000 Prices................ | 99b.p | 129,004 | 141,170 | 156,080 | 166,880 | 158,430 | 136,409 | 140,645 | .... | .... | .... | .... | .... |
| GDP Volume 2005 Prices................ | 99b.p | .... | † 174,956 | 192,622 | 207,054 | 199,453 | 171,016 | 174,887 | .... | .... | .... | .... | .... |
| GDP Volume 2010 Ref., Chained..... | 99b.p | .... | .... | .... | .... | .... | .... | .... | † 15,925 | 16,665 | 16,937 | 17,290 | 17,611 |
| GDP Volume (2010=100)............... | 99bvp | 91.4 | † 100.0 | 110.1 | 118.4 | 114.0 | 97.8 | 100.0 | † 109.5 | 114.6 | 116.5 | 118.9 | 121.1 |
| GDP Deflator (2010=100).............. | 99bip | 74.0 | 78.0 | 84.9 | 93.3 | 99.4 | 98.3 | 100.0 | 104.6 | 107.4 | 112.3 | 114.6 | 117.9 |
| | | *Millions: Midyear Estimates* | | | | | | | | | | | |
| Population................................ | 99z | 1.36 | 1.36 | 1.35 | 1.34 | 1.34 | 1.34 | 1.33 | 1.33 | 1.32 | 1.32 | 1.32 | 1.31 |

# Ethiopia 644

| | | 2004 | 2005 | 2006 | 2007 | 2008 | 2009 | 2010 | 2011 | 2012 | 2013 | 2014 | 2015 |
|---|---|---|---|---|---|---|---|---|---|---|---|---|---|
| **Exchange Rates** | | | | | | *Birr per SDR: End of Period* | | | | | | | |
| Official Rate | aa | 13.44 | 12.41 | 13.20 | 14.54 | 15.33 | 19.82 | 25.49 | 26.42 | 27.95 | .... | .... | .... |
| | | | | | | *Birr per US Dollar: End of Period (ae) Period Average (rf)* | | | | | | | |
| Official Rate | ae | 8.65 | 8.68 | 8.78 | 9.20 | 9.96 | 12.64 | 16.55 | 17.21 | 18.18 | .... | .... | .... |
| Official Rate | rf | 8.64 | 8.67 | 8.70 | 8.97 | 9.60 | 11.78 | 14.41 | 16.90 | 17.70 | .... | .... | .... |
| **Fund Position** | | | | | | *Millions of SDRs: End of Period* | | | | | | | |
| Quota | 2f.s | 133.70 | 133.70 | 133.70 | 133.70 | 133.70 | 133.70 | 133.70 | 133.70 | 133.70 | 133.70 | 133.70 | 133.70 |
| SDR Holdings | 1b.s | .33 | .13 | .04 | .06 | .03 | 17.46 | 97.41 | 97.27 | 97.24 | 97.21 | 93.84 | 68.41 |
| Reserve Position in the Fund | 1c.s | 7.19 | 7.19 | 7.33 | 7.37 | 7.44 | 7.51 | 7.51 | 7.51 | 7.51 | 7.51 | 7.51 | 7.51 |
| Total Fund Cred.&Loans Outstg. | 2tl | 117.97 | 112.07 | — | — | — | 106.96 | 187.18 | 187.18 | 187.18 | 187.18 | 183.84 | 158.43 |
| SDR Allocations | 1bd | 11.16 | 11.16 | 11.16 | 11.16 | 11.16 | 127.93 | 127.93 | 127.93 | 127.93 | 127.93 | 127.93 | 127.93 |
| **International Liquidity** | | | | | | *Millions of US Dollars Unless Otherwise Indicated: End of Period* | | | | | | | |
| Total Reserves minus Gold | 1l.d | 1,496.8 | 1,042.6 | 867.4 | 1,289.9 | 870.5 | 1,780.9 | .... | .... | .... | .... | .... | .... |
| SDR Holdings | 1b.d | .5 | .2 | .1 | .1 | — | 27.4 | 150.0 | 149.3 | 149.4 | 149.7 | 136.0 | 94.8 |
| Reserve Position in the Fund | 1c.d | 11.2 | 10.3 | 11.0 | 11.6 | 11.5 | 11.8 | 11.6 | 11.5 | 11.5 | 11.6 | 10.9 | 10.4 |
| Foreign Exchange | 1d.d | 1,485.1 | 1,032.1 | 856.3 | 1,278.1 | 859.0 | 1,741.7 | .... | .... | .... | .... | .... | .... |
| Gold (Million Fine Troy Ounces) | 1ad | — | — | — | — | — | — | .... | .... | .... | .... | .... | .... |
| Gold (National Valuation) | 1and | — | — | — | — | — | — | .... | .... | .... | .... | .... | .... |
| Monetary Authorities: Other Liabs. | 4..d | .3 | .4 | .3 | .3 | .3 | .... | .... | .... | .... | .... | .... | .... |
| Deposit Money Banks: Assets | 7a.d | 607.8 | 851.0 | 900.9 | 691.8 | 698.2 | .... | .... | .... | .... | .... | .... | .... |
| Deposit Money Banks: Liabs. | 7b.d | 190.6 | 189.9 | 201.3 | 239.6 | 284.9 | .... | .... | .... | .... | .... | .... | .... |
| Other Banking Insts.: Assets | 7e.d | 6.3 | 6.6 | 1.0 | .... | .... | .... | .... | .... | .... | .... | .... | .... |
| Other Banking Insts.: Liabs. | 7f.d | 32.9 | 36.8 | 41.6 | .... | .... | .... | .... | .... | .... | .... | .... | .... |
| **Monetary Authorities** | | | | | | *Millions of Birr: End of Period* | | | | | | | |
| Foreign Assets | 11 | 13,184.7 | 10,583.4 | 7,756.9 | 12,282.0 | 9,178.1 | .... | .... | .... | .... | .... | .... | .... |
| Claims on Central Government | 12a | 22,726.2 | 28,151.1 | 28,165.7 | 31,995.3 | 42,949.0 | .... | .... | .... | .... | .... | .... | .... |
| Claims on Other Financial Insts. | 12f | 395.3 | 1.0 | 1.0 | 1.0 | 1.0 | .... | .... | .... | .... | .... | .... | .... |
| Reserve Money | 14 | 22,472.8 | 24,494.5 | 22,465.5 | 29,081.5 | 40,084.7 | .... | .... | .... | .... | .... | .... | .... |
| of which: Currency Outside DMBs. | 14a | 8,274.5 | 9,623.3 | 11,606.4 | 14,445.8 | 17,432.9 | .... | .... | .... | .... | .... | .... | .... |
| Foreign Liabilities | 16c | 1,737.5 | 1,532.8 | 150.0 | 164.9 | 173.8 | .... | .... | .... | .... | .... | .... | .... |
| Central Government Deposits | 16d | 7,440.9 | 8,989.8 | 10,795.6 | 11,580.8 | 10,330.2 | .... | .... | .... | .... | .... | .... | .... |
| Central Govt. Lending Funds | 16f | 736.9 | 855.3 | 55.5 | 57.7 | 59.3 | .... | .... | .... | .... | .... | .... | .... |
| Capital Accounts | 17a | 3,302.7 | 3,267.4 | 2,104.2 | 2,952.7 | 1,914.6 | .... | .... | .... | .... | .... | .... | .... |
| Other Items (Net) | 17r | 615.4 | -404.3 | 352.7 | 440.8 | -434.6 | .... | .... | .... | .... | .... | .... | .... |
| **Deposit Money Banks** | | | | | | *Millions of Birr: End of Period* | | | | | | | |
| Reserves | 20 | 14,239.6 | 14,491.5 | 10,058.4 | 14,355.5 | 20,659.3 | .... | .... | .... | .... | .... | .... | .... |
| Foreign Assets | 21 | 5,258.3 | 7,387.9 | 7,905.7 | 6,364.8 | 6,950.6 | .... | .... | .... | .... | .... | .... | .... |
| Claims on Central Government | 22a | 6,060.0 | 7,847.0 | 12,287.6 | 16,074.0 | 5,547.2 | .... | .... | .... | .... | .... | .... | .... |
| Claims on Nonfin.Pub.Enterprises | 22c | 2,592.5 | 2,768.3 | 2,411.6 | 3,479.9 | 9,337.2 | .... | .... | .... | .... | .... | .... | .... |
| Claims on Private Sector | 22d | 14,432.6 | 20,234.5 | 27,122.3 | 32,100.5 | 44,148.1 | .... | .... | .... | .... | .... | .... | .... |
| Claims on Other Financial Insts. | 22f | 570.9 | 1,002.1 | 1,174.9 | 1,627.3 | 1,576.5 | .... | .... | .... | .... | .... | .... | .... |
| Demand Deposits | 24 | 13,933.1 | 16,132.1 | 20,207.0 | 24,175.9 | 31,391.6 | .... | .... | .... | .... | .... | .... | .... |
| Time, Savings,& Fgn.Currency Dep. | 25 | 17,292.9 | 20,987.5 | 24,302.7 | 29,974.2 | 35,882.2 | .... | .... | .... | .... | .... | .... | .... |
| Foreign Liabilities | 26c | 1,649.3 | 1,648.4 | 1,766.7 | 2,204.5 | 2,836.6 | .... | .... | .... | .... | .... | .... | .... |
| Central Government Deposits | 26d | 858.6 | 1,465.2 | 1,602.0 | 1,186.2 | 1,160.2 | .... | .... | .... | .... | .... | .... | .... |
| Central Govt. Lending Funds | 26f | 26.2 | 22.4 | 17.0 | 17.3 | 18.0 | .... | .... | .... | .... | .... | .... | .... |
| Capital Accounts | 27a | 3,087.6 | 3,645.1 | 4,595.6 | 8,502.6 | 10,537.1 | .... | .... | .... | .... | .... | .... | .... |
| Other Items (Net) | 27r | 6,306.2 | 9,830.5 | 8,469.5 | 7,941.3 | 6,393.2 | .... | .... | .... | .... | .... | .... | .... |
| **Monetary Survey** | | | | | | *Millions of Birr: End of Period* | | | | | | | |
| Foreign Assets (Net) | 31n | 15,056.2 | 14,790.2 | 13,745.8 | 16,277.5 | 13,118.3 | .... | .... | .... | .... | .... | .... | .... |
| Domestic Credit | 32 | 38,479.6 | 49,555.4 | 58,769.6 | 72,516.0 | 92,232.5 | .... | .... | .... | .... | .... | .... | .... |
| Claims on Central Govt. (Net) | 32an | 20,486.7 | 25,543.0 | 28,055.7 | 35,302.2 | 37,005.8 | .... | .... | .... | .... | .... | .... | .... |
| Claims on Nonfin.Pub.Enterprises | 32c | 2,592.5 | 2,768.3 | 2,411.6 | 3,479.9 | 9,337.2 | .... | .... | .... | .... | .... | .... | .... |
| Claims on Private Sector | 32d | 14,434.2 | 20,241.0 | 27,126.4 | 32,105.6 | 44,311.9 | .... | .... | .... | .... | .... | .... | .... |
| Claims on Other Financial Insts. | 32f | 966.2 | 1,003.1 | 1,175.9 | 1,628.3 | 1,577.5 | .... | .... | .... | .... | .... | .... | .... |
| Money | 34 | 22,312.0 | 25,980.7 | 32,056.2 | 38,903.5 | 49,105.8 | .... | .... | .... | .... | .... | .... | .... |
| Quasi-Money | 35 | 17,292.9 | 20,987.5 | 24,302.7 | 29,974.2 | 35,882.2 | .... | .... | .... | .... | .... | .... | .... |
| Central Government Lending Funds | 36f | 763.1 | 877.7 | 72.5 | 75.0 | 77.3 | .... | .... | .... | .... | .... | .... | .... |
| Capital Accounts | 37a | 6,390.3 | 6,912.5 | 6,699.7 | 11,455.3 | 12,451.7 | .... | .... | .... | .... | .... | .... | .... |
| Other Items (Net) | 37r | 6,777.5 | 9,587.2 | 9,384.2 | 8,385.5 | 7,833.8 | .... | .... | .... | .... | .... | .... | .... |
| Money plus Quasi-Money | 35l | 39,604.9 | 46,968.2 | 56,358.9 | 68,877.7 | 84,988.0 | .... | .... | .... | .... | .... | .... | .... |
| **Other Banking Institutions** | | | | | | *Millions of Birr: End of Period* | | | | | | | |
| Reserves | 40 | 72.6 | 10.7 | 17.1 | .... | .... | .... | .... | .... | .... | .... | .... | .... |
| Foreign Assets | 41 | 54.7 | 57.2 | 8.4 | .... | .... | .... | .... | .... | .... | .... | .... | .... |
| Claims on Central Government | 42a | 96.6 | 88.7 | 88.7 | .... | .... | .... | .... | .... | .... | .... | .... | .... |
| Claims on Nonfin.Pub.Enterprises | 42c | 179.5 | 179.0 | 175.6 | .... | .... | .... | .... | .... | .... | .... | .... | .... |
| Claims on Private Sector | 42d | 2,330.5 | 4,235.8 | 4,260.3 | .... | .... | .... | .... | .... | .... | .... | .... | .... |
| Claims on Deposit Money Banks | 42e | 156.4 | 237.2 | 551.9 | .... | .... | .... | .... | .... | .... | .... | .... | .... |
| Demand Deposits | 44 | 13.5 | 5.9 | 15.5 | .... | .... | .... | .... | .... | .... | .... | .... | .... |
| Time and Savings Deposits | 45 | 685.1 | 674.7 | 580.1 | .... | .... | .... | .... | .... | .... | .... | .... | .... |
| Foreign Liabilities | 46c | 284.3 | 319.9 | 365.2 | .... | .... | .... | .... | .... | .... | .... | .... | .... |
| Central Govt. Lending Funds | 46f | 72.6 | 73.1 | 72.7 | .... | .... | .... | .... | .... | .... | .... | .... | .... |
| Credit from Monetary Authorities | 46g | 381.4 | 381.4 | 381.4 | .... | .... | .... | .... | .... | .... | .... | .... | .... |
| Credit from Deposit Money Banks | 46h | 565.3 | 901.0 | 1,129.5 | .... | .... | .... | .... | .... | .... | .... | .... | .... |
| Capital Accounts | 47a | 520.3 | 1,859.4 | 1,880.1 | .... | .... | .... | .... | .... | .... | .... | .... | .... |
| Other Items (Net) | 47r | 367.9 | 593.2 | 677.6 | .... | .... | .... | .... | .... | .... | .... | .... | .... |

| | | 2004 | 2005 | 2006 | 2007 | 2008 | 2009 | 2010 | 2011 | 2012 | 2013 | 2014 | 2015 |
|---|---|---|---|---|---|---|---|---|---|---|---|---|---|
| **Banking Survey** | | | | | *Millions of Birr: End of Period* | | | | | | | | |
| Foreign Assets (Net) | 51n | 14,826.6 | 14,527.5 | 13,389.0 | .... | .... | .... | .... | .... | .... | .... | .... | .... |
| Domestic Credit | 52 | 40,120.1 | 53,055.8 | 62,118.3 | .... | .... | .... | .... | .... | .... | .... | .... | .... |
| Claims on Central Govt. (Net) | 52an | 20,583.3 | 25,631.7 | 28,144.4 | .... | .... | .... | .... | .... | .... | .... | .... | .... |
| Claims on Nonfin.Pub.Enterprises | 52c | 2,772.1 | 2,947.3 | 2,587.2 | .... | .... | .... | .... | .... | .... | .... | .... | .... |
| Claims on Private Sector | 52d | 16,764.7 | 24,476.8 | 31,386.7 | .... | .... | .... | .... | .... | .... | .... | .... | .... |
| Liquid Liabilities | 55l | 40,230.9 | 47,638.2 | 56,937.3 | .... | .... | .... | .... | .... | .... | .... | .... | .... |
| Central Govt. Lending Funds | 56f | 835.7 | 950.8 | 145.2 | .... | .... | .... | .... | .... | .... | .... | .... | .... |
| Capital Accounts | 57a | 6,910.6 | 8,771.9 | 8,579.8 | .... | .... | .... | .... | .... | .... | .... | .... | .... |
| Other Items (Net) | 57r | 6,969.5 | 10,222.4 | 9,845.0 | .... | .... | .... | .... | .... | .... | .... | .... | .... |
| **Money (National Definitions)** | | | | | *Millions of Birr: End of Period* | | | | | | | | |
| Base Money | 19ma | 22,705.6 | 24,269.2 | 22,222.8 | .... | .... | .... | .... | .... | .... | .... | .... | .... |
| M1 | 59ma | 18,662.9 | 21,205.8 | 25,592.7 | .... | .... | .... | .... | .... | .... | .... | .... | .... |
| M2 | 59mb | 35,882.0 | 42,098.9 | 49,811.3 | .... | .... | .... | .... | .... | .... | .... | .... | .... |
| **Interest Rates** | | | | | *Percent Per Annum* | | | | | | | | |
| Treasury Bill Rate | 60c | .56 | .25 | .08 | .93 | .68 | .... | .... | .... | .... | .... | .... | .... |
| Savings Rate | 60k | 3.00 | 3.00 | 3.00 | 3.50 | 4.00 | .... | .... | .... | .... | .... | .... | .... |
| Deposit Rate | 60l | 3.38 | 3.46 | 3.56 | 4.11 | 4.68 | .... | .... | .... | .... | .... | .... | .... |
| Lending Rate | 60p | 7.00 | 7.00 | 7.00 | 7.50 | 8.00 | .... | .... | .... | .... | .... | .... | .... |
| Government Bond Yield | 61 | 3.91 | 3.98 | 4.00 | 4.00 | 4.00 | .... | .... | .... | .... | .... | .... | .... |
| **Prices and Labor** | | | | | *Index Numbers (2010=100): Period Averages* | | | | | | | | |
| Producer Prices (2007=100) | 63 | .... | .... | 56.1 | 71.7 | 105.4 | 102.0 | 100.0 | .... | .... | .... | .... | .... |
| Consumer Prices | 64 | 39.7 | † 44.8 | 50.4 | 59.0 | 85.3 | 92.5 | 100.0 | 133.2 | † 163.6 | 176.8 | 189.8 | 209.1 |
| | | | | | *Number in Thousands: Period Averages* | | | | | | | | |
| Labor Force | 67d | .... | 33,089 | .... | .... | .... | .... | .... | .... | .... | .... | .... | .... |
| **Intl. Transactions & Positions** | | | | | *Millions of Birr* | | | | | | | | |
| Exports | 70 | 5,309.3 | 8,028.3 | 9,082.2 | 11,474.8 | 14,946.0 | 17,732.3 | 32,259.9 | 50,183.0 | 56,276.3 | 55,501.1 | 64,763.2 | .... |
| Imports, c.i.f. | 71 | 24,830.6 | 35,365.9 | 46,141.9 | 52,007.4 | 79,453.0 | 90,310.2 | 123,270.8 | 150,434.7 | 211,124.5 | 212,684.3 | 301,047.7 | .... |
| **Balance of Payments** | | | | | *Millions of US Dollars* | | | | | | | | |
| A. Current Account* | 109bx | −667.8 | −1,567.8 | −1,785.9 | −828.0 | −1,805.7 | −2,190.7 | −425.4 | −783.1 | −2,985.3 | .... | .... | |
| Goods, credit (exports) | 1a9cx | 678.3 | 917.3 | 1,055.5 | 1,350.8 | 1,718.6 | 1,694.7 | 2,479.5 | 3,029.0 | 3,258.0 | .... | .... | |
| Goods, debit (imports) | 1a9dx | 2,768.5 | 3,700.9 | 4,105.6 | 5,155.6 | 7,206.3 | 6,819.0 | 7,364.5 | 8,328.9 | 10,547.3 | .... | .... | |
| Balance on goods | 1a9bx | −2,090.2 | −2,783.5 | −3,050.0 | −3,804.9 | −5,487.7 | −5,124.4 | −4,885.0 | −5,299.8 | −7,289.3 | .... | .... | |
| Services, credit (exports) | 1b9cx | 1,005.5 | 1,012.1 | 1,142.9 | 1,298.8 | 1,776.7 | 1,735.2 | 2,164.7 | 2,785.8 | 2,735.9 | .... | .... | |
| Services, debit (imports) | 1b9dx | 958.3 | 1,193.8 | 1,170.6 | 1,748.9 | 2,391.6 | 2,223.8 | 2,546.3 | 3,321.8 | 3,582.6 | .... | .... | |
| Balance on Goods & Services | 1z9bx | −2,043.0 | −2,965.2 | −3,077.6 | −4,254.9 | −6,102.6 | −5,612.9 | −5,266.6 | −5,835.8 | −8,136.0 | .... | .... | |
| Primary income: credit | 1c9cx | 31.7 | 43.4 | 55.8 | 76.5 | 37.5 | 6.5 | 8.1 | 8.8 | 8.7 | .... | .... | |
| Primary income: debit | 1c9dx | 60.3 | 48.0 | 37.8 | 36.9 | 35.9 | 43.3 | 71.7 | 85.6 | 105.5 | .... | .... | |
| Balance on gds, serv. & prim. inc. | 1y9bx | −2,071.6 | −2,969.8 | −3,059.7 | −4,215.3 | −6,101.0 | −5,649.7 | −5,330.1 | −5,912.7 | −8,232.9 | .... | .... | |
| Secondary income: credit | 1d9ca | 1,420.6 | 1,426.0 | 1,297.2 | 3,414.9 | 4,343.8 | 3,499.7 | 4,987.9 | 5,172.9 | 5,326.8 | .... | .... | |
| Secondary income: debit | 1d9da | 16.8 | 23.9 | 23.4 | 27.5 | 48.5 | 40.7 | 83.2 | 43.3 | 79.3 | .... | .... | |
| B. Capital Account* | 209ba | — | — | — | — | — | — | — | — | — | .... | .... | |
| Capital account: credit | 209ca | — | — | — | — | — | — | — | — | — | .... | .... | |
| Capital account: debit | 209da | — | — | — | — | — | — | — | — | — | .... | .... | |
| Balance on current & capital acct. | 129ba | −667.8 | −1,567.8 | −1,785.9 | −828.0 | −1,805.7 | −2,190.7 | −425.4 | −783.1 | −2,985.3 | .... | .... | |
| C. Financial Account* | 309na | −73.2 | −758.6 | −976.3 | −447.7 | −736.7 | −1,654.3 | −2,368.5 | −1,869.9 | −666.7 | .... | .... | |
| Direct investment: assets | 3a9aa | — | — | — | — | — | — | — | — | — | .... | .... | |
| Equity & investment fund shares | 3aaaa | — | — | — | — | — | — | — | — | — | .... | .... | |
| Debt instruments | 3abaa | — | — | — | — | — | — | — | — | — | .... | .... | |
| Direct investment: liabilities | 3a9la | — | 265.1 | 545.3 | 222.0 | 108.5 | 221.5 | 288.3 | 626.5 | 278.6 | .... | .... | |
| Equity & investment fund shares | 3aala | — | — | — | — | — | — | — | — | — | .... | .... | |
| Debt instruments | 3abla | — | 265.1 | 545.3 | 222.0 | 108.5 | 221.5 | 288.3 | 626.5 | 278.6 | .... | .... | |
| Portfolio investment: assets | 3b9aa | — | — | — | — | — | — | — | — | — | .... | .... | |
| Equity & investment fund shares | 3baaa | — | — | — | — | — | — | — | — | — | .... | .... | |
| Debt securities | 3bbaa | — | — | — | — | — | — | — | — | — | .... | .... | |
| Portfolio investment: liabilities | 3b9la | — | — | — | — | — | — | — | — | — | .... | .... | |
| Equity & investment fund shares | 3bala | — | — | — | — | — | — | — | — | — | .... | .... | |
| Debt securities | 3bbla | — | — | — | — | — | — | — | — | — | .... | .... | |
| Fin. der.& empl.stk.ops.(ESOs): net | 3c9na | .... | .... | .... | .... | — | — | .... | .... | .... | .... | .... | |
| Fin. der. & ESOs.: assets | 3c9aa | .... | .... | .... | .... | .... | .... | .... | .... | .... | .... | .... | |
| Fin. der. & ESOs.: liabilities | 3c9la | .... | .... | .... | .... | .... | .... | .... | .... | .... | .... | .... | |
| Other investment: assets | 3d9aa | 261.8 | −302.2 | −73.3 | 108.1 | −113.0 | −420.3 | −1,084.6 | −171.3 | 142.7 | .... | .... | |
| Other equity | 3daaa | .... | .... | .... | .... | .... | .... | .... | .... | .... | .... | .... | |
| Debt instruments | 3dzaa | 261.8 | −302.2 | −73.3 | 108.1 | −113.0 | −420.3 | −1,084.6 | −171.3 | 142.7 | .... | .... | |
| Other investment: liabilities | 3d9la | 335.0 | 191.2 | 357.7 | 333.8 | 515.2 | 1,012.6 | 995.6 | 1,072.1 | 530.8 | .... | .... | |
| Other equity | 3dala | .... | .... | .... | .... | .... | .... | .... | .... | .... | .... | .... | |
| Debt instruments | 3dzla | 335.0 | 191.2 | 357.7 | 333.8 | 515.2 | 1,012.6 | 995.6 | 1,072.1 | 530.8 | .... | .... | |
| Curr.+ cap.− finan. acct. balance | 4y9na | −594.7 | −809.2 | −809.6 | −380.3 | −1,069.1 | −536.4 | 1,943.1 | 1,086.9 | −2,318.5 | .... | .... | |
| D. Net Errors and Omissions | 409na | −354.1 | 486.3 | 1,161.3 | −156.5 | 1,450.7 | −793.1 | −2,929.9 | −1,795.8 | 2,648.6 | .... | .... | |
| E. Reserves and Related Items | 4z9na | −948.8 | −322.9 | 351.7 | −536.8 | 381.6 | −1,329.5 | −986.8 | −708.9 | 330.0 | .... | .... | |
| Reserve assets | 3e9aa | −544.3 | −330.3 | 189.6 | −536.8 | 381.6 | −1,163.8 | −865.3 | −708.9 | 330.0 | .... | .... | |
| Credit and loans from the IMF | 3dcla | 17.8 | −8.7 | −162.2 | — | — | 165.7 | 121.5 | — | — | .... | .... | |
| Exceptional financing | 409la | 386.8 | 1.2 | — | — | — | — | — | — | — | .... | .... | |

*Excludes components in group E

# Ethiopia   644

| | | 2004 | 2005 | 2006 | 2007 | 2008 | 2009 | 2010 | 2011 | 2012 | 2013 | 2014 | 2015 |
|---|---|---|---|---|---|---|---|---|---|---|---|---|---|
| **Government Finance** | | | | | | | | | | | | | |
| **Cash Flow Statement** | | | | | | | | | | | | | |
| **Budgetary Central Government** | | | | | | *Millions of Birr: Fiscal Year Ends July 7* | | | | | | | |
| Cash Receipts:Operating Activities... | c1 | 16,086.6 | 17,072.8 | 13,646.5 | 16,878.5 | 36,789.9 | 47,749.0 | 60,382.1 | 77,455.4 | .... | .... | .... | .... |
| Taxes............................................. | c11 | 8,453.8 | 9,360.4 | 10,960.8 | 13,539.8 | 19,551.5 | 22,242.1 | 31,500.8 | 47,435.4 | .... | .... | .... | .... |
| Social Contributions...................... | c12 | — | — | — | — | — | — | — | — | .... | .... | .... | .... |
| Grants.......................................... | c13 | 5,691.3 | 5,339.1 | 1,878.4 | 2,550.4 | 11,411.2 | 15,973.9 | 18,854.7 | 21,433.1 | .... | .... | .... | .... |
| Other Receipts.............................. | c14 | 1,941.5 | 2,373.3 | 807.3 | 788.3 | 5,827.2 | 9,533.0 | 10,026.6 | 8,587.0 | .... | .... | .... | .... |
| Cash Payments:Operating Activities. | c2 | 14,118.0 | 15,934.3 | 12,622.9 | 13,333.0 | 32,221.8 | 41,073.3 | 48,246.9 | 54,515.6 | .... | .... | .... | .... |
| Compensation of Employees.......... | c21 | 1,941.4 | 1,966.8 | 2,699.1 | 3,662.4 | 5,108.2 | 6,149.2 | 6,978.6 | 6,978.6 | .... | .... | .... | .... |
| Purchases of Goods & Services....... | c22 | 3,268.9 | 2,999.8 | 4,313.2 | 4,706.0 | 5,039.8 | 8,588.0 | 10,364.0 | 10,820.1 | .... | .... | .... | .... |
| Interest......................................... | c24 | 1,104.3 | 1,114.0 | 2,427.8 | 2,427.8 | 1,578.2 | 1,383.8 | 1,577.7 | 2,004.2 | .... | .... | .... | .... |
| Subsidies...................................... | c25 | — | — | 2,823.1 | 637.3 | 19,059.8 | 18,152.4 | 23,661.9 | 27,732.0 | .... | .... | .... | .... |
| Grants.......................................... | c26 | 5,528.1 | 6,653.2 | 353.5 | 510.0 | 335.2 | 5,570.4 | 5,526.0 | 6,980.6 | .... | .... | .... | .... |
| Social Benefits.............................. | c27 | .9 | .9 | — | — | — | — | — | — | .... | .... | .... | .... |
| Other Payments............................ | c28 | 2,274.4 | 3,199.6 | 6.2 | 1,389.5 | 1,100.6 | 1,229.5 | 138.7 | — | .... | .... | .... | .... |
| Net Cash Inflow:Operating Act.[1-2] | ccio | 1,968.6 | 1,138.5 | 1,023.6 | 3,545.5 | 4,568.2 | 6,675.7 | 12,135.2 | 22,939.9 | .... | .... | .... | .... |
| Net Cash Outflow:Invest. in NFA...... | c31 | 4,869.5 | 5,941.7 | 6,607.4 | 8,325.1 | 9,376.1 | 14,187.2 | 22,684.9 | 29,892.6 | .... | .... | .... | .... |
| Purchases of Nonfinancial Assets... | c31.1 | 4,869.5 | 5,941.7 | 6,607.4 | 8,325.1 | 9,376.1 | 14,187.2 | 22,684.9 | 29,892.6 | .... | .... | .... | .... |
| Sales of Nonfinancial Assets.......... | c31.2 | | | | | | | | | .... | .... | .... | .... |
| Cash Surplus/Deficit [1-2-31=1-2M] | ccsd | −2,900.9 | −4,803.2 | −5,583.8 | −4,779.6 | −4,807.9 | −7,511.5 | −10,549.7 | −6,952.7 | .... | .... | .... | .... |
| Net Acq. Fin. Assets, excl. Cash....... | c32x | | 47.4 | 3,268.3 | 5,010.6 | 8,795.6 | 13,454.6 | 64,069.3 | 24,600.3 | .... | .... | .... | .... |
| Domestic....................................... | c321x | — | — | 3,220.9 | 4,963.2 | 6,927.8 | 8,763.7 | 55,019.3 | 13,149.3 | .... | .... | .... | .... |
| Foreign......................................... | c322x | — | 47.4 | 47.4 | 47.4 | 1,867.8 | 4,690.9 | 9,050.0 | 11,451.0 | .... | .... | .... | .... |
| Net Incurrence of Liabilities.............. | c33 | 4,227.5 | 5,713.3 | 29,856.8 | 36,105.5 | 40,850.6 | 49,378.5 | 51,199.9 | 62,383.0 | .... | .... | .... | .... |
| Domestic....................................... | c331 | 2,824.3 | 4,606.1 | 29,638.4 | 34,397.8 | 40,376.2 | 44,791.6 | 51,029.6 | 60,808.0 | .... | .... | .... | .... |
| Foreign......................................... | c332 | 1,403.2 | 1,107.2 | 218.4 | 1,707.7 | 474.4 | 4,586.9 | 170.3 | 1,575.0 | .... | .... | .... | .... |
| Net Cash Inflow, Fin.Act.[-32x+33].. | cnfb | 4,227.5 | 5,665.9 | 26,588.5 | 31,094.9 | 32,055.0 | 35,923.9 | −12,869.4 | 37,782.6 | .... | .... | .... | .... |
| Net Change in Stock of Cash........... | cncb | 1,326.6 | 910.0 | 4,493.9 | 5,036.1 | 4,785.9 | 22,772.2 | 5,735.1 | 24,907.7 | .... | .... | .... | .... |
| Stat. Discrep. [32X-33+NCB-CSD].... | ccsdz | | 47.3 | −16,510.8 | −21,279.2 | −22,461.2 | −5,640.2 | 29,154.2 | −5,922.2 | .... | .... | .... | .... |
| Memo Item:Cash Expenditure[2+31] | c2m | 18,987.5 | 21,876.0 | 19,230.3 | 21,658.1 | 41,597.9 | 55,260.5 | 70,931.8 | 84,408.2 | .... | .... | .... | .... |
| Memo Item: Gross Debt................... | c63 | .... | | | | | | | | .... | .... | .... | .... |
| **National Accounts** | | | | | | *Millions of Birr: Fiscal Year Ends July 7* | | | | | | | |
| Househ.Cons.Expend.,incl.NPISHs.... | 96f | 65,026 | 87,012 | 109,546 | 139,012 | 210,958 | 286,320 | 330,262 | 373,089 | 541,536 | 626,774 | 728,373 | .... |
| Government Consumption Expend... | 91f | 11,315 | 13,203 | 16,080 | 18,072 | 24,364 | 29,810 | 32,888 | 53,147 | 62,045 | 71,704 | 83,305 | .... |
| Gross Capital Formation................... | 93e | 22,979 | 25,293 | 33,176 | 38,044 | 55,512 | 76,185 | 94,497 | 165,380 | 277,244 | 309,527 | 421,786 | .... |
| Exports of Goods and Services......... | 90c | 12,914 | 16,077 | 18,205 | 21,854 | 28,317 | 35,233 | 52,168 | 85,950 | 102,887 | 108,777 | 123,660 | .... |
| Imports of Goods and Services (-)..... | 98c | 27,367 | 37,776 | 48,092 | 55,088 | 76,564 | 96,285 | 126,319 | 162,487 | 236,385 | 252,255 | 311,599 | .... |
| Statistical Discrepancy..................... | 99bs | 1,794 | 2,664 | 2,726 | 10,096 | 5,716 | 4,128 | −557 | .... | .... | .... | .... | .... |
| Gross Domestic Product (GDP)......... | 99b | 86,661 | 106,473 | 131,641 | 171,989 | 248,303 | 335,392 | 382,939 | 515,079 | 747,327 | 864,673 | 1,047,393 | .... |
| Net Primary Income from Abroad..... | 98.n | −335 | 107 | 238 | 415 | 431 | −34 | −366 | −1,120 | −1,660 | −1,943 | −2,915 | .... |
| Gross National Income (GNI)........... | 99a | 86,326 | 106,580 | 131,879 | 172,404 | 248,733 | 335,346 | 382,998 | 513,958 | 745,667 | 862,731 | 1,044,478 | .... |
| Gross Saving.................................. | 99s | 19,421 | 21,700 | 24,416 | 40,765 | 47,605 | 65,607 | 80,276 | 161,984 | 228,936 | 257,608 | 332,068 | .... |
| GDP Volume 2000 Prices................. | 99b.p | 81,421 | 91,044 | 100,908 | 112,468 | 124,602 | 135,557 | 152,405 | 159,737 | .... | .... | .... | .... |
| GDP Volume (2010=100).............. | 99bvp | 53.4 | 59.7 | 66.2 | 73.8 | 81.8 | 88.9 | 100.0 | 104.8 | .... | .... | .... | .... |
| GDP Deflator (2010=100)............... | 99bip | 42.4 | 46.5 | 51.9 | 60.9 | 79.3 | 98.5 | 100.0 | 128.3 | .... | .... | .... | .... |
| | | | | | | *Millions: Midyear Estimates* | | | | | | | |
| **Population**................................ | 99z | 74.51 | 76.61 | 78.74 | 80.89 | 83.08 | 85.30 | 87.56 | 89.86 | 92.19 | 94.56 | 96.96 | 99.39 |

| | | 2004 | 2005 | 2006 | 2007 | 2008 | 2009 | 2010 | 2011 | 2012 | 2013 | 2014 | 2015 |
|---|---|---|---|---|---|---|---|---|---|---|---|---|---|
| **Exchange Rates** | | *Euros per SDR: End of Period* | | | | | | | | | | | |
| Market Rate.................................. | aa | 1.1402 | 1.2116 | 1.1423 | 1.0735 | 1.1525 | 1.1068 | 1.0882 | 1.1525 | 1.1865 | 1.1649 | 1.1167 | 1.1933 | 1.2728 |
| | | *Euros per US Dollar: End of Period (ae) Period Average (rf)* | | | | | | | | | | | |
| Market Rate.................................. | ae | .7342 | .8477 | .7593 | .6793 | .7185 | .6942 | .7484 | .7729 | .7579 | .7251 | .8237 | .9185 |
| Market Rate.................................. | rf | .8054 | .8041 | .7971 | .7306 | .6827 | .7198 | .7550 | .7194 | .7783 | .7532 | .7537 | .9017 |
| | | *Index Numbers (2010=100): Period Averages* | | | | | | | | | | | |
| Nominal Effective Exchange Rate..... | nec | 99.51 | 97.92 | 97.82 | 101.19 | 105.75 | 107.86 | 100.00 | 100.48 | 95.47 | 100.45 | 102.36 | 94.90 |
| CPI-Based Real Effect. Ex. Rate........ | rec | 105.68 | 103.36 | 102.52 | 104.78 | 107.96 | 109.33 | 100.00 | 99.45 | 94.30 | 98.29 | 98.41 | 89.93 |
| ULC-Based Real Effect. Ex. Rate....... | rel | 94.41 | 93.73 | 93.63 | 98.38 | 105.90 | 105.15 | 100.00 | 98.24 | 93.49 | 97.98 | 98.67 | 89.91 |
| **International Liquidity** | | *Millions of US Dollars Unless Otherwise Indicated: End of Period* | | | | | | | | | | | |
| Tot.Res.minus Gold (Eurosyst.Def).... | 1l.d | 211,971 | 184,714 | 197,006 | 215,296 | 218,717 | 282,824 | 300,242 | 316,706 | 332,541 | 330,961 | 327,597 | 333,872 |
| SDR Holdings............................. | 1b.d | 5,323 | 5,106 | 6,079 | 6,868 | 6,564 | 73,221 | 72,078 | 69,845 | 69,590 | 68,998 | 65,503 | 62,610 |
| Reserve Position in the Fund......... | 1c.d | 25,452 | 12,457 | 6,893 | 5,239 | 10,182 | 15,189 | 21,036 | 38,721 | 42,092 | 39,817 | 29,688 | 20,947 |
| Foreign Exchange........................ | 1d.d | 181,196 | 167,150 | 184,034 | 203,189 | 201,969 | 194,411 | 207,127 | 208,138 | 220,036 | 220,817 | 227,926 | 245,646 |
| of which: Fin.Deriv.rel.to Res....... | 1ddd | 497 | −188 | 375 | 473 | 57 | −120 | −43 | −544 | 769 | 540 | −360 | −163 |
| Other Reserve Assets................... | 1e.d | — | — | — | — | 2 | 2 | 2 | 1 | 822 | 1,329 | 4,480 | 4,669 |
| Gold (Million Fine Troy Ounces)....... | 1ad | 390.00 | 375.86 | 365.21 | 353.69 | 349.21 | 347.18 | 346.96 | 346.85 | 346.69 | 346.57 | 346.72 | 346.87 |
| Gold (Eurosystem Valuation)............ | 1and | 170,819 | 192,816 | 232,166 | 295,860 | 302,064 | 383,287 | 489,303 | 546,109 | 576,897 | 416,399 | 415,804 | 367,524 |
| Memo:Euro Cl. on Non-EA Res.......... | 1dgd | .... | .... | .... | .... | .... | .... | .... | .... | .... | .... | .... | .... |
| Non-Euro Cl. on EA Res.............. | 1dhd | 26,069 | 30,142 | 32,340 | 65,239 | 365,727 | 46,184 | 35,207 | 125,984 | 43,322 | 30,985 | 33,208 | 34,520 |
| Central Bank: Other Liabs............... | 4..d | 29 | 25 | 48 | 170 | 525 | 201 | 204 | 368 | 394 | 279 | 171 | 165 |
| Other Depository Corps.: Assets...... | 7a.d | 4,009 | 4,307 | 5,704 | 7,172 | 6,606 | 6,126 | 5,774 | 5,504 | 5,338 | 5,316 | 5,182 | 4,638 |
| Other Depository Corps.: Liabs....... | 7b.d | 3,834 | 4,159 | 5,257 | 6,682 | 6,129 | 5,907 | 5,633 | 4,932 | 4,618 | 4,293 | 4,094 | 3,766 |
| Other Financial Corps.: Assets........ | 7e.d | .... | .... | .... | .... | .... | 3,786 | 4,359 | 4,189 | 5,001 | 5,675 | 5,930 | 5,927 |
| Other Financial Corps.: Liabs............ | 7f.d | .... | .... | .... | .... | .... | 239 | 253 | 266 | 303 | 287 | 315 | 309 |
| **Central Bank** | | *Billions of Euros: End of Period* | | | | | | | | | | | |
| Net Foreign Assets.......................... | 11n | 266.1 | 308.7 | 314.2 | † 310.0 | † 100.7 | † 364.6 | 475.2 | † 437.2 | 444.0 | 375.0 | 504.6 | 546.9 |
| Claims on Non Residents............... | 11 | 292.7 | 335.5 | 356.5 | † 430.7 | † 483.6 | † 555.4 | 682.4 | † 777.5 | 797.6 | 629.8 | 701.4 | 758.8 |
| Liabilities to Non Residents............ | 16c | 26.6 | 26.8 | 42.3 | † 120.7 | † 382.9 | † 190.8 | 207.3 | † 340.3 | 353.6 | 254.8 | 196.8 | 211.9 |
| Claims on Other Depository Corps.... | 12e | 371.4 | 443.3 | 509.5 | 753.4 | 1,226.1 | 916.3 | 751.4 | 1,237.8 | 1,506.6 | 969.2 | 846.6 | 925.8 |
| Net Claims on Central Government.. | 12an | 135.4 | 160.5 | 187.2 | 235.6 | 238.4 | 248.9 | 375.2 | 510.0 | 502.2 | 518.4 | 543.7 | 893.1 |
| Claims on Central Govt.................. | 12a | 160.1 | 184.9 | 221.2 | 259.5 | 309.9 | 352.5 | 443.1 | 573.7 | 583.6 | 580.7 | 582.4 | 957.6 |
| Liabs. to Central Govt.................... | 16d | 24.7 | 24.4 | 34.0 | 23.9 | 71.6 | 103.6 | 68.0 | 63.8 | 81.4 | 62.3 | 38.7 | 64.5 |
| Claims on Other Sectors.................. | 12s | 13.5 | 14.4 | 17.8 | 17.8 | 15.5 | 21.4 | 23.9 | 25.4 | 28.1 | 44.4 | 40.0 | 94.9 |
| Claims on Other Financial Corps.... | 12g | 5.8 | 6.0 | 8.1 | 8.5 | 8.4 | 13.1 | 15.4 | 17.0 | 19.1 | 34.0 | 28.7 | 82.0 |
| Claims on State & Local Govts....... | 12b | 1.4 | 1.3 | 1.4 | 1.1 | 1.2 | 1.2 | .9 | 1.2 | 1.7 | 1.8 | 1.6 | 2.2 |
| Claims on Public Nonfin. Corps...... | 12c | | | | | | | | | | | | |
| Claims on Private Sector............... | 12d | 6.3 | 7.0 | 8.2 | 8.2 | 5.9 | 7.1 | 7.6 | 7.1 | 7.2 | 8.6 | 9.7 | 10.7 |
| Monetary Base................................ | 14 | 668.1 | 749.7 | 826.9 | 1,087.1 | 1,312.0 | 1,252.3 | 1,248.8 | 1,777.5 | 1,941.1 | 1,494.3 | 1,430.3 | 1,930.5 |
| Currency in Circulation.................. | 14a | 516.7 | 582.1 | 646.4 | † 696.4 | † 783.9 | † 828.5 | 862.9 | † 912.7 | 937.3 | 981.5 | 1,042.8 | 1,110.8 |
| Liabs. to Other Depository Corps.... | 14c | 136.4 | 153.1 | 165.1 | 372.2 | 511.4 | 401.7 | 377.3 | 852.6 | 939.4 | 472.7 | 353.3 | 747.6 |
| Liabs. to Other Sectors.................. | 14d | 15.0 | 14.5 | 15.3 | 18.5 | 16.6 | 22.1 | 8.7 | 12.1 | 64.5 | 40.1 | 34.1 | 72.1 |
| Other Liabs. to Other Dep. Corps..... | 14n | — | — | — | — | — | — | — | — | — | — | — | — |
| Dep. & Sec. Excl. f/Monetary Base..... | 14o | .5 | .1 | .1 | .1 | .1 | .1 | — | — | — | — | — | — |
| Deposits Included in Broad Money. | 15 | — | — | — | — | — | — | — | — | — | — | — | — |
| Sec.Oth.th.Shares Inc.in.Brd.Money. | 16a | .5 | .1 | .1 | .1 | .1 | .1 | — | — | — | — | — | — |
| Deposits Excl. from Broad Money... | 16b | — | — | — | — | — | — | — | — | — | — | — | — |
| Sec.Oth.th.Shares Excl.f/Brd.Money | 16s | — | — | — | — | — | — | — | — | — | — | — | — |
| Loans.......................................... | 16l | — | — | — | — | — | — | — | — | — | — | — | — |
| Financial Derivatives...................... | 16m | — | — | — | — | — | — | — | — | — | — | — | — |
| Shares and Other Equity................. | 17a | 138.4 | 202.3 | 210.6 | † 239.4 | † 277.6 | † 325.5 | 433.0 | † 486.8 | 544.6 | 412.4 | 496.4 | 520.7 |
| Other Items (Net)........................... | 17r | −20.6 | −25.1 | −6.3 | † −7.4 | † −4.3 | † −20.9 | −51.9 | † −48.7 | 3.0 | 6.5 | 8.2 | 9.5 |
| Memorandum Item | | | | | | | | | | | | | |
| Total Assets.................................. | 10ra | 1,026.3 | 1,210.9 | 1,340.8 | † 1,719.3 | † 2,327.0 | † 2,160.5 | 2,271.0 | † 3,018.3 | 3,307.8 | 2,642.9 | 2,636.4 | 3,246.0 |
| **Other Depository Corporations** | | *Billions of Euros: End of Period* | | | | | | | | | | | |
| Net Foreign Assets.......................... | 21n | 128.4 | 125.6 | 339.0 | † 333.1 | † 342.8 | † 152.1 | 105.3 | 441.9 | 545.9 | 741.7 | 896.8 | 800.8 |
| Claims on Nonresidents............... | 21 | 2,943.4 | 3,651.2 | 4,330.7 | † 4,872.0 | † 4,746.9 | † 4,252.4 | 4,321.1 | 4,253.5 | 4,045.7 | 3,854.9 | 4,268.5 | 4,260.3 |
| Liabilities to Nonresidents............. | 26c | 2,815.0 | 3,525.6 | 3,991.7 | † 4,538.9 | † 4,404.0 | † 4,100.3 | 4,215.8 | 3,811.5 | 3,499.8 | 3,113.2 | 3,371.7 | 3,459.5 |
| Claims on Eurosystem..................... | 20 | 188.6 | 207.9 | 228.7 | 438.7 | 544.7 | 463.7 | 440.7 | 912.4 | 1,000.2 | 544.4 | 436.8 | 836.5 |
| Currency.................................... | 20a | 48.3 | 49.3 | 54.3 | 57.9 | 61.2 | 58.6 | 54.3 | 55.3 | 60.5 | 60.2 | 62.2 | 61.8 |
| Reserve Deposits and Securities...... | 20b | 139.8 | 158.5 | 174.3 | 380.7 | 483.4 | 405.0 | 386.4 | 857.1 | 939.8 | 484.1 | 374.6 | 774.7 |
| Other Claims............................... | 20n | .5 | .1 | .1 | .1 | .1 | .1 | — | — | — | — | — | — |
| Net Claims on Central Government.. | 22an | 1,099.8 | 1,193.5 | 1,033.4 | 1,059.1 | 1,043.0 | 1,318.6 | 1,448.9 | 1,259.1 | 1,464.1 | 1,491.9 | 1,644.0 | 1,582.0 |
| Claims on Central Government...... | 22a | 1,238.8 | 1,343.1 | 1,157.7 | 1,187.3 | 1,234.8 | 1,465.8 | 1,645.4 | 1,454.6 | 1,634.8 | 1,644.5 | 1,822.2 | 1,745.3 |
| Liabilities to Central Government... | 26d | 139.1 | 149.5 | 124.3 | 128.1 | 191.8 | 147.2 | 196.5 | 195.6 | 170.8 | 152.6 | 178.2 | 163.3 |
| Claims on Other Sectors.................. | 22s | 9,603.1 | 10,500.1 | 11,919.7 | 13,599.8 | 14,884.5 | 14,800.9 | 16,338.1 | 16,827.7 | 16,622.3 | 15,403.7 | 15,937.9 | 15,616.2 |
| Claims on Other Financial Corps.... | 22g | 1,140.1 | 1,318.4 | 1,889.0 | 2,697.6 | 3,455.5 | 3,451.9 | 4,917.6 | 5,315.9 | 5,225.1 | 4,226.8 | 4,907.7 | 4,517.7 |
| Claims on State & Local Govts....... | 22b | 872.9 | 918.1 | 934.4 | 968.7 | 983.8 | 1,018.0 | 1,096.7 | 1,100.9 | 1,145.5 | 1,132.1 | 1,149.8 | 1,132.5 |
| Claims on Public Nonfin. Corps...... | 22c | | | | | | | | | | | | |
| Claims on Private Sector............... | 22d | 7,590.1 | 8,263.5 | 9,096.3 | 9,933.5 | 10,445.2 | 10,331.0 | 10,323.8 | 10,410.9 | 10,251.6 | 10,044.9 | 9,880.4 | 9,966.0 |
| Liabilities to Eurosystem.................. | 26g | 371.6 | 439.6 | 510.9 | 762.3 | 1,193.0 | 918.0 | 797.5 | 1,272.4 | 1,492.3 | 970.7 | 856.8 | 940.7 |
| Transf.Dep.Included in Broad Money | 24 | 2,390.9 | 2,850.1 | 3,062.5 | 3,155.6 | 3,214.2 | 3,678.4 | 3,847.3 | 3,906.1 | 4,114.7 | 4,378.6 | 4,837.6 | 5,407.5 |
| Other.Dep.Included in Broad Money. | 25 | 3,379.2 | 3,366.6 | 3,668.2 | 4,407.5 | 5,004.7 | 4,516.8 | 4,415.2 | 4,436.4 | 4,451.8 | 4,307.9 | 4,239.6 | 4,112.0 |
| Sec.Oth.th.Shares Inc.in.Brd. Money. | 26a | 102.3 | 124.2 | 195.6 | 311.7 | 264.3 | 131.7 | 123.2 | 206.9 | 180.2 | 87.6 | 106.0 | 70.7 |
| Deposits Excl. from Broad Money..... | 26b | 1,475.7 | 1,636.8 | 1,807.1 | 2,033.4 | 2,206.8 | 2,494.1 | 2,847.4 | 2,937.2 | 2,770.3 | 2,655.3 | 2,533.7 | 2,477.8 |
| Sec.Oth.th.Shares Excl.f/Brd. Money. | 26s | 1,958.0 | 2,173.8 | 2,356.0 | 2,513.5 | 2,528.7 | 2,586.0 | 2,699.5 | 2,799.4 | 2,671.9 | 2,498.9 | 2,373.8 | 2,247.2 |
| Loans.......................................... | 26l | | | | | | | | | | | | |
| Financial Derivatives...................... | 26m | 48.4 | 57.1 | 396.6 | 628.2 | 938.4 | 697.4 | 1,885.4 | 2,318.1 | 2,274.6 | 1,520.4 | 2,161.8 | 1,783.1 |
| Insurance Technical Reserves........... | 26r | — | — | — | — | — | — | — | — | — | — | — | — |
| Shares and Other Equity................. | 27a | 1,178.5 | 1,277.4 | 1,416.4 | † 1,641.1 | † 1,718.1 | † 1,862.4 | 1,897.5 | 2,037.5 | 2,121.6 | 2,132.8 | 2,105.9 | 2,121.6 |
| Other Items (Net)........................... | 27r | 115.3 | 101.5 | 107.5 | † −22.6 | † −253.3 | † −149.7 | −179.9 | −469.6 | −447.9 | −369.9 | −298.5 | −320.8 |
| Memorandum Item | | | | | | | | | | | | | |
| Total Assets.................................. | 20ra | 21,355.4 | 23,635.4 | 25,954.0 | † 29,494.4 | † 31,830.7 | † 31,144.2 | 32,206.8 | 33,508.7 | 32,659.4 | 30,398.5 | 31,194.5 | 30,803.9 |

# Euro Area 163

| | | 2004 | 2005 | 2006 | 2007 | 2008 | 2009 | 2010 | 2011 | 2012 | 2013 | 2014 | 2015 |
|---|---|---|---|---|---|---|---|---|---|---|---|---|---|
| **Depository Corporations** | | | | | | *Billions of Euros: End of Period* | | | | | | | |
| Net Foreign Assets............. | 31n | 394.5 | 434.3 | 653.2 | 643.2 | 443.5 | 516.7 | 580.5 | 879.2 | 989.9 | 1,116.7 | 1,401.3 | 1,347.7 |
| Claims on Nonresidents.............. | 31 | 3,236.1 | 3,986.7 | 4,687.2 | 5,302.7 | 5,230.4 | 4,807.8 | 5,003.5 | 5,030.9 | 4,843.3 | 4,484.7 | 4,969.9 | 5,019.1 |
| Liabilities to Nonresidents............ | 36c | 2,841.6 | 3,552.4 | 4,034.0 | 4,659.6 | 4,786.9 | 4,291.0 | 4,423.0 | 4,151.8 | 3,853.4 | 3,368.0 | 3,568.5 | 3,671.4 |
| Domestic Claims............................ | 32 | 10,851.8 | 11,868.4 | 13,158.0 | 14,912.3 | 16,181.3 | 16,389.8 | 18,186.0 | 18,622.1 | 18,616.6 | 17,458.5 | 18,165.6 | 18,186.2 |
| Net Claims on Central Government | 32an | 1,235.2 | 1,354.0 | 1,220.6 | 1,294.7 | 1,281.4 | 1,567.5 | 1,824.0 | 1,769.0 | 1,966.3 | 2,010.3 | 2,187.7 | 2,475.1 |
| Claims on Central Government.... | 32a | 1,399.0 | 1,528.0 | 1,378.9 | 1,446.7 | 1,544.7 | 1,818.3 | 2,088.5 | 2,028.4 | 2,218.4 | 2,225.2 | 2,404.6 | 2,702.9 |
| Liabilities to Central Government. | 36d | 163.8 | 173.9 | 158.3 | 152.0 | 263.4 | 250.8 | 264.5 | 259.3 | 252.1 | 214.9 | 216.9 | 227.8 |
| Claims on Other Sectors............... | 32s | 9,616.6 | 10,514.4 | 11,937.4 | 13,617.5 | 14,899.9 | 14,822.3 | 16,362.0 | 16,853.0 | 16,650.3 | 15,448.2 | 15,977.9 | 15,711.1 |
| Claims on Other Financial Corps.. | 32g | 1,145.9 | 1,324.4 | 1,897.1 | 2,706.1 | 3,463.8 | 3,465.0 | 4,932.9 | 5,333.0 | 5,244.2 | 4,260.8 | 4,936.4 | 4,599.7 |
| Claims on State & Local Govts..... | 32b | 874.3 | 919.5 | 935.8 | 969.8 | 985.1 | 1,019.2 | 1,097.7 | 1,102.1 | 1,147.3 | 1,133.9 | 1,151.5 | 1,134.7 |
| Claims on Public Nonfin. Corps.... | 32c | — | — | — | — | — | — | — | — | — | — | — | — |
| Claims on Private Sector.............. | 32d | 7,596.4 | 8,270.5 | 9,104.6 | 9,941.6 | 10,451.0 | 10,338.1 | 10,331.4 | 10,418.0 | 10,258.8 | 10,053.5 | 9,890.1 | 9,976.7 |
| Broad Money Liabilities.................. | 35l | 6,356.3 | 6,888.3 | 7,533.9 | 8,532.0 | 9,222.7 | 9,119.0 | 9,202.9 | 9,419.0 | 9,688.0 | 9,735.4 | 10,198.0 | 10,711.3 |
| Currency Outside Depository Corps | 34a | 468.4 | 532.7 | 592.1 | 638.6 | 722.7 | 769.9 | 808.6 | 857.5 | 876.8 | 921.2 | 980.6 | 1,048.9 |
| Transferable Deposits.................... | 34 | 2,405.8 | 2,864.5 | 3,077.8 | 3,174.0 | 3,230.8 | 3,700.4 | 3,855.8 | 3,918.0 | 4,178.9 | 4,413.3 | 4,866.5 | 5,479.3 |
| Other Deposits............................ | 35 | 3,379.3 | 3,366.7 | 3,668.2 | 4,407.6 | 5,004.9 | 4,517.0 | 4,415.3 | 4,436.6 | 4,452.1 | 4,313.3 | 4,244.8 | 4,112.4 |
| Securities Other than Shares........ | 36a | 102.8 | 124.3 | 195.7 | 311.8 | 264.4 | 131.8 | 123.2 | 206.9 | 180.2 | 87.6 | 106.0 | 70.7 |
| Deposits Excl. from Broad Money..... | 36b | 1,475.7 | 1,636.8 | 1,807.1 | 2,033.4 | 2,206.8 | 2,494.1 | 2,847.4 | 2,937.3 | 2,770.4 | 2,655.3 | 2,533.8 | 2,477.8 |
| Sec.Oth.th.Shares Excl.f/Brd. Money. | 36s | 1,958.0 | 2,173.8 | 2,356.0 | 2,513.5 | 2,528.7 | 2,586.0 | 2,699.5 | 2,799.4 | 2,671.9 | 2,498.9 | 2,373.8 | 2,247.2 |
| Loans.......................................... | 36l | — | — | — | — | — | — | — | — | — | — | — | — |
| Financial Derivatives...................... | 36m | 48.4 | 57.1 | 396.6 | 628.2 | 938.4 | 697.4 | 1,885.4 | 2,318.1 | 2,274.6 | 1,520.4 | 2,161.8 | 1,783.1 |
| Insurance Technical Reserves........... | 36r | | | | | | | | | | | | |
| Shares and Other Equity................. | 37a | 1,316.9 | 1,479.7 | 1,627.0 | 1,880.5 | 1,995.7 | 2,188.0 | 2,330.5 | 2,524.3 | 2,666.2 | 2,545.2 | 2,602.2 | 2,642.2 |
| Other Items (Net)......................... | 37r | 91.0 | 67.1 | 93.5 | −29.7 | −262.8 | −172.3 | −194.9 | −488.2 | −459.6 | −373.4 | −301.4 | −323.5 |
| Broad Money Liabs., Seasonally Adj. | 35l.b | 6,318.0 | 6,847.2 | 7,491.2 | 8,488.2 | 9,182.4 | 9,086.1 | 9,176.7 | 9,397.7 | 9,673.9 | 9,727.5 | 10,197.2 | 10,714.7 |
| **Other Financial Corporations** | | | | | | *Billions of Euros: End of Period* | | | | | | | |
| Net Foreign Assets.......................... | 41n | .... | .... | .... | .... | .... | 2,462.2 | 3,072.9 | 3,031.9 | 3,560.8 | 3,907.2 | 4,624.8 | 5,160.0 |
| Claims on Nonresidents.................. | 41 | .... | .... | .... | .... | .... | 2,628.0 | 3,262.1 | 3,237.8 | 3,790.1 | 4,115.3 | 4,884.2 | 5,444.0 |
| Liabilities to Nonresidents............... | 46c | .... | .... | .... | .... | .... | 165.7 | 189.1 | 205.9 | 229.3 | 208.1 | 259.4 | 284.1 |
| Claims on Depository Corporations.. | 40 | .... | .... | .... | .... | .... | 3,171.8 | 3,188.3 | 3,207.5 | 3,155.7 | 3,052.7 | 3,118.7 | 3,050.3 |
| Net Claims on Central Government.. | 42an | .... | .... | .... | .... | .... | 1,949.7 | 2,078.5 | 2,085.8 | 2,281.6 | 2,416.0 | 2,823.2 | 2,863.0 |
| Claims on Central Government...... | 42a | .... | .... | .... | .... | .... | 1,957.9 | 2,086.8 | 2,094.1 | 2,289.8 | 2,424.2 | 2,831.4 | 2,871.4 |
| Liabilities to Central Government... | 46d | .... | .... | .... | .... | .... | 8.2 | 8.3 | 8.3 | 8.2 | 8.1 | 8.2 | 8.4 |
| Claims on Other Sectors................ | 42s | .... | .... | .... | .... | .... | 2,475.6 | 2,540.5 | 2,528.8 | 2,642.4 | 2,785.0 | 2,889.7 | 3,099.0 |
| Claims on State & Local Govts....... | 42b | .... | .... | .... | .... | .... | | | | | | | |
| Claims on Pub. Nonfin. Corps....... | 42c | .... | .... | .... | .... | .... | — | — | — | — | — | — | — |
| Claims on Private Sector................ | 42d | .... | .... | .... | .... | .... | 2,475.6 | 2,540.5 | 2,528.8 | 2,642.4 | 2,785.0 | 2,889.7 | 3,099.0 |
| Deposits....................................... | 46b | .... | .... | .... | .... | .... | | | | | | | |
| Securities Other than Shares............ | 46s | .... | .... | .... | .... | .... | 924.2 | 965.9 | 1,077.2 | 951.0 | 867.1 | 819.5 | 769.0 |
| Loans........................................... | 46l | .... | .... | .... | .... | .... | 288.0 | 289.3 | 308.5 | 328.7 | 335.1 | 390.7 | 424.7 |
| Financial Derivatives....................... | 46m | .... | .... | .... | .... | .... | | | | | | | |
| Insurance Technical Reserves.......... | 46r | .... | .... | .... | .... | .... | 5,148.8 | 5,546.2 | 5,749.9 | 6,038.1 | 6,239.2 | 6,784.0 | 7,081.3 |
| Shares and Other Equity.................. | 47a | .... | .... | .... | .... | .... | 5,670.7 | 6,418.4 | 6,206.9 | 7,393.1 | 8,159.8 | 9,588.6 | 10,421.6 |
| Other Items (Net)............................ | 47r | .... | .... | .... | .... | .... | −1,972.5 | −2,339.7 | −2,488.4 | −3,070.4 | −3,440.1 | −4,130.3 | −4,524.6 |
| Memorandum Item | | | | | | | | | | | | | |
| Total Assets.................................. | 40ra | .... | .... | .... | .... | .... | 14,433.6 | 15,701.8 | 15,696.7 | 17,047.9 | 17,924.4 | 20,195.6 | 21,467.7 |
| **Financial Corporations** | | | | | | *Billions of Euros: End of Period* | | | | | | | |
| Net Foreign Assets.......................... | 51n | .... | .... | .... | .... | .... | 2,979.0 | 3,653.4 | 3,911.1 | 4,550.7 | 5,023.9 | 6,026.1 | 6,507.6 |
| Claims on Nonresidents.................. | 51 | .... | .... | .... | .... | .... | 7,435.7 | 8,265.6 | 8,268.7 | 8,633.4 | 8,600.0 | 9,854.1 | 10,463.1 |
| Liabilities to Nonresidents............... | 56c | .... | .... | .... | .... | .... | 4,456.8 | 4,612.2 | 4,357.6 | 4,082.7 | 3,576.1 | 3,827.9 | 3,955.5 |
| Domestic Claims............................ | 52 | .... | .... | .... | .... | .... | 17,350.0 | 17,872.0 | 17,903.7 | 18,296.4 | 18,398.8 | 18,942.2 | 19,548.4 |
| Net Claims on Central Government | 52an | .... | .... | .... | .... | .... | 3,517.2 | 3,902.5 | 3,854.8 | 4,247.9 | 4,426.4 | 5,010.9 | 5,338.1 |
| Claims on Central Government.... | 52a | .... | .... | .... | .... | .... | 3,776.2 | 4,175.3 | 4,122.5 | 4,508.2 | 4,649.4 | 5,236.0 | 5,574.3 |
| Liabilities to Central Government. | 56d | .... | .... | .... | .... | .... | 259.0 | 272.8 | 267.6 | 260.3 | 223.0 | 225.1 | 236.2 |
| Claims on Other Sectors................ | 52s | .... | .... | .... | .... | .... | 13,832.8 | 13,969.5 | 14,048.8 | 14,048.5 | 13,972.4 | 13,931.3 | 14,210.4 |
| Claims on State & Local Govts..... | 52b | .... | .... | .... | .... | .... | 1,019.2 | 1,097.7 | 1,102.1 | 1,147.3 | 1,133.9 | 1,151.5 | 1,134.7 |
| Claims on Pub. Nonfin. Corps...... | 52c | .... | .... | .... | .... | .... | — | — | — | — | — | — | — |
| Claims on Private Sector.............. | 52d | .... | .... | .... | .... | .... | 12,813.6 | 12,871.9 | 12,946.8 | 12,901.2 | 12,838.5 | 12,779.8 | 13,075.7 |
| Currency Outside Fin. Corporations.. | 54a | .... | .... | .... | .... | .... | 768.6 | 807.0 | 855.8 | 875.1 | 919.6 | 978.9 | 1,047.1 |
| Deposits....................................... | 55l | .... | .... | .... | .... | .... | 8,100.6 | 8,200.7 | 8,352.5 | 8,643.0 | 8,833.8 | 9,121.8 | 9,477.4 |
| Securities Other than Shares........... | 56a | .... | .... | .... | .... | .... | — | — | — | — | — | — | — |
| Loans........................................... | 56l | .... | .... | .... | .... | .... | — | — | — | — | — | — | — |
| Financial Derivatives....................... | 56m | .... | .... | .... | .... | .... | | | | | | | |
| Insurance Technical Reserves.......... | 56r | .... | .... | .... | .... | .... | 5,145.7 | 5,543.0 | 5,746.4 | 6,034.9 | 6,235.8 | 6,779.6 | 7,077.8 |
| Shares and Other Equity.................. | 57a | .... | .... | .... | .... | .... | 7,858.6 | 8,749.0 | 8,731.3 | 10,059.3 | 10,705.0 | 12,190.8 | 13,063.8 |
| Other Items (Net)............................ | 57r | .... | .... | .... | .... | .... | −1,538.8 | −1,769.9 | −1,862.4 | −2,760.2 | −3,265.0 | −4,105.6 | −4,606.0 |
| **Monetary Aggregates** | | | | | | *Billions of Euros: End of Period* | | | | | | | |
| Broad Money.................................. | 59m | 6,549.2 | 7,110.9 | 7,778.3 | 8,659.8 | 9,337.8 | 9,236.2 | 9,320.8 | 9,535.0 | 9,808.0 | 9,849.5 | 10,310.3 | 10,834.2 |
| o/w: Currency Issued by Cent.Gov | 59m.a | — | — | — | — | — | — | — | — | — | — | — | — |
| o/w: Dep.in Nonfin. Corporations. | 59m.b | 192.8 | 222.6 | 244.4 | 127.8 | 115.1 | 117.2 | 117.9 | 116.0 | 120.0 | 114.1 | 112.3 | 123.0 |
| o/w: Secs. Issued by Central Govt. | 59m.c | — | — | — | — | — | — | — | — | — | — | — | — |
| Money (Eurosystem Definitions) | | | | | | | | | | | | | |
| M1, Seasonally Adjusted.............. | 59mau | 2,948.9 | 3,482.1 | 3,758.6 | † 3,901.3 | † 4,035.7 | † 4,556.2 | 4,754.4 | 4,866.6 | 5,151.4 | 5,386.1 | 5,921.1 | 6,630.8 |
| M1,Seas.Adj.Annual Growth Rate | 59max | 8.6 | 11.4 | 8.0 | 3.9 | 3.4 | 12.3 | 4.4 | 2.0 | 6.5 | 5.8 | 8.1 | 10.8 |
| M2, Seasonally Adjusted.............. | 59mbu | 5,632.3 | 6,168.7 | 6,743.8 | † 7,436.9 | † 8,103.1 | † 8,275.1 | 8,472.3 | 8,670.6 | 9,044.6 | 9,212.1 | 9,668.7 | 10,234.5 |
| M2,Seas.Adj.Annual Growth Rate | 59mbx | 6.6 | 8.5 | 9.6 | 10.2 | 8.4 | 1.6 | 2.2 | 1.9 | 4.5 | 2.5 | 3.8 | 5.3 |
| M3, Seasonally Adjusted.............. | 59mcu | 6,568.2 | 7,130.7 | 7,801.7 | † 8,691.4 | † 9,423.8 | † 9,382.2 | 9,320.8 | 9,535.0 | 9,808.0 | 9,838.1 | 10,325.0 | 10,966.0 |
| M3,Seas.Adj.Annual Growth Rate | 59mcx | 6.6 | 7.3 | 10.1 | 11.6 | 7.7 | −.3 | 1.1 | 1.7 | 3.5 | 1.0 | 3.8 | 4.7 |

|  |  | 2004 | 2005 | 2006 | 2007 | 2008 | 2009 | 2010 | 2011 | 2012 | 2013 | 2014 | 2015 |
|---|---|---|---|---|---|---|---|---|---|---|---|---|---|
| **Interest Rates** |  |  |  |  |  | *Percent Per Annum* |  |  |  |  |  |  |  |
| Central Bank Policy Rate (EOP) | 60 | 2.00 | 2.25 | 3.50 | 4.00 | † 2.50 | 1.00 | 1.00 | 1.00 | .75 | .25 | .05 | .05 |
| Discount Rate (End of Period) | 60.a | 3.00 | 3.25 | 4.50 | 5.00 | 3.00 | 1.75 | 1.75 | 1.75 | 1.50 | .75 | .30 | .30 |
| Eurosyst. Refinancing Rate | 60r | 2.02 | 2.09 | 2.86 | 3.97 | .... | .... | .... | .... | .... | .... | .... | .... |
| Eurosyst. Deposit Facility Rate | 60x | 1.00 | 1.02 | 1.94 | 2.94 | 2.98 | .40 | .25 | .50 | .13 | — | −.09 | −.21 |
| Interbank Rate (Overnight) | 60a | 2.05 | 2.09 | 2.84 | 3.86 | 3.86 | .72 | .44 | .87 | .23 | .09 | .10 | −.11 |
| Eurepo Rate (3-month) | 60b | 2.05 | 2.12 | 3.01 | 3.98 | 3.78 | .70 | .48 | .82 | .06 | .05 | .05 | −.24 |
| Deposit Rate |  |  |  |  |  |  |  |  |  |  |  |  |  |
| Households: Stocks, up to 2 years | 60lhs | 1.91 | 1.93 | 2.41 | 3.45 | 4.25 | 3.20 | 2.16 | 2.51 | 2.71 | 2.29 | 1.61 | .97 |
| New Business, up to 1 year | 60lhn | 1.90 | 1.97 | 2.67 | 3.79 | 4.34 | 2.01 | 2.11 | 2.60 | 2.76 | 1.97 | 1.33 | .79 |
| Corporations: Stocks, up to 2 years | 60lcs | 2.10 | 2.13 | 2.80 | 3.89 | 4.43 | 2.25 | 1.53 | 2.04 | 1.93 | 1.51 | 1.12 | .68 |
| New Business, up to 1 year | 60lcn | 2.00 | 2.04 | 2.79 | 3.90 | 4.12 | 1.07 | .95 | 1.58 | 1.15 | .87 | .56 | .28 |
| REPOS, Stocks | 60lcr | 1.98 | 2.02 | 2.69 | 3.75 | 4.05 | 1.77 | 1.22 | 1.90 | 2.54 | 1.74 | .92 | .50 |
| Lending Rate |  |  |  |  |  |  |  |  |  |  |  |  |  |
| Households: Stocks, up to 1 year | 60phs | 8.18 | 7.94 | 8.16 | 8.76 | 9.14 | 7.99 | 7.68 | 8.07 | 7.95 | 7.69 | 7.50 | 7.15 |
| New Bus., Floating & up to 1 year | 60pns | 6.78 | 6.69 | 7.20 | 7.99 | 8.53 | 7.43 | 5.86 | 5.22 | 5.36 | 5.54 | 5.51 | 5.11 |
| House Purch., Stocks,Over 5 yrs | 60phm | 4.96 | 4.66 | 4.58 | 4.88 | 5.08 | 4.46 | 3.88 | 3.86 | 3.72 | 3.41 | 3.25 | 2.96 |
| House Purch., New Bus., 5-10 yrs | 60phn | 4.81 | 4.17 | 4.43 | 4.91 | 5.12 | 4.57 | 4.04 | 4.09 | 3.40 | 3.04 | 2.81 | 2.26 |
| Corporations: Stocks, up to 1 year | 60pcs | 4.43 | 4.32 | 4.79 | 5.68 | 6.13 | 3.98 | 3.47 | 3.99 | 3.96 | 3.68 | 3.47 | 2.90 |
| New Bus., Over € 1 mil.,up to 1 yr | 60pcn | 2.99 | 3.02 | 3.81 | 4.88 | 5.21 | 2.53 | 2.18 | 2.83 | 2.41 | 2.18 | 2.04 | 1.58 |
| Government Bond Yield | 61 | 4.14 | 3.44 | 3.86 | 4.33 | 4.36 | 4.03 | 3.78 | 4.31 | 3.05 | 3.01 | 2.28 | 1.27 |
| **Prices, Production, Labor** |  |  |  |  | *Index Numbers (2010=100): Period Averages* |  |  |  |  |  |  |  |  |
| Producer Prices | 63 | 85.5 | 89.2 | 94.1 | 96.5 | 102.6 | 97.5 | 100.0 | 105.7 | 108.7 | 108.5 | 106.8 | 103.9 |
| Harmonized CPI (hcpi) | 64h | 89.1 | 91.0 | 93.0 | 95.0 | 98.1 | 98.4 | 100.0 | 102.7 | 105.3 | 106.7 | 107.2 | 107.2 |
| Wages/Labor Costs | 65..c | 84.9 | 87.0 | 89.4 | 92.5 | 96.2 | 98.9 | 100.0 | 102.8 | 105.4 | 107.5 | 109.3 | .... |
| Employment | 67..c | 112.0 | 110.6 | 109.6 | 110.2 | 110.3 | 103.7 | 100.0 | 100.2 | 99.6 | .... | .... | .... |
|  |  |  |  |  | *Number in Thousands: Period Averages* |  |  |  |  |  |  |  |  |
| Employment | 67e | 135,030 | 136,693 | 139,476 | 142,206 | 143,514 | 140,716 | 139,901 | 140,238 | 139,127 | 138,085 | 140,224 | .... |
| Unemployment | 67c | 13,806 | 13,993 | 12,985 | 11,722 | 11,951 | 15,233 | 16,156 | 16,186 | 18,189 | 19,232 | 18,631 | 17,445 |
| Unemployment Rate (%) | 67r | 9.2 | 9.3 | 8.4 | 7.5 | 7.6 | 9.6 | 10.2 | 10.2 | 11.4 | 12.0 | 11.6 | 10.9 |
| **Intl. Transactions & Positions** |  |  |  |  |  | *Billions of Euros* |  |  |  |  |  |  |  |
| Exports | 70 | 1,145.5 | 1,236.4 | 1,383.5 | 1,503.1 | 1,566.4 | 1,286.3 | 1,545.3 | 1,746.7 | 1,879.1 | 1,897.4 | 1,939.3 | 2,043.8 |
| Imports, c.i.f | 71 | 1,086.6 | 1,237.1 | 1,416.9 | 1,509.5 | 1,628.9 | 1,274.6 | 1,557.7 | 1,768.5 | 1,798.4 | 1,745.0 | 1,757.3 | 1,796.2 |
|  |  |  |  |  |  | *2010=100* |  |  |  |  |  |  |  |
| Volume of Exports | 72 | 84.1 | 88.7 | 96.3 | 102.1 | 103.8 | 87.2 | 100.0 | 107.4 | 111.2 | 113.0 | 114.8 | 116.9 |
| Volume of Imports | 73 | 88.4 | 93.6 | 99.8 | 105.2 | 104.9 | 90.6 | 100.0 | 103.0 | 99.8 | 99.3 | 102.2 | 106.0 |
| Unit Value of Exports | 74 | 87.4 | 90.1 | 93.1 | 95.2 | 97.5 | 95.5 | 100.0 | 105.3 | 109.5 | 108.9 | 109.4 | 112.9 |
| Unit Value of Imports | 75 | 78.2 | 84.4 | 90.9 | 92.0 | 99.3 | 90.3 | 100.0 | 110.5 | 116.1 | 113.2 | 110.6 | 108.9 |
| **Balance of Payments** |  |  |  |  |  | *Billions of US Dollars* |  |  |  |  |  |  |  |
| A. Current Account* | 109bx | 81.2 | 19.2 | −.3 | 24.9 | −195.9 | −12.5 | 12.2 | 16.0 | 171.4 | 305.4 | † 329.2 | 364.8 |
| Goods, credit (exports) | 1a9cx | 1,412.8 | 1,529.2 | 1,760.2 | 2,086.3 | 2,328.9 | 1,816.1 | 2,087.2 | 2,491.7 | 2,467.4 | 2,569.1 | † 2,613.2 | 2,302.7 |
| Goods, debit (imports) | 1a9dx | 1,287.5 | 1,463.8 | 1,730.9 | 2,010.5 | 2,349.4 | 1,770.9 | 2,066.0 | 2,488.4 | 2,350.5 | 2,346.1 | † 2,286.3 | 1,946.4 |
| Balance on goods | 1a9bx | 125.4 | 65.4 | 29.3 | 75.8 | −20.5 | 45.2 | 21.1 | 3.3 | 116.9 | 223.0 | † 326.9 | 356.3 |
| Services, credit (exports) | 1b9cx | 447.3 | 497.5 | 548.7 | 671.6 | 752.8 | 697.1 | 723.2 | 819.9 | 811.6 | 878.7 | † 938.3 | 848.2 |
| Services, debit (imports) | 1b9dx | 413.0 | 456.4 | 502.7 | 613.7 | 691.1 | 634.2 | 641.5 | 712.9 | 691.3 | 729.8 | † 837.8 | 774.7 |
| Balance on Goods & Services | 1z9bx | 159.6 | 106.4 | 75.3 | 133.7 | 41.2 | 108.1 | 102.8 | 110.4 | 237.2 | 371.9 | † 427.4 | 429.8 |
| Primary income: credit | 1c9cx | 374.7 | 482.1 | 630.4 | 828.9 | 774.1 | 597.1 | 660.6 | 763.6 | 730.9 | 726.8 | † 841.1 | 717.6 |
| Primary income: debit | 1c9dx | 379.4 | 477.2 | 605.8 | 817.6 | 869.2 | 582.3 | 606.2 | 709.4 | 658.0 | 633.1 | † 750.4 | 634.4 |
| Balance on gds, serv. & prim. inc. | 1y9bx | 154.9 | 111.3 | 99.9 | 145.0 | −53.9 | 122.9 | 157.2 | 164.6 | 310.1 | 465.6 | † 518.2 | 512.9 |
| Secondary income: credit | 1d9ca | 100.5 | 104.0 | 110.1 | 119.9 | 132.0 | 130.0 | 117.0 | 131.1 | 125.7 | 131.5 | † 123.4 | 114.4 |
| Secondary income: debit | 1d9da | 174.2 | 196.1 | 210.4 | 240.0 | 274.0 | 265.4 | 262.0 | 279.7 | 264.5 | 291.7 | † 312.4 | 262.5 |
| B. Capital Account* | 209ba | 20.5 | 14.2 | 11.7 | 5.4 | 14.2 | 11.1 | 7.3 | 14.0 | 7.3 | 27.9 | † 25.3 | −15.9 |
| Capital account: credit | 209ca | 30.4 | 30.3 | 29.8 | 35.0 | 35.8 | 27.0 | 27.2 | 34.9 | 38.5 | 44.4 | † 49.4 | 48.3 |
| Capital account: debit | 209da | 9.9 | 16.1 | 18.1 | 29.6 | 21.6 | 15.8 | 19.9 | 20.9 | 31.2 | 16.5 | † 24.1 | 64.1 |
| Balance on current & capital acct. | 129ba | 101.7 | 33.4 | 11.4 | 30.3 | −181.7 | −1.4 | 19.5 | 30.0 | 178.6 | 333.3 | † 354.5 | 349.0 |
| C. Financial Account* | 309na | 123.6 | 71.4 | 28.5 | 3.4 | −175.3 | −73.8 | 12.2 | 103.3 | 213.6 | 345.1 | † 470.5 | 294.9 |
| Direct investment: assets | 3a9aa | 215.3 | 453.6 | 542.7 | 706.0 | 504.0 | 488.2 | 462.0 | 688.9 | 526.5 | 483.2 | † 256.4 | 669.3 |
| Equity & investment fund shares | 3aaaa | 225.0 | 382.7 | 435.5 | 538.0 | 289.8 | 368.3 | 304.4 | 591.0 | 353.4 | 437.9 | † 122.9 | 452.0 |
| Debt instruments | 3abaa | −9.7 | 70.8 | 107.2 | 168.0 | 214.2 | 119.9 | 157.7 | 97.9 | 173.1 | 45.2 | † 133.5 | 217.3 |
| Direct investment: liabilities | 3a9la | 114.8 | 194.1 | 328.6 | 581.9 | 178.7 | 399.9 | 362.5 | 545.4 | 432.9 | 439.0 | † 175.0 | 541.0 |
| Equity & investment fund shares | 3aala | 115.2 | 154.2 | 287.0 | 433.6 | 93.4 | 382.3 | 389.0 | 497.9 | 324.0 | 422.1 | † 121.2 | 344.9 |
| Debt instruments | 3abla | −.4 | 39.9 | 41.6 | 148.2 | 85.3 | 17.7 | −26.5 | 47.5 | 108.8 | 16.9 | † 53.8 | 196.2 |
| Portfolio investment: assets | 3b9aa | 428.8 | 514.6 | 650.5 | 601.3 | 46.2 | 139.4 | 174.7 | −72.5 | 252.8 | 332.7 | † 606.2 | 437.6 |
| Equity & investment fund shares | 3baaa | 132.4 | 166.0 | 193.2 | 86.9 | −130.6 | 78.9 | 102.6 | −90.3 | 75.6 | 217.7 | † 192.7 | 15.3 |
| Debt securities | 3bbaa | 296.4 | 348.7 | 457.2 | 514.5 | 176.8 | 60.4 | 72.2 | 17.8 | 177.2 | 115.0 | † 413.4 | 422.3 |
| Portfolio investment: liabilities | 3b9la | 486.1 | 660.6 | 889.5 | 768.6 | 385.7 | 488.1 | 278.1 | 263.8 | 372.3 | 483.3 | † 470.7 | 182.5 |
| Equity & investment fund shares | 3bala | 132.0 | 292.3 | 310.1 | 222.2 | −158.3 | 120.5 | 230.5 | 85.8 | 213.0 | 321.3 | † 353.3 | 262.2 |
| Debt securities | 3bbla | 354.1 | 368.3 | 579.4 | 546.4 | 544.0 | 367.6 | 47.6 | 178.0 | 159.3 | 162.0 | † 117.4 | −79.7 |
| Fin. der.& empl.stk.ops.(ESOs): net. | 3c9na | 10.5 | 21.6 | −.2 | 92.9 | 121.7 | −24.9 | −13.2 | 6.9 | −7.0 | −22.9 | † 56.3 | 78.0 |
| Fin. der. & ESOs.: assets | 3c9aa | .... | .... | .... | .... | .... | .... | .... | .... | .... | .... | .... | .... |
| Fin. der. & ESOs.: liabilities | 3c9la | −10.5 | −21.6 | .2 | −92.9 | −121.7 | 24.9 | 13.2 | −6.9 | 7.0 | 22.9 | .... | .... |
| Other investment: assets | 3d9aa | 426.0 | 738.0 | 999.0 | 1,236.5 | 32.7 | −688.6 | 206.5 | 286.0 | −44.0 | −87.2 | † 294.8 | −284.9 |
| Other equity | 3daaa | .... | .... | .... | .... | .... | .... | .... | .... | .... | .... | † 2.0 | 2.2 |
| Debt instruments | 3dzaa | 426.0 | 738.0 | 999.0 | 1,236.5 | 32.7 | −688.6 | 206.5 | 286.0 | −44.0 | −87.2 | † 292.8 | −287.1 |
| Other investment: liabilities | 3d9la | 356.1 | 801.7 | 945.4 | 1,283.0 | 315.4 | −900.2 | 177.2 | −3.1 | −290.5 | −561.6 | † 97.4 | −118.5 |
| Other equity | 3dala | .... | .... | .... | .... | .... | .... | .... | .... | .... | .... | † — | .1 |
| Debt instruments | 3dzla | 356.1 | 801.7 | 945.4 | 1,283.0 | 315.4 | −900.2 | 177.2 | −3.1 | −290.5 | −561.6 | † 97.3 | −118.6 |
| Curr.+ cap.− finan. acct. balance... | 4y9na | −22.0 | −38.0 | −17.0 | 26.9 | −6.4 | 72.4 | 7.3 | −73.3 | −35.0 | −11.8 | † −116.1 | 54.0 |
| D. Net Errors and Omissions | 409na | 6.4 | 15.1 | 19.6 | −21.2 | 11.3 | −12.6 | −7.2 | 38.5 | 33.7 | 1.8 | † 135.3 | −11.9 |
| E. Reserves and Related Items | 4z9na | −15.6 | −22.9 | 2.6 | 5.7 | 4.9 | 59.7 | .1 | −34.8 | −1.3 | −10.1 | † 19.2 | 42.2 |
| Reserve assets | 3e9aa | −15.6 | −22.9 | 2.6 | 5.7 | 4.9 | 59.7 | 13.9 | 13.8 | 19.9 | 5.8 | † 5.9 | 12.1 |
| Credit and loans from the IMF | 3dcla | — | — | — | — | — | — | 13.7 | 48.6 | 21.2 | 15.9 | † −13.3 | −30.1 |
| Exceptional financing | 409la | .... | .... | .... | .... | .... | .... | .... | .... | .... | .... | .... | .... |

*Excludes components in group E

| | | 2004 | 2005 | 2006 | 2007 | 2008 | 2009 | 2010 | 2011 | 2012 | 2013 | 2014 | 2015 |
|---|---|---|---|---|---|---|---|---|---|---|---|---|---|
| **International Investment Position** | | | | | | | *Billions of US Dollars* | | | | | | |
| Assets............................................ | 809aa | 12,025.3 | 13,047.6 | 16,650.5 | 21,158.3 | 19,364.3 | 20,596.2 | 22,527.8 | 23,708.7 | 25,484.6 | 25,970.9 | † 27,042.3 | 25,971.0 |
| Direct investment.......................... | 8a9aa | 3,112.7 | 3,327.4 | 4,204.7 | 5,502.7 | 5,472.4 | 6,355.5 | 6,586.9 | 7,388.4 | 8,084.4 | 8,818.9 | † 10,307.2 | 10,554.8 |
| Equity & investment fund shares.. | 8aaaa | 2,535.3 | 2,706.3 | 3,432.6 | 4,386.6 | 4,233.6 | 4,944.3 | 5,135.3 | 5,541.3 | 6,021.5 | 6,592.5 | † 7,093.9 | 7,197.8 |
| Debt instruments......................... | 8abaa | 577.4 | 621.1 | 772.1 | 1,116.1 | 1,238.9 | 1,411.1 | 1,451.6 | 1,847.1 | 2,062.9 | 2,226.4 | † 3,213.3 | 3,357.0 |
| Portfolio investment...................... | 8b9aa | 4,137.8 | 4,568.4 | 5,730.5 | 6,829.5 | 5,329.6 | 6,253.8 | 6,544.5 | 6,130.9 | 6,933.3 | 7,658.7 | † 7,946.2 | 7,805.4 |
| Equity & investment fund shares.. | 8baaa | 1,702.6 | 2,035.6 | 2,549.2 | 2,894.7 | 1,592.7 | 2,170.5 | 2,541.1 | 2,204.6 | 2,575.5 | 3,162.2 | † 3,465.7 | 3,314.1 |
| Debt securities............................. | 8bbaa | 2,435.3 | 2,532.8 | 3,181.4 | 3,934.7 | 3,736.9 | 4,083.3 | 4,003.4 | 3,926.3 | 4,357.8 | 4,496.6 | † 4,480.5 | 4,491.3 |
| Fin. der.(oth.than reserves) & ESOs | 8c9aa | 217.1 | 228.1 | 289.6 | 519.2 | 888.9 | 789.1 | 2,191.7 | 2,958.1 | 3,102.9 | 2,320.5 | † 2,415.2 | 1,862.8 |
| Other investment........................... | 8d9aa | 4,174.8 | 4,546.1 | 5,996.5 | 7,795.8 | 7,152.7 | 6,531.7 | 6,415.2 | 6,368.4 | 6,454.6 | 6,425.5 | † 5,630.2 | 5,046.6 |
| Other equity................................ | 8daaa | . . . . | . . . . | . . . . | . . . . | . . . . | . . . . | . . . . | . . . . | . . . . | . . . . | † 82.2 | 78.5 |
| Debt instruments......................... | 8dzaa | 4,174.8 | 4,546.1 | 5,996.5 | 7,795.8 | 7,152.7 | 6,531.7 | 6,415.2 | 6,368.4 | 6,454.6 | 6,425.5 | † 5,548.0 | 4,968.0 |
| Reserve assets............................. | 8e9aa | 382.8 | 377.5 | 429.2 | 511.2 | 520.8 | 666.1 | 789.6 | 862.8 | 909.4 | 747.2 | † 743.4 | 701.4 |
| Liabilities....................................... | 809la | 13,346.5 | 14,043.5 | 17,894.6 | 22,831.3 | 21,444.5 | 22,783.5 | 24,268.9 | 25,614.1 | 27,189.9 | 27,610.4 | † 28,263.4 | 26,426.6 |
| Direct investment.......................... | 8a9la | 2,980.7 | 2,832.4 | 3,533.6 | 4,610.5 | 4,458.1 | 5,079.8 | 5,191.5 | 5,705.5 | 6,107.0 | 6,796.6 | † 8,104.7 | 8,188.3 |
| Equity & investment fund shares.. | 8aala | 2,246.2 | 2,111.3 | 2,693.9 | 3,463.2 | 3,222.4 | 3,738.5 | 3,896.6 | 4,051.5 | 4,257.9 | 4,846.5 | † 5,251.5 | 5,264.8 |
| Debt instruments......................... | 8abla | 734.6 | 721.1 | 839.7 | 1,147.3 | 1,235.7 | 1,341.2 | 1,294.9 | 1,654.0 | 1,849.1 | 1,950.0 | † 2,853.2 | 2,923.5 |
| Portfolio investment...................... | 8b9la | 5,744.6 | 6,191.1 | 7,840.9 | 9,634.9 | 8,294.7 | 9,868.7 | 9,935.2 | 9,991.9 | 11,115.1 | 12,184.7 | † 11,830.2 | 11,058.5 |
| Equity & investment fund shares.. | 8bala | 2,583.5 | 3,037.4 | 3,995.0 | 4,872.7 | 3,039.9 | 4,041.0 | 4,319.9 | 3,979.0 | 4,651.2 | 5,478.4 | † 5,776.4 | 5,639.7 |
| Debt securities............................. | 8bbla | 3,161.1 | 3,153.7 | 3,846.0 | 4,762.2 | 5,254.9 | 5,827.7 | 5,615.4 | 6,012.9 | 6,464.0 | 6,706.3 | † 6,053.8 | 5,418.8 |
| Fin. der.(oth.than reserves) & ESOs | 8c9la | 267.5 | 253.3 | 315.0 | 528.5 | 889.8 | 815.4 | 2,250.9 | 3,028.6 | 3,164.3 | 2,374.7 | † 2,471.5 | 1,909.1 |
| Other investment........................... | 8d9la | 4,353.7 | 4,766.7 | 6,205.0 | 8,057.4 | 7,801.8 | 7,019.7 | 6,891.4 | 6,888.0 | 6,803.5 | 6,254.5 | † 5,857.1 | 5,270.7 |
| Other equity................................ | 8dala | . . . . | . . . . | . . . . | . . . . | . . . . | . . . . | . . . . | . . . . | . . . . | . . . . | † 5.9 | 5.1 |
| Debt instruments......................... | 8dzla | 4,353.7 | 4,766.7 | 6,205.0 | 8,057.4 | 7,801.8 | 7,019.7 | 6,891.4 | 6,888.0 | 6,803.5 | 6,254.5 | † 5,851.2 | 5,265.6 |

|  |  | 2004 | 2005 | 2006 | 2007 | 2008 | 2009 | 2010 | 2011 | 2012 | 2013 | 2014 | 2015 |
|---|---|---|---|---|---|---|---|---|---|---|---|---|---|
| **Government Finance Operations Statement General Government** | | | | | | *Billions of Euros: Fiscal Year Ends December 31* | | | | | | | |
| Revenue | a1 | 3,575.71 | 3,728.37 | 3,966.90 | 4,198.85 | 4,277.76 | 4,124.38 | 4,229.43 | 4,401.10 | 4,530.02 | 4,631.11 | 4,729.01 | 4,848.36 |
| Taxes | a11 | 1,972.59 | 2,072.60 | 2,236.12 | 2,388.93 | 2,388.64 | 2,233.84 | 2,298.29 | 2,404.49 | 2,492.46 | 2,555.64 | 2,620.05 | 2,709.75 |
| Social Contributions | a12 | 1,225.13 | 1,256.84 | 1,307.96 | 1,363.74 | 1,417.63 | 1,414.93 | 1,440.31 | 1,483.45 | 1,509.59 | 1,535.27 | 1,568.14 | 1,602.25 |
| Grants | a13 | .... | .... | .... | .... | .... | .... | .... | .... | .... | .... | .... | .... |
| Other Revenue | a14 | .... | .... | .... | .... | .... | .... | .... | .... | .... | .... | .... | .... |
| Expense | a2 | 3,759.83 | 3,892.09 | 4,041.26 | 4,189.87 | 4,409.49 | 4,615.35 | 4,756.82 | 4,776.73 | 4,876.17 | 4,924.96 | 4,994.01 | 5,065.20 |
| Compensation of Employees | a21 | 839.33 | 870.23 | 900.76 | 930.61 | 973.51 | 1,009.89 | 1,020.85 | 1,024.10 | 1,020.84 | 1,032.63 | 1,045.17 | 1,057.75 |
| Use of Goods & Services | a22 | 385.20 | 407.52 | 425.22 | 449.11 | 476.97 | 504.32 | 514.26 | 519.10 | 527.25 | 531.55 | 536.47 | 546.24 |
| Consumption of Fixed Capital | a23 | 200.55 | 210.40 | 221.47 | 232.97 | 245.22 | 251.40 | 259.53 | 266.93 | 274.09 | 279.35 | 282.08 | 284.60 |
| Interest | a24 | 246.31 | 246.43 | 250.55 | 268.71 | 282.78 | 259.99 | 262.47 | 292.29 | 296.62 | 277.96 | 268.12 | 250.77 |
| Subsidies | a25 | 102.10 | 100.98 | 105.51 | 111.34 | 116.33 | 135.02 | 137.85 | 134.57 | 132.20 | 135.12 | 150.98 | 158.56 |
| Grants | a26 | .... | .... | .... | .... | .... | .... | .... | .... | .... | .... | .... | .... |
| Social Benefits | a27 | 1,691.37 | 1,748.60 | 1,817.35 | 1,880.75 | 1,969.15 | 2,097.68 | 2,149.69 | 2,178.66 | 2,226.00 | 2,281.53 | 2,333.55 | 2,392.55 |
| Other Expense | a28 | .... | .... | .... | .... | .... | .... | .... | .... | .... | .... | .... | .... |
| Gross Operating Balance [1-2+23] | agob | 16.43 | 46.67 | 147.12 | 241.96 | 113.48 | −239.57 | −267.86 | −108.70 | −72.06 | −14.50 | 17.09 | 67.76 |
| Net Operating Balance [1-2] | anob | −184.12 | −163.72 | −74.36 | 8.99 | −131.73 | −490.97 | −527.39 | −375.62 | −346.15 | −293.85 | −264.99 | −216.84 |
| Net Acq. of Nonfinancial Assets | a31 | 57.11 | 54.80 | 57.99 | 68.77 | 76.07 | 90.45 | 61.87 | 33.92 | 13.64 | 1.74 | −3.51 | −1.60 |
| Aquisition of Nonfin. Assets | a31.1 | .... | .... | .... | .... | .... | .... | .... | .... | .... | .... | .... | .... |
| Disposal of Nonfin. Assets | a31.2 | .... | .... | .... | .... | .... | .... | .... | .... | .... | .... | .... | .... |
| Net Lending/Borrowing [1-2-31] | anlb | −241.22 | −218.53 | −132.35 | −59.78 | −207.81 | −581.42 | −589.26 | −409.55 | −359.79 | −295.59 | −261.49 | −215.24 |
| Net Acq. of Financial Assets | a32 | 17.62 | 67.23 | 37.80 | 77.87 | 288.83 | 107.66 | 171.20 | 39.60 | 243.75 | −4.88 | 23.67 | −53.12 |
| By instrument | | | | | | | | | | | | | |
| Monetary Gold & SDRs | a3201 | — | — | — | — | — | — | — | — | — | — | — | — |
| Currency & Deposits | a3202 | 13.98 | 25.76 | 26.63 | 20.04 | 73.16 | 28.47 | 1.68 | 20.70 | 31.72 | −44.52 | 26.96 | 5.36 |
| Securities other than Shares | a3203 | 9.66 | 16.55 | 20.02 | 23.00 | 70.10 | 25.14 | 90.30 | −24.06 | −8.54 | −10.02 | −22.15 | −14.62 |
| Loans | a3204 | −5.33 | −2.82 | −15.00 | 3.07 | 60.75 | −3.05 | 65.52 | 25.07 | 129.19 | 24.84 | −14.33 | −20.84 |
| Shares & Other Equity | a3205 | −.12 | 13.54 | −18.41 | 4.42 | 76.79 | 37.95 | 18.16 | −13.68 | 70.17 | 2.13 | 2.73 | −13.49 |
| Insurance Technical Reserves | a3206 | .31 | .24 | .26 | .28 | .10 | .46 | .13 | — | −.10 | −.06 | .20 | .10 |
| Financial Derivatives | a3207 | −1.71 | −1.70 | −.66 | .78 | 1.67 | 2.12 | −20.82 | 1.31 | 3.12 | 4.65 | 4.87 | −3.19 |
| Other Accounts Receivable | a3208 | .82 | 15.66 | 24.96 | 26.28 | 6.27 | 16.57 | 16.23 | 30.28 | 18.19 | 18.10 | 25.38 | −6.44 |
| By debtor | | | | | | | | | | | | | |
| Domestic | a321 | .... | .... | .... | .... | .... | .... | .... | .... | .... | .... | .... | .... |
| Foreign | a322 | .... | .... | .... | .... | .... | .... | .... | .... | .... | .... | .... | .... |
| Net Incurrence of Liabilities | a33 | 251.05 | 284.77 | 174.75 | 149.02 | 496.71 | 688.32 | 755.12 | 449.72 | 601.24 | 291.70 | 284.78 | 153.63 |
| By instrument | | | | | | | | | | | | | |
| Special Drawing Rights (SDRs) | a3301 | — | — | — | — | — | — | — | −.03 | .01 | .02 | — | — |
| Currency & Deposits | a3302 | 18.61 | 21.32 | 10.91 | −7.65 | 6.61 | 9.28 | 3.50 | −1.20 | 9.69 | −32.88 | 11.58 | 10.62 |
| Securities other than Shares | a3303 | 230.67 | 219.30 | 98.38 | 119.88 | 426.10 | 607.39 | 425.19 | 332.10 | 285.50 | 312.73 | 259.05 | 181.90 |
| Loans | a3304 | 8.40 | 20.59 | 22.83 | −1.88 | 49.78 | 62.97 | 301.61 | 97.91 | 319.02 | 22.14 | 2.77 | −57.49 |
| Shares & Other Equity | a3305 | −.03 | .26 | .01 | −.05 | .01 | 2.50 | — | .01 | .35 | −.34 | .02 | −.07 |
| Insurance Technical Reserves | a3306 | .24 | .25 | .26 | .24 | .22 | .57 | 1.01 | .49 | .10 | .50 | .60 | .79 |
| Financial Derivatives | a3307 | 1.21 | 1.54 | .95 | 2.22 | 3.75 | −.21 | 1.35 | .13 | −2.67 | 3.26 | −3.21 | −4.11 |
| Other Accounts Payable | a3308 | −8.05 | 21.51 | 41.42 | 36.26 | 10.23 | 5.82 | 22.45 | 20.30 | −10.76 | −13.72 | 13.98 | 21.99 |
| By creditor | | | | | | | | | | | | | |
| Domestic | a331 | .... | .... | .... | .... | .... | .... | .... | .... | .... | .... | .... | .... |
| Foreign | a332 | .... | .... | .... | .... | .... | .... | .... | .... | .... | .... | .... | .... |
| Stat. Discrepancy [32-33-NLB] | anlbz | 7.79 | .99 | −4.60 | −11.37 | −.07 | .77 | 5.34 | −.57 | 2.30 | −.99 | .37 | 8.49 |
| Memo Item: Expenditure [2+31] | a2m | 3,816.93 | 3,946.90 | 4,099.25 | 4,258.64 | 4,485.56 | 4,705.80 | 4,818.69 | 4,810.65 | 4,889.81 | 4,926.70 | 4,990.50 | 5,063.60 |
| **Balance Sheet** | | | | | | | | | | | | | |
| Net Worth | a6 | .... | .... | .... | .... | .... | .... | .... | .... | .... | .... | .... | .... |
| Nonfinancial Assets | a61 | .... | .... | .... | .... | .... | .... | .... | .... | .... | .... | .... | .... |
| Financial Assets | a62 | 2,223.77 | 2,439.74 | 2,604.10 | 2,821.75 | 2,920.52 | 3,122.79 | 3,423.61 | 3,477.33 | 3,835.51 | 3,880.48 | 4,022.34 | 4,024.65 |
| By instrument | | | | | | | | | | | | | |
| Monetary Gold & SDRs | a6201 | — | — | — | — | — | — | — | — | — | — | — | — |
| Currency & Deposits | a6202 | 408.42 | 433.56 | 458.03 | 480.23 | 548.60 | 591.31 | 591.47 | 613.07 | 648.75 | 606.26 | 657.76 | 669.32 |
| Securities other than Shares | a6203 | 96.21 | 108.54 | 125.09 | 145.12 | 214.22 | 247.31 | 341.35 | 314.09 | 317.57 | 305.04 | 307.90 | 298.33 |
| Loans | a6204 | 323.95 | 320.64 | 305.62 | 307.17 | 368.74 | 367.32 | 435.26 | 480.48 | 606.30 | 638.07 | 636.40 | 619.44 |
| Shares and Other Equity | a6205 | 889.98 | 1,049.99 | 1,166.48 | 1,308.71 | 1,205.26 | 1,307.63 | 1,439.21 | 1,410.48 | 1,560.39 | 1,610.64 | 1,666.06 | 1,698.11 |
| Insurance Technical Reserves | a6206 | 6.70 | 6.94 | 7.24 | 7.52 | 7.61 | 8.07 | 8.19 | 8.18 | 8.08 | 8.02 | 8.31 | 8.41 |
| Financial Derivatives | a6207 | 2.77 | 4.48 | 4.73 | 7.00 | 6.06 | 5.01 | −8.92 | .70 | 1.02 | −2.09 | 14.87 | 11.46 |
| Other Accounts Receivable | a6208 | 495.75 | 515.58 | 536.91 | 565.99 | 570.04 | 596.15 | 617.05 | 650.32 | 693.40 | 714.53 | 731.04 | 719.58 |
| By debtor | | | | | | | | | | | | | |
| Domestic | a621 | .... | .... | .... | .... | .... | .... | .... | .... | .... | .... | .... | .... |
| Foreign | a622 | .... | .... | .... | .... | .... | .... | .... | .... | .... | .... | .... | .... |
| Liabilities | a63 | 6,356.61 | 6,679.42 | 6,719.61 | 6,755.43 | 7,413.17 | 8,152.97 | 8,790.84 | 9,145.53 | 10,222.55 | 10,437.74 | 11,319.36 | 11,436.64 |
| By instrument | | | | | | | | | | | | | |
| Special Drawing Rights (SDRs) | a6301 | — | — | — | — | — | .13 | .14 | .11 | .12 | .14 | .14 | 1.15 |
| Currency & Deposits | a6302 | 255.08 | 276.27 | 287.57 | 279.92 | 287.09 | 305.07 | 310.04 | 351.85 | 361.84 | 328.76 | 339.73 | 351.87 |
| Securities other than Shares | a6303 | 4,721.29 | 4,959.43 | 4,903.79 | 4,912.83 | 5,496.28 | 6,142.54 | 6,422.82 | 6,631.53 | 7,355.86 | 7,583.55 | 8,421.05 | 8,560.34 |
| Loans | a6304 | 1,013.04 | 1,044.87 | 1,083.81 | 1,080.20 | 1,130.05 | 1,192.93 | 1,523.55 | 1,593.49 | 1,921.98 | 1,950.40 | 1,968.25 | 1,929.13 |
| Shares and Other Equity | a6305 | 3.67 | 11.48 | 13.82 | 13.96 | 13.61 | 16.39 | 16.91 | 16.88 | 16.91 | 16.73 | 17.14 | 17.54 |
| Insurance Technical Reserves | a6306 | 1.33 | 1.59 | 1.85 | 2.09 | 2.32 | 2.89 | 2.56 | 3.06 | 3.17 | 3.67 | 4.28 | 5.09 |
| Financial Derivatives | a6307 | 27.17 | 23.96 | 27.07 | 26.72 | 33.70 | 27.19 | 23.91 | 34.74 | 42.37 | 37.83 | 49.30 | 37.69 |
| Other Accounts Payable | a6308 | 335.04 | 361.82 | 401.70 | 439.71 | 450.12 | 465.83 | 490.91 | 513.86 | 520.29 | 516.67 | 519.46 | 533.83 |
| By creditor | | | | | | | | | | | | | |
| Domestic | a631 | .... | .... | .... | .... | .... | .... | .... | .... | .... | .... | .... | .... |
| Foreign | a632 | .... | .... | .... | .... | .... | .... | .... | .... | .... | .... | .... | .... |
| Net Financial Worth [62-63] | a6m2 | −4,132.84 | −4,239.68 | −4,115.51 | −3,933.68 | −4,492.65 | −5,030.18 | −5,367.24 | −5,668.20 | −6,387.04 | −6,557.26 | −7,297.02 | −7,411.99 |
| Memo Item: Debt at Market Value | a6m3 | 6,325.77 | 6,643.98 | 6,678.72 | 6,714.75 | 7,365.86 | 8,109.39 | 8,750.02 | 9,093.91 | 10,163.26 | 10,383.18 | 11,252.91 | 11,381.41 |
| Memo Item: Debt at Face Value | a6m35 | 5,920.19 | 6,212.37 | 6,393.11 | 6,540.80 | 7,049.83 | 7,740.91 | 8,493.00 | 8,938.10 | 9,305.98 | 9,563.58 | 9,826.93 | 9,975.23 |
| Memo Item: Maastricht Debt | a6m36 | 5,585,151.06 | 5,850,551.63 | 5,991,407.93 | 6,101,084.26 | 6,599,715.41 | 7,274,941.79 | 8,001,947.42 | 8,424,128.27 | 8,785,570.40 | 9,046,774.29 | 9,307,327.57 | 9,440,247.50 |
| Memo Item: Debt at Nominal Value. | a6m4 | .... | .... | .... | .... | .... | .... | .... | .... | .... | .... | .... | .... |

|  | | 2004 | 2005 | 2006 | 2007 | 2008 | 2009 | 2010 | 2011 | 2012 | 2013 | 2014 | 2015 |
|---|---|---|---|---|---|---|---|---|---|---|---|---|---|
| **National Accounts** | | | | | | | *Billions of Euros:* | | | | | | |
| Househ.Cons.Expend.,incl.NPISHs.... | 96f.c | 4,428.5 | 4,597.0 | 4,794.9 | 4,994.3 | 5,158.5 | 5,129.3 | 5,263.4 | 5,413.6 | 5,447.5 | 5,482.7 | 5,629.9 | 5,734.4 |
| Government Consumption Expend... | 91f.c | 1,584.8 | 1,648.3 | 1,716.0 | 1,790.3 | 1,884.4 | 1,985.6 | 2,013.4 | 2,029.6 | 2,040.1 | 2,069.4 | 2,123.2 | 2,174.7 |
| Gross Fixed Capital Formation......... | 93e.c | 1,560.7 | 1,653.1 | 1,800.9 | 1,948.8 | 1,966.0 | 1,727.0 | 1,731.2 | 1,790.7 | 1,740.5 | 1,696.8 | 1,967.8 | 2,050.7 |
| Changes in Inventories.................... | 93i.c | 26.6 | 23.1 | 46.7 | 73.4 | 61.0 | −53.1 | 19.7 | 58.1 | 6.9 | −2.9 | −32.8 | −31.1 |
| Exports of Goods and Services......... | 90c.c | 2,819.0 | 3,034.8 | 3,384.0 | 3,683.7 | 3,811.8 | 3,277.8 | 3,762.8 | 4,169.8 | 4,352.0 | 4,389.9 | 4,456.7 | 4,746.3 |
| Imports of Goods and Services (-)..... | 98c.c | 2,659.6 | 2,913.0 | 3,282.8 | 3,548.0 | 3,725.7 | 3,161.7 | 3,645.3 | 4,042.1 | 4,103.0 | 4,055.8 | 4,062.4 | 4,281.3 |
| Gross National Income (GNI)........... | 99a.c | 7,772.4 | 8,053.6 | 8,503.0 | 8,955.8 | 9,118.4 | 8,903.0 | 9,165.1 | 9,435.6 | 9,514.0 | 9,617.7 | . . . . | . . . . |
| Gross Domestic Product (GDP)......... | 99b.c | 7,760.0 | 8,043.3 | 8,459.7 | 8,942.5 | 9,156.0 | 8,904.9 | 9,145.2 | 9,419.7 | 9,484.1 | 9,580.1 | 10,082.4 | 10,393.7 |
| Net Primary Income from Abroad..... | 98.nc | 12.4 | 10.3 | 43.3 | 13.3 | −37.6 | −1.9 | 19.9 | 16.0 | 29.8 | 35.1 | . . . . | . . . . |
| GDP Volume 2010 Ref., Chained..... | 99b.r | 8,833.5 | 8,983.3 | 9,280.0 | 9,590.9 | 9,649.9 | 9,287.4 | 9,470.9 | 9,643.2 | 9,577.7 | 9,536.4 | 9,633.6 | 9,819.0 |
| GDP Volume (2010=100)............... | 99bvr | 93.3 | 94.9 | 98.0 | 101.3 | 101.9 | 98.1 | 100.0 | 101.8 | 101.1 | 100.7 | 101.7 | 103.7 |
| GDP Deflator (2010=100)............... | 99bir | 91.0 | 92.7 | 94.4 | 96.6 | 98.3 | 99.3 | 100.0 | 101.2 | 102.5 | 104.0 | 108.4 | 109.6 |

# Fiji   819

| | | 2004 | 2005 | 2006 | 2007 | 2008 | 2009 | 2010 | 2011 | 2012 | 2013 | 2014 | 2015 |
|---|---|---|---|---|---|---|---|---|---|---|---|---|---|
| **Exchange Rates** | | *Fiji Dollars per SDR: End of Period* | | | | | | | | | | | |
| Official Rate | aa | 2.5547 | 2.4939 | 2.5036 | 2.4511 | 2.7170 | 3.0234 | 2.8021 | 2.7950 | 2.7470 | 2.9228 | 2.8798 | 2.9477 |
| | | *Fiji Dollars per US Dollar: End of Period (ae) Period Average (rf)* | | | | | | | | | | | |
| Official Rate | ae | 1.6450 | 1.7449 | 1.6642 | 1.5511 | 1.7640 | 1.9286 | 1.8195 | 1.8205 | 1.7873 | 1.8979 | 1.9877 | 2.1272 |
| Official Rate | rf | 1.7330 | 1.6910 | 1.7312 | 1.6103 | 1.5937 | 1.9557 | 1.9183 | 1.7932 | 1.7899 | 1.8414 | 1.8873 | 2.0976 |
| | | *Index Numbers (2010=100): Period Averages* | | | | | | | | | | | |
| Official Rate | ahx | 110.7 | 113.4 | 110.8 | 119.1 | 121.0 | 98.3 | 100.0 | 106.9 | 107.1 | 104.2 | 101.6 | 91.4 |
| Nominal Effective Exchange Rate | nec | 125.5 | 126.1 | 123.9 | 123.4 | 122.5 | 106.1 | 100.0 | 99.7 | 101.5 | 101.6 | 102.1 | 105.4 |
| CPI-Based Real Effect. Ex. Rate | rec | 116.0 | 116.2 | 113.7 | 115.6 | 118.7 | 104.8 | 100.0 | 103.4 | 106.6 | 107.6 | 106.6 | 110.4 |
| **Fund Position** | | *Millions of SDRs: End of Period* | | | | | | | | | | | |
| Quota | 2f.s | 70.30 | 70.30 | 70.30 | 70.30 | 70.30 | 70.30 | 70.30 | 70.30 | 70.30 | 70.30 | 70.30 | 70.30 |
| SDR Holdings | 1b.s | 5.35 | 5.59 | 5.94 | 6.39 | 6.86 | 67.06 | 51.10 | 51.09 | 51.09 | 51.08 | 51.08 | 51.08 |
| Reserve Position in the Fund | 1c.s | 15.26 | 15.31 | 15.49 | 15.69 | 15.81 | 16.01 | 16.25 | 16.39 | 16.46 | 16.54 | 16.61 | 16.68 |
| Total Fund Cred.&Loans Outstg. | 2tl | — | — | — | — | — | — | — | — | — | — | — | — |
| SDR Allocations | 1bd | 6.96 | 6.96 | 6.96 | 6.96 | 6.96 | 67.09 | 67.09 | 67.09 | 67.09 | 67.09 | 67.09 | 67.09 |
| **International Liquidity** | | *Millions of US Dollars Unless Otherwise Indicated: End of Period* | | | | | | | | | | | |
| Total Reserves minus Gold | 1l.d | 482.73 | 320.89 | 312.79 | 527.61 | 321.49 | 569.14 | 719.40 | 832.23 | 919.97 | 940.86 | 915.20 | 917.90 |
| SDR Holdings | 1b.d | 8.31 | 7.99 | 8.93 | 10.10 | 10.57 | 105.13 | 78.69 | 78.44 | 78.51 | 78.67 | 74.00 | 70.78 |
| Reserve Position in the Fund | 1c.d | 23.70 | 21.89 | 23.30 | 24.79 | 24.36 | 25.09 | 25.02 | 25.16 | 25.30 | 25.47 | 24.06 | 23.11 |
| Foreign Exchange | 1d.d | 450.72 | 291.02 | 280.56 | 492.71 | 286.56 | 438.91 | 615.69 | 728.63 | 816.16 | 836.73 | 817.14 | 824.01 |
| Gold (Million Fine Troy Ounces) | 1ad | .001 | .001 | .001 | .001 | .001 | .001 | .001 | .001 | .001 | .001 | .001 | .001 |
| Gold (National Valuation) | 1and | .38 | .43 | .53 | .70 | .70 | .91 | 1.17 | 1.28 | 1.39 | 1.00 | 1.01 | .88 |
| Central Bank: Other Assets | 3..d | † 4.43 | 3.33 | 13.27 | 12.56 | 9.43 | 9.46 | 9.66 | 8.26 | 14.25 | 12.50 | 13.61 | 15.75 |
| Central Bank: Other Liabs | 4..d | † 1.42 | 1.43 | 1.44 | 4.09 | 1.26 | .24 | .27 | .53 | .39 | .43 | .52 | .20 |
| Other Depository Corps.: Assets | 7a.d | 125.20 | 137.27 | 78.84 | 99.37 | 131.86 | † 118.51 | 95.28 | 113.87 | 136.73 | 212.15 | 140.16 | 353.18 |
| Other Depository Corps.: Liabs | 7b.d | 57.32 | 105.70 | 70.89 | 82.01 | 119.71 | † 153.05 | 116.30 | 98.43 | 142.18 | 128.48 | 155.47 | 337.47 |
| Other Financial Corps.: Assets | 7e.d | 130.7 | 146.8 | 53.2 | 54.9 | 41.8 | 43.0 | 34.1 | 123.8 | 193.1 | 245.3 | 186.4 | 222.0 |
| Other Financial Corps.: Liabs | 7f.d | 5.4 | 4.1 | 3.4 | 3.2 | 5.0 | 7.6 | 9.7 | 14.8 | 24.7 | 20.7 | 17.4 | 14.4 |
| **Central Bank** | | *Millions of Fiji Dollars: End of Period* | | | | | | | | | | | |
| Net Foreign Assets | 11n | † 781.6 | 546.6 | 527.3 | 815.3 | 563.9 | 914.1 | 1,140.1 | 1,343.9 | 1,482.3 | 1,614.6 | 1,653.5 | 1,789.7 |
| Claims on Nonresidents | 11 | † 801.7 | 566.5 | 547.1 | 838.7 | 585.0 | 1,117.4 | 1,328.5 | 1,532.4 | 1,667.3 | 1,811.5 | 1,847.8 | 1,987.9 |
| Liabilities to Nonresidents | 16c | † 20.1 | 19.8 | 19.8 | 23.4 | 21.1 | 203.3 | 188.5 | 188.5 | 185.0 | 196.9 | 194.2 | 198.2 |
| Claims on Other Depository Corps. | 12e | † .7 | 3.6 | 3.7 | 3.5 | .7 | 4.1 | 5.9 | 26.7 | 45.8 | 78.9 | 97.5 | 92.2 |
| Net Claims on Central Government | 12an | † 32.8 | 111.7 | 174.5 | 151.3 | 124.8 | 200.0 | 150.5 | 107.5 | 98.4 | 39.2 | 58.5 | 58.2 |
| Claims on Central Government | 12a | † 75.8 | 137.4 | 191.5 | 177.0 | 162.3 | 202.7 | 162.1 | 149.3 | 129.6 | 105.8 | 99.0 | 94.2 |
| Liabilities to Central Government | 16d | † 43.0 | 25.7 | 17.1 | 25.7 | 37.5 | 2.7 | 11.7 | 41.8 | 31.2 | 66.5 | 40.5 | 36.0 |
| Claims on Other Sectors | 12s | † 4.2 | 6.1 | 5.4 | 1.3 | 1.4 | 27.4 | 25.2 | 24.9 | 24.6 | 24.3 | 1.7 | 1.3 |
| Claims on Other Financial Corps. | 12g | † — | — | — | — | — | — | — | — | — | — | — | — |
| Claims on State & Local Govts. | 12b | † — | — | — | — | — | — | — | — | — | — | — | — |
| Claims on Public Nonfin. Corps. | 12c | † 2.4 | 4.6 | 4.3 | — | — | 25.6 | 23.5 | 23.2 | 23.0 | 22.7 | — | — |
| Claims on Private Sector | 12d | † 1.8 | 1.5 | 1.0 | 1.3 | 1.4 | 1.7 | 1.7 | 1.6 | 1.6 | 1.6 | 1.7 | 1.3 |
| Monetary Base | 14 | † 519.6 | 531.2 | 660.2 | 921.9 | 634.4 | 955.0 | 1,164.8 | 1,392.6 | 1,551.7 | 1,667.4 | 1,737.9 | 1,883.4 |
| Currency in Circulation | 14a | † 303.5 | 339.8 | 354.2 | 381.5 | 390.3 | 431.0 | 479.5 | 496.3 | 558.4 | 572.1 | 640.6 | 732.0 |
| Liabs. to Other Depository Corps. | 14c | † 216.1 | 191.4 | 306.0 | 540.4 | 244.1 | 524.1 | 685.4 | 896.4 | 993.3 | 1,095.3 | 1,097.3 | 1,151.4 |
| Liabilities to Other Sectors | 14d | † — | — | — | — | — | — | — | — | — | — | — | — |
| Other Liabs. to Other Dep. Corps. | 14n | † 96.6 | 35.2 | 6.3 | — | .2 | — | .2 | .3 | .2 | .2 | — | .1 |
| Dep. & Sec. Excl. f/Monetary Base | 14o | † 157.0 | 48.3 | — | — | — | .2 | .2 | .2 | .4 | .4 | .4 | .4 |
| Deposits Included in Broad Money | 15 | † — | — | — | — | — | — | — | — | — | — | — | — |
| Sec.Ot.th.Shares Incl.in Brd.Money | 16a | † — | — | — | — | — | — | — | — | — | — | — | — |
| Deposits Excl. from Broad Money | 16b | † — | — | — | — | — | .2 | .2 | .2 | .4 | .4 | .4 | .4 |
| Sec.Ot.th.Shares Excl.f/Brd.Money | 16s | † 157.0 | 48.3 | — | — | — | — | — | — | — | — | — | — |
| Loans | 16l | † — | — | — | — | — | — | — | — | — | — | — | — |
| Financial Derivatives | 16m | † — | — | — | — | — | — | — | — | — | — | — | — |
| Shares and Other Equity | 17a | † 57.3 | 63.5 | 55.6 | 62.3 | 76.6 | 213.3 | 176.8 | 130.9 | 115.3 | 103.6 | 90.7 | 95.1 |
| Other Items (Net) | 17r | † −11.3 | −10.2 | −11.3 | −12.7 | −20.5 | −23.0 | −20.4 | −21.1 | −16.3 | −14.6 | −17.8 | −37.6 |
| Memo Item: | | | | | | | | | | | | | |
| Total Assets | 10ra | † 1,048.6 | 875.9 | 912.4 | 1,181.9 | 929.3 | 1,550.6 | 1,709.5 | 1,921.2 | 2,054.0 | 2,216.5 | 2,244.6 | 2,389.6 |

# Fiji 819

|  |  | 2004 | 2005 | 2006 | 2007 | 2008 | 2009 | 2010 | 2011 | 2012 | 2013 | 2014 | 2015 |
|---|---|---|---|---|---|---|---|---|---|---|---|---|---|
| **Other Depository Corporations** |  | *Millions of Fiji Dollars: End of Period* | | | | | | | | | | | |
| Net Foreign Assets | 21n | 111.7 | 55.1 | 13.2 | 26.9 | 21.4 | † −66.6 | −38.2 | 28.1 | −9.7 | 158.8 | −30.4 | 33.4 |
| Claims on Nonresidents | 21 | 206.0 | 239.5 | 131.2 | 154.1 | 232.6 | † 228.6 | 173.4 | 207.3 | 244.4 | 402.6 | 278.6 | 751.3 |
| Liabilities to Nonresidents | 26c | 94.3 | 184.4 | 118.0 | 127.2 | 211.2 | † 295.2 | 211.6 | 179.2 | 254.1 | 243.8 | 309.0 | 717.9 |
| Claims on Central Bank | 20 | 364.4 | 288.5 | 366.3 | 632.2 | 320.2 | † 600.1 | 780.3 | 988.0 | 1,118.7 | 1,225.8 | 1,247.6 | 1,335.5 |
| Currency | 20a | 51.4 | 59.9 | 60.3 | 91.9 | 76.2 | † 76.1 | 95.6 | 91.8 | 121.4 | 130.5 | 150.4 | 184.2 |
| Reserve Deposits and Securities | 20b | 216.0 | 191.3 | 305.8 | 540.3 | 244.0 | † 524.0 | 684.7 | 896.2 | 997.2 | 1,095.3 | 1,097.3 | 1,151.3 |
| Other Claims | 20n | 97.0 | 37.2 | .2 | — | — | † — | — | — | — | — | — | — |
| Net Claims on Central Government | 22an | 109.0 | 169.9 | 179.5 | 144.1 | 43.9 | † 120.1 | 63.2 | 16.3 | −67.8 | −29.3 | −26.7 | −29.1 |
| Claims on Central Government | 22a | 200.6 | 258.4 | 265.0 | 245.5 | 175.4 | † 269.1 | 231.2 | 206.2 | 192.6 | 145.9 | 186.3 | 267.4 |
| Liabilities to Central Government | 26d | 91.6 | 88.5 | 85.5 | 101.3 | 131.5 | † 149.1 | 168.0 | 189.9 | 260.3 | 175.2 | 213.0 | 296.5 |
| Claims on Other Sectors | 22s | 2,336.2 | 2,865.4 | 3,461.2 | 3,521.3 | 3,802.3 | † 3,884.7 | 3,953.0 | 4,043.8 | 4,267.5 | 4,871.7 | 5,723.2 | 6,495.9 |
| Claims on Other Financial Corps | 22g | .5 | 1.5 | 6.3 | 12.6 | 8.6 | † 2.2 | 3.8 | 3.4 | .3 | 4.4 | 5.1 | 6.8 |
| Claims on State & Local Govts | 22b | 9.7 | 8.5 | 3.1 | 8.2 | 10.9 | † 11.6 | 13.0 | 16.3 | 17.5 | 16.3 | 17.9 | 16.3 |
| Claims on Public Nonfin. Corps | 22c | 91.1 | 87.5 | 116.7 | 125.6 | 160.3 | † 222.2 | 161.3 | 100.2 | 76.9 | 294.3 | 438.2 | 462.6 |
| Claims on Private Sector | 22d | 2,234.9 | 2,767.9 | 3,335.0 | 3,375.0 | 3,622.4 | † 3,648.6 | 3,774.8 | 3,923.9 | 4,172.8 | 4,556.7 | 5,262.1 | 6,010.2 |
| Liabilities to Central Bank | 26g | 102.8 | 98.7 | 3.7 | 3.1 | .2 | † 2.4 | 2.9 | 26.9 | 39.1 | 72.7 | 90.0 | 85.6 |
| Transf.Dep.Included in Broad Money | 24 | 737.2 | 925.2 | 856.0 | 1,331.8 | 1,043.1 | † 907.2 | 1,027.1 | 1,595.6 | 1,660.9 | 3,068.0 | 3,213.6 | 3,653.2 |
| Other Dep.Included in Broad Money | 25 | 1,407.7 | 1,522.5 | 2,125.7 | 1,956.1 | 2,025.6 | † 2,371.2 | 2,375.1 | 2,347.1 | 2,529.1 | 2,094.2 | 2,493.7 | 2,872.4 |
| Sec.Ot.th.Shares Incl.in Brd. Money | 26a | 180.9 | 241.2 | 354.3 | 353.3 | 293.7 | † 303.6 | 288.9 | 194.8 | 182.9 | 119.2 | 120.4 | 124.9 |
| Deposits Excl. from Broad Money | 26b | .8 | 1.4 | 1.2 | .8 | 2.2 | † .5 | .1 | .5 | .7 | .7 | .8 | 1.5 |
| Sec.Ot.th.Shares Excl.f/Brd.Money | 26s | 92.6 | 103.1 | 13 .9 | 95.0 | 104.2 | † 89.6 | 76.2 | 52.2 | 44.6 | 28.9 | .4 | — |
| Loans | 26l | 10.4 | 11.6 | 27.0 | 21.0 | 11.6 | † 8.0 | 7.0 | 9.0 | 35.0 | 39.4 | 13.9 | 12.4 |
| Financial Derivatives | 26m | — | — | — | — | — | † — | — | — | — | — | — | — |
| Insurance Technical Reserves | 26r | — | — | — | — | — | † — | — | — | — | — | — | — |
| Shares and Other Equity | 27a | 387.7 | 445.4 | 537.0 | 605.3 | 683.3 | † 774.0 | 837.3 | 762.8 | 772.8 | 843.5 | 981.2 | 1,118.9 |
| Other Items (Net) | 27r | 1.1 | 29.7 | −18.5 | −41.7 | 23.9 | † 81.7 | 143.5 | 87.2 | 43.6 | −39.6 | −.3 | −33.2 |
| Memo Item: |  |  |  |  |  |  |  |  |  |  |  |  |  |
| Total Assets | 20ra | 3,355.6 | 3,896.3 | 4,555.4 | 4,981.6 | 4,949.6 | † 5,412.4 | 5,526.9 | 5,904.4 | 6,380.0 | 7,277.7 | 8,076.0 | 9,545.8 |
| **Depository Corporations** |  | *Millions of Fiji Dollars: End of Period* | | | | | | | | | | | |
| Net Foreign Assets | 31n | † 893.3 | 601.7 | 540.5 | 842.3 | 585.3 | † 847.4 | 1,101.8 | 1,372.0 | 1,472.6 | 1,773.4 | 1,623.1 | 1,823.1 |
| Claims on Nonresidents | 31 | † 1,007.7 | 806.0 | 678.3 | 992.9 | 817.6 | † 1,345.9 | 1,501.9 | 1,739.7 | 1,911.7 | 2,214.1 | 2,126.4 | 2,739.2 |
| Liabilities to Nonresidents | 36c | † 114.4 | 204.3 | 137.8 | 150.6 | 232.3 | † 498.5 | 400.1 | 367.7 | 439.1 | 440.8 | 503.3 | 916.1 |
| Domestic Claims | 32 | † 2,482.1 | 3,153.1 | 3,820.6 | 3,818.0 | 3,972.4 | † 4,232.1 | 4,191.8 | 4,192.5 | 4,322.8 | 4,906.0 | 5,756.7 | 6,526.3 |
| Net Claims on Central Government | 32an | † 141.8 | 281.6 | 354.0 | 295.4 | 168.7 | † 320.1 | 213.7 | 123.8 | 30.7 | 10.0 | 31.8 | 29.1 |
| Claims on Central Government | 32a | † 276.4 | 395.7 | 456.5 | 422.5 | 337.7 | † 471.9 | 393.3 | 355.5 | 322.2 | 251.7 | 285.3 | 361.6 |
| Liabilities to Central Government | 36d | † 134.7 | 114.2 | 102.5 | 127.1 | 169.0 | † 151.8 | 179.7 | 231.7 | 291.5 | 241.7 | 253.5 | 332.5 |
| Claims on Other Sectors | 32s | † 2,340.3 | 2,871.5 | 3,466.6 | 3,522.6 | 3,803.7 | † 3,912.0 | 3,978.2 | 4,068.7 | 4,292.1 | 4,896.0 | 5,724.9 | 6,497.2 |
| Claims on Other Financial Corps | 32g | † .5 | 1.5 | 6.3 | 12.6 | 8.6 | † 2.2 | 3.8 | 3.4 | .3 | 4.4 | 5.1 | 6.8 |
| Claims on State & Local Govts | 32b | † 9.7 | 8.5 | 3.1 | 8.2 | 10.9 | † 11.6 | 13.0 | 16.3 | 17.5 | 16.3 | 17.9 | 16.3 |
| Claims on Public Nonfin. Corps | 32c | † 93.4 | 92.0 | 121.1 | 125.6 | 160.3 | † 247.8 | 184.8 | 123.4 | 99.9 | 317.0 | 438.2 | 462.6 |
| Claims on Private Sector | 32d | † 2,236.7 | 2,769.4 | 3,336.0 | 3,376.3 | 3,623.8 | † 3,650.4 | 3,776.5 | 3,925.6 | 4,174.5 | 4,558.3 | 5,263.7 | 6,011.4 |
| Broad Money Liabilities | 35l | † 2,577.8 | 2,968.8 | 3,629.9 | 3,930.8 | 3,676.6 | † 3,937.0 | 4,075.0 | 4,542.0 | 4,809.8 | 5,723.0 | 6,317.9 | 7,198.3 |
| Currency Outside Depository Corps | 34a | † 252.1 | 279.9 | 293.9 | 289.6 | 314.2 | † 354.9 | 383.9 | 404.5 | 436.9 | 441.6 | 490.3 | 547.8 |
| Transferable Deposits | 34 | † 737.2 | 925.2 | 856.0 | 1,331.8 | 1,043.1 | † 907.2 | 1,027.1 | 1,595.6 | 1,660.9 | 3,068.0 | 3,213.6 | 3,653.2 |
| Other Deposits | 35 | † 1,407.7 | 1,522.5 | 2,125.7 | 1,956.1 | 2,025.6 | † 2,371.2 | 2,375.1 | 2,347.1 | 2,529.1 | 2,094.2 | 2,493.7 | 2,872.4 |
| Securities Other than Shares | 36a | † 180.9 | 241.2 | 354.3 | 353.3 | 293.7 | † 303.6 | 288.9 | 194.8 | 182.9 | 119.2 | 120.4 | 124.9 |
| Deposits Excl. from Broad Money | 36b | † .8 | 1.4 | 1.2 | .8 | 2.2 | † .7 | .1 | .7 | 1.0 | 1.0 | 1.2 | 1.9 |
| Sec.Ot.th.Shares Excl.f/Brd.Money | 36s | † 249.6 | 151.4 | 133.9 | 95.0 | 104.2 | † 89.6 | 76.2 | 52.2 | 44.6 | 28.9 | .4 | — |
| Loans | 36l | † 10.4 | 11.6 | 27.0 | 21.0 | 11.6 | † 8.0 | 7.0 | 9.0 | 35.0 | 39.4 | 13.9 | 12.4 |
| Financial Derivatives | 36m | † — | — | — | — | — | † — | — | — | — | — | — | — |
| Insurance Technical Reserves | 36r | † — | — | — | — | — | † — | — | — | — | — | — | — |
| Shares and Other Equity | 37a | † 445.1 | 508.9 | 592.6 | 667.5 | 759.9 | † 987.3 | 1,014.1 | 893.7 | 888.1 | 947.1 | 1,071.9 | 1,214.0 |
| Other Items (Net) | 37r | † 91.6 | 112.6 | −23.5 | −54.8 | 3.2 | † 57.0 | 121.0 | 66.8 | 16.8 | −60.1 | −25.5 | −77.2 |
| Broad Money Liabs., Seasonally Adj. | 35l.b | † 2,548.0 | 2,935.5 | 3,592.1 | 3,891.0 | 3,641.4 | † 3,918.3 | 4,052.4 | 4,516.8 | 4,783.1 | 5,691.7 | 6,277.6 | 7,158.7 |
| **Other Financial Corporations** |  | *Millions of Fiji Dollars: End of Period* | | | | | | | | | | | |
| Net Foreign Assets | 41n | 206.0 | 249.0 | 82.9 | 80.2 | 64.9 | 68.4 | 44.4 | 198.4 | 301.0 | 426.2 | 336.0 | 441.5 |
| Claims on Nonresidents | 41 | 215.0 | 256.2 | 88.5 | 85.2 | 73.7 | 83.0 | 62.1 | 225.4 | 345.1 | 465.5 | 370.5 | 472.2 |
| Liabilities to Nonresidents | 46c | 9.0 | 7.1 | 5.6 | 5.0 | 8.8 | 14.6 | 17.7 | 26.9 | 44.1 | 39.4 | 34.5 | 30.7 |
| Claims on Depository Corporations | 40 | 723.4 | 714.8 | 876.0 | 1,047.4 | 848.0 | 797.6 | 784.8 | 992.5 | 1,007.9 | 1,203.4 | 1,454.8 | 1,494.1 |
| Net Claims on Central Government | 42an | 1,606.4 | 1,659.6 | 1,732.0 | 1,716.5 | 1,854.0 | 2,023.5 | 2,296.7 | 2,277.2 | 2,354.9 | 2,385.6 | 2,372.0 | 2,479.2 |
| Claims on Central Government | 42a | 1,747.3 | 1,800.3 | 1,869.9 | 1,854.1 | 1,992.4 | 2,161.6 | 2,435.0 | 2,415.9 | 2,493.4 | 2,525.9 | 2,512.6 | 2,618.7 |
| Liabilities to Central Government | 46d | 140.9 | 140.7 | 137.9 | 137.5 | 138.4 | 138.2 | 138.3 | 138.7 | 138.5 | 140.3 | 140.6 | 139.5 |
| Claims on Other Sectors | 42s | 738.1 | 862.2 | 994.7 | 1,056.3 | 1,367.4 | 1,613.1 | 1,485.3 | 1,357.2 | 1,469.4 | 1,356.0 | 1,547.3 | 1,947.4 |
| Claims on State & Local Govts | 42b | 15.5 | 14.3 | 12.7 | 11.2 | 10.0 | 8.4 | 6.9 | 6.6 | 4.9 | 4.4 | 1.7 | 1.3 |
| Claims on Public Nonfin. Corps | 42c | 80.4 | 124.0 | 100.9 | 131.0 | 153.4 | 223.5 | 225.9 | 171.5 | 178.7 | 131.7 | 154.4 | 214.9 |
| Claims on Private Sector | 42d | 642.2 | 723.9 | 881.1 | 914.0 | 1,203.9 | 1,381.3 | 1,252.6 | 1,179.2 | 1,285.7 | 1,219.9 | 1,391.3 | 1,731.2 |
| Deposits | 46b | — | — | — | — | — | — | — | — | — | — | — | — |
| Securities Other than Shares | 46s | — | — | — | — | — | — | — | — | — | — | — | — |
| Loans | 46l | 3.9 | .4 | — | .2 | 9.8 | 9.8 | 9.3 | .5 | .6 | .6 | .6 | .6 |
| Financial Derivatives | 46m | — | — | — | — | — | — | — | — | — | — | — | — |
| Insurance Technical Reserves | 46r | 2,554.3 | 2,748.4 | 2,923.9 | 3,083.1 | 3,238.0 | 3,403.5 | 3,563.1 | 3,804.1 | 4,162.8 | 4,478.9 | 4,777.5 | 5,196.2 |
| Shares and Other Equity | 47a | 888.1 | 915.8 | 958.1 | 989.6 | 1,075.9 | 1,214.8 | 944.0 | 1,054.4 | 1,011.2 | 956.9 | 1,075.7 | 1,360.9 |
| Other Items (Net) | 47r | −172.4 | −178.9 | −196.5 | −172.6 | −189.4 | −125.7 | 95.0 | −33.7 | −41.5 | −65.3 | −143.8 | −195.6 |
| Memo Item: |  |  |  |  |  |  |  |  |  |  |  |  |  |
| Total Assets | 40ra | 3,635.6 | 3,853.1 | 4,077.3 | 4,279.2 | 4,533.3 | 4,905.2 | 5,017.9 | 5,285.5 | 5,616.2 | 5,881.0 | 6,254.1 | 6,958.6 |

|  |  | 2004 | 2005 | 2006 | 2007 | 2008 | 2009 | 2010 | 2011 | 2012 | 2013 | 2014 | 2015 |
|---|---|---|---|---|---|---|---|---|---|---|---|---|---|
| **Financial Corporations** | | | | | | *Millions of Fiji Dollars: End of Period* | | | | | | | |
| Net Foreign Assets | 51n | † 1,099.3 | 850.7 | 623.4 | 922.4 | 650.2 | † 915.8 | 1,146.2 | 1,570.4 | 1,773.6 | 2,199.5 | 1,959.1 | 2,264.6 |
| Claims on Nonresidents | 51 | † 1,222.7 | 1,062.2 | 766.7 | 1,078.1 | 891.3 | † 1,429.0 | 1,564.0 | 1,965.1 | 2,256.8 | 2,679.6 | 2,496.9 | 3,211.4 |
| Liabilities to Nonresidents | 56c | † 123.4 | 211.4 | 143.4 | 155.6 | 241.0 | † 513.2 | 417.8 | 394.6 | 483.2 | 480.1 | 537.8 | 946.8 |
| Domestic Claims | 52 | † 4,826.0 | 5,673.4 | 6,540.9 | 6,578.3 | 7,185.2 | † 7,866.4 | 7,970.1 | 7,823.5 | 8,146.8 | 8,643.2 | 9,670.9 | 10,946.1 |
| Net Claims on Central Government | 52an | † 1,748.1 | 1,941.2 | 2,086.0 | 2,011.9 | 2,022.7 | † 2,343.5 | 2,510.4 | 2,401.0 | 2,385.6 | 2,395.5 | 2,403.8 | 2,508.3 |
| Claims on Central Government | 52a | † 2,023.7 | 2,196.1 | 2,326.4 | 2,276.6 | 2,330.2 | † 2,633.5 | 2,828.3 | 2,771.4 | 2,815.6 | 2,777.6 | 2,797.9 | 2,980.3 |
| Liabilities to Central Government | 56d | † 275.5 | 254.9 | 240.5 | 264.6 | 307.4 | † 290.0 | 317.9 | 370.4 | 430.0 | 382.0 | 394.1 | 472.0 |
| Claims on Other Sectors | 52s | † 3,077.9 | 3,732.2 | 4,454.9 | 4,566.3 | 5,162.4 | † 5,522.9 | 5,459.7 | 5,422.5 | 5,761.2 | 6,247.6 | 7,267.1 | 8,437.8 |
| Claims on State & Local Govts | 52b | † 25.2 | 22.8 | 15.8 | 19.4 | 21.0 | † 20.0 | 19.9 | 22.9 | 22.4 | 20.7 | 19.5 | 17.7 |
| Claims on Public Nonfin. Corps | 52c | † 173.8 | 216.1 | 222.0 | 256.6 | 313.8 | † 471.3 | 410.8 | 294.9 | 278.6 | 448.7 | 592.6 | 677.5 |
| Claims on Private Sector | 52d | † 2,878.9 | 3,493.3 | 4,217.1 | 4,290.4 | 4,827.7 | † 5,031.6 | 5,029.0 | 5,104.7 | 5,460.2 | 5,778.2 | 6,655.0 | 7,742.6 |
| Currency Outside Financial Corps | 54a | † 228.7 | 222.1 | 264.7 | 226.4 | 275.0 | † 322.0 | 338.4 | 346.0 | 318.1 | 304.3 | 424.1 | 474.2 |
| Deposits | 55l | † 1,915.0 | 2,244.3 | 2,628.4 | 2,653.9 | 2,600.1 | † 2,862.4 | 2,943.5 | 3,210.1 | 3,339.8 | 3,829.5 | 4,252.9 | 4,974.2 |
| Securities Other than Shares | 56a | † 47.4 | 45.5 | 73.0 | 68.9 | 46.9 | † 48.7 | 32.4 | 28.2 | 35.3 | 22.4 | 25.5 | 20.4 |
| Loans | 56l | † 3.9 | .4 | — | .2 | 9.8 | † 9.8 | 9.2 | .5 | .6 | .6 | .6 | .6 |
| Financial Derivatives | 56m | † — | — | — | — | — | † — | | | | | | |
| Insurance Technical Reserves | 56r | † 2,554.3 | 2,748.4 | 2,923.9 | 3,083.1 | 3,238.0 | † 3,403.5 | 3,563.1 | 3,804.1 | 4,162.8 | 4,478.9 | 4,777.5 | 5,196.2 |
| Shares and Other Equity | 57a | † 1,333.1 | 1,424.7 | 1,550.6 | 1,657.1 | 1,835.8 | † 2,202.1 | 1,958.1 | 1,948.1 | 1,899.3 | 1,904.1 | 2,147.6 | 2,574.9 |
| Other Items (Net) | 57r | † −157.2 | −161.3 | −276.4 | −189.0 | −170.2 | † −66.3 | 271.6 | 56.8 | 164.6 | 303.0 | 1.8 | −29.7 |
| **Monetary Aggregates** | | | | | | *Millions of Fiji Dollars: End of Period* | | | | | | | |
| Broad Money | 59m | 2,577.8 | 2,968.8 | 3,629.9 | 3,930.8 | 3,676.6 | 3,937.0 | 4,075.0 | 4,542.0 | 4,809.8 | 5,723.0 | 6,317.9 | 7,198.3 |
| o/w: Currency Issued by Cent.Govt | 59m.a | — | — | — | — | — | — | — | — | — | — | — | — |
| o/w: Dep.in Nonfin. Corporations | 59m.b | — | — | — | — | — | — | — | — | — | — | — | — |
| o/w: Secs. Issued by Central Govt. | 59m.c | — | — | — | — | — | — | — | — | — | — | — | — |
| Money (National Definitions) | | | | | | | | | | | | | |
| Narrow Money (M1) | 59mak | 961.9 | 1,156.5 | 1,111.0 | 1,572.6 | 1,273.2 | 1,213.4 | 1,367.9 | 1,941.7 | 2,035.0 | 3,447.3 | 3,622.7 | 4,108.5 |
| Quasi Money | 59mal | 1,435.1 | 1,571.2 | 2,164.6 | 2,004.9 | 2,109.7 | 2,420.0 | 2,418.1 | 2,405.6 | 2,591.8 | 2,156.5 | 2,574.8 | 2,964.9 |
| M2 | 59mb | 2,397.0 | 2,727.6 | 3,275.6 | 3,577.5 | 3,382.9 | 3,633.4 | 3,786.1 | 4,347.2 | 4,626.9 | 5,603.8 | 6,197.5 | 7,073.4 |
| Broad Money (M3) | 59mea | 2,577.8 | 2,968.8 | 3,629.9 | 3,930.8 | 3,676.6 | 3,937.0 | 4,075.0 | 4,542.0 | 4,809.8 | 5,723.0 | 6,317.9 | 7,198.3 |
| **Interest Rates** | | | | | | *Percent Per Annum* | | | | | | | |
| Central Bank Policy Rate (EOP) | 60 | 1.75 | 2.25 | 4.25 | .... | .... | .... | † 2.50 | .50 | .50 | .50 | .50 | .50 |
| Discount Rate (End of Period) | 60.a | 2.25 | 2.75 | 5.25 | 9.25 | 6.32 | 3.50 | 3.00 | 1.00 | 1.00 | 1.00 | 1.00 | 1.00 |
| Money Market Rate | 60b | .89 | 1.28 | 4.42 | 5.00 | 1.25 | 1.31 | 1.00 | .... | .... | .... | .... | .... |
| Treasury Bill Rate | 60c | 1.52 | 1.94 | 7.45 | 4.55 | .22 | 6.07 | 3.45 | 2.20 | .57 | .15 | 1.17 | 1.19 |
| Savings Rate | 60k | .38 | .38 | .71 | .90 | .67 | .77 | .99 | 1.06 | .82 | .76 | .90 | .87 |
| Deposit Rate | 60l | 1.72 | 1.83 | 5.56 | 7.04 | 2.75 | 4.91 | 5.41 | 3.75 | 2.42 | 2.07 | 1.86 | 2.52 |
| Lending Rate | 60p | 7.17 | 6.78 | 7.35 | 9.01 | 8.00 | 7.85 | 7.49 | 7.47 | 6.97 | 6.10 | 5.76 | 5.79 |
| Government Bond Yield | 61 | 2.55 | 2.74 | 5.75 | 6.87 | 5.91 | 8.13 | .... | .... | 4.00 | 4.00 | † 4.58 | 5.17 |
| **Prices, Production, Labor** | | | | | | *Index Numbers (2010=100): Period Averages* | | | | | | | |
| Share Prices | 62 | 125.9 | 144.7 | 137.5 | 106.7 | 129.7 | 118.7 | 100.0 | 94.7 | 102.9 | 92.3 | 92.3 | 135.2 |
| Share Prices (End of Month) | 62.ep | 105.7 | 120.0 | 133.0 | 106.9 | 107.7 | 113.2 | 100.0 | 89.5 | 89.8 | 91.6 | 92.5 | 112.5 |
| Consumer Prices | 64 | 78.9 | † 80.8 | 82.8 | 86.7 | † 93.4 | 96.5 | 100.0 | 107.3 | 110.9 | 114.2 | 114.8 | 116.4 |
| Wage Rates (2000=100) | 65 | .... | .... | .... | .... | .... | .... | .... | .... | .... | .... | .... | .... |
| Industrial Production (2005=100) | 66 | 116.3 | 100.0 | 102.6 | 101.0 | 100.0 | .... | .... | .... | .... | .... | .... | .... |
| Tourist Arrivals | 66.t | 79.8 | 86.3 | 86.8 | 85.4 | 92.6 | 85.8 | 100.0 | 106.8 | 104.5 | 104.1 | 109.6 | .... |
| Industrial Employment (2005=100) | 67 | 97.6 | 100.0 | .... | .... | .... | .... | .... | .... | .... | .... | .... | .... |
| | | | | | | *Number in Thousands: Period Averages* | | | | | | | |
| Labor Force | 67d | .... | .... | .... | .... | .... | .... | .... | .... | .... | .... | .... | .... |
| Employment | 67e | 119 | 122 | .... | .... | .... | .... | .... | .... | .... | .... | .... | .... |
| Unemployment | 67c | .... | .... | .... | .... | .... | .... | .... | .... | .... | .... | .... | .... |
| Unemployment Rate (%) | 67r | .... | .... | .... | .... | .... | .... | .... | .... | .... | .... | .... | .... |
| **Intl. Transactions & Positions** | | | | | | *Millions of Fiji Dollars* | | | | | | | |
| Exports | 70 | 1,205.52 | 1,192.58 | 1,201.57 | 1,209.81 | 1,470.97 | 1,230.34 | 1,605.22 | 1,916.35 | 2,191.27 | 2,044.90 | .... | .... |
| Imports, c.i.f. | 71 | 2,501.64 | 2,722.79 | 3,124.34 | 2,890.07 | 3,601.40 | 2,807.95 | 3,464.61 | 3,911.25 | 4,033.99 | 5,206.23 | .... | .... |
| Imports, f.o.b. | 71.v | 2,505.99 | 2,717.52 | 3,123.58 | 2,899.49 | 3,608.72 | 2,813.81 | 2,896.94 | .... | .... | .... | .... | .... |

# Fiji  819

| | | 2004 | 2005 | 2006 | 2007 | 2008 | 2009 | 2010 | 2011 | 2012 | 2013 | 2014 | 2015 |
|---|---|---|---|---|---|---|---|---|---|---|---|---|---|
| **Balance of Payments** | | | | | | *Millions of US Dollars* | | | | | | | |
| A. Current Account* | 109bx | −253.2 | † −212.3 | −505.7 | −387.2 | −529.3 | −123.9 | −141.8 | −195.3 | −55.9 | −560.8 | .... | .... |
| Goods, credit (exports) | 1a9cx | 634.4 | † 680.6 | 659.2 | 722.7 | 902.2 | 615.6 | 826.5 | 1,062.5 | 1,213.3 | 1,047.5 | .... | .... |
| Goods, debit (imports) | 1a9dx | 1,274.1 | † 1,365.3 | 1,555.6 | 1,575.6 | 1,983.6 | 1,245.9 | 1,560.0 | 1,912.7 | 1,976.2 | 2,379.7 | .... | .... |
| Balance on goods | 1a9bx | −639.8 | † −684.7 | −896.4 | −852.8 | −1,081.5 | −630.3 | −733.6 | −850.3 | −762.9 | −1,332.2 | .... | .... |
| Services, credit (exports) | 1b9cx | 768.0 | † 930.5 | 883.7 | 926.7 | 1,115.3 | 805.9 | 993.5 | 1,168.6 | 1,221.7 | 1,223.7 | .... | .... |
| Services, debit (imports) | 1b9dx | 475.8 | † 537.2 | 536.7 | 520.3 | 626.5 | 466.2 | 449.9 | 539.0 | 574.8 | 564.3 | .... | .... |
| Balance on Goods & Services | 1z9bx | −347.6 | † −291.4 | −549.5 | −446.4 | −592.7 | −290.5 | −190.0 | −220.7 | −115.9 | −672.9 | .... | .... |
| Primary income: credit | 1c9cx | 146.7 | † 81.8 | 66.0 | 67.1 | 72.3 | 61.2 | 78.2 | 99.1 | 75.4 | 62.1 | .... | .... |
| Primary income: debit | 1c9dx | 157.2 | † 143.6 | 176.2 | 160.7 | 157.9 | 73.3 | 179.3 | 216.6 | 226.9 | 155.6 | .... | .... |
| Balance on gds, serv. & prim. inc. | 1y9bx | −358.2 | † −353.1 | −659.6 | −540.0 | −678.2 | −302.6 | −291.1 | −338.2 | −267.5 | −766.4 | .... | .... |
| Secondary income: credit | 1d9ca | 188.2 | † 230.1 | 251.8 | 214.4 | 221.1 | 227.8 | 202.2 | 202.1 | 277.3 | 279.3 | .... | .... |
| Secondary income: debit | 1d9da | 83.2 | † 89.3 | 97.9 | 61.7 | 73.2 | 49.1 | 53.0 | 59.2 | 65.7 | 73.8 | .... | .... |
| B. Capital Account* | 209ba | 28.3 | † 3.1 | 2.0 | 2.9 | 5.2 | 2.4 | 2.9 | 5.9 | 4.0 | 4.8 | .... | .... |
| Capital account: credit | 209ca | 28.3 | † 3.1 | 2.0 | 2.9 | 5.2 | 2.4 | 2.9 | 5.9 | 4.0 | 4.8 | .... | .... |
| Capital account: debit | 209da | — | .... | .... | .... | .... | .... | .... | .... | .... | .... | .... | .... |
| Balance on current & capital acct. | 129ba | −224.9 | † −209.2 | −503.6 | −384.3 | −524.1 | −121.5 | −138.9 | −189.4 | −51.9 | −556.0 | .... | .... |
| C. Financial Account* | 309na | −297.0 | † −221.6 | −501.2 | −560.6 | −270.4 | −447.7 | −291.2 | −508.2 | −275.7 | −333.8 | .... | .... |
| Direct investment: assets | 3a9aa | 3.2 | † 10.3 | .6 | −6.4 | −8.8 | 3.0 | 5.8 | 1.2 | 1.6 | 4.7 | .... | .... |
| Equity & investment fund shares | 3aaaa | 3.2 | † 10.3 | .6 | −6.4 | −8.8 | 3.0 | 5.8 | 1.2 | 1.6 | 4.7 | .... | .... |
| Debt instruments | 3abaa | — | .... | .... | .... | .... | .... | .... | .... | .... | .... | .... | .... |
| Direct investment: liabilities | 3a9la | 250.6 | † 159.6 | 370.2 | 377.1 | 350.2 | 140.2 | 356.7 | 416.7 | 267.1 | 158.2 | .... | .... |
| Equity & investment fund shares | 3aala | 256.9 | † 155.5 | 369.4 | 379.5 | 350.5 | 136.9 | 350.3 | 404.6 | 261.0 | 127.7 | .... | .... |
| Debt instruments | 3abla | −6.2 | † 4.1 | .9 | −2.5 | −.3 | 3.2 | 6.4 | 12.1 | 6.2 | 30.5 | .... | .... |
| Portfolio investment: assets | 3b9aa | — | .... | .1 | −.1 | .... | .... | .... | .... | .... | .... | .... | .... |
| Equity & investment fund shares | 3baaa | — | .... | .1 | −.1 | .... | .... | .... | .... | .... | .... | .... | .... |
| Debt securities | 3bbaa | — | .... | .... | .... | .... | .... | .... | .... | .... | .... | .... | .... |
| Portfolio investment: liabilities | 3b9la | −.3 | † 1.7 | 145.5 | 4.8 | 1.4 | −1.1 | .1 | 97.5 | .... | .... | .... | .... |
| Equity & investment fund shares | 3bala | −.3 | † 1.7 | −1.6 | 4.8 | 1.4 | −1.1 | .1 | −.1 | .... | .... | .... | .... |
| Debt securities | 3bbla | — | .... | 147.1 | .... | .... | .... | .... | 97.6 | .... | .... | .... | .... |
| Fin. der.& empl.stk.ops.(ESOs): net | 3c9na | — | .... | .... | .... | .... | .... | .... | .... | .... | .... | .... | .... |
| Fin. der. & ESOs.: assets | 3c9aa | .... | .... | .... | .... | .... | .... | .... | .... | .... | .... | .... | .... |
| Fin. der. & ESOs.: liabilities | 3c9la | .... | .... | .... | .... | .... | .... | .... | .... | .... | .... | .... | .... |
| Other investment: assets | 3d9aa | −68.5 | † −6.6 | 92.8 | −92.5 | 170.2 | −.5 | −38.3 | 5.6 | 82.5 | 77.5 | .... | .... |
| Other equity | 3daaa | .... | .... | .... | .... | .... | .... | .... | .... | .... | .... | .... | .... |
| Debt instruments | 3dzaa | −68.5 | † −6.6 | 92.8 | −92.5 | 170.2 | −.5 | −38.3 | 5.6 | 82.5 | 77.5 | .... | .... |
| Other investment: liabilities | 3d9la | −18.5 | † 64.0 | 78.9 | 79.7 | 80.2 | 311.2 | −98.1 | .7 | 92.7 | 257.8 | .... | .... |
| Other equity | 3dala | .... | .... | .... | .... | .... | .... | .... | .... | .... | .... | .... | .... |
| Debt instruments | 3dzla | −18.5 | † 64.0 | 78.9 | 79.7 | 80.2 | 311.2 | −98.1 | .7 | 92.7 | 257.8 | .... | .... |
| Curr.+ cap.− finan. acct. balance | 4y9na | 72.1 | † 12.4 | −2.5 | 176.3 | −253.7 | 326.2 | 152.3 | 318.8 | 223.8 | −222.2 | .... | .... |
| D. Net Errors and Omissions | 409na | 28.5 | † −117.2 | −163.3 | 16.3 | 86.5 | −137.8 | −14.0 | −100.6 | −122.7 | 296.3 | .... | .... |
| E. Reserves and Related Items | 4z9na | 100.6 | † −104.8 | −165.8 | 192.6 | −167.2 | 188.4 | 138.3 | 218.2 | 101.1 | 74.1 | .... | .... |
| Reserve assets | 3e9aa | 75.6 | † −104.8 | −165.8 | 192.6 | −167.2 | 188.4 | 138.3 | 218.2 | 101.1 | 74.1 | .... | .... |
| Credit and loans from the IMF | 3dcla | — | † — | — | — | — | — | — | — | — | — | .... | .... |
| Exceptional financing | 409la | −25.0 | .... | .... | .... | .... | .... | .... | .... | .... | .... | .... | .... |
| *Excludes components in group E | | | | | | | | | | | | | |
| | | | | | | | | | | | | | |
| **International Investment Position** | | | | | | *Millions of US Dollars* | | | | | | | |
| Assets | 809aa | .... | † 849.1 | 817.2 | 943.3 | 869.4 | 1,033.7 | 1,147.6 | 1,280.8 | 1,487.6 | 1,779.1 | 1,603.5 | .... |
| Direct investment | 8a9aa | .... | † 68.4 | 48.1 | 44.9 | 34.1 | 36.3 | 47.2 | 48.3 | 51.1 | 157.0 | 186.6 | .... |
| Equity & investment fund shares | 8aaaa | .... | † 68.4 | 48.1 | 44.9 | 34.1 | 36.3 | 46.8 | 47.8 | 50.6 | 52.1 | 86.2 | .... |
| Debt instruments | 8abaa | .... | .... | .... | .... | .... | .... | .4 | .5 | .4 | 104.9 | 100.4 | .... |
| Portfolio investment | 8b9aa | .... | .... | .1 | .... | .... | .... | 14.8 | 21.7 | 55.8 | 70.8 | 73.7 | .... |
| Equity & investment fund shares | 8baaa | .... | .... | .1 | .... | .... | .... | 14.8 | 21.7 | 55.8 | 70.8 | 73.7 | .... |
| Debt securities | 8bbaa | .... | .... | .... | .... | .... | .... | .... | .... | .... | .... | .... | .... |
| Fin. der.(oth.than reserves) & ESOs | 8c9aa | .... | .... | .... | .... | .... | .... | .... | .... | .... | .... | .... | .... |
| Other investment | 8d9aa | .... | † 260.3 | 399.1 | 310.0 | 469.0 | 409.5 | 386.8 | 410.0 | 504.3 | 653.3 | 471.0 | .... |
| Other equity | 8daaa | .... | .... | .... | .... | .... | .... | .... | .... | .... | .... | .4 | .... |
| Debt instruments | 8dzaa | .... | † 260.3 | 399.1 | 310.0 | 469.0 | 409.5 | 386.8 | 410.0 | 504.3 | 653.3 | 470.7 | .... |
| Reserve assets | 8e9aa | .... | † 520.4 | 369.9 | 588.4 | 366.3 | 587.9 | 698.7 | 800.8 | 876.4 | 898.0 | 872.1 | .... |
| Liabilities | 809la | .... | † 1,499.1 | 2,089.3 | 2,707.5 | 2,771.3 | 3,132.3 | 3,652.3 | 3,974.2 | 4,486.6 | 4,772.1 | 5,026.0 | .... |
| Direct investment | 8a9la | .... | † 1,067.8 | 1,474.6 | 1,947.8 | 2,003.5 | 2,047.3 | 2,692.2 | 3,103.7 | 3,541.1 | 3,559.1 | 3,746.5 | .... |
| Equity & investment fund shares | 8aala | .... | † 1,059.3 | 1,470.1 | 1,942.9 | 1,991.9 | 2,033.5 | 2,510.3 | 2,907.9 | 3,297.9 | 3,298.2 | 3,525.2 | .... |
| Debt instruments | 8abla | .... | † 8.5 | 4.5 | 4.8 | 11.6 | 13.8 | 181.9 | 195.7 | 243.3 | 260.9 | 221.3 | .... |
| Portfolio investment | 8b9la | .... | † 2.9 | 156.3 | 170.1 | 147.2 | 132.9 | 252.6 | 199.8 | 177.9 | 169.6 | 169.2 | .... |
| Equity & investment fund shares | 8bala | .... | † 2.9 | 3.1 | 5.7 | 2.6 | .7 | .... | .... | .... | .... | .... | .... |
| Debt securities | 8bbla | .... | .... | 153.2 | 164.4 | 144.6 | 132.2 | 252.6 | 199.8 | 177.9 | 169.6 | 169.2 | .... |
| Fin. der.(oth.than reserves) & ESOs | 8c9la | .... | .... | .... | .... | .... | .... | .... | .... | .... | .... | .... | .... |
| Other investment | 8d9la | .... | † 428.4 | 458.4 | 589.6 | 620.6 | 952.0 | 707.5 | 670.7 | 767.5 | 1,043.4 | 1,110.3 | .... |
| Other equity | 8dala | .... | .... | .... | .... | .... | .... | .9 | .8 | .8 | .6 | 1.6 | .... |
| Debt instruments | 8dzla | .... | † 428.4 | 458.4 | 589.6 | 620.6 | 952.0 | 706.6 | 669.9 | 766.7 | 1,042.8 | 1,108.7 | .... |

| | | 2004 | 2005 | 2006 | 2007 | 2008 | 2009 | 2010 | 2011 | 2012 | 2013 | 2014 | 2015 |
|---|---|---|---|---|---|---|---|---|---|---|---|---|---|
| **Government Finance** | | | | | | | | | | | | | |
| **Cash Flow Statement** | | | | | | | | | | | | | |
| **Budgetary Central Government** | | *Millions of Fiji Dollars: Fiscal Year Ends December 31* | | | | | | | | | | | |
| Cash Receipts:Operating Activities... | c1 | 1,176.02 | 1,223.24 | 1,373.12 | .... | .... | .... | 1,464.22 | 1,732.40 | 1,819.25 | 2,012.70 | .... | .... |
| Taxes............................................. | c11 | 1,048.87 | 1,085.40 | 1,245.48 | .... | .... | .... | 1,312.07 | 1,558.30 | 1,651.77 | 1,824.43 | .... | .... |
| Social Contributions...................... | c12 | — | — | — | .... | .... | .... | .... | .... | .... | .... | .... | .... |
| Grants........................................... | c13 | 22.70 | 7.14 | 6.40 | .... | .... | .... | 16.79 | 21.33 | 19.79 | 28.87 | .... | .... |
| Other Receipts................................ | c14 | 104.45 | 130.69 | 121.24 | .... | .... | .... | 135.37 | 152.77 | 147.68 | 159.41 | .... | .... |
| Cash Payments:Operating Activities. | c2 | 1,177.97 | 1,245.44 | 1,412.87 | .... | .... | .... | 1,429.17 | 1,608.43 | 1,686.88 | 1,882.70 | .... | .... |
| Compensation of Employees......... | c21 | 519.26 | 525.26 | 632.48 | .... | .... | .... | 551.42 | 553.32 | 585.55 | 606.49 | .... | .... |
| Purchases of Goods & Services....... | c22 | 182.70 | 200.74 | 234.17 | .... | .... | .... | 197.45 | 206.77 | 236.53 | 260.31 | .... | .... |
| Interest.......................................... | c24 | 119.02 | 128.09 | 141.48 | .... | .... | .... | 222.55 | 262.79 | 257.65 | 260.21 | .... | .... |
| Subsidies....................................... | c25 | 8.21 | 8.51 | 8.42 | .... | .... | .... | 106.19 | 188.11 | 119.50 | 83.86 | .... | .... |
| Grants........................................... | c26 | 194.24 | 212.58 | 212.92 | .... | .... | .... | 159.06 | 198.26 | 281.71 | 467.38 | .... | .... |
| Social Benefits............................... | c27 | 59.41 | 66.77 | 67.39 | .... | .... | .... | 86.94 | 112.03 | 111.13 | 106.82 | .... | .... |
| Other Payments............................. | c28 | 95.13 | 103.50 | 116.01 | .... | .... | .... | 105.56 | 87.15 | 94.80 | 97.64 | .... | .... |
| Net Cash Inflow:Operating Act.[1-2] | ccio | −1.95 | −22.19 | −39.75 | .... | .... | .... | 35.06 | 123.97 | 132.38 | 130.00 | .... | .... |
| Net Cash Outflow:Invest. in NFA...... | c31 | 144.55 | 145.02 | 116.85 | .... | .... | .... | 194.70 | 238.20 | 234.65 | 196.00 | .... | .... |
| Purchases of Nonfinancial Assets... | c31.1 | 144.55 | 145.02 | 144.85 | .... | .... | .... | .... | .... | .... | .... | .... | .... |
| Sales of Nonfinancial Assets.......... | c31.2 | — | — | 28.00 | .... | .... | .... | .... | .... | .... | .... | .... | .... |
| Cash Surplus/Deficit [1-2-31=1-2M] | ccsd | −146.50 | −167.21 | −156.60 | .... | .... | .... | −159.64 | −114.23 | −102.27 | −66.00 | .... | .... |
| Net Acq. Fin. Assets, excl. Cash...... | c32x | .... | .... | .40 | .... | .... | .... | .... | .... | .... | .... | .... | .... |
| Domestic....................................... | c321x | .... | .... | .40 | .... | .... | .... | .... | .... | .... | .... | .... | .... |
| Foreign.......................................... | c322x | .... | .... | — | .... | .... | .... | .... | .... | .... | .... | .... | .... |
| Net Incurrence of Liabilities............. | c33 | .... | .... | 220.14 | .... | .... | .... | 260.50 | 142.10 | 127.40 | 93.40 | .... | .... |
| Domestic....................................... | c331 | .... | .... | 202.27 | .... | .... | .... | 231.40 | −136.00 | 9.10 | 13.20 | .... | .... |
| Foreign.......................................... | c332 | .... | .... | 17.87 | .... | .... | .... | 29.10 | 278.10 | 118.30 | 80.30 | .... | .... |
| Net Cash Inflow, Fin.Act.[-32x+33].. | cnfb | .... | .... | 219.74 | .... | .... | .... | 281.90 | 158.30 | 149.40 | 108.60 | .... | .... |
| Net Change in Stock of Cash........... | cncb | .... | .... | 63.14 | .... | .... | .... | 122.30 | 44.10 | 47.10 | 42.60 | .... | .... |
| Stat. Discrep. [32X-33+NCB-CSD].... | ccsdz | .... | .... | — | .... | .... | .... | .04 | .03 | −.03 | — | .... | .... |
| Memo Item:Cash Expenditure[2+31] | c2m | .... | .... | .... | .... | .... | .... | 1,623.87 | 1,846.63 | 1,921.53 | 2,078.70 | .... | .... |
| Memo Item: Gross Debt.................. | c63 | .... | .... | .... | .... | .... | .... | .... | .... | .... | .... | .... | .... |
| **National Accounts** | | *Millions of Fiji Dollars* | | | | | | | | | | | |
| Househ.Cons.Expend.,incl.NPISHs.... | 96f | 2,319.0 | 3,878.9 | 4,064.9 | 3,951.1 | 4,620.8 | 4,237.3 | 4,357.5 | 4,575.1 | 4,778.0 | 5,065.6 | 5,399.6 | .... |
| Government Consumption Expend... | 91f | 738.9 | 803.3 | 989.1 | 934.5 | 877.4 | 949.6 | 902.3 | 1,172.4 | 1,331.5 | 1,461.2 | 1,735.7 | .... |
| Gross Fixed Capital Formation.......... | 93e | 873.2 | 989.3 | 912.3 | 726.9 | 1,171.3 | 909.3 | 956.9 | 1,223.5 | 1,031.1 | 2,005.5 | 1,577.3 | .... |
| Changes in Inventories.................... | 93i | 31.1 | 71.2 | 80.9 | 122.4 | 143.9 | 158.4 | 172.0 | 197.1 | 166.8 | 106.6 | | .... |
| Exports of Goods and Services.......... | 90c | 2,543.7 | 2,569.6 | 2,512.8 | 2,509.9 | 2,931.2 | 2,776.4 | 3,484.4 | 4,012.4 | 4,344.7 | 4,372.4 | 4,689.4 | .... |
| Imports of Goods and Services (-)..... | 98c | 3,328.4 | 3,221.6 | 3,638.9 | 3,404.0 | 4,129.7 | 3,336.6 | 3,849.2 | 4,412.8 | 4,562.4 | 5,361.2 | 5,368.9 | .... |
| Gross Domestic Product (GDP)......... | 99b | 4,693.1 | 5,040.0 | 5,325.7 | 5,440.1 | 5,614.9 | 5,614.1 | 6,024.4 | 6,768.5 | 7,119.6 | 7,726.7 | 8,552.9 | .... |
| Net National Income....................... | 99e | 3,420.4 | 4,693.4 | .... | .... | .... | .... | .... | .... | .... | .... | .... | .... |
| GDP at Factor Cost......................... | 99ba | 3,989.5 | 4,327.3 | 4,545.0 | 4,648.6 | 4,900.7 | 4,858.5 | 5,218.7 | 5,738.8 | 6,010.1 | 6,440.0 | 7,129.8 | .... |
| Net Primary Income from Abroad..... | 98.n | 136.7 | 246.8 | .... | .... | .... | .... | .... | .... | .... | .... | .... | .... |
| Gross National Income (GNI)............ | 99a | .... | .... | .... | .... | .... | .... | .... | .... | .... | .... | .... | .... |
| Consumption of Fixed Capital.......... | 99cf | 408 | 449 | .... | .... | .... | .... | .... | .... | .... | .... | .... | .... |
| GDP at Fact.Cost,Vol.'95 Prices....... | 99bap | 2,959.4 | 2,979.9 | 3,087.5 | .... | .... | .... | .... | .... | .... | .... | .... | .... |
| GDP at Fact.Cost,Vol.'05 Prices....... | 99bap | | 4,327.3 | 4,407.5 | 4,370.0 | 4,415.1 | 4,358.9 | 4,351.8 | 4,445.3 | .... | .... | .... | .... |
| GDP at Fact.Cost,Vol.'08 Prices....... | 99bap | .... | .... | .... | .... | 4,730.6 | 4,665.0 | 4,802.9 | 4,932.8 | 5,016.3 | .... | .... | .... |
| GDP Volume (2010=100)................ | 99bvp | 95.9 | † 96.5 | 98.3 | 97.5 | † 98.5 | 97.1 | 100.0 | † 102.7 | 104.2 | 109.1 | 114.9 | .... |
| GDP Deflator (2010=100)............... | 99bip | 79.7 | 85.9 | 88.6 | 91.4 | 95.3 | 95.8 | 100.0 | 107.1 | 110.6 | 113.1 | 118.9 | .... |
| | | *Millions: Midyear Estimates* | | | | | | | | | | | |
| Population................................. | 99z | .82 | .82 | .83 | .83 | .84 | .85 | .86 | .87 | .87 | .88 | .89 | .89 |

# Finland 172

| | | 2004 | 2005 | 2006 | 2007 | 2008 | 2009 | 2010 | 2011 | 2012 | 2013 | 2014 | 2015 |
|---|---|---|---|---|---|---|---|---|---|---|---|---|---|
| **Exchange Rates** | | \multicolumn{12}{c}{*Euros per SDR: End of Period*} | | | | | | | | | | | |
| Market Rate.................................. | aa | 1.1402 | 1.2116 | 1.1423 | 1.0735 | 1.1068 | 1.0882 | 1.1525 | 1.1865 | 1.1649 | 1.1167 | 1.1933 | 1.2728 |
| | | \multicolumn{12}{c}{*Euros per US Dollar: End of Period (ae) Period Average (rf)*} | | | | | | | | | | | |
| Market Rate.................................. | ae | .7342 | .8477 | .7593 | .6793 | .7185 | .6942 | .7484 | .7729 | .7579 | .7251 | .8237 | .9185 |
| Market Rate.................................. | rf | .8054 | .8041 | .7971 | .7306 | .6827 | .7198 | .7550 | .7194 | .7783 | .7532 | .7537 | .9017 |
| | | \multicolumn{12}{c}{*Index Numbers (2010=100): Period Averages*} | | | | | | | | | | | |
| Nominal Effective Exchange Rate..... | nec | 99.0 | 98.3 | 98.0 | 100.2 | 102.7 | 104.6 | 100.0 | 100.0 | 96.6 | 99.1 | 101.0 | 98.6 |
| CPI-Based Real Effect. Ex. Rate........ | rec | 104.1 | 101.8 | 100.7 | 102.4 | 104.6 | 105.7 | 100.0 | 100.0 | 97.1 | 99.3 | 100.6 | 96.6 |
| ULC-Based Real Effect. Ex. Rate....... | rel | 109.2 | 109.4 | 104.1 | 100.1 | 101.4 | 102.9 | 100.0 | 100.0 | 98.9 | 100.4 | 101.1 | 97.3 |
| **Fund Position** | | \multicolumn{12}{c}{*Millions of SDRs: End of Period*} | | | | | | | | | | | |
| Quota...................................... | 2f.s | 1,263.80 | 1,263.80 | 1,263.80 | 1,263.80 | 1,263.80 | 1,263.80 | 1,263.80 | 1,263.80 | 1,263.80 | 1,263.80 | 1,263.80 | 1,263.80 |
| SDR Holdings............................. | 1b.s | 106.72 | 113.27 | 128.40 | 153.72 | 155.19 | 1,201.71 | 1,195.41 | 1,118.76 | 1,125.26 | 1,125.64 | 1,126.08 | 1,123.41 |
| Reserve Position in the Fund............ | 1c.s | 405.99 | 198.27 | 110.66 | 82.90 | 161.05 | 270.10 | 367.44 | 541.87 | 667.98 | 616.81 | 496.76 | 359.79 |
| Total Fund Cred.&Loans Outstg....... | 2tl | — | — | — | — | — | — | — | — | — | — | — | — |
| SDR Allocations........................... | 1bd | 142.69 | 142.69 | 142.69 | 142.69 | 142.69 | 1,189.51 | 1,189.51 | 1,189.51 | 1,189.51 | 1,189.51 | 1,189.51 | 1,189.51 |
| **International Liquidity** | | \multicolumn{12}{c}{*Millions of US Dollars Unless Otherwise Indicated: End of Period*} | | | | | | | | | | | |
| Total Res.Min.Gold (Eurosys.Def)..... | 1l.d | 12,221.5 | 10,521.1 | 6,494.2 | 7,063.1 | 6,979.4 | 9,710.6 | 7,326.7 | 7,857.1 | 8,453.2 | 9,369.2 | 8,773.8 | 8,341.5 |
| SDR Holdings............................. | 1b.d | 165.7 | 161.9 | 193.2 | 242.9 | 239.0 | 1,883.9 | 1,841.0 | 1,717.6 | 1,729.4 | 1,733.5 | 1,631.5 | 1,556.7 |
| Reserve Position in the Fund.......... | 1c.d | 630.5 | 283.4 | 166.5 | 131.0 | 248.1 | 423.4 | 565.9 | 831.9 | 1,026.6 | 949.9 | 719.7 | 498.6 |
| Foreign Exchange......................... | 1d.d | 11,425.3 | 10,075.8 | 6,134.6 | 6,689.2 | 6,492.3 | 7,403.2 | 4,919.9 | 5,307.6 | 5,697.2 | 6,685.9 | 6,414.1 | 6,228.5 |
| o/w:Fin.Deriv.Rel.to Reserves...... | 1ddd | 1.36 | −1.18 | 3.95 | — | −5.57 | 14.41 | −1.34 | −5.18 | 6.60 | 4.14 | −3.64 | 1.09 |
| Other Reserve Assets..................... | 1e.d | — | — | — | — | — | — | — | — | — | — | 8 | 58 |
| Gold (Million Fine Troy Ounces)....... | 1ad | 1.580 | 1.580 | 1.580 | 1.580 | 1.580 | 1.580 | 1.580 | 1.580 | 1.580 | 1.580 | 1.580 | 1.580 |
| Gold (Eurosystem Valuation)............ | 1and | 692.0 | 810.5 | 1,004.4 | 1,321.7 | 1,366.7 | 1,744.3 | 2,228.2 | 2,487.7 | 2,629.1 | 1,898.4 | 1,894.8 | 1,674.1 |
| Memo:Euro Cl. on Non-EA Res....... | 1dgd | 311 | 312 | 846 | 1,010 | 1,201 | 1,879 | 2,806 | 3,304 | 3,655 | 2,577 | 1,428 | . . . . |
| Non-Euro Cl. on EA Res............ | 1dhd | 947 | 919 | 1,270 | 1,743 | 3,424 | 1,154 | 677 | 640 | 286 | 178 | 266 | 311 |
| Central Bank: Other Assets.............. | 3..d | 2,482 | 4,183 | 10,944 | 17,250 | 20,241 | 28,188 | 44,879 | 106,154 | 112,215 | 47,335 | 39,083 | 35,234 |
| Central Bank: Other Liabs.............. | 4..d | 223 | 205 | 219 | 228 | 285 | 2,215 | 3,545 | 2,948 | 4,208 | 2,634 | 1,728 | 2,390 |
| Other Depository Corps.: Assets......... | 7a.d | 66,722 | 61,343 | 82,530 | 98,952 | 101,327 | 129,890 | 159,419 | 170,605 | 163,670 | 187,911 | 155,229 | 128,616 |
| Other Depository Corps.: Liabs......... | 7b.d | 45,392 | 52,083 | 62,941 | 84,041 | 97,845 | 128,862 | 153,203 | 223,206 | 215,591 | 179,207 | 158,372 | 117,441 |
| **Central Bank** | | \multicolumn{12}{c}{*Millions of Euros: End of Period*} | | | | | | | | | | | |
| *Euro Area Wide Residency Criterion* | | | | | | | | | | | | | |
| Net Foreign Assets.......................... | 11n.u | 8,623 | 9,094 | 6,105 | 6,085 | 6,605 | 7,192 | 6,529 | 8,138 | 7,785 | 8,132 | 8,501 | 8,606 |
| Claims on Nonresidents............... | 11..u | 9,716 | 9,776 | 6,271 | 6,328 | 6,810 | 9,093 | 9,205 | 10,569 | 11,114 | 10,109 | 9,983 | 10,847 |
| Liabilities to Nonresidents.............. | 16c.u | 1,093 | 683 | 166 | 243 | 205 | 1,900 | 2,676 | 2,431 | 3,329 | 1,976 | 1,481 | 2,241 |
| Claims on Other Depository Corps.... | 12e.u | 2,850 | 3,822 | 3,117 | 4,884 | 10,819 | 14,180 | 2,096 | 4,772 | 5,836 | 4,621 | 3,596 | 4,941 |
| Net Claims on Central Government.. | 12anu | 76 | 101 | 4,762 | 5,975 | 3,130 | 6,313 | 9,006 | 10,097 | 8,560 | 6,985 | 8,115 | 14,645 |
| Claims on Central Govt................. | 12a.u | 76 | 101 | 4,762 | 5,975 | 6,130 | 6,313 | 9,006 | 10,097 | 8,560 | 6,985 | 8,115 | 14,719 |
| Liabs. to Central Govt.................... | 16d.u | — | — | — | — | 3,000 | — | — | — | — | — | — | 74 |
| Claims on Other Sectors.................. | 12s.u | 400 | 433 | 528 | 564 | 639 | 882 | 1,317 | 1,478 | 1,286 | 1,161 | 1,317 | 1,503 |
| Claims on Other Financial Corps.... | 12g.u | 214 | 216 | 313 | 204 | 188 | 326 | 679 | 841 | 767 | 637 | 719 | 931 |
| Claims on State & Local Govts.... | 12b.u | 54 | 38 | 56 | 174 | 261 | 167 | 93 | 227 | 219 | 168 | 192 | 236 |
| Claims on Public Nonfin. Corps...... | 12c.u | — | — | — | — | — | — | — | — | — | — | — | — |
| Claims on Private Sector............... | 12d.u | 132 | 179 | 159 | 186 | 190 | 389 | 545 | 410 | 300 | 356 | 406 | 336 |
| Monetary Base.............................. | 14..u | 12,320 | 13,273 | 14,583 | 17,488 | 21,102 | 27,614 | 36,090 | 87,631 | 89,397 | 40,131 | 37,093 | 45,947 |
| Currency in Circulation.................. | 14a.u | 8,643 | 9,738 | 10,817 | 11,578 | 12,992 | 13,817 | 14,392 | 15,184 | 15,598 | 16,328 | 17,380 | 18,388 |
| Liabs. to Other Depository Corps..... | 14c.u | 3,677 | 3,535 | 3,766 | 5,910 | 8,110 | 13,792 | 21,698 | 71,697 | 73,799 | 23,803 | 19,713 | 27,559 |
| Liabs. to Other Sectors.................. | 14d.u | — | — | — | — | — | 5 | — | — | 750 | — | — | — |
| Other Liabs. to Other Dep. Corps..... | 14n.u | — | — | — | — | — | — | — | — | — | — | — | — |
| Dep. & Sec. Excl. f/Monetary Base.... | 14o.u | — | — | — | — | — | — | — | — | — | — | — | — |
| Deposits Included in Broad Money. | 15..u | — | — | — | — | — | — | — | — | — | — | — | — |
| Sec.Ot.th.Shares Inc.in.Brd.Money.. | 16a.u | — | — | — | — | — | — | — | — | — | — | — | — |
| Deposits Excl. from Broad Money... | 16b.u | — | — | — | — | — | — | — | — | — | — | — | — |
| Sec.Oh.th.Shares Excl. f/Brd.Money | 16s.u | — | — | — | — | — | — | — | — | — | — | — | — |
| Loans...................................... | 16l.u | — | — | — | — | — | — | — | — | — | — | — | — |
| Financial Derivatives...................... | 16m.u | — | — | — | — | — | — | — | — | — | — | — | — |
| Shares and Other Equity.................. | 17a.u | 4,670 | 5,073 | 5,096 | 5,189 | 5,853 | 5,802 | 6,630 | 7,260 | 7,802 | 7,888 | 9,431 | 9,421 |
| Other Items (Net)........................... | 17r.u | −5,041 | −4,898 | −5,169 | −5,169 | −5,763 | −4,850 | −23,979 | −70,688 | −73,911 | −27,122 | −24,996 | −25,682 |
| *Memorandum Items* | | | | | | | | | | | | | |
| *National Residency Criterion* | | | | | | | | | | | | | |
| Net Foreign Assets.......................... | 11n | 9,688 | 12,467 | 13,836 | 17,169 | 20,334 | 25,366 | 38,058 | 87,601 | 90,116 | 40,513 | 39,493 | 39,318 |
| Claims on Nonresidents............... | 11 | 11,302 | 13,150 | 14,002 | 17,412 | 20,539 | 27,516 | 40,734 | 90,032 | 93,445 | 42,490 | 40,975 | 41,559 |
| Liabilities to Nonresidents.............. | 16c | 1,614 | 684 | 166 | 243 | 205 | 2,149 | 2,676 | 2,431 | 3,329 | 1,976 | 1,481 | 2,241 |
| Claims on Other Depository Corps.... | 12e | 2,450 | 1,692 | 1,075 | 629 | 4,155 | 2,961 | 498 | 2,845 | 4,190 | 3,008 | 1,887 | 3,524 |
| Net Claims on Central Government.. | 12an | — | — | 311 | 420 | −2,595 | 420 | 153 | 235 | 111 | 141 | 390 | 7,428 |
| Claims on Central Government....... | 12a | — | — | 311 | 420 | 405 | 420 | 153 | 235 | 111 | 141 | 390 | 7,502 |
| Liabilities to Central Government... | 16d | — | — | — | — | 3,000 | — | — | — | — | — | — | 74 |
| Claims on Other Sectors.................. | 12s | 7 | 7 | 7 | 7 | 16 | 293 | 647 | 534 | 376 | 199 | 220 | 297 |
| Claims on Other Fin. Corps............ | 12g | — | — | — | — | 13 | 73 | 278 | 349 | 244 | 44 | 54 | 163 |
| Claims on State & Local Govts....... | 12b | — | — | — | — | — | — | — | — | — | — | — | 14 |
| Claims on Private Sector............... | 12d | 7 | 7 | 7 | 7 | 3 | 220 | 369 | 185 | 132 | 155 | 166 | 120 |
| Liabs.to ODCs, Inc.in Mon.Base....... | 14c | 3,156 | 3,535 | 3,766 | 5,910 | 8,110 | 13,543 | 21,698 | 71,697 | 73,799 | 23,803 | 19,713 | 27,559 |
| Liabs.to Ot.Sectors, Inc.in Mon.Base | 14d | — | — | — | — | — | 5 | — | — | 750 | — | — | — |
| Liabs.to ODCs,Excl.f/Mon.Base........ | 14n | — | — | — | — | — | — | — | — | — | — | — | — |
| Net Claims on Eurosystem............... | 12e.s | 791 | 790 | 791 | 790 | 790 | 800 | 20,507 | 66,850 | 71,467 | 23,103 | 20,605 | 21,016 |

# Finland   172

2016, International Monetary Fund : *International Financial Statistics Yearbook*

| | | 2004 | 2005 | 2006 | 2007 | 2008 | 2009 | 2010 | 2011 | 2012 | 2013 | 2014 | 2015 |
|---|---|---|---|---|---|---|---|---|---|---|---|---|---|
| **Other Depository Corporations** | | | | | | | *Millions of Euros: End of Period* | | | | | | |
| Euro Area Wide Residency Criterion | | | | | | | | | | | | | |
| Net Foreign Assets.......................... | **21n.u** | 15,660 | 7,850 | 14,874 | 10,129 | 2,502 | 714 | 4,652 | −40,653 | −39,352 | 6,311 | −2,589 | 10,264 |
| Claims on Nonresidents................ | **21..u** | 48,985 | 51,999 | 62,665 | 67,218 | 72,808 | 90,164 | 119,308 | 131,853 | 124,049 | 136,256 | 127,855 | 118,137 |
| Liabilities to Nonresidents............. | **26c.u** | 33,325 | 44,149 | 47,791 | 57,089 | 70,306 | 89,450 | 114,656 | 172,506 | 163,401 | 129,945 | 130,444 | 107,873 |
| Claims on Eurosystem..................... | **20..u** | 3,457 | 3,841 | 4,067 | 6,217 | 8,411 | 13,835 | 22,169 | 72,143 | 74,151 | 23,831 | 20,359 | 27,751 |
| Currency......................................... | **20a.u** | 301 | 306 | 301 | 307 | 301 | 292 | 271 | 262 | 260 | 234 | 211 | 205 |
| Reserve Deposits and Securities..... | **20b.u** | 3,156 | 3,535 | 3,766 | 5,910 | 8,110 | 13,543 | 21,898 | 71,881 | 73,891 | 23,597 | 20,148 | 27,546 |
| Other Claims................................ | **20n.u** | — | — | — | — | — | — | — | — | — | — | — | — |
| Net Claims on Central Government.. | **22anu** | −1,466 | −1,704 | −115 | −130 | 7 | 329 | 3,936 | 2,433 | 3,155 | 6,881 | 10,352 | 6,600 |
| Claims on Central Government...... | **22a.u** | 3,025 | 2,480 | 2,271 | 2,078 | 2,165 | 2,668 | 5,560 | 6,131 | 6,217 | 8,598 | 13,320 | 10,403 |
| Liabilities to Central Government... | **26d.u** | 4,491 | 4,184 | 2,386 | 2,208 | 2,158 | 2,339 | 1,624 | 3,698 | 3,062 | 1,717 | 2,968 | 3,803 |
| Claims on Other Sectors................... | **22s.u** | 135,857 | 153,805 | 163,460 | 188,048 | 258,388 | 249,105 | 286,422 | 379,251 | 340,903 | 303,983 | 355,479 | 334,934 |
| Claims on Other Financial Corps.... | **22g.u** | 29,590 | 34,030 | 30,049 | 38,121 | 95,168 | 83,919 | 111,193 | 190,782 | 142,628 | 98,472 | 145,933 | 115,913 |
| Claims on State & Local Govts....... | **22b.u** | 4,178 | 4,961 | 5,451 | 5,892 | 6,321 | 7,262 | 8,649 | 9,892 | 12,082 | 14,148 | 15,649 | 17,548 |
| Claims on Public Nonfin. Corps...... | **22c.u** | — | — | — | — | — | — | — | — | — | — | — | — |
| Claims on Private Sector................ | **22d.u** | 102,089 | 114,814 | 127,960 | 144,035 | 156,899 | 157,924 | 166,580 | 178,577 | 186,193 | 191,363 | 193,897 | 201,473 |
| Liabilities to Eurosystem.................. | **26g.u** | 2,690 | 1,998 | 1,727 | 1,767 | 5,470 | 4,346 | 1,961 | 4,345 | 5,627 | 4,480 | 4,233 | 5,408 |
| Transf.Dep.Included in Broad Money | **24..u** | 46,156 | 49,367 | 51,500 | 53,652 | 55,545 | 65,777 | 70,273 | 73,772 | 81,875 | 90,992 | 97,850 | 111,465 |
| Other.Dep.Included in Broad Money. | **25..u** | 34,408 | 37,517 | 43,187 | 56,315 | 59,258 | 49,531 | 51,022 | 53,948 | 45,267 | 39,118 | 36,184 | 34,897 |
| Sec.Ot.th.Shares Inc.in.Brd. Money... | **26a.u** | 7,622 | 8,799 | 8,265 | 12,816 | 14,441 | 12,285 | 16,012 | 15,128 | 13,121 | 15,060 | 14,187 | 10,406 |
| Deposits Excl. from Broad Money..... | **26b.u** | 2,602 | 2,404 | 2,523 | 2,387 | 1,990 | 2,770 | 4,595 | 6,377 | 12,258 | 17,451 | 17,308 | 8,530 |
| Sec.Ot.th.Shares Excl.f/Brd. Money... | **26s.u** | 10,064 | 12,988 | 17,692 | 16,791 | 21,966 | 22,272 | 29,721 | 39,940 | 53,372 | 55,179 | 62,687 | 69,405 |
| Loans............................................... | **26l.u** | — | — | — | — | — | — | — | — | — | — | — | — |
| Financial Derivatives....................... | **26m.u** | 27,178 | 28,480 | 25,229 | 33,963 | 90,889 | 76,035 | 100,454 | 175,783 | 124,750 | 74,738 | 113,374 | 93,105 |
| Insurance Technical Reserves.......... | **26r.u** | — | — | — | — | — | — | — | — | — | — | — | — |
| Shares and Other Equity................. | **27a.u** | 18,368 | 21,290 | 23,410 | 22,248 | 22,892 | 24,043 | 24,984 | 25,891 | 24,878 | 26,391 | 28,857 | 33,587 |
| Other Items (Net)............................ | **27r.u** | 4,418 | 945 | 8,755 | 4,324 | −3,146 | 6,919 | 18,163 | 17,993 | 17,703 | 17,594 | 8,932 | 13,238 |
| Memorandum Items | | | | | | | | | | | | | |
| Total Assets.................................... | **20ra** | 222,744 | 246,887 | 271,443 | 306,524 | 396,240 | 399,397 | 480,418 | 644,357 | 600,303 | 525,316 | 579,303 | 555,988 |
| National Residency Criterion | | | | | | | | | | | | | |
| Net Foreign Assets.......................... | **21n** | 15,495 | 9,552 | 13,778 | 16,686 | 7,413 | 5,932 | 3,677 | −34,702 | −42,070 | 2,586 | 4,593 | 13,407 |
| Claims on Nonresidents................ | **21** | 57,021 | 61,621 | 73,986 | 81,178 | 86,016 | 105,806 | 135,689 | 153,760 | 148,441 | 168,408 | 168,255 | 148,796 |
| Liabilities to Nonresidents............. | **26c** | 41,526 | 52,069 | 60,208 | 64,492 | 78,603 | 99,874 | 132,012 | 188,462 | 190,511 | 165,822 | 163,662 | 135,389 |
| Net Claims on Central Government.. | **22an** | −2,650 | −1,667 | −73 | −817 | −971 | −1,263 | 1,380 | −376 | 441 | 1,898 | 1,866 | 1,306 |
| Claims on Central Government...... | **22a** | 1,840 | 1,616 | 1,232 | 1,101 | 974 | 775 | 2,837 | 2,995 | 2,630 | 3,314 | 4,333 | 4,118 |
| Liabilities to Central Government... | **26d** | 4,490 | 3,283 | 1,305 | 1,918 | 1,945 | 2,038 | 1,457 | 3,371 | 2,189 | 1,416 | 2,467 | 2,812 |
| Claims on Other Sectors................... | **22s** | 134,009 | 151,825 | 160,728 | 184,754 | 255,557 | 246,619 | 282,669 | 372,536 | 329,747 | 286,622 | 335,327 | 319,692 |
| Claims on Other Fin. Corps........... | **22g** | 28,685 | 32,852 | 28,383 | 36,203 | 93,647 | 82,736 | 108,826 | 186,450 | 134,928 | 85,528 | 130,580 | 106,240 |
| Claims on State & Local Govts....... | **22b** | 4,161 | 4,941 | 5,448 | 5,864 | 6,306 | 7,250 | 8,401 | 9,303 | 10,452 | 11,359 | 12,701 | 13,938 |
| Claims on Private Sector................ | **22d** | 101,163 | 114,032 | 126,897 | 142,687 | 155,604 | 156,633 | 165,442 | 176,783 | 184,367 | 189,735 | 192,046 | 199,514 |
| Transf.Dep.Included in Broad Money | **24** | 46,040 | 49,216 | 51,362 | 53,430 | 54,893 | 65,434 | 69,957 | 73,335 | 80,985 | 89,648 | 97,111 | 110,799 |
| Other.Dep.Included in Broad Money. | **25** | 34,034 | 37,009 | 42,734 | 55,697 | 58,820 | 48,745 | 49,583 | 52,241 | 42,487 | 37,428 | 34,060 | 31,042 |
| Sec.Ot.th.Shares Inc.in.Brd. Money... | **26a** | 6,708 | 6,385 | 6,163 | 11,058 | 12,823 | 10,361 | 7,906 | 10,030 | 7,008 | 6,257 | 5,208 | 3,234 |
| Deposits Excl. from Broad Money..... | **26b** | 2,280 | 2,011 | 1,895 | 1,546 | 1,160 | 1,660 | 3,049 | 3,638 | 3,286 | 2,933 | 2,340 | 2,309 |
| Sec.Ot.th.Shares Excl.f/Brd. Money... | **26s** | 12,696 | 16,898 | 24,258 | 25,211 | 28,267 | 31,029 | 38,540 | 48,537 | 60,706 | 62,393 | 70,166 | 77,275 |

# Finland 172

| | | 2004 | 2005 | 2006 | 2007 | 2008 | 2009 | 2010 | 2011 | 2012 | 2013 | 2014 | 2015 |
|---|---|---|---|---|---|---|---|---|---|---|---|---|---|
| **Depository Corporations** | | | | | | *Millions of Euros: End of Period* | | | | | | | |
| Euro Area Wide Residency Criterion | | | | | | | | | | | | | |
| Net Foreign Assets.......................... | 31n.u | 24,283 | 16,944 | 20,979 | 16,214 | 9,107 | 7,906 | 11,181 | −32,515 | −31,567 | 14,443 | 5,912 | 18,870 |
| Claims on Nonresidents............... | 31..u | 58,701 | 61,775 | 68,936 | 73,546 | 79,618 | 99,257 | 128,513 | 142,422 | 135,163 | 146,365 | 137,838 | 128,984 |
| Liabilities to Nonresidents............. | 36c.u | 34,418 | 44,832 | 47,957 | 57,332 | 70,511 | 91,350 | 117,332 | 174,937 | 166,730 | 131,921 | 131,925 | 110,114 |
| Domestic Claims............................ | 32..u | 134,867 | 152,635 | 168,635 | 194,457 | 262,164 | 256,629 | 300,681 | 393,259 | 353,904 | 319,010 | 375,263 | 357,682 |
| Net Claims on Central Government.. | 32anu | −1,390 | −1,603 | 4,647 | 5,845 | 3,137 | 6,642 | 12,942 | 12,530 | 11,715 | 13,866 | 18,467 | 21,245 |
| Claims on Central Government...... | 32a.u | 3,101 | 2,581 | 7,033 | 8,053 | 8,295 | 8,981 | 14,566 | 16,228 | 14,777 | 15,583 | 21,435 | 25,122 |
| Liabilities to Central Government... | 36d.u | 4,491 | 4,184 | 2,386 | 2,208 | 5,158 | 2,339 | 1,624 | 3,698 | 3,062 | 1,717 | 2,968 | 3,877 |
| Claims on Other Sectors................ | 32s.u | 136,257 | 154,238 | 163,988 | 188,612 | 259,027 | 249,987 | 287,739 | 380,729 | 342,189 | 305,144 | 356,796 | 336,437 |
| Claims on Other Financial Corps.... | 32g.u | 29,804 | 34,246 | 30,362 | 38,325 | 95,356 | 84,245 | 111,872 | 191,623 | 143,395 | 99,109 | 146,652 | 116,844 |
| Claims on State & Local Govts....... | 32b.u | 4,232 | 4,999 | 5,507 | 6,066 | 6,582 | 7,429 | 8,742 | 10,119 | 12,301 | 14,316 | 15,841 | 17,784 |
| Claims on Public Nonfin. Corps...... | 32c.u | — | — | — | — | — | — | — | — | — | — | — | — |
| Claims on Private Sector................ | 32d.u | 102,221 | 114,993 | 128,119 | 144,221 | 157,089 | 158,313 | 167,125 | 178,987 | 186,493 | 191,719 | 194,303 | 201,809 |
| Broad Money Liabilities................. | 35l.u | 96,528 | 105,115 | 113,468 | 134,054 | 141,935 | 141,123 | 151,428 | 158,520 | 155,601 | 161,264 | 165,390 | 174,951 |
| Currency Outside Depository Corps | 34a.u | 8,342 | 9,432 | 10,516 | 11,271 | 12,691 | 13,525 | 14,121 | 14,922 | 15,338 | 16,094 | 17,169 | 18,183 |
| Transferable Deposits................... | 34..u | 46,156 | 49,367 | 51,500 | 53,652 | 55,545 | 65,782 | 70,273 | 74,522 | 81,875 | 90,992 | 97,850 | 111,465 |
| Other Deposits........................... | 35..u | 34,408 | 37,517 | 43,187 | 56,315 | 59,258 | 49,531 | 51,022 | 53,948 | 45,267 | 39,118 | 36,184 | 34,897 |
| Securities Other than Shares.......... | 36a.u | 7,622 | 8,799 | 8,265 | 12,816 | 14,441 | 12,285 | 16,012 | 15,128 | 13,121 | 15,060 | 14,187 | 10,406 |
| Deposits Excl. from Broad Money..... | 36b.u | 2,602 | 2,404 | 2,523 | 2,387 | 1,990 | 2,770 | 4,595 | 6,377 | 12,258 | 17,451 | 17,308 | 8,530 |
| Sec.Oth.th.Shares Excl.f/Brd. Money. | 36s.u | 10,064 | 12,988 | 17,692 | 16,791 | 21,966 | 22,272 | 29,721 | 39,940 | 53,372 | 55,179 | 62,687 | 69,405 |
| Loans...................................... | 36l.u | — | — | — | — | — | — | — | — | — | — | — | — |
| Financial Derivatives...................... | 36m.u | 27,178 | 28,480 | 25,229 | 33,963 | 90,889 | 76,035 | 100,454 | 175,783 | 124,750 | 74,738 | 113,374 | 93,105 |
| Insurance Technical Reserves........... | 36r.u | — | — | — | — | — | — | — | — | — | — | — | — |
| Shares and Other Equity................. | 37a.u | 23,038 | 26,363 | 28,506 | 27,437 | 28,745 | 29,845 | 31,614 | 33,151 | 32,680 | 34,279 | 38,288 | 43,008 |
| Other Items (Net)........................ | 37r.u | −262 | −5,777 | 2,196 | −3,962 | −14,258 | −7,516 | −6,151 | −53,306 | −56,509 | −9,463 | −15,862 | −11,964 |
| Broad Money Liabs., Seasonally Adj. | 35lub | 95,715 | 104,319 | 112,654 | 133,126 | 140,862 | 140,029 | 150,234 | 157,313 | 154,550 | 160,369 | 164,684 | 174,255 |
| Memorandum Items | | | | | | | | | | | | | |
| National Residency Criterion | | | | | | | | | | | | | |
| Net Foreign Assets........................ | 31n | 25,183 | 22,019 | 27,614 | 33,855 | 27,747 | 31,298 | 41,735 | 52,899 | 48,046 | 43,099 | 44,086 | 52,725 |
| Claims on Nonresidents................ | 31 | 68,323 | 74,771 | 87,988 | 98,590 | 106,555 | 133,322 | 176,423 | 243,792 | 241,886 | 210,898 | 209,230 | 190,355 |
| Liabilities to Nonresidents............. | 36c | 43,140 | 52,753 | 60,374 | 64,735 | 78,808 | 102,023 | 134,688 | 190,893 | 193,840 | 167,798 | 165,143 | 137,630 |
| Domestic Claims............................ | 32 | 131,366 | 150,165 | 160,973 | 184,364 | 252,007 | 246,069 | 284,849 | 372,929 | 330,675 | 288,860 | 337,803 | 328,723 |
| Net Claims on Central Government | 32an | −2,650 | −1,667 | 238 | −397 | −3,566 | −843 | 1,533 | −141 | 552 | 2,039 | 2,256 | 8,734 |
| Claims on Central Government..... | 32a | 1,840 | 1,616 | 1,543 | 1,521 | 1,379 | 1,195 | 2,990 | 3,230 | 2,741 | 3,455 | 4,723 | 11,620 |
| Liabilities to Central Government. | 36d | 4,490 | 3,283 | 1,305 | 1,918 | 4,945 | 2,038 | 1,457 | 3,371 | 2,189 | 1,416 | 2,467 | 2,886 |
| Claims on Other Sectors................ | 32s | 134,016 | 151,832 | 160,735 | 184,761 | 255,573 | 246,912 | 283,316 | 373,070 | 330,123 | 286,821 | 335,547 | 319,989 |
| Claims on Other Financial Corps.. | 32g | 28,685 | 32,852 | 28,383 | 36,203 | 93,660 | 82,809 | 109,104 | 186,799 | 135,172 | 85,572 | 130,634 | 106,403 |
| Claims on State & Local Govts..... | 32b | 4,161 | 4,941 | 5,448 | 5,864 | 6,306 | 7,250 | 8,401 | 9,303 | 10,452 | 11,359 | 12,701 | 13,952 |
| Claims on Private Sector................ | 32d | 101,170 | 114,039 | 126,904 | 142,694 | 155,607 | 156,853 | 165,811 | 176,968 | 184,499 | 189,890 | 192,212 | 199,634 |
| Transf.Dep.Included in Broad Money | 34 | 46,040 | 49,216 | 51,362 | 53,430 | 54,893 | 65,439 | 69,957 | 74,085 | 80,985 | 89,648 | 97,111 | 110,799 |
| Other Dep.Included in Broad Money. | 35 | 34,034 | 37,009 | 42,734 | 55,697 | 58,820 | 48,745 | 49,583 | 52,241 | 42,487 | 37,428 | 34,060 | 31,042 |
| Sec.Ot.th.Shares Inc.in.Brd. Money... | 36a | 6,708 | 6,385 | 6,163 | 11,058 | 12,823 | 10,361 | 7,906 | 10,030 | 7,008 | 6,257 | 5,208 | 3,234 |
| Deposits Excl. from Broad Money..... | 36b | 2,280 | 2,011 | 1,895 | 1,546 | 1,160 | 1,660 | 3,049 | 3,638 | 3,286 | 2,933 | 2,340 | 2,309 |
| Sec.Ot.th.Shares Excl./f.Brd. Money.. | 36s | 12,696 | 16,898 | 24,258 | 25,211 | 28,267 | 31,029 | 38,540 | 48,537 | 60,706 | 62,393 | 70,166 | 77,275 |
| **Interest Rates** | | | | | | | *Percent Per Annum* | | | | | | | |
| Money Market Rate....................... | 60b | 2.11 | 2.18 | 3.08 | 4.28 | 4.63 | 1.23 | .81 | 1.39 | .57 | .22 | .21 | −.02 |
| Deposit Rate | | | | | | | | | | | | | |
| Households: Stocks, up to 2 years.. | 60lhs | 2.06 | 2.10 | 2.63 | 3.74 | 4.53 | 2.80 | 1.82 | 2.11 | 2.11 | 1.41 | 1.19 | 1.06 |
| New Business, up to 1 year.......... | 60lhn | 1.96 | 2.06 | 2.92 | 4.12 | 4.54 | 1.46 | 1.52 | 2.00 | 1.50 | 1.08 | 1.08 | .97 |
| Corporations: Stocks, up to 2 years | 60lcs | 1.93 | 1.99 | 2.75 | 3.91 | 4.45 | 1.69 | 1.09 | 1.61 | 1.23 | .72 | .71 | .56 |
| New Business, up to 1 year.......... | 60lcn | 1.92 | 1.99 | 2.80 | 3.88 | 4.02 | .69 | .47 | .94 | .43 | .27 | .39 | .26 |
| Lending Rate | | | | | | | | | | | | | |
| Households: Stocks, up to 1 year.... | 60phs | 7.87 | 8.01 | 8.77 | 10.22 | 11.00 | 7.92 | 6.75 | 6.89 | 6.43 | 6.26 | 6.39 | 6.27 |
| New Bus., Floating & up to 1 year | 60pns | 4.90 | 4.04 | 4.46 | 5.62 | 5.79 | 3.51 | 3.25 | 3.78 | 3.75 | 3.99 | 3.98 | 4.21 |
| House Purch., Stocks,Over 5 years | 60phm | 3.42 | 3.27 | 3.69 | 4.70 | 5.18 | 2.93 | 1.98 | 2.34 | 2.05 | 1.49 | 1.49 | 1.32 |
| House Purch., New Bus., 5-10 yrs | 60phn | 4.38 | 3.89 | 4.39 | 5.08 | 5.03 | 4.13 | 3.42 | 3.37 | 2.93 | 3.16 | 2.71 | 2.48 |
| Corporations: Stocks, up to 1 year.. | 60pcs | 3.58 | 3.41 | 4.06 | 4.98 | 5.33 | 2.55 | 2.27 | 2.68 | 2.06 | 2.11 | 2.20 | 2.00 |
| New Bus., Over € 1 mil.,up to 1 yr | 60pcn | 3.02 | 2.97 | 3.74 | 4.81 | 5.08 | 2.21 | 1.85 | 2.58 | 2.06 | 1.88 | 1.92 | 1.46 |
| Government Bond Yield................. | 61 | 4.11 | 3.35 | 3.78 | 4.29 | 4.29 | 3.74 | 3.01 | 3.01 | 1.88 | 1.86 | 1.45 | .72 |
| **Prices, Production, Labor** | | | | | | *Index Numbers (2010=100): Period Averages* | | | | | | | |
| Share Prices............................... | 62 | 88.5 | 103.7 | 129.6 | 161.2 | 122.5 | 82.3 | 100.0 | 94.2 | 80.6 | 93.8 | 109.1 | 123.2 |
| Prices: Domestic Supply.................. | 63 | 85.1 | 88.3 | 93.3 | 97.1 | 102.6 | 96.0 | 100.0 | 106.4 | 109.7 | 109.9 | 108.4 | 104.9 |
| Producer, Manufacturing......... | 63ey | 90.2 | 92.2 | 95.7 | 98.0 | 102.1 | 95.1 | 100.0 | 105.6 | 107.0 | 106.6 | 105.6 | 103.6 |
| Consumer Prices........................ | 64 | 90.4 | † 91.2 | 92.6 | 94.9 | 98.8 | 98.8 | 100.0 | 103.4 | 106.3 | 107.9 | 109.0 | 108.8 |
| Harmonized CPI............................ | 64h | 89.8 | 90.5 | 91.7 | 93.1 | 96.8 | 98.3 | 100.0 | 103.3 | 106.6 | 109.0 | 110.3 | 110.1 |
| Wages: Hourly Earnings.................. | 65ey | 82.3 | † 85.6 | 87.7 | 90.8 | 95.1 | 98.3 | 100.0 | 102.7 | 106.0 | 107.5 | 108.7 | 110.3 |
| Industrial Production..................... | 66 | 99.9 | 100.0 | 109.6 | 114.7 | 115.6 | 94.7 | 100.0 | 101.7 | 99.6 | 96.5 | 94.7 | 93.9 |
| Industrial Employment, Seas.Adj... | 67eyc | 126.7 | 114.7 | 115.7 | 116.8 | 115.3 | 104.8 | 100.0 | 99.4 | 98.5 | 96.8 | 91.6 | 90.7 |
| | | | | | | *Number in Thousands: Period Averages* | | | | | | | |
| Labor Force................................ | 67d | 2,593 | 2,597 | 2,620 | 2,642 | 2,669 | 2,644 | 2,634 | 2,637 | 2,637 | 2,622 | 2,617 | 2,619 |
| Employment................................ | 67e | 2,374 | 2,378 | 2,416 | 2,459 | 2,497 | 2,424 | 2,410 | 2,429 | 2,431 | 2,403 | 2,386 | 2,368 |
| Unemployment............................ | 67c | 229 | 220 | 204 | 183 | 172 | 221 | 224 | 209 | 207 | 219 | 232 | 252 |
| Unemployment Rate (%)................ | 67r | 8.8 | 8.4 | 7.7 | 6.9 | 6.4 | 8.2 | 8.4 | 7.8 | 7.7 | 8.2 | 8.7 | 9.4 |
| **Intl. Transactions & Positions** | | | | | | | *Millions of Euros* | | | | | | |
| Exports........................................ | 70 | 48,917 | 52,453 | 61,489 | 65,688 | 65,581 | 45,064 | 52,439 | 56,854 | 56,878 | 56,047 | 55,974 | 53,870 |
| Imports, c.i.f.............................. | 71 | 40,729 | 47,028 | 55,253 | 59,615 | 62,402 | 43,654 | 51,899 | 60,537 | 59,519 | 58,407 | 57,770 | 54,427 |
| | | | | | | | *2010=100* | | | | | | |
| Export Prices................................ | 76 | 100.6 | 101.6 | 103.7 | 104.3 | 104.7 | 95.8 | 100.0 | 104.9 | 105.3 | 103.6 | 102.5 | 101.1 |
| Import Prices............................... | 76.x | 87.3 | 92.0 | 98.1 | 99.9 | 103.3 | 94.3 | 100.0 | 108.3 | 111.3 | 108.9 | 106.5 | 100.1 |

## Balance of Payments

*Millions of US Dollars*

| | | 2004 | 2005 | 2006 | 2007 | 2008 | 2009 | 2010 | 2011 | 2012 | 2013 | 2014 | 2015 |
|---|---|---|---|---|---|---|---|---|---|---|---|---|---|
| A. Current Account* | 109bx | 12,542.4 | †7,788.4 | 8,208.5 | 9,940.2 | 6,151.0 | 5,121.5 | 3,167.7 | −4,900.1 | −5,019.4 | −4,312.2 | −2,685.6 | 315.3 |
| Goods, credit (exports) | 1a9cx | 65,651.1 | †70,074.7 | 75,550.5 | 88,924.2 | 96,503.2 | 63,641.8 | 68,165.0 | 77,435.9 | 73,104.2 | 75,409.5 | 75,597.5 | 61,292.4 |
| Goods, debit (imports) | 1a9dx | 47,440.4 | †55,294.5 | 65,354.7 | 76,952.1 | 86,314.5 | 58,218.7 | 65,220.6 | 79,653.1 | 73,611.5 | 75,080.8 | 74,431.4 | 58,504.0 |
| Balance on goods | 1a9bx | 18,210.7 | †14,780.1 | 10,195.8 | 11,972.1 | 10,188.7 | 5,423.1 | 2,944.4 | −2,217.2 | −507.4 | 328.7 | 1,166.0 | 2,788.4 |
| Services, credit (exports) | 1b9cx | 9,590.6 | †12,265.3 | 18,035.5 | 23,666.3 | 32,171.6 | 28,348.3 | 27,839.4 | 29,412.0 | 28,742.6 | 29,742.5 | 28,109.0 | 24,351.0 |
| Services, debit (imports) | 1b9dx | 14,425.8 | †17,343.7 | 19,002.1 | 22,960.1 | 31,532.9 | 27,852.6 | 27,316.9 | 29,626.3 | 31,125.4 | 31,536.2 | 30,538.8 | 25,769.3 |
| Balance on Goods & Services | 1z9bx | 13,375.4 | †9,701.7 | 9,229.2 | 12,678.3 | 10,827.4 | 5,918.8 | 3,467.0 | −2,431.5 | −2,890.1 | −1,465.0 | −1,263.8 | 1,370.1 |
| Primary income: credit | 1c9cx | 13,128.7 | †14,406.7 | 19,810.4 | 25,356.9 | 24,944.8 | 16,424.4 | 19,200.7 | 20,342.7 | 18,882.1 | 18,731.2 | 21,855.5 | 17,889.2 |
| Primary income: debit | 1c9dx | 12,884.1 | †14,750.4 | 18,637.4 | 25,693.6 | 26,729.9 | 14,262.2 | 16,775.9 | 20,166.7 | 18,820.2 | 18,416.8 | 20,080.4 | 16,561.4 |
| Balance on gds, serv. & prim. inc. | 1y9bx | 13,620.1 | †9,358.0 | 10,402.3 | 12,341.6 | 9,042.3 | 8,080.9 | 5,891.8 | −2,255.5 | −2,828.3 | −1,150.5 | 511.3 | 2,697.9 |
| Secondary income: credit | 1d9ca | 2,040.1 | †1,987.1 | 995.5 | 1,193.3 | 1,203.9 | 1,103.7 | 1,220.8 | 1,870.4 | 2,070.0 | 1,629.4 | 1,538.6 | 1,298.7 |
| Secondary income: debit | 1d9da | 3,117.8 | †3,556.7 | 3,189.3 | 3,594.7 | 4,095.2 | 4,063.2 | 3,944.9 | 4,515.0 | 4,261.1 | 4,791.1 | 4,735.5 | 3,681.4 |
| B. Capital Account* | 209ba | 187.6 | †323.8 | 212.2 | 209.7 | 272.1 | 227.0 | 234.2 | 264.3 | 264.8 | 308.2 | 247.2 | 224.1 |
| Capital account: credit | 209ca | 188.9 | †337.5 | 224.7 | 237.1 | 300.0 | 249.2 | 244.0 | 297.7 | 275.1 | 326.8 | 268.4 | 241.8 |
| Capital account: debit | 209da | 1.2 | †13.7 | 12.6 | 27.4 | 27.9 | 22.3 | 9.8 | 33.4 | 10.3 | 18.6 | 21.2 | 17.7 |
| Balance on current & capital acct. | 129ba | 12,730.0 | †8,112.2 | 8,420.6 | 10,149.9 | 6,423.1 | 5,348.4 | 3,401.9 | −4,635.8 | −4,754.6 | −4,004.0 | −2,438.4 | 539.5 |
| C. Financial Account* | 309na | 9,474.9 | †3,966.4 | 11,252.3 | −383.5 | −6,407.0 | −9,140.6 | 6,482.2 | −11,918.9 | −22,841.6 | −10,428.3 | −10,128.0 | −2,455.8 |
| Direct investment: assets | 3a9aa | 2,754.4 | †10,485.4 | 1,792.9 | 16,523.1 | 30,137.9 | −3,908.0 | 14,992.6 | −3,552.3 | 8,378.1 | −7,243.5 | −1,864.4 | −187.8 |
| Equity & investment fund shares.. | 3aaaa | 4,901.2 | †4,213.2 | 9,165.4 | 10,755.2 | 22,478.7 | 7,574.0 | 6,915.9 | 511.7 | 4,772.5 | −5,516.3 | 1,589.7 | 1,152.3 |
| Debt instruments | 3abaa | −2,146.8 | †6,272.2 | −7,372.4 | 5,767.9 | 7,659.2 | −11,482.0 | 8,076.7 | −4,064.0 | 3,605.6 | −1,727.2 | −3,454.0 | −1,340.1 |
| Direct investment: liabilities | 3a9la | 6,771.3 | †10,875.8 | 4,631.6 | 21,985.1 | 19,403.2 | −8,826.5 | 12,226.4 | −6,008.2 | 4,932.8 | −4,940.7 | 16,322.2 | 18,710.8 |
| Equity & investment fund shares . | 3aala | 1,927.7 | †2,466.9 | 5,946.2 | 9,311.3 | 2,501.1 | 1,265.8 | 8,249.3 | 660.0 | 1,648.4 | 1,405.5 | 5,880.1 | 3,346.9 |
| Debt instruments | 3abla | 4,843.6 | †8,408.9 | −1,314.5 | 12,673.7 | 16,902.0 | −10,092.3 | 3,977.1 | −6,668.2 | 3,284.5 | −6,346.2 | 10,442.0 | 15,363.9 |
| Portfolio investment: assets | 3b9aa | 24,503.2 | †17,917.1 | 30,417.9 | 16,101.8 | 798.7 | 38,016.9 | 28,542.6 | 6,232.7 | 20,364.8 | 11,399.8 | 18,622.1 | −987.6 |
| Equity & investment fund shares | 3baaa | 10,219.5 | †9,412.2 | 14,789.5 | 13,530.4 | −5,712.8 | 19,521.3 | 15,294.1 | −3,240.7 | 11,318.5 | 9,445.2 | 5,395.0 | 1,205.8 |
| Debt securities | 3bbaa | 14,283.7 | †8,504.9 | 15,628.4 | 2,571.4 | 6,511.5 | 18,495.6 | 13,248.5 | 9,473.3 | 9,046.3 | 1,954.6 | 13,227.1 | −2,193.4 |
| Portfolio investment: liabilities | 3b9la | 13,110.1 | †10,414.4 | 18,990.9 | 10,483.7 | 649.5 | 28,200.2 | 14,996.8 | 17,111.5 | 32,432.9 | 16,105.4 | 12,284.4 | −1,806.5 |
| Equity & investment fund shares . | 3bala | 102.8 | †4,988.7 | 5,373.8 | 5,295.7 | −1,766.1 | −601.6 | −1,259.3 | −881.0 | 3,161.7 | 3,662.2 | 3,965.5 | 1,875.5 |
| Debt securities | 3bbla | 13,007.3 | †5,425.6 | 13,617.1 | 5,188.0 | 2,415.5 | 28,801.8 | 16,256.1 | 17,992.5 | 29,271.2 | 12,443.1 | 8,318.9 | −3,682.0 |
| Fin. der.− & empl.stk.ops.(ESOs): net. | 3c9na | −522.3 | †−1,815.9 | −152.3 | 877.9 | −1,670.3 | −3,019.4 | 114.3 | −1,660.2 | −1,381.9 | −2,645.6 | −868.4 | −5,686.0 |
| Fin. der. & ESOs.: assets | 3c9aa | — | .... | 10,570.3 | 15,546.7 | 21,875.9 | 13,250.2 | −75,838.3 | −6,869.0 | −7,591.2 | −87,393.6 | −91,604.3 | −99,604.8 |
| Fin. der. & ESOs.: liabilities | 3c9la | 522.3 | .... | 10,722.6 | 14,668.8 | 23,546.2 | 16,269.7 | −75,952.5 | −5,208.8 | −6,209.3 | −84,748.0 | −90,735.9 | −93,918.8 |
| Other investment: assets | 3d9aa | 11,851.1 | †3,556.0 | 15,151.7 | 13,544.4 | 16,620.7 | 12,797.0 | 38,153.6 | 116,140.8 | 2,002.3 | −37,227.9 | −2,284.0 | −2,756.8 |
| Other equity | 3daaa | .... | .... | .... | .... | .... | .... | .... | .... | .... | 18.3 | 2.0 | 12.0 |
| Debt instruments | 3dzaa | 11,851.1 | †3,556.0 | 15,151.7 | 13,544.4 | 16,620.7 | 12,797.0 | 38,164.9 | 116,132.8 | 405.5 | −37,246.2 | −2,286.0 | −2,768.8 |
| Other investment: liabilities | 3d9la | 9,230.1 | †4,886.0 | 12,335.4 | 14,961.8 | 32,241.3 | 33,653.2 | 48,097.8 | 117,976.6 | 14,839.1 | −36,453.5 | −4,873.2 | −24,066.7 |
| Other equity | 3dala | .... | .... | −7.5 | .... | .... | .... | .... | .... | .... | .... | .... | .... |
| Debt instruments | 3dzla | 9,230.1 | †4,886.0 | 12,342.9 | 14,966.4 | 32,241.3 | 33,653.2 | 48,097.8 | 117,976.6 | 14,839.1 | −36,453.5 | −4,873.2 | −24,066.7 |
| Curr.+ cap.− finan. acct. balance... | 4y9na | 3,255.1 | †4,145.8 | −2,831.7 | 10,533.4 | 12,830.1 | 14,489.0 | −3,080.3 | 7,283.2 | 18,087.0 | 6,424.3 | 7,689.6 | 2,995.3 |
| D. Net Errors and Omissions | 409na | −2,440.7 | †−4,325.3 | −1,488.9 | −10,213.7 | −12,591.7 | −11,972.6 | 962.3 | −6,767.4 | −17,399.5 | −5,372.7 | −7,973.7 | −3,237.6 |
| E. Reserves and Related Items | 4z9na | 814.4 | †−179.5 | −4,320.6 | 319.6 | 238.4 | 2,516.3 | −2,118.0 | 515.7 | 687.5 | 1,051.6 | −284.0 | −242.3 |
| Reserve assets | 3e9aa | 814.4 | †−179.5 | −4,320.6 | 319.6 | 238.4 | 2,516.3 | −2,118.0 | 515.7 | 687.5 | 1,051.6 | −284.0 | −242.3 |
| Credit and loans from the IMF | 3dcla | — | † — | .... | .... | .... | .... | .... | .... | .... | .... | .... | .... |
| Exceptional financing | 409la | — | .... | .... | .... | .... | .... | .... | .... | .... | .... | .... | .... |

*Excludes components in group E

## International Investment Position

*Millions of US Dollars*

| | | 2004 | 2005 | 2006 | 2007 | 2008 | 2009 | 2010 | 2011 | 2012 | 2013 | 2014 | 2015 |
|---|---|---|---|---|---|---|---|---|---|---|---|---|---|
| Assets | 809aa | 391,144.0 | †387,118.2 | 481,911.4 | 599,260.3 | 627,269.6 | 713,360.6 | 812,161.9 | 943,174.7 | 954,983.3 | 894,893.1 | 873,015.1 | 759,653.5 |
| Direct investment | 8a9aa | 106,812.0 | †105,982.8 | 120,004.7 | 152,087.1 | 167,383.3 | 176,862.6 | 187,187.1 | 173,000.6 | 191,796.9 | 187,802.9 | 155,072.3 | 141,115.9 |
| Equity & investment fund shares.. | 8aaaa | 57,331.3 | †57,080.2 | 74,068.4 | 95,912.7 | 108,558.0 | 125,651.8 | 131,459.6 | 123,525.3 | 137,572.5 | 137,167.1 | 113,793.2 | 104,264.0 |
| Debt instruments | 8abaa | 49,480.7 | †48,902.5 | 45,936.3 | 56,174.5 | 58,825.3 | 51,210.8 | 55,727.4 | 49,475.3 | 54,224.3 | 50,635.8 | 41,279.2 | 36,851.9 |
| Portfolio investment | 8b9aa | 146,344.1 | †154,338.8 | 213,937.8 | 256,021.5 | 182,184.9 | 254,314.2 | 286,956.0 | 272,402.0 | 316,574.4 | 347,038.4 | 347,360.3 | 317,097.6 |
| Equity & investment fund shares.. | 8baaa | 53,281.6 | †64,511.2 | 96,258.5 | 122,330.0 | 63,345.5 | 103,086.1 | 131,659.4 | 113,492.8 | 139,731.9 | 164,838.7 | 170,447.1 | 162,556.2 |
| Debt securities | 8bbaa | 93,062.5 | †89,827.6 | 117,679.3 | 133,691.5 | 118,839.4 | 151,228.1 | 155,296.5 | 158,909.2 | 176,842.6 | 182,199.7 | 176,913.2 | 154,541.4 |
| Fin. der.(oth.than reserves) & ESOs | 8c9aa | 38,805.8 | †34,927.1 | 36,687.3 | 53,394.4 | 129,755.3 | 116,823.6 | 144,757.2 | 238,756.1 | 178,905.6 | 117,631.2 | 156,826.4 | 109,222.9 |
| Other investment | 8d9aa | 86,270.0 | †80,539.1 | 103,784.1 | 129,374.1 | 139,603.8 | 153,909.5 | 183,710.8 | 248,676.8 | 256,629.5 | 231,156.1 | 203,091.7 | 182,203.8 |
| Other equity | 8daaa | .... | .... | .... | .... | .... | .... | .... | .... | .... | 3,915.8 | 3,469.9 | 3,163.3 |
| Debt instruments | 8dzaa | 86,270.0 | †80,539.1 | 103,784.1 | 129,374.1 | 139,603.8 | 153,909.5 | 183,710.8 | 248,676.8 | 256,629.5 | 227,240.3 | 199,621.7 | 179,040.5 |
| Reserve assets | 8e9aa | 12,912.1 | †11,330.4 | 7,497.5 | 8,383.3 | 8,342.3 | 11,450.7 | 9,550.8 | 10,339.1 | 11,076.9 | 11,264.4 | 10,664.4 | 10,013.3 |
| Liabilities | 809la | 412,103.7 | †415,723.7 | 512,255.3 | 673,368.3 | 634,421.6 | 698,529.3 | 762,909.8 | 896,950.0 | 910,140.5 | 884,091.1 | 880,435.4 | 768,410.3 |
| Direct investment | 8a9la | 79,168.6 | †78,924.1 | 94,365.8 | 127,258.5 | 136,778.2 | 131,796.1 | 136,221.6 | 128,451.5 | 137,053.3 | 131,245.2 | 131,659.4 | 135,933.4 |
| Equity & investment fund shares.. | 8aala | 43,844.9 | †41,231.0 | 54,992.3 | 71,539.0 | 67,055.4 | 68,628.3 | 72,887.2 | 71,722.0 | 76,364.7 | 77,403.1 | 75,422.2 | 70,611.3 |
| Debt instruments | 8abla | 35,323.7 | †37,693.1 | 39,373.5 | 55,719.4 | 69,722.8 | 63,167.8 | 63,334.3 | 56,729.5 | 60,688.7 | 53,842.1 | 56,237.2 | 65,322.1 |
| Portfolio investment | 8b9la | 221,820.1 | †230,331.3 | 289,489.9 | 379,635.3 | 231,078.5 | 278,409.0 | 277,198.3 | 262,871.8 | 311,822.2 | 363,959.8 | 354,082.4 | 324,073.5 |
| Equity & investment fund shares.. | 8bala | 102,974.3 | †119,952.0 | 154,812.8 | 229,908.3 | 96,964.2 | 104,051.7 | 97,396.5 | 66,877.8 | 77,234.1 | 113,430.7 | 110,523.1 | 111,301.8 |
| Debt securities | 8bbla | 118,845.7 | †110,379.3 | 134,677.1 | 149,727.0 | 134,114.3 | 174,357.3 | 179,801.8 | 195,994.1 | 234,588.1 | 250,529.1 | 243,559.3 | 212,771.8 |
| Fin. der.(oth.than reserves) & ESOs | 8c9la | 37,544.4 | †34,019.0 | 35,643.6 | 51,095.4 | 129,389.7 | 113,675.0 | 138,005.0 | 228,671.8 | 167,773.6 | 110,706.5 | 147,746.9 | 105,709.9 |
| Other investment | 8d9la | 73,570.7 | †72,449.3 | 92,756.0 | 115,378.7 | 137,175.2 | 174,649.2 | 211,485.0 | 276,954.8 | 293,491.4 | 278,179.5 | 246,946.7 | 202,693.4 |
| Other equity | 8dala | .... | .... | .... | .... | .... | .... | .... | .... | .... | .... | — | .... |
| Debt instruments | 8dzla | 73,570.7 | †72,449.3 | 92,756.0 | 115,378.7 | 137,175.2 | 174,649.2 | 211,485.0 | 276,954.8 | 293,491.4 | 278,179.5 | 246,946.7 | 202,693.4 |

# Finland 172

Government Finance

| | | 2004 | 2005 | 2006 | 2007 | 2008 | 2009 | 2010 | 2011 | 2012 | 2013 | 2014 | 2015 |
|---|---|---|---|---|---|---|---|---|---|---|---|---|---|
| **Government Finance** | | | | | | | | | | | | | |
| **Operations Statement** | | | | | | | | | | | | | |
| **General Government** | | *Millions of Euros: Fiscal Year Ends December 31; Data Reported through Eurostat* | | | | | | | | | | | |
| Revenue | a1 | 81,640 | 85,265 | 90,228 | 96,890 | 101,581 | 94,551 | 97,563 | 105,010 | 107,929 | 111,607 | 112,695 | 115,025 |
| Taxes | a11 | 48,385 | 50,197 | 52,311 | 55,863 | 57,282 | 51,895 | 53,515 | 58,784 | 59,823 | 62,889 | 63,839 | 65,268 |
| Social Contributions | a12 | 17,988 | 19,108 | 20,505 | 21,612 | 22,559 | 22,275 | 22,902 | 24,037 | 25,528 | 25,902 | 26,288 | 26,996 |
| Grants | a13 | .... | .... | .... | .... | .... | .... | .... | .... | .... | .... | .... | .... |
| Other Revenue | a14 | .... | .... | .... | .... | .... | .... | .... | .... | .... | .... | .... | .... |
| Expense | a2 | 76,684 | 80,114 | 83,043 | 86,539 | 92,537 | 97,992 | 101,733 | 106,115 | 111,108 | 115,686 | 118,037 | 119,804 |
| Compensation of Employees | a21 | 20,896 | 21,846 | 22,543 | 23,455 | 24,942 | 25,800 | 26,433 | 27,449 | 28,561 | 29,128 | 29,161 | 29,046 |
| Use of Goods & Services | a22 | 13,654 | 14,406 | 15,350 | 16,523 | 18,263 | 19,562 | 20,540 | 21,418 | 22,483 | 23,438 | 23,633 | 23,863 |
| Consumption of Fixed Capital | a23 | 4,691 | 4,988 | 5,246 | 5,553 | 5,942 | 6,039 | 6,172 | 6,532 | 6,883 | 7,167 | 7,216 | 7,309 |
| Interest | a24 | 2,686 | 2,653 | 2,581 | 2,650 | 2,713 | 2,414 | 2,497 | 2,745 | 2,840 | 2,560 | 2,544 | 2,521 |
| Subsidies | a25 | 2,017 | 2,075 | 2,256 | 2,319 | 2,463 | 2,477 | 2,650 | 2,724 | 2,740 | 2,697 | 2,689 | 2,834 |
| Grants | a26 | .... | .... | .... | .... | .... | .... | .... | .... | .... | .... | .... | .... |
| Social Benefits | a27 | 28,389 | 29,309 | 30,123 | 30,954 | 32,749 | 35,824 | 37,446 | 38,929 | 41,342 | 43,928 | 45,885 | 47,439 |
| Other Expense | a28 | .... | .... | .... | .... | .... | .... | .... | .... | .... | .... | .... | .... |
| Gross Operating Balance [1-2+23] | agob | 9,647 | 10,139 | 12,431 | 15,904 | 14,986 | 2,598 | 2,002 | 5,427 | 3,704 | 3,088 | 1,874 | 2,530 |
| Net Operating Balance [1-2] | anob | 4,956 | 5,151 | 7,185 | 10,351 | 9,044 | –3,441 | –4,170 | –1,105 | –3,179 | –4,079 | –5,342 | –4,779 |
| Net Acq. of Nonfinancial Assets | a31 | 1,454 | 888 | 399 | 774 | 946 | 1,136 | 713 | 951 | 1,183 | 1,236 | 1,204 | 917 |
| Aquisition of Nonfin. Assets | a31.1 | .... | .... | .... | .... | .... | .... | .... | .... | .... | .... | .... | .... |
| Disposal of Nonfin. Assets | a31.2 | .... | .... | .... | .... | .... | .... | .... | .... | .... | .... | .... | .... |
| Net Lending/Borrowing [1-2-31] | anlb | 3,502 | 4,263 | 6,786 | 9,577 | 8,098 | –4,577 | –4,883 | –2,056 | –4,362 | –5,315 | –6,546 | –5,696 |
| Net Acq. of Financial Assets | a32 | 7,060 | 1,587 | 6,751 | 8,664 | 8,384 | 9,592 | 6,501 | 4,363 | 7,216 | 5,035 | –374 | 2,932 |
| By instrument | | | | | | | | | | | | | |
| Monetary Gold & SDRs | a3201 | — | — | — | — | — | — | — | — | — | — | — | — |
| Currency & Deposits | a3202 | 1,331 | –487 | 1,289 | 641 | 765 | –1,559 | 4,953 | 2,502 | –2,215 | –1,578 | –1,648 | 5,653 |
| Securities other than Shares | a3203 | 5,078 | 1,883 | –141 | –1,164 | 3,484 | 3,593 | –7,410 | 1,738 | –1,007 | 2,615 | –1,170 | 136 |
| Loans | a3204 | –656 | 336 | 693 | 81 | 3,498 | 2,681 | 893 | –649 | 3,716 | 932 | –1,495 | –478 |
| Shares & Other Equity | a3205 | 1,157 | 766 | 4,827 | 8,094 | 414 | 6,024 | 6,751 | 518 | 6,509 | 4,931 | 1,926 | –2,374 |
| Insurance Technical Reserves | a3206 | 6 | –13 | –6 | 26 | — | — | — | — | –10 | — | 18 | 6 |
| Financial Derivatives | a3207 | — | — | — | — | — | — | — | — | — | — | — | — |
| Other Accounts Receivable | a3208 | 144 | –899 | 89 | 988 | 223 | –1,147 | 1,313 | 254 | 223 | –1,865 | 1,995 | –11 |
| By debtor | | | | | | | | | | | | | |
| Domestic | a321 | .... | .... | .... | .... | .... | .... | .... | .... | .... | .... | .... | .... |
| Foreign | a322 | .... | .... | .... | .... | .... | .... | .... | .... | .... | .... | .... | .... |
| Net Incurrence of Liabilities | a33 | 3,183 | –1,844 | 79 | –710 | 308 | 14,349 | 12,029 | 6,415 | 11,506 | 9,974 | 6,892 | 8,070 |
| By instrument | | | | | | | | | | | | | |
| Special Drawing Rights (SDRs) | a3301 | — | — | — | — | — | — | — | — | — | — | — | — |
| Currency & Deposits | a3302 | 35 | 55 | 33 | 30 | 27 | 43 | –43 | 106 | –212 | 59 | 138 | 79 |
| Securities other than Shares | a3303 | 2,888 | –2,354 | 683 | –2,462 | –1,388 | 11,083 | 12,108 | 3,868 | 6,537 | 5,758 | 7,316 | 5,194 |
| Loans | a3304 | –245 | 189 | –684 | 614 | 1,091 | 1,136 | 691 | 2,484 | 4,008 | 1,391 | 2,161 | 2,362 |
| Shares & Other Equity | a3305 | — | — | — | — | — | — | — | 5 | 1 | — | — | — |
| Insurance Technical Reserves | a3306 | — | — | 1 | –1 | 2 | 2 | 2 | –2 | 5 | 5 | 11 | — |
| Financial Derivatives | a3307 | 213 | 272 | –23 | –244 | 749 | –377 | –692 | –49 | 369 | 1,593 | –1,441 | –840 |
| Other Accounts Payable | a3308 | 292 | –6 | 69 | 1,353 | –173 | 2,462 | –42 | 7 | 799 | 1,168 | –1,295 | 1,275 |
| By creditor | | | | | | | | | | | | | |
| Domestic | a331 | .... | .... | .... | .... | .... | .... | .... | .... | .... | .... | .... | .... |
| Foreign | a332 | .... | .... | .... | .... | .... | .... | .... | .... | .... | .... | .... | .... |
| Stat. Discrepancy [32-33-NLB] | anlbz | 375 | –832 | –114 | –203 | –22 | –180 | –645 | 4 | 72 | 376 | –720 | 558 |
| Memo Item: Expenditure [2+31] | a2m | 78,138 | 81,002 | 83,442 | 87,313 | 93,483 | 99,128 | 102,446 | 107,066 | 112,291 | 116,922 | 119,241 | 120,721 |
| **Balance Sheet** | | | | | | | | | | | | | |
| Net Worth | a6 | .... | .... | .... | .... | .... | .... | .... | .... | .... | .... | .... | .... |
| Nonfinancial Assets | a61 | .... | .... | .... | .... | .... | .... | .... | .... | .... | .... | .... | .... |
| Financial Assets | a62 | 149,445 | 168,432 | 190,666 | 204,876 | 171,977 | 197,642 | 220,176 | 208,405 | 226,137 | 239,528 | 256,632 | 267,636 |
| By instrument | | | | | | | | | | | | | |
| Monetary Gold & SDRs | a6201 | — | — | — | — | — | — | — | — | — | — | — | — |
| Currency & Deposits | a6202 | 9,752 | 9,346 | 10,458 | 11,262 | 12,040 | 10,483 | 15,469 | 18,001 | 16,341 | 14,743 | 13,097 | 18,750 |
| Securities other than Shares | a6203 | 41,903 | 44,540 | 43,554 | 41,519 | 42,423 | 47,030 | 39,267 | 41,028 | 42,117 | 42,507 | 43,598 | 44,227 |
| Loans | a6204 | 19,190 | 19,552 | 20,244 | 20,325 | 23,825 | 26,572 | 27,485 | 26,468 | 30,184 | 31,091 | 30,739 | 30,278 |
| Shares and Other Equity | a6205 | 70,281 | 87,447 | 106,879 | 120,151 | 83,066 | 105,030 | 126,835 | 111,926 | 125,749 | 141,473 | 157,397 | 162,695 |
| Insurance Technical Reserves | a6206 | 85 | 72 | 66 | 92 | 93 | 94 | 94 | 94 | 84 | 84 | 176 | 176 |
| Financial Derivatives | a6207 | 205 | 162 | 2,142 | 3,216 | 1,998 | 1,048 | 2,231 | 1,805 | 2,355 | 2,188 | 2,173 | 2,177 |
| Other Accounts Receivable | a6208 | 8,029 | 7,313 | 7,323 | 8,311 | 8,532 | 7,385 | 8,795 | 9,083 | 9,307 | 7,442 | 9,452 | 9,333 |
| By debtor | | | | | | | | | | | | | |
| Domestic | a621 | .... | .... | .... | .... | .... | .... | .... | .... | .... | .... | .... | .... |
| Foreign | a622 | .... | .... | .... | .... | .... | .... | .... | .... | .... | .... | .... | .... |
| Liabilities | a63 | 78,539 | 76,345 | 75,843 | 74,756 | 75,184 | 89,666 | 104,623 | 112,378 | 125,760 | 130,193 | 145,005 | 153,239 |
| By instrument | | | | | | | | | | | | | |
| Special Drawing Rights (SDRs) | a6301 | — | — | — | — | — | — | — | — | — | — | — | — |
| Currency & Deposits | a6302 | 299 | 354 | 387 | 417 | 444 | 704 | 661 | 767 | 555 | 614 | 752 | 831 |
| Securities other than Shares | a6303 | 59,754 | 57,728 | 56,180 | 52,763 | 53,067 | 64,396 | 77,183 | 83,630 | 92,545 | 94,004 | 107,848 | 113,232 |
| Loans | a6304 | 11,127 | 11,318 | 10,635 | 11,249 | 12,336 | 13,471 | 14,664 | 18,264 | 22,273 | 23,543 | 25,615 | 27,904 |
| Shares and Other Equity | a6305 | 35 | 95 | 15 | 16 | 16 | 16 | 500 | 521 | 521 | 521 | 521 | 521 |
| Insurance Technical Reserves | a6306 | 70 | 70 | 71 | 70 | 72 | 74 | 76 | 74 | 79 | 84 | 95 | 102 |
| Financial Derivatives | a6307 | 221 | –242 | 1,463 | 1,797 | 1,017 | 528 | 1,097 | –1,383 | –1,517 | –1,039 | –1,003 | –1,941 |
| Other Accounts Payable | a6308 | 7,033 | 7,022 | 7,092 | 8,444 | 8,232 | 10,477 | 10,442 | 10,505 | 11,304 | 12,466 | 11,177 | 12,590 |
| By creditor | | | | | | | | | | | | | |
| Domestic | a631 | .... | .... | .... | .... | .... | .... | .... | .... | .... | .... | .... | .... |
| Foreign | a632 | .... | .... | .... | .... | .... | .... | .... | .... | .... | .... | .... | .... |
| Net Financial Worth [62-63] | a6m2 | 70,906 | 92,087 | 114,823 | 130,120 | 96,793 | 107,976 | 115,553 | 96,027 | 100,377 | 109,335 | 111,627 | 114,397 |
| Memo Item: Debt at Market Value | a6m3 | 78,283 | 76,492 | 74,365 | 72,943 | 74,151 | 89,122 | 103,026 | 113,240 | 126,756 | 130,711 | 145,487 | 154,659 |
| Memo Item: Debt at Face Value | a6m35 | 74,730 | 72,781 | 72,986 | 71,869 | 71,486 | 85,959 | 98,602 | 105,995 | 117,092 | 125,263 | 132,960 | 143,336 |
| Memo Item: Maastricht Debt | a6m36 | 67,697 | 65,759 | 65,894 | 63,425 | 63,254 | 75,482 | 88,160 | 95,490 | 105,788 | 112,797 | 121,783 | 130,746 |
| Memo Item: Debt at Nominal Value | a6m4 | .... | .... | .... | .... | .... | .... | .... | .... | .... | .... | .... | .... |

# Finland   172

|  | | 2004 | 2005 | 2006 | 2007 | 2008 | 2009 | 2010 | 2011 | 2012 | 2013 | 2014 | 2015 |
|---|---|---|---|---|---|---|---|---|---|---|---|---|---|
| **National Accounts** | | | | | | | *Billions of Euros* | | | | | | |
| Househ.Cons.Expend.,incl.NPISHs.... | 96f | 78.04 | 81.10 | 85.77 | 90.71 | 95.64 | 94.17 | 99.22 | 104.99 | 109.53 | 111.28 | 113.69 | 115.59 |
| Government Consumption Expend... | 91f | 33.70 | 35.34 | 36.94 | 38.94 | 41.99 | 43.84 | 44.70 | 46.49 | 48.68 | 50.31 | 50.78 | 50.92 |
| Gross Fixed Capital Formation.......... | 93e | 35.33 | 37.74 | 39.33 | 45.10 | 47.25 | 41.19 | 40.93 | 43.78 | 44.61 | 43.08 | 42.20 | 42.12 |
| Changes in Inventories.................... | 93i | .97 | 2.78 | 2.13 | 2.48 | 1.38 | −2.76 | −.45 | 2.50 | .40 | .47 | 1.49 | −.64 |
| Exports of Goods and Services.......... | 90c | 61.16 | 66.18 | 74.52 | 82.09 | 87.32 | 65.66 | 72.37 | 77.09 | 78.88 | 78.92 | 77.60 | 77.28 |
| Imports of Goods and Services (-)..... | 98c | 51.35 | 59.79 | 67.34 | 73.10 | 80.26 | 62.02 | 70.00 | 78.77 | 81.76 | 80.72 | 79.46 | 76.63 |
| Gross Domestic Product (GDP)......... | 99b | 158.48 | 164.39 | 172.61 | 186.58 | 193.71 | 181.03 | 187.10 | 196.87 | 199.79 | 203.34 | 205.27 | 207.53 |
| Net Primary Income from Abroad..... | 98.n | −5.06 | −6.23 | −5.28 | −6.68 | −7.25 | −5.96 | −5.72 | −7.63 | −6.54 | −8.51 | . . . . | . . . . |
| Gross National Income (GNI)............ | 99a | 153.42 | 158.15 | 167.34 | 179.91 | 186.47 | 175.07 | 181.38 | 189.24 | 193.25 | 194.83 | . . . . | . . . . |
| Net Current Transf.from Abroad....... | 98t | −1.49 | −1.69 | −1.73 | −1.73 | −1.97 | −2.14 | −2.06 | −1.91 | −1.71 | −2.47 | . . . . | . . . . |
| Gross Nat'l Disposable Inc.(GNDI).... | 99i | 151.92 | 156.46 | 165.61 | 178.18 | 184.50 | 172.93 | 179.36 | 188.41 | 192.44 | 192.11 | . . . . | . . . . |
| Gross Saving................................... | 99s | 40.03 | 39.87 | 42.98 | 48.72 | 47.13 | 35.40 | 35.91 | 37.24 | 34.63 | 32.95 | . . . . | . . . . |
| Consumption of Fixed Capital.......... | 99cf | 23.33 | 24.58 | 25.67 | 27.63 | 29.52 | 29.22 | 28.96 | 30.03 | 31.39 | 31.98 | . . . . | . . . . |
| GDP Volume 2010 Ref., Chained..... | 99b.p | 174.79 | 179.65 | 186.93 | 196.62 | 198.04 | 181.66 | 187.10 | 191.91 | 189.17 | 186.67 | 186.46 | 186.83 |
| GDP Volume (2010=100)............... | 99bvp | 93.4 | 96.0 | 99.9 | 105.1 | 105.8 | 97.1 | 100.0 | 102.6 | 101.1 | 99.8 | 99.7 | 99.9 |
| GDP Deflator (2010=100)............... | 99bip | 90.7 | 91.5 | 92.3 | 94.9 | 97.8 | 99.7 | 100.0 | 102.6 | 105.6 | 108.9 | 110.1 | 111.1 |
| | | | | | | | *Millions: Midyear Estimates* | | | | | | |
| Population................................. | 99z | 5.23 | 5.25 | 5.27 | 5.29 | 5.31 | 5.34 | 5.37 | 5.40 | 5.42 | 5.45 | 5.48 | 5.50 |

2016, International Monetary Fund : *International Financial Statistics Yearbook*

| | | 2004 | 2005 | 2006 | 2007 | 2008 | 2009 | 2010 | 2011 | 2012 | 2013 | 2014 | 2015 |
|---|---|---|---|---|---|---|---|---|---|---|---|---|---|
| **Exchange Rates** | | | | | | *Euros per SDR: End of Period* | | | | | | | |
| Market Rate | aa | 1.1402 | 1.2116 | 1.1423 | 1.0735 | 1.1068 | 1.0882 | 1.1525 | 1.1865 | 1.1649 | 1.1167 | 1.1933 | 1.2728 |
| | | | | | | *Euros per US Dollar: End of Period (ae) Period Average (rf)* | | | | | | | |
| Market Rate | ae | .7342 | .8477 | .7593 | .6793 | .7185 | .6942 | .7484 | .7729 | .7579 | .7251 | .8237 | .9185 |
| Market Rate | rf | .8054 | .8041 | .7971 | .7306 | .6827 | .7198 | .7550 | .7194 | .7783 | .7532 | .7537 | .9017 |
| | | | | | | *Index Numbers (2010=100): Period Averages* | | | | | | | |
| Nominal Effective Exchange Rate | nec | 98.5 | 98.4 | 98.6 | 100.4 | 102.6 | 102.8 | 100.0 | 100.3 | 97.6 | 99.7 | 99.8 | 95.3 |
| CPI-Based Real Effect. Ex. Rate | rec | 101.8 | 101.3 | 100.9 | 101.6 | 102.9 | 103.1 | 100.0 | 99.4 | 96.4 | 97.7 | 97.1 | 92.4 |
| ULC-Based Real Effect. Ex. Rate | rel | 96.0 | 95.9 | 97.9 | 100.8 | 101.4 | 99.3 | 100.0 | 101.0 | 100.4 | 104.5 | 106.8 | 104.8 |
| **Fund Position** | | | | | | *Millions of SDRs: End of Period* | | | | | | | |
| Quota | 2f.s | 10,738.50 | 10,738.50 | 10,738.50 | 10,738.50 | 10,738.50 | 10,738.50 | 10,738.50 | 10,738.50 | 10,738.50 | 10,738.50 | 10,738.50 | 10,738.50 |
| SDR Holdings | 1b.s | 563.26 | 614.38 | 629.89 | 629.62 | 626.92 | 9,717.51 | 9,739.85 | 9,558.59 | 9,490.46 | 9,185.30 | 9,371.43 | 9,422.93 |
| Reserve Position in the Fund | 1c.s | 3,453.00 | 2,013.94 | 941.91 | 713.39 | 1,473.55 | 2,341.52 | 2,979.99 | 5,073.61 | 5,513.45 | 5,168.96 | 4,002.99 | 2,968.18 |
| Total Fund Cred. & Loans Outstg. | 2tl | — | — | — | — | — | — | — | — | — | — | — | — |
| SDR Allocations | 1bd | 1,079.87 | 1,079.87 | 1,079.87 | 1,079.87 | 1,079.87 | 10,134.20 | 10,134.20 | 10,134.20 | 10,134.20 | 10,134.20 | 10,134.20 | 10,134.20 |
| **International Liquidity** | | | | | | *Millions of US Dollars Unless Otherwise Indicated: End of Period* | | | | | | | |
| Total Res.Min.Gold (Eurosys.Def) | 1l.d | 35,314 | 27,753 | 42,652 | 45,710 | 33,617 | 46,633 | 55,800 | 48,612 | 54,231 | 50,849 | 49,547 | 55,192 |
| SDR Holdings | 1b.d | 875 | 878 | 948 | 995 | 966 | 15,234 | 15,000 | 14,675 | 14,586 | 14,145 | 13,577 | 13,058 |
| Reserve Position in the Fund | 1c.d | 5,363 | 2,878 | 1,417 | 1,127 | 2,270 | 3,671 | 4,589 | 7,789 | 8,474 | 7,960 | 5,800 | 4,113 |
| Foreign Exchange | 1d.d | 29,077 | 23,996 | 40,287 | 43,587 | 30,382 | 27,729 | 36,211 | 26,147 | 30,350 | 27,414 | 28,658 | 36,372 |
| o/w:Fin.Deriv.Rel.to Reserves | 1ddd | — | — | — | — | — | — | — | — | 821 | 1,329 | 1.21 | 1.09 |
| Other Reserve Assets | 1e.d | — | — | — | — | — | — | — | — | 821 | 1,329 | 1,513 | 1,649 |
| Gold (Million Fine Troy Ounces) | 1ad | 95.98 | 90.85 | 87.44 | 83.69 | 80.13 | 78.30 | 78.30 | 78.30 | 78.30 | 78.30 | 78.30 | 78.31 |
| Gold (Eurosystem Valuation) | 1and | 42,039 | 46,607 | 55,588 | 70,008 | 69,308 | 86,444 | 110,424 | 123,285 | 130,291 | 94,077 | 93,901 | 82,971 |
| Memo:Euro Cl. on Non-EA Res. | 1dgd | — | — | — | — | — | — | — | — | — | — | — | — |
| Non-Euro Cl. on EA Res. | 1dhd | 4,171 | 8,043 | 10,275 | 23,446 | 90,488 | 26,670 | 21,932 | 61,430 | 20,643 | 19,812 | 19,643 | 19,972 |
| Central Bank: Other Liabs. | 4..d | 11,633 | 11,236 | 12,840 | 17,055 | 33,080 | 48,053 | 42,352 | 39,781 | 40,765 | 29,600 | 32,427 | 30,403 |
| Other Depository Corps.: Assets | 7a.d | 829,479 | 1,003,062 | 1,268,935 | 1,478,577 | 1,288,895 | 1,221,964 | 1,286,778 | 1,262,449 | 1,175,816 | 1,279,877 | 1,251,493 | 1,103,449 |
| Other Depository Corps.: Liabs. | 7b.d | 756,952 | 960,703 | 1,320,979 | 1,711,350 | 1,465,673 | 1,355,674 | 1,382,092 | 1,083,755 | 1,025,811 | 1,098,055 | 1,054,976 | 941,115 |
| **Central Bank** | | | | | | *Millions of Euros: End of Period* | | | | | | | |
| Euro Area Wide Residency Criterion | | | | | | | | | | | | | |
| Net Foreign Assets | 11n.u | 49,806 | 55,946 | 62,454 | 65,310 | 62,152 | 45,743 | 61,767 | 67,791 | 73,393 | 48,612 | 54,632 | 67,007 |
| Claims on Nonresidents | 11..u | 58,346 | 65,470 | 87,618 | 142,342 | 162,783 | 169,461 | 196,387 | 223,190 | 231,162 | 172,561 | 184,159 | 189,936 |
| Liabilities to Nonresidents | 16c.u | 8,540 | 9,524 | 25,165 | 77,031 | 100,631 | 123,718 | 134,620 | 155,399 | 157,770 | 123,949 | 129,527 | 122,929 |
| Claims on Other Depository Corps. | 12e.u | 18,145 | 27,752 | 33,068 | 109,113 | 247,098 | 178,884 | 110,438 | 270,439 | 278,091 | 161,419 | 180,678 | 199,370 |
| Net Claims on Central Government | 12anu | 5,385 | 6,576 | 23,415 | 31,656 | 38,988 | 50,886 | 85,091 | 114,282 | 122,546 | 117,935 | 108,706 | 181,410 |
| Claims on Central Govt | 12a.u | 5,680 | 6,896 | 23,650 | 31,964 | 52,024 | 69,890 | 86,578 | 123,220 | 127,429 | 121,201 | 111,148 | 195,283 |
| Liabs. to Central Govt | 16d.u | 295 | 320 | 235 | 308 | 13,036 | 19,004 | 1,487 | 8,938 | 4,883 | 3,266 | 2,442 | 13,873 |
| Claims on Other Sectors | 12s.u | 258 | 230 | 694 | 679 | 620 | 621 | 668 | 677 | 288 | 288 | 293 | 21,364 |
| Claims on Other Financial Corps. | 12g.u | — | — | — | — | — | — | — | — | — | — | — | 21,085 |
| Claims on State & Local Govts | 12b.u | — | — | — | — | — | — | — | — | — | — | — | — |
| Claims on Public Nonfin. Corps. | 12c.u | — | — | — | — | — | — | — | — | — | — | — | — |
| Claims on Private Sector | 12d.u | 258 | 230 | 694 | 679 | 620 | 621 | 668 | 677 | 288 | 288 | 293 | 279 |
| Monetary Base | 14..u | 126,872 | 139,492 | 152,380 | 210,569 | 247,036 | 223,318 | 210,175 | 347,852 | 388,050 | 312,395 | 320,095 | 429,061 |
| Currency in Circulation | 14a.u | 97,834 | 110,171 | 122,377 | 131,196 | 147,302 | 153,733 | 160,097 | 168,950 | 173,530 | 181,735 | 192,600 | 203,980 |
| Liabs. to Other Depository Corps. | 14c.u | 28,675 | 28,553 | 29,788 | 79,239 | 99,249 | 67,965 | 49,647 | 178,428 | 197,372 | 112,175 | 112,692 | 222,863 |
| Liabs. to Other Sectors | 14d.u | 363 | 768 | 215 | 134 | 485 | 1,620 | 431 | 474 | 17,148 | 18,485 | 14,803 | 2,218 |
| Other Liabs. to Other Dep. Corps. | 14n.u | — | — | — | — | — | — | — | — | — | — | — | — |
| Dep. & Sec. Excl. f/Monetary Base | 14o.u | — | — | — | — | — | — | — | — | — | — | — | — |
| Deposits Included in Broad Money | 15..u | — | — | — | — | — | — | — | — | — | — | — | — |
| Sec.Ot.th.Shares Inc.in.Brd.Money | 16a.u | — | — | — | — | — | — | — | — | — | — | — | — |
| Deposits Excl. from Broad Money | 16b.u | — | — | — | — | — | — | — | — | — | — | — | — |
| Sec.Oh.th.Shares Excl. f/Brd.Money | 16s.u | — | — | — | — | — | — | — | — | — | — | — | — |
| Loans | 16l.u | — | — | — | — | — | — | — | — | — | — | — | — |
| Financial Derivatives | 16m.u | — | — | — | — | — | — | — | — | — | — | — | — |
| Shares and Other Equity | 17a.u | 32,949 | 45,655 | 50,699 | 57,640 | 63,414 | 76,349 | 102,065 | 117,964 | 125,059 | 92,724 | 106,624 | 110,874 |
| Other Items (Net) | 17r.u | −86,227 | −94,643 | −80,738 | −58,994 | 43,212 | −17,799 | −49,778 | −7,082 | −30,754 | −70,773 | −82,410 | −70,784 |
| Memorandum Items | | | | | | | | | | | | | |
| National Residency Criterion | | | | | | | | | | | | | |
| Net Foreign Assets | 11n | 73,707 | 76,367 | 103,635 | 94,823 | 6,523 | 61,188 | 135,926 | 94,915 | 87,105 | 105,898 | 110,518 | 140,799 |
| Claims on Nonresidents | 11 | 82,247 | 85,891 | 128,799 | 184,112 | 224,838 | 246,914 | 298,895 | 329,943 | 318,773 | 263,925 | 270,904 | 293,045 |
| Liabilities to Nonresidents | 16c | 8,540 | 9,524 | 25,165 | 89,288 | 218,315 | 185,726 | 162,969 | 235,028 | 231,669 | 158,027 | 160,386 | 152,246 |
| Claims on Other Depository Corps. | 12e | 17,315 | 27,054 | 27,301 | 98,665 | 231,064 | 162,901 | 80,376 | 252,233 | 266,169 | 152,130 | 171,105 | 190,649 |
| Net Claims on Central Government | 12an | 5,385 | 6,576 | 6,880 | 8,622 | 1,255 | −2,392 | 20,837 | 33,927 | 55,049 | 44,051 | 39,751 | 116,324 |
| Claims on Central Government | 12a | 5,680 | 6,896 | 7,115 | 8,930 | 14,291 | 16,612 | 22,324 | 42,865 | 59,932 | 47,317 | 42,193 | 130,197 |
| Liabilities to Central Government | 16d | 295 | 320 | 235 | 308 | 13,036 | 19,004 | 1,487 | 8,938 | 4,883 | 3,266 | 2,442 | 13,873 |
| Claims on Other Sectors | 12s | 258 | 230 | 694 | 679 | 620 | 621 | 668 | 677 | 288 | 288 | 293 | 279 |
| Claims on Other Fin. Corps. | 12g | — | — | — | — | — | — | — | — | — | — | — | — |
| Claims on State & Local Govts. | 12b | — | — | — | — | — | — | — | — | — | — | — | — |
| Claims on Private Sector | 12d | 258 | 230 | 694 | 679 | 620 | 621 | 668 | 677 | 288 | 288 | 293 | 279 |
| Liabs.to ODCs, Inc.in Mon.Base | 14c | 28,675 | 28,553 | 29,788 | 78,917 | 99,249 | 67,965 | 49,647 | 176,223 | 194,772 | 112,175 | 112,692 | 222,863 |
| Liabs.to Ot.Sectors, Inc.in Mon.Base | 14d | 363 | 768 | 215 | 134 | 485 | 1,620 | 431 | 474 | 648 | 595 | 953 | 2,218 |
| Liabs.to ODCs,Excl.f/Mon.Base | 14n | — | — | — | — | — | — | — | — | — | — | — | — |
| Net Claims on Eurosystem | 12e.s | 23,901 | 20,553 | 19,709 | −2,816 | −108,565 | −52,997 | −19,101 | −67,939 | −45,077 | −6,467 | −7,252 | −19,560 |

# France 132

| Other Depository Corporations | | 2004 | 2005 | 2006 | 2007 | 2008 | 2009 | 2010 | 2011 | 2012 | 2013 | 2014 | 2015 |
|---|---|---|---|---|---|---|---|---|---|---|---|---|---|
| Euro Area Wide Residency Criterion | | *Millions of Euros: End of Period* | | | | | | | | | | | |
| Net Foreign Assets | 21n.u | 53,247 | 35,907 | −39,517 | −158,123 | −127,023 | −92,815 | −71,332 | 138,105 | 113,692 | 131,841 | 161,862 | 149,108 |
| Claims on Nonresidents | 21..u | 608,971 | 850,269 | 963,504 | 1,004,400 | 926,130 | 848,233 | 963,013 | 975,693 | 891,175 | 928,052 | 1,030,799 | 1,013,547 |
| Liabilities to Nonresidents | 26c.u | 555,724 | 814,362 | 1,003,021 | 1,162,523 | 1,053,153 | 941,048 | 1,034,345 | 837,588 | 777,483 | 796,211 | 868,937 | 864,439 |
| Claims on Eurosystem | 20..u | 32,793 | 32,306 | 33,470 | 80,757 | 98,724 | 69,285 | 53,353 | 180,890 | 202,887 | 120,676 | 122,259 | 229,505 |
| Currency | 20a.u | 6,409 | 6,614 | 7,150 | 7,147 | 7,962 | 8,241 | 7,081 | 7,652 | 8,115 | 8,501 | 9,567 | 9,572 |
| Reserve Deposits and Securities | 20b.u | 26,384 | 25,692 | 26,320 | 73,610 | 90,762 | 61,044 | 46,272 | 173,238 | 194,772 | 112,175 | 112,692 | 219,933 |
| Other Claims | 20n.u | — | — | — | — | — | — | — | — | — | — | — | — |
| Net Claims on Central Government | 22anu | 221,243 | 279,704 | 284,906 | 296,802 | 297,991 | 318,664 | 275,511 | 163,799 | 223,118 | 227,579 | 247,514 | 221,140 |
| Claims on Central Government | 22a.u | 267,614 | 329,770 | 305,380 | 316,267 | 322,643 | 348,578 | 313,944 | 203,477 | 253,956 | 253,512 | 268,836 | 243,180 |
| Liabilities to Central Government | 26d.u | 46,371 | 50,066 | 20,474 | 19,465 | 24,652 | 29,914 | 38,433 | 39,678 | 30,838 | 25,933 | 21,322 | 22,040 |
| Claims on Other Sectors | 22s.u | 1,760,285 | 1,896,837 | 2,410,461 | 2,845,985 | 3,042,239 | 2,887,103 | 3,045,838 | 3,105,626 | 3,114,950 | 3,068,362 | 3,170,156 | 3,205,963 |
| Claims on Other Financial Corps | 22g.u | 246,653 | 245,492 | 591,691 | 818,510 | 870,998 | 711,579 | 779,140 | 792,535 | 766,038 | 700,478 | 814,023 | 785,123 |
| Claims on State & Local Govts | 22b.u | 140,323 | 161,994 | 172,411 | 188,782 | 197,294 | 215,771 | 230,730 | 209,911 | 221,689 | 226,995 | 231,864 | 227,656 |
| Claims on Public Nonfin. Corps | 22c.u | — | — | — | — | — | — | — | — | — | — | — | — |
| Claims on Private Sector | 22d.u | 1,373,309 | 1,489,351 | 1,646,359 | 1,838,693 | 1,973,947 | 1,959,753 | 2,035,968 | 2,103,180 | 2,127,223 | 2,140,889 | 2,124,269 | 2,193,184 |
| Liabilities to Eurosystem | 26g.u | 17,315 | 27,054 | 30,493 | 105,605 | 244,859 | 177,666 | 93,604 | 261,903 | 273,944 | 158,574 | 177,276 | 191,833 |
| Transf.Dep.Included in Broad Money | 24..u | 364,054 | 404,132 | 431,589 | 456,873 | 449,479 | 481,399 | 521,767 | 546,962 | 560,060 | 587,485 | 643,182 | 741,587 |
| Other.Dep.Included in Broad Money. | 25..u | 771,802 | 812,177 | 893,026 | 1,013,593 | 1,164,945 | 1,129,871 | 1,134,890 | 1,106,113 | 1,157,112 | 1,126,327 | 1,123,462 | 1,105,617 |
| Sec.Ot.th.Shares Inc.in.Brd. Money | 26a.u | 8,328 | 25,177 | 55,790 | 132,602 | 83,231 | −4,463 | 59,869 | 99,686 | 52,655 | 58,713 | 77,875 | 43,250 |
| Deposits Excl. from Broad Money | 26b.u | 310,903 | 313,208 | 308,670 | 295,887 | 285,502 | 390,836 | 412,385 | 519,339 | 523,621 | 545,823 | 516,143 | 581,721 |
| Sec.Ot.th.Shares Excl.f/Brd. Money. | 26s.u | 296,603 | 317,642 | 328,340 | 423,274 | 466,463 | 497,903 | 509,161 | 593,314 | 641,836 | 618,794 | 620,293 | 624,096 |
| Loans | 26l.u | — | — | — | — | — | — | — | — | — | — | — | — |
| Financial Derivatives | 26m.u | — | — | 275,996 | 374,159 | 449,462 | 299,275 | 305,235 | 340,132 | 317,166 | 288,165 | 358,018 | 306,303 |
| Insurance Technical Reserves | 26r.u | — | — | — | — | — | — | — | — | — | — | — | — |
| Shares and Other Equity | 27a.u | 313,812 | 318,664 | 367,924 | 392,549 | 416,145 | 454,651 | 476,657 | 498,331 | 518,166 | 509,400 | 523,897 | 548,306 |
| Other Items (Net) | 27r.u | −15,249 | 26,700 | −2,508 | −129,120 | −248,155 | −244,901 | −210,198 | −377,360 | −389,913 | −344,823 | −338,359 | −336,993 |
| Memorandum Items | | | | | | | | | | | | | |
| Total Assets | 20ra | 4,783,758 | 5,471,901 | 6,172,270 | 7,120,412 | 7,710,573 | 7,656,744 | 7,827,084 | 8,398,744 | 8,075,875 | 7,881,631 | 8,176,956 | 8,150,043 |
| National Residency Criterion | | | | | | | | | | | | | |
| Net Foreign Assets | 21n | 352,890 | 467,563 | 445,414 | 410,609 | 452,012 | 535,974 | 520,305 | 542,251 | 490,620 | 442,908 | 444,330 | 390,618 |
| Claims on Nonresidents | 21 | 1,164,087 | 1,577,276 | 1,812,451 | 2,015,929 | 1,932,482 | 1,882,590 | 1,983,247 | 1,790,698 | 1,671,482 | 1,645,444 | 1,786,648 | 1,747,125 |
| Liabilities to Nonresidents | 26c | 811,197 | 1,109,713 | 1,367,037 | 1,605,320 | 1,480,470 | 1,346,616 | 1,462,942 | 1,248,447 | 1,180,862 | 1,202,536 | 1,342,318 | 1,356,507 |
| Net Claims on Central Government | 22an | 116,654 | 124,195 | 137,584 | 134,339 | 128,056 | 132,897 | 123,313 | 112,295 | 149,975 | 154,070 | 165,867 | 154,732 |
| Claims on Central Government | 22a | 160,591 | 169,380 | 153,614 | 150,685 | 151,434 | 161,158 | 152,012 | 148,877 | 179,814 | 178,644 | 185,674 | 174,028 |
| Liabilities to Central Government | 26d | 43,937 | 45,185 | 16,030 | 16,346 | 23,378 | 28,261 | 28,699 | 36,582 | 29,839 | 24,574 | 19,807 | 19,296 |
| Claims on Other Sectors | 22s | 1,634,491 | 1,741,918 | 2,202,334 | 2,527,322 | 2,723,935 | 2,590,903 | 2,725,368 | 2,855,832 | 2,879,302 | 2,846,396 | 2,949,376 | 2,969,472 |
| Claims on Other Fin. Corps | 22g | 194,490 | 176,711 | 490,994 | 635,982 | 709,130 | 556,039 | 597,993 | 664,465 | 653,098 | 601,726 | 705,300 | 660,185 |
| Claims on State & Local Govts | 22b | 134,690 | 150,084 | 154,781 | 167,807 | 171,974 | 194,566 | 214,862 | 199,001 | 209,655 | 212,029 | 221,671 | 219,076 |
| Claims on Private Sector | 22d | 1,305,311 | 1,415,123 | 1,556,559 | 1,723,533 | 1,842,831 | 1,840,298 | 1,912,513 | 1,992,366 | 2,016,549 | 2,032,641 | 2,022,405 | 2,090,211 |
| Transf.Dep.Included in Broad Money | 24 | 357,103 | 395,266 | 419,076 | 445,771 | 434,367 | 463,103 | 502,062 | 532,456 | 542,700 | 568,758 | 621,659 | 713,190 |
| Other.Dep.Included in Broad Money. | 25 | 741,945 | 776,837 | 842,775 | 931,495 | 1,088,940 | 1,046,468 | 1,029,234 | 1,034,999 | 1,082,785 | 1,054,567 | 1,033,449 | 1,006,355 |
| Sec.Ot.th.Shares Inc.in.Brd. Money | 26a | 46,443 | 66,128 | 81,243 | 142,205 | 120,491 | 51,645 | 104,228 | 110,935 | 88,521 | 49,595 | 65,933 | 57,908 |
| Deposits Excl. from Broad Money | 26b | 306,386 | 307,073 | 297,297 | 277,238 | 260,869 | 362,437 | 376,966 | 483,743 | 483,522 | 499,255 | 456,482 | 495,375 |
| Sec.Ot.th.Shares Excl.f/Brd. Money. | 26s | 351,517 | 401,196 | 457,764 | 518,985 | 553,525 | 582,463 | 596,125 | 656,707 | 687,738 | 663,128 | 678,061 | 687,888 |

# France   132

| | | 2004 | 2005 | 2006 | 2007 | 2008 | 2009 | 2010 | 2011 | 2012 | 2013 | 2014 | 2015 |
|---|---|---|---|---|---|---|---|---|---|---|---|---|---|
| **Depository Corporations** | | colspan... | | | | | *Millions of Euros: End of Period* | | | | | | |
| Euro Area Wide Residency Criterion | | | | | | | | | | | | | |
| Net Foreign Assets | 31n.u | 103,053 | 91,853 | 22,937 | −92,813 | −64,871 | −47,072 | −9,565 | 205,896 | 187,085 | 180,453 | 216,494 | 216,115 |
| Claims on Nonresidents | 31..u | 667,317 | 915,739 | 1,051,122 | 1,146,742 | 1,088,913 | 1,017,694 | 1,159,400 | 1,198,883 | 1,122,337 | 1,100,613 | 1,214,958 | 1,203,483 |
| Liabilities to Nonresidents | 36c.u | 564,264 | 823,886 | 1,028,186 | 1,239,554 | 1,153,784 | 1,064,766 | 1,168,965 | 992,987 | 935,253 | 920,160 | 998,464 | 987,368 |
| Domestic Claims | 32..u | 1,987,171 | 2,183,347 | 2,719,476 | 3,175,122 | 3,379,838 | 3,257,274 | 3,407,108 | 3,384,384 | 3,460,902 | 3,414,164 | 3,526,669 | 3,629,877 |
| Net Claims on Central Government | 32anu | 226,628 | 286,280 | 308,321 | 328,458 | 336,979 | 369,550 | 360,602 | 278,081 | 345,664 | 345,514 | 356,220 | 402,550 |
| Claims on Central Government | 32a.u | 273,294 | 336,666 | 329,030 | 348,231 | 374,667 | 418,468 | 400,522 | 326,697 | 381,385 | 374,713 | 379,984 | 438,463 |
| Liabilities to Central Government | 36d.u | 46,666 | 50,386 | 20,709 | 19,773 | 37,688 | 48,918 | 39,920 | 48,616 | 35,721 | 29,199 | 23,764 | 35,913 |
| Claims on Other Sectors | 32s.u | 1,760,543 | 1,897,067 | 2,411,155 | 2,846,664 | 3,042,859 | 2,887,724 | 3,046,506 | 3,106,303 | 3,115,238 | 3,068,650 | 3,170,449 | 3,227,327 |
| Claims on Other Financial Corps | 32g.u | 246,653 | 245,492 | 591,691 | 818,510 | 870,998 | 711,579 | 779,140 | 792,535 | 766,038 | 700,478 | 814,023 | 806,208 |
| Claims on State & Local Govts | 32b.u | 140,323 | 161,994 | 172,411 | 188,782 | 197,294 | 215,771 | 230,730 | 209,911 | 221,689 | 226,995 | 231,864 | 227,656 |
| Claims on Public Nonfin. Corps. | 32c.u | — | — | — | — | — | — | — | — | — | — | — | — |
| Claims on Private Sector | 32d.u | 1,373,567 | 1,489,581 | 1,647,053 | 1,839,372 | 1,974,567 | 1,960,374 | 2,036,636 | 2,103,857 | 2,127,511 | 2,141,177 | 2,124,562 | 2,193,463 |
| Broad Money Liabilities | 35l.u | 1,235,972 | 1,345,811 | 1,495,847 | 1,727,251 | 1,837,480 | 1,753,919 | 1,869,973 | 1,914,533 | 1,952,390 | 1,964,244 | 2,042,355 | 2,087,080 |
| Currency Outside Depository Corps | 34a.u | 91,425 | 103,557 | 115,227 | 124,049 | 139,340 | 145,492 | 153,016 | 161,298 | 165,415 | 173,234 | 183,033 | 194,408 |
| Transferable Deposits | 34..u | 364,417 | 404,900 | 431,804 | 457,007 | 449,964 | 483,019 | 522,198 | 547,436 | 577,208 | 605,970 | 657,985 | 743,805 |
| Other Deposits | 35..u | 771,802 | 812,177 | 893,026 | 1,013,593 | 1,164,945 | 1,129,871 | 1,134,890 | 1,106,113 | 1,157,112 | 1,126,327 | 1,123,462 | 1,105,617 |
| Securities Other than Shares | 36a.u | 8,328 | 25,177 | 55,790 | 132,602 | 83,231 | −4,463 | 59,869 | 99,686 | 52,655 | 58,713 | 77,875 | 43,250 |
| Deposits Excl. from Broad Money | 36b.u | 310,903 | 313,208 | 308,670 | 295,887 | 285,502 | 390,836 | 412,385 | 519,339 | 523,621 | 545,823 | 516,143 | 581,721 |
| Sec.Oth.th.Shares Excl.f/Brd. Money. | 36s.u | 296,603 | 317,642 | 328,340 | 423,274 | 466,463 | 497,903 | 509,161 | 593,314 | 641,836 | 618,794 | 620,293 | 624,096 |
| Loans | 36l.u | — | — | — | — | — | — | — | — | — | — | — | — |
| Financial Derivatives | 36m.u | — | — | 275,996 | 374,159 | 449,462 | 299,275 | 305,235 | 340,132 | 317,166 | 288,165 | 358,018 | 306,303 |
| Insurance Technical Reserves | 36r.u | — | — | — | — | — | — | — | — | — | — | — | — |
| Shares and Other Equity | 37a.u | 346,761 | 364,319 | 418,623 | 450,189 | 479,559 | 531,000 | 578,722 | 616,295 | 643,225 | 602,124 | 630,521 | 659,180 |
| Other Items (Net) | 37r.u | −100,015 | −65,780 | −82,353 | −185,993 | −198,695 | −256,997 | −273,435 | −387,788 | −422,214 | −418,441 | −424,171 | −412,384 |
| Broad Money Liabs., Seasonally Adj. | 35lub | 1,245,324 | 1,354,647 | 1,503,035 | 1,731,957 | 1,838,924 | 1,753,504 | 1,869,514 | 1,915,428 | 1,955,729 | 1,969,683 | 2,049,770 | 2,095,391 |
| *Memorandum Items* | | | | | | | | | | | | | |
| National Residency Criterion | | | | | | | | | | | | | |
| Net Foreign Assets | 31n | 426,597 | 543,930 | 549,049 | 505,432 | 458,535 | 597,162 | 656,231 | 637,166 | 577,725 | 548,806 | 554,848 | 531,417 |
| Claims on Nonresidents | 31 | 1,246,334 | 1,663,167 | 1,941,250 | 2,200,041 | 2,157,320 | 2,129,504 | 2,282,142 | 2,120,641 | 1,990,255 | 1,909,369 | 2,057,552 | 2,040,170 |
| Liabilities to Nonresidents | 36c | 819,737 | 1,119,237 | 1,392,202 | 1,694,608 | 1,698,785 | 1,532,342 | 1,625,911 | 1,483,475 | 1,412,531 | 1,360,563 | 1,502,704 | 1,508,753 |
| Domestic Claims | 32 | 1,756,788 | 1,872,919 | 2,347,492 | 2,670,962 | 2,853,866 | 2,722,029 | 2,870,186 | 3,002,731 | 3,084,614 | 3,155,287 | 3,155,287 | 3,240,807 |
| Net Claims on Central Government | 32an | 122,039 | 130,771 | 144,464 | 142,961 | 129,311 | 130,505 | 144,150 | 146,222 | 205,024 | 198,121 | 205,618 | 271,056 |
| Claims on Central Government | 32a | 166,271 | 176,276 | 160,729 | 159,615 | 165,725 | 177,770 | 174,336 | 191,742 | 239,746 | 225,961 | 227,867 | 304,225 |
| Liabilities to Central Government | 36d | 44,232 | 45,505 | 16,265 | 16,654 | 36,414 | 47,265 | 30,186 | 45,520 | 34,722 | 27,840 | 22,249 | 33,169 |
| Claims on Other Sectors | 32s | 1,634,749 | 1,742,148 | 2,203,028 | 2,528,001 | 2,724,555 | 2,591,524 | 2,726,036 | 2,856,509 | 2,879,590 | 2,846,684 | 2,949,669 | 2,969,751 |
| Claims on Other Financial Corps | 32g | 194,490 | 176,711 | 490,994 | 635,982 | 709,130 | 556,039 | 597,993 | 664,465 | 653,098 | 601,726 | 705,300 | 660,185 |
| Claims on State & Local Govts | 32b | 134,690 | 150,084 | 154,781 | 167,807 | 171,974 | 194,566 | 214,862 | 199,001 | 209,655 | 212,029 | 221,671 | 219,076 |
| Claims on Private Sector | 32d | 1,305,569 | 1,415,353 | 1,557,253 | 1,724,212 | 1,843,451 | 1,840,919 | 1,913,181 | 1,993,043 | 2,016,837 | 2,032,929 | 2,022,698 | 2,090,490 |
| Transf.Dep.Included in Broad Money | 34 | 357,466 | 396,034 | 419,291 | 445,905 | 434,852 | 464,723 | 502,493 | 532,930 | 543,348 | 569,353 | 622,612 | 715,408 |
| Other Dep.Included in Broad Money. | 35 | 741,945 | 776,837 | 842,775 | 931,495 | 1,088,940 | 1,046,468 | 1,029,234 | 1,034,999 | 1,082,785 | 1,054,561 | 1,033,449 | 1,006,355 |
| Sec.Ot.th.Shares Inc.in.Brd. Money | 36a | 46,443 | 66,128 | 81,243 | 142,205 | 120,491 | 51,645 | 104,228 | 110,935 | 88,521 | 49,595 | 65,933 | 57,908 |
| Deposits Excl. from Broad Money | 36b | 306,386 | 307,073 | 297,297 | 277,238 | 260,869 | 362,437 | 376,966 | 483,743 | 483,522 | 499,255 | 456,482 | 495,375 |
| Sec.Ot.th.Shares Excl./f.Brd. Money | 36s | 351,517 | 401,196 | 457,764 | 518,985 | 553,525 | 582,463 | 596,125 | 656,707 | 687,738 | 663,128 | 678,061 | 687,888 |
| **Interest Rates** | | | | | | | | *Percent Per Annum* | | | | | | |
| Treasury Bill Rate | 60c | 2.02 | 2.07 | 2.89 | 3.86 | 3.62 | .65 | .38 | .69 | .05 | .04 | .06 | −.20 |
| Deposit Rate | | | | | | | | | | | | | |
| Households: Stocks, up to 2 years | 60lhs | 2.52 | 2.49 | 2.85 | 3.69 | 4.31 | 3.49 | 2.83 | 2.78 | 2.90 | 2.94 | 2.76 | 1.88 |
| New Business, up to 1 year | 60lhn | 2.06 | 2.15 | 2.76 | 3.77 | 4.17 | 1.68 | 1.60 | 2.10 | 1.92 | 1.63 | 1.68 | 1.39 |
| Corporations: Stocks, up to 2 years | 60lcs | 2.46 | 2.47 | 3.01 | 3.79 | 4.48 | 2.63 | 1.68 | 2.08 | 2.01 | 1.70 | 1.51 | .88 |
| New Business, up to 1 year | 60lcn | 2.01 | 2.06 | 2.82 | 3.93 | 4.23 | 1.10 | .81 | 1.55 | 1.10 | .66 | .62 | .22 |
| REPOS, Stocks | 60lcr | 2.63 | 2.27 | 2.86 | 3.59 | 3.45 | 1.86 | 1.06 | 1.04 | .46 | .11 | .18 | .13 |
| Lending Rate | | | | | | | | | | | | | |
| Households: Stocks, up to 1 year | 60phs | 8.25 | 8.29 | 8.42 | 8.60 | 8.68 | 8.26 | 7.50 | 7.40 | 6.83 | 6.16 | 5.82 | 5.06 |
| New Bus., Floating & up to 1 year | 60pns | 5.29 | 4.84 | 5.97 | 7.28 | 8.13 | 7.46 | 6.66 | 6.04 | 6.25 | 5.82 | 6.07 | 6.05 |
| House Purch., Stocks,Over 5 years | 60phm | 5.03 | 4.68 | 4.41 | 4.40 | 4.48 | 4.35 | 4.09 | 3.94 | 3.88 | 3.67 | 3.53 | 3.21 |
| House Purch., New Bus., 5-10 yrs | 60phn | 4.04 | 3.58 | 3.73 | 4.31 | 4.81 | 4.25 | 3.37 | 3.43 | 3.44 | 2.84 | 2.60 | 1.93 |
| Corporations: Stocks, up to 1 year | 60pcs | 3.69 | 3.89 | 4.35 | 5.22 | 5.47 | 3.32 | 2.64 | 2.87 | 2.42 | 1.99 | 1.98 | 1.82 |
| New Bus., Over € 1 mil.,up to 1 yr | 60pcn | 2.78 | 2.75 | 3.68 | 4.75 | 5.11 | 2.08 | 1.89 | 2.67 | 2.14 | 1.81 | 1.77 | 1.45 |
| Government Bond Yield | 61 | 4.10 | 3.41 | 3.80 | 4.30 | 4.23 | 3.65 | 3.12 | 3.32 | 2.54 | 2.20 | 1.67 | .84 |
| **Prices, Production, Labor** | | | | | | | | *Index Numbers (2010=100): Period Averages* | | | | | | |
| Share Prices | 62 | 98.3 | 113.8 | 136.4 | 152.9 | 115.8 | 89.2 | 100.0 | 95.9 | 89.4 | 105.4 | 115.7 | 128.9 |
| Share Prices (End of Month) | 62.ep | 99.7 | 116.0 | 139.6 | 155.9 | 116.6 | 90.6 | 100.0 | 98.5 | 90.9 | 107.5 | 118.0 | 131.1 |
| Producer Prices | 63 | 90.1 | † 92.9 | 95.8 | 97.9 | 102.4 | 97.6 | 100.0 | 104.6 | 107.0 | 107.0 | 105.5 | 103.8 |
| Intermediate Indust. Goods | 63a | 89.7 | † 92.3 | 95.7 | 99.6 | 103.1 | 97.3 | † 100.0 | 105.7 | 106.3 | 106.6 | 105.6 | 104.9 |
| Imported Raw Materials | 63b | 61.0 | 68.7 | 86.3 | 91.3 | 89.9 | 74.5 | 100.0 | 108.7 | 112.2 | 105.5 | 106.1 | 110.1 |
| Consumer Prices | 64 | 91.2 | 92.7 | 94.3 | 95.7 | 98.4 | 98.5 | 100.0 | 102.1 | 104.1 | 105.0 | 105.5 | † 105.6 |
| Harmonized CPI | 64h | 90.2 | 91.9 | 93.7 | 95.2 | 98.2 | 98.3 | 100.0 | 102.3 | 104.6 | 105.6 | 106.2 | 106.3 |
| Labor Costs | 65 | 86.3 | 88.7 | 91.2 | 93.6 | † 96.6 | 97.5 | 100.0 | 105.0 | 108.0 | 109.6 | 111.2 | 112.9 |
| Industrial Production | 66 | 111.9 | 111.5 | 112.4 | 113.7 | 110.3 | 95.8 | 100.0 | 102.6 | 100.3 | 99.6 | 98.8 | 100.8 |
| Industrial Employment,Seas. Adj. | 67..c | 115.9 | 113.2 | 111.4 | 110.0 | 107.7 | 102.6 | 100.0 | 99.5 | 98.9 | 97.7 | 96.5 | 95.5 |
| | | | | | | | *Number in Thousands: Period Averages* | | | | | | | |
| Labor Force | 67d | 27,103 | 27,303 | 27,471 | 27,708 | 27,897 | 28,132 | † 28,236 | 28,248 | 28,474 | 28,590 | 29,123 | 29,118 |
| Employment | 67e | 24,808 | 24,984 | 25,150 | 25,587 | 25,926 | 25,674 | † 25,731 | 25,759 | 25,800 | 25,764 | 26,110 | 26,079 |
| Unemployment | 67c | 2,459 | 2,478 | 2,482 | 2,268 | 2,121 | 2,622 | 2,680 | 2,665 | 2,852 | 3,014 | 3,026 | 3,047 |
| Unemployment Rate (%) | 67r | 8.9 | 8.9 | 8.8 | 8.0 | 7.4 | 9.1 | 9.3 | 9.2 | 9.8 | 10.3 | 10.3 | 10.4 |

|  |  | 2004 | 2005 | 2006 | 2007 | 2008 | 2009 | 2010 | 2011 | 2012 | 2013 | 2014 | 2015 |
|---|---|---|---|---|---|---|---|---|---|---|---|---|---|
| **Intl. Transactions & Positions** | | | | | | | *Billions of Euros* | | | | | | |
| Exports............................ | 70 | 339.69 | 356.54 | 390.91 | 401.46 | 412.97 | 341.59 | 390.00 | 420.69 | 434.43 | 428.15 | 427.72 | 445.31 |
| Imports, c.i.f........................... | 71 | 359.86 | 394.29 | 435.31 | 460.26 | 485.61 | 402.07 | 459.21 | 512.35 | 518.87 | 507.10 | 503.61 | 507.91 |
| Imports, f.o.b......................... | 71.v | 351.00 | 384.59 | 424.55 | 450.82 | 475.26 | 391.25 | 442.57 | 496.83 | 507.81 | .... | .... | .... |
| | | | | | | | *2010=100* | | | | | | |
| Volume of Exports.................. | 72 | 91.2 | 94.2 | 101.3 | 103.3 | 103.2 | 89.9 | 100.0 | 103.3 | 105.5 | 104.4 | 95.8 | 100.0 |
| Volume of Imports................. | 73 | 87.8 | 92.8 | 97.6 | 101.2 | 101.3 | 90.8 | 100.0 | 102.0 | 101.0 | 101.4 | 105.6 | 113.5 |
| Unit Value of Exports (2005=100)... | 74 | 100.8 | 100.0 | 99.5 | 99.6 | 97.9 | .... | .... | .... | .... | .... | .... | .... |
| Unit Value of Imports (2005=100)... | 75 | 100.6 | 100.0 | 101.1 | 102.0 | 102.0 | .... | .... | .... | .... | .... | .... | .... |
| Export Price Index.................. | 76 | 94.9 | 96.4 | 97.7 | 99.6 | 102.8 | 97.8 | 100.0 | 104.3 | 105.6 | 105.2 | 114.8 | 114.7 |
| Import Price Index.................. | 76.x | 88.3 | 91.8 | 96.1 | 97.6 | 102.8 | 93.6 | 100.0 | 108.1 | 111.1 | 108.7 | 102.7 | 97.5 |
| **Balance of Payments** | | | | | | | *Billions of US Dollars* | | | | | | |
| A. Current Account*.............. | 109bx | 9.2 | −.1 | .5 | −8.7 | −28.2 | −22.1 | −22.0 | −29.5 | −32.2 | −22.5 | −27.5 | −4.8 |
| Goods, credit (exports)............ | 1a9cx | 416.4 | 439.9 | 484.9 | 544.4 | 603.0 | 470.6 | 507.8 | 586.5 | 561.1 | 582.5 | 584.5 | 510.5 |
| Goods, debit (imports)............ | 1a9dx | 416.3 | 459.1 | 512.1 | 590.3 | 674.4 | 521.3 | 571.3 | 676.8 | 630.8 | 639.6 | 631.1 | 537.5 |
| Balance on goods................ | 1a9bx | .2 | −19.2 | −27.3 | −45.9 | −71.4 | −50.7 | −63.5 | −90.3 | −69.6 | −57.0 | −46.5 | −27.0 |
| Services, credit (exports)........ | 1b9cx | 142.8 | 153.3 | 165.4 | 196.8 | 224.3 | 194.0 | 201.7 | 236.7 | 234.4 | 256.5 | 276.1 | 241.1 |
| Services, debit (imports)........ | 1b9dx | 125.6 | 134.4 | 146.3 | 169.4 | 194.9 | 176.2 | 181.7 | 203.0 | 202.6 | 226.8 | 252.3 | 231.0 |
| Balance on Goods & Services....... | 1z9bx | 17.4 | −.3 | −8.2 | −18.5 | −41.9 | −32.8 | −43.5 | −56.6 | −37.8 | −27.3 | −22.7 | −16.9 |
| Primary income: credit.................. | 1c9cx | 136.8 | 175.3 | 220.0 | 276.1 | 285.0 | 212.3 | 222.1 | 237.8 | 214.2 | 210.3 | 208.5 | 181.8 |
| Primary income: debit................... | 1c9dx | 108.3 | 135.9 | 171.9 | 221.4 | 221.1 | 151.1 | 150.7 | 158.7 | 153.2 | 146.6 | 149.7 | 123.9 |
| Balance on gds, serv. & prim. inc. | 1y9bx | 45.9 | 39.1 | 39.9 | 36.2 | 21.9 | 28.4 | 27.8 | 22.5 | 23.2 | 36.4 | 36.0 | 41.0 |
| Secondary income: credit......... | 1d9ca | 11.0 | 11.2 | 12.7 | 14.9 | 15.9 | 15.7 | 15.3 | 17.1 | 14.7 | 16.0 | 17.6 | 19.0 |
| Secondary income: debit.............. | 1d9da | 47.8 | 50.4 | 52.1 | 59.9 | 66.0 | 66.2 | 65.1 | 69.1 | 70.0 | 74.9 | 81.1 | 64.7 |
| B. Capital Account*................. | 209ba | 2.5 | 1.2 | 1.2 | 3.4 | 2.3 | 3.2 | 1.6 | 1.6 | .7 | 2.6 | 2.9 | 2.3 |
| Capital account: credit................. | 209ca | 3.8 | 2.6 | 2.9 | 3.8 | 2.9 | 3.8 | 2.6 | 3.1 | 2.0 | 3.2 | 3.8 | 2.7 |
| Capital account: debit................. | 209da | 1.3 | 1.5 | 1.7 | .4 | .6 | .6 | .9 | 1.5 | 1.3 | .6 | .8 | .5 |
| Balance on current & capital acct. | 129ba | 11.6 | 1.0 | 1.7 | −5.3 | −25.8 | −18.9 | −20.4 | −27.9 | −31.5 | −19.9 | −24.5 | −2.5 |
| C. Financial Account*  .............. | 309na | 7.5 | −2.1 | −40.8 | 3.0 | −32.7 | −61.7 | −7.0 | −65.1 | −58.0 | −21.2 | −18.2 | −20.9 |
| Direct investment: assets.............. | 3a9aa | 61.1 | 118.9 | 130.4 | 132.2 | 136.0 | 88.6 | 72.6 | 64.5 | 55.9 | 15.6 | 34.8 | 36.7 |
| Equity & investment fund shares.. | 3aaaa | 45.1 | 61.5 | 106.0 | 114.1 | 102.2 | 69.3 | 64.1 | 51.7 | 65.8 | 14.9 | 19.1 | 33.6 |
| Debt instruments...................... | 3abaa | 16.0 | 57.4 | 24.4 | 18.1 | 33.7 | 19.3 | 8.5 | 12.7 | −9.9 | .7 | 15.8 | 3.1 |
| Direct investment: liabilities .......... | 3a9la | 35.6 | 85.2 | 78.9 | 83.8 | 68.0 | 18.4 | 38.9 | 44.2 | 41.5 | 33.6 | 8.0 | 44.2 |
| Equity & investment fund shares . | 3aala | 11.1 | 40.6 | 39.2 | 45.6 | 23.6 | 17.0 | 23.5 | 29.8 | 18.9 | 34.5 | 17.7 | 44.2 |
| Debt instruments...................... | 3abla | 24.5 | 44.6 | 39.7 | 38.2 | 44.4 | 1.3 | 15.4 | 14.4 | 22.6 | −1.0 | −9.7 | −.1 |
| Portfolio investment: assets .......... | 3b9aa | 232.5 | 243.6 | 325.4 | 281.8 | 157.8 | 106.8 | −37.8 | −229.8 | −23.7 | 57.9 | 105.9 | 58.6 |
| Equity & investment fund shares | 3baaa | 60.8 | 54.0 | 72.2 | 40.1 | 57.0 | 43.7 | 18.2 | −53.6 | 52.7 | 44.6 | 15.8 | −.8 |
| Debt securities...................... | 3bbaa | 171.6 | 189.6 | 253.2 | 241.7 | 100.7 | 63.1 | −56.0 | −176.2 | −76.4 | 13.3 | 90.1 | 59.5 |
| Portfolio investment: liabilities....... | 3b9la | 166.3 | 225.2 | 191.2 | 113.3 | 184.8 | 433.8 | 115.8 | 105.1 | 28.9 | 138.8 | 118.8 | 17.0 |
| Equity & investment fund shares . | 3bala | 31.8 | 64.2 | 94.0 | −10.4 | −18.1 | 67.0 | −5.0 | 8.3 | 37.1 | 36.5 | 15.3 | 7.0 |
| Debt securities...................... | 3bbla | 134.5 | 161.1 | 97.2 | 123.7 | 202.9 | 366.8 | 120.9 | 96.8 | −8.2 | 102.3 | 103.5 | 10.0 |
| Fin. der.& empl.stk.ops.(ESOs): net. | 3c9na | −6.2 | −6.5 | −4.2 | −6.8 | 35.1 | −16.2 | −3.5 | −19.6 | −18.5 | −22.4 | −31.4 | 12.2 |
| Fin. der. & ESOs.: assets............ | 3c9aa | 38.8 | 24.9 | 18.2 | −26.8 | −6.2 | −49.7 | −19.2 | 61.5 | −139.2 | −287.3 | 16.2 | 156.0 |
| Fin. der. & ESOs.: liabilities.......... | 3c9la | 45.0 | 31.3 | 22.5 | −20.1 | −41.3 | −33.6 | −15.6 | 81.0 | −120.7 | −265.0 | 47.6 | 143.8 |
| Other investment: assets.............. | 3d9aa | 116.1 | 265.7 | 145.9 | 275.0 | −57.6 | −10.7 | 260.0 | 94.4 | −60.0 | −6.3 | 120.8 | −47.6 |
| Other equity............................ | 3daaa | — | — | — | — | .... | — | .3 | .9 | 8.9 | 11.2 | 4.6 | — |
| Debt instruments...................... | 3dzaa | 116.1 | 265.7 | 145.9 | 275.0 | −57.6 | −10.7 | 259.7 | 93.5 | −68.9 | −17.5 | 116.2 | −47.6 |
| Other investment: liabilities........... | 3d9la | 194.0 | 313.4 | 368.0 | 482.2 | 51.1 | −222.0 | 143.5 | −174.7 | −58.7 | −106.3 | 121.5 | 19.7 |
| Other equity............................ | 3dala | .... | .... | .... | .... | .... | .... | .... | .5 | −.1 | −.1 | −.1 | −.1 |
| Debt instruments...................... | 3dzla | 194.0 | 313.4 | 368.0 | 482.2 | 51.1 | −222.0 | 143.5 | −175.2 | −58.6 | −106.2 | 121.6 | 19.8 |
| Curr.+ cap.− finan. acct. balance... | 4y9na | 4.1 | 3.1 | 42.5 | −8.3 | 6.9 | 42.8 | −13.4 | 37.3 | 26.5 | 1.3 | −6.4 | 18.4 |
| D. Net Errors and Omissions............ | 409na | — | −12.2 | −30.7 | 8.0 | −18.9 | −33.5 | 21.2 | −45.7 | −21.0 | −3.3 | 7.5 | −10.4 |
| E. Reserves and Related Items......... | 4z9na | 4.1 | −9.0 | 11.8 | −.3 | −12.0 | 9.3 | 7.8 | −8.4 | 5.5 | −2.0 | 1.1 | 8.0 |
| Reserve assets...................... | 3e9aa | 4.1 | −9.0 | 11.8 | −.3 | −12.0 | 9.3 | 7.8 | −8.4 | 5.5 | −2.0 | 1.1 | 8.0 |
| Credit and loans from the IMF....... | 3dcla | — | — | — | — | — | — | — | — | — | — | — | — |
| Exceptional financing.................. | 409la | .... | .... | .... | .... | .... | .... | .... | .... | .... | .... | .... | .... |
| *Excludes components in group E | | | | | | | | | | | | | |
| **International Investment Position** | | | | | | | *Billions of US Dollars* | | | | | | |
| Assets.................................. | 809aa | 4,362.6 | 4,640.1 | 5,969.1 | 7,347.8 | 7,351.9 | 7,848.1 | 7,692.5 | 7,719.9 | 8,070.9 | 8,064.4 | 7,862.8 | 7,007.3 |
| Direct investment........................ | 8a9aa | 868.3 | 911.9 | 1,143.2 | 1,382.7 | 1,320.4 | 1,504.8 | 1,557.0 | 1,608.5 | 1,709.9 | 1,764.1 | 1,636.0 | 1,560.4 |
| Equity & investment fund shares.. | 8aaaa | 600.0 | 624.7 | 815.6 | 1,005.0 | 936.1 | 1,090.4 | 1,154.9 | 1,137.4 | 1,249.4 | 1,289.6 | 1,192.8 | 1,147.8 |
| Debt instruments...................... | 8abaa | 268.4 | 287.2 | 327.6 | 377.7 | 384.3 | 414.4 | 402.2 | 471.1 | 460.5 | 474.5 | 443.1 | 412.6 |
| Portfolio investment...................... | 8b9aa | 1,750.7 | 1,873.3 | 2,437.7 | 2,965.0 | 2,605.3 | 2,983.2 | 2,806.2 | 2,413.9 | 2,626.8 | 2,875.1 | 2,749.1 | 2,534.1 |
| Equity & investment fund shares.. | 8baaa | 442.7 | 524.9 | 716.8 | 826.9 | 474.8 | 646.0 | 665.8 | 519.3 | 652.6 | 814.1 | 767.4 | 725.0 |
| Debt securities...................... | 8bbaa | 1,308.1 | 1,348.4 | 1,720.9 | 2,138.1 | 2,130.6 | 2,337.1 | 2,140.4 | 1,894.6 | 1,974.2 | 2,060.9 | 1,981.7 | 1,809.1 |
| Fin. der.(oth.than reserves) & ESOs | 8c9aa | 585.0 | 539.9 | 770.7 | 865.0 | 1,476.1 | 1,334.9 | 1,103.4 | 1,413.1 | 1,425.3 | 1,106.9 | 1,256.0 | 895.6 |
| Other investment........................ | 8d9aa | 1,081.1 | 1,240.7 | 1,519.3 | 2,019.4 | 1,847.2 | 1,892.3 | 2,059.7 | 2,112.5 | 2,124.4 | 2,173.4 | 2,078.3 | 1,879.1 |
| Other equity............................ | 8daaa | 12.2 | 17.4 | 18.2 | 21.9 | 23.8 | 25.3 | 25.1 | 26.0 | 35.2 | 47.8 | 46.2 | 43.4 |
| Debt instruments...................... | 8dzaa | 1,069.0 | 1,223.4 | 1,501.1 | 1,997.4 | 1,823.4 | 1,867.0 | 2,034.6 | 2,086.4 | 2,089.2 | 2,125.6 | 2,032.1 | 1,835.7 |
| Reserve assets........................ | 8e9aa | 77.4 | 74.4 | 98.2 | 115.7 | 102.9 | 133.1 | 166.2 | 171.9 | 184.5 | 144.9 | 143.4 | 138.2 |
| Liabilities.................................. | 809la | 4,434.3 | 4,674.2 | 6,076.6 | 7,587.0 | 7,720.1 | 8,242.8 | 7,919.1 | 7,920.7 | 8,425.9 | 8,574.0 | 8,370.7 | 7,421.7 |
| Direct investment........................ | 8a9la | 653.9 | 644.7 | 813.4 | 996.3 | 949.2 | 1,032.3 | 1,014.8 | 1,055.0 | 1,119.5 | 1,200.3 | 1,086.0 | 1,032.8 |
| Equity & investment fund shares.. | 8aala | 428.1 | 414.8 | 517.2 | 627.2 | 562.0 | 625.4 | 615.8 | 578.7 | 613.6 | 677.8 | 627.0 | 612.7 |
| Debt instruments...................... | 8abla | 225.7 | 229.9 | 296.2 | 369.1 | 387.2 | 406.9 | 399.0 | 476.2 | 505.9 | 522.5 | 459.1 | 420.1 |
| Portfolio investment...................... | 8b9la | 1,988.4 | 2,081.9 | 2,585.3 | 2,926.4 | 2,592.3 | 3,299.0 | 3,234.8 | 3,121.1 | 3,482.3 | 3,891.0 | 3,758.9 | 3,370.2 |
| Equity & investment fund shares.. | 8bala | 593.9 | 690.4 | 990.3 | 1,060.4 | 624.8 | 825.8 | 774.0 | 647.7 | 811.0 | 1,022.7 | 919.5 | 848.2 |
| Debt securities...................... | 8bbla | 1,394.5 | 1,391.4 | 1,594.9 | 1,866.0 | 1,967.5 | 2,473.2 | 2,460.8 | 2,473.4 | 2,671.3 | 2,868.3 | 2,839.4 | 2,522.0 |
| Fin. der.(oth.than reserves) & ESOs | 8c9la | 556.5 | 520.1 | 744.3 | 983.3 | 1,547.1 | 1,438.1 | 1,167.3 | 1,470.7 | 1,484.9 | 1,192.5 | 1,327.7 | 947.0 |
| Other investment........................ | 8d9la | 1,235.6 | 1,427.5 | 1,933.6 | 2,681.1 | 2,631.6 | 2,473.4 | 2,502.3 | 2,273.9 | 2,339.2 | 2,290.2 | 2,198.0 | 2,071.7 |
| Other equity............................ | 8dala | .... | .... | .... | .... | .... | .... | .... | .4 | .3 | .3 | .2 | .1 |
| Debt instruments...................... | 8dzla | 1,235.6 | 1,427.5 | 1,933.6 | 2,681.1 | 2,631.6 | 2,473.4 | 2,502.3 | 2,273.5 | 2,338.9 | 2,289.9 | 2,197.8 | 2,071.6 |

|  |  | 2004 | 2005 | 2006 | 2007 | 2008 | 2009 | 2010 | 2011 | 2012 | 2013 | 2014 | 2015 |
|---|---|---|---|---|---|---|---|---|---|---|---|---|---|
| **Government Finance Operations Statement General Government** | | | | | *Millions of Euros: Fiscal Year Ends December 31; Data Reported through Eurostat* | | | | | | | | |
| Revenue | a1 | 838,870 | 880,900 | 929,437 | 966,674 | 994,077 | 961,731 | 992,228 | 1,046,576 | 1,085,572 | 1,119,879 | 1,141,796 | 1,165,977 |
| Taxes | a11 | 452,610 | 475,907 | 504,129 | 523,831 | 535,644 | 500,792 | 521,522 | 559,236 | 586,046 | 608,611 | 617,840 | 634,522 |
| Social Contributions | a12 | 299,109 | 312,241 | 328,749 | 341,169 | 350,663 | 354,284 | 361,844 | 376,154 | 387,116 | 398,880 | 408,804 | 412,814 |
| Grants | a13 | .... | .... | .... | .... | .... | .... | .... | .... | .... | .... | .... | .... |
| Other Revenue | a14 | .... | .... | .... | .... | .... | .... | .... | .... | .... | .... | .... | .... |
| Expense | a2 | 881,155 | 918,336 | 955,688 | 997,481 | 1,040,407 | 1,080,351 | 1,110,886 | 1,139,159 | 1,173,023 | 1,191,721 | 1,219,199 | 1,240,246 |
| Compensation of Employees | a21 | 219,223 | 226,730 | 232,932 | 240,576 | 246,622 | 254,106 | 259,843 | 263,635 | 268,491 | 273,114 | 278,637 | 281,531 |
| Use of Goods & Services | a22 | 82,782 | 86,706 | 89,091 | 90,925 | 93,061 | 99,057 | 102,492 | 104,161 | 107,285 | 109,755 | 109,675 | 111,230 |
| Consumption of Fixed Capital | a23 | 52,522 | 54,948 | 57,888 | 60,764 | 64,410 | 65,858 | 68,002 | 70,928 | 72,987 | 74,244 | 74,731 | 74,731 |
| Interest | a24 | 45,808 | 46,470 | 46,753 | 50,968 | 56,154 | 46,522 | 47,667 | 53,628 | 53,851 | 48,189 | 46,403 | 44,112 |
| Subsidies | a25 | 24,120 | 24,013 | 25,094 | 26,868 | 29,050 | 34,500 | 36,411 | 34,735 | 36,290 | 36,437 | 47,609 | 55,348 |
| Grants | a26 | .... | .... | .... | .... | .... | .... | .... | .... | .... | .... | .... | .... |
| Social Benefits | a27 | 386,880 | 403,569 | 423,499 | 443,084 | 459,031 | 483,503 | 498,624 | 512,849 | 530,008 | 545,082 | 557,268 | 567,388 |
| Other Expense | a28 | .... | .... | .... | .... | .... | .... | .... | .... | .... | .... | .... | .... |
| Gross Operating Balance [1-2+23] | agob | 10,237 | 17,512 | 31,637 | 29,957 | 18,080 | −52,762 | −50,656 | −21,655 | −14,464 | 2,402 | −2,672 | 462 |
| Net Operating Balance [1-2] | anob | −42,285 | −37,436 | −26,251 | −30,807 | −46,330 | −118,620 | −118,658 | −92,583 | −87,451 | −71,842 | −77,403 | −74,269 |
| Net Acq. of Nonfinancial Assets | a31 | 17,403 | 18,654 | 17,150 | 18,685 | 17,205 | 20,258 | 17,136 | 12,379 | 12,996 | 13,533 | 7,444 | 3,158 |
| Aquisition of Nonfin. Assets | a31.1 | .... | .... | .... | .... | .... | .... | .... | .... | .... | .... | .... | .... |
| Disposal of Nonfin. Assets | a31.2 | .... | .... | .... | .... | .... | .... | .... | .... | .... | .... | .... | .... |
| Net Lending/Borrowing [1-2-31] | anlb | −59,688 | −56,090 | −43,401 | −49,492 | −63,535 | −138,878 | −135,794 | −104,962 | −100,447 | −85,375 | −84,847 | −77,427 |
| Net Acq. of Financial Assets | a32 | −3,630 | 19,980 | −28,877 | 13,710 | 36,400 | 42,104 | −13,364 | 23,303 | 42,669 | 2,730 | 13,117 | 12,550 |
| By instrument | | | | | | | | | | | | | |
| Monetary Gold & SDRs | a3201 | — | — | — | — | — | — | — | — | — | — | — | — |
| Currency & Deposits | a3202 | 4,186 | −1,999 | −30,824 | 896 | 16,665 | 16,289 | −17,935 | 16,576 | −3,915 | −8,919 | −2,550 | 9,914 |
| Securities other than Shares | a3203 | −1,654 | 1,690 | 7,079 | 5,548 | 13,252 | −6,162 | 981 | −4,637 | −7,462 | 2,062 | 6,902 | −2,961 |
| Loans | a3204 | 1,114 | −4,034 | −4,352 | −2,290 | −4,279 | 6,189 | −299 | 5,396 | 25,763 | 7,292 | 346 | −3,450 |
| Shares & Other Equity | a3205 | 6,674 | 9,678 | −10,946 | −487 | 5,489 | 12,492 | −8,146 | −3,984 | 19,937 | −6,756 | −3,633 | 857 |
| Insurance Technical Reserves | a3206 | 130 | 160 | 154 | 236 | 169 | 428 | 163 | −62 | 8 | −59 | 170 | 64 |
| Financial Derivatives | a3207 | — | 211 | −372 | −725 | 2,006 | 987 | 1,720 | 829 | 1,110 | −188 | 544 | 1,047 |
| Other Accounts Receivable | a3208 | −14,081 | 14,272 | 10,383 | 10,530 | 3,095 | 11,879 | 10,151 | 9,184 | 7,230 | 9,296 | 11,337 | 7,080 |
| By debtor | | | | | | | | | | | | | |
| Domestic | a321 | .... | .... | .... | .... | .... | .... | .... | .... | .... | .... | .... | .... |
| Foreign | a322 | .... | .... | .... | .... | .... | .... | .... | .... | .... | .... | .... | .... |
| Net Incurrence of Liabilities | a33 | 55,948 | 72,439 | 17,684 | 67,085 | 104,682 | 180,466 | 120,692 | 127,302 | 141,834 | 86,574 | 98,639 | 88,036 |
| By instrument | | | | | | | | | | | | | |
| Special Drawing Rights (SDRs) | a3301 | — | — | — | — | — | — | — | — | — | — | — | — |
| Currency & Deposits | a3302 | −1,321 | 461 | 5,518 | 2,322 | 3,507 | −2,365 | 2,249 | 6,965 | 4,639 | −1,107 | −744 | 1,052 |
| Securities other than Shares | a3303 | 70,306 | 62,799 | −5,585 | 38,655 | 96,952 | 162,432 | 91,275 | 124,166 | 84,681 | 72,954 | 78,095 | 72,468 |
| Loans | a3304 | −870 | 4,074 | 4,207 | 15,435 | 307 | 18,902 | 16,287 | −9,291 | 35,883 | 10,236 | 11,602 | 1,717 |
| Shares & Other Equity | a3305 | | | | | | | | | | | | |
| Insurance Technical Reserves | a3306 | 12 | 6 | 18 | 26 | −24 | −3 | 10 | 10 | 11 | 2 | 28 | — |
| Financial Derivatives | a3307 | 203 | — | −138 | 311 | 338 | 1,771 | 1,561 | 1,337 | 1,006 | 1,115 | 864 | 172 |
| Other Accounts Payable | a3308 | −12,381 | 5,098 | 13,663 | 10,335 | 3,600 | −272 | 9,310 | 4,115 | 15,614 | 3,376 | 8,796 | 12,626 |
| By creditor | | | | | | | | | | | | | |
| Domestic | a331 | .... | .... | .... | .... | .... | .... | .... | .... | .... | .... | .... | .... |
| Foreign | a332 | .... | .... | .... | .... | .... | .... | .... | .... | .... | .... | .... | .... |
| Stat. Discrepancy [32-33-NLB] | anlbz | 110 | 3,631 | −3,160 | −3,883 | −4,747 | 516 | 1,738 | 963 | 1,282 | 1,531 | −675 | 1,941 |
| Memo Item: Expenditure [2+31] | a2m | 898,558 | 936,990 | 972,838 | 1,016,166 | 1,057,612 | 1,100,609 | 1,128,022 | 1,151,538 | 1,186,019 | 1,205,254 | 1,226,643 | 1,243,404 |
| **Balance Sheet** | | | | | | | | | | | | | |
| Net Worth | a6 | .... | .... | .... | .... | .... | .... | .... | .... | .... | .... | .... | .... |
| Nonfinancial Assets | a61 | .... | .... | .... | .... | .... | .... | .... | .... | .... | .... | .... | .... |
| Financial Assets | a62 | 638,352 | 724,612 | 771,119 | 849,496 | 781,600 | 838,130 | 849,875 | 853,050 | 897,865 | 944,633 | 978,682 | 988,062 |
| By instrument | | | | | | | | | | | | | |
| Monetary Gold & SDRs | a6201 | — | — | — | — | — | — | — | — | — | — | — | — |
| Currency & Deposits | a6202 | 59,884 | 56,396 | 25,467 | 26,525 | 43,188 | 59,662 | 42,200 | 58,794 | 55,108 | 46,520 | 39,771 | 49,538 |
| Securities other than Shares | a6203 | 22,663 | 24,353 | 31,432 | 36,407 | 50,396 | 45,550 | 46,413 | 41,789 | 36,216 | 37,250 | 47,553 | 43,530 |
| Loans | a6204 | 75,881 | 70,220 | 65,871 | 63,780 | 59,539 | 65,233 | 64,962 | 70,923 | 95,699 | 103,271 | 102,862 | 99,454 |
| Shares and Other Equity | a6205 | 304,671 | 383,200 | 448,916 | 510,426 | 412,870 | 438,708 | 455,554 | 428,779 | 451,187 | 485,168 | 507,269 | 506,107 |
| Insurance Technical Reserves | a6206 | 4,504 | 4,664 | 4,818 | 5,054 | 5,223 | 5,651 | 5,814 | 5,752 | 5,760 | 5,701 | 5,870 | 5,934 |
| Financial Derivatives | a6207 | — | 726 | — | — | — | — | 1,061 | 3,292 | 951 | 951 | 951 | 951 |
| Other Accounts Receivable | a6208 | 170,750 | 185,053 | 194,616 | 207,305 | 210,384 | 223,326 | 233,871 | 243,721 | 252,945 | 265,773 | 274,406 | 282,548 |
| By debtor | | | | | | | | | | | | | |
| Domestic | a621 | .... | .... | .... | .... | .... | .... | .... | .... | .... | .... | .... | .... |
| Foreign | a622 | .... | .... | .... | .... | .... | .... | .... | .... | .... | .... | .... | .... |
| Liabilities | a63 | 1,373,500 | 1,450,553 | 1,428,851 | 1,476,198 | 1,632,138 | 1,811,530 | 1,939,784 | 2,078,607 | 2,304,633 | 2,347,700 | 2,575,228 | 2,635,739 |
| By instrument | | | | | | | | | | | | | |
| Special Drawing Rights (SDRs) | a6301 | — | — | — | — | — | — | — | — | — | — | — | — |
| Currency & Deposits | a6302 | 16,636 | 17,096 | 22,976 | 25,296 | 29,456 | 27,091 | 29,132 | 37,305 | 42,339 | 41,228 | 40,358 | 39,330 |
| Securities other than Shares | a6303 | 1,007,414 | 1,075,722 | 1,030,818 | 1,046,799 | 1,193,136 | 1,356,909 | 1,460,139 | 1,594,852 | 1,770,241 | 1,784,079 | 1,991,295 | 2,038,217 |
| Loans | a6304 | 188,034 | 192,127 | 195,049 | 210,719 | 210,865 | 229,781 | 245,862 | 236,119 | 271,259 | 285,649 | 297,510 | 299,164 |
| Shares and Other Equity | a6305 | — | — | — | — | — | — | — | — | — | — | — | — |
| Insurance Technical Reserves | a6306 | 121 | 127 | 145 | 171 | 147 | 144 | 154 | 164 | 175 | 177 | 203 | 203 |
| Financial Derivatives | a6307 | 921 | — | 798 | 1,894 | 1,288 | 812 | — | — | — | — | — | — |
| Other Accounts Payable | a6308 | 160,373 | 165,482 | 179,066 | 191,319 | 197,246 | 196,794 | 204,497 | 210,166 | 220,618 | 236,568 | 245,861 | 258,825 |
| By creditor | | | | | | | | | | | | | |
| Domestic | a631 | .... | .... | .... | .... | .... | .... | .... | .... | .... | .... | .... | .... |
| Foreign | a632 | .... | .... | .... | .... | .... | .... | .... | .... | .... | .... | .... | .... |
| Net Financial Worth [62-63] | a6m2 | −735,148 | −725,941 | −657,732 | −626,702 | −850,538 | −973,400 | −1,089,909 | −1,225,557 | −1,406,768 | −1,403,067 | −1,596,546 | −1,647,677 |
| Memo Item: Debt at Market Value | a6m3 | 1,372,578 | 1,450,554 | 1,428,054 | 1,474,304 | 1,630,850 | 1,810,719 | 1,939,784 | 2,078,606 | 2,304,632 | 2,347,701 | 2,575,227 | 2,635,739 |
| Memo Item: Debt at Face Value | a6m35 | 1,284,953 | 1,356,369 | 1,373,444 | 1,444,433 | 1,555,644 | 1,728,564 | 1,837,241 | 1,964,850 | 2,090,296 | 2,191,107 | 2,286,321 | 2,355,928 |
| Memo Item: Maastricht Debt | a6m36 | 1,124,580 | 1,190,887 | 1,194,378 | 1,253,114 | 1,358,398 | 1,531,770 | 1,632,744 | 1,754,684 | 1,869,678 | 1,954,539 | 2,040,460 | 2,097,103 |
| Memo Item: Debt at Nominal Value | a6m4 | .... | .... | .... | .... | .... | .... | .... | .... | .... | .... | .... | .... |

| National Accounts | | 2004 | 2005 | 2006 | 2007 | 2008 | 2009 | 2010 | 2011 | 2012 | 2013 | 2014 | 2015 |
|---|---|---|---|---|---|---|---|---|---|---|---|---|---|
| | | | | | | | *Billions of Euros:* | | | | | | |
| Househ.Cons.Expend.,incl.NPISHs.... | 96f.c | 935.8 | 976.4 | 1,021.6 | 1,068.3 | 1,102.1 | 1,089.9 | 1,121.8 | 1,147.3 | 1,161.0 | 1,176.0 | 1,185.8 | 1,201.6 |
| Government Consumption Expend... | 91f.c | 390.4 | 405.2 | 418.7 | 433.3 | 447.0 | 463.9 | 476.0 | 486.1 | 497.6 | 507.7 | 515.7 | 521.8 |
| Gross Fixed Capital Formation.......... | 93e.c | 363.3 | 384.1 | 415.2 | 450.8 | 469.7 | 427.4 | 440.2 | 461.0 | 469.5 | 467.4 | 466.2 | 469.1 |
| Changes in Inventories.................... | 93i.c | 8.4 | 11.5 | 14.4 | 19.4 | 10.7 | −14.3 | −4.2 | 16.3 | 3.7 | 5.6 | 16.6 | 18.8 |
| Exports of Goods and Services.......... | 90c.c | 441.3 | 466.4 | 504.3 | 528.6 | 545.4 | 466.8 | 519.0 | 572.2 | 595.7 | 605.4 | 620.4 | 654.8 |
| Imports of Goods and Services (-)..... | 98c.c | 431.0 | 473.6 | 519.9 | 554.0 | 580.5 | 494.4 | 555.5 | 624.2 | 640.7 | 646.4 | 663.3 | 685.1 |
| Gross Domestic Product (GDP)......... | 99b.c | 1,708.2 | 1,769.9 | 1,854.4 | 1,946.5 | 1,994.5 | 1,939.3 | 1,997.3 | 2,058.6 | 2,086.8 | 2,115.8 | 2,141.3 | 2,181.0 |
| Net Primary Income from Abroad..... | 98.nc | 27.4 | 33.1 | 36.2 | 39.7 | 43.9 | 34.4 | 42.0 | 48.2 | 29.7 | 33.9 | 33.2 | .... |
| Gross National Income (GNI)............ | 99a.c | 1,735.6 | 1,803.0 | 1,890.5 | 1,986.2 | 2,038.5 | 1,973.6 | 2,039.3 | 2,106.7 | 2,116.5 | 2,149.7 | 2,174.5 | .... |
| Net Current Transf.from Abroad....... | 98t.c | −24.4 | −26.8 | −28.2 | −29.4 | −30.0 | −33.6 | −32.7 | −32.7 | −34.2 | .... | .... | .... |
| Gross Nat'l Disposable Inc.(GNDI).... | 99i.c | 1,650.4 | 1,716.2 | 1,803.3 | 1,890.9 | 1,935.8 | 1,887.3 | 1,941.4 | 2,004.0 | 2,032.3 | 2,060.5 | .... | .... |
| Gross Saving................................ | 99s.c | 320.9 | 331.7 | 360.3 | 389.4 | 387.0 | 324.4 | 335.5 | 364.2 | 362.7 | .... | .... | .... |
| Consumption of Fixed Capital.......... | 99cfc | 204.0 | 215.1 | 229.9 | 243.0 | 259.5 | 262.9 | 269.7 | 282.8 | 288.5 | .... | .... | .... |
| GDP Volume 2010 Ref., Chained..... | 99b.r | 1,889.8 | 1,920.8 | 1,970.5 | 2,016.1 | 2,017.9 | 1,960.1 | 1,997.1 | 2,038.7 | 2,046.2 | 2,054.1 | 2,062.1 | 2,084.9 |
| GDP Volume (2010=100)................ | 99bvr | 94.6 | 96.2 | 98.7 | 101.0 | 101.0 | 98.1 | 100.0 | 102.1 | 102.5 | 102.9 | 103.3 | 104.4 |
| GDP Deflator (2010=100)............... | 99bir | 90.4 | 92.1 | 94.1 | 96.5 | 98.8 | 98.9 | 100.0 | 101.0 | 102.0 | 103.0 | 103.8 | 104.6 |
| | | .... | .... | .... | .... | .... | .... | .... | .... | .... | .... | .... | .... |
| | | | | | | | *Millions: Midyear Estimates* | | | | | | |
| Population.............................. | 99z | 60.86 | 61.24 | 61.61 | 61.97 | 62.31 | 62.64 | 62.96 | 63.27 | 63.56 | 63.84 | 64.12 | 64.40 |

# Gabon  646

| | | 2004 | 2005 | 2006 | 2007 | 2008 | 2009 | 2010 | 2011 | 2012 | 2013 | 2014 | 2015 |
|---|---|---|---|---|---|---|---|---|---|---|---|---|---|
| **Exchange Rates** | | | | | | *CFA Francs per SDR: End of Period* | | | | | | | |
| Official Rate........................... | aa | 747.90 | 794.73 | 749.30 | 704.15 | 725.98 | 713.83 | 756.02 | 778.32 | 764.10 | 732.49 | 782.77 | 834.92 |
| | | | | | | *CFA Francs per US Dollar: End of Period (ae) Period Average (rf)* | | | | | | | |
| Official Rate........................... | ae | 481.58 | 556.04 | 498.07 | 445.59 | 471.34 | 455.34 | 490.91 | 506.96 | 497.16 | 475.64 | 540.28 | 602.51 |
| Official Rate........................... | rf | 528.28 | 527.47 | 522.89 | 479.27 | 447.81 | 472.19 | 495.28 | 471.87 | 510.53 | 494.04 | 494.41 | 591.45 |
| | | | | | | *Index Numbers (2010=100): Period Averages* | | | | | | | |
| Official Rate........................... | ahx | 93.7 | 93.9 | 94.6 | 103.3 | 110.9 | 105.0 | 100.0 | 104.9 | 96.9 | 100.1 | 100.1 | 83.6 |
| Nominal Effective Exchange Rate..... | nec | 100.7 | 100.2 | 100.2 | 102.4 | 104.3 | 103.5 | 100.0 | 100.3 | 97.8 | 100.7 | 102.0 | 98.9 |
| CPI-Based Real Effect. Ex. Rate........ | rec | 97.7 | 98.7 | 95.2 | 99.7 | 103.1 | 103.9 | 100.0 | 98.6 | 96.5 | 98.2 | 102.8 | 99.4 |
| **Fund Position** | | | | | | *Millions of SDRs: End of Period* | | | | | | | |
| Quota................................... | 2f.s | 154.30 | 154.30 | 154.30 | 154.30 | 154.30 | 154.30 | 154.30 | 154.30 | 154.30 | 154.30 | 154.30 | 154.30 |
| SDR Holdings................................... | 1b.s | 4.03 | .08 | .58 | .42 | .30 | 132.81 | 132.81 | 132.81 | 132.80 | 132.80 | 132.80 | 132.80 |
| Reserve Position in the Fund............ | 1c.s | .18 | .22 | .24 | .35 | .45 | .51 | .54 | .61 | .66 | .69 | .88 | 1.00 |
| Total Fund Cred.&Loans Outstg........ | 2tl | 64.36 | 47.64 | 37.84 | 15.62 | 1.74 | — | — | — | — | — | — | — |
| SDR Allocations........................ | 1bd | 14.09 | 14.09 | 14.09 | 14.09 | 14.09 | 146.72 | 146.72 | 146.72 | 146.72 | 146.72 | 146.72 | 146.72 |
| **International Liquidity** | | | | | | *Millions of US Dollars Unless Otherwise Indicated: End of Period* | | | | | | | |
| Total Reserves minus Gold............... | 1l.d | 443.42 | 668.56 | 1,113.43 | 1,227.24 | 1,923.49 | 1,993.24 | 1,735.88 | 2,157.32 | 2,351.56 | 3,003.57 | 2,478.48 | 1,863.12 |
| SDR Holdings........................... | 1b.d | 6.26 | .12 | .88 | .66 | .47 | 208.20 | 204.53 | 203.89 | 204.11 | 204.52 | 192.40 | 184.02 |
| Reserve Position in the Fund.......... | 1c.d | .28 | .31 | .37 | .55 | .70 | .80 | .83 | .93 | 1.02 | 1.06 | 1.27 | 1.39 |
| Foreign Exchange........................ | 1d.d | 436.88 | 668.13 | 1,112.19 | 1,226.03 | 1,922.33 | 1,784.24 | 1,530.53 | 1,952.49 | 2,146.44 | 2,798.00 | 2,284.81 | 1,677.71 |
| Gold (Million Fine Troy Ounces)........ | 1ad | .013 | .013 | .013 | .013 | .013 | . . . . | . . . . | . . . . | . . . . | . . . . | . . . . | . . . . |
| Gold (National Valuation)............... | 1and | 5.63 | 6.59 | 8.14 | 10.80 | 1.86 | — | 9.64 | 19.62 | 21.61 | . . . . | . . . . | . . . . |
| Central Bank: Other Assets............. | 3..d | — | — | — | — | — | — | — | — | — | — | — | — |
| Central Bank: Other Liabs............... | 4..d | 7.42 | 6.41 | 4.80 | 20.51 | 6.76 | 11.87 | 5.71 | 10.71 | 7.50 | 26.66 | 20.08 | 11.89 |
| Other Depository Corps.: Assets....... | 7a.d | 403.92 | 477.64 | 495.53 | 1,605.32 | 344.45 | 657.51 | 469.08 | 511.87 | 670.85 | 611.60 | 327.09 | 477.66 |
| Other Depository Corps.: Liabs......... | 7b.d | 154.53 | 114.76 | 133.94 | 313.33 | 184.72 | 269.88 | 156.88 | 388.50 | 603.65 | 392.18 | 168.34 | 281.84 |
| **Central Bank** | | | | | | *Billions of CFA Francs: End of Period* | | | | | | | |
| Net Foreign Assets........................... | 11n | 154.01 | 322.79 | 517.32 | 521.60 | 892.45 | 797.46 | 743.17 | 984.00 | 1,064.02 | 1,315.84 | 1,221.75 | 1,001.11 |
| Claims on Nonresidents................ | 11 | 216.26 | 375.41 | 558.62 | 551.66 | 907.12 | 907.59 | 856.90 | 1,103.62 | 1,179.86 | 1,435.99 | 1,347.45 | 1,130.77 |
| Liabilities to Nonresidents............. | 16c | 62.25 | 52.62 | 41.30 | 30.06 | 14.68 | 110.14 | 113.72 | 119.62 | 115.84 | 120.15 | 125.69 | 129.66 |
| Claims on Other Depository Corps.... | 12e | — | — | — | — | — | — | — | — | — | — | 11.50 | 32.56 |
| Net Claims on Central Government.. | 12an | 97.15 | 54.79 | −61.06 | −15.66 | −204.11 | −140.87 | −10.08 | −39.73 | −16.63 | −412.13 | −315.25 | −46.98 |
| Claims on Central Government...... | 12a | 197.18 | 174.08 | 89.92 | 110.41 | .36 | 90.18 | 244.50 | 242.64 | 242.78 | 257.70 | 257.72 | 452.87 |
| Liabilities to Central Government... | 16d | 100.03 | 119.30 | 150.98 | 126.06 | 204.46 | 231.05 | 254.58 | 282.37 | 259.41 | 669.83 | 572.97 | 499.85 |
| Claims on Other Sectors.................. | 12s | — | — | — | — | .66 | .62 | 1.18 | 1.50 | 2.15 | 2.48 | 2.59 | 2.65 |
| Claims on Other Financial Corps.... | 12g | — | — | — | — | — | — | — | — | — | — | — | — |
| Claims on State & Local Govts....... | 12b | — | — | — | — | — | — | — | — | — | — | — | — |
| Claims on Public Nonfin. Corps...... | 12c | — | — | — | — | — | — | — | — | — | — | — | — |
| Claims on Private Sector................ | 12d | — | — | — | — | .66 | .62 | 1.18 | 1.50 | 2.15 | 2.48 | 2.59 | 2.65 |
| Monetary Base........................... | 14 | 264.92 | 382.44 | 461.74 | 515.03 | 701.20 | 674.53 | 743.91 | 950.19 | 993.25 | 899.53 | 891.20 | 980.85 |
| Currency in Circulation................... | 14a | 168.94 | 237.96 | 270.54 | 290.25 | 317.03 | 340.44 | 334.62 | 403.01 | 426.00 | 467.46 | 479.57 | 462.32 |
| Liabs. to Other Depository Corps.... | 14c | 95.59 | 140.34 | 189.42 | 214.52 | 370.93 | 325.68 | 405.92 | 545.01 | 567.24 | 432.05 | 411.62 | 503.57 |
| Liabilities to Other Sectors............. | 14d | .39 | 4.14 | 1.78 | 10.26 | 13.24 | 8.40 | 3.36 | 2.17 | .01 | .01 | .01 | 14.96 |
| Other Liabs. to Other Dep. Corps..... | 14n | — | — | — | — | — | — | — | — | — | — | — | — |
| Dep. & Sec. Excl. f/Monetary Base.... | 14o | — | — | — | — | — | — | — | — | — | — | — | — |
| Deposits Included in Broad Money. | 15 | — | — | — | — | — | — | — | — | — | — | — | — |
| Sec.Ot.th.Shares Incl.in Brd. Money | 16a | — | — | — | — | — | — | — | — | — | — | — | — |
| Deposits Excl. from Broad Money... | 16b | — | — | — | — | — | — | — | — | — | — | — | — |
| Sec.Ot.th.Shares Excl.f/Brd.Money.. | 16s | — | — | — | — | — | — | — | — | — | — | — | — |
| Loans....................................... | 16l | — | — | — | — | — | — | — | — | — | — | — | — |
| Financial Derivatives........................ | 16m | — | — | — | — | — | — | — | — | — | — | — | — |
| Shares and Other Equity................... | 17a | −1.96 | −2.28 | .03 | −3.17 | −10.28 | −11.27 | −10.11 | −5.07 | −2.16 | −.06 | −4.55 | −1.21 |
| Other Items (Net)........................... | 17r | −11.81 | −2.59 | −5.51 | −5.92 | −1.91 | −6.05 | .48 | .66 | 58.45 | 6.72 | 33.94 | 9.71 |
| Memo Item: | | | | | | | | | | | | | |
| Total Assets.................................... | 10ra | 448.47 | 583.74 | 682.98 | 701.98 | 943.12 | 1,033.14 | 1,135.97 | 1,380.71 | 1,456.64 | 1,729.03 | 1,653.88 | 1,656.02 |

|  |  | 2004 | 2005 | 2006 | 2007 | 2008 | 2009 | 2010 | 2011 | 2012 | 2013 | 2014 | 2015 |
|---|---|---|---|---|---|---|---|---|---|---|---|---|---|
| **Other Depository Corporations** |  | *Billions of CFA Francs: End of Period* | | | | | | | | | | | |
| Net Foreign Assets | 21n | 120.10 | 201.77 | 180.09 | 575.70 | 75.29 | 176.51 | 153.26 | 62.54 | 33.41 | 104.36 | 85.77 | 117.99 |
| Claims on Nonresidents | 21 | 194.52 | 265.58 | 246.81 | 715.32 | 162.35 | 299.39 | 230.28 | 259.50 | 333.52 | 290.90 | 176.72 | 287.80 |
| Liabilities to Nonresidents | 26c | 74.42 | 63.81 | 66.71 | 139.62 | 87.06 | 122.89 | 77.01 | 196.96 | 300.11 | 186.54 | 90.95 | 169.81 |
| Claims on Central Bank | 20 | 102.42 | 171.02 | 200.10 | 251.87 | 399.27 | 362.41 | 443.55 | 583.24 | 625.51 | 448.34 | 452.83 | 568.15 |
| Currency | 20a | 20.59 | 22.34 | 27.14 | 27.18 | 44.84 | 45.74 | 46.83 | 51.78 | 68.15 | 55.47 | 69.98 | 64.73 |
| Reserve Deposits and Securities | 20b | 81.83 | 148.68 | 172.96 | 203.62 | 344.43 | 316.66 | 396.72 | 531.46 | 557.36 | 392.87 | 382.85 | 503.42 |
| Other Claims | 20n | — | — | — | 21.06 | 10.00 | — | — | — | — | — | — | — |
| Net Claims on Central Government | 22an | 20.71 | −16.08 | −10.21 | −474.26 | 3.06 | −10.92 | 131.56 | 171.57 | 186.09 | 101.01 | 173.36 | 135.29 |
| Claims on Central Government | 22a | 91.62 | 89.79 | 90.92 | 121.15 | 89.69 | 89.95 | 205.64 | 288.11 | 303.04 | 303.93 | 448.96 | 431.97 |
| Liabilities to Central Government | 26d | 70.91 | 105.87 | 101.12 | 595.41 | 86.63 | 100.87 | 74.08 | 116.54 | 116.95 | 202.92 | 275.61 | 296.68 |
| Claims on Other Sectors | 22s | 411.08 | 448.88 | 536.58 | 628.01 | 621.31 | 600.99 | 622.72 | 849.53 | 1,064.79 | 1,426.29 | 1,381.92 | 1,344.43 |
| Claims on Other Financial Corps | 22g | 14.50 | 13.45 | 17.06 | 32.76 | 19.08 | 25.57 | 27.36 | 23.18 | 35.74 | 37.49 | 34.02 | 67.47 |
| Claims on State & Local Govts | 22b | — | — | — | — | — | — | — | — | — | — | — | — |
| Claims on Public Nonfin. Corps | 22c | 16.69 | 7.80 | 4.10 | 1.94 | 1.38 | 1.15 | 12.69 | 10.23 | 40.40 | 86.58 | 43.43 | 45.23 |
| Claims on Private Sector | 22d | 379.88 | 427.63 | 515.42 | 593.31 | 600.85 | 574.27 | 582.67 | 816.13 | 988.65 | 1,302.22 | 1,304.47 | 1,231.73 |
| Liabilities to Central Bank | 26g | — | 8.23 | 1.72 | — | 10.50 | .45 | .31 | .19 | .10 | — | 11.50 | 43.03 |
| Transf.Dep.Included in Broad Money | 24 | 207.83 | 300.26 | 344.44 | 388.81 | 473.83 | 461.66 | 641.95 | 883.19 | 863.94 | 1,020.13 | 920.59 | 962.32 |
| Other Dep.Included in Broad Money | 25 | 263.29 | 302.36 | 350.55 | 348.57 | 360.91 | 393.41 | 465.07 | 540.01 | 731.99 | 734.55 | 779.39 | 742.23 |
| Sec.Ot.th.Shares Incl.in Brd. Money | 26a | — | — | — | — | — | — | — | — | — | — | — | — |
| Deposits Excl. from Broad Money | 26b | 11.53 | 9.57 | 25.13 | 14.97 | 10.19 | 22.11 | 8.03 | 8.97 | 9.46 | 6.26 | 8.66 | 7.71 |
| Sec.Ot.th.Shares Excl.f/Brd.Money | 26s | — | — | — | — | — | — | — | — | — | — | — | — |
| Loans | 26l | — | — | — | — | — | — | — | — | — | — | — | — |
| Financial Derivatives | 26m | — | — | — | — | — | — | — | — | — | — | — | — |
| Insurance Technical Reserves | 26r | — | — | — | — | — | — | — | — | — | — | — | — |
| Shares and Other Equity | 27a | 152.17 | 168.39 | 173.38 | 208.01 | 221.56 | 238.16 | 221.84 | 213.92 | 222.64 | 258.68 | 254.25 | 250.79 |
| Other Items (Net) | 27r | 19.48 | 16.78 | 11.36 | 20.96 | 21.95 | 13.19 | 13.90 | 20.61 | 81.67 | 60.37 | 119.49 | 159.79 |
| Memo Item: |  |  |  |  |  |  |  |  |  |  |  |  |  |
| Total Assets | 20ra | 900.66 | 1,080.49 | 1,203.24 | 1,842.70 | 1,439.45 | 1,522.04 | 1,666.24 | 2,188.86 | 2,522.06 | 2,806.44 | 2,684.39 | 2,826.78 |
| **Depository Corporations** |  | *Billions of CFA Francs: End of Period* | | | | | | | | | | | |
| Net Foreign Assets | 31n | 274.11 | 524.56 | 697.42 | 1,097.30 | 967.73 | 973.96 | 896.44 | 1,046.54 | 1,097.43 | 1,420.20 | 1,307.52 | 1,119.10 |
| Claims on Nonresidents | 31 | 410.77 | 640.99 | 805.43 | 1,266.98 | 1,069.47 | 1,206.98 | 1,087.17 | 1,363.12 | 1,513.38 | 1,726.89 | 1,524.17 | 1,418.57 |
| Liabilities to Nonresidents | 36c | 136.67 | 116.44 | 108.01 | 169.68 | 101.74 | 233.02 | 190.74 | 316.58 | 415.95 | 306.69 | 216.65 | 299.47 |
| Domestic Claims | 32 | 528.93 | 487.59 | 465.31 | 138.10 | 420.92 | 449.82 | 745.38 | 982.87 | 1,236.39 | 1,117.64 | 1,242.61 | 1,435.39 |
| Net Claims on Central Government | 32an | 117.85 | 38.71 | −71.27 | −489.91 | −201.04 | −151.79 | 121.48 | 131.85 | 169.46 | −311.13 | −141.89 | 88.31 |
| Claims on Central Government | 32a | 288.79 | 263.87 | 180.84 | 231.56 | 90.05 | 180.13 | 450.14 | 530.75 | 545.82 | 561.63 | 706.68 | 884.84 |
| Liabilities to Central Government | 36d | 170.94 | 225.16 | 252.10 | 721.47 | 291.09 | 331.92 | 328.67 | 398.91 | 376.36 | 872.75 | 848.57 | 796.53 |
| Claims on Other Sectors | 32s | 411.08 | 448.88 | 536.58 | 628.01 | 621.97 | 601.61 | 623.91 | 851.03 | 1,066.93 | 1,428.77 | 1,384.51 | 1,347.08 |
| Claims on Other Financial Corps | 32g | 14.50 | 13.45 | 17.06 | 32.76 | 19.08 | 25.57 | 27.36 | 23.18 | 35.74 | 37.49 | 34.02 | 67.47 |
| Claims on State & Local Govts | 32b | — | — | — | — | — | — | — | — | — | — | — | — |
| Claims on Public Nonfin. Corps | 32c | 16.69 | 7.80 | 4.10 | 1.94 | 1.38 | 1.15 | 12.69 | 10.23 | 40.40 | 86.58 | 43.43 | 45.23 |
| Claims on Private Sector | 32d | 379.88 | 427.63 | 515.42 | 593.31 | 601.50 | 574.89 | 583.85 | 817.63 | 990.80 | 1,304.69 | 1,307.06 | 1,234.38 |
| Broad Money Liabilities | 35l | 619.86 | 822.38 | 940.17 | 1,010.71 | 1,120.17 | 1,158.17 | 1,398.17 | 1,776.59 | 1,953.79 | 2,166.69 | 2,109.58 | 2,117.10 |
| Currency Outside Depository Corps | 34a | 148.35 | 215.62 | 243.40 | 263.07 | 272.19 | 294.70 | 287.80 | 351.22 | 357.85 | 411.99 | 409.60 | 397.58 |
| Transferable Deposits | 34 | 208.22 | 304.40 | 346.22 | 399.07 | 487.07 | 470.07 | 645.31 | 885.35 | 863.95 | 1,020.14 | 920.60 | 977.28 |
| Other Deposits | 35 | 263.29 | 302.36 | 350.55 | 348.57 | 360.91 | 393.41 | 465.07 | 540.01 | 731.99 | 734.55 | 779.39 | 742.23 |
| Securities Other than Shares | 36a | — | — | — | — | — | — | — | — | — | — | — | — |
| Deposits Excl. from Broad Money | 36b | 11.53 | 9.57 | 25.13 | 14.97 | 10.19 | 22.11 | 8.03 | 8.97 | 9.46 | 6.26 | 8.66 | 7.71 |
| Sec.Ot.th.Shares Excl.f/Brd.Money | 36s | — | — | — | — | — | — | — | — | — | — | — | — |
| Loans | 36l | — | — | — | — | — | — | — | — | — | — | — | — |
| Financial Derivatives | 36m | — | — | — | — | — | — | — | — | — | — | — | — |
| Insurance Technical Reserves | 36r | — | — | — | — | — | — | — | — | — | — | — | — |
| Shares and Other Equity | 37a | 150.21 | 166.11 | 173.41 | 204.85 | 211.27 | 226.89 | 211.73 | 208.85 | 220.48 | 258.62 | 249.71 | 249.57 |
| Other Items (Net) | 37r | 21.44 | 14.08 | 24.02 | 4.88 | 47.03 | 16.61 | 23.89 | 35.01 | 150.10 | 106.28 | 182.19 | 180.11 |
| Broad Money Liabs., Seasonally Adj. | 35l.b | 621.14 | 823.68 | 940.92 | 1,008.85 | 1,111.22 | 1,141.40 | 1,368.02 | 1,730.52 | 1,899.79 | 2,110.85 | 2,059.94 | 2,069.34 |
| **Monetary Aggregates** |  | *Billions of CFA Francs: End of Period* | | | | | | | | | | | |
| Broad Money | 59m | 619.86 | 822.38 | 940.17 | 1,010.71 | 1,120.17 | 1,158.17 | 1,398.17 | 1,776.59 | 1,953.79 | 2,166.69 | 2,109.58 | 2,117.10 |
| o/w:Currency Issued by Cent.Govt | 59m.a | — | — | — | — | — | — | — | — | — | — | — | — |
| o/w: Dep.in Nonfin. Corporations | 59m.b | — | — | — | — | — | — | — | — | — | — | — | — |
| o/w: Secs. Issued by Central Govt. | 59m.c | — | — | — | — | — | — | — | — | — | — | — | — |
| Money (National Definitions) |  |  |  |  |  |  |  |  |  |  |  |  |  |
| M1 | 59ma | 347.14 | 494.81 | 565.33 | 625.34 | 716.71 | 721.38 | 869.28 | 1,176.82 | 1,221.80 | 1,432.13 | 1,322.70 | 1,356.32 |
| M2 | 59mb | 610.43 | 797.18 | 915.88 | 973.90 | 1,077.61 | 1,114.78 | 1,334.35 | 1,716.84 | 1,891.86 | 2,102.76 | 2,102.09 | 2,098.54 |
| **Interest Rates** |  | *Percent Per Annum* | | | | | | | | | | | |
| Discount Rate (End of Period) | 60.a | 6.00 | 5.50 | 5.25 | 5.25 | 4.75 | 4.25 | 4.00 | 4.00 | 4.00 | 3.25 | 2.95 | 2.45 |
| Deposit Rate | 60l | 5.00 | 4.92 | 4.33 | 4.25 | 3.75 | 3.25 | 3.25 | 3.25 | 3.25 | 3.21 | 2.60 | 2.45 |
| **Prices and Production** |  | *Index Numbers (2010=100): Period Averages* | | | | | | | | | | | |
| Consumer Prices | 64 | † 85.6 | 88.7 | 87.5 | 91.9 | 96.7 | 98.6 | 100.0 | 101.3 | 104.0 | 104.5 | 109.3 | 110.0 |
| Crude Petroleum | 66aa | 109.5 | 120.8 | 119.7 | 118.9 | 117.7 | 96.4 | 100.0 | 114.5 | 147.4 | 143.7 | 145.4 | 151.2 |
| **Intl. Transactions & Positions** |  | *Billions of CFA Francs* | | | | | | | | | | | |
| Exports | 70 | 1,969.2 | 2,671.6 | 2,849.8 | 3,023.7 | 4,256.8 | 2,532.7 | 4,262.0 | 4,605.0 | 3,936.6 | .... | .... | .... |
| Imports, c.i.f. | 71 | 711.8 | 775.9 | 901.9 | 1,033.8 | 1,160.3 | 1,179.2 | 1,475.5 | 1,730.9 | 1,850.5 | .... | .... | .... |

# Gabon 646

| | | 2004 | 2005 | 2006 | 2007 | 2008 | 2009 | 2010 | 2011 | 2012 | 2013 | 2014 | 2015 |
|---|---|---|---|---|---|---|---|---|---|---|---|---|---|
| **Balance of Payments** | | | | | | *Millions of US Dollars* | | | | | | | |
| A. Current Account* | 109bx | 924.5 | 1,983.0 | .... | .... | .... | .... | .... | .... | .... | .... | .... | .... |
| Goods, credit (exports) | 1a9cx | 4,069.2 | 5,456.9 | .... | .... | .... | .... | .... | .... | .... | .... | .... | .... |
| Goods, debit (imports) | 1a9dx | 1,215.6 | 1,358.8 | .... | .... | .... | .... | .... | .... | .... | .... | .... | .... |
| Balance on goods | 1a9bx | 2,853.5 | 4,098.0 | .... | .... | .... | .... | .... | .... | .... | .... | .... | .... |
| Services, credit (exports) | 1b9cx | 154.3 | 145.5 | .... | .... | .... | .... | .... | .... | .... | .... | .... | .... |
| Services, debit (imports) | 1b9dx | 934.7 | 1,034.0 | .... | .... | .... | .... | .... | .... | .... | .... | .... | .... |
| Balance on Goods & Services | 1z9bx | 2,073.1 | 3,209.6 | .... | .... | .... | .... | .... | .... | .... | .... | .... | .... |
| Primary income: credit | 1c9cx | 13.3 | 36.5 | .... | .... | .... | .... | .... | .... | .... | .... | .... | .... |
| Primary income: debit | 1c9dx | 978.1 | 994.1 | .... | .... | .... | .... | .... | .... | .... | .... | .... | .... |
| Balance on gds, serv. & prim. inc. | 1y9bx | 1,108.3 | 2,252.0 | .... | .... | .... | .... | .... | .... | .... | .... | .... | .... |
| Secondary income: credit | 1d9ca | 9.9 | 17.7 | .... | .... | .... | .... | .... | .... | .... | .... | .... | .... |
| Secondary income: debit | 1d9da | 193.7 | 286.7 | .... | .... | .... | .... | .... | .... | .... | .... | .... | .... |
| B. Capital Account* | 209ba | — | — | .... | .... | .... | .... | .... | .... | .... | .... | .... | .... |
| Capital account: credit | 209ca | — | — | .... | .... | .... | .... | .... | .... | .... | .... | .... | .... |
| Capital account: debit | 209da | — | — | .... | .... | .... | .... | .... | .... | .... | .... | .... | .... |
| Balance on current & capital acct. | 129ba | 924.5 | 1,983.0 | .... | .... | .... | .... | .... | .... | .... | .... | .... | .... |
| C. Financial Account* | 309na | 499.2 | 1,342.0 | .... | .... | .... | .... | .... | .... | .... | .... | .... | .... |
| Direct investment: assets | 3a9aa | −30.3 | 159.2 | .... | .... | .... | .... | .... | .... | .... | .... | .... | .... |
| Equity & investment fund shares | 3aaaa | −3.0 | −15.6 | .... | .... | .... | .... | .... | .... | .... | .... | .... | .... |
| Debt instruments | 3abaa | −27.4 | 174.8 | .... | .... | .... | .... | .... | .... | .... | .... | .... | .... |
| Direct investment: liabilities | 3a9la | 314.0 | 326.2 | .... | .... | .... | .... | .... | .... | .... | .... | .... | .... |
| Equity & investment fund shares | 3aala | 318.2 | 320.6 | .... | .... | .... | .... | .... | .... | .... | .... | .... | .... |
| Debt instruments | 3abla | −4.2 | 5.5 | .... | .... | .... | .... | .... | .... | .... | .... | .... | .... |
| Portfolio investment: assets | 3b9aa | 9.4 | −7.6 | .... | .... | .... | .... | .... | .... | .... | .... | .... | .... |
| Equity & investment fund shares | 3baaa | 7.6 | −8.3 | .... | .... | .... | .... | .... | .... | .... | .... | .... | .... |
| Debt securities | 3bbaa | 1.9 | .7 | .... | .... | .... | .... | .... | .... | .... | .... | .... | .... |
| Portfolio investment: liabilities | 3b9la | −1.4 | .7 | .... | .... | .... | .... | .... | .... | .... | .... | .... | .... |
| Equity & investment fund shares | 3bala | .... | .... | .... | .... | .... | .... | .... | .... | .... | .... | .... | .... |
| Debt securities | 3bbla | −1.4 | .7 | .... | .... | .... | .... | .... | .... | .... | .... | .... | .... |
| Fin. der.& empl.stk.ops.(ESOs): net. | 3c9na | .... | .... | .... | .... | .... | .... | .... | .... | .... | .... | .... | .... |
| Fin. der. & ESOs.: assets | 3c9aa | .... | .... | .... | .... | .... | .... | .... | .... | .... | .... | .... | .... |
| Fin. der. & ESOs.: liabilities | 3c9la | .... | .... | .... | .... | .... | .... | .... | .... | .... | .... | .... | .... |
| Other investment: assets | 3d9aa | 511.8 | 1,079.1 | .... | .... | .... | .... | .... | .... | .... | .... | .... | .... |
| Other equity | 3daaa | .... | .... | .... | .... | .... | .... | .... | .... | .... | .... | .... | .... |
| Debt instruments | 3dzaa | 511.8 | 1,079.1 | .... | .... | .... | .... | .... | .... | .... | .... | .... | .... |
| Other investment: liabilities | 3d9la | −320.9 | −438.1 | .... | .... | .... | .... | .... | .... | .... | .... | .... | .... |
| Other equity | 3dala | .... | .... | .... | .... | .... | .... | .... | .... | .... | .... | .... | .... |
| Debt instruments | 3dzla | −320.9 | −438.1 | .... | .... | .... | .... | .... | .... | .... | .... | .... | .... |
| Curr.+ cap.− finan. acct. balance | 4y9na | 425.2 | 641.0 | .... | .... | .... | .... | .... | .... | .... | .... | .... | .... |
| D. Net Errors and Omissions | 409na | −357.0 | −415.1 | .... | .... | .... | .... | .... | .... | .... | .... | .... | .... |
| E. Reserves and Related Items | 4z9na | 68.2 | 225.9 | .... | .... | .... | .... | .... | .... | .... | .... | .... | .... |
| Reserve assets | 3e9aa | 210.9 | 299.5 | .... | .... | .... | .... | .... | .... | .... | .... | .... | .... |
| Credit and loans from the IMF | 3dcla | 37.2 | −24.5 | .... | .... | .... | .... | .... | .... | .... | .... | .... | .... |
| Exceptional financing | 409la | 105.5 | 98.1 | .... | .... | .... | .... | .... | .... | .... | .... | .... | .... |

*Excludes components in group E

| | | 2004 | 2005 | 2006 | 2007 | 2008 | 2009 | 2010 | 2011 | 2012 | 2013 | 2014 | 2015 |
|---|---|---|---|---|---|---|---|---|---|---|---|---|---|
| **National Accounts** | | | | | | *Billions of CFA Francs* | | | | | | | |
| Househ.Cons.Expend.,incl.NPISHs | 96f | 1,455.2 | 1,628.3 | 1,739.6 | 1,844.0 | 1,942.8 | 2,031.1 | .... | .... | .... | .... | .... | .... |
| Government Consumption Expend | 91f | 351.4 | 381.0 | 419.6 | 492.2 | 532.9 | 570.4 | .... | .... | .... | .... | .... | .... |
| Gross Fixed Capital Formation | 93e | 959.2 | 1,021.7 | 1,158.9 | 1,240.9 | 1,405.3 | 1,376.4 | .... | .... | .... | .... | .... | .... |
| Changes in Inventories | 93i | 10.0 | 14.0 | 16.0 | 16.0 | 17.0 | 17.0 | .... | .... | .... | .... | .... | .... |
| Exports of Goods and Services | 90c | 2,233.0 | 2,957.5 | 3,243.9 | 3,472.4 | 4,370.8 | 2,904.2 | .... | .... | .... | .... | .... | .... |
| Imports of Goods and Services (-) | 98c | 1,138.3 | 1,353.6 | 1,460.3 | 1,514.3 | 1,670.6 | 1,390.2 | .... | .... | .... | .... | .... | .... |
| Gross Domestic Product (GDP) | 99b | 3,870.4 | 4,648.8 | 5,117.7 | 5,551.2 | 6,598.2 | 5,509.0 | .... | .... | .... | .... | .... | .... |
| Gross National Income (GNI) | 99a | 3,184.7 | .... | .... | .... | .... | .... | .... | .... | .... | .... | .... | .... |
| | | | | | | *Millions: Midyear Estimates* | | | | | | | |
| Population | 99z | 1.35 | 1.38 | 1.41 | 1.44 | 1.47 | 1.51 | 1.54 | 1.58 | 1.61 | 1.65 | 1.69 | 1.73 |

| | | 2004 | 2005 | 2006 | 2007 | 2008 | 2009 | 2010 | 2011 | 2012 | 2013 | 2014 | 2015 |
|---|---|---|---|---|---|---|---|---|---|---|---|---|---|
| **Exchange Rates** | | | | | | *Dalasis per SDR: End of Period* | | | | | | | |
| Market Rate.................. | aa | 46.084 | 40.212 | 42.194 | 35.618 | 40.882 | 42.235 | 43.720 | 46.427 | 52.132 | 58.381 | 65.602 | .... |
| | | | | | *Dalasis per US Dollar: End of Period (ae) Period Average (rf)* | | | | | | | | |
| Market Rate.................. | ae | 29.674 | 28.135 | 28.047 | 22.539 | 26.542 | 26.941 | 28.389 | 30.240 | 33.920 | 37.910 | 45.280 | .... |
| Market Rate.................. | rf | 30.030 | 28.575 | 28.066 | 24.873 | 22.192 | 26.644 | 28.012 | 29.462 | 32.077 | 35.958 | 41.733 | .... |
| | | | | | *Index Numbers (2010=100): Period Averages* | | | | | | | | |
| Market Rate.................. | ahx | 93.20 | 97.98 | 99.72 | 114.47 | 127.16 | 105.05 | 100.00 | 95.08 | 87.41 | 78.01 | 67.26 | .... |
| Nominal Effective Exchange Rate..... | nec | 99.27 | 103.55 | 104.13 | 112.15 | 120.20 | 105.16 | 100.00 | 91.72 | 88.14 | 79.09 | 69.48 | 66.27 |
| CPI-Based Real Effect. Ex. Rate........ | rec | 93.11 | 98.89 | 98.31 | 107.07 | 113.54 | 103.13 | 100.00 | 92.44 | 90.09 | 83.39 | 76.05 | 75.80 |
| **Fund Position** | | | | | | *Millions of SDRs: End of Period* | | | | | | | |
| Quota.................. | 2f.s | 31.10 | 31.10 | 31.10 | 31.10 | 31.10 | 31.10 | 31.10 | 31.10 | 31.10 | 31.10 | 31.10 | 31.10 |
| SDR Holdings.................. | 1b.s | .48 | .11 | .97 | .15 | .07 | 24.61 | 24.60 | 24.57 | 24.37 | 23.36 | 21.24 | 17.40 |
| Reserve Position in the Fund............ | 1c.s | 1.48 | 1.48 | 1.48 | 1.48 | 1.48 | 1.48 | 1.54 | 1.54 | 1.54 | 1.54 | 1.54 | 1.54 |
| Total Fund Cred.&Loans Outstg....... | 2tl | 15.94 | 14.57 | 11.82 | 4.00 | 8.00 | 18.22 | 20.22 | 22.55 | 31.68 | 32.23 | 30.12 | 34.05 |
| SDR Allocations.................. | 1bd | 5.12 | 5.12 | 5.12 | 5.12 | 5.12 | 29.77 | 29.77 | 29.77 | 29.77 | 29.77 | 29.77 | 29.77 |
| **International Liquidity** | | | | | | *Millions of US Dollars Unless Otherwise Indicated: End of Period* | | | | | | | |
| Total Reserves minus Gold.............. | 1l.d | 83.77 | 98.31 | 120.62 | 142.78 | 116.52 | 224.18 | 201.63 | 223.24 | 236.24 | 210.55 | 159.33 | .... |
| SDR Holdings.................. | 1b.d | .75 | .16 | 1.46 | .23 | .10 | 38.58 | 37.88 | 37.73 | 37.45 | 35.98 | 30.78 | 24.11 |
| Reserve Position in the Fund.......... | 1c.d | 2.31 | 2.12 | 2.23 | 2.35 | 2.29 | 2.33 | 2.37 | 2.37 | 2.37 | 2.37 | 2.23 | 2.14 |
| Foreign Exchange.................. | 1d.d | 80.72 | 96.03 | 116.92 | 140.20 | 114.13 | 183.26 | 161.37 | 183.15 | 196.42 | 172.20 | 126.32 | .... |
| Gold (Million Fine Troy Ounces)........ | 1ad | .... | .... | .... | .... | .... | .... | .... | .... | .... | .... | .... | .... |
| Gold (National Valuation)............... | 1and | .... | .... | .... | .... | .... | .... | .... | .... | .... | .... | .... | .... |
| Central Bank: Other Assets.............. | 3..d | 4.91 | 5.03 | 6.79 | 8.35 | 7.21 | 7.70 | 5.73 | 12.73 | 11.34 | 9.20 | 7.69 | .... |
| Central Bank: Other Liabs.............. | 4..d | .62 | .65 | .65 | 1.21 | 1.97 | 2.19 | .99 | 1.30 | 1.76 | .07 | 3.61 | .... |
| Other Depository Corps.: Assets.......... | 7a.d | 50.79 | 39.31 | 48.37 | 64.73 | 49.03 | 54.53 | 65.02 | 64.59 | 80.58 | 77.90 | 91.47 | .... |
| Other Depository Corps.: Liabs.......... | 7b.d | 4.42 | 4.73 | 6.59 | 26.78 | 25.33 | 50.54 | 24.87 | 23.36 | 46.29 | 45.88 | 42.70 | .... |
| **Central Bank** | | | | | | *Millions of Dalasis: End of Period* | | | | | | | |
| Net Foreign Assets.................. | 11n | 1,479.75 | 1,938.90 | 2,605.67 | 2,859.88 | 2,457.49 | 2,916.65 | 2,430.51 | 3,061.74 | 3,390.19 | 2,836.05 | 1,325.60 | .... |
| Claims on Nonresidents.............. | 11 | 2,468.80 | 2,749.02 | 3,338.85 | 3,212.09 | 3,046.12 | 4,999.34 | 4,644.82 | 5,526.76 | 6,651.10 | 6,457.27 | 5,419.81 | .... |
| Liabilities to Nonresidents.............. | 16c | 989.06 | 810.11 | 733.18 | 352.21 | 588.64 | 2,082.70 | 2,214.30 | 2,465.02 | 3,260.91 | 3,621.22 | 4,094.22 | .... |
| Claims on Other Depository Corps.... | 12e | 33.62 | 33.62 | 33.62 | 33.62 | 33.62 | — | — | — | — | — | 300.00 | .... |
| Net Claims on Central Government.. | 12an | 178.53 | −262.40 | −413.62 | −1,157.12 | −428.60 | −589.60 | 520.50 | 525.40 | 527.50 | 2,517.80 | 4,386.20 | .... |
| Claims on Central Government....... | 12a | 1,167.53 | 1,140.63 | 560.73 | 519.15 | 479.31 | 334.70 | 2,283.50 | 2,308.90 | 2,477.50 | 4,489.80 | 6,794.80 | .... |
| Liabilities to Central Government... | 16d | 989.00 | 1,403.03 | 974.36 | 1,676.27 | 907.91 | 924.30 | 1,763.00 | 1,783.50 | 1,950.00 | 1,972.00 | 2,408.60 | .... |
| Claims on Other Sectors.................. | 12s | 28.93 | 30.95 | 30.77 | 38.65 | 59.91 | 57.80 | 68.10 | 76.60 | 109.80 | 114.50 | 146.00 | .... |
| Claims on Other Financial Corps.... | 12g | −.01 | −.01 | −.01 | .24 | 11.55 | 12.20 | 21.30 | 11.80 | 12.90 | 13.80 | 14.60 | .... |
| Claims on State & Local Govts....... | 12b | — | — | — | — | — | — | — | → | — | — | — | .... |
| Claims on Public Nonfin. Corps...... | 12c | — | — | — | — | — | — | — | — | — | — | — | .... |
| Claims on Private Sector.............. | 12d | 28.93 | 30.96 | 30.78 | 38.41 | 48.36 | 45.60 | 46.80 | 64.80 | 96.90 | 100.70 | 131.40 | .... |
| Monetary Base.................. | 14 | 2,379.00 | 2,306.59 | 2,866.47 | 2,744.55 | 2,902.14 | 3,171.40 | 3,503.30 | 3,933.00 | 4,202.90 | 5,382.60 | 6,021.30 | .... |
| Currency in Circulation.................. | 14a | 1,703.32 | 1,537.55 | 2,087.17 | 1,893.50 | 2,050.17 | 2,216.70 | 2,436.40 | 2,700.50 | 3,183.80 | 3,635.50 | 3,908.60 | .... |
| Liabs. to Other Depository Corps.... | 14c | 675.67 | 769.04 | 779.30 | 851.04 | 851.97 | 954.70 | 1,066.90 | 1,232.50 | 1,019.10 | 1,747.10 | 2,112.70 | .... |
| Liabilities to Other Sectors............. | 14d | — | — | — | — | — | — | — | — | — | — | — | .... |
| Other Liabs. to Other Dep. Corps..... | 14n | — | — | — | — | — | — | — | 9.90 | 14.70 | 26.20 | 29.70 | .... |
| Dep. & Sec. Excl. f/Monetary Base.... | 14o | .17 | .36 | .93 | 25.40 | 4.19 | 4.50 | 4.90 | 5.70 | 9.30 | 12.40 | 16.90 | .... |
| Deposits Included in Broad Money. | 15 | .04 | .15 | .32 | 22.86 | .45 | .40 | .50 | .60 | .70 | .30 | .20 | .... |
| Sec.Ot.th.Shares Incl.in Brd. Money | 16a | — | — | — | — | — | — | — | — | — | — | — | .... |
| Deposits Excl. from Broad Money... | 16b | .13 | .20 | .61 | 2.54 | 3.73 | 4.10 | 4.40 | 5.10 | 8.60 | 12.10 | 16.70 | .... |
| Sec.Ot.th.Shares Excl.f/Brd.Money.. | 16s | — | — | — | — | — | — | — | — | — | — | — | .... |
| Loans.................. | 16l | — | — | — | — | — | — | — | — | — | — | — | .... |
| Financial Derivatives.................. | 16m | — | — | — | — | — | — | — | — | — | — | — | .... |
| Shares and Other Equity.................. | 17a | −547.00 | −525.56 | −361.26 | −837.07 | −476.80 | −222.10 | 143.20 | 241.80 | 500.90 | 893.10 | 1,027.60 | .... |
| Other Items (Net).......................... | 17r | −111.34 | −40.31 | −249.69 | −157.84 | −307.10 | −569.25 | −632.49 | −526.56 | −700.31 | −846.05 | −937.50 | .... |
| Memo Item: | | | | | | | | | | | | | |
| Total Assets.................. | 10ra | 4,906.31 | 5,641.61 | 5,728.26 | 5,557.90 | 5,124.52 | 7,168.60 | 8,837.60 | 9,855.80 | 11,085.10 | 13,305.70 | 15,234.40 | .... |

|  |  | 2004 | 2005 | 2006 | 2007 | 2008 | 2009 | 2010 | 2011 | 2012 | 2013 | 2014 | 2015 |
|---|---|---|---|---|---|---|---|---|---|---|---|---|---|
| **Other Depository Corporations** | | | | | | *Millions of Dalasis: End of Period* | | | | | | | |
| Net Foreign Assets | 21n | 1,375.99 | 972.64 | 1,171.90 | 855.43 | 629.14 | 107.50 | 1,139.99 | 1,246.88 | 1,163.09 | 1,213.94 | 2,209.30 | .... |
| Claims on Nonresidents | 21 | 1,507.24 | 1,105.85 | 1,356.62 | 1,458.97 | 1,301.41 | 1,469.09 | 1,845.95 | 1,953.19 | 2,733.32 | 2,953.31 | 4,143.50 | .... |
| Liabilities to Nonresidents | 26c | 131.25 | 133.20 | 184.73 | 603.54 | 672.27 | 1,361.60 | 705.96 | 706.31 | 1,570.23 | 1,739.36 | 1,934.20 | .... |
| Claims on Central Bank | 20 | 744.97 | 882.39 | 927.50 | 1,055.33 | 1,069.23 | 1,166.62 | 1,438.69 | 1,556.68 | 1,384.36 | 2,127.39 | 2,513.30 | .... |
| Currency | 20a | 69.30 | 113.35 | 148.20 | 204.29 | 217.26 | 211.91 | 371.77 | 324.16 | 365.22 | 380.28 | 400.60 | .... |
| Reserve Deposits and Securities | 20b | 675.67 | 769.04 | 779.30 | 851.04 | 851.97 | 954.71 | 1,066.93 | 1,232.52 | 1,019.14 | 1,747.11 | 2,112.70 | .... |
| Other Claims | 20n | — | — | — | — | — | — | — | — | — | — | — | .... |
| Net Claims on Central Government.. | 22an | 1,289.84 | 1,912.04 | 2,450.08 | 2,804.55 | 3,089.45 | 3,836.27 | 4,873.43 | 5,929.95 | 7,031.08 | 7,781.16 | 9,410.10 | .... |
| Claims on Central Government | 22a | 1,289.84 | 1,912.04 | 2,450.08 | 2,804.55 | 3,089.45 | 3,836.27 | 4,873.43 | 5,929.95 | 7,031.08 | 7,781.16 | 9,410.10 | .... |
| Liabilities to Central Government... | 26d | — | — | — | — | — | — | — | — | — | — | — | .... |
| Claims on Other Sectors | 22s | 1,511.23 | 1,810.51 | 2,233.75 | 2,455.99 | 3,303.99 | 4,176.07 | 4,926.63 | 5,068.92 | 5,243.11 | 5,643.40 | 5,120.50 | .... |
| Claims on Other Financial Corps... | 22g | — | — | — | — | — | — | — | — | — | — | — | .... |
| Claims on State & Local Govts | 22b | — | — | — | — | — | — | — | — | — | — | — | .... |
| Claims on Public Nonfin. Corps | 22c | 86.46 | 122.85 | 130.63 | 91.66 | 325.66 | 679.92 | 870.37 | 811.28 | 764.92 | 807.13 | 720.70 | .... |
| Claims on Private Sector | 22d | 1,424.78 | 1,687.67 | 2,103.12 | 2,364.33 | 2,978.33 | 3,496.15 | 4,056.26 | 4,257.64 | 4,478.18 | 4,836.26 | 4,399.80 | .... |
| Liabilities to Central Bank | 26g | — | — | — | — | — | — | 40.00 | — | — | — | — | .... |
| Transf.Dep.Included in Broad Money | 24 | 1,674.97 | 1,857.68 | 2,187.81 | 2,491.30 | 3,247.17 | 3,151.04 | 3,915.51 | 4,250.58 | 4,523.76 | 6,128.13 | 6,736.00 | .... |
| Other Dep.Included in Broad Money. | 25 | 2,288.69 | 2,766.30 | 3,532.84 | 3,975.79 | 4,583.63 | 5,940.76 | 7,096.12 | 7,913.64 | 8,254.87 | 8,493.36 | 9,242.50 | .... |
| Sec.Ot.th.Shares Incl.in Brd. Money.. | 26a | — | — | — | — | — | — | — | — | — | — | — | .... |
| Deposits Excl. from Broad Money..... | 26b | — | — | — | — | — | — | — | — | — | — | — | .... |
| Sec.Ot.th.Shares Excl.f/Brd.Money.... | 26s | — | — | — | — | — | — | — | — | — | — | — | .... |
| Loans | 26l | 1.30 | 1.30 | — | — | — | — | — | — | — | — | — | .... |
| Financial Derivatives | 26m | — | — | — | — | — | — | — | — | — | — | — | .... |
| Insurance Technical Reserves | 26r | — | — | — | — | — | — | — | — | — | — | — | .... |
| Shares and Other Equity | 27a | 652.55 | 904.39 | 1,066.75 | 1,219.20 | 1,447.99 | 1,586.09 | 2,580.43 | 2,657.90 | 3,064.63 | 3,025.97 | 3,897.00 | .... |
| Other Items (Net) | 27r | 304.53 | 47.92 | −4.18 | −514.99 | −1,186.98 | −1,391.44 | −1,253.31 | −1,019.69 | −1,021.61 | −881.57 | −622.30 | .... |
| Memo Item: | | | | | | | | | | | | | |
| Total Assets | 20ra | 6,593.18 | 7,667.69 | 9,213.47 | 10,427.70 | 12,468.25 | 14,805.60 | 17,806.84 | 18,655.01 | 20,618.91 | 23,775.62 | 28,208.40 | .... |
| **Depository Corporations** | | | | | | *Millions of Dalasis: End of Period* | | | | | | | |
| Net Foreign Assets | 31n | 2,855.74 | 2,911.55 | 3,777.57 | 3,715.32 | 3,086.63 | 3,024.14 | 3,570.51 | 4,308.63 | 4,553.28 | 4,049.99 | 3,534.90 | .... |
| Claims on Nonresidents | 31 | 3,976.04 | 3,854.86 | 4,695.47 | 4,671.06 | 4,347.53 | 6,468.44 | 6,490.77 | 7,479.95 | 9,384.41 | 9,410.58 | 9,563.31 | .... |
| Liabilities to Nonresidents | 36c | 1,120.31 | 943.31 | 917.91 | 955.74 | 1,260.90 | 3,444.29 | 2,920.26 | 3,171.32 | 4,831.14 | 5,360.59 | 6,028.42 | .... |
| Domestic Claims | 32 | 3,008.53 | 3,491.10 | 4,300.98 | 4,142.07 | 6,024.75 | 7,480.53 | 10,388.66 | 11,600.87 | 12,911.49 | 16,056.86 | 19,062.80 | .... |
| Net Claims on Central Government | 32an | 1,468.37 | 1,649.63 | 2,036.46 | 1,647.43 | 2,660.84 | 3,246.67 | 5,393.93 | 6,455.35 | 7,558.58 | 10,298.96 | 13,796.30 | .... |
| Claims on Central Government.... | 32a | 2,457.37 | 3,052.66 | 3,010.81 | 3,323.70 | 3,568.76 | 4,170.97 | 7,156.93 | 8,238.85 | 9,508.58 | 12,270.96 | 16,204.90 | .... |
| Liabilities to Central Government. | 36d | 989.00 | 1,403.03 | 974.36 | 1,676.27 | 907.91 | 924.30 | 1,763.00 | 1,783.50 | 1,950.00 | 1,972.00 | 2,408.60 | .... |
| Claims on Other Sectors | 32s | 1,540.16 | 1,841.47 | 2,264.53 | 2,494.64 | 3,363.90 | 4,233.87 | 4,994.73 | 5,145.52 | 5,352.91 | 5,757.90 | 5,266.50 | .... |
| Claims on Other Financial Corps.. | 32g | −.01 | −.01 | −.01 | .24 | 11.55 | 12.20 | 21.30 | 11.80 | 12.90 | 13.80 | 14.60 | .... |
| Claims on State & Local Govts..... | 32b | — | — | — | — | — | — | — | — | — | — | — | .... |
| Claims on Public Nonfin. Corps.... | 32c | 86.46 | 122.85 | 130.63 | 91.66 | 325.66 | 679.92 | 870.37 | 811.28 | 764.92 | 807.13 | 720.70 | .... |
| Claims on Private Sector | 32d | 1,453.71 | 1,718.63 | 2,133.90 | 2,402.74 | 3,026.69 | 3,541.75 | 4,103.06 | 4,322.44 | 4,575.08 | 4,936.96 | 4,531.20 | .... |
| Broad Money Liabilities | 35l | 5,597.73 | 6,048.33 | 7,659.95 | 8,179.16 | 9,664.16 | 11,096.99 | 13,076.76 | 14,541.16 | 15,597.90 | 17,877.01 | 19,486.70 | .... |
| Currency Outside Depository Corps | 34a | 1,634.02 | 1,424.20 | 1,938.97 | 1,689.21 | 1,832.91 | 2,004.79 | 2,064.63 | 2,376.34 | 2,818.58 | 3,255.22 | 3,508.00 | .... |
| Transferable Deposits | 34 | 1,675.02 | 1,857.84 | 2,188.14 | 2,514.16 | 3,247.62 | 3,151.44 | 3,916.01 | 4,251.18 | 4,524.46 | 6,128.43 | 6,736.20 | .... |
| Other Deposits | 35 | 2,288.69 | 2,766.30 | 3,532.84 | 3,975.79 | 4,583.63 | 5,940.76 | 7,096.12 | 7,913.64 | 8,254.87 | 8,493.36 | 9,242.50 | .... |
| Securities Other than Shares | 36a | — | — | — | — | — | — | — | — | — | — | — | .... |
| Deposits Excl. from Broad Money..... | 36b | .13 | .20 | .61 | 2.54 | 3.73 | 4.10 | 4.40 | 5.10 | 8.60 | 12.10 | 16.70 | .... |
| Sec.Ot.th.Shares Excl.f/Brd.Money.... | 36s | — | — | — | — | — | — | — | — | — | — | — | .... |
| Loans | 36l | 1.30 | 1.30 | — | — | — | — | — | — | — | — | — | .... |
| Financial Derivatives | 36m | — | — | — | — | — | — | — | — | — | — | — | .... |
| Insurance Technical Reserves | 36r | — | — | — | — | — | — | — | — | — | — | — | .... |
| Shares and Other Equity | 37a | 105.55 | 378.83 | 705.49 | 382.13 | 971.18 | 1,363.99 | 2,723.63 | 2,899.70 | 3,565.53 | 3,919.07 | 4,924.60 | .... |
| Other Items (Net) | 37r | 159.56 | −26.02 | −287.50 | −706.45 | −1,527.70 | −1,960.70 | −1,845.83 | −1,536.37 | −1,707.26 | −1,701.43 | −1,830.10 | .... |
| Broad Money Liabs., Seasonally Adj. | 35l.b | 5,392.20 | 5,829.68 | 7,393.61 | 7,912.87 | 9,380.32 | 10,817.73 | 12,798.58 | 14,281.93 | 15,342.30 | 17,601.17 | 19,155.03 | .... |
| **Monetary Aggregates** | | | | | | *Millions of Dalasis: End of Period* | | | | | | | |
| Broad Money | 59m | 5,597.73 | 6,048.33 | 7,659.95 | 8,179.16 | 9,664.16 | 11,096.99 | 13,076.76 | 14,541.16 | 15,597.90 | 17,877.01 | 19,486.70 | |
| o/w:Currency Issued by Cent.Govt | 59m.a | — | — | — | — | — | — | — | — | — | — | — | |
| o/w: Dep.in Nonfin. Corporations. | 59m.b | — | — | — | — | — | — | — | — | — | — | — | |
| o/w: Secs. Issued by Central Govt. | 59m.c | — | — | — | — | — | — | — | — | — | — | — | |
| Money (National Definitions) | | | | | | | | | | | | | |
| M0 (Reserve Money) | 19ma | 2,379.00 | 2,306.59 | 2,866.47 | 2,744.55 | 2,902.14 | 3,171.40 | 3,503.30 | 3,933.00 | 4,202.90 | 5,382.60 | 6,021.30 | .... |
| M1 (Narrow Money) | 59ma | 3,107.61 | 3,320.61 | 4,185.40 | 4,208.52 | 5,119.60 | 5,599.77 | 6,021.96 | 6,666.82 | 7,395.77 | 9,518.38 | 10,482.49 | .... |
| Quasi-Money | 59mal | 2,324.35 | 2,824.59 | 3,572.22 | 4,065.39 | 4,676.76 | 6,095.22 | 7,270.26 | 8,086.58 | 8,506.18 | 8,790.64 | 9,882.12 | .... |
| M2 (Broad Money) | 59mb | 5,431.96 | 6,145.20 | 7,757.62 | 8,273.90 | 9,796.37 | 11,694.99 | 13,292.22 | 14,753.40 | 15,901.95 | 18,309.02 | 20,364.61 | .... |
| **Interest Rates** | | | | | | *Percent Per Annum* | | | | | | | |
| Central Bank Policy Rate (EOP) | 60 | 33.00 | 19.00 | 14.00 | 15.00 | 16.00 | 14.00 | 15.00 | 14.00 | 12.00 | 20.00 | 22.00 | 23.00 |
| Discount Rate (End of Period) | 60.a | .... | .... | .... | .... | .... | .... | .... | .... | 10.95 | 18.54 | 19.08 | .... |
| Treasury Bill Rate | 60c | 30.75 | 22.50 | 14.14 | 13.46 | 13.32 | 14.33 | 13.16 | 11.81 | 12.46 | | | .... |
| Savings Rate | 60k | 17.00 | 14.17 | 8.75 | 7.00 | 7.00 | 7.25 | 8.00 | 8.00 | 8.00 | 8.00 | 7.33 | .... |
| Deposit Rate | 60l | 22.00 | 17.33 | 12.67 | 12.89 | 12.87 | 15.50 | 14.63 | 11.75 | 11.50 | 13.44 | 16.51 | .... |
| Lending Rate | 60p | 36.50 | 34.92 | 29.75 | 27.92 | 27.00 | 27.00 | 27.00 | 28.00 | 28.00 | 28.00 | 28.50 | .... |
| **Prices** | | | | | | *Index Numbers (2010=100): Period Averages* | | | | | | | |
| Consumer Prices | 64 | 77.3 | † 81.1 | 82.7 | 87.2 | 91.0 | 95.2 | 100.0 | 104.8 | 109.3 | 115.5 | 122.4 | |
| **Intl. Transactions & Positions** | | | | | | *Millions of Dalasis* | | | | | | | |
| Exports | 70 | 300.4 | 228.6 | 321.7 | 311.4 | 303.4 | 399.7 | 420.2 | 334.3 | 587.5 | 296.4 | .... | .... |
| Imports, c.i.f | 71 | 6,872.9 | 7,417.6 | 7,277.1 | 7,983.5 | 7,150.6 | 8,098.3 | 8,403.6 | 9,899.3 | 12,158.5 | 12,549.1 | .... | .... |

# Gambia, The   648

| Balance of Payments | | 2004 | 2005 | 2006 | 2007 | 2008 | 2009 | 2010 | 2011 | 2012 | 2013 | 2014 | 2015 |
|---|---|---|---|---|---|---|---|---|---|---|---|---|---|
| | | | | | | *Millions of US Dollars* | | | | | | | |
| A. Current Account* | 109bx | −43.5 | −50.5 | −72.3 | −65.7 | 2.9 | 29.2 | 21.1 | 47.3 | −15.4 | .... | .... | .... |
| Goods, credit (exports) | 1a9cx | 106.8 | 104.3 | 108.9 | 134.3 | 205.5 | 174.2 | 139.9 | 162.1 | 182.5 | .... | .... | .... |
| Goods, debit (imports) | 1a9dx | 202.8 | 222.6 | 222.2 | 279.6 | 274.6 | 260.0 | 245.8 | 295.6 | 358.8 | .... | .... | .... |
| Balance on goods | 1a9bx | −96.0 | −118.3 | −113.4 | −145.2 | −69.1 | −85.8 | −105.8 | −133.5 | −176.4 | .... | .... | .... |
| Services, credit (exports) | 1b9cx | 71.6 | 82.2 | 92.1 | 127.9 | 117.6 | 104.2 | 130.6 | 143.7 | 151.5 | .... | .... | .... |
| Services, debit (imports) | 1b9dx | 44.7 | 46.9 | 94.1 | 86.8 | 85.6 | 82.6 | 73.2 | 68.4 | 80.3 | .... | .... | .... |
| Balance on Goods & Services | 1z9bx | −69.1 | −83.0 | −115.3 | −104.0 | −37.1 | −64.1 | −48.4 | −58.1 | −105.2 | .... | .... | .... |
| Primary income: credit | 1c9cx | 1.7 | 3.2 | 4.5 | 9.0 | 12.7 | 11.7 | 14.3 | 13.0 | 9.8 | .... | .... | .... |
| Primary income: debit | 1c9dx | 28.9 | 35.6 | 42.4 | 53.5 | 47.2 | 19.8 | 22.4 | 28.8 | 28.5 | .... | .... | .... |
| Balance on gds, serv. & prim. inc. | 1y9bx | −96.3 | −115.3 | −153.2 | −148.6 | −71.6 | −72.2 | −56.4 | −73.9 | −123.8 | .... | .... | .... |
| Secondary income: credit | 1d9ca | 76.5 | 90.9 | 107.6 | 105.8 | 96.5 | 160.2 | 212.7 | 181.6 | 163.1 | .... | .... | .... |
| Secondary income: debit | 1d9da | 23.7 | 26.1 | 26.7 | 23.0 | 22.0 | 58.8 | 135.3 | 60.4 | 54.7 | .... | .... | .... |
| B. Capital Account* | 209ba | — | — | — | .5 | — | — | — | 4.2 | — | .... | .... | .... |
| Capital account: credit | 209ca | — | — | — | .5 | — | — | — | 7.8 | — | .... | .... | .... |
| Capital account: debit | 209da | .... | .... | .... | — | — | — | — | 3.7 | — | .... | .... | .... |
| Balance on current & capital acct. | 129ba | −43.5 | −50.5 | −72.3 | −65.3 | 2.9 | 29.2 | 21.1 | 51.5 | −15.4 | .... | .... | .... |
| C. Financial Account* | 309na | −45.9 | −42.6 | −78.6 | −93.0 | −11.9 | −18.9 | 24.6 | −1.0 | 24.0 | .... | .... | .... |
| Direct investment: assets | 3a9aa | .... | .... | .... | — | — | — | — | — | — | .... | .... | .... |
| Equity & investment fund shares | 3aaaa | .... | .... | .... | — | — | — | — | — | — | .... | .... | .... |
| Debt instruments | 3abaa | .... | .... | .... | — | — | — | — | — | — | .... | .... | .... |
| Direct investment: liabilities | 3a9la | 55.5 | 53.7 | 82.2 | 78.1 | 78.6 | 39.4 | 37.4 | 36.2 | 33.5 | .... | .... | .... |
| Equity & investment fund shares | 3aala | 55.5 | 53.7 | 82.2 | 78.1 | 78.6 | 39.4 | 37.4 | 36.2 | 33.5 | .... | .... | .... |
| Debt instruments | 3abla | .... | .... | .... | — | — | — | — | — | — | .... | .... | .... |
| Portfolio investment: assets | 3b9aa | .... | .... | .... | — | — | — | — | — | — | .... | .... | .... |
| Equity & investment fund shares | 3baaa | .... | .... | .... | — | — | — | — | — | — | .... | .... | .... |
| Debt securities | 3bbaa | .... | .... | .... | — | — | — | — | — | — | .... | .... | .... |
| Portfolio investment: liabilities | 3b9la | .... | .... | .... | — | — | — | — | — | — | .... | .... | .... |
| Equity & investment fund shares | 3bala | .... | .... | .... | — | — | — | — | — | — | .... | .... | .... |
| Debt securities | 3bbla | .... | .... | .... | — | — | — | — | — | — | .... | .... | .... |
| Fin. der.& empl.stk.ops.(ESOs): net | 3c9na | .... | .... | .... | — | — | — | — | — | — | .... | .... | .... |
| Fin. der. & ESOs: assets | 3c9aa | .... | .... | .... | — | — | — | — | — | — | .... | .... | .... |
| Fin. der. & ESOs: liabilities | 3c9la | .... | .... | .... | — | — | — | — | — | — | .... | .... | .... |
| Other investment: assets | 3d9aa | 15.0 | 14.0 | 14.1 | −34.2 | −1.3 | −20.1 | −20.3 | .3 | −24.9 | .... | .... | .... |
| Other equity | 3daaa | .... | .... | .... | — | — | — | — | — | — | .... | .... | .... |
| Debt instruments | 3dzaa | 15.0 | 14.0 | 14.1 | −34.2 | −1.3 | −20.1 | −20.3 | .3 | −24.9 | .... | .... | .... |
| Other investment: liabilities | 3d9la | 5.4 | 3.0 | 10.5 | −19.3 | −68.0 | −40.6 | −82.2 | −34.9 | −82.5 | .... | .... | .... |
| Other equity | 3dala | .... | .... | .... | — | — | — | — | — | — | .... | .... | .... |
| Debt instruments | 3dzla | 5.4 | 3.0 | 10.5 | −19.3 | −68.0 | −40.6 | −82.2 | −34.9 | −82.5 | .... | .... | .... |
| Curr.+ cap.− finan. acct. balance | 4y9na | 2.4 | −7.9 | 6.2 | 27.7 | 14.8 | 48.1 | −3.5 | 52.5 | −39.4 | .... | .... | .... |
| D. Net Errors and Omissions | 409na | −3.3 | −34.1 | −5.1 | −33.7 | −37.4 | −8.5 | −89.8 | −101.9 | −25.3 | .... | .... | .... |
| E. Reserves and Related Items | 4z9na | −.9 | −42.0 | 1.1 | −5.9 | −22.6 | 39.6 | −93.3 | −49.4 | −64.8 | .... | .... | .... |
| Reserve assets | 3e9aa | 30.3 | 10.1 | 20.6 | −12.8 | −6.3 | 108.8 | −9.8 | 23.1 | 34.2 | .... | .... | .... |
| Credit and loans from the IMF | 3dcla | −11.2 | −2.0 | −4.1 | −12.4 | 6.3 | 15.6 | 3.1 | 3.6 | 13.8 | .... | .... | .... |
| Exceptional financing | 409la | 42.3 | 54.1 | 23.5 | 5.6 | 10.0 | 53.6 | 80.4 | 68.9 | 85.1 | .... | .... | .... |

*Excludes components in group E

| National Accounts | | 2004 | 2005 | 2006 | 2007 | 2008 | 2009 | 2010 | 2011 | 2012 | 2013 | 2014 | 2015 |
|---|---|---|---|---|---|---|---|---|---|---|---|---|---|
| | | | | | *Millions of Dalasis: Fiscal Year Ends June 30* | | | | | | | | |
| Househ.Cons.Expend.,incl.NPISHs | 96f | 13,857.8 | 16,460.0 | 17,548.5 | 18,017.5 | 18,704.7 | 19,575.6 | 23,032.0 | 20,797.7 | 24,469.6 | 27,454.2 | .... | .... |
| Government Consumption Expend | 91f | 1,404.1 | 1,261.5 | 1,164.0 | 1,439.6 | 2,085.6 | 2,510.6 | 2,676.3 | 2,694.3 | 2,201.2 | 2,395.4 | .... | .... |
| Gross Fixed Capital Formation | 93e | 5,120.8 | 5,254.4 | 5,643.3 | 5,843.6 | 5,723.2 | 6,421.1 | 4,902.6 | 6,755.3 | 6,838.5 | 6,649.5 | .... | .... |
| Changes in Inventories | 93i | 625 | 653 | 640 | 699 | 626 | .... | .... | .... | .... | .... | .... | .... |
| Exports of Goods and Services | 90c | 342.4 | 211.8 | 321.8 | 332.8 | 300.6 | 1,847.2 | 1,184.9 | 2,789.6 | 3,793.9 | 3,550.7 | .... | .... |
| Imports of Goods and Services (-) | 98c | 6,089.2 | 6,361.1 | 6,236.6 | 6,809.2 | 6,094.8 | 6,928.5 | 6,890.3 | 8,636.0 | 10,450.5 | 10,780.4 | .... | .... |
| Gross Domestic Product (GDP) | 99b | †17,381.0 | 17,836.0 | 18,385.0 | 19,870.6 | 21,432.7 | 23,997.0 | 26,662.5 | 26,640.8 | 29,268.1 | 32,047.0 | .... | .... |
| Statistical Discrepancy | 99bs | 1,314.2 | 1,509.1 | 44.1 | 167.0 | 290.7 | .... | 171.7 | .... | .... | .... | .... | .... |
| GDP Volume 2004 Prices | 99b.p | 17,381.0 | 17,217.3 | 17,410.8 | 18,043.0 | 19,077.7 | 20,308.2 | 21,633.2 | 20,696.8 | 21,910.1 | 22,962.3 | .... | .... |
| GDP Volume (2010=100) | 99bvp | 80.3 | 79.6 | 80.5 | 83.4 | 88.2 | 93.9 | 100.0 | 95.7 | 101.3 | 106.1 | .... | .... |
| GDP Deflator (2010=100) | 99bip | 81.1 | 84.1 | 85.7 | 89.4 | 91.2 | 95.9 | 100.0 | 104.4 | 108.4 | 113.2 | .... | .... |
| | | | | | *Millions: Midyear Estimates* | | | | | | | | |
| Population | 99z | 1.39 | 1.44 | 1.49 | 1.54 | 1.59 | 1.64 | 1.69 | 1.75 | 1.81 | 1.87 | 1.93 | 1.99 |

# Georgia 915

| | | 2004 | 2005 | 2006 | 2007 | 2008 | 2009 | 2010 | 2011 | 2012 | 2013 | 2014 | 2015 |
|---|---|---|---|---|---|---|---|---|---|---|---|---|---|
| **Exchange Rates** | | | | | | *Lari per SDR: End of Period* | | | | | | | |
| Official Rate.................... | aa | 2.8342 | 2.5620 | 2.5778 | 2.5151 | 2.5676 | 2.6428 | 2.7302 | 2.5644 | 2.5462 | 2.6739 | 2.7000 | 3.3187 |
| | | | | | | *Lari per US Dollar: End of Period (ae) Period Average (rf)* | | | | | | | |
| Official Rate.................... | ae | 1.8250 | 1.7925 | 1.7135 | 1.5916 | 1.6670 | 1.6858 | 1.7728 | 1.6703 | 1.6567 | 1.7363 | 1.8636 | 2.3949 |
| Official Rate.................... | rf | 1.9167 | 1.8127 | 1.7804 | 1.6705 | 1.4908 | 1.6705 | 1.7823 | 1.6865 | 1.6513 | 1.6634 | 1.7657 | 2.2693 |
| | | | | | | *Index Numbers (2010=100): Period Averages* | | | | | | | |
| Nominal Effective Exchange Rate..... | nec | 91.83 | 94.20 | 96.07 | 96.02 | 107.94 | 107.53 | 100.00 | 105.32 | 112.34 | 113.07 | 113.40 | 107.08 |
| CPI-Based Real Effect. Ex. Rate....... | rec | 83.30 | 87.63 | 92.87 | 96.21 | 110.54 | 104.75 | 100.00 | 109.29 | 111.29 | 107.69 | 106.92 | 99.80 |
| **Fund Position** | | | | | | *Millions of SDRs: End of Period* | | | | | | | |
| Quota................................. | 2f.s | 150.30 | 150.30 | 150.30 | 150.30 | 150.30 | 150.30 | 150.30 | 150.30 | 150.30 | 150.30 | 150.30 | 150.30 |
| SDR Holdings.................................. | 1b.s | 7.22 | .71 | .60 | 9.37 | 7.99 | 139.53 | 144.42 | 145.42 | 143.98 | 144.09 | 143.98 | 144.09 |
| Reserve Position in the Fund............ | 1c.s | .01 | .01 | .01 | .01 | .01 | .01 | .01 | .01 | .01 | .01 | .01 | .01 |
| Total Fund Cred.&Loans Outstg....... | 2tl | 171.26 | 162.54 | 157.11 | 159.17 | 298.76 | 501.60 | 682.10 | 643.99 | 484.09 | 232.98 | 146.23 | 94.00 |
| SDR Allocations............................. | 1bd | — | — | — | — | — | 143.96 | 143.96 | 143.96 | 143.96 | 143.96 | 143.96 | 143.96 |
| **International Liquidity** | | | | | | *Millions of US Dollars Unless Otherwise Indicated: End of Period* | | | | | | | |
| Total Reserves minus Gold............ | 1l.d | 386.68 | 478.64 | 930.83 | 1,361.16 | 1,480.16 | 2,110.32 | 2,263.79 | 2,818.19 | 2,872.95 | 2,823.38 | 2,699.17 | 2,520.72 |
| SDR Holdings......................... | 1b.d | 11.22 | 1.02 | .90 | 14.80 | 12.31 | 218.73 | 222.41 | 223.27 | 221.29 | 221.90 | 208.61 | 199.67 |
| Reserve Position in the Fund......... | 1c.d | .02 | .01 | .02 | .02 | .02 | .02 | .02 | .02 | .02 | .02 | .01 | .01 |
| Foreign Exchange........................ | 1d.d | 375.44 | 477.61 | 929.91 | 1,346.34 | 1,467.84 | 1,891.58 | 2,041.36 | 2,594.91 | 2,651.65 | 2,601.47 | 2,490.55 | 2,321.04 |
| Gold(Millions Fine Troy Ounces)....... | 1ad | — | — | — | — | — | — | — | — | — | — | — | — |
| Gold (National Valuation)................ | 1and | — | — | — | — | — | — | — | — | — | — | — | — |
| Central Bank: Other Assets............. | 3..d | — | .62 | 2.82 | 51.47 | 24.88 | 3.44 | 4.86 | 1.26 | .79 | .86 | 1.52 | 1.36 |
| Central Bank: Other Liabs............... | 4..d | 62.81 | 55.68 | 61.83 | 68.33 | 1.90 | .19 | .15 | .37 | .98 | 1.00 | .75 | 1.22 |
| Other Depository Corps.: Assets....... | 7a.d | 161.98 | 162.33 | 226.07 | 447.15 | 1,856.65 | 1,494.04 | 1,588.54 | 2,021.36 | 2,470.25 | 2,748.89 | 2,802.42 | 2,666.77 |
| Other Depository Corps.: Liabs......... | 7b.d | 136.53 | 316.81 | 564.13 | 1,305.67 | 1,856.65 | 1,494.04 | 1,588.54 | 2,021.36 | 2,470.25 | 2,748.89 | 2,802.42 | 2,666.77 |
| **Central Bank** | | | | | | *Millions of Lari: End of Period* | | | | | | | |
| Net Foreign Assets........................ | 11n | 105.66 | 342.85 | 1,088.89 | 1,739.25 | 1,738.63 | 1,856.97 | 1,766.33 | 2,688.13 | 3,160.16 | 3,894.11 | 4,248.11 | 5,247.50 |
| Claims on Nonresidents................. | 11 | 705.68 | 859.07 | 1,599.82 | 2,248.34 | 2,508.90 | 3,563.38 | 4,021.88 | 4,709.33 | 4,760.93 | 4,903.73 | 5,033.01 | 6,040.14 |
| Liabilities to Nonresidents............. | 16c | 600.03 | 516.22 | 510.93 | 509.09 | 770.27 | 1,706.41 | 2,255.55 | 2,021.20 | 1,600.77 | 1,009.62 | 784.89 | 792.64 |
| Claims on Other Depository Corps... | 12e | — | — | 20.00 | 73.13 | 209.41 | 45.00 | 190.04 | 13.51 | 391.08 | 400.20 | 712.50 | 1,067.00 |
| Net Claims on Central Government.. | 12an | 734.66 | 647.40 | 427.15 | 412.08 | −99.25 | 177.73 | −85.70 | −70.40 | −416.78 | 35.31 | −66.31 | −350.91 |
| Claims on Central Government...... | 12a | 841.41 | 832.85 | 787.14 | 778.47 | 779.67 | 760.88 | 716.40 | 687.36 | 530.48 | 523.58 | 521.63 | 502.47 |
| Liabilities to Central Government... | 16d | 106.75 | 185.45 | 359.98 | 366.39 | 878.91 | 583.15 | 802.11 | 757.76 | 947.26 | 488.28 | 587.94 | 853.38 |
| Claims on Other Sectors.................. | 12s | 112.57 | 96.91 | 105.18 | 102.56 | 3.99 | 3.67 | 2.67 | 2.67 | 2.06 | 4.92 | 4.48 | 4.46 |
| Claims on Other Financial Corps.... | 12g | .04 | .04 | .04 | .04 | .04 | .04 | .04 | — | — | — | — | — |
| Claims on State & Local Govts....... | 12b | — | — | — | — | — | — | — | — | — | — | — | — |
| Claims on Public Nonfin. Corps.... | 12c | 110.10 | 94.80 | 101.39 | 98.94 | — | — | — | — | — | — | — | — |
| Claims on Private Sector................ | 12d | 2.44 | 2.07 | 3.76 | 3.58 | 3.95 | 3.63 | 2.63 | 2.67 | 2.06 | 4.92 | 4.48 | 4.46 |
| Monetary Base.............................. | 14 | 866.66 | 1,007.37 | 1,272.10 | 1,793.80 | 1,642.08 | 1,874.96 | 2,081.13 | 2,901.07 | 3,255.31 | 3,989.08 | 4,501.01 | 4,948.16 |
| Currency in Circulation.................. | 14a | 676.16 | 811.40 | 929.54 | 1,310.49 | 1,290.70 | 1,457.94 | 1,618.18 | 1,753.58 | 1,918.06 | 2,351.55 | 2,462.11 | 2,503.73 |
| Liabs. to Other Depository Corps.... | 14c | 190.50 | 195.97 | 342.56 | 483.31 | 351.38 | 417.02 | 462.95 | 1,147.49 | 1,337.25 | 1,637.53 | 2,038.90 | 2,444.43 |
| Liabilities to Other Sectors.............. | 14d | | | | | | | | | | | | |
| Other Liabs. to Other Dep. Corps.... | 14n | 17.04 | — | 274.60 | 376.54 | 77.35 | 219.05 | 355.12 | 442.13 | 562.87 | 684.72 | 500.85 | 353.65 |
| Dep. & Sec. Excl. f/Monetary Base.... | 14o | 14.37 | 2.12 | 3.75 | .34 | 1.38 | .01 | .01 | — | — | — | — | — |
| Deposits Included in Broad Money. | 15 | 1.42 | .55 | 3.45 | .34 | 1.38 | .01 | .01 | — | — | — | — | — |
| Sec.Ot.th.Shares Incl.in Brd. Money | 16a | — | — | — | — | — | — | — | — | — | — | — | — |
| Deposits Excl. from Broad Money... | 16b | 12.94 | 1.56 | .29 | — | — | — | — | — | — | — | — | — |
| Sec.Ot.th.Shares Excl.f/Brd.Money.. | 16s | — | — | — | — | — | — | — | — | — | — | — | — |
| Loans........................................... | 16l | — | — | — | — | — | — | — | — | — | — | — | — |
| Financial Derivatives....................... | 16m | — | — | — | — | — | — | — | — | — | — | — | — |
| Shares and Other Equity.................. | 17a | 98.09 | 117.24 | 107.68 | 109.74 | 157.86 | 190.17 | 171.76 | 27.93 | 28.25 | 143.29 | 258.87 | 983.47 |
| Other Items (Net).......................... | 17r | −43.26 | −39.57 | −16.90 | 46.60 | −25.90 | −200.83 | −734.68 | −737.22 | −709.91 | −482.55 | −361.95 | −317.23 |
| Memo Item: | | | | | | | | | | | | | |
| Total Assets..................................... | 10ra | 1,727.85 | 1,858.64 | 2,574.55 | 3,265.73 | 3,560.55 | 4,426.46 | 4,988.63 | 5,512.00 | 5,792.60 | 5,918.58 | 6,357.40 | 7,701.68 |

# Georgia 915

| | | 2004 | 2005 | 2006 | 2007 | 2008 | 2009 | 2010 | 2011 | 2012 | 2013 | 2014 | 2015 |
|---|---|---|---|---|---|---|---|---|---|---|---|---|---|
| **Other Depository Corporations** | | | | | | *Millions of Lari: End of Period* | | | | | | | |
| Net Foreign Assets | 21n | 46.43 | −276.91 | −579.27 | −1,366.42 | −1,907.70 | −1,515.40 | −1,262.38 | −2,450.60 | −2,824.00 | −3,122.59 | −3,640.77 | −3,308.81 |
| Claims on Nonresidents | 21 | 295.61 | 290.97 | 387.36 | 711.69 | 1,187.34 | 1,003.25 | 1,553.79 | 925.68 | 1,268.47 | 1,650.30 | 1,581.83 | 3,077.83 |
| Liabilities to Nonresidents | 26c | 249.17 | 567.88 | 966.64 | 2,078.11 | 3,095.04 | 2,518.64 | 2,816.16 | 3,376.28 | 4,092.47 | 4,772.89 | 5,222.60 | 6,386.64 |
| Claims on Central Bank | 20 | 244.46 | 269.01 | 717.01 | 1,004.40 | 635.93 | 864.45 | 1,063.44 | 1,904.68 | 2,268.76 | 2,775.33 | 3,063.19 | 3,321.18 |
| Currency | 20a | 60.16 | 75.12 | 102.18 | 158.42 | 208.15 | 228.50 | 245.19 | 314.59 | 368.03 | 451.93 | 519.53 | 521.80 |
| Reserve Deposits and Securities | 20b | 184.29 | 193.90 | 340.23 | 469.44 | 350.43 | 416.89 | 463.13 | 1,147.96 | 1,337.89 | 1,638.77 | 2,042.97 | 2,445.99 |
| Other Claims | 20n | — | — | 274.60 | 376.54 | 77.35 | 219.05 | 355.12 | 442.13 | 562.84 | 684.63 | 500.69 | 353.40 |
| Net Claims on Central Government | 22an | 35.71 | −3.16 | 12.63 | −10.16 | −48.14 | 146.70 | 318.05 | 355.42 | 473.00 | 718.91 | 959.44 | 1,177.65 |
| Claims on Central Government | 22a | 53.13 | 26.46 | 52.42 | 55.23 | 35.96 | 288.21 | 477.16 | 580.03 | 578.66 | 876.27 | 1,419.11 | 1,696.63 |
| Liabilities to Central Government | 26d | 17.42 | 29.62 | 39.79 | 65.39 | 84.10 | 141.51 | 159.11 | 224.61 | 105.66 | 157.35 | 459.67 | 518.99 |
| Claims on Other Sectors | 22s | 978.35 | 1,753.37 | 2,729.97 | 4,775.02 | 6,375.15 | 5,595.19 | 6,648.14 | 8,019.44 | 9,083.88 | 10,760.02 | 13,258.64 | 15,831.84 |
| Claims on Other Financial Corps. | 22g | — | — | — | — | — | — | — | — | — | — | — | — |
| Claims on State & Local Govts | 22b | .24 | .02 | — | — | — | — | — | .53 | .29 | — | — | — |
| Claims on Public Nonfin. Corps. | 22c | 23.47 | 50.21 | 62.04 | 47.97 | 74.86 | 36.25 | 52.68 | 65.67 | 74.46 | 66.46 | 74.94 | 67.68 |
| Claims on Private Sector | 22d | 954.64 | 1,703.14 | 2,667.93 | 4,727.04 | 6,300.29 | 5,558.94 | 6,595.45 | 7,953.24 | 9,009.14 | 10,693.55 | 13,183.70 | 15,764.16 |
| Liabilities to Central Bank | 26g | | 2.53 | 21.08 | 53.11 | 209.44 | 45.00 | 190.04 | 13.59 | 391.28 | 400.40 | 713.15 | 1,067.10 |
| Transf.Dep.Included in Broad Money | 24 | 490.68 | 593.47 | 1,025.04 | 1,453.87 | 1,556.69 | 1,557.45 | 2,321.81 | 2,629.58 | 2,711.79 | 3,678.83 | 4,178.57 | 4,967.24 |
| Other Dep.Included in Broad Money. | 25 | 426.11 | 631.20 | 943.93 | 1,492.58 | 1,781.07 | 1,976.71 | 2,504.20 | 3,029.20 | 3,641.92 | 4,258.16 | 5,068.68 | 6,394.74 |
| Sec.Ot.th.Shares Incl.in Brd. Money.. | 26a | — | — | — | — | — | — | — | — | — | — | — | — |
| Deposits Excl. from Broad Money.. | 26b | 17.27 | 15.24 | 24.68 | 49.28 | 23.89 | 51.46 | 70.92 | 158.55 | 136.05 | 184.43 | 244.20 | 113.85 |
| Sec.Ot.th.Shares Excl.f/Brd.Money.... | 26s | — | — | — | — | — | — | — | — | — | — | — | — |
| Loans | 26l | 73.71 | 92.43 | 134.54 | 225.49 | 236.24 | 237.97 | 250.77 | 153.20 | 151.12 | 160.49 | 148.11 | 203.97 |
| Financial Derivatives | 26m | — | — | — | — | — | — | — | — | — | — | — | — |
| Insurance Technical Reserves | 26r | — | — | — | — | — | — | — | — | — | — | — | — |
| Shares and Other Equity | 27a | 372.51 | 479.49 | 898.37 | 1,471.05 | 1,517.25 | 1,516.99 | 1,787.65 | 2,104.36 | 2,390.06 | 2,893.39 | 3,586.80 | 3,512.74 |
| Other Items (Net) | 27r | −75.34 | −72.05 | −167.30 | −342.55 | −269.32 | −294.63 | −358.14 | −259.54 | −420.57 | −444.04 | −299.01 | 762.23 |
| Memo Item: | | | | | | | | | | | | | |
| Total Assets | 20ra | 1,805.49 | 2,682.82 | 4,381.63 | 7,454.87 | 9,555.73 | 9,208.14 | 11,500.43 | 13,658.72 | 15,480.69 | 18,590.84 | 22,109.69 | 26,980.22 |
| **Depository Corporations** | | | | | | *Millions of Lari: End of Period* | | | | | | | |
| Net Foreign Assets | 31n | 152.09 | 65.94 | 509.62 | 372.82 | −169.07 | 341.57 | 503.95 | 237.53 | 336.16 | 771.51 | 607.35 | 1,938.69 |
| Claims on Nonresidents | 31 | 1,001.29 | 1,150.04 | 1,987.19 | 2,960.03 | 3,696.23 | 4,566.63 | 5,575.67 | 5,635.01 | 6,029.40 | 6,554.03 | 6,614.84 | 9,117.97 |
| Liabilities to Nonresidents | 36c | 849.20 | 1,084.10 | 1,477.57 | 2,587.20 | 3,865.31 | 4,225.06 | 5,071.71 | 5,397.48 | 5,693.24 | 5,782.52 | 6,007.49 | 7,179.28 |
| Domestic Claims | 32 | 1,861.31 | 2,494.52 | 3,274.94 | 5,279.49 | 6,231.76 | 5,923.29 | 6,883.15 | 8,307.14 | 9,142.17 | 11,519.16 | 14,156.25 | 16,663.03 |
| Net Claims on Central Government | 32an | 770.38 | 644.24 | 439.79 | 401.92 | −147.38 | 324.43 | 232.35 | 285.03 | 56.23 | 754.22 | 893.13 | 826.73 |
| Claims on Central Government | 32a | 894.54 | 859.31 | 839.56 | 833.70 | 815.63 | 1,049.09 | 1,193.56 | 1,267.39 | 1,109.15 | 1,399.85 | 1,940.74 | 2,199.10 |
| Liabilities to Central Government. | 36d | 124.17 | 215.07 | 399.77 | 431.78 | 963.01 | 724.66 | 961.21 | 982.37 | 1,052.92 | 645.63 | 1,047.61 | 1,372.37 |
| Claims on Other Sectors | 32s | 1,090.93 | 1,850.28 | 2,835.16 | 4,877.57 | 6,379.15 | 5,598.86 | 6,650.81 | 8,022.11 | 9,085.95 | 10,764.94 | 13,263.11 | 15,836.30 |
| Claims on Other Financial Corps.. | 32g | .04 | .04 | .04 | .04 | .04 | .04 | .04 | — | — | — | — | — |
| Claims on State & Local Govts..... | 32b | .24 | .02 | — | — | — | — | — | .53 | .29 | — | — | — |
| Claims on Public Nonfin. Corps... | 32c | 133.57 | 145.01 | 163.43 | 146.92 | 74.86 | 36.25 | 52.68 | 65.67 | 74.46 | 66.46 | 74.94 | 67.68 |
| Claims on Private Sector | 32d | 957.08 | 1,705.21 | 2,671.68 | 4,730.62 | 6,304.25 | 5,562.58 | 6,598.09 | 7,955.91 | 9,011.20 | 10,698.48 | 13,188.18 | 15,768.62 |
| Broad Money Liabilities | 35l | 1,534.21 | 1,961.50 | 2,799.78 | 4,098.86 | 4,421.70 | 4,763.61 | 6,199.01 | 7,097.78 | 7,903.74 | 9,836.62 | 11,189.84 | 13,343.92 |
| Currency Outside Depository Corps | 34a | 615.99 | 736.28 | 827.36 | 1,152.07 | 1,082.55 | 1,229.44 | 1,372.99 | 1,438.99 | 1,550.03 | 1,899.63 | 1,942.58 | 1,981.94 |
| Transferable Deposits | 34 | 492.11 | 594.02 | 1,028.49 | 1,454.20 | 1,558.07 | 1,557.46 | 2,321.82 | 2,629.58 | 2,711.79 | 3,678.83 | 4,178.57 | 4,967.24 |
| Other Deposits | 35 | 426.11 | 631.20 | 943.93 | 1,492.58 | 1,781.07 | 1,976.71 | 2,504.20 | 3,029.20 | 3,641.92 | 4,258.16 | 5,068.68 | 6,394.74 |
| Securities Other than Shares | 36a | — | — | — | — | — | — | — | — | — | — | — | — |
| Deposits Excl. from Broad Money..... | 36b | 30.22 | 16.81 | 24.97 | 49.28 | 23.89 | 51.46 | 70.92 | 158.55 | 136.05 | 184.43 | 244.20 | 113.85 |
| Sec.Ot.th.Shares Excl.f/Brd.Money.... | 36s | — | — | — | — | — | — | — | — | — | — | — | — |
| Loans | 36l | 73.71 | 92.43 | 134.54 | 225.49 | 236.24 | 237.97 | 250.77 | 153.20 | 151.12 | 160.49 | 148.11 | 203.97 |
| Financial Derivatives | 36m | — | — | — | — | — | — | — | — | — | — | — | — |
| Insurance Technical Reserves | 36r | — | — | — | — | — | — | — | — | — | — | — | — |
| Shares and Other Equity | 37a | 470.60 | 596.72 | 1,006.05 | 1,580.78 | 1,675.12 | 1,707.15 | 1,959.41 | 2,132.30 | 2,418.32 | 3,036.68 | 3,845.67 | 4,496.21 |
| Other Items (Net) | 37r | −95.34 | −107.02 | −180.79 | −302.10 | −294.25 | −495.33 | −1,093.00 | −997.15 | −1,130.88 | −927.54 | −664.22 | 443.78 |
| Broad Money Liabs., Seasonally Adj. | 35l.b | 1,492.01 | 1,899.34 | 2,700.68 | 3,934.82 | 4,231.81 | 4,552.70 | 5,930.35 | 6,812.96 | 7,623.45 | 9,540.54 | 10,890.58 | 13,004.97 |
| **Monetary Aggregates** | | | | | | *Millions of Lari: End of Period* | | | | | | | |
| Broad Money | 59m | 1,534.21 | 1,961.50 | 2,799.78 | 4,098.86 | 4,421.70 | 4,763.61 | 6,199.01 | 7,097.78 | 7,903.74 | 9,836.62 | 11,189.84 | 13,343.92 |
| o/w:Currency Issued by Cent.Govt | 59m.a | — | — | — | — | — | — | — | — | — | — | — | |
| o/w: Dep.in Nonfin. Corporations. | 59m.b | — | — | — | — | — | — | — | — | — | — | — | |
| o/w:Secs. Issued by Central Govt. | 59m.c | — | — | — | — | — | — | — | — | — | — | — | |
| Money (National Definitions) | | | | | | | | | | | | | |
| Reserve Money | 19mb | 866.66 | 1,007.37 | 1,272.10 | 1,793.80 | 1,642.08 | 1,874.96 | 2,081.13 | 2,901.07 | 3,255.31 | 3,989.08 | 4,501.01 | 4,948.16 |
| M2 | 59mb | 856.52 | 1,104.13 | 1,473.17 | 2,262.96 | 1,999.22 | 2,330.49 | 2,960.25 | 3,783.18 | 4,069.16 | 5,418.40 | 5,911.31 | 5,762.93 |
| M3 | 59mc | 1,534.21 | 1,961.50 | 2,799.78 | 4,098.86 | 4,421.70 | 4,763.61 | 6,199.01 | 7,097.78 | 7,903.74 | 9,836.62 | 11,189.84 | 13,343.92 |
| **Interest Rates** | | | | | | *Percent Per Annum* | | | | | | | |
| Central Bank Policy Rate (EOP) | 60 | .... | .... | .... | .... | 8.00 | 5.00 | 7.50 | 6.75 | 5.25 | 3.75 | 4.00 | 8.00 |
| Money Market Rate | 60b | 11.87 | 7.71 | 9.46 | 7.42 | † 14.77 | 5.55 | 5.45 | 7.64 | 5.59 | 3.94 | 3.85 | 5.97 |
| Money Market Rate (Fgn. Currency). | 60b.f | 8.75 | 6.30 | 8.64 | 12.47 | † 15.40 | 14.36 | 11.00 | 11.00 | .... | .... | .... | .... |
| Treasury Bill Rate | 60c | 19.16 | 11.62 | .... | .... | | 5.98 | 9.55 | 9.68 | 6.76 | 5.16 | 6.17 | 8.78 |
| Deposit Rate | 60l | 7.07 | 7.48 | 10.13 | 10.19 | 11.24 | 10.81 | 10.06 | 11.54 | 10.71 | 9.73 | 8.43 | 8.91 |
| Deposit Rate (Fgn. Currency) | 60l.f | 8.10 | 7.02 | 7.66 | 8.22 | 10.83 | 9.49 | 7.67 | 8.16 | 8.17 | 6.04 | 4.83 | 4.22 |
| Lending Rate | 60p | 22.09 | 17.55 | 17.06 | 17.09 | 18.04 | 17.87 | 15.85 | 15.00 | 14.81 | 13.59 | 11.91 | 12.49 |
| Lending Rate (Fgn. Currency) | 60p.f | 17.74 | 15.05 | 16.24 | 15.97 | 17.56 | 17.56 | 18.54 | 15.66 | 13.80 | 13.73 | 12.64 | 10.90 | 10.45 |
| **Prices and Labor** | | | | | | *Index Numbers (2010=100): Period Averages* | | | | | | | |
| Producer Prices | 63 | 65.1 | 70.0 | 77.6 | 86.6 | 95.0 | 89.8 | 100.0 | 112.8 | 114.6 | 112.4 | 115.6 | 125.6 |
| Consumer Prices | 64 | 64.6 | 70.0 | 76.4 | 83.4 | 91.8 | † 93.4 | 100.0 | 108.5 | 107.5 | 107.0 | 110.3 | 114.7 |
| | | | | | | *Number in Thousands: Period Averages* | | | | | | | |
| Labor Force | 67d | 2,041 | 2,024 | 2,022 | 1,965 | 1,918 | 1,992 | 1,945 | 1,959 | 2,029 | 2,004 | 1,991 | .... |
| Employment | 67e | 1,783 | 1,745 | 1,747 | 1,704 | 1,602 | 1,656 | 1,628 | 1,664 | 1,724 | 1,712 | 1,745 | .... |
| Unemployment | 67c | 258 | 279 | 275 | 261 | 316 | 336 | 317 | 295 | 305 | 292 | 246 | .... |
| Unemployment Rate (%) | 67r | 12.6 | 13.8 | 13.6 | 13.3 | 16.5 | 16.9 | 16.3 | 15.1 | 15.0 | 14.6 | 12.4 | .... |

# Georgia   915

| | | 2004 | 2005 | 2006 | 2007 | 2008 | 2009 | 2010 | 2011 | 2012 | 2013 | 2014 | 2015 |
|---|---|---|---|---|---|---|---|---|---|---|---|---|---|
| **Intl. Transactions & Positions** | | *Millions of US Dollars* | | | | | | | | | | | |
| Exports | 70..d | 647 | 865 | 936 | 1,232 | 1,495 | 1,134 | 1,677 | 2,187 | 2,376 | 2,910 | 2,861 | 2,204 |
| Imports, c.i.f. | 71..d | 1,844 | 2,488 | 3,675 | 5,212 | 6,302 | 4,500 | 5,257 | 7,038 | 8,037 | 8,012 | 8,593 | 7,724 |
| Imports, f.o.b. | 71.v | .... | .... | .... | .... | .... | .... | .... | .... | .... | .... | .... | .... |
| **Balance of Payments** | | *Millions of US Dollars* | | | | | | | | | | | |
| A. Current Account* | 109bx | −432.3 | −756.8 | −1,271.7 | −2,104.1 | −3,132.5 | −1,248.8 | −1,329.7 | −1,961.8 | −1,914.7 | −1,013.6 | −1,828.5 | −1,749.4 |
| Goods, credit (exports) | 1a9cx | 1,055.1 | 1,413.9 | 1,586.4 | 2,055.6 | 2,387.6 | 1,853.7 | 2,393.3 | 3,223.0 | 3,459.1 | 4,190.8 | 3,995.1 | 3,042.6 |
| Goods, debit (imports) | 1a9dx | 1,985.9 | 2,631.4 | 3,642.9 | 4,944.4 | 6,224.5 | 4,270.4 | 5,021.3 | 6,722.6 | 7,685.2 | 7,697.0 | 8,290.1 | 7,362.8 |
| Balance on goods | 1a9bx | −930.8 | −1,217.5 | −2,056.5 | −2,888.8 | −3,836.9 | −2,416.7 | −2,628.1 | −3,499.6 | −4,226.1 | −3,506.2 | −4,295.1 | −4,320.3 |
| Services, credit (exports) | 1b9cx | 570.6 | 737.9 | 913.5 | 1,107.0 | 1,270.9 | 1,329.3 | 1,640.8 | 2,018.9 | 2,562.0 | 2,983.8 | 3,043.3 | 3,154.7 |
| Services, debit (imports) | 1b9dx | 485.9 | 635.8 | 733.3 | 934.7 | 1,246.2 | 977.6 | 1,092.5 | 1,265.2 | 1,447.4 | 1,561.8 | 1,725.4 | 1,685.4 |
| Balance on Goods & Services | 1z9bx | −846.1 | −1,115.4 | −1,876.4 | −2,716.4 | −3,812.2 | −2,065.1 | −2,079.8 | −2,745.9 | −3,111.5 | −2,084.2 | −2,977.2 | −2,851.0 |
| Primary income: credit | 1c9cx | 251.8 | 263.3 | 341.2 | 482.5 | 585.8 | 489.3 | 556.6 | 758.0 | 1,077.5 | 922.1 | 1,027.2 | 843.9 |
| Primary income: debit | 1c9dx | 178.0 | 201.8 | 179.1 | 445.7 | 644.3 | 532.0 | 773.3 | 1,183.0 | 1,226.5 | 1,238.2 | 1,231.7 | 1,245.6 |
| Balance on gds, serv. & prim. inc. | 1y9bx | −772.3 | −1,053.8 | −1,714.3 | −2,679.6 | −3,870.7 | −2,107.8 | −2,296.4 | −3,170.9 | −3,260.6 | −2,400.3 | −3,181.7 | −3,252.6 |
| Secondary income: credit | 1d9ca | 391.4 | 351.5 | 505.6 | 655.6 | 819.8 | 930.0 | 1,051.7 | 1,339.0 | 1,454.1 | 1,505.7 | 1,488.7 | 1,604.9 |
| Secondary income: debit | 1d9da | 51.5 | 54.4 | 63.0 | 80.0 | 81.7 | 71.0 | 85.0 | 129.9 | 108.3 | 119.0 | 135.5 | 101.7 |
| B. Capital Account* | 209ba | 31.9 | 53.8 | 124.5 | 82.3 | 82.9 | 148.7 | 154.5 | 127.1 | 125.6 | 123.3 | 107.9 | 61.5 |
| Capital account: credit | 209ca | 31.9 | 53.8 | 124.5 | 82.3 | 82.9 | 148.7 | 154.5 | 127.1 | 125.6 | 123.3 | 107.9 | 61.5 |
| Capital account: debit | 209da | .... | .... | .... | .... | .... | .... | .... | .... | .... | .... | .... | .... |
| Balance on current & capital acct. | 129ba | −400.4 | −703.0 | −1,147.3 | −2,021.8 | −3,049.6 | −1,100.1 | −1,175.2 | −1,834.7 | −1,789.1 | −890.3 | −1,720.5 | −1,687.9 |
| C. Financial Account* | 309na | −594.0 | −725.4 | −1,607.9 | −2,403.2 | −2,210.8 | −1,442.9 | −995.8 | −1,960.4 | −1,282.1 | −762.9 | −1,619.6 | −1,451.6 |
| Direct investment: assets | 3a9aa | 10.0 | −89.1 | −13.2 | 201.3 | 173.6 | −24.5 | 190.4 | 182.7 | 216.9 | 127.3 | 406.6 | 137.3 |
| Equity & investment fund shares.. | 3aaaa | 9.6 | −89.5 | −15.6 | 76.2 | 146.6 | −19.8 | 134.5 | 137.2 | 126.7 | 111.9 | 399.2 | 133.3 |
| Debt instruments | 3abaa | .4 | .4 | 2.4 | 125.1 | 27.0 | −4.7 | 55.9 | 45.6 | 90.2 | 15.4 | 7.3 | 4.0 |
| Direct investment: liabilities | 3a9la | 492.7 | 453.1 | 1,170.3 | 1,865.8 | 1,583.3 | 647.4 | 866.3 | 861.3 | 425.9 | 705.4 | 1,647.3 | 1,246.0 |
| Equity & investment fund shares . | 3aala | 440.3 | 383.4 | 922.6 | 909.9 | 1,173.8 | 564.5 | 695.6 | 798.4 | 508.2 | 744.7 | 1,416.8 | 1,200.8 |
| Debt instruments | 3abla | 52.4 | 69.8 | 247.7 | 955.9 | 409.5 | 82.9 | 170.7 | 62.9 | −82.3 | −39.3 | 230.5 | 45.2 |
| Portfolio investment: assets | 3b9aa | 13.1 | −13.1 | 2.2 | 12.7 | −.7 | 1.1 | .6 | — | 33.1 | −6.0 | 37.5 | 78.8 |
| Equity & investment fund shares | 3baaa | — | — | 2.2 | 5.1 | — | 1.1 | .6 | −.1 | 31.1 | −8.0 | −8.6 | −3.7 |
| Debt securities | 3bbaa | 13.1 | −13.1 | .... | 7.6 | −.7 | .... | .... | .1 | 2.1 | 2.0 | 46.2 | 82.4 |
| Portfolio investment: liabilities | 3b9la | −.6 | 2.4 | 142.4 | 33.7 | 122.5 | 11.7 | 251.1 | 108.5 | 881.5 | −42.6 | 244.9 | −77.2 |
| Equity & investment fund shares . | 3bala | .... | 2.5 | 142.5 | 33.7 | 114.7 | 11.7 | −22.0 | −7.2 | 73.6 | 1.3 | 209.6 | 4.9 |
| Debt securities | 3bbla | −.6 | −.1 | −.1 | .... | 7.8 | — | 273.1 | 115.6 | 807.9 | −43.9 | 35.3 | −82.1 |
| Fin. der.& empl.stk.ops.(ESOs): net | 3c9na | .... | .... | .... | −1.1 | −7.8 | −.6 | −.8 | −5.1 | −5.4 | 2.4 | −8.2 | 1.8 |
| Fin. der. & ESOs.: assets | 3c9aa | .... | .... | .... | −1.2 | −11.1 | −1.1 | −1.8 | −12.1 | −10.7 | −5.1 | −11.6 | −12.3 |
| Fin. der. & ESOs.: liabilities | 3c9la | .... | .... | .... | −.2 | −3.3 | −.5 | −1.0 | −7.0 | −5.2 | −7.5 | −3.4 | −14.1 |
| Other investment: assets | 3d9aa | 26.6 | 12.6 | 40.5 | 172.7 | 276.7 | −117.2 | 411.0 | −205.2 | 349.2 | 173.6 | 253.8 | 754.1 |
| Other equity | 3daaa | .... | .... | .... | .... | .... | .... | .... | .... | .... | .... | .... | .... |
| Debt instruments | 3dzaa | 26.6 | 12.6 | 40.5 | 172.7 | 276.7 | −117.2 | 411.0 | −205.2 | 349.2 | 173.6 | 253.8 | 754.1 |
| Other investment: liabilities | 3d9la | 151.5 | 180.3 | 324.7 | 889.3 | 946.8 | 642.6 | 479.6 | 963.0 | 568.6 | 397.4 | 417.1 | 1,254.8 |
| Other equity | 3dala | .... | .... | .... | .... | −.8 | −.7 | −2.3 | −41.8 | −399.6 | −223.4 | −86.6 | −99.4 |
| Debt instruments | 3dzla | 151.5 | 180.3 | 324.7 | 889.3 | 947.6 | 643.3 | 482.0 | 1,004.8 | 968.2 | 620.9 | 503.8 | 1,354.2 |
| Curr.+ cap.– finan. acct. balance... | 4y9na | 193.6 | 22.4 | 460.6 | 381.4 | −838.8 | 342.8 | −179.4 | 125.7 | −507.0 | −127.4 | −101.0 | −236.2 |
| D. Net Errors and Omissions | 409na | 15.2 | 26.3 | −59.5 | −36.0 | −54.0 | 32.5 | −32.1 | 14.9 | −55.0 | −43.0 | −74.7 | −86.0 |
| E. Reserves and Related Items | 4z9na | 208.8 | 48.8 | 401.1 | 345.5 | −892.7 | 375.2 | −211.5 | 140.7 | −562.0 | −170.4 | −175.7 | −322.2 |
| Reserve assets | 3e9aa | 177.9 | 110.6 | 438.6 | 377.1 | 130.6 | 616.2 | 208.2 | 572.6 | 37.8 | −45.7 | −33.8 | −99.4 |
| Credit and loans from the IMF | 3dcla | −34.2 | −12.5 | −7.9 | 3.2 | 216.4 | 308.8 | 276.4 | −59.4 | −245.0 | −381.5 | −136.0 | −73.1 |
| Exceptional financing | 409la | 3.3 | 74.3 | 45.4 | 28.4 | 807.0 | −67.8 | 143.4 | 491.4 | 844.9 | 506.2 | 277.8 | 295.9 |

*Excludes components in group E

| | | 2004 | 2005 | 2006 | 2007 | 2008 | 2009 | 2010 | 2011 | 2012 | 2013 | 2014 | 2015 |
|---|---|---|---|---|---|---|---|---|---|---|---|---|---|
| **International Investment Position** | | *Millions of US Dollars* | | | | | | | | | | | |
| Assets | 809aa | 1,079.9 | 1,149.0 | 1,670.1 | 2,764.0 | 3,363.7 | 3,928.2 | 4,808.2 | 5,269.6 | 5,924.0 | 6,178.3 | 6,597.8 | 7,044.9 |
| Direct investment | 8a9aa | 213.4 | 154.2 | 142.1 | 561.8 | 773.0 | 802.2 | 1,082.6 | 1,182.8 | 1,407.0 | 1,524.8 | 1,867.1 | 1,772.9 |
| Equity & investment fund shares.. | 8aaaa | 207.6 | 148.0 | 133.5 | 428.1 | 612.3 | 636.9 | 845.9 | 946.5 | 1,095.1 | 1,204.4 | 1,541.3 | 1,451.5 |
| Debt instruments | 8abaa | 5.8 | 6.1 | 8.6 | 133.7 | 160.7 | 165.4 | 236.8 | 236.2 | 311.9 | 320.4 | 326.5 | 321.4 |
| Portfolio investment | 8b9aa | 13.1 | — | 2.2 | 7.7 | .2 | 1.4 | 2.0 | 1.9 | 34.5 | 27.4 | 61.7 | 118.6 |
| Equity & investment fund shares.. | 8baaa | — | — | 2.2 | .2 | .2 | 1.3 | 1.9 | 1.7 | 32.2 | 23.1 | 13.4 | 7.3 |
| Debt instruments | 8bbaa | 13.1 | — | — | 7.6 | .1 | .1 | .1 | .2 | 2.3 | 4.3 | 48.4 | 111.3 |
| Fin. der.(oth.than reserves) & ESOs | 8c9aa | .... | .... | .... | .1 | .2 | .7 | 1.5 | 4.2 | — | .1 | 1.1 | .1 |
| Other investment | 8d9aa | 466.8 | 516.3 | 594.9 | 833.2 | 1,110.1 | 1,013.5 | 1,458.3 | 1,262.6 | 1,609.6 | 1,802.7 | 1,968.1 | 2,632.6 |
| Other equity | 8daaa | .... | .... | .... | .... | .... | .... | .... | .... | .... | .... | .... | .... |
| Debt instruments | 8dzaa | 466.8 | 516.3 | 594.9 | 833.2 | 1,110.1 | 1,013.5 | 1,458.3 | 1,262.6 | 1,609.6 | 1,802.7 | 1,968.1 | 2,632.6 |
| Reserve assets | 8e9aa | 386.7 | 478.5 | 930.8 | 1,361.2 | 1,480.2 | 2,110.3 | 2,263.8 | 2,818.2 | 2,873.0 | 2,823.4 | 2,699.2 | 2,520.7 |
| Liabilities | 809la | 4,492.6 | 5,033.4 | 6,738.9 | 9,813.7 | 12,902.2 | 14,637.4 | 16,627.4 | 19,034.4 | 21,667.4 | 22,283.4 | 23,997.5 | 24,963.8 |
| Direct investment | 8a9la | 1,914.0 | 2,379.7 | 3,565.6 | 5,505.4 | 6,947.0 | 7,630.4 | 8,585.0 | 9,774.5 | 10,519.7 | 11,546.9 | 12,898.6 | 12,641.2 |
| Equity & investment fund shares.. | 8aala | 1,428.0 | 1,822.4 | 2,738.8 | 3,706.7 | 4,844.7 | 5,415.1 | 6,116.2 | 7,049.5 | 7,856.9 | 8,898.6 | 9,894.6 | 9,649.8 |
| Debt instruments | 8abla | 486.1 | 557.4 | 826.7 | 1,798.7 | 2,102.2 | 2,215.3 | 2,468.8 | 2,724.9 | 2,662.9 | 2,648.4 | 3,004.1 | 2,991.4 |
| Portfolio investment | 8b9la | 14.0 | 24.2 | 207.0 | 329.8 | 734.1 | 904.9 | 1,221.8 | 1,389.6 | 2,496.5 | 1,938.6 | 2,220.8 | 2,085.6 |
| Equity & investment fund shares.. | 8bala | 13.9 | 24.1 | 207.0 | 329.8 | 401.6 | 395.4 | 404.8 | 401.0 | 530.6 | 106.3 | 379.3 | 351.3 |
| Debt securities | 8bbla | .2 | .1 | .... | .... | 332.5 | 509.5 | 817.0 | 988.6 | 1,966.0 | 1,832.3 | 1,841.5 | 1,734.2 |
| Fin. der.(oth.than reserves) & ESOs | 8c9la | .... | .... | .... | — | .1 | .3 | .2 | .4 | .4 | .3 | — | .1 |
| Other investment | 8d9la | 2,564.6 | 2,629.5 | 2,966.4 | 3,978.5 | 5,221.0 | 6,101.7 | 6,820.4 | 7,870.0 | 8,650.8 | 8,797.6 | 8,878.0 | 10,237.0 |
| Other equity | 8dala | .... | .... | .... | .... | .... | .... | .... | .... | .... | .... | .... | .... |
| Debt instruments | 8dzla | 2,564.6 | 2,629.5 | 2,966.4 | 3,978.5 | 5,221.0 | 6,101.7 | 6,820.4 | 7,870.0 | 8,650.8 | 8,797.6 | 8,878.0 | 10,237.0 |

| | | 2004 | 2005 | 2006 | 2007 | 2008 | 2009 | 2010 | 2011 | 2012 | 2013 | 2014 | 2015 |
|---|---|---|---|---|---|---|---|---|---|---|---|---|---|
| **Government Finance** | | | | | | | | | | | | | |
| **Cash Flow Statement** | | | | | | | | | | | | | |
| **General Government** | | | | | *Millions of Lari: Fiscal Year Ends December 31* | | | | | | | |
| Cash Receipts:Operating Activities... | c1 | 2,266.9 | 2,828.9 | † 3,850.2 | 4,972.7 | 5,854.2 | 5,264.5 | 5,865.9 | 6,873.4 | 7,560.0 | 7,402.9 | 8,392.7 | 8,938.3 |
| Taxes............................................. | c11 | 1,530.2 | 1,982.8 | † 2,646.6 | 3,669.0 | 4,752.7 | 4,388.8 | 4,867.5 | 6,134.8 | 6,671.0 | 6,659.3 | 7,483.4 | 8,010.8 |
| Social Contributions...................... | c12 | 402.2 | 428.8 | † 502.8 | 722.1 | — | — | — | — | — | — | — | — |
| Grants.......................................... | c13 | 124.7 | 104.5 | † 195.7 | 102.0 | 617.2 | 388.6 | 472.1 | 223.5 | 270.8 | 207.6 | 291.5 | 293.9 |
| Other Receipts.............................. | c14 | 209.8 | 312.8 | † 505.1 | 479.6 | 484.3 | 487.1 | 526.3 | 515.1 | 618.2 | 536.0 | 617.8 | 633.6 |
| Cash Payments:Operating Activities. | c2 | 1,835.8 | 2,425.9 | † 2,978.7 | 4,379.0 | 5,410.9 | 5,397.0 | 5,480.3 | 5,786.6 | 6,495.7 | 6,692.0 | 8,186.5 | 8,155.6 |
| Compensation of Employees.......... | c21 | 472.9 | 549.6 | † 563.3 | 696.9 | 1,008.1 | 1,048.3 | 1,120.2 | 1,136.2 | 1,202.6 | 1,395.1 | 1,571.8 | 1,601.7 |
| Purchases of Goods & Services....... | c22 | 428.7 | 572.0 | † 786.6 | 1,590.8 | 1,606.4 | 1,105.2 | 1,138.6 | 1,211.0 | 1,297.8 | 1,010.9 | 1,250.4 | 1,203.2 |
| Interest......................................... | c24 | 153.0 | 121.9 | † 105.2 | 98.6 | 120.5 | 171.2 | 206.1 | 287.6 | 253.5 | 237.6 | 244.7 | 329.8 |
| Subsidies...................................... | c25 | 217.4 | 436.3 | † 419.0 | 267.3 | 362.5 | 613.4 | 380.0 | 426.0 | 514.1 | 547.6 | 671.3 | 670.9 |
| Grants.......................................... | c26 | — | 4.7 | † 6.8 | 18.7 | 12.2 | 8.7 | 10.5 | 13.4 | 16.7 | 14.8 | 11.2 | 83.8 |
| Social Benefits.............................. | c27 | 547.6 | 558.1 | † 661.4 | 933.7 | 1,347.4 | 1,505.9 | 1,623.6 | 1,655.5 | 1,857.6 | 2,294.9 | 2,855.6 | 3,036.7 |
| Other Payments............................ | c28 | 16.2 | 183.3 | † 436.4 | 773.0 | 953.8 | 944.3 | 1,001.3 | 1,056.9 | 1,353.4 | 1,191.1 | 1,581.5 | 1,229.5 |
| Net Cash Inflow:Operating Act.[1-2] | ccio | 431.1 | 403.0 | † 871.5 | 593.7 | 443.3 | −132.5 | 385.6 | 1,086.8 | 1,064.3 | 710.9 | 206.2 | 782.7 |
| Net Cash Outflow:Invest. in NFA..... | c31 | 352.8 | 240.8 | † 505.1 | 541.0 | 826.7 | 1,041.4 | 1,320.8 | 1,298.0 | 1,219.0 | 1,012.1 | 1,149.2 | 1,123.8 |
| Purchases of Nonfinancial Assets... | c31.1 | 425.5 | 660.2 | † 1,069.6 | 1,429.4 | 1,524.2 | 1,252.8 | 1,540.8 | 1,675.3 | 1,498.5 | 1,137.8 | 1,274.1 | 1,479.0 |
| Sales of Nonfinancial Assets.......... | c31.2 | 72.7 | 419.4 | † 564.5 | 888.4 | 697.5 | 211.4 | 220.0 | 377.3 | 279.5 | 125.7 | 124.9 | 355.2 |
| Cash Surplus/Deficit [1-2-31=1-2M] | ccsd | 78.3 | 162.2 | † 366.4 | 52.7 | −383.4 | −1,173.9 | −935.2 | −211.2 | −154.7 | −301.2 | −943.0 | −341.1 |
| Net Acq. Fin. Assets, excl. Cash....... | c32x | 58.8 | 25.8 | † 159.6 | 56.3 | 184.3 | −114.3 | 251.7 | 266.1 | 293.2 | 233.8 | 228.0 | 447.1 |
| Domestic..................................... | c321x | 58.8 | 25.8 | † 159.6 | 56.3 | 184.3 | −114.3 | 251.7 | 266.1 | 293.2 | 233.8 | 228.0 | 447.1 |
| Foreign........................................ | c322x | — | — | † — | — | — | — | — | — | — | — | — | — |
| Net Incurrence of Liabilities............. | c33 | 40.1 | −67.1 | † −82.3 | 12.2 | 951.2 | 691.9 | 1,308.1 | 557.8 | 600.0 | 209.2 | 1,345.9 | 933.1 |
| Domestic..................................... | c331 | 11.6 | −32.6 | † −27.4 | −22.3 | −63.4 | 9.2 | 102.8 | 24.0 | 5.3 | 77.6 | 515.7 | 256.8 |
| Foreign........................................ | c332 | 28.5 | −34.5 | † −54.9 | 34.5 | 1,014.6 | 682.7 | 1,205.3 | 533.8 | 594.7 | 131.6 | 830.2 | 676.3 |
| Net Cash Inflow, Fin.Act.[-32x+33].. | cnfb | −18.7 | −92.9 | † −241.9 | −44.1 | 766.9 | 806.2 | 1,056.4 | 291.7 | 306.8 | −24.6 | 1,117.9 | 486.0 |
| Net Change in Stock of Cash........... | cncb | 59.6 | 69.3 | † 124.5 | 8.6 | 383.5 | −367.7 | 121.2 | 80.8 | 152.1 | −325.8 | 174.9 | 144.9 |
| Stat. Discrep. [32X-33+NCB-CSD].... | ccsdz | — | — | † — | — | — | — | — | .3 | — | — | — | — |
| Memo Item:Cash Expenditure[2+31] | c2m | 2,188.6 | 2,666.7 | † 3,483.8 | 4,920.0 | 6,237.6 | 6,438.4 | 6,801.1 | 7,084.6 | 7,714.7 | 7,704.1 | 9,335.7 | 9,279.4 |
| Memo Item: Gross Debt.................. | c63 | . . . . | . . . . | . . . . | . . . . | . . . . | . . . . | . . . . | . . . . | . . . . | . . . . | . . . . | . . . . |
| **National Accounts** | | | | | | *Millions of Lari* | | | | | | | |
| Househ.Cons.Expend.,incl.NPISHs..... | 96f | 7,195 | 7,780 | 10,856 | 12,014 | 14,660 | 14,676 | 15,527 | 18,018 | 18,875 | 19,054 | 20,320 | . . . . |
| Government Consumption Expend... | 91f | 1,379 | 2,014 | 2,116 | 3,718 | 4,936 | 4,399 | 4,371 | 4,431 | 4,633 | 4,479 | 4,866 | . . . . |
| Gross Fixed Capital Formation......... | 93e | 2,697 | 3,261 | 3,524 | 4,370 | 4,099 | 2,755 | 4,009 | 5,474 | 6,497 | 5,893 | 7,535 | . . . . |
| Changes in Inventories.................... | 93i | 437 | 630 | 731 | 1,077 | 853 | −412 | 469 | 894 | 1,079 | 760 | 1,154 | . . . . |
| Exports of Goods and Services......... | 90c | 3,100 | 3,922 | 4,532 | 5,303 | 5,459 | 5,349 | 7,250 | 8,823 | 9,983 | 11,998 | 12,518 | . . . . |
| Imports of Goods and Services (-)..... | 98c | 4,734 | 5,993 | 7,863 | 9,848 | 11,140 | 8,801 | 10,945 | 13,334 | 15,124 | 15,475 | 17,627 | . . . . |
| Gross Domestic Product (GDP)........ | 99b | 9,824 | 11,621 | 13,790 | 16,994 | 19,075 | 17,986 | 20,743 | 24,344 | 26,167 | 26,847 | 29,187 | . . . . |
| Statistical Discrepancy..................... | 99bs | −251 | 6 | −107 | 359 | 209 | 20 | 63 | 39 | 225 | 139 | 422 | . . . . |
| GDP Volume 2003 Prices................ | 99b.p | 9,066 | 9,936 | 10,868 | 12,236 | 12,555 | 12,086 | 12,835 | 13,757 | 14,638 | 15,124 | 15,845 | . . . . |
| GDP Volume (2010=100)................ | 99bvp | 70.6 | 77.4 | 84.7 | 95.3 | 97.8 | 94.2 | 100.0 | 107.2 | 114.0 | 117.8 | 123.4 | . . . . |
| GDP Deflator (2010=100)............... | 99bip | 67.1 | 72.4 | 78.5 | 85.9 | 94.0 | 92.1 | 100.0 | 109.5 | 110.6 | 109.8 | 114.0 | . . . . |
| | | | | | | *Millions: Midyear Estimates* | | | | | | | |
| **Population**................................. | 99z | 4.52 | 4.48 | 4.43 | 4.39 | 4.34 | 4.30 | 4.25 | 4.20 | 4.14 | 4.08 | 4.03 | 4.00 |

| | | 2004 | 2005 | 2006 | 2007 | 2008 | 2009 | 2010 | 2011 | 2012 | 2013 | 2014 | 2015 |
|---|---|---|---|---|---|---|---|---|---|---|---|---|---|
| **Exchange Rates** | | | | | | *Euros per SDR: End of Period* | | | | | | | |
| Market Rate.................................. | aa | 1.1402 | 1.2116 | 1.1423 | 1.0735 | 1.1068 | 1.0882 | 1.1525 | 1.1865 | 1.1649 | 1.1167 | 1.1933 | 1.2728 |
| | | | | | | *Euros per US Dollar: End of Period (ae) Period Average (rf)* | | | | | | | |
| Market Rate.................................. | ae | .7342 | .8477 | .7593 | .6793 | .7185 | .6942 | .7484 | .7729 | .7579 | .7251 | .8237 | .9185 |
| Market Rate.................................. | rf | .8054 | .8041 | .7971 | .7306 | .6827 | .7198 | .7550 | .7194 | .7783 | .7532 | .7537 | .9017 |
| | | | | | | *Index Numbers (2010=100): Period Averages* | | | | | | | |
| Nominal Effective Exchange Rate..... | nec | 99.9 | 98.9 | 98.9 | 101.2 | 103.2 | 104.0 | 100.0 | 100.3 | 97.2 | 99.9 | 100.8 | 95.9 |
| CPI-Based Real Effect. Ex. Rate........ | rec | 104.6 | 102.8 | 102.0 | 103.8 | 104.4 | 105.1 | 100.0 | 99.2 | 95.6 | 98.2 | 98.6 | 93.4 |
| ULC-Based Real Effect. Ex. Rate....... | rel | 100.6 | 97.4 | 94.0 | 94.9 | 99.4 | 101.3 | 100.0 | 96.1 | 94.1 | 97.0 | 97.2 | 92.4 |
| **Fund Position** | | | | | | *Millions of SDRs: End of Period* | | | | | | | |
| Quota..................................... | 2f.s | 13,008.20 | 13,008.20 | 13,008.20 | 13,008.20 | 13,008.20 | 13,008.20 | 13,008.20 | 14,565.50 | 14,565.50 | 14,565.50 | 14,565.50 | 14,565.50 |
| SDR Holdings.............................. | 1b.s | 1,326.98 | 1,323.65 | 1,335.86 | 1,368.05 | 1,426.90 | 12,184.18 | 12,187.67 | 11,896.91 | 11,652.16 | 11,478.94 | 11,959.22 | 11,930.72 |
| Reserve Position in the Fund............ | 1c.s | 4,419.30 | 2,436.60 | 1,301.50 | 883.61 | 1,546.70 | 2,485.15 | 4,005.99 | 6,891.18 | 7,514.64 | 7,118.46 | 5,336.84 | 4,032.18 |
| Total Fund Cred. & Loans Outstg...... | 2tl | — | — | — | — | — | — | — | — | — | — | — | — |
| SDR Allocations............................ | 1bd | 1,210.76 | 1,210.76 | 1,210.76 | 1,210.76 | 1,210.76 | 12,059.17 | 12,059.17 | 12,059.17 | 12,059.17 | 12,059.17 | 12,059.17 | 12,059.17 |
| **International Liquidity** | | | | | | *Millions of US Dollars Unless Otherwise Indicated: End of Period* | | | | | | | |
| Total Res.Min.Gold (Eurosys.Def)..... | 1l.d | 48,823 | 45,140 | 41,687 | 44,327 | 43,137 | 59,925 | 62,295 | 66,928 | 67,422 | 67,365 | 62,266 | 58,507 |
| SDR Holdings.......................... | 1b.d | 2,061 | 1,892 | 2,010 | 2,162 | 2,198 | 19,101 | 18,769 | 18,265 | 17,908 | 17,678 | 17,327 | 16,533 |
| Reserve Position in the Fund......... | 1c.d | 6,863 | 3,483 | 1,958 | 1,396 | 2,382 | 3,896 | 6,169 | 10,580 | 11,549 | 10,962 | 7,732 | 5,588 |
| Foreign Exchange...................... | 1d.d | 39,899 | 39,765 | 37,719 | 40,768 | 38,557 | 36,928 | 37,356 | 38,083 | 37,964 | 38,725 | 37,207 | 36,387 |
| o/w:Fin.Deriv.Rel.to Reserves....... | 1ddd | — | — | — | — | — | — | — | — | — | — | — | — |
| Other Reserve Assets................. | 1e.d | — | — | — | — | — | — | — | — | — | — | — | — |
| Gold (Million Fine Troy Ounces)........ | 1ad | 110.38 | 110.21 | 110.04 | 109.87 | 109.72 | 109.53 | 109.34 | 109.19 | 109.04 | 108.90 | 108.81 | 108.70 |
| Gold (Eurosystem Valuation)........... | 1and | 48,347 | 56,536 | 69,951 | 91,908 | 94,906 | 120,922 | 154,202 | 171,926 | 181,434 | 130,843 | 130,484 | 115,175 |
| Memo:Euro Cl. on Non-EA Res........ | 1dgd | 409 | 354 | 395 | 442 | 418 | 432 | — | — | — | — | — | — |
| Non-Euro Cl. on EA Res.......... | 1dhd | — | — | — | 10,380 | 88,043 | 6,356 | — | 23,456 | 4,408 | 172 | — | — |
| Central Bank: Other Assets.............. | 3..d | 28,027 | 50,604 | 23,976 | 125,027 | 179,979 | 281,178 | 482,459 | 683,591 | 963,605 | 793,926 | 629,039 | 695,932 |
| Central Bank: Other Liabs................ | 4..d | 9,919 | 5,786 | 6,755 | 22,589 | 14,703 | 32,049 | 37,890 | 78,748 | 128,416 | 90,349 | 32,359 | 46,301 |
| Other Depository Corps.: Assets....... | 7a.d | 1,223,212 | 1,172,697 | 1,544,898 | 1,972,333 | 1,780,805 | 1,531,286 | 1,364,906 | 1,288,398 | 1,281,234 | 1,270,711 | 1,275,156 | 1,096,109 |
| Other Depository Corps.: Liabs......... | 7b.d | 842,189 | 790,810 | 909,918 | 1,085,329 | 1,043,357 | 924,217 | 946,028 | 821,907 | 900,562 | 751,585 | 735,724 | 671,209 |
| **Central Bank** | | | | | | *Millions of Euros: End of Period* | | | | | | | |
| Euro Area Wide Residency Criterion | | | | | | | | | | | | | |
| Net Foreign Assets.......................... | 11n.u | 62,348 | 78,798 | 78,926 | 75,597 | 86,435 | 103,639 | 133,556 | 123,789 | 91,256 | 78,223 | 131,369 | 116,484 |
| Claims on Nonresidents................ | 11..u | 71,652 | 86,537 | 85,116 | 92,893 | 99,541 | 125,886 | 162,073 | 184,650 | 188,664 | 143,772 | 158,810 | 159,583 |
| Liabilities to Nonresidents............ | 16c.u | 9,303 | 7,739 | 6,190 | 17,296 | 13,106 | 22,247 | 28,517 | 60,861 | 97,407 | 65,549 | 27,440 | 43,099 |
| Claims on Other Depository Corps.... | 12e.u | 194,273 | 207,983 | 263,340 | 299,026 | 374,550 | 260,191 | 145,068 | 116,085 | 110,860 | 85,491 | 100,066 | 136,853 |
| Net Claims on Central Government.. | 12anu | 4,427 | 4,432 | 4,432 | 4,432 | 4,363 | −5,444 | 18,112 | 46,545 | 56,186 | 48,049 | 41,146 | 108,622 |
| Claims on Central Govt................. | 12a.u | 4,440 | 4,440 | 4,440 | 4,440 | 4,440 | 4,440 | 18,141 | 47,142 | 56,474 | 49,445 | 41,863 | 119,945 |
| Liabs. to Central Govt................. | 16d.u | 13 | 8 | 8 | 8 | 77 | 9,884 | 29 | 597 | 288 | 1,396 | 717 | 11,323 |
| Claims on Other Sectors................. | 12s.u | 2 | 2 | 2 | 2 | 2 | 1 | 2 | 3 | 2 | 215 | 214 | 200 |
| Claims on Other Financial Corps.... | 12g.u | 2 | 2 | 2 | 2 | 2 | 1 | 1 | 1 | 1 | 1 | 1 | 2 |
| Claims on State & Local Govts....... | 12b.u | — | — | — | — | — | — | — | — | — | — | — | — |
| Claims on Public Nonfin. Corps...... | 12c.u | — | — | — | — | — | — | — | — | — | — | — | — |
| Claims on Private Sector................ | 12d.u | — | — | — | — | — | — | 1 | 2 | 1 | 214 | 213 | 198 |
| Monetary Base.............................. | 14..u | 182,664 | 205,454 | 224,460 | 299,420 | 398,979 | 320,360 | 363,757 | 462,196 | 574,344 | 397,439 | 348,072 | 532,746 |
| Currency in Circulation................ | 14a.u | 140,807 | 158,553 | 176,106 | 189,464 | 212,632 | 207,693 | 216,413 | 228,412 | 234,739 | 245,080 | 248,689 | 263,406 |
| Liabs. to Other Depository Corps.... | 14c.u | 41,476 | 46,504 | 47,959 | 109,517 | 185,340 | 112,200 | 146,437 | 228,878 | 299,963 | 143,288 | 90,230 | 208,775 |
| Liabs. to Other Sectors................. | 14d.u | 381 | 397 | 395 | 439 | 1,007 | 467 | 907 | 4,906 | 39,642 | 9,071 | 9,153 | 60,565 |
| Other Liabs. to Other Dep. Corps..... | 14n.u | — | — | — | — | — | — | — | — | — | — | — | — |
| Dep. & Sec. Excl. f/Monetary Base..... | 14o.u | — | — | — | — | — | — | — | — | — | — | — | — |
| Deposits Included in Broad Money. | 15..u | — | — | — | — | — | — | — | — | — | — | — | — |
| Sec.Ot.th.Shares Inc.in.Brd.Money.. | 16a.u | — | — | — | — | — | — | — | — | — | — | — | — |
| Deposits Excl. from Broad Money... | 16b.u | — | — | — | — | — | — | — | — | — | — | — | — |
| Sec.Oh.th.Shares Excl. f/Brd.Money | 16s.u | — | — | — | — | — | — | — | — | — | — | — | — |
| Loans......................................... | 16l.u | — | — | — | — | — | — | — | — | — | — | — | — |
| Financial Derivatives....................... | 16m.u | — | — | — | — | — | — | — | — | — | — | — | — |
| Shares and Other Equity.................. | 17a.u | 32,801 | 49,274 | 50,933 | 60,044 | 68,171 | 82,163 | 113,774 | 126,621 | 140,997 | 97,106 | 114,822 | 114,897 |
| Other Items (Net)........................... | 17r.u | 45,585 | 36,487 | 71,306 | 19,593 | −1,801 | −44,136 | −180,793 | −302,394 | −457,037 | −282,567 | −190,099 | −285,484 |
| Memorandum Items | | | | | | | | | | | | | |
| National Residency Criterion | | | | | | | | | | | | | |
| Net Foreign Assets.......................... | 11n | 82,591 | 121,321 | 96,746 | 160,118 | 215,392 | 298,462 | 494,571 | 652,052 | 798,406 | 648,726 | 642,168 | 697,293 |
| Claims on Nonresidents................ | 11 | 91,915 | 129,084 | 102,972 | 177,475 | 228,513 | 320,717 | 523,092 | 712,918 | 918,950 | 719,407 | 676,872 | 798,764 |
| Liabilities to Nonresidents............ | 16c | 9,323 | 7,763 | 6,226 | 17,357 | 13,121 | 22,255 | 28,521 | 60,866 | 120,543 | 70,681 | 34,703 | 101,471 |
| Claims on Other Depository Corps.... | 12e | 193,784 | 207,273 | 262,647 | 297,314 | 372,697 | 253,992 | 134,213 | 104,563 | 99,188 | 75,935 | 90,704 | 123,409 |
| Net Claims on Central Government.. | 12an | 4,427 | 4,432 | 4,432 | 4,432 | 4,363 | −5,444 | 4,411 | 3,843 | 4,152 | 3,044 | 3,723 | 77,527 |
| Claims on Central Government...... | 12a | 4,440 | 4,440 | 4,440 | 4,440 | 4,440 | 4,440 | 4,440 | 4,440 | 4,440 | 4,440 | 4,440 | 88,850 |
| Liabilities to Central Government... | 16d | 13 | 8 | 8 | 8 | 77 | 9,884 | 29 | 597 | 288 | 1,396 | 717 | 11,323 |
| Claims on Other Sectors................. | 12s | — | — | — | — | — | — | 1 | 2 | 1 | 214 | 213 | 198 |
| Claims on Other Fin. Corps............ | 12g | — | — | — | — | — | — | — | — | — | — | — | — |
| Claims on State & Local Govts....... | 12b | — | — | — | — | — | — | — | — | — | — | — | — |
| Claims on Private Sector................ | 12d | — | — | — | — | — | — | 1 | 2 | 1 | 214 | 213 | 198 |
| Liabs.to ODCs, Inc.in Mon.Base....... | 14c | 41,456 | 46,481 | 47,923 | 109,456 | 185,325 | 112,192 | 146,433 | 228,875 | 299,961 | 143,285 | 90,228 | 208,773 |
| Liabs.to Ot.Sectors, Inc.in Mon.Base | 14d | 381 | 396 | 395 | 439 | 1,007 | 467 | 907 | 4,904 | 16,508 | 3,942 | 1,892 | 2,195 |
| Liabs.to ODCs,Excl.f/Mon.Base........ | 14n | — | — | — | — | — | — | — | — | — | — | — | — |
| Net Claims on Eurosystem............... | 12e.s | 20,955 | 43,018 | 18,344 | 84,064 | 128,313 | 189,722 | 337,869 | 475,765 | 668,617 | 523,104 | 473,263 | 596,588 |

| Other Depository Corporations | | 2004 | 2005 | 2006 | 2007 | 2008 | 2009 | 2010 | 2011 | 2012 | 2013 | 2014 | 2015 |
|---|---|---|---|---|---|---|---|---|---|---|---|---|---|
| Euro Area Wide Residency Criterion | | | | | | *Millions of Euros: End of Period* | | | | | | | |
| Net Foreign Assets.......................... | **21n.u** | 279,732 | 323,716 | 482,141 | 602,543 | 529,890 | 421,400 | 313,484 | 360,531 | 288,519 | 376,424 | 444,306 | 390,282 |
| Claims on Nonresidents............... | **21..u** | 898,034 | 994,064 | 1,173,043 | 1,339,809 | 1,279,590 | 1,062,950 | 1,021,483 | 995,748 | 971,073 | 921,406 | 1,050,289 | 1,006,805 |
| Liabilities to Nonresidents............. | **26c.u** | 618,302 | 670,348 | 690,902 | 737,266 | 749,700 | 641,550 | 707,999 | 635,217 | 682,554 | 544,982 | 605,983 | 616,523 |
| Claims on Eurosystem.................... | **20..u** | 56,953 | 64,319 | 66,115 | 126,492 | 184,008 | 131,588 | 164,143 | 246,221 | 321,478 | 160,909 | 110,769 | 229,010 |
| Currency....................................... | **20a.u** | 14,917 | 15,087 | 16,035 | 17,491 | 17,420 | 16,891 | 16,032 | 15,793 | 18,477 | 18,517 | 18,943 | 19,243 |
| Reserve Deposits and Securities..... | **20b.u** | 42,036 | 49,232 | 50,080 | 109,001 | 166,588 | 114,697 | 148,111 | 230,428 | 303,001 | 142,392 | 91,826 | 209,767 |
| Other Claims............................... | **20n.u** | — | — | — | — | — | — | — | — | — | — | — | — |
| Net Claims on Central Government.. | **22anu** | 179,799 | 168,396 | 135,063 | 97,344 | 81,853 | 106,491 | 191,706 | 116,738 | 123,557 | 130,359 | 161,544 | 159,466 |
| Claims on Central Government...... | **22a.u** | 223,591 | 209,985 | 180,570 | 137,474 | 118,498 | 129,283 | 231,515 | 156,264 | 152,497 | 147,977 | 172,116 | 170,759 |
| Liabilities to Central Government... | **26d.u** | 43,792 | 41,589 | 45,507 | 40,130 | 36,645 | 22,792 | 39,809 | 39,526 | 28,940 | 17,618 | 10,572 | 11,293 |
| Claims on Other Sectors.................. | **22s.u** | 3,135,091 | 3,197,619 | 3,281,544 | 3,349,810 | 3,519,664 | 3,508,985 | 4,476,265 | 4,658,975 | 4,596,867 | 4,125,731 | 4,347,913 | 4,267,553 |
| Claims on Other Financial Corps.... | **22g.u** | 122,976 | 162,396 | 202,419 | 276,959 | 395,690 | 442,315 | 1,536,692 | 1,707,158 | 1,602,016 | 1,127,635 | 1,340,721 | 1,216,768 |
| Claims on State & Local Govts...... | **22b.u** | 514,831 | 523,992 | 517,433 | 499,192 | 484,669 | 493,924 | 534,649 | 530,990 | 565,602 | 562,464 | 550,923 | 545,559 |
| Claims on Public Nonfin. Corps..... | **22c.u** | — | — | — | — | — | — | — | — | — | — | — | — |
| Claims on Private Sector............... | **22d.u** | 2,497,284 | 2,511,231 | 2,561,692 | 2,573,659 | 2,639,305 | 2,572,746 | 2,404,924 | 2,420,827 | 2,429,249 | 2,435,632 | 2,456,269 | 2,505,226 |
| Liabilities to Eurosystem................. | **26g.u** | 193,548 | 207,292 | 262,841 | 301,706 | 370,387 | 265,987 | 146,101 | 117,604 | 108,908 | 84,805 | 99,178 | 135,313 |
| Transf.Dep.Included in Broad Money | **24..u** | 654,991 | 725,394 | 759,646 | 789,258 | 831,823 | 1,015,470 | 1,108,359 | 1,169,171 | 1,326,065 | 1,439,075 | 1,548,630 | 1,705,488 |
| Other.Dep.Included in Broad Money. | **25..u** | 800,667 | 797,337 | 840,658 | 972,805 | 1,066,456 | 862,880 | 846,760 | 905,910 | 870,966 | 856,362 | 854,199 | 850,449 |
| Sec.Ot.th.Shares Inc.in.Brd.Money.... | **26a.u** | 50,000 | 53,938 | 58,511 | 72,046 | 79,327 | 40,116 | 42,784 | 32,481 | 26,285 | 14,849 | 17,949 | 35,583 |
| Deposits Excl. from Broad Money..... | **26b.u** | 810,052 | 814,413 | 849,691 | 879,073 | 935,802 | 1,006,038 | 1,026,026 | 1,020,710 | 950,169 | 828,065 | 790,946 | 745,746 |
| Sec.Ot.th.Shares Excl.f/Brd. Money.... | **26s.u** | 800,163 | 829,409 | 830,175 | 794,849 | 739,765 | 663,175 | 665,691 | 658,577 | 600,717 | 535,111 | 529,388 | 497,779 |
| Loans............................................. | **26l.u** | — | — | — | — | — | — | — | — | — | — | — | — |
| Financial Derivatives..................... | **26m.u** | — | — | — | — | — | — | 967,869 | 1,123,859 | 1,034,420 | 645,116 | 826,307 | 673,667 |
| Insurance Technical Reserves.......... | **26r.u** | — | — | — | — | — | — | — | — | — | — | — | — |
| Shares and Other Equity.................. | **27a.u** | 288,134 | 302,681 | 337,229 | 351,952 | 378,240 | 378,842 | 380,644 | 394,406 | 416,168 | 437,559 | 464,624 | 479,020 |
| Other Items (Net)............................ | **27r.u** | 54,020 | 23,586 | 26,110 | 14,500 | −86,385 | −64,044 | −38,636 | −40,252 | −3,277 | −47,519 | −66,689 | −76,464 |
| Memorandum Items | | | | | | | | | | | | | |
| Total Assets.................................... | **20ra** | 6,617,357 | 6,859,403 | 7,154,390 | 7,592,390 | 7,892,671 | 7,436,089 | 8,304,802 | 8,393,335 | 8,226,623 | 7,528,947 | 7,802,346 | 7,664,936 |
| National Residency Criterion | | | | | | | | | | | | | |
| Net Foreign Assets.......................... | **21n** | 602,504 | 785,408 | 1,060,272 | 1,288,118 | 1,346,823 | 1,212,837 | 959,537 | 971,978 | 848,832 | 954,353 | 1,039,464 | 989,459 |
| Claims on Nonresidents............... | **21** | 1,598,304 | 1,831,135 | 2,146,024 | 2,441,085 | 2,446,853 | 2,181,179 | 2,017,621 | 1,949,129 | 1,866,638 | 1,804,080 | 1,957,631 | 1,914,138 |
| Liabilities to Nonresidents............. | **26c** | 995,800 | 1,045,727 | 1,085,752 | 1,152,967 | 1,100,030 | 968,342 | 1,058,084 | 977,151 | 1,017,806 | 849,727 | 918,167 | 924,679 |
| Net Claims on Central Government.. | **22an** | 65,751 | 40,448 | 17,874 | −350 | −10,831 | 10,414 | 89,088 | 18,677 | 26,021 | 30,704 | 38,555 | 43,369 |
| Claims on Central Government...... | **22a** | 107,188 | 79,203 | 59,759 | 37,940 | 24,004 | 32,625 | 127,816 | 56,528 | 51,955 | 46,663 | 49,030 | 53,012 |
| Liabilities to Central Government... | **26d** | 41,437 | 38,755 | 41,885 | 38,290 | 34,835 | 22,211 | 38,728 | 37,851 | 25,934 | 15,959 | 10,475 | 9,643 |
| Claims on Other Sectors.................. | **22s** | 2,976,226 | 3,006,023 | 3,025,778 | 3,023,861 | 3,139,036 | 3,155,284 | 4,158,376 | 4,355,634 | 4,298,224 | 3,834,774 | 4,055,956 | 3,967,840 |
| Claims on Other Fin. Corps........... | **22g** | 71,400 | 91,554 | 101,595 | 128,249 | 216,693 | 277,229 | 1,383,129 | 1,564,321 | 1,455,424 | 987,769 | 1,205,295 | 1,082,144 |
| Claims on State & Local Govts....... | **22b** | 496,567 | 501,463 | 489,723 | 467,834 | 452,125 | 462,412 | 505,977 | 504,529 | 542,037 | 539,147 | 528,990 | 521,800 |
| Claims on Private Sector............... | **22d** | 2,408,259 | 2,413,006 | 2,434,460 | 2,427,778 | 2,470,218 | 2,415,643 | 2,269,270 | 2,286,784 | 2,300,763 | 2,307,858 | 2,321,671 | 2,363,896 |
| Transf.Dep.Included in Broad Money | **24** | 646,154 | 715,843 | 745,757 | 769,631 | 809,453 | 997,783 | 1,089,071 | 1,143,270 | 1,294,861 | 1,405,254 | 1,514,257 | 1,670,232 |
| Other.Dep.Included in Broad Money. | **25** | 783,442 | 781,297 | 825,795 | 949,454 | 1,037,928 | 842,143 | 825,164 | 882,049 | 853,421 | 830,873 | 832,754 | 828,797 |
| Sec.Ot.th.Shares Inc.in.Brd.Money... | **26a** | 25,065 | 40,088 | 57,391 | 77,823 | 85,795 | 38,316 | 32,788 | 25,405 | 20,857 | 19,459 | 14,774 | 20,449 |
| Deposits Excl. from Broad Money..... | **26b** | 756,382 | 768,590 | 808,600 | 844,795 | 909,658 | 975,525 | 991,410 | 986,423 | 921,649 | 800,205 | 764,102 | 718,858 |
| Sec.Ot.th.Shares Excl.f/Brd. Money... | **26s** | 886,428 | 949,983 | 996,477 | 992,155 | 931,204 | 850,008 | 847,314 | 821,794 | 750,142 | 676,485 | 665,460 | 633,790 |

| | | 2004 | 2005 | 2006 | 2007 | 2008 | 2009 | 2010 | 2011 | 2012 | 2013 | 2014 | 2015 |
|---|---|---|---|---|---|---|---|---|---|---|---|---|---|
| **Depository Corporations** | | | | | | | *Millions of Euros: End of Period* | | | | | | |
| Euro Area Wide Residency Criterion | | | | | | | | | | | | | |
| Net Foreign Assets | 31n.u | 342,080 | 402,514 | 561,067 | 678,140 | 616,325 | 525,039 | 447,040 | 484,320 | 379,775 | 454,647 | 575,675 | 506,766 |
| Claims on Nonresidents | 31..u | 969,686 | 1,080,601 | 1,258,159 | 1,432,702 | 1,379,131 | 1,188,836 | 1,183,556 | 1,180,398 | 1,159,737 | 1,065,178 | 1,209,099 | 1,166,388 |
| Liabilities to Nonresidents | 36c.u | 627,605 | 678,087 | 697,092 | 754,562 | 762,806 | 663,797 | 736,516 | 696,078 | 779,961 | 610,531 | 633,423 | 659,622 |
| Domestic Claims | 32..u | 3,319,319 | 3,370,449 | 3,421,041 | 3,451,588 | 3,605,882 | 3,610,033 | 4,686,085 | 4,822,261 | 4,776,612 | 4,304,354 | 4,550,817 | 4,535,841 |
| Net Claims on Central Government | 32anu | 184,226 | 172,828 | 139,495 | 101,776 | 86,216 | 101,047 | 209,818 | 163,283 | 179,743 | 178,408 | 202,690 | 268,088 |
| Claims on Central Government | 32a.u | 228,031 | 214,425 | 185,010 | 141,914 | 122,938 | 133,723 | 249,656 | 203,406 | 208,971 | 197,422 | 213,979 | 290,704 |
| Liabilities to Central Government | 36d.u | 43,805 | 41,597 | 45,515 | 40,138 | 36,722 | 32,676 | 39,838 | 40,123 | 29,228 | 19,014 | 11,289 | 22,616 |
| Claims on Other Sectors | 32s.u | 3,135,093 | 3,197,621 | 3,281,546 | 3,349,812 | 3,519,666 | 3,508,986 | 4,476,267 | 4,658,978 | 4,596,869 | 4,125,946 | 4,348,127 | 4,267,753 |
| Claims on Other Financial Corps | 32g.u | 122,978 | 162,398 | 202,421 | 276,961 | 395,692 | 442,316 | 1,536,693 | 1,707,159 | 1,602,017 | 1,127,636 | 1,340,722 | 1,216,770 |
| Claims on State & Local Govts | 32b.u | 514,831 | 523,992 | 517,433 | 499,192 | 484,669 | 493,924 | 534,649 | 530,990 | 565,602 | 562,464 | 550,923 | 545,559 |
| Claims on Public Nonfin. Corps | 32c.u | | | | | | | | | | | | |
| Claims on Private Sector | 32d.u | 2,497,284 | 2,511,231 | 2,561,692 | 2,573,659 | 2,639,305 | 2,572,746 | 2,404,925 | 2,420,829 | 2,429,250 | 2,435,846 | 2,456,482 | 2,505,424 |
| Broad Money Liabilities | 35l.u | 1,631,929 | 1,720,532 | 1,819,281 | 2,006,521 | 2,173,825 | 2,109,735 | 2,199,191 | 2,325,087 | 2,479,220 | 2,545,920 | 2,659,677 | 2,896,248 |
| Currency Outside Depository Corps | 34..u | 125,890 | 143,466 | 160,071 | 171,973 | 195,212 | 190,802 | 200,381 | 212,619 | 216,262 | 226,563 | 229,746 | 244,163 |
| Transferable Deposits | 34..u | 655,372 | 725,791 | 760,041 | 789,697 | 832,830 | 1,015,937 | 1,109,266 | 1,174,077 | 1,365,707 | 1,448,146 | 1,557,783 | 1,766,053 |
| Other Deposits | 35..u | 800,667 | 797,337 | 840,658 | 972,805 | 1,066,456 | 862,880 | 846,760 | 905,910 | 870,966 | 856,362 | 854,199 | 850,449 |
| Securities Other than Shares | 36a.u | 50,000 | 53,938 | 58,511 | 72,046 | 79,327 | 40,116 | 42,784 | 32,481 | 26,285 | 14,849 | 17,949 | 35,583 |
| Deposits Excl. from Broad Money | 36b.u | 810,052 | 814,413 | 849,691 | 879,073 | 935,802 | 1,006,038 | 1,026,026 | 1,020,710 | 950,169 | 828,065 | 790,946 | 745,746 |
| Sec.Oth.th.Shares Excl.f/Brd. Money | 36s.u | 800,163 | 829,409 | 830,175 | 794,849 | 739,765 | 663,175 | 665,691 | 658,577 | 600,717 | 535,111 | 529,388 | 497,779 |
| Loans | 36l.u | — | — | — | — | — | — | | | | | | |
| Financial Derivatives | 36m.u | — | — | — | — | — | — | 967,869 | 1,123,859 | 1,034,420 | 645,116 | 826,307 | 673,667 |
| Insurance Technical Reserves | 36r.u | — | — | — | — | — | — | | | | | | |
| Shares and Other Equity | 37a.u | 320,935 | 351,955 | 388,162 | 411,996 | 446,411 | 461,005 | 494,418 | 521,027 | 557,165 | 534,665 | 579,446 | 593,917 |
| Other Items (Net) | 37r.u | 98,320 | 56,654 | 94,796 | 37,289 | −73,597 | −104,881 | −220,070 | −342,677 | −465,304 | −329,876 | −259,272 | −364,480 |
| Broad Money Liabs., Seasonally Adj. | 35lub | 1,617,462 | 1,705,172 | 1,803,342 | 1,989,212 | 2,156,309 | 2,094,064 | 2,185,230 | 2,313,158 | 2,470,238 | 2,540,265 | 2,656,832 | 2,894,736 |
| Memorandum Items | | | | | | | | | | | | | |
| National Residency Criterion | | | | | | | | | | | | | |
| Net Foreign Assets | 31n | 685,095 | 906,729 | 1,157,018 | 1,448,236 | 1,562,215 | 1,511,299 | 1,454,108 | 1,624,030 | 1,647,238 | 1,603,079 | 1,681,632 | 1,686,752 |
| Claims on Nonresidents | 31 | 1,690,219 | 1,960,219 | 2,248,996 | 2,618,560 | 2,675,366 | 2,501,896 | 2,540,713 | 2,662,047 | 2,785,588 | 2,523,487 | 2,634,503 | 2,712,902 |
| Liabilities to Nonresidents | 36c | 1,005,123 | 1,053,490 | 1,091,978 | 1,170,324 | 1,113,151 | 990,597 | 1,086,605 | 1,038,017 | 1,138,349 | 920,408 | 952,870 | 1,026,150 |
| Domestic Claims | 32 | 3,046,404 | 3,050,903 | 3,048,084 | 3,027,943 | 3,132,568 | 3,160,254 | 4,251,876 | 4,378,156 | 4,328,398 | 3,868,736 | 4,098,447 | 4,088,934 |
| Net Claims on Central Government | 32an | 70,178 | 44,880 | 22,306 | 4,082 | −6,468 | 4,970 | 93,499 | 22,520 | 30,173 | 33,748 | 42,278 | 120,896 |
| Claims on Central Government | 32a | 111,628 | 83,643 | 64,199 | 42,380 | 28,444 | 37,065 | 132,256 | 60,968 | 56,395 | 51,103 | 53,470 | 141,862 |
| Liabilities to Central Government | 36d | 41,450 | 38,763 | 41,893 | 38,298 | 34,912 | 32,095 | 38,757 | 38,448 | 26,222 | 17,355 | 11,192 | 20,966 |
| Claims on Other Sectors | 32s | 2,976,226 | 3,006,023 | 3,025,778 | 3,023,861 | 3,139,036 | 3,155,284 | 4,158,377 | 4,355,636 | 4,298,225 | 3,834,988 | 4,056,169 | 3,968,038 |
| Claims on Other Financial Corps | 32g | 71,440 | 91,554 | 101,595 | 128,249 | 216,693 | 277,229 | 1,383,129 | 1,564,321 | 1,455,424 | 987,769 | 1,205,295 | 1,082,144 |
| Claims on State & Local Govts | 32b | 496,567 | 501,463 | 489,723 | 467,834 | 452,125 | 462,412 | 505,977 | 504,529 | 542,037 | 539,147 | 528,990 | 521,800 |
| Claims on Private Sector | 32d | 2,408,259 | 2,413,006 | 2,434,460 | 2,427,778 | 2,470,218 | 2,415,643 | 2,269,271 | 2,286,786 | 2,300,764 | 2,308,072 | 2,321,884 | 2,364,094 |
| Transf.Dep.Included in Broad Money | 34 | 646,535 | 716,239 | 746,152 | 770,070 | 810,460 | 998,250 | 1,089,978 | 1,148,174 | 1,311,369 | 1,409,196 | 1,516,149 | 1,672,427 |
| Other Dep.Included in Broad Money | 35 | 783,442 | 781,297 | 825,795 | 949,454 | 1,037,928 | 842,143 | 825,164 | 882,049 | 853,421 | 830,873 | 832,754 | 828,797 |
| Sec.Ot.th.Shares Inc.in.Brd. Money | 36a | 25,065 | 40,088 | 57,391 | 77,823 | 85,795 | 38,316 | 32,788 | 25,405 | 20,857 | 19,459 | 14,774 | 20,449 |
| Deposits Excl. from Broad Money | 36b | 756,382 | 768,590 | 808,600 | 844,795 | 909,658 | 975,525 | 991,410 | 986,423 | 921,649 | 800,205 | 764,102 | 718,858 |
| Sec.Ot.th.Shares Excl./f.Brd. Money | 36s | 886,428 | 949,983 | 996,477 | 992,155 | 931,204 | 850,008 | 847,314 | 821,794 | 750,142 | 676,485 | 665,460 | 633,790 |
| **Interest Rates** | | | | | | | *Percent Per Annum* | | | | | | |
| Money Market Rate | 60b | 2.05 | 2.09 | 2.84 | 3.86 | 3.82 | .63 | .38 | .81 | .26 | .... | .... | .... |
| Treasury Bill Rate | 60c | 2.00 | 2.03 | 3.08 | 3.81 | .... | .... | .... | .... | .... | .... | .... | .... |
| Deposit Rate | | | | | | | | | | | | | |
| Households: Stocks, up to 2 years | 60lhs | 1.92 | 1.98 | 2.56 | 3.61 | 4.25 | 3.14 | 1.62 | 1.61 | 1.64 | 1.14 | .81 | .55 |
| New Business, up to 1 year | 60lhn | 1.93 | 1.91 | 2.61 | 3.75 | 4.13 | 1.38 | 1.10 | 1.40 | 1.16 | .72 | .58 | .37 |
| Corporations: Stocks, up to 2 years | 60lcs | 2.00 | 2.06 | 2.81 | 3.94 | 4.36 | 1.62 | .91 | 1.37 | 1.11 | .57 | .42 | .28 |
| New Business, up to 1 year | 60lcn | 1.94 | 2.01 | 2.79 | 3.88 | 4.04 | .80 | .57 | 1.11 | .44 | .21 | .20 | .13 |
| Lending Rate | | | | | | | | | | | | | |
| Households: Stocks, up to 1 year | 60phs | 8.79 | 8.75 | 9.23 | 10.07 | 10.40 | 8.85 | 8.58 | 8.86 | 8.48 | 7.97 | 7.84 | 7.50 |
| New Bus., Floating & up to 1 year | 60pns | 5.12 | 5.16 | 5.40 | 5.96 | 5.97 | 4.96 | 3.87 | 3.68 | 3.99 | 5.17 | 4.95 | 5.08 |
| House Purch., Stocks,Over 5 years | 60phm | 5.71 | 5.50 | 5.26 | 5.13 | 5.07 | 4.95 | 4.74 | 4.55 | 4.35 | 4.07 | 3.80 | 3.49 |
| House Purch., New Bus., 5-10 yrs | 60phn | 4.93 | 4.29 | 4.55 | 4.96 | 5.04 | 4.42 | 3.90 | 3.95 | 3.05 | 2.75 | 2.47 | 1.84 |
| Corporations: Stocks, up to 1 year | 60pcs | 4.73 | 4.60 | 5.08 | 5.93 | 6.16 | 4.13 | 3.90 | 4.23 | 3.62 | 3.31 | 3.22 | 2.88 |
| New Bus., Over € 1 mil.,up to 1 yr | 60pcn | 3.26 | 3.23 | 3.97 | 5.06 | 5.26 | 2.88 | 2.45 | 2.86 | 2.24 | 1.77 | 1.72 | 1.40 |
| Government Bond Yield | 61 | 4.04 | 3.35 | 3.76 | 4.22 | 3.98 | 3.22 | 2.74 | 2.61 | 1.50 | 1.57 | 1.16 | .50 |
| **Prices, Production, Labor** | | | | | | | *Index Numbers (2010=100): Period Averages* | | | | | | |
| Share Prices (End of Month) | 62.ep | 77.3 | 90.0 | 112.8 | 140.2 | 109.1 | 83.0 | 100.0 | 106.4 | 106.4 | 126.1 | 141.1 | 158.9 |
| Producer Prices | 63 | 87.4 | 91.2 | 96.2 | 97.5 | 102.8 | 98.5 | 100.0 | 105.3 | 107.0 | 106.9 | 105.8 | 103.9 |
| Consumer Prices | 64 | 91.0 | 92.5 | 93.9 | 96.1 | 98.6 | 98.9 | 100.0 | 102.1 | 104.1 | 105.7 | 106.7 | 106.9 |
| Harmonized CPI | 64h | 90.4 | 92.2 | 93.9 | 96.0 | 98.6 | 98.9 | 100.0 | 102.5 | 104.7 | 106.3 | 107.2 | 107.3 |
| Industrial Production | 66 | 92.0 | 95.0 | 100.5 | 107.1 | 108.1 | 89.3 | 100.0 | 107.9 | 106.7 | 107.7 | 109.8 | 110.4 |
| Wages:Hourly Earnings.,s.a. | 65..c | 91.0 | 92.3 | 93.4 | 94.9 | 97.5 | 100.6 | 100.0 | 102.9 | 106.3 | 109.5 | 112.5 | 116.1 |
| | | | | | | | *Number in Thousands: Period Averages* | | | | | | |
| Labor Force | 67d | 39,968 | 40,411 | 40,875 | † 40,992 | 41,032 | 41,030 | 40,178 | 40,438 | 40,538 | 40,814 | 40,990 | 41,117 |
| Employment | 67e | 35,841 | 35,845 | 36,633 | † 37,397 | 37,902 | 37,808 | 37,337 | 38,045 | 38,321 | 38,640 | 38,908 | 39,176 |
| Unemployment | 67c | 4,387 | 4,861 | 4,487 | † 3,601 | 3,136 | 3,415 | 3,239 | 2,976 | 2,897 | 2,950 | 2,899 | 2,606 |
| Unemployment Rate (%) | 67r | 10.6 | 11.7 | 10.8 | † 8.7 | 7.5 | 8.1 | 7.7 | 7.1 | 6.8 | 6.9 | 6.7 | 6.0 |
| **Intl. Transactions & Positions** | | | | | | | *Billions of Euros* | | | | | | |
| Exports | 70 | 731.54 | 786.27 | 893.04 | 965.24 | 984.14 | 803.31 | 951.96 | 1,061.23 | 1,095.77 | 1,093.11 | 1,123.75 | 1,196.38 |
| Imports, c.i.f | 71 | 575.45 | 628.09 | 733.99 | 769.89 | 805.84 | 664.62 | 797.10 | 902.52 | 905.93 | 898.16 | 910.15 | 948.50 |
| Imports, f.o.b | 71.v | 558.69 | 609.79 | 712.62 | 747.46 | 782.37 | 645.26 | 773.88 | 876.24 | 879.54 | 872.00 | .... | .... |
| | | | | | | | *2010=100* | | | | | | |
| Volume of Exports | 72 | 82.8 | † 88.6 | 99.9 | 105.6 | † 107.0 | 87.5 | 100.0 | 108.4 | 108.9 | 109.5 | 112.1 | 115.1 |
| Volume of Imports | 73 | 80.9 | † 86.0 | 96.9 | 100.0 | † 101.4 | 88.2 | 100.0 | 106.8 | 104.3 | 105.4 | 109.2 | 111.9 |
| Unit Value of Exports | 74 | 99.4 | † 99.9 | 100.7 | 102.9 | † 103.6 | 102.1 | 100.0 | 103.1 | 107.1 | 106.1 | 107.7 | 110.2 |
| Unit Value of Imports | 75 | 94.4 | † 96.6 | 100.2 | 101.9 | † 105.2 | 98.6 | 100.0 | 106.8 | 111.9 | 109.8 | 108.4 | 109.3 |
| Export Prices | 76 | 93.8 | 94.7 | 96.3 | 97.5 | 99.2 | 97.0 | 100.0 | 103.3 | 104.9 | 104.3 | 107.1 | 110.0 |
| Import Prices | 76.x | 89.9 | 92.9 | 97.0 | 97.6 | 102.1 | 93.4 | 100.0 | 106.4 | 108.7 | 105.9 | 108.3 | 109.1 |

| | | 2004 | 2005 | 2006 | 2007 | 2008 | 2009 | 2010 | 2011 | 2012 | 2013 | 2014 | 2015 |
|---|---|---|---|---|---|---|---|---|---|---|---|---|---|
| **Balance of Payments** | | | | | | | *Billions of US Dollars* | | | | | | |
| A. Current Account* | 109bx | 126.1 | 131.7 | 171.3 | 233.3 | 210.9 | 198.9 | 193.0 | 228.0 | 248.9 | 253.5 | 281.3 | 285.4 |
| Goods, credit (exports) | 1a9cx | 852.7 | 920.1 | 1,057.3 | 1,270.9 | 1,398.4 | 1,074.4 | 1,217.1 | 1,432.9 | 1,377.1 | 1,434.1 | 1,480.2 | 1,309.0 |
| Goods, debit (imports) | 1a9dx | 662.8 | 724.0 | 854.4 | 994.1 | 1,124.6 | 876.4 | 1,003.3 | 1,205.6 | 1,119.7 | 1,153.1 | 1,179.8 | 1,016.9 |
| Balance on goods | 1a9bx | 189.9 | 196.1 | 202.9 | 276.9 | 273.8 | 198.0 | 213.7 | 227.3 | 257.4 | 281.1 | 300.4 | 292.1 |
| Services, credit (exports) | 1b9cx | 147.8 | 159.4 | 181.5 | 211.8 | 241.4 | 222.8 | 227.6 | 250.4 | 252.5 | 271.9 | 291.3 | 264.5 |
| Services, debit (imports) | 1b9dx | 195.6 | 209.9 | 225.0 | 259.4 | 288.6 | 250.2 | 263.0 | 296.0 | 294.3 | 329.1 | 338.2 | 297.9 |
| Balance on Goods & Services | 1z9bx | 142.1 | 145.7 | 159.4 | 229.2 | 226.6 | 170.6 | 178.3 | 181.7 | 215.6 | 223.8 | 253.4 | 258.7 |
| Primary income: credit | 1c9cx | 177.2 | 207.9 | 262.5 | 336.4 | 290.6 | 255.5 | 265.0 | 306.4 | 263.2 | 255.9 | 253.8 | 216.0 |
| Primary income: debit | 1c9dx | 155.8 | 182.2 | 210.2 | 286.0 | 256.4 | 178.2 | 196.9 | 211.1 | 178.5 | 168.0 | 172.0 | 145.3 |
| Balance on gds, serv. & prim. inc. | 1y9bx | 163.5 | 171.3 | 211.8 | 279.6 | 260.8 | 247.9 | 246.4 | 277.0 | 300.4 | 311.6 | 335.3 | 329.3 |
| Secondary income: credit | 1d9ca | 48.0 | 52.5 | 49.4 | 57.3 | 65.9 | 56.5 | 56.1 | 72.8 | 67.9 | 79.4 | 81.6 | 71.0 |
| Secondary income: debit | 1d9da | 85.4 | 92.1 | 89.9 | 103.6 | 115.8 | 105.4 | 109.5 | 121.9 | 119.3 | 137.5 | 135.6 | 115.0 |
| B. Capital Account* | 209ba | −.2 | −3.0 | −1.7 | −2.3 | −1.2 | −2.6 | 1.6 | 2.2 | −.6 | −.9 | 1.8 | −.1 |
| Capital account: credit | 209ca | 4.6 | 6.3 | 6.1 | 7.4 | 8.6 | 16.9 | 16.3 | 17.3 | 18.9 | 21.8 | 22.9 | 24.6 |
| Capital account: debit | 209da | 4.8 | 9.3 | 7.8 | 9.7 | 9.8 | 19.4 | 14.6 | 15.1 | 19.5 | 22.7 | 21.1 | 24.8 |
| Balance on current & capital acct. | 129ba | 125.9 | 128.7 | 169.6 | 231.0 | 209.7 | 196.3 | 194.7 | 230.2 | 248.3 | 252.6 | 283.1 | 285.2 |
| C. Financial Account* | 309na | 140.3 | 123.1 | 200.3 | 252.2 | 177.1 | 172.1 | 121.6 | 163.8 | 184.1 | 290.2 | 327.2 | 259.4 |
| Direct investment: assets | 3a9aa | 9.1 | 89.0 | 147.9 | 140.7 | 98.0 | 99.7 | 146.7 | 107.8 | 99.1 | 90.8 | 115.0 | 108.8 |
| Equity & investment fund shares | 3aaaa | 3.2 | 59.6 | 125.1 | 109.1 | 48.7 | 88.6 | 102.1 | 87.4 | 79.6 | 57.9 | 88.7 | 77.2 |
| Debt instruments | 3abaa | 5.9 | 29.3 | 22.8 | 31.5 | 49.3 | 11.0 | 44.6 | 20.5 | 19.6 | 32.8 | 26.3 | 31.6 |
| Direct investment: liabilities | 3a9la | −20.4 | 59.9 | 87.4 | 50.8 | 30.9 | 56.7 | 86.1 | 97.5 | 65.5 | 62.7 | 9.4 | 46.2 |
| Equity & investment fund shares | 3aala | 38.9 | 40.0 | 37.4 | 63.7 | 5.6 | −1.8 | 29.9 | 28.2 | 19.8 | 1.1 | 31.2 | 20.6 |
| Debt instruments | 3abla | −59.3 | 19.8 | 50.0 | −12.9 | 25.3 | 58.4 | 56.1 | 69.3 | 45.7 | 61.6 | −21.7 | 25.6 |
| Portfolio investment: assets | 3b9aa | 128.6 | 257.3 | 203.4 | 199.0 | −14.7 | 110.2 | 230.2 | 25.6 | 136.2 | 186.0 | 198.4 | 138.3 |
| Equity & investment fund shares | 3baaa | 4.8 | 78.5 | 28.6 | 27.9 | −39.9 | 11.2 | 30.0 | −1.8 | 41.6 | 68.0 | 71.4 | 61.3 |
| Debt securities | 3bbaa | 123.8 | 178.9 | 174.8 | 171.0 | 25.2 | 99.0 | 200.2 | 27.3 | 94.6 | 118.0 | 127.0 | 77.0 |
| Portfolio investment: liabilities | 3b9la | 147.8 | 221.7 | 181.0 | 414.3 | 29.8 | −9.0 | 76.1 | 77.0 | 69.3 | −26.8 | 17.8 | −82.1 |
| Equity & investment fund shares | 3bala | −7.9 | 22.1 | 35.7 | 77.0 | −68.6 | 20.8 | 4.8 | −5.5 | −2.5 | 14.9 | .4 | 17.5 |
| Debt securities | 3bbla | 155.7 | 199.6 | 145.4 | 337.4 | 98.4 | −29.9 | 71.3 | 82.5 | 71.8 | −41.7 | 17.4 | −99.6 |
| Fin. der.& empl.stk.ops.(ESOs): net | 3c9na | 8.3 | 10.3 | 5.5 | 116.4 | 44.0 | −7.5 | 17.6 | 39.8 | 30.9 | 31.9 | 42.1 | 28.7 |
| Fin. der. & ESOs.: assets | 3c9aa | 8.3 | 10.3 | 5.5 | 116.4 | 44.0 | −7.5 | 17.6 | 39.8 | 30.9 | 31.9 | 42.1 | 28.7 |
| Fin. der. & ESOs.: liabilities | 3c9la | .... | .... | .... | .... | .... | .... | .... | .... | .... | .... | .... | .... |
| Other investment: assets | 3d9aa | 185.8 | 162.9 | 254.6 | 462.8 | 220.0 | −145.5 | 156.9 | 194.5 | 217.6 | −231.5 | 53.8 | 16.8 |
| Other equity | 3daaa | 2.1 | 2.3 | 3.0 | 8.7 | 5.9 | 3.0 | 4.1 | 5.3 | 17.2 | 13.3 | 8.0 | 2.5 |
| Debt instruments | 3dzaa | 183.6 | 160.6 | 251.6 | 454.2 | 214.0 | −148.5 | 152.8 | 189.1 | 200.3 | −244.8 | 45.8 | 14.3 |
| Other investment: liabilities | 3d9la | 64.1 | 114.9 | 142.6 | 201.5 | 109.4 | −162.9 | 267.6 | 29.4 | 164.9 | −248.9 | 54.8 | 69.1 |
| Other equity | 3dala | .3 | .2 | .4 | 1.0 | 1.5 | .6 | −.3 | .4 | .3 | .3 | — | .1 |
| Debt instruments | 3dzla | 63.8 | 114.7 | 142.2 | 200.5 | 107.9 | −163.5 | 267.9 | 29.0 | 164.6 | −249.2 | 54.8 | 68.9 |
| Curr.+ cap.− finan. acct. balance | 4y9na | −14.4 | 5.6 | −30.7 | −21.2 | 32.6 | 24.2 | 73.0 | 66.4 | 64.2 | −37.5 | −44.1 | 25.8 |
| D. Net Errors and Omissions | 409na | 12.6 | −8.2 | 27.1 | 22.4 | −29.8 | −11.8 | −70.9 | −62.5 | −62.5 | 38.7 | 40.8 | −28.3 |
| E. Reserves and Related Items | 4z9na | −1.8 | −2.6 | −3.7 | 1.2 | 2.7 | 12.4 | 2.1 | 3.9 | 1.7 | 1.2 | −3.3 | −2.4 |
| Reserve assets | 3e9aa | −1.8 | −2.6 | −3.7 | 1.2 | 2.7 | 12.4 | 2.1 | 3.9 | 1.7 | 1.2 | −3.3 | −2.4 |
| Credit and loans from the IMF | 3dcla | — | — | — | — | — | — | — | — | — | — | — | — |
| Exceptional financing | 409la | .... | .... | .... | .... | .... | .... | .... | .... | .... | .... | .... | .... |
| *Excludes components in group E | | | | | | | | | | | | | |
| | | | | | | | | | | | | | |
| **International Investment Position** | | | | | | | *Billions of US Dollars* | | | | | | |
| Assets | 809aa | 4,960.0 | 5,015.5 | 6,245.7 | 7,676.3 | † 7,096.3 | 7,554.1 | 8,739.3 | 8,862.6 | 9,630.4 | 9,566.7 | 9,295.4 | 8,604.8 |
| Direct investment | 8a9aa | 982.5 | 996.7 | 1,236.0 | 1,545.3 | † 1,459.6 | 1,605.3 | 1,634.9 | 1,696.2 | 1,931.1 | 2,083.1 | 2,001.6 | 1,971.9 |
| Equity & investment fund shares | 8aaaa | 809.7 | 824.8 | 1,036.9 | 1,309.8 | † 1,179.9 | 1,291.8 | 1,320.5 | 1,358.8 | 1,482.8 | 1,577.4 | 1,522.2 | 1,502.0 |
| Debt instruments | 8abaa | 172.7 | 171.9 | 199.0 | 235.5 | † 279.7 | 313.5 | 314.4 | 337.4 | 448.2 | 505.8 | 479.4 | 469.9 |
| Portfolio investment | 8b9aa | 1,676.5 | 1,817.9 | 2,266.4 | 2,624.8 | † 2,149.2 | 2,507.9 | 2,555.7 | 2,380.4 | 2,760.1 | 3,083.6 | 3,075.7 | 2,905.6 |
| Equity & investment fund shares | 8baaa | 668.2 | 771.4 | 884.2 | 954.0 | † 589.5 | 707.1 | 739.7 | 647.2 | 747.4 | 919.6 | 939.8 | 952.0 |
| Debt securities | 8bbaa | 1,008.2 | 1,046.5 | 1,382.1 | 1,670.8 | † 1,559.6 | 1,800.8 | 1,816.0 | 1,733.2 | 2,012.7 | 2,164.0 | 2,136.0 | 1,953.6 |
| Fin. der.(oth.than reserves) & ESOs | 8c9aa | .... | .... | .... | .... | .... | .... | 1,047.8 | 1,185.3 | 1,259.8 | 868.5 | 960.9 | 728.9 |
| Other investment | 8d9aa | 2,203.9 | 2,099.2 | 2,631.8 | 3,370.0 | † 3,349.5 | 3,260.1 | 3,284.4 | 3,361.9 | 3,430.6 | 3,333.3 | 3,064.4 | 2,824.7 |
| Other equity | 8daaa | 25.5 | 24.5 | 30.2 | 41.6 | † 43.3 | 47.8 | 48.1 | 49.9 | 67.5 | 83.6 | 80.6 | 74.6 |
| Debt instruments | 8dzaa | 2,178.4 | 2,074.7 | 2,601.6 | 3,328.4 | † 3,306.2 | 3,212.3 | 3,236.3 | 3,312.0 | 3,363.1 | 3,249.6 | 2,983.9 | 2,750.1 |
| Reserve assets | 8e9aa | 97.2 | 101.7 | 111.6 | 136.2 | † 138.0 | 180.8 | 216.5 | 238.9 | 248.9 | 198.2 | 192.8 | 173.7 |
| Liabilities | 809la | 4,821.1 | 4,654.8 | 5,620.9 | 6,983.1 | † 6,447.1 | 6,667.0 | 7,851.5 | 8,046.9 | 8,611.5 | 8,252.9 | 7,843.5 | 6,984.6 |
| Direct investment | 8a9la | 887.1 | 813.2 | 1,029.9 | 1,246.9 | † 1,137.2 | 1,212.4 | 1,210.5 | 1,252.0 | 1,448.0 | 1,594.8 | 1,436.0 | 1,360.1 |
| Equity & investment fund shares | 8aala | 423.5 | 401.8 | 513.5 | 649.6 | † 571.7 | 593.2 | 584.7 | 592.9 | 627.6 | 668.7 | 625.6 | 595.4 |
| Debt instruments | 8abla | 463.6 | 411.4 | 516.4 | 597.3 | † 565.5 | 619.2 | 625.8 | 659.1 | 820.3 | 926.1 | 810.4 | 764.7 |
| Portfolio investment | 8b9la | 2,082.8 | 2,114.0 | 2,508.0 | 3,259.0 | † 2,839.7 | 3,042.7 | 3,015.5 | 3,044.9 | 3,361.8 | 3,393.7 | 3,210.9 | 2,803.8 |
| Equity & investment fund shares | 8bala | 399.7 | 445.2 | 622.9 | 908.9 | † 472.3 | 647.3 | 667.6 | 565.8 | 702.5 | 855.1 | 754.6 | 725.2 |
| Debt securities | 8bbla | 1,683.1 | 1,668.9 | 1,885.1 | 2,350.0 | † 2,367.5 | 2,395.4 | 2,347.9 | 2,479.1 | 2,659.3 | 2,538.6 | 2,456.3 | 2,078.7 |
| Fin. der.(oth.than reserves) & ESOs | 8c9la | .... | .... | .... | .... | .... | .... | 1,050.8 | 1,202.2 | 1,251.0 | 852.8 | 988.9 | 741.8 |
| Other investment | 8d9la | 1,851.2 | 1,727.6 | 2,083.1 | 2,477.2 | † 2,470.2 | 2,411.9 | 2,574.6 | 2,547.7 | 2,550.7 | 2,411.6 | 2,207.6 | 2,078.9 |
| Other equity | 8dala | 2.9 | 2.8 | 3.5 | 5.0 | † 6.2 | 7.0 | 6.4 | 6.6 | 6.8 | 7.5 | 6.6 | 6.1 |
| Debt instruments | 8dzla | 1,848.3 | 1,724.9 | 2,079.5 | 2,472.2 | † 2,464.0 | 2,404.9 | 2,568.2 | 2,541.2 | 2,543.9 | 2,404.1 | 2,201.1 | 2,072.8 |

# Germany 134

| | | 2004 | 2005 | 2006 | 2007 | 2008 | 2009 | 2010 | 2011 | 2012 | 2013 | 2014 | 2015 |
|---|---|---|---|---|---|---|---|---|---|---|---|---|---|

**Government Finance**
**Operations Statement**
**General Government**

*Millions of Euros: Fiscal Year Ends December 31; Data Reported through Eurostat*

| | | 2004 | 2005 | 2006 | 2007 | 2008 | 2009 | 2010 | 2011 | 2012 | 2013 | 2014 | 2015 |
|---|---|---|---|---|---|---|---|---|---|---|---|---|---|
| Revenue | a1 | 966,631 | 984,380 | 1,028,495 | 1,080,805 | 1,111,692 | 1,090,918 | 1,110,315 | 1,182,702 | 1,222,079 | 1,252,410 | 1,299,553 | 1,349,905 |
| Taxes | a11 | 471,322 | 483,087 | 520,063 | 567,228 | 585,911 | 554,747 | 556,189 | 598,771 | 623,906 | 642,017 | 665,063 | 697,150 |
| Social Contributions | a12 | 400,721 | 399,730 | 404,212 | 404,271 | 412,449 | 415,615 | 426,180 | 442,255 | 454,204 | 464,928 | 481,948 | 501,154 |
| Grants | a13 | .... | .... | .... | .... | .... | .... | .... | .... | .... | .... | .... | .... |
| Other Revenue | a14 | .... | .... | .... | .... | .... | .... | .... | .... | .... | .... | .... | .... |
| Expense | a2 | 1,056,762 | 1,068,721 | 1,072,893 | 1,081,332 | 1,118,755 | 1,168,840 | 1,222,194 | 1,207,492 | 1,225,210 | 1,257,429 | 1,294,707 | 1,332,003 |
| Compensation of Employees | a21 | 182,235 | 182,233 | 183,180 | 184,175 | 189,079 | 197,812 | 203,528 | 208,645 | 212,889 | 218,647 | 224,620 | 230,710 |
| Use of Goods & Services | a22 | 84,373 | 88,702 | 92,340 | 96,030 | 103,336 | 111,733 | 118,049 | 124,076 | 131,463 | 134,996 | 138,557 | 143,715 |
| Consumption of Fixed Capital | a23 | 47,696 | 48,271 | 49,434 | 51,885 | 53,804 | 55,246 | 56,610 | 58,791 | 61,141 | 63,416 | 65,412 | 67,212 |
| Interest | a24 | 63,221 | 63,118 | 64,684 | 66,994 | 68,469 | 64,962 | 63,850 | 67,500 | 63,085 | 56,010 | 51,477 | 48,549 |
| Subsidies | a25 | 26,760 | 25,084 | 25,349 | 24,552 | 24,268 | 32,313 | 29,666 | 27,422 | 24,101 | 24,375 | 25,485 | 26,815 |
| Grants | a26 | .... | .... | .... | .... | .... | .... | .... | .... | .... | .... | .... | .... |
| Social Benefits | a27 | 576,323 | 581,739 | 582,585 | 582,028 | 592,394 | 624,836 | 634,483 | 633,852 | 644,369 | 665,682 | 691,081 | 721,635 |
| Other Expense | a28 | .... | .... | .... | .... | .... | .... | .... | .... | .... | .... | .... | .... |
| Gross Operating Balance [1-2+23] | agob | −42,435 | −36,070 | 5,036 | 51,358 | 46,741 | −22,676 | −55,269 | 34,001 | 58,010 | 58,397 | 70,258 | 85,114 |
| Net Operating Balance [1-2] | anob | −90,131 | −84,341 | −44,398 | −527 | −7,063 | −77,922 | −111,879 | −24,790 | −3,131 | −5,019 | 4,846 | 17,902 |
| Net Acq. of Nonfinancial Assets | a31 | −5,192 | −5,722 | −3,198 | −5,233 | −2,532 | 1,668 | −2,975 | 1,073 | −391 | −1,194 | −3,506 | −3,302 |
| Aquisition of Nonfin. Assets | a31.1 | .... | .... | .... | .... | .... | .... | .... | .... | .... | .... | .... | .... |
| Disposal of Nonfin. Assets | a31.2 | .... | .... | .... | .... | .... | .... | .... | .... | .... | .... | .... | .... |
| Net Lending/Borrowing [1-2-31] | anlb | −84,939 | −78,619 | −41,200 | 4,706 | −4,531 | −79,590 | −108,904 | −25,863 | −2,740 | −3,825 | 8,352 | 21,204 |
| Net Acq. of Financial Assets | a32 | −13,314 | −8,794 | 7,263 | 16,638 | 65,008 | 31,387 | 175,512 | −738 | 74,745 | −15,347 | 14,024 | 2,929 |
| By instrument | | | | | | | | | | | | | |
| Monetary Gold & SDRs | a3201 | — | — | — | — | — | — | — | — | — | — | — | — |
| Currency & Deposits | a3202 | −5,172 | 5,425 | 31,961 | 10,680 | 6,861 | −3,870 | 35,999 | 27,474 | 13,724 | −19,199 | 19,205 | 2,132 |
| Securities other than Shares | a3203 | 757 | −447 | −570 | 1,205 | 40,200 | 2,504 | 103,201 | −12,374 | −9,781 | −7,270 | −10,560 | 3,427 |
| Loans | a3204 | −7,494 | −10,949 | −4,342 | 2,193 | 8,611 | 2,698 | 53,095 | −8,405 | 51,232 | −1,470 | −7,162 | −2,432 |
| Shares & Other Equity | a3205 | −8,012 | 5,571 | −4,391 | −1,613 | 12,831 | 33,489 | 8,612 | −8,003 | 14,462 | 10,709 | 5,559 | 658 |
| Insurance Technical Reserves | a3206 | 19 | 36 | 24 | 24 | 24 | 24 | 24 | 24 | 24 | 24 | 24 | 24 |
| Financial Derivatives | a3207 | −8 | −200 | −304 | −216 | 130 | −205 | −21,525 | −896 | −976 | 1,265 | 1,775 | 909 |
| Other Accounts Receivable | a3208 | 6,596 | −8,230 | −15,115 | 4,365 | −3,649 | −3,253 | −3,894 | 1,442 | 6,060 | 594 | 5,183 | −1,789 |
| By debtor | | | | | | | | | | | | | |
| Domestic | a321 | .... | .... | .... | .... | .... | .... | .... | .... | .... | .... | .... | .... |
| Foreign | a322 | .... | .... | .... | .... | .... | .... | .... | .... | .... | .... | .... | .... |
| Net Incurrence of Liabilities | a33 | 71,625 | 69,825 | 48,463 | 11,932 | 69,539 | 110,977 | 284,416 | 25,125 | 77,485 | −11,522 | 5,672 | −18,275 |
| By instrument | | | | | | | | | | | | | |
| Special Drawing Rights (SDRs) | a3301 | — | — | — | — | — | — | — | — | — | — | — | — |
| Currency & Deposits | a3302 | 490 | 431 | 499 | 511 | 3,592 | 576 | 1,067 | −1,735 | −689 | 847 | 1,559 | 2,153 |
| Securities other than Shares | a3303 | 69,225 | 69,856 | 52,748 | 30,570 | 40,757 | 117,378 | 93,738 | 66,080 | 89,836 | 8,229 | 17,733 | −7,907 |
| Loans | a3304 | 2,897 | 859 | −5,619 | −21,089 | 21,059 | 664 | 193,598 | −39,165 | −14,625 | −22,388 | −21,967 | −19,393 |
| Shares & Other Equity | a3305 | — | — | — | — | — | — | — | — | — | — | — | — |
| Insurance Technical Reserves | a3306 | 144 | 148 | 144 | 126 | 129 | 152 | 168 | — | — | — | — | — |
| Financial Derivatives | a3307 | — | — | — | — | — | — | — | — | — | — | — | — |
| Other Accounts Payable | a3308 | −1,131 | −1,469 | 691 | 1,814 | 4,002 | −7,793 | −4,155 | −55 | 2,963 | 1,790 | 8,347 | 6,872 |
| By creditor | | | | | | | | | | | | | |
| Domestic | a331 | .... | .... | .... | .... | .... | .... | .... | .... | .... | .... | .... | .... |
| Foreign | a332 | .... | .... | .... | .... | .... | .... | .... | .... | .... | .... | .... | .... |
| Stat. Discrepancy [32-33-NLB] | anlbz | — | — | — | — | — | — | — | — | — | — | — | — |
| Memo Item: Expenditure [2+31] | a2m | 1,051,570 | 1,062,999 | 1,069,695 | 1,076,099 | 1,116,223 | 1,170,508 | 1,219,219 | 1,208,565 | 1,224,819 | 1,256,235 | 1,291,201 | 1,328,701 |

**Balance Sheet**

| | | 2004 | 2005 | 2006 | 2007 | 2008 | 2009 | 2010 | 2011 | 2012 | 2013 | 2014 | 2015 |
|---|---|---|---|---|---|---|---|---|---|---|---|---|---|
| Net Worth | a6 | .... | .... | .... | .... | .... | .... | .... | .... | .... | .... | .... | .... |
| Nonfinancial Assets | a61 | .... | .... | .... | .... | .... | .... | .... | .... | .... | .... | .... | .... |
| Financial Assets | a62 | 494,540 | 500,238 | 513,935 | 567,619 | 629,168 | 674,187 | 911,374 | 916,061 | 1,018,587 | 1,011,806 | 1,060,735 | 1,068,392 |
| By instrument | | | | | | | | | | | | | |
| Monetary Gold & SDRs | a6201 | | | | | | | | | | | | |
| Currency & Deposits | a6202 | 147,866 | 153,610 | 185,541 | 197,366 | 198,958 | 196,754 | 232,782 | 260,664 | 276,723 | 259,737 | 301,424 | 304,700 |
| Securities other than Shares | a6203 | 9,577 | 10,002 | 5,707 | 6,877 | 46,430 | 47,676 | 151,259 | 137,232 | 134,392 | 125,423 | 130,997 | 134,743 |
| Loans | a6204 | 78,502 | 67,554 | 63,088 | 65,238 | 74,450 | 77,326 | 130,332 | 121,949 | 173,383 | 171,918 | 164,795 | 162,384 |
| Shares and Other Equity | a6205 | 137,375 | 152,872 | 158,289 | 192,668 | 209,936 | 247,650 | 310,725 | 308,324 | 342,161 | 362,184 | 369,759 | 380,560 |
| Insurance Technical Reserves | a6206 | 571 | 600 | 654 | 678 | 702 | 726 | 750 | 774 | 798 | 822 | 846 | 870 |
| Financial Derivatives | a6207 | 2,199 | 2,979 | 2,313 | 1,727 | 1,594 | 2,445 | −16,258 | −17,114 | −18,090 | −16,816 | −15,041 | −14,132 |
| Other Accounts Receivable | a6208 | 118,450 | 112,621 | 98,343 | 103,065 | 97,098 | 101,610 | 101,784 | 104,232 | 109,220 | 108,538 | 107,955 | 99,267 |
| By debtor | | | | | | | | | | | | | |
| Domestic | a621 | .... | .... | .... | .... | .... | .... | .... | .... | .... | .... | .... | .... |
| Foreign | a622 | .... | .... | .... | .... | .... | .... | .... | .... | .... | .... | .... | .... |
| Liabilities | a63 | 1,531,616 | 1,610,110 | 1,629,750 | 1,610,018 | 1,738,281 | 1,853,107 | 2,180,155 | 2,266,933 | 2,387,461 | 2,306,899 | 2,398,776 | 2,360,076 |
| By instrument | | | | | | | | | | | | | |
| Special Drawing Rights (SDRs) | a6301 | — | — | — | — | — | — | — | — | — | — | — | — |
| Currency & Deposits | a6302 | 5,493 | 5,924 | 6,423 | 6,934 | 10,526 | 11,101 | 12,168 | 10,430 | 9,744 | 10,593 | 12,151 | 14,304 |
| Securities other than Shares | a6303 | 1,049,431 | 1,127,051 | 1,151,726 | 1,153,257 | 1,256,202 | 1,369,382 | 1,482,861 | 1,608,831 | 1,739,040 | 1,682,105 | 1,791,657 | 1,769,843 |
| Loans | a6304 | 472,426 | 472,759 | 467,114 | 445,248 | 466,877 | 467,827 | 681,585 | 644,146 | 635,165 | 610,703 | 591,487 | 572,466 |
| Shares and Other Equity | a6305 | — | — | — | — | — | — | — | — | — | — | — | — |
| Insurance Technical Reserves | a6306 | 532 | 681 | 825 | 951 | 1,080 | 1,232 | — | — | — | — | — | — |
| Financial Derivatives | a6307 | — | — | — | — | — | — | — | — | — | — | — | — |
| Other Accounts Payable | a6308 | 3,734 | 3,695 | 3,662 | 3,628 | 3,596 | 3,565 | 3,541 | 3,526 | 3,512 | 3,498 | 3,481 | 3,463 |
| By creditor | | | | | | | | | | | | | |
| Domestic | a631 | .... | .... | .... | .... | .... | .... | .... | .... | .... | .... | .... | .... |
| Foreign | a632 | .... | .... | .... | .... | .... | .... | .... | .... | .... | .... | .... | .... |
| Net Financial Worth [62-63] | a6m2 | −1,037,076 | −1,109,872 | −1,115,815 | −1,042,399 | −1,109,113 | −1,178,920 | −1,268,781 | −1,350,872 | −1,368,874 | −1,295,093 | −1,338,041 | −1,291,684 |
| Memo Item: Debt at Market Value | a6m3 | 1,531,616 | 1,610,110 | 1,629,750 | 1,610,018 | 1,738,281 | 1,853,107 | 2,180,155 | 2,266,933 | 2,387,461 | 2,306,899 | 2,398,776 | 2,360,076 |
| Memo Item: Debt at Face Value | a6m35 | 1,472,584 | 1,543,186 | 1,591,188 | 1,600,592 | 1,666,833 | 1,785,552 | 2,093,487 | 2,120,358 | 2,196,770 | 2,181,328 | 2,181,216 | 2,156,406 |
| Memo Item: Maastricht Debt | a6m36 | 1,468,850 | 1,539,491 | 1,587,526 | 1,596,964 | 1,663,237 | 1,781,987 | 2,089,946 | 2,116,832 | 2,193,258 | 2,177,830 | 2,177,735 | 2,152,943 |
| Memo Item: Debt at Nominal Value | a6m4 | .... | .... | .... | .... | .... | .... | .... | .... | .... | .... | .... | .... |

|  |  | 2004 | 2005 | 2006 | 2007 | 2008 | 2009 | 2010 | 2011 | 2012 | 2013 | 2014 | 2015 |
|---|---|---|---|---|---|---|---|---|---|---|---|---|---|
| **National Accounts** | | | | | | | | | | | | | |
| Househ.Cons.Expend.,incl.NPISHs..... | **96f.c** | 1,300.4 | 1,327.5 | 1,362.7 | 1,385.3 | 1,415.4 | 1,413.7 | 1,445.6 | 1,494.7 | 1,532.4 | 1,563.2 | 1,593.9 | 1,635.5 |
| Government Consumption Expend... | **91f.c** | 419.0 | 423.0 | 430.4 | 439.7 | 457.6 | 481.2 | 493.3 | 505.7 | 522.7 | 541.9 | 564.0 | 586.8 |
| Gross Fixed Capital Formation......... | **93e.c** | 432.1 | 436.9 | 475.0 | 507.4 | 519.4 | 470.4 | 498.8 | 545.9 | 557.2 | 559.1 | 586.8 | 604.7 |
| Changes in Inventories.................... | **93i.c** | −.9 | −5.2 | −1.5 | 15.7 | 14.2 | −27.7 | 5.1 | 22.8 | −24.8 | −10.4 | −22.6 | −39.0 |
| Exports of Goods and Services......... | **90c.c** | 799.4 | 864.8 | 986.4 | 1,084.9 | 1,110.4 | 927.7 | 1,083.9 | 1,206.5 | 1,269.5 | 1,288.0 | 1,336.8 | 1,416.3 |
| Imports of Goods and Services (-)..... | **98c.c** | 686.8 | 749.7 | 859.2 | 916.3 | 958.8 | 807.1 | 952.3 | 1,076.5 | 1,100.8 | 1,116.6 | 1,139.2 | 1,181.4 |
| Gross Domestic Product (GDP)......... | **99b.c** | 2,267.6 | 2,297.8 | 2,390.2 | 2,510.1 | 2,558.0 | 2,456.7 | 2,576.2 | 2,699.1 | 2,749.9 | 2,809.5 | 2,903.8 | 3,023.0 |
| Net Primary Income from Abroad..... | **98.nc** | −53.1 | −48.2 | −29.2 | −39.8 | −55.4 | −23.2 | −26.8 | −30.2 | −19.8 | .... | .... | .... |
| Gross National Income (GNI)............ | **99a.c** | 2,214.5 | 2,249.6 | 2,361.0 | 2,470.3 | 2,502.6 | 2,433.5 | 2,549.4 | 2,668.9 | 2,730.1 | .... | .... | .... |
| Net Current Transf.from Abroad....... | **98t.c** | −27.1 | −27.8 | −27.2 | −29.3 | −32.5 | −30.8 | −35.2 | −31.5 | −33.7 | .... | .... | .... |
| Gross Nat'l Disposable Inc.(GNDI).... | **99i.c** | 2,187.4 | 2,221.8 | 2,333.9 | 2,441.0 | 2,470.1 | 2,402.6 | 2,514.2 | 2,637.5 | 2,696.4 | .... | .... | .... |
| Gross Saving................................ | **99s.c** | 489.6 | 497.5 | 569.6 | 650.3 | 628.6 | 534.1 | 590.6 | 620.3 | 627.0 | .... | .... | .... |
| Consumption of Fixed Capital.......... | **99cfc** | 322.9 | 328.0 | 335.8 | 352.3 | 366.5 | 374.8 | 380.2 | 391.1 | 402.1 | .... | .... | .... |
| GDP Volume 2010 Ref., Chained..... | **99b.r** | 2,401.6 | 2,422.7 | 2,516.7 | 2,601.9 | 2,622.9 | 2,476.9 | 2,574.6 | 2,670.2 | 2,686.7 | 2,697.6 | 2,740.3 | 2,780.0 |
| GDP Volume (2010=100)............... | **99bvr** | 93.3 | 94.1 | 97.8 | 101.1 | 101.9 | 96.2 | 100.0 | 103.7 | 104.4 | 104.8 | 106.4 | 108.0 |
| GDP Deflator (2010=100)............... | **99bir** | 94.4 | 94.8 | 94.9 | 96.4 | 97.5 | 99.1 | 100.0 | 101.0 | 102.3 | 104.1 | 105.9 | 108.7 |
| | | | | | | ***Millions: Midyear Estimates*** | | | | | | | |
| Population................................. | **99z** | 81.42 | 81.25 | 81.06 | 80.85 | 80.67 | 80.52 | 80.44 | 80.42 | 80.48 | 80.57 | 80.65 | 80.69 |

# Ghana 652

| | | 2004 | 2005 | 2006 | 2007 | 2008 | 2009 | 2010 | 2011 | 2012 | 2013 | 2014 | 2015 |
|---|---|---|---|---|---|---|---|---|---|---|---|---|---|
| **Exchange Rates** | | | | | *Cedis per SDR: End of Period* | | | | | | | | |
| Market Rate............................ | aa | 1.4061 | 1.3050 | 1.3894 | 1.5335 | 1.8700 | 2.2239 | 2.2697 | 2.3804 | 2.8894 | 3.3880 | 4.6363 | 5.2588 |
| | | | | | *Cedis per US Dollar: End of Period (ae) Period Average (rf)* | | | | | | | | |
| Market Rate............................ | ae | .9054 | .9131 | .9235 | .9704 | 1.2141 | 1.4186 | 1.4738 | 1.5505 | 1.8800 | 2.2000 | 3.2001 | 3.7950 |
| Market Rate............................ | rf | .8995 | .9063 | .9165 | .9352 | 1.0579 | 1.4088 | 1.4310 | 1.5119 | 1.7958 | 1.9541 | . . . . | . . . . |
| | | | | | *Index Numbers (2010=100): Period Averages* | | | | | | | | |
| Nominal Effective Exchange Rate..... | nec | 169.90 | 166.07 | 162.40 | 150.13 | 128.95 | 101.10 | 100.00 | 90.83 | 80.41 | 74.39 | 51.10 | 44.85 |
| CPI-Based Real Effect. Ex. Rate........ | rec | 93.67 | 102.33 | 107.73 | 107.01 | 101.87 | 93.75 | 100.00 | 95.03 | 88.99 | 89.57 | 69.46 | 70.43 |
| **Fund Position** | | | | | *Millions of SDRs: End of Period* | | | | | | | | |
| Quota................................. | 2f.s | 369.00 | 369.00 | 369.00 | 369.00 | 369.00 | 369.00 | 369.00 | 369.00 | 369.00 | 369.00 | 369.00 | 369.00 |
| SDR Holdings........................... | 1b.s | 13.34 | .77 | .78 | .37 | .29 | 290.51 | 291.31 | 280.48 | 259.29 | 238.13 | 216.92 | 174.07 |
| Reserve Position in the Fund............ | 1c.s | — | — | — | — | — | — | — | — | — | — | .12 | .21 |
| Total Fund Cred.&Loans Outstg........ | 2tl | 301.65 | 291.74 | 105.45 | 105.45 | 105.45 | 173.10 | 254.60 | 363.22 | 461.27 | 440.18 | 419.09 | 542.37 |
| SDR Allocations.......................... | 1bd | 62.98 | 62.98 | 62.98 | 62.98 | 62.98 | 353.87 | 353.87 | 353.87 | 353.87 | 353.87 | 353.87 | 353.87 |
| **International Liquidity** | | | | *Millions of US Dollars Unless Otherwise Indicated: End of Period* | | | | | | | | | |
| Total Reserves minus Gold.............. | 1l.d | 1,626.7 | 1,752.9 | 2,090.3 | 1,984.0 | 1,769.8 | 3,386.2 | 4,763.2 | 5,483.4 | 5,367.5 | 5,249.3 | . . . . | . . . . |
| SDR Holdings.............................. | 1b.d | 20.7 | 1.1 | 1.2 | .6 | .4 | 455.4 | 448.6 | 430.6 | 398.5 | 366.7 | 314.3 | 241.2 |
| Reserve Position in the Fund......... | 1c.d | | | | | | | | | | | .2 | .3 |
| Foreign Exchange........................ | 1d.d | 1,605.9 | 1,751.8 | 2,089.1 | 1,983.4 | 1,769.4 | 2,930.8 | 4,314.6 | 5,052.8 | 4,969.0 | 4,882.6 | . . . . | . . . . |
| Gold (Million Fine Troy Ounces)........ | 1ad | .281 | .281 | .281 | .281 | .281 | .281 | .281 | .281 | .281 | .281 | . . . . | . . . . |
| Gold (National Valuation).............. | 1and | 122.6 | 144.5 | 177.9 | 177.7 | 242.2 | 237.4 | 303.4 | 321.7 | 337.2 | 200.1 | . . . . | . . . . |
| Central Bank: Other Assets............. | 3..d | 7.49 | 7.31 | † 7.34 | 6.79 | 529.83 | 9.09 | 7.20 | 25.29 | 56.12 | 34.87 | 24.11 | 20.53 |
| Central Bank: Other Liabs............... | 4..d | 83.87 | 61.99 | † 79.27 | 69.33 | 272.51 | 133.32 | 143.70 | 69.82 | 881.16 | 1,182.89 | 1,020.62 | 1,445.84 |
| Other Depository Corps.: Assets....... | 7a.d | 414.23 | 382.48 | † 537.33 | 651.29 | 806.20 | 1,087.17 | 902.20 | 1,262.66 | 1,133.69 | 1,299.35 | 1,481.07 | 1,398.81 |
| Other Depository Corps.: Liabs......... | 7b.d | 149.43 | 91.06 | † 220.01 | 587.01 | 596.30 | 778.76 | 755.75 | 735.72 | 597.22 | 1,514.21 | 1,446.21 | 1,110.70 |
| **Central Bank** | | | | | *Millions of Cedis: End of Period* | | | | | | | | |
| Net Foreign Assets.......................... | 11n | 1,010.8 | 1,211.8 | † 1,794.7 | 2,368.8 | 2,431.6 | 3,162.6 | 5,220.5 | 6,519.1 | 5,967.9 | 5,928.2 | 8,768.5 | 10,294.6 |
| Claims on Nonresidents................ | 11 | 1,599.4 | 1,731.4 | † 2,102.0 | 2,694.4 | 3,077.4 | 4,523.7 | 6,813.3 | 8,334.3 | 9,979.8 | 11,124.6 | 15,618.3 | 20,508.2 |
| Liabilities to Nonresidents.............. | 16c | 588.7 | 519.5 | † 307.2 | 325.6 | 645.8 | 1,361.1 | 1,592.8 | 1,815.2 | 4,011.8 | 5,196.4 | 6,849.8 | 10,213.6 |
| Claims on Other Depository Corps.... | 12e | 3.9 | 10.3 | † 3.4 | 2.5 | 64.1 | 499.2 | 113.4 | 105.1 | 59.6 | 752.7 | 331.7 | 2,021.0 |
| Net Claims on Central Government.. | 12an | 613.5 | 495.1 | † 464.0 | 248.6 | 1,436.8 | 1,344.2 | 1,383.9 | 1,873.9 | 4,104.4 | 5,364.3 | 7,206.8 | 6,646.3 |
| Claims on Central Government...... | 12a | 1,228.1 | 1,244.7 | † 1,522.0 | 2,367.1 | 3,496.1 | 2,570.6 | 2,770.1 | 3,179.5 | 4,473.2 | 6,613.2 | 13,082.3 | 10,110.1 |
| Liabilities to Central Government... | 16d | 614.5 | 749.6 | † 1,058.0 | 2,118.5 | 2,059.3 | 1,226.4 | 1,386.1 | 1,305.6 | 368.8 | 1,248.9 | 5,875.5 | 3,463.8 |
| Claims on Other Sectors................ | 12s | 56.4 | 11.5 | † 14.2 | 16.5 | 16.5 | 145.3 | 497.5 | 849.6 | 1,860.0 | 3,384.3 | 3,983.4 | 3,877.2 |
| Claims on Other Financial Corps.... | 12g | — | — | † — | — | — | — | 65.4 | 70.4 | 76.5 | 80.5 | 80.5 | 79.5 |
| Claims on State & Local Govts....... | 12b | — | — | † — | — | — | — | — | — | — | — | — | — |
| Claims on Public Nonfin. Corps...... | 12c | 47.2 | .3 | † .3 | .1 | .1 | 103.4 | 105.6 | 381.2 | 1,099.6 | 2,371.5 | 2,691.3 | 2,303.4 |
| Claims on Private Sector.............. | 12d | 9.1 | 11.1 | † 13.9 | 16.4 | 16.5 | 41.8 | 326.6 | 398.0 | 683.9 | 932.2 | 1,211.5 | 1,494.4 |
| Monetary Base........................... | 14 | 1,003.6 | 1,074.3 | † 1,463.5 | 1,998.9 | 2,553.8 | 3,552.2 | 4,779.0 | 6,256.1 | 8,508.1 | 11,394.7 | 16,547.8 | 17,338.3 |
| Currency in Circulation................. | 14a | 767.4 | 852.1 | † 1,090.8 | 1,470.6 | 1,872.3 | 2,343.8 | 3,262.7 | 4,244.3 | 5,555.5 | 6,197.4 | 7,742.2 | 9,536.5 |
| Liabs. to Other Depository Corps.... | 14c | 236.2 | 222.2 | † 372.7 | 490.0 | 636.5 | 1,121.1 | 1,354.0 | 1,835.8 | 2,677.8 | 4,773.4 | 8,037.6 | 6,727.8 |
| Liabilities to Other Sectors.............. | 14d | — | — | † — | 38.3 | 45.0 | 87.3 | 162.3 | 176.1 | 274.8 | 423.8 | 768.0 | 1,074.0 |
| Other Liabs. to Other Dep. Corps..... | 14n | 613.1 | 694.2 | † 548.4 | 465.9 | 198.5 | 864.6 | 1,491.2 | 1,925.8 | 1,745.7 | 1,861.4 | 3,209.7 | 2,810.3 |
| Dep. & Sec. Excl. f/Monetary Base.... | 14o | 113.0 | 63.6 | † 82.0 | 289.3 | 269.8 | 317.1 | 534.0 | 722.7 | 768.4 | 3,824.0 | 2,378.6 | 2,522.9 |
| Deposits Included in Broad Money. | 15 | 78.7 | 16.3 | † 20.8 | 20.2 | 12.0 | 15.2 | — | — | 11.7 | 13.3 | 21.1 | 25.5 |
| Sec.Ot.th.Shares Incl.in Brd. Money | 16a | — | — | † — | — | — | — | — | — | — | — | — | — |
| Deposits Excl. from Broad Money... | 16b | 34.2 | 47.3 | † 61.4 | 269.1 | 257.8 | 301.8 | 534.0 | 722.7 | 730.2 | 1,760.3 | 2,329.1 | 2,497.5 |
| Sec.Ot.th.Shares Excl.f/Brd.Money.. | 16s | — | — | † — | — | — | — | — | — | 26.4 | 2,050.4 | 28.4 | — |
| Loans.................................... | 16l | — | — | † — | — | — | — | — | — | — | — | — | — |
| Financial Derivatives........................ | 16m | — | — | † — | — | — | — | — | — | — | — | — | — |
| Shares and Other Equity................. | 17a | 2.0 | 58.2 | † 147.3 | 354.3 | 449.0 | 190.7 | 324.2 | 852.6 | 1,965.0 | 985.1 | 5,609.2 | 3,503.5 |
| Other Items (Net)......................... | 17r | −47.1 | −161.5 | † 35.0 | −471.8 | 477.9 | 226.7 | 86.9 | −409.5 | −995.3 | −2,635.6 | −7,454.9 | −3,335.9 |
| Memo Item: | | | | | | | | | | | | | |
| Total Assets..................... | 10ra | 3,062.8 | 3,272.0 | † 3,900.9 | 5,469.0 | 6,771.8 | 9,013.7 | 11,636.9 | 14,411.3 | 19,505.4 | 26,609.1 | 43,057.8 | 42,882.8 |

# Ghana 652

| | | 2004 | 2005 | 2006 | 2007 | 2008 | 2009 | 2010 | 2011 | 2012 | 2013 | 2014 | 2015 |
|---|---|---|---|---|---|---|---|---|---|---|---|---|---|
| **Other Depository Corporations** | | *Millions of Cedis: End of Period* | | | | | | | | | | | |
| Net Foreign Assets............................ | 21n | 239.8 | 266.1 | † 293.1 | 62.4 | 254.8 | 437.5 | 215.8 | 817.0 | 1,008.6 | −464.1 | 111.5 | 1,094.8 |
| Claims on Nonresidents................. | 21 | 375.1 | 349.2 | † 496.2 | 631.8 | 978.8 | 1,542.3 | 1,329.7 | 1,957.7 | 2,131.3 | 2,806.6 | 4,739.6 | 5,315.5 |
| Liabilities to Nonresidents.............. | 26c | 135.3 | 83.1 | † 203.2 | 569.4 | 724.0 | 1,104.8 | 1,113.8 | 1,140.7 | 1,122.8 | 3,270.7 | 4,628.0 | 4,220.7 |
| Claims on Central Bank................... | 20 | 376.8 | 389.1 | † 572.4 | 846.3 | 1,135.0 | 1,593.3 | 2,141.7 | 3,036.1 | 4,043.6 | 5,274.5 | 6,681.8 | 8,898.9 |
| Currency................................. | 20a | 37.1 | 48.8 | † 71.2 | 168.4 | 208.4 | 260.3 | 333.5 | 477.0 | 632.4 | 696.9 | 844.2 | 1,027.5 |
| Reserve Deposits and Securities..... | 20b | 244.7 | 233.0 | † 358.5 | 590.8 | 853.1 | 1,142.9 | 1,435.9 | 1,932.8 | 2,662.8 | 2,851.9 | 4,642.6 | 6,169.5 |
| Other Claims.............................. | 20n | 95.0 | 107.2 | † 142.7 | 87.1 | 73.4 | 190.0 | 372.3 | 626.3 | 748.4 | 1,725.7 | 1,195.0 | 1,702.0 |
| Net Claims on Central Government.. | 22an | 733.2 | 734.0 | † 1,069.2 | 1,074.0 | 1,203.9 | 2,232.6 | 3,403.3 | 4,414.7 | 5,636.0 | 8,044.7 | 9,571.2 | 9,455.8 |
| Claims on Central Government...... | 22a | 931.9 | 864.7 | † 1,178.4 | 1,471.5 | 1,711.8 | 2,859.9 | 4,369.5 | 5,542.3 | 7,170.4 | 9,692.6 | 11,738.7 | 13,074.1 |
| Liabilities to Central Government... | 26d | 198.8 | 130.7 | † 109.2 | 397.5 | 507.9 | 627.3 | 966.2 | 1,127.6 | 1,534.4 | 1,647.9 | 2,167.5 | 3,618.4 |
| Claims on Other Sectors.................. | 22s | 1,107.5 | 1,758.9 | † 2,400.1 | 3,954.5 | 5,762.7 | 6,781.6 | 7,777.5 | 9,299.5 | 12,000.2 | 15,829.2 | 22,544.0 | 29,073.6 |
| Claims on Other Financial Corps.... | 22g | 4.0 | 8.7 | † 27.7 | 35.7 | 167.1 | 98.9 | 147.1 | 82.8 | 82.3 | 219.5 | 491.1 | 1,345.9 |
| Claims on State & Local Govts...... | 22b | — | — | † — | | | | | | | | | |
| Claims on Public Nonfin. Corps...... | 22c | 60.3 | 249.5 | † 311.1 | 580.4 | 819.1 | 994.0 | 917.4 | 612.3 | 818.9 | 594.8 | 701.2 | 855.4 |
| Claims on Private Sector............... | 22d | 1,043.2 | 1,500.7 | † 2,061.2 | 3,338.3 | 4,776.5 | 5,688.6 | 6,713.1 | 8,604.5 | 11,099.0 | 15,014.9 | 21,351.8 | 26,872.3 |
| Liabilities to Central Bank............... | 26g | 6.0 | 50.8 | † 43.1 | 52.7 | 13.1 | 443.9 | 134.8 | 80.7 | 175.1 | 333.9 | 241.2 | 1,524.4 |
| Transf.Dep.Included in Broad Money | 24 | 1,115.4 | 1,341.3 | † 1,921.9 | 2,607.8 | 3,810.2 | 4,197.0 | 5,547.5 | 8,113.9 | 10,606.0 | 12,723.3 | 17,879.8 | 21,512.6 |
| Other Dep.Included in Broad Money. | 25 | 689.7 | 962.2 | † 1,389.4 | 1,986.1 | 2,756.4 | 3,954.7 | 4,998.3 | 6,216.1 | 7,051.5 | 8,665.3 | 11,950.1 | 15,990.4 |
| Sec.Ot.th.Shares Incl.in Brd. Money.. | 26a | | | † — | | | | | | | | | |
| Deposits Excl. from Broad Money..... | 26b | 51.7 | 62.9 | † 151.1 | 213.4 | 171.8 | 330.7 | 317.5 | 294.8 | 264.5 | 501.2 | 867.8 | 556.4 |
| Sec.Ot.th.Shares Excl.f/Brd.Money.... | 26s | 27.3 | 28.5 | † 25.7 | 33.1 | 36.3 | 47.0 | 51.3 | 55.9 | 57.3 | 67.1 | 84.9 | 68.1 |
| Loans.......................................... | 26l | 56.3 | 87.6 | † 130.6 | 187.4 | 189.1 | 314.6 | 444.5 | 580.2 | 725.0 | 556.6 | 1,391.6 | 2,303.2 |
| Financial Derivatives...................... | 26m | | | † — | | | | | | | | | |
| Insurance Technical Reserves.......... | 26r | — | — | † — | — | — | — | — | — | — | — | — | — |
| Shares and Other Equity.................. | 27a | 408.3 | 490.7 | † 616.9 | 833.9 | 1,195.8 | 1,789.6 | 2,336.3 | 3,048.2 | 4,037.2 | 5,331.2 | 7,526.5 | 9,184.4 |
| Other Items (Net).......................... | 27r | 102.6 | 124.1 | † 56.1 | 22.6 | 183.7 | −32.5 | −291.7 | −822.4 | −228.3 | 505.7 | −1,033.3 | −2,616.4 |
| Memo Item: | | | | | | | | | | | | | |
| Total Assets................................... | 20ra | 3,246.7 | 3,835.1 | † 5,328.6 | 7,977.7 | 10,997.9 | 14,691.3 | 18,167.1 | 22,777.5 | 28,074.0 | 37,011.4 | 52,546.1 | 65,124.8 |
| **Depository Corporations** | | *Millions of Cedis: End of Period* | | | | | | | | | | | |
| Net Foreign Assets.......................... | 31n | 1,250.5 | 1,477.9 | † 2,087.8 | 2,431.2 | 2,686.4 | 3,600.1 | 5,436.3 | 7,336.1 | 6,976.5 | 5,464.1 | 8,880.1 | 11,389.4 |
| Claims on Nonresidents................. | 31 | 1,974.5 | 2,080.6 | † 2,598.2 | 3,326.1 | 4,056.2 | 6,066.0 | 8,142.9 | 10,292.1 | 12,111.1 | 13,931.2 | 20,357.9 | 25,823.6 |
| Liabilities to Nonresidents.............. | 36c | 724.0 | 602.7 | † 510.4 | 895.0 | 1,369.8 | 2,465.8 | 2,706.7 | 2,956.0 | 5,134.6 | 8,467.1 | 11,477.8 | 14,434.3 |
| Domestic Claims............................ | 32 | 2,510.6 | 2,999.5 | † 3,947.6 | 5,293.7 | 8,419.9 | 10,503.6 | 13,062.3 | 16,437.6 | 23,600.6 | 32,622.5 | 43,305.4 | 49,052.9 |
| Net Claims on Central Government | 32an | 1,346.7 | 1,229.1 | † 1,533.3 | 1,322.7 | 2,640.7 | 3,576.8 | 4,787.3 | 6,288.5 | 9,740.4 | 13,409.0 | 16,778.1 | 16,102.1 |
| Claims on Central Government.... | 32a | 2,160.0 | 2,109.4 | † 2,700.5 | 3,838.6 | 5,207.9 | 5,430.5 | 7,139.5 | 8,721.8 | 11,643.6 | 16,305.8 | 24,821.0 | 23,184.3 |
| Liabilities to Central Government. | 36d | 813.3 | 880.3 | † 1,167.2 | 2,515.9 | 2,567.2 | 1,853.7 | 2,352.3 | 2,433.3 | 1,903.2 | 2,896.8 | 8,042.9 | 7,082.2 |
| Claims on Other Sectors................. | 32s | 1,163.9 | 1,770.4 | † 2,414.3 | 3,971.0 | 5,779.2 | 6,926.9 | 8,275.1 | 10,149.1 | 13,860.2 | 19,213.4 | 26,527.4 | 32,950.9 |
| Claims on Other Financial Corps.. | 32g | 4.0 | 8.7 | † 27.8 | 35.8 | 167.1 | 99.0 | 212.5 | 153.2 | 158.8 | 300.0 | 571.6 | 1,425.3 |
| Claims on State & Local Govts...... | 32b | | | † — | | | | | | | | | |
| Claims on Public Nonfin. Corps..... | 32c | 107.5 | 249.9 | † 311.4 | 580.6 | 819.1 | 1,097.4 | 1,022.9 | 993.5 | 1,918.5 | 2,966.4 | 3,392.5 | 3,158.8 |
| Claims on Private Sector............... | 32d | 1,052.3 | 1,511.8 | † 2,075.1 | 3,354.7 | 4,793.0 | 5,730.5 | 7,039.7 | 9,002.4 | 11,782.9 | 15,947.1 | 22,563.3 | 28,366.7 |
| Broad Money Liabilities................... | 35l | 2,614.1 | 3,123.0 | † 4,351.7 | 5,954.6 | 8,287.5 | 10,337.7 | 13,637.3 | 18,273.3 | 22,867.1 | 27,326.3 | 37,516.9 | 47,111.5 |
| Currency Outside Depository Corps | 34a | 730.3 | 803.2 | † 1,019.6 | 1,302.2 | 1,663.8 | 2,083.5 | 2,929.2 | 3,767.3 | 4,923.0 | 5,500.5 | 6,898.0 | 8,509.1 |
| Transferable Deposits.................... | 34 | 1,194.1 | 1,357.6 | † 1,942.7 | 2,666.3 | 3,867.2 | 4,299.6 | 5,709.8 | 8,290.0 | 10,892.5 | 13,160.4 | 18,668.9 | 22,612.1 |
| Other Deposits............................. | 35 | 689.7 | 962.2 | † 1,389.4 | 1,986.1 | 2,756.4 | 3,954.7 | 4,998.3 | 6,216.1 | 7,051.5 | 8,665.3 | 11,950.1 | 15,990.4 |
| Securities Other than Shares.......... | 36a | — | — | † — | — | — | — | — | — | — | — | — | — |
| Deposits Excl. from Broad Money..... | 36b | 85.9 | 110.3 | † 212.5 | 482.5 | 429.6 | 632.5 | 851.5 | 1,017.5 | 994.8 | 2,261.5 | 3,196.8 | 3,053.9 |
| Sec.Ot.th.Shares Excl.f/Brd.Money... | 36s | 27.3 | 28.5 | † 25.7 | 33.1 | 36.3 | 47.0 | 51.3 | 55.9 | 83.7 | 2,117.5 | 113.3 | 68.1 |
| Loans.......................................... | 36l | 56.3 | 87.6 | † 130.6 | 187.4 | 189.1 | 314.6 | 444.5 | 580.2 | 725.0 | 556.6 | 1,391.6 | 2,303.2 |
| Financial Derivatives...................... | 36m | — | — | † — | — | — | — | — | — | — | — | — | — |
| Insurance Technical Reserves.......... | 36r | — | — | † — | — | — | — | — | — | — | — | — | — |
| Shares and Other Equity.................. | 37a | 410.3 | 548.9 | † 764.2 | 1,188.2 | 1,644.8 | 1,980.4 | 2,660.4 | 3,900.7 | 6,002.2 | 6,316.3 | 13,135.7 | 12,687.9 |
| Other Items (Net).......................... | 37r | 567.2 | 579.1 | † 550.7 | −120.9 | 519.2 | 791.6 | 853.7 | −53.8 | −95.7 | −491.6 | −3,168.9 | −4,782.3 |
| Broad Money Liabs., Seasonally Adj. | 35l.b | 2,445.0 | 2,920.9 | † 4,122.0 | 5,646.4 | 7,873.4 | 9,847.6 | 13,038.1 | 17,526.5 | 21,975.4 | 26,280.8 | 36,097.8 | 45,349.1 |
| **Monetary Aggregates** | | *Millions of Cedis: End of Period* | | | | | | | | | | | |
| Broad Money.................................. | 59m | 2,614.1 | 3,123.1 | 4,351.7 | 5,954.6 | 8,287.5 | 10,337.7 | 13,637.3 | 18,273.3 | 22,867.1 | 27,326.3 | 37,516.9 | 47,111.5 |
| o/w:Currency Issued by Cent.Govt | 59m.a | — | — | — | — | — | — | — | — | — | — | — | — |
| o/w: Dep.in Nonfin. Corporations. | 59m.b | — | — | — | — | — | — | — | — | — | — | — | — |
| o/w: Secs. Issued by Central Govt. | 59m.c | — | — | — | — | — | — | — | — | — | — | — | — |
| Money (National Definitions) | | | | | | | | | | | | | |
| Reserve Money........................... | 19mb | 900.1 | 1,002.9 | 1,320.2 | 1,781.5 | 2,224.6 | 3,039.5 | 4,409.6 | 5,779.5 | 7,860.1 | 9,058.0 | 11,783.8 | 14,634.1 |
| M1................................................ | 59ma | 1,448.3 | 1,684.1 | 2,282.5 | 3,029.7 | 4,173.6 | 4,484.6 | 6,675.4 | 9,189.8 | 11,562.3 | 13,463.4 | 18,114.1 | 21,756.3 |
| M2................................................ | 59mb | 2,015.1 | 2,476.2 | 3,425.6 | 4,671.4 | 6,458.6 | 7,887.0 | 11,208.6 | 14,716.5 | 17,906.8 | 21,257.4 | 28,386.6 | 35,599.0 |
| M2+.............................................. | 59mba | 2,614.1 | 3,123.0 | 4,351.7 | 5,954.6 | 8,287.5 | 10,337.7 | 13,637.3 | 18,273.3 | 22,867.1 | 27,326.3 | 37,516.9 | 47,111.5 |
| **Interest Rates** | | *Percent Per Annum* | | | | | | | | | | | |
| Central Bank Policy Rate (EOP)........ | 60 | 18.50 | 15.50 | 12.50 | 13.50 | 17.00 | 18.00 | 13.50 | 12.50 | 15.00 | 16.00 | 21.00 | 26.00 |
| Money Market Rate....................... | 60b | 15.73 | 14.70 | 10.57 | 12.00 | 15.64 | 21.50 | 13.56 | 10.71 | 14.48 | 17.57 | 21.81 | 24.16 |
| Treasury Bill Rate........................... | 60c | 16.57 | 14.89 | 9.95 | 9.66 | 16.96 | 23.76 | 13.28 | 10.40 | 17.79 | 20.82 | 22.57 | 23.61 |
| Savings Rate................................. | 60k | 9.50 | 8.35 | 6.13 | 4.65 | 5.80 | 9.17 | 7.92 | 5.18 | 4.86 | 5.35 | 5.44 | 5.24 |
| Deposit Rate................................. | 60l | 13.63 | 10.16 | 8.89 | 8.90 | 11.29 | 17.06 | 12.88 | 8.91 | 10.05 | 12.35 | 12.90 | 13.34 |
| Government Bond Yield.................. | 61 | 21.50 | 20.54 | 16.42 | 12.71 | 14.89 | . . . . | 15.14 | 13.43 | 20.41 | 18.24 | 24.34 | 23.52 |
| **Prices and Labor** | | *Index Numbers (2010=100): Period Averages* | | | | | | | | | | | |
| Consumer Prices............................. | 64 | 46.0 | 52.9 | † 58.7 | 65.0 | 75.7 | 90.3 | 100.0 | 108.7 | † 118.7 | 132.5 | 153.0 | 179.2 |
| | | *Number in Thousands: Period Averages* | | | | | | | | | | | |
| **Intl. Transactions & Positions** | | *Millions of Cedis* | | | | | | | | | | | |
| Exports........................................... | 70 | . . . . | 2,540 | 3,415 | 4,041 | . . . . | . . . . | . . . . | . . . . | . . . . | . . . . | . . . . | . . . . |
| Cocoa Beans................................. | 70r | . . . . | 743 | 923 | . . . . | . . . . | . . . . | . . . . | . . . . | . . . . | . . . . | . . . . | . . . . |
| Imports, c.i.f.................................... | 71 | 3,664 | 4,846 | 6,189 | 7,539 | 10,863 | 11,336 | 15,799 | 19,065 | 24,421 | 25,002 | . . . . | . . . . |
| Volume of Exports | | *2010=100* | | | | | | | | | | | |
| Cocoa Beans................................. | 72r | . . . . | 100.0 | 122.4 | . . . . | . . . . | . . . . | . . . . | . . . . | . . . . | . . . . | . . . . | . . . . |
| Export Prices | | | | | | | | | | | | | |
| Cocoa Beans (1995=100)............. | 74r | . . . . | 764.9 | 776.8 | . . . . | . . . . | . . . . | . . . . | . . . . | . . . . | . . . . | . . . . | . . . . |

# Ghana 652

## Balance of Payments

*Millions of US Dollars*

| | | 2004 | 2005 | 2006 | 2007 | 2008 | 2009 | 2010 | 2011 | 2012 | 2013 | 2014 | 2015 |
|---|---|---|---|---|---|---|---|---|---|---|---|---|---|
| A. Current Account* | 109bx | −590.2 | −1,104.6 | −1,056.1 | −2,378.8 | −3,327.4 | −1,897.2 | −2,747.3 | †−3,541.3 | −4,911.7 | −5,704.0 | −3,694.6 | −2,809.3 |
| Goods, credit (exports) | 1a9cx | 2,704.5 | 2,802.2 | 3,726.7 | 4,172.1 | 5,269.7 | 5,839.7 | 7,960.1 | †12,785.4 | 13,552.3 | 13,751.9 | 13,216.8 | 10,355.7 |
| Goods, debit (imports) | 1a9dx | 4,297.3 | 5,347.3 | 6,753.7 | 8,066.1 | 10,268.5 | 8,046.3 | 10,922.1 | †15,837.7 | 17,763.2 | 17,600.2 | 14,600.0 | 13,465.1 |
| Balance on goods | 1a9bx | −1,592.8 | −2,545.1 | −3,027.0 | −3,894.0 | −4,998.8 | −2,206.6 | −2,962.0 | †−3,052.3 | −4,210.8 | −3,848.3 | −1,383.3 | −3,109.3 |
| Services, credit (exports) | 1b9cx | 702.3 | 1,106.5 | 1,382.8 | 1,831.9 | 1,800.9 | 1,769.7 | 1,477.5 | †1,810.1 | 3,259.7 | 2,454.0 | 2,044.7 | 6,143.0 |
| Services, debit (imports) | 1b9dx | 1,081.8 | 1,273.1 | 1,532.8 | 1,998.6 | 2,298.1 | 2,943.1 | 3,003.2 | †3,666.4 | 4,235.9 | 4,897.8 | 4,647.1 | 7,308.8 |
| Balance on Goods & Services | 1z9bx | −1,972.3 | −2,711.7 | −3,177.0 | −4,060.7 | −5,495.9 | −3,380.0 | −4,488.0 | †−4,908.6 | −5,187.1 | −6,292.1 | −3,985.6 | −4,275.1 |
| Primary income: credit | 1c9cx | 44.5 | 43.3 | 73.3 | 84.0 | 85.6 | 125.2 | 52.9 | †55.4 | 55.3 | 284.5 | 110.8 | 394.4 |
| Primary income: debit | 1c9dx | 242.3 | 230.4 | 200.6 | 445.2 | 128.6 | 720.4 | 634.7 | †1,285.5 | 2,185.2 | 1,635.9 | 1,828.2 | 1,526.3 |
| Balance on gds, serv. & prim. inc. | 1y9bx | −2,170.1 | −2,898.8 | −3,304.3 | −4,422.0 | −5,538.9 | −3,975.2 | −5,069.8 | †−6,138.7 | −7,317.0 | −7,643.5 | −5,703.0 | −5,407.0 |
| Secondary income: credit | 1d9ca | 1,579.9 | 1,794.2 | 2,248.3 | 2,043.2 | 2,211.5 | 2,078.0 | 2,322.4 | †2,597.4 | 2,413.3 | 1,944.3 | 2,017.4 | 5,204.8 |
| Secondary income: debit | 1d9da | — | — | — | — | — | — | — | †— | 8.0 | 4.8 | 8.9 | 2,607.1 |
| B. Capital Account* | 209ba | 251.0 | 331.2 | 229.9 | 188.1 | 463.3 | 563.9 | 337.5 | †445.1 | 283.4 | 349.3 | — | 473.9 |
| Capital account: credit | 209ca | 251.0 | 331.2 | 229.9 | 188.1 | 463.3 | 563.9 | 337.5 | †445.1 | 283.4 | 349.3 | — | 473.9 |
| Capital account: debit | 209da | — | — | — | — | — | — | — | †— | | | | |
| Balance on current & capital acct. | 129ba | −339.1 | −773.4 | −826.1 | −2,190.6 | −2,864.1 | −1,333.3 | −2,409.8 | †−3,096.3 | −4,628.3 | −5,354.8 | −3,694.6 | −2,335.4 |
| C. Financial Account* | 309na | −201.6 | −834.5 | −1,255.0 | −2,641.0 | −2,297.1 | −4,156.4 | −4,146.2 | †−4,034.3 | −3,367.9 | −5,426.9 | −3,752.8 | −2,639.5 |
| Direct investment: assets | 3a9aa | — | — | — | — | — | 6.9 | — | †25.3 | 1.1 | .7 | 6.4 | 221.4 |
| Equity & investment fund shares | 3aaaa | — | — | — | — | — | — | — | †25.3 | 1.1 | .7 | 6.4 | 221.4 |
| Debt instruments | 3abaa | .... | .... | .... | .... | .... | 6.9 | — | †— | | | | |
| Direct investment: liabilities | 3a9la | 139.3 | 145.0 | 636.0 | 1,383.2 | 2,714.9 | 2,372.5 | 2,527.4 | †3,247.6 | 3,294.5 | 3,227.0 | 3,363.4 | 3,192.3 |
| Equity & investment fund shares | 3aala | 139.3 | 145.0 | 636.0 | 605.8 | 1,429.4 | 1,939.5 | 2,527.4 | †3,247.6 | 3,294.5 | 3,227.0 | 3,363.4 | 3,192.3 |
| Debt instruments | 3abla | .... | .... | .... | 777.4 | 1,285.6 | 433.0 | — | †— | — | — | — | — |
| Portfolio investment: assets | 3b9aa | — | — | −65.8 | 373.3 | — | −41.3 | −723.0 | .... | .... | .... | .... | .... |
| Equity & investment fund shares | 3baaa | .... | .... | .... | .... | .... | .... | .... | .... | .... | .... | .... | .... |
| Debt securities | 3bbaa | .... | .... | −65.8 | 373.3 | .... | −41.3 | −723.0 | .... | .... | .... | .... | .... |
| Portfolio investment: liabilities | 3b9la | — | — | — | 685.7 | −127.4 | 450.5 | 52.5 | †117.6 | 1,121.8 | 658.9 | 835.9 | 900.0 |
| Equity & investment fund shares | 3bala | .... | .... | .... | .... | .... | 534.5 | 18.1 | .... | | | | |
| Debt securities | 3bbla | .... | .... | .... | 685.7 | −127.4 | −84.0 | 34.4 | †117.6 | 1,121.8 | 658.9 | 835.9 | 900.0 |
| Fin. der.& empl.stk.ops.(ESOs): net | 3c9na | — | — | — | — | — | — | — | .... | .... | .... | .... | .... |
| Fin. der. & ESOs.: assets | 3c9aa | — | — | — | — | — | — | — | .... | .... | .... | .... | .... |
| Fin. der. & ESOs.: liabilities | 3c9la | — | — | — | — | — | — | — | .... | .... | .... | .... | .... |
| Other investment: assets | 3d9aa | — | — | — | 76.6 | 349.1 | 370.2 | — | †367.0 | 761.5 | −331.2 | 338.4 | 178.2 |
| Other equity | 3daaa | .... | .... | .... | .... | .... | .... | .... | .... | .... | .... | .... | .... |
| Debt instruments | 3dzaa | — | — | — | 76.6 | 349.1 | 370.2 | — | †367.0 | 761.5 | −331.2 | 338.4 | 178.2 |
| Other investment: liabilities | 3d9la | 62.3 | 689.5 | 553.2 | 1,022.0 | 58.6 | 1,669.2 | 843.3 | †1,061.4 | −285.9 | 1,210.4 | −101.7 | −1,053.1 |
| Other equity | 3dala | .... | .... | .... | .... | .... | .... | .... | .... | .... | .... | .... | .... |
| Debt instruments | 3dzla | 62.3 | 689.5 | 553.2 | 1,022.0 | 58.6 | 1,669.2 | 843.3 | †1,061.4 | −285.9 | 1,210.4 | −101.7 | −1,053.1 |
| Curr.+ cap.− finan. acct. balance | 4y9na | −137.6 | 61.1 | 428.8 | 450.3 | −567.0 | 2,823.1 | 1,736.3 | †938.0 | −1,260.5 | 72.1 | 58.2 | 304.1 |
| D. Net Errors and Omissions | 409na | 132.6 | 63.6 | −10.4 | −37.9 | −373.8 | −1,793.8 | −1,175.7 | †−487.3 | 25.5 | −1,262.1 | −143.5 | −476.4 |
| E. Reserves and Related Items | 4z9na | −4.9 | 124.6 | 418.5 | 412.5 | −940.8 | 1,029.4 | 560.6 | †450.7 | −1,234.9 | −1,190.0 | −85.2 | −172.3 |
| Reserve assets | 3e9aa | 185.8 | 334.6 | 272.9 | 412.5 | −940.8 | 1,134.4 | 680.3 | †621.7 | −1,087.7 | −1,222.1 | −117.1 | −.5 |
| Credit and loans from the IMF | 3dcla | −5.3 | −15.1 | −267.2 | — | — | 105.0 | 119.7 | †171.0 | 147.2 | −32.1 | −31.9 | 171.8 |
| Exceptional financing | 409la | 196.0 | 225.0 | 121.6 | — | — | — | — | .... | .... | .... | .... | .... |

*Excludes components in group E

## International Investment Position

*Millions of US Dollars*

| | | 2004 | 2005 | 2006 | 2007 | 2008 | 2009 | 2010 | 2011 | 2012 | 2013 | 2014 | 2015 |
|---|---|---|---|---|---|---|---|---|---|---|---|---|---|
| Assets | 809aa | .... | .... | 3,684.2 | 4,670.7 | 4,065.9 | 5,805.1 | †7,616.5 | 9,915.5 | 9,183.9 | 9,783.8 | 7,596.6 | .... |
| Direct investment | 8a9aa | .... | .... | .... | 67.2 | 55.5 | 71.8 | †212.1 | 544.2 | 428.7 | 433.6 | 573.4 | .... |
| Equity & investment fund shares | 8aaaa | .... | .... | .... | 67.2 | 55.5 | 71.8 | †154.8 | 188.9 | 202.9 | 210.4 | 331.9 | .... |
| Debt instruments | 8abaa | .... | .... | .... | .... | .... | .... | †57.3 | 355.3 | 225.8 | 223.2 | 241.5 | .... |
| Portfolio investment | 8b9aa | .... | .... | 65.8 | 439.1 | 439.1 | 613.1 | †759.4 | 1,194.0 | 703.4 | 108.8 | 53.2 | .... |
| Equity & investment fund shares | 8baaa | .... | .... | .... | .... | .... | 130.8 | †235.8 | 116.3 | 376.6 | 52.2 | 20.8 | .... |
| Debt securities | 8bbaa | .... | .... | 65.8 | 439.1 | 439.1 | 482.3 | †523.5 | 1,077.6 | 326.8 | 56.6 | 32.4 | .... |
| Fin. der.(oth.than reserves) & ESOs | 8c9aa | .... | .... | .... | .... | .... | .... | .... | — | — | — | — | .... |
| Other investment | 8d9aa | .... | .... | 1,342.4 | 1,381.0 | 1,555.2 | 1,820.5 | †1,862.0 | 2,627.9 | 2,707.2 | 3,934.5 | 1,979.0 | .... |
| Other equity | 8daaa | .... | .... | .... | .... | .... | .... | .... | .... | .... | .... | .... | .... |
| Debt instruments | 8dzaa | .... | .... | 1,342.4 | 1,381.0 | 1,555.2 | 1,820.5 | †1,862.0 | 2,627.9 | 2,707.2 | 3,934.5 | 1,979.0 | .... |
| Reserve assets | 8e9aa | .... | .... | 2,276.1 | 2,783.4 | 2,016.1 | 3,299.7 | †4,783.1 | 5,549.5 | 5,344.5 | 5,306.9 | 4,991.0 | .... |
| Liabilities | 809la | .... | .... | 7,813.5 | 11,766.7 | 14,820.5 | 18,941.4 | †23,982.8 | 27,587.2 | 28,182.5 | 30,062.4 | 28,666.6 | .... |
| Direct investment | 8a9la | .... | .... | 3,001.5 | 4,384.6 | 7,099.6 | 8,523.5 | †11,476.4 | 13,174.2 | 13,262.9 | 11,941.8 | 11,588.0 | .... |
| Equity & investment fund shares | 8aala | .... | .... | 1,500.7 | 2,106.5 | 3,535.8 | 4,526.7 | †4,906.7 | 5,869.1 | 5,257.3 | 2,405.7 | 3,363.7 | .... |
| Debt instruments | 8abla | .... | .... | 1,500.8 | 2,278.2 | 3,563.8 | 3,996.7 | †6,569.8 | 7,305.1 | 8,005.7 | 9,536.1 | 8,224.3 | .... |
| Portfolio investment | 8b9la | .... | .... | .... | 750.0 | 750.0 | 908.5 | †1,150.4 | 1,274.2 | 1,080.0 | 1,312.6 | 1,020.9 | .... |
| Equity & investment fund shares | 8bala | .... | .... | .... | .... | .... | 701.0 | †832.3 | 835.8 | 632.6 | 562.9 | 32.1 | .... |
| Debt securities | 8bbla | .... | .... | .... | 750.0 | 750.0 | 207.6 | †318.0 | 438.4 | 447.4 | 749.6 | 988.8 | .... |
| Fin. der.(oth.than reserves) & ESOs | 8c9la | .... | .... | .... | .... | .... | .... | .... | — | — | — | — | .... |
| Other investment | 8d9la | .... | .... | 4,812.1 | 6,632.1 | 6,971.0 | 9,509.4 | †11,356.0 | 13,138.8 | 13,839.5 | 16,808.1 | 16,057.6 | .... |
| Other equity | 8dala | .... | .... | .... | .... | .... | .... | .... | .... | .... | .... | .... | .... |
| Debt instruments | 8dzla | .... | .... | 4,812.1 | 6,632.1 | 6,971.0 | 9,509.4 | †11,356.0 | 13,138.8 | 13,839.5 | 16,808.1 | 16,057.6 | .... |

| | | 2004 | 2005 | 2006 | 2007 | 2008 | 2009 | 2010 | 2011 | 2012 | 2013 | 2014 | 2015 |
|---|---|---|---|---|---|---|---|---|---|---|---|---|---|
| **Government Finance** | | | | | | | | | | | | | |
| **Cash Flow Statement** | | | | | | | | | | | | | |
| **Budgetary Central Government** | | | | *Millions of Cedis: Fiscal Year Ends December 31* | | | | | | | | | |
| Cash Receipts:Operating Activities... | c1 | 2,407.8 | .... | 3,270.2 | 4,576.6 | 5,634.6 | 6,802.7 | 8,858.9 | 12,934.8 | 15,889.5 | 18,629.6 | 26,277.3 | 32,939.9 |
| Taxes............................................ | c11 | 1,786.2 | .... | 2,395.6 | 3,213.4 | 4,193.6 | 4,615.9 | 6,236.8 | 8,892.2 | 11,024.3 | 12,583.4 | 17,004.7 | 21,601.9 |
| Social Contributions...................... | c12 | — | .... | — | — | — | — | — | 78.5 | 137.9 | 159.1 | 218.2 | 289.3 |
| Grants......................................... | c13 | 508.0 | .... | 727.6 | 949.0 | 898.3 | 1,159.9 | 1,173.7 | 1,347.3 | 1,160.3 | 739.4 | 814.1 | 2,688.8 |
| Other Receipts........................... | c14 | 113.6 | .... | 147.2 | 414.2 | 542.7 | 1,026.9 | 1,448.4 | 2,616.8 | 3,567.0 | 5,147.7 | 8,240.3 | 8,360.0 |
| Cash Payments:Operating Activities. | c2 | 1,669.6 | .... | 2,921.9 | 4,136.6 | 6,225.8 | 6,597.8 | 9,280.9 | 12,645.7 | 16,069.5 | 19,955.6 | 28,851.3 | 33,880.8 |
| Compensation of Employees.......... | c21 | 748.3 | .... | 1,234.7 | 1,551.8 | 2,147.3 | 2,635.6 | 3,315.6 | 4,855.3 | 6,665.5 | 8,115.4 | 9,448.6 | 10,555.9 |
| Purchases of Goods & Services....... | c22 | .... | .... | 457.2 | 615.8 | 769.1 | 1,087.5 | 1,371.7 | 2,001.9 | 1,321.8 | 938.5 | 3,874.8 | 2,933.2 |
| Interest......................................... | c24 | 347.2 | .... | 393.4 | 440.0 | 679.2 | 1,032.3 | 1,439.4 | 1,611.2 | 2,436.2 | 4,397.0 | 7,080.9 | 9,075.3 |
| Subsidies...................................... | c25 | .... | .... | 267.3 | 3.7 | 19.8 | — | 131.1 | — | 809.0 | 1,158.1 | 473.7 | 25.0 |
| Grants.......................................... | c26 | .... | .... | 393.0 | 1,111.3 | 1,594.1 | 1,230.5 | 2,332.4 | 3,092.5 | 3,765.0 | 4,547.9 | 5,737.4 | 7,677.5 |
| Social Benefits.............................. | c27 | 78.5 | .... | 176.4 | 413.9 | 725.3 | 612.0 | 690.8 | 1,084.9 | — | 1.1 | 2,235.9 | 3,613.9 |
| Other Payments............................ | c28 | — | .... | — | — | 291.0 | — | — | — | 1,072.1 | 797.7 | — | — |
| Net Cash Inflow:Operating Act.[1-2] | ccio | 738.2 | .... | 348.3 | 440.0 | −591.2 | 204.9 | −422.1 | 289.1 | −180.0 | −1,326.0 | −2,574.0 | −940.9 |
| Net Cash Outflow:Invest. in NFA...... | c31 | 970.5 | .... | 1,135.0 | 1,525.3 | 1,206.7 | 2,271.4 | 2,892.9 | 2,632.6 | 3,584.2 | 4,649.6 | 6,327.4 | 7,455.8 |
| Purchases of Nonfinancial Assets... | c31.1 | 970.5 | .... | 1,135.6 | 1,640.5 | 2,245.1 | 2,276.9 | 2,892.9 | 2,632.6 | 3,584.2 | 4,649.6 | 6,327.4 | 7,455.8 |
| Sales of Nonfinancial Assets........... | c31.2 | — | .... | .6 | 115.2 | 1,038.4 | 5.5 | — | — | — | — | — | — |
| Cash Surplus/Deficit [1-2-31=1-2M] | ccsd | −232.3 | .... | −786.6 | −1,085.3 | −1,797.9 | −2,066.6 | −3,315.0 | −2,343.5 | −3,764.2 | −5,975.6 | −8,901.4 | −8,396.8 |
| Net Acq. Fin. Assets, excl. Cash....... | c32x | 17.6 | .... | .7 | .9 | — | — | — | — | .... | .... | — | .... |
| Domestic...................................... | c321x | 17.6 | .... | .7 | .9 | — | — | — | — | .... | .... | .... | .... |
| Foreign......................................... | c322x | — | .... | — | — | — | — | — | — | .... | .... | .... | .... |
| Net Incurrence of Liabilities.............. | c33 | .... | .... | 804.4 | 1,040.4 | 1,905.3 | 1,997.5 | 2,906.4 | 2,375.7 | .... | .... | 10,636.3 | 9,329.0 |
| Domestic...................................... | c331 | .... | .... | 579.4 | 881.6 | .... | .... | .... | .... | .... | .... | .... | .... |
| Foreign......................................... | c332 | 261.1 | .... | 225.0 | 158.8 | .... | .... | .... | .... | .... | .... | .... | .... |
| Net Cash Inflow, Fin.Act.[-32x+33].. | cnfb | .... | .... | 803.6 | 1,039.5 | 1,905.3 | 1,997.5 | 2,906.4 | 2,375.7 | .... | .... | 10,636.3 | 9,329.0 |
| Net Change in Stock of Cash........... | cncb | .... | .... | 17.0 | −45.9 | 107.4 | −69.0 | −408.6 | 32.2 | .... | .... | 1,734.9 | 932.2 |
| Stat. Discrep. [32X-33+NCB-CSD].... | ccsdz | .... | .... | — | — | — | — | — | — | .... | .... | — | — |
| Memo Item:Cash Expenditure[2+31] | c2m | 2,640.1 | .... | 4,056.9 | 5,661.9 | 7,432.5 | 8,869.2 | 12,173.8 | 15,278.3 | 19,653.7 | 24,605.2 | 35,178.7 | 41,336.7 |
| Memo Item: Gross Debt.................. | c63 | .... | .... | .... | .... | .... | .... | .... | .... | .... | .... | .... | .... |
| **National Accounts** | | | | *Millions of Cedis: End of Period* | | | | | | | | | |
| Househ.Cons.Expend.,incl.NPISHs.... | 96f | .... | .... | 15,450 | 18,945 | 25,729 | 28,349 | 35,860 | 39,045 | 44,329 | 60,436p | 75,542 | .... |
| Government Consumption Expend... | 91f | .... | .... | 2,114 | 2,676 | 3,393 | 4,294 | 4,768 | 9,955 | 15,732 | 18,606p | 20,374 | .... |
| Gross Fixed Capital Formation......... | 93e | .... | .... | 4,047 | 4,656 | 6,474 | 7,216 | 11,354 | 15,317 | 23,293 | 25,311p | 29,741 | .... |
| Changes in Inventories.................... | 93i | .... | .... | .... | .... | .... | 349 | 615 | 498 | 646 | 595p | 1,020 | .... |
| Exports of Goods and Services........ | 90c | .... | .... | 4,712 | 5,679 | 7,554 | 10,720 | 13,572 | 22,094 | 30,397 | 31,938p | 44,797 | .... |
| Imports of Goods and Services (-)..... | 98c | .... | .... | 7,619 | 9,454 | 13,425 | 15,482 | 19,918 | 29,525 | 39,773 | 44,338p | 55,457 | .... |
| Statistical Discrepancy.................... | 99bs | .... | .... | — | 653 | 455 | 1,151 | −209 | 2,431 | 692 | 867p | −2,674 | .... |
| Gross Domestic Product (GDP)........ | 99b | .... | .... | 18,706 | 23,154 | 30,179 | 36,598 | 46,042 | 59,816 | 75,315 | 93,416p | 113,343p | .... |
| GDP, Production Based................... | 99bp | .... | .... | 17,810 | 21,755 | 28,664 | 36,598 | 46,042 | 59,816 | 75,315 | 93,416p | 113,343 | .... |
| | | | | *Millions: Midyear Estimates* | | | | | | | | | |
| **Population.............................** | 99z | 20.84 | 21.39 | 21.95 | 22.53 | 23.12 | 23.71 | 24.32 | 24.93 | 25.54 | 26.16 | 26.79 | 27.41 |

# Greece 174

|  |  | 2004 | 2005 | 2006 | 2007 | 2008 | 2009 | 2010 | 2011 | 2012 | 2013 | 2014 | 2015 |
|---|---|---|---|---|---|---|---|---|---|---|---|---|---|
| **Exchange Rates** | | | | | | *Drachmas per SDR through 2000; Euros per SDR Thereafter: End of Period* | | | | | | | |
| Market Rate | aa | 1.1402 | 1.2116 | 1.1423 | 1.0735 | 1.1068 | 1.0882 | 1.1525 | 1.1865 | 1.1649 | 1.1167 | 1.1933 | 1.2728 |
| | | | | | | *Drachmas per US Dollar through 2000; Euros per US Dollar Thereafter: End of Period (ae) Period Average (rf)* | | | | | | | |
| Market Rate | ae | .73416 | .84767 | .75930 | .67930 | .71855 | .69416 | .74839 | .77286 | .75792 | .72511 | .82366 | .91853 |
| Market Rate | rf | .80537 | .80412 | .79714 | .73064 | .68267 | .71984 | .75504 | .71936 | .77829 | .75316 | .75373 | .90166 |
| | | | | | *Drachmas per ECU through 1998; Drachmas per Euro through 2000: End of Period (ea) Period Average (eb)* | | | | | | | | |
| | | | | | | *Index Numbers (2010=100): Period Averages* | | | | | | | |
| Nominal Effective Exchange Rate | nec | 98.6 | 97.9 | 97.9 | 99.3 | 101.9 | 102.7 | 100.0 | 100.4 | 98.3 | 100.1 | 100.3 | 96.9 |
| CPI-Based Real Effect. Ex. Rate | rec | 93.4 | 93.7 | 94.5 | 96.0 | 98.8 | 100.1 | 100.0 | 100.7 | 97.6 | 96.8 | 94.7 | 89.5 |
| ULC-Based Real Effect. Ex. Rate | rel | 101.1 | 96.9 | 99.9 | 102.4 | 100.9 | 101.1 | 100.0 | 99.7 | 90.3 | 85.5 | 84.8 | 81.8 |
| **Fund Position** | | | | | | *Millions of SDRs: End of Period* | | | | | | | |
| Quota | 2f.s | 823.00 | 823.00 | 823.00 | 823.00 | 823.00 | 823.00 | 823.00 | 1,101.80 | 1,101.80 | 1,101.80 | 1,101.80 | 1,101.80 |
| SDR Holdings | 1b.s | 17.41 | 20.33 | 19.61 | 17.42 | 15.46 | 694.20 | 609.06 | 553.20 | 553.50 | 554.67 | 553.99 | 258.62 |
| Reserve Position in the Fund | 1c.s | 270.60 | 117.72 | 85.16 | 54.03 | 104.73 | 170.77 | 170.95 | 240.74 | 240.82 | 240.91 | 240.99 | 241.03 |
| Total Fund Cred.&Loans Outstg | 2tl | — | — | — | — | — | — | 9,131.30 | 17,541.80 | 18,940.90 | 23,280.89 | 20,016.70 | 12,717.61 |
| SDR Allocations | 1bd | 103.54 | 103.54 | 103.54 | 103.54 | 103.54 | 782.36 | 782.36 | 782.36 | 782.36 | 782.36 | 782.36 | 782.36 |
| **International Liquidity** | | | | | | *Millions of US Dollars Unless Otherwise Indicated: End of Period* | | | | | | | |
| Total Res.Min.Gold(Eurosys.Def.) | 1l.d | 1,191.0 | 506.4 | 565.9 | 631.1 | 343.8 | 1,554.8 | 1,309.5 | 1,248.7 | 1,269.6 | 1,419.6 | 1,876.6 | 2,189.3 |
| SDR Holdings | 1b.d | 27.0 | 29.1 | 29.5 | 27.5 | 23.8 | 1,088.3 | 938.0 | 849.3 | 850.7 | 854.2 | 802.6 | 358.4 |
| Reserve Position in the Fund | 1c.d | 420.2 | 168.3 | 128.1 | 85.4 | 161.3 | 267.7 | 263.3 | 369.6 | 370.1 | 371.0 | 349.2 | 334.0 |
| Foreign Exchange | 1d.d | 743.7 | 309.1 | 408.3 | 518.2 | 158.7 | 198.8 | 108.2 | 29.8 | 48.8 | 194.5 | 724.8 | 1,497.0 |
| o/w:Fin.Deriv.Rel.to Reserves | 1ddd | | | | | | | | | | | | |
| Other Reserve Assets | 1e.d | | | | | | | | | | | | |
| Gold (Million Fine Troy Ounces) | 1ad | 3.463 | 3.471 | 3.593 | 3.618 | 3.617 | 3.615 | 3.588 | 3.589 | 3.597 | 3.606 | 3.615 | 3.621 |
| Gold (Eurosystem Valuation) | 1and | 1,516.8 | 1,780.6 | 2,284.1 | 3,026.5 | 3,128.7 | 3,991.0 | 5,060.0 | 5,650.9 | 5,985.4 | 4,332.6 | 4,335.3 | 3,836.6 |
| Memo:Euro Cl. on Non-EA Res. | 1dgd | | | | | | | | | | | | |
| Non-Euro Cl. on EA Res | 1dhd | 1,834.7 | 1,129.0 | 738.8 | 984.8 | 3,452.8 | 400.5 | 376.8 | 1,304.3 | 453.9 | 446.8 | 728.5 | 543.3 |
| Central Bank: Other Assets | 3..d | 15,081.2 | 14,223.6 | 16,807.6 | 24,930.0 | 19,539.5 | 26,285.2 | 22,893.1 | 20,087.8 | 22,140.9 | 23,454.4 | 32,809.8 | 39,566.6 |
| Central Bank: Other Liabs | 4..d | 174.4 | 158.6 | 166.3 | 178.3 | 170.6 | 1,240.9 | 1,218.2 | 1,571.2 | 1,859.5 | 1,880.6 | 1,641.0 | 1,227.8 |
| Other Depository Corps.: Assets | 7a.d | 39,507.7 | 41,059.5 | 63,327.9 | 94,463.2 | 117,403.8 | 136,218.8 | 99,839.5 | 85,753.2 | 80,333.0 | 73,290.9 | 60,941.7 | 47,244.1 |
| Other Depository Corps.: Liabs | 7b.d | 44,526 | 53,216 | 77,599 | 115,969 | 104,076 | 91,534 | 109,369 | 81,961 | 72,099 | 78,602 | 72,981 | 29,477 |
| **Central Bank** | | | | | | *Millions of Euros: End of Period* | | | | | | | |
| *Euro Area Wide Residency Criterion* | | | | | | | | | | | | | |
| Net Foreign Assets | 11n.u | 3,089 | 3,140 | 2,759 | 3,392 | 3,274 | 3,032 | 3,907 | 4,156 | 4,162 | 2,867 | 3,812 | 11,233 |
| Claims on Nonresidents | 11..u | 3,217 | 3,274 | 2,886 | 3,513 | 3,397 | 3,893 | 4,819 | 5,370 | 5,571 | 4,230 | 5,164 | 12,361 |
| Liabilities to Nonresidents | 16c.u | 128 | 134 | 126 | 121 | 123 | 861 | 912 | 1,214 | 1,409 | 1,364 | 1,352 | 1,128 |
| Claims on Other Depository Corps | 12e.u | 1,544 | 4,110 | 6,493 | 10,532 | 41,000 | 51,089 | 100,717 | 130,942 | 123,135 | 74,810 | 58,753 | 113,055 |
| Net Claims on Central Government | 12anu | 21,570 | 20,851 | 22,084 | 24,624 | 22,023 | 27,193 | 27,394 | 23,026 | 21,396 | 21,507 | 32,025 | 24,510 |
| Claims on Central Govt | 12a.u | 22,055 | 21,687 | 22,493 | 25,297 | 23,245 | 28,061 | 29,534 | 27,823 | 26,911 | 26,688 | 35,758 | 28,091 |
| Liabs. to Central Govt | 16d.u | 485 | 836 | 409 | 673 | 1,222 | 868 | 2,140 | 4,797 | 5,515 | 5,181 | 3,733 | 3,581 |
| Claims on Other Sectors | 12s.u | 251 | 274 | 302 | 325 | 346 | 364 | 380 | 397 | 603 | 410 | 444 | 6,763 |
| Claims on Other Financial Corps | 12g.u | 12 | 9 | 8 | 8 | 8 | 8 | 8 | 8 | 211 | 8 | 41 | 6,350 |
| Claims on State & Local Govts | 12c.u | — | — | — | — | — | — | — | — | — | — | — | — |
| Claims on Public Nonfin. Corps | 12c.u | | | | | | | | | | | | |
| Claims on Private Sector | 12d.u | 239 | 265 | 294 | 317 | 338 | 356 | 372 | 389 | 392 | 402 | 403 | 413 |
| Monetary Base | 14..u | 18,814 | 19,077 | 21,049 | 24,657 | 27,226 | 30,168 | 33,184 | 28,864 | 27,651 | 29,703 | 31,600 | 33,052 |
| Currency in Circulation | 14a.u | 12,726 | 14,328 | 15,909 | 16,893 | 18,953 | 21,574 | 22,448 | 23,656 | 24,262 | 25,325 | 27,872 | 29,513 |
| Liabs. to Other Depository Corps | 14c.u | 5,387 | 4,354 | 4,625 | 7,248 | 7,936 | 8,187 | 10,613 | 5,054 | 3,113 | 4,022 | 3,487 | 1,674 |
| Liabs. to Other Sectors | 14d.u | 701 | 395 | 515 | 516 | 337 | 407 | 123 | 154 | 276 | 356 | 241 | 1,865 |
| Other Liabs. to Other Dep. Corps | 14n.u | 536 | 110 | 112 | 102 | 79 | 85 | — | — | — | — | — | — |
| Dep. & Sec. Excl. f/Monetary Base | 14o.u | | | | | | | | | | | | |
| Deposits Included in Broad Money | 15..u | — | — | — | — | — | — | — | — | — | — | — | — |
| Sec.Ot.th.Shares Inc.in.Brd.Money | 16a.u | — | — | — | — | — | — | — | — | — | — | — | — |
| Deposits Excl. from Broad Money | 16b.u | — | — | — | — | — | — | — | — | — | — | — | — |
| Sec.Oh.th.Shares Excl. f/Brd.Money | 16s.u | — | — | — | — | — | — | — | — | — | — | — | — |
| Loans | 16l.u | | | | | | | | | | | | |
| Financial Derivatives | 16m.u | | | | | | | | | | | | |
| Shares and Other Equity | 17a.u | 874 | 753 | 789 | 881 | 943 | 1,194 | 1,480 | 1,702 | 2,786 | 5,322 | 5,323 | 10,086 |
| Other Items (Net) | 17r.u | 6,230 | 8,435 | 9,688 | 13,233 | 38,395 | 50,231 | 97,734 | 127,955 | 118,859 | 64,569 | 58,111 | 112,423 |
| *Memorandum Items* | | | | | | | | | | | | | |
| *National Residency Criterion* | | | | | | | | | | | | | |
| Net Foreign Assets | 11n | 6,386 | 6,645 | 6,616 | 8,503 | −18,935 | −27,802 | −66,100 | −85,107 | −77,484 | −31,302 | −18,530 | −53,637 |
| Claims on Nonresidents | 11 | 13,060 | 13,996 | 14,927 | 19,421 | 16,536 | 22,095 | 21,900 | 20,857 | 22,280 | 21,177 | 32,141 | 41,878 |
| Liabilities to Nonresidents | 16c | 6,674 | 7,351 | 8,310 | 10,918 | 35,471 | 49,897 | 88,000 | 105,964 | 99,764 | 52,480 | 50,671 | 95,515 |
| Claims on Other Depository Corps | 12e | 272 | 2,425 | 4,866 | 8,795 | 40,594 | 50,080 | 99,114 | 129,298 | 121,606 | 73,429 | 56,457 | 108,051 |
| Net Claims on Central Government | 12an | 14,056 | 12,871 | 12,727 | 11,501 | 10,338 | 11,133 | 13,048 | 10,315 | 7,551 | 7,070 | 8,552 | 7,514 |
| Claims on Central Government | 12a | 14,541 | 13,707 | 13,136 | 12,174 | 11,560 | 12,001 | 15,188 | 15,112 | 13,066 | 12,251 | 12,285 | 11,095 |
| Liabilities to Central Government | 16d | 485 | 836 | 409 | 673 | 1,222 | 868 | 2,140 | 4,797 | 5,515 | 5,181 | 3,733 | 3,581 |
| Claims on Other Sectors | 12s | 251 | 274 | 302 | 325 | 346 | 364 | 380 | 397 | 400 | 410 | 414 | 424 |
| Claims on Other Fin. Corps | 12g | 12 | 9 | 8 | 8 | 8 | 8 | 8 | 8 | 8 | 8 | 11 | 11 |
| Claims on State & Local Govts | 12b | — | — | — | — | — | — | — | — | — | — | — | — |
| Claims on Private Sector | 12d | 239 | 265 | 294 | 317 | 338 | 356 | 372 | 389 | 392 | 402 | 403 | 413 |
| Liabs.to ODCs, Inc.in Mon.Base | 14c | 5,387 | 4,354 | 4,625 | 7,248 | 7,936 | 8,187 | 10,613 | 5,054 | 3,113 | 4,022 | 3,487 | 1,674 |
| Liabs.to Ot.Sectors, Inc.in Mon.Base | 14d | 701 | 395 | 515 | 516 | 337 | 407 | 123 | 154 | 276 | 356 | 241 | 1,865 |
| Liabs.to ODCs,Excl.f/Mon.Base | 14n | 536 | 110 | 112 | 102 | 79 | 85 | — | — | — | — | — | — |
| Net Claims on Eurosystem | 12e.s | −5,096 | −5,767 | −6,734 | −9,359 | −33,910 | −47,468 | −85,488 | −103,117 | −96,689 | −49,456 | −47,576 | −92,644 |

# Greece   174

|  |  | 2004 | 2005 | 2006 | 2007 | 2008 | 2009 | 2010 | 2011 | 2012 | 2013 | 2014 | 2015 |
|---|---|---|---|---|---|---|---|---|---|---|---|---|---|
| **Other Depository Corporations** | | | | | | *Millions of Euros: End of Period* | | | | | | | |
| Euro Area Wide Residency Criterion | | | | | | | | | | | | | |
| Net Foreign Assets............................ | **21n.u** | −3,684 | −10,305 | −10,836 | −14,609 | 9,577 | 31,018 | −7,132 | 2,931 | 6,241 | −3,851 | −9,916 | 16,320 |
| Claims on Nonresidents................. | **21..u** | 29,005 | 34,805 | 48,085 | 64,169 | 84,360 | 94,557 | 74,719 | 66,275 | 60,886 | 53,144 | 50,195 | 43,395 |
| Liabilities to Nonresidents............. | **26c.u** | 32,689 | 45,110 | 58,921 | 78,778 | 74,783 | 63,539 | 81,851 | 63,344 | 54,645 | 56,995 | 60,111 | 27,075 |
| Claims on Eurosystem...................... | **20..u** | 7,814 | 6,580 | 7,269 | 9,996 | 10,650 | 10,724 | 12,712 | 7,743 | 5,740 | 6,046 | 5,309 | 3,359 |
| Currency...................................... | **20a.u** | 1,891 | 2,116 | 2,532 | 2,646 | 2,635 | 2,452 | 2,065 | 2,286 | 2,442 | 1,959 | 1,822 | 1,685 |
| Reserve Deposits and Securities..... | **20b.u** | 5,387 | 4,354 | 4,625 | 7,248 | 7,936 | 8,187 | 10,647 | 5,457 | 3,298 | 4,087 | 3,487 | 1,674 |
| Other Claims................................. | **20n.u** | 536 | 110 | 112 | 102 | 79 | 85 | — | — | — | — | — | — |
| Net Claims on Central Government.. | **22anu** | 30,626 | 40,114 | 36,772 | 31,647 | 31,432 | 38,529 | 52,793 | 53,880 | 20,381 | 12,977 | 15,104 | 16,870 |
| Claims on Central Government...... | **22a.u** | 33,953 | 43,777 | 40,483 | 35,601 | 35,662 | 41,586 | 61,753 | 57,979 | 27,501 | 20,512 | 22,243 | 22,578 |
| Liabilities to Central Government... | **26d.u** | 3,327 | 3,663 | 3,711 | 3,954 | 4,230 | 3,057 | 8,960 | 4,099 | 7,120 | 7,535 | 7,139 | 5,708 |
| Claims on Other Sectors.................. | **22s.u** | 138,820 | 164,591 | 189,150 | 222,233 | 244,250 | 232,601 | 274,582 | 265,039 | 277,608 | 270,017 | 264,942 | 261,518 |
| Claims on Other Financial Corps.... | **22g.u** | 15,673 | 18,922 | 20,888 | 23,288 | 24,454 | 19,544 | 17,452 | 18,172 | 51,220 | 53,642 | 54,537 | 59,776 |
| Claims on State & Local Govts....... | **22b.u** | 1,871 | 1,804 | 1,562 | 1,538 | 1,539 | 1,699 | 2,636 | 2,187 | 1,811 | 1,581 | 1,562 | 1,343 |
| Claims on Public Nonfin. Corps...... | **22c.u** | | | | | | | | | | | | |
| Claims on Private Sector................ | **22d.u** | 121,276 | 143,865 | 166,700 | 197,407 | 218,257 | 211,358 | 254,494 | 244,680 | 224,577 | 214,794 | 208,843 | 200,399 |
| Liabilities to Eurosystem.................. | **26g.u** | 355 | 2,694 | 4,987 | 9,666 | 40,594 | 50,640 | 100,219 | 130,367 | 122,543 | 74,223 | 57,876 | 112,183 |
| Transf.Dep.Included in Broad Money | **24..u** | 91,100 | 98,956 | 99,666 | 98,395 | 90,359 | 102,823 | 90,718 | 74,428 | 65,149 | 68,340 | 68,967 | 77,761 |
| Other.Dep.Included in Broad Money. | **25..u** | 59,999 | 63,657 | 79,569 | 108,351 | 142,257 | 138,808 | 121,648 | 103,257 | 101,003 | 101,120 | 97,358 | 50,970 |
| Sec.Ot.th.Shares Inc.in.Brd. Money... | **26a.u** | 466 | 419 | 490 | −1,587 | 2,126 | −69 | 6 | −1 | 181 | 7 | 26 | — |
| Deposits Excl. from Broad Money..... | **26b.u** | 4,187 | 4,552 | 4,363 | 2,991 | 3,237 | 4,147 | 4,207 | 3,041 | 2,469 | 2,115 | 1,952 | 1,197 |
| Sec.Ot.th.Shares Excl.f/Brd. Money... | **26s.u** | −453 | −1,218 | −1,450 | −2,245 | −2,906 | −1,525 | −865 | −1,247 | 848 | −67 | −153 | 511 |
| Loans........................................... | **26l.u** | | | | | | | | | | | | |
| Financial Derivatives...................... | **26m.u** | 4,227 | 6,585 | 6,558 | 6,913 | 9,940 | 7,514 | 4,325 | 5,955 | 5,221 | 3,312 | 5,344 | 4,552 |
| Insurance Technical Reserves........... | **26r.u** | — | — | — | — | — | — | — | — | — | — | — | — |
| Shares and Other Equity................. | **27a.u** | 14,143 | 17,342 | 19,426 | 22,005 | 20,257 | 28,730 | 30,027 | 32,713 | 25,113 | 24,597 | 34,350 | 35,468 |
| Other Items (Net).......................... | **27r.u** | −448 | 7,990 | 8,745 | 4,776 | −9,957 | −18,194 | −17,330 | −18,923 | −12,563 | 11,534 | 9,885 | 15,429 |
| Memorandum Items | | | | | | | | | | | | | |
| Total Assets................................... | **20ra** | 246,004 | 286,047 | 321,409 | 391,500 | 464,748 | 492,609 | 514,967 | 476,914 | 442,215 | 407,414 | 397,801 | 386,022 |
| National Residency Criterion | | | | | | | | | | | | | |
| Net Foreign Assets......................... | **21n** | 6,401 | −1,092 | −4,636 | −6,445 | 24,409 | 55,155 | 13,375 | 20,676 | 49,450 | 36,590 | 26,845 | 61,850 |
| Claims on Nonresidents................. | **21** | 44,063 | 51,419 | 64,656 | 91,437 | 134,741 | 167,850 | 129,813 | 111,948 | 124,954 | 107,342 | 100,261 | 96,971 |
| Liabilities to Nonresidents............. | **26c** | 37,662 | 52,511 | 69,292 | 97,882 | 110,332 | 112,695 | 116,438 | 91,272 | 75,504 | 70,752 | 73,416 | 35,121 |
| Net Claims on Central Government.. | **22an** | 29,267 | 37,492 | 35,388 | 30,960 | 30,866 | 37,087 | 51,453 | 52,856 | 19,309 | 12,704 | 14,864 | 16,669 |
| Claims on Central Government...... | **22a** | 32,594 | 41,155 | 39,099 | 34,914 | 35,096 | 40,143 | 60,412 | 56,954 | 26,428 | 20,234 | 22,001 | 22,375 |
| Liabilities to Central Government... | **26d** | 3,327 | 3,663 | 3,711 | 3,954 | 4,230 | 3,056 | 8,959 | 4,098 | 7,119 | 7,530 | 7,137 | 5,706 |
| Claims on Other Sectors.................. | **22s** | 136,013 | 161,929 | 185,835 | 218,046 | 237,902 | 226,147 | 268,649 | 259,417 | 238,741 | 227,405 | 222,329 | 213,813 |
| Claims on Other Fin. Corps............ | **22g** | 13,713 | 16,925 | 18,388 | 20,104 | 20,628 | 15,731 | 14,143 | 15,074 | 13,968 | 12,863 | 13,590 | 13,963 |
| Claims on State & Local Govts....... | **22b** | 1,871 | 1,804 | 1,562 | 1,538 | 1,539 | 1,699 | 2,636 | 2,187 | 1,811 | 1,581 | 1,562 | 1,343 |
| Claims on Private Sector............... | **22d** | 120,429 | 143,200 | 165,885 | 196,404 | 215,735 | 208,717 | 251,870 | 242,156 | 222,962 | 212,961 | 207,177 | 198,507 |
| Transf.Dep.Included in Broad Money | **24** | 90,895 | 98,710 | 99,403 | 98,123 | 89,837 | 102,081 | 90,185 | 73,829 | 64,108 | 67,709 | 68,494 | 76,792 |
| Other.Dep.Included in Broad Money. | **25** | 59,414 | 63,457 | 79,194 | 107,718 | 140,829 | 137,894 | 120,467 | 102,469 | 100,353 | 100,368 | 96,388 | 50,784 |
| Sec.Ot.th.Shares Inc.in.Brd. Money... | **26a** | 472 | 443 | 515 | 376 | 2,310 | 16 | 7 | 3 | 181 | 7 | 26 | — |
| Deposits Excl. from Broad Money..... | **26b** | 4,176 | 4,541 | 4,347 | 2,985 | 3,222 | 3,967 | 4,192 | 3,034 | 2,460 | 2,110 | 1,952 | 995 |
| Sec.Ot.th.Shares Excl.f/Brd. Money... | **26s** | 738 | 115 | 384 | 794 | 698 | 1,956 | 1,934 | 965 | 2,457 | 984 | 1,436 | 4,844 |

# Greece  174

| | | 2004 | 2005 | 2006 | 2007 | 2008 | 2009 | 2010 | 2011 | 2012 | 2013 | 2014 | 2015 |
|---|---|---|---|---|---|---|---|---|---|---|---|---|---|
| **Depository Corporations** | | | | | | | *Millions of Euros: End of Period* | | | | | | |
| Euro Area Wide Residency Criterion | | | | | | | | | | | | | |
| Net Foreign Assets | 31n.u | −595 | −7,165 | −8,077 | −11,217 | 12,851 | 34,050 | −3,225 | 7,087 | 10,403 | −984 | −6,104 | 27,553 |
| Claims on Nonresidents | 31..u | 32,222 | 38,079 | 50,971 | 67,682 | 87,757 | 98,450 | 79,538 | 71,645 | 66,457 | 57,374 | 55,359 | 55,756 |
| Liabilities to Nonresidents | 36c.u | 32,817 | 45,244 | 59,047 | 78,899 | 74,906 | 64,400 | 82,763 | 64,558 | 56,054 | 58,359 | 61,463 | 28,203 |
| Domestic Claims | 32..u | 191,267 | 225,830 | 248,308 | 278,829 | 298,051 | 298,687 | 355,149 | 342,342 | 319,988 | 304,911 | 312,515 | 309,661 |
| Net Claims on Central Government | 32anu | 52,196 | 60,965 | 58,856 | 56,271 | 53,455 | 65,722 | 80,187 | 76,906 | 41,777 | 34,484 | 47,129 | 41,380 |
| Claims on Central Government | 32a.u | 56,008 | 65,464 | 62,976 | 60,898 | 58,907 | 69,647 | 91,287 | 85,802 | 54,412 | 47,200 | 58,001 | 50,669 |
| Liabilities to Central Government | 36d.u | 3,812 | 4,499 | 4,120 | 4,627 | 5,452 | 3,925 | 11,100 | 8,896 | 12,635 | 12,716 | 10,872 | 9,289 |
| Claims on Other Sectors | 32s.u | 139,071 | 164,865 | 189,452 | 222,558 | 244,596 | 232,965 | 274,962 | 265,436 | 278,211 | 270,427 | 265,386 | 268,281 |
| Claims on Other Financial Corps | 32g.u | 15,685 | 18,931 | 20,896 | 23,296 | 24,462 | 19,552 | 17,460 | 18,180 | 51,431 | 53,650 | 54,578 | 66,126 |
| Claims on State & Local Govts | 32b.u | 1,871 | 1,804 | 1,562 | 1,538 | 1,539 | 1,699 | 2,636 | 2,187 | 1,811 | 1,581 | 1,562 | 1,343 |
| Claims on Public Nonfin. Corps | 32c.u | — | — | — | — | — | — | — | — | — | — | — | — |
| Claims on Private Sector | 32d.u | 121,515 | 144,130 | 166,994 | 197,724 | 218,595 | 211,714 | 254,866 | 245,069 | 224,969 | 215,196 | 209,246 | 200,812 |
| Broad Money Liabilities | 35l.u | 163,101 | 175,639 | 193,617 | 219,922 | 251,397 | 261,091 | 232,878 | 199,208 | 188,443 | 193,239 | 192,642 | 158,424 |
| Currency Outside Depository Corps | 34a.u | 10,835 | 12,212 | 13,377 | 14,247 | 16,318 | 19,122 | 20,383 | 21,370 | 21,820 | 23,366 | 26,050 | 27,828 |
| Transferable Deposits | 34..u | 91,696 | 99,207 | 100,107 | 98,835 | 90,599 | 103,167 | 90,831 | 74,573 | 65,416 | 68,680 | 69,208 | 79,626 |
| Other Deposits | 35..u | 60,104 | 63,801 | 79,643 | 108,427 | 142,354 | 138,871 | 121,658 | 103,266 | 101,026 | 101,186 | 97,358 | 50,970 |
| Securities Other than Shares | 36a.u | 466 | 419 | 490 | −1,587 | 2,126 | −69 | 6 | −1 | 181 | 7 | 26 | — |
| Deposits Excl. from Broad Money | 36b.u | 4,187 | 4,552 | 4,363 | 2,991 | 3,237 | 4,147 | 4,207 | 3,041 | 2,469 | 2,115 | 1,952 | 1,197 |
| Sec.Oth.th.Shares Excl.f/Brd. Money | 36s.u | −453 | −1,218 | −1,450 | −2,245 | −2,906 | −1,525 | −865 | −1,247 | 848 | −67 | −153 | 511 |
| Loans | 36l.u | — | — | — | — | — | — | — | — | — | — | — | — |
| Financial Derivatives | 36m.u | 4,227 | 6,585 | 6,558 | 6,913 | 9,940 | 7,514 | 4,325 | 5,955 | 5,221 | 3,312 | 5,344 | 4,552 |
| Insurance Technical Reserves | 36r.u | — | — | — | — | — | — | — | — | — | — | — | — |
| Shares and Other Equity | 37a.u | 15,017 | 18,095 | 20,215 | 22,886 | 21,200 | 29,924 | 31,507 | 34,415 | 27,899 | 29,919 | 39,673 | 45,554 |
| Other Items (Net) | 37r.u | 4,593 | 15,009 | 16,927 | 17,143 | 28,032 | 31,588 | 79,872 | 108,054 | 105,519 | 75,451 | 67,119 | 126,980 |
| Broad Money Liabs., Seasonally Adj. | 35lub | 160,866 | 173,192 | 190,808 | 216,696 | 247,718 | 257,342 | 229,491 | 196,057 | 185,115 | 189,430 | 188,560 | 154,964 |
| Memorandum Items | | | | | | | | | | | | | |
| National Residency Criterion | | | | | | | | | | | | | |
| Net Foreign Assets | 31n | 12,787 | 5,553 | 1,980 | 2,058 | 5,474 | 27,353 | −52,725 | −64,431 | −28,034 | 5,288 | 8,315 | 8,213 |
| Claims on Nonresidents | 31 | 57,123 | 65,415 | 79,583 | 110,858 | 151,277 | 189,945 | 151,713 | 132,805 | 147,234 | 128,519 | 132,402 | 138,849 |
| Liabilities to Nonresidents | 36c | 44,336 | 59,862 | 77,602 | 108,800 | 145,803 | 162,592 | 204,438 | 197,236 | 175,268 | 123,232 | 124,087 | 130,636 |
| Domestic Claims | 32 | 179,587 | 212,566 | 234,252 | 260,832 | 279,452 | 274,731 | 333,530 | 322,985 | 266,001 | 247,589 | 246,159 | 238,420 |
| Net Claims on Central Government | 32an | 43,323 | 50,363 | 48,115 | 42,461 | 41,204 | 48,220 | 64,501 | 63,171 | 26,860 | 19,774 | 23,416 | 24,183 |
| Claims on Central Government | 32a | 47,135 | 54,862 | 52,235 | 47,088 | 46,656 | 52,144 | 75,600 | 72,066 | 39,494 | 32,485 | 34,286 | 33,470 |
| Liabilities to Central Government | 36d | 3,812 | 4,499 | 4,120 | 4,627 | 5,452 | 3,924 | 11,099 | 8,895 | 12,634 | 12,711 | 10,870 | 9,287 |
| Claims on Other Sectors | 32s | 136,264 | 162,203 | 186,137 | 218,371 | 238,248 | 226,511 | 269,029 | 259,814 | 239,141 | 227,815 | 222,743 | 214,237 |
| Claims on Other Financial Corps | 32g | 13,725 | 16,934 | 18,396 | 20,112 | 20,636 | 15,739 | 14,151 | 15,082 | 13,976 | 12,871 | 13,601 | 13,974 |
| Claims on State & Local Govts | 32b | 1,871 | 1,804 | 1,562 | 1,538 | 1,539 | 1,699 | 2,636 | 2,187 | 1,811 | 1,581 | 1,562 | 1,343 |
| Claims on Private Sector | 32d | 120,668 | 143,465 | 166,179 | 196,721 | 216,073 | 209,073 | 252,242 | 242,545 | 223,354 | 213,363 | 207,580 | 198,920 |
| Transf.Dep.Included in Broad Money | 34 | 91,491 | 98,961 | 99,844 | 98,563 | 90,077 | 102,425 | 90,298 | 73,974 | 64,361 | 67,999 | 68,735 | 78,657 |
| Other Dep.Included in Broad Money | 35 | 59,519 | 63,601 | 79,268 | 107,794 | 140,926 | 137,957 | 120,477 | 102,478 | 100,376 | 100,434 | 96,388 | 50,784 |
| Sec.Ot.th.Shares Inc.in.Brd. Money | 36a | 472 | 443 | 515 | 376 | 2,310 | 16 | 7 | 3 | 181 | 7 | 26 | — |
| Deposits Excl. from Broad Money | 36b | 4,176 | 4,541 | 4,347 | 2,985 | 3,222 | 3,967 | 4,192 | 3,034 | 2,460 | 2,110 | 1,952 | 995 |
| Sec.Ot.th.Shares Excl./f.Brd. Money | 36s | 738 | 115 | 384 | 794 | 698 | 1,956 | 1,934 | 965 | 2,457 | 984 | 1,436 | 4,844 |
| **Interest Rates** | | | | | | | *Percent Per Annum* | | | | | | |
| Treasury Bill Rate | 60c | 2.27 | 2.33 | 3.44 | 4.45 | 4.81 | 1.62 | 1.35 | 2.01 | 1.11 | .54 | .48 | .17 |
| Deposit Rate | 60l | 2.29 | 2.23 | . . . . | . . . . | . . . . | . . . . | . . . . | . . . . | . . . . | . . . . | . . . . | . . . . |
| Households: Stocks, up to 2 years | 60lhs | 2.42 | 2.34 | 2.80 | 3.85 | 4.70 | 3.48 | 2.98 | 3.79 | 4.49 | 3.91 | 2.55 | 1.66 |
| New Business, up to 1 year | 60lhn | 2.29 | 2.23 | 2.86 | 3.95 | 4.87 | 2.74 | 3.25 | 4.17 | 4.77 | 3.66 | 2.34 | 1.46 |
| Corporations: Stocks, up to 2 years | 60lcs | 2.16 | 2.10 | 2.88 | 4.01 | 4.82 | 2.62 | 2.97 | 3.91 | 4.54 | 3.73 | 2.49 | 1.57 |
| New Business, up to 1 year | 60lcn | 2.17 | 2.09 | 2.81 | 3.94 | 4.48 | 1.65 | 2.53 | 3.55 | 4.19 | 3.35 | 2.33 | 1.55 |
| REPOS, Stocks | 60lcr | 2.01 | 2.03 | 2.67 | 3.70 | 4.26 | 1.40 | 1.49 | . . . . | . . . . | . . . . | . . . . | . . . . |
| Households: Stocks, up to 1 year | 60phs | 13.02 | 12.61 | 12.68 | 13.31 | 13.68 | 13.13 | 12.52 | 13.23 | 13.32 | 12.89 | 12.76 | 12.91 |
| New Bus., Floating & up to 1 year | 60pns | 9.55 | 8.47 | 7.89 | 7.70 | 8.65 | 8.59 | 9.79 | 10.16 | 8.19 | 7.62 | 7.29 | . . . . |
| House Purch., Stocks,Over 5 years | 60phm | 5.07 | 4.84 | 4.89 | 5.12 | 5.09 | 4.28 | 3.75 | 3.82 | 3.40 | 3.13 | 2.94 | 2.82 |
| House Purch., New Bus., 5-10 yrs | 60phm | 6.09 | 5.91 | 5.24 | 4.89 | 5.22 | 4.84 | 4.54 | . . . . | . . . . | . . . . | . . . . | . . . . |
| Corporations: Stocks, up to 1 year | 60pcs | 5.77 | 5.76 | 6.34 | 7.05 | 7.43 | 6.06 | 5.98 | 7.15 | 7.33 | 7.00 | 6.52 | 5.89 |
| New Bus., Over € 1 mil.,up to 1 yr | 60pcn | 3.67 | 3.62 | 4.37 | 5.32 | 5.71 | 3.52 | 4.23 | 5.74 | 5.92 | 5.77 | 5.55 | 4.82 |
| Government Bond Yield | 61 | 4.26 | 3.59 | 4.07 | 4.50 | 4.80 | 5.17 | 9.09 | 15.75 | 22.50 | 10.05 | 6.93 | 9.81 |
| **Prices, Production, Labor** | | | | | | | *Index Numbers (2010=100): Period Averages* | | | | | | |
| Share Prices (End of Month) | 62.ep | 147.4 | 190.8 | 241.2 | 295.0 | 198.3 | 131.3 | 100.0 | 69.2 | 43.1 | 60.3 | 68.0 | 44.4 |
| Producer Prices | 63 | 76.8 | 81.4 | 87.3 | 90.9 | 100.0 | 94.3 | 100.0 | 107.4 | 112.7 | 112.0 | 111.1 | 104.6 |
| Consumer Prices | 64 | 82.4 | 85.3 | 88.0 | 90.6 | 94.4 | 95.5 | 100.0 | 103.3 | 104.9 | 103.9 | 102.6 | 100.8 |
| Harmonized CPI | 64h | 82.1 | 85.0 | 87.8 | 90.4 | 94.2 | 95.5 | 100.0 | 103.1 | 104.2 | 103.3 | 101.9 | 100.7 |
| Wages: Monthly Earnings | 65 | 87.3 | 88.6 | †90.5 | 95.2 | 99.6 | 99.3 | 100.0 | 95.2 | 87.3 | 78.5 | 78.9 | 78.2 |
| Industrial Production | 66 | 120.3 | 118.4 | 119.4 | 122.2 | 117.3 | 106.3 | 100.0 | 94.3 | 92.4 | 89.5 | 87.8 | 88.4 |
| | | | | | | | *Number in Thousands: Period Averages* | | | | | | |
| Labor Force | 67d | 4,902 | 4,853 | 4,888 | 4,894 | 4,910 | 4,953 | 4,945 | 4,859 | 4,829 | 4,784 | 4,747 | 4,738 |
| Employment | 67e | 4,382 | 4,361 | 4,440 | 4,476 | 4,523 | 4,469 | 4,306 | 3,979 | 3,636 | 3,459 | 3,480 | 3,548 |
| Unemployment | 67c | 520 | 493 | 448 | 418 | 388 | 485 | 639 | 882 | 1,195 | 1,330 | 1,274 | 1,197 |
| Unemployment Rate (%) | 67r | 10.6 | 10.0 | 9.0 | 8.4 | 7.8 | 9.6 | 12.7 | 17.9 | 24.5 | 27.5 | 26.5 | 25.0 |
| **Intl. Transactions & Positions** | | | | | | | *Millions of US Dollars through 2000; Millions of Euros Beginning 2001* | | | | | | |
| Exports | 70 | †13,366.2 | 14,856.8 | 17,131.0 | 19,317.2 | 21,227.7 | 18,015.1 | 21,300.2 | 24,377.3 | 27,579.7 | 27,295.5 | 27,120.5 | 25,892.7 |
| Imports, c.i.f. | 71 | †45,148.3 | 46,437.1 | 53,574.3 | 61,858.6 | 65,529.4 | 53,138.2 | 52,147.8 | 48,892.3 | 49,537.6 | 46,996.6 | 48,322.7 | 43,575.2 |
| | | | | | | | *2010=100* | | | | | | |
| Export Prices | 76 | 82.1 | 85.1 | 89.2 | 91.9 | 97.8 | 91.9 | 100.0 | 108.8 | 113.2 | 111.3 | 108.3 | 96.0 |
| Import Prices | 76.x | 76.6 | 83.4 | 86.9 | 89.1 | 95.5 | 93.8 | 100.0 | 107.6 | 112.4 | 109.4 | 105.3 | 94.2 |

# Greece 174

| | | 2004 | 2005 | 2006 | 2007 | 2008 | 2009 | 2010 | 2011 | 2012 | 2013 | 2014 | 2015 |
|---|---|---|---|---|---|---|---|---|---|---|---|---|---|
| **Balance of Payments** | | | | | | | *Millions of US Dollars* | | | | | | |
| A. Current Account* | 109bx | −13,476.1 | −18,233.2 | −29,565.3 | −44,587.3 | −51,312.8 | † −35,913.2 | −30,275.1 | −28,582.9 | −6,172.1 | −4,946.5 | −4,871.8 | −118.7 |
| Goods, credit (exports) | 1a9cx | 15,616.7 | 17,468.9 | 20,130.1 | 23,751.9 | 28,865.7 | † 20,976.4 | 22,249.2 | 27,453.6 | 27,894.8 | 35,701.2 | 35,567.5 | 27,489.1 |
| Goods, debit (imports) | 1a9dx | 47,203.7 | 51,704.5 | 64,163.5 | 80,677.5 | 93,758.5 | † 63,833.0 | 59,801.2 | 65,337.2 | 53,175.9 | 63,317.4 | 65,144.9 | 46,626.1 |
| Balance on goods | 1a9bx | −31,587.0 | −34,235.7 | −44,033.5 | −56,925.6 | −64,892.8 | † −42,856.7 | −37,552.0 | −37,883.6 | −25,281.1 | −27,616.2 | −29,577.4 | −19,137.0 |
| Services, credit (exports) | 1b9cx | 33,191.2 | 34,052.9 | 35,900.9 | 43,288.6 | 50,727.4 | † 38,046.9 | 37,667.0 | 40,168.7 | 35,343.7 | 37,204.1 | 41,258.8 | 30,975.2 |
| Services, debit (imports) | 1b9dx | 14,159.9 | 14,913.2 | 16,756.5 | 20,602.9 | 25,311.7 | † 20,244.7 | 20,375.0 | 19,624.1 | 16,058.7 | 16,329.5 | 16,965.7 | 12,198.0 |
| Balance on Goods & Services | 1z9bx | −12,555.8 | −15,096.0 | −24,889.1 | −34,239.8 | −39,477.1 | † −25,054.4 | −20,260.0 | −17,339.0 | −5,996.1 | −6,741.6 | −5,284.3 | −359.8 |
| Primary income: credit | 1c9cx | 3,495.1 | 4,071.6 | 4,566.1 | 6,344.6 | 8,427.0 | † 9,502.1 | 8,398.8 | 7,972.5 | 8,533.0 | 8,567.5 | 9,192.5 | 6,608.2 |
| Primary income: debit | 1c9dx | 8,919.7 | 11,101.5 | 13,524.0 | 18,813.7 | 24,442.3 | † 19,004.4 | 16,026.5 | 17,115.4 | 7,484.3 | 9,166.5 | 8,377.2 | 5,788.1 |
| Balance on gds, serv. & prim. inc. | 1y9bx | −17,980.3 | −22,126.0 | −33,847.0 | −46,708.9 | −55,492.4 | † −34,556.8 | −27,887.8 | −26,481.9 | −4,947.5 | −7,340.7 | −4,469.1 | 460.3 |
| Secondary income: credit | 1d9ca | 7,900.6 | 8,615.2 | 8,586.9 | 9,052.8 | 10,189.4 | † 3,758.2 | 2,974.0 | 2,761.6 | 3,019.4 | 6,179.3 | 3,425.2 | 2,124.0 |
| Secondary income: debit | 1d9da | 3,396.3 | 4,722.3 | 4,305.3 | 6,931.1 | 6,009.8 | † 5,114.6 | 5,361.4 | 4,862.5 | 4,244.0 | 3,785.1 | 3,828.0 | 2,703.0 |
| B. Capital Account* | 209ba | 2,989.9 | 2,563.0 | 3,821.9 | 5,956.9 | 5,995.1 | † 2,817.7 | 2,776.3 | 3,659.7 | 3,009.7 | 4,031.9 | 3,354.6 | 2,192.0 |
| Capital account: credit | 209ca | 3,278.0 | 2,904.9 | 4,172.6 | 6,426.2 | 6,812.8 | † 3,250.9 | 3,154.9 | 4,022.3 | 3,314.7 | 4,483.0 | 3,825.3 | 2,614.4 |
| Capital account: debit | 209da | 288.1 | 342.0 | 350.7 | 469.3 | 817.7 | † 433.3 | 378.7 | 362.6 | 305.0 | 451.2 | 470.7 | 422.3 |
| Balance on current & capital acct. | 129ba | −10,486.3 | −15,670.2 | −25,743.4 | −38,630.4 | −45,317.7 | † −33,095.5 | −27,498.9 | −24,923.2 | −3,162.5 | −914.6 | −1,517.2 | 2,073.3 |
| C. Financial Account* | 309na | −6,836.4 | −15,633.2 | −25,660.7 | −38,027.4 | −44,243.5 | † −34,930.4 | −14,180.3 | −11,918.3 | −1,616.1 | 9,794.3 | −4,394.5 | −7,230.2 |
| Direct investment: assets | 3a9aa | 1,070.6 | 1,508.3 | 4,234.2 | 5,260.8 | 3,206.0 | † 2,439.9 | 1,696.9 | 1,817.4 | 678.5 | −697.8 | 901.6 | 383.2 |
| Equity & investment fund shares | 3aaaa | 967.7 | 1,453.6 | 4,263.3 | 5,161.6 | 3,158.0 | † 2,451.2 | 1,691.5 | 1,767.3 | 699.6 | −729.3 | 884.8 | 371.3 |
| Debt instruments | 3abaa | 102.9 | 54.7 | −29.1 | 99.2 | 48.0 | † −11.3 | 5.4 | 50.2 | −21.2 | 31.6 | 16.8 | 11.8 |
| Direct investment: liabilities | 3a9la | 2,147.4 | 690.0 | 5,409.2 | 1,957.7 | 5,733.4 | † 2,762.6 | 533.7 | 1,092.1 | 1,663.3 | 2,945.4 | 1,682.6 | −289.4 |
| Equity & investment fund shares | 3aala | 2,503.5 | 1,011.8 | 5,665.4 | 3,402.4 | 6,205.4 | † 2,895.5 | 718.0 | 1,079.4 | 2,096.0 | 2,951.2 | 1,574.5 | −426.2 |
| Debt instruments | 3abla | −356.0 | −321.9 | −256.2 | −1,444.7 | −472.0 | † −132.9 | −184.3 | 12.7 | −432.7 | −5.8 | 108.1 | 136.8 |
| Portfolio investment: assets | 3b9aa | 13,835.3 | 23,193.7 | 9,374.4 | 21,635.8 | −143.8 | † 10,915.0 | −17,061.1 | −6,845.1 | 74,030.8 | −2,373.7 | 11,094.1 | 7,285.0 |
| Equity & investment fund shares | 3baaa | 830.0 | 2,189.3 | 2,922.6 | 593.0 | −4,030.2 | † 949.6 | 1,551.0 | −88.7 | 156.9 | −363.8 | 998.5 | 7,178.4 |
| Debt securities | 3bbaa | 13,005.2 | 21,004.4 | 6,451.8 | 21,042.8 | 3,886.4 | † 9,965.4 | −18,612.1 | −6,756.4 | 73,873.9 | −2,010.0 | 10,095.6 | 106.6 |
| Portfolio investment: liabilities | 3b9la | 31,300.7 | 32,307.9 | 18,737.9 | 45,545.5 | 24,890.9 | † 43,144.1 | −43,932.6 | −33,419.5 | −54,284.0 | −10,036.2 | 3,019.6 | −1,578.2 |
| Equity & investment fund shares | 3bala | 4,290.4 | 6,292.6 | 7,529.4 | 10,865.1 | −5,259.9 | † 763.7 | −1,459.9 | −354.3 | −66.4 | 3,134.8 | 11,266.8 | 6,997.3 |
| Debt securities | 3bbla | 27,010.3 | 26,015.3 | 11,208.5 | 34,680.3 | 30,150.8 | † 42,380.4 | −42,472.7 | −33,065.2 | −54,217.6 | −13,171.0 | −8,247.2 | −8,575.4 |
| Fin. der.& empl.stk.ops.(ESOs): net | 3c9na | 429.3 | −13.1 | −919.7 | 622.5 | 661.2 | † 1,151.1 | −432.5 | 986.0 | 1,077.7 | 856.3 | 490.2 | 364.2 |
| Fin. der. & ESOs.: assets | 3c9aa | 429.3 | −13.1 | −919.7 | 622.5 | 661.2 | † 1,151.1 | −432.5 | 986.0 | 1,077.7 | 856.3 | 490.2 | 364.2 |
| Fin. der. & ESOs.: liabilities | 3c9la | — | | | .... | .... | | | | | | | |
| Other investment: assets | 3d9aa | 7,463.5 | 8,739.9 | 7,336.2 | 22,117.7 | 40,678.7 | † 29,715.2 | 97.2 | 4,519.5 | −23,071.6 | −28,048.4 | −9,463.3 | 18,757.2 |
| Other equity | 3daaa | .... | .... | .... | .... | .... | † 169.2 | 44.8 | 44.5 | 1,212.0 | 1,241.8 | 663.6 | 34.2 |
| Debt instruments | 3dzaa | 7,463.5 | 8,739.9 | 7,336.2 | 22,117.7 | 40,678.7 | † 29,546.0 | 52.3 | 4,475.0 | −24,283.6 | −29,290.2 | −10,126.9 | 18,722.9 |
| Other investment: liabilities | 3d9la | −3,813.0 | 16,064.2 | 21,538.7 | 40,161.1 | 58,021.4 | † 33,244.9 | 41,879.7 | 44,723.6 | 106,952.2 | −32,967.1 | 2,714.9 | 35,887.2 |
| Other equity | 3dala | .... | | | | | | | | | | | |
| Debt instruments | 3dzla | −3,813.0 | 16,064.2 | 21,538.7 | 40,161.1 | 58,021.4 | † 33,244.9 | 41,879.7 | 44,723.6 | 106,952.2 | −32,967.1 | 2,714.9 | 35,887.2 |
| Curr.+ cap.− finan. acct. balance | 4y9na | −3,649.9 | −37.0 | −82.7 | −603.0 | −1,074.2 | † 1,835.0 | −13,318.6 | −13,004.9 | −1,546.4 | −10,708.9 | 2,877.3 | 9,303.4 |
| D. Net Errors and Omissions | 409na | 372.8 | −66.9 | 361.2 | 1,059.7 | 1,112.7 | † −625.2 | −617.9 | −305.1 | −590.5 | 4,253.0 | 2,595.1 | 1,280.8 |
| E. Reserves and Related Items | 4z9na | −3,277.0 | −103.9 | 278.5 | 456.8 | 38.5 | † 1,209.8 | −13,936.4 | −13,310.0 | −2,136.9 | −6,455.9 | 5,472.5 | 10,584.2 |
| Reserve assets | 3e9aa | −3,277.0 | −103.9 | 278.5 | 456.8 | 38.5 | † 1,209.8 | −201.1 | −44.1 | 18.7 | 140.1 | 626.1 | 382.4 |
| Credit and loans from the IMF | 3dcla | — | — | — | — | — | † — | 13,735.3 | 13,266.0 | 2,155.6 | 6,596.0 | −4,846.4 | −10,201.8 |
| Exceptional financing | 409la | .... | .... | .... | .... | .... | .... | .... | .... | .... | .... | .... | .... |

*Excludes components in group E

| | | 2004 | 2005 | 2006 | 2007 | 2008 | 2009 | 2010 | 2011 | 2012 | 2013 | 2014 | 2015 |
|---|---|---|---|---|---|---|---|---|---|---|---|---|---|
| **International Investment Position** | | | | | | | *Millions of US Dollars* | | | | | | |
| Assets | 809aa | 139,964.5 | 153,463.9 | 196,273.4 | 279,777.2 | † 320,323.3 | 374,874.2 | 315,792.2 | 306,288.1 | 348,183.5 | 316,583.7 | 279,283.0 | 268,437.4 |
| Direct investment | 8a9aa | 13,791.3 | 13,601.9 | 22,418.0 | 31,650.2 | † 39,584.1 | 48,899.7 | 49,376.6 | 51,677.1 | 48,865.3 | 40,380.0 | 34,491.4 | 30,074.9 |
| Equity & investment fund shares | 8aaaa | 12,968.6 | 13,055.7 | 21,897.8 | 30,578.5 | † 35,740.2 | 40,348.3 | 40,561.7 | 46,337.1 | 43,534.9 | 36,213.8 | 30,776.2 | 26,731.5 |
| Debt instruments | 8abaa | 822.7 | 546.2 | 520.2 | 1,071.7 | † 3,843.9 | 8,551.4 | 8,814.9 | 5,339.9 | 5,330.4 | 4,166.3 | 3,715.1 | 3,343.4 |
| Portfolio investment | 8b9aa | 52,665.6 | 69,978.6 | 88,495.8 | 127,848.9 | † 122,198.2 | 129,155.6 | 95,337.9 | 82,073.4 | 147,362.1 | 148,855.9 | 141,519.1 | 127,933.1 |
| Equity & investment fund shares | 8baaa | 6,200.3 | 8,326.3 | 13,355.7 | 20,602.0 | † 15,432.6 | 13,728.9 | 12,246.3 | 11,603.7 | 6,853.0 | 7,094.1 | 8,155.1 | 14,272.9 |
| Debt securities | 8bbaa | 46,465.3 | 61,652.3 | 75,140.1 | 107,246.9 | † 106,765.7 | 115,426.6 | 83,091.6 | 70,469.7 | 140,509.2 | 141,761.8 | 133,364.0 | 113,660.3 |
| Fin. der.(oth.than reserves) & ESOs | 8c9aa | 821.3 | 659.5 | 13.2 | 740.5 | † 1,349.9 | 2,551.3 | 1,864.0 | 2,722.4 | 3,872.4 | 4,934.4 | 4,798.1 | 4,662.9 |
| Other investment | 8d9aa | 69,977.9 | 66,937.4 | 82,496.9 | 115,879.9 | † 153,690.8 | 188,720.9 | 162,845.4 | 162,916.1 | 140,827.9 | 116,660.6 | 92,262.2 | 99,740.5 |
| Other equity | 8daaa | .... | .... | .... | .... | † 572.0 | 592.1 | 653.4 | 675.4 | 1,902.6 | 3,406.4 | 3,605.9 | 3,266.1 |
| Debt instruments | 8dzaa | 69,977.9 | 66,937.4 | 82,496.9 | 115,879.9 | † 153,118.9 | 188,128.8 | 162,192.0 | 162,240.7 | 138,925.3 | 113,254.2 | 88,656.3 | 96,474.4 |
| Reserve assets | 8e9aa | 2,708.4 | 2,286.6 | 2,849.6 | 3,657.7 | † 3,500.2 | 5,546.7 | 6,368.3 | 6,899.1 | 7,255.7 | 5,752.8 | 6,212.1 | 6,025.9 |
| Liabilities | 809la | 309,199.5 | 329,615.8 | 431,078.2 | 595,668.0 | † 568,685.6 | 669,018.1 | 607,827.9 | 535,263.7 | 627,510.5 | 622,751.5 | 549,205.4 | 510,680.3 |
| Direct investment | 8a9la | 28,481.5 | 29,189.3 | 41,288.0 | 53,220.8 | † 40,470.6 | 47,381.4 | 41,779.0 | 32,691.7 | 29,111.2 | 29,949.9 | 26,535.4 | 21,280.8 |
| Equity & investment fund shares | 8aala | 27,420.4 | 26,966.8 | 38,592.1 | 49,655.4 | † 34,164.8 | 39,145.4 | 30,855.5 | 22,925.3 | 18,945.3 | 19,325.3 | 16,929.4 | 12,532.2 |
| Debt instruments | 8abla | 1,061.1 | 2,222.6 | 2,695.9 | 3,565.4 | † 6,305.8 | 8,235.9 | 10,923.4 | 9,766.4 | 10,166.0 | 10,624.6 | 9,606.0 | 8,748.6 |
| Portfolio investment | 8b9la | 188,456.1 | 202,113.3 | 255,982.7 | 348,059.1 | † 290,836.1 | 343,676.7 | 213,793.3 | 105,628.8 | 78,784.0 | 79,720.3 | 68,822.5 | 55,055.6 |
| Equity & investment fund shares | 8bala | 28,386.2 | 37,962.7 | 60,247.5 | 93,547.5 | † 23,892.7 | 28,114.7 | 17,106.0 | 7,480.0 | 10,391.6 | 13,300.0 | 16,945.2 | 16,539.5 |
| Debt securities | 8bbla | 160,069.9 | 164,150.5 | 195,735.2 | 254,511.5 | † 266,943.4 | 315,562.0 | 196,687.3 | 98,148.8 | 68,392.4 | 66,420.2 | 51,877.3 | 38,516.0 |
| Fin. der.(oth.than reserves) & ESOs | 8c9la | .... | .... | .... | .... | .... | .... | .... | .... | .... | .... | .... | .... |
| Other investment | 8d9la | 92,261.9 | 98,313.2 | 133,807.6 | 194,388.1 | † 237,378.9 | 277,960.0 | 352,255.6 | 396,943.2 | 519,615.2 | 513,081.3 | 453,847.5 | 434,344.0 |
| Other equity | 8dala | .... | .... | .... | .... | .... | .... | .... | .... | .... | .... | .... | .... |
| Debt instruments | 8dzla | 92,261.9 | 98,313.2 | 133,807.6 | 194,388.1 | † 237,378.9 | 277,960.0 | 352,255.6 | 396,943.2 | 519,615.2 | 513,081.3 | 453,847.5 | 434,344.0 |

| | | 2004 | 2005 | 2006 | 2007 | 2008 | 2009 | 2010 | 2011 | 2012 | 2013 | 2014 | 2015 |
|---|---|---|---|---|---|---|---|---|---|---|---|---|---|

**Government Finance**
**Operations Statement**
**General Government**

*Millions of Euros: Fiscal Year Ends December 31;  Data Reported through Eurostat*

| | | 2004 | 2005 | 2006 | 2007 | 2008 | 2009 | 2010 | 2011 | 2012 | 2013 | 2014 | 2015 |
|---|---|---|---|---|---|---|---|---|---|---|---|---|---|
| Revenue | a1 | 75,136 | 78,449 | 85,338 | 93,921 | 98,351 | 92,422 | 93,253 | 91,077 | 88,805 | 88,565 | 83,463 | 84,662 |
| Taxes | a11 | 38,386 | 41,904 | 45,022 | 48,743 | 50,667 | 48,642 | 47,386 | 47,323 | 46,706 | 44,539 | 45,118 | 45,020 |
| Social Contributions | a12 | 23,440 | 24,537 | 25,891 | 28,892 | 30,641 | 29,344 | 29,700 | 27,272 | 26,621 | 24,455 | 24,088 | 24,428 |
| Grants | a13 | .... | .... | .... | .... | .... | .... | .... | .... | .... | .... | .... | .... |
| Other Revenue | a14 | .... | .... | .... | .... | .... | .... | .... | .... | .... | .... | .... | .... |
| Expense | a2 | 85,914 | 87,314 | 94,142 | 104,515 | 116,409 | 123,694 | 118,109 | 114,569 | 107,868 | 110,256 | 89,298 | 95,531 |
| Compensation of Employees | a21 | 21,890 | 22,700 | 23,988 | 25,777 | 28,001 | 31,013 | 28,020 | 25,962 | 24,360 | 21,954 | 21,832 | 21,447 |
| Use of Goods & Services | a22 | 12,335 | 11,727 | 13,629 | 15,639 | 14,973 | 15,821 | 13,742 | 10,075 | 9,652 | 8,408 | 8,558 | 8,194 |
| Consumption of Fixed Capital | a23 | 5,615 | 5,892 | 6,399 | 6,820 | 7,344 | 7,822 | 7,978 | 7,456 | 7,114 | 6,793 | 6,459 | 6,311 |
| Interest | a24 | 9,269 | 9,353 | 9,623 | 10,469 | 11,653 | 11,972 | 13,239 | 15,067 | 9,743 | 7,275 | 7,181 | 6,703 |
| Subsidies | a25 | 189 | 169 | 80 | 195 | 99 | 234 | 343 | 1,342 | 1,294 | 1,952 | 1,644 | 1,659 |
| Grants | a26 | .... | .... | .... | .... | .... | .... | .... | .... | .... | .... | .... | .... |
| Social Benefits | a27 | 29,257 | 31,968 | 35,966 | 39,996 | 45,772 | 48,987 | 47,378 | 47,529 | 44,387 | 38,702 | 38,399 | 38,995 |
| Other Expense | a28 | .... | .... | .... | .... | .... | .... | .... | .... | .... | .... | .... | .... |
| Gross Operating Balance [1-2+23] | agob | −5,163 | −2,973 | −2,405 | −3,774 | −10,714 | −23,450 | −16,878 | −16,036 | −11,949 | −14,898 | 624 | −4,558 |
| Net Operating Balance [1-2] | anob | −10,778 | −8,865 | −8,804 | −10,594 | −18,058 | −31,272 | −24,856 | −23,492 | −19,063 | −21,691 | −5,835 | −10,869 |
| Net Acq. of Nonfinancial Assets | a31 | 6,323 | 3,464 | 4,150 | 5,013 | 6,548 | 4,718 | 477 | −2,287 | −2,193 | 1,812 | 641 | 1,888 |
| Aquisition of Nonfin. Assets | a31.1 | .... | .... | .... | .... | .... | .... | .... | .... | .... | .... | .... | .... |
| Disposal of Nonfin. Assets | a31.2 | .... | .... | .... | .... | .... | .... | .... | .... | .... | .... | .... | .... |
| Net Lending/Borrowing [1-2-31] | anlb | −17,101 | −12,329 | −12,954 | −15,607 | −24,606 | −35,990 | −25,333 | −21,205 | −16,870 | −23,503 | −6,476 | −12,757 |
| Net Acq. of Financial Assets | a32 | .... | .... | .... | .... | .... | .... | .... | .... | .... | .... | .... | .... |
| By instrument | | | | | | | | | | | | | |
| Monetary Gold & SDRs | a3201 | .... | .... | .... | .... | .... | .... | .... | .... | .... | .... | | |
| Currency & Deposits | a3202 | .... | .... | .... | .... | .... | .... | .... | .... | .... | .... | | |
| Securities other than Shares | a3203 | .... | .... | .... | .... | .... | .... | .... | .... | .... | .... | | |
| Loans | a3204 | .... | .... | .... | .... | .... | .... | .... | .... | .... | .... | | |
| Shares & Other Equity | a3205 | .... | .... | .... | .... | .... | .... | .... | .... | .... | .... | | |
| Insurance Technical Reserves | a3206 | .... | .... | .... | .... | .... | .... | .... | .... | .... | .... | | |
| Financial Derivatives | a3207 | .... | .... | .... | .... | .... | .... | .... | .... | .... | .... | | |
| Other Accounts Receivable | a3208 | .... | .... | .... | .... | .... | .... | .... | .... | .... | .... | | |
| By debtor | | | | | | | | | | | | | |
| Domestic | a321 | .... | .... | .... | .... | .... | .... | .... | .... | .... | .... | | |
| Foreign | a322 | .... | .... | .... | .... | .... | .... | .... | .... | .... | .... | | |
| Net Incurrence of Liabilities | a33 | .... | .... | .... | .... | .... | .... | .... | .... | .... | .... | | |
| By instrument | | | | | | | | | | | | | |
| Special Drawing Rights (SDRs) | a3301 | .... | .... | .... | .... | .... | .... | .... | .... | .... | .... | | |
| Currency & Deposits | a3302 | .... | .... | .... | .... | .... | .... | .... | .... | .... | .... | | |
| Securities other than Shares | a3303 | .... | .... | .... | .... | .... | .... | .... | .... | .... | .... | | |
| Loans | a3304 | .... | .... | .... | .... | .... | .... | .... | .... | .... | .... | | |
| Shares & Other Equity | a3305 | .... | .... | .... | .... | .... | .... | .... | .... | .... | .... | | |
| Insurance Technical Reserves | a3306 | .... | .... | .... | .... | .... | .... | .... | .... | .... | .... | | |
| Financial Derivatives | a3307 | .... | .... | .... | .... | .... | .... | .... | .... | .... | .... | | |
| Other Accounts Payable | a3308 | .... | .... | .... | .... | .... | .... | .... | .... | .... | .... | | |
| By creditor | | | | | | | | | | | | | |
| Domestic | a331 | .... | .... | .... | .... | .... | .... | .... | .... | .... | .... | | |
| Foreign | a332 | .... | .... | .... | .... | .... | .... | .... | .... | .... | .... | | |
| Stat. Discrepancy [32-33-NLB] | anlbz | .... | .... | .... | .... | .... | .... | .... | .... | .... | .... | | |
| Memo Item: Expenditure [2+31] | a2m | 92,237 | 90,778 | 98,292 | 109,528 | 122,957 | 128,412 | 118,586 | 112,282 | 105,675 | 112,068 | 89,939 | 97,419 |

**Balance Sheet**

| | | 2004 | 2005 | 2006 | 2007 | 2008 | 2009 | 2010 | 2011 | 2012 | 2013 | 2014 | 2015 |
|---|---|---|---|---|---|---|---|---|---|---|---|---|---|
| Net Worth | a6 | .... | .... | .... | .... | .... | .... | .... | .... | .... | .... | | |
| Nonfinancial Assets | a61 | .... | .... | .... | .... | .... | .... | .... | .... | .... | .... | | |
| Financial Assets | a62 | .... | .... | .... | .... | .... | .... | .... | .... | .... | .... | | |
| By instrument | | | | | | | | | | | | | |
| Monetary Gold & SDRs | a6201 | .... | .... | .... | .... | .... | .... | .... | .... | .... | .... | | |
| Currency & Deposits | a6202 | .... | .... | .... | .... | .... | .... | .... | .... | .... | .... | | |
| Securities other than Shares | a6203 | .... | .... | .... | .... | .... | .... | .... | .... | .... | .... | | |
| Loans | a6204 | .... | .... | .... | .... | .... | .... | .... | .... | .... | .... | | |
| Shares and Other Equity | a6205 | .... | .... | .... | .... | .... | .... | .... | .... | .... | .... | | |
| Insurance Technical Reserves | a6206 | .... | .... | .... | .... | .... | .... | .... | .... | .... | .... | | |
| Financial Derivatives | a6207 | .... | .... | .... | .... | .... | .... | .... | .... | .... | .... | | |
| Other Accounts Receivable | a6208 | .... | .... | .... | .... | .... | .... | .... | .... | .... | .... | | |
| By debtor | | | | | | | | | | | | | |
| Domestic | a621 | .... | .... | .... | .... | .... | .... | .... | .... | .... | .... | | |
| Foreign | a622 | .... | .... | .... | .... | .... | .... | .... | .... | .... | .... | | |
| Liabilities | a63 | .... | .... | .... | .... | .... | .... | .... | .... | .... | .... | | |
| By instrument | | | | | | | | | | | | | |
| Special Drawing Rights (SDRs) | a6301 | .... | .... | .... | .... | .... | .... | .... | .... | .... | .... | | |
| Currency & Deposits | a6302 | .... | .... | .... | .... | .... | .... | .... | .... | .... | .... | | |
| Securities other than Shares | a6303 | .... | .... | .... | .... | .... | .... | .... | .... | .... | .... | | |
| Loans | a6304 | .... | .... | .... | .... | .... | .... | .... | .... | .... | .... | | |
| Shares and Other Equity | a6305 | .... | .... | .... | .... | .... | .... | .... | .... | .... | .... | | |
| Insurance Technical Reserves | a6306 | .... | .... | .... | .... | .... | .... | .... | .... | .... | .... | | |
| Financial Derivatives | a6307 | .... | .... | .... | .... | .... | .... | .... | .... | .... | .... | | |
| Other Accounts Payable | a6308 | .... | .... | .... | .... | .... | .... | .... | .... | .... | .... | | |
| By creditor | | | | | | | | | | | | | |
| Domestic | a631 | .... | .... | .... | .... | .... | .... | .... | .... | .... | .... | | |
| Foreign | a632 | .... | .... | .... | .... | .... | .... | .... | .... | .... | .... | | |
| Net Financial Worth [62-63] | a6m2 | .... | .... | .... | .... | .... | .... | .... | .... | .... | .... | | |
| Memo Item: Debt at Market Value | a6m3 | | | | | | | | | | | | |
| Memo Item: Debt at Face Value | a6m35 | .... | .... | .... | .... | .... | .... | .... | .... | .... | .... | | |
| Memo Item: Maastricht Debt | a6m36 | 199,276 | 213,970 | 225,648 | 239,915 | 264,775 | 301,062 | 330,570 | 356,289 | 305,094 | 320,510 | 319,718 | 311,452 |
| Memo Item: Debt at Nominal Value | a6m4 | .... | .... | .... | .... | .... | .... | .... | .... | .... | .... | | |

# Greece   174

| National Accounts | | 2004 | 2005 | 2006 | 2007 | 2008 | 2009 | 2010 | 2011 | 2012 | 2013 | 2014 | 2015 |
|---|---|---|---|---|---|---|---|---|---|---|---|---|---|
| | | *Billions of Drachmas through 2000; Billions of Euros Beginning 2001* | | | | | | | | | | | |
| Househ.Cons.Expend.,incl.NPISHs.... | 96f | 130.3 | 134.7 | 145.4 | 155.3 | 168.7 | 167.2 | 163.1 | 155.6 | 133.7 | 127.9 | 125.0 | 123.8 |
| Government Consumption Expend... | 91f | 37.1 | 39.9 | 43.9 | 47.7 | 50.1 | 55.4 | 50.2 | 45.1 | 41.6 | 36.9 | 35.4 | 35.2 |
| Gross Fixed Capital Formation......... | 93e | 47.3 | 41.5 | 51.6 | 60.5 | 57.6 | 49.4 | 39.7 | 31.6 | 24.1 | 21.7 | 20.6 | 20.5 |
| Changes in Inventories................... | 93i | 1.8 | 2.5 | 5.4 | 2.6 | 1.7 | −5.8 | −1.2 | −.3 | .3 | −1.0 | 1.1 | −3.2 |
| Exports of Goods and Services......... | 90c | 40.1 | 42.5 | 46.1 | 52.4 | 56.5 | 45.1 | 50.0 | 52.9 | 54.8 | 55.2 | 58.0 | 53.0 |
| Imports of Goods and Services (-)..... | 98c | 56.5 | 59.0 | 69.0 | 81.5 | 87.0 | 68.3 | 69.5 | 66.9 | 63.4 | 60.2 | 62.6 | 53.3 |
| Gross Domestic Product (GDP)......... | 99b | 193.7 | 199.2 | 217.9 | 232.7 | 242.0 | 237.5 | 226.0 | 207.0 | 191.2 | 180.4 | 177.6 | 176.0 |
| Net Primary Income from Abroad..... | 98.n | −9.8 | −9.0 | −4.3 | −6.2 | −7.7 | −5.6 | −4.8 | −5.7 | 1.2 | −.4 | .4 | .4 |
| Gross National Income (GNI)............ | 99a | 184.0 | 190.2 | 213.5 | 226.5 | 234.3 | 232.0 | 221.3 | 201.3 | 192.4 | 180.0 | 177.9 | 176.4 |
| Net Current Transf.from Abroad....... | 98t | .5 | −.2 | .1 | −1.2 | −.6 | −1.2 | −1.5 | −1.3 | −.8 | 1.4 | −.6 | −1.1 |
| Gross Nat'l Disposable Inc.(GNDI).... | 99i | 184.5 | 190.0 | 213.7 | 225.2 | 233.7 | 230.8 | 219.8 | 200.0 | 191.7 | 181.4 | 177.3 | 175.3 |
| Gross Saving................................... | 99s | 22.3 | 20.4 | 29.9 | 26.6 | 20.5 | 13.6 | 12.8 | 10.4 | 16.6 | 16.8 | 16.4 | 16.3 |
| Consumption of Fixed Capital.......... | 99cf | 22.8 | 23.6 | 31.2 | 33.6 | 36.4 | 37.7 | 37.9 | 36.9 | 37.0 | 34.6 | 32.6 | 31.4 |
| GDP Vol. Ref., Chained 2010 Prices. | 99b.p | 227.4 | 229.4 | 242.8 | 250.7 | 249.9 | 239.1 | 226.0 | 205.4 | 190.4 | 184.3 | 185.5 | 185.1 |
| GDP Volume (2010=100)............... | 99bvp | 100.6 | 101.5 | 107.4 | 110.9 | 110.6 | 105.8 | 100.0 | 90.9 | 84.2 | 81.5 | 82.1 | 81.9 |
| GDP Deflator (2010=100)............... | 99bip | 85.2 | 86.8 | 89.7 | 92.8 | 96.8 | 99.3 | 100.0 | 100.8 | 100.4 | 97.9 | 95.7 | 95.1 |
| | | *Millions: Midyear Estimates* | | | | | | | | | | | |
| Population................................. | 99z | 11.05 | 11.07 | 11.10 | 11.13 | 11.16 | 11.18 | 11.18 | 11.15 | 11.11 | 11.06 | 11.00 | 10.95 |

# Grenada 328

| | | 2004 | 2005 | 2006 | 2007 | 2008 | 2009 | 2010 | 2011 | 2012 | 2013 | 2014 | 2015 |
|---|---|---|---|---|---|---|---|---|---|---|---|---|---|
| **Exchange Rates** | | *E.Caribbean Dollars per SDR: End of Period* | | | | | | | | | | | |
| Official Rate................................. | aa | 4.1931 | 3.8590 | 4.0619 | 4.2667 | 4.1587 | 4.2328 | 4.1581 | 4.1452 | 4.1497 | 4.1580 | 3.9118 | 3.7415 |
| | | *E.Caribbean Dollars per US Dollar: End of Period (ae) Period Average (rf)* | | | | | | | | | | | |
| Official Rate................................. | ae | 2.7000 | 2.7000 | 2.7000 | 2.7000 | 2.7000 | 2.7000 | 2.7000 | 2.7000 | 2.7000 | 2.7000 | 2.7000 | 2.7000 |
| Official Rate................................. | rf | 2.7000 | 2.7000 | 2.7000 | 2.7000 | 2.7000 | 2.7000 | 2.7000 | 2.7000 | 2.7000 | 2.7000 | 2.7000 | 2.7000 |
| | | *Index Numbers (2010=100): Period Averages* | | | | | | | | | | | |
| Official Rate................................. | ahx | 100.0 | 100.0 | 100.0 | 100.0 | 100.0 | 100.0 | 100.0 | 100.0 | 100.0 | 100.0 | 100.0 | 100.0 |
| Nominal Effective Exchange Rate..... | nec | 98.7 | 99.6 | 100.3 | 98.4 | 97.7 | 100.2 | 100.0 | 99.4 | 101.9 | 104.7 | 105.8 | 112.6 |
| CPI-Based Real Effect. Ex. Rate........ | rec | 101.1 | 101.6 | 102.2 | 100.0 | 101.0 | 101.0 | 100.0 | 97.9 | 98.7 | 98.2 | 94.7 | 96.4 |
| **Fund Position** | | *Millions of SDRs: End of Period* | | | | | | | | | | | |
| Quota............................................. | 2f.s | 11.70 | 11.70 | 11.70 | 11.70 | 11.70 | 11.70 | 11.70 | 11.70 | 11.70 | 11.70 | 11.70 | 11.70 |
| SDR Holdings................................. | 1b.s | .01 | .01 | .11 | .08 | .83 | 10.65 | 10.64 | 10.39 | 10.07 | 9.85 | 8.07 | 6.83 |
| Reserve Position in the Fund........... | 1c.s | — | — | — | — | — | — | — | — | — | — | — | — |
| Total Fund Cred.&Loans Outstg....... | 2tl | 5.86 | 5.86 | 6.32 | 4.85 | 8.41 | 14.70 | 18.91 | 18.75 | 18.44 | 18.13 | 20.39 | 21.15 |
| SDR Allocations............................. | 1bd | .93 | .93 | .93 | .93 | .93 | 11.17 | 11.17 | 11.17 | 11.17 | 11.17 | 11.17 | 11.17 |
| **International Liquidity** | | *Millions of US Dollars Unless Otherwise Indicated: End of Period* | | | | | | | | | | | |
| Total Reserves minus Gold.............. | 1l.d | 121.73 | 94.25 | 99.96 | 110.57 | 105.34 | 129.08 | 119.15 | 120.71 | 119.49 | 150.57 | 169.95 | 197.98 |
| SDR Holdings................................. | 1b.d | .01 | .02 | .17 | .12 | 1.28 | 16.69 | 16.39 | 15.95 | 15.48 | 15.16 | 11.69 | 9.46 |
| Reserve Position in the Fund......... | 1c.d | — | — | — | — | — | — | — | — | — | — | — | — |
| Foreign Exchange........................... | 1d.d | 121.72 | 94.23 | 99.79 | 110.45 | 104.06 | 112.39 | 102.76 | 104.77 | 104.00 | 135.41 | 158.26 | 188.51 |
| Central Bank: Other Assets............. | 3..d | — | — | — | — | — | — | — | — | — | — | — | — |
| Central Bank: Other Liabs............... | 4..d | — | — | — | — | — | — | — | — | — | — | — | — |
| Other Depository Corps.: Assets....... | 7a.d | 311.16 | 277.89 | 254.37 | 238.54 | 212.32 | 203.45 | 190.55 | 189.58 | 177.03 | 202.31 | 249.16 | 317.01 |
| Other Depository Corps.: Liabs........ | 7b.d | 170.29 | 175.23 | 198.06 | 198.76 | 224.23 | 210.77 | 203.57 | 232.93 | 238.90 | 207.20 | 191.81 | 189.78 |
| **Central Bank** | | *Millions of E.Caribbean Dollars: End of Period* | | | | | | | | | | | |
| Net Foreign Assets.......................... | 11n | 301.63 | 230.21 | 242.47 | 276.81 | 248.05 | 241.99 | 199.76 | 205.12 | 199.90 | 284.89 | 335.57 | 413.75 |
| Claims on Nonresidents................. | 11 | 330.08 | 256.40 | 271.90 | 301.47 | 286.90 | 351.48 | 324.80 | 329.12 | 322.74 | 406.67 | 459.00 | 534.67 |
| Liabilities to Nonresidents............. | 16c | 28.45 | 26.18 | 29.43 | 24.67 | 38.85 | 109.48 | 125.03 | 124.00 | 122.84 | 121.79 | 123.43 | 120.91 |
| Claims on Other Depository Corps.... | 12e | .02 | .01 | .01 | .02 | .01 | .01 | .02 | — | .02 | .05 | .09 | .12 |
| Net Claims on Central Government.. | 12an | −.76 | −1.93 | −7.53 | 4.37 | 6.49 | −30.42 | −7.71 | 27.88 | 30.14 | 17.71 | −9.78 | −55.81 |
| Claims on Central Government...... | 12a | 2.03 | 2.03 | 2.03 | 6.41 | 8.26 | 4.15 | 4.00 | 31.25 | 31.89 | 19.84 | 25.05 | 8.32 |
| Liabilities to Central Government... | 16d | 2.79 | 3.96 | 9.56 | 2.05 | 1.77 | 34.57 | 11.71 | 3.37 | 1.75 | 2.14 | 34.83 | 64.13 |
| Claims on Other Sectors................. | 12s | — | — | — | — | — | — | — | — | — | — | — | — |
| Claims on Other Financial Corps.... | 12g | — | — | — | — | — | — | — | — | — | — | — | — |
| Claims on State & Local Govts....... | 12b | — | — | — | — | — | — | — | — | — | — | — | — |
| Claims on Public Nonfin. Corps...... | 12c | — | — | — | — | — | — | — | — | — | — | — | — |
| Claims on Private Sector............... | 12d | — | — | — | — | — | — | — | — | — | — | — | — |
| Monetary Base................................ | 14 | 327.86 | 252.74 | 261.90 | 303.25 | 287.42 | 272.99 | 269.76 | 310.75 | 307.63 | 378.86 | 392.94 | 421.30 |
| Currency in Circulation.................. | 14a | 133.91 | 141.32 | 140.59 | 149.11 | 149.40 | 148.97 | 142.26 | 154.36 | 156.44 | 162.10 | 182.94 | 188.61 |
| Liabs. to Other Depository Corps.... | 14c | 193.66 | 111.42 | 121.30 | 154.15 | 138.02 | 124.02 | 127.00 | 156.24 | 151.19 | 216.75 | 210.00 | 232.69 |
| Liabilities to Other Sectors........... | 14d | .28 | — | .01 | — | — | — | — | .50 | .15 | — | — | — |
| Other Liabs. to Other Dep. Corps..... | 14n | 1.45 | 1.69 | 2.01 | 2.28 | 2.40 | 2.90 | 2.96 | 3.07 | 3.34 | 4.51 | 24.68 | 32.00 |
| Dep. & Sec. Excl. f/Monetary Base..... | 14o | — | — | — | — | — | — | — | — | — | — | — | — |
| Deposits Included in Broad Money. | 15 | — | — | — | — | — | — | — | — | — | — | — | — |
| Sec.Ot.th.Shares Incl.in Brd. Money | 16a | — | — | — | — | — | — | — | — | — | — | — | — |
| Deposits Excl. from Broad Money.. | 16b | — | — | — | — | — | — | — | — | — | — | — | — |
| Sec.Ot.th.Shares Excl.f/Brd.Money.. | 16s | — | — | — | — | — | — | — | — | — | — | — | — |
| Loans............................................. | 16l | — | — | — | — | — | — | — | — | — | — | — | — |
| Financial Derivatives...................... | 16m | — | — | — | — | — | — | — | — | — | — | — | — |
| Shares and Other Equity................. | 17a | — | — | — | — | — | — | — | — | — | — | — | — |
| Other Items (Net)........................... | 17r | −28.42 | −26.13 | −28.97 | −24.34 | −35.28 | −64.30 | −80.65 | −80.82 | −80.91 | −80.72 | −91.74 | −95.23 |
| Memo Item: | | | | | | | | | | | | | |
| Total Assets................................... | 10ra | 332.10 | 258.39 | 273.48 | 307.58 | 291.71 | 310.57 | 284.56 | 317.32 | 312.86 | 385.63 | 452.58 | 517.56 |
| **Other Depository Corporations** | | *Millions of E.Caribbean Dollars: End of Period* | | | | | | | | | | | |
| Net Foreign Assets.......................... | 21n | 380.35 | 277.16 | 152.04 | 107.42 | −32.17 | −19.78 | −35.16 | −117.04 | −167.03 | −13.21 | 154.85 | 343.50 |
| Claims on Nonresidents................. | 21 | 840.14 | 750.29 | 686.80 | 644.07 | 573.26 | 549.31 | 514.48 | 511.86 | 477.99 | 546.23 | 672.74 | 855.91 |
| Liabilities to Nonresidents............. | 26c | 459.79 | 473.13 | 534.76 | 536.65 | 605.42 | 569.09 | 549.63 | 628.90 | 645.02 | 559.44 | 517.89 | 512.42 |
| Claims on Central Bank.................. | 20 | 237.62 | 148.81 | 152.28 | 175.02 | 177.27 | 168.61 | 172.88 | 200.23 | 196.01 | 262.77 | 273.20 | 296.41 |
| Currency....................................... | 20a | 31.82 | 36.06 | 36.10 | 41.33 | 46.00 | 42.31 | 43.45 | 45.70 | 43.57 | 46.42 | 58.84 | 57.06 |
| Reserve Deposits and Securities...... | 20b | 205.81 | 112.76 | 116.18 | 133.69 | 131.27 | 126.31 | 129.44 | 154.53 | 152.44 | 216.35 | 214.36 | 239.35 |
| Other Claims.................................. | 20n | — | — | — | — | — | — | — | — | — | — | — | — |
| Net Claims on Central Government.. | 22an | 72.43 | 16.80 | 44.88 | 99.32 | 116.45 | 129.31 | 117.73 | 122.52 | 77.37 | 34.59 | 27.38 | −9.82 |
| Claims on Central Government...... | 22a | 124.15 | 101.98 | 113.71 | 142.77 | 161.87 | 168.88 | 154.16 | 156.15 | 118.84 | 101.95 | 86.24 | 67.95 |
| Liabilities to Central Government... | 26d | 51.72 | 85.18 | 68.83 | 43.45 | 45.42 | 39.57 | 36.43 | 33.64 | 41.47 | 67.36 | 58.87 | 77.76 |
| Claims on Other Sectors.................. | 22s | 1,036.93 | 1,138.48 | 1,280.16 | 1,451.02 | 1,653.57 | 1,730.36 | 1,822.40 | 1,860.73 | 1,862.17 | 1,753.24 | 1,666.53 | 1,597.82 |
| Claims on Other Financial Corps.... | 22g | 17.46 | 17.99 | 11.96 | 13.41 | 33.86 | 15.78 | 13.91 | 15.91 | 14.90 | 11.01 | 9.11 | 9.34 |
| Claims on State & Local Govts....... | 22b | — | — | — | — | — | — | — | — | — | — | — | — |
| Claims on Public Nonfin. Corps...... | 22c | 22.72 | 32.17 | 44.31 | 28.41 | 56.89 | 61.60 | 60.25 | 60.41 | 58.95 | 52.83 | 52.67 | 45.43 |
| Claims on Private Sector............... | 22d | 996.75 | 1,088.32 | 1,223.89 | 1,409.20 | 1,562.81 | 1,652.98 | 1,748.24 | 1,784.41 | 1,788.32 | 1,689.39 | 1,604.75 | 1,543.05 |
| Liabilities to Central Bank.............. | 26g | .02 | .58 | .01 | .03 | .02 | .02 | .02 | .01 | .03 | .05 | .09 | .12 |
| Transf.Dep.Included in Broad Money | 24 | 429.59 | 361.76 | 333.09 | 432.64 | 405.39 | 372.96 | 374.42 | 351.67 | 333.29 | 376.73 | 478.27 | 632.56 |
| Other Dep.Included in Broad Money. | 25 | 1,186.35 | 1,143.94 | 1,210.25 | 1,308.03 | 1,433.80 | 1,527.80 | 1,597.02 | 1,617.78 | 1,528.32 | 1,556.44 | 1,572.83 | 1,570.38 |
| Sec.Ot.th.Shares Incl.in Brd. Money.. | 26a | — | — | — | — | — | — | — | — | — | — | — | — |
| Deposits Excl. from Broad Money..... | 26b | — | — | — | — | — | — | — | — | — | — | — | — |
| Sec.Ot.th.Shares Excl.f/Brd.Money.... | 26s | — | — | — | — | — | — | — | — | — | — | — | — |
| Loans............................................. | 26l | — | — | — | — | — | — | — | — | — | — | — | — |
| Financial Derivatives...................... | 26m | — | — | — | — | — | — | — | — | — | — | — | — |
| Insurance Technical Reserves........... | 26r | — | — | — | — | — | — | — | — | — | — | — | — |
| Shares and Other Equity................. | 27a | 146.26 | 141.19 | 167.66 | 176.47 | 194.86 | 200.78 | 221.61 | 194.85 | 182.93 | 150.70 | 137.58 | 143.92 |
| Other Items (Net)........................... | 27r | −34.89 | −66.21 | −81.65 | −84.39 | −118.96 | −93.06 | −115.23 | −97.87 | −76.05 | −46.54 | −66.81 | −119.06 |
| Memo Item: | | | | | | | | | | | | | |
| Total Assets................................... | 20ra | 2,397.55 | 2,327.40 | 2,437.59 | 2,627.33 | 2,826.84 | 2,875.87 | 2,940.30 | 3,012.16 | 2,943.06 | 2,970.91 | 3,023.68 | 3,182.16 |

| | | 2004 | 2005 | 2006 | 2007 | 2008 | 2009 | 2010 | 2011 | 2012 | 2013 | 2014 | 2015 |
|---|---|---|---|---|---|---|---|---|---|---|---|---|---|
| **Depository Corporations** | | *Millions of E.Caribbean Dollars: End of Period* | | | | | | | | | | | |
| Net Foreign Assets............................ | 31n | 681.98 | 507.37 | 394.50 | 384.23 | 215.88 | 222.22 | 164.61 | 88.08 | 32.87 | 271.67 | 490.41 | 757.25 |
| Claims on Nonresidents................ | 31 | 1,170.22 | 1,006.69 | 958.70 | 945.55 | 860.16 | 900.79 | 839.28 | 840.98 | 800.73 | 952.90 | 1,131.74 | 1,390.58 |
| Liabilities to Nonresidents............. | 36c | 488.24 | 499.32 | 564.19 | 561.32 | 644.27 | 678.57 | 674.67 | 752.90 | 767.86 | 681.23 | 641.32 | 633.33 |
| Domestic Claims............................ | 32 | 1,108.60 | 1,153.36 | 1,317.51 | 1,554.71 | 1,776.50 | 1,829.25 | 1,932.41 | 2,011.13 | 1,969.68 | 1,805.53 | 1,684.13 | 1,532.19 |
| Net Claims on Central Government | 32an | 71.67 | 14.87 | 37.35 | 103.69 | 122.93 | 98.89 | 110.01 | 150.40 | 107.51 | 52.30 | 17.60 | −65.63 |
| Claims on Central Government.... | 32a | 126.18 | 104.01 | 115.75 | 149.19 | 170.12 | 173.03 | 158.16 | 187.41 | 150.73 | 121.79 | 111.30 | 76.27 |
| Liabilities to Central Government. | 36d | 54.51 | 89.14 | 78.40 | 45.50 | 47.19 | 74.14 | 48.14 | 37.00 | 43.22 | 69.50 | 93.69 | 141.90 |
| Claims on Other Sectors................ | 32s | 1,036.93 | 1,138.48 | 1,280.16 | 1,451.02 | 1,653.57 | 1,730.36 | 1,822.40 | 1,860.73 | 1,862.17 | 1,753.24 | 1,666.53 | 1,597.82 |
| Claims on Other Financial Corps.. | 32g | 17.46 | 17.99 | 11.96 | 13.41 | 33.86 | 15.78 | 13.91 | 15.91 | 14.90 | 11.01 | 9.11 | 9.34 |
| Claims on State & Local Govts..... | 32b | — | — | — | — | — | — | — | — | — | — | — | — |
| Claims on Public Nonfin. Corps.... | 32c | 22.72 | 32.17 | 44.31 | 28.41 | 56.89 | 61.60 | 60.25 | 60.41 | 58.95 | 52.83 | 52.67 | 45.43 |
| Claims on Private Sector.............. | 32d | 996.75 | 1,088.32 | 1,223.89 | 1,409.20 | 1,562.81 | 1,652.98 | 1,748.24 | 1,784.41 | 1,788.32 | 1,689.39 | 1,604.75 | 1,543.05 |
| Broad Money Liabilities.................. | 35l | 1,718.32 | 1,610.96 | 1,647.84 | 1,848.45 | 1,942.60 | 2,007.43 | 2,070.76 | 2,078.26 | 1,974.49 | 2,048.86 | 2,175.19 | 2,334.48 |
| Currency Outside Depository Corps | 34a | 102.10 | 105.26 | 104.50 | 107.77 | 103.40 | 106.66 | 98.82 | 108.66 | 112.88 | 115.69 | 124.09 | 131.55 |
| Transferable Deposits.................... | 34 | 429.87 | 361.76 | 333.10 | 432.64 | 405.39 | 372.97 | 374.92 | 351.81 | 333.30 | 376.73 | 478.27 | 632.56 |
| Other Deposits............................. | 35 | 1,186.35 | 1,143.94 | 1,210.25 | 1,308.03 | 1,433.80 | 1,527.80 | 1,597.02 | 1,617.78 | 1,528.32 | 1,556.44 | 1,572.83 | 1,570.38 |
| Securities Other than Shares.......... | 36a | — | — | — | — | — | — | — | — | — | — | — | — |
| Deposits Excl. from Broad Money..... | 36b | — | — | — | — | — | — | — | — | — | — | — | — |
| Sec.Ot.th.Shares Excl.f/Brd.Money.... | 36s | — | — | — | — | — | — | — | — | — | — | — | — |
| Loans...................................... | 36l | — | — | — | — | — | — | — | — | — | — | — | — |
| Financial Derivatives...................... | 36m | — | — | — | — | — | — | — | — | — | — | — | — |
| Insurance Technical Reserves.......... | 36r | — | — | — | — | — | — | — | — | — | — | — | — |
| Shares and Other Equity................ | 37a | 146.26 | 141.19 | 167.66 | 176.47 | 194.86 | 200.78 | 221.61 | 194.85 | 182.93 | 150.70 | 137.58 | 143.92 |
| Other Items (Net)......................... | 37r | −74.00 | −91.43 | −103.49 | −85.99 | −145.07 | −156.74 | −195.35 | −173.89 | −154.87 | −122.36 | −138.22 | −188.95 |
| Broad Money Liabs., Seasonally Adj. | 35l.b | 1,698.02 | 1,594.67 | 1,636.01 | 1,842.05 | 1,942.49 | 2,013.12 | 2,081.49 | 2,093.91 | 1,993.16 | 2,072.20 | 2,202.09 | 2,364.06 |
| **Monetary Aggregates** | | *Millions of E.Caribbean Dollars: End of Period* | | | | | | | | | | | |
| Broad Money.............................. | 59m | 1,718.32 | 1,610.96 | 1,647.84 | 1,848.45 | 1,942.60 | 2,007.43 | 2,070.76 | 2,078.26 | 1,974.49 | 2,048.86 | 2,175.19 | 2,334.48 |
| o/w:Currency Issued by Cent.Govt | 59m.a | — | — | — | — | — | — | — | — | — | — | — | — |
| o/w: Dep.in Nonfin. Corporations. | 59m.b | — | — | — | — | — | — | — | — | — | — | — | — |
| o/w:Secs. Issued by Central Govt.. | 59m.c | — | — | — | — | — | — | — | — | — | — | — | — |
| Money (National Definitions) | | | | | | | | | | | | | |
| M1............................................. | 59ma | 340.46 | 315.34 | 309.46 | 355.76 | 355.52 | 332.26 | 342.29 | 324.53 | 333.00 | 381.04 | 466.47 | 543.00 |
| M2............................................. | 59mb | 1,484.13 | 1,469.02 | 1,482.38 | 1,644.71 | 1,753.65 | 1,820.03 | 1,837.39 | 1,849.67 | 1,862.25 | 1,938.72 | 2,017.98 | 2,122.37 |
| **Interest Rates** | | *Percent Per Annum* | | | | | | | | | | | |
| Discount Rate (End of Period).......... | 60.a | 6.50 | 6.50 | 6.50 | 6.50 | 6.50 | 6.50 | 6.50 | 6.50 | 6.50 | 6.50 | 6.50 | 6.50 |
| Money Market Rate........................ | 60b | 4.67 | 4.01 | 4.76 | 5.24 | 4.94 | 6.03 | 6.36 | 5.68 | 5.19 | 6.28 | 6.19 | 6.44 |
| Treasury Bill Rate.......................... | 60c | 5.50 | 5.50 | 6.25 | 6.38 | 6.25 | 6.33 | 6.21 | 5.94 | 6.00 | 5.96 | 6.00 | 6.00 |
| Savings Rate................................ | 60k | 3.53 | 3.28 | 3.26 | 3.28 | 3.28 | 3.16 | 2.98 | 3.13 | 3.06 | 3.04 | 3.03 | 2.41 |
| Savings Rate (Fgn. Currency)........... | 60k.f | 1.17 | 1.00 | 1.72 | 2.10 | 1.27 | 1.28 | .71 | .62 | .57 | .53 | .58 | .44 |
| Deposit Rate................................. | 60l | 3.32 | 2.87 | 2.95 | 3.13 | 3.23 | 3.27 | 3.08 | 3.11 | 2.86 | 2.64 | 2.40 | 1.83 |
| Deposit Rate (Fgn. Currency)........... | 60l.f | 1.37 | 1.03 | 1.48 | 1.79 | 1.03 | .86 | .42 | .36 | .60 | .73 | .64 | .50 |
| Lending Rate................................ | 60p | 10.18 | 10.07 | 9.85 | 9.76 | 9.53 | 10.99 | 10.58 | 10.69 | 9.73 | 9.27 | 9.19 | 8.96 |
| Lending Rate (Fgn. Currency).......... | 60p.f | 7.85 | 6.94 | 7.80 | 8.09 | 6.61 | 4.66 | 4.73 | 5.12 | 5.47 | 6.24 | 6.48 | 5.82 |
| **Prices** | | *Index Numbers (2010=100): Period Averages* | | | | | | | | | | | |
| Consumer Prices............................ | 64 | 80.1 | 82.9 | 86.4 | 89.8 | 97.0 | † 96.7 | 100.0 | 103.0 | 105.5 | 105.5 | 104.5 | 103.0 |
| **Intl. Transactions & Positions** | | *Millions of E. Caribbean Dollars* | | | | | | | | | | | |
| Exports...................................... | 70 | 86.50 | 74.64 | 68.50 | 90.21 | 81.68 | 78.81 | 65.23 | 74.48 | 93.43 | 88.61 | 109.25 | 91.17 |
| Imports, c.i.f................................. | 71 | 681.76 | 901.89 | 893.24 | 985.86 | 1,018.55 | 790.39 | 855.15 | 889.07 | 906.51 | 994.78 | 908.54 | 953.75 |

# Grenada 328

## Balance of Payments

*Millions of US Dollars*

| | | 2004 | 2005 | 2006 | 2007 | 2008 | 2009 | 2010 | 2011 | 2012 | 2013 | 2014 | 2015 |
|---|---|---|---|---|---|---|---|---|---|---|---|---|---|
| A. Current Account* | 109bx | −65.7 | −193.3 | −226.7 | −241.7 | −251.9 | −197.2 | −203.9 | −207.0 | −193.2 | −212.8 | .... | .... |
| Goods, credit (exports) | 1a9cx | 37.5 | 32.9 | 32.3 | 40.7 | 40.5 | 35.3 | 31.1 | 37.2 | 42.8 | 46.5 | .... | .... |
| Goods, debit (imports) | 1a9dx | 226.7 | 300.0 | 297.1 | 327.9 | 338.8 | 262.9 | 285.6 | 295.3 | 300.3 | 324.2 | .... | .... |
| Balance on goods | 1a9bx | −189.2 | −267.1 | −264.8 | −287.2 | −298.3 | −227.6 | −254.4 | −258.1 | −257.5 | −277.7 | .... | .... |
| Services, credit (exports) | 1b9cx | 160.2 | 116.0 | 130.0 | 168.8 | 167.3 | 151.9 | 152.6 | 159.0 | 163.7 | 163.2 | .... | .... |
| Services, debit (imports) | 1b9dx | 92.4 | 96.2 | 105.3 | 108.5 | 113.0 | 98.1 | 94.0 | 100.2 | 95.4 | 99.0 | .... | .... |
| Balance on Goods & Services | 1z9bx | −121.4 | −247.3 | −240.1 | −226.8 | −243.9 | −173.7 | −195.8 | −199.3 | −189.2 | −213.5 | .... | .... |
| Primary income: credit | 1c9cx | 5.7 | 11.4 | 13.3 | 13.7 | 8.1 | 8.1 | 7.2 | 5.8 | 7.0 | 7.0 | .... | .... |
| Primary income: debit | 1c9dx | 70.9 | 39.7 | 42.1 | 54.8 | 50.8 | 71.2 | 47.0 | 37.5 | 41.3 | 32.7 | .... | .... |
| Balance on gds, serv. & prim. inc. | 1y9bx | −186.6 | −275.6 | −269.0 | −267.9 | −286.6 | −236.8 | −235.7 | −231.1 | −223.5 | −239.2 | .... | .... |
| Secondary income: credit | 1d9ca | 125.9 | 87.6 | 54.9 | 40.6 | 49.2 | 54.8 | 46.2 | 38.1 | 42.6 | 39.2 | .... | .... |
| Secondary income: debit | 1d9da | 5.0 | 5.3 | 12.7 | 14.4 | 14.5 | 15.2 | 14.5 | 14.0 | 12.3 | 12.8 | .... | .... |
| B. Capital Account* | 209ba | 17.8 | 24.3 | 38.3 | 14.7 | 16.8 | 15.0 | 36.2 | 28.5 | 35.6 | 36.3 | .... | .... |
| Capital account: credit | 209ca | 17.8 | 24.3 | 38.3 | 14.7 | 16.8 | 15.0 | 36.2 | 28.5 | 35.6 | 36.3 | .... | .... |
| Capital account: debit | 209ca | — | — | — | — | — | — | — | — | — | — | .... | .... |
| Balance on current & capital acct. | 129ba | −47.9 | −169.0 | −188.4 | −227.0 | −235.2 | −182.2 | −167.7 | −178.5 | −157.6 | −176.5 | .... | .... |
| C. Financial Account* | 309na | −68.4 | −143.7 | −165.9 | −227.1 | −204.2 | −204.0 | −125.3 | −157.0 | −114.7 | −155.0 | .... | .... |
| Direct investment: assets | 3a9aa | — | — | — | — | — | — | — | — | — | — | .... | .... |
| Equity & investment fund shares | 3aaaa | — | — | — | — | — | — | — | — | — | — | .... | .... |
| Debt instruments | 3abaa | .... | .... | .... | .... | .... | .... | .... | .... | .... | .... | .... | .... |
| Direct investment: liabilities | 3a9la | 65.0 | 70.2 | 89.8 | 156.6 | 134.8 | 102.6 | 60.4 | 42.6 | 31.5 | 74.7 | .... | .... |
| Equity & investment fund shares | 3aala | 46.5 | 49.6 | 67.3 | 124.3 | 115.7 | 82.8 | 42.3 | 29.4 | 16.5 | 58.0 | .... | .... |
| Debt instruments | 3abla | 18.5 | 20.5 | 22.5 | 32.2 | 19.2 | 19.8 | 18.1 | 13.3 | 15.0 | 16.7 | .... | .... |
| Portfolio investment: assets | 3b9aa | 7.4 | −.6 | 5.3 | 3.2 | 3.0 | −6.8 | .6 | 4.3 | 1.5 | .4 | .... | .... |
| Equity & investment fund shares | 3baaa | .... | .... | .... | .... | .... | .... | .... | .... | .... | .... | .... | .... |
| Debt securities | 3bbaa | .... | .... | .... | .... | .... | .... | .... | .... | .... | .... | .... | .... |
| Portfolio investment: liabilities | 3b9la | 37.5 | 17.2 | 4.6 | .6 | 2.8 | 7.2 | 3.5 | 14.3 | −1.6 | 14.7 | .... | .... |
| Equity & investment fund shares | 3bala | .... | .... | .... | .... | .... | .... | .... | .... | .... | .... | .... | .... |
| Debt securities | 3bbla | .... | .... | .... | .... | .... | .... | .... | .... | .... | .... | .... | .... |
| Fin. der.& empl.stk.ops.(ESOs): net | 3c9na | .... | .... | .... | .... | .... | .... | .... | .... | .... | .... | .... | .... |
| Fin. der. & ESOs.: assets | 3c9aa | .... | .... | .... | .... | .... | .... | .... | .... | .... | .... | .... | .... |
| Fin. der. & ESOs.: liabilities | 3c9la | .... | .... | .... | .... | .... | .... | .... | .... | .... | .... | .... | .... |
| Other investment: assets | 3d9aa | 100.1 | 228.4 | 17.8 | 19.6 | 14.3 | 27.6 | 20.4 | 58.2 | 52.2 | 104.4 | .... | .... |
| Other equity | 3daaa | .... | .... | .... | .... | .... | .... | .... | .... | .... | .... | .... | .... |
| Debt instruments | 3dzaa | 100.1 | 228.4 | 17.8 | 19.6 | 14.3 | 27.6 | 20.4 | 58.2 | 52.2 | 104.4 | .... | .... |
| Other investment: liabilities | 3d9la | 73.4 | 284.2 | 94.6 | 92.7 | 83.9 | 115.0 | 82.4 | 162.4 | 138.5 | 170.4 | .... | .... |
| Other equity | 3dala | .... | .... | .... | .... | .... | .... | .... | .... | .... | .... | .... | .... |
| Debt instruments | 3dzla | 73.4 | 284.2 | 94.6 | 92.7 | 83.9 | 115.0 | 82.4 | 162.4 | 138.5 | 170.4 | .... | .... |
| Curr.+ cap.− finan. acct. balance | 4y9na | 20.5 | −25.2 | −22.5 | .1 | −31.0 | 21.8 | −42.4 | −21.5 | −42.9 | −21.5 | .... | .... |
| D. Net Errors and Omissions | 409na | 21.4 | −2.2 | 27.6 | 12.9 | 18.6 | −7.6 | 26.4 | 23.4 | 41.0 | 53.0 | .... | .... |
| E. Reserves and Related Items | 4z9na | 41.9 | −27.4 | 5.1 | 12.9 | −12.4 | 14.2 | −16.0 | 1.9 | −1.9 | 31.5 | .... | .... |
| Reserve assets | 3e9aa | 46.3 | −27.4 | 5.7 | 10.7 | −6.7 | 23.9 | −9.6 | 1.6 | −2.4 | 31.1 | .... | .... |
| Credit and loans from the IMF | 3dcla | 4.4 | — | .7 | −2.2 | 5.7 | 9.7 | 6.4 | −.2 | −.5 | −.5 | .... | .... |
| Exceptional financing | 409la | .... | .... | .... | .... | .... | .... | .... | .... | .... | .... | .... | .... |

*Excludes components in group E

## Government Finance
## Cash Flow Statement
## Budgetary Central Government

*Millions of E. Caribbean Dollars: Fiscal Year Ends December 31*

| | | 2004 | 2005 | 2006 | 2007 | 2008 | 2009 | 2010 | 2011 | 2012 | 2013 | 2014 | 2015 |
|---|---|---|---|---|---|---|---|---|---|---|---|---|---|
| Cash Receipts:Operating Activities | c1 | .... | .... | .... | .... | 516.06 | 430.67 | 465.52 | 480.36 | 435.31 | 468.50 | 602.20 | .... |
| Taxes | c11 | .... | .... | .... | .... | 433.77 | 379.91 | 389.88 | 403.84 | 403.19 | 419.00 | 478.04 | .... |
| Social Contributions | c12 | .... | .... | .... | .... | — | — | — | — | — | — | — | .... |
| Grants | c13 | .... | .... | .... | .... | 51.54 | 28.88 | 50.64 | 42.01 | 10.03 | 31.26 | 100.00 | .... |
| Other Receipts | c14 | .... | .... | .... | .... | 30.75 | 21.88 | 25.00 | 34.51 | 22.09 | 18.24 | 24.16 | .... |
| Cash Payments:Operating Activities. | c2 | .... | .... | .... | .... | 413.60 | 422.85 | 408.52 | 414.36 | 433.63 | 462.14 | 488.51 | .... |
| Compensation of Employees | c21 | .... | .... | .... | .... | 200.81 | 191.24 | 199.42 | 222.22 | 226.07 | 243.49 | 241.47 | .... |
| Purchases of Goods & Services | c22 | .... | .... | .... | .... | 84.67 | 85.96 | 91.90 | 70.33 | 75.12 | 75.89 | 70.46 | .... |
| Interest | c24 | .... | .... | .... | .... | 34.89 | 51.51 | 43.00 | 49.77 | 63.48 | 70.59 | 87.34 | .... |
| Subsidies | c25 | .... | .... | .... | .... | 68.30 | 70.79 | 51.53 | 48.47 | 42.48 | 43.18 | 55.82 | .... |
| Grants | c26 | .... | .... | .... | .... | — | — | — | — | — | — | — | .... |
| Social Benefits | c27 | .... | .... | .... | .... | 24.93 | 23.35 | 22.67 | 23.57 | 26.48 | 28.99 | 33.42 | .... |
| Other Payments | c28 | .... | .... | .... | .... | — | — | — | — | — | — | — | .... |
| Net Cash Inflow:Operating Act.[1-2] | ccio | .... | .... | .... | .... | 102.46 | 7.82 | 57.00 | 66.00 | 1.68 | 6.36 | 113.69 | .... |
| Net Cash Outflow:Invest. in NFA | c31 | .... | .... | .... | .... | 213.77 | 117.27 | 107.76 | 101.22 | 108.28 | 154.28 | 226.66 | .... |
| Purchases of Nonfinancial Assets | c31.1 | .... | .... | .... | .... | 213.87 | 117.42 | 107.94 | 101.27 | 108.36 | 154.33 | 226.75 | .... |
| Sales of Nonfinancial Assets | c31.2 | .... | .... | .... | .... | .10 | .15 | .18 | .05 | .08 | .05 | .09 | .... |
| Cash Surplus/Deficit [1-2-31=1-2M] | ccsd | .... | .... | .... | .... | −111.31 | −109.45 | −50.76 | −35.22 | −106.60 | −147.92 | −112.97 | .... |
| Net Acq. Fin. Assets, excl. Cash | c32x | .... | .... | .... | .... | — | — | — | — | — | — | — | .... |
| Domestic | c321x | .... | .... | .... | .... | — | — | — | — | — | — | — | .... |
| Foreign | c322x | .... | .... | .... | .... | — | — | — | — | — | — | — | .... |
| Net Incurrence of Liabilities | c33 | .... | .... | .... | .... | 35.74 | −10.88 | 40.49 | 26.97 | −65.54 | −17.88 | 133.83 | .... |
| Domestic | c331 | .... | .... | .... | .... | 18.55 | −24.05 | 11.17 | 40.39 | −75.60 | −55.26 | −9.85 | .... |
| Foreign | c332 | .... | .... | .... | .... | 17.19 | 13.17 | 29.32 | −13.42 | 10.06 | 37.38 | 143.68 | .... |
| Net Cash Inflow, Fin.Act.[-32x+33] | cnfb | .... | .... | .... | .... | 35.74 | −10.88 | 40.49 | 26.97 | −65.54 | −17.88 | 133.83 | .... |
| Net Change in Stock of Cash | cncb | .... | .... | .... | .... | −75.57 | −120.33 | −10.27 | −8.25 | −172.14 | −165.80 | 20.86 | .... |
| Stat. Discrep. [32X-33+NCB-CSD] | ccsdz | .... | .... | .... | .... | | | | | | | | .... |
| Memo Item:Cash Expenditure[2+31] | c2m | .... | .... | .... | .... | 627.37 | 540.12 | 516.28 | 515.58 | 541.91 | 616.42 | 715.17 | .... |
| Memo Item: Gross Debt | c63 | .... | .... | .... | .... | .... | .... | .... | .... | 2,014.74 | 2,079.79 | 2,179.03 | .... |

# Grenada 328

| | | 2004 | 2005 | 2006 | 2007 | 2008 | 2009 | 2010 | 2011 | 2012 | 2013 | 2014 | 2015 |
|---|---|---|---|---|---|---|---|---|---|---|---|---|---|
| **National Accounts** | | | | | | *Millions of E. Caribbean Dollars* | | | | | | | |
| Househ.Cons.Expend.,incl.NPISHs.... | 96f | 1,158.2 | 1,431.1 | 1,616.7 | 1,663.4 | 1,861.8 | 1,728.4 | 1,815.8 | 1,888.6 | 1,964.9 | 1,991.0 | 2,040.5 | .... |
| Government Consumption Expend... | 91f | 218.6 | 245.0 | 246.1 | 272.1 | 334.4 | 324.9 | 336.4 | 333.4 | 352.6 | 379.3 | 374.8 | .... |
| Gross Fixed Capital Formation.......... | 93e | 568.5 | 869.1 | 672.0 | 725.4 | 692.6 | 498.2 | 458.2 | 418.6 | 353.0 | 453.0 | 434.0 | .... |
| Exports of Goods and Services......... | 90c | 533.9 | 402.0 | 438.2 | 565.8 | 561.1 | 505.5 | 496.2 | 529.7 | 557.5 | 578.4 | 631.9 | .... |
| Imports of Goods and Services (-)..... | 98c | 861.6 | 1,069.6 | 1,086.5 | 1,178.2 | 1,219.7 | 974.7 | 1,024.8 | 1,067.8 | 1,068.4 | 1,145.6 | 1,099.4 | .... |
| Gross Domestic Product (GDP)......... | 99b | 1,617.6 | 1,877.5 | 1,886.5 | 2,048.5 | 2,230.1 | 2,082.5 | 2,081.7 | 2,102.4 | 2,159.7 | 2,256.1 | 2,381.8 | .... |
| Net Primary Income from Abroad..... | 98.n | −176.0 | −76.4 | −78.0 | −110.9 | −115.3 | −170.2 | −107.7 | −85.8 | −92.6 | −79.9 | −58.4 | .... |
| Gross National Income (GNI)............ | 99a | 1,441.6 | 1,801.1 | 1,808.5 | 1,937.5 | 2,114.8 | 1,912.2 | 1,974.1 | 2,016.6 | 2,067.1 | 2,176.2 | 2,323.4 | .... |
| Net Current Transf.from Abroad....... | 98t | 326.4 | 222.2 | 114.1 | 70.8 | 93.7 | 107.0 | 85.8 | 65.0 | 81.7 | 49.4 | 49.4 | .... |
| Gross Nat'l Disposable Inc.(GNDI).... | 99i | 1,768.0 | 2,023.4 | 1,922.6 | 2,008.3 | 2,208.5 | 2,019.2 | 2,059.9 | 2,081.6 | 2,148.9 | 2,225.6 | 2,372.9 | .... |
| Gross Saving................................... | 99s | 391.1 | 347.3 | 59.9 | 72.8 | 12.3 | −34.1 | −92.3 | −140.3 | −168.6 | −144.6 | −42.4 | .... |
| | | | | | | *Millions: Midyear Estimates* | | | | | | | |
| **Population**................................. | 99z | .10 | .10 | .10 | .10 | .10 | .10 | .10 | .11 | .11 | .11 | .11 | .11 |

# Guatemala 258

| | | 2004 | 2005 | 2006 | 2007 | 2008 | 2009 | 2010 | 2011 | 2012 | 2013 | 2014 | 2015 |
|---|---|---|---|---|---|---|---|---|---|---|---|---|---|
| **Exchange Rates** | | | | | | *Quetzales per SDR: End of Period* | | | | | | | |
| Market Rate....................aa=........ | wa | 12.033 | 10.877 | 11.470 | 12.059 | 11.975 | 13.086 | 12.345 | 11.985 | 12.134 | 12.092 | 11.004 | 10.605 |
| | | | | | *Quetzales per US Dollar: End of Period (we) Period Average (wf)* | | | | | | | | |
| Market Rate....................ae=........ | we | 7.7484 | 7.6103 | 7.6245 | 7.6308 | 7.7744 | 8.3471 | 8.0160 | 7.8066 | 7.8949 | 7.8521 | 7.5955 | 7.6528 |
| Market Rate....................rf=.......... | wf | 7.9465 | 7.6339 | 7.6026 | 7.6733 | 7.5600 | 8.1616 | 8.0578 | 7.7854 | 7.8336 | 7.8568 | 7.7322 | 7.6548 |
| **Fund Position** | | | | | | *Millions of SDRs: End of Period* | | | | | | | |
| Quota.............................................. | 2f.s | 210.20 | 210.20 | 210.20 | 210.20 | 210.20 | 210.20 | 210.20 | 210.20 | 210.20 | 210.20 | 210.20 | 210.20 |
| SDR Holdings.................................. | 1b.s | 5.14 | 4.58 | 3.75 | 2.75 | 2.27 | 174.35 | 173.64 | 173.52 | 174.10 | 175.63 | 175.60 | 175.59 |
| Reserve Position in the Fund........... | 1c.s | — | — | — | — | — | — | — | — | — | — | — | — |
| Total Fund Cred.&Loans Outstg........ | 2tl | — | — | — | — | — | — | — | — | — | — | — | — |
| SDR Allocations.............................. | 1bd | 27.68 | 27.68 | 27.68 | 27.68 | 27.68 | 200.91 | 200.91 | 200.91 | 200.91 | 200.91 | 200.91 | 200.91 |
| **International Liquidity** | | | | | *Millions of US Dollars Unless Otherwise Indicated: End of Period* | | | | | | | | |
| Total Reserves minus Gold.............. | 1l.d | 3,426.3 | 3,663.8 | 3,914.9 | 4,129.9 | 4,461.9 | 4,963.6 | 5,636.8 | 5,834.9 | 6,325.0 | 7,002.3 | 7,063.6 | 7,511.0 |
| SDR Holdings................................ | 1b.d | 8.0 | 6.5 | 5.6 | 4.3 | 3.5 | 273.3 | 267.4 | 266.4 | 267.6 | 270.5 | 254.4 | 243.3 |
| Reserve Position in the Fund.......... | 1c.d | — | — | — | — | — | — | — | — | — | — | — | — |
| Foreign Exchange.......................... | 1d.d | 3,418.3 | 3,657.3 | 3,909.3 | 4,125.6 | 4,458.4 | 4,690.3 | 5,369.4 | 5,568.5 | 6,057.4 | 6,731.8 | 6,809.2 | 7,267.7 |
| Gold (Million Fine Troy Ounces)........ | 1ad | .219 | .221 | .221 | .221 | .221 | .222 | .222 | .222 | .222 | .222 | .222 | .222 |
| Gold (National Valuation)................ | 1and | 9.3 | 9.3 | 9.3 | 9.3 | † 191.0 | 244.9 | 312.9 | 348.9 | 368.8 | 266.3 | 265.8 | 235.4 |
| Central Bank: Other Assets.............. | 3..d | 147.9 | 149.0 | 166.0 | 149.6 | 143.4 | 149.3 | 149.3 | 150.9 | 152.9 | 366.9 | 371.3 | 375.5 |
| Central Bank: Other Liabs................ | 4..d | 336.7 | 308.8 | 323.9 | 339.1 | 329.2 | 335.1 | 329.6 | 327.7 | 327.7 | 331.5 | 314.8 | 300.5 |
| Other Depository Corps.: Assets....... | 7a.d | 1,277.4 | 1,377.2 | 1,211.4 | 1,502.1 | 1,447.2 | 1,722.4 | 1,906.7 | 2,262.3 | 2,504.0 | 2,668.0 | 2,937.8 | 3,221.1 |
| Other Depository Corps.: Liabs......... | 7b.d | 1,410.1 | 1,622.1 | 1,396.3 | 1,851.5 | 1,773.4 | 1,383.0 | 1,473.8 | 2,596.8 | 3,462.9 | 4,087.3 | 4,718.0 | 5,300.7 |
| Other Financial Corps.: Assets.......... | 7e.d | .1 | — | .4 | .6 | .7 | 1.5 | 2.9 | 3.6 | 2.8 | 2.8 | 7.6 | 9.2 |
| Other Financial Corps.: Liabs........... | 7f.d | .7 | .6 | .8 | .6 | .6 | .7 | .7 | .8 | .9 | 1.5 | 1.6 | 1.6 |
| **Central Bank** | | | | | | *Millions of Quetzales: End of Period* | | | | | | | |
| Net Foreign Assets........................... | 11n | 25,505.7 | 27,224.1 | 29,327.3 | 31,150.8 | 34,475.4 | 39,363.5 | 43,785.7 | 44,542.0 | 49,074.7 | 54,877.9 | 53,928.5 | 57,607.0 |
| Claims on Nonresidents................. | 11 | 28,447.5 | 29,875.6 | 32,114.6 | 34,071.9 | 37,368.8 | 44,794.2 | 48,906.5 | 49,511.0 | 54,104.5 | 59,903.5 | 58,530.9 | 62,025.7 |
| Liabilities to Nonresidents............. | 16c | 2,941.8 | 2,651.5 | 2,787.3 | 2,921.1 | 2,893.5 | 5,430.7 | 5,120.8 | 4,969.0 | 5,029.8 | 5,025.6 | 4,602.4 | 4,418.7 |
| Claims on Other Depository Corps.... | 12e | 2,520.1 | 2,569.2 | 2,636.5 | 3,036.2 | 3,693.6 | 2,955.5 | 3,024.2 | 3,099.5 | 3,151.1 | 3,229.0 | 3,299.9 | 2,059.7 |
| Net Claims on Central Government.. | 12an | 5,082.5 | 6,507.2 | 6,927.9 | 5,178.8 | 7,143.5 | 11,089.8 | 9,933.9 | 11,104.7 | 12,131.0 | 13,902.6 | 16,665.3 | 18,568.6 |
| Claims on Central Government...... | 12a | 16,944.4 | 18,104.7 | 18,773.8 | 19,573.9 | 19,588.5 | 19,631.2 | 19,610.7 | 19,935.0 | 20,963.7 | 22,291.1 | 23,803.0 | 25,515.8 |
| Liabilities to Central Government... | 16d | 11,862.0 | 11,597.6 | 11,846.0 | 14,395.1 | 12,445.1 | 8,541.4 | 9,676.9 | 8,830.3 | 8,832.7 | 8,388.6 | 7,137.7 | 6,947.2 |
| Claims on Other Sectors.................. | 12s | 37.0 | 33.1 | 33.2 | 33.2 | 33.7 | 176.7 | 193.6 | 250.4 | 275.0 | 299.6 | 313.9 | 335.3 |
| Claims on Other Financial Corps.... | 12g | 14.4 | 7.0 | 7.0 | 7.0 | 7.0 | 148.0 | 166.0 | 223.6 | 247.8 | 272.7 | 287.8 | 311.7 |
| Claims on State & Local Govts....... | 12b | 22.5 | 26.1 | 26.2 | 26.2 | 26.7 | 28.7 | 27.5 | 26.8 | 27.2 | 26.9 | 26.1 | 23.6 |
| Claims on Public Nonfin. Corps...... | 12c | — | — | — | — | — | — | — | — | — | — | — | — |
| Claims on Private Sector............... | 12d | — | — | — | — | — | — | — | — | — | — | — | — |
| Monetary Base................................ | 14 | 27,027.5 | 27,186.5 | 31,332.0 | 31,551.8 | 37,736.0 | 42,945.8 | 44,921.6 | 48,996.4 | 52,024.7 | 57,301.9 | 59,833.4 | 62,498.7 |
| Currency in Circulation................... | 14a | 12,626.4 | 14,261.9 | 15,772.0 | 20,010.8 | 19,665.9 | 21,232.6 | 23,390.3 | 24,532.5 | 26,552.1 | 27,130.3 | 29,164.4 | 33,308.1 |
| Liabs. to Other Depository Corps.... | 14c | 14,401.1 | 12,924.6 | 15,560.0 | 11,541.0 | 18,070.1 | 21,713.3 | 21,531.4 | 24,463.9 | 25,472.5 | 30,171.6 | 30,669.0 | 29,190.6 |
| Liabilities to Other Sectors............. | 14d | — | — | — | — | — | — | — | — | — | — | — | — |
| Other Liabs. to Other Dep. Corps..... | 14n | 4,498.1 | 6,771.8 | 5,567.4 | 5,172.4 | 3,474.0 | 3,138.2 | 5,768.4 | 5,185.7 | 7,008.4 | 8,814.8 | 9,286.6 | 12,067.7 |
| Dep. & Sec. Excl. f/Monetary Base.... | 14o | 1,899.9 | 2,106.8 | 1,464.3 | 797.2 | 779.8 | 986.3 | 1,216.7 | 1,079.0 | 1,798.3 | 2,246.7 | 2,754.6 | 2,530.9 |
| Deposits Included in Broad Money. | 15 | 85.6 | 109.5 | 57.3 | 79.3 | 60.2 | — | — | — | — | — | — | — |
| Sec.Ot.th.Shares Incl.in Brd. Money | 16a | 339.7 | 416.2 | 253.4 | 51.4 | 59.8 | 61.7 | 58.9 | 68.1 | 2.6 | 2.0 | .4 | — |
| Deposits Excl. from Broad Money... | 16b | .3 | .1 | .2 | .1 | — | 76.9 | 123.5 | 95.3 | 119.8 | 114.8 | 92.7 | 128.9 |
| Sec.Ot.th.Shares Excl.f/Brd.Money.. | 16s | 1,474.4 | 1,581.0 | 1,153.4 | 666.4 | 659.8 | 847.7 | 1,034.3 | 915.6 | 1,675.9 | 2,129.9 | 2,661.5 | 2,402.0 |
| Loans.............................................. | 16l | — | — | — | — | — | — | — | — | — | — | — | — |
| Financial Derivatives........................ | 16m | — | — | — | — | — | — | — | — | — | — | — | — |
| Shares and Other Equity.................. | 17a | 2,467.1 | 2,692.2 | 2,819.2 | 4,158.6 | 5,579.7 | 8,415.2 | 6,534.0 | 5,036.0 | 5,262.1 | 5,308.7 | 3,468.9 | 3,500.3 |
| Other Items (Net)............................ | 17r | –2,747.4 | –2,423.7 | –2,258.1 | –2,280.9 | –2,223.4 | –1,899.9 | –1,503.3 | –1,300.4 | –1,461.7 | –1,363.0 | –1,135.8 | –2,027.1 |
| Memo Item: | | | | | | | | | | | | | |
| Total Assets.................................... | 10ra | 51,574.7 | 53,972.8 | 56,905.2 | 60,316.1 | 64,194.5 | 71,068.8 | 75,006.0 | 76,005.8 | 82,123.4 | 89,348.7 | 89,304.1 | 94,460.8 |
| **Other Depository Corporations** | | | | | | *Millions of Quetzales: End of Period* | | | | | | | |
| Net Foreign Assets........................... | 21n | –1,028.5 | –1,864.1 | –1,410.0 | –2,666.6 | –2,538.3 | 2,835.6 | 3,469.1 | –2,612.5 | –7,577.5 | –11,129.4 | –13,524.1 | –15,872.2 |
| Claims on Nonresidents................. | 21 | 9,897.7 | 10,480.6 | 9,236.4 | 11,462.4 | 11,261.6 | 14,389.7 | 15,279.9 | 17,670.7 | 19,787.3 | 20,920.7 | 22,317.4 | 24,584.5 |
| Liabilities to Nonresidents............. | 26c | 10,926.2 | 12,344.7 | 10,646.4 | 14,129.0 | 13,799.9 | 11,554.1 | 11,810.8 | 20,283.2 | 27,364.9 | 32,050.1 | 35,841.6 | 40,456.7 |
| Claims on Central Bank................... | 20 | 19,934.6 | 20,953.6 | 20,038.9 | 18,323.0 | 24,334.7 | 27,567.5 | 30,568.1 | 33,360.2 | 36,861.6 | 42,457.1 | 43,890.4 | 47,128.9 |
| Currency........................................ | 20a | 1,433.7 | 1,771.4 | 1,063.7 | 2,876.7 | 2,970.9 | 3,124.1 | 3,653.8 | 4,022.0 | 5,325.1 | 5,165.4 | 5,102.6 | 6,244.7 |
| Reserve Deposits and Securities..... | 20b | 7,479.6 | 7,935.6 | 10,935.6 | 9,973.7 | 10,514.9 | 13,623.3 | 14,476.9 | 16,018.6 | 18,227.9 | 21,958.7 | 22,950.6 | 23,535.3 |
| Other Claims................................ | 20n | 11,021.3 | 11,246.7 | 8,039.5 | 5,472.6 | 10,849.0 | 10,820.1 | 12,437.5 | 13,319.6 | 13,308.6 | 15,333.0 | 15,837.1 | 17,348.9 |
| Net Claims on Central Government.. | 22an | 4,061.9 | 5,995.8 | 8,547.7 | 8,880.2 | 7,114.2 | 11,861.8 | 16,284.0 | 18,252.9 | 13,727.8 | 16,321.2 | 19,416.5 | 19,148.6 |
| Claims on Central Government...... | 22a | 10,046.6 | 14,120.3 | 18,258.6 | 18,335.0 | 18,266.5 | 24,014.3 | 28,074.9 | 30,845.8 | 27,939.9 | 32,488.3 | 37,124.7 | 40,371.2 |
| Liabilities to Central Government... | 26d | 5,984.7 | 8,124.5 | 9,710.8 | 9,454.8 | 11,152.3 | 12,152.5 | 11,790.9 | 12,592.8 | 14,212.1 | 16,167.0 | 17,708.3 | 21,222.6 |
| Claims on Other Sectors.................. | 22s | 51,676.5 | 60,588.2 | 77,406.8 | 91,436.7 | 100,828.2 | 97,683.2 | 101,345.5 | 113,363.2 | 135,738.0 | 150,254.7 | 163,391.8 | 181,596.7 |
| Claims on Other Financial Corps.... | 22g | 2,694.7 | 3,764.0 | 5,731.4 | 7,207.1 | 8,710.9 | 8,170.7 | 9,069.9 | 10,445.2 | 11,760.3 | 13,637.3 | 15,207.7 | 16,158.7 |
| Claims on State & Local Govts....... | 22b | .3 | 928.1 | 975.0 | 670.5 | 573.6 | 381.1 | 428.1 | 318.0 | 1,070.9 | 1,002.9 | 812.6 | 474.0 |
| Claims on Public Nonfin. Corps...... | 22c | 259.3 | 4,528.1 | 6,939.2 | 11,311.4 | 12,297.6 | 12,601.4 | 14,060.0 | 17,165.0 | .1 | 1.4 | — | — |
| Claims on Private Sector............... | 22d | 48,722.2 | 51,367.9 | 63,761.2 | 72,247.8 | 79,246.1 | 76,530.0 | 77,787.5 | 85,434.9 | 122,906.6 | 135,613.0 | 147,371.5 | 164,964.0 |
| Liabilities to Central Bank............... | 26g | 11.1 | — | — | — | 2.3 | 3.9 | 5.9 | 7.2 | 10.2 | 7.4 | 7.2 | 7.9 |
| Transf.Dep.Included in Broad Money | 24 | 24,509.0 | 27,580.1 | 32,128.3 | 36,402.6 | 39,700.0 | 42,563.4 | 48,111.5 | 52,147.5 | 56,665.6 | 60,713.5 | 65,362.2 | 69,143.5 |
| Other Dep.Included in Broad Money. | 25 | 42,578.7 | 49,072.8 | 53,933.8 | 59,166.6 | 66,382.3 | 76,172.8 | 82,367.5 | 88,477.4 | 98,176.5 | 110,332.2 | 118,921.3 | 130,491.7 |
| Sec.Ot.th.Shares Incl.in Brd. Money.. | 26a | 4,435.6 | 4,752.5 | 5,612.4 | 4,839.0 | 4,797.6 | 5,257.5 | 4,776.9 | 5,067.3 | 5,763.4 | 6,177.7 | 6,556.1 | 7,703.4 |
| Deposits Excl. from Broad Money..... | 26b | 243.9 | 250.1 | 257.8 | 241.4 | 312.5 | 294.4 | 319.8 | 449.9 | 474.2 | 561.0 | 596.5 | 960.9 |
| Sec.Ot.th.Shares Excl.f/Brd.Money.... | 26s | — | — | — | — | 1.0 | 1.0 | 1.0 | 1.0 | 3.2 | 2.1 | 2.1 | 2.2 |
| Loans.............................................. | 26l | — | — | — | — | — | — | — | — | — | — | — | — |
| Financial Derivatives........................ | 26m | — | — | — | — | — | — | — | — | — | — | — | — |
| Insurance Technical Reserves........... | 26r | — | — | — | — | — | — | — | — | — | — | — | — |
| Shares and Other Equity.................. | 27a | 5,232.4 | 6,906.4 | 11,611.4 | 14,116.2 | 16,848.7 | 18,613.6 | 19,638.4 | 20,287.1 | 22,161.3 | 25,078.8 | 26,984.2 | 29,276.7 |
| Other Items (Net)............................ | 27r | –2,366.1 | –2,888.3 | 1,039.7 | 1,207.5 | 1,694.6 | –2,958.5 | –3,554.4 | –4,073.5 | –4,504.5 | –4,969.0 | –5,255.0 | –5,584.2 |
| Memo Item: | | | | | | | | | | | | | |
| Total Assets.................................... | 20ra | 103,170.7 | 120,006.1 | 138,269.6 | 152,000.8 | 166,957.4 | 180,108.7 | 192,959.5 | 216,083.1 | 242,501.1 | 269,340.4 | 291,145.6 | 318,774.6 |

# Guatemala 258


| | | 2004 | 2005 | 2006 | 2007 | 2008 | 2009 | 2010 | 2011 | 2012 | 2013 | 2014 | 2015 |
|---|---|---|---|---|---|---|---|---|---|---|---|---|---|
| **Depository Corporations** | | | | | | *Millions of Quetzales: End of Period* | | | | | | | |
| Net Foreign Assets | 31n | 24,477.2 | 25,360.0 | 27,917.3 | 28,484.2 | 31,937.0 | 42,199.1 | 47,254.8 | 41,929.5 | 41,497.2 | 43,748.5 | 40,404.3 | 41,734.8 |
| Claims on Nonresidents | 31 | 38,345.2 | 40,356.2 | 41,351.0 | 45,534.3 | 48,630.4 | 59,183.9 | 64,186.4 | 67,181.7 | 73,891.9 | 80,824.3 | 80,848.3 | 86,610.3 |
| Liabilities to Nonresidents | 36c | 13,868.0 | 14,996.2 | 13,433.7 | 17,050.0 | 16,693.4 | 16,984.8 | 16,931.6 | 25,252.2 | 32,394.7 | 37,075.7 | 40,444.0 | 44,875.5 |
| Domestic Claims | 32 | 60,857.9 | 73,124.3 | 92,915.6 | 105,529.0 | 115,119.7 | 120,811.5 | 127,757.0 | 142,971.2 | 161,871.8 | 180,778.1 | 199,787.4 | 219,649.3 |
| Net Claims on Central Government | 32an | 9,144.4 | 12,503.0 | 15,475.6 | 14,059.0 | 14,257.7 | 22,951.5 | 26,217.9 | 29,357.6 | 25,858.8 | 30,223.8 | 36,081.8 | 37,717.3 |
| Claims on Central Government | 32a | 26,991.0 | 32,225.0 | 37,032.4 | 37,908.9 | 37,855.0 | 43,645.5 | 47,685.7 | 50,780.8 | 48,903.6 | 54,779.4 | 60,927.8 | 65,887.0 |
| Liabilities to Central Government | 36d | 17,846.7 | 19,722.1 | 21,556.8 | 23,849.9 | 23,597.3 | 20,694.0 | 21,467.8 | 21,423.2 | 23,044.8 | 24,555.6 | 24,846.0 | 28,169.8 |
| Claims on Other Sectors | 32s | 51,713.5 | 60,621.3 | 77,440.0 | 91,470.0 | 100,862.0 | 97,860.0 | 101,539.1 | 113,613.6 | 136,013.0 | 150,554.3 | 163,705.6 | 181,932.0 |
| Claims on Other Financial Corps. | 32g | 2,709.2 | 3,771.0 | 5,738.4 | 7,214.1 | 8,717.9 | 8,318.7 | 9,235.9 | 10,668.8 | 12,008.1 | 13,910.0 | 15,495.4 | 16,470.4 |
| Claims on State & Local Govts. | 32b | 22.8 | 954.2 | 1,001.2 | 696.7 | 600.3 | 409.8 | 455.6 | 344.8 | 1,098.1 | 1,029.9 | 838.7 | 497.6 |
| Claims on Public Nonfin. Corps. | 32c | 259.3 | 4,528.1 | 6,939.2 | 11,311.4 | 12,297.6 | 12,601.4 | 14,060.0 | 17,165.0 | .1 | 1.4 | — | — |
| Claims on Private Sector | 32d | 48,722.2 | 51,367.9 | 63,761.2 | 72,247.8 | 79,246.1 | 76,530.0 | 77,787.5 | 85,434.9 | 122,906.6 | 135,613.0 | 147,371.5 | 164,964.0 |
| Broad Money Liabilities | 35l | 83,021.7 | 94,411.7 | 106,679.4 | 117,652.2 | 127,673.0 | 142,158.4 | 155,044.1 | 166,261.5 | 181,824.7 | 199,182.8 | 214,867.8 | 234,399.4 |
| Currency Outside Depository Corps | 34a | 11,192.7 | 12,490.5 | 14,708.2 | 17,134.1 | 16,695.1 | 18,108.5 | 19,736.5 | 20,510.5 | 21,227.0 | 21,964.9 | 24,061.8 | 27,063.4 |
| Transferable Deposits | 34 | 24,474.7 | 27,679.3 | 32,170.4 | 36,460.8 | 39,737.8 | 42,557.9 | 48,104.3 | 52,138.2 | 56,655.2 | 60,706.0 | 65,328.2 | 69,140.9 |
| Other Deposits | 35 | 42,579.1 | 49,073.2 | 53,935.0 | 59,167.0 | 66,382.8 | 76,172.8 | 82,367.5 | 88,477.4 | 98,176.5 | 110,332.2 | 118,921.3 | 130,491.7 |
| Securities Other than Shares | 36a | 4,775.3 | 5,168.7 | 5,865.8 | 4,890.3 | 4,857.4 | 5,319.2 | 4,835.8 | 5,135.4 | 5,766.0 | 6,179.7 | 6,556.5 | 7,703.4 |
| Deposits Excl. from Broad Money | 36b | 244.2 | 250.2 | 258.0 | 241.6 | 312.5 | 371.3 | 443.3 | 545.2 | 593.9 | 675.8 | 689.2 | 1,089.8 |
| Sec.Ot.th.Shares Excl.f/Brd.Money | 36s | 1,474.4 | 1,581.0 | 1,153.4 | 666.4 | 660.8 | 848.6 | 1,035.3 | 916.5 | 1,679.1 | 2,132.0 | 2,663.6 | 2,404.2 |
| Loans | 36l | — | — | — | — | — | — | — | — | — | — | — | — |
| Financial Derivatives | 36m | — | — | — | — | — | — | — | — | — | — | — | — |
| Insurance Technical Reserves | 36r | — | — | — | — | — | — | — | — | — | — | — | — |
| Shares and Other Equity | 37a | 7,699.6 | 9,598.6 | 14,430.6 | 18,274.8 | 22,428.4 | 27,028.7 | 26,172.4 | 25,323.0 | 27,423.4 | 30,387.5 | 30,453.0 | 32,777.1 |
| Other Items (Net) | 37r | –7,104.7 | –7,357.3 | –1,688.5 | –2,821.8 | –4,017.9 | –7,396.4 | –7,683.3 | –8,145.6 | –8,152.2 | –7,851.4 | –8,481.8 | –9,286.4 |
| Broad Money Liabs., Seasonally Adj. | 35l.b | 81,058.7 | 92,509.6 | 104,916.2 | 115,751.3 | 125,527.3 | 139,664.4 | 152,380.7 | 163,556.3 | 179,087.0 | 196,496.4 | 212,300.9 | 231,803.0 |
| **Other Financial Corporations** | | | | | | *Millions of Quetzales: End of Period* | | | | | | | |
| Net Foreign Assets | 41n | –4.8 | –4.7 | –3.2 | — | .7 | 6.5 | 17.7 | 21.7 | 14.6 | 10.3 | 44.9 | 57.9 |
| Claims on Nonresidents | 41 | .5 | .1 | 2.8 | 4.9 | 5.6 | 12.2 | 22.9 | 27.8 | 21.9 | 21.9 | 57.4 | 70.1 |
| Liabilities to Nonresidents | 46c | 5.3 | 4.8 | 6.0 | 4.9 | 4.9 | 5.7 | 5.3 | 6.1 | 7.3 | 11.6 | 12.5 | 12.2 |
| Claims on Depository Corporations | 40 | 559.9 | 681.4 | 721.0 | 817.0 | 914.1 | 1,074.3 | 1,293.3 | 1,397.7 | 1,470.1 | 1,584.1 | 1,638.4 | 1,650.8 |
| Net Claims on Central Government | 42an | 804.0 | 845.8 | 944.4 | 1,073.4 | 1,212.1 | 1,478.1 | 1,622.0 | 2,084.6 | 2,234.6 | 2,534.0 | 2,896.8 | 2,936.8 |
| Claims on Central Government | 42a | 848.4 | 910.0 | 1,016.1 | 1,141.0 | 1,287.6 | 1,555.3 | 1,723.6 | 2,185.6 | 2,338.7 | 2,628.3 | 2,985.7 | 3,060.9 |
| Liabilities to Central Government | 46d | 44.4 | 64.3 | 71.7 | 67.6 | 75.5 | 77.2 | 101.5 | 101.0 | 104.1 | 94.3 | 88.9 | 124.1 |
| Claims on Other Sectors | 42s | 1,172.5 | 1,314.9 | 1,430.0 | 1,524.7 | 1,564.2 | 1,513.6 | 1,590.2 | 2,021.3 | 2,081.7 | 2,338.7 | 2,465.6 | 2,892.1 |
| Claims on State & Local Govts. | 42b | — | — | — | — | .1 | — | — | — | — | — | — | — |
| Claims on Public Nonfin. Corps. | 42c | — | — | — | — | — | — | — | — | — | — | — | — |
| Claims on Private Sector | 42d | 1,172.5 | 1,314.9 | 1,430.0 | 1,524.7 | 1,564.2 | 1,513.6 | 1,590.2 | 2,021.3 | 2,081.7 | 2,338.7 | 2,465.6 | 2,892.1 |
| Deposits | 46b | — | — | — | — | .1 | — | — | — | — | — | — | — |
| Securities Other than Shares | 46s | .1 | .1 | .2 | .1 | .6 | .1 | .1 | .1 | — | — | — | .1 |
| Loans | 46l | 3.0 | 9.8 | 26.7 | 32.7 | 31.0 | 20.1 | 30.0 | 11.6 | 12.7 | 20.0 | 16.9 | 18.9 |
| Financial Derivatives | 46m | — | — | — | — | — | — | — | — | — | — | — | — |
| Insurance Technical Reserves | 46r | 1,800.6 | 2,234.5 | 2,236.5 | 2,499.2 | 2,857.4 | 3,027.3 | 3,504.6 | 3,682.5 | 3,726.1 | 3,813.9 | 4,066.7 | 4,524.9 |
| Shares and Other Equity | 47a | 903.1 | 986.3 | 1,229.1 | 1,344.5 | 1,456.6 | 1,715.2 | 1,873.8 | 2,113.9 | 2,330.6 | 2,658.0 | 3,002.2 | 3,300.0 |
| Other Items (Net) | 47r | –175.3 | –393.4 | –400.1 | –461.5 | –654.5 | –690.2 | –885.4 | –282.8 | –268.5 | –24.9 | –40.1 | –306.3 |
| Memo Item: | | | | | | | | | | | | | |
| Total Assets | 40ra | 3,495.0 | 4,238.4 | 4,691.9 | 5,022.3 | 5,517.7 | 6,010.0 | 6,712.0 | 7,927.0 | 7,710.2 | 8,296.9 | 8,963.1 | 9,900.5 |
| **Financial Corporations** | | | | | | *Millions of Quetzales: End of Period* | | | | | | | |
| Net Foreign Assets | 51n | 24,472.4 | 25,355.3 | 27,914.1 | 28,484.2 | 31,937.8 | 42,205.6 | 47,272.5 | 41,951.2 | 41,511.8 | 43,758.8 | 40,449.3 | 41,792.7 |
| Claims on Nonresidents | 51 | 38,345.7 | 40,356.3 | 41,353.8 | 45,539.1 | 48,636.0 | 59,196.1 | 64,209.3 | 67,209.5 | 73,913.8 | 80,846.2 | 80,905.8 | 86,680.3 |
| Liabilities to Nonresidents | 56c | 13,873.3 | 15,001.0 | 13,439.7 | 17,055.0 | 16,698.3 | 16,990.5 | 16,936.8 | 25,258.3 | 32,402.0 | 37,087.4 | 40,456.5 | 44,887.6 |
| Domestic Claims | 52 | 60,125.1 | 71,513.9 | 89,551.7 | 100,913.0 | 109,178.2 | 115,484.5 | 121,733.3 | 136,408.3 | 154,180.0 | 171,740.7 | 189,654.4 | 209,007.8 |
| Net Claims on Central Government | 52an | 9,948.4 | 13,348.8 | 16,420.1 | 15,132.4 | 15,469.9 | 24,429.6 | 27,839.9 | 31,442.3 | 28,093.4 | 32,757.8 | 38,978.6 | 40,654.0 |
| Claims on Central Government | 52a | 27,839.5 | 33,135.1 | 38,048.5 | 39,049.9 | 39,142.6 | 45,200.8 | 49,409.3 | 52,966.4 | 51,242.3 | 57,407.7 | 63,913.5 | 68,947.9 |
| Liabilities to Central Government | 56d | 17,891.1 | 19,786.3 | 21,628.5 | 23,917.5 | 23,672.8 | 20,771.2 | 21,569.3 | 21,524.2 | 23,148.9 | 24,649.9 | 24,934.9 | 28,293.9 |
| Claims on Other Sectors | 52s | 50,176.8 | 58,165.2 | 73,131.6 | 85,780.5 | 93,708.3 | 91,054.9 | 93,893.3 | 104,966.1 | 126,086.5 | 138,983.0 | 150,675.8 | 168,353.8 |
| Claims on State & Local Govts. | 52b | 22.8 | 954.2 | 1,001.2 | 696.7 | 600.4 | 409.8 | 455.6 | 344.8 | 1,098.1 | 1,029.9 | 838.7 | 497.6 |
| Claims on Pub. Nonfin. Corps. | 52c | 259.3 | 4,528.1 | 6,939.2 | 11,311.4 | 12,297.6 | 12,601.4 | 14,060.0 | 17,165.0 | .1 | 1.4 | — | — |
| Claims on Private Sector | 52d | 49,894.7 | 52,682.8 | 65,191.2 | 73,772.5 | 80,810.3 | 78,043.6 | 79,377.7 | 87,456.2 | 124,988.3 | 137,951.7 | 149,837.1 | 167,856.1 |
| Currency Outside Fin. Corporations | 54a | 11,187.2 | 12,486.3 | 14,698.6 | 17,128.7 | 16,690.8 | 18,102.7 | 19,727.5 | 20,496.1 | 21,217.0 | 21,960.5 | 24,055.4 | 27,056.4 |
| Deposits | 55l | 66,654.1 | 76,287.8 | 85,466.1 | 94,762.3 | 105,043.3 | 117,157.3 | 128,414.3 | 138,503.9 | 152,853.6 | 168,360.6 | 181,240.2 | 195,991.9 |
| Securities Other than Shares | 56a | 4,407.0 | 4,803.0 | 5,003.7 | 4,526.3 | 4,648.2 | 5,204.2 | 4,748.8 | 5,065.7 | 5,594.1 | 5,976.4 | 6,418.6 | 7,554.5 |
| Loans | 56l | — | — | — | — | — | — | — | — | — | — | — | — |
| Financial Derivatives | 56m | — | — | — | — | — | — | — | — | — | — | — | — |
| Insurance Technical Reserves | 56r | 1,800.6 | 2,234.5 | 2,236.5 | 2,499.2 | 2,857.4 | 3,027.3 | 3,504.6 | 3,682.5 | 3,726.1 | 3,813.9 | 4,066.7 | 4,524.9 |
| Shares and Other Equity | 57a | 8,602.6 | 10,585.0 | 15,659.7 | 19,619.3 | 23,885.0 | 28,743.9 | 28,046.2 | 27,437.0 | 29,754.0 | 33,045.5 | 33,455.2 | 36,077.1 |
| Other Items (Net) | 57r | –8,054.0 | –9,527.4 | –5,598.7 | –9,138.7 | –12,008.8 | –14,545.3 | –15,435.7 | –16,825.6 | –17,453.1 | –17,657.3 | –19,132.4 | –20,404.3 |
| **Monetary Aggregates** | | | | | | *Millions of Quetzales: End of Period* | | | | | | | |
| Broad Money | 59m | 83,021.7 | 94,411.7 | 106,679.4 | 117,652.2 | 127,673.0 | 142,158.4 | 155,044.1 | 166,261.5 | 181,824.7 | 199,182.8 | 214,867.8 | 234,399.4 |
| o/w:Currency Issued by Cent.Govt | 59m.a | — | — | — | — | — | — | — | — | — | — | — | — |
| o/w: Dep.in Nonfin. Corporations | 59m.b | — | — | — | — | — | — | — | — | — | — | — | — |
| o/w:Secs. Issued by Central Govt. | 59m.c | — | — | — | — | — | — | — | — | — | — | — | — |
| Money (National Definitions) | | | | | | | | | | | | | |
| Base Money | 19ma | 20,130.2 | 22,330.5 | 27,020.3 | 31,551.8 | 37,736.0 | 42,945.8 | 44,921.6 | 48,996.4 | 52,024.7 | 57,301.9 | 59,833.4 | 62,498.7 |
| M1 | 59ma | 28,817.7 | 33,643.9 | 40,016.1 | 44,911.6 | 47,505.9 | 50,027.9 | 54,557.2 | 58,593.6 | 62,962.1 | 65,258.0 | 69,800.8 | 76,929.3 |
| M2 | 59mb | 58,478.8 | 69,149.2 | 80,945.0 | 88,616.9 | 95,135.2 | 103,083.5 | 113,523.5 | 123,980.3 | 176,058.7 | 193,003.1 | 208,311.3 | 226,696.0 |
| M3 | 59mc | 83,021.7 | 94,411.7 | 106,679.4 | 117,652.2 | 127,673.0 | 142,180.6 | 155,044.1 | 166,261.5 | 181,824.7 | 199,182.8 | 214,867.8 | 234,399.4 |
| **Interest Rates** | | | | | | *Percent Per Annum* | | | | | | | |
| Central Bank Policy Rate (EOP) | 60 | .... | 4.25 | 5.00 | 6.50 | 7.25 | 4.50 | 4.50 | 5.50 | 5.00 | 5.00 | 4.00 | 3.00 |
| Money Market Rate | 60b | 6.16 | 6.54 | 6.56 | .... | .... | .... | .... | .... | .... | .... | .... | .... |
| Savings Rate | 60k | 1.77 | 1.71 | 1.73 | 1.66 | 1.63 | 1.69 | 1.72 | 1.77 | 1.77 | 1.70 | 1.70 | 1.69 |
| Deposit Rate | 60l | 4.19 | 4.35 | 4.50 | 4.76 | 5.08 | 5.58 | 5.45 | 5.24 | 5.29 | 5.45 | 5.48 | 5.47 |
| Lending Rate | 60p | 13.81 | 13.03 | 12.76 | 12.84 | 13.39 | 13.85 | 13.34 | 13.43 | 13.49 | 13.60 | 13.77 | 13.23 |

| | | 2004 | 2005 | 2006 | 2007 | 2008 | 2009 | 2010 | 2011 | 2012 | 2013 | 2014 | 2015 |
|---|---|---|---|---|---|---|---|---|---|---|---|---|---|
| **Prices and Labor** | | *Index Numbers (2010=100): Period Averages* | | | | | | | | | | | |
| Consumer Prices.................... | 64 | 68.3 | 74.6 | 79.5 | 84.9 | 94.5 | 96.3 | † 100.0 | 106.2 | 110.2 | 115.0 | 119.0 | 121.8 |
| **Intl. Transactions & Positions** | | *Millions of US Dollars* | | | | | | | | | | | |
| Exports................................ | 70..d | 2,938.7 | 3,476.9 | 3,664.9 | 4,489.5 | 5,411.8 | 3,834.6 | 5,906.7 | 7,200.6 | 7,139.2 | 6,975.4 | 7,366.4 | 7,175.9 |
| Imports, c.i.f........................ | 71..d | 7,811.6 | 8,809.8 | 10,156.5 | 11,860.6 | 12,834.5 | 10,066.4 | 12,051.3 | 14,517.9 | 14,873.4 | 14,367.7 | 14,921.1 | 14,997.7 |
| Imports, f.o.b....................... | 71.vd | 7,279.0 | 8,174.2 | 9,472.5 | 10,981.1 | 11,947.9 | 9,226.3 | 11,289.9 | 13,662.4 | 13,946.3 | 14,813.3 | 15,897.7 | 14,575.8 |
| **Balance of Payments** | | *Millions of US Dollars* | | | | | | | | | | | |
| A. Current Account*................. | 109bx | −1,235.7 | −1,300.6 | −1,585.3 | −1,842.8 | † −1,484.3 | 272.8 | −563.3 | −1,598.7 | −1,309.6 | −1,351.1 | −1,229.7 | −202.8 |
| Goods, credit (exports)............. | 1a9cx | 5,105.1 | 5,459.5 | 6,082.1 | 6,983.2 | † 7,846.6 | 7,294.9 | 8,535.6 | 10,518.7 | 10,102.7 | 10,182.6 | 10,991.8 | 10,830.8 |
| Goods, debit (imports)............. | 1a9dx | 8,737.0 | 9,650.1 | 10,934.4 | 12,470.2 | † 13,421.2 | 10,643.1 | 12,806.5 | 15,482.0 | 15,837.7 | 16,358.8 | 17,055.9 | 16,379.6 |
| Balance on goods................. | 1a9bx | −3,631.9 | −4,190.6 | −4,852.3 | −5,487.0 | † −5,574.7 | −3,348.3 | −4,270.9 | −4,963.4 | −5,735.0 | −6,176.2 | −6,064.1 | −5,548.7 |
| Services, credit (exports)......... | 1b9cx | 1,100.4 | 1,307.8 | 1,518.9 | 1,731.2 | † 2,118.6 | 2,088.7 | 2,267.7 | 2,238.8 | 2,435.0 | 2,533.6 | 2,830.1 | 2,764.4 |
| Services, debit (imports)......... | 1b9dx | 1,344.3 | 1,449.6 | 1,778.4 | 2,041.2 | † 2,043.3 | 2,131.5 | 2,407.2 | 2,516.8 | 2,539.4 | 2,756.9 | 3,033.1 | 3,074.1 |
| Balance on Goods & Services....... | 1z9bx | −3,875.8 | −4,332.4 | −5,111.8 | −5,797.0 | † −5,499.4 | −3,391.1 | −4,410.4 | −5,241.4 | −5,839.5 | −6,399.5 | −6,267.1 | −5,858.5 |
| Primary income: credit................ | 1c9cx | 219.9 | 301.5 | 434.6 | 556.0 | † 583.3 | 408.4 | 361.6 | 413.6 | 447.0 | 461.8 | 553.9 | 545.8 |
| Primary income: debit................ | 1c9dx | 630.0 | 786.5 | 1,115.0 | 1,398.7 | † 1,423.8 | 1,370.1 | 1,460.1 | 1,904.7 | 1,562.2 | 1,526.0 | 1,961.6 | 1,969.0 |
| Balance on gds, serv. & prim. inc. | 1y9bx | −4,285.9 | −4,817.4 | −5,792.2 | −6,639.7 | † −6,339.9 | −4,352.8 | −5,508.9 | −6,732.5 | −6,954.7 | −7,463.8 | −7,674.8 | −7,281.7 |
| Secondary income: credit............. | 1d9ca | 3,085.6 | 3,555.3 | 4,244.4 | 4,808.0 | † 5,078.7 | 4,644.1 | 4,970.0 | 5,165.8 | 5,674.6 | 6,152.0 | 6,481.5 | 7,113.8 |
| Secondary income: debit............. | 1d9da | 35.4 | 38.5 | 37.5 | 11.1 | † 223.1 | 18.4 | 24.4 | 32.0 | 29.6 | 39.3 | 36.4 | 34.9 |
| B. Capital Account*...................... | 209ba | — | — | 142.2 | — | † 1.1 | 1.0 | 2.5 | 2.6 | .... | .... | .... | .... |
| Capital account: credit.............. | 209ca | — | — | 142.2 | — | † 1.1 | 1.0 | 2.5 | 2.6 | .... | .... | .... | .... |
| Capital account: debit.............. | 209da | — | — | — | — | .... | .... | .... | .... | .... | .... | .... | .... |
| Balance on current & capital acct. | 129ba | −1,235.7 | −1,300.6 | −1,443.1 | −1,842.8 | † −1,483.2 | 273.9 | −560.7 | −1,596.0 | −1,309.6 | −1,351.1 | −1,229.7 | −202.8 |
| C. Financial Account*................. | 309na | −402.4 | −611.7 | −1,045.0 | −1,551.2 | † −1,379.4 | −474.8 | −1,584.0 | −2,026.5 | −2,262.0 | −2,619.9 | −1,796.9 | −1,061.5 |
| Direct investment: assets............. | 3a9aa | 66.6 | 69.8 | 83.5 | 139.5 | † 13.7 | 122.8 | 63.3 | 130.8 | 58.1 | 91.5 | −116.7 | 31.6 |
| Equity & investment fund shares.. | 3aaaa | 38.2 | 40.2 | 40.0 | 25.4 | † 16.4 | 26.4 | 23.5 | 17.2 | 39.2 | 32.4 | 102.6 | 85.3 |
| Debt instruments........................ | 3abaa | 28.4 | 29.6 | 43.5 | 114.1 | † −2.7 | 96.4 | 39.8 | 113.6 | 18.9 | 59.2 | −219.3 | −53.7 |
| Direct investment: liabilities......... | 3a9la | 321.4 | 540.0 | 635.3 | 859.2 | † 751.1 | 696.5 | 845.6 | 1,139.7 | 1,263.6 | 1,353.1 | 1,165.8 | 1,147.5 |
| Equity & investment fund shares . | 3aala | 254.6 | 392.0 | 612.5 | 775.0 | † 679.2 | 581.2 | 907.5 | 968.4 | 1,025.6 | 879.9 | 957.5 | 1,705.8 |
| Debt instruments........................ | 3abla | 66.8 | 148.0 | 22.8 | 84.2 | † 71.9 | 115.3 | −61.9 | 171.2 | 238.1 | 473.2 | 208.3 | −558.5 |
| Portfolio investment: assets.......... | 3b9aa | −11.6 | 39.8 | 59.8 | −16.7 | † 10.6 | −22.7 | 45.7 | 143.7 | 8.7 | −6.3 | 38.4 | −5.5 |
| Equity & investment fund shares | 3baaa | | .4 | | .4 | † .4 | .4 | −.1 | 4.5 | — | .... | .... | .... |
| Debt securities ........................... | 3bbaa | −11.6 | 39.4 | 59.8 | −17.1 | † 10.6 | −23.1 | 45.8 | 139.2 | 8.7 | −6.3 | 38.4 | −5.5 |
| Portfolio investment: liabilities....... | 3b9la | −143.8 | −106.0 | −131.3 | −245.0 | † −12.4 | −147.8 | 33.8 | −248.6 | 730.9 | 926.4 | 832.8 | −57.3 |
| Equity & investment fund shares . | 3bala | | .... | | .... | .... | .... | .... | .... | .... | .... | .... | .... |
| Debt securities ........................... | 3bbla | −143.8 | −106.0 | −131.3 | −245.0 | † −12.4 | −147.8 | 33.8 | −248.6 | 30.9 | 526.4 | 832.8 | −57.3 |
| Fin. der.& empl.stk.ops.(ESOs): net. | 3c9na | — | — | — | — | .... | .... | .... | .... | .... | .... | .... | .... |
| Fin. der. & ESOs.: assets.............. | 3c9aa | — | — | — | — | .... | .... | .... | .... | .... | .... | .... | .... |
| Fin. der. & ESOs.: liabilities.......... | 3c9la | — | — | — | — | .... | .... | .... | .... | .... | .... | .... | .... |
| Other investment: assets.............. | 3d9aa | 340.3 | 434.5 | 508.9 | 597.5 | † 2.4 | 260.7 | −131.4 | 648.7 | −78.0 | 405.7 | 572.4 | 378.1 |
| Other equity............................. | 3daaa | .... | .... | .... | .... | .... | .... | .... | .... | .... | .... | .... | .... |
| Debt instruments........................ | 3dzaa | 340.3 | 434.5 | 508.9 | 597.5 | † 2.4 | 260.7 | −131.4 | 648.7 | −78.0 | 405.7 | 572.4 | 378.1 |
| Other investment: liabilities........... | 3d9la | 620.1 | 721.8 | 1,193.2 | 1,657.3 | † 667.3 | 286.9 | 682.2 | 2,058.7 | 256.4 | 831.3 | 292.5 | 375.6 |
| Other equity............................. | 3dala | .... | .... | .... | .... | .... | .... | .... | .... | .... | .... | .... | .... |
| Debt instruments........................ | 3dzla | 620.1 | 721.8 | 1,193.2 | 1,657.3 | † 667.3 | 286.9 | 682.2 | 2,058.7 | 256.4 | 831.3 | 292.5 | 375.6 |
| Curr.+ cap.− finan. acct. balance... | 4y9na | −833.3 | −688.9 | −398.1 | −291.6 | † −103.9 | 748.7 | 1,023.2 | 430.5 | 952.4 | 1,268.8 | 567.2 | 858.7 |
| D. Net Errors and Omissions............ | 409na | 835.0 | 798.3 | 479.8 | 405.9 | † 280.4 | −278.1 | −346.3 | −224.5 | −453.5 | −566.7 | −494.7 | −383.6 |
| E. Reserves and Related Items......... | 4z9na | 1.7 | 109.4 | 81.7 | 114.3 | † 176.5 | 470.6 | 677.0 | 206.0 | 499.0 | 702.1 | 72.5 | 475.4 |
| Reserve assets......................... | 3e9aa | 604.0 | 238.0 | 250.7 | 214.9 | † 332.0 | 470.6 | 677.0 | 206.0 | 499.0 | 702.1 | 72.5 | 475.4 |
| Credit and loans from the IMF....... | 3dcla | — | — | — | — | † — | .... | .... | — | .... | — | .... | — |
| Exceptional financing.................. | 409la | 602.3 | 128.6 | 169.0 | 100.6 | † 155.5 | .... | .... | .... | .... | .... | .... | .... |

*Excludes components in group E

| **International Investment Position** | | *Millions of US Dollars* | | | | | | | | | | | |
|---|---|---|---|---|---|---|---|---|---|---|---|---|---|
| Assets................................. | 809aa | .... | 9,400.7 | 10,359.9 | 11,164.5 | 11,176.1 | 12,180.4 | 13,060.2 | 14,445.5 | 15,038.1 | † 15,283.6 | 16,054.6 | 16,783.1 |
| Direct investment..................... | 8a9aa | .... | 792.8 | 877.6 | 1,010.2 | 1,034.6 | 1,105.1 | 1,178.4 | 1,334.5 | 1,385.3 | † 472.1 | 578.4 | 671.1 |
| Equity & investment fund shares.. | 8aaaa | .... | 250.3 | 293.4 | 315.6 | 331.9 | 358.3 | 381.7 | 398.9 | 438.1 | † 472.1 | 578.4 | 671.1 |
| Debt instruments..................... | 8abaa | .... | 542.5 | 584.3 | 694.6 | 702.6 | 746.9 | 796.7 | 935.6 | 947.2 | .... | .... | .... |
| Portfolio investment.................... | 8b9aa | .... | 163.8 | 223.5 | 205.0 | 215.5 | 192.3 | 238.0 | 381.3 | 390.0 | † 383.9 | 422.3 | 416.9 |
| Equity & investment fund shares.. | 8baaa | .... | .... | .... | .... | .... | .... | .... | .... | .... | .... | .... | .... |
| Debt securities..................... | 8bbaa | .... | 163.8 | 223.5 | 205.0 | 215.5 | 192.3 | 238.0 | 381.3 | 390.0 | † 383.9 | 422.3 | 416.9 |
| Fin. der.(oth.than reserves) & ESOs | 8c9aa | .... | .... | .... | .... | .... | .... | .... | .... | .... | .... | .... | .... |
| Other investment..................... | 8d9aa | .... | 4,667.0 | 5,203.5 | 5,634.7 | 5,273.2 | 5,674.5 | 5,694.1 | 6,545.9 | 6,573.0 | † 7,159.1 | 7,724.4 | 7,948.7 |
| Other equity......................... | 8daaa | .... | .... | .... | .... | .... | .... | .... | .... | .... | .... | .... | .... |
| Debt instruments..................... | 8dzaa | .... | 4,667.0 | 5,203.5 | 5,634.7 | 5,273.2 | 5,674.5 | 5,694.1 | 6,545.9 | 6,573.0 | † 7,159.1 | 7,724.4 | 7,948.7 |
| Reserve assets....................... | 8e9aa | .... | 3,777.1 | 4,055.3 | 4,314.6 | 4,652.9 | 5,208.5 | 5,949.7 | 6,183.8 | 6,689.8 | † 7,268.6 | 7,329.4 | 7,746.4 |
| Liabilities................................. | 809la | .... | 12,317.0 | 13,930.5 | 15,746.6 | 16,749.8 | 16,961.9 | 18,648.2 | 21,776.7 | 24,054.2 | † 25,944.5 | 29,606.4 | 32,127.1 |
| Direct investment..................... | 8a9la | .... | 3,861.7 | 4,482.1 | 5,312.2 | 6,142.0 | 6,382.9 | 7,314.2 | 8,686.8 | 9,874.8 | † 10,254.6 | 11,976.9 | 13,176.3 |
| Equity & investment fund shares.. | 8aala | .... | 3,445.8 | 4,044.7 | 4,793.5 | 5,543.6 | 5,713.9 | 6,622.9 | 7,756.1 | 8,714.8 | † 8,619.0 | 10,075.2 | 11,826.9 |
| Debt instruments..................... | 8abla | .... | 415.9 | 437.3 | 518.7 | 598.4 | 668.9 | 691.3 | 930.7 | 1,160.0 | † 1,635.6 | 1,901.7 | 1,349.5 |
| Portfolio investment.................... | 8b9la | .... | 1,601.8 | 1,387.4 | 1,347.0 | 1,254.9 | 1,270.6 | 1,327.9 | 1,026.5 | 1,853.5 | † 2,117.4 | 3,077.7 | 2,950.9 |
| Equity & investment fund shares.. | 8bala | .... | .... | .... | .... | .... | .... | .... | .... | .... | .... | .... | .... |
| Debt securities..................... | 8bbla | .... | 1,601.8 | 1,387.4 | 1,347.0 | 1,254.9 | 1,270.6 | 1,327.9 | 1,026.5 | 1,853.5 | † 2,117.4 | 3,077.7 | 2,950.9 |
| Fin. der.(oth.than reserves) & ESOs | 8c9la | .... | .... | .... | .... | .... | .... | .... | .... | .... | .... | .... | .... |
| Other investment..................... | 8d9la | .... | 6,853.5 | 8,061.1 | 9,087.4 | 9,352.9 | 9,308.5 | 10,006.1 | 12,063.4 | 12,325.9 | † 13,572.5 | 14,551.8 | 15,999.8 |
| Other equity......................... | 8dala | .... | .... | .... | .... | .... | .... | .... | .... | .... | .... | .... | .... |
| Debt instruments..................... | 8dzla | .... | 6,853.5 | 8,061.1 | 9,087.4 | 9,352.9 | 9,308.5 | 10,006.1 | 12,063.4 | 12,325.9 | † 13,572.5 | 14,551.8 | 15,999.8 |

| | | 2004 | 2005 | 2006 | 2007 | 2008 | 2009 | 2010 | 2011 | 2012 | 2013 | 2014 | 2015 |
|---|---|---|---|---|---|---|---|---|---|---|---|---|---|
| **Government Finance** | | | | | | | | | | | | | |
| **Cash Flow Statement** | | | | | | | | | | | | | |
| **Budgetary Central Government** | | | | | | | *Millions of Quetzales: Fiscal Year Ends December 31* | | | | | | |
| Cash Receipts:Operating Activities... | c1 | † 23,461 | 24,881 | 29,215 | 33,584 | 35,547 | 34,026 | 37,397 | 43,141 | 45,855 | 49,240 | 52,217 | 52,858 |
| Taxes................................... | c11 | † 19,711 | 22,233 | 24,624 | 28,695 | 30,192 | 29,035 | 31,905 | 37,021 | 39,663 | 43,170 | 46,033 | 46,608 |
| Social Contributions...................... | c12 | † 540 | 550 | 585 | 659 | 747 | 922 | 1,069 | 1,214 | 1,274 | 1,427 | 1,617 | 1,651 |
| Grants...................................... | c13 | † 312 | 360 | 370 | 425 | 362 | 490 | 417 | 571 | 407 | 385 | 179 | 105 |
| Other Receipts.............................. | c14 | † 2,899 | 1,738 | 3,636 | 3,805 | 4,247 | 3,580 | 4,006 | 4,334 | 4,512 | 4,258 | 4,388 | 4,494 |
| Cash Payments:Operating Activities. | c2 | † 23,326 | 25,894 | 29,959 | 32,649 | 34,618 | 38,087 | 42,231 | 46,681 | 51,314 | 54,466 | 56,503 | 57,811 |
| Compensation of Employees.......... | c21 | † 6,816 | 6,829 | 7,650 | 8,226 | 9,260 | 11,154 | 12,529 | 14,156 | 15,081 | 16,968 | 18,466 | 20,304 |
| Purchases of Goods & Services....... | c22 | † 2,051 | 2,259 | 2,870 | 3,497 | 5,235 | 5,686 | 6,262 | 7,184 | 8,722 | 8,661 | 9,346 | 7,997 |
| Interest................................... | c24 | † 2,601 | 2,923 | 3,182 | 3,892 | 4,026 | 4,374 | 4,940 | 5,476 | 6,022 | 6,569 | 6,583 | 7,617 |
| Subsidies.................................. | c25 | † 4,008 | 4,644 | 5,255 | 6,625 | 6,106 | 7,026 | 7,772 | 8,537 | 8,900 | 9,426 | 9,076 | 9,342 |
| Grants...................................... | c26 | † 412 | 513 | 776 | 479 | 74 | 72 | 58 | 72 | 79 | 91 | 84 | 75 |
| Social Benefits............................. | c27 | † 1,516 | 1,665 | 1,829 | 2,005 | 2,347 | 2,776 | 2,979 | 3,147 | 3,306 | 3,581 | 3,774 | 3,898 |
| Other Payments............................ | c28 | † 5,923 | 7,061 | 8,396 | 7,926 | 7,571 | 6,999 | 7,692 | 8,110 | 9,205 | 9,169 | 9,174 | 8,578 |
| Net Cash Inflow:Operating Act.[1-2] | ccio | † 135 | −1,013 | −744 | 935 | 929 | −4,061 | −4,834 | −3,540 | −5,459 | −5,226 | −4,286 | −4,953 |
| Net Cash Outflow:Invest. in NFA...... | c31 | † 2,081 | 2,508 | 3,669 | 4,646 | 5,555 | 5,609 | 6,126 | 6,811 | 3,984 | 3,791 | 4,302 | 2,054 |
| Net Cash Outflow: Invest. in NFA..... | c31 | † 2,081 | 2,508 | 3,669 | 4,646 | 5,555 | 5,609 | 6,126 | 6,811 | 3,984 | 3,791 | 4,302 | 2,054 |
| Purchases of Nonfinancial Assets... | c31.1 | .... | .... | .... | .... | .... | .... | .... | .... | .... | .... | .... | .... |
| Sales of Nonfinancial Assets.......... | c31.2 | .... | .... | .... | .... | .... | .... | .... | .... | .... | .... | .... | .... |
| Cash Surplus/Deficit [1-2-31=1-2M] | ccsd | † −1,946 | −3,521 | −4,413 | −3,711 | −4,626 | −9,670 | −10,959 | −10,351 | −9,443 | −9,017 | −8,588 | −7,007 |
| Net Acq. Fin. Assets, excl. Cash....... | c32x | † 134 | 73 | 58 | 60 | 152 | 26 | 1 | 6 | 2 | 4 | 6 | — |
| Domestic.................................. | c321x | † 134 | 73 | 58 | 60 | 152 | 26 | 1 | 6 | 2 | 4 | 6 | — |
| Foreign.................................... | c322x | .... | .... | .... | .... | .... | .... | .... | .... | .... | .... | .... | .... |
| Net Incurrence of Liabilities.............. | c33 | † 5,166 | 2,285 | 5,470 | 5,566 | 2,475 | 8,506 | 11,281 | 11,069 | 7,426 | 12,506 | 8,346 | 7,632 |
| Domestic.................................. | c331 | † 1,804 | 2,621 | 2,603 | 2,525 | 1,626 | 4,388 | 6,171 | 10,690 | 1,683 | 6,142 | 8,223 | 3,994 |
| Foreign.................................... | c332 | † 3,362 | −337 | 2,867 | 3,040 | 850 | 4,117 | 5,110 | 378 | 5,743 | 6,364 | 123 | 3,638 |
| Net Cash Inflow, Fin.Act.[-32x+33].. | cnfb | † 5,032 | 2,212 | 5,412 | 5,506 | 2,324 | 8,480 | 11,280 | 11,062 | 7,424 | 12,503 | 8,340 | 7,632 |
| Net Change in Stock of Cash........... | cncb | † 3,086 | −1,309 | 999 | 1,794 | −2,302 | −1,191 | 320 | 712 | −2,019 | 3,486 | −249 | 624 |
| Stat. Discrep. [32X-33+NCB-CSD].... | ccsdz | .... | .... | .... | .... | .... | .... | .... | .... | .... | .... | .... | .... |
| Memo Item:Cash Expenditure[2+31] | c2m | † 25,407 | 28,402 | 33,628 | 37,295 | 40,173 | 43,696 | 48,357 | 53,492 | 55,299 | 58,257 | 60,805 | 59,865 |
| Memo Item: Gross Debt................ | c63 | .... | .... | .... | .... | .... | .... | .... | .... | .... | .... | .... | .... |
| **National Accounts** | | | | | | | *Millions of Quetzales* | | | | | | |
| Househ.Cons.Expend.,incl.NPISHs.... | 96f | 162,861 | 182,231 | 201,706 | 228,461 | 264,134 | 264,615 | 286,760 | 316,528 | 339,236 | 366,020 | 389,427 | 414,864 |
| Government Consumption Expend... | 91f | 16,687 | 17,611 | 19,237 | 22,663 | 26,668 | 31,348 | 34,894 | 37,803 | 40,845 | 44,290 | 49,278 | 50,619 |
| Gross Fixed Capital Formation.......... | 93e | 34,924 | 38,009 | 46,215 | 51,273 | 53,056 | 46,595 | 49,324 | 54,910 | 58,379 | 60,463 | 62,862 | 64,642 |
| Changes in Inventories................... | 93i | 4,776 | 2,988 | 1,647 | 3,255 | −4,527 | −6,396 | −2,900 | 1,592 | 650 | −802 | −1,170 | 955 |
| Exports of Goods and Services.......... | 90c | 51,372 | 52,046 | 57,302 | 66,920 | 73,134 | 73,836 | 85,957 | 98,783 | 98,162 | 100,249 | 104,674 | 103,966 |
| Imports of Goods and Services (-)..... | 98c | 80,180 | 85,156 | 96,270 | 110,812 | 116,594 | 102,031 | 120,943 | 138,605 | 142,549 | 147,105 | 150,972 | 146,712 |
| Gross Domestic Product (GDP)......... | 99b | 190,440 | 207,729 | 229,836 | 261,760 | 295,871 | 307,967 | 333,093 | 371,012 | 394,723 | 423,115 | 454,098 | 488,333 |
| Net Primary Income from Abroad..... | 98.n | −2,689 | −2,568 | −2,413 | −6,485 | −7,105 | −9,109 | −9,785 | −12,885 | −10,182 | .... | .... | .... |
| Gross National Income (GNI)........... | 99a | 187,751 | 205,161 | 227,423 | 255,275 | 288,767 | 298,858 | 323,309 | 358,127 | 384,541 | .... | .... | .... |
| Consumption of Fixed Capital.......... | 99cf | 6,890 | 6,003 | 6,252 | 7,375 | .... | .... | .... | .... | .... | .... | .... | .... |
| GDP Volume 2001 Prices................. | 99b.p | 161,458 | 166,722 | 175,691 | 186,767 | 192,895 | 193,910 | 199,474 | 207,776 | 213,947 | 221,838 | 231,268 | 240,707 |
| GDP Volume (2010=100)............... | 99bvp | 80.9 | 83.6 | 88.1 | 93.6 | 96.7 | 97.2 | 100.0 | 104.2 | 107.3 | 111.2 | 115.9 | 120.7 |
| GDP Deflator (2010=100)............... | 99bip | 70.6 | 74.6 | 78.3 | 83.9 | 91.9 | 95.1 | 100.0 | 106.9 | 110.5 | 114.2 | 117.6 | 121.5 |
| | | | | | | *Millions: Midyear Estimates* | | | | | | | |
| Population................................ | 99z | 12.88 | 13.18 | 13.49 | 13.80 | 14.11 | 14.42 | 14.73 | 15.05 | 15.37 | 15.69 | 16.02 | 16.34 |

# Guinea 656

|  |  | 2004 | 2005 | 2006 | 2007 | 2008 | 2009 | 2010 | 2011 | 2012 | 2013 | 2014 | 2015 |
|---|---|---|---|---|---|---|---|---|---|---|---|---|---|
| **Exchange Rates** | | *Francs per US Dollar: End of Period (ae) Period Average (rf)* | | | | | | | | | | | |
| Official Rate | ae | 2,550.0 | 4,500.0 | 5,650.0 | 4,181.7 | 5,161.0 | 4,924.4 | 6,083.9 | 7,089.5 | 6,969.8 | 7,005.8 | 7,227.7 | 8,003.7 |
| Official Rate | rf | 2,243.9 | 3,644.3 | 5,148.8 | 4,197.8 | 4,601.7 | 4,801.1 | 5,726.1 | 6,658.0 | 6,985.8 | 6,907.9 | 7,014.1 | 7,485.5 |
| **Fund Position** | | *Millions of SDRs: End of Period* | | | | | | | | | | | |
| Quota | 2f.s | 107.10 | 107.10 | 107.10 | 107.10 | 107.10 | 107.10 | 107.10 | 107.10 | 107.10 | 107.10 | 107.10 | 107.10 |
| SDR Holdings | 1b.s | — | .01 | — | 7.72 | 1.57 | 82.21 | 75.43 | 61.45 | 78.47 | 96.82 | 160.32 | 145.48 |
| Reserve Position in the Fund | 1c.s | .08 | .08 | .08 | .08 | .08 | .08 | .08 | .08 | .08 | .08 | .08 | .08 |
| Total Fund Cred.&Loans Outstg | 2tl | 78.52 | 61.11 | 47.90 | 40.93 | 45.91 | 37.62 | 30.91 | 27.05 | 37.22 | 55.58 | 119.08 | 142.79 |
| SDR Allocations | 1bd | 17.60 | 17.60 | 17.60 | 17.60 | 17.60 | 102.47 | 102.47 | 102.47 | 102.47 | 102.47 | 102.47 | 102.47 |
| **International Liquidity** | | *Millions of US Dollars Unless Otherwise Indicated: End of Period* | | | | | | | | | | | |
| Total Reserves minus Gold | 1l.d | 110.48 | 95.06 | .... | .... | .... | .... | .... | 103.16 | 154.95 | 174.03 | 293.03 | 249.19 |
| SDR Holdings | 1b.d | — | .02 | — | 12.20 | 2.43 | 128.88 | 116.16 | 94.34 | 120.60 | 149.10 | 232.27 | 201.59 |
| Reserve Position in the Fund | 1c.d | .12 | .11 | .11 | .12 | .12 | .12 | .12 | .12 | .12 | .12 | .11 | .10 |
| Foreign Exchange | 1d.d | 110.37 | 94.93 | .... | .... | .... | .... | .... | 8.70 | 34.23 | 24.81 | 60.65 | 47.50 |
| Gold (Million Fine Troy Ounces) | 1ad | .003 | .002 | .018 | .003 | .007 | .007 | .007 | .007 | .007 | .007 | .007 | .077 |
| Gold (National Valuation) | 1and | 1.26 | 1.27 | 18.26 | 2.92 | 6.16 | 7.84 | 10.02 | 8.60 | 11.12 | 8.47 | 9.35 | 90.08 |
| Monetary Authorities: Other Liabs | 4..d | 13.04 | 7.27 | 10.99 | 15.48 | 12.68 | 7.84 | 165.19 | 16.48 | 66.48 | 95.20 | 146.20 | 157.61 |
| Deposit Money Banks: Assets | 7a.d | 110.60 | 88.61 | 146.82 | 156.39 | 218.02 | 166.10 | 139.93 | 216.04 | 287.78 | 241.18 | 139.58 | 162.68 |
| Deposit Money Banks: Liabs | 7b.d | 38.04 | 27.62 | 20.81 | 29.72 | 35.12 | 35.11 | 53.78 | 162.55 | 58.42 | 49.24 | 121.92 | 99.92 |
| **Monetary Authorities** | | *Millions of Francs: End of Period* | | | | | | | | | | | |
| Foreign Assets | 11 | 285,007 | 433,471 | 330,553 | 175,813 | 312,637 | 1,644,935 | 1,529,810 | 6,019,113 | 4,480,844 | 4,940,037 | 5,436,139 | 3,623,244 |
| Claims on Central Government | 12a | 1,304,367 | 2,513,388 | 4,436,037 | 2,587,477 | 3,421,751 | 6,692,257 | 10,100,315 | 10,032,264 | 6,270,947 | 6,270,589 | 6,268,127 | 7,871,957 |
| Claims on Nonfin.Pub.Enterprises | 12c | 2,660 | 4,793 | 1,702 | 25,079 | 49,290 | 42,262 | 28,958 | 39,515 | 22,103 | 15,003 | 7,668 | 1,568 |
| Claims on Private Sector | 12d | 31,941 | 131,308 | 182,514 | 122,041 | 151,627 | 10,522 | 6,478 | 10,061 | 48,330 | 55,409 | 52,011 | 120,143 |
| Claims on Deposit Money Banks | 12e | 2,009 | 14,548 | 14,174 | 3,206 | 56,144 | 2,475 | — | 521 | — | — | — | — |
| Claims on Other Banking Insts | 12f | — | 56 | 64 | 56 | 56 | | | | | | | |
| Reserve Money | 14 | 861,418 | 986,111 | 2,011,985 | 2,126,058 | 2,475,603 | 4,334,002 | 6,990,326 | 7,494,516 | 6,587,917 | 7,607,872 | 8,712,616 | 8,878,510 |
| of which: Currency Outside DMBs | 14a | 536,169 | 786,587 | 1,170,526 | 1,418,181 | 1,627,923 | 2,123,925 | 3,987,512 | 3,296,217 | 3,705,537 | 4,052,007 | 4,317,733 | 5,178,033 |
| Foreign Liabilities | 16c | 413,911 | 539,002 | 618,861 | 451,528 | 570,314 | 1,120,076 | 2,254,644 | 1,526,525 | 1,959,685 | 2,372,125 | 3,376,584 | 3,981,626 |
| Central Government Deposits | 16d | 613,880 | 1,640,583 | 2,657,460 | 620,224 | 1,272,554 | 3,220,963 | 3,522,703 | 4,547,085 | 2,419,784 | 1,716,520 | 744,447 | 379,332 |
| Capital Accounts | 17a | 62,017 | 119,459 | 34,509 | 54,398 | 9,079 | 81,074 | 82,620 | 20,236 | 353,299 | 338,496 | 327,104 | 273,583 |
| Other Items (Net) | 17r | −325,242 | −187,591 | −357,771 | −338,536 | −336,046 | −363,666 | −1,184,732 | 2,513,112 | −498,460 | −753,975 | −1,396,806 | −1,896,141 |
| **Deposit Money Banks** | | *Millions of Francs: End of Period* | | | | | | | | | | | |
| Reserves | 20 | 232,320 | 142,830 | 954,442 | 648,496 | 753,526 | 1,630,114 | 2,929,273 | 3,163,429 | 2,321,547 | 2,729,036 | 3,475,279 | 3,172,831 |
| Foreign Assets | 21 | 282,018 | 398,734 | 829,557 | 653,987 | 1,125,215 | 817,958 | 851,302 | 1,531,601 | 2,005,790 | 1,689,683 | 1,008,841 | 1,302,027 |
| Claims on Central Government | 22a | 386,175 | 502,955 | 692,174 | 368,172 | 825,344 | 453,801 | 1,984,533 | 2,321,829 | 1,856,102 | 2,024,544 | 2,027,405 | 2,544,744 |
| Claims on Nonfin.Pub.Enterprises | 22c | 1 | 65 | 4 | 7 | 1,097 | 185 | 42,644 | 58,207 | 48,085 | 89,696 | 62,496 | 39,931 |
| Claims on Private Sector | 22d | 276,869 | 474,102 | 818,000 | 738,315 | 886,514 | 847,244 | 1,540,774 | 3,069,967 | 2,900,139 | 3,873,635 | 5,622,681 | 7,093,256 |
| Demand Deposits | 24 | 518,469 | 590,420 | 1,440,767 | 969,728 | 1,424,405 | 1,944,782 | 4,785,300 | 5,490,842 | 4,529,989 | 5,170,892 | 6,425,160 | 7,810,059 |
| Time, Savings,& Fgn.Currency Dep | 25 | 356,870 | 606,326 | 1,262,095 | 1,001,437 | 1,615,854 | 1,203,057 | 1,561,738 | 2,485,029 | 2,960,166 | 3,426,841 | 3,515,588 | 4,191,258 |
| Foreign Liabilities | 26c | 97,008 | 124,307 | 117,602 | 124,264 | 181,270 | 172,908 | 327,214 | 1,152,427 | 407,192 | 344,937 | 881,173 | 799,711 |
| Central Government Deposits | 26d | 60,652 | 88,526 | 144,170 | 114,191 | 111,724 | 143,142 | 71,309 | 115,757 | 182,894 | 117,010 | 85,122 | 87,374 |
| Credit from Monetary Authorities | 26g | 2,903 | 2,176 | — | 2,812 | 38,329 | — | 1,168 | — | 3,357 | — | — | 90,000 |
| Capital Accounts | 27a | 177,045 | 196,757 | 398,758 | 268,161 | 323,678 | 408,388 | 644,171 | 924,496 | 1,223,263 | 1,428,429 | 1,717,221 | 1,911,198 |
| Other Items (Net) | 27r | −35,565 | −89,826 | −69,214 | −71,616 | −103,566 | −122,974 | −42,373 | −23,517 | −175,197 | −81,515 | −427,560 | −736,812 |
| **Monetary Survey** | | *Millions of Francs: End of Period* | | | | | | | | | | | |
| Foreign Assets (Net) | 31n | 56,105 | 168,896 | 423,647 | 254,008 | 686,268 | 1,169,908 | −200,745 | 4,871,762 | 4,119,758 | 3,912,658 | 2,187,223 | 143,933 |
| Domestic Credit | 32 | 1,331,455 | 1,899,268 | 3,331,271 | 3,106,731 | 3,951,887 | 4,682,363 | 10,116,304 | 10,869,001 | 8,543,028 | 10,495,346 | 13,210,820 | 17,204,891 |
| Claims on Central Govt. (Net) | 32an | 1,016,010 | 1,287,234 | 2,326,581 | 2,221,234 | 2,862,817 | 3,781,953 | 8,490,836 | 7,691,250 | 5,524,371 | 6,461,603 | 7,465,963 | 9,949,994 |
| Claims on Nonfin.Pub.Enterprises | 32c | 2,661 | 4,858 | 1,705 | 25,086 | 50,386 | 42,447 | 71,602 | 97,722 | 70,188 | 104,699 | 70,164 | 41,498 |
| Claims on Private Sector | 32d | 308,810 | 605,410 | 1,000,514 | 860,356 | 1,038,141 | 857,766 | 1,547,252 | 3,080,028 | 2,948,470 | 3,929,044 | 5,674,693 | 7,213,399 |
| Claims on Other Banking Insts | 32f | — | 56 | 64 | 56 | 56 | | | | | | | |
| Money | 34 | 1,143,312 | 1,394,203 | 2,626,506 | 2,409,293 | 3,105,311 | 4,398,032 | 8,814,784 | 9,783,878 | 8,647,130 | 9,807,727 | 11,348,545 | 13,592,695 |
| Quasi-Money | 35 | 356,870 | 606,326 | 1,262,095 | 1,001,437 | 1,615,854 | 1,203,057 | 1,561,738 | 2,485,029 | 2,960,166 | 3,426,841 | 3,515,588 | 4,191,258 |
| Capital Accounts | 37a | 239,062 | 316,216 | 433,267 | 322,559 | 332,757 | 489,462 | 726,790 | 944,732 | 1,576,561 | 1,766,925 | 2,044,324 | 2,184,781 |
| Other Items (Net) | 37r | −351,684 | −248,581 | −566,950 | −372,550 | −415,768 | −238,280 | −1,187,754 | 2,527,125 | −521,071 | −593,488 | −1,510,414 | −2,619,910 |
| Money plus Quasi-Money | 35l | 1,500,182 | 2,000,529 | 3,888,601 | 3,410,730 | 4,721,164 | 5,601,089 | 10,376,522 | 12,268,907 | 11,607,296 | 13,234,568 | 14,864,132 | 17,783,954 |
| **Interest Rates** | | *Percent Per Annum* | | | | | | | | | | | |
| Refinancing Rate (End of Period) | 60.b | 16.25 | 22.25 | 22.25 | 22.25 | 25.25 | 9.00 | 16.75 | 22.00 | 22.00 | 16.00 | 13.00 | 11.00 |
| Deposit Rate | 60l | 8.85 | 14.35 | 17.50 | 17.50 | 17.50 | 17.50 | 17.50 | 17.50 | 16.73 | 15.62 | 13.13 | 6.69 |
| **Prices** | | *Index Numbers (2010=100): Period Averages* | | | | | | | | | | | |
| Consumer Prices | 64 | 32.1 | 42.2 | 56.9 | 69.9 | 82.7 | 86.6 | 100.0 | 121.4 | 139.8 | 156.4 | 171.6 | 185.6 |
| Industrial Production (2006=100) | 66 | .... | .... | 100.0 | 100.0 | 110.3 | 98.9 | .... | .... | .... | .... | .... | .... |

# Guinea 656

| Balance of Payments | | 2004 | 2005 | 2006 | 2007 | 2008 | 2009 | 2010 | 2011 | 2012 | 2013 | 2014 | 2015 |
|---|---|---|---|---|---|---|---|---|---|---|---|---|---|
| | | | | | | *Millions of US Dollars* | | | | | | | |
| A. Current Account* | 109bx | −174.8 | −160.3 | −221.4 | −462.4 | −440.1 | −426.7 | −329.2 | −1,215.2 | −1,101.5 | −1,240.3 | .... | .... |
| Goods, credit (exports) | 1a9cx | 725.6 | 842.8 | 1,032.6 | 1,203.2 | 1,342.0 | 1,049.7 | 1,471.2 | 1,428.4 | 1,927.6 | 1,886.3 | .... | .... |
| Goods, debit (imports) | 1a9dx | 680.7 | 739.5 | 950.6 | 1,206.4 | 1,364.2 | 1,054.5 | 1,398.5 | 2,097.1 | 2,244.0 | 2,136.5 | .... | .... |
| Balance on goods | 1a9bx | 44.9 | 103.3 | 81.9 | −3.2 | −22.2 | −4.8 | 72.7 | −668.8 | −316.4 | −250.3 | .... | .... |
| Services, credit (exports) | 1b9cx | 85.4 | 82.9 | 63.5 | 48.7 | 102.9 | 72.2 | 62.4 | 77.4 | 159.1 | 103.5 | .... | .... |
| Services, debit (imports) | 1b9dx | 283.0 | 288.1 | 305.4 | 306.3 | 446.2 | 336.3 | 402.0 | 576.1 | 891.8 | 696.9 | .... | .... |
| Balance on Goods & Services | 1z9bx | −152.7 | −101.9 | −159.9 | −260.9 | −365.5 | −268.8 | −266.9 | −1,167.5 | −1,049.1 | −843.6 | .... | .... |
| Primary income: credit | 1c9cx | 9.8 | 3.2 | 1.4 | 61.0 | 9.9 | 22.2 | 14.9 | 22.2 | 31.5 | 3.6 | .... | .... |
| Primary income: debit | 1c9dx | 37.1 | 51.6 | 42.2 | 124.1 | 101.1 | 190.4 | 92.0 | 155.6 | 153.5 | 408.8 | .... | .... |
| Balance on gds, serv. & prim. inc. | 1y9bx | −180.0 | −150.3 | −200.7 | −324.0 | −456.7 | −437.1 | −344.0 | −1,300.8 | −1,171.1 | −1,248.8 | .... | .... |
| Secondary income: credit | 1d9ca | 55.1 | 49.2 | 56.0 | 35.3 | 102.6 | 61.9 | 81.5 | 353.7 | 242.4 | 230.4 | .... | .... |
| Secondary income: debit | 1d9da | 49.9 | 59.3 | 76.6 | 173.7 | 86.0 | 51.5 | 66.8 | 268.0 | 172.9 | 221.8 | .... | .... |
| B. Capital Account* | 209ba | −30.2 | 20.6 | 2.8 | 51.3 | 24.5 | 4.7 | 5.2 | 129.3 | 56.4 | 29.4 | .... | .... |
| Capital account: credit | 209ca | — | 13.0 | 20.0 | 51.8 | 30.6 | 4.7 | 5.2 | 129.3 | 56.6 | 31.3 | .... | .... |
| Capital account: debit | 209da | 30.2 | −7.6 | 17.2 | .5 | 6.1 | — | — | — | .2 | 1.9 | .... | .... |
| Balance on current & capital acct. | 129ba | −205.0 | −139.8 | −218.5 | −411.1 | −415.6 | −422.0 | −324.0 | −1,085.9 | −1,045.2 | −1,210.8 | .... | .... |
| C. Financial Account* | 309na | −77.7 | −90.7 | −239.2 | −457.8 | −436.5 | −515.9 | −313.4 | −1,735.9 | −23.4 | −666.4 | .... | .... |
| Direct investment: assets | 3a9aa | — | — | — | — | 63.6 | — | — | .8 | 1.9 | −.1 | .... | .... |
| Equity & investment fund shares.. | 3aaaa | — | — | — | — | 63.6 | — | — | .8 | 2.9 | 1.8 | .... | .... |
| Debt instruments | 3abaa | — | — | — | — | — | — | — | — | −1.1 | −1.9 | .... | .... |
| Direct investment: liabilities | 3a9la | — | 105.0 | 125.0 | 385.9 | 381.9 | 49.8 | 101.4 | 956.0 | .1 | 3.3 | .... | .... |
| Equity & investment fund shares . | 3aala | — | 105.0 | 125.0 | 385.9 | 378.5 | 49.8 | 101.4 | 955.1 | .1 | 3.3 | .... | .... |
| Debt instruments | 3abla | .... | — | — | — | 3.4 | — | — | .9 | — | — | .... | .... |
| Portfolio investment: assets | 3b9aa | −14.8 | — | −22.4 | −8.3 | — | — | .1 | −211.6 | 3.1 | — | .... | .... |
| Equity & investment fund shares | 3baaa | — | — | — | — | — | — | — | .... | .... | — | .... | .... |
| Debt securities | 3bbaa | −14.8 | — | −22.4 | −8.3 | — | — | .1 | −211.6 | 3.1 | — | .... | .... |
| Portfolio investment: liabilities | 3b9la | — | — | — | — | — | — | — | — | .... | — | .... | .... |
| Equity & investment fund shares . | 3bala | — | — | — | — | — | — | — | — | .... | — | .... | .... |
| Debt securities | 3bbla | — | — | — | — | — | — | — | .... | .... | — | .... | .... |
| Fin. der.& empl.stk.ops.(ESOs): net. | 3c9na | .... | — | — | — | — | — | — | — | .... | — | .... | .... |
| Fin. der. & ESOs.: assets | 3c9aa | .... | — | — | — | — | — | — | — | .... | — | .... | .... |
| Fin. der. & ESOs.: liabilities | 3c9la | — | — | — | — | — | — | — | — | .... | — | .... | .... |
| Other investment: assets | 3d9aa | −49.5 | 89.7 | −37.4 | −33.2 | 44.1 | −56.1 | 77.4 | 186.5 | 98.4 | 98.7 | .... | .... |
| Other equity | 3daaa | .... | .... | .... | .... | .... | .... | .... | .... | .... | .... | .... | .... |
| Debt instruments | 3dzaa | −49.5 | 89.7 | −37.4 | −33.2 | 44.1 | −56.1 | 77.4 | 186.5 | 98.4 | 98.7 | .... | .... |
| Other investment: liabilities | 3d9la | 13.4 | 75.4 | 54.4 | 30.4 | 162.4 | 409.9 | 289.5 | 755.6 | 126.6 | 761.7 | .... | .... |
| Other equity | 3dala | .... | .... | .... | .... | .... | .... | .... | .... | .... | .... | .... | .... |
| Debt instruments | 3dzla | 13.4 | 75.4 | 54.4 | 30.4 | 162.4 | 409.9 | 289.5 | 755.6 | 126.6 | 761.7 | .... | .... |
| Curr.+ cap.− finan. acct. balance.. | 4y9na | −127.3 | −49.0 | 20.7 | 46.7 | 20.9 | 93.9 | −10.7 | 650.1 | −1,021.8 | −544.5 | .... | .... |
| D. Net Errors and Omissions | 409na | 68.6 | 120.2 | 61.7 | 143.5 | −5.9 | 60.2 | 50.5 | −30.4 | 257.9 | 360.3 | .... | .... |
| E. Reserves and Related Items | 4z9na | −58.6 | 71.2 | 82.4 | 190.2 | 15.0 | 154.1 | 39.8 | 619.6 | −763.9 | −184.2 | .... | .... |
| Reserve assets | 3e9aa | −11.8 | −16.5 | −15.0 | −8.7 | 10.6 | 223.5 | −35.5 | 626.6 | 57.6 | 73.7 | .... | .... |
| Credit and loans from the IMF | 3dcla | −19.5 | −25.7 | −19.5 | −10.4 | 8.0 | −12.9 | −10.2 | −6.1 | 15.8 | 27.5 | .... | .... |
| Exceptional financing | 409la | 66.3 | −61.9 | −77.9 | −188.6 | −12.4 | 82.2 | −65.1 | 13.1 | 805.7 | 230.3 | .... | .... |

*Excludes components in group E

| International Investment Position | | | | | | | | | | | | | |
|---|---|---|---|---|---|---|---|---|---|---|---|---|---|
| | | | | | | *Millions of US Dollars* | | | | | | | |
| Assets | 809aa | .... | .... | .... | .... | 338.0 | 508.9 | 548.5 | 1,151.6 | 1,313.6 | 1,402.4 | .... | .... |
| Direct investment | 8a9aa | .... | .... | .... | .... | 143.6 | 143.6 | 143.6 | 145.0 | 148.0 | 67.3 | .... | .... |
| Equity & investment fund shares.. | 8aaaa | .... | .... | .... | .... | 62.5 | 62.5 | 62.5 | 63.3 | 66.2 | 67.3 | .... | .... |
| Debt instruments | 8abaa | .... | .... | .... | .... | 81.1 | 81.1 | 81.1 | 81.8 | 81.8 | .... | .... | .... |
| Portfolio investment | 8b9aa | .... | .... | .... | .... | .... | .... | .1 | .1 | 3.2 | .... | .... | .... |
| Equity & investment fund shares.. | 8baaa | .... | .... | .... | .... | .... | .... | .... | .... | .... | .... | .... | .... |
| Debt securities | 8bbaa | .... | .... | .... | .... | .... | .... | .1 | .1 | 3.2 | .... | .... | .... |
| Fin. der.(oth.than reserves) & ESOs | 8c9aa | .... | .... | .... | .... | .... | .... | .... | .... | .... | .... | .... | .... |
| Other investment | 8d9aa | .... | .... | .... | .... | 149.6 | 93.5 | 170.9 | 357.4 | 455.7 | 553.7 | .... | .... |
| Other equity | 8daaa | .... | .... | .... | .... | .... | .... | .... | .... | .... | .... | .... | .... |
| Debt instruments | 8dzaa | .... | .... | .... | .... | 149.6 | 93.5 | 170.9 | 357.4 | 455.7 | 553.7 | .... | .... |
| Reserve assets | 8e9aa | .... | .... | .... | .... | 44.8 | 271.9 | 234.0 | 649.1 | 706.7 | 781.4 | .... | .... |
| Liabilities | 809la | .... | .... | .... | .... | 686.3 | 970.1 | 1,108.6 | 2,213.2 | 2,485.4 | 2,943.8 | .... | .... |
| Direct investment | 8a9la | .... | .... | .... | .... | 243.9 | 384.7 | 486.1 | 1,442.2 | 1,884.2 | 2,018.1 | .... | .... |
| Equity & investment fund shares.. | 8aala | .... | .... | .... | .... | 243.9 | 384.7 | 486.1 | 1,441.3 | 1,883.3 | 2,015.3 | .... | .... |
| Debt instruments | 8abla | .... | .... | .... | .... | .... | .... | .... | .9 | .9 | 2.8 | .... | .... |
| Portfolio investment | 8b9la | .... | .... | .... | .... | 42.9 | 42.9 | 44.3 | 44.3 | 44.3 | 44.3 | .... | .... |
| Equity & investment fund shares.. | 8bala | .... | .... | .... | .... | 42.9 | 42.9 | 42.9 | 42.9 | 42.9 | 42.9 | .... | .... |
| Debt securities | 8bbla | .... | .... | .... | .... | .... | .... | 1.4 | 1.4 | 1.4 | 1.4 | .... | .... |
| Fin. der.(oth.than reserves) & ESOs | 8c9la | .... | .... | .... | .... | .... | .... | .... | .... | .... | .... | .... | .... |
| Other investment | 8d9la | .... | .... | .... | .... | 399.5 | 542.5 | 578.3 | 726.7 | 557.0 | 881.4 | .... | .... |
| Other equity | 8dala | .... | .... | .... | .... | .... | .... | .... | .... | .... | .... | .... | .... |
| Debt instruments | 8dzla | .... | .... | .... | .... | 399.5 | 542.5 | 578.3 | 726.7 | 557.0 | 881.4 | .... | .... |

| National Accounts | | | | | | | | | | | | | |
|---|---|---|---|---|---|---|---|---|---|---|---|---|---|
| | | | | | | *Millions of Francs* | | | | | | | |
| Hous      Cons.Expend.,incl.NPISHs.... | 96f | 8,298,830 | 10,665,360 | 12,787,300 | .... | .... | .... | .... | .... | .... | .... | .... | .... |
| Government Consumption Expend. | 91f | 566,220 | 670,730 | 821,160 | .... | .... | .... | .... | .... | .... | .... | .... | .... |
| Gross Fixed Capital Formation | 93e | 806,260 | 1,039,120 | 1,561,330 | .... | .... | .... | .... | .... | .... | .... | .... | .... |
| Changes in Inventories | 93i | 18,840 | 30,280 | 47,160 | .... | .... | .... | .... | .... | .... | .... | .... | .... |
| Exports of Goods and Services | 90c | 2,034,870 | 3,237,030 | 4,521,320 | .... | .... | .... | .... | .... | .... | .... | .... | .... |
| Imports of Goods and Services (-) | 98c | 2,707,930 | 3,655,140 | 4,807,140 | .... | .... | .... | .... | .... | .... | .... | .... | .... |
| Gross Domestic Product (GDP) | 99b | 9,017,100 | 11,987,370 | 14,931,130 | .... | .... | .... | .... | .... | .... | .... | .... | .... |
| | | | | | | *Millions: Midyear Estimates* | | | | | | | |
| Population | 99z | 9.46 | 9.67 | 9.90 | 10.15 | 10.43 | 10.72 | 11.01 | 11.32 | 11.63 | 11.95 | 12.28 | 12.61 |

| | | 2004 | 2005 | 2006 | 2007 | 2008 | 2009 | 2010 | 2011 | 2012 | 2013 | 2014 | 2015 |
|---|---|---|---|---|---|---|---|---|---|---|---|---|---|
| **Exchange Rates** | | | | | | *CFA Francs per SDR: End of Period* | | | | | | | |
| Official Rate | aa | 747.90 | 794.73 | 749.30 | 704.15 | 725.98 | 713.83 | 756.02 | 778.32 | 764.10 | 732.49 | 782.77 | 834.92 |
| | | | | | *CFA Francs per US Dollar: End of Period (ae) Period Average (rf)* | | | | | | | | |
| Official Rate | ae | 481.58 | 556.04 | 498.07 | 445.59 | 471.34 | 455.34 | 490.91 | 506.96 | 497.16 | 475.64 | 540.28 | 602.51 |
| Official Rate | rf | 528.28 | 527.47 | 522.89 | 479.27 | 447.81 | 472.19 | 495.28 | 471.87 | 510.53 | 494.04 | 494.41 | 591.45 |
| **Fund Position** | | | | | | *Millions of SDRs: End of Period* | | | | | | | |
| Quota | 2f.s | 14.20 | 14.20 | 14.20 | 14.20 | 14.20 | 14.20 | 14.20 | 14.20 | 14.20 | 14.20 | 14.20 | 14.20 |
| SDR Holdings | 1b.s | .44 | .40 | .34 | .03 | .05 | 11.89 | 12.39 | 12.39 | 12.39 | 12.38 | 12.38 | 12.38 |
| Reserve Position in the Fund | 1c.s | — | — | — | .01 | .05 | .09 | .13 | .21 | .25 | .29 | .32 | .34 |
| Total Fund Cred.&Loans Outstg | 2tl | 10.17 | 8.05 | 5.46 | 3.28 | 5.58 | 6.34 | 2.41 | 7.24 | 7.24 | 7.24 | 10.79 | 13.63 |
| SDR Allocations | 1bd | 1.21 | 1.21 | 1.21 | 1.21 | 1.21 | 13.60 | 13.60 | 13.60 | 13.60 | 13.60 | 13.60 | 13.60 |
| **International Liquidity** | | | | *Millions of US Dollars Unless Otherwise Indicated: End of Period* | | | | | | | | | |
| Total Reserves minus Gold | 1l.d | 71.61 | 79.78 | 82.02 | 112.91 | 124.56 | 168.59 | 156.43 | 220.00 | 164.59 | 186.25 | 286.95 | 332.10 |
| SDR Holdings | 1b.d | .68 | .57 | .50 | .05 | .08 | 18.64 | 19.09 | 19.02 | 19.04 | 19.07 | 17.94 | 17.16 |
| Reserve Position in the Fund | 1c.d | — | — | — | .02 | .08 | .15 | .20 | .32 | .39 | .44 | .47 | .47 |
| Foreign Exchange | 1d.d | 70.93 | 79.21 | 81.52 | 112.83 | 124.40 | 149.80 | 137.15 | 200.66 | 145.16 | 166.74 | 268.54 | 314.47 |
| Gold (Million Fine Troy Ounces) | 1ad | — | — | — | — | — | — | — | — | — | — | — | .... |
| Gold (National Valuation) | 1and | — | — | — | — | — | — | — | — | — | — | — | .... |
| Monetary Authorities: Other Liabs | 4..d | .63 | 2.04 | 3.65 | 5.13 | 3.09 | 2.11 | 1.00 | 1.49 | 1.71 | 1.97 | 2.06 | 1.58 |
| Deposit Money Banks: Assets | 7a.d | 13.42 | 7.78 | 20.00 | 22.80 | 53.97 | 67.02 | 83.71 | 87.41 | 57.88 | 62.39 | 67.66 | 71.92 |
| Deposit Money Banks: Liabs | 7b.d | 1.08 | 8.20 | 1.40 | 6.97 | 25.21 | 24.84 | 24.93 | 18.43 | 18.57 | 14.47 | 21.08 | 39.03 |
| **Monetary Authorities** | | | | | | *Millions of CFA Francs: End of Period* | | | | | | | |
| Foreign Assets | 11 | 34,484 | 44,361 | 40,854 | 50,311 | 58,710 | 76,766 | 76,795 | 111,531 | 81,828 | 88,589 | 155,035 | 200,094 |
| Claims on Central Government | 12a | 15,098 | 13,879 | 11,688 | 9,583 | 10,584 | 18,356 | 15,521 | 20,475 | 20,232 | 15,177 | 17,919 | 21,147 |
| Claims on Other Financial Insts | 12f | — | — | — | — | — | — | — | — | — | — | — | — |
| Reserve Money | 14 | 37,019 | 50,072 | 44,498 | 53,778 | 62,231 | 63,452 | 75,951 | 110,663 | 96,934 | 102,090 | 164,359 | 206,851 |
| of which: Currency Outside DMBs | 14a | 32,570 | 40,544 | 39,679 | 43,452 | 53,320 | 56,318 | 64,086 | 85,912 | 83,385 | 90,956 | 151,826 | 194,471 |
| Foreign Liabilities | 16c | 8,814 | 8,492 | 6,813 | 5,453 | 6,389 | 15,199 | 12,601 | 16,98i | 16,780 | 16,206 | 20,210 | 23,693 |
| Central Government Deposits | 16d | 4,638 | 737 | 1,178 | 175 | 2,457 | 19,350 | 4,470 | 9,283 | 80 | 162 | 5,873 | 5,870 |
| Other Items (Net) | 17r | −888 | −1,061 | 53 | 489 | −783 | −86 | −706 | −1,922 | −1,331 | −1,692 | −3,088 | −174 |
| **Deposit Money Banks** | | | | | | *Millions of CFA Francs: End of Period* | | | | | | | |
| Reserves | 20 | 4,467 | 6,542 | 4,702 | 9,756 | 8,261 | 5,947 | 10,833 | 23,684 | 15,864 | 12,543 | 18,080 | 14,113 |
| Foreign Assets | 21 | 6,464 | 4,326 | 9,960 | 10,160 | 25,436 | 30,515 | 41,095 | 44,315 | 28,777 | 29,673 | 36,558 | 43,332 |
| Claims on Central Government | 22a | 1,008 | 3,003 | 3,581 | 8,743 | 8,417 | 5,931 | 8,675 | 243 | 4,061 | 11,115 | 15,125 | 51,074 |
| Claims on Private Sector | 22d | 2,251 | 3,370 | 6,329 | 10,469 | 18,312 | 21,761 | 25,756 | 54,110 | 64,224 | 66,561 | 61,090 | 62,580 |
| Claims on Other Financial Insts | 22f | — | — | — | — | — | — | — | — | — | — | — | — |
| Demand Deposits | 24 | 10,277 | 10,185 | 13,436 | 19,954 | 27,181 | 30,850 | 40,400 | 69,032 | 48,195 | 65,752 | 60,114 | 79,172 |
| Time & Foreign Currency Deposits | 25 | 577 | 1,503 | 1,892 | 5,367 | 8,481 | 7,807 | 13,637 | 28,253 | 31,020 | 29,988 | 32,195 | 35,725 |
| Foreign Liabilities | 26c | 521 | 4,559 | 698 | 3,107 | 11,384 | 9,812 | 12,240 | 6,343 | 6,231 | 6,883 | 11,391 | 23,518 |
| Long-Term Foreign Liabilities | 26cl | — | — | — | — | 500 | 1,500 | — | 3,000 | 3,000 | — | — | — |
| Central Government Deposits | 26d | 1,742 | 3,673 | 3,688 | 7,927 | 7,106 | 7,320 | 13,502 | 3,484 | 3,068 | 4,412 | 1,765 | 4,528 |
| Credit from Monetary Authorities | 26g | — | — | — | — | 1,000 | 2,793 | — | — | 7,403 | 13,000 | 7,720 | 2,700 |
| Capital Accounts | 27a | 1,788 | 3,874 | 6,207 | 8,293 | 10,405 | 16,653 | 21,029 | 21,100 | 22,116 | 22,258 | 22,530 | 22,050 |
| Other Items (Net) | 27r | −715 | −6,553 | −1,349 | −5,520 | −5,631 | −12,581 | −14,449 | −8,860 | −8,107 | −22,401 | −4,862 | 3,406 |
| **Monetary Survey** | | | | | | *Millions of CFA Francs: End of Period* | | | | | | | |
| Foreign Assets (Net) | 31n | 31,614 | 35,636 | 43,303 | 51,911 | 66,373 | 82,270 | 93,048 | 132,522 | 87,594 | 95,173 | 159,992 | 196,214 |
| Domestic Credit | 32 | 11,977 | 15,842 | 16,732 | 20,693 | 27,750 | 19,378 | 31,980 | 62,060 | 85,369 | 88,280 | 86,496 | 124,403 |
| Claims on Central Govt. (Net) | 32an | 9,726 | 12,472 | 10,403 | 10,224 | 9,129 | −2,692 | 6,224 | 7,950 | 21,145 | 21,719 | 25,406 | 61,822 |
| Claims on Private Sector | 32d | 2,251 | 3,370 | 6,329 | 10,469 | 18,621 | 22,070 | 25,756 | 54,110 | 64,224 | 66,561 | 61,090 | 62,580 |
| Claims on Other Financial Insts | 32f | — | — | — | — | — | — | — | — | — | — | — | — |
| Money | 34 | 42,964 | 50,879 | 53,260 | 63,509 | 80,688 | 87,483 | 104,871 | 156,519 | 131,731 | 156,936 | 212,080 | 274,026 |
| Quasi-Money | 35 | 577 | 1,503 | 1,892 | 5,367 | 8,481 | 7,807 | 13,637 | 28,253 | 31,020 | 29,988 | 32,195 | 35,725 |
| Long-Term Foreign Liabilities | 36cl | — | — | — | — | 500 | 1,500 | — | 3,000 | 3,000 | — | — | — |
| Other Items (Net) | 37r | 49 | −904 | 4,883 | 3,729 | 4,454 | 4,859 | 6,521 | 6,810 | 7,212 | −3,472 | 2,213 | 10,866 |
| Money plus Quasi-Money | 35l | 43,541 | 52,382 | 55,152 | 68,876 | 89,169 | 95,290 | 118,508 | 184,772 | 162,751 | 186,924 | 244,275 | 309,751 |
| **Interest Rates** | | | | | | *Percent Per Annum* | | | | | | | |
| Repurchase Agreement Rate | 60.q | 4.00 | 4.00 | 4.25 | 4.25 | 4.75 | 4.25 | 4.25 | 4.25 | 4.00 | 3.50 | 3.50 | 3.50 |
| Deposit Rate | 60l | 3.50 | 3.50 | 3.50 | 3.50 | 3.50 | 3.50 | 3.50 | 3.50 | 3.50 | 3.50 | 3.50 | 3.50 |
| **Prices** | | | | | | *Index Numbers (2010=100): Period Averages* | | | | | | | |
| Consumer Prices | 64 | 81.5 | 84.2 | 85.8 | 89.8 | 99.2 | † 97.5 | 100.0 | 105.0 | 107.3 | 108.6 | 106.9 | 108.4 |
| **Intl. Transactions & Positions** | | | | | | *Millions of CFA Francs* | | | | | | | |
| Exports | 70 | 40,150 | 47,200 | 38,694 | 51,299 | 57,400 | 56,662 | 59,433 | .... | .... | .... | .... | .... |
| Imports, c.i.f. | 71 | 50,700 | 63,300 | 57,518 | 52,719 | .... | .... | .... | .... | .... | .... | .... | .... |

# Guinea-Bissau 654

| Balance of Payments | | 2004 | 2005 | 2006 | 2007 | 2008 | 2009 | 2010 | 2011 | 2012 | 2013 | 2014 | 2015 |
|---|---|---|---|---|---|---|---|---|---|---|---|---|---|
| | | | | | | *Millions of US Dollars* | | | | | | | |
| A. Current Account* | 109bx | −13.22 | −45.55 | −74.15 | † −66.12 | −92.87 | −113.59 | −99.48 | −14.05 | −83.24 | −52.51 | .... | .... |
| Goods, credit (exports) | 1a9cx | 75.75 | 89.62 | 74.14 | † 107.04 | 128.13 | 121.64 | 126.60 | 237.99 | 131.36 | 152.79 | .... | .... |
| Goods, debit (imports) | 1a9dx | 82.87 | 105.93 | 127.05 | † 167.90 | 198.79 | 202.32 | 196.57 | 240.21 | 181.76 | 182.83 | .... | .... |
| Balance on goods | 1a9bx | −7.12 | −16.31 | −52.91 | † −60.86 | −70.66 | −80.68 | −69.97 | −2.22 | −50.40 | −30.04 | .... | .... |
| Services, credit (exports) | 1b9cx | 7.70 | 5.17 | 3.43 | † 33.39 | 43.77 | 33.12 | 43.99 | 44.65 | 21.69 | 38.14 | .... | .... |
| Services, debit (imports) | 1b9dx | 44.30 | 41.74 | 39.58 | † 68.24 | 85.18 | 86.88 | 102.56 | 99.71 | 72.51 | 87.23 | .... | .... |
| Balance on Goods & Services | 1z9bx | −43.73 | −52.88 | −89.06 | † −95.71 | −112.07 | −134.44 | −128.54 | −57.27 | −101.23 | −79.12 | .... | .... |
| Primary income: credit | 1c9cx | 1.30 | .44 | .29 | † .44 | .18 | 8.64 | 13.20 | 15.26 | 3.23 | 10.24 | .... | .... |
| Primary income: debit | 1c9dx | 10.94 | 9.26 | 9.13 | † 10.34 | 14.88 | 19.75 | 15.52 | 33.77 | 36.26 | 18.26 | .... | .... |
| Balance on gds, serv. & prim. inc. | 1y9bx | −53.36 | −61.69 | −97.89 | † −105.61 | −126.77 | −145.55 | −130.86 | −75.78 | −134.26 | −87.15 | .... | .... |
| Secondary income: credit | 1d9ca | 47.36 | 25.07 | 32.46 | † 43.71 | 50.37 | 52.24 | 50.87 | 90.47 | 73.06 | 62.69 | .... | .... |
| Secondary income: debit | 1d9da | 7.21 | 8.93 | 8.72 | † 4.22 | 16.47 | 20.28 | 19.49 | 28.73 | 22.04 | 28.05 | .... | .... |
| B. Capital Account* | 209ba | 27.40 | 36.07 | 22.39 | † 20.95 | 32.29 | 65.82 | 63.76 | 57.13 | 31.07 | 31.95 | .... | .... |
| Capital account: credit | 209ca | 27.44 | 36.07 | 22.39 | † 20.95 | 32.29 | 65.82 | 63.76 | 57.13 | 31.14 | 32.03 | .... | .... |
| Capital account: debit | 209da | .05 | — | — | † 20.95 | .... | .... | .... | .... | .07 | .07 | .... | .... |
| Balance on current & capital acct. | 129ba | 14.18 | −9.48 | −51.76 | † −45.17 | −60.58 | −47.77 | −35.72 | 43.08 | −52.17 | −20.56 | .... | .... |
| C. Financial Account* | 309na | −1.18 | 8.78 | 5.17 | † 8.98 | 55.51 | −12.10 | 907.90 | −28.29 | −1.71 | −27.19 | .... | .... |
| Direct investment: assets | 3a9aa | −7.31 | .70 | .67 | † .21 | .66 | 1.35 | −1.47 | .86 | −.15 | .... | .... | .... |
| Equity & investment fund shares | 3aaaa | −8.04 | — | .10 | † .02 | .... | 1.41 | −1.17 | .86 | −.15 | .... | .... | .... |
| Debt instruments | 3abaa | .73 | .70 | .56 | † .19 | .66 | −.06 | −.30 | — | — | — | .... | .... |
| Direct investment: liabilities | 3a9la | 1.92 | 8.69 | 17.89 | † 18.77 | 6.63 | 18.89 | 26.24 | 25.02 | 6.62 | 19.64 | .... | .... |
| Equity & investment fund shares | 3aala | 1.84 | 5.92 | 17.89 | † 18.77 | 5.14 | 18.89 | 26.24 | 25.02 | 6.62 | 19.64 | .... | .... |
| Debt instruments | 3abla | .08 | 2.77 | — | .... | 1.49 | .... | .... | .... | .... | .... | .... | .... |
| Portfolio investment: assets | 3b9aa | −.95 | 4.55 | −.97 | † 5.22 | 8.37 | 19.15 | 8.27 | 4.48 | 1.96 | 15.98 | .... | .... |
| Equity & investment fund shares | 3baaa | −.91 | −2.09 | −1.34 | † −1.04 | .... | .... | 8.30 | .... | .... | −.04 | .... | .... |
| Debt securities | 3bbaa | −.04 | 6.64 | .37 | † 6.26 | 8.37 | 19.15 | −.03 | 4.48 | 1.96 | 16.02 | .... | .... |
| Portfolio investment: liabilities | 3b9la | — | — | — | † .21 | — | −.21 | 2.66 | .03 | .... | .... | .... | .... |
| Equity & investment fund shares | 3bala | — | — | — | † .21 | .... | −.21 | 2.66 | .03 | .... | .... | .... | .... |
| Debt securities | 3bbla | — | — | — | .... | .... | .... | .... | .... | .... | .... | .... | .... |
| Fin. der.& empl.stk.ops.(ESOs): net. | 3c9na | — | — | — | .... | .... | .... | .... | .... | .... | .... | .... | .... |
| Fin. der. & ESOs.: assets | 3c9aa | .... | .... | .... | .... | .... | .... | .... | .... | .... | .... | .... | .... |
| Fin. der. & ESOs.: liabilities | 3c9la | .... | .... | .... | .... | .... | .... | .... | .... | .... | .... | .... | .... |
| Other investment: assets | 3d9aa | 7.65 | −4.33 | 6.66 | † 5.03 | 28.17 | −3.70 | 24.11 | 38.74 | −2.80 | 1.21 | .... | .... |
| Other equity | 3daaa | .... | .... | .... | .... | .... | .... | .... | .... | .... | .... | .... | .... |
| Debt instruments | 3dzaa | 7.65 | −4.33 | 6.66 | † 5.03 | 28.17 | −3.70 | 24.11 | 38.74 | −2.80 | 1.21 | .... | .... |
| Other investment: liabilities | 3d9la | −1.35 | −16.55 | −16.69 | † −17.50 | −24.94 | 10.22 | −905.95 | 47.31 | −5.90 | 24.74 | .... | .... |
| Other equity | 3dala | .... | .... | .... | .... | .... | .... | .... | .... | .... | .... | .... | .... |
| Debt instruments | 3dzla | −1.35 | −16.55 | −16.69 | † −17.50 | −24.94 | 10.22 | −905.95 | 47.31 | −5.90 | 24.74 | .... | .... |
| Curr.+ cap.− finan. acct. balance | 4y9na | 15.35 | −18.26 | −56.93 | † −54.15 | −116.09 | −35.67 | −943.68 | 71.37 | −50.46 | 6.63 | .... | .... |
| D. Net Errors and Omissions | 409na | −4.16 | −4.57 | 1.20 | † 5.70 | −7.58 | −7.53 | −2.49 | −5.93 | −7.37 | 7.87 | .... | .... |
| E. Reserves and Related Items | 4z9na | 11.19 | −22.83 | −55.73 | † −48.45 | −123.67 | −43.21 | −946.16 | 65.43 | −57.83 | 14.50 | .... | .... |
| Reserve assets | 3e9aa | 32.94 | 18.41 | −6.27 | † 20.71 | 18.75 | 38.84 | −.95 | 73.02 | −57.83 | 14.50 | .... | .... |
| Credit and loans from the IMF | 3dcla | −5.33 | −3.16 | −3.82 | † −3.32 | 3.73 | 1.15 | −6.14 | 7.59 | — | — | .... | .... |
| Exceptional financing | 409la | 27.08 | 44.40 | 53.28 | † 72.48 | 138.70 | 80.89 | 951.36 | .... | .... | .... | .... | .... |

*Excludes components in group E

| International Investment Position | | 2004 | 2005 | 2006 | 2007 | 2008 | 2009 | 2010 | 2011 | 2012 | 2013 | 2014 | 2015 |
|---|---|---|---|---|---|---|---|---|---|---|---|---|---|
| | | | | | | *Millions of US Dollars* | | | | | | | |
| Assets | 809aa | 88.82 | 95.68 | 103.56 | † 153.46 | 170.49 | 207.64 | 212.64 | 374.74 | 252.98 | 304.79 | .... | .... |
| Direct investment | 8a9aa | .92 | .66 | 1.34 | † 1.83 | .... | .... | .... | 8.50 | 8.58 | 6.58 | .... | .... |
| Equity & investment fund shares | 8aaaa | .31 | .... | .... | .... | .... | .... | .... | 8.16 | 8.17 | 6.58 | .... | .... |
| Debt instruments | 8abaa | .61 | .66 | 1.34 | † 1.83 | .... | .... | .... | .35 | .42 | — | .... | .... |
| Portfolio investment | 8b9aa | .... | 6.29 | 7.03 | † 15.69 | 12.20 | .03 | .22 | 8.89 | .... | 19.21 | .... | .... |
| Equity & investment fund shares | 8baaa | .... | .... | .... | .... | 3.19 | .... | .... | .09 | .... | .... | .... | .... |
| Debt securities | 8bbaa | .... | 6.29 | 7.03 | † 15.69 | 9.01 | .03 | .22 | 8.81 | .... | 19.21 | .... | .... |
| Fin. der.(oth.than reserves) & ESOs | 8c9aa | .... | .... | .... | .... | .... | .... | .... | .... | .... | .... | .... | .... |
| Other investment | 8d9aa | 16.29 | 9.21 | 14.08 | † 14.51 | 39.93 | 33.47 | 54.76 | 137.35 | 85.38 | 106.09 | .... | .... |
| Other equity | 8daaa | .... | .... | .... | .... | .... | .... | .... | .... | .... | .... | .... | .... |
| Debt instruments | 8dzaa | 16.29 | 9.21 | 14.08 | † 14.51 | 39.93 | 33.47 | 54.76 | 137.35 | 85.38 | 106.09 | .... | .... |
| Reserve assets | 8e9aa | 71.61 | 79.52 | 81.11 | † 121.43 | 118.36 | 174.14 | 157.65 | 220.00 | 159.02 | 172.91 | .... | .... |
| Liabilities | 809la | 1,514.29 | 1,177.36 | 1,323.62 | † 1,766.96 | 1,238.03 | 1,399.60 | 348.50 | 547.62 | 570.24 | 589.24 | .... | .... |
| Direct investment | 8a9la | 1.17 | 5.93 | 25.42 | † 183.88 | 92.72 | 123.63 | 139.80 | 148.41 | 145.52 | 167.47 | .... | .... |
| Equity & investment fund shares | 8aala | 1.17 | 5.93 | 25.42 | † 183.88 | 92.72 | 123.63 | 138.31 | 148.29 | 145.52 | 167.47 | .... | .... |
| Debt instruments | 8abla | — | .... | .... | .... | .... | .... | 1.49 | .12 | .... | .... | .... | .... |
| Portfolio investment | 8b9la | 1.36 | 1.17 | 2.72 | † 3.51 | 8.76 | .82 | 2.70 | .27 | .... | .... | .... | .... |
| Equity & investment fund shares | 8bala | 1.36 | 1.17 | 2.72 | † 3.51 | .69 | .82 | 2.70 | .27 | .... | .... | .... | .... |
| Debt securities | 8bbla | .... | .... | .... | .... | 8.07 | .... | .... | .... | .... | .... | .... | .... |
| Fin. der.(oth.than reserves) & ESOs | 8c9la | .... | .... | .... | .... | .... | .... | .... | .... | .... | .... | .... | .... |
| Other investment | 8d9la | 1,511.76 | 1,170.26 | 1,295.49 | † 1,579.57 | 1,136.55 | 1,275.15 | 205.99 | 398.94 | 424.72 | 421.77 | .... | .... |
| Other equity | 8dala | .... | .... | .... | .... | .... | .... | .... | .... | .... | .... | .... | .... |
| Debt instruments | 8dzla | 1,511.76 | 1,170.26 | 1,295.49 | † 1,579.57 | 1,136.55 | 1,275.15 | 205.99 | 398.94 | 424.72 | 421.77 | .... | .... |

| National Accounts | | 2004 | 2005 | 2006 | 2007 | 2008 | 2009 | 2010 | 2011 | 2012 | 2013 | 2014 | 2015 |
|---|---|---|---|---|---|---|---|---|---|---|---|---|---|
| | | | | | | *Millions of CFA Francs* | | | | | | | |
| Househ.Cons.Expend.,incl.NPISHs | 96f | 242,220 | 271,620 | 289,470 | 304,510 | 373,020 | 375,230 | 397,740 | 455,330 | 509,770 | 535,210 | 547,030 | .... |
| Government Consumption Expend | 91f | 41,000 | 46,000 | 46,000 | 48,500 | 40,500 | 54,000 | 57,500 | 58,650 | 61,580 | 49,210 | 64,530 | .... |
| Gross Fixed Capital Formation | 93e | 20,140 | 18,750 | 21,550 | 25,770 | 23,240 | 23,220 | 27,240 | 32,420 | 27,370 | 26,480 | 35,070 | .... |
| Changes in Inventories | 93i | 300 | 1,100 | −1,900 | 500 | 300 | 1,400 | 900 | 1,400 | 100 | 100 | 100 | .... |
| Exports of Goods and Services | 90c | 44,030 | 49,970 | 39,760 | 67,350 | 76,860 | 73,590 | 84,460 | 133,370 | 78,160 | 94,430 | 102,180 | .... |
| Imports of Goods and Services (-) | 98c | 67,110 | 77,920 | 85,410 | 113,250 | 126,970 | 137,510 | 148,100 | 160,390 | 129,790 | 133,390 | 153,410 | .... |
| Gross Domestic Product (GDP) | 99b | 280,580 | 309,510 | 309,460 | 333,380 | 386,950 | 389,930 | 419,740 | 520,780 | 547,180 | 572,030 | 595,500 | .... |
| GDP Volume 2008 Prices | 99b.p | 332,610 | 346,910 | 354,330 | 365,670 | 386,950 | 399,780 | 417,500 | 455,190 | 445,020 | 449,030 | 462,230 | .... |
| GDP Volume (2010=100) | 99bvp | 79.7 | 83.1 | 84.9 | 87.6 | 92.7 | 95.8 | 100.0 | 109.0 | 106.6 | 107.6 | 110.7 | .... |
| GDP Deflator (2010=100) | 99bip | 83.9 | 88.7 | 86.9 | 90.7 | 99.5 | 97.0 | 100.0 | 113.8 | 122.3 | 126.7 | 128.1 | .... |

| | | 2004 | 2005 | 2006 | 2007 | 2008 | 2009 | 2010 | 2011 | 2012 | 2013 | 2014 | 2015 |
|---|---|---|---|---|---|---|---|---|---|---|---|---|---|
| | | | | | | *Millions: Midyear Estimates* | | | | | | | |
| Population | 99z | 1.43 | 1.46 | 1.49 | 1.53 | 1.56 | 1.60 | 1.63 | 1.67 | 1.71 | 1.76 | 1.80 | 1.84 |

# Guyana 336

| | | 2004 | 2005 | 2006 | 2007 | 2008 | 2009 | 2010 | 2011 | 2012 | 2013 | 2014 | 2015 |
|---|---|---|---|---|---|---|---|---|---|---|---|---|---|
| **Exchange Rates** | | | | | *Guyana Dollars per SDR: End of Period* | | | | | | | | |
| Market Rate.................................. | aa | 310.2 | 286.2 | 302.4 | 321.6 | 316.1 | 318.6 | 313.4 | 312.8 | 313.9 | 317.6 | 299.2 | 286.2 |
| | | | | *Guyana Dollars per US Dollar: End of Period (ae) Period Average (rf)* | | | | | | | | | |
| Market Rate.................................. | ae | 199.8 | 200.3 | 201.0 | 203.5 | 205.3 | 203.3 | 203.5 | 203.8 | 204.3 | 206.3 | 206.5 | 206.5 |
| Market Rate.................................. | rf | 198.3 | 199.9 | 200.2 | 202.3 | 203.6 | 203.6 | 204.0 | 203.6 | 204.4 | 205.4 | 206.4 | 206.5 |
| | | | | *Index Numbers (2010=100): Period Averages* | | | | | | | | | |
| Market Rate.................................. | ahx | 102.7 | 101.9 | 101.7 | 100.6 | 100.0 | 99.8 | 100.0 | 99.8 | 99.6 | 99.1 | 98.6 | 98.6 |
| Nominal Effective Exchange Rate..... | nec | 108.2 | 106.9 | 105.7 | 99.8 | 96.6 | 100.8 | 100.0 | 96.5 | 100.0 | 100.5 | 101.4 | 112.9 |
| CPI-Based Real Effect. Ex. Rate....... | rec | 88.3 | 90.4 | 92.4 | 95.0 | 95.3 | 101.2 | 100.0 | 97.7 | 100.9 | 101.1 | 100.8 | 109.7 |
| **Fund Position** | | | | | *Millions of SDRs: End of Period* | | | | | | | | |
| Quota........................................ | 2f.s | 90.90 | 90.90 | 90.90 | 90.90 | 90.90 | 90.90 | 90.90 | 90.90 | 90.90 | 90.90 | 90.90 | 90.90 |
| SDR Holdings................................ | 1b.s | 4.60 | .34 | 1.06 | .30 | .02 | 2.49 | 1.33 | 2.43 | 1.18 | 4.37 | 1.58 | 1.75 |
| Reserve Position in the Fund........... | 1c.s | — | — | — | — | — | — | — | — | — | — | — | — |
| Total Fund Cred.&Loans Outstg....... | 2tl | 56.71 | 63.60 | 37.06 | 37.06 | 37.06 | 37.06 | 36.13 | 31.50 | 24.09 | 16.67 | 9.26 | 2.78 |
| SDR Allocations............................. | 1bd | 14.53 | 14.53 | 14.53 | 14.53 | 14.53 | 87.09 | 87.09 | 87.09 | 87.09 | 87.09 | 87.09 | 87.09 |
| **International Liquidity** | | | | *Millions of US Dollars Unless Otherwise Indicated: End of Period* | | | | | | | | | |
| Total Reserves minus Gold.............. | 1l.d | 231.84 | 251.87 | 279.64 | 313.01 | 355.91 | 631.41 | 782.06 | 801.78 | 864.03 | 783.62 | 667.93 | 600.93 |
| SDR Holdings............................... | 1b.d | 7.15 | .49 | 1.59 | .48 | .03 | 3.90 | 2.04 | 3.73 | 1.81 | 6.73 | 2.29 | 2.43 |
| Reserve Position in the Fund.......... | 1c.d | — | — | — | — | — | — | — | — | — | — | — | — |
| Foreign Exchange.......................... | 1d.d | 224.70 | 251.39 | 278.05 | 312.53 | 355.89 | 627.51 | 780.02 | 798.05 | 862.22 | 776.89 | 665.64 | 598.51 |
| Central Bank: Other Assets............. | 3..d | 1.09 | .65 | — | 1.83 | .25 | 2.57 | 3.30 | 3.33 | 4.05 | 3.23 | 2.27 | 1.99 |
| Central Bank: Other Liabs............... | 4..d | 55.53 | 55.43 | 53.18 | 50.04 | 60.47 | 59.77 | 49.49 | 50.34 | 51.53 | 54.79 | 26.98 | 29.01 |
| Other Depository Corps.: Assets...... | 7a.d | 116.30 | 150.72 | 168.88 | 270.27 | 272.99 | 244.22 | 252.87 | 279.77 | 329.79 | 314.83 | 371.17 | 357.24 |
| Other Depository Corps.: Liabs........ | 7b.d | 36.13 | 58.09 | 61.12 | 63.21 | 54.88 | 66.13 | 92.98 | 87.09 | 77.00 | 84.30 | 85.79 | 83.41 |
| Other Financial Corps.: Assets......... | 7e.d | 92.10 | 90.78 | 83.63 | 100.99 | 106.60 | 85.90 | 85.59 | 93.12 | 101.77 | 106.65 | 108.52 | 123.08 |
| Other Financial Corps.: Liabs............ | 7f.d | 5.45 | 5.20 | 5.31 | .38 | .42 | .51 | .69 | .98 | .77 | .83 | .53 | .60 |
| **Central Bank** | | | | | *Millions of Guyana Dollars: End of Period* | | | | | | | | |
| Net Foreign Assets......................... | 11n | 12,046 | 17,180 | 29,497 | 37,198 | 44,583 | 76,358 | 110,733 | 115,942 | 130,313 | 117,054 | 103,527 | 92,294 |
| Claims on Nonresidents................. | 11 | 45,237 | 50,641 | 55,786 | 63,971 | 73,303 | 128,064 | 159,421 | 163,293 | 175,792 | 161,312 | 137,924 | 123,998 |
| Liabilities to Nonresidents............... | 16c | 33,191 | 33,461 | 26,288 | 26,773 | 28,720 | 51,706 | 48,688 | 47,351 | 45,479 | 44,258 | 34,396 | 31,704 |
| Claims on Other Depository Corps.... | 12e | 37 | 37 | 37 | 37 | 45 | 53 | — | — | — | — | — | — |
| Net Claims on Central Government.. | 12an | 23,054 | 24,429 | 12,104 | 7,922 | 5,382 | −15,224 | −24,831 | −16,104 | −13,446 | −5,917 | 21,847 | 44,666 |
| Claims on Central Government...... | 12a | 48,133 | 46,776 | 48,927 | 45,798 | 46,796 | 46,826 | 45,557 | 45,186 | 45,184 | 46,863 | 43,728 | 56,148 |
| Liabilities to Central Government... | 16d | 25,079 | 22,347 | 36,823 | 37,876 | 41,415 | 62,050 | 70,389 | 61,290 | 58,630 | 52,779 | 21,881 | 11,482 |
| Claims on Other Sectors.................. | 12s | 4,827 | 4,823 | 6,093 | 6,151 | 5,713 | 5,582 | 5,239 | 5,019 | 4,192 | 3,991 | 3,972 | 3,027 |
| Claims on Other Financial Corps..... | 12g | — | — | — | — | — | — | — | — | — | — | — | — |
| Claims on State & Local Govts....... | 12b | — | — | — | — | — | — | — | — | — | — | — | — |
| Claims on Public Nonfin. Corps...... | 12c | 4,710 | 4,710 | 5,963 | 5,887 | 5,512 | 5,371 | 4,971 | 4,497 | 3,791 | 3,563 | 3,602 | 2,883 |
| Claims on Private Sector................ | 12d | 117 | 112 | 131 | 265 | 201 | 212 | 268 | 523 | 401 | 428 | 370 | 144 |
| Monetary Base............................. | 14 | 42,678 | 48,085 | 50,310 | 54,084 | 57,902 | 71,848 | 91,668 | 98,076 | 113,011 | 114,664 | 125,460 | 134,374 |
| Currency in Circulation.................. | 14a | 21,226 | 23,468 | 28,408 | 32,876 | 37,626 | 41,905 | 50,328 | 61,392 | 67,782 | 67,199 | 78,447 | 83,203 |
| Liabs. to Other Depository Corps.... | 14c | 21,452 | 24,617 | 21,902 | 21,208 | 20,276 | 29,943 | 41,341 | 36,684 | 45,229 | 47,466 | 47,013 | 51,171 |
| Liabilities to Other Sectors............. | 14d | — | — | — | — | — | — | — | — | — | — | — | — |
| Other Liabs. to Other Dep. Corps..... | 14n | 62 | 62 | 62 | 62 | 62 | 62 | 61 | 77 | 78 | 78 | 61 | 3,365 |
| Dep. & Sec. Excl. f/Monetary Base.... | 14o | 241 | 576 | 427 | 481 | 572 | 778 | 840 | 130 | 303 | 1,224 | 1,102 | 908 |
| Deposits Included in Broad Money. | 15 | 1 | 9 | 8 | 84 | 11 | 8 | 11 | 14 | 131 | 31 | 92 | 51 |
| Sec.Ot.th.Shares Incl.in Brd. Money | 16a | — | — | — | — | — | — | — | — | — | — | — | — |
| Deposits Excl. from Broad Money... | 16b | 240 | 567 | 419 | 398 | 560 | 770 | 828 | 116 | 172 | 1,193 | 1,010 | 858 |
| Sec.Ot.th.Shares Excl.f/Brd.Money.. | 16s | — | — | — | — | — | — | — | — | — | — | — | — |
| Loans......................................... | 16l | — | — | — | — | — | — | — | — | — | — | — | — |
| Financial Derivatives...................... | 16m | — | — | — | — | — | — | — | — | — | — | — | — |
| Shares and Other Equity................. | 17a | 4,021 | 2,813 | 3,197 | 3,293 | 5,531 | 1,279 | 5,477 | 13,712 | 17,136 | 7,767 | 9,477 | 7,748 |
| Other Items (Net).......................... | 17r | −7,039 | −5,066 | −6,265 | −6,612 | −8,344 | −7,197 | −6,906 | −7,138 | −9,469 | −8,605 | −6,754 | −6,409 |
| Memo Item: | | | | | | | | | | | | | |
| Total Assets................................. | 10ra | 105,639 | 111,024 | 119,787 | 125,286 | 138,569 | 189,871 | 220,021 | 228,985 | 240,728 | 227,088 | 201,366 | 196,521 |

| | | 2004 | 2005 | 2006 | 2007 | 2008 | 2009 | 2010 | 2011 | 2012 | 2013 | 2014 | 2015 |
|---|---|---|---|---|---|---|---|---|---|---|---|---|---|
| **Other Depository Corporations** | | *Millions of Guyana Dollars: End of Period* | | | | | | | | | | | |
| Net Foreign Assets | 21n | 16,014 | 18,549 | 21,660 | 42,138 | 44,766 | 36,197 | 32,536 | 39,258 | 51,696 | 47,548 | 58,931 | 56,546 |
| Claims on Nonresidents | 21 | 23,230 | 30,182 | 33,945 | 55,000 | 56,031 | 49,637 | 51,458 | 57,004 | 67,442 | 64,934 | 76,646 | 73,771 |
| Liabilities to Nonresidents | 26c | 7,217 | 11,633 | 12,285 | 12,862 | 11,265 | 13,440 | 18,922 | 17,746 | 15,746 | 17,386 | 17,715 | 17,225 |
| Claims on Central Bank | 20 | 24,014 | 27,210 | 29,150 | 24,955 | 26,114 | 36,554 | 46,069 | 41,753 | 49,637 | 54,395 | 54,149 | 61,508 |
| Currency | 20a | 2,244 | 2,421 | 2,671 | 3,425 | 3,314 | 3,710 | 4,493 | 4,800 | 7,675 | 6,582 | 6,365 | 7,840 |
| Reserve Deposits and Securities | 20b | 21,770 | 24,789 | 26,479 | 21,530 | 22,800 | 32,844 | 41,576 | 36,953 | 41,962 | 47,812 | 47,784 | 53,668 |
| Other Claims | 20n | — | — | — | — | — | — | — | — | — | — | — | — |
| Net Claims on Central Government | 22an | 40,697 | 36,994 | 46,811 | 42,392 | 46,308 | 56,910 | 67,189 | 73,122 | 60,693 | 65,089 | 46,040 | 43,224 |
| Claims on Central Government | 22a | 49,345 | 53,308 | 58,825 | 55,809 | 61,501 | 67,596 | 77,935 | 86,887 | 79,071 | 83,242 | 65,681 | 63,704 |
| Liabilities to Central Government | 26d | 8,648 | 16,314 | 12,014 | 13,418 | 15,193 | 10,685 | 10,745 | 13,764 | 18,379 | 18,152 | 19,641 | 20,480 |
| Claims on Other Sectors | 22s | 66,471 | 71,711 | 81,398 | 93,988 | 112,837 | 120,780 | 140,160 | 166,468 | 198,404 | 226,845 | 248,366 | 217,277 |
| Claims on Other Financial Corps | 22g | 1,037 | 1,350 | 1,116 | 496 | 834 | 599 | 548 | 608 | 811 | 1,329 | 1,409 | 1,069 |
| Claims on State & Local Govts | 22b | 50 | 81 | 91 | 89 | 54 | 53 | 47 | 60 | 50 | 7 | 1 | 44 |
| Claims on Public Nonfin. Corps | 22c | 1,265 | 1,486 | 967 | 1,240 | 2,998 | 2,641 | 3,085 | 4,031 | 3,661 | 2,585 | 2,399 | 1,954 |
| Claims on Private Sector | 22d | 64,118 | 68,795 | 79,225 | 92,163 | 108,951 | 117,487 | 136,480 | 161,770 | 193,882 | 222,924 | 244,557 | 214,210 |
| Liabilities to Central Bank | 26g | — | — | — | — | — | — | — | — | — | — | — | — |
| Transf.Dep.Included in Broad Money | 24 | 23,710 | 24,652 | 33,232 | 38,028 | 41,233 | 41,472 | 51,480 | 57,122 | 71,947 | 77,182 | 82,523 | 81,227 |
| Other Dep.Included in Broad Money | 25 | 108,894 | 114,968 | 129,422 | 144,920 | 162,922 | 183,741 | 207,720 | 232,072 | 258,173 | 275,914 | 272,537 | 237,104 |
| Sec.Ot.th.Shares Incl.in Brd.Money | 26a | — | — | — | — | — | — | — | — | — | — | — | — |
| Deposits Excl. from Broad Money | 26b | 721 | 724 | 724 | 724 | 724 | — | — | — | — | — | — | — |
| Sec.Ot.th.Shares Excl.f/Brd.Money | 26s | — | — | — | — | — | — | — | — | — | — | — | — |
| Loans | 26l | 662 | 597 | 160 | 5 | 4 | 10 | — | — | — | — | — | — |
| Financial Derivatives | 26m | — | — | — | — | — | — | — | — | — | — | — | — |
| Insurance Technical Reserves | 26r | — | — | — | — | — | — | — | — | — | — | — | — |
| Shares and Other Equity | 27a | 15,129 | 17,090 | 19,169 | 22,043 | 26,901 | 31,410 | 36,680 | 41,814 | 48,042 | 55,634 | 66,026 | 60,096 |
| Other Items (Net) | 27r | −1,921 | −3,568 | −3,689 | −2,248 | −1,757 | −6,191 | −9,924 | −10,406 | −17,733 | −14,852 | −13,600 | 129 |
| Memo Item: | | | | | | | | | | | | | |
| Total Assets | 20ra | 183,950 | 203,328 | 223,036 | 250,191 | 281,931 | 302,936 | 349,564 | 385,716 | 440,315 | 481,142 | 493,451 | 451,301 |
| **Depository Corporations** | | *Millions of Guyana Dollars: End of Period* | | | | | | | | | | | |
| Net Foreign Assets | 31n | 28,059 | 35,729 | 51,158 | 79,336 | 89,349 | 112,555 | 143,269 | 155,200 | 182,009 | 164,601 | 162,458 | 148,840 |
| Claims on Nonresidents | 31 | 68,467 | 80,822 | 89,731 | 118,971 | 129,334 | 177,701 | 210,879 | 220,297 | 243,234 | 226,246 | 214,569 | 197,768 |
| Liabilities to Nonresidents | 36c | 40,408 | 45,093 | 38,573 | 39,635 | 39,985 | 65,146 | 67,610 | 65,096 | 61,225 | 61,644 | 52,111 | 48,929 |
| Domestic Claims | 32 | 135,048 | 137,958 | 146,406 | 150,453 | 170,240 | 168,049 | 187,757 | 228,506 | 249,842 | 290,008 | 320,225 | 308,195 |
| Net Claims on Central Government | 32an | 63,750 | 61,424 | 58,915 | 50,314 | 51,690 | 41,686 | 42,358 | 57,018 | 47,247 | 59,173 | 67,887 | 87,891 |
| Claims on Central Government | 32a | 97,477 | 100,084 | 107,752 | 101,608 | 108,297 | 114,422 | 123,492 | 132,073 | 124,255 | 130,104 | 109,410 | 119,852 |
| Liabilities to Central Government | 36d | 33,727 | 38,661 | 48,838 | 51,294 | 56,608 | 72,736 | 81,134 | 75,055 | 77,009 | 70,932 | 41,522 | 31,961 |
| Claims on Other Sectors | 32s | 71,298 | 76,534 | 87,491 | 100,139 | 118,550 | 126,362 | 145,400 | 171,488 | 202,596 | 230,836 | 252,338 | 220,304 |
| Claims on Other Financial Corps | 32g | 1,037 | 1,350 | 1,116 | 496 | 834 | 599 | 548 | 608 | 811 | 1,329 | 1,409 | 1,069 |
| Claims on State & Local Govts | 32b | 50 | 81 | 91 | 89 | 54 | 53 | 47 | 60 | 50 | 7 | 1 | 44 |
| Claims on Public Nonfin. Corps | 32c | 5,976 | 6,196 | 6,929 | 7,126 | 8,510 | 8,012 | 8,056 | 8,527 | 7,452 | 6,148 | 6,001 | 4,837 |
| Claims on Private Sector | 32d | 64,235 | 68,907 | 79,356 | 92,428 | 109,152 | 117,698 | 136,748 | 162,293 | 194,283 | 223,352 | 244,927 | 214,354 |
| Broad Money Liabilities | 35l | 151,536 | 160,644 | 187,936 | 212,447 | 238,447 | 263,379 | 305,020 | 345,660 | 390,228 | 412,335 | 427,204 | 393,742 |
| Currency Outside Depository Corps | 34a | 18,982 | 21,047 | 25,737 | 29,452 | 34,311 | 38,195 | 45,835 | 56,592 | 60,107 | 60,616 | 72,083 | 75,363 |
| Transferable Deposits | 34 | 23,660 | 24,629 | 32,778 | 38,075 | 41,214 | 41,443 | 51,465 | 56,996 | 71,948 | 75,805 | 82,585 | 81,275 |
| Other Deposits | 35 | 108,894 | 114,968 | 129,422 | 144,920 | 162,922 | 183,741 | 207,720 | 232,072 | 258,173 | 275,914 | 272,537 | 237,104 |
| Securities Other than Shares | 36a | — | — | — | — | — | — | — | — | — | — | — | — |
| Deposits Excl. from Broad Money | 36b | 961 | 1,292 | 1,143 | 1,122 | 1,285 | 770 | 828 | 116 | 172 | 1,193 | 1,010 | 858 |
| Sec.Ot.th.Shares Excl.f/Brd.Money | 36s | — | — | — | — | — | — | — | — | — | — | — | — |
| Loans | 36l | 662 | 597 | 160 | 5 | 4 | 10 | — | — | — | — | — | — |
| Financial Derivatives | 36m | — | — | — | — | — | — | — | — | — | — | — | — |
| Insurance Technical Reserves | 36r | — | — | — | — | — | — | — | — | — | — | — | — |
| Shares and Other Equity | 37a | 19,150 | 19,903 | 22,367 | 25,336 | 32,432 | 32,690 | 42,157 | 55,526 | 65,178 | 63,400 | 75,503 | 67,844 |
| Other Items (Net) | 37r | −9,202 | −8,749 | −14,043 | −9,121 | −12,578 | −16,245 | −16,979 | −17,596 | −23,728 | −22,319 | −21,034 | −5,409 |
| Broad Money Liabs., Seasonally Adj. | 35l.b | 149,830 | 159,007 | 186,200 | 210,381 | 235,662 | 259,482 | 299,608 | 338,832 | 382,373 | 404,554 | 419,887 | 387,391 |
| **Other Financial Corporations** | | *Millions of Guyana Dollars: End of Period* | | | | | | | | | | | |
| Net Foreign Assets | 41n | 17,308 | 17,137 | 15,743 | 20,473 | 21,793 | 17,357 | 17,276 | 18,773 | 20,655 | 21,827 | 22,301 | 25,292 |
| Claims on Nonresidents | 41 | 18,396 | 18,179 | 16,810 | 20,551 | 21,879 | 17,460 | 17,417 | 18,974 | 20,813 | 21,997 | 22,410 | 25,416 |
| Liabilities to Nonresidents | 46c | 1,088 | 1,042 | 1,067 | 78 | 86 | 103 | 141 | 200 | 158 | 170 | 109 | 123 |
| Claims on Depository Corporations | 40 | 7,868 | 7,660 | 6,639 | 6,061 | 5,539 | 9,404 | 10,004 | 9,496 | 12,243 | 12,691 | 12,827 | 15,145 |
| Net Claims on Central Government | 42an | 925 | 1,131 | 1,125 | 1,072 | 1,031 | 2,021 | 3,306 | 3,185 | 1,038 | 319 | 132 | 705 |
| Claims on Central Government | 42a | 925 | 1,131 | 1,125 | 1,072 | 1,031 | 2,021 | 3,306 | 3,185 | 1,038 | 319 | 132 | 705 |
| Liabilities to Central Government | 46d | — | — | — | — | — | — | — | — | — | — | — | — |
| Claims on Other Sectors | 42s | 18,881 | 25,272 | 28,591 | 31,269 | 25,535 | 33,195 | 34,769 | 36,958 | 44,733 | 50,353 | 67,470 | 63,375 |
| Claims on State & Local Govts | 42b | — | — | — | 150 | 150 | 150 | 150 | 150 | 150 | — | — | — |
| Claims on Public Nonfin. Corps | 42c | — | — | — | — | — | — | — | — | — | — | — | — |
| Claims on Private Sector | 42d | 18,881 | 25,272 | 28,591 | 31,119 | 25,385 | 33,045 | 34,619 | 36,808 | 44,583 | 50,353 | 67,470 | 63,375 |
| Deposits | 46b | — | — | — | — | — | — | — | — | — | — | — | — |
| Securities Other than Shares | 46s | — | — | — | — | — | — | — | — | — | — | — | — |
| Loans | 46l | 342 | 2,770 | 3,117 | 4,081 | 3,946 | 530 | 574 | 610 | 2,066 | 1,846 | 2,045 | 2,076 |
| Financial Derivatives | 46m | — | — | — | — | — | — | — | — | — | — | — | — |
| Insurance Technical Reserves | 46r | 39,520 | 32,662 | 32,263 | 35,966 | 37,517 | 28,064 | 31,215 | 32,864 | 36,363 | 40,950 | 43,194 | 45,107 |
| Shares and Other Equity | 47a | 5,676 | 6,268 | 5,985 | 7,125 | 6,657 | 12,310 | 12,889 | 13,512 | 14,126 | 14,889 | 16,495 | 17,096 |
| Other Items (Net) | 47r | −557 | 9,501 | 10,733 | 11,704 | 5,778 | 21,073 | 20,676 | 21,427 | 26,114 | 27,504 | 40,996 | 40,237 |
| Memo Item: | | | | | | | | | | | | | |
| Total Assets | 40ra | 57,149 | 70,739 | 73,488 | 81,254 | 77,359 | 82,559 | 86,631 | 92,227 | 106,048 | 112,895 | 132,405 | 135,897 |

# Guyana 336

| | | 2004 | 2005 | 2006 | 2007 | 2008 | 2009 | 2010 | 2011 | 2012 | 2013 | 2014 | 2015 |
|---|---|---|---|---|---|---|---|---|---|---|---|---|---|
| **Financial Corporations** | | | | | | *Millions of Guyana Dollars: End of Period* | | | | | | | |
| Net Foreign Assets.......................... | 51n | 45,368 | 52,866 | 66,901 | 99,809 | 111,142 | 129,912 | 160,545 | 173,973 | 202,664 | 186,428 | 184,759 | 174,132 |
| Claims on Nonresidents.............. | 51 | 86,863 | 99,001 | 106,541 | 139,522 | 151,213 | 195,161 | 228,296 | 239,270 | 264,047 | 248,243 | 236,980 | 223,184 |
| Liabilities to Nonresidents............. | 56c | 41,496 | 46,135 | 39,640 | 39,713 | 40,071 | 65,249 | 67,751 | 65,297 | 61,383 | 61,815 | 52,220 | 49,052 |
| Domestic Claims........................... | 52 | 153,817 | 163,011 | 175,005 | 182,298 | 195,972 | 202,666 | 225,284 | 268,041 | 294,803 | 339,352 | 386,418 | 371,206 |
| Net Claims on Central Government | 52an | 64,675 | 62,555 | 60,039 | 51,386 | 52,721 | 43,708 | 45,663 | 60,204 | 48,284 | 59,492 | 68,019 | 88,596 |
| Claims on Central Government.... | 52a | 98,402 | 101,216 | 108,877 | 102,680 | 109,329 | 116,443 | 126,797 | 135,258 | 125,293 | 130,423 | 109,542 | 120,558 |
| Liabilities to Central Government. | 56d | 33,727 | 38,661 | 48,838 | 51,294 | 56,608 | 72,736 | 81,134 | 75,055 | 77,009 | 70,932 | 41,522 | 31,961 |
| Claims on Other Sectors................ | 52s | 89,141 | 100,456 | 114,966 | 130,913 | 143,252 | 158,959 | 179,621 | 207,838 | 246,519 | 279,860 | 318,399 | 282,610 |
| Claims on State & Local Govts..... | 52b | 50 | 81 | 91 | 239 | 204 | 203 | 197 | 210 | 200 | 7 | 1 | 44 |
| Claims on Public Nonfin. Corps.... | 52c | 5,976 | 6,196 | 6,929 | 7,126 | 8,510 | 8,012 | 8,056 | 8,527 | 7,452 | 6,148 | 6,001 | 4,837 |
| Claims on Private Sector............. | 52d | 83,116 | 94,179 | 107,946 | 123,547 | 134,537 | 150,744 | 171,367 | 199,100 | 238,867 | 273,705 | 312,398 | 277,729 |
| Currency Outside Financial Corps..... | 54a | 18,661 | 20,644 | 25,501 | 28,945 | 33,698 | 37,606 | 44,900 | 55,857 | 59,251 | 59,541 | 70,848 | 72,995 |
| Deposits.......................................... | 55l | 127,151 | 136,635 | 159,579 | 180,261 | 201,351 | 219,768 | 252,814 | 280,884 | 321,416 | 341,156 | 345,364 | 307,273 |
| Securities Other than Shares........... | 56a | — | — | — | — | — | — | — | — | — | — | — | — |
| Loans.............................................. | 56l | 831 | 3,270 | 3,273 | 4,085 | 3,839 | 464 | 574 | 610 | 2,066 | 1,846 | 2,045 | 2,076 |
| Financial Derivatives....................... | 56m | — | — | — | — | — | — | — | — | — | — | — | — |
| Insurance Technical Reserves.......... | 56r | 39,520 | 32,662 | 32,263 | 35,966 | 37,517 | 28,064 | 31,215 | 32,864 | 36,363 | 40,950 | 43,194 | 45,107 |
| Shares and Other Equity.................. | 57a | 24,827 | 26,171 | 28,352 | 32,461 | 39,089 | 45,000 | 55,046 | 69,038 | 79,304 | 78,290 | 91,999 | 84,940 |
| Other Items (Net)............................ | 57r | −11,806 | −3,504 | −7,060 | 388 | −8,380 | 1,677 | 1,280 | 2,762 | −933 | 3,996 | 17,728 | 32,947 |
| **Monetary Aggregates** | | | | | | *Millions of Guyana Dollars: End of Period* | | | | | | | |
| Broad Money................................ | 59m | 151,536 | 160,644 | 187,936 | 212,447 | 238,447 | 263,379 | 305,020 | 345,660 | 390,228 | 412,335 | 427,204 | 393,742 |
| o/w:Currency Issued by Cent.Govt | 59m.a | — | — | — | — | — | — | — | — | — | — | — | — |
| o/w: Dep.in Nonfin. Corporations. | 59m.b | — | — | — | — | — | — | — | — | — | — | — | — |
| o/w:Secs. Issued by Central Govt.. | 59m.c | — | — | — | — | — | — | — | — | — | — | — | — |
| Money (National Definitions) | | | | | | | | | | | | | |
| Base Money................................ | 19ma | 19,546 | 21,527 | 25,952 | 29,801 | 34,552 | 38,437 | 45,999 | 56,869 | 60,332 | 60,901 | 72,454 | 75,754 |
| Reserve Money........................... | 19mb | 43,283 | 48,085 | 50,309 | 54,084 | 57,902 | 71,848 | 91,668 | 98,076 | 113,011 | 114,664 | 131,186 | 130,295 |
| M1.............................................. | 59ma | 34,606 | 37,839 | 48,070 | 54,241 | 61,035 | 66,365 | 80,832 | 97,268 | 112,419 | 115,196 | 329,640 | 334,471 |
| M2.............................................. | 59mb | 114,495 | 124,011 | 143,777 | 163,399 | 184,153 | 202,094 | 233,362 | 270,691 | 304,356 | 313,421 | 329,640 | 334,471 |
| **Interest Rates** | | | | | | *Percent Per Annum* | | | | | | | |
| Central Bank Policy Rate (EOP)........ | 60 | 6.00 | 6.00 | 6.75 | 6.50 | 6.75 | 6.75 | 6.25 | 5.50 | 5.25 | 5.00 | 5.00 | 5.00 |
| Treasury Bill Rate............................ | 60c | 3.62 | 3.79 | 3.95 | 3.94 | 3.99 | 4.31 | 3.87 | 2.48 | 1.73 | 1.32 | 1.57 | 1.84 |
| Savings Rate................................... | 60k | 3.43 | 3.36 | 3.27 | 3.19 | 3.17 | 2.83 | 2.72 | 2.30 | 1.77 | 1.37 | 1.26 | 1.26 |
| Deposit Rate................................... | 60l | 2.68 | 2.59 | 2.54 | 2.47 | 2.37 | 2.32 | 2.27 | 1.94 | 1.52 | 1.13 | 1.07 | 1.11 |
| Lending Rate.................................. | 60p | 14.54 | 14.54 | 14.54 | 14.61 | 14.58 | 14.54 | 14.54 | 14.45 | 13.86 | 13.50 | 12.83 | 12.83 |
| **Prices** | | | | | | *Index Numbers (2010=100): Period Averages* | | | | | | | |
| Consumer Prices.............................. | 64 | 68.8 | 73.6 | 78.4 | 88.1 | 95.2 | † 98.0 | 100.0 | 105.0 | 107.5 | 109.5 | 110.5 | 109.4 |
| **Intl. Transactions & Positions** | | | | | | *Millions of Guyana Dollars* | | | | | | | |
| Exports............................................ | 70 | 117,705.8 | 110,535.9 | 117,709.9 | 137,418.7 | 161,819.3 | 155,510.6 | 179,122.1 | 227,777.9 | 289,278.4 | . . . . | . . . . | . . . . |
| Imports, c.i.f..................................... | 71 | 129,267.9 | 157,564.4 | 178,065.0 | 214,468.9 | 267,224.9 | 236,700.0 | 284,494.3 | 359,765.4 | 408,064.6 | . . . . | . . . . | . . . . |
| | | | | | | | *2010=100* | | | | | | |
| Volume of Exports......................... | 72 | 108 | 97 | 98 | 127 | 110 | 99 | 100 | 116 | 129 | . . . . | . . . . | . . . . |

| | | 2004 | 2005 | 2006 | 2007 | 2008 | 2009 | 2010 | 2011 | 2012 | 2013 | 2014 | 2015 |
|---|---|---|---|---|---|---|---|---|---|---|---|---|---|
| **Balance of Payments** | | | | | | *Millions of US Dollars* | | | | | | | |
| A. Current Account* | 109bx | −19.9 | −96.3 | −180.6 | −165.7 | −321.4 | −230.6 | −246.4 | −372.3 | −366.7 | −456.0 | −385.2 | −144.2 |
| Goods, credit (exports) | 1a9cx | 584.0 | 545.6 | 579.6 | 674.9 | 801.5 | 768.2 | 885.0 | 1,129.1 | 1,415.5 | 1,375.1 | 1,167.2 | 1,170.0 |
| Goods, debit (imports) | 1a9dx | 591.8 | 717.1 | 809.8 | 982.9 | 1,323.6 | 1,179.4 | 1,419.1 | 1,770.5 | 1,996.7 | 1,874.9 | 1,791.3 | 1,474.9 |
| Balance on goods | 1a9bx | −7.8 | −171.4 | −230.2 | −308.0 | −522.1 | −411.2 | −534.1 | −641.4 | −581.3 | −499.8 | −624.1 | −304.9 |
| Services, credit (exports) | 1b9cx | 160.9 | 147.9 | 147.6 | 172.9 | 211.9 | 170.3 | 248.1 | 297.6 | 297.8 | 164.7 | 180.8 | 142.9 |
| Services, debit (imports) | 1b9dx | 207.6 | 200.9 | 245.4 | 272.5 | 325.2 | 272.4 | 343.8 | 433.8 | 526.3 | 502.7 | 426.2 | 423.4 |
| Balance on Goods & Services | 1z9bx | −54.5 | −224.5 | −327.9 | −407.6 | −635.4 | −513.3 | −629.9 | −777.6 | −809.9 | −837.8 | −869.5 | −585.4 |
| Primary income: credit | 1c9cx | 4.0 | 3.3 | 2.8 | 2.9 | 41.3 | 39.8 | 64.0 | 51.9 | 50.8 | 53.7 | 55.0 | 57.2 |
| Primary income: debit | 1c9dx | 43.4 | 42.3 | 71.8 | 47.7 | 56.1 | 56.7 | 51.2 | 61.2 | 26.9 | 25.2 | 28.4 | 32.5 |
| Balance on gds, serv. & prim. inc. | 1y9bx | −93.9 | −263.5 | −396.9 | −452.5 | −650.2 | −530.2 | −617.1 | −786.9 | −785.9 | −809.3 | −842.8 | −560.7 |
| Secondary income: credit | 1d9ca | 193.9 | 261.9 | 310.9 | 423.8 | 470.0 | 471.7 | 555.5 | 623.0 | 790.1 | 623.6 | 672.8 | 610.9 |
| Secondary income: debit | 1d9da | 119.9 | 94.6 | 94.6 | 137.0 | 141.1 | 172.1 | 184.8 | 208.4 | 370.9 | 270.3 | 215.2 | 194.3 |
| B. Capital Account* | 209ba | 45.9 | 52.1 | 350.5 | 426.6 | 38.7 | 37.2 | 27.1 | 30.1 | 29.3 | 7.3 | 4.4 | 18.5 |
| Capital account: credit | 209ca | 45.9 | 52.1 | 350.5 | 426.6 | 38.7 | 37.2 | 27.1 | 30.1 | 29.3 | 7.3 | 4.4 | 18.5 |
| Capital account: debit | 209da | — | — | — | — | — | — | — | — | — | — | — | — |
| Balance on current & capital acct. | 129ba | 26.0 | −44.2 | 169.9 | 260.9 | −282.7 | −193.4 | −219.3 | −342.2 | −337.3 | −448.8 | −380.8 | −125.8 |
| C. Financial Account* | 309na | −38.5 | −126.7 | 52.4 | 226.6 | −296.7 | −166.2 | −159.8 | −319.8 | −362.1 | −289.7 | −382.4 | 38.6 |
| Direct investment: assets | 3a9aa | .... | .... | .... | .... | .... | .... | .... | .... | .... | .... | .... | .... |
| Equity & investment fund shares | 3aaaa | .... | .... | .... | .... | .... | .... | .... | .... | .... | .... | .... | .... |
| Debt instruments | 3abaa | .... | .... | .... | .... | .... | .... | .... | .... | .... | .... | .... | .... |
| Direct investment: liabilities | 3a9la | 30.0 | 76.8 | 102.4 | 152.4 | 178.0 | 164.0 | 198.0 | 246.8 | 277.9 | 200.6 | 237.8 | 117.0 |
| Equity & investment fund shares | 3aala | 7.0 | 17.9 | 23.8 | 25.4 | 34.4 | 31.1 | 39.5 | 45.5 | 42.1 | 28.5 | 32.5 | 19.1 |
| Debt instruments | 3abla | 23.0 | 58.9 | 78.6 | 127.0 | 143.6 | 132.9 | 158.5 | 201.3 | 235.9 | 172.1 | 205.2 | 97.9 |
| Portfolio investment: assets | 3b9aa | 16.2 | 34.1 | 5.5 | 95.3 | −2.7 | −19.9 | −2.9 | 32.3 | 65.0 | 18.9 | −57.8 | 22.7 |
| Equity & investment fund shares | 3baaa | .... | .... | .... | .... | .... | .... | .... | .... | .... | .... | .... | .... |
| Debt securities | 3bbaa | 16.2 | 34.1 | 5.5 | 95.3 | −2.7 | −19.9 | −2.9 | 32.3 | 65.0 | 18.9 | −57.8 | 22.7 |
| Portfolio investment: liabilities | 3b9la | 10.6 | 17.3 | 1.4 | .2 | 18.5 | 11.0 | 24.7 | −16.0 | −18.7 | 21.8 | 58.7 | −34.9 |
| Equity & investment fund shares | 3bala | .... | .... | .... | .... | .... | .... | .... | .... | .... | .... | .... | .... |
| Debt securities | 3bbla | 10.6 | 17.3 | 1.4 | .2 | 18.5 | 11.0 | 24.7 | −16.0 | −18.7 | 21.8 | 58.7 | −34.9 |
| Fin. der.& empl.stk.ops.(ESOs): net. | 3c9na | — | — | — | — | — | — | — | — | — | — | — | — |
| Fin. der. & ESOs.: assets | 3c9aa | .... | .... | .... | .... | .... | .... | .... | .... | .... | .... | .... | .... |
| Fin. der. & ESOs.: liabilities | 3c9la | .... | .... | .... | .... | .... | .... | .... | .... | .... | .... | .... | .... |
| Other investment: assets | 3d9aa | .... | .... | .... | .... | — | — | — | — | — | — | — | — |
| Other equity | 3daaa | .... | .... | .... | .... | — | — | — | .... | .... | .... | .... | .... |
| Debt instruments | 3dzaa | .... | .... | .... | .... | — | — | — | .... | .... | .... | .... | .... |
| Other investment: liabilities | 3d9la | 14.1 | 66.7 | −150.7 | −283.9 | 97.6 | −28.7 | −65.8 | 121.2 | 168.0 | 86.3 | 28.1 | −98.0 |
| Other equity | 3dala | .... | .... | .... | .... | .... | .... | .... | .... | .... | .... | .... | .... |
| Debt instruments | 3dzla | 14.1 | 66.7 | −150.7 | −283.9 | 97.6 | −28.7 | −65.8 | 121.2 | 168.0 | 86.3 | 28.1 | −98.0 |
| Curr.+ cap.− finan. acct. balance | 4y9na | 64.5 | 82.5 | 117.5 | 34.3 | 14.1 | −27.2 | −59.5 | −22.4 | 24.8 | −159.0 | 1.6 | −164.4 |
| D. Net Errors and Omissions | 409na | −43.4 | −68.2 | −84.1 | −37.4 | −96.1 | −274.8 | −135.9 | −32.3 | −135.6 | 208.4 | 20.8 | 189.1 |
| E. Reserves and Related Items | 4z9na | 21.1 | 14.3 | 33.3 | −3.1 | −82.0 | −302.0 | −195.3 | −54.7 | −110.8 | 49.4 | 22.3 | 24.7 |
| Reserve assets | 3e9aa | 9.8 | 24.9 | 25.3 | 35.6 | −44.2 | −265.0 | −158.4 | −21.7 | −79.5 | 83.6 | 59.5 | 67.6 |
| Credit and loans from the IMF | 3dcla | −11.2 | 10.5 | −38.2 | — | — | — | −1.4 | −7.4 | −11.4 | −11.3 | −11.3 | −9.1 |
| Exceptional financing | 409la | .... | .... | 30.2 | 38.7 | 37.8 | 37.0 | 38.4 | 40.4 | 42.6 | 45.5 | 48.5 | 52.0 |
| *Excludes components in group E | | | | | | | | | | | | | |
| | | | | | | | | | | | | | |
| **National Accounts** | | | | | | *Millions of Guyana Dollars* | | | | | | | |
| Househ.Cons.Expend.,incl.NPISHs | 96f | 85,100 | 121,006 | 237,160 | 311,304 | 365,540 | 340,133 | 399,063 | 477,028 | 526,634 | .... | .... | .... |
| Government Consumption Expend | 91f | 37,732 | 44,374 | 44,284 | 53,381 | 60,438 | 66,811 | 69,533 | 81,206 | 76,872 | .... | .... | .... |
| Gross Domestic Product (GDP) | 99b | 156,358 | 165,028 | 183,087 | 217,552 | 236,059 | 255,823 | 460,072 | 525,672 | 582,657 | .... | .... | .... |
| Net Primary Income from Abroad | 98.n | 6,320 | 4,088 | 8,792 | 7,228 | 2,985 | 3,417 | −2,601 | 1,895 | −256 | .... | .... | .... |
| Gross National Income (GNI) | 99a | 124,085 | 133,545 | 145,208 | 163,962 | 187,743 | 198,841 | 403,523 | 458,213 | 511,090 | .... | .... | .... |
| GDP Volume 1988 Prices | 99b.p | 5,639 | .... | .... | .... | .... | .... | .... | .... | .... | .... | .... | .... |
| GDP Volume (2000=100) | 99bvp | 105.4 | .... | .... | .... | .... | .... | .... | .... | .... | .... | .... | .... |
| GDP Deflator (2000=100) | 99bip | 114.1 | .... | .... | .... | .... | .... | .... | .... | .... | .... | .... | .... |
| | | | | | | | | | | | | | |
| | | | | | | *Millions: Midyear Estimates* | | | | | | | |
| Population | 99z | .74 | .74 | .74 | .75 | .75 | .75 | .75 | .76 | .76 | .76 | .76 | .77 |

# Haiti 263

| | | 2004 | 2005 | 2006 | 2007 | 2008 | 2009 | 2010 | 2011 | 2012 | 2013 | 2014 | 2015 |
|---|---|---|---|---|---|---|---|---|---|---|---|---|---|
| **Exchange Rates** | | | | | | *Gourdes per SDR: End of Period* | | | | | | | |
| Market Rate | aa | 57.821 | 61.459 | 56.553 | 58.129 | 61.330 | 65.873 | 61.419 | 62.911 | 65.401 | 67.578 | 67.729 | 78.567 |
| | | | | | | *Gourdes per US Dollar: End of Period (ae) Period Average (rf)* | | | | | | | |
| Market Rate | ae | 37.232 | 43.000 | 37.591 | 36.784 | 39.818 | 42.019 | 39.882 | 40.977 | 42.553 | 43.882 | 46.748 | 56.697 |
| Market Rate | rf | 38.352 | 40.449 | 40.409 | 36.861 | 39.108 | 41.198 | 39.797 | 40.523 | 41.950 | 43.463 | 45.216 | 50.706 |
| **Fund Position** | | | | | | *Millions of SDRs: End of Period* | | | | | | | |
| Quota | 2f.s | 81.90 | 81.90 | 81.90 | 81.90 | 81.90 | 81.90 | 81.90 | 81.90 | 81.90 | 81.90 | 81.90 | 81.90 |
| SDR Holdings | 1b.s | .12 | 8.61 | 5.19 | 4.74 | 4.56 | 68.92 | 68.88 | 68.84 | 68.83 | 68.82 | 68.81 | 68.80 |
| Reserve Position in the Fund | 1c.s | .07 | .07 | .07 | .07 | .07 | .07 | .07 | .07 | .07 | .07 | .07 | .07 |
| Total Fund Cred.&Loans Outstg. | 2tl | 6.07 | 23.51 | 28.10 | 35.70 | 67.28 | 105.00 | 8.19 | 16.38 | 31.12 | 37.67 | 40.95 | 47.97 |
| SDR Allocations | 1bd | 13.70 | 13.70 | 13.70 | 13.70 | 13.70 | 78.51 | 78.51 | 78.51 | 78.51 | 78.51 | 78.51 | 78.51 |
| **International Liquidity** | | | | | | *Millions of US Dollars Unless Otherwise Indicated: End of Period* | | | | | | | |
| Total Reserves minus Gold | 1l.d | 188.5 | 218.4 | 367.0 | 580.9 | 704.2 | 1,051.9 | 1,891.3 | 1,880.1 | 2,163.5 | 2,447.9 | 1,964.7 | 1,915.9 |
| SDR Holdings | 1b.d | .2 | 12.3 | 7.8 | 7.5 | 7.0 | 108.0 | 106.1 | 105.7 | 105.8 | 106.0 | 99.7 | 95.3 |
| Reserve Position in the Fund | 1c.d | .1 | .1 | .1 | .1 | .1 | .1 | .1 | .1 | .1 | .1 | .1 | .1 |
| Foreign Exchange | 1d.d | 188.2 | 206.0 | 359.1 | 573.3 | 697.1 | 943.8 | 1,785.1 | 1,774.3 | 2,057.6 | 2,341.9 | 1,864.9 | 1,820.5 |
| Gold (Million Fine Troy Ounces) | 1ad | .001 | .001 | .001 | .001 | .001 | .001 | .001 | .001 | .001 | .058 | .058 | .058 |
| Central Bank: Other Assets | 3..d | 50.8 | 52.6 | † 50.0 | 49.9 | 52.7 | 52.3 | 54.5 | 254.4 | 158.8 | 60.2 | 61.0 | 65.8 |
| Central Bank: Other Liabs. | 4..d | 65.9 | 97.7 | † 84.3 | 96.4 | 81.7 | 87.1 | 89.0 | 88.6 | 92.2 | 487.6 | 92.8 | 128.8 |
| Other Depository Corps.: Assets | 7a.d | 120.9 | 116.0 | † 116.5 | 236.4 | 287.9 | 442.5 | 499.5 | 469.3 | 431.1 | 352.0 | 344.8 | 475.6 |
| Other Depository Corps.: Liabs. | 7b.d | 33.0 | 27.1 | † 36.1 | 31.8 | 40.9 | 57.2 | 60.0 | 72.3 | 103.6 | 112.5 | 142.0 | 140.4 |
| **Central Bank** | | | | | | *Millions of Gourdes: End of Period* | | | | | | | |
| Net Foreign Assets | 11n | 7,122.6 | 6,653.6 | † 11,680.2 | 18,340.0 | 23,703.2 | 28,286.2 | 64,959.2 | 75,750.5 | 85,709.5 | 73,703.8 | 74,768.2 | 86,261.6 |
| Claims on Nonresidents | 11 | 10,720.0 | 13,139.9 | † 17,211.3 | 24,758.7 | 31,921.2 | 44,034.9 | 73,835.3 | 85,352.0 | 96,804.6 | 102,950.0 | 87,195.1 | 103,502.9 |
| Liabilities to Nonresidents | 16c | 3,597.3 | 6,486.3 | † 5,531.1 | 6,418.7 | 8,218.0 | 15,748.7 | 8,876.1 | 9,601.5 | 11,095.1 | 29,246.2 | 12,426.9 | 17,241.3 |
| Claims on Other Depository Corps. | 12e | 49.2 | 205.7 | † 2,076.1 | 529.1 | 458.4 | 895.1 | 465.7 | 640.9 | 5,447.4 | 1,519.7 | 1,472.7 | 4,298.2 |
| Net Claims on Central Government | 12an | 20,808.1 | 22,527.5 | † 22,486.2 | 20,585.0 | 22,217.5 | 24,293.3 | 15,275.2 | 9,287.8 | 11,720.9 | 16,803.5 | 22,447.3 | 32,637.8 |
| Claims on Central Government | 12a | 24,618.8 | 25,812.0 | † 31,974.2 | 37,384.9 | 42,812.7 | 49,714.4 | 58,473.8 | 55,957.4 | 61,815.2 | 48,732.1 | 51,646.0 | 58,089.5 |
| Liabilities to Central Government | 16d | 3,810.7 | 3,284.5 | † 9,488.0 | 16,800.0 | 20,595.3 | 25,421.1 | 43,198.6 | 46,669.5 | 50,094.3 | 31,928.7 | 29,198.6 | 25,451.7 |
| Claims on Other Sectors | 12s | 3,120.2 | 3,228.6 | † 3,660.4 | 4,322.4 | 4,769.4 | 4,723.2 | 4,625.3 | 4,642.5 | 4,988.2 | 5,220.0 | 5,761.8 | 6,018.8 |
| Claims on Other Financial Corps. | 12g | — | — | † 42.6 | 65.6 | 121.3 | 144.8 | 261.8 | 159.8 | 151.9 | 153.1 | 162.3 | 189.5 |
| Claims on State & Local Govts. | 12b | — | — | † — | | | | | | | | | |
| Claims on Public Nonfin. Corps. | 12c | 2,116.8 | 2,108.6 | † 2,044.3 | 2,404.9 | 2,531.6 | 2,454.6 | 1,945.0 | 1,945.0 | 1,945.0 | 1,945.0 | 1,945.0 | 1,945.0 |
| Claims on Private Sector | 12d | 1,003.4 | 1,120.0 | † 1,573.5 | 1,851.9 | 2,116.4 | 2,123.9 | 2,418.5 | 2,537.7 | 2,891.2 | 3,121.9 | 3,654.6 | 3,884.4 |
| Monetary Base | 14 | 31,850.3 | 35,377.4 | † 39,000.1 | 42,551.4 | 50,143.7 | 55,958.5 | 80,519.8 | 82,815.9 | 90,293.2 | 86,774.4 | 97,856.8 | 122,710.4 |
| Currency in Circulation | 14a | 11,839.0 | 14,205.5 | † 14,271.6 | 15,082.7 | 17,927.4 | 18,358.1 | 23,749.1 | 24,503.6 | 26,766.4 | 28,951.6 | 32,489.5 | 39,077.2 |
| Liabs. to Other Depository Corps. | 14c | 19,032.8 | 20,119.3 | † 24,228.1 | 26,923.4 | 31,600.2 | 36,534.9 | 55,109.1 | 56,072.3 | 61,579.6 | 55,379.5 | 64,207.2 | 82,682.6 |
| Liabilities to Other Sectors | 14d | 978.4 | 1,052.6 | † 500.3 | 545.4 | 616.0 | 1,065.5 | 1,661.6 | 2,239.9 | 1,947.3 | 2,443.4 | 1,160.1 | 950.6 |
| Other Liabs. to Other Dep. Corps. | 14n | — | — | † 634.1 | 630.0 | — | .3 | 19.5 | 11.7 | 19.6 | 376.5 | 40.1 | 115.9 |
| Dep. & Sec. Excl. f/Monetary Base | 14o | — | — | † 1,171.4 | 2,040.6 | 2,384.7 | 3,178.9 | 4,894.8 | 7,572.6 | 9,093.3 | 8,768.1 | 3,355.2 | 1,648.2 |
| Deposits Included in Broad Money. | 15 | — | — | † — | — | — | — | — | — | — | — | — | — |
| Sec.Ot.th.Shares Incl.in Brd. Money | 16a | — | — | † — | — | — | — | — | — | — | — | — | — |
| Deposits Excl. from Broad Money | 16b | — | — | † 1,171.4 | 2,040.6 | 2,384.7 | 3,178.9 | 4,894.8 | 7,572.6 | 9,093.3 | 8,768.1 | 3,355.2 | 1,648.2 |
| Sec.Ot.th.Shares Excl.f/Brd.Money | 16s | — | — | † — | — | — | — | — | — | — | — | — | — |
| Loans | 16l | — | — | † — | — | — | — | — | — | — | — | — | — |
| Financial Derivatives | 16m | — | — | † — | — | — | — | — | — | — | — | — | — |
| Shares and Other Equity | 17a | 1,530.9 | 983.6 | † 823.8 | 509.4 | 812.2 | 1,008.8 | 507.2 | 1,654.3 | 5,630.6 | 2,325.8 | 5,196.4 | 7,332.7 |
| Other Items (Net) | 17r | −2,281.1 | −3,745.7 | † −1,726.5 | −1,955.0 | −2,192.2 | −1,948.5 | −616.0 | −1,732.7 | 2,829.2 | −997.9 | −1,998.5 | −2,590.9 |
| Memo Item: | | | | | | | | | | | | | |
| Total Assets | 10ra | 41,158.7 | 45,355.5 | † 62,166.6 | 74,550.3 | 88,313.8 | 108,545.8 | 146,247.4 | 155,494.5 | 178,584.5 | 168,327.7 | 158,182.1 | 185,794.9 |
| **Other Depository Corporations** | | | | | | *Millions of Gourdes: End of Period* | | | | | | | |
| Net Foreign Assets | 21n | 3,272.1 | 3,820.3 | † 3,020.4 | 7,525.8 | 9,836.5 | 16,193.0 | 17,529.5 | 16,263.8 | 13,940.1 | 10,509.8 | 9,479.8 | 19,008.9 |
| Claims on Nonresidents | 21 | 4,502.4 | 4,986.2 | † 4,378.3 | 8,695.2 | 11,465.1 | 18,595.1 | 19,921.5 | 19,226.9 | 18,346.5 | 15,445.4 | 16,119.3 | 26,967.5 |
| Liabilities to Nonresidents | 26c | 1,230.4 | 1,165.9 | † 1,357.9 | 1,169.4 | 1,628.6 | 2,402.0 | 2,392.0 | 2,963.1 | 4,406.4 | 4,935.6 | 6,639.6 | 7,958.6 |
| Claims on Central Bank | 20 | 20,684.4 | 21,558.8 | † 26,057.9 | 28,158.2 | 34,178.5 | 38,498.0 | 58,011.6 | 58,799.0 | 60,204.8 | 58,993.6 | 64,269.7 | 80,166.9 |
| Currency | 20a | 1,620.7 | 1,987.1 | † 1,900.4 | 1,448.8 | 2,622.6 | 2,503.4 | 3,401.3 | 2,802.2 | 3,503.2 | 3,896.2 | 4,091.3 | 4,627.0 |
| Reserve Deposits and Securities | 20b | 15,519.7 | 13,516.6 | † 16,129.2 | 17,825.1 | 21,765.0 | 29,092.7 | 45,511.3 | 51,137.8 | 50,806.1 | 48,238.4 | 53,565.4 | 69,324.9 |
| Other Claims | 20n | 3,544.0 | 6,055.0 | † 8,028.3 | 8,884.3 | 9,791.0 | 6,902.0 | 9,099.0 | 4,859.0 | 5,895.6 | 6,859.0 | 6,613.0 | 6,215.0 |
| Net Claims on Central Government | 22an | 4,251.8 | 6,664.6 | † 3,748.4 | 2,906.7 | −2,342.9 | −6,813.5 | −5,069.6 | −12,645.4 | −18,365.4 | −4,718.9 | −4,937.0 | 2,464.4 |
| Claims on Central Government | 22a | 4,574.1 | 7,594.6 | † 4,339.2 | 3,640.6 | 3,543.7 | 4,110.7 | 8,435.2 | 6,267.9 | 5,331.3 | 6,443.4 | 8,689.2 | 13,558.8 |
| Liabilities to Central Government | 26d | 322.3 | 930.0 | † 590.8 | 733.9 | 5,886.6 | 10,924.2 | 13,504.8 | 18,913.3 | 23,696.7 | 11,162.3 | 13,626.2 | 11,094.4 |
| Claims on Other Sectors | 22s | 20,597.1 | 25,191.5 | † 27,336.5 | 29,493.9 | 36,188.3 | 42,074.9 | 41,935.3 | 53,582.7 | 70,625.1 | 78,257.5 | 90,087.8 | 95,204.4 |
| Claims on Other Financial Corps. | 22g | 1,595.6 | 2,022.1 | † 2,054.8 | 3,480.6 | 3,604.9 | 5,421.8 | 7,073.6 | 11,424.5 | 11,723.8 | 12,141.4 | 16,498.4 | 18,499.8 |
| Claims on State & Local Govts. | 22b | — | — | † — | — | — | — | — | — | — | — | — | — |
| Claims on Public Nonfin. Corps. | 22c | — | — | † — | — | — | — | — | — | — | — | — | — |
| Claims on Private Sector | 22d | 19,001.4 | 23,169.4 | † 25,281.8 | 26,013.3 | 32,583.4 | 36,653.0 | 34,861.7 | 42,158.2 | 58,901.3 | 66,116.1 | 73,589.4 | 76,704.6 |
| Liabilities to Central Bank | 26g | 3.0 | 3.0 | † 3.0 | 278.0 | 278.0 | 342.0 | 3.0 | 3.0 | 29.9 | 369.6 | 210.1 | 1,980.3 |
| Transf.Dep.Included in Broad Money | 24 | 14,097.8 | 18,245.9 | † 19,213.6 | 21,282.4 | 24,921.9 | 32,668.9 | 48,448.2 | 51,104.8 | 56,148.2 | 60,992.1 | 64,905.7 | 76,014.4 |
| Other Dep.Included in Broad Money. | 25 | 35,175.3 | 39,728.0 | † 40,900.1 | 45,892.8 | 50,961.8 | 54,693.5 | 61,059.4 | 65,470.6 | 69,226.7 | 73,488.0 | 80,050.9 | 104,598.8 |
| Sec.Ot.th.Shares Incl.in Brd. Money | 26a | — | — | † — | — | — | — | — | — | — | — | — | — |
| Deposits Excl. from Broad Money | 26b | 18.1 | 19.5 | † 904.2 | 129.0 | 151.7 | 177.5 | 217.0 | 207.0 | 177.6 | 348.1 | 1,080.5 | 1,309.2 |
| Sec.Ot.th.Shares Excl.f/Brd.Money | 26s | — | — | † — | — | — | — | — | — | — | — | — | — |
| Loans | 26l | — | — | † — | 496.6 | 634.0 | 394.4 | 833.6 | 360.9 | 844.8 | 881.7 | 1,273.4 | 625.2 |
| Financial Derivatives | 26m | — | — | † — | — | — | — | — | — | — | — | — | — |
| Insurance Technical Reserves | 26r | — | — | † — | — | — | — | — | — | — | — | — | — |
| Shares and Other Equity | 27a | 3,112.9 | 3,761.6 | † 6,833.0 | 7,058.5 | 7,741.9 | 9,020.8 | 10,449.1 | 11,227.2 | 13,210.3 | 15,824.9 | 17,504.4 | 21,284.5 |
| Other Items (Net) | 27r | −3,601.7 | −4,522.9 | † −7,690.6 | −7,052.7 | −6,828.8 | −7,344.7 | −8,603.4 | −12,373.5 | −13,232.9 | −8,862.4 | −6,124.8 | −8,967.9 |
| Memo Item: | | | | | | | | | | | | | |
| Total Assets | 20ra | 57,369.0 | 68,582.0 | † 75,593.4 | 85,344.6 | 101,504.7 | 119,780.3 | 145,661.9 | 160,236.1 | 183,028.1 | 181,322.5 | 201,376.2 | 240,343.3 |

| | | 2004 | 2005 | 2006 | 2007 | 2008 | 2009 | 2010 | 2011 | 2012 | 2013 | 2014 | 2015 |
|---|---|---|---|---|---|---|---|---|---|---|---|---|---|
| **Depository Corporations** | | | | | *Millions of Gourdes: End of Period* | | | | | | | | |
| Net Foreign Assets | 31n | 10,394.7 | 10,473.9 † 14,700.7 | 25,865.8 | 33,539.6 | 44,479.2 | 82,488.7 | 92,014.2 | 99,649.6 | 84,213.6 | 84,247.9 | 105,270.5 |
| Claims on Nonresidents | 31 | 15,222.4 | 18,126.1 † 21,589.7 | 33,453.9 | 43,386.3 | 62,630.0 | 93,756.8 | 104,578.8 | 115,151.1 | 118,395.3 | 103,314.4 | 130,470.3 |
| Liabilities to Nonresidents | 36c | 4,827.7 | 7,652.2 † 6,889.0 | 7,588.1 | 9,846.6 | 18,150.7 | 11,268.1 | 12,564.6 | 15,501.6 | 34,181.8 | 19,066.5 | 25,199.9 |
| Domestic Claims | 32 | 48,777.2 | 57,612.2 † 57,231.4 | 57,308.0 | 60,832.2 | 64,277.9 | 56,766.2 | 54,867.6 | 68,968.7 | 95,562.1 | 113,359.9 | 136,325.3 |
| Net Claims on Central Government | 32an | 25,059.9 | 29,192.1 † 26,234.5 | 23,491.7 | 19,874.6 | 17,479.8 | 10,205.6 | −3,357.6 | −6,644.5 | 12,084.5 | 17,510.3 | 35,102.2 |
| Claims on Central Government | 32a | 29,192.9 | 33,406.6 † 36,313.4 | 41,025.5 | 46,356.4 | 53,825.1 | 66,908.9 | 62,225.3 | 67,146.4 | 55,175.5 | 60,335.1 | 71,648.3 |
| Liabilities to Central Government | 36d | 4,133.0 | 4,214.5 † 10,078.8 | 17,533.9 | 26,481.9 | 36,345.2 | 56,703.4 | 65,582.9 | 73,791.0 | 43,091.0 | 42,824.8 | 36,546.2 |
| Claims on Other Sectors | 32s | 23,717.3 | 28,420.1 † 30,996.9 | 33,816.3 | 40,957.6 | 46,798.1 | 46,560.6 | 58,225.2 | 75,613.2 | 83,477.6 | 95,849.6 | 101,223.2 |
| Claims on Other Financial Corps.. | 32g | 1,595.6 | 2,022.1 † 2,097.3 | 3,546.1 | 3,726.2 | 5,566.6 | 7,335.4 | 11,584.3 | 11,875.7 | 12,294.6 | 16,660.7 | 18,689.2 |
| Claims on State & Local Govts..... | 32b | — | — † — | | | | | | | | | |
| Claims on Public Nonfin. Corps.... | 32c | 2,116.8 | 2,108.6 † 2,044.3 | 2,404.9 | 2,531.6 | 2,454.6 | 1,945.0 | 1,945.0 | 1,945.0 | 1,945.0 | 1,945.0 | 1,945.0 |
| Claims on Private Sector | 32d | 20,004.8 | 24,289.4 † 26,855.2 | 27,865.2 | 34,699.8 | 38,776.9 | 37,280.2 | 44,695.9 | 61,792.5 | 69,238.0 | 77,243.9 | 80,589.0 |
| Broad Money Liabilities | 35l | 60,469.8 | 71,244.9 † 72,985.2 | 81,354.5 | 91,804.5 | 104,282.6 | 131,517.0 | 140,516.8 | 150,585.4 | 161,978.9 | 174,514.9 | 216,014.0 |
| Currency Outside Depository Corps | 34a | 10,218.3 | 12,218.3 † 12,371.2 | 13,633.9 | 15,304.8 | 15,854.7 | 20,347.8 | 21,701.5 | 23,263.3 | 25,055.4 | 28,398.2 | 34,450.2 |
| Transferable Deposits | 34 | 15,072.0 | 19,272.0 † 19,412.7 | 21,411.8 | 25,122.3 | 32,878.3 | 48,772.2 | 51,455.3 | 56,447.1 | 61,314.3 | 65,219.0 | 76,392.5 |
| Other Deposits | 35 | 35,179.6 | 39,754.6 † 41,201.3 | 46,308.8 | 51,377.4 | 55,549.6 | 62,397.0 | 67,360.0 | 70,875.0 | 75,609.1 | 80,897.7 | 105,171.4 |
| Securities Other than Shares | 36a | — | — | † — | | | | | | | | | |
| Deposits Excl. from Broad Money..... | 36b | 18.1 | 19.5 † 2,075.5 | 2,169.6 | 2,536.4 | 3,356.4 | 5,111.8 | 7,779.7 | 9,271.0 | 9,116.2 | 4,435.7 | 2,957.4 |
| Sec.Ot.th.Shares Excl.f/Brd.Money.... | 36s | — | — | † — | | | | | | | | | |
| Loans | 36l | — | — | † — | 496.6 | 634.0 | 394.4 | 833.6 | 360.9 | 844.8 | 881.7 | 1,273.4 | 625.2 |
| Financial Derivatives | 36m | — | — | † — | — | — | — | — | — | — | — | — | — |
| Insurance Technical Reserves | 36r | — | — | † — | | | | | | | | | |
| Shares and Other Equity | 37a | 4,643.8 | 4,745.3 † 7,656.8 | 7,568.0 | 8,554.1 | 10,029.6 | 10,956.4 | 12,881.5 | 18,840.9 | 18,150.7 | 22,700.8 | 28,617.3 |
| Other Items (Net) | 37r | −5,959.8 | −7,923.5 † −10,785.4 | −8,414.9 | −9,157.1 | −9,305.8 | −9,163.9 | −14,657.1 | −10,923.8 | −10,351.8 | −5,317.0 | −6,618.0 |
| Broad Money Liabs., Seasonally Adj. | 35l.b | 60,014.5 | 70,653.4 † 72,318.6 | 80,623.0 | 90,997.3 | 103,406.9 | 130,455.4 | 139,426.9 | 149,407.0 | 160,751.5 | 173,188.0 | 214,382.0 |
| **Monetary Aggregates** | | | | | *Millions of Gourdes: End of Period* | | | | | | | | |
| Broad Money | 59m | .... | .... | 72,985.2 | 81,354.5 | 91,804.5 | 104,282.6 | 131,517.0 | 140,516.8 | 150,585.4 | 161,978.9 | 174,514.9 | 216,014.0 |
| o/w:Currency Issued by Cent.Govt | 59m.a | .... | .... | — | — | — | — | — | — | — | — | — | — |
| o/w: Dep.in Nonfin. Corporations. | 59m.b | .... | .... | — | — | — | — | — | — | — | — | — | — |
| o/w:Secs. Issued by Central Govt.. | 59m.c | .... | .... | — | — | — | — | — | — | — | — | — | — |
| Money (National Definitions) | | | | | | | | | | | | | |
| Monetary Base | 19ma | 31,865.8 | 35,372.5 | 39,000.1 | 42,551.4 | 50,143.7 | 55,958.5 | 80,519.8 | 82,815.9 | 90,293.2 | 86,774.4 | 97,856.8 | 122,710.4 |
| M1 | 59ma | 17,361.2 | 20,488.4 | 20,424.7 | 23,682.2 | 27,331.5 | 29,575.3 | 39,300.7 | 41,089.2 | 47,095.8 | 49,662.3 | 57,743.8 | 60,860.9 |
| M2 | 59mb | 36,445.6 | 40,489.3 | 40,885.8 | 46,128.6 | 51,968.4 | 55,319.2 | 69,108.7 | 72,129.4 | 78,357.6 | 83,940.1 | 91,739.3 | 101,609.5 |
| M3 | 59mc | 59,702.6 | 70,754.7 | 72,985.2 | 81,354.5 | 91,804.5 | 104,282.6 | 131,517.0 | 140,516.8 | 150,585.4 | 161,978.9 | 174,514.9 | 215,990.3 |
| **Interest Rates** | | | | | *Percent per Annum* | | | | | | | | |
| Central Bank Bill Rate | 60ag | 7.60 | † 18.90 | 16.90 | 4.00 | 8.00 | 4.00 | 1.20 | 1.00 | 3.00 | 3.00 | 8.20 | 16.70 |
| Savings Rate | 60k | .46 | † 1.10 | .77 | .56 | .42 | .19 | .16 | .34 | .14 | .10 | .20 | .08 |
| Savings Rate (Fgn. Currency) | 60k.f | .11 | † .65 | .68 | .53 | .40 | .18 | .10 | .08 | .06 | .06 | .06 | .06 |
| Deposit Rate | 60l | 18.54 | † 4.62 | 7.81 | 5.92 | 2.15 | 1.13 | .74 | .28 | .45 | .68 | 2.61 | 4.29 |
| Deposit Rate (Fgn. Currency) | 60l.f | .10 | † 3.30 | 3.41 | 3.35 | 1.63 | .58 | .35 | .16 | .26 | .20 | .90 | 2.35 |
| Lending Rate | 60p | 48.00 | † 22.25 | 26.37 | 23.08 | 17.81 | 17.33 | 17.48 | 11.61 | 8.93 | 8.72 | 10.77 | 12.92 |
| Lending Rate (Fgn. Currency) | 60p.f | 20.00 | † 11.47 | 12.10 | 11.95 | 10.94 | 11.12 | 10.82 | 8.23 | 7.37 | 7.03 | 8.25 | 10.56 |
| **Prices** | | | | | *Index Numbers (2010=100): Period Averages* | | | | | | | | |
| Consumer Prices | 64 | † 57.7 | 66.8 | 75.5 | 81.9 | 94.6 | 94.6 | 100.0 | 108.4 | 115.2 | 122.0 | 127.5 | 139.0 |
| **Intl. Transactions & Positions** | | | | | *Millions of Gourdes* | | | | | | | | |
| Exports | 70 | 15,006.8 | 19,016.9 | 19,226.0 | 19,232.4 | 18,625.8 | 23,741.4 | 23,045.1 | 31,076.5 | 34,196.6 | 38,485.0 | 43,002.2 | .... |
| Imports, c.i.f | 71 | 50,087.8 | 58,801.7 | 75,779.1 | 61,982.8 | 90,552.8 | 87,497.5 | 125,206.6 | 122,360.7 | 132,961.3 | 147,903.0 | 168,790.4 | .... |

| | | 2004 | 2005 | 2006 | 2007 | 2008 | 2009 | 2010 | 2011 | 2012 | 2013 | 2014 | 2015 |
|---|---|---|---|---|---|---|---|---|---|---|---|---|---|
| **Balance of Payments** | | | | | | | *Millions of US Dollars* | | | | | | |
| A. Current Account* | 109bx | −168.3 | −356.4 | −458.5 | −477.4 | −678.4 | −516.7 | −1,941.8 | −1,769.6 | −1,418.7 | −1,287.2 | −1,364.8 | −723.0 |
| Goods, credit (exports) | 1a9cx | 376.9 | 459.6 | 495.2 | 522.1 | 490.2 | 551.0 | 563.4 | 768.1 | 778.8 | 914.9 | 960.9 | 1,029.0 |
| Goods, debit (imports) | 1a9dx | 1,210.0 | 1,308.5 | 1,548.2 | 1,704.2 | 2,107.7 | 2,032.1 | 3,010.1 | 3,314.5 | 3,079.3 | 3,329.2 | 3,666.2 | 3,445.3 |
| Balance on goods | 1a9bx | −833.1 | −848.9 | −1,053.0 | −1,182.1 | −1,617.5 | −1,481.1 | −2,446.7 | −2,546.4 | −2,300.5 | −2,414.3 | −2,705.2 | −2,416.4 |
| Services, credit (exports) | 1b9cx | 135.7 | 145.5 | 193.9 | 257.1 | 427.0 | 483.0 | 453.0 | 543.6 | 549.0 | 652.0 | 701.2 | 723.5 |
| Services, debit (imports) | 1b9dx | 351.6 | 544.4 | 593.4 | 680.3 | 746.0 | 772.1 | 1,277.3 | 1,119.0 | 1,116.0 | 1,090.2 | 1,096.4 | 986.4 |
| Balance on Goods & Services | 1z9bx | −1,049.0 | −1,247.8 | −1,452.5 | −1,605.3 | −1,936.6 | −1,770.2 | −3,270.9 | −3,121.7 | −2,867.5 | −2,852.5 | −3,100.4 | −2,679.2 |
| Primary income: credit | 1c9cx | — | — | 20.8 | 21.8 | 28.0 | 31.1 | 32.7 | 44.2 | 72.4 | 45.4 | 21.6 | 24.9 |
| Primary income: debit | 1c9dx | 12.3 | 35.0 | 14.2 | 19.6 | 22.5 | 18.3 | 10.4 | 3.2 | 4.0 | 13.3 | 14.4 | 17.0 |
| Balance on gds, serv. & prim. inc. | 1y9bx | −1,061.3 | −1,282.8 | −1,445.8 | −1,603.1 | −1,931.0 | −1,757.4 | −3,248.7 | −3,080.8 | −2,799.1 | −2,820.5 | −3,093.2 | −2,671.3 |
| Secondary income: credit | 1d9ca | 931.5 | 986.2 | 1,062.9 | 1,222.1 | 1,369.8 | 1,375.5 | 1,473.8 | 1,551.4 | 1,612.3 | 1,781.0 | 1,977.0 | 2,195.6 |
| Secondary income: debit | 1d9da | 38.5 | 59.7 | 75.5 | 96.4 | 117.1 | 134.8 | 167.0 | 240.2 | 231.9 | 247.7 | 248.6 | 247.3 |
| B. Capital Account* | 209ba | — | — | — | — | — | — | 658.0 | 170.0 | 75.7 | 20.0 | 25.9 | 25.0 |
| Capital account: credit | 209ca | — | — | — | — | — | — | 658.0 | 170.0 | 75.7 | 20.0 | 25.9 | 25.0 |
| Capital account: debit | 209da | — | — | — | — | — | — | — | — | — | — | — | — |
| Balance on current & capital acct. | 129ba | −168.3 | −356.4 | −458.5 | −477.4 | −678.4 | −516.7 | −1,283.8 | −1,599.6 | −1,343.0 | −1,267.2 | −1,338.9 | −698.0 |
| C. Financial Account* | 309na | −39.6 | −15.0 | −140.3 | −142.8 | −308.9 | 473.1 | 752.3 | 140.4 | −605.7 | −1,495.0 | −226.4 | −150.6 |
| Direct investment: assets | 3a9aa | — | — | — | — | — | — | — | — | — | — | — | — |
| Equity & investment fund shares.. | 3aaaa | — | — | — | — | — | — | — | — | — | — | — | — |
| Debt instruments | 3abaa | — | — | — | — | — | — | — | — | — | — | — | — |
| Direct investment: liabilities | 3a9la | 5.9 | 26.0 | 160.6 | 74.5 | 29.8 | 55.5 | 178.0 | 119.0 | 156.0 | 160.4 | 99.0 | 109.4 |
| Equity & investment fund shares . | 3aala | 5.9 | 26.0 | 160.6 | 74.5 | 29.8 | 55.5 | 178.0 | 119.0 | 156.0 | 160.4 | 99.0 | 109.4 |
| Debt instruments | 3abla | — | — | — | — | — | — | — | — | — | — | — | — |
| Portfolio investment: assets | 3b9aa | — | — | — | — | — | — | — | — | — | — | — | — |
| Equity & investment fund shares | 3baaa | — | — | — | — | — | — | — | — | — | — | — | — |
| Debt securities | 3bbaa | — | — | — | — | — | — | — | — | — | — | — | — |
| Portfolio investment: liabilities | 3b9la | — | — | — | — | — | — | — | — | — | — | — | — |
| Equity & investment fund shares . | 3bala | — | — | — | — | — | — | — | — | — | — | — | — |
| Debt securities | 3bbla | — | — | — | — | — | — | — | — | — | — | — | — |
| Fin. der.& empl.stk.ops.(ESOs): net | 3c9na | — | — | — | — | — | — | — | — | — | — | — | — |
| Fin. der. & ESOs: assets | 3c9aa | — | — | — | — | — | — | — | — | — | — | — | — |
| Fin. der. & ESOs.: liabilities | 3c9la | — | — | — | — | — | — | — | — | — | — | — | — |
| Other investment: assets | 3d9aa | −5.7 | 51.6 | 55.1 | 5.1 | 89.9 | −56.5 | 334.7 | 55.6 | −93.4 | −182.6 | −6.2 | 31.2 |
| Other equity | 3daaa | .... | .... | .... | .... | .... | .... | .... | .... | .... | .... | .... | .... |
| Debt instruments | 3dzaa | −5.7 | 51.6 | 55.1 | 5.1 | 89.9 | −56.5 | 334.7 | 55.6 | −93.4 | −182.6 | −6.2 | 31.2 |
| Other investment: liabilities | 3d9la | 28.0 | 40.6 | 34.8 | 73.3 | 369.0 | −585.1 | −595.6 | −203.8 | 356.3 | 1,152.1 | 121.2 | 72.4 |
| Other equity | 3dala | .... | .... | .... | .... | .... | .... | .... | .... | .... | .... | .... | .... |
| Debt instruments | 3dzla | 28.0 | 40.6 | 34.8 | 73.3 | 369.0 | −585.1 | −595.6 | −203.8 | 356.3 | 1,152.1 | 121.2 | 72.4 |
| Curr.+ cap.– finan. acct. balance... | 4y9na | −128.7 | −341.4 | −318.2 | −334.6 | −369.4 | −989.8 | −2,036.2 | −1,740.1 | −737.3 | 227.8 | −1,112.5 | −547.5 |
| D. Net Errors and Omissions | 409na | 62.6 | 10.8 | 40.9 | 144.0 | −15.0 | −138.2 | 365.8 | −74.1 | 7.6 | −966.8 | 66.4 | −108.6 |
| E. Reserves and Related Items | 4z9na | −66.1 | −330.6 | −277.3 | −190.7 | −384.4 | −1,128.1 | −1,670.4 | −1,814.1 | −729.8 | −739.0 | −1,046.0 | −656.0 |
| Reserve assets | 3e9aa | 50.0 | 21.8 | 108.2 | 208.4 | 163.3 | 238.3 | 846.8 | 208.9 | 285.9 | 32.9 | −469.9 | −149.3 |
| Credit and loans from the IMF | 3dcla | −7.2 | 11.1 | 10.4 | 20.9 | 51.2 | 57.0 | −141.1 | 13.1 | 22.5 | 9.9 | 2.5 | 12.2 |
| Exceptional financing | 409la | 123.3 | 341.4 | 375.2 | 378.2 | 496.5 | 1,309.4 | 2,658.3 | 2,009.9 | 993.1 | 762.0 | 573.6 | 494.5 |
| *Excludes components in group E | | | | | | | | | | | | | |
| | | | | | | | | | | | | | |
| **International Investment Position** | | | | | | | *Millions of US Dollars* | | | | | | |
| Assets | 809aa | 536.9 | 662.2 | 1,036.1 | 1,246.7 | 1,647.1 | 1,814.2 | 2,994.3 | 3,286.8 | 3,524.3 | 3,332.8 | 2,855.7 | .... |
| Direct investment | 8a9aa | .... | .... | .... | .... | .... | .... | .... | .... | .... | .... | .... | .... |
| Equity & investment fund shares.. | 8aaaa | .... | .... | .... | .... | .... | .... | .... | .... | .... | .... | .... | .... |
| Debt instruments | 8abaa | .... | .... | .... | .... | .... | .... | .... | .... | .... | .... | .... | .... |
| Portfolio investment | 8b9aa | .... | .... | .... | .... | .... | .... | .... | .... | .... | .... | .... | .... |
| Equity & investment fund shares.. | 8baaa | .... | .... | .... | .... | .... | .... | .... | .... | .... | .... | .... | .... |
| Debt securities | 8bbaa | .... | .... | .... | .... | .... | .... | .... | .... | .... | .... | .... | .... |
| Fin. der.(oth.than reserves) & ESOs | 8c9aa | .... | .... | .... | .... | .... | .... | .... | .... | .... | .... | .... | .... |
| Other investment | 8d9aa | 280.8 | 371.4 | 651.5 | 651.0 | 888.6 | 867.0 | 1,201.7 | 1,286.8 | 1,238.2 | 1,013.6 | 1,000.5 | .... |
| Other equity | 8daaa | .... | .... | .... | .... | .... | .... | .... | .... | .... | .... | .... | .... |
| Debt instruments | 8dzaa | 280.8 | 371.4 | 651.5 | 651.0 | 888.6 | 867.0 | 1,201.7 | 1,286.8 | 1,238.2 | 1,013.6 | 1,000.5 | .... |
| Reserve assets | 8e9aa | 256.1 | 290.8 | 384.6 | 595.7 | 758.5 | 947.3 | 1,792.6 | 2,000.0 | 2,286.1 | 2,319.2 | 1,855.2 | .... |
| Liabilities | 809la | 1,690.2 | 1,743.3 | 1,987.6 | 2,217.1 | 2,718.1 | 2,295.4 | 1,867.9 | 1,785.2 | 2,356.8 | 3,602.0 | 3,531.8 | .... |
| Direct investment | 8a9la | 124.5 | 150.5 | 310.5 | 385.0 | 415.4 | 447.2 | 625.2 | 744.2 | 900.2 | 1,060.5 | 1,159.5 | .... |
| Equity & investment fund shares.. | 8aala | 124.5 | 150.5 | 310.5 | 385.0 | 415.4 | 447.2 | 625.2 | 744.2 | 900.2 | 1,060.5 | 1,159.5 | .... |
| Debt instruments | 8abla | .... | .... | .... | .... | .... | .... | .... | .... | .... | .... | .... | .... |
| Portfolio investment | 8b9la | .... | .... | .... | .... | .... | .... | .... | .... | .... | .... | .... | .... |
| Equity & investment fund shares.. | 8bala | .... | .... | .... | .... | .... | .... | .... | .... | .... | .... | .... | .... |
| Debt securities | 8bbla | .... | .... | .... | .... | .... | .... | .... | .... | .... | .... | .... | .... |
| Fin. der.(oth.than reserves) & ESOs | 8c9la | .... | .... | .... | .... | .... | .... | .... | .... | .... | .... | .... | .... |
| Other investment | 8d9la | 1,565.8 | 1,592.8 | 1,677.2 | 1,832.1 | 2,302.7 | 1,848.3 | 1,242.7 | 1,041.1 | 1,456.7 | 2,541.5 | 2,372.3 | .... |
| Other equity | 8dala | .... | .... | .... | .... | .... | .... | .... | .... | .... | .... | .... | .... |
| Debt instruments | 8dzla | 1,565.8 | 1,592.8 | 1,677.2 | 1,832.1 | 2,302.7 | 1,848.3 | 1,242.7 | 1,041.1 | 1,456.7 | 2,541.5 | 2,372.3 | .... |
| | | | | | | | | | | | | | |
| **National Accounts** | | | | | | *Millions of Gourdes: Fiscal Year Ends September 30* | | | | | | | |
| Househ.Cons.Expend.,incl.NPISHs.... | 96f | 142,230 | 170,525 | 199,482 | 209,590 | 257,145 | 266,197 | 331,020 | 344,247 | 350,070 | .... | .... | .... |
| Gross Fixed Capital Formation | 93e | 38,386 | 46,072 | 57,861 | 67,092 | 72,281 | 73,647 | 67,825 | 84,364 | 96,925 | .... | .... | .... |
| Exports of Goods and Services | 90c | 21,555 | 23,592 | 28,563 | 29,142 | 31,903 | 42,084 | 40,956 | 52,848 | 55,466 | .... | .... | .... |
| Imports of Goods and Services (-) | 98c | 61,784 | 72,154 | 88,769 | 85,715 | 110,739 | 114,048 | 172,849 | 178,605 | 174,400 | .... | .... | .... |
| Gross Domestic Product (GDP) | 99b | 140,387 | 168,035 | 197,183 | 220,110 | 250,590 | 267,880 | 266,952 | 302,854 | 328,061 | 364,526 | .... | .... |
| GDP Volume 1987 Prices | 99b.p | 12,558 | 12,783 | 13,071 | 13,508 | 13,622 | 14,042 | 13,270 | 14,003 | 14,407 | .... | .... | .... |
| GDP Volume (2010=100) | 99bvp | 94.6 | 96.3 | 98.5 | 101.8 | 102.7 | 105.8 | 100.0 | 105.5 | 108.6 | .... | .... | .... |
| GDP Deflator (2010=100) | 99bip | 55.6 | 65.3 | 75.0 | 81.0 | 91.4 | 94.8 | 100.0 | 107.5 | 113.2 | .... | .... | .... |
| | | | | | | | | | | | | | |
| | | | | | | | *Millions: Midyear Estimates* | | | | | | |
| Population | 99z | 9.12 | 9.26 | 9.41 | 9.56 | 9.71 | 9.85 | 10.00 | 10.14 | 10.29 | 10.43 | 10.57 | 10.71 |

| | | 2004 | 2005 | 2006 | 2007 | 2008 | 2009 | 2010 | 2011 | 2012 | 2013 | 2014 | 2015 |
|---|---|---|---|---|---|---|---|---|---|---|---|---|---|
| **Exchange Rates** | | | | | *Lempiras per SDR: End of Period* | | | | | | | | |
| Market Rate | aa | 28.937 | 27.006 | 28.426 | 29.859 | 29.104 | 29.622 | 29.099 | 29.244 | 30.680 | 31.720 | 31.167 | 30.995 |
| | | | | | *Lempiras per US Dollar: End of Period (ae) Period Average (rf)* | | | | | | | | |
| Market Rate | ae | 18.633 | 18.895 | 18.895 | 18.895 | 18.895 | 18.895 | 18.895 | 19.048 | 19.962 | 20.598 | 21.512 | 22.368 |
| Market Rate | rf | 18.206 | 18.832 | 18.895 | 18.895 | 18.904 | 18.895 | 18.895 | 18.917 | 19.502 | .... | .... | .... |
| **Fund Position** | | | | | *Millions of SDRs: End of Period* | | | | | | | | |
| Quota | 2f.s | 129.50 | 129.50 | 129.50 | 129.50 | 129.50 | 129.50 | 129.50 | 129.50 | 129.50 | 129.50 | 129.50 | 129.50 |
| SDR Holdings | 1b.s | .06 | .20 | — | .06 | .06 | 104.78 | 103.63 | 100.44 | 96.35 | 92.26 | 88.10 | 84.95 |
| Reserve Position in the Fund | 1c.s | 8.63 | 8.63 | 8.63 | 8.63 | 8.63 | 8.63 | 8.63 | 8.63 | 8.63 | 8.63 | 8.63 | 8.63 |
| Total Fund Cred.&Loans Outstg | 2tl | 125.71 | 117.63 | 20.34 | 20.34 | 20.34 | 20.34 | 19.32 | 16.27 | 12.21 | 8.14 | 4.07 | 1.02 |
| SDR Allocations | 1bd | 19.06 | 19.06 | 19.06 | 19.06 | 19.06 | 123.85 | 123.85 | 123.85 | 123.85 | 123.85 | 123.85 | 123.85 |
| **International Liquidity** | | | | | *Millions of US Dollars Unless Otherwise Indicated: End of Period* | | | | | | | | |
| Total Reserves minus Gold | 1l.d | 1,970.38 | 2,327.21 | 2,628.48 | 2,528.03 | 2,473.37 | 2,086.48 | 2,670.79 | 2,749.74 | 2,495.24 | 2,981.87 | 3,431.76 | 3,730.88 |
| SDR Holdings | 1b.d | .09 | .28 | — | .09 | .09 | 164.26 | 159.60 | 154.20 | 148.08 | 142.08 | 127.65 | 117.72 |
| Reserve Position in the Fund | 1c.d | 13.40 | 12.33 | 12.98 | 13.63 | 13.29 | 13.52 | 13.29 | 13.24 | 13.26 | 13.28 | 12.50 | 11.95 |
| Foreign Exchange | 1d.d | 1,956.90 | 2,314.60 | 2,615.50 | 2,514.30 | 2,460.00 | 1,908.70 | 2,497.90 | 2,582.30 | 2,333.90 | 2,826.50 | 3,291.62 | 3,601.21 |
| Gold (Million Fine Troy Ounces) | 1ad | .021 | .021 | .021 | .021 | .021 | .021 | .021 | .022 | .022 | .022 | .022 | .022 |
| Gold (National Valuation) | 1and | 9.93 | 11.34 | 13.95 | 18.19 | 19.11 | 24.04 | 31.15 | 34.74 | 36.72 | 26.57 | 26.56 | 23.71 |
| Central Bank: Other Assets | 3..d | 228.86 | 235.20 | 241.98 | 233.59 | 228.64 | 222.94 | 223.06 | 223.36 | 225.45 | 261.55 | 160.29 | 195.39 |
| Central Bank: Other Liabs | 4..d | 215.04 | 200.41 | 198.34 | 196.59 | 196.69 | 172.72 | 171.19 | 170.46 | 160.11 | 155.19 | 152.64 | 148.57 |
| Other Depository Corps.: Assets | 7a.d | 663.69 | 730.64 | 717.35 | 767.28 | 812.84 | 641.91 | 559.13 | 598.88 | 473.46 | 491.31 | 563.52 | 472.47 |
| Other Depository Corps.: Liabs | 7b.d | 370.26 | 478.87 | 609.42 | 749.93 | 748.66 | 470.14 | 496.23 | 539.59 | 746.63 | 990.24 | 1,114.12 | 1,183.55 |
| Other Financial Corps.: Assets | 7e.d | 12.52 | 15.42 | 17.80 | 38.45 | 59.71 | 78.77 | 63.82 | 66.98 | 77.85 | 81.28 | 91.80 | 87.33 |
| Other Financial Corps.: Liabs | 7f.d | 23.08 | 19.31 | 14.82 | 19.71 | 23.14 | 33.75 | 31.23 | 38.58 | 39.40 | 41.00 | 45.99 | 71.94 |
| **Central Bank** | | | | | *Millions of Lempiras: End of Period* | | | | | | | | |
| Net Foreign Assets | 11n | 36,544 | 44,934 | 53,308 | 51,415 | 50,546 | 41,107 | 52,509 | 54,963 | 52,825 | 65,322 | 75,996 | 86,725 |
| Claims on Nonresidents | 11 | 44,739 | 52,412 | 58,176 | 56,306 | 55,409 | 48,642 | 59,909 | 62,308 | 60,195 | 72,705 | 83,267 | 93,919 |
| Liabilities to Nonresidents | 16c | 8,196 | 7,478 | 4,868 | 4,891 | 4,863 | 7,535 | 7,401 | 7,345 | 7,370 | 7,383 | 7,270 | 7,193 |
| Claims on Other Depository Corps. | 12e | — | 100 | — | — | 94 | — | 340 | — | 710 | — | — | 1,910 |
| Net Claims on Central Government | 12an | −1,520 | −835 | −4,539 | −1,562 | 566 | 6,666 | 8,524 | 12,909 | 12,961 | 7,479 | 6,353 | 3,577 |
| Claims on Central Government | 12a | 10,819 | 11,635 | 11,784 | 11,950 | 13,125 | 16,771 | 21,726 | 23,488 | 24,619 | 24,447 | 24,225 | 23,916 |
| Liabilities to Central Government | 16d | 12,340 | 12,470 | 16,324 | 13,512 | 12,559 | 10,104 | 13,202 | 10,579 | 11,658 | 16,968 | 17,872 | 20,340 |
| Claims on Other Sectors | 12s | 222 | 181 | 143 | 78 | 50 | 6,522 | 9,005 | 9,000 | 9,000 | 9,850 | 10,200 | 10,200 |
| Claims on Other Financial Corps. | 12g | 196 | 159 | 125 | 64 | 41 | 6,518 | 9,005 | 9,000 | 9,000 | 9,850 | 10,200 | 10,200 |
| Claims on State & Local Govts | 12b | 26 | 22 | 18 | 13 | 9 | 4 | — | — | — | — | — | — |
| Claims on Public Nonfin. Corps. | 12c | — | — | — | — | — | — | — | — | — | — | — | — |
| Claims on Private Sector | 12d | — | — | — | — | — | — | — | — | — | — | — | — |
| Monetary Base | 14 | 29,775 | 38,738 | 43,530 | 43,483 | 43,972 | 47,383 | 63,648 | 69,033 | 68,731 | 76,106 | 88,491 | 97,822 |
| Currency in Circulation | 14a | 9,379 | 11,113 | 13,593 | 16,363 | 16,468 | 17,706 | 19,933 | 21,358 | 22,149 | 23,600 | 26,395 | 29,452 |
| Liabs. to Other Depository Corps. | 14c | 15,083 | 21,392 | 23,571 | 22,965 | 23,874 | 27,436 | 40,286 | 44,592 | 43,328 | 49,112 | 58,135 | 65,121 |
| Liabilities to Other Sectors | 14d | 5,313 | 6,233 | 6,366 | 4,155 | 3,630 | 2,241 | 3,429 | 3,083 | 3,253 | 3,394 | 3,962 | 3,248 |
| Other Liabs. to Other Dep. Corps. | 14n | — | — | — | — | — | — | — | — | — | — | — | — |
| Dep. & Sec. Excl. f/Monetary Base | 14o | 3 | 33 | 47 | 20 | 23 | 12 | 3 | 1 | 15 | 7 | 8 | 8 |
| Deposits Included in Broad Money | 15 | 3 | 33 | 47 | 20 | 23 | 12 | 2 | 1 | 15 | 7 | 8 | 8 |
| Sec.Ot.th.Shares Incl.in Brd. Money | 16a | — | — | — | — | — | — | — | — | — | — | — | — |
| Deposits Excl. from Broad Money | 16b | — | — | — | — | — | — | 1 | — | — | — | — | — |
| Sec.Ot.th.Shares Excl.f/Brd.Money | 16s | — | — | — | — | — | — | — | — | — | — | — | — |
| Loans | 16l | — | — | — | — | — | — | — | — | — | — | — | — |
| Financial Derivatives | 16m | — | — | — | — | — | — | — | — | — | — | — | — |
| Shares and Other Equity | 17a | 2,827 | 2,259 | 2,460 | 2,956 | 3,423 | 2,913 | 2,991 | 3,738 | 2,552 | 2,831 | 1,170 | 2,182 |
| Other Items (Net) | 17r | 2,641 | 3,350 | 2,874 | 3,473 | 3,837 | 3,988 | 3,736 | 4,101 | 4,198 | 3,707 | 2,880 | 2,400 |
| Memo Item: | | | | | | | | | | | | | |
| Total Assets | 10ra | 56,815 | 65,868 | 71,377 | 69,194 | 69,588 | 72,553 | 91,914 | 96,622 | 96,209 | 109,463 | 120,150 | 132,410 |
| **Other Depository Corporations** | | | | | *Millions of Lempiras: End of Period* | | | | | | | | |
| Net Foreign Assets | 21n | 5,467 | 4,757 | 2,040 | 328 | 1,213 | 3,246 | 1,189 | 1,129 | −5,453 | −10,277 | −11,845 | −15,905 |
| Claims on Nonresidents | 21 | 12,366 | 13,806 | 13,555 | 14,498 | 15,359 | 12,129 | 10,565 | 11,408 | 9,451 | 10,120 | 12,123 | 10,568 |
| Liabilities to Nonresidents | 26c | 6,899 | 9,048 | 11,515 | 14,170 | 14,146 | 8,883 | 9,376 | 10,278 | 14,905 | 20,397 | 23,967 | 26,473 |
| Claims on Central Bank | 20 | 16,878 | 23,451 | 26,633 | 27,572 | 28,494 | 31,889 | 45,610 | 50,072 | 49,392 | 56,378 | 66,000 | 74,930 |
| Currency | 20a | 1,791 | 2,209 | 3,150 | 4,457 | 4,612 | 4,735 | 5,247 | 5,159 | 5,723 | 6,538 | 7,245 | 7,876 |
| Reserve Deposits and Securities | 20b | 8,644 | 9,326 | 10,676 | 14,272 | 18,597 | 20,434 | 21,910 | 24,928 | 28,103 | 31,404 | 38,412 | 40,798 |
| Other Claims | 20n | 6,443 | 11,915 | 12,807 | 8,843 | 5,286 | 6,721 | 18,452 | 19,985 | 15,566 | 18,437 | 20,343 | 26,256 |
| Net Claims on Central Government | 22an | −1,633 | −3,067 | −4,404 | −7,330 | −5,994 | −5,313 | −5,230 | −3,534 | −3,705 | −8,618 | −9,968 | −12,954 |
| Claims on Central Government | 22a | 1,141 | 1,176 | 1,470 | 915 | 2,797 | 7,086 | 8,123 | 13,728 | 15,872 | 16,721 | 17,893 | 19,199 |
| Liabilities to Central Government | 26d | 2,774 | 4,243 | 5,875 | 8,245 | 8,791 | 12,400 | 13,353 | 17,262 | 19,578 | 25,340 | 27,861 | 32,153 |
| Claims on Other Sectors | 22s | 64,677 | 75,049 | 97,368 | 127,595 | 140,771 | 144,275 | 148,964 | 163,787 | 191,041 | 215,565 | 240,220 | 265,097 |
| Claims on Other Financial Corps. | 22g | 3,367 | 3,066 | 3,125 | 2,959 | 2,834 | 2,422 | 1,989 | 1,744 | 1,472 | 1,415 | 1,377 | 1,716 |
| Claims on State & Local Govts | 22b | 551 | 767 | 1,873 | 2,268 | 2,557 | 2,537 | 2,764 | 4,050 | 4,425 | 4,067 | 4,025 | 4,028 |
| Claims on Public Nonfin. Corps. | 22c | 671 | 921 | 1,321 | 1,738 | 648 | 656 | 752 | 731 | 1,227 | 5,640 | 8,469 | 9,460 |
| Claims on Private Sector | 22d | 60,088 | 70,296 | 91,048 | 120,630 | 134,732 | 138,660 | 143,460 | 157,263 | 183,916 | 204,443 | 226,349 | 249,894 |
| Liabilities to Central Bank | 26g | — | — | — | — | 94 | 375 | 340 | 500 | 639 | — | — | 735 |
| Transf.Dep.Included in Broad Money | 24 | 15,322 | 15,265 | 18,954 | 22,862 | 23,376 | 23,837 | 27,218 | 30,061 | 28,483 | 29,023 | 39,555 | 40,506 |
| Other Dep.Included in Broad Money | 25 | 51,440 | 63,102 | 77,919 | 93,693 | 100,207 | 100,813 | 108,230 | 123,235 | 136,460 | 150,411 | 163,496 | 178,466 |
| Sec.Ot.th.Shares Incl.in Brd. Money | 26a | 59 | — | — | — | — | — | — | — | — | — | — | — |
| Deposits Excl. from Broad Money | 26b | 1,147 | 174 | 137 | 171 | 294 | 421 | 386 | 638 | 526 | 655 | 708 | 681 |
| Sec.Ot.th.Shares Excl.f/Brd.Money | 26s | — | 278 | 428 | 782 | 2,414 | 2,266 | 2,102 | 2,615 | 2,645 | 2,998 | 3,162 | 3,536 |
| Loans | 26l | 7,480 | 7,036 | 6,282 | 7,987 | 10,642 | 17,788 | 20,554 | 21,756 | 23,769 | 26,359 | 28,305 | 30,770 |
| Financial Derivatives | 26m | — | — | — | — | — | — | — | — | — | — | — | — |
| Insurance Technical Reserves | 26r | — | — | — | — | — | — | — | — | — | — | — | — |
| Shares and Other Equity | 27a | 14,426 | 18,199 | 21,822 | 26,146 | 32,421 | 35,399 | 38,550 | 43,364 | 49,365 | 55,315 | 62,592 | 67,447 |
| Other Items (Net) | 27r | −4,485 | −3,864 | −3,907 | −3,476 | −4,965 | −6,801 | −6,848 | −10,715 | −10,613 | −11,714 | −13,411 | −10,972 |
| Memo Item: | | | | | | | | | | | | | |
| Total Assets | 20ra | 106,495 | 125,396 | 151,409 | 184,007 | 202,437 | 211,920 | 230,884 | 260,634 | 289,730 | 324,987 | 368,819 | 404,516 |

# Honduras 268

| | | 2004 | 2005 | 2006 | 2007 | 2008 | 2009 | 2010 | 2011 | 2012 | 2013 | 2014 | 2015 |
|---|---|---|---|---|---|---|---|---|---|---|---|---|---|
| **Depository Corporations** | | *Millions of Lempiras: End of Period* | | | | | | | | | | | |
| Net Foreign Assets.......................... | 31n | 42,011 | 49,691 | 55,347 | 51,743 | 51,758 | 44,352 | 53,697 | 56,093 | 47,371 | 55,045 | 64,152 | 70,820 |
| Claims on Nonresidents................ | 31 | 57,106 | 66,217 | 71,730 | 70,804 | 70,767 | 60,771 | 70,474 | 73,716 | 69,646 | 82,825 | 95,390 | 104,487 |
| Liabilities to Nonresidents............. | 36c | 15,095 | 16,527 | 16,383 | 19,061 | 19,009 | 16,418 | 16,777 | 17,623 | 22,275 | 27,780 | 31,238 | 33,667 |
| Domestic Claims............................. | 32 | 61,746 | 71,328 | 88,567 | 118,782 | 135,392 | 152,151 | 161,263 | 182,162 | 209,296 | 224,276 | 246,805 | 265,920 |
| Net Claims on Central Government | 32an | −3,153 | −3,902 | −8,944 | −8,891 | −5,428 | 1,353 | 3,294 | 9,375 | 9,255 | −1,139 | −3,615 | −9,377 |
| Claims on Central Government.... | 32a | 11,960 | 12,811 | 13,255 | 12,865 | 15,923 | 23,857 | 29,849 | 37,216 | 40,491 | 41,169 | 42,118 | 43,115 |
| Liabilities to Central Government. | 36d | 15,113 | 16,713 | 22,198 | 21,757 | 21,351 | 22,504 | 26,555 | 27,841 | 31,236 | 42,308 | 45,734 | 52,492 |
| Claims on Other Sectors................ | 32s | 64,899 | 75,230 | 97,510 | 127,673 | 140,820 | 150,798 | 157,969 | 172,787 | 200,041 | 225,415 | 250,420 | 275,297 |
| Claims on Other Financial Corps.. | 32g | 3,563 | 3,225 | 3,250 | 3,024 | 2,875 | 8,940 | 10,993 | 10,744 | 10,472 | 11,265 | 11,577 | 11,916 |
| Claims on State & Local Govts..... | 32b | 577 | 788 | 1,891 | 2,282 | 2,566 | 2,541 | 2,764 | 4,050 | 4,425 | 4,067 | 4,025 | 4,028 |
| Claims on Public Nonfin. Corps.... | 32c | 671 | 921 | 1,321 | 1,738 | 648 | 656 | 752 | 731 | 1,227 | 5,640 | 8,469 | 9,460 |
| Claims on Private Sector.............. | 32d | 60,088 | 70,296 | 91,048 | 120,630 | 134,732 | 138,660 | 143,460 | 157,263 | 183,916 | 204,443 | 226,349 | 249,894 |
| Broad Money Liabilities................... | 35l | 79,725 | 93,538 | 113,729 | 132,636 | 139,093 | 139,873 | 153,565 | 172,579 | 184,638 | 199,897 | 226,170 | 243,805 |
| Currency Outside Depository Corps | 34a | 7,588 | 8,904 | 10,443 | 11,906 | 11,857 | 12,971 | 14,686 | 16,199 | 16,426 | 17,062 | 19,150 | 21,577 |
| Transferable Deposits................... | 34 | 16,113 | 16,319 | 19,918 | 23,585 | 24,032 | 24,476 | 28,422 | 30,804 | 29,102 | 29,795 | 40,758 | 42,245 |
| Other Deposits............................. | 35 | 51,501 | 63,177 | 78,009 | 93,764 | 100,328 | 100,912 | 108,322 | 123,354 | 136,698 | 150,581 | 163,675 | 178,635 |
| Securities Other than Shares.......... | 36a | 4,523 | 5,138 | 5,359 | 3,380 | 2,876 | 1,514 | 2,135 | 2,222 | 2,411 | 2,458 | 2,588 | 1,348 |
| Deposits Excl. from Broad Money..... | 36b | 1,147 | 174 | 137 | 171 | 294 | 421 | 387 | 638 | 526 | 655 | 708 | 681 |
| Sec.Ot.th.Shares Excl.f/Brd.Money.... | 36s | — | 278 | 428 | 782 | 2,414 | 2,266 | 2,102 | 2,615 | 2,645 | 2,998 | 3,162 | 3,536 |
| Loans............................................ | 36l | 7,480 | 7,036 | 6,282 | 7,987 | 10,642 | 17,788 | 20,554 | 21,756 | 23,769 | 26,359 | 28,305 | 30,770 |
| Financial Derivatives....................... | 36m | — | — | — | — | — | — | — | — | — | — | — | — |
| Insurance Technical Reserves.......... | 36r | — | — | — | — | — | — | — | — | — | — | — | — |
| Shares and Other Equity.................. | 37a | 17,253 | 20,457 | 24,283 | 29,102 | 35,844 | 38,312 | 41,541 | 47,102 | 51,917 | 58,146 | 63,762 | 69,629 |
| Other Items (Net)............................ | 37r | −1,848 | −465 | −944 | −153 | −1,137 | −2,157 | −3,188 | −6,435 | −6,827 | −8,735 | −11,151 | −11,680 |
| Broad Money Liabs., Seasonally Adj. | 35l.b | 78,302 | 91,986 | 111,998 | 130,813 | 137,381 | 138,418 | 152,216 | 171,275 | 183,307 | 198,468 | 224,440 | 241,830 |
| **Other Financial Corporations** | | *Millions of Lempiras: End of Period* | | | | | | | | | | | |
| Net Foreign Assets.......................... | 41n | −197 | −74 | 56 | 354 | 691 | 851 | 616 | 541 | 767 | 830 | 986 | 344 |
| Claims on Nonresidents................ | 41 | 233 | 291 | 336 | 727 | 1,128 | 1,488 | 1,206 | 1,276 | 1,554 | 1,674 | 1,975 | 1,953 |
| Liabilities to Nonresidents............. | 46c | 430 | 365 | 280 | 372 | 437 | 638 | 590 | 735 | 787 | 845 | 989 | 1,609 |
| Claims on Depository Corporations.. | 40 | 9,661 | 10,181 | 10,414 | 10,861 | 12,513 | 18,948 | 23,052 | 23,671 | 25,772 | 27,970 | 29,965 | 32,761 |
| Net Claims on Central Government.. | 42an | 37 | 262 | 258 | −88 | −666 | −432 | −616 | −441 | −262 | −698 | 171 | 438 |
| Claims on Central Government...... | 42a | 1,634 | 1,323 | 1,145 | 666 | 735 | 954 | 703 | 723 | 1,021 | 590 | 1,433 | 1,554 |
| Liabilities to Central Government... | 46d | 1,597 | 1,060 | 887 | 754 | 1,401 | 1,386 | 1,319 | 1,164 | 1,282 | 1,288 | 1,262 | 1,116 |
| Claims on Other Sectors.................. | 42s | 1,934 | 2,169 | 2,270 | 2,751 | 3,399 | 3,730 | 3,337 | 3,542 | 3,798 | 4,114 | 5,560 | 5,551 |
| Claims on State & Local Govts....... | 42b | — | — | — | — | — | — | — | — | — | — | — | — |
| Claims on Public Nonfin. Corps..... | 42c | — | — | — | 15 | — | — | — | — | — | — | 1,065 | 453 |
| Claims on Private Sector................ | 42d | 1,934 | 2,169 | 2,270 | 2,736 | 3,399 | 3,730 | 3,337 | 3,542 | 3,798 | 4,114 | 4,495 | 5,098 |
| Deposits......................................... | 46b | 80 | 71 | 132 | 121 | 599 | 609 | 630 | 644 | 862 | 678 | 1,166 | 1,109 |
| Securities Other than Shares............ | 46s | 3,523 | 3,435 | 3,216 | 2,653 | 2,614 | 2,262 | 1,905 | 1,200 | 1,306 | 970 | 760 | 761 |
| Loans............................................. | 46l | 146 | 102 | 73 | 99 | 247 | 310 | 261 | 313 | 438 | 460 | 383 | 508 |
| Financial Derivatives....................... | 46m | — | — | — | — | — | — | — | — | — | — | — | — |
| Insurance Technical Reserves........... | 46r | 1,651 | 1,783 | 1,987 | 2,388 | 2,697 | 2,726 | 2,949 | 3,319 | 3,622 | 3,782 | 4,040 | 4,349 |
| Shares and Other Equity.................. | 47a | 5,979 | 7,098 | 7,548 | 8,281 | 9,142 | 16,335 | 19,912 | 21,054 | 22,685 | 24,421 | 28,438 | 30,166 |
| Other Items (Net)............................ | 47r | 57 | 48 | 42 | 336 | 638 | 856 | 731 | 784 | 1,163 | 1,906 | 1,895 | 2,202 |
| Memo Item: | | | | | | | | | | | | | |
| Total Assets.................................... | 40ra | 15,031 | 15,354 | 15,617 | 16,350 | 19,260 | 26,806 | 29,879 | 30,720 | 33,735 | 36,025 | 40,755 | 44,028 |
| **Monetary Aggregates** | | *Millions of Lempiras: End of Period* | | | | | | | | | | | |
| Broad Money............................ | 59m | 79,725 | 93,538 | 113,729 | 132,636 | 139,093 | 139,873 | 153,565 | 172,579 | 184,638 | 199,897 | 226,170 | 243,805 |
| o/w:Currency Issued by Cent.Govt | 59m.a | — | — | — | — | — | — | — | — | — | — | — | — |
| o/w: Dep.in Nonfin. Corporations. | 59m.b | — | — | — | — | — | — | — | — | — | — | — | — |
| o/w:Secs. Issued by Central Govt.. | 59m.c | — | — | — | — | — | — | — | — | — | — | — | — |
| Money (National Definitions) | | | | | | | | | | | | | |
| Base Money................................. | 19ma | 29,775 | 38,738 | 43,530 | 43,483 | 43,972 | 47,383 | 63,648 | 69,033 | 68,731 | 76,106 | 88,491 | 97,822 |
| M1................................................ | 59ma | 18,555 | 21,238 | 26,236 | 30,248 | 30,864 | 32,394 | 37,375 | 41,225 | 38,400 | 40,120 | 45,522 | 52,221 |
| M2................................................ | 59mb | 57,399 | 68,782 | 85,271 | 99,891 | 102,378 | 102,200 | 115,759 | 130,773 | 136,501 | 147,467 | 163,053 | 180,535 |
| M3................................................ | 59mc | 79,725 | 93,538 | 113,729 | 132,636 | 139,093 | 139,873 | 153,565 | 172,578 | 184,638 | 199,890 | 226,162 | 243,797 |
| **Interest Rates** | | *Percent Per Annum* | | | | | | | | | | | |
| Central Bank Policy Rate (EOP)........ | 60 | .... | 7.00 | 6.00 | 7.50 | 7.75 | 4.50 | 4.50 | 5.50 | 7.00 | 7.00 | 7.00 | 6.25 |
| Savings Rate................................... | 60k | 6.04 | 6.00 | 5.08 | 4.14 | 3.92 | 4.13 | 4.11 | 3.84 | 3.84 | 4.00 | 3.91 | 3.97 |
| Savings Rate (Fgn. Currency)........... | 60k.f | 1.16 | 1.23 | 1.41 | 1.50 | 1.59 | 1.77 | 1.50 | 1.30 | 1.21 | 1.29 | 1.25 | 1.60 |
| Deposit Rate................................... | 60l | 11.09 | 10.90 | 9.33 | 7.78 | 9.49 | 10.82 | 9.81 | 8.18 | 8.93 | 11.65 | 10.82 | 9.70 |
| Deposit Rate (Fgn. Currency)........... | 60l.f | 2.59 | 2.61 | 3.35 | 3.94 | 4.47 | 4.77 | 4.12 | 3.59 | 3.79 | 4.23 | 4.08 | 4.00 |
| Lending Rate.................................. | 60p | 19.88 | 18.83 | 17.44 | 16.61 | 17.94 | 19.45 | 18.86 | 18.56 | 18.45 | 20.08 | 20.61 | 20.66 |
| Lending Rate (Fgn. Currency)......... | 60p.f | 8.77 | 8.63 | 8.98 | 9.58 | 10.04 | 10.43 | 10.09 | 9.33 | 8.77 | 8.59 | 8.56 | 8.56 |
| Government Bond Yield.................... | 61 | 11.67 | 11.32 | 7.87 | 7.70 | .... | .... | .... | .... | .... | .... | .... | .... |
| **Prices and Labor** | | *Index Numbers (2010=100): Period Averages* | | | | | | | | | | | |
| Consumer Prices............................. | 64 | 66.2 | 72.0 | 76.0 | 81.3 | 90.5 | 95.5 | 100.0 | 106.8 | 112.3 | 118.1 | 125.3 | 129.3 |
| | | *Number in Thousands: Period Averages* | | | | | | | | | | | |
| Labor Force.................................... | 67d | 2,592 | 2,651 | 2,812 | .... | .... | .... | 3,427 | .... | .... | .... | .... | .... |
| Employment................................... | 67e | 2,439 | 2,543 | 2,724 | .... | .... | .... | 3,281 | .... | .... | .... | .... | .... |
| Unemployment................................ | 67c | 153 | 108 | 87 | .... | .... | .... | 146 | .... | .... | .... | .... | .... |
| Unemployment Rate (%)................. | 67r | 5.9 | .... | .... | .... | .... | .... | 4.3 | .... | .... | .... | .... | .... |
| **Intl. Transactions & Positions** | | *Millions of US Dollars* | | | | | | | | | | | |
| Exports.......................................... | 70..d | 1,640.4 | 1,892.4 | 2,053.9 | 2,120.1 | 2,882.7 | 2,304.2 | 2,712.0 | 3,892.5 | 4,426.6 | 3,923.5 | 4,063.5 | 3,911.2 |
| Imports, c.i.f.................................. | 71..d | 4,212.3 | 4,852.5 | 5,694.6 | 6,761.8 | 8,830.9 | 6,133.3 | 7,078.5 | 8,953.0 | 9,463.5 | 9,169.0 | 9,310.9 | 9,424.3 |
| Imports, f.o.b................................. | 71.vd | 3,804.9 | 4,383.2 | 5,153.5 | 6,119.3 | 7,991.8 | 5,527.6 | 6,594.3 | 8,629.2 | 9,072.5 | 8,892.8 | 9,061.4 | 9,145.1 |
| | | *2010=100* | | | | | | | | | | | |
| Volume of Exports.......................... | 72 | 97.2 | 90.2 | 94.6 | 101.9 | 105.4 | 96.8 | 100.0 | 112.3 | 141.8 | 123.8 | 124.5 | 140.4 |
| Export Prices.................................. | 74..d | 47.9 | 68.5 | 70.1 | 74.0 | 88.6 | 83.3 | 100.0 | 143.7 | 122.8 | 95.0 | 100.4 | 100.7 |

# Honduras 268

| | | 2004 | 2005 | 2006 | 2007 | 2008 | 2009 | 2010 | 2011 | 2012 | 2013 | 2014 | 2015 |
|---|---|---|---|---|---|---|---|---|---|---|---|---|---|
| **Balance of Payments** | | | | | | *Millions of US Dollars* | | | | | | | |
| A. Current Account* | 109bx | −683.4 | −304.3 | −403.9 | −1,116.2 | −2,129.9 | −556.7 | −681.5 | −1,408.7 | −1,580.8 | −1,762.5 | −1,444.2 | −1,291.4 |
| Goods, credit (exports) | 1a9cx | 1,646.9 | 1,900.3 | 2,108.7 | 2,542.7 | 2,848.2 | 2,375.0 | 2,831.7 | 3,977.6 | 4,419.8 | 3,915.8 | 4,092.2 | 3,953.8 |
| Goods, debit (imports) | 1a9dx | 3,885.7 | 4,468.3 | 5,218.9 | 6,707.6 | 8,209.2 | 5,845.7 | 6,606.3 | 8,357.6 | 8,547.7 | 8,393.0 | 8,508.4 | 8,582.7 |
| Balance on goods | 1a9bx | −2,238.8 | −2,567.9 | −3,110.1 | −4,164.9 | −5,361.0 | −3,470.6 | −3,774.6 | −4,380.0 | −4,128.0 | −4,477.2 | −4,416.2 | −4,628.9 |
| Services, credit (exports) | 1b9cx | 1,590.5 | 1,771.3 | 1,828.6 | 1,841.5 | 2,017.0 | 1,871.4 | 2,107.6 | 2,253.9 | 2,247.1 | 2,343.0 | 2,505.6 | 2,676.9 |
| Services, debit (imports) | 1b9dx | 849.3 | 929.2 | 1,035.9 | 1,068.8 | 1,238.5 | 964.0 | 1,168.9 | 1,446.2 | 1,722.1 | 1,680.6 | 1,784.4 | 1,794.0 |
| Balance on Goods & Services | 1z9bx | −1,497.5 | −1,725.8 | −2,317.4 | −3,392.2 | −4,582.5 | −2,563.2 | −2,835.9 | −3,572.3 | −3,603.0 | −3,814.8 | −3,695.0 | −3,746.0 |
| Primary income: credit | 1c9cx | 87.5 | 145.1 | 198.2 | 257.2 | 148.1 | 71.8 | 53.6 | 58.6 | 62.1 | 48.2 | 46.7 | 59.0 |
| Primary income: debit | 1c9dx | 538.7 | 618.7 | 735.0 | 652.4 | 668.9 | 703.3 | 780.9 | 1,032.7 | 1,327.6 | 1,401.2 | 1,368.2 | 1,439.3 |
| Balance on gds, serv. & prim. inc. | 1y9bx | −1,948.7 | −2,199.5 | −2,854.2 | −3,787.4 | −5,103.3 | −3,194.7 | −3,563.2 | −4,546.4 | −4,868.5 | −5,167.8 | −5,016.5 | −5,126.2 |
| Secondary income: credit | 1d9ca | 1,374.0 | 2,042.4 | 2,588.7 | 2,825.2 | 3,044.4 | 2,697.0 | 2,949.3 | 3,220.5 | 3,369.0 | 3,540.9 | 3,751.5 | 4,018.4 |
| Secondary income: debit | 1d9da | 108.6 | 147.3 | 138.4 | 154.0 | 71.0 | 58.9 | 67.7 | 82.8 | 81.3 | 135.6 | 179.3 | 183.6 |
| B. Capital Account* | 209ba | 44.8 | 581.1 | 1,454.6 | 1,171.6 | 53.1 | 95.9 | 47.6 | 102.1 | 35.0 | 28.0 | 32.4 | 20.8 |
| Capital account: credit | 209ca | 44.8 | 581.1 | 1,454.6 | 1,171.6 | 53.1 | 95.9 | 47.6 | 102.1 | 35.0 | 28.0 | 32.4 | 20.8 |
| Capital account: debit | 209da | — | — | — | — | — | — | — | — | — | — | — | — |
| Balance on current & capital acct. | 129ba | −638.6 | 276.8 | 1,050.7 | 55.4 | −2,076.7 | −460.8 | −634.0 | −1,306.6 | −1,545.8 | −1,734.5 | −1,411.9 | −1,270.7 |
| C. Financial Account* | 309na | −987.9 | −689.4 | 513.0 | −77.7 | −1,439.1 | −206.2 | −1,341.4 | −1,121.5 | −1,435.0 | −2,501.3 | −1,657.6 | −1,384.1 |
| Direct investment: assets | 3a9aa | 39.2 | .3 | 49.1 | 40.8 | 193.5 | −10.8 | −363.2 | 30.3 | 216.6 | 77.4 | 174.1 | 203.8 |
| Equity & investment fund shares | 3aaaa | — | — | — | — | — | — | — | 2.0 | — | — | 14.5 | 73.4 |
| Debt instruments | 3abaa | 39.2 | .3 | 49.1 | 40.8 | 193.5 | −10.8 | −363.2 | 28.3 | 216.6 | 77.4 | 159.6 | 130.5 |
| Direct investment: liabilities | 3a9la | 592.3 | 601.1 | 717.6 | 966.9 | 1,200.8 | 494.5 | 484.8 | 1,042.6 | 1,067.6 | 1,069.0 | 1,294.1 | 1,316.7 |
| Equity & investment fund shares | 3aala | 462.9 | 536.6 | 623.5 | 724.5 | 1,046.4 | 443.4 | 469.1 | 958.3 | 1,006.2 | 819.6 | 789.2 | 974.3 |
| Debt instruments | 3abla | 129.4 | 64.5 | 94.1 | 242.4 | 154.4 | 51.1 | 15.7 | 84.3 | 61.4 | 249.5 | 504.9 | 342.4 |
| Portfolio investment: assets | 3b9aa | 11.8 | 23.1 | 20.9 | 22.4 | 26.8 | −3.3 | 18.9 | −45.8 | 11.8 | .1 | −20.1 | 8.8 |
| Equity & investment fund shares | 3baaa | 1.2 | 11.7 | −1.8 | −.6 | 4.1 | −.4 | −2.4 | .4 | −.5 | — | .3 | — |
| Debt securities | 3bbaa | 10.6 | 11.4 | 22.7 | 23.0 | 22.6 | −2.9 | 21.3 | −46.2 | 12.3 | .1 | −20.4 | 8.7 |
| Portfolio investment: liabilities | 3b9la | .2 | — | — | — | — | 33.8 | −22.1 | 41.9 | 12.9 | 1,007.0 | 20.4 | −.6 |
| Equity & investment fund shares | 3bala | .2 | — | — | — | — | — | — | — | — | — | — | — |
| Debt securities | 3bbla | — | — | — | — | — | 33.8 | −22.1 | 41.9 | 12.9 | 1,007.0 | 20.4 | −.6 |
| Fin. der.& empl.stk.ops.(ESOs): net | 3c9na | — | — | — | — | — | — | — | — | — | — | — | — |
| Fin. der. & ESOs.: assets | 3c9aa | — | — | — | — | — | — | — | — | — | — | — | — |
| Fin. der. & ESOs.: liabilities | 3c9la | — | — | — | — | — | — | — | — | — | — | — | — |
| Other investment: assets | 3d9aa | 59.3 | −12.3 | −84.4 | 29.2 | −17.1 | −149.7 | −65.8 | 436.6 | −217.2 | 78.5 | −38.1 | 90.3 |
| Other equity | 3daaa | .... | .... | .... | .... | .... | .... | .... | .... | .... | .... | .... | .... |
| Debt instruments | 3dzaa | 59.3 | −12.3 | −84.4 | 29.2 | −17.1 | −149.7 | −65.8 | 436.6 | −217.2 | 78.5 | −38.1 | 90.3 |
| Other investment: liabilities | 3d9la | 505.7 | 99.4 | −1,245.0 | −796.8 | 441.4 | −485.9 | 468.5 | 458.2 | 365.8 | 581.4 | 459.0 | 370.9 |
| Other equity | 3dala | .... | .... | .... | .... | .... | .... | .... | .... | .... | .... | .... | .... |
| Debt instruments | 3dzla | 505.7 | 99.4 | −1,245.0 | −796.8 | 441.4 | −485.9 | 468.5 | 458.2 | 365.8 | 581.4 | 459.0 | 370.9 |
| Curr.+ cap.– finan. acct. balance | 4y9na | 349.3 | 966.1 | 537.6 | 133.1 | −637.7 | −254.6 | 707.5 | −185.1 | −110.8 | 766.8 | 245.7 | 113.5 |
| D. Net Errors and Omissions | 409na | 52.6 | −178.0 | −274.6 | −319.3 | 482.7 | −279.2 | −140.3 | 228.5 | −182.9 | −284.2 | 210.3 | 167.4 |
| E. Reserves and Related Items | 4z9na | 401.9 | 788.2 | 263.0 | −186.2 | −155.0 | −533.8 | 567.2 | 43.4 | −293.6 | 482.6 | 456.0 | 280.9 |
| Reserve assets | 3e9aa | 510.4 | 346.4 | 282.1 | −108.5 | −77.8 | −346.8 | 590.9 | 72.6 | −282.7 | 484.7 | 458.6 | 303.0 |
| Credit and loans from the IMF | 3dcla | 15.1 | −11.5 | −140.8 | — | — | — | −1.6 | −4.8 | −6.2 | −6.2 | −6.2 | −4.3 |
| Exceptional financing | 409la | 93.4 | −430.3 | 159.9 | 77.6 | 77.2 | 187.0 | 25.3 | 34.1 | 17.2 | 8.3 | 8.9 | 26.4 |

*Excludes components in group E

| | | 2004 | 2005 | 2006 | 2007 | 2008 | 2009 | 2010 | 2011 | 2012 | 2013 | 2014 | 2015 |
|---|---|---|---|---|---|---|---|---|---|---|---|---|---|
| **International Investment Position** | | | | | | *Millions of US Dollars* | | | | | | | |
| Assets | 809aa | 3,310.2 | 3,785.5 | 4,809.8 | 5,003.5 | 5,042.6 | 4,563.9 | 5,078.0 | 5,664.1 | 5,571.2 | 6,310.7 | 6,792.0 | 7,213.2 |
| Direct investment | 8a9aa | 25.6 | 27.8 | 30.0 | 35.5 | 43.9 | 74.6 | 49.0 | 109.2 | 316.8 | 497.2 | 510.5 | 627.0 |
| Equity & investment fund shares | 8aaaa | .... | .... | .... | .... | .... | .... | .... | .... | .... | 115.8 | 102.5 | 160.6 |
| Debt instruments | 8abaa | 25.6 | 27.8 | 30.0 | 35.5 | 43.9 | 74.6 | 49.0 | 109.2 | 316.8 | 381.4 | 408.0 | 466.4 |
| Portfolio investment | 8b9aa | 117.0 | 190.2 | 216.2 | 243.9 | 266.9 | 258.2 | 272.0 | 227.4 | 239.0 | 240.2 | 225.9 | 257.5 |
| Equity & investment fund shares | 8baaa | 1.2 | 12.9 | 13.1 | 12.5 | 16.8 | 16.3 | 13.9 | 14.6 | 14.1 | 14.1 | 14.3 | 14.8 |
| Debt securities | 8bbaa | 115.8 | 177.3 | 203.1 | 231.4 | 250.1 | 241.9 | 258.1 | 212.8 | 224.9 | 226.1 | 211.5 | 242.7 |
| Fin. der.(oth.than reserves) & ESOs | 8c9aa | .... | .... | .... | .... | .... | .... | .... | .... | .... | .... | .... | .... |
| Other investment | 8d9aa | 1,218.2 | 1,262.4 | 1,956.6 | 2,216.0 | 2,282.2 | 2,120.6 | 2,055.1 | 2,543.0 | 2,483.4 | 2,564.8 | 2,597.4 | 2,574.1 |
| Other equity | 8daaa | .... | .... | .... | .... | .... | .... | .... | .... | .... | .... | .... | .... |
| Debt instruments | 8dzaa | 1,218.2 | 1,262.4 | 1,956.6 | 2,216.0 | 2,282.2 | 2,120.6 | 2,055.1 | 2,543.0 | 2,483.4 | 2,564.8 | 2,597.4 | 2,574.1 |
| Reserve assets | 8e9aa | 1,949.3 | 2,305.2 | 2,607.0 | 2,508.1 | 2,449.6 | 2,110.5 | 2,701.9 | 2,784.5 | 2,532.0 | 3,008.4 | 3,458.3 | 3,754.6 |
| Liabilities | 809la | 8,734.0 | 8,411.3 | 7,842.6 | 7,907.9 | 9,480.5 | 9,988.9 | 11,322.9 | 12,954.8 | 14,719.1 | 17,491.4 | 19,555.7 | 21,386.9 |
| Direct investment | 8a9la | 2,270.1 | 2,869.8 | 3,538.9 | 4,466.5 | 5,472.8 | 5,981.7 | 6,950.9 | 7,965.3 | 9,023.8 | 10,083.5 | 11,227.6 | 12,431.1 |
| Equity & investment fund shares | 8aala | 1,921.6 | 2,458.2 | 3,081.7 | 3,806.2 | 4,852.6 | 5,296.1 | 5,887.7 | 6,846.0 | 7,852.1 | 8,671.7 | 9,460.9 | 10,435.1 |
| Debt instruments | 8abla | 348.5 | 411.6 | 457.2 | 660.3 | 620.2 | 685.6 | 1,063.2 | 1,119.3 | 1,171.7 | 1,411.8 | 1,766.7 | 1,995.9 |
| Portfolio investment | 8b9la | .... | .... | .... | .... | 78.3 | 112.1 | 90.0 | 132.0 | 144.8 | 1,117.4 | 1,253.9 | 1,252.8 |
| Equity & investment fund shares | 8bala | .... | .... | .... | .... | .... | .... | .... | .... | .... | .... | .... | .... |
| Debt securities | 8bbla | .... | .... | .... | .... | 78.3 | 112.1 | 90.0 | 132.0 | 144.8 | 1,117.4 | 1,253.9 | 1,252.8 |
| Fin. der.(oth.than reserves) & ESOs | 8c9la | .... | .... | .... | .... | .... | .... | .... | .... | .... | .... | .... | .... |
| Other investment | 8d9la | 6,464.0 | 5,541.5 | 4,303.6 | 3,441.4 | 3,929.4 | 3,895.1 | 4,282.0 | 4,857.5 | 5,550.5 | 6,290.5 | 7,074.2 | 7,703.0 |
| Other equity | 8dala | .... | .... | .... | .... | .... | .... | .... | .... | .... | .... | .... | .... |
| Debt instruments | 8dzla | 6,464.0 | 5,541.5 | 4,303.6 | 3,441.4 | 3,929.4 | 3,895.1 | 4,282.0 | 4,857.5 | 5,550.5 | 6,290.5 | 7,074.2 | 7,703.0 |

| | | 2004 | 2005 | 2006 | 2007 | 2008 | 2009 | 2010 | 2011 | 2012 | 2013 | 2014 | 2015 |
|---|---|---|---|---|---|---|---|---|---|---|---|---|---|
| **Government Finance** | | | | | | | | | | | | | |
| **Operations Statement** | | | | | | | | | | | | | |
| **Budgetary Central Government** | | | | | | *Millions of Lempiras: Fiscal Year Ends December 31* | | | | | | | |
| Revenue.......... | a1 | 27,706.3 | 32,195.6 | 37,242.4 | 44,694.6 | 52,297.3 | 47,006.8 | 50,494.4 | 56,824.7 | 60,356.6 | 64,119.3 | 76,768.3 | .... |
| Taxes.......... | a11 | 23,411.9 | 26,707.6 | 31,434.9 | 38,270.0 | 42,329.2 | 39,035.0 | 43,172.3 | 49,543.8 | 53,289.8 | 56,719.0 | 68,591.3 | .... |
| Social Contributions.......... | a12 | — | — | — | — | — | — | — | — | — | — | — | .... |
| Grants.......... | a13 | 1,352.1 | 2,127.6 | 3,059.7 | 3,721.9 | 5,472.6 | 5,020.0 | 4,078.2 | 3,594.7 | 3,471.0 | 2,948.6 | 3,294.8 | .... |
| Other Revenue.......... | a14 | 2,942.4 | 3,360.4 | 2,747.9 | 2,702.7 | 4,495.5 | 2,951.8 | 3,243.9 | 3,686.2 | 3,595.9 | 4,451.7 | 4,882.1 | .... |
| Expense.......... | a2 | 28,281.4 | 32,742.2 | 36,386.9 | 46,911.9 | 51,882.5 | 57,866.0 | 59,894.1 | 66,665.6 | 75,798.6 | 84,732.7 | 86,298.5 | .... |
| Compensation of Employees.......... | a21 | 13,720.6 | 15,045.4 | 16,900.9 | 21,423.3 | 24,439.8 | 29,765.9 | 31,744.7 | 31,968.0 | 34,594.7 | 36,033.0 | 36,404.0 | .... |
| Use of Goods & Services.......... | a22 | 3,248.5 | 4,583.0 | 5,614.9 | 7,134.4 | 6,885.3 | 8,482.9 | 7,762.3 | 8,562.5 | 10,487.9 | 11,919.5 | 10,969.8 | .... |
| Consumption of Fixed Capital.......... | a23 | .... | .... | .... | .... | .... | .... | .... | .... | .... | .... | .... | .... |
| Interest.......... | a24 | 2,160.9 | 2,246.2 | 1,760.7 | 1,388.3 | 1,611.8 | 1,760.8 | 2,538.2 | 4,017.9 | 5,512.9 | 7,763.7 | 9,390.8 | .... |
| Subsidies.......... | a25 | 523.5 | 635.5 | 999.4 | 3,037.4 | 857.4 | 363.3 | 318.2 | 557.5 | 1,091.4 | 351.0 | 180.6 | .... |
| Grants.......... | a26 | 5,460.7 | 7,020.7 | 6,437.2 | 8,117.7 | 10,095.2 | 8,419.9 | 7,675.5 | 9,551.4 | 10,652.7 | 14,297.5 | 11,728.2 | .... |
| Social Benefits.......... | a27 | 97.7 | 64.5 | 186.2 | 136.6 | 71.2 | 172.5 | 163.2 | 176.5 | 52.3 | 498.7 | 734.1 | .... |
| Other Expense.......... | a28 | 3,069.5 | 3,146.9 | 4,487.5 | 5,674.2 | 7,921.8 | 8,900.8 | 9,692.0 | 11,831.9 | 13,406.6 | 13,869.5 | 16,891.0 | .... |
| Gross Operating Balance [1-2+23]... | agob | −575.1 | −546.6 | 855.6 | −2,217.3 | 414.9 | −10,859.3 | −9,399.7 | −9,841.0 | −15,441.9 | −20,613.4 | −9,530.2 | .... |
| Net Operating Balance [1-2].......... | anob | .... | .... | .... | .... | .... | .... | .... | .... | .... | .... | .... | .... |
| Net Acq. of Nonfinancial Assets.......... | a31 | 4,063.9 | 4,164.2 | 3,487.1 | 5,023.0 | 6,978.6 | 7,629.7 | 4,959.7 | 5,460.2 | 5,610.7 | 9,463.0 | 8,470.1 | .... |
| Aquisition of Nonfin. Assets.......... | a31.1 | .... | .... | .... | .... | .... | .... | .... | .... | .... | .... | .... | |
| Disposal of Nonfin. Assets.......... | a31.2 | .... | .... | .... | .... | .... | .... | .... | .... | .... | .... | .... | |
| Net Lending/Borrowing [1-2-31]...... | anlb | −4,639.0 | −4,710.8 | −2,631.5 | −7,240.3 | −6,563.7 | −18,489.0 | −14,359.4 | −15,301.1 | −21,052.6 | −30,076.3 | −18,000.3 | .... |
| Net Acq. of Financial Assets.......... | a32 | 423.3 | −2,420.4 | 1,819.5 | −1,058.8 | 889.3 | 804.0 | 827.9 | −607.0 | 2,481.4 | 5,692.0 | −1,103.0 | .... |
| By instrument | | | | | | | | | | | | | |
| Monetary Gold & SDRs.......... | a3201 | — | — | — | — | — | — | — | — | — | — | — | .... |
| Currency & Deposits.......... | a3202 | 2,732.1 | −1,398.8 | 2,236.5 | −219.8 | 2,461.7 | 1,587.2 | 1,733.8 | −2,357.5 | 1,501.0 | 6,340.5 | −1,126.8 | .... |
| Securities other than Shares.......... | a3203 | −1,277.7 | −41.2 | 252.4 | −143.0 | 53.5 | 337.6 | −117.6 | 348.2 | 504.9 | −227.0 | −32.1 | .... |
| Loans.......... | a3204 | −550.1 | −857.5 | −659.0 | −601.4 | −348.4 | −1,962.5 | −721.6 | −97.6 | 445.1 | −444.3 | −17.4 | .... |
| Shares & Other Equity.......... | a3205 | −528.5 | — | −252.2 | −150.0 | −50.0 | — | — | — | — | — | — | .... |
| Insurance Technical Reserves.......... | a3206 | — | — | — | — | — | — | — | — | — | — | — | .... |
| Financial Derivatives.......... | a3207 | — | — | — | — | — | — | — | — | — | — | — | .... |
| Other Accounts Receivable.......... | a3208 | 47.5 | −122.9 | 241.8 | 55.4 | −1,227.5 | 841.7 | −66.7 | 1,500.0 | 30.5 | 22.7 | 73.4 | .... |
| By debtor | | | | | | | | | | | | | |
| Domestic.......... | a321 | 345.0 | −2,506.4 | 1,727.9 | −1,156.0 | 786.2 | 694.7 | 712.0 | −730.1 | 2,347.0 | 5,543.0 | −1,265.7 | .... |
| Foreign.......... | a322 | 78.3 | 86.0 | 91.6 | 97.2 | 103.1 | 109.3 | 115.9 | 123.1 | 134.4 | 149.0 | 162.7 | .... |
| Net Incurrence of Liabilities.......... | a33 | 5,062.3 | 2,290.4 | 4,451.1 | 6,181.5 | 7,453.0 | 19,293.0 | 15,187.3 | 14,694.2 | 23,534.0 | 35,768.3 | 16,897.3 | .... |
| By instrument | | | | | | | | | | | | | |
| Special Drawing Rights (SDRs).......... | a3301 | — | — | — | — | — | — | — | — | — | — | — | .... |
| Currency & Deposits.......... | a3302 | — | — | — | — | — | — | — | — | — | — | — | .... |
| Securities other than Shares.......... | a3303 | −47.1 | −159.0 | 57.5 | 72.2 | 6,387.3 | 7,614.0 | 14,469.8 | 10,701.6 | 6,800.6 | 3,855.2 | 6,347.5 | .... |
| Loans.......... | a3304 | 4,432.2 | 2,431.6 | 1,480.3 | 2,164.6 | 6,956.0 | 5,393.5 | 7,522.0 | 9,066.8 | 8,467.4 | 31,384.0 | 12,108.5 | .... |
| Shares & Other Equity.......... | a3305 | — | — | — | — | — | — | — | — | — | — | — | .... |
| Insurance Technical Reserves.......... | a3306 | — | — | — | — | — | — | — | — | — | — | — | .... |
| Financial Derivatives.......... | a3307 | — | — | — | — | — | — | — | — | — | — | — | .... |
| Other Accounts Payable.......... | a3308 | 677.1 | 17.7 | 2,913.3 | 3,944.7 | −5,890.3 | 6,285.5 | −6,804.5 | −5,074.3 | 8,266.0 | 529.1 | −1,558.6 | .... |
| By creditor | | | | | | | | | | | | | |
| Domestic.......... | a331 | −903.2 | −768.7 | 2,774.4 | 3,650.8 | 402.9 | 16,678.7 | 7,621.3 | 5,583.2 | 14,695.1 | 4,201.7 | 6,339.2 | .... |
| Foreign.......... | a332 | 5,965.4 | 3,059.0 | 1,676.7 | 2,530.7 | 7,050.1 | 2,614.3 | 7,566.0 | 9,111.0 | 8,838.9 | 31,566.6 | 10,558.2 | .... |
| Stat. Discrepancy [32-33-NLB].......... | anlbz | — | — | — | — | — | — | — | — | — | — | — | .... |
| Memo Item: Expenditure [2+31]...... | a2m | 32,345.3 | 36,906.4 | 39,874.0 | 51,934.9 | 58,861.1 | 65,495.7 | 64,853.8 | 72,125.8 | 81,409.2 | 94,195.7 | 94,768.5 | .... |
| **National Accounts** | | | | | | *Millions of Lempiras* | | | | | | | |
| Househ.Cons.Expend.,incl.NPISHs.... | 96f | 119,418 | 138,421 | 160,238 | 181,680 | 209,717 | 216,496 | 233,796 | 260,106 | 284,080 | 308,495 | 332,199 | 354,800 |
| Government Consumption Expend... | 91f | 24,244 | 28,522 | 30,951 | 38,778 | 44,912 | 51,543 | 53,651 | 53,820 | 58,545 | 63,009 | 64,350 | 67,471 |
| Gross Fixed Capital Formation.......... | 93e | 43,737 | 45,780 | 56,371 | 75,193 | 88,165 | 60,661 | 64,514 | 81,883 | 88,064 | 88,808 | 91,245 | 102,706 |
| Changes in Inventories.......... | 93i | 4,175 | 4,977 | 2,095 | 3,438 | 6,478 | −3,882 | 970 | 5,224 | 698 | −6,872 | −886 | 4,580 |
| Exports of Goods and Services.......... | 90c | 94,358 | 108,422 | 115,634 | 124,980 | 134,686 | 108,958 | 136,950 | 171,728 | 183,937 | 180,519 | 191,982 | 200,778 |
| Imports of Goods and Services (-).......... | 98c | 124,423 | 142,375 | 159,001 | 190,501 | 221,542 | 158,143 | 190,594 | 237,733 | 253,975 | 257,420 | 269,278 | 284,999 |
| Gross Domestic Product (GDP).......... | 99b | 161,508 | 183,747 | 206,288 | 233,567 | 262,417 | 275,632 | 299,286 | 335,028 | 361,348 | 376,540 | 409,612 | 445,336 |
| Net Primary Income from Abroad.......... | 98.n | −8,289 | −8,606 | −10,061 | −7,558 | −7,695 | −5,457 | −13,772 | −17,812 | −24,994 | −26,536 | −27,951 | −30,524 |
| Gross National Income (GNI).......... | 99a | 153,219 | 175,141 | 196,228 | 226,009 | 254,721 | 270,174 | 285,514 | 317,216 | 336,355 | 350,004 | 381,660 | 414,812 |
| Consumption of Fixed Capital.......... | 99cf | 8,430 | 10,211 | 11,194 | 12,803 | 14,553 | 16,145 | 17,613 | 18,356 | 19,273 | 20,556 | 19,161 | 21,568 |
| GDP Volume 2000 Prices.......... | 99b.p | 126,247 | 133,886 | 142,678 | 151,508 | 157,919 | 154,079 | 159,828 | 165,958 | 172,810 | 177,634 | 183,115 | 189,771 |
| GDP Volume (2010=100).......... | 99bvp | 79.0 | 83.8 | 89.3 | 94.8 | 98.8 | 96.4 | 100.0 | 103.8 | 108.1 | 111.1 | 114.6 | 118.7 |
| GDP Deflator (2010=100).......... | 99bip | 68.3 | 73.3 | 77.2 | 82.3 | 88.7 | 95.5 | 100.0 | 107.8 | 111.7 | 113.2 | 119.5 | 125.3 |
| | | | | | | *Millions: Midyear Estimates* | | | | | | | |
| Population.......... | 99z | 6.75 | 6.88 | 7.01 | 7.13 | 7.26 | 7.38 | 7.50 | 7.62 | 7.74 | 7.85 | 7.96 | 8.08 |

| | | 2004 | 2005 | 2006 | 2007 | 2008 | 2009 | 2010 | 2011 | 2012 | 2013 | 2014 | 2015 |
|---|---|---|---|---|---|---|---|---|---|---|---|---|---|
| **Exchange Rates** | | | | | | *Forint per SDR: End of Period* | | | | | | | |
| Official Rate.................................. | aa | 279.99 | 305.26 | 288.27 | 272.77 | 289.43 | 294.84 | 321.33 | 369.51 | 339.55 | 332.13 | 375.43 | 397.19 |
| | | | | | | *Forint per US Dollar: End of Period (ae) Period Average (rf)* | | | | | | | |
| Official Rate.................................. | ae | 180.29 | 213.58 | 191.62 | 172.61 | 187.91 | 188.07 | 208.65 | 240.68 | 220.93 | 215.67 | 259.13 | 286.63 |
| Official Rate.................................. | rf | 202.75 | 199.58 | 210.39 | 183.63 | 172.11 | 202.34 | 207.94 | 201.06 | 225.10 | 223.70 | 232.60 | 279.33 |
| | | | | | | *Index Numbers (2010=100): Period Averages* | | | | | | | |
| Official Rate.................................. | ahx | 102.4 | 104.0 | 98.6 | 113.0 | 121.6 | 103.2 | 100.0 | 103.7 | 92.1 | 92.7 | 89.2 | 74.2 |
| Nominal Effective Exchange Rate....... | nec | 108.7 | 109.5 | 102.9 | 109.1 | 110.5 | 100.6 | 100.0 | 99.1 | 93.9 | 92.9 | 90.0 | 87.6 |
| CPI-Based Real Effect. Ex. Rate........ | rec | 92.3 | 94.2 | 89.9 | 100.2 | 103.9 | 97.8 | 100.0 | 100.0 | 97.7 | 96.6 | 92.3 | 89.1 |
| **Fund Position** | | | | | | *Millions of SDRs: End of Period* | | | | | | | |
| Quota.......................................... | 2f.s | 1,038.40 | 1,038.40 | 1,038.40 | 1,038.40 | 1,038.40 | 1,038.40 | 1,038.40 | 1,038.40 | 1,038.40 | 1,038.40 | 1,038.40 | 1,038.40 |
| SDR Holdings................................. | 1b.s | 37.56 | 44.62 | 49.22 | 52.83 | 35.16 | 943.42 | 749.64 | 548.53 | 237.21 | 13.76 | 12.86 | 12.36 |
| Reserve Position in the Fund............ | 1c.s | 346.26 | 134.56 | 91.05 | 71.68 | 73.83 | 73.83 | 73.83 | 73.83 | 73.83 | 73.83 | 73.84 | 73.84 |
| Total Fund Cred.&Loans Outstg....... | 2tl | — | — | — | — | 4,215.00 | 7,637.00 | 7,637.00 | 7,637.00 | 4,416.81 | — | — | — |
| SDR Allocations.............................. | 1bd | — | — | — | — | — | 991.05 | 991.05 | 991.05 | 991.05 | 991.05 | 991.05 | 991.05 |
| **International Liquidity** | | | | | | *Millions of US Dollars Unless Otherwise Indicated: End of Period* | | | | | | | |
| Total Reserves minus Gold............... | 1l.d | 15,922 | 18,552 | 21,527 | 23,970 | 33,788 | 44,074 | 44,849 | 48,681 | 44,506 | 46,389 | 41,901 | 33,019 |
| SDR Holdings.............................. | 1b.d | 58 | 64 | 74 | 83 | 54 | 1,479 | 1,154 | 842 | 365 | 21 | 19 | 17 |
| Reserve Position in the Fund.......... | 1c.d | 538 | 192 | 137 | 113 | 114 | 116 | 114 | 113 | 113 | 114 | 107 | 102 |
| Foreign Exchange........................ | 1d.d | 15,326 | 18,296 | 21,316 | 23,773 | 33,620 | 42,479 | 43,581 | 47,725 | 44,028 | 46,254 | 41,775 | 32,900 |
| Gold (Million Fine Troy Ounces)....... | 1ad | .099 | .099 | .099 | .099 | .099 | .099 | .099 | .099 | .099 | .099 | .099 | .099 |
| Gold (National Valuation)................ | 1and | 43 | 51 | 63 | 82 | 86 | 109 | 139 | 154 | 164 | 119 | 118 | 105 |
| Central Bank: Other Assets............. | 3..d | 3,203.5 | 4,668.7 | 3,240.1 | 4,070.6 | 6,945.3 | 4,564.8 | 4,734.2 | 9,333.6 | 9,728.3 | 7,456.9 | 5,988.4 | 4,430.6 |
| Central Bank: Other Liabs.............. | 4..d | 1,427.7 | 1,584.7 | 1,815.7 | 1,858.2 | 2,658.2 | 5,808.4 | 8,910.4 | 7,509.1 | 4,479.8 | 2,776.4 | 2,596.0 | 1,910.9 |
| Other Depository Corps.: Assets....... | 7a.d | 7,199.7 | 6,968.2 | 12,434.1 | 17,041.4 | 19,863.3 | 20,029.8 | 17,612.0 | 15,644.5 | 12,881.2 | 11,966.9 | 10,393.2 | 12,946.9 |
| Other Depository Corps.: Liabs........ | 7b.d | 16,393.6 | 18,999.9 | 25,804.2 | 35,000.4 | 48,005.3 | 45,580.8 | 40,677.1 | 34,646.0 | 27,330.0 | 22,937.1 | 18,749.1 | 14,951.5 |
| **Central Bank** | | | | | | *Billions of Forint: End of Period* | | | | | | | |
| Net Foreign Assets........................ | 11n | 2,787.7 | 3,875.1 | 4,013.6 | 4,038.8 | 4,864.6 | 4,848.8 | 4,966.5 | 6,974.0 | 7,266.2 | 9,334.5 | 10,140.8 | 8,682.4 |
| Claims on Nonresidents................ | 11 | 3,045.1 | 4,213.6 | 4,361.5 | 4,359.5 | 6,584.1 | 8,485.0 | 9,598.1 | 11,969.4 | 10,092.2 | 10,262.5 | 11,185.6 | 9,623.8 |
| Liabilities to Nonresidents............. | 16c | 257.4 | 338.5 | 347.9 | 320.8 | 1,719.5 | 3,636.2 | 4,631.6 | 4,995.4 | 2,826.0 | 928.0 | 1,044.8 | 941.4 |
| Claims on Other Depository Corps.... | 12e | 11.7 | 4.7 | .9 | .6 | 177.2 | .6 | 36.9 | 119.3 | 184.4 | 821.6 | 1,037.9 | 1,401.1 |
| Net Claims on Central Government.... | 12an | 211.0 | −36.9 | −140.6 | −108.2 | −1,285.9 | −709.4 | −827.3 | −1,214.6 | −1,235.7 | −613.5 | −848.8 | −620.4 |
| Claims on Central Government...... | 12a | 525.5 | 246.6 | 232.6 | 146.7 | 360.0 | 279.0 | 249.5 | 168.5 | 142.2 | 138.4 | 139.5 | 39.2 |
| Liabilities to Central Government.... | 16d | 314.6 | 283.5 | 373.2 | 254.9 | 1,645.9 | 988.4 | 1,076.8 | 1,383.1 | 1,377.9 | 751.9 | 988.3 | 659.6 |
| Claims on Other Sectors................. | 12s | 13.1 | 12.9 | 12.0 | 11.9 | 10.5 | 9.9 | 9.9 | 9.9 | 9.9 | 10.6 | 47.1 | 69.6 |
| Claims on Other Financial Corps..... | 12g | .4 | .4 | .4 | .4 | .4 | .4 | .4 | .4 | .4 | .6 | 31.9 | 56.6 |
| Claims on State & Local Govts...... | 12b | — | — | — | — | — | — | — | — | — | — | — | — |
| Claims on Public Nonfin. Corps...... | 12c | — | — | — | — | — | — | — | — | — | — | — | — |
| Claims on Private Sector.............. | 12d | 12.7 | 12.6 | 11.7 | 11.5 | 10.1 | 9.5 | 9.5 | 9.5 | 9.5 | 9.9 | 15.2 | 13.1 |
| Monetary Base............................. | 14 | 2,582.1 | 3,522.7 | 3,662.5 | 3,265.7 | 3,438.2 | 2,964.8 | 3,239.7 | 4,031.2 | 3,751.1 | 4,069.0 | 9,767.9 | 9,132.8 |
| Currency in Circulation................. | 14a | 1,452.6 | 1,714.1 | 1,967.9 | 2,202.2 | 2,308.7 | 2,187.9 | 2,378.1 | 2,709.6 | 2,737.7 | 3,202.7 | 3,749.1 | 4,318.4 |
| Liabs. to Other Depository Corps..... | 14c | 1,120.0 | 1,803.5 | 1,689.6 | 1,063.5 | 1,129.6 | 776.9 | 861.6 | 1,317.6 | 1,009.2 | 864.5 | 6,013.6 | 4,807.3 |
| Liabilities to Other Sectors............. | 14d | 9.5 | 5.1 | 5.1 | — | — | — | — | 4.0 | 4.3 | 1.8 | 5.2 | 7.2 |
| Other Liabs. to Other Dep. Corps..... | 14n | 410.0 | 244.3 | 183.4 | 652.7 | 1,346.9 | 3,230.5 | 3,124.2 | 3,445.7 | 3,600.8 | 5,182.7 | 14.4 | — |
| Dep. & Sec. Excl. f/Monetary Base..... | 14o | — | — | — | — | — | — | — | — | — | — | — | — |
| Deposits Included in Broad Money... | 15 | — | — | — | — | — | — | — | — | — | — | — | — |
| Sec.Ot.th.Shares Incl.in Brd. Money | 16a | — | — | — | — | — | — | — | — | — | — | — | — |
| Deposits Excl. from Broad Money... | 16b | — | — | — | — | — | — | — | — | — | — | — | — |
| Sec.Ot.th.Shares Excl.f/Brd.Money.. | 16s | — | — | — | — | — | — | — | — | — | — | — | — |
| Loans....................................... | 16l | — | — | — | — | — | — | — | — | — | — | — | — |
| Financial Derivatives...................... | 16m | — | — | — | — | — | — | — | — | — | — | — | — |
| Shares and Other Equity................. | 17a | 44.6 | 132.0 | 92.2 | 80.9 | 320.9 | 345.1 | 463.4 | 1,381.8 | 543.9 | 445.9 | 630.9 | 456.3 |
| Other Items (Net)........................... | 17r | −13.2 | −43.2 | −52.1 | −56.3 | −1,339.7 | −2,390.6 | −2,642.6 | −2,970.1 | −1,671.1 | −144.4 | −36.3 | 161.3 |
| **Other Depository Corporations** | | | | | | *Billions of Forint: End of Period* | | | | | | | |
| Net Foreign Assets........................ | 21n | −1,657.6 | −2,569.7 | −2,562.0 | −3,099.9 | −5,288.2 | −4,805.4 | −4,812.5 | −4,573.3 | −3,192.2 | −2,365.9 | −2,165.3 | −574.6 |
| Claims on Nonresidents................ | 21 | 1,298.0 | 1,488.3 | 2,382.6 | 2,941.5 | 3,732.5 | 3,767.0 | 3,674.8 | 3,765.3 | 2,845.8 | 2,580.9 | 2,693.2 | 3,711.0 |
| Liabilities to Nonresidents............. | 26c | 2,955.6 | 4,058.0 | 4,944.6 | 6,041.4 | 9,020.7 | 8,572.4 | 8,487.3 | 8,338.6 | 6,038.0 | 4,946.8 | 4,858.5 | 4,285.5 |
| Claims on Central Bank................. | 20 | 1,259.4 | 147.6 | 1,819.1 | 1,748.0 | 2,546.2 | 4,048.4 | 4,027.6 | 4,856.9 | 4,751.9 | 6,234.6 | 6,189.6 | 4,988.1 |
| Currency.................................. | 20a | 111.0 | 113.9 | 129.5 | 134.3 | 171.5 | 148.6 | 159.7 | 158.1 | 183.7 | 201.7 | 200.7 | 209.3 |
| Reserve Deposits and Securities..... | 20b | 1,114.7 | — | 1,689.6 | 1,063.2 | 1,129.5 | 769.1 | 843.2 | 1,295.5 | 1,004.5 | 863.8 | 5,988.9 | 4,778.8 |
| Other Claims............................. | 20n | 33.7 | 33.7 | — | 550.5 | 1,245.2 | 3,130.7 | 3,024.7 | 3,403.3 | 3,563.7 | 5,169.0 | — | — |
| Net Claims on Central Government.. | 22an | 2,149.1 | 2,219.5 | 2,796.2 | 2,829.4 | 3,498.1 | 2,936.9 | 3,073.0 | 3,280.0 | 3,745.3 | 4,434.9 | 5,096.8 | 6,585.2 |
| Claims on Central Government...... | 22a | 2,209.3 | 2,288.7 | 2,874.3 | 2,947.1 | 3,594.3 | 3,508.5 | 3,472.9 | 3,588.1 | 3,911.1 | 4,599.7 | 5,390.1 | 6,866.5 |
| Liabilities to Central Government.... | 26d | 60.2 | 69.2 | 78.1 | 117.7 | 96.1 | 571.6 | 399.9 | 308.1 | 165.9 | 164.8 | 293.3 | 281.3 |
| Claims on Other Sectors................. | 22s | 9,628.7 | 11,650.3 | 13,700.2 | 16,476.4 | 19,888.0 | 18,959.4 | 19,600.2 | 19,664.3 | 17,103.6 | 15,866.0 | 15,446.1 | 13,982.9 |
| Claims on Other Financial Corps..... | 22g | 1,278.8 | 1,656.0 | 1,842.7 | 2,251.0 | 2,989.3 | 2,306.9 | 2,047.4 | 2,048.7 | 1,687.8 | 1,550.1 | 1,432.3 | 1,678.8 |
| Claims on State & Local Govts...... | 22b | 148.8 | 243.3 | 369.9 | 549.0 | 743.1 | 807.0 | 1,017.8 | 972.3 | 845.2 | 338.5 | 32.9 | 38.3 |
| Claims on Public Nonfin. Corps...... | 22c | — | — | — | — | — | — | — | — | — | — | — | — |
| Claims on Private Sector.............. | 22d | 8,201.1 | 9,751.0 | 11,487.5 | 13,676.5 | 16,155.6 | 15,845.5 | 16,535.1 | 16,643.3 | 14,570.6 | 13,977.4 | 13,980.8 | 12,265.8 |
| Liabilities to Central Bank.............. | 26g | 10.7 | — | .4 | — | 175.8 | — | 36.3 | 118.6 | 183.7 | 827.2 | 1,042.7 | 1,404.9 |
| Transf.Dep.Included in Broad Money | 24 | 2,823.1 | 3,588.5 | 3,995.0 | 4,280.4 | 4,024.8 | 4,082.3 | 4,416.6 | 4,787.2 | 4,739.1 | 5,893.2 | 7,184.7 | 9,109.8 |
| Other Dep.Included in Broad Money. | 25 | 5,574.7 | 5,997.6 | 6,926.9 | 7,660.2 | 8,969.5 | 9,392.3 | 9,088.6 | 9,363.6 | 9,086.0 | 8,378.0 | 7,902.2 | 6,541.0 |
| Sec.Ot.th.Shares Incl. in Brd. Money.. | 26a | 57.3 | 56.2 | 34.9 | 201.1 | 315.7 | 497.0 | 970.5 | 1,100.6 | 597.9 | 1,033.4 | 123.7 | 80.8 |
| Deposits Excl. from Broad Money..... | 26b | 263.3 | 327.4 | 595.9 | 764.5 | 811.7 | 724.8 | 911.5 | 1,041.6 | 1,247.9 | 1,367.9 | 1,365.8 | 1,453.2 |
| Sec.Ot.th.Shares Excl.f/Brd.Money... | 26s | 1,293.1 | 1,439.0 | 2,098.2 | 2,444.1 | 2,820.1 | 2,616.5 | 2,225.8 | 1,674.9 | 1,603.3 | 1,673.3 | 1,697.7 | 1,812.2 |
| Loans....................................... | 26l | — | — | — | — | — | — | — | — | — | — | — | — |
| Financial Derivatives...................... | 26m | — | 114.3 | 173.3 | 279.8 | 814.0 | 513.4 | 448.9 | 450.1 | 357.9 | 393.9 | 263.3 | 216.3 |
| Insurance Technical Reserves.......... | 26r | — | — | — | — | — | — | — | — | — | — | — | — |
| Shares and Other Equity................. | 27a | 1,463.8 | 694.6 | 760.2 | 836.5 | 759.0 | 796.8 | 2,749.7 | 2,787.0 | 2,915.7 | 3,103.5 | 2,855.8 | 2,881.0 |
| Other Items (Net)........................... | 27r | −106.4 | −770.1 | 1,168.9 | 1,487.2 | 1,953.5 | 2,516.3 | 1,267.6 | 1,904.4 | 1,677.1 | 1,499.2 | 2,150.3 | 1,482.6 |
| Memo Item: | | | | | | | | | | | | | |
| Total Assets................................. | 20ra | 17,076.9 | 20,298.3 | 24,370.9 | 28,536.2 | 34,127.4 | 35,268.7 | 36,014.5 | 37,919.3 | 34,467.1 | 34,466.2 | 35,821.0 | 35,527.5 |

# Hungary 944

| | | 2004 | 2005 | 2006 | 2007 | 2008 | 2009 | 2010 | 2011 | 2012 | 2013 | 2014 | 2015 |
|---|---|---|---|---|---|---|---|---|---|---|---|---|---|
| **Depository Corporations** | | | | | | *Billions of Forint: End of Period* | | | | | | | |
| Net Foreign Assets | 31n | 1,130.1 | 1,305.4 | 1,451.6 | 938.8 | −423.6 | 43.4 | 154.0 | 2,400.7 | 4,074.0 | 6,968.6 | 7,975.5 | 8,107.9 |
| Claims on Nonresidents | 31 | 4,343.1 | 5,701.8 | 6,744.2 | 7,301.0 | 10,316.6 | 12,252.0 | 13,272.9 | 15,734.7 | 12,938.0 | 12,843.4 | 13,878.8 | 13,334.8 |
| Liabilities to Nonresidents | 36c | 3,213.0 | 4,396.5 | 5,292.5 | 6,362.2 | 10,740.1 | 12,208.6 | 13,118.9 | 13,334.0 | 8,864.0 | 5,874.8 | 5,903.2 | 5,226.9 |
| Domestic Claims | 32 | 12,001.9 | 13,845.8 | 16,367.9 | 19,209.5 | 22,110.6 | 21,196.8 | 21,855.7 | 21,739.6 | 19,623.1 | 19,698.0 | 19,741.2 | 20,017.3 |
| Net Claims on Central Government | 32an | 2,360.1 | 2,182.6 | 2,655.6 | 2,721.2 | 2,212.2 | 2,227.5 | 2,245.6 | 2,065.4 | 2,509.6 | 3,821.4 | 4,248.1 | 5,964.8 |
| Claims on Central Government | 32a | 2,734.9 | 2,535.3 | 3,106.9 | 3,093.8 | 3,954.3 | 3,787.6 | 3,722.3 | 3,756.6 | 4,053.3 | 4,738.0 | 5,529.6 | 6,905.7 |
| Liabilities to Central Government | 36d | 374.8 | 352.7 | 451.3 | 372.6 | 1,742.1 | 1,560.0 | 1,476.7 | 1,691.2 | 1,543.7 | 916.7 | 1,281.5 | 940.9 |
| Claims on Other Sectors | 32s | 9,641.8 | 11,663.2 | 13,712.2 | 16,488.3 | 19,898.4 | 18,969.3 | 19,610.1 | 19,674.1 | 17,113.5 | 15,876.6 | 15,493.1 | 14,052.5 |
| Claims on Other Financial Corps. | 32g | 1,279.2 | 1,656.3 | 1,843.1 | 2,251.3 | 2,989.7 | 2,307.3 | 2,047.7 | 2,049.1 | 1,688.2 | 1,550.8 | 1,464.2 | 1,735.4 |
| Claims on State & Local Govts. | 32b | 148.8 | 243.3 | 369.9 | 549.0 | 743.1 | 807.0 | 1,017.8 | 972.3 | 845.2 | 338.5 | 32.9 | 38.3 |
| Claims on Public Nonfin. Corps. | 32c | — | — | — | — | — | — | — | — | — | — | — | — |
| Claims on Private Sector | 32d | 8,213.8 | 9,763.6 | 11,499.2 | 13,688.0 | 16,165.7 | 15,855.0 | 16,544.6 | 16,652.8 | 14,580.1 | 13,987.3 | 13,996.0 | 12,278.9 |
| Broad Money Liabilities | 35l | 9,806.2 | 11,247.7 | 12,800.1 | 14,209.6 | 15,447.2 | 16,010.8 | 16,694.0 | 17,807.0 | 16,981.3 | 18,307.4 | 18,764.2 | 19,847.8 |
| Currency Outside Depository Corps | 34a | 1,341.5 | 1,600.3 | 1,838.3 | 2,067.9 | 2,137.2 | 2,039.3 | 2,218.3 | 2,551.5 | 2,553.9 | 3,001.0 | 3,548.5 | 4,109.1 |
| Transferable Deposits | 34 | 2,827.7 | 3,588.5 | 3,995.0 | 4,280.4 | 4,024.8 | 4,082.3 | 4,416.7 | 4,791.3 | 4,743.4 | 5,895.0 | 7,189.8 | 9,116.9 |
| Other Deposits | 35 | 5,579.6 | 6,002.7 | 6,932.0 | 7,660.2 | 8,969.5 | 9,392.3 | 9,088.6 | 9,363.6 | 9,086.0 | 8,378.0 | 7,902.2 | 6,541.0 |
| Securities Other than Shares | 36a | 57.3 | 56.2 | 34.9 | 201.1 | 315.7 | 497.0 | 970.5 | 1,100.6 | 597.9 | 1,033.4 | 123.7 | 80.8 |
| Deposits Excl. from Broad Money | 36b | 263.3 | 327.4 | 595.9 | 764.5 | 811.7 | 724.8 | 911.5 | 1,041.6 | 1,247.9 | 1,367.9 | 1,365.8 | 1,453.2 |
| Sec.Ot.th.Shares Excl.f/Brd.Money | 36s | 1,293.1 | 1,439.0 | 2,098.2 | 2,444.1 | 2,820.1 | 2,616.5 | 2,225.8 | 1,674.9 | 1,603.3 | 1,673.3 | 1,697.7 | 1,812.2 |
| Loans | 36l | — | — | — | — | — | — | — | — | — | — | — | — |
| Financial Derivatives | 36m | — | 114.3 | 173.3 | 279.8 | 814.0 | 513.4 | 448.9 | 450.1 | 357.9 | 393.9 | 263.3 | 216.3 |
| Insurance Technical Reserves | 36r | — | — | — | — | — | — | — | — | — | — | — | — |
| Shares and Other Equity | 37a | 1,508.4 | 826.6 | 852.4 | 917.5 | 1,079.9 | 1,142.0 | 3,213.1 | 4,168.8 | 3,459.6 | 3,549.4 | 3,486.7 | 3,337.3 |
| Other Items (Net) | 37r | 261.1 | 1,196.1 | 1,299.6 | 1,532.8 | 714.2 | 232.8 | −1,257.6 | −1,002.0 | 47.1 | 1,374.7 | 2,157.9 | 1,676.1 |
| Broad Money Liabs., Seasonally Adj. | 35l.b | 9,643.1 | 11,077.1 | 12,636.0 | 14,065.1 | 15,315.0 | 15,876.6 | 16,515.1 | 17,553.4 | 16,659.4 | 17,896.9 | 18,293.5 | 19,330.8 |
| **Monetary Aggregates** | | | | | | *Billions of Forint: End of Period* | | | | | | | |
| Broad Money | 59m | 9,806.2 | 11,247.7 | 12,800.1 | 14,209.6 | 15,447.2 | 16,010.8 | 16,694.0 | 17,807.0 | 16,981.3 | 18,307.4 | 18,764.2 | 19,847.8 |
| o/w:Currency Issued by Cent.Govt | 59m.a | — | — | — | — | — | — | — | — | — | — | — | — |
| o/w: Dep.in Nonfin. Corporations. | 59m.b | — | — | — | — | — | — | — | — | — | — | — | — |
| o/w:Secs. Issued by Central Govt. | 59m.c | — | — | — | — | — | — | — | — | — | — | — | — |
| Money (National Definitions) | | | | | | | | | | | | | |
| Monetary Base | 19ma | 2,014.7 | 2,405.0 | 2,737.8 | 3,051.1 | 3,647.4 | 2,801.3 | 3,205.6 | 3,872.6 | 3,412.1 | 3,795.9 | 4,517.0 | 4,781.4 |
| M1 | 59ma | 4,169.3 | 5,188.8 | 5,833.3 | 6,355.3 | 6,158.3 | 6,123.1 | 6,635.0 | 7,341.6 | 7,289.0 | 8,898.6 | 10,740.6 | 13,219.6 |
| M2 | 59mb | 9,427.3 | 10,652.8 | 11,913.2 | 12,953.4 | 14,240.6 | 14,367.2 | 14,350.8 | 15,366.8 | 15,177.1 | 15,847.8 | 17,342.8 | 18,638.9 |
| M3 | 59mc | 9,808.0 | 11,230.7 | 12,785.1 | 14,202.0 | 15,421.2 | 15,972.9 | 16,441.0 | 17,415.7 | 16,834.9 | 17,930.5 | 18,764.6 | 19,944.3 |
| M4 | 59md | 14,508.1 | 16,542.6 | .... | .... | .... | .... | .... | .... | .... | .... | .... | .... |
| **Interest Rates** | | | | | | *Percent Per Annum* | | | | | | | |
| Discount Rate (End of Period) | 60.a | 9.50 | 6.00 | 8.00 | 7.50 | 10.00 | 6.25 | 5.75 | 7.00 | 5.75 | 3.00 | 2.10 | 1.35 |
| Treasury Bill Rate | 60c | 11.32 | 6.95 | 6.87 | 7.67 | 8.90 | 8.48 | 5.37 | 6.02 | 6.90 | 4.18 | 2.17 | 1.16 |
| Deposit Rate | 60l | 9.09 | 5.17 | 7.45 | 6.81 | 9.92 | 5.82 | 4.92 | 6.19 | 5.29 | 2.46 | 1.42 | .87 |
| Lending Rate | 60p | 12.82 | 8.54 | 8.08 | 9.09 | 10.18 | 11.04 | 7.59 | 8.32 | 9.00 | 6.30 | 4.45 | 2.90 |
| Government Bond Yield | 61 | 8.19 | 6.60 | 7.12 | 6.74 | 8.24 | 9.12 | 7.28 | 7.64 | 7.89 | 5.92 | 4.81 | 3.43 |
| **Prices, Production, Labor** | | | | | | *Index Numbers (2010=100): Period Averages* | | | | | | | |
| Share Prices | 62 | 52.2 | 84.5 | 100.2 | 116.0 | 87.9 | 71.4 | 100.0 | 91.3 | 80.3 | 83.0 | 79.8 | 93.5 |
| Producer Prices | 63 | 76.3 | 79.9 | 85.1 | 87.1 | 90.2 | 95.9 | 100.0 | 105.4 | 109.7 | 110.5 | 110.1 | 109.0 |
| Consumer Prices | 64 | 74.3 | 76.9 | 79.9 | 86.3 | 91.5 | 95.3 | † 100.0 | 103.9 | 109.8 | 111.7 | 111.5 | 111.4 |
| Harmonized CPI | 64h | 74.5 | 77.1 | 80.2 | 86.6 | 91.8 | 95.5 | † 100.0 | 103.9 | 109.8 | 111.7 | 111.7 | 111.8 |
| Wages: Average Earnings | 65 | 68.2 | 74.3 | 80.1 | 82.4 | 87.5 | 91.2 | 100.0 | 107.9 | 113.6 | 120.3 | 125.5 | 130.4 |
| Industrial Production | 66 | 86.8 | 92.7 | 101.9 | 109.9 | 109.9 | 90.5 | 100.0 | 105.6 | 103.7 | 104.8 | 112.9 | 121.4 |
| Industrial Employment | 67 | 119.1 | 115.6 | 114.0 | 112.9 | 112.1 | 101.1 | 100.0 | 102.8 | 100.6 | 101.0 | 103.6 | 106.2 |
| | | | | | | *Number in Thousands: Period Averages* | | | | | | | |
| Labor Force | 67d | 4,135 | 4,180 | 4,222 | 4,185 | 4,144 | 4,135 | 4,171 | 4,190 | 4,265 | 4,300 | 4,413 | 4,483 |
| Employment | 67e | 3,894 | 3,879 | 3,904 | 3,872 | 3,818 | 3,718 | 3,701 | 3,724 | 3,793 | 3,860 | 4,070 | 4,176 |
| Unemployment | 67c | 252 | 302 | 317 | 312 | 326 | 418 | 469 | 468 | 474 | 441 | 343 | 308 |
| Unemployment Rate (%) | 67r | 6.1 | 7.2 | 7.5 | 7.4 | 7.8 | 10.0 | 11.2 | 11.0 | 11.0 | 10.2 | 7.7 | 6.8 |
| **Intl. Transactions & Positions** | | | | | | *Billions of Forint* | | | | | | | |
| Exports | 70 | 11,093.9 | 12,425.5 | 15,591.1 | 17,207.8 | 18,301.7 | 16,946.1 | 19,688.6 | 22,262.9 | 23,183.3 | 24,244.0 | 26,120.5 | 28,037.8 |
| Imports, c.i.f. | 71 | 12,063.7 | 13,145.5 | 16,224.7 | 17,285.3 | 18,102.1 | 15,634.9 | 18,205.7 | 20,283.9 | 21,211.9 | 22,154.0 | 24,143.6 | 25,520.1 |
| Imports, f.o.b. | 71.v | 11,869.4 | 12,949.9 | 15,976.1 | 17,060.9 | 18,325.5 | 15,618.3 | 17,965.4 | 20,051.0 | 20,947.3 | 21,924.5 | 23,907.6 | 25,315.0 |
| | | | | | | *2010=100* | | | | | | | |
| Volume of Exports | 72 | 63.0 | 70.1 | 82.7 | 95.8 | 99.9 | 87.8 | 100.0 | 109.9 | 110.8 | 115.5 | 123.5 | 133.0 |
| Volume of Imports | 73 | 75.2 | 79.6 | 91.1 | 102.1 | 106.8 | 88.8 | 100.0 | 106.8 | 106.9 | 112.3 | 122.1 | 130.4 |
| Export Prices | 76 | 94.4 | 93.7 | 99.7 | 95.2 | 95.6 | 98.4 | 100.0 | 103.3 | 106.3 | 106.2 | 107.4 | 107.1 |
| Import Prices | 76.x | 91.1 | 92.3 | 99.7 | 95.3 | 97.2 | 98.3 | 100.0 | 105.0 | 109.5 | 108.9 | 108.9 | 107.7 |

# Hungary 944

| | | 2004 | 2005 | 2006 | 2007 | 2008 | 2009 | 2010 | 2011 | 2012 | 2013 | 2014 | 2015 |
|---|---|---|---|---|---|---|---|---|---|---|---|---|---|
| **Balance of Payments** | | | | | | | *Millions of US Dollars* | | | | | | |
| A. Current Account* | 109bx | −8,848.2 | −7,883.4 | −8,119.0 | −9,950.1 | −10,931.1 | −992.2 | 346.3 | 1,132.4 | 2,188.7 | 5,273.7 | 2,710.2 | 5,034.7 |
| Goods, credit (exports) | 1a9cx | 50,961.0 | 58,646.1 | 70,187.9 | 89,603.5 | 105,858.5 | 79,380.3 | 87,665.9 | 99,910.6 | 89,883.3 | 95,632.0 | 99,185.1 | 89,443.1 |
| Goods, debit (imports) | 1a9dx | 55,423.2 | 61,106.0 | 72,767.1 | 90,157.3 | 107,216.7 | 75,641.8 | 84,193.8 | 95,839.1 | 86,152.3 | 91,115.5 | 95,806.6 | 84,703.6 |
| Balance on goods | 1a9bx | −4,462.3 | −2,459.9 | −2,579.2 | −553.9 | −1,358.2 | 3,738.5 | 3,472.1 | 4,071.5 | 3,731.0 | 4,516.4 | 3,378.5 | 4,739.6 |
| Services, credit (exports) | 1b9cx | 11,459.6 | 12,642.1 | 13,577.4 | 17,064.9 | 20,494.0 | 18,561.4 | 19,396.9 | 22,340.7 | 20,617.6 | 22,630.2 | 24,676.7 | 21,684.8 |
| Services, debit (imports) | 1b9dx | 10,393.7 | 11,535.0 | 12,145.2 | 15,831.5 | 18,513.1 | 16,940.0 | 15,909.6 | 17,736.1 | 15,752.6 | 17,348.4 | 18,139.2 | 16,036.0 |
| Balance on Goods & Services | 1z9bx | −3,396.3 | −1,352.8 | −1,147.0 | 679.5 | 622.7 | 5,360.0 | 6,959.3 | 8,676.2 | 8,595.9 | 9,798.3 | 9,916.0 | 10,388.4 |
| Primary income: credit | 1c9cx | 3,770.0 | 4,610.3 | 9,513.8 | 14,235.1 | 18,161.0 | 18,785.3 | 19,304.8 | 16,279.6 | 16,272.6 | 16,621.3 | 14,009.7 | 12,368.2 |
| Primary income: debit | 1c9dx | 8,741.9 | 9,969.9 | 15,236.9 | 23,287.2 | 27,810.2 | 24,777.4 | 25,401.4 | 22,997.1 | 21,655.2 | 20,440.6 | 20,237.9 | 16,878.8 |
| Balance on gds, serv. & prim. inc. | 1y9bx | −8,368.2 | −6,712.3 | −6,870.1 | −8,372.6 | −9,026.4 | −632.2 | 862.8 | 1,958.7 | 3,213.4 | 5,979.0 | 3,687.8 | 5,877.7 |
| Secondary income: credit | 1d9ca | 1,799.4 | 2,002.8 | 2,313.6 | 2,901.3 | 1,272.1 | 1,969.8 | 1,970.4 | 2,037.8 | 2,168.1 | 3,013.6 | 2,643.2 | 2,478.3 |
| Secondary income: debit | 1d9da | 2,279.4 | 3,174.0 | 3,562.5 | 4,478.9 | 3,176.7 | 2,329.8 | 2,486.8 | 2,864.1 | 3,192.8 | 3,719.0 | 3,620.7 | 3,321.3 |
| B. Capital Account* | 209ba | 98.2 | 740.3 | 747.7 | 978.7 | 1,673.3 | 2,285.8 | 2,364.9 | 3,267.0 | 3,249.8 | 4,895.4 | 5,030.0 | 5,424.8 |
| Capital account: credit | 209ca | 288.2 | 858.1 | 1,285.8 | 1,422.6 | 1,705.6 | 2,426.6 | 3,043.0 | 3,416.3 | 3,382.5 | 5,168.3 | 5,233.3 | 5,714.5 |
| Capital account: debit | 209da | 190.0 | 117.8 | 538.1 | 443.9 | 32.3 | 140.8 | 678.1 | 149.3 | 132.7 | 272.9 | 203.3 | 289.7 |
| Balance on current & capital acct. | 129ba | −8,749.9 | −7,143.2 | −7,371.3 | −8,971.4 | −9,257.8 | 1,293.6 | 2,711.3 | 4,399.4 | 5,438.5 | 10,169.0 | 7,740.2 | 10,459.4 |
| C. Financial Account* | 309na | −12,817.1 | −14,976.7 | −11,076.4 | −8,962.0 | −16,662.1 | −3,861.7 | −2,782.6 | −4,622.2 | 5,317.6 | −49.4 | 5,041.8 | 14,407.5 |
| Direct investment: assets | 3a9aa | 1,578.5 | 3,100.7 | 18,227.5 | 68,145.5 | 73,613.8 | −3,792.4 | −24,773.0 | 8,646.7 | 7,854.3 | −3,944.3 | 8,809.6 | 1,631.0 |
| Equity & investment fund shares | 3aaaa | 1,236.5 | 2,429.4 | 17,728.4 | 66,995.9 | 71,728.6 | 4,787.0 | −41,334.3 | 18,458.2 | 17,799.9 | −3,722.7 | 4,523.8 | −4,909.2 |
| Debt instruments | 3abaa | 342.0 | 671.3 | 499.2 | 1,149.6 | 1,885.1 | −8,579.4 | 16,561.2 | −9,811.5 | −9,945.5 | −221.6 | 4,285.8 | 6,540.2 |
| Direct investment: liabilities | 3a9la | 4,538.1 | 8,505.4 | 18,678.7 | 70,631.3 | 75,013.0 | −2,967.2 | −20,933.5 | 10,506.2 | 10,618.9 | −3,777.8 | 12,521.7 | 2,790.0 |
| Equity & investment fund shares | 3aala | 4,150.9 | 7,141.1 | 13,012.3 | 60,447.2 | 42,159.5 | −5,848.6 | 197.6 | −6,223.8 | 11,006.6 | −2,981.5 | 9,062.6 | 5,050.4 |
| Debt instruments | 3abla | 387.2 | 1,364.3 | 5,666.4 | 10,184.1 | 32,853.5 | 2,881.5 | −21,131.1 | 16,730.0 | −387.7 | −796.2 | 3,459.1 | −2,260.3 |
| Portfolio investment: assets | 3b9aa | 526.3 | 1,283.3 | 2,426.5 | 2,868.7 | 3,854.3 | 1,036.9 | 448.9 | −2,185.5 | −960.3 | −468.7 | 2,325.4 | 434.2 |
| Equity & investment fund shares | 3baaa | 523.7 | 746.8 | 1,906.9 | 2,573.6 | 3,295.4 | 1,108.1 | 689.6 | −2,191.0 | −888.7 | −399.0 | 1,225.4 | 399.0 |
| Debt securities | 3bbaa | 2.6 | 536.5 | 519.6 | 295.1 | 558.9 | −71.2 | −240.6 | 5.4 | −71.6 | −69.7 | 1,100.0 | 35.2 |
| Portfolio investment: liabilities | 3b9la | 7,352.5 | 5,784.3 | 8,750.7 | 525.7 | 841.4 | −4,083.6 | 337.1 | 6,772.1 | 944.7 | 3,558.9 | −1,765.9 | −5,852.8 |
| Equity & investment fund shares | 3bala | 1,490.8 | −16.3 | 911.8 | −5,009.8 | −197.1 | 665.2 | −325.2 | 177.6 | 746.2 | 25.0 | −341.2 | 793.1 |
| Debt securities | 3bbla | 5,861.7 | 5,800.6 | 7,839.0 | 5,535.6 | 1,038.6 | −4,748.8 | 662.3 | 6,594.4 | 198.5 | 3,533.8 | −1,424.8 | −6,645.9 |
| Fin. der.& empl.stk.ops.(ESOs): net | 3c9na | −411.8 | 150.9 | −187.1 | −1,120.9 | 1,063.2 | −1,015.9 | −912.0 | 1,037.0 | −424.3 | −837.8 | 330.3 | −776.0 |
| Fin. der. & ESOs: assets | 3c9aa | −4,214.1 | −3,620.5 | −4,570.1 | −6,335.6 | −12,980.9 | −7,765.4 | −6,592.9 | −7,016.2 | −6,051.8 | −5,264.6 | −5,281.9 | −6,915.2 |
| Fin. der. & ESOs: liabilities | 3c9la | −3,802.3 | −3,771.4 | −4,383.1 | −5,214.6 | −14,044.1 | −6,749.5 | −5,680.9 | −8,053.2 | −5,627.4 | −4,426.9 | −5,612.2 | −6,139.2 |
| Other investment: assets | 3d9aa | 1,542.8 | 2,323.8 | 3,603.7 | 7,977.3 | 3,898.6 | 1,059.0 | 1,071.3 | −3,113.2 | −2,312.6 | −1,144.6 | −814.1 | 5,906.3 |
| Other equity | 3daaa | 33.4 | 64.2 | 39.4 | 73.3 | 80.2 | 59.9 | 384.2 | −3.9 | −10.9 | 58.8 | 45.9 | 45.5 |
| Debt instruments | 3dzaa | 1,509.4 | 2,259.6 | 3,564.3 | 7,904.0 | 3,818.4 | 999.1 | 687.2 | −3,109.4 | −2,301.7 | −1,203.4 | −860.0 | 5,860.8 |
| Other investment: liabilities | 3d9la | 4,162.1 | 7,545.8 | 7,717.6 | 15,675.6 | 23,237.5 | 8,200.1 | −785.6 | −8,271.1 | −12,724.0 | −6,127.0 | −5,146.3 | −4,149.2 |
| Other equity | 3dala | .... | .... | .... | .... | .2 | .2 | 118.8 | −380.4 | 489.2 | — | 3.3 | — |
| Debt instruments | 3dzla | 4,162.1 | 7,545.8 | 7,717.6 | 15,675.6 | 23,237.3 | 8,199.9 | −904.4 | −7,890.7 | −13,213.3 | −6,127.0 | −5,149.7 | −4,149.2 |
| Curr.+ cap.− finan. acct. balance | 4y9bx | 4,067.1 | 7,833.5 | 3,705.1 | −9.4 | 7,404.3 | 5,155.3 | 5,493.9 | 9,021.6 | 120.9 | 10,218.5 | 2,698.4 | −3,948.0 |
| D. Net Errors and Omissions | 409na | −2,081.2 | −2,929.4 | −2,602.7 | 163.2 | −3,231.5 | −1,190.7 | −1,331.5 | −3,471.8 | 500.5 | −1,876.8 | −1,495.9 | −1,430.8 |
| E. Reserves and Related Items | 4z9na | 1,985.9 | 4,904.1 | 1,102.4 | 153.8 | 4,172.8 | 3,964.6 | 4,162.4 | 5,549.8 | 621.4 | 8,341.6 | 1,202.5 | −5,378.9 |
| Reserve assets | 3e9aa | 1,985.9 | 4,904.1 | 1,102.4 | 153.8 | 10,423.6 | 9,122.7 | 4,162.4 | 5,549.8 | −4,310.0 | 1,644.1 | 1,202.5 | −5,378.9 |
| Credit and loans from the IMF | 3dcla | — | — | — | — | 6,250.8 | 5,158.2 | — | — | −4,931.5 | −6,697.5 | — | — |
| Exceptional financing | 409la | .... | .... | .... | .... | .... | .... | .... | .... | .... | .... | .... | .... |

*Excludes components in group E

| **International Investment Position** | | | | | | | *Millions of US Dollars* | | | | | | |
|---|---|---|---|---|---|---|---|---|---|---|---|---|---|
| Assets | 809aa | 53,603.9 | 58,442.8 | 181,064.3 | 279,427.7 | 326,383.2 | 332,884.3 | 305,858.9 | 305,663.4 | 320,880.9 | 320,879.0 | 297,943.4 | 285,151.4 |
| Direct investment | 8a9aa | 12,409.2 | 14,375.7 | 121,503.6 | 202,118.9 | 250,443.1 | 242,538.0 | 213,945.0 | 217,140.7 | 238,323.2 | 238,671.9 | 220,810.3 | 213,085.1 |
| Equity & investment fund shares | 8aaaa | 6,400.1 | 8,462.2 | 56,397.4 | 131,044.4 | 188,019.8 | 186,720.1 | 145,406.6 | 160,836.8 | 191,166.0 | 190,695.3 | 171,991.1 | 159,830.2 |
| Debt instruments | 8abaa | 6,009.1 | 5,913.4 | 65,106.2 | 71,074.5 | 62,423.3 | 55,817.9 | 68,538.4 | 56,303.8 | 47,157.2 | 47,976.6 | 48,819.1 | 53,254.9 |
| Portfolio investment | 8b9aa | 1,692.0 | 2,800.1 | 5,567.9 | 9,468.1 | 8,433.6 | 11,771.8 | 12,422.2 | 8,053.1 | 8,054.8 | 8,035.9 | 9,664.6 | 9,135.9 |
| Equity & investment fund shares | 8baaa | 1,016.6 | 1,663.1 | 3,828.3 | 7,255.8 | 6,211.8 | 9,550.6 | 10,640.1 | 6,527.3 | 6,437.9 | 6,282.8 | 6,981.1 | 6,588.6 |
| Debt securities | 8bbaa | 675.4 | 1,137.0 | 1,739.7 | 2,212.3 | 2,221.8 | 2,221.2 | 1,782.2 | 1,525.7 | 1,616.9 | 1,753.1 | 2,683.5 | 2,547.3 |
| Fin. der.(oth.than reserves) & ESOs | 8c9aa | 2,480.5 | 1,447.0 | 2,069.5 | 2,438.0 | 5,132.6 | 3,433.2 | 3,827.1 | 5,286.8 | 5,147.9 | 3,736.1 | 4,732.7 | 4,769.2 |
| Other investment | 8d9aa | 21,057.0 | 21,217.0 | 30,334.0 | 41,351.2 | 28,500.4 | 30,958.1 | 30,676.5 | 26,348.3 | 24,684.7 | 23,927.2 | 20,716.9 | 25,036.8 |
| Other equity | 8daaa | 224.9 | 246.2 | 311.1 | 425.5 | 456.6 | 528.3 | 876.8 | 837.8 | 834.2 | 521.9 | 513.0 | 517.3 |
| Debt instruments | 8dzaa | 20,832.0 | 20,970.7 | 30,022.8 | 40,925.7 | 28,043.8 | 30,429.8 | 29,799.8 | 25,510.4 | 23,850.6 | 23,405.3 | 20,203.9 | 24,519.5 |
| Reserve assets | 8e9aa | 15,965.3 | 18,603.1 | 21,589.3 | 24,051.6 | 33,873.6 | 44,183.1 | 44,988.0 | 48,834.6 | 44,670.1 | 46,507.9 | 42,018.9 | 33,124.4 |
| Liabilities | 809la | 150,892.5 | 155,177.7 | 300,911.1 | 410,462.8 | 473,565.4 | 494,447.8 | 447,062.3 | 429,995.5 | 442,831.9 | 437,334.5 | 391,690.8 | 367,373.9 |
| Direct investment | 8a9la | 67,160.8 | 66,849.5 | 182,916.8 | 262,837.2 | 315,504.7 | 318,837.8 | 279,583.1 | 277,843.9 | 295,862.2 | 296,455.1 | 272,385.9 | 265,244.0 |
| Equity & investment fund shares | 8aala | 55,144.1 | 55,225.0 | 147,597.7 | 214,553.6 | 234,525.4 | 231,272.0 | 216,641.2 | 201,260.2 | 217,630.6 | 217,598.2 | 195,486.3 | 193,863.6 |
| Debt instruments | 8abla | 12,016.7 | 11,624.5 | 35,319.2 | 48,283.5 | 80,979.2 | 87,565.8 | 62,941.9 | 76,583.8 | 78,231.6 | 78,856.9 | 76,899.6 | 71,380.4 |
| Portfolio investment | 8b9la | 43,153.3 | 46,067.8 | 63,018.8 | 70,395.4 | 58,577.1 | 62,038.7 | 56,806.2 | 52,194.0 | 63,135.6 | 68,638.8 | 60,622.9 | 53,821.7 |
| Equity & investment fund shares | 8bala | 11,359.0 | 13,156.5 | 18,376.3 | 15,267.3 | 8,518.9 | 15,584.8 | 13,978.2 | 9,355.5 | 11,666.8 | 11,337.7 | 7,860.3 | 10,849.6 |
| Debt securities | 8bbla | 31,794.3 | 32,911.3 | 44,642.5 | 55,128.2 | 50,058.2 | 46,453.9 | 42,828.0 | 42,838.6 | 51,468.8 | 57,301.2 | 52,762.7 | 42,972.1 |
| Fin. der.(oth.than reserves) & ESOs | 8c9la | 2,605.3 | 1,652.1 | 2,403.4 | 3,192.0 | 6,355.9 | 4,290.9 | 5,838.5 | 5,977.0 | 4,979.7 | 5,452.5 | 4,206.8 | 2,312.9 |
| Other investment | 8d9la | 37,973.0 | 40,608.3 | 52,572.1 | 74,038.2 | 93,127.7 | 109,280.3 | 104,834.5 | 93,980.5 | 78,854.4 | 66,788.1 | 54,475.2 | 45,995.3 |
| Other equity | 8dala | .... | .... | .... | .... | 515.9 | 516.1 | 681.3 | 874.8 | 1,377.1 | 39.6 | 36.0 | 29.1 |
| Debt instruments | 8dzla | 37,973.0 | 40,608.3 | 52,572.1 | 74,038.2 | 92,611.8 | 108,764.2 | 104,153.2 | 93,105.7 | 77,477.3 | 66,748.5 | 54,439.2 | 45,966.2 |

# Hungary 944

|  |  | 2004 | 2005 | 2006 | 2007 | 2008 | 2009 | 2010 | 2011 | 2012 | 2013 | 2014 | 2015 |
|---|---|---|---|---|---|---|---|---|---|---|---|---|---|
| **Government Finance** | | | | | | | | | | | | | |
| **Operations Statement** | | | | | | | | | | | | | |
| **General Government** | | | | | | *Billions of Forint: Fiscal Year Ends December 31; Data Reported through Eurostat* | | | | | | | |
| Revenue | a1 | 8,889.2 | 9,375.7 | 10,222.4 | 11,503.1 | 12,206.6 | 12,103.1 | 12,181.1 | 12,458.1 | 13,254.0 | 14,142.8 | 15,298.5 | 16,417.5 |
| Taxes | a11 | 5,228.7 | 5,446.6 | 5,830.4 | 6,612.4 | 7,010.3 | 6,852.8 | 6,874.5 | 6,657.1 | 7,278.3 | 7,545.8 | 8,170.5 | 8,738.1 |
| Social Contributions | a12 | 2,559.3 | 2,781.1 | 2,996.9 | 3,465.4 | 3,668.0 | 3,411.9 | 3,247.1 | 3,686.0 | 3,734.0 | 3,907.5 | 4,204.1 | 4,482.6 |
| Grants | a13 | .... | .... | .... | .... | .... | .... | .... | .... | .... | .... | .... | .... |
| Other Revenue | a14 | .... | .... | .... | .... | .... | .... | .... | .... | .... | .... | .... | .... |
| Expense | a2 | 10,215.0 | 10,963.0 | 12,072.7 | 12,583.1 | 13,317.3 | 13,385.5 | 13,424.7 | 14,093.5 | 13,930.6 | 14,700.4 | 15,534.0 | 16,007.6 |
| Compensation of Employees | a21 | 2,612.8 | 2,772.7 | 2,889.0 | 2,921.0 | 3,082.4 | 2,958.1 | 2,935.9 | 2,866.7 | 2,849.5 | 3,028.3 | 3,339.5 | 3,595.2 |
| Use of Goods & Services | a22 | 1,327.6 | 1,412.7 | 1,552.8 | 1,603.5 | 1,884.1 | 1,996.8 | 2,062.6 | 2,044.3 | 2,080.1 | 2,246.0 | 2,563.7 | 2,409.6 |
| Consumption of Fixed Capital | a23 | 720.3 | 748.9 | 812.7 | 882.1 | 943.9 | 977.1 | 1,014.2 | 1,038.7 | 1,057.6 | 1,074.3 | 1,126.5 | 1,167.2 |
| Interest | a24 | 912.7 | 915.9 | 934.7 | 1,035.3 | 1,100.3 | 1,185.2 | 1,115.3 | 1,172.4 | 1,314.4 | 1,363.5 | 1,301.0 | 1,209.4 |
| Subsidies | a25 | 329.9 | 298.0 | 340.0 | 354.9 | 300.1 | 248.7 | 292.7 | 348.1 | 397.1 | 397.6 | 437.5 | 421.4 |
| Grants | a26 | .... | .... | .... | .... | .... | .... | .... | .... | .... | .... | .... | .... |
| Social Benefits | a27 | 3,498.6 | 3,914.3 | 4,399.8 | 4,597.3 | 4,944.7 | 4,971.6 | 4,926.1 | 5,039.0 | 4,994.6 | 5,126.0 | 5,142.2 | 5,190.4 |
| Other Expense | a28 | .... | .... | .... | .... | .... | .... | .... | .... | .... | .... | .... | .... |
| Gross Operating Balance [1-2+23] | agob | −605.5 | −838.4 | −1,037.6 | −198.0 | −166.7 | −305.3 | −229.4 | −596.7 | 381.0 | 516.6 | 891.1 | 1,577.2 |
| Net Operating Balance [1-2] | anob | −1,325.8 | −1,587.3 | −1,850.3 | −1,080.1 | −1,110.7 | −1,282.4 | −1,243.6 | −1,635.4 | −676.6 | −557.6 | −235.4 | 409.9 |
| Net Acq. of Nonfinancial Assets | a31 | 9.1 | 168.8 | 402.0 | 213.2 | −126.7 | −77.4 | −19.8 | −97.3 | −14.3 | 225.1 | 503.9 | 1,089.6 |
| Aquisition of Nonfin. Assets | a31.1 | .... | .... | .... | .... | .... | .... | .... | .... | .... | .... | .... | .... |
| Disposal of Nonfin. Assets | a31.2 | .... | .... | .... | .... | .... | .... | .... | .... | .... | .... | .... | .... |
| Net Lending/Borrowing [1-2-31] | anlb | −1,334.9 | −1,756.1 | −2,252.3 | −1,293.3 | −983.9 | −1,205.0 | −1,223.7 | −1,538.1 | −662.3 | −782.7 | −739.4 | −679.7 |
| Net Acq. of Financial Assets | a32 | 404.2 | −449.9 | −124.7 | 12.5 | 1,336.4 | −117.3 | −416.1 | 1,156.4 | −346.9 | −245.2 | 254.0 | −43.9 |
| By instrument | | | | | | | | | | | | | |
| Monetary Gold & SDRs | a3201 | — | — | — | — | — | — | — | — | — | — | — | — |
| Currency & Deposits | a3202 | 304.1 | −96.6 | 151.8 | 204.6 | 1,495.2 | −683.1 | −203.7 | 130.7 | 106.6 | −432.9 | 241.3 | −317.8 |
| Securities other than Shares | a3203 | — | −.6 | −.4 | 1.3 | −1.2 | −.1 | 9.1 | 49.0 | 33.0 | 79.4 | −115.8 | −.7 |
| Loans | a3204 | 9.2 | 138.0 | −34.5 | −173.1 | −15.4 | 529.0 | −189.9 | −144.1 | −124.9 | −8.2 | 1.8 | 1.7 |
| Shares & Other Equity | a3205 | −109.1 | −515.9 | −288.4 | −74.1 | −165.8 | 25.3 | −1.8 | 1,211.5 | −212.4 | −105.5 | 122.5 | 116.7 |
| Insurance Technical Reserves | a3206 | .5 | .7 | — | −.2 | .1 | — | −.1 | −.1 | .2 | −.4 | −.1 | — |
| Financial Derivatives | a3207 | −14.6 | −18.2 | −21.0 | −14.5 | −10.5 | −119.5 | −84.9 | −74.4 | −130.5 | −114.1 | −97.5 | −267.6 |
| Other Accounts Receivable | a3208 | 214.0 | 42.7 | 67.8 | 68.6 | 34.0 | 131.0 | 55.3 | −16.1 | −18.9 | 336.5 | 101.8 | 423.9 |
| By debtor | | | | | | | | | | | | | |
| Domestic | a321 | .... | .... | .... | .... | .... | .... | .... | .... | .... | .... | .... | .... |
| Foreign | a322 | .... | .... | .... | .... | .... | .... | .... | .... | .... | .... | .... | .... |
| Net Incurrence of Liabilities | a33 | 1,774.0 | 1,312.7 | 2,121.4 | 1,248.8 | 2,241.5 | 1,092.9 | 818.8 | 2,691.5 | 323.7 | 496.0 | 970.9 | 643.2 |
| By instrument | | | | | | | | | | | | | |
| Special Drawing Rights (SDRs) | a3301 | — | — | — | — | — | — | — | — | — | — | — | — |
| Currency & Deposits | a3302 | .2 | −.1 | 3.2 | 3.4 | 3.2 | 6.7 | 3.6 | 3.1 | 10.1 | .1 | 1.3 | 6.2 |
| Securities other than Shares | a3303 | 1,662.5 | 1,266.5 | 1,533.0 | 1,368.9 | 505.8 | −791.7 | 469.7 | −257.1 | 1,342.6 | 1,562.9 | 1,811.6 | 617.1 |
| Loans | a3304 | −108.6 | −7.6 | 479.4 | −163.7 | 1,861.7 | 1,886.2 | 390.0 | −180.3 | −960.2 | −1,110.0 | −849.7 | 200.5 |
| Shares & Other Equity | a3305 | — | — | — | — | — | — | — | — | — | — | — | — |
| Insurance Technical Reserves | a3306 | 1.0 | 7.9 | 16.1 | 9.5 | 1.0 | −.1 | −6.5 | −1.0 | −3.2 | −7.0 | −1.8 | −.5 |
| Financial Derivatives | a3307 | −39.3 | −29.8 | −32.9 | −34.2 | −23.0 | −293.3 | −25.5 | −27.9 | −18.5 | −32.4 | −68.6 | −19.3 |
| Other Accounts Payable | a3308 | 258.3 | 75.8 | 122.7 | 64.8 | −107.1 | 285.0 | −12.6 | 3,154.7 | −47.2 | 82.4 | 78.1 | −160.7 |
| By creditor | | | | | | | | | | | | | |
| Domestic | a331 | .... | .... | .... | .... | .... | .... | .... | .... | .... | .... | .... | .... |
| Foreign | a332 | .... | .... | .... | .... | .... | .... | .... | .... | .... | .... | .... | .... |
| Stat. Discrepancy [32-33-NLB] | anlbz | −34.9 | −6.5 | 6.1 | 57.0 | 78.9 | −5.2 | −11.1 | 2.9 | −8.4 | 41.5 | 22.5 | −7.4 |
| Memo Item: Expenditure [2+31] | a2m | 10,224.1 | 11,131.8 | 12,474.7 | 12,796.3 | 13,190.5 | 13,308.1 | 13,404.8 | 13,996.2 | 13,916.3 | 14,925.5 | 16,037.9 | 17,097.2 |
| **Balance Sheet** | | | | | | *Billions of Forint: Fiscal Year Ends December 31* | | | | | | | |
| Net Worth | a6 | .... | .... | .... | .... | .... | .... | .... | .... | .... | .... | .... | .... |
| Nonfinancial Assets | a61 | .... | .... | .... | .... | .... | .... | .... | .... | .... | .... | .... | .... |
| Financial Assets | a62 | 4,854.5 | 5,170.2 | 4,781.3 | 4,927.4 | 6,728.7 | 6,858.8 | 6,952.7 | 9,281.6 | 8,159.3 | 7,894.2 | 8,967.8 | 9,676.4 |
| By instrument | | | | | | | | | | | | | |
| Monetary Gold & SDRs | a6201 | — | — | — | — | — | — | — | — | — | — | — | — |
| Currency & Deposits | a6202 | 693.7 | 601.8 | 771.8 | 979.7 | 2,383.4 | 1,770.0 | 1,652.7 | 1,926.1 | 1,959.5 | 1,556.3 | 1,838.3 | 1,517.9 |
| Securities other than Shares | a6203 | 1.8 | 1.2 | .8 | 2.2 | 1.0 | .8 | 10.6 | 57.9 | 92.6 | 180.3 | 69.1 | 74.2 |
| Loans | a6204 | 170.7 | 314.3 | 323.7 | 149.2 | 134.3 | 604.1 | 434.4 | 297.9 | 160.5 | 152.1 | 120.3 | 122.5 |
| Shares and Other Equity | a6205 | 2,943.6 | 3,140.4 | 2,536.2 | 2,598.0 | 2,910.8 | 2,991.9 | 3,127.1 | 4,948.7 | 4,119.8 | 4,067.8 | 4,432.1 | 4,599.4 |
| Insurance Technical Reserves | a6206 | 1.5 | 2.2 | 2.2 | 2.0 | 2.1 | 2.1 | 2.0 | 1.9 | 2.1 | 1.7 | 1.6 | 1.5 |
| Financial Derivatives | a6207 | 37.2 | 61.9 | 30.2 | 20.9 | 81.8 | 99.7 | 278.7 | 604.2 | 397.2 | 154.3 | 579.5 | 1,014.8 |
| Other Accounts Receivable | a6208 | 1,005.8 | 1,048.5 | 1,116.5 | 1,175.4 | 1,215.2 | 1,390.3 | 1,447.1 | 1,444.9 | 1,427.7 | 1,781.8 | 1,926.9 | 2,346.1 |
| By debtor | | | | | | | | | | | | | |
| Domestic | a621 | .... | .... | .... | .... | .... | .... | .... | .... | .... | .... | .... | .... |
| Foreign | a622 | .... | .... | .... | .... | .... | .... | .... | .... | .... | .... | .... | .... |
| Liabilities | a63 | 13,577.9 | 15,160.8 | 17,206.5 | 18,426.9 | 20,465.4 | 22,281.4 | 23,425.1 | 26,880.7 | 28,148.1 | 29,104.8 | 32,058.7 | 33,109.6 |
| By instrument | | | | | | | | | | | | | |
| Special Drawing Rights (SDRs) | a6301 | — | — | — | — | — | — | — | — | — | — | — | — |
| Currency & Deposits | a6302 | .2 | .1 | 3.3 | 6.7 | 9.9 | 16.6 | 20.2 | 23.3 | 33.4 | 33.5 | 34.7 | 40.9 |
| Securities other than Shares | a6303 | 11,031.9 | 12,506.6 | 13,901.1 | 15,145.4 | 15,457.5 | 15,141.2 | 15,656.4 | 15,473.5 | 18,149.8 | 19,968.0 | 23,625.4 | 24,676.6 |
| Loans | a6304 | 1,371.8 | 1,422.3 | 1,880.8 | 1,714.0 | 3,539.9 | 5,359.1 | 6,042.4 | 6,525.3 | 5,186.3 | 4,127.8 | 3,501.3 | 3,694.6 |
| Shares and Other Equity | a6305 | .... | .... | .... | .... | .... | .... | .... | .... | .... | .... | .... | .... |
| Insurance Technical Reserves | a6306 | 6.0 | 13.9 | 30.0 | 39.4 | 40.4 | 40.4 | 33.9 | 32.9 | 29.7 | 22.7 | 20.9 | 20.4 |
| Financial Derivatives | a6307 | 112.8 | 85.4 | 132.6 | 176.5 | 181.3 | 195.4 | 158.7 | 151.8 | 124.3 | 245.2 | 87.6 | 47.7 |
| Other Accounts Payable | a6308 | 1,055.3 | 1,132.4 | 1,258.7 | 1,344.8 | 1,236.4 | 1,528.7 | 1,513.5 | 4,673.9 | 4,624.6 | 4,707.6 | 4,788.7 | 4,629.4 |
| By creditor | | | | | | | | | | | | | |
| Domestic | a631 | .... | .... | .... | .... | .... | .... | .... | .... | .... | .... | .... | .... |
| Foreign | a632 | .... | .... | .... | .... | .... | .... | .... | .... | .... | .... | .... | .... |
| Net Financial Worth [62-63] | a6m2 | −8,723.5 | −9,990.6 | −12,425.1 | −13,499.5 | −13,736.7 | −15,422.6 | −16,472.4 | −17,599.0 | −19,988.8 | −21,210.6 | −23,090.9 | −23,433.2 |
| Memo Item: Debt at Market Value | a6m3 | 13,465.1 | 15,075.4 | 17,073.9 | 18,250.4 | 20,284.2 | 22,086.0 | 23,266.4 | 26,728.9 | 28,023.8 | 28,859.6 | 31,971.1 | 33,061.9 |
| Memo Item: Debt at Face Value | a6m35 | 13,351.7 | 14,717.1 | 16,870.3 | 18,102.2 | 20,608.5 | 21,999.6 | 23,312.3 | 27,394.7 | 27,038.1 | 27,783.9 | 29,302.9 | 30,023.4 |
| Memo Item: Maastricht Debt | a6m36 | 12,296.4 | 13,584.7 | 15,611.5 | 16,757.4 | 19,372.1 | 20,470.9 | 21,798.8 | 22,720.7 | 22,414.1 | 23,076.2 | 24,514.2 | 25,393.9 |
| Memo Item: Debt at Nominal Value | a6m4 | .... | .... | .... | .... | .... | .... | .... | .... | .... | .... | .... | .... |

# Hungary   944

| | | 2004 | 2005 | 2006 | 2007 | 2008 | 2009 | 2010 | 2011 | 2012 | 2013 | 2014 | 2015 |
|---|---|---|---|---|---|---|---|---|---|---|---|---|---|
| **National Accounts** | | | | | | | *Billions of Forint* | | | | | | | |
| Househ.Cons.Expend.,incl.NPISHs.... | 96f | 14,011.3 | 14,971.1 | 15,737.8 | 16,655.0 | 17,477.0 | 17,042.9 | 17,138.0 | 17,775.8 | 18,304.0 | 18,694.8 | 19,401.2 | 20,024.8 |
| Government Consumption Expend... | 91f | 2,138.8 | 2,277.9 | 2,448.6 | 2,512.1 | 2,768.5 | 2,803.9 | 2,858.8 | 2,856.0 | 2,814.5 | 2,972.2 | 3,292.0 | 3,381.9 |
| Gross Fixed Capital Formation.......... | 93e | 5,058.3 | 5,364.1 | 5,694.6 | 6,048.6 | 6,296.3 | 5,999.6 | 5,511.2 | 5,568.7 | 5,547.7 | 6,160.0 | 6,971.3 | 7,192.3 |
| Changes in Inventories.................... | 93i | 632.5 | 356.8 | 524.2 | 150.1 | 400.8 | −650.8 | 99.2 | 206.2 | 37.6 | 42.6 | 176.9 | 213.9 |
| Exports of Goods and Services......... | 90c | 12,553.8 | 14,102.9 | 17,936.4 | 20,004.1 | 21,547.5 | 19,647.5 | 22,263.7 | 24,540.1 | 24,855.5 | 26,445.0 | 28,721.7 | 31,047.2 |
| Imports of Goods and Services (-)..... | 98c | 13,381.9 | 14,613.6 | 18,202.7 | 19,831.2 | 21,452.0 | 18,584.3 | 20,819.1 | 22,812.9 | 22,931.5 | 24,249.7 | 26,383.3 | 28,148.2 |
| Gross Domestic Product (GDP)........ | 99b | 21,012.8 | 22,459.2 | 24,138.8 | 25,538.6 | 27,038.1 | 26,258.7 | 27,051.7 | 28,133.8 | 28,627.9 | 30,065.0 | 32,179.7 | 33,711.8 |
| GDP Volume 2005 Prices................ | 99b.p | 21,522.0 | 22,459.2 | 23,314.1 | 23,413.4 | 23,609.9 | 22,061.3 | 22,225.2 | 22,615.9 | 22,233.9 | 22,654.1 | 23,486.0 | 24,176.2 |
| GDP Volume (2010=100)............... | 99bvp | 96.8 | 101.1 | 104.9 | 105.3 | 106.2 | 99.3 | 100.0 | 101.8 | 100.0 | 101.9 | 105.7 | 108.8 |
| GDP Deflator (2010=100)............... | 99bip | 80.2 | 82.2 | 85.1 | 89.6 | 94.1 | 97.8 | 100.0 | 102.2 | 105.8 | 109.0 | 112.6 | 114.6 |
| | | | | | | | *Millions: Midyear Estimates* | | | | | | | |
| **Population................................** | 99z | 10.12 | 10.10 | 10.08 | 10.06 | 10.05 | 10.03 | 10.01 | 9.99 | 9.96 | 9.92 | 9.89 | 9.86 |

# Iceland 176

| | | 2004 | 2005 | 2006 | 2007 | 2008 | 2009 | 2010 | 2011 | 2012 | 2013 | 2014 | 2015 |
|---|---|---|---|---|---|---|---|---|---|---|---|---|---|
| **Exchange Rates** | | | | | | *Kronur per SDR: End of Period* | | | | | | | |
| Official Rate | aa | 94.80 | 90.02 | 107.81 | 97.74 | 185.73 | 195.80 | 177.18 | 188.39 | 198.25 | 177.95 | 183.85 | 179.58 |
| | | | | | | *Kronur per US Dollar: End of Period (ae) Period Average (rf)* | | | | | | | |
| Official Rate | ae | 61.04 | 62.98 | 71.66 | 61.85 | 120.58 | 124.90 | 115.05 | 122.71 | 128.99 | 115.55 | 126.90 | 129.59 |
| Official Rate | rf | 70.19 | 62.98 | 70.18 | 64.06 | 87.95 | 123.64 | 122.24 | 115.95 | 125.08 | 122.18 | 116.77 | 131.92 |
| | | | | | | *Index Numbers (2010=100): Period Averages* | | | | | | | |
| Official Rate | ahx | 174.0 | 193.7 | 174.1 | 190.7 | 146.5 | 98.7 | 100.0 | 105.2 | 97.5 | 99.8 | 104.5 | 92.4 |
| Nominal Effective Exchange Rate | nec | 186.3 | 205.5 | 183.2 | 188.2 | 137.1 | 98.5 | 100.0 | 100.3 | 97.0 | 99.2 | 105.0 | 106.4 |
| CPI-Based Real Effect. Ex. Rate | rec | 135.9 | 152.8 | 142.1 | 149.9 | 117.8 | 95.2 | 100.0 | 101.4 | 101.0 | 105.7 | 112.7 | 115.3 |
| **Fund Position** | | | | | | *Millions of SDRs: End of Period* | | | | | | | |
| Quota | 2f.s | 117.60 | 117.60 | 117.60 | 117.60 | 117.60 | 117.60 | 117.60 | 117.60 | 117.60 | 117.60 | 117.60 | 117.60 |
| SDR Holdings | 1b.s | .08 | .03 | .08 | .11 | .28 | 92.73 | 73.47 | 463.23 | 8.92 | 5.37 | 5.52 | 111.72 |
| Reserve Position in the Fund | 1c.s | 18.58 | 18.59 | 18.59 | 18.59 | 18.59 | 18.63 | 18.66 | 18.71 | 18.74 | 18.75 | 18.75 | 18.75 |
| Total Fund Cred.&Loans Outstg. | 2tl | — | — | — | — | 560.00 | 665.00 | 875.00 | 1,400.00 | 511.88 | 511.88 | 236.88 | — |
| SDR Allocations | 1bd | 16.41 | 16.41 | 16.41 | 16.41 | 16.41 | 112.18 | 112.18 | 112.18 | 112.18 | 112.18 | 112.18 | 112.18 |
| **International Liquidity** | | | | | | *Millions of US Dollars Unless Otherwise Indicated: End of Period* | | | | | | | |
| Total Reserves minus Gold | 1l.d | 1,046.2 | 1,035.7 | 2,301.3 | 2,578.7 | 3,515.2 | 3,813.2 | 5,698.9 | 8,450.4 | 4,085.3 | 4,160.8 | 4,100.1 | 4,972.9 |
| SDR Holdings | 1b.d | .1 | — | .1 | .2 | .4 | 145.4 | 113.1 | 711.2 | 13.7 | 8.3 | 8.0 | 154.8 |
| Reserve Position in the Fund | 1c.d | 28.9 | 26.6 | 28.0 | 29.4 | 28.6 | 29.2 | 28.7 | 28.7 | 28.8 | 28.9 | 27.2 | 26.0 |
| Foreign Exchange | 1d.d | 1,017.3 | 1,009.1 | 2,273.2 | 2,549.1 | 3,486.2 | 3,638.7 | 5,557.0 | 7,710.5 | 4,042.8 | 4,123.6 | 4,065.0 | 4,792.1 |
| Gold (Million Fine Troy Ounces) | 1ad | .064 | .064 | .064 | .064 | .064 | .064 | .064 | .064 | .064 | .064 | .064 | .064 |
| Gold (National Valuation) | 1and | 28.0 | 32.9 | 40.9 | 53.4 | 55.2 | 69.4 | 90.6 | 99.8 | 106.9 | 76.6 | 75.6 | 67.8 |
| Central Bank: Other Assets | 3..d | 2 | 3 | 3 | 153 | 1,556 | 1,196 | 1,715 | 3,413 | 411 | 279 | 1 | 1 |
| Central Bank: Other Liabs | 4..d | 2 | 2 | 1 | 2 | 1,115 | 412 | 905 | 925 | 546 | 535 | 196 | 137 |
| Other Depository Corps.: Assets | 7a.d | 2,857 | 8,549 | 18,584 | † 76,333 | 6,091 | 3,076 | 3,281 | 3,624 | 3,629 | 4,813 | 3,161 | 2,793 |
| Other Depository Corps.: Liabs | 7b.d | 3,660 | 5,343 | 9,502 | † 100,638 | 6,074 | 2,500 | 1,835 | 1,278 | 966 | 1,273 | 1,202 | 2,189 |
| **Central Bank** | | | | | | *Millions of Kronur: End of Period* | | | | | | | |
| Net Foreign Assets | 11n | 64,008 | 65,874 | 166,200 | 161,876 | 188,024 | 281,941 | 387,902 | 649,723 | 346,508 | 315,930 | 441,142 | 615,091 |
| Claims on Nonresidents | 11 | 65,706 | 67,501 | 168,063 | 163,579 | 429,481 | 485,075 | 666,321 | 1,047,229 | 539,876 | 487,609 | 530,237 | 652,997 |
| Liabilities to Nonresidents | 16c | 1,698 | 1,627 | 1,864 | 1,703 | 241,457 | 203,134 | 278,419 | 397,506 | 193,368 | 171,679 | 89,095 | 37,906 |
| Claims on Other Depository Corps. | 12e | 31,771 | 77,772 | 119,863 | 258,165 | 466,540 | 28,869 | 90,037 | 4,312 | 17,823 | 53,327 | 57,048 | 55,993 |
| Net Claims on Central Government | 12an | −17,782 | −75,916 | −211,036 | −211,177 | −133,241 | −281,270 | −254,123 | −336,911 | −304,468 | −225,175 | −385,312 | −298,340 |
| Claims on Central Government | 12a | 32 | — | — | — | 270,005 | 165,398 | 170,525 | 191,905 | 184,547 | 179,531 | 153,362 | 98,413 |
| Liabilities to Central Government | 12d | 17,815 | 75,916 | 211,036 | 211,177 | 403,246 | 446,668 | 424,648 | 528,816 | 489,016 | 404,706 | 538,675 | 396,753 |
| Claims on Other Sectors | 12s | 9,038 | 11,940 | 28,642 | 50,178 | 16,423 | 493,797 | 394,528 | 332,404 | 316,539 | 253,279 | 211,933 | 128,698 |
| Claims on Other Financial Corps. | 12g | 8,993 | 11,902 | 28,547 | 50,102 | 16,423 | 493,797 | 394,528 | 332,404 | 316,539 | 253,279 | 211,933 | 128,698 |
| Claims on State & Local Govts. | 12b | 45 | 38 | 95 | 76 | — | — | — | — | — | — | — | — |
| Claims on Public Nonfin. Corps. | 12c | — | — | — | — | — | — | — | — | — | — | — | — |
| Claims on Private Sector | 12d | — | — | — | — | — | — | — | — | — | — | — | — |
| Monetary Base | 14 | 47,832 | 45,303 | 57,871 | 169,272 | 119,470 | 159,303 | 130,845 | 88,389 | 113,244 | 116,931 | 228,833 | 410,916 |
| Currency in Circulation | 14a | 11,632 | 13,202 | 14,513 | 15,735 | 24,436 | 28,958 | 38,269 | 43,205 | 45,142 | 47,016 | 49,955 | 55,671 |
| Liabs. to Other Depository Corps. | 14c | 22,519 | 31,956 | 43,228 | 152,112 | 90,618 | 94,933 | 55,660 | 31,286 | 53,215 | 51,643 | 133,546 | 288,063 |
| Liabilities to Other Sectors | 14d | 13,681 | 145 | 131 | 1,425 | 4,415 | 35,412 | 36,916 | 13,898 | 14,887 | 18,273 | 45,331 | 67,182 |
| Other Liabs. to Other Dep. Corps. | 14n | 4,407 | 2,294 | 1,777 | — | 295,891 | 114,595 | 114,878 | 86,828 | 105,163 | 134,020 | 973 | 1 |
| Dep. & Sec. Excl. f/Monetary Base | 14o | — | — | — | — | 9,827 | 153,142 | 279,999 | 344,326 | 27,448 | 29,747 | 24,402 | 22,798 |
| Deposits Included in Broad Money. | 15 | — | — | — | — | — | — | — | — | — | — | — | — |
| Sec.Ot.th.Shares Incl.in Brd. Money | 16a | — | — | — | — | — | — | — | — | — | — | — | — |
| Deposits Excl. from Broad Money | 16b | — | — | — | — | 9,827 | 153,142 | 279,999 | 344,326 | 27,448 | 29,747 | 24,402 | 22,798 |
| Sec.Ot.th.Shares Excl.f/Brd.Money | 16s | — | — | — | — | — | — | — | — | — | — | — | — |
| Loans | 16l | — | — | — | — | — | — | — | — | — | — | — | — |
| Financial Derivatives | 16m | — | — | — | — | — | — | — | — | — | — | — | — |
| Shares and Other Equity | 17a | 34,198 | 36,370 | 48,336 | 91,003 | 82,378 | 82,878 | 69,379 | 83,777 | 98,531 | 89,807 | 75,027 | 78,760 |
| Other Items (Net) | 17r | 598 | −4,296 | −4,316 | −1,234 | 30,181 | 13,419 | 23,243 | 46,207 | 32,017 | 26,857 | −4,102 | −10,496 |
| Memo Item: | | | | | | | | | | | | | |
| Total Assets | 10ra | 106,591 | 162,294 | 321,842 | 476,859 | 1,187,460 | 1,178,082 | 1,328,240 | 1,585,775 | 1,068,887 | 1,003,777 | 957,277 | 948,340 |

# Iceland  176

| | Code | 2004 | 2005 | 2006 | 2007 | 2008 | 2009 | 2010 | 2011 | 2012 | 2013 | 2014 | 2015 |
|---|---|---|---|---|---|---|---|---|---|---|---|---|---|
| **Other Depository Corporations** | | | | | | *Millions of Kronur: End of Period* | | | | | | | |
| Net Foreign Assets | 21n | −49,052 | 201,881 | 650,796 | †−1,503,312 | 2,024 | 71,836 | 166,054 | 287,242 | 342,885 | 406,166 | 248,599 | 78,269 |
| Claims on Nonresidents | 21 | 174,366 | 538,385 | 1,331,724 | †4,721,174 | 734,424 | 383,303 | 376,622 | 443,667 | 467,249 | 552,295 | 401,113 | 361,973 |
| Liabilities to Nonresidents | 26c | 223,418 | 336,504 | 680,928 | †6,224,485 | 732,401 | 311,467 | 210,568 | 156,425 | 124,364 | 146,129 | 152,514 | 283,704 |
| Claims on Central Bank | 20 | 29,413 | 36,906 | 47,359 | †163,798 | 208,044 | 133,772 | 117,766 | 121,303 | 159,955 | 184,184 | 139,069 | 294,599 |
| Currency | 20a | 2,489 | 2,702 | 3,041 | †3,307 | 4,085 | 3,233 | 3,604 | 3,814 | 4,280 | 5,399 | 5,928 | 6,767 |
| Reserve Deposits and Securities | 20b | 26,923 | 34,204 | 44,318 | †160,491 | 202,501 | 129,472 | 114,162 | 117,490 | 155,675 | 178,707 | 133,141 | 287,829 |
| Other Claims | 20n | — | — | — | †— | 1,457 | 1,066 | — | — | — | 78 | — | 2 |
| Net Claims on Central Government | 22an | 4,594 | 7,686 | 8,202 | †13,563 | 3,511 | 235,825 | 213,561 | 200,848 | 197,077 | 189,837 | 137,050 | 171,799 |
| Claims on Central Government | 22a | 4,594 | 7,686 | 8,202 | †56,483 | 50,479 | 255,718 | 238,158 | 221,939 | 217,492 | 214,347 | 218,438 | 211,214 |
| Liabilities to Central Government | 26d | — | — | — | †42,920 | 46,968 | 19,893 | 24,597 | 21,091 | 20,415 | 24,511 | 81,388 | 39,416 |
| Claims on Other Sectors | 22s | 1,531,303 | 2,542,777 | 3,733,226 | †4,255,562 | 4,692,481 | 4,106,810 | 3,732,073 | 2,945,042 | 2,567,318 | 2,430,032 | 2,345,071 | 2,362,702 |
| Claims on Other Financial Corps. | 22g | — | — | — | †786,029 | 1,589,340 | 1,262,304 | 1,008,791 | 485,098 | 347,373 | 279,796 | 297,893 | 255,363 |
| Claims on State & Local Govts. | 22b | — | — | — | †12,415 | 15,364 | 15,300 | 22,714 | 18,802 | 15,430 | 12,844 | 19,012 | 19,626 |
| Claims on Public Nonfin. Corps. | 22c | — | — | — | †36,767 | 22,617 | 22,290 | 18,009 | 33,891 | 30,249 | 25,882 | 62,088 | 71,874 |
| Claims on Private Sector | 22d | 1,531,303 | 2,542,777 | 3,733,226 | †3,420,351 | 3,065,160 | 2,806,916 | 2,682,559 | 2,407,251 | 2,174,266 | 2,111,510 | 1,966,078 | 2,015,839 |
| Liabilities to Central Bank | 26g | 33,256 | 79,059 | 120,388 | †281,360 | 359,662 | 13,669 | 42,815 | 4,655 | 18,011 | 538 | 2,151 | 139 |
| Transf.Dep.Included in Broad Money | 24 | 132,517 | 163,517 | 191,111 | †379,388 | 400,171 | 393,862 | 393,507 | 408,395 | 368,868 | 374,140 | 363,686 | 380,549 |
| Other Dep.Included in Broad Money | 25 | 405,590 | 533,769 | 930,819 | †805,473 | 1,160,011 | 1,169,113 | 996,269 | 1,082,864 | 1,049,370 | 1,108,557 | 1,224,142 | 1,293,338 |
| Sec.Ot.th.Shares Incl.in Brd. Money | 26a | — | — | — | †— | | | | | | | | |
| Deposits Excl. from Broad Money | 26b | — | — | — | †— | | | | | | | | |
| Sec.Ot.th.Shares Excl.f/Brd.Money | 26s | 999,662 | 1,992,413 | 3,074,738 | †424,522 | 119,895 | 41,023 | 22,521 | 156,015 | 189,259 | 208,887 | 179,938 | 233,303 |
| Loans | 26l | — | — | — | †165,937 | 583,558 | 467,370 | 453,040 | 506,350 | 477,768 | 387,741 | 228,368 | 166,000 |
| Financial Derivatives | 26m | — | — | — | †23,601 | 1,716 | 1,578 | 215 | 669 | 2,481 | 2,339 | 3,024 | 7,544 |
| Insurance Technical Reserves | 26r | — | — | — | †4,956 | 3,317 | 1,859 | 325 | 506 | 512 | 456 | 1,013 | 1,073 |
| Shares and Other Equity | 27a | 335,787 | 586,673 | 967,342 | †922,122 | 369,070 | 309,740 | 415,117 | 444,925 | 508,519 | 550,732 | 603,604 | 636,589 |
| Other Items (Net) | 27r | −390,553 | −566,181 | −844,816 | †−77,748 | 1,908,659 | 2,150,026 | 1,905,644 | 950,056 | 652,447 | 576,829 | 263,866 | 188,833 |
| Memo Item: | | | | | | | | | | | | | |
| Total Assets | 20ra | .... | .... | .... | †9,699,061 | 6,474,806 | 5,166,511 | 4,631,814 | 3,875,362 | 3,522,493 | 3,476,042 | 3,183,005 | 3,309,599 |
| **Depository Corporations** | | | | | | *Millions of Kronur: End of Period* | | | | | | | |
| Net Foreign Assets | 31n | 14,956 | 267,755 | 816,996 | †−1,341,436 | 190,048 | 353,777 | 553,956 | 936,964 | 689,393 | 722,095 | 689,742 | 693,360 |
| Claims on Nonresidents | 31 | 240,072 | 605,886 | 1,499,788 | †4,884,753 | 1,163,905 | 868,378 | 1,042,943 | 1,490,896 | 1,007,124 | 1,039,904 | 931,350 | 1,014,971 |
| Liabilities to Nonresidents | 36c | 225,116 | 338,131 | 682,792 | †6,226,189 | 973,858 | 514,600 | 488,987 | 553,932 | 317,731 | 317,808 | 241,609 | 321,610 |
| Domestic Claims | 32 | 1,527,153 | 2,486,487 | 3,559,034 | †4,108,126 | 4,579,174 | 4,555,162 | 4,086,038 | 3,141,383 | 2,776,466 | 2,647,973 | 2,308,742 | 2,364,858 |
| Net Claims on Central Government | 32an | −13,189 | −68,229 | −202,834 | †−197,614 | −129,730 | −45,445 | −40,562 | −136,063 | −107,391 | −35,338 | −248,262 | −126,542 |
| Claims on Central Government | 32a | 4,626 | 7,686 | 8,202 | †56,483 | 320,484 | 421,116 | 408,682 | 413,844 | 402,040 | 393,879 | 371,800 | 309,627 |
| Liabilities to Central Government | 36d | 17,815 | 75,916 | 211,036 | †254,097 | 450,214 | 466,561 | 449,245 | 549,907 | 509,431 | 429,217 | 620,062 | 436,169 |
| Claims on Other Sectors | 32s | 1,540,341 | 2,554,717 | 3,761,868 | †4,305,739 | 4,708,904 | 4,600,607 | 4,126,600 | 3,277,446 | 2,883,857 | 2,683,311 | 2,557,004 | 2,491,400 |
| Claims on Other Financial Corps. | 32g | 8,993 | 11,902 | 28,547 | †836,131 | 1,605,763 | 1,756,101 | 1,403,319 | 817,503 | 663,912 | 533,075 | 509,825 | 384,061 |
| Claims on State & Local Govts. | 32b | 45 | 38 | 95 | †12,491 | 15,364 | 15,300 | 22,714 | 18,802 | 15,430 | 12,844 | 19,012 | 19,626 |
| Claims on Public Nonfin. Corps. | 32c | — | — | — | †36,767 | 22,617 | 22,290 | 18,009 | 33,891 | 30,249 | 25,882 | 62,088 | 71,874 |
| Claims on Private Sector | 32d | 1,531,303 | 2,542,777 | 3,733,226 | †3,420,351 | 3,065,160 | 2,806,916 | 2,682,559 | 2,407,251 | 2,174,266 | 2,111,510 | 1,966,078 | 2,015,839 |
| Broad Money Liabilities | 35l | 560,930 | 707,930 | 1,133,532 | †1,198,715 | 1,584,949 | 1,624,112 | 1,461,358 | 1,544,549 | 1,473,987 | 1,542,587 | 1,677,186 | 1,789,974 |
| Currency Outside Depository Corps | 34a | 9,143 | 10,500 | 11,471 | †12,429 | 20,352 | 25,725 | 34,666 | 39,391 | 40,862 | 41,617 | 44,028 | 48,904 |
| Transferable Deposits | 34 | 146,197 | 163,662 | 191,242 | †380,813 | 404,586 | 429,275 | 430,423 | 422,293 | 383,755 | 392,413 | 403,958 | 444,717 |
| Other Deposits | 35 | 405,590 | 533,769 | 930,819 | †805,473 | 1,160,011 | 1,169,113 | 996,269 | 1,082,864 | 1,049,370 | 1,108,557 | 1,229,201 | 1,296,353 |
| Securities Other than Shares | 36a | — | — | — | †— | | | | | | | | |
| Deposits Excl. from Broad Money | 36b | — | — | — | †— | 9,827 | 153,142 | 279,999 | 344,326 | 27,448 | 29,747 | 24,402 | 22,798 |
| Sec.Ot.th.Shares Excl.f/Brd.Money | 36s | 999,662 | 1,992,413 | 3,074,738 | †424,522 | 119,895 | 41,023 | 22,521 | 156,015 | 189,259 | 208,887 | 179,938 | 233,303 |
| Loans | 36l | — | — | — | †165,937 | 583,558 | 467,370 | 453,040 | 506,350 | 477,768 | 387,741 | 228,368 | 166,000 |
| Financial Derivatives | 36m | — | — | — | †23,601 | 1,716 | 1,578 | 215 | 669 | 2,481 | 2,339 | 3,024 | 7,544 |
| Insurance Technical Reserves | 36r | — | — | — | †4,956 | 3,317 | 1,859 | 325 | 506 | 512 | 456 | 1,013 | 1,073 |
| Shares and Other Equity | 37a | 369,985 | 623,043 | 1,015,679 | †1,013,125 | 451,448 | 392,618 | 484,496 | 528,702 | 607,050 | 640,539 | 678,631 | 715,349 |
| Other Items (Net) | 37r | −388,468 | −569,144 | −847,918 | †−64,166 | 2,014,512 | 2,227,235 | 1,938,040 | 997,231 | 687,355 | 557,773 | 206,244 | 122,715 |
| Broad Money Liabs., Seasonally Adj. | 35l.b | 572,791 | 723,280 | 1,158,987 | †1,188,448 | 1,573,067 | 1,615,352 | 1,457,588 | 1,546,309 | 1,481,394 | 1,555,535 | 1,695,978 | 1,812,856 |
| **Monetary Aggregates** | | | | | | *Millions of Kronur: End of Period* | | | | | | | |
| Broad Money | 59m | 560,930 | 707,930 | 1,133,532 | 1,199,895 | 1,584,949 | 1,624,112 | 1,461,358 | 1,544,549 | 1,473,987 | 1,542,587 | 1,677,186 | 1,789,974 |
| o/w:Currency Issued by Cent.Govt | 59m.a | — | — | — | — | — | — | — | — | — | — | — | — |
| o/w: Dep.in Nonfin. Corporations. | 59m.b | — | — | — | 1,180 | — | — | — | — | — | — | — | — |
| o/w:Secs. Issued by Central Govt.. | 59m.c | — | — | — | — | — | — | — | — | — | — | — | — |
| Money (National Definitions) | | | | | | | | | | | | | |
| Base Money | 19ma | 34,151 | 45,158 | 57,741 | 167,847 | 115,054 | 116,565 | 93,929 | 74,491 | 98,357 | 98,658 | 183,502 | 343,734 |
| M1 | 59ma | 135,909 | 169,831 | 207,491 | 391,816 | 513,702 | 503,983 | 496,087 | 499,409 | 462,552 | 476,238 | 407,685 | 429,457 |
| M2 | 59mb | 234,710 | 298,081 | 357,059 | 627,914 | 1,049,110 | 996,054 | 915,431 | 990,370 | 900,222 | 920,114 | 968,762 | 968,139 |
| M3 | 59mc | 518,421 | 647,018 | 775,608 | 1,198,469 | 1,580,533 | 1,588,700 | 1,424,442 | 1,530,650 | 1,459,100 | 1,524,314 | 1,632,017 | 1,725,299 |
| M4 | 59md | 629,521 | 803,746 | 1,037,629 | 1,636,809 | .... | .... | .... | .... | .... | .... | .... | .... |
| **Interest Rates** | | | | | | *Percent Per Annum* | | | | | | | |
| Discount Rate (End of Period) | 60.a | 10.25 | 12.00 | 15.25 | 15.25 | 22.00 | 14.55 | 5.50 | 5.75 | 7.00 | 7.00 | 6.25 | 7.50 |
| Money Market Rate | 60b | 6.22 | 9.05 | 12.41 | 13.96 | 16.05 | 11.15 | 6.92 | 3.94 | 4.80 | 5.35 | 5.17 | 5.00 |
| Treasury Bill Rate | 60c | 6.04 | 8.80 | 13.41 | 15.13 | 17.88 | 11.38 | 6.65 | 4.28 | 5.56 | 6.19 | 6.03 | 5.93 |
| Deposit Rate | 60l | 4.85 | .... | .... | .... | .... | .... | .... | .... | .... | .... | .... | .... |
| Housing Bond Rate | 60m | 4.64 | 5.16 | 6.99 | 8.99 | .... | .... | .... | .... | .... | .... | .... | .... |
| Lending Rate | 60p | 12.02 | 14.78 | 17.91 | 19.29 | 20.14 | 18.99 | 10.26 | 7.70 | 8.32 | 8.15 | 7.74 | 7.61 |
| Government Bond Yield | 61 | 3.88 | 3.73 | 4.32 | 4.96 | 4.30 | 4.30 | 3.49 | 2.95 | 2.28 | 2.55 | 3.20 | 2.66 |

# Iceland 176

| | | 2004 | 2005 | 2006 | 2007 | 2008 | 2009 | 2010 | 2011 | 2012 | 2013 | 2014 | 2015 |
|---|---|---|---|---|---|---|---|---|---|---|---|---|---|
| **Prices, Production, Labor** | | | | | | *Index Numbers (2010=100): Period Averages* | | | | | | | |
| Share Prices................................... | 62 | 908.1 | 1,303.5 | 1,821.3 | 2,337.7 | 1,149.2 | † 84.3 | 100.0 | 104.0 | 110.6 | 128.5 | 133.7 | 182.2 |
| Consumer Prices............................. | 64 | 64.5 | 67.1 | 71.6 | 75.2 | † 84.7 | 94.9 | 100.0 | 104.0 | 109.4 | 113.6 | 116.0 | 117.8 |
| Wages............................................ | 65a | 66.6 | 71.1 | 77.9 | 84.9 | 91.8 | 95.4 | 100.0 | 106.8 | 115.1 | 121.6 | 128.7 | 137.9 |
| Industrial Production........................ | 66 | 47.7 | 53.6 | 62.6 | 63.0 | 85.4 | 88.6 | 100.0 | 112.1 | 117.1 | 112.4 | 113.6 | 124.4 |
| Total Fish Catch.............................. | 66al | 161.5 | 155.9 | 123.8 | 130.7 | 120.3 | 106.0 | 100.0 | 107.7 | 136.1 | 128.0 | . . . . | . . . . |
| | | | | | | *Number in Thousands: Period Averages* | | | | | | | |
| Labor Force.................................... | 67d | 163 | 158 | 167 | 174 | 176 | 173 | 172 | 172 | 171 | 175 | 178 | 182 |
| Employment.................................... | 67e | 156 | 154 | 162 | 170 | 171 | 160 | 159 | 159 | 161 | 166 | 169 | 174 |
| Unemployment................................ | 67c | 5 | 4 | 5 | 4 | 6 | 13 | † 14 | 13 | 11 | 10 | 9 | 8 |
| Unemployment Rate (%)................. | 67r | 3.1 | 2.6 | 2.9 | 2.3 | 3.0 | 7.2 | † 7.6 | 7.1 | 6.0 | 5.4 | 5.0 | 4.0 |
| **Intl. Transactions & Positions** | | | | | | *Millions of Kronur* | | | | | | | |
| Exports.......................................... | 70 | 202,824 | 185,286 | 227,785 | 277,420 | 452,428 | 500,855 | 561,032 | 619,682 | 633,029 | 609,788 | 582,123 | 626,022 |
| Fish............................................... | 70al | 64,711 | 61,010 | 69,916 | 72,859 | 91,790 | 113,723 | 121,162 | 142,531 | 142,402 | 139,696 | 131,432 | 120,466 |
| Fishmeal........................................ | 70z | 12,605 | 8,580 | 10,001 | 10,428 | 13,581 | 16,686 | 14,114 | 17,078 | 22,291 | 26,624 | 15,914 | 29,477 |
| Imports, c.i.f.................................. | 71 | 249,063 | 287,257 | 357,965 | 389,234 | 468,598 | 446,128 | 477,222 | 560,692 | 597,262 | 584,224 | 611,530 | 699,961 |
| | | | | | | *2010=100* | | | | | | | |
| Volume of Exports.......................... | 72 | 74.1 | 70.7 | 68.9 | 75.9 | 94.7 | 98.1 | 100.0 | . . . . | . . . . | . . . . | . . . . | . . . . |
| Volume of Imports.......................... | 73 | 111.6 | 138.4 | 152.6 | 151.9 | 130.2 | 94.5 | 100.0 | . . . . | . . . . | . . . . | . . . . | . . . . |
| Unit Value of Exports...................... | 74 | 49.1 | 47.1 | 59.2 | 60.7 | 82.9 | 87.7 | 100.0 | . . . . | . . . . | . . . . | . . . . | . . . . |
| Unit Value of Imports...................... | 75 | 47.7 | 45.9 | 54.1 | 55.5 | 80.8 | 96.2 | 100.0 | . . . . | . . . . | . . . . | . . . . | . . . . |
| **Balance of Payments** | | | | | | *Millions of US Dollars* | | | | | | | |
| A. Current Account*........................ | 109bx | −1,270.2 | −2,339.0 | −3,523.5 | −3,473.8 | −4,149.5 | −669.1 | −308.4 | −605.4 | −936.9 | 887.9 | 615.9 | 709.1 |
| Goods, credit (exports).................. | 1a9cx | 2,740.6 | 2,885.6 | 3,098.7 | 4,118.5 | 4,652.8 | 3,716.0 | 4,121.7 | 4,851.8 | 4,607.9 | 4,592.7 | 4,861.3 | 4,653.2 |
| Goods, debit (imports).................. | 1a9dx | 3,458.3 | 4,672.4 | 5,790.6 | 6,215.6 | 5,644.9 | 3,264.2 | 3,599.4 | 4,537.2 | 4,510.3 | 4,532.9 | 4,960.8 | 4,924.2 |
| Balance on goods........................ | 1a9bx | −717.8 | −1,786.8 | −2,691.9 | −2,097.1 | −992.1 | 451.8 | 522.3 | 314.6 | 97.6 | 59.9 | −99.5 | −271.0 |
| Services, credit (exports)............... | 1b9cx | 123.3 | 191.5 | 330.6 | 734.5 | 582.8 | 437.2 | 611.2 | 651.6 | 572.8 | 3,995.2 | 4,277.0 | 4,265.6 |
| Services, debit (imports)............... | 1b9dx | 17.0 | 11.9 | 31.3 | 79.7 | 102.6 | 28.7 | 105.4 | 191.6 | 168.5 | 2,823.7 | 3,116.7 | 2,821.2 |
| Balance on Goods & Services....... | 1z9bx | −611.4 | −1,607.2 | −2,392.6 | −1,442.3 | −511.9 | 860.4 | 1,028.1 | 774.6 | 501.9 | 1,231.4 | 1,060.8 | 1,173.4 |
| Primary income: credit................... | 1c9cx | 366.0 | 1,342.5 | 2,427.0 | 3,136.5 | 1,224.1 | 555.7 | 382.9 | 1,026.1 | 884.2 | 1,054.5 | 909.6 | 831.1 |
| Primary income: debit................... | 1c9dx | 1,020.6 | 2,078.2 | 3,569.3 | 5,182.3 | 4,827.1 | 2,016.8 | 1,626.9 | 2,292.4 | 2,211.6 | 1,264.4 | 1,211.8 | 992.6 |
| Balance on gds, serv. & prim. inc. | 1y9bx | −1,266.0 | −2,342.9 | −3,534.8 | −3,488.2 | −4,114.9 | −600.8 | −215.9 | −491.7 | −825.5 | 1,021.5 | 758.7 | 1,011.9 |
| Secondary income: credit............... | 1d9ca | 51.4 | 73.2 | 93.5 | 135.7 | 107.7 | 55.2 | 52.0 | 73.5 | 75.5 | 78.7 | 102.1 | 84.1 |
| Secondary income: debit............... | 1d9da | 55.5 | 69.4 | 82.2 | 121.2 | 142.3 | 123.5 | 144.6 | 187.2 | 186.9 | 212.4 | 244.8 | 386.9 |
| B. Capital Account*........................ | 209ba | −5.7 | −6.5 | −7.3 | −14.0 | −11.6 | −11.3 | −11.3 | −12.7 | −9.9 | −10.5 | −13.6 | −11.2 |
| Capital account: credit.................. | 209ca | . . . . | . . . . | . . . . | . . . . | . . . . | . . . . | . . . . | . . . . | . . . . | . . . . | . . . . | . . . . |
| Capital account: debit.................... | 209da | 5.7 | 6.5 | 7.3 | 14.0 | 11.6 | 11.3 | 11.3 | 12.7 | 9.9 | 10.5 | 13.6 | 11.2 |
| Balance on current & capital acct. | 129ba | −1,275.9 | −2,345.5 | −3,530.8 | −3,487.8 | −4,161.1 | −680.3 | −319.7 | −618.1 | −946.8 | 877.4 | 602.3 | 697.9 |
| C. Financial Account*................. | 309na | −3,725.7 | −6,286.1 | −8,216.2 | −4,606.6 | −7,367.3 | 21,038.6 | 11,966.6 | 7,348.1 | −1,046.8 | 942.0 | −3,009.5 | −70,111.2 |
| Direct investment: assets.............. | 3a9aa | 2,183.5 | 5,993.4 | 4,766.7 | 10,582.0 | −2,641.1 | 2,456.8 | −1,260.4 | 451.1 | −5,315.2 | 527.1 | 21.3 | −133.3 |
| Equity & investment fund shares.. | 3aaaa | 2,183.5 | 5,993.4 | 4,766.7 | 10,582.0 | −2,641.1 | 2,456.8 | −1,260.4 | 451.1 | −5,315.2 | 479.0 | 6.7 | −666.6 |
| Debt instruments........................ | 3abaa | . . . . | . . . . | . . . . | . . . . | . . . . | . . . . | . . . . | . . . . | . . . . | 48.1 | 14.6 | 533.3 |
| Direct investment: liabilities.......... | 3a9la | 556.6 | 2,641.1 | 3,190.0 | 3,129.5 | −220.8 | −382.1 | −93.1 | 137.1 | 238.7 | 472.6 | 766.8 | 386.6 |
| Equity & investment fund shares . | 3aala | 556.6 | 2,641.1 | 3,190.0 | 3,129.5 | −220.8 | −382.1 | −93.1 | 137.1 | 238.7 | −98.7 | −180.7 | 3,412.8 |
| Debt instruments........................ | 3abla | . . . . | . . . . | . . . . | . . . . | . . . . | . . . . | . . . . | . . . . | . . . . | 571.3 | 947.5 | −3,026.1 |
| Portfolio investment: assets.......... | 3b9aa | 63.1 | 1,417.4 | 1,954.6 | 4,768.6 | −3,217.9 | −678.4 | 828.4 | 1,020.3 | 625.6 | 1,213.4 | −55.9 | −3,014.0 |
| Equity & investment fund shares | 3baaa | . . . . | . . . . | . . . . | . . . . | . . . . | . . . . | . . . . | . . . . | −85.3 | −33.5 | −73.2 | 283.0 |
| Debt securities........................... | 3bbaa | 63.1 | 1,417.4 | 1,954.6 | 4,768.6 | −3,217.9 | −678.4 | 828.4 | 1,020.3 | 710.8 | 1,246.9 | 17.3 | −3,297.0 |
| Portfolio investment: liabilities....... | 3b9la | 8,382.5 | 16,851.8 | 14,320.2 | 417.1 | −1,210.6 | −10,924.8 | −10,773.3 | −7,358.1 | 413.4 | −309.7 | 713.4 | 31,916.0 |
| Equity & investment fund shares . | 3bala | 300.9 | 82.7 | 1,164.8 | 211.2 | −1,989.2 | −76.8 | 17.7 | 3.1 | −15.5 | −18.8 | −60.6 | −107.6 |
| Debt securities........................... | 3bbla | 8,081.6 | 16,769.0 | 13,155.4 | 205.8 | 778.6 | −10,848.1 | −10,791.0 | −7,361.2 | 428.9 | −290.9 | 774.1 | 32,023.7 |
| Fin. der.& empl.stk.ops.(ESOs): net | 3c9na | . . . . | . . . . | . . . . | −.6 | −1.5 | −.5 | −.6 | −7.5 | −.1 | −5.4 | −6.3 | 16.8 |
| Fin. der. & ESOs.: assets............. | 3c9aa | . . . . | . . . . | . . . . | −.6 | −1.5 | −.5 | −.6 | −7.5 | −.1 | −5.4 | −6.3 | 16.8 |
| Fin. der. & ESOs.: liabilities........... | 3c9la | . . . . | . . . . | . . . . | . . . . | . . . . | . . . . | . . . . | . . . . | . . . . | . . . . | . . . . | . . . . |
| Other investment: assets.............. | 3d9aa | 3,489.5 | 10,846.7 | 11,318.2 | 17,115.0 | 2,697.3 | 1,093.0 | −2,408.6 | −4,168.8 | 2,118.3 | −955.9 | −3,026.3 | −545.0 |
| Other equity............................... | 3daaa | 3.3 | 3.4 | 3.0 | 3.9 | 3.4 | 2.9 | 2.1 | 2.6 | 2.0 | 1.9 | 3.0 | . . . . |
| Debt instruments........................ | 3dzaa | 3,486.1 | 10,843.4 | 11,315.2 | 17,111.1 | 2,693.9 | 1,090.0 | −2,410.7 | −4,171.4 | 2,116.3 | −957.9 | −3,029.3 | −545.0 |
| Other investment: liabilities........... | 3d9la | 522.7 | 5,050.8 | 8,745.6 | 33,525.1 | 5,635.5 | −6,860.8 | −3,941.2 | −2,832.0 | −2,176.8 | −325.7 | −1,537.8 | 34,133.0 |
| Other equity............................... | 3dala | . . . . | . . . . | . . . . | . . . . | . . . . | . . . . | . . . . | . . . . | . . . . | . . . . | . . . . | . . . . |
| Debt instruments........................ | 3dzla | 522.7 | 5,050.8 | 8,745.6 | 33,525.1 | 5,635.5 | −6,860.8 | −3,941.2 | −2,832.0 | −2,176.8 | −325.7 | −1,537.8 | 34,133.0 |
| Curr.+ cap.− finan. acct. balance... | 4y9na | 2,449.8 | 3,940.6 | 4,685.3 | 1,118.8 | 3,206.2 | −21,718.9 | −12,286.3 | −7,966.2 | 100.0 | −64.6 | 3,611.8 | 70,809.1 |
| D. Net Errors and Omissions............ | 409na | −2,248.4 | −3,869.6 | −3,435.1 | −1,022.1 | −4,619.4 | 6,571.4 | 2,262.9 | 2,839.0 | −1,090.5 | 196.7 | −23.5 | 368.1 |
| E. Reserves and Related Items......... | 4z9na | 201.4 | 71.0 | 1,250.2 | 96.7 | −1,413.2 | −15,147.5 | −10,023.4 | −5,127.2 | −990.6 | 132.0 | 3,588.4 | 71,177.2 |
| Reserve assets............................. | 3e9aa | 201.4 | 71.0 | 1,250.2 | 96.7 | 1,183.1 | 212.3 | 1,982.1 | 2,848.9 | −4,371.7 | 14.9 | 315.2 | 1,089.0 |
| Credit and loans from the IMF....... | 3dcla | — | — | — | — | 830.5 | 166.9 | 320.5 | 838.8 | −1,357.4 | — | −400.6 | −333.1 |
| Exceptional financing.................... | 409la | . . . . | . . . . | . . . . | . . . . | 1,765.8 | 15,192.9 | 11,684.9 | 7,137.3 | −2,023.7 | −117.1 | −2,872.5 | −69,755.1 |

*Excludes components in group E

# Iceland 176

| International Investment Position | | 2004 | 2005 | 2006 | 2007 | 2008 | 2009 | 2010 | 2011 | 2012 | 2013 | 2014 | 2015 |
|---|---|---|---|---|---|---|---|---|---|---|---|---|---|
| | | | | | | *Millions of US Dollars* | | | | | | | |
| Assets.............................................. | 809aa | 19,774.7 | 40,628.1 | 67,026.0 | 115,747.9 | 40,403.6 | 38,261.6 | 37,670.9 | 37,983.9 | 39,628.1 | 47,030.3 | 41,059.9 | 36,962.5 |
| Direct investment.......................... | 8a9aa | 4,427.2 | 10,648.5 | 14,906.3 | 29,528.3 | 13,438.0 | 14,682.9 | 12,819.8 | 12,764.5 | 13,648.9 | 18,648.7 | 16,337.7 | 15,413.9 |
| Equity & investment fund shares.. | 8aaaa | 3,463.4 | 8,544.4 | 11,816.9 | 23,414.3 | 9,109.9 | 7,799.9 | 6,796.8 | 6,676.8 | 4,134.6 | 7,979.1 | 7,809.1 | 7,192.5 |
| Debt instruments........................ | 8abaa | 963.8 | 2,104.1 | 3,089.4 | 6,114.1 | 4,328.0 | 6,883.0 | 6,023.0 | 6,087.8 | 9,514.4 | 10,669.6 | 8,528.6 | 8,221.3 |
| Portfolio investment...................... | 8b9aa | 6,296.2 | 11,021.0 | 18,617.4 | 31,175.9 | 8,499.2 | 7,089.3 | 6,834.3 | 7,493.1 | 8,298.6 | 10,584.2 | 10,432.0 | 7,143.7 |
| Equity & investment fund shares.. | 8baaa | 5,841.6 | 9,339.4 | 13,392.6 | 20,630.7 | 6,706.3 | 5,893.0 | 4,810.6 | 4,659.2 | 4,885.6 | 5,887.9 | 6,020.6 | 6,282.0 |
| Debt securities............................ | 8bbaa | 454.6 | 1,681.5 | 5,224.9 | 10,545.2 | 1,792.9 | 1,196.3 | 2,023.7 | 2,833.8 | 3,413.0 | 4,696.3 | 4,411.4 | 861.7 |
| Fin. der.(oth.than reserves) & ESOs | 8c9aa | .... | .... | .... | 2,171.7 | 12.6 | 7.7 | .2 | 2.6 | 9.5 | 41.2 | 97.4 | 80.8 |
| Other investment.......................... | 8d9aa | 7,977.0 | 17,890.1 | 31,160.1 | 50,240.0 | 14,888.9 | 12,599.1 | 12,239.3 | 9,189.3 | 13,486.4 | 13,537.7 | 10,015.8 | 9,286.6 |
| Other equity.............................. | 8daaa | 56.4 | 56.6 | 60.1 | 68.5 | 61.2 | 64.3 | 66.4 | 67.3 | 68.6 | 79.9 | 75.9 | 68.9 |
| Debt instruments........................ | 8dzaa | 7,920.6 | 17,833.5 | 31,100.0 | 50,171.5 | 14,827.7 | 12,534.8 | 12,172.9 | 9,122.0 | 13,417.9 | 13,457.8 | 9,939.9 | 9,217.8 |
| Reserve assets............................. | 8e9aa | 1,074.2 | 1,068.5 | 2,342.2 | 2,632.1 | 3,564.9 | 3,882.6 | 5,777.2 | 8,534.4 | 4,184.6 | 4,218.6 | 4,176.9 | 5,037.5 |
| Liabilities........................................ | 809la | 29,791.4 | 54,336.5 | 83,398.8 | 138,354.0 | 125,762.3 | 123,168.0 | 122,891.6 | 113,538.5 | 103,627.1 | 112,723.2 | 102,509.8 | 37,943.9 |
| Direct investment.......................... | 8a9la | 2,475.4 | 5,265.7 | 8,610.5 | 20,824.9 | 13,239.9 | 13,124.4 | 13,137.5 | 13,899.6 | 11,711.1 | 16,538.0 | 15,844.8 | 15,590.2 |
| Equity & investment fund shares.. | 8aala | 1,542.5 | 3,760.8 | 5,962.7 | 10,680.2 | 2,167.7 | 911.9 | 1,461.0 | 1,707.7 | 597.1 | 4,581.7 | 3,913.8 | 7,441.3 |
| Debt instruments........................ | 8abla | 932.9 | 1,504.9 | 2,647.8 | 10,144.6 | 11,072.2 | 12,212.5 | 11,676.5 | 12,191.9 | 11,114.0 | 11,956.4 | 11,931.0 | 8,149.0 |
| Portfolio investment...................... | 8b9la | 20,697.2 | 37,915.1 | 54,687.5 | 59,842.7 | 50,953.2 | 53,086.9 | 50,999.1 | 46,887.2 | 46,374.4 | 48,749.4 | 47,565.1 | 7,522.6 |
| Equity & investment fund shares.. | 8bala | 781.3 | 3,722.0 | 4,992.3 | 5,845.4 | 103.7 | 493.9 | 466.0 | 465.2 | 464.0 | 590.8 | 626.5 | 775.0 |
| Debt securities............................ | 8bbla | 19,915.9 | 34,193.1 | 49,695.2 | 53,997.3 | 50,849.5 | 52,593.0 | 50,533.1 | 46,421.9 | 45,910.3 | 48,158.7 | 46,938.6 | 6,747.6 |
| Fin. der.(oth.than reserves) & ESOs | 8c9la | .... | .... | .... | 2,034.6 | 104.2 | 6.1 | 15.2 | 31.4 | 12.2 | 49.4 | 139.0 | 105.9 |
| Other investment.......................... | 8d9la | 6,618.9 | 11,155.6 | 20,100.8 | 55,651.8 | 61,465.0 | 56,950.7 | 58,739.8 | 52,720.3 | 45,529.5 | 47,386.3 | 38,960.9 | 14,725.2 |
| Other equity.............................. | 8dala | .... | .... | .... | .... | — | — | — | — | — | — | — | — |
| Debt instruments........................ | 8dzla | 6,618.9 | 11,155.6 | 20,100.8 | 55,651.8 | 61,465.0 | 56,950.7 | 58,739.8 | 52,720.3 | 45,529.5 | 47,386.3 | 38,960.9 | 14,725.2 |

# Iceland 176

| | | 2004 | 2005 | 2006 | 2007 | 2008 | 2009 | 2010 | 2011 | 2012 | 2013 | 2014 | 2015 |
|---|---|---|---|---|---|---|---|---|---|---|---|---|---|

**Government Finance Operations Statement**
**General Government**

*Millions of Kronur: Fiscal Year Ends December 31*

| | | 2004 | 2005 | 2006 | 2007 | 2008 | 2009 | 2010 | 2011 | 2012 | 2013 | 2014 | 2015 |
|---|---|---|---|---|---|---|---|---|---|---|---|---|---|
| Revenue | a1 | 409,478 | 560,510 | 560,510 | 623,894 | 653,473 | 636,055 | 641,204 | 682,425 | 741,081 | 795,864 | 906,988 | 931,116 |
| Taxes | a11 | 323,275 | 445,445 | 445,445 | 489,413 | 501,389 | 469,742 | 477,979 | 519,116 | 561,567 | 606,243 | 700,831 | 733,779 |
| Social Contributions | a12 | 28,364 | 38,414 | 38,414 | 40,684 | 41,644 | 42,933 | 63,599 | 66,820 | 64,882 | 69,899 | 73,432 | 78,927 |
| Grants | a13 | 1,286 | 1,443 | 1,443 | 1,220 | 1,416 | 1,711 | 2,404 | 2,943 | 3,733 | 2,881 | 2,534 | 2,900 |
| Other Revenue | a14 | 56,553 | 75,208 | 75,208 | 92,577 | 109,025 | 121,669 | 97,223 | 93,546 | 110,899 | 116,842 | 130,191 | 115,509 |
| Expense | a2 | 390,411 | 461,931 | 461,931 | 521,192 | 814,920 | 746,589 | 778,811 | 767,920 | 797,669 | 813,420 | 886,095 | 918,257 |
| Compensation of Employees | a21 | 145,491 | 178,792 | 178,792 | 193,582 | 216,200 | 224,175 | 220,037 | 229,655 | 242,673 | 256,819 | 275,652 | 304,935 |
| Use of Goods & Services | a22 | 102,692 | 123,362 | 123,362 | 141,440 | 171,386 | 187,972 | 193,633 | 200,444 | 209,941 | 218,096 | 230,033 | 239,003 |
| Consumption of Fixed Capital | a23 | 17,157 | 20,822 | 20,822 | 22,829 | 27,215 | 31,993 | 33,601 | 35,076 | 37,090 | 38,274 | 39,617 | 40,471 |
| Interest | a24 | 22,570 | 25,201 | 25,201 | 33,937 | 49,488 | 101,939 | 80,245 | 77,480 | 89,428 | 90,598 | 94,799 | 97,314 |
| Subsidies | a25 | 16,991 | 20,257 | 20,257 | 23,316 | 27,386 | 29,407 | 27,762 | 29,154 | 30,485 | 31,070 | 29,477 | 29,422 |
| Grants | a26 | 1,249 | 2,094 | 2,094 | 2,335 | 3,447 | 3,903 | 4,890 | 4,514 | 3,838 | 4,342 | 5,159 | 3,702 |
| Social Benefits | a27 | 63,488 | 66,651 | 66,651 | 75,377 | 89,778 | 122,869 | 120,619 | 138,347 | 133,922 | 132,563 | 139,441 | 141,767 |
| Other Expense | a28 | 20,773 | 24,751 | 24,751 | 28,377 | 230,020 | 44,332 | 98,024 | 53,250 | 50,293 | 41,658 | 71,916 | 61,644 |
| Gross Operating Balance [1-2+23] | agob | 36,224 | 119,402 | 119,402 | 125,531 | −134,232 | −78,542 | −104,006 | −50,419 | −19,498 | 20,717 | 60,510 | 53,330 |
| Net Operating Balance [1-2] | anob | 19,067 | 98,580 | 98,580 | 102,702 | −161,447 | −110,535 | −137,607 | −85,495 | −56,588 | −17,556 | 20,893 | 12,858 |
| Net Acq. of Nonfinancial Assets | a31 | 18,786 | 24,741 | 24,741 | 31,916 | 38,788 | 26,453 | 20,155 | 9,490 | 8,618 | 14,484 | 22,110 | 23,593 |
| Aquisition of Nonfin. Assets | a31.1 | .... | .... | .... | .... | .... | .... | .... | .... | .... | .... | .... | .... |
| Disposal of Nonfin. Assets | a31.2 | .... | .... | .... | .... | .... | .... | .... | .... | .... | .... | .... | .... |
| Net Lending/Borrowing [1-2-31] | anlb | 281 | 73,839 | 73,839 | 70,786 | −200,234 | −136,988 | −157,762 | −94,984 | −65,206 | −32,040 | −1,217 | −10,735 |
| Net Acq. of Financial Assets | a32 | −9,645 | 143,457 | 143,457 | 95,888 | 257,537 | 66,484 | −52,188 | 51,963 | −72,571 | −46,700 | 13,266 | −166,696 |
| *By instrument* | | | | | | | | | | | | | |
| Monetary Gold & SDRs | a3201 | — | — | — | — | — | — | — | — | — | — | — | — |
| Currency & Deposits | a3202 | 8,298 | 24,334 | 40,182 | 10,457 | 55,357 | 41,971 | 110,155 | 191,811 | −76,884 | −47,328 | 89,872 | −113,037 |
| Securities other than Shares | a3203 | — | — | — | — | — | — | 199 | 4 | −205 | — | — | — |
| Loans | a3204 | −18,296 | 82,699 | 94,833 | 29,157 | 200,310 | −112,007 | −92,512 | −104,643 | 7,286 | −7,614 | −26,387 | −13,334 |
| Shares & Other Equity | a3205 | 386 | −68,200 | 1,221 | 68,578 | 2,922 | 136,655 | 44,468 | 1,016 | 5,872 | 13,715 | −12,681 | 845 |
| Insurance Technical Reserves | a3206 | — | — | — | — | — | — | — | — | — | — | — | — |
| Financial Derivatives | a3207 | — | — | — | — | — | — | — | — | — | — | — | — |
| Other Accounts Receivable | a3208 | 1,296 | 7,221 | 7,221 | −12,304 | 182,023 | −136 | −88,663 | −37,631 | −24,747 | −5,473 | −37,538 | −41,170 |
| *By debtor* | | | | | | | | | | | | | |
| Domestic | a321 | −9,645 | 143,457 | 143,457 | 95,888 | 257,537 | 66,484 | −52,188 | 51,963 | −72,571 | −46,700 | 13,266 | −166,696 |
| Foreign | a322 | — | — | — | — | — | — | — | 5 | 6 | 3 | 1 | — |
| Net Incurrence of Liabilities | a33 | −9,926 | 69,618 | 69,618 | 25,102 | 457,771 | 203,472 | 105,574 | 146,947 | −7,365 | −14,660 | 14,483 | −155,961 |
| *By instrument* | | | | | | | | | | | | | |
| Special Drawing Rights (SDRs) | a3301 | — | — | — | — | — | — | — | — | — | — | — | — |
| Currency & Deposits | a3302 | — | — | — | — | — | — | — | — | — | — | — | — |
| Securities other than Shares | a3303 | 2,573 | 2,775 | 2,775 | 10,028 | 184,597 | 309,623 | 96,879 | 61,688 | 43,760 | 25,837 | 30,663 | 7,671 |
| Loans | a3304 | −9,183 | 66,843 | 66,843 | 15,074 | 273,174 | −106,152 | 60,511 | 90,584 | −59,069 | −40,497 | −16,180 | −163,632 |
| Shares & Other Equity | a3305 | — | — | — | — | — | — | — | — | — | — | — | — |
| Insurance Technical Reserves | a3306 | −3,316 | — | — | — | — | — | 1,113 | 4,856 | 4,586 | — | — | — |
| Financial Derivatives | a3307 | — | — | — | — | — | — | — | — | — | — | — | — |
| Other Accounts Payable | a3308 | — | — | — | — | — | — | 30,348 | −801 | 1,554 | — | — | — |
| *By creditor* | | | | | | | | | | | | | |
| Domestic | a331 | −867 | 2,669 | 2,669 | 36,462 | 430,159 | 164,645 | 121,029 | 43,170 | 7,488 | 30,268 | −10,866 | −44,809 |
| Foreign | a332 | −9,059 | 66,949 | 66,949 | −11,360 | 27,612 | 38,826 | −15,455 | 103,777 | −14,853 | −44,928 | 25,349 | −111,152 |
| Stat. Discrepancy [32-33-NLB] | anlbz | — | — | — | — | — | — | — | — | — | — | — | — |
| Memo Item: Expenditure [2+31] | a2m | 409,197 | 486,672 | 486,672 | 553,108 | 853,708 | 773,043 | 798,966 | 777,410 | 806,287 | 827,904 | 908,205 | 941,851 |

**Balance Sheet**

| | | 2004 | 2005 | 2006 | 2007 | 2008 | 2009 | 2010 | 2011 | 2012 | 2013 | 2014 | 2015 |
|---|---|---|---|---|---|---|---|---|---|---|---|---|---|
| Net Worth | a6 | .... | .... | .... | .... | .... | .... | .... | .... | .... | .... | .... | .... |
| Nonfinancial Assets | a61 | .... | .... | .... | .... | .... | .... | .... | .... | .... | .... | .... | .... |
| Financial Assets | a62 | 341,838 | 400,534 | 578,662 | 711,083 | 1,127,972 | 1,204,463 | 1,196,238 | 1,282,511 | 1,236,519 | 1,198,590 | 1,290,951 | .... |
| *By instrument* | | | | | | | | | | | | | |
| Monetary Gold & SDRs | a6201 | — | — | — | — | — | — | — | — | — | — | — | .... |
| Currency & Deposits | a6202 | 31,225 | 61,678 | 106,124 | 133,193 | 219,226 | 263,764 | 364,768 | 568,430 | 511,313 | 427,316 | 533,292 | .... |
| Securities other than Shares | a6203 | 70 | 34 | 27 | 22 | 18 | 21 | 220 | 17 | 19 | 22 | 32 | .... |
| Loans | a6204 | 72,040 | 91,062 | 184,624 | 196,862 | 497,927 | 396,577 | 271,808 | 177,211 | 193,639 | 196,556 | 196,940 | .... |
| Shares and Other Equity | a6205 | 136,814 | 131,786 | 149,504 | 225,928 | 230,863 | 369,224 | 378,708 | 367,985 | 362,506 | 400,940 | 385,223 | .... |
| Insurance Technical Reserves | a6206 | — | — | — | — | — | — | — | — | — | — | — | .... |
| Financial Derivatives | a6207 | — | — | — | — | — | — | — | — | — | — | — | .... |
| Other Accounts Receivable | a6208 | 101,689 | 115,974 | 138,385 | 155,078 | 179,937 | 174,877 | 180,735 | 168,868 | 169,042 | 173,752 | 175,463 | .... |
| *By debtor* | | | | | | | | | | | | | |
| Domestic | a621 | 341,838 | 400,534 | 578,662 | 711,083 | 1,127,972 | 1,204,463 | 1,196,238 | 1,282,511 | 1,236,519 | 1,198,590 | 1,290,951 | .... |
| Foreign | a622 | — | — | — | — | — | — | — | — | — | — | — | .... |
| Liabilities | a63 | 598,928 | 539,791 | 670,563 | 700,381 | 1,421,482 | 1,801,362 | 1,936,725 | 2,155,359 | 2,240,775 | 2,169,420 | 2,291,379 | .... |
| *By instrument* | | | | | | | | | | | | | |
| Special Drawing Rights (SDRs) | a6301 | — | — | — | — | — | — | — | — | — | — | — | .... |
| Currency & Deposits | a6302 | — | — | — | — | — | — | — | — | — | — | — | .... |
| Securities other than Shares | a6303 | 106,913 | 106,466 | 112,996 | 125,286 | 308,697 | 624,684 | 722,456 | 788,758 | 848,720 | 842,604 | 877,939 | .... |
| Loans | a6304 | 210,948 | 152,718 | 237,422 | 248,128 | 733,556 | 692,430 | 705,769 | 828,872 | 800,320 | 759,609 | 775,251 | .... |
| Shares and Other Equity | a6305 | — | — | — | — | — | — | — | — | — | — | — | .... |
| Insurance Technical Reserves | a6306 | 238,342 | 244,700 | 273,086 | 267,980 | 290,584 | 378,239 | 383,089 | 416,894 | 453,229 | 457,269 | 490,028 | .... |
| Financial Derivatives | a6307 | — | — | — | — | — | — | — | — | — | — | — | .... |
| Other Accounts Payable | a6308 | 42,724 | 35,906 | 47,060 | 58,987 | 88,645 | 106,009 | 125,412 | 120,835 | 138,505 | 109,937 | 148,160 | .... |
| *By creditor* | | | | | | | | | | | | | |
| Domestic | a631 | 432,428 | 433,495 | 474,731 | 526,028 | 1,056,945 | 1,396,707 | 1,555,902 | 1,676,635 | 1,784,457 | 1,766,930 | 1,872,685 | .... |
| Foreign | a632 | 166,499 | 106,296 | 195,832 | 174,353 | 364,537 | 404,656 | 380,824 | 478,724 | 456,318 | 402,490 | 418,694 | .... |
| Net Financial Worth [62-63] | a6m2 | −257,089 | −139,257 | −91,901 | 10,701 | −293,510 | −596,900 | −740,487 | −867,761 | −1,004,256 | −970,833 | −1,000,429 | .... |
| Memo Item: Debt at Market Value | a6m3 | 598,928 | 539,791 | 670,563 | 700,381 | 1,421,482 | 1,801,362 | 1,936,725 | 2,155,359 | 2,240,775 | 2,169,419 | 2,291,379 | .... |
| Memo Item: Debt at Face Value | a6m35 | .... | .... | .... | .... | .... | .... | .... | .... | .... | .... | .... | .... |
| Memo Item: Debt at Nominal Value | a6m4 | .... | .... | .... | .... | .... | .... | .... | .... | .... | .... | .... | .... |

# Iceland 176

|  |  | 2004 | 2005 | 2006 | 2007 | 2008 | 2009 | 2010 | 2011 | 2012 | 2013 | 2014 | 2015 |
|---|---|---|---|---|---|---|---|---|---|---|---|---|---|
| **National Accounts** | | | | | | | *Millions of Kronur* | | | | | | |
| Househ.Cons.Expend.,incl.NPISHs.... | 96f | 547,643 | 623,383 | 689,580 | 771,675 | 814,867 | 811,624 | 827,393 | 878,950 | 946,707 | 984,308 | 1,048,471 | 1,106,060 |
| Government Consumption Expend... | 91f | 229,976 | 249,340 | 282,268 | 314,404 | 364,592 | 394,597 | 398,341 | 419,389 | 435,213 | 457,518 | 484,262 | 517,175 |
| Gross Fixed Capital Formation......... | 93e | 239,578 | 311,922 | 428,701 | 401,875 | 393,252 | 240,382 | 228,455 | 263,693 | 287,389 | 290,467 | 331,341 | 412,421 |
| Changes in Inventories................... | 93i | −1,284 | −1,972 | 3,927 | 5,949 | 7,581 | −2,282 | −2,611 | 3,357 | 1,800 | −4,953 | 1,434 | 3,489 |
| Exports of Goods and Services......... | 90c | 314,362 | 321,931 | 372,958 | 458,422 | 637,902 | 787,875 | 867,765 | 959,867 | 1,009,937 | 1,045,937 | 1,065,915 | 1,177,967 |
| Imports of Goods and Services (-)..... | 98c | 366,053 | 446,607 | 577,284 | 578,554 | 670,349 | 646,679 | 698,293 | 822,105 | 900,800 | 892,383 | 938,088 | 1,023,319 |
| Gross Domestic Product (GDP)......... | 99b | 964,222 | 1,057,998 | 1,200,152 | 1,373,771 | 1,547,845 | 1,585,516 | 1,621,049 | 1,703,151 | 1,780,245 | 1,880,894 | 1,993,336 | 2,193,793 |
| Net Primary Income from Abroad..... | 98.n | −37,744 | −36,954 | −68,186 | −64,551 | −319,088 | −291,906 | −269,498 | −231,110 | −184,296 | −50,084 | .... | .... |
| Gross National Income (GNI)............ | 99a | 892,396 | 988,786 | 1,100,416 | 1,243,979 | 1,161,258 | 1,206,028 | 1,266,435 | 1,397,210 | 1,515,105 | 1,736,160 | .... | .... |
| Consumption of Fixed Capital.......... | 99cf | 107,354 | 119,389 | 144,742 | 170,082 | 219,629 | 255,665 | 251,099 | 250,704 | 261,513 | 266,193 | .... | .... |
| GDP Volume 2005 Prices................. | 99b.p | 998,094 | 1,057,998 | 1,102,782 | 1,210,002 | 1,223,925 | 1,160,898 | 1,125,292 | 1,152,309 | 1,167,402 | 1,208,966 | 1,231,592 | .... |
| GDP Volume 2010 Ref., Chained..... | 99b.p | 1,435,159 | 1,520,699 | 1,584,666 | 1,735,096 | 1,760,754 | 1,678,330 | 1,618,101 | 1,650,270 | 1,669,792 | 1,734,847 | 1,766,537 | 1,841,502 |
| GDP Volume (2010=100)................ | 99bvp | 88.7 | 94.0 | 97.9 | 107.2 | 108.8 | 103.7 | 100.0 | 102.0 | 103.2 | 107.2 | 109.2 | 113.8 |
| GDP Deflator (2010=100)............... | 99bip | 67.1 | 69.4 | 75.6 | 79.0 | 87.7 | 94.3 | 100.0 | 103.0 | 106.4 | 108.2 | 112.6 | 118.9 |
| | | | | | | | *Millions: Midyear Estimates* | | | | | | |
| Population................................. | 99z | .29 | .30 | .30 | .31 | .31 | .31 | .32 | .32 | .32 | .33 | .33 | .33 |

# India 534

| | | 2004 | 2005 | 2006 | 2007 | 2008 | 2009 | 2010 | 2011 | 2012 | 2013 | 2014 | 2015 |
|---|---|---|---|---|---|---|---|---|---|---|---|---|---|
| **Exchange Rates** | | | | | *Rupees per SDR: End of Period* | | | | | | | | |
| Market Rate.................... | aa | 67.688 | 64.410 | 66.562 | 62.286 | 74.634 | 73.180 | 69.009 | 81.768 | 84.188 | 95.321 | 91.755 | 91.910 |
| | | | | | *Rupees per US Dollar: End of Period (ae) Period Average (rf)* | | | | | | | | |
| Market Rate.................... | ae | 43.585 | 45.065 | 44.245 | 39.415 | 48.455 | 46.680 | 44.810 | 53.260 | 54.777 | 61.897 | 63.332 | 66.326 |
| Market Rate.................... | rf | 45.316 | 44.100 | 45.307 | 41.349 | 43.505 | 48.405 | 45.726 | 46.670 | 53.437 | 58.598 | 61.030 | 64.152 |
| **Fund Position** | | | | | *Millions of SDRs: End of Period* | | | | | | | | |
| Quota.................... | 2f.s | 4,158.20 | 4,158.20 | 4,158.20 | 4,158.20 | 4,158.20 | 4,158.20 | 4,158.20 | 5,821.50 | 5,821.50 | 5,821.50 | 5,821.50 | 5,821.50 |
| SDR Holdings.................... | 1b.s | 3.24 | 3.15 | .64 | 2.07 | 1.78 | 3,297.14 | 3,297.07 | 2,884.84 | 2,886.38 | 2,887.50 | 2,888.77 | 2,889.00 |
| Reserve Position in the Fund........... | 1c.s | 917.09 | 630.97 | 365.61 | 273.42 | 527.94 | 912.06 | 1,548.35 | 2,555.38 | 2,924.21 | 2,820.66 | 2,293.38 | 1,780.67 |
| Total Fund Cred.&Loans Outstg....... | 2tl | — | — | — | — | — | — | — | — | — | — | — | — |
| SDR Allocations.................... | 1bd | 681.17 | 681.17 | 681.17 | 681.17 | 681.17 | 3,978.26 | 3,978.26 | 3,978.26 | 3,978.26 | 3,978.26 | 3,978.26 | 3,978.26 |
| **International Liquidity** | | | | | *Millions of US Dollars Unless Otherwise Indicated: End of Period* | | | | | | | | |
| Total Reserves minus Gold.............. | 1l.d | 126,593 | 131,924 | 170,738 | 266,988 | 247,419 | 265,182 | 275,277 | 271,285 | 270,587 | 276,493 | 303,455 | 334,311 |
| SDR Holdings.................... | 1b.d | 5 | 4 | 1 | 3 | 3 | 5,169 | 5,078 | 4,429 | 4,436 | 4,447 | 4,185 | 4,003 |
| Reserve Position in the Fund.......... | 1c.d | 1,424 | 902 | 550 | 432 | 813 | 1,430 | 2,385 | 3,923 | 4,494 | 4,344 | 3,323 | 2,468 |
| Foreign Exchange.................... | 1d.d | 125,164 | 131,018 | 170,187 | 266,553 | 246,603 | 258,583 | 267,814 | 262,933 | 261,656 | 267,703 | 295,947 | 327,840 |
| Gold (Million Fine Troy Ounces)....... | 1ad | 11.502 | 11.502 | 11.502 | 11.502 | 11.502 | 17.932 | 17.932 | 17.932 | 17.932 | 17.932 | 17.932 | 17.932 |
| Gold (National Valuation)................ | 1and | 3,808 | 4,102 | 5,367 | 6,871 | 6,605 | 9,486 | † 22,470 | 26,620 | 27,220 | 19,725 | 19,378 | 17,240 |
| **Monetary Authorities** | | | | | *Billions of Rupees: Last Friday of Period* | | | | | | | | |
| Foreign Assets.................... | 11 | 5,706.7 | 6,467.2 | 7,806.1 | 10,731.8 | 11,908.7 | 12,889.7 | 12,873.9 | 15,214.6 | 15,697.6 | 17,948.0 | 20,004.6 | 23,049.3 |
| Claims on Central Government........ | 12a | 857.3 | 760.9 | 1,008.9 | 997.1 | 994.9 | 1,633.0 | 3,648.8 | 4,520.0 | 6,323.6 | 6,776.9 | 5,378.0 | 5,550.0 |
| Claims on Deposit Money Banks...... | 12e | 6.7 | 4.8 | 36.2 | 8.4 | 116.3 | 1.6 | 50.8 | 59.1 | 245.4 | 429.3 | 920.8 | 1,932.7 |
| Claims on Other Financial Insts........ | 12f | 82.6 | 70.0 | 70.5 | 29.2 | 28.3 | 61.7 | 16.5 | 32.9 | 37.5 | 73.6 | 57.7 | 64.8 |
| Reserve Money.................... | 14 | 4,549.6 | 5,228.1 | 6,193.9 | 8,079.1 | 8,864.8 | 10,171.0 | 12,418.3 | 13,942.6 | 14,580.0 | 16,136.9 | 17,659.8 | 20,182.3 |
| of which: Currency Outside DMBs.. | 14a | 3,418.4 | 3,946.5 | 4,616.2 | 5,344.0 | 6,265.5 | 7,382.5 | 8,686.7 | 9,774.4 | 10,914.6 | 12,136.6 | 13,264.6 | 14,997.9 |
| Foreign Liabilities.................... | 16c | 46.1 | 43.9 | 45.3 | 42.4 | 50.8 | 291.1 | 274.5 | 325.3 | 334.9 | 379.2 | 365.0 | 365.6 |
| Central Government Deposits........... | 16d | 752.0 | 812.6 | 924.2 | 2,283.5 | 1,201.9 | 672.1 | 945.8 | 1.4 | 826.0 | 509.7 | 1.4 | 3.3 |
| Capital Accounts.................... | 17a | 67.1 | 67.1 | 67.1 | 67.1 | 67.1 | 67.2 | 67.2 | 67.2 | 67.2 | 67.2 | 67.3 | 67.3 |
| Other Items (Net).................... | 17r | 1,238.6 | 1,151.2 | 1,691.1 | 1,294.4 | 2,863.5 | 3,384.7 | 2,884.2 | 5,490.0 | 6,495.9 | 8,134.7 | 8,267.6 | 9,978.3 |
| Memo Item: | | | | | | | | | | | | | |
| Total Assets.................... | 10ra | 6,765.41 | 7,410.26 | 9,014.74 | 11,865.38 | 13,251.83 | 15,135.44 | 17,115.53 | 20,556.69 | 23,075.05 | 26,095.09 | 27,023.01 | 31,310.98 |
| **Deposit Money Banks** | | | | | *Billions of Rupees: Last Friday of Period* | | | | | | | | |
| Reserves.................... | 20 | 1,182.7 | 1,298.0 | 1,692.2 | 2,796.4 | 2,460.6 | 2,761.1 | 3,503.2 | 3,926.9 | 3,453.2 | 3,750.4 | 4,055.9 | 4,758.6 |
| Claims on Central Government........ | 22a | 6,950.0 | 6,983.7 | 7,426.8 | 9,232.2 | 10,951.8 | 13,781.1 | 14,687.0 | 17,164.2 | 19,614.3 | 22,339.7 | 24,521.3 | 27,087.8 |
| Claims on Private Sector................. | 22d | 11,531.9 | 14,553.2 | 18,562.0 | 22,351.5 | 27,327.8 | 30,638.0 | 38,596.4 | 44,808.0 | 51,598.0 | 58,847.6 | 64,686.5 | 71,431.3 |
| Demand Deposits.................... | 24 | 2,602.0 | 3,221.7 | 3,928.9 | 4,498.2 | 4,639.7 | 5,558.8 | 6,518.5 | 6,486.9 | 6,455.0 | 6,948.3 | 7,722.7 | 8,580.0 |
| Time Deposits.................... | 25 | 14,527.4 | 16,595.0 | 20,361.1 | 25,517.9 | 31,634.4 | 37,351.3 | 44,063.4 | 52,591.3 | 59,098.0 | 68,716.3 | 76,055.9 | 83,716.1 |
| Credit from Monetary Authorities..... | 26g | 1.5 | .1 | .2 | 23.1 | 135.4 | — | 49.8 | 58.8 | 244.3 | 427.5 | 920.7 | 1,932.8 |
| Other Items (Net).................... | 27r | 2,533.6 | 3,018.1 | 3,390.8 | 4,341.0 | 4,330.7 | 4,270.0 | 6,154.9 | 6,762.1 | 8,868.2 | 8,845.6 | 8,564.4 | 9,048.8 |
| Memo Item: | | | | | | | | | | | | | |
| Total Assets.................... | 20ra | 19,664.60 | 22,834.90 | 27,681.03 | 34,380.11 | 40,740.13 | 47,180.17 | 56,786.55 | 65,899.08 | 74,665.50 | 84,937.70 | 93,263.70 | 103,277.70 |
| **Monetary Survey** | | | | | *Billions of Rupees: Last Friday of Period* | | | | | | | | |
| Foreign Assets (Net).................... | 31n | 5,660.6 | 6,423.3 | 7,760.7 | 10,689.4 | 11,857.8 | 12,598.6 | 12,599.4 | 14,889.3 | 15,362.7 | 17,568.8 | 19,639.6 | 22,683.7 |
| Domestic Credit.................... | 32 | 18,669.9 | 21,555.2 | 26,144.0 | 30,326.6 | 38,100.8 | 45,441.7 | 56,002.8 | 66,523.6 | 76,747.4 | 87,528.1 | 94,642.0 | 104,130.6 |
| Claims on Central Govt. (Net)........ | 32an | 7,055.3 | 6,932.0 | 7,511.5 | 7,945.6 | 10,744.7 | 14,742.0 | 17,390.0 | 21,682.8 | 25,111.9 | 28,606.9 | 29,897.8 | 32,634.5 |
| Claims on Private Sector................ | 32d | 11,531.9 | 14,553.2 | 18,562.0 | 22,351.5 | 27,327.8 | 30,638.0 | 38,596.4 | 44,808.0 | 51,598.0 | 58,847.6 | 64,686.5 | 71,431.3 |
| Claims on Other Financial Insts...... | 32f | 82.6 | 70.0 | 70.5 | 29.2 | 28.3 | 61.7 | 16.5 | 32.9 | 37.5 | 73.6 | 57.7 | 64.8 |
| Money.................... | 34 | 6,067.7 | 7,212.9 | 8,597.2 | 9,889.9 | 11,030.2 | 12,991.2 | 15,241.2 | 16,283.5 | 17,384.6 | 19,109.8 | 21,068.7 | 23,721.4 |
| Quasi-Money.................... | 35 | 14,527.4 | 16,595.0 | 20,361.1 | 25,517.9 | 31,634.4 | 37,351.3 | 44,063.4 | 52,591.3 | 59,098.0 | 68,716.3 | 76,055.9 | 83,716.1 |
| Other Items (Net).................... | 37r | 3,735.4 | 4,170.6 | 4,946.4 | 5,608.2 | 7,294.0 | 7,697.8 | 9,297.7 | 12,538.0 | 15,627.5 | 17,270.7 | 17,157.0 | 19,376.8 |
| Money plus Quasi-Money.................... | 35l | 20,595.1 | 23,807.9 | 28,958.3 | 35,407.7 | 42,664.6 | 50,342.5 | 59,304.5 | 68,874.9 | 76,482.6 | 87,826.1 | 97,124.6 | 107,437.5 |
| **Money (National Definitions)** | | | | | *Billions of Rupees: End of Period* | | | | | | | | |
| M0.................... | 19mb | .... | .... | 6,193.9 | 8,079.1 | 8,864.8 | 10,171.0 | 12,418.3 | 13,942.6 | 14,580.0 | 16,136.9 | 17,659.8 | 20,182.3 |
| M1.................... | 59ma | .... | .... | 8,663.6 | 10,223.3 | 11,287.1 | 13,309.9 | 15,918.0 | 16,987.1 | 18,122.6 | 19,896.7 | 21,885.7 | 24,576.2 |
| M3.................... | 59mc | .... | .... | 30,163.1 | 36,987.5 | 44,440.3 | 52,453.5 | 62,252.5 | 72,221.6 | 80,299.7 | 92,229.8 | 102,107.4 | 113,004.4 |
| **Interest Rates** | | | | | *Percent Per Annum* | | | | | | | | |
| Discount Rate (End of Period).......... | 60.a | 6.00 | 6.00 | 6.00 | 6.00 | 6.00 | 6.00 | 6.00 | 6.00 | 9.00 | 8.75 | 9.00 | 7.75 |
| Money Market Rate.................... | 60b | .... | .... | .... | 15.29 | 11.55 | 4.49 | 6.51 | 8.80 | 9.34 | 8.58 | 8.64 | 8.14 |
| Lending Rate.................... | 60p | 10.92 | 10.75 | 11.19 | 13.02 | 13.31 | 12.19 | † 8.33 | 10.17 | 10.60 | 10.29 | 10.25 | 10.01 |
| Government Bond Yield.................... | 61 | .... | † 6.96 | 7.66 | 7.97 | 7.85 | 6.95 | 7.85 | 8.37 | 8.29 | 8.15 | 8.56 | 7.77 |
| **Prices, Production, Labor** | | | | | *Index Numbers (2010=100): Period Averages* | | | | | | | | |
| Share Prices.................... | 62 | 29.9 | 39.6 | 61.4 | 85.7 | 82.3 | 77.0 | 100.0 | 97.4 | 94.9 | 105.8 | 132.4 | 146.8 |
| Wholesale Prices.................... | 63 | 71.3 | 74.7 | † 78.2 | 82.1 | 89.2 | 91.3 | 100.0 | 108.9 | 117.7 | 125.1 | 130.0 | 126.4 |
| Consumer Prices.................... | 64 | 63.1 | 65.8 | † 69.9 | 74.3 | 80.5 | 89.3 | 100.0 | 108.9 | 119.0 | † 132.0 | 140.8 | 147.7 |
| Industrial Production.................... | 66 | 61.1 | 65.9 | 72.7 | 80.2 | 83.6 | 89.1 | † 100.0 | 104.8 | 105.5 | 106.2 | 108.1 | 111.6 |
| | | | | | *Number in Thousands: Period Averages* | | | | | | | | |
| Employment.................... | 67e | .... | † 371,990 | .... | .... | .... | .... | 374,286 | .... | .... | .... | .... | .... |
| Unemployment.................... | 67c | 40,458 | 39,348 | 41,466 | 39,974 | .... | .... | .... | .... | .... | .... | .... | .... |
| **Intl. Transactions & Positions** | | | | | *Billions of Rupees* | | | | | | | | |
| Exports.................... | 70 | 3,473 | 4,393 | 5,522 | 6,190 | 8,412 | 7,967 | 10,341 | 14,121 | 15,840 | 18,448 | 19,677 | 17,163 |
| Imports, c.i.f.................... | 71 | 4,521 | 6,300 | 8,091 | 9,435 | 13,939 | 12,398 | 16,002 | 21,698 | 26,150 | 27,136 | 28,239 | 25,257 |
| | | | | | *2010=100* | | | | | | | | |
| Unit Value of Exports.................... | 74 | 60 | 66 | † 71 | 74 | 87 | 88 | 100 | 120 | 127 | 140 | 135 | .... |
| Unit Value of Imports.................... | 75 | 92 | 83 | † 85 | 86 | 98 | 88 | 100 | 175 | 189 | 213 | 213 | .... |

## Balance of Payments

*Millions of US Dollars*

| | | 2004 | 2005 | 2006 | 2007 | 2008 | 2009 | 2010 | 2011 | 2012 | 2013 | 2014 | 2015 |
|---|---|---|---|---|---|---|---|---|---|---|---|---|---|
| A. Current Account* | 109bx | 780.2 | −10,283.5 | −9,299.1 | −8,075.7 | −30,972.0 | † −26,186.4 | −54,515.9 | −62,517.6 | −91,471.2 | −49,226.0 | −27,451.6 | . . . . |
| Goods, credit (exports) | 1a9cx | 77,921.9 | 102,403.1 | 123,876.2 | 153,529.6 | 199,065.1 | † 167,957.7 | 230,967.1 | 307,847.5 | 298,320.6 | 319,109.8 | 329,633.3 | . . . . |
| Goods, debit (imports) | 1a9dx | 95,539.1 | 134,692.0 | 166,571.9 | 208,610.9 | 291,740.3 | † 247,907.7 | 324,320.5 | 428,021.2 | 450,249.4 | 433,760.3 | 415,528.7 | . . . . |
| Balance on goods | 1a9bx | −17,617.2 | −32,288.9 | −42,695.6 | −55,081.3 | −92,675.2 | † −79,950.0 | −93,353.4 | −120,173.7 | −151,928.8 | −114,650.6 | −85,895.3 | . . . . |
| Services, credit (exports) | 1b9cx | 38,097.9 | 52,179.0 | 69,439.8 | 86,552.5 | 106,054.2 | † 92,889.5 | 117,068.3 | 138,527.9 | 145,524.6 | 148,649.0 | 156,252.3 | . . . . |
| Services, debit (imports) | 1b9dx | 35,441.0 | 47,166.4 | 58,514.2 | 70,174.9 | 87,739.1 | † 80,349.5 | 114,738.5 | 125,041.0 | 129,659.2 | 126,255.7 | 137,596.6 | . . . . |
| Balance on Goods & Services | 1z9bx | −14,960.3 | −27,276.3 | −31,770.0 | −38,703.7 | −74,360.0 | † −67,410.0 | −91,023.7 | −106,686.8 | −136,063.4 | −92,257.3 | −67,239.7 | . . . . |
| Primary income: credit | 1c9cx | 4,689.9 | 5,645.9 | 8,199.4 | 12,649.8 | 15,593.4 | † 13,732.8 | 9,961.1 | 10,147.3 | 9,899.0 | 11,229.8 | 11,003.8 | . . . . |
| Primary income: debit | 1c9dx | 8,742.1 | 12,295.9 | 14,444.8 | 19,165.6 | 20,957.7 | † 21,271.7 | 25,563.1 | 26,190.5 | 30,741.9 | 33,013.2 | 36,818.5 | . . . . |
| Balance on gds, serv. & prim. inc. | 1y9bx | −19,012.4 | −33,926.3 | −38,015.3 | −45,219.5 | −79,724.4 | † −74,949.0 | −106,625.6 | −122,730.0 | −156,906.3 | −114,040.8 | −93,054.3 | . . . . |
| Secondary income: credit | 1d9ca | 20,614.7 | 24,512.0 | 30,015.2 | 38,885.4 | 52,065.2 | † 50,526.4 | 54,379.9 | 62,735.3 | 68,611.5 | 69,441.2 | 69,786.1 | . . . . |
| Secondary income: debit | 1d9da | 822.1 | 869.3 | 1,299.0 | 1,741.6 | 3,312.8 | † 1,763.9 | 2,270.1 | 2,522.9 | 3,176.4 | 4,626.4 | 4,183.4 | . . . . |
| B. Capital Account* | 209ba | . . . . | . . . . | . . . . | . . . . | — | † 293.0 | 49.7 | 67.9 | −597.2 | 961.8 | −194.9 | . . . . |
| Capital account: credit | 209ca | . . . . | . . . . | . . . . | . . . . | — | † 639.0 | 693.3 | 938.9 | 1,080.2 | 2,123.9 | 669.3 | . . . . |
| Capital account: debit | 209da | . . . . | . . . . | . . . . | . . . . | — | † 346.0 | 643.6 | 871.0 | 1,677.4 | 1,162.1 | 864.3 | . . . . |
| Balance on current & capital acct. | 129ba | 780.2 | −10,283.5 | −9,299.1 | −8,075.7 | −30,972.0 | † −25,893.4 | −54,466.2 | −62,449.7 | −92,068.5 | −48,264.1 | −27,646.6 | . . . . |
| C. Financial Account* | 309na | −22,228.8 | −25,283.9 | −37,774.7 | −94,363.5 | −34,436.8 | † −42,920.8 | −69,596.6 | −59,326.1 | −85,645.7 | −59,178.0 | −68,338.1 | . . . . |
| Direct investment: assets | 3a9aa | 1,837.1 | 2,640.8 | 14,036.8 | 17,026.1 | 19,256.5 | † 16,095.6 | 15,968.1 | 12,608.0 | 8,553.2 | 1,764.9 | 9,950.6 | . . . . |
| Equity & investment fund shares | 3aaaa | 1,925.1 | 2,348.8 | 12,820.8 | 15,048.9 | 15,210.7 | † 12,747.7 | 9,253.1 | 6,011.9 | 3,416.5 | −1,348.6 | 6,877.8 | . . . . |
| Debt instruments | 3abaa | −88.0 | 291.9 | 1,216.0 | 1,977.2 | 4,045.8 | † 3,347.9 | 6,715.0 | 6,596.1 | 5,136.7 | 3,113.5 | 3,072.8 | . . . . |
| Direct investment: liabilities | 3a9la | 5,429.3 | 7,269.4 | 20,029.1 | 25,227.7 | 43,406.3 | † 35,581.4 | 27,396.9 | 36,498.7 | 23,995.7 | 28,153.0 | 33,871.4 | . . . . |
| Equity & investment fund shares | 3aala | 5,429.3 | 7,269.4 | 20,029.1 | 24,928.2 | 42,690.1 | † 34,111.3 | 27,356.6 | 34,642.5 | 23,171.9 | 26,712.7 | 31,601.6 | . . . . |
| Debt instruments | 3abla | — | — | — | 299.6 | 716.2 | † 1,470.0 | 40.3 | 1,856.1 | 823.8 | 1,440.3 | 2,269.8 | . . . . |
| Portfolio investment: assets | 3b9aa | 16.9 | 7.1 | −36.6 | −153.5 | 44.8 | † 174.1 | 1,110.8 | 46.0 | 824.9 | 169.2 | 267.9 | . . . . |
| Equity & investment fund shares | 3baaa | 16.9 | 7.1 | −36.6 | −153.5 | 44.8 | † 174.1 | 1,110.8 | 46.0 | 824.9 | 169.2 | 267.9 | . . . . |
| Debt securities | 3bbaa | . . . . | . . . . | . . . . | . . . . | | † — | . . . . | . . . . | . . . . | . . . . | . . . . | . . . . |
| Portfolio investment: liabilities | 3b9la | 9,054.0 | 12,151.2 | 9,509.1 | 32,862.8 | −15,030.0 | † 17,930.9 | 37,986.3 | 2,710.8 | 30,110.1 | 7,027.2 | 38,008.3 | . . . . |
| Equity & investment fund shares | 3bala | 9,054.0 | 12,151.2 | 9,509.1 | 32,862.8 | −15,030.0 | † 24,688.9 | 30,442.2 | −4,048.3 | 22,809.1 | 19,891.6 | 12,369.3 | . . . . |
| Debt securities | 3bbla | . . . . | . . . . | . . . . | . . . . | — | † −6,758.0 | 7,544.1 | 6,759.1 | 7,301.0 | −12,864.4 | 25,639.0 | . . . . |
| Fin. der.& empl.stk.ops.(ESOs): net. | 3c9na | . . . . | . . . . | . . . . | . . . . | . . . . | . . . . | . . . . | — | 1,403.7 | 2,255.7 | −981.5 | . . . . |
| Fin. der. & ESOs.: assets | 3c9aa | . . . . | . . . . | . . . . | . . . . | . . . . | . . . . | . . . . | — | 3,629.6 | 8,082.7 | 13,565.6 | . . . . |
| Fin. der. & ESOs.: liabilities | 3c9la | . . . . | . . . . | . . . . | . . . . | . . . . | . . . . | . . . . | — | 2,225.9 | 5,827.0 | 14,547.0 | . . . . |
| Other investment: assets | 3d9aa | −2,898.8 | 4,431.9 | 2,789.4 | −13,065.3 | −1,009.7 | † 727.6 | 19,106.2 | 17,672.8 | 16,802.8 | 22,829.9 | 15,058.0 | . . . . |
| Other equity | 3daaa | . . . . | . . . . | . . . . | . . . . | . . . . | . . . . | . . . . | . . . . | . . . . | . . . . | . . . . | . . . . |
| Debt instruments | 3dzaa | −2,898.8 | 4,431.9 | 2,789.4 | −13,065.3 | −1,009.7 | † 727.6 | 19,106.2 | 17,672.8 | 16,802.8 | 22,829.9 | 15,058.0 | . . . . |
| Other investment: liabilities | 3d9la | 6,700.8 | 12,943.0 | 25,026.1 | 40,080.3 | 24,352.1 | † 6,405.7 | 40,398.5 | 50,443.4 | 59,124.5 | 51,017.5 | 20,753.5 | . . . . |
| Other equity | 3dala | . . . . | . . . . | . . . . | . . . . | . . . . | † 3,182.0 | 1,985.0 | 777.3 | 217.2 | 20.0 | . . . . | . . . . |
| Debt instruments | 3dzla | 6,700.8 | 12,943.0 | 25,026.1 | 40,080.3 | 24,352.1 | † 3,223.7 | 38,413.5 | 49,666.1 | 58,907.2 | 50,997.5 | 20,753.5 | . . . . |
| Curr.+ cap.– finan. acct. balance... | 4y9na | 23,009.0 | 15,000.4 | 28,475.6 | 86,287.8 | 3,464.8 | † 17,027.3 | 15,130.3 | −3,123.6 | −6,422.8 | 10,913.9 | 40,691.6 | . . . . |
| D. Net Errors and Omissions | 409na | 640.2 | −446.3 | 694.3 | 1,200.4 | 21,907.9 | † 8.6 | −1,003.5 | −1,014.9 | 2,400.0 | 14.6 | −3,108.1 | . . . . |
| E. Reserves and Related Items | 4z9na | 23,649.2 | 14,554.1 | 29,169.9 | 87,488.2 | 25,372.7 | † 17,036.0 | 14,126.8 | −4,138.6 | −4,022.8 | 10,928.5 | 37,583.5 | . . . . |
| Reserve assets | 3e9aa | 23,649.2 | 14,554.1 | 29,169.9 | 87,488.2 | 25,372.7 | † 17,036.0 | 14,126.8 | −4,138.6 | −4,022.8 | 10,928.5 | 37,583.5 | . . . . |
| Credit and loans from the IMF | 3dcla | — | — | — | — | — | † — | — | — | — | — | — | . . . . |
| Exceptional financing | 409la | . . . . | . . . . | . . . . | . . . . | — | † — | . . . . | . . . . | . . . . | . . . . | . . . . | . . . . |

*Excludes components in group E

## International Investment Position

*Millions of US Dollars*

| | | 2004 | 2005 | 2006 | 2007 | 2008 | 2009 | 2010 | 2011 | 2012 | 2013 | 2014 | 2015 |
|---|---|---|---|---|---|---|---|---|---|---|---|---|---|
| Assets | 809aa | 167,482.2 | 182,468.1 | † 231,642.2 | 335,779.8 | 337,527.2 | 385,877.8 | 426,203.6 | 434,475.5 | 445,685.3 | 460,537.9 | 492,967.4 | . . . . |
| Direct investment | 8a9aa | 10,072.1 | 15,738.4 | † 27,035.6 | 44,080.4 | 63,337.8 | 80,839.2 | 96,900.6 | 109,508.8 | 118,072.3 | 119,837.5 | 131,524.0 | . . . . |
| Equity & investment fund shares.. | 8aaaa | 9,120.9 | 13,801.5 | † 24,110.2 | 38,948.5 | 54,160.4 | 65,316.4 | 74,644.9 | 80,657.4 | 84,081.5 | 82,732.8 | 91,145.0 | . . . . |
| Debt instruments | 8abaa | 951.1 | 1,936.9 | † 2,925.4 | 5,131.9 | 9,177.4 | 15,522.9 | 22,255.7 | 28,851.4 | 33,990.8 | 37,104.7 | 40,379.0 | . . . . |
| Portfolio investment | 8b9aa | 471.3 | 1,223.5 | † 1,114.6 | 723.9 | 514.3 | 1,029.1 | 1,818.4 | 1,322.6 | 1,440.1 | 1,232.2 | 1,360.6 | . . . . |
| Equity & investment fund shares.. | 8baaa | 244.4 | 754.2 | † 656.1 | 566.0 | 494.3 | 986.7 | 1,766.0 | 1,301.2 | 1,360.3 | 1,079.0 | 983.8 | . . . . |
| Debt securities | 8bbaa | 226.9 | 469.3 | † 458.5 | 157.8 | 20.0 | 42.5 | 52.3 | 21.3 | 79.8 | 153.1 | 376.8 | . . . . |
| Fin. der.(oth.than reserves) & ESOs | 8c9aa | . . . . | . . . . | . . . . | . . . . | . . . . | . . . . | . . . . | . . . . | . . . . | . . . . | . . . . | . . . . |
| Other investment | 8d9aa | 14,909.1 | 15,259.8 | † 26,296.8 | 15,694.7 | 17,797.8 | 20,535.8 | 29,732.4 | 25,693.7 | 28,367.4 | 43,249.3 | 37,558.1 | . . . . |
| Other equity | 8daaa | . . . . | . . . . | . . . . | . . . . | . . . . | . . . . | . . . . | . . . . | . . . . | . . . . | . . . . | . . . . |
| Debt instruments | 8dzaa | 14,909.1 | 15,259.8 | † 26,296.8 | 15,694.7 | 17,797.8 | 20,535.8 | 29,732.4 | 25,693.7 | 28,367.4 | 43,249.3 | 37,558.1 | . . . . |
| Reserve assets | 8e9aa | 142,029.7 | 150,246.4 | † 177,195.1 | 275,281.0 | 255,877.3 | 283,473.6 | 297,752.3 | 297,950.4 | 297,805.5 | 296,218.9 | 322,524.7 | . . . . |
| Liabilities | 809la | 211,785.9 | 242,641.8 | † 292,349.1 | 411,622.3 | 426,108.9 | 517,770.6 | 637,701.8 | 661,056.1 | 746,851.4 | 783,707.6 | 854,917.3 | . . . . |
| Direct investment | 8a9la | 44,668.6 | 51,836.0 | † 70,870.3 | 105,790.5 | 125,211.7 | 171,217.9 | 205,580.2 | 206,353.8 | 224,987.5 | 226,542.6 | 252,818.5 | . . . . |
| Equity & investment fund shares.. | 8aala | 41,392.4 | 48,567.1 | † 67,320.3 | 101,568.1 | 120,123.7 | 164,374.1 | 199,164.7 | 197,681.7 | 215,009.1 | 215,631.3 | 241,930.8 | . . . . |
| Debt instruments | 8abla | 3,276.2 | 3,268.9 | † 3,550.0 | 4,222.4 | 5,088.0 | 6,843.8 | 6,415.5 | 8,672.2 | 9,978.4 | 10,911.3 | 10,887.7 | . . . . |
| Portfolio investment | 8b9la | 55,906.6 | 63,621.6 | † 74,179.0 | 122,599.0 | 91,602.7 | 117,085.5 | 166,980.0 | 161,054.2 | 185,788.6 | 179,669.4 | 215,193.4 | . . . . |
| Equity & investment fund shares.. | 8bala | 43,323.4 | 54,184.4 | † 60,512.4 | 101,679.6 | 69,025.3 | 93,319.6 | 133,968.8 | 109,717.2 | 128,932.4 | 132,347.5 | 145,045.0 | . . . . |
| Debt securities | 8bbla | 12,583.2 | 9,437.2 | † 13,666.6 | 20,919.4 | 22,577.4 | 23,765.9 | 33,011.2 | 51,337.0 | 56,856.2 | 47,321.9 | 70,148.4 | . . . . |
| Fin. der.(oth.than reserves) & ESOs | 8c9la | . . . . | . . . . | . . . . | . . . . | . . . . | . . . . | . . . . | . . . . | . . . . | . . . . | . . . . | . . . . |
| Other investment | 8d9la | 111,210.8 | 127,184.1 | † 147,299.8 | 183,232.8 | 209,294.6 | 229,467.2 | 265,141.7 | 293,648.0 | 336,075.4 | 377,495.6 | 386,905.4 | . . . . |
| Other equity | 8dala | . . . . | . . . . | . . . . | . . . . | . . . . | . . . . | . . . . | . . . . | . . . . | . . . . | . . . . | . . . . |
| Debt instruments | 8dzla | 111,210.8 | 127,184.1 | † 147,299.8 | 183,232.8 | 209,294.6 | 229,467.2 | 265,141.7 | 293,648.0 | 336,075.4 | 377,495.6 | 386,905.4 | . . . . |

# India   534

| | | 2004 | 2005 | 2006 | 2007 | 2008 | 2009 | 2010 | 2011 | 2012 | 2013 | 2014 | 2015 |
|---|---|---|---|---|---|---|---|---|---|---|---|---|---|
| **Government Finance** | | | | | | | | | | | | | |
| **Cash Flow Statement** | | | | | | | | | | | | | |
| **Budgetary Central Government** | | | | | | *Billions of Rupees: Fiscal Year Begins April 1* | | | | | | | |
| Cash Receipts:Operating Activities... | c1 | 3,875.6 | 4,510.5 | 5,691.1 | 5,398.9 | 5,446.5 | 5,755.3 | 7,942.8 | 7,561.9 | 8,788.0 | 10,152.8 | 10,994.4 | 12,031.3 |
| Taxes...................................... | c11 | 3,049.6 | 3,661.5 | 4,735.1 | 4,375.2 | 4,477.3 | 4,594.4 | 5,727.9 | 6,318.9 | 7,410.6 | 8,160.5 | 9,024.8 | 9,445.6 |
| Social Contributions...................... | c12 | 9.2 | 8.2 | 8.2 | — | — | — | — | — | — | — | — | — |
| Grants...................................... | c13 | 25.6 | 30.2 | 25.3 | 27.2 | 27.9 | 31.4 | 26.7 | 29.6 | 23.6 | 36.2 | 12.7 | 29.4 |
| Other Receipts............................. | c14 | 791.3 | 810.5 | 922.5 | 996.6 | 941.3 | 1,129.4 | 2,188.1 | 1,213.4 | 1,353.8 | 1,956.2 | 1,956.9 | 2,556.4 |
| Cash Payments:Operating Activities. | c2 | 4,822.0 | 5,511.4 | 6,462.6 | 5,954.3 | 7,906.9 | 9,061.0 | 10,391.3 | 11,409.2 | 12,422.6 | 13,755.9 | 14,577.5 | 15,476.7 |
| Compensation of Employees.......... | c21 | 428.0 | 464.7 | 493.4 | .... | .... | .... | .... | .... | .... | .... | .... | .... |
| Purchases of Goods & Services....... | c22 | 628.9 | 698.3 | 722.7 | .... | .... | .... | .... | .... | .... | .... | .... | .... |
| Interest.................................... | c24 | 1,236.6 | 1,288.7 | 1,459.1 | 1,714.9 | 1,904.9 | 2,116.4 | 2,347.4 | 2,724.6 | 3,120.0 | 3,775.0 | 4,040.2 | 4,426.2 |
| Subsidies................................... | c25 | 1,025.7 | 1,167.3 | 1,465.6 | .... | .... | .... | .... | .... | .... | .... | .... | .... |
| Grants...................................... | c26 | 1,134.6 | 1,475.5 | 1,864.2 | .... | .... | .... | .... | .... | .... | .... | .... | .... |
| Social Benefits............................ | c27 | — | — | — | .... | .... | .... | .... | .... | .... | .... | .... | .... |
| Other Payments........................... | c28 | 368.2 | 416.8 | 457.6 | .... | .... | .... | .... | .... | .... | .... | .... | .... |
| Net Cash Inflow:Operating Act.[1-2] | ccio | −946.4 | −1,000.9 | −771.5 | −555.4 | −2,460.4 | −3,305.7 | −2,448.5 | −3,847.2 | −3,634.6 | −3,603.1 | −3,583.1 | −3,445.4 |
| Net Cash Outflow:Invest. in NFA...... | c31 | 91.1 | 172.8 | 191.8 | 725.2 | 756.1 | 951.7 | 1,343.4 | 1,398.0 | 1,463.6 | 1,687.1 | 1,614.1 | 2,112.1 |
| Purchases of Nonfinancial Assets... | c31.1 | 140.1 | 191.9 | 200.4 | 1,069.3 | 756.6 | 951.7 | 1,348.0 | 1,398.0 | 1,463.6 | 1,687.1 | 1,665.2 | 2,112.1 |
| Sales of Nonfinancial Assets.......... | c31.2 | 48.9 | 19.1 | 8.6 | 344.1 | .4 | | 4.7 | | | | 51.2 | |
| Cash Surplus/Deficit [1-2-31=1-2M] | ccsd | −1,037.5 | −1,173.7 | −963.3 | −1,280.6 | −3,216.6 | −4,257.4 | −3,791.9 | −5,245.2 | −5,098.1 | −5,290.2 | −5,197.1 | −5,557.4 |
| Net Acq. Fin. Assets, excl. Cash....... | c32x | −129.4 | 168.5 | 106.3 | 20.9 | 84.6 | −135.0 | −101.5 | −147.9 | −199.2 | −208.8 | −178.3 | −177.0 |
| Domestic................................... | c321x | −135.3 | 164.6 | 104.9 | 20.9 | 84.6 | −135.0 | −101.5 | −147.9 | −199.2 | −208.8 | −178.3 | −177.0 |
| Foreign..................................... | c322x | 5.9 | 3.9 | 1.4 | — | — | — | — | — | — | — | — | — |
| Net Incurrence of Liabilities.............. | c33 | 1,631.5 | 1,551.1 | 1,024.4 | 1,590.4 | 2,730.1 | 4,155.3 | 3,608.6 | 5,674.0 | 5,380.7 | 5,190.7 | 5,223.0 | 5,571.7 |
| Domestic................................... | c331 | 595.5 | 1,891.1 | 1,318.6 | 1,497.2 | 2,620.2 | 4,044.9 | 3,372.7 | 5,582.4 | 5,343.2 | 5,124.2 | 5,139.1 | 5,456.9 |
| Foreign..................................... | c332 | 1,036.0 | −340.1 | −294.2 | 93.2 | 110.0 | 110.4 | 235.9 | 91.6 | 37.5 | 66.5 | 83.9 | 114.8 |
| Net Cash Inflow, Fin.Act.[-32x+33].. | cnfb | 1,760.9 | 1,382.6 | 918.1 | 1,569.5 | 2,645.6 | 4,290.3 | 3,710.0 | 5,821.9 | 5,580.0 | 5,399.5 | 5,401.3 | 5,748.8 |
| Net Change in Stock of Cash........... | cncb | 723.4 | 208.9 | −45.2 | 289.0 | −571.0 | 32.7 | −81.9 | 576.7 | 481.8 | 109.2 | 204.2 | 564.6 |
| Stat. Discrep. [32X-33+NCB-CSD].... | ccsdz | — | — | — | — | — | −.2 | — | — | — | — | — | 373.3 |
| Memo Item:Cash Expenditure[2+31] | c2m | 4,913.2 | 5,684.2 | 6,654.4 | 6,679.5 | 8,663.1 | 10,012.7 | 11,734.7 | 12,807.1 | 13,886.2 | 15,443.0 | 16,191.5 | 17,588.8 |
| Memo Item: Gross Debt.................. | c63 | 19,944.2 | 22,601.5 | 22,540.1 | 24,740.7 | 28,408.9 | 31,897.7 | 35,610.6 | 41,733.7 | 47,399.6 | 53,110.8 | 57,945.3 | .... |
| **National Accounts** | | | | | | *Billions of Rupees: Fiscal Year Begins April 1* | | | | | | | |
| Househ.Cons.Expend.,incl.NPISHs.... | 96f | 19,175.1 | 21,527.0 | 24,766.7 | 28,407.3 | 32,492.8 | 37,075.7 | 43,603.2 | 49,104.5 | 56,709.3 | 65,079.3 | 71,930.5 | .... |
| Government Consumption Expend... | 91f | 3,545.2 | 4,016.2 | 4,434.8 | 5,130.2 | 6,153.3 | 7,711.5 | 8,901.4 | 9,683.8 | 10,613.6 | 11,529.9 | 13,654.6 | .... |
| Gross Fixed Capital Formation........ | 93e | 9,310.3 | 11,202.9 | 13,437.7 | 16,416.7 | 18,211.0 | 20,557.7 | 24,070.7 | 29,976.2 | 33,214.1 | 35,643.2 | 38,443.7 | .... |
| Changes in Inventories.................... | 93i | 801.5 | 1,043.9 | 1,471.0 | 2,015.3 | 1,067.9 | 1,791.7 | 2,735.1 | 2,068.5 | 2,123.6 | 1,799.7 | 2,205.6 | .... |
| Exports of Goods and Services........ | 90c | 5,690.5 | 7,120.9 | 9,048.7 | 10,189.1 | 13,287.7 | 12,987.8 | 17,101.9 | 21,439.3 | 24,397.1 | 28,547.1 | 28,610.7 | .... |
| Imports of Goods and Services (-).... | 98c | 6,259.5 | 8,134.7 | 10,405.4 | 12,191.1 | 16,140.4 | 16,471.4 | 20,501.8 | 27,155.5 | 31,084.3 | 31,903.5 | 32,331.2 | .... |
| Gross Domestic Product (GDP)........ | 99b | 32,422.1 | 36,933.7 | 42,947.1 | 49,870.9 | 56,300.6 | 64,778.3 | 77,841.2 | 87,360.4 | 99,513.4 | 112,727.6 | 124,882.0 | .... |
| Net Primary Income from Abroad..... | 98.n | −223.8 | −261.2 | −332.3 | −205.1 | −329.2 | −380.0 | −818.1 | −768.3 | −1,167.7 | −1,285.0 | .... | .... |
| Gross National Income (GNI).......... | 99a | 29,490.9 | 33,643.9 | 39,200.4 | 45,615.7 | 52,706.4 | 60,709.0 | 71,670.5 | 86,592.2 | 98,345.8 | 111,328.8 | 123,407.7 | .... |
| Gross Nat'l Disposable Inc.(GNDI).... | 99i | 33,118.1 | 37,758.2 | 43,960.8 | 51,340.8 | 58,003.5 | 66,869.4 | 79,555.1 | 89,641.2 | 101,846.6 | 115,288.0 | 127,459.3 | .... |
| Gross Saving............................... | 99s | 10,507.0 | 12,351.5 | 14,859.1 | 18,363.3 | 18,026.2 | 21,823.4 | 26,217.4 | 30,267.2 | 33,648.2 | 37,250.5 | 41,167.0 | .... |
| Consumption of Fixed Capital.......... | 99cf | 3,198.9 | 3,637.2 | 4,187.3 | 4,847.0 | 5,652.0 | 6,598.0 | 7,602.2 | 9,171.4 | 10,599.7 | 11,984.7 | 13,331.8 | .... |
| GDP at Factor Cost....................... | 99ba | 29,714.6 | 33,905.0 | 39,532.8 | 45,820.9 | 53,035.7 | 61,089.0 | 72,488.6 | 81,066.6 | 92,100.2 | 103,808.1 | 114,724.1 | .... |
| GDP at Fact.Cost,Vol.'04/05 Prices.. | 99bap | 29,714.6 | 32,530.7 | 35,643.6 | 38,966.4 | 41,586.8 | 45,160.7 | 49,370.1 | 52,475.3 | 54,821.1 | 57,485.6 | .... | .... |
| GDP Volume 2004/05 Prices........... | 99b.p | 32,422.1 | 35,432.4 | 38,714.9 | 42,509.5 | 44,163.5 | 47,908.5 | 52,961.1 | 56,330.5 | 58,998.5 | 61,735.3 | .... | .... |
| GDP Volume 2011/12 Prices........... | 99b.p | .... | .... | .... | .... | .... | .... | .... | 87,360.4 | 92,268.8 | 98,394.3 | 105,521.5 | .... |
| GDP at Fact.Cost,Vol.'11/12 Prices.. | 99bap | .... | .... | .... | .... | .... | .... | .... | 81,066.6 | 85,465.5 | 90,843.7 | 97,274.9 | .... |
| GDP Volume (2010=100)................ | 99bvp | 60.2 | 65.9 | 72.2 | 78.9 | 84.2 | 91.5 | 100.0 | 106.3 | 112.1 | 119.1 | 127.5 | .... |
| GDP Deflator (2010=100)............... | 99bip | 68.1 | 71.0 | 75.5 | 80.1 | 86.9 | 92.1 | 100.0 | 105.2 | 113.4 | 120.2 | 124.1 | .... |
| | | | | | | *Millions: Midyear Estimates* | | | | | | | |
| Population................................. | 99z | 1,126.42 | 1,144.33 | 1,162.09 | 1,179.69 | 1,197.07 | 1,214.18 | 1,230.98 | 1,247.45 | 1,263.59 | 1,279.50 | 1,295.29 | 1,311.05 |

# Indonesia 536

| | | 2004 | 2005 | 2006 | 2007 | 2008 | 2009 | 2010 | 2011 | 2012 | 2013 | 2014 | 2015 |
|---|---|---|---|---|---|---|---|---|---|---|---|---|---|
| **Exchange Rates** | | | | | | *Rupiah per SDR: End of Period* | | | | | | | |
| Market Rate | aa | 14,427.5 | 14,049.7 | 13,569.7 | 14,884.4 | 16,866.0 | 14,736.3 | 13,846.4 | 13,921.8 | 14,862.0 | 18,771.1 | 18,023.2 | 19,116.1 |
| | | | | | | *Rupiah per US Dollar: End of Period (ae) Period Average (rf)* | | | | | | | |
| Market Rate | ae | 9,290.0 | 9,830.0 | 9,020.0 | 9,419.0 | 10,950.0 | 9,400.0 | 8,991.0 | 9,068.0 | 9,670.0 | 12,189.0 | 12,440.0 | 13,795.0 |
| Market Rate | rf | 8,938.9 | 9,704.7 | 9,159.3 | 9,141.0 | 9,699.0 | 10,389.9 | 9,090.4 | 8,770.4 | 9,386.6 | 10,461.2 | 11,865.2 | 13,389.4 |
| **Fund Position** | | | | | | *Millions of SDRs: End of Period* | | | | | | | |
| Quota | 2f.s | 2,079.30 | 2,079.30 | 2,079.30 | 2,079.30 | 2,079.30 | 2,079.30 | 2,079.30 | 2,079.30 | 2,079.30 | 2,079.30 | 2,079.30 | 2,079.30 |
| SDR Holdings | 1b.s | 1.58 | 4.91 | 12.13 | 5.85 | 21.88 | 1,762.58 | 1,762.19 | 1,761.57 | 1,761.37 | 1,761.26 | 1,761.11 | 1,761.00 |
| Reserve Position in the Fund | 1c.s | 145.50 | 145.50 | 145.50 | 145.50 | 145.50 | 145.50 | 145.50 | 145.50 | 145.50 | 145.50 | 145.50 | 145.50 |
| Total Fund Cred.&Loans Outstg | 2tl | 6,237.01 | 5,462.20 | — | — | — | — | — | — | — | — | — | — |
| SDR Allocations | 1bd | 238.96 | 238.96 | 238.96 | 238.96 | 238.96 | 1,980.44 | 1,980.44 | 1,980.44 | 1,980.44 | 1,980.44 | 1,980.44 | 1,980.44 |
| **International Liquidity** | | | | | | *Millions of US Dollars Unless Otherwise Indicated: End of Period* | | | | | | | |
| Total Reserves minus Gold | 1l.d | 34,952 | 33,140 | 41,103 | 54,976 | 49,597 | 63,563 | 92,908 | 106,539 | 108,837 | 96,364 | 108,836 | 103,268 |
| SDR Holdings | 1b.d | 2 | 7 | 18 | 9 | 34 | 2,763 | 2,714 | 2,704 | 2,707 | 2,712 | 2,552 | 2,440 |
| Reserve Position in the Fund | 1c.d | 226 | 208 | 219 | 230 | 224 | 228 | 224 | 223 | 224 | 224 | 211 | 202 |
| Foreign Exchange | 1d.d | 34,724 | 32,926 | 40,866 | 54,737 | 49,339 | 60,572 | 89,970 | 103,611 | 105,907 | 93,427 | 106,073 | 100,626 |
| Gold (Million Fine Troy Ounces) | 1ad | 3.101 | 3.100 | 2.350 | 2.350 | 2.350 | 2.350 | 2.350 | 2.350 | 2.380 | 2.510 | 2.510 | 2.510 |
| Gold (National Valuation) | 1and | 1,351 | 1,590 | 1,485 | 1,948 | 2,044 | 2,556 | 3,303 | 3,598 | 3,940 | 3,023 | 3,027 | 2,661 |
| Central Bank: Other Assets | 3..d | † 686 | 575 | 677 | 925 | 861 | 715 | 709 | 451 | 217 | 248 | 223 | 195 |
| Central Bank: Other Liabs | 4..d | † 1,918 | 1,370 | 769 | 730 | 1,465 | 5,325 | 6,695 | 1,383 | 403 | 577 | 400 | 225 |
| Other Depository Corps.: Assets | 7a.d | † 7,414 | 12,182 | 10,548 | 7,724 | 13,543 | 20,131 | † 18,920 | 13,219 | 12,201 | 13,423 | 13,808 | 15,359 |
| Other Depository Corps.: Liabs | 7b.d | † 6,480 | 6,927 | 7,847 | 9,863 | 10,349 | 10,111 | † 14,934 | 19,141 | 21,574 | 26,413 | 33,552 | 33,178 |
| Other Financial Corps.: Assets | 7e.d | .... | .... | .... | .... | .... | 278 | 237 | 242 | 549 | 311 | 275 | 370 |
| Other Financial Corps.: Liabs | 7f.d | .... | .... | .... | .... | .... | 4,779 | 6,699 | 8,683 | 8,959 | 8,313 | 9,198 | 8,466 |
| **Central Bank** | | | | | | *Billions of Rupiah: End of Period* | | | | | | | |
| Net Foreign Assets | 11n | † 232,871 | 252,379 | 377,616 | 530,510 | 549,336 | 544,818 | 777,378 | 961,089 | 1,058,850 | 1,169,683 | 1,353,167 | 1,422,445 |
| Claims on Nonresidents | 11 | † 344,125 | 345,942 | 387,794 | 540,942 | 569,412 | 624,053 | 864,994 | 1,001,199 | 1,092,180 | 1,213,893 | 1,393,831 | 1,463,410 |
| Liabilities to Nonresidents | 16c | † 111,254 | 93,563 | 10,179 | 10,431 | 20,076 | 79,235 | 87,616 | 40,110 | 33,329 | 44,210 | 40,664 | 40,965 |
| Claims on Other Depository Corps | 12e | † 10,111 | 9,389 | 9,603 | 7,908 | 8,771 | 6,732 | 5,023 | 4,399 | 3,226 | 2,535 | 1,489 | 7,433 |
| Net Claims on Central Government | 12an | † 226,620 | 249,486 | 274,249 | 264,527 | 191,159 | 225,751 | 187,414 | 240,408 | 299,848 | 295,173 | 298,149 | 210,862 |
| Claims on Central Government | 12a | † 273,670 | 297,275 | 289,136 | 279,931 | 283,381 | 280,293 | 278,985 | 329,956 | 351,497 | 354,846 | 367,010 | 360,614 |
| Liabilities to Central Government | 16d | † 47,050 | 47,789 | 14,887 | 15,404 | 92,222 | 54,542 | 91,572 | 89,548 | 51,649 | 59,674 | 68,861 | 149,752 |
| Claims on Other Sectors | 12s | † 39,845 | 26,123 | 26,092 | 13,030 | 14,311 | 14,508 | 13,344 | 12,065 | 6,465 | 8,115 | 7,926 | 7,864 |
| Claims on Other Financial Corps | 12g | † 1,494 | 1,473 | 1,449 | 1,472 | 1,591 | 1,442 | 1,000 | 5,743 | 202 | 6 | 1 | — |
| Claims on State & Local Govts | 12b | † — | — | — | — | — | — | — | — | — | — | — | — |
| Claims on Public Nonfin. Corps | 12c | † — | — | — | — | — | — | — | — | — | — | — | — |
| Claims on Private Sector | 12d | † 38,351 | 24,649 | 24,644 | 11,558 | 12,721 | 13,066 | 12,345 | 6,322 | 6,263 | 8,109 | 7,925 | 7,864 |
| Monetary Base | 14 | † 206,180 | 269,971 | 346,492 | 438,460 | 425,847 | 498,979 | 525,145 | 657,337 | 755,251 | 891,612 | 993,320 | 1,029,906 |
| Currency in Circulation | 14a | † 126,895 | 144,869 | 178,572 | 220,785 | 264,391 | 279,029 | 318,575 | 372,972 | 439,720 | 500,020 | 528,537 | 586,763 |
| Liabs. to Other Depository Corps | 14c | † 78,789 | 124,720 | 167,829 | 217,330 | 160,806 | 219,349 | 206,086 | 284,249 | 315,397 | 391,141 | 463,385 | 442,777 |
| Liabilities to Other Sectors | 14d | † 496 | 381 | 91 | 345 | 650 | 601 | 484 | 116 | 133 | 451 | 1,397 | 366 |
| Other Liabs. to Other Dep. Corps | 14n | † 130,652 | 85,305 | 176,417 | 201,748 | 161,469 | 177,743 | 375,266 | 470,103 | 447,965 | 300,248 | 376,959 | 325,883 |
| Dep. & Sec. Excl. f/Monetary Base | 14o | † 13,593 | 24,457 | 32,266 | 45,410 | 8,163 | 6,519 | 7,441 | 1,582 | 35 | 15 | 17 | 192 |
| Deposits Included in Broad Money | 15 | † — | | | | | | | | | | | |
| Sec.Ot.th.Shares Incl.in Brd. Money | 16a | † — | | | | | | | | | | | |
| Deposits Excl. from Broad Money | 16b | † 12 | 10 | 10 | 10 | 10 | 10 | 10 | 32 | 35 | 15 | 17 | 191 |
| Sec.Ot.th.Shares Excl.f/Brd.Money | 16s | † 13,581 | 24,447 | 32,256 | 45,400 | 8,153 | 6,509 | 7,431 | 1,550 | — | — | — | — |
| Loans | 16l | † — | | | | | | | | | | | |
| Financial Derivatives | 16m | † — | | | | | | | | | | | |
| Shares and Other Equity | 17a | † 116,950 | 115,727 | 97,082 | 111,596 | 150,786 | 92,464 | 60,213 | 79,087 | 169,783 | 284,545 | 288,822 | 313,331 |
| Other Items (Net) | 17r | † 42,072 | 41,916 | 35,302 | 18,761 | 17,312 | 16,105 | 15,094 | 9,852 | −4,644 | −915 | 1,612 | −20,707 |
| Memo Item: | | | | | | | | | | | | | |
| Total Assets | 10ra | † 672,681 | 684,214 | 718,423 | 847,700 | 881,654 | 931,898 | 1,169,361 | 1,361,542 | 1,476,910 | 1,600,431 | 1,790,143 | 1,910,784 |
| **Other Depository Corporations** | | | | | | *Billions of Rupiah: End of Period* | | | | | | | |
| Net Foreign Assets | 21n | † 8,679 | 51,664 | 24,368 | −20,146 | 34,984 | 94,188 | † 35,837 | −53,699 | −90,642 | −158,328 | −245,619 | −245,807 |
| Claims on Nonresidents | 21 | † 68,874 | 119,752 | 95,147 | 72,756 | 148,301 | 189,230 | † 170,107 | 119,870 | 117,980 | 163,614 | 171,773 | 211,879 |
| Liabilities to Nonresidents | 26c | † 60,195 | 68,088 | 70,779 | 92,902 | 113,317 | 95,042 | † 134,270 | 173,570 | 208,622 | 321,942 | 417,392 | 457,686 |
| Claims on Central Bank | 20 | † 240,889 | 255,351 | 372,111 | 456,941 | 375,020 | 530,454 | † 640,118 | 819,564 | 841,185 | 795,540 | 951,480 | 885,902 |
| Currency | 20a | † 17,867 | 20,879 | 27,918 | 37,819 | 54,644 | 53,023 | † 58,349 | 65,212 | 77,823 | 100,414 | 109,275 | 117,228 |
| Reserve Deposits and Securities | 20b | † 119,512 | 160,242 | 167,829 | 217,330 | 160,806 | 219,349 | † 480,407 | 608,546 | 608,813 | 574,271 | 660,552 | 728,589 |
| Other Claims | 20n | † 103,509 | 74,231 | 176,363 | 201,793 | 159,570 | 258,082 | † 101,363 | 145,806 | 154,550 | 120,854 | 181,652 | 40,085 |
| Net Claims on Central Government | 22an | † 273,698 | 256,718 | 241,418 | 258,051 | 215,236 | 228,450 | † 187,267 | 162,140 | 170,844 | 197,648 | 221,599 | 359,893 |
| Claims on Central Government | 22a | † 324,674 | 321,006 | 311,364 | 317,219 | 308,455 | 303,761 | † 240,356 | 236,452 | 258,997 | 307,605 | 349,992 | 472,900 |
| Liabilities to Central Government | 26d | † 50,975 | 64,287 | 69,947 | 59,169 | 93,219 | 75,311 | † 53,089 | 74,313 | 88,154 | 109,957 | 128,394 | 113,007 |
| Claims on Other Sectors | 22s | † 599,100 | 749,527 | 849,338 | 1,067,673 | 1,398,936 | 1,529,441 | † 1,896,677 | 2,370,080 | 2,910,987 | 3,518,415 | 3,953,656 | 4,310,261 |
| Claims on Other Financial Corps | 22g | † 16,909 | 23,291 | 24,102 | 32,916 | 48,675 | 66,183 | † 123,852 | 161,023 | 174,750 | 217,462 | 252,741 | 271,704 |
| Claims on State & Local Govts | 22b | † 708 | 483 | 583 | 686 | 1,017 | 1,594 | † 1,594 | 2,790 | 4,726 | 6,635 | 6,516 |
| Claims on Public Nonfin. Corps | 22c | † 13,908 | 17,220 | 27,647 | 39,891 | 47,949 | 66,589 | † 99,369 | 102,594 | 158,383 | 206,111 | 213,528 | 217,778 |
| Claims on Private Sector | 22d | † 567,576 | 708,534 | 797,005 | 994,181 | 1,301,328 | 1,395,652 | † 1,671,863 | 2,105,054 | 2,575,064 | 3,090,116 | 3,480,752 | 3,814,263 |
| Liabilities to Central Bank | 26g | † 10,111 | 9,388 | 9,603 | 7,908 | 8,771 | 6,732 | † 5,023 | 4,399 | 3,226 | 2,535 | 1,489 | 7,433 |
| Transf.Dep.Included in Broad Money | 24 | † 204,204 | 227,571 | 276,196 | 355,272 | 359,291 | 413,672 | † 483,879 | 568,436 | 661,963 | 729,440 | 766,567 | 858,218 |
| Other Dep.Included in Broad Money | 25 | † 717,478 | 848,539 | 952,937 | 1,107,591 | 1,322,871 | 1,497,601 | † 1,717,541 | 1,986,520 | 2,273,094 | 2,577,895 | 2,964,470 | 3,207,283 |
| Sec.Ot.th.Shares Incl.in Brd. Money | 26a | † 2,670 | 2,280 | 2,615 | 3,487 | 3,279 | 3,504 | † 9,075 | 14,388 | 10,420 | 22,805 | 21,630 | 13,399 |
| Deposits Excl. from Broad Money | 26b | † 5,627 | 5,950 | 6,636 | 9,375 | 11,516 | 15,005 | † 112,108 | 192,557 | 243,013 | 288,438 | 297,433 | 281,811 |
| Sec.Ot.th.Shares Excl.f/Brd.Money | 26s | † 7,347 | 8,047 | 9,834 | 12,809 | 12,649 | 15,478 | † 16,010 | 17,040 | 26,825 | 25,671 | 23,705 | 22,728 |
| Loans | 26l | † 2,723 | 3,353 | 3,494 | 4,058 | 2,630 | 6,945 | † 11,557 | 7,819 | 15,298 | 7,342 | 10,058 | 9,831 |
| Financial Derivatives | 26m | † 4 | — | — | 37 | 191 | — | † 1,081 | 1,960 | 2,360 | 12,814 | 6,909 | 11,206 |
| Insurance Technical Reserves | 26r | † — | — | — | — | — | — | † — | — | — | — | — | — |
| Shares and Other Equity | 27a | † 134,239 | 147,821 | 176,222 | 206,741 | 220,150 | 266,913 | † 358,241 | 446,761 | 536,861 | 636,214 | 738,492 | 859,670 |
| Other Items (Net) | 27r | † 37,963 | 60,312 | 49,697 | 55,241 | 82,828 | 156,683 | † 45,384 | 58,204 | 59,312 | 50,120 | 50,361 | 38,669 |
| Memo Item: | | | | | | | | | | | | | |
| Total Assets | 20ra | † 1,334,833 | 1,541,466 | 1,774,787 | 2,075,711 | 2,413,422 | 2,666,922 | † 3,184,565 | 3,807,097 | 4,420,802 | 5,144,519 | 5,847,145 | 6,390,982 |

# Indonesia 536

| | | 2004 | 2005 | 2006 | 2007 | 2008 | 2009 | 2010 | 2011 | 2012 | 2013 | 2014 | 2015 |
|---|---|---|---|---|---|---|---|---|---|---|---|---|---|
| **Depository Corporations** | | | | | | | *Billions of Rupiah: End of Period* | | | | | | | |
| Net Foreign Assets | 31n | † 241,550 | 304,044 | 401,983 | 510,364 | 584,320 | 639,006 | † 813,215 | 907,390 | 968,208 | 1,011,355 | 1,107,547 | 1,176,638 |
| Claims on Nonresidents | 31 | † 412,999 | 465,695 | 482,941 | 613,698 | 717,713 | 813,283 | † 1,035,100 | 1,121,069 | 1,210,160 | 1,377,508 | 1,565,604 | 1,675,290 |
| Liabilities to Nonresidents | 36c | † 171,450 | 161,651 | 80,958 | 103,334 | 133,393 | 174,277 | † 221,886 | 213,679 | 241,952 | 366,152 | 458,056 | 498,652 |
| Domestic Claims | 32 | † 1,139,263 | 1,281,854 | 1,391,096 | 1,603,281 | 1,819,642 | 1,998,150 | † 2,284,703 | 2,784,693 | 3,388,143 | 4,019,351 | 4,481,330 | 4,888,880 |
| Net Claims on Central Government | 32an | † 500,318 | 506,204 | 515,666 | 522,577 | 406,395 | 454,201 | † 374,681 | 402,548 | 470,692 | 492,821 | 519,747 | 570,755 |
| Claims on Central Government | 32a | † 598,344 | 618,281 | 600,500 | 597,150 | 591,836 | 584,054 | † 519,341 | 566,408 | 610,494 | 662,452 | 717,002 | 833,514 |
| Liabilities to Central Government | 36d | † 98,025 | 112,076 | 84,834 | 74,573 | 185,441 | 129,853 | † 144,660 | 163,860 | 139,803 | 169,631 | 197,255 | 262,759 |
| Claims on Other Sectors | 32s | † 638,945 | 775,650 | 875,430 | 1,080,703 | 1,413,247 | 1,543,950 | † 1,910,022 | 2,382,145 | 2,917,451 | 3,526,530 | 3,961,582 | 4,318,125 |
| Claims on Other Financial Corps | 32g | † 18,403 | 24,764 | 25,550 | 34,388 | 50,265 | 67,625 | † 124,852 | 166,766 | 174,952 | 217,469 | 252,742 | 271,704 |
| Claims on State & Local Govts | 32b | † 708 | 483 | 583 | 686 | 984 | 1,017 | † 1,594 | 1,410 | 2,790 | 4,726 | 6,635 | 6,516 |
| Claims on Public Nonfin. Corps | 32c | † 13,908 | 17,220 | 27,647 | 39,891 | 47,949 | 66,589 | † 99,369 | 102,594 | 158,383 | 206,111 | 213,528 | 217,778 |
| Claims on Private Sector | 32d | † 605,927 | 733,183 | 821,649 | 1,005,739 | 1,314,049 | 1,408,718 | † 1,684,207 | 2,111,376 | 2,581,327 | 3,098,225 | 3,488,677 | 3,822,127 |
| Broad Money Liabilities | 35l | † 1,033,877 | 1,202,762 | 1,382,493 | 1,649,662 | 1,895,839 | 2,141,384 | † 2,471,206 | 2,877,220 | 3,307,508 | 3,730,197 | 4,173,327 | 4,548,800 |
| Currency Outside Depository Corps | 34a | † 109,028 | 123,991 | 150,654 | 182,967 | 209,747 | 226,006 | † 260,227 | 307,760 | 361,897 | 399,606 | 419,262 | 469,534 |
| Transferable Deposits | 34 | † 204,429 | 227,638 | 276,228 | 355,555 | 359,890 | 414,211 | † 484,312 | 568,499 | 662,060 | 729,838 | 767,879 | 858,539 |
| Other Deposits | 35 | † 717,749 | 848,854 | 952,996 | 1,107,653 | 1,322,922 | 1,497,663 | † 1,717,592 | 1,986,573 | 2,273,130 | 2,577,948 | 2,964,556 | 3,207,328 |
| Securities Other than Shares | 36a | † 2,670 | 2,280 | 2,615 | 3,487 | 3,279 | 3,504 | † 9,075 | 14,388 | 10,420 | 22,805 | 21,630 | 13,399 |
| Deposits Excl. from Broad Money | 36b | † 5,639 | 5,961 | 6,646 | 9,385 | 11,526 | 15,015 | † 112,118 | 192,590 | 243,048 | 288,454 | 297,450 | 282,003 |
| Sec.Ot.th.Shares Excl.f/Brd.Money | 36s | † 20,928 | 32,493 | 42,090 | 58,209 | 20,802 | 21,986 | † 23,441 | 18,590 | 26,825 | 25,671 | 23,705 | 22,728 |
| Loans | 36l | † 2,723 | 3,353 | 3,494 | 4,058 | 2,630 | 6,945 | † 11,557 | 7,819 | 15,298 | 7,342 | 10,058 | 9,831 |
| Financial Derivatives | 36m | † 4 | — | — | 37 | 191 | — | † 1,081 | 1,960 | 2,360 | 12,814 | 6,909 | 11,206 |
| Insurance Technical Reserves | 36r | † — | | | | | | | | | | | |
| Shares and Other Equity | 37a | † 251,189 | 263,548 | 273,303 | 318,337 | 370,936 | 359,377 | † 418,454 | 525,849 | 706,644 | 920,759 | 1,027,315 | 1,173,001 |
| Other Items (Net) | 37r | † 66,453 | 77,781 | 85,053 | 73,957 | 102,038 | 92,450 | † 60,061 | 68,056 | 54,668 | 45,469 | 50,113 | 17,949 |
| Broad Money Liabs., Seasonally Adj. | 35l.b | † 1,004,031 | 1,166,748 | 1,341,097 | 1,600,266 | 1,839,150 | 2,075,735 | † 2,400,284 | 2,796,053 | 3,218,462 | 3,636,345 | 4,074,465 | 4,444,235 |
| **Other Financial Corporations** | | | | | | | *Billions of Rupiah: End of Period* | | | | | | | |
| Net Foreign Assets | 41n | .... | .... | .... | .... | .... | † –42,311 | –58,094 | –76,540 | –81,323 | –97,542 | –110,999 | –111,692 |
| Claims on Nonresidents | 41 | .... | .... | .... | .... | .... | † 2,612 | 2,135 | 2,198 | 5,309 | 3,789 | 3,425 | 5,098 |
| Liabilities to Nonresidents | 46c | .... | .... | .... | .... | .... | † 44,923 | 60,228 | 78,738 | 86,633 | 101,331 | 114,424 | 116,790 |
| Claims on Depository Corporations | 40 | .... | .... | .... | .... | .... | † 8,847 | 8,277 | 12,378 | 13,996 | 13,907 | — | 178,565 |
| Net Claims on Central Government | 42an | .... | .... | .... | .... | .... | † — | — | — | — | — | — | 87,322 |
| Claims on Central Government | 42a | .... | .... | .... | .... | .... | † — | — | — | — | — | — | 87,732 |
| Liabilities to Central Government | 46d | .... | .... | .... | .... | .... | † — | — | — | — | — | — | 410 |
| Claims on Other Sectors | 42s | .... | .... | .... | .... | .... | † 141,886 | 186,478 | 244,580 | 299,263 | 343,934 | 361,184 | 686,836 |
| Claims on State & Local Govts | 42b | .... | .... | .... | .... | .... | † — | — | — | — | — | — | — |
| Claims on Public Nonfin. Corps | 42c | .... | .... | .... | .... | .... | † — | — | — | — | — | — | — |
| Claims on Private Sector | 42d | .... | .... | .... | .... | .... | † 141,886 | 186,478 | 244,580 | 299,263 | 343,934 | 361,184 | 686,836 |
| Deposits | 46b | .... | .... | .... | .... | .... | † — | — | — | — | — | — | — |
| Securities Other Than Shares | 46s | .... | .... | .... | .... | .... | † 13,595 | 18,389 | 30,290 | 43,765 | 53,211 | 53,160 | 95,261 |
| Loans | 46l | .... | .... | .... | .... | .... | † 53,225 | 79,485 | 101,597 | 115,600 | 138,050 | 136,216 | 182,418 |
| Financial Derivatives | 46m | .... | .... | .... | .... | .... | † — | — | — | — | — | — | 4 |
| Insurance Technical Reserves | 46r | .... | .... | .... | .... | .... | † — | — | — | — | — | — | 511,143 |
| Shares and Other Equity | 47a | .... | .... | .... | .... | .... | † 40,088 | 47,831 | 56,142 | 66,516 | 82,568 | 87,413 | 241,787 |
| Other Items (Net) | 47r | .... | .... | .... | .... | .... | † 1,514 | –9,044 | –7,611 | 6,055 | –13,530 | –10,515 | –189,582 |
| Memo Item: | | | | | | | | | | | | | |
| Total Assets | 40ra | .... | .... | .... | .... | .... | 177,156 | 234,643 | 296,467 | 346,162 | 405,984 | 427,183 | 1,228,185 |
| **Financial Corporations** | | | | | | | *Billions of Rupiah: End of Period* | | | | | | | |
| Net Foreign Assets | 51n | .... | .... | .... | .... | .... | 596,695 | † 755,121 | 830,850 | 886,884 | 913,813 | 996,548 | 1,064,946 |
| Claims on Nonresidents | 51 | .... | .... | .... | .... | .... | 815,895 | † 1,037,235 | 1,123,267 | 1,215,469 | 1,381,297 | 1,569,029 | 1,680,387 |
| Liabilities to Nonresidents | 56c | .... | .... | .... | .... | .... | 219,200 | † 282,114 | 292,417 | 328,585 | 467,483 | 572,481 | 615,441 |
| Domestic Claims | 52 | .... | .... | .... | .... | .... | 2,072,411 | † 2,346,328 | 2,862,507 | 3,512,453 | 4,145,816 | 4,589,772 | 5,391,335 |
| Net Claims on Central Government | 52an | .... | .... | .... | .... | .... | 454,201 | † 374,681 | 402,548 | 470,692 | 492,821 | 519,747 | 658,078 |
| Claims on Central Government | 52a | .... | .... | .... | .... | .... | 584,054 | † 519,341 | 566,408 | 610,494 | 662,452 | 717,002 | 921,247 |
| Liabilities to Central Government | 56d | .... | .... | .... | .... | .... | 129,853 | † 144,660 | 163,860 | 139,803 | 169,631 | 197,255 | 263,169 |
| Claims on Other Sectors | 52s | .... | .... | .... | .... | .... | 1,618,210 | † 1,971,648 | 2,459,959 | 3,041,762 | 3,652,995 | 4,070,025 | 4,733,257 |
| Claims on State & Local Govts | 52b | .... | .... | .... | .... | .... | 1,017 | † 1,594 | 1,410 | 2,790 | 4,726 | 6,635 | 6,516 |
| Claims on Public Nonfin. Corps | 52c | .... | .... | .... | .... | .... | 66,589 | † 99,369 | 102,594 | 158,383 | 206,111 | 213,528 | 217,778 |
| Claims on Private Sector | 52d | .... | .... | .... | .... | .... | 1,550,604 | † 1,870,685 | 2,355,955 | 2,880,589 | 3,442,158 | 3,849,861 | 4,508,963 |
| Currency Outside Financial Corps | 54a | .... | .... | .... | .... | .... | 225,630 | † 259,680 | 307,086 | 360,824 | 398,761 | 418,634 | 468,842 |
| Deposits | 55l | .... | .... | .... | .... | .... | 1,830,898 | † 2,166,721 | 2,556,963 | 2,953,084 | 3,346,253 | 3,708,863 | 4,007,964 |
| Securities Other than Shares | 56a | .... | .... | .... | .... | .... | 31,280 | † 37,484 | 45,196 | 59,840 | 74,920 | 70,425 | 70,645 |
| Loans | 56l | .... | .... | .... | .... | .... | 6,188 | † 7,320 | 4,668 | 10,661 | 1,255 | 2,920 | 2,003 |
| Financial Derivatives | 56m | .... | .... | .... | .... | .... | — | † 880 | 754 | 845 | 5,808 | 2,468 | 3,688 |
| Insurance Technical Reserves | 56r | .... | .... | .... | .... | .... | — | † — | — | — | — | — | 511,143 |
| Shares and Other Equity | 57a | .... | .... | .... | .... | .... | 399,465 | † 466,285 | 581,991 | 773,160 | 1,003,327 | 1,114,728 | 1,414,788 |
| Other Items (Net) | 57r | .... | .... | .... | .... | .... | 175,646 | † 163,079 | 196,700 | 240,923 | 229,305 | 268,282 | –22,792 |
| **Monetary Aggregates** | | | | | | | *Billions of Rupiah: End of Period* | | | | | | | |
| Broad Money | 59m | 1,033,877 | 1,202,762 | 1,382,493 | 1,649,662 | 1,895,839 | 2,141,384 | 2,471,206 | 2,877,220 | 3,307,508 | 3,730,197 | 4,173,327 | 4,548,800 |
| o/w:Currency Issued by Cent.Govt | 59m.a | — | — | — | — | — | — | — | — | — | — | — | — |
| o/w: Dep.in Nonfin. Corporations | 59m.b | — | — | — | — | — | — | — | — | — | — | — | — |
| o/w:Secs. Issued by Central Govt | 59m.c | — | — | — | — | — | — | — | — | — | — | — | — |
| Money (National Definitions) | | | | | | | | | | | | | |
| Base Money | 19ma | 206,180 | 269,971 | 346,492 | 438,460 | 425,847 | 466,393 | 525,145 | 657,337 | 755,251 | 890,552 | 993,320 | 1,029,906 |
| M1 | 59ma | 245,946 | 271,166 | 347,013 | 450,055 | 456,787 | 515,824 | 483,879 | 722,938 | 841,652 | 887,081 | 942,221 | 1,055,440 |
| M2 | 59mb | 1,033,877 | 1,202,762 | 1,382,493 | 1,649,662 | 1,895,839 | 2,141,384 | 2,471,206 | 2,877,220 | 3,307,508 | 3,730,197 | 4,173,327 | 4,548,800 |
| **Interest Rates** | | | | | | | *Percent Per Annum* | | | | | | | |
| Central Bank Policy Rate (EOP) | 60 | 7.43 | 12.75 | 9.75 | 8.00 | 9.25 | 6.50 | 6.50 | 6.00 | 5.75 | 7.50 | 7.75 | 7.50 |
| Money Market Rate | 60b | 5.38 | 6.78 | 9.18 | 6.02 | 8.48 | 7.16 | 6.01 | 5.62 | 4.01 | 4.83 | 5.85 | 5.83 |
| Deposit Rate | 60l | 6.44 | 8.08 | 11.41 | 7.98 | 8.49 | 9.28 | 7.02 | 6.93 | 5.95 | 6.26 | 8.75 | 8.34 |
| Deposit Rate (Fgn. Currency) | 60l.f | 1.74 | 2.63 | 4.01 | 4.17 | 3.75 | 3.30 | 2.30 | 1.48 | 1.96 | 1.93 | 2.20 | 1.61 |
| Lending Rate | 60p | 14.12 | 14.05 | 15.98 | 13.86 | 13.60 | 14.50 | 13.25 | 12.40 | 11.80 | 11.66 | 12.61 | 12.66 |
| Lending Rate (Fgn. Currency) | 60p.f | 5.70 | 6.36 | 7.57 | 7.21 | 6.41 | 6.34 | 4.97 | 3.93 | 4.04 | 3.95 | 4.24 | 4.00 |

| | | 2004 | 2005 | 2006 | 2007 | 2008 | 2009 | 2010 | 2011 | 2012 | 2013 | 2014 | 2015 |
|---|---|---|---|---|---|---|---|---|---|---|---|---|---|
| **Prices, Production, Labor** | | *Index Numbers (2010=100): Period Averages* | | | | | | | | | | | |
| Share Prices (End of Month)............ | 62.ep | 26.0 | 35.1 | 46.6 | 71.4 | 67.4 | 65.0 | 100.0 | 121.0 | 133.1 | 148.8 | 159.5 | 157.5 |
| Wholesale Prices: Incl. Petroleum..... | 63 | 50.8 | 59.3 | † 66.7 | 76.5 | 97.1 | 95.4 | 100.0 | 107.4 | 112.9 | 119.6 | † 130.8 | 136.5 |
| Wholesale Prices: Excl. Petrol........... | 63a | 159.9 | 100.0 | .... | .... | .... | 95.3 | 100.0 | 105.3 | 110.3 | 121.5 | † 134.5 | .... |
| Consumer Prices........................... | 64 | 62.2 | 68.7 | † 77.7 | 82.7 | 90.7 | 95.1 | 100.0 | 105.4 | † 109.9 | 116.9 | 124.4 | 132.3 |
| Crude Petroleum Production............ | 66aa | 51.9 | 48.4 | 47.1 | 43.8 | 44.1 | 41.4 | 100.0 | 42.9 | 40.8 | 40.8 | 40.0 | 33.3 |
| Manufacturing Production................ | 66ey | 87.2 | 88.3 | 86.9 | 91.7 | 94.5 | 95.6 | † 100.0 | 104.1 | 108.3 | .... | .... | .... |
| | | *Number in Thousands: Period Averages* | | | | | | | | | | | |
| Employment................................... | 67e | 93,722 | 94,453 | 95,317 | 98,757 | 102,301 | 104,678 | 107,588 | 110,476 | 111,805 | 112,413 | 116,400 | 117,833 |
| Unemployment............................... | 67c | 10,251 | 11,377 | 11,018 | 10,280 | 9,411 | 9,111 | 8,456 | 7,909 | 7,430 | 7,280 | 7,196 | 7,508 |
| Unemployment Rate (%)................. | 67r | 9.9 | 10.8 | 10.4 | 9.4 | 8.4 | 8.0 | 7.3 | 6.7 | 6.2 | 6.1 | 5.8 | 6.0 |
| **Intl. Transactions & Positions** | | *Millions of US Dollars* | | | | | | | | | | | |
| Exports........................................ | 70..d | 70,767 | 86,995 | 103,528 | 118,014 | 139,606 | 119,646 | 158,074 | 200,587 | 188,516 | 182,659 | 176,341 | 150,358 |
| Imports, c.i.f................................ | 71..d | 55,009 | 75,725 | 80,650 | 93,101 | 127,538 | 93,786 | 135,323 | 176,881 | 190,992 | 186,351 | 178,182 | 142,691 |
| | | | | *2005=100* | | | | | | | | | |
| Volume of Exports......................... | 72 | 157.7 | 100.0 | .... | .... | .... | .... | .... | .... | .... | .... | .... | .... |
| Crude Petroleum........................ | 72aa | 187.4 | 100.0 | .... | .... | .... | .... | .... | .... | .... | .... | .... | .... |
| Export Prices | | | | *2005=100: Indices of Unit Values in US Dollars* | | | | | | | | | |
| Exports (Unit Value)..................... | 74..d | 147.9 | 100.0 | .... | .... | .... | .... | .... | .... | .... | .... | .... | .... |
| Crude Petrol.(Unit Val.)2000=100. | 74aad | 129.0 | .... | .... | .... | .... | .... | .... | .... | .... | .... | .... | .... |
| Crude Petrol.(Ofc.Price)................ | 76aad | 69.2 | 100.0 | .... | .... | .... | .... | .... | .... | .... | .... | .... | .... |
| **Balance of Payments** | | *Millions of US Dollars* | | | | | | | | | | | |
| A. Current Account*...................... | 109bx | 1,563.0 | 277.5 | 10,859.5 | 10,491.0 | 126.0 | 10,628.5 | † 5,144.3 | 1,685.1 | −24,418.1 | −29,109.5 | −27,515.6 | .... |
| Goods, credit (exports)................ | 1a9cx | 66,084.1 | 81,682.4 | 98,251.0 | 111,301.2 | 132,209.7 | 113,266.4 | † 149,965.8 | 191,108.7 | 187,346.5 | 182,089.2 | 175,292.8 | .... |
| Goods, debit (imports)................ | 1a9dx | 46,615.9 | 64,071.5 | 66,053.1 | 76,775.5 | 107,667.3 | 80,979.0 | † 118,963.2 | 157,283.7 | 178,667.0 | 176,256.0 | 168,310.2 | .... |
| Balance on goods................... | 1a9bx | 19,468.3 | 17,610.9 | 32,197.9 | 34,525.7 | 24,542.4 | 32,287.4 | † 31,002.7 | 33,825.0 | 8,679.6 | 5,833.2 | 6,982.6 | .... |
| Services, credit (exports)............. | 1b9cx | 12,729.4 | 12,997.2 | 9,149.1 | 10,964.4 | 13,845.5 | 12,055.6 | † 16,670.5 | 21,888.2 | 23,660.2 | 22,944.1 | 23,530.9 | .... |
| Services, debit (imports)............. | 1b9dx | 20,856.3 | 22,196.8 | 21,560.9 | 24,578.4 | 28,470.1 | 23,152.0 | † 26,461.0 | 31,691.4 | 34,224.4 | 35,014.6 | 33,540.6 | .... |
| Balance on Goods & Services....... | 1z9bx | 11,341.4 | 8,411.2 | 19,786.0 | 20,911.7 | 9,917.8 | 21,191.0 | † 21,212.2 | 24,021.7 | −1,884.6 | −6,237.3 | −3,027.1 | .... |
| Primary income: credit................. | 1c9cx | 1,995.0 | 2,337.7 | 2,587.2 | 3,469.2 | 3,591.8 | 1,921.1 | † 1,933.9 | 2,581.1 | 2,649.6 | 2,601.8 | 2,129.6 | .... |
| Primary income: debit................. | 1c9dx | 12,912.3 | 15,264.3 | 16,376.8 | 18,993.9 | 18,747.2 | 17,061.2 | † 22,632.0 | 29,128.3 | 29,277.5 | 29,652.1 | 31,837.9 | .... |
| Balance on gds, serv. & prim. inc. | 1y9bx | 424.2 | −4,515.4 | 5,996.4 | 5,387.0 | −5,237.6 | 6,050.9 | † 514.0 | −2,525.4 | −28,512.4 | −33,287.6 | −32,735.5 | .... |
| Secondary income: credit.............. | 1d9ca | 2,432.8 | 5,992.5 | 6,078.8 | 6,800.5 | 7,352.2 | 7,240.7 | † 7,571.3 | 7,635.6 | 8,066.7 | 8,508.3 | 9,373.5 | .... |
| Secondary income: debit............... | 1d9da | 1,293.9 | 1,199.6 | 1,215.7 | 1,696.5 | 1,988.5 | 2,663.2 | † 2,941.0 | 3,425.1 | 3,972.4 | 4,330.1 | 4,153.7 | .... |
| B. Capital Account*...................... | 209ba | — | 333.9 | 350.3 | 546.2 | 294.5 | 95.8 | † 49.8 | 32.9 | 50.6 | 45.3 | 26.6 | .... |
| Capital account: credit.................. | 209ca | — | 333.9 | 350.3 | 546.2 | 294.5 | 95.8 | † 49.8 | 32.9 | 50.6 | 45.3 | 26.6 | .... |
| Capital account: debit................... | 209da | — | — | — | — | — | — | .... | .... | .... | .... | .... | .... |
| Balance on current & capital acct. | 129ba | 1,563.0 | 611.5 | 11,209.8 | 11,037.2 | 420.4 | 10,724.3 | † 5,194.1 | 1,718.0 | −24,367.5 | −29,064.2 | −27,489.0 | .... |
| C. Financial Account*.................... | 309na | 667.0 | 2,586.6 | −2,674.5 | −3,044.7 | 2,126.3 | −4,757.0 | † −26,476.1 | −13,603.3 | −24,858.1 | −21,925.6 | −45,340.0 | .... |
| Direct investment: assets.............. | 3a9aa | 3,408.0 | 3,065.0 | 2,725.8 | 4,675.2 | 5,899.7 | 2,249.1 | † 4,185.7 | 9,036.5 | 7,484.6 | 11,111.7 | 10,387.5 | .... |
| Equity & investment fund shares.. | 3aaaa | 470.0 | 331.0 | 608.8 | 997.5 | 1,419.7 | 1,523.9 | † 1,019.7 | 5,064.4 | 4,377.3 | 10,952.9 | 9,565.6 | .... |
| Debt instruments..................... | 3abaa | 2,938.0 | 2,734.0 | 2,117.0 | 3,677.7 | 4,480.0 | 725.2 | † 3,165.9 | 3,972.2 | 3,107.2 | 158.8 | 822.0 | .... |
| Direct investment: liabilities .......... | 3a9la | 1,896.1 | 8,336.3 | 4,914.2 | 6,928.5 | 9,318.5 | 4,877.4 | † 15,292.0 | 20,564.9 | 21,200.8 | 23,281.7 | 26,277.4 | .... |
| Equity & investment fund shares . | 3aala | 2,138.1 | 7,812.2 | 4,616.2 | 7,549.1 | 9,105.0 | 4,981.8 | † 12,446.7 | 16,278.0 | 18,614.6 | 20,004.0 | 22,293.3 | .... |
| Debt instruments..................... | 3abla | −242.0 | 524.1 | 298.0 | −620.6 | 213.4 | −104.4 | † 2,845.3 | 4,286.9 | 2,586.2 | 3,277.7 | 3,984.1 | .... |
| Portfolio investment: assets.......... | 3b9aa | −353.0 | 1,080.0 | 1,830.5 | 4,415.3 | 1,294.4 | 143.7 | † 2,511.3 | 1,189.4 | 5,467.0 | 1,272.8 | −2,586.7 | .... |
| Equity & investment fund shares | 3baaa | 106.0 | −38.0 | −10.5 | 216.7 | 297.9 | 363.1 | † 96.1 | 311.8 | 465.4 | 709.5 | 752.7 | .... |
| Debt securities ......................... | 3bbaa | −459.0 | 1,118.0 | 1,841.0 | 4,198.5 | 996.5 | −219.3 | † 2,415.2 | 877.7 | 5,001.6 | 563.2 | −3,339.5 | .... |
| Portfolio investment: liabilities....... | 3b9la | 4,056.2 | 5,269.6 | 6,107.1 | 9,981.4 | 3,058.6 | 10,480.0 | † 15,713.3 | 4,995.8 | 14,673.4 | 12,145.4 | 23,556.3 | .... |
| Equity & investment fund shares . | 3bala | 2,042.5 | −165.3 | 1,897.6 | 3,559.0 | 322.5 | 787.3 | † 2,131.6 | −326.1 | 1,697.6 | −1,856.0 | 3,259.3 | .... |
| Debt securities......................... | 3bbla | 2,013.6 | 5,434.9 | 4,209.5 | 6,422.4 | 2,736.2 | 9,692.7 | † 13,581.7 | 5,321.9 | 12,975.8 | 14,001.4 | 20,297.1 | .... |
| Fin. der.& empl.stk.ops.(ESOs): net. | 3c9na | .... | .... | .... | .... | .... | .... | † 94.4 | −69.4 | −13.0 | 334.4 | 213.3 | .... |
| Fin. der. & ESOs.: assets.............. | 3c9aa | .... | .... | .... | .... | .... | .... | † −1,128.0 | −527.0 | −333.3 | −344.8 | −159.0 | .... |
| Fin. der. & ESOs.: liabilities........ | 3c9la | .... | .... | .... | .... | .... | .... | † −1,222.4 | −457.7 | −320.3 | −679.1 | −372.3 | .... |
| Other investment: assets.............. | 3d9aa | −985.0 | 8,646.0 | 1,586.8 | 4,485.6 | 10,754.9 | 12,002.3 | † 1,725.3 | 6,754.5 | 5,353.0 | 3,427.4 | 4,293.0 | .... |
| Other equity........................... | 3daaa | .... | .... | .... | .... | .... | .... | .... | .... | .... | .... | .... | .... |
| Debt instruments..................... | 3dzaa | −985.0 | 8,646.0 | 1,586.8 | 4,485.6 | 10,754.9 | 12,002.3 | † 1,725.3 | 6,754.5 | 5,353.0 | 3,427.4 | 4,293.0 | .... |
| Other investment: liabilities........... | 3d9la | −4,549.3 | −3,401.5 | −2,203.8 | −289.1 | 3,445.7 | 3,794.8 | † 3,987.5 | 4,953.7 | 7,275.4 | 2,644.7 | 7,813.4 | .... |
| Other equity........................... | 3dala | .... | .... | .... | .... | .... | .... | .... | .... | .... | .... | .... | .... |
| Debt instruments..................... | 3dzla | −4,549.3 | −3,401.5 | −2,203.8 | −289.1 | 3,445.7 | 3,794.8 | † 3,987.5 | 4,953.7 | 7,275.4 | 2,644.7 | 7,813.4 | .... |
| Curr.+ cap.− finan. acct. balance... | 4y9na | 896.0 | −1,975.1 | 13,884.3 | 14,082.0 | −1,705.8 | 15,481.3 | † 31,670.3 | 15,321.3 | 490.6 | −7,138.6 | 17,851.0 | .... |
| D. Net Errors and Omissions.......... | 409na | −3,094.0 | −136.1 | 1,073.5 | −1,377.7 | −211.9 | −2,975.7 | † −1,327.8 | −3,465.7 | −275.8 | −186.6 | −2,602.7 | .... |
| E. Reserves and Related Items.......... | 4z9na | −2,198.0 | −2,111.2 | 14,957.8 | 12,705.8 | −1,918.2 | 12,505.6 | † 30,342.5 | 11,855.6 | 214.8 | −7,325.2 | 15,248.3 | .... |
| Reserve assets.............................. | 3e9aa | −686.0 | −657.3 | 6,903.3 | 12,705.8 | −1,918.2 | 12,505.6 | † 30,342.5 | 11,855.6 | 214.8 | −7,325.2 | 15,248.3 | .... |
| Credit and loans from the IMF....... | 3dcla | −1,007.0 | −1,144.2 | −8,054.5 | — | — | — | † — | .... | .... | .... | .... | .... |
| Exceptional financing.................... | 409la | 2,519.1 | 2,598.1 | — | — | — | — | .... | .... | .... | .... | .... | .... |

*Excludes components in group E

# Indonesia 536

| | | 2004 | 2005 | 2006 | 2007 | 2008 | 2009 | 2010 | 2011 | 2012 | 2013 | 2014 | 2015 |
|---|---|---|---|---|---|---|---|---|---|---|---|---|---|
| **International Investment Position** | | | | | | | | *Millions of US Dollars* | | | | | |
| Assets | 809aa | 57,450.9 | 64,289.7 | 82,664.0 | 104,522.1 | 88,034.7 | 116,248.8 | 149,981.2 | 166,852.3 | 187,256.4 | † 190,289.9 | 202,819.5 | .... |
| Direct investment | 8a9aa | 834.9 | 1,914.3 | 9,274.3 | 10,176.4 | 10,512.8 | 16,742.0 | 19,293.4 | 19,997.7 | 27,985.2 | † 39,737.9 | 37,514.6 | .... |
| Equity & investment fund shares.. | 8aaaa | 214.6 | 308.1 | 3,046.0 | 4,171.6 | 4,404.4 | 9,182.0 | 10,359.3 | 10,183.3 | 15,335.4 | † 26,464.4 | 25,005.7 | .... |
| Debt instruments | 8abaa | 620.3 | 1,606.1 | 6,228.3 | 6,004.8 | 6,108.4 | 7,560.0 | 8,934.2 | 9,814.4 | 12,649.7 | † 13,273.5 | 12,509.0 | .... |
| Portfolio investment | 8b9aa | 2,802.1 | 2,509.8 | 3,744.4 | 3,598.1 | 4,311.5 | 4,192.0 | 6,828.6 | 8,018.1 | 13,486.1 | † 14,758.9 | 12,172.1 | .... |
| Equity & investment fund shares.. | 8baaa | 50.8 | 93.7 | 354.4 | 865.0 | 488.3 | 851.0 | 947.1 | 1,258.9 | 1,724.4 | † 2,433.9 | 3,186.6 | .... |
| Debt securities | 8bbaa | 2,751.3 | 2,416.0 | 3,390.0 | 2,733.1 | 3,823.2 | 3,341.0 | 5,881.5 | 6,759.1 | 11,761.7 | † 12,325.0 | 8,985.5 | .... |
| Fin. der.(oth.than reserves) & ESOs | 8c9aa | 40.3 | 26.7 | 18.8 | 37.9 | 170.0 | 76.0 | 80.9 | 101.4 | 57.3 | † 168.1 | 151.9 | .... |
| Other investment | 8d9aa | 17,452.4 | 25,115.2 | 27,040.0 | 33,787.7 | 21,402.4 | 29,123.1 | 27,571.4 | 28,603.0 | 32,955.4 | † 36,238.4 | 41,118.4 | .... |
| Other equity | 8daaa | .... | .... | .... | .... | .... | .... | .... | .... | .... | .... | .... | .... |
| Debt instruments | 8dzaa | 17,452.4 | 25,115.2 | 27,040.0 | 33,787.7 | 21,402.4 | 29,123.1 | 27,571.4 | 28,603.0 | 32,955.4 | † 36,238.4 | 41,118.4 | .... |
| Reserve assets | 8e9aa | 36,321.2 | 34,723.7 | 42,586.5 | 56,922.1 | 51,638.1 | 66,115.7 | 96,206.8 | 110,132.1 | 112,772.5 | † 99,386.7 | 111,862.5 | .... |
| Liabilities | 809la | 174,580.4 | 189,486.4 | 219,880.1 | 274,067.8 | 236,157.8 | 329,973.3 | 441,042.8 | 485,124.9 | 548,480.2 | † 561,722.6 | 589,049.3 | .... |
| Direct investment | 8a9la | 16,794.7 | 44,862.5 | 62,766.8 | 86,910.3 | 79,937.5 | 121,625.0 | 173,356.3 | 198,597.9 | 227,218.7 | † 251,186.8 | 232,496.0 | .... |
| Equity & investment fund shares.. | 8aala | 9,795.0 | 37,762.5 | 51,828.5 | 74,274.4 | 65,164.7 | 103,122.0 | 151,017.6 | 170,882.6 | 196,405.0 | † 216,196.4 | 192,908.7 | .... |
| Debt instruments | 8abla | 6,999.7 | 7,100.0 | 10,938.3 | 12,635.9 | 14,772.8 | 18,503.0 | 22,338.7 | 27,715.3 | 30,813.7 | † 34,990.3 | 39,587.3 | .... |
| Portfolio investment | 8b9la | 25,732.3 | 34,591.7 | 56,161.5 | 71,421.2 | 45,347.9 | 95,641.0 | 146,148.5 | 152,782.3 | 178,393.4 | † 161,974.6 | 204,826.4 | .... |
| Equity & investment fund shares.. | 8bala | 15,594.4 | 15,854.0 | 31,518.7 | 41,416.5 | 14,982.8 | 53,293.0 | 88,846.6 | 89,252.9 | 100,910.8 | † 77,691.6 | 102,141.8 | .... |
| Debt securities | 8bbla | 10,137.9 | 18,737.7 | 24,642.8 | 30,004.8 | 30,365.1 | 42,348.0 | 57,301.8 | 63,529.4 | 77,482.6 | † 84,283.0 | 102,684.7 | .... |
| Fin. der.(oth.than reserves) & ESOs | 8c9la | 39.9 | 43.2 | 22.5 | 22.5 | 221.4 | 78.0 | 56.7 | 87.1 | 94.8 | † 136.1 | 122.0 | .... |
| Other investment | 8d9la | 132,013.5 | 109,989.0 | 100,929.4 | 115,713.8 | 110,650.9 | 112,629.3 | 121,481.4 | 133,657.7 | 142,773.3 | † 148,425.2 | 151,604.8 | .... |
| Other equity | 8dala | .... | .... | .... | .... | .... | .... | .... | .... | .... | .... | .... | .... |
| Debt instruments | 8dzla | 132,013.5 | 109,989.0 | 100,929.4 | 115,713.8 | 110,650.9 | 112,629.3 | 121,481.4 | 133,657.7 | 142,773.3 | † 148,425.2 | 151,604.8 | .... |
| **Government Finance** | | | | | | | | | | | | | |
| **Cash Flow Statement** | | | | | | | | | | | | | |
| **Budgetary Central Government** | | | | | | | *Billions of Rupiah: Fiscal Year Ends December 31* | | | | | | |
| Cash Receipts:Operating Activities... | c1 | 407,860 | 495,444 | 637,796 | 711,909 | 949,300 | 868,946 | 1,017,258 | 1,194,505 | 1,335,663 | 1,429,453 | 1,549,889 | .... |
| Taxes | c11 | 280,898 | 346,834 | 409,054 | 491,666 | 632,125 | 641,380 | 744,401 | 873,735 | 980,065 | 1,072,119 | 1,146,472 | .... |
| Social Contributions | c12 | — | — | — | — | — | — | — | — | — | — | — | .... |
| Grants | c13 | 278 | 1,296 | 1,857 | 1,695 | 2,245 | 1,116 | 2,859 | 2,582 | 3,966 | 4,484 | 4,596 | .... |
| Other Receipts | c14 | 126,684 | 147,315 | 226,885 | 218,548 | 314,570 | 226,449 | 269,998 | 318,188 | 351,632 | 352,851 | 398,821 | .... |
| Cash Payments:Operating Activities. | c2 | 368,389 | 468,747 | 611,606 | 673,201 | 909,954 | 881,844 | 977,969 | 1,174,520 | 1,341,506 | 1,189,343 | 1,629,399 | .... |
| Compensation of Employees | c21 | 54,391 | 55,589 | 72,873 | 89,767 | 109,671 | 127,656 | 147,903 | 175,526 | 197,670 | 221,399 | 243,692 | .... |
| Purchases of Goods & Services | c22 | 16,649 | 33,060 | 47,066 | 51,200 | 52,356 | 79,628 | 97,467 | 121,796 | 137,174 | 167,767 | 176,300 | .... |
| Interest | c24 | 62,351 | 53,832 | 79,026 | 79,364 | 87,269 | 93,802 | 88,345 | 93,273 | 100,550 | 112,770 | 133,400 | .... |
| Subsidies | c25 | 85,469 | 120,708 | 107,399 | 133,999 | 275,282 | 159,545 | 214,138 | 294,874 | 346,363 | 77,118 | 391,963 | .... |
| Grants | c26 | 129,681 | 150,516 | 226,394 | 253,257 | 299,082 | 308,569 | 344,805 | 411,652 | 480,483 | 514,569 | 574,584 | .... |
| Social Benefits | c27 | — | — | — | — | — | — | — | — | 74,506 | 90,356 | 97,822 | .... |
| Other Payments | c28 | 19,848 | 55,041 | 78,848 | 65,614 | 86,293 | 112,644 | 85,311 | 77,399 | 4,761 | 5,364 | 11,637 | .... |
| Net Cash Inflow:Operating Act.[1-2] | ccio | 39,471 | 26,698 | 26,190 | 38,708 | 39,346 | −12,898 | 39,289 | 19,985 | −5,842 | 240,110 | −79,510 | .... |
| Net Cash Outflow:Invest. in NFA | c31 | 69,352 | 36,529 | 58,931 | 64,652 | 70,753 | 74,535 | 78,994 | 115,903 | 140,169 | 171,758 | 141,655 | .... |
| Purchases of Nonfinancial Assets... | c31.1 | .... | .... | .... | .... | .... | .... | .... | .... | .... | .... | .... | .... |
| Sales of Nonfinancial Assets | c31.2 | .... | .... | .... | .... | .... | .... | .... | .... | .... | .... | .... | .... |
| Cash Surplus/Deficit [1-2-31=1-2M] | ccsd | −29,882 | −9,832 | −32,741 | −25,944 | −31,407 | −87,433 | −39,705 | −95,919 | −146,011 | 68,351 | −221,166 | .... |
| Net Acq. Fin. Assets, excl. Cash | c32x | .... | .... | .... | .... | .... | .... | .... | .... | .... | .... | .... | .... |
| Domestic | c321x | .... | .... | .... | .... | .... | .... | .... | .... | .... | .... | .... | .... |
| Foreign | c322x | .... | .... | .... | .... | .... | .... | .... | .... | .... | .... | .... | .... |
| Net Incurrence of Liabilities | c33 | 31,774 | 14,401 | 30,604 | 49,809 | 42,062 | 114,489 | 10,794 | −24,268 | 204,331 | 267,539 | 235,782 | .... |
| Domestic | c331 | 50,076 | 26,007 | 52,894 | 72,603 | 59,710 | 137,337 | 6,130 | −13,737 | 220,429 | 273,242 | 261,287 | .... |
| Foreign | c332 | −18,301 | −11,606 | −22,289 | −22,794 | −17,648 | −22,848 | 4,664 | −10,531 | −16,098 | −5,704 | −25,505 | .... |
| Net Cash Inflow, Fin.Act.[-32x+33].. | cnfb | .... | .... | .... | .... | .... | .... | .... | .... | .... | .... | .... | .... |
| Net Change in Stock of Cash | cncb | .... | .... | .... | .... | .... | .... | .... | .... | .... | .... | .... | .... |
| Stat. Discrep. [32X-33+NCB-CSD] | ccsdz | −1,893 | −4,569 | 2,137 | −23,864 | −10,296 | −27,056 | 28,911 | 120,187 | −58,320 | −335,890 | −14,616 | .... |
| Memo Item:Cash Expenditure[2+31] | c2m | 437,742 | 505,276 | 670,537 | 737,853 | 980,707 | 956,379 | 1,056,963 | 1,290,423 | 1,481,674 | 1,361,102 | 1,771,054 | .... |
| Memo Item: Gross Debt | c63 | 1,299,500 | 1,313,290 | 1,302,160 | 1,389,410 | 1,636,740 | 1,590,656 | 1,676,681 | 1,803,490 | 1,975,420 | | | |
| **National Accounts** | | | | | | | | *Billions of Rupiah* | | | | | |
| Househ.Cons.Expend.,incl.NPISHs.. | 96f | 1,532,888 | 1,785,596 | 2,092,656 | 2,510,504 | 2,999,957 | 3,290,996 | 3,858,822 | 4,340,605 | 4,858,331 | 5,425,017 | 6,039,984 | 6,584,142 |
| Government Consumption Expend... | 91f | 191,056 | 224,981 | 288,080 | 329,760 | 416,867 | 537,589 | 618,178 | 709,451 | 796,848 | 908,574 | 996,197 | 1,125,542 |
| Gross Fixed Capital Formation | 93e | 515,381 | 655,854 | 805,786 | 985,627 | 1,370,717 | 1,744,357 | 2,127,841 | 2,451,914 | 2,819,026 | 3,051,496 | 3,442,027 | 3,829,978 |
| Changes in Inventories | 93i | 36,911 | 39,975 | 42,382 | −1,053 | 5,822 | −7,264 | 129,095 | 131,329 | 202,638 | 178,091 | 210,407 | 158,754 |
| Exports of Goods and Services | 90c | 739,639 | 945,122 | 1,036,316 | 1,162,974 | 1,475,119 | 1,354,409 | 1,667,918 | 2,061,886 | 2,118,979 | 2,283,777 | 2,497,116 | 2,434,181 |
| Imports of Goods and Services (-).... | 98c | 632,376 | 830,083 | 855,588 | 1,003,271 | 1,422,902 | 1,197,093 | 1,537,720 | 1,868,075 | 2,152,937 | 2,359,212 | 2,580,527 | 2,405,762 |
| Gross Domestic Product (GDP) | 99b | 2,295,826 | 2,774,281 | 3,339,217 | 3,950,893 | 4,948,688 | 5,606,203 | 6,864,133 | 7,831,726 | 8,615,705 | 9,546,134 | 10,565,817 | 11,540,790 |
| Statistical Discrepancy | 99bs | −87,673 | −47,163 | −70,416 | −33,647 | 103,109 | −116,791 | — | 4,616 | −27,181 | 58,392 | −39,387 | −186,045 |
| Net Primary Income from Abroad | 98.n | −105,350 | −135,000 | −142,269 | −162,485 | −175,865 | −196,220 | −182,771 | −216,893 | −243,193 | −285,326 | −354,474 | −386,258 |
| Gross National Income (GNI) | 99a | 2,127,942 | 2,585,561 | 3,098,805 | 3,676,220 | 4,703,177 | 5,409,984 | 6,681,362 | 7,614,833 | 8,372,512 | 9,260,808 | 10,211,343 | 11,154,532 |
| Consumption of Fixed Capital | 99cf | 114,791 | 138,714 | 166,961 | 197,545 | 247,434 | 280,310 | 1,270,479 | 1,429,984 | 1,603,812 | 1,766,892 | 1,970,519 | 2,129,438 |
| GDP Volume 2010 Prices | 99b.p | .... | .... | | | | | 6,864,133 | 7,287,635 | 7,727,083 | 8,156,498 | 8,566,271 | 8,976,932 |
| GDP Volume (2010=100) | 99bvp | 71.6 | 75.6 | 79.8 | 84.9 | 90.0 | 94.1 | † 100.0 | 106.2 | 112.6 | 118.8 | 124.8 | 130.8 |
| GDP Deflator (2010=100) | 99bip | 46.7 | 53.4 | 61.0 | 67.8 | 80.1 | 86.8 | 100.0 | 107.5 | 111.5 | 117.0 | 123.3 | 128.6 |
| | | | | | | | *Millions: Midyear Estimates* | | | | | | |
| Population | 99z | 223.27 | 226.25 | 229.26 | 232.30 | 235.36 | 238.47 | 241.61 | 244.81 | 248.04 | 251.27 | 254.45 | 257.56 |

# Iran, Islamic Republic of   429

| | | 2004 | 2005 | 2006 | 2007 | 2008 | 2009 | 2010 | 2011 | 2012 | 2013 | 2014 | 2015 |
|---|---|---|---|---|---|---|---|---|---|---|---|---|---|
| **Exchange Rates** | | | | | | | | | | | | | |
| Official Rate | aa | 13,656 | 12,993 | 13,875 | 14,668 | 15,133 | 15,652 | 15,944 | 17,141 | 18,843 | 38,152 | 39,318 | 41,752 |
| Official Rate | ae | 8,793 | 9,091 | 9,223 | 9,282 | 9,825 | 9,984 | 10,353 | 11,165 | 12,260 | 24,774 | 27,138 | 30,130 |
| Official Rate | rf | 8,614 | 8,964 | 9,171 | 9,281 | 9,429 | 9,864 | 10,254 | 10,616 | 12,176 | 18,414 | 25,942 | 29,011 |
| Nominal Effective Exchange Rate | nec | 125.30 | 118.27 | 115.14 | 107.27 | 102.42 | 104.14 | 100.00 | 93.62 | 85.22 | 63.39 | 40.76 | 41.36 |
| CPI-Based Real Effect. Ex. Rate | rec | 65.93 | 68.46 | 71.95 | 75.24 | 85.52 | 97.07 | 100.00 | 109.25 | 123.15 | 122.35 | 91.92 | 103.80 |
| **Fund Position** | | | | | | | | | | | | | |
| Quota | 2f.s | 1,497.20 | 1,497.20 | 1,497.20 | 1,497.20 | 1,497.20 | 1,497.20 | 1,497.20 | 1,497.20 | 1,497.20 | 1,497.20 | 1,497.20 | 1,497.20 |
| SDR Holdings | 1b.s | 273.91 | 274.66 | 275.76 | 282.19 | 283.32 | 1,535.53 | 1,535.81 | 1,536.27 | 1,540.79 | 1,551.87 | 1,551.98 | 1,536.63 |
| Reserve Position in the Fund | 1c.s | — | — | — | — | .01 | .01 | .01 | .01 | .01 | .01 | .01 | .01 |
| Total Fund Cred.&Loans Outstg. | 2tl | — | — | — | — | — | — | — | — | — | — | — | — |
| SDR Allocations | 1bd | 244.06 | 244.06 | 244.06 | 244.06 | 244.06 | 1,426.06 | 1,426.06 | 1,426.06 | 1,426.06 | 1,426.06 | 1,426.06 | 1,426.06 |
| **International Liquidity** | | | | | | | | | | | | | |
| SDR Holdings | 1b.d | 425 | 393 | 415 | 446 | 436 | 2,407 | 2,365 | 2,359 | 2,368 | 2,390 | 2,249 | 2,129 |
| Reserve Position in the Fund | 1c.d | — | — | — | — | — | — | — | — | — | — | — | — |
| Monetary Authorities: Other Liabs. | 4..d | 9,357 | 18,927 | 22,039 | 24,966 | 34,418 | 14,220 | 16,164 | 33,152 | .... | .... | .... | .... |
| Deposit Money Banks: Assets | 7a.d | 27,670 | 30,378 | 32,159 | 35,806 | 35,646 | 41,771 | 12,294 | 77,838 | 80,050 | 73,160 | 79,453 | .... |
| Deposit Money Banks: Liabs. | 7b.d | 27,926 | 31,183 | 31,895 | 40,698 | 48,676 | 44,731 | 65,875 | 72,287 | 71,562 | 60,536 | 64,268 | .... |
| **Monetary Authorities** | | | | | | | | | | | | | |
| Foreign Assets | 11 | 263,305 | 396,520 | 538,583 | 689,585 | 905,405 | 795,581 | 827,934 | .... | .... | .... | .... | |
| Claims on Central Government | 12a | 107,594 | 103,416 | 109,627 | 107,118 | 101,418 | 91,861 | 162,647 | 154,510 | .... | .... | .... | |
| Claims on Official Entities | 12bx | .... | .... | .... | .... | .... | .... | .... | .... | .... | .... | .... | |
| Claims on Deposit Money Banks | 12e | 35,424 | 33,017 | 52,273 | 135,117 | 216,276 | 188,042 | 284,286 | 472,220 | 478,959 | 565,432 | 773,526 | |
| Reserve Money | 14 | 145,986 | 178,490 | 245,012 | 345,823 | 453,978 | 506,968 | 669,230 | 683,787 | .... | .... | .... | |
| of which: Currency Outside DMBs | 14a | 33,638 | 38,479 | 48,413 | 59,540 | 117,920 | 141,556 | 176,192 | 201,491 | .... | .... | .... | |
| Nonfin.Pub.Ent. Deps. | 14e | 8,611 | 10,915 | 12,091 | 15,995 | 16,978 | 15,496 | 18,353 | 17,258 | .... | .... | .... | |
| Restricted Deposits | 16b | 1,216 | 879 | 1,078 | 1,344 | 612 | 560 | 559 | 306 | .... | .... | .... | |
| Foreign Liabilities | 16c | 85,607 | 175,235 | 206,654 | 235,315 | 341,847 | 164,297 | 190,087 | 394,583 | .... | .... | .... | |
| Central Government Deposits | 16d | 92,882 | 108,358 | 161,002 | 213,296 | 282,446 | 254,741 | 248,321 | 354,504 | .... | .... | .... | |
| Capital Accounts | 17a | 1,681 | 3,325 | 5,173 | 13,693 | 19,436 | 27,029 | 34,555 | 34,555 | .... | .... | .... | |
| Other Items (Net) | 17r | .... | .... | .... | .... | .... | .... | .... | .... | .... | .... | .... | |
| **Deposit Money Banks** | | | | | | | | | | | | | |
| Reserves | 20 | 103,737 | 129,096 | 184,508 | 270,328 | 319,080 | 349,915 | 474,684 | 465,037 | 623,829 | 717,371 | 912,267 | .... |
| Foreign Assets | 21 | 243,304 | 276,165 | 296,601 | 332,352 | 350,219 | 417,038 | 127,283 | 869,064 | 981,416 | 1,812,456 | 2,156,196 | .... |
| Claims on Central Government | 22a | 31,102 | 33,590 | 48,252 | 90,937 | 101,021 | 139,602 | 247,333 | 330,539 | 509,436 | 686,100 | 932,978 | .... |
| Claims on Private Sector | 22d | 574,125 | 778,432 | 1,093,984 | 1,527,768 | 1,761,725 | 2,021,376 | 2,619,778 | 3,396,108 | 3,917,624 | 4,742,837 | 6,002,905 | .... |
| Demand Deposits | 24 | 188,497 | 234,577 | 301,472 | 401,618 | 352,575 | 365,760 | 468,618 | 569,160 | 722,214 | 803,319 | 864,871 | .... |
| Time and Savings Deposits | 25 | 403,844 | 559,067 | 787,513 | 1,062,009 | 1,234,449 | 1,664,607 | 2,061,952 | 2,486,737 | 3,324,069 | 4,428,324 | 6,268,022 | .... |
| Foreign Liabilities | 26c | 245,555 | 283,481 | 294,172 | 377,759 | 478,240 | 446,593 | 682,001 | 807,084 | 877,353 | 1,499,730 | 1,744,097 | .... |
| Credit from Monetary Authorities | 26g | 35,424 | 33,017 | 52,273 | 135,117 | 216,276 | 188,042 | 284,286 | 472,220 | 478,959 | 565,432 | 773,526 | .... |
| Capital Accounts | 27a | 22,999 | 86,026 | 108,404 | 140,813 | 147,732 | 165,932 | 195,732 | 236,175 | 303,082 | 442,561 | 586,631 | .... |
| Other Items (Net) | 27r | 87,333 | 60,144 | 135,213 | 188,714 | 227,043 | 229,894 | 380,370 | 489,373 | 326,629 | 219,397 | −232,800 | .... |
| **Monetary Survey** | | | | | | | | | | | | | |
| Foreign Assets (Net) | 31n | 175,447 | 213,969 | 334,359 | 408,863 | 435,537 | 601,728 | 83,131 | .... | .... | .... | .... | |
| Domestic Credit | 32 | .... | .... | .... | .... | .... | .... | .... | .... | .... | .... | .... | |
| Claims on Central Govt. (Net) | 32an | 21,250 | −16,655 | −71,127 | −98,267 | −178,427 | −141,785 | 29,850 | 34,371 | .... | .... | .... | |
| Claims on Official Entities | 32bx | .... | .... | .... | .... | .... | .... | .... | .... | .... | .... | .... | |
| Claims on Private Sector | 32d | 574,125 | 778,432 | 1,093,984 | 1,527,768 | 1,761,725 | 2,021,376 | 2,619,778 | 3,396,108 | 3,917,624 | 4,742,837 | 6,002,905 | .... |
| Money | 34 | 230,746 | 283,971 | 361,976 | 477,113 | 487,473 | 522,812 | 663,163 | 787,910 | .... | .... | .... | |
| Quasi-Money | 35 | 403,844 | 559,067 | 787,513 | 1,062,009 | 1,234,449 | 1,664,607 | 2,061,952 | 2,486,737 | 3,324,069 | 4,428,324 | 6,268,022 | .... |
| Restricted Deposits | 36b | 1,216 | 879 | 1,078 | 1,344 | 612 | 560 | 559 | 306 | .... | .... | .... | |
| Other Items (Net) | 37r | .... | .... | .... | .... | .... | .... | .... | .... | .... | .... | .... | |
| Money plus Quasi-Money | 35l | 634,589 | 843,039 | 1,149,489 | 1,539,122 | 1,721,922 | 2,187,419 | 2,725,114 | 3,274,647 | .... | .... | .... | |
| **Interest Rates** | | | | | | | | | | | | | |
| Deposit Rate (End of Period) | 60l | 11.70 | 11.78 | 11.56 | 11.60 | 13.30 | 13.14 | 11.94 | 11.16 | 14.81 | 14.76 | 16.94 | .... |
| Lending Rate (End of Period) | 60p | 16.65 | 16.00 | 14.00 | 12.00 | 12.00 | 12.00 | 12.00 | 11.00 | 11.00 | 11.00 | 14.00 | .... |
| **Prices and Production** | | | | | | | | | | | | | |
| Share Prices | 62 | 80.9 | 75.3 | 62.8 | 63.6 | 70.0 | 64.4 | 100.0 | 160.8 | 179.1 | 359.5 | 492.5 | .... |
| Producer Prices | 63b | 46.3 | 50.7 | 56.8 | 69.0 | † 78.0 | 85.2 | 94.1 | 129.7 | 161.7 | † 222.0 | 260.3 | 278.5 |
| Consumer Prices | 64 | 42.8 | 48.6 | † 54.4 | 63.7 | 80.0 | 90.8 | 100.0 | 120.6 | † 153.6 | 214.0 | 250.8 | 285.2 |
| Crude Petroleum Production | 66aa | 109.5 | 109.5 | 106.4 | 107.7 | 107.7 | 100.0 | 100.0 | 100.2 | 80.1 | 72.0 | 72.4 | 78.9 |
| **Intl. Transactions & Positions** | | | | | | | | | | | | | |
| Exports | 70..d | 41,697 | 56,252 | 77,012 | 83,000 | 113,668 | 78,830 | 101,316 | 130,500 | 95,500 | 82,000 | 88,800 | 63,000 |
| Imports, c.i.f. | 71..d | 31,976 | 40,041 | 40,772 | 45,000 | 57,401 | 50,768 | 65,404 | 61,808 | 53,451 | 49,709 | 53,569 | 42,500 |
| **National Accounts** | | | | | | | | | | | | | |
| Househ.Cons.Expend.,incl.NPISHs. | 96f | 645,860 | 786,920 | 938,888 | 1,185,508 | 1,420,657 | 1,540,628 | 1,767,132 | 2,778,553 | 3,546,398 | 4,690,756 | 5,586,451 | .... |
| Government Consumption Expend. | 91f | 192,649 | 251,216 | 310,392 | 309,098 | 391,519 | 445,320 | 481,350 | 631,222 | 708,139 | 983,406 | 1,181,023 | .... |
| Gross Fixed Capital Formation | 93e | 409,175 | 474,983 | 544,249 | 685,452 | 957,271 | 949,354 | 1,146,917 | 1,648,671 | 1,973,068 | 2,528,109 | 2,886,932 | .... |
| Changes in Inventories | 93i | 127,479 | 100,651 | 138,844 | 336,305 | 313,386 | 475,472 | 639,312 | 553,658 | 758,470 | 494,883 | 797,279 | .... |
| Exports of Goods and Services | 90c | 411,607 | 613,102 | 738,427 | 944,163 | 1,015,562 | 923,411 | 1,194,391 | 1,612,985 | 1,598,714 | 2,588,373 | 2,666,704 | .... |
| Imports of Goods and Services (-) | 98c | 379,076 | 441,236 | 529,766 | 606,663 | 741,949 | 756,788 | 896,016 | 1,039,833 | 1,482,252 | 1,864,313 | 2,084,724 | .... |
| Gross Domestic Product (GDP) | 99b | 1,468,989 | 1,831,737 | 2,224,093 | 2,853,863 | 3,356,447 | 3,577,397 | 4,333,087 | † 6,285,255 | 7,149,595 | 9,421,214 | 11,033,666 | .... |
| Net Primary Income from Abroad | 98.n | −26,933 | −28,333 | −25,742 | −28,347 | −23,212 | −33,823 | −32,555 | 3,535 | 29,286 | 47,479 | 41,532 | .... |
| Gross National Income (GNI) | 99a | 1,442,056 | 1,803,405 | 2,198,350 | 2,825,516 | 3,333,235 | 3,543,574 | 4,300,531 | 6,288,790 | 7,178,882 | 9,468,693 | 11,075,198 | .... |
| GDP Volume 1997 Prices | 99b.p | 414,179 | 433,463 | 460,387 | 489,699 | 492,520 | 511,975 | 542,174 | .... | .... | .... | .... | |
| GDP Volume (2010=100) | 99bvp | 76.4 | 79.9 | 84.9 | 90.3 | 90.8 | 94.4 | 100.0 | .... | .... | .... | .... | |
| GDP Deflator (2010=100) | 99bip | 44.4 | 52.9 | 60.4 | 72.9 | 85.3 | 87.4 | 100.0 | .... | .... | .... | .... | |
| Population | 99z | 69.32 | 70.12 | 70.92 | 71.72 | 72.53 | 73.37 | 74.25 | 75.18 | 76.16 | 77.15 | 78.14 | 79.11 |

*Rials per SDR: End of Period*
*Rials per US Dollar: End of Period (ae) Period Average (rf)*
*Index Numbers (2010=100): Period Averages*
*Millions of SDRs: End of Period*
*Millions of US Dollars Unless Otherwise Indicated: End of Period*
*Billions of Rials: Months Ending the 20th*
*Billions of Rials: Months Ending the 20th*
*Billions of Rials: Months Ending the 20th*
*Percent Per Annum*
*Index Numbers (2010=100)*
*Millions of US Dollars Fiscal Year Ends March 20*
*Billions of Rials: Fiscal Year Begins March 21*
*Millions: Midyear Estimates*

# Iraq  433

|  |  | 2004 | 2005 | 2006 | 2007 | 2008 | 2009 | 2010 | 2011 | 2012 | 2013 | 2014 | 2015 |
|---|---|---|---|---|---|---|---|---|---|---|---|---|---|
| **Exchange Rates** | | *New Iraqi dinars per SDR* | | | | | | | | | | | |
| Market Rate.................................. | aa | 2,281.4 | 2,125.3 | 1,993.3 | 1,920.0 | 1,805.2 | 1,834.2 | 1,801.8 | 1,796.3 | 1,792.0 | 1,795.6 | 1,689.3 | 1,637.9 |
| | | *New Iraqi dinars per US Dollar: End of Period (ae) Period Average (rf)* | | | | | | | | | | | |
| Market Rate.................................. | ae | 1,469.0 | 1,487.0 | 1,325.0 | 1,215.0 | 1,172.0 | 1,170.0 | 1,170.0 | 1,170.0 | 1,166.0 | 1,166.0 | 1,166.0 | 1,182.0 |
| Market Rate.................................. | rf | 1,453.4 | 1,472.0 | 1,467.4 | 1,254.6 | 1,193.1 | 1,170.0 | 1,170.0 | 1,170.0 | 1,166.2 | 1,166.0 | 1,166.0 | 1,167.3 |
| | | *Index Numbers (2010=100): Period Averages* | | | | | | | | | | | |
| Principal Rate............................... | ahx | 80.5 | 79.5 | 79.6 | 93.3 | 98.1 | 100.0 | 100.0 | 100.0 | 100.3 | 100.3 | 100.3 | 100.2 |
| Nominal Effective Exchange Rate..... | nec | 81.9 | 78.9 | 79.6 | 89.9 | 93.0 | 100.0 | 100.0 | 101.0 | 107.0 | 114.3 | 123.6 | 137.8 |
| **Fund Position** | | *Millions of SDRs: End of Period* | | | | | | | | | | | |
| Quota......................................... | 2f.s | 1,188.40 | 1,188.40 | 1,188.40 | 1,188.40 | 1,188.40 | 1,188.40 | 1,188.40 | 1,188.40 | 1,188.40 | 1,188.40 | 1,188.40 | 1,188.40 |
| SDR Holdings............................... | 1b.s | 296.12 | 293.58 | 291.65 | 88.43 | 92.93 | 1,159.86 | 1,151.87 | 1,135.82 | 1,121.96 | 1,008.04 | 501.56 | 67.95 |
| Reserve Position in the Fund............ | 1c.s | 171.10 | 171.10 | 171.10 | 171.10 | 171.10 | 171.10 | 171.10 | 171.10 | 171.10 | 171.10 | 171.10 | 171.10 |
| Total Fund Cred.&Loans Outstg....... | 2tl | 297.10 | 297.10 | 297.10 | — | — | 1,134.50 | 1,134.50 | 1,069.56 | 1,069.56 | 1,069.56 | 958.15 | 928.44 |
| SDR Allocations............................. | 1bd | 68.46 | 68.46 | 68.46 | 68.46 | 68.46 | 1,134.50 | 1,134.50 | 1,134.50 | 1,134.50 | 1,134.50 | 1,134.50 | 1,134.50 |
| **International Liquidity** | | *Millions of US Dollars Unless Otherwise Indicated: End of Period* | | | | | | | | | | | |
| Total Reserves minus Gold.............. | 1l.d | 7,824.1 | 12,104.1 | 19,931.9 | 31,297.6 | 49,937.8 | 44,127.5 | 50,357.0 | 60,744.4 | 68,733.4 | 76,112.2 | 62,885.9 | 50,990.8 |
| SDR Holdings............................... | 1b.d | 459.9 | 419.6 | 438.8 | 139.7 | 143.1 | 1,818.3 | 1,773.9 | 1,743.8 | 1,724.4 | 1,552.4 | 726.7 | 94.2 |
| Reserve Position in the Fund.......... | 1c.d | 265.7 | 244.5 | 257.4 | 270.4 | 263.5 | 268.2 | 263.5 | 262.7 | 263.0 | 263.5 | 247.9 | 237.1 |
| Foreign Exchange......................... | 1d.d | 7,098.5 | 11,439.9 | 19,235.7 | 30,887.5 | 49,531.1 | 42,041.0 | 48,319.6 | 58,737.9 | 66,746.1 | 74,296.3 | 61,911.4 | 50,659.6 |
| Gold (Million Fine Troy Ounces)....... | 1ad | .189 | .189 | .189 | .189 | .189 | .189 | .189 | .189 | .958 | 1.357 | 2.888 | 2.888 |
| Gold (National Valuation).............. | 1and | 79.0 | 96.8 | 121.8 | 157.8 | 163.1 | 208.2 | 266.0 | 296.9 | 1,593.6 | 1,631.0 | 3,463.2 | 3,067.6 |
| Central Bank: Other Assets.............. | 3..d | 9,135.4 | 1,389.2 | 1,408.8 | 1,446.7 | 1,486.6 | 1,456.5 | 1,353.1 | 1,340.6 | 1,341.9 | 1,348.6 | 1,331.8 | 308.5 |
| Central Bank: Other Liabs................ | 4..d | 8,967.1 | 9,105.9 | 9,240.8 | 2,027.2 | 548.1 | 161.4 | 164.8 | 8.3 | 9.4 | 11.2 | 12.9 | 14.7 |
| Other Depository Corps.: Assets....... | 7a.d | 3,134.1 | 3,659.5 | 5,859.0 | 7,531.1 | 7,792.6 | 13,707.1 | 10,849.4 | 9,861.4 | 13,315.4 | 18,987.4 | 23,390.5 | 13,683.5 |
| Other Depository Corps.: Liabs......... | 7b.d | 7,196.3 | 7,492.1 | 8,285.5 | 8,759.6 | 7,559.0 | 9,109.8 | 7,614.9 | 7,822.4 | 1,271.0 | 1,238.2 | 1,182.7 | 1,299.5 |
| **Central Bank** | | *Billions of New Iraqi Dinars: End of Period* | | | | | | | | | | | |
| Net Foreign Assets.......................... | 11n | 9,527.5 | 5,602.3 | 15,051.8 | 37,655.6 | 60,128.0 | 51,919.2 | 57,540.4 | 69,244.3 | 78,410.3 | 88,543.6 | 76,563.2 | 60,378.4 |
| Claims on Nonresidents................. | 11 | 23,534.2 | 19,919.7 | 28,024.6 | 40,250.1 | 60,913.6 | 54,189.0 | 61,169.3 | 73,213.1 | 82,371.0 | 92,314.3 | 79,272.6 | 63,728.8 |
| Liabilities to Nonresidents............. | 16c | 14,006.7 | 14,317.4 | 12,972.8 | 2,594.5 | 785.5 | 2,269.7 | 3,628.9 | 3,968.8 | 3,960.7 | 3,770.7 | 2,709.4 | 3,350.4 |
| Claims on Other Depository Corps.... | 12e | 18.5 | 19.0 | 20.6 | 15.6 | 12.2 | 10.4 | 7.8 | 6.5 | 39.8 | 29.2 | 6.7 | 14.2 |
| Net Claims on Central Government.. | 12an | 5,717.2 | 2,210.2 | 1,092.6 | −1,428.3 | −9,348.7 | 2,722.3 | 2,569.9 | −2,386.3 | −3,622.0 | 751.5 | 512.6 | 2,936.6 |
| Claims on Central Government...... | 12a | 6,405.7 | 6,505.9 | 6,480.7 | 5,687.1 | 3,973.2 | 3,973.5 | 4,494.4 | 3,561.7 | 3,155.5 | 2,755.5 | 2,486.5 | 8,691.2 |
| Liabilities to Central Government... | 16d | 688.4 | 4,295.8 | 5,388.1 | 7,115.4 | 13,321.9 | 1,251.3 | 1,924.4 | 5,948.0 | 6,777.5 | 2,004.1 | 1,973.9 | 5,754.6 |
| Claims on Other Sectors.................. | 12s | .5 | 3.2 | 4.7 | 5.1 | 3.1 | 1.2 | .4 | 59.4 | 73.5 | 83.0 | 80.3 | 88.3 |
| Claims on Other Financial Corps.... | 12g | — | — | — | — | — | — | — | — | — | — | — | 7.5 |
| Claims on State & Local Govts....... | 12b | — | — | — | — | — | — | — | — | — | — | — | — |
| Claims on Public Nonfin. Corps...... | 12c | — | — | — | — | — | — | — | — | — | — | — | — |
| Claims on Private Sector................ | 12d | .5 | 3.2 | 4.7 | 5.1 | 3.1 | 1.2 | .4 | 59.4 | 73.5 | 83.0 | 80.3 | 80.8 |
| Monetary Base............................... | 14 | 11,799.5 | 13,794.7 | 17,521.5 | 28,808.4 | 42,858.6 | 45,270.9 | 54,524.3 | 60,059.3 | 65,055.2 | 73,259.3 | 66,230.8 | 57,887.6 |
| Currency in Circulation.................. | 14a | 7,592.0 | 10,256.5 | 11,916.6 | 15,632.2 | 21,304.4 | 24,169.4 | 27,507.3 | 32,157.4 | 35,784.8 | 40,630.0 | 39,883.7 | 38,585.1 |
| Liabs. to Other Depository Corps.... | 14c | 4,207.6 | 3,538.2 | 5,604.9 | 13,176.2 | 21,554.2 | 21,101.5 | 27,017.0 | 27,901.9 | 29,270.4 | 32,629.2 | 26,347.1 | 19,302.5 |
| Liabilities to Other Sectors.......... | 14d | — | — | — | — | — | — | — | — | — | — | — | — |
| Other Liabs. to Other Dep. Corps..... | 14n | 1,970.5 | 3,334.1 | 7,221.7 | 8,212.4 | 6,963.5 | 5,914.3 | 4,336.2 | 5,609.6 | 6,901.5 | 10,797.0 | 6,566.9 | 6,455.2 |
| Dep. & Sec. Excl. f/Monetary Base.... | 14o | 315.5 | 311.9 | 994.7 | 131.5 | 262.5 | 58.0 | 58.1 | 66.6 | 65.6 | 19.8 | 22.0 | 24.4 |
| Deposits Included in Broad Money. | 15 | 314.7 | 311.2 | 994.0 | 131.4 | 262.4 | 57.9 | 57.9 | 66.5 | 65.5 | 19.7 | 21.9 | 24.3 |
| Sec.Ot.th.Shares Incl.in Brd. Money | 16a | — | — | — | — | — | — | — | — | — | — | — | — |
| Deposits Excl. from Broad Money... | 16b | .8 | .7 | .7 | .1 | .1 | .1 | .1 | .1 | .1 | .1 | .1 | .1 |
| Sec.Ot.th.Shares Excl.f/Brd.Money.. | 16s | — | — | — | — | — | — | — | — | — | — | — | — |
| Loans.......................................... | 16l | — | — | — | — | — | — | — | — | — | — | — | — |
| Financial Derivatives...................... | 16m | — | — | — | — | — | — | — | — | — | — | — | — |
| Shares and Other Equity.................. | 17a | −128.1 | −129.0 | 145.0 | 8,645.6 | 1,106.4 | 3,658.5 | 204.0 | 1,256.5 | 3,133.2 | 5,462.6 | 3,280.0 | 2,167.6 |
| Other Items (Net)........................... | 17r | 1,306.4 | −9,477.1 | −9,713.2 | −9,549.9 | −396.4 | −248.6 | 995.9 | −68.1 | −253.9 | −131.4 | 1,063.2 | −3,117.3 |
| Memo Item: | | | | | | | | | | | | | |
| Total Assets.................................. | 10ra | 29,958.1 | 41,738.8 | 49,920.0 | 61,095.6 | 70,502.4 | 62,441.4 | 67,599.2 | 78,966.4 | 87,602.0 | 97,168.1 | 83,773.6 | 72,404.7 |

| | | 2004 | 2005 | 2006 | 2007 | 2008 | 2009 | 2010 | 2011 | 2012 | 2013 | 2014 | 2015 |
|---|---|---|---|---|---|---|---|---|---|---|---|---|---|
| **Other Depository Corporations** | | | | | | | *Billions of New Iraqi Dinars: End of Period* | | | | | | | |
| Net Foreign Assets........................ | 21n | −5,967.5 | −5,699.1 | −3,215.1 | −1,492.7 | 280.8 | 5,379.4 | 3,784.4 | 2,385.6 | 14,043.7 | 20,695.5 | 25,894.3 | 14,439.8 |
| Claims on Nonresidents................ | 21 | 4,603.9 | 5,441.7 | 7,763.1 | 9,150.3 | 9,366.7 | 16,038.0 | 12,693.8 | 11,537.8 | 15,525.7 | 22,139.3 | 27,273.3 | 15,954.9 |
| Liabilities to Nonresidents............. | 26c | 10,571.4 | 11,140.7 | 10,978.2 | 10,643.0 | 9,085.9 | 10,658.5 | 8,909.4 | 9,152.2 | 1,482.0 | 1,443.7 | 1,379.0 | 1,515.2 |
| Claims on Central Bank.................. | 20 | 6,349.4 | 9,663.0 | 10,062.5 | 18,278.1 | 26,011.5 | 29,902.7 | 35,087.0 | 38,246.7 | 41,482.5 | 45,231.0 | 41,985.0 | 34,671.9 |
| Currency...................................... | 20a | 857.6 | 1,143.7 | 948.5 | 1,400.5 | 2,811.9 | 2,393.7 | 3,165.1 | 3,861.4 | 5,191.2 | 5,634.6 | 3,812.4 | 3,729.9 |
| Reserve Deposits and Securities..... | 20b | 5,491.8 | 8,519.3 | 9,114.0 | 16,877.5 | 23,199.6 | 27,509.0 | 31,921.9 | 34,385.2 | 36,291.4 | 39,596.5 | 38,172.6 | 30,942.0 |
| Other Claims................................. | 20n | — | — | — | — | — | — | — | — | — | — | — | — |
| Net Claims on Central Government.. | 22an | −2,732.3 | −4,630.1 | −7,452.0 | −13,935.5 | −20,772.3 | −20,421.1 | −13,524.5 | −11,410.1 | −21,464.0 | −27,772.2 | −25,088.4 | −11,166.6 |
| Claims on Central Government...... | 22a | 1,041.2 | 1,325.5 | 2,141.5 | 3,506.3 | 2,851.6 | 3,411.9 | 8,322.5 | 11,725.5 | 11,589.7 | 9,100.1 | 13,405.6 | 19,824.5 |
| Liabilities to Central Government... | 26d | 3,773.5 | 5,955.6 | 9,593.5 | 17,441.8 | 23,623.9 | 23,833.1 | 21,847.0 | 23,135.5 | 33,053.7 | 36,872.3 | 38,494.0 | 30,991.1 |
| Claims on Other Sectors.................. | 22s | 794.0 | 1,711.1 | 2,851.4 | 2,842.2 | 4,399.9 | 5,136.1 | 8,934.2 | 12,611.1 | 20,388.3 | 23,237.3 | 25,441.1 | 26,457.6 |
| Claims on Other Financial Corps.... | 22g | — | — | — | — | — | — | — | — | — | — | — | — |
| Claims on State & Local Govts....... | 22b | — | — | — | — | — | — | — | — | — | — | — | — |
| Claims on Public Nonfin. Corps...... | 22c | 120.0 | 570.0 | 692.0 | 87.9 | 191.2 | 200.6 | 194.3 | 903.5 | 5,377.4 | 5,903.8 | 7,325.3 | 7,217.8 |
| Claims on Private Sector............... | 22d | 674.0 | 1,141.1 | 2,159.4 | 2,754.3 | 4,208.7 | 4,935.5 | 8,739.9 | 11,707.7 | 15,011.0 | 17,333.5 | 18,115.8 | 19,239.8 |
| Liabilities to Central Bank.............. | 26g | — | — | — | — | 4.0 | 2.0 | — | — | — | — | — | — |
| Transf.Dep.Included in Broad Money | 24 | 5,972.8 | 3,628.6 | 5,768.4 | 9,680.1 | 13,055.8 | 18,614.3 | 30,035.5 | 37,979.6 | 37,047.9 | 43,322.7 | 41,326.6 | 34,635.0 |
| Other Dep.Included in Broad Money. | 25 | 1,334.0 | 1,835.4 | 2,189.8 | 3,268.5 | 5,118.9 | 6,343.3 | 6,957.4 | 7,755.9 | 9,435.1 | 11,041.0 | 15,218.0 | 14,757.3 |
| Sec.Ot.th.Shares Incl.in Brd.Money.. | 26a | — | — | — | — | — | — | — | — | — | — | — | — |
| Deposits Excl. from Broad Money..... | 26b | 753.2 | 1,431.0 | 3,400.6 | 2,057.0 | 1,665.6 | 1,809.4 | 1,690.2 | 1,936.6 | 2,246.5 | 2,720.3 | 2,695.5 | 2,296.8 |
| Sec.Ot.th.Shares Excl.f/Brd.Money.... | 26s | — | — | — | — | — | — | — | — | — | — | — | — |
| Loans........................................... | 26l | 150.4 | 151.2 | 153.2 | 166.3 | 375.5 | 377.5 | 472.1 | 679.6 | 729.6 | 613.8 | 499.2 | 477.2 |
| Financial Derivatives..................... | 26m | — | — | — | — | — | — | — | — | — | — | — | — |
| Insurance Technical Reserves........... | 26r | — | — | — | — | — | — | — | — | — | — | — | — |
| Shares and Other Equity................... | 27a | −9,897.5 | −6,367.5 | −6,100.1 | −3,720.9 | −7,498.4 | −3,499.9 | −3,389.5 | −1,936.8 | 8,198.6 | 11,246.3 | 11,806.9 | 12,314.9 |
| Other Items (Net)............................ | 27r | 130.7 | 366.3 | −3,165.0 | −5,758.9 | −2,801.5 | −3,649.6 | −1,484.7 | −4,581.7 | −3,207.1 | −7,552.4 | −3,314.2 | −78.6 |
| Memo Item: | | | | | | | | | | | | | |
| Total Assets.................................... | 20ra | 16,129.1 | 23,289.1 | 30,161.1 | 44,823.3 | 59,616.2 | 81,219.2 | 102,275.4 | 104,179.1 | 125,436.4 | 175,573.2 | 192,586.2 | 190,663.3 |
| **Depository Corporations** | | | | | | | *Billions of New Iraqi Dinars: End of Period* | | | | | | | |
| Net Foreign Assets........................ | 31n | 3,560.1 | −96.8 | 11,836.7 | 36,162.9 | 60,408.8 | 57,298.7 | 61,324.7 | 71,629.9 | 92,454.0 | 109,239.1 | 102,457.5 | 74,818.2 |
| Claims on Nonresidents................ | 31 | 28,138.2 | 25,361.4 | 35,787.7 | 49,400.3 | 70,280.3 | 70,226.9 | 73,863.0 | 84,750.9 | 97,896.7 | 114,453.6 | 106,545.9 | 79,683.8 |
| Liabilities to Nonresidents............. | 36c | 24,578.1 | 25,458.2 | 23,951.0 | 13,237.4 | 9,871.5 | 12,928.2 | 12,538.3 | 13,121.0 | 5,442.7 | 5,214.5 | 4,088.4 | 4,865.6 |
| Domestic Claims............................ | 32 | 3,779.4 | −705.6 | −3,503.3 | −12,516.4 | −25,718.0 | −12,561.6 | −2,020.0 | −1,125.8 | −4,624.1 | −3,700.5 | 945.6 | 18,315.8 |
| Net Claims on Central Government | 32an | 2,984.9 | −2,419.9 | −6,359.4 | −15,363.8 | −30,121.0 | −17,698.9 | −10,954.6 | −13,796.4 | −25,086.0 | −27,020.7 | −24,575.8 | −8,230.0 |
| Claims on Central Government..... | 32a | 7,446.9 | 7,831.4 | 8,622.2 | 9,193.4 | 6,824.9 | 7,385.5 | 12,816.9 | 15,287.2 | 14,745.3 | 11,855.7 | 15,892.0 | 28,515.7 |
| Liabilities to Central Government. | 36d | 4,462.0 | 10,251.3 | 14,981.6 | 24,557.2 | 36,945.8 | 25,084.3 | 23,771.4 | 29,083.5 | 39,831.2 | 38,876.4 | 40,467.8 | 36,745.7 |
| Claims on Other Sectors................. | 32s | 794.5 | 1,714.4 | 2,856.2 | 2,847.4 | 4,402.9 | 5,137.3 | 8,934.6 | 12,670.5 | 20,461.9 | 23,320.3 | 25,521.4 | 26,545.9 |
| Claims on Other Financial Corps.. | 32g | — | — | — | — | — | — | — | — | — | — | — | 7.5 |
| Claims on State & Local Govts..... | 32b | — | — | — | — | — | — | — | — | — | — | — | — |
| Claims on Public Nonfin. Corps.... | 32c | 120.0 | 570.0 | 692.0 | 87.9 | 191.2 | 200.6 | 194.3 | 903.5 | 5,377.4 | 5,903.8 | 7,325.3 | 7,217.8 |
| Claims on Private Sector.............. | 32d | 674.5 | 1,144.3 | 2,164.1 | 2,759.4 | 4,211.8 | 4,936.7 | 8,740.3 | 11,767.1 | 15,084.5 | 17,416.5 | 18,196.1 | 19,320.5 |
| Broad Money Liabilities................. | 35l | 14,355.9 | 14,888.0 | 19,920.3 | 27,311.7 | 36,929.6 | 46,791.2 | 61,393.1 | 74,098.0 | 77,142.2 | 89,378.9 | 92,637.7 | 84,271.9 |
| Currency Outside Depository Corps | 34a | 6,734.4 | 9,112.8 | 10,968.1 | 14,231.7 | 18,492.5 | 21,775.7 | 24,342.2 | 28,296.0 | 30,593.7 | 34,995.5 | 36,071.3 | 34,855.3 |
| Transferable Deposits.................... | 34 | 6,287.5 | 3,871.0 | 6,701.0 | 9,755.2 | 13,263.9 | 18,618.0 | 30,039.2 | 37,991.9 | 37,059.4 | 43,342.4 | 41,348.5 | 34,659.3 |
| Other Deposits.............................. | 35 | 1,334.0 | 1,904.2 | 2,251.2 | 3,324.8 | 5,173.2 | 6,397.6 | 7,011.6 | 7,810.1 | 9,489.1 | 11,041.0 | 15,218.0 | 14,757.3 |
| Securities Other than Shares......... | 36a | — | — | — | — | — | — | — | — | — | — | — | — |
| Deposits Excl. from Broad Money.... | 36b | 754.0 | 1,431.7 | 3,401.3 | 2,057.1 | 1,665.7 | 1,809.5 | 1,690.3 | 1,936.7 | 2,246.6 | 2,720.4 | 2,695.6 | 2,296.9 |
| Sec.Ot.th.Shares Excl.f/Brd.Money.... | 36s | — | — | — | — | — | — | — | — | — | — | — | — |
| Loans........................................... | 36l | 150.4 | 151.2 | 153.2 | 166.3 | 375.5 | 377.5 | 472.1 | 679.6 | 729.6 | 613.8 | 499.2 | 477.2 |
| Financial Derivatives..................... | 36m | — | — | — | — | — | — | — | — | — | — | — | — |
| Insurance Technical Reserves........... | 36r | — | — | — | — | — | — | — | — | — | — | — | — |
| Shares and Other Equity................. | 37a | −10,025.6 | −6,496.5 | −5,955.1 | 4,924.7 | −6,392.0 | 158.6 | −3,185.5 | −680.3 | 11,331.8 | 16,708.8 | 15,086.9 | 14,482.5 |
| Other Items (Net)........................... | 37r | 2,104.8 | −10,776.8 | −9,186.2 | −10,813.5 | 2,112.0 | −4,399.7 | −1,065.2 | −5,530.0 | −3,620.3 | −3,883.2 | −7,516.4 | −8,394.4 |
| Broad Money Liabs., Seasonally Adj. | 35l.b | 13,819.1 | 14,347.9 | 19,229.3 | 26,439.2 | 35,878.8 | 45,657.0 | 60,129.7 | 72,779.3 | 75,966.2 | 88,231.6 | 91,617.9 | 83,423.7 |
| **Monetary Aggregates** | | | | | | | *Billions of New Iraqi Dinars: End of Period* | | | | | | | |
| Broad Money................................. | 59m | 14,355.9 | 14,888.0 | 19,920.3 | 27,311.7 | 36,929.6 | 46,791.2 | 61,393.1 | 74,098.0 | 77,142.2 | 89,378.9 | 92,637.7 | 84,271.9 |
| o/w:Currency Issued by Cent.Govt | 59m.a | — | — | — | — | — | — | — | — | — | — | — | — |
| o/w: Dep.in Nonfin. Corporations. | 59m.b | — | — | — | — | — | — | — | — | — | — | — | — |
| o/w:Secs. Issued by Central Govt.. | 59m.c | — | — | — | — | — | — | — | — | — | — | — | — |
| Money (National Definitions) | | | | | | | | | | | | | |
| M0................................................ | 19mc | 12,219 | 13,795 | 17,521 | 28,808 | 42,859 | 45,270 | 53,810 | 58,698 | 63,391 | 73,259 | 66,047 | 57,888 |
| M1................................................ | 59ma | 10,149 | 11,399 | 15,460 | 21,721 | 28,190 | 37,300 | 51,743 | 62,476 | 63,736 | 73,831 | 72,651 | .... |
| M2................................................ | 59mb | 12,254 | 14,684 | 21,080 | 26,956 | 34,920 | 45,438 | 60,386 | 72,180 | 75,466 | 87,679 | 91,704 | 82,600 |
| **Interest Rates** | | | | | | | *Percent Per Annum* | | | | | | | |
| Central Bank Policy Rate (EOP)........ | 60 | 6.00 | 7.00 | 16.00 | 20.00 | 15.00 | 7.00 | 6.00 | 6.00 | 6.00 | 6.00 | 6.00 | 6.00 |
| Treasury Bill Rate............................ | 60c | 5.33 | 7.07 | 9.49 | 21.00 | 17.67 | 7.43 | † 8.94 | 9.49 | 6.15 | .... | .... | .... |
| Savings Rate.................................. | 60k | 6.50 | 5.59 | 5.66 | 9.18 | 9.47 | 6.84 | 5.52 | 5.24 | 5.06 | 4.88 | .... | .... |
| Savings Rate (Fgn. Currency)............ | 60k.f | 3.10 | 2.71 | 2.82 | 3.51 | 3.41 | 2.82 | 2.62 | 2.77 | 2.88 | 2.79 | .... | .... |
| Deposit Rate................................... | 60l | 8.00 | 6.56 | 6.62 | 10.43 | 10.54 | 7.82 | 6.06 | 5.91 | 5.87 | 5.75 | .... | .... |
| Deposit Rate (Fgn. Currency)............ | 60l.f | 4.10 | 3.32 | 3.47 | 4.10 | 4.60 | 3.31 | 2.87 | 2.93 | 3.03 | 3.01 | .... | .... |
| Lending Rate.................................. | 60p | 13.28 | 13.65 | 14.48 | 19.47 | 19.50 | 15.63 | 13.33 | 13.61 | 13.03 | 13.13 | .... | .... |
| Lending Rate (Fgn. Currency).......... | 60p.f | 8.60 | 9.97 | 11.40 | 14.59 | 16.60 | 16.01 | 13.89 | 13.11 | 12.67 | 12.86 | .... | .... |
| **Prices and Production** | | | | | | | *Index Numbers (2010=100): Period Averages* | | | | | | | |
| Consumer Prices............................. | 64 | 42.8 | 58.6 | 89.8 | 80.7 | 91.0 | † 97.2 | 100.0 | 105.8 | 112.2 | 114.4 | 116.9 | 115.5 |
| Crude Petroleum............................ | 66aa | 85.9 | 79.3 | 78.8 | 84.9 | 92.3 | 98.7 | 100.0 | 109.6 | 122.7 | 124.3 | 135.6 | 164.3 |

# Iraq   433

| | | 2004 | 2005 | 2006 | 2007 | 2008 | 2009 | 2010 | 2011 | 2012 | 2013 | 2014 | 2015 |
|---|---|---|---|---|---|---|---|---|---|---|---|---|---|
| **Balance of Payments** | | | | | | *Millions of US Dollars* | | | | | | | |
| A. Current Account*...................... | 109bx | .... | −7,513.0 | 1,252.1 | 14,056.4 | 28,280.3 | −1,151.8 | 6,488.3 | 26,126.0 | 29,541.0 | .... | .... | .... |
| Goods, credit (exports)................... | 1a9cx | .... | 23,697.4 | 30,529.4 | 39,587.0 | 63,728.2 | 39,429.3 | 51,760.3 | 79,684.0 | 94,207.0 | .... | .... | .... |
| Goods, debit (imports)................... | 1a9dx | .... | 20,002.2 | 18,707.5 | 16,622.5 | 29,761.4 | 35,284.8 | 37,328.0 | 40,633.0 | 50,155.0 | .... | .... | .... |
| Balance on goods................. | 1a9bx | .... | 3,695.2 | 11,821.9 | 22,964.5 | 33,966.8 | 4,144.5 | 14,432.3 | 39,051.0 | 44,052.0 | .... | .... | .... |
| Services, credit (exports)............... | 1b9cx | .... | 355.2 | 357.1 | 867.9 | 1,496.4 | 2,193.4 | 2,833.6 | 2,822.0 | 2,833.0 | .... | .... | .... |
| Services, debit (imports)................ | 1b9dx | .... | 6,094.5 | 5,490.0 | 4,865.6 | 7,572.0 | 8,563.1 | 9,863.5 | 11,124.0 | 13,291.0 | .... | .... | .... |
| Balance on Goods & Services....... | 1z9bx | .... | −2,044.1 | 6,689.0 | 18,966.8 | 27,891.2 | −2,225.2 | 7,402.4 | 30,749.0 | 33,594.0 | .... | .... | .... |
| Primary income: credit.................. | 1c9cx | .... | 680.2 | 1,205.5 | 1,923.4 | 4,038.8 | 3,412.2 | 2,079.9 | 1,172.0 | 2,080.0 | .... | .... | .... |
| Primary income: debit.................. | 1c9dx | .... | 5,207.4 | 4,751.0 | 4,990.4 | 553.6 | 317.1 | 486.7 | 1,409.0 | 1,021.0 | .... | .... | .... |
| Balance on gds, serv. & prim. inc. | 1y9bx | .... | −6,571.3 | 3,143.5 | 15,899.8 | 31,376.4 | 869.9 | 8,995.6 | 30,512.0 | 34,653.0 | .... | .... | .... |
| Secondary income: credit.............. | 1d9ca | .... | 551.6 | 261.2 | 88.5 | 188.0 | 221.4 | 240.8 | 371.0 | 413.0 | .... | .... | .... |
| Secondary income: debit............... | 1d9da | .... | 1,493.3 | 2,152.6 | 1,931.9 | 3,284.1 | 2,243.1 | 2,748.1 | 4,757.0 | 5,525.0 | .... | .... | .... |
| B. Capital Account*.................... | 209ba | .... | 3,888.9 | 2,769.0 | 675.1 | 440.8 | 10.2 | 25.3 | 11.0 | 7.0 | .... | .... | .... |
| Capital account: credit.................. | 209ca | .... | 3,888.9 | 2,769.0 | 675.1 | 440.8 | 11.7 | 25.3 | 11.0 | 7.0 | .... | .... | .... |
| Capital account: debit.................. | 209da | .... | — | — | — | — | 1.5 | — | — | — | .... | .... | .... |
| Balance on current & capital acct. | 129bx | .... | −3,624.1 | 4,021.1 | 14,731.5 | 28,721.1 | −1,141.6 | 6,513.6 | 26,137.0 | 29,548.0 | .... | .... | .... |
| C. Financial Account* ................. | 309na | .... | 1,349.6 | 3,067.5 | 5,274.3 | 986.0 | −3,083.6 | −7,703.1 | 12,474.0 | 16,177.0 | .... | .... | .... |
| Direct investment: assets............. | 3a9aa | .... | 88.7 | 305.0 | 7.9 | 33.6 | 71.9 | 124.9 | 366.0 | 490.0 | .... | .... | .... |
| Equity & investment fund shares.. | 3aaaa | .... | 88.7 | 305.0 | 7.9 | 33.6 | 71.9 | 124.9 | 366.0 | 490.0 | .... | .... | .... |
| Debt instruments....................... | 3abaa | .... | | | | | | | | | .... | .... | .... |
| Direct investment: liabilities .......... | 3a9la | .... | 515.3 | 383.0 | 971.8 | 1,855.7 | 1,598.3 | 1,396.2 | 2,082.0 | 3,400.0 | .... | .... | .... |
| Equity & investment fund shares . | 3aala | .... | 515.3 | 383.0 | 971.8 | 1,855.7 | 1,598.3 | 1,396.2 | 2,082.0 | 3,400.0 | .... | .... | .... |
| Debt instruments....................... | 3abla | .... | | | | | | | | | .... | .... | .... |
| Portfolio investment: assets .......... | 3b9aa | .... | 1,967.7 | 3,669.6 | 1,773.5 | 2,807.2 | −3,646.3 | −727.1 | 6,573.0 | 5,679.0 | .... | .... | .... |
| Equity & investment fund shares | 3baaa | .... | | | | | | | | | .... | .... | .... |
| Debt securities .......................... | 3bbaa | .... | 1,967.7 | 3,669.6 | 1,773.5 | 2,807.2 | −3,646.3 | −727.1 | 6,573.0 | 5,679.0 | .... | .... | .... |
| Portfolio investment: liabilities....... | 3b9la | .... | — | — | — | 8.5 | 2.9 | 56.5 | 43.0 | 7.0 | .... | .... | .... |
| Equity & investment fund shares . | 3bala | .... | — | .... | .... | 8.5 | 2.9 | 56.5 | 169.0 | 7.0 | .... | .... | .... |
| Debt securities.......................... | 3bbla | .... | — | .... | .... | — | — | — | −126.0 | — | .... | .... | .... |
| Fin. der.& empl.stk.ops.(ESOs): net. | 3c9na | .... | — | — | — | — | — | — | — | — | .... | .... | .... |
| Fin. der. & ESOs.: assets.............. | 3c9aa | .... | — | — | — | — | — | — | — | — | .... | .... | .... |
| Fin. der. & ESOs.: liabilities.......... | 3c9la | .... | — | — | — | — | — | — | — | — | .... | .... | .... |
| Other investment: assets................ | 3d9aa | .... | 282.5 | −1,846.5 | 4,938.9 | −41.9 | 5,362.4 | −5,310.4 | 8,226.0 | 4,967.0 | .... | .... | .... |
| Other equity............................. | 3daaa | .... | .... | .... | .... | .... | .... | .... | .... | .... | .... | .... | .... |
| Debt instruments....................... | 3dzaa | .... | 282.5 | −1,846.5 | 4,938.9 | −41.9 | 5,362.4 | −5,310.4 | 8,226.0 | 4,967.0 | .... | .... | .... |
| Other investment: liabilities............ | 3d9la | .... | 474.0 | −1,322.3 | 474.2 | −51.3 | 3,270.4 | 337.8 | 566.0 | −8,448.0 | .... | .... | .... |
| Other equity............................. | 3dala | .... | | | | | | | | | .... | .... | .... |
| Debt instruments....................... | 3dzla | .... | 474.0 | −1,322.3 | 474.2 | −51.3 | 3,270.4 | 337.8 | 566.0 | −8,448.0 | .... | .... | .... |
| Curr.+ cap.– finan. acct. balance... | 4y9na | .... | −4,973.7 | 953.6 | 9,457.2 | 27,735.1 | 1,942.0 | 14,216.7 | 13,663.0 | 13,371.0 | .... | .... | .... |
| D. Net Errors and Omissions............ | 409na | .... | 450.9 | 579.1 | −3,662.2 | −9,244.5 | −7,787.4 | −9,150.6 | −3,738.8 | −4,116.2 | .... | .... | .... |
| E. Reserves and Related Items.......... | 4z9na | .... | −4,522.8 | 1,532.8 | 5,795.1 | 18,490.6 | −5,845.4 | 5,066.1 | 9,924.2 | 9,254.8 | .... | .... | .... |
| Reserve assets............................ | 3e9aa | .... | 4,337.8 | 7,362.8 | 11,339.8 | 18,650.6 | −5,822.1 | 6,266.2 | 10,393.6 | 9,254.8 | .... | .... | .... |
| Credit and loans from the IMF....... | 3dcla | .... | — | — | −468.2 | — | — | 1,200.1 | 469.5 | — | .... | .... | .... |
| Exceptional financing.................... | 409la | .... | 8,860.6 | 5,830.0 | 6,012.9 | 160.0 | 23.3 | — | — | — | .... | .... | .... |
| *Excludes components in group E | | | | | | | | | | | | | |

| | | 2004 | 2005 | 2006 | 2007 | 2008 | 2009 | 2010 | 2011 | 2012 | 2013 | 2014 | 2015 |
|---|---|---|---|---|---|---|---|---|---|---|---|---|---|
| **International Investment Position** | | | | | | *Millions of US Dollars* | | | | | | | |
| Assets............................................ | 809aa | .... | .... | 33,907.9 | 48,743.8 | 68,391.3 | 67,820.4 | 68,963.3 | 86,838.5 | † 102,629.8 | .... | .... | .... |
| Direct investment....................... | 8a9aa | .... | .... | .... | .... | .... | .... | .... | .... | .... | .... | .... | .... |
| Equity & investment fund shares.. | 8aaaa | .... | .... | .... | .... | .... | .... | .... | .... | .... | .... | .... | .... |
| Debt instruments........................ | 8abaa | .... | .... | .... | .... | .... | .... | .... | .... | .... | .... | .... | .... |
| Portfolio investment...................... | 8b9aa | .... | .... | 8,116.7 | 7,466.1 | 10,273.5 | 6,627.4 | 5,925.0 | 12,573.0 | † 18,167.7 | .... | .... | .... |
| Equity & investment fund shares.. | 8baaa | .... | .... | .... | .... | .... | .... | .... | .... | † 14.7 | .... | .... | .... |
| Debt securities............................ | 8bbaa | .... | .... | 8,116.7 | 7,466.1 | 10,273.5 | 6,627.4 | 5,925.0 | 12,573.0 | † 18,153.0 | .... | .... | .... |
| Fin. der.(oth.than reserves) & ESOs | 8c9aa | .... | .... | .... | .... | .... | .... | .... | .... | .... | .... | .... | .... |
| Other investment....................... | 8d9aa | .... | .... | 5,750.6 | 9,822.3 | 7,912.2 | 16,857.3 | 12,395.3 | 13,224.0 | † 14,135.8 | .... | .... | .... |
| Other equity............................. | 8daaa | .... | .... | .... | .... | .... | .... | .... | .... | .... | .... | .... | .... |
| Debt instruments....................... | 8dzaa | .... | .... | 5,750.6 | 9,822.3 | 7,912.2 | 16,857.3 | 12,395.3 | 13,224.0 | † 14,135.8 | .... | .... | .... |
| Reserve assets............................ | 8e9aa | .... | .... | 20,040.6 | 31,455.4 | 50,205.6 | 44,335.7 | 50,643.0 | 61,041.5 | † 70,326.3 | .... | .... | .... |
| Liabilities..................................... | 809la | .... | .... | 83,995.5 | 84,777.8 | 75,587.0 | 80,875.5 | 73,537.7 | 75,150.8 | † 76,457.2 | .... | .... | .... |
| Direct investment....................... | 8a9la | .... | .... | 898.0 | 1,870.0 | 3,726.0 | 5,581.7 | 7,033.2 | 8,803.0 | † 12,203.0 | .... | .... | .... |
| Equity & investment fund shares.. | 8aala | .... | .... | 898.0 | 1,870.0 | 3,726.0 | 5,581.7 | 7,033.2 | 8,803.0 | † 12,203.0 | .... | .... | .... |
| Debt instruments........................ | 8abla | .... | .... | .... | .... | .... | .... | .... | .... | .... | .... | .... | .... |
| Portfolio investment...................... | 8b9la | .... | .... | 1,177.0 | 799.0 | 889.0 | 1,338.0 | 1,152.0 | 1,472.0 | † 1,890.0 | .... | .... | .... |
| Equity & investment fund shares.. | 8bala | .... | .... | 16.0 | 40.0 | 40.0 | 117.0 | 117.0 | 409.0 | † 287.0 | .... | .... | .... |
| Debt securities............................ | 8bbla | .... | .... | 1,161.0 | 759.0 | 849.0 | 1,221.0 | 1,035.0 | 1,063.0 | † 1,603.0 | .... | .... | .... |
| Fin. der.(oth.than reserves) & ESOs | 8c9la | .... | .... | .... | .... | .... | .... | .... | .... | .... | .... | .... | .... |
| Other investment.......................... | 8d9la | .... | .... | 81,920.5 | 82,108.8 | 70,972.0 | 73,955.8 | 65,352.5 | 64,875.8 | † 62,364.2 | .... | .... | .... |
| Other equity............................. | 8dala | .... | .... | .... | .... | .... | .... | .... | .... | .... | .... | .... | .... |
| Debt instruments....................... | 8dzla | .... | .... | 81,920.5 | 82,108.8 | 70,972.0 | 73,955.8 | 65,352.5 | 64,875.8 | † 62,364.2 | .... | .... | .... |

| | | 2004 | 2005 | 2006 | 2007 | 2008 | 2009 | 2010 | 2011 | 2012 | 2013 | 2014 | 2015 |
|---|---|---|---|---|---|---|---|---|---|---|---|---|---|
| **National Accounts** | | | | | | *Billions of Iraqi Dinar* | | | | | | | |
| Gross Domestic Product (GDP)........ | 99b | 53,235 | 73,533 | 95,588 | 111,456 | 157,026 | 130,642 | 158,522 | 211,310 | 214,768 | 235,550 | .... | .... |
| GDP Volume 1988 Prices................ | 99b.p | 42.0 | 43.0 | 48.0 | 49.0 | 51.7 | 54.7 | 57.9 | 62.9 | .... | .... | .... | .... |
| GDP Volume (2010=100)............... | 99bvp | 72.5 | 74.2 | 82.9 | 84.6 | 89.3 | 94.5 | 100.0 | 108.6 | .... | .... | .... | .... |
| GDP Deflator (2010=100).............. | 99bip | 46 | 62 | 73 | 83 | 111 | 87 | 100 | 123 | .... | .... | .... | .... |
| | | | | | | *Millions: Midyear Estimates* | | | | | | | |
| Population................................ | 99z | 26.32 | 27.02 | 27.72 | 28.42 | 29.16 | 29.97 | 30.87 | 31.87 | 32.96 | 34.11 | 35.27 | 36.42 |

# Ireland 178

| | | 2004 | 2005 | 2006 | 2007 | 2008 | 2009 | 2010 | 2011 | 2012 | 2013 | 2014 | 2015 |
|---|---|---|---|---|---|---|---|---|---|---|---|---|---|
| **Exchange Rates** | | | | | | *Euros per SDR: End of Period* | | | | | | | |
| Market Rate.............................. | aa | 1.1402 | 1.2116 | 1.1423 | 1.0735 | 1.1068 | 1.0882 | 1.1525 | 1.1865 | 1.1649 | 1.1167 | 1.1933 | 1.2728 |
| | | | | | | *Euros per US Dollar: End of Period (ae) Period Average (rf)* | | | | | | | |
| Market Rate.............................. | ae | .7342 | .8477 | .7593 | .6793 | .7185 | .6942 | .7484 | .7729 | .7579 | .7251 | .8237 | .9185 |
| Market Rate.............................. | rf | .8054 | .8041 | .7971 | .7306 | .6827 | .7198 | .7550 | .7194 | .7783 | .7532 | .7537 | .9017 |
| | | | | | | *Index Numbers (2010=100): Period Averages* | | | | | | | |
| Nominal Effective Exchange Rate..... | nec | 97.03 | 96.86 | 97.10 | 100.31 | 104.45 | 104.12 | 100.00 | 100.52 | 96.24 | 99.32 | 99.26 | 92.18 |
| CPI-Based Real Effect. Ex. Rate........ | rec | 99.82 | 99.81 | 101.74 | 107.45 | 112.52 | 107.18 | 100.00 | 100.11 | 95.42 | 97.36 | 96.17 | 88.65 |
| ULC-Based Real Effect. Ex. Rate....... | rel | 130.77 | 139.76 | 140.44 | 137.88 | 137.09 | 116.87 | 100.00 | 91.42 | 87.50 | 89.53 | 89.47 | 83.60 |
| **Fund Position** | | | | | | *Millions of SDRs: End of Period* | | | | | | | |
| Quota.......................................... | 2f.s | 838.40 | 838.40 | 838.40 | 838.40 | 838.40 | 838.40 | 838.40 | 1,257.60 | 1,257.60 | 1,257.60 | 1,257.60 | 1,257.60 |
| SDR Holdings................................. | 1b.s | 57.33 | 61.64 | 63.11 | 63.60 | 63.74 | 752.21 | 717.00 | 635.52 | 641.26 | 650.00 | 651.18 | 650.94 |
| Reserve Position in the Fund............ | 1c.s | 269.23 | 123.25 | 87.28 | 55.34 | 106.29 | 156.22 | 153.69 | 258.53 | 258.61 | 258.66 | 258.70 | 258.70 |
| Total Fund Cred.&Loans Outstg....... | 2tl | — | — | — | — | — | — | — | 11,050.43 | 16,543.43 | 19,465.80 | 11,821.85 | 3,772.80 |
| SDR Allocations.............................. | 1bd | 87.26 | 87.26 | 87.26 | 87.26 | 87.26 | 775.42 | 775.42 | 775.42 | 775.42 | 775.42 | 775.42 | 775.42 |
| **International Liquidity** | | | | | | *Millions of US Dollars Unless Otherwise Indicated: End of Period* | | | | | | | |
| Total Res.Min.Gold (Eurosys.Def)..... | 1l.d | 2,831 | 779 | 720 | 779 | 871 | 1,941 | 1,843 | 1,399 | 1,386 | 1,403 | 1,517 | 1,999 |
| SDR Holdings.............................. | 1b.d | 89 | 88 | 95 | 101 | 98 | 1,179 | 1,104 | 976 | 986 | 1,001 | 943 | 902 |
| Reserve Position in the Fund.......... | 1c.d | 418 | 176 | 131 | 87 | 164 | 245 | 237 | 397 | 397 | 398 | 375 | 358 |
| Foreign Exchange......................... | 1d.d | 2,324 | 514 | 494 | 591 | 609 | 517 | 502 | 27 | 3 | 4 | 198 | 738 |
| o/w:Fin.Deriv.Rel.to Reserves...... | 1ddd | — | — | — | — | — | — | — | — | -.01 | .23 | — | — |
| Other Reserve Assets.................... | 1e.d | — | — | — | — | — | — | — | — | — | — | — | — |
| Gold (Million Fine Troy Ounces)....... | 1ad | .176 | .176 | .176 | .176 | .193 | .193 | .193 | .193 | .193 | .193 | .193 | .193 |
| Gold (Eurosystem Valuation)........... | 1and | 77 | 90 | 112 | 147 | 167 | 213 | 272 | 304 | 321 | 232 | 231 | 204 |
| Memo:Euro Cl. on Non-EA Res........ | 1dgd | 1,472.43 | 2,531.64 | .... | .... | .... | .... | .... | .... | .... | .... | .... | .... |
| Non-Euro Cl. on EA Res........ | 1dhd | 111.69 | 50.62 | 42.58 | 658.28 | 7,378.13 | 10.50 | 56.57 | 1,457.79 | 664.54 | — | — | .... |
| Central Bank: Other Assets.............. | 3..d | 9,200 | 10,209 | 12,988 | 13,357 | 21,753 | 23,940 | 23,725 | 26,593 | 26,141 | 27,699 | 24,620 | 21,255 |
| Central Bank: Other Liabs................. | 4..d | 610 | 137 | 143 | 141 | 144 | 1,226 | 1,208 | 1,219 | 1,221 | 1,218 | 1,125 | 1,076 |
| Other Depository Corps.: Assets....... | 7a.d | 433,678 | 509,694 | 747,608 | 991,468 | 957,974 | 916,969 | 776,443 | 627,742 | 593,483 | 532,888 | 537,888 | 520,595 |
| Other Depository Corps.: Liabs......... | 7b.d | 476,946 | 553,957 | 786,197 | 1,047,649 | 927,255 | 887,158 | 670,199 | 514,260 | 505,589 | 485,771 | 509,660 | 526,396 |
| **Central Bank** | | | | | | *Millions of Euros: End of Period* | | | | | | | |
| Euro Area Wide Residency Criterion | | | | | | | | | | | | | |
| Net Foreign Assets........................... | 11n.u | 3,194 | 2,784 | 3,507 | 1,620 | 1,895 | 1,895 | 1,579 | 1,620 | 1,617 | 1,836 | 2,681 | 3,869 |
| Claims on Nonresidents................ | 11..u | 3,642 | 2,901 | 3,616 | 1,716 | 1,998 | 2,746 | 2,483 | 2,563 | 2,542 | 2,719 | 3,608 | 4,857 |
| Liabilities to Nonresidents............. | 16c.u | 448 | 117 | 109 | 96 | 104 | 851 | 904 | 943 | 925 | 883 | 926 | 988 |
| Claims on Other Depository Corps.... | 12e.u | 18,752 | 22,983 | 29,302 | 41,005 | 96,247 | 96,727 | 135,429 | 110,517 | 114,761 | 42,390 | 24,250 | 16,518 |
| Net Claims on Central Government.. | 12anu | −382 | −147 | −1,184 | −1,857 | −14,158 | −14,318 | −293 | 2,526 | −1,574 | 38,376 | 44,860 | 40,449 |
| Claims on Central Govt................. | 12a.u | 3,495 | 4,093 | 4,279 | 6,168 | 11,659 | 11,942 | 15,597 | 18,098 | 18,062 | 48,637 | 51,671 | 54,167 |
| Liabs. to Central Govt.................. | 16d.u | 3,877 | 4,240 | 5,463 | 8,025 | 25,817 | 26,260 | 15,890 | 15,572 | 19,636 | 10,261 | 6,811 | 13,718 |
| Claims on Other Sectors............... | 12s.u | 6 | 4 | 4 | 3 | 3 | 2 | 1 | 1 | 1 | 12,639 | 426 | 253 |
| Claims on Other Financial Corps... | 12g.u | — | — | — | — | — | — | — | — | — | 12,638 | 426 | 253 |
| Claims on State & Local Govts...... | 12b.u | — | — | — | — | — | — | — | — | — | — | — | — |
| Claims on Public Nonfin. Corps...... | 12c.u | — | — | — | — | — | — | — | — | — | — | — | — |
| Claims on Private Sector............... | 12d.u | 6 | 4 | 4 | 3 | 3 | 2 | 1 | 1 | 1 | 1 | — | — |
| Monetary Base............................ | 14..u | 10,779 | 15,499 | 20,936 | 30,450 | 29,092 | 27,388 | 24,380 | 19,702 | 17,517 | 17,969 | 20,260 | 27,154 |
| Currency in Circulation................. | 14a.u | 6,437 | 7,247 | 8,021 | 8,611 | 9,645 | 12,480 | 12,966 | 13,673 | 13,999 | 14,726 | 16,205 | 17,136 |
| Liabs. to Other Depository Corps.... | 14c.u | 4,342 | 8,252 | 12,915 | 21,839 | 19,447 | 14,908 | 11,414 | 6,029 | 3,518 | 3,243 | 4,055 | 10,018 |
| Liabs. to Other Sectors................. | 14d.u | — | — | — | — | — | — | — | — | — | — | — | — |
| Other Liabs. to Other Dep. Corps...... | 14n.u | — | — | — | — | — | — | — | — | — | — | — | — |
| Dep. & Sec. Excl. f/Monetary Base.... | 14o.u | — | — | — | — | — | — | — | — | — | — | — | — |
| Deposits Included in Broad Money. | 15..u | — | — | — | — | — | — | — | — | — | — | — | — |
| Sec.Ot.th.Shares Inc.in.Brd.Money. | 16a.u | — | — | — | — | — | — | — | — | — | — | — | — |
| Deposits Excl. from Broad Money... | 16b.u | — | — | — | — | — | — | — | — | — | — | — | — |
| Sec.Oh.th.Shares Excl. f/Brd.Money | 16s.u | — | — | — | — | — | — | — | — | — | — | — | — |
| Loans........................................... | 16l.u | — | — | — | — | — | — | — | — | — | — | — | — |
| Financial Derivatives....................... | 16m.u | — | — | — | — | — | — | — | — | — | — | — | — |
| Shares and Other Equity................. | 17a.u | 1,488 | 1,526 | 1,172 | 1,184 | 1,408 | 1,528 | 1,760 | 2,026 | 2,213 | 5,388 | 12,065 | 13,478 |
| Other Items (Net)............................ | 17r.u | 9,305 | 8,599 | 9,520 | 9,135 | 53,486 | 55,388 | 110,575 | 92,939 | 95,076 | 71,883 | 39,891 | 20,458 |
| Memorandum Items | | | | | | | | | | | | | |
| National Residency Criterion | | | | | | | | | | | | | |
| Net Foreign Assets........................... | 11n | 1,765 | 4,772 | 7,848 | 9,421 | −28,091 | −36,256 | −126,750 | −99,508 | −59,077 | −34,729 | −1,944 | 17,522 |
| Claims on Nonresidents................ | 11 | 8,894 | 9,398 | 10,502 | 9,713 | 16,376 | 18,114 | 19,339 | 21,869 | 21,107 | 21,271 | 21,719 | 21,547 |
| Liabilities to Nonresidents............. | 16c | 7,129 | 4,626 | 2,654 | 292 | 44,468 | 54,370 | 146,089 | 121,377 | 80,184 | 56,000 | 23,662 | 4,025 |
| Claims on Other Depository Corps.... | 12e | 17,508 | 21,070 | 27,171 | 39,597 | 93,543 | 92,952 | 132,306 | 107,386 | 112,434 | 39,777 | 21,712 | 12,738 |
| Net Claims on Central Government.. | 12an | −3,877 | −4,218 | −5,426 | −7,934 | −25,320 | −25,271 | −13,386 | −13,009 | −17,172 | 23,081 | 29,974 | 28,225 |
| Claims on Central Government....... | 12a | — | 22 | 37 | 91 | 497 | 989 | 2,504 | 2,563 | 2,464 | 33,342 | 36,785 | 41,943 |
| Liabilities to Central Government.... | 16d | 3,877 | 4,240 | 5,463 | 8,025 | 25,817 | 26,260 | 15,890 | 15,572 | 19,636 | 10,261 | 6,811 | 13,718 |
| Claims on Other Sectors............... | 12s | 6 | 4 | 4 | 3 | 3 | 2 | 1 | 1 | 1 | 12,639 | 426 | 253 |
| Claims on Other Fin. Corps........... | 12g | — | — | — | — | — | — | — | — | — | 12,638 | 426 | 253 |
| Claims on State & Local Govts....... | 12b | — | — | — | — | — | — | — | — | — | — | — | — |
| Claims on Private Sector............... | 12d | 6 | 4 | 4 | 3 | 3 | 2 | 1 | 1 | 1 | 1 | — | — |
| Liabs.to ODCs, Inc.in Mon.Base....... | 14c | 4,342 | 8,252 | 12,915 | 21,839 | 19,447 | 14,908 | 11,414 | 6,029 | 3,518 | 3,243 | 4,055 | 10,018 |
| Liabs.to Ot.Sectors, Inc.in Mon.Base | 14d | — | — | — | — | — | — | — | — | — | — | — | — |
| Liabs.to ODCs,Excl.f/Mon.Base........ | 14n | — | — | — | — | — | — | — | — | — | — | — | — |
| Net Claims on Eurosystem.............. | 12e.s | −6,111 | −3,939 | −1,975 | 373 | −43,795 | −52,758 | −144,406 | −119,636 | −78,443 | −54,294 | −21,850 | −2,152 |

# Ireland 178

| | | 2004 | 2005 | 2006 | 2007 | 2008 | 2009 | 2010 | 2011 | 2012 | 2013 | 2014 | 2015 |
|---|---|---|---|---|---|---|---|---|---|---|---|---|---|
| **Other Depository Corporations** | | | | | | | *Millions of Euros: End of Period* | | | | | | | |
| Euro Area Wide Residency Criterion | | | | | | | | | | | | | |
| Net Foreign Assets | 21n.u | −31,766 | −37,521 | −29,301 | −38,163 | 22,073 | 20,694 | 79,512 | 87,706 | 66,617 | 34,165 | 23,250 | −5,329 |
| Claims on Nonresidents | 21..u | 318,389 | 432,054 | 567,660 | 673,506 | 688,348 | 636,519 | 581,083 | 485,155 | 449,813 | 386,403 | 443,034 | 478,180 |
| Liabilities to Nonresidents | 26c.u | 350,155 | 469,575 | 596,961 | 711,669 | 666,275 | 615,825 | 501,571 | 397,449 | 383,196 | 352,238 | 419,784 | 483,509 |
| Claims on Eurosystem | 20..u | 5,890 | 10,013 | 14,860 | 24,183 | 21,887 | 17,529 | 13,551 | 7,970 | 4,994 | 4,827 | 5,603 | 11,599 |
| Currency | 20a.u | 1,130 | 1,143 | 1,247 | 1,629 | 1,561 | 1,308 | 1,232 | 1,205 | 1,095 | 1,206 | 1,161 | 1,189 |
| Reserve Deposits and Securities | 20b.u | 4,760 | 8,870 | 13,613 | 22,554 | 20,326 | 16,221 | 12,319 | 6,765 | 3,899 | 3,621 | 4,442 | 10,410 |
| Other Claims | 20n.u | — | — | — | — | — | — | — | — | — | — | — | — |
| Net Claims on Central Government | 22anu | 55,266 | 62,665 | 52,239 | 45,199 | 49,581 | 64,488 | 88,129 | 85,973 | 62,753 | 28,986 | 56,309 | 49,926 |
| Claims on Central Government | 22a.u | 56,791 | 65,550 | 54,154 | 47,743 | 52,958 | 66,493 | 108,706 | 102,974 | 74,084 | 45,286 | 65,330 | 54,271 |
| Liabilities to Central Government | 26d.u | 1,525 | 2,885 | 1,915 | 2,544 | 3,377 | 2,005 | 20,577 | 17,001 | 11,331 | 16,300 | 9,021 | 4,345 |
| Claims on Other Sectors | 22s.u | 264,099 | 335,656 | 423,403 | 570,256 | 554,977 | 505,392 | 430,518 | 421,803 | 388,425 | 348,953 | 321,448 | 284,350 |
| Claims on Other Financial Corps | 22g.u | 55,872 | 78,471 | 96,724 | 205,315 | 189,826 | 167,712 | 177,129 | 190,275 | 165,372 | 140,165 | 134,843 | 114,382 |
| Claims on State & Local Govts | 22b.u | 16,891 | 17,986 | 27,185 | 21,506 | 20,659 | 19,950 | 10,691 | 15,430 | 11,468 | 7,194 | 9,331 | 13,916 |
| Claims on Public Nonfin. Corps | 22c.u | | | | | | | | | | | | |
| Claims on Private Sector | 22d.u | 191,336 | 239,199 | 299,494 | 343,435 | 344,492 | 317,730 | 242,698 | 216,098 | 211,585 | 201,594 | 177,274 | 156,052 |
| Liabilities to Eurosystem | 26g.u | 19,934 | 23,086 | 29,790 | 42,305 | 101,776 | 108,598 | 185,079 | 153,932 | 115,050 | 41,778 | 23,850 | 16,195 |
| Transf.Dep.Included in Broad Money | 24..u | 55,370 | 65,794 | 79,099 | 84,995 | 71,798 | 91,237 | 87,263 | 80,539 | 83,075 | 101,698 | 103,118 | 118,830 |
| Other.Dep.Included in Broad Money. | 25..u | 88,608 | 100,667 | 133,176 | 160,300 | 175,490 | 155,183 | 147,874 | 134,321 | 126,541 | 118,538 | 134,760 | 124,798 |
| Sec.Ot.th.Shares Inc.in.Brd. Money | 26a.u | −12,130 | −9,966 | −5,726 | −21,638 | −26,496 | −34,778 | −72,858 | −27,832 | −40,017 | −44,503 | −51,617 | −63,038 |
| Deposits Excl. from Broad Money | 26b.u | 21,410 | 26,390 | 27,938 | 27,229 | 28,964 | 28,822 | 30,340 | 31,210 | 33,579 | 30,456 | 29,150 | 33,792 |
| Sec.Ot.th.Shares Excl.f/Brd. Money | 26s.u | 18,291 | 51,742 | 72,561 | 65,363 | 40,563 | 30,881 | 47,144 | 38,973 | 24,251 | 14,982 | 14,208 | 9,076 |
| Loans | 26l.u | — | — | — | — | — | — | — | — | — | — | — | — |
| Financial Derivatives | 26m.u | — | — | — | 90,963 | 59,584 | 40,807 | 35,478 | 44,284 | 34,869 | 24,748 | 39,143 | 30,737 |
| Insurance Technical Reserves | 26r.u | — | — | — | — | — | — | — | — | — | — | — | — |
| Shares and Other Equity | 27a.u | 44,257 | 53,732 | 62,765 | 74,576 | 73,705 | 90,017 | 82,064 | 81,085 | 82,501 | 70,976 | 71,405 | 73,750 |
| Other Items (Net) | 27r.u | 57,745 | 59,365 | 61,593 | 77,382 | 123,131 | 97,335 | 69,325 | 66,941 | 62,941 | 58,260 | 41,127 | −3,067 |
| Memorandum Items | | | | | | | | | | | | | |
| Total Assets | 20ra | 898,030 | 1,155,081 | 1,454,201 | 1,663,527 | 1,731,539 | 1,634,012 | 1,527,021 | 1,313,507 | 1,170,003 | 1,016,951 | 1,079,762 | 1,086,739 |
| National Residency Criterion | | | | | | | | | | | | | |
| Net Foreign Assets | 21n | 46,963 | 54,320 | 85,806 | 43,869 | 50,758 | 66,932 | 165,834 | 152,658 | 126,056 | 101,661 | 103,197 | 98,096 |
| Claims on Nonresidents | 21 | 545,645 | 704,983 | 877,547 | 1,006,166 | 1,021,253 | 955,465 | 882,779 | 737,341 | 666,330 | 585,373 | 683,157 | 722,508 |
| Liabilities to Nonresidents | 26c | 498,682 | 650,663 | 791,741 | 962,297 | 970,495 | 888,533 | 716,945 | 584,683 | 540,274 | 483,712 | 579,960 | 624,412 |
| Net Claims on Central Government | 22an | 3,250 | 2,341 | 1,985 | −423 | 890 | 6,828 | 41,146 | 40,614 | 42,716 | 8,102 | 13,053 | 15,914 |
| Claims on Central Government | 22a | 4,075 | 3,548 | 3,212 | 721 | 2,218 | 8,300 | 42,841 | 42,061 | 46,950 | 20,296 | 20,518 | 19,084 |
| Liabilities to Central Government | 22d | 825 | 1,207 | 1,227 | 1,144 | 1,328 | 1,472 | 1,695 | 1,447 | 4,234 | 12,194 | 7,465 | 3,170 |
| Claims on Other Sectors | 22s | 200,983 | 261,768 | 322,725 | 469,994 | 457,480 | 415,792 | 367,957 | 363,513 | 333,900 | 302,242 | 269,749 | 236,176 |
| Claims on Other Fin. Corps | 22g | 36,397 | 48,442 | 54,433 | 157,468 | 144,761 | 127,649 | 144,221 | 164,218 | 137,889 | 114,572 | 112,104 | 96,467 |
| Claims on State & Local Govts | 22b | 676 | 1,059 | 961 | 964 | 1,228 | 1,229 | 574 | 655 | 604 | 364 | 278 | 268 |
| Claims on Private Sector | 22d | 163,910 | 212,267 | 267,331 | 311,562 | 311,491 | 286,914 | 223,162 | 198,640 | 195,407 | 187,306 | 157,367 | 139,441 |
| Transf.Dep.Included in Broad Money | 24 | 54,259 | 64,587 | 77,308 | 82,826 | 69,956 | 88,735 | 85,501 | 77,719 | 79,376 | 99,870 | 100,894 | 116,959 |
| Other.Dep.Included in Broad Money. | 25 | 60,909 | 67,542 | 92,688 | 107,248 | 116,584 | 97,715 | 85,483 | 87,691 | 84,702 | 78,746 | 67,645 | 71,100 |
| Sec.Ot.th.Shares Inc.in.Brd. Money | 26a | 2,583 | 1,790 | 4,985 | −57 | −1,868 | 2,269 | −4,601 | 671 | 877 | −119 | 1,305 | 1,828 |
| Deposits Excl. from Broad Money | 26b | 16,424 | 19,175 | 18,515 | 10,858 | 11,843 | 10,189 | 10,527 | 11,769 | 15,492 | 15,212 | 12,889 | 11,772 |
| Sec.Ot.th.Shares Excl.f/Brd. Money | 26s | 59,182 | 99,395 | 134,491 | 127,118 | 102,141 | 86,089 | 86,799 | 69,247 | 51,470 | 40,317 | 39,522 | 32,452 |

| | | 2004 | 2005 | 2006 | 2007 | 2008 | 2009 | 2010 | 2011 | 2012 | 2013 | 2014 | 2015 |
|---|---|---|---|---|---|---|---|---|---|---|---|---|---|
| **Depository Corporations** | | | | | | *Millions of Euros: End of Period* | | | | | | | |
| Euro Area Wide Residency Criterion | | | | | | | | | | | | | |
| Net Foreign Assets | 31n.u | −28,572 | −34,736 | −25,794 | −36,543 | 23,968 | 22,589 | 81,091 | 89,326 | 68,234 | 36,001 | 25,932 | −1,460 |
| Claims on Nonresidents | 31..u | 322,031 | 434,955 | 571,276 | 675,222 | 690,346 | 639,265 | 583,566 | 487,718 | 452,355 | 389,122 | 446,642 | 483,037 |
| Liabilities to Nonresidents | 36c.u | 350,603 | 469,691 | 597,069 | 711,765 | 666,378 | 616,676 | 502,475 | 398,392 | 384,121 | 353,121 | 420,710 | 484,497 |
| Domestic Claims | 32..u | 318,989 | 398,178 | 474,462 | 613,601 | 590,403 | 555,564 | 518,355 | 510,303 | 449,605 | 428,954 | 423,043 | 374,978 |
| Net Claims on Central Government | 32anu | 54,884 | 62,518 | 51,055 | 43,342 | 35,423 | 50,170 | 87,836 | 88,499 | 61,179 | 67,362 | 101,169 | 90,375 |
| Claims on Central Government | 32a.u | 60,286 | 69,643 | 58,433 | 53,911 | 64,617 | 78,435 | 124,303 | 121,072 | 92,146 | 93,923 | 117,001 | 108,438 |
| Liabilities to Central Government | 36d.u | 5,402 | 7,125 | 7,378 | 10,569 | 29,194 | 28,265 | 36,467 | 32,573 | 30,967 | 26,561 | 15,832 | 18,063 |
| Claims on Other Sectors | 32s.u | 264,105 | 335,660 | 423,407 | 570,259 | 554,980 | 505,394 | 430,519 | 421,804 | 388,426 | 361,592 | 321,874 | 284,603 |
| Claims on Other Financial Corps | 32g.u | 55,872 | 78,471 | 96,724 | 205,315 | 189,826 | 167,712 | 177,129 | 190,275 | 165,372 | 152,803 | 135,269 | 114,635 |
| Claims on State & Local Govts | 32b.u | 16,891 | 17,986 | 27,185 | 21,506 | 20,659 | 19,950 | 10,691 | 15,430 | 11,468 | 7,194 | 9,331 | 13,916 |
| Claims on Public Nonfin. Corps | 32c.u | — | — | — | — | — | — | — | — | — | — | — | — |
| Claims on Private Sector | 32d.u | 191,342 | 239,203 | 299,498 | 343,438 | 344,495 | 317,732 | 242,699 | 216,099 | 211,586 | 201,595 | 177,274 | 156,052 |
| Broad Money Liabilities | 35l.u | 137,155 | 162,599 | 213,323 | 230,639 | 228,876 | 222,814 | 174,013 | 199,496 | 182,503 | 189,253 | 201,305 | 196,537 |
| Currency Outside Depository Corps | 34a.u | 5,307 | 6,104 | 6,774 | 6,982 | 8,084 | 11,172 | 11,734 | 12,468 | 12,904 | 13,520 | 15,044 | 15,947 |
| Transferable Deposits | 34..u | 55,370 | 65,794 | 79,099 | 84,995 | 71,798 | 91,237 | 87,263 | 80,539 | 83,075 | 101,698 | 103,118 | 118,830 |
| Other Deposits | 35..u | 88,608 | 100,667 | 133,176 | 160,300 | 175,490 | 155,183 | 147,874 | 134,321 | 126,541 | 118,538 | 134,760 | 124,798 |
| Securities Other than Shares | 36a.u | −12,130 | −9,966 | −5,726 | −21,638 | −26,496 | −34,778 | −72,858 | −27,832 | −40,017 | −44,503 | −51,617 | −63,038 |
| Deposits Excl. from Broad Money | 36b.u | 21,410 | 26,390 | 27,938 | 27,229 | 28,964 | 28,822 | 30,340 | 31,210 | 33,579 | 30,456 | 29,150 | 33,792 |
| Sec.Oth.th.Shares Excl.f/Brd. Money. | 36s.u | 18,291 | 51,742 | 72,561 | 65,363 | 40,563 | 30,881 | 47,144 | 38,973 | 24,251 | 14,982 | 14,208 | 9,076 |
| Loans | 36l.u | — | — | — | — | — | — | — | — | — | — | — | — |
| Financial Derivatives | 36m.u | — | — | — | 90,963 | 59,584 | 40,807 | 35,478 | 44,284 | 34,869 | 24,748 | 39,143 | 30,737 |
| Insurance Technical Reserves | 36r.u | — | — | — | — | — | — | — | — | — | — | — | — |
| Shares and Other Equity | 37a.u | 45,745 | 55,258 | 63,937 | 75,760 | 75,113 | 91,545 | 83,824 | 83,111 | 84,714 | 76,364 | 83,470 | 87,228 |
| Other Items (Net) | 37r.u | 67,814 | 67,449 | 70,903 | 87,102 | 181,267 | 163,281 | 228,645 | 202,559 | 157,925 | 129,153 | 80,231 | 16,676 |
| Broad Money Liabs., Seasonally Adj. | 35lub | 137,990 | 163,453 | 214,555 | 232,473 | 231,424 | 225,325 | 175,592 | 200,291 | 182,117 | 187,571 | 198,681 | 193,643 |
| Memorandum Items | | | | | | | | | | | | | |
| National Residency Criterion | | | | | | | | | | | | | |
| Net Foreign Assets | 31n | 48,728 | 59,093 | 93,654 | 53,290 | 22,666 | 30,676 | 39,084 | 53,150 | 66,979 | 66,931 | 101,253 | 115,618 |
| Claims on Nonresidents | 31 | 554,539 | 714,381 | 888,049 | 1,015,879 | 1,037,629 | 973,579 | 902,118 | 759,210 | 687,437 | 606,644 | 704,876 | 744,055 |
| Liabilities to Nonresidents | 36c | 505,812 | 655,289 | 794,395 | 962,589 | 1,014,963 | 942,903 | 863,033 | 706,060 | 620,458 | 539,712 | 603,623 | 628,437 |
| Domestic Claims | 32 | 200,362 | 259,895 | 319,288 | 461,640 | 433,053 | 397,351 | 395,718 | 391,119 | 359,445 | 346,064 | 313,202 | 280,568 |
| Net Claims on Central Government | 32an | −627 | −1,877 | −3,441 | −8,357 | −24,430 | −18,443 | 27,760 | 27,605 | 25,544 | 31,183 | 43,027 | 44,139 |
| Claims on Central Government | 32a | 4,075 | 3,570 | 3,249 | 812 | 2,715 | 9,289 | 45,345 | 44,624 | 49,414 | 53,638 | 57,303 | 61,027 |
| Liabilities to Central Government. | 36d | 4,702 | 5,447 | 6,690 | 9,169 | 27,145 | 27,732 | 17,585 | 17,019 | 23,870 | 22,455 | 14,276 | 16,888 |
| Claims on Other Sectors | 32s | 200,989 | 261,772 | 322,729 | 469,997 | 457,483 | 415,794 | 367,958 | 363,514 | 333,901 | 314,881 | 270,175 | 236,429 |
| Claims on Other Financial Corps | 32g | 36,397 | 48,442 | 54,433 | 157,468 | 144,761 | 127,649 | 144,221 | 164,218 | 137,889 | 127,210 | 112,530 | 96,720 |
| Claims on State & Local Govts | 32b | 676 | 1,059 | 961 | 964 | 1,228 | 1,229 | 574 | 655 | 604 | 364 | 278 | 268 |
| Claims on Private Sector | 32d | 163,916 | 212,271 | 267,335 | 311,565 | 311,494 | 286,916 | 223,163 | 198,641 | 195,408 | 187,307 | 157,367 | 139,441 |
| Transf.Dep.Included in Broad Money | 34 | 54,259 | 64,587 | 77,308 | 82,826 | 69,956 | 88,735 | 85,501 | 77,719 | 79,376 | 99,870 | 100,894 | 116,959 |
| Other Dep.Included in Broad Money. | 35 | 60,909 | 67,542 | 92,688 | 107,248 | 116,584 | 97,715 | 85,483 | 87,691 | 84,702 | 78,746 | 67,645 | 71,100 |
| Sec.Oth.th.Shares Inc.in.Brd. Money... | 36a | 2,583 | 1,790 | 4,985 | −57 | −1,868 | 2,269 | −4,601 | 671 | 877 | −119 | 1,305 | 1,828 |
| Deposits Excl. from Broad Money | 36b | 16,424 | 19,175 | 18,515 | 10,858 | 11,843 | 10,189 | 10,527 | 11,769 | 15,492 | 15,212 | 12,889 | 11,772 |
| Sec.Ot.th.Shares Excl./f.Brd. Money.. | 36s | 59,182 | 99,395 | 134,491 | 127,118 | 102,141 | 86,089 | 86,799 | 69,247 | 51,470 | 40,317 | 39,522 | 32,452 |
| **Interest Rates** | | | | | | *Percent Per Annum* | | | | | | | |
| Money Market Rate | 60b | 2.13 | 2.40 | 3.64 | 4.71 | 2.99 | .48 | .81 | 1.14 | .11 | .21 | .02 | −.19 |
| Deposit Rate | 60l | .01 | .01 | .... | .... | .... | .... | .... | .... | .... | .... | .... | .... |
| Households: Stocks, up to 2 years | 60lhs | 1.91 | 2.00 | 2.64 | 3.81 | 4.48 | 3.61 | 2.93 | 3.17 | 3.54 | 2.67 | 1.92 | 1.27 |
| Corporations: Stocks, up to 2 years | 60lcs | 2.02 | 2.10 | 2.84 | 3.98 | 4.47 | 2.45 | 2.05 | 2.74 | 2.90 | 1.84 | 1.22 | .50 |
| Lending Rate | | | | | | | | | | | | | |
| Households: Stocks, up to 1 year | 60phs | 9.38 | 8.39 | 8.48 | 9.08 | 9.52 | 7.23 | 7.31 | 8.34 | 8.02 | 7.19 | 7.15 | 7.95 |
| New Bus., Floating & up to 1 year | 60pns | 5.19 | 4.98 | 5.53 | 6.52 | 6.75 | 4.28 | 5.39 | 5.88 | 6.11 | 6.66 | 7.62 | 9.04 |
| House Purch., Stocks,Over 5 years | 60phm | 3.51 | 3.41 | 3.96 | 4.94 | 5.04 | 2.99 | 2.80 | 3.19 | 2.95 | 2.93 | 2.77 | 2.68 |
| Corporations: Stocks, up to 1 year. | 60pcs | 4.92 | 4.72 | 5.35 | 6.37 | 6.69 | 3.62 | 3.17 | 3.81 | 3.55 | 3.28 | 3.41 | 3.36 |
| New Bus., Over € 1 mil.,up to 1 yr | 60pcn | 4.13 | 4.05 | 4.77 | 5.95 | 6.17 | 3.22 | 2.85 | 3.32 | 2.80 | 2.70 | 2.96 | 2.43 |
| Government Bond Yield | 61 | 4.08 | 3.33 | 3.77 | 4.31 | 4.53 | 5.23 | 5.74 | 9.60 | 6.17 | 3.79 | 2.37 | 1.18 |
| **Prices, Production, Labor** | | | | | | *Index Numbers (2010=100): Period Averages* | | | | | | | |
| Share Prices (End of Month) | 62.ep | 189.8 | 226.4 | 279.4 | 297.8 | 164.7 | 93.5 | 100.0 | 97.5 | 110.6 | 141.2 | 168.9 | 216.0 |
| Wholesale Prices (2005=100) | 63 | 97.8 | 100.0 | 102.1 | 102.3 | 102.7 | 102.1 | .... | .... | .... | .... | .... | .... |
| Output Manufacturing Industry | 63a | 102.5 | † 102.5 | 102.9 | 100.5 | 99.2 | 99.9 | 100.0 | † 100.5 | 102.3 | 101.9 | 100.6 | 106.1 |
| Consumer Prices | 64 | 91.0 | 93.2 | † 96.8 | 101.6 | 105.7 | 101.0 | † 100.0 | 102.6 | 104.3 | 104.8 | 105.0 | 104.7 |
| Harmonized CPI | 64h | 92.9 | 94.9 | 97.5 | 100.3 | 103.4 | 101.6 | 100.0 | 101.2 | 103.1 | 103.7 | 104.0 | 104.0 |
| Wages: Weekly Earnings | 65ey | 86.9 | 93.1 | 94.7 | 100.2 | 98.1 | 99.0 | 100.0 | 99.2 | 101.4 | 98.2 | 102.0 | 102.4 |
| Industrial Production | 66 | 87.5 | 90.9 | 93.7 | 98.6 | 96.5 | 92.2 | 100.0 | 99.6 | 98.1 | 95.9 | 116.0 | 136.4 |
| Industrial Employment | 67ey | † 121.1 | 119.6 | 120.9 | 121.9 | 117.4 | 105.6 | 100.0 | 98.0 | 95.4 | 98.0 | 97.4 | 101.2 |
| | | | | | | *Number in Thousands: Period Averages* | | | | | | | |
| Labor Force | 67d | 1,923 | 2,004 | 2,099 | 2,204 | 2,226 | 2,184 | 2,139 | 2,120 | 2,106 | 2,109 | 2,098 | 2,102 |
| Employment | 67e | 1,836 | 1,915 | 2,005 | 2,099 | 2,081 | 1,917 | 1,838 | 1,804 | 1,790 | 1,828 | 1,857 | 1,900 |
| Unemployment | 67c | 88 | 90 | 97 | 105 | 146 | 268 | 303 | 317 | 316 | 282 | 243 | 204 |
| Unemployment Rate (%) | 67r | 4.5 | 4.4 | 4.5 | 4.7 | 6.4 | 12.0 | 13.9 | 14.7 | 14.7 | 13.1 | 11.3 | 9.5 |
| **Intl. Transactions & Positions** | | | | | | *Millions of Euros* | | | | | | | |
| Exports | 70 | 83,807 | 86,732 | 86,772 | 89,226 | 86,395 | 85,804 | 89,703 | 91,227 | 91,688 | 86,886 | 89,352 | 110,132 |
| Imports, c.i.f. | 71 | 49,347 | 57,465 | 60,857 | 63,486 | 57,585 | 45,061 | 45,764 | 48,302 | 49,151 | 49,672 | 53,320 | 64,494 |
| | | | | | | *2010=100* | | | | | | | |
| Volume of Exports | 72 | 91.7 | 93.8 | 94.0 | 98.7 | 99.1 | 95.1 | 100.0 | 104.0 | 97.8 | 93.9 | 96.8 | .... |
| Volume of Imports | 73 | 116.7 | 130.1 | 133.8 | 136.9 | 123.4 | 101.6 | 100.0 | 95.8 | 94.1 | 96.5 | 103.6 | .... |
| Unit Value of Exports | 74 | 103.0 | 103.4 | 103.3 | 100.6 | 97.4 | 97.9 | 100.0 | 99.6 | 105.0 | 103.5 | 102.9 | .... |
| Unit Value of Imports | 75 | 95.2 | 96.0 | 98.7 | 98.4 | 100.4 | 95.5 | 100.0 | 106.0 | 112.1 | 110.9 | 111.4 | .... |

# Ireland  178

## Balance of Payments

*Millions of US Dollars*

| | | 2004 | 2005 | 2006 | 2007 | 2008 | 2009 | 2010 | 2011 | 2012 | 2013 | 2014 | 2015 |
|---|---|---|---|---|---|---|---|---|---|---|---|---|---|
| A. Current Account* | 109bx | .... | −7,150.4 | −7,858.8 | −13,850.4 | −15,296.9 | −5,001.4 | 2,318.7 | 2,827.8 | 9,245.2 | 14,437.7 | †8,914.3 | 10,561.7 |
| Goods, credit (exports) | 1a9cx | .... | 107,764.6 | 111,171.5 | 127,364.6 | 129,849.0 | 118,214.7 | 118,792.0 | 127,471.4 | 119,320.8 | 116,091.2 | †151,785.3 | 160,870.0 |
| Goods, debit (imports) | 1a9dx | .... | 67,729.6 | 73,075.0 | 88,121.6 | 84,326.2 | 62,768.0 | 62,124.3 | 67,194.8 | 63,627.9 | 66,101.1 | †94,034.4 | 87,793.5 |
| Balance on goods | 1a9bx | .... | 40,034.9 | 38,096.5 | 39,243.0 | 45,522.8 | 55,446.7 | 56,667.7 | 60,276.7 | 55,693.0 | 49,990.1 | †57,750.9 | 73,076.5 |
| Services, credit (exports) | 1b9cx | .... | 54,980.8 | 65,069.6 | 81,172.0 | 89,061.3 | 83,959.6 | 89,095.7 | 104,146.2 | 107,041.2 | 118,404.9 | †133,371.6 | 128,003.0 |
| Services, debit (imports) | 1b9dx | .... | 71,436.6 | 80,288.8 | 94,911.8 | 110,873.6 | 103,787.5 | 107,301.1 | 115,640.9 | 111,955.2 | 117,703.7 | †144,956.4 | 151,435.3 |
| Balance on Goods & Services | 1z9bx | .... | 23,579.1 | 22,877.3 | 25,503.2 | 23,710.5 | 35,618.8 | 38,462.3 | 48,782.0 | 50,779.0 | 50,691.3 | †46,166.0 | 49,644.3 |
| Primary income: credit | 1c9cx | .... | 53,862.0 | 83,138.4 | 116,528.1 | 123,774.4 | 76,469.9 | 75,668.8 | 79,470.7 | 73,559.4 | 73,495.8 | †83,288.7 | 75,840.3 |
| Primary income: debit | 1c9dx | .... | 84,875.6 | 113,282.7 | 154,621.6 | 160,908.8 | 115,255.8 | 109,972.8 | 123,734.1 | 113,555.4 | 107,900.0 | †116,897.5 | 111,753.6 |
| Balance on gds, serv. & prim. inc. | 1y9bx | .... | −7,434.5 | −7,267.0 | −12,590.3 | −13,423.9 | −3,167.2 | 4,158.4 | 4,518.7 | 10,783.0 | 16,287.1 | †12,557.2 | 13,731.1 |
| Secondary income: credit | 1d9ca | .... | 6,963.2 | 6,645.3 | 6,703.7 | 8,012.7 | 7,551.8 | 6,615.1 | 7,448.4 | 7,163.5 | 6,004.8 | †6,806.4 | 6,598.3 |
| Secondary income: debit | 1d9da | .... | 6,679.2 | 7,237.1 | 7,963.9 | 9,885.7 | 9,386.0 | 8,454.8 | 9,139.3 | 8,701.3 | 7,854.1 | †10,449.2 | 9,767.6 |
| B. Capital Account* | 209ba | .... | 417.6 | 378.6 | 155.2 | 180.5 | −1,754.1 | −827.2 | −273.1 | −2,557.1 | 100.0 | †179.8 | 62.6 |
| Capital account: credit | 209ca | .... | 534.0 | 392.3 | 167.5 | 196.6 | 102.6 | 131.4 | 492.7 | 112.1 | 134.6 | †179.8 | 62.6 |
| Capital account: debit | 209da | .... | 116.5 | 13.8 | 12.3 | 16.1 | 1,856.8 | 958.6 | 765.8 | 2,669.2 | 34.6 | †— | — |
| Balance on current & capital acct. | 129ba | .... | −6,732.8 | −7,480.3 | −13,695.2 | −15,116.4 | −6,755.5 | 1,491.5 | 2,554.7 | 6,688.2 | 14,537.7 | †9,094.1 | 10,624.3 |
| C. Financial Account* | 309na | .... | 2,500.7 | −6,139.1 | −16,813.4 | −25,300.3 | 964.3 | −8,377.6 | 3,844.8 | 7,334.0 | 17,725.8 | †−2,526.3 | 3,151.9 |
| Direct investment: assets | 3a9aa | .... | 91,852.7 | 42,897.9 | 55,926.7 | 58,164.0 | 54,480.7 | 16,831.9 | −1,536.4 | 21,340.2 | 37,588.2 | †98,451.3 | 128,285.2 |
| Equity & investment fund shares | 3aaaa | .... | 8,970.3 | 19,304.1 | .... | .... | 20,982.7 | 14,458.7 | .... | .... | .... | †16,814.4 | 80,371.8 |
| Debt instruments | 3abaa | .... | 82,882.4 | 23,593.8 | 42,201.2 | 44,381.9 | 33,498.0 | 2,373.3 | .... | .... | .... | †81,636.9 | 47,913.4 |
| Direct investment: liabilities | 3a9la | .... | 47,028.5 | 22,080.9 | 59,941.1 | 23,258.6 | 53,935.3 | 37,763.6 | 23,664.9 | 40,961.6 | 49,960.1 | †86,765.6 | 125,710.2 |
| Equity & investment fund shares | 3aala | .... | 10,383.0 | 6,421.5 | 21,932.2 | 17,421.9 | 32,444.2 | 28,725.5 | −7,188.0 | 42,873.7 | 36,115.9 | †49,589.4 | 81,794.1 |
| Debt instruments | 3abla | .... | 36,645.5 | 15,659.4 | 38,008.8 | 5,836.6 | 21,491.0 | 9,038.1 | 30,853.0 | −1,912.0 | 13,844.2 | †37,176.3 | 43,916.1 |
| Portfolio investment: assets | 3b9aa | .... | 151,138.6 | 267,083.0 | 232,630.8 | 45,302.9 | 749.0 | −17,740.0 | 4,170.2 | 95,816.3 | 125,796.9 | †203,415.6 | 137,900.2 |
| Equity & investment fund shares | 3baaa | .... | 59,601.9 | 74,005.7 | 29,414.6 | −32,388.3 | 13,643.5 | 38,839.3 | −8,731.2 | 15,106.3 | 78,370.5 | †90,575.8 | 52,726.9 |
| Debt securities | 3bbaa | .... | 91,536.7 | 193,077.3 | 203,216.1 | 77,691.2 | −12,894.5 | −56,579.3 | 12,901.5 | 80,710.0 | 47,426.5 | †112,839.8 | 85,173.3 |
| Portfolio investment: liabilities | 3b9la | .... | 215,055.6 | 279,048.7 | 222,284.6 | −17,189.8 | 35,184.3 | 101,615.0 | 41,378.9 | 94,077.5 | 68,733.8 | †231,217.9 | 237,342.6 |
| Equity & investment fund shares | 3bala | .... | 93,590.0 | 160,467.3 | 138,387.0 | −7,843.6 | 30,814.8 | 152,336.4 | 85,211.3 | 105,421.9 | 109,125.8 | †230,002.8 | 204,783.2 |
| Debt securities | 3bbla | .... | 121,465.6 | 118,581.4 | 83,897.7 | −9,346.1 | 4,369.4 | −50,721.4 | −43,832.3 | −11,344.4 | −40,392.0 | †1,215.2 | 32,559.4 |
| Fin. der.& empl.stk.ops.(ESOs): net. | 3c9na | .... | 8,041.4 | −374.1 | 16,331.4 | −1,388.2 | 3,357.7 | 16,023.5 | −554.2 | 14,535.8 | 3,803.7 | †32,522.7 | 35,816.8 |
| Fin. der. & ESOs.: assets | 3c9aa | .... | 5,347.0 | −3,045.9 | 18,724.8 | −6,210.3 | −16,553.1 | 7,947.6 | −14,439.0 | −6,828.0 | −10,376.4 | .... | .... |
| Fin. der. & ESOs.: liabilities | 3c9la | .... | −2,694.4 | −2,671.7 | 2,393.4 | −4,822.1 | −19,910.8 | −8,075.9 | −13,884.8 | −21,363.9 | −14,180.1 | .... | .... |
| Other investment: assets | 3d9aa | .... | 133,298.4 | 154,940.9 | 196,846.2 | 106,455.4 | −72,037.0 | 35,407.8 | −4,234.4 | −91,753.8 | −65,971.3 | †58,667.6 | 60,445.4 |
| Other equity | 3daaa | .... | .... | .... | .... | .... | .... | .... | .... | .... | .... | †368.2 | 6.7 |
| Debt instruments | 3dzaa | .... | 133,298.4 | 154,940.9 | 196,846.2 | 106,455.4 | −72,037.0 | 35,407.8 | −4,234.4 | −91,753.8 | −65,971.3 | †58,299.4 | 60,438.7 |
| Other investment: liabilities | 3d9la | .... | 119,746.3 | 169,557.1 | 236,322.8 | 227,765.5 | −103,533.5 | −80,477.8 | −71,043.4 | −102,434.6 | −35,202.2 | †77,600.0 | −3,757.0 |
| Other equity | 3dala | .... | .... | .... | .... | .... | .... | .... | .... | .... | .... | †— | — |
| Debt instruments | 3dzla | .... | 119,746.3 | 169,557.1 | 236,322.8 | 227,765.5 | −103,533.5 | −80,477.8 | −71,043.4 | −102,434.6 | −35,202.2 | †77,600.0 | −3,757.0 |
| Curr.+ cap.– finan. acct. balance | 4y9na | .... | −9,233.5 | −1,341.2 | 3,118.1 | 10,183.9 | −7,719.8 | 9,869.1 | −1,290.1 | −645.8 | −3,188.1 | †11,620.5 | 7,472.4 |
| D. Net Errors and Omissions | 409na | .... | 7,457.3 | 1,229.1 | −3,102.2 | −10,027.4 | 8,753.3 | −9,910.9 | −16,350.0 | −7,824.4 | −1,233.1 | †−311.1 | 4,318.7 |
| E. Reserves and Related Items | 4z9na | .... | −1,776.3 | −112.1 | 16.0 | 156.5 | 1,033.5 | −41.8 | −17,640.1 | −8,470.3 | −4,421.2 | †11,309.3 | 11,791.1 |
| Reserve assets | 3e9aa | .... | −1,776.3 | −112.1 | 16.0 | 156.5 | 1,033.5 | −41.8 | −442.2 | −17.1 | 14.7 | †173.2 | 565.6 |
| Credit and loans from the IMF | 3dcla | .... | — | — | — | — | — | — | 17,197.9 | 8,453.1 | 4,435.9 | †−11,136.1 | −11,225.5 |
| Exceptional financing | 409la | .... | .... | .... | .... | .... | .... | .... | .... | .... | .... | .... | .... |

*Excludes components in group E

## International Investment Position

*Millions of US Dollars*

| | | 2004 | 2005 | 2006 | 2007 | 2008 | 2009 | 2010 | 2011 | 2012 | 2013 | 2014 | 2015 |
|---|---|---|---|---|---|---|---|---|---|---|---|---|---|
| Assets | 809aa | .... | 2,221,851.7 | 2,930,135.1 | 3,677,270.0 | 3,393,336.4 | 3,715,430.7 | 3,714,692.8 | 3,871,745.8 | 4,104,265.8 | 4,490,902.2 | †4,535,606.6 | 4,745,514.6 |
| Direct investment | 8a9aa | .... | 342,409.1 | 401,918.1 | 485,584.0 | 522,536.0 | 672,185.4 | 700,103.3 | 709,704.2 | 766,017.3 | 913,708.9 | †1,124,303.9 | 1,321,283.3 |
| Equity & investment fund shares | 8aaaa | .... | 87,691.8 | 108,474.7 | 130,693.0 | 139,687.7 | 232,280.9 | 266,359.4 | 276,591.8 | 318,392.3 | 400,108.6 | †545,540.1 | 714,709.8 |
| Debt instruments | 8abaa | .... | 254,717.3 | 293,443.4 | 354,890.9 | 382,848.3 | 439,904.5 | 433,743.9 | 433,112.3 | 447,624.9 | 513,600.3 | †578,763.9 | 606,573.6 |
| Portfolio investment | 8b9aa | .... | 1,182,211.6 | 1,620,218.2 | 1,970,467.7 | 1,621,054.9 | 1,802,055.2 | 1,764,343.9 | 1,853,175.3 | 2,096,504.2 | 2,347,828.1 | †2,349,426.8 | 2,346,474.0 |
| Equity & investment fund shares | 8baaa | .... | 383,154.8 | 573,199.2 | 649,172.5 | 427,868.4 | 539,873.5 | 603,914.3 | 563,101.4 | 664,738.8 | 830,590.6 | †902,954.1 | 920,264.0 |
| Debt securities | 8bbaa | .... | 799,056.8 | 1,047,019.0 | 1,321,295.1 | 1,193,186.5 | 1,262,181.7 | 1,160,429.6 | 1,290,073.9 | 1,431,765.4 | 1,517,237.6 | †1,446,472.7 | 1,426,210.1 |
| Fin. der.(oth.than reserves) & ESOs | 8c9aa | .... | 11,047.9 | 11,326.2 | 37,793.2 | 51,324.5 | 67,473.4 | 82,565.1 | 100,885.4 | 91,200.9 | 84,002.4 | †50,297.7 | 40,516.0 |
| Other investment | 8d9aa | .... | 685,304.2 | 895,830.0 | 1,182,484.9 | 1,197,382.5 | 1,171,562.2 | 1,165,565.9 | 1,206,278.4 | 1,148,837.2 | 1,143,727.6 | †1,009,844.7 | 1,035,050.0 |
| Other equity | 8daaa | .... | .... | .... | .... | .... | .... | .... | .... | .... | .... | †1,579.5 | 1,422.9 |
| Debt instruments | 8dzaa | .... | 685,304.2 | 895,830.0 | 1,182,484.9 | 1,197,382.5 | 1,171,562.2 | 1,165,565.9 | 1,206,278.4 | 1,148,837.2 | 1,143,727.6 | †1,008,265.1 | 1,033,627.0 |
| Reserve assets | 8e9aa | .... | 878.9 | 842.6 | 940.2 | 1,038.5 | 2,154.5 | 2,114.5 | 1,702.6 | 1,706.3 | 1,635.2 | †1,733.5 | 2,191.4 |
| Liabilities | 809la | .... | 2,269,149.1 | 2,942,714.9 | 3,731,771.5 | 3,572,411.2 | 3,942,927.7 | 3,915,352.9 | 4,108,925.8 | 4,347,670.1 | 4,729,504.7 | †4,776,029.7 | 4,914,504.1 |
| Direct investment | 8a9la | .... | 401,786.9 | 437,681.2 | 539,206.7 | 546,858.8 | 642,821.7 | 628,190.4 | 669,386.2 | 725,757.1 | 788,523.9 | †867,742.8 | 963,353.6 |
| Equity & investment fund shares | 8aala | .... | 217,612.2 | 226,458.2 | 267,016.9 | 257,538.3 | 305,747.2 | 291,985.1 | 296,294.0 | 339,325.9 | 374,890.4 | †417,294.7 | 455,430.4 |
| Debt instruments | 8abla | .... | 184,174.8 | 211,223.1 | 272,189.8 | 289,320.5 | 337,074.5 | 336,205.3 | 373,092.2 | 386,431.1 | 413,633.5 | †450,448.1 | 507,923.2 |
| Portfolio investment | 8b9la | .... | 1,210,256.6 | 1,611,590.5 | 1,957,757.6 | 1,643,931.7 | 1,948,581.5 | 2,074,155.2 | 2,235,635.4 | 2,514,144.4 | 2,835,653.0 | †2,746,220.1 | 2,916,078.6 |
| Equity & investment fund shares | 8bala | .... | 712,330.0 | 950,795.0 | 1,155,092.1 | 889,190.5 | 1,177,526.3 | 1,407,712.1 | 1,482,030.5 | 1,759,906.8 | 2,080,721.3 | †2,353,565.6 | 2,520,992.6 |
| Debt securities | 8bbla | .... | 497,926.6 | 660,795.5 | 802,665.5 | 754,741.2 | 771,055.2 | 666,443.1 | 753,604.9 | 754,237.6 | 754,931.8 | †392,654.5 | 395,086.0 |
| Fin. der.(oth.than reserves) & ESOs | 8c9la | .... | 2,895.0 | .... | 42,138.9 | 65,606.1 | 73,706.9 | 73,372.1 | 92,380.6 | 76,696.7 | 60,039.1 | †44,084.0 | 28,721.0 |
| Other investment | 8d9la | .... | 654,210.6 | .... | 1,192,668.4 | 1,316,014.6 | 1,277,817.7 | 1,139,635.2 | 1,111,523.6 | 1,031,071.9 | 1,045,288.7 | †1,117,982.8 | 1,006,350.9 |
| Other equity | 8dala | .... | .... | .... | .... | .... | .... | .... | .... | .... | .... | †— | — |
| Debt instruments | 8dzla | .... | 654,210.6 | .... | 1,192,668.4 | 1,316,014.6 | 1,277,817.7 | 1,139,635.2 | 1,111,523.6 | 1,031,071.9 | 1,045,288.7 | †1,117,982.8 | 1,006,350.9 |

# Ireland   178

| | | 2004 | 2005 | 2006 | 2007 | 2008 | 2009 | 2010 | 2011 | 2012 | 2013 | 2014 | 2015 |
|---|---|---|---|---|---|---|---|---|---|---|---|---|---|
| **Government Finance** | | | | | | | | | | | | | |
| **Operations Statement** | | | | | | | | | | | | | |
| **General Government** | | *Millions of Euros: Fiscal Year Ends December 31; Data Reported through Eurostat* | | | | | | | | | | | |
| Revenue............................... | a1 | 53,852 | 59,478 | 67,808 | 71,266 | 65,400 | 56,511 | 55,407 | 57,319 | 59,082 | 61,049 | 65,709 | 70,492 |
| Taxes............................ | a11 | 40,057 | 44,395 | 50,687 | 52,374 | 45,867 | 38,728 | 37,891 | 38,863 | 40,929 | 42,500 | 46,450 | 50,748 |
| Social Contributions................. | a12 | 8,025 | 8,730 | 9,556 | 10,697 | 10,984 | 10,243 | 9,485 | 9,972 | 9,651 | 10,301 | 10,931 | 11,429 |
| Grants.............................. | a13 | .... | .... | .... | .... | .... | .... | .... | .... | .... | .... | .... | .... |
| Other Revenue....................... | a14 | .... | .... | .... | .... | .... | .... | .... | .... | .... | .... | .... | .... |
| Expense............................... | a2 | 49,130 | 53,827 | 58,950 | 65,234 | 71,925 | 76,966 | 106,785 | 78,179 | 72,803 | 71,988 | 72,370 | 74,993 |
| Compensation of Employees.......... | a21 | 14,494 | 16,566 | 18,164 | 19,904 | 21,206 | 20,713 | 19,293 | 19,175 | 18,907 | 18,653 | 18,807 | 19,543 |
| Use of Goods & Services.............. | a22 | 8,137 | 7,894 | 8,780 | 9,732 | 10,036 | 9,982 | 8,991 | 8,582 | 8,242 | 8,186 | 8,785 | 9,324 |
| Consumption of Fixed Capital....... | a23 | 2,786 | 3,028 | 3,314 | 3,521 | 3,416 | 3,254 | 3,186 | 3,266 | 3,356 | 3,407 | 3,528 | 3,528 |
| Interest............................ | a24 | 1,709 | 1,737 | 1,846 | 1,979 | 2,398 | 3,412 | 4,921 | 5,888 | 7,157 | 7,667 | 7,485 | 6,747 |
| Subsidies........................... | a25 | 1,540 | 1,726 | 1,677 | 1,798 | 1,922 | 1,889 | 1,828 | 1,725 | 1,921 | 1,815 | 1,857 | 1,840 |
| Grants.............................. | a26 | .... | .... | .... | .... | .... | .... | .... | .... | .... | .... | .... | .... |
| Social Benefits..................... | a27 | 16,163 | 18,351 | 20,472 | 23,186 | 26,281 | 28,848 | 28,774 | 28,808 | 29,436 | 28,549 | 28,122 | 27,988 |
| Other Expense....................... | a28 | .... | .... | .... | .... | .... | .... | .... | .... | .... | .... | .... | .... |
| Gross Operating Balance [1-2+23]... | agob | 7,508 | 8,678 | 12,172 | 9,553 | −3,109 | −17,201 | −48,193 | −17,593 | −10,365 | −7,531 | −3,133 | −973 |
| Net Operating Balance [1-2]........... | anob | 4,722 | 5,651 | 8,858 | 6,032 | −6,525 | −20,455 | −51,379 | −20,859 | −13,721 | −10,938 | −6,661 | −4,501 |
| Net Acq. of Nonfinancial Assets....... | a31 | 2,641 | 2,914 | 3,659 | 5,493 | 6,574 | 2,986 | 2,298 | 982 | 294 | −746 | 534 | 436 |
| Aquisition of Nonfin. Assets......... | a31.1 | .... | .... | .... | .... | .... | .... | .... | .... | .... | .... | .... | .... |
| Disposal of Nonfin. Assets........... | a31.2 | .... | .... | .... | .... | .... | .... | .... | .... | .... | .... | .... | .... |
| Net Lending/Borrowing [1-2-31]...... | anlb | 2,081 | 2,737 | 5,199 | 539 | −13,099 | −23,441 | −53,676 | −21,842 | −14,015 | −10,193 | −7,195 | −4,937 |
| Net Acq. of Financial Assets............. | a32 | 3,025 | 3,764 | 4,083 | 4,009 | 19,385 | 2,950 | −11,637 | 3,665 | 6,058 | −5,518 | −19,005 | −7,332 |
| By instrument | | | | | | | | | | | | | |
| Monetary Gold & SDRs................ | a3201 | — | — | — | — | — | — | — | — | — | — | — | 1 |
| Currency & Deposits.................... | a3202 | 617 | 1,053 | 374 | 1,277 | 18,192 | 1,041 | −11,288 | −651 | 5,838 | −1,259 | −6,329 | −218 |
| Securities other than Shares.......... | a3203 | 222 | 229 | 2,014 | 1,256 | −68 | 4,124 | 1,858 | −648 | 956 | −758 | −1,429 | −5,834 |
| Loans.................................. | a3204 | 102 | 142 | −62 | 125 | 309 | 128 | 447 | 1,228 | −2,415 | −2,356 | −11,826 | −892 |
| Shares & Other Equity................. | a3205 | 1,306 | 914 | 1,101 | 1,169 | 1,402 | −2,357 | −2,388 | 3,703 | 1,826 | −1,307 | −91 | 100 |
| Insurance Technical Reserves........ | a3206 | — | — | — | — | — | 1 | — | — | −1 | — | 1 | −1 |
| Financial Derivatives.................... | a3207 | — | — | −44 | 80 | −160 | 16 | 254 | −271 | −76 | 196 | 97 | −367 |
| Other Accounts Receivable............ | a3208 | 778 | 1,426 | 700 | 102 | −290 | −3 | −520 | 304 | −70 | −34 | 572 | −121 |
| By debtor | | | | | | | | | | | | | |
| Domestic........................... | a321 | .... | .... | .... | .... | .... | .... | .... | .... | .... | .... | .... | .... |
| Foreign............................. | a322 | .... | .... | .... | .... | .... | .... | .... | .... | .... | .... | .... | .... |
| Net Incurrence of Liabilities.............. | a33 | 358 | 658 | −655 | 3,834 | 33,478 | 26,443 | 41,756 | 25,554 | 19,882 | 4,569 | −11,643 | −1,354 |
| By instrument | | | | | | | | | | | | | |
| Special Drawing Rights (SDRs)....... | a3301 | — | — | — | — | — | — | — | — | — | — | — | — |
| Currency & Deposits.................... | a3302 | 166 | 244 | −246 | −397 | 1,169 | 1,395 | 3,422 | 2,893 | 3,802 | −30,707 | −10,474 | −256 |
| Securities other than Shares........... | a3303 | −305 | −10 | −514 | 3,777 | 30,163 | 24,829 | 5,972 | −9,007 | −7,570 | 25,512 | 6,421 | 6,998 |
| Loans................................. | a3304 | 105 | 75 | 50 | 82 | 1,864 | −4 | 31,250 | 31,304 | 23,277 | 10,635 | −8,229 | −8,339 |
| Shares & Other Equity.................. | a3305 | — | — | — | — | — | — | — | — | — | — | — | — |
| Insurance Technical Reserves........ | a3306 | — | — | — | — | — | — | — | 1 | −1 | — | — | — |
| Financial Derivatives.................... | a3307 | 3 | 2 | 5 | — | — | — | — | 3 | 1 | −1 | −1 | — |
| Other Accounts Payable............... | a3308 | 389 | 347 | 50 | 372 | 282 | 223 | 1,112 | 361 | 371 | −869 | 640 | 243 |
| By creditor | | | | | | | | | | | | | |
| Domestic........................... | a331 | .... | .... | .... | .... | .... | .... | .... | .... | .... | .... | .... | .... |
| Foreign............................. | a332 | .... | .... | .... | .... | .... | .... | .... | .... | .... | .... | .... | .... |
| Stat. Discrepancy [32-33-NLB]........ | anlbz | 586 | 369 | −461 | −364 | −994 | −52 | 283 | −47 | 191 | 106 | −167 | −1,041 |
| Memo Item: Expenditure [2+31]...... | a2m | 51,771 | 56,741 | 62,609 | 70,727 | 78,499 | 79,952 | 109,083 | 79,161 | 73,097 | 71,242 | 72,904 | 75,429 |
| **Balance Sheet** | | | | | | | | | | | | | |
| Net Worth............................. | a6 | .... | .... | .... | .... | .... | .... | .... | .... | .... | .... | .... | .... |
| Nonfinancial Assets........................ | a61 | .... | .... | .... | .... | .... | .... | .... | .... | .... | .... | .... | .... |
| Financial Assets.............................. | a62 | 37,267 | 44,102 | 49,791 | 55,833 | 67,382 | 73,395 | 62,231 | 88,281 | 93,068 | 94,813 | 84,442 | 85,118 |
| By instrument | | | | | | | | | | | | | |
| Monetary Gold & SDRs................. | a6201 | — | — | — | — | — | — | — | — | — | — | — | 1 |
| Currency & Deposits.................... | a6202 | 8,894 | 9,579 | 10,181 | 11,639 | 29,643 | 30,690 | 19,662 | 19,284 | 25,283 | 24,022 | 17,765 | 17,768 |
| Securities other than Shares........... | a6203 | 1,696 | 2,143 | 4,252 | 4,619 | 4,609 | 8,700 | 10,114 | 7,919 | 9,470 | 10,249 | 9,646 | 3,289 |
| Loans.................................. | a6204 | 2,712 | 2,851 | 2,781 | 2,907 | 3,217 | 3,293 | 3,740 | 27,965 | 23,965 | 20,326 | 9,327 | 8,845 |
| Shares and Other Equity................. | a6205 | 17,766 | 21,391 | 23,838 | 27,372 | 21,044 | 21,788 | 20,130 | 22,975 | 25,098 | 30,795 | 38,445 | 45,618 |
| Insurance Technical Reserves......... | a6206 | — | 3 | 8 | 9 | — | 1 | 1 | 1 | — | — | — | — |
| Financial Derivatives.................... | a6207 | — | 86 | — | 458 | 332 | 410 | 606 | 1,694 | 897 | 1,135 | 352 | 812 |
| Other Accounts Receivable............ | a6208 | 6,199 | 8,049 | 8,731 | 8,829 | 8,537 | 8,513 | 7,978 | 8,443 | 8,355 | 8,286 | 8,906 | 8,785 |
| By debtor | | | | | | | | | | | | | |
| Domestic........................... | a621 | .... | .... | .... | .... | .... | .... | .... | .... | .... | .... | .... | .... |
| Foreign............................. | a622 | .... | .... | .... | .... | .... | .... | .... | .... | .... | .... | .... | .... |
| Liabilities..................................... | a63 | 49,206 | 53,354 | 51,072 | 54,187 | 89,181 | 114,938 | 140,608 | 192,906 | 229,846 | 240,013 | 237,523 | 235,078 |
| By instrument | | | | | | | | | | | | | |
| Special Drawing Rights (SDRs)....... | a6301 | — | — | — | — | — | — | — | — | — | — | — | — |
| Currency & Deposits.................... | a6302 | 8,076 | 8,319 | 8,073 | 7,676 | 8,845 | 10,308 | 13,711 | 58,388 | 62,099 | 31,356 | 20,918 | 20,704 |
| Securities other than Shares........... | a6303 | 36,084 | 37,454 | 35,298 | 38,388 | 70,587 | 94,787 | 84,112 | 85,194 | 94,295 | 126,293 | 142,394 | 146,741 |
| Loans.................................. | a6304 | 1,697 | 1,969 | 2,021 | 2,095 | 3,369 | 3,367 | 35,175 | 38,275 | 62,202 | 73,854 | 65,535 | 58,102 |
| Shares and Other Equity................. | a6305 | — | — | — | — | — | — | — | — | — | — | — | — |
| Insurance Technical Reserves......... | a6306 | 1 | — | — | — | — | — | — | — | 1 | — | — | — |
| Financial Derivatives.................... | a6307 | 42 | 22 | 40 | 119 | 144 | 16 | 38 | 2,974 | 2,802 | 932 | 457 | 1,068 |
| Other Accounts Payable................ | a6308 | 3,306 | 5,590 | 5,640 | 5,909 | 6,236 | 6,460 | 7,572 | 8,075 | 8,447 | 7,578 | 8,219 | 8,463 |
| By creditor | | | | | | | | | | | | | |
| Domestic........................... | a631 | .... | .... | .... | .... | .... | .... | .... | .... | .... | .... | .... | .... |
| Foreign............................. | a632 | .... | .... | .... | .... | .... | .... | .... | .... | .... | .... | .... | .... |
| Net Financial Worth [62-63]........... | a6m2 | −11,939 | −9,252 | −1,281 | 1,646 | −21,799 | −41,543 | −78,377 | −104,625 | −136,778 | −145,200 | −153,081 | −149,960 |
| Memo Item: Debt at Market Value... | a6m | 49,164 | 53,332 | 51,032 | 54,068 | 89,037 | 114,922 | 140,570 | 189,932 | 227,044 | 239,081 | 237,066 | 234,010 |
| Memo Item: Debt at Face Value....... | a6m35 | 47,362 | 49,969 | 49,332 | 53,057 | 85,841 | 111,127 | 151,799 | 197,782 | 218,433 | 222,876 | 211,514 | 209,729 |
| Memo Item: Maastricht Debt.......... | a6m36 | 44,056 | 44,379 | 43,692 | 47,148 | 79,605 | 104,667 | 144,227 | 189,707 | 209,986 | 215,298 | 203,295 | 201,266 |
| Memo Item: Debt at Nominal Value. | a6m4 | .... | .... | .... | .... | .... | .... | .... | .... | .... | .... | .... | .... |

# Ireland 178

| National Accounts | | 2004 | 2005 | 2006 | 2007 | 2008 | 2009 | 2010 | 2011 | 2012 | 2013 | 2014 | 2015 |
|---|---|---|---|---|---|---|---|---|---|---|---|---|---|
| | | | | | | | *Millions of Euros* | | | | | | |
| Househ.Cons.Expend.,incl.NPISHs.... | 96f | 68,551 | 74,521 | 81,432 | 89,469 | 90,655 | 79,439 | 77,987 | 78,499 | 77,730 | 78,938 | 80,192 | 87,160 |
| Government Consumption Expend... | 91f | 24,849 | 26,902 | 29,706 | 32,926 | 34,832 | 33,776 | 30,897 | 30,581 | 30,659 | 30,352 | 31,394 | 32,620 |
| Gross Fixed Capital Formation........ | 93e | 41,289 | 48,909 | 53,518 | 54,287 | 45,219 | 33,049 | 26,047 | 24,864 | 27,013 | 26,527 | 30,386 | 47,116 |
| Changes in Inventories.................... | 93i | 419 | 819 | 1,676 | 1,066 | −328 | −1,457 | −509 | 756 | 199 | 851 | 1,863 | 1,197 |
| Exports of Goods and Services......... | 90c | 125,049 | 132,530 | 140,709 | 152,415 | 150,180 | 146,363 | 157,811 | 167,086 | 182,506 | 184,056 | 207,792 | 260,593 |
| Imports of Goods and Services (-).... | 98c | 102,693 | 113,435 | 123,576 | 135,000 | 133,876 | 121,555 | 129,023 | 132,398 | 147,079 | 147,694 | 168,083 | 215,830 |
| Statistical Discrepancy.................... | 99bs | −1,994 | −1,092 | 295 | 1,585 | 189 | −1,501 | 1,719 | 1,654 | 1,728 | 1,761 | 1,868 | −269 |
| Gross Domestic Product (GDP)........ | 99b | 156,176 | 169,978 | 184,923 | 197,054 | 187,547 | 169,432 | 166,157 | 173,940 | 174,845 | 179,448 | 189,046 | 214,623 |
| Net Primary Income from Abroad..... | 98.n | −29,029 | −31,342 | −30,614 | −33,919 | −32,613 | −35,512 | −34,345 | −43,278 | −42,197 | −41,532 | .... | .... |
| Gross National Income (GNI)............ | 99a | 127,147 | 138,636 | 154,309 | 163,135 | 154,934 | 133,920 | 131,812 | 130,662 | 132,648 | 137,916 | .... | .... |
| Gross Nat'l Disposable Inc. (GNDI)... | 99i | 128,075 | 139,470 | 154,524 | 162,427 | 153,520 | 131,033 | 126,982 | 122,975 | 131,443 | 146,433 | .... | .... |
| Gross Saving................................. | 99s | 35,461 | 38,949 | 44,354 | 40,951 | 28,987 | 18,434 | 18,586 | 14,894 | 23,713 | 37,143 | .... | .... |
| Net National Income....................... | 99e | 113,699 | 123,969 | 137,034 | 144,251 | 136,717 | 117,429 | 115,317 | 112,494 | 119,378 | 132,266 | .... | .... |
| GDP Volume 2010 Ref., Chained..... | 99b.p | 150,251 | 159,768 | 169,849 | 179,263 | 175,387 | 165,498 | 166,157 | 170,458 | 170,715 | 173,164 | 182,167 | 196,397 |
| GDP Volume (2010=100)............... | 99bvp | 90.4 | 96.2 | 102.2 | 107.9 | 105.6 | 99.6 | 100.0 | 102.6 | 102.7 | 104.2 | 109.6 | 118.2 |
| GDP Deflator (2010=100).............. | 99bip | 103.9 | 106.4 | 108.9 | 109.9 | 106.9 | 102.4 | 100.0 | 102.0 | 102.4 | 103.6 | 103.8 | 109.3 |
| | | | | | | | *Millions: Midyear Estimates* | | | | | | |
| Population................................. | 99z | 4.12 | 4.20 | 4.29 | 4.39 | 4.48 | 4.56 | 4.62 | 4.65 | 4.67 | 4.67 | 4.68 | 4.69 |

# Israel 436

| | | 2004 | 2005 | 2006 | 2007 | 2008 | 2009 | 2010 | 2011 | 2012 | 2013 | 2014 | 2015 |
|---|---|---|---|---|---|---|---|---|---|---|---|---|---|
| **Exchange Rates** | | | | | | *New Sheqalim per SDR: End of Period* | | | | | | | |
| Market Rate | aa | 6.6904 | 6.5789 | 6.3561 | 6.0776 | 5.8561 | 5.9180 | 5.4656 | 5.8663 | 5.7373 | 5.3453 | 5.6344 | 5.4071 |
| | | | | *New Sheqalim per US Dollar: End of Period (ae) Period Average (rf)* | | | | | | | | | |
| Market Rate | ae | 4.3080 | 4.6030 | 4.2250 | 3.8460 | 3.8020 | 3.7750 | 3.5490 | 3.8210 | 3.7330 | 3.4710 | 3.8890 | 3.9020 |
| Market Rate | rf | 4.4820 | 4.4877 | 4.4558 | 4.1081 | 3.5880 | 3.9323 | 3.7390 | 3.5781 | 3.8559 | 3.6108 | 3.5779 | 3.8868 |
| | | | | | *Index Numbers (2010=100): Period Averages* | | | | | | | | |
| Nominal Effective Exchange Rate | nec | 87.68 | 86.86 | 87.06 | 90.00 | 99.98 | 95.40 | 100.00 | 101.14 | 97.14 | 104.12 | 106.41 | 107.99 |
| CPI-Based Real Effect. Ex. Rate | rec | 88.65 | 86.65 | 86.37 | 87.21 | 97.20 | 95.22 | 100.00 | 101.18 | 96.25 | 102.54 | 103.33 | 103.09 |
| ULC-Based Real Effect. Ex. Rate | rel | 80.80 | 82.69 | 84.40 | 88.21 | 97.30 | 90.99 | 100.00 | 101.52 | 98.33 | 105.06 | 107.30 | 110.10 |
| **Fund Position** | | | | | | *Millions of SDRs: End of Period* | | | | | | | |
| Quota | 2f.s | 928.20 | 928.20 | 928.20 | 928.20 | 928.20 | 928.20 | 928.20 | 1,061.10 | 1,061.10 | 1,061.10 | 1,061.10 | 1,061.10 |
| SDR Holdings | 1b.s | 9.77 | 13.04 | 12.76 | 10.55 | 8.56 | 785.51 | 859.30 | 826.90 | 830.66 | 999.47 | 782.24 | 849.00 |
| Reserve Position in the Fund | 1c.s | 298.26 | 141.17 | 81.79 | 60.65 | 114.30 | 184.30 | 207.11 | 359.93 | 384.51 | 425.54 | 432.04 | 329.45 |
| Total Fund Cred.&Loans Outstg. | 2tl | — | — | — | — | — | — | — | — | — | — | — | — |
| SDR Allocations | 1bd | 106.36 | 106.36 | 106.36 | 106.36 | 106.36 | 883.39 | 883.39 | 883.39 | 883.39 | 883.39 | 883.39 | 883.39 |
| **International Liquidity** | | | | | *Millions of US Dollars Unless Otherwise Indicated: End of Period* | | | | | | | | |
| Total Reserves minus Gold | 1l.d | 27,094.4 | 28,059.4 | 29,153.2 | 28,518.5 | 42,513.2 | 60,611.4 | 70,907.3 | 74,874.1 | 75,907.6 | 81,785.5 | 86,101.3 | 90,575.0 |
| SDR Holdings | 1b.d | 15.2 | 18.6 | 19.2 | 16.7 | 13.2 | 1,231.4 | 1,323.4 | 1,269.5 | 1,276.7 | 1,539.2 | 1,133.3 | 1,176.5 |
| Reserve Position in the Fund | 1c.d | 463.2 | 201.8 | 123.0 | 95.8 | 176.1 | 288.9 | 319.0 | 552.6 | 591.0 | 655.3 | 625.9 | 456.5 |
| Foreign Exchange | 1d.d | 26,616.0 | 27,839.0 | 29,011.0 | 28,406.0 | 42,324.0 | 59,091.0 | 69,265.0 | 73,052.0 | 74,040.0 | 79,591.0 | 84,342.0 | 88,942.0 |
| Gold (Million Fine Troy Ounces) | 1ad | — | — | — | — | — | — | — | — | — | — | — | — |
| Gold (National Valuation) | 1and | — | — | — | — | — | — | — | — | — | — | — | — |
| Central Bank: Other Liabs | 4..d | 121.2 | 3,284.5 | 4,306.8 | 3,832.3 | 1,684.5 | 2,493.2 | 17,151.9 | 11,433.3 | 7,973.6 | 4,809.9 | 13,471.9 | 23,055.8 |
| Other Depository Corps.: Assets | 7a.d | 21,753.2 | 25,395.4 | 33,215.4 | † 37,001.1 | 30,088.3 | 25,275.4 | 24,608.7 | 23,495.7 | 23,772.0 | 25,570.3 | 28,134.9 | 27,172.0 |
| Other Depository Corps.: Liabs | 7b.d | 21,432.9 | 21,073.4 | 22,923.8 | † 26,676.8 | 28,270.7 | 27,157.5 | 28,820.8 | 30,684.5 | 25,991.5 | 24,393.6 | 20,994.6 | 16,644.3 |
| **Central Bank** | | | | | | *Millions of New Sheqalim: End of Period* | | | | | | | |
| Net Foreign Assets | 11n | 116,015.6 | 128,489.0 | 122,342.3 | 109,218.1 | 161,064.8 | 220,003.6 | 209,353.5 | 267,129.2 | 278,343.1 | 278,662.8 | 326,567.9 | 348,037.3 |
| Claims on Nonresidents | 11 | 117,249.5 | 144,307.1 | 141,214.7 | 124,603.5 | 168,092.3 | 234,643.3 | 275,053.6 | 315,997.8 | 313,176.8 | 300,080.1 | 383,937.4 | 442,729.1 |
| Liabilities to Nonresidents | 16c | 1,233.9 | 15,818.1 | 18,872.4 | 15,385.4 | 7,027.5 | 14,639.6 | 65,700.1 | 48,867.7 | 34,833.7 | 21,417.3 | 57,369.5 | 94,691.8 |
| Claims on Other Depository Corps. | 12e | 2,190.5 | 1,063.8 | 8,320.2 | 481.2 | 2,001.0 | 420.0 | — | — | — | — | — | — |
| Net Claims on Central Government | 12an | 2,083.7 | −270.0 | −297.0 | 1,368.7 | −4,661.4 | 514.2 | 5,464.5 | 7,018.4 | 443.0 | −5,433.1 | −3,681.4 | −12,450.0 |
| Claims on Central Government | 12a | 8,758.2 | 6,832.1 | 5,947.8 | 5,002.5 | 3,871.5 | 20,971.7 | 19,789.2 | 19,721.6 | 17,225.8 | 15,208.6 | 12,096.7 | 10,220.9 |
| Liabilities to Central Government | 16d | 6,674.5 | 7,102.1 | 6,244.7 | 3,633.8 | 8,532.9 | 20,457.4 | 14,324.7 | 12,703.2 | 16,782.8 | 20,641.7 | 15,778.1 | 22,671.0 |
| Claims on Other Sectors | 12s | — | — | — | — | — | — | — | — | — | 101.3 | 83.4 | 79.0 |
| Claims on Other Financial Corps. | 12g | — | — | — | — | — | — | — | — | — | — | — | — |
| Claims on State & Local Govts. | 12b | — | — | — | — | — | — | — | — | — | — | — | — |
| Claims on Public Nonfin. Corps. | 12c | — | — | — | — | — | — | — | — | — | — | — | — |
| Claims on Private Sector | 12d | — | — | — | — | — | — | — | — | — | 101.3 | 83.4 | 79.0 |
| Monetary Base | 14 | 95,163.2 | 107,071.7 | 121,905.2 | 107,266.7 | 107,110.2 | 111,205.8 | 127,877.3 | 136,507.8 | 132,191.8 | 135,884.7 | 171,794.9 | 161,248.7 |
| Currency in Circulation | 14a | 20,778.5 | 24,410.5 | 25,539.2 | 28,966.3 | 34,359.7 | 41,490.1 | 44,828.1 | 48,975.4 | 54,772.7 | 57,535.5 | 63,194.1 | 73,486.9 |
| Liabs. to Other Depository Corps. | 14c | 10,425.7 | 14,150.7 | 11,845.8 | 12,397.8 | 15,300.8 | 13,312.0 | 21,482.8 | 23,414.3 | 18,369.2 | 22,049.0 | 28,089.9 | 26,224.4 |
| Liabilities to Other Sectors | 14d | 63,959.0 | 68,510.5 | 84,520.2 | 65,902.6 | 57,449.7 | 56,403.7 | 61,566.3 | 64,118.1 | 59,050.0 | 56,300.2 | 80,510.9 | 61,537.4 |
| Other Liabs. to Other Dep. Corps. | 14n | 25,081.7 | 19,146.0 | 12,232.7 | 11,910.3 | 60,238.2 | 117,837.7 | 114,908.0 | 150,944.7 | 164,935.1 | 174,352.4 | 165,241.6 | 197,730.3 |
| Dep. & Sec. Excl. f/Monetary Base | 14o | — | — | — | — | — | — | — | — | — | — | — | — |
| Deposits Included in Broad Money. | 15 | — | — | — | — | — | — | — | — | — | — | — | — |
| Sec.Ot.th.Shares Incl.in Brd. Money | 16a | — | — | — | — | — | — | — | — | — | — | — | — |
| Deposits Excl. from Broad Money | 16b | — | — | — | — | — | — | — | — | — | — | — | — |
| Sec.Ot.th.Shares Excl.f/Brd.Money | 16s | — | — | — | — | — | — | — | — | — | — | — | — |
| Loans | 16l | — | — | — | — | — | — | — | — | — | — | — | — |
| Financial Derivatives | 16m | — | — | — | — | — | — | — | — | — | — | — | — |
| Shares and Other Equity | 17a | −2,837.2 | 429.3 | −6,681.0 | −11,169.0 | −12,150.0 | −11,935.9 | −31,756.5 | −18,056.7 | −23,362.2 | −41,571.0 | −18,631.3 | −29,428.4 |
| Other Items (Net) | 17r | 2,882.3 | 2,635.8 | 2,908.6 | 3,060.0 | 3,205.9 | 3,830.3 | 3,789.2 | 4,751.8 | 5,021.3 | 4,664.9 | 4,564.7 | 6,118.7 |
| Memo Item: | | | | | | | | | | | | | |
| Total Assets | 10ra | 132,761.5 | 157,906.1 | 161,392.0 | 135,899.2 | 179,276.3 | 261,023.3 | 299,410.6 | 340,446.4 | 334,933.7 | 319,400.7 | 400,281.8 | 457,634.8 |

# Israel 436

| | | 2004 | 2005 | 2006 | 2007 | 2008 | 2009 | 2010 | 2011 | 2012 | 2013 | 2014 | 2015 |
|---|---|---|---|---|---|---|---|---|---|---|---|---|---|
| **Other Depository Corporations** | | | | | | *Millions of New Sheqalim: End of Period* | | | | | | | |
| Net Foreign Assets | 21n | 1,380.0 | 19,894.0 | 43,482.0 | † 39,707.0 | 6,910.5 | −7,104.9 | −14,948.5 | −27,468.5 | −8,285.4 | 4,084.1 | 27,768.3 | 41,584.7 |
| Claims on Nonresidents | 21 | 93,713.0 | 116,895.0 | 140,335.0 | † 142,306.1 | 114,395.6 | 95,414.6 | 87,336.4 | 89,777.0 | 88,740.8 | 88,754.4 | 109,416.5 | 107,329.5 |
| Liabilities to Nonresidents | 26c | 92,333.0 | 97,001.0 | 96,853.0 | † 102,599.2 | 107,485.1 | 102,519.5 | 102,284.9 | 117,245.5 | 97,026.1 | 84,670.2 | 81,648.2 | 65,744.8 |
| Claims on Central Bank | 20 | 30,872.0 | 22,346.0 | 18,954.0 | † 29,342.4 | 79,390.4 | 137,470.7 | 144,023.9 | 179,971.0 | 190,251.7 | 202,704.5 | 201,118.2 | 233,638.1 |
| Currency | 20a | 3,025.0 | 3,453.0 | 3,884.0 | † 4,697.9 | 4,180.5 | 5,883.9 | 6,547.1 | 5,879.9 | 6,534.9 | 6,793.3 | 6,544.6 | 8,848.0 |
| Reserve Deposits and Securities | 20b | 27,847.0 | 18,893.0 | 15,070.0 | † 15,439.3 | 63,646.5 | 106,880.9 | 101,484.3 | 131,956.3 | 127,315.8 | 129,578.6 | 149,729.6 | 172,216.8 |
| Other Claims | 20n | — | — | — | † 9,205.2 | 11,563.4 | 24,705.8 | 35,992.5 | 42,134.8 | 56,401.0 | 66,332.6 | 44,843.9 | 52,573.4 |
| Net Claims on Central Government | 22an | 23,154.0 | 13,524.0 | 14,674.0 | † 36,810.4 | 44,500.9 | 44,899.7 | 44,203.5 | 53,743.8 | 52,178.2 | 57,739.3 | 63,153.2 | 73,538.3 |
| Claims on Central Government | 22a | 55,939.0 | 61,985.0 | 62,023.0 | † 55,550.7 | 57,229.4 | 55,299.5 | 56,254.3 | 67,195.4 | 63,477.4 | 68,001.8 | 73,221.6 | 83,440.6 |
| Liabilities to Central Government | 26d | 32,785.0 | 48,461.0 | 47,349.0 | † 18,740.3 | 12,728.5 | 10,399.8 | 12,050.8 | 13,451.6 | 11,299.1 | 10,262.5 | 10,068.3 | 9,902.2 |
| Claims on Other Sectors | 22s | 482,871.0 | 540,180.0 | 560,533.0 | † 616,713.0 | 673,702.4 | 670,036.3 | 727,005.4 | 780,600.5 | 800,280.4 | 837,622.5 | 876,825.3 | 896,053.0 |
| Claims on Other Financial Corps | 22g | 30,850.0 | 46,358.0 | 46,419.0 | † 98,058.7 | 105,079.4 | 102,435.4 | 104,574.9 | 112,144.0 | 104,420.6 | 118,663.8 | 122,478.2 | 99,521.7 |
| Claims on State & Local Govts | 22b | — | — | — | † 19,706.4 | 20,562.4 | 21,397.0 | 22,473.6 | 22,056.1 | 22,216.0 | 21,960.5 | 22,480.1 | 21,450.3 |
| Claims on Public Nonfin. Corps. | 22c | — | — | — | † — | | | | | | | | |
| Claims on Private Sector | 22d | 452,021.0 | 493,822.0 | 514,114.0 | † 498,947.9 | 548,060.6 | 546,204.0 | 599,956.9 | 646,400.4 | 673,643.9 | 696,998.1 | 731,867.1 | 775,081.0 |
| Liabilities to Central Bank | 26g | 2,187.0 | 1,098.0 | 8,350.0 | † 481.2 | .6 | 420.9 | 3.2 | — | — | 32.4 | 179.8 | 261.3 |
| Transf.Dep.Included in Broad Money | 24 | 35,012.0 | 39,942.0 | 43,140.0 | † 70,312.2 | 92,619.0 | 129,953.2 | 130,384.7 | 130,820.3 | 153,761.3 | 197,825.0 | 263,843.8 | 367,742.2 |
| Other Dep.Included in Broad Money. | 25 | 450,464.0 | 494,679.0 | 518,116.0 | † 361,022.0 | 414,121.2 | 407,119.1 | 417,232.4 | 483,238.5 | 508,322.5 | 529,426.2 | 534,057.0 | 480,721.6 |
| Sec.Ot.th.Shares Incl.in Brd. Money. | 26a | — | — | — | † — | | | | | | | | |
| Deposits Excl. from Broad Money | 26b | 5,930.0 | 5,816.0 | 5,838.0 | † 185,475.7 | 181,439.6 | 177,789.2 | 200,624.4 | 227,193.4 | 233,462.7 | 217,938.4 | 209,449.6 | 214,969.7 |
| Sec.Ot.th.Shares Excl.f/Brd.Money | 26s | 27,977.0 | 34,970.0 | 37,985.0 | † 31,380.1 | 34,696.2 | 40,490.0 | 43,712.8 | 47,140.7 | 42,410.9 | 42,361.3 | 39,166.6 | 52,788.5 |
| Loans | 26l | — | — | — | † 173.3 | 1,419.8 | 287.2 | 884.5 | 1,604.3 | 1,645.9 | 791.7 | 2,237.6 | 1,546.3 |
| Financial Derivatives | 26m | — | — | — | † 8,282.5 | 17,701.7 | 11,846.4 | 13,416.1 | 13,227.4 | 10,534.9 | 21,694.4 | 26,947.6 | 19,038.0 |
| Insurance Technical Reserves | 26r | — | — | — | † — | | | | | | | | |
| Shares and Other Equity | 27a | 52,195.0 | 52,556.0 | 52,521.0 | † 55,455.7 | 56,199.0 | 66,033.3 | 78,268.6 | 69,785.3 | 69,413.7 | 77,211.3 | 78,859.3 | 90,473.6 |
| Other Items (Net) | 27r | −35,488.0 | −33,117.0 | −28,307.0 | † 9,989.9 | 6,306.9 | 11,362.6 | 15,757.5 | 13,836.9 | 14,873.1 | 14,869.9 | 14,123.8 | 17,273.1 |
| Memo Item: | | | | | | | | | | | | | |
| Total Assets | 20ra | 730,866.0 | 814,700.0 | 858,687.0 | † 919,498.2 | 1,028,128.5 | 1,053,336.1 | 1,120,748.0 | 1,243,524.7 | 1,218,261.6 | 1,276,878.0 | 1,344,139.7 | 1,392,625.0 |
| **Depository Corporations** | | | | | | *Millions of New Sheqalim: End of Period* | | | | | | | |
| Net Foreign Assets | 31n | 117,395.6 | 148,383.0 | 165,824.3 | † 148,925.1 | 167,975.3 | 212,898.7 | 194,405.0 | 239,660.7 | 270,057.7 | 282,746.9 | 354,336.2 | 389,622.0 |
| Claims on Nonresidents | 31 | 210,962.5 | 261,202.1 | 281,549.7 | † 266,909.6 | 282,487.8 | 330,057.8 | 362,390.0 | 405,774.9 | 401,917.6 | 388,834.4 | 493,353.9 | 550,058.7 |
| Liabilities to Nonresidents | 36c | 93,566.9 | 112,819.1 | 115,725.4 | † 117,984.5 | 114,512.6 | 117,159.2 | 167,985.0 | 166,114.2 | 131,859.9 | 106,087.5 | 139,017.7 | 160,436.6 |
| Domestic Claims | 32 | 508,108.7 | 553,434.0 | 574,910.0 | † 654,892.2 | 713,541.8 | 715,450.3 | 776,673.4 | 841,362.8 | 852,901.6 | 890,029.9 | 936,380.5 | 957,220.4 |
| Net Claims on Central Government | 32an | 25,237.7 | 13,254.0 | 14,377.0 | † 38,179.2 | 39,839.4 | 45,413.9 | 49,668.0 | 60,762.2 | 52,621.2 | 52,306.2 | 59,471.8 | 61,088.3 |
| Claims on Central Government | 32a | 64,697.2 | 68,817.1 | 67,970.8 | † 60,553.2 | 61,100.8 | 76,271.2 | 76,043.5 | 86,917.0 | 80,703.1 | 83,210.4 | 85,318.3 | 93,661.5 |
| Liabilities to Central Government | 36d | 39,459.5 | 55,563.1 | 53,593.7 | † 22,374.0 | 21,261.4 | 30,857.2 | 26,375.5 | 26,154.8 | 28,081.9 | 30,904.2 | 25,846.5 | 32,573.2 |
| Claims on Other Sectors | 32s | 482,871.0 | 540,180.0 | 560,533.0 | † 616,713.0 | 673,702.4 | 670,036.3 | 727,005.4 | 780,600.5 | 800,280.4 | 837,723.7 | 876,908.8 | 896,132.1 |
| Claims on Other Financial Corps | 32g | 30,850.0 | 46,358.0 | 46,419.0 | † 98,058.7 | 105,079.4 | 102,435.4 | 104,574.9 | 112,144.0 | 104,420.6 | 118,663.8 | 122,478.2 | 99,521.7 |
| Claims on State & Local Govts | 32b | — | — | — | † 19,706.4 | 20,562.4 | 21,397.0 | 22,473.6 | 22,056.1 | 22,216.0 | 21,960.5 | 22,480.1 | 21,450.3 |
| Claims on Public Nonfin. Corps. | 32c | — | — | — | † — | | | | | | | | |
| Claims on Private Sector | 32d | 452,021.0 | 493,822.0 | 514,114.0 | † 498,947.9 | 548,060.6 | 546,204.0 | 599,956.9 | 646,400.4 | 673,643.9 | 697,099.4 | 731,950.5 | 775,160.1 |
| Broad Money Liabilities | 35l | 567,188.5 | 624,089.0 | 667,431.4 | † 521,505.3 | 594,369.1 | 629,082.0 | 647,464.4 | 721,272.4 | 769,371.4 | 834,293.5 | 935,061.2 | 974,640.2 |
| Currency Outside Depository Corps | 34a | 17,753.5 | 20,957.5 | 21,655.2 | † 24,268.4 | 30,179.1 | 35,606.1 | 38,281.0 | 43,095.5 | 48,237.8 | 50,742.2 | 56,649.5 | 64,638.9 |
| Transferable Deposits | 34 | 35,012.0 | 39,942.0 | 43,140.0 | † 70,312.2 | 92,619.0 | 129,953.2 | 130,384.7 | 130,820.3 | 153,761.3 | 197,825.0 | 263,843.8 | 367,742.2 |
| Other Deposits | 35 | 450,464.0 | 494,679.0 | 518,116.0 | † 361,022.0 | 414,121.2 | 407,119.1 | 417,232.4 | 483,238.5 | 508,322.5 | 529,426.2 | 534,057.0 | 480,721.6 |
| Securities Other than Shares | 36a | 63,959.0 | 68,510.5 | 84,520.2 | † 65,902.6 | 57,449.7 | 56,403.7 | 61,566.3 | 64,118.1 | 59,050.0 | 56,300.2 | 80,510.9 | 61,537.4 |
| Deposits Excl. from Broad Money | 36b | 5,930.0 | 5,816.0 | 5,838.0 | † 185,475.7 | 181,439.6 | 177,789.2 | 200,624.4 | 227,193.4 | 233,462.7 | 217,938.4 | 209,449.6 | 214,969.7 |
| Sec.Ot.th.Shares Excl.f/Brd.Money | 36s | 27,977.0 | 34,970.0 | 37,985.0 | † 31,380.1 | 34,696.2 | 40,490.0 | 43,712.8 | 47,140.7 | 42,410.9 | 42,361.3 | 39,166.6 | 52,788.5 |
| Loans | 36l | — | — | — | † 173.3 | 1,419.8 | 287.2 | 884.5 | 1,604.3 | 1,645.9 | 791.7 | 2,237.6 | 1,546.3 |
| Financial Derivatives | 36m | — | — | — | † 8,282.5 | 17,701.7 | 11,846.4 | 13,416.1 | 13,227.4 | 10,534.9 | 21,694.4 | 26,947.6 | 19,038.0 |
| Insurance Technical Reserves | 36r | — | — | — | † — | | | | | | | | |
| Shares and Other Equity | 37a | 49,357.8 | 52,985.3 | 45,840.0 | † 44,286.6 | 44,049.0 | 54,097.3 | 46,512.1 | 51,728.6 | 46,051.5 | 35,640.3 | 60,228.0 | 61,045.2 |
| Other Items (Net) | 37r | −24,948.9 | −16,043.4 | −16,360.1 | † 12,713.6 | 7,841.8 | 14,756.8 | 18,463.9 | 18,856.6 | 19,481.9 | 20,057.4 | 17,626.3 | 22,817.6 |
| Broad Money Liabs., Seasonally Adj. | 35l.b | 557,262.9 | 607,167.4 | 643,337.3 | 512,928.4 | 584,231.6 | 617,932.4 | 635,685.1 | 708,062.7 | 755,551.8 | 819,935.6 | 919,623.6 | 958,826.5 |
| **Monetary Aggregates** | | | | | | *Millions of New Sheqalim: End of Period* | | | | | | | |
| Broad Money | 59n | 567,188.5 | 624,089.0 | 667,431.4 | 1,053,358.7 | 1,192,891.8 | 1,262,339.1 | 1,300,688.8 | 1,450,046.8 | 1,544,254.7 | 1,675,300.9 | 1,875,662.6 | 976,972.7 |
| o/w:Currency Issued by Cent.Govt | 59m.a | — | — | — | 531,077.6 | 597,562.4 | 632,155.5 | 651,958.7 | 727,301.0 | 773,125.2 | 839,047.6 | 938,268.9 | — |
| o/w: Dep.in Nonfin. Corporations. | 59m.b | — | — | — | | | | | | | | | 2,332.6 |
| o/w:Secs. Issued by Central Govt. | 59m.c | — | — | — | 775.8 | 960.4 | 1,101.6 | 1,265.7 | 1,473.3 | 1,758.0 | 1,959.8 | 2,332.6 | — |
| Money (National Definitions) | | | | | | | | | | | | | |
| M1 | 59ma | . . . . | . . . . | . . . . | 61,347.9 | 72,064.0 | 109,615.5 | 114,672.0 | 116,518.1 | 126,618.8 | 145,838.0 | 197,761.1 | 278,202.4 |
| M2 | 59mb | . . . . | . . . . | . . . . | 330,688.4 | 375,249.3 | 426,196.2 | 441,510.4 | 487,757.5 | 527,619.3 | 562,252.5 | 609,642.7 | . . . . |
| M3 | 59mc | . . . . | . . . . | . . . . | 61,347.9 | 72,064.0 | 109,615.5 | 114,672.0 | 116,518.1 | 126,618.8 | 145,838.0 | 197,761.1 | 278,202.4 |
| **Interest Rates** | | | | | | *Percent Per Annum* | | | | | | | |
| Central Bank Policy Rate (EOP) | 60 | 3.900 | 4.500 | 5.000 | 4.000 | 2.500 | 1.000 | 2.000 | 2.750 | 2.000 | 1.000 | .250 | .100 |
| Discount Rate | 60.a | 3.977 | 4.602 | 5.127 | 4.081 | 2.531 | 1.005 | 2.020 | 2.788 | 2.020 | 1.005 | .250 | .100 |
| Treasury Bill Rate | 60c | 4.294 | 5.206 | 4.980 | 4.612 | 2.050 | 1.863 | 2.442 | 2.591 | 1.812 | .882 | .251 | .154 |
| Deposit Rate | 60l | 3.514 | 3.662 | 4.310 | 3.496 | 2.310 | 1.107 | 1.851 | 2.482 | 1.923 | † 1.084 | .565 | .452 |
| Lending Rate | 60p | 7.111 | 7.550 | 7.763 | 6.914 | 5.744 | 4.376 | 5.241 | 5.922 | 5.227 | † 4.195 | 3.587 | 3.449 |
| **Prices, Production, Labor** | | | | | | *Index Numbers (2010=100): Period Averages* | | | | | | | |
| Share Prices (End of Month) | 62.ep | 54.3 | 66.6 | 78.6 | 96.6 | 78.8 | 77.9 | 100.0 | 95.3 | 87.5 | 95.3 | 110.7 | 122.8 |
| Prices: Industrial Products | 63 | 80.7 | † 85.7 | 90.6 | 93.7 | 102.7 | 96.2 | 100.0 | 107.8 | † 112.4 | 112.9 | 111.4 | 104.8 |
| Consumer Prices | 64 | 86.6 | 87.8 | 89.6 | 90.1 | † 94.2 | 97.4 | † 100.0 | 103.5 | † 105.2 | 106.8 | † 107.3 | 106.7 |
| Wages: Daily Earnings | 65 | 79.9 | 82.1 | 85.8 | 89.6 | 92.7 | 96.2 | 100.0 | 102.9 | 105.6 | 109.4 | 112.2 | 114.1 |
| Industrial Production | 66 | 77.3 | 80.1 | 88.0 | 91.9 | 98.7 | 92.7 | 100.0 | † 102.0 | 106.1 | 106.7 | 107.9 | 110.3 |
| Industrial Employment | 67 | 92.7 | 94.3 | 97.2 | 101.1 | 103.1 | 98.2 | 100.0 | † 101.5 | 102.3 | 102.6 | 102.7 | 102.6 |
| | | | | | | *Number in Thousands: Period Averages* | | | | | | | |
| Labor Force | 67d | 2,679 | 2,740 | 2,810 | 2,894 | 2,957 | 3,073 | 3,147 | 3,204 | 3,606 | 3,678 | 3,778 | 3,846 |
| Employment | 67e | 2,401 | 2,493 | 2,573 | 2,682 | 2,777 | 2,841 | 2,970 | 3,025 | 3,359 | 3,450 | 3,556 | 3,644 |
| Unemployment | 67c | 278 | 246 | 236 | 212 | 180 | 232 | 209 | 180 | 247 | 228 | 223 | 202 |
| Unemployment Rate (%) | 67r | 10.4 | 9.0 | 8.4 | 7.3 | 6.1 | 7.5 | 6.7 | 5.6 | 6.8 | 6.2 | 5.9 | 5.2 |

Israel 436

| | | 2004 | 2005 | 2006 | 2007 | 2008 | 2009 | 2010 | 2011 | 2012 | 2013 | 2014 | 2015 |
|---|---|---|---|---|---|---|---|---|---|---|---|---|---|
| **Intl. Transactions & Positions** | | | | | | | *Millions of US Dollars* | | | | | | |
| Exports | 70..d | 38,618 | 42,770 | 46,789 | 54,065 | 60,825 | 47,934 | 58,392 | 67,648 | 63,191 | 66,607 | 68,553 | 63,607 |
| Imports, c.i.f. | 71..d | 42,864 | 47,142 | 50,334 | 59,039 | 67,656 | 49,278 | 61,209 | 75,830 | 75,392 | 74,861 | 75,483 | 64,990 |
| Imports,c.i.f.,excl. Military Gds | 71.md | 40,969 | 44,944 | 47,841 | 56,621 | 65,171 | 47,355 | 59,140 | 73,536 | 72,932 | 71,999 | 72,302 | 62,071 |
| | | | | | | | *2010=100* | | | | | | |
| Volume of Exports | 72 | 87.7 | 90.0 | 93.8 | 103.1 | 101.1 | 84.8 | 100.0 | † 109.0 | 97.1 | 85.9 | 105.2 | 103.2 |
| Volume of Imports | 73 | 89.0 | 91.2 | 91.4 | 99.0 | 100.8 | 85.8 | 100.0 | † 109.0 | 110.9 | 110.1 | 112.9 | 112.9 |
| Unit Value of Exports(US$) | 74..d | 74.8 | 80.8 | 84.4 | 89.6 | 103.6 | 96.3 | 100.0 | † 106.5 | 110.7 | 113.0 | 112.0 | 106.0 |
| Unit Value of Imports(US$) | 75..d | 77.7 | 83.3 | 88.3 | 95.9 | 109.4 | 93.0 | 100.0 | † 114.5 | 111.3 | 110.2 | 108.3 | 93.1 |
| **Balance of Payments** | | | | | | | *Millions of US Dollars* | | | | | | |
| A. Current Account* | 109bx | 6,891.9 | 4,043.1 | 6,848.2 | 5,525.6 | 3,181.5 | 7,963.0 | 7,854.5 | 6,678.5 | 1,524.3 | 9,704.4 | 12,207.5 | † 14,455.3 |
| Goods, credit (exports) | 1a9cx | 36,915.2 | 40,375.6 | 43,492.4 | 50,758.2 | 58,011.4 | 46,805.0 | 56,413.6 | 64,985.7 | 61,282.4 | 62,997.5 | 63,760.8 | † 56,289.7 |
| Goods, debit (imports) | 1a9dx | 39,507.4 | 43,887.1 | 47,346.6 | 55,998.4 | 64,422.7 | 46,072.3 | 58,316.5 | 72,467.4 | 70,265.1 | 70,035.5 | 70,357.2 | † 59,493.1 |
| Balance on goods | 1a9bx | −2,592.2 | −3,511.5 | −3,854.2 | −5,240.2 | −6,411.3 | 732.7 | −1,902.9 | −7,481.7 | −8,982.7 | −7,038.0 | −6,596.4 | † −3,203.4 |
| Services, credit (exports) | 1b9cx | 20,649.8 | 16,872.9 | 19,058.3 | 21,402.9 | 25,031.2 | 22,533.9 | 25,370.0 | 29,444.8 | 31,800.4 | 34,899.5 | 35,629.5 | † 35,608.9 |
| Services, debit (imports) | 1b9dx | 13,398.0 | 13,826.1 | 15,093.9 | 17,716.8 | 19,862.5 | 17,439.9 | 18,670.2 | 20,299.4 | 22,135.7 | 21,247.9 | 23,065.9 | † 22,573.5 |
| Balance on Goods & Services | 1z9bx | 4,659.6 | −464.7 | 110.2 | −1,554.1 | −1,242.6 | 5,826.7 | 4,796.9 | 1,663.7 | 682.0 | 6,613.6 | 5,967.2 | † 9,832.0 |
| Primary income: credit | 1c9cx | 3,003.5 | 5,600.8 | 8,408.2 | 10,908.2 | 7,358.9 | 5,722.5 | 6,266.2 | 7,766.0 | 7,571.7 | 8,108.7 | 9,536.4 | † 9,474.7 |
| Primary income: debit | 1c9dx | 7,045.7 | 7,095.2 | 9,177.6 | 11,155.1 | 11,389.8 | 10,811.8 | 11,444.2 | 11,345.9 | 14,626.0 | 13,985.5 | 13,130.3 | † 13,881.5 |
| Balance on gds, serv. & prim. inc. | 1y9bx | 617.4 | −1,959.1 | −659.2 | −1,801.0 | −5,273.5 | 737.4 | −381.1 | −1,916.2 | −6,372.3 | 736.8 | 2,373.3 | † 5,425.2 |
| Secondary income: credit | 1d9ca | 7,355.3 | 7,039.7 | 8,665.4 | 8,668.8 | 9,486.4 | 8,687.7 | 9,734.6 | 11,059.2 | 10,313.2 | 11,517.2 | 12,349.1 | † 11,593.2 |
| Secondary income: debit | 1d9da | 1,080.8 | 1,037.5 | 1,158.0 | 1,342.2 | 1,031.4 | 1,462.1 | 1,499.0 | 2,464.5 | 2,416.6 | 2,549.6 | 2,514.9 | † 2,563.1 |
| B. Capital Account* | 209ba | 249.9 | 253.4 | 305.1 | 324.9 | 229.6 | 147.7 | 142.9 | 336.0 | 259.3 | 306.8 | 355.4 | † 332.3 |
| Capital account: credit | 209ca | 249.9 | 253.4 | 305.1 | 324.9 | 229.6 | 147.7 | 142.9 | 336.0 | 259.3 | 306.8 | 355.4 | † 332.3 |
| Capital account: debit | 209da | — | — | — | — | — | — | — | — | .... | .... | .... | .... |
| Balance on current & capital acct. | 129ba | 7,141.8 | 4,296.5 | 7,153.3 | 5,850.5 | 3,411.1 | 8,110.7 | 7,997.4 | 7,014.5 | 1,783.6 | 10,011.2 | 12,562.9 | † 14,787.6 |
| C. Financial Account* | 309na | 6,762.5 | 8,282.4 | 10,362.9 | 4,540.0 | −12,853.7 | −5,718.5 | 17.1 | 8,429.6 | 6,613.0 | 5,161.5 | 8,572.8 | † 6,684.4 |
| Direct investment: assets | 3a9aa | 4,533.3 | 2,945.9 | 15,461.8 | 8,603.7 | 7,209.5 | 1,694.6 | 9,088.1 | 9,165.6 | 3,256.4 | 5,502.0 | 3,667.2 | † 9,884.1 |
| Equity & investment fund shares | 3aaaa | 4,149.3 | 2,745.9 | 12,740.8 | 6,755.4 | 6,535.9 | 908.9 | 5,423.1 | 8,621.4 | 4,204.6 | 6,737.3 | 4,532.5 | † 5,534.6 |
| Debt instruments | 3abaa | 384.0 | 200.0 | 2,721.0 | 1,848.3 | 673.6 | 785.7 | 3,665.0 | 544.2 | −948.2 | −1,235.3 | −865.3 | † 4,349.5 |
| Direct investment: liabilities | 3a9la | 2,946.9 | 4,818.4 | 15,295.5 | 8,798.1 | 10,874.1 | 4,438.1 | 5,509.6 | 8,727.6 | 8,467.6 | 12,448.1 | 6,738.0 | † 11,510.2 |
| Equity & investment fund shares | 3aala | 2,771.6 | 4,588.4 | 15,002.1 | 8,754.1 | 10,473.4 | 3,961.8 | 5,887.1 | 7,378.4 | 6,254.5 | 11,122.9 | 8,889.2 | † 10,443.5 |
| Debt instruments | 3abla | 175.3 | 230.0 | 293.4 | 44.0 | 400.7 | 476.3 | −377.5 | 1,349.2 | 2,213.1 | 1,325.2 | −2,151.2 | † 1,066.7 |
| Portfolio investment: assets | 3b9aa | 2,853.6 | 7,974.5 | 6,346.9 | 3,137.7 | 1,634.2 | 8,254.0 | 9,370.2 | 3,449.2 | 7,530.4 | 9,347.9 | 10,336.7 | † 9,901.7 |
| Equity & investment fund shares | 3baaa | 1,149.4 | 3,373.3 | 2,906.3 | 2,034.4 | 2,289.7 | 7,126.1 | 7,251.1 | 3,617.0 | 3,907.7 | 5,960.5 | 3,078.8 | † 1,612.0 |
| Debt securities | 3bbaa | 1,704.2 | 4,601.2 | 3,440.6 | 1,103.3 | −655.5 | 1,127.9 | 2,119.1 | −167.8 | 3,622.7 | 3,387.4 | 7,257.9 | † 8,289.7 |
| Portfolio investment: liabilities | 3b9la | 3,827.5 | 2,755.6 | 9,083.7 | 1,636.0 | 995.9 | 2,389.1 | 8,985.5 | −5,370.0 | −3,323.3 | 1,770.9 | 9,555.1 | † 3,140.9 |
| Equity & investment fund shares | 3bala | 3,940.0 | 2,255.0 | 3,970.0 | 3,620.0 | 2,153.0 | 2,122.0 | −622.0 | −739.0 | 290.0 | 2,712.0 | 3,600.0 | † 4,521.0 |
| Debt securities | 3bbla | −112.5 | 500.6 | 5,113.7 | −1,984.0 | −1,157.1 | 267.1 | 9,607.5 | −4,631.0 | −3,613.3 | −941.1 | 5,955.1 | † −1,380.1 |
| Fin. der.& empl.stk.ops.(ESOs): net | 3c9na | −49.8 | −34.5 | 88.7 | −29.0 | 115.5 | −230.3 | −29.7 | 12.3 | −296.6 | −458.0 | −421.2 | † −273.5 |
| Fin. der. & ESOs.: assets | 3c9aa | −49.8 | −34.5 | 88.7 | −29.0 | 115.5 | −230.3 | −29.7 | 12.3 | −296.6 | −458.0 | −421.2 | † −273.5 |
| Fin. der. & ESOs.: liabilities | 3c9la | — | — | — | — | — | — | — | — | .... | .... | .... | .... |
| Other investment: assets | 3d9aa | 6,583.7 | 5,314.5 | 16,853.4 | 7,673.0 | −11,331.3 | −4,654.1 | −242.4 | 683.3 | −2,409.1 | 4,176.5 | 4,686.8 | † −3,381.7 |
| Other equity | 3daaa | .... | .... | .... | .... | .... | .... | .... | .... | .... | .... | .... | .... |
| Debt instruments | 3dzaa | 6,583.7 | 5,314.5 | 16,853.4 | 7,673.0 | −11,331.3 | −4,654.1 | −242.4 | 683.3 | −2,409.1 | 4,176.5 | 4,686.8 | † −3,381.7 |
| Other investment: liabilities | 3d9la | 383.9 | 344.0 | 4,008.7 | 4,411.3 | −1,388.4 | 3,955.5 | 3,674.0 | 1,523.2 | −3,676.2 | −812.1 | −6,596.4 | † −5,204.9 |
| Other equity | 3dala | .... | .... | .... | .... | .... | .... | .... | .... | .... | .... | .... | .... |
| Debt instruments | 3dzla | 383.9 | 344.0 | 4,008.7 | 4,411.3 | −1,388.4 | 3,955.5 | 3,674.0 | 1,523.2 | −3,676.2 | −812.1 | −6,596.4 | † −5,204.9 |
| Curr.+ cap.– finan. acct. balance | 4y9na | 379.3 | −3,985.9 | −3,209.6 | 1,310.5 | 16,264.8 | 13,829.2 | 7,980.3 | −1,415.1 | −4,829.4 | 4,849.7 | 3,990.1 | † 8,103.2 |
| D. Net Errors and Omissions | 409na | −3,252.4 | 5,608.8 | 3,546.8 | −3,031.8 | −2,011.7 | 2,912.9 | 4,095.3 | 6,147.4 | 4,694.2 | −177.5 | 3,168.6 | † −767.5 |
| E. Reserves and Related Items | 4z9na | −2,873.1 | 1,622.9 | 337.2 | −1,721.3 | 14,253.1 | 16,742.1 | 12,075.6 | 4,732.3 | −135.2 | 4,672.2 | 7,158.7 | † 7,335.7 |
| Reserve assets | 3e9aa | 362.6 | 1,622.9 | 337.2 | −1,721.3 | 14,253.1 | 16,742.1 | 12,075.6 | 4,732.3 | −135.2 | 4,672.2 | 7,158.7 | † 7,335.7 |
| Credit and loans from the IMF | 3dcla | — | — | — | — | — | — | — | — | — | — | — | † — |
| Exceptional financing | 409la | 3,235.7 | — | — | — | — | — | — | — | .... | .... | .... | .... |

*Excludes components in group E

| | | 2004 | 2005 | 2006 | 2007 | 2008 | 2009 | 2010 | 2011 | 2012 | 2013 | 2014 | 2015 |
|---|---|---|---|---|---|---|---|---|---|---|---|---|---|
| **International Investment Position** | | | | | | | *Millions of US Dollars* | | | | | | |
| Assets | 809aa | 108,300.3 | 125,429.6 | 170,085.1 | 197,622.5 | 194,595.2 | 227,144.1 | 260,935.5 | 265,727.9 | 277,029.2 | 313,735.0 | 335,828.8 | † 353,818.3 |
| Direct investment | 8a9aa | 18,493.2 | 23,083.0 | 39,322.0 | 49,833.4 | 54,410.0 | 57,371.4 | 68,972.5 | 70,782.6 | 71,171.5 | 76,726.0 | 79,685.5 | † 89,385.2 |
| Equity & investment fund shares | 8aaaa | 13,527.2 | 17,554.0 | 30,689.0 | 39,107.9 | 43,045.8 | 45,013.3 | 52,577.5 | 57,433.5 | 60,178.5 | 67,145.3 | 70,970.5 | † 76,320.6 |
| Debt instruments | 8abaa | 4,966.0 | 5,529.0 | 8,633.0 | 10,725.5 | 11,364.2 | 12,358.1 | 16,395.0 | 13,349.1 | 10,993.0 | 9,580.7 | 8,715.0 | † 13,064.6 |
| Portfolio investment | 8b9aa | 18,576.1 | 26,589.4 | 35,373.4 | 42,121.8 | 33,395.0 | 49,425.0 | 62,397.6 | 62,365.1 | 76,191.6 | 95,528.0 | 106,188.4 | † 114,121.9 |
| Equity & investment fund shares | 8baaa | 5,002.5 | 8,663.1 | 13,348.1 | 16,930.5 | 12,869.7 | 25,336.5 | 35,434.1 | 33,092.5 | 41,640.6 | 56,174.4 | 60,429.4 | † 60,640.9 |
| Debt securities | 8bbaa | 13,573.6 | 17,926.3 | 22,025.3 | 25,191.3 | 20,525.3 | 24,088.5 | 26,963.5 | 29,272.6 | 34,551.0 | 39,353.6 | 45,759.0 | † 53,481.0 |
| Fin. der.(oth.than reserves) & ESOs | 8c9aa | 37.2 | 10.0 | 132.0 | 72.9 | −66.5 | −67.7 | −134.6 | −294.1 | −326.5 | −81.7 | −302.8 | † −619.7 |
| Other investment | 8d9aa | 43,786.0 | 47,619.1 | 66,098.2 | 77,094.6 | 64,318.5 | 59,667.9 | 58,509.9 | 57,533.7 | 53,575.4 | 58,941.6 | 63,677.4 | † 59,947.1 |
| Other equity | 8daaa | .... | .... | .... | .... | .... | .... | .... | .... | .... | .... | .... | .... |
| Debt instruments | 8dzaa | 43,786.0 | 47,619.1 | 66,098.2 | 77,094.6 | 64,318.5 | 59,667.9 | 58,509.9 | 57,533.7 | 53,575.4 | 58,941.6 | 63,677.4 | † 59,947.1 |
| Reserve assets | 8e9aa | 27,407.8 | 28,128.1 | 29,159.5 | 28,499.8 | 42,538.2 | 60,747.5 | 71,190.1 | 75,340.6 | 76,417.2 | 82,621.1 | 86,580.3 | † 90,983.8 |
| Liabilities | 809la | 130,955.5 | 147,425.5 | 170,142.9 | 198,593.2 | 180,497.3 | 214,780.9 | 235,457.2 | 223,047.9 | 223,750.0 | 250,312.0 | 270,606.0 | † 284,869.2 |
| Direct investment | 8a9la | 24,876.3 | 30,811.0 | 44,272.5 | 49,988.5 | 49,747.5 | 55,797.0 | 60,237.1 | 65,327.0 | 76,527.0 | 88,161.0 | 93,279.0 | † 104,102.0 |
| Equity & investment fund shares | 8aala | 22,045.0 | 27,750.0 | 40,918.0 | 46,590.0 | 45,948.0 | 51,521.0 | 56,345.0 | 55,688.0 | 64,094.0 | 75,592.0 | 82,860.0 | † 92,618.0 |
| Debt instruments | 8abla | 2,831.3 | 3,061.0 | 3,354.5 | 3,398.5 | 3,799.5 | 4,276.0 | 3,892.1 | 9,639.0 | 12,433.0 | 12,569.0 | 10,419.0 | † 11,484.0 |
| Portfolio investment | 8b9la | 53,865.5 | 65,077.1 | 69,522.6 | 87,053.1 | 71,366.9 | 95,146.0 | 108,015.8 | 89,818.0 | 84,777.0 | 99,987.5 | 122,105.0 | † 131,595.5 |
| Equity & investment fund shares | 8bala | 30,444.0 | 41,494.0 | 40,535.0 | 59,670.0 | 44,961.0 | 68,650.0 | 71,276.0 | 58,063.0 | 57,626.0 | 73,464.0 | 91,582.0 | † 102,815.0 |
| Debt securities | 8bbla | 23,421.5 | 23,583.1 | 28,987.6 | 27,383.1 | 26,405.9 | 26,496.0 | 36,739.8 | 31,755.0 | 27,151.0 | 26,523.5 | 30,523.0 | † 28,780.5 |
| Fin. der.(oth.than reserves) & ESOs | 8c9la | .... | .... | .... | .... | .... | .... | .... | .... | .... | .... | .... | .... |
| Other investment | 8d9la | 52,213.7 | 51,537.4 | 56,347.8 | 61,551.6 | 59,382.9 | 63,837.9 | 67,204.3 | 67,902.9 | 62,446.0 | 62,163.5 | 55,222.0 | † 49,171.7 |
| Other equity | 8dala | .... | .... | .... | .... | .... | .... | .... | .... | .... | .... | .... | .... |
| Debt instruments | 8dzla | 52,213.7 | 51,537.4 | 56,347.8 | 61,551.6 | 59,382.9 | 63,837.9 | 67,204.3 | 67,902.9 | 62,446.0 | 62,163.5 | 55,222.0 | † 49,171.7 |

| | | 2004 | 2005 | 2006 | 2007 | 2008 | 2009 | 2010 | 2011 | 2012 | 2013 | 2014 | 2015 |
|---|---|---|---|---|---|---|---|---|---|---|---|---|---|
| **Government Finance** | | | | | | | | | | | | | |
| **Operations Statement** | | | | | | | | | | | | | |
| **Budgetary Central Government** | | | | | *Millions of New Sheqalim: Fiscal Year Ends December 31* | | | | | | | | |
| Revenue........................... | a1 | .... | .... | 251,345 | 262,430 | 258,454 | 249,636 | 275,106 | 296,739 | 307,752 | 333,750 | 352,545 | 373,342 |
| Taxes............................ | a11 | .... | .... | 178,959 | 191,280 | 184,204 | 178,285 | 196,819 | 212,766 | 219,435 | 242,298 | 256,862 | 271,581 |
| Social Contributions..................... | a12 | .... | .... | 41,871 | 43,612 | 46,585 | 47,453 | 51,870 | 55,577 | 57,326 | 60,668 | 63,291 | 66,781 |
| Grants.......................... | a13 | .... | .... | 16,990 | 12,813 | 12,347 | 10,773 | 12,866 | 13,004 | 14,605 | 14,029 | 14,824 | 16,297 |
| Other Revenue........................ | a14 | .... | .... | 13,526 | 14,725 | 15,319 | 13,125 | 13,551 | 15,393 | 16,386 | 16,754 | 17,569 | 18,683 |
| Expense........................... | a2 | .... | .... | 259,070 | 265,268 | 273,585 | 290,155 | 305,336 | 319,218 | 343,437 | 366,772 | 379,310 | 399,156 |
| Compensation of Employees.......... | a21 | .... | .... | 44,226 | 45,775 | 47,838 | 50,136 | 53,183 | 56,362 | 59,861 | 63,997 | 66,263 | 68,881 |
| Use of Goods & Services................ | a22 | .... | .... | 40,834 | 40,398 | 41,468 | 41,813 | 44,157 | 46,370 | 50,043 | 52,092 | 56,016 | 58,132 |
| Consumption of Fixed Capital....... | a23 | .... | .... | 2,481 | 2,603 | 2,776 | 2,891 | 2,953 | 3,072 | 3,205 | 3,155 | 3,180 | 3,359 |
| Interest.............................. | a24 | .... | .... | 28,631 | 29,610 | 24,440 | 26,472 | 26,785 | 24,688 | 26,676 | 27,394 | 26,699 | 30,773 |
| Subsidies............................. | a25 | .... | .... | 6,435 | 5,075 | 4,870 | 5,002 | 4,768 | 5,438 | 6,046 | 7,862 | 8,421 | 8,097 |
| Grants.............................. | a26 | .... | .... | 53,492 | 55,480 | 58,783 | 59,874 | 65,141 | 70,661 | 75,630 | 82,279 | 85,727 | 91,752 |
| Social Benefits....................... | a27 | .... | .... | 66,082 | 68,466 | 72,706 | 80,219 | 85,699 | 90,945 | 97,229 | 101,865 | 105,952 | 110,455 |
| Other Expense......................... | a28 | .... | .... | 16,889 | 17,861 | 20,706 | 23,747 | 22,650 | 21,681 | 24,747 | 28,129 | 27,052 | 27,707 |
| Gross Operating Balance [1-2+23]... | agob | .... | .... | −5,243 | −234 | −12,355 | −37,628 | −27,277 | −19,406 | −32,480 | −29,867 | −23,585 | −22,455 |
| Net Operating Balance [1-2]............ | anob | .... | .... | −7,724 | −2,838 | −15,131 | −40,519 | −30,230 | −22,479 | −35,685 | −33,023 | −26,765 | −25,814 |
| Net Acq. of Nonfinancial Assets....... | a31 | .... | .... | −834 | −790 | −1,165 | −713 | −1,328 | −929 | −1,063 | −1,898 | −1,149 | −1,792 |
| Aquisition of Nonfin. Assets.......... | a31.1 | .... | .... | 1,729 | 1,869 | 1,657 | 2,226 | 1,746 | 2,203 | 2,215 | 1,321 | 2,105 | 1,612 |
| Disposal of Nonfin. Assets............ | a31.2 | .... | .... | 82 | 56 | 47 | 49 | 121 | 59 | 73 | 63 | 74 | 45 |
| Net Lending/Borrowing [1-2-31]...... | anlb | .... | .... | −6,890 | −2,047 | −13,965 | −39,806 | −28,903 | −21,550 | −34,622 | −31,125 | −25,616 | −24,021 |
| Net Acq. of Financial Assets............. | a32 | .... | .... | −13,388 | −11,887 | −3,184 | 3,334 | −19,365 | −15,873 | −1,718 | 1,845 | −11,465 | −5,044 |
| By instrument | | | | | | | | | | | | | |
| Monetary Gold & SDRs.............. | a3201 | .... | .... | — | — | — | — | — | — | — | — | — | — |
| Currency & Deposits..................... | a3202 | .... | .... | −4,555 | −932 | 5,856 | 11,092 | −9,047 | −3,169 | 3,570 | 7,480 | −5,250 | 4,352 |
| Securities other than Shares........... | a3203 | .... | .... | — | — | — | — | — | — | — | — | — | — |
| Loans.............................. | a3204 | .... | .... | −2,765 | −3,368 | −6,162 | −5,362 | −5,861 | −5,579 | −4,430 | −4,597 | −3,964 | −6,050 |
| Shares & Other Equity..................... | a3205 | .... | .... | −6,079 | −7,552 | −2,891 | −2,245 | −4,457 | −7,124 | −858 | −1,039 | −2,251 | −3,346 |
| Insurance Technical Reserves......... | a3206 | .... | .... | — | — | — | — | — | — | — | — | — | — |
| Financial Derivatives..................... | a3207 | .... | .... | — | — | — | — | — | — | — | — | — | — |
| Other Accounts Receivable............. | a3208 | .... | .... | 11 | −35 | 13 | −152 | — | — | — | — | — | — |
| By debtor | | | | | | | | | | | | | |
| Domestic............................ | a321 | .... | .... | −11,042 | −2,325 | 7,180 | 3,984 | −9,296 | −17,478 | −4,278 | −506 | −11,834 | −6,429 |
| Foreign............................... | a322 | .... | .... | −2,346 | −9,562 | −10,365 | −650 | −10,069 | 1,605 | 2,559 | 2,351 | 369 | 1,385 |
| Net Incurrence of Liabilities.............. | a33 | .... | .... | −7,707 | −11,811 | 8,946 | 38,045 | 10,114 | 6,785 | 31,505 | 30,219 | 15,870 | 18,866 |
| By instrument | | | | | | | | | | | | | |
| Special Drawing Rights (SDRs)........ | a3301 | .... | .... | — | — | — | — | — | — | — | — | — | — |
| Currency & Deposits..................... | a3302 | .... | .... | — | — | — | — | — | — | — | — | — | — |
| Securities other than Shares........... | a3303 | .... | .... | −5,278 | −10,461 | 10,285 | 37,451 | 11,972 | 8,633 | 32,741 | 30,725 | 16,446 | 19,424 |
| Loans.............................. | a3304 | .... | .... | −2,149 | −765 | −1,587 | 785 | −1,404 | −906 | −646 | −275 | −291 | −273 |
| Shares & Other Equity.................... | a3305 | .... | .... | — | — | — | — | — | — | — | — | — | — |
| Insurance Technical Reserves......... | a3306 | .... | .... | — | — | — | — | — | — | — | — | — | — |
| Financial Derivatives..................... | a3307 | .... | .... | — | — | — | — | — | — | — | — | — | — |
| Other Accounts Payable................. | a3308 | .... | .... | −280 | −585 | 249 | −192 | −453 | −942 | −590 | −231 | −285 | −285 |
| By creditor | | | | | | | | | | | | | |
| Domestic............................ | a331 | .... | .... | −15,126 | −4,255 | 21,641 | 33,952 | 11,098 | −6,691 | 35,490 | 38,473 | 10,411 | 22,419 |
| Foreign............................... | a332 | .... | .... | 7,419 | −7,556 | −12,695 | 4,093 | −983 | 13,476 | −3,985 | −8,254 | 5,459 | −3,554 |
| Stat. Discrepancy [32-33-NLB]......... | anlbz | .... | .... | 1,209 | 1,972 | 1,835 | 5,095 | −577 | −1,107 | 1,399 | 2,751 | −1,719 | 112 |
| Memo Item: Expenditure [2+31]...... | a2m | .... | .... | 258,235 | 264,478 | 272,419 | 289,442 | 304,009 | 318,289 | 342,374 | 364,874 | 378,161 | 397,364 |
| **National Accounts** | | | | | *Millions of New Sheqalim* | | | | | | | | |
| Househ.Cons.Expend.,incl.NPISHs.... | 96f | 339,980 | 357,158 | 384,184 | 421,829 | 451,088 | 463,327 | 501,467 | 534,343 | 555,235 | 586,421 | 611,072 | 636,858 |
| Government Consumption Expend... | 91f | 147,334 | 152,496 | 161,874 | 166,652 | 176,212 | 183,957 | 195,684 | 206,974 | 222,830 | 237,630 | 246,552 | 256,980 |
| Gross Fixed Capital Formation.......... | 93e | 112,833 | 121,116 | 130,464 | 146,157 | 152,281 | 150,352 | 163,123 | 189,688 | 206,134 | 212,762 | 211,709 | 212,975 |
| Changes in Inventories..................... | 93i | 5,352 | 9,827 | 9,387 | 7,817 | 973 | −3,142 | −3,583 | −457 | 4,093 | 129 | 6,296 | 10,470 |
| Exports of Goods and Services......... | 90c | 237,912 | 261,347 | 280,500 | 298,173 | 299,138 | 272,803 | 306,775 | 337,753 | 368,988 | 350,698 | 353,118 | 358,557 |
| Imports of Goods and Services (-)..... | 98c | 236,466 | 260,933 | 277,937 | 302,961 | 301,955 | 249,108 | 287,337 | 331,682 | 356,237 | 331,813 | 335,073 | 325,377 |
| Gross Domestic Product (GDP)......... | 99b | 606,946 | 641,012 | 688,472 | 737,668 | 777,736 | 818,189 | 876,129 | 936,619 | 1,001,044 | 1,055,828 | 1,093,674 | 1,150,464 |
| Net Primary Income from Abroad.... | 98.n | −17,749 | −5,588 | −2,657 | −1,036 | −15,073 | −19,929 | −19,294 | −12,283 | −26,769 | −20,928 | −13,111 | −15,420 |
| Gross National Income (GNI)........... | 99a | 589,197 | 635,424 | 685,815 | 736,632 | 762,663 | 798,260 | 856,835 | 924,336 | 974,275 | 1,034,900 | 1,080,563 | 1,135,044 |
| Consumption of Fixed Capital.......... | 99cf | 92,646 | 99,176 | 103,562 | 109,320 | 111,955 | 117,962 | 119,533 | 124,996 | 135,842 | 138,576 | 145,660 | 154,039 |
| Net National Income..................... | 99e | 496,550 | 536,248 | 582,253 | 627,311 | 650,708 | 680,298 | 737,302 | 799,340 | 838,432 | 896,324 | 934,903 | 981,005 |
| GDP Volume 2010 Ref., Chained...... | 99b.p | 678,692 | 708,486 | 749,591 | 795,579 | 819,918 | 830,321 | 876,130 | 920,201 | 946,702 | 977,481 | 1,002,450 | 1,002,450 |
| GDP Volume (2010=100)................ | 99bvp | 77.5 | 80.9 | 85.6 | 90.8 | 93.6 | 94.8 | 100.0 | 105.0 | 108.1 | 111.6 | 114.4 | 114.4 |
| GDP Deflator (2010=100).............. | 99bip | 89.4 | 90.5 | 91.8 | 92.7 | 94.9 | 98.5 | 100.0 | 101.8 | 105.7 | 108.0 | 109.1 | 114.8 |
| | | | | | | *Millions: Midyear Estimates* | | | | | | | |
| **Population................................** | 99z | 6.47 | 6.60 | 6.75 | 6.92 | 7.09 | 7.26 | 7.42 | 7.56 | 7.69 | 7.82 | 7.94 | 8.06 |

|  |  | 2004 | 2005 | 2006 | 2007 | 2008 | 2009 | 2010 | 2011 | 2012 | 2013 | 2014 | 2015 |
|---|---|---|---|---|---|---|---|---|---|---|---|---|---|
| **Exchange Rates** |  | *Euros per SDR: End of Period* | | | | | | | | | | | |
| Market Rate.................................. | aa | 1.1402 | 1.2116 | 1.1423 | 1.0735 | 1.1068 | 1.0882 | 1.1525 | 1.1865 | 1.1649 | 1.1167 | 1.1933 | 1.2728 |
|  |  | *Euros per US Dollar: End of Period (ae) Period Average (rf)* | | | | | | | | | | | |
| Market Rate.................................. | ae | .7342 | .8477 | .7593 | .6793 | .7185 | .6942 | .7484 | .7729 | .7579 | .7251 | .8237 | .9185 |
| Market Rate.................................. | rf | .8054 | .8041 | .7971 | .7306 | .6827 | .7198 | .7550 | .7194 | .7783 | .7532 | .7537 | .9017 |
|  |  | *Index Numbers (2010=100): Period Averages* | | | | | | | | | | | |
| Nominal Effective Exchange Rate..... | nec | 99.5 | 98.7 | 98.6 | 100.4 | 102.4 | 103.3 | 100.0 | 100.3 | 97.8 | 100.0 | 100.7 | 96.9 |
| CPI-Based Real Effect. Ex. Rate........ | rec | 101.8 | 100.6 | 100.2 | 101.1 | 102.6 | 103.8 | 100.0 | 100.0 | 98.2 | 99.9 | 99.5 | 95.0 |
| ULC-Based Real Effect. Ex. Rate....... | rel | 87.5 | 89.8 | 91.1 | 95.1 | 100.7 | 101.0 | 100.0 | 107.2 | 107.6 | 109.2 | 108.8 | 103.7 |
| **Fund Position** |  | *Millions of SDRs: End of Period* | | | | | | | | | | | |
| Quota........................................ | 2f.s | 7,055.50 | 7,055.50 | 7,055.50 | 7,055.50 | 7,055.50 | 7,055.50 | 7,055.50 | 7,882.30 | 7,882.30 | 7,882.30 | 7,882.30 | 7,882.30 |
| SDR Holdings................................ | 1b.s | 93.14 | 159.88 | 180.62 | 209.42 | 169.75 | 6,005.19 | 6,200.67 | 5,982.00 | 6,153.58 | 6,125.86 | 6,130.70 | 5,994.36 |
| Reserve Position in the Fund............ | 1c.s | 2,384.59 | 1,230.20 | 649.28 | 464.99 | 986.90 | 1,170.51 | 1,595.44 | 3,806.20 | 4,050.29 | 3,782.59 | 3,069.77 | 2,175.39 |
| Total Fund Cred.&Loans Outstg....... | 2tl | — | — | — | — | — | — | — | — | — | — | — | — |
| SDR Allocations............................. | 1bd | 702.40 | 702.40 | 702.40 | 702.40 | 702.40 | 6,576.11 | 6,576.11 | 6,576.11 | 6,576.11 | 6,576.11 | 6,576.11 | 6,576.11 |
| **International Liquidity** |  | *Millions of US Dollars Unless Otherwise Indicated: End of Period* | | | | | | | | | | | |
| Total Res.Min.Gold (Eurosys.Def)..... | 1l.d | 27,859 | 25,515 | 25,662 | 28,385 | 37,088 | 45,770 | 47,684 | 49,185 | 50,499 | 50,775 | 47,689 | 47,034 |
| SDR Holdings........................... | 1b.d | 145 | 229 | 272 | 331 | 261 | 9,414 | 9,549 | 9,184 | 9,458 | 9,434 | 8,882 | 8,307 |
| Reserve Position in the Fund......... | 1c.d | 3,703 | 1,758 | 977 | 735 | 1,520 | 1,835 | 2,457 | 5,844 | 6,225 | 5,825 | 4,448 | 3,014 |
| Foreign Exchange...................... | 1d.d | 24,011 | 23,528 | 24,413 | 27,319 | 35,306 | 34,521 | 35,678 | 34,158 | 34,816 | 35,516 | 33,314 | 34,441 |
| o/w:Fin.Deriv.Rel.to Reserves....... | 1ddd | .... | .... | .... | — | — | — | — | — | — | — | — | — |
| Other Reserve Assets................... | 1e.d | .... | .... | .... | — | — | — | — | — | — | — | 1,045 | 1,272 |
| Gold (Million Fine Troy Ounces)....... | 1ad | 78.83 | 78.83 | 78.83 | 78.83 | 78.83 | 78.83 | 78.83 | 78.83 | 78.83 | 78.83 | 78.83 | 78.83 |
| Gold (Eurosystem Valuation)........... | 1and | 34,527 | 40,439 | 50,112 | 65,940 | 68,187 | 87,027 | 111,169 | 124,116 | 131,171 | 94,713 | 94,536 | 83,523 |
| Memo:Euro Cl. on Non-EA Res........ | 1dgd | 139 | 215 | 237 | 269 | 13 | 16 | 8 | — | — | — | — | — |
| Non-Euro Cl. on EA Res............. | 1dhd | .... | .... | .... | 7,437 | 9,675 | 2,389 | 2,759 | 3,668 | 3,888 | 1,222 | 1,507 | 1,320 |
| Central Bank: Other Assets............. | 3..d | 26,997 | 26,572 | 65,972 | 97,403 | 77,411 | 141,990 | 99,158 | 102,117 | 99,328 | 96,857 | 83,097 | 73,872 |
| Central Bank: Other Liabs............... | 4..d | 1,132 | 1,111 | 1,174 | 1,240 | 1,362 | 10,759 | 14,068 | 13,578 | 11,426 | 10,893 | 9,555 | 9,138 |
| Other Depository Corps.: Assets....... | 7a.d | 122,626 | 110,304 | 140,814 | 156,306 | 128,777 | 138,148 | 140,985 | 167,578 | 171,380 | 154,571 | 144,611 | 137,436 |
| Other Depository Corps.: Liabs......... | 7b.d | 214,790 | 212,727 | 256,534 | 317,492 | 277,235 | 281,930 | 251,779 | 203,454 | 205,759 | 172,931 | 155,931 | 137,663 |
| **Central Bank** |  | *Millions of Euros: End of Period* | | | | | | | | | | | |
| Euro Area Wide Residency Criterion |  |  |  |  |  |  |  |  |  |  |  |  |  |
| Net Foreign Assets......................... | 11n.u | 44,073 | 53,525 | 56,247 | 63,887 | 75,194 | 85,751 | 109,740 | 124,701 | 130,780 | 100,983 | 112,925 | 115,492 |
| Claims on Nonresidents................ | 11..u | 45,553 | 56,094 | 58,004 | 64,731 | 76,174 | 93,222 | 120,270 | 135,198 | 139,443 | 108,883 | 120,798 | 123,889 |
| Liabilities to Nonresidents............ | 16c.u | 1,480 | 2,569 | 1,757 | 844 | 980 | 7,470 | 10,530 | 10,497 | 8,663 | 7,900 | 7,873 | 8,396 |
| Claims on Other Depository Corps.... | 12e.u | 21,078 | 29,206 | 28,707 | 34,055 | 58,391 | 34,695 | 62,607 | 226,009 | 285,340 | 244,023 | 192,063 | 156,251 |
| Net Claims on Central Government.. | 12anu | 44,665 | 52,690 | 57,872 | 71,404 | 64,422 | 62,909 | 76,561 | 119,756 | 123,244 | 127,583 | 157,866 | 230,790 |
| Claims on Central Govt................ | 12a.u | 60,524 | 67,352 | 80,817 | 81,119 | 84,246 | 94,355 | 119,673 | 143,834 | 157,424 | 155,095 | 166,105 | 235,984 |
| Liabs. to Central Govt................. | 16d.u | 15,859 | 14,662 | 22,945 | 9,715 | 19,824 | 31,446 | 43,112 | 24,078 | 34,180 | 27,512 | 8,239 | 5,194 |
| Claims on Other Sectors................. | 12s.u | 6,937 | 7,329 | 8,238 | 8,474 | 5,207 | 7,144 | 7,641 | 5,929 | 7,157 | 8,637 | 9,609 | 12,195 |
| Claims on Other Financial Corps..... | 12g.u | 2,247 | 2,349 | 2,654 | 2,973 | 1,909 | 3,147 | 3,606 | 2,436 | 2,919 | 3,133 | 3,688 | 5,492 |
| Claims on State & Local Govts....... | 12b.u | — | — | — | — | — | — | — | — | — | — | — | — |
| Claims on Public Nonfin. Corps...... | 12c.u | — | — | — | — | — | — | — | — | — | — | — | — |
| Claims on Private Sector............... | 12d.u | 4,690 | 4,980 | 5,584 | 5,501 | 3,298 | 3,997 | 4,035 | 3,493 | 4,238 | 5,504 | 5,921 | 6,703 |
| Monetary Base............................... | 14..u | 93,793 | 101,286 | 111,667 | 142,167 | 151,922 | 160,560 | 157,997 | 177,650 | 185,119 | 189,350 | 190,293 | 205,637 |
| Currency in Circulation................. | 14a.u | 86,790 | 97,889 | 108,698 | 115,623 | 129,794 | 136,605 | 142,321 | 150,155 | 154,156 | 161,775 | 168,780 | 178,609 |
| Liabs. to Other Depository Corps.... | 14c.u | 6,894 | 3,352 | 2,950 | 26,378 | 22,128 | 23,955 | 15,647 | 27,285 | 30,270 | 20,797 | 15,436 | 24,139 |
| Liabs. to Other Sectors.................. | 14d.u | 109 | 45 | 19 | 166 | — | — | 29 | 210 | 693 | 6,778 | 6,077 | 2,889 |
| Other Liabs. to Other Dep. Corps..... | 14n.u | — | — | — | — | — | — | — | — | — | — | — | — |
| Dep. & Sec. Excl. f/Monetary Base.... | 14o.u | — | — | — | — | — | — | — | — | — | — | — | — |
| Deposits Included in Broad Money. | 15..u | — | — | — | — | — | — | — | — | — | — | — | — |
| Sec.Ot.th.Shares Inc.in.Brd.Money.. | 16a.u | — | — | — | — | — | — | — | — | — | — | — | — |
| Deposits Excl. from Broad Money... | 16b.u | — | — | — | — | — | — | — | — | — | — | — | — |
| Sec.Oh.th.Shares Excl. f/Brd.Money | 16s.u | — | — | — | — | — | — | — | — | — | — | — | — |
| Loans........................................ | 16l.u | — | — | — | — | — | — | — | — | — | — | — | — |
| Financial Derivatives...................... | 16m.u | — | — | — | — | — | — | — | — | — | — | — | — |
| Shares and Other Equity.................. | 17a.u | 26,648 | 42,243 | 43,579 | 48,712 | 56,395 | 71,193 | 93,095 | 98,118 | 120,279 | 90,964 | 115,198 | 118,935 |
| Other Items (Net)........................... | 17r.u | −3,687 | −781 | −4,182 | −13,057 | −5,103 | −41,255 | 5,458 | 200,628 | 241,122 | 200,911 | 166,974 | 190,158 |
| Memorandum Items |  |  |  |  |  |  |  |  |  |  |  |  |  |
| National Residency Criterion |  |  |  |  |  |  |  |  |  |  |  |  |  |
| Net Foreign Assets......................... | 11n | 64,141 | 75,862 | 105,871 | 129,393 | 130,287 | 183,274 | 182,562 | 11,463 | −49,488 | −66,387 | −36,036 | −69,316 |
| Claims on Nonresidents................ | 11 | 65,621 | 78,431 | 107,628 | 130,241 | 131,267 | 190,745 | 193,092 | 212,859 | 212,974 | 175,726 | 185,587 | 187,969 |
| Liabilities to Nonresidents............ | 16c | 1,480 | 2,569 | 1,757 | 848 | 980 | 7,470 | 10,530 | 201,396 | 262,462 | 242,113 | 221,623 | 257,284 |
| Claims on Other Depository Corps.... | 12e | 15,612 | 22,265 | 22,041 | 29,660 | 57,206 | 29,978 | 55,270 | 218,608 | 281,258 | 250,373 | 208,172 | 178,568 |
| Net Claims on Central Government.. | 12an | 44,665 | 52,690 | 45,915 | 54,658 | 42,626 | 35,398 | 25,871 | 59,487 | 68,250 | 80,706 | 113,486 | 192,952 |
| Claims on Central Government...... | 12a | 60,524 | 67,352 | 68,860 | 64,373 | 62,450 | 66,844 | 68,983 | 83,565 | 102,430 | 108,218 | 121,725 | 198,146 |
| Liabilities to Central Government... | 16d | 15,859 | 14,662 | 22,945 | 9,715 | 19,824 | 31,446 | 43,112 | 24,078 | 34,180 | 27,512 | 8,239 | 5,194 |
| Claims on Other Sectors................. | 12s | 6,856 | 6,749 | 7,356 | 7,127 | 3,765 | 4,324 | 3,744 | 3,137 | 3,505 | 3,153 | 2,961 | 3,379 |
| Claims on Other Fin. Corps........... | 12g | 2,208 | 2,348 | 2,553 | 2,549 | 1,321 | 1,354 | 1,060 | 854 | 1,012 | 920 | 951 | 919 |
| Claims on State & Local Govts....... | 12b | — | — | — | — | — | — | — | — | — | — | — | — |
| Claims on Private Sector............... | 12d | 4,648 | 4,401 | 4,803 | 4,578 | 2,444 | 2,970 | 2,684 | 2,283 | 2,493 | 2,233 | 2,010 | 2,460 |
| Liabs.to ODCs, Inc.in Mon.Base....... | 14c | 12,971 | 11,453 | 17,159 | 42,619 | 35,441 | 34,313 | 22,740 | 33,878 | 27,665 | 20,797 | 15,436 | 24,110 |
| Liabs.to Ot.Sectors, Inc.in Mon.Base | 14d | 109 | 45 | 19 | 166 | — | — | 29 | 210 | 693 | 1,693 | 1,272 | 2,889 |
| Liabs.to ODCs,Excl.f/Mon.Base........ | 14n | — | — | — | — | — | — | — | — | — | — | — | — |
| Net Claims on Eurosystem.............. | 12e.s | 9,170 | 7,441 | 16,636 | 27,499 | 18,079 | 52,853 | 4,750 | −189,140 | −239,030 | −206,919 | −177,742 | −207,783 |

|  |  | 2004 | 2005 | 2006 | 2007 | 2008 | 2009 | 2010 | 2011 | 2012 | 2013 | 2014 | 2015 |
|---|---|---|---|---|---|---|---|---|---|---|---|---|---|
| **Other Depository Corporations** | | | | | | *Millions of Euros: End of Period* | | | | | | | |
| Euro Area Wide Residency Criterion | | | | | | | | | | | | | |
| Net Foreign Assets........................ | **21n.u** | −67,663 | −86,821 | −87,867 | −109,494 | −106,674 | −99,807 | −82,917 | −27,727 | −26,057 | −13,313 | −9,323 | −208 |
| Claims on Nonresidents................ | **21..u** | 90,027 | 93,502 | 106,920 | 106,179 | 92,532 | 95,896 | 105,512 | 129,514 | 129,892 | 112,081 | 119,110 | 126,239 |
| Liabilities to Nonresidents............. | **26c.u** | 157,690 | 180,323 | 194,787 | 215,673 | 199,206 | 195,703 | 188,429 | 157,241 | 155,949 | 125,394 | 128,433 | 126,447 |
| Claims on Eurosystem...................... | **20..u** | 21,959 | 20,604 | 25,300 | 53,590 | 48,156 | 46,446 | 34,189 | 45,040 | 40,636 | 33,395 | 27,800 | 35,534 |
| Currency........................................ | **20a.u** | 8,802 | 8,949 | 10,553 | 11,657 | 12,851 | 11,328 | 10,787 | 11,153 | 12,939 | 12,629 | 12,419 | 11,323 |
| Reserve Deposits and Securities..... | **20b.u** | 13,157 | 11,655 | 14,747 | 41,933 | 35,305 | 35,118 | 23,402 | 33,887 | 27,697 | 20,766 | 15,381 | 24,211 |
| Other Claims................................ | **20n.u** | — | — | — | — | — | — | — | — | — | — | — | — |
| Net Claims on Central Government.. | **22anu** | 195,713 | 188,962 | 178,551 | 303,389 | 304,733 | 344,340 | 391,591 | 395,926 | 515,540 | 562,521 | 567,869 | 583,940 |
| Claims on Central Government...... | **22a.u** | 202,944 | 198,097 | 188,481 | 316,943 | 318,201 | 360,534 | 408,556 | 411,097 | 528,463 | 584,788 | 617,803 | 628,444 |
| Liabilities to Central Government... | **26d.u** | 7,231 | 9,135 | 9,930 | 13,554 | 13,468 | 16,194 | 16,965 | 15,171 | 12,923 | 22,267 | 49,934 | 44,504 |
| Claims on Other Sectors................. | **22s.u** | 1,266,541 | 1,372,737 | 1,519,617 | 1,729,000 | 1,981,538 | 2,006,541 | 2,238,437 | 2,309,605 | 2,346,552 | 2,188,377 | 2,164,563 | 2,100,282 |
| Claims on Other Financial Corps.... | **22g.u** | 239,745 | 264,271 | 287,157 | 309,806 | 504,686 | 515,336 | 627,586 | 647,938 | 714,033 | 625,492 | 629,219 | 564,780 |
| Claims on State & Local Govts....... | **22b.u** | 38,457 | 43,950 | 48,024 | 89,135 | 94,320 | 97,261 | 97,595 | 98,698 | 96,691 | 89,224 | 83,877 | 79,725 |
| Claims on Public Nonfin. Corps...... | **22c.u** | — | — | — | — | — | — | — | — | — | — | — | — |
| Claims on Private Sector............... | **22d.u** | 988,339 | 1,064,516 | 1,184,436 | 1,330,059 | 1,382,532 | 1,393,944 | 1,513,256 | 1,562,969 | 1,535,828 | 1,473,661 | 1,451,467 | 1,455,777 |
| Liabilities to Eurosystem................... | **26g.u** | 18,703 | 25,597 | 24,556 | 30,481 | 56,638 | 33,619 | 59,759 | 223,798 | 284,647 | 253,339 | 211,861 | 186,585 |
| Transf.Dep.Included in Broad Money | **24..u** | 549,462 | 593,889 | 633,140 | 651,207 | 697,722 | 774,939 | 762,149 | 740,697 | 737,888 | 759,406 | 828,833 | 897,975 |
| Other.Dep.Included in Broad Money. | **25..u** | 281,851 | 275,158 | 282,215 | 449,324 | 459,314 | 428,515 | 415,339 | 420,487 | 471,063 | 472,648 | 445,438 | 426,279 |
| Sec.Ot.th.Shares Inc.in.Brd. Money... | **26a.u** | 3,480 | 3,495 | 13,713 | 31,873 | 52,299 | 59,226 | 43,607 | 48,968 | 49,906 | 27,002 | 15,824 | 9,081 |
| Deposits Excl. from Broad Money..... | **26b.u** | 5,539 | 7,856 | 14,622 | 19,418 | 40,883 | 60,056 | 314,586 | 258,428 | 302,276 | 303,194 | 279,401 | 301,894 |
| Sec.Ot.th.Shares Excl.f/Brd. Money... | **26s.u** | 366,318 | 388,132 | 428,599 | 470,353 | 503,700 | 516,345 | 521,967 | 528,823 | 492,366 | 472,181 | 417,800 | 354,512 |
| Loans............................................. | **26l.u** | — | — | — | — | — | — | — | — | — | — | — | — |
| Financial Derivatives....................... | **26m.u** | 14,038 | 17,964 | 18,997 | 20,449 | 168,436 | 150,176 | 163,276 | 214,379 | 246,877 | 163,344 | 206,755 | 160,845 |
| Insurance Technical Reserves........... | **26r.u** | | | | | | | | | | | | |
| Shares and Other Equity.................. | **27a.u** | 163,181 | 191,407 | 195,372 | 264,679 | 276,427 | 293,936 | 290,028 | 300,434 | 284,759 | 277,653 | 272,466 | 277,445 |
| Other Items (Net)............................ | **27r.u** | 13,980 | −8,013 | 24,393 | 38,701 | −27,671 | −19,287 | 10,592 | −13,173 | 6,896 | 42,204 | 71,857 | 104,931 |
| Memorandum Items | | | | | | | | | | | | | |
| Total Assets.................................... | **20ra** | 2,379,065 | 2,599,140 | 2,870,510 | 3,407,400 | 3,693,945 | 3,746,463 | 3,798,277 | 4,062,717 | 4,220,479 | 4,048,229 | 4,022,304 | 3,920,747 |
| National Residency Criterion | | | | | | | | | | | | | |
| Net Foreign Assets......................... | **21n** | −38,171 | −49,199 | −77,627 | −123,344 | −103,732 | −93,513 | −97,296 | −30,562 | −7,573 | −17,311 | 3,669 | 12,849 |
| Claims on Nonresidents................ | **21** | 259,499 | 293,064 | 345,525 | 390,196 | 373,441 | 337,117 | 333,266 | 367,782 | 345,073 | 305,215 | 311,817 | 335,822 |
| Liabilities to Nonresidents............. | **26c** | 297,670 | 342,263 | 423,152 | 513,540 | 477,173 | 430,630 | 430,562 | 398,344 | 352,646 | 322,526 | 308,148 | 322,973 |
| Net Claims on Central Government.. | **22an** | 169,795 | 168,420 | 161,987 | 286,029 | 293,845 | 333,698 | 384,855 | 390,069 | 511,306 | 557,068 | 554,978 | 551,982 |
| Claims on Central Government...... | **22a** | 177,013 | 176,634 | 170,125 | 299,553 | 307,280 | 349,862 | 401,802 | 405,201 | 524,187 | 579,301 | 604,884 | 596,462 |
| Liabilities to Central Government... | **26d** | 7,218 | 8,214 | 8,138 | 13,524 | 13,435 | 16,164 | 16,947 | 15,132 | 12,881 | 22,233 | 49,906 | 44,480 |
| Claims on Other Sectors................. | **22s** | 1,231,797 | 1,332,177 | 1,466,661 | 1,661,226 | 1,905,820 | 1,927,527 | 2,160,099 | 2,234,719 | 2,278,736 | 2,130,459 | 2,120,510 | 2,055,835 |
| Claims on Other Fin. Corps............ | **22g** | 214,516 | 234,593 | 247,326 | 256,576 | 444,793 | 453,331 | 567,620 | 589,372 | 663,040 | 579,991 | 597,686 | 533,932 |
| Claims on State & Local Govts....... | **22b** | 38,303 | 43,735 | 47,638 | 88,291 | 92,901 | 96,044 | 95,852 | 96,805 | 95,206 | 87,652 | 82,147 | 78,270 |
| Claims on Private Sector............... | **22d** | 978,978 | 1,053,849 | 1,171,697 | 1,316,359 | 1,368,126 | 1,378,152 | 1,496,627 | 1,548,542 | 1,520,490 | 1,462,816 | 1,440,677 | 1,443,633 |
| Transf.Dep.Included in Broad Money | **24** | 546,142 | 590,517 | 629,210 | 647,499 | 692,596 | 769,841 | 757,720 | 736,085 | 731,945 | 753,282 | 821,435 | 890,750 |
| Other.Dep.Included in Broad Money. | **25** | 273,927 | 266,833 | 272,161 | 440,380 | 451,273 | 424,204 | 410,183 | 417,417 | 467,834 | 466,286 | 440,946 | 419,851 |
| Sec.Ot.th.Shares Inc.in.Brd. Money... | **26a** | 7,323 | 7,710 | 16,455 | 32,603 | 53,779 | 60,126 | 42,017 | 49,790 | 49,997 | 27,333 | 16,456 | 10,063 |
| Deposits Excl. from Broad Money..... | **26b** | 4,011 | 5,759 | 11,192 | 16,378 | 27,932 | 45,858 | 300,583 | 243,712 | 286,829 | 288,864 | 275,648 | 294,512 |
| Sec.Ot.th.Shares Excl.f/Brd. Money... | **26s** | 373,906 | 398,726 | 439,091 | 483,458 | 524,723 | 540,199 | 546,799 | 553,535 | 512,971 | 490,708 | 437,065 | 376,622 |

Italy 136

| | | 2004 | 2005 | 2006 | 2007 | 2008 | 2009 | 2010 | 2011 | 2012 | 2013 | 2014 | 2015 |
|---|---|---|---|---|---|---|---|---|---|---|---|---|---|
| **Depository Corporations** | | | | | | *Millions of Euros: End of Period* | | | | | | | |
| Euro Area Wide Residency Criterion | | | | | | | | | | | | | |
| Net Foreign Assets | 31n.u | −23,590 | −33,296 | −31,620 | −45,607 | −31,480 | −14,056 | 26,823 | 96,974 | 104,723 | 87,670 | 103,602 | 115,284 |
| Claims on Nonresidents | 31..u | 135,580 | 149,596 | 164,924 | 170,910 | 168,706 | 189,118 | 225,782 | 264,712 | 269,335 | 220,964 | 239,908 | 250,128 |
| Liabilities to Nonresidents | 36c.u | 159,170 | 182,892 | 196,544 | 216,517 | 200,186 | 203,173 | 198,959 | 167,738 | 164,612 | 133,294 | 136,306 | 134,843 |
| Domestic Claims | 32..u | 1,513,856 | 1,621,718 | 1,764,278 | 2,112,267 | 2,355,900 | 2,420,934 | 2,714,230 | 2,831,216 | 2,992,493 | 2,887,118 | 2,899,907 | 2,927,207 |
| Net Claims on Central Government | 32anu | 240,378 | 241,652 | 236,423 | 374,793 | 369,155 | 407,249 | 468,152 | 515,682 | 638,784 | 690,104 | 725,735 | 814,730 |
| Claims on Central Government | 32a.u | 263,468 | 265,449 | 269,298 | 398,062 | 402,447 | 454,889 | 528,229 | 554,931 | 685,887 | 739,883 | 783,908 | 864,428 |
| Liabilities to Central Government | 36d.u | 23,090 | 23,797 | 32,875 | 23,269 | 33,292 | 47,640 | 60,077 | 39,249 | 47,103 | 49,779 | 58,173 | 49,698 |
| Claims on Other Sectors | 32s.u | 1,273,478 | 1,380,066 | 1,527,855 | 1,737,474 | 1,986,745 | 2,013,685 | 2,246,078 | 2,315,534 | 2,353,709 | 2,197,014 | 2,174,172 | 2,112,477 |
| Claims on Other Financial Corps. | 32g.u | 241,992 | 266,620 | 289,811 | 312,779 | 506,595 | 518,483 | 631,192 | 650,374 | 716,952 | 628,625 | 632,907 | 570,272 |
| Claims on State & Local Govts. | 32b.u | 38,457 | 43,950 | 48,024 | 89,135 | 94,320 | 97,261 | 97,595 | 98,698 | 96,691 | 89,224 | 83,877 | 79,725 |
| Claims on Public Nonfin. Corps. | 32c.u | — | — | — | — | — | — | — | — | — | — | — | — |
| Claims on Private Sector | 32d.u | 993,029 | 1,069,496 | 1,190,020 | 1,335,560 | 1,385,830 | 1,397,941 | 1,517,291 | 1,566,462 | 1,540,066 | 1,479,165 | 1,457,388 | 1,462,480 |
| Broad Money Liabilities | 35l.u | 912,890 | 961,527 | 1,027,232 | 1,236,536 | 1,326,278 | 1,387,957 | 1,352,658 | 1,349,364 | 1,400,767 | 1,414,980 | 1,452,533 | 1,503,510 |
| Currency Outside Depository Corps | 34a.u | 77,988 | 88,940 | 98,145 | 103,966 | 116,943 | 125,277 | 131,534 | 139,002 | 141,217 | 149,146 | 156,361 | 167,286 |
| Transferable Deposits | 34..u | 549,571 | 593,934 | 633,159 | 651,373 | 697,722 | 774,939 | 762,178 | 740,907 | 738,581 | 761,099 | 830,105 | 900,864 |
| Other Deposits | 35..u | 281,851 | 275,158 | 282,215 | 449,324 | 459,314 | 428,515 | 415,339 | 420,487 | 471,063 | 477,733 | 450,243 | 426,279 |
| Securities Other than Shares | 36a.u | 3,480 | 3,495 | 13,713 | 31,873 | 52,299 | 59,226 | 43,607 | 48,968 | 49,906 | 27,002 | 15,824 | 9,081 |
| Deposits Excl. from Broad Money | 36b.u | 5,539 | 7,856 | 14,622 | 19,418 | 40,883 | 60,056 | 314,586 | 258,428 | 302,276 | 303,194 | 279,401 | 301,894 |
| Sec.Oth.th.Shares Excl.f/Brd. Money | 36s.u | 366,318 | 388,132 | 428,599 | 470,353 | 503,700 | 516,345 | 521,967 | 528,823 | 492,366 | 472,181 | 417,800 | 354,512 |
| Loans | 36l.u | — | — | — | — | — | — | — | — | — | — | — | — |
| Financial Derivatives | 36m.u | 14,038 | 17,964 | 18,997 | 20,449 | 168,436 | 150,176 | 163,276 | 214,379 | 246,877 | 163,344 | 206,755 | 160,845 |
| Insurance Technical Reserves | 36r.u | — | — | — | — | — | — | — | — | — | — | — | — |
| Shares and Other Equity | 37a.u | 189,829 | 233,650 | 238,951 | 313,391 | 332,822 | 365,129 | 383,123 | 398,552 | 405,038 | 368,617 | 387,664 | 396,380 |
| Other Items (Net) | 37r.u | 1,655 | −20,706 | 4,263 | 6,515 | −47,704 | −72,781 | 5,447 | 178,642 | 249,898 | 252,462 | 258,684 | 325,351 |
| Broad Money Liabs., Seasonally Adj. | 35lub | 894,188 | 940,614 | 1,003,818 | 1,209,235 | 1,299,132 | 1,363,241 | 1,332,244 | 1,332,758 | 1,386,192 | 1,402,270 | 1,440,771 | 1,492,242 |
| Memorandum Items | | | | | | | | | | | | | |
| National Residency Criterion | | | | | | | | | | | | | |
| Net Foreign Assets | 31n | 25,970 | 26,663 | 28,244 | 6,049 | 26,555 | 89,761 | 85,266 | −19,099 | −57,061 | −83,698 | −32,367 | −56,467 |
| Claims on Nonresidents | 31 | 325,120 | 371,495 | 453,153 | 520,437 | 504,708 | 527,862 | 526,358 | 580,641 | 558,047 | 480,941 | 497,404 | 523,791 |
| Liabilities to Nonresidents | 36c | 299,150 | 344,832 | 424,909 | 514,388 | 478,153 | 438,100 | 441,092 | 599,740 | 615,108 | 564,639 | 529,771 | 580,257 |
| Domestic Claims | 32 | 1,453,113 | 1,560,036 | 1,681,919 | 2,009,040 | 2,246,056 | 2,300,947 | 2,574,569 | 2,687,412 | 2,861,797 | 2,771,386 | 2,791,935 | 2,804,148 |
| Net Claims on Central Government | 32an | 214,460 | 221,110 | 207,902 | 340,687 | 336,471 | 369,096 | 410,726 | 449,556 | 579,556 | 637,774 | 668,464 | 744,934 |
| Claims on Central Government | 32a | 237,537 | 243,986 | 238,985 | 363,926 | 369,730 | 416,706 | 470,785 | 488,766 | 626,617 | 687,519 | 726,609 | 794,608 |
| Liabilities to Central Government | 36d | 23,077 | 22,876 | 31,083 | 23,239 | 33,259 | 47,610 | 60,059 | 39,210 | 47,061 | 49,745 | 58,145 | 49,674 |
| Claims on Other Sectors | 32s | 1,238,653 | 1,338,926 | 1,474,017 | 1,668,353 | 1,909,585 | 1,931,851 | 2,163,843 | 2,237,856 | 2,282,241 | 2,133,612 | 2,123,471 | 2,059,214 |
| Claims on Other Financial Corps. | 32g | 216,724 | 236,941 | 249,879 | 259,125 | 446,114 | 454,685 | 568,680 | 590,226 | 664,052 | 580,911 | 598,637 | 534,851 |
| Claims on State & Local Govts. | 32b | 38,303 | 43,735 | 47,638 | 88,291 | 92,901 | 96,044 | 95,852 | 96,805 | 95,206 | 87,652 | 82,147 | 78,270 |
| Claims on Private Sector | 32d | 983,626 | 1,058,250 | 1,176,500 | 1,320,937 | 1,370,570 | 1,381,122 | 1,499,311 | 1,550,825 | 1,522,983 | 1,465,049 | 1,442,687 | 1,446,093 |
| Transf.Dep.Included in Broad Money | 34 | 546,251 | 590,562 | 629,229 | 647,665 | 692,596 | 769,841 | 757,749 | 736,295 | 732,638 | 754,975 | 822,707 | 893,639 |
| Other Dep.Included in Broad Money | 35 | 273,927 | 266,833 | 272,161 | 440,380 | 451,273 | 424,204 | 410,183 | 417,417 | 467,834 | 466,286 | 440,946 | 419,851 |
| Sec.Ot.th.Shares Inc.in.Brd. Money | 36a | 7,323 | 7,710 | 16,455 | 32,603 | 53,779 | 60,126 | 42,017 | 49,790 | 49,997 | 27,333 | 16,456 | 10,063 |
| Deposits Excl. from Broad Money | 36b | 4,011 | 5,759 | 11,192 | 16,378 | 27,932 | 45,858 | 300,583 | 243,712 | 286,829 | 288,864 | 275,648 | 294,512 |
| Sec.Ot.th.Shares Excl./f.Brd. Money | 36s | 373,906 | 398,726 | 439,091 | 483,458 | 524,723 | 540,199 | 546,799 | 553,535 | 512,971 | 490,708 | 437,065 | 376,622 |
| **Interest Rates** | | | | | | *Percent Per Annum* | | | | | | | |
| Money Market Rate | 60b | 2.10 | 2.18 | 3.09 | 4.29 | 4.67 | 1.28 | 1.02 | 2.73 | 2.12 | .... | .... | .... |
| Treasury Bill Rate | 60c | 2.08 | 2.17 | 3.18 | 4.04 | 3.76 | .96 | 1.13 | 2.79 | 1.90 | .86 | .42 | .05 |
| Deposit Rate | | | | | | | | | | | | | |
| Households: Stocks, up to 2 years | 60lhs | 1.52 | 1.45 | 1.65 | 2.25 | 2.79 | 2.02 | 1.33 | 1.95 | 3.25 | 2.71 | 2.04 | 1.47 |
| New Business, up to 1 year | 60lhn | 1.49 | 1.51 | 1.88 | 2.64 | 3.14 | 1.40 | 1.17 | 2.24 | 2.87 | 2.15 | 1.61 | 1.20 |
| REPOS, Stocks | 60lcr | 1.92 | 1.99 | 2.69 | 3.77 | 4.13 | 2.03 | 1.35 | 2.08 | 3.11 | 2.31 | 1.80 | 1.15 |
| Lending Rate | | | | | | | | | | | | | |
| Households: Stocks, up to 1 year | 60phs | 8.00 | 7.80 | 7.95 | 8.36 | 8.66 | 7.01 | 6.44 | 6.75 | 7.09 | 7.00 | 6.63 | 5.97 |
| New Bus., Floating & up to 1 year | 60pns | 10.40 | 10.08 | 10.49 | 10.50 | 10.85 | 9.73 | 7.49 | 5.72 | 6.04 | 5.96 | 5.82 | 5.20 |
| House Purch., Stocks,Over 5 years | 60phm | 4.48 | 4.24 | 4.60 | 5.38 | 5.80 | 4.28 | 3.57 | 3.64 | 3.30 | 3.01 | 3.00 | 2.74 |
| House Purch., New Bus., 5-10 yrs | 60phn | 4.96 | 4.19 | 4.84 | 5.57 | 5.63 | 4.41 | 4.02 | 4.29 | 4.82 | 4.47 | 3.98 | 2.95 |
| Corporations: Stocks, up to 1 year | 60pcs | 5.03 | 4.85 | 5.22 | 6.01 | 6.56 | 4.38 | 3.66 | 4.21 | 4.88 | 4.80 | 4.53 | 3.76 |
| New Bus., Over € 1 mil.,up to 1 yi | 60pcn | 2.93 | 3.02 | 3.80 | 4.59 | 5.12 | 2.34 | 1.93 | 2.93 | 3.02 | 2.89 | 2.42 | 1.63 |
| Government Bond Yield | 61 | 4.26 | 3.56 | 4.05 | 4.49 | 4.68 | 4.31 | 4.04 | 5.42 | 5.49 | 4.32 | 2.89 | 1.71 |
| Govt. Bond Yield (Medium-Term) | 61b | 3.34 | 2.90 | 3.71 | 4.27 | 4.29 | 3.17 | 2.90 | 4.68 | 4.51 | 3.11 | 1.57 | .76 |
| **Prices, Production, Labor** | | | | | | *Index Numbers (2010=100): Period Averages* | | | | | | | |
| Share Prices | 62 | 125.6 | 149.5 | 172.9 | 189.9 | 131.7 | 94.2 | 100.0 | 91.3 | 77.1 | 88.5 | 104.8 | 115.6 |
| Producer Prices | 63 | 85.5 | 88.9 | 93.9 | † 97.2 | 101.9 | 97.1 | 100.0 | † 104.7 | 108.5 | 107.3 | 105.7 | 102.9 |
| Consumer Prices | 64 | 89.2 | 91.0 | 92.9 | 94.6 | 97.8 | 98.5 | 100.0 | 102.7 | 105.9 | 107.2 | 107.4 | † 107.5 |
| Harmonized CPI | 64h | 88.5 | 90.5 | 92.5 | 94.4 | 97.7 | 98.4 | 100.0 | 102.9 | 106.3 | 107.7 | 107.9 | 108.0 |
| Wages: Contractual | 65 | 85.1 | 87.7 | 90.5 | 93.0 | † 95.0 | 97.9 | † 100.0 | 101.7 | 103.2 | 104.7 | 105.9 | 107.2 |
| Industrial Production | 66 | 114.4 | 112.4 | 115.9 | 118.8 | 115.0 | 93.5 | 100.0 | 100.3 | 94.2 | 91.4 | 90.3 | 92.0 |
| Industrial Employment | 67 | 101.0 | 99.6 | 101.1 | 101.7 | 102.5 | 100.8 | 100.0 | 100.3 | 100.0 | 98.2 | 98.5 | 99.2 |
| | | | | | | *Number in Thousands: Period Averages* | | | | | | | |
| Labor Force | 67d | † 24,307 | 23,934 | 24,038 | 23,996 | 24,357 | 24,227 | 24,203 | 24,272 | 24,833 | 24,816 | 25,040 | 24,997 |
| Employment | 67e | † 22,363 | 22,060 | 22,388 | 22,518 | 22,699 | 22,324 | 22,152 | 22,215 | 22,149 | 21,755 | 21,810 | 21,973 |
| Unemployment | 67c | † 1,941 | 1,874 | 1,659 | 1,483 | 1,663 | 1,905 | 2,058 | 2,056 | 2,691 | 3,069 | 3,230 | 3,033 |
| Unemployment Rate (%) | 67r | † 8.0 | 7.7 | 6.8 | 6.1 | 6.7 | 7.8 | 8.4 | 8.4 | 10.6 | 12.1 | 12.7 | 11.9 |
| **Intl. Transactions & Positions** | | | | | | *Millions of Euros* | | | | | | | |
| Exports | 70 | 284,413 | 299,923 | 332,013 | 364,743 | 369,015 | 291,732 | 337,344 | 375,904 | 390,182 | 389,858 | 397,572 | 413,630 |
| Imports, c.i.f. | 71 | 285,635 | 309,292 | 352,465 | 373,341 | 382,049 | 297,608 | 367,390 | 401,428 | 380,293 | 359,455 | 353,972 | 367,778 |
| | | | | | | | *2010=100* | | | | | | |
| Volume of Exports | 72 | 107.2 | 108.0 | 113.7 | 118.9 | 114.0 | 91.8 | † 100.0 | 104.1 | 103.3 | 102.1 | 102.8 | 105.1 |
| Volume of Imports | 73 | 102.2 | 103.0 | 107.2 | 110.3 | 103.6 | 89.6 | † 100.0 | 98.7 | 89.6 | 86.3 | 87.5 | 94.2 |
| Unit Value of Exports | 74 | 78.8 | 82.4 | 86.7 | 91.1 | 96.1 | 94.3 | † 100.0 | 107.1 | 112.2 | 113.4 | 114.8 | 116.7 |
| Unit Value of Imports | 75 | 76.0 | 81.8 | 89.6 | 92.3 | 100.6 | 90.5 | † 100.0 | 110.8 | 115.7 | 113.5 | 110.5 | 106.4 |

| | | 2004 | 2005 | 2006 | 2007 | 2008 | 2009 | 2010 | 2011 | 2012 | 2013 | 2014 | 2015 |
|---|---|---|---|---|---|---|---|---|---|---|---|---|---|
| **Balance of Payments** | | | | | | | *Millions of US Dollars* | | | | | | |
| A. Current Account* | **109bx** | –16,454.6 | –29,743.9 | –47,828.0 | –51,574.3 | † –67,989.2 | –41,404.6 | –74,384.8 | –70,097.2 | –9,228.6 | 18,967.4 | 38,512.1 | 39,480.5 |
| Goods, credit (exports) | **1a9cx** | 339,400.9 | 358,592.4 | 401,717.6 | 481,639.4 | † 532,671.1 | 397,022.2 | 435,466.4 | 506,292.7 | 485,102.2 | 503,488.7 | 518,317.0 | 450,074.8 |
| Goods, debit (imports) | **1a9dx** | 328,071.1 | 358,049.7 | 414,510.9 | 476,848.1 | † 536,638.1 | 397,351.8 | 464,542.0 | 532,125.1 | 463,660.4 | 455,530.7 | 455,182.0 | 390,473.7 |
| Balance on goods | **1a9bx** | 11,329.8 | 542.7 | –12,793.4 | 4,791.2 | † –3,965.5 | –328.0 | –29,072.9 | –25,833.8 | 21,443.1 | 47,957.9 | 63,133.7 | 59,600.1 |
| Services, credit (exports) | **1b9cx** | 84,439.9 | 89,700.5 | 99,990.7 | 113,134.0 | † 116,478.5 | 97,335.8 | 100,678.0 | 110,586.7 | 108,391.8 | 111,704.8 | 114,028.2 | 98,759.3 |
| Services, debit (imports) | **1b9dx** | 83,598.2 | 90,544.0 | 101,235.1 | 123,005.2 | † 132,046.5 | 109,575.3 | 113,054.0 | 118,994.3 | 108,674.6 | 111,423.3 | 115,139.6 | 100,319.9 |
| Balance on Goods & Services | **1z9bx** | 12,171.5 | –300.9 | –14,037.9 | –5,080.0 | † –19,535.0 | –12,569.0 | –41,451.6 | –34,240.0 | 21,159.0 | 48,239.4 | 62,023.7 | 58,040.6 |
| Primary income: credit | **1c9cx** | 53,117.5 | 61,321.1 | 72,350.0 | 88,212.2 | † 110,639.4 | 90,421.2 | 79,426.3 | 89,778.4 | 74,193.5 | 75,160.1 | 80,386.0 | 63,702.4 |
| Primary income: debit | **1c9dx** | 71,456.0 | 78,429.3 | 89,426.5 | 115,011.1 | † 132,659.1 | 93,810.9 | 85,637.4 | 98,969.9 | 79,421.2 | 80,525.1 | 82,760.1 | 65,956.6 |
| Balance on gds, serv. & prim. inc. | **1y9bx** | –6,167.0 | –17,409.0 | –31,114.4 | –31,879.0 | † –41,554.7 | –15,958.7 | –47,662.7 | –43,431.5 | 15,931.3 | 42,874.5 | 59,649.5 | 55,786.5 |
| Secondary income: credit | **1d9ca** | 21,832.8 | 23,541.0 | 22,223.5 | 26,617.2 | † 21,028.1 | 20,174.8 | 16,033.5 | 19,468.7 | 17,848.8 | 18,942.1 | 20,172.8 | 16,634.1 |
| Secondary income: debit | **1d9da** | 32,120.4 | 35,876.0 | 38,937.1 | 46,312.5 | † 47,462.6 | 45,620.8 | 42,755.6 | 46,134.3 | 43,008.7 | 42,849.2 | 41,310.3 | 32,940.0 |
| B. Capital Account* | **209ba** | 2,163.1 | 1,627.8 | 2,384.1 | 3,149.5 | † –341.2 | 396.2 | 69.5 | 1,298.4 | 5,131.5 | 329.4 | 4,226.1 | 2,873.3 |
| Capital account: credit | **209ca** | 4,030.8 | 5,041.4 | 5,417.1 | 5,077.1 | † 3,655.2 | 3,387.0 | 3,908.1 | 7,877.5 | 9,302.3 | 8,678.6 | 8,596.5 | 7,227.4 |
| Capital account: debit | **209da** | 1,867.7 | 3,413.7 | 3,032.9 | 1,927.6 | † 3,996.4 | 2,990.9 | 3,838.6 | 6,579.1 | 4,170.8 | 8,349.2 | 4,370.4 | 4,354.1 |
| Balance on current & capital acct. | **129ba** | –14,291.4 | –28,116.2 | –45,443.9 | –48,424.8 | † –68,330.4 | –41,008.5 | –74,315.3 | –68,798.8 | –4,097.1 | 19,296.8 | 42,738.2 | 42,353.9 |
| C. Financial Account* | **309na** | –8,347.0 | –25,285.9 | –30,939.2 | –37,738.7 | † –53,298.8 | –59,567.8 | –114,150.2 | –94,071.8 | –17,181.0 | 12,233.4 | 57,473.3 | 53,544.6 |
| Direct investment: assets | **3a9aa** | 19,248.1 | 40,780.6 | 42,477.6 | 92,118.7 | † 67,431.2 | 18,258.7 | 30,699.1 | 51,784.3 | 6,770.5 | 20,251.7 | 20,408.9 | 15,370.4 |
| Equity & investment fund shares | **3aaaa** | 3,829.4 | 29,237.6 | 32,949.8 | 73,721.8 | † 38,823.7 | 25,360.5 | 19,085.4 | 29,915.2 | 11,926.4 | 15,318.2 | 22,742.2 | 12,500.2 |
| Debt instruments | **3abaa** | 15,418.7 | 11,543.0 | 9,527.9 | 18,396.9 | † 28,609.2 | –7,104.6 | 11,613.8 | 21,870.5 | –5,155.9 | 4,934.9 | –2,336.1 | 2,869.0 |
| Direct investment: liabilities | **3a9la** | 16,791.1 | 19,636.8 | 39,007.0 | 40,042.9 | † –9,500.3 | 16,574.4 | 9,937.5 | 34,443.6 | 34.8 | 19,530.6 | 17,028.0 | 2,742.9 |
| Equity & investment fund shares | **3aala** | 12,385.8 | 13,676.8 | 28,161.0 | 24,962.1 | † 146.1 | 14,731.4 | 2,331.0 | 30,837.8 | 114.9 | 19,404.0 | 24,582.7 | 13,064.8 |
| Debt instruments | **3abla** | 4,405.3 | 5,960.0 | 10,846.0 | 15,080.8 | † –9,647.8 | 1,843.0 | 7,606.4 | 3,608.5 | –81.3 | 127.9 | –7,554.7 | –10,321.9 |
| Portfolio investment: assets | **3b9aa** | 26,379.6 | 108,090.5 | 61,724.9 | –1,587.2 | † –95,614.9 | 56,070.5 | 43,303.0 | –47,689.8 | –78,977.0 | 27,250.3 | 122,389.8 | 136,291.2 |
| Equity & investment fund shares | **3baaa** | 16,169.1 | 24,883.6 | 23,036.6 | –17,023.0 | † –118,450.6 | 18,975.7 | 54,638.1 | –4,335.9 | 19,566.3 | 63,072.1 | 93,262.9 | 90,708.2 |
| Debt securities | **3bbaa** | 10,210.5 | 83,206.9 | 38,688.3 | 15,435.8 | † 22,835.7 | 37,093.2 | –11,333.7 | –43,354.0 | –98,542.0 | –35,823.1 | 29,125.6 | 45,584.1 |
| Portfolio investment: liabilities | **3b9la** | 58,554.8 | 164,403.5 | 115,291.4 | 24,057.9 | † 11,251.4 | 105,837.7 | –14,097.8 | –61,902.6 | –47,428.7 | 47,508.2 | 135,373.4 | 26,493.9 |
| Equity & investment fund shares | **3bala** | 17,182.7 | 2,630.8 | 13,558.3 | –14,873.0 | † –29,028.4 | 20,910.1 | 3,819.5 | 6,046.5 | 20,846.4 | 17,444.1 | 26,675.9 | 12,899.0 |
| Debt securities | **3bbla** | 41,372.1 | 161,772.7 | 101,733.1 | 38,930.9 | † 40,276.7 | 84,924.8 | –17,918.7 | –67,947.7 | –68,273.7 | 30,065.4 | 108,697.5 | 13,594.8 |
| Fin. der.& empl.stk.ops.(ESOs): net | **3c9na** | –2,276.1 | –3,117.5 | 591.2 | –741.7 | † –225.3 | –6,700.6 | 6,951.2 | –10,006.6 | 7,564.7 | 3,995.7 | –4,774.8 | 3,663.8 |
| Fin. der. & ESOs.: assets | **3c9aa** | — | — | — | — | .... | .... | .... | .... | .... | .... | .... | .... |
| Fin. der. & ESOs.: liabilities | **3c9la** | 2,276.1 | 3,117.5 | –591.2 | 741.7 | .... | .... | .... | .... | .... | .... | .... | .... |
| Other investment: assets | **3d9aa** | 47,935.7 | 100,277.8 | 142,422.9 | 82,668.9 | † –41,804.8 | –62,103.9 | –69,531.0 | 61,843.1 | 42,217.6 | –34,197.7 | 24,522.9 | –21,527.3 |
| Other equity | **3daaa** | .... | .... | .... | .... | † –32.5 | 37.6 | 281.4 | 283.3 | 7,713.4 | 9,611.9 | 3,834.1 | 19.2 |
| Debt instruments | **3dzaa** | 47,935.7 | 100,277.8 | 142,422.9 | 82,668.9 | † –41,772.3 | –62,141.5 | –69,812.4 | 61,559.8 | 34,504.2 | –43,809.6 | 20,688.8 | –21,546.5 |
| Other investment: liabilities | **3d9la** | 24,288.5 | 87,277.0 | 123,857.4 | 146,096.6 | † –18,664.7 | –57,319.8 | 129,731.6 | 177,457.7 | 42,149.5 | –61,973.6 | –47,330.6 | 51,015.6 |
| Other equity | **3dala** | .... | .... | .... | .... | † — | — | — | — | — | –53.1 | –5.3 | — |
| Debt instruments | **3dzla** | 24,288.5 | 87,277.0 | 123,857.4 | 146,096.6 | † –18,664.7 | –57,319.8 | 129,731.6 | 177,457.7 | 42,149.5 | –61,920.4 | –47,325.3 | 51,015.6 |
| Curr.+ cap.– finan. acct. balance | **4y9na** | –5,944.4 | –2,830.3 | –14,504.7 | –10,686.2 | † –15,031.6 | 18,559.4 | 39,834.9 | 25,273.0 | 13,083.9 | 7,063.4 | –14,735.1 | –11,190.7 |
| D. Net Errors and Omissions | **409na** | 3,100.9 | 1,800.6 | 13,938.9 | 12,579.3 | † 23,235.3 | –9,556.9 | –38,504.9 | –24,099.9 | –11,202.7 | –5,063.5 | 13,523.8 | 11,783.8 |
| E. Reserves and Related Items | **4z9na** | –2,843.6 | –1,029.7 | –565.9 | 1,893.1 | † 8,203.8 | 9,002.8 | 1,335.3 | 1,167.5 | 1,879.9 | 1,998.6 | –1,214.1 | 593.0 |
| Reserve assets | **3e9aa** | –2,843.6 | –1,029.7 | –565.9 | 1,893.1 | † 8,203.8 | 9,002.8 | 1,335.3 | 1,167.5 | 1,879.9 | 1,998.6 | –1,214.1 | 593.0 |
| Credit and loans from the IMF | **3dcla** | — | — | — | — | † — | — | — | — | — | — | — | — |
| Exceptional financing | **409la** | .... | .... | .... | .... | .... | .... | .... | .... | .... | .... | .... | .... |

*Excludes components in group E

| | | 2004 | 2005 | 2006 | 2007 | 2008 | 2009 | 2010 | 2011 | 2012 | 2013 | 2014 | 2015 |
|---|---|---|---|---|---|---|---|---|---|---|---|---|---|
| **International Investment Position** | | | | | | | *Millions of US Dollars* | | | | | | |
| Assets | **809aa** | 1,829,149.1 | 1,920,148.3 | 2,397,605.1 | 2,755,124.9 | † 2,476,239.5 | 2,715,300.1 | 2,583,667.4 | 2,568,385.2 | 2,718,437.8 | 2,758,655.8 | 2,674,235.1 | 2,522,950.9 |
| Direct investment | **8a9aa** | 280,480.9 | 293,478.7 | 378,932.5 | 535,545.6 | † 524,517.8 | 608,291.9 | 579,686.3 | 600,106.9 | 646,259.3 | 695,121.6 | 632,285.1 | 592,484.7 |
| Equity & investment fund shares | **8aaaa** | 248,474.3 | 253,038.6 | 320,725.1 | 421,057.4 | † 424,457.4 | 474,218.1 | 465,298.2 | 483,311.8 | 507,201.1 | 556,327.6 | 501,865.2 | 462,689.9 |
| Debt instruments | **8abaa** | 32,006.6 | 40,440.1 | 58,207.4 | 114,488.2 | † 100,060.4 | 134,073.8 | 114,388.1 | 116,795.2 | 139,058.2 | 138,794.0 | 130,419.8 | 129,793.7 |
| Portfolio investment | **8b9aa** | 933,583.3 | 982,073.1 | 1,153,000.6 | 1,295,660.0 | † 1,003,534.0 | 1,174,659.5 | 1,155,921.2 | 1,030,661.2 | 1,045,722.1 | 1,146,211.4 | 1,162,589.4 | 1,175,114.5 |
| Equity & investment fund shares | **8baaa** | 399,682.4 | 416,449.4 | 534,842.9 | 589,975.0 | † 318,134.3 | 401,158.1 | 455,610.8 | 409,421.0 | 480,472.7 | 603,389.3 | 649,329.8 | 679,500.1 |
| Debt securities | **8bbaa** | 533,901.0 | 565,623.7 | 618,157.7 | 705,685.0 | † 685,399.7 | 773,499.9 | 700,310.4 | 621,238.9 | 565,249.4 | 542,822.0 | 513,259.6 | 495,614.3 |
| Fin. der.(oth.than reserves) & ESOs | **8c9aa** | 28,489.7 | 30,228.6 | 31,281.4 | 34,297.0 | † 161,511.0 | 146,813.0 | 149,836.1 | 182,130.7 | 198,003.7 | 143,023.7 | 152,588.1 | 111,260.8 |
| Other investment | **8d9aa** | 524,209.6 | 548,415.4 | 758,618.3 | 795,297.6 | † 681,402.8 | 652,738.7 | 539,369.2 | 582,185.1 | 646,784.4 | 628,810.3 | 584,549.1 | 513,321.0 |
| Other equity | **8daaa** | .... | .... | .... | .... | † 1,482.2 | 1,574.6 | 1,737.1 | 1,953.8 | 10,119.8 | 20,740.3 | 22,279.9 | 20,183.4 |
| Debt instruments | **8dzaa** | 524,209.6 | 548,415.4 | 758,618.3 | 795,297.6 | † 679,920.6 | 651,164.2 | 537,632.1 | 580,231.3 | 636,664.6 | 608,070.0 | 562,269.1 | 493,137.6 |
| Reserve assets | **8e9aa** | 62,385.6 | 65,952.5 | 75,772.3 | 94,324.7 | † 105,273.9 | 132,797.0 | 158,854.6 | 173,301.3 | 181,668.3 | 145,487.4 | 142,223.4 | 130,771.0 |
| Liabilities | **809la** | 2,138,816.9 | 2,185,394.2 | 2,801,143.6 | 3,317,150.7 | † 3,011,632.4 | 3,278,888.1 | 3,085,454.5 | 3,032,244.1 | 3,289,984.9 | 3,402,564.3 | 3,228,441.7 | 2,997,839.2 |
| Direct investment | **8a9la** | 220,717.4 | 224,080.5 | 294,875.0 | 494,188.4 | † 409,649.7 | 485,706.9 | 421,400.1 | 439,435.6 | 493,348.7 | 526,183.2 | 493,767.2 | 457,992.1 |
| Equity & investment fund shares | **8aala** | 184,944.6 | 185,650.6 | 240,700.2 | 277,203.8 | † 246,255.7 | 274,512.1 | 234,949.4 | 262,126.0 | 278,942.3 | 309,494.9 | 308,630.3 | 293,910.9 |
| Debt instruments | **8abla** | 35,772.8 | 38,429.9 | 54,174.8 | 216,984.6 | † 163,393.9 | 211,194.8 | 186,450.7 | 177,309.6 | 214,406.5 | 216,688.3 | 185,136.9 | 164,081.2 |
| Portfolio investment | **8b9la** | 1,286,363.2 | 1,308,238.9 | 1,657,761.9 | 1,862,078.4 | † 1,572,483.2 | 1,813,840.7 | 1,593,429.2 | 1,326,731.4 | 1,439,790.0 | 1,607,074.9 | 1,611,546.6 | 1,512,006.2 |
| Equity & investment fund shares | **8bala** | 285,346.3 | 292,199.9 | 412,911.1 | 419,413.1 | † 186,156.6 | 245,736.1 | 203,909.5 | 150,488.3 | 195,545.6 | 255,050.8 | 240,089.5 | 268,746.7 |
| Debt securities | **8bbla** | 1,001,016.8 | 1,016,039.0 | 1,244,850.8 | 1,442,665.4 | † 1,386,325.3 | 1,568,104.6 | 1,389,519.7 | 1,176,243.1 | 1,244,244.3 | 1,352,024.1 | 1,371,458.3 | 1,243,259.5 |
| Fin. der.(oth.than reserves) & ESOs | **8c9la** | 26,345.7 | 37,733.9 | 47,599.0 | 29,034.2 | † 206,815.0 | 185,048.0 | 189,974.2 | 247,224.2 | 274,795.4 | 202,010.6 | 228,328.5 | 166,811.7 |
| Other investment | **8d9la** | 605,390.6 | 615,341.0 | 800,907.7 | 931,849.6 | † 822,684.5 | 794,292.5 | 880,652.4 | 1,018,852.9 | 1,082,050.8 | 1,067,295.6 | 894,799.5 | 861,030.3 |
| Other equity | **8dala** | .... | .... | .... | .... | † 71.0 | 73.5 | 68.1 | 66.0 | 69.9 | 19.3 | 10.9 | 9.8 |
| Debt instruments | **8dzla** | 605,390.6 | 615,341.0 | 800,907.7 | 931,849.6 | † 822,613.5 | 794,219.0 | 880,584.2 | 1,018,786.9 | 1,081,980.9 | 1,067,276.3 | 894,788.6 | 861,020.5 |

| | | 2004 | 2005 | 2006 | 2007 | 2008 | 2009 | 2010 | 2011 | 2012 | 2013 | 2014 | 2015 |
|---|---|---|---|---|---|---|---|---|---|---|---|---|---|
| **Government Finance Operations Statement General Government** | | | | | | *Millions of Euros: Fiscal Year Ends December 31; Data Reported through Eurostat* | | | | | | | |
| Revenue | a1 | 626,726 | 640,146 | 681,982 | 728,559 | 736,729 | 721,779 | 732,371 | 747,782 | 771,685 | 772,024 | 776,597 | 784,040 |
| Taxes | a11 | 392,657 | 400,401 | 438,617 | 465,104 | 461,782 | 446,095 | 453,912 | 464,907 | 487,394 | 483,749 | 487,718 | 492,753 |
| Social Contributions | a12 | 176,614 | 181,958 | 184,337 | 203,069 | 212,925 | 212,133 | 213,702 | 216,294 | 215,838 | 215,290 | 214,340 | 218,535 |
| Grants | a13 | .... | .... | .... | .... | .... | .... | .... | .... | .... | .... | .... | .... |
| Other Revenue | a14 | .... | .... | .... | .... | .... | .... | .... | .... | .... | .... | .... | .... |
| Expense | a2 | 668,501 | 693,562 | 729,446 | 745,715 | 773,198 | 792,482 | 796,424 | 805,857 | 821,079 | 824,465 | 832,174 | 832,450 |
| Compensation of Employees | a21 | 150,145 | 156,644 | 163,798 | 164,330 | 170,271 | 171,677 | 172,548 | 169,616 | 166,143 | 164,783 | 163,622 | 161,746 |
| Use of Goods & Services | a22 | 72,377 | 76,396 | 75,114 | 78,282 | 82,593 | 85,610 | 87,355 | 87,166 | 87,022 | 89,579 | 88,564 | 88,832 |
| Consumption of Fixed Capital | a23 | 34,287 | 35,912 | 37,692 | 38,888 | 40,680 | 42,159 | 42,817 | 42,683 | 43,412 | 44,428 | 44,149 | 43,817 |
| Interest | a24 | 66,723 | 67,175 | 68,869 | 76,660 | 80,461 | 69,458 | 68,836 | 76,417 | 83,566 | 77,568 | 74,341 | 68,439 |
| Subsidies | a25 | 18,350 | 17,306 | 17,992 | 18,569 | 18,800 | 21,612 | 23,235 | 23,521 | 25,864 | 27,547 | 30,428 | 27,711 |
| Grants | a26 | .... | .... | .... | .... | .... | .... | .... | .... | .... | .... | .... | .... |
| Social Benefits | a27 | 273,083 | 283,031 | 293,977 | 306,913 | 320,642 | 337,193 | 344,976 | 349,086 | 354,786 | 363,240 | 370,647 | 377,180 |
| Other Expense | a28 | | | | | | | | | | | | |
| Gross Operating Balance [1-2+23] | agob | −7,488 | −17,504 | −9,772 | 21,732 | 4,211 | −28,544 | −21,236 | −15,392 | −5,982 | −8,013 | −11,428 | −4,592 |
| Net Operating Balance [1-2] | anob | −41,775 | −53,416 | −47,464 | −17,156 | −36,469 | −70,703 | −64,053 | −58,075 | −49,394 | −52,441 | −55,577 | −48,409 |
| Net Acq. of Nonfinancial Assets | a31 | 9,887 | 8,753 | 8,088 | 7,410 | 7,464 | 12,182 | 4,067 | −1,120 | −1,859 | −5,483 | −6,640 | −6,020 |
| Aquisition of Nonfin. Assets | a31.1 | .... | .... | .... | .... | .... | .... | .... | .... | .... | .... | .... | .... |
| Disposal of Nonfin. Assets | a31.2 | .... | .... | .... | .... | .... | .... | .... | .... | .... | .... | .... | .... |
| Net Lending/Borrowing [1-2-31] | anlb | −51,662 | −62,169 | −55,552 | −24,566 | −43,933 | −82,885 | −68,120 | −56,955 | −47,535 | −46,958 | −48,938 | −42,389 |
| Net Acq. of Financial Assets | a32 | 13,196 | 23,137 | 17,891 | −4,917 | 14,748 | 20,065 | 19,967 | −4,690 | 34,772 | 22,969 | 21,047 | −9,507 |
| By instrument | | | | | | | | | | | | | |
| Monetary Gold & SDRs | a3201 | — | — | — | — | — | — | — | — | — | — | — | — |
| Currency & Deposits | a3202 | 3,804 | 6,656 | 11,329 | −11,055 | 7,688 | 11,783 | 11,146 | −19,136 | 1,539 | 504 | 9,358 | −9,937 |
| Securities other than Shares | a3203 | 4,817 | 8,156 | 1,045 | 3,034 | 1,667 | 2,494 | 2,693 | 2,874 | 2,675 | 573 | 770 | 3,241 |
| Loans | a3204 | 4,697 | 8,041 | −10,287 | 1,838 | 2,175 | 1,119 | 3,271 | 7,750 | 24,568 | 7,459 | 1,700 | −2,519 |
| Shares & Other Equity | a3205 | 692 | −2,661 | 1,210 | −2,785 | 644 | 3,612 | 383 | −1,442 | −1,708 | 8,178 | 897 | −3,232 |
| Insurance Technical Reserves | a3206 | 148 | 48 | 56 | −4 | −92 | 12 | −64 | 32 | −124 | −20 | −12 | 4 |
| Financial Derivatives | a3207 | −1,183 | −1,311 | 165 | 182 | 868 | 763 | 2,029 | 2,193 | 3,876 | 2,714 | 3,621 | 3,190 |
| Other Accounts Receivable | a3208 | 224 | 4,208 | 14,372 | 3,876 | 1,801 | 283 | 508 | 3,039 | 3,947 | 3,560 | 4,712 | −254 |
| By debtor | | | | | | | | | | | | | |
| Domestic | a321 | .... | .... | .... | .... | .... | .... | .... | .... | .... | .... | .... | .... |
| Foreign | a322 | .... | .... | .... | .... | .... | .... | .... | .... | .... | .... | .... | .... |
| Net Incurrence of Liabilities | a33 | 62,911 | 85,336 | 68,972 | 24,537 | 56,380 | 101,542 | 86,128 | 51,785 | 79,823 | 71,467 | 66,616 | 31,843 |
| By instrument | | | | | | | | | | | | | |
| Special Drawing Rights (SDRs) | a3301 | — | — | — | — | — | — | — | — | — | — | — | — |
| Currency & Deposits | a3302 | 18,849 | 17,690 | 3,455 | −11,199 | −816 | 9,570 | 1,060 | −6,153 | 6,043 | −1,777 | 14,735 | 5,055 |
| Securities other than Shares | a3303 | 45,351 | 45,438 | 38,225 | 29,898 | 64,527 | 87,099 | 79,943 | 47,745 | 50,823 | 83,050 | 64,955 | 33,084 |
| Loans | a3304 | −4,769 | 10,103 | 23,966 | −1,736 | −3,482 | 2,826 | 2,145 | 5,799 | 27,010 | −804 | −7,632 | 129 |
| Shares & Other Equity | a3305 | — | — | — | — | — | — | — | — | — | — | — | — |
| Insurance Technical Reserves | a3306 | 44 | 44 | 68 | 104 | 104 | 248 | 468 | 376 | 316 | 532 | 608 | 820 |
| Financial Derivatives | a3307 | 164 | 116 | 24 | 40 | — | — | — | −221 | −1,689 | −800 | −1,829 | −3,562 |
| Other Accounts Payable | a3308 | 3,272 | 11,942 | 3,232 | 7,433 | −3,953 | 1,802 | 2,512 | 4,240 | −2,678 | −8,733 | −4,221 | −3,682 |
| By creditor | | | | | | | | | | | | | |
| Domestic | a331 | .... | .... | .... | .... | .... | .... | .... | .... | .... | .... | .... | .... |
| Foreign | a332 | .... | .... | .... | .... | .... | .... | .... | .... | .... | .... | .... | .... |
| Stat. Discrepancy [32-33-NLB] | anlbz | 1,947 | −30 | 4,471 | −4,888 | 2,301 | 1,408 | 1,959 | 480 | 2,484 | −1,540 | 3,369 | 1,039 |
| Memo Item: Expenditure [2+31] | a2m | 678,388 | 702,315 | 737,534 | 753,125 | 780,662 | 804,664 | 800,491 | 804,737 | 819,220 | 818,982 | 825,534 | 826,430 |
| **Balance Sheet** | | | | | | | | | | | | | |
| Net Worth | a6 | .... | .... | .... | .... | .... | .... | .... | .... | .... | .... | .... | .... |
| Nonfinancial Assets | a61 | .... | .... | .... | .... | .... | .... | .... | .... | .... | .... | .... | .... |
| Financial Assets | a62 | 315,770 | 345,151 | 371,749 | 368,236 | 369,402 | 388,725 | 400,099 | 388,737 | 428,785 | 435,246 | 451,493 | 443,222 |
| By instrument | | | | | | | | | | | | | |
| Monetary Gold & SDRs | a6201 | — | — | — | — | — | — | — | — | — | — | — | — |
| Currency & Deposits | a6202 | 51,305 | 58,018 | 69,369 | 58,323 | 66,737 | 81,049 | 92,377 | 73,446 | 76,155 | 75,996 | 85,617 | 75,877 |
| Securities other than Shares | a6203 | 7,257 | 9,432 | 10,704 | 13,727 | 15,700 | 18,298 | 21,027 | 23,732 | 26,328 | 27,149 | 27,884 | 30,851 |
| Loans | a6204 | 49,923 | 59,063 | 49,411 | 51,199 | 53,593 | 54,700 | 58,017 | 62,672 | 87,211 | 94,680 | 96,440 | 94,020 |
| Shares and Other Equity | a6205 | 130,260 | 137,357 | 146,561 | 145,409 | 132,089 | 133,105 | 126,659 | 123,795 | 130,177 | 124,966 | 124,397 | 125,568 |
| Insurance Technical Reserves | a6206 | 1,496 | 1,543 | 1,601 | 1,596 | 1,502 | 1,513 | 1,450 | 1,482 | 1,357 | 1,338 | 1,326 | 1,330 |
| Financial Derivatives | a6207 | — | — | — | — | — | — | — | — | — | — | — | — |
| Other Accounts Receivable | a6208 | 75,529 | 79,737 | 94,104 | 97,981 | 99,781 | 100,060 | 100,569 | 103,610 | 107,557 | 111,117 | 115,828 | 115,576 |
| By debtor | | | | | | | | | | | | | |
| Domestic | a621 | .... | .... | .... | .... | .... | .... | .... | .... | .... | .... | .... | .... |
| Foreign | a622 | .... | .... | .... | .... | .... | .... | .... | .... | .... | .... | .... | .... |
| Liabilities | a63 | 1,681,645 | 1,772,279 | 1,802,381 | 1,797,979 | 1,868,997 | 2,002,567 | 2,022,070 | 1,958,504 | 2,231,797 | 2,333,851 | 2,566,806 | 2,620,173 |
| By instrument | | | | | | | | | | | | | |
| Special Drawing Rights (SDRs) | a6301 | — | — | — | — | — | — | — | — | — | — | — | — |
| Currency & Deposits | a6302 | 202,059 | 219,750 | 223,204 | 212,005 | 211,189 | 220,759 | 221,819 | 215,665 | 221,708 | 219,932 | 234,667 | 239,722 |
| Securities other than Shares | a6303 | 1,282,797 | 1,327,430 | 1,327,554 | 1,332,851 | 1,403,503 | 1,526,347 | 1,542,692 | 1,466,013 | 1,701,883 | 1,819,914 | 2,037,527 | 2,097,262 |
| Loans | a6304 | 112,364 | 126,281 | 150,943 | 149,809 | 146,331 | 149,156 | 151,304 | 157,104 | 184,114 | 183,625 | 176,074 | 176,136 |
| Shares and Other Equity | a6305 | | | | | | | | | | | | |
| Insurance Technical Reserves | a6306 | 165 | 210 | 278 | 381 | 485 | 732 | 1,201 | 1,576 | 1,890 | 2,422 | 3,031 | 3,849 |
| Financial Derivatives | a6307 | 20,456 | 22,864 | 21,427 | 16,524 | 25,033 | 21,316 | 18,679 | 27,528 | 34,265 | 28,752 | 40,522 | 31,899 |
| Other Accounts Payable | a6308 | 63,804 | 75,743 | 78,975 | 86,409 | 82,456 | 84,257 | 86,376 | 90,617 | 87,937 | 79,206 | 74,985 | 71,304 |
| By creditor | | | | | | | | | | | | | |
| Domestic | a631 | .... | .... | .... | .... | .... | .... | .... | .... | .... | .... | .... | .... |
| Foreign | a632 | .... | .... | .... | .... | .... | .... | .... | .... | .... | .... | .... | .... |
| Net Financial Worth [62-63] | a6m2 | −1,365,875 | −1,427,128 | −1,430,632 | −1,429,743 | −1,499,595 | −1,613,842 | −1,621,971 | −1,569,767 | −1,803,012 | −1,898,605 | −2,115,313 | −2,176,951 |
| Memo Item: Debt at Market Value | a6m3 | 1,661,189 | 1,749,414 | 1,780,954 | 1,781,455 | 1,843,964 | 1,981,251 | 2,003,392 | 1,930,975 | 2,197,532 | 2,305,099 | 2,526,284 | 2,588,273 |
| Memo Item: Debt at Face Value | a6m35 | 1,513,461 | 1,594,377 | 1,667,047 | 1,692,354 | 1,753,586 | 1,854,245 | 1,937,876 | 1,998,398 | 2,077,718 | 2,149,053 | 2,211,189 | 2,242,975 |
| Memo Item: Maastricht Debt | a6m36 | 1,449,657 | 1,518,634 | 1,588,072 | 1,605,945 | 1,671,130 | 1,769,988 | 1,851,500 | 1,907,781 | 1,989,781 | 2,069,847 | 2,136,204 | 2,171,671 |
| Memo Item: Debt at Nominal Value | a6m4 | .... | .... | .... | .... | .... | .... | .... | .... | .... | .... | .... | .... |

# Italy    136

|  | | 2004 | 2005 | 2006 | 2007 | 2008 | 2009 | 2010 | 2011 | 2012 | 2013 | 2014 | 2015 |
|---|---|---|---|---|---|---|---|---|---|---|---|---|---|
| **National Accounts** | | | | | *Billions of Euros: Quarterly Data Seasonally Adjusted* | | | | | | | | |
| Househ.Cons.Expend.,incl.NPISHs.... | **96f.c** | 856.5 | 886.1 | 922.2 | 954.2 | 973.2 | 954.5 | 980.1 | 1,008.6 | 995.1 | 977.9 | 983.2 | 996.7 |
| Government Consumption Expend... | **91f.c** | 277.5 | 291.6 | 300.9 | 304.8 | 317.1 | 324.4 | 327.6 | 320.9 | 315.9 | 315.7 | 314.5 | 314.5 |
| Gross Fixed Capital Formation......... | **93e.c** | 301.8 | 315.2 | 332.7 | 347.2 | 346.7 | 314.4 | 320.0 | 321.8 | 296.1 | 280.3 | 271.3 | 270.7 |
| Changes in Inventories.................... | **93i.c** | 4.8 | −.8 | 6.3 | 9.9 | 8.8 | −9.3 | 9.5 | 13.2 | −8.1 | −1.8 | −4.0 | .2 |
| Exports of Goods and Services.......... | **90c.c** | 348.5 | 367.2 | 406.1 | 441.5 | 440.1 | 353.5 | 404.1 | 442.2 | 461.2 | 463.8 | 474.6 | 493.6 |
| Imports of Goods and Services (-)..... | **98c.c** | 340.1 | 368.9 | 419.1 | 447.2 | 453.0 | 363.8 | 435.7 | 467.9 | 445.0 | 426.4 | 423.3 | 441.4 |
| Gross Domestic Product (GDP)......... | **99b.c** | 1,449.0 | 1,490.4 | 1,549.2 | 1,610.3 | 1,632.9 | 1,573.7 | 1,605.7 | 1,638.9 | 1,615.1 | 1,609.5 | 1,616.3 | 1,634.2 |
| Net Primary Income from Abroad..... | **98.nc** | −57.6 | −52.9 | −49.9 | −57.3 | −75.3 | −61.9 | −62.7 | −67.9 | −56.0 | −58.6 | . . . . | . . . . |
| Gross National Income (GNI)............ | **99a.c** | 1,391.4 | 1,437.5 | 1,499.3 | 1,553.0 | 1,557.6 | 1,511.8 | 1,543.0 | 1,571.0 | 1,559.1 | 1,550.8 | . . . . | . . . . |
| Net Current Transf.from Abroad....... | **98t.c** | −9.8 | −12.4 | −14.6 | −15.4 | −14.6 | −15.1 | −17.0 | −16.8 | −15.8 | −15.4 | . . . . | . . . . |
| Net National Income....................... | **99e.c** | 1,179.4 | 1,215.1 | 1,266.6 | 1,309.6 | 1,303.0 | 1,252.7 | 1,277.3 | 1,297.3 | 1,280.2 | 1,270.2 | . . . . | . . . . |
| Gross Nat'l Disposable Inc.(GNDI).... | **99i.c** | 1,381.5 | 1,425.1 | 1,484.7 | 1,537.7 | 1,543.0 | 1,496.7 | 1,526.1 | 1,554.2 | 1,543.4 | 1,535.4 | . . . . | . . . . |
| Gross Saving................................... | **99s.c** | 287.0 | 288.0 | 305.2 | 323.3 | 295.6 | 255.3 | 254.9 | 264.5 | 275.4 | 282.6 | . . . . | . . . . |
| Consumption of Fixed Capital.......... | **99cfc** | 212.0 | 222.4 | 232.7 | 243.4 | 254.6 | 259.1 | 265.7 | 273.7 | 278.9 | 280.6 | . . . . | . . . . |
| GDP Volume 2010 Ref., Chained..... | **99b.r** | 1,612.5 | 1,631.2 | 1,665.6 | 1,687.6 | 1,669.6 | 1,577.6 | 1,604.0 | 1,615.7 | 1,578.4 | 1,547.9 | 1,537.9 | 1,545.8 |
| GDP Volume (2010=100)................ | **99bvr** | 100.5 | 101.7 | 103.8 | 105.2 | 104.1 | 98.4 | 100.0 | 100.7 | 98.4 | 96.5 | 95.9 | 96.4 |
| GDP Deflator (2010=100)............... | **99bir** | 89.8 | 91.3 | 92.9 | 95.3 | 97.7 | 99.6 | 100.0 | 101.3 | 102.2 | 103.9 | 105.0 | 105.6 |
| | | | | | | *Millions: Midyear Estimates* | | | | | | | | |
| **Population................................** | **99z** | 58.35 | 58.66 | 58.92 | 59.14 | 59.32 | 59.47 | 59.59 | 59.68 | 59.74 | 59.77 | 59.79 | 59.80 |

| | | 2004 | 2005 | 2006 | 2007 | 2008 | 2009 | 2010 | 2011 | 2012 | 2013 | 2014 | 2015 |
|---|---|---|---|---|---|---|---|---|---|---|---|---|---|
| **Exchange Rates** | | | | | | *Jamaica Dollars per SDR: End of Period* | | | | | | | |
| Market Rate........aa=........ | wa | 95.432 | 92.017 | 100.843 | 111.244 | 123.555 | 140.038 | 131.828 | 132.598 | 142.263 | 163.313 | 165.729 | 166.327 |
| | | | | | *Jamaica Dollars per US Dollar: End of Period (we) Period Average (wf)* | | | | | | | | |
| Market Rate..........ae=........ | we | 61.450 | 64.381 | 67.032 | 70.397 | 80.217 | 89.328 | 85.601 | 86.368 | 92.564 | 106.047 | 114.390 | 120.028 |
| Market Rate..........rf=........ | wf | 61.197 | 62.281 | 65.744 | 69.192 | 72.756 | 87.894 | 87.196 | 85.892 | 88.751 | 100.241 | 110.935 | 116.898 |
| **Fund Position** | | | | | | *Millions of SDRs: End of Period* | | | | | | | |
| Quota................................ | 2f.s | 273.50 | 273.50 | 273.50 | 273.50 | 273.50 | 273.50 | 273.50 | 273.50 | 273.50 | 273.50 | 273.50 | 273.50 |
| SDR Holdings...................... | 1b.s | .05 | — | .19 | .21 | .05 | 221.01 | 214.07 | 205.73 | 199.44 | 192.27 | 185.80 | 180.68 |
| Reserve Position in the Fund........... | 1c.s | — | — | — | — | — | — | — | — | — | — | — | — |
| Total Fund Cred.&Loans Outstg....... | 2tl | .58 | — | — | — | — | — | 509.90 | 541.80 | 541.80 | 543.22 | 460.10 | 477.76 |
| SDR Allocations......................... | 1bd | 40.61 | 40.61 | 40.61 | 40.61 | 40.61 | 261.64 | 261.64 | 261.64 | 261.64 | 261.64 | 261.64 | 261.64 |
| **International Liquidity** | | | | | *Millions of US Dollars Unless Otherwise Indicated: End of Period* | | | | | | | | |
| Total Reserves minus Gold.............. | 1l.d | 1,846.5 | 2,169.8 | 2,318.4 | 1,878.5 | 1,772.7 | 2,075.8 | 2,501.1 | 2,281.9 | 1,996.4 | 1,818.4 | 2,473.0 | 2,913.8 |
| SDR Holdings....................... | 1b.d | .1 | — | .3 | .3 | .1 | 346.5 | 329.7 | 315.9 | 306.5 | 296.1 | 269.2 | 250.4 |
| Reserve Position in the Fund......... | 1c.d | — | — | — | — | — | — | — | — | — | — | — | — |
| Foreign Exchange................... | 1d.d | 1,846.4 | 2,169.8 | 2,318.2 | 1,878.2 | 1,772.6 | 1,729.4 | 2,171.4 | 1,966.1 | 1,689.9 | 1,522.3 | 2,203.8 | 2,663.5 |
| Central Bank: Other Assets............. | 3..d | — | .2 | — | — | — | .8 | — | — | — | — | 10.4 | — |
| Central Bank: Other Liabs............. | 4..d | 6.9 | 5.4 | 4.4 | 4.0 | 2.3 | 2.3 | 9.6 | 1.8 | 29.9 | 64.8 | — | 2.6 |
| Other Depository Corps.: Assets....... | 7a.d | 1,294.0 | 1,053.2 | 1,283.4 | 1,382.7 | 920.2 | 882.9 | 1,011.3 | 1,164.2 | 1,137.0 | 1,397.3 | 2,052.6 | 2,131.7 |
| Other Depository Corps.: Liabs....... | 7b.d | 1,138.9 | 960.4 | 1,228.3 | 1,231.7 | 1,435.8 | 1,195.3 | 984.8 | 817.2 | 782.2 | 575.2 | 645.0 | 868.6 |
| **Central Bank** | | | | | | *Millions of Jamaica Dollars: End of Period* | | | | | | | |
| Net Foreign Assets...................... | 11n | 111,423 | 135,592 | 156,226 | 129,446 | 138,327 | 121,773 | 152,428 | 135,990 | 68,699 | 55,100 | 164,769 | 226,948 |
| Claims on Nonresidents........... | 11 | 115,779 | 139,676 | 160,617 | 134,247 | 143,529 | 158,620 | 254,964 | 242,677 | 185,765 | 193,412 | 284,383 | 350,237 |
| Liabilities to Nonresidents............. | 16c | 4,356 | 4,084 | 4,391 | 4,801 | 5,202 | 36,847 | 102,536 | 106,686 | 117,066 | 138,311 | 119,615 | 123,289 |
| Claims on Other Depository Corps.... | 12e | — | — | — | — | — | — | 2,295 | 9 | — | — | — | 3 |
| Net Claims on Central Government.. | 12an | 81,648 | 78,049 | 67,113 | 55,539 | 102,601 | 126,542 | 83,572 | 84,214 | 86,373 | 104,513 | 156,577 | 124,358 |
| Claims on Central Government...... | 12a | 85,131 | 81,357 | 86,791 | 73,757 | 107,105 | 132,625 | 89,632 | 92,988 | 93,617 | 111,805 | 166,305 | 140,817 |
| Liabilities to Central Government... | 16d | 3,483 | 3,308 | 19,678 | 18,218 | 4,504 | 6,083 | 6,060 | 8,774 | 7,244 | 7,292 | 9,728 | 16,459 |
| Claims on Other Sectors.................. | 12s | 83 | 79 | 58 | 43 | 22 | 2 | — | — | — | — | — | — |
| Claims on Other Financial Corps.... | 12g | 83 | 79 | 58 | 43 | 22 | 2 | — | — | — | — | — | — |
| Claims on State & Local Govts...... | 12b | — | — | — | — | — | — | — | — | — | — | — | — |
| Claims on Public Nonfin. Corps...... | 12c | — | — | — | — | — | — | — | — | — | — | — | — |
| Claims on Private Sector............... | 12d | — | — | — | — | — | — | — | — | — | — | — | — |
| Monetary Base............................. | 14 | 65,849 | 69,966 | 80,765 | 84,551 | 110,018 | 132,096 | 128,503 | 140,518 | 128,499 | 169,863 | 361,205 | 380,442 |
| Currency in Circulation.................. | 14a | 32,398 | 35,645 | 42,317 | 47,221 | 49,026 | 51,856 | 56,711 | 62,647 | 64,684 | 69,802 | 74,937 | 84,295 |
| Liabs. to Other Depository Corps.... | 14c | 29,187 | 26,227 | 27,912 | 32,677 | 53,951 | 76,176 | 47,522 | 44,996 | 60,091 | 65,227 | 117,115 | 97,612 |
| Liabilities to Other Sectors............. | 14d | 4,265 | 8,094 | 10,536 | 4,653 | 7,041 | 4,064 | 24,270 | 32,875 | 3,724 | 34,834 | 169,153 | 198,536 |
| Other Liabs. to Other Dep. Corps..... | 14n | 25,095 | 30,599 | 42,204 | 37,100 | 35,443 | 25,499 | 56,678 | 28,333 | 7,838 | 7,620 | 13,150 | 12,866 |
| Dep. & Sec. Excl. f/Monetary Base... | 14o | 105,597 | 119,207 | 112,553 | 77,641 | 97,286 | 86,513 | 72,502 | 70,567 | 40,837 | 42,328 | 12,331 | 26,593 |
| Deposits Included in Broad Money. | 15 | — | — | — | — | — | — | — | — | — | — | — | — |
| Sec.Ot.th.Shares Incl.in Brd. Money | 16a | 105,597 | 119,207 | 112,553 | 77,641 | 97,286 | 86,513 | 72,502 | 70,567 | 40,837 | 42,328 | 12,331 | 26,593 |
| Deposits Excl. from Broad Money... | 16b | — | — | — | — | — | — | — | — | — | — | — | — |
| Sec.Ot.th.Shares Excl.f/Brd.Money.. | 16s | — | — | — | — | — | — | — | — | — | — | — | — |
| Loans......................................... | 16l | — | — | — | — | — | — | — | — | — | — | — | — |
| Financial Derivatives...................... | 16m | — | — | — | — | — | — | — | — | — | — | — | — |
| Shares and Other Equity.................. | 17a | 2,313 | 2,890 | 3,403 | 5,128 | 5,709 | 6,606 | 10,015 | 12,869 | 11,731 | 7,051 | 8,813 | 8,972 |
| Other Items (Net)........................... | 17r | −5,700 | −8,942 | −15,529 | −19,392 | −7,505 | −2,396 | −29,402 | −32,073 | −33,834 | −67,248 | −74,153 | −77,564 |
| Memo Item: | | | | | | | | | | | | | |
| Total Assets.................................. | 10ra | 212,755 | 240,298 | 269,734 | 233,606 | 273,951 | 310,103 | 371,175 | 370,875 | 315,455 | 356,368 | 506,910 | 546,755 |
| **Other Depository Corporations** | | | | | | *Millions of Jamaica Dollars: End of Period* | | | | | | | |
| Net Foreign Assets.......................... | 21n | 9,532 | 5,972 | 3,694 | 10,634 | −41,361 | −27,909 | 2,273 | 29,967 | 32,843 | 87,186 | 161,012 | 151,608 |
| Claims on Nonresidents........... | 21 | 79,517 | 67,806 | 86,027 | 97,341 | 73,813 | 78,868 | 86,571 | 100,548 | 105,243 | 148,183 | 234,793 | 255,861 |
| Liabilities to Nonresidents............. | 26c | 69,984 | 61,834 | 82,333 | 86,707 | 115,174 | 106,778 | 84,298 | 70,581 | 72,400 | 60,997 | 73,781 | 104,253 |
| Claims on Central Bank.................. | 20 | 66,320 | 66,694 | 82,142 | 80,509 | 98,791 | 108,002 | 117,768 | 98,147 | 88,024 | 90,639 | 91,610 | 95,182 |
| Currency................................. | 20a | 6,648 | 6,939 | 7,573 | 7,824 | 8,460 | 8,485 | 9,696 | 11,142 | 11,182 | 12,764 | 12,968 | 12,137 |
| Reserve Deposits and Securities..... | 20b | 33,918 | 29,156 | 32,365 | 35,585 | 54,887 | 74,018 | 51,394 | 58,672 | 69,005 | 70,255 | 65,492 | 70,179 |
| Other Claims........................... | 20n | 25,755 | 30,599 | 42,204 | 37,100 | 35,443 | 25,499 | 56,678 | 28,333 | 7,838 | 7,620 | 13,150 | 12,866 |
| Net Claims on Central Government.. | 22an | 99,274 | 110,763 | 110,627 | 116,321 | 116,283 | 142,988 | 139,337 | 140,001 | 157,998 | 146,578 | 121,326 | 136,931 |
| Claims on Central Government...... | 22a | 116,482 | 125,889 | 130,413 | 141,666 | 140,220 | 160,579 | 161,725 | 169,273 | 189,863 | 178,720 | 156,296 | 172,792 |
| Liabilities to Central Government... | 26d | 17,208 | 15,126 | 19,786 | 25,344 | 23,936 | 17,591 | 22,388 | 29,272 | 31,865 | 32,142 | 34,971 | 35,862 |
| Claims on Other Sectors.................. | 22s | 177,454 | 203,933 | 243,348 | 294,829 | 356,686 | 370,483 | 366,698 | 391,664 | 436,040 | 489,567 | 531,739 | 564,601 |
| Claims on Other Financial Corps..... | 22g | 31,609 | 30,895 | 35,901 | 26,140 | 29,064 | 42,215 | 40,526 | 43,291 | 35,721 | 37,655 | 50,227 | 39,621 |
| Claims on State & Local Govts....... | 22b | 4 | 5 | 1 | 1 | 5 | 7 | 1 | — | — | — | — | — |
| Claims on Public Nonfin. Corps...... | 22c | 21,273 | 26,130 | 23,605 | 26,852 | 26,476 | 23,544 | 21,772 | 15,917 | 19,376 | 25,581 | 29,380 | 26,588 |
| Claims on Private Sector............... | 22d | 124,568 | 146,904 | 183,841 | 241,837 | 301,142 | 304,718 | 304,399 | 332,455 | 380,943 | 426,332 | 452,131 | 498,392 |
| Liabilities to Central Bank............... | 26g | 230 | 234 | 183 | 783 | 6,211 | 5,844 | 457 | 603 | 1,711 | 11,839 | 44,710 | 17,887 |
| Transf.Dep.Included in Broad Money | 24 | 45,473 | 49,477 | 56,452 | 70,542 | 64,540 | 73,075 | 82,566 | 85,033 | 102,227 | 110,172 | 129,852 | 154,413 |
| Other Dep.Included in Broad Money. | 25 | 219,361 | 233,559 | 268,792 | 302,667 | 328,767 | 360,411 | 373,907 | 391,282 | 418,009 | 480,061 | 499,122 | 556,938 |
| Sec.Ot.th.Shares Incl.in Brd. Money.. | 26a | — | — | — | — | — | — | — | — | — | — | — | — |
| Deposits Excl. from Broad Money..... | 26b | — | — | — | — | — | — | — | — | — | — | — | — |
| Sec.Ot.th.Shares Excl.f/Brd.Money.... | 26s | — | — | — | — | — | — | — | — | — | — | — | — |
| Loans......................................... | 26l | 36,585 | 46,845 | 44,608 | 52,218 | 50,078 | 58,878 | 61,898 | 53,107 | 72,529 | 73,750 | 84,056 | 69,148 |
| Financial Derivatives...................... | 26m | — | — | — | — | — | — | — | — | — | — | — | — |
| Insurance Technical Reserves........... | 26r | — | — | — | — | — | — | — | — | — | — | — | — |
| Shares and Other Equity.................. | 27a | 63,306 | 69,068 | 79,534 | 86,505 | 89,269 | 106,199 | 115,995 | 137,684 | 131,842 | 144,880 | 157,883 | 177,991 |
| Other Items (Net)........................... | 27r | −12,375 | −11,821 | −9,757 | −10,422 | −8,465 | −10,843 | −8,748 | −7,933 | −11,411 | −6,732 | −9,936 | −28,056 |
| Memo Item: | | | | | | | | | | | | | |
| Total Assets.................................. | 20ra | 474,949 | 504,043 | 583,444 | 663,200 | 727,127 | 774,413 | 792,101 | 827,046 | 897,220 | 990,099 | 1,098,801 | 1,201,771 |

| | | 2004 | 2005 | 2006 | 2007 | 2008 | 2009 | 2010 | 2011 | 2012 | 2013 | 2014 | 2015 |
|---|---|---|---|---|---|---|---|---|---|---|---|---|---|
| **Depository Corporations** | | *Millions of Jamaica Dollars: End of Period* | | | | | | | | | | | |
| Net Foreign Assets...................... | 31n | 120,955 | 141,564 | 159,920 | 140,080 | 96,966 | 93,864 | 154,701 | 165,957 | 101,542 | 142,286 | 325,781 | 378,556 |
| Claims on Nonresidents................ | 31 | 195,295 | 207,482 | 246,644 | 231,588 | 217,342 | 237,489 | 341,535 | 343,224 | 291,008 | 341,595 | 519,176 | 606,098 |
| Liabilities to Nonresidents............. | 36c | 74,340 | 65,918 | 86,724 | 91,508 | 120,376 | 143,625 | 186,834 | 177,267 | 189,466 | 199,309 | 193,395 | 227,542 |
| Domestic Claims............................ | 32 | 358,460 | 392,825 | 421,145 | 466,733 | 575,593 | 640,015 | 589,608 | 615,878 | 680,411 | 740,658 | 809,641 | 825,890 |
| Net Claims on Central Government | 32an | 180,922 | 188,812 | 177,739 | 171,860 | 218,884 | 269,530 | 222,909 | 224,215 | 244,371 | 251,091 | 277,902 | 261,289 |
| Claims on Central Government.... | 32a | 201,613 | 207,246 | 217,204 | 215,422 | 247,324 | 293,203 | 251,357 | 262,261 | 283,480 | 290,525 | 322,601 | 313,609 |
| Liabilities to Central Government. | 36d | 20,690 | 18,434 | 39,465 | 43,562 | 28,440 | 23,673 | 28,447 | 38,047 | 39,109 | 39,434 | 44,699 | 52,321 |
| Claims on Other Sectors................ | 32s | 177,538 | 204,013 | 243,406 | 294,873 | 356,709 | 370,486 | 366,698 | 391,664 | 436,040 | 489,567 | 531,739 | 564,601 |
| Claims on Other Financial Corps.. | 32g | 31,692 | 30,974 | 35,959 | 26,183 | 29,087 | 42,217 | 40,526 | 43,291 | 35,721 | 37,655 | 50,227 | 39,621 |
| Claims on State & Local Govts..... | 32b | 4 | 5 | 1 | 1 | 5 | 7 | 1 | — | — | — | — | — |
| Claims on Public Nonfin. Corps.... | 32c | 21,273 | 26,130 | 23,605 | 26,852 | 26,476 | 23,544 | 21,772 | 15,917 | 19,376 | 25,581 | 29,380 | 26,588 |
| Claims on Private Sector............. | 32d | 124,568 | 146,904 | 183,841 | 241,837 | 301,142 | 304,718 | 304,399 | 332,455 | 380,943 | 426,332 | 452,131 | 498,392 |
| Broad Money Liabilities.................... | 35l | 400,447 | 439,043 | 483,077 | 494,900 | 538,199 | 567,433 | 600,260 | 631,262 | 618,299 | 724,433 | 872,427 | 1,008,638 |
| Currency Outside Depository Corps | 34a | 25,750 | 28,705 | 34,745 | 39,396 | 40,565 | 43,371 | 47,015 | 51,505 | 53,502 | 57,038 | 61,969 | 72,158 |
| Transferable Deposits................... | 34 | 49,738 | 57,571 | 66,988 | 75,195 | 71,581 | 77,139 | 106,836 | 117,908 | 105,951 | 145,006 | 299,006 | 352,949 |
| Other Deposits........................... | 35 | 219,361 | 233,559 | 268,792 | 302,667 | 328,767 | 360,411 | 373,907 | 391,282 | 418,009 | 480,061 | 499,122 | 556,938 |
| Securities Other than Shares.......... | 36a | 105,597 | 119,207 | 112,553 | 77,641 | 97,286 | 86,513 | 72,502 | 70,567 | 40,837 | 42,328 | 12,331 | 26,593 |
| Deposits Excl. from Broad Money..... | 36b | — | — | — | — | — | — | — | — | — | — | — | — |
| Sec.Ot.th.Shares Excl.f/Brd.Money.... | 36s | — | — | — | — | — | — | — | — | — | — | — | — |
| Loans........................................ | 36l | 36,585 | 46,845 | 44,608 | 52,218 | 50,078 | 58,878 | 61,898 | 53,107 | 72,529 | 73,750 | 84,056 | 69,148 |
| Financial Derivatives.................... | 36m | — | — | — | — | — | — | — | — | — | — | — | — |
| Insurance Technical Reserves.......... | 36r | — | — | — | — | — | — | — | — | — | — | — | — |
| Shares and Other Equity.................. | 37a | 65,619 | 71,958 | 82,937 | 91,633 | 94,978 | 112,804 | 126,010 | 150,553 | 143,573 | 151,931 | 166,696 | 186,963 |
| Other Items (Net)........................... | 37r | −23,236 | −23,457 | −29,557 | −31,938 | −10,695 | −5,237 | −43,859 | −53,087 | −52,448 | −67,170 | 12,243 | −60,302 |
| Broad Money Liabs., Seasonally Adj. | 35l.b | 401,486 | 440,975 | 486,380 | 498,096 | 540,897 | 568,975 | 600,681 | 630,469 | 617,168 | 723,831 | 872,675 | 1,009,117 |
| **Monetary Aggregates** | | *Millions of Jamaica Dollars: End of Period* | | | | | | | | | | | |
| Broad Money............................... | 59m | 400,447 | 439,043 | 483,077 | 494,900 | 538,199 | 567,433 | 600,260 | 631,262 | 618,299 | 724,433 | 872,427 | 1,008,638 |
| o/w:Currency Issued by Cent.Govt | 59m.a | — | — | — | — | — | — | — | — | — | — | — | — |
| o/w: Dep.in Nonfin. Corporations. | 59m.b | — | — | — | — | — | — | — | — | — | — | — | — |
| o/w:Secs. Issued by Central Govt.. | 59m.c | — | — | — | — | — | — | — | — | — | — | — | — |
| Money (National Definitions) | | | | | | | | | | | | | |
| Base Money............................... | 19ma | 45,055 | 49,418 | 57,975 | 65,257 | 71,499 | 81,116 | 85,093 | 91,710 | 97,648 | 103,633 | 108,883 | 122,212 |
| M1........................................... | 59ma | 55,308 | 62,573 | 77,619 | 89,073 | 91,018 | 97,592 | 103,256 | 112,757 | 118,752 | 120,249 | 132,667 | 159,477 |
| M2........................................... | 59mb | 141,590 | 155,398 | 181,230 | 202,301 | 210,583 | 216,662 | 230,236 | 245,020 | 254,692 | 265,300 | 276,864 | 316,954 |
| **Interest Rates** | | *Percent Per Annum* | | | | | | | | | | | |
| Money Market Rate........................ | 60b | 12.79 | 10.96 | 9.37 | 9.04 | 10.78 | 8.79 | 5.44 | 3.59 | 4.70 | 5.26 | 6.71 | 3.31 |
| Treasury Bill Rate........................... | 60c | 15.47 | 13.39 | 12.79 | 12.56 | 15.89 | 19.95 | 9.26 | 6.59 | 6.62 | 7.29 | 8.29 | 6.59 |
| Savings Rate................................. | 60k | 1.25 | 1.00 | 1.00 | 1.00 | 1.00 | 1.00 | .48 | .10 | .10 | .10 | .10 | .10 |
| Deposit Rate................................. | 60l | 7.98 | 7.50 | 7.04 | 7.14 | 7.56 | 6.97 | 6.35 | 3.86 | 3.53 | 3.66 | 5.27 | 4.90 |
| Lending Rate................................. | 60p | 18.14 | 17.36 | 17.64 | 17.20 | 16.83 | 16.43 | 20.45 | 19.51 | 17.63 | 17.72 | 17.22 | 16.98 |
| **Prices and Labor** | | *Index Numbers (2010=100): Period Averages* | | | | | | | | | | | |
| Industrial Share Prices..................... | 62a | 115.9 | 130.0 | 107.4 | 114.1 | 127.1 | 97.1 | 100.0 | 107.8 | 106.4 | 100.1 | 88.4 | 120.2 |
| Consumer Prices............................. | 64 | 48.5 | 56.0 | † 60.8 | 66.4 | 81.0 | 88.8 | 100.0 | 107.5 | 114.9 | 125.7 | 136.1 | 141.1 |
| | | *Number in Thousands: Period Averages* | | | | | | | | | | | |
| Labor Force................................... | 67d | 1,195 | 1,191 | 1,253 | 1,277 | 1,296 | 1,270 | 1,249 | .... | 1,282 | 1,309 | 1,307 | 1,316 |
| Employment.................................. | 67e | 1,050 | 1,057 | 1,124 | 1,153 | 1,159 | 1,126 | 1,095 | .... | 1,103 | 1,109 | 1,128 | 1,139 |
| Unemployment.............................. | 67c | 146 | 134 | 129 | 124 | 137 | 144 | 155 | .... | 179 | 200 | 180 | 178 |
| Unemployment Rate (%)................. | 67r | 12.2 | 11.3 | 10.3 | 9.7 | 10.6 | 11.4 | 12.4 | .... | 13.9 | 15.2 | 13.8 | 13.5 |
| **Intl. Transactions & Positions** | | *Millions of Jamaica Dollars* | | | | | | | | | | | |
| Exports........................................ | 70 | 85,017 | 93,441 | 123,220 | 142,858 | 183,976 | 115,838 | 116,061 | 137,660 | 151,648 | 157,132 | 159,997 | .... |
| Imports, c.i.f.................................. | 71 | 230,964 | 277,869 | 349,303 | 442,859 | 559,908 | 426,608 | 452,907 | 557,482 | 575,761 | 620,963 | 648,098 | .... |
| | | *2010=100* | | | | | | | | | | | |
| Volume of Exports.......................... | 72 | 205.7 | 215.8 | 217.2 | 197.2 | 214.2 | 110.0 | 100.0 | 122.7 | 110.7 | 113.4 | 111.4 | .... |

# Jamaica   343

| Balance of Payments | | 2004 | 2005 | 2006 | 2007 | 2008 | 2009 | 2010 | 2011 | 2012 | 2013 | 2014 | 2015 |
|---|---|---|---|---|---|---|---|---|---|---|---|---|---|
| | | | | | | | *Millions of US Dollars* | | | | | | |
| A. Current Account* | 109bx | −501.6 | −1,071.3 | −1,182.9 | −2,038.1 | −2,793.3 | −1,127.5 | −934.0 | † −2,063.2 | −1,376.1 | −1,281.0 | −1,128.2 | −326.2 |
| Goods, credit (exports) | 1a9cx | 1,601.6 | 1,664.3 | 2,133.6 | 2,362.6 | 2,743.9 | 1,387.7 | 1,370.4 | † 1,666.1 | 1,728.5 | 1,580.5 | 1,448.6 | 1,261.1 |
| Goods, debit (imports) | 1a9dx | 3,545.3 | 4,245.5 | 5,077.0 | 6,203.9 | 7,546.8 | 4,475.7 | 4,629.4 | † 5,881.4 | 5,634.2 | 5,458.2 | 5,207.6 | 4,414.4 |
| Balance on goods | 1a9bx | −1,943.7 | −2,581.2 | −2,943.4 | −3,841.3 | −4,802.9 | −3,087.9 | −3,259.0 | † −4,215.3 | −3,905.7 | −3,877.7 | −3,759.0 | −3,153.3 |
| Services, credit (exports) | 1b9cx | 2,297.1 | 2,329.7 | 2,648.7 | 2,706.6 | 2,795.2 | 2,650.6 | 2,634.0 | † 2,620.2 | 2,694.3 | 2,674.0 | 2,859.4 | 2,943.2 |
| Services, debit (imports) | 1b9dx | 1,718.7 | 1,722.0 | 2,021.1 | 2,281.7 | 2,367.1 | 1,880.6 | 1,824.4 | † 1,946.0 | 2,162.5 | 2,042.0 | 2,233.2 | 2,137.1 |
| Balance on Goods & Services | 1z9bx | −1,365.3 | −1,973.5 | −2,315.8 | −3,416.4 | −4,374.8 | −2,318.0 | −2,449.4 | † −3,541.2 | −3,373.9 | −3,245.7 | −3,132.9 | −2,347.1 |
| Primary income: credit | 1c9cx | 269.6 | 327.9 | 378.4 | 520.7 | 487.9 | 235.0 | 243.2 | † 221.5 | 492.1 | 407.6 | 296.7 | 295.2 |
| Primary income: debit | 1c9dx | 852.1 | 1,004.1 | 994.0 | 1,182.3 | 1,056.2 | 902.9 | 737.8 | † 739.9 | 605.5 | 663.4 | 583.2 | 607.6 |
| Balance on gds, serv. & prim. inc. | 1y9bx | −1,947.8 | −2,649.8 | −2,931.4 | −4,078.0 | −4,943.1 | −2,985.9 | −2,944.0 | † −4,059.6 | −3,487.4 | −3,501.5 | −3,419.4 | −2,659.5 |
| Secondary income: credit | 1d9ca | 1,892.1 | 1,935.5 | 2,088.5 | 2,385.7 | 2,488.8 | 2,122.0 | 2,292.9 | † 2,284.0 | 2,381.9 | 2,463.7 | 2,522.6 | 2,569.8 |
| Secondary income: debit | 1d9da | 445.9 | 357.0 | 339.9 | 345.8 | 339.0 | 263.6 | 282.9 | † 287.6 | 270.7 | 243.2 | 231.4 | 236.5 |
| B. Capital Account* | 209ba | 13.8 | .3 | 4.1 | .7 | 48.6 | 45.3 | 4.2 | † −9.1 | 5.9 | 18.9 | 9.1 | 1,466.7 |
| Capital account: credit | 209ca | 13.8 | .3 | 4.1 | .7 | 48.6 | 45.3 | 4.2 | † 46.1 | 5.9 | 18.9 | 9.1 | 1,466.7 |
| Capital account: debit | 209da | — | — | — | — | — | — | — | † 55.3 | .... | .... | .... | .... |
| Balance on current & capital acct. | 129ba | −487.8 | −1,071.0 | −1,178.8 | −2,037.4 | −2,744.7 | −1,082.2 | −929.8 | † −2,072.3 | −1,370.2 | −1,262.1 | −1,119.1 | 1,140.5 |
| C. Financial Account* | 309na | −1,215.8 | −1,309.7 | −1,338.1 | −1,294.4 | −3,020.5 | −1,280.8 | −437.0 | † −1,309.7 | 245.9 | −966.7 | −2,142.4 | −74.8 |
| Direct investment: assets | 3a9aa | 17.7 | 56.4 | 45.6 | 60.4 | 15.9 | 5.4 | 16.3 | † 29.1 | 2.8 | −85.9 | −2.1 | 4.4 |
| Equity & investment fund shares | 3aaaa | 17.7 | 56.4 | 45.6 | 60.4 | 15.9 | 5.4 | 16.3 | † 29.1 | .... | .... | .... | .... |
| Debt instruments | 3abaa | — | — | — | — | — | — | — | † — | .... | .... | .... | .... |
| Direct investment: liabilities | 3a9la | 559.4 | 637.9 | 842.3 | 811.9 | 1,376.6 | 485.2 | 185.8 | † 172.8 | 413.3 | 594.7 | 591.5 | 794.5 |
| Equity & investment fund shares | 3aala | 514.3 | 659.8 | 872.2 | 717.8 | 1,321.7 | 440.3 | 183.3 | † 198.6 | .... | .... | .... | .... |
| Debt instruments | 3abla | 45.0 | −21.9 | −29.8 | 94.1 | 54.9 | 44.9 | 2.5 | † −25.8 | .... | .... | .... | .... |
| Portfolio investment: assets | 3b9aa | 1,132.8 | 1,406.4 | 506.4 | 1,768.6 | 813.8 | 352.1 | 352.2 | † 70.8 | 174.1 | 122.5 | 316.3 | 522.6 |
| Equity & investment fund shares | 3baaa | — | — | — | — | — | — | — | † — | 43.1 | −13.5 | −7.3 | 29.8 |
| Debt securities | 3bbaa | 1,132.8 | 1,406.4 | 506.4 | 1,768.6 | 813.8 | 352.1 | 352.2 | † 70.8 | 131.0 | 136.0 | 323.6 | 492.8 |
| Portfolio investment: liabilities | 3b9la | 1,228.8 | 1,280.4 | 377.9 | 1,128.1 | 781.1 | −290.9 | −61.1 | † 240.5 | −313.3 | 99.0 | 786.0 | 1,840.8 |
| Equity & investment fund shares | 3bala | — | — | — | — | — | — | — | † — | 78.3 | −13.9 | 140.8 | 95.2 |
| Debt securities | 3bbla | 1,228.8 | 1,280.4 | 377.9 | 1,128.1 | 781.1 | −290.9 | −61.1 | † 240.5 | −391.6 | 112.9 | 645.3 | 1,745.6 |
| Fin. der.& empl.stk.ops.(ESOs): net | 3c9na | — | — | — | — | — | — | — | † — | −8.7 | 66.0 | −178.1 | 26.4 |
| Fin. der. & ESOs: assets | 3c9aa | — | — | — | — | — | — | — | † — | 29.0 | −21.8 | −221.0 | 6.4 |
| Fin. der. & ESOs: liabilities | 3c9la | — | — | — | — | — | — | — | † — | 37.7 | −87.8 | −42.9 | −20.0 |
| Other investment: assets | 3d9aa | 127.4 | 290.8 | 269.0 | 238.3 | 242.2 | −21.0 | 1,143.4 | † 274.4 | 234.1 | 218.0 | −315.5 | −141.3 |
| Other equity | 3daaa | .... | .... | .... | .... | .... | .... | .... | .... | .1 | .... | −.1 | .... |
| Debt instruments | 3dzaa | 127.4 | 290.8 | 269.0 | 238.3 | 242.2 | −21.0 | 1,143.4 | † 274.4 | 234.0 | 218.0 | −315.4 | −141.3 |
| Other investment: liabilities | 3d9la | 705.6 | 1,145.0 | 938.9 | 1,421.6 | 1,934.7 | 1,423.0 | 1,824.2 | † 1,270.8 | 56.3 | 593.7 | 585.5 | −2,148.5 |
| Other equity | 3dala | .... | .... | .... | .... | .... | .... | .... | .... | .... | .... | .... | .... |
| Debt instruments | 3dzla | 705.6 | 1,145.0 | 938.9 | 1,421.6 | 1,934.7 | 1,423.0 | 1,824.2 | † 1,270.8 | 56.3 | 593.7 | 585.5 | −2,148.5 |
| Curr.+ cap.− finan. acct. balance | 4y9na | 728.0 | 238.7 | 159.4 | −743.1 | 275.8 | 198.5 | −492.8 | † −762.7 | −1,616.2 | −295.4 | 1,023.3 | 1,215.3 |
| D. Net Errors and Omissions | 409na | −33.3 | −8.8 | 71.0 | 303.3 | −380.8 | −227.8 | 144.7 | † 494.9 | 792.9 | 116.0 | −223.0 | −787.1 |
| E. Reserves and Related Items | 4z9na | 694.7 | 229.9 | 230.3 | −439.8 | −105.0 | −29.3 | −348.1 | † −267.8 | −823.2 | −179.4 | 800.3 | 428.2 |
| Reserve assets | 3e9aa | 685.6 | 227.9 | 230.3 | −439.8 | −105.0 | −29.3 | 431.4 | † −218.4 | −823.2 | −178.9 | 672.6 | 451.9 |
| Credit and loans from the IMF | 3dcla | −8.0 | −.9 | — | — | — | — | 779.5 | † 49.3 | — | .5 | −127.8 | 23.6 |
| Exceptional financing | 409la | −1.1 | −1.1 | — | — | — | — | — | † — | .... | .... | .... | .... |

*Excludes components in group E

| International Investment Position | | 2004 | 2005 | 2006 | 2007 | 2008 | 2009 | 2010 | 2011 | 2012 | 2013 | 2014 | 2015 |
|---|---|---|---|---|---|---|---|---|---|---|---|---|---|
| | | | | | | | *Millions of US Dollars* | | | | | | |
| Assets | 809aa | .... | 3,616.4 | 4,463.6 | 5,105.5 | 5,181.7 | † 3,187.0 | 4,910.2 | 5,180.9 | 6,041.7 | 6,293.9 | 6,991.7 | 7,736.0 |
| Direct investment | 8a9aa | .... | 48.6 | 96.0 | 69.0 | 62.2 | † 220.1 | 176.2 | 420.8 | 402.5 | 316.6 | 314.5 | 318.9 |
| Equity & investment fund shares | 8aaaa | .... | .... | .... | .... | .... | .... | .... | .... | .... | .... | .... | .... |
| Debt instruments | 8abaa | .... | .... | .... | .... | .... | .... | .... | .... | .... | .... | .... | .... |
| Portfolio investment | 8b9aa | .... | 602.6 | 1,114.8 | 1,895.5 | 2,072.2 | † 361.1 | 701.1 | 752.4 | 1,357.2 | 1,557.3 | 2,096.5 | 2,432.5 |
| Equity & investment fund shares | 8baaa | .... | .... | .... | .... | .... | † 55.8 | 56.7 | 48.9 | 128.9 | 176.4 | 227.4 | 286.8 |
| Debt securities | 8bbaa | .... | .... | .... | .... | .... | † 305.3 | 644.4 | 703.5 | 1,228.3 | 1,380.9 | 1,869.0 | 2,145.7 |
| Fin. der.(oth.than reserves) & ESOs | 8c9aa | .... | 19.4 | 2.8 | 31.0 | 61.2 | † 2.4 | 8.9 | 68.8 | 120.1 | 97.1 | 13.8 | 44.1 |
| Other investment | 8d9aa | .... | 858.5 | 932.3 | 1,232.0 | 1,213.0 | † 851.4 | 1,046.0 | 1,119.1 | 2,165.1 | 2,504.5 | 2,093.1 | 2,026.4 |
| Other equity | 8daaa | .... | .... | .... | .... | .... | .... | .... | .... | .... | .... | .... | .... |
| Debt instruments | 8dzaa | .... | 858.5 | 932.3 | 1,232.0 | 1,213.0 | † 851.4 | 1,046.0 | 1,119.1 | 2,165.1 | 2,504.5 | 2,093.1 | 2,026.4 |
| Reserve assets | 8e9aa | .... | 2,087.4 | 2,317.8 | 1,878.1 | 1,773.0 | † 1,752.0 | 2,977.9 | 2,819.7 | 1,996.8 | 1,818.4 | 2,473.9 | 2,914.1 |
| Liabilities | 809la | .... | 14,498.9 | 16,757.4 | 18,614.9 | 20,551.2 | † 20,294.2 | 22,081.9 | 23,800.0 | 25,588.2 | 26,303.0 | 27,694.3 | 28,398.9 |
| Direct investment | 8a9la | .... | 6,918.5 | 7,800.7 | 8,667.2 | 10,103.8 | † 10,627.5 | 10,855.2 | 11,110.4 | 12,119.0 | 12,712.0 | 13,303.0 | 13,906.9 |
| Equity & investment fund shares | 8aala | .... | .... | .... | .... | .... | .... | .... | .... | .... | .... | .... | .... |
| Debt instruments | 8abla | .... | .... | .... | .... | .... | .... | .... | .... | .... | .... | .... | .... |
| Portfolio investment | 8b9la | .... | 357.5 | 518.5 | 633.4 | 422.5 | † 2,899.6 | 2,462.7 | 3,552.3 | 3,611.2 | 3,070.1 | 3,860.7 | 6,415.7 |
| Equity & investment fund shares | 8bala | .... | .... | .... | .... | .... | † 414.4 | 507.0 | 705.3 | 987.8 | 324.0 | 442.9 | 1,238.4 |
| Debt securities | 8bbla | .... | .... | .... | .... | .... | † 2,485.2 | 1,955.7 | 2,847.0 | 2,623.5 | 2,746.0 | 3,417.8 | 5,177.2 |
| Fin. der.(oth.than reserves) & ESOs | 8c9la | .... | 11.3 | — | 23.3 | 70.3 | † 19.4 | 20.6 | 66.9 | 115.7 | 91.9 | 12.9 | 16.9 |
| Other investment | 8d9la | .... | 7,211.5 | 8,438.2 | 9,291.0 | 9,954.7 | † 6,747.7 | 8,743.5 | 9,070.5 | 9,742.2 | 10,429.1 | 10,517.6 | 8,059.4 |
| Other equity | 8dala | .... | .... | .... | .... | .... | .... | .... | .... | .... | .... | .... | .... |
| Debt instruments | 8dzla | .... | 7,211.5 | 8,438.2 | 9,291.0 | 9,954.7 | † 6,747.7 | 8,743.5 | 9,070.5 | 9,742.2 | 10,429.1 | 10,517.6 | 8,059.4 |

# Jamaica  343

| | | 2004 | 2005 | 2006 | 2007 | 2008 | 2009 | 2010 | 2011 | 2012 | 2013 | 2014 | 2015 |
|---|---|---|---|---|---|---|---|---|---|---|---|---|---|
| **Government Finance** | | | | | | | | | | | | | |
| **Cash Flow Statement** | | | | | | | | | | | | | |
| **Budgetary Central Government** | | | | *Millions of Jamaica Dollars: Fiscal Year Ends March 31* | | | | | | | | | |
| Cash Receipts:Operating Activities... | c1 | 169,700.8 | .... | 208,018.1 | 247,290.5 | 274,321.2 | 294,984.9 | 310,893.7 | 311,872.4 | 339,368.2 | 388,295.4 | 410,207.4 | 455,183.8 |
| Taxes... | c11 | 150,481.6 | .... | 188,300.5 | 219,517.6 | 246,216.5 | 265,860.6 | 279,873.6 | 289,882.1 | 315,483.4 | 335,810.2 | 370,878.0 | 411,854.8 |
| Social Contributions... | c12 | — | .... | | | | | | | | | | |
| Grants... | c13 | 5,392.6 | .... | 1,499.2 | 4,539.5 | 7,576.7 | 6,296.7 | 10,124.9 | 3,448.6 | 3,935.4 | 10,428.5 | 5,017.8 | 5,463.4 |
| Other Receipts... | c14 | 13,826.7 | .... | 18,218.4 | 23,233.4 | 20,528.0 | 22,827.6 | 20,895.2 | 18,541.7 | 19,949.4 | 42,056.7 | 34,311.6 | 37,865.6 |
| Cash Payments:Operating Activities. | c2 | 195,100.1 | .... | 224,505.5 | 252,877.7 | 310,149.2 | 387,044.2 | 333,174.0 | 350,440.2 | 361,601.7 | 358,252.8 | 395,967.9 | 427,972.3 |
| Compensation of Employees... | c21 | 26,380.8 | .... | 78,713.2 | 86,235.8 | 111,534.0 | 126,286.4 | 127,956.7 | 140,011.7 | 147,108.6 | 156,361.6 | 158,758.5 | 168,787.4 |
| Purchases of Goods & Services... | c22 | 9,098.9 | .... | .... | .... | .... | .... | .... | .... | .... | .... | .... | .... |
| Interest... | c24 | 93,636.3 | .... | 97,818.0 | 101,723.3 | 125,305.0 | 188,715.7 | 128,354.8 | 120,883.7 | 127,018.6 | 109,919.5 | 124,512.7 | 125,679.7 |
| Subsidies... | c25 | — | .... | .... | .... | .... | .... | .... | .... | .... | .... | .... | .... |
| Grants... | c26 | — | .... | .... | .... | .... | .... | .... | .... | .... | .... | .... | .... |
| Social Benefits... | c27 | 7,517.2 | .... | .... | .... | .... | .... | .... | .... | .... | .... | .... | .... |
| Other Payments... | c28 | 58,467.0 | .... | .... | .... | .... | .... | .... | .... | .... | .... | .... | .... |
| Net Cash Inflow:Operating Act.[1-2] | ccio | −25,399.3 | .... | −16,487.4 | −5,587.2 | −35,828.0 | −92,059.3 | −22,280.3 | −38,567.8 | −22,233.5 | 30,042.6 | 14,239.5 | 27,211.5 |
| Net Cash Outflow:Invest. in NFA... | c31 | 6,475.2 | .... | 20,213.1 | 36,655.7 | 39,493.6 | 29,205.5 | 51,929.4 | 42,645.8 | 36,571.7 | 36,330.7 | 21,510.1 | 32,094.8 |
| Purchases of Nonfinancial Assets... | c31.1 | .... | .... | 23,506.4 | 41,401.5 | 41,372.0 | 34,414.2 | 55,594.0 | 53,230.9 | 37,758.0 | 36,988.9 | 23,019.2 | 32,747.4 |
| Sales of Nonfinancial Assets... | c31.2 | .... | .... | 3,293.3 | 4,745.8 | 1,878.4 | 5,208.7 | 3,664.6 | 10,585.1 | 1,186.3 | 658.2 | 1,509.1 | 652.6 |
| Cash Surplus/Deficit [1-2-31=1-2M] | ccsd | −31,874.5 | .... | −36,700.5 | −42,242.9 | −75,321.6 | −121,264.8 | −74,209.7 | −81,213.6 | −58,805.2 | −6,288.1 | −7,270.6 | −4,883.3 |
| Net Acq. Fin. Assets, excl. Cash... | c32x | −2,251.7 | .... | — | — | — | — | — | — | — | — | — | −6,071.2 |
| Domestic... | c321x | −2,251.7 | .... | — | — | — | — | — | — | — | — | — | −6,071.2 |
| Foreign... | c322x | .... | .... | — | — | — | — | — | — | — | — | — | — |
| Net Incurrence of Liabilities... | c33 | 21,588.4 | .... | 39,247.3 | 29,124.6 | 63,415.3 | 130,085.4 | 110,811.0 | 35,324.9 | 55,501.4 | −13,112.8 | 81,070.3 | −44,125.3 |
| Domestic... | c331 | −13,548.2 | .... | 23,833.4 | 49,582.6 | 56,879.1 | 104,800.6 | 43,084.9 | 74,930.5 | 95,045.3 | −36,484.5 | 9,496.3 | −48,714.3 |
| Foreign... | c332 | 35,136.7 | .... | 15,413.9 | −20,458.0 | 6,536.2 | 25,284.8 | 67,726.1 | −39,605.6 | −39,543.9 | 23,371.7 | 71,574.0 | 4,589.0 |
| Net Cash Inflow, Fin.Act.[-32x+33].. | cnfb | 23,840.1 | .... | 39,247.3 | 29,124.6 | 63,415.3 | 130,085.4 | 110,811.0 | 35,324.9 | 55,501.4 | −13,112.8 | 81,070.3 | −38,054.1 |
| Net Change in Stock of Cash... | cncb | −8,034.4 | .... | 2,546.8 | −13,118.3 | −11,906.3 | 8,820.6 | 36,601.3 | −45,888.7 | −3,303.8 | −19,400.9 | 73,799.7 | −42,937.4 |
| Stat. Discrep. [32X-33+NCB-CSD]... | ccsdz | .... | .... | | | | | | | | | | |
| Memo Item:Cash Expenditure[2+31] | c2m | 201,575.3 | .... | 244,718.6 | 289,533.4 | 349,642.8 | 416,249.7 | 385,103.4 | 393,086.0 | 398,173.4 | 394,583.5 | 417,478.0 | 460,067.1 |
| Memo Item: Gross Debt... | c63 | 731,213.1 | .... | .... | .... | .... | .... | .... | .... | .... | .... | .... | .... |
| **National Accounts** | | | | | *Millions of Jamaica Dollars* | | | | | | | | |
| Househ.Cons.Expend.,incl.NPISHs.... | 96f | 466,231 | 551,731 | 613,118 | 711,413 | 889,064 | 855,780 | 944,301 | 1,064,229 | 1,122,026 | 1,219,908 | 1,312,997 | .... |
| Government Consumption Expend... | 91f | 80,234 | 99,518 | 108,943 | 131,849 | 161,646 | 176,189 | 185,829 | 196,091 | 213,901 | 221,980 | 228,307 | .... |
| Gross Fixed Capital Formation... | 93e | 164,173 | 187,221 | 220,129 | 231,392 | 239,066 | 222,197 | 229,408 | 259,834 | 258,093 | 300,554 | 339,502 | .... |
| Changes in Inventories... | 93i | 628 | 1,450 | 2,799 | 3,932 | 3,813 | 2,000 | 3,429 | 5,535 | 3,069 | 3,832 | 6,982 | .... |
| Exports of Goods and Services... | 90c | 233,772 | 247,010 | 314,766 | 351,850 | 418,361 | 367,317 | 361,227 | 376,784 | 396,652 | 437,876 | 481,916 | .... |
| Imports of Goods and Services (-)... | 98c | 322,377 | 386,655 | 475,418 | 544,803 | 714,510 | 558,285 | 571,608 | 663,195 | 681,458 | 754,481 | 824,708 | .... |
| Gross Domestic Product (GDP)... | 99b | 622,661 | 700,276 | 784,336 | 885,632 | 997,440 | 1,065,196 | 1,152,587 | 1,239,278 | 1,312,284 | 1,429,669 | 1,544,997 | 1,637,204 |
| Net Primary Income from Abroad... | 98.n | −35,642 | −42,147 | −40,428 | −45,477 | −41,023 | −58,732 | −43,121 | −44,536 | −19,778 | −36,633 | −40,597 | .... |
| Gross National Income (GNI)... | 99a | 587,019 | 658,129 | 743,908 | 840,154 | 956,417 | 1,006,465 | 1,109,465 | 1,194,742 | 1,292,507 | 1,393,036 | 1,504,399 | .... |
| GDP Volume 2007 Prices... | 99b.p | 728,509 | 735,020 | 756,328 | 767,251 | †760,966 | 735,015 | 724,325 | 734,642 | 730,829 | 732,255 | 736,133 | 742,449 |
| GDP Volume (2010=100)... | 99bvp | 100.6 | 101.5 | 104.4 | 105.9 | 105.1 | 101.5 | 100.0 | 101.4 | 100.9 | 101.1 | 101.6 | 102.5 |
| GDP Deflator (2010=100)... | 99bip | 53.7 | 59.9 | 65.2 | 72.5 | 82.4 | 91.1 | 100.0 | 106.0 | 112.8 | 122.7 | 131.9 | 138.6 |
| | | | | | | *Millions: Midyear Estimates* | | | | | | | |
| Population... | 99z | 2.66 | 2.68 | 2.69 | 2.70 | 2.72 | 2.73 | 2.74 | 2.75 | 2.76 | 2.77 | 2.78 | 2.79 |

# Japan 158

| | | 2004 | 2005 | 2006 | 2007 | 2008 | 2009 | 2010 | 2011 | 2012 | 2013 | 2014 | 2015 |
|---|---|---|---|---|---|---|---|---|---|---|---|---|---|
| **Exchange Rates** | | | | | | *Yen per SDR: End of Period* | | | | | | | |
| Market Rate................................... | aa | 161.70 | 168.61 | 178.95 | 180.15 | 139.78 | 144.32 | 125.44 | 119.32 | 133.02 | 162.16 | 174.78 | 166.98 |
| | | | | | | *Yen per US Dollar: End of Period (ae) Period Average (rf)* | | | | | | | |
| Market Rate................................... | ae | 104.120 | 117.970 | 118.950 | 114.000 | 90.750 | 92.060 | 81.450 | 77.720 | 86.550 | 105.300 | 120.640 | 120.500 |
| Market Rate................................... | rf | 108.193 | 110.218 | 116.299 | 117.754 | 103.359 | 93.570 | 87.780 | 79.807 | 79.790 | 97.596 | 105.945 | 121.044 |
| | | | | | | *Index Numbers (2010=100): Period Averages* | | | | | | | |
| Market Rate................................... | ahx | 81.0 | 79.6 | 75.3 | 74.5 | 85.0 | 93.7 | 100.0 | 109.9 | 109.9 | 89.9 | 82.9 | 72.4 |
| Nominal Effective Exchange Rate..... | nec | 88.3 | 85.4 | 79.1 | 74.9 | 83.7 | 95.8 | 100.0 | 105.8 | 107.1 | 87.0 | 80.6 | 75.2 |
| CPI-Based Real Effect. Ex. Rate........ | rec | 103.8 | 97.4 | 88.2 | 81.0 | 87.7 | 98.8 | 100.0 | 101.7 | 100.6 | 80.3 | 75.1 | 70.1 |
| ULC-Based Real Effect. Ex. Rate....... | rel | 99.4 | 91.1 | 82.9 | 74.5 | 81.7 | 98.5 | 100.0 | 108.0 | 109.0 | 88.1 | 80.7 | 77.3 |
| **Fund Position** | | | | | | *Millions of SDRs: End of Period* | | | | | | | |
| Quota................................... | 2f.s | 13,312.80 | 13,312.80 | 13,312.80 | 13,312.80 | 13,312.80 | 13,312.80 | 13,312.80 | 15,628.50 | 15,628.50 | 15,628.50 | 15,628.50 | 15,628.50 |
| SDR Holdings................................... | 1b.s | 1,827.75 | 1,808.24 | 1,869.06 | 1,919.61 | 1,968.71 | 13,375.01 | 13,392.96 | 12,860.97 | 12,954.62 | 13,071.29 | 13,042.37 | 13,023.79 |
| Reserve Position in the Fund............ | 1c.s | 4,371.38 | 2,013.20 | 1,285.35 | 882.77 | 1,725.95 | 2,751.25 | 2,992.34 | 11,189.15 | 8,887.15 | 9,197.40 | 8,253.64 | 6,834.47 |
| Total Fund Cred. & Loans Outstg..... | 2tl | — | — | — | — | — | — | — | — | — | — | — | — |
| SDR Allocations............................. | 1bd | 891.69 | 891.69 | 891.69 | 891.69 | 891.69 | 12,284.97 | 12,284.97 | 12,284.97 | 12,284.97 | 12,284.97 | 12,284.97 | 12,284.97 |
| **International Liquidity** | | | | | | *Millions of US Dollars Unless Otherwise Indicated: End of Period* | | | | | | | |
| Total Reserves minus Gold.............. | 1l.d | 833,891 | 834,275 | 879,682 | 952,784 | 1,009,365 | 1,022,236 | 1,061,490 | 1,258,172 | 1,227,147 | 1,237,218 | 1,231,010 | 1,207,019 |
| SDR Holdings............................... | 1b.d | 2,839 | 2,584 | 2,812 | 3,033 | 3,032 | 20,968 | 20,626 | 19,745 | 19,910 | 20,130 | 18,896 | 18,047 |
| Reserve Position in the Fund......... | 1c.d | 6,789 | 2,877 | 1,934 | 1,395 | 2,658 | 4,313 | 4,608 | 17,178 | 13,659 | 14,164 | 11,958 | 9,471 |
| Foreign Exchange....................... | 1d.d | 824,264 | 828,813 | 874,936 | 948,356 | 1,003,674 | 996,955 | 1,036,256 | 1,221,249 | 1,193,578 | 1,202,924 | 1,200,156 | 1,179,501 |
| Gold (Million Fine Troy Ounces)..... | 1ad | 24.60 | 24.60 | 24.60 | 24.60 | 24.60 | 24.60 | 24.60 | 24.60 | 24.60 | 24.60 | 24.60 | 24.60 |
| Gold (National Valuation)............... | 1and | 10,776 | 12,621 | 15,639 | 20,580 | 21,281 | 27,161 | 34,695 | 37,666 | 40,939 | 29,560 | 29,504 | 26,134 |
| Central Bank: Other Assets.............. | 3..d | 43,803 | 42,641 | 45,992 | 50,018 | 52,413 | 54,636 | 55,390 | 58,200 | 57,080 | 52,460 | 47,001 | 46,877 |
| Central Bank: Other Liabs................ | 4..d | 20,721 | 36,680 | 10,844 | 13,171 | 147,759 | 32,994 | 24,259 | 43,248 | 23,380 | 33,368 | 42,599 | 53,040 |
| Other Depository Corps.: Assets....... | 7a.d | 1,149,742 | 1,258,431 | 1,259,448 | 1,546,246 | 2,036,642 | 1,835,223 | 2,201,055 | 2,407,385 | 2,509,041 | 2,234,930 | 2,104,709 | 2,228,281 |
| Other Depository Corps.: Liabs........ | 7b.d | 782,001 | 729,487 | 705,903 | 743,629 | 1,158,194 | 1,188,959 | 1,374,465 | 1,446,951 | 1,581,846 | 1,291,398 | 1,306,057 | 1,240,826 |
| Other Financial Corps.: Assets.......... | 7e.d | 1,129,159 | 1,220,282 | 1,420,811 | 1,663,113 | 1,615,285 | 1,683,896 | 1,946,451 | 2,146,498 | 1,981,306 | 1,906,273 | 1,984,630 | 1,996,230 |
| Other Financial Corps.: Liabs............ | 7f.d | 171,065 | 304,661 | 237,262 | 270,707 | 266,306 | 248,712 | 329,387 | 448,055 | 457,797 | 583,654 | 597,073 | 589,131 |
| **Central Bank** | | | | | | *Trillions of Yen: End of Period* | | | | | | | |
| Net Foreign Assets......................... | 11n | 3.471 | 2.119 | 5.956 | 6.423 | −6.819 | 4.381 | 5.235 | 3.952 | 6.290 | 4.984 | 3.906 | 2.262 |
| Claims on Nonresidents................ | 11 | 5.628 | 6.446 | 7.246 | 7.924 | 6.590 | 7.418 | 7.211 | 7.313 | 8.314 | 8.498 | 9.045 | 8.653 |
| Liabilities to Nonresidents............. | 16c | 2.158 | 4.327 | 1.290 | 1.502 | 13.409 | 3.037 | 1.976 | 3.361 | 2.024 | 3.514 | 5.139 | 6.391 |
| Claims on Other Depository Corps.... | 12e | 24.367 | 32.448 | 11.381 | 12.759 | 21.546 | 15.857 | 18.327 | 25.682 | 19.643 | 23.909 | 29.219 | 33.434 |
| Net Claims on Central Government.. | 12an | 79.188 | 79.194 | 65.375 | 62.691 | 59.422 | 64.876 | 64.771 | 77.035 | 96.089 | 159.203 | 222.029 | 288.555 |
| Claims on Central Government...... | 12a | 94.341 | 96.662 | 77.963 | 69.209 | 63.180 | 72.315 | 76.396 | 89.245 | 108.997 | 172.498 | 238.237 | 305.599 |
| Liabilities to Central Government... | 16d | 15.154 | 17.468 | 12.588 | 6.518 | 3.758 | 7.439 | 11.625 | 12.210 | 12.908 | 13.295 | 16.208 | 17.044 |
| Claims on Other Sectors............... | 12s | 25.595 | 26.907 | 25.922 | 29.845 | 37.721 | 33.913 | 33.505 | 27.902 | 30.737 | 31.073 | 40.272 | 52.651 |
| Claims on Other Financial Corps.... | 12g | 23.015 | 23.322 | 22.547 | 27.003 | 36.372 | 31.978 | 31.472 | 22.059 | 22.218 | 19.326 | 26.348 | 34.893 |
| Claims on State & Local Govts....... | 12b | — | — | — | — | — | — | — | — | — | — | — | — |
| Claims on Public Nonfin. Corps...... | 12c | — | — | — | — | — | — | — | — | — | — | — | — |
| Claims on Private Sector............... | 12d | 2.580 | 3.585 | 3.375 | 2.841 | 1.349 | 1.934 | 2.033 | 5.843 | 8.519 | 11.747 | 13.924 | 17.758 |
| Monetary Base............................. | 14 | 115.627 | 116.641 | 94.778 | 95.979 | 101.261 | 105.848 | 109.507 | 125.079 | 138.475 | 201.847 | 275.874 | 356.134 |
| Currency in Circulation................. | 14a | 82.448 | 83.773 | 84.365 | 85.855 | 86.069 | 85.511 | 86.856 | 88.547 | 91.231 | 94.770 | 97.738 | 103.120 |
| Liabs. to Other Depository Corps.... | 14c | 31.508 | 30.382 | 9.781 | 9.712 | 13.993 | 18.335 | 20.215 | 33.064 | 44.452 | 102.619 | 172.050 | 244.713 |
| Liabilities to Other Sectors............. | 14d | 1.671 | 2.486 | .631 | .412 | 1.199 | 2.002 | 2.437 | 3.469 | 2.792 | 4.458 | 6.086 | 8.301 |
| Other Liabs. to Other Dep. Corps...... | 14n | — | 3.664 | — | — | — | — | — | — | — | — | — | — |
| Dep. & Sec. Excl. f/Monetary Base.... | 14o | — | — | — | — | — | — | — | — | — | — | — | — |
| Deposits Included in Broad Money. | 15 | — | — | — | — | — | — | — | — | — | — | — | — |
| Sec.Ot.th.Shares Incl.in Brd. Money | 16a | — | — | — | — | — | — | — | — | — | — | — | — |
| Deposits Excl. from Broad Money. | 16b | — | — | — | — | — | — | — | — | — | — | — | — |
| Sec.Ot.th.Shares Excl.f/Brd.Money.. | 16s | — | — | — | — | — | — | — | — | — | — | — | — |
| Loans............................................... | 16l | 9.964 | 11.921 | 5.333 | 5.355 | 2.219 | 4.088 | 3.499 | .194 | 2.999 | 3.388 | .211 | — |
| Financial Derivatives....................... | 16m | — | — | — | — | — | — | — | — | — | — | — | — |
| Shares and Other Equity.................. | 17a | 7.990 | 8.991 | 8.971 | 10.778 | 8.793 | 9.532 | 9.365 | 9.805 | 11.808 | 14.433 | 19.889 | 21.335 |
| Other Items (Net)............................ | 17r | −.960 | −.549 | −.448 | −.395 | −.402 | −.442 | −.533 | −.507 | −.523 | −.498 | −.547 | −.566 |
| Memo Item: | | | | | | | | | | | | | |
| Total Assets...................................... | 10ra | 150.902 | 163.021 | 122.970 | 120.142 | 129.461 | 129.968 | 135.993 | 150.670 | 168.223 | 236.487 | 317.334 | 400.920 |

| | | 2004 | 2005 | 2006 | 2007 | 2008 | 2009 | 2010 | 2011 | 2012 | 2013 | 2014 | 2015 |
|---|---|---|---|---|---|---|---|---|---|---|---|---|---|
| **Other Depository Corporations** | | | | | | *Trillions of Yen: End of Period* | | | | | | | |
| Net Foreign Assets | 21n | 38.289 | 62.400 | 65.844 | 91.498 | 79.719 | 59.495 | 67.326 | 74.645 | 80.249 | 99.354 | 96.349 | 118.988 |
| Claims on Nonresidents | 21 | 119.711 | 148.457 | 149.811 | 176.272 | 184.825 | 168.951 | 179.276 | 187.102 | 217.158 | 235.338 | 253.912 | 268.508 |
| Liabilities to Nonresidents | 26c | 81.422 | 86.058 | 83.967 | 84.774 | 105.106 | 109.456 | 111.950 | 112.457 | 136.909 | 135.984 | 157.563 | 149.520 |
| Claims on Central Bank | 20 | 41.106 | 42.960 | 17.989 | 18.147 | 23.461 | 27.122 | 28.670 | 41.639 | 52.616 | 112.113 | 181.625 | 254.214 |
| Currency | 20a | 9.598 | 8.914 | 8.207 | 8.435 | 9.468 | 8.787 | 8.456 | 8.576 | 8.164 | 9.493 | 9.575 | 9.501 |
| Reserve Deposits and Securities | 20b | 31.508 | 30.382 | 9.781 | 9.712 | 13.993 | 18.335 | 20.215 | 33.064 | 44.452 | 102.619 | 172.050 | 244.713 |
| Other Claims | 20n | — | 3.664 | — | — | — | — | — | — | — | — | — | — |
| Net Claims on Central Government | 22an | 206.638 | 212.476 | 217.653 | 216.502 | 247.449 | 279.805 | 309.303 | 320.078 | 316.390 | 295.427 | 266.411 | 207.566 |
| Claims on Central Government | 22a | 229.907 | 236.933 | 243.889 | 241.353 | 268.019 | 296.591 | 322.358 | 334.217 | 328.643 | 307.823 | 284.903 | 234.663 |
| Liabilities to Central Government | 26d | 23.269 | 24.457 | 26.236 | 24.851 | 20.570 | 16.786 | 13.055 | 14.139 | 12.252 | 12.396 | 18.492 | 27.097 |
| Claims on Other Sectors | 22s | 852.330 | 846.643 | 826.487 | 800.910 | 781.551 | 763.284 | 747.653 | 736.981 | 758.967 | 772.991 | 781.024 | 788.463 |
| Claims on Other Financial Corps | 22g | 310.312 | 283.105 | 262.081 | 238.131 | 211.407 | 192.004 | 174.696 | 167.399 | 173.862 | 166.721 | 167.615 | 164.196 |
| Claims on State & Local Govts | 22b | 37.210 | 42.167 | 42.946 | 45.063 | 47.780 | 51.507 | 56.599 | 59.878 | 63.053 | 64.513 | 65.506 | 66.530 |
| Claims on Public Nonfin. Corps | 22c | 18.321 | 15.969 | 14.120 | 12.949 | 12.056 | 12.109 | 10.392 | 10.060 | 9.314 | 8.644 | 8.547 | 8.034 |
| Claims on Private Sector | 22d | 486.487 | 505.402 | 507.340 | 504.767 | 510.309 | 507.664 | 505.968 | 499.644 | 512.738 | 533.114 | 539.356 | 549.704 |
| Liabilities to Central Bank | 26g | 24.367 | 32.448 | 11.381 | 12.759 | 21.546 | 15.857 | 18.327 | 25.682 | 19.643 | 23.909 | 29.219 | 33.434 |
| Transf.Dep.Included in Broad Money | 24 | 395.027 | 417.453 | 418.694 | 418.929 | 412.714 | 418.441 | 431.024 | 456.385 | 473.526 | 500.213 | 524.592 | 545.008 |
| Other Dep.Included in Broad Money | 25 | 566.845 | 546.749 | 538.370 | 543.620 | 557.400 | 572.394 | 576.366 | 579.861 | 584.746 | 594.233 | 600.849 | 610.415 |
| Sec.Ot.th.Shares Incl.in Brd. Money | 26a | — | — | — | — | — | — | — | — | — | — | — | — |
| Deposits Excl. from Broad Money | 26b | 11.332 | 11.666 | 10.898 | 12.160 | 12.718 | 14.108 | 14.956 | 14.394 | 14.251 | 18.657 | 19.647 | 18.911 |
| Sec.Ot.th.Shares Excl.f/Brd.Money | 26s | 38.013 | 32.748 | 28.790 | 27.007 | 24.456 | 26.452 | 25.324 | 23.184 | 22.211 | 22.564 | 22.104 | 24.547 |
| Loans | 26l | 80.717 | 76.463 | 68.548 | 61.850 | 58.558 | 40.551 | 39.836 | 39.374 | 40.748 | 55.273 | 59.160 | 75.585 |
| Financial Derivatives | 26m | — | — | — | — | — | — | — | — | — | — | — | — |
| Insurance Technical Reserves | 26r | — | — | — | — | — | — | — | — | — | — | — | — |
| Shares and Other Equity | 27a | 45.840 | 55.894 | 54.763 | 57.252 | 22.241 | 22.427 | 25.923 | 14.203 | 29.135 | 55.313 | 70.046 | 76.072 |
| Other Items (Net) | 27r | −23.779 | −8.943 | −3.470 | −6.520 | 22.548 | 19.477 | 21.197 | 20.260 | 23.962 | 9.722 | −.209 | −14.737 |
| Memo Item: | | | | | | | | | | | | | |
| Total Assets | 20ra | 1,480.707 | 1,481.771 | 1,447.090 | 1,456.034 | 1,489.668 | 1,482.320 | 1,503.103 | 1,536.376 | 1,599.922 | 1,669.848 | 1,764.974 | 1,803.931 |
| **Depository Corporations** | | | | | | *Trillions of Yen: End of Period* | | | | | | | |
| Net Foreign Assets | 31n | 41.760 | 64.518 | 71.800 | 97.921 | 72.901 | 63.876 | 72.561 | 78.597 | 86.539 | 104.338 | 100.255 | 121.250 |
| Claims on Nonresidents | 31 | 125.339 | 154.903 | 157.057 | 184.196 | 191.416 | 176.369 | 186.487 | 194.415 | 225.471 | 243.836 | 262.957 | 277.161 |
| Liabilities to Nonresidents | 36c | 83.579 | 90.385 | 85.257 | 86.275 | 118.515 | 112.493 | 113.926 | 115.818 | 138.932 | 139.498 | 162.702 | 155.911 |
| Domestic Claims | 32 | 1,163.750 | 1,165.220 | 1,135.437 | 1,109.947 | 1,126.144 | 1,141.877 | 1,155.232 | 1,161.996 | 1,202.183 | 1,258.695 | 1,309.737 | 1,337.235 |
| Net Claims on Central Government | 32an | 285.826 | 291.670 | 283.028 | 279.193 | 306.872 | 344.681 | 374.074 | 397.113 | 412.479 | 454.630 | 488.440 | 496.121 |
| Claims on Central Government | 32a | 324.248 | 333.595 | 321.852 | 310.562 | 331.199 | 368.906 | 398.754 | 423.462 | 437.640 | 480.321 | 523.140 | 540.262 |
| Liabilities to Central Government | 36d | 38.423 | 41.924 | 38.824 | 31.369 | 24.327 | 24.225 | 24.680 | 26.349 | 25.161 | 25.690 | 34.700 | 44.141 |
| Claims on Other Sectors | 32s | 877.924 | 873.550 | 852.409 | 830.754 | 819.272 | 797.196 | 781.158 | 764.883 | 789.704 | 804.065 | 821.296 | 841.114 |
| Claims on Other Financial Corps | 32g | 333.327 | 306.427 | 284.628 | 265.135 | 247.779 | 223.982 | 206.168 | 189.459 | 196.080 | 186.047 | 193.964 | 199.088 |
| Claims on State & Local Govts | 32b | 37.210 | 42.167 | 42.946 | 45.063 | 47.780 | 51.507 | 56.599 | 59.878 | 63.053 | 64.513 | 65.506 | 66.530 |
| Claims on Public Nonfin. Corps | 32c | 18.321 | 15.969 | 14.120 | 12.949 | 12.056 | 12.109 | 10.392 | 10.060 | 9.314 | 8.644 | 8.547 | 8.034 |
| Claims on Private Sector | 32d | 489.067 | 508.987 | 510.715 | 507.608 | 511.657 | 509.598 | 508.000 | 505.487 | 521.257 | 544.861 | 553.280 | 567.462 |
| Broad Money Liabilities | 35l | 1,036.393 | 1,041.547 | 1,033.853 | 1,040.381 | 1,047.913 | 1,069.561 | 1,088.226 | 1,119.685 | 1,144.131 | 1,184.181 | 1,219.690 | 1,257.343 |
| Currency Outside Depository Corps | 34a | 72.851 | 74.859 | 76.158 | 77.420 | 76.600 | 76.724 | 78.400 | 79.971 | 83.067 | 85.276 | 88.163 | 93.619 |
| Transferable Deposits | 34 | 396.697 | 419.940 | 419.325 | 419.341 | 413.913 | 420.443 | 433.460 | 459.854 | 476.318 | 504.672 | 530.678 | 553.309 |
| Other Deposits | 35 | 566.845 | 546.749 | 538.370 | 543.620 | 557.400 | 572.394 | 576.366 | 579.861 | 584.746 | 594.233 | 600.849 | 610.415 |
| Securities Other than Shares | 36a | — | — | — | — | — | — | — | — | — | — | — | — |
| Deposits Excl. from Broad Money | 36b | 11.332 | 11.666 | 10.898 | 12.160 | 12.718 | 14.108 | 14.956 | 14.394 | 14.251 | 18.657 | 19.647 | 18.911 |
| Sec.Ot.th.Shares Excl.f/Brd.Money | 36s | 38.013 | 32.748 | 28.790 | 27.007 | 24.456 | 26.452 | 25.324 | 23.184 | 22.211 | 22.564 | 22.104 | 24.547 |
| Loans | 36l | 90.681 | 88.384 | 73.882 | 67.204 | 60.777 | 44.639 | 43.335 | 39.568 | 43.747 | 58.661 | 59.371 | 75.585 |
| Financial Derivatives | 36m | — | — | — | — | — | — | — | — | — | — | — | — |
| Insurance Technical Reserves | 36r | — | — | — | — | — | — | — | — | — | — | — | — |
| Shares and Other Equity | 37a | 53.830 | 64.885 | 63.734 | 68.030 | 31.034 | 31.959 | 35.288 | 24.008 | 40.943 | 69.746 | 89.935 | 97.406 |
| Other Items (Net) | 37r | −24.739 | −9.492 | −3.918 | −6.915 | 22.146 | 19.034 | 20.663 | 19.753 | 23.439 | 9.225 | −.756 | −15.302 |
| Broad Money Liabs., Seasonally Adj. | 35l.b | 1,032.132 | 1,037.375 | 1,030.022 | 1,036.928 | 1,045.099 | 1,067.325 | 1,086.603 | 1,118.222 | 1,142.464 | 1,182.107 | 1,217.404 | 1,255.019 |
| **Other Financial Corporations** | | | | | | *Trillions of Yen: End of Period* | | | | | | | |
| Net Foreign Assets | 41n | 99.757 | 108.016 | 140.783 | 158.734 | 122.420 | 132.123 | 131.710 | 132.003 | 131.860 | 139.272 | 167.395 | 169.555 |
| Claims on Nonresidents | 41 | 117.568 | 143.957 | 169.006 | 189.595 | 146.587 | 155.020 | 158.538 | 166.826 | 171.482 | 200.731 | 239.426 | 240.546 |
| Liabilities to Nonresidents | 46c | 17.811 | 35.941 | 28.222 | 30.861 | 24.167 | 22.896 | 26.829 | 34.823 | 39.622 | 61.459 | 72.031 | 70.990 |
| Claims on Depository Corporations | 40 | 140.500 | 179.887 | 157.255 | 140.388 | 121.050 | 110.681 | 107.168 | 102.311 | 108.842 | 140.549 | 140.955 | 162.872 |
| Net Claims on Central Government | 42an | 120.740 | 116.268 | 112.664 | 118.072 | 126.764 | 143.670 | 161.274 | 170.148 | 192.905 | 201.329 | 221.380 | 218.005 |
| Claims on Central Government | 42a | 256.268 | 240.105 | 221.217 | 211.360 | 203.835 | 210.886 | 224.657 | 224.188 | 243.360 | 247.967 | 261.058 | 252.658 |
| Liabilities to Central Government | 46d | 135.53 | 123.84 | 108.55 | 93.29 | 77.07 | 67.22 | 63.38 | 54.04 | 50.45 | 46.64 | 39.68 | 34.65 |
| Claims on Other Sectors | 42s | 603.205 | 639.048 | 621.300 | 581.083 | 533.869 | 508.159 | 491.990 | 473.932 | 473.010 | 487.517 | 498.385 | 523.297 |
| Claims on State & Local Govts | 42b | 124.047 | 118.353 | 112.841 | 109.040 | 104.065 | 101.350 | 99.128 | 98.347 | 97.277 | 96.284 | 94.273 | 92.931 |
| Claims on Public Nonfin. Corps | 42c | 64.157 | 38.051 | 37.275 | 38.581 | 35.714 | 34.191 | 32.617 | 31.419 | 30.423 | 29.314 | 29.943 | 28.089 |
| Claims on Private Sector | 42d | 415.001 | 482.644 | 471.183 | 433.462 | 394.091 | 372.618 | 360.245 | 344.167 | 345.310 | 361.919 | 374.169 | 402.277 |
| Deposits | 46b | — | — | — | — | — | — | — | — | — | — | — | — |
| Securities Other than Shares | 46s | 113.233 | 137.401 | 139.650 | 137.347 | 134.080 | 133.596 | 136.040 | 131.469 | 132.875 | 129.662 | 130.961 | 133.057 |
| Loans | 46l | 127.944 | 109.495 | 108.770 | 114.546 | 120.808 | 115.115 | 98.077 | 85.451 | 91.273 | 82.771 | 86.895 | 87.286 |
| Financial Derivatives | 46m | — | — | — | — | — | — | — | — | — | — | — | — |
| Insurance Technical Reserves | 46r | 415.872 | 482.969 | 484.512 | 479.236 | 469.246 | 464.769 | 465.684 | 468.439 | 480.998 | 493.180 | 506.275 | 513.836 |
| Shares and Other Equity | 47a | 128.106 | 224.382 | 243.635 | 238.131 | 160.494 | 184.592 | 198.843 | 192.987 | 205.286 | 268.446 | 306.365 | 340.487 |
| Other Items (Net) | 47r | 179.047 | 88.972 | 55.435 | 29.017 | 19.474 | −3.439 | −6.502 | .049 | −3.814 | −5.393 | −2.380 | −.938 |
| Memo Item: | | | | | | | | | | | | | |
| Total Assets | 40ra | 1,348.398 | 1,481.211 | 1,441.376 | 1,396.466 | 1,235.602 | 1,217.288 | 1,217.774 | 1,189.352 | 1,227.679 | 1,314.456 | 1,383.083 | 1,418.399 |

| | | 2004 | 2005 | 2006 | 2007 | 2008 | 2009 | 2010 | 2011 | 2012 | 2013 | 2014 | 2015 |
|---|---|---|---|---|---|---|---|---|---|---|---|---|---|
| **Financial Corporations** | | *Trillions of Yen: End of Period* | | | | | | | | | | | |
| Net Foreign Assets | 51n | 141.517 | 172.534 | 212.583 | 256.655 | 195.320 | 195.999 | 204.271 | 210.600 | 218.399 | 243.610 | 267.650 | 290.806 |
| Claims on Nonresidents | 51 | 242.907 | 298.860 | 326.063 | 373.791 | 338.003 | 331.388 | 345.025 | 361.241 | 396.953 | 444.566 | 502.383 | 517.707 |
| Liabilities to Nonresidents | 56c | 101.391 | 126.326 | 113.479 | 117.136 | 142.683 | 135.389 | 140.755 | 150.641 | 178.555 | 200.957 | 234.733 | 226.901 |
| Domestic Claims | 52 | 1,554.367 | 1,614.108 | 1,584.773 | 1,543.967 | 1,538.997 | 1,569.723 | 1,602.328 | 1,616.618 | 1,672.018 | 1,761.494 | 1,835.539 | 1,879.449 |
| Net Claims on Central Government | 52an | 406.565 | 407.938 | 395.692 | 397.265 | 433.636 | 488.351 | 535.348 | 567.261 | 605.384 | 655.959 | 709.821 | 714.126 |
| Claims on Central Government | 52a | 580.516 | 573.699 | 543.069 | 521.922 | 535.034 | 579.792 | 623.411 | 647.650 | 680.999 | 728.288 | 784.199 | 792.920 |
| Liabilities to Central Government | 56d | 173.951 | 165.761 | 147.377 | 124.657 | 101.399 | 91.442 | 88.064 | 80.388 | 75.615 | 72.329 | 74.378 | 78.794 |
| Claims on Other Sectors | 52s | 1,147.802 | 1,206.170 | 1,189.081 | 1,146.702 | 1,105.362 | 1,081.373 | 1,066.980 | 1,049.356 | 1,066.634 | 1,105.535 | 1,125.718 | 1,165.323 |
| Claims on State & Local Govts | 52b | 161.256 | 160.520 | 155.787 | 154.102 | 151.845 | 152.857 | 155.726 | 158.224 | 160.330 | 160.796 | 159.779 | 159.461 |
| Claims on Public Nonfin. Corps | 52c | 82.478 | 54.020 | 51.396 | 51.529 | 47.769 | 46.300 | 43.008 | 41.478 | 39.737 | 37.958 | 38.489 | 36.123 |
| Claims on Private Sector | 52d | 904.068 | 991.630 | 981.898 | 941.071 | 905.748 | 882.216 | 868.246 | 849.654 | 866.567 | 906.781 | 927.449 | 969.738 |
| Currency Outside Financial Corps | 54a | 71.804 | 73.564 | 74.192 | 75.442 | 75.089 | 75.808 | 78.051 | 79.565 | 82.619 | 84.351 | 87.143 | 92.039 |
| Deposits | 55l | 944.866 | 949.026 | 942.725 | 947.230 | 955.115 | 975.472 | 995.037 | 1,022.896 | 1,045.976 | 1,080.347 | 1,110.368 | 1,139.423 |
| Securities Other than Shares | 56a | 35.962 | 37.565 | 29.748 | 22.009 | 19.004 | 25.000 | 24.815 | 22.678 | 21.351 | 21.356 | 20.914 | 23.532 |
| Loans | 56l | 24.964 | 18.454 | 16.434 | 18.332 | 16.111 | 17.813 | 16.845 | 16.529 | 18.930 | 20.456 | 22.703 | 22.729 |
| Financial Derivatives | 56m | — | — | — | — | — | — | — | — | — | — | — | — |
| Insurance Technical Reserves | 56r | 415.872 | 482.969 | 484.512 | 479.236 | 469.246 | 464.769 | 465.684 | 468.439 | 480.998 | 493.180 | 506.275 | 513.836 |
| Shares and Other Equity | 57a | 181.936 | 289.266 | 307.369 | 306.161 | 191.528 | 216.551 | 234.131 | 216.995 | 246.228 | 338.192 | 396.299 | 437.893 |
| Other Items (Net) | 57r | 20.481 | −64.201 | −57.623 | −47.786 | 8.224 | −9.693 | −7.964 | .115 | −5.685 | −32.778 | −40.514 | −59.194 |
| **Monetary Aggregates** | | *Trillions of Yen: End of Period* | | | | | | | | | | | |
| Broad Money | 59m | 1,036.393 | 1,041.547 | 1,033.853 | 1,040.381 | 1,047.913 | 1,069.561 | 1,088.226 | 1,119.685 | 1,144.131 | 1,184.181 | 1,219.690 | 1,257.343 |
| o/w:Currency Issued by Cent.Govt | 59m.a | — | — | — | — | — | — | — | — | — | — | — | — |
| o/w: Dep.in Nonfin. Corporations | 59m.b | — | — | — | — | — | — | — | — | — | — | — | — |
| o/w:Secs. Issued by Central Govt | 59m.c | — | — | — | — | — | — | — | — | — | — | — | — |
| Money (National Definitions) | | | | | | | | | | | | | |
| M1 | 59ma | 470.91 | 495.14 | 495.28 | 498.68 | 493.92 | 498.57 | 515.31 | 541.40 | 560.28 | 592.04 | 618.73 | 646.05 |
| M1, Seasonally Adjusted | 59mac | 464.56 | 486.22 | 480.13 | 492.68 | 488.70 | 494.35 | 510.56 | 533.13 | 554.07 | 586.47 | 611.87 | 639.69 |
| M2 (Period Average) | 59mb | 688.93 | 701.37 | 708.43 | 719.58 | 734.60 | 754.49 | 775.39 | 796.61 | 816.53 | 845.97 | 874.84 | 907.13 |
| M2, Seas. Adj. (Period Average) | 59mbc | 688.91 | 701.39 | 708.46 | 719.61 | 734.60 | 754.46 | 775.35 | 796.59 | 816.53 | 845.97 | 874.82 | 907.12 |
| M3 | 59mc | 1,037.71 | 1,041.61 | 1,037.20 | 1,045.19 | 1,053.15 | 1,074.26 | 1,095.02 | 1,123.51 | 1,148.62 | 1,187.63 | 1,221.28 | 1,252.30 |
| M3, Seasonally Adjusted | 59mcc | 1,030.83 | 1,031.21 | 1,026.91 | 1,038.76 | 1,047.72 | 1,068.85 | 1,089.36 | 1,113.04 | 1,141.23 | 1,180.38 | 1,213.48 | 1,244.19 |
| L (Period Average) | 59mf | 1,273.11 | 1,303.13 | 1,344.01 | 1,382.08 | 1,399.25 | 1,404.06 | 1,427.78 | 1,441.23 | 1,452.61 | 1,499.08 | 1,550.88 | 1,614.01 |
| L, Seas. Adj. (Period Average) | 59mfc | 1,273.11 | 1,303.15 | 1,344.04 | 1,382.12 | 1,399.27 | 1,404.07 | 1,427.76 | 1,441.18 | 1,452.54 | 1,498.96 | 1,550.74 | 1,613.88 |
| **Interest Rates** | | *Percent Per Annum* | | | | | | | | | | | |
| Discount Rate (End of Period) | 60.a | .100 | .100 | .400 | .750 | .300 | .300 | .300 | .300 | .300 | .300 | .300 | .300 |
| Money Market Rate | 60b | .001 | .001 | .125 | .473 | .461 | .105 | .094 | .078 | .083 | .075 | .068 | .073 |
| Treasury Bill Rate | 60c | .003 | .003 | .419 | .553 | .357 | .121 | .130 | .100 | .094 | .057 | −.006 | −.021 |
| Deposit Rate | 60l | .080 | .271 | .683 | .808 | .589 | .435 | .500 | .462 | .478 | .542 | .415 | .406 |
| Certificates of Deposit Rate | 60la | .006 | .009 | .414 | .687 | .718 | .172 | .095 | .094 | .092 | .064 | .052 | .038 |
| Lending Rate | 60p | 1.767 | 1.677 | 1.665 | 1.883 | 1.910 | 1.723 | 1.598 | 1.501 | 1.408 | 1.304 | 1.219 | . . . . |
| Government Bond Yield | 61 | 1.499 | 1.360 | 1.731 | 1.653 | 1.449 | 1.343 | 1.151 | 1.118 | .839 | .700 | .526 | .347 |
| **Prices, Production, Labor** | | *Index Numbers (2010=100): Period Averages* | | | | | | | | | | | |
| Share Prices | 62 | 126.3 | 143.3 | 183.7 | 187.8 | 134.0 | 98.0 | 100.0 | 92.8 | 86.8 | 126.8 | 142.7 | 175.2 |
| Wholesale Prices | 63 | 95.6 | 97.2 | 99.3 | 101.1 | 105.7 | 100.1 | † 100.0 | 101.5 | 100.6 | 101.8 | 105.1 | 102.7 |
| Consumer Prices | 64 | 100.7 | 100.4 | 100.7 | 100.7 | 102.1 | 100.7 | 100.0 | 99.7 | 99.7 | 100.0 | 102.8 | 103.6 |
| Wages: Monthly Earnings | 65 | 101.7 | 102.4 | 103.0 | 103.0 | 102.2 | 99.4 | 100.0 | 99.8 | 99.8 | 99.0 | 99.2 | 99.6 |
| Industrial Production | 66 | 104.6 | 106.1 | 110.7 | 113.8 | 110.1 | 87.0 | 100.0 | 97.1 | 97.7 | 96.9 | 98.7 | 98.1 |
| Mfg. Employment, Seas. Adj | 67eyc | 100.8 | 100.9 | 101.9 | 102.6 | 103.6 | 101.2 | 100.0 | 99.3 | 98.5 | 97.1 | 96.2 | 96.2 |
| | | *Number in Thousands: Period Averages* | | | | | | | | | | | |
| Labor Force | 67d | 66,420 | 66,500 | 66,570 | 66,690 | 66,500 | 66,170 | 65,900 | 64,028 | 65,550 | 65,770 | 65,870 | 65,980 |
| Employment | 67e | 63,290 | 63,560 | 63,820 | 64,120 | 63,850 | 62,820 | 62,570 | 61,113 | 62,700 | 63,110 | 63,510 | 63,760 |
| Unemployment | 67c | 3,130 | 2,940 | 2,750 | 2,570 | 2,650 | 3,360 | 3,340 | 2,914 | 2,850 | 2,650 | 2,360 | 2,220 |
| Unemployment Rate (%) | 67r | 4.7 | 4.4 | 4.1 | 3.9 | 4.0 | 5.1 | 5.1 | 4.6 | 4.3 | 4.0 | 3.6 | 3.4 |
| **Intl. Transactions & Positions** | | *Billions of Yen* | | | | | | | | | | | |
| Exports | 70 | 61,170 | 65,657 | 75,246 | 83,931 | 81,018 | 54,171 | 67,400 | 65,546 | 63,748 | 69,774 | 73,093 | 75,614 |
| Imports, c.i.f. | 71 | 49,147 | 56,852 | 67,408 | 72,854 | 78,959 | 51,366 | 60,623 | 68,037 | 70,655 | 81,249 | 85,876 | 78,446 |
| | | *2010=100* | | | | | | | | | | | |
| Volume of Exports | 72 | 96.8 | 97.6 | 105.2 | † 111.4 | 109.6 | 80.6 | † 100.0 | 96.1 | 91.5 | 90.1 | 90.6 | 89.7 |
| Volume of Imports | 73 | 99.3 | 101.9 | 106.6 | † 103.1 | 102.5 | 87.7 | † 100.0 | 102.5 | 105.0 | 105.3 | 105.9 | 102.9 |
| Unit Value of Exports | 74 | 93.7 | 99.7 | 106.0 | † 111.8 | 109.5 | 99.9 | † 100.0 | 101.1 | 103.3 | 114.7 | 119.5 | 125.0 |
| Unit Value of Imports | 75 | 81.5 | 91.7 | 103.6 | † 116.6 | 126.6 | 96.5 | † 100.0 | 109.3 | 110.8 | 126.9 | 133.4 | 125.3 |
| Export Prices | 76 | 113.6 | 115.8 | 119.3 | 122.0 | 114.6 | 102.5 | † 100.0 | 97.8 | 95.8 | 106.9 | 110.4 | 111.7 |
| Import Prices | 76.x | 83.1 | 94.1 | 107.1 | 115.2 | 125.1 | 93.4 | † 100.0 | 107.5 | 107.2 | 122.7 | 127.9 | 113.6 |

# Japan 158

| | | 2004 | 2005 | 2006 | 2007 | 2008 | 2009 | 2010 | 2011 | 2012 | 2013 | 2014 | 2015 |
|---|---|---|---|---|---|---|---|---|---|---|---|---|---|
| **Balance of Payments** | | | | | | | *Billions of US Dollars* | | | | | | |
| A. Current Account* | 109bx | 182.0 | 170.1 | 174.7 | 211.7 | 142.1 | 145.7 | 220.9 | 129.6 | 60.1 | 46.4 | 36.0 | 135.6 |
| Goods, credit (exports) | 1a9cx | 533.5 | 571.0 | 619.2 | 680.6 | 749.1 | 548.1 | 735.4 | 790.0 | 776.6 | 694.9 | 699.2 | 622.0 |
| Goods, debit (imports) | 1a9dx | 400.2 | 464.0 | 524.1 | 560.0 | 693.8 | 490.1 | 626.9 | 794.4 | 830.1 | 784.6 | 799.0 | 627.2 |
| Balance on goods | 1a9bx | 133.3 | 107.0 | 95.1 | 120.6 | 55.3 | 58.1 | 108.5 | −4.5 | −53.5 | −89.6 | −99.8 | −5.2 |
| Services, credit (exports) | 1b9cx | 97.8 | 102.0 | 109.3 | 121.6 | 141.0 | 120.9 | 134.6 | 140.7 | 137.0 | 135.4 | 163.8 | 162.5 |
| Services, debit (imports) | 1b9dx | 136.9 | 139.0 | 141.4 | 158.7 | 179.0 | 155.8 | 164.9 | 175.8 | 184.7 | 170.9 | 192.6 | 176.4 |
| Balance on Goods & Services | 1z9bx | 94.2 | 69.9 | 63.0 | 83.5 | 17.3 | 23.3 | 78.2 | −39.5 | −101.2 | −125.1 | −128.6 | −19.1 |
| Primary income: credit | 1c9cx | 123.0 | 146.5 | 172.2 | 199.4 | 192.8 | 175.4 | 201.8 | 233.6 | 229.9 | 241.5 | 255.1 | 242.0 |
| Primary income: debit | 1c9dx | 27.4 | 38.8 | 49.9 | 59.7 | 55.0 | 40.6 | 46.7 | 50.6 | 54.2 | 59.9 | 71.5 | 71.3 |
| Balance on gds, serv. & prim. inc. | 1y9bx | 189.9 | 177.7 | 185.4 | 223.2 | 155.2 | 158.1 | 233.3 | 143.4 | 74.5 | 56.5 | 55.0 | 151.6 |
| Secondary income: credit | 1d9ca | 6.9 | 9.7 | 6.2 | 6.8 | 9.1 | 9.5 | 10.1 | 13.1 | 14.9 | 15.9 | 16.6 | 17.2 |
| Secondary income: debit | 1d9da | 14.8 | 17.3 | 16.9 | 18.3 | 22.1 | 21.9 | 22.5 | 26.9 | 29.2 | 26.0 | 35.5 | 33.2 |
| B. Capital Account* | 209na | −4.8 | −4.9 | −4.8 | −4.0 | −5.5 | −5.0 | −5.0 | .5 | −1.0 | −7.7 | −2.0 | −2.3 |
| Capital account: credit | 209ca | .4 | .8 | .8 | .7 | .6 | 1.1 | .9 | 7.6 | 6.0 | 1.2 | .5 | .2 |
| Capital account: debit | 209da | 5.2 | 5.7 | 5.5 | 4.7 | 6.1 | 6.1 | 5.8 | 7.1 | 7.0 | 8.9 | 2.4 | 2.5 |
| Balance on current & capital acct. | 129ba | 177.2 | 165.2 | 169.9 | 207.7 | 136.6 | 140.7 | 215.9 | 130.1 | 59.1 | 38.7 | 34.0 | 133.4 |
| C. Financial Account* | 309na | −12.6 | 126.7 | 105.9 | 187.3 | 149.6 | 140.7 | 203.0 | −19.0 | 91.3 | −43.0 | 49.9 | 169.7 |
| Direct investment: assets | 3a9aa | 40.6 | 51.7 | 58.2 | 73.0 | 113.6 | 73.7 | 79.7 | 116.8 | 117.6 | 155.7 | 136.3 | 130.7 |
| Equity & investment fund shares | 3aaaa | 36.6 | 47.3 | 51.0 | 70.2 | 99.5 | 64.9 | 76.9 | 108.6 | 103.8 | 144.7 | 117.2 | 117.1 |
| Debt instruments | 3abaa | 4.0 | 4.4 | 7.2 | 2.8 | 14.2 | 8.8 | 2.8 | 8.2 | 13.8 | 11.0 | 19.1 | 13.6 |
| Direct investment: liabilities | 3a9la | 7.5 | 5.5 | −2.4 | 21.6 | 24.6 | 12.2 | 7.4 | −.9 | .5 | 10.6 | 18.4 | — |
| Equity & investment fund shares | 3aala | 8.7 | 6.6 | −4.4 | 13.1 | 23.9 | 8.7 | 11.1 | −2.4 | 1.1 | 10.4 | 20.5 | 9.9 |
| Debt instruments | 3abla | −1.2 | −1.2 | 2.0 | 8.5 | .7 | 3.6 | −3.7 | 1.5 | −.5 | .3 | −2.1 | −9.9 |
| Portfolio investment: assets | 3b9aa | 173.8 | 196.4 | 71.0 | 123.5 | 183.9 | 154.3 | 256.4 | 95.7 | 141.6 | −89.6 | 116.7 | 305.4 |
| Equity & investment fund shares | 3baaa | 31.5 | 23.0 | 25.0 | 26.1 | 65.6 | 29.7 | 21.5 | 12.5 | −22.5 | −69.7 | 61.6 | 166.7 |
| Debt securities | 3bbaa | 142.3 | 173.4 | 46.0 | 97.4 | 118.4 | 124.6 | 235.0 | 83.2 | 164.1 | −19.9 | 55.1 | 138.8 |
| Portfolio investment: liabilities | 3b9la | 196.7 | 183.1 | 198.6 | 196.6 | −98.8 | −56.3 | 111.6 | 264.1 | 109.4 | 185.0 | 157.0 | 172.7 |
| Equity & investment fund shares | 3bala | 98.3 | 131.3 | 71.4 | 45.5 | −69.7 | 12.4 | 40.3 | 5.6 | 34.9 | 169.8 | 33.0 | 10.8 |
| Debt instruments | 3bbla | 98.4 | 51.8 | 127.1 | 151.1 | −29.1 | −68.7 | 71.3 | 258.5 | 74.5 | 15.3 | 124.1 | 162.0 |
| Fin. der.& empl.stk.ops.(ESOs): net. | 3c9na | −2.4 | 6.5 | −2.5 | −2.8 | −24.8 | −10.5 | −11.9 | −17.1 | 7.1 | 58.2 | 34.3 | 17.9 |
| Fin. der. & ESOs.: assets | 3c9aa | −56.4 | −230.6 | −143.5 | −188.5 | −271.9 | −333.9 | −403.5 | −407.5 | −235.7 | −208.5 | −342.3 | −130.3 |
| Fin. der. & ESOs.: liabilities | 3c9la | −54.0 | −237.1 | −141.0 | −185.7 | −247.2 | −323.3 | −391.5 | −390.4 | −242.8 | −266.7 | −376.7 | −148.2 |
| Other investment: assets | 3d9aa | 48.0 | 106.6 | 86.2 | 260.8 | −135.3 | −202.7 | 130.1 | 92.7 | 121.1 | 185.1 | 107.4 | −44.1 |
| Other equity | 3daaa | .9 | .9 | 2.5 | .1 | 1.4 | .2 | 3.1 | 2.1 | 1.6 | 1.4 | 2.2 | 1.9 |
| Debt instruments | 3dzaa | 47.1 | 105.7 | 83.7 | 260.6 | −136.7 | −202.9 | 127.1 | 90.6 | 119.5 | 183.7 | 105.2 | −46.0 |
| Other investment: liabilities | 3d9la | 68.3 | 45.9 | −89.1 | 48.9 | 62.0 | −81.9 | 132.2 | 43.9 | 186.2 | 156.7 | 169.3 | 67.5 |
| Other equity | 3dala | .... | .... | .... | .... | .... | .... | .... | .... | .... | .... | .8 | .6 |
| Debt instruments | 3dzla | 68.3 | 45.9 | −89.1 | 48.9 | 62.0 | −81.9 | 132.2 | 43.9 | 186.2 | 156.7 | 168.6 | 67.0 |
| Curr.+ cap.− finan. acct. balance | 4y9na | 189.8 | 38.6 | 64.0 | 20.4 | −13.0 | — | 12.9 | 149.1 | −32.2 | 81.7 | −15.9 | −36.4 |
| D. Net Errors and Omissions | 409na | −28.9 | −16.3 | −32.0 | 16.1 | 43.9 | 26.9 | 30.9 | 27.5 | −6.0 | −42.9 | 24.4 | 41.5 |
| E. Reserves and Related Items | 4z9na | 160.9 | 22.3 | 32.0 | 36.5 | 30.9 | 26.9 | 43.9 | 176.6 | −38.3 | 38.8 | 8.5 | 5.1 |
| Reserve assets | 3e9aa | 160.9 | 22.3 | 32.0 | 36.5 | 30.9 | 26.9 | 43.9 | 176.6 | −38.3 | 38.8 | 8.5 | 5.1 |
| Credit and loans from the IMF | 3dcla | — | — | — | — | — | — | — | — | — | — | — | — |
| Exceptional financing | 409la | .... | .... | .... | .... | .... | .... | .... | .... | .... | .... | .... | .... |
| *Excludes components in group E | | | | | | | | | | | | | |
| | | | | | | | | | | | | | |
| **International Investment Position** | | | | | | | *Millions of US Dollars* | | | | | | |
| Assets | 809aa | 4,172.1 | 4,294.9 | 4,697.2 | 5,360.1 | 5,731.5 | 6,039.0 | 6,893.1 | 7,502.6 | 7,613.3 | 7,575.3 | 7,811.7 | 7,873.2 |
| Direct investment | 8a9aa | 375.7 | 390.6 | 454.8 | 547.5 | 690.8 | 753.2 | 846.2 | 972.1 | 1,054.1 | 1,133.0 | 1,177.2 | 1,258.2 |
| Equity & investment fund shares | 8aaaa | 351.4 | 368.7 | 429.5 | 519.3 | 644.7 | 704.4 | 796.4 | 916.0 | 991.0 | 1,070.3 | 1,075.6 | 1,146.5 |
| Debt instruments | 8abaa | 24.3 | 21.9 | 25.3 | 28.2 | 46.2 | 48.8 | 49.8 | 56.3 | 63.1 | 62.7 | 101.6 | 111.7 |
| Portfolio investment | 8b9aa | 2,009.7 | 2,114.9 | 2,343.5 | 2,523.6 | 2,376.7 | 2,845.9 | 3,305.2 | 3,379.3 | 3,559.8 | 3,430.7 | 3,398.0 | 3,511.7 |
| Equity & investment fund shares | 8baaa | 364.7 | 408.6 | 510.4 | 573.5 | 394.7 | 594.0 | 678.5 | 665.8 | 687.2 | 1,198.7 | 1,190.1 | 1,275.0 |
| Debt securities | 8bbaa | 1,645.0 | 1,706.3 | 1,833.1 | 1,950.1 | 1,982.0 | 2,251.8 | 2,626.7 | 2,713.4 | 2,872.6 | 2,232.0 | 2,207.9 | 2,236.6 |
| Fin. der.(oth.than reserves) & ESOs | 8c9aa | 5.7 | 26.3 | 23.0 | 39.0 | 77.4 | 46.2 | 52.6 | 53.9 | 53.4 | 77.9 | 466.6 | 373.2 |
| Other investment | 8d9aa | 938.5 | 920.1 | 981.1 | 1,282.7 | 1,562.0 | 1,342.6 | 1,592.4 | 1,803.8 | 1,681.2 | 1,665.7 | 1,517.4 | 1,497.4 |
| Other equity | 8daaa | 45.1 | 41.4 | 45.3 | 45.3 | 56.7 | 56.2 | 65.9 | 70.8 | 65.9 | 56.7 | 64.8 | 66.7 |
| Debt instruments | 8dzaa | 893.4 | 878.7 | 937.5 | 1,237.4 | 1,505.3 | 1,286.4 | 1,526.5 | 1,733.0 | 1,615.3 | 1,609.0 | 1,452.6 | 1,430.6 |
| Reserve assets | 8e9aa | 842.5 | 843.0 | 894.8 | 967.4 | 1,024.6 | 1,051.2 | 1,096.7 | 1,293.4 | 1,264.8 | 1,268.0 | 1,252.5 | 1,232.8 |
| Liabilities | 809la | 2,387.7 | 2,763.1 | 2,889.0 | 3,165.2 | 3,242.1 | 3,125.2 | 3,751.3 | 4,083.4 | 4,155.2 | 4,482.0 | 4,799.3 | 5,057.8 |
| Direct investment | 8a9la | 102.1 | 104.9 | 112.9 | 137.7 | 213.9 | 212.4 | 230.0 | 242.2 | 222.2 | 185.7 | 196.9 | 202.4 |
| Equity & investment fund shares | 8aala | 76.5 | 82.8 | 91.1 | 107.9 | 174.2 | 174.6 | 204.0 | 215.1 | 196.6 | 163.5 | 170.4 | 176.4 |
| Debt instruments | 8abla | 25.6 | 22.2 | 21.9 | 29.8 | 39.7 | 37.8 | 26.0 | 27.1 | 25.5 | 22.2 | 26.5 | 25.9 |
| Portfolio investment | 8b9la | 1,153.4 | 1,542.4 | 1,762.9 | 1,942.9 | 1,541.7 | 1,537.0 | 1,866.8 | 2,026.3 | 2,085.5 | 2,393.2 | 2,363.1 | 2,660.2 |
| Equity & investment fund shares | 8bala | 743.3 | 1,126.1 | 1,255.0 | 1,245.9 | 756.2 | 829.6 | 988.8 | 847.2 | 965.4 | 1,446.6 | 1,402.1 | 1,551.2 |
| Debt securities | 8bbla | 410.1 | 416.4 | 507.9 | 697.0 | 785.5 | 707.4 | 878.0 | 1,179.1 | 1,120.1 | 946.7 | 961.0 | 1,109.0 |
| Fin. der.(oth.than reserves) & ESOs. | 8c9la | 10.8 | 33.2 | 30.2 | 43.5 | 85.5 | 56.6 | 64.7 | 72.6 | 61.5 | 82.2 | 493.7 | 378.0 |
| Other investment | 8d9la | 1,121.4 | 1,082.6 | 983.1 | 1,041.0 | 1,401.1 | 1,319.2 | 1,589.8 | 1,742.4 | 1,785.9 | 1,820.9 | 1,745.7 | 1,817.3 |
| Other equity | 8dala | .... | .... | .... | .... | .... | .... | .... | .... | .... | .... | 6.5 | 7.1 |
| Debt instruments | 8dzla | 1,121.4 | 1,082.6 | 983.1 | 1,041.0 | 1,401.1 | 1,319.2 | 1,589.8 | 1,742.4 | 1,785.9 | 1,820.9 | 1,739.2 | 1,810.1 |

|  |  | 2004 | 2005 | 2006 | 2007 | 2008 | 2009 | 2010 | 2011 | 2012 | 2013 | 2014 | 2015 |
|---|---|---|---|---|---|---|---|---|---|---|---|---|---|
| **Government Finance** | | | | | | | | | | | | | |
| **Operations Statement** | | | | | | | | | | | | | |
| **General Government** | | | | | | *Billions of Yen: Fiscal Year Begins April 1* | | | | | | | |
| Revenue | a1 | 155,637 | 219,972 | 235,194 | 223,705 | 227,053 | 219,941 | 220,374 | 226,181 | 227,345 | 236,666 | 249,151 | .... |
| Taxes | a11 | 82,792 | 88,231 | 92,192 | 94,248 | 86,141 | 75,744 | 78,608 | 80,440 | 82,610 | 87,774 | 95,995 | .... |
| Social Contributions | a12 | 52,159 | 53,500 | 55,413 | 56,817 | 57,588 | 55,644 | 57,526 | 59,422 | 61,167 | 62,663 | 64,879 | .... |
| Grants | a13 | — | 57,275 | 56,766 | 53,169 | 55,068 | 65,694 | 65,007 | 69,408 | 69,065 | 70,038 | 69,808 | .... |
| Other Revenue | a14 | 20,686 | 20,966 | 30,822 | 19,471 | 28,257 | 22,858 | 19,233 | 16,911 | 14,503 | 16,191 | 18,468 | .... |
| Expense | a2 | 177,590 | 234,653 | 234,250 | 233,863 | 241,091 | 258,777 | 258,394 | 265,875 | 266,463 | 269,288 | 270,956 | .... |
| Compensation of Employees | a21 | 31,732 | 31,592 | 31,572 | 31,698 | 31,096 | 30,342 | 29,647 | 29,672 | 29,089 | 28,366 | 29,347 | .... |
| Use of Goods & Services | a22 | 17,244 | 16,895 | 16,336 | 16,521 | 16,236 | 17,245 | 17,850 | 17,903 | 18,201 | 19,194 | 19,574 | .... |
| Consumption of Fixed Capital | a23 | 15,237 | 13,852 | 14,032 | 14,271 | 14,501 | 14,402 | 14,321 | 14,281 | 14,296 | 14,499 | 14,786 | .... |
| Interest | a24 | 12,356 | 11,682 | 12,019 | 12,290 | 12,118 | 11,540 | 11,518 | 11,492 | 11,296 | 11,216 | 11,108 | .... |
| Subsidies | a25 | 3,843 | 2,974 | 2,938 | 2,686 | 2,680 | 3,473 | 3,012 | 3,011 | 3,030 | 2,967 | 2,854 | .... |
| Grants | a26 | 485 | 58,330 | 57,602 | 53,750 | 55,789 | 66,340 | 65,661 | 70,014 | 69,762 | 70,887 | 70,435 | .... |
| Social Benefits | a27 | 86,909 | 89,210 | 90,636 | 93,660 | 95,681 | 100,960 | 104,490 | 106,568 | 108,436 | 109,652 | 110,874 | .... |
| Other Expense | a28 | 9,784 | 10,117 | 9,114 | 8,988 | 12,990 | 14,475 | 11,897 | 12,933 | 12,353 | 12,508 | 11,978 | .... |
| Gross Operating Balance [1-2+23] | agob | −6,717 | −829 | 14,976 | 4,112 | 463 | −24,434 | −23,700 | −25,413 | −24,823 | −18,123 | −7,019 | .... |
| Net Operating Balance [1-2] | anob | −21,954 | −14,681 | 944 | −10,159 | −14,038 | −38,836 | −38,021 | −39,694 | −39,118 | −32,622 | −21,805 | .... |
| Net Acq. of Nonfinancial Assets | a31 | 5,342 | 6,189 | 4,583 | 3,333 | 2,462 | 4,057 | 2,421 | 2,249 | 1,871 | 4,189 | 3,620 | .... |
| Aquisition of Nonfin. Assets | a31.1 | .... | .... | .... | .... | .... | .... | .... | .... | .... | .... | .... | .... |
| Disposal of Nonfin. Assets | a31.2 | .... | .... | .... | .... | .... | .... | .... | .... | .... | .... | .... | .... |
| Net Lending/Borrowing [1-2-31] | anlb | −27,296 | −20,870 | −3,640 | −13,492 | −16,500 | −42,893 | −40,442 | −41,943 | −40,989 | −36,811 | −25,425 | .... |
| Net Acq. of Financial Assets | a32 | 16,361 | −212 | −1,318 | −5,946 | −12,253 | 25,620 | 1,169 | −2,324 | −3,610 | 3,944 | 11,042 | .... |
| By instrument | | | | | | | | | | | | | |
| Monetary Gold & SDRs | a3201 | — | — | — | — | — | 1,681 | — | — | — | — | — | .... |
| Currency & Deposits | a3202 | .... | −15,796 | −13,332 | −18,944 | −13,939 | −4,433 | −704 | −191 | 1,271 | −1,844 | 9,552 | .... |
| Securities other than Shares | a3203 | .... | 16,629 | 12,978 | 7,414 | −9,007 | −7,148 | 8,118 | −16,438 | −111 | 1,378 | −13,611 | .... |
| Loans | a3204 | .... | −5,485 | −7,553 | −2,310 | −942 | 8,161 | −958 | 1,057 | −67 | −375 | 6,811 | .... |
| Shares & Other Equity | a3205 | .... | −312 | 207 | 8,611 | 9,422 | 3,343 | 19 | 2,359 | −1,092 | −57 | 3,445 | .... |
| Insurance Technical Reserves | a3206 | .... | — | — | — | — | — | — | — | — | — | — | .... |
| Financial Derivatives | a3207 | .... | — | — | — | — | — | — | — | — | — | — | .... |
| Other Accounts Receivable | a3208 | .... | 4,752 | 6,383 | −718 | 2,213 | 24,015 | −5,306 | 10,890 | −3,611 | 4,842 | 4,845 | .... |
| By debtor | | | | | | | | | | | | | |
| Domestic | a321 | .... | .... | .... | .... | .... | .... | .... | .... | .... | .... | .... | .... |
| Foreign | a322 | .... | .... | .... | .... | .... | .... | .... | .... | .... | .... | .... | .... |
| Net Incurrence of Liabilities | a33 | 50,291 | 22,197 | 2,320 | 1,403 | −450 | 55,576 | 36,302 | 39,153 | 33,734 | 38,109 | 33,974 | .... |
| By instrument | | | | | | | | | | | | | |
| Special Drawing Rights (SDRs) | a3301 | .... | — | — | — | — | 1,681 | — | — | — | — | — | .... |
| Currency & Deposits | a3302 | .... | — | — | — | — | — | — | — | — | — | — | .... |
| Securities other than Shares | a3303 | .... | 28,944 | 8,004 | 18,365 | 5,428 | 47,555 | 49,311 | 40,844 | 35,164 | 39,490 | 31,321 | .... |
| Loans | a3304 | .... | −4,924 | −7,238 | −10,235 | −5,205 | −3,106 | −1,778 | −3,207 | −282 | 56 | −570 | .... |
| Shares & Other Equity | a3305 | .... | −2,852 | −11 | −169 | 76 | 276 | 739 | 56 | 397 | −66 | 24 | .... |
| Insurance Technical Reserves | a3306 | .... | — | — | — | — | — | — | — | — | — | — | .... |
| Financial Derivatives | a3307 | .... | — | — | — | — | — | — | — | — | — | — | .... |
| Other Accounts Payable | a3308 | .... | 1,029 | 1,565 | −6,558 | −749 | 9,171 | −11,971 | 1,460 | −1,546 | −1,371 | 3,198 | .... |
| By creditor | | | | | | | | | | | | | |
| Domestic | a331 | .... | .... | .... | .... | .... | .... | .... | .... | .... | .... | .... | .... |
| Foreign | a332 | .... | .... | .... | .... | .... | .... | .... | .... | .... | .... | .... | .... |
| Stat. Discrepancy [32-33-NLB] | anlbz | −6,634 | −1,539 | 2 | 6,143 | 4,697 | 12,936 | 5,309 | 466 | 3,645 | 2,646 | 2,493 | .... |
| Memo Item: Expenditure [2+31] | a2m | 182,933 | 240,842 | 238,833 | 237,197 | 243,553 | 262,833 | 260,816 | 268,124 | 268,334 | 273,477 | 274,576 | .... |
| **Balance Sheet** | | | | | | *Billions of Yen: Fiscal Year Begins April 1* | | | | | | | |
| Net Worth | a6 | 47,197 | 144,174 | 154,269 | 169,989 | 108,568 | 72,560 | 34,231 | −17,591 | −41,923 | −5,908 | −13,502 | .... |
| Nonfinancial Assets | a61 | 459,229 | 558,453 | 565,169 | 583,202 | 586,399 | 574,750 | 579,339 | 582,153 | 572,244 | 589,256 | 601,171 | .... |
| Financial Assets | a62 | 475,311 | 525,484 | 531,864 | 525,924 | 483,822 | 490,239 | 493,873 | 492,571 | 515,119 | 576,088 | 598,191 | .... |
| By instrument | | | | | | | | | | | | | |
| Monetary Gold & SDRs | a6201 | .... | — | 420 | 422 | 372 | 1,988 | 1,863 | 1,794 | 3,062 | 3,759 | 3,862 | .... |
| Currency & Deposits | a6202 | .... | 134,798 | 123,587 | 106,275 | 89,638 | 80,216 | 79,216 | 77,783 | 76,103 | 78,668 | 93,950 | .... |
| Securities other than Shares | a6203 | .... | 111,604 | 125,457 | 128,808 | 140,859 | 126,308 | 127,875 | 123,529 | 122,683 | 114,831 | 89,796 | .... |
| Loans | a6204 | .... | 40,585 | 33,653 | 25,649 | 21,232 | 28,245 | 31,844 | 32,143 | 33,859 | 35,574 | 30,944 | .... |
| Shares and Other Equity | a6205 | .... | 99,353 | 100,563 | 115,214 | 99,950 | 107,522 | 114,099 | 110,588 | 120,630 | 153,652 | 160,329 | .... |
| Insurance Technical Reserves | a6206 | .... | — | — | — | — | — | — | — | — | — | — | .... |
| Financial Derivatives | a6207 | .... | — | 2 | — | — | — | — | — | — | 461 | 47 | .... |
| Other Accounts Receivable | a6208 | .... | 138,783 | 148,182 | 149,555 | 131,770 | 145,960 | 138,976 | 146,734 | 158,782 | 189,142 | 219,264 | .... |
| By debtor | | | | | | | | | | | | | |
| Domestic | a621 | .... | .... | .... | .... | .... | .... | .... | .... | .... | .... | .... | .... |
| Foreign | a622 | .... | .... | .... | .... | .... | .... | .... | .... | .... | .... | .... | .... |
| Liabilities | a63 | 887,343 | 939,763 | 942,764 | 939,137 | 961,653 | 992,429 | 1,038,980 | 1,092,310 | 1,129,286 | 1,171,251 | 1,212,863 | .... |
| By instrument | | | | | | | | | | | | | |
| Special Drawing Rights (SDRs) | a6301 | .... | 305 | 340 | 329 | 273 | 1,875 | 1,737 | 1,577 | 1,630 | 1,994 | 2,133 | .... |
| Currency & Deposits | a6302 | .... | — | — | — | — | — | — | — | — | — | — | .... |
| Securities other than Shares | a6303 | .... | 686,108 | 691,296 | 704,095 | 733,198 | 760,921 | 819,598 | 877,655 | 915,584 | 953,256 | 994,365 | .... |
| Loans | a6304 | .... | 194,644 | 188,605 | 178,594 | 171,839 | 169,439 | 165,920 | 163,877 | 163,249 | 164,238 | 163,836 | .... |
| Shares and Other Equity | a6305 | .... | 23,794 | 23,878 | 22,791 | 22,855 | 23,027 | 22,854 | 23,963 | 24,365 | 24,316 | 24,361 | .... |
| Insurance Technical Reserves | a6306 | .... | — | — | — | — | — | — | — | — | — | — | .... |
| Financial Derivatives | a6307 | .... | — | — | 9 | 28 | 39 | 47 | 51 | 58 | 54 | 43 | .... |
| Other Accounts Payable | a6308 | .... | 34,912 | 38,645 | 33,318 | 33,459 | 37,127 | 28,825 | 25,192 | 24,401 | 27,395 | 28,125 | .... |
| By creditor | | | | | | | | | | | | | |
| Domestic | a631 | .... | .... | .... | .... | .... | .... | .... | .... | .... | .... | .... | .... |
| Foreign | a632 | .... | .... | .... | .... | .... | .... | .... | .... | .... | .... | .... | .... |
| Net Financial Worth [62-63] | a6m2 | −412,032 | −414,279 | −410,900 | −413,213 | −477,832 | −502,190 | −545,107 | −599,744 | −614,167 | −595,164 | −614,672 | .... |
| Memo Item: Debt at Market Value | a6m3 | .... | 915,970 | 918,886 | 916,337 | 938,769 | 969,363 | 1,016,080 | 1,068,301 | 1,104,864 | 1,146,882 | 1,188,459 | .... |
| Memo Item: Debt at Face Value | a6m35 | .... | .... | .... | .... | .... | .... | .... | .... | .... | .... | .... | .... |
| Memo Item: Debt at Nominal Value | a6m4 | .... | .... | .... | .... | .... | .... | .... | .... | .... | .... | .... | .... |

| National Accounts | | 2004 | 2005 | 2006 | 2007 | 2008 | 2009 | 2010 | 2011 | 2012 | 2013 | 2014 | 2015 |
|---|---|---|---|---|---|---|---|---|---|---|---|---|---|
| | | | | | | | *Billions of Yen* | | | | | | |
| Househ.Cons.Expend.,incl.NPISHs.... | 96fac | 288,599 | 291,133 | 293,433 | 294,122 | 292,055 | 282,942 | 285,867 | 284,244 | 288,195 | 295,661 | 293,217 | . . . . |
| Government Consumption Expend... | 91fac | 91,909 | 92,468 | 91,966 | 92,793 | 93,019 | 93,820 | 95,129 | 96,117 | 97,145 | 98,823 | 100,954 | . . . . |
| Gross Fixed Capital Formation......... | 93eac | 111,787 | 112,574 | 114,896 | 115,781 | 112,462 | 97,991 | 96,431 | 97,107 | 100,020 | 106,709 | 106,515 | . . . . |
| Changes in Inventories.................... | 93iac | 1,571 | 635 | 24 | 1,606 | 2,700 | −5,340 | −806 | −1,883 | −858 | −2,825 | 282 | . . . . |
| Exports of Goods and Services......... | 90cac | 66,544 | 72,122 | 81,939 | 91,037 | 88,770 | 59,814 | 73,183 | 71,298 | 69,765 | 79,989 | 88,351 | . . . . |
| Imports of Goods and Services (-)..... | 98cac | 56,684 | 65,028 | 75,572 | 82,363 | 87,798 | 58,088 | 67,419 | 75,572 | 79,157 | 95,926 | 99,696 | . . . . |
| Gross Domestic Product (GDP)........ | 99bac | 503,725 | 503,903 | 506,687 | 512,975 | 501,209 | 471,139 | 482,384 | 471,311 | 475,110 | 482,430 | 489,623 | . . . . |
| Net Primary Income from Abroad..... | 98nac | 9,387 | 11,749 | 14,465 | 17,338 | 16,793 | 13,078 | 12,974 | 14,675 | 15,054 | 15,344 | 21,047 | . . . . |
| Gross National Income (GNI)........... | 99aac | 513,112 | 515,652 | 521,152 | 530,313 | 518,002 | 484,216 | 495,359 | 485,986 | 490,165 | 497,774 | 510,670 | . . . . |
| GDP Volume 2005 Prices................ | 99bar | 497,541 | 504,076 | 512,533 | 523,630 | 518,012 | 489,406 | 512,619 | 510,518 | 519,371 | 526,439 | 525,848 | 528,985 |
| GDP Volume (2010=100)............... | 99bvr | 97.1 | 98.3 | 100.0 | 102.1 | 101.1 | 95.5 | 100.0 | 99.6 | 101.3 | 102.7 | 102.6 | 103.2 |
| GDP Deflator (2010=100)............... | 99bir | 107.6 | 106.2 | 105.1 | 104.1 | 102.8 | 102.3 | 100.0 | 98.1 | 97.2 | 97.4 | 98.9 | . . . . |
| | | | | | | | *Millions: Midyear Estimates* | | | | | | |
| Population............................... | 99z | 126.77 | 126.98 | 127.14 | 127.25 | 127.32 | 127.34 | 127.32 | 127.25 | 127.14 | 126.98 | 126.79 | 126.57 |

| | | 2004 | 2005 | 2006 | 2007 | 2008 | 2009 | 2010 | 2011 | 2012 | 2013 | 2014 | 2015 |
|---|---|---|---|---|---|---|---|---|---|---|---|---|---|
| **Exchange Rates** | | | | | | *Dinars per SDR: End of Period* | | | | | | | |
| Official Rate | aa | 1.1011 | 1.0134 | 1.0666 | 1.1204 | 1.0924 | 1.1131 | 1.0934 | 1.0900 | 1.0912 | 1.0934 | 1.0287 | .9839 |
| | | | | | | *Dinars per US Dollar: End of Period (ae) Period Average (rf)* | | | | | | | |
| Official Rate | ae | .7090 | .7090 | .7090 | .7090 | .7092 | .7100 | .7100 | .7100 | .7100 | .7100 | .7100 | .7100 |
| Official Rate | rf | .7090 | .7090 | .7090 | .7090 | .7097 | .7100 | .7100 | .7100 | .7100 | .7100 | .7100 | .7100 |
| **Fund Position** | | | | | | *Millions of SDRs: End of Period* | | | | | | | |
| Quota | 2f.s | 170.50 | 170.50 | 170.50 | 170.50 | 170.50 | 170.50 | 170.50 | 170.50 | 170.50 | 170.50 | 170.50 | 170.50 |
| SDR Holdings | 1b.s | 1.08 | .43 | .84 | 1.39 | 2.09 | 146.72 | 146.59 | 146.45 | 143.35 | 138.67 | 123.49 | 98.59 |
| Reserve Position in the Fund | 1c.s | .09 | .14 | .20 | .26 | .26 | .31 | .31 | .33 | .33 | .33 | .38 | .38 |
| Total Fund Cred.&Loans Outstg | 2tl | 217.47 | 165.30 | 105.21 | 55.41 | 17.89 | 7.61 | 5.07 | 5.07 | 255.75 | 682.00 | 937.75 | 1,332.03 |
| SDR Allocations | 1bd | 16.89 | 16.89 | 16.89 | 16.89 | 16.89 | 162.07 | 162.07 | 162.07 | 162.07 | 162.07 | 162.07 | 162.07 |
| **International Liquidity** | | | | | | *Millions of US Dollars Unless Otherwise Indicated: End of Period* | | | | | | | |
| Total Reserves minus Gold | 1l.d | 5,266.6 | 5,250.3 | 6,722.0 | 7,542.0 | 8,561.6 | 11,689.3 | 13,056.7 | 11,467.3 | 8,089.5 | 13,223.8 | 15,299.5 | 15,162.1 |
| SDR Holdings | 1b.d | 1.7 | .6 | 1.3 | 2.2 | 3.2 | 230.0 | 225.8 | 224.8 | 220.3 | 213.5 | 178.9 | 136.6 |
| Reserve Position in the Fund | 1c.d | .1 | .2 | .3 | .4 | .4 | .5 | .5 | .5 | .5 | .5 | .5 | .5 |
| Foreign Exchange | 1d.d | 5,264.8 | 5,249.5 | 6,720.4 | 7,539.4 | 8,558.0 | 11,458.8 | 12,830.5 | 11,241.9 | 7,868.7 | 13,009.7 | 15,120.0 | 15,025.0 |
| Gold (Million Fine Troy Ounces) | 1ad | .411 | .411 | .409 | .459 | .410 | .410 | .410 | .410 | .445 | .500 | .620 | 1.330 |
| Gold (National Valuation) | 1and | 179.6 | 212.3 | 257.1 | 387.0 | 356.6 | 450.5 | 589.3 | 637.7 | 739.9 | 600.3 | 744.7 | 1,407.5 |
| Monetary Authorities: Other Liabs | 4..d | 158.3 | 158.3 | 256.1 | 258.0 | 362.5 | 166.6 | 654.3 | 154.3 | 863.2 | 1,899.8 | 1,685.1 | 1,399.6 |
| Deposit Money Banks: Assets | 7a.d | 6,947.5 | 7,448.7 | 8,654.8 | 9,055.6 | 8,015.3 | 7,340.4 | 8,436.7 | 8,662.9 | 8,540.0 | 6,920.1 | 6,367.1 | 6,429.0 |
| Deposit Money Banks: Liabs | 7b.d | 4,892.5 | 5,233.7 | 5,946.3 | 6,760.5 | 7,786.4 | 7,992.6 | 8,437.8 | 8,681.7 | 8,207.3 | 9,459.3 | 9,490.6 | 9,530.6 |
| **Monetary Authorities** | | | | | | *Millions of Dinars: End of Period* | | | | | | | |
| Foreign Assets | 11 | 4,628.2 | 4,639.9 | 5,714.4 | 6,388.6 | 7,089.9 | 9,374.2 | 10,435.8 | 9,346.2 | 7,027.2 | 10,568.3 | 12,187.3 | 12,513.4 |
| Claims on Central Government | 12a | 633.0 | 880.4 | 633.8 | 604.0 | 1,246.3 | 1,191.2 | 1,092.5 | 1,217.9 | 2,057.8 | 1,637.4 | 1,169.7 | 1,003.7 |
| Claims on State & Local Govts | 12b | — | — | — | — | — | — | — | — | — | — | — | — |
| Claims on Nonfin.Pub.Enterprises | 12c | — | — | — | — | — | — | — | — | — | — | — | — |
| Claims on Private Sector | 12d | 18.3 | 18.2 | 17.7 | 17.8 | 19.0 | 19.0 | 19.0 | 19.6 | 20.0 | 20.6 | 22.4 | 23.3 |
| Claims on Deposit Money Banks | 12e | 401.9 | 571.5 | 560.1 | 514.4 | 465.3 | 423.5 | 475.3 | 507.9 | 508.7 | 530.0 | 587.5 | 431.9 |
| Claims on Nonbank Financial Insts | 12g | — | — | — | — | — | — | — | — | — | — | — | — |
| Reserve Money | 14 | 2,676.6 | 3,170.2 | 3,826.4 | 4,128.0 | 5,092.7 | 5,084.6 | 5,480.7 | 6,006.2 | 6,108.2 | 6,666.4 | 7,782.0 | 7,920.3 |
| of which: Currency Outside DMBs | 14a | 1,414.4 | 1,657.3 | 2,027.4 | 2,172.4 | 2,664.8 | 2,679.5 | 2,843.7 | 3,019.3 | 3,215.0 | 3,606.6 | 3,804.4 | 3,933.2 |
| Time, Savings,& Fgn.Currency Dep | 15 | 148.2 | 366.1 | 42.9 | 263.8 | 1,261.0 | 4,067.5 | 4,118.4 | 2,997.4 | 1,791.3 | 3,230.9 | 3,424.0 | 2,960.4 |
| Liabs. of Central Bank: Securities | 16ac | 2,534.0 | 2,279.5 | 2,153.0 | 1,977.0 | 1,166.0 | 150.0 | 196.5 | 230.0 | 230.9 | 230.9 | 259.3 | 1,076.5 |
| Foreign Liabilities | 16c | 370.3 | 296.9 | 311.8 | 263.9 | 295.1 | 307.1 | 647.3 | 291.7 | 1,068.8 | 2,271.8 | 2,327.8 | 2,429.0 |
| Central Government Deposits | 16d | 218.2 | 132.9 | 592.3 | 491.2 | 281.7 | 518.4 | 691.8 | 773.5 | 759.1 | 1,125.0 | 956.9 | 914.1 |
| Capital Accounts | 17a | 160.8 | 43.1 | 166.6 | 235.6 | 241.2 | 309.7 | 317.8 | 451.8 | 464.4 | 290.8 | 154.1 | 240.1 |
| Other Items (Net) | 17r | −426.7 | −178.6 | −167.0 | 165.2 | 482.9 | 570.6 | 570.2 | 341.0 | −809.1 | −1,059.5 | −937.1 | −1,568.1 |
| **Deposit Money Banks** | | | | | | *Millions of Dinars: End of Period* | | | | | | | |
| Reserves | 20 | 1,250.1 | 1,907.1 | 1,855.7 | 2,125.9 | 3,420.4 | 6,268.3 | 6,692.5 | 5,936.4 | 4,611.1 | 6,266.0 | 7,331.7 | 6,895.9 |
| Claims on Mon.Author.:Securities | 20c | 2,534.0 | 2,279.5 | 2,153.0 | 1,977.0 | 1,166.0 | 150.0 | 196.5 | 230.0 | 230.9 | 230.9 | 259.3 | 1,076.5 |
| Foreign Assets | 21 | 4,925.8 | 5,281.1 | 6,136.2 | 6,420.4 | 5,684.6 | 5,211.7 | 5,990.1 | 6,150.7 | 6,063.4 | 4,913.3 | 4,520.6 | 4,500.3 |
| Claims on Central Government | 22a | 1,101.8 | 1,337.4 | 1,791.8 | 2,451.7 | 3,700.5 | 4,721.4 | 5,169.8 | 6,888.9 | 8,540.3 | 10,013.9 | 10,635.0 | 11,160.6 |
| Claims on State & Local Govts | 22b | — | — | .1 | 2.0 | 49.9 | 71.5 | 173.2 | 180.9 | 184.9 | 187.8 | 232.4 | 225.7 |
| Claims on Nonfin.Pub.Enterprises | 22c | 472.6 | 528.1 | 520.6 | 621.2 | 602.7 | 410.5 | 343.3 | 332.9 | 298.6 | 257.2 | 148.0 | 127.8 |
| Claims on Private Sector | 22d | 6,025.5 | 7,844.5 | 9,779.0 | 11,098.3 | 12,593.4 | 12,754.7 | 13,708.3 | 15,036.7 | 15,991.9 | 17,232.2 | 17,838.6 | 18,690.1 |
| Claims on Nonbank Financial Insts | 22g | 45.5 | 62.8 | 108.4 | 167.8 | 235.7 | 155.7 | 144.5 | 126.2 | 121.2 | 89.0 | 89.3 | 87.8 |
| Demand Deposits | 24 | 1,721.1 | 2,362.8 | 2,491.6 | 2,629.6 | 2,857.4 | 3,293.2 | 3,657.2 | 4,206.3 | 3,934.5 | 4,711.7 | 5,358.8 | 5,867.3 |
| Time, Savings,& Fgn.Currency Dep | 25 | 6,922.7 | 8,007.0 | 9,422.0 | 10,657.6 | 12,255.9 | 13,617.3 | 15,226.8 | 16,321.6 | 17,061.5 | 18,134.5 | 19,277.7 | 20,782.5 |
| Money Market Instruments | 26aa | 699.4 | 809.0 | 777.6 | 794.8 | 805.0 | 1,027.9 | 1,316.6 | 1,406.3 | 1,617.0 | 1,818.6 | 2,244.4 | 2,335.0 |
| Foreign Liabilities | 26c | 3,468.8 | 3,710.7 | 4,215.9 | 4,793.2 | 5,522.4 | 5,674.8 | 5,990.8 | 6,164.0 | 5,827.2 | 6,716.1 | 6,738.3 | 6,671.4 |
| Central Government Deposits | 26d | 757.3 | 754.0 | 624.3 | 611.9 | 872.2 | 1,123.6 | 1,213.0 | 1,188.8 | 1,362.0 | 1,633.9 | 2,171.9 | 2,310.2 |
| Credit from Monetary Authorities | 26g | 388.2 | 432.0 | 492.9 | 436.3 | 373.1 | 371.7 | 414.6 | 449.0 | 998.3 | 842.7 | 645.6 | 500.6 |
| Capital Accounts | 27a | 1,255.4 | 1,541.6 | 2,473.3 | 2,823.9 | 3,072.2 | 3,449.1 | 3,742.2 | 4,107.4 | 4,329.6 | 4,450.3 | 4,655.7 | 4,930.1 |
| Other Items (Net) | 27r | 1,142.4 | 1,623.4 | 1,846.9 | 2,117.1 | 1,695.2 | 1,186.3 | 857.0 | 1,039.3 | 912.4 | 882.6 | −37.5 | −632.4 |
| **Monetary Survey** | | | | | | *Millions of Dinars: End of Period* | | | | | | | |
| Foreign Assets (Net) | 31n | 5,715.0 | 5,913.4 | 7,322.9 | 7,751.8 | 6,957.2 | 8,603.9 | 9,787.7 | 9,041.1 | 6,194.6 | 6,493.7 | 7,641.8 | 7,913.3 |
| Domestic Credit | 32 | 7,339.1 | 9,795.0 | 11,643.9 | 13,868.5 | 17,304.0 | 17,692.4 | 18,747.6 | 21,842.6 | 25,094.9 | 26,680.5 | 27,008.4 | 28,096.3 |
| Claims on Central Govt. (Net) | 32an | 759.2 | 1,330.9 | 1,209.0 | 1,952.6 | 3,792.9 | 4,270.6 | 4,357.5 | 6,144.5 | 8,476.9 | 8,892.4 | 8,675.9 | 8,940.2 |
| Claims on State & Local Govts | 32b | — | — | .1 | 2.0 | 49.9 | 71.5 | 173.2 | 180.9 | 184.9 | 187.8 | 232.4 | 225.7 |
| Claims on Nonfin.Pub.Enterprises | 32c | 472.6 | 528.1 | 520.6 | 621.2 | 602.7 | 410.5 | 343.3 | 332.9 | 298.6 | 257.2 | 148.0 | 127.8 |
| Claims on Private Sector | 32d | 6,043.8 | 7,862.7 | 9,796.7 | 11,116.2 | 12,612.4 | 12,773.7 | 13,727.2 | 15,056.3 | 16,011.9 | 17,252.8 | 17,861.0 | 18,713.4 |
| Claims on Nonbank Financial Insts | 32g | 45.5 | 62.8 | 108.4 | 167.8 | 235.7 | 155.7 | 144.5 | 126.2 | 121.2 | 89.0 | 89.3 | 87.8 |
| Money | 34 | 3,138.5 | 4,022.6 | 4,521.8 | 4,803.3 | 5,524.7 | 5,982.0 | 6,504.4 | 7,228.0 | 7,152.1 | 8,320.5 | 9,165.3 | 9,803.2 |
| Quasi-Money | 35 | 7,070.9 | 8,373.1 | 9,464.9 | 10,921.4 | 13,516.9 | 17,684.8 | 19,345.2 | 19,318.9 | 18,852.8 | 21,365.4 | 22,701.8 | 23,743.0 |
| Money Market Instruments | 36aa | 699.4 | 809.0 | 777.6 | 794.8 | 805.0 | 1,027.9 | 1,316.6 | 1,406.3 | 1,617.0 | 1,818.6 | 2,244.4 | 2,335.0 |
| Liabs. of Central Bank:Securities | 36ac | — | — | — | — | — | — | — | — | — | — | — | — |
| Capital Accounts | 37a | 1,416.2 | 1,584.7 | 2,640.0 | 3,059.5 | 3,313.4 | 3,758.8 | 4,059.9 | 4,559.2 | 4,793.9 | 4,741.2 | 4,809.7 | 5,170.3 |
| Other Items (Net) | 37r | 729.1 | 919.1 | 1,562.6 | 2,041.4 | 1,101.3 | −2,157.0 | −2,690.7 | −1,628.7 | −1,126.3 | −3,071.4 | −4,270.9 | −5,041.7 |
| Money plus Quasi-Money | 35l | 10,209.4 | 12,395.6 | 13,986.7 | 15,724.6 | 19,041.6 | 23,666.7 | 25,849.6 | 26,547.0 | 26,004.8 | 29,685.9 | 31,867.0 | 33,546.1 |
| **Money (National Definitions)** | | | | | | *Millions of Dinars: End of Period* | | | | | | | |
| Reserve Money | 19mb | 2,241.3 | 2,678.4 | 3,385.6 | 3,652.6 | 4,512.9 | 4,664.0 | 5,059.3 | 5,485.3 | 5,229.2 | 5,952.4 | 7,041.9 | 7,299.8 |
| M1 | 59ma | 3,192.9 | 4,061.3 | 4,566.4 | 4,833.2 | 5,573.0 | 6,039.5 | 6,550.0 | 7,271.6 | 7,211.1 | 8,408.4 | 9,231.7 | 9,880.3 |
| M2 | 59mb | 10,571.4 | 12,364.0 | 14,109.7 | 15,606.9 | 18,304.2 | 20,013.3 | 22,306.7 | 24,118.9 | 24,945.1 | 27,363.4 | 29,240.5 | 31,605.7 |
| **Interest Rates** | | | | | | *Percent Per Annum* | | | | | | | |
| Central Bank Policy Rate (EOP) | 60 | 2.25 | 4.50 | 5.25 | 4.75 | 4.00 | 2.50 | 2.00 | 2.25 | 4.00 | 3.50 | 2.75 | 1.50 |
| Discount Rate (End of Period) | 60.a | 3.75 | 6.50 | 7.50 | 7.00 | 6.25 | 4.75 | 4.25 | 4.50 | 5.00 | 4.50 | 4.25 | 3.75 |
| Money Market Rate | 60b | 2.18 | 3.59 | 5.55 | 5.70 | 4.94 | 3.33 | 2.19 | 2.56 | 3.62 | 4.10 | 3.16 | 2.29 |
| Savings Rate | 60k | .76 | .74 | 1.04 | 1.06 | 1.08 | .89 | .78 | .69 | .71 | .79 | .84 | .72 |
| Deposit Rate | 60l | 2.49 | 2.91 | 4.62 | 5.45 | 5.46 | 4.94 | 3.53 | 3.40 | 3.77 | 4.85 | 4.52 | 3.50 |
| Lending Rate | 60p | 8.26 | 7.61 | 8.18 | 8.68 | 9.03 | 9.25 | 9.02 | 8.71 | 8.78 | 9.01 | 8.99 | 8.48 |

| | | 2004 | 2005 | 2006 | 2007 | 2008 | 2009 | 2010 | 2011 | 2012 | 2013 | 2014 | 2015 |
|---|---|---|---|---|---|---|---|---|---|---|---|---|---|
| **Prices and Production** | | | | | | *Index Numbers (2010=100): Period Averages* | | | | | | | |
| Producer Prices | 63 | 56.9 | 62.3 | 72.1 | 78.7 | 122.9 | 102.4 | 100.0 | 114.7 | 120.1 | 117.0 | 115.1 | † 103.9 |
| Wholesale Prices | 63a | 64.7 | 69.2 | 73.7 | 80.0 | 95.6 | 96.4 | 100.0 | .... | .... | .... | .... | .... |
| Consumer Prices | 64 | 72.0 | 74.5 | 79.2 | 83.4 | † 95.9 | 95.2 | † 100.0 | 104.2 | 108.9 | 114.1 | 117.4 | 116.4 |
| Industrial Production | 66 | 86.1 | 94.9 | 100.4 | 103.6 | 105.0 | 103.2 | 100.0 | 99.7 | 99.9 | 101.4 | 103.2 | † 104.5 |
| **Intl. Transactions & Positions** | | | | | | *Millions of Dinars* | | | | | | | |
| Exports | 70 | 2,780.5 | 3,050.0 | 3,668.9 | 4,059.3 | 5,527.3 | 4,637.2 | 4,986.4 | 5,654.1 | 5,627.5 | 5,606.4 | 5,946.7 | 5,572.9 |
| Imports, c.i.f. | 71 | 5,762.9 | 7,448.9 | 8,115.8 | 9,579.2 | 11,897.1 | 10,318.9 | 10,710.4 | 13,108.5 | 14,690.8 | 15,407.4 | 16,295.9 | 14,211.1 |
| | | | | | | | *2010=100* | | | | | | |
| Volume of Exports | 72 | 101.0 | 96.9 | 100.0 | 92.4 | 83.9 | 75.7 | 100.0 | 101.1 | 93.2 | 103.8 | 108.9 | 105.1 |
| Volume of Imports | 73 | 98.3 | 112.2 | 112.0 | 117.7 | 120.5 | 112.3 | 100.0 | 95.6 | 109.7 | 112.4 | 112.4 | 111.1 |
| Unit Value of Exports | 74 | 54.8 | 63.1 | 69.1 | 81.9 | 125.9 | 114.4 | 100.0 | 112.4 | 121.4 | 111.1 | 111.1 | 109.7 |
| Unit Value of Imports | 75 | 53.6 | 60.9 | 66.7 | 75.7 | 91.2 | 103.2 | 100.0 | 125.5 | 123.9 | 125.1 | 132.5 | 117.0 |
| **Balance of Payments** | | | | | | *Millions of US Dollars* | | | | | | | |
| A. Current Account* | 109bx | 39.2 | −2,271.2 | −1,725.9 | −2,874.7 | −2,054.1 | −1,243.2 | † −1,881.9 | −2,956.0 | −4,711.1 | −3,504.0 | −2,607.9 | −3,331.7 |
| Goods, credit (exports) | 1a9cx | 3,882.9 | 4,301.4 | 5,204.6 | 5,731.5 | 7,937.1 | 6,375.1 | † 7,028.3 | 8,006.3 | 7,886.6 | 7,912.5 | 8,385.4 | 7,828.6 |
| Goods, debit (imports) | 1a9dx | 7,261.1 | 9,317.3 | 10,260.3 | 12,183.3 | 15,101.9 | 12,641.1 | † 13,822.4 | 16,825.6 | 18,431.1 | 19,560.6 | 20,351.0 | 18,038.9 |
| Balance on goods | 1a9bx | −3,378.2 | −5,015.9 | −5,056.0 | −6,451.8 | −7,164.8 | −6,266.1 | † −6,794.1 | −8,819.3 | −10,544.5 | −11,648.0 | −11,965.6 | −10,210.3 |
| Services, credit (exports) | 1b9cx | 2,115.7 | 2,412.4 | 2,996.9 | 3,656.1 | 4,761.9 | 4,686.1 | † 5,723.5 | 5,737.5 | 6,420.8 | 6,315.1 | 7,139.6 | 6,307.9 |
| Services, debit (imports) | 1b9dx | 2,145.8 | 2,542.0 | 2,970.7 | 3,517.3 | 4,126.5 | 3,817.6 | † 4,419.0 | 4,475.5 | 4,544.4 | 4,611.5 | 4,634.1 | 4,495.9 |
| Balance on Goods & Services | 1z9bx | −3,408.4 | −5,145.5 | −5,029.7 | −6,313.1 | −6,529.5 | −5,397.6 | † −5,489.6 | −7,557.3 | −8,668.0 | −9,944.5 | −9,460.1 | −8,398.3 |
| Primary income: credit | 1c9cx | 606.4 | 712.5 | 942.6 | 1,296.1 | 1,051.7 | 961.1 | † 887.2 | 710.4 | 690.1 | 793.5 | 880.1 | 736.0 |
| Primary income: debit | 1c9dx | 374.9 | 454.6 | 578.8 | 720.3 | 640.1 | 585.2 | † 1,101.7 | 974.9 | 1,078.1 | 1,132.3 | 1,296.8 | 1,225.9 |
| Balance on gds, serv. & prim. inc. | 1y9bx | −3,176.9 | −4,887.6 | −4,666.0 | −5,737.3 | −6,117.8 | −5,021.6 | † −5,704.1 | −7,821.8 | −9,056.0 | −10,283.3 | −9,876.8 | −8,888.2 |
| Secondary income: credit | 1d9ca | 3,562.3 | 3,029.9 | 3,378.8 | 3,594.8 | 4,698.1 | 4,433.8 | † 4,372.5 | 5,365.5 | 4,977.6 | 7,261.4 | 7,886.5 | 6,100.4 |
| Secondary income: debit | 1d9da | 346.3 | 413.5 | 438.8 | 732.2 | 634.3 | 655.4 | † 550.4 | 499.7 | 632.7 | 482.1 | 617.6 | 543.9 |
| B. Capital Account* | 209na | 2.1 | 8.5 | 62.8 | 12.8 | 283.9 | .6 | † .3 | — | 2.5 | 2.4 | 4.4 | 6.8 |
| Capital account: credit | 209ca | 2.1 | 8.5 | 62.8 | 12.8 | 283.9 | .6 | † .3 | — | 2.5 | 2.4 | 4.4 | 6.8 |
| Capital account: debit | 209da | — | — | — | — | — | — | † — | — | — | — | — | — |
| Balance on current & capital acct. | 129ba | 41.3 | −2,262.8 | −1,663.2 | −2,861.9 | −1,770.1 | −1,242.6 | † −1,881.7 | −2,956.0 | −4,708.6 | −3,501.6 | −2,603.6 | −3,325.0 |
| C. Financial Account* | 309na | −17.2 | −1,848.7 | −3,318.9 | −3,220.2 | −2,746.8 | −3,978.0 | † −2,577.3 | −1,586.9 | −1,705.5 | −7,134.8 | −3,249.8 | −2,454.9 |
| Direct investment: assets | 3a9aa | 18.2 | 163.2 | −138.1 | 48.1 | 12.8 | 72.4 | † 28.5 | 30.8 | 5.4 | 15.7 | 83.4 | 1.0 |
| Equity & investment fund shares | 3aaaa | .... | .... | .... | .... | .... | .... | † 28.5 | 30.8 | 5.4 | 15.7 | 83.4 | 1.0 |
| Debt instruments | 3abaa | .... | .... | .... | .... | .... | .... | † — | — | — | — | — | — |
| Direct investment: liabilities | 3a9la | 936.8 | 1,984.5 | 3,544.0 | 2,622.1 | 2,826.7 | 2,413.1 | † 1,688.4 | 1,486.1 | 1,513.2 | 1,805.6 | 2,009.3 | 1,274.8 |
| Equity & investment fund shares | 3aala | .... | .... | .... | .... | .... | 2,413.1 | † 1,688.4 | 1,486.1 | 1,513.2 | 1,805.6 | 2,009.3 | 1,274.8 |
| Debt instruments | 3abla | .... | .... | .... | .... | .... | .... | † — | — | — | — | — | — |
| Portfolio investment: assets | 3b9aa | 199.0 | −143.6 | 180.4 | −494.4 | −51.9 | 600.0 | † −41.0 | −282.5 | −221.7 | 19.6 | 103.9 | 70.4 |
| Equity & investment fund shares | 3baaa | 199.0 | −143.6 | 180.4 | −494.4 | −51.9 | 600.0 | † −3.4 | 8.7 | 1.7 | 4.4 | 23.7 | .4 |
| Debt securities | 3bbaa | — | — | — | — | — | — | † −37.6 | −291.3 | −223.4 | 15.2 | 80.3 | 70.0 |
| Portfolio investment: liabilities | 3b9la | −89.8 | 169.1 | 143.6 | 346.0 | 521.1 | −29.6 | † 729.4 | −44.4 | 223.7 | 1,671.0 | 1,265.8 | 1,363.9 |
| Equity & investment fund shares | 3bala | −89.8 | 169.1 | 143.6 | 346.0 | 521.1 | −29.6 | † −20.6 | 109.4 | 53.1 | 158.5 | −31.1 | 14.6 |
| Debt securities | 3bbla | — | — | — | — | — | — | † 750.0 | −153.8 | 170.6 | 1,512.5 | 1,296.9 | 1,349.3 |
| Fin. der.& empl.stk.ops.(ESOs): net. | 3c9na | .... | .... | .... | .... | — | — | † — | — | — | — | — | — |
| Fin. der. & ESOs.: assets | 3c9aa | .... | .... | .... | .... | — | — | † — | — | — | — | — | — |
| Fin. der. & ESOs.: liabilities | 3c9la | .... | .... | .... | .... | — | — | † — | — | — | — | — | — |
| Other investment: assets | 3d9aa | 680.8 | 615.9 | 1,148.0 | 939.6 | −734.6 | −1,503.4 | † 1,228.5 | 496.5 | 1,014.6 | −901.1 | −236.4 | −425.3 |
| Other equity | 3daaa | .... | .... | .... | .... | .... | .... | † 5.8 | 4.8 | 5.7 | 5.7 | 3.2 | 17.2 |
| Debt instruments | 3dzaa | 680.8 | 615.9 | 1,148.0 | 939.6 | −734.6 | −1,503.4 | † 1,222.7 | 491.7 | 1,008.9 | −906.8 | −239.6 | −442.5 |
| Other investment: liabilities | 3d9la | 68.3 | 330.6 | 821.6 | 745.4 | −1,374.8 | 763.5 | † 1,375.4 | 390.0 | 766.9 | 2,792.4 | −74.4 | −537.7 |
| Other equity | 3dala | .... | .... | .... | .... | .... | .... | † — | — | — | — | — | — |
| Debt instruments | 3dzla | 68.3 | 330.6 | 821.6 | 745.4 | −1,374.8 | 763.5 | † 1,375.4 | 390.0 | 766.9 | 2,792.4 | −74.4 | −537.7 |
| Curr.+ cap.− finan. acct. balance | 4y9na | 58.5 | −414.1 | 1,655.7 | 358.3 | 976.7 | 2,735.3 | † 695.6 | −1,369.1 | −3,003.1 | 3,633.2 | 646.2 | −870.1 |
| D. Net Errors and Omissions | 409na | 121.3 | 674.9 | −214.0 | 531.7 | 220.4 | 392.2 | † 764.2 | −283.5 | −650.6 | 951.2 | 1,339.9 | 1,097.7 |
| E. Reserves and Related Items | 4z9na | 179.8 | 260.8 | 1,441.7 | 890.0 | 1,197.1 | 3,127.5 | † 1,459.8 | −1,652.6 | −3,653.7 | 4,584.4 | 1,986.1 | 227.6 |
| Reserve assets | 3e9aa | 81.8 | 183.5 | 1,353.3 | 813.6 | 1,137.6 | 3,112.0 | † 1,455.9 | −1,652.6 | −3,274.6 | 5,230.0 | 2,375.1 | 778.6 |
| Credit and loans from the IMF | 3dcla | −98.1 | −77.2 | −88.4 | −76.4 | −59.4 | −15.5 | † −3.9 | — | 379.1 | 645.5 | 389.0 | 550.9 |
| Exceptional financing | 409la | — | — | — | — | — | — | † — | — | — | — | — | — |
| *Excludes components in group E | | | | | | | | | | | | | |
| **International Investment Position** | | | | | | *Millions of US Dollars* | | | | | | | |
| Assets | 809aa | 13,849.4 | 14,452.6 | 17,138.0 | 18,681.5 | 18,972.5 | 21,323.2 | † 24,017.5 | 22,913.9 | 20,442.7 | 24,727.3 | 26,108.1 | 26,278.3 |
| Direct investment | 8a9aa | 286.6 | 449.6 | 311.6 | 359.7 | 372.4 | 444.4 | † 473.1 | 503.9 | 509.3 | 524.9 | 608.3 | 609.3 |
| Equity & investment fund shares | 8aaaa | 286.6 | 449.6 | 311.6 | 359.7 | 372.4 | 444.4 | † 473.1 | 503.9 | 509.3 | 524.9 | 608.3 | 609.3 |
| Debt instruments | 8abaa | .... | .... | .... | .... | .... | .... | † — | — | — | — | — | — |
| Portfolio investment | 8b9aa | 862.6 | 719.2 | 902.0 | 410.7 | 353.6 | 960.1 | † 930.6 | 648.0 | 426.2 | 445.8 | 549.6 | 620.0 |
| Equity & investment fund shares | 8baaa | 49.1 | 92.1 | 61.2 | 71.1 | 69.1 | 88.0 | † 96.1 | 104.8 | 106.3 | 110.7 | 134.2 | 134.6 |
| Debt securities | 8bbaa | 813.5 | 627.1 | 840.8 | 339.6 | 284.5 | 872.1 | † 834.5 | 543.2 | 319.9 | 335.1 | 415.4 | 485.4 |
| Fin. der.(oth.than reserves) & ESOs | 8c9aa | .... | .... | .... | .... | .... | .... | † — | — | — | — | — | — |
| Other investment | 8d9aa | 7,253.9 | 7,835.8 | 8,946.1 | 9,982.1 | 9,331.0 | 7,795.8 | † 8,996.5 | 9,678.5 | 10,689.9 | 9,951.8 | 8,928.9 | 8,503.2 |
| Other equity | 8daaa | .... | .... | .... | .... | .... | .... | † 221.4 | 408.3 | 416.9 | 427.9 | 423.7 | 443.7 |
| Debt instruments | 8dzaa | 7,253.9 | 7,835.8 | 8,946.1 | 9,982.1 | 9,331.0 | 7,795.8 | † 8,775.1 | 9,270.1 | 10,273.0 | 9,523.9 | 8,505.3 | 8,059.5 |
| Reserve assets | 8e9aa | 5,446.3 | 5,447.9 | 6,978.3 | 7,929.0 | 8,915.5 | 12,122.9 | † 13,617.4 | 12,083.5 | 8,817.3 | 13,804.8 | 16,021.3 | 16,545.9 |
| Liabilities | 809la | 24,629.2 | 34,366.7 | 32,618.4 | 40,572.6 | 38,662.0 | 38,640.4 | † 42,390.9 | 44,230.7 | 46,922.8 | 54,400.5 | 57,910.4 | 60,585.3 |
| Direct investment | 8a9la | 8,315.7 | 13,228.6 | 12,713.1 | 19,012.7 | 20,405.8 | 20,761.4 | † 21,898.6 | 23,384.6 | 24,897.9 | 26,769.7 | 28,714.1 | 29,957.7 |
| Equity & investment fund shares | 8aala | 8,315.7 | 13,228.6 | 12,713.1 | 19,012.7 | 20,405.8 | 20,761.4 | † 21,898.6 | 23,384.6 | 24,897.9 | 26,769.7 | 28,714.1 | 29,957.7 |
| Debt instruments | 8abla | .... | .... | .... | .... | .... | .... | † — | — | — | — | — | — |
| Portfolio investment | 8b9la | 3,260.4 | 8,210.0 | 5,896.5 | 6,531.9 | 4,385.1 | 3,329.6 | † 4,247.0 | 4,005.9 | 4,128.7 | 6,494.8 | 8,200.9 | 9,534.0 |
| Equity & investment fund shares | 8bala | 3,260.4 | 8,210.0 | 5,896.5 | 6,531.9 | 4,385.1 | 3,329.6 | † 3,397.0 | 3,293.7 | 3,263.7 | 3,997.6 | 4,356.3 | 4,351.3 |
| Debt securities | 8bbla | — | — | — | — | — | — | † 850.0 | 712.2 | 865.0 | 2,497.2 | 3,844.5 | 5,182.8 |
| Fin. der.(oth.than reserves) & ESOs | 8c9la | .... | .... | .... | .... | .... | .... | † — | — | — | — | — | — |
| Other investment | 8d9la | 13,053.1 | 12,927.8 | 14,008.8 | 15,028.0 | 13,871.1 | 14,549.4 | † 16,245.3 | 16,840.2 | 17,896.2 | 21,144.8 | 20,995.5 | 21,093.6 |
| Other equity | 8dala | .... | .... | .... | .... | .... | .... | † — | — | — | — | — | — |
| Debt instruments | 8dzla | 13,053.1 | 12,927.8 | 14,008.8 | 15,028.0 | 13,871.1 | 14,549.4 | † 16,245.3 | 16,840.2 | 17,896.2 | 21,144.8 | 20,995.5 | 21,093.6 |

| | | 2004 | 2005 | 2006 | 2007 | 2008 | 2009 | 2010 | 2011 | 2012 | 2013 | 2014 | 2015 |
|---|---|---|---|---|---|---|---|---|---|---|---|---|---|
| **Government Finance** | | | | | | | | | | | | | |
| **Cash Flow Statement** | | | | | | | | | | | | | |
| **Budgetary Central Government** | | | | | *Millions of Dinars: Fiscal Year Ends December 31* | | | | | | | |
| Cash Receipts:Operating Activities... | c1 | .... | 3,064.0 | 3,687.3 | 3,602.2 | 4,676.1 | 4,526.7 | 4,661.6 | 5,420.8 | 5,054.5 | 5,758.8 | 7,267.6 | 6,796.0 |
| Taxes......................... | c11 | .... | 2,179.2 | 2,268.6 | 2,593.0 | 2,922.4 | 2,925.7 | 2,985.2 | 3,057.5 | 3,351.4 | 3,652.4 | 4,037.1 | 4,096.0 |
| Social Contributions....................... | c12 | .... | 18.1 | 16.4 | 18.2 | 21.2 | 20.5 | 20.7 | 25.4 | 24.3 | 22.1 | 21.0 | 18.6 |
| Grants........................... | c13 | .... | 501.1 | 547.4 | 88.4 | 720.8 | 344.1 | 401.3 | 1,215.0 | 327.1 | 639.0 | 1,236.5 | 886.2 |
| Other Receipts........................ | c14 | .... | 365.6 | 854.9 | 902.6 | 1,011.7 | 1,236.4 | 1,254.4 | 1,122.9 | 1,351.7 | 1,445.3 | 1,973.0 | 1,795.2 |
| Cash Payments:Operating Activities. | c2 | .... | 3,181.8 | 3,285.9 | 3,943.7 | 4,537.6 | 5,013.7 | 4,745.4 | 3,914.8 | 4,441.5 | 4,277.4 | 4,793.5 | 4,629.3 |
| Compensation of Employees.......... | c21 | .... | 1,254.1 | 1,342.7 | 1,733.3 | 2,239.6 | 2,665.8 | 2,594.7 | 1,013.5 | 1,176.4 | 1,267.1 | 1,320.1 | 1,344.6 |
| Purchases of Goods & Services....... | c22 | .... | 144.8 | 327.6 | 355.5 | 616.9 | 429.3 | 303.1 | 265.4 | 236.2 | 270.5 | 479.5 | 403.1 |
| Interest................................. | c24 | .... | 207.1 | 343.2 | 367.3 | 377.4 | 378.6 | 397.6 | 429.5 | 582.8 | 736.5 | 925.9 | 914.4 |
| Subsidies............................... | c25 | .... | 82.7 | 82.8 | 254.4 | 260.6 | 186.2 | 295.2 | 151.3 | 67.3 | 79.5 | 79.5 | 94.8 |
| Grants............................. | c26 | .... | 18.1 | 238.9 | 224.4 | 64.5 | 134.7 | 91.0 | 101.5 | 183.5 | 192.7 | 205.8 | 117.2 |
| Social Benefits................... | c27 | .... | 1,117.9 | 542.4 | 546.2 | 710.1 | 913.2 | 969.6 | 1,866.9 | 2,093.9 | 1,618.1 | 1,691.0 | 1,641.0 |
| Other Payments................... | c28 | .... | 357.1 | 408.3 | 462.6 | 268.5 | 305.9 | 94.2 | 86.7 | 101.4 | 113.0 | 91.7 | 114.2 |
| Net Cash Inflow:Operating Act.[1-2] | ccio | .... | −117.8 | 401.5 | −341.5 | 138.5 | −487.0 | −83.8 | 1,506.0 | 613.0 | 1,481.4 | 2,474.1 | 2,166.7 |
| Net Cash Outflow:Invest. in NFA...... | c31 | .... | 339.4 | 723.4 | 744.5 | 875.6 | 954.7 | 962.8 | 2,854.8 | 2,420.7 | 2,799.7 | 3,057.6 | 3,094.6 |
| Purchases of Nonfinancial Assets... | c31.1 | .... | 339.4 | 723.4 | 744.5 | 875.6 | 954.7 | 962.8 | 2,854.8 | 2,420.7 | 2,799.7 | 3,057.6 | 3,094.6 |
| Sales of Nonfinancial Assets.......... | c31.2 | .... | — | — | — | — | — | — | — | — | — | — | — |
| Cash Surplus/Deficit [1-2-31=1-2M] | ccsd | .... | −457.2 | −321.9 | −1,086.0 | −737.1 | −1,441.7 | −1,046.6 | −1,348.8 | −1,807.7 | −1,318.3 | −583.5 | −927.9 |
| Net Acq. Fin. Assets, excl. Cash....... | c32x | .... | .... | 48.8 | 46.0 | 19.8 | −16.3 | — | — | — | — | — | — |
| Domestic.......................... | c321x | .... | .... | 48.8 | 46.0 | 19.8 | −15.9 | — | — | — | — | — | — |
| Foreign............................. | c322x | .... | — | — | — | — | — | — | — | — | — | — | — |
| Net Incurrence of Liabilities............. | c33 | .... | .... | 262.8 | 799.8 | 384.1 | 1,530.2 | 1,048.1 | 1,151.2 | 2,012.1 | 3,356.7 | 2,296.6 | 1,274.3 |
| Domestic...................... | c331 | .... | .... | 348.5 | 965.4 | 2,000.4 | 1,324.7 | 395.1 | 1,282.0 | 1,728.0 | 1,134.0 | 1,518.0 | −139.0 |
| Foreign........................ | c332 | .... | .... | −87.1 | −165.6 | −1,616.3 | 205.2 | 653.0 | −130.8 | 284.1 | 2,222.7 | 778.6 | 1,413.3 |
| Net Cash Inflow, Fin.Act.[-32x+33].. | cnfb | .... | .... | 214.0 | 753.8 | 364.3 | 1,546.5 | 1,048.1 | 1,151.2 | 2,012.1 | 3,356.7 | 2,296.6 | 1,274.3 |
| Net Change in Stock of Cash........... | cncb | .... | .... | −107.9 | −332.2 | −372.8 | 104.8 | 1.5 | −197.6 | 204.4 | 2,038.4 | 1,713.1 | 346.4 |
| Stat. Discrep. [32X-33+NCB-CSD].... | ccsdz | .... | — | — | — | — | — | — | — | — | — | — | — |
| Memo Item:Cash Expenditure[2+31] | c2m | .... | 3,521.2 | 4,009.3 | 4,688.2 | 5,413.2 | 5,968.4 | 5,708.2 | 6,769.6 | 6,862.2 | 7,077.1 | 7,851.1 | 7,723.9 |
| Memo Item: Gross Debt.................. | c63 | .... | 7,136.0 | .... | .... | .... | 10,317.5 | 11,514.9 | 12,666.0 | 14,678.1 | 18,034.8 | 20,331.4 | 21,605.7 |
| **National Accounts** | | | | | | *Millions of Dinars* | | | | | | |
| Househ.Cons.Expend.,incl.NPISHs.... | 96f | 6,587.1 | 7,838.3 | 9,076.2 | 10,512.3 | 12,403.0 | 12,688.4 | .... | .... | .... | .... | .... | .... |
| Government Consumption Expend... | 91f | 1,723.1 | 1,743.2 | 2,203.3 | 2,499.4 | 3,363.6 | 3,699.5 | .... | .... | .... | .... | .... | .... |
| Gross Fixed Capital Formation.......... | 93e | 2,005.4 | 2,733.7 | 2,717.1 | 3,334.1 | 4,342.9 | 4,254.2 | .... | .... | .... | .... | .... | .... |
| Changes in Inventories................. | 93i | 210.2 | 314.2 | 308.3 | 337.8 | 318.7 | 193.7 | .... | .... | .... | .... | .... | .... |
| Exports of Goods and Services........ | 90c | 4,222.6 | 4,704.2 | 5,751.3 | 6,579.4 | 8,811.2 | 7,758.6 | .... | .... | .... | .... | .... | .... |
| Imports of Goods and Services (-).... | 98c | 6,669.5 | 8,408.3 | 9,380.8 | 11,131.6 | 13,646.0 | 11,682.2 | .... | .... | .... | .... | .... | .... |
| Gross Domestic Product (GDP)........ | 99b | 8,078.9 | 8,925.3 | 10,675.4 | 12,131.4 | 15,593.4 | 16,912.2 | 19,527.8 | 20,476.5 | 21,965.5 | 23,851.6 | 25,437.1 | .... |
| Net Primary Income from Abroad..... | 98.n | 229.6 | 289.7 | 411.7 | 572.3 | .... | .... | .... | .... | .... | .... | .... | .... |
| Gross National Income (GNI)........... | 99a | 8,308.3 | 9,215.1 | 10,789.9 | 12,629.2 | .... | .... | .... | .... | .... | .... | .... | .... |
| Net National Income...................... | 99e | 7,472.9 | 8,290.8 | 9,768.0 | 11,503.0 | .... | .... | .... | .... | .... | .... | .... | .... |
| GDP Volume 1994 Prices................ | 99b.p | 6,823.7 | 7,379.6 | 7,973.8 | 8,676.9 | 9,345.1 | 9,514.4 | 9,808.7 | 10,244.0 | .... | .... | .... | .... |
| GDP Volume (2010=100)................ | 99bvp | 69.6 | 75.2 | 81.3 | 88.5 | 95.3 | 97.0 | 100.0 | 104.4 | .... | .... | .... | .... |
| GDP Deflator (2010=100)............... | 99bip | 59.5 | 60.8 | 67.2 | 70.2 | 83.8 | 89.3 | 100.0 | 100.4 | .... | .... | .... | .... |
| | | | | | | *Millions: Midyear Estimates* | | | | | | |
| Population.............................. | 99z | 5.17 | 5.33 | 5.53 | 5.76 | 6.01 | 6.27 | 6.52 | 6.76 | 6.99 | 7.21 | 7.42 | 7.59 |

# Kazakhstan 916

| | | 2004 | 2005 | 2006 | 2007 | 2008 | 2009 | 2010 | 2011 | 2012 | 2013 | 2014 | 2015 |
|---|---|---|---|---|---|---|---|---|---|---|---|---|---|
| **Exchange Rates** | | | | | | | *Tenge per SDR: End of Period* | | | | | | | |
| Official Rate | aa | 201.89 | 191.49 | 191.06 | 190.10 | 186.05 | 232.74 | 227.15 | 227.83 | 231.68 | 237.25 | 264.19 | 471.16 |
| | | | | | | | *Tenge per US Dollar: End of Period (ae) Period Average (rf)* | | | | | | | |
| Official Rate | ae | 130.00 | 133.98 | 127.00 | 120.30 | 120.79 | 148.46 | 147.50 | 148.40 | 150.74 | 154.06 | 182.35 | 340.01 |
| Official Rate | rf | 136.04 | 132.88 | 126.09 | 122.55 | 120.30 | 147.50 | 147.36 | 146.62 | 149.11 | 152.13 | 179.19 | 221.73 |
| **Fund Position** | | | | | | | *Millions of SDRs: End of Period* | | | | | | | |
| Quota | 2f.s | 365.70 | 365.70 | 365.70 | 365.70 | 365.70 | 365.70 | 365.70 | 365.70 | 365.70 | 365.70 | 365.70 | 427.80 |
| SDR Holdings | 1b.s | .79 | .81 | .84 | .87 | .90 | 344.56 | 344.56 | 344.56 | 345.63 | 348.32 | 348.32 | 348.31 |
| Reserve Position in the Fund | 1c.s | .01 | .01 | .01 | .01 | .01 | .01 | .01 | .01 | .01 | .01 | .01 | 15.53 |
| Total Fund Cred.&Loans Outstg | 2tl | — | — | — | — | — | | | | | | | |
| SDR Allocations | 1bd | — | — | — | — | — | 343.65 | 343.65 | 343.65 | 343.65 | 343.65 | 343.65 | 343.65 |
| **International Liquidity** | | | | | | | *Millions of US Dollars Unless Otherwise Indicated: End of Period* | | | | | | | |
| Total Reserves minus Gold | 1l.d | 8,473.1 | 6,084.2 | 17,750.8 | 15,776.8 | 17,871.5 | 20,719.8 | 25,222.7 | 25,179.1 | 22,131.5 | 19,126.6 | 21,814.0 | 20,496.8 |
| SDR Holdings | 1b.d | 1.2 | 1.2 | 1.3 | 1.4 | 1.4 | 540.2 | 530.6 | 529.0 | 531.2 | 536.4 | 504.6 | 482.7 |
| Reserve Position in the Fund | 1c.d | .01 | .01 | .01 | .01 | .01 | .01 | .01 | .01 | .01 | .01 | .01 | 21.52 |
| Foreign Exchange | 1d.d | 8,471.9 | 6,083.0 | 17,749.5 | 15,775.4 | 17,870.1 | 20,179.6 | 24,692.1 | 24,650.1 | 21,600.3 | 18,590.2 | 21,309.3 | 19,992.6 |
| Gold (Million Fine Troy Ounces) | 1ad | 1.83 | 1.92 | 2.16 | 2.24 | 2.31 | 2.27 | 2.16 | 2.64 | 3.71 | 4.62 | 6.17 | 7.13 |
| Gold (National Valuation) | 1and | 803.6 | 985.5 | 1,376.2 | 1,852.5 | 2,000.7 | 2,500.7 | 3,052.2 | 4,150.8 | 6,148.4 | 5,551.2 | 7,394.7 | 7,576.1 |
| Central Bank: Other Assets | 3..d | 6.2 | 16.6 | 24.7 | 110.4 | 40.7 | 419.7 | 125.1 | 184.3 | 68.0 | 1,901.6 | 1,216.6 | 1,932.8 |
| Central Bank: Other Liabs | 4..d | 4.3 | 87.2 | 4.0 | 10.6 | 28.4 | 121.6 | 269.9 | 46.4 | 91.7 | 33.5 | 454.3 | 419.4 |
| Other Depository Corps.: Assets | 7a.d | 3,861.5 | 8,888.8 | 16,695.4 | 22,975.9 | 25,214.3 | 23,902.7 | 20,839.6 | 22,058.0 | 21,401.6 | 26,113.0 | 19,686.3 | 5,101.2 |
| Other Depository Corps.: Liabs | 7b.d | 7,485.0 | 15,065.3 | 31,835.5 | 45,308.7 | 38,386.2 | 27,754.0 | 17,939.3 | 15,372.4 | 10,672.8 | 8,697.6 | 7,572.0 | 5,686.5 |
| Other Financial Corps.: Assets | 7e.d | .... | .... | .... | .... | .... | .... | .... | .... | .... | .... | .... | 1,653.23 |
| Other Financial Corps.: Liabs | 7f.d | .... | .... | .... | .... | .... | .... | .... | .... | .... | .... | .... | 4,350.33 |
| **Central Bank** | | | | | | | *Millions of Tenge: End of Period* | | | | | | | |
| Net Foreign Assets | 11n | 1,206,077 | 947,165 | 2,430,389 | 2,132,816 | 2,401,847 | 3,392,717 | 4,071,145 | 4,294,737 | 4,178,070 | 4,013,927 | 5,374,433 | 9,830,457 |
| Claims on Nonresidents | 11 | 1,206,630 | 958,843 | 2,430,892 | 2,134,087 | 2,405,275 | 3,490,749 | 4,189,017 | 4,379,917 | 4,271,513 | 4,100,617 | 5,548,057 | 10,134,982 |
| Liabilities to Nonresidents | 16c | 553 | 11,679 | 503 | 1,272 | 3,429 | 98,032 | 117,872 | 85,180 | 93,443 | 86,690 | 173,624 | 304,525 |
| Claims on Other Depository Corps. | 12e | 26,126 | 95 | — | 76,885 | 143,347 | 406,424 | 483,448 | 446,799 | 587,390 | 556,762 | 727,885 | 70,283 |
| Net Claims on Central Government | 12an | −72,664 | −44,988 | −262,581 | −275,529 | 14,038 | −313,145 | −381,867 | −660,103 | −788,097 | −1,137,329 | −1,469,862 | −2,310,300 |
| Claims on Central Government | 12a | 4,999 | 5,223 | 16,233 | 17,113 | 75,376 | 5,164 | 3,975 | 437 | 32,831 | 203,710 | 437,199 | 346,822 |
| Liabilities to Central Government | 16d | 77,663 | 50,212 | 278,814 | 292,643 | 61,338 | 318,309 | 385,842 | 660,541 | 820,927 | 1,341,039 | 1,907,062 | 2,657,122 |
| Claims on Other Sectors | 12s | 13,993 | 21,058 | 9,755 | 30,726 | 117,808 | 310,556 | 141,724 | 162,422 | 242,768 | 251,140 | 312,187 | 1,210,964 |
| Claims on Other Financial Corps. | 12g | 5,885 | 3,231 | 3,441 | 24,227 | 111,253 | 120,143 | 131,282 | 146,208 | 169,044 | 177,912 | 234,214 | 387,025 |
| Claims on State & Local Govts | 12b | — | | | | | | | | | | | |
| Claims on Public Nonfin. Corps | 12c | 7,766 | 17,362 | 5,255 | 6,103 | 6,124 | 189,740 | 9,824 | 13,924 | 71,013 | 71,693 | 72,615 | 822,518 |
| Claims on Private Sector | 12d | 343 | 464 | 1,059 | 396 | 431 | 673 | 617 | 2,289 | 2,711 | 1,535 | 5,358 | 1,421 |
| Monetary Base | 14 | 577,841 | 649,835 | 1,501,328 | 1,464,136 | 1,525,238 | 2,450,836 | 2,572,217 | 2,837,356 | 2,890,061 | 2,825,961 | 3,413,841 | 4,750,422 |
| Currency in Circulation | 14a | 410,898 | 458,518 | 687,257 | 859,852 | 986,856 | 1,047,795 | 1,306,208 | 1,548,166 | 1,736,646 | 1,762,907 | 1,382,183 | 1,494,930 |
| Liabs. to Other Depository Corps. | 14c | 164,208 | 184,151 | 796,942 | 567,694 | 328,216 | 949,494 | 721,590 | 728,243 | 724,145 | 843,830 | 1,500,115 | 2,835,665 |
| Liabilities to Other Sectors | 14d | 2,735 | 7,167 | 17,129 | 36,589 | 210,166 | 453,548 | 544,419 | 560,947 | 429,271 | 219,224 | 531,543 | 419,827 |
| Other Liabs. to Other Dep. Corps. | 14n | 407,674 | 174,838 | 535,084 | 233,875 | 316,519 | 474,770 | 901,452 | 511,237 | 187,229 | 3,796 | 75,626 | 991,771 |
| Dep. & Sec. Excl. f/Monetary Base | 14o | 112,465 | 10,082 | 6,584 | 27,582 | 612,244 | 200,779 | 37,863 | 9,197 | 101,424 | 27,676 | 28,982 | 427,917 |
| Deposits Included in Broad Money | 15 | 112,465 | 10,082 | 6,584 | 27,582 | 612,244 | 200,779 | 37,863 | 9,197 | 101,424 | 27,676 | 28,982 | 72,865 |
| Sec.Ot.th.Shares Incl.in Brd. Money | 16a | — | — | — | — | — | — | — | — | — | — | — | — |
| Deposits Excl. from Broad Money | 16b | — | — | — | — | — | — | — | — | — | — | — | — |
| Sec.Ot.th.Shares Excl.f/Brd.Money | 16s | — | — | — | — | — | — | — | — | — | — | — | 355,052 |
| | 16l | — | — | — | — | — | — | — | — | — | — | — | 100 |
| Loans | 16l | — | — | — | — | — | — | — | — | — | — | — | 49,799 |
| Financial Derivatives | 16m | — | — | — | — | 72 | — | — | — | — | — | — | — |
| Shares and Other Equity | 17a | 89,684 | 97,647 | 143,779 | 226,894 | 242,982 | 688,769 | 801,550 | 900,756 | 1,060,879 | 858,396 | 1,369,707 | 2,616,472 |
| Other Items (Net) | 17r | −14,132 | −9,074 | −9,212 | 12,411 | −20,015 | −18,602 | 1,367 | −14,693 | −19,464 | −31,329 | 56,487 | −35,078 |
| Memo Item: | | | | | | | | | | | | | |
| Total Assets | 10ra | 1,267,225 | 995,873 | 2,468,242 | 2,284,991 | 2,764,147 | 4,320,810 | 4,920,262 | 5,094,290 | 5,243,222 | 5,235,971 | 7,161,803 | 12,002,387 |
| **Other Depository Corporations** | | | | | | | *Millions of Tenge: End of Period* | | | | | | | |
| Net Foreign Assets | 21n | −471,063 | −827,528 | −1,922,793 | −2,686,629 | −1,591,037 | −571,763 | 427,794 | 992,145 | 1,617,267 | 2,683,025 | 2,209,045 | −199,011 |
| Claims on Nonresidents | 21 | 501,993 | 1,190,918 | 2,120,315 | 2,764,006 | 3,045,630 | 3,548,590 | 3,073,846 | 3,273,406 | 3,226,080 | 4,022,973 | 3,589,791 | 1,734,460 |
| Liabilities to Nonresidents | 26c | 973,055 | 2,018,446 | 4,043,108 | 5,450,635 | 4,636,666 | 4,120,353 | 2,646,052 | 2,281,261 | 1,608,813 | 1,339,947 | 1,380,746 | 1,933,471 |
| Claims on Central Bank | 20 | 392,299 | 311,094 | 1,203,539 | 842,655 | 616,427 | 1,442,202 | 1,542,353 | 1,230,854 | 1,018,426 | 1,097,108 | 1,933,783 | 4,153,738 |
| Currency | 20a | 31,625 | 46,705 | 86,425 | 120,165 | 129,014 | 134,352 | 157,719 | 182,468 | 208,569 | 250,646 | 259,864 | 257,957 |
| Reserve Deposits and Securities | 20b | 164,179 | 178,461 | 774,891 | 567,733 | 328,154 | 949,493 | 724,539 | 727,145 | 723,678 | 842,603 | 1,561,201 | 2,933,348 |
| Other Claims | 20n | 196,494 | 85,927 | 342,223 | 154,757 | 159,259 | 358,358 | 660,095 | 321,241 | 86,179 | 3,859 | 112,718 | 962,433 |
| Net Claims on Central Government | 22an | 121,743 | 127,157 | 136,481 | 141,480 | 208,861 | 240,809 | 399,043 | 462,989 | 599,706 | 655,924 | 701,424 | 819,310 |
| Claims on Central Government | 22a | 125,696 | 129,700 | 138,298 | 149,007 | 243,731 | 288,784 | 443,947 | 518,487 | 657,804 | 709,713 | 768,372 | 855,291 |
| Liabilities to Central Government | 26d | 3,954 | 2,544 | 1,817 | 7,526 | 34,870 | 47,975 | 44,904 | 55,498 | 58,098 | 53,788 | 66,948 | 35,981 |
| Claims on Other Sectors | 22s | 1,642,216 | 2,854,816 | 5,219,589 | 7,881,143 | 8,354,075 | 9,047,066 | 9,747,245 | 11,144,349 | 12,427,549 | 14,015,895 | 14,763,717 | 17,536,836 |
| Claims on Other Financial Corps. | 22g | 59,633 | 114,007 | 310,164 | 269,287 | 352,735 | 350,201 | 345,777 | 315,671 | 378,164 | 562,739 | 516,955 | 3,317,776 |
| Claims on State & Local Govts | 22b | 3,360 | 2,676 | 1,683 | 791 | 424 | 1,460 | 6,934 | 8,015 | 7,331 | 7,035 | 5,342 | — |
| Claims on Public Nonfin. Corps | 22c | 18,502 | 29,847 | 28,279 | 37,600 | 31,487 | 146,348 | 822,544 | 897,205 | 915,418 | 895,980 | 944,804 | 316,279 |
| Claims on Private Sector | 22d | 1,560,721 | 2,708,285 | 4,879,463 | 7,573,464 | 7,969,430 | 8,549,057 | 8,571,990 | 9,923,458 | 11,126,636 | 12,550,141 | 13,296,617 | 13,902,782 |
| Liabilities to Central Bank | 26g | 39,592 | 15,068 | 8,786 | 2,406 | 19,628 | 3,312 | 468,588 | 430,937 | 563,637 | 555,121 | 778,173 | 30,204 |
| Transf.Dep.Included in Broad Money | 24 | 373,288 | 523,838 | 883,537 | 924,610 | 1,149,313 | 1,812,653 | 2,067,940 | 2,761,632 | 2,600,105 | 2,635,936 | 2,971,137 | 3,785,499 |
| Other Dep.Included in Broad Money | 25 | 782,354 | 1,112,448 | 2,169,478 | 2,901,362 | 3,437,636 | 4,106,883 | 4,684,117 | 5,054,761 | 5,863,935 | 7,203,022 | 8,162,574 | 11,692,290 |
| Sec.Ot.th.Shares Incl.in Brd. Money | 26a | — | — | — | — | — | — | — | — | — | — | — | — |
| Deposits Excl. from Broad Money | 26b | — | — | — | — | — | — | — | — | — | — | — | — |
| Sec.Ot.th.Shares Excl.f/Brd.Money | 26s | 31,097 | 149,280 | 272,628 | 268,737 | 310,716 | 404,292 | 268,111 | 307,948 | 311,664 | 447,675 | 631,459 | 1,176,630 |
| Loans | 26l | 82,057 | 48,158 | 221,777 | 150,542 | 268,189 | 720,361 | 225,787 | 297,603 | 522,907 | 473,203 | 736,245 | 795,806 |
| Financial Derivatives | 26m | 10 | 1 | 154 | 3,204 | 15,452 | 6,737 | 25,839 | 7,248 | 52,624 | 95,578 | 8,063 | 242,191 |
| Insurance Technical Reserves | 26r | — | — | — | — | — | — | — | — | — | — | — | — |
| Shares and Other Equity | 27a | 405,326 | 642,169 | 1,185,445 | 1,979,040 | 2,533,984 | 3,098,818 | 4,558,191 | 5,259,105 | 6,143,399 | 2,128,861 | 2,424,421 | 2,589,790 |
| Other Items (Net) | 27r | −28,531 | −25,425 | −104,990 | −51,251 | −146,590 | 5,259 | −182,139 | −288,896 | −395,324 | 4,912,558 | 3,895,898 | 1,998,464 |
| Memo Item: | | | | | | | | | | | | | |
| Total Assets | 20ra | 2,819,553 | 4,717,743 | 9,167,862 | 12,206,880 | 12,958,178 | 15,610,703 | 15,266,192 | 16,764,243 | 18,015,318 | 20,706,619 | 22,435,538 | 25,759,688 |

| | | 2004 | 2005 | 2006 | 2007 | 2008 | 2009 | 2010 | 2011 | 2012 | 2013 | 2014 | 2015 |
|---|---|---|---|---|---|---|---|---|---|---|---|---|---|
| **Depository Corporations** | | | | | | *Millions of Tenge: End of Period* | | | | | | | |
| Net Foreign Assets | 31n | 735,014 | 119,637 | 507,596 | −553,813 | 810,810 | 2,820,954 | 4,498,939 | 5,286,882 | 5,795,337 | 6,696,952 | 7,583,478 | 9,631,446 |
| Claims on Nonresidents | 31 | 1,708,622 | 2,149,761 | 4,551,207 | 4,898,093 | 5,450,905 | 7,039,339 | 7,262,863 | 7,653,322 | 7,497,593 | 8,123,589 | 9,137,848 | 11,869,442 |
| Liabilities to Nonresidents | 36c | 973,608 | 2,030,125 | 4,043,611 | 5,451,906 | 4,640,095 | 4,218,384 | 2,763,924 | 2,366,440 | 1,702,256 | 1,426,637 | 1,554,370 | 2,237,996 |
| Domestic Claims | 32 | 1,705,288 | 2,958,041 | 5,103,245 | 7,777,820 | 8,694,782 | 9,285,286 | 9,906,144 | 11,109,657 | 12,481,926 | 13,785,631 | 14,307,466 | 17,256,810 |
| Net Claims on Central Government | 32an | 49,079 | 82,168 | −126,100 | −134,049 | 222,899 | −72,335 | 17,176 | −197,114 | −188,391 | −481,405 | −768,438 | −1,490,990 |
| Claims on Central Government | 32a | 130,695 | 134,924 | 154,532 | 166,120 | 319,107 | 293,948 | 447,922 | 518,925 | 690,635 | 913,423 | 1,205,572 | 1,202,113 |
| Liabilities to Central Government | 36d | 81,617 | 52,755 | 280,631 | 300,169 | 96,208 | 366,283 | 430,747 | 716,039 | 879,026 | 1,394,828 | 1,974,010 | 2,693,103 |
| Claims on Other Sectors | 32s | 1,656,209 | 2,875,873 | 5,229,344 | 7,911,869 | 8,471,883 | 9,357,622 | 9,888,969 | 11,306,771 | 12,670,317 | 14,267,036 | 15,075,904 | 18,747,800 |
| Claims on Other Financial Corps. | 32g | 65,518 | 117,238 | 313,604 | 293,514 | 463,988 | 470,344 | 477,059 | 461,879 | 547,208 | 740,651 | 751,168 | 3,704,801 |
| Claims on State & Local Govts | 32b | 3,360 | 2,676 | 1,683 | 791 | 424 | 1,460 | 6,934 | 8,015 | 7,331 | 7,035 | 5,342 | — |
| Claims on Public Nonfin. Corps. | 32c | 26,267 | 47,209 | 33,534 | 43,703 | 37,611 | 336,087 | 832,368 | 911,129 | 986,431 | 967,674 | 1,017,419 | 1,138,797 |
| Claims on Private Sector | 32d | 1,561,064 | 2,708,750 | 4,880,523 | 7,573,860 | 7,969,861 | 8,549,731 | 8,572,607 | 9,925,748 | 11,129,347 | 12,551,677 | 13,301,975 | 13,904,203 |
| Broad Money Liabilities | 35l | 1,650,115 | 2,065,348 | 3,677,561 | 4,629,829 | 6,267,201 | 7,487,306 | 8,482,828 | 9,752,236 | 10,522,812 | 11,598,118 | 12,816,554 | 17,207,454 |
| Currency Outside Depository Corps | 34a | 379,273 | 411,813 | 600,832 | 739,687 | 857,842 | 913,443 | 1,148,489 | 1,365,698 | 1,528,077 | 1,512,261 | 1,122,319 | 1,236,973 |
| Transferable Deposits | 34 | 376,117 | 531,028 | 900,667 | 961,207 | 1,359,522 | 2,266,473 | 2,612,523 | 3,324,220 | 3,059,781 | 2,857,373 | 3,504,732 | 4,206,621 |
| Other Deposits | 35 | 894,726 | 1,122,508 | 2,176,062 | 2,928,936 | 4,049,837 | 4,307,390 | 4,721,817 | 5,062,317 | 5,934,954 | 7,228,485 | 8,189,503 | 11,763,860 |
| Securities Other than Shares | 36a | — | — | — | — | — | — | — | — | — | — | — | — |
| Deposits Excl. from Broad Money | 36b | — | — | — | — | — | — | — | — | — | — | — | — |
| Sec.Ot.th.Shares Excl.f/Brd.Money | 36s | 31,097 | 149,280 | 272,628 | 268,737 | 310,716 | 404,292 | 268,111 | 307,948 | 311,664 | 447,675 | 631,459 | 1,531,682 |
| Loans | 36l | 82,057 | 48,158 | 221,777 | 150,542 | 268,189 | 720,361 | 225,787 | 297,603 | 522,907 | 473,203 | 736,245 | 795,906 |
| Financial Derivatives | 36m | 10 | 1 | 154 | 3,204 | 15,525 | 6,737 | 25,839 | 7,248 | 52,624 | 95,578 | 8,063 | 291,990 |
| Insurance Technical Reserves | 36r | — | — | — | — | — | — | — | — | — | — | — | — |
| Shares and Other Equity | 37a | 495,010 | 739,815 | 1,329,224 | 2,205,934 | 2,776,965 | 3,787,587 | 5,359,742 | 6,159,861 | 7,204,278 | 2,987,257 | 3,794,128 | 5,206,263 |
| Other Items (Net) | 37r | 182,011 | 75,074 | 109,497 | −34,239 | −133,003 | −300,042 | 42,776 | −128,356 | −337,024 | 4,880,753 | 3,904,495 | 1,854,962 |
| Broad Money Liabs., Seasonally Adj. | 35l.b | 1,618,684 | 2,028,035 | 3,624,442 | 4,584,552 | 6,250,015 | 7,514,227 | 8,565,268 | 9,881,045 | 10,673,166 | 11,753,371 | 12,971,019 | 17,409,597 |
| **Other Financial Corporations** | | | | | | *Millions of Tenge: End of Period* | | | | | | | |
| Net Foreign Assets | 41n | .... | .... | .... | .... | .... | .... | .... | .... | .... | .... | .... | −917,041.00 |
| Claims on Nonresidents | 41 | .... | .... | .... | .... | .... | .... | .... | .... | .... | .... | .... | 562,116.30 |
| Liabilities to Nonresidents | 46c | .... | .... | .... | .... | .... | .... | .... | .... | .... | .... | .... | 1,479,157.30 |
| Claims on Depository Corporations | 40 | .... | .... | .... | .... | .... | .... | .... | .... | .... | .... | .... | 3,077,113.20 |
| Net Claims on Central Government | 42an | .... | .... | .... | .... | .... | .... | .... | .... | .... | .... | .... | 2,660,650.20 |
| Claims on Central Government | 42a | .... | .... | .... | .... | .... | .... | .... | .... | .... | .... | .... | 2,683,208.59 |
| Liabilities to Central Government | 46d | .... | .... | .... | .... | .... | .... | .... | .... | .... | .... | .... | 22,558.40 |
| Claims on Other Sectors | 42s | .... | .... | .... | .... | .... | .... | .... | .... | .... | .... | .... | 2,123,878.03 |
| Claims on State & Local Govts | 42b | .... | .... | .... | .... | .... | .... | .... | .... | .... | .... | .... | 18.32 |
| Claims on Public Nonfin. Corps. | 42c | .... | .... | .... | .... | .... | .... | .... | .... | .... | .... | .... | 602,786.24 |
| Claims on Private Sector | 42d | .... | .... | .... | .... | .... | .... | .... | .... | .... | .... | .... | 1,521,073.47 |
| Deposits | 46b | .... | .... | .... | .... | .... | .... | .... | .... | .... | .... | .... | 44,454.12 |
| Securities Other than Shares | 46s | .... | .... | .... | .... | .... | .... | .... | .... | .... | .... | .... | 25,482.22 |
| Loans | 46l | .... | .... | .... | .... | .... | .... | .... | .... | .... | .... | .... | 211,110.29 |
| Financial Derivatives | 46m | .... | .... | .... | .... | .... | .... | .... | .... | .... | .... | .... | 33.66 |
| Insurance Technical Reserves | 46r | .... | .... | .... | .... | .... | .... | .... | .... | .... | .... | .... | 6,147,709.74 |
| Shares and Other Equity | 47a | .... | .... | .... | .... | .... | .... | .... | .... | .... | .... | .... | 885,639.45 |
| Other Items (Net) | 47r | .... | .... | .... | .... | .... | .... | .... | .... | .... | .... | .... | −369,829.05 |
| Memo Item: | | | | | | | | | | | | | |
| Total Assets | 40ra | .... | .... | .... | .... | .... | .... | .... | .... | .... | .... | .... | 9,151,659.13 |
| **Financial Corporations** | | | | | | *Millions of Tenge: End of Period* | | | | | | | |
| Net Foreign Assets | 51n | .... | .... | .... | .... | .... | .... | .... | .... | .... | .... | .... | 8,714,405.13 |
| Claims on Nonresidents | 51 | .... | .... | .... | .... | .... | .... | .... | .... | .... | .... | .... | 12,431,558.73 |
| Liabilities to Nonresidents | 56c | .... | .... | .... | .... | .... | .... | .... | .... | .... | .... | .... | 3,717,153.60 |
| Domestic Claims | 52 | .... | .... | .... | .... | .... | .... | .... | .... | .... | .... | .... | 18,336,537.58 |
| Net Claims on Central Government | 52an | .... | .... | .... | .... | .... | .... | .... | .... | .... | .... | .... | 1,169,660.06 |
| Claims on Central Government | 52a | .... | .... | .... | .... | .... | .... | .... | .... | .... | .... | .... | 3,885,321.11 |
| Liabilities to Central Government | 56d | .... | .... | .... | .... | .... | .... | .... | .... | .... | .... | .... | 2,715,661.05 |
| Claims on Other Sectors | 52s | .... | .... | .... | .... | .... | .... | .... | .... | .... | .... | .... | 17,166,877.52 |
| Claims on State & Local Govts | 52b | .... | .... | .... | .... | .... | .... | .... | .... | .... | .... | .... | 18.33 |
| Claims on Pub. Nonfin. Corps. | 52c | .... | .... | .... | .... | .... | .... | .... | .... | .... | .... | .... | 1,741,583.09 |
| Claims on Private Sector | 52d | .... | .... | .... | .... | .... | .... | .... | .... | .... | .... | .... | 15,425,276.10 |
| Currency Outside Fin. Corporations | 54a | .... | .... | .... | .... | .... | .... | .... | .... | .... | .... | .... | 1,236,032.63 |
| Deposits | 55l | .... | .... | .... | .... | .... | .... | .... | .... | .... | .... | .... | 14,120,447.66 |
| Securities Other than Shares | 56a | .... | .... | .... | .... | .... | .... | .... | .... | .... | .... | .... | 43,433.56 |
| Loans | 56l | .... | .... | .... | .... | .... | .... | .... | .... | .... | .... | .... | 404,255.53 |
| Financial Derivatives | 56m | .... | .... | .... | .... | .... | .... | .... | .... | .... | .... | .... | 10,508.68 |
| Insurance Technical Reserves | 56r | .... | .... | .... | .... | .... | .... | .... | .... | .... | .... | .... | 6,142,344.40 |
| Shares and Other Equity | 57a | .... | .... | .... | .... | .... | .... | .... | .... | .... | .... | .... | 6,091,902.00 |
| Other Items (Net) | 57r | .... | .... | .... | .... | .... | .... | .... | .... | .... | .... | .... | −997,981.77 |
| **Monetary Aggregates** | | | | | | *Millions of Tenge: End of Period* | | | | | | | |
| Broad Money | 59m | 1,650,115 | 2,065,348 | 3,677,561 | 4,629,829 | 6,267,201 | 7,487,306 | 8,482,828 | 9,752,236 | 10,522,812 | 11,598,118 | 12,816,554 | 17,207,454 |
| o/w:Currency Issued by Cent.Govt | 59m.a | — | — | — | — | — | — | — | — | — | — | — | — |
| o/w: Dep.in Nonfin. Corporations | 59m.b | — | — | — | — | — | — | — | — | — | — | — | — |
| o/w:Secs. Issued by Central Govt. | 59m.c | — | — | — | — | — | — | — | — | — | — | — | — |
| Money (National Definitions) | | | | | | | | | | | | | |
| M1 | 59ma | 680,632 | 799,440 | 1,281,549 | 1,532,688 | 1,946,604 | 2,457,677 | 3,116,049 | 3,844,996 | 3,880,611 | 3,518,418 | 2,980,974 | 3,032,362 |
| M2 | 59mb | 1,175,491 | 1,515,970 | 2,814,551 | 3,553,643 | 4,619,524 | 5,335,204 | 6,570,099 | 7,967,502 | 8,546,937 | 8,677,614 | 7,967,715 | 8,600,161 |
| M3 | 59mc | 1,650,146 | 2,065,348 | 3,677,561 | 4,629,829 | 6,267,201 | 7,487,306 | 8,482,828 | 9,752,236 | 10,522,812 | 11,598,118 | 12,816,554 | 17,207,454 |
| **Interest Rates** | | | | | | *Percent Per Annum* | | | | | | | |
| Central Bank Policy Rate (EOP) | 60 | .... | 8.00 | 9.00 | 11.00 | 10.50 | 7.00 | 7.00 | 7.50 | 5.50 | 5.50 | 5.50 | 16.00 |
| Refinancing Rate (End of Period) | 60.b | 7.00 | 8.00 | 9.00 | 11.00 | 10.50 | 7.00 | 7.00 | 7.50 | 5.50 | 5.50 | 5.50 | 5.50 |
| Treasury Bill Rate | 60c | 3.28 | 3.28 | 3.28 | 7.01 | .... | .... | .... | .... | .... | .... | .... | .... |

# Kazakhstan 916

| | | 2004 | 2005 | 2006 | 2007 | 2008 | 2009 | 2010 | 2011 | 2012 | 2013 | 2014 | 2015 |
|---|---|---|---|---|---|---|---|---|---|---|---|---|---|
| **Prices and Labor** | | | | | | *Index Numbers (2010=100): Period Averages* | | | | | | | |
| Producer Prices | 63 | 46.1 | 57.0 | 67.5 | † 74.9 | 102.5 | 79.9 | 100.0 | 127.2 | 131.7 | 131.3 | 143.7 | 114.2 |
| Consumer Prices | 64 | 57.4 | 61.7 | 67.0 | 74.3 | 87.0 | 93.4 | 100.0 | 108.3 | 113.9 | 120.5 | 128.6 | 137.2 |
| Wages: Monthly Earnings | 65 | 36.5 | 43.8 | 52.8 | 67.6 | 78.5 | 87.1 | 100.0 | 115.9 | 131.6 | 140.4 | .... | 162.3 |
| Total Employment | 67 | 96.4 | 100.0 | .... | .... | .... | .... | .... | .... | .... | .... | .... | .... |
| | | | | | | *Number in Thousands: Period Averages* | | | | | | | |
| Employment | 67e | 7,166 | 7,244 | 7,404 | 7,632 | 7,855 | 7,905 | 8,115 | 8,283 | 8,507 | 8,580 | 8,652 | 8,542 |
| Unemployment | 67c | 657 | 639 | 625 | 598 | 558 | 555 | 497 | 472 | 475 | 470 | 461 | 448 |
| Unemployment Rate (%) | 67r | 8.4 | 8.1 | 7.8 | 7.3 | 6.6 | 6.6 | 5.8 | 5.4 | 5.3 | 5.2 | 5.1 | 5.0 |
| **Intl. Transactions & Positions** | | | | | | *Millions of US Dollars* | | | | | | | |
| Exports | 70..d | 20,603.0 | 28,301.0 | 38,762.0 | 48,351.0 | 71,971.0 | 43,195.8 | 57,243.9 | 83,315.9 | 88,575.4 | 81,911.5 | 79,117.4 | 45,722.1 |
| Imports, c.i.f. | 71..d | 13,818.0 | 17,979.0 | 24,120.0 | 33,260.0 | 38,452.0 | 28,408.7 | 24,023.5 | 29,999.9 | 35,307.2 | 45,966.4 | 41,202.0 | 30,179.3 |
| **Balance of Payments** | | | | | | *Millions of US Dollars* | | | | | | | |
| A. Current Account* | 109bx | 335.4 | −1,036.0 | −1,999.9 | −8,372.3 | 6,250.1 | −4,120.8 | 1,385.7 | 10,198.6 | 1,057.7 | 926.6 | 4,643.5 | .... |
| Goods, credit (exports) | 1a9cx | 20,595.7 | 28,299.2 | 38,761.4 | 48,348.1 | 71,964.2 | 43,923.4 | 61,391.7 | 85,193.9 | 86,931.1 | 85,595.4 | 79,060.3 | .... |
| Goods, debit (imports) | 1a9dx | 13,804.9 | 17,937.7 | 24,069.7 | 33,121.9 | 38,352.2 | 28,919.5 | 32,891.5 | 40,349.8 | 48,785.8 | 50,803.2 | 43,429.0 | .... |
| Balance on goods | 1a9bx | 6,790.8 | 10,361.5 | 14,691.7 | 15,226.2 | 33,612.0 | 15,003.9 | 28,500.2 | 44,844.1 | 38,145.2 | 34,792.3 | 35,631.3 | .... |
| Services, credit (exports) | 1b9cx | 1,874.1 | 2,087.3 | 2,676.9 | 3,424.8 | 4,292.4 | 4,103.7 | 4,119.0 | 4,337.7 | 4,828.2 | 5,120.3 | 6,348.1 | .... |
| Services, debit (imports) | 1b9dx | 5,120.7 | 7,521.3 | 8,811.1 | 11,868.1 | 11,218.9 | 10,081.7 | 11,368.5 | 10,972.9 | 12,758.1 | 12,214.9 | 12,783.3 | .... |
| Balance on Goods & Services | 1z9bx | 3,544.2 | 4,927.6 | 8,557.5 | 6,783.0 | 26,685.5 | 9,025.9 | 21,250.6 | 38,208.8 | 30,215.3 | 27,697.6 | 29,196.1 | .... |
| Primary income: credit | 1c9cx | 602.7 | 993.4 | 1,776.4 | 3,815.1 | 3,740.2 | 3,178.1 | 2,701.3 | 2,232.0 | 2,089.6 | 2,320.4 | 2,027.0 | .... |
| Primary income: debit | 1c9dx | 3,323.3 | 6,549.0 | 11,126.5 | 16,760.8 | 23,115.6 | 15,595.6 | 22,076.9 | 29,977.1 | 30,206.6 | 27,464.9 | 24,887.2 | .... |
| Balance on gds, serv. & prim. inc. | 1y9bx | 823.6 | −628.0 | −792.5 | −6,162.7 | 7,310.2 | −3,391.6 | 1,875.0 | 10,463.8 | 2,098.3 | 2,553.1 | 6,335.9 | .... |
| Secondary income: credit | 1d9ca | 352.9 | 810.0 | 898.3 | 850.8 | 1,028.2 | 945.9 | 1,459.3 | 2,745.9 | 2,628.5 | 2,721.2 | 2,227.7 | .... |
| Secondary income: debit | 1d9da | 841.1 | 1,218.0 | 2,105.7 | 3,060.4 | 2,088.2 | 1,675.1 | 1,948.6 | 3,011.1 | 3,669.1 | 4,347.6 | 3,920.1 | .... |
| B. Capital Account* | 209ba | 4.5 | 4.5 | 30.8 | 35.8 | 19.3 | 31.4 | 7,898.0 | 31.8 | 15.4 | −6.4 | 31.1 | .... |
| Capital account: credit | 209ca | 4.6 | 4.5 | 30.8 | 36.3 | 19.5 | 31.8 | 7,903.2 | 33.9 | 32.4 | 7.1 | 36.7 | .... |
| Capital account: debit | 209da | .1 | — | — | .5 | .2 | .4 | 5.2 | 2.1 | 17.0 | 13.5 | 5.6 | .... |
| Balance on current & capital acct. | 129ba | 339.9 | −1,031.5 | −1,969.1 | −8,336.5 | 6,269.4 | −4,089.4 | 9,283.7 | 10,230.4 | 1,073.1 | 920.2 | 4,674.6 | .... |
| C. Financial Account* | 309na | −4,700.7 | 2,293.8 | −11,803.4 | −1,993.6 | 1,680.5 | −3,915.1 | 10,631.8 | 9,531.1 | 4,319.3 | −338.4 | −7,362.2 | .... |
| Direct investment: assets | 3a9aa | 179.1 | 427.0 | 921.8 | 3,942.3 | 3,704.1 | 4,192.6 | 3,790.9 | 5,177.6 | 1,792.3 | 2,012.4 | 1,660.0 | .... |
| Equity & investment fund shares | 3aaaa | 96.5 | 104.8 | 830.9 | 2,167.9 | 4,112.0 | 1,809.6 | 6,271.3 | 4,503.8 | 2,347.7 | 2,109.7 | 155.9 | .... |
| Debt instruments | 3abaa | 82.6 | 322.2 | 90.9 | 1,774.4 | −407.8 | 2,383.0 | −2,480.4 | 673.8 | −555.5 | −97.2 | 1,504.1 | .... |
| Direct investment: liabilities | 3a9la | 5,615.3 | 2,546.1 | 7,611.2 | 11,972.8 | 16,818.9 | 14,275.9 | 7,456.1 | 13,760.3 | 13,648.1 | 9,946.8 | 7,597.7 | .... |
| Equity & investment fund shares | 3aala | 909.4 | 236.7 | 1,374.9 | 7,321.6 | 6,949.3 | 4,183.4 | 4,162.4 | 5,906.6 | 7,116.6 | 4,818.0 | 5,126.0 | .... |
| Debt instruments | 3abla | 4,705.9 | 2,309.4 | 6,236.2 | 4,651.2 | 9,869.6 | 10,092.4 | 3,293.7 | 7,853.7 | 6,531.6 | 5,128.7 | 2,471.7 | .... |
| Portfolio investment: assets | 3b9aa | 1,092.1 | 5,157.1 | 9,176.7 | 4,101.3 | 7,277.6 | −1,868.8 | 7,202.1 | 13,590.3 | 15,068.2 | 8,503.0 | 6,238.2 | .... |
| Equity & investment fund shares | 3baaa | 362.8 | 423.8 | 1,847.4 | 1,531.6 | −593.5 | 619.6 | 832.9 | 500.0 | 1,420.2 | 2,604.0 | 518.6 | .... |
| Debt securities | 3bbaa | 729.3 | 4,733.3 | 7,329.3 | 2,569.7 | 7,871.1 | −2,488.3 | 6,369.2 | 13,090.3 | 13,648.0 | 5,899.0 | 5,719.6 | .... |
| Portfolio investment: liabilities | 3b9la | 675.0 | 1,204.4 | 4,675.4 | −481.8 | −2,099.9 | 1,224.3 | 15,672.4 | 722.1 | −2,319.7 | 2,469.4 | 5,434.9 | .... |
| Equity & investment fund shares | 3bala | −12.8 | 149.7 | 2,788.9 | 828.3 | −1,280.4 | 37.8 | 133.9 | 7.9 | −418.2 | 65.4 | −135.2 | .... |
| Debt securities | 3bbla | 687.7 | 1,054.7 | 1,886.5 | −1,310.2 | −819.5 | 1,186.5 | 15,538.4 | 714.2 | −1,901.5 | 2,404.0 | 5,570.2 | .... |
| Fin. der.& empl.stk.ops.(ESOs): net | 3c9na | 46.4 | 112.6 | 67.8 | 369.1 | −163.7 | −66.2 | 3.9 | −126.7 | 108.9 | 103.7 | −37.1 | .... |
| Fin. der. & ESOs.: assets | 3c9aa | 52.3 | 152.9 | 91.6 | 615.3 | 364.4 | −369.8 | −262.0 | −226.2 | −63.2 | −4.5 | −18.7 | .... |
| Fin. der. & ESOs.: liabilities | 3c9la | 5.9 | 40.2 | 23.8 | 246.2 | 528.1 | −303.7 | −265.8 | −99.5 | −172.1 | −108.2 | 18.4 | .... |
| Other investment: assets | 3d9aa | 4,534.4 | 7,521.4 | 12,424.6 | 18,214.5 | 6,909.6 | 4,555.9 | 9,296.9 | 7,044.6 | 5,820.9 | 8,578.7 | 1,717.3 | .... |
| Other equity | 3daaa | .... | 3.7 | 217.3 | 193.7 | 96.8 | 104.3 | 4.5 | 8.2 | 14.7 | 215.2 | 200.1 | .... |
| Debt instruments | 3dzaa | 4,534.4 | 7,517.7 | 12,207.2 | 18,020.8 | 6,812.8 | 4,451.5 | 9,292.4 | 7,036.3 | 5,806.2 | 8,363.5 | 1,517.2 | .... |
| Other investment: liabilities | 3d9la | 4,262.5 | 7,173.8 | 22,107.7 | 17,129.8 | 1,328.1 | −4,771.6 | −13,466.6 | 1,672.3 | 7,142.6 | 7,120.1 | 3,908.0 | .... |
| Other equity | 3dala | .... | .... | .... | .... | .... | .... | .... | .... | .... | 20.1 | −17.1 | .... |
| Debt instruments | 3dzla | 4,262.5 | 7,173.8 | 22,107.7 | 17,129.8 | 1,328.1 | −4,771.6 | −13,466.6 | 1,672.3 | 7,142.6 | 7,100.1 | 3,925.1 | .... |
| Curr.+ cap.– finan. acct. balance | 4y9na | 5,040.7 | −3,325.3 | 9,834.3 | −6,342.9 | 4,588.9 | −174.3 | −1,348.1 | 699.3 | −3,246.1 | 1,258.6 | 12,036.8 | .... |
| D. Net Errors and Omissions | 409na | −1,041.7 | 1,381.5 | 1,240.3 | 3,314.2 | −2,423.7 | 2,638.2 | 6,054.4 | −398.9 | −1,060.3 | −3,638.4 | −8,117.0 | .... |
| E. Reserves and Related Items | 4z9na | 3,999.0 | −1,943.8 | 11,074.6 | −3,028.7 | 2,165.2 | 2,463.9 | 4,706.4 | 300.4 | −4,306.5 | −2,379.7 | 3,919.8 | .... |
| Reserve assets | 3e9aa | 3,999.0 | −1,943.8 | 11,074.6 | −3,028.7 | 2,165.2 | 2,463.9 | 4,706.4 | 300.4 | −4,306.5 | −2,379.7 | 3,919.8 | .... |
| Credit and loans from the IMF | 3dcla | — | — | — | — | — | — | — | — | — | — | — | .... |
| Exceptional financing | 409la | — | — | — | — | — | — | — | — | — | — | — | .... |

*Excludes components in group E

| | | 2004 | 2005 | 2006 | 2007 | 2008 | 2009 | 2010 | 2011 | 2012 | 2013 | 2014 | 2015 |
|---|---|---|---|---|---|---|---|---|---|---|---|---|---|
| **International Investment Position** | | | | | | *Millions of US Dollars* | | | | | | | |
| Assets | 809aa | 24,978.2 | 32,722.5 | 63,326.9 | 82,428.7 | 98,662.7 | 104,039.9 | 120,221.8 | 145,535.2 | 162,809.3 | 176,789.5 | 178,668.7 | .... |
| Direct investment | 8a9aa | 986.3 | 1,400.8 | 2,857.0 | 6,873.3 | 9,055.0 | 14,008.7 | 19,294.0 | 27,805.3 | 28,229.9 | 28,841.5 | 30,555.3 | .... |
| Equity & investment fund shares | 8aaaa | 577.4 | 680.8 | 2,012.2 | 4,166.6 | 8,131.4 | 10,692.0 | 18,443.4 | 24,726.5 | 25,560.3 | 26,360.5 | 26,055.6 | .... |
| Debt instruments | 8abaa | 408.9 | 720.0 | 844.8 | 2,706.6 | 923.6 | 3,316.7 | 850.6 | 3,078.8 | 2,669.6 | 2,481.0 | 4,499.7 | .... |
| Portfolio investment | 8b9aa | 5,903.3 | 10,962.2 | 20,104.8 | 24,842.0 | 31,591.1 | 28,076.2 | 33,989.4 | 47,095.1 | 62,811.8 | 72,797.6 | 76,849.3 | .... |
| Equity & investment fund shares | 8baaa | 1,075.2 | 1,512.7 | 3,271.1 | 4,901.2 | 3,491.7 | 4,400.2 | 5,143.1 | 5,246.6 | 7,047.9 | 11,234.9 | 11,668.6 | .... |
| Debt securities | 8bbaa | 4,828.1 | 9,449.5 | 16,833.6 | 19,940.8 | 28,099.4 | 23,676.1 | 28,846.3 | 41,848.5 | 55,763.9 | 61,562.7 | 65,180.8 | .... |
| Fin. der.(oth.than reserves) & ESOs | 8c9aa | 15.2 | 164.3 | 258.1 | 865.4 | 1,296.9 | 581.6 | 213.7 | 116.9 | 136.7 | 161.7 | 96.0 | .... |
| Other investment | 8d9aa | 8,792.9 | 13,125.5 | 20,980.0 | 32,218.7 | 36,871.1 | 38,296.9 | 38,479.1 | 41,216.6 | 43,362.1 | 50,273.5 | 42,294.5 | .... |
| Other equity | 8daaa | .... | 3.7 | 221.0 | 414.8 | 511.6 | 615.9 | 620.4 | 628.6 | 645.0 | 860.2 | 1,158.2 | .... |
| Debt instruments | 8dzaa | 8,792.9 | 13,121.8 | 20,759.0 | 31,803.9 | 36,359.5 | 37,680.9 | 37,858.7 | 40,588.0 | 42,717.1 | 49,413.3 | 41,136.3 | .... |
| Reserve assets | 8e9aa | 9,280.5 | 7,069.7 | 19,127.1 | 17,629.3 | 19,848.6 | 23,076.6 | 28,245.6 | 29,301.2 | 28,268.8 | 24,715.2 | 28,873.6 | .... |
| Liabilities | 809la | 40,680.4 | 52,996.1 | 92,285.3 | 126,736.1 | 137,493.1 | 147,064.1 | 155,783.9 | 178,352.4 | 198,151.6 | 210,082.5 | 213,863.8 | .... |
| Direct investment | 8a9la | 24,334.5 | 28,152.0 | 36,773.8 | 49,399.0 | 64,923.1 | 78,771.4 | 85,730.2 | 112,457.9 | 125,245.7 | 130,550.9 | 132,599.7 | .... |
| Equity & investment fund shares | 8aala | 7,659.5 | 8,930.1 | 11,260.8 | 19,318.4 | 24,724.3 | 29,139.4 | 33,455.4 | 49,881.7 | 57,637.4 | 56,620.7 | 53,398.5 | .... |
| Debt instruments | 8abla | 16,675.0 | 19,222.0 | 25,513.0 | 30,080.6 | 40,198.8 | 49,632.0 | 52,274.7 | 62,576.2 | 67,608.3 | 73,930.2 | 79,201.2 | .... |
| Portfolio investment | 8b9la | 1,310.8 | 2,721.1 | 11,142.1 | 14,313.3 | 7,077.6 | 8,568.1 | 23,790.2 | 21,036.8 | 21,199.6 | 22,144.8 | 25,753.6 | .... |
| Equity & investment fund shares | 8bala | 291.5 | 593.2 | 6,942.5 | 10,212.2 | 3,923.4 | 4,486.2 | 3,761.3 | 2,814.6 | 3,415.6 | 3,414.9 | 3,249.0 | .... |
| Debt securities | 8bbla | 1,019.3 | 2,127.9 | 4,199.6 | 4,101.1 | 3,154.2 | 4,081.9 | 20,028.9 | 18,222.2 | 17,783.9 | 18,729.9 | 22,504.6 | .... |
| Fin. der.(oth.than reserves) & ESOs | 8c9la | 5.6 | 44.3 | 67.9 | 312.5 | 912.0 | 569.7 | 344.4 | 333.6 | 182.0 | 89.6 | 133.7 | .... |
| Other investment | 8d9la | 15,029.5 | 22,078.7 | 44,301.5 | 62,711.3 | 64,580.4 | 59,155.0 | 45,919.1 | 44,524.0 | 51,524.4 | 57,297.2 | 55,376.8 | .... |
| Other equity | 8dala | .... | — | — | — | — | — | — | — | — | 31.9 | 25.8 | .... |
| Debt instruments | 8dzla | 15,029.5 | 22,078.7 | 44,301.5 | 62,711.3 | 64,580.4 | 59,155.0 | 45,919.1 | 44,524.0 | 51,524.4 | 57,265.2 | 55,351.0 | .... |

# Kazakhstan 916

|  |  | 2004 | 2005 | 2006 | 2007 | 2008 | 2009 | 2010 | 2011 | 2012 | 2013 | 2014 | 2015 |
|---|---|---|---|---|---|---|---|---|---|---|---|---|---|
| **Government Finance** | | | | | | | | | | | | | |
| **Cash Flow Statement** | | | | | | | | | | | | | |
| **General Government** | | | | | | *Billions of Tenge: Fiscal Year Ends December 31* | | | | | | |
| Cash Receipts:Operating Activities... | c1 | 1,286.73 | 2,111.01 | 2,353.30 | 2,890.49 | 3,977.47 | 3,469.46 | 4,238.48 | 5,320.93 | 5,760.51 | 8,753.48 | 8,773.24 | .... |
| Taxes........................................ | c11 | .... | .... | .... | .... | 2,568.29 | 1,995.84 | 2,680.25 | 3,685.49 | 3,754.37 | 7,795.04 | 8,155.15 | .... |
| Social Contributions...................... | c12 | .... | .... | .... | .... | 251.22 | 232.84 | 253.83 | 296.84 | 341.00 | 380.48 | 427.98 | .... |
| Grants....................................... | c13 | .... | .... | .... | .... | 1,073.38 | 1,105.74 | 1,200.82 | 1,200.54 | 1,380.58 | .06 | .71 | .... |
| Other Receipts........................... | c14 | .... | .... | .... | .... | 84.58 | 135.03 | 103.57 | 138.05 | 284.57 | 577.90 | 189.39 | .... |
| Cash Payments:Operating Activities. | c2 | 1,305.43 | 2,064.34 | 2,271.68 | 3,105.79 | 2,315.67 | 2,793.83 | 3,326.18 | 4,074.28 | 4,865.15 | 5,459.40 | 6,082.88 | .... |
| Compensation of Employees.......... | c21 | .... | .... | .... | .... | 467.05 | 591.01 | 681.23 | 823.55 | 948.15 | 1,040.16 | 1,107.98 | .... |
| Purchases of Goods & Services....... | c22 | .... | .... | .... | .... | 980.04 | 1,194.08 | 1,442.83 | 1,827.69 | 2,330.89 | 2,590.84 | 2,792.36 | .... |
| Interest..................................... | c24 | .... | .... | .... | .... | 61.39 | 69.04 | 94.62 | 121.68 | 130.52 | 178.03 | 232.74 | .... |
| Subsidies................................... | c25 | .... | .... | .... | .... | 87.41 | 89.45 | 117.44 | 148.59 | 193.86 | 223.21 | 311.42 | .... |
| Grants....................................... | c26 | .... | .... | .... | .... | 1.70 | 17.47 | 3.64 | 3.59 | 5.96 | 36.35 | 38.06 | .... |
| Social Benefits............................ | c27 | .... | .... | .... | .... | 583.17 | 694.65 | 835.96 | 1,061.12 | 1,156.61 | 1,278.35 | 1,476.99 | .... |
| Other Payments.......................... | c28 | .... | .... | .... | .... | 134.91 | 138.14 | 150.47 | 88.06 | 99.15 | 112.44 | 123.32 | .... |
| Net Cash Inflow:Operating Act.[1-2] | ccio | .... | .... | .... | .... | 1,661.80 | 675.63 | 912.30 | 1,246.66 | 895.36 | 3,294.08 | 2,690.36 | .... |
| Net Cash Outflow:Invest. in NFA...... | c31 | .... | .... | .... | .... | 890.46 | 904.77 | 1,066.88 | 1,288.59 | 1,351.33 | 1,341.78 | 1,642.56 | .... |
| Purchases of Nonfinancial Assets... | c31.1 | .... | .... | .... | .... | 947.40 | 940.66 | 1,127.53 | 1,338.48 | 1,403.82 | 1,399.12 | 1,717.67 | .... |
| Sales of Nonfinancial Assets.......... | c31.2 | .... | .... | .... | .... | 56.94 | 35.89 | 60.65 | 49.89 | 52.49 | 57.35 | 75.12 | .... |
| Cash Surplus/Deficit [1-2-31=1-2M] | ccsd | −18.70 | 46.66 | 81.62 | −215.30 | 771.34 | −229.15 | −154.58 | −41.94 | −455.97 | 1,952.30 | 1,047.80 | .... |
| Net Acq. Fin. Assets, excl. Cash....... | c32x | .... | .... | .... | .... | 1,104.57 | 263.55 | 372.68 | 526.68 | 434.34 | 230.95 | 616.08 | .... |
| Domestic................................... | c321x | .... | .... | .... | .... | 1,094.15 | 264.08 | 373.32 | 527.34 | 435.21 | 228.64 | 614.88 | .... |
| Foreign..................................... | c322x | .... | .... | .... | .... | 10.43 | −.53 | −.64 | −.66 | −.87 | 2.31 | 1.20 | .... |
| Net Incurrence of Liabilities............. | c33 | 18.70 | −46.66 | −81.62 | 215.30 | 309.70 | 560.37 | .... | 504.83 | 904.63 | 776.92 | 1,004.90 | .... |
| Domestic................................... | c331 | 68.06 | 66.68 | −81.65 | 264.27 | 304.70 | 468.70 | .... | 412.21 | 826.17 | 713.91 | 536.84 | .... |
| Foreign..................................... | c332 | −49.37 | −113.34 | .03 | −48.98 | 5.00 | 91.67 | .... | 92.62 | 78.46 | 63.01 | 468.06 | .... |
| Net Cash Inflow, Fin.Act.[-32x+33].. | cnfb | .... | .... | .... | .... | −794.88 | 296.82 | 219.44 | −21.85 | 470.29 | 545.96 | 388.82 | .... |
| Net Change in Stock of Cash........... | cncb | .... | .... | .... | .... | −23.54 | 67.68 | 64.86 | −63.79 | 14.32 | 2,498.66 | 1,436.62 | .... |
| Stat. Discrep. [32X-33+NCB-CSD].... | ccsdz | .... | .... | .... | .... | — | — | .... | — | — | .46 | — | .... |
| Memo Item:Cash Expenditure[2+31] | c2m | .... | .... | .... | .... | 3,206.14 | 3,698.60 | 4,393.06 | 5,362.87 | 6,216.48 | 6,801.18 | 7,725.44 | .... |
| Memo Item: Gross Debt.................. | c63 | .... | .... | .... | .... | .... | .... | 74.3 | 227.1 | 419.4 | 360.2 | 413.9 | .... |
| **National Accounts** | | | | | | *Billions of Tenge* | | | | | | | |
| Househ.Cons.Expend.,incl.NPISHs... | 96f | 3,142.46 | 3,784.44 | 4,669.90 | 5,795.44 | 7,129.39 | 8,082.51 | 9,899.99 | 11,791.86 | 13,900.65 | 17,881.17 | 19,995.21 | 21,338.95 |
| Government Consumption Expend... | 91f | 681.79 | 853.83 | 1,039.85 | 1,420.41 | 1,635.55 | 1,983.59 | 2,358.77 | 2,941.97 | 3,543.80 | 3,634.36 | 4,210.26 | 4,755.94 |
| Gross Fixed Capital Formation......... | 93e | 1,472.42 | 2,122.68 | 3,084.39 | 3,857.19 | 4,308.79 | 4,726.72 | 5,307.14 | 5,771.55 | 6,761.45 | 7,472.85 | 8,122.52 | 8,754.39 |
| Changes in Inventories................... | 93i | 72.07 | 228.11 | 378.15 | 707.92 | 106.80 | 276.01 | 228.23 | 433.09 | 752.58 | 967.44 | 1,680.01 | 2,055.00 |
| Exports of Goods and Services........ | 90c | 3,081.84 | 4,064.19 | 5,224.45 | 6,352.92 | 9,173.66 | 7,115.73 | 9,652.10 | 13,123.05 | 13,680.51 | 13,801.13 | 15,640.55 | 11,634.15 |
| Imports of Goods and Services (-)..... | 98c | 2,577.50 | 3,394.97 | 4,134.34 | 5,493.38 | 5,963.41 | 5,770.29 | 6,521.55 | 7,527.61 | 9,246.63 | 9,563.33 | 10,136.47 | 10,092.28 |
| Statistical Discrepancy.................... | 99bs | −2.95 | −67.69 | −48.66 | 209.30 | −337.87 | 593.38 | 890.84 | 2,845.87 | 2,801.39 | 2,891.70 | 1,242.74 | 2,431.83 |
| Gross Domestic Product (GDP)......... | 99b | 5,873.08 | 7,658.28 | 10,262.39 | 12,640.49 | 16,390.79 | 16,414.27 | 20,924.67 | 26,533.91 | 29,392.36 | 34,193.63 | 39,512.09 | 38,446.14 |
| Net Primary Income from Abroad..... | 98.n | −388.06 | −713.09 | −1,191.91 | −1,587.89 | −2,324.93 | −1,861.49 | −2,854.39 | −4,064.89 | −4,195.99 | −3,828.60 | .... | .... |
| Gross National Income (GNI)........... | 99a | 5,482.07 | 6,877.51 | 9,021.82 | 11,261.91 | 13,727.99 | 15,146.16 | 18,961.12 | 23,507.00 | 26,150.97 | 31,446.55 | .... | .... |
| Net Current Transf.from Abroad....... | 98t | −65.95 | −55.27 | −151.93 | −261.35 | −118.38 | −107.66 | −72.01 | −39.07 | −151.14 | −244.39 | .... | .... |
| Gross Nat'l Disposable Inc.(GNDI).... | 99i | 5,416.12 | 6,822.24 | 8,869.89 | 11,000.55 | 13,609.61 | 15,038.50 | 18,889.11 | 23,467.93 | 25,999.83 | 31,202.16 | .... | .... |
| Gross Saving................................ | 99s | 1,591.88 | 2,183.97 | 3,160.14 | 3,784.71 | 4,885.89 | 5,001.14 | 6,630.36 | 8,734.10 | 8,555.38 | 9,686.64 | .... | .... |
| Consumption of Fixed Capital......... | 99cf | 822.51 | 1,049.15 | 1,422.05 | 1,744.05 | 2,124.97 | 2,382.55 | 3,001.71 | 3,588.24 | 3,732.52 | 4,352.76 | 4,869.37 | 5,118.48 |
| GDP, Production Based.................. | 99bp | 5,870.13 | 7,590.59 | 10,213.73 | 12,849.79 | 16,052.92 | 17,007.65 | 21,815.52 | 29,379.78 | 32,193.75 | 37,085.33 | 40,754.83 | 40,877.97 |
| GDP Volume (2005=100)................ | 99bvp | 91.2 | 100.0 | 110.7 | 120.6 | 124.5 | 126.0 | .... | .... | .... | .... | .... | .... |
| GDP Deflator (2005=100)............... | 99bip | 84.1 | 100.0 | 121.1 | 136.9 | 171.9 | 171.9 | .... | .... | .... | .... | .... | .... |
| | | | | | | *Millions: Midyear Estimates* | | | | | | | |
| Population................................ | 99z | 15.29 | 15.45 | 15.60 | 15.76 | 15.92 | 16.10 | 16.31 | 16.55 | 16.82 | 17.10 | 17.37 | 17.63 |

# Kenya   664

| | | 2004 | 2005 | 2006 | 2007 | 2008 | 2009 | 2010 | 2011 | 2012 | 2013 | 2014 | 2015 |
|---|---|---|---|---|---|---|---|---|---|---|---|---|---|
| **Exchange Rates** | | | | | | *Shillings per SDR: End of Period* | | | | | | | |
| Principal Rate | aa | 120.117 | 103.432 | 104.400 | 99.042 | 119.696 | 118.862 | 124.360 | 130.603 | 132.176 | 132.917 | 131.120 | 141.776 |
| | | | | | | *Shillings per US Dollar: End of Period (ae) Period Average (rf)* | | | | | | | |
| Principal Rate | ae | 77.344 | 72.367 | 69.397 | 62.675 | 77.711 | 75.820 | 80.752 | 85.068 | 86.001 | 86.310 | 90.502 | 102.311 |
| Principal Rate | rf | 79.174 | 75.554 | 72.101 | 67.318 | 69.175 | 77.352 | 79.233 | 88.811 | 84.530 | 86.123 | 87.922 | 98.178 |
| **Fund Position** | | | | | | *Millions of SDRs: End of Period* | | | | | | | |
| Quota | 2f.s | 271.40 | 271.40 | 271.40 | 271.40 | 271.40 | 271.40 | 271.40 | 271.40 | 271.40 | 271.40 | 271.40 | 271.40 |
| SDR Holdings | 1b.s | .39 | .01 | .33 | .11 | 1.98 | 223.66 | 206.80 | 11.01 | 5.95 | 19.76 | 8.97 | 10.51 |
| Reserve Position in the Fund | 1c.s | 12.70 | 12.74 | 12.78 | 12.80 | 12.83 | 12.89 | 12.96 | 13.00 | 13.01 | 13.29 | 13.29 | 13.29 |
| Total Fund Cred.&Loans Outstg | 2tl | 66.08 | 111.09 | 101.88 | 170.16 | 163.44 | 287.42 | 270.70 | 456.54 | 581.63 | 695.47 | 656.90 | 609.76 |
| SDR Allocations | 1bd | 36.99 | 36.99 | 36.99 | 36.99 | 36.99 | 259.65 | 259.65 | 259.65 | 259.65 | 259.65 | 259.65 | 259.65 |
| **International Liquidity** | | | | | | *Millions of US Dollars Unless Otherwise Indicated: End of Period* | | | | | | | |
| Total Reserves minus Gold | 1l.d | 1,519.3 | 1,798.8 | 2,415.8 | 3,355.0 | 2,878.5 | 3,849.0 | 4,320.2 | 4,264.4 | 5,711.0 | 6,598.2 | 7,910.5 | 7,547.8 |
| SDR Holdings | 1b.d | .6 | — | .5 | .2 | 3.1 | 350.6 | 318.5 | 16.9 | 9.1 | 30.4 | 13.0 | 14.6 |
| Reserve Position in the Fund | 1c.d | 19.7 | 18.2 | 19.2 | 20.2 | 19.8 | 20.2 | 20.0 | 20.0 | 20.0 | 20.5 | 19.3 | 18.4 |
| Foreign Exchange | 1d.d | 1,499.0 | 1,780.6 | 2,396.0 | 3,334.6 | 2,855.7 | 3,478.1 | 3,981.7 | 4,227.5 | 5,681.9 | 6,547.3 | 7,878.3 | 7,514.8 |
| Gold (Million Fine Troy Ounces) | 1ad | .001 | .001 | .001 | .001 | .001 | .001 | .001 | .001 | .001 | .001 | .001 | .001 |
| Gold (National Valuation) | 1and | .2 | .2 | .3 | .4 | .4 | .5 | .8 | .9 | .7 | .7 | .7 | .6 |
| Central Bank: Other Assets | 3..d | 10.2 | 329.5 | — | — | .2 | .2 | .2 | .2 | .2 | .2 | .2 | .1 |
| Central Bank: Other Liabs | 4..d | 45.2 | 105.9 | 97.6 | 210.4 | 194.8 | 43.5 | 17.0 | 302.3 | 494.9 | 671.2 | 575.5 | 485.2 |
| Other Depository Corps.: Assets | 7a.d | 620.3 | 736.7 | 925.4 | 1,217.0 | † 1,765.4 | 1,218.0 | 1,123.6 | 1,826.7 | 1,493.4 | 1,928.0 | 1,853.7 | 2,273.5 |
| Other Depository Corps.: Liabs | 7b.d | 152.1 | 111.1 | 135.4 | 417.1 | † 995.1 | 939.9 | 904.8 | 1,398.3 | 1,936.8 | 2,452.2 | 3,061.8 | 3,564.2 |
| **Central Bank** | | | | | | *Millions of Shillings: End of Period* | | | | | | | |
| Net Foreign Assets | 11n | 104,406 | 137,635 | 152,217 | 205,183 | 198,536 | 222,366 | 251,747 | 257,852 | 366,454 | 435,383 | 592,716 | 625,025 |
| Claims on Nonresidents | 11 | 116,809 | 153,056 | 167,207 | 225,831 | 222,696 | 286,705 | 320,925 | 352,815 | 478,927 | 562,640 | 713,718 | 748,330 |
| Liabilities to Nonresidents | 16c | 12,403 | 15,421 | 14,990 | 20,648 | 24,160 | 64,339 | 69,178 | 94,963 | 112,473 | 127,257 | 121,002 | 123,305 |
| Claims on Other Depository Corps | 12e | 10,014 | 9,543 | 9,404 | 19,579 | 11,010 | 7,756 | 6,414 | 23,413 | 17,157 | 26,246 | 15,077 | 67,533 |
| Net Claims on Central Government | 12an | 12,200 | −3,343 | −16,027 | −39,115 | −9,382 | −16,289 | 10,076 | 42,773 | 9,076 | −52,467 | −121,255 | −106,559 |
| Claims on Central Government | 12a | 51,297 | 46,891 | 48,541 | 38,771 | 49,949 | 61,500 | 68,775 | 56,482 | 55,372 | 63,075 | 58,708 | 71,346 |
| Liabilities to Central Government | 16d | 39,097 | 50,234 | 64,569 | 77,885 | 59,330 | 77,789 | 58,700 | 13,709 | 46,296 | 115,542 | 179,963 | 177,905 |
| Claims on Other Sectors | 12s | 1,985 | 2,061 | 2,256 | 2,407 | 2,472 | 2,657 | 3,005 | 5,679 | 2,306 | 3,822 | 3,674 | 4,171 |
| Claims on Other Financial Corps | 12g | — | — | — | 2 | 17 | 24 | 9 | 45 | 33 | 28 | 23 | 27 |
| Claims on State & Local Govts | 12b | — | — | — | — | — | — | — | — | — | — | — | — |
| Claims on Public Nonfin. Corps | 12c | — | — | — | — | — | — | — | — | — | — | — | — |
| Claims on Private Sector | 12d | 1,985 | 2,061 | 2,256 | 2,405 | 2,456 | 2,633 | 2,996 | 5,634 | 2,273 | 3,795 | 3,651 | 4,143 |
| Monetary Base | 14 | 101,054 | 107,236 | 124,676 | 156,929 | 163,589 | 181,957 | 222,634 | 255,006 | 298,874 | 320,762 | 380,040 | 401,130 |
| Currency in Circulation | 14a | 70,962 | 76,820 | 89,326 | 115,924 | 115,731 | 124,284 | 147,209 | 172,234 | 187,737 | 209,990 | 221,930 | 240,931 |
| Liabs. to Other Depository Corps | 14c | 30,092 | 30,415 | 35,350 | 41,005 | 47,858 | 57,673 | 75,425 | 82,771 | 111,137 | 110,773 | 158,111 | 160,199 |
| Liabilities to Other Sectors | 14d | — | — | — | — | — | — | — | — | — | — | — | — |
| Other Liabs. to Other Dep. Corps | 14n | 8,243 | 9,564 | 5,970 | 14,125 | 6,564 | 4,318 | 2,608 | 9,055 | 30,982 | 10,748 | 16,805 | 44,628 |
| Dep. & Sec. Excl. f/Monetary Base | 14o | 165 | 240 | 246 | 193 | 236 | 1,432 | 12,252 | 13,504 | 14,736 | 31,223 | 26,994 | 29,908 |
| Deposits Included in Broad Money | 15 | 109 | 185 | 193 | 110 | 92 | 1,269 | 12,073 | 13,329 | 14,446 | 30,948 | 26,729 | 29,634 |
| Sec.Ot.th.Shares Incl.in Brd. Money | 16a | — | — | — | — | — | — | — | — | — | — | — | — |
| Deposits Excl. from Broad Money | 16b | 55 | 55 | 53 | 83 | 144 | 162 | 179 | 175 | 290 | 275 | 265 | 275 |
| Sec.Ot.th.Shares Excl.f/Brd.Money | 16s | — | — | — | — | — | — | — | — | — | — | — | — |
| Loans | 16l | — | — | — | — | — | — | — | — | — | — | — | — |
| Financial Derivatives | 16m | — | — | — | — | — | — | — | — | — | — | — | — |
| Shares and Other Equity | 17a | 12,560 | 18,137 | 9,505 | 11,435 | 23,126 | 26,303 | 33,514 | 49,297 | 62,608 | 61,329 | 73,646 | 134,735 |
| Other Items (Net) | 17r | 6,583 | 10,720 | 7,452 | 5,373 | 9,121 | 2,481 | 234 | 2,855 | −12,206 | −11,076 | −7,274 | −20,230 |
| Memo Item: | | | | | | | | | | | | | |
| Total Assets | 10ra | 183,467 | 215,543 | 232,756 | 295,132 | 291,792 | 367,847 | 409,595 | 449,335 | 555,952 | 682,634 | 823,884 | 927,528 |
| **Other Depository Corporations** | | | | | | *Millions of Shillings: End of Period* | | | | | | | |
| Net Foreign Assets | 21n | 36,174 | 45,201 | 54,751 | 50,081 | † 59,855 | 21,083 | 17,665 | 36,443 | −38,147 | −45,248 | −109,454 | −132,063 |
| Claims on Nonresidents | 21 | 47,922 | 53,227 | 64,133 | 76,191 | † 137,188 | 92,346 | 90,731 | 155,390 | 128,473 | 166,405 | 167,938 | 232,600 |
| Liabilities to Nonresidents | 26c | 11,747 | 8,025 | 9,382 | 26,110 | † 77,332 | 71,262 | 73,066 | 118,947 | 166,621 | 211,652 | 277,392 | 364,663 |
| Claims on Central Bank | 20 | 45,993 | 46,463 | 53,735 | 74,616 | † 78,837 | 85,373 | 106,606 | 128,127 | 183,738 | 164,061 | 224,940 | 233,040 |
| Currency | 20a | 8,288 | 10,534 | 12,931 | 19,939 | † 21,992 | 23,434 | 24,284 | 35,251 | 39,984 | 46,810 | 48,711 | 49,968 |
| Reserve Deposits and Securities | 20b | 31,833 | 31,913 | 36,637 | 44,647 | † 52,966 | 61,923 | 82,308 | 92,876 | 135,251 | 117,092 | 170,635 | 176,080 |
| Other Claims | 20n | 5,872 | 4,017 | 4,167 | 10,030 | † 3,880 | 16 | 15 | — | 8,504 | 159 | 5,594 | 6,992 |
| Net Claims on Central Government | 22an | 102,455 | 114,821 | 140,027 | 168,314 | † 163,750 | 244,415 | 351,749 | 271,886 | 410,777 | 461,666 | 516,215 | 581,696 |
| Claims on Central Government | 22a | 113,350 | 131,766 | 160,440 | 194,651 | † 213,682 | 305,295 | 434,998 | 373,340 | 522,100 | 587,817 | 666,348 | 742,415 |
| Liabilities to Central Government | 26d | 10,894 | 16,945 | 20,414 | 26,338 | † 49,932 | 60,880 | 83,249 | 101,454 | 111,323 | 126,151 | 150,133 | 160,719 |
| Claims on Other Sectors | 22s | 385,186 | 415,388 | 469,649 | 537,314 | † 684,979 | 788,031 | 937,148 | 1,232,558 | 1,377,716 | 1,624,469 | 1,990,077 | 2,334,295 |
| Claims on Other Financial Corps | 22g | 27,581 | 32,223 | 26,464 | 27,261 | † 41,247 | 52,363 | 51,499 | 63,326 | 66,765 | 79,376 | 100,421 | 118,646 |
| Claims on State & Local Govts | 22b | 338 | 630 | 1,089 | 973 | † 1,478 | 2,107 | 3,055 | 6,389 | 6,552 | 3,548 | 278 | 1,149 |
| Claims on Public Nonfin. Corps | 22c | 11,519 | 12,587 | 18,162 | 15,707 | † 14,495 | 19,653 | 22,639 | 29,366 | 48,027 | 40,527 | 48,904 | 47,177 |
| Claims on Private Sector | 22d | 345,748 | 369,948 | 423,934 | 493,373 | † 627,760 | 713,908 | 859,954 | 1,133,478 | 1,256,372 | 1,501,018 | 1,840,475 | 2,167,323 |
| Liabilities to Central Bank | 26g | 57 | — | — | 6,155 | † — | 6,129 | 13,730 | 1,677 | 914 | 9,825 | 9,135 | 18,391 |
| Transf.Dep.Included in Broad Money | 24 | 190,647 | 208,615 | 268,563 | 348,677 | † 430,097 | 427,532 | 557,124 | 621,196 | 706,679 | 804,639 | 909,584 | 1,018,747 |
| Other Dep.Included in Broad Money | 25 | 247,677 | 275,546 | 299,065 | 330,932 | † 372,593 | 514,412 | 585,412 | 750,700 | 872,306 | 966,036 | 1,190,259 | 1,386,210 |
| Sec.Ot.th.Shares Incl.in Brd. Money | 26a | 48 | 180 | 79 | 175 | † — | — | — | — | 105 | 106 | 106 | 106 |
| Deposits Excl. from Broad Money | 26b | 1,940 | 2,916 | 6,684 | 4,724 | † 3,438 | 8,837 | 3,171 | 4,074 | 3,664 | 3,776 | 7,907 | 10,079 |
| Sec.Ot.th.Shares Excl.f/Brd.Money | 26s | — | — | — | — | † 2,965 | 2,978 | 10,007 | 7,844 | 11,870 | 12,946 | 18,140 | 17,481 |
| Loans | 26l | 5,592 | 5,031 | 2,847 | 2,752 | † 1,489 | 4,433 | 7,194 | 6,975 | 7,685 | 11,466 | 11,195 | 25,802 |
| Financial Derivatives | 26m | — | — | — | — | † 1,334 | 1,518 | 673 | 8,746 | 3,375 | 3,400 | 2,352 | 1,474 |
| Insurance Technical Reserves | 26r | — | — | — | — | † — | — | — | — | — | — | — | — |
| Shares and Other Equity | 27a | 69,361 | 82,151 | 96,321 | 130,187 | † 165,050 | 195,543 | 261,799 | 294,958 | 361,921 | 430,386 | 528,638 | 585,639 |
| Other Items (Net) | 27r | 54,486 | 47,434 | 44,603 | 6,722 | † 10,456 | −22,481 | −25,942 | −27,156 | −34,111 | −37,631 | −55,537 | −46,962 |
| Memo Item: | | | | | | | | | | | | | |
| Total Assets | 20ra | 836,790 | 942,723 | 1,039,844 | 1,254,953 | † 1,363,717 | 1,549,523 | 1,776,327 | 2,146,651 | 2,475,355 | 2,880,579 | 3,439,060 | 3,962,934 |

# Kenya   664

| | | 2004 | 2005 | 2006 | 2007 | 2008 | 2009 | 2010 | 2011 | 2012 | 2013 | 2014 | 2015 |
|---|---|---|---|---|---|---|---|---|---|---|---|---|---|
| **Depository Corporations** | | | | | | *Millions of Shillings: End of Period* | | | | | | | |
| Net Foreign Assets | 31n | 140,580 | 182,836 | 206,968 | 255,265 | † 258,391 | 243,450 | 269,412 | 294,295 | 328,307 | 390,135 | 483,262 | 492,963 |
| Claims on Nonresidents | 31 | 164,731 | 206,282 | 231,340 | 302,023 | † 359,883 | 379,050 | 411,656 | 508,204 | 607,400 | 729,044 | 881,657 | 980,931 |
| Liabilities to Nonresidents | 36c | 24,150 | 23,446 | 24,372 | 46,758 | † 101,492 | 135,601 | 142,244 | 213,910 | 279,093 | 338,909 | 398,395 | 487,968 |
| Domestic Claims | 32 | 501,826 | 528,927 | 595,905 | 668,920 | † 841,819 | 1,018,813 | 1,301,978 | 1,552,896 | 1,799,875 | 2,037,491 | 2,388,711 | 2,813,604 |
| Net Claims on Central Government | 32an | 114,655 | 111,478 | 123,999 | 129,199 | † 154,368 | 228,125 | 361,825 | 314,659 | 419,853 | 409,199 | 394,960 | 475,138 |
| Claims on Central Government | 32a | 164,647 | 178,657 | 208,982 | 233,422 | † 263,631 | 366,795 | 503,773 | 429,822 | 577,472 | 650,892 | 725,056 | 813,762 |
| Liabilities to Central Government | 36d | 49,992 | 67,179 | 84,982 | 104,223 | † 109,263 | 138,670 | 141,948 | 115,163 | 157,619 | 241,693 | 330,096 | 338,624 |
| Claims on Other Sectors | 32s | 387,170 | 417,449 | 471,905 | 539,721 | † 687,451 | 790,688 | 940,153 | 1,238,237 | 1,380,022 | 1,628,292 | 1,993,751 | 2,338,466 |
| Claims on Other Financial Corps | 32g | 27,581 | 32,223 | 26,464 | 27,263 | † 41,264 | 52,387 | 51,508 | 63,371 | 66,799 | 79,403 | 100,443 | 118,673 |
| Claims on State & Local Govts | 32b | 338 | 630 | 1,089 | 973 | † 1,478 | 2,107 | 3,055 | 6,389 | 6,552 | 3,548 | 278 | 1,149 |
| Claims on Public Nonfin. Corps | 32c | 11,519 | 12,587 | 18,162 | 15,707 | † 14,495 | 19,653 | 22,639 | 29,366 | 48,027 | 40,527 | 48,904 | 47,177 |
| Claims on Private Sector | 32d | 347,733 | 372,008 | 426,190 | 495,778 | † 630,215 | 716,541 | 862,950 | 1,139,112 | 1,258,645 | 1,504,813 | 1,844,126 | 2,171,467 |
| Broad Money Liabilities | 35l | 501,156 | 550,812 | 644,295 | 775,880 | † 896,520 | 1,044,064 | 1,277,534 | 1,522,208 | 1,741,289 | 1,964,909 | 2,299,897 | 2,625,659 |
| Currency Outside Depository Corps | 34a | 62,675 | 66,286 | 76,395 | 95,985 | † 93,739 | 100,850 | 122,925 | 136,983 | 147,753 | 163,180 | 173,219 | 190,963 |
| Transferable Deposits | 34 | 190,647 | 208,615 | 268,563 | 348,677 | † 430,097 | 427,532 | 557,124 | 621,196 | 706,679 | 804,639 | 909,584 | 1,018,747 |
| Other Deposits | 35 | 247,786 | 275,731 | 299,258 | 331,042 | † 372,685 | 515,682 | 597,485 | 764,029 | 886,752 | 996,984 | 1,216,988 | 1,415,843 |
| Securities Other than Shares | 36a | 48 | 180 | 79 | 175 | † — | — | — | — | 105 | 106 | 106 | 106 |
| Deposits Excl. from Broad Money | 36b | 1,995 | 2,971 | 6,737 | 4,807 | † 3,582 | 8,999 | 3,350 | 4,249 | 3,954 | 4,050 | 8,171 | 10,353 |
| Sec.Ot.th.Shares Excl.f/Brd.Money | 36s | — | — | — | — | † 2,965 | 2,978 | 10,007 | 7,844 | 11,870 | 12,946 | 18,140 | 17,481 |
| Loans | 36l | 5,592 | 5,031 | 2,847 | 2,752 | † 1,489 | 4,433 | 7,194 | 6,975 | 7,685 | 11,466 | 11,195 | 25,802 |
| Financial Derivatives | 36m | — | — | — | — | † 1,334 | 1,518 | 673 | 8,746 | 3,375 | 3,400 | 2,352 | 1,474 |
| Insurance Technical Reserves | 36r | — | — | — | — | † — | | | | | | | |
| Shares and Other Equity | 37a | 81,921 | 100,288 | 105,826 | 141,622 | † 188,176 | 221,847 | 295,313 | 344,256 | 424,528 | 491,715 | 602,285 | 720,374 |
| Other Items (Net) | 37r | 51,742 | 52,661 | 43,167 | −877 | † 6,144 | −21,576 | −22,682 | −47,087 | −64,519 | −60,860 | −70,066 | −94,579 |
| Broad Money Liabs., Seasonally Adj. | 35l.b | 495,860 | 546,261 | 640,071 | 771,581 | † 893,728 | 1,040,664 | 1,273,167 | 1,516,828 | 1,734,510 | 1,956,901 | 2,290,313 | 2,614,811 |
| **Monetary Aggregates** | | | | | | *Millions of Shillings: End of Period* | | | | | | | |
| Broad Money | 59m | 501,156 | 550,812 | 644,295 | 775,880 | 896,520 | 1,044,064 | 1,277,534 | 1,522,208 | 1,741,289 | 1,964,909 | 2,299,897 | 2,625,659 |
| o/w:Currency Issued by Cent.Govt | 59m.a | — | — | — | — | — | — | — | — | — | — | — | — |
| o/w: Dep.in Nonfin. Corporations | 59m.b | — | — | — | — | — | — | — | — | — | — | — | — |
| o/w: Secs. Issued by Central Govt. | 59m.c | — | — | — | — | — | — | — | — | — | — | — | — |
| Money (National Definitions) | | | | | | | | | | | | | |
| Reserve Money | 19mb | 101,054 | 107,202 | 124,676 | 156,929 | 163,589 | 181,957 | 222,634 | 255,006 | 298,874 | 320,762 | 380,040 | 392,421 |
| M1 | 59ma | 210,599 | 231,122 | 291,789 | 373,310 | 392,856 | 442,245 | 577,206 | 622,731 | 710,744 | 788,319 | 936,440 | 1,015,688 |
| M2 | 59mb | 432,567 | 474,490 | 553,907 | 666,875 | 766,471 | 898,099 | 1,099,234 | 1,253,958 | 1,469,037 | 1,632,845 | 1,981,860 | 2,226,813 |
| M3 | 59mc | 501,156 | 550,812 | 644,295 | 775,880 | 896,520 | 1,044,064 | 1,277,534 | 1,522,208 | 1,741,289 | 1,964,909 | 2,299,897 | 2,625,659 |
| **Interest Rates** | | | | | | *Percent Per Annum* | | | | | | | |
| Central Bank Policy Rate (EOP) | 60 | .... | .... | 10.00 | 8.75 | 8.50 | 7.00 | 6.00 | 18.00 | 11.00 | 8.50 | 8.50 | 11.50 |
| Treasury Bill Rate | 60c | 2.96 | 8.44 | 6.81 | 6.80 | 7.70 | 7.38 | 3.60 | 8.72 | 12.58 | 8.93 | 8.93 | 10.93 |
| Savings Rate | 60k | 1.17 | 1.19 | 1.34 | 1.55 | 1.70 | 1.84 | 1.63 | 1.38 | 1.60 | 1.59 | 1.62 | 1.59 |
| Savings Rate (Fgn. Currency) | 60k.f | .91 | 1.23 | 1.14 | 1.33 | 1.19 | 1.22 | .77 | .82 | .90 | .61 | .82 | .52 |
| Deposit Rate | 60l | † 2.43 | 5.08 | 5.14 | 5.16 | 5.30 | 5.97 | 4.56 | 5.63 | 11.57 | 8.64 | 8.37 | 9.19 |
| Deposit Rate (Fgn. Currency) | 60l.f | 1.62 | 2.29 | 3.39 | 3.50 | 3.20 | 1.97 | 1.08 | 1.21 | 1.27 | 2.08 | 2.58 | 2.46 |
| Lending Rate | 60p | † 12.53 | 12.88 | 13.64 | 13.34 | 14.02 | 14.80 | 14.37 | 15.05 | 19.72 | 17.31 | 16.51 | 16.09 |
| Lending Rate (Fgn. Currency) | 60p.f | 5.83 | 6.36 | 7.62 | 7.57 | 8.19 | 9.28 | 7.89 | 7.57 | 7.91 | 7.66 | 7.58 | 7.39 |
| **Prices, Production, Labor** | | | | | | *Index Numbers (2010=100): Period Averages* | | | | | | | |
| Share Prices (End of Month) | 62.ep | 65.9 | 85.8 | 108.0 | 123.6 | 106.2 | 71.1 | 100.0 | 88.1 | 87.4 | 112.5 | 117.9 | 108.5 |
| Consumer Prices | 64 | 50.3 | 55.5 | 63.6 | 69.8 | † 88.1 | 96.2 | 100.0 | 114.0 | 124.7 | 131.8 | 140.9 | 150.2 |
| **Intl. Transactions & Positions** | | | | | | *Millions of Shillings* | | | | | | | |
| Exports | 70 | 212,602 | 248,929 | 247,900 | 274,596 | 342,954 | 344,949 | 408,103 | 511,036 | 517,804 | 504,300 | 531,190 | 581,001 |
| Imports, c.i.f | 71 | 360,812 | 464,495 | 526,870 | 605,121 | 766,743 | 788,097 | 957,949 | 1,315,671 | 1,376,678 | 1,408,807 | 1,618,454 | 1,580,330 |

# Kenya  664

| | | 2004 | 2005 | 2006 | 2007 | 2008 | 2009 | 2010 | 2011 | 2012 | 2013 | 2014 | 2015 |
|---|---|---|---|---|---|---|---|---|---|---|---|---|---|
| **Balance of Payments** | | | | | | | *Millions of US Dollars* | | | | | | |
| A. Current Account* | 109bx | −131.8 | −252.3 | −510.4 | −1,032.0 | −1,982.6 | −1,688.5 | −2,368.7 | −3,830.4 | −4,255.0 | −4,871.7 | −6,339.4 | .... |
| Goods, credit (exports) | 1a9cx | 2,723.4 | 3,459.5 | 3,509.0 | 4,123.2 | 5,028.6 | 4,492.1 | 5,210.9 | 5,791.8 | 6,164.7 | 5,803.0 | 6,173.8 | .... |
| Goods, debit (imports) | 1a9dx | 4,334.6 | 5,586.5 | 6,752.1 | 8,368.7 | 10,635.6 | 9,461.2 | 11,442.2 | 14,162.1 | 15,472.4 | 16,024.0 | 17,609.6 | .... |
| Balance on goods | 1a9bx | −1,611.1 | −2,127.1 | −3,243.1 | −4,245.5 | −5,607.0 | −4,969.1 | −6,231.3 | −8,370.3 | −9,307.8 | −10,221.0 | −11,435.8 | .... |
| Services, credit (exports) | 1b9cx | 1,559.1 | 1,882.8 | 2,436.8 | 2,939.6 | 3,261.9 | 2,893.0 | 3,772.2 | 4,114.5 | 4,861.0 | 4,973.6 | 4,935.2 | .... |
| Services, debit (imports) | 1b9dx | 955.2 | 1,152.3 | 1,418.9 | 1,690.3 | 1,923.6 | 1,840.4 | 2,089.1 | 2,186.5 | 2,447.3 | 2,422.1 | 2,933.6 | .... |
| Balance on Goods & Services | 1z9bx | −1,007.3 | −1,396.6 | −2,225.3 | −2,996.2 | −4,268.6 | −3,916.5 | −4,548.3 | −6,442.2 | −6,894.1 | −7,669.6 | −9,434.2 | .... |
| Primary income: credit | 1c9cx | 45.0 | 73.3 | 99.4 | 160.6 | 176.2 | 181.9 | 144.2 | 223.2 | 179.8 | 174.0 | 181.2 | .... |
| Primary income: debit | 1c9dx | 171.5 | 181.7 | 169.5 | 304.8 | 221.4 | 212.4 | 291.9 | 282.5 | 350.4 | 512.8 | 863.7 | .... |
| Balance on gds, serv. & prim. inc. | 1y9bx | −1,133.8 | −1,505.0 | −2,295.3 | −3,140.4 | −4,313.8 | −3,947.0 | −4,695.9 | −6,501.5 | −7,064.7 | −8,008.3 | −10,116.6 | .... |
| Secondary income: credit | 1d9ca | 1,044.7 | 1,319.2 | 1,832.8 | 2,148.8 | 2,419.3 | 2,341.3 | 2,370.4 | 2,717.6 | 2,849.3 | 3,183.3 | 3,980.3 | .... |
| Secondary income: debit | 1d9da | 42.6 | 66.6 | 47.9 | 40.4 | 88.1 | 82.8 | 43.2 | 46.4 | 39.7 | 46.7 | 203.1 | .... |
| B. Capital Account* | 209ba | 145.2 | 103.3 | 168.4 | 156.8 | 94.5 | 260.9 | 240.2 | 234.9 | 235.3 | 97.7 | 23.9 | .... |
| Capital account: credit | 209ca | 145.2 | 103.3 | 168.4 | 156.8 | 94.5 | 260.9 | 240.2 | 234.9 | 235.3 | 97.7 | 23.9 | .... |
| Capital account: debit | 209da | — | — | — | — | — | — | — | — | — | — | — | .... |
| Balance on current & capital acct. | 129ba | 13.4 | −149.0 | −342.0 | −875.2 | −1,888.1 | −1,427.7 | −2,128.5 | −3,595.5 | −4,019.7 | −4,774.0 | −6,315.5 | .... |
| C. Financial Account* | 309na | −40.2 | −511.4 | −673.6 | −1,936.4 | −1,095.4 | −2,465.8 | −2,128.2 | −2,367.4 | −4,713.0 | −4,924.0 | −6,832.7 | .... |
| Direct investment: assets | 3a9aa | 4.4 | 9.7 | 24.0 | 36.0 | 43.8 | 46.0 | 1.6 | −186.0 | −79.1 | −136.9 | −78.5 | .... |
| Equity & investment fund shares | 3aaaa | 4.4 | 9.7 | 24.0 | 36.0 | 43.8 | 46.0 | 1.6 | 9.4 | 16.1 | 5.6 | 27.8 | .... |
| Debt instruments | 3abaa | .... | — | — | — | — | — | — | −195.4 | −95.2 | −142.5 | −106.3 | .... |
| Direct investment: liabilities | 3a9la | 46.1 | 21.2 | 50.7 | 729.0 | 95.6 | 116.3 | 178.1 | 139.9 | 163.4 | 371.8 | 944.3 | .... |
| Equity & investment fund shares | 3aala | 29.9 | 5.6 | 3.0 | 665.3 | 22.8 | 31.6 | 89.4 | 39.6 | 48.7 | 71.0 | 467.0 | .... |
| Debt instruments | 3abla | 16.2 | 15.6 | 47.7 | 63.7 | 72.8 | 84.7 | 88.7 | 100.3 | 114.7 | 300.8 | 477.4 | .... |
| Portfolio investment: assets | 3b9aa | 71.7 | 45.9 | 23.6 | 25.5 | 35.9 | 23.7 | 51.2 | 81.2 | 40.8 | 38.1 | 55.4 | .... |
| Equity & investment fund shares | 3baaa | 25.8 | 27.9 | 20.5 | 24.8 | 6.3 | 8.8 | 8.5 | 68.6 | 22.1 | 11.8 | 3.5 | .... |
| Debt securities | 3bbaa | 45.9 | 18.0 | 3.1 | .7 | 29.6 | 14.8 | 42.7 | 12.6 | 18.8 | 26.3 | 51.9 | .... |
| Portfolio investment: liabilities | 3b9la | 5.4 | 15.4 | 3.0 | .8 | 9.8 | 2.8 | 22.2 | 23.8 | 27.2 | 271.8 | 3,564.7 | .... |
| Equity & investment fund shares | 3bala | 3.2 | 3.1 | 1.8 | .5 | 5.0 | 2.6 | 22.1 | 20.1 | 25.8 | 259.9 | 954.3 | .... |
| Debt securities | 3bbla | 2.1 | 12.3 | 1.2 | .3 | 4.8 | .2 | .1 | 3.7 | 1.4 | 11.8 | 2,610.3 | .... |
| Fin. der.& empl.stk.ops.(ESOs): net. | 3c9na | .... | — | — | — | — | — | — | — | — | — | — | .... |
| Fin. der. & ESOs.: assets | 3c9aa | .... | — | — | — | — | — | — | — | — | — | — | .... |
| Fin. der. & ESOs.: liabilities | 3c9la | .... | — | — | — | — | — | — | — | — | — | — | .... |
| Other investment: assets | 3d9aa | 307.1 | 200.6 | 259.6 | 346.7 | 631.6 | −544.6 | −94.7 | 668.5 | −347.6 | 464.8 | −71.8 | .... |
| Other equity | 3daaa | .... | .... | .... | .... | .... | .... | .... | .... | .... | .... | .... | .... |
| Debt instruments | 3dzaa | 307.1 | 200.6 | 259.6 | 346.7 | 631.6 | −544.6 | −94.7 | 668.5 | −347.6 | 464.8 | −71.8 | .... |
| Other investment: liabilities | 3d9la | 372.0 | 730.9 | 927.1 | 1,614.8 | 1,701.3 | 1,871.9 | 1,886.0 | 2,767.4 | 4,136.4 | 4,646.3 | 2,228.8 | .... |
| Other equity | 3dala | .... | .... | .... | .... | .... | .... | .... | .... | .... | .... | .... | .... |
| Debt instruments | 3dzla | 372.0 | 730.9 | 927.1 | 1,614.8 | 1,701.3 | 1,871.9 | 1,886.0 | 2,767.4 | 4,136.4 | 4,646.3 | 2,228.8 | .... |
| Curr.+ cap.− finan. acct. balance | 4y9na | 53.7 | 362.4 | 331.6 | 1,061.2 | −792.7 | 1,038.2 | −.3 | −1,228.1 | 693.2 | 150.0 | 517.2 | .... |
| D. Net Errors and Omissions | 409na | −66.8 | −245.4 | 249.7 | −249.9 | 297.4 | 79.8 | 141.9 | 16.4 | 522.6 | 243.8 | 860.7 | .... |
| E. Reserves and Related Items | 4z9na | −13.1 | 117.0 | 581.3 | 811.3 | −495.3 | 1,118.0 | 141.6 | −1,211.7 | 1,215.9 | 393.7 | 1,377.9 | .... |
| Reserve assets | 3e9aa | 36.6 | 281.2 | 615.8 | 938.2 | −475.9 | 1,317.7 | 129.1 | −63.2 | 1,446.6 | 879.3 | 1,320.1 | .... |
| Credit and loans from the IMF | 3dcla | −14.1 | 69.1 | −13.5 | 106.2 | −10.6 | 191.5 | −25.4 | 290.1 | 192.4 | 173.2 | −57.8 | .... |
| Exceptional financing | 409la | 63.8 | 95.1 | 48.1 | 20.7 | 30.0 | 8.2 | 12.8 | 858.4 | 38.4 | 312.4 | — | .... |

*Excludes components in group E

**Government Finance**
**Cash Flow Statement**
**Budgetary Central Government**

| | | 2004 | 2005 | 2006 | 2007 | 2008 | 2009 | 2010 | 2011 | 2012 | 2013 | 2014 | 2015 |
|---|---|---|---|---|---|---|---|---|---|---|---|---|---|
| | | | | | | *Millions of Shillings: Fiscal Year Ends June 30* | | | | | | | |
| Cash Receipts:Operating Activities... | c1 | 270,920 | 301,299 | 317,855 | 359,027 | 442,180 | 484,939 | † 538,928 | 641,013 | 764,113 | 805,571 | .... | .... |
| Taxes | c11 | 216,290 | 264,322 | 281,940 | 326,185 | 396,386 | 445,167 | † 498,637 | 594,198 | 676,601 | 734,582 | .... | .... |
| Social Contributions | c12 | 239 | 558 | — | — | — | — | † — | — | 660 | 584 | | |
| Grants | c13 | 16,224 | 14,905 | 20,070 | 15,494 | 33,153 | 19,669 | † 20,710 | 23,893 | 15,286 | 20,723 | | |
| Other Receipts | c14 | 38,168 | 21,514 | 15,845 | 17,348 | 12,641 | 20,103 | † 19,581 | 22,922 | 71,566 | 49,681 | | |
| Cash Payments:Operating Activities. | c2 | 265,813 | 257,493 | 320,405 | 357,205 | 450,777 | 493,772 | † 571,828 | 682,121 | 833,400 | 919,187 | | |
| Compensation of Employees | c21 | 131,673 | 154,062 | 145,538 | 155,425 | 169,892 | 184,224 | † 217,671 | 236,372 | 211,123 | 279,425 | | |
| Purchases of Goods & Services | c22 | 76,055 | 60,198 | 49,236 | 55,212 | 89,276 | 99,837 | † 82,150 | 99,360 | 82,377 | 111,968 | | |
| Interest | c24 | 27,743 | 26,875 | 31,453 | 38,997 | 49,853 | 50,640 | † 55,786 | 68,678 | 84,458 | 92,951 | | |
| Subsidies | c25 | 10,253 | 8,790 | 421 | 45 | 33 | 37 | † 77 | 18,118 | 86 | 52 | | |
| Grants | c26 | 13,897 | 2,333 | 69,692 | 80,188 | 116,296 | 128,892 | † 182,056 | 228,522 | 421,855 | 400,568 | | |
| Social Benefits | c27 | 866 | 974 | 17,051 | 27,338 | 24,616 | 25,677 | † 29,296 | 25,007 | 31,497 | 29,116 | | |
| Other Payments | c28 | 5,324 | 4,262 | 7,014 | — | 811 | 4,465 | † 4,552 | 6,064 | 2,004 | 5,107 | | |
| Net Cash Inflow:Operating Act.[1-2] | ccio | 5,108 | 43,806 | −2,550 | 1,822 | −8,597 | −8,833 | † −32,900 | −41,108 | −69,287 | −113,616 | | |
| Net Cash Outflow:Invest. in NFA | c31 | 23,781 | 22,644 | 35,247 | 56,465 | 77,328 | 116,945 | † 116,959 | 94,828 | 94,535 | 139,720 | | |
| Purchases of Nonfinancial Assets... | c31.1 | 23,916 | 22,644 | 35,247 | 56,465 | 77,328 | 116,945 | † 116,959 | 94,828 | 97,173 | .... | | |
| Sales of Nonfinancial Assets | c31.2 | 135 | — | — | — | — | — | † — | — | 2,637 | .... | | |
| Cash Surplus/Deficit [1-2-31=1-2M] | ccsd | −18,673 | 21,162 | −32,189 | −33,993 | −67,234 | −109,981 | † −149,859 | −135,935 | −163,822 | −253,336 | | |
| Net Acq. Fin. Assets, excl. Cash | c32x | 5,312 | 8,697 | 1,192 | 1,915 | 46,265 | 9,109 | † 5,660 | 6,395 | 6,395 | .... | | |
| Domestic | c321x | 5,312 | 8,697 | 1,192 | 1,703 | 46,265 | 9,109 | † 5,660 | 6,395 | 6,395 | .... | | |
| Foreign | c322x | — | — | — | 212 | — | — | † — | — | — | .... | | |
| Net Incurrence of Liabilities | c33 | 17,618 | −6,673 | 29,396 | 32,624 | −12,945 | 68,737 | † 174,268 | 121,657 | 108,743 | .... | | |
| Domestic | c331 | 8,809 | −6,673 | 28,251 | 34,661 | −19,171 | 57,173 | † 126,060 | 98,135 | 81,520 | — | | |
| Foreign | c332 | −8,860 | — | 1,145 | −2,037 | 6,226 | 11,564 | † 48,208 | 23,522 | 27,223 | — | | |
| Net Cash Inflow, Fin.Act.[-32x+33].. | cnfb | 12,306 | −15,370 | 35,255 | 36,696 | −60,156 | 101,461 | † 168,608 | 115,262 | 102,348 | .... | | |
| Net Change in Stock of Cash | cncb | −6,368 | 5,793 | −2,542 | −17,948 | −146,081 | −24,317 | † 18,749 | −20,673 | −61,474 | .... | | |
| Stat. Discrep. [32X-33+NCB-CSD].... | ccsdz | — | — | 2,793 | 1,369 | −10,991 | −9,763 | † — | | | | | |
| Memo Item:Cash Expenditure[2+31] | c2m | 289,594 | 280,137 | 355,652 | 413,671 | 528,104 | 610,717 | † 688,786 | 776,948 | 925,297 | 1,058,907 | .... | .... |
| Memo Item: Gross Debt | c63 | 747,416 | 749,548 | 789,076 | 801,255 | 870,579 | 1,053,650 | .... | .... | .... | .... | .... | .... |

# Kenya 664

| National Accounts | | 2004 | 2005 | 2006 | 2007 | 2008 | 2009 | 2010 | 2011 | 2012 | 2013 | 2014 | 2015 |
|---|---|---|---|---|---|---|---|---|---|---|---|---|---|
| | | | | | | *Millions of Shillings* | | | | | | | |
| Househ.Cons.Expend.,incl.NPISHs.... | 96f | 962,399 | 1,067,432 | 1,222,652 | 1,383,603 | 1,583,651 | 1,849,582 | 1,982,955 | 2,351,534 | 2,660,565 | .... | .... | .... |
| Government Consumption Expend... | 91f | 227,596 | 246,056 | 285,056 | 327,918 | 347,262 | 383,847 | 439,667 | 498,881 | 592,388 | .... | .... | .... |
| Gross Fixed Capital Formation.......... | 93e | 207,196 | 264,728 | 309,592 | 355,090 | 409,597 | 465,111 | 518,538 | 609,255 | 701,398 | .... | .... | .... |
| Changes in Inventories.................... | 93i | 10,565 | −25,282 | −18,383 | −6,240 | −4,120 | 6,365 | −14,015 | 16,228 | −10,346 | .... | .... | .... |
| Exports of Goods and Services......... | 90c | 335,743 | 395,208 | 439,906 | 490,987 | 581,806 | 571,305 | 709,209 | 870,168 | 939,116 | .... | .... | .... |
| Imports of Goods and Services (-)..... | 98c | 435,844 | 523,970 | 613,856 | 691,220 | 879,821 | 886,480 | 1,021,873 | 1,374,101 | 1,530,664 | .... | .... | .... |
| Gross Domestic Product (GDP)........ | 99b | 1,274,322 | 1,415,811 | 1,622,565 | 1,833,511 | 2,107,589 | 2,366,984 | 2,553,733 | 3,048,867 | 3,440,115 | 4,730,801 | 5,357,672 | .... |
| Net Primary Income from Abroad..... | 98.n | −10,017 | −8,194 | −5,053 | −9,706 | −3,127 | −2,926 | −12,493 | .... | .... | .... | .... | .... |
| Gross National Income (GNI)............ | 99a | 1,264,305 | 1,407,617 | 1,617,512 | 1,823,805 | 2,108,046 | 2,362,527 | 2,538,668 | .... | .... | .... | .... | .... |
| GDP Volume 2001 Prices................ | 99b.p | 1,109,771 | 1,175,248 | 1,249,470 | 1,336,846 | 1,357,263 | 1,394,387 | 1,475,302 | 1,539,912 | 1,610,116 | .... | .... | .... |
| GDP Volume (2010=100)................ | 99bvp | 75.2 | 79.7 | 84.7 | 90.6 | 92.0 | 94.5 | 100.0 | 104.4 | 109.1 | .... | .... | .... |
| GDP Deflator (2010=100).............. | 99bip | 66.3 | 69.6 | 75.0 | 79.2 | 89.7 | 98.1 | 100.0 | 114.4 | 123.4 | .... | .... | .... |
| | | | | | | *Millions: Midyear Estimates* | | | | | | | |
| Population............................... | 99z | 34.44 | 35.35 | 36.29 | 37.25 | 38.24 | 39.27 | 40.33 | 41.42 | 42.54 | 43.69 | 44.86 | 46.05 |

2016, International Monetary Fund : *International Financial Statistics Yearbook*

# Kiribati 826

| | | 2004 | 2005 | 2006 | 2007 | 2008 | 2009 | 2010 | 2011 | 2012 | 2013 | 2014 | 2015 |
|---|---|---|---|---|---|---|---|---|---|---|---|---|---|
| **Exchange Rates** | | | | | *Australian Dollars per SDR: End of Period* | | | | | | | | |
| Market Rate | aa | 1.9936 | 1.9480 | 1.9012 | 1.7925 | 2.2233 | 1.7479 | 1.5153 | 1.5117 | 1.4771 | 1.7372 | 1.7664 | 1.8967 |
| | | | | *Australian Dollars per US Dollar: End of Period (ae) Period Average (rf)* | | | | | | | | | |
| Market Rate | ae | 1.2837 | 1.3630 | 1.2637 | 1.1343 | 1.4434 | 1.1150 | .9840 | .9846 | .9611 | 1.1280 | 1.2192 | 1.3687 |
| Market Rate | rf | 1.3598 | 1.3095 | 1.3280 | 1.1951 | 1.1922 | 1.2822 | 1.0902 | .9695 | .9658 | 1.0358 | 1.1094 | 1.3311 |
| **Fund Position** | | | | | | *Millions of SDRs: End of Period* | | | | | | | |
| Quota | 2f.s | 5.60 | 5.60 | 5.60 | 5.60 | 5.60 | 5.60 | 5.60 | 5.60 | 5.60 | 5.60 | 5.60 | 5.60 |
| SDR Holdings | 1b.s | .01 | .01 | .01 | .01 | .01 | 5.34 | 5.34 | 5.34 | 5.35 | 5.39 | 5.39 | 5.39 |
| Reserve Position in the Fund | 1c.s | — | — | — | — | — | — | — | — | — | — | — | — |
| Total Fund Cred.&Loans Outstg. | 2tl | — | — | — | — | — | — | — | — | — | — | — | — |
| SDR Allocations | 1bd | — | — | — | — | — | 5.32 | 5.32 | 5.32 | 5.32 | 5.32 | 5.32 | 5.32 |
| **Balance of Payments** | | | | | | *Millions of US Dollars* | | | | | | | |
| A. Current Account* | 109bx | .... | .... | † −14.19 | −7.08 | −9.11 | −17.56 | −3.38 | −23.76 | −8.42 | 15.47 | 44.74 | .... |
| Goods, credit (exports) | 1a9cx | .... | .... | † 3.27 | 11.26 | 9.18 | 7.42 | 6.66 | 11.48 | 10.19 | 9.94 | 11.08 | .... |
| Goods, debit (imports) | 1a9dx | .... | .... | † 60.52 | 68.23 | 72.06 | 66.86 | 70.49 | 88.68 | 104.08 | 104.20 | 116.07 | .... |
| Balance on goods | 1a9bx | .... | .... | † −57.25 | −56.97 | −62.88 | −59.45 | −63.83 | −77.20 | −93.89 | −94.26 | −104.98 | .... |
| Services, credit (exports) | 1b9cx | .... | .... | † 9.02 | 10.93 | 12.70 | 13.05 | 13.40 | 15.20 | 14.24 | 13.74 | 12.02 | .... |
| Services, debit (imports) | 1b9dx | .... | .... | † 38.17 | 47.61 | 51.86 | 47.15 | 52.14 | 63.91 | 70.88 | 69.89 | 53.73 | .... |
| Balance on Goods & Services | 1z9bx | .... | .... | † −86.39 | −93.65 | −102.04 | −93.55 | −102.57 | −125.92 | −150.53 | −150.41 | −146.69 | .... |
| Primary income: credit | 1c9cx | .... | .... | † 48.43 | 60.70 | 70.54 | 53.77 | 75.80 | 73.79 | 101.25 | 128.12 | 161.63 | .... |
| Primary income: debit | 1c9dx | .... | .... | † 1.13 | 2.31 | 5.98 | 3.17 | 3.31 | 2.64 | 3.50 | 2.42 | 3.16 | .... |
| Balance on gds, serv. & prim. inc. | 1y9bx | .... | .... | † −39.10 | −35.26 | −37.47 | −42.95 | −30.08 | −54.77 | −52.78 | −24.71 | 11.78 | .... |
| Secondary income: credit | 1d9ca | .... | .... | † 25.84 | 29.62 | 29.86 | 26.71 | 28.47 | 33.12 | 46.81 | 41.71 | 34.20 | .... |
| Secondary income: debit | 1d9da | .... | .... | † .93 | 1.44 | 1.50 | 1.32 | 1.77 | 2.12 | 2.45 | 1.54 | 1.24 | .... |
| B. Capital Account* | 209ba | .... | .... | † 7.64 | 8.74 | 8.28 | 12.50 | 13.03 | 15.11 | 22.28 | 23.10 | 31.89 | .... |
| Capital account: credit | 209ca | .... | .... | † 7.64 | 8.74 | 8.28 | 12.50 | 13.03 | 15.11 | 22.28 | 23.59 | 32.67 | .... |
| Capital account: debit | 209da | .... | .... | .... | .... | .... | .... | .... | .... | .... | .49 | .78 | .... |
| Balance on current & capital acct. | 129ba | .... | .... | † −6.55 | 1.66 | −.83 | −5.06 | 9.65 | −8.65 | 13.86 | 38.57 | 76.63 | .... |
| C. Financial Account* | 309na | .... | .... | † −.56 | 4.62 | −10.23 | −4.47 | −7.39 | −1.14 | 24.30 | 15.05 | 96.77 | .... |
| Direct investment: assets | 3a9aa | .... | .... | † .01 | .01 | .03 | −.19 | .... | .56 | .08 | .... | 7.87 | .... |
| Equity & investment fund shares | 3aaaa | .... | .... | † .01 | .01 | .03 | −.19 | .... | .56 | .08 | .... | 7.87 | .... |
| Debt instruments | 3abaa | .... | .... | .... | .... | .... | .... | .... | .... | .... | .... | .... | .... |
| Direct investment: liabilities | 3a9la | .... | .... | † .57 | 1.15 | −1.27 | 5.00 | −6.60 | .68 | −3.42 | 1.17 | 8.27 | .... |
| Equity & investment fund shares | 3aala | .... | .... | † .57 | 1.15 | −1.27 | 5.00 | −6.60 | .68 | −3.42 | 1.17 | 2.46 | .... |
| Debt instruments | 3abla | .... | .... | .... | .... | .... | .... | .... | .... | .... | .... | 5.81 | .... |
| Portfolio investment: assets | 3b9aa | .... | .... | .... | 3.34 | 3.86 | 3.65 | .76 | −5.31 | 4.51 | 6.97 | 9.27 | .... |
| Equity & investment fund shares | 3baaa | .... | .... | .... | 3.3 | 3.9 | 3.7 | .8 | −5.3 | 4.5 | 7.0 | 9.3 | .... |
| Debt securities | 3bbaa | .... | .... | .... | .... | .... | .... | .... | .... | .... | .... | .... | .... |
| Portfolio investment: liabilities | 3b9la | .... | .... | .... | .... | .... | .... | .... | .... | .... | .... | .... | .... |
| Equity & investment fund shares | 3bala | .... | .... | .... | .... | .... | .... | .... | .... | .... | .... | .... | .... |
| Debt securities | 3bbla | .... | .... | .... | .... | .... | .... | .... | .... | .... | .... | .... | .... |
| Fin. der.& empl.stk.ops.(ESOs): net | 3c9na | .... | .... | .... | .... | .... | .... | .... | .... | .... | .... | .... | .... |
| Fin. der. & ESOs: assets | 3c9aa | .... | .... | .... | .... | .... | .... | .... | .... | .... | .... | .... | .... |
| Fin. der. & ESOs: liabilities | 3c9la | .... | .... | .... | .... | .... | .... | .... | .... | .... | .... | .... | .... |
| Other investment: assets | 3d9aa | .... | .... | .... | 2.37 | −15.38 | 6.04 | −15.73 | 3.85 | 16.26 | 9.09 | 95.20 | .... |
| Other equity | 3daaa | .... | .... | .... | .... | .... | .... | .... | .... | .... | .... | .... | .... |
| Debt instruments | 3dzaa | .... | .... | .... | 2.37 | −15.38 | 6.04 | −15.73 | 3.85 | 16.26 | 9.09 | 95.20 | .... |
| Other investment: liabilities | 3d9la | .... | .... | † — | −.05 | — | 8.97 | −.98 | −.45 | −.03 | −.16 | 7.30 | .... |
| Other equity | 3dala | .... | .... | .... | .... | .... | .... | .... | .... | .... | .... | .... | .... |
| Debt instruments | 3dzla | .... | .... | † — | −.05 | — | 8.97 | −.98 | −.45 | −.03 | −.16 | 7.30 | .... |
| Curr.+ cap.− finan. acct. balance | 4y9na | .... | .... | † −5.99 | −2.95 | 9.40 | −.59 | 17.04 | −7.51 | −10.44 | 23.52 | −20.14 | .... |
| D. Net Errors and Omissions | 409na | .... | .... | † −3.54 | −11.15 | −2.87 | 10.48 | −7.54 | 9.48 | −6.63 | −11.06 | 21.86 | .... |
| E. Reserves and Related Items | 4z9na | .... | .... | † −9.53 | −14.10 | 6.53 | 9.89 | 9.50 | 1.97 | −17.08 | 12.46 | 1.72 | .... |
| Reserve assets | 3e9aa | .... | .... | † −9.53 | −14.10 | 6.53 | 9.89 | 9.50 | 1.97 | −17.08 | 12.46 | 1.72 | .... |
| Credit and loans from the IMF | 3dcla | .... | .... | † — | — | — | — | — | — | — | — | — | .... |
| Exceptional financing | 409la | .... | .... | .... | .... | .... | .... | .... | .... | .... | .... | .... | .... |

*Excludes components in group E

| **International Investment Position** | | | | | | *Millions of US Dollars* | | | | | | | |
|---|---|---|---|---|---|---|---|---|---|---|---|---|---|
| Assets | 809aa | .... | .... | .... | † 689.4 | 468.1 | 635.4 | 709.8 | 706.5 | 779.8 | 678.8 | 776.2 | .... |
| Direct investment | 8a9aa | .... | .... | .... | † 1.2 | 2.1 | 1.6 | 1.6 | 2.0 | 2.2 | 1.9 | 1.4 | .... |
| Equity & investment fund shares | 8aaaa | .... | .... | .... | † 1.2 | 2.1 | 1.6 | 1.6 | 2.0 | 2.2 | 1.9 | 1.4 | .... |
| Debt instruments | 8abaa | .... | .... | .... | .... | .... | .... | .... | .... | .... | .... | .... | .... |
| Portfolio investment | 8b9aa | .... | .... | .... | † 84.7 | 53.3 | 79.3 | 90.7 | 85.4 | 92.0 | 85.1 | 85.7 | .... |
| Equity & investment fund shares | 8baaa | .... | .... | .... | † 84.7 | 53.3 | 79.3 | 90.7 | 85.4 | 92.0 | 85.1 | 85.7 | .... |
| Debt securities | 8bbaa | .... | .... | .... | .... | .... | .... | .... | .... | .... | .... | .... | .... |
| Fin. der.(oth.than reserves) & ESOs | 8c9aa | .... | .... | .... | .... | .... | .... | .... | .... | .... | .... | .... | .... |
| Other investment | 8d9aa | .... | .... | .... | † 38.7 | 18.0 | 30.4 | 17.1 | 20.8 | 37.7 | 41.0 | 124.4 | .... |
| Other equity | 8daaa | .... | .... | .... | .... | .... | .... | .... | .... | .... | .... | .... | .... |
| Debt instruments | 8dzaa | .... | .... | .... | † 38.7 | 18.0 | 30.4 | 17.1 | 20.8 | 37.7 | 41.0 | 124.4 | .... |
| Reserve assets | 8e9aa | .... | .... | .... | † 564.7 | 394.7 | 524.1 | 600.4 | 598.2 | 647.9 | 550.9 | 564.7 | .... |
| Liabilities | 809la | .... | .... | .... | † 21.0 | 15.4 | 32.8 | 27.1 | 27.4 | 29.0 | 37.8 | 47.0 | .... |
| Direct investment | 8a9la | .... | .... | .... | † 8.2 | 5.2 | 10.4 | 4.6 | 4.9 | 6.9 | 6.9 | 11.5 | .... |
| Equity & investment fund shares | 8aala | .... | .... | .... | † 8.2 | 5.2 | 10.4 | 4.6 | 4.9 | 6.9 | 6.9 | 6.4 | .... |
| Debt instruments | 8abla | .... | .... | .... | .... | .... | .... | .... | .... | .... | .... | 5.1 | .... |
| Portfolio investment | 8b9la | .... | .... | .... | .... | .... | .... | .... | .... | .... | .... | .... | .... |
| Equity & investment fund shares | 8bala | .... | .... | .... | .... | .... | .... | .... | .... | .... | .... | .... | .... |
| Debt securities | 8bbla | .... | .... | .... | .... | .... | .... | .... | .... | .... | .... | .... | .... |
| Fin. der.(oth.than reserves) & ESOs | 8c9la | .... | .... | .... | .... | .... | .... | .... | .... | .... | .... | .... | .... |
| Other investment | 8d9la | .... | .... | .... | † 12.9 | 10.1 | 22.3 | 22.5 | 22.4 | 22.0 | 30.9 | 35.4 | .... |
| Other equity | 8dala | .... | .... | .... | .... | .... | .... | .... | .... | .... | .... | .... | .... |
| Debt instruments | 8dzla | .... | .... | .... | † 12.9 | 10.1 | 22.3 | 22.5 | 22.4 | 22.0 | 30.9 | 35.4 | .... |

# Kiribati 826

Thousands of Australian Dollars: Fiscal Year Ends June 30

**Government Finance**
**Cash Flow Statement**
**General Government**

| | | 2004 | 2005 | 2006 | 2007 | 2008 | 2009 | 2010 | 2011 | 2012 | 2013 | 2014 | 2015 |
|---|---|---|---|---|---|---|---|---|---|---|---|---|---|
| Cash Receipts:Operating Activities... | c1 | .... | .... | .... | .... | .... | .... | .... | 113,370.8 | 143,125.9 | 175,410.8 | 238,275.6 | .... |
| Taxes............................................. | c11 | .... | .... | .... | .... | .... | .... | .... | 32,162.9 | 34,854.2 | 35,070.3 | 34,421.4 | .... |
| Social Contributions...................... | c12 | .... | .... | .... | .... | .... | .... | .... | — | — | — | — | .... |
| Grants........................................... | c13 | .... | .... | .... | .... | .... | .... | .... | 13,836.6 | 15,128.0 | 12,180.8 | 26,086.0 | .... |
| Other Receipts.............................. | c14 | .... | .... | .... | .... | .... | .... | .... | 67,371.3 | 93,143.7 | 128,159.8 | 177,768.2 | .... |
| Cash Payments:Operating Activities. | c2 | .... | .... | .... | .... | .... | .... | .... | 115,464.6 | 127,691.5 | 132,277.2 | 139,044.5 | .... |
| Compensation of Employees.......... | c21 | .... | .... | .... | .... | .... | .... | .... | 52,562.5 | 53,320.7 | 55,106.8 | 56,604.1 | .... |
| Purchases of Goods & Services....... | c22 | .... | .... | .... | .... | .... | .... | .... | 41,928.4 | 45,940.4 | 50,996.2 | 52,154.2 | .... |
| Interest......................................... | c24 | .... | .... | .... | .... | .... | .... | .... | 3,875.4 | 6,428.6 | 1,837.6 | 222.8 | .... |
| Subsidies....................................... | c25 | .... | .... | .... | .... | .... | .... | .... | 11,666.2 | 10,628.9 | 11,759.1 | 7,911.1 | .... |
| Grants........................................... | c26 | .... | .... | .... | .... | .... | .... | .... | 1,231.3 | 1,886.3 | 1,043.5 | 1,708.2 | .... |
| Social Benefits.............................. | c27 | .... | .... | .... | .... | .... | .... | .... | 1,894.1 | 5,051.6 | 5,922.9 | 5,110.5 | .... |
| Other Payments............................ | c28 | .... | .... | .... | .... | .... | .... | .... | 2,306.7 | 4,435.1 | 5,611.1 | 15,333.5 | .... |
| Net Cash Inflow:Operating Act.[1-2] | ccio | .... | .... | .... | .... | .... | .... | .... | −2,093.8 | 15,434.4 | 43,133.6 | 99,231.1 | .... |
| Net Cash Outflow:Invest. in NFA...... | c31 | .... | .... | .... | .... | .... | .... | .... | 10,058.9 | 9,044.7 | 7,977.3 | 10,563.7 | .... |
| Purchases of Nonfinancial Assets... | c31.1 | .... | .... | .... | .... | .... | .... | .... | .... | .... | .... | .... | .... |
| Sales of Nonfinancial Assets.......... | c31.2 | .... | .... | .... | .... | .... | .... | .... | .... | .... | .... | .... | .... |
| Cash Surplus/Deficit [1-2-31=1-2M] | ccsd | .... | .... | .... | .... | .... | .... | .... | −12,152.7 | 6,389.7 | 35,156.3 | 88,667.4 | .... |
| Net Acq. Fin. Assets, excl. Cash....... | c32x | .... | .... | .... | .... | .... | .... | .... | .... | .... | .... | .... | .... |
| Domestic....................................... | c321x | .... | .... | .... | .... | .... | .... | .... | .... | .... | .... | .... | .... |
| Foreign.......................................... | c322x | .... | .... | .... | .... | .... | .... | .... | .... | .... | .... | .... | .... |
| Net Incurrence of Liabilities.............. | c33 | .... | .... | .... | .... | .... | .... | .... | 2,017.7 | −678.8 | −539.7 | −16,414.8 | .... |
| Domestic....................................... | c331 | .... | .... | .... | .... | .... | .... | .... | 2,560.4 | 79.7 | 347.2 | −15,675.6 | .... |
| Foreign.......................................... | c332 | .... | .... | .... | .... | .... | .... | .... | −542.7 | −758.6 | −887.0 | −739.2 | .... |
| Net Cash Inflow, Fin.Act.[-32x+33].. | cnfb | .... | .... | .... | .... | .... | .... | .... | 33,571.0 | 6,976.0 | −13,744.3 | 200,435.9 | .... |
| Net Change in Stock of Cash............ | cncb | .... | .... | .... | .... | .... | .... | .... | 21,418.3 | 13,365.7 | 21,412.0 | 289,103.3 | .... |
| Stat. Discrep. [32X-33+NCB-CSD].... | ccsdz | .... | .... | .... | .... | .... | .... | .... | — | — | — | — | .... |
| Memo Item:Cash Expenditure[2+31] | c2m | .... | .... | .... | .... | .... | .... | .... | 125,523.5 | 136,736.2 | 140,254.5 | 149,608.2 | .... |
| Memo Item: Gross Debt.................. | c63 | .... | .... | .... | .... | .... | .... | .... | .... | .... | .... | .... | .... |

| | | 2004 | 2005 | 2006 | 2007 | 2008 | 2009 | 2010 | 2011 | 2012 | 2013 | 2014 | 2015 |
|---|---|---|---|---|---|---|---|---|---|---|---|---|---|
| **Exchange Rates** | | | | | | | *Won per SDR: End of Period* | | | | | | | |
| Market Rate............................ | aa | 1,607.5 | 1,445.8 | 1,398.8 | 1,479.3 | 1,940.0 | 1,825.6 | 1,747.6 | 1,768.3 | 1,645.4 | 1,625.3 | 1,592.7 | 1,624.8 |
| | | | | | | *Won per US Dollar: End of Period (ae) Period Average (rf)* | | | | | | | | |
| Market Rate............................ | ae | 1,035.1 | 1,011.6 | 929.8 | 936.1 | 1,259.5 | 1,164.5 | 1,134.8 | 1,151.8 | 1,070.6 | 1,055.4 | 1,099.3 | 1,172.5 |
| Market Rate............................ | rf | 1,145.3 | 1,024.1 | 954.8 | 929.3 | 1,102.0 | 1,276.9 | 1,156.1 | 1,108.3 | 1,126.5 | 1,094.9 | 1,053.0 | 1,131.2 |
| | | | | | | *Index Numbers (2010=100): Period Averages* | | | | | | | | |
| ULC-Based Real Effect. Ex. Rate....... | rel | 108.51 | 127.83 | 136.33 | 136.13 | 107.27 | 91.73 | 100.00 | 95.09 | 98.46 | 105.28 | 112.02 | 115.48 |
| **Fund Position** | | | | | | | *Millions of SDRs: End of Period* | | | | | | | |
| Quota................................... | 2f.s | 1,633.60 | 1,633.60 | 2,927.30 | 2,927.30 | 2,927.30 | 2,927.30 | 2,927.30 | 3,366.40 | 3,366.40 | 3,366.40 | 3,366.40 | 3,366.40 |
| SDR Holdings............................ | 1b.s | 21.14 | 30.54 | 35.93 | 43.45 | 55.58 | 2,389.16 | 2,298.65 | 2,252.17 | 2,293.99 | 2,266.18 | 2,264.89 | 2,337.19 |
| Reserve Position in the Fund........... | 1c.s | 507.68 | 213.97 | 292.71 | 196.67 | 376.41 | 628.41 | 665.41 | 1,670.29 | 1,811.20 | 1,631.37 | 1,313.57 | 1,007.97 |
| Total Fund Cred.&Loans Outstg....... | 2tl | — | — | — | — | — | — | — | — | — | — | — | — |
| SDR Allocations........................ | 1bd | 72.91 | 72.91 | 72.91 | 72.91 | 72.91 | 2,404.45 | 2,404.45 | 2,404.45 | 2,404.45 | 2,404.45 | 2,404.45 | 2,404.45 |
| **International Liquidity** | | | | | | *Millions of US Dollars Unless Otherwise Indicated: End of Period* | | | | | | | | |
| Total Reserves minus Gold.............. | 1l.d | 198,996.6 | 210,317.2 | 238,882.3 | 262,150.2 | 201,144.5 | 269,932.9 | 291,491.1 | 304,255.0 | 323,207.1 | 341,649.7 | 358,785.0 | 363,149.3 |
| SDR Holdings............................ | 1b.d | 32.8 | 43.7 | 54.1 | 68.7 | 85.6 | 3,745.5 | 3,540.0 | 3,457.1 | 3,525.7 | 3,489.9 | 3,281.4 | 3,238.7 |
| Reserve Position in the Fund.......... | 1c.d | 788.4 | 305.8 | 440.4 | 310.8 | 579.8 | 985.2 | 1,024.8 | 2,564.3 | 2,783.7 | 2,512.3 | 1,903.1 | 1,396.8 |
| Foreign Exchange...................... | 1d.d | 198,175.3 | 209,967.7 | 238,387.9 | 261,770.7 | 200,479.1 | 265,202.3 | 286,926.4 | 298,232.9 | 316,897.7 | 335,647.5 | 353,600.5 | 358,513.8 |
| Gold (Million Fine Troy Ounces)....... | 1ad | .454 | .458 | .418 | .459 | .460 | .464 | .464 | 1.750 | 2.715 | 3.358 | 3.358 | 3.357 |
| Gold (National Valuation)............... | 1and | 72.3 | 73.6 | 74.2 | 74.3 | 75.7 | 79.0 | 79.6 | 2,166.6 | 3,761.4 | 4,794.5 | 4,794.7 | 4,794.8 |
| Central Bank: Other Assets............. | 3..d | 2.5 | 3.0 | 5.0 | 5.2 | 4.3 | 5.2 | 4.7 | 4.0 | 4.4 | 4.8 | 1.5 | 1.9 |
| Central Bank: Other Liabs.............. | 4..d | 21.0 | 18.4 | 33.6 | 45.7 | 35.4 | 34.7 | 33.5 | 78.8 | 87.1 | 89.8 | 81.9 | 66.3 |
| Other Depository Corps.: Assets....... | 7a.d | 65.0 | 61.0 | 88.3 | 169.2 | 157.8 | 149.2 | 143.7 | 149.6 | 156.0 | 171.6 | 209.8 | 228.5 |
| Other Depository Corps.: Liabs........ | 7b.d | 86.6 | 86.7 | 133.9 | 189.6 | 220.9 | 194.9 | 184.3 | 194.7 | 188.0 | 176.9 | 209.7 | 197.6 |
| **Central Bank** | | | | | | | *Billions of Won: End of Period* | | | | | | | |
| Net Foreign Assets...................... | 11n | 209,578 | 213,607 | 218,336 | 233,493 | 214,004 | 279,072 | 300,584 | 267,202 | 258,526 | 265,195 | 284,209 | 318,228 |
| Claims on Nonresidents................. | 11 | 231,439 | 232,347 | 249,682 | 276,400 | 258,698 | 323,823 | 342,837 | 362,231 | 355,727 | 363,906 | 378,065 | 399,844 |
| Liabilities to Nonresidents............. | 16c | 21,861 | 18,740 | 31,346 | 42,906 | 44,694 | 44,752 | 42,253 | 95,028 | 97,201 | 98,711 | 93,856 | 81,616 |
| Claims on Other Depository Corps.... | 12e | 10,775 | 11,078 | 11,059 | 8,101 | 30,731 | 16,682 | 14,208 | 9,198 | 9,033 | 9,953 | 15,406 | 19,970 |
| Net Claims on Central Government.. | 12an | −35,082 | −42,280 | −46,696 | −64,220 | −13,850 | −62,882 | −70,809 | −78,765 | −68,473 | −65,732 | −54,471 | −52,947 |
| Claims on Central Government...... | 12a | 3,589 | 6,084 | 8,906 | 12,947 | 12,369 | 15,216 | 16,062 | 15,211 | 20,716 | 18,876 | 21,365 | 17,713 |
| Liabilities to Central Government... | 16d | 38,672 | 48,364 | 55,602 | 77,167 | 26,219 | 78,098 | 86,871 | 93,976 | 89,189 | 84,608 | 75,836 | 70,660 |
| Claims on Other Sectors.................. | 12s | 310 | 453 | 453 | 453 | 453 | 310 | 310 | 1,921 | 2,056 | 2,056 | 1,562 | 1,925 |
| Claims on Other Financial Corps.... | 12g | — | — | — | — | — | — | — | — | — | — | — | — |
| Claims on State & Local Govts....... | 12b | — | — | — | — | — | — | — | — | — | — | — | — |
| Claims on Public Nonfin. Corps...... | 12c | 310 | 453 | 453 | 453 | 453 | 310 | 310 | 1,921 | 2,056 | 2,056 | 1,562 | 1,925 |
| Claims on Private Sector............... | 12d | — | — | — | — | — | — | — | — | — | — | — | — |
| Monetary Base............................ | 14 | 38,792 | 43,249 | 51,870 | 56,399 | 64,846 | 67,779 | 74,546 | 80,056 | 88,342 | 104,262 | 116,794 | 131,439 |
| Currency in Circulation.................. | 14a | 24,789 | 26,037 | 27,742 | 29,219 | 30,652 | 37,239 | 43,197 | 48,543 | 54,216 | 63,242 | 74,815 | 86,618 |
| Liabs. to Other Depository Corps.... | 14c | 14,003 | 17,212 | 24,128 | 27,180 | 34,194 | 30,540 | 31,349 | 31,513 | 34,126 | 41,020 | 41,979 | 44,821 |
| Liabilities to Other Sectors............. | 14d | — | — | — | — | — | — | — | — | — | — | — | — |
| Other Liabs. to Other Dep. Corps..... | 14n | 89,291 | 95,619 | 103,125 | 87,203 | 93,696 | 86,881 | 91,477 | 101,125 | 91,415 | 83,293 | 99,450 | 108,546 |
| Dep. & Sec. Excl. f/Monetary Base.... | 14o | 56,069 | 58,455 | 54,234 | 53,060 | 37,081 | 49,857 | 58,921 | 55,826 | 63,427 | 72,533 | 82,511 | 78,479 |
| Deposits Included in Broad Money. | 15 | — | — | — | — | — | — | — | — | — | — | — | — |
| Sec.Ot.th.Shares Incl.in Brd.Money. | 16a | 14,464 | 14,039 | 12,006 | 10,683 | 7,747 | 12,734 | 12,222 | 13,594 | 16,596 | 18,503 | 23,578 | 22,189 |
| Deposits Excl. from Broad Money... | 16b | — | — | — | — | — | — | — | — | — | — | — | — |
| Sec.Ot.th.Shares Excl.f/Brd.Money.. | 16s | 41,604 | 44,416 | 42,228 | 42,377 | 29,334 | 37,123 | 46,699 | 42,232 | 46,831 | 54,030 | 58,933 | 56,290 |
| Loans..................................... | 16l | — | — | — | — | — | — | — | — | — | — | — | — |
| Financial Derivatives..................... | 16m | — | — | — | — | — | — | — | — | — | — | — | — |
| Shares and Other Equity................. | 17a | 5,817 | 3,830 | 2,015 | 1,553 | 4,896 | 6,208 | 8,558 | 9,630 | 11,578 | 10,082 | 10,619 | 11,946 |
| Other Items (Net)......................... | 17r | −4,388 | −18,296 | −28,091 | −20,387 | 30,819 | 22,457 | 10,792 | −47,080 | −53,619 | −58,698 | −62,668 | −43,234 |
| Memo Item: | | | | | | | | | | | | | |
| Total Assets.............................. | 10ra | 253,034 | 271,259 | 303,005 | 323,460 | 312,340 | 364,033 | 383,188 | 456,341 | 446,491 | 458,481 | 485,799 | 488,897 |
| **Other Depository Corporations** | | | | | | | *Billions of Won: End of Period* | | | | | | | |
| Net Foreign Assets...................... | 21n | −22,352 | −25,977 | −42,434 | −19,037 | −79,489 | −53,272 | −46,088 | −51,935 | −34,283 | −5,599 | 93 | 36,280 |
| Claims on Nonresidents................. | 21 | 67,313 | 61,717 | 82,092 | 158,433 | 198,771 | 173,734 | 163,028 | 172,288 | 166,986 | 181,071 | 230,610 | 267,834 |
| Liabilities to Nonresidents............. | 26c | 89,665 | 87,694 | 124,526 | 177,471 | 278,260 | 227,005 | 209,116 | 224,223 | 201,269 | 186,671 | 230,516 | 231,553 |
| Claims on Central Bank.................. | 20 | 122,058 | 130,694 | 144,325 | 138,037 | 162,624 | 158,044 | 156,856 | 162,789 | 168,624 | 172,608 | 186,546 | 196,798 |
| Currency................................ | 20a | 5,582 | 5,625 | 6,106 | 7,179 | 7,215 | 8,033 | 8,248 | 8,934 | 10,042 | 9,926 | 10,375 | 10,275 |
| Reserve Deposits and Securities..... | 20b | 16,511 | 17,241 | 26,932 | 27,172 | 46,897 | 41,586 | 40,240 | 43,885 | 57,275 | 67,546 | 75,625 | 80,097 |
| Other Claims............................ | 20n | 99,965 | 107,828 | 111,287 | 103,686 | 108,512 | 108,425 | 108,368 | 109,970 | 101,307 | 95,136 | 100,544 | 106,426 |
| Net Claims on Central Government.. | 22an | 13,509 | 16,780 | 13,578 | −9,023 | −62,158 | 5,787 | 19,590 | 16,477 | 31,404 | 42,473 | 46,633 | 45,158 |
| Claims on Central Government...... | 22a | 73,893 | 78,970 | 85,817 | 74,997 | 75,686 | 91,011 | 96,114 | 87,313 | 93,961 | 106,017 | 113,225 | 121,779 |
| Liabilities to Central Government... | 26d | 60,384 | 62,190 | 72,239 | 84,020 | 137,844 | 85,224 | 76,523 | 70,836 | 62,557 | 63,544 | 66,592 | 76,622 |
| Claims on Other Sectors.................. | 22s | 1,085,049 | 1,178,949 | 1,370,773 | 1,570,691 | 1,828,886 | 1,869,004 | 1,962,040 | 2,101,573 | 2,181,710 | 2,248,326 | 2,418,099 | 2,601,640 |
| Claims on Other Financial Corps.... | 22g | 115,270 | 113,982 | 128,564 | 145,332 | 168,779 | 180,528 | 218,679 | 231,877 | 270,875 | 290,331 | 329,761 | 373,750 |
| Claims on State & Local Govts....... | 22b | 2,722 | 2,769 | 4,852 | 6,458 | 6,617 | 6,793 | 7,254 | 8,748 | 12,513 | 13,925 | 19,066 | 24,224 |
| Claims on Public Nonfin. Corps...... | 22c | 5,385 | 6,097 | 8,330 | 11,755 | 15,081 | 17,159 | 16,201 | 20,072 | 15,435 | 15,636 | 13,160 | 12,746 |
| Claims on Private Sector............... | 22d | 961,673 | 1,056,100 | 1,229,027 | 1,407,146 | 1,638,409 | 1,664,524 | 1,719,905 | 1,840,876 | 1,882,887 | 1,928,433 | 2,056,112 | 2,190,920 |
| Liabilities to Central Bank............... | 26g | 9,215 | 9,522 | 9,506 | 6,551 | 22,581 | 11,665 | 10,107 | 8,562 | 8,499 | 11,828 | 15,773 | 19,633 |
| Transf.Dep.Included in Broad Money | 24 | 247,953 | 281,338 | 308,683 | 294,343 | 307,187 | 360,189 | 392,843 | 402,468 | 425,837 | 462,327 | 521,384 | 632,110 |
| Other Dep.Included in Broad Money. | 25 | 619,801 | 633,532 | 717,958 | 821,514 | 936,267 | 1,015,462 | 1,121,962 | 1,213,119 | 1,276,591 | 1,305,671 | 1,383,076 | 1,428,197 |
| Sec.Ot.th.Shares Incl.in Brd. Money.... | 26a | 53,297 | 72,128 | 88,979 | 125,033 | 151,249 | 149,260 | 98,554 | 82,668 | 72,445 | 80,977 | 84,757 | 88,536 |
| Deposits Excl. from Broad Money.... | 26b | 120,832 | 128,195 | 131,405 | 129,314 | 150,099 | 158,395 | 181,817 | 199,581 | 218,577 | 238,591 | 273,101 | 308,359 |
| Sec.Ot.th.Shares Excl.f/Brd.Money..... | 26s | 34,461 | 43,555 | 60,728 | 94,523 | 106,216 | 86,589 | 73,567 | 77,869 | 80,211 | 84,123 | 114,086 | 120,234 |
| Loans..................................... | 26l | 16,974 | 18,845 | 19,903 | 19,441 | 22,417 | 20,705 | 23,225 | 29,174 | 31,042 | 34,819 | 30,960 | 28,487 |
| Financial Derivatives..................... | 26m | 14,021 | 7,552 | 9,130 | 9,694 | 49,131 | 23,989 | 17,245 | 13,299 | 16,229 | 13,466 | 13,382 | 14,928 |
| Insurance Technical Reserves.......... | 26r | — | — | — | — | — | — | — | — | — | — | — | — |
| Shares and Other Equity................. | 27a | 70,837 | 93,493 | 108,687 | 122,367 | 129,564 | 144,415 | 152,512 | 162,800 | 184,549 | 189,460 | 201,541 | 215,752 |
| Other Items (Net)......................... | 27r | 10,872 | 12,287 | 31,264 | 57,887 | −24,847 | 8,894 | 20,565 | 39,364 | 33,477 | 36,545 | 13,311 | 23,640 |
| Memo Item: | | | | | | | | | | | | | |
| Total Assets.............................. | 20ra | 1,718,222 | 1,830,327 | 2,125,284 | 2,458,416 | 2,992,329 | 2,952,117 | 3,036,905 | 3,162,554 | 3,323,163 | 3,450,628 | 3,786,255 | 4,100,548 |

# Korea, Republic of  542

| | | 2004 | 2005 | 2006 | 2007 | 2008 | 2009 | 2010 | 2011 | 2012 | 2013 | 2014 | 2015 |
|---|---|---|---|---|---|---|---|---|---|---|---|---|---|
| **Depository Corporations** | | | | | | *Billions of Won: End of Period* | | | | | | | |
| Net Foreign Assets | 31n | 187,226 | 187,630 | 175,902 | 214,456 | 134,515 | 225,800 | 254,496 | 215,268 | 224,243 | 259,595 | 284,302 | 354,508 |
| Claims on Nonresidents | 31 | 298,752 | 294,064 | 331,774 | 434,833 | 457,469 | 497,557 | 505,865 | 534,519 | 522,714 | 544,977 | 608,675 | 667,677 |
| Liabilities to Nonresidents | 36c | 111,527 | 106,434 | 155,871 | 220,377 | 322,954 | 271,757 | 251,369 | 319,251 | 298,470 | 285,382 | 324,372 | 313,169 |
| Domestic Claims | 32 | 1,063,786 | 1,153,902 | 1,338,107 | 1,497,902 | 1,753,332 | 1,812,219 | 1,911,132 | 2,041,206 | 2,146,698 | 2,227,123 | 2,411,823 | 2,595,775 |
| Net Claims on Central Government | 32an | −21,573 | −25,500 | −33,119 | −73,243 | −76,007 | −57,095 | −51,218 | −62,288 | −37,069 | −23,258 | −7,838 | −7,789 |
| Claims on Central Government | 32a | 77,482 | 85,054 | 94,722 | 87,944 | 88,055 | 106,227 | 112,176 | 102,524 | 114,677 | 124,894 | 134,590 | 139,492 |
| Liabilities to Central Government | 36d | 99,055 | 110,554 | 127,841 | 161,187 | 164,063 | 163,322 | 163,394 | 164,812 | 151,746 | 148,152 | 142,428 | 147,281 |
| Claims on Other Sectors | 32s | 1,085,359 | 1,179,402 | 1,371,226 | 1,571,144 | 1,829,339 | 1,869,314 | 1,962,350 | 2,103,494 | 2,183,766 | 2,250,382 | 2,419,661 | 2,603,565 |
| Claims on Other Financial Corps | 32g | 115,270 | 113,982 | 128,564 | 145,332 | 168,779 | 180,528 | 218,679 | 231,877 | 270,875 | 290,331 | 329,761 | 373,750 |
| Claims on State & Local Govts | 32b | 2,722 | 2,769 | 4,852 | 6,458 | 6,617 | 6,793 | 7,254 | 8,748 | 12,513 | 13,925 | 19,066 | 24,224 |
| Claims on Public Nonfin. Corps | 32c | 5,695 | 6,550 | 8,783 | 12,208 | 15,534 | 17,469 | 16,511 | 21,993 | 17,491 | 17,692 | 14,723 | 14,671 |
| Claims on Private Sector | 32d | 961,673 | 1,056,100 | 1,229,027 | 1,407,146 | 1,638,409 | 1,664,524 | 1,719,905 | 1,840,876 | 1,882,887 | 1,928,433 | 2,056,112 | 2,190,920 |
| Broad Money Liabilities | 35l | 954,723 | 1,021,449 | 1,149,262 | 1,273,612 | 1,425,887 | 1,566,850 | 1,660,530 | 1,751,458 | 1,835,642 | 1,920,795 | 2,077,234 | 2,247,375 |
| Currency Outside Depository Corps | 34a | 19,207 | 20,412 | 21,636 | 22,039 | 23,437 | 29,206 | 34,949 | 39,609 | 44,174 | 53,316 | 64,438 | 76,343 |
| Transferable Deposits | 34 | 247,953 | 281,338 | 308,683 | 294,343 | 307,187 | 360,189 | 392,843 | 402,468 | 425,837 | 462,327 | 521,384 | 632,110 |
| Other Deposits | 35 | 619,801 | 633,532 | 717,958 | 821,514 | 936,267 | 1,015,462 | 1,121,962 | 1,213,119 | 1,276,591 | 1,305,671 | 1,383,076 | 1,428,197 |
| Securities Other than Shares | 36a | 67,761 | 86,166 | 100,986 | 135,716 | 158,996 | 161,994 | 110,776 | 96,262 | 89,041 | 99,481 | 108,335 | 110,725 |
| Deposits Excl. from Broad Money | 36b | 120,832 | 128,195 | 131,405 | 129,314 | 150,099 | 158,395 | 181,817 | 199,581 | 218,577 | 238,591 | 273,101 | 308,359 |
| Sec.Ot.th.Shares Excl.f/Brd.Money | 36s | 76,066 | 87,971 | 102,955 | 136,900 | 135,550 | 123,712 | 120,266 | 120,101 | 127,042 | 138,152 | 173,019 | 176,524 |
| Loans | 36l | 16,974 | 18,845 | 19,903 | 19,441 | 22,417 | 20,705 | 23,225 | 29,174 | 31,042 | 34,819 | 30,960 | 28,487 |
| Financial Derivatives | 36m | 14,021 | 7,552 | 9,130 | 9,694 | 49,131 | 23,989 | 17,245 | 13,299 | 16,229 | 13,466 | 13,382 | 14,928 |
| Insurance Technical Reserves | 36r | — | — | — | — | — | — | — | — | — | — | — | — |
| Shares and Other Equity | 37a | 76,654 | 97,323 | 110,702 | 123,919 | 134,460 | 150,623 | 161,070 | 172,429 | 196,127 | 199,542 | 212,161 | 227,698 |
| Other Items (Net) | 37r | −8,258 | −19,803 | −9,347 | 19,476 | −29,698 | −6,255 | 1,474 | −29,570 | −53,718 | −58,646 | −83,731 | −53,087 |
| Broad Money Liabs., Seasonally Adj. | 35l.b | 954,597 | 1,021,817 | 1,150,601 | 1,276,505 | 1,430,204 | 1,572,002 | 1,665,788 | 1,756,988 | 1,841,416 | 1,927,208 | 2,084,305 | 2,258,579 |
| **Monetary Aggregates** | | | | | | *Billions of Won: End of Period* | | | | | | | |
| Broad Money | 59m | 954,723 | 1,021,449 | 1,149,262 | 1,273,612 | 1,425,887 | 1,566,850 | 1,660,530 | 1,751,458 | 1,835,642 | 1,920,795 | 2,077,234 | 2,247,375 |
| o/w:Currency Issued by Cent.Govt | 59m.a | — | — | — | — | — | — | — | — | — | — | — | — |
| o/w: Dep.in Nonfin. Corporations | 59m.b | — | — | — | — | — | — | — | — | — | — | — | — |
| o/w: Secs. Issued by Central Govt | 59m.c | — | — | — | — | — | — | — | — | — | — | — | — |
| Money (National Definitions) | | | | | | | | | | | | | |
| M1 | 59ma | 321,728 | 332,345 | 371,088 | 316,383 | 330,624 | 389,395 | 427,792 | 442,078 | 470,011 | 515,643 | 585,823 | 708,453 |
| M2 | 59mb | 954,723 | 1,021,449 | 1,149,262 | 1,273,612 | 1,425,887 | 1,566,850 | 1,660,530 | 1,751,458 | 1,835,642 | 1,920,795 | 2,077,234 | 2,247,375 |
| Lf | 59mfa | 1,295,822 | 1,391,560 | 1,538,300 | 1,691,565 | 1,845,199 | 2,018,785 | 2,137,198 | 2,277,679 | 2,456,121 | 2,615,094 | 2,841,785 | 3,098,949 |
| L | 59mf | 1,517,011 | 1,654,005 | 1,830,671 | 2,037,174 | 2,243,277 | 2,486,672 | 2,665,004 | 2,889,658 | 3,121,879 | 3,350,483 | 3,635,489 | 3,946,828 |
| **Interest Rates** | | | | | | *Percent Per Annum* | | | | | | | |
| Central Bank Policy Rate (EOP) | 60 | 3.25 | 3.75 | 4.50 | 5.00 | 3.00 | 2.00 | 2.50 | 3.25 | 2.75 | 2.50 | 2.00 | 1.50 |
| Discount Rate (End of Period) | 60.a | 2.00 | 2.00 | 2.75 | 3.25 | 1.75 | 1.25 | 1.25 | 1.50 | 1.25 | 1.00 | 1.00 | .75 |
| Money Market Rate | 60b | 3.65 | 3.33 | 4.19 | 4.77 | 4.78 | 1.98 | 2.16 | 3.09 | 3.08 | 2.59 | 2.34 | 1.65 |
| Corporate Bond Rate | 60bc | 4.73 | 4.68 | 5.17 | 5.70 | 7.02 | 5.81 | 4.66 | 4.41 | 3.77 | 3.19 | 2.99 | 2.09 |
| Deposit Rate | 60l | 3.87 | 3.72 | 4.50 | 5.17 | 5.87 | 3.48 | 3.86 | 4.15 | 3.70 | 2.89 | 2.54 | 1.81 |
| Lending Rate | 60p | 5.90 | 5.59 | 5.99 | 6.55 | 7.17 | 5.65 | 5.51 | 5.76 | 5.40 | 4.64 | 4.26 | 3.53 |
| Government Bond Yield | 61 | 4.45 | 4.66 | 5.07 | 5.43 | 5.79 | 5.10 | 4.59 | 4.11 | 3.43 | 3.16 | 2.98 | 2.11 |
| **Prices, Production, Labor** | | | | | | *Index Numbers (2010=100): Period Averages* | | | | | | | |
| Share Prices | 62 | 47.3 | 60.8 | 76.8 | 97.3 | 87.0 | 80.9 | 100.0 | 112.6 | 109.6 | 111.3 | 112.5 | 114.1 |
| Share Prices (End of Month) | 62.ep | 47.4 | 61.6 | 77.5 | 98.4 | 86.0 | 81.3 | 100.0 | 112.9 | 110.0 | 112.1 | 112.8 | 114.3 |
| Producer Prices | 63 | 85.1 | 86.9 | 87.7 | 88.9 | 96.5 | 96.3 | 100.0 | 106.7 | 107.5 | 105.7 | 105.2 | 101.0 |
| Consumer Prices | 64 | 83.8 | 86.1 | 88.1 | 90.3 | 94.5 | 97.1 | 100.0 | 104.0 | 106.3 | 107.7 | 109.0 | 109.8 |
| Wages: Monthly Earnings | 65ey | 71.6 | 77.4 | 81.8 | 87.1 | 90.1 | 91.8 | 100.0 | 100.5 | 106.5 | 111.5 | 115.7 | 119.0 |
| Industrial Production | 66 | 67.6 | 71.8 | 77.9 | 83.3 | 86.1 | 86.0 | 100.0 | 105.9 | 106.8 | 106.8 | 107.8 | 107.5 |
| Manufacturing Employment | 67ey | 103.7 | 102.5 | 100.7 | 99.7 | 98.4 | 95.3 | 100.0 | 101.6 | 101.9 | 103.9 | 107.5 | 111.4 |
| | | | | | | *Number in Thousands: Period Averages* | | | | | | | |
| Labor Force | 67d | 23,417 | 23,743 | 23,978 | 24,216 | 24,347 | 24,394 | 24,748 | 25,099 | 25,501 | 25,873 | 26,536 | 26,913 |
| Employment | 67e | 22,557 | 22,856 | 23,151 | 23,433 | 23,577 | 23,506 | 23,829 | 24,244 | 24,681 | 25,066 | 25,599 | 25,936 |
| Unemployment | 67c | 860 | 887 | 827 | 783 | 769 | 889 | 920 | 855 | 820 | 807 | 937 | 976 |
| Unemployment Rate (%) | 67r | 3.7 | 3.7 | 3.5 | 3.2 | 3.2 | 3.6 | 3.7 | 3.4 | 3.2 | 3.1 | 3.5 | 3.6 |
| **Intl. Transactions & Positions** | | | | | | *Millions of US Dollars* | | | | | | | |
| Exports | 70..d | 253,847 | 284,422 | 325,468 | 371,492 | 422,007 | 363,534 | 466,384 | 555,216 | 547,879 | 559,632 | 572,665 | 526,756 |
| Imports, c.i.f. | 71..d | 224,454 | 267,559 | 309,350 | 356,852 | 435,275 | 323,085 | 425,212 | 524,413 | 519,585 | 515,586 | 525,515 | 436,499 |
| | | | | | | *2010=100* | | | | | | | |
| Volume of Exports | 72 | 56.3 | 59.9 | 69.3 | 78.3 | 82.0 | 82.0 | 100.0 | 113.9 | 120.2 | 126.0 | 131.4 | 134.9 |
| Volume of Imports | 73 | 77.0 | 78.3 | 85.7 | 90.9 | 97.7 | 85.8 | 100.0 | 105.5 | 106.1 | 110.6 | 115.8 | 119.7 |
| Export Prices | 76 | 100.7 | 94.0 | 86.3 | 84.4 | 102.8 | 102.6 | 100.0 | 100.2 | 97.9 | 93.7 | 88.1 | 83.5 |
| Import Prices | 76.x | 67.0 | 69.0 | 69.6 | 72.7 | 99.1 | 95.0 | 100.0 | 111.6 | 110.8 | 102.7 | 94.9 | 80.4 |

# Korea, Republic of  542

| | | 2004 | 2005 | 2006 | 2007 | 2008 | 2009 | 2010 | 2011 | 2012 | 2013 | 2014 | 2015 |
|---|---|---|---|---|---|---|---|---|---|---|---|---|---|
| **Balance of Payments** | | | | | | | *Millions of US Dollars* | | | | | | |
| A. Current Account* | 109bx | 29,743.4 | 12,654.8 | 3,569.2 | 11,794.5 | 3,189.7 | 33,593.3 | 28,850.4 | 18,655.8 | 50,835.0 | 81,148.2 | 84,373.0 | 105,870.7 |
| Goods, credit (exports) | 1a9cx | 256,049.9 | 285,254.1 | 329,102.5 | 382,789.0 | 432,894.0 | 363,900.9 | 463,769.6 | 587,099.7 | 603,509.2 | 618,156.9 | 613,020.6 | 548,837.8 |
| Goods, debit (imports) | 1a9dx | 216,772.4 | 252,941.6 | 303,928.4 | 349,951.4 | 420,696.5 | 316,086.9 | 415,854.2 | 558,009.8 | 554,103.2 | 535,375.9 | 524,135.2 | 428,547.8 |
| Balance on goods | 1a9bx | 39,277.5 | 32,312.5 | 25,174.1 | 32,837.6 | 12,197.5 | 47,814.0 | 47,915.4 | 29,089.9 | 49,406.0 | 82,781.0 | 88,885.4 | 120,290.0 |
| Services (exports) | 1b9cx | 45,465.6 | 50,730.3 | 57,212.5 | 71,650.5 | 91,333.3 | 72,752.1 | 83,260.3 | 90,900.1 | 103,533.2 | 103,739.2 | 112,105.9 | 97,877.0 |
| Services, debit (imports) | 1b9dx | 50,628.3 | 59,860.6 | 70,426.1 | 84,897.5 | 97,876.2 | 82,342.0 | 97,498.7 | 103,179.2 | 108,746.8 | 110,238.4 | 115,784.4 | 113,585.1 |
| Balance on Goods & Services | 1z9bx | 34,114.8 | 23,182.2 | 11,960.5 | 19,590.6 | 5,654.6 | 38,224.1 | 33,677.0 | 16,810.8 | 44,192.4 | 76,281.8 | 85,206.9 | 104,581.9 |
| Primary income: credit | 1c9cx | 11,042.5 | 12,007.7 | 15,450.9 | 20,949.7 | 21,686.3 | 15,371.5 | 22,737.4 | 27,436.2 | 30,160.5 | 30,108.3 | 26,817.1 | 28,023.6 |
| Primary income: debit | 1c9dx | 12,375.6 | 19,276.8 | 19,460.4 | 24,358.4 | 22,884.4 | 17,807.7 | 22,247.5 | 20,875.6 | 18,043.8 | 21,052.6 | 22,666.3 | 22,121.9 |
| Balance on gds, serv. & prim. inc. | 1y9bx | 32,781.7 | 15,913.1 | 7,951.0 | 16,181.9 | 4,456.5 | 35,787.9 | 34,166.9 | 23,371.4 | 56,309.1 | 85,337.5 | 89,357.7 | 110,483.6 |
| Secondary income: credit | 1d9ca | 6,162.0 | 6,251.6 | 6,065.0 | 6,609.4 | 9,275.4 | 7,901.9 | 7,049.6 | 8,432.2 | 8,558.0 | 8,778.6 | 8,873.9 | 8,922.5 |
| Secondary income: debit | 1d9da | 9,200.3 | 9,509.9 | 10,446.8 | 10,996.8 | 10,542.2 | 10,096.5 | 12,366.1 | 13,147.8 | 14,032.1 | 12,967.9 | 13,858.6 | 13,535.4 |
| B. Capital Account* | 209ba | 9.7 | −.6 | −69.0 | 5.7 | 26.4 | −69.6 | −63.2 | −112.0 | −41.7 | −27.0 | −8.9 | −64.7 |
| Capital account: credit | 209ca | 22.6 | 113.4 | 64.0 | 156.2 | 103.8 | 15.5 | 61.8 | 23.6 | 20.7 | 59.0 | 53.7 | 87.6 |
| Capital account: debit | 209da | 12.9 | 114.0 | 133.0 | 150.5 | 77.4 | 85.1 | 125.0 | 135.6 | 62.4 | 86.0 | 62.6 | 152.3 |
| Balance on current & capital acct. | 129bx | 29,753.1 | 12,654.2 | 3,500.2 | 11,800.2 | 3,216.1 | 33,523.7 | 28,787.2 | 18,543.8 | 50,793.3 | 81,121.2 | 84,364.1 | 105,806.0 |
| C. Financial Account* | 309na | −4,378.2 | −1,035.1 | −9,567.4 | 2,365.5 | 49,854.4 | −41,503.7 | −3,780.6 | 10,363.0 | 38,397.9 | 63,808.5 | 71,448.2 | 97,677.4 |
| Direct investment: assets | 3a9aa | 7,195.6 | 8,330.0 | 12,769.3 | 22,074.3 | 19,632.6 | 17,435.9 | 28,279.9 | 29,704.7 | 30,632.1 | 28,359.8 | 28,039.2 | 27,639.8 |
| Equity & investment fund shares.. | 3aaaa | 6,758.0 | 7,936.3 | 11,422.9 | 20,380.8 | 17,581.8 | 15,064.2 | 25,211.4 | 26,688.9 | 27,542.1 | 24,830.2 | 22,812.2 | 23,959.9 |
| Debt instruments | 3abaa | 437.6 | 393.7 | 1,346.4 | 1,693.5 | 2,050.8 | 2,371.7 | 3,068.5 | 3,015.8 | 3,090.0 | 3,529.6 | 5,227.0 | 3,679.9 |
| Direct investment: liabilities | 3a9la | 13,294.4 | 13,643.2 | 9,161.9 | 8,826.9 | 11,187.5 | 9,021.9 | 9,497.4 | 9,773.0 | 9,495.9 | 12,766.6 | 9,273.6 | 5,042.0 |
| Equity & investment fund shares . | 3aala | 11,928.2 | 13,109.6 | 7,975.6 | 7,718.1 | 9,158.6 | 8,548.7 | 8,429.5 | 9,492.6 | 7,977.1 | 9,919.4 | 7,886.9 | 7,766.8 |
| Debt instruments | 3abla | 1,366.2 | 533.6 | 1,186.3 | 1,108.8 | 2,028.9 | 473.2 | 1,067.9 | 280.4 | 1,518.8 | 2,847.2 | 1,386.7 | −2,724.8 |
| Portfolio investment: assets | 3b9aa | 11,775.8 | 17,631.6 | 31,285.9 | 56,444.0 | −23,480.5 | −1,400.9 | 1,265.4 | 4,138.4 | 26,079.5 | 27,494.2 | 39,816.8 | 41,305.4 |
| Equity & investment fund shares | 3baaa | 3,621.6 | 3,685.6 | 15,261.7 | 52,558.0 | −7,120.2 | 2,103.7 | 2,954.0 | 988.8 | 14,619.5 | 13,759.1 | 13,963.3 | 16,072.3 |
| Debt securities | 3bbaa | 8,154.2 | 13,946.0 | 16,024.2 | 3,886.0 | −16,360.3 | −3,504.6 | −1,688.6 | 3,149.6 | 11,460.0 | 13,735.1 | 25,853.5 | 25,233.1 |
| Portfolio investment: liabilities | 3b9la | 18,374.8 | 14,113.5 | 7,900.2 | 29,366.0 | −25,901.9 | 49,786.6 | 43,630.1 | 17,281.1 | 32,827.3 | 18,149.7 | 9,207.9 | −7,287.4 |
| Equity & investment fund shares . | 3bala | 9,468.8 | 3,282.1 | −7,949.2 | −28,324.0 | −33,412.6 | 24,743.9 | 23,595.3 | −6,851.4 | 16,572.5 | 4,383.2 | 6,753.2 | −1,987.0 |
| Debt securities | 3bbla | 8,906.0 | 10,831.4 | 15,849.4 | 57,690.0 | 7,510.7 | 25,042.7 | 20,034.8 | 24,132.5 | 16,254.8 | 13,766.5 | 2,454.7 | −5,300.4 |
| Fin. der.& empl.stk.ops.(ESOs): net. | 3c9na | −2,020.3 | −1,789.9 | −484.4 | −5,444.8 | 14,369.4 | 3,093.0 | −828.9 | 1,031.3 | −2,627.8 | −4,410.3 | −3,826.9 | 2,532.5 |
| Fin. der. & ESOs.: assets | 3c9aa | −4,380.3 | −6,956.5 | −8,932.9 | −12,109.4 | −95,182.9 | −74,846.1 | −49,483.2 | −43,553.9 | −33,454.3 | −29,795.5 | −35,773.1 | −46,061.6 |
| Fin. der. & ESOs.: liabilities | 3c9la | −2,360.0 | −5,166.6 | −8,448.5 | −6,664.6 | −109,552.3 | −77,939.1 | −48,654.3 | −44,585.2 | −30,826.5 | −25,385.2 | −31,946.2 | −48,594.1 |
| Other investment: assets | 3d9aa | 9,459.9 | 6,175.7 | 10,282.6 | 16,965.8 | 13,518.1 | −4,267.9 | 11,741.5 | 22,166.4 | 8,600.1 | 37,096.7 | 38,410.0 | 15,499.7 |
| Other equity | 3daaa | 62.7 | 17.4 | 1,330.5 | 132.4 | 98.8 | 103.5 | 153.0 | 385.8 | 222.1 | 231.2 | 243.8 | 245.0 |
| Debt instruments | 3dzaa | 9,397.2 | 6,158.3 | 8,952.1 | 16,833.4 | 13,419.3 | −4,371.4 | 11,588.5 | 21,780.6 | 8,378.0 | 36,865.5 | 38,166.2 | 15,254.7 |
| Other investment: liabilities | 3d9la | −880.0 | 3,625.8 | 46,358.7 | 49,480.9 | −11,100.4 | −2,444.7 | −8,889.0 | 19,623.7 | −18,037.2 | −6,184.4 | 12,509.4 | −8,454.6 |
| Other equity | 3dala | −18.9 | 106.6 | −84.6 | −6.5 | 48.7 | −6.4 | −14.4 | 57.5 | 99.7 | 29.1 | 37.7 | 6.7 |
| Debt instruments | 3dzla | −861.1 | 3,519.2 | 46,443.3 | 49,487.4 | −11,149.1 | −2,438.3 | −8,874.6 | 19,566.2 | −18,136.9 | −6,213.5 | 12,471.7 | −8,461.3 |
| Curr.+ cap.− finan. acct. balance... | 4y9na | 34,131.3 | 13,689.3 | 13,067.6 | 9,434.7 | −46,638.3 | 75,027.4 | 32,567.8 | 8,180.8 | 12,395.4 | 17,312.7 | 12,915.9 | 8,128.6 |
| D. Net Errors and Omissions | 409na | 4,543.7 | 6,174.7 | 9,022.5 | 5,674.6 | −9,808.4 | −6,361.0 | −5,597.2 | 5,772.0 | 789.1 | −1,016.6 | 4,969.9 | 3,924.0 |
| E. Reserves and Related Items | 4z9na | 38,675.0 | 19,864.0 | 22,090.1 | 15,109.3 | −56,446.7 | 68,666.4 | 26,970.6 | 13,952.8 | 13,184.5 | 16,296.1 | 17,885.8 | 12,052.6 |
| Reserve assets | 3e9aa | 38,675.0 | 19,864.0 | 22,090.1 | 15,109.3 | −56,446.7 | 68,666.4 | 26,970.6 | 13,952.8 | 13,184.5 | 16,296.1 | 17,885.8 | 12,052.6 |
| Credit and loans from the IMF | 3dcla | — | — | — | — | — | — | — | — | — | — | — | — |
| Exceptional financing | 409la | .... | .... | .... | .... | .... | .... | .... | .... | .... | .... | .... | .... |
| *Excludes components in group E | | | | | | | | | | | | | |
| **International Investment Position** | | | | | | | *Millions of US Dollars* | | | | | | |
| Assets | 809aa | 329,595.4 | 370,181.0 | 466,733.1 | 594,961.4 | 537,236.3 | 630,427.3 | 697,092.5 | 759,545.6 | 861,041.5 | 967,522.3 | 1,081,941.3 | 1,134,902.3 |
| Direct investment | 8a9aa | 32,165.6 | 38,683.1 | 49,187.0 | 74,776.5 | 97,953.1 | 121,278.8 | 144,031.9 | 172,413.2 | 202,875.3 | 238,812.1 | 265,728.9 | 278,395.0 |
| Equity & investment fund shares.. | 8aaaa | 30,041.2 | 35,740.8 | 45,652.0 | 68,073.6 | 88,384.4 | 109,174.5 | 132,308.7 | 157,719.1 | 186,002.8 | 205,127.3 | 221,164.0 | 233,034.7 |
| Debt instruments | 8abaa | 2,124.4 | 2,942.3 | 3,535.0 | 6,702.9 | 9,568.7 | 12,104.4 | 11,723.2 | 14,694.1 | 16,872.5 | 33,684.7 | 44,564.9 | 45,360.3 |
| Portfolio investment | 8b9aa | 33,086.3 | 52,133.9 | 97,765.8 | 158,606.1 | 75,112.9 | 101,146.1 | 112,230.9 | 103,447.2 | 137,695.3 | 168,759.9 | 203,014.1 | 235,871.9 |
| Equity & investment fund shares.. | 8baaa | 9,009.0 | 13,913.5 | 36,818.7 | 104,857.6 | 47,878.9 | 72,319.6 | 81,930.1 | 71,663.2 | 99,121.1 | 123,774.8 | 140,299.6 | 152,523.0 |
| Debt securities | 8bbaa | 24,077.3 | 38,220.4 | 60,947.1 | 53,748.5 | 27,234.0 | 28,826.5 | 30,300.7 | 31,784.0 | 38,574.1 | 44,985.1 | 62,714.5 | 83,348.9 |
| Fin. der.(oth.than reserves) & ESOs | 8c9aa | 1,078.3 | 1,009.1 | 1,392.0 | 2,338.3 | 56,007.2 | 28,682.2 | 27,581.6 | 26,747.5 | 31,717.3 | 23,590.1 | 30,569.0 | 29,457.5 |
| Other investment | 8d9aa | 64,196.3 | 67,964.1 | 79,431.8 | 97,015.9 | 106,942.9 | 109,308.4 | 121,677.3 | 150,516.0 | 161,785.0 | 189,916.1 | 219,049.7 | 223,233.7 |
| Other equity | 8daaa | 2,521.5 | 3,047.2 | 5,009.6 | 5,266.6 | 4,380.4 | 5,150.4 | 4,691.0 | 4,728.4 | 5,620.9 | 6,156.7 | 6,353.7 | 2,346.8 |
| Debt instruments | 8dzaa | 61,674.8 | 64,916.9 | 74,422.2 | 91,749.3 | 102,562.5 | 104,158.0 | 116,986.3 | 145,787.6 | 156,164.1 | 183,759.4 | 212,696.0 | 220,886.9 |
| Reserve assets | 8e9aa | 199,068.9 | 210,390.8 | 238,956.5 | 262,224.5 | 201,220.2 | 270,011.8 | 291,570.8 | 306,421.6 | 326,968.6 | 346,444.2 | 363,579.6 | 367,944.2 |
| Liabilities | 809la | 390,023.1 | 514,082.4 | 621,950.0 | 782,409.2 | 606,566.7 | 730,298.3 | 828,196.6 | 840,567.9 | 955,411.1 | 1,004,762.1 | 994,381.0 | 939,640.0 |
| Direct investment | 8a9la | 87,766.4 | 100,879.1 | 115,773.5 | 121,956.5 | 94,721.5 | 121,933.4 | 135,499.7 | 135,178.3 | 157,876.1 | 180,859.7 | 179,205.1 | 174,573.2 |
| Equity & investment fund shares.. | 8aala | 83,914.3 | 100,767.6 | 113,392.9 | 118,202.5 | 90,164.5 | 115,453.4 | 127,358.3 | 126,120.9 | 151,034.7 | 165,641.9 | 163,447.6 | 162,364.2 |
| Debt instruments | 8abla | 3,852.1 | 4,111.5 | 2,380.6 | 3,754.0 | 4,557.0 | 6,480.0 | 8,141.4 | 9,057.4 | 6,841.4 | 15,217.8 | 15,757.5 | 12,209.0 |
| Portfolio investment | 8b9la | 210,313.2 | 310,456.3 | 352,392.9 | 456,653.6 | 252,151.1 | 391,579.7 | 489,149.1 | 477,017.7 | 578,102.3 | 615,574.4 | 591,306.0 | 551,939.4 |
| Equity & investment fund shares.. | 8bala | 156,416.4 | 249,475.5 | 276,388.1 | 320,065.4 | 124,639.7 | 237,083.2 | 317,029.0 | 284,242.7 | 363,305.6 | 387,922.1 | 369,461.4 | 344,070.9 |
| Debt securities | 8bbla | 53,896.8 | 60,980.8 | 76,004.9 | 136,588.2 | 127,512.4 | 154,496.5 | 172,120.0 | 192,775.0 | 214,796.7 | 227,652.2 | 221,844.5 | 207,868.5 |
| Fin. der.(oth.than reserves) & ESOs | 8c9la | 904.4 | 1,319.2 | 2,423.2 | 4,911.0 | 75,321.2 | 32,598.8 | 27,361.0 | 29,073.0 | 30,910.7 | 26,419.7 | 35,833.3 | 37,807.7 |
| Other investment | 8d9la | 91,039.2 | 97,427.8 | 151,360.3 | 198,888.0 | 184,372.0 | 184,186.3 | 176,186.9 | 199,298.9 | 188,522.0 | 181,908.4 | 188,036.7 | 175,319.7 |
| Other equity | 8dala | 504.8 | 564.0 | 521.7 | 523.2 | 498.1 | 541.7 | 537.2 | 1,085.7 | 1,232.0 | 1,273.7 | 1,246.8 | — |
| Debt instruments | 8dzla | 90,534.4 | 96,863.8 | 150,838.6 | 198,364.8 | 183,873.9 | 183,644.6 | 175,649.7 | 198,213.2 | 187,290.0 | 180,634.7 | 186,789.9 | 175,319.7 |

# Korea, Republic of  542

| | | 2004 | 2005 | 2006 | 2007 | 2008 | 2009 | 2010 | 2011 | 2012 | 2013 | 2014 | 2015 |
|---|---|---|---|---|---|---|---|---|---|---|---|---|---|
| **Government Finance** | | | | | | | | | | | | | |
| **Operations Statement** | | | | | | | | | | | | | |
| **General Government** | | | | | | *Billions of Korean Won: Fiscal Year Ends December 31* | | | | | | | |
| Revenue.......................... | a1 | .... | .... | .... | .... | .... | .... | .... | .... | 479,727 | 484,435 | 504,923 | .... |
| Taxes................................ | a11 | .... | .... | .... | .... | .... | .... | .... | .... | 258,649 | 260,176 | 270,524 | .... |
| Social Contributions...................... | a12 | .... | .... | .... | .... | .... | .... | .... | .... | 90,422 | 95,717 | 102,600 | .... |
| Grants............................... | a13 | .... | .... | .... | .... | .... | .... | .... | .... | 49 | — | — | .... |
| Other Revenue............................... | a14 | .... | .... | .... | .... | .... | .... | .... | .... | 130,607 | 128,541 | 131,799 | .... |
| Expense........................... | a2 | .... | .... | .... | .... | .... | .... | .... | .... | 418,814 | 421,085 | 442,842 | .... |
| Compensation of Employees.......... | a21 | .... | .... | .... | .... | .... | .... | .... | .... | 82,171 | 86,316 | 90,415 | .... |
| Use of Goods & Services................ | a22 | .... | .... | .... | .... | .... | .... | .... | .... | 82,490 | 86,311 | 92,234 | .... |
| Consumption of Fixed Capital........ | a23 | .... | .... | .... | .... | .... | .... | .... | .... | 21,458 | 23,952 | 24,692 | .... |
| Interest............................ | a24 | .... | .... | .... | .... | .... | .... | .... | .... | 21,754 | 21,580 | 22,613 | .... |
| Subsidies......................... | a25 | .... | .... | .... | .... | .... | .... | .... | .... | 58,381 | 70,602 | 70,005 | .... |
| Grants............................... | a26 | .... | .... | .... | .... | .... | .... | .... | .... | 488 | 536 | 597 | .... |
| Social Benefits............................. | a27 | .... | .... | .... | .... | .... | .... | .... | .... | 91,156 | 85,565 | 92,593 | .... |
| Other Expense....................... | a28 | .... | .... | .... | .... | .... | .... | .... | .... | 60,917 | 46,223 | 49,694 | .... |
| Gross Operating Balance [1-2+23]... | agob | .... | .... | .... | .... | .... | .... | .... | .... | 82,371 | 87,302 | 86,773 | .... |
| Net Operating Balance [1-2]........... | anob | .... | .... | .... | .... | .... | .... | .... | .... | 60,913 | 63,350 | 62,081 | .... |
| Net Acq. of Nonfinancial Assets....... | a31 | .... | .... | .... | .... | .... | .... | .... | .... | 44,452 | 42,184 | 41,284 | .... |
| Aquisition of Nonfin. Assets......... | a31.1 | .... | .... | .... | .... | .... | .... | .... | .... | .... | .... | .... | .... |
| Disposal of Nonfin. Assets.......... | a31.2 | .... | .... | .... | .... | .... | .... | .... | .... | .... | .... | .... | .... |
| Net Lending/Borrowing [1-2-31]...... | anlb | .... | .... | .... | .... | .... | .... | .... | .... | 16,461 | 21,166 | 20,797 | .... |
| Net Acq. of Financial Assets............. | a32 | .... | .... | .... | .... | .... | .... | .... | .... | 55,316 | 75,051 | 71,758 | .... |
| By instrument | | | | | | | | | | | | | |
| Monetary Gold & SDRs................. | a3201 | .... | .... | .... | .... | .... | .... | .... | .... | — | — | — | .... |
| Currency & Deposits...................... | a3202 | .... | .... | .... | .... | .... | .... | .... | .... | 10,843 | 3,716 | −4,899 | .... |
| Securities other than Shares.......... | a3203 | .... | .... | .... | .... | .... | .... | .... | .... | 3,873 | 12,398 | 17,359 | .... |
| Loans.............................. | a3204 | .... | .... | .... | .... | .... | .... | .... | .... | 9,444 | −7,182 | 696 | .... |
| Shares & Other Equity.................. | a3205 | .... | .... | .... | .... | .... | .... | .... | .... | 26,673 | 41,828 | 32,690 | .... |
| Insurance Technical Reserves.......... | a3206 | .... | .... | .... | .... | .... | .... | .... | .... | — | — | — | .... |
| Financial Derivatives...................... | a3207 | .... | .... | .... | .... | .... | .... | .... | .... | −2,760 | −2,686 | −2,008 | .... |
| Other Accounts Receivable............. | a3208 | .... | .... | .... | .... | .... | .... | .... | .... | 7,245 | 26,977 | 27,921 | .... |
| By debtor | | | | | | | | | | | | | |
| Domestic........................... | a321 | .... | .... | .... | .... | .... | .... | .... | .... | .... | 61,104 | .... | .... |
| Foreign............................. | a322 | .... | .... | .... | .... | .... | .... | .... | .... | .... | 13,947 | .... | .... |
| Net Incurrence of Liabilities............. | a33 | .... | .... | .... | .... | .... | .... | .... | .... | 37,234 | 53,886 | 50,960 | .... |
| By instrument | | | | | | | | | | | | | |
| Special Drawing Rights (SDRs)....... | a3301 | .... | .... | .... | .... | .... | .... | .... | .... | — | — | — | .... |
| Currency & Deposits...................... | a3302 | .... | .... | .... | .... | .... | .... | .... | .... | −4 | — | — | .... |
| Securities other than Shares.......... | a3303 | .... | .... | .... | .... | .... | .... | .... | .... | 40,553 | 47,713 | 35,044 | .... |
| Loans.............................. | a3304 | .... | .... | .... | .... | .... | .... | .... | .... | −2,810 | 8,007 | 11,575 | .... |
| Shares & Other Equity.................. | a3305 | .... | .... | .... | .... | .... | .... | .... | .... | — | −3 | — | .... |
| Insurance Technical Reserves.......... | a3306 | .... | .... | .... | .... | .... | .... | .... | .... | — | — | — | .... |
| Financial Derivatives...................... | a3307 | .... | .... | .... | .... | .... | .... | .... | .... | — | −2,111 | −2,413 | .... |
| Other Accounts Payable................. | a3308 | .... | .... | .... | .... | .... | .... | .... | .... | −505 | 281 | 6,754 | .... |
| By creditor | | | | | | | | | | | | | |
| Foreign............................. | a332 | .... | .... | .... | .... | .... | .... | .... | .... | .... | 58,799 | .... | .... |
| Stat. Discrepancy [32-33-NLB]........ | anlbz | .... | .... | .... | .... | .... | .... | .... | .... | 1,621 | — | — | .... |
| Memo Item: Expenditure [2+31]...... | a2m | .... | .... | .... | .... | .... | .... | .... | .... | 463,266 | 463,269 | 484,126 | .... |
| **Balance Sheet** | | | | | | *Billions of Korean Won: Fiscal Year Ends December 31* | | | | | | | |
| Net Worth........................... | a6 | .... | .... | .... | .... | .... | .... | .... | .... | 2,256,690 | 2,309,650 | 2,393,483 | .... |
| Nonfinancial Assets......................... | a61 | .... | .... | .... | .... | .... | .... | .... | .... | 1,828,550 | 1,869,910 | 1,912,783 | .... |
| Financial Assets........................... | a62 | .... | .... | .... | .... | .... | .... | .... | .... | 932,746 | 1,007,120 | 1,102,400 | .... |
| By instrument | | | | | | | | | | | | | |
| Monetary Gold & SDRs................. | a6201 | .... | .... | .... | .... | .... | .... | .... | .... | — | — | — | .... |
| Currency & Deposits...................... | a6202 | .... | .... | .... | .... | .... | .... | .... | .... | 197,005 | 196,803 | 198,362 | .... |
| Securities other than Shares.......... | a6203 | .... | .... | .... | .... | .... | .... | .... | .... | 113,110 | 122,824 | 143,174 | .... |
| Loans.............................. | a6204 | .... | .... | .... | .... | .... | .... | .... | .... | 161,130 | 159,150 | 161,560 | .... |
| Shares and Other Equity................. | a6205 | .... | .... | .... | .... | .... | .... | .... | .... | 359,249 | 398,453 | 435,942 | .... |
| Insurance Technical Reserves........ | a6206 | .... | .... | .... | .... | .... | .... | .... | .... | — | — | — | .... |
| Financial Derivatives...................... | a6207 | .... | .... | .... | .... | .... | .... | .... | .... | 800 | 560 | 2,866 | .... |
| Other Accounts Receivable............. | a6208 | .... | .... | .... | .... | .... | .... | .... | .... | 101,453 | 129,330 | 160,495 | .... |
| By debtor | | | | | | | | | | | | | |
| Domestic........................... | a621 | .... | .... | .... | .... | .... | .... | .... | .... | .... | .... | .... | .... |
| Foreign............................. | a622 | .... | .... | .... | .... | .... | .... | .... | .... | .... | .... | .... | .... |
| Liabilities.............................. | a63 | .... | .... | .... | .... | .... | .... | .... | .... | 504,607 | 567,382 | 621,700 | .... |
| By instrument | | | | | | | | | | | | | |
| Special Drawing Rights (SDRs)....... | a6301 | .... | .... | .... | .... | .... | .... | .... | .... | — | — | — | .... |
| Currency & Deposits...................... | a6302 | .... | .... | .... | .... | .... | .... | .... | .... | — | — | — | .... |
| Securities other than Shares.......... | a6303 | .... | .... | .... | .... | .... | .... | .... | .... | 399,386 | 449,283 | 484,831 | .... |
| Loans.............................. | a6304 | .... | .... | .... | .... | .... | .... | .... | .... | 44,175 | 56,591 | 69,682 | .... |
| Shares and Other Equity............... | a6305 | .... | .... | .... | .... | .... | .... | .... | .... | — | 371 | 405 | .... |
| Insurance Technical Reserves........ | a6306 | .... | .... | .... | .... | .... | .... | .... | .... | — | — | — | .... |
| Financial Derivatives...................... | a6307 | .... | .... | .... | .... | .... | .... | .... | .... | — | 1,367 | 723 | .... |
| Other Accounts Payable................. | a6308 | .... | .... | .... | .... | .... | .... | .... | .... | 61,048 | 59,771 | 66,058 | .... |
| By creditor | | | | | | | | | | | | | |
| Domestic........................... | a631 | .... | .... | .... | .... | .... | .... | .... | .... | .... | .... | .... | .... |
| Foreign............................. | a632 | .... | .... | .... | .... | .... | .... | .... | .... | .... | .... | .... | .... |
| Net Financial Worth [62-63]........... | a6m2 | .... | .... | .... | .... | .... | .... | .... | .... | 428,139 | 439,737 | 480,700 | .... |
| Memo Item: Debt at Market Value... | a6m3 | .... | .... | .... | .... | .... | .... | .... | .... | 504,607 | | | |
| Memo Item: Debt at Face Value....... | a6m35 | 203,700 | 247,900 | 282,700 | 299,200 | 309,000 | 359,600 | 392,200 | 420,500 | 443,100 | .... | .... | .... |
| Memo Item: Debt at Nominal Value. | a6m4 | .... | .... | .... | .... | .... | .... | .... | .... | .... | .... | .... | .... |

# Korea, Republic of  542

| National Accounts | | 2004 | 2005 | 2006 | 2007 | 2008 | 2009 | 2010 | 2011 | 2012 | 2013 | 2014 | 2015 |
|---|---|---|---|---|---|---|---|---|---|---|---|---|---|
| | | | | | | | *Billions of Won* | | | | | | |
| Househ.Cons.Expend.,incl.NPISHs.... | 96f | 449,981 | 480,170 | 509,907 | 546,429 | 579,053 | 594,883 | 636,713 | 679,142 | 707,614 | 727,800 | 748,201 | 771,212 |
| Government Consumption Expend... | 91f | 112,039 | 122,175 | 133,501 | 145,311 | 161,751 | 174,706 | 183,109 | 194,381 | 204,324 | 214,467 | 224,724 | 237,135 |
| Gross Fixed Capital Formation......... | 93e | 273,320 | 283,859 | 296,970 | 318,339 | 346,612 | 360,697 | 385,924 | 403,045 | 407,307 | 418,289 | 433,266 | 453,290 |
| Changes in Inventories................... | 93i | 8,036 | 11,976 | 18,937 | 21,550 | 18,075 | −32,856 | 19,264 | 36,191 | 19,722 | −2,288 | 1,813 | −9,275 |
| Exports of Goods and Services......... | 90c | 335,477 | 338,574 | 359,046 | 408,797 | 551,820 | 547,634 | 625,309 | 742,936 | 776,062 | 770,115 | 747,134 | 715,411 |
| Imports of Goods and Services (-)..... | 98c | 301,934 | 316,177 | 351,500 | 397,047 | 551,939 | 493,655 | 585,010 | 723,014 | 737,572 | 698,937 | 669,058 | 606,942 |
| Statistical Discrepancy.................... | 99bs | −886 | −780 | −807 | −122 | −881 | 299 | — | — | — | — | — | −2,240 |
| Gross Domestic Product (GDP)......... | 99b | 876,033 | 919,797 | 966,055 | 1,043,258 | 1,104,492 | 1,151,708 | 1,265,308 | 1,332,681 | 1,377,457 | 1,429,445 | 1,486,079 | 1,558,592 |
| Net Primary Income from Abroad..... | 98.n | −1,794 | −7,189 | −3,608 | −3,166 | −78 | −2,726 | 1,272 | 7,849 | 14,139 | 10,199 | 4,685 | 7,224 |
| Gross National Income (GNI)............ | 99a | 874,239 | 912,609 | 962,447 | 1,040,092 | 1,104,414 | 1,148,982 | 1,266,580 | 1,340,530 | 1,391,596 | 1,439,644 | 1,490,764 | 1,565,816 |
| Consumption of Fixed Capital.......... | 99cf | 150,834 | 158,964 | 167,364 | 178,020 | 203,034 | 221,748 | 232,133 | 252,382 | 267,390 | 279,102 | 291,307 | 305,774 |
| GDP Volume 2010 Prices................. | 99b.p | 995,286 | 1,034,338 | 1,087,876 | 1,147,311 | 1,179,771 | 1,188,118 | 1,265,308 | 1,311,893 | 1,341,967 | 1,380,833 | 1,426,972 | 1,464,244 |
| GDP Volume (2010=100)................ | 99bvp | 78.7 | 81.7 | 86.0 | 90.7 | 93.2 | 93.9 | 100.0 | 103.7 | 106.1 | 109.1 | 112.8 | 115.7 |
| GDP Deflator (2010=100)................ | 99bip | 88.0 | 88.9 | 88.8 | 90.9 | 93.6 | 96.9 | 100.0 | 101.6 | 102.6 | 103.5 | 104.1 | 106.4 |
| | | | | | | | *Millions: Midyear Estimates* | | | | | | |
| Population................................. | 99z | 47.32 | 47.61 | 47.90 | 48.21 | 48.51 | 48.81 | 49.09 | 49.36 | 49.61 | 49.85 | 50.07 | 50.29 |

# Kosovo 967

|  |  | 2004 | 2005 | 2006 | 2007 | 2008 | 2009 | 2010 | 2011 | 2012 | 2013 | 2014 | 2015 |
|---|---|---|---|---|---|---|---|---|---|---|---|---|---|
| **Exchange Rates** | | | | | | | *Euros per SDR: End of Period* | | | | | | | |
| Market Rate | aa | 1.1402 | 1.2116 | 1.1423 | 1.0735 | 1.1068 | 1.0882 | 1.1525 | 1.1865 | 1.1649 | 1.1167 | 1.1933 | 1.2728 |
| | | | | | | | *Euros per US Dollar: End of Period (ae) Period Average (rf)* | | | | | | | |
| Market Rate | ae | .7342 | .8477 | .7593 | .6793 | .7185 | .6942 | .7484 | .7729 | .7579 | .7251 | .8237 | .9185 |
| Market Rate | rf | .8054 | .8041 | .7971 | .7306 | .6827 | .7198 | .7550 | .7194 | .7783 | .7532 | .7537 | .9017 |
| **Fund Position** | | | | | | | *Millions of SDRs: End of Period* | | | | | | | |
| Quota | 2f.s | — | — | — | — | — | 59.00 | 59.00 | 59.00 | 59.00 | 59.00 | 59.00 | 59.00 |
| SDR Holdings | 1b.s | — | — | — | — | — | 55.37 | 55.18 | 54.91 | 54.34 | 53.34 | 52.34 | 51.17 |
| Reserve Position in the Fund | 1c.s | — | — | — | — | — | 14.16 | 14.17 | 14.17 | 14.17 | 14.17 | 14.17 | 14.17 |
| Total Fund Cred.&Loans Outstg. | 2tl | — | — | — | — | — | — | 18.76 | 18.76 | 96.98 | 94.63 | 85.25 | 100.36 |
| SDR Allocations | 1bd | — | — | — | — | — | 55.37 | 55.37 | 55.37 | 55.37 | 55.37 | 55.37 | 55.37 |
| **International Liquidity** | | | | | | | *Millions of US Dollars Unless Otherwise Indicated: End of Period* | | | | | | | |
| Total Reserves minus Gold | 1l.d | .... | .... | .... | 951.73 | 892.06 | 830.21 | 846.41 | 741.54 | 1,108.09 | 1,102.92 | 906.31 | 938.27 |
| SDR Holdings | 1b.d | — | — | — | — | — | 86.8 | 85.0 | 84.3 | 83.5 | 82.1 | 75.8 | 70.9 |
| Reserve Position in the Fund | 1c.d | — | — | — | — | — | 22.2 | 21.8 | 21.7 | 21.8 | 21.8 | 20.5 | 19.6 |
| Foreign Exchange | 1d.d | .... | .... | .... | 951.73 | 892.06 | 721.21 | 739.61 | 635.49 | 1,002.81 | 998.96 | 809.95 | 847.73 |
| Gold (Million Fine Troy Ounces) | 1ad | .... | .... | .... | — | — | — | — | — | — | — | — | — |
| Gold (National Valuation) | 1and | .... | .... | .... | — | — | — | — | — | — | — | — | — |
| Central Bank: Other Assets | 3..d | .28 | .18 | 1.93 | 8.13 | .94 | .16 | .83 | 2.23 | .12 | .14 | .36 | .57 |
| Central Bank: Other Liabs. | 4..d | 7.05 | 3.66 | .14 | .03 | — | 1.15 | 2.24 | .94 | .54 | .36 | .37 | .90 |
| Other Depository Corps.: Assets | 7a.d | 460.34 | 409.28 | 519.51 | 542.48 | 558.53 | 840.50 | 947.92 | 861.24 | 830.47 | 1,026.48 | 865.82 | 801.65 |
| Other Depository Corps.: Liabs. | 7b.d | 46.29 | 54.54 | 79.15 | 71.57 | 105.37 | 201.57 | 270.14 | 201.00 | 181.85 | 238.34 | 216.59 | 225.04 |
| Other Financial Corps.: Assets | 7e.d | 114.63 | 172.67 | 276.61 | 409.96 | 298.83 | 365.57 | 575.27 | 704.00 | 885.05 | 904.35 | 1,249.77 | 1,187.90 |
| Other Financial Corps.: Liabs. | 7f.d | 13.71 | 16.82 | 15.66 | 49.49 | 80.28 | 122.20 | 119.23 | 105.65 | 83.42 | 86.66 | 75.03 | 68.13 |
| **Central Bank** | | | | | | | *Millions of Euros: End of Period* | | | | | | | |
| Net Foreign Assets | 11n | 344.71 | 394.44 | 641.07 | 1,057.60 | 1,110.68 | 1,088.50 | 1,107.30 | 1,092.74 | 1,238.87 | 1,392.12 | 1,146.48 | 1,201.03 |
| Claims on Nonresidents | 11 | 349.89 | 397.55 | 641.17 | 1,057.62 | 1,110.68 | 1,149.55 | 1,194.41 | 1,181.42 | 1,416.74 | 1,559.88 | 1,314.59 | 1,400.08 |
| Liabilities to Nonresidents | 16c | 5.18 | 3.11 | .11 | .02 | — | 61.05 | 87.11 | 88.69 | 177.87 | 167.76 | 168.11 | 199.05 |
| Claims on Other Depository Corps. | 12e | — | — | — | — | — | 1.00 | — | — | — | — | — | — |
| Net Claims on Central Government | 12an | −216.84 | −225.66 | −472.91 | −849.41 | −870.48 | −681.46 | −813.14 | −797.16 | −837.89 | −773.26 | −730.50 | −753.97 |
| Claims on Central Government | 12a | — | — | — | — | — | — | — | — | — | — | — | — |
| Liabilities to Central Government | 16d | 216.84 | 225.66 | 472.91 | 849.41 | 870.48 | 681.46 | 813.14 | 797.16 | 837.89 | 773.26 | 730.50 | 753.97 |
| Claims on Other Sectors | 12s | — | — | — | — | — | — | — | — | — | — | — | — |
| Claims on Other Financial Corps. | 12g | — | — | — | — | — | — | — | — | — | — | — | — |
| Claims on State & Local Govts. | 12b | — | — | — | — | — | — | — | — | — | — | — | — |
| Claims on Public Nonfin. Corps. | 12c | — | — | — | — | — | — | — | — | — | — | — | — |
| Claims on Private Sector | 12d | — | — | — | — | — | — | — | — | — | — | — | — |
| Monetary Base | 14 | 110.57 | 149.13 | 144.33 | 170.79 | 201.10 | 364.09 | 247.55 | 246.76 | 351.93 | 569.79 | 366.54 | 399.05 |
| Currency in Circulation | 14a | — | — | — | — | — | — | — | — | — | — | — | — |
| Liabs. to Other Depository Corps. | 14c | 72.90 | 82.52 | 94.47 | 113.55 | 137.16 | 233.25 | 203.57 | 209.70 | 302.15 | 333.17 | 315.93 | 316.41 |
| Liabilities to Other Sectors | 14d | 37.67 | 66.61 | 49.86 | 57.24 | 63.95 | 130.84 | 43.98 | 37.06 | 49.78 | 236.62 | 50.61 | 82.65 |
| Other Liabs. to Other Dep. Corps. | 14n | — | — | — | — | — | 2.00 | — | — | — | — | — | — |
| Dep. & Sec. Excl. f/Monetary Base. | 14o | — | — | — | — | — | — | 1.67 | 2.43 | 1.67 | 2.43 | 2.43 | .76 |
| Deposits Included in Broad Money. | 15 | — | — | — | — | — | — | — | — | — | — | — | — |
| Sec.Ot.th.Shares Incl.in Brd. Money | 16a | — | — | — | — | — | — | — | — | — | — | — | — |
| Deposits Excl. from Broad Money | 16b | — | — | — | — | — | — | 1.67 | 2.43 | 1.67 | 2.43 | 2.43 | .76 |
| Sec.Ot.th.Shares Excl.f/Brd.Money | 16s | — | — | — | — | — | — | — | — | — | — | — | — |
| Loans | 16l | — | — | — | — | — | — | — | — | — | — | — | — |
| Financial Derivatives | 16m | — | — | — | — | — | — | — | — | — | — | — | — |
| Shares and Other Equity | 17a | 17.98 | 20.40 | 25.52 | 33.78 | 41.44 | 44.93 | 47.94 | 50.03 | 50.35 | 50.47 | 51.02 | 51.64 |
| Other Items (Net) | 17r | −.68 | −.75 | −1.69 | 3.61 | −2.35 | −2.98 | −3.01 | −3.64 | −2.97 | −3.83 | −4.00 | −4.39 |
| Memo Item: | | | | | | | | | | | | | |
| Total Assets | 10ra | 350.67 | 398.83 | 643.12 | 1,060.14 | 1,113.18 | 1,203.01 | 1,250.05 | 1,238.22 | 1,472.62 | 1,614.42 | 1,372.46 | 1,462.19 |
| **Other Depository Corporations** | | | | | | | *Millions of Euros: End of Period* | | | | | | | |
| Net Foreign Assets | 21n | 303.98 | 300.70 | 334.37 | 319.89 | 325.62 | 443.52 | 507.24 | 510.27 | 491.60 | 571.49 | 534.75 | 529.63 |
| Claims on Nonresidents | 21 | 337.96 | 346.94 | 394.47 | 368.50 | 401.33 | 583.44 | 709.41 | 665.62 | 629.43 | 744.31 | 713.14 | 736.33 |
| Liabilities to Nonresidents | 26c | 33.98 | 46.23 | 60.10 | 48.62 | 75.71 | 139.92 | 202.17 | 155.35 | 137.83 | 172.83 | 178.40 | 206.70 |
| Claims on Central Bank | 20 | 73.24 | 81.64 | 88.76 | 107.53 | 136.81 | 233.14 | 203.45 | 219.96 | 301.07 | 331.75 | 315.93 | 315.69 |
| Currency | 20a | — | — | — | — | — | — | — | — | — | — | — | — |
| Reserve Deposits and Securities | 20b | 73.24 | 81.64 | 88.76 | 107.53 | 136.81 | 233.14 | 203.45 | 219.96 | 301.07 | 331.75 | 315.93 | 315.69 |
| Other Claims | 20n | — | — | — | — | — | — | — | — | — | — | — | — |
| Net Claims on Central Government | 22an | — | −.03 | −2.06 | −3.93 | −1.35 | −164.87 | −11.62 | −1.23 | 59.18 | 99.36 | 192.45 | 225.18 |
| Claims on Central Government | 22a | — | — | — | — | — | — | .01 | .05 | 59.81 | 100.08 | 192.72 | 226.14 |
| Liabilities to Central Government | 26d | — | .03 | 2.06 | 3.93 | 1.35 | 164.87 | 11.63 | 1.28 | .64 | .73 | .27 | .96 |
| Claims on Other Sectors | 22s | 373.66 | 513.86 | 636.61 | 892.10 | 1,183.42 | 1,289.03 | 1,457.07 | 1,665.60 | 1,740.93 | 1,785.95 | 1,881.89 | 2,019.20 |
| Claims on Other Financial Corps. | 22g | — | — | — | — | .60 | 2.28 | 9.89 | 17.35 | 19.85 | 20.44 | 7.14 | 8.67 |
| Claims on State & Local Govts. | 22b | — | — | — | — | — | — | — | — | — | — | — | — |
| Claims on Public Nonfin. Corps. | 22c | — | — | .05 | .17 | .15 | .31 | 6.27 | 1.54 | 1.42 | .24 | .63 | .61 |
| Claims on Private Sector | 22d | 373.66 | 513.86 | 636.56 | 891.93 | 1,182.68 | 1,286.44 | 1,440.92 | 1,646.71 | 1,719.66 | 1,765.28 | 1,874.11 | 2,009.91 |
| Liabilities to Central Bank | 26g | — | — | — | — | — | — | — | — | — | — | — | — |
| Transf.Dep.Included in Broad Money | 24 | 270.93 | 283.05 | 294.53 | 367.06 | 397.88 | 490.50 | 628.59 | 665.86 | 708.05 | 857.31 | 1,146.92 | 1,397.00 |
| Other Dep.Included in Broad Money. | 25 | 410.94 | 515.77 | 568.37 | 702.28 | 925.84 | 916.77 | 1,073.38 | 1,196.69 | 1,277.09 | 1,290.45 | 1,092.74 | 948.23 |
| Sec.Ot.th.Shares Incl.in Brd. Money. | 26a | — | — | — | — | — | — | — | — | — | — | — | — |
| Deposits Excl. from Broad Money | 26b | — | 19.94 | 40.62 | 53.72 | 80.16 | 108.36 | 138.45 | 175.97 | 206.39 | 211.40 | 208.74 | 251.18 |
| Sec.Ot.th.Shares Excl.f/Brd.Money | 26s | — | — | — | — | — | — | — | — | — | — | — | — |
| Loans | 26l | — | — | — | — | — | — | — | — | — | — | — | — |
| Financial Derivatives | 26m | — | — | — | — | — | — | — | — | — | — | — | — |
| Insurance Technical Reserves | 26r | — | — | — | — | — | — | — | — | — | — | — | — |
| Shares and Other Equity | 27a | 69.12 | 73.99 | 103.30 | 152.68 | 182.28 | 205.59 | 230.42 | 252.85 | 270.73 | 278.47 | 323.12 | 392.72 |
| Other Items (Net) | 27r | −.10 | 3.42 | 50.86 | 39.84 | 58.45 | 79.39 | 85.30 | 103.24 | 130.52 | 150.92 | 153.51 | 100.50 |
| Memo Item: | | | | | | | | | | | | | |
| Total Assets | 20ra | 816.54 | 984.41 | 1,161.22 | 1,435.03 | 1,808.29 | 2,204.58 | 2,455.12 | 2,649.73 | 2,829.32 | 3,059.52 | 3,186.62 | 3,384.73 |

# Kosovo   967

| | | 2004 | 2005 | 2006 | 2007 | 2008 | 2009 | 2010 | 2011 | 2012 | 2013 | 2014 | 2015 |
|---|---|---|---|---|---|---|---|---|---|---|---|---|---|
| **Depository Corporations** | | | | | | | *Millions of Euros: End of Period* | | | | | | |
| Net Foreign Assets............... | 31n | 648.69 | 695.15 | 975.43 | 1,377.49 | 1,436.30 | 1,532.02 | 1,614.54 | 1,603.01 | 1,730.47 | 1,963.61 | 1,681.23 | 1,730.66 |
| Claims on Nonresidents................ | 31 | 687.85 | 744.49 | 1,035.64 | 1,426.12 | 1,512.01 | 1,732.99 | 1,903.83 | 1,847.04 | 2,046.17 | 2,304.19 | 2,027.73 | 2,136.41 |
| Liabilities to Nonresidents............. | 36c | 39.16 | 49.34 | 60.21 | 48.64 | 75.71 | 200.97 | 289.29 | 244.03 | 315.70 | 340.58 | 346.50 | 405.75 |
| Domestic Claims...................... | 32 | 156.82 | 288.16 | 161.64 | 38.76 | 311.59 | 442.71 | 632.31 | 867.21 | 962.21 | 1,112.05 | 1,343.85 | 1,490.41 |
| Net Claims on Central Government | 32an | −216.84 | −225.69 | −474.97 | −853.34 | −871.83 | −846.33 | −824.77 | −798.39 | −778.72 | −673.90 | −538.04 | −528.79 |
| Claims on Central Government..... | 32a | — | — | — | — | — | — | .01 | .05 | 59.81 | 100.08 | 192.72 | 226.14 |
| Liabilities to Central Government. | 36d | 216.84 | 225.69 | 474.97 | 853.34 | 871.83 | 846.33 | 824.77 | 798.44 | 838.53 | 773.99 | 730.76 | 754.93 |
| Claims on Other Sectors................ | 32s | 373.66 | 513.86 | 636.61 | 892.10 | 1,183.42 | 1,289.03 | 1,457.07 | 1,665.60 | 1,740.93 | 1,785.95 | 1,881.89 | 2,019.20 |
| Claims on Other Financial Corps.. | 32g | — | — | — | — | .60 | 2.28 | 9.89 | 17.35 | 19.85 | 20.44 | 7.14 | 8.67 |
| Claims on State & Local Govts..... | 32b | — | — | — | — | — | — | — | — | — | — | — | — |
| Claims on Public Nonfin. Corps.... | 32c | — | — | .05 | .17 | .15 | .31 | 6.27 | 1.54 | 1.42 | .24 | .63 | .61 |
| Claims on Private Sector............. | 32d | 373.66 | 513.86 | 636.56 | 891.93 | 1,182.68 | 1,286.44 | 1,440.92 | 1,646.71 | 1,719.66 | 1,765.28 | 1,874.11 | 2,009.91 |
| Broad Money Liabilities............... | 35l | 719.53 | 865.43 | 912.76 | 1,126.58 | 1,387.66 | 1,538.12 | 1,745.95 | 1,899.60 | 2,034.92 | 2,384.37 | 2,290.26 | 2,427.88 |
| Currency Outside Depository Corps | 34a | — | — | — | — | — | — | — | — | — | — | — | — |
| Transferable Deposits................... | 34 | 303.49 | 345.56 | 336.42 | 413.74 | 454.63 | 621.35 | 672.57 | 702.91 | 757.83 | 1,093.92 | 1,197.52 | 1,479.65 |
| Other Deposits.......................... | 35 | 416.04 | 519.87 | 576.34 | 712.84 | 933.04 | 916.77 | 1,073.38 | 1,196.69 | 1,277.09 | 1,290.45 | 1,092.74 | 948.23 |
| Securities Other than Shares.......... | 36a | — | — | — | — | — | — | — | — | — | — | — | — |
| Deposits Excl. from Broad Money..... | 36b | — | 19.94 | 40.62 | 53.72 | 80.16 | 108.36 | 140.12 | 178.40 | 208.06 | 213.82 | 211.17 | 251.94 |
| Sec.Ot.th.Shares Excl.f/Brd.Money.... | 36s | — | — | — | — | — | — | — | — | — | — | — | — |
| Loans....................................... | 36l | — | — | — | — | — | — | — | — | — | — | — | — |
| Financial Derivatives.................... | 36m | — | — | — | — | — | — | — | — | — | — | — | — |
| Insurance Technical Reserves............ | 36r | — | — | — | — | — | — | — | — | — | — | — | — |
| Shares and Other Equity............... | 37a | 87.10 | 94.39 | 128.82 | 186.46 | 223.72 | 250.52 | 278.36 | 302.88 | 321.09 | 328.94 | 374.14 | 444.37 |
| Other Items (Net)........................ | 37r | −1.13 | 3.54 | 54.87 | 49.48 | 56.45 | 77.51 | 82.42 | 89.33 | 128.62 | 148.52 | 149.51 | 96.83 |
| Broad Money Liabs., Seasonally Adj. | 35l.b | 702.73 | 846.43 | 892.78 | 1,101.15 | 1,353.96 | 1,497.26 | 1,694.80 | 1,843.28 | 1,977.17 | 2,323.27 | 2,235.51 | 2,370.70 |
| **Other Financial Corporations** | | | | | | | *Millions of Euros: End of Period* | | | | | | |
| Net Foreign Assets........................ | 41n | 74.09 | 132.12 | 198.14 | 244.86 | 157.04 | 168.93 | 341.30 | 462.44 | 607.57 | 592.92 | 967.58 | 1,028.53 |
| Claims on Nonresidents................ | 41 | 84.15 | 146.37 | 210.03 | 278.49 | 214.72 | 253.76 | 430.53 | 544.09 | 670.80 | 655.76 | 1,029.38 | 1,091.11 |
| Liabilities to Nonresidents............. | 46c | 10.07 | 14.26 | 11.89 | 33.62 | 57.69 | 84.83 | 89.23 | 81.65 | 63.22 | 62.84 | 61.80 | 62.58 |
| Claims on Depository Corporations.. | 40 | 48.87 | 54.77 | 66.94 | 72.76 | 112.96 | 200.03 | 142.70 | 131.43 | 154.00 | 313.79 | 119.45 | 162.78 |
| Net Claims on Central Government.. | 42an | — | — | — | — | — | — | — | — | 13.93 | 53.12 | 54.70 | 100.45 |
| Claims on Central Government...... | 42a | — | — | — | — | — | — | — | — | 13.93 | 53.12 | 54.70 | 100.45 |
| Liabilities to Central Government... | 46d | — | — | — | — | — | — | — | — | — | — | — | — |
| Claims on Other Sectors................. | 42s | 39.86 | 51.70 | 57.72 | 73.84 | 93.99 | 111.15 | 118.67 | 106.23 | 98.34 | 95.82 | 96.80 | 106.41 |
| Claims on State & Local Govts....... | 42b | — | — | — | — | — | — | — | — | — | — | — | — |
| Claims on Public Nonfin. Corps...... | 42c | — | — | — | — | — | — | — | — | — | — | — | — |
| Claims on Private Sector............... | 42d | 39.86 | 51.70 | 57.72 | 73.84 | 93.99 | 111.15 | 118.67 | 106.23 | 98.34 | 95.82 | 96.80 | 106.41 |
| Deposits................................... | 46b | — | — | — | — | — | — | — | — | — | — | — | — |
| Securities Other than Shares............ | 46s | — | — | — | — | — | — | — | — | — | — | — | — |
| Loans....................................... | 46l | 2.33 | 3.02 | 3.37 | — | 1.01 | .22 | 3.21 | 3.26 | 7.22 | 6.98 | 3.20 | 1.04 |
| Financial Derivatives.................... | 46m | — | — | — | — | — | — | — | — | — | — | — | — |
| Insurance Technical Reserves.......... | 46r | 106.54 | 174.54 | 251.42 | 316.11 | 288.59 | 422.28 | 540.86 | 647.81 | 814.93 | 988.36 | 1,173.81 | 1,329.61 |
| Shares and Other Equity.................. | 47a | 57.95 | 71.39 | 80.49 | 87.37 | 77.39 | 76.97 | 81.34 | 78.98 | 78.13 | 77.21 | 79.07 | 86.09 |
| Other Items (Net)........................... | 47r | −4.01 | −10.37 | −12.50 | −12.02 | −3.01 | −19.35 | −22.74 | −29.94 | −26.45 | −16.91 | −17.53 | −18.57 |
| Memo Item: | | | | | | | | | | | | | |
| Total Assets..................................... | 40ra | 186.22 | 267.60 | 354.62 | 446.70 | 448.88 | 600.39 | 735.59 | 827.64 | 992.54 | 1,164.91 | 1,348.26 | 1,510.83 |
| **Financial Corporations** | | | | | | | *Millions of Euros: End of Period* | | | | | | |
| Net Foreign Assets........................... | 51n | 722.78 | 827.26 | 1,173.57 | 1,622.35 | 1,593.33 | 1,700.95 | 1,955.84 | 2,065.44 | 2,338.04 | 2,556.53 | 2,648.81 | 2,759.19 |
| Claims on Nonresidents................ | 51 | 772.01 | 890.86 | 1,245.67 | 1,704.61 | 1,726.74 | 1,986.75 | 2,334.36 | 2,391.13 | 2,716.96 | 2,959.95 | 3,057.11 | 3,227.52 |
| Liabilities to Nonresidents............. | 56c | 49.23 | 63.60 | 72.10 | 82.26 | 133.40 | 285.80 | 378.52 | 325.68 | 378.92 | 403.42 | 408.30 | 468.33 |
| Domestic Claims........................... | 52 | 196.68 | 339.86 | 219.36 | 112.59 | 404.98 | 551.58 | 741.09 | 956.09 | 1,054.63 | 1,240.55 | 1,488.21 | 1,688.60 |
| Net Claims on Central Government | 52an | −216.84 | −225.69 | −474.97 | −853.34 | −871.83 | −846.33 | −824.77 | −798.39 | −764.79 | −620.78 | −483.34 | −428.34 |
| Claims on Central Government.... | 52a | — | — | — | — | — | — | .01 | .05 | 73.74 | 153.21 | 247.42 | 326.59 |
| Liabilities to Central Government. | 56d | 216.84 | 225.69 | 474.97 | 853.34 | 871.83 | 846.33 | 824.77 | 798.44 | 838.53 | 773.99 | 730.76 | 754.93 |
| Claims on Other Sectors................. | 52s | 413.52 | 565.55 | 694.34 | 965.93 | 1,276.81 | 1,397.90 | 1,565.85 | 1,754.48 | 1,819.42 | 1,861.33 | 1,971.55 | 2,116.94 |
| Claims on State & Local Govts..... | 52b | — | — | — | — | — | — | — | — | — | — | — | — |
| Claims on Public Nonfin. Corps..... | 52c | — | — | .05 | .17 | .15 | .31 | 6.27 | 1.54 | 1.42 | .24 | .63 | .61 |
| Claims on Private Sector............. | 52d | 413.52 | 565.55 | 694.29 | 965.76 | 1,276.66 | 1,397.60 | 1,559.58 | 1,752.94 | 1,818.00 | 1,861.09 | 1,970.92 | 2,116.33 |
| Currency Outside Financial Corps..... | 54a | — | — | — | — | — | — | — | — | — | — | — | — |
| Deposits.................................... | 55l | 670.66 | 830.60 | 886.44 | 1,110.89 | 1,351.91 | 1,444.19 | 1,744.17 | 1,942.65 | 2,094.01 | 2,297.88 | 2,359.69 | 2,527.32 |
| Securities Other than Shares............ | 56a | — | — | — | — | — | — | — | — | — | — | — | — |
| Loans....................................... | 56l | 2.33 | 3.02 | 3.37 | — | — | — | — | — | — | — | — | — |
| Financial Derivatives.................... | 56m | — | — | — | — | — | — | — | — | — | — | — | — |
| Insurance Technical Reserves.......... | 56r | 106.54 | 174.54 | 251.42 | 316.11 | 288.59 | 422.28 | 540.86 | 647.81 | 814.93 | 988.36 | 1,173.81 | 1,329.61 |
| Shares and Other Equity.................. | 57a | 145.06 | 165.78 | 209.32 | 273.83 | 301.12 | 327.49 | 359.69 | 381.86 | 399.22 | 406.15 | 453.20 | 530.45 |
| Other Items (Net)........................... | 57r | −5.14 | −6.83 | 42.37 | 34.11 | 56.80 | 58.36 | 52.20 | 49.22 | 84.52 | 104.68 | 150.32 | 60.35 |
| **Interest Rates** | | | | | | | *Percent Per Annum* | | | | | | |
| Treasury Bill Rate.......................... | 60c | .... | .... | .... | .... | .... | .... | .... | 2.19 | 1.72 | 2.20 | 1.34 | |
| Deposit Rate................................. | 60l | 2.75 | 3.12 | 3.11 | 4.00 | 4.42 | 3.98 | 3.38 | 3.62 | 3.72 | 2.40 | 1.11 | 1.15 |
| Lending Rate................................ | 60p | 14.77 | 14.00 | 14.57 | 14.06 | 13.79 | 14.09 | 13.97 | 13.30 | 12.24 | 10.90 | 9.29 | 7.69 |
| **Prices** | | | | | | | *Index Numbers (2010=100): Period Averages* | | | | | | |
| Consumer Prices............................ | 64 | 87.5 | 86.2 | 86.8 | 90.6 | 99.0 | 96.6 | 100.0 | 107.3 | 110.0 | 111.9 | 112.4 | † 111.8 |
| **Intl. Transactions & Positions** | | | | | | | *Millions of Euros* | | | | | | |
| Exports........................................ | 70 | 56.57 | 56.28 | 110.77 | 165.11 | 195.94 | 165.33 | 294.03 | 313.11 | 268.84 | 293.92 | 324.55 | 325.31 |
| Imports, c.i.f................................... | 71 | 1,063.35 | 1,157.49 | 1,305.88 | 1,576.19 | 1,927.92 | 1,935.54 | 2,144.93 | 2,479.61 | 2,489.62 | 2,443.67 | 2,538.23 | 2,634.87 |
| | | | | | | | *2008=100* | | | | | | |
| Import Prices.................................. | 76.x | .... | .... | 88.1 | 91.3 | 99.1 | 95.0 | † 100.0 | 109.3 | 115.0 | 115.2 | .... | .... |

# Kosovo 967

| | | 2004 | 2005 | 2006 | 2007 | 2008 | 2009 | 2010 | 2011 | 2012 | 2013 | 2014 | 2015 |
|---|---|---|---|---|---|---|---|---|---|---|---|---|---|
| **Balance of Payments** | | | | | | *Millions of US Dollars* | | | | | | | |
| Goods, credit (exports)............... | 1a9cx | 76.1 | 79.6 | 123.6 | 181.6 | 175.7 | 243.0 | 394.9 | 441.2 | 362.1 | † 386.9 | 429.5 | 357.7 |
| Goods, debit (imports)................. | 1a9dx | 1,294.8 | 1,422.7 | 1,583.5 | 2,075.4 | 2,714.8 | 2,549.2 | 2,695.6 | 3,289.1 | 2,990.3 | † 3,038.5 | 3,157.9 | 2,694.0 |
| Balance on goods................ | 1a9bx | −1,218.7 | −1,343.1 | −1,459.9 | −1,893.8 | −2,539.1 | −2,306.2 | −2,300.7 | −2,847.9 | −2,628.2 | † −2,651.6 | −2,728.4 | −2,336.3 |
| Services, credit (exports)............ | 1b9cx | 309.2 | 333.2 | 391.2 | 486.5 | 620.3 | 673.0 | 703.9 | 893.1 | 818.6 | † 830.6 | 1,015.2 | 883.1 |
| Services, debit (imports)............. | 1b9dx | 333.9 | 341.7 | 366.6 | 384.9 | 406.0 | 412.4 | 527.9 | 535.6 | 407.0 | † 417.3 | 568.3 | 490.3 |
| Balance on Goods & Services...... | 1z9bx | −1,243.4 | −1,351.6 | −1,435.2 | −1,792.2 | −2,324.9 | −2,045.6 | −2,124.7 | −2,490.4 | −2,216.6 | † −2,238.4 | −2,281.6 | −1,943.5 |
| Primary income: credit................ | 1c9cx | 196.6 | 212.0 | 235.6 | 322.5 | 341.8 | 253.8 | 234.3 | 336.1 | 296.4 | † 302.5 | 286.4 | 246.0 |
| Primary income: debit................. | 1c9dx | 25.0 | 39.0 | 36.4 | 67.6 | 101.5 | 139.2 | 153.9 | 193.7 | 97.5 | † 140.4 | 134.9 | 159.2 |
| Balance on gds, serv. & prim. inc. | 1y9bx | −1,071.8 | −1,178.7 | −1,236.1 | −1,537.3 | −2,084.6 | −1,931.0 | −2,044.2 | −2,348.0 | −2,017.7 | † −2,076.2 | −2,130.1 | −1,856.7 |
| Secondary income: credit.............. | 1d9ca | 1,022.9 | 1,068.2 | 1,110.4 | 1,180.1 | 1,316.8 | 1,556.4 | 1,415.7 | 1,476.2 | 1,664.8 | † 1,733.2 | 1,685.4 | 1,352.5 |
| Secondary income: debit............... | 1d9da | 209.7 | 197.3 | 157.9 | 127.4 | 153.1 | 172.3 | 139.3 | 156.5 | 131.5 | † 108.3 | 119.7 | 77.8 |
| B. Capital Account*..................... | 209ba | 24.0 | 19.6 | 23.5 | 21.9 | 17.7 | 10.7 | 26.7 | 31.6 | 19.1 | † 38.8 | 27.0 | 28.3 |
| Capital account: credit.................. | 209ca | 24.0 | 19.6 | 23.5 | 21.9 | 17.7 | 10.7 | 26.7 | 31.6 | 19.1 | † 54.8 | 43.3 | 49.6 |
| Capital account: debit................... | 209da | — | — | — | — | — | — | — | — | — | † 16.0 | 16.3 | 21.2 |
| Balance on current & capital acct. | 129ba | −234.6 | −288.1 | −260.1 | −462.8 | −903.3 | −536.3 | −741.1 | −996.7 | −465.4 | † −412.6 | −537.4 | −553.7 |
| C. Financial Account*................... | 309na | 68.5 | −26.6 | −52.9 | −499.6 | −696.5 | −30.3 | −442.0 | −566.5 | −399.0 | † −156.5 | −131.3 | −380.8 |
| Direct investment: assets.............. | 3a9aa | — | — | 7.0 | 13.3 | 36.6 | 14.6 | 32.4 | 6.9 | 20.2 | † 23.8 | 35.5 | 41.1 |
| Equity & investment fund shares.. | 3aaaa | — | — | 7.0 | 13.3 | 36.6 | 14.6 | 3.1 | 6.9 | 20.2 | † 23.8 | 35.3 | 40.6 |
| Debt instruments.......................... | 3abaa | .... | .... | .... | .... | .... | .... | 29.3 | | | | .2 | .5 |
| Direct investment: liabilities .......... | 3a9la | 53.3 | 133.8 | 369.8 | 603.2 | 536.8 | 408.1 | 486.6 | 546.2 | 293.2 | † 343.2 | 199.8 | 360.3 |
| Equity & investment fund shares . | 3aala | 48.9 | 102.5 | 271.0 | 448.6 | 407.9 | 375.9 | 439.2 | 477.6 | 260.1 | † 223.1 | 154.0 | 270.4 |
| Debt instruments.......................... | 3abla | 4.3 | 31.3 | 98.8 | 154.6 | 128.9 | 32.1 | 47.4 | 68.7 | 33.1 | † 120.1 | 45.8 | 89.9 |
| Portfolio investment: assets.......... | 3b9aa | 39.8 | 21.8 | 82.0 | 50.1 | −24.6 | 85.6 | 37.9 | 83.2 | 234.9 | † 170.7 | 27.6 | 54.0 |
| Equity & investment fund shares | 3baaa | — | — | — | — | — | — | 58.5 | 133.5 | 147.8 | † −72.9 | 408.7 | −4.1 |
| Debt securities ............................ | 3bbaa | 39.8 | 21.8 | 82.0 | 50.1 | −24.6 | 85.6 | −20.6 | −50.4 | 87.1 | † 243.6 | −381.2 | 58.2 |
| Portfolio investment: liabilities....... | 3b9la | — | — | — | — | — | — | — | — | .9 | † −1.3 | .... | .... |
| Equity & investment fund shares . | 3bala | — | — | — | — | — | — | — | — | .9 | † −1.3 | .... | .... |
| Debt securities............................ | 3bbla | — | — | — | — | — | — | — | — | — | .... | .... | .... |
| Fin. der.& empl.stk.ops.(ESOs): net. | 3c9na | — | — | — | — | — | — | — | — | — | .... | .... | .... |
| Fin. der. & ESOs.: assets.............. | 3c9aa | — | — | — | — | — | — | — | — | — | .... | .... | .... |
| Fin. der. & ESOs.: liabilities.......... | 3c9la | — | — | — | — | — | — | — | — | — | .... | .... | .... |
| Other investment: assets................ | 3d9aa | 159.0 | 175.8 | 274.3 | 148.3 | 29.0 | 344.9 | 365.9 | 132.8 | −186.8 | † 102.0 | 131.1 | −21.3 |
| Other equity.............................. | 3daaa | .... | .... | .... | .... | .... | .... | .... | .... | .... | .... | .... | .... |
| Debt instruments........................ | 3dzaa | 159.0 | 175.8 | 274.3 | 148.3 | 29.0 | 344.9 | 365.9 | 132.8 | −186.8 | † 102.0 | 131.1 | −21.3 |
| Other investment: liabilities........... | 3d9la | 77.0 | 90.3 | 46.4 | 108.0 | 200.7 | 67.3 | 391.6 | 243.2 | 173.2 | † 111.1 | 125.7 | 94.3 |
| Other equity.............................. | 3dala | .... | .... | .... | .... | .... | .... | .... | .... | .... | .... | .2 | .1 |
| Debt instruments........................ | 3dzla | 77.0 | 90.3 | 46.4 | 108.0 | 200.7 | 67.3 | 391.6 | 243.2 | 173.2 | † 111.1 | 125.5 | 94.2 |
| Curr.+ cap.− finan. acct. balance.. | 4y9na | −303.1 | −261.5 | −207.2 | 36.8 | −206.8 | −506.0 | −299.2 | −430.2 | −66.3 | † −256.1 | −406.1 | −172.9 |
| D. Net Errors and Omissions........... | 409na | 163.1 | 221.2 | 304.9 | 360.4 | 240.6 | 228.3 | 344.9 | 348.0 | 281.9 | † 219.0 | 348.1 | 275.1 |
| E. Reserves and Related Items.......... | 4z9na | −140.0 | −40.2 | 97.7 | 397.3 | 33.8 | −277.7 | 45.7 | −82.2 | 215.6 | † −29.6 | −58.0 | 102.2 |
| Reserve assets............................ | 3e9aa | −140.0 | −40.2 | 97.7 | 397.3 | 33.8 | −146.0 | 59.0 | −84.2 | 336.2 | † −33.2 | −72.3 | 123.2 |
| Credit and loans from the IMF....... | 3dcla | — | — | — | — | — | — | 28.5 | — | 119.1 | † −3.6 | −14.3 | 21.0 |
| Exceptional financing................... | 409la | — | — | — | — | — | 131.7 | −15.2 | −2.1 | 1.5 | .... | .... | .... |

*Excludes components in group E

| **International Investment Position** | | | | | | *Millions of US Dollars* | | | | | | | |
|---|---|---|---|---|---|---|---|---|---|---|---|---|---|
| Assets......................................... | 809aa | .... | .... | .... | 3,528.9 | 3,526.1 | 4,047.3 | 4,337.6 | 4,302.6 | 4,888.4 | † 5,641.9 | 5,193.4 | 4,921.6 |
| Direct investment........................ | 8a9aa | .... | .... | .... | 22.4 | 56.2 | 74.4 | 115.4 | 132.0 | 155.5 | † 186.7 | 211.9 | 230.3 |
| Equity & investment fund shares.. | 8aaaa | .... | .... | .... | 22.4 | 56.2 | 74.4 | 115.4 | 132.0 | 155.5 | † 186.7 | 196.6 | 216.2 |
| Debt instruments........................ | 8abaa | .... | .... | .... | .... | .... | .... | .... | .... | .... | .... | 15.3 | 14.1 |
| Portfolio investment..................... | 8b9aa | .... | .... | .... | 654.1 | 645.6 | 896.0 | 927.0 | 957.8 | 1,301.8 | † 1,644.7 | 1,547.6 | 1,512.0 |
| Equity & investment fund shares.. | 8baaa | .... | .... | .... | 233.9 | 156.6 | 201.8 | 259.5 | 383.0 | 467.2 | † 562.4 | 1,243.7 | 1,182.7 |
| Debt securities............................ | 8bbaa | .... | .... | .... | 420.2 | 489.1 | 694.2 | 667.5 | 574.8 | 834.6 | † 1,082.3 | 303.9 | 329.3 |
| Fin. der.(oth.than reserves) & ESOs | 8c9aa | .... | .... | .... | .... | .... | .... | .... | .... | .... | .... | .... | .... |
| Other investment......................... | 8d9aa | .... | .... | .... | 1,892.5 | 1,891.5 | 2,246.5 | 2,447.9 | 2,469.0 | 2,323.0 | † 2,707.5 | 2,527.2 | 2,240.5 |
| Other equity.............................. | 8daaa | .... | .... | .... | .... | .... | .... | .... | .... | .... | .... | .... | .... |
| Debt instruments........................ | 8dzaa | .... | .... | .... | 1,892.5 | 1,891.5 | 2,246.5 | 2,447.9 | 2,469.0 | 2,323.0 | † 2,707.5 | 2,527.2 | 2,240.5 |
| Reserve assets............................ | 8e9aa | .... | .... | .... | 959.9 | 932.8 | 830.4 | 847.2 | 743.8 | 1,108.2 | † 1,103.1 | 906.7 | 938.8 |
| Liabilities.................................... | 809la | .... | .... | .... | 1,682.7 | 2,256.3 | 3,350.9 | 3,764.5 | 4,170.1 | 4,560.0 | † 5,088.9 | 4,831.3 | 4,817.1 |
| Direct investment........................ | 8a9la | .... | .... | .... | 1,360.9 | 1,796.6 | 2,279.6 | 2,620.1 | 3,050.7 | 3,330.6 | † 3,816.9 | 3,595.4 | 3,560.2 |
| Equity & investment fund shares.. | 8aala | .... | .... | .... | 914.5 | 1,233.8 | 1,641.4 | 1,944.5 | 2,319.2 | 2,557.6 | † 2,886.9 | 2,721.3 | 2,713.3 |
| Debt instruments........................ | 8abla | .... | .... | .... | 446.4 | 562.8 | 638.1 | 675.6 | 731.5 | 773.0 | † 930.0 | 874.2 | 846.8 |
| Portfolio investment..................... | 8b9la | .... | .... | .... | 1.7 | 2.1 | 2.8 | 1.7 | 2.7 | .7 | † 1.0 | .... | .... |
| Equity & investment fund shares.. | 8bala | .... | .... | .... | 1.7 | 2.1 | 2.8 | 1.7 | 2.7 | .7 | † 1.0 | .... | .... |
| Debt securities............................ | 8bbla | .... | .... | .... | .... | .... | .... | .... | .... | .... | .... | .... | .... |
| Fin. der.(oth.than reserves) & ESOs | 8c9la | .... | .... | .... | .... | .... | .... | .... | .... | .... | .... | .... | .... |
| Other investment........................ | 8d9la | .... | .... | .... | 320.0 | 457.6 | 1,068.6 | 1,142.7 | 1,116.7 | 1,228.7 | † 1,270.9 | 1,235.9 | 1,257.0 |
| Other equity.............................. | 8dala | .... | .... | .... | .... | .... | .... | .... | .... | .... | .... | 1.0 | 1.0 |
| Debt instruments........................ | 8dzla | .... | .... | .... | 320.0 | 457.6 | 1,068.6 | 1,142.7 | 1,116.7 | 1,228.7 | † 1,270.9 | 1,234.8 | 1,256.0 |

| **National Accounts** | | | | | | *Millions of Euros* | | | | | | | |
|---|---|---|---|---|---|---|---|---|---|---|---|---|---|
| Househ.Cons.Expend.,incl.NPISHs.... | 96f | 2,511.2 | 2,662.1 | 2,795.6 | 3,169.0 | 3,512.5 | 3,553.5 | 3,794.2 | 4,173.4 | 4,478.3 | 4,675.4 | 4,945.0 | .... |
| Government Consumption Expend... | 91f | 701.5 | 705.5 | 670.6 | 641.6 | 659.8 | 668.1 | 722.3 | 802.1 | 842.1 | 863.9 | 910.4 | .... |
| Gross Fixed Capital Formation.......... | 93e | 583.6 | 592.8 | 657.1 | 744.3 | 1,052.7 | 1,129.6 | 1,301.2 | 1,475.9 | 1,316.8 | 1,322.6 | 1,293.8 | .... |
| Changes in Inventories................... | 93i | 117.7 | 129.4 | 141.2 | 148.3 | 156.0 | 137.6 | 149.4 | 156.5 | 148.3 | 148.3 | 141.0 | .... |
| Exports of Goods and Services......... | 90c | 310.0 | 332.8 | 441.4 | 547.1 | 608.9 | 694.9 | 876.0 | 943.4 | 922.1 | 927.1 | 1,091.5 | .... |
| Imports of Goods and Services (-)..... | 98c | 1,312.1 | 1,419.8 | 1,585.5 | 1,789.5 | 2,107.1 | 2,114.2 | 2,443.1 | 2,736.7 | 2,648.8 | 2,610.7 | 2,814.1 | .... |
| Gross Domestic Product (GDP)......... | 99b | 2,911.8 | 3,002.8 | 3,120.4 | 3,460.8 | 3,882.8 | 4,069.6 | 4,402.0 | 4,814.5 | 5,058.7 | 5,326.6 | 5,567.5 | .... |
| | | | | | | *Millions: Midyear Estimates* | | | | | | | |
| Population................................. | 99z | 2.04 | 2.07 | 2.10 | 2.13 | .... | .... | .... | .... | .... | .... | .... | .... |

# Kuwait 443

| | | 2004 | 2005 | 2006 | 2007 | 2008 | 2009 | 2010 | 2011 | 2012 | 2013 | 2014 | 2015 |
|---|---|---|---|---|---|---|---|---|---|---|---|---|---|
| **Exchange Rates** | | | | | | *SDRs per Dinar: End of Period* | | | | | | | |
| Official Rate............................. | ac | 2.1850 | 2.3961 | 2.2989 | 2.3180 | 2.3527 | 2.2242 | 2.3141 | 2.3384 | 2.3135 | 2.3023 | 2.3573 | 2.3777 |
| | | | | | | *US Dollars per Dinar: End of Period (ag) Period Average (rh)* | | | | | | | |
| Official Rate............................. | ag | 3.3933 | 3.4247 | 3.4585 | 3.6630 | 3.6238 | 3.4868 | 3.5638 | 3.5900 | 3.5556 | 3.5455 | 3.4153 | 3.2949 |
| Official Rate............................. | rh | 3.3933 | 3.4247 | 3.4463 | 3.5198 | 3.7204 | 3.4750 | 3.6237 | 3.5724 | 3.5263 | 3.5147 | 3.3242 |
| **Fund Position** | | | | | | *Millions of SDRs: End of Period* | | | | | | | |
| Quota...................................... | 2f.s | 1,381.10 | 1,381.10 | 1,381.10 | 1,381.10 | 1,381.10 | 1,381.10 | 1,381.10 | 1,381.10 | 1,381.10 | 1,381.10 | 1,381.10 | 1,381.10 |
| SDR Holdings.............................. | 1b.s | 117.07 | 128.70 | 137.79 | 146.15 | 152.03 | 1,442.43 | 1,443.39 | 1,445.35 | 1,446.01 | 1,446.43 | 1,446.98 | 1,447.23 |
| Reserve Position in the Fund........... | 1c.s | 458.94 | 208.82 | 120.38 | 90.82 | 173.77 | 253.77 | 253.77 | 426.45 | 454.95 | 504.55 | 510.13 | 437.33 |
| Total Fund Cred. & Loans Outstg...... | 2tl | — | — | — | — | — | — | — | — | — | — | — | — |
| SDR Allocations........................... | 1bd | 26.74 | 26.74 | 26.74 | 26.74 | 26.74 | 1,315.57 | 1,315.57 | 1,315.57 | 1,315.57 | 1,315.57 | 1,315.57 | 1,315.57 |
| **International Liquidity** | | | | | *Millions of US Dollars Unless Otherwise Indicated: End of Period* | | | | | | | | |
| Total Reserves minus Gold.............. | 1l.d | 8,241.9 | 8,862.8 | 12,566.0 | 16,660.0 | 17,112.8 | 20,267.5 | 21,236.7 | 25,795.2 | 28,885.7 | 29,352.5 | 32,113.9 | 28,270.0 |
| SDR Holdings........................... | 1b.d | 181.8 | 183.9 | 207.3 | 231.0 | 234.2 | 2,261.3 | 2,222.9 | 2,219.0 | 2,222.4 | 2,227.5 | 2,096.4 | 2,005.5 |
| Reserve Position in the Fund......... | 1c.d | 712.7 | 298.5 | 181.1 | 143.5 | 267.7 | 397.8 | 390.8 | 654.7 | 699.2 | 777.0 | 739.1 | 606.0 |
| Foreign Exchange...................... | 1d.d | 7,347.4 | 8,380.4 | 12,177.6 | 16,285.6 | 16,611.0 | 17,608.4 | 18,623.0 | 22,921.4 | 25,964.1 | 26,348.0 | 29,278.5 | 25,658.5 |
| Gold (Million Fine Troy Ounces)....... | 1ad | 2.539 | 2.539 | 2.539 | 2.539 | 2.539 | 2.539 | 2.539 | 2.539 | 2.539 | 2.539 | 2.539 | 2.539 |
| Gold (National Valuation)............... | 1and | 107.7 | 108.7 | 109.8 | 116.3 | 115.0 | 110.7 | .... | 113.9 | 112.8 | 112.5 | 108.4 | 104.6 |
| Central Bank: Other Assets............. | 3..d | — | — | — | — | — | — | — | — | — | — | — | — |
| Central Bank: Other Liabs............... | 4..d | 107.5 | 367.5 | 465.9 | 543.0 | 373.8 | 245.3 | 252.8 | 53.4 | 41.3 | 37.1 | 28.7 | 81.9 |
| Other Depository Corps.: Assets....... | 7a.d | 10,831.5 | 12,993.6 | 18,142.7 | 27,958.3 | 31,875.1 | 25,642.3 | 25,923.3 | 29,226.6 | 33,734.6 | 36,084.6 | 39,892.7 | 41,356.0 |
| Other Depository Corps.: Liabs....... | 7b.d | 6,199.1 | 7,741.3 | 10,777.7 | 22,793.8 | 20,651.0 | 10,187.9 | 10,660.8 | 11,341.4 | 10,606.9 | 10,792.5 | 14,676.8 | 15,462.3 |
| Other Financial Corps.: Assets......... | 7e.d | 9,728.1 | 10,700.7 | 15,715.8 | 20,711.7 | 23,043.4 | 19,836.4 | 20,764.1 | 19,266.5 | 19,593.9 | 16,805.1 | 15,736.6 | 14,740.4 |
| Other Financial Corps.: Liabs............ | 7f.d | 5,540.8 | 5,657.3 | 8,241.1 | 11,447.3 | 12,929.3 | 10,639.4 | 11,621.7 | 8,304.4 | 9,221.8 | 6,308.2 | 6,131.1 | 5,609.0 |
| **Central Bank** | | | | | | *Millions of Dinars: End of Period* | | | | | | | |
| Net Foreign Assets....................... | 11n | 2,415.4 | 2,500.4 | 3,517.1 | 4,417.5 | 4,637.1 | 5,179.8 | 5,347.6 | 6,635.4 | 7,570.5 | 8,521.1 | 8,860.3 | 8,014.0 |
| Claims on Nonresidents............. | 11 | 2,459.4 | 2,618.5 | 3,663.4 | 4,577.2 | 4,751.6 | 5,841.7 | 5,987.1 | 7,212.8 | 8,150.8 | 9,103.0 | 9,426.8 | 8,592.1 |
| Liabilities to Nonresidents.............. | 16c | 43.9 | 118.5 | 146.3 | 159.8 | 114.5 | 661.8 | 639.4 | 577.5 | 580.3 | 581.9 | 566.5 | 578.2 |
| Claims on Other Depository Corps.... | 12e | 1.0 | — | — | — | 311.0 | — | — | — | — | — | — | — |
| Net Claims on Central Government.. | 12an | −681.2 | −543.4 | −658.5 | −984.9 | −1,200.4 | −1,344.4 | −715.7 | −858.9 | −707.3 | −750.2 | −696.0 | −995.0 |
| Claims on Central Government...... | 12a | — | 14.5 | — | — | — | — | — | — | — | — | — | — |
| Liabilities to Central Government... | 16d | 681.2 | 557.9 | 658.5 | 984.9 | 1,200.4 | 1,344.4 | 715.7 | 858.9 | 707.3 | 750.2 | 696.0 | 995.0 |
| Claims on Other Sectors.................. | 12s | — | — | — | — | — | — | — | — | — | — | — | — |
| Claims on Other Financial Corps.... | 12g | — | — | — | — | — | — | — | — | — | — | — | — |
| Claims on State & Local Govts....... | 12b | — | — | — | — | — | — | — | — | — | — | — | — |
| Claims on Public Nonfin. Corps...... | 12c | — | — | — | — | — | — | — | — | — | — | — | — |
| Claims on Private Sector............... | 12d | — | — | — | — | — | — | — | — | — | — | — | — |
| Monetary Base............................ | 14 | 912.2 | 1,240.4 | 1,763.5 | 2,063.3 | 1,330.3 | 2,979.5 | 3,804.1 | 4,890.9 | 5,787.6 | 6,831.9 | 7,279.9 | 6,193.2 |
| Currency in Circulation.................. | 14a | 606.3 | 684.6 | 804.9 | 756.7 | 869.1 | 943.8 | 1,006.7 | 1,205.1 | 1,339.9 | 1,481.3 | 1,492.6 | 1,496.5 |
| Liabs. to Other Depository Corps.... | 14c | 305.9 | 555.7 | 958.6 | 1,306.6 | 461.2 | 2,035.7 | 2,797.4 | 3,685.8 | 4,447.6 | 5,350.7 | 5,787.3 | 4,696.7 |
| Liabilities to Other Sectors............. | 14d | — | — | — | — | — | — | — | — | — | — | — | — |
| Other Liabs. to Other Dep. Corps..... | 14n | — | 124.0 | 356.0 | 590.6 | 374.5 | — | — | — | — | — | — | — |
| Dep. & Sec. Excl. f/Monetary Base.... | 14o | — | — | — | — | — | — | — | — | — | — | — | — |
| Deposits Included in Broad Money. | 15 | — | — | — | — | — | — | — | — | — | — | — | — |
| Sec.Ot.th.Shares Incl.in Brd. Money | 16a | — | — | — | — | — | — | — | — | — | — | — | — |
| Deposits Excl. from Broad Money... | 16b | — | — | — | — | — | — | — | — | — | — | — | — |
| Sec.Ot.th.Shares Excl.f/Brd.Money.. | 16s | — | — | — | — | — | — | — | — | — | — | — | — |
| Loans...................................... | 16l | — | — | — | — | — | — | — | — | — | — | — | — |
| Financial Derivatives...................... | 16m | — | — | — | — | — | — | — | — | — | — | — | — |
| Shares and Other Equity................ | 17a | 457.3 | 482.8 | 433.7 | 606.0 | 412.0 | 399.8 | 567.1 | 615.4 | 580.2 | 701.6 | 400.1 | 384.1 |
| Other Items (Net)......................... | 17r | 365.7 | 109.4 | 305.4 | 172.7 | 1,630.8 | 456.2 | 260.7 | 270.2 | 495.4 | 237.4 | 484.3 | 441.7 |
| Memo Item: | | | | | | | | | | | | | |
| Total Assets.............................. | 10ra | 2,904.4 | 3,244.6 | 4,252.4 | 5,313.8 | 5,815.2 | 6,416.1 | 6,546.3 | 7,829.2 | 8,626.5 | 9,855.0 | 9,905.2 | 9,094.7 |
| **Other Depository Corporations** | | | | | | *Millions of Dinars: End of Period* | | | | | | | |
| Net Foreign Assets....................... | 21n | 1,365.2 | 1,533.6 | 2,129.6 | 1,409.9 | 3,097.3 | 4,432.6 | 4,282.6 | 4,981.9 | 6,504.6 | 7,133.6 | 7,383.2 | 7,858.7 |
| Claims on Nonresidents............. | 21 | 3,192.0 | 3,794.1 | 5,245.8 | 7,632.6 | 8,796.0 | 7,354.1 | 7,274.1 | 8,141.1 | 9,487.7 | 10,177.6 | 11,680.6 | 12,551.5 |
| Liabilities to Nonresidents.............. | 26c | 1,826.9 | 2,260.4 | 3,116.3 | 6,222.7 | 5,698.7 | 2,921.8 | 2,991.4 | 3,159.2 | 2,983.2 | 3,044.0 | 4,297.4 | 4,692.8 |
| Claims on Central Bank.................. | 20 | 376.2 | 782.0 | 1,480.9 | 2,002.4 | 1,004.4 | 2,282.5 | 2,959.6 | 3,868.4 | 4,658.3 | 5,654.3 | 6,133.1 | 4,995.9 |
| Currency.................................. | 20a | 75.3 | 105.9 | 148.6 | 115.2 | 161.4 | 168.1 | 163.7 | 185.9 | 219.2 | 308.6 | 352.2 | 301.2 |
| Reserve Deposits and Securities..... | 20b | 300.9 | 552.1 | 1,332.3 | 1,887.2 | 843.1 | 2,114.4 | 2,795.8 | 3,682.5 | 4,439.2 | 5,345.7 | 5,780.9 | 4,694.7 |
| Other Claims............................. | 20n | — | 124.0 | — | — | — | — | — | — | — | — | — | — |
| Net Claims on Central Government.. | 22an | 1,938.0 | 1,467.3 | 2,165.1 | 1,911.8 | 1,996.4 | 1,921.7 | −1,908.1 | −2,123.4 | −3,271.1 | −3,554.3 | −3,723.4 | −4,299.4 |
| Claims on Central Government...... | 22a | 2,750.0 | 2,463.1 | 2,165.1 | 1,911.8 | 1,996.4 | 1,921.7 | 1,910.3 | 1,887.1 | 1,684.3 | 1,502.4 | 1,562.6 | 1,579.6 |
| Liabilities to Central Government... | 26d | 812.0 | 995.8 | — | — | — | — | 3,818.3 | 4,010.5 | 4,955.4 | 5,056.7 | 5,286.0 | 5,879.0 |
| Claims on Other Sectors.................. | 22s | 10,145.3 | 12,128.1 | 16,148.2 | 21,820.0 | 25,450.3 | 27,017.6 | 27,527.2 | 28,229.5 | 29,016.0 | 31,124.8 | 32,705.9 | 35,176.7 |
| Claims on Other Financial Corps.... | 22g | 272.1 | 111.5 | 1,427.0 | 2,408.7 | 2,762.1 | 2,903.7 | 2,837.2 | 2,379.8 | 1,856.6 | 1,612.0 | 1,398.4 | 1,342.4 |
| Claims on State & Local Govts....... | 22b | — | — | — | — | — | — | — | — | — | — | — | — |
| Claims on Public Nonfin. Corps...... | 22c | — | — | — | — | — | — | — | — | — | — | — | — |
| Claims on Private Sector............... | 22d | 9,873.2 | 12,016.6 | 14,721.2 | 19,411.3 | 22,688.3 | 24,113.9 | 24,690.0 | 25,849.7 | 27,159.4 | 29,512.7 | 31,307.5 | 33,834.3 |
| Liabilities to Central Bank............... | 26g | — | — | — | — | — | — | — | — | — | — | — | — |
| Transf.Dep.Included in Broad Money | 24 | 2,703.7 | 3,234.7 | 3,128.5 | 3,788.2 | 4,192.8 | 4,383.5 | 5,285.1 | 5,839.0 | 6,889.2 | 7,911.6 | 8,813.6 | 8,526.0 |
| Other Dep.Included in Broad Money. | 25 | 8,450.5 | 9,272.8 | 12,135.7 | 14,530.2 | 17,049.7 | 19,736.5 | 19,506.2 | 20,888.5 | 21,530.8 | 23,339.5 | 23,666.5 | 24,369.6 |
| Sec.Ot.th.Shares Incl.in Brd. Money.. | 26a | — | — | — | — | — | — | — | — | — | — | — | — |
| Deposits Excl. from Broad Money..... | 26b | 1,199.7 | 827.8 | 1,434.4 | 2,004.3 | 3,535.1 | 3,984.3 | — | — | — | — | — | — |
| Sec.Ot.th.Shares Excl.f/Brd.Money.... | 26s | 90.0 | 90.0 | 50.0 | — | — | — | — | — | 100.0 | 100.0 | 100.0 | 224.0 |
| Loans...................................... | 26l | — | — | — | — | — | — | — | — | — | — | — | — |
| Financial Derivatives...................... | 26m | — | — | — | — | — | — | — | — | — | — | — | — |
| Insurance Technical Reserves........... | 26r | — | — | — | — | — | — | — | — | — | — | — | — |
| Shares and Other Equity................ | 27a | 2,311.3 | 2,800.1 | 3,170.0 | 4,495.8 | 4,599.9 | 4,903.8 | 5,879.4 | 6,265.0 | 6,357.3 | 6,995.0 | 7,524.8 | 7,583.9 |
| Other Items (Net).......................... | 27r | −930.6 | −314.4 | 2,005.1 | 2,325.5 | 2,171.1 | 2,646.0 | 2,190.7 | 1,964.0 | 2,030.5 | 2,012.4 | 2,393.9 | 3,028.4 |
| Memo Item: | | | | | | | | | | | | | |
| Total Assets.............................. | 20ra | 19,144.2 | 21,611.6 | 26,990.0 | 35,553.3 | 39,241.0 | 40,319.6 | 41,381.8 | 44,081.5 | 47,207.7 | 51,486.4 | 55,452.3 | 58,595.1 |

| | | 2004 | 2005 | 2006 | 2007 | 2008 | 2009 | 2010 | 2011 | 2012 | 2013 | 2014 | 2015 |
|---|---|---|---|---|---|---|---|---|---|---|---|---|---|
| **Depository Corporations** | | *Millions of Dinars: End of Period* | | | | | | | | | | | |
| Net Foreign Assets | 31n | 3,780.6 | 4,033.7 | 5,646.6 | 5,827.4 | 7,734.4 | 9,612.1 | 9,630.3 | 11,617.3 | 14,075.1 | 15,654.7 | 16,243.5 | 15,872.7 |
| Claims on Nonresidents | 31 | 5,651.4 | 6,412.6 | 8,909.3 | 12,209.8 | 13,547.6 | 13,195.8 | 13,261.1 | 15,354.0 | 17,638.5 | 19,280.6 | 21,107.4 | 21,143.6 |
| Liabilities to Nonresidents | 36c | 1,870.8 | 2,378.9 | 3,262.6 | 6,382.5 | 5,813.2 | 3,583.7 | 3,630.9 | 3,736.7 | 3,563.4 | 3,625.9 | 4,863.9 | 5,271.0 |
| Domestic Claims | 32 | 11,402.1 | 13,052.0 | 17,654.8 | 22,746.9 | 26,246.3 | 27,594.9 | 24,903.4 | 25,247.2 | 25,037.6 | 26,820.4 | 28,286.4 | 29,882.3 |
| Net Claims on Central Government | 32an | 1,256.8 | 923.9 | 1,506.6 | 926.9 | 796.0 | 577.3 | −2,623.8 | −2,982.3 | −3,978.4 | −4,304.4 | −4,419.4 | −5,294.4 |
| Claims on Central Government | 32a | 2,750.0 | 2,477.6 | 2,165.1 | 1,911.8 | 1,996.4 | 1,921.7 | 1,910.3 | 1,887.1 | 1,684.3 | 1,502.4 | 1,562.6 | 1,579.6 |
| Liabilities to Central Government | 36d | 1,493.2 | 1,553.8 | 658.5 | 984.9 | 1,200.4 | 1,344.4 | 4,534.1 | 4,869.3 | 5,662.7 | 5,806.8 | 5,982.0 | 6,873.9 |
| Claims on Other Sectors | 32s | 10,145.3 | 12,128.1 | 16,148.2 | 21,820.0 | 25,450.3 | 27,017.6 | 27,527.2 | 28,229.5 | 29,016.0 | 31,124.8 | 32,705.9 | 35,176.7 |
| Claims on Other Financial Corps. | 32g | 272.1 | 111.5 | 1,427.0 | 2,408.7 | 2,762.1 | 2,903.7 | 2,837.2 | 2,379.8 | 1,856.6 | 1,612.0 | 1,398.4 | 1,342.4 |
| Claims on State & Local Govts | 32b | — | — | — | — | — | — | — | — | — | — | — | — |
| Claims on Public Nonfin. Corps. | 32c | — | — | — | — | — | — | — | — | — | — | — | — |
| Claims on Private Sector | 32d | 9,873.2 | 12,016.6 | 14,721.2 | 19,411.3 | 22,688.3 | 24,113.9 | 24,690.0 | 25,849.7 | 27,159.4 | 29,512.7 | 31,307.5 | 33,834.3 |
| Broad Money Liabilities | 35l | 11,685.2 | 13,086.2 | 15,920.6 | 18,959.9 | 21,950.2 | 24,895.8 | 25,634.2 | 27,746.6 | 29,540.7 | 32,423.7 | 33,620.4 | 34,090.9 |
| Currency Outside Depository Corps | 34a | 531.0 | 578.7 | 656.3 | 641.5 | 707.8 | 775.7 | 842.9 | 1,019.2 | 1,120.7 | 1,172.7 | 1,140.4 | 1,195.2 |
| Transferable Deposits | 34 | 2,703.7 | 3,234.7 | 3,128.5 | 3,788.2 | 4,192.8 | 4,383.5 | 5,285.1 | 5,839.0 | 6,889.2 | 7,911.6 | 8,813.6 | 8,526.0 |
| Other Deposits | 35 | 8,450.5 | 9,272.8 | 12,135.7 | 14,530.2 | 17,049.7 | 19,736.5 | 19,506.2 | 20,888.5 | 21,530.8 | 23,339.5 | 23,666.5 | 24,369.6 |
| Securities Other than Shares | 36a | — | — | — | — | — | — | — | — | — | — | — | — |
| Deposits Excl. from Broad Money | 36b | 1,199.7 | 827.8 | 1,434.4 | 2,004.3 | 3,535.1 | 3,984.3 | — | — | — | — | — | — |
| Sec.Ot.th.Shares Excl.f/Brd.Money | 36s | 90.0 | 90.0 | 50.0 | — | — | — | — | — | 100.0 | 100.0 | 100.0 | 224.0 |
| Loans | 36l | — | — | — | — | — | — | — | — | — | — | — | — |
| Financial Derivatives | 36m | — | — | — | — | — | — | — | — | — | — | — | — |
| Insurance Technical Reserves | 36r | — | — | — | — | — | — | — | — | — | — | — | — |
| Shares and Other Equity | 37a | 2,768.7 | 3,282.9 | 3,603.7 | 5,101.8 | 5,011.9 | 5,303.6 | 6,446.5 | 6,880.4 | 6,937.5 | 7,696.6 | 7,924.9 | 7,968.0 |
| Other Items (Net) | 37r | −560.9 | −201.3 | 2,292.7 | 2,508.2 | 3,483.5 | 3,023.4 | 2,453.0 | 2,237.5 | 2,534.4 | 2,254.7 | 2,884.6 | 3,472.1 |
| Broad Money Liabs., Seasonally Adj. | 35l.b | 11,900.8 | 13,335.7 | 16,241.6 | 19,324.3 | 22,325.5 | 25,233.3 | 25,879.5 | 27,901.3 | 29,619.8 | 32,473.1 | 33,657.9 | 34,125.8 |
| **Other Financial Corporations** | | *Millions of Dinars: End of Period* | | | | | | | | | | | |
| Net Foreign Assets | 41n | 1,234.0 | 1,472.6 | 2,161.3 | 2,529.2 | 2,791.0 | 2,637.7 | 2,565.4 | 3,053.5 | 2,917.1 | 2,960.6 | 2,812.5 | 2,771.4 |
| Claims on Nonresidents | 41 | 2,866.9 | 3,124.6 | 4,544.1 | 5,654.3 | 6,358.9 | 5,689.0 | 5,826.4 | 5,366.7 | 5,510.7 | 4,739.8 | 4,607.7 | 4,473.7 |
| Liabilities to Nonresidents | 46c | 1,632.9 | 1,651.9 | 2,382.9 | 3,125.1 | 3,567.9 | 3,051.3 | 3,261.0 | 2,313.2 | 2,593.6 | 1,779.2 | 1,795.2 | 1,702.3 |
| Claims on Depository Corporations | 40 | 465.2 | 1,170.8 | 1,900.2 | 2,946.0 | 2,479.5 | 2,048.8 | 1,904.2 | 1,572.8 | 1,430.3 | 1,303.9 | 1,105.0 | 1,073.2 |
| Net Claims on Central Government | 42an | −79.4 | −102.2 | −53.8 | −28.6 | −88.7 | −77.3 | −69.0 | −65.4 | −63.9 | −50.9 | −55.2 | −60.4 |
| Claims on Central Government | 42a | 2.7 | 3.5 | 7.3 | 34.8 | — | .8 | — | — | — | — | — | — |
| Liabilities to Central Government | 46d | 82.1 | 105.7 | 61.1 | 63.4 | 88.7 | 78.1 | 69.0 | 65.4 | 63.9 | 50.9 | 55.2 | 60.4 |
| Claims on Other Sectors | 42s | 1,239.3 | 1,780.5 | 2,204.6 | 2,119.2 | 2,486.3 | 1,845.4 | 1,523.3 | 1,555.3 | 1,439.3 | 1,190.6 | 1,086.4 | 1,083.0 |
| Claims on State & Local Govts | 42b | — | — | — | — | — | — | — | — | — | — | — | — |
| Claims on Public Nonfin. Corps. | 42c | — | — | — | — | — | — | — | — | — | — | — | — |
| Claims on Private Sector | 42d | 1,239.3 | 1,780.5 | 2,204.6 | 2,119.2 | 2,486.3 | 1,845.4 | 1,523.3 | 1,555.3 | 1,439.3 | 1,190.6 | 1,086.4 | 1,083.0 |
| Deposits | 46b | — | — | — | — | — | — | — | — | — | — | — | — |
| Securities Other than Shares | 46s | — | — | — | — | — | — | — | — | — | — | — | — |
| Loans | 46l | 1,456.6 | 2,239.5 | 3,437.9 | 4,733.3 | 4,480.0 | 3,838.8 | 3,542.3 | 3,217.7 | 2,846.6 | 2,319.3 | 2,004.2 | 1,939.3 |
| Financial Derivatives | 46m | — | — | — | — | — | — | — | — | — | — | — | — |
| Insurance Technical Reserves | 46r | — | — | — | — | — | — | — | — | — | — | — | — |
| Shares and Other Equity | 47a | 2,017.8 | 3,410.8 | 4,625.3 | 5,393.9 | 5,828.4 | 4,832.7 | 4,953.4 | 4,338.0 | 4,194.1 | 4,444.6 | 4,480.7 | 4,264.8 |
| Other Items (Net) | 47r | −615.3 | −1,328.6 | −1,850.9 | −2,561.4 | −2,640.3 | −2,217.0 | −2,571.8 | −1,439.5 | −1,317.9 | −1,359.6 | −1,575.7 | −1,381.5 |
| Memo Item: | | | | | | | | | | | | | |
| Total Assets | 40ra | 6,359.6 | 9,429.1 | 13,135.3 | 16,042.0 | 16,981.7 | 13,634.0 | 13,735.3 | 12,155.8 | 11,913.2 | 10,604.7 | 10,104.2 | 9,654.0 |
| **Monetary Aggregates** | | *Millions of Dinars: End of Period* | | | | | | | | | | | |
| Broad Money | 59m | 11,685.2 | 13,086.2 | 15,920.6 | 18,959.9 | 21,950.2 | 24,895.8 | 25,634.2 | 27,746.6 | 29,540.7 | 32,423.7 | 33,620.4 | 34,090.9 |
| o/w:Currency Issued by Cent.Govt | 59m.a | — | — | — | — | — | — | — | — | — | — | — | — |
| o/w: Dep.in Nonfin. Corporations. | 59m.b | — | — | — | — | — | — | — | — | — | — | — | — |
| o/w:Secs. Issued by Central Govt. | 59m.c | — | — | — | — | — | — | — | — | — | — | — | — |
| Money (National Definitions) | | | | | | | | | | | | | |
| Monetary Base | 19ma | 912.2 | 1,364.4 | 2,119.5 | 2,653.9 | 1,704.8 | 2,979.5 | 3,804.1 | 4,890.9 | 5,787.6 | 6,831.9 | 7,279.9 | 6,193.2 |
| M1 | 59ma | 3,174.2 | 3,727.4 | 3,550.3 | 4,146.7 | 4,370.3 | 4,714.0 | 5,625.0 | 6,365.4 | 7,525.8 | 8,676.5 | 9,253.0 | 8,942.8 |
| M2 | 59mb | 11,685.2 | 13,086.2 | 15,920.6 | 18,959.9 | 21,950.2 | 24,895.8 | 25,634.2 | 27,746.6 | 29,540.7 | 32,423.7 | 33,620.4 | 34,090.9 |
| M3 | 59mc | 11,678.4 | 13,100.4 | 15,946.7 | 18,986.0 | 22,007.0 | 24,919.4 | 25,662.8 | 27,760.7 | 29,568.7 | 32,614.8 | 33,640.4 | 34,126.4 |
| **Interest Rates** | | *Percent Per Annum* | | | | | | | | | | | |
| Discount Rate (End of Period) | 60.a | 4.75 | 6.00 | 6.25 | 6.25 | 3.75 | 3.00 | 2.50 | 2.50 | 2.00 | 2.00 | 2.00 | 2.25 |
| Money Market Rate | 60b | 2.14 | 2.83 | 5.62 | 4.88 | 2.80 | 1.60 | .91 | .94 | .81 | .65 | 1.04 | 1.14 |
| Treasury Bill Rate | 60c | 1.75 | 1.99 | . . . . | . . . . | . . . . | .92 | .64 | .83 | . . . . | . . . . | . . . . | . . . . |
| Deposit Rate | 60l | 2.65 | 3.47 | 4.92 | 5.45 | 4.81 | 2.83 | 2.34 | 2.16 | 2.04 | 2.02 | 2.02 | 2.03 |
| Lending Rate | 60p | 5.64 | 7.50 | 8.58 | 8.54 | 7.61 | 6.16 | 4.91 | 5.19 | 4.98 | 4.56 | 4.27 | 4.28 |
| **Prices, Production, Labor** | | *Index Numbers (2010=100): Period Averages* | | | | | | | | | | | |
| Share Prices (End of Month) | 62.ep | 80.8 | 132.0 | 146.9 | 166.6 | 185.9 | 105.6 | 100.0 | 88.3 | 85.7 | 107.1 | 104.5 | 87.5 |
| Wholesale Prices | 63 | 81.0 | 84.6 | 86.4 | † 89.8 | 95.6 | 95.7 | 100.0 | 103.8 | 106.0 | 109.7 | 112.3 | 115.7 |
| Consumer Prices | 64 | 73.1 | 76.1 | 78.4 | 82.7 | † 91.5 | 95.7 | 100.0 | 104.9 | 108.3 | 111.2 | 114.4 | 118.2 |
| Crude Petroleum Production | 66aa | 98.3 | 111.1 | 106.6 | 105.5 | 114.1 | 98.6 | 100.0 | 115.4 | 131.6 | 130.3 | 130.8 | 137.9 |
| **Intl. Transactions & Positions** | | *Millions of Dinars* | | | | | | | | | | | |
| Exports | 70 | 8,436.9 | 13,101.6 | 16,357.0 | 17,770.1 | 23,481.6 | 15,529.4 | 19,082.2 | 28,159.6 | 32,051.3 | 32,363.3 | 28,636.5 | 16,591.3 |
| Oil Exports | 70a | 7,861.1 | 12,392.6 | 15,429.7 | 16,780.0 | 22,200.1 | 14,073.4 | 17,711.3 | 26,688.6 | 31,607.8 | 30,789.5 | 27,753.0 | 14,683.0 |
| Imports, c.i.f. | 71 | 3,724.7 | 4,613.9 | 5,000.5 | 6,061.5 | 6,678.7 | 5,722.5 | 6,498.6 | 6,938.1 | 7,631.7 | 8,308.8 | 8,829.3 | 9,600.1 |

|  |  | 2004 | 2005 | 2006 | 2007 | 2008 | 2009 | 2010 | 2011 | 2012 | 2013 | 2014 | 2015 |
|---|---|---|---|---|---|---|---|---|---|---|---|---|---|
| **Balance of Payments** | | | | | | | *Millions of US Dollars* | | | | | | |
| A. Current Account* | 109bx | 15,508.0 | 30,070.5 | 45,311.8 | 41,330.1 | 60,239.3 | † 28,972.2 | 36,989.2 | 66,145.8 | 79,122.1 | 69,492.8 | 53,966.4 | 8,584.2 |
| Goods, credit (exports) | 1a9cx | 29,000.7 | 45,302.7 | 56,453.3 | 62,526.1 | 86,943.6 | † 54,422.9 | 67,130.1 | 102,854.7 | 119,642.8 | 115,745.1 | 104,792.2 | 55,335.4 |
| Goods, debit (imports) | 1a9dx | 12,402.4 | 15,053.4 | 16,240.1 | 19,962.1 | 22,939.2 | † 18,528.7 | 19,569.2 | 22,597.2 | 24,241.4 | 25,576.3 | 27,384.9 | 27,342.8 |
| Balance on goods | 1a9bx | 16,598.2 | 30,249.3 | 40,213.1 | 42,564.1 | 64,004.4 | † 35,894.3 | 47,560.9 | 80,257.5 | 95,401.3 | 90,168.9 | 77,407.3 | 27,992.6 |
| Services, credit (exports) | 1b9cx | 3,771.0 | 4,774.7 | 8,444.2 | 10,168.7 | 11,959.1 | † 11,466.2 | 9,009.4 | 10,097.0 | 8,836.5 | 6,179.5 | 6,268.3 | 6,055.6 |
| Services, debit (imports) | 1b9dx | 7,495.1 | 8,714.7 | 10,638.4 | 13,343.8 | 15,777.4 | † 13,742.6 | 15,784.9 | 19,013.2 | 21,097.2 | 21,004.0 | 23,787.0 | 23,796.4 |
| Balance on Goods & Services | 1z9bx | 12,874.1 | 26,309.2 | 38,019.0 | 39,389.0 | 60,186.2 | † 33,617.9 | 40,785.4 | 71,341.4 | 83,140.6 | 75,344.4 | 59,888.6 | 10,251.8 |
| Primary income: credit | 1c9cx | 5,888.4 | 8,022.6 | 12,499.3 | 16,326.8 | 13,961.7 | † 8,861.3 | 9,727.9 | 10,602.9 | 13,999.0 | 14,649.1 | 16,145.9 | 16,993.9 |
| Primary income: debit | 1c9dx | 700.4 | 840.8 | 1,532.5 | 3,932.2 | 3,219.2 | † 1,178.3 | 1,265.9 | 1,422.5 | 1,303.6 | 1,394.2 | 1,394.0 | 2,139.5 |
| Balance on gds, serv. & prim. inc. | 1y9bx | 18,062.1 | 33,491.1 | 48,985.7 | 51,783.5 | 70,928.7 | † 41,300.9 | 49,247.4 | 80,521.8 | 95,836.0 | 88,599.3 | 74,640.5 | 25,106.3 |
| Secondary income: credit | 1d9ca | — | — | — | — | — | . . . . | 1.7 | 2.3 | 1.9 | 2.0 | 2.6 | 3.2 |
| Secondary income: debit | 1d9da | 2,554.1 | 3,420.5 | 3,674.0 | 10,453.4 | 10,689.3 | † 12,328.7 | 12,259.8 | 14,378.2 | 16,715.8 | 19,108.5 | 20,676.7 | 16,525.3 |
| B. Capital Account* | 209ba | 348.5 | 709.9 | 743.7 | 1,487.6 | 1,728.6 | † 1,007.0 | 2,096.3 | 3,409.6 | 4,243.0 | 4,460.8 | 3,991.0 | −288.3 |
| Capital account: credit | 209ca | 430.6 | 780.8 | 850.5 | 1,554.1 | 1,855.5 | † 1,191.7 | 2,263.3 | 3,643.2 | 4,414.0 | 4,723.7 | 4,266.2 | . . . . |
| Capital account: debit | 209da | 82.1 | 70.9 | 106.8 | 66.5 | 126.8 | † 184.7 | 167.0 | 233.6 | 171.0 | 262.9 | 275.2 | 288.3 |
| Balance on current & capital acct. | 129bx | 15,856.5 | 30,780.5 | 46,055.5 | 42,817.7 | 61,968.0 | † 29,979.2 | 39,085.5 | 69,555.4 | 83,365.0 | 73,953.6 | 57,957.4 | 8,295.9 |
| C. Financial Account* | 309na | 16,764.8 | 32,762.0 | 49,558.8 | 34,862.5 | 51,280.6 | † 26,526.9 | 45,576.7 | 60,066.6 | 80,717.3 | 68,675.8 | 57,004.0 | 14,370.6 |
| Direct investment: assets | 3a9aa | 2,581.3 | 5,141.8 | 8,210.5 | 9,784.2 | 9,090.6 | † 8,581.8 | 5,889.8 | 10,772.9 | 6,741.3 | 16,648.0 | 13,108.0 | 5,439.6 |
| Equity & investment fund shares | 3aaaa | 2,581.3 | 5,157.2 | 8,210.5 | 9,784.2 | 9,099.1 | † 8,363.1 | 5,732.3 | 11,623.5 | 9,845.3 | 16,350.3 | 12,685.7 | 4,411.9 |
| Debt instruments | 3abaa | | −15.4 | | | −8.6 | † 218.7 | 157.5 | −850.6 | −3,104.0 | 297.7 | 422.3 | 1,027.7 |
| Direct investment: liabilities | 3a9la | 23.8 | 233.9 | 121.3 | 111.5 | −6.0 | † 1,113.6 | 1,304.6 | 3,259.1 | 2,872.6 | 1,433.6 | 485.8 | 284.6 |
| Equity & investment fund shares | 3aala | 23.8 | 233.9 | 121.3 | 111.5 | −6.0 | † 1,041.5 | 1,403.9 | 3,207.8 | 2,901.4 | 1,393.6 | 486.4 | 278.0 |
| Debt instruments | 3abla | — | — | — | — | — | † 72.1 | −99.2 | 51.2 | −28.8 | 40.1 | −.6 | 6.6 |
| Portfolio investment: assets | 3b9aa | 14,168.0 | 12,675.3 | 29,170.5 | 35,580.9 | 32,084.7 | † 8,674.2 | 20,613.7 | 8,448.7 | 25,425.1 | 21,916.4 | 42,200.6 | 33,018.3 |
| Equity & investment fund shares | 3baaa | 1,513.1 | 2,088.0 | 3,249.1 | 3,848.9 | 2,182.4 | † 3,919.8 | 15,950.8 | 9,737.9 | 8,000.6 | 19,359.2 | 29,224.9 | 25,819.8 |
| Debt securities | 3bbaa | 12,654.9 | 10,587.3 | 25,921.5 | 31,732.1 | 29,902.3 | † 4,754.4 | 4,662.9 | −1,289.2 | 17,424.5 | 2,557.1 | 12,975.7 | 7,198.5 |
| Portfolio investment: liabilities | 3b9la | 287.8 | −458.9 | 44.5 | 677.0 | 3,954.9 | † 480.2 | 89.6 | 786.1 | 1,507.3 | 682.5 | 498.0 | 350.0 |
| Equity & investment fund shares | 3bala | — | — | 44.5 | 677.0 | 3,954.9 | † 500.7 | −25.3 | 832.4 | 638.5 | 65.1 | 585.6 | — |
| Debt securities | 3bbla | 287.8 | −458.9 | — | — | — | † −20.5 | 114.9 | −46.3 | 868.7 | 617.4 | −87.6 | 350.0 |
| Fin. der.& empl.stk.ops.(ESOs): net | 3c9na | — | — | — | — | — | † 47.9 | 115.7 | −624.5 | −63.8 | 55.1 | −96.8 | −113.1 |
| Fin. der. & ESOs.: assets | 3c9aa | — | — | — | — | — | † 252.2 | −7.4 | −24.4 | 90.9 | 307.5 | 1,144.7 | 972.7 |
| Fin. der. & ESOs.: liabilities | 3c9la | — | — | — | — | — | † 204.3 | −123.2 | 600.1 | 154.7 | 252.4 | 1,241.6 | 1,085.7 |
| Other investment: assets | 3d9aa | 559.2 | 19,322.9 | 22,735.5 | 14,482.8 | 18,281.2 | † −2,911.1 | 15,521.1 | 47,737.5 | 47,179.7 | 35,503.5 | 7,997.7 | −23,143.3 |
| Other equity | 3daaa | . . . . | . . . . | . . . . | . . . . | . . . . | . . . . | . . . . | . . . . | . . . . | . . . . | . . . . | . . . . |
| Debt instruments | 3dzaa | 559.2 | 19,322.9 | 22,735.5 | 14,482.8 | 18,281.2 | † −2,911.1 | 15,521.1 | 47,737.5 | 47,179.7 | 35,503.5 | 7,997.7 | −23,143.3 |
| Other investment: liabilities | 3d9la | 232.1 | 4,603.1 | 10,392.0 | 24,196.9 | 4,226.9 | † −13,727.8 | −4,830.5 | 2,223.0 | −5,814.9 | 3,331.1 | 5,221.6 | 196.2 |
| Other equity | 3dala | . . . . | . . . . | . . . . | . . . . | . . . . | . . . . | . . . . | . . . . | . . . . | . . . . | . . . . | . . . . |
| Debt instruments | 3dzla | 232.1 | 4,603.1 | 10,392.0 | 24,196.9 | 4,226.9 | † −13,727.8 | −4,830.5 | 2,223.0 | −5,814.9 | 3,331.1 | 5,221.6 | 196.2 |
| Curr.+ cap.− finan. acct. balance | 4y9na | −908.4 | −1,981.5 | −3,503.4 | 7,955.3 | 10,687.3 | † 3,452.3 | −6,491.1 | 9,488.8 | 2,647.7 | 5,277.8 | 953.4 | −6,074.7 |
| D. Net Errors and Omissions | 409na | 1,534.4 | 2,600.8 | 7,087.0 | −4,736.7 | −10,040.0 | † 306.3 | 7,101.9 | −5,017.6 | 710.1 | −1,922.2 | 299.2 | 3,246.1 |
| E. Reserves and Related Items | 4z9na | 626.1 | 619.3 | 3,583.6 | 3,218.5 | 647.4 | † 3,758.6 | 610.8 | 4,471.3 | 3,357.8 | 3,355.6 | 1,252.6 | −2,828.6 |
| Reserve assets | 3e9aa | 626.1 | 619.3 | 3,583.6 | 3,218.5 | 647.4 | † 3,758.6 | 610.8 | 4,471.3 | 3,357.8 | 3,355.6 | 1,252.6 | −2,828.6 |
| Credit and loans from the IMF | 3dcla | | | | | | † — | | | | | | |
| Exceptional financing | 409la | — | . . . . | . . . . | . . . . | . . . . | . . . . | . . . . | . . . . | . . . . | . . . . | . . . . | . . . . |
| *Excludes components in group E | | | | | | | | | | | | | |
| | | | | | | | | | | | | | |
| **International Investment Position** | | | | | | | *Millions of US Dollars* | | | | | | |
| Assets | 809aa | 53,624.9 | 70,770.6 | 96,641.0 | 131,611.7 | 172,998.9 | † 168,313.9 | 152,116.1 | 170,885.9 | 175,713.9 | 179,368.6 | 173,390.6 | 169,567.4 |
| Direct investment | 8a9aa | 1,467.6 | 5,893.5 | 10,845.2 | 14,665.2 | 22,436.5 | † 29,414.0 | 28,189.2 | 32,250.3 | 31,023.3 | 37,153.2 | 34,310.2 | 31,577.1 |
| Equity & investment fund shares | 8aaaa | 1,467.6 | 5,893.5 | 10,845.2 | 14,665.2 | 20,709.7 | † 22,567.6 | 21,024.3 | 25,861.7 | 27,898.0 | 33,732.6 | 30,997.9 | 27,587.1 |
| Debt instruments | 8abaa | . . . . | . . . . | . . . . | . . . . | 1,726.8 | † 6,846.4 | 7,164.9 | 6,388.6 | 3,125.3 | 3,420.6 | 3,312.3 | 3,989.9 |
| Portfolio investment | 8b9aa | 11,406.9 | 18,642.1 | 27,423.8 | 37,915.3 | 59,168.7 | † 48,441.5 | 35,069.7 | 33,255.0 | 32,723.7 | 20,578.1 | 14,391.4 | 14,609.6 |
| Equity & investment fund shares | 8baaa | 5,874.8 | 8,017.1 | 11,357.0 | 16,035.5 | 50,887.0 | † 41,556.2 | 29,227.4 | 27,891.4 | 25,986.4 | 17,192.4 | 10,167.5 | 9,349.8 |
| Debt securities | 8bbaa | 5,532.1 | 10,625.0 | 16,066.8 | 21,879.8 | 8,281.8 | † 6,885.3 | 5,842.3 | 5,363.6 | 6,737.3 | 3,385.7 | 4,223.9 | 5,259.8 |
| Fin. der.(oth.than reserves) & ESOs | 8c9aa | . . . . | . . . . | . . . . | . . . . | 13.8 | † 958.5 | 963.8 | 931.8 | 1,019.5 | 1,313.8 | 2,771.6 | 3,623.9 |
| Other investment | 8d9aa | 32,405.0 | 37,267.5 | 45,702.0 | 62,264.8 | 74,161.2 | † 69,131.1 | 66,556.8 | 78,554.6 | 81,966.6 | 88,048.8 | 89,722.0 | 91,446.6 |
| Other equity | 8daaa | . . . . | . . . . | . . . . | . . . . | . . . . | . . . . | . . . . | . . . . | . . . . | . . . . | . . . . | . . . . |
| Debt instruments | 8dzaa | 32,405.0 | 37,267.5 | 45,702.0 | 62,264.8 | 74,161.2 | † 69,131.1 | 66,556.8 | 78,554.6 | 81,966.6 | 88,048.8 | 89,722.0 | 91,446.6 |
| Reserve assets | 8e9aa | 8,345.4 | 8,967.5 | 12,670.0 | 16,766.4 | 17,218.8 | † 20,368.7 | 21,336.7 | 25,894.1 | 28,980.8 | 32,274.7 | 32,195.3 | 28,310.2 |
| Liabilities | 809la | 17,077.9 | 21,609.5 | 32,421.2 | 60,034.8 | 68,714.6 | † 66,416.6 | 52,737.8 | 59,576.4 | 57,090.0 | 55,053.8 | 56,564.3 | 61,319.6 |
| Direct investment | 8a9la | 407.5 | 645.2 | 773.3 | 945.4 | 8,721.6 | † 10,332.2 | 11,883.5 | 15,176.0 | 18,144.3 | 16,097.1 | 13,540.2 | 12,637.7 |
| Equity & investment fund shares | 8aala | 407.5 | 645.2 | 773.3 | 945.4 | 8,525.9 | † 10,114.7 | 11,781.4 | 15,022.0 | 18,098.0 | 16,012.6 | 13,523.1 | 12,620.7 |
| Debt instruments | 8abla | . . . . | . . . . | . . . . | . . . . | 195.7 | † 217.4 | 102.1 | 154.0 | 46.3 | 84.5 | 17.1 | 17.0 |
| Portfolio investment | 8b9la | 1,170.0 | 721.9 | 780.2 | 1,360.4 | 7,042.5 | † 10,188.6 | 5,786.5 | 6,278.4 | 7,796.3 | 3,126.9 | 3,447.7 | 3,473.1 |
| Equity & investment fund shares | 8bala | . . . . | . . . . | . . . . | . . . . | 6,924.7 | † 9,273.3 | 4,738.5 | 5,269.0 | 5,889.0 | 636.2 | 1,151.3 | 1,030.4 |
| Debt securities | 8bbla | 1,170.0 | 721.9 | 780.2 | 1,360.4 | 117.8 | † 915.3 | 1,048.0 | 1,009.4 | 1,907.3 | 2,490.7 | 2,296.4 | 2,442.7 |
| Fin. der.(oth.than reserves) & ESOs | 8c9la | . . . . | . . . . | . . . . | . . . . | 23.7 | † 414.6 | 292.5 | 880.7 | 1,032.3 | 1,271.8 | 2,458.5 | 3,475.1 |
| Other investment | 8d9la | 15,500.4 | 20,242.4 | 30,867.6 | 57,729.0 | 52,926.8 | † 45,481.3 | 34,775.3 | 37,241.3 | 30,117.0 | 34,558.0 | 37,117.9 | 41,733.7 |
| Other equity | 8dala | . . . . | . . . . | . . . . | . . . . | . . . . | . . . . | . . . . | . . . . | . . . . | . . . . | . . . . | . . . . |
| Debt instruments | 8dzla | 15,500.4 | 20,242.4 | 30,867.6 | 57,729.0 | 52,926.8 | † 45,481.3 | 34,775.3 | 37,241.3 | 30,117.0 | 34,558.0 | 37,117.9 | 41,733.7 |

| | | 2004 | 2005 | 2006 | 2007 | 2008 | 2009 | 2010 | 2011 | 2012 | 2013 | 2014 | 2015 |
|---|---|---|---|---|---|---|---|---|---|---|---|---|---|
| **Government Finance** | | | | | | | | | | | | | |
| **Cash Flow Statement** | | | | | | | | | | | | | |
| **Budgetary Central Government** | | *Millions of Dinars: Fiscal Year Ends March 31* | | | | | | | | | | | |
| Cash Receipts:Operating Activities... | c1 | 6,721.0 | 8,737.0 | 15,240.8 | 15,490.3 | 21,417.1 | 17,813.7 | 19,658.7 | 22,934.8 | 31,700.9 | 30,985.8 | 31,953.8 | 21,878.1 |
| Taxes........................................ | c11 | 189.0 | 232.0 | 243.0 | 330.0 | 301.9 | 300.0 | 306.1 | 310.2 | 233.8 | 196.6 | 401.1 | 456.4 |
| Social Contributions...................... | c12 | — | — | — | — | — | — | — | — | — | — | — | — |
| Grants....................................... | c13 | — | — | — | — | — | — | — | — | — | — | — | — |
| Other Receipts............................ | c14 | 6,532.0 | 8,505.0 | 13,314.0 | 15,160.3 | 21,115.2 | 17,513.7 | 19,352.6 | 22,624.6 | 31,467.1 | 30,789.2 | 31,552.7 | 21,421.7 |
| Cash Payments:Operating Activities. | c2 | 4,889.0 | 5,632.0 | 4,075.4 | 4,873.5 | 5,462.2 | 6,857.8 | 7,341.6 | 7,762.2 | 10,863.3 | 12,356.6 | 13,127.2 | 15,124.9 |
| Compensation of Employees.......... | c21 | 1,512.0 | 1,625.0 | 1,792.0 | 1,726.1 | 1,975.5 | 2,214.0 | 2,956.2 | 2,516.0 | 3,836.2 | 4,838.7 | 5,200.8 | 5,215.7 |
| Purchases of Goods & Services....... | c22 | 1,350.0 | 1,335.0 | 1,351.0 | 1,081.8 | 1,558.0 | 2,400.4 | 2,252.6 | 1,669.5 | 3,115.0 | 4,600.2 | 3,213.0 | 3,032.8 |
| Interest...................................... | c24 | 18.0 | 13.0 | 13.0 | — | — | — | — | — | — | — | — | — |
| Subsidies................................... | c25 | 775.0 | 1,228.0 | 793.0 | — | — | — | — | — | — | — | — | — |
| Grants....................................... | c26 | 63.0 | 132.0 | 109.0 | 132.0 | 171.8 | 290.3 | 144.3 | 213.4 | 422.5 | 539.1 | 270.0 | 1,024.0 |
| Social Benefits............................ | c27 | 558.0 | 567.0 | 776.0 | 70.2 | 92.5 | 122.2 | 132.4 | 119.9 | 85.7 | 41.0 | 76.4 | 158.5 |
| Other Payments........................... | c28 | 613.0 | 732.0 | 1,320.0 | 1,863.4 | 1,664.4 | 1,830.9 | 1,856.1 | 3,243.4 | 3,403.9 | 2,337.6 | 4,367.0 | 5,693.9 |
| Net Cash Inflow:Operating Act.[1-2] | ccio | 1,832.0 | 3,105.0 | 7,403.0 | 10,616.8 | 15,954.9 | 10,955.9 | 12,317.1 | 15,172.6 | 20,837.6 | 18,629.2 | 18,826.6 | 6,753.2 |
| Net Cash Outflow:Invest. in NFA...... | c31 | 573.0 | 664.0 | 548.0 | 3,570.5 | 3,259.5 | 7,388.8 | 2,936.4 | 4,225.6 | 6,200.3 | 9,411.8 | 7,726.3 | 6,757.5 |
| Purchases of Nonfinancial Assets... | c31.1 | 610.0 | 724.0 | 546.0 | 3,583.9 | 3,271.4 | 7,390.9 | 2,940.8 | 4,232.0 | 6,215.7 | 9,411.1 | 7,751.6 | 6,759.2 |
| Sales of Nonfinancial Assets.......... | c31.2 | 37.0 | 60.0 | — | 13.4 | 11.9 | 2.1 | 4.4 | 6.4 | 15.4 | −.7 | 25.3 | 1.7 |
| Cash Surplus/Deficit [1-2-31=1-2M] | ccsd | 1,259.0 | 2,441.0 | 10,407.6 | 7,046.3 | 12,695.4 | 3,567.1 | 9,380.7 | 10,947.0 | 14,637.3 | 9,217.4 | 11,100.3 | −4.3 |
| Net Acq. Fin. Assets, excl. Cash...... | c32x | .... | .... | .... | .... | .... | .... | .... | .... | .... | .... | .... | .... |
| Domestic................................... | c321x | .... | .... | .... | .... | .... | .... | .... | .... | .... | .... | .... | .... |
| Foreign..................................... | c322x | .... | .... | .... | .... | .... | .... | .... | .... | .... | .... | .... | .... |
| Net Incurrence of Liabilities............. | c33 | .... | .... | .... | .... | .... | .... | .... | .... | .... | .... | .... | .... |
| Domestic................................... | c331 | .... | .... | .... | .... | .... | .... | .... | .... | .... | .... | .... | .... |
| Foreign..................................... | c332 | .... | .... | .... | .... | .... | .... | .... | .... | .... | .... | .... | .... |
| Net Cash Inflow, Fin.Act.[-32x+33].. | cnfb | .... | .... | .... | .... | .... | .... | .... | .... | .... | .... | .... | .... |
| Net Change in Stock of Cash........... | cncb | .... | .... | .... | .... | .... | .... | .... | .... | .... | .... | .... | .... |
| Stat. Discrep. [32X-33+NCB-CSD].... | ccsdz | .... | .... | .... | .... | .... | .... | .... | .... | .... | .... | .... | .... |
| Memo Item:Cash Expenditure[2+31] | c2m | 5,462.0 | 6,296.0 | 6,702.0 | 8,444.0 | 8,721.7 | 14,246.6 | 10,278.0 | 11,987.8 | 17,063.6 | 21,768.4 | 20,853.5 | 21,882.4 |
| Memo Item: Gross Debt.................. | c63 | .... | .... | .... | .... | .... | .... | .... | .... | .... | .... | .... | .... |
| **National Accounts** | | *Millions of Dinars* | | | | | | | | | | | |
| Househ.Cons.Expend.,incl.NPISHs.. | 96f | 6,555 | 7,586 | 8,419 | 9,918 | 11,148 | 10,216 | 9,557 | 10,310 | 11,524 | 12,420p | 13,147 | .... |
| Government Consumption Expend... | 91f | 3,478 | 3,707 | 4,095 | 4,563 | 5,308 | 5,635 | 5,667 | 6,327 | 7,337 | 8,094p | 9,011 | .... |
| Gross Capital Formation.................. | 93 | 3,186 | 3,876 | 4,762 | 6,665 | 6,985 | 5,479 | 5,841 | 5,760 | 6,254 | 7,089 | 7,364 | .... |
| Gross Fixed Capital Formation.......... | 93e | 2,623 | 3,450 | 4,762 | 6,665 | 6,985 | 5,479 | 5,931 | 5,740 | 6,238 | .... | .... | .... |
| Changes in Inventories.................... | 93i | 562 | 425 | — | — | — | — | — | — | — | .... | .... | .... |
| Exports of Goods and Services......... | 90c | 9,970 | 15,094 | 19,316 | 20,661 | 26,450 | 18,125 | 22,055 | 31,126 | 36,411 | 35,000p | 31,604 | .... |
| Imports of Goods and Services (-)..... | 98c | 5,672 | 6,669 | 7,122 | 9,226 | 10,271 | 8,959 | 10,041 | 11,010 | 12,804 | 13,210p | 14,562 | .... |
| Gross Domestic Product (GDP)........ | 99b | 17,517 | 23,593 | 29,470 | 32,581 | 39,620 | 30,496 | 33,079 | 42,512 | 48,722 | 49,392p | 46,564 | .... |
| Net Primary Income from Abroad..... | 98.n | 1,529 | 2,097 | 3,182 | 3,523 | 2,888 | 2,700 | 2,700 | 2,481 | 3,554 | 3,450p | .... | .... |
| Gross National Income (GNI)........... | 99a | 19,046 | 25,690 | 32,652 | 36,103 | 42,508 | 37,069 | 47,385 | 51,290 | .... | .... | .... | .... |
| Consumption of Fixed Capital.......... | 99cf | 1,277 | 1,601 | 1,726 | 2,002 | 2,400 | 2,603 | 2,814 | 2,930 | .... | .... | .... | .... |
| GDP Volume 2000 Prices................. | 99b.p | 15,449 | 17,088 | 18,372 | 19,473 | 19,956 | 18,544 | 18,104 | 19,245 | .... | .... | .... | .... |
| GDP Volume 2010 Prices................. | 99b.p | .... | .... | .... | .... | .... | .... | 33,079 | 36,264 | 38,667 | 39,111 | 38,477 | .... |
| GDP Volume (2010=100)............... | 99bvp | 85.3 | 94.4 | 101.5 | 107.6 | 110.2 | 102.4 | † 100.0 | 109.6 | 116.9 | 118.2 | 116.3 | .... |
| GDP Deflator (2010=100)............... | 99bip | 62.1 | 75.6 | 87.8 | 91.6 | 108.7 | 90.0 | 100.0 | 117.2 | 126.0 | 126.3 | 121.0 | .... |
| | | *Millions: Midyear Estimates* | | | | | | | | | | | |
| **Population**............................... | 99z | 2.17 | 2.26 | 2.39 | 2.54 | 2.71 | 2.88 | 3.06 | 3.24 | 3.42 | 3.59 | 3.75 | 3.89 |

# Kyrgyz Republic   917

| | | 2004 | 2005 | 2006 | 2007 | 2008 | 2009 | 2010 | 2011 | 2012 | 2013 | 2014 | 2015 |
|---|---|---|---|---|---|---|---|---|---|---|---|---|---|
| **Exchange Rates** | | | | | | *Soms per SDR: End of Period* | | | | | | | |
| Official Rate | aa | 64.643 | 59.030 | 57.353 | 56.097 | 60.715 | 69.122 | 72.534 | 71.367 | 72.852 | 75.840 | 85.315 | 105.176 |
| | | | | | | *Soms per US Dollar: End of Period (ae) Period Average (rf)* | | | | | | | |
| Official Rate | ae | 41.625 | 41.301 | 38.124 | 35.499 | 39.418 | 44.092 | 47.099 | 46.485 | 47.401 | 49.247 | 58.887 | 75.899 |
| Official Rate | rf | 42.650 | 41.012 | 40.153 | 37.316 | 36.575 | 42.904 | 45.964 | 46.144 | 47.004 | 48.438 | 53.654 | 64.462 |
| **Fund Position** | | | | | | *Millions of SDRs: End of Period* | | | | | | | |
| Quota | 2f.s | 88.80 | 88.80 | 88.80 | 88.80 | 88.80 | 88.80 | 88.80 | 88.80 | 88.80 | 88.80 | 88.80 | 88.80 |
| SDR Holdings | 1b.s | 12.80 | 3.69 | 22.13 | 8.74 | 35.88 | 103.38 | 111.50 | 115.32 | 120.90 | 128.60 | 124.82 | 132.83 |
| Reserve Position in the Fund | 1c.s | — | — | — | — | — | — | — | — | — | — | — | — |
| Total Fund Cred.&Loans Outstg | 2tl | 133.25 | 124.47 | 108.39 | 94.81 | 106.82 | 106.61 | 114.71 | 118.42 | 123.97 | 131.64 | 127.83 | 135.82 |
| SDR Allocations | 1bd | — | — | — | — | — | 84.74 | 84.74 | 84.74 | 84.74 | 84.74 | 84.74 | 84.74 |
| **International Liquidity** | | | | | | *Millions of US Dollars Unless Otherwise Indicated: End of Period* | | | | | | | |
| Total Reserves minus Gold | 1l.d | 528.2 | 569.7 | 764.3 | 1,107.2 | 1,152.9 | 1,494.0 | 1,603.6 | 1,703.0 | 1,903.2 | 2,098.6 | 1,804.8 | 1,633.9 |
| SDR Holdings | 1b.d | 19.9 | 5.3 | 33.3 | 13.8 | 55.3 | 162.1 | 171.7 | 177.0 | 185.8 | 198.0 | 180.8 | 184.1 |
| Reserve Position in the Fund | 1c.d | — | — | — | — | — | — | — | — | — | — | — | — |
| Foreign Exchange | 1d.d | 508.3 | 564.5 | 731.1 | 1,093.4 | 1,097.6 | 1,331.9 | 1,431.9 | 1,525.9 | 1,717.3 | 1,900.6 | 1,623.9 | 1,449.9 |
| Gold (Million Fine Troy Ounces) | 1ad | .0831 | .0831 | .0831 | .0831 | .0831 | .0831 | .0831 | .0839 | .0983 | .1161 | .1266 | .1359 |
| Gold (National Valuation) | 1and | 36.39 | 42.63 | 52.82 | 69.50 | 71.87 | 90.78 | 116.78 | 132.08 | 162.89 | 139.80 | 152.70 | 144.01 |
| Central Bank: Other Assets | 3..d | .01 | 27.89 | 43.68 | 1.74 | 2.44 | 1.64 | 8.27 | 16.67 | 41.67 | 193.02 | 238.71 | 310.14 |
| Central Bank: Other Liabs | 4..d | 58.14 | † 56.86 | 61.03 | 58.88 | 54.94 | 53.46 | 52.32 | 50.99 | .04 | .30 | .37 | † — |
| Other Depository Corps.: Assets | 7a.d | 193.52 | † 223.13 | 250.92 | 644.48 | 361.88 | 612.18 | 275.29 | 289.79 | 305.43 | 388.16 | 400.22 | 582.55 |
| Other Depository Corps.: Liabs | 7b.d | 101.42 | † 177.53 | 182.68 | 218.09 | 410.00 | 480.51 | 140.51 | 165.14 | 243.80 | 270.51 | 335.22 | 433.24 |
| **Central Bank** | | | | | | *Millions of Soms: End of Period* | | | | | | | |
| Net Foreign Assets | 11n | 21,119.63 | † 15,608.53 | 22,691.29 | 34,490.89 | 39,745.52 | 54,203.51 | 65,883.80 | 71,513.99 | 87,277.87 | 100,063.10 | 104,852.66 | † 123,185.60 |
| Claims on Nonresidents | 11 | 23,539.59 | † 25,303.52 | 31,229.51 | 41,856.06 | 48,410.45 | 69,938.77 | 81,145.49 | 85,423.31 | 98,108.54 | 110,474.36 | 115,435.11 | † 135,047.42 |
| Liabilities to Nonresidents | 16c | 2,419.96 | † 9,694.99 | 8,538.22 | 7,365.18 | 8,664.93 | 15,735.26 | 15,261.69 | 13,909.32 | 10,830.67 | 10,411.26 | 10,582.44 | † 11,861.82 |
| Claims on Other Depository Corps. | 12e | 412.22 | † 348.44 | 275.44 | 1,045.26 | 390.22 | 329.39 | 349.07 | 1,671.54 | 1,157.07 | 1,212.05 | 4,123.28 | † 6,322.68 |
| Net Claims on Central Government | 12an | 521.50 | † 5,603.33 | 1,518.82 | 310.44 | 565.11 | −1,649.04 | −2,056.76 | −1,170.93 | −2,978.34 | −6,973.85 | −18,190.85 | † −13,714.16 |
| Claims on Central Government | 12a | 6,671.81 | † 6,554.01 | 6,147.80 | 5,874.48 | 5,478.14 | 5,103.63 | 5,359.93 | 5,409.37 | 2,311.27 | 1,511.56 | 1,453.62 | † 1,401.97 |
| Liabilities to Central Government | 16d | 6,150.31 | † 950.69 | 4,628.98 | 5,564.04 | 4,913.03 | 6,752.67 | 7,416.69 | 6,580.30 | 5,289.61 | 8,485.41 | 19,644.47 | † 15,116.13 |
| Claims on Other Sectors | 12s | 43.65 | † 55.67 | 74.54 | 374.70 | 363.16 | 2,466.27 | 2,615.25 | 703.51 | 675.73 | 708.89 | 794.03 | † 519.49 |
| Claims on Other Financial Corps. | 12g | — | † 15.00 | 15.00 | 80.91 | 87.89 | 95.43 | 100.92 | 139.53 | 86.47 | 89.83 | 107.42 | † — |
| Claims on State & Local Govts | 12b | — | † — | — | — | — | — | — | — | — | — | — | † — |
| Claims on Public Nonfin. Corps. | 12c | — | † — | — | 34.37 | 34.17 | 34.03 | 33.77 | 33.31 | 32.81 | 30.47 | 20.95 | † — |
| Claims on Private Sector | 12d | 43.65 | † 40.67 | 59.54 | 259.43 | 241.10 | 2,336.81 | 2,480.57 | 530.66 | 556.46 | 588.59 | 665.66 | † 519.49 |
| Monetary Base | 14 | 12,391.90 | † 20,002.30 | 22,729.70 | 31,582.00 | 35,161.50 | 41,603.30 | 48,821.50 | 55,316.50 | 65,634.00 | 73,665.90 | 65,985.80 | 72,252.80 |
| Currency in Circulation | 14a | 11,425.06 | † 13,413.80 | 19,909.75 | 27,568.02 | 30,813.99 | 35,754.26 | 43,307.29 | 49,884.00 | 58,269.22 | 66,973.44 | 57,107.42 | † 58,398.02 |
| Liabs. to Other Depository Corps. | 14c | 966.83 | † 6,588.53 | 2,819.92 | 4,014.00 | 4,347.51 | 5,849.00 | 5,514.24 | 5,432.51 | 7,364.79 | 6,692.49 | 8,878.35 | † 13,854.79 |
| Liabilities to Other Sectors | 14d | — | † — | — | — | — | — | — | — | — | — | — | † — |
| Other Liabs. to Other Dep. Corps. | 14n | — | † 23.30 | 569.05 | 1,622.01 | 1,741.75 | 1,059.54 | 1,469.57 | 1,566.63 | 3,843.61 | 7,220.38 | 1,325.72 | † 2,126.45 |
| Dep. & Sec. Excl. f/Monetary Base | 14o | — | † — | — | — | 36.82 | 1,478.58 | 530.33 | 164.16 | 6.49 | .74 | 1.63 | † 5,639.62 |
| Deposits Included in Broad Money | 15 | — | † — | — | — | — | — | — | — | — | — | — | † — |
| Sec.Ot.th.Shares Incl.in Brd. Money | 16a | — | † — | — | — | — | — | — | — | — | — | — | † — |
| Deposits Excl. from Broad Money | 16b | — | † — | — | — | 36.82 | 1,478.58 | 530.33 | 164.16 | 6.49 | .74 | 1.63 | † 5,639.62 |
| Sec.Ot.th.Shares Excl.f/Brd.Money | 16s | — | † — | — | — | — | — | — | — | — | — | — | † — |
| Loans | 16l | — | † — | — | — | — | — | — | — | — | — | — | † — |
| Financial Derivatives | 16m | — | † — | — | — | — | — | — | — | — | — | — | † — |
| Shares and Other Equity | 17a | 1,227.29 | † 1,462.73 | 1,529.29 | 2,413.64 | 3,903.84 | 11,252.50 | 16,596.49 | 15,605.71 | 17,140.71 | 14,860.73 | 25,103.82 | † 37,928.14 |
| Other Items (Net) | 17r | 8,477.83 | † 127.61 | −267.92 | 603.62 | 220.10 | −43.75 | −626.56 | 65.09 | −492.49 | −737.58 | −837.81 | † −1,633.41 |
| Memo Item: | | | | | | | | | | | | | |
| Total Assets | 10ra | 36,348.70 | 38,264.76 | 43,715.83 | 55,166.92 | 60,908.59 | 85,047.10 | 96,767.55 | 100,414.24 | 110,110.66 | 122,286.69 | 131,230.98 | 155,434.37 |
| **Other Depository Corporations** | | | | | | *Millions of Soms: End of Period* | | | | | | | |
| Net Foreign Assets | 21n | 3,833.52 | † 1,883.17 | 2,601.93 | 15,136.44 | −1,896.79 | 5,805.46 | 6,348.22 | 5,794.34 | 2,921.14 | 5,793.74 | 3,828.11 | † 11,333.13 |
| Claims on Nonresidents | 21 | 8,055.13 | † 9,215.34 | 9,566.20 | 22,878.39 | 14,264.64 | 26,992.02 | 12,965.92 | 13,470.77 | 14,477.54 | 19,115.57 | 23,567.83 | † 44,215.39 |
| Liabilities to Nonresidents | 26c | 4,221.61 | † 7,332.18 | 6,964.27 | 7,741.96 | 16,161.44 | 21,186.56 | 6,617.70 | 7,676.44 | 11,556.40 | 13,321.83 | 19,739.72 | † 32,882.26 |
| Claims on Central Bank | 20 | 1,319.38 | † 2,474.36 | 3,974.88 | 6,279.18 | 7,086.70 | 8,801.92 | 8,458.91 | 9,326.06 | 14,868.89 | 16,220.14 | 14,870.68 | † 20,765.01 |
| Currency | 20a | 315.60 | † 356.55 | 517.73 | 932.10 | 1,418.17 | 1,856.31 | 1,819.14 | 2,647.37 | 3,731.00 | 5,046.92 | 5,170.47 | † 5,280.06 |
| Reserve Deposits and Securities | 20b | 1,003.78 | † 2,051.83 | 2,889.02 | 4,013.98 | 4,347.42 | 5,848.39 | 5,554.56 | 5,431.10 | 7,361.33 | 6,685.49 | 8,426.53 | † 13,408.62 |
| Other Claims | 20n | — | † 65.97 | 568.13 | 1,333.10 | 1,321.10 | 1,097.15 | 1,085.20 | 1,247.59 | 3,776.56 | 4,487.73 | 1,273.69 | † 2,076.32 |
| Net Claims on Central Government | 22an | 712.16 | † 221.45 | −354.66 | −1,564.91 | −1,854.45 | −4,348.06 | −2,142.78 | −1,868.76 | −730.83 | −1,333.87 | −2,639.13 | † −3,300.98 |
| Claims on Central Government | 22a | 937.61 | † 1,143.78 | 1,141.35 | 1,619.45 | 2,394.12 | 3,376.07 | 3,809.03 | 4,497.78 | 5,829.18 | 6,280.09 | 5,143.38 | † 5,773.86 |
| Liabilities to Central Government | 26d | 225.45 | † 922.34 | 1,496.01 | 3,184.36 | 4,248.57 | 7,724.13 | 5,951.81 | 6,366.53 | 6,560.01 | 7,613.96 | 7,782.51 | † 9,074.84 |
| Claims on Other Sectors | 22s | 6,633.22 | † 8,086.68 | 11,965.35 | 8,752.60 | 26,893.16 | 26,128.12 | 29,075.48 | 34,277.60 | 42,668.69 | 58,140.40 | 83,709.82 | † 97,011.36 |
| Claims on Other Financial Corps. | 22g | — | † .03 | .03 | .03 | 1,228.97 | 840.48 | 1,487.80 | 1,953.06 | 1,711.70 | 3,080.96 | 4,028.46 | † 2,345.06 |
| Claims on State & Local Govts | 22b | — | † 109.16 | 10.36 | — | 11.56 | — | — | — | — | — | — | † — |
| Claims on Public Nonfin. Corps. | 22c | — | † — | — | — | — | — | — | — | — | — | — | † — |
| Claims on Private Sector | 22d | 6,633.22 | † 7,977.49 | 11,954.96 | 8,752.57 | 25,652.62 | 25,287.64 | 27,587.67 | 32,324.54 | 40,956.99 | 55,059.43 | 79,681.35 | † 94,666.30 |
| Liabilities to Central Bank | 26g | 545.22 | † 421.65 | 393.84 | 399.05 | 7.57 | 2.87 | 721.29 | 910.81 | 742.88 | 853.02 | 3,763.49 | † 4,729.04 |
| Transf.Dep.Included in Broad Money | 24 | 7,621.71 | † 5,997.06 | 9,375.63 | 10,616.55 | 12,787.62 | 11,677.45 | 13,482.94 | 13,068.48 | 18,507.15 | 21,309.98 | 24,943.61 | † 29,237.80 |
| Other Dep.Included in Broad Money | 25 | 685.09 | † 2,284.06 | 3,277.90 | 6,137.40 | 4,568.72 | 11,566.63 | 14,253.63 | 19,239.75 | 25,454.53 | 37,686.23 | 47,696.62 | † 60,787.23 |
| Sec.Ot.th.Shares Incl.in Brd. Money | 26a | — | † — | — | — | — | — | — | — | — | — | — | † — |
| Deposits Excl. from Broad Money | 26b | — | † — | — | 345.32 | 6.37 | — | — | 1.64 | .29 | .11 | .95 | † 6.30 |
| Sec.Ot.th.Shares Excl.f/Brd.Money | 26s | — | † — | — | — | — | — | — | — | — | — | — | † — |
| Loans | 26l | — | † — | — | — | — | 345.64 | 1,258.29 | 614.16 | 234.31 | 233.49 | 549.21 | † 1,563.43 |
| Financial Derivatives | 26m | — | † — | — | — | — | — | 2.67 | 1,391.17 | 861.96 | 518.53 | 761.02 | † 234.14 |
| Insurance Technical Reserves | 26r | — | † — | — | — | — | — | — | — | — | — | — | † — |
| Shares and Other Equity | 27a | 2,053.83 | † 2,667.51 | 4,220.47 | 8,576.52 | 13,388.26 | 14,080.10 | 13,488.25 | 13,635.41 | 15,944.41 | 18,754.54 | 21,766.82 | † 26,437.02 |
| Other Items (Net) | 27r | 1,592.43 | † 1,300.54 | 635.71 | 2,528.44 | −529.93 | −1,287.92 | −2,855.76 | −802.97 | −1,674.22 | −777.99 | −154.41 | † 2,813.56 |
| Memo Item: | | | | | | | | | | | | | |
| Total Assets | 20ra | 19,535.76 | 23,168.02 | 29,592.57 | 44,624.38 | 59,567.77 | 75,430.37 | 66,539.99 | 70,700.62 | 90,931.57 | 114,822.70 | 143,824.84 | 187,952.52 |

| | | 2004 | 2005 | 2006 | 2007 | 2008 | 2009 | 2010 | 2011 | 2012 | 2013 | 2014 | 2015 |
|---|---|---|---|---|---|---|---|---|---|---|---|---|---|
| **Depository Corporations** | | | | | | *Millions of Soms: End of Period* | | | | | | | |
| Net Foreign Assets.......................... | **31n** | 24,953.15 | † 17,491.70 | 25,293.22 | 49,627.32 | 37,848.72 | 60,008.97 | 72,232.02 | 77,308.33 | 90,199.01 | 105,856.84 | 108,680.77 | † 134,518.73 |
| Claims on Nonresidents................. | **31** | 31,594.72 | † 34,518.86 | 40,795.71 | 64,734.46 | 62,675.09 | 96,930.79 | 94,111.41 | 98,894.09 | 112,586.08 | 129,589.92 | 139,002.94 | † 179,262.81 |
| Liabilities to Nonresidents............. | **36c** | 6,641.57 | † 17,027.16 | 15,502.49 | 15,107.13 | 24,826.37 | 36,921.82 | 21,879.39 | 21,585.76 | 22,387.07 | 23,733.08 | 30,322.17 | † 44,744.08 |
| Domestic Claims........................... | **32** | 7,910.53 | † 13,967.12 | 13,204.04 | 7,872.83 | 25,966.98 | 22,597.29 | 27,491.19 | 31,941.42 | 39,635.26 | 50,541.57 | 63,673.86 | † 80,515.72 |
| Net Claims on Central Government | **32an** | 1,233.66 | † 5,824.77 | 1,164.16 | −1,254.47 | −1,289.34 | −5,997.10 | −4,199.54 | −3,039.69 | −3,709.17 | −8,307.72 | −20,829.99 | † −17,015.13 |
| Claims on Central Government..... | **32a** | 7,609.42 | † 7,697.80 | 7,289.14 | 7,493.93 | 7,872.26 | 8,479.70 | 9,168.96 | 9,907.15 | 8,140.45 | 7,791.65 | 6,596.99 | † 7,175.83 |
| Liabilities to Central Government. | **36d** | 6,375.76 | † 1,873.02 | 6,124.99 | 8,748.40 | 9,161.60 | 14,476.80 | 13,368.50 | 12,946.83 | 11,849.62 | 16,099.37 | 27,426.98 | † 24,190.96 |
| Claims on Other Sectors................. | **32s** | 6,676.87 | † 8,142.35 | 12,039.89 | 9,127.30 | 27,256.32 | 28,594.39 | 31,690.73 | 34,981.11 | 43,344.43 | 58,849.29 | 84,503.85 | † 97,530.85 |
| Claims on Other Financial Corps.. | **32g** | — | † 15.03 | 15.03 | 80.93 | 1,316.86 | 935.91 | 1,588.72 | 2,092.59 | 1,798.17 | 3,170.80 | 4,135.88 | † 2,345.06 |
| Claims on State & Local Govts..... | **32b** | — | † — | — | — | — | — | — | — | — | — | — | † — |
| Claims on Public Nonfin. Corps.... | **32c** | — | † 109.16 | 10.36 | 34.37 | 45.73 | 34.03 | 33.77 | 33.31 | 32.81 | 30.47 | 20.95 | † — |
| Claims on Private Sector.............. | **32d** | 6,676.87 | † 8,018.16 | 12,014.50 | 9,012.00 | 25,893.73 | 27,624.45 | 30,068.25 | 32,855.21 | 41,513.45 | 55,648.03 | 80,347.01 | † 95,185.79 |
| Broad Money Liabilities.................... | **35l** | 19,416.30 | † 21,338.40 | 32,045.60 | 43,389.90 | 46,752.20 | 57,142.00 | 69,224.70 | 79,544.90 | 98,499.90 | 120,922.70 | 124,577.20 | 143,142.99 |
| Currency Outside Depository Corps | **34a** | 11,109.46 | † 13,057.25 | 19,392.02 | 26,635.91 | 29,395.82 | 33,897.90 | 41,488.15 | 47,236.63 | 54,538.23 | 61,926.52 | 51,936.96 | † 53,117.96 |
| Transferable Deposits................... | **34** | 7,621.71 | † 5,997.06 | 9,375.63 | 10,616.55 | 12,787.62 | 11,677.45 | 13,482.94 | 13,068.48 | 18,507.15 | 21,309.98 | 24,943.61 | † 29,237.80 |
| Other Deposits........................... | **35** | 685.09 | † 2,284.06 | 3,277.90 | 6,137.40 | 4,568.72 | 11,566.63 | 14,253.63 | 19,239.75 | 25,454.53 | 37,686.23 | 47,696.62 | † 60,787.23 |
| Securities Other than Shares.......... | **36a** | — | † — | — | — | — | — | — | — | — | — | — | † — |
| Deposits Excl. from Broad Money..... | **36b** | — | † — | — | 345.32 | 43.19 | 1,478.58 | 530.33 | 165.80 | 6.78 | .85 | 2.58 | † 5,645.93 |
| Sec.Ot.th.Shares Excl.f/Brd.Money.... | **36s** | — | † — | — | — | — | — | — | — | — | — | — | † — |
| Loans......................................... | **36l** | — | † — | — | — | — | 345.64 | 1,258.29 | 614.16 | 234.31 | 233.49 | 549.21 | † 1,563.43 |
| Financial Derivatives..................... | **36m** | — | † — | — | — | — | 2.67 | 1,391.17 | 861.96 | 518.53 | 761.02 | 1,203.20 | † 234.14 |
| Insurance Technical Reserves.......... | **36r** | — | † — | — | — | — | — | — | — | — | — | — | † — |
| Shares and Other Equity................. | **37a** | 3,281.12 | † 4,130.24 | 5,749.75 | 10,990.16 | 17,292.10 | 25,332.60 | 30,084.75 | 29,241.12 | 33,085.11 | 33,615.27 | 46,870.64 | † 64,365.16 |
| Other Items (Net)........................... | **37r** | 10,166.30 | † 5,995.39 | 418.01 | 2,774.79 | −271.74 | −1,695.20 | −2,766.04 | −1,178.16 | −2,510.38 | 865.06 | −848.17 | † 82.80 |
| Broad Money Liabs., Seasonally Adj. | **35l.b** | 18,734.89 | 20,625.71 | 30,750.10 | 41,375.73 | 44,388.76 | 54,263.37 | 66,159.20 | 76,782.09 | 95,986.61 | 118,424.21 | 122,183.99 | 139,758.95 |
| **Monetary Aggregates** | | | | | | *Millions of Soms: End of Period* | | | | | | | |
| Broad Money............................. | **59m** | 19,416.26 | † 21,338.37 | 32,045.55 | 43,389.86 | 46,752.16 | 57,141.98 | 69,224.72 | 79,544.86 | 98,499.91 | 120,922.73 | 124,577.19 | 143,142.99 |
| o/w:Currency Issued by Cent.Govt | **59m.a** | — | — | — | — | — | — | — | — | — | — | — | — |
| o/w: Dep.in Nonfin. Corporations. | **59m.b** | — | — | — | — | — | — | — | — | — | — | — | — |
| o/w:Secs. Issued by Central Govt.. | **59m.c** | — | — | — | — | — | — | — | — | — | — | — | — |
| Money (National Definitions) | | | | | | | | | | | | | |
| M1............................................. | **59ma** | 13,044.50 | 15,007.30 | 22,501.41 | 31,407.90 | 36,134.59 | 38,612.45 | 47,976.63 | 53,532.55 | 65,046.35 | 72,625.58 | 62,537.93 | 70,452.70 |
| M2............................................. | **59mb** | 13,729.59 | 15,972.06 | 23,949.74 | 34,688.84 | 38,094.43 | 43,505.52 | 53,762.42 | 62,142.39 | 77,477.62 | 90,981.95 | 82,419.22 | 82,267.20 |
| M2x........................................... | **59mba** | 19,416.26 | 21,338.37 | 32,045.55 | 43,389.86 | 46,752.16 | 57,141.98 | 69,224.72 | 79,544.86 | 98,499.91 | 120,922.73 | 124,577.19 | 143,143.00 |
| **Interest Rates** | | | | | | *Percent per Annum* | | | | | | | |
| Central Bank Policy Rate (EOP)........ | **60** | 4.00 | 4.13 | 3.15 | 8.79 | 15.22 | .90 | 5.50 | 13.61 | 2.64 | 4.17 | 10.50 | 10.00 |
| Lombard Rate................................. | **60.a** | 4.80 | 6.20 | 4.73 | 13.19 | 18.26 | 1.08 | 6.60 | 16.33 | 3.19 | . . . . | 11.50 | 12.00 |
| Central Bank Bill Rate.................... | **60aa** | . . . . | . . . . | . . . . | 8.64 | 13.80 | .92 | 4.89 | 11.79 | 2.79 | 3.98 | 10.00 | 9.99 |
| Money Market Rate........................ | **60b** | 4.00 | 1.01 | 2.12 | 4.29 | 13.39 | 2.89 | . . . . | 11.31 | 7.74 | 6.05 | 18.50 | 11.23 |
| Treasury Bill Rate.......................... | **60c** | 6.37 | 6.82 | 6.63 | † 8.67 | 19.53 | 6.37 | 11.07 | 13.39 | 8.98 | 7.91 | 11.13 | 13.48 |
| Savings Rate................................... | **60k** | 8.65 | 9.65 | 3.63 | 5.28 | 5.39 | 8.09 | 9.53 | 11.45 | 10.51 | 10.13 | 14.14 | 15.36 |
| Savings Rate (Fgn. Currency)........... | **60k.f** | 4.23 | 5.87 | 5.05 | 5.66 | 8.28 | 6.63 | 7.35 | 5.87 | 6.77 | 6.41 | 5.41 | 5.73 |
| Deposit Rate.................................. | **60l** | 1.48 | 1.74 | 1.59 | 2.96 | 2.56 | 3.17 | 2.00 | 2.25 | 2.55 | 2.24 | 2.71 | 2.69 |
| Deposit Rate (Fgn. Currency)............ | **60l.f** | .18 | .13 | .46 | .75 | 1.53 | 1.65 | 1.01 | .77 | .94 | .93 | 1.10 | .94 |
| Lending Rate................................. | **60p** | 29.27 | 26.60 | 23.20 | † 25.83 | 25.69 | 26.36 | 23.11 | 25.27 | 23.90 | 21.73 | 22.36 | 24.25 |
| Lending Rate (Fgn. Currency).......... | **60p.f** | 10.30 | 19.07 | 13.30 | † 18.30 | 20.39 | 20.72 | 18.14 | 19.04 | 18.04 | 15.09 | 15.10 | 13.60 |
| Government Bond Yield.................. | **61** | . . . . | . . . . | . . . . | | | 9.00 | 18.90 | 16.00 | 14.53 | 13.40 | 14.42 | 15.70 |
| **Prices and Labor** | | | | | | *Index Numbers (2010=100): Period Averages* | | | | | | | |
| Producer Prices.............................. | **63** | 43.6 | 44.9 | 52.1 | 58.2 | 73.0 | 81.3 | † 100.0 | 121.8 | 119.2 | 111.9 | 112.2 | 122.4 |
| Consumer Prices............................. | **64** | 57.3 | 59.8 | 63.2 | 69.6 | 86.6 | † 92.6 | 100.0 | 116.5 | 119.6 | 127.5 | 137.1 | 146.1 |
| Wages: Average Earnings............... | **65** | 31.2 | 36.3 | 45.5 | 55.2 | 74.8 | 85.7 | 100.0 | 129.4 | 151.4 | 158.9 | 172.9 | 184.6 |
| | | | | | | *Number in Thousands: Period Averages* | | | | | | | |
| Employment.................................. | **67e** | 555 | 550 | 533 | 560 | 574 | 563 | 559 | 571 | 514 | 518 | 521 | 526 |
| Unemployment.............................. | **67c** | 58 | 62 | 73 | 72 | 70 | 66 | 65 | 64 | 62 | 60 | 58 | 57 |
| Unemployment Rate (%)................. | **67r** | 2.7 | 3.0 | 3.2 | 3.0 | 2.8 | 2.5 | 2.6 | 2.5 | 2.4 | 2.4 | 2.4 | 2.3 |
| **Intl. Transactions & Positions** | | | | | | *Millions of US Dollars* | | | | | | | |
| Exports........................................ | **70..d** | 733.2 | 686.8 | 905.9 | 1,337.9 | 1,874.3 | 1,693.8 | 1,778.8 | 2,267.0 | 1,954.5 | 2,058.2 | 1,896.5 | 1,441.4 |
| Imports, c.i.f................................... | **71..d** | 941.0 | 1,101.5 | 1,718.2 | 2,416.9 | 4,072.3 | 3,040.3 | 3,223.1 | 4,261.1 | 5,576.4 | 6,069.7 | 5,732.4 | 4,069.6 |

| | | 2004 | 2005 | 2006 | 2007 | 2008 | 2009 | 2010 | 2011 | 2012 | 2013 | 2014 | 2015 |
|---|---|---|---|---|---|---|---|---|---|---|---|---|---|
| **Balance of Payments** | | | | | | | *Millions of US Dollars* | | | | | | |
| A. Current Account* | 109bx | 3.7 | −62.1 | −303.2 | −262.0 | −713.2 | −202.3 | −317.1 | −593.0 | −1,675.1 | −1,807.0 | † −1,891.8 | −813.4 |
| Goods, credit (exports) | 1a9cx | 733.2 | 686.8 | 906.0 | 1,337.8 | 1,874.4 | 1,693.8 | 1,778.7 | 2,267.0 | 1,954.4 | 2,058.2 | † 1,793.9 | 1,609.5 |
| Goods, debit (imports) | 1a9dx | 903.8 | 1,105.5 | 1,792.4 | 2,613.6 | 3,753.5 | 2,813.6 | 2,980.9 | 3,935.9 | 5,165.1 | 5,613.6 | † 5,203.5 | 3,648.0 |
| Balance on goods | 1a9bx | −170.6 | −418.7 | −886.5 | −1,275.8 | −1,879.2 | −1,119.8 | −1,202.2 | −1,669.0 | −3,210.7 | −3,555.4 | † −3,409.6 | −2,038.5 |
| Services, credit (exports) | 1b9cx | 209.8 | 259.4 | 378.7 | 684.8 | 805.6 | 638.2 | 600.1 | 860.2 | 966.6 | 1,042.7 | † 896.8 | 843.8 |
| Services, debit (imports) | 1b9dx | 222.6 | 290.3 | 459.7 | 604.5 | 909.8 | 746.4 | 801.3 | 963.9 | 1,323.1 | 1,109.2 | † 1,246.6 | 971.7 |
| Balance on Goods & Services | 1z9bx | −183.5 | −449.5 | −967.4 | −1,195.5 | −1,982.5 | −1,228.0 | −1,403.4 | −1,772.6 | −3,567.2 | −3,622.0 | † −3,759.7 | −2,166.5 |
| Primary income: credit | 1c9cx | 7.8 | 16.5 | 41.6 | 42.6 | 41.7 | 21.7 | 29.7 | 31.6 | 29.7 | 40.1 | † 41.0 | 33.7 |
| Primary income: debit | 1c9dx | 109.9 | 104.7 | 89.8 | 93.2 | 248.4 | 203.1 | 334.7 | 690.8 | 199.0 | 463.1 | † 348.9 | 308.7 |
| Balance on gds, serv. & prim. inc. | 1y9bx | −285.6 | −537.7 | −1,015.6 | −1,246.1 | −2,189.3 | −1,409.4 | −1,708.5 | −2,431.7 | −3,736.6 | −4,045.0 | † −4,067.6 | −2,441.5 |
| Secondary income: credit | 1d9ca | 306.9 | 513.6 | 762.4 | 1,063.1 | 1,556.3 | 1,292.1 | 1,532.7 | 2,044.1 | 2,339.2 | 2,610.7 | † 2,610.3 | 1,976.7 |
| Secondary income: debit | 1d9da | 17.6 | 37.9 | 50.0 | 79.0 | 80.2 | 85.1 | 141.4 | 205.4 | 277.7 | 372.7 | † 434.6 | 348.7 |
| B. Capital Account* | 209ba | 23.8 | 42.9 | 29.7 | 44.9 | 83.7 | 86.2 | 108.6 | 157.3 | 183.8 | 297.4 | † 65.8 | 99.4 |
| Capital account: credit | 209ca | 24.1 | 42.9 | 29.7 | 44.9 | 83.7 | 86.2 | 108.6 | 157.3 | 183.9 | 298.7 | † 90.5 | 117.9 |
| Capital account: debit | 209da | .2 | — | — | — | — | — | — | — | .1 | 1.3 | † 24.7 | 18.4 |
| Balance on current & capital acct. | 129ba | 27.5 | −19.2 | −273.5 | −217.0 | −629.5 | −116.1 | −208.6 | −435.8 | −1,491.3 | −1,509.6 | † −1,826.1 | −714.0 |
| C. Financial Account* | 309na | −180.1 | −85.4 | −339.4 | −986.4 | −397.8 | −539.9 | −496.0 | −860.6 | −868.5 | −859.5 | † −986.9 | −1,020.1 |
| Direct investment: assets | 3a9aa | 43.9 | — | — | −1.0 | −.1 | −.3 | −17.6 | 3.8 | 16.1 | 7.0 | † 2.4 | 53.0 |
| Equity & investment fund shares.. | 3aaaa | 43.9 | — | — | −1.0 | −.1 | −.3 | | −.1 | .3 | 7.0 | † — | 50.0 |
| Debt instruments | 3abaa | — | — | — | — | — | — | −17.6 | 3.9 | 15.9 | 7.0 | † 2.5 | 3.0 |
| Direct investment: liabilities | 3a9la | 175.5 | 42.6 | 182.0 | 207.9 | 377.0 | 189.4 | 420.0 | 697.4 | 308.5 | 633.1 | † 352.9 | 760.4 |
| Equity & investment fund shares . | 3aala | 197.5 | 46.9 | 52.6 | 50.0 | 178.2 | 177.7 | 230.8 | 547.1 | 112.3 | 162.3 | † 354.9 | 872.7 |
| Debt instruments | 3abla | −22.1 | −4.3 | 129.5 | 157.9 | 198.8 | 11.7 | 189.2 | 150.3 | 196.2 | 470.8 | † −2.0 | −112.3 |
| Portfolio investment: assets | 3b9aa | 9.5 | −2.3 | 3.0 | 15.8 | 10.8 | 14.6 | −45.2 | 5.8 | −5.6 | −6.2 | † — | — |
| Equity & investment fund shares | 3baaa | — | — | — | 10.8 | −21.1 | −7.0 | −22.9 | — | — | — | † — | — |
| Debt securities | 3bbaa | 9.5 | −2.3 | 3.0 | 5.1 | 31.8 | 21.7 | −22.3 | 5.8 | −5.6 | −6.2 | † — | — |
| Portfolio investment: liabilities | 3b9la | — | — | — | 1.5 | 6.2 | .7 | −18.2 | 5.5 | .1 | −1.4 | † .1 | 2.0 |
| Equity & investment fund shares . | 3bala | — | — | — | 1.5 | 6.2 | .7 | −18.2 | 5.5 | — | −1.6 | † — | .1 |
| Debt securities | 3bbla | — | — | — | — | — | — | — | — | .1 | .2 | † — | 1.9 |
| Fin. der.& empl.stk.ops.(ESOs): net. | 3c9na | 20.5 | — | — | — | — | — | — | — | .4 | .1 | † .5 | −5.3 |
| Fin. der. & ESOs.: assets | 3c9aa | 20.5 | — | — | — | — | — | — | — | .4 | .1 | † 5.5 | −1.0 |
| Fin. der. & ESOs.: liabilities | 3c9la | .... | .... | .... | .... | — | — | — | — | — | — | † 5.0 | 4.3 |
| Other investment: assets | 3d9aa | 35.8 | 47.5 | 24.0 | −19.4 | 352.0 | 237.5 | −128.7 | 231.8 | −137.8 | 68.4 | † 298.8 | 259.1 |
| Other equity | 3daaa | .... | .... | .... | .... | .... | .... | .... | .... | .... | .... | .... | .... |
| Debt instruments | 3dzaa | 35.8 | 47.5 | 24.0 | −19.4 | 352.0 | 237.5 | −128.7 | 231.8 | −137.8 | 68.4 | † 298.8 | 259.1 |
| Other investment: liabilities | 3d9la | 114.3 | 88.1 | 184.4 | 772.3 | 377.2 | 601.7 | −97.4 | 399.2 | 433.0 | 297.2 | † 935.6 | 564.3 |
| Other equity | 3dala | .... | .... | .... | .... | .... | .... | .... | .... | .... | .... | .... | .... |
| Debt instruments | 3dzla | 114.3 | 88.1 | 184.4 | 772.3 | 377.2 | 601.7 | −97.4 | 399.2 | 433.0 | 297.2 | † 935.6 | 564.3 |
| Curr.+ cap.− finan. acct. balance | 4y9na | 207.7 | 66.3 | 65.9 | 769.3 | −231.7 | 423.8 | 287.5 | 424.8 | −622.8 | −650.0 | † −839.2 | 306.0 |
| D. Net Errors and Omissions | 409na | −63.1 | 2.1 | 110.8 | −476.2 | 334.4 | −159.0 | −184.2 | −317.6 | 814.5 | 915.6 | † 712.2 | −346.3 |
| E. Reserves and Related Items | 4z9na | 144.5 | 68.4 | 176.7 | 293.1 | 102.7 | 264.8 | 103.2 | 107.3 | 191.7 | 265.5 | † −127.0 | −40.3 |
| Reserve assets | 3e9aa | 166.2 | 80.5 | 170.3 | 306.7 | 121.0 | 264.6 | 115.7 | 113.1 | 200.4 | 277.3 | † −132.4 | −29.3 |
| Credit and loans from the IMF | 3dcla | −3.9 | −12.5 | −23.5 | −20.7 | 18.3 | −.2 | 12.4 | 5.8 | 8.6 | 11.8 | † −5.4 | 10.9 |
| Exceptional financing | 409la | 25.6 | 24.6 | 17.1 | 34.3 | — | — | — | — | — | — | † — | — |

*Excludes components in group E

| | | 2004 | 2005 | 2006 | 2007 | 2008 | 2009 | 2010 | 2011 | 2012 | 2013 | 2014 | 2015 |
|---|---|---|---|---|---|---|---|---|---|---|---|---|---|
| **International Investment Position** | | | | | | | *Millions of US Dollars* | | | | | | |
| Assets | 809aa | 985.3 | 1,154.7 | 1,257.9 | 1,680.8 | 2,086.4 | 3,446.7 | 4,138.8 | 4,321.5 | 3,745.7 | 3,610.3 | † 3,541.3 | 3,405.1 |
| Direct investment | 8a9aa | 77.0 | 137.1 | −9.0 | 2.6 | 10.9 | 820.8 | 1,564.1 | 1,404.4 | 748.4 | 341.7 | † 418.3 | 331.4 |
| Equity & investment fund shares.. | 8aaaa | 83.2 | 147.5 | 3.4 | 17.9 | 1.3 | 797.1 | 1,522.3 | 1,366.3 | 725.7 | 320.4 | † 404.7 | 321.3 |
| Debt instruments | 8abaa | −6.2 | −10.5 | −12.4 | −15.3 | 9.7 | 23.7 | 41.8 | 38.1 | 22.7 | 21.2 | † 13.6 | 10.1 |
| Portfolio investment | 8b9aa | 17.4 | 14.9 | 19.3 | 50.5 | 66.9 | 81.5 | 36.2 | 37.1 | 31.5 | 25.1 | † 25.1 | 25.1 |
| Equity & investment fund shares.. | 8baaa | .... | .... | .... | 27.7 | 34.8 | 27.7 | 4.7 | .... | .... | .... | † — | — |
| Debt securities | 8bbaa | 17.4 | 14.9 | 19.3 | 22.8 | 32.2 | 53.8 | 31.5 | 37.1 | 31.5 | 25.1 | † 25.1 | 25.1 |
| Fin. der.(oth.than reserves) & ESOs | 8c9aa | .... | .... | .... | .... | .... | .... | .... | .... | .... | .4 | † .5 | 46.9 |
| Other investment | 8d9aa | 347.0 | 394.3 | 433.3 | 433.8 | 786.0 | 963.4 | 822.0 | 1,048.9 | 903.3 | 1,008.0 | † 1,139.1 | 1,228.1 |
| Other equity | 8daaa | .... | .... | .... | .... | .... | .... | .... | .... | .... | .... | .... | .... |
| Debt instruments | 8dzaa | 347.0 | 394.3 | 433.3 | 433.8 | 786.0 | 963.4 | 822.0 | 1,048.9 | 903.3 | 1,008.0 | † 1,139.1 | 1,228.1 |
| Reserve assets | 8e9aa | 543.9 | 608.5 | 814.3 | 1,193.8 | 1,222.5 | 1,580.9 | 1,716.5 | 1,831.2 | 2,062.2 | 2,235.1 | † 1,953.4 | 1,773.8 |
| Liabilities | 809la | 2,939.3 | 2,787.8 | 3,048.6 | 3,489.9 | 4,911.4 | 5,723.1 | 5,959.7 | 7,076.7 | 7,702.3 | 8,848.1 | † 9,595.0 | 10,561.3 |
| Direct investment | 8a9la | 706.2 | 507.2 | 607.5 | 803.3 | 1,389.2 | 1,452.6 | 1,739.4 | 2,451.4 | 2,696.5 | 3,451.4 | † 3,666.9 | 4,347.3 |
| Equity & investment fund shares.. | 8aala | 459.0 | 257.9 | 301.3 | 316.4 | 696.0 | 888.0 | 1,075.3 | 1,623.0 | 1,733.2 | 1,957.4 | † 2,287.1 | 3,108.0 |
| Debt instruments | 8abla | 247.2 | 249.3 | 306.2 | 486.9 | 693.2 | 564.6 | 664.1 | 828.4 | 963.3 | 1,494.0 | † 1,379.8 | 1,239.3 |
| Portfolio investment | 8b9la | 6.0 | 6.1 | 6.6 | 8.7 | 21.2 | 20.1 | .3 | 6.4 | 6.4 | 8.7 | † 10.2 | 6.7 |
| Equity & investment fund shares.. | 8bala | 6.0 | 6.1 | 6.6 | 8.7 | 21.2 | 20.1 | .3 | 6.4 | 6.4 | 8.7 | † 3.2 | 3.2 |
| Debt securities | 8bbla | .... | .... | .... | .... | .... | .... | .... | .... | .... | .... | † 7.0 | 3.5 |
| Fin. der.(oth.than reserves) & ESOs | 8c9la | .... | .... | .... | .... | .... | .... | .... | .... | .... | .... | † 5.6 | 46.9 |
| Other investment | 8d9la | 2,227.1 | 2,274.5 | 2,434.5 | 2,677.9 | 3,501.0 | 4,250.4 | 4,220.0 | 4,618.8 | 4,999.5 | 5,388.0 | † 5,912.3 | 6,160.5 |
| Other equity | 8dala | .... | .... | .... | .... | .... | .... | .... | .... | .... | .... | .... | .... |
| Debt instruments | 8dzla | 2,227.1 | 2,274.5 | 2,434.5 | 2,677.9 | 3,501.0 | 4,250.4 | 4,220.0 | 4,618.8 | 4,999.5 | 5,388.0 | † 5,912.3 | 6,160.5 |

# Kyrgyz Republic 917

| | | 2004 | 2005 | 2006 | 2007 | 2008 | 2009 | 2010 | 2011 | 2012 | 2013 | 2014 | 2015 |
|---|---|---|---|---|---|---|---|---|---|---|---|---|---|
| **Government Finance** | | | | | | | | | | | | | |
| **Cash Flow Statement** | | | | | | | | | | | | | |
| **Budgetary Central Government** | | | | | | *Millions of Soms: Fiscal Year Ends December 31* | | | | | | | |
| Cash Receipts:Operating Activities... | c1 | 18,335.9 | 20,368.0 | 25,081.0 | 35,994.9 | 46,596.4 | 47,971.0 | 49,822.8 | 68,941.8 | 77,497.1 | 89,252.3 | 105,258.9 | .... |
| Taxes............................... | c11 | .... | .... | .... | .... | .... | 30,256.0 | 33,122.2 | 46,125.2 | 56,247.1 | 62,414.4 | 70,945.4 | .... |
| Social Contributions..................... | c12 | .... | .... | .... | .... | .... | — | — | — | — | — | — | .... |
| Grants................................ | c13 | .... | .... | .... | .... | .... | 10,163.0 | 7,022.1 | 8,672.3 | 5,608.4 | 9,189.2 | 9,959.1 | .... |
| Other Receipts........................ | c14 | .... | .... | .... | .... | .... | 7,552.0 | 9,678.5 | 14,144.3 | 15,641.7 | 17,648.7 | 24,354.4 | .... |
| Cash Payments:Operating Activities. | c2 | 18,841.7 | 20,143.7 | 25,297.5 | 35,864.9 | 45,031.7 | 43,453.0 | 54,927.1 | 75,138.0 | 91,511.7 | .... | 84,145.4 | .... |
| Compensation of Employees.......... | c21 | .... | .... | .... | .... | .... | 10,948.6 | 12,852.9 | 16,124.2 | 18,809.7 | 24,223.8 | 34,291.6 | .... |
| Purchases of Goods & Services....... | c22 | .... | .... | .... | .... | .... | 11,342.8 | 11,710.1 | 14,092.5 | 16,425.8 | 18,208.9 | 19,542.0 | .... |
| Interest............................... | c24 | .... | .... | .... | .... | .... | 1,592.5 | 1,761.4 | 2,725.4 | 2,899.0 | 2,961.9 | 3,452.5 | .... |
| Subsidies............................. | c25 | .... | .... | .... | .... | .... | 1,099.2 | 1,265.6 | 1,566.6 | 1,297.8 | 1,627.0 | 1,992.3 | .... |
| Grants................................ | c26 | .... | .... | .... | .... | .... | 6,514.7 | 7,698.1 | 13,163.4 | 14,453.9 | 8,736.4 | 2,154.5 | .... |
| Social Benefits........................ | c27 | .... | .... | .... | .... | .... | 5,147.4 | 10,416.8 | 13,494.9 | 16,287.2 | 19,681.0 | 22,236.0 | .... |
| Other Payments...................... | c28 | .... | .... | .... | .... | .... | 6,807.8 | 9,222.2 | 13,971.0 | 21,318.2 | .... | 476.5 | .... |
| Net Cash Inflow:Operating Act.[1-2] | ccio | .... | .... | .... | .... | .... | 4,518.0 | −5,104.3 | −6,196.2 | −14,014.6 | .... | 21,113.5 | .... |
| Net Cash Outflow:Invest. in NFA...... | c31 | .... | .... | .... | .... | .... | 7,154.8 | 5,575.8 | 7,526.0 | 6,218.7 | 16,153.9 | 23,239.6 | .... |
| Purchases of Nonfinancial Assets... | c31.1 | .... | .... | .... | .... | .... | 7,224.0 | 6,072.2 | 7,741.8 | 6,320.9 | 16,165.6 | 23,241.9 | .... |
| Sales of Nonfinancial Assets.......... | c31.2 | .... | .... | .... | .... | .... | 69.2 | 496.4 | 215.8 | 102.5 | 11.6 | 2.4 | .... |
| Cash Surplus/Deficit [1-2-31=1-2M] | ccsd | −505.8 | 224.4 | −216.5 | 130.0 | 1,564.7 | −2,636.8 | −10,680.1 | −13,722.2 | −20,233.3 | .... | −2,126.1 | .... |
| Net Acq. Fin. Assets, excl. Cash.... | c32x | .... | .... | .... | .... | .... | 13,820.0 | −5,060.6 | −2,658.5 | −1,453.8 | 10,699.4 | 15,848.0 | .... |
| Domestic.............................. | c321x | .... | .... | .... | .... | .... | 13,721.4 | −5,060.6 | −2,658.8 | −1,453.8 | 10,699.5 | 15,848.0 | .... |
| Foreign............................... | c322x | .... | .... | .... | .... | .... | 98.6 | — | .3 | — | — | — | .... |
| Net Incurrence of Liabilities............. | c33 | 505.8 | −224.4 | 216.5 | −130.0 | −1,564.7 | 16,194.3 | 6,447.5 | 13,382.6 | 15,921.8 | 16,452.5 | 22,519.8 | .... |
| Domestic.............................. | c331 | 209.8 | −460.5 | .... | 353.5 | −838.7 | 1,036.9 | −191.9 | 4,085.0 | 339.8 | −1,257.1 | 381.9 | .... |
| Foreign............................... | c332 | 296.0 | 236.1 | .... | −483.5 | −726.0 | 15,157.4 | 6,639.4 | 9,297.6 | 15,581.9 | 17,709.7 | 22,137.9 | .... |
| Net Cash Inflow, Fin.Act.[-32x+33].. | cnfb | .... | .... | .... | .... | .... | 2,374.3 | 11,508.1 | 16,041.1 | 17,375.6 | .... | 6,671.8 | .... |
| Net Change in Stock of Cash........... | cncb | .... | .... | .... | .... | .... | −262.5 | 828.0 | 2,318.9 | −2,857.6 | .... | 4,545.7 | .... |
| Stat. Discrep. [32X-33+NCB-CSD].... | ccsdz | .... | .... | .... | .... | .... | — | — | — | .1 | .... | — | .... |
| Memo Item:Cash Expenditure[2+31] | c2m | .... | .... | .... | .... | .... | 50,607.8 | 60,502.9 | 82,664.0 | 97,632.4 | .... | 107,385.0 | .... |
| Memo Item: Gross Debt.................. | c63 | .... | .... | .... | .... | .... | .... | .... | .... | .... | .... | .... | .... |
| **National Accounts** | | | | | | *Millions of Soms* | | | | | | | |
| Househ.Cons.Expend.,incl.NPISHs.... | 96f | 71,747 | 85,305 | 108,253 | 124,141 | 173,965 | 157,518 | 186,423 | 238,522 | 297,433 | 345,278 | 384,662 | 373,663 |
| Government Consumption Expend... | 91f | 17,146 | 17,667 | 20,470 | 24,269 | 32,938 | 37,089 | 39,947 | 52,129 | 62,423 | 65,541 | 70,015 | 74,179 |
| Gross Fixed Capital Formation......... | 93e | 13,925 | 16,357 | 26,667 | 35,495 | 51,098 | 57,546 | 61,950 | 68,635 | 98,510 | 106,291 | 131,598 | 145,039 |
| Changes in Inventories.................... | 93i | −256 | 209 | 868 | 2,311 | 3,324 | −2,672 | −1,565 | 4,215 | 10,034 | 14,150 | 15,684 | 2,092 |
| Exports of Goods and Services......... | 90c | 40,152 | 38,650 | 47,478 | 75,082 | 100,668 | 110,066 | 113,610 | 155,974 | 137,862 | 150,113 | 150,055 | 153,164 |
| Imports of Goods and Services (-)..... | 98c | 48,364 | 57,289 | 89,936 | 119,400 | 174,000 | 158,324 | 179,994 | 233,485 | 295,791 | 326,078 | 351,319 | 305,983 |
| Statistical Discrepancy..................... | 99bs | — | — | — | — | — | — | — | — | — | — | — | −18,518 |
| Gross Domestic Product (GDP)......... | 99b | 94,351 | 100,899 | 113,800 | 141,898 | 187,992 | 201,223 | 220,369 | 285,989 | 310,471 | 355,295 | 400,694 | 423,635 |
| Net Primary Income from Abroad..... | 98.n | −4,210 | −3,320 | −1,394 | −1,986 | −3,710 | −8,188 | −15,701 | −24,541 | −7,951 | −20,070 | .... | .... |
| Gross National Income (GNI).......... | 99a | 90,141 | 97,579 | 112,407 | 139,912 | 184,282 | 193,035 | 204,668 | 261,448 | 302,520 | 335,225 | .... | .... |
| Net Current Transf.from Abroad....... | 98t | 8,551 | 13,617 | 28,619 | 37,911 | 53,959 | 52,119 | 67,479 | 85,711 | 96,975 | 108,598 | .... | .... |
| Gross Nat'l Disposable Inc.(GNDI).... | 99i | 98,691 | 111,196 | 141,026 | 177,824 | 238,240 | 245,154 | 272,147 | 347,159 | 399,495 | 443,823 | .... | .... |
| Gross Saving............................. | 99s | 9,798 | 8,224 | 12,303 | 29,414 | 31,338 | 50,547 | 45,777 | 56,508 | 39,639 | 33,004 | .... | .... |
| Consumption of Fixed Capital.......... | 99cf | 9,983 | 10,095 | 10,781 | 12,676 | 19,525 | 20,194 | 22,511 | 25,261 | 34,177 | 49,070 | .... | .... |
| GDP Volume 2000 Prices............... | 99b.p | 78,841 | 78,681 | 81,134 | 88,018 | 95,444 | 98,258 | 97,757 | 103,612 | 103,506 | 114,416 | .... | .... |
| GDP Volume 2010 Prices................ | 99b.p | .... | .... | .... | .... | .... | .... | 220,369 | 233,495 | 234,921 | 260,376 | 271,693 | 281,314 |
| GDP Volume (2010=100)............... | 99bvp | 80.7 | 80.5 | 83.0 | 90.0 | 97.6 | 100.5 | † 100.0 | 106.0 | 106.6 | 118.2 | 123.3 | 127.7 |
| GDP Deflator (2010=100)............... | 99bip | 53.1 | 56.9 | 62.2 | 71.5 | 87.4 | 90.8 | 100.0 | 122.5 | 132.2 | 136.5 | 147.5 | 150.6 |
| | | | | | | *Millions: Midyear Estimates* | | | | | | | |
| Population.................................. | 99z | 5.08 | 5.12 | 5.17 | 5.23 | 5.30 | 5.38 | 5.46 | 5.55 | 5.65 | 5.75 | 5.84 | 5.94 |

# Lao People's Democratic Republic  544

| | | 2004 | 2005 | 2006 | 2007 | 2008 | 2009 | 2010 | 2011 | 2012 | 2013 | 2014 | 2015 |
|---|---|---|---|---|---|---|---|---|---|---|---|---|---|
| **Exchange Rates** | | | | | | *Kip per SDR: End of Period* | | | | | | | |
| Official Rate | aa | 16,115 | 15,355 | 14,587 | 14,769 | 13,058 | 13,301 | 12,411 | 12,318 | 12,276 | 12,363 | 11,732 | 11,325 |
| | | | | | | *Kip per US Dollar: End of Period (ae) Period Average (rf)* | | | | | | | |
| Official Rate | ae | 10,376.5 | 10,743.0 | 9,696.5 | 9,346.0 | 8,477.8 | 8,484.3 | 8,058.8 | 8,023.2 | 7,987.5 | 8,027.8 | 8,097.8 | 8,172.6 |
| Official Rate | rf | 10,585.4 | 10,655.2 | 10,159.9 | 9,603.2 | 8,744.2 | 8,516.1 | 8,258.8 | 8,030.1 | 8,007.8 | 7,860.1 | 8,049.0 | 8,147.9 |
| **Fund Position** | | | | | | *Millions of SDRs: End of Period* | | | | | | | |
| Quota | 2f.s | 52.90 | 52.90 | 52.90 | 52.90 | 52.90 | 52.90 | 52.90 | 52.90 | 52.90 | 52.90 | 52.90 | 52.90 |
| SDR Holdings | 1b.s | 9.90 | 9.86 | 9.78 | 9.79 | 9.80 | 51.07 | 51.07 | 51.07 | 51.07 | 51.07 | 51.07 | 51.07 |
| Reserve Position in the Fund | 1c.s | — | — | — | — | — | — | — | — | — | — | — | .02 |
| Total Fund Cred.&Loans Outstg | 2tl | 24.57 | 20.47 | 18.25 | 16.31 | 13.59 | 9.97 | 6.34 | 3.17 | .91 | — | — | — |
| SDR Allocations | 1bd | 9.41 | 9.41 | 9.41 | 9.41 | 9.41 | 50.68 | 50.68 | 50.68 | 50.68 | 50.68 | 50.68 | 50.68 |
| **International Liquidity** | | | | | *Millions of US Dollars Unless Otherwise Indicated: End of Period* | | | | | | | | |
| Total Reserves minus Gold | 1l.d | 223.25 | 234.29 | 328.43 | 532.56 | 628.74 | 608.60 | 703.35 | 741.21 | 799.09 | 721.63 | 875.10 | 1,043.07 |
| SDR Holdings | 1b.d | 15.37 | 14.09 | 14.71 | 15.47 | 15.10 | 80.06 | 78.65 | 78.41 | 78.50 | 78.65 | 74.00 | 70.77 |
| Reserve Position in the Fund | 1c.d | — | — | — | — | — | — | — | — | — | — | — | .03 |
| Foreign Exchange | 1d.d | 207.87 | 220.21 | 313.73 | 517.09 | 613.64 | 528.54 | 624.70 | 662.80 | 720.59 | 642.98 | 801.10 | 972.27 |
| Gold (Million Fine Troy Ounces) | 1ad | .1171 | .1457 | .2100 | .2100 | .2854 | .2854 | .2854 | † .2854 | .2854 | .2850 | .2850 | . . . . |
| Gold (National Valuation) | 1and | 4.10 | 5.10 | 7.35 | 7.35 | 9.99 | 9.99 | 9.99 | 16.00 | 19.05 | 18.92 | 14.60 | 14.53 |
| Monetary Authorities: Other Liabs | 4..d | — | .76 | .72 | .68 | .25 | .16 | .17 | . . . . | . . . . | . . . . | . . . . | . . . . |
| Deposit Money Banks: Assets | 7a.d | 218.87 | 221.73 | 331.47 | 470.27 | 474.29 | 326.68 | 555.42 | . . . . | . . . . | . . . . | . . . . | . . . . |
| Deposit Money Banks: Liabs | 7b.d | 95.28 | 108.62 | 132.64 | 151.80 | 222.12 | 215.35 | 418.00 | . . . . | . . . . | . . . . | . . . . | . . . . |
| **Monetary Authorities** | | | | | | *Billions of Kip: End of Period* | | | | | | | |
| Foreign Assets | 11 | 2,359.91 | 2,573.17 | 3,258.39 | 5,051.06 | 5,415.86 | 5,369.35 | 5,866.31 | . . . . | . . . . | . . . . | . . . . | . . . . |
| Claims on Central Government | 12a | 185.86 | 260.85 | 619.93 | 907.00 | 972.85 | 925.09 | 925.63 | . . . . | . . . . | . . . . | . . . . | . . . . |
| Claims on Nonfin.Pub.Enterprises | 12c | 575.14 | 228.40 | 176.11 | 160.73 | 685.07 | 2,312.23 | 3,367.06 | . . . . | . . . . | . . . . | . . . . | . . . . |
| Claims on Private Sector | 12d | 153.59 | 126.52 | 70.39 | — | — | — | — | . . . . | . . . . | . . . . | . . . . | . . . . |
| Claims on Deposit Money Banks | 12e | 131.04 | 221.94 | 143.38 | 192.06 | 537.92 | 1,173.34 | 1,966.67 | . . . . | . . . . | . . . . | . . . . | . . . . |
| Reserve Money | 14 | 1,545.29 | 1,823.23 | 2,501.97 | 3,973.61 | 4,776.04 | 6,302.23 | 9,371.79 | . . . . | . . . . | . . . . | . . . . | . . . . |
| of which: Currency Outside DMBs | 14a | 666.42 | 948.55 | 1,230.59 | 1,837.92 | 2,223.23 | 3,085.78 | 3,790.53 | . . . . | . . . . | . . . . | . . . . | . . . . |
| Time, Savings,& Fgn.Currency Dep | 15 | — | — | — | — | — | 133.33 | 188.59 | . . . . | . . . . | . . . . | . . . . | . . . . |
| Liabs. of Central Bank: Securities | 16ac | — | — | — | — | 222.52 | 660.18 | 1,023.30 | . . . . | . . . . | . . . . | . . . . | . . . . |
| Restricted Deposits | 16b | — | — | — | — | — | — | — | . . . . | . . . . | . . . . | . . . . | . . . . |
| Foreign Liabilities | 16c | 547.59 | 466.93 | 410.51 | 386.22 | 302.40 | 807.97 | 709.00 | . . . . | . . . . | . . . . | . . . . | . . . . |
| Central Government Deposits | 16d | 940.49 | 1,033.55 | 1,178.60 | 1,623.81 | 2,213.18 | 1,902.49 | 1,804.16 | . . . . | . . . . | . . . . | . . . . | . . . . |
| Capital Accounts | 17a | 802.44 | 279.43 | 308.87 | 564.40 | 464.79 | 514.99 | 682.80 | . . . . | . . . . | . . . . | . . . . | . . . . |
| Other Items (Net) | 17r | −430.27 | −192.26 | −131.75 | −237.12 | −367.35 | −541.26 | −1,654.09 | . . . . | . . . . | . . . . | . . . . | . . . . |
| **Deposit Money Banks** | | | | | | *Billions of Kip: End of Period* | | | | | | | |
| Reserves | 20 | 982.05 | 962.67 | 1,265.06 | 2,162.37 | 2,357.59 | 3,414.80 | 5,691.00 | . . . . | . . . . | . . . . | . . . . | . . . . |
| Claims on Mon.Author.:Securities | 20c | — | — | — | — | 210.28 | 645.70 | 835.90 | . . . . | . . . . | . . . . | . . . . | . . . . |
| Foreign Assets | 21 | 2,271.14 | 2,382.04 | 3,214.06 | 4,395.18 | 4,020.98 | 2,771.60 | 4,476.00 | . . . . | . . . . | . . . . | . . . . | . . . . |
| Claims on Central Government | 22a | 355.84 | 464.04 | 549.14 | 838.19 | 681.26 | 742.30 | 1,052.00 | . . . . | . . . . | . . . . | . . . . | . . . . |
| Claims on Nonfin.Pub.Enterprises | 22c | 423.46 | 508.08 | 380.15 | 352.15 | 605.67 | 266.30 | 588.60 | . . . . | . . . . | . . . . | . . . . | . . . . |
| Claims on Private Sector | 22d | 1,528.05 | 2,017.24 | 1,990.22 | 2,653.54 | 4,553.82 | 8,564.60 | 12,314.50 | . . . . | . . . . | . . . . | . . . . | . . . . |
| Demand Deposits | 24 | 537.54 | 610.26 | 767.66 | 1,226.74 | 1,491.68 | 1,704.00 | 2,555.30 | . . . . | . . . . | . . . . | . . . . | . . . . |
| Time, Savings,& Fgn.Currency Dep | 25 | 3,947.56 | 4,001.43 | 5,047.80 | 6,709.51 | 7,848.62 | 10,387.60 | 14,764.20 | . . . . | . . . . | . . . . | . . . . | . . . . |
| Restricted Deposits | 26b | 23.63 | 27.74 | 31.21 | 36.39 | 51.98 | 8.70 | 8.40 | . . . . | . . . . | . . . . | . . . . | . . . . |
| Foreign Liabilities | 26c | 988.65 | 1,166.92 | 1,286.18 | 1,418.77 | 1,883.10 | 1,827.10 | 3,368.60 | . . . . | . . . . | . . . . | . . . . | . . . . |
| Central Government Deposits | 26d | 114.94 | 222.75 | 355.94 | 616.92 | 267.53 | 554.10 | 730.90 | . . . . | . . . . | . . . . | . . . . | . . . . |
| Credit from Monetary Authorities | 26g | 98.39 | 150.10 | 164.90 | 174.56 | 419.59 | 923.50 | 1,440.80 | . . . . | . . . . | . . . . | . . . . | . . . . |
| Capital Accounts | 27a | 60.18 | 191.97 | 159.15 | 684.27 | 1,189.92 | 2,093.80 | 3,815.30 | . . . . | . . . . | . . . . | . . . . | . . . . |
| Other Items (Net) | 27r | −210.35 | −37.10 | −414.21 | −465.71 | −722.78 | −1,093.20 | −1,725.20 | . . . . | . . . . | . . . . | . . . . | . . . . |
| **Monetary Survey** | | | | | | *Billions of Kip: End of Period* | | | | | | | |
| Foreign Assets (Net) | 31n | 3,094.81 | 3,321.36 | 4,775.76 | 7,641.26 | 7,251.33 | 5,505.88 | 6,264.71 | . . . . | . . . . | . . . . | . . . . | . . . . |
| Domestic Credit | 32 | 2,166.51 | 2,348.83 | 2,251.40 | 2,670.88 | 5,017.96 | 10,353.93 | 15,712.73 | . . . . | . . . . | . . . . | . . . . | . . . . |
| Claims on Central Govt. (Net) | 32an | −513.73 | −531.41 | −365.47 | −495.54 | −826.60 | −789.20 | −557.43 | . . . . | . . . . | . . . . | . . . . | . . . . |
| Claims on Nonfin.Pub.Enterprises | 32c | 998.60 | 736.48 | 556.26 | 512.88 | 1,290.74 | 2,578.53 | 3,955.66 | . . . . | . . . . | . . . . | . . . . | . . . . |
| Claims on Private Sector | 32d | 1,681.64 | 2,143.76 | 2,060.61 | 2,653.54 | 4,553.82 | 8,564.60 | 12,314.50 | . . . . | . . . . | . . . . | . . . . | . . . . |
| Money | 34 | 1,207.29 | 1,558.91 | 1,998.32 | 3,064.72 | 3,715.33 | 4,790.49 | 6,349.83 | . . . . | . . . . | . . . . | . . . . | . . . . |
| Quasi-Money | 35 | 3,947.56 | 4,001.43 | 5,047.80 | 6,709.51 | 7,848.62 | 10,520.93 | 14,952.79 | . . . . | . . . . | . . . . | . . . . | . . . . |
| Liabs. of Central Bank: Securities | 36ac | — | — | — | — | 12.24 | 14.48 | 187.40 | . . . . | . . . . | . . . . | . . . . | . . . . |
| Restricted Deposits | 36b | 23.63 | 27.74 | 31.21 | 36.39 | 51.98 | 8.70 | 8.40 | . . . . | . . . . | . . . . | . . . . | . . . . |
| Capital Accounts | 37a | 862.62 | 471.40 | 468.02 | 1,248.67 | 1,654.71 | 2,608.79 | 4,498.10 | . . . . | . . . . | . . . . | . . . . | . . . . |
| Other Items (Net) | 37r | −779.78 | −389.29 | −518.19 | −747.07 | −1,013.66 | −2,083.36 | −4,018.90 | . . . . | . . . . | . . . . | . . . . | . . . . |
| Money plus Quasi-Money | 35l | 5,154.85 | 5,560.34 | 7,046.12 | 9,774.23 | 11,563.95 | 15,311.42 | 21,302.62 | . . . . | . . . . | . . . . | . . . . | . . . . |
| **Interest Rates** | | | | | | *Percent Per Annum* | | | | | | | |
| Discount Rate (End of Period) | 60.a | 20.00 | 20.00 | 20.00 | 12.67 | 7.67 | 4.75 | 4.33 | . . . . | . . . . | . . . . | . . . . | . . . . |
| Treasury Bill Rate | 60c | 20.37 | 18.61 | 18.34 | 18.36 | 12.26 | 9.52 | 7.97 | . . . . | . . . . | . . . . | . . . . | . . . . |
| Deposit Rate | 60l | 7.85 | 4.75 | 5.00 | 5.00 | 4.67 | 3.25 | 3.00 | . . . . | . . . . | . . . . | . . . . | . . . . |
| Lending Rate | 60p | 29.25 | 26.83 | 30.00 | 28.50 | 24.00 | 24.78 | 22.61 | . . . . | . . . . | . . . . | . . . . | . . . . |
| **Prices** | | | | | | *Index Numbers (2010=100): Period Averages* | | | | | | | |
| Consumer Prices | 64 | 73.3 | † 78.5 | 83.8 | 87.6 | 94.3 | 94.4 | † 100.0 | 107.6 | 112.2 | 119.3 | 124.2 | 125.8 |
| **Intl. Transactions & Positions** | | | | | | *Millions of US Dollars* | | | | | | | |
| Exports | 70..d | 363.3 | 553.1 | 882.0 | 841.6 | 1,085.0 | 1,052.7 | 1,746.4 | 2,189.6 | 2,270.7 | 2,263.9 | 2,650.0 | 2,340.0 |
| Imports, c.i.f | 71..d | 712.7 | 882.0 | 1,059.5 | 1,066.9 | 1,404.6 | 1,461.1 | 2,060.4 | 2,404.2 | 3,055.1 | 3,019.7 | 3,300.0 | 3,860.0 |

## Balance of Payments

*Millions of US Dollars*

| | | 2004 | 2005 | 2006 | 2007 | 2008 | 2009 | 2010 | 2011 | 2012 | 2013 | 2014 | 2015 |
|---|---|---|---|---|---|---|---|---|---|---|---|---|---|
| A. Current Account* | 109bx | −178.2 | −173.8 | 75.3 | 139.4 | 77.5 | −60.9 | 29.3 | −206.3 | −412.7 | −376.1 | −1,178.3 | −2,264.5 |
| Goods, credit (exports) | 1a9cx | 363.3 | 553.1 | 882.0 | 922.7 | 1,091.9 | 1,052.7 | 1,746.4 | 1,854.0 | 2,270.7 | 2,263.9 | 2,662.0 | 2,769.0 |
| Goods, debit (imports) | 1a9dx | 712.7 | 882.0 | 1,060.2 | 1,064.6 | 1,403.2 | 1,461.1 | 2,060.4 | 2,422.9 | 3,055.1 | 3,019.7 | 4,271.2 | 5,232.8 |
| Balance on goods | 1a9bx | −349.4 | −328.9 | −178.2 | −141.9 | −311.3 | −408.4 | −314.0 | −568.9 | −784.4 | −755.8 | −1,609.2 | −2,463.8 |
| Services, credit (exports) | 1b9cx | 178.8 | 204.2 | 223.4 | 278.1 | 401.6 | 397.3 | 511.0 | 549.6 | 577.2 | 781.2 | 764.5 | 799.3 |
| Services, debit (imports) | 1b9dx | 31.4 | 39.0 | 37.4 | 43.8 | 107.9 | 135.6 | 263.1 | 330.7 | 339.2 | 533.8 | 497.3 | 585.1 |
| Balance on Goods & Services | 1z9bx | −202.0 | −163.6 | 7.8 | 92.4 | −17.5 | −146.8 | −66.1 | −350.0 | −546.4 | −508.4 | −1,342.0 | −2,249.7 |
| Primary income: credit | 1c9cx | 4.0 | 5.0 | 16.2 | 43.6 | 32.1 | 41.7 | 50.3 | 48.3 | 69.1 | 72.7 | 47.1 | 102.3 |
| Primary income: debit | 1c9dx | 58.8 | 82.4 | 75.4 | 94.0 | 77.7 | 88.8 | 133.5 | 127.5 | 187.4 | 178.0 | 171.9 | 302.5 |
| Balance on gds, serv. & prim. inc. | 1y9bx | −256.9 | −240.9 | −51.3 | 42.0 | −63.2 | −193.8 | −149.3 | −429.1 | −664.7 | −613.7 | −1,466.8 | −2,450.0 |
| Secondary income: credit | 1d9ca | 119.2 | 124.2 | 151.5 | 139.1 | 198.9 | 178.4 | 218.7 | 333.2 | 308.1 | 297.9 | 336.0 | 308.2 |
| Secondary income: debit | 1d9da | 40.6 | 57.0 | 24.9 | 41.7 | 58.2 | 45.5 | 40.1 | 110.4 | 56.1 | 60.3 | 47.6 | 122.7 |
| B. Capital Account* | 209ba | — | — | — | — | — | — | — | — | — | — | — | — |
| Capital account: credit | 209ca | — | — | — | — | — | — | — | — | — | — | — | — |
| Capital account: debit | 209da | — | — | — | — | — | — | — | — | — | — | — | — |
| Balance on current & capital acct. | 129ba | −178.2 | −173.8 | 75.3 | 139.4 | 77.5 | −60.9 | 29.3 | −206.3 | −412.7 | −376.1 | −1,178.3 | −2,264.5 |
| C. Financial Account* | 309na | −100.5 | −161.8 | −231.8 | −399.2 | −433.4 | −635.1 | −476.5 | −477.2 | −714.6 | −776.9 | −1,724.7 | −2,819.2 |
| Direct investment: assets | 3a9aa | — | — | — | — | — | — | — | — | — | — | — | — |
| Equity & investment fund shares | 3aaaa | — | — | — | — | — | — | — | — | — | — | — | — |
| Debt instruments | 3abaa | — | — | — | — | — | — | — | — | — | — | — | — |
| Direct investment: liabilities | 3a9la | 16.9 | 27.7 | 187.3 | 323.5 | 227.8 | 318.6 | 278.8 | 300.7 | 294.4 | 426.7 | 913.2 | 1,079.1 |
| Equity & investment fund shares | 3aala | 16.9 | 27.7 | 187.3 | 323.5 | 227.8 | 318.6 | 278.8 | 300.7 | 294.4 | 426.7 | 913.2 | 1,079.1 |
| Debt instruments | 3abla | — | — | — | — | — | — | — | — | — | — | — | — |
| Portfolio investment: assets | 3b9aa | — | — | — | — | — | — | — | — | — | — | — | 10.5 |
| Equity & investment fund shares | 3baaa | — | — | — | — | — | — | — | — | — | — | — | — |
| Debt securities | 3bbaa | — | — | — | — | — | — | — | — | — | — | — | 10.5 |
| Portfolio investment: liabilities | 3b9la | — | — | — | — | — | — | 53.8 | 11.5 | 5.7 | 6.7 | 360.7 | 541.8 |
| Equity & investment fund shares | 3bala | — | — | — | — | — | — | 53.8 | 11.5 | 5.7 | 6.7 | 4.3 | −.1 |
| Debt securities | 3bbla | — | — | — | — | — | — | — | — | — | — | 356.4 | 541.9 |
| Fin. der.& empl.stk.ops.(ESOs): net | 3c9na | | | | | | | | | | | .... | .... |
| Fin. der. & ESOs.: assets | 3c9aa | — | — | — | — | — | — | — | — | — | — | .... | .... |
| Fin. der. & ESOs.: liabilities | 3c9la | .... | .... | .... | .... | — | | | | | | .... | .... |
| Other investment: assets | 3d9aa | 53.0 | 3.4 | 111.0 | 134.9 | 3.0 | −142.7 | 173.9 | 194.7 | −107.2 | 105.1 | 363.2 | −117.1 |
| Other equity | 3daaa | .... | .... | .... | .... | .... | .... | .... | .... | .... | .... | .... | .... |
| Debt instruments | 3dzaa | 53.0 | 3.4 | 111.0 | 134.9 | 3.0 | −142.7 | 173.9 | 194.7 | −107.2 | 105.1 | 363.2 | −117.1 |
| Other investment: liabilities | 3d9la | 136.6 | 137.5 | 155.5 | 210.7 | 208.7 | 173.7 | 317.8 | 359.7 | 307.3 | 448.5 | 814.0 | 1,091.7 |
| Other equity | 3dala | .... | .... | .... | .... | .... | .... | .... | .... | .... | .... | .... | .... |
| Debt instruments | 3dzla | 136.6 | 137.5 | 155.5 | 210.7 | 208.7 | 173.7 | 317.8 | 359.7 | 307.3 | 448.5 | 814.0 | 1,091.7 |
| Curr.+ cap.− finan. acct. balance | 4y9na | −77.7 | −12.0 | 307.1 | 538.7 | 511.0 | 574.1 | 505.8 | 270.9 | 301.9 | 400.8 | 546.4 | 554.7 |
| D. Net Errors and Omissions | 409na | 65.3 | 5.9 | −400.7 | −750.2 | −407.8 | −507.9 | −403.2 | −322.9 | −408.5 | −477.1 | −386.7 | −380.1 |
| E. Reserves and Related Items | 4z9na | −12.4 | −6.0 | −93.6 | −211.5 | 103.2 | 66.3 | 102.6 | −52.1 | −106.5 | −76.3 | 159.6 | 174.6 |
| Reserve assets | 3e9aa | −20.3 | −12.1 | −96.9 | −214.5 | 98.9 | 60.7 | 97.0 | −57.1 | −110.0 | −77.7 | 159.6 | 174.6 |
| Credit and loans from the IMF | 3dcla | −7.9 | −6.1 | −3.3 | −3.0 | −4.3 | −5.5 | −5.6 | −5.0 | −3.5 | −1.4 | — | — |
| Exceptional financing | 409la | — | — | — | — | — | — | — | — | — | — | — | — |

*Excludes components in group E

## Government Finance
### Cash Flow Statement
### Budgetary Central Government

*Billions of Lao Kip: Fiscal Year Ends September 30*

| | | 2004 | 2005 | 2006 | 2007 | 2008 | 2009 | 2010 | 2011 | 2012 | 2013 | 2014 | 2015 |
|---|---|---|---|---|---|---|---|---|---|---|---|---|---|
| Cash Receipts:Operating Activities | c1 | .... | .... | 5,312 | 6,435 | 7,708 | 8,174 | 12,129 | 13,754 | 16,991 | 19,711 | 22,733 | .... |
| Taxes | c11 | .... | .... | 3,680 | 4,699 | 5,761 | 6,337 | 7,669 | 9,101 | 11,116 | 12,928 | 15,175 | .... |
| Social Contributions | c12 | .... | .... | — | — | — | — | — | — | — | — | — | .... |
| Grants | c13 | .... | .... | 1,046 | 1,094 | 1,269 | 1,143 | 3,591 | 3,709 | 4,552 | 4,913 | 4,870 | .... |
| Other Receipts | c14 | .... | .... | 586 | 642 | 678 | 694 | 870 | 945 | 1,323 | 1,871 | 2,688 | .... |
| Cash Payments:Operating Activities | c2 | .... | .... | 3,510 | 4,146 | 5,134 | 5,720 | 6,499 | 7,516 | 9,007 | 15,782 | 15,785 | .... |
| Compensation of Employees | c21 | .... | .... | 1,447 | 1,589 | 2,435 | 2,803 | 2,825 | 3,468 | 4,121 | 8,884 | 8,562 | .... |
| Purchases of Goods & Services | c22 | .... | .... | 1,190 | 1,637 | 1,404 | 1,535 | 1,859 | 2,095 | 2,346 | 3,709 | 3,962 | .... |
| Interest | c24 | .... | .... | 277 | 198 | 361 | 264 | 398 | 431 | 561 | 1,005 | 881 | .... |
| Subsidies | c25 | .... | .... | 261 | 343 | 492 | 551 | 799 | 872 | 953 | 1,096 | 1,100 | .... |
| Grants | c26 | .... | .... | 26 | 26 | 27 | 19 | 19 | 28 | 27 | 23 | 25 | .... |
| Social Benefits | c27 | .... | .... | — | — | — | — | — | — | — | — | — | .... |
| Other Payments | c28 | .... | .... | 309 | 352 | 414 | 548 | 600 | 622 | 998 | 1,065 | 1,255 | .... |
| Net Cash Inflow:Operating Act.[1-2] | ccio | .... | .... | 1,803 | 2,289 | 2,575 | 2,453 | 5,630 | 6,239 | 7,984 | 3,929 | 6,949 | .... |
| Net Cash Outflow:Invest. in NFA | c31 | .... | .... | 2,929 | 3,381 | 3,608 | 3,276 | 6,128 | 6,870 | 8,589 | 8,379 | 9,280 | .... |
| Purchases of Nonfinancial Assets | c31.1 | .... | .... | 2,945 | 3,388 | 3,642 | 3,324 | 6,406 | 7,139 | 8,612 | .... | .... | .... |
| Sales of Nonfinancial Assets | c31.2 | .... | .... | 16 | 7 | 34 | 49 | 277 | 269 | 23 | .... | .... | .... |
| Cash Surplus/Deficit [1-2-31=1-2M] | ccsd | .... | .... | −1,126 | −1,092 | −1,033 | −823 | −498 | −631 | −605 | −4,450 | −2,331 | .... |
| Net Acq. Fin. Assets, excl. Cash | c32x | .... | .... | −130 | −112 | −144 | −143 | −139 | −149 | −248 | .... | .... | .... |
| Domestic | c321x | .... | .... | −130 | −112 | −144 | −143 | −139 | −149 | −248 | .... | .... | .... |
| Foreign | c322x | .... | .... | — | — | — | — | — | — | — | .... | .... | .... |
| Net Incurrence of Liabilities | c33 | .... | .... | 1,358 | 1,511 | 1,159 | 912 | 1,107 | 1,307 | 739 | 381 | 3,826 | .... |
| Domestic | c331 | .... | .... | −32 | 27 | −204 | −132 | 97 | 44 | −270 | −542 | 2,800 | .... |
| Foreign | c332 | .... | .... | 1,390 | 1,484 | 1,363 | 1,044 | 1,010 | 1,262 | 1,008 | 923 | 1,027 | .... |
| Net Cash Inflow, Fin.Act.[-32x+33] | cnfb | .... | .... | 1,488 | 1,623 | 1,303 | 1,055 | 1,247 | 1,455 | 986 | 573 | 3,922 | .... |
| Net Change in Stock of Cash | cncb | .... | .... | 305 | 363 | 230 | −465 | 328 | 182 | −1,454 | −2,559 | 1,059 | .... |
| Stat. Discrep. [32X-33+NCB-CSD] | ccsdz | .... | .... | −56 | −168 | −40 | −697 | −420 | −643 | −1,836 | 1,318 | −532 | .... |
| Memo Item:Cash Expenditure[2+31] | c2m | .... | .... | 6,438 | 7,527 | 8,741 | 8,996 | 12,628 | 14,386 | 17,596 | 24,162 | 25,065 | .... |
| Memo Item: Gross Debt | c63 | .... | .... | .... | .... | .... | .... | .... | .... | .... | .... | .... | .... |

# Lao People's Democratic Republic   544

| | | 2004 | 2005 | 2006 | 2007 | 2008 | 2009 | 2010 | 2011 | 2012 | 2013 | 2014 | 2015 |
|---|---|---|---|---|---|---|---|---|---|---|---|---|---|
| **National Accounts** | | | | | | *Billions of Kip* | | | | | | | |
| Gross Domestic Product (GDP)......... | **99b** | 26,590.1 | 30,594.1 | 35,407.3 | 39,284.2 | 45,578.3 | 46,796.9 | 55,694.0 | 64,727.1 | 72,727.5 | 82,736.5 | . . . . | . . . . |
| GDP Volume 1990 Prices................. | **99b.p** | 1,428.0 | 1,532.0 | 1,658.9 | 1,783.1 | . . . . | . . . . | . . . . | . . . . | . . . . | . . . . | . . . . | . . . . |
| GDP Volume 2002 Prices................. | **99b.p** | 20,098.6 | 21,458.6 | 23,317.1 | 24,909.8 | 27,099.2 | 29,132.2 | 31,500.9 | 34,033.2 | 36,731.5 | 39,652.7 | . . . . | . . . . |
| GDP Volume (2010=100)................. | **99bvp** | 63.8 | 68.1 | 74.0 | 79.1 | 86.0 | 92.5 | 100.0 | 108.0 | 116.6 | 125.9 | . . . . | . . . . |
| GDP Deflator (2010=100)............... | **99bip** | 74.8 | 80.6 | 85.9 | 89.2 | 95.1 | 90.9 | 100.0 | 107.6 | 112.0 | 118.0 | . . . . | . . . . |
| | | | | | | *Millions: Midyear Estimates* | | | | | | | |
| Population............................... | **99z** | 5.66 | 5.75 | 5.84 | 5.94 | 6.05 | 6.15 | 6.26 | 6.37 | 6.47 | 6.58 | 6.69 | 6.80 |

# Latvia 941

| | | 2004 | 2005 | 2006 | 2007 | 2008 | 2009 | 2010 | 2011 | 2012 | 2013 | 2014 | 2015 |
|---|---|---|---|---|---|---|---|---|---|---|---|---|---|
| **Exchange Rates** | | | | | | | | | | | | | |
| | | *Lats per SDR through 2013; Euros per SDR Thereafter: End of Period* | | | | | | | | | | | |
| Official Rate | aa | .8014 | .8476 | .8064 | .7648 | .7624 | .7666 | .8239 | .8352 | .8161 | .7931 | 1.1933 | 1.2728 |
| | | *Lats per US Dollar through 2013; Euros per US Dollar Thereafter: End of Period (ae) Period Average (rf)* | | | | | | | | | | | |
| Official Rate | ae | .5160 | .5930 | .5360 | .4840 | .4950 | .4890 | .5350 | .5440 | .5310 | .5150 | .8237 | .9185 |
| Official Rate | rf | .5402 | .5647 | .5604 | .5138 | .4808 | .5056 | .5305 | .5012 | .5469 | .5294 | .7537 | .9017 |
| | | *Index Numbers (2010=100): Period Averages* | | | | | | | | | | | |
| Nominal Effective Exchange Rate | nec | 102.7 | 97.4 | 96.9 | 98.3 | 99.6 | 103.5 | 100.0 | 101.8 | 99.6 | 101.7 | 104.5 | 105.3 |
| CPI-Based Real Effect. Ex. Rate | rec | 83.8 | 82.2 | 84.8 | 91.5 | 101.4 | 107.1 | 100.0 | 102.0 | 98.8 | 98.8 | 100.2 | 99.0 |
| **Fund Position** | | *Millions of SDRs: End of Period* | | | | | | | | | | | |
| Quota | 2f.s | 126.80 | 126.80 | 126.80 | 126.80 | 126.80 | 126.80 | 126.80 | 142.10 | 142.10 | 142.10 | 142.10 | 142.10 |
| SDR Holdings | 1b.s | .10 | .10 | .11 | .11 | .24 | 119.11 | 121.17 | 94.24 | 101.92 | 120.82 | 120.82 | 120.82 |
| Reserve Position in the Fund | 1c.s | .06 | .06 | .06 | .06 | .06 | .06 | .06 | .06 | .06 | .06 | .06 | .06 |
| Total Fund Cred.&Loans Outstg. | 2tl | — | — | — | — | 535.34 | 713.79 | 982.24 | 982.24 | — | — | — | — |
| SDR Allocations | 1bd | — | — | — | — | — | 120.82 | 120.82 | 120.82 | 120.82 | 120.82 | 120.82 | 120.82 |
| **International Liquidity** | | *Millions of US Dollars Unless Otherwise Indicated: End of Period* | | | | | | | | | | | |
| Total Res. Min. Gold (Eurosys.Def) | 1l.d | 1,911.98 | 2,232.13 | 4,353.37 | 5,553.37 | 5,027.63 | 6,631.80 | 7,256.16 | 5,997.27 | 7,110.87 | 7,595.71 | † 2,971.20 | 3,220.22 |
| SDR Holdings | 1b.d | .15 | .14 | .16 | .17 | .38 | 186.72 | 186.60 | 144.69 | 156.64 | 186.07 | 175.05 | 167.42 |
| Reserve Position in the Fund | 1c.d | .09 | .08 | .08 | .09 | .09 | .09 | .09 | .09 | .09 | .09 | .08 | .08 |
| Foreign Exchange | 1d.d | 1,911.74 | 2,231.91 | 4,353.13 | 5,553.11 | 5,027.17 | 6,444.99 | 7,069.48 | 5,852.50 | 6,954.15 | 7,409.56 | † 2,796.07 | 3,052.71 |
| o/w:Fin. Deriv. Rel to Reserves | 1ddd | .... | .... | .... | .... | .... | .... | .... | .... | .... | .... | | — |
| Other Reserve Assets | | .... | .... | .... | .... | .... | .... | .... | .... | .... | .... | | — |
| Gold (Million Fine Troy Ounces) | 1ad | .2486 | .2487 | .2487 | .2487 | .2487 | .2487 | .2487 | .2487 | .2487 | .2487 | .2130 | .2130 |
| Gold (Eurosystem Valuation) | 1and | 110.27 | 128.45 | 156.10 | 204.81 | 220.20 | 274.78 | 349.87 | 386.15 | 411.96 | 297.39 | † 255.44 | 225.68 |
| Memo:Euro Cl. On Non-EA Res. | 1dgd | .... | .... | .... | .... | .... | .... | .... | .... | .... | .... | .... | .... |
| Non-Euro Cl. on EA Res. | 1dhd | .... | .... | .... | .... | .... | .... | .... | .... | .... | .... | 531.78 | 629.27 |
| Central Bank: Other Assets | 3..d | .... | .... | .... | .... | .... | .... | 95 | 18 | −9 | 116 | 2,593 | 3,852 |
| Central Bank: Other Liabs | 4..d | .... | .... | .... | .... | .... | .... | 226 | 229 | 203 | 201 | 203 | 176 |
| Other Depository Corps.: Assets | 7a.d | .... | .... | .... | .... | .... | .... | 7,086 | 6,894 | 7,709 | 8,003 | 9,470 | 8,981 |
| Other Depository Corps.: Liabs. | 7b.d | .... | .... | .... | .... | .... | .... | 15,235 | 13,666 | 13,724 | 14,354 | 14,693 | 14,808 |
| **Central Bank** | | *Millions of Euros: End of Period* | | | | | | | | | | | |
| Euro Area Wide Residency Criterion | | | | | | | | | | | | | |
| Net Foreign Assets | 11n.u | .... | .... | .... | .... | .... | .... | 2,871 | 2,419 | 2,609 | 2,917 | 2,727 | 3,195 |
| Claims on Nonresidents | 11..u | .... | .... | .... | .... | .... | .... | 3,042 | 2,602 | 2,771 | 3,066 | 2,895 | 3,359 |
| Liabilities to Nonresidents | 16c.u | .... | .... | .... | .... | .... | .... | 170 | 183 | 162 | 149 | 168 | 164 |
| Claims on Other Depository Corps. | 12e.u | .... | .... | .... | .... | .... | .... | 696 | 451 | 315 | 324 | 506 | 709 |
| Net Claims on Central Government | 12anu | .... | .... | .... | .... | .... | .... | −787 | −390 | −638 | −117 | 36 | 864 |
| Claims on Central Govt | 12a.u | .... | .... | .... | .... | .... | .... | 751 | 659 | 445 | 223 | 231 | 1,057 |
| Liabs. to Central Govt | 16d.u | .... | .... | .... | .... | .... | .... | 1,538 | 1,049 | 1,083 | 340 | 195 | 193 |
| Claims on Other Sectors | 12s.u | .... | .... | .... | .... | .... | .... | 673 | 613 | 1,018 | 1,046 | 1,049 | 2,172 |
| Claims on Other Financial Corps. | 12g.u | .... | .... | .... | .... | .... | .... | 373 | 388 | 706 | 858 | 880 | 1,994 |
| Claims on State & Local Govts | 12b.u | .... | .... | .... | .... | .... | .... | 74 | 30 | 40 | 7 | 15 | 41 |
| Claims on Public Nonfin. Corps. | 12c.u | .... | .... | .... | .... | .... | .... | — | — | — | — | — | — |
| Claims on Private Sector | 12d.u | .... | .... | .... | .... | .... | .... | 226 | 195 | 272 | 181 | 154 | 137 |
| Monetary Base | 14..u | .... | .... | .... | .... | .... | .... | 3,799 | 3,397 | 4,170 | 5,050 | 6,458 | 8,946 |
| Currency in Circulation | 14a.u | .... | .... | .... | .... | .... | .... | 1,312 | 1,631 | 1,738 | 898 | 3,958 | 4,045 |
| Liabs. to Other Depository Corps. | 14c.u | .... | .... | .... | .... | .... | .... | 2,406 | 1,706 | 2,416 | 4,138 | 2,424 | 4,793 |
| Liabs. to Other Sectors | 14d.u | .... | .... | .... | .... | .... | .... | 81 | 60 | 16 | 14 | 76 | 108 |
| Other Liabs. to Other Dep. Corps. | 14n.u | .... | .... | .... | .... | .... | .... | — | — | — | — | — | — |
| Dep. & Sec. Excl. f/Monetary Base | 14o.u | .... | .... | .... | .... | .... | .... | — | — | — | — | — | — |
| Deposits Included in Broad Money | 15..u | .... | .... | .... | .... | .... | .... | — | — | — | — | — | — |
| Sec.Ot.th.Shares Inc.in.Brd.Money. | 16a.u | .... | .... | .... | .... | .... | .... | — | — | — | — | — | — |
| Deposits Excl. from Broad Money | 16b.u | .... | .... | .... | .... | .... | .... | — | — | — | — | — | — |
| Sec.Oh.th.Shares Excl. f/Brd.Money | 16s.u | .... | .... | .... | .... | .... | .... | — | — | — | — | — | — |
| Loans | 16l.u | .... | .... | .... | .... | .... | .... | — | — | — | — | — | — |
| Financial Derivatives | 16m.u | .... | .... | .... | .... | .... | .... | — | — | — | — | — | — |
| Shares and Other Equity | 17a.u | .... | .... | .... | .... | .... | .... | 423 | 465 | 515 | 470 | 494 | 501 |
| Other Items (Net) | 17r.u | .... | .... | .... | .... | .... | .... | −1,899 | −1,933 | −1,380 | −1,348 | −2,633 | −2,509 |
| Memorandum Items | | | | | | | | | | | | | |
| National Residency Criterion | | | | | | | | | | | | | |
| Net Foreign Assets | 11n | .... | .... | .... | .... | .... | .... | 5,596 | 4,764 | 5,519 | 5,651 | 3,828 | 5,219 |
| Claims on Nonresidents | 11 | .... | .... | .... | .... | .... | .... | 5,768 | 4,948 | 5,695 | 5,810 | 4,794 | 6,704 |
| Liabilities to Nonresidents | 16c | .... | .... | .... | .... | .... | .... | 171 | 184 | 176 | 159 | 966 | 1,485 |
| Claims on Other Depository Corps. | 12e | .... | .... | .... | .... | .... | .... | — | — | — | — | 14 | 264 |
| Net Claims on Central Government | 12an | .... | .... | .... | .... | .... | .... | −1,538 | −1,049 | −1,083 | −340 | −195 | 328 |
| Claims on Central Government | 12a | .... | .... | .... | .... | .... | .... | — | — | — | — | — | 521 |
| Liabilities to Central Government | 16d | .... | .... | .... | .... | .... | .... | 1,538 | 1,049 | 1,083 | 340 | 195 | 193 |
| Claims on Other Sectors | 12s | .... | .... | .... | .... | .... | .... | — | — | — | — | — | — |
| Claims on Other Fin. Corps. | 12g | .... | .... | .... | .... | .... | .... | — | — | — | — | — | — |
| Claims on State & Local Govts | 12b | .... | .... | .... | .... | .... | .... | — | — | — | — | — | — |
| Claims on Private Sector | 12d | .... | .... | .... | .... | .... | .... | — | — | — | — | — | — |
| Liabs.to ODCs, Inc.in Mon.Base | 14c | .... | .... | .... | .... | .... | .... | 2,405 | 1,705 | 2,402 | 4,128 | 2,423 | 4,784 |
| Liabs.to Ot.Sectors, Inc.in Mon.Base | 14d | .... | .... | .... | .... | .... | .... | 81 | 60 | 16 | 14 | 76 | 108 |
| Liabs.to ODCs,Excl.f/Mon.Base | 14n | .... | .... | .... | .... | .... | .... | — | — | — | — | — | — |
| Net Claims on Eurosystem | 12e.s | .... | .... | .... | .... | .... | .... | .... | .... | .... | .... | −483 | −1,005 |

# Latvia   941

| | | 2004 | 2005 | 2006 | 2007 | 2008 | 2009 | 2010 | 2011 | 2012 | 2013 | 2014 | 2015 |
|---|---|---|---|---|---|---|---|---|---|---|---|---|---|
| **Other Depository Corporations** | | | | | *Millions of Euros: End of Period* | | | | | | | | |
| Euro Area Wide Residency Criterion | | | | | | | | | | | | | |
| Net Foreign Assets | 21n.u | .... | .... | .... | .... | .... | .... | −6,099 | −5,234 | −4,559 | −4,605 | −4,302 | −5,353 |
| Claims on Nonresidents | 21..u | .... | .... | .... | .... | .... | .... | 5,303 | 5,328 | 5,843 | 5,803 | 7,800 | 8,249 |
| Liabilities to Nonresidents | 26c.u | .... | .... | .... | .... | .... | .... | 11,402 | 10,562 | 10,402 | 10,408 | 12,102 | 13,602 |
| Claims on Eurosystem | 20..u | .... | .... | .... | .... | .... | .... | 2,649 | 1,970 | 2,673 | 4,414 | 2,635 | 4,984 |
| Currency | 20a.u | .... | .... | .... | .... | .... | .... | 249 | 269 | 271 | 286 | 211 | 200 |
| Reserve Deposits and Securities | 20b.u | .... | .... | .... | .... | .... | .... | 2,400 | 1,701 | 2,402 | 4,128 | 2,424 | 4,784 |
| Other Claims | 20n.u | .... | .... | .... | .... | .... | .... | — | — | — | — | — | — |
| Net Claims on Central Government | 22anu | .... | .... | .... | .... | .... | .... | −136 | 448 | 24 | −187 | −218 | 961 |
| Claims on Central Government | 22a.u | .... | .... | .... | .... | .... | .... | 878 | 762 | 774 | 750 | 870 | 1,272 |
| Liabilities to Central Government | 26d.u | .... | .... | .... | .... | .... | .... | 1,014 | 314 | 750 | 937 | 1,088 | 311 |
| Claims on Other Sectors | 22s.u | .... | .... | .... | .... | .... | .... | 18,761 | 17,451 | 15,775 | 15,065 | 14,023 | 13,937 |
| Claims on Other Financial Corps. | 22g.u | .... | .... | .... | .... | .... | .... | 1,052 | 1,022 | 1,012 | 1,191 | 1,330 | 1,437 |
| Claims on State & Local Govts. | 22b.u | .... | .... | .... | .... | .... | .... | 87 | 94 | 100 | 117 | 22 | 36 |
| Claims on Public Nonfin. Corps. | 22c.u | .... | .... | .... | .... | .... | .... | — | — | — | — | — | — |
| Claims on Private Sector | 22d.u | .... | .... | .... | .... | .... | .... | 17,622 | 16,335 | 14,663 | 13,757 | 12,671 | 12,464 |
| Liabilities to Eurosystem | 26g.u | .... | .... | .... | .... | .... | .... | 345 | 302 | 299 | 303 | 383 | 589 |
| Transf.Dep.Included in Broad Money | 24..u | .... | .... | .... | .... | .... | .... | 4,577 | 5,129 | 6,104 | 7,887 | 8,230 | 9,347 |
| Other.Dep.Included in Broad Money. | 25..u | .... | .... | .... | .... | .... | .... | 3,937 | 3,168 | 2,807 | 2,396 | 2,258 | 2,052 |
| Sec.Ot.th.Shares Inc.in.Brd. Money. | 26a.u | .... | .... | .... | .... | .... | .... | −33 | 184 | −23 | 2 | 34 | 65 |
| Deposits Excl. from Broad Money. | 26b.u | .... | .... | .... | .... | .... | .... | 389 | 425 | 436 | 445 | 446 | 440 |
| Sec.Ot.th.Shares Excl.f/Brd. Money | 26s.u | .... | .... | .... | .... | .... | .... | −187 | 12 | −535 | −548 | −776 | −775 |
| Loans | 26l.u | .... | .... | .... | .... | .... | .... | — | — | — | — | — | — |
| Financial Derivatives | 26m.u | .... | .... | .... | .... | .... | .... | 63 | 77 | 99 | 81 | 75 | 153 |
| Insurance Technical Reserves | 26r.u | .... | .... | .... | .... | .... | .... | — | — | — | — | — | — |
| Shares and Other Equity | 27a.u | .... | .... | .... | .... | .... | .... | 2,334 | 2,305 | 2,719 | 2,907 | 3,054 | 3,339 |
| Other Items (Net) | 27r.u | .... | .... | .... | .... | .... | .... | 3,748 | 3,040 | 2,014 | 1,218 | −1,563 | −677 |
| Memorandum Items | | | | | | | | | | | | | |
| Total Assets | 20ra | .... | .... | .... | .... | .... | .... | 30,653 | 29,323 | 28,344 | 29,254 | 30,851 | 31,931 |
| National Residency Criterion | | | | | | | | | | | | | |
| Net Foreign Assets | 21n | .... | .... | .... | .... | .... | .... | −7,518 | −5,389 | −5,050 | −4,762 | −1,785 | −3,675 |
| Claims on Nonresidents | 21 | .... | .... | .... | .... | .... | .... | 7,666 | 8,276 | 8,689 | 8,773 | 13,154 | 11,849 |
| Liabilities to Nonresidents | 26c | .... | .... | .... | .... | .... | .... | 15,184 | 13,665 | 13,739 | 13,535 | 14,939 | 15,524 |
| Net Claims on Central Government | 22an | .... | .... | .... | .... | .... | .... | −298 | 285 | −61 | −275 | −369 | 638 |
| Claims on Central Government | 22a | .... | .... | .... | .... | .... | .... | 715 | 598 | 688 | 661 | 718 | 948 |
| Liabilities to Central Government | 26d | .... | .... | .... | .... | .... | .... | 1,013 | 313 | 749 | 936 | 1,087 | 310 |
| Claims on Other Sectors | 22s | .... | .... | .... | .... | .... | .... | 18,154 | 16,847 | 15,128 | 14,346 | 13,296 | 13,167 |
| Claims on Other Fin. Corps. | 22g | .... | .... | .... | .... | .... | .... | 942 | 909 | 845 | 982 | 1,145 | 1,261 |
| Claims on State & Local Govts. | 22b | .... | .... | .... | .... | .... | .... | 87 | 92 | 100 | 117 | 22 | 36 |
| Claims on Private Sector | 22d | .... | .... | .... | .... | .... | .... | 17,125 | 15,846 | 14,183 | 13,247 | 12,129 | 11,870 |
| Transf.Dep.Included in Broad Money | 24 | .... | .... | .... | .... | .... | .... | 4,215 | 4,664 | 5,323 | 6,753 | 7,138 | 8,231 |
| Other.Dep.Included in Broad Money. | 25 | .... | .... | .... | .... | .... | .... | 3,843 | 3,085 | 2,751 | 2,352 | 2,227 | 1,984 |
| Sec.Ot.th.Shares Inc.in.Brd. Money | 26a | .... | .... | .... | .... | .... | .... | 29 | 190 | 2 | 4 | 27 | 35 |
| Deposits Excl. from Broad Money | 26b | .... | .... | .... | .... | .... | .... | 290 | 368 | 359 | 324 | 337 | 332 |
| Sec.Ot.th.Shares Excl.f/Brd. Money | 26s | .... | .... | .... | .... | .... | .... | 190 | 567 | 88 | 114 | 156 | 196 |

| | | 2004 | 2005 | 2006 | 2007 | 2008 | 2009 | 2010 | 2011 | 2012 | 2013 | 2014 | 2015 |
|---|---|---|---|---|---|---|---|---|---|---|---|---|---|
| **Depository Corporations** | | | | | | *Millions of Euros: End of Period* | | | | | | | |
| Euro Area Wide Residency Criterion | | | | | | | | | | | | | |
| Net Foreign Assets........................ | 31n.u | .... | .... | .... | .... | .... | .... | −3,228 | −2,815 | −1,950 | −1,688 | −1,575 | −2,158 |
| Claims on Nonresidents................ | 31..u | .... | .... | .... | .... | .... | .... | 8,345 | 7,930 | 8,614 | 8,869 | 10,695 | 11,608 |
| Liabilities to Nonresidents............. | 36c.u | .... | .... | .... | .... | .... | .... | 11,572 | 10,745 | 10,564 | 10,557 | 12,270 | 13,766 |
| Domestic Claims............................. | 32..u | .... | .... | .... | .... | .... | .... | 18,511 | 18,122 | 16,179 | 15,807 | 14,890 | 17,934 |
| Net Claims on Central Government.. | 32anu | .... | .... | .... | .... | .... | .... | −923 | 58 | −614 | −304 | −182 | 1,825 |
| Claims on Central Government....... | 32a.u | .... | .... | .... | .... | .... | .... | 1,629 | 1,421 | 1,219 | 973 | 1,101 | 2,329 |
| Liabilities to Central Government... | 36d.u | .... | .... | .... | .... | .... | .... | 2,552 | 1,363 | 1,833 | 1,277 | 1,283 | 504 |
| Claims on Other Sectors.................. | 32s.u | .... | .... | .... | .... | .... | .... | 19,434 | 18,064 | 16,793 | 16,111 | 15,072 | 16,109 |
| Claims on Other Financial Corps..... | 32g.u | .... | .... | .... | .... | .... | .... | 1,425 | 1,410 | 1,718 | 2,049 | 2,210 | 3,431 |
| Claims on State & Local Govts...... | 32b.u | .... | .... | .... | .... | .... | .... | 161 | 124 | 140 | 124 | 37 | 77 |
| Claims on Public Nonfin. Corps... | 32c.u | .... | .... | .... | .... | .... | .... | — | — | — | — | — | — |
| Claims on Private Sector............... | 32d.u | .... | .... | .... | .... | .... | .... | 17,848 | 16,530 | 14,935 | 13,938 | 12,825 | 12,601 |
| Broad Money Liabilities................... | 35l.u | .... | .... | .... | .... | .... | .... | 9,625 | 9,903 | 10,371 | 10,911 | 14,345 | 15,417 |
| Currency Outside Depository Corps | 34a.u | .... | .... | .... | .... | .... | .... | 1,063 | 1,362 | 1,467 | 612 | 3,747 | 3,845 |
| Transferable Deposits.................... | 34..u | .... | .... | .... | .... | .... | .... | 4,578 | 5,186 | 6,117 | 7,901 | 8,306 | 9,455 |
| Other Deposits............................. | 35..u | .... | .... | .... | .... | .... | .... | 4,017 | 3,171 | 2,810 | 2,396 | 2,258 | 2,052 |
| Securities Other than Shares.......... | 36a.u | .... | .... | .... | .... | .... | .... | −33 | 184 | −23 | 2 | 34 | 65 |
| Deposits Excl. from Broad Money..... | 36b.u | .... | .... | .... | .... | .... | .... | 389 | 425 | 436 | 445 | 446 | 440 |
| Sec.Oth.th.Shares Excl.f/Brd. Money. | 36s.u | .... | .... | .... | .... | .... | .... | −187 | 12 | −535 | −548 | −776 | −775 |
| Loans........................................... | 36l.u | .... | .... | .... | .... | .... | .... | — | — | — | — | — | — |
| Financial Derivatives...................... | 36m.u | .... | .... | .... | .... | .... | .... | 63 | 77 | 99 | 81 | 75 | 153 |
| Insurance Technical Reserves........... | 36r.u | .... | .... | .... | .... | .... | .... | — | — | — | — | — | — |
| Shares and Other Equity.................. | 37a.u | .... | .... | .... | .... | .... | .... | 2,757 | 2,770 | 3,234 | 3,377 | 3,548 | 3,840 |
| Other Items (Net)............................ | 37r.u | .... | .... | .... | .... | .... | .... | 1,504 | 963 | 632 | −141 | −4,319 | −3,297 |
| Broad Money Liabs., Seasonally Adj. | 35lub | .... | .... | .... | .... | .... | .... | 9,532 | 9,803 | 10,266 | 10,801 | 14,200 | 15,263 |
| Memorandum Items | | | | | | | | | | | | | |
| National Residency Criterion | | | | | | | | | | | | | |
| Net Foreign Assets.......................... | 31n | .... | .... | .... | .... | .... | .... | −1,922 | −625 | 469 | 889 | 2,043 | 1,544 |
| Claims on Nonresidents................ | 31 | .... | .... | .... | .... | .... | .... | 13,434 | 13,224 | 14,384 | 14,583 | 17,948 | 18,553 |
| Liabilities to Nonresidents............. | 36c | .... | .... | .... | .... | .... | .... | 15,355 | 13,849 | 13,915 | 13,694 | 15,905 | 17,009 |
| Domestic Claims............................. | 32 | .... | .... | .... | .... | .... | .... | 16,318 | 16,083 | 13,984 | 13,731 | 12,732 | 14,133 |
| Net Claims on Central Government | 32an | .... | .... | .... | .... | .... | .... | −1,836 | −764 | −1,144 | −615 | −564 | 966 |
| Claims on Central Government.... | 32a | .... | .... | .... | .... | .... | .... | 715 | 598 | 688 | 661 | 718 | 1,469 |
| Liabilities to Central Government. | 36d | .... | .... | .... | .... | .... | .... | 2,551 | 1,362 | 1,832 | 1,276 | 1,282 | 503 |
| Claims on Other Sectors................. | 32s | .... | .... | .... | .... | .... | .... | 18,154 | 16,847 | 15,128 | 14,346 | 13,296 | 13,167 |
| Claims on Other Financial Corps.. | 32g | .... | .... | .... | .... | .... | .... | 942 | 909 | 845 | 982 | 1,145 | 1,261 |
| Claims on State & Local Govts..... | 32b | .... | .... | .... | .... | .... | .... | 87 | 92 | 100 | 117 | 22 | 36 |
| Claims on Private Sector............. | 32d | .... | .... | .... | .... | .... | .... | 17,125 | 15,846 | 14,183 | 13,247 | 12,129 | 11,870 |
| Transf.Dep.Included in Broad Money | 34 | .... | .... | .... | .... | .... | .... | 4,216 | 4,721 | 5,336 | 6,767 | 7,214 | 8,339 |
| Other Dep.Included in Broad Money. | 35 | .... | .... | .... | .... | .... | .... | 3,923 | 3,088 | 2,754 | 2,352 | 2,227 | 1,984 |
| Sec.Ot.th.Shares Inc.in.Brd. Money... | 36a | .... | .... | .... | .... | .... | .... | 29 | 190 | 2 | 4 | 27 | 35 |
| Deposits Excl. from Broad Money..... | 36b | .... | .... | .... | .... | .... | .... | 290 | 368 | 359 | 324 | 337 | 332 |
| Sec.Ot.th.Shares Excl./f.Brd. Money.. | 36s | .... | .... | .... | .... | .... | .... | 190 | 567 | 88 | 114 | 156 | 196 |
| **Monetary Aggregates** | | | | | | | *Millions of Lati: End of Period* | | | | | | |
| Money (National Definitions) | | | | | | | | | | | | | |
| M1........................................... | 59ma | 2,000 | 2,870 | 4,066 | 3,935 | 3,345 | 2,979 | 3,771 | 4,357 | 4,832 | 7,426 | .... | .... |
| M2........................................... | 59mb | 2,817 | 3,906 | 5,456 | 6,242 | 5,965 | 5,796 | 6,446 | 6,462 | 6,706 | 9,723 | .... | .... |
| M3........................................... | 59mc | 2,817 | 3,925 | 5,507 | 6,312 | 6,039 | 5,873 | 6,548 | 6,660 | 6,846 | 10,010 | .... | .... |
| **Interest Rates** | | | | | | | *Percent Per Annum* | | | | | | |
| Discount Rate (End of Period).......... | 60.a | 4.00 | 4.00 | 5.00 | 6.00 | 6.00 | 4.00 | 3.50 | 3.50 | 2.50 | .25 | | |
| Money Market Rate........................ | 60b | 3.25 | 2.49 | 3.24 | 5.07 | 4.09 | 3.92 | .73 | .31 | .24 | .07 | .... | .... |
| Treasury Bill Rate.......................... | 60c | 3.43 | 2.56 | 4.13 | 4.23 | 6.99 | 10.42 | 2.22 | 1.12 | .54 | .... | .... | .... |
| Deposit Rate................................. | 60l | 3.27 | 2.78 | 3.53 | 6.06 | 6.34 | 8.04 | 1.87 | .51 | .37 | .13 | .... | .... |
| Households: Stocks, up to 2 years.. | 60lhs | .... | .... | .... | .... | .... | .... | .... | .... | .... | .... | .84 | .83 |
| New Business, up to 1 year.......... | 60lhn | .... | .... | .... | .... | .... | .... | .... | .... | .... | .... | .61 | .43 |
| Corporations: Stocks, up to 2 years | 60lcs | .... | .... | .... | .... | .... | .... | .... | .... | .... | .... | .39 | .21 |
| New Business, up to 1 year.......... | 60lcn | .... | .... | .... | .... | .... | .... | .... | .... | .... | .... | .05 | .06 |
| Lending Rate................................. | 60p | 7.45 | 6.11 | 7.29 | 10.91 | 11.85 | 16.23 | 9.56 | 6.39 | 5.52 | 5.92 | | |
| Households: Stocks, up to 1 year.... | 60phs | .... | .... | .... | .... | .... | .... | .... | .... | .... | .... | 20.27 | 20.28 |
| New Bus., Floating & up to 1 year | 60pns | .... | .... | .... | .... | .... | .... | .... | .... | .... | .... | 20.94 | 20.13 |
| House Purch., Stocks,Over 5 years | 60phm | .... | .... | .... | .... | .... | .... | .... | .... | .... | .... | 2.43 | 2.31 |
| House Purch., New Bus., 5-10 yrs | 60phn | .... | .... | .... | .... | .... | .... | .... | .... | .... | .... | 5.02 | 12.93 |
| Corporations: Stocks, up to 1 year.. | 60pcs | .... | .... | .... | .... | .... | .... | .... | .... | .... | .... | 3.20 | 3.21 |
| New Bus., Over € 1 mil.,up to 1 yr | 60pcn | .... | .... | .... | .... | .... | .... | .... | .... | .... | .... | 3.34 | 3.42 |
| Government Bond Yield.................. | 61 | 4.86 | 3.88 | 4.13 | 5.28 | 6.43 | 12.35 | 10.34 | 5.91 | 4.57 | 3.34 | 2.51 | .96 |
| **Prices and Labor** | | | | | | | *Index Numbers (2010=100): Period Averages* | | | | | | |
| Share Prices.................................. | 62 | 93.4 | 140.3 | 170.4 | 190.8 | 132.2 | 71.8 | 100.0 | 112.8 | 106.3 | 119.6 | 120.8 | 132.0 |
| Producer Prices............................. | 63 | 65.9 | 71.1 | 78.4 | † 91.0 | 101.7 | 97.0 | 100.0 | 107.7 | 111.6 | 113.4 | 113.8 | 112.7 |
| Consumer Prices............................ | 64 | 67.6 | 72.2 | 76.8 | 84.6 | 97.7 | 101.1 | 100.0 | 104.4 | 106.7 | 106.7 | 107.4 | 107.6 |
| Harmonized CPI.............................. | 64h | 67.8 | 72.5 | 77.3 | 85.1 | 98.0 | 101.2 | 100.0 | 104.2 | 106.6 | 106.6 | 107.4 | 107.6 |
| Wages: Average Earnings................. | 65 | 47.4 | 55.2 | 67.9 | 89.4 | 107.9 | 103.5 | 100.0 | 104.4 | 107.6 | 110.7 | .... | .... |
| Industrial Production....................... | 66 | 95.3 | 102.1 | 108.7 | 109.9 | 106.4 | 87.1 | 100.0 | 109.0 | 115.8 | 114.7 | 113.5 | 117.6 |
| Industrial Employment..................... | 67 | 132.9 | 127.5 | 130.5 | 134.0 | 161.0 | 134.8 | 100.0 | 106.2 | 111.3 | 114.7 | 112.3 | 109.8 |
| | | | | | | | *Number in Thousands: Period Averages* | | | | | | |
| Labor Force................................... | 67d | 1,092 | 1,081 | 1,109 | 1,126 | 1,143 | 1,101 | 1,057 | 1,028 | 1,031 | 1,014 | 992 | 994 |
| Employment.................................. | 67e | 964 | 972 | 1,031 | 1,057 | 1,055 | 909 | 851 | 862 | 876 | 894 | 885 | 896 |
| Unemployment.............................. | 67c | 128 | 108 | 78 | 68 | 88 | 193 | 206 | 167 | 155 | 120 | 108 | 98 |
| Unemployment Rate (%)................. | 67r | 11.7 | 10.0 | 7.0 | 6.1 | 7.7 | 17.5 | 19.5 | 16.2 | 15.0 | 11.9 | 10.8 | 9.9 |

# Latvia 941

| | | 2004 | 2005 | 2006 | 2007 | 2008 | 2009 | 2010 | 2011 | 2012 | 2013 | 2014 | 2015 |
|---|---|---|---|---|---|---|---|---|---|---|---|---|---|
| **Intl. Transactions & Positions** | | | | | *Millions of Lats through 2013; Millions of Euros Beginning 2014: End of Period* | | | | | | | | |
| Exports............................................. | 70 | 2,121.6 | 2,888.2 | 3,293.2 | 4,040.3 | 4,428.9 | 3,602.2 | 4,694.9 | 5,998.5 | 6,937.4 | 7,043.0 | 10,248.6 | 10,369.6 |
| Imports, c.i.f. ................................... | 71 | 3,781.8 | 4,866.9 | 6,378.5 | 7,780.2 | 7,527.7 | 4,709.8 | 5,911.9 | 7,719.1 | 8,793.7 | 8,880.0 | 12,654.3 | 12,536.0 |
| | | | | | | *(2010=100) Period Averages* | | | | | | | |
| Volume of Exports (2000=100)....... | 72 | .... | .... | .... | .... | .... | .... | .... | .... | .... | .... | .... | .... |
| Unit Value of Exports..................... | 74 | 69.4 | 76.6 | 84.0 | 95.2 | 102.4 | 92.3 | 100.0 | † 112.2 | 116.3 | 118.5 | 116.8 | 117.1 |
| **Balance of Payments** | | | | | | *Millions of US Dollars* | | | | | | | |
| A. Current Account*........................ | 109bx | −1,681.0 | −1,987.5 | −4,519.6 | −6,427.8 | −4,482.7 | 2,146.5 | 563.5 | −801.3 | −924.1 | −720.2 | −628.6 | −333.6 |
| Goods, credit (exports)................... | 1a9cx | 3,353.1 | 4,804.8 | 5,619.1 | 7,762.8 | 9,082.7 | 7,014.0 | 8,814.5 | 11,546.2 | 12,387.6 | 13,037.8 | 13,495.7 | 11,399.9 |
| Goods, debit (imports)................... | 1a9dx | 6,248.1 | 7,994.7 | 10,899.6 | 14,834.1 | 15,273.1 | 9,111.0 | 10,787.4 | 14,944.7 | 15,682.1 | 16,409.7 | 16,521.4 | 13,744.5 |
| Balance on goods..................... | 1a9bx | −2,895.0 | −3,188.6 | −5,281.8 | −7,075.5 | −6,190.4 | −2,096.9 | −1,974.3 | −3,397.0 | −3,293.2 | −3,371.8 | −3,028.2 | −2,344.6 |
| Services, credit (exports)............... | 1b9cx | 2,023.6 | 2,467.6 | 3,034.1 | 4,374.5 | 5,370.8 | 4,386.7 | 4,041.2 | 4,828.2 | 4,838.7 | 5,181.7 | 5,111.7 | 4,481.5 |
| Services, debit (imports)............... | 1b9dx | 1,173.4 | 1,602.8 | 2,044.5 | 2,815.2 | 3,321.1 | 2,402.8 | 2,317.1 | 2,770.2 | 2,753.4 | 2,826.6 | 2,793.6 | 2,525.5 |
| Balance on Goods & Services....... | 1z9bx | −2,046.0 | −2,325.1 | −4,292.2 | −5,516.1 | −4,142.2 | −110.1 | −248.8 | −1,337.7 | −1,209.2 | −1,016.7 | −710.1 | −387.4 |
| Primary income: credit.................. | 1c9cx | 473.0 | 839.8 | 1,127.0 | 1,471.3 | 1,852.9 | 1,443.8 | 1,256.2 | 1,556.4 | 1,620.1 | 1,639.1 | 1,646.8 | 1,540.2 |
| Primary income: debit................... | 1c9dx | 757.4 | 1,009.0 | 1,735.1 | 2,662.8 | 2,738.3 | −165.6 | 1,000.5 | 1,567.8 | 1,781.5 | 1,739.4 | 1,697.5 | 1,616.2 |
| Balance on gds, serv. & prim. inc. | 1y9bx | −2,330.3 | −2,494.3 | −4,900.3 | −6,707.6 | −5,027.6 | 1,499.3 | 6.9 | −1,349.1 | −1,370.6 | −1,117.0 | −760.8 | −463.4 |
| Secondary income: credit............... | 1d9ca | 1,190.7 | 1,225.5 | 1,621.7 | 1,822.4 | 1,860.5 | 1,685.0 | 1,277.2 | 1,427.6 | 1,351.4 | 1,440.4 | 1,288.1 | 1,063.2 |
| Secondary income: debit............... | 1d9da | 541.4 | 718.7 | 1,241.0 | 1,542.5 | 1,315.7 | 1,037.8 | 720.7 | 879.8 | 904.9 | 1,043.7 | 1,156.0 | 933.4 |
| B. Capital Account*........................ | 209ba | 136.0 | 212.0 | 237.9 | 577.8 | 506.9 | 623.0 | 469.7 | 599.2 | 825.4 | 762.6 | 1,006.1 | 758.3 |
| Capital account: credit.................. | 209ca | 143.4 | 218.2 | 247.9 | 587.4 | 530.2 | 638.4 | 484.3 | 613.0 | 835.7 | 769.2 | 1,012.7 | 764.9 |
| Capital account: debit................... | 209da | 7.5 | 6.2 | 10.1 | 9.6 | 23.4 | 15.4 | 14.6 | 13.9 | 10.3 | 6.6 | 6.7 | 6.7 |
| Balance on current & capital acct. | 129ba | −1,545.1 | −1,775.5 | −4,281.7 | −5,849.9 | −3,975.9 | 2,769.5 | 1,033.2 | −202.1 | −98.7 | 42.4 | 377.5 | 424.7 |
| C. Financial Account* ................... | 309na | −1,923.1 | −2,593.0 | −6,122.8 | −7,052.8 | −3,247.7 | 1,754.7 | 899.5 | 1,080.8 | −2,327.7 | −226.8 | 1,235.0 | −519.3 |
| Direct investment: assets............. | 3a9aa | 85.0 | 225.8 | 212.4 | 769.5 | 342.3 | −193.3 | 79.9 | 107.7 | 161.4 | 493.8 | 573.8 | 92.8 |
| Equity & investment fund shares.. | 3aaaa | 33.7 | 106.1 | 97.3 | 288.4 | 178.6 | 74.8 | −40.7 | 77.2 | 57.9 | 348.9 | 449.1 | 39.6 |
| Debt instruments..................... | 3abaa | 48.8 | 120.8 | 115.1 | 481.1 | 163.7 | −271.0 | 122.0 | 27.7 | 100.8 | 144.9 | 124.7 | 51.0 |
| Direct investment: liabilities ......... | 3a9la | 591.0 | 810.4 | 1,705.0 | 2,713.7 | 1,432.7 | −32.4 | 435.5 | 1,500.5 | 1,078.7 | 989.5 | 712.2 | 634.0 |
| Equity & investment fund shares . | 3aala | 498.2 | 593.9 | 1,250.4 | 1,942.1 | 583.0 | −580.2 | 278.9 | 1,153.6 | 786.8 | 1,026.5 | 164.6 | 85.0 |
| Debt instruments..................... | 3abla | 90.4 | 217.7 | 455.8 | 769.0 | 848.2 | 549.3 | 156.6 | 349.7 | 290.5 | −35.7 | 712.2 | 634.0 |
| Portfolio investment: assets........... | 3b9aa | 16.7 | 267.4 | 248.3 | 609.9 | −238.2 | −157.1 | 380.0 | 858.6 | 955.2 | 624.4 | 2,126.1 | 2,389.8 |
| Equity & investment fund shares | 3baaa | 27.8 | 72.8 | 73.7 | 171.2 | −432.9 | 165.5 | 294.9 | 254.7 | 167.1 | 106.8 | 172.3 | 12.8 |
| Debt securities .......................... | 3bbaa | −9.8 | 194.5 | 173.4 | 440.0 | 193.1 | −322.6 | 85.0 | 601.1 | 790.7 | 516.3 | 1,955.2 | 2,375.9 |
| Portfolio investment: liabilities....... | 3b9la | 237.7 | 136.3 | 291.8 | −50.6 | 122.9 | 11.9 | −33.0 | 238.5 | 2,241.9 | 363.7 | 2,278.1 | 100.1 |
| Equity & investment fund shares . | 3bala | 31.5 | 12.1 | 23.1 | −12.7 | −49.4 | −7.3 | 8.8 | 38.4 | 3.9 | 47.3 | 57.9 | 113.2 |
| Debt securities.......................... | 3bbla | 207.4 | 122.9 | 268.7 | −39.3 | 172.3 | 19.2 | −43.2 | 200.1 | 2,237.9 | 315.1 | 2,220.2 | −13.1 |
| Fin. der.& empl.stk.ops.(ESOs): net. | 3c9na | 45.8 | 76.0 | −58.9 | −230.6 | 75.0 | −399.4 | 270.8 | −119.7 | −74.8 | −288.7 | 193.0 | 199.6 |
| Fin. der. & ESOs.: assets............. | 3c9aa | .... | .... | .... | .... | .... | .... | .... | .... | .... | .... | .... | .... |
| Fin. der. & ESOs.: liabilities......... | 3c9la | .... | .... | .... | .... | .... | .... | .... | .... | .... | .... | .... | .... |
| Other investment: assets............... | 3d9aa | 1,692.0 | 406.9 | 1,949.8 | 6,014.5 | 480.4 | 1,078.5 | 803.5 | 398.1 | 359.6 | −15.0 | 1,985.9 | −3,800.3 |
| Other equity............................... | 3daaa | 31.3 | 24.9 | — | — | — | — | — | — | — | — | 217.8 | 50.7 |
| Debt instruments..................... | 3dzaa | 1,660.7 | 382.0 | 1,949.8 | 6,014.5 | 480.4 | 1,078.5 | 803.5 | 398.1 | 359.6 | −15.0 | 1,768.1 | −3,851.0 |
| Other investment: liabilities............ | 3d9la | 2,935.1 | 2,621.2 | 6,477.6 | 11,554.2 | 2,353.1 | −1,407.1 | 236.1 | −1,575.1 | 411.1 | −311.9 | 489.0 | −1,419.0 |
| Other equity............................... | 3dala | — | — | — | — | — | — | — | — | — | −2.7 | 4.2 | −6.6 |
| Debt instruments..................... | 3dzla | 2,935.1 | 2,621.2 | 6,477.6 | 11,554.2 | 2,353.1 | −1,407.1 | 236.1 | −1,575.1 | 411.1 | −309.2 | 484.8 | −1,412.5 |
| Curr.+ cap.− finan. acct. balance... | 4y9na | 378.1 | 817.5 | 1,841.1 | 1,202.8 | −728.2 | 1,014.8 | 133.7 | −1,282.9 | 2,229.0 | 269.2 | −857.5 | 944.0 |
| D. Net Errors and Omissions........... | 409na | 3.4 | −292.5 | 134.6 | −215.5 | −625.4 | 312.3 | 443.9 | 84.6 | 307.3 | 255.2 | 701.4 | −598.5 |
| E. Reserves and Related Items.......... | 4z9na | 385.2 | 525.0 | 1,976.9 | 984.5 | −1,352.1 | 1,329.8 | 578.8 | −1,199.8 | 2,538.9 | 520.5 | −154.6 | 347.7 |
| Reserve assets.............................. | 3e9aa | 379.5 | 525.0 | 1,976.9 | 984.5 | −537.9 | 1,608.2 | 989.8 | −1,199.8 | 1,029.1 | 520.5 | −154.6 | 347.7 |
| Credit and loans from the IMF....... | 3dcla | −5.6 | — | — | — | 814.2 | 278.4 | 411.1 | — | −1,509.8 | — | — | .... |
| Exceptional financing.................... | 409la | .... | .... | .... | .... | .... | .... | .... | .... | .... | .... | .... | .... |
| *Excludes components in group E | | | | | | | | | | | | | |
| **International Investment Position** | | | | | | *Millions of US Dollars* | | | | | | | |
| Assets............................................. | 809aa | 9,569.0 | 10,210.5 | 15,509.2 | 25,688.4 | 25,059.4 | 28,226.6 | 29,179.6 | 28,369.9 | 31,282.7 | 33,916.2 | 35,012.5 | 33,184.5 |
| Direct investment.......................... | 8a9aa | 427.7 | 491.9 | 744.1 | 1,740.0 | 1,927.5 | 1,759.0 | 1,762.4 | 1,847.7 | 2,030.6 | 2,664.4 | 2,567.8 | 2,390.8 |
| Equity & investment fund shares.. | 8aaaa | 179.8 | 195.8 | 305.5 | 649.2 | 688.9 | 672.8 | 614.7 | 619.8 | 740.2 | 1,158.4 | 1,092.7 | 990.7 |
| Debt instruments..................... | 8abaa | 247.9 | 296.1 | 438.6 | 1,092.3 | 1,238.6 | 1,086.2 | 1,146.5 | 1,227.9 | 1,290.4 | 1,504.6 | 1,475.1 | 1,400.1 |
| Portfolio investment..................... | 8b9aa | 1,343.0 | 1,596.1 | 2,053.2 | 2,848.5 | 2,864.1 | 2,997.9 | 3,261.7 | 3,789.8 | 4,946.4 | 5,732.9 | 9,524.6 | 11,989.9 |
| Equity & investment fund shares.. | 8baaa | 85.5 | 168.7 | 302.9 | 538.8 | 513.5 | 775.0 | 1,034.2 | 1,181.3 | 1,451.3 | 1,690.8 | 1,688.8 | 1,589.5 |
| Debt securities.......................... | 8bbaa | 1,257.2 | 1,427.4 | 1,749.0 | 2,308.3 | 2,350.6 | 2,222.8 | 2,227.4 | 2,608.5 | 3,495.1 | 4,040.8 | 7,837.0 | 10,401.4 |
| Fin. der.(oth.than reserves) & ESOs | 8c9aa | 51.8 | 21.2 | 21.2 | 101.6 | 407.8 | 134.0 | 89.5 | 146.2 | 168.9 | 110.3 | 125.1 | 402.8 |
| Other investment......................... | 8d9aa | 5,723.5 | 5,751.0 | 8,100.9 | 15,159.7 | 14,715.8 | 16,415.6 | 16,332.4 | 16,191.9 | 16,636.3 | 17,436.0 | 19,566.4 | 14,954.4 |
| Other equity............................... | 8daaa | 55.8 | 72.0 | 79.0 | 86.9 | 84.9 | 87.9 | 85.5 | 84.1 | 84.4 | 88.3 | 289.0 | 302.7 |
| Debt instruments..................... | 8dzaa | 5,667.7 | 5,679.1 | 8,021.8 | 15,072.8 | 14,630.9 | 16,327.8 | 16,246.9 | 16,107.8 | 16,551.9 | 17,347.7 | 19,277.5 | 14,651.7 |
| Reserve assets.............................. | 8e9aa | 2,023.0 | 2,350.2 | 4,529.4 | 5,837.1 | 5,145.6 | 6,921.6 | 7,733.5 | 6,394.3 | 7,499.2 | 7,973.9 | 3,227.4 | 3,445.6 |
| Liabilities....................................... | 809la | 17,088.9 | 19,219.7 | 30,092.1 | 48,732.4 | 50,239.7 | 50,562.5 | 48,866.6 | 47,815.9 | 50,854.6 | 54,817.7 | 52,799.0 | 48,924.9 |
| Direct investment.......................... | 8a9la | 4,718.3 | 5,117.5 | 7,776.9 | 11,793.0 | 12,203.8 | 12,494.3 | 11,802.7 | 13,093.0 | 14,451.4 | 17,019.5 | 15,896.2 | 15,711.0 |
| Equity & investment fund shares.. | 8aala | 3,461.1 | 3,847.0 | 5,827.7 | 8,725.1 | 8,407.3 | 8,100.5 | 8,323.2 | 9,110.3 | 10,499.8 | 12,114.0 | 11,550.9 | 11,688.3 |
| Debt instruments..................... | 8abla | 1,257.2 | 1,270.5 | 1,949.2 | 3,067.9 | 3,796.6 | 4,393.8 | 3,478.1 | 3,982.6 | 3,951.6 | 4,906.8 | 4,345.3 | 4,022.7 |
| Portfolio investment..................... | 8b9la | 1,035.2 | 1,113.6 | 1,606.7 | 1,812.2 | 1,700.7 | 1,744.6 | 1,644.9 | 1,753.2 | 4,330.3 | 4,648.9 | 6,750.4 | 6,644.3 |
| Equity & investment fund shares.. | 8bala | 152.6 | 232.4 | 330.6 | 393.1 | 222.7 | 203.1 | 224.5 | 270.4 | 275.8 | 333.7 | 373.9 | 542.2 |
| Debt securities.......................... | 8bbla | 882.6 | 881.2 | 1,276.2 | 1,417.6 | 1,478.0 | 1,542.9 | 1,419.0 | 1,482.8 | 4,054.5 | 4,315.2 | 6,376.5 | 6,102.2 |
| Fin. der.(oth.than reserves) & ESOs | 8c9la | 27.2 | 30.7 | 60.6 | 111.9 | 175.4 | 155.6 | 93.5 | 141.0 | 162.3 | 270.3 | 114.1 | 123.0 |
| Other investment......................... | 8d9la | 11,309.5 | 12,957.8 | 20,647.9 | 35,016.8 | 36,161.2 | 36,168.1 | 35,326.9 | 32,827.3 | 31,910.7 | 32,879.0 | 30,038.3 | 26,447.6 |
| Other equity............................... | 8dala | — | — | — | — | — | — | — | — | — | 38.6 | 36.4 | 27.2 |
| Debt instruments..................... | 8dzla | 11,309.5 | 12,957.8 | 20,647.9 | 35,016.8 | 36,161.2 | 36,168.1 | 35,326.9 | 32,827.3 | 31,910.7 | 32,840.4 | 30,001.8 | 26,420.3 |

# Latvia 941

Millions of Euros: Fiscal Year Ends December 31; Data Reported through Eurostat

## Government Finance Operations Statement
### General Government

| | | 2004 | 2005 | 2006 | 2007 | 2008 | 2009 | 2010 | 2011 | 2012 | 2013 | 2014 | 2015 |
|---|---|---|---|---|---|---|---|---|---|---|---|---|---|
| Revenue | a1 | 3,729.5 | 4,603.2 | 6,076.1 | 7,530.7 | 8,075.7 | 6,519.6 | 6,509.6 | 7,240.8 | 7,930.1 | 8,220.6 | 8,472.0 | 8,757.5 |
| Taxes | a11 | 2,126.0 | 2,692.1 | 3,504.2 | 4,562.2 | 4,789.9 | 3,371.7 | 3,431.7 | 3,854.8 | 4,316.4 | 4,553.0 | 4,825.4 | 4,998.8 |
| Social Contributions | a12 | 935.8 | 1,105.9 | 1,416.3 | 1,825.0 | 2,037.8 | 1,806.5 | 1,590.0 | 1,794.9 | 1,947.7 | 1,991.9 | 2,053.8 | 2,109.8 |
| Grants | a13 | .... | .... | .... | .... | .... | .... | .... | .... | .... | .... | .... | .... |
| Other Revenue | a14 | .... | .... | .... | .... | .... | .... | .... | .... | .... | .... | .... | .... |
| Expense | a2 | 3,893.1 | 4,757.4 | 6,021.6 | 7,171.1 | 8,865.0 | 8,132.4 | 7,976.3 | 7,848.1 | 8,041.3 | 8,378.7 | 8,748.9 | 8,930.4 |
| Compensation of Employees | a21 | 1,111.3 | 1,295.4 | 1,598.4 | 2,241.6 | 2,773.2 | 2,255.5 | 1,854.9 | 1,940.0 | 2,005.2 | 2,140.2 | 2,267.9 | 2,414.6 |
| Use of Goods & Services | a22 | 890.8 | 881.0 | 1,041.1 | 1,227.5 | 1,508.8 | 1,151.8 | 1,181.2 | 1,342.7 | 1,339.4 | 1,427.4 | 1,452.5 | 1,570.4 |
| Consumption of Fixed Capital | a23 | 482.6 | 565.2 | 740.7 | 934.3 | 1,003.0 | 697.9 | 752.2 | 896.6 | 969.3 | 964.0 | 957.2 | 951.0 |
| Interest | a24 | 77.1 | 69.8 | 73.0 | 79.5 | 134.1 | 285.6 | 313.2 | 361.1 | 359.3 | 337.4 | 337.3 | 324.5 |
| Subsidies | a25 | 64.4 | 70.3 | 105.6 | 167.3 | 265.1 | 207.4 | 137.6 | 98.4 | 121.1 | 134.4 | 160.3 | 104.4 |
| Grants | a26 | .... | .... | .... | .... | .... | .... | .... | .... | .... | .... | .... | .... |
| Social Benefits | a27 | 1,073.0 | 1,234.6 | 1,467.1 | 1,750.1 | 2,167.8 | 2,628.5 | 2,564.5 | 2,490.9 | 2,485.6 | 2,608.3 | 2,664.2 | 2,812.6 |
| Other Expense | a28 | .... | .... | .... | .... | .... | .... | .... | .... | .... | .... | .... | .... |
| Gross Operating Balance [1-2+23] | agob | 319.0 | 410.9 | 795.2 | 1,293.9 | 213.7 | −915.0 | −714.5 | 289.3 | 858.0 | 805.9 | 680.2 | 778.0 |
| Net Operating Balance [1-2] | anob | −163.6 | −154.2 | 54.5 | 359.6 | −789.3 | −1,612.9 | −1,466.7 | −607.3 | −111.3 | −158.1 | −276.9 | −173.0 |
| Net Acq. of Nonfinancial Assets | a31 | −49.7 | −95.6 | 159.1 | 508.3 | 213.6 | 89.7 | 51.7 | 74.9 | 67.9 | 45.4 | 89.2 | 133.3 |
| Aquisition of Nonfin. Assets | a31.1 | .... | .... | .... | .... | .... | .... | .... | .... | .... | .... | .... | .... |
| Disposal of Nonfin. Assets | a31.2 | .... | .... | .... | .... | .... | .... | .... | .... | .... | .... | .... | .... |
| Net Lending/Borrowing [1-2-31] | anlb | −113.9 | −58.7 | −104.6 | −148.7 | −1,002.9 | −1,702.5 | −1,518.4 | −682.2 | −179.2 | −203.4 | −366.1 | −306.2 |
| Net Acq. of Financial Assets | a32 | 149.0 | −43.0 | 409.0 | 342.0 | 1,683.0 | 686.0 | −313.0 | −559.0 | 160.0 | −336.0 | 279.0 | −1,257.0 |
| **By instrument** | | | | | | | | | | | | | |
| Monetary Gold & SDRs | a3201 | .... | .... | .... | .... | .... | .... | .... | .... | .... | .... | .... | .... |
| Currency & Deposits | a3202 | 97.0 | −125.0 | 226.0 | 240.0 | 653.0 | 651.0 | −96.0 | −624.0 | 545.0 | −351.0 | 198.0 | −1,187.0 |
| Securities other than Shares | a3203 | −36.0 | — | — | — | −2.0 | — | −89.0 | −79.0 | −6.0 | 60.0 | −49.0 | — |
| Loans | a3204 | −5.0 | −2.0 | −33.0 | 33.0 | 961.0 | −24.0 | −377.0 | 30.0 | −296.0 | −67.0 | −82.0 | −96.0 |
| Shares & Other Equity | a3205 | 11.0 | 40.0 | −81.0 | 12.0 | 48.0 | 18.0 | 158.0 | 3.0 | −9.0 | 18.0 | 29.0 | −1.0 |
| Insurance Technical Reserves | a3206 | — | — | — | — | — | −4.0 | — | — | — | — | — | 1.0 |
| Financial Derivatives | a3207 | −30.0 | −5.0 | — | — | — | −8.0 | −35.0 | −5.0 | −3.0 | −2.0 | −2.0 | −18.0 |
| Other Accounts Receivable | a3208 | 111.0 | 47.0 | 298.0 | 56.0 | 25.0 | 55.0 | 124.0 | 115.0 | −71.0 | 8.0 | 184.0 | 44.0 |
| **By debtor** | | | | | | | | | | | | | |
| Domestic | a321 | .... | .... | .... | .... | .... | .... | .... | .... | .... | .... | .... | .... |
| Foreign | a322 | .... | .... | .... | .... | .... | .... | .... | .... | .... | .... | .... | .... |
| Net Incurrence of Liabilities | a33 | 289.0 | 28.0 | 503.0 | 438.0 | 2,741.0 | 2,349.0 | 1,190.0 | 121.0 | 339.0 | −121.0 | 637.0 | −969.0 |
| **By instrument** | | | | | | | | | | | | | |
| Special Drawing Rights (SDRs) | a3301 | .... | .... | .... | .... | .... | .... | 2.0 | −30.0 | 9.0 | 21.0 | — | — |
| Currency & Deposits | a3302 | 29.0 | — | −8.0 | −10.0 | 178.0 | 42.0 | −212.0 | 54.0 | −164.0 | −101.0 | 23.0 | −107.0 |
| Securities other than Shares | a3303 | 243.0 | −3.0 | −6.0 | −52.0 | 1,446.0 | −638.0 | −1.0 | 230.0 | 1,677.0 | 12.0 | 1,691.0 | 618.0 |
| Loans | a3304 | −64.0 | 13.0 | 110.0 | 274.0 | 1,009.0 | 2,979.0 | 1,436.0 | −76.0 | −1,166.0 | −55.0 | −1,170.0 | −1,268.0 |
| Shares & Other Equity | a3305 | — | — | — | 4.0 | — | −3.0 | — | — | — | 2.0 | 2.0 | — |
| Insurance Technical Reserves | a3306 | — | — | — | — | — | — | — | — | — | — | — | — |
| Financial Derivatives | a3307 | — | — | — | — | −2.0 | −15.0 | 17.0 | −15.0 | −23.0 | −9.0 | −22.0 | −59.0 |
| Other Accounts Payable | a3308 | 84.0 | 20.0 | 406.0 | 223.0 | 111.0 | −17.0 | −52.0 | −45.0 | 6.0 | 10.0 | 114.0 | −153.0 |
| **By creditor** | | | | | | | | | | | | | |
| Domestic | a331 | .... | .... | .... | .... | .... | .... | .... | .... | .... | .... | .... | .... |
| Foreign | a332 | .... | .... | .... | .... | .... | .... | .... | .... | .... | .... | .... | .... |
| Stat. Discrepancy [32-33-NLB] | anlbz | −26.1 | −12.4 | 10.6 | 52.7 | −55.1 | 39.5 | 15.4 | 2.2 | .2 | −11.6 | 8.1 | 18.2 |
| Memo Item: Expenditure [2+31] | a2m | 3,843.4 | 4,661.8 | 6,180.7 | 7,679.3 | 9,078.6 | 8,222.1 | 8,028.0 | 7,923.0 | 8,109.3 | 8,424.0 | 8,838.0 | 9,063.7 |

### Balance Sheet

| | | 2004 | 2005 | 2006 | 2007 | 2008 | 2009 | 2010 | 2011 | 2012 | 2013 | 2014 | 2015 |
|---|---|---|---|---|---|---|---|---|---|---|---|---|---|
| Net Worth | a6 | .... | .... | .... | .... | .... | .... | .... | .... | .... | .... | .... | .... |
| Nonfinancial Assets | a61 | .... | .... | .... | .... | .... | .... | .... | .... | .... | .... | .... | .... |
| Financial Assets | a62 | 2,543.0 | 2,648.0 | 3,130.0 | 3,792.0 | 5,878.0 | 6,618.0 | 7,096.0 | 6,740.0 | 7,486.0 | 6,887.0 | 7,396.0 | 6,024.0 |
| **By instrument** | | | | | | | | | | | | | |
| Monetary Gold & SDRs | a6201 | .... | .... | .... | .... | .... | .... | .... | .... | .... | .... | .... | .... |
| Currency & Deposits | a6202 | 346.0 | 226.0 | 464.0 | 704.0 | 1,338.0 | 1,989.0 | 2,097.0 | 1,418.0 | 1,995.0 | 1,645.0 | 1,901.0 | 723.0 |
| Securities other than Shares | a6203 | — | — | — | — | — | — | 86.0 | 7.0 | — | 60.0 | 16.0 | 12.0 |
| Loans | a6204 | 232.0 | 212.0 | 168.0 | 192.0 | 1,132.0 | 1,104.0 | 956.0 | 1,173.0 | 758.0 | 547.0 | 634.0 | 544.0 |
| Shares and Other Equity | a6205 | 1,485.0 | 1,687.0 | 1,679.0 | 2,038.0 | 2,492.0 | 2,554.0 | 2,858.0 | 2,912.0 | 3,574.0 | 3,557.0 | 3,563.0 | 3,348.0 |
| Insurance Technical Reserves | a6206 | 4.0 | 5.0 | 6.0 | 7.0 | 8.0 | 2.0 | 2.0 | 1.0 | 2.0 | 3.0 | 4.0 | 4.0 |
| Financial Derivatives | a6207 | 6.0 | — | 2.0 | 6.0 | 25.0 | 9.0 | 1.0 | — | 1.0 | 3.0 | — | 53.0 |
| Other Accounts Receivable | a6208 | 470.0 | 518.0 | 810.0 | 845.0 | 884.0 | 959.0 | 1,096.0 | 1,228.0 | 1,156.0 | 1,075.0 | 1,277.0 | 1,339.0 |
| **By debtor** | | | | | | | | | | | | | |
| Domestic | a621 | .... | .... | .... | .... | .... | .... | .... | .... | .... | .... | .... | .... |
| Foreign | a622 | .... | .... | .... | .... | .... | .... | .... | .... | .... | .... | .... | .... |
| Liabilities | a63 | 1,954.0 | 1,992.0 | 2,511.0 | 2,932.0 | 5,623.0 | 7,869.0 | 9,559.0 | 9,737.0 | 10,125.0 | 10,029.0 | 11,109.0 | 10,177.0 |
| **By instrument** | | | | | | | | | | | | | |
| Special Drawing Rights (SDRs) | a6301 | .... | .... | .... | .... | .... | 130.0 | 141.0 | 113.0 | 119.0 | 136.0 | 144.0 | 154.0 |
| Currency & Deposits | a6302 | 44.0 | 43.0 | 35.0 | 25.0 | 186.0 | 229.0 | 442.0 | 497.0 | 335.0 | 233.0 | 327.0 | 220.0 |
| Securities other than Shares | a6303 | 1,206.0 | 1,202.0 | 1,196.0 | 1,166.0 | 2,620.0 | 1,982.0 | 2,005.0 | 2,212.0 | 3,896.0 | 3,924.0 | 5,570.0 | 6,163.0 |
| Loans | a6304 | 330.0 | 352.0 | 468.0 | 737.0 | 1,744.0 | 4,766.0 | 6,241.0 | 6,154.0 | 4,998.0 | 4,951.0 | 3,945.0 | 2,649.0 |
| Shares and Other Equity | a6305 | 2.0 | 2.0 | 12.0 | 21.0 | 6.0 | 7.0 | 8.0 | 8.0 | 44.0 | 38.0 | 28.0 | 37.0 |
| Insurance Technical Reserves | a6306 | — | — | — | — | — | — | — | — | — | — | — | — |
| Financial Derivatives | a6307 | — | — | — | 4.0 | 21.0 | 13.0 | 16.0 | 83.0 | 77.0 | 95.0 | 256.0 | 260.0 |
| Other Accounts Payable | a6308 | 373.0 | 392.0 | 800.0 | 978.0 | 1,045.0 | 742.0 | 706.0 | 669.0 | 658.0 | 652.0 | 838.0 | 695.0 |
| **By creditor** | | | | | | | | | | | | | |
| Domestic | a631 | .... | .... | .... | .... | .... | .... | .... | .... | .... | .... | .... | .... |
| Foreign | a632 | .... | .... | .... | .... | .... | .... | .... | .... | .... | .... | .... | .... |
| Net Financial Worth [62-63] | a6m2 | 589.0 | 656.0 | 619.0 | 860.0 | 255.0 | −1,251.0 | −2,463.0 | −2,997.0 | −2,639.0 | −3,142.0 | −3,713.0 | −4,153.0 |
| Memo Item: Debt at Market Value | a6m3 | 1,953.0 | 1,989.0 | 2,499.0 | 2,906.0 | 5,595.0 | 7,849.0 | 9,535.0 | 9,645.0 | 10,006.0 | 9,896.0 | 10,824.0 | 9,881.0 |
| Memo Item: Debt at Face Value | a6m35 | 1,952.9 | 1,989.2 | 2,498.7 | 2,882.5 | 5,590.7 | 7,759.9 | 9,355.5 | 9,449.0 | 9,797.1 | 9,680.7 | 10,598.3 | 9,720.7 |
| Memo Item: Maastricht Debt | a6m36 | 1,579.9 | 1,597.2 | 1,698.7 | 1,904.5 | 4,545.9 | 6,887.9 | 8,508.5 | 8,667.0 | 9,020.1 | 8,892.7 | 9,616.3 | 8,871.7 |
| Memo Item: Debt at Nominal Value | a6m4 | .... | .... | .... | .... | .... | .... | .... | .... | .... | .... | .... | .... |

# Latvia 941

| | | 2004 | 2005 | 2006 | 2007 | 2008 | 2009 | 2010 | 2011 | 2012 | 2013 | 2014 | 2015 |
|---|---|---|---|---|---|---|---|---|---|---|---|---|---|
| **National Accounts** | | | | | *Millions of Lats through 2013; Millions of Euros Beginning 2014* | | | | | | | | |
| Househ.Cons.Expend.,incl.NPISHs.... | 96f | 4,688.1 | 5,666.1 | 7,280.5 | 9,213.2 | 9,524.2 | 8,137.4 | 8,162.5 | 8,909.1 | 9,482.0 | 10,103.4 | 14,430.4 | 14,962.6 |
| Government Consumption Expend... | 91f | 1,538.5 | 1,699.9 | 2,068.9 | 2,800.9 | 3,395.0 | 2,515.7 | 2,315.4 | 2,601.0 | 2,667.8 | 2,654.0 | 4,151.8 | 4,403.5 |
| Gross Fixed Capital Formation......... | 93e | 2,241.8 | 2,991.9 | 4,107.9 | 5,780.7 | 5,481.3 | 2,981.9 | 2,437.8 | 3,158.7 | 3,899.3 | 3,795.9 | 5,393.6 | 5,560.2 |
| Changes in Inventories.................... | 93i | 360.1 | 334.0 | 471.9 | 562.8 | 357.3 | −142.0 | 37.5 | 306.6 | 126.8 | 284.8 | 135.0 | −201.4 |
| Exports of Goods and Services......... | 90c | 3,034.7 | 4,125.9 | 4,804.5 | 6,105.2 | 6,767.3 | 5,637.0 | 6,764.5 | 8,249.8 | 9,430.2 | 9,698.6 | 14,031.7 | 14,324.3 |
| Imports of Goods and Services (-)..... | 98c | 4,242.2 | 5,509.9 | 7,289.1 | 9,125.3 | 8,977.9 | 5,851.4 | 6,950.3 | 8,960.1 | 10,114.2 | 10,216.2 | 14,561.7 | 14,671.5 |
| Gross Domestic Product (GDP)......... | 99b | 7,806.5 | 9,561.2 | 12,002.4 | 15,838.8 | 17,148.1 | 13,278.5 | 12,767.3 | 14,265.1 | 15,491.9 | 16,320.4 | 23,580.9 | 24,377.7 |
| Net Primary Income from Abroad..... | 98.n | −160.9 | −99.3 | −302.2 | −473.9 | −218.7 | 935.8 | 158.5 | −3.9 | −104.4 | −58.5 | −39.9 | −69.7 |
| Gross National Income (GNI)............ | 99a | 7,645.6 | 9,461.9 | 11,700.2 | 15,364.9 | 16,929.4 | 14,214.3 | 12,925.8 | 14,261.2 | 15,387.5 | 16,261.9 | 23,541.0 | 24,308.1 |
| Net Current Transf.from Abroad....... | 98t | 366.2 | 287.5 | 214.8 | 138.5 | 255.3 | 323.6 | 295.0 | 275.5 | 246.1 | 210.2 | 103.1 | 117.3 |
| Gross Nat'l Disposable Inc.(GNDI).... | 99i | 8,011.8 | 9,749.4 | 11,915.0 | 15,503.4 | 17,184.7 | 14,537.9 | 13,220.8 | 14,536.8 | 15,633.6 | 16,472.1 | 23,644.0 | 24,425.4 |
| Gross Saving................................... | 99s | 1,599.6 | 2,130.2 | 2,007.8 | 2,988.0 | 3,664.6 | 3,884.8 | 2,742.9 | 3,026.6 | 3,483.8 | 3,714.7 | 5,061.8 | 5,063.2 |
| Consumption of Fixed Capital.......... | 99cf | 1,762.1 | 2,090.9 | 2,730.3 | 3,421.4 | 3,781.9 | 3,120.4 | 3,190.8 | 3,489.2 | 3,834.7 | 3,934.9 | 5,556.5 | 5,562.7 |
| GDP Volume 2010 Ref., Chained..... | 99b.p | .... | .... | .... | .... | .... | .... | .... | .... | .... | .... | 20,876.4 | 21,448.7 |
| GDP Volume (2010=100)............... | 99bvp | 91.8 | 101.1 | 112.9 | 123.9 | 120.0 | 103.0 | 100.0 | 105.0 | 110.1 | 114.7 | 114.9 | 118.1 |
| GDP Deflator (2010=100)............... | 99bip | 66.6 | 74.1 | 83.3 | 100.1 | 111.9 | 101.0 | 100.0 | 106.4 | 110.2 | 111.4 | 113.0 | 113.7 |
| | | | | | | *Millions: Midyear Estimates* | | | | | | | |
| **Population**............................... | 99z | 2.26 | 2.23 | 2.20 | 2.17 | 2.14 | 2.12 | 2.09 | 2.06 | 2.04 | 2.01 | 1.99 | 1.97 |

|  |  | 2004 | 2005 | 2006 | 2007 | 2008 | 2009 | 2010 | 2011 | 2012 | 2013 | 2014 | 2015 |
|---|---|---|---|---|---|---|---|---|---|---|---|---|---|
| **Exchange Rates** | | | | | | *Pounds per SDR: End of Period* | | | | | | | | |
| Market Rate | aa | 2,341.2 | 2,154.6 | 2,267.9 | 2,382.2 | 2,322.0 | 2,363.3 | 2,321.6 | 2,314.4 | 2,316.9 | 2,321.6 | 2,184.1 | 2,089.0 |
| | | | | | | *Pounds per US Dollar: End of Period (ae) Period Average (rf)* | | | | | | | | |
| Market Rate | ae | 1,507.5 | 1,507.5 | 1,507.5 | 1,507.5 | 1,507.5 | 1,507.5 | 1,507.5 | 1,507.5 | 1,507.5 | 1,507.5 | 1,507.5 | 1,507.5 |
| Market Rate | rf | 1,507.5 | 1,507.5 | 1,507.5 | 1,507.5 | 1,507.5 | 1,507.5 | 1,507.5 | 1,507.5 | 1,507.5 | 1,507.5 | 1,507.5 | 1,507.5 |
| | | | | | | *Index Numbers (2010=100): Period Averages* | | | | | | | | |
| Market Rate | ahx | 99.95 | 99.95 | 99.96 | 100.00 | 100.00 | 100.00 | 100.00 | 100.00 | 100.00 | 100.00 | 100.00 | 100.00 |
| Nominal Effective Exchange Rate | nec | 108.56 | 106.75 | 105.98 | 101.10 | 96.33 | 99.54 | 100.00 | 98.48 | 109.25 | 124.64 | 137.63 | 162.24 |
| **Fund Position** | | | | | | *Millions of SDRs: End of Period* | | | | | | | | |
| Quota | 2f.s | 203.00 | 203.00 | 203.00 | 203.00 | 203.00 | 203.00 | 203.00 | 266.40 | 266.40 | 266.40 | 266.40 | 266.40 |
| SDR Holdings | 1b.s | 21.19 | 22.00 | 23.17 | 22.82 | 21.89 | 209.81 | 208.95 | 192.61 | 192.36 | 192.29 | 192.32 | 192.33 |
| Reserve Position in the Fund | 1c.s | 18.83 | 18.83 | 18.83 | 18.83 | 18.83 | 18.83 | 18.83 | 34.68 | 34.68 | 34.68 | 34.68 | 34.68 |
| Total Fund Cred.&Loans Outstg | 2tl | — | — | — | 50.75 | 76.13 | 76.13 | 63.44 | 38.06 | 12.69 | | — | — |
| SDR Allocations | 1bd | 4.39 | 4.39 | 4.39 | 4.39 | 4.39 | 193.29 | 193.29 | 193.29 | 193.29 | 193.29 | 193.29 | 193.29 |
| **International Liquidity** | | | | | | *Millions of US Dollars Unless Otherwise Indicated: End of Period* | | | | | | | | |
| Total Reserves minus Gold | 1l.d | 11,734.6 | 11,887.1 | 13,376.4 | 12,909.9 | 20,244.5 | 29,102.9 | 31,514.1 | 33,740.6 | 37,185.6 | 36,748.0 | 39,547.1 | 38,756.1 |
| SDR Holdings | 1b.d | 32.9 | 31.4 | 34.9 | 36.1 | 33.7 | 328.9 | 321.8 | 295.7 | 295.6 | 296.1 | 278.6 | 266.5 |
| Reserve Position in the Fund | 1c.d | 29.2 | 26.9 | 28.3 | 29.8 | 29.0 | 29.5 | 29.0 | 53.2 | 53.3 | 53.4 | 50.2 | 48.1 |
| Foreign Exchange | 1d.d | 11,672.4 | 11,828.7 | 13,313.3 | 12,844.1 | 20,181.8 | 28,744.5 | 31,163.3 | 33,391.6 | 36,836.6 | 36,398.5 | 39,218.3 | 38,441.5 |
| Gold (Million Fine Troy Ounces) | 1ad | 9.222 | 9.222 | 9.222 | 9.222 | 9.222 | 9.222 | 9.222 | 9.222 | 9.222 | 9.222 | 9.222 | 9.222 |
| Gold (National Valuation) | 1and | 4,006.0 | 4,736.4 | 5,807.3 | 7,639.8 | 8,031.7 | 10,062.0 | 13,010.0 | 14,400.7 | 15,312.3 | 11,103.7 | 10,951.0 | 9,848.2 |
| Monetary Authorities: Other Liabs | 4..d | 765.9 | 2,431.4 | 4,185.3 | 4,544.9 | 4,341.8 | 4,184.5 | 3,992.0 | 3,937.1 | 3,695.8 | 3,206.0 | 2,514.0 | 1,073.6 |
| Deposit Money Banks: Assets | 7a.d | 13,552.9 | 13,261.9 | 16,415.3 | 20,709.7 | 19,127.1 | 23,680.0 | 25,727.7 | 25,496.7 | 26,167.1 | 26,625.1 | 24,192.4 | 23,794.3 |
| Deposit Money Banks: Liabs | 7b.d | 12,096.3 | 11,633.4 | 12,181.6 | 13,640.0 | 15,810.6 | 21,173.5 | 22,985.7 | 27,076.3 | 29,988.9 | 33,491.6 | 36,136.0 | 38,401.2 |
| **Monetary Authorities** | | | | | | *Billions of Pounds: End of Period* | | | | | | | | |
| Foreign Assets | 11 | 20,473.2 | 22,080.7 | 24,248.1 | 26,367.3 | 37,935.3 | 54,476.5 | 63,284.1 | 68,699.8 | 71,050.3 | 67,761.5 | 72,486.8 | 69,423.5 |
| Claims on Central Government | 12a | 13,641.6 | 14,518.0 | 13,791.1 | 12,975.9 | 12,812.8 | 14,157.7 | 16,061.2 | 17,757.5 | 20,501.5 | 18,197.2 | 20,807.0 | 26,859.5 |
| Claims on Private Sector | 12d | 900.4 | 779.2 | 749.6 | 974.2 | 1,731.9 | 1,876.4 | 2,126.6 | 2,569.4 | 2,637.7 | 3,383.7 | 2,826.4 | 3,267.2 |
| Claims on Deposit Money Banks | 12e | 1,859.2 | 1,795.7 | 1,843.0 | 1,690.4 | 1,543.1 | 1,788.8 | 1,122.3 | 2,047.2 | 2,386.3 | 3,363.3 | 5,780.7 | 6,833.8 |
| Reserve Money | 14 | 30,906.2 | 30,268.4 | 29,102.1 | 29,538.9 | 38,728.6 | 52,809.2 | 60,518.8 | 72,118.0 | 79,739.2 | 84,690.0 | 100,954.3 | 113,229.2 |
| of which: Currency Outside DMBs | 14a | 1,586.5 | 1,534.7 | 1,809.2 | 1,929.0 | 2,174.6 | 2,383.0 | 2,712.9 | 2,891.0 | 3,213.2 | 3,407.5 | 3,647.1 | 4,013.8 |
| Time, Savings,& Fgn.Currency Dep | 15 | 1,250.2 | 1,131.9 | 916.9 | 1,152.7 | 1,304.3 | 1,906.0 | 2,173.7 | 959.5 | 1,059.2 | 1,376.3 | 1,345.8 | 1,470.7 |
| Foreign Liabilities | 16c | 1,164.9 | 3,674.4 | 6,319.3 | 6,862.0 | 6,555.5 | 6,764.9 | 6,466.6 | 6,382.6 | 6,019.3 | 5,281.7 | 4,212.0 | 2,022.2 |
| Central Government Deposits | 16d | 2,879.5 | 3,885.2 | 2,864.5 | 3,363.9 | 6,994.5 | 8,931.6 | 9,311.7 | 7,984.6 | 8,907.9 | 11,032.5 | 9,123.2 | 8,153.6 |
| Capital Accounts | 17a | 2,272.2 | 3,007.8 | 5,099.9 | 5,755.9 | 6,012.2 | 10,102.9 | 15,449.5 | 17,840.5 | 19,788.0 | 13,560.3 | 13,319.8 | 11,740.8 |
| Other Items (Net) | 17r | −1,598.7 | −2,794.6 | −3,670.8 | −4,665.6 | −5,572.1 | −8,215.1 | −11,326.1 | −14,211.2 | −18,937.9 | −23,235.2 | −27,054.2 | −30,232.4 |
| **Deposit Money Banks** | | | | | | *Billions of Pounds: End of Period* | | | | | | | | |
| Reserves | 20 | 29,878.7 | 30,917.3 | 29,337.8 | 29,851.4 | 39,113.4 | 53,574.9 | 61,153.5 | 71,535.4 | 79,604.0 | 82,533.1 | 96,314.0 | 107,021.2 |
| Foreign Assets | 21 | 20,430.9 | 19,992.3 | 24,746.0 | 31,219.8 | 28,834.1 | 35,697.6 | 38,784.5 | 38,436.3 | 39,446.9 | 40,137.3 | 36,470.0 | 35,869.8 |
| Claims on Central Government | 22a | 24,155.4 | 26,696.5 | 31,192.8 | 32,423.5 | 38,313.7 | 43,811.6 | 44,192.3 | 44,055.1 | 46,930.5 | 56,785.6 | 56,308.4 | 56,983.7 |
| Claims on Private Sector | 22d | 24,020.4 | 21,798.8 | 23,091.2 | 26,761.8 | 31,750.5 | 36,570.1 | 45,702.1 | 51,594.4 | 57,052.4 | 62,565.3 | 68,390.6 | 72,427.4 |
| Demand Deposits | 24 | 1,389.3 | 1,358.5 | 1,450.0 | 1,601.8 | 2,057.5 | 2,410.3 | 2,950.8 | 3,200.6 | 3,808.1 | 4,144.4 | 4,563.7 | 4,906.9 |
| Time & Foreign Currency Deposits | 25 | 66,879.0 | 70,273.7 | 75,916.4 | 85,378.9 | 97,850.4 | 116,972.9 | 130,792.6 | 139,184.9 | 148,316.0 | 158,251.5 | 167,477.1 | 175,581.9 |
| Money Market Instruments | 26aa | 150.5 | 88.3 | 95.5 | 90.6 | 92.9 | 142.9 | 411.8 | 661.4 | 395.9 | 398.4 | 351.8 | 411.6 |
| Foreign Liabilities | 26c | 18,235.2 | 17,537.4 | 18,363.8 | 20,562.3 | 23,834.4 | 31,919.1 | 34,650.9 | 40,817.6 | 45,208.3 | 50,488.5 | 54,475.1 | 57,889.8 |
| Central Government Deposits | 26d | 1,480.0 | 1,704.9 | 1,579.0 | 1,163.4 | 1,331.2 | 1,589.9 | 2,107.4 | 2,999.1 | 4,008.0 | 4,462.6 | 4,842.2 | 5,074.1 |
| Credit from Monetary Authorities | 26g | 1,859.2 | 1,795.7 | 1,843.0 | 1,690.4 | 1,543.1 | 1,788.8 | 1,122.3 | 2,047.2 | 2,386.3 | 3,363.3 | 5,780.7 | 6,833.8 |
| Capital Accounts | 27a | 5,808.5 | 6,410.7 | 8,717.7 | 9,438.7 | 10,705.3 | 11,977.2 | 13,901.0 | 16,161.5 | 19,057.8 | 21,409.9 | 23,719.1 | 25,131.1 |
| Other Items (Net) | 27r | 2,683.8 | 235.7 | 402.4 | 330.3 | 597.0 | 2,853.4 | 3,895.5 | 549.0 | −146.5 | −497.2 | −3,726.6 | −3,527.2 |
| **Monetary Survey** | | | | | | *Billions of Pounds: End of Period* | | | | | | | | |
| Foreign Assets (Net) | 31n | 21,504.0 | 20,860.9 | 24,311.0 | 30,162.8 | 36,379.5 | 51,490.2 | 60,951.1 | 59,935.9 | 59,269.7 | 52,128.6 | 50,269.7 | 45,381.3 |
| Domestic Credit | 32 | 58,358.4 | 58,202.3 | 64,381.2 | 68,608.1 | 76,283.2 | 85,894.5 | 96,663.1 | 104,992.7 | 114,206.2 | 125,436.6 | 134,367.0 | 146,310.1 |
| Claims on Central Govt. (Net) | 32an | 33,437.5 | 35,624.3 | 40,540.5 | 40,872.1 | 42,800.8 | 47,447.9 | 48,834.4 | 50,828.9 | 54,516.0 | 59,487.7 | 63,150.0 | 70,615.5 |
| Claims on Private Sector | 32d | 24,920.9 | 22,578.0 | 23,840.7 | 27,736.0 | 33,482.4 | 38,446.6 | 47,828.7 | 54,163.8 | 59,690.2 | 65,949.0 | 71,217.0 | 75,694.6 |
| Money | 34 | 3,030.6 | 2,952.1 | 3,321.7 | 3,578.1 | 4,269.3 | 4,839.7 | 5,728.3 | 6,138.4 | 7,103.6 | 7,620.4 | 8,301.0 | 9,042.4 |
| Quasi-Money | 35 | 68,129.2 | 71,405.6 | 76,833.3 | 86,531.6 | 99,154.7 | 118,878.9 | 132,966.3 | 140,144.3 | 149,375.2 | 159,627.8 | 168,822.9 | 177,052.6 |
| Money Market Instruments | 36aa | 150.5 | 88.3 | 95.5 | 90.6 | 92.9 | 142.9 | 411.8 | 661.4 | 395.9 | 398.4 | 351.8 | 411.6 |
| Capital Accounts | 37a | 8,080.7 | 9,418.6 | 13,817.6 | 15,194.6 | 16,717.5 | 22,080.0 | 29,350.5 | 34,002.0 | 38,845.8 | 34,970.2 | 37,038.9 | 36,871.9 |
| Other Items (Net) | 37r | 471.3 | −4,801.4 | −5,375.9 | −6,624.0 | −7,571.7 | −8,556.8 | −10,842.9 | −16,017.4 | −22,244.7 | −25,051.6 | −29,877.9 | −31,687.1 |
| Money plus Quasi-Money | 35l | 71,159.8 | 74,357.7 | 80,155.0 | 90,109.8 | 103,424.0 | 123,718.6 | 138,694.7 | 146,282.7 | 156,478.8 | 167,248.2 | 177,123.9 | 186,095.0 |
| **Money (National Definitions)** | | | | | | *Billions of Pounds: End of Period* | | | | | | | | |
| M1 | 59ma | 3,030.6 | 2,952.1 | 3,321.7 | 3,578.1 | 4,269.3 | 4,839.7 | 5,728.3 | 6,138.4 | 7,103.6 | 7,620.4 | 8,301.0 | 9,042.4 |
| M1, Seasonally Adjusted | 59mac | 3,018.2 | 2,954.2 | 3,321.5 | 3,559.3 | 4,186.5 | 4,653.7 | 5,442.3 | 5,806.0 | 6,850.8 | 7,358.5 | .... | .... |
| M2 | 59mb | 25,978.0 | 24,464.5 | 23,477.3 | 24,830.7 | 37,324.7 | 51,489.4 | 59,401.9 | 58,643.0 | 65,077.0 | 68,749.4 | 73,400.3 | 78,620.2 |
| M2, Seasonally Adjusted | 59mbc | 25,797.6 | 24,470.2 | 23,570.8 | 24,913.4 | 37,327.0 | 51,252.1 | 58,887.5 | 57,989.1 | 64,602.6 | 68,220.6 | .... | .... |
| M3 | 59mc | 71,310.3 | 74,446.0 | 80,244.4 | 90,196.7 | 103,505.7 | 123,731.6 | 138,909.8 | 146,575.6 | 156,797.0 | 167,571.0 | 177,396.6 | 186,360.4 |
| M3, Seasonally Adjusted | 59mcc | 70,482.0 | 73,777.4 | 79,703.6 | 89,770.4 | 103,034.1 | 123,237.5 | 138,347.1 | 146,042.0 | 156,298.2 | 167,027.9 | .... | .... |
| M4 | 59md | 74,810.0 | 77,771.0 | 84,545.1 | 95,809.7 | 109,411.7 | 131,084.6 | 146,820.8 | 154,364.6 | 164,679.0 | 176,807.0 | 187,825.6 | 197,369.4 |
| **Interest Rates** | | | | | | *Percent Per Annum* | | | | | | | | |
| Discount Rate (End of Period) | 60.a | 20.00 | 12.00 | 12.00 | 12.00 | 12.00 | 10.00 | 10.00 | 10.00 | 10.00 | 10.00 | 10.00 | 10.00 |
| Treasury Bill Rate | 60c | 5.25 | 5.22 | 5.22 | 5.22 | 5.21 | 4.91 | 4.10 | 3.93 | 4.35 | 4.44 | 4.44 | 4.44 |
| Deposit Rate | 60l | 7.37 | 8.15 | 7.98 | 7.97 | 7.70 | 7.32 | 6.20 | 5.88 | 5.77 | 5.83 | 5.91 | 5.98 |
| Lending Rate | 60p | 10.81 | 10.64 | 10.26 | 10.26 | 9.96 | 9.57 | 8.34 | 7.53 | 7.25 | 7.35 | 7.27 | 7.09 |
| **Prices** | | | | | | *Index Numbers (2010=100): Period Averages* | | | | | | | | |
| Share Prices (End of Month) | 62.ep | 12.9 | 32.9 | 86.7 | 67.1 | 133.3 | 89.4 | 100.0 | 71.7 | 49.8 | 44.3 | .... | .... |
| Consumer Prices (2008=100) | 64 | .... | .... | .... | .... | 95.0 | 96.2 | 100.0 | .... | 111.9 | 118.1 | † 119.0 | 114.5 |
| **Intl. Transactions & Positions** | | | | | | *Millions of US Dollars* | | | | | | | | |
| Exports | 70..d | 2,199 | 2,337 | 2,814 | 3,574 | 4,454 | 4,187 | 5,021 | 4,267 | 4,485 | 4,059 | 4,548 | 3,982 |
| Imports, c.i.f. | 71..d | 9,609 | 9,633 | 9,647 | 12,251 | 16,754 | 16,574 | 18,460 | 20,165 | 21,287 | 21,236 | 21,137 | 18,439 |

# Lebanon  446

|  |  | 2004 | 2005 | 2006 | 2007 | 2008 | 2009 | 2010 | 2011 | 2012 | 2013 | 2014 | 2015 |
|---|---|---|---|---|---|---|---|---|---|---|---|---|---|
| **Balance of Payments** |  |  |  |  |  | *Millions of US Dollars* |  |  |  |  |  |  |  |
| A. Current Account*........................ | 109bx | −4,405.6 | −2,748.0 | −1,220.9 | −1,604.8 | −4,102.7 | −6,740.9 | −7,552.1 | −4,858.8 | −9,548.7 | −11,471.2 | −11,667.1 | −8,145.5 |
| Goods, credit (exports)................. | 1a9cx | 2,096.0 | 2,361.0 | 2,813.9 | 3,574.3 | 4,453.6 | 4,187.1 | 4,688.7 | 5,385.5 | 5,008.4 | 4,498.8 | 4,099.9 | 3,551.4 |
| Goods, debit (imports)................. | 1a9dx | 8,908.0 | 8,959.2 | 9,025.0 | 11,463.1 | 15,530.7 | 15,394.3 | 17,187.8 | 19,304.4 | 19,839.5 | 19,672.3 | 19,163.2 | 16,710.5 |
| Balance on goods...................... | 1a9bx | −6,812.1 | −6,598.2 | −6,211.2 | −7,888.8 | −11,077.1 | −11,207.2 | −12,499.0 | −13,918.9 | −14,831.1 | −15,173.5 | −15,063.3 | −13,159.1 |
| Services, credit (exports).............. | 1b9cx | 9,736.9 | 10,864.1 | 11,672.8 | 12,758.5 | 17,635.6 | 16,909.9 | 16,040.1 | 19,672.6 | 15,124.8 | 15,476.0 | 14,751.1 | 15,815.4 |
| Services, debit (imports).............. | 1b9dx | 8,228.6 | 7,890.2 | 8,730.5 | 9,983.2 | 13,458.7 | 14,042.7 | 13,034.0 | 12,963.3 | 11,444.9 | 12,853.4 | 13,142.7 | 13,565.0 |
| Balance on Goods & Services...... | 1z9bx | −5,303.8 | −3,624.3 | −3,269.0 | −5,113.5 | −6,900.3 | −8,340.0 | −9,492.9 | −7,209.6 | −11,151.2 | −12,550.9 | −13,454.9 | −10,908.7 |
| Primary income: credit................. | 1c9cx | 1,060.3 | 1,732.5 | 2,439.6 | 3,112.8 | 2,723.3 | 2,040.2 | 1,448.1 | 1,629.1 | 1,678.7 | 1,968.2 | 2,498.3 | 2,399.5 |
| Primary income: debit................. | 1c9dx | 1,877.9 | 1,918.9 | 2,256.0 | 2,372.7 | 2,286.1 | 2,268.3 | 1,957.0 | 1,803.4 | 1,870.4 | 2,245.6 | 2,990.9 | 3,017.8 |
| Balance on gds, serv. & prim. inc. | 1y9bx | −6,121.5 | −3,810.7 | −3,085.3 | −4,373.4 | −6,463.0 | −8,568.1 | −10,001.8 | −7,383.9 | −11,343.0 | −12,828.4 | −13,947.5 | −11,527.1 |
| Secondary income: credit.............. | 1d9ca | 5,325.2 | 4,399.4 | 5,052.9 | 5,218.5 | 6,069.5 | 6,642.0 | 7,956.6 | 7,859.9 | 8,149.8 | 8,297.2 | 9,725.1 | 8,887.0 |
| Secondary income: debit.............. | 1d9da | 3,609.4 | 3,336.7 | 3,188.5 | 2,449.9 | 3,709.2 | 4,814.9 | 5,506.8 | 5,334.8 | 6,355.6 | 6,940.0 | 7,444.7 | 5,505.4 |
| B. Capital Account*..................... | 209ba | 50.4 | 27.4 | 1,940.4 | 589.7 | 409.5 | 18.0 | 38.8 | 32.8 | 73.1 | 1,538.8 | 1,392.1 | 1,801.0 |
| Capital account: credit................. | 209ca | 53.7 | 27.4 | 1,944.4 | 590.7 | 409.9 | 24.8 | 404.4 | 236.7 | 235.2 | 1,814.2 | 1,684.0 | 2,712.9 |
| Capital account: debit................. | 209da | 3.3 | — | 4.0 | 1.0 | .4 | 6.9 | 365.6 | 203.9 | 162.1 | 275.3 | 291.9 | 911.9 |
| Balance on current & capital acct. | 129ba | −4,355.2 | −2,720.6 | 719.5 | −1,015.1 | −3,693.1 | −6,722.9 | −7,513.2 | −4,826.0 | −9,475.7 | −9,932.4 | −10,275.0 | −6,344.5 |
| C. Financial Account* .................. | 309na | −4,308.9 | −3,786.2 | −2,240.3 | −6,424.2 | −12,693.3 | −18,700.4 | −3,516.2 | −8,986.3 | −10,045.7 | −9,220.1 | −13,931.8 | −8,783.0 |
| Direct investment: assets.............. | 3a9aa | 827.1 | 715.5 | 874.7 | 848.1 | 986.6 | 1,125.8 | 486.7 | 754.3 | 1,012.2 | 1,965.4 | 1,213.0 | 619.7 |
| Equity & investment fund shares.. | 3aaaa | 827.1 | 715.5 | 874.7 | 848.1 | 986.6 | 1,125.8 | 486.7 | 754.3 | 1,013.5 | 1,956.0 | 1,213.4 | 620.1 |
| Debt instruments........................ | 3abaa | — | .... | .... | .... | — | .... | .... | — | −1.3 | 9.4 | −.3 | −.3 |
| Direct investment: liabilities .......... | 3a9la | 1,898.8 | 2,623.5 | 2,674.5 | 3,376.0 | 4,333.0 | 4,803.6 | 4,279.9 | 3,490.2 | 3,158.6 | 2,700.7 | 2,906.1 | 2,341.9 |
| Equity & investment fund shares . | 3aala | 1,898.8 | 2,623.5 | 2,674.5 | 3,376.0 | 4,333.0 | 4,803.6 | 4,279.9 | 3,490.2 | 3,154.5 | 2,701.8 | 2,904.2 | 2,340.0 |
| Debt instruments........................ | 3abla | — | .... | .... | .... | — | .... | .... | — | 4.1 | −1.1 | 1.9 | 1.9 |
| Portfolio investment: assets .......... | 3b9aa | 614.3 | 111.8 | 358.3 | 1,560.0 | 565.9 | 825.9 | 1,910.6 | 444.6 | −594.5 | −640.3 | 201.2 | −1,247.6 |
| Equity & investment fund shares | 3baaa | 348.9 | 151.7 | 205.8 | 472.5 | 403.2 | 707.0 | −293.5 | 1,069.5 | −789.4 | 114.5 | 270.8 | −875.6 |
| Debt securities.......................... | 3bbaa | 265.4 | −39.9 | 152.5 | 1,087.6 | 162.7 | 118.9 | 2,204.1 | −624.8 | 194.9 | −754.8 | −69.6 | −372.0 |
| Portfolio investment: liabilities....... | 3b9la | −93.0 | 647.7 | 2,023.7 | 1,730.4 | 1,203.2 | 2,690.5 | −724.7 | −305.4 | 600.0 | 727.1 | 2,161.5 | −463.3 |
| Equity & investment fund shares . | 3bala | 147.6 | 1,435.6 | 550.8 | 791.1 | 465.7 | 929.1 | 153.9 | −145.4 | −191.3 | 37.7 | 99.6 | −553.1 |
| Debt securities.......................... | 3bbla | −240.6 | −788.0 | 1,472.9 | 939.3 | 737.5 | 1,761.4 | −878.6 | −160.0 | 791.3 | 689.4 | 2,061.9 | 89.8 |
| Fin. der.& empl.stk.ops.(ESOs): net. | 3c9na | .... | .... | .... | .... | .... | .... | .... | .... | .... | .... | .... | .... |
| Fin. der. & ESOs.: assets.............. | 3c9aa | .... | .... | .... | .... | .... | .... | .... | .... | .... | .... | .... | .... |
| Fin. der. & ESOs.: liabilities.......... | 3c9la | .... | .... | .... | .... | .... | .... | .... | .... | .... | .... | .... | .... |
| Other investment: assets................ | 3d9aa | −3,125.5 | −2,637.9 | 1,598.3 | −528.7 | −7,819.3 | −5,083.0 | −2,025.7 | −3,131.9 | −4,105.6 | −4,242.4 | −6,284.0 | −4,286.8 |
| Other equity............................ | 3daaa | .... | .... | .... | .... | .... | .... | .... | .... | .... | .... | .... | .... |
| Debt instruments........................ | 3dzaa | −3,125.5 | −2,637.9 | 1,598.3 | −528.7 | −7,819.3 | −5,083.0 | −2,025.7 | −3,131.9 | −4,105.6 | −4,242.4 | −6,284.0 | −4,286.8 |
| Other investment: liabilities........... | 3d9la | 819.0 | −1,295.6 | 373.2 | 3,197.3 | 890.3 | 8,075.0 | 332.6 | 3,868.6 | 2,599.2 | 2,875.0 | 3,994.5 | 1,989.9 |
| Other equity............................ | 3dala | .... | .... | .... | .... | .... | .... | .... | .... | .... | .... | .... | .... |
| Debt instruments........................ | 3dzla | 819.0 | −1,295.6 | 373.2 | 3,197.3 | 890.3 | 8,075.0 | 332.6 | 3,868.6 | 2,599.2 | 2,875.0 | 3,994.5 | 1,989.9 |
| Curr.+ cap.− finan. acct. balance... | 4y9na | −46.3 | 1,065.6 | 2,959.8 | 5,409.1 | 9,000.2 | 11,977.4 | −3,997.0 | 4,160.3 | 570.0 | −712.2 | 3,656.9 | 2,438.6 |
| D. Net Errors and Omissions............ | 409na | −733.6 | −608.1 | −2,814.2 | −6,073.9 | −1,663.7 | −3,042.1 | 7,056.4 | −1,866.1 | 47.3 | 2,767.6 | −349.0 | −3,353.5 |
| E. Reserves and Related Items......... | 4z9na | −780.0 | 457.5 | 145.5 | −664.8 | 7,336.4 | 8,935.4 | 3,059.4 | 2,294.2 | 617.3 | 2,055.3 | 3,307.9 | −915.0 |
| Reserve assets........................ | 3e9aa | −780.0 | 457.5 | 250.1 | −587.7 | 7,374.1 | 8,935.4 | 3,039.9 | 2,254.2 | 578.3 | 2,036.1 | 3,307.9 | −915.0 |
| Credit and loans from the IMF....... | 3dcla | — | — | — | 77.1 | 37.6 | — | −19.5 | −40.0 | −39.0 | −19.3 | — | — |
| Exceptional financing................... | 409la | — | — | 104.5 | — | — | — | — | — | — | — | — | — |

*Excludes components in group E

| | | 2004 | 2005 | 2006 | 2007 | 2008 | 2009 | 2010 | 2011 | 2012 | 2013 | 2014 | 2015 |
|---|---|---|---|---|---|---|---|---|---|---|---|---|---|
| **Government Finance Operations Statement** | | | | | | | | | | | | | |
| **Budgetary Central Government** | | | | | *Billions of Pounds: Fiscal Year Ends December 31* | | | | | | | | |
| Revenue | a1 | 7,000.3 | 6,852.2 | 7,779.2 | 8,389.6 | 9,887.3 | 11,877.0 | 11,668.8 | 13,163.5 | 13,234.7 | 13,085.9 | 14,467.0 | .... |
| Taxes | a11 | 5,266.0 | 4,915.6 | 4,982.6 | 5,593.2 | 7,207.1 | 8,995.3 | 9,762.1 | 9,857.5 | 10,084.7 | 9,940.8 | 10,229.9 | .... |
| Social Contributions | a12 | 85.6 | 83.9 | 85.3 | 77.1 | 85.2 | 95.2 | 107.3 | 206.4 | 156.0 | 128.2 | 136.2 | .... |
| Grants | a13 | .2 | — | 1,049.7 | 496.0 | 398.0 | 165.9 | 34.6 | 5.8 | .7 | 7.7 | 26.0 | .... |
| Other Revenue | a14 | 1,648.5 | 1,852.8 | 1,661.6 | 2,223.3 | 2,196.9 | 2,620.5 | 1,764.8 | 3,093.7 | 2,993.3 | 3,009.2 | 4,074.8 | .... |
| Expense | a2 | 8,563.5 | 8,699.4 | 10,528.3 | 11,816.2 | 13,410.1 | 15,361.2 | 14,977.3 | 15,888.4 | 17,782.7 | 18,863.7 | 18,812.4 | .... |
| Compensation of Employees | a21 | 1,997.5 | 2,000.9 | 2,113.8 | 2,296.5 | 2,563.5 | 3,263.8 | 3,180.4 | 3,486.0 | 3,954.1 | 4,002.0 | 4,143.8 | .... |
| Use of Goods & Services | a22 | 250.8 | 232.2 | 291.9 | 331.0 | 459.1 | 494.1 | 527.7 | 582.0 | 539.3 | 792.4 | 767.2 | .... |
| Consumption of Fixed Capital | a23 | .... | .... | .... | .... | .... | .... | .... | .... | .... | .... | .... | .... |
| Interest | a24 | 3,922.1 | 3,408.7 | 4,334.5 | 4,694.6 | 4,957.4 | 5,784.1 | 5,893.3 | 5,654.8 | 5,457.2 | 5,713.8 | 6,314.3 | .... |
| Subsidies | a25 | 280.3 | 869.8 | 1,217.7 | 1,496.5 | 2,434.8 | 2,304.3 | 1,894.1 | 2,772.4 | 3,604.4 | 3,282.5 | 3,341.9 | .... |
| Grants | a26 | 505.6 | 493.9 | 444.9 | 379.0 | 469.3 | 1,014.6 | 669.4 | 249.7 | 711.9 | 803.9 | 516.8 | .... |
| Social Benefits | a27 | 1,410.0 | 1,491.5 | 1,734.3 | 1,655.7 | 2,071.4 | 2,242.5 | 2,501.2 | 2,534.1 | 3,178.1 | 3,731.3 | 3,248.5 | .... |
| Other Expense | a28 | 197.2 | 202.3 | 391.2 | 962.9 | 454.5 | 257.7 | 311.2 | 609.5 | 337.8 | 537.9 | 480.0 | .... |
| Gross Operating Balance [1-2+23] | agob | −1,563.2 | −1,847.2 | −2,749.0 | −3,426.6 | −3,522.8 | −3,484.3 | −3,308.4 | −2,725.0 | −4,548.1 | −5,777.8 | −4,345.4 | .... |
| Net Operating Balance [1-2] | anob | .... | .... | .... | .... | .... | .... | .... | .... | .... | .... | .... | .... |
| Net Acq. of Nonfinancial Assets | a31 | 1,171.5 | 735.1 | 951.2 | 783.0 | 890.1 | 851.3 | 1,039.7 | 1,153.7 | 1,171.5 | 1,325.5 | 1,620.8 | .... |
| Aquisition of Nonfin. Assets | a31.1 | .... | .... | .... | .... | .... | .... | .... | .... | .... | .... | .... | .... |
| Disposal of Nonfin. Assets | a31.2 | .... | .... | .... | .... | .... | .... | .... | .... | .... | .... | .... | .... |
| Net Lending/Borrowing [1-2-31] | anlb | −2,734.6 | −2,582.3 | −3,700.2 | −4,209.7 | −4,413.0 | −4,335.6 | −4,348.2 | −3,878.7 | −5,719.5 | −7,103.3 | −5,966.1 | .... |
| Net Acq. of Financial Assets | a32 | 851.8 | 1,184.2 | −1,102.6 | −1,757.7 | 3,089.3 | 1,923.3 | −1,651.9 | −1,435.6 | 609.2 | 1,734.8 | −615.3 | .... |
| By instrument | | | | | | | | | | | | | |
| Monetary Gold & SDRs | a3201 | — | — | — | — | — | — | — | — | — | — | — | .... |
| Currency & Deposits | a3202 | 851.8 | 1,184.2 | −1,102.6 | 622.3 | 3,089.3 | 1,923.3 | −1,651.9 | −1,435.6 | 609.2 | 1,734.8 | −615.3 | .... |
| Securities other than Shares | a3203 | — | — | — | — | — | — | — | — | — | — | — | .... |
| Loans | a3204 | — | — | — | — | — | — | — | — | — | — | — | .... |
| Shares & Other Equity | a3205 | — | — | — | −2,380.0 | — | — | — | — | — | — | — | .... |
| Insurance Technical Reserves | a3206 | — | — | — | — | — | — | — | — | — | — | — | .... |
| Financial Derivatives | a3207 | — | — | — | — | — | — | — | — | — | — | — | .... |
| Other Accounts Receivable | a3208 | — | — | — | — | — | — | — | — | — | — | — | .... |
| By debtor | | | | | | | | | | | | | |
| Domestic | a321 | 255.9 | 1,151.2 | −1,507.6 | −2,000.3 | 4,036.3 | 4,593.8 | −1,651.9 | −1,435.6 | 609.2 | 4,861.8 | 4,242.7 | .... |
| Foreign | a322 | 595.9 | 33.0 | 405.0 | 242.7 | −947.0 | −2,670.5 | — | — | — | −3,127.0 | −4,858.0 | .... |
| Net Incurrence of Liabilities | a33 | 3,586.4 | 3,766.5 | 2,597.6 | 2,452.0 | 7,502.3 | 6,258.8 | 2,696.3 | 2,443.1 | 6,328.7 | 8,838.0 | 5,350.8 | .... |
| By instrument | | | | | | | | | | | | | |
| Special Drawing Rights (SDRs) | a3301 | — | — | — | — | — | — | — | — | — | — | — | .... |
| Currency & Deposits | a3302 | −185.7 | −81.8 | −142.3 | −39.6 | 78.5 | 101.3 | 257.2 | 127.4 | 322.7 | −654.7 | −13.0 | .... |
| Securities other than Shares | a3303 | 3,554.4 | 3,780.0 | 2,478.0 | 1,689.7 | 7,134.7 | 6,395.5 | 2,715.0 | 2,048.0 | 6,281.0 | 8,771.0 | 4,581.0 | .... |
| Loans | a3304 | 40.4 | 64.0 | 153.0 | 455.7 | 207.8 | −200.0 | −420.0 | −304.0 | −203.0 | −170.0 | −43.0 | .... |
| Shares & Other Equity | a3305 | — | — | — | — | — | — | — | — | — | — | — | .... |
| Insurance Technical Reserves | a3306 | — | — | — | — | — | — | — | — | — | — | — | .... |
| Financial Derivatives | a3307 | — | — | — | — | — | — | — | — | — | — | — | .... |
| Other Accounts Payable | a3308 | 177.3 | 4.3 | 108.9 | 346.2 | 81.3 | −38.0 | 144.1 | 571.6 | −72.0 | 891.8 | 825.8 | .... |
| By creditor | | | | | | | | | | | | | |
| Domestic | a331 | −417.8 | 2,530.5 | 862.6 | 1,446.6 | 7,554.8 | 6,123.3 | 3,815.3 | 1,863.1 | 1,107.7 | 6,263.0 | 6,100.8 | .... |
| Foreign | a332 | 4,004.2 | 1,236.0 | 1,735.0 | 1,005.4 | −52.5 | 135.5 | −1,119.0 | 580.0 | 5,221.0 | 2,575.0 | −750.0 | .... |
| Stat. Discrepancy [32-33-NLB] | anlbz | — | — | — | — | — | — | — | — | — | — | — | .... |
| Memo Item: Expenditure [2+31] | a2m | 9,734.9 | 9,434.5 | 11,479.4 | 12,599.2 | 14,300.2 | 16,212.5 | 16,017.0 | 17,042.1 | 18,954.2 | 20,189.2 | 20,433.2 | .... |
| **National Accounts** | | | | | | *Billions of Pounds* | | | | | | | |
| Househ.Cons.Expend.,incl.NPISHs | 96f | 26,539 | 26,523 | 28,160 | 32,096 | 38,749 | 44,982 | 50,711 | 53,384 | 60,788 | 62,534 | .... | .... |
| Government Consumption Expend | 91f | 4,411 | 4,522 | 4,638 | 4,925 | 5,686 | 6,566 | 6,763 | 7,306 | 8,730 | 8,879 | .... | .... |
| Gross Fixed Capital Formation | 93e | 7,200 | 7,195 | 7,352 | 9,261 | 12,111 | 15,104 | 14,657 | 15,430 | 16,493 | 19,355 | .... | .... |
| Changes in Inventories | 93i | 223 | 317 | −454 | −76 | 298 | −598 | −57 | 753 | −339 | 423 | .... | .... |
| Exports of Goods and Services | 90c | 11,388 | 12,084 | 12,012 | 14,114 | 17,171 | 18,023 | 20,731 | 22,318 | 21,250 | 20,095 | .... | .... |
| Imports of Goods and Services (-) | 98c | 17,884 | 18,246 | 18,469 | 22,824 | 29,954 | 30,594 | 34,887 | 38,776 | 40,442 | 40,102 | .... | .... |
| Gross Domestic Product (GDP) | 99b | 31,877 | 32,396 | 33,238 | 37,497 | 44,061 | 53,482 | 57,918 | 60,414 | 66,481 | 71,185 | .... | .... |
| Net Primary Income from Abroad | 98.n | −531 | 787 | 567 | 636 | 406 | 1,287 | .... | .... | .... | .... | .... | .... |
| Gross National Income | 99a | 32,317 | 33,742 | 34,394 | 38,410 | 45,530 | 53,937 | .... | .... | .... | .... | .... | .... |
| | | | | | | *Millions: Midyear Estimates* | | | | | | | |
| **Population** | 99z | 3.86 | 3.99 | 4.06 | 4.09 | 4.11 | 4.18 | 4.34 | 4.59 | 4.92 | 5.29 | 5.61 | 5.85 |

# Lesotho 666

| | | 2004 | 2005 | 2006 | 2007 | 2008 | 2009 | 2010 | 2011 | 2012 | 2013 | 2014 | 2015 |
|---|---|---|---|---|---|---|---|---|---|---|---|---|---|
| **Exchange Rates** | | \multicolumn{12}{c}{*Maloti per SDR: End of Period*} | | | | | | | | | | | |
| Principal Rate | aa | 8.743 | 9.040 | 10.486 | 10.762 | 14.332 | 11.570 | 10.213 | 12.502 | 13.066 | 16.154 | 16.779 | 21.541 |
| | | \multicolumn{12}{c}{*Maloti per US Dollar: End of Period (ae) Period Average (rf)*} | | | | | | | | | | | |
| Principal Rate | ae | 5.6300 | 6.3250 | 6.9700 | 6.8100 | 9.3050 | 7.3800 | 6.6316 | 8.1429 | 8.5012 | 10.4899 | 11.5810 | 15.5450 |
| Principal Rate | rf | 6.4597 | 6.3593 | 6.7715 | 7.0454 | 8.2612 | 8.4737 | 7.3212 | 7.2611 | 8.2100 | 9.6551 | 10.8527 | 12.7589 |
| | | \multicolumn{12}{c}{*Index Numbers (2010=100): Period Averages*} | | | | | | | | | | | |
| Principal Rate | ahx | 113.5 | 115.2 | 108.7 | 103.8 | 89.7 | 87.5 | 100.0 | 101.2 | 89.2 | 75.9 | 67.4 | 57.7 |
| Nominal Effective Exchange Rate | nec | 113.7 | 116.3 | 110.3 | 104.1 | 89.6 | 89.2 | 100.0 | 98.8 | 89.8 | 78.1 | 70.8 | 64.5 |
| CPI-Based Real Effect. Ex. Rate | rec | 91.5 | 94.0 | 91.9 | 90.7 | 82.5 | 87.8 | 100.0 | 100.6 | 94.7 | 84.7 | 79.1 | 73.7 |
| **Fund Position** | | \multicolumn{12}{c}{*Millions of SDRs: End of Period*} | | | | | | | | | | | |
| Quota | 2f.s | 34.90 | 34.90 | 34.90 | 34.90 | 34.90 | 34.90 | 34.90 | 34.90 | 34.90 | 34.90 | 34.90 | 34.90 |
| SDR Holdings | 1b.s | .40 | .31 | .14 | 3.97 | 3.59 | 31.26 | 34.16 | 35.32 | 37.90 | 47.52 | 46.48 | 45.71 |
| Reserve Position in the Fund | 1c.s | 3.56 | 3.60 | 3.62 | 3.61 | 3.61 | 3.61 | 3.61 | 3.61 | 3.71 | 3.80 | 3.81 | 3.84 |
| Total Fund Cred.&Loans Outstg | 2tl | 24.50 | 24.50 | 24.15 | 22.40 | 19.25 | 15.40 | 18.30 | 19.43 | 42.05 | 51.66 | 50.61 | 49.83 |
| SDR Allocations | 1bd | 3.74 | 3.74 | 3.74 | 3.74 | 3.74 | 32.88 | 32.88 | 32.88 | 32.88 | 32.88 | 32.88 | 32.88 |
| **International Liquidity** | | \multicolumn{12}{c}{*Millions of US Dollars Unless Otherwise Indicated: End of Period*} | | | | | | | | | | | |
| Total Reserves minus Gold | 1l.d | 501.50 | 519.11 | 658.40 | 1,002.76 | 971.53 | 1,179.80 | 1,070.96 | 919.09 | 1,027.91 | 1,055.24 | 1,070.83 | 904.16 |
| SDR Holdings | 1b.d | .62 | .44 | .22 | 6.28 | 5.53 | 49.00 | 52.61 | 54.22 | 58.25 | 73.18 | 67.35 | 63.34 |
| Reserve Position in the Fund | 1c.d | 5.53 | 5.64 | 5.15 | 5.45 | 5.71 | 5.57 | 5.66 | 5.56 | 5.55 | 5.71 | 5.85 | 5.53 | 5.32 |
| Foreign Exchange | 1d.d | 495.35 | 513.52 | 652.74 | 990.77 | 960.43 | 1,125.13 | 1,012.78 | 859.32 | 963.95 | 976.20 | 997.96 | 835.50 |
| Central Bank: Other Assets | 3..d | 544.63 | 527.71 | 658.16 | 947.03 | 911.96 | 1,076.26 | 964.57 | — | — | — | — | — |
| Central Bank: Other Liabs | 4..d | — | — | — | — | — | — | 2.11 | .07 | — | — | — | — |
| Other Depository Corps.: Assets | 7a.d | 224.07 | 199.54 | 273.26 | 338.34 | 329.94 | 455.70 | 599.55 | 416.42 | 302.26 | 345.79 | 287.51 | 273.02 |
| Other Depository Corps.: Liabs | 7b.d | 24.14 | 16.89 | 10.47 | 10.77 | 9.96 | 42.07 | 17.75 | 22.27 | 9.74 | 37.24 | 25.04 | 24.76 |
| **Central Bank** | | \multicolumn{12}{c}{*Millions of Maloti: End of Period*} | | | | | | | | | | | |
| Net Foreign Assets | 11n | 2,854.16 | 3,117.91 | 4,334.43 | 6,249.62 | 8,259.74 | 7,787.89 | 6,246.01 | 6,696.09 | 7,654.35 | 9,598.84 | 10,924.12 | 12,273.62 |
| Claims on Nonresidents | 11 | 3,101.08 | 3,373.21 | 4,626.88 | 6,530.94 | 8,589.25 | 8,346.47 | 6,782.66 | 7,350.58 | 8,633.27 | 10,964.44 | 12,324.74 | 14,055.15 |
| Liabilities to Nonresidents | 16c | 246.92 | 255.30 | 292.45 | 281.32 | 329.51 | 558.58 | 536.65 | 654.49 | 978.92 | 1,365.60 | 1,400.62 | 1,781.52 |
| Claims on Other Depository Corps | 12e | — | — | — | — | — | — | — | — | — | — | — | — |
| Net Claims on Central Government | 12an | −1,197.75 | −1,199.85 | −1,973.93 | −3,728.81 | −4,232.60 | −4,353.35 | −3,639.68 | −3,292.81 | −3,986.06 | −4,829.95 | −5,559.87 | −5,507.73 |
| Claims on Central Government | 12a | 214.09 | 222.16 | 257.56 | 263.48 | 529.86 | 308.33 | 250.07 | 242.92 | 479.78 | 834.58 | 849.79 | 1,073.81 |
| Liabilities to Central Government | 16d | 1,411.84 | 1,422.01 | 2,231.49 | 3,992.30 | 4,762.46 | 4,661.68 | 3,889.75 | 3,535.73 | 4,465.84 | 5,664.53 | 6,409.66 | 6,581.53 |
| Claims on Other Sectors | 12s | 16.30 | 19.48 | 20.10 | 22.19 | 26.11 | 27.03 | 27.08 | 32.63 | 42.26 | 50.90 | 60.99 | 69.46 |
| Claims on Other Financial Corps | 12g | — | — | — | — | — | — | — | — | — | — | — | — |
| Claims on State & Local Govts | 12b | — | — | — | — | — | — | — | — | — | — | — | — |
| Claims on Public Nonfin. Corps | 12c | — | — | — | — | — | — | — | — | — | — | — | — |
| Claims on Private Sector | 12d | 16.30 | 19.48 | 20.10 | 22.19 | 26.11 | 27.03 | 27.08 | 32.63 | 42.26 | 50.90 | 60.99 | 69.46 |
| Monetary Base | 14 | 559.07 | 734.14 | 680.69 | 687.18 | 718.45 | 1,015.99 | 1,048.68 | 1,049.49 | 1,203.54 | 1,506.30 | 1,712.02 | 1,723.85 |
| Currency in Circulation | 14a | 256.93 | 297.97 | 377.71 | 402.22 | 481.25 | 584.24 | 637.79 | 843.59 | 998.55 | 1,197.97 | 1,163.71 | 1,321.98 |
| Liabs. to Other Depository Corps | 14c | 112.26 | 244.78 | 110.78 | 130.49 | 96.50 | 232.52 | 234.26 | 169.61 | 184.65 | 298.73 | 490.27 | 363.87 |
| Liabilities to Other Sectors | 14d | 189.88 | 191.39 | 192.19 | 154.46 | 140.70 | 199.23 | 176.63 | 36.29 | 20.33 | 9.60 | 58.04 | 38.00 |
| Other Liabs. to Other Dep. Corps | 14n | — | — | — | — | — | — | — | — | — | — | — | — |
| Dep. & Sec. Excl. f/Monetary Base | 14o | — | — | — | — | — | — | — | — | — | — | — | — |
| Deposits Included in Broad Money | 15 | — | — | — | — | — | — | — | — | — | — | — | — |
| Sec.Ot.th.Shares Incl.in Brd. Money | 16a | — | — | — | — | — | — | — | — | — | — | — | — |
| Deposits Excl. from Broad Money | 16b | — | — | — | — | — | — | — | — | — | — | — | — |
| Sec.Ot.th.Shares Excl.f/Brd.Money | 16s | — | — | — | — | — | — | — | — | — | — | — | — |
| Loans | 16l | — | — | — | — | — | — | — | — | — | — | — | — |
| Financial Derivatives | 16m | — | — | — | — | — | — | — | — | — | — | — | — |
| Shares and Other Equity | 17a | 1,171.55 | 1,304.53 | 1,819.78 | 1,922.22 | 3,095.50 | 1,709.12 | 1,361.41 | 2,217.68 | 2,655.04 | 3,389.54 | 3,936.52 | 5,535.76 |
| Other Items (Net) | 17r | −57.91 | −101.14 | −119.87 | −66.39 | 239.29 | 736.46 | 223.33 | 168.74 | −148.02 | −76.04 | −223.30 | −424.24 |
| Memo Item: | | | | | | | | | | | | | |
| Total Assets | 10ra | 3,791.86 | 4,127.63 | 5,418.53 | 7,351.18 | 9,827.66 | 8,931.32 | 7,391.33 | 7,867.96 | 9,360.27 | 12,096.73 | 13,595.71 | 15,757.67 |
| **Other Depository Corporations** | | \multicolumn{12}{c}{*Millions of Maloti: End of Period*} | | | | | | | | | | | |
| Net Foreign Assets | 21n | 1,125.61 | 1,155.21 | 1,831.69 | 2,230.71 | 2,977.41 | 3,052.56 | 3,858.26 | 3,209.50 | 2,486.70 | 3,236.64 | 3,039.45 | 3,859.15 |
| Claims on Nonresidents | 21 | 1,261.50 | 1,262.07 | 1,904.64 | 2,304.07 | 3,070.08 | 3,363.04 | 3,975.95 | 3,390.87 | 2,569.52 | 3,627.33 | 3,329.38 | 4,244.11 |
| Liabilities to Nonresidents | 26c | 135.90 | 106.86 | 72.94 | 73.36 | 92.67 | 310.48 | 117.69 | 181.37 | 82.82 | 390.69 | 289.93 | 384.96 |
| Claims on Central Bank | 20 | 164.76 | 255.15 | 179.07 | 188.98 | 154.41 | 281.42 | 313.08 | 292.06 | 419.23 | 533.05 | 771.89 | 681.87 |
| Currency | 20a | 52.40 | 85.19 | 68.29 | 62.91 | 79.17 | 97.06 | 98.83 | 154.90 | 229.50 | 244.64 | 222.22 | 307.47 |
| Reserve Deposits and Securities | 20b | 112.36 | 169.95 | 110.77 | 126.07 | 75.24 | 184.36 | 214.25 | 137.16 | 189.73 | 288.41 | 549.67 | 374.40 |
| Other Claims | 20n | — | — | — | — | — | — | — | — | — | — | — | — |
| Net Claims on Central Government | 22an | 485.67 | 289.77 | 475.17 | 404.50 | 259.90 | 357.35 | 442.05 | 720.62 | 837.12 | 652.12 | 597.31 | 717.61 |
| Claims on Central Government | 22a | 543.43 | 461.65 | 598.26 | 559.28 | 453.96 | 384.12 | 466.31 | 722.17 | 839.09 | 664.89 | 610.75 | 825.42 |
| Liabilities to Central Government | 26d | 57.76 | 171.88 | 123.09 | 154.79 | 194.06 | 26.77 | 24.26 | 1.55 | 1.97 | 12.78 | 13.45 | 107.81 |
| Claims on Other Sectors | 22s | 548.95 | 790.10 | 901.84 | 1,231.07 | 1,480.87 | 1,832.76 | 2,169.73 | 2,667.00 | 3,746.50 | 4,516.90 | 5,072.85 | 5,463.58 |
| Claims on Other Financial Corps | 22g | — | 2.37 | 7.32 | 17.57 | — | — | — | 11.27 | 10.60 | 11.70 | 12.53 | 31.39 |
| Claims on State & Local Govts | 22b | — | — | — | — | — | — | — | — | — | — | — | — |
| Claims on Public Nonfin. Corps | 22c | 52.16 | 33.37 | 17.39 | 51.47 | 43.83 | — | 2.98 | 1.37 | — | — | — | — |
| Claims on Private Sector | 22d | 496.79 | 754.36 | 877.14 | 1,162.03 | 1,437.04 | 1,832.76 | 2,166.75 | 2,654.37 | 3,735.90 | 4,505.21 | 5,060.31 | 5,432.19 |
| Liabilities to Central Bank | 26g | — | — | — | — | — | — | — | — | — | — | — | — |
| Transf.Dep.Included in Broad Money | 24 | 1,197.50 | 1,427.86 | 2,187.20 | 2,496.89 | 3,334.62 | 3,492.83 | 4,273.42 | 2,132.83 | 2,707.35 | 3,034.88 | 3,155.13 | 4,280.81 |
| Other Dep.Included in Broad Money | 25 | 783.63 | 760.54 | 819.10 | 1,090.79 | 1,006.16 | 1,567.63 | 1,588.82 | 3,822.29 | 3,652.10 | 4,663.80 | 4,849.18 | 4,803.63 |
| Sec.Ot.th.Shares Incl.in Brd. Money | 26a | — | — | — | — | — | — | — | — | — | — | — | — |
| Deposits Excl. from Broad Money | 26b | — | — | — | — | — | — | — | — | — | .02 | 2.63 | 63.37 |
| Sec.Ot.th.Shares Excl.f/Brd.Money | 26s | — | — | — | — | — | — | — | — | — | — | — | — |
| Loans | 26l | — | — | — | — | — | — | — | — | — | — | — | — |
| Financial Derivatives | 26m | — | — | — | — | — | — | — | — | — | — | — | — |
| Insurance Technical Reserves | 26r | — | — | — | — | — | — | — | — | — | — | — | — |
| Shares and Other Equity | 27a | 345.75 | 403.50 | 315.84 | 413.07 | 464.69 | 631.69 | 713.59 | 815.27 | 954.99 | 1,117.44 | 1,271.03 | 1,457.33 |
| Other Items (Net) | 27r | −1.90 | −101.66 | 65.64 | 54.50 | 67.11 | −168.07 | 207.28 | 118.79 | 175.11 | 122.57 | 203.54 | 117.06 |
| Memo Item: | | | | | | | | | | | | | |
| Total Assets | 20ra | 3,348.42 | 3,924.07 | 4,177.47 | 4,985.85 | 6,164.60 | 7,360.03 | 8,293.46 | 8,545.13 | 8,989.55 | 11,776.44 | 12,653.06 | 14,308.43 |

# Lesotho 666

| Depository Corporations | | 2004 | 2005 | 2006 | 2007 | 2008 | 2009 | 2010 | 2011 | 2012 | 2013 | 2014 | 2015 |
|---|---|---|---|---|---|---|---|---|---|---|---|---|---|
| | | | | | | *Millions of Maloti: End of Period* | | | | | | | |
| Net Foreign Assets | 31n | 3,979.76 | 4,273.12 | 6,166.12 | 8,480.34 | 11,237.15 | 10,840.45 | 10,104.27 | 9,905.59 | 10,141.05 | 12,835.48 | 13,963.58 | 16,132.77 |
| Claims on Nonresidents | 31 | 4,362.58 | 4,635.28 | 6,531.52 | 8,835.01 | 11,659.33 | 11,709.51 | 10,758.61 | 10,741.45 | 11,202.79 | 14,591.77 | 15,654.12 | 18,299.26 |
| Liabilities to Nonresidents | 36c | 382.82 | 362.16 | 365.40 | 354.67 | 422.18 | 869.06 | 654.34 | 835.85 | 1,061.73 | 1,756.29 | 1,690.54 | 2,166.48 |
| Domestic Claims | 32 | −146.83 | −100.49 | −576.82 | −2,071.06 | −2,465.73 | −2,136.21 | −1,000.82 | 127.45 | 639.81 | 389.98 | 171.28 | 742.93 |
| Net Claims on Central Government | 32an | −712.08 | −910.08 | −1,498.76 | −3,324.32 | −3,972.70 | −3,996.00 | −3,197.63 | −2,572.19 | −3,148.94 | −4,177.83 | −4,962.56 | −4,790.12 |
| Claims on Central Government | 32a | 757.52 | 683.81 | 855.82 | 822.77 | 983.82 | 692.45 | 716.38 | 965.09 | 1,318.87 | 1,499.48 | 1,460.54 | 1,899.23 |
| Liabilities to Central Government | 36d | 1,469.60 | 1,593.89 | 2,354.58 | 4,147.08 | 4,956.52 | 4,688.45 | 3,914.01 | 3,537.28 | 4,467.82 | 5,677.31 | 6,423.11 | 6,689.34 |
| Claims on Other Sectors | 32s | 565.25 | 809.59 | 921.94 | 1,253.25 | 1,506.98 | 1,859.79 | 2,196.81 | 2,699.64 | 3,788.76 | 4,567.81 | 5,133.84 | 5,533.05 |
| Claims on Other Financial Corps. | 32g | — | 2.37 | 7.32 | 17.57 | — | — | — | 11.27 | 10.60 | 11.70 | 12.53 | 31.39 |
| Claims on State & Local Govts. | 32b | — | — | — | — | — | — | — | — | — | — | — | — |
| Claims on Public Nonfin. Corps. | 32c | 52.16 | 33.37 | 17.39 | 51.47 | 43.83 | — | 2.98 | 1.37 | — | — | — | — |
| Claims on Private Sector | 32d | 513.09 | 773.84 | 897.24 | 1,184.22 | 1,463.15 | 1,859.79 | 2,193.83 | 2,687.00 | 3,778.16 | 4,556.11 | 5,121.30 | 5,501.66 |
| Broad Money Liabilities | 35l | 2,375.55 | 2,592.57 | 3,507.90 | 4,081.46 | 4,883.56 | 5,746.87 | 6,577.83 | 6,680.10 | 7,148.83 | 8,661.61 | 9,003.84 | 10,136.94 |
| Currency Outside Depository Corps | 34a | 204.54 | 212.78 | 309.42 | 339.31 | 402.08 | 487.18 | 538.96 | 688.70 | 769.05 | 953.33 | 941.49 | 1,014.50 |
| Transferable Deposits | 34 | 1,387.38 | 1,619.26 | 2,379.39 | 2,651.35 | 3,475.32 | 3,692.06 | 4,450.05 | 2,132.83 | 2,707.35 | 3,034.88 | 3,155.13 | 4,280.81 |
| Other Deposits | 35 | 783.63 | 760.54 | 819.10 | 1,090.79 | 1,006.16 | 1,567.63 | 1,588.82 | 3,858.58 | 3,672.43 | 4,673.40 | 4,907.22 | 4,841.63 |
| Securities Other than Shares | 36a | — | — | — | — | — | — | — | — | — | — | — | — |
| Deposits Excl. from Broad Money | 36b | — | — | — | — | — | — | — | — | — | .02 | 2.63 | 63.37 |
| Sec.Ot.th.Shares Excl.f/Brd.Money | 36s | — | — | — | — | — | — | — | — | — | — | — | — |
| Loans | 36l | — | — | — | — | — | — | — | — | — | — | — | — |
| Financial Derivatives | 36m | — | — | — | — | — | — | — | — | — | — | — | — |
| Insurance Technical Reserves | 36r | — | — | — | — | — | — | — | — | — | — | — | — |
| Shares and Other Equity | 37a | 1,517.30 | 1,708.03 | 2,135.61 | 2,335.29 | 3,560.19 | 2,340.81 | 2,074.99 | 3,032.96 | 3,610.03 | 4,506.98 | 5,207.55 | 6,993.09 |
| Other Items (Net) | 37r | −59.91 | −127.97 | −54.22 | −7.47 | 327.67 | 616.56 | 450.62 | 319.98 | 22.01 | 56.85 | −79.17 | −317.70 |
| Broad Money Liabs., Seasonally Adj. | 35l.b | 2,359.89 | 2,576.46 | 3,494.34 | 4,078.24 | 4,881.49 | 5,732.95 | 6,535.14 | 6,587.16 | 7,003.00 | 8,440.50 | 8,764.87 | 9,859.87 |
| **Monetary Aggregates** | | | | | | *Millions of Maloti: End of Period* | | | | | | | |
| Broad Money | 59m | 2,375.55 | 2,592.57 | 3,507.90 | 4,081.46 | 4,883.56 | 5,746.87 | 6,577.83 | 6,680.10 | 7,148.83 | 8,661.61 | 9,003.84 | 10,136.94 |
| o/w:Currency Issued by Cent.Govt | 59m.a | — | — | — | — | — | — | — | — | — | — | — | — |
| o/w: Dep.in Nonfin. Corporations | 59m.b | — | — | — | — | — | — | — | — | — | — | — | — |
| o/w:Secs. Issued by Central Govt. | 59m.c | — | — | — | — | — | — | — | — | — | — | — | — |
| Money (National Definitions) | | | | | | | | | | | | | |
| M1 | 59ma | 1,591.92 | 1,832.03 | 2,688.81 | 2,990.67 | 3,877.39 | 4,179.24 | 4,989.01 | † 2,821.52 | 3,476.40 | 3,988.21 | 4,096.62 | 5,295.31 |
| Quasi-Money | 59mal | 783.63 | 760.54 | 819.10 | 1,090.79 | 1,006.16 | 1,567.63 | 1,588.82 | † 3,858.58 | 3,672.43 | 4,673.40 | 4,907.22 | 4,841.63 |
| M2 | 59mb | 2,375.55 | 2,592.57 | 3,507.90 | 4,156.48 | 4,883.56 | 5,746.87 | 6,577.83 | † 6,680.10 | 7,148.83 | 8,661.61 | 9,003.84 | 10,136.94 |
| **Interest Rates** | | | | | | *Percent Per Annum* | | | | | | | |
| Discount Rate (End of Period) | 60.a | 13.00 | 13.00 | 10.76 | 12.82 | 14.05 | 10.66 | 9.52 | 9.28 | 9.37 | 9.18 | 10.25 | 10.49 |
| Treasury Bill Rate | 60c | 8.52 | 7.23 | 6.87 | 7.81 | 9.75 | 7.75 | 6.24 | 5.35 | 5.46 | 5.30 | 5.99 | 6.31 |
| Savings Rate | 60k | 1.89 | 1.75 | 2.91 | 5.48 | 7.10 | 5.13 | 3.92 | 1.66 | 1.75 | 1.75 | 1.90 | 1.43 |
| Deposit Rate | 60l | 4.24 | 3.95 | 4.54 | 6.46 | 7.64 | 4.85 | 3.68 | 2.70 | 2.85 | 2.85 | 2.73 | 2.34 |
| Lending Rate | 60p | 12.38 | 11.72 | 12.16 | 14.13 | 16.19 | 13.00 | 11.22 | 10.43 | 10.12 | 9.92 | 10.34 | 10.59 |
| **Prices** | | | | | | *Index Numbers (2010=100): Period Averages* | | | | | | | |
| Consumer Prices | 64 | 68.5 | 70.9 | 75.2 | 81.2 | 89.9 | 96.5 | 100.0 | 105.0 | 111.4 | 116.9 | 123.2 | 127.1 |
| **Intl. Transactions & Positions** | | | | | | *Millions of Maloti* | | | | | | | |
| Exports | 70 | 4,573.5 | 4,137.2 | 4,697.0 | 5,420.8 | 7,289.5 | 6,066.1 | 5,857.0 | 5,595.6 | 5,577.2 | .... | .... | .... |
| Imports, c.i.f. | 71 | 9,302.1 | 8,967.3 | 10,157.3 | 12,244.8 | 16,563.8 | 16,523.7 | 16,106.7 | 10,630.6 | 13,127.3 | .... | .... | .... |

# Lesotho 666

| | | 2004 | 2005 | 2006 | 2007 | 2008 | 2009 | 2010 | 2011 | 2012 | 2013 | 2014 | 2015 |
|---|---|---|---|---|---|---|---|---|---|---|---|---|---|
| **Balance of Payments** | | | | | | | *Millions of US Dollars* | | | | | | |
| A. Current Account* | 109bx | 100.7 | 165.7 | 283.2 | 373.2 | 344.7 | 55.2 | −158.3 | −294.5 | −380.6 | −164.7 | −230.5 | −197.3 |
| Goods, credit (exports) | 1a9cx | 664.4 | 634.3 | 718.2 | 829.7 | 884.0 | 734.1 | 877.7 | 1,174.8 | 972.4 | 847.1 | 826.4 | 844.1 |
| Goods, debit (imports) | 1a9dx | 1,234.2 | 1,289.4 | 1,359.1 | 1,506.2 | 1,531.7 | 1,583.3 | 1,968.7 | 2,155.4 | 2,254.1 | 1,884.2 | 1,857.8 | 1,737.0 |
| Balance on goods | 1a9bx | −569.7 | −655.1 | −640.9 | −676.5 | −647.6 | −849.2 | −1,091.0 | −980.6 | −1,281.8 | −1,037.2 | −1,031.3 | −892.9 |
| Services, credit (exports) | 1b9cx | 34.4 | 33.8 | 38.8 | 42.6 | 48.3 | 41.5 | 46.1 | 46.0 | 41.4 | 32.8 | 29.9 | 25.6 |
| Services, debit (imports) | 1b9dx | 373.9 | 367.6 | 377.8 | 375.7 | 403.9 | 430.3 | 446.9 | 487.8 | 454.6 | 372.6 | 333.5 | 315.4 |
| Balance on Goods & Services | 1z9bx | −909.2 | −989.0 | −979.8 | −1,009.6 | −1,003.2 | −1,238.0 | −1,491.8 | −1,422.4 | −1,695.0 | −1,376.9 | −1,335.0 | −1,182.7 |
| Primary income: credit | 1c9cx | 758.7 | 723.1 | 744.8 | 795.5 | 748.5 | 698.0 | 743.9 | 642.9 | 618.2 | 540.2 | 459.8 | 449.7 |
| Primary income: debit | 1c9dx | 189.7 | 45.1 | 59.3 | 106.9 | 99.2 | 124.8 | 83.9 | 195.7 | 183.1 | 164.1 | 155.2 | 139.5 |
| Balance on gds, serv. & prim. inc. | 1y9bx | −340.1 | −311.0 | −294.4 | −321.0 | −353.9 | −664.8 | −831.8 | −975.2 | −1,259.8 | −1,000.8 | −1,030.4 | −872.5 |
| Secondary income: credit | 1d9ca | 465.1 | 497.2 | 598.7 | 719.6 | 723.5 | 747.9 | 701.0 | 710.6 | 908.9 | 867.9 | 828.2 | 700.8 |
| Secondary income: debit | 1d9da | 24.2 | 20.5 | 21.1 | 25.5 | 24.8 | 27.9 | 27.6 | 29.9 | 29.7 | 31.8 | 28.3 | 25.6 |
| B. Capital Account* | 209ba | 33.4 | 21.3 | 11.0 | 32.0 | 23.6 | 79.6 | 155.7 | 214.8 | 223.5 | 132.7 | 61.2 | 65.2 |
| Capital account: credit | 209ca | 33.4 | 21.3 | 11.0 | 32.0 | 23.6 | 79.6 | 155.7 | 214.8 | 223.5 | 132.7 | 61.2 | 65.2 |
| Capital account: debit | 209da | — | — | — | — | — | — | — | — | — | — | — | — |
| Balance on current & capital acct. | 129ba | 134.1 | 187.1 | 294.2 | 405.3 | 368.3 | 134.7 | −2.6 | −79.7 | −157.1 | −32.0 | −169.2 | −132.1 |
| C. Financial Account* | 309na | 164.9 | 116.3 | 285.2 | 113.6 | 145.0 | −94.7 | 178.7 | −97.7 | −252.9 | −130.0 | −280.5 | −226.6 |
| Direct investment: assets | 3a9aa | .9 | — | — | — | — | — | — | — | — | — | — | — |
| Equity & investment fund shares | 3aaaa | .8 | — | — | — | — | — | — | — | — | — | — | — |
| Debt instruments | 3abaa | .1 | — | — | — | — | — | — | — | — | — | — | — |
| Direct investment: liabilities | 3a9la | 55.7 | 27.4 | 24.3 | 75.6 | 11.0 | 91.4 | 30.4 | 61.2 | 56.6 | 50.4 | 94.5 | 113.3 |
| Equity & investment fund shares | 3aala | 55.7 | 29.0 | 25.3 | 76.1 | 62.4 | 85.6 | 46.6 | −60.2 | −55.7 | −49.6 | 2.2 | 31.8 |
| Debt instruments | 3abla | — | −1.5 | −1.0 | −.5 | −51.4 | 5.7 | −16.2 | 121.4 | 112.4 | 100.0 | 92.3 | 81.5 |
| Portfolio investment: assets | 3b9aa | 2.1 | 21.5 | 1.9 | 3.6 | — | .1 | 2.1 | — | — | — | — | — |
| Equity & investment fund shares | 3baaa | 1.6 | 2.0 | −.2 | −.2 | — | — | — | — | — | — | — | — |
| Debt securities | 3bbaa | .6 | 19.4 | 2.1 | 3.8 | — | .1 | 2.1 | — | — | — | — | — |
| Portfolio investment: liabilities | 3b9la | .8 | 6.9 | 2.8 | 7.5 | −1.0 | −2.1 | — | −3.3 | −3.1 | −2.7 | −2.5 | −2.2 |
| Equity & investment fund shares | 3bala | .7 | — | 1.3 | — | — | — | — | .4 | .4 | .3 | .3 | .3 |
| Debt securities | 3bbla | .1 | 6.9 | 1.5 | 7.5 | −1.0 | −2.1 | — | −3.7 | −3.5 | −3.1 | −2.8 | −2.5 |
| Fin. der.& empl.stk.ops.(ESOs): net. | 3c9na | .... | .... | .... | .... | −.2 | .7 | — | .... | .... | .... | .... | .... |
| Fin. der. & ESOs.: assets | 3c9aa | .... | .... | .... | .... | .... | .... | .... | .... | .... | .... | .... | .... |
| Fin. der. & ESOs.: liabilities | 3c9la | .... | .... | .... | .... | .... | .... | .... | .... | .... | .... | .... | .... |
| Other investment: assets | 3d9aa | 218.2 | 148.3 | 261.0 | 227.6 | 198.9 | 102.0 | 172.3 | 21.7 | −82.8 | 70.9 | −114.9 | −14.0 |
| Other equity | 3daaa | .... | .... | .... | .... | .... | .... | .... | .... | .... | .... | .... | .... |
| Debt instruments | 3dzaa | 218.2 | 148.3 | 261.0 | 227.6 | 198.9 | 102.0 | 172.3 | 21.7 | −82.8 | 70.9 | −114.9 | −14.0 |
| Other investment: liabilities | 3d9la | −.1 | 19.1 | −49.5 | 34.5 | 43.6 | 108.3 | −34.8 | 61.5 | 116.6 | 153.2 | 73.7 | 101.5 |
| Other equity | 3dala | .... | .... | .... | .... | .... | .... | .... | .... | .... | .... | .... | .... |
| Debt instruments | 3dzla | −.1 | 19.1 | −49.5 | 34.5 | 43.6 | 108.3 | −34.8 | 61.5 | 116.6 | 153.2 | 73.7 | 101.5 |
| Curr.+ cap.− finan. acct. balance | 4y9na | −30.8 | 70.7 | 9.0 | 291.6 | 223.3 | 229.5 | −181.3 | 17.9 | 95.8 | 98.0 | 111.2 | 94.5 |
| D. Net Errors and Omissions | 409na | 34.5 | −27.1 | 181.8 | −21.7 | 50.1 | −257.0 | −28.0 | 47.8 | 13.4 | 113.6 | 13.3 | 18.9 |
| E. Reserves and Related Items | 4z9na | 3.8 | 43.7 | 190.8 | 269.9 | 273.4 | −27.5 | −209.4 | 65.7 | 109.3 | 211.6 | 124.5 | 113.3 |
| Reserve assets | 3e9aa | 13.6 | 43.7 | 190.3 | 267.2 | 268.4 | −33.5 | −205.4 | 67.6 | 144.2 | 226.1 | 122.9 | 112.2 |
| Credit and loans from the IMF | 3dcla | 9.8 | — | −.5 | −2.7 | −5.0 | −5.9 | 4.0 | 1.9 | 34.9 | 14.5 | −1.6 | −1.1 |
| Exceptional financing | 409la | — | .... | .... | .... | .... | .... | .... | .... | .... | .... | | |

*Excludes components in group E

| **International Investment Position** | | | | | | | | *Millions of US Dollars* | | | | | |
|---|---|---|---|---|---|---|---|---|---|---|---|---|---|
| Assets | 809aa | 818.0 | 769.4 | 970.4 | 1,336.6 | 1,295.4 | 1,626.6 | 1,666.5 | 1,348.6 | 1,317.5 | 1,391.0 | .... | .... |
| Direct investment | 8a9aa | .... | .... | .... | .... | .... | .... | .... | .... | .... | .... | .... | .... |
| Equity & investment fund shares | 8aaaa | .... | .... | .... | .... | .... | .... | .... | .... | .... | .... | .... | .... |
| Debt instruments | 8abaa | .... | .... | .... | .... | .... | .... | .... | .... | .... | .... | .... | .... |
| Portfolio investment | 8b9aa | .... | .... | .... | .... | .... | .... | .... | .... | .... | .... | .... | .... |
| Equity & investment fund shares | 8baaa | .... | .... | .... | .... | .... | .... | .... | .... | .... | .... | .... | .... |
| Debt securities | 8bbaa | .... | .... | .... | .... | .... | .... | .... | .... | .... | .... | .... | .... |
| Fin. der.(oth.than reserves) & ESOs | 8c9aa | .... | .... | .... | .... | .... | .... | .... | .... | .... | .... | .... | .... |
| Other investment | 8d9aa | 222.7 | 196.3 | 264.8 | 333.9 | 323.9 | 446.8 | 590.7 | 398.1 | 302.3 | 345.8 | .... | .... |
| Other equity | 8daaa | .... | .... | .... | .... | .... | .... | .... | .... | .... | .... | .... | .... |
| Debt instruments | 8dzaa | 222.7 | 196.3 | 264.8 | 333.9 | 323.9 | 446.8 | 590.7 | 398.1 | 302.3 | 345.8 | .... | .... |
| Reserve assets | 8e9aa | 595.3 | 573.1 | 705.6 | 1,002.8 | 971.5 | 1,179.8 | 1,075.8 | 950.4 | 1,015.3 | 1,045.2 | .... | .... |
| Liabilities | 809la | 886.8 | 778.4 | 777.8 | 828.8 | 818.6 | 906.9 | 935.3 | 863.0 | 1,043.7 | 1,047.3 | .... | .... |
| Direct investment | 8a9la | .... | .... | .... | .... | .... | .... | .... | .... | .... | .... | .... | .... |
| Equity & investment fund shares | 8aala | .... | .... | .... | .... | .... | .... | .... | .... | .... | .... | .... | .... |
| Debt instruments | 8abla | .... | .... | .... | .... | .... | .... | .... | .... | .... | .... | .... | .... |
| Portfolio investment | 8b9la | .... | .... | .... | .... | .... | .... | .... | .... | .... | .... | .... | .... |
| Equity & investment fund shares | 8bala | .... | .... | .... | .... | .... | .... | .... | .... | .... | .... | .... | .... |
| Debt securities | 8bbla | .... | .... | .... | .... | .... | .... | .... | .... | .... | .... | .... | .... |
| Fin. der.(oth.than reserves) & ESOs | 8c9la | .... | .... | .... | .... | .... | .... | .... | .... | .... | .... | .... | .... |
| Other investment | 8d9la | 886.8 | 778.4 | 777.8 | 828.8 | 818.6 | 906.9 | 935.3 | 863.0 | 1,043.7 | 1,047.3 | .... | .... |
| Other equity | 8dala | .... | .... | .... | .... | .... | .... | .... | .... | .... | .... | .... | .... |
| Debt instruments | 8dzla | 886.8 | 778.4 | 777.8 | 828.8 | 818.6 | 906.9 | 935.3 | 863.0 | 1,043.7 | 1,047.3 | .... | .... |

# Lesotho   666

| | | 2004 | 2005 | 2006 | 2007 | 2008 | 2009 | 2010 | 2011 | 2012 | 2013 | 2014 | 2015 |
|---|---|---|---|---|---|---|---|---|---|---|---|---|---|
| **Government Finance** | | | | | | | | | | | | | |
| **Cash Flow Statement** | | | | | | | | | | | | | |
| **Budgetary Central Government** | | *Millions of Maloti: Fiscal Year Begins April 1* | | | | | | | | | | | |
| Cash Receipts:Operating Activities... | c1 | 4,442.4 | 4,662.4 | 6,479.5 | 7,176.0 | 8,878.6 | 10,667.2 | 8,725.9 | 9,337.3 | 13,159.7 | 13,385.6 | .... | .... |
| Taxes............................... | c11 | 3,693.2 | 3,998.7 | 5,852.3 | 6,330.7 | 7,906.5 | 9,235.2 | 6,493.5 | 7,035.5 | 10,759.5 | 11,855.5 | .... | .... |
| Social Contributions..................... | c12 | — | — | — | — | — | — | — | — | — | — | .... | .... |
| Grants................................... | c13 | 238.4 | 171.4 | 92.4 | 178.4 | 122.0 | 635.4 | 828.0 | 1,146.9 | 1,507.1 | 455.0 | .... | .... |
| Other Receipts........................ | c14 | 510.8 | 492.3 | 534.8 | 666.9 | 850.1 | 796.5 | 1,404.4 | 1,154.9 | 893.2 | 1,075.1 | .... | .... |
| Cash Payments:Operating Activities. | c2 | 3,315.6 | 3,601.1 | 4,598.5 | 4,956.3 | 7,074.2 | 8,338.4 | 7,460.9 | 8,698.6 | 9,104.4 | 9,810.1 | .... | .... |
| Compensation of Employees.......... | c21 | 1,178.6 | 1,283.4 | 1,574.0 | 1,792.2 | 2,428.5 | 3,144.3 | 3,193.6 | 3,637.6 | 3,769.5 | 4,307.4 | .... | .... |
| Purchases of Goods & Services....... | c22 | 991.0 | 965.7 | 1,654.9 | 1,539.8 | 2,893.4 | 2,559.2 | 1,928.8 | 2,199.0 | 2,783.5 | 2,728.6 | .... | .... |
| Interest............................... | c24 | 157.1 | 225.1 | 308.1 | 292.5 | 118.4 | 137.0 | 96.0 | 137.1 | 165.9 | 231.5 | .... | .... |
| Subsidies................................. | c25 | 409.6 | 690.1 | — | 3.4 | 204.0 | 273.6 | 218.3 | 210.4 | 229.8 | 235.0 | .... | .... |
| Grants................................... | c26 | 133.4 | 140.7 | 606.2 | 701.0 | 757.3 | 997.1 | 704.8 | 958.4 | 873.7 | 828.0 | .... | .... |
| Social Benefits........................... | c27 | 446.0 | 296.1 | 170.9 | 188.5 | 226.9 | 555.7 | 609.5 | 613.3 | 630.0 | 742.4 | .... | .... |
| Other Payments......................... | c28 | — | — | 284.4 | 438.9 | 445.7 | 671.6 | 709.8 | 942.8 | 652.1 | 737.3 | .... | .... |
| Net Cash Inflow:Operating Act.[1-2] | ccio | 1,126.8 | 1,061.4 | 1,881.0 | 2,219.8 | 1,804.4 | 2,328.7 | 1,265.0 | 638.7 | 4,055.3 | 3,575.5 | .... | .... |
| Net Cash Outflow:Invest. in NFA...... | c31 | 457.4 | 698.6 | 573.6 | 1,204.1 | 1,251.9 | 1,728.4 | 1,933.5 | 2,831.9 | 3,395.1 | 2,709.2 | .... | .... |
| Purchases of Nonfinancial Assets... | c31.1 | 457.4 | 698.6 | 573.6 | 1,204.1 | 1,253.1 | .... | .... | .... | .... | .... | .... | .... |
| Sales of Nonfinancial Assets.......... | c31.2 | — | — | — | — | 1.2 | .... | .... | .... | .... | .... | .... | .... |
| Cash Surplus/Deficit [1-2-31=1-2M] | ccsd | 669.4 | 362.7 | 1,307.4 | 1,015.7 | 552.5 | 600.3 | −668.5 | −2,193.2 | 660.2 | 866.3 | .... | .... |
| Net Acq. Fin. Assets, excl. Cash....... | c32x | −89.3 | 6.4 | −9.4 | — | — | — | — | — | — | — | .... | .... |
| Domestic............................... | c321x | −89.3 | 6.4 | −9.4 | — | — | — | — | — | — | — | .... | .... |
| Foreign................................... | c322x | — | — | — | — | — | — | — | — | — | — | .... | .... |
| Net Incurrence of Liabilities............. | c33 | −38.3 | −276.6 | 64.1 | 17.1 | 151.4 | −341.4 | −30.2 | 530.0 | 1,062.6 | 1,538.0 | .... | .... |
| Domestic............................... | c331 | — | — | 126.1 | 39.0 | −53.7 | −360.9 | −198.1 | 364.3 | 247.0 | 13.7 | .... | .... |
| Foreign................................... | c332 | −38.3 | −276.6 | −62.0 | −21.9 | 205.1 | 19.5 | 167.9 | 165.7 | 815.6 | 1,524.3 | .... | .... |
| Net Cash Inflow, Fin.Act.[-32x+33].. | cnfb | 51.0 | −283.0 | 73.5 | 17.1 | 151.4 | −341.4 | −30.2 | 530.0 | 1,062.6 | 1,539.0 | .... | .... |
| Net Change in Stock of Cash........... | cncb | 720.4 | 79.7 | 1,377.2 | 998.5 | 703.8 | 258.9 | −698.7 | −1,663.3 | 1,722.7 | 2,404.3 | .... | .... |
| Stat. Discrep. [32X-33+NCB-CSD].... | ccsdz | — | — | −3.7 | −34.3 | −.1 | | | | | | .... | .... |
| Memo Item:Cash Expenditure[2+31] | c2m | 3,773.0 | 4,299.7 | 5,172.1 | 6,160.4 | 8,326.1 | 10,066.9 | 9,394.4 | 11,530.5 | 12,499.6 | 12,519.3 | .... | .... |
| Memo Item: Gross Debt.................. | c63 | .... | .... | .... | .... | 6,884.1 | .... | .... | .... | .... | .... | .... | .... |
| **National Accounts** | | *Millions of Maloti* | | | | | | | | | | | |
| Househ.Cons.Expend.,incl.NPISHs.... | 96f | 8,858.7 | 9,543.2 | 10,445.1 | 11,862.7 | 13,808.4 | 14,884.1 | 16,409.3 | 18,173.6 | 19,389.7 | 20,287.7 | .... | .... |
| Government Consumption Expend... | 91f | 2,839.8 | 3,193.4 | 3,425.6 | 4,017.1 | 4,958.8 | 5,740.2 | 6,069.8 | 6,420.3 | 7,361.4 | 7,525.6 | .... | .... |
| Gross Fixed Capital Formation......... | 93e | 2,108.4 | 1,837.6 | 2,083.4 | 2,471.4 | 3,756.0 | 3,697.4 | 4,413.2 | 4,630.4 | 5,936.7 | 7,537.7 | .... | .... |
| Changes in Inventories................... | 93i | 13.3 | 74.9 | −84.9 | 253.4 | −35.6 | −.8 | 243.5 | −526.4 | −609.5 | −445.5 | .... | .... |
| Exports of Goods and Services......... | 90c | 4,493.5 | 4,253.0 | 5,181.2 | 5,863.7 | 7,546.8 | 6,632.2 | 7,106.6 | 8,864.0 | 8,596.9 | 8,656.9 | .... | .... |
| Imports of Goods and Services (-)..... | 98c | 10,347.2 | 10,518.2 | 11,523.5 | 13,281.0 | 16,237.0 | 16,347.8 | 17,838.0 | 18,959.9 | 20,192.5 | 21,677.4 | .... | .... |
| Gross Domestic Product (GDP)........ | 99b | 7,972.7 | 8,701.8 | 9,675.5 | 11,254.9 | 13,471.3 | 14,502.5 | 16,014.5 | 18,322.3 | 19,572.8 | 21,416.0 | 23,673.0 | .... |
| Net Primary Income from Abroad..... | 98.n | 3,702.0 | 3,147.9 | 2,992.0 | 2,980.2 | 3,301.2 | 3,383.9 | 3,062.8 | 4,624.0 | 4,378.4 | 3,628.8 | .... | .... |
| Gross National Income (GNI)............ | 99a | 11,674.7 | 11,849.7 | 12,667.5 | 14,235.1 | 16,772.5 | 17,886.4 | 19,077.4 | 22,946.4 | 23,951.3 | 24,364.8 | .... | .... |
| Net Current Trans.from Abroad...... | 98t | 2,888.8 | 3,180.3 | 4,549.7 | 5,100.8 | 5,743.9 | 6,150.7 | 4,916.7 | 4,475.0 | 7,176.1 | 7,821.5 | .... | .... |
| Gross Nat'l Disposable Inc.(GNDI).... | 99i | 14,563.5 | 15,030.0 | 17,217.2 | 19,335.8 | 22,516.4 | 24,037.1 | 23,994.1 | 27,421.4 | 31,127.4 | 32,186.3 | .... | .... |
| Net National Income...................... | 99e | 12,262.4 | 13,181.7 | 14,297.8 | .... | .... | .... | .... | .... | .... | .... | .... | .... |
| GDP Volume 1995 Prices................ | 99b.p | 4,405.3 | 4,531.1 | 4,856.1 | | | | | | | | | |
| GDP Volume 2004 Prices................ | 99b.p | 7,972.7 | 8,188.2 | 8,540.9 | 8,945.1 | 9,458.0 | 9,778.1 | 10,547.3 | 10,974.0 | 11,522.2 | 12,036.0 | 12,474.0 | .... |
| GDP Volume (2005=100)................ | 99bvp | 97.4 | 100.0 | 104.3 | 109.2 | 115.5 | 119.4 | 128.8 | 134.0 | 140.7 | 147.0 | 152.3 | .... |
| GDP Deflator (2005=100)............... | 99bip | 94.1 | 100.0 | 106.6 | 118.4 | 134.0 | 139.6 | 142.9 | 157.1 | 159.8 | 167.4 | 178.6 | .... |
| | | *Millions: Midyear Estimates* | | | | | | | | | | | |
| **Population.............................** | 99z | 1.91 | 1.93 | 1.94 | 1.96 | 1.97 | 1.99 | 2.01 | 2.03 | 2.06 | 2.08 | 2.11 | 2.14 |

# Liberia   668

| | | 2004 | 2005 | 2006 | 2007 | 2008 | 2009 | 2010 | 2011 | 2012 | 2013 | 2014 | 2015 |
|---|---|---|---|---|---|---|---|---|---|---|---|---|---|
| **Exchange Rates** | | | | | | *Liberian Dollars per SDR: End of Period* | | | | | | | |
| Market Rate.............................. | aa | 84.639 | 80.754 | 89.512 | 98.766 | 98.577 | 110.522 | 110.112 | 111.307 | 111.427 | 127.050 | 119.527 | . . . . |
| | | | | | | *Liberian Dollars per US Dollar: End of Period (ae) Period Average (rf)* | | | | | | | |
| Market Rate.............................. | ae | 54.500 | 56.500 | 59.500 | 62.500 | 64.000 | 70.500 | 71.500 | 72.500 | 72.500 | 82.500 | 82.500 | . . . . |
| Market Rate.............................. | rf | 54.906 | 57.096 | 58.013 | 61.272 | 63.208 | 68.287 | 71.403 | 72.227 | 73.515 | 77.520 | 83.893 | . . . . |
| **Fund Position** | | | | | | *Millions of SDRs: End of Period* | | | | | | | |
| Quota...................................... | 2f.s | 71.30 | 71.30 | 71.30 | 71.30 | 129.20 | 129.20 | 129.20 | 129.20 | 129.20 | 129.20 | 129.20 | 129.20 |
| SDR Holdings............................ | 1b.s | — | — | — | — | 14.18 | 128.49 | 136.68 | 145.62 | 157.46 | 173.20 | 178.53 | 185.94 |
| Reserve Position in the Fund.......... | 1c.s | .03 | .03 | .03 | .03 | .03 | .03 | .03 | .03 | .03 | .03 | .03 | .03 |
| Total Fund Cred.&Loans Outstg........ | 2tl | 223.67 | 223.63 | 223.14 | 222.67 | 557.03 | 568.47 | 28.82 | 37.70 | 49.52 | 64.28 | 101.87 | 115.71 |
| SDR Allocations......................... | 1bd | 21.01 | 21.01 | 21.01 | 21.01 | 21.01 | 123.98 | 123.98 | 123.98 | 123.98 | 123.98 | 123.98 | 123.98 |
| **International Liquidity** | | | | | | *Millions of US Dollars: End of Period* | | | | | | | |
| Total Reserves minus Gold.............. | 1l.d | 18.74 | 25.40 | 71.99 | 119.36 | 160.86 | 372.46 | 465.90 | 512.83 | 497.22 | 493.10 | 499.01 | . . . . |
| SDR Holdings.......................... | 1b.d | — | — | — | — | 21.84 | 201.43 | 210.49 | 223.56 | 242.01 | 266.73 | 258.66 | 257.66 |
| Reserve Position in the Fund......... | 1c.d | .05 | .04 | .05 | .05 | .05 | .05 | .05 | .05 | .05 | .05 | .04 | .04 |
| Foreign Exchange...................... | 1d.d | 18.69 | 25.35 | 71.94 | 119.31 | 138.97 | 170.97 | 255.36 | 289.22 | 255.16 | 226.32 | 240.30 | . . . . |
| Monetary Authorities: Other Liabs.... | 4..d | 7.09 | 7.40 | 8.14 | 7.53 | 7.62 | 7.24 | 12.04 | 11.91 | 11.69 | 11.47 | 11.47 | 11.47 |
| Banking Institutions: Assets............ | 7a.d | 35.73 | 47.38 | 52.48 | 64.31 | 99.78 | 96.45 | 153.25 | 147.91 | 161.01 | 146.72 | 202.31 | 137.29 |
| Banking Institutions: Liabs.............. | 7b.d | 22.54 | 25.56 | 22.20 | 13.26 | 9.55 | 11.63 | 14.12 | 14.33 | 33.07 | 21.28 | 29.54 | 28.20 |
| **Monetary Authorities** | | | | | | *Millions of Liberian Dollars: End of Period* | | | | | | | |
| Foreign Assets.......................... | 11 | 1,021.7 | 1,434.8 | 4,283.4 | 7,459.9 | 10,295.0 | 26,258.2 | 33,311.8 | 37,180.2 | 36,066.7 | 40,701.3 | 41,993.9 | 47,068.6 |
| Claims on Central Government........ | 12a | 56,911.6 | 56,360.4 | 62,992.3 | 70,062.8 | 71,994.2 | 81,299.5 | 21,893.4 | 23,172.8 | 25,267.6 | 29,943.7 | 33,622.2 | 37,129.3 |
| Claims on Nonfin.Pub.Enterprises..... | 12c | .5 | .6 | .6 | | | | | | | | — | — |
| Claims on Private Sector................. | 12d | 100.0 | 119.8 | 220.5 | 133.0 | 113.0 | 123.5 | 350.7 | 421.6 | 137.5 | 174.9 | 263.1 | 346.0 |
| Claims on Banking Institutions......... | 12e | 81.1 | 77.8 | 46.5 | 56.6 | 78.5 | 242.3 | 615.6 | 930.6 | 1,947.1 | 2,320.8 | 2,371.9 | 2,494.6 |
| Claims on Nonbank Financial Insts... | 12g | — | | | | | | | | | | | |
| Reserve Money........................... | 14 | 2,910.3 | 3,698.1 | 4,842.4 | 6,568.8 | 8,681.9 | 10,581.2 | 14,267.5 | 22,333.6 | 23,006.8 | 22,669.8 | 23,655.8 | 23,125.4 |
| of which: Currency Outside Banks.. | 14a | 1,754.9 | 2,168.9 | 2,647.6 | 3,317.4 | 3,637.1 | 4,161.8 | 5,007.9 | 6,704.3 | 7,291.3 | 8,271.7 | 8,359.0 | 9,656.2 |
| Other Liabs. to Banking Insts........... | 14n | 767.0 | 796.3 | 846.3 | 846.4 | 872.4 | 1,053.9 | 1,071.5 | 1,194.7 | 1,054.5 | 1,228.3 | 130.7 | 135.7 |
| Time Deposits............................ | 15 | 70.2 | 15.7 | 19.4 | — | — | — | — | — | — | — | | |
| Restricted Deposits..................... | 16b | 18.8 | 18.8 | 18.8 | 18.8 | 18.8 | 18.8 | 18.8 | 18.8 | 18.8 | 18.8 | — | — |
| Foreign Liabilities....................... | 16c | 45,244.2 | 43,838.2 | 49,604.0 | 55,903.3 | 57,469.1 | 77,041.3 | 17,685.5 | 18,859.1 | 20,179.7 | 24,865.1 | 27,940.7 | 30,409.4 |
| Central Government Deposits.......... | 16d | 63.2 | 86.2 | 1,773.9 | 2,975.1 | 2,243.9 | 3,239.3 | 6,519.8 | 3,100.9 | 3,422.0 | 5,497.1 | 8,553.0 | 15,263.9 |
| Capital Accounts........................ | 17a | 10,398.6 | 10,687.0 | 11,204.0 | 13,638.8 | 14,131.2 | 11,189.5 | 10,965.7 | 10,397.6 | 9,713.5 | 10,729.4 | 10,097.9 | 10,127.6 |
| Other Items (Net)........................ | 17r | −1,338.6 | −1,128.0 | −746.7 | −2,220.0 | −917.6 | 4,818.3 | 5,661.6 | 5,819.4 | 6,042.4 | 8,151.3 | 7,872.9 | 7,976.4 |
| **Banking Institutions** | | | | | | *Millions of Liberian Dollars: End of Period* | | | | | | | |
| Reserves.................................. | 20 | 1,531.5 | 1,763.7 | 2,398.4 | 2,852.9 | 3,922.0 | 5,791.6 | 8,209.6 | 12,780.4 | 14,568.2 | 15,075.7 | 11,817.4 | 12,298.2 |
| Other Claims on Monetary Author.... | 20n | 715.6 | 741.9 | 781.3 | 787.1 | 803.3 | 883.7 | 895.6 | 906.0 | 907.0 | 956.4 | 1,068.9 | 11.0 |
| Foreign Assets.......................... | 21 | 1,947.2 | 2,676.8 | 3,122.4 | 4,019.7 | 6,385.6 | 6,799.4 | 10,957.1 | 10,723.2 | 11,673.0 | 12,104.6 | 16,691.0 | 12,150.5 |
| Claims on Central Government........ | 22a | 738.7 | 787.6 | 822.9 | 735.4 | 593.3 | 677.7 | 461.2 | 424.2 | 433.5 | 1,800.2 | 3,153.6 | 3,809.8 |
| Claims on Nonfin.Pub.Enterprises..... | 22c | 105.8 | 82.8 | 146.0 | 131.8 | 64.4 | 1,264.2 | 500.5 | 719.2 | 1,614.4 | 1,862.6 | 1,874.7 | 2,908.1 |
| Claims on Private Sector................. | 22d | 1,550.9 | 1,944.4 | 2,859.2 | 4,370.0 | 6,533.1 | 9,501.1 | 13,325.7 | 17,934.2 | 20,277.4 | 29,373.1 | 30,939.4 | 35,837.0 |
| Claims on Nonbank Financial Insts... | 22g | 186.7 | 109.7 | 89.9 | 81.3 | .5 | .1 | 94.7 | 100.4 | 158.2 | 114.6 | 126.1 | 199.5 |
| Demand Deposits....................... | 24 | 1,971.9 | 2,701.9 | 3,973.2 | 5,541.7 | 9,110.8 | 14,189.1 | 18,596.7 | 25,274.9 | 23,633.3 | 31,533.2 | 29,521.5 | 32,572.3 |
| Time and Savings Deposits.............. | 25 | 960.3 | 1,491.0 | 1,928.0 | 3,118.0 | 4,183.2 | 5,884.4 | 7,572.7 | 11,355.8 | 13,273.2 | 16,252.3 | 17,011.4 | 19,496.3 |
| Restricted Deposits..................... | 26b | 432.6 | 445.8 | 465.6 | 29.2 | 28.6 | 28.6 | 34.4 | 35.3 | 24.9 | 25.2 | — | — |
| Foreign Liabilities....................... | 26c | 1,228.3 | 1,444.2 | 1,321.1 | 828.6 | 611.4 | 820.1 | 1,009.2 | 1,039.0 | 2,397.6 | 1,755.4 | 2,437.3 | 2,495.6 |
| Central Government Deposits.......... | 26d | 161.9 | 166.0 | 257.6 | 215.9 | 101.6 | 186.6 | 648.2 | 1,016.7 | 1,233.3 | 771.0 | 665.5 | 832.5 |
| Credit from Monetary Authorities..... | 26g | 29.9 | 67.0 | 11.6 | 3.2 | — | — | 53.6 | 108.8 | 982.4 | 2,853.3 | 1,892.2 | 3,066.2 |
| Capital Accounts........................ | 27a | 885.4 | 1,283.7 | 1,585.6 | 2,697.4 | 3,408.9 | 857.8 | 7,434.7 | 8,464.5 | 9,613.7 | 10,258.5 | 10,740.4 | 9,823.7 |
| Other Items (Net)........................ | 27r | 1,106.1 | 507.4 | 677.4 | 544.3 | 857.8 | −2,289.9 | −905.2 | −3,707.5 | −1,526.8 | −2,161.5 | 3,390.3 | −1,089.3 |
| **Banking Survey** | | | | | | *Millions of Liberian Dollars: End of Period* | | | | | | | |
| Foreign Assets (Net)...................... | 31n | −43,503.6 | −41,170.8 | −43,519.3 | −45,252.3 | −41,399.8 | −44,803.7 | 25,574.1 | 28,005.3 | 25,162.3 | 26,185.4 | 28,306.8 | 26,314.1 |
| Domestic Credit.......................... | 32 | 59,369.1 | 59,153.1 | 65,099.9 | 72,323.4 | 76,953.0 | 89,441.3 | 29,458.1 | 38,654.7 | 43,233.4 | 57,001.1 | 60,760.4 | 64,133.2 |
| Claims on Central Govt. (Net)........ | 32an | 57,425.2 | 56,895.8 | 61,783.6 | 67,607.2 | 70,242.0 | 78,551.3 | 15,186.6 | 19,479.4 | 21,045.8 | 25,475.9 | 27,557.2 | 24,842.6 |
| Claims on Nonfin.Pub.Enterprises.. | 32c | 106.3 | 83.3 | 146.6 | 131.8 | 64.4 | 1,264.2 | 500.5 | 719.2 | 1,614.4 | 1,862.6 | 1,874.7 | 2,908.1 |
| Claims on Private Sector.............. | 32d | 1,650.9 | 2,064.2 | 3,079.7 | 4,503.0 | 6,646.1 | 9,625.7 | 13,676.3 | 18,355.8 | 20,414.9 | 29,548.0 | 31,202.4 | 36,183.0 |
| Claims on Nonbank Financial Insts. | 32g | 186.7 | 109.7 | 89.9 | 81.3 | .5 | .1 | 94.7 | 100.4 | 158.2 | 114.6 | 126.1 | 199.5 |
| Money..................................... | 34 | 3,727.5 | 4,871.6 | 6,635.4 | 9,099.9 | 13,243.7 | 19,113.7 | 24,562.1 | 33,205.5 | 31,261.3 | 39,972.2 | 40,401.8 | 43,100.1 |
| Quasi-Money.............................. | 35 | 1,030.4 | 1,506.8 | 1,947.4 | 3,118.0 | 4,183.2 | 5,884.4 | 7,572.7 | 11,355.8 | 13,273.2 | 16,252.3 | 17,011.4 | 19,496.3 |
| Restricted Deposits..................... | 36b | 451.4 | 464.6 | 484.3 | 48.0 | 47.4 | 47.4 | 53.2 | 54.1 | 43.7 | 44.0 | — | — |
| Capital Accounts......................... | 37a | 11,284.0 | 11,970.6 | 12,789.6 | 16,336.2 | 17,540.1 | 17,289.6 | 18,400.3 | 18,862.1 | 19,327.2 | 20,987.9 | 20,838.3 | 19,951.3 |
| Other Items (Net)........................ | 37r | −627.9 | −831.2 | −276.1 | −1,531.0 | 538.9 | 2,302.6 | 4,443.9 | 3,182.5 | 4,490.3 | 5,930.4 | 10,803.4 | 7,882.8 |
| Money plus Quasi-Money............... | 35l | 4,757.9 | 6,378.4 | 8,582.8 | 12,217.9 | 17,426.9 | 24,998.0 | 32,134.8 | 44,561.3 | 44,534.5 | 56,224.5 | 57,413.2 | 62,596.4 |
| **Money (National Definitions)** | | | | | | *Millions of Liberian Dollars: End of Period* | | | | | | | |
| M1......................................... | 59ma | 3,726.8 | 4,870.9 | 6,485.1 | 8,514.4 | 12,443.5 | 16,847.8 | 23,212.7 | 30,069.0 | 30,132.7 | 38,666.5 | 36,634.5 | 41,036.5 |
| M2......................................... | 59mb | 4,687.1 | 6,361.9 | 8,455.7 | 11,673.7 | 16,717.9 | 22,855.4 | 31,103.9 | 43,398.2 | 44,742.4 | 54,956.4 | 53,696.9 | 60,627.3 |
| **Interest Rates** | | | | | | *Percent Per Annum* | | | | | | | |
| Savings Rate.............................. | 60k | 4.60 | 3.69 | 3.00 | 2.32 | 2.12 | 2.03 | 2.07 | 2.03 | 2.02 | 2.01 | 2.00 | 2.00 |
| Deposit Rate.............................. | 60l | 3.84 | 3.43 | 3.44 | 3.77 | 4.00 | 4.11 | 3.54 | 3.03 | 3.50 | 3.87 | 4.16 | 4.05 |
| Lending Rate.............................. | 60p | 18.10 | 17.03 | 15.50 | 15.05 | 14.40 | 14.19 | 14.24 | 13.75 | 13.52 | 13.49 | 13.50 | 13.61 |
| **Prices** | | | | | | *Index Numbers (2010=100): Period Averages* | | | | | | | |
| Consumer Prices.......................... | 64 | 55.7 | 61.8 | † 66.3 | 73.8 | 86.8 | 93.2 | 100.0 | 108.5 | 115.9 | 124.7 | 136.9 | . . . . |

| | | 2004 | 2005 | 2006 | 2007 | 2008 | 2009 | 2010 | 2011 | 2012 | 2013 | 2014 | 2015 |
|---|---|---|---|---|---|---|---|---|---|---|---|---|---|
| **Balance of Payments** | | | | | | **Millions of US Dollars** | | | | | | | |
| A. Current Account*............... | 109bx | −172.5 | −207.5 | −368.9 | −395.1 | −618.2 | −541.1 | −736.9 | −953.0 | −479.9 | −535.8 | −1,217.4 | .... |
| Goods, credit (exports)............... | 1a9cx | 104.8 | 132.3 | 154.6 | 196.2 | 249.0 | 180.0 | 241.2 | 645.7 | 507.2 | 624.3 | 624.1 | .... |
| Goods, debit (imports)............... | 1a9dx | 278.9 | 306.4 | 441.1 | 498.5 | 728.8 | 559.0 | 719.1 | 2,068.4 | 1,011.0 | 1,019.6 | 2,167.4 | .... |
| Balance on goods............... | 1a9bx | −174.1 | −174.1 | −286.5 | −302.3 | −479.8 | −379.0 | −477.9 | −1,422.8 | −503.8 | −395.2 | −1,543.3 | .... |
| Services, credit (exports)......... | 1b9cx | 212.4 | 213.2 | 336.5 | 346.2 | 509.6 | 274.1 | 158.0 | 604.1 | 178.9 | 203.1 | 237.8 | .... |
| Services, debit (imports)......... | 1b9dx | 779.8 | 855.5 | 1,274.6 | 1,248.8 | 1,411.1 | 1,145.2 | 1,078.6 | 1,242.8 | 940.7 | 942.2 | 1,165.3 | .... |
| Balance on Goods & Services...... | 1z9bx | −741.5 | −816.4 | −1,224.6 | −1,204.9 | −1,381.4 | −1,250.1 | −1,398.5 | −2,061.5 | −1,265.7 | −1,134.3 | −2,470.8 | .... |
| Primary income: credit............... | 1c9cx | 5.0 | 9.2 | 18.3 | 19.9 | 22.4 | 18.1 | 31.2 | 102.1 | 23.5 | 22.5 | 31.6 | .... |
| Primary income: debit............... | 1c9dx | 167.6 | 155.8 | 166.7 | 176.9 | 170.7 | 145.9 | 7.0 | 14.1 | 365.4 | 400.3 | 209.2 | .... |
| Balance on gds, serv. & prim. inc. | 1y9bx | −904.1 | −963.0 | −1,372.9 | −1,361.9 | −1,529.7 | −1,377.9 | −1,374.2 | −1,973.5 | −1,607.5 | −1,512.1 | −2,648.4 | .... |
| Secondary income: credit............... | 1d9ca | 731.6 | 755.4 | 1,004.1 | 966.8 | 911.5 | 836.8 | 637.3 | 1,020.4 | 1,496.2 | 1,300.4 | 1,747.5 | .... |
| Secondary income: debit............... | 1d9da | — | — | — | — | — | — | — | — | 368.6 | 324.1 | 316.5 | .... |
| B. Capital Account*............... | 209ba | .... | .... | .... | .... | 1,197.0 | 1,526.0 | 1,594.3 | .... | 37.4 | 32.5 | 116.7 | .... |
| Capital account: credit............... | 209ca | .... | .... | .... | .... | 1,197.0 | 1,526.0 | 1,594.3 | .... | 37.4 | 32.5 | 116.7 | .... |
| Capital account: debit............... | 209da | .... | .... | .... | .... | .... | .... | .... | .... | .... | .... | .... | .... |
| Balance on current & capital acct. | 129ba | −172.5 | −207.5 | −368.9 | −395.1 | 578.8 | 984.9 | 857.4 | −953.0 | −442.5 | −503.3 | −1,100.7 | .... |
| C. Financial Account*............... | 309na | −52.2 | −61.1 | −86.6 | −113.5 | −347.9 | −576.7 | −446.9 | −683.9 | −796.3 | −794.3 | −450.6 | .... |
| Direct investment: assets............... | 3a9aa | — | — | — | — | −111.0 | −90.0 | — | — | .... | .... | −1.0 | .... |
| Equity & investment fund shares.. | 3aaaa | — | — | — | — | — | — | — | — | .... | .... | −1.0 | .... |
| Debt instruments............... | 3abaa | — | — | — | — | −111.0 | −90.0 | — | — | .... | .... | .... | .... |
| Direct investment: liabilities............ | 3a9la | 75.4 | 82.8 | 107.9 | 131.6 | 283.5 | 127.8 | 452.3 | 1,312.7 | 646.6 | 700.3 | 363.0 | .... |
| Equity & investment fund shares . | 3aala | 2.8 | 3.5 | 7.0 | 7.3 | 11.3 | 2.9 | — | 30.5 | 646.6 | 700.3 | 363.0 | .... |
| Debt instruments............... | 3abla | 72.5 | 79.3 | 100.8 | 124.3 | 272.3 | 124.9 | 452.3 | 1,282.3 | .... | .... | .... | .... |
| Portfolio investment: assets............... | 3b9aa | — | — | — | — | — | — | — | .... | .... | .... | .... | .... |
| Equity & investment fund shares | 3baaa | — | — | — | — | — | — | — | .... | .... | .... | .... | .... |
| Debt securities............... | 3bbaa | — | — | — | — | — | — | — | .... | .... | .... | .... | .... |
| Portfolio investment: liabilities....... | 3b9la | — | — | — | — | — | — | — | .... | .... | .... | .... | .... |
| Equity & investment fund shares . | 3bala | — | — | — | — | — | — | — | .... | .... | .... | .... | .... |
| Debt securities............... | 3bbla | — | — | — | — | — | — | — | .... | .... | .... | .... | .... |
| Fin. der.& empl.stk.ops.(ESOs): net. | 3c9na | — | — | — | — | — | — | — | — | .... | .... | .... | .... |
| Fin. der. & ESOs.: assets............... | 3c9aa | — | — | — | — | — | — | — | — | .... | .... | .... | .... |
| Fin. der. & ESOs.: liabilities............ | 3c9la | — | — | — | — | — | — | — | — | .... | .... | .... | .... |
| Other investment: assets............... | 3d9aa | 3.3 | 3.1 | 15.5 | 13.2 | 33.2 | −200.4 | −1.4 | 626.5 | −32.4 | 13.4 | −57.6 | .... |
| Other equity............... | 3daaa | .... | .... | .... | .... | .... | .... | .... | .... | .... | .... | .... | .... |
| Debt instruments............... | 3dzaa | 3.3 | 3.1 | 15.5 | 13.2 | 33.2 | −200.4 | −1.4 | 626.5 | −32.4 | 13.4 | −57.6 | .... |
| Other investment: liabilities............ | 3d9la | −19.9 | −18.7 | −5.7 | −4.9 | −13.4 | 158.5 | −6.8 | −2.3 | 117.3 | 107.4 | 29.1 | .... |
| Other equity............... | 3dala | .... | .... | .... | .... | .... | .... | .... | .... | .... | .... | .... | .... |
| Debt instruments............... | 3dzla | −19.9 | −18.7 | −5.7 | −4.9 | −13.4 | 158.5 | −6.8 | −2.3 | 117.3 | 107.4 | 29.1 | .... |
| Curr.+ cap.− finan. acct. balance... | 4y9na | −120.4 | −146.5 | −282.2 | −281.6 | 926.7 | 1,561.6 | 1,304.3 | −269.1 | 353.8 | 291.1 | −650.1 | .... |
| D. Net Errors and Omissions............ | 409na | −57.5 | −39.2 | −97.7 | −75.2 | −565.3 | −288.6 | 698.3 | −21.8 | −322.5 | −272.0 | 550.1 | .... |
| E. Reserves and Related Items.......... | 4z9na | −177.9 | −185.7 | −379.9 | −356.9 | 361.4 | 1,273.0 | 2,002.5 | −291.0 | 31.2 | 19.1 | −99.9 | .... |
| Reserve assets............... | 3e9aa | −5.3 | −2.3 | −38.6 | −38.8 | −27.7 | 28.6 | −62.0 | −79.6 | 49.3 | 41.6 | −38.4 | .... |
| Credit and loans from the IMF....... | 3dcla | — | −.1 | −.7 | −.7 | 545.0 | 17.7 | −791.9 | 13.9 | 18.1 | 22.5 | 56.3 | .... |
| Exceptional financing............... | 409la | 172.6 | 183.4 | 342.1 | 318.7 | −934.1 | −1,262.1 | −1,272.6 | 197.4 | .... | .... | 5.3 | .... |
| *Excludes components in group E | | | | | | | | | | | | | |

**Government Finance**
**Cash Flow Statement**
**Budgetary Central Government**

| | | 2004 | 2005 | 2006 | 2007 | 2008 | 2009 | 2010 | 2011 | 2012 | 2013 | 2014 | 2015 |
|---|---|---|---|---|---|---|---|---|---|---|---|---|---|
| | | | | | | **Thousands of US Dollars: Fiscal Year Ends June 30** | | | | | | | |
| Cash Receipts:Operating Activities... | c1 | .... | 82,344.5 | 85,473.3 | 148,341.2 | 206,891.5 | 234,905.2 | 287,962.1 | 359,947.9 | 458,931.6 | 517,197.0 | .... | .... |
| Taxes............... | c11 | .... | 72,529.8 | 80,975.7 | 140,053.3 | 169,865.3 | 204,658.5 | 223,878.9 | 267,347.9 | 362,116.3 | 395,924.2 | .... | .... |
| Social Contributions............... | c12 | .... | — | — | — | — | — | — | — | 2,350.0 | — | .... | .... |
| Grants............... | c13 | .... | 3,000.0 | 1,000.0 | 1,500.0 | 5,687.8 | 23,637.8 | 13,008.9 | 40,300.0 | 28,250.3 | 36,372.8 | .... | .... |
| Other Receipts............... | c14 | .... | 6,814.7 | 3,497.6 | 6,787.9 | 31,338.4 | 6,608.9 | 51,074.3 | 52,300.0 | 66,215.0 | 84,900.0 | .... | .... |
| Cash Payments:Operating Activities. | c2 | .... | 65,851.0 | 62,774.6 | 105,383.7 | 179,963.5 | 201,641.7 | 280,129.4 | 322,407.7 | 436,206.7 | 505,591.5 | .... | .... |
| Compensation of Employees.......... | c21 | .... | 31,874.5 | 36,421.8 | 50,199.6 | 65,441.7 | 60,489.9 | 88,264.7 | 137,443.1 | 181,500.0 | 206,856.2 | .... | .... |
| Purchases of Goods & Services....... | c22 | .... | 23,995.1 | 15,600.6 | 36,133.8 | 66,566.7 | 71,268.4 | 74,517.9 | 85,600.2 | 121,000.0 | .... | .... | .... |
| Interest............... | c24 | .... | 846.2 | 1,199.2 | 1,350.8 | 4,429.8 | 3,097.1 | 14,462.1 | 17,650.1 | 3,405.7 | .... | .... | .... |
| Subsidies............... | c25 | .... | — | — | — | — | 65,240.9 | 76,746.9 | 14,501.3 | 37,310.9 | .... | .... | .... |
| Grants............... | c26 | .... | 9,135.2 | 9,553.0 | 17,699.5 | 43,525.3 | — | — | 66,700.7 | 87,204.5 | 110,274.3 | .... | .... |
| Social Benefits............... | c27 | .... | — | — | — | — | — | — | 512.1 | 450.2 | 1,067.3 | .... | .... |
| Other Payments............... | c28 | .... | — | — | — | — | 1,545.3 | 26,137.8 | — | — | — | .... | .... |
| Net Cash Inflow:Operating Act.[1-2] | ccio | .... | 16,493.4 | 22,698.7 | 42,957.5 | 26,928.1 | 33,263.5 | 14,884.0 | 37,540.3 | 22,724.9 | 11,605.6 | .... | .... |
| Net Cash Outflow:Invest. in NFA...... | c31 | .... | 9,568.9 | 3,663.4 | 17,899.9 | 21,295.3 | .... | 26,227.1 | 62,310.8 | 52,012.4 | 24,890.9 | .... | .... |
| Purchases of Nonfinancial Assets... | c31.1 | .... | 9,568.9 | 3,663.4 | 17,899.9 | 21,295.3 | .... | 26,227.1 | 62,310.8 | 72,600.0 | .... | .... | .... |
| Sales of Nonfinancial Assets.......... | c31.2 | .... | — | — | — | — | .... | — | — | .... | .... | .... | .... |
| Cash Surplus/Deficit [1-2-31=1-2M] | ccsd | .... | 6,924.5 | 19,035.3 | 25,057.7 | 5,632.7 | .... | −11,343.1 | −24,770.5 | −29,287.4 | −13,285.3 | .... | .... |
| Net Acq. Fin. Assets, excl. Cash... | c32x | .... | — | — | — | — | .... | .... | .... | .... | .... | .... | .... |
| Domestic............... | c321x | .... | — | — | — | — | .... | .... | .... | .... | .... | .... | .... |
| Foreign............... | c322x | .... | — | — | — | — | .... | .... | .... | .... | .... | .... | .... |
| Net Incurrence of Liabilities............ | c33 | .... | −2,983.3 | −1,462.0 | −2,055.4 | −1,828.6 | .... | .... | .... | 45,500.0 | .... | .... | .... |
| Domestic............... | c331 | .... | −2,333.1 | −492.0 | −855.4 | −1,036.8 | .... | .... | .... | — | — | .... | .... |
| Foreign............... | c332 | .... | −650.0 | −970.0 | −1,200.0 | −791.8 | .... | .... | .... | — | — | .... | .... |
| Net Cash Inflow, Fin.Act.[-32x+33].. | cnfb | .... | −2,983.3 | −1,462.0 | −2,055.4 | −1,828.6 | .... | .... | .... | 45,500.0 | .... | .... | .... |
| Net Change in Stock of Cash........... | cncb | .... | 3,941.3 | 17,573.3 | 23,002.2 | 3,804.2 | .... | .... | .... | 960.3 | .... | .... | .... |
| Stat. Discrep. [32X-33+NCB-CSD].... | ccsdz | .... | — | — | — | — | .... | .... | .... | — | .... | .... | .... |
| Memo Item:Cash Expenditure[2+31] | c2m | .... | 75,419.9 | 66,438.0 | 123,283.6 | 201,258.8 | .... | 297,319.8 | 384,718.5 | 488,219.0 | 530,482.4 | .... | .... |
| Memo Item: Gross Debt............... | c63 | .... | .... | .... | .... | .... | .... | .... | .... | .... | .... | .... | .... |
| | | | | | | **Millions: Midyear Estimates** | | | | | | | |
| Population............... | 99z | 3.18 | 3.27 | 3.38 | 3.52 | 3.67 | 3.82 | 3.96 | 4.08 | 4.19 | 4.29 | 4.40 | 4.50 |

# Libya   672

| | | 2004 | 2005 | 2006 | 2007 | 2008 | 2009 | 2010 | 2011 | 2012 | 2013 | 2014 | 2015 |
|---|---|---|---|---|---|---|---|---|---|---|---|---|---|
| **Exchange Rates** | | *SDRs per Dinar: End of Period (ac) US Dollars per Dinar: End of Period (ag)* | | | | | | | | | | | |
| Official Rate | ac | .5175 | .5175 | .5175 | .5175 | .5175 | .5175 | .5175 | .5175 | .5175 | .5175 | .5175 | .... |
| Official Rate | ag | .8037 | .7396 | .7785 | .8178 | .7971 | .8113 | .7970 | .7945 | .7953 | .7969 | .7497 | .... |
| **Fund Position** | | *Millions of SDRs: End of Period* | | | | | | | | | | | |
| Quota | 2f.s | 1,123.70 | 1,123.70 | 1,123.70 | 1,123.70 | 1,123.70 | 1,123.70 | 1,123.70 | 1,123.70 | 1,123.70 | 1,123.70 | 1,123.70 | 1,123.70 |
| SDR Holdings | 1b.s | 475.41 | 494.88 | 523.12 | 558.29 | 584.69 | 1,603.57 | 1,605.80 | 1,609.28 | 1,613.60 | 1,622.46 | 1,623.23 | 1,623.62 |
| Reserve Position in the Fund | 1c.s | 395.51 | 395.51 | 395.51 | 395.51 | 395.53 | 379.64 | 241.83 | 295.83 | 295.83 | 295.83 | 295.83 | 295.83 |
| Total Fund Cred.&Loans Outstg | 2tl | — | — | — | — | — | — | — | — | — | — | — | — |
| SDR Allocations | 1bd | 58.77 | 58.77 | 58.77 | 58.77 | 58.77 | 1,072.70 | 1,072.70 | 1,072.70 | 1,072.70 | 1,072.70 | 1,072.70 | 1,072.70 |
| **International Liquidity** | | *Millions of US Dollars Unless Otherwise Indicated: End of Period* | | | | | | | | | | | |
| Total Reserves minus Gold | 1l.d | 25,689 | 39,508 | 59,289 | 79,405 | 92,313 | 98,725 | 99,645 | 104,797 | 118,408 | 115,197 | 89,093 | .... |
| SDR Holdings | 1b.d | 738 | 707 | 787 | 882 | 901 | 2,514 | 2,473 | 2,471 | 2,480 | 2,499 | 2,352 | 2,250 |
| Reserve Position in the Fund | 1c.d | 614 | 565 | 595 | 625 | 609 | 595 | 372 | 454 | 455 | 456 | 429 | 410 |
| Foreign Exchange | 1d.d | 24,336 | 38,235 | 57,907 | 77,897 | 90,803 | 95,616 | 96,800 | 101,872 | 115,473 | 112,243 | 86,313 | .... |
| Gold (Million Fine Troy Ounces) | 1ad | 4.624 | 4.624 | 4.624 | 4.624 | 4.624 | 4.624 | 4.624 | 3.750 | 3.750 | 3.750 | 3.750 | .... |
| Gold (National Valuation) | 1and | 194 | 194 | 194 | 194 | 194 | 194 | 194 | 158 | 158 | 158 | 158 | .... |
| Monetary Authorities: Other Liabs | 4..d | 6 | 9 | 10 | 14 | 10 | 36 | 247 | 164 | 164 | 164 | 155 | 147 |
| Deposit Money Banks: Assets | 7a.d | 1,629.9 | 2,764.6 | 2,947.8 | 3,004.2 | 4,643.2 | 5,167.5 | 4,492.0 | 5,645.2 | 4,564.1 | 5,188.2 | 7,490.9 | 9,392.3 |
| Deposit Money Banks: Liabs | 7b.d | 113 | 53 | 81 | 220 | 105 | 116 | 95 | 265 | 151 | 126 | 371 | 723 |
| **Monetary Authorities** | | *Millions of Dinars: End of Period* | | | | | | | | | | | |
| Foreign Assets | 11 | 33,072.7 | 54,459.7 | 77,253.3 | 98,322.4 | 121,279.6 | 126,862.2 | 133,099.7 | 138,280.4 | 157,389.2 | 152,535.2 | 127,206.0 | 111,035.9 |
| Claims on Central Government | 12a | 828.2 | 828.2 | 828.2 | 3,163.1 | 905.0 | 1,477.2 | 1,522.7 | 4,616.7 | 2,388.0 | 2,743.2 | 24,807.3 | 43,949.5 |
| Claims on Nonfin.Pub.Enterprises | 12c | 1,842.1 | 3,075.0 | 3,716.1 | 4,099.0 | 3,102.7 | 5,947.6 | 7,898.6 | 6,796.6 | 6,787.3 | 6,789.9 | 7,033.3 | 7,208.1 |
| Claims on Private Sector | 12d | 14.7 | 16.4 | 18.0 | 24.3 | 29.7 | 30.5 | 32.6 | 32.1 | 33.7 | 29.8 | 28.4 | 30.0 |
| Claims on Deposit Money Banks | 12e | 1.0 | 1.8 | 61.5 | 52.9 | 52.2 | 51.9 | | | | | | |
| Reserve Money | 14 | 9,920.7 | 14,388.0 | 16,562.7 | 24,458.8 | 39,024.2 | 46,641.4 | 53,311.2 | 62,853.8 | 68,779.6 | 81,469.0 | 75,693.9 | 67,727.4 |
| of which: Currency Outside DMBs | 14a | 2,612.7 | 3,310.6 | 3,932.9 | 4,581.2 | 5,608.3 | 6,962.9 | 7,609.0 | 14,840.1 | 13,391.1 | 13,419.9 | 17,242.5 | 23,007.3 |
| Time & Foreign Currency Deposits | 15 | 44.9 | 34.5 | 93.9 | 13.9 | — | 2,032.0 | 37.0 | 635.0 | 1,137.3 | — | — | — |
| Restricted Deposits | 16b | 1,351.6 | 1,548.9 | 2,607.8 | 4,591.1 | 2,902.3 | 2,553.5 | 2,054.2 | 1,836.7 | 2,080.0 | 2,007.9 | 2,282.5 | 2,724.1 |
| Foreign Liabilities | 16c | 120.5 | 125.4 | 126.2 | 130.7 | 125.7 | 2,117.0 | 2,383.2 | 2,279.1 | 2,279.1 | 2,279.0 | 2,279.0 | 2,287.2 |
| Central Government Deposits | 16d | 18,755.0 | 35,128.5 | 52,956.6 | 63,584.3 | 70,281.1 | 66,843.2 | 69,822.3 | 64,055.1 | 72,764.1 | 53,813.1 | 54,913.1 | 64,211.3 |
| Capital Accounts | 17a | 4,200.9 | 5,520.8 | 5,161.8 | 4,787.1 | 6,379.4 | 6,905.5 | 4,875.8 | 4,798.7 | 6,453.5 | 7,892.5 | 9,123.4 | 8,294.2 |
| Other Items (Net) | 17r | 1,364.9 | 1,635.0 | 4,368.1 | 8,088.9 | 6,657.0 | 7,258.0 | 10,048.9 | 13,265.9 | 13,104.6 | 14,636.6 | 14,783.1 | 16,979.3 |
| **Deposit Money Banks** | | *Millions of Dinars: End of Period* | | | | | | | | | | | |
| Reserves | 20 | 6,341.6 | 9,154.4 | 11,473.9 | 18,522.5 | 32,882.1 | 39,079.8 | 44,784.7 | 46,932.9 | 54,374.5 | 65,294.5 | 58,304.4 | 45,866.5 |
| Foreign Assets | 21 | 1,309.9 | 2,044.8 | 2,294.9 | 2,456.8 | 3,701.0 | 4,192.3 | 3,580.0 | 4,485.0 | 3,630.0 | 4,134.7 | 5,616.3 | 6,708.8 |
| Claims on Central Government | 22a | 373.0 | 373.0 | 373.0 | 328.0 | 174.0 | — | — | — | — | — | — | 1,000.0 |
| Claims on Nonfin.Pub.Enterprises | 22c | 1,995.1 | 1,775.1 | 2,311.2 | 2,840.1 | 2,796.2 | 3,914.3 | 4,310.1 | 4,594.5 | 5,386.2 | 5,270.8 | 5,712.3 | 6,006.4 |
| Claims on Private Sector | 22d | 4,437.6 | 4,556.9 | 4,724.3 | 5,261.8 | 7,714.4 | 8,490.2 | 8,810.1 | 8,330.5 | 10,869.0 | 13,133.4 | 14,074.4 | 14,450.6 |
| Claims on Other Banking Insts | 22f | 27.9 | .6 | — | — | — | — | 20.3 | 61.9 | 9.4 | 8.6 | 7.8 | 7.4 |
| Claims on Nonbank Financial Insts | 22g | 214.7 | 6.9 | 7.3 | 7.9 | 9.6 | 10.0 | 539.4 | 531.1 | 562.7 | 539.4 | 926.5 | 509.5 |
| Demand Deposits | 24 | 6,801.6 | 8,666.2 | 10,506.9 | 16,375.1 | 27,055.8 | 29,582.9 | 31,602.2 | 35,435.3 | 42,461.4 | 47,153.7 | 44,975.6 | 48,257.3 |
| Time & Foreign Currency Deposits | 25 | 2,554.0 | 3,033.6 | 3,219.0 | 3,880.5 | 5,329.9 | 5,959.9 | 4,992.5 | 3,868.8 | 4,517.8 | 4,706.5 | 2,680.9 | 1,823.4 |
| Restricted Deposits | 26b | 856.5 | 1,154.4 | 1,403.5 | 2,926.9 | 6,612.3 | 7,197.3 | 6,922.5 | 7,516.8 | 6,823.3 | 6,609.0 | 8,538.7 | 9,738.7 |
| Foreign Liabilities | 26c | 141.1 | 71.5 | 104.5 | 269.4 | 131.9 | 143.2 | 119.4 | 333.1 | 189.6 | 157.6 | 494.6 | 1,012.3 |
| Central Government Deposits | 26d | 1,146.7 | 1,210.0 | 1,912.2 | 867.8 | 1,439.9 | 4,586.9 | 10,531.0 | 9,629.1 | 12,618.6 | 22,963.6 | 19,662.5 | 7,852.9 |
| Credit from Monetary Authorities | 26g | 1.0 | 1.3 | 56.2 | 53.0 | 52.2 | 51.9 | | | | | | |
| Capital Accounts | 27a | 1,566.4 | 1,842.4 | 1,975.1 | 2,309.3 | 2,497.1 | 3,979.3 | 4,885.1 | 4,787.0 | 5,082.5 | 5,228.2 | 5,458.7 | 5,692.7 |
| Other Items (Net) | 27r | 1,632.5 | 1,932.3 | 2,007.2 | 2,735.1 | 4,158.2 | 4,185.2 | 2,991.9 | 3,365.9 | 3,138.6 | 1,562.8 | 2,830.7 | 171.9 |
| **Monetary Survey** | | *Millions of Dinars: End of Period* | | | | | | | | | | | |
| Foreign Assets (Net) | 31n | 34,121.1 | 56,307.6 | 79,317.6 | 100,379.1 | 124,723.0 | 128,794.2 | 134,177.1 | 140,153.3 | 158,550.5 | 154,233.3 | 130,048.7 | 114,445.2 |
| Domestic Credit | 32 | −10,168.4 | −25,706.4 | −42,890.7 | −48,727.9 | −56,989.4 | −51,560.3 | −57,219.5 | −48,720.7 | −59,346.4 | −48,261.6 | −21,985.6 | 1,097.3 |
| Claims on Central Govt. (Net) | 32an | −18,700.5 | −35,137.3 | −53,667.6 | −60,961.0 | −70,642.0 | −69,952.9 | −78,830.6 | −69,067.5 | −82,994.7 | −74,033.5 | −49,768.3 | −27,114.7 |
| Claims on Nonfin.Pub.Enterprises | 32c | 3,837.2 | 4,850.1 | 6,027.3 | 6,939.1 | 5,898.9 | 9,861.9 | 12,208.7 | 11,391.1 | 12,173.5 | 12,060.7 | 12,745.6 | 13,214.5 |
| Claims on Private Sector | 32d | 4,452.3 | 4,573.3 | 4,742.3 | 5,286.1 | 7,744.1 | 8,520.7 | 8,842.7 | 8,362.6 | 10,902.7 | 13,163.2 | 14,102.8 | 14,480.6 |
| Claims on Other Banking Insts | 32f | 27.9 | .6 | — | — | — | — | 20.3 | 61.9 | 9.4 | 8.6 | 7.8 | 7.4 |
| Claims on Nonbank Financial Insts | 32g | 214.7 | 6.9 | 7.3 | 7.9 | 9.6 | 10.0 | 539.4 | 531.1 | 562.7 | 539.4 | 926.5 | 509.5 |
| Money | 34 | 10,154.0 | 13,383.9 | 15,455.3 | 22,013.8 | 33,323.1 | 37,391.7 | 40,093.9 | 51,449.4 | 57,338.5 | 62,252.2 | 64,051.0 | 73,254.7 |
| Quasi-Money | 35 | 2,598.9 | 3,068.1 | 3,312.9 | 3,894.4 | 5,329.9 | 7,991.9 | 5,029.5 | 4,503.8 | 5,655.1 | 4,706.5 | 2,680.9 | 1,823.4 |
| Restricted Deposits | 36b | 2,208.1 | 2,703.3 | 4,011.3 | 7,518.0 | 9,514.6 | 9,750.8 | 8,976.7 | 9,353.5 | 8,903.3 | 8,616.9 | 10,821.2 | 12,462.8 |
| Capital Accounts | 37a | 5,767.3 | 7,363.2 | 7,136.9 | 7,096.4 | 8,876.5 | 10,884.8 | 9,760.9 | 9,585.7 | 11,536.0 | 13,120.7 | 14,582.1 | 13,986.9 |
| Other Items (Net) | 37r | 3,224.1 | 4,082.7 | 6,510.4 | 11,121.7 | 10,690.0 | 11,196.0 | 13,075.6 | 16,538.6 | 15,771.2 | 17,275.4 | 15,927.9 | 14,014.7 |
| Money plus Quasi-Money | 35l | 12,752.9 | 16,452.0 | 18,768.2 | 25,908.2 | 38,653.0 | 45,383.6 | 45,123.4 | 55,953.2 | 62,993.6 | 66,958.7 | 66,731.9 | 75,078.1 |
| **Other Banking Institutions** | | *Millions of Dinars: End of Period* | | | | | | | | | | | |
| Cash | 40 | .8 | .... | .... | .... | .... | .... | .... | .... | .... | .... | .... | .... |
| Claims on Private Sector | 42d | 1,955.8 | .... | .... | .... | .... | .... | .... | .... | .... | .... | .... | .... |
| Claims on Deposit Money Banks | 42e | 918.2 | .... | .... | .... | .... | .... | .... | .... | .... | .... | .... | .... |
| Deposits | 45 | 103.7 | .... | .... | .... | .... | .... | .... | .... | .... | .... | .... | .... |
| Central Government Deposits | 46d | 32.0 | .... | .... | .... | .... | .... | .... | .... | .... | .... | .... | .... |
| Capital Accounts | 47a | 2,206.9 | .... | .... | .... | .... | .... | .... | .... | .... | .... | .... | .... |
| Other Items (Net) | 47r | 532.2 | .... | .... | .... | .... | .... | .... | .... | .... | .... | .... | .... |
| **Money (National Definitions)** | | *Millions of Dinars: End of Period* | | | | | | | | | | | |
| Monetary Base | 19ma | 9,920.7 | 14,387.9 | 16,562.7 | 24,458.8 | 17,759.6 | 20,462.8 | 22,604.2 | 32,404.5 | 35,438.2 | 36,886.5 | 38,130.3 | 41,926.2 |
| Money | 59ma | .... | .... | 16,491.2 | 22,844.9 | 27,035.0 | 38,169.4 | 41,321.2 | 53,437.1 | 58,708.9 | 64,299.4 | 66,740.2 | 76,783.0 |
| Quasi-Money | 59mal | .... | .... | 7,343.6 | 11,382.0 | 10,660.2 | 5,991.9 | 5,029.5 | 4,503.8 | 5,131.6 | 4,706.5 | 2,680.9 | 1,823.3 |
| **Interest Rates** | | *Percent Per Annum* | | | | | | | | | | | |
| Discount Rate (End of Period) | 60.a | 4.00 | 4.00 | 4.00 | 4.00 | 5.00 | 3.00 | 3.00 | 3.00 | 3.00 | 3.00 | 3.00 | .... |
| Money Market Rate | 60b | 4.00 | .... | .... | .... | .... | .... | .... | .... | .... | .... | .... | .... |
| Deposit Rate | 60l | 2.08 | 2.13 | 2.50 | 2.50 | 2.50 | 2.50 | 2.50 | 2.50 | 2.50 | 2.50 | 2.50 | .... |
| Lending Rate | 60p | 6.08 | 6.13 | 6.33 | 6.00 | 6.00 | 6.00 | 6.00 | 6.00 | 6.00 | 6.00 | 6.00 | .... |

# Libya   672

| | | 2004 | 2005 | 2006 | 2007 | 2008 | 2009 | 2010 | 2011 | 2012 | 2013 | 2014 | 2015 |
|---|---|---|---|---|---|---|---|---|---|---|---|---|---|
| **Prices** | | | | | | *Index Numbers (2010=100): Period Averages* | | | | | | | |
| Consumer Prices.............................. | 64 | † 77.7 | 79.8 | 81.0 | 86.0 | 94.9 | 97.3 | 100.0 | 115.5 | 122.5 | 125.7 | .... | .... |
| **Intl. Transactions & Positions** | | | | | | *Millions of Dinars* | | | | | | | |
| Exports............................................ | 70 | 26,634.4 | 41,028.3 | 52,885.0 | 59,306.4 | 75,959.3 | 46,583.3 | 58,335.7 | .... | .... | .... | .... | .... |
| Imports, c.i.f.................................... | 71 | 8,255.2 | 7,953.7 | 7,934.7 | 8,501.4 | 11,195.2 | 12,535.3 | 13,301.3 | .... | .... | .... | .... | .... |
| **Balance of Payments** | | | | | | *Millions of US Dollars* | | | | | | | |
| A. Current Account*........................ | 109bx | 4,616.0 | 14,945.0 | 22,170.0 | 28,510.3 | 35,701.7 | 9,380.6 | 16,800.7 | 3,192.4 | 23,836.3 | −108.1 | .... | .... |
| Goods, credit (exports)................. | 1a9cx | 17,425.0 | 28,849.0 | 37,473.0 | 46,929.0 | 61,950.1 | 37,055.0 | 48,935.0 | 19,060.0 | 61,026.1 | 46,017.9 | .... | .... |
| Goods, debit (imports)................. | 1a9dx | 8,768.0 | 11,174.0 | 13,219.0 | 17,701.4 | 21,658.3 | 22,002.0 | 24,559.0 | 11,200.0 | 25,590.0 | 34,049.5 | .... | .... |
| Balance on goods.................. | 1a9bx | 8,657.0 | 17,675.0 | 24,254.0 | 29,227.6 | 40,291.8 | 15,053.0 | 24,376.0 | 7,860.0 | 35,436.1 | 11,968.4 | .... | .... |
| Services, credit (exports)............. | 1b9cx | 437.0 | 534.0 | 489.0 | 108.5 | 207.7 | 385.0 | 410.1 | 40.2 | 152.2 | 179.9 | .... | .... |
| Services, debit (imports)............. | 1b9dx | 1,914.0 | 2,349.0 | 2,564.0 | 2,624.1 | 4,344.2 | 5,063.0 | 6,127.4 | 4,386.4 | 6,995.9 | 8,471.5 | .... | .... |
| Balance on Goods & Services....... | 1z9bx | 7,180.0 | 15,860.0 | 22,179.0 | 26,712.0 | 36,155.3 | 10,375.0 | 18,658.7 | 3,513.8 | 28,592.4 | 3,676.8 | .... | .... |
| Primary income: credit.................. | 1c9cx | 1,339.0 | 1,837.0 | 2,180.0 | 4,517.0 | 4,471.1 | 2,460.9 | 2,318.0 | 1,209.6 | 2,391.9 | 2,275.3 | .... | .... |
| Primary income: debit.................... | 1c9dx | 1,394.0 | 2,118.0 | 2,775.0 | 2,500.0 | 3,884.7 | 1,883.3 | 2,348.0 | 1,154.0 | 4,323.8 | 2,808.0 | .... | .... |
| Balance on gds, serv. & prim. inc. | 1y9bx | 7,125.0 | 15,579.0 | 21,584.0 | 28,729.0 | 36,741.7 | 10,952.6 | 18,628.7 | 3,569.4 | 26,660.5 | 3,144.1 | .... | .... |
| Secondary income: credit.............. | 1d9ca | 254.0 | 418.0 | 1,646.0 | 598.0 | 45.2 | — | — | 303.8 | — | — | .... | .... |
| Secondary income: debit.............. | 1d9da | 2,763.0 | 1,052.0 | 1,060.0 | 816.7 | 1,085.2 | 1,572.0 | 1,828.0 | 680.8 | 2,824.2 | 3,252.2 | .... | .... |
| B. Capital Account*........................ | 209ba | — | — | — | — | — | — | — | — | — | — | .... | .... |
| Capital account: credit.................. | 209ca | — | — | — | — | — | — | — | — | — | — | .... | .... |
| Capital account: debit.................... | 209da | — | — | — | — | — | — | — | — | — | — | .... | .... |
| Balance on current & capital acct. | 129ba | 4,616.0 | 14,945.0 | 22,170.0 | 28,510.3 | 35,701.7 | 9,380.6 | 16,800.7 | 3,192.4 | 23,836.3 | −108.1 | .... | .... |
| C. Financial Account* .................... | 309na | 238.0 | −392.0 | 4,731.0 | 9,542.4 | 21,039.4 | 5,525.0 | 10,338.8 | 2,373.6 | 7,890.3 | 4,108.8 | .... | .... |
| Direct investment: assets.............. | 3a9aa | 286.0 | 128.0 | 474.0 | 3,932.8 | 5,888.2 | 1,165.0 | 2,722.0 | 131.0 | 2,508.8 | 881.8 | .... | .... |
| Equity & investment fund shares.. | 3aaaa | 286.0 | 128.0 | 474.0 | 3,932.8 | 5,888.2 | 1,165.0 | 2,722.0 | 131.0 | 2,508.8 | 881.8 | .... | .... |
| Debt instruments....................... | 3abaa | .... | .... | .... | .... | .... | .... | .... | .... | .... | .... | .... | .... |
| Direct investment: liabilities....... | 3a9la | 357.0 | 1,038.0 | 2,064.0 | 4,689.0 | 4,111.3 | 1,371.0 | 1,784.0 | — | — | — | .... | .... |
| Equity & investment fund shares . | 3aala | 213.0 | 163.0 | 250.0 | 4,689.0 | 4,111.3 | 1,371.0 | 1,784.0 | — | — | — | .... | .... |
| Debt instruments....................... | 3abla | 144.0 | 875.0 | 1,814.0 | — | — | — | — | — | — | — | .... | .... |
| Portfolio investment: assets ......... | 3b9aa | 187.0 | 393.0 | 5,198.0 | 1,440.1 | 10,963.6 | 3,352.0 | 4,396.0 | 324.1 | 540.3 | 1,697.6 | .... | .... |
| Equity & investment fund shares | 3baaa | −27.0 | 47.0 | 60.0 | 1,440.1 | 10,963.6 | 3,352.0 | 4,396.0 | 324.1 | 540.3 | 1,697.6 | .... | .... |
| Debt securities .......................... | 3bbaa | 214.0 | 346.0 | 5,138.0 | — | — | — | — | — | — | — | .... | .... |
| Portfolio investment: liabilities....... | 3b9la | — | — | — | — | — | — | — | — | — | — | .... | .... |
| Equity & investment fund shares . | 3bala | — | — | — | — | — | — | — | — | — | — | .... | .... |
| Debt securities........................... | 3bbla | — | — | — | — | — | — | — | — | — | — | .... | .... |
| Fin. der.& empl.stk.ops.(ESOs): net. | 3c9na | .... | .... | .... | .... | .... | .... | .... | .... | .... | .... | .... | .... |
| Fin. der. & ESOs.: assets.............. | 3c9aa | .... | .... | .... | .... | .... | .... | .... | .... | .... | .... | .... | .... |
| Fin. der. & ESOs.: liabilities.......... | 3c9la | .... | .... | .... | .... | .... | .... | .... | .... | .... | .... | .... | .... |
| Other investment: assets............... | 3d9aa | 1,767.0 | 416.0 | 1,194.0 | 8,946.9 | 8,279.6 | 3,951.7 | 4,889.0 | 2,389.0 | 4,500.5 | 1,675.6 | .... | .... |
| Other equity.............................. | 3daaa | .... | .... | .... | .... | .... | .... | .... | .... | .... | .... | .... | .... |
| Debt instruments....................... | 3dzaa | 1,767.0 | 416.0 | 1,194.0 | 8,946.9 | 8,279.6 | 3,951.7 | 4,889.0 | 2,389.0 | 4,500.5 | 1,675.6 | .... | .... |
| Other investment: liabilities........... | 3d9la | 1,645.0 | 291.0 | 71.0 | 88.4 | −19.3 | 1,572.7 | −115.8 | 470.5 | −340.7 | 146.2 | .... | .... |
| Other equity.............................. | 3dala | .... | .... | .... | .... | .... | .... | .... | .... | .... | .... | .... | .... |
| Debt instruments....................... | 3dzla | 1,645.0 | 291.0 | 71.0 | 88.4 | −19.3 | 1,572.7 | −115.8 | 470.5 | −340.7 | 146.2 | .... | .... |
| Curr.+ cap.− finan. acct. balance... | 4y9na | 4,378.0 | 15,337.0 | 17,439.0 | 18,967.9 | 14,662.3 | 3,855.6 | 6,461.9 | 818.8 | 15,946.0 | −4,216.9 | .... | .... |
| D. Net Errors and Omissions............ | 409na | 1,732.9 | −1,497.3 | 2,007.7 | 1,076.4 | −1,714.8 | 1,332.5 | −2,292.0 | 2,549.7 | −2,537.5 | −2,694.8 | .... | .... |
| E. Reserves and Related Items.......... | 4z9na | 6,110.9 | 13,839.7 | 19,446.7 | 20,044.3 | 12,947.5 | 5,188.2 | 4,169.9 | 3,368.5 | 13,408.5 | −6,911.7 | .... | .... |
| Reserve assets............................ | 3e9aa | 6,039.9 | 13,839.7 | 19,446.7 | 20,044.3 | 12,947.5 | 5,188.2 | 4,169.9 | 3,368.5 | 13,408.5 | −6,911.7 | .... | .... |
| Credit and loans from the IMF....... | 3dcla | — | — | — | — | — | — | — | — | — | — | .... | .... |
| Exceptional financing.................... | 409la | −71.0 | — | — | — | — | — | — | — | — | — | .... | .... |

*Excludes components in group E

| **National Accounts** | | | | | | *Millions of Dinars* | | | | | | | |
|---|---|---|---|---|---|---|---|---|---|---|---|---|---|
| Househ.Cons.Expend.,incl.NPISHs.... | 96f | 15,669 | 18,149 | .... | .... | .... | .... | .... | .... | .... | .... | .... | .... |
| Government Consumption Expend... | 91f | 5,132 | 6,713 | .... | .... | .... | .... | .... | .... | .... | .... | .... | .... |
| Gross Fixed Capital Formation.......... | 93e | 3,988 | 4,807 | .... | .... | .... | .... | .... | .... | .... | .... | .... | .... |
| Changes in Inventories.................... | 93i | 167 | 202 | .... | .... | .... | .... | .... | .... | .... | .... | .... | .... |
| Exports of Goods and Services......... | 90c | 27,928 | 40,613 | .... | .... | .... | .... | .... | .... | .... | .... | .... | .... |
| Imports of Goods and Services (-)..... | 98c | 11,398 | 14,458 | .... | .... | .... | .... | .... | .... | .... | .... | .... | .... |
| Gross Domestic Product (GDP)......... | 99b | 48,159 | 66,619 | 79,030 | 92,694 | 116,640 | 86,289 | .... | .... | .... | .... | .... | .... |
| Net Primary Income from Abroad..... | 98.n | .... | .... | .... | .... | .... | .... | .... | .... | .... | .... | .... | .... |
| Gross National Income (GNI)........... | 99a | .... | .... | .... | .... | .... | .... | .... | .... | .... | .... | .... | .... |
| GDP Volume 2003 Prices.......... | 99b.p | 39,679 | 44,087 | 46,584 | 48,898 | 50,229 | 49,854 | .... | .... | .... | .... | .... | .... |
| GDP Volume (2005=100)................ | 99bvp | 90.0 | 100.0 | 105.7 | 110.9 | 113.9 | 113.1 | .... | .... | .... | .... | .... | .... |
| GDP Deflator (2005=100)............... | 99bip | 80.3 | 100.0 | 112.3 | 125.5 | 153.7 | 114.5 | .... | .... | .... | .... | .... | .... |
| | | | | | | *Millions: Midyear Estimates* | | | | | | | |
| **Population**................................. | 99z | 5.70 | 5.80 | 5.91 | 6.02 | 6.12 | 6.21 | 6.27 | 6.29 | 6.28 | 6.27 | 6.26 | 6.28 |

# Lithuania 946

| | | 2004 | 2005 | 2006 | 2007 | 2008 | 2009 | 2010 | 2011 | 2012 | 2013 | 2014 | 2015 |
|---|---|---|---|---|---|---|---|---|---|---|---|---|---|
| **Exchange Rates** | | *Litai per SDR through 2014; Euros per SDR Thereafter: End of Period* | | | | | | | | | | | |
| Official Rate | aa | 3.9361 | 4.1595 | 3.9572 | 3.7250 | 3.7747 | 3.7706 | 4.0193 | 4.0982 | 4.0052 | 3.8651 | 4.1127 | 1.2728 |
| | | *Litai per US Dollar through 2014; Euros per US Dollar Thereafter: End of Period (ae) Period Average (rf)* | | | | | | | | | | | |
| Official Rate | ae | 2.5345 | 2.9102 | 2.6304 | 2.3572 | 2.4507 | 2.4052 | 2.6099 | 2.6694 | 2.6060 | 2.5098 | 2.8387 | .9185 |
| Official Rate | rf | 2.7806 | 2.7740 | 2.7522 | 2.5237 | 2.3571 | 2.4840 | 2.6063 | 2.4811 | 2.6863 | 2.6010 | 2.6003 | .9017 |
| **Fund Position** | | *Millions of SDRs: End of Period* | | | | | | | | | | | |
| Quota | 2f.s | 144.20 | 144.20 | 144.20 | 144.20 | 144.20 | 144.20 | 144.20 | 183.90 | 183.90 | 183.90 | 183.90 | 183.90 |
| SDR Holdings | 1b.s | .06 | .05 | .07 | .07 | .07 | 137.31 | 137.31 | 137.31 | 137.31 | 137.31 | 137.31 | 137.30 |
| Reserve Position in the Fund | 1c.s | .02 | .02 | .03 | .03 | .03 | .03 | .03 | .03 | .03 | .03 | .03 | .03 |
| Total Fund Cred.&Loans Outstg. | 2tl | 16.82 | — | — | — | — | — | — | — | — | — | — | — |
| SDR Allocations | 1bd | — | — | — | — | — | 137.24 | 137.24 | 137.24 | 137.24 | 137.24 | 137.24 | 137.24 |
| **International Liquidity** | | *Millions of US Dollars Unless Otherwise Indicated: End of Period* | | | | | | | | | | | |
| Total Res.Min.Gold (Eurosys.Def.) | 1l.d | 3,512.58 | 3,720.24 | 5,654.41 | 7,556.62 | 6,280.46 | 6,419.82 | 6,335.52 | 7,915.37 | 8,218.17 | 7,847.28 | 8,503.94 | † 1,498.93 |
| SDR Holdings | 1b.d | .09 | .08 | .10 | .11 | .11 | 215.26 | 211.46 | 210.81 | 211.03 | 211.45 | 198.93 | 190.27 |
| Reserve Position in the Fund | 1c.d | .02 | .02 | .05 | .05 | .05 | .05 | .05 | .05 | .05 | .05 | .05 | .05 |
| Foreign Exchange | 1d.d | 3,512.47 | 3,720.14 | 5,654.26 | 7,556.46 | 6,280.30 | 6,204.51 | 6,124.01 | 7,704.51 | 8,007.09 | 7,635.78 | 8,304.96 | † 1,308.62 |
| o/w:Fin.Deriv.Rel.to Reserves | 1ddd | .... | .... | .... | .... | .... | .... | .... | .... | .... | .... | .... | — |
| Other Reserve Assets | 1e.d | .... | .... | .... | .... | .... | .... | .... | .... | .... | .... | .... | — |
| Gold (Million Fine Troy Ounces) | 1ad | .1858 | .1858 | .1858 | .1863 | .1867 | .1870 | .1870 | .1870 | .1870 | .1870 | .1870 | .1870 |
| Gold (Eurosystem Valuation) | 1and | 81.40 | 95.34 | 118.14 | 155.36 | 161.47 | 206.43 | 263.71 | 294.45 | 311.21 | 224.71 | 224.44 | † 198.14 |
| Memo:Euro Cl. on Non-EA Res. | 1dgd | .... | .... | .... | .... | .... | .... | .... | .... | .... | .... | .... | |
| Non-Euro Cl. on EA Res. | 1dhd | .... | .... | .... | .... | .... | .... | .... | .... | .... | .... | .... | 1,197.57 |
| Central Bank: Other Assets | 3..d | .... | .... | .... | .... | .... | .... | 292 | 74 | −72 | 167 | 866 | 5,103 |
| Central Bank: Other Liabs. | 4..d | .... | .... | .... | .... | .... | .... | 408 | 618 | 233 | 240 | 257 | 191 |
| Other Depository Corps.: Assets | 7a.d | .... | .... | .... | .... | .... | .... | 3,224 | 3,135 | 2,763 | 2,615 | 1,149 | 1,392 |
| Other Depository Corps.: Liabs. | 7b.d | .... | .... | .... | .... | .... | .... | 8,526 | 6,577 | 5,915 | 5,858 | 3,764 | 2,648 |
| **Central Bank** | | *Millions of Euros: End of Period* | | | | | | | | | | | |
| Euro Area Wide Residency Criterion | | | | | | | | | | | | | |
| Net Foreign Assets | 11n.u | .... | .... | .... | .... | .... | .... | 527 | 1,228 | 1,952 | 1,909 | 4,666 | 2,654 |
| Claims on Nonresidents | 11..u | .... | .... | .... | .... | .... | .... | 852 | 1,705 | 2,129 | 2,082 | 4,878 | 2,882 |
| Liabilities to Nonresidents | 16c.u | .... | .... | .... | .... | .... | .... | 325 | 477 | 177 | 173 | 212 | 228 |
| Claims on Other Depository Corps. | 12e.u | .... | .... | .... | .... | .... | .... | 381 | 608 | 394 | 347 | 220 | 694 |
| Net Claims on Central Government | 12anu | .... | .... | .... | .... | .... | .... | 2,892 | 3,341 | 824 | 1,583 | 646 | −176 |
| Claims on Central Govt. | 12a.u | .... | .... | .... | .... | .... | .... | 3,601 | 3,834 | 1,959 | 2,102 | 1,906 | 1,100 |
| Liabs. to Central Govt. | 16d.u | .... | .... | .... | .... | .... | .... | 709 | 493 | 1,135 | 519 | 1,260 | 1,276 |
| Claims on Other Sectors | 12s.u | .... | .... | .... | .... | .... | .... | 5 | 25 | 417 | 718 | 888 | 2,299 |
| Claims on Other Financial Corps. | 12g.u | .... | .... | .... | .... | .... | .... | — | 21 | 131 | 304 | 594 | 2,139 |
| Claims on State & Local Govts. | 12b.u | .... | .... | .... | .... | .... | .... | — | — | 283 | 387 | 252 | 140 |
| Claims on Public Nonfin. Corps. | 12c.u | .... | .... | .... | .... | .... | .... | — | — | — | — | — | — |
| Claims on Private Sector | 12d.u | .... | .... | .... | .... | .... | .... | 5 | 4 | 3 | 27 | 42 | 20 |
| Monetary Base | 14..u | .... | .... | .... | .... | .... | .... | 3,666 | 5,007 | 4,695 | 4,920 | 5,952 | 8,997 |
| Currency in Circulation | 14a.u | .... | .... | .... | .... | .... | .... | 2,552 | 3,132 | 3,302 | 3,442 | 1,676 | 6,053 |
| Liabs. to Other Depository Corps. | 14c.u | .... | .... | .... | .... | .... | .... | 1,089 | 1,873 | 1,383 | 1,472 | 4,276 | 2,944 |
| Liabs. to Other Sectors | 14d.u | .... | .... | .... | .... | .... | .... | 25 | 2 | 10 | 6 | — | — |
| Other Liabs. to Other Dep. Corps. | 14n.u | .... | .... | .... | .... | .... | .... | — | — | — | — | — | — |
| Dep. & Sec. Excl. f/Monetary Base | 14o.u | .... | .... | .... | .... | .... | .... | — | — | — | — | — | — |
| Deposits Included in Broad Money | 15..u | .... | .... | .... | .... | .... | .... | — | — | — | — | — | — |
| Sec.Ot.th.Shares Inc.in.Brd.Money | 16a.u | .... | .... | .... | .... | .... | .... | — | — | — | — | — | — |
| Deposits Excl. from Broad Money | 16b.u | .... | .... | .... | .... | .... | .... | — | — | — | — | — | — |
| Sec.Oh.th.Shares Excl. f/Brd.Money | 16s.u | .... | .... | .... | .... | .... | .... | — | — | — | — | — | — |
| Loans | 16l.u | .... | .... | .... | .... | .... | .... | — | — | — | — | — | — |
| Financial Derivatives | 16m.u | .... | .... | .... | .... | .... | .... | — | — | — | — | — | — |
| Shares and Other Equity | 17a.u | .... | .... | .... | .... | .... | .... | 558 | 588 | 551 | 482 | 555 | 656 |
| Other Items (Net) | 17r.u | .... | .... | .... | .... | .... | .... | −418 | −393 | −1,659 | −845 | −89 | −4,182 |
| Memorandum Items | | | | | | | | | | | | | |
| National Residency Criterion | | | | | | | | | | | | | |
| Net Foreign Assets | 11n | .... | .... | .... | .... | .... | .... | 4,834 | 5,926 | 6,232 | 5,801 | 7,663 | 5,803 |
| Claims on Nonresidents | 11 | .... | .... | .... | .... | .... | .... | 5,159 | 6,403 | 6,409 | 5,974 | 7,903 | 6,246 |
| Liabilities to Nonresidents | 16c | .... | .... | .... | .... | .... | .... | 325 | 477 | 177 | 173 | 240 | 443 |
| Claims on Other Depository Corps. | 12e | .... | .... | .... | .... | .... | .... | — | — | — | — | — | 346 |
| Net Claims on Central Government | 12an | .... | .... | .... | .... | .... | .... | −709 | −420 | −1,056 | −465 | −1,204 | −414 |
| Claims on Central Government | 12a | .... | .... | .... | .... | .... | .... | — | 73 | 79 | 54 | 56 | 862 |
| Liabilities to Central Government | 16d | .... | .... | .... | .... | .... | .... | 709 | 493 | 1,135 | 519 | 1,260 | 1,276 |
| Claims on Other Sectors | 12s | .... | .... | .... | .... | .... | .... | 5 | 4 | 3 | 3 | 1 | 1 |
| Claims on Other Fin. Corps. | 12g | .... | .... | .... | .... | .... | .... | — | — | — | — | — | — |
| Claims on State & Local Govts. | 12b | .... | .... | .... | .... | .... | .... | — | — | — | — | — | — |
| Claims on Private Sector | 12d | .... | .... | .... | .... | .... | .... | 5 | 4 | 3 | 3 | 1 | 1 |
| Liabs.to ODCs, Inc.in Mon.Base | 14c | .... | .... | .... | .... | .... | .... | 1,089 | 1,873 | 1,383 | 1,472 | 4,267 | 2,842 |
| Liabs.to Ot.Sectors, Inc.in Mon.Base | 14d | .... | .... | .... | .... | .... | .... | 25 | 2 | 10 | 6 | — | — |
| Liabs.to ODCs,Excl.f/Mon.Base | 14n | .... | .... | .... | .... | .... | .... | — | — | — | — | — | — |
| Net Claims on Eurosystem | 12e.s | .... | .... | .... | .... | .... | .... | .... | .... | .... | .... | .... | 367 |

# Lithuania 946

| | | 2004 | 2005 | 2006 | 2007 | 2008 | 2009 | 2010 | 2011 | 2012 | 2013 | 2014 | 2015 |
|---|---|---|---|---|---|---|---|---|---|---|---|---|---|
| **Other Depository Corporations** | | | | | | | _Millions of Euros: End of Period_ | | | | | | |
| Euro Area Wide Residency Criterion | | | | | | | | | | | | | |
| Net Foreign Assets.......................... | **21n.u** | .... | .... | .... | .... | .... | .... | −3,968 | −2,660 | −2,389 | −2,352 | −2,154 | −1,153 |
| Claims on Nonresidents................ | **21..u** | .... | .... | .... | .... | .... | .... | 2,413 | 2,423 | 2,094 | 1,896 | 946 | 1,279 |
| Liabilities to Nonresidents............. | **26c.u** | .... | .... | .... | .... | .... | .... | 6,381 | 5,083 | 4,483 | 4,248 | 3,100 | 2,432 |
| Claims on Eurosystem..................... | **20..u** | .... | .... | .... | .... | .... | .... | 1,432 | 2,301 | 1,785 | 1,830 | 4,759 | 3,299 |
| Currency......................................... | **20a.u** | .... | .... | .... | .... | .... | .... | 353 | 399 | 374 | 331 | 405 | 361 |
| Reserve Deposits and Securities..... | **20b.u** | .... | .... | .... | .... | .... | .... | 1,079 | 1,902 | 1,411 | 1,499 | 4,354 | 2,938 |
| Other Claims.................................. | **20n.u** | .... | .... | .... | .... | .... | .... | — | — | — | — | — | — |
| Net Claims on Central Government.. | **22anu** | .... | .... | .... | .... | .... | .... | 759 | 712 | 495 | 1,431 | 858 | 867 |
| Claims on Central Government...... | **22a.u** | .... | .... | .... | .... | .... | .... | 1,534 | 1,005 | 1,059 | 1,813 | 1,714 | 1,585 |
| Liabilities to Central Government... | **26d.u** | .... | .... | .... | .... | .... | .... | 775 | 293 | 564 | 382 | 856 | 718 |
| Claims on Other Sectors................. | **22s.u** | .... | .... | .... | .... | .... | .... | 18,596 | 17,726 | 18,110 | 17,321 | 17,132 | 17,597 |
| Claims on Other Financial Corps.... | **22g.u** | .... | .... | .... | .... | .... | .... | 1,281 | 1,176 | 1,487 | 1,202 | 1,163 | 1,049 |
| Claims on State & Local Govts....... | **22b.u** | .... | .... | .... | .... | .... | .... | 689 | 955 | 970 | 964 | 933 | 885 |
| Claims on Public Nonfin. Corps...... | **22c.u** | .... | .... | .... | .... | .... | .... | — | — | — | — | — | — |
| Claims on Private Sector................ | **22d.u** | .... | .... | .... | .... | .... | .... | 16,626 | 15,595 | 15,653 | 15,155 | 15,036 | 15,663 |
| Liabilities to Eurosystem................. | **26g.u** | .... | .... | .... | .... | .... | .... | 379 | 296 | 392 | 344 | 192 | 538 |
| Transf.Dep.Included in Broad Money | **24..u** | .... | .... | .... | .... | .... | .... | 5,753 | 6,317 | 7,467 | 8,416 | 10,814 | 12,131 |
| Other.Dep.Included in Broad Money. | **25..u** | .... | .... | .... | .... | .... | .... | 5,931 | 5,425 | 5,079 | 4,767 | 4,436 | 4,141 |
| Sec.Ot.th.Shares Inc.in.Brd. Money... | **26a.u** | .... | .... | .... | .... | .... | .... | 44 | 74 | 118 | 63 | 27 | 28 |
| Deposits Excl. from Broad Money..... | **26b.u** | .... | .... | .... | .... | .... | .... | 291 | 338 | 373 | 330 | 294 | 343 |
| Sec.Ot.th.Shares Excl.f/Brd. Money... | **26s.u** | .... | .... | .... | .... | .... | .... | −343 | −301 | −469 | −522 | −365 | −266 |
| Loans............................................. | **26l.u** | .... | .... | .... | .... | .... | .... | — | — | — | — | — | — |
| Financial Derivatives....................... | **26m.u** | .... | .... | .... | .... | .... | .... | 217 | 185 | 206 | 144 | 275 | 132 |
| Insurance Technical Reserves........... | **26r.u** | .... | .... | .... | .... | .... | .... | — | — | — | — | — | — |
| Shares and Other Equity................. | **27a.u** | .... | .... | .... | .... | .... | .... | 1,894 | 2,181 | 2,340 | 2,507 | 2,580 | 2,615 |
| Other Items (Net)........................... | **27r.u** | .... | .... | .... | .... | .... | .... | 2,652 | 3,563 | 2,492 | 2,172 | 2,338 | 951 |
| Memorandum Items | | | | | | | | | | | | | |
| Total Assets................................... | **20ra** | .... | .... | .... | .... | .... | .... | 25,670 | 24,695 | 24,405 | 24,038 | 25,488 | 24,781 |
| National Residency Criterion | | | | | | | | | | | | | |
| Net Foreign Assets.......................... | **21n** | .... | .... | .... | .... | .... | .... | −4,663 | −4,599 | −3,633 | −3,118 | −3,404 | −882 |
| Claims on Nonresidents................ | **21** | .... | .... | .... | .... | .... | .... | 3,947 | 3,226 | 3,142 | 3,068 | 1,726 | 2,241 |
| Liabilities to Nonresidents............. | **26c** | .... | .... | .... | .... | .... | .... | 8,610 | 7,825 | 6,775 | 6,186 | 5,130 | 3,123 |
| Net Claims on Central Government.. | **22an** | .... | .... | .... | .... | .... | .... | 210 | 687 | 465 | 1,221 | 788 | 643 |
| Claims on Central Government...... | **22a** | .... | .... | .... | .... | .... | .... | 984 | 979 | 1,028 | 1,603 | 1,644 | 1,361 |
| Liabilities to Central Government... | **26d** | .... | .... | .... | .... | .... | .... | 774 | 292 | 563 | 382 | 856 | 718 |
| Claims on Other Sectors................. | **22s** | .... | .... | .... | .... | .... | .... | 18,367 | 17,545 | 17,912 | 17,051 | 16,984 | 17,427 |
| Claims on Other Fin. Corps............ | **22g** | .... | .... | .... | .... | .... | .... | 1,252 | 1,144 | 1,452 | 1,068 | 1,152 | 1,024 |
| Claims on State & Local Govts....... | **22b** | .... | .... | .... | .... | .... | .... | 685 | 903 | 921 | 913 | 902 | 884 |
| Claims on Private Sector................ | **22d** | .... | .... | .... | .... | .... | .... | 16,430 | 15,498 | 15,539 | 15,070 | 14,930 | 15,519 |
| Transf.Dep.Included in Broad Money | **24** | .... | .... | .... | .... | .... | .... | 5,660 | 6,255 | 7,394 | 8,348 | 10,722 | 12,035 |
| Other.Dep.Included in Broad Money. | **25** | .... | .... | .... | .... | .... | .... | 5,868 | 5,419 | 5,069 | 4,752 | 4,415 | 4,138 |
| Sec.Ot.th.Shares Inc.in.Brd. Money... | **26a** | .... | .... | .... | .... | .... | .... | 103 | 138 | 143 | 88 | 37 | 28 |
| Deposits Excl. from Broad Money..... | **26b** | .... | .... | .... | .... | .... | .... | 257 | 308 | 344 | 330 | 293 | 299 |
| Sec.Ot.th.Shares Excl.f/Brd. Money... | **26s** | .... | .... | .... | .... | .... | .... | 240 | 195 | 183 | 35 | 20 | 16 |

# Lithuania 946

| | | 2004 | 2005 | 2006 | 2007 | 2008 | 2009 | 2010 | 2011 | 2012 | 2013 | 2014 | 2015 |
|---|---|---|---|---|---|---|---|---|---|---|---|---|---|
| **Depository Corporations** | | | | | | | *Millions of Euros: End of Period* | | | | | | |
| Euro Area Wide Residency Criterion | | | | | | | | | | | | | |
| Net Foreign Assets | 31n.u | .... | .... | .... | .... | .... | .... | −3,441 | −1,432 | −437 | −443 | 2,512 | 1,501 |
| Claims on Nonresidents | 31..u | .... | .... | .... | .... | .... | .... | 3,265 | 4,128 | 4,223 | 3,978 | 5,824 | 4,161 |
| Liabilities to Nonresidents | 36c.u | .... | .... | .... | .... | .... | .... | 6,706 | 5,560 | 4,660 | 4,421 | 3,312 | 2,660 |
| Domestic Claims | 32..u | .... | .... | .... | .... | .... | .... | 22,252 | 21,804 | 19,846 | 21,053 | 19,524 | 20,587 |
| Net Claims on Central Government | 32anu | .... | .... | .... | .... | .... | .... | 3,651 | 4,053 | 1,319 | 3,014 | 1,504 | 691 |
| Claims on Central Government | 32a.u | .... | .... | .... | .... | .... | .... | 5,135 | 4,839 | 3,018 | 3,915 | 3,620 | 2,685 |
| Liabilities to Central Government | 36d.u | .... | .... | .... | .... | .... | .... | 1,484 | 786 | 1,699 | 901 | 2,116 | 1,994 |
| Claims on Other Sectors | 32s.u | .... | .... | .... | .... | .... | .... | 18,601 | 17,751 | 18,527 | 18,039 | 18,020 | 19,896 |
| Claims on Other Financial Corps | 32g.u | .... | .... | .... | .... | .... | .... | 1,281 | 1,197 | 1,618 | 1,506 | 1,757 | 3,188 |
| Claims on State & Local Govts | 32b.u | .... | .... | .... | .... | .... | .... | 689 | 955 | 1,253 | 1,351 | 1,185 | 1,025 |
| Claims on Public Nonfin. Corps | 32c.u | .... | .... | .... | .... | .... | .... | — | — | — | — | — | — |
| Claims on Private Sector | 32d.u | .... | .... | .... | .... | .... | .... | 16,631 | 15,599 | 15,656 | 15,182 | 15,078 | 15,683 |
| Broad Money Liabilities | 35l.u | .... | .... | .... | .... | .... | .... | 13,952 | 14,551 | 15,602 | 16,363 | 16,548 | 21,992 |
| Currency Outside Depository Corps | 34a.u | .... | .... | .... | .... | .... | .... | 2,199 | 2,733 | 2,928 | 3,111 | 1,271 | 5,692 |
| Transferable Deposits | 34..u | .... | .... | .... | .... | .... | .... | 5,755 | 6,319 | 7,477 | 8,419 | 10,814 | 12,131 |
| Other Deposits | 35..u | .... | .... | .... | .... | .... | .... | 5,954 | 5,425 | 5,079 | 4,770 | 4,436 | 4,141 |
| Securities Other than Shares | 36a.u | .... | .... | .... | .... | .... | .... | 44 | 74 | 118 | 63 | 27 | 28 |
| Deposits Excl. from Broad Money | 36b.u | .... | .... | .... | .... | .... | .... | 291 | 338 | 373 | 330 | 294 | 343 |
| Sec.Oth.th.Shares Excl.f/Brd. Money | 36s.u | .... | .... | .... | .... | .... | .... | −343 | −301 | −469 | −522 | −365 | −266 |
| Loans | 36l.u | .... | .... | .... | .... | .... | .... | — | — | — | — | — | — |
| Financial Derivatives | 36m.u | .... | .... | .... | .... | .... | .... | 217 | 185 | 206 | 144 | 275 | 132 |
| Insurance Technical Reserves | 36r.u | .... | .... | .... | .... | .... | .... | — | — | — | — | — | — |
| Shares and Other Equity | 37a.u | .... | .... | .... | .... | .... | .... | 2,452 | 2,769 | 2,891 | 2,989 | 3,135 | 3,271 |
| Other Items (Net) | 37r.u | .... | .... | .... | .... | .... | .... | 2,242 | 2,829 | 803 | 1,297 | 2,143 | −3,381 |
| Broad Money Liabs., Seasonally Adj. | 35lub | .... | .... | .... | .... | .... | .... | 13,782 | 14,379 | 15,418 | 16,170 | 16,352 | 21,740 |
| Memorandum Items | | | | | | | | | | | | | |
| National Residency Criterion | | | | | | | | | | | | | |
| Net Foreign Assets | 31n | .... | .... | .... | .... | .... | .... | 171 | 1,327 | 2,599 | 2,683 | 4,259 | 4,921 |
| Claims on Nonresidents | 31 | .... | .... | .... | .... | .... | .... | 9,106 | 9,629 | 9,551 | 9,042 | 9,629 | 8,487 |
| Liabilities to Nonresidents | 36c | .... | .... | .... | .... | .... | .... | 8,935 | 8,302 | 6,952 | 6,359 | 5,370 | 3,566 |
| Domestic Claims | 32 | .... | .... | .... | .... | .... | .... | 17,873 | 17,816 | 17,324 | 17,810 | 16,569 | 17,657 |
| Net Claims on Central Government | 32an | .... | .... | .... | .... | .... | .... | −499 | 267 | −591 | 756 | −416 | 229 |
| Claims on Central Government | 32a | .... | .... | .... | .... | .... | .... | 984 | 1,052 | 1,107 | 1,657 | 1,700 | 2,223 |
| Liabilities to Central Government | 36d | .... | .... | .... | .... | .... | .... | 1,483 | 785 | 1,698 | 901 | 2,116 | 1,994 |
| Claims on Other Sectors | 32s | .... | .... | .... | .... | .... | .... | 18,372 | 17,549 | 17,915 | 17,054 | 16,985 | 17,428 |
| Claims on Other Financial Corps | 32g | .... | .... | .... | .... | .... | .... | 1,252 | 1,144 | 1,452 | 1,068 | 1,152 | 1,024 |
| Claims on State & Local Govts | 32b | .... | .... | .... | .... | .... | .... | 685 | 903 | 921 | 913 | 902 | 884 |
| Claims on Private Sector | 32d | .... | .... | .... | .... | .... | .... | 16,435 | 15,502 | 15,542 | 15,073 | 14,931 | 15,520 |
| Transf.Dep.Included in Broad Money | 34 | .... | .... | .... | .... | .... | .... | 5,662 | 6,257 | 7,404 | 8,351 | 10,722 | 12,035 |
| Other Dep.Included in Broad Money | 35 | .... | .... | .... | .... | .... | .... | 5,891 | 5,419 | 5,069 | 4,755 | 4,415 | 4,138 |
| Sec.Ot.th.Shares Inc.in.Brd. Money | 36a | .... | .... | .... | .... | .... | .... | 103 | 138 | 143 | 88 | 37 | 28 |
| Deposits Excl. from Broad Money | 36b | .... | .... | .... | .... | .... | .... | 257 | 308 | 344 | 330 | 293 | 299 |
| Sec.Ot.th.Shares Excl./f.Brd. Money | 36s | .... | .... | .... | .... | .... | .... | 240 | 195 | 183 | 35 | 20 | 16 |
| **Monetary Aggregates** | | | | | | | *Millions of Litai: End of Period* | | | | | | |
| Money (National Definitions) | | | | | | | | | | | | | |
| Monetary Base | 19ma | 6,979 | 8,919 | 10,642 | 12,886 | 12,708 | 10,523 | 12,564 | 17,280 | 16,172 | 16,967 | 20,520 | .... |
| M1 | 59ma | † 15,126 | 20,903 | 24,834 | 27,938 | 23,322 | 22,050 | 27,399 | 31,285 | 35,894 | 39,808 | 41,712 | 17,823 |
| M2 | 59mb | † 22,354 | 29,488 | 35,819 | 43,470 | 43,313 | 43,634 | 47,727 | 50,001 | 53,623 | 56,280 | 57,065 | 21,993 |
| M3 | 59mc | 22,542 | 29,851 | 36,346 | 44,228 | 44,063 | 44,182 | 48,117 | 50,487 | 54,150 | 56,582 | 57,192 | 22,021 |
| **Interest Rates** | | | | | | | *Percent Per Annum* | | | | | | |
| Repurchase Agreement Rate (EOP) | 60.q | 3.00 | 3.25 | 4.50 | 5.00 | 3.00 | 1.75 | 1.75 | 1.75 | 1.50 | .75 | .30 | .30 |
| Money Market Rate | 60b | 1.53 | 1.97 | 2.76 | 4.18 | 3.95 | .88 | .22 | .75 | .14 | .12 | .07 | .02 |
| Money Market Rate (Fgn. Cur.) | 60b.f | 1.73 | 2.59 | 3.06 | 4.25 | 2.92 | .44 | .28 | .41 | .11 | .19 | .26 | .... |
| Treasury Bill Rate | 60c | 2.25 | 2.36 | 2.95 | 4.23 | 5.35 | 8.54 | 2.80 | 2.40 | 1.33 | .61 | .... | .... |
| Savings Rate | 60k | 2.03 | .... | .... | .... | .... | .... | .... | .... | .... | .... | .... | .... |
| Savings Rate (Fgn. Cur.) | 60k.f | 1.45 | .... | .... | .... | .... | .... | .... | .... | .... | .... | .... | .... |
| Deposit Rate | 60l | 1.22 | † 2.40 | 2.97 | 5.40 | 7.65 | 4.81 | 1.71 | .... | .... | .... | .... | .... |
| Deposit Rate (Fgn. Currency) | 60l.f | 1.44 | † 2.11 | 2.49 | 3.45 | 3.95 | 2.32 | .96 | .... | .... | .... | .... | .... |
| Lending Rate | 60p | 5.74 | † 5.27 | 5.11 | 6.86 | 8.41 | 8.39 | 5.99 | .... | .... | .... | .... | .... |
| Lending Rate (Fgn. Currency) | 60p.f | 3.95 | † 3.86 | 4.60 | 5.65 | 6.29 | 4.57 | 4.07 | .... | .... | .... | .... | .... |
| Government Bond Yield | 61 | 4.50 | 3.70 | 4.08 | 4.55 | 5.61 | 14.00 | 5.57 | 5.16 | 4.83 | 3.83 | 2.79 | 1.38 |
| **Prices, Production, Labor** | | | | | | | *Index Numbers (2010=100): Period Averages* | | | | | | |
| Share Prices | 62 | 65.4 | 122.3 | 125.0 | 156.4 | 115.0 | 64.2 | 100.0 | 111.2 | 100.1 | 119.4 | 136.4 | 145.4 |
| Producer Prices | 63 | 71.0 | 80.5 | 86.3 | 91.5 | 107.4 | 89.8 | 100.0 | 114.7 | 119.5 | 115.9 | 110.8 | 101.0 |
| Consumer Prices | 64 | 75.7 | 77.7 | 80.6 | 85.2 | 94.5 | 98.7 | 100.0 | 104.1 | 107.3 | 108.5 | 108.6 | 107.6 |
| Harmonized CPI | 64h | 75.8 | 77.8 | 80.7 | 85.4 | 94.9 | 98.8 | 100.0 | 104.1 | 107.4 | 108.7 | 108.9 | 108.2 |
| Wages: Average Earnings | 65 | 58.0 | 62.3 | 72.8 | 88.2 | 103.8 | 100.2 | 100.0 | 101.9 | 105.6 | 110.7 | 115.8 | 122.9 |
| Industrial Production | 66 | 88.3 | 95.7 | 101.9 | 103.5 | 109.8 | 93.8 | 100.0 | 110.1 | 115.5 | 121.0 | 121.9 | 128.8 |
| Manufacturing Employment | 67 | 124.1 | † 127.4 | 127.2 | 128.7 | † 127.9 | 109.5 | 100.0 | 101.5 | 105.0 | 105.1 | 103.3 | 104.7 |
| | | | | | | | *Number in Thousands: Period Averages* | | | | | | |
| Labor Force | 67d | 1,594 | 1,544 | 1,492 | 1,487 | 1,484 | 1,500 | 1,495 | 1,454 | 1,441 | 1,437 | 1,446 | 1,434 |
| Employment | 67e | 1,420 | 1,414 | 1,405 | 1,422 | 1,397 | 1,290 | 1,224 | 1,226 | 1,244 | 1,264 | 1,288 | 1,301 |
| Unemployment | 67c | 173 | † 130 | 88 | 64 | 88 | 211 | 270 | 228 | 197 | 173 | 158 | 134 |
| Unemployment Rate (%) | 67r | 10.9 | † 8.3 | 5.8 | 4.3 | 5.8 | 13.8 | 17.8 | 15.4 | 13.4 | 11.8 | 10.7 | 9.1 |
| **Intl. Transactions & Positions** | | | | | | *Millions of Litai through 2014: Millions of Euros Beginning 2015; End of Period* | | | | | | | |
| Exports | 70 | 25,819 | 32,767 | 38,888 | 43,192 | 55,511 | 40,732 | 54,039 | 69,577 | 79,578 | 84,748 | 84,252 | 22,984 |
| Imports, c.i.f | 71 | 34,384 | 43,152 | 53,275 | 61,504 | 73,006 | 45,311 | 60,953 | 78,812 | 85,902 | 90,490 | 91,605 | 25,397 |

# Lithuania   946

| | | 2004 | 2005 | 2006 | 2007 | 2008 | 2009 | 2010 | 2011 | 2012 | 2013 | 2014 | 2015 |
|---|---|---|---|---|---|---|---|---|---|---|---|---|---|
| **Balance of Payments** | | | | | | | *Millions of US Dollars* | | | | | | |
| A. Current Account* | 109bx | † −1,714.8 | −1,877.8 | −3,190.1 | −5,996.1 | −6,565.8 | 848.7 | −119.2 | −1,682.5 | −510.3 | 726.0 | 1,684.6 | −720.4 |
| Goods, credit (exports) | 1a9cx | † 7,977.2 | 10,973.9 | 13,200.7 | 15,836.3 | 22,497.4 | 15,445.6 | 19,720.5 | 27,018.3 | 28,808.5 | 31,884.0 | 31,497.7 | 24,813.8 |
| Goods, debit (imports) | 1a9dx | † 10,653.3 | 13,800.8 | 17,373.2 | 21,868.3 | 28,970.7 | 17,065.8 | 21,903.3 | 29,895.2 | 30,230.1 | 33,109.7 | 32,750.8 | 26,932.6 |
| Balance on goods | 1a9bx | † −2,676.1 | −2,826.8 | −4,172.5 | −6,032.1 | −6,473.3 | −1,620.2 | −2,182.8 | −2,876.9 | −1,421.6 | −1,225.7 | −1,253.1 | −2,116.6 |
| Services, credit (exports) | 1b9cx | † 2,765.3 | 3,039.5 | 3,630.3 | 4,242.9 | 5,068.2 | 4,093.9 | 4,525.3 | 5,620.8 | 6,151.2 | 7,162.1 | 7,762.0 | 6,646.3 |
| Services, debit (imports) | 1b9dx | † 1,668.2 | 2,072.5 | 2,562.4 | 3,426.3 | 4,238.6 | 3,094.6 | 3,043.4 | 3,848.1 | 4,369.7 | 5,360.7 | 5,590.5 | 4,670.2 |
| Balance on Goods & Services | 1z9bx | † −1,579.0 | −1,859.9 | −3,104.6 | −5,215.4 | −5,643.7 | −620.9 | −700.9 | −1,104.2 | 359.9 | 575.7 | 918.4 | −142.7 |
| Primary income: credit | 1c9cx | † 453.5 | 672.1 | 785.3 | 934.4 | 1,166.5 | 908.2 | 1,143.1 | 1,362.3 | 1,133.6 | 1,258.6 | 985.2 | 757.5 |
| Primary income: debit | 1c9dx | † 960.5 | 1,084.2 | 1,448.7 | 2,489.1 | 2,933.7 | 155.2 | 1,827.9 | 2,975.9 | 2,503.3 | 2,388.5 | 1,724.9 | 2,356.4 |
| Balance on gds, serv. & prim. inc. | 1y9bx | † −2,086.0 | −2,271.9 | −3,768.0 | −6,770.1 | −7,410.9 | 132.0 | −1,385.8 | −2,717.9 | −1,009.8 | −554.1 | 178.7 | −1,741.7 |
| Secondary income: credit | 1d9ca | † 746.7 | 837.4 | 1,214.3 | 1,599.7 | 1,893.9 | 1,739.8 | 2,259.6 | 2,507.1 | 1,932.4 | 2,528.6 | 2,747.9 | 1,944.3 |
| Secondary income: debit | 1d9da | † 375.6 | 443.2 | 636.4 | 825.7 | 1,048.8 | 1,023.1 | 993.1 | 1,471.7 | 1,432.9 | 1,248.5 | 1,242.0 | 923.0 |
| B. Capital Account* | 209ba | † 170.2 | 260.9 | 467.0 | 873.3 | 910.0 | 1,657.0 | 1,422.2 | 1,392.8 | 1,240.4 | 1,454.5 | 1,286.9 | 1,242.3 |
| Capital account: credit | 209ca | † 171.2 | 261.0 | 467.2 | 873.3 | 910.1 | 1,657.5 | 1,422.2 | 1,392.9 | 1,288.2 | 1,454.6 | 1,287.5 | 1,243.2 |
| Capital account: debit | 209da | † 1.0 | .1 | .2 | — | .1 | .5 | — | .1 | 47.8 | — | .6 | 1.0 |
| Balance on current & capital acct. | 129ba | † −1,544.6 | −1,616.9 | −2,723.1 | −5,122.8 | −5,655.8 | 2,505.7 | 1,303.0 | −289.7 | 730.1 | 2,180.5 | 2,971.4 | 521.9 |
| C. Financial Account* | 309na | † −1,312.4 | −1,950.7 | −4,442.7 | −6,291.0 | −4,342.9 | 2,467.5 | 447.6 | −2,171.9 | 463.4 | 2,217.3 | −802.1 | 2,096.8 |
| Direct investment: assets | 3a9aa | † 297.5 | 499.5 | 501.7 | 917.1 | 271.1 | 253.0 | 57.0 | 139.8 | 274.8 | 426.9 | 550.5 | −250.2 |
| Equity & investment fund shares | 3aaaa | † 202.3 | 205.7 | 107.1 | 656.1 | 399.5 | 158.3 | 1.2 | 1.4 | 329.2 | 267.9 | 30.7 | 48.5 |
| Debt instruments | 3abaa | † 95.2 | 293.8 | 394.6 | 260.9 | −128.5 | 94.7 | 55.9 | 138.4 | −54.4 | 159.0 | 519.7 | −299.2 |
| Direct investment: liabilities | 3a9la | † 796.1 | 845.9 | 2,067.1 | 2,293.5 | 1,907.5 | 18.0 | 865.3 | 1,538.0 | 575.6 | 708.3 | 350.9 | 627.3 |
| Equity & investment fund shares | 3aala | † 727.3 | 728.7 | 1,754.2 | 1,484.8 | 1,042.6 | −125.2 | 318.5 | 1,248.6 | 416.1 | 577.4 | 893.2 | 946.9 |
| Debt instruments | 3abla | † 68.8 | 117.1 | 312.9 | 808.6 | 865.0 | 143.2 | 546.8 | 289.4 | 159.6 | 130.8 | −542.3 | −320.2 |
| Portfolio investment: assets | 3b9aa | † 217.8 | 777.7 | 1,105.7 | 838.3 | 100.3 | 1,018.8 | 249.4 | −273.0 | 301.4 | 754.0 | 163.2 | −265.3 |
| Equity & investment fund shares | 3baaa | † 16.7 | 184.9 | 286.3 | 357.2 | −26.6 | 353.6 | 439.5 | 247.8 | 216.8 | 119.9 | 156.4 | 87.6 |
| Debt securities | 3bbaa | † 201.0 | 592.7 | 819.3 | 481.1 | 126.9 | 665.2 | −190.1 | −520.8 | 84.6 | 634.1 | 6.8 | −352.6 |
| Portfolio investment: liabilities | 3b9la | † 430.9 | 542.0 | 852.2 | 609.4 | −236.1 | 2,294.2 | 2,459.0 | 1,376.1 | 1,520.6 | −1,118.4 | 1,648.3 | −90.6 |
| Equity & investment fund shares | 3bala | † 8.0 | 130.0 | 72.0 | −166.1 | 2.5 | −2.0 | 36.7 | 8.6 | −53.0 | −14.7 | 16.2 | 19.9 |
| Debt securities | 3bbla | † 423.0 | 412.0 | 780.2 | 775.5 | −238.7 | 2,296.3 | 2,422.3 | 1,367.5 | 1,573.6 | −1,103.7 | 1,632.1 | −110.5 |
| Fin. der.& empl.stk.ops.(ESOs): net. | 3c9na | † 2.6 | 12.8 | −11.0 | −2.4 | 14.7 | 38.1 | −89.1 | 5.5 | 6.5 | −6.5 | 1.3 | −135.1 |
| Fin. der. & ESOs.: assets | 3c9aa | .... | .... | .... | .... | .... | .... | .... | .... | .... | .... | .... | .... |
| Fin. der. & ESOs.: liabilities | 3c9la | .... | .... | .... | .... | .... | .... | .... | .... | .... | .... | .... | .... |
| Other investment: assets | 3d9aa | † 710.0 | 788.0 | 529.0 | 1,899.0 | 875.8 | 698.1 | 1,088.7 | 605.9 | −301.9 | −1.3 | −537.0 | 5,620.0 |
| Other equity | 3daaa | † 2.1 | — | — | −.1 | — | .1 | −.1 | — | — | — | .1 | 308.4 |
| Debt instruments | 3dzaa | † 708.0 | 788.0 | 529.0 | 1,899.0 | 875.8 | 698.0 | 1,088.7 | 605.9 | −301.9 | −1.3 | −537.2 | 5,311.6 |
| Other investment: liabilities | 3d9la | † 1,313.2 | 2,640.9 | 3,648.8 | 7,040.1 | 3,933.4 | −2,771.8 | −2,465.8 | −263.9 | −2,278.8 | −634.0 | −1,019.1 | 2,335.8 |
| Other equity | 3dala | † — | — | — | — | — | — | — | — | 2.1 | −3.7 | — | — |
| Debt instruments | 3dzla | † 1,313.2 | 2,640.9 | 3,648.8 | 7,040.1 | 3,933.4 | −2,771.8 | −2,465.8 | −263.9 | −2,280.9 | −630.3 | −1,019.1 | 2,335.8 |
| Curr.+ cap.− finan. acct. balance | 4y9na | † −232.2 | 333.8 | 1,719.6 | 1,168.2 | −1,312.9 | 38.2 | 855.4 | 1,882.2 | 266.7 | −36.8 | 3,773.5 | −1,574.9 |
| D. Net Errors and Omissions | 409na | † 127.8 | 378.0 | −212.4 | 39.3 | 155.2 | 84.9 | −364.1 | −8.2 | −146.5 | −538.6 | −2,158.5 | 92.7 |
| E. Reserves and Related Items | 4z9na | † −104.4 | 711.8 | 1,507.2 | 1,207.6 | −1,157.7 | 123.1 | 491.3 | 1,873.9 | 120.2 | −575.3 | 1,615.0 | −1,481.3 |
| Reserve assets | 3e9aa | † −124.2 | 686.3 | 1,507.2 | 1,207.6 | −1,157.7 | 123.1 | 491.3 | 1,873.9 | 120.2 | −575.3 | 1,615.0 | −1,481.3 |
| Credit and loans from the IMF | 3dcla | † −19.8 | −25.5 | — | — | — | — | — | — | — | — | — | — |
| Exceptional financing | 409la | .... | .... | .... | .... | .... | .... | .... | .... | .... | .... | .... | .... |
| *Excludes components in group E | | | | | | | | | | | | | |
| | | | | | | | | | | | | | |
| **International Investment Position** | | | | | | | *Millions of US Dollars* | | | | | | |
| Assets | 809aa | † 7,619.0 | 9,410.7 | 14,127.7 | 20,637.3 | 19,383.7 | 22,253.9 | 22,694.1 | 23,167.5 | 23,798.2 | 25,346.5 | 24,227.9 | 24,975.7 |
| Direct investment | 8a9aa | † 591.8 | 1,011.2 | 1,575.8 | 2,495.9 | 2,781.1 | 3,407.7 | 3,153.1 | 3,146.6 | 3,436.3 | 4,393.9 | 4,403.5 | 3,427.2 |
| Equity & investment fund shares | 8aaaa | † 289.9 | 488.0 | 561.2 | 1,079.7 | 1,528.5 | 1,750.0 | 1,630.7 | 1,545.7 | 1,919.8 | 2,704.9 | 2,356.4 | 1,907.4 |
| Debt instruments | 8abaa | † 301.9 | 523.2 | 1,014.6 | 1,416.2 | 1,252.6 | 1,657.8 | 1,522.4 | 1,600.9 | 1,516.4 | 1,689.1 | 2,047.0 | 1,519.8 |
| Portfolio investment | 8b9aa | † 514.3 | 1,246.1 | 2,523.3 | 3,632.6 | 3,406.9 | 4,508.6 | 4,490.6 | 3,258.6 | 3,676.7 | 4,555.2 | 4,112.7 | 7,206.1 |
| Equity & investment fund shares | 8baaa | † 33.8 | 217.2 | 561.0 | 1,041.3 | 820.9 | 1,294.5 | 1,747.8 | 1,618.7 | 1,902.7 | 2,129.8 | 2,138.0 | 2,678.2 |
| Debt securities | 8bbaa | † 480.4 | 1,028.9 | 1,962.3 | 2,591.3 | 2,585.9 | 3,214.1 | 2,742.7 | 1,639.8 | 1,774.0 | 2,425.4 | 1,974.6 | 4,527.9 |
| Fin. der.(oth.than reserves) & ESOs | 8c9aa | † — | 9.5 | 69.2 | 223.1 | 38.8 | 46.4 | 151.0 | 148.6 | 179.3 | 113.8 | 272.2 | 118.7 |
| Other investment | 8d9aa | † 2,919.6 | 3,350.1 | 4,167.6 | 6,535.2 | 6,793.8 | 7,642.3 | 8,236.3 | 8,401.2 | 8,011.4 | 8,192.3 | 6,726.9 | 12,526.6 |
| Other equity | 8daaa | † 2.4 | 2.0 | 2.3 | 2.5 | 2.4 | 2.6 | 2.3 | 2.2 | 2.3 | 23.2 | 20.6 | 317.9 |
| Debt instruments | 8dzaa | † 2,917.2 | 3,348.1 | 4,165.3 | 6,532.7 | 6,791.5 | 7,639.7 | 8,234.0 | 8,399.0 | 8,009.2 | 8,169.1 | 6,706.3 | 12,208.7 |
| Reserve assets | 8e9aa | † 3,593.4 | 3,793.9 | 5,791.7 | 7,750.5 | 6,363.3 | 6,648.8 | 6,663.2 | 8,212.5 | 8,494.6 | 8,091.3 | 8,712.7 | 1,697.1 |
| Liabilities | 809la | † 16,430.8 | 19,893.8 | 29,350.0 | 43,965.4 | 42,836.6 | 44,924.1 | 43,642.1 | 44,427.3 | 47,275.3 | 48,020.1 | 44,684.4 | 43,240.6 |
| Direct investment | 8a9la | † 6,563.0 | 8,137.4 | 11,210.1 | 15,647.8 | 13,605.8 | 14,362.2 | 14,449.7 | 15,337.1 | 16,824.6 | 18,665.0 | 17,193.8 | 15,632.6 |
| Equity & investment fund shares | 8aala | † 5,498.9 | 7,101.8 | 9,707.9 | 13,033.5 | 9,586.0 | 10,809.0 | 10,686.0 | 11,398.7 | 12,485.7 | 13,656.4 | 13,002.1 | 12,369.8 |
| Debt instruments | 8abla | † 1,064.1 | 1,035.6 | 1,502.2 | 2,614.4 | 4,019.7 | 3,553.2 | 3,763.7 | 3,938.4 | 4,339.0 | 5,008.6 | 4,191.6 | 3,263.9 |
| Portfolio investment | 8b9la | † 2,811.5 | 2,964.6 | 4,587.5 | 5,733.5 | 3,958.4 | 7,201.1 | 9,977.8 | 10,774.2 | 13,929.5 | 12,647.3 | 13,887.9 | 13,014.3 |
| Equity & investment fund shares | 8bala | † 172.5 | 317.7 | 812.1 | 747.2 | 230.3 | 336.3 | 498.1 | 372.8 | 326.8 | 349.2 | 377.9 | 296.1 |
| Debt securities | 8bbla | † 2,639.1 | 2,646.9 | 3,775.4 | 4,986.3 | 3,728.1 | 6,864.8 | 9,479.8 | 10,401.4 | 13,602.6 | 12,298.1 | 13,510.0 | 12,718.2 |
| Fin. der.(oth.than reserves) & ESOs | 8c9la | † 2.9 | 4.0 | 30.2 | 41.2 | 130.0 | 156.6 | 152.4 | 116.3 | 113.9 | 95.3 | 74.1 | 90.4 |
| Other investment | 8d9la | † 7,053.3 | 8,787.8 | 13,522.2 | 22,542.9 | 25,142.5 | 23,204.1 | 19,062.2 | 18,199.7 | 16,407.3 | 16,612.5 | 13,528.6 | 14,503.3 |
| Other equity | 8dala | † — | — | — | — | — | — | — | — | 3.3 | — | — | — |
| Debt instruments | 8dzla | † 7,053.3 | 8,787.8 | 13,522.2 | 22,542.9 | 25,142.5 | 23,204.1 | 19,062.2 | 18,199.7 | 16,404.1 | 16,612.5 | 13,528.6 | 14,503.3 |

# Lithuania   946

| | | 2004 | 2005 | 2006 | 2007 | 2008 | 2009 | 2010 | 2011 | 2012 | 2013 | 2014 | 2015 |
|---|---|---|---|---|---|---|---|---|---|---|---|---|---|
| **Government Finance Operations Statement General Government** | | | | | | *Millions of Litai through 2009;  Millions of Euros Thereafter:  Fiscal Year Ends December 31* | | | | | | | | |
| Revenue | a1 | 19,932.0 | 23,662.3 | 27,644.6 | 33,504.6 | †38,125.4 | 31,918.7 | 9,615.9 | 10,191.2 | 10,700.1 | 11,268.6 | 12,200.2 | .... |
| Taxes | a11 | 12,386.7 | 14,439.1 | 17,143.9 | 20,523.7 | †23,185.3 | 15,992.4 | 4,589.0 | 4,970.6 | 5,305.7 | 5,632.0 | 5,975.8 | .... |
| Social Contributions | a12 | 5,440.0 | 6,080.3 | 7,584.1 | 9,135.5 | †10,778.6 | 11,749.8 | 3,295.7 | 3,480.8 | 3,622.8 | 3,806.6 | 4,078.5 | .... |
| Grants | a13 | .... | .... | 1,094.9 | 1,760.4 | †1,642.0 | 1,976.4 | 977.8 | 994.2 | 914.7 | 878.7 | 796.0 | .... |
| Other Revenue | a14 | 2,105.3 | 3,142.9 | 1,821.7 | 2,085.0 | †2,519.5 | 2,200.1 | 753.4 | 745.5 | 856.9 | 951.2 | 1,349.9 | .... |
| Expense | a2 | 20,480.9 | 23,465.8 | 25,743.3 | 30,771.9 | †38,950.4 | 39,720.0 | 11,136.8 | 12,625.9 | 11,521.6 | 12,135.9 | 12,414.3 | .... |
| Compensation of Employees | a21 | 6,796.8 | 7,433.6 | 8,307.4 | 9,373.4 | †11,536.0 | 11,312.1 | 2,942.0 | 3,074.2 | 3,111.3 | 3,195.4 | 3,307.0 | .... |
| Use of Goods & Services | a22 | 3,575.2 | 4,095.7 | 4,721.3 | 5,299.8 | †6,357.7 | 5,318.5 | 1,737.7 | 1,576.4 | 1,616.1 | 1,615.6 | 1,672.3 | .... |
| Consumption of Fixed Capital | a23 | 1,684.6 | 1,829.9 | 1,018.1 | 1,133.7 | †2,649.6 | 2,638.4 | 812.6 | 873.4 | 947.8 | 1,009.0 | 1,073.3 | .... |
| Interest | a24 | 586.5 | 582.5 | 618.9 | 698.0 | †777.9 | 1,226.8 | 526.1 | 591.1 | 693.9 | 661.1 | 649.9 | .... |
| Subsidies | a25 | 433.7 | 489.5 | 584.6 | 890.2 | †762.9 | 588.4 | 138.0 | 122.6 | 104.8 | 88.2 | 98.1 | .... |
| Grants | a26 | .... | .... | 627.2 | 679.6 | †874.3 | 898.0 | 195.9 | 228.9 | 192.0 | 361.3 | 312.2 | .... |
| Social Benefits | a27 | 6,568.3 | 7,504.5 | 8,898.0 | 11,175.0 | †14,783.8 | 16,723.3 | 4,504.9 | 4,501.4 | 4,540.6 | 4,524.4 | 4,550.1 | .... |
| Other Expense | a28 | 835.9 | 1,530.2 | 967.8 | 1,522.2 | †1,208.2 | 1,014.5 | 279.5 | 1,658.0 | 315.0 | 681.0 | 751.4 | .... |
| Gross Operating Balance [1-2+23] | agob | 1,135.7 | 2,026.4 | 2,919.4 | 3,866.4 | †1,824.6 | −5,162.9 | −708.4 | −1,561.3 | 126.2 | 141.7 | 859.3 | .... |
| Net Operating Balance [1-2] | anob | −548.9 | 196.5 | 1,901.3 | 2,732.7 | †−825.0 | −7,801.3 | −1,521.0 | −2,434.7 | −821.6 | −867.3 | −214.1 | .... |
| Net Acq. of Nonfinancial Assets | a31 | 414.6 | 558.5 | 2,333.9 | 3,908.0 | †2,861.8 | 874.4 | 413.1 | 361.2 | 227.4 | 49.6 | 28.9 | .... |
| Aquisition of Nonfin. Assets | a31.1 | .... | .... | .... | .... | †5,720.3 | 3,684.7 | 1,271.4 | 1,359.2 | 1,525.8 | 1,448.4 | 1,545.2 | .... |
| Disposal of Nonfin. Assets | a31.2 | .... | .... | .... | .... | †208.9 | 171.9 | 45.7 | 124.5 | 350.6 | 389.8 | 443.0 | .... |
| Net Lending/Borrowing [1-2-31] | anlb | −963.5 | −362.0 | −432.6 | −1,175.3 | †−3,686.8 | −8,675.7 | −1,934.1 | −2,795.9 | −1,049.0 | −916.9 | −243.0 | .... |
| Net Acq. of Financial Assets | a32 | −699.7 | 401.0 | 409.3 | 92.9 | †−2,249.5 | 1,863.1 | 691.1 | −1,230.9 | 550.2 | −379.8 | 1,396.0 | .... |
| *By instrument* | | | | | | | | | | | | | |
| Monetary Gold & SDRs | a3201 | .... | .... | .... | .... | .... | .... | .... | .... | .... | .... | .... | .... |
| Currency & Deposits | a3202 | −314.0 | 344.6 | 2,503.3 | −73.8 | †−2,546.5 | 2,463.1 | 400.4 | −1,091.0 | 849.6 | −486.5 | 1,211.4 | .... |
| Securities other than Shares | a3203 | — | — | — | — | †— | — | 30.1 | −113.4 | −11.6 | — | 50.0 | .... |
| Loans | a3204 | −214.3 | −166.1 | −148.5 | −62.2 | †−104.3 | −115.8 | −57.8 | −182.5 | −3.4 | 3.2 | 5.3 | .... |
| Shares & Other Equity | a3205 | −398.5 | −229.6 | −2,276.5 | −59.3 | †−2.5 | −763.6 | −65.7 | −7.0 | −66.7 | −3.5 | −1.2 | .... |
| Insurance Technical Reserves | a3206 | 3.6 | 2.4 | — | — | †— | — | .... | .... | .... | .... | .... | .... |
| Financial Derivatives | a3207 | .... | .... | — | — | †51.8 | 93.7 | −22.4 | −10.1 | −42.2 | −18.8 | −10.5 | .... |
| Other Accounts Receivable | a3208 | 223.5 | 449.7 | 331.0 | 288.2 | †352.0 | 185.7 | 406.4 | 173.2 | −175.5 | 125.8 | 141.0 | .... |
| *By debtor* | | | | | | | | | | | | | |
| Domestic | a321 | .... | .... | 276.4 | 86.4 | †−2,980.3 | 1,315.8 | 201.7 | −949.5 | 659.2 | −564.6 | 1,345.0 | .... |
| Foreign | a322 | .... | .... | 132.9 | 6.5 | †730.8 | 547.3 | 489.5 | −281.4 | −109.0 | 184.8 | 51.0 | .... |
| Net Incurrence of Liabilities | a33 | 175.1 | 766.7 | 841.9 | 1,268.2 | †1,437.3 | 10,538.8 | 2,625.2 | 1,565.0 | 1,599.2 | 537.2 | 1,639.0 | .... |
| *By instrument* | | | | | | | | | | | | | |
| Special Drawing Rights (SDRs) | a3301 | .... | .... | — | — | †— | — | — | — | — | — | — | .... |
| Currency & Deposits | a3302 | −286.2 | −87.8 | −796.4 | −1,358.7 | †−357.3 | −30.8 | −2.1 | −6.7 | 184.6 | 55.9 | 55.3 | .... |
| Securities other than Shares | a3303 | 1,086.7 | 1,692.7 | 2,379.7 | 1,910.3 | †−312.4 | 7,328.5 | 1,994.0 | 1,212.9 | 1,128.7 | −42.1 | 1,175.7 | .... |
| Loans | a3304 | −656.8 | −484.2 | −455.6 | −123.6 | †883.0 | 2,133.7 | 636.5 | 248.1 | 301.4 | 283.4 | 24.0 | .... |
| Shares & Other Equity | a3305 | — | — | — | — | †— | — | — | — | — | — | — | .... |
| Insurance Technical Reserves | a3306 | — | — | — | — | †— | — | — | — | — | — | — | .... |
| Financial Derivatives | a3307 | — | — | — | — | †— | — | — | — | — | — | — | .... |
| Other Accounts Payable | a3308 | 31.3 | −354.1 | −285.8 | 840.2 | †1,224.0 | 1,107.4 | −3.2 | 110.8 | −15.6 | 240.0 | 383.9 | .... |
| *By creditor* | | | | | | | | | | | | | |
| Domestic | a331 | .... | .... | −2,496.8 | −460.8 | †1,587.8 | 1,996.1 | 269.0 | 499.3 | 209.5 | 1,016.6 | 411.3 | .... |
| Foreign | a332 | .... | .... | 3,338.7 | 1,729.0 | †−150.5 | 8,542.7 | 2,356.3 | 1,065.7 | 1,389.7 | −479.4 | 1,227.6 | .... |
| Stat. Discrepancy [32-33-NLB] | anlbz | −88.7 | 3.7 | — | — | †— | .... | .... | .... | .... | .... | .... | .... |
| Memo Item: Expenditure [2+31] | a2m | 20,895.5 | 24,024.2 | 28,077.2 | 34,679.9 | †41,812.2 | 40,594.4 | 11,550.0 | 12,987.1 | 11,749.0 | 12,185.5 | 12,443.2 | .... |
| **Balance Sheet** | | | | | | | | | | | | | |
| Net Worth | a6 | .... | .... | .... | .... | .... | .... | .... | .... | .... | .... | .... | .... |
| Nonfinancial Assets | a61 | .... | .... | .... | .... | .... | .... | .... | .... | .... | .... | .... | .... |
| Financial Assets | a62 | 23,501.6 | 25,592.8 | 29,118.7 | 31,051.8 | †25,553.6 | 28,204.5 | 8,922.2 | 7,713.1 | 8,820.8 | 8,450.2 | 9,628.6 | .... |
| *By instrument* | | | | | | | | | | | | | |
| Monetary Gold & SDRs | a6201 | .... | .... | .... | .... | .... | .... | .... | .... | .... | .... | .... | .... |
| Currency & Deposits | a6202 | 3,476.2 | 3,820.8 | 6,336.9 | 6,278.1 | †2,581.5 | 5,036.2 | 2,089.5 | 1,050.3 | 1,885.2 | 1,375.8 | 2,575.2 | .... |
| Securities other than Shares | a6203 | — | — | — | — | †— | — | 132.6 | 10.8 | 1.0 | 1.0 | 51.0 | .... |
| Loans | a6204 | 1,613.8 | 1,563.8 | 1,347.2 | 1,243.1 | †1,121.7 | 1,003.5 | 253.1 | 65.0 | 64.6 | 65.6 | 65.2 | .... |
| Shares and Other Equity | a6205 | 16,386.5 | 17,731.0 | 18,594.7 | 20,394.7 | †18,247.2 | 18,228.3 | 4,783.8 | 4,716.1 | 5,215.7 | 5,285.6 | 5,228.6 | .... |
| Insurance Technical Reserves | a6206 | 11.5 | 14.0 | 20.4 | 9.8 | †— | — | .... | .... | .... | .... | .... | .... |
| Financial Derivatives | a6207 | — | — | — | — | †51.8 | 145.5 | 19.7 | 9.6 | −32.6 | −51.4 | −61.9 | .... |
| Other Accounts Receivable | a6208 | 2,013.6 | 2,463.3 | 2,819.6 | 3,126.2 | †3,551.4 | 3,791.0 | 1,643.4 | 1,861.4 | 1,686.9 | 1,773.5 | 1,770.5 | .... |
| *By debtor* | | | | | | | | | | | | | |
| Domestic | a621 | .... | .... | .... | .... | †23,598.3 | 25,701.9 | 7,595.1 | 6,685.5 | 7,917.4 | 7,361.9 | 8,489.4 | .... |
| Foreign | a622 | .... | .... | .... | .... | †1,955.3 | 2,502.6 | 1,327.1 | 1,027.6 | 903.4 | 1,088.2 | 1,139.2 | .... |
| Liabilities | a63 | 16,706.0 | 17,537.0 | 18,373.8 | 19,709.4 | †22,199.2 | 33,361.1 | 12,279.7 | 14,093.0 | 15,936.5 | 15,934.7 | 18,071.2 | .... |
| *By instrument* | | | | | | | | | | | | | |
| Special Drawing Rights (SDRs) | a6301 | — | — | — | — | †— | — | — | — | — | — | — | .... |
| Currency & Deposits | a6302 | 331.3 | 243.5 | — | — | †421.2 | 387.8 | 25.6 | 106.3 | 293.2 | 350.4 | 405.8 | .... |
| Securities other than Shares | a6303 | 9,931.3 | 11,624.0 | 14,212.2 | 16,136.3 | †15,145.9 | 22,622.1 | 8,394.6 | 9,750.3 | 11,140.2 | 10,800.2 | 12,698.4 | .... |
| Loans | a6304 | 2,235.0 | 1,815.1 | 1,365.9 | 1,242.7 | †2,139.9 | 4,260.1 | 1,886.9 | 2,143.7 | 2,521.1 | 2,876.1 | 2,833.6 | .... |
| Shares and Other Equity | a6305 | — | — | — | — | †— | — | — | — | — | — | — | .... |
| Insurance Technical Reserves | a6306 | — | — | — | — | †— | — | — | — | — | — | — | .... |
| Financial Derivatives | a6307 | .... | .... | — | — | †— | — | — | — | — | — | — | .... |
| Other Accounts Payable | a6308 | 4,208.4 | 3,854.3 | 2,795.6 | 2,330.3 | †4,492.2 | 6,091.1 | 1,972.6 | 2,092.8 | 1,982.0 | 1,908.0 | 2,133.4 | .... |
| *By creditor* | | | | | | | | | | | | | |
| Domestic | a631 | .... | .... | .... | .... | †8,381.5 | 10,802.0 | 3,206.1 | 3,805.0 | 5,192.0 | 6,132.4 | 6,318.0 | .... |
| Foreign | a632 | .... | .... | .... | .... | †13,817.7 | 22,559.1 | 9,073.5 | 10,288.0 | 10,744.4 | 9,802.4 | 11,753.1 | .... |
| Net Financial Worth [62-63] | a6m2 | 6,795.6 | 8,055.8 | 10,745.0 | 11,342.5 | †3,354.4 | −5,156.6 | −3,357.5 | −6,379.9 | −7,115.6 | −7,484.5 | −8,442.5 | .... |
| Memo Item: Debt at Market Value | a6m3 | 12,155.3 | 13,276.1 | 18,373.8 | 19,709.4 | 22,199.2 | 33,361.1 | 12,279.7 | 14,093.0 | 15,936.5 | 15,934.7 | 18,071.2 | .... |
| Memo Item: Debt at Face Value | a6m35 | 12,155.4 | 13,276.2 | 16,138.4 | 19,722.7 | †21,867.0 | 33,197.3 | .... | .... | .... | .... | .... | .... |
| Memo Item: Maastricht Debt | a6m36 | 7,947.0 | 9,421.9 | 13,387.8 | 17,392.4 | 17,374.8 | 27,106.2 | 10,305.8 | 11,900.2 | 13,439.3 | 13,501.2 | 15,471.1 | .... |
| Memo Item: Debt at Nominal Value | a6m4 | .... | .... | .... | .... | †17,374.8 | 27,106.2 | 10,305.8 | 11,900.2 | 13,439.3 | 13,501.2 | 15,471.1 | .... |

# Lithuania  946

| National Accounts | | 2004 | 2005 | 2006 | 2007 | 2008 | 2009 | 2010 | 2011 | 2012 | 2013 | 2014 | 2015 |
|---|---|---|---|---|---|---|---|---|---|---|---|---|---|
| | | *Millions of Litai through 2014; Millions of Euros Beginning 2015* | | | | | | | | | | | |
| Househ.Cons.Expend.,incl.NPISHs.... | 96f | 41,050.6 | 46,899.7 | 53,552.4 | 63,740.8 | 73,409.4 | 63,308.4 | 61,962.4 | 67,481.0 | 72,040.0 | 75,802.5 | 80,113.5 | † 23,806.6 |
| Government Consumption Expend... | 91f | 11,937.6 | 13,260.4 | 15,691.9 | 17,302.7 | 20,808.8 | 19,525.7 | 19,003.1 | 19,587.3 | 19,922.2 | 20,297.8 | 21,367.6 | † 6,503.0 |
| Gross Fixed Capital Formation.......... | 93e | 14,419.4 | 16,961.6 | 21,577.3 | 28,700.5 | 29,391.6 | 16,662.5 | 16,353.5 | 19,890.5 | 19,946.6 | 21,958.6 | 24,077.2 | † 7,705.7 |
| Changes in Inventories.................... | 93i | −12.8 | 599.7 | 803.8 | 3,641.6 | 2,347.3 | −4,933.5 | 1,180.8 | 3,685.9 | 2,127.2 | 1,126.1 | −618.5 | † −781.0 |
| Exports of Goods and Services......... | 90c | 29,845.3 | 39,100.9 | 46,304.7 | 50,554.2 | 64,506.4 | 48,303.7 | 63,234.2 | 80,985.6 | 93,985.5 | 101,470.4 | 102,435.6 | † 28,744.5 |
| Imports of Goods and Services (-)..... | 98c | 34,268.8 | 44,305.3 | 54,789.5 | 63,668.2 | 77,569.7 | 49,866.3 | 65,051.1 | 83,739.8 | 92,995.0 | 99,960.7 | 102,080.5 | † 28,789.1 |
| Gross Domestic Product (GDP)........ | 99b | 62,971.2 | 72,516.9 | 83,140.6 | 100,271.6 | 112,893.7 | 93,000.5 | 96,682.9 | 107,890.6 | 115,026.5 | 120,694.7 | 125,294.8 | † 37,189.7 |
| Net Primary Income from Abroad..... | 98.n | −1,226.0 | −969.6 | −1,586.5 | −3,775.3 | −3,849.1 | 1,736.1 | −1,802.6 | −3,963.9 | −3,456.4 | −3,141.0 | −3,746.5 | † −1,476.8 |
| Gross National Income (GNI)............ | 99a | 61,745.2 | 71,547.3 | 81,554.1 | 96,496.3 | 109,044.6 | 94,736.6 | 94,880.2 | 103,926.6 | 111,570.1 | 117,553.7 | 121,548.3 | † 35,713.0 |
| Net Current Transf.from Abroad....... | 98t | 999 | 1,107 | 1,637 | 1,975 | 2,058 | 1,811 | 3,314 | 2,605 | 1,382 | 3,467 | 4,116 | † 940 |
| Gross Nat'l Disposable Inc.(GNDI).... | 99i | 62,745 | 72,655 | 83,191 | 98,471 | 111,102 | 96,548 | 98,194 | 106,532 | 112,952 | 121,020 | 125,664 | † 36,652 |
| Gross Saving................................. | 99s | 9,756.3 | 12,494.6 | 13,947.1 | 17,427.5 | 16,884.2 | 13,713.8 | 17,228.5 | 19,463.6 | 20,989.5 | 24,920.1 | 24,183.2 | † 6,342.9 |
| Consumption of Fixed Capital.......... | 99cf | 8,073.6 | 8,948.8 | 10,047.0 | 11,692.0 | 13,610.4 | 13,757.4 | 13,919.4 | 14,333.1 | 15,217.1 | 16,042.8 | 17,018.8 | † 4,926.9 |
| GDP Volume 2010 Ref., Chained..... | 99b.p | 84,731 | 91,278 | 98,039 | 108,908 | 111,770 | 95,213 | 96,774 | 102,624 | 106,560 | 110,337 | 113,683 | † 33,450 |
| GDP Volume (2010=100)............... | 99bvp | 87.6 | 94.3 | 101.3 | 112.5 | 115.5 | 98.4 | 100.0 | 106.0 | 110.1 | 114.0 | 117.5 | 119.3 |
| GDP Deflator (2010=100)............... | 99bip | 74.4 | 79.5 | 84.9 | 92.2 | 101.1 | 97.8 | 100.0 | 105.2 | 108.0 | 109.5 | 110.3 | 111.3 |
| | | *Millions: Midyear Estimates* | | | | | | | | | | | |
| Population................................. | 99z | 3.38 | 3.34 | 3.31 | 3.26 | 3.22 | 3.17 | 3.12 | 3.07 | 3.02 | 2.96 | 2.92 | 2.88 |

# Luxembourg 137

| | | 2004 | 2005 | 2006 | 2007 | 2008 | 2009 | 2010 | 2011 | 2012 | 2013 | 2014 | 2015 |
|---|---|---|---|---|---|---|---|---|---|---|---|---|---|
| **Exchange Rates** | | | | | | | *Euros per SDR: End of Period* | | | | | | |
| Market Rate | aa | 1.1402 | 1.2116 | 1.1423 | 1.0735 | 1.1068 | 1.0882 | 1.1525 | 1.1865 | 1.1649 | 1.1167 | 1.1933 | 1.2728 |
| | | | | | | *Euros per US Dollar: End of Period (ae) Period Average (rf)* | | | | | | | |
| Market Rate | ae | .7342 | .8477 | .7593 | .6793 | .7185 | .6942 | .7484 | .7729 | .7579 | .7251 | .8237 | .9185 |
| Market Rate | rf | .8054 | .8041 | .7971 | .7306 | .6827 | .7198 | .7550 | .7194 | .7783 | .7532 | .7537 | .9017 |
| | | | | | | *Index Numbers (2010=100): Period Averages* | | | | | | | |
| Nominal Effective Exchange Rate | nec | 98.6 | 98.0 | 98.2 | 99.4 | 101.8 | 102.8 | 100.0 | 100.5 | 98.1 | 100.2 | 100.5 | 97.0 |
| CPI-Based Real Effect. Ex. Rate | rec | 98.4 | 98.2 | 98.8 | 99.7 | 101.6 | 102.6 | 100.0 | 100.8 | 98.6 | 100.7 | 100.3 | 96.6 |
| **Fund Position** | | | | | | *Millions of SDRs: End of Period* | | | | | | | |
| Quota | 2f.s | 279.10 | 279.10 | 279.10 | 279.10 | 279.10 | 279.10 | 279.10 | 418.70 | 418.70 | 418.70 | 418.70 | 418.70 |
| SDR Holdings | 1b.s | 9.83 | 11.43 | 12.23 | 12.76 | 13.41 | 243.23 | 243.34 | 243.83 | 244.10 | 244.25 | 244.43 | 244.49 |
| Reserve Position in the Fund | 1c.s | 89.66 | 40.65 | 29.01 | 18.72 | 36.10 | 52.10 | 66.10 | 224.12 | 224.34 | 204.83 | 161.66 | 119.92 |
| Total Fund Cred. & Loans Outstg. | 2tl | — | — | — | — | — | — | — | — | — | — | — | — |
| SDR Allocations | 1bd | 16.96 | 16.96 | 16.96 | 16.96 | 16.96 | 246.62 | 246.62 | 246.62 | 246.62 | 246.62 | 246.62 | 246.62 |
| **International Liquidity** | | | | | | *Millions of US Dollars Unless Otherwise Indicated: End of Period* | | | | | | | |
| Total Res.Min.Gold (Eurosys.Def) | 1l.d | 298.37 | 241.10 | 218.08 | 143.55 | 334.63 | 730.52 | 747.12 | 900.50 | 871.00 | 876.42 | 776.83 | 694.43 |
| SDR Holdings | 1b.d | 15.26 | 16.33 | 18.40 | 20.16 | 20.66 | 381.30 | 374.75 | 374.34 | 375.16 | 376.15 | 354.13 | 338.80 |
| Reserve Position in the Fund | 1c.d | 139.25 | 58.10 | 43.65 | 29.59 | 55.60 | 81.67 | 101.79 | 344.08 | 344.79 | 315.43 | 234.21 | 166.17 |
| Foreign Exchange | 1d.d | 143.87 | 166.68 | 156.03 | 93.81 | 258.37 | 267.54 | 270.58 | 182.08 | 151.05 | 184.84 | 188.48 | 189.46 |
| o/w:Fin.Deriv.Rel.to Reserves | 1ddd | — | — | — | — | — | — | — | — | — | — | — | — |
| Other Reserve Assets | 1e.d | — | — | — | — | — | — | — | — | — | — | — | — |
| Gold (Million Fine Troy Ounces) | 1ad | .074 | .074 | .074 | .074 | .073 | .072 | .072 | .072 | .072 | .072 | .072 | .072 |
| Gold (Eurosystem Valuation) | 1and | 32.41 | 37.96 | 47.04 | † 62.00 | 63.15 | 79.49 | 101.54 | 113.36 | 119.81 | 86.51 | 86.35 | 76.29 |
| Memo:Euro Cl. on Non-EA Res | 1dgd | . . . . | . . . . | — | . . . . | . . . . | . . . . | . . . . | . . . . | . . . . | . . . . | . . . . | . . . . |
| Non-Euro Cl. on EA Res | 1dhd | — | — | 49.00 | 1,921.86 | 15,448.61 | 102.38 | 97.41 | 4,596.75 | 2,063.09 | 1,878.20 | 2,553.28 | 1,703.01 |
| Central Bank: Other Assets | 3..d | 8,072 | 13,592 | 13,690 | 34,590 | 67,062 | 84,592 | 99,342 | 151,235 | 150,121 | 153,914 | 136,841 | 167,095 |
| Central Bank: Other Liabs. | 4..d | 105 | 395 | 69 | 148 | 1,435 | 2,405 | 2,363 | 2,700 | 2,792 | 4,317 | 1,136 | 849 |
| Other Depository Corps.: Assets | 7a.d | 332,241 | 355,928 | 471,586 | 595,360 | 616,362 | 531,011 | 466,904 | 497,215 | 443,115 | 461,694 | 441,895 | 409,213 |
| Other Depository Corps.: Liabs. | 7b.d | 340,855 | 343,585 | 407,133 | 499,553 | 521,634 | 543,112 | 489,129 | 470,800 | 386,905 | 383,528 | 361,418 | 348,260 |
| **Central Bank** | | | | | | *Millions of Euros: End of Period* | | | | | | | |
| Euro Area Wide Residency Criterion | | | | | | | | | | | | | |
| Net Foreign Assets | 11n.u | 827 | 1,147 | 1,727 | 1,633 | 1,432 | 519 | 451 | 737 | −1,534 | −2,646 | −655 | −176 |
| Claims on Nonresidents | 11..u | 956 | 1,529 | 1,816 | 2,029 | 2,521 | 2,262 | 2,295 | 3,010 | 2,130 | 1,851 | 2,390 | 2,172 |
| Liabilities to Nonresidents | 16c.u | 129 | 383 | 89 | 396 | 1,089 | 1,743 | 1,843 | 2,274 | 3,663 | 4,497 | 3,044 | 2,348 |
| Claims on Other Depository Corps. | 12e.u | 29,269 | 33,330 | 43,781 | 37,349 | 53,080 | 17,318 | 5,122 | 11,791 | 9,588 | 10,356 | 6,538 | 6,125 |
| Net Claims on Central Government | 12anu | −472 | −453 | −287 | −308 | 555 | 1,752 | 1,812 | 1,088 | 1,240 | 1,108 | 985 | 1,507 |
| Claims on Central Govt | 12a.u | 83 | 62 | 186 | 126 | 942 | 2,096 | 2,160 | 1,590 | 1,793 | 1,684 | 1,564 | 2,066 |
| Liabs. to Central Govt | 16d.u | 555 | 515 | 473 | 434 | 387 | 344 | 348 | 502 | 553 | 576 | 579 | 559 |
| Claims on Other Sectors | 12s.u | 853 | 895 | 1,118 | 745 | 1,279 | 739 | 611 | 652 | 759 | 802 | 1,328 | 872 |
| Claims on Other Financial Corps. | 12g.u | 853 | 895 | 1,118 | 745 | 1,279 | 739 | 611 | 652 | 759 | 802 | 784 | 542 |
| Claims on State & Local Govts | 12b.u | — | — | — | — | — | — | — | — | — | — | 50 | 6 |
| Claims on Public Nonfin. Corps. | 12c.u | — | — | — | — | — | — | — | — | — | — | — | — |
| Claims on Private Sector | 12d.u | — | — | — | — | — | — | — | — | — | — | 494 | 324 |
| Monetary Base | 14..u | 6,180 | 8,076 | 11,154 | 12,355 | 47,295 | 15,314 | 11,553 | 53,287 | 40,722 | 26,907 | 21,363 | 62,044 |
| Currency in Circulation | 14a.u | 1,117 | 1,266 | 1,412 | 1,575 | 1,763 | 2,053 | 2,143 | 2,260 | 2,331 | 2,448 | 2,974 | 3,148 |
| Liabs. to Other Depository Corps. | 14c.u | 5,063 | 6,810 | 9,742 | 10,780 | 45,532 | 13,261 | 9,410 | 50,827 | 38,321 | 24,459 | 16,550 | 57,031 |
| Liabs. to Other Sectors | 14d.u | — | — | — | — | — | — | — | 200 | 70 | — | 1,839 | 1,865 |
| Other Liabs. to Other Dep. Corps. | 14n.u | — | — | — | — | — | — | — | — | — | — | — | — |
| Dep. & Sec. Excl. f/Monetary Base | 14o.u | — | — | — | — | — | — | — | — | — | — | — | — |
| Deposits Included in Broad Money | 15..u | — | — | — | — | — | — | — | — | — | — | — | — |
| Sec.Ot.th.Shares Inc.in.Brd.Money | 16a.u | — | — | — | — | — | — | — | — | — | — | — | — |
| Deposits Excl. from Broad Money | 16b.u | — | — | — | — | — | — | — | — | — | — | — | — |
| Sec.Oh.th.Shares Excl. f/Brd.Money | 16s.u | — | — | — | — | — | — | — | — | — | — | — | — |
| Loans | 16l.u | — | — | — | — | — | — | — | — | — | — | — | — |
| Financial Derivatives | 16m.u | — | — | — | — | — | — | — | — | — | — | — | — |
| Shares and Other Equity | 17a.u | 527 | 601 | 649 | 655 | 520 | 925 | 984 | 890 | 1,250 | 1,362 | 1,530 | 1,608 |
| Other Items (Net) | 17r.u | 23,770 | 26,242 | 34,535 | 26,409 | 8,532 | 4,089 | −4,540 | −39,909 | −31,920 | −18,650 | −14,698 | −55,324 |
| Memorandum Items | | | | | | | | | | | | | |
| National Residency Criterion | | | | | | | | | | | | | |
| Net Foreign Assets | 11n | 6,040 | 11,376 | 10,507 | 23,241 | 47,384 | 57,539 | 73,138 | 115,394 | 110,867 | 107,806 | 108,538 | 150,002 |
| Claims on Nonresidents | 11 | 6,169 | 11,758 | 10,596 | 23,637 | 48,473 | 59,282 | 74,982 | 117,667 | 114,531 | 112,303 | 113,422 | 154,189 |
| Liabilities to Nonresidents | 16c | 129 | 383 | 89 | 396 | 1,089 | 1,743 | 1,843 | 2,274 | 3,663 | 4,497 | 4,883 | 4,187 |
| Claims on Other Depository Corps. | 12e | 28,470 | 31,947 | 41,632 | 35,040 | 51,574 | 15,731 | 3,180 | 8,858 | 5,818 | 5,996 | 3,372 | 3,658 |
| Net Claims on Central Government | 12an | −555 | −515 | −473 | −434 | −387 | −344 | −348 | −502 | −553 | −576 | −579 | 452 |
| Claims on Central Government | 12a | — | — | — | — | — | — | — | — | — | — | — | 1,011 |
| Liabilities to Central Government | 16d | 555 | 515 | 473 | 434 | 387 | 344 | 348 | 502 | 553 | 576 | 579 | 559 |
| Claims on Other Sectors | 12s | 23 | — | — | — | — | 20 | 69 | 65 | 208 | 187 | 228 | 65 |
| Claims on Other Fin. Corps. | 12g | 23 | — | — | — | — | 20 | 69 | 65 | 208 | 187 | 228 | 65 |
| Claims on State & Local Govts | 12b | — | — | — | — | — | — | — | — | — | — | — | — |
| Claims on Private Sector | 12d | — | — | — | — | — | — | — | — | — | — | — | — |
| Liabs.to ODCs, Inc.in Mon.Base | 14c | 5,063 | 6,810 | 9,742 | 10,780 | 45,532 | 13,261 | 9,410 | 50,827 | 38,321 | 24,459 | 16,550 | 57,031 |
| Liabs.to Ot.Sectors, Inc.in Mon.Base | 14d | — | — | — | — | — | — | — | 200 | 70 | — | — | 26 |
| Liabs.to ODCs,Excl.f/Mon.Base | 14n | — | — | — | — | — | — | — | — | — | — | — | — |
| Net Claims on Eurosystem | 12e.s | 3,510 | 7,898 | 5,336 | 18,439 | 42,236 | 52,634 | 68,062 | 109,569 | 106,312 | 103,818 | 105,238 | 147,724 |

| | | 2004 | 2005 | 2006 | 2007 | 2008 | 2009 | 2010 | 2011 | 2012 | 2013 | 2014 | 2015 |
|---|---|---|---|---|---|---|---|---|---|---|---|---|---|
| **Other Depository Corporations** | | | | | | *Millions of Euros: End of Period* | | | | | | | |
| Euro Area Wide Residency Criterion | | | | | | | | | | | | | |
| Net Foreign Assets | 21n.u | −6,324 | 10,463 | 48,939 | 65,082 | 68,066 | −8,400 | −16,633 | 20,415 | 42,603 | 56,679 | 66,285 | 55,987 |
| Claims on Nonresidents | 21..u | 243,918 | 301,711 | 358,076 | 404,429 | 442,884 | 368,604 | 349,427 | 384,276 | 335,846 | 334,779 | 363,969 | 375,873 |
| Liabilities to Nonresidents | 26c.u | 250,242 | 291,248 | 309,137 | 339,347 | 374,818 | 377,004 | 366,060 | 363,861 | 293,243 | 278,100 | 297,684 | 319,886 |
| Claims on Eurosystem | 20..u | 5,302 | 7,019 | 9,963 | 11,015 | 45,775 | 13,524 | 9,700 | 51,056 | 38,542 | 24,785 | 16,700 | 57,280 |
| Currency | 20a.u | 239 | 209 | 221 | 235 | 243 | 263 | 290 | 229 | 221 | 326 | 706 | 472 |
| Reserve Deposits and Securities | 20b.u | 5,063 | 6,810 | 9,742 | 10,780 | 45,532 | 13,261 | 9,410 | 50,827 | 38,321 | 24,459 | 15,994 | 56,808 |
| Other Claims | 20n.u | — | — | — | — | — | — | — | — | — | — | — | — |
| Net Claims on Central Government | 22anu | 49,280 | 55,786 | 41,735 | 31,232 | 42,781 | 71,224 | 49,359 | 44,003 | 37,270 | 35,290 | 46,820 | 41,305 |
| Claims on Central Government | 22a.u | 53,724 | 59,277 | 44,790 | 33,579 | 45,396 | 72,688 | 52,206 | 46,122 | 39,205 | 37,832 | 49,252 | 43,730 |
| Liabilities to Central Government | 26d.u | 4,444 | 3,491 | 3,055 | 2,347 | 2,615 | 1,464 | 2,847 | 2,119 | 1,935 | 2,542 | 2,432 | 2,425 |
| Claims on Other Sectors | 22s.u | 122,356 | 153,167 | 178,465 | 213,840 | 228,355 | 205,004 | 218,444 | 214,460 | 203,278 | 185,710 | 200,996 | 215,485 |
| Claims on Other Financial Corps | 22g.u | 38,899 | 58,586 | 71,610 | 89,511 | 84,421 | 79,382 | 100,975 | 100,013 | 91,022 | 77,600 | 82,946 | 86,384 |
| Claims on State & Local Govts | 22b.u | 13,016 | 14,347 | 15,401 | 13,931 | 19,105 | 11,827 | 12,890 | 16,845 | 18,901 | 14,389 | 16,098 | 16,191 |
| Claims on Public Nonfin. Corps | 22c.u | — | — | — | — | — | — | — | — | — | — | — | — |
| Claims on Private Sector | 22d.u | 70,441 | 80,234 | 91,454 | 110,398 | 124,829 | 113,795 | 104,579 | 97,602 | 93,355 | 93,721 | 101,952 | 112,910 |
| Liabilities to Eurosystem | 26g.u | 29,204 | 33,251 | 43,697 | 36,529 | 52,412 | 16,303 | 4,096 | 10,658 | 8,124 | 7,598 | 4,060 | 4,643 |
| Transf.Dep.Included in Broad Money | 24..u | 56,007 | 70,497 | 75,771 | 83,225 | 86,170 | 90,259 | 111,714 | 120,175 | 133,672 | 148,491 | 169,172 | 196,958 |
| Other.Dep.Included in Broad Money | 25..u | 184,858 | 190,547 | 215,106 | 264,538 | 270,889 | 199,946 | 155,465 | 191,787 | 157,575 | 126,999 | 122,827 | 130,241 |
| Sec.Ot.th.Shares Inc.in.Brd. Money | 26a.u | −24,849 | −26,463 | −24,515 | −41,310 | −51,908 | −67,599 | −54,680 | −49,071 | −41,644 | −24,897 | −28,174 | −28,389 |
| Deposits Excl. from Broad Money | 26b.u | 12,628 | 18,323 | 19,091 | 20,476 | 16,668 | 17,119 | 17,573 | 18,378 | 14,641 | 15,521 | 17,768 | 18,991 |
| Sec.Ot.th.Shares Excl.f/Brd. Money | 26s.u | −18,578 | −6,825 | −12,117 | −15,704 | −8,455 | −7,091 | −8,894 | −1,877 | 4,396 | 799 | −2,004 | −1,177 |
| Loans | 26l.u | — | — | — | — | — | — | — | — | — | — | — | — |
| Financial Derivatives | 26m.u | — | — | — | — | — | — | 18,922 | 24,065 | 22,778 | 17,643 | 18,848 | 16,555 |
| Insurance Technical Reserves | 26r.u | — | — | — | — | — | — | — | — | — | — | — | — |
| Shares and Other Equity | 27a.u | 33,256 | 35,371 | 39,045 | 42,050 | 41,148 | 47,611 | 45,716 | 46,631 | 49,409 | 52,349 | 59,062 | 58,893 |
| Other Items (Net) | 27r.u | −101,910 | −88,267 | −76,973 | −68,631 | −21,945 | −15,202 | −29,041 | −30,814 | −27,256 | −42,037 | −33,960 | −26,657 |
| Memorandum Items | | | | | | | | | | | | | |
| Total Assets | 20ra | 857,175 | 973,131 | 1,029,808 | 1,169,089 | 1,271,783 | 1,116,836 | 1,053,808 | 1,099,344 | 961,934 | 914,814 | 957,742 | 1,002,752 |
| National Residency Criterion | | | | | | | | | | | | | |
| Net Foreign Assets | 21n | 193,858 | 229,684 | 248,437 | 253,073 | 254,338 | 195,688 | 178,717 | 149,223 | 149,768 | 179,971 | 210,591 | 177,319 |
| Claims on Nonresidents | 21 | 715,448 | 810,607 | 858,948 | 953,220 | 1,005,523 | 920,151 | 872,108 | 883,943 | 775,152 | 743,998 | 789,713 | 791,355 |
| Liabilities to Nonresidents | 26c | 521,590 | 580,923 | 610,511 | 700,147 | 751,185 | 724,463 | 693,391 | 734,720 | 625,384 | 564,027 | 579,122 | 614,036 |
| Net Claims on Central Government | 22an | −2,283 | −727 | −1,359 | −1,142 | −504 | 237 | −637 | 90 | 485 | 274 | 639 | 634 |
| Claims on Central Government | 22a | 558 | 492 | 667 | 794 | 1,836 | 1,695 | 2,080 | 2,134 | 2,415 | 2,786 | 3,041 | 3,029 |
| Liabilities to Central Government | 26d | 2,841 | 1,219 | 2,026 | 1,936 | 2,340 | 1,458 | 2,717 | 2,044 | 1,930 | 2,512 | 2,402 | 2,395 |
| Claims on Other Sectors | 22s | 29,745 | 39,832 | 53,253 | 70,148 | 73,280 | 71,067 | 89,756 | 90,925 | 90,144 | 87,642 | 94,803 | 98,500 |
| Claims on Other Fin. Corps | 22g | 10,510 | 17,489 | 26,919 | 37,168 | 31,921 | 30,583 | 52,066 | 52,476 | 50,174 | 44,107 | 48,970 | 47,718 |
| Claims on State & Local Govts | 22b | 631 | 761 | 797 | 867 | 888 | 1,053 | 1,174 | 1,139 | 1,082 | 989 | 1,031 | 1,087 |
| Claims on Private Sector | 22d | 18,604 | 21,582 | 25,537 | 32,113 | 40,471 | 39,431 | 36,516 | 37,310 | 38,888 | 42,546 | 44,802 | 49,695 |
| Transf.Dep.Included in Broad Money | 24 | 40,614 | 51,197 | 55,756 | 68,198 | 68,585 | 71,012 | 92,618 | 92,392 | 107,810 | 122,511 | 145,626 | 170,558 |
| Other.Dep.Included in Broad Money | 25 | 59,277 | 70,346 | 87,488 | 102,823 | 116,311 | 64,584 | 47,054 | 54,709 | 35,196 | 38,184 | 39,870 | 33,625 |
| Sec.Ot.th.Shares Inc.in.Brd. Money | 26a | 4,591 | 5,038 | 7,116 | 5,360 | 5,269 | 6,126 | 6,046 | 6,406 | 6,730 | 8,028 | 7,329 | 8,997 |
| Deposits Excl. from Broad Money | 26b | 4,742 | 10,716 | 11,499 | 13,544 | 12,376 | 10,807 | 11,493 | 11,850 | 7,842 | 9,319 | 9,598 | 10,685 |
| Sec.Ot.th.Shares Excl.f/Brd. Money | 26s | 49,417 | 63,457 | 62,075 | 61,657 | 59,608 | 56,634 | 49,824 | 44,645 | 39,578 | 33,550 | 30,007 | 30,227 |

| | | 2004 | 2005 | 2006 | 2007 | 2008 | 2009 | 2010 | 2011 | 2012 | 2013 | 2014 | 2015 |
|---|---|---|---|---|---|---|---|---|---|---|---|---|---|
| **Depository Corporations** | | | | | | *Millions of Euros: End of Period* | | | | | | | |
| Euro Area Wide Residency Criterion | | | | | | | | | | | | | |
| Net Foreign Assets............................ | 31n.u | −5,497 | 11,610 | 50,666 | 66,715 | 69,498 | −7,881 | −16,182 | 21,152 | 41,069 | 54,033 | 65,630 | 55,811 |
| Claims on Nonresidents................. | 31..u | 244,874 | 303,240 | 359,892 | 406,458 | 445,405 | 370,866 | 351,722 | 387,286 | 337,976 | 336,630 | 366,359 | 378,045 |
| Liabilities to Nonresidents.............. | 36c.u | 250,371 | 291,631 | 309,226 | 339,743 | 375,907 | 378,747 | 367,903 | 366,135 | 296,906 | 282,597 | 300,728 | 322,234 |
| Domestic Claims............................ | 32..u | 172,017 | 209,395 | 221,031 | 245,509 | 272,970 | 278,719 | 270,226 | 260,203 | 242,547 | 222,910 | 250,129 | 259,169 |
| Net Claims on Central Government.. | 32anu | 48,808 | 55,333 | 41,448 | 30,924 | 43,336 | 72,976 | 51,171 | 45,091 | 38,510 | 36,398 | 47,805 | 42,812 |
| Claims on Central Government...... | 32a.u | 53,807 | 59,339 | 44,976 | 33,705 | 46,338 | 74,784 | 54,366 | 47,712 | 40,998 | 39,516 | 50,816 | 45,796 |
| Liabilities to Central Government... | 36d.u | 4,999 | 4,006 | 3,528 | 2,781 | 3,002 | 1,808 | 3,195 | 2,621 | 2,488 | 3,118 | 3,011 | 2,984 |
| Claims on Other Sectors.................. | 32s.u | 123,209 | 154,062 | 179,583 | 214,585 | 229,634 | 205,743 | 219,055 | 215,112 | 204,037 | 186,512 | 202,324 | 216,357 |
| Claims on Other Financial Corps..... | 32g.u | 39,752 | 59,481 | 72,728 | 90,256 | 85,700 | 80,121 | 101,586 | 100,665 | 91,781 | 78,402 | 83,730 | 86,926 |
| Claims on State & Local Govts....... | 32b.u | 13,016 | 14,347 | 15,401 | 13,931 | 19,105 | 11,827 | 12,890 | 16,845 | 18,901 | 14,389 | 16,148 | 16,197 |
| Claims on Public Nonfin. Corps...... | 32c.u | — | — | — | — | — | — | — | — | — | — | — | — |
| Claims on Private Sector............... | 32d.u | 70,441 | 80,234 | 91,454 | 110,398 | 124,829 | 113,795 | 104,579 | 97,602 | 93,355 | 93,721 | 102,446 | 113,234 |
| Broad Money Liabilities................... | 35l.u | 216,894 | 235,638 | 267,553 | 307,793 | 306,671 | 224,396 | 214,352 | 265,122 | 251,783 | 252,715 | 267,932 | 303,351 |
| Currency Outside Depository Corps | 34a.u | 878 | 1,057 | 1,191 | 1,340 | 1,520 | 1,790 | 1,853 | 2,031 | 2,110 | 2,122 | 2,268 | 2,676 |
| Transferable Deposits................... | 34..u | 56,007 | 70,497 | 75,771 | 83,225 | 86,170 | 90,259 | 111,714 | 120,375 | 133,742 | 148,491 | 171,011 | 198,823 |
| Other Deposits.............................. | 35..u | 184,858 | 190,547 | 215,106 | 264,538 | 270,889 | 199,946 | 155,465 | 191,787 | 157,575 | 126,999 | 122,827 | 130,241 |
| Securities Other than Shares.......... | 36a.u | −24,849 | −26,463 | −24,515 | −41,310 | −51,908 | −67,599 | −54,680 | −49,071 | −41,644 | −24,897 | −28,174 | −28,389 |
| Deposits Excl. from Broad Money..... | 36b.u | 12,628 | 18,323 | 19,091 | 20,476 | 16,668 | 17,119 | 17,573 | 18,378 | 14,641 | 15,521 | 17,768 | 18,991 |
| Sec.Oth.th.Shares Excl.f/Brd. Money. | 36s.u | −18,578 | −6,825 | −12,117 | −15,704 | −8,455 | −7,091 | −8,894 | −1,877 | 4,396 | 799 | −2,004 | −1,177 |
| Loans........................................ | 36l.u | — | — | — | — | — | — | — | — | — | — | — | — |
| Financial Derivatives...................... | 36m.u | — | — | — | — | — | — | 18,922 | 24,065 | 22,778 | 17,643 | 18,848 | 16,555 |
| Insurance Technical Reserves.......... | 36r.u | — | — | — | — | — | — | — | — | — | — | — | — |
| Shares and Other Equity.................. | 37a.u | 33,783 | 35,972 | 39,694 | 42,705 | 41,668 | 48,536 | 46,700 | 47,521 | 50,659 | 53,711 | 60,592 | 60,501 |
| Other Items (Net)........................... | 37r.u | −78,205 | −62,104 | −42,522 | −43,042 | −14,081 | −12,128 | −34,607 | −71,856 | −60,640 | −63,445 | −50,580 | −83,240 |
| Broad Money Liabs., Seasonally Adj. | 35lub | 218,095 | 237,603 | 271,018 | 312,988 | 312,908 | 229,258 | 219,374 | 271,718 | 258,493 | 259,861 | 276,034 | 313,092 |
| Memorandum Items | | | | | | | | | | | | | |
| National Residency Criterion | | | | | | | | | | | | | |
| Net Foreign Assets........................ | 31n | 199,898 | 241,060 | 258,944 | 276,314 | 301,722 | 253,227 | 251,855 | 264,617 | 260,635 | 287,777 | 319,129 | 327,321 |
| Claims on Nonresidents............... | 31 | 721,617 | 822,365 | 869,544 | 976,857 | 1,053,996 | 979,433 | 947,090 | 1,001,610 | 889,683 | 856,301 | 903,135 | 945,544 |
| Liabilities to Nonresidents............. | 36c | 521,719 | 581,306 | 610,600 | 700,543 | 752,274 | 726,206 | 695,234 | 736,994 | 629,047 | 568,524 | 584,005 | 618,223 |
| Domestic Claims............................ | 32 | 26,930 | 38,590 | 51,421 | 68,572 | 72,389 | 70,980 | 88,840 | 90,578 | 90,284 | 87,527 | 95,091 | 99,651 |
| Net Claims on Central Government | 32an | −2,838 | −1,242 | −1,832 | −1,576 | −891 | −107 | −985 | −412 | −68 | −302 | 60 | 1,086 |
| Claims on Central Government..... | 32a | 558 | 492 | 667 | 794 | 1,836 | 1,695 | 2,080 | 2,134 | 2,415 | 2,786 | 3,041 | 4,040 |
| Liabilities to Central Government. | 36d | 3,396 | 1,734 | 2,499 | 2,370 | 2,727 | 1,802 | 3,065 | 2,546 | 2,483 | 3,088 | 2,981 | 2,954 |
| Claims on Other Sectors............... | 32s | 29,768 | 39,832 | 53,253 | 70,148 | 73,280 | 71,087 | 89,825 | 90,990 | 90,352 | 87,829 | 95,031 | 98,565 |
| Claims on Other Financial Corps.. | 32g | 10,533 | 17,489 | 26,919 | 37,168 | 31,921 | 30,603 | 52,135 | 52,541 | 50,382 | 44,294 | 49,198 | 47,783 |
| Claims on State & Local Govts..... | 32b | 631 | 761 | 797 | 867 | 888 | 1,053 | 1,174 | 1,139 | 1,082 | 989 | 1,031 | 1,087 |
| Claims on Private Sector............. | 32d | 18,604 | 21,582 | 25,537 | 32,113 | 40,471 | 39,431 | 36,516 | 37,310 | 38,888 | 42,546 | 44,802 | 49,695 |
| Transf.Dep.Included in Broad Money | 34 | 40,614 | 51,197 | 55,756 | 68,198 | 68,585 | 71,012 | 92,618 | 92,592 | 107,880 | 122,511 | 145,626 | 170,584 |
| Other Dep.Included in Broad Money. | 35 | 59,277 | 70,346 | 87,488 | 102,823 | 116,311 | 64,584 | 47,054 | 54,709 | 35,196 | 38,184 | 39,870 | 33,625 |
| Sec.Ot.th.Shares Inc.in.Brd. Money... | 36a | 4,591 | 5,038 | 7,116 | 5,360 | 5,269 | 6,126 | 6,046 | 6,406 | 6,730 | 8,028 | 7,329 | 8,997 |
| Deposits Excl. from Broad Money..... | 36b | 4,742 | 10,716 | 11,499 | 13,544 | 12,376 | 10,807 | 11,493 | 11,850 | 7,842 | 9,319 | 9,598 | 10,685 |
| Sec.Ot.th.Shares Excl./f.Brd. Money.. | 36s | 49,417 | 63,457 | 62,075 | 61,657 | 59,608 | 56,634 | 49,824 | 44,645 | 39,578 | 33,550 | 30,007 | 30,227 |
| **Interest Rates** | | | | | | *Percent Per Annum* | | | | | | | |
| Deposit Rate | | | | | | | | | | | | | |
| Households: Stocks, up to 2 years.. | 60lhs | 1.72 | 1.81 | 2.50 | 3.57 | 4.14 | 1.43 | .78 | 1.20 | 1.13 | .87 | .64 | .59 |
| New Business, up to 1 year.......... | 60lhn | 1.78 | 1.86 | 2.56 | 3.58 | 3.93 | .77 | .60 | 1.03 | .64 | .50 | .32 | .35 |
| Corporations: Stocks, up to 2 years | 60lcs | 2.03 | 2.07 | 2.78 | 3.94 | 4.18 | 1.30 | .66 | 1.10 | .61 | .47 | .45 | .15 |
| New Business, up to 1 year.......... | 60lcn | 2.05 | 2.06 | 2.83 | 3.84 | 3.86 | .79 | .54 | 1.01 | .33 | .24 | .19 | .06 |
| Lending Rate | | | | | | | | | | | | | |
| House Purch., Stocks,Over 5 years.. | 60phm | 3.56 | 3.45 | 3.97 | 4.82 | 4.98 | 2.69 | 2.29 | 2.35 | 2.23 | 2.24 | 2.15 | 2.03 |
| Corporations: Stocks, up to 1 year.. | 60pcs | 3.20 | 3.30 | 4.01 | 5.05 | 5.34 | 3.12 | 2.52 | 2.65 | 2.07 | 1.86 | 1.93 | 1.64 |
| New Bus., Over € 1 mil.,up to 1 yr | 60pcn | 3.15 | 3.16 | 3.93 | 4.93 | 5.00 | 2.49 | 2.31 | 2.61 | 1.87 | 1.63 | 1.49 | 1.21 |
| Government Bond Yield.................. | 61 | 2.84 | 2.41 | 3.30 | 4.46 | 4.61 | 4.23 | 3.17 | 2.92 | 1.75 | 1.85 | 1.34 | .37 |
| **Prices, Production, Labor** | | | | | | *Index Numbers (2010=100): Period Averages* | | | | | | | |
| Producer Prices in Industry.............. | 63a | 75.9 | 82.1 | 88.1 | 96.5 | † 105.1 | 96.4 | 100.0 | 108.6 | † 111.3 | 108.5 | 105.3 | 104.1 |
| Consumer Prices............................ | 64 | 87.5 | 89.7 | 92.1 | 94.2 | 97.4 | 97.8 | 100.0 | 103.4 | 106.2 | 108.0 | 108.7 | † 109.2 |
| Harmonized CPI............................. | 64h | 85.2 | 88.4 | 91.0 | 93.4 | 97.3 | 97.3 | 100.0 | 103.7 | 106.7 | 108.5 | 109.3 | 109.4 |
| Industrial Production...................... | 66 | 116.6 | 118.1 | 120.6 | 120.3 | 114.2 | 95.9 | 100.0 | 102.2 | 96.9 | 93.9 | 97.6 | 99.5 |
| Employment.................................. | 67 | 83.3 | 85.7 | 88.8 | 92.7 | 97.4 | 98.4 | 100.0 | 102.9 | 105.4 | 107.5 | 110.0 | . . . . |
| | | | | | | *Number in Thousands: Period Averages* | | | | | | | |
| Employment.................................. | 67e | 188 | 193 | 195 | 203 | 202 | 215 | 219 | 222 | 234 | 236 | 243 | 255 |
| Unemployment.............................. | 67c | 10 | 10 | 10 | 9 | 11 | 12 | 11 | 11 | 13 | 15 | 16 | 18 |
| Unemployment Rate (%)................. | 67r | 5.0 | 4.6 | 4.6 | 4.2 | 4.9 | 5.1 | 4.6 | 4.8 | 5.1 | 5.9 | 6.0 | 6.4 |
| **Intl. Transactions & Positions** | | | | | | *Millions of Euros* | | | | | | | |
| Exports...................................... | 70 | 9.79 | 10.18 | 11.14 | 11.95 | 11.99 | 9.25 | 10.79 | 12.06 | 10.88 | 10.60 | 11.33 | 11.81 |
| Imports, c.i.f................................. | 71 | 13.68 | 14.40 | 15.71 | 16.47 | 17.52 | 13.80 | 16.42 | 18.90 | 18.80 | 18.01 | 17.74 | 17.42 |

## Balance of Payments

| | | 2004 | 2005 | 2006 | 2007 | 2008 | 2009 | 2010 | 2011 | 2012 | 2013 | 2014 | 2015 |
|---|---|---|---|---|---|---|---|---|---|---|---|---|---|
| | | | | | | | *Millions of US Dollars* | | | | | | |
| A. Current Account* | 109bx | 4,142.6 | 4,107.0 | 4,211.3 | 4,991.3 | 4,355.3 | 3,544.6 | 3,585.1 | 3,584.5 | 3,401.0 | 3,502.0 | 3,548.8 | 3,193.8 |
| Goods, credit (exports) | 1a9cx | 13,646.8 | 14,401.5 | 16,840.9 | 19,197.0 | 23,112.7 | 17,564.2 | 19,718.0 | 23,655.4 | 22,447.1 | 24,190.3 | 24,564.8 | 17,811.5 |
| Goods, debit (imports) | 1a9dx | 17,259.8 | 18,739.3 | 20,535.8 | 22,940.7 | 27,476.5 | 19,850.5 | 21,771.3 | 26,592.7 | 24,356.4 | 25,423.4 | 24,811.7 | 20,218.5 |
| Balance on goods | 1a9bx | −3,613.0 | −4,337.9 | −3,694.9 | −3,743.8 | −4,363.8 | −2,286.3 | −2,053.3 | −2,937.4 | −1,909.3 | −1,233.1 | −246.8 | −2,407.0 |
| Services, credit (exports) | 1b9cx | 34,720.3 | 40,416.8 | 50,079.5 | 63,719.2 | 68,198.9 | 57,645.1 | 62,501.9 | 72,678.3 | 75,998.9 | 89,101.4 | 99,016.5 | 94,215.0 |
| Services, debit (imports) | 1b9dx | 23,134.2 | 27,385.0 | 34,407.3 | 44,131.2 | 46,115.3 | 39,641.3 | 45,627.8 | 53,580.6 | 56,675.5 | 67,516.9 | 76,704.9 | 71,293.0 |
| Balance on Goods & Services | 1z9bx | 7,973.1 | 8,694.0 | 11,977.3 | 15,844.2 | 17,719.8 | 15,717.4 | 14,820.8 | 16,160.2 | 17,414.1 | 20,351.4 | 22,064.7 | 20,515.0 |
| Primary income: credit | 1c9cx | 75,031.1 | 97,659.0 | 128,567.3 | 164,782.2 | 202,230.1 | 140,940.9 | 146,583.5 | 211,011.5 | 238,119.9 | 281,947.1 | 216,692.8 | 203,334.4 |
| Primary income: debit | 1c9dx | 78,758.9 | 102,337.0 | 136,486.8 | 175,920.3 | 215,837.2 | 152,276.7 | 157,983.8 | 223,732.0 | 251,850.5 | 299,291.2 | 235,746.0 | 221,009.0 |
| Balance on gds, serv. & prim. inc. | 1y9bx | 4,245.3 | 4,016.0 | 4,057.8 | 4,706.1 | 4,112.6 | 4,381.7 | 3,420.5 | 3,439.7 | 3,683.5 | 3,007.3 | 3,011.5 | 2,840.3 |
| Secondary income: credit | 1d9ca | 5,806.1 | 6,160.1 | 6,251.0 | 7,440.6 | 9,451.1 | 8,536.9 | 8,748.6 | 9,281.7 | 8,914.6 | 10,321.1 | 10,433.3 | 9,154.0 |
| Secondary income: debit | 1d9da | 5,908.9 | 6,069.0 | 6,097.5 | 7,155.5 | 9,208.4 | 9,374.0 | 8,584.0 | 9,136.8 | 9,197.0 | 9,826.2 | 9,896.0 | 8,800.5 |
| B. Capital Account* | 209ba | −670.3 | 1,278.4 | −306.0 | −198.5 | −364.9 | −573.3 | −262.8 | −249.9 | −502.6 | −1,012.1 | −1,303.3 | −647.2 |
| Capital account: credit | 209ca | 61.2 | 1,615.6 | 87.0 | 101.7 | 200.9 | 1,493.3 | 831.6 | 143.4 | 56.7 | 224.6 | 236.5 | 440.5 |
| Capital account: debit | 209da | 731.5 | 337.1 | 393.0 | 300.2 | 565.8 | 2,066.6 | 1,094.4 | 393.3 | 559.3 | 1,236.7 | 1,539.7 | 1,087.7 |
| Balance on current & capital acct. | 129ba | 3,472.3 | 5,385.5 | 3,905.4 | 4,792.8 | 3,990.4 | 2,971.3 | 3,322.4 | 3,334.7 | 2,898.4 | 2,489.9 | 2,245.5 | 2,546.6 |
| C. Financial Account* | 309na | 3,514.6 | 5,453.2 | 3,920.6 | 4,808.1 | 3,831.5 | 2,560.2 | 3,264.2 | 3,280.6 | 2,922.0 | 2,419.5 | 2,375.8 | 2,575.7 |
| Direct investment: assets | 3a9aa | 85,137.0 | 121,688.1 | 118,373.5 | 267,148.0 | 130,004.0 | 230,768.2 | 209,368.3 | 371,351.1 | 455,973.7 | 515,313.0 | 231,659.2 | 313,733.5 |
| Equity & investment fund shares | 3aaaa | 104,512.4 | 110,131.9 | 90,254.6 | 229,522.2 | 88,708.2 | 121,509.4 | 180,721.4 | 328,935.9 | 272,836.8 | 422,605.4 | 81,879.2 | 284,805.2 |
| Debt instruments | 3abaa | −19,375.4 | 11,556.2 | 28,118.9 | 37,625.7 | 41,295.8 | 109,258.9 | 28,646.8 | 42,415.2 | 183,136.9 | 92,707.6 | 149,780.0 | 28,928.3 |
| Direct investment: liabilities | 3a9la | 80,079.9 | 113,254.2 | 130,282.8 | 192,466.7 | 98,351.2 | 211,552.2 | 228,175.2 | 404,012.4 | 547,675.4 | 707,596.6 | 189,477.5 | 260,370.1 |
| Equity & investment fund shares | 3aala | 67,881.5 | 45,771.4 | 115,441.7 | 158,433.8 | 48,382.1 | 236,037.7 | 309,495.8 | 345,253.1 | 364,783.0 | 624,861.1 | 145,739.7 | 315,351.3 |
| Debt instruments | 3abla | 12,198.4 | 67,482.8 | 14,841.2 | 34,032.9 | 49,969.1 | −24,485.5 | −81,320.6 | 58,759.4 | 182,892.4 | 82,735.4 | 43,737.8 | −54,981.2 |
| Portfolio investment: assets | 3b9aa | 87,514.4 | 266,975.6 | 176,127.9 | 174,516.2 | −164,735.9 | 247,795.2 | 130,918.9 | −61,391.8 | 129,727.0 | 212,359.0 | 324,679.6 | 285,179.5 |
| Equity & investment fund shares | 3baaa | 45,834.9 | 123,620.5 | 102,722.6 | 52,572.3 | −85,754.4 | 98,702.8 | 57,786.0 | −41,403.4 | 4,159.9 | 110,826.4 | 128,396.9 | 164,167.9 |
| Debt securities | 3bbaa | 41,679.5 | 143,355.1 | 73,405.3 | 121,944.0 | −78,981.4 | 149,092.4 | 73,132.9 | −19,988.4 | 125,567.1 | 101,532.6 | 196,282.4 | 121,011.6 |
| Portfolio investment: liabilities | 3b9la | 139,609.5 | 315,138.7 | 250,697.5 | 307,664.1 | −126,991.8 | 196,106.1 | 200,155.9 | 55,805.7 | 467,413.4 | 321,913.5 | 446,136.9 | 395,387.1 |
| Equity & investment fund shares | 3bala | 121,545.8 | 275,561.2 | 220,261.9 | 279,316.2 | −132,109.0 | 154,680.6 | 218,741.3 | 39,814.6 | 177,558.3 | 258,763.0 | 383,260.8 | 360,659.9 |
| Debt securities | 3bbla | 18,063.6 | 39,577.4 | 30,435.6 | 28,348.0 | 5,117.2 | 41,425.5 | −18,585.3 | 15,991.1 | 289,855.0 | 63,150.5 | 62,876.1 | 34,727.2 |
| Fin. der.& empl.stk.ops.(ESOs): net | 3c9na | 2,997.7 | 3,189.9 | −9,850.4 | −14,177.0 | 21,729.6 | 14,016.9 | −23,240.6 | −14,846.2 | −8,987.6 | −25,894.8 | 232.2 | −6,863.4 |
| Fin. der. & ESOs.: assets | 3c9aa | .... | .... | .... | .... | .... | .... | .... | .... | .... | .... | .... | .... |
| Fin. der. & ESOs.: liabilities | 3c9la | .... | .... | .... | .... | .... | .... | .... | .... | .... | .... | .... | .... |
| Other investment: assets | 3d9aa | 127,918.4 | 199,914.3 | 272,336.6 | 256,725.6 | 60,574.5 | −69,876.8 | 218,439.5 | 339,890.8 | 393,558.4 | 332,689.7 | 144,060.3 | 35,226.2 |
| Other equity | 3daaa | — | — | — | — | — | — | — | — | 103.9 | 107.7 | — | 939.0 |
| Debt instruments | 3dzaa | 127,918.4 | 199,914.3 | 272,336.6 | 256,725.6 | 60,574.5 | −69,876.8 | 218,439.5 | 339,890.8 | 393,454.5 | 332,582.0 | 144,060.3 | 34,287.2 |
| Other investment: liabilities | 3d9la | 80,363.6 | 157,921.8 | 172,086.6 | 179,273.9 | 72,381.5 | 12,485.2 | 103,890.8 | 171,905.2 | −47,739.2 | 2,537.2 | 62,640.8 | −31,057.1 |
| Other equity | 3dala | — | — | — | — | — | — | — | — | — | — | — | −3.7 |
| Debt instruments | 3dzla | 80,363.6 | 157,921.8 | 172,086.6 | 179,273.9 | 72,381.5 | 12,485.2 | 103,890.8 | 171,905.2 | −47,739.2 | 2,537.2 | 62,640.8 | −31,053.5 |
| Curr.+ cap.− finan. acct. balance | 4y9na | −42.3 | −67.7 | −15.3 | −15.3 | 159.0 | 411.1 | 58.2 | 54.1 | −23.6 | 70.4 | −130.3 | −29.1 |
| D. Net Errors and Omissions | 409na | −1.4 | −1.4 | −.1 | .5 | .5 | −16.0 | −23.9 | 110.0 | 1.7 | 3.8 | .3 | −26.2 |
| E. Reserves and Related Items | 4z9na | −43.7 | −69.0 | −15.3 | −14.8 | 159.5 | 395.1 | 34.3 | 164.1 | −21.9 | 74.2 | −129.9 | −55.3 |
| Reserve assets | 3e9aa | −43.7 | −69.0 | −15.3 | −14.8 | 159.5 | 395.1 | 34.3 | 164.1 | −21.9 | 74.2 | −129.9 | −55.3 |
| Credit and loans from the IMF | 3dcla | — | — | — | — | — | — | — | — | — | — | — | — |
| Exceptional financing | 409la | .... | .... | .... | .... | .... | .... | .... | .... | .... | .... | .... | .... |

*Excludes components in group E

## International Investment Position

| | | 2004 | 2005 | 2006 | 2007 | 2008 | 2009 | 2010 | 2011 | 2012 | 2013 | 2014 | 2015 |
|---|---|---|---|---|---|---|---|---|---|---|---|---|---|
| | | | | | | | *Millions of US Dollars* | | | | | | |
| Assets | 809aa | 3,422,609.0 | 3,781,346.6 | 4,917,399.3 | 6,211,746.7 | 5,420,539.4 | 6,088,929.8 | 6,394,748.7 | 6,941,924.3 | 8,148,385.8 | 9,245,094.8 | 10,148,354.3 | 10,310,512.2 |
| Direct investment | 8a9aa | 889,495.5 | 900,630.5 | 1,098,758.8 | 1,473,765.1 | 1,622,541.9 | 1,902,963.4 | 2,009,052.8 | 2,900,072.6 | 3,594,664.6 | 4,124,358.3 | 4,795,086.4 | 4,989,877.8 |
| Equity & investment fund shares | 8aaaa | 764,302.9 | 780,091.5 | 930,071.2 | 1,250,437.2 | 1,375,896.9 | 1,531,706.7 | 1,624,522.0 | 1,822,888.5 | 2,227,839.5 | 2,582,968.2 | 3,189,107.5 | 3,414,290.2 |
| Debt instruments | 8abaa | 125,192.6 | 120,539.0 | 168,687.5 | 223,328.0 | 246,645.0 | 371,256.7 | 384,530.8 | 1,077,184.1 | 1,366,825.1 | 1,541,390.1 | 1,605,978.9 | 1,575,587.6 |
| Portfolio investment | 8b9aa | 1,616,313.5 | 1,840,921.2 | 2,432,432.5 | 2,882,606.8 | 2,157,361.8 | 2,705,576.7 | 2,876,744.7 | 2,687,945.4 | 3,072,072.5 | 3,509,014.8 | 3,770,493.9 | 3,805,432.2 |
| Equity & investment fund shares | 8baaa | 637,836.6 | 807,865.9 | 1,149,651.7 | 1,413,235.5 | 755,186.0 | 1,068,481.4 | 1,228,710.7 | 1,073,023.9 | 1,231,209.4 | 1,563,416.6 | 1,722,758.0 | 1,809,401.4 |
| Debt securities | 8bbaa | 978,476.9 | 1,033,055.4 | 1,282,780.8 | 1,469,371.2 | 1,402,175.8 | 1,637,095.3 | 1,648,034.0 | 1,614,921.5 | 1,840,863.0 | 1,945,598.2 | 2,047,735.9 | 1,996,030.8 |
| Fin. der.(oth.than reserves) & ESOs | 8c9aa | 23,733.9 | 31,076.6 | 26,678.3 | 30,258.7 | 93,265.3 | 76,905.8 | 91,429.4 | 228,457.0 | 220,610.1 | 228,421.8 | 152,218.3 | 205,462.1 |
| Other investment | 8d9aa | 892,735.2 | 1,008,439.9 | 1,359,264.3 | 1,824,910.4 | 1,546,972.7 | 1,402,673.4 | 1,416,672.8 | 1,124,435.3 | 1,260,047.9 | 1,382,336.4 | 1,429,692.0 | 1,308,968.8 |
| Other equity | 8daaa | | | | | | | | | | 101.3 | 1,446.4 | 2,392.9 |
| Debt instruments | 8dzaa | 892,735.2 | 1,008,439.9 | 1,359,264.3 | 1,824,910.4 | 1,546,972.7 | 1,402,673.4 | 1,416,672.8 | 1,124,435.3 | 1,260,047.9 | 1,382,235.0 | 1,428,245.6 | 1,306,575.9 |
| Reserve assets | 8e9aa | 330.9 | 278.4 | 265.4 | 205.7 | 397.7 | 810.5 | 849.0 | 1,014.0 | 990.9 | 963.4 | 863.7 | 771.2 |
| Liabilities | 809la | 3,415,828.1 | 3,774,406.3 | 4,907,927.0 | 6,221,686.1 | 5,411,884.6 | 6,104,334.8 | 6,405,705.5 | 6,925,779.9 | 8,127,871.8 | 9,222,548.1 | 10,137,272.6 | 10,292,576.1 |
| Direct investment | 8a9la | 954,753.1 | 917,480.2 | 1,155,614.8 | 1,509,175.1 | 1,575,053.0 | 1,867,272.5 | 1,954,564.6 | 2,605,987.5 | 3,084,202.4 | 3,600,404.1 | 4,254,068.2 | 4,443,303.5 |
| Equity & investment fund shares | 8aala | 834,063.6 | 749,493.2 | 953,252.8 | 1,257,612.4 | 1,221,105.4 | 1,505,686.3 | 1,658,821.4 | 1,612,073.4 | 1,803,986.6 | 2,118,935.3 | 2,581,952.0 | 2,918,587.2 |
| Debt instruments | 8abla | 120,689.5 | 167,987.0 | 202,362.0 | 251,562.7 | 353,947.5 | 361,586.2 | 295,743.2 | 993,914.1 | 1,280,215.8 | 1,481,468.8 | 1,672,116.1 | 1,524,716.3 |
| Portfolio investment | 8b9la | 1,661,113.3 | 1,944,048.7 | 2,530,490.3 | 3,166,600.7 | 2,431,770.4 | 3,031,074.5 | 3,238,784.8 | 3,156,317.7 | 3,893,949.5 | 4,392,882.0 | 4,633,584.1 | 4,641,630.7 |
| Equity & investment fund shares | 8bala | 1,436,257.5 | 1,698,464.4 | 2,233,555.3 | 2,821,021.4 | 2,058,013.2 | 2,575,507.8 | 2,819,569.2 | 2,585,188.4 | 2,993,127.3 | 3,406,094.1 | 3,561,295.9 | 3,586,146.4 |
| Debt securities | 8bbla | 224,855.8 | 245,584.3 | 296,935.0 | 345,579.3 | 373,757.2 | 455,566.7 | 419,215.7 | 571,129.3 | 900,822.2 | 986,787.8 | 1,072,288.1 | 1,055,484.3 |
| Fin. der.(oth.than reserves) & ESOs | 8c9la | 30,890.8 | 26,094.6 | 28,582.1 | 41,229.4 | 72,068.3 | 42,234.1 | 73,071.7 | 220,967.5 | 214,732.1 | 228,501.6 | 136,320.3 | 201,054.9 |
| Other investment | 8d9la | 769,070.9 | 886,782.8 | 1,193,239.8 | 1,504,680.9 | 1,332,992.9 | 1,163,753.8 | 1,139,284.4 | 942,507.2 | 934,987.8 | 1,000,760.4 | 1,113,300.1 | 1,006,587.0 |
| Other equity | 8dala | — | — | — | — | — | — | — | — | — | — | 879.0 | 856.4 |
| Debt instruments | 8dzla | 769,070.9 | 886,782.8 | 1,193,239.8 | 1,504,680.9 | 1,332,992.9 | 1,163,753.8 | 1,139,284.4 | 942,507.2 | 934,987.8 | 1,000,760.4 | 1,112,421.1 | 1,005,730.6 |

# Luxembourg 137

| | | 2004 | 2005 | 2006 | 2007 | 2008 | 2009 | 2010 | 2011 | 2012 | 2013 | 2014 | 2015 |
|---|---|---|---|---|---|---|---|---|---|---|---|---|---|

**Government Finance Operations Statement**
**General Government**

*Millions of Euros: Fiscal Year Ends December 31; Data Reported through Eurostat*

| | | 2004 | 2005 | 2006 | 2007 | 2008 | 2009 | 2010 | 2011 | 2012 | 2013 | 2014 | 2015 |
|---|---|---|---|---|---|---|---|---|---|---|---|---|---|
| Revenue | a1 | 11,884 | 13,110 | 14,063 | 15,599 | 16,401 | 16,443 | 17,464 | 18,509 | 19,533 | 20,487 | 21,573 | 22,295 |
| Taxes | a11 | 7,273 | 8,192 | 8,729 | 9,738 | 10,020 | 9,915 | 10,696 | 11,346 | 12,006 | 12,640 | 13,394 | 13,724 |
| Social Contributions | a12 | 3,335 | 3,584 | 3,797 | 4,151 | 4,452 | 4,741 | 4,886 | 5,234 | 5,531 | 5,736 | 6,025 | 6,242 |
| Grants | a13 | .... | .... | .... | .... | .... | .... | .... | .... | .... | .... | .... | .... |
| Other Revenue | a14 | .... | .... | .... | .... | .... | .... | .... | .... | .... | .... | .... | .... |
| Expense | a2 | 11,477 | 12,211 | 12,789 | 13,449 | 14,481 | 15,840 | 16,654 | 17,402 | 18,635 | 19,500 | 20,100 | 20,823 |
| Compensation of Employees | a21 | 2,549 | 2,714 | 2,852 | 3,001 | 3,155 | 3,390 | 3,596 | 3,788 | 3,997 | 4,177 | 4,350 | 4,559 |
| Use of Goods & Services | a22 | 1,047 | 1,128 | 1,138 | 1,179 | 1,313 | 1,475 | 1,545 | 1,568 | 1,698 | 1,732 | 1,734 | 1,864 |
| Consumption of Fixed Capital | a23 | 546 | 591 | 639 | 685 | 736 | 785 | 833 | 912 | 987 | 1,080 | 1,123 | 1,149 |
| Interest | a24 | 60 | 67 | 84 | 118 | 145 | 149 | 166 | 202 | 208 | 201 | 190 | 189 |
| Subsidies | a25 | 339 | 379 | 399 | 460 | 472 | 481 | 504 | 527 | 613 | 619 | 709 | 728 |
| Grants | a26 | .... | .... | .... | .... | .... | .... | .... | .... | .... | .... | .... | .... |
| Social Benefits | a27 | 5,619 | 6,059 | 6,358 | 6,641 | 7,263 | 8,018 | 8,345 | 8,610 | 9,183 | 9,726 | 10,125 | 10,316 |
| Other Expense | a28 | .... | .... | .... | .... | .... | .... | .... | .... | .... | .... | .... | .... |
| Gross Operating Balance [1-2+23] | agob | 954 | 1,491 | 1,913 | 2,836 | 2,656 | 1,388 | 1,644 | 2,019 | 1,885 | 2,067 | 2,595 | 2,622 |
| Net Operating Balance [1-2] | anob | 407 | 900 | 1,273 | 2,150 | 1,920 | 603 | 811 | 1,107 | 898 | 987 | 1,472 | 1,472 |
| Net Acq. of Nonfinancial Assets | a31 | 766 | 876 | 619 | 607 | 654 | 853 | 1,075 | 885 | 783 | 624 | 638 | 824 |
| Aquisition of Nonfin. Assets | a31.1 | .... | .... | .... | .... | .... | .... | .... | .... | .... | .... | .... | .... |
| Disposal of Nonfin. Assets | a31.2 | .... | .... | .... | .... | .... | .... | .... | .... | .... | .... | .... | .... |
| Net Lending/Borrowing [1-2-31] | anlb | −358 | 23 | 655 | 1,543 | 1,266 | −249 | −264 | 221 | 115 | 363 | 834 | 648 |
| Net Acq. of Financial Assets | a32 | 188 | −71 | 897 | 1,860 | 4,165 | −673 | 3,183 | 728 | 1,840 | 1,274 | 1,879 | 165 |
| By instrument | | | | | | | | | | | | | |
| Monetary Gold & SDRs | a3201 | — | — | — | — | — | — | — | — | — | — | — | — |
| Currency & Deposits | a3202 | 341 | −141 | 1,139 | −3,960 | 1,483 | −2,235 | 1,358 | 66 | 61 | 368 | 566 | 107 |
| Securities other than Shares | a3203 | −252 | −270 | −34 | 5,113 | 439 | 747 | −1,129 | 12 | 765 | 349 | 670 | 778 |
| Loans | a3204 | −24 | −7 | 24 | 179 | −105 | 194 | 24 | −223 | 229 | 149 | 338 | −71 |
| Shares & Other Equity | a3205 | 56 | −10 | −350 | 381 | 2,289 | 1,111 | 1,651 | 324 | 880 | 978 | 955 | 73 |
| Insurance Technical Reserves | a3206 | | | | | | | | | | | | |
| Financial Derivatives | a3207 | — | — | — | 2 | — | 1 | 5 | 3 | −5 | −4 | 2 | — |
| Other Accounts Receivable | a3208 | 68 | 356 | 118 | 146 | 59 | −491 | 1,274 | 546 | −90 | −567 | −653 | −723 |
| By debtor | | | | | | | | | | | | | |
| Domestic | a321 | .... | .... | .... | .... | .... | .... | .... | .... | .... | .... | .... | .... |
| Foreign | a322 | .... | .... | .... | .... | .... | .... | .... | .... | .... | .... | .... | .... |
| Net Incurrence of Liabilities | a33 | 547 | −94 | 243 | 317 | 2,899 | −423 | 3,447 | 506 | 1,725 | 910 | 1,044 | −483 |
| By instrument | | | | | | | | | | | | | |
| Special Drawing Rights (SDRs) | a3301 | — | — | — | — | — | — | — | — | — | — | — | — |
| Currency & Deposits | a3302 | 22 | 20 | 19 | 18 | 16 | 17 | 13 | 14 | 16 | 12 | 11 | 11 |
| Securities other than Shares | a3303 | −25 | −97 | −139 | −74 | 2,000 | — | 2,000 | — | 1,000 | 1,050 | 200 | — |
| Loans | a3304 | 235 | 273 | 527 | 294 | 801 | 113 | 122 | 110 | 492 | 217 | 138 | −47 |
| Shares & Other Equity | a3305 | — | — | — | — | — | — | — | — | — | — | — | — |
| Insurance Technical Reserves | a3306 | — | — | — | — | — | — | — | — | — | — | — | — |
| Financial Derivatives | a3307 | — | — | — | — | — | — | — | — | — | — | — | — |
| Other Accounts Payable | a3308 | 315 | −291 | −163 | 79 | 83 | −553 | 1,312 | 383 | 217 | −369 | 695 | −448 |
| By creditor | | | | | | | | | | | | | |
| Domestic | a331 | .... | .... | .... | .... | .... | .... | .... | .... | .... | .... | .... | .... |
| Foreign | a332 | .... | .... | .... | .... | .... | .... | .... | .... | .... | .... | .... | .... |
| Stat. Discrepancy [32-33-NLB] | anlbz | | | | | | | | | | | | |
| Memo Item: Expenditure [2+31] | a2m | 12,243 | 13,087 | 13,408 | 14,056 | 15,135 | 16,692 | 17,729 | 18,287 | 19,418 | 20,124 | 20,739 | 21,647 |

**Balance Sheet**

*Millions of Euros: Fiscal Year Ends December 31*

| | | 2004 | 2005 | 2006 | 2007 | 2008 | 2009 | 2010 | 2011 | 2012 | 2013 | 2014 | 2015 |
|---|---|---|---|---|---|---|---|---|---|---|---|---|---|
| Net Worth | a6 | .... | .... | .... | .... | .... | .... | .... | .... | .... | .... | .... | .... |
| Nonfinancial Assets | a61 | .... | .... | .... | .... | .... | .... | .... | .... | .... | .... | .... | .... |
| Financial Assets | a62 | 18,635 | 19,237 | 21,352 | 25,022 | 27,586 | 27,896 | 30,977 | 30,823 | 34,398 | 36,350 | 38,491 | 38,429 |
| By instrument | | | | | | | | | | | | | |
| Monetary Gold & SDRs | a6201 | — | — | — | — | — | — | — | — | — | — | — | — |
| Currency & Deposits | a6202 | 8,044 | 7,904 | 9,043 | 5,082 | 6,565 | 4,331 | 5,689 | 5,754 | 5,815 | 6,183 | 6,749 | 6,857 |
| Securities other than Shares | a6203 | 1,200 | 954 | 885 | 6,011 | 6,459 | 7,234 | 6,077 | 6,090 | 6,851 | 7,195 | 7,864 | 8,639 |
| Loans | a6204 | 1,122 | 1,115 | 1,140 | 1,319 | 1,213 | 1,461 | 1,486 | 1,262 | 1,492 | 1,641 | 1,979 | 1,908 |
| Shares and Other Equity | a6205 | 5,451 | 6,091 | 6,993 | 9,170 | 9,850 | 11,862 | 13,439 | 12,881 | 15,499 | 17,158 | 18,376 | 18,225 |
| Insurance Technical Reserves | a6206 | — | — | — | — | — | — | — | — | — | — | — | — |
| Financial Derivatives | a6207 | — | — | — | 2 | 1 | 2 | 7 | 10 | 5 | 5 | 7 | 8 |
| Other Accounts Receivable | a6208 | 2,817 | 3,174 | 3,292 | 3,438 | 3,497 | 3,006 | 4,280 | 4,826 | 4,736 | 4,169 | 3,516 | 2,793 |
| By debtor | | | | | | | | | | | | | |
| Domestic | a621 | .... | .... | .... | .... | .... | .... | .... | .... | .... | .... | .... | .... |
| Foreign | a622 | .... | .... | .... | .... | .... | .... | .... | .... | .... | .... | .... | .... |
| Liabilities | a63 | 4,251 | 4,151 | 4,387 | 4,703 | 7,647 | 7,269 | 10,758 | 11,429 | 13,314 | 13,965 | 15,711 | 15,228 |
| By instrument | | | | | | | | | | | | | |
| Special Drawing Rights (SDRs) | a6301 | — | — | — | — | — | — | — | — | — | — | — | — |
| Currency & Deposits | a6302 | 104 | 124 | 143 | 161 | 177 | 194 | 207 | 221 | 237 | 249 | 260 | 272 |
| Securities other than Shares | a6303 | 324 | 221 | 74 | — | 2,044 | 2,090 | 4,131 | 4,296 | 5,456 | 6,247 | 7,149 | 7,149 |
| Loans | a6304 | 1,612 | 1,885 | 2,412 | 2,706 | 3,507 | 3,620 | 3,742 | 3,852 | 4,344 | 4,561 | 4,699 | 4,652 |
| Shares and Other Equity | a6305 | — | — | — | — | — | — | — | — | — | — | — | — |
| Insurance Technical Reserves | a6306 | 1 | 1 | 1 | 1 | 1 | 1 | 1 | — | — | — | — | — |
| Financial Derivatives | a6307 | — | — | — | — | — | — | — | — | — | — | — | — |
| Other Accounts Payable | a6308 | 2,211 | 1,920 | 1,757 | 1,835 | 1,918 | 1,365 | 2,676 | 3,059 | 3,277 | 2,908 | 3,603 | 3,156 |
| By creditor | | | | | | | | | | | | | |
| Domestic | a631 | .... | .... | .... | .... | .... | .... | .... | .... | .... | .... | .... | .... |
| Foreign | a632 | .... | .... | .... | .... | .... | .... | .... | .... | .... | .... | .... | .... |
| Net Financial Worth [62-63] | a6m2 | 14,384 | 15,086 | 16,965 | 20,319 | 19,939 | 20,627 | 20,220 | 19,395 | 21,084 | 22,385 | 22,780 | 23,201 |
| Memo Item: Debt at Market Value | a6m3 | 4,251 | 4,151 | 4,387 | 4,703 | 7,647 | 7,269 | 10,758 | 11,429 | 13,314 | 13,965 | 15,711 | 15,228 |
| Memo Item: Debt at Face Value | a6m35 | 4,237 | 4,143 | 4,386 | 4,703 | 7,602 | 7,179 | 10,626 | 11,133 | 12,857 | 13,768 | 14,812 | 14,329 |
| Memo Item: Maastricht Debt | a6m36 | 2,026 | 2,223 | 2,629 | 2,867 | 5,684 | 5,814 | 7,950 | 8,073 | 9,581 | 10,860 | 11,209 | 11,174 |
| Memo Item: Debt at Nominal Value | a6m4 | .... | .... | .... | .... | .... | .... | .... | .... | .... | .... | .... | .... |

| | | 2004 | 2005 | 2006 | 2007 | 2008 | 2009 | 2010 | 2011 | 2012 | 2013 | 2014 | 2015 |
|---|---|---|---|---|---|---|---|---|---|---|---|---|---|
| **National Accounts** | | | | | | | *Billions of Euros* | | | | | | |
| Househ.Cons.Expend.,incl.NPISHs..... | 96f | 10.1 | 10.8 | 11.5 | 12.0 | 12.3 | 12.5 | 12.8 | 13.3 | 13.8 | 14.1 | 14.6 | 15.3 |
| Government Consumption Expend... | 91f | 4.6 | 5.0 | 5.1 | 5.4 | 5.7 | 6.2 | 6.6 | 6.9 | 7.4 | 7.8 | 8.2 | 8.9 |
| Gross Fixed Capital Formation.......... | 93e | 5.7 | 5.7 | 5.9 | 6.5 | 7.3 | 6.5 | 6.6 | 7.6 | 8.0 | 7.7 | 8.5 | 9.0 |
| Changes in Inventories.................... | 93i | .1 | .4 | .2 | .4 | — | −1.0 | .2 | .5 | −.3 | −.3 | −.5 | .3 |
| Exports of Goods and Services.......... | 90c | 42.4 | 48.3 | 58.9 | 67.3 | 71.8 | 60.7 | 71.1 | 78.5 | 84.7 | 92.1 | 97.7 | 111.6 |
| Imports of Goods and Services (-)..... | 98c | 35.3 | 40.3 | 48.3 | 55.6 | 59.5 | 48.8 | 57.9 | 64.5 | 69.9 | 76.1 | 80.4 | 92.6 |
| Gross Domestic Product (GDP)......... | 99b | 27.6 | 29.8 | 33.3 | 36.0 | 37.5 | 36.1 | 39.4 | 42.4 | 43.8 | 45.3 | 48.1 | 52.5 |
| Net Primary Income from Abroad..... | 98.n | −3.6 | −3.8 | −7.5 | −5.8 | −8.0 | −12.6 | −12.2 | −13.7 | −14.6 | .... | .... | .... |
| Gross National Income (GNI)............ | 99a | 24.0 | 26.0 | 25.8 | 30.2 | 29.5 | 23.5 | 27.2 | 28.7 | 29.2 | .... | .... | .... |
| Net Current Transf.from Abroad....... | 98t | −2.6 | −2.8 | −1.3 | −1.6 | −1.9 | −1.1 | −.9 | −1.4 | −1.2 | .... | .... | .... |
| Net National Income...................... | 99e | 20.8 | 22.6 | 22.3 | 25.7 | 25.6 | .... | .... | .... | .... | .... | .... | .... |
| Gross Nat'l Disposable Inc.(GNDI).... | 99i | .... | .... | .... | .... | .... | .... | .... | .... | .... | .... | .... | .... |
| Consumption of Fixed Capital......... | 99cf | 3.2 | 3.4 | 3.7 | 4.0 | 4.5 | 5.2 | 5.4 | 5.2 | 5.4 | .... | .... | .... |
| GDP Volume 2010 Ref., Chained..... | 99b.p | 33.9 | 35.3 | 37.0 | 39.4 | 39.6 | 37.4 | 39.4 | 40.4 | 40.3 | 41.1 | 44.4 | 45.9 |
| GDP Volume (2010=100)............... | 99bvp | 86.0 | 89.5 | 93.9 | 100.0 | 100.5 | 95.1 | 100.0 | 102.6 | 102.4 | 104.5 | 112.8 | 116.5 |
| GDP Deflator (2010=100)............... | 99bip | 81.4 | 84.5 | 90.1 | 91.3 | 94.9 | 96.4 | 100.0 | 105.0 | 108.6 | 110.1 | 108.4 | 114.4 |
| | | | | | | | *Millions: Midyear Estimates* | | | | | | |
| Population................................. | 99z | .45 | .46 | .47 | .47 | .49 | .50 | .51 | .52 | .53 | .54 | .56 | .57 |

# Macedonia, FYR 962

| | | 2004 | 2005 | 2006 | 2007 | 2008 | 2009 | 2010 | 2011 | 2012 | 2013 | 2014 | 2015 |
|---|---|---|---|---|---|---|---|---|---|---|---|---|---|
| **Exchange Rates** | | | | | | *Denar per SDR: End of Period* | | | | | | | |
| Market Rate.................................. | aa | 69.990 | 74.120 | 69.879 | 65.828 | 67.096 | 66.886 | 71.325 | 72.978 | 71.699 | 68.728 | 73.252 | 78.120 |
| | | | | | | *Denar per US Dollar: End of Period (ae) Period Average (rf)* | | | | | | | |
| Market Rate.................................. | ae | 45.068 | 51.859 | 46.450 | 41.656 | 43.561 | 42.665 | 46.314 | 47.535 | 46.651 | 44.628 | 50.560 | 56.374 |
| Market Rate.................................. | rf | 49.410 | 49.284 | 48.802 | 44.730 | 41.868 | 44.101 | 46.485 | 44.231 | 47.890 | 46.395 | 46.437 | 55.537 |
| | | | | | | *Index Numbers (2010=100): Period Averages* | | | | | | | |
| Nominal Effective Exchange Rate..... | nec | 96.88 | 97.82 | 97.89 | 98.63 | 99.67 | 101.62 | 100.00 | 101.27 | 100.34 | 101.79 | 102.94 | 101.61 |
| CPI-Based Real Effect. Ex. Rate........ | rec | 102.04 | 99.54 | 99.42 | 98.95 | 103.09 | 102.79 | 100.00 | 101.62 | 101.11 | 103.44 | 103.19 | 100.80 |
| **Fund Position** | | | | | | *Millions of SDRs: End of Period* | | | | | | | |
| Quota........................................ | 2f.s | 68.90 | 68.90 | 68.90 | 68.90 | 68.90 | 68.90 | 68.90 | 68.90 | 68.90 | 68.90 | 68.90 | 68.90 |
| SDR Holdings................................ | 1b.s | .49 | .55 | 1.98 | .92 | .89 | 58.08 | .81 | .49 | 1.04 | 2.98 | 3.57 | 3.78 |
| Reserve Position in the Fund............ | 1c.s | — | — | — | — | — | — | — | — | — | — | — | — |
| Total Fund Cred.&Loans Outstg........ | 2tl | 40.27 | 43.50 | 37.00 | — | — | — | — | 197.00 | 197.00 | 197.00 | 123.13 | — |
| SDR Allocations............................. | 1bd | 8.38 | 8.38 | 8.38 | 8.38 | 8.38 | 65.62 | 65.62 | 65.62 | 65.62 | 65.62 | 65.62 | 65.62 |
| **International Liquidity** | | | | | | *Millions of US Dollars Unless Otherwise Indicated: End of Period* | | | | | | | |
| Total Reserves minus Gold.............. | 1l.d | 904.97 | 1,228.51 | 1,750.60 | 2,082.25 | 1,920.34 | 2,050.91 | 1,970.03 | 2,331.41 | 2,528.17 | 2,484.61 | 2,700.54 | 2,238.72 |
| SDR Holdings........................... | 1b.d | .8 | .8 | 3.0 | 1.5 | 1.4 | 91.1 | 1.2 | .8 | 1.6 | 4.6 | 5.2 | 5.2 |
| Reserve Position in the Fund......... | 1c.d | — | — | — | — | — | — | — | — | — | — | — | — |
| Foreign Exchange......................... | 1d.d | 904.21 | 1,227.73 | 1,747.62 | 2,080.80 | 1,918.97 | 1,959.85 | 1,968.79 | 2,330.66 | 2,526.57 | 2,480.03 | 2,695.37 | 2,233.49 |
| Gold (Million Fine Troy Ounces)....... | 1ad | .197 | .218 | .218 | .218 | .218 | .218 | .218 | .219 | .218 | .218 | .219 | .219 |
| Gold (National Valuation)................. | 1and | 86.47 | 111.98 | 138.76 | 182.59 | 188.81 | 240.98 | 307.79 | 345.53 | 363.30 | 262.34 | 262.22 | 232.47 |
| Central Bank: Other Assets.............. | 3..d | 9.06 | 17.16 | 30.96 | 40.51 | 2.30 | 1.94 | .96 | 302.45 | 180.75 | 1.44 | 1.33 | .87 |
| Central Bank: Other Liabs............... | 4..d | 1.15 | .39 | 1.49 | .07 | 9.02 | 4.03 | 4.06 | 301.00 | 207.85 | .09 | .24 | .29 |
| Other Depository Corps.: Assets....... | 7a.d | 823.34 | 728.84 | 855.38 | 923.70 | 548.75 | 718.21 | 763.18 | 784.42 | 763.34 | 783.66 | 791.07 | 710.83 |
| Other Depository Corps.: Liabs......... | 7b.d | 238.71 | 281.24 | 367.30 | 572.16 | 548.13 | 682.64 | 779.17 | 738.26 | 824.28 | 859.53 | 764.91 | 653.58 |
| Other Financial Corps.: Assets......... | 7e.d | .... | .... | .... | .... | .... | .... | .... | .... | 95 | 159 | 221 | 242 |
| Other Financial Corps.: Liabs........... | 7f.d | .... | .... | .... | .... | .... | .... | .... | .... | 15 | 16 | 57 | 43 |
| **Central Bank** | | | | | | *Millions of Denar: End of Period* | | | | | | | |
| Net Foreign Assets.......................... | 11n | 41,370 | 65,723 | 84,861 | 94,425 | 90,952 | 93,246 | 100,627 | 108,151 | 114,797 | 104,603 | 136,028 | 134,219 |
| Claims on Nonresidents................. | 11 | 44,827 | 69,587 | 88,101 | 94,979 | 91,908 | 97,807 | 105,495 | 141,624 | 143,322 | 122,656 | 149,866 | 139,361 |
| Liabilities to Nonresidents.............. | 16c | 3,457 | 3,865 | 3,240 | 555 | 955 | 4,561 | 4,868 | 33,473 | 28,526 | 18,053 | 13,838 | 5,142 |
| Claims on Other Depository Corps.... | 12e | 991 | 29 | 22 | 14 | 14 | 16 | 16 | 16 | 2,717 | 16 | 16 | 16 |
| Net Claims on Central Government.. | 12an | −9,370 | −20,475 | −32,128 | −19,562 | −11,030 | −11,365 | −3,516 | −13,443 | −24,889 | −24,104 | −31,362 | −20,217 |
| Claims on Central Government...... | 12a | 3,495 | 3,549 | 2,519 | 1,271 | 1,304 | 1,327 | 5,493 | 20,098 | 19,727 | 18,901 | 14,730 | 6,039 |
| Liabilities to Central Government... | 16d | 12,865 | 24,025 | 34,648 | 20,833 | 12,334 | 12,692 | 9,009 | 33,541 | 44,616 | 43,005 | 46,092 | 26,255 |
| Claims on Other Sectors................... | 12s | 47 | 1,066 | 1,095 | 1,415 | 1,511 | 1,514 | 1,456 | 74 | 89 | 46 | 77 | 138 |
| Claims on Other Financial Corps... | 12g | 3 | 3 | 3 | 3 | 3 | 1 | 1 | — | — | — | — | — |
| Claims on State & Local Govts....... | 12b | — | — | — | — | — | — | — | — | — | — | — | — |
| Claims on Public Nonfin. Corps...... | 12c | — | — | — | — | — | — | — | — | — | — | — | — |
| Claims on Private Sector................ | 12d | 44 | 1,063 | 1,092 | 1,412 | 1,508 | 1,512 | 1,455 | 74 | 89 | 46 | 77 | 138 |
| Monetary Base............................... | 14 | 22,683 | 28,374 | 34,018 | 41,468 | 48,035 | 51,892 | 53,917 | 58,879 | 61,310 | 58,934 | 74,223 | 73,364 |
| Currency in Circulation................. | 14a | 15,071 | 15,813 | 17,732 | 19,894 | 20,799 | 19,482 | 20,173 | 22,767 | 23,979 | 25,045 | 28,081 | 31,951 |
| Liabs. to Other Depository Corps.... | 14c | 6,043 | 10,307 | 13,769 | 17,966 | 21,619 | 26,639 | 28,830 | 30,877 | 33,115 | 31,227 | 42,930 | 38,184 |
| Liabilities to Other Sectors............. | 14d | 1,569 | 2,254 | 2,517 | 3,608 | 5,617 | 5,771 | 4,914 | 5,235 | 4,216 | 2,661 | 3,211 | 3,230 |
| Other Liabs. to Other Dep. Corps..... | 14n | 4,713 | 8,945 | 9,480 | 21,040 | 17,451 | 16,676 | 26,867 | 32,230 | 27,636 | 25,466 | 25,468 | 25,046 |
| Dep. & Sec. Excl. f/Monetary Base.... | 14o | — | — | — | — | 11 | — | — | — | 32 | 73 | 20 | 9 |
| Deposits Included in Broad Money. | 15 | — | — | — | — | — | — | — | — | — | — | — | — |
| Sec.Ot.th.Shares Incl.in Brd. Money. | 16a | — | — | — | — | — | — | — | — | — | — | — | — |
| Deposits Excl. from Broad Money... | 16b | — | — | — | — | 11 | — | — | — | 32 | 73 | 20 | 9 |
| Sec.Ot.th.Shares Excl.f/Brd.Money.. | 16s | — | — | — | — | — | — | — | — | — | — | — | — |
| Loans........................................ | 16l | — | — | — | — | — | — | — | — | — | — | — | — |
| Financial Derivatives....................... | 16m | — | — | — | — | — | — | — | — | — | — | — | — |
| Shares and Other Equity.................. | 17a | 5,746 | 8,167 | 8,367 | 9,257 | 11,780 | 12,748 | 16,448 | 18,378 | 18,151 | 9,802 | 13,354 | 15,634 |
| Other Items (Net)............................ | 17r | −104 | 856 | 1,985 | 4,527 | 4,171 | 2,095 | 1,350 | −14,689 | −14,415 | −13,713 | −8,306 | 102 |
| Memo Item: | | | | | | | | | | | | | |
| Total Assets.................................. | 10ra | 51,352 | 75,272 | 95,647 | 99,990 | 96,111 | 102,010 | 114,473 | 164,498 | 169,084 | 146,545 | 168,794 | 149,627 |

# Macedonia, FYR   962

| | | 2004 | 2005 | 2006 | 2007 | 2008 | 2009 | 2010 | 2011 | 2012 | 2013 | 2014 | 2015 |
|---|---|---|---|---|---|---|---|---|---|---|---|---|---|
| **Other Depository Corporations** | | *Millions of Denar: End of Period* | | | | | | | | | | | |
| Net Foreign Assets | 21n | 26,348 | 23,212 | 22,671 | 14,644 | 27 | 1,518 | −740 | 2,194 | −2,843 | −3,386 | 1,323 | 3,227 |
| Claims on Nonresidents | 21 | 37,106 | 37,797 | 39,732 | 38,478 | 23,904 | 30,643 | 35,346 | 37,287 | 35,611 | 34,974 | 39,997 | 40,073 |
| Liabilities to Nonresidents | 26c | 10,758 | 14,585 | 17,061 | 23,834 | 23,877 | 29,125 | 36,086 | 35,093 | 38,453 | 38,359 | 38,674 | 36,845 |
| Claims on Central Bank | 20 | 11,657 | 20,386 | 24,704 | 40,912 | 42,020 | 45,492 | 57,736 | 66,483 | 64,354 | 60,903 | 73,180 | 69,064 |
| Currency | 20a | 921 | 1,389 | 1,545 | 1,986 | 3,198 | 3,216 | 3,215 | 3,460 | 3,862 | 4,339 | 4,860 | 5,651 |
| Reserve Deposits and Securities | 20b | 6,271 | 10,065 | 13,702 | 17,926 | 21,385 | 26,401 | 28,561 | 30,778 | 34,506 | 31,088 | 42,852 | 38,366 |
| Other Claims | 20n | 4,465 | 8,932 | 9,457 | 21,000 | 17,437 | 15,876 | 25,960 | 32,246 | 25,987 | 25,476 | 25,469 | 25,047 |
| Net Claims on Central Government | 22an | 5,238 | 5,204 | 10,865 | 10,640 | 5,500 | 8,957 | 15,027 | 13,960 | 29,096 | 37,011 | 31,387 | 36,496 |
| Claims on Central Government | 22a | 7,333 | 7,542 | 13,646 | 12,995 | 9,380 | 13,059 | 18,060 | 16,737 | 31,656 | 38,756 | 33,252 | 37,964 |
| Liabilities to Central Government | 26d | 2,095 | 2,338 | 2,781 | 2,355 | 3,880 | 4,103 | 3,033 | 2,777 | 2,560 | 1,745 | 1,865 | 1,468 |
| Claims on Other Sectors | 22s | 59,297 | 71,437 | 93,080 | 129,321 | 173,768 | 179,720 | 193,039 | 209,414 | 220,604 | 234,806 | 258,331 | 282,811 |
| Claims on Other Financial Corps. | 22g | — | 3 | 6 | 52 | 337 | 586 | 668 | 715 | 900 | 962 | 1,368 | 1,428 |
| Claims on State & Local Govts. | 22b | 20 | 13 | — | — | 24 | 20 | 15 | 253 | 412 | 636 | 739 | 794 |
| Claims on Public Nonfin. Corps. | 22c | 682 | 517 | 363 | 315 | 133 | 431 | 417 | 321 | 392 | 507 | 811 | 904 |
| Claims on Private Sector | 22d | 58,595 | 70,904 | 92,711 | 128,954 | 173,274 | 178,684 | 191,939 | 208,124 | 218,901 | 232,701 | 255,413 | 279,686 |
| Liabilities to Central Bank | 26g | 779 | 937 | 2,301 | 1,560 | 842 | 30 | 22 | 23 | 2,722 | 21 | 24 | 23 |
| Transf.Dep.Included in Broad Money | 24 | 19,910 | 21,326 | 26,544 | 37,688 | 46,524 | 50,673 | 57,972 | 60,623 | 64,405 | 70,537 | 87,427 | 107,494 |
| Other Dep.Included in Broad Money. | 25 | 58,921 | 71,399 | 91,294 | 118,181 | 128,606 | 136,913 | 155,229 | 172,212 | 179,845 | 188,564 | 198,600 | 197,058 |
| Sec.Ot.th.Shares Incl.in Brd. Money.. | 26a | — | — | — | — | — | — | — | — | — | — | — | — |
| Deposits Excl. from Broad Money | 26b | 324 | 150 | 98 | 85 | 58 | 6,123 | 6,477 | 7,826 | 8,164 | 8,684 | 10,000 | 11,322 |
| Sec.Ot.th.Shares Excl.f/Brd.Money | 26s | — | — | — | — | 40 | — | — | — | — | — | — | — |
| Loans | 26l | 28 | 38 | 44 | 393 | 102 | 419 | 437 | 659 | 806 | 735 | 657 | 642 |
| Financial Derivatives | 26m | — | — | — | — | — | 1 | 1 | — | 3 | 2 | — | 14 |
| Insurance Technical Reserves | 26r | — | — | — | — | — | — | — | — | — | — | — | — |
| Shares and Other Equity | 27a | 34,981 | 37,589 | 39,277 | 43,313 | 49,694 | 52,806 | 56,454 | 64,140 | 70,824 | 75,834 | 81,141 | 87,574 |
| Other Items (Net) | 27r | −12,403 | −11,200 | −8,238 | −5,703 | −4,551 | −11,280 | −11,530 | −13,432 | −15,557 | −15,043 | −13,628 | −12,528 |
| *Memo Item:* | | | | | | | | | | | | | |
| Total Assets | 20ra | 146,283 | 171,189 | 204,745 | 254,348 | 283,710 | 306,469 | 349,758 | 383,002 | 424,660 | 447,852 | 484,568 | 524,146 |
| **Depository Corporations** | | *Millions of Denar: End of Period* | | | | | | | | | | | |
| Net Foreign Assets | 31n | 67,718 | 88,935 | 107,532 | 109,069 | 90,979 | 94,764 | 99,887 | 110,345 | 111,954 | 101,218 | 137,351 | 137,446 |
| Claims on Nonresidents | 31 | 81,933 | 107,384 | 127,833 | 133,457 | 115,812 | 128,450 | 140,841 | 178,911 | 178,933 | 157,630 | 189,863 | 179,434 |
| Liabilities to Nonresidents | 36c | 14,215 | 18,450 | 20,301 | 24,389 | 24,832 | 33,686 | 40,955 | 68,566 | 66,979 | 56,412 | 52,512 | 41,987 |
| Domestic Claims | 32 | 55,212 | 57,232 | 72,912 | 121,814 | 169,749 | 178,825 | 206,007 | 210,005 | 224,901 | 247,760 | 258,433 | 299,228 |
| Net Claims on Central Government | 32an | −4,132 | −15,271 | −21,263 | −8,922 | −5,530 | −2,408 | 11,511 | 518 | 4,208 | 12,907 | 25 | 16,279 |
| Claims on Central Government | 32a | 10,828 | 11,091 | 16,165 | 14,266 | 10,684 | 14,386 | 23,553 | 36,835 | 51,383 | 57,657 | 47,982 | 44,003 |
| Liabilities to Central Government | 36d | 14,960 | 26,363 | 37,429 | 23,188 | 16,214 | 16,795 | 12,041 | 36,317 | 47,176 | 44,750 | 47,957 | 27,724 |
| Claims on Other Sectors | 32s | 59,344 | 72,503 | 94,175 | 130,736 | 175,279 | 181,234 | 194,495 | 209,487 | 220,693 | 234,852 | 258,408 | 282,949 |
| Claims on Other Financial Corps. | 32g | 3 | 6 | 9 | 55 | 340 | 587 | 669 | 715 | 900 | 962 | 1,368 | 1,428 |
| Claims on State & Local Govts. | 32b | 20 | 13 | — | — | 24 | 20 | 15 | 253 | 412 | 636 | 739 | 794 |
| Claims on Public Nonfin. Corps. | 32c | 682 | 517 | 363 | 315 | 133 | 431 | 417 | 321 | 392 | 507 | 811 | 904 |
| Claims on Private Sector | 32d | 58,639 | 71,967 | 93,803 | 130,366 | 174,782 | 180,196 | 193,394 | 208,198 | 218,990 | 232,748 | 255,490 | 279,823 |
| Broad Money Liabilities | 35l | 94,550 | 109,403 | 136,542 | 177,385 | 198,348 | 209,623 | 235,074 | 257,379 | 268,583 | 282,469 | 312,460 | 334,082 |
| Currency Outside Depository Corps | 34a | 14,150 | 14,424 | 16,187 | 17,908 | 17,601 | 16,266 | 16,958 | 19,308 | 20,118 | 20,706 | 23,221 | 26,300 |
| Transferable Deposits | 34 | 21,479 | 23,580 | 29,061 | 41,296 | 52,141 | 56,444 | 62,887 | 65,859 | 68,621 | 73,199 | 90,638 | 110,723 |
| Other Deposits | 35 | 58,921 | 71,399 | 91,294 | 118,181 | 128,606 | 136,913 | 155,229 | 172,212 | 179,845 | 188,564 | 198,600 | 197,058 |
| Securities Other than Shares | 36a | — | — | — | — | — | — | — | — | — | — | — | — |
| Deposits Excl. from Broad Money | 36b | 324 | 150 | 98 | 85 | 69 | 6,124 | 6,477 | 7,826 | 8,196 | 8,757 | 10,020 | 11,331 |
| Sec.Ot.th.Shares Excl.f/Brd.Money | 36s | — | — | — | — | 40 | — | — | — | — | — | — | — |
| Loans | 36l | 28 | 38 | 44 | 393 | 102 | 419 | 437 | 659 | 806 | 735 | 657 | 642 |
| Financial Derivatives | 36m | — | — | — | — | — | 1 | 1 | — | 3 | 2 | — | 14 |
| Insurance Technical Reserves | 36r | — | — | — | — | — | — | — | — | — | — | — | — |
| Shares and Other Equity | 37a | 40,727 | 45,756 | 47,644 | 52,570 | 61,474 | 65,554 | 72,902 | 82,518 | 88,975 | 85,637 | 94,495 | 103,208 |
| Other Items (Net) | 37r | −12,699 | −9,180 | −3,884 | 450 | 695 | −8,132 | −8,997 | −28,031 | −29,708 | −28,622 | −21,849 | −12,602 |
| Broad Money Liabs., Seasonally Adj. | 35l.b | 93,637 | 108,308 | 135,111 | 175,493 | 196,177 | 207,432 | 232,788 | 254,966 | 266,010 | 279,672 | 309,321 | 330,686 |
| **Other Financial Corporations** | | *Millions of Denar: End of Period* | | | | | | | | | | | |
| Net Foreign Assets | 41n | .... | .... | .... | .... | .... | .... | .... | .... | 3,751 | 6,358 | 8,301 | 11,200 |
| Claims on Nonresidents | 41 | .... | .... | .... | .... | .... | .... | .... | .... | 4,437 | 7,079 | 11,198 | 13,637 |
| Liabilities to Nonresidents | 46c | .... | .... | .... | .... | .... | .... | .... | .... | 686 | 721 | 2,897 | 2,437 |
| Claims on Depository Corporations.. | 40 | .... | .... | .... | .... | .... | .... | .... | .... | 7,479 | 8,697 | 11,019 | 10,902 |
| Net Claims on Central Government.. | 42an | .... | .... | .... | .... | .... | .... | .... | .... | 18,127 | 21,291 | 24,888 | 31,186 |
| Claims on Central Government | 42a | .... | .... | .... | .... | .... | .... | .... | .... | 18,167 | 21,327 | 24,941 | 31,253 |
| Liabilities to Central Government | 46d | .... | .... | .... | .... | .... | .... | .... | .... | 40 | 36 | 53 | 66 |
| Claims on Other Sectors | 42s | .... | .... | .... | .... | .... | .... | .... | .... | 1,173 | 1,452 | 5,301 | 5,123 |
| Claims on State & Local Govts. | 42b | .... | .... | .... | .... | .... | .... | .... | .... | — | — | 32 | 24 |
| Claims on Public Nonfin. Corps. | 42c | .... | .... | .... | .... | .... | .... | .... | .... | — | — | 34 | 25 |
| Claims on Private Sector | 42d | .... | .... | .... | .... | .... | .... | .... | .... | 1,173 | 1,452 | 5,236 | 5,074 |
| Deposits | 46b | .... | .... | .... | .... | .... | .... | .... | .... | — | — | — | — |
| Securities Other than Shares | 46s | .... | .... | .... | .... | .... | .... | .... | .... | — | — | — | — |
| Loans | 46l | .... | .... | .... | .... | .... | .... | .... | .... | 32 | 44 | 521 | 480 |
| Financial Derivatives | 46m | .... | .... | .... | .... | .... | .... | .... | .... | — | — | — | — |
| Insurance Technical Reserves | 46r | .... | .... | .... | .... | .... | .... | .... | .... | 24,386 | 28,610 | 34,540 | 40,528 |
| Shares and Other Equity | 47a | .... | .... | .... | .... | .... | .... | .... | .... | 9,299 | 11,877 | 17,982 | 21,127 |
| Other Items (Net) | 47r | .... | .... | .... | .... | .... | .... | .... | .... | −3,188 | −2,733 | −3,534 | −3,723 |
| *Memo Item:* | | | | | | | | | | | | | |
| Total Assets | 40ra | .... | .... | .... | .... | .... | .... | .... | .... | 35,891 | 43,000 | 58,308 | 67,027 |

# Macedonia, FYR  962

| | | 2004 | 2005 | 2006 | 2007 | 2008 | 2009 | 2010 | 2011 | 2012 | 2013 | 2014 | 2015 |
|---|---|---|---|---|---|---|---|---|---|---|---|---|---|
| **Financial Corporations** | | | | | | *Millions of Denar: End of Period* | | | | | | | |
| Net Foreign Assets | 51n | .... | .... | .... | .... | .... | .... | .... | .... | 115,705 | 107,576 | 145,651 | 148,647 |
| Claims on Nonresidents | 51 | .... | .... | .... | .... | .... | .... | .... | .... | 183,370 | 164,709 | 201,060 | 193,071 |
| Liabilities to Nonresidents | 56c | .... | .... | .... | .... | .... | .... | .... | .... | 67,665 | 57,133 | 55,409 | 44,424 |
| Domestic Claims | 52 | .... | .... | .... | .... | .... | .... | .... | .... | 243,301 | 269,540 | 287,254 | 334,110 |
| Net Claims on Central Government | 52an | .... | .... | .... | .... | .... | .... | .... | .... | 22,335 | 34,198 | 24,913 | 47,466 |
| Claims on Central Government | 52a | .... | .... | .... | .... | .... | .... | .... | .... | 69,551 | 78,984 | 72,923 | 75,255 |
| Liabilities to Central Government | 56d | .... | .... | .... | .... | .... | .... | .... | .... | 47,216 | 44,786 | 48,010 | 27,790 |
| Claims on Other Sectors | 52s | .... | .... | .... | .... | .... | .... | .... | .... | 220,966 | 235,342 | 262,341 | 286,644 |
| Claims on State & Local Govts | 52b | .... | .... | .... | .... | .... | .... | .... | .... | 412 | 636 | 771 | 818 |
| Claims on Public Nonfin. Corps | 52c | .... | .... | .... | .... | .... | .... | .... | .... | 392 | 507 | 844 | 929 |
| Claims on Private Sector | 52d | .... | .... | .... | .... | .... | .... | .... | .... | 220,162 | 234,199 | 260,726 | 284,898 |
| Currency Outside Financial Corps | 54a | .... | .... | .... | .... | .... | .... | .... | .... | 20,117 | 20,705 | 23,216 | 26,279 |
| Deposits | 55l | .... | .... | .... | .... | .... | .... | .... | .... | 246,403 | 260,629 | 288,040 | 307,853 |
| Securities Other than Shares | 56a | .... | .... | .... | .... | .... | .... | .... | .... | — | — | — | — |
| Loans | 56l | .... | .... | .... | .... | .... | .... | .... | .... | 46 | 45 | 363 | 420 |
| Financial Derivatives | 56m | .... | .... | .... | .... | .... | .... | .... | .... | 3 | 2 | — | 14 |
| Insurance Technical Reserves | 56r | .... | .... | .... | .... | .... | .... | .... | .... | 24,386 | 28,610 | 34,540 | 40,528 |
| Shares and Other Equity | 57a | .... | .... | .... | .... | .... | .... | .... | .... | 98,274 | 97,514 | 112,477 | 124,336 |
| Other Items (Net) | 57r | .... | .... | .... | .... | .... | .... | .... | .... | −30,225 | −30,389 | −25,731 | −16,673 |
| **Monetary Aggregates** | | | | | | *Millions of Denar: End of Period* | | | | | | | |
| Broad Money | 59m | 94,550 | 109,403 | 136,542 | 177,385 | 198,348 | 209,623 | 235,074 | 257,379 | 268,583 | 282,469 | 312,460 | 334,082 |
| o/w:Currency Issued by Cent.Govt | 59m.a | — | — | — | — | — | — | — | — | — | — | — | — |
| o/w:Dep.in Nonfin. Corporations | 59m.b | — | — | — | — | — | — | — | — | — | — | — | — |
| o/w:Secs. Issued by Central Govt | 59m.c | — | — | — | — | — | — | — | — | — | — | — | — |
| Money (National Definitions) | | | | | | | | | | | | | |
| M1 | 59ma | 28,842 | 30,675 | 36,153 | 47,257 | 54,119 | 52,223 | 57,362 | 61,301 | 65,936 | 70,005 | 85,548 | 101,282 |
| M2 | 59mb | 49,787 | 55,763 | 73,388 | 104,592 | 103,703 | 97,958 | 108,515 | 119,593 | 123,479 | 127,117 | 142,698 | 154,836 |
| M4 | 59md | 94,550 | 108,724 | 135,907 | 175,783 | 195,525 | 207,262 | 232,569 | 255,038 | 266,284 | 280,363 | 309,878 | 331,007 |
| **Interest Rates** | | | | | | *Percent Per Annum* | | | | | | | |
| Discount Rate (End of Period) | 60.a | 6.50 | 6.50 | 6.50 | 6.50 | 6.50 | 6.50 | †5.00 | 4.00 | 3.75 | 3.50 | 3.25 | 3.25 |
| Deposit Rate | 60l | 6.54 | †5.23 | 4.66 | 4.88 | 5.89 | 7.05 | 7.07 | 5.91 | 5.09 | 4.42 | 3.70 | 2.89 |
| Deposit Rate (Fgn. Currency) | 60l.f | .... | 1.28 | 1.53 | 1.89 | 2.43 | 3.27 | 3.10 | 2.72 | 2.23 | 1.82 | 1.36 | 1.28 |
| Lending Rate | 60p | 12.44 | †12.13 | 11.29 | 10.23 | 9.68 | 10.07 | 9.48 | 8.87 | 8.50 | 8.04 | 7.46 | 7.08 |
| Lending Rate (Fgn. Currency) | 60p.f | .... | 7.73 | 8.08 | 8.44 | 8.01 | 7.42 | 7.37 | 7.40 | 6.97 | 6.54 | 6.26 | 5.89 |
| **Prices, Production, Labor** | | | | | | *Index Numbers (2010=100): Period Averages* | | | | | | | |
| Producer Prices | 63 | 79.7 | 82.2 | 87.9 | 90.1 | 99.2 | 92.0 | 100.0 | 112.4 | 117.6 | 118.1 | 116.7 | 112.1 |
| Consumer Prices | 64 | 86.7 | †86.8 | 89.6 | 91.6 | 99.2 | 98.5 | 100.0 | 103.9 | 107.4 | 110.3 | 110.0 | 109.7 |
| Wages: Average Monthly | 65 | 59.8 | 61.3 | 65.8 | 71.0 | 78.3 | 97.1 | 100.0 | 101.4 | 101.7 | 102.9 | 104.1 | 106.6 |
| Industrial Production | 66 | 92.9 | †99.5 | 105.4 | 109.5 | 115.1 | 105.1 | 100.0 | 106.9 | 104.0 | 107.3 | 112.5 | 118.0 |
| | | | | | | *Number in Thousands: Period Averages* | | | | | | | |
| Labor Force | 67d | 832 | 869 | 892 | 907 | 919 | 929 | 938 | 940 | 943 | 956 | 959 | 955 |
| Employment | 67e | 523 | 545 | 570 | 590 | 609 | 630 | 638 | 645 | 651 | 679 | 690 | 706 |
| Unemployment | 67c | 309 | 324 | 321 | 317 | 310 | 299 | 300 | 295 | 293 | 277 | 269 | 249 |
| Unemployment Rate (%) | 67r | 37.2 | 37.3 | 36.0 | 34.9 | 33.8 | 32.2 | 32.0 | 31.4 | 31.0 | 29.0 | 28.0 | 26.1 |
| **Intl. Transactions & Positions** | | | | | | *Millions of US Dollars* | | | | | | | |
| Exports | 70..d | 1,675.9 | 2,041.3 | 2,400.7 | 3,356.1 | 3,920.5 | 2,691.6 | 3,351.4 | 4,478.3 | 4,015.4 | 4,298.8 | 4,933.8 | 4,489.9 |
| Imports, c.i.f. | 71..d | 2,931.6 | 3,228.0 | 3,762.7 | 5,216.0 | 6,843.1 | 5,037.5 | 5,474.5 | 7,027.2 | 6,522.4 | 6,619.6 | 7,276.7 | 6,399.8 |

# Macedonia, FYR   962

| | | 2004 | 2005 | 2006 | 2007 | 2008 | 2009 | 2010 | 2011 | 2012 | 2013 | 2014 | 2015 |
|---|---|---|---|---|---|---|---|---|---|---|---|---|---|
| **Balance of Payments** | | | | | | | *Millions of US Dollars* | | | | | | |
| A. Current Account* | 109bx | −451.6 | −159.3 | −28.5 | −605.7 | −1,235.8 | −609.6 | −198.3 | −261.7 | −319.1 | −177.2 | −104.1 | −137.1 |
| Goods, credit (exports) | 1a9cx | 1,047.0 | 1,406.7 | 1,788.0 | 2,558.7 | 2,996.4 | 1,891.9 | 2,617.2 | 3,338.6 | 2,965.1 | 3,155.7 | 3,681.6 | 3,371.5 |
| Goods, debit (imports) | 1a9dx | 2,357.3 | 2,642.1 | 3,206.1 | 4,434.4 | 5,838.8 | 4,313.8 | 4,648.9 | 5,980.1 | 5,549.0 | 5,629.9 | 6,149.8 | 5,392.5 |
| Balance on goods | 1a9bx | −1,310.3 | −1,235.4 | −1,418.1 | −1,875.7 | −2,842.5 | −2,421.9 | −2,031.7 | −2,641.5 | −2,583.9 | −2,474.1 | −2,468.2 | −2,021.0 |
| Services, credit (exports) | 1b9cx | 621.9 | 686.7 | 757.8 | 1,053.1 | 1,260.8 | 1,103.7 | 989.2 | 1,455.6 | 1,367.1 | 1,533.5 | 1,695.3 | 1,519.1 |
| Services, debit (imports) | 1b9dx | 501.3 | 545.2 | 566.2 | 765.7 | 980.7 | 818.4 | 814.5 | 954.4 | 973.6 | 1,035.8 | 1,223.5 | 1,139.1 |
| Balance on Goods & Services | 1z9bx | −1,189.7 | −1,093.9 | −1,226.5 | −1,588.3 | −2,562.4 | −2,136.5 | −1,857.0 | −2,140.4 | −2,190.3 | −1,976.4 | −1,996.4 | −1,641.1 |
| Primary income: credit | 1c9cx | 83.7 | 96.4 | 132.7 | 209.2 | 267.0 | 179.4 | 194.3 | 225.0 | 188.7 | 226.9 | 210.0 | 133.6 |
| Primary income: debit | 1c9dx | 119.0 | 205.6 | 160.2 | 598.5 | 386.7 | 246.2 | 325.5 | 412.3 | 399.8 | 483.2 | 422.6 | 379.4 |
| Balance on gds, serv. & prim. inc. | 1y9bx | −1,225.0 | −1,203.1 | −1,254.0 | −1,977.6 | −2,682.2 | −2,203.4 | −1,988.1 | −2,327.7 | −2,401.3 | −2,232.7 | −2,209.0 | −1,886.8 |
| Secondary income: credit | 1d9ca | 829.1 | 1,099.8 | 1,285.0 | 1,486.5 | 1,535.6 | 1,677.2 | 1,873.8 | 2,153.1 | 2,174.7 | 2,158.0 | 2,219.2 | 1,849.3 |
| Secondary income: debit | 1d9da | 55.7 | 56.0 | 59.5 | 114.6 | 89.2 | 83.3 | 83.9 | 87.1 | 92.5 | 104.4 | 114.2 | 99.6 |
| B. Capital Account* | 209ba | — | — | — | 5.4 | −15.4 | 15.5 | 4.5 | −3.9 | 12.0 | 19.5 | 4.0 | 6.2 |
| Capital account: credit | 209ca | .... | .... | .... | .... | .... | 4.5 | 3.8 | 13.8 | 12.8 | 19.8 | 14.1 | 6.6 |
| Capital account: debit | 209da | — | — | — | −5.4 | 15.4 | −11.0 | −.7 | 17.7 | .8 | .3 | 10.1 | .4 |
| Balance on current & capital acct. | 129ba | −451.6 | −159.3 | −28.5 | −600.3 | −1,251.2 | −594.1 | −193.8 | −265.6 | −307.1 | −157.7 | −100.1 | −130.9 |
| C. Financial Account* | 309na | −462.2 | −575.6 | −408.4 | −841.4 | −1,202.1 | −700.8 | −271.5 | −382.9 | −469.6 | −90.1 | −717.4 | −54.2 |
| Direct investment: assets | 3a9aa | −12.7 | 51.1 | 3.5 | 33.3 | 11.2 | 74.0 | 94.6 | 34.0 | 172.4 | 97.5 | −200.5 | −.7 |
| Equity & investment fund shares | 3aaaa | 1.2 | 2.8 | .2 | −1.1 | −13.5 | 11.6 | 1.9 | −.1 | −28.4 | 23.4 | 44.1 | 9.0 |
| Debt instruments | 3abaa | −13.9 | 48.3 | 3.3 | 34.4 | 24.7 | 62.4 | 92.7 | 34.1 | 200.8 | 74.1 | −244.6 | −9.7 |
| Direct investment: liabilities | 3a9la | 309.1 | 145.3 | 427.4 | 733.5 | 611.7 | 259.5 | 301.4 | 507.9 | 337.9 | 402.5 | 60.9 | 192.7 |
| Equity & investment fund shares | 3aala | 153.8 | 154.7 | 373.4 | 510.4 | 324.1 | 56.9 | 201.8 | 571.5 | 142.3 | 195.9 | −140.6 | −73.5 |
| Debt instruments | 3abla | 155.3 | −9.4 | 54.0 | 223.1 | 287.6 | 202.6 | 99.6 | −63.6 | 195.6 | 206.6 | 201.5 | 266.2 |
| Portfolio investment: assets | 3b9aa | .9 | −.8 | .5 | 2.8 | 1.1 | 51.3 | 29.0 | 33.5 | 9.4 | 43.8 | 44.0 | 43.5 |
| Equity & investment fund shares | 3baaa | −.2 | −.1 | −.1 | 2.3 | .4 | 29.2 | 18.5 | 38.5 | 10.3 | 41.6 | 43.4 | 33.8 |
| Debt securities | 3bbaa | 1.1 | −.7 | .5 | .5 | .7 | 22.1 | 10.5 | −5.0 | −.9 | 2.2 | .6 | 9.7 |
| Portfolio investment: liabilities | 3b9la | 12.4 | 237.8 | 92.8 | 157.9 | −71.4 | 198.5 | −46.9 | −72.7 | 108.1 | −165.0 | 694.1 | 107.0 |
| Equity & investment fund shares | 3bala | 13.0 | 53.8 | 86.3 | 169.8 | −49.4 | −14.0 | −4.0 | −8.1 | −6.4 | −.7 | −4.0 | −9.4 |
| Debt securities | 3bbla | −.7 | 184.0 | 6.5 | −11.9 | −22.0 | 212.5 | −42.9 | −64.5 | 114.5 | −164.3 | 698.1 | 116.4 |
| Fin. der.& empl.stk.ops.(ESOs): net | 3c9na | .... | .... | .... | .... | .... | .... | .... | .... | .... | .... | .... | .... |
| Fin. der. & ESOs.: assets | 3c9na | .... | .... | .... | .... | .... | .... | .... | .... | .... | .... | .... | .... |
| Fin. der. & ESOs.: liabilities | 3c9la | .... | .... | .... | .... | .... | .... | .... | .... | .... | .... | .... | .... |
| Other investment: assets | 3d9aa | −3.9 | 49.1 | 149.7 | 81.4 | −295.6 | 131.5 | 195.4 | 560.3 | 99.3 | 77.6 | 465.1 | 297.2 |
| Other equity | 3daaa | .... | .... | .... | .... | .... | .... | .... | .... | −.3 | — | — | — |
| Debt instruments | 3dzaa | −3.9 | 49.1 | 149.7 | 81.4 | −295.6 | 131.5 | 195.4 | 560.3 | 99.6 | 77.6 | 465.1 | 297.1 |
| Other investment: liabilities | 3d9la | 125.0 | 291.9 | 41.9 | 67.4 | 378.4 | 499.6 | 335.9 | 575.4 | 304.7 | 71.5 | 271.1 | 94.5 |
| Other equity | 3dala | .... | .... | .... | .... | .... | .... | .... | .... | .... | .... | .... | .1 |
| Debt instruments | 3dzla | 125.0 | 291.9 | 41.9 | 67.4 | 378.4 | 499.6 | 335.9 | 575.4 | 304.7 | 71.5 | 271.0 | 94.4 |
| Curr.+ cap.− finan. acct. balance | 4y9na | 10.6 | 416.3 | 379.9 | 241.0 | −49.1 | 106.7 | 77.7 | 117.3 | 162.5 | −67.5 | 617.3 | −76.7 |
| D. Net Errors and Omissions | 409na | 17.5 | −5.8 | 3.8 | −51.8 | −30.8 | 40.2 | .4 | 15.5 | 22.2 | 20.0 | 42.7 | 31.1 |
| E. Reserves and Related Items | 4z9na | 28.0 | 410.6 | 383.7 | 189.2 | −80.0 | 146.9 | 78.1 | 132.8 | 184.7 | −47.5 | 660.0 | −45.6 |
| Reserve assets | 3e9aa | 19.4 | 415.3 | 374.1 | 133.1 | −80.0 | 146.9 | 78.1 | 444.1 | 184.7 | −47.5 | 549.4 | −219.5 |
| Credit and loans from the IMF | 3dcla | −8.6 | 4.7 | −9.6 | −56.1 | — | — | — | 311.3 | — | — | −110.6 | −173.9 |
| Exceptional financing | 409la | .... | .... | .... | .... | .... | .... | .... | .... | .... | .... | .... | .... |
| *Excludes components in group E | | | | | | | | | | | | | |
| | | | | | | | | | | | | | |
| **International Investment Position** | | | | | | | *Millions of US Dollars* | | | | | | |
| Assets | 809aa | 2,216.7 | 2,550.3 | 3,379.1 | 4,112.3 | 3,637.0 | 3,993.9 | 4,327.1 | 5,322.1 | 5,612.7 | 5,626.9 | 5,635.0 | 4,940.3 |
| Direct investment | 8a9aa | 109.2 | 156.7 | 162.3 | 232.4 | 256.9 | 350.1 | 443.0 | 509.2 | 703.4 | 851.5 | 578.4 | 529.4 |
| Equity & investment fund shares | 8aaaa | 43.9 | 43.6 | 36.4 | 51.6 | 69.0 | 71.1 | 67.2 | 90.5 | 60.9 | 108.9 | 140.3 | 135.0 |
| Debt instruments | 8abaa | 65.3 | 113.1 | 125.9 | 180.9 | 187.9 | 279.0 | 375.7 | 418.7 | 642.5 | 742.6 | 438.1 | 394.4 |
| Portfolio investment | 8b9aa | 4.9 | 4.4 | 5.0 | 6.4 | 6.2 | 9.3 | 34.4 | 58.9 | 83.2 | 148.5 | 188.4 | 221.1 |
| Equity & investment fund shares | 8baaa | 4.9 | 4.4 | 5.0 | 6.4 | 6.2 | 9.3 | 26.5 | 58.9 | 83.2 | 148.5 | 188.4 | 212.2 |
| Debt securities | 8bbaa | .... | .... | .... | .... | .... | .... | 7.9 | .... | .... | .... | .... | 8.8 |
| Fin. der.(oth.than reserves) & ESOs | 8c9aa | .... | .... | .... | .... | .... | .... | .... | .... | .... | .... | .... | .... |
| Other investment | 8d9aa | 1,127.3 | 1,064.5 | 1,346.1 | 1,633.9 | 1,266.3 | 1,344.1 | 1,572.9 | 2,077.0 | 1,934.6 | 1,879.9 | 1,905.5 | 1,718.6 |
| Other equity | 8daaa | .... | .... | .... | .... | .... | .... | .... | .... | .... | 1.2 | 1.1 | 1.0 |
| Debt instruments | 8dzaa | 1,127.3 | 1,064.5 | 1,346.1 | 1,633.9 | 1,266.3 | 1,344.1 | 1,572.9 | 2,077.0 | 1,934.6 | 1,878.7 | 1,904.3 | 1,717.5 |
| Reserve assets | 8e9aa | 975.2 | 1,324.7 | 1,865.7 | 2,239.6 | 2,107.6 | 2,290.5 | 2,276.9 | 2,676.9 | 2,891.5 | 2,746.9 | 2,962.8 | 2,471.2 |
| Liabilities | 809la | 4,728.3 | 4,898.8 | 5,864.8 | 7,640.2 | 8,240.1 | 9,173.5 | 9,146.7 | 10,450.7 | 11,118.5 | 11,909.8 | 11,166.3 | 10,343.4 |
| Direct investment | 8a9la | 2,245.5 | 2,181.5 | 2,887.7 | 3,904.2 | 4,356.4 | 4,758.5 | 4,667.7 | 5,064.8 | 5,466.8 | 6,182.6 | 5,324.1 | 4,998.1 |
| Equity & investment fund shares | 8aala | 1,858.5 | 1,863.5 | 2,454.0 | 3,271.3 | 3,394.0 | 3,557.6 | 3,509.3 | 4,024.2 | 4,151.2 | 4,570.9 | 3,750.3 | 3,294.1 |
| Debt instruments | 8abla | 387.1 | 318.0 | 433.7 | 632.9 | 962.5 | 1,200.9 | 1,158.4 | 1,040.6 | 1,315.6 | 1,611.8 | 1,573.7 | 1,704.0 |
| Portfolio investment | 8b9la | 71.6 | 273.9 | 364.7 | 445.2 | 373.5 | 590.7 | 529.4 | 420.1 | 538.3 | 348.9 | 944.4 | 929.4 |
| Equity & investment fund shares | 8bala | 40.0 | 52.8 | 114.0 | 194.8 | 187.9 | 195.6 | 185.5 | 158.2 | 151.0 | 138.9 | 124.3 | 102.4 |
| Debt securities | 8bbla | 31.6 | 221.2 | 250.7 | 250.5 | 185.6 | 395.1 | 343.9 | 262.0 | 387.3 | 210.1 | 820.1 | 827.0 |
| Fin. der.(oth.than reserves) & ESOs | 8c9la | .... | .... | .... | .... | .... | .... | .... | .... | .... | .... | .... | .... |
| Other investment | 8d9la | 2,411.2 | 2,443.4 | 2,612.4 | 3,290.7 | 3,510.2 | 3,824.3 | 3,949.7 | 4,965.8 | 5,113.5 | 5,378.2 | 4,897.8 | 4,416.0 |
| Other equity | 8dala | .... | .... | .... | .... | .... | .... | .... | .... | .... | 5.6 | 5.3 | 4.9 |
| Debt instruments | 8dzla | 2,411.2 | 2,443.4 | 2,612.4 | 3,290.7 | 3,510.2 | 3,824.3 | 3,949.7 | 4,965.8 | 5,113.5 | 5,372.7 | 4,892.4 | 4,411.1 |
| | | | | | | | | | | | | | |
| **National Accounts** | | | | | | | *Millions of Denar* | | | | | | |
| Househ.Cons.Expend.,incl.NPISHs | 96f | 213,884 | 227,944 | 250,309 | 279,880 | 330,399 | 314,376 | 324,096 | 345,262 | 342,809 | 364,666 | 367,297 | 379,290 |
| Government Consumption Expend | 91f | 53,499 | 54,378 | 58,019 | 62,481 | 75,088 | 78,536 | 82,957 | 84,188 | 84,764 | 82,912 | 88,431 | 93,555 |
| Gross Capital Formation | 93 | 59,902 | 62,913 | 68,809 | 89,928 | 110,405 | 107,600 | 108,218 | 120,548 | 134,962 | 115,886 | 160,764 | 178,492 |
| Exports of Goods and Services | 90c | 108,815 | 130,220 | 149,219 | 191,111 | 209,557 | 160,933 | 202,166 | 252,229 | 245,866 | 254,906 | 251,668 | 271,814 |
| Imports of Goods and Services (-) | 98c | 163,637 | 180,403 | 206,296 | 258,410 | 313,721 | 250,710 | 283,324 | 342,438 | 349,781 | 344,174 | 342,316 | 363,002 |
| Gross Domestic Product (GDP) | 99b | 272,462 | 295,052 | 320,059 | 364,989 | 411,728 | 410,735 | 434,112 | 459,789 | 458,621 | 474,196 | 525,843 | 560,148 |
| GDP Volume 2005 Prices | 99b.p | 282,748 | 295,052 | 309,895 | 328,951 | 345,239 | 342,062 | 351,963 | 361,714 | 360,322 | 371,504 | 407,049 | 422,111 |
| GDP Deflator (2010=100) | 99bip | 78.1 | 81.1 | 83.7 | 90.0 | 96.7 | 97.4 | 100.0 | 103.1 | 103.2 | 103.5 | 104.7 | 107.6 |
| GDP Volume (2010=100) | 99bvp | 80.3 | 83.8 | 88.0 | 93.5 | 98.1 | 97.2 | 100.0 | 102.8 | 102.4 | 105.6 | 115.7 | 119.9 |
| | | | | | | | *Millions: Midyear Estimates* | | | | | | |
| Population | 99z | 2.04 | 2.04 | 2.05 | 2.05 | 2.06 | 2.06 | 2.06 | 2.07 | 2.07 | 2.07 | 2.08 | 2.08 |

# Madagascar 674

| | | 2004 | 2005 | 2006 | 2007 | 2008 | 2009 | 2010 | 2011 | 2012 | 2013 | 2014 | 2015 |
|---|---|---|---|---|---|---|---|---|---|---|---|---|---|
| **Exchange Rates** | | | | | | *Ariary per SDR: End of Period* | | | | | | | |
| Official Rate...................... | aa | 2,903.2 | 3,087.0 | 3,029.8 | 2,823.4 | 2,865.5 | 3,064.3 | 3,305.1 | 3,450.5 | 3,489.7 | 3,443.6 | 3,762.2 | 4,433.2 |
| | | | | | | *Ariary per US Dollar: End of Period (ae) Period Average (rf)* | | | | | | | |
| Official Rate...................... | ae | 1,869.4 | 2,159.8 | 2,014.0 | 1,786.7 | 1,860.4 | 1,954.6 | 2,146.1 | 2,247.5 | 2,270.6 | 2,236.1 | 2,596.7 | 3,199.2 |
| Official Rate...................... | rf | 1,868.9 | 2,003.0 | 2,142.3 | 1,873.9 | 1,708.4 | 1,956.2 | 2,090.0 | 2,025.1 | 2,195.0 | 2,206.9 | 2,414.8 | 2,933.5 |
| **Fund Position** | | | | | | *Millions of SDRs: End of Period* | | | | | | | |
| Quota............................. | 2f.s | 122.20 | 122.20 | 122.20 | 122.20 | 122.20 | 122.20 | 122.20 | 122.20 | 122.20 | 122.20 | 122.20 | 122.20 |
| SDR Holdings.................... | 1b.s | .12 | .03 | .03 | .02 | .14 | 97.69 | 96.50 | 94.14 | 89.84 | 83.73 | 70.81 | 59.05 |
| Reserve Position in the Fund...... | 1c.s | .03 | .03 | .03 | .03 | .03 | .03 | .03 | .03 | .03 | .05 | .07 | .07 |
| Total Fund Cred.&Loans Outstg... | 2tl | 145.42 | 148.63 | 19.20 | 27.06 | 63.45 | 64.38 | 63.24 | 60.97 | 56.35 | 49.36 | 67.04 | 85.85 |
| SDR Allocations.................. | 1bd | 19.27 | 19.27 | 19.27 | 19.27 | 19.27 | 117.09 | 117.09 | 117.09 | 117.09 | 117.09 | 117.09 | 117.09 |
| **International Liquidity** | | | | | *Millions of US Dollars Unless Otherwise Indicated: End of Period* | | | | | | | | |
| Total Reserves minus Gold...... | 1l.d | 503.5 | 481.3 | 583.2 | 846.7 | 982.3 | 982.1 | 1,023.0 | 1,134.6 | 1,052.8 | 776.1 | 773.8 | 832.0 |
| SDR Holdings.................. | 1b.d | .2 | — | — | — | .2 | 153.2 | 148.6 | 144.5 | 138.1 | 128.9 | 102.6 | 81.8 |
| Reserve Position in the Fund...... | 1c.d | — | — | — | — | — | — | — | — | — | .1 | .1 | .1 |
| Foreign Exchange............... | 1d.d | 503.3 | 481.2 | 583.1 | 846.6 | 982.0 | 828.9 | 874.3 | 990.0 | 914.7 | 647.1 | 671.1 | 750.1 |
| Monetary Authorities: Other Liabs... | 4..d | 27.3 | 26.8 | 23.1 | 17.7 | 13.9 | 10.5 | 6.8 | 3.3 | .7 | .7 | 1.3 | .4 |
| Deposit Money Banks: Assets...... | 7a.d | 260.8 | 229.3 | 304.1 | 331.7 | 344.4 | 363.7 | 399.7 | 374.0 | 383.5 | 341.5 | 355.8 | 306.7 |
| Deposit Money Banks: Liabs...... | 7b.d | 61.4 | 40.9 | 39.2 | 50.6 | 68.0 | 65.7 | 61.2 | 64.5 | 52.8 | 63.8 | 59.4 | 41.9 |
| **Monetary Authorities** | | | | | | *Billions of Ariary: End of Period* | | | | | | | |
| Foreign Assets.................. | 11 | 932.06 | 1,013.86 | 1,155.21 | 1,506.33 | 1,846.85 | 1,918.72 | 2,191.99 | 2,552.12 | 2,386.05 | 1,733.16 | 2,013.51 | 2,665.32 |
| Claims on Central Government...... | 12a | 379.53 | 397.00 | 385.10 | 387.64 | 341.09 | 388.30 | 403.70 | 485.76 | 486.34 | 540.89 | 918.53 | 1,262.70 |
| Claims on Nonfin.Pub.Enterprises... | 12c | 3.86 | 4.46 | 4.55 | 4.70 | 5.02 | 5.59 | 6.79 | 7.75 | 8.64 | 9.04 | 8.28 | 5.87 |
| Claims on Deposit Money Banks...... | 12e | — | 1.07 | 5.50 | | | | | | | | | |
| Reserve Money.................. | 14 | 847.46 | 937.54 | 1,062.67 | 1,395.02 | 1,584.97 | 1,642.74 | 1,893.55 | 2,377.79 | 2,611.55 | 2,452.21 | 2,798.20 | 3,066.11 |
| of which: Currency Outside DMBs.. | 14a | 591.38 | 599.12 | 715.05 | 840.64 | 936.33 | 1,010.72 | 1,174.61 | 1,477.52 | 1,516.74 | 1,607.54 | 1,825.52 | 2,115.44 |
| Other Liabs. to DMBs.......... | 14n | — | — | 55.00 | 175.95 | 256.05 | 203.00 | 111.50 | 278.10 | 110.50 | 110.80 | 24.00 | 110.00 |
| Time, Savings,& Fgn.Currency Dep... | 15 | .2 | .3 | .3 | 9.6 | .4 | .4 | .5 | .5 | .6 | .6 | .6 | .6 |
| Foreign Liabilities.............. | 16c | 529.17 | 576.17 | 163.02 | 162.45 | 262.85 | 576.59 | 610.58 | 621.86 | 606.93 | 574.72 | 696.17 | 900.99 |
| Central Government Deposits...... | 16d | 114.72 | 71.73 | 463.85 | 450.27 | 482.11 | 364.19 | 597.03 | 420.42 | 327.74 | 111.28 | 266.68 | 213.40 |
| Capital Accounts................ | 17a | 18.95 | 17.76 | 18.73 | 181.53 | 150.76 | 176.10 | 193.90 | 212.59 | 212.90 | 211.99 | 211.22 | 229.73 |
| Other Items (Net).............. | 17r | −193.82 | −186.17 | −213.22 | −476.19 | −544.21 | −650.45 | −804.53 | −865.60 | −989.14 | −1,178.53 | −1,056.55 | −586.92 |
| **Deposit Money Banks** | | | | | | *Billions of Ariary: End of Period* | | | | | | | |
| Reserves........................ | 20 | 258.35 | 338.37 | 400.34 | 554.32 | 672.93 | 724.92 | 808.32 | 1,010.94 | 1,094.65 | 844.48 | 971.52 | 950.66 |
| Other Claims on Monetary Author.... | 20n | — | | | 175.95 | 216.05 | 110.00 | 22.00 | 167.30 | 110.50 | 110.80 | 24.00 | 110.00 |
| Foreign Assets.................. | 21 | 487.58 | 495.29 | 612.41 | 592.70 | 640.75 | 710.85 | 857.78 | 840.62 | 870.83 | 763.64 | 924.02 | 981.25 |
| Claims on Central Government...... | 22a | 271.10 | 192.84 | 252.58 | 314.70 | 359.97 | 484.69 | 480.13 | 636.91 | 855.28 | 810.36 | 694.90 | 772.61 |
| Claims on Private Sector.......... | 22d | 814.70 | 997.07 | 1,191.33 | 1,397.75 | 1,796.36 | 1,926.17 | 2,133.74 | 2,206.14 | 2,398.53 | 2,792.64 | 3,319.05 | 3,809.54 |
| Demand Deposits................ | 24 | 808.05 | 815.57 | 1,035.75 | 1,234.18 | 1,326.55 | 1,392.18 | 1,444.17 | 1,768.94 | 1,869.96 | 1,943.36 | 2,083.89 | 2,282.60 |
| Time Deposits.................. | 25 | 587.55 | 616.89 | 817.93 | 1,022.04 | 1,240.82 | 1,497.37 | 1,661.12 | 1,749.39 | 1,963.29 | 2,026.09 | 2,320.00 | 2,776.91 |
| Bonds.......................... | 26ab | 28.35 | 29.07 | 31.15 | 31.69 | 33.56 | 31.11 | 31.09 | 35.13 | 32.83 | 36.48 | 42.62 | 33.83 |
| Foreign Liabilities.............. | 26c | 114.76 | 88.37 | 79.03 | 90.44 | 126.48 | 128.34 | 131.24 | 144.92 | 119.86 | 142.70 | 154.16 | 134.03 |
| Central Government Deposits...... | 26d | 130.14 | 223.98 | 231.42 | 283.20 | 512.64 | 489.03 | 515.63 | 547.68 | 593.14 | 379.21 | 368.99 | 374.61 |
| Credit from Monetary Authorities..... | 26g | 2.33 | 1.07 | 5.50 | | | | | | | | | |
| Capital Accounts................ | 27a | 102.01 | 148.46 | 189.48 | 236.70 | 283.11 | 319.81 | 376.99 | 405.95 | 446.27 | 459.55 | 519.47 | 562.70 |
| Other Items (Net).............. | 27r | 58.54 | 100.16 | 66.40 | 137.17 | 162.90 | 98.80 | 141.74 | 209.91 | 304.43 | 334.53 | 444.36 | 459.40 |
| Treasury Claims: Private Sector...... | 22d.i | .11 | — | — | — | — | — | — | — | — | — | 22.63 | .... |
| Post Office: Checking Deposits...... | 24..i | 3.09 | 2.73 | 5.22 | 2.74 | 3.17 | 2.99 | 4.85 | 3.98 | 3.06 | 1.85 | 1.81 | 1.97 |
| Treasury: Checking Deposits...... | 24..r | 1.95 | 1.95 | — | — | — | — | — | — | — | — | | |
| **Monetary Survey** | | | | | | *Billions of Ariary: End of Period* | | | | | | | |
| Foreign Assets (Net)............ | 31n | 775.72 | 844.60 | 1,525.58 | 1,846.14 | 2,098.27 | 1,924.64 | 2,307.95 | 2,625.96 | 2,530.09 | 1,779.37 | 2,087.20 | 2,611.55 |
| Domestic Credit................ | 32 | 1,224.33 | 1,295.66 | 1,138.30 | 1,371.32 | 1,507.69 | 1,951.52 | 1,911.70 | 2,368.45 | 2,827.92 | 3,662.43 | 4,305.08 | 5,262.71 |
| Claims on Central Govt. (Net)...... | 32an | 405.77 | 294.13 | −57.58 | −31.13 | −293.69 | 19.76 | −228.82 | 154.57 | 420.74 | 860.75 | 977.75 | 1,447.31 |
| Claims on Nonfin.Pub.Enterprises.. | 32c | 3.86 | 4.46 | 4.55 | 4.70 | 5.02 | 5.59 | 6.79 | 7.75 | 8.64 | 9.04 | 8.28 | 5.87 |
| Claims on Private Sector.......... | 32d | 814.70 | 997.07 | 1,191.33 | 1,397.75 | 1,796.36 | 1,926.17 | 2,133.74 | 2,206.14 | 2,398.53 | 2,792.64 | 3,319.05 | 3,809.54 |
| Money.......................... | 34 | 1,399.43 | 1,414.69 | 1,750.81 | 2,074.83 | 2,262.88 | 2,402.91 | 2,618.79 | 3,246.47 | 3,386.70 | 3,550.90 | 3,909.41 | 4,398.05 |
| Quasi-Money.................... | 35 | 587.79 | 617.17 | 818.25 | 1,031.68 | 1,241.24 | 1,497.80 | 1,661.58 | 1,749.86 | 1,963.86 | 2,026.70 | 2,320.60 | 2,777.49 |
| Bonds.......................... | 36ab | 28.35 | 29.07 | 31.15 | 31.69 | 33.56 | 31.11 | 31.09 | 35.13 | 32.83 | 36.48 | 42.62 | 33.83 |
| Capital Accounts................ | 37a | 120.96 | 166.21 | 208.21 | 418.22 | 433.87 | 495.91 | 570.88 | 618.54 | 659.17 | 671.54 | 730.69 | 792.43 |
| Other Items (Net).............. | 37r | −135.23 | −85.96 | −144.54 | −338.96 | −365.59 | −551.56 | −662.68 | −655.58 | −684.56 | −843.81 | −611.04 | −127.53 |
| Money plus Quasi-Money......... | 35l | 1,987.22 | 2,031.87 | 2,569.06 | 3,106.50 | 3,504.13 | 3,900.70 | 4,280.36 | 4,996.32 | 5,350.56 | 5,577.60 | 6,230.01 | 7,175.54 |
| **Interest Rates** | | | | | | *Percent Per Annum* | | | | | | | |
| Base Rate (End of Period)........ | 60.k | 16.00 | 16.00 | 12.00 | 12.00 | 12.00 | 9.50 | 9.50 | 9.50 | 9.50 | 9.50 | 9.50 | 8.70 |
| Money Market Rate............. | 60b | 16.50 | 16.50 | 14.50 | 11.00 | 11.50 | 9.50 | 9.50 | 9.50 | .... | .... | .... | .... |
| Treasury Bill Rate.............. | 60c | 12.95 | 18.84 | 21.16 | 11.84 | 8.81 | 7.62 | 9.33 | 9.58 | 6.92 | 6.64 | 8.43 | 8.96 |
| Deposit Rate................... | 60l | 15.19 | 18.75 | 22.30 | 16.50 | 11.50 | 11.50 | 10.50 | 10.65 | 10.50 | 10.75 | 12.40 | 15.00 |
| Lending Rate.................. | 60p | 25.50 | 27.00 | 29.50 | 45.00 | 45.00 | 45.00 | 49.00 | 52.50 | 60.00 | 60.00 | 60.00 | 60.00 |
| **Prices and Labor** | | | | | | *Index Numbers (2010=100): Period Averages* | | | | | | | |
| Consumer Prices............... | 64 | 53.1 | 63.0 | 69.7 | 76.9 | 84.0 | 91.5 | 100.0 | 109.5 | 116.4 | 123.2 | 130.7 | 140.4 |
| **Intl. Transactions & Positions** | | | | | | *Billions of Ariary* | | | | | | | |
| Exports........................ | 70 | 1,853.18 | 1,703.63 | 2,112.39 | 2,518.41 | 2,865.56 | 2,146.11 | 2,245.58 | 2,534.44 | 2,713.36 | .... | .... | .... |
| Imports, c.i.f.................. | 71 | 3,139.69 | 3,408.10 | 3,723.95 | 4,528.41 | 6,532.11 | 6,188.99 | 5,305.22 | 5,303.83 | 5,438.55 | .... | .... | .... |

# Madagascar 674

| Balance of Payments | | 2004 | 2005 | 2006 | 2007 | 2008 | 2009 | 2010 | 2011 | 2012 | 2013 | 2014 | 2015 |
|---|---|---|---|---|---|---|---|---|---|---|---|---|---|
| | | | | | | | *Millions of US Dollars* | | | | | | |
| A. Current Account* | 109bx | −541.2 | −766.9 | −663.1 | −951.8 | −1,875.6 | −1,817.8 | −895.7 | −702.2 | −758.7 | −622.1 | .... | .... |
| Goods, credit (exports) | 1a9cx | 449.3 | 830.2 | 965.6 | 1,245.3 | 1,319.4 | 1,060.9 | 1,166.7 | 1,474.4 | 1,518.5 | 1,922.2 | .... | .... |
| Goods, debit (imports) | 1a9dx | 929.3 | 1,451.2 | 1,536.4 | 2,247.1 | 3,215.6 | 2,704.5 | 2,197.0 | 2,472.8 | 2,630.0 | 2,773.4 | .... | .... |
| Balance on goods | 1a9bx | −480.0 | −621.0 | −570.8 | −1,001.8 | −1,896.3 | −1,643.6 | −1,030.3 | −998.3 | −1,111.6 | −851.3 | .... | .... |
| Services, credit (exports) | 1b9cx | 467.1 | 499.3 | 672.9 | 999.3 | 1,296.3 | 859.6 | 1,011.8 | 1,173.0 | 1,314.5 | 1,264.5 | .... | .... |
| Services, debit (imports) | 1b9dx | 636.3 | 656.8 | 786.6 | 1,176.3 | 1,579.5 | 1,214.1 | 1,226.2 | 1,302.3 | 1,245.1 | 1,334.1 | .... | .... |
| Balance on Goods & Services | 1z9bx | −649.3 | −778.6 | −684.5 | −1,178.7 | −2,179.5 | −1,998.0 | −1,244.7 | −1,127.7 | −1,042.2 | −920.8 | .... | .... |
| Primary income: credit | 1c9cx | 15.2 | 23.2 | 29.5 | 51.8 | 62.8 | 33.9 | 62.5 | 85.2 | 34.0 | 18.0 | .... | .... |
| Primary income: debit | 1c9dx | 89.4 | 143.2 | 176.2 | 126.4 | 141.0 | 147.4 | 192.7 | 240.6 | 348.3 | 353.6 | .... | .... |
| Balance on gds, serv. & prim. inc. | 1y9bx | −723.4 | −898.6 | −831.2 | −1,253.4 | −2,257.7 | −2,111.4 | −1,374.9 | −1,283.1 | −1,356.5 | −1,256.5 | .... | .... |
| Secondary income: credit | 1d9ca | 244.6 | 170.7 | 209.6 | 355.4 | 445.8 | 369.1 | 530.5 | 616.8 | 673.5 | 739.2 | .... | .... |
| Secondary income: debit | 1d9da | 62.4 | 38.9 | 41.5 | 53.8 | 63.8 | 75.5 | 51.3 | 35.9 | 75.6 | 104.9 | .... | .... |
| B. Capital Account* | 209ba | 182.0 | 286.4 | 2,587.9 | 274.2 | 247.4 | 75.5 | 74.9 | 183.9 | 119.9 | 133.6 | .... | .... |
| Capital account: credit | 209ca | 182.0 | 286.4 | 2,587.9 | 274.2 | 247.4 | 75.5 | 74.9 | 183.9 | 119.9 | 133.6 | .... | .... |
| Capital account: debit | 209da | .... | — | — | — | — | — | — | — | — | — | .... | .... |
| Balance on current & capital acct. | 129ba | −359.2 | −480.5 | 1,924.8 | −677.5 | −1,628.2 | −1,742.4 | −820.8 | −518.3 | −638.7 | −488.5 | .... | .... |
| C. Financial Account* | 309na | −251.3 | −15.5 | 1,914.4 | −706.1 | −1,255.4 | −1,631.4 | −943.1 | −649.6 | −678.1 | −274.4 | .... | .... |
| Direct investment: assets | 3a9aa | .... | 34.9 | 11.2 | 38.5 | 44.6 | 26.2 | 43.5 | 42.3 | 36.4 | 15.6 | .... | .... |
| Equity & investment fund shares | 3aaaa | .... | 34.9 | 11.2 | 38.5 | 44.6 | 26.2 | 43.5 | 42.3 | 36.4 | 15.6 | .... | .... |
| Debt instruments | 3abaa | .... | .... | .... | .... | .... | .... | .... | .... | .... | .... | .... | .... |
| Direct investment: liabilities | 3a9la | 52.9 | 85.4 | 294.7 | 789.4 | 1,134.5 | 1,293.3 | 809.7 | 738.5 | 810.5 | 566.5 | .... | .... |
| Equity & investment fund shares | 3aala | 52.9 | 52.8 | 69.7 | 71.0 | 78.1 | 72.4 | 65.4 | 40.8 | 40.5 | 32.2 | .... | .... |
| Debt instruments | 3abla | .... | 32.7 | 225.0 | 718.4 | 1,056.4 | 1,221.0 | 744.3 | 697.7 | 770.0 | 534.4 | .... | .... |
| Portfolio investment: assets | 3b9aa | .... | .... | — | .... | −.3 | .... | −1.9 | — | .... | .... | .... | .... |
| Equity & investment fund shares | 3baaa | .... | .... | .... | .... | −.3 | .... | −1.9 | — | .... | .... | .... | .... |
| Debt securities | 3bbaa | .... | .... | .... | .... | .... | .... | .... | .... | .... | .... | .... | .... |
| Portfolio investment: liabilities | 3b9la | .... | .... | .... | .... | — | .... | — | .... | .... | .... | .... | .... |
| Equity & investment fund shares | 3bala | .... | .... | .... | .... | — | .... | — | .... | .... | .... | .... | .... |
| Debt securities | 3bbla | .... | .... | .... | .... | .... | .... | .... | .... | .... | .... | .... | .... |
| Fin. der. & empl.stk.ops.(ESOs): net | 3c9na | .... | .... | .... | .... | .... | .... | .... | .... | .... | .... | .... | .... |
| Fin. der. & ESOs.: assets | 3c9aa | .... | .... | .... | .... | .... | .... | .... | .... | .... | .... | .... | .... |
| Fin. der. & ESOs.: liabilities | 3c9la | .... | .... | .... | .... | .... | .... | .... | .... | .... | .... | .... | .... |
| Other investment: assets | 3d9aa | −295.4 | −36.2 | 108.6 | 157.4 | 58.7 | 192.1 | −218.6 | 7.5 | 19.3 | 249.8 | .... | .... |
| Other equity | 3daaa | .... | .... | .... | .... | .... | .... | .... | .... | .... | .... | .... | .... |
| Debt instruments | 3dzaa | −295.4 | −36.2 | 108.6 | 157.4 | 58.7 | 192.1 | −218.6 | 7.5 | 19.3 | 249.8 | .... | .... |
| Other investment: liabilities | 3d9la | −97.0 | −71.2 | −2,089.3 | 112.5 | 223.9 | 556.4 | −43.5 | −39.0 | −76.7 | −26.7 | .... | .... |
| Other equity | 3dala | .... | .... | .... | .... | .... | .... | .... | .... | .... | .... | .... | .... |
| Debt instruments | 3dzla | −97.0 | −71.2 | −2,089.3 | 112.5 | 223.9 | 556.4 | −43.5 | −39.0 | −76.7 | −26.7 | .... | .... |
| Curr.+ cap.− finan. acct. balance | 4y9na | −107.9 | −465.0 | 10.4 | 28.5 | −372.8 | −110.9 | 122.4 | 131.3 | 39.4 | −214.1 | .... | .... |
| D. Net Errors and Omissions | 409na | −34.9 | 86.9 | −107.0 | −106.2 | −16.9 | −21.5 | −163.4 | −102.3 | −199.9 | −182.7 | .... | .... |
| E. Reserves and Related Items | 4z9na | −142.9 | −378.1 | −96.6 | −77.7 | −389.7 | −132.4 | −41.1 | 29.0 | −160.5 | −396.8 | .... | .... |
| Reserve assets | 3e9aa | 384.1 | 9.5 | 79.5 | 239.0 | 166.7 | −18.5 | 56.3 | 123.6 | −90.8 | −272.9 | .... | .... |
| Credit and loans from the IMF | 3dcla | 43.8 | 5.3 | −187.0 | 11.7 | 58.7 | 1.4 | −1.7 | −3.6 | −7.1 | −10.6 | .... | .... |
| Exceptional financing | 409la | 483.2 | 382.4 | 363.0 | 305.0 | 497.7 | 112.5 | 99.1 | 98.2 | 76.7 | 134.6 | .... | .... |

*Excludes components in group E

# Madagascar   674

| | | 2004 | 2005 | 2006 | 2007 | 2008 | 2009 | 2010 | 2011 | 2012 | 2013 | 2014 | 2015 |
|---|---|---|---|---|---|---|---|---|---|---|---|---|---|
| **Government Finance** | | | | | | | | | | | | | |
| **Operations Statement** | | | | | | | | | | | | | |
| **Central Government** | | | | | *Billions of Ariary: Fiscal Year Ends December 31* | | | | | | | | |
| Revenue.................................. | a1 | 1,656.8 | 1,685.1 | 2,537.7 | 2,229.4 | 3,257.7 | 1,842.2 | 2,404.0 | 2,449.3 | .... | .... | .... | .... |
| Taxes..................................... | a11 | 887.1 | 1,019.9 | 1,260.8 | 1,573.1 | 2,087.2 | 1,569.8 | 1,780.7 | 2,022.7 | .... | .... | .... | .... |
| Social Contributions..................... | a12 | — | — | — | — | 137.1 | — | — | — | .... | .... | .... | .... |
| Grants.................................... | a13 | 671.1 | 579.5 | 1,160.6 | 593.3 | 980.4 | 192.3 | 354.9 | 390.3 | .... | .... | .... | .... |
| Other Revenue............................ | a14 | 98.5 | 85.7 | 116.3 | 63.0 | 53.0 | 80.2 | 268.3 | 36.3 | .... | .... | .... | .... |
| Expense................................... | a2 | 1,027.6 | 1,114.7 | 1,370.4 | 1,546.1 | 1,890.9 | 1,539.4 | 1,646.6 | 1,943.6 | .... | .... | .... | .... |
| Compensation of Employees.......... | a21 | 400.0 | 456.4 | 589.9 | 711.2 | 758.9 | 803.2 | 944.9 | 1,060.4 | .... | .... | .... | .... |
| Use of Goods & Services............... | a22 | 147.1 | 295.6 | 190.4 | 215.6 | 276.7 | 198.5 | 198.4 | 214.9 | .... | .... | .... | .... |
| Consumption of Fixed Capital........ | a23 | .... | .... | .... | .... | .... | — | — | — | .... | .... | .... | .... |
| Interest.................................... | a24 | 239.5 | 266.6 | 284.8 | 155.7 | 127.3 | 128.5 | 147.9 | 143.2 | .... | .... | .... | .... |
| Subsidies.................................. | a25 | 110.3 | — | 190.6 | 216.8 | 468.7 | — | — | — | .... | .... | .... | .... |
| Grants..................................... | a26 | — | — | — | — | — | 49.1 | 42.9 | 57.4 | .... | .... | .... | .... |
| Social Benefits............................ | a27 | — | — | — | — | — | — | — | — | .... | .... | .... | .... |
| Other Expense............................ | a28 | 130.7 | 96.1 | 114.6 | 246.8 | 259.3 | 360.1 | 312.5 | 467.7 | .... | .... | .... | .... |
| Gross Operating Balance [1-2+23]... | agob | 629.2 | 570.4 | 1,167.3 | 683.3 | 1,366.8 | 302.8 | 757.4 | 505.8 | .... | .... | .... | .... |
| Net Operating Balance [1-2]............ | anob | .... | .... | .... | .... | .... | .... | .... | .... | .... | .... | .... | .... |
| Net Acq. of Nonfinancial Assets....... | a31 | 996.6 | 1,039.5 | 1,213.9 | 1,049.9 | 1,676.8 | 727.8 | 914.5 | 841.8 | 595.2 | 730.4 | 999.0 | .... |
| Aquisition of Nonfin. Assets........... | a31.1 | .... | .... | .... | .... | .... | .... | .... | .... | .... | .... | .... | .... |
| Disposal of Nonfin. Assets............. | a31.2 | .... | .... | .... | .... | .... | .... | .... | .... | .... | .... | .... | .... |
| Net Lending/Borrowing [1-2-31]...... | anlb | −367.4 | −469.1 | −46.6 | −366.6 | −310.0 | −425.0 | −157.1 | −336.1 | .... | .... | .... | .... |
| Net Acq. of Financial Assets............ | a32 | 92.5 | 53.7 | 403.3 | 40.2 | 260.2 | −140.5 | 324.2 | −55.3 | 61.4 | −337.3 | 315.5 | .... |
| By instrument | | | | | | | | | | | | | |
| Monetary Gold & SDRs................. | a3201 | — | — | — | — | — | — | — | — | — | — | — | .... |
| Currency & Deposits..................... | a3202 | 26.3 | 53.7 | 403.3 | 40.2 | 260.2 | −141.5 | 323.1 | −56.9 | 22.1 | −367.0 | 278.0 | .... |
| Securities other than Shares........... | a3203 | — | — | — | — | — | — | — | — | — | — | — | .... |
| Loans...................................... | a3204 | 63.2 | — | — | — | — | — | — | — | — | — | — | .... |
| Shares & Other Equity................... | a3205 | — | — | — | — | — | 1.1 | 1.0 | 1.6 | 32.5 | 29.7 | 30.7 | .... |
| Insurance Technical Reserves......... | a3206 | — | — | — | — | — | — | — | — | — | — | — | .... |
| Financial Derivatives..................... | a3207 | — | — | — | — | — | — | — | — | 6.8 | — | 6.8 | .... |
| Other Accounts Receivable............. | a3208 | 3.0 | — | — | — | — | — | — | — | — | — | — | .... |
| By debtor | | | | | | | | | | | | | |
| Domestic................................... | a321 | 92.5 | 53.7 | 403.3 | 40.2 | 260.2 | −140.5 | 263.8 | −141.9 | −7.9 | −400.7 | 182.7 | .... |
| Foreign..................................... | a322 | — | — | — | — | — | — | 60.4 | 86.6 | 69.3 | 63.4 | 132.8 | .... |
| Net Incurrence of Liabilities............. | a33 | 459.9 | 522.8 | 450.0 | 406.9 | 570.2 | 284.5 | 484.4 | 280.8 | 296.6 | 50.4 | 855.2 | .... |
| By instrument | | | | | | | | | | | | | |
| Special Drawing Rights (SDRs)....... | a3301 | — | — | — | — | — | — | — | — | .... | .... | — | .... |
| Currency & Deposits..................... | a3302 | 17.3 | 41.0 | 358.7 | 95.8 | 331.8 | 32.3 | 228.2 | −108.4 | 38.7 | −268.1 | 183.2 | .... |
| Securities other than Shares........... | a3303 | 107.9 | 120.0 | 300.8 | 74.2 | — | 85.1 | 99.3 | 119.6 | 117.8 | 18.5 | −98.9 | .... |
| Loans...................................... | a3304 | 334.6 | 361.8 | −209.5 | 236.9 | 238.4 | 166.0 | 194.4 | 255.9 | 160.1 | 339.7 | 820.3 | .... |
| Shares & Other Equity................... | a3305 | — | — | — | — | — | — | — | — | — | — | — | .... |
| Insurance Technical Reserves......... | a3306 | — | — | — | — | — | — | — | — | — | — | — | .... |
| Financial Derivatives..................... | a3307 | — | — | — | — | — | — | — | — | — | — | — | .... |
| Other Accounts Payable................. | a3308 | — | — | — | — | — | 1.1 | −37.6 | 13.7 | −20.0 | −39.7 | −49.3 | .... |
| By creditor | | | | | | | | | | | | | |
| Domestic................................... | a331 | −58.3 | 134.6 | 84.1 | 99.6 | 91.9 | 161.4 | 291.5 | 98.3 | 128.9 | −246.7 | 412.5 | .... |
| Foreign..................................... | a332 | 518.2 | 388.3 | 365.8 | 307.3 | 478.3 | 123.1 | 192.8 | 182.5 | 167.7 | 297.1 | 442.7 | .... |
| Stat. Discrepancy [32-33-NLB]........ | anlbz | — | — | — | — | — | — | — | — | 6.8 | — | 6.8 | .... |
| Memo Item: Expenditure [2+31]...... | a2m | 2,024.1 | 2,154.2 | 2,584.3 | 2,596.0 | 3,567.7 | 2,267.2 | 2,564.2 | 2,785.4 | 2,753.2 | 3,164.0 | 3,756.5 | .... |
| **National Accounts** | | | | | *Billions of Ariary* | | | | | | | | |
| Househ.Cons.Expend.,incl.NPISHs.... | 96f | 6,965.5 | 8,698.4 | 9,688.0 | 11,030.0 | 11,885.8 | 13,707.5 | 15,706.2 | 16,882.4 | 17,882.4 | 19,324.9 | 20,188.1 | 21,603.9 |
| Government Consumption Expend... | 91f | 745.1 | 904.0 | 1,033.6 | 1,691.2 | 1,626.6 | 1,668.7 | 1,699.8 | 1,998.7 | 2,178.8 | 2,381.2 | 2,676.1 | 3,303.0 |
| Gross Fixed Capital Formation.......... | 93e | 1,906.6 | 2,240.3 | 2,988.6 | 4,030.0 | 6,483.0 | 5,309.0 | 3,435.9 | 3,501.4 | 3,823.6 | 3,720.0 | 4,020.7 | 4,750.6 |
| Exports of Goods and Services.......... | 90c | 2,855.4 | 2,847.7 | 3,512.9 | 4,172.5 | 4,268.1 | 3,741.0 | 4,556.6 | 5,357.6 | 6,316.5 | 7,031.1 | 8,446.3 | 9,650.2 |
| Imports of Goods and Services (-)..... | 98c | 4,317.2 | 4,598.0 | 5,408.3 | 7,164.0 | 8,182.6 | 7,696.8 | 7,153.4 | 7,598.6 | 8,427.8 | 9,060.3 | 9,556.6 | 10,689.4 |
| Gross Domestic Product (GDP)........ | 99b | 8,155.6 | 10,092.4 | 11,815.3 | 13,759.7 | 16,080.9 | 16,729.4 | 18,245.1 | 20,033.9 | 21,773.6 | 23,397.0 | 25,774.5 | 28,563.8 |
| GDP Volume 1984 Prices.............. | 99b.p | 498.8 | 521.7 | 547.9 | 582.1 | 623.7 | 597.9 | 600.2 | 608.9 | 627.3 | 641.5 | 662.8 | 682.9 |
| GDP Volume (2010=100).............. | 99bvp | 83.1 | 86.9 | 91.3 | 97.0 | 103.9 | 99.6 | 100.0 | 101.4 | 104.5 | 106.9 | 110.4 | 113.8 |
| GDP Deflator (2010=100).............. | 99bip | 53.8 | 63.6 | 70.9 | 77.8 | 84.8 | 92.0 | 100.0 | 108.2 | 114.2 | 120.0 | 127.9 | 137.6 |
| | | | | | *Millions: Midyear Estimates* | | | | | | | | |
| **Population**............................... | 99z | 17.76 | 18.29 | 18.83 | 19.37 | 19.93 | 20.50 | 21.08 | 21.68 | 22.29 | 22.92 | 23.57 | 24.24 |

| | | 2004 | 2005 | 2006 | 2007 | 2008 | 2009 | 2010 | 2011 | 2012 | 2013 | 2014 | 2015 |
|---|---|---|---|---|---|---|---|---|---|---|---|---|---|
| **Exchange Rates** | | | | | | *Kwacha per SDR: End of Period* | | | | | | | |
| Official Rate..................................... | aa | 169.19 | 176.92 | 209.63 | 221.73 | 216.56 | 228.88 | 232.24 | 251.40 | 515.06 | 669.83 | 682.07 | .... |
| | | | | | | *Kwacha per US Dollar: End of Period (ae) Period Average (rf)* | | | | | | | |
| Official Rate..................................... | ae | 108.94 | 123.78 | 139.34 | 140.32 | 140.60 | 146.00 | 150.80 | 163.75 | 335.13 | 434.96 | 470.78 | .... |
| Official Rate..................................... | rf | 108.90 | 118.42 | 136.01 | 139.96 | 140.52 | 141.17 | 150.49 | 156.52 | 249.11 | 364.41 | 424.90 | .... |
| | | | | | | *Index Numbers (2010=100): Period Averages* | | | | | | | |
| Official Rate..................................... | ahx | 138.2 | 127.4 | 110.8 | 107.5 | 107.1 | 106.6 | 100.0 | 96.3 | 65.0 | 41.6 | 35.6 | .... |
| Nominal Effective Exchange Rate..... | nec | 136.5 | 123.5 | 108.8 | 103.3 | 105.4 | 110.3 | 100.0 | 94.3 | 67.7 | 45.4 | 41.3 | 40.4 |
| CPI-Based Real Effect. Ex. Rate........ | rec | 98.4 | 99.7 | 96.3 | 94.1 | 97.1 | 106.3 | 100.0 | 96.7 | 79.0 | 66.8 | 72.6 | 83.2 |
| **Fund Position** | | | | | | *Millions of SDRs: End of Period* | | | | | | | |
| Quota.............................................. | 2f.s | 69.40 | 69.40 | 69.40 | 69.40 | 69.40 | 69.40 | 69.40 | 69.40 | 69.40 | 69.40 | 69.40 | 69.40 |
| SDR Holdings................................... | 1b.s | .77 | .74 | .45 | .02 | .05 | 1.23 | 1.05 | .28 | .58 | 5.66 | 6.55 | 3.66 |
| Reserve Position in the Fund............ | 1c.s | 2.29 | 2.29 | 2.31 | 2.31 | 2.33 | 2.42 | 2.42 | 2.42 | 2.44 | 2.44 | 2.44 | 2.44 |
| Total Fund Cred.&Loans Outstg........ | 2tl | 59.55 | 52.60 | 12.94 | 19.62 | 80.95 | 80.95 | 94.83 | 94.34 | 117.74 | 125.38 | 121.73 | 117.40 |
| SDR Allocations................................ | 1bd | 10.98 | 10.98 | 10.98 | 10.98 | 10.98 | 66.37 | 66.37 | 66.37 | 66.37 | 66.37 | 66.37 | 66.37 |
| **International Liquidity** | | | | | | *Millions of US Dollars Unless Otherwise Indicated: End of Period* | | | | | | | |
| Total Reserves minus Gold............... | 1l.d | 128.05 | 158.65 | 133.77 | 216.61 | 242.78 | 149.36 | 307.36 | 197.43 | 223.18 | 413.10 | 602.39 | .... |
| SDR Holdings................................ | 1b.d | 1.20 | 1.05 | .68 | .03 | .08 | 1.93 | 1.62 | .43 | .89 | 8.72 | 9.48 | 5.08 |
| Reserve Position in the Fund.......... | 1c.d | 3.56 | 3.27 | 3.48 | 3.66 | 3.59 | 3.80 | 3.73 | 3.72 | 3.75 | 3.76 | 3.54 | 3.38 |
| Foreign Exchange.......................... | 1d.d | 123.30 | 154.32 | 129.61 | 212.92 | 239.10 | 143.63 | 302.01 | 193.29 | 218.54 | 400.63 | 589.37 | .... |
| Gold (Million Fine Troy Ounces)........ | 1ad | .013 | .013 | .013 | .013 | .013 | .013 | .013 | .013 | .013 | .013 | .013 | .... |
| Gold (National Valuation)................. | 1and | .54 | .54 | .54 | .54 | .54 | † 14.03 | 15.68 | 15.68 | 22.85 | 22.78 | 22.78 | .... |
| Monetary Authorities: Other Liabs.... | 4..d | .02 | .09 | .07 | 2.49 | .17 | .32 | .21 | .55 | 11.42 | 58.31 | 4.88 | .... |
| Deposit Money Banks: Assets........... | 7a.d | 52.61 | 38.89 | 59.13 | 39.95 | 52.87 | 77.87 | 96.09 | 106.68 | 199.54 | 242.27 | 238.14 | .... |
| Deposit Money Banks: Liabs............. | 7b.d | 15.60 | 14.80 | 18.90 | 41.66 | 29.65 | 27.17 | 10.58 | 36.88 | 46.28 | 29.80 | 34.79 | .... |
| Other Banking Institutions: Assets.... | 7e.d | 14.67 | 11.68 | 15.51 | 15.04 | .... | .... | .... | .... | .... | .... | .... | .... |
| Other Banking Insts.: Liabs.............. | 7f.d | 8.43 | .08 | .07 | .09 | .... | .... | .... | .... | .... | .... | .... | .... |
| **Monetary Authorities** | | | | | | *Millions of Kwacha: End of Period* | | | | | | | |
| Foreign Assets................................. | 11 | 13,824.5 | 19,576.3 | 18,520.7 | 35,215.6 | 36,151.9 | 24,014.8 | 45,522.6 | 32,792.6 | 79,566.0 | 175,689.2 | 275,786.7 | .... |
| Claims on Central Government.......... | 12a | 18,990.0 | 22,879.9 | 14,219.7 | 22,300.0 | 85,459.9 | 109,139.1 | 102,234.8 | 142,697.8 | 138,631.3 | 185,781.1 | 107,995.7 | .... |
| Claims on Nonfin.Pub.Enterprises..... | 12c | — | — | — | 1,266.3 | 1,972.8 | 978.1 | 699.0 | — | — | — | — | .... |
| Claims on Deposit Money Banks...... | 12e | — | .2 | 20.0 | 107.0 | — | 1.1 | 10.7 | — | — | — | — | .... |
| Claims on Other Banking Insts......... | 12f | 1.7 | 1.9 | 1.9 | 1.5 | 1.2 | 1.2 | 1.2 | 1.2 | 9.8 | 1.2 | 64.5 | .... |
| Reserve Money................................. | 14 | 17,967.5 | 20,610.6 | 21,522.3 | 27,057.7 | 36,047.4 | 50,393.0 | 57,417.4 | 73,219.8 | 113,198.7 | 156,899.4 | 212,252.4 | .... |
| of which: Currency Outside DMBs.. | 14a | 10,992.8 | 11,947.0 | 15,470.9 | 20,587.5 | 25,261.3 | 27,493.1 | 30,663.0 | 42,251.0 | 55,377.5 | 76,000.1 | 98,110.3 | .... |
| Liabs. of Central Bank: Securities..... | 16ac | 4,555.9 | 5,044.3 | 2,914.4 | 4,309.6 | 4,066.3 | | | | | | | .... |
| Restricted Deposits.......................... | 16b | — | — | — | — | — | | | | | | | .... |
| Foreign Liabilities............................ | 16c | 11,933.6 | 11,259.1 | 5,021.7 | 7,132.3 | 19,931.3 | 33,763.9 | 37,466.9 | 40,491.4 | 98,654.8 | 153,800.3 | 130,596.4 | .... |
| Central Government Deposits........... | 16d | 6,944.4 | 11,422.7 | 7,696.9 | 24,053.2 | 29,691.2 | 24,330.3 | 30,656.9 | 40,705.9 | 29,127.2 | 90,583.4 | 91,122.1 | .... |
| Capital Accounts.............................. | 17a | 570.9 | 795.8 | 374.2 | 306.0 | 19,772.7 | 20,550.0 | 20,550.0 | 22,468.4 | 22,590.7 | 23,665.8 | 31,547.2 | .... |
| Other Items (Net)............................. | 17r | −9,156.0 | −6,674.2 | −4,767.1 | −3,968.4 | 14,076.7 | 5,097.0 | 2,377.0 | −1,393.9 | −45,364.3 | −63,477.4 | −81,671.2 | .... |
| **Deposit Money Banks** | | | | | | *Millions of Kwacha: End of Period* | | | | | | | |
| Reserves.......................................... | 20 | 7,033.9 | 7,860.9 | 4,811.0 | 5,320.8 | 10,421.0 | 20,620.4 | 24,009.9 | 37,280.8 | 42,000.5 | 77,081.8 | 108,998.2 | .... |
| Claims on Mon.Author.:Securities..... | 20c | 210.0 | 210.0 | 320.0 | 500.0 | 3,611.7 | | | 3,500.0 | | | | .... |
| Foreign Assets................................. | 21 | 5,731.3 | 4,813.8 | 8,239.7 | 5,605.6 | 7,433.8 | 11,368.2 | 14,490.4 | 17,469.8 | 66,872.1 | 105,376.1 | 112,111.0 | .... |
| Claims on Central Government........ | 22a | 10,711.0 | 12,363.5 | 12,117.6 | 21,585.6 | 29,858.3 | 29,036.6 | 30,092.6 | 44,410.4 | 36,970.9 | 65,537.0 | 88,771.4 | .... |
| Claims on Nonfin.Pub.Enterprises.... | 22c | 299.5 | 307.2 | 1,210.4 | 2,470.2 | 4,070.6 | 5,261.3 | 3,963.3 | 20,024.0 | 19,357.4 | 17,839.8 | 3,871.0 | .... |
| Claims on Private Sector.................. | 22d | 13,926.3 | 17,502.1 | 27,746.6 | 33,988.0 | 68,143.5 | 95,043.6 | 144,842.5 | 174,538.0 | 218,866.4 | 250,445.7 | 293,038.2 | .... |
| Demand Deposits............................. | 24 | 14,730.2 | 19,356.1 | 20,217.8 | 30,142.3 | 45,335.5 | 54,407.1 | 76,206.7 | 99,683.5 | 97,976.0 | 121,772.6 | 169,261.3 | .... |
| Time, Savings,& Fgn.Currency Dep... | 25 | 20,725.3 | 22,691.4 | 27,170.4 | 35,130.4 | 69,046.6 | 92,132.0 | 124,841.0 | 172,396.2 | 233,082.1 | 324,189.8 | 348,781.7 | .... |
| Foreign Liabilities............................ | 26c | 1,699.2 | 1,832.2 | 2,633.1 | 5,845.6 | 4,168.3 | 3,966.8 | 1,595.0 | 6,039.6 | 15,508.0 | 12,961.0 | 16,376.2 | .... |
| Central Government Deposits........... | 26d | 434.5 | 422.2 | 519.3 | 668.7 | 2,708.1 | 1,328.3 | 7,574.5 | 6,645.9 | 6,802.2 | 7,477.5 | 13,459.3 | .... |
| Credit from Monetary Authorities..... | 26g | | | | | | | | | 84.3 | | | .... |
| Capital Accounts.............................. | 27a | 7,317.1 | 8,722.7 | 11,760.2 | 13,866.6 | 25,232.4 | 32,757.4 | 45,158.9 | 54,911.6 | 69,719.7 | 100,512.1 | 142,762.5 | .... |
| Other Items (Net)............................. | 27r | −6,994.4 | −9,967.3 | −7,855.6 | −16,183.4 | −22,952.0 | −23,261.6 | −37,977.4 | −42,453.7 | −39,105.1 | −50,632.7 | −83,851.1 | .... |
| **Monetary Survey** | | | | | | *Millions of Kwacha: End of Period* | | | | | | | |
| Foreign Assets (Net)......................... | 31n | 5,923.0 | 11,298.8 | 19,105.5 | 27,843.4 | 19,486.0 | −2,347.8 | 20,951.2 | 3,731.5 | 32,275.3 | 114,304.0 | 240,925.1 | .... |
| Domestic Credit............................... | 32 | 36,549.6 | 41,209.6 | 47,079.9 | 56,889.7 | 157,106.8 | 213,801.2 | 243,601.9 | 334,319.7 | 377,906.6 | 421,543.8 | 389,159.5 | .... |
| Claims on Central Govt. (Net)........ | 32an | 22,322.1 | 23,398.5 | 18,121.0 | 19,163.7 | 82,918.8 | 112,517.0 | 94,095.9 | 139,756.5 | 139,672.9 | 153,257.2 | 92,185.8 | .... |
| Claims on Nonfin.Pub.Enterprises.. | 32c | 299.5 | 307.2 | 1,210.4 | 3,736.5 | 6,043.4 | 6,239.3 | 4,662.4 | 20,024.0 | 19,357.4 | 17,839.8 | 3,871.0 | .... |
| Claims on Private Sector................ | 32d | 13,926.3 | 17,502.1 | 27,746.6 | 33,988.0 | 68,143.5 | 95,043.6 | 144,842.5 | 174,538.0 | 218,866.4 | 250,445.7 | 293,038.2 | .... |
| Claims on Other Banking Insts....... | 32f | 1.7 | 1.9 | 1.9 | 1.5 | 1.2 | 1.2 | 1.2 | 1.2 | 9.8 | 1.2 | 64.5 | .... |
| Money............................................. | 34 | 25,723.0 | 31,303.1 | 35,688.7 | 50,729.8 | 70,596.7 | 81,900.3 | 106,869.7 | 141,934.5 | 153,353.5 | 197,772.7 | 267,371.5 | .... |
| Quasi-Money.................................... | 35 | 20,725.3 | 22,691.4 | 27,170.4 | 35,130.4 | 69,046.6 | 92,132.0 | 124,841.0 | 172,396.2 | 233,082.1 | 324,189.8 | 348,781.7 | .... |
| Liabs. of Central Bank:Securities..... | 36ac | 4,345.9 | 4,834.3 | 2,594.4 | 3,809.6 | 454.6 | — | — | −3,500.0 | — | — | — | .... |
| Restricted Deposits.......................... | 36b | — | — | — | — | — | | | | | | | .... |
| Capital Accounts.............................. | 37a | 7,888.0 | 9,518.5 | 12,134.4 | 14,172.6 | 45,005.1 | 53,307.4 | 65,708.9 | 77,380.0 | 92,310.5 | 124,177.8 | 174,309.7 | .... |
| Other Items (Net)............................. | 37r | −16,209.7 | −15,838.9 | −11,402.4 | −19,109.4 | −8,510.2 | −15,886.2 | −32,866.5 | −50,159.5 | −68,564.2 | −110,292.6 | −160,378.3 | .... |
| Money plus Quasi-Money................. | 35l | 46,448.3 | 53,994.5 | 62,859.1 | 85,860.3 | 139,643.3 | 174,032.2 | 231,710.7 | 314,330.7 | 386,435.6 | 521,962.5 | 616,153.2 | .... |

# Malawi   676

| | | 2004 | 2005 | 2006 | 2007 | 2008 | 2009 | 2010 | 2011 | 2012 | 2013 | 2014 | 2015 |
|---|---|---|---|---|---|---|---|---|---|---|---|---|---|
| **Other Banking Institutions** | | *Millions of Kwacha: End of Period* | | | | | | | | | | | |
| Reserves | 40 | 939.7 | 1,391.9 | 2,545.7 | 3,207.7 | .... | .... | .... | .... | .... | .... | .... | .... |
| Claims on Mon.Author.:Securities | 40c | 386.3 | 651.5 | 95.8 | — | .... | .... | .... | .... | .... | .... | .... | .... |
| Foreign Assets | 41 | 1,598.3 | 1,446.0 | 2,161.9 | 2,110.6 | .... | .... | .... | .... | .... | .... | .... | .... |
| Claims on Central Government | 42a | 5,964.7 | 4,742.8 | 2,812.0 | 4,836.0 | .... | .... | .... | .... | .... | .... | .... | .... |
| Claims on Nonfin.Pub.Enterprises | 42c | 5.7 | — | 355.3 | .2 | .... | .... | .... | .... | .... | .... | .... | .... |
| Claims on Private Sector | 42d | 3,346.1 | 8,312.4 | 9,696.6 | 18,649.9 | .... | .... | .... | .... | .... | .... | .... | .... |
| Claims on Deposit Money Banks | 42e | 817.8 | 703.4 | 1,571.4 | 2,793.2 | .... | .... | .... | .... | .... | .... | .... | .... |
| Demand Deposits | 44 | 1,336.7 | 2,198.5 | 2,484.6 | 5,213.2 | .... | .... | .... | .... | .... | .... | .... | .... |
| Time, Savings,& Fgn.Currency Dep | 45 | 9,400.8 | 13,303.4 | 16,148.1 | 22,408.4 | .... | .... | .... | .... | .... | .... | .... | .... |
| Foreign Liabilities | 46c | 918.0 | 10.3 | 9.4 | 13.2 | .... | .... | .... | .... | .... | .... | .... | .... |
| Credit from Monetary Authorities | 46g | — | — | — | — | .... | .... | .... | .... | .... | .... | .... | .... |
| Credit from Deposit Money Banks | 46h | 174.5 | 512.4 | 111.0 | 508.4 | .... | .... | .... | .... | .... | .... | .... | .... |
| Capital Accounts | 47a | 2,127.8 | 2,414.3 | 2,740.6 | 3,484.7 | .... | .... | .... | .... | .... | .... | .... | .... |
| Other Items (Net) | 47r | −899.2 | −1,191.1 | −2,255.1 | −30.3 | .... | .... | .... | .... | .... | .... | .... | .... |
| **Banking Survey** | | *Millions of Kwacha: End of Period* | | | | | | | | | | | |
| Foreign Assets (Net) | 51n | 6,603.2 | 12,734.5 | 21,258.0 | 29,940.8 | .... | .... | .... | .... | .... | .... | .... | .... |
| Domestic Credit | 52 | 45,864.4 | 54,262.9 | 59,941.9 | 80,374.2 | .... | .... | .... | .... | .... | .... | .... | .... |
| Claims on Central Govt. (Net) | 52an | 28,286.8 | 28,141.2 | 20,933.0 | 23,999.6 | .... | .... | .... | .... | .... | .... | .... | .... |
| Claims on Nonfin.Pub.Enterprises | 52c | 305.2 | 307.2 | 1,565.7 | 3,736.7 | .... | .... | .... | .... | .... | .... | .... | .... |
| Claims on Private Sector | 52d | 17,272.4 | 25,814.5 | 37,443.2 | 52,637.9 | .... | .... | .... | .... | .... | .... | .... | .... |
| Liquid Liabilities | 55l | 56,246.1 | 68,104.6 | 78,946.0 | 110,274.2 | .... | .... | .... | .... | .... | .... | .... | .... |
| Liabs. of Central Bank:Securities | 56ac | 3,959.5 | 4,182.8 | 2,498.6 | 3,809.6 | .... | .... | .... | .... | .... | .... | .... | .... |
| Restricted Deposits | 56b | — | — | — | — | — | — | — | — | — | — | — | — |
| Capital Accounts | 57a | 10,015.8 | 11,932.8 | 14,875.0 | 17,657.3 | .... | .... | .... | .... | .... | .... | .... | .... |
| Other Items (Net) | 57r | −17,753.8 | −17,222.9 | −15,119.7 | −21,426.0 | .... | .... | .... | .... | .... | .... | .... | .... |
| **Nonbank Financial Institutions** | | *Millions of Kwacha: End of Period* | | | | | | | | | | | |
| Claims on Central Government | 42a.s | 826.83 | 3,490.87 | 3,472.32 | 5,800.03 | .... | .... | .... | .... | .... | .... | .... | .... |
| Claims on Private Sector | 42d.s | 2,301.06 | 6,206.46 | 15,544.06 | 29,992.14 | .... | .... | .... | .... | .... | .... | .... | .... |
| of which: Policy Loans | 42dxs | 61.77 | 107.95 | 184.13 | 255.69 | .... | .... | .... | .... | .... | .... | .... | .... |
| Incr.in Total Assets(Within Per.) | 49z.s | 8,589.81 | 8,938.56 | 11,641.30 | 18,265.41 | .... | .... | .... | .... | .... | .... | .... | .... |
| **Money (National Definitions)** | | *Millions of Kwacha: End of Period* | | | | | | | | | | | |
| Reserve Money | 19mb | 17,967.5 | 20,610.6 | 21,522.3 | 27,057.1 | 36,047.4 | 50,393.0 | 57,417.4 | 73,219.8 | 113,198.7 | 156,899.4 | 212,252.4 | .... |
| M1 | 59ma | 25,443.5 | 30,204.0 | 35,007.7 | 49,089.0 | 70,596.7 | 81,900.3 | 125,193.3 | 163,962.2 | 222,365.1 | 201,052.6 | 271,525.2 | .... |
| M2 | 59mb | 45,666.0 | 52,208.0 | 61,316.9 | 83,456.8 | 139,643.3 | 174,032.2 | 231,710.7 | 314,330.7 | 386,435.6 | 521,962.5 | 616,153.2 | .... |
| **Interest Rates** | | *Percent Per Annum* | | | | | | | | | | | |
| Discount Rate (End of Period) | 60.a | 25.00 | 25.00 | 20.00 | 15.00 | 15.00 | 15.00 | 13.00 | 13.00 | 25.00 | 25.00 | 25.00 | 27.00 |
| Treasury Bill Rate | 60c | 28.58 | 24.40 | 19.27 | 13.95 | 11.29 | 10.15 | 7.16 | 6.56 | 14.33 | 29.56 | 20.66 | 23.90 |
| Deposit Rate | 60l | 13.73 | 10.92 | 11.00 | 5.97 | 3.50 | 3.50 | 3.60 | 4.11 | 11.08 | 18.41 | 13.17 | 11.59 |
| Lending Rate | 60p | 36.83 | 33.08 | 32.25 | 27.72 | 25.28 | 25.25 | 24.63 | 23.75 | 32.33 | 46.01 | 44.29 | 44.39 |
| **Prices, Production, Labor** | | *Index Numbers (2010=100): Period Averages* | | | | | | | | | | | |
| Consumer Prices | 64 | 55.6 | 64.2 | 73.2 | 79.0 | 85.9 | 93.1 | 100.0 | 107.6 | † 130.5 | 166.1 | 205.6 | 250.6 |
| Industrial Production (2005=100) | 66 | 102.9 | 100.0 | 102.9 | 116.0 | .... | .... | .... | .... | .... | .... | .... | .... |
| **Intl. Transactions & Positions** | | *Millions of Kwacha* | | | | | | | | | | | |
| Exports | 70 | 52,621 | 60,251 | 73,800 | 99,259 | 120,850 | 152,460 | 170,050 | 220,446 | 292,716 | 435,222 | .... | .... |
| Imports, c.i.f | 71 | 101,549 | 137,982 | 164,463 | 193,141 | .... | .... | 325,579 | 380,171 | 594,760 | 1,029,795 | .... | .... |

# Malawi 676

| Balance of Payments | | 2004 | 2005 | 2006 | 2007 | 2008 | 2009 | 2010 | 2011 | 2012 | 2013 | 2014 | 2015 |
|---|---|---|---|---|---|---|---|---|---|---|---|---|---|
| | | | | | | | *Millions of US Dollars* | | | | | | |
| A. Current Account* | 109bx | −379.0 | −506.7 | −306.6 | −418.0 | −664.1 | −481.6 | −969.3 | −1,136.7 | −744.7 | −1,263.9 | −1,077.8 | .... |
| Goods, credit (exports) | 1a9cx | 517.5 | 541.4 | 721.0 | 803.2 | 950.1 | 1,268.4 | 1,142.5 | 1,518.0 | 1,276.6 | 1,295.2 | 1,527.8 | .... |
| Goods, debit (imports) | 1a9dx | 906.3 | 1,150.0 | 1,160.7 | 1,385.3 | 1,818.6 | 2,008.4 | 2,402.6 | 2,632.5 | 2,327.1 | 2,751.0 | 2,743.9 | .... |
| Balance on goods | 1a9bx | −388.8 | −608.6 | −439.6 | −582.1 | −868.5 | −740.0 | −1,260.1 | −1,114.5 | −1,050.5 | −1,455.8 | −1,216.1 | .... |
| Services, credit (exports) | 1b9cx | 54.8 | 67.3 | 64.5 | 74.0 | 74.4 | 79.1 | 80.1 | 86.3 | 105.3 | 111.0 | 100.4 | .... |
| Services, debit (imports) | 1b9dx | 149.6 | 159.4 | 159.3 | 152.6 | 159.1 | 167.1 | 239.9 | 249.8 | 227.4 | 245.3 | 268.8 | .... |
| Balance on Goods & Services | 1z9bx | −483.7 | −700.6 | −534.4 | −660.7 | −953.2 | −828.0 | −1,419.9 | −1,278.0 | −1,172.7 | −1,590.0 | −1,384.4 | .... |
| Primary income: credit | 1c9cx | 1.5 | .6 | 7.2 | 1.6 | 1.7 | .4 | 1.8 | 1.8 | 2.9 | 2.2 | 3.4 | .... |
| Primary income: debit | 1c9dx | 102.4 | 80.6 | 80.3 | 80.7 | 149.8 | 122.5 | 192.3 | 379.3 | 44.7 | 268.5 | 302.8 | .... |
| Balance on gds, serv. & prim. inc. | 1y9bx | −584.6 | −780.7 | −607.5 | −739.9 | −1,101.3 | −950.2 | −1,610.4 | −1,655.6 | −1,214.5 | −1,856.3 | −1,683.9 | .... |
| Secondary income: credit | 1d9ca | 214.5 | 285.5 | 315.1 | 326.0 | 443.2 | 476.8 | 651.7 | 532.9 | 484.1 | 605.5 | 620.8 | .... |
| Secondary income: debit | 1d9da | 8.9 | 11.5 | 14.2 | 4.1 | 6.1 | 8.2 | 10.6 | 14.0 | 14.2 | 13.1 | 14.8 | .... |
| B. Capital Account* | 209ba | 268.4 | 363.3 | 2,480.8 | 190.8 | 438.7 | 408.7 | 710.0 | 458.3 | 359.6 | 611.0 | 574.0 | .... |
| Capital account: credit | 209ca | 268.6 | 363.5 | 2,481.0 | 190.9 | 438.9 | 408.8 | 710.2 | 458.5 | 359.8 | 611.2 | 574.1 | .,,. |
| Capital account: debit | 209da | .2 | .1 | .1 | .1 | .1 | .1 | .1 | .1 | .2 | .1 | .2 | .... |
| Balance on current & capital acct. | 129ba | −110.6 | −143.4 | 2,174.3 | −227.2 | −225.4 | −72.9 | −259.2 | −678.4 | −385.0 | −652.9 | −503.9 | .... |
| C. Financial Account* | 309na | −35.6 | −149.9 | 2,164.2 | −253.1 | −334.1 | −217.7 | −120.5 | −972.5 | −67.9 | −1,104.7 | −1,010.5 | .... |
| Direct investment: assets | 3a9aa | 1.8 | 3.0 | 5.9 | 13.6 | 18.6 | −1.3 | 42.3 | .9 | −4.5 | −4.2 | −4.7 | .... |
| Equity & investment fund shares | 3aaaa | 1.3 | .7 | .9 | 1.5 | 2.0 | 2.6 | .3 | −.1 | −1.1 | −1.0 | −1.2 | .... |
| Debt instruments | 3abaa | .5 | 2.3 | 5.0 | 12.2 | 16.6 | −3.9 | 42.0 | 1.1 | −3.4 | −3.2 | −3.6 | .... |
| Direct investment: liabilities | 3a9la | 107.8 | 139.7 | 35.6 | 124.4 | 195.4 | 49.1 | 97.0 | 1,128.3 | −52.3 | 634.7 | 715.7 | .... |
| Equity & investment fund shares | 3aala | 38.8 | 88.2 | −44.7 | −20.5 | 145.9 | 69.2 | 132.8 | 757.0 | −263.1 | 439.8 | 495.9 | .... |
| Debt instruments | 3abla | 69.0 | 51.5 | 80.3 | 144.9 | 49.5 | −20.0 | −35.8 | 371.3 | 210.8 | 194.9 | 219.8 | .... |
| Portfolio investment: assets | 3b9aa | .... | .1 | .1 | .1 | .1 | .1 | −.1 | −.1 | −.1 | −.1 | −.1 | .... |
| Equity & investment fund shares | 3baaa | .... | .1 | .1 | .1 | .1 | .1 | −.1 | −.1 | −.1 | −.1 | −.1 | .... |
| Debt securities | 3bbaa | .... | .... | .... | .... | .... | .... | .... | .... | .... | .... | .... | .... |
| Portfolio investment: liabilities | 3b9la | −.1 | −3.9 | −2.5 | −1.7 | −1.5 | −.3 | 1.0 | 1.7 | .4 | .4 | .4 | .... |
| Equity & investment fund shares | 3bala | −.1 | −3.9 | −2.5 | −1.7 | −1.5 | −.3 | 1.0 | 1.7 | .4 | .4 | .4 | .... |
| Debt securities | 3bbla | .... | .... | .... | .... | .... | .... | .... | .... | .... | .... | .... | .... |
| Fin. der.& empl.stk.ops.(ESOs): net. | 3c9na | .... | .... | .... | .... | .... | .... | .... | .... | .... | .... | .... | .... |
| Fin. der. & ESOs: assets | 3c9aa | .... | .... | .... | .... | .... | .... | .... | .... | .... | .... | .... | .... |
| Fin. der. & ESOs: liabilities | 3c9la | .... | .... | .... | .... | .... | .... | .... | .... | .... | .... | .... | .... |
| Other investment: assets | 3d9aa | 40.0 | −32.8 | 29.6 | −19.8 | −38.4 | 40.5 | 32.4 | 29.1 | −3.1 | 32.7 | 18.6 | .... |
| Other equity | 3daaa | .... | .... | .... | .... | .... | .... | .... | .... | .... | .... | .... | .... |
| Debt instruments | 3dzaa | 40.0 | −32.8 | 29.6 | −19.8 | −38.4 | 40.5 | 32.4 | 29.1 | −3.1 | 32.7 | 18.6 | .... |
| Other investment: liabilities | 3d9la | −30.3 | −15.6 | −2,161.7 | 124.4 | 120.4 | 208.1 | 97.1 | −127.7 | 112.0 | 497.9 | 308.0 | .... |
| Other equity | 3dala | .... | .... | .... | .... | .... | .... | .... | .... | .... | .... | .... | .... |
| Debt instruments | 3dzla | −30.3 | −15.6 | −2,161.7 | 124.4 | 120.4 | 208.1 | 97.1 | −127.7 | 112.0 | 497.9 | 308.0 | .... |
| Curr.+ cap.− finan. acct. balance. | 4y9na | −75.0 | 6.6 | 10.0 | 25.9 | 108.7 | 144.8 | −138.7 | 294.1 | −317.1 | 451.8 | 506.6 | .... |
| D. Net Errors and Omissions | 409na | 94.6 | 34.8 | 23.7 | 81.9 | −198.2 | −253.9 | 252.9 | −402.1 | 306.9 | −274.6 | −318.9 | .... |
| E. Reserves and Related Items | 4z9na | 19.6 | 41.3 | 33.7 | 107.8 | −89.5 | −109.1 | 114.2 | −108.0 | −10.2 | 177.1 | 187.6 | .... |
| Reserve assets | 3e9aa | 5.9 | 31.2 | −25.4 | 117.9 | 6.2 | −109.1 | 135.5 | −108.8 | 25.4 | 188.6 | 182.3 | .... |
| Credit and loans from the IMF. | 3dcla | −13.7 | −10.1 | −59.1 | 10.1 | 95.7 | — | 21.3 | −.8 | 35.6 | 11.4 | −5.3 | .... |
| Exceptional financing | 409la | .... | .... | .... | .... | .... | .... | .... | .... | .... | .... | .... | .... |
| *Excludes components in group E | | | | | | | | | | | | | |

| International Investment Position | | 2004 | 2005 | 2006 | 2007 | 2008 | 2009 | 2010 | 2011 | 2012 | 2013 | 2014 | 2015 |
|---|---|---|---|---|---|---|---|---|---|---|---|---|---|
| | | | | | | | *Millions of US Dollars* | | | | | | |
| Assets | 809aa | 379.6 | 389.0 | 395.0 | 537.3 | 505.6 | 468.4 | 674.8 | 559.6 | 690.1 | 897.0 | 1,157.9 | .... |
| Direct investment | 8a9aa | 4.9 | 8.4 | 15.1 | 28.9 | 49.5 | 48.1 | 9.1 | 7.2 | 12.6 | 13.1 | 16.0 | .... |
| Equity & investment fund shares.. | 8aaaa | 2.1 | 2.9 | 3.9 | 5.4 | 7.8 | 10.5 | 5.9 | 5.3 | 4.5 | 4.7 | 5.7 | .... |
| Debt instruments | 8abaa | 2.8 | 5.5 | 11.2 | 23.5 | 41.7 | 37.6 | 3.2 | 1.9 | 8.1 | 8.4 | 10.3 | .... |
| Portfolio investment | 8b9aa | .1 | .... | .... | .... | .... | .... | .1 | .1 | .1 | .1 | .1 | .... |
| Equity & investment fund shares.. | 8baaa | .1 | .... | .... | .... | .... | .... | .1 | .1 | .1 | .1 | .1 | .... |
| Debt securities | 8bbaa | .... | .... | .... | .... | .... | .... | .... | .... | .... | .... | .... | .... |
| Fin. der.(oth.than reserves) & ESOs | 8c9aa | .... | .... | .... | .... | .... | .... | .... | .... | .... | .... | .... | .... |
| Other investment | 8d9aa | 246.1 | 221.2 | 245.5 | 256.1 | 197.6 | 253.7 | 363.5 | 359.0 | 458.7 | 478.7 | 555.1 | .... |
| Other equity | 8daaa | .... | .... | .... | .... | .... | .... | .... | .... | .... | .... | .... | .... |
| Debt instruments | 8dzaa | 246.1 | 221.2 | 245.5 | 256.1 | 197.6 | 253.7 | 363.5 | 359.0 | 458.7 | 478.7 | 555.1 | .... |
| Reserve assets | 8e9aa | 128.6 | 159.5 | 134.3 | 252.3 | 258.4 | 166.6 | 302.0 | 193.3 | 218.6 | 405.1 | 586.7 | .... |
| Liabilities | 809la | 3,909.4 | 3,692.8 | 1,349.7 | 1,597.9 | 2,057.6 | 2,310.3 | 4,540.4 | 4,958.1 | 2,868.6 | 3,144.3 | 3,539.8 | .... |
| Direct investment | 8a9la | 645.1 | 614.4 | 655.1 | 780.3 | 977.4 | 1,028.5 | 2,091.2 | 2,731.5 | 932.7 | 972.0 | 1,180.8 | .... |
| Equity & investment fund shares.. | 8aala | 454.0 | 363.7 | 312.6 | 292.0 | 440.1 | 512.0 | 1,075.2 | 1,430.2 | 299.6 | 312.3 | 379.3 | .... |
| Debt instruments | 8abla | 191.0 | 250.7 | 342.5 | 488.4 | 537.3 | 516.5 | 1,016.0 | 1,301.3 | 633.1 | 659.8 | 801.4 | .... |
| Portfolio investment | 8b9la | 12.0 | 7.5 | 4.7 | 6.0 | 4.1 | 5.7 | 5.1 | 7.5 | 13.1 | 13.6 | 16.5 | .... |
| Equity & investment fund shares.. | 8bala | 12.0 | 7.5 | 4.7 | 2.9 | 1.4 | 1.1 | 2.2 | 7.1 | 7.1 | 7.4 | 8.9 | .... |
| Debt securities | 8bbla | .... | .... | .... | 3.1 | 2.7 | 4.5 | 2.9 | .5 | 6.0 | 6.3 | 7.6 | .... |
| Fin. der.(oth.than reserves) & ESOs | 8c9la | .... | .... | .... | .... | .... | .... | .... | .... | .... | .... | .... | .... |
| Other investment | 8d9la | 3,252.3 | 3,071.0 | 690.0 | 811.6 | 1,076.1 | 1,276.2 | 2,444.0 | 2,219.1 | 1,922.9 | 2,158.7 | 2,342.5 | .... |
| Other equity | 8dala | .... | .... | .... | .... | .... | .... | .... | .... | .... | .... | .... | .... |
| Debt instruments | 8dzla | 3,252.3 | 3,071.0 | 690.0 | 811.6 | 1,076.1 | 1,276.2 | 2,444.0 | 2,219.1 | 1,922.9 | 2,158.7 | 2,342.5 | .... |

# Malawi 676

|  |  | 2004 | 2005 | 2006 | 2007 | 2008 | 2009 | 2010 | 2011 | 2012 | 2013 | 2014 | 2015 |
|---|---|---|---|---|---|---|---|---|---|---|---|---|---|
| **Government Finance** | | | | | | | | | | | | | |
| **Cash Flow Statement** | | | | | | | | | | | | | |
| **Budgetary Central Government** | | | | | | *Millions of Kwacha: Fiscal Year Ends June 30* | | | | | | | |
| Cash Receipts:Operating Activities... | c1 | .... | .... | .... | .... | .... | 207,874 | 256,372 | 272,176 | 257,480 | 469,979 | 521,731 | .... |
| Taxes............................. | c11 | .... | .... | .... | .... | .... | 126,429 | 161,006 | 193,573 | 203,591 | 284,318 | 409,458 | .... |
| Social Contributions..................... | c12 | .... | .... | .... | .... | .... | — | — | — | — | — | — | .... |
| Grants................................ | c13 | .... | .... | .... | .... | .... | 75,980 | 78,448 | 64,329 | 42,815 | 174,188 | 80,586 | .... |
| Other Receipts......................... | c14 | .... | .... | .... | .... | .... | 5,465 | 16,918 | 14,274 | 11,075 | 11,473 | 31,688 | .... |
| Cash Payments:Operating Activities. | c2 | .... | .... | .... | .... | .... | 199,529 | 193,562 | 228,365 | 259,448 | 378,124 | 542,592 | .... |
| Compensation of Employees.......... | c21 | .... | .... | .... | .... | .... | 37,595 | 44,792 | 58,092 | 70,178 | 97,166 | 140,233 | .... |
| Purchases of Goods & Services....... | c22 | .... | .... | .... | .... | .... | 58,512 | 64,252 | 69,540 | 84,009 | 123,503 | 130,559 | .... |
| Interest............................... | c24 | .... | .... | .... | .... | .... | 17,864 | 21,498 | 22,819 | 23,765 | 33,397 | 97,939 | .... |
| Subsidies.............................. | c25 | .... | .... | .... | .... | .... | 40,601 | 21,938 | 22,359 | 23,661 | 52,102 | 59,990 | .... |
| Grants................................ | c26 | .... | .... | .... | .... | .... | 37,349 | 33,074 | 40,474 | 41,365 | 50,480 | 83,940 | .... |
| Social Benefits........................ | c27 | .... | .... | .... | .... | .... | 5,106 | 6,376 | 12,042 | 10,413 | 15,618 | 19,581 | .... |
| Other Payments........................ | c28 | .... | .... | .... | .... | .... | 2,503 | 1,633 | 3,038 | 6,057 | 5,857 | 10,351 | .... |
| Net Cash Inflow:Operating Act.[1-2] | ccio | .... | .... | .... | .... | .... | 8,345 | 62,811 | 43,812 | −1,968 | 91,855 | −20,861 | .... |
| Net Cash Outflow:Invest. in NFA...... | c31 | .... | .... | .... | .... | .... | 48,770 | 62,386 | 66,851 | 78,170 | 107,563 | 113,352 | .... |
| Purchases of Nonfinancial Assets... | c31.1 | .... | .... | .... | .... | .... | 48,770 | 62,386 | 66,851 | 78,170 | 107,563 | 113,352 | .... |
| Sales of Nonfinancial Assets.......... | c31.2 | .... | .... | .... | .... | .... | — | — | — | — | — | — | .... |
| Cash Surplus/Deficit [1-2-31=1-2M] | ccsd | .... | .... | .... | .... | .... | −40,425 | 425 | −23,039 | −80,138 | −15,708 | −134,212 | .... |
| Net Acq. Fin. Assets, excl. Cash...... | c32x | .... | .... | .... | .... | .... | −453 | 23 | 1,000 | — | — | — | .... |
| Domestic........................... | c321x | .... | .... | .... | .... | .... | −453 | 23 | 1,000 | — | — | — | .... |
| Foreign.............................. | c322x | .... | .... | .... | .... | .... | — | — | — | — | — | — | .... |
| Net Incurrence of Liabilities............. | c33 | .... | .... | .... | .... | .... | 39,838 | 2,772 | 27,374 | 83,611 | 33,938 | 147,036 | .... |
| Domestic........................... | c331 | .... | .... | .... | .... | .... | 24,075 | −6,753 | 14,037 | 64,629 | −3,799 | 93,147 | .... |
| Foreign.............................. | c332 | .... | .... | .... | .... | .... | 15,764 | 9,526 | 13,337 | 18,982 | 37,737 | 53,889 | .... |
| Net Cash Inflow, Fin.Act.[-32x+33].. | cnfb | .... | .... | .... | .... | .... | 40,291 | 2,749 | 26,374 | 83,611 | 33,938 | 147,036 | .... |
| Net Change in Stock of Cash.......... | cncb | .... | .... | .... | .... | .... | −134 | 3,174 | 3,335 | 3,472 | 18,230 | 12,823 | .... |
| Stat. Discrep. [32X-33+NCB-CSD].... | ccsdz | .... | .... | .... | .... | .... | — | — | — | — | — | — | .... |
| Memo Item:Cash Expenditure[2+31] | c2m | .... | .... | .... | .... | .... | 248,299 | 255,948 | 295,215 | 337,618 | 485,687 | 655,944 | .... |
| Memo Item: Gross Debt.................. | c63 | .... | .... | .... | .... | 149,808 | 139,826 | 160,989 | 167,602 | 222,975 | 292,444 | 434,782 | .... |
| **National Accounts** | | | | | | *Millions of Kwacha* | | | | | | | |
| Government Consumption Expend... | 91f | 46,348.4 | 54,990.5 | 59,481.4 | 75,780.6 | 92,269.8 | 107,992.8 | 95,280.9 | 100,997.8 | 146,446.7 | 207,954.4 | .... | .... |
| Gross Fixed Capital Formation.......... | 93e | 43,909.4 | 61,709.7 | 90,108.8 | 95,537.3 | 156,278.6 | 144,201.1 | 105,304.4 | 146,053.7 | 197,916.1 | 317,697.7 | .... | .... |
| Changes in Inventories..................... | 93i | 20,176.5 | 22,183.0 | 20,045.5 | −21,687.6 | 24,896.7 | −25,795.6 | 64,559.4 | −35,309.9 | 75,260.3 | 127,763.8 | .... | .... |
| Exports of Goods and Services.......... | 90c | 66,945.8 | 73,000.2 | 91,310.4 | 124,099.8 | 140,931.7 | 187,363.2 | 183,055.4 | 255,036.8 | 345,598.2 | 554,759.1 | .... | .... |
| Imports of Goods and Services (-)..... | 98c | 123,413.3 | 170,160.9 | 199,613.8 | 212,686.6 | 333,898.9 | 351,356.7 | 422,425.2 | 439,457.0 | 644,011.0 | 1,101,865.4 | .... | .... |
| Gross Domestic Product (GDP)........ | 99b | 378,564.1 | 432,929.9 | 543,784.7 | 620,421.9 | 747,723.0 | 873,982.3 | 1,047,335.6 | 1,120,391.2 | 1,384,799.2 | 1,875,333.9 | 2,534,700.0 | .... |
| Net Primary Income from Abroad..... | 98.n | −10,989.8 | −9,478.3 | −9,937.3 | −11,077.7 | −20,813.8 | −17,246.8 | −28,666.2 | −16,703.4 | −27,616.1 | −39,491.7 | .... | .... |
| Gross National Income (GNI)........... | 99a | 202,216.2 | 240,587.6 | 533,847.4 | 609,344.2 | 726,909.2 | 856,735.5 | 1,018,669.4 | 1,103,687.8 | 1,357,183.2 | 1,835,842.2 | .... | .... |
| GDP Volume 2009 Prices................. | 99b.p | 632,503.3 | 653,178.1 | 683,877.5 | 749,529.7 | 806,791.8 | 873,982.3 | 934,060.4 | 961,167.1 | 979,345.5 | 1,032,106.8 | .... | .... |
| GDP Volume (2010=100)............... | 99bvp | 67.7 | 69.9 | 73.2 | 80.2 | 86.4 | 93.6 | 100.0 | 102.9 | 104.8 | 110.5 | .... | .... |
| GDP Deflator (2010=100)............... | 99bip | 53.4 | 59.1 | 70.9 | 73.8 | 82.7 | 89.2 | 100.0 | 104.0 | 126.1 | 162.0 | .... | .... |
| | | | | | | *Millions: Midyear Estimates* | | | | | | | |
| Population................................ | 99z | 12.41 | 12.75 | 13.11 | 13.50 | 13.90 | 14.33 | 14.77 | 15.23 | 15.70 | 16.19 | 16.70 | 17.22 |

# Malaysia 548

| | | 2004 | 2005 | 2006 | 2007 | 2008 | 2009 | 2010 | 2011 | 2012 | 2013 | 2014 | 2015 |
|---|---|---|---|---|---|---|---|---|---|---|---|---|---|
| **Exchange Rates** | | *Ringgit per SDR: End of Period* | | | | | | | | | | | |
| Official Rate.................... | aa | 5.9014 | 5.4026 | 5.3128 | 5.2251 | 5.3355 | 5.3686 | 4.7487 | 4.8776 | 4.7003 | 5.0535 | 5.0636 | 5.9476 |
| | | *Ringgit per US Dollar: End of Period (ae) Period Average (rf)* | | | | | | | | | | | |
| Official Rate.................... | ae | 3.8000 | 3.7800 | 3.5315 | 3.3065 | 3.4640 | 3.4245 | 3.0835 | 3.1770 | 3.0583 | 3.2815 | 3.4950 | 4.2920 |
| Official Rate.................... | rf | 3.8000 | 3.7871 | 3.6682 | 3.4376 | 3.3358 | 3.5245 | 3.2211 | 3.0600 | 3.0888 | 3.1509 | 3.2729 | 3.9055 |
| | | *Index Numbers (2010=100): Period Averages* | | | | | | | | | | | |
| Official Rate.................... | ahx | 84.7 | 85.0 | 87.7 | 93.6 | 96.7 | 91.4 | 100.0 | 105.2 | 104.2 | 102.2 | 98.4 | 82.9 |
| Nominal Effective Exchange Rate..... | nec | 93.8 | 93.1 | 95.2 | 97.8 | 97.4 | 94.3 | 100.0 | 100.5 | 100.9 | 101.3 | 99.5 | 90.5 |
| CPI-Based Real Effect. Ex. Rate........ | rec | 92.0 | 91.9 | 95.0 | 97.0 | 97.6 | 94.8 | 100.0 | 100.4 | 100.1 | 100.6 | 99.9 | 91.9 |
| **Fund Position** | | *Millions of SDRs: End of Period* | | | | | | | | | | | |
| Quota.......................... | 2f.s | 1,486.60 | 1,486.60 | 1,486.60 | 1,486.60 | 1,486.60 | 1,486.60 | 1,486.60 | 1,773.90 | 1,773.90 | 1,773.90 | 1,773.90 | 1,773.90 |
| SDR Holdings.................... | 1b.s | 128.18 | 137.16 | 142.13 | 145.21 | 147.02 | 1,355.00 | 1,355.66 | 1,285.31 | 1,285.83 | 1,286.16 | 1,286.64 | 1,286.83 |
| Reserve Position in the Fund........... | 1c.s | 499.76 | 199.43 | 129.55 | 97.94 | 205.99 | 282.19 | 305.89 | 549.33 | 564.43 | 631.05 | 650.50 | 553.20 |
| Total Fund Cred.&Loans Outstg....... | 2tl | — | — | — | — | — | — | — | — | — | — | — | — |
| SDR Allocations................. | 1bd | 139.05 | 139.05 | 139.05 | 139.05 | 139.05 | 1,346.14 | 1,346.14 | 1,346.14 | 1,346.14 | 1,346.14 | 1,346.14 | 1,346.14 |
| **International Liquidity** | | *Millions of US Dollars Unless Otherwise Indicated: End of Period* | | | | | | | | | | | |
| Total Reserves minus Gold.............. | 1l.d | 65,881 | 69,858 | 82,132 | 101,019 | 91,149 | 95,432 | 104,884 | 131,780 | 137,784 | 133,444 | 114,572 | 93,979 |
| SDR Holdings.................... | 1b.d | 199 | 196 | 214 | 229 | 226 | 2,124 | 2,088 | 1,973 | 1,976 | 1,981 | 1,864 | 1,783 |
| Reserve Position in the Fund......... | 1c.d | 776 | 285 | 195 | 155 | 317 | 442 | 471 | 843 | 867 | 972 | 942 | 767 |
| Foreign Exchange.................... | 1d.d | 64,906 | 69,377 | 81,724 | 100,635 | 90,605 | 92,865 | 102,325 | 128,964 | 134,940 | 130,492 | 111,765 | 91,429 |
| Gold (Million Fine Troy Ounces)........ | 1ad | 1.170 | 1.170 | 1.170 | 1.170 | 1.170 | 1.170 | 1.170 | 1.170 | 1.170 | 1.170 | 1.150 | 1.230 |
| Gold (National Valuation)................ | 1and | 295 | 295 | 294 | 294 | 379 | † 1,281 | 1,641 | 1,838 | 1,940 | 1,410 | 1,365 | 1,309 |
| Central Bank: Other Assets........ | 3..d | 32.7 | 30.5 | 32.1 | 34.6 | 10.8 | 4.2 | 5.1 | 5.4 | 2.9 | 3.4 | 3.4 | 2.3 |
| Central Bank: Other Liabs.............. | 4..d | 2,988.2 | 2,435.3 | 4,368.3 | 16,461.4 | 7,725.8 | 4,596.1 | 16,278.4 | 19,761.7 | 26,557.4 | 24,010.4 | 17,626.0 | 5,586.0 |
| Other Depository Corps.: Assets....... | 7a.d | 10,686.6 | 8,653.6 | 14,320.6 | 28,289.7 | 16,491.5 | 19,068.3 | 29,869.8 | 37,049.6 | 43,476.8 | 40,975.5 | 49,720.3 | 42,803.7 |
| Other Depository Corps.: Liabs......... | 7b.d | 16,843.6 | 18,370.8 | 17,469.2 | 25,415.6 | 25,781.1 | 24,971.0 | 25,921.1 | 36,155.3 | 40,924.0 | 46,753.2 | 52,908.0 | 46,846.1 |
| **Central Bank** | | *Millions of Ringgit: End of Period* | | | | | | | | | | | |
| Net Foreign Assets......................... | 11n | 241,328 | 256,337 | 274,238 | 280,567 | 289,342 | 308,384 | 272,014 | 354,127 | 339,574 | 356,316 | 337,115 | 377,150 |
| Claims on Nonresidents................ | 11 | 253,504 | 266,294 | 290,404 | 335,724 | 316,846 | 331,350 | 328,601 | 423,476 | 427,120 | 441,909 | 405,534 | 409,132 |
| Liabilities to Nonresidents.............. | 16c | 12,176 | 9,957 | 16,166 | 55,156 | 27,504 | 22,966 | 56,587 | 69,349 | 87,546 | 85,593 | 68,419 | 31,981 |
| Claims on Other Depository Corps..... | 12e | 9,189 | 10,096 | 12,172 | 70,306 | 11,969 | 16,497 | 48,245 | 36,031 | 34,447 | 21,518 | 9,203 | 20,567 |
| Net Claims on Central Government.. | 12an | −20,184 | −21,073 | −7,914 | −11,338 | −8,627 | −15,957 | −11,940 | −8,799 | −12,524 | −5,255 | −2,809 | −8,297 |
| Claims on Central Government...... | 12a | 221 | 961 | 1,504 | 2,468 | 2,526 | 2,683 | 2,286 | 2,017 | 2,183 | 1,852 | 2,455 | 1,917 |
| Liabilities to Central Government... | 16d | 20,405 | 22,034 | 9,418 | 13,806 | 11,153 | 18,640 | 14,226 | 10,816 | 14,707 | 7,107 | 5,264 | 10,214 |
| Claims on Other Sectors................ | 12s | 21,224 | 16,943 | 17,839 | 15,290 | 12,292 | 12,535 | 10,442 | 11,029 | 11,929 | 8,686 | 8,232 | 6,611 |
| Claims on Other Financial Corps.... | 12g | 13,595 | 11,133 | 13,580 | 11,536 | 11,185 | 11,397 | 9,741 | 10,382 | 11,247 | 7,598 | 7,679 | 6,068 |
| Claims on State & Local Govts....... | 12b | — | — | — | — | — | — | — | — | — | — | — | — |
| Claims on Public Nonfin. Corps...... | 12c | 6,164 | 4,551 | 3,217 | 2,691 | — | — | — | — | — | — | — | — |
| Claims on Private Sector.............. | 12d | 1,464 | 1,258 | 1,042 | 1,063 | 1,106 | 1,138 | 701 | 647 | 682 | 1,088 | 553 | 543 |
| Monetary Base.......................... | 14 | 50,085 | 52,623 | 58,216 | 63,899 | 68,513 | 54,814 | 61,261 | 96,339 | 105,832 | 115,825 | 124,760 | 137,325 |
| Currency in Circulation.................. | 14a | 32,354 | 34,397 | 37,895 | 42,192 | 48,043 | 51,138 | 55,787 | 61,874 | 67,124 | 73,031 | 77,735 | 88,157 |
| Liabs. to Other Depository Corps.... | 14c | 17,732 | 18,226 | 20,321 | 21,707 | 20,470 | 3,676 | 5,474 | 34,465 | 38,708 | 42,795 | 47,025 | 49,168 |
| Liabilities to Other Sectors............. | 14d | — | — | — | — | — | — | — | — | — | — | — | — |
| Other Liabs. to Other Dep. Corps.... | 14n | 133,456 | 154,558 | 191,667 | 254,838 | 201,062 | 209,021 | 226,620 | 244,820 | 231,593 | 205,592 | 154,640 | 126,969 |
| Dep. & Sec. Excl. f/Monetary Base.... | 14o | 12,406 | 13,262 | 11,601 | 3,840 | 2,425 | 5,267 | 7,602 | 15,567 | 4,260 | 3,040 | 2,182 | 736 |
| Deposits Included in Broad Money. | 15 | 12,406 | 13,262 | 11,599 | 3,829 | 2,422 | 4,357 | 4,476 | 3,245 | 4,131 | 2,916 | 2,022 | 639 |
| Sec.Ot.th.Shares Incl.in Brd. Money | 16a | — | — | — | — | — | — | — | — | — | — | — | — |
| Deposits Excl. from Broad Money... | 16b | — | — | 2 | 10 | 3 | 910 | 3,126 | 12,323 | 129 | 124 | 159 | 97 |
| Sec.Ot.th.Shares Excl.f/Brd.Money.. | 16s | — | — | — | — | — | — | — | — | — | — | — | — |
| Loans.......................... | 16l | — | — | — | — | — | — | — | — | — | — | — | 90 |
| Financial Derivatives...................... | 16m | — | — | — | — | — | — | — | — | — | — | — | — |
| Shares and Other Equity................. | 17a | 53,022 | 39,354 | 33,825 | 29,747 | 32,463 | 50,745 | 20,135 | 34,004 | 28,563 | 54,472 | 69,404 | 129,134 |
| Other Items (Net)........................ | 17r | 2,587 | 2,507 | 1,026 | 2,502 | 513 | 1,612 | 3,143 | 1,657 | 3,177 | 2,335 | 754 | 1,777 |
| Memo Item: | | | | | | | | | | | | | |
| Total Assets..................... | 10ra | 284,189 | 294,343 | 321,965 | 423,833 | 343,685 | 363,092 | 389,601 | 472,554 | 475,701 | 473,972 | 427,568 | 440,377 |

# Malaysia   548

| | | 2004 | 2005 | 2006 | 2007 | 2008 | 2009 | 2010 | 2011 | 2012 | 2013 | 2014 | 2015 |
|---|---|---|---|---|---|---|---|---|---|---|---|---|---|
| **Other Depository Corporations** | | *Millions of Ringgit: End of Period* | | | | | | | | | | | |
| Net Foreign Assets | 21n | −23,397 | −36,731 | −11,119 | 9,503 | −32,179 | −20,214 | 12,176 | 2,841 | 7,807 | −18,960 | −11,141 | −17,350 |
| Claims on Nonresidents | 21 | 40,609 | 32,710 | 50,573 | 93,540 | 57,126 | 65,299 | 92,104 | 117,707 | 132,963 | 134,461 | 173,773 | 183,714 |
| Liabilities to Nonresidents | 26c | 64,006 | 69,442 | 61,692 | 84,037 | 89,306 | 85,513 | 79,928 | 114,865 | 125,156 | 153,421 | 184,913 | 201,063 |
| Claims on Central Bank | 20 | 144,784 | 173,865 | 216,031 | 237,257 | 229,126 | 218,555 | 216,035 | 266,579 | 258,167 | 241,766 | 210,634 | 189,716 |
| Currency | 20a | 3,817 | 4,230 | 4,395 | 5,946 | 7,611 | 7,700 | 8,103 | 8,386 | 10,326 | 10,321 | 9,705 | 11,514 |
| Reserve Deposits and Securities | 20b | 17,789 | 18,328 | 20,336 | 22,169 | 20,636 | 4,200 | 6,552 | 34,604 | 38,710 | 42,894 | 47,196 | 49,422 |
| Other Claims | 20n | 123,177 | 151,307 | 191,300 | 209,142 | 200,878 | 206,656 | 201,380 | 223,589 | 209,131 | 188,551 | 153,733 | 128,779 |
| Net Claims on Central Government | 22an | 13,262 | 8,482 | 5,077 | −1,471 | 27,861 | 65,364 | 59,154 | 60,006 | 61,011 | 77,581 | 103,771 | 113,301 |
| Claims on Central Government | 22a | 36,899 | 34,556 | 35,266 | 33,696 | 67,249 | 105,639 | 107,041 | 111,993 | 112,307 | 128,382 | 160,077 | 162,679 |
| Liabilities to Central Government | 26d | 23,637 | 26,074 | 30,189 | 35,167 | 39,388 | 40,275 | 47,887 | 51,987 | 51,295 | 50,801 | 56,306 | 49,378 |
| Claims on Other Sectors | 22s | 590,032 | 635,198 | 668,772 | 725,587 | 821,951 | 872,283 | 955,100 | 1,072,037 | 1,200,728 | 1,328,345 | 1,445,477 | 1,564,015 |
| Claims on Other Financial Corps | 22g | 54,721 | 53,385 | 46,036 | 46,059 | 69,704 | 71,365 | 66,307 | 71,466 | 71,612 | 87,499 | 91,710 | 98,789 |
| Claims on State & Local Govts | 22b | 785 | 322 | 545 | 611 | 635 | 618 | 648 | 863 | 1,595 | 1,597 | 1,430 | 1,230 |
| Claims on Public Nonfin. Corps | 22c | 5,352 | 3,706 | 4,584 | 4,126 | 7,806 | 5,840 | 8,904 | 11,800 | 19,766 | 19,022 | 18,756 | 15,590 |
| Claims on Private Sector | 22d | 529,174 | 577,785 | 617,607 | 674,790 | 743,806 | 794,460 | 879,242 | 987,908 | 1,107,755 | 1,220,227 | 1,333,581 | 1,448,405 |
| Liabilities to Central Bank | 26g | 7,928 | 7,676 | 8,180 | 8,561 | 9,913 | 12,086 | 21,472 | 14,025 | 11,997 | 9,305 | 9,004 | 21,762 |
| Transf.Dep.Included in Broad Money | 24 | 90,303 | 101,388 | 113,803 | 137,022 | 150,765 | 170,428 | 192,075 | 219,397 | 252,114 | 284,799 | 306,352 | 322,314 |
| Other Dep.Included in Broad Money | 25 | 467,650 | 492,048 | 551,195 | 607,368 | 679,560 | 745,200 | 794,527 | 916,537 | 989,783 | 1,050,474 | 1,109,669 | 1,141,481 |
| Sec.Ot.th.Shares Incl.in Brd. Money | 26a | 25,479 | 42,414 | 61,773 | 48,556 | 47,606 | 28,628 | 26,183 | 28,058 | 25,885 | 26,101 | 30,887 | 22,076 |
| Deposits Excl. from Broad Money | 26b | — | — | — | — | — | — | — | — | — | 310 | 1,953 | 722 |
| Sec.Ot.th.Shares Excl.f/Brd.Money | 26s | — | — | — | — | — | — | — | — | — | — | — | — |
| Loans | 26l | 3,801 | 5,942 | 5,961 | 20,999 | 18,145 | 18,269 | 26,922 | 35,667 | 34,599 | 30,473 | 32,843 | 32,801 |
| Financial Derivatives | 26m | — | — | — | — | — | — | — | — | — | — | — | — |
| Insurance Technical Reserves | 26r | — | — | — | — | — | — | — | — | — | — | — | — |
| Shares and Other Equity | 27a | 75,117 | 77,583 | 86,649 | 94,359 | 111,961 | 131,969 | 144,429 | 157,459 | 178,915 | 196,026 | 223,551 | 246,229 |
| Other Items (Net) | 27r | 54,403 | 53,764 | 51,201 | 54,010 | 28,809 | 29,407 | 36,858 | 30,321 | 34,421 | 31,245 | 34,483 | 62,296 |
| Memo Item: | | | | | | | | | | | | | |
| Total Assets | 20ra | 891,365 | 972,279 | 1,082,411 | 1,209,413 | 1,323,317 | 1,411,976 | 1,533,745 | 1,767,890 | 1,898,392 | 2,057,193 | 2,241,540 | 2,379,086 |
| **Depository Corporations** | | *Millions of Ringgit: End of Period* | | | | | | | | | | | |
| Net Foreign Assets | 31n | 217,932 | 219,606 | 263,119 | 290,070 | 257,163 | 288,170 | 284,190 | 356,968 | 347,381 | 337,357 | 325,974 | 359,801 |
| Claims on Nonresidents | 31 | 294,113 | 299,005 | 340,977 | 429,263 | 373,973 | 396,650 | 420,705 | 541,182 | 560,083 | 576,370 | 579,307 | 592,845 |
| Liabilities to Nonresidents | 36c | 76,181 | 79,398 | 77,858 | 139,193 | 116,810 | 108,480 | 136,514 | 184,214 | 212,702 | 239,014 | 253,333 | 233,045 |
| Domestic Claims | 32 | 604,333 | 639,550 | 683,773 | 728,068 | 853,477 | 934,225 | 1,012,756 | 1,134,273 | 1,261,145 | 1,409,357 | 1,554,671 | 1,675,630 |
| Net Claims on Central Government | 32an | −6,922 | −12,591 | −2,837 | −12,809 | 19,234 | 49,407 | 47,214 | 51,207 | 48,487 | 72,327 | 100,962 | 105,004 |
| Claims on Central Government | 32a | 37,120 | 35,517 | 36,770 | 36,164 | 69,775 | 108,322 | 109,327 | 114,010 | 114,489 | 130,234 | 162,532 | 164,596 |
| Liabilities to Central Government | 36d | 44,042 | 48,108 | 39,607 | 48,973 | 50,541 | 58,916 | 62,113 | 62,803 | 66,002 | 57,908 | 61,570 | 59,592 |
| Claims on Other Sectors | 32s | 611,256 | 652,141 | 686,611 | 740,876 | 834,243 | 884,818 | 965,542 | 1,083,066 | 1,212,658 | 1,337,031 | 1,453,709 | 1,570,626 |
| Claims on Other Financial Corps | 32g | 68,316 | 64,518 | 59,616 | 57,595 | 80,889 | 82,762 | 76,048 | 81,848 | 82,860 | 95,097 | 99,390 | 104,857 |
| Claims on State & Local Govts | 32b | 785 | 322 | 545 | 611 | 635 | 618 | 648 | 863 | 1,595 | 1,597 | 1,430 | 1,230 |
| Claims on Public Nonfin. Corps | 32c | 11,516 | 8,257 | 7,800 | 6,818 | 7,806 | 5,840 | 8,904 | 11,800 | 19,766 | 19,022 | 18,756 | 15,590 |
| Claims on Private Sector | 32d | 530,638 | 579,043 | 618,649 | 675,853 | 744,912 | 795,598 | 879,943 | 988,555 | 1,108,437 | 1,221,315 | 1,334,134 | 1,448,948 |
| Broad Money Liabilities | 35l | 624,375 | 679,277 | 771,870 | 833,022 | 920,784 | 992,052 | 1,064,945 | 1,220,725 | 1,328,710 | 1,427,000 | 1,516,959 | 1,563,153 |
| Currency Outside Depository Corps | 34a | 28,537 | 30,166 | 33,500 | 36,246 | 40,431 | 43,438 | 47,685 | 53,488 | 56,798 | 62,710 | 68,029 | 76,643 |
| Transferable Deposits | 34 | 97,697 | 108,362 | 121,632 | 138,059 | 150,840 | 170,431 | 192,100 | 219,454 | 252,156 | 284,852 | 306,433 | 322,370 |
| Other Deposits | 35 | 472,663 | 498,336 | 554,965 | 610,161 | 681,907 | 749,555 | 798,978 | 919,724 | 993,871 | 1,053,337 | 1,111,610 | 1,142,064 |
| Securities Other than Shares | 36a | 25,479 | 42,414 | 61,773 | 48,556 | 47,606 | 28,628 | 26,183 | 28,058 | 25,885 | 26,101 | 30,887 | 22,076 |
| Deposits Excl. from Broad Money | 36b | — | — | 2 | 10 | 3 | 910 | 3,126 | 12,323 | 129 | 434 | 2,112 | 819 |
| Sec.Ot.th.Shares Excl.f/Brd.Money | 36s | — | — | — | — | — | — | — | — | — | — | — | — |
| Loans | 36l | 3,801 | 5,942 | 5,961 | 20,999 | 18,145 | 18,269 | 26,922 | 35,667 | 34,599 | 30,473 | 32,843 | 32,891 |
| Financial Derivatives | 36m | — | — | — | — | — | — | — | — | — | — | — | — |
| Insurance Technical Reserves | 36r | — | — | — | — | — | — | — | — | — | — | — | — |
| Shares and Other Equity | 37a | 128,139 | 116,938 | 120,474 | 124,106 | 144,424 | 182,714 | 164,564 | 191,463 | 207,478 | 250,498 | 292,955 | 375,363 |
| Other Items (Net) | 37r | 65,951 | 56,999 | 48,586 | 40,001 | 27,284 | 28,450 | 37,390 | 31,063 | 37,610 | 38,308 | 35,775 | 63,204 |
| Broad Money Liabs., Seasonally Adj. | 35l.b | 626,037 | 679,618 | 770,468 | 829,894 | 916,409 | 987,080 | 1,060,121 | 1,216,176 | 1,324,949 | 1,423,805 | 1,514,073 | 1,560,497 |
| **Monetary Aggregates** | | *Millions of Ringgit: End of Period* | | | | | | | | | | | |
| Broad Money | 59m | 624,375 | 679,277 | 771,870 | 833,022 | 920,784 | 992,052 | 1,064,945 | 1,220,725 | 1,328,710 | 1,427,000 | 1,516,959 | 1,563,153 |
| o/w:Currency Issued by Cent.Govt | 59m.a | — | — | — | — | — | — | — | — | — | — | — | — |
| o/w: Dep.in Nonfin. Corporations | 59m.b | — | — | — | — | — | — | — | — | — | — | — | — |
| o/w:Secs. Issued by Central Govt | 59m.c | — | — | — | — | — | — | — | — | — | — | — | — |
| Money (National Definitions) | | | | | | | | | | | | | |
| Reserve Money | 19mb | 50,087 | 52,623 | 58,219 | 63,902 | 68,513 | 54,816 | 61,262 | 96,339 | 105,832 | 115,826 | 124,760 | 137,327 |
| M1 | 59ma | 114,269 | 124,023 | 141,124 | 169,007 | 182,839 | 200,917 | 224,384 | 258,210 | 289,736 | 327,503 | 346,416 | 360,458 |
| M2 | 59mb | 534,163 | 616,178 | 718,216 | 796,926 | 903,222 | 989,343 | 1,060,154 | 1,214,857 | 1,333,388 | 1,444,851 | 1,544,657 | 1,588,523 |
| M3 | 59mc | 617,639 | 667,327 | 749,691 | 832,788 | 931,656 | 1,017,303 | 1,086,094 | 1,240,929 | 1,352,886 | 1,462,390 | 1,553,807 | 1,594,583 |
| **Interest Rates** | | *Percent Per Annum* | | | | | | | | | | | |
| Central Bank Policy Rate (EOP) | 60 | 2.70 | 3.00 | 3.50 | 3.50 | 3.25 | 2.00 | 2.75 | 3.00 | 3.00 | 3.00 | 3.25 | 3.25 |
| Money Market Rate | 60b | 2.70 | 2.72 | 3.38 | 3.50 | 3.47 | 2.12 | 2.45 | 2.88 | 2.99 | 2.99 | 3.10 | 3.21 |
| Treasury Bill Rate | 60c | 2.40 | 2.48 | 3.23 | 3.43 | 3.39 | 2.05 | 2.58 | 2.92 | 3.04 | 3.00 | 3.12 | 3.12 |
| Savings Rate | 60k | 1.71 | 1.47 | 1.46 | 1.44 | 1.42 | .94 | .94 | 1.08 | 1.04 | 1.01 | 1.03 | 1.06 |
| Deposit Rate | 60l | 3.00 | 3.00 | 3.15 | 3.17 | 3.13 | 2.08 | 2.50 | 2.91 | 2.98 | 2.97 | 3.05 | 3.13 |
| Lending Rate | 60p | 6.05 | 5.95 | 6.49 | 6.41 | 6.08 | 5.08 | 5.00 | 4.92 | 4.79 | 4.61 | 4.59 | 4.59 |
| Government Bond Yield | 61 | 4.09 | 3.57 | 4.01 | 3.57 | 3.73 | 3.59 | 3.52 | 3.45 | 3.25 | 3.42 | 3.69 | 3.67 |

# Malaysia   548

| | | 2004 | 2005 | 2006 | 2007 | 2008 | 2009 | 2010 | 2011 | 2012 | 2013 | 2014 | 2015 |
|---|---|---|---|---|---|---|---|---|---|---|---|---|---|
| **Prices, Production, Labor** | | *Index Numbers (2010=100): Period Averages* | | | | | | | | | | | |
| Share Prices.................................. | 62 | 62.0 | 65.9 | 69.7 | 95.5 | 83.7 | 78.7 | 100.0 | 109.7 | 116.8 | 126.9 | 133.9 | 125.8 |
| Share Prices (End of Month)............ | 62.ep | 62.0 | 65.3 | 69.9 | 96.0 | 82.3 | 79.0 | 100.0 | 109.4 | 116.7 | 126.6 | 133.7 | 125.0 |
| Producer Prices............................. | 63 | 77.1 | 82.4 | † 87.9 | 92.7 | 102.2 | 94.7 | † 100.0 | 109.6 | 109.7 | 107.8 | 109.3 | 104.0 |
| Consumer Prices............................ | 64 | † 85.2 | 87.7 | 90.9 | 92.7 | 97.7 | 98.3 | † 100.0 | 103.2 | 104.9 | 107.1 | 110.5 | 112.8 |
| Industrial Production....................... | 66 | 96.1 | † 100.0 | 105.0 | 107.3 | 108.1 | 99.9 | † 100.0 | 102.4 | 106.7 | 110.3 | 116.0 | 121.2 |
| Total Employment.......................... | 67 | 88.4 | 89.1 | 91.5 | 93.1 | 94.9 | 97.6 | 100.0 | 108.2 | 111.1 | 118.3 | 120.4 | .... |
| | | *Number in Thousands: Period Averages* | | | | | | | | | | | |
| Labor Force.................................... | 67d | 10,016 | 10,135 | 10,403 | 10,604 | 10,880 | 11,319 | 11,679 | 12,609 | 12,938 | 13,785 | 13,999 | .... |
| Employment................................... | 67e | 9,987 | 10,065 | 10,328 | 10,514 | 10,715 | 11,020 | 11,291 | 12,220 | 12,545 | 13,352 | 13,599 | .... |
| Unemployment............................... | 67c | 29 | 70 | 75 | 91 | 165 | 299 | 388 | 389 | 393 | 433 | 399 | .... |
| Unemployment Rate (%)................. | 67r | 3.6 | 3.6 | 3.3 | 3.3 | 3.3 | 3.6 | 3.3 | 3.1 | 3.0 | 3.1 | 2.9 | .... |
| **Intl. Transactions & Positions** | | *Millions of Ringgit* | | | | | | | | | | | |
| Exports.......................................... | 70 | 477,829 | 533,372 | 588,588 | 604,300 | 663,014 | 552,518 | 638,822 | 697,862 | 702,641 | 719,992 | 766,128 | 779,975 |
| Rubber....................................... | 70l | 5,205 | 5,787 | 8,235 | 7,334 | 8,112 | 4,460 | 9,210 | 13,481 | 7,864 | 7,027 | 4,574 | .... |
| Palm Oil..................................... | 70dg | 20,842 | 19,091 | 22,070 | 32,027 | 45,951 | 36,329 | 44,730 | 60,310 | 53,067 | 41,737 | 42,312 | .... |
| Tin............................................. | 70q | 954 | 935 | 583 | 795 | 1,698 | 1,047 | 2,084 | 3,234 | 2,410 | 2,526 | 2,450 | .... |
| Imports, c.i.f................................. | 71 | 400,133 | 433,196 | 480,506 | 502,045 | 519,804 | 434,670 | 528,828 | 573,626 | 606,677 | 648,695 | 683,016 | 685,654 |
| Volume of Exports | | *2010=100* | | | | | | | | | | | |
| Rubber....................................... | 72l | 123.0 | 127.8 | 131.9 | 113.2 | 101.6 | 78.1 | 100.0 | 105.0 | 85.6 | 93.9 | 80.0 | .... |
| Palm Oil..................................... | 72dg | 72.1 | 76.1 | 83.5 | 79.2 | 87.9 | 95.9 | 100.0 | 108.9 | 105.6 | 105.2 | 102.6 | .... |
| Tin............................................. | 72q | 89.3 | 99.7 | 57.5 | 50.0 | 81.8 | 67.9 | 100.0 | 125.6 | 110.4 | 107.9 | 101.4 | .... |
| Export Prices | | | | | | | | | | | | | |
| Rubber (Wholesale Price).............. | 76l | 45.9 | 49.2 | 67.8 | 70.4 | 86.7 | 62.0 | 100.0 | 139.4 | 99.7 | 81.2 | 61.2 | .... |
| Palm Oil (Unit Value)................... | 74dg | 64.6 | 56.1 | 59.1 | 90.5 | 116.9 | 84.7 | 100.0 | 123.8 | 112.4 | 88.7 | 92.2 | .... |
| Tin (Unit Value)........................... | 76q | 51.3 | 45.0 | 48.7 | 76.4 | 99.6 | 74.0 | 100.0 | 123.7 | 104.8 | 112.3 | 116.4 | .... |
| **Balance of Payments** | | *Millions of US Dollars* | | | | | | | | | | | |
| A. Current Account*...................... | 109bx | 15,079.4 | 19,979.9 | 26,199.5 | 29,770.1 | 38,914.4 | 31,801.0 | † 25,643.8 | 32,491.6 | 16,315.7 | 11,205.2 | 14,846.5 | 8,959.6 |
| Goods, credit (exports)................. | 1a9cx | 126,589.2 | 141,603.0 | 161,484.9 | 176,545.2 | 199,222.4 | 158,058.0 | † 187,335.6 | 215,164.0 | 208,795.1 | 202,285.3 | 207,482.7 | 175,730.5 |
| Goods, debit (imports)................. | 1a9dx | 99,217.1 | 108,621.4 | 123,443.1 | 138,432.2 | 148,391.4 | 117,327.0 | † 148,932.5 | 169,225.6 | 172,152.0 | 171,707.9 | 172,877.6 | 147,679.7 |
| Balance on goods...................... | 1a9bx | 27,372.1 | 32,981.6 | 38,041.8 | 38,113.0 | 50,831.1 | 40,731.0 | † 38,403.1 | 45,938.4 | 36,643.1 | 30,577.4 | 34,605.1 | 28,050.8 |
| Services, credit (exports)............. | 1b9cx | 17,311.2 | 19,749.7 | 21,080.9 | 29,075.8 | 30,751.4 | 28,291.5 | † 34,676.1 | 38,842.7 | 40,581.1 | 42,100.1 | 42,056.1 | 34,677.0 |
| Services, debit (imports)............... | 1b9dx | 19,268.6 | 21,955.7 | 23,651.0 | 28,668.4 | 30,269.8 | 27,471.5 | † 32,644.6 | 38,344.5 | 43,348.5 | 45,137.2 | 45,319.7 | 40,003.8 |
| Balance on Goods & Services....... | 1z9bx | 25,414.7 | 30,775.5 | 35,471.7 | 38,520.5 | 51,312.7 | 41,551.0 | † 40,434.6 | 46,436.6 | 33,875.6 | 27,540.3 | 31,341.6 | 22,724.0 |
| Primary income: credit.................. | 1c9cx | 4,329.1 | 5,372.7 | 8,494.1 | 11,379.8 | 12,081.2 | 11,212.7 | † 11,995.7 | 17,143.6 | 13,700.0 | 15,091.7 | 16,049.3 | 12,605.5 |
| Primary income: debit................... | 1c9dx | 10,750.8 | 11,690.7 | 13,206.0 | 15,462.1 | 19,217.8 | 15,382.3 | † 20,016.8 | 24,204.5 | 25,282.2 | 25,870.2 | 27,217.4 | 20,728.6 |
| Balance on gds, serv. & prim. inc. | 1y9bx | 18,993.0 | 24,457.4 | 30,759.8 | 34,438.1 | 44,176.1 | 37,381.3 | † 32,413.5 | 39,375.6 | 22,293.5 | 16,761.8 | 20,173.5 | 14,600.8 |
| Secondary income: credit.............. | 1d9ca | 421.8 | 298.6 | 313.7 | 390.9 | 419.1 | 1,077.0 | † 598.5 | 1,528.4 | 2,156.0 | 2,409.3 | 3,212.1 | 3,036.0 |
| Secondary income: debit............... | 1d9da | 4,335.3 | 4,776.1 | 4,874.0 | 5,058.9 | 5,680.9 | 6,657.4 | † 7,368.2 | 8,412.4 | 8,133.8 | 7,965.9 | 8,539.1 | 8,677.3 |
| B. Capital Account*....................... | 209ba | — | — | −72.4 | −54.3 | 186.6 | −44.9 | † −34.4 | −43.5 | 78.9 | −4.7 | 103.3 | −311.5 |
| Capital account: credit.................. | 209ca | — | — | 9.2 | 13.9 | 267.6 | 3.4 | † 21.8 | 14.3 | 133.9 | 5.3 | 114.9 | 1.6 |
| Capital account: debit.................. | 209da | — | — | 81.7 | 68.2 | 81.0 | 48.3 | † 56.2 | 57.8 | 55.0 | 10.0 | 11.5 | 313.1 |
| Balance on current & capital acct. | 129bx | 15,079.4 | 19,979.9 | 26,127.1 | 29,715.8 | 39,101.0 | 31,756.1 | † 25,609.4 | 32,448.2 | 16,394.6 | 11,200.5 | 14,949.8 | 8,648.1 |
| C. Financial Account*..................... | 309na | −5,091.1 | 9,805.7 | 11,812.4 | 11,377.4 | 33,973.5 | 22,638.8 | † 5,961.5 | −7,726.8 | 7,501.5 | 6,174.7 | 24,169.5 | 13,321.0 |
| Direct investment: assets.............. | 3a9aa | 1,813.2 | 2,931.1 | 7,637.6 | 11,815.6 | 15,400.0 | 6,740.8 | † 15,349.5 | 18,108.4 | 16,896.9 | 13,408.2 | 16,059.9 | 9,887.5 |
| Equity & investment fund shares.. | 3aaaa | 957.4 | 1,867.3 | 4,582.9 | 9,216.1 | 8,774.3 | 5,404.9 | .... | .... | .... | .... | .... | .... |
| Debt instruments...................... | 3abaa | 855.8 | 1,063.8 | 3,054.7 | 2,599.4 | 6,625.7 | 1,335.9 | .... | .... | .... | .... | .... | .... |
| Direct investment: liabilities ......... | 3a9la | 4,376.1 | 3,924.8 | 7,690.7 | 9,071.4 | 7,572.5 | 114.7 | † 10,885.6 | 15,119.4 | 8,895.8 | 11,296.3 | 10,619.4 | 10,962.7 |
| Equity & investment fund shares . | 3aala | 4,437.9 | 4,232.4 | 7,608.7 | 8,687.6 | 5,166.5 | 706.1 | .... | .... | .... | .... | .... | .... |
| Debt instruments....................... | 3abla | −61.8 | −307.6 | 82.0 | 383.7 | 2,406.0 | −591.4 | .... | .... | .... | .... | .... | .... |
| Portfolio investment: assets.......... | 3b9aa | 286.6 | 715.0 | 2,120.9 | 3,931.6 | 2,878.2 | 6,339.4 | † 7,276.2 | 6,099.4 | 6,954.1 | 10,195.0 | 8,689.6 | 2,747.3 |
| Equity & investment fund shares | 3baaa | −22.6 | −7.0 | 1,887.1 | 4,093.0 | 2,291.1 | 3,759.7 | .... | .... | .... | .... | .... | .... |
| Debt securities ......................... | 3bbaa | 309.2 | 722.1 | 233.7 | −161.4 | 587.1 | 2,579.7 | .... | .... | .... | .... | .... | .... |
| Portfolio investment: liabilities....... | 3b9la | 8,675.3 | −2,985.3 | 5,556.8 | 9,319.8 | −21,082.5 | 6,048.0 | † 22,270.2 | 14,777.6 | 27,634.7 | 9,381.4 | −3,193.7 | −4,960.7 |
| Equity & investment fund shares . | 3bala | 4,509.5 | −1,199.6 | 2,355.2 | −669.1 | −10,715.6 | −448.6 | .... | .... | .... | .... | .... | .... |
| Debt securities.......................... | 3bbla | 4,165.8 | −1,785.7 | 3,201.6 | 9,988.9 | −10,367.0 | 6,496.6 | .... | .... | .... | .... | .... | .... |
| Fin. der.& empl.stk.ops.(ESOs): net. | 3c9na | −293.9 | 58.2 | −29.4 | 48.0 | 659.2 | −682.8 | † 211.6 | 20.8 | −312.5 | 97.8 | 295.1 | 174.0 |
| Fin. der. & ESOs.: assets................ | 3c9aa | 1,520.0 | 59.4 | −8.4 | −198.0 | 1,164.9 | −32.0 | .... | .... | .... | .... | .... | .... |
| Fin. der. & ESOs.: liabilities.......... | 3c9la | 1,813.9 | 1.2 | 21.0 | −246.1 | 505.7 | 650.8 | .... | .... | .... | .... | .... | .... |
| Other investment: assets................ | 3d9aa | 10,756.1 | 4,877.3 | 8,562.3 | 17,400.4 | −3,825.7 | 17,667.3 | .... | .... | .... | .... | .... | .... |
| Other equity.............................. | 3daaa | .... | .... | .... | .... | .... | .... | .... | .... | .... | .... | .... | .... |
| Debt instruments....................... | 3dzaa | 10,756.1 | 4,877.3 | 8,562.3 | 17,400.4 | −3,825.7 | 17,667.3 | .... | .... | .... | .... | .... | .... |
| Other investment: liabilities.......... | 3d9la | 4,601.6 | −2,163.6 | −6,768.5 | 3,427.0 | −5,351.7 | 1,263.3 | .... | .... | .... | .... | .... | .... |
| Other equity.............................. | 3dala | .... | .... | .... | .... | .... | .... | .... | .... | .... | .... | .... | .... |
| Debt instruments....................... | 3dzla | 4,601.6 | −2,163.6 | −6,768.5 | 3,427.0 | −5,351.7 | 1,263.3 | .... | .... | .... | .... | .... | .... |
| Curr.+ cap.− finan. acct. balance.. | 4y9na | 20,170.5 | 10,174.2 | 14,314.6 | 18,338.4 | 5,127.5 | 9,117.3 | † 19,648.0 | 40,175.0 | 8,893.2 | 5,025.8 | −9,219.7 | −4,672.9 |
| D. Net Errors and Omissions........... | 409na | 1,879.6 | −6,554.6 | −7,450.8 | −5,194.6 | −8,577.8 | −5,199.4 | † −19,684.9 | −9,018.8 | −7,549.8 | −627.1 | −1,860.6 | 5,019.3 |
| E. Reserves and Related Items......... | 4z9na | 22,050.0 | 3,619.6 | 6,863.8 | 13,143.7 | −3,450.3 | 3,917.9 | † −36.9 | 31,156.2 | 1,343.3 | 4,398.8 | −11,080.2 | 346.4 |
| Reserve assets.............................. | 3e9aa | 22,050.0 | 3,619.6 | 6,863.8 | 13,143.7 | −3,450.3 | 3,917.9 | † −36.9 | 31,156.2 | 1,343.3 | 4,398.8 | −11,080.2 | 346.4 |
| Credit and loans from the IMF....... | 3dcla | | | | | | | † | | | | | |
| Exceptional financing.................... | 409la | — | — | — | — | .... | .... | † .... | .... | .... | .... | .... | .... |

*Excludes components in group E

| | | 2004 | 2005 | 2006 | 2007 | 2008 | 2009 | 2010 | 2011 | 2012 | 2013 | 2014 | 2015 |
|---|---|---|---|---|---|---|---|---|---|---|---|---|---|
| **International Investment Position** | | | | | | | *Millions of US Dollars* | | | | | | |
| Assets................................................ | 809aa | 109,182.1 | † 120,305.7 | 166,038.5 | 237,994.5 | 233,024.6 | 264,218.2 | 310,712.0 | 360,372.8 | 403,623.0 | 415,595.9 | 417,963.0 | . . . . |
| Direct investment.......................... | 8a9aa | 15,844.7 | † 24,982.8 | 44,429.6 | 71,114.8 | 80,945.8 | 92,328.0 | 112,226.6 | 125,072.3 | 138,799.6 | 146,003.0 | 152,855.8 | . . . . |
| Equity & investment fund shares.. | 8aaaa | 8,007.9 | † 13,498.7 | 20,188.6 | 34,318.5 | 43,001.5 | 54,032.5 | 65,594.8 | 70,822.2 | 77,077.4 | 80,591.5 | 86,856.1 | . . . . |
| Debt instruments........................ | 8abaa | 7,836.8 | † 11,484.1 | 24,241.0 | 36,796.3 | 37,944.3 | 38,295.5 | 46,631.8 | 54,250.1 | 61,722.2 | 65,411.5 | 65,999.8 | . . . . |
| Portfolio investment...................... | 8b9aa | 2,509.2 | † 4,183.1 | 8,269.4 | 15,319.9 | 16,289.1 | 27,781.6 | 35,892.7 | 40,152.7 | 50,690.1 | 59,993.0 | 67,846.8 | . . . . |
| Equity & investment fund shares.. | 8baaa | 917.4 | † 1,714.8 | 5,511.7 | 12,524.2 | 11,674.5 | 20,133.2 | 25,049.6 | 26,508.3 | 32,857.2 | 40,253.6 | 45,456.6 | . . . . |
| Debt securities............................ | 8bbaa | 1,591.8 | † 2,468.3 | 2,757.8 | 2,795.7 | 4,614.6 | 7,648.4 | 10,843.1 | 13,644.4 | 17,832.8 | 19,739.5 | 22,390.2 | . . . . |
| Fin. der.(oth.than reserves) & ESOs | 8c9aa | 166.1 | † 233.3 | 585.9 | 541.1 | 2,234.7 | 2,273.4 | 1,700.3 | 2,139.3 | 3,433.7 | 2,116.8 | 2,816.4 | . . . . |
| Other investment.......................... | 8d9aa | 24,461.6 | † 20,256.3 | 30,114.1 | 49,108.7 | 41,370.1 | 42,531.3 | 51,750.4 | 56,943.2 | 68,166.9 | 69,880.9 | 75,658.8 | . . . . |
| Other equity.............................. | 8daaa | . . . . | . . . . | . . . . | . . . . | . . . . | . . . . | . . . . | . . . . | . . . . | . . . . | . . . . | . . . . |
| Debt instruments........................ | 8dzaa | 24,461.6 | † 20,256.3 | 30,114.1 | 49,108.7 | 41,370.1 | 42,531.3 | 51,750.4 | 56,943.2 | 68,166.9 | 69,880.9 | 75,658.8 | . . . . |
| Reserve assets.............................. | 8e9aa | 66,200.6 | † 70,650.2 | 82,639.5 | 101,910.0 | 92,185.0 | 99,303.9 | 109,142.0 | 136,065.3 | 142,532.7 | 137,602.2 | 118,785.2 | . . . . |
| Liabilities........................................... | 809la | 142,695.0 | † 139,647.1 | 172,249.6 | 242,150.1 | 202,230.3 | 230,758.4 | 303,956.5 | 346,050.7 | 406,587.3 | 426,987.0 | 418,907.9 | . . . . |
| Direct investment.......................... | 8a9la | 46,097.1 | † 47,407.4 | 62,012.5 | 88,441.9 | 87,620.9 | 91,660.0 | 116,883.1 | 133,688.1 | 151,100.9 | 153,816.5 | 150,938.4 | . . . . |
| Equity & investment fund shares.. | 8aala | 39,754.2 | † 41,346.0 | 51,245.9 | 71,666.7 | 68,605.4 | 73,141.0 | 95,434.7 | 107,793.8 | 125,124.6 | 126,195.2 | 122,794.1 | . . . . |
| Debt instruments........................ | 8abla | 6,342.9 | † 6,061.4 | 10,766.6 | 16,775.2 | 19,015.6 | 18,519.0 | 21,448.4 | 25,894.3 | 25,976.4 | 27,621.3 | 28,144.3 | . . . . |
| Portfolio investment...................... | 8b9la | 50,938.2 | † 46,054.2 | 65,927.3 | 103,207.7 | 64,349.2 | 84,773.7 | 128,527.8 | 142,200.0 | 182,305.9 | 188,870.5 | 176,924.6 | . . . . |
| Equity & investment fund shares.. | 8bala | 31,285.0 | † 30,497.9 | 46,030.7 | 68,162.5 | 27,678.5 | 41,716.0 | 65,901.8 | 66,562.1 | 81,027.8 | 86,194.2 | 79,408.8 | . . . . |
| Debt securities............................ | 8bbla | 19,653.2 | † 15,556.3 | 19,896.6 | 35,045.2 | 36,670.6 | 43,057.7 | 62,626.0 | 75,637.9 | 101,278.1 | 102,676.3 | 97,515.8 | . . . . |
| Fin. der.(oth.than reserves) & ESOs | 8c9la | 223.4 | † 316.5 | 515.4 | 535.9 | 2,134.9 | 2,538.7 | 1,498.3 | 2,008.5 | 3,570.8 | 2,319.2 | 2,832.4 | . . . . |
| Other investment.......................... | 8d9la | 45,436.3 | † 45,868.5 | 43,794.4 | 49,964.6 | 48,125.2 | 51,786.0 | 57,047.4 | 68,154.2 | 69,609.7 | 81,980.8 | 88,212.6 | . . . . |
| Other equity.............................. | 8dala | . . . . | . . . . | . . . . | . . . . | . . . . | . . . . | . . . . | . . . . | . . . . | . . . . | . . . . |
| Debt instruments........................ | 8dzla | 45,436.3 | † 45,868.5 | 43,794.4 | 49,964.6 | 48,125.2 | 51,786.0 | 57,047.4 | 68,154.2 | 69,609.7 | 81,980.8 | 88,212.6 | . . . . |
| | | | | | | | | | | | | | |
| **Government Finance** | | | | | | | | | | | | | |
| **Cash Flow Statement** | | | | | | | | | | | | | |
| **Budgetary Central Government** | | | | | | *Billions of Ringgit: Fiscal Year Ends December 31* | | | | | | | |
| Cash Receipts:Operating Activities... | c1 | 99,398 | 106,303 | 123,544 | 139,885 | 159,793 | 158,639 | 159,653 | 185,420 | 194,487 | 226,599 | 220,625 | . . . . |
| Taxes........................................ | c11 | 72,051 | 80,593 | 86,631 | 95,168 | 112,897 | 106,504 | 109,515 | 134,885 | 140,209 | 161,340 | 164,205 | . . . . |
| Social Contributions...................... | c12 | — | — | — | — | — | — | — | — | — | — | — | . . . . |
| Grants......................................... | c13 | — | — | — | — | — | — | — | — | — | — | — | . . . . |
| Other Receipts.............................. | c14 | 27,347 | 25,710 | 36,913 | 44,717 | 46,896 | 52,135 | 50,138 | 50,535 | 54,278 | 65,259 | 56,421 | . . . . |
| Cash Payments:Operating Activities. | c2 | 89,532 | 96,143 | 105,745 | 120,552 | 150,664 | 154,485 | 149,763 | 179,928 | 193,101 | 213,186 | 217,787 | . . . . |
| Compensation of Employees.......... | c21 | 23,779 | 25,588 | 28,522 | 32,587 | 41,011 | 42,778 | 46,663 | 50,148 | 55,749 | 63,173 | 66,947 | . . . . |
| Purchases of Goods & Services....... | c22 | 16,632 | 17,984 | 20,923 | 23,622 | 25,197 | 26,372 | 23,841 | 28,949 | 24,273 | 36,813 | 34,259 | . . . . |
| Interest...................................... | c24 | 10,920 | 11,603 | 12,496 | 12,911 | 12,797 | 14,222 | 15,621 | 17,716 | 18,765 | 22,190 | 22,588 | . . . . |
| Subsidies.................................... | c25 | 5,795 | 13,388 | 10,112 | 10,481 | 35,165 | 20,345 | 23,106 | 36,256 | 37,328 | 40,984 | 39,703 | . . . . |
| Grants........................................ | c26 | 21,263 | 20,428 | 26,294 | 31,501 | 25,623 | 39,937 | 27,862 | 32,157 | 40,966 | 34,531 | 34,587 | . . . . |
| Social Benefits............................. | c27 | 6,060 | 6,809 | 7,008 | 8,251 | 10,022 | 10,146 | 11,515 | 13,565 | 14,931 | 14,515 | 18,218 | . . . . |
| Other Payments............................ | c28 | 5,083 | 343 | 391 | 1,197 | 849 | 685 | 1,155 | 1,138 | 1,089 | 980 | 1,484 | . . . . |
| Net Cash Inflow:Operating Act.[1-2] | ccio | 9,866 | 10,160 | 17,799 | 19,334 | 9,130 | 4,154 | 9,890 | 5,491 | 1,386 | 13,413 | 2,839 | . . . . |
| Net Cash Outflow:Invest. in NFA...... | c31 | 29,416 | 30,605 | 35,463 | 40,455 | 43,076 | 47,876 | 50,966 | 47,583 | 38,708 | 41,776 | 39,426 | . . . . |
| Purchases of Nonfinancial Assets... | c31.1 | 29,416 | 30,605 | 35,463 | 40,455 | 43,076 | 47,876 | 50,966 | 47,583 | 38,708 | 41,776 | 39,426 | . . . . |
| Sales of Nonfinancial Assets.......... | c31.2 | | | | | | | | | | | | |
| Cash Surplus/Deficit [1-2-31=1-2M] | ccsd | −19,550 | −20,445 | −17,664 | −21,122 | −33,946 | −43,722 | −41,076 | −42,091 | −37,322 | −28,363 | −36,588 | . . . . |
| Net Acq. Fin. Assets, excl. Cash....... | c32x | −135 | −1,717 | 1,446 | −463 | 1,648 | 3,702 | 2,199 | 418 | −1,510 | 721 | 827 | . . . . |
| By instrument | | | | | | | | | | | | | |
| Monetary Gold & SDRs................. | c3201 | — | — | — | — | — | — | — | — | — | — | — | . . . . |
| Securities Other Than Shares.......... | c3203 | — | — | — | — | — | — | — | — | — | — | — | . . . . |
| Loans........................................ | c3204 | −135 | −1,717 | 1,446 | −463 | 1,648 | 3,702 | 2,199 | 418 | −1,510 | 721 | 827 | . . . . |
| Shares and Other Equity................. | c3205 | — | — | — | — | — | — | — | — | — | — | — | . . . . |
| Insurance Technical Reserves.......... | c3206 | . . . . | . . . . | . . . . | . . . . | . . . . | . . . . | . . . . | . . . . | . . . . | . . . . | . . . . | . . . . |
| Financial Derivatives..................... | c3207 | — | — | — | — | — | — | — | — | — | — | — | . . . . |
| By debtor | | | | | | | | | | | | | |
| Domestic...................................... | c321x | −135 | −1,717 | 1,446 | −463 | 1,648 | 3,702 | 2,199 | 418 | −1,510 | 721 | 827 | . . . . |
| Foreign........................................ | c322x | — | — | — | — | — | — | — | — | — | — | — | . . . . |
| Net Incurrence of Liabilities.............. | c33 | 25,771 | 9,197 | 14,696 | 21,486 | 35,180 | 50,593 | 40,120 | 45,619 | 33,546 | 42,073 | 37,201 | . . . . |
| By instrument | | | | | | | | | | | | | |
| Special Drawing Rights (SDRs)........ | c3301 | — | — | — | — | — | — | — | — | — | — | — | . . . . |
| Currency and Deposits.................. | c3302 | — | — | — | — | — | — | — | — | — | — | — | . . . . |
| Securities Other Than Shares.......... | c3303 | 25,650 | 12,700 | 17,750 | 25,800 | 35,654 | 56,879 | 36,456 | 45,069 | 34,125 | 42,001 | 37,557 | . . . . |
| Loans........................................ | c3304 | 121 | −3,503 | −3,054 | −4,314 | −474 | −6,286 | 3,664 | 550 | −580 | 72 | −356 | . . . . |
| Shares and Other Equity................. | c3305 | — | — | — | — | — | — | — | — | — | — | — | . . . . |
| Insurance Technical Reserves.......... | c3306 | — | — | — | — | — | — | — | — | — | — | — | . . . . |
| Financial Derivatives..................... | c3307 | — | — | — | — | — | — | — | — | — | — | — | . . . . |
| By creditor | | | | | | | | | | | | | |
| Domestic...................................... | c331 | 14,362 | 15,648 | 10,291 | 10,698 | 37,799 | 44,365 | 3,567 | 15,811 | 8,142 | 50,446 | 28,459 | . . . . |
| Foreign........................................ | c332 | 11,409 | −6,451 | 4,405 | 10,788 | −2,619 | 6,227 | 36,553 | 29,808 | 25,403 | −8,373 | 8,742 | . . . . |
| Net Cash Inflow, Fin.Act.[-32x+33].. | cnfb | 25,906 | 10,914 | 13,250 | 21,949 | 33,532 | 46,890 | 37,921 | 45,201 | 35,056 | 41,352 | 36,374 | . . . . |
| Net Change in Stock of Cash.......... | cncb | 6,356 | −9,531 | −4,414 | 827 | −414 | 3,168 | −3,156 | 3,110 | −2,266 | 12,989 | −214 | . . . . |
| Stat. Discrep. [32X-33+NCB-CSD].... | ccsdz | — | — | — | — | — | — | — | — | — | — | — | . . . . |
| Memo Item:Cash Expenditure[2+31] | c2m | 118,948 | 126,748 | 141,208 | 161,007 | 193,739 | 202,361 | 200,729 | 227,511 | 231,810 | 254,962 | 257,213 | . . . . |
| Memo Item: Gross Debt................... | c63 | 216,624 | 228,670 | 242,225 | 266,722 | 306,437 | 362,386 | 407,101 | 456,128 | 501,617 | 539,858 | 582,828 | . . . . |

| | | 2004 | 2005 | 2006 | 2007 | 2008 | 2009 | 2010 | 2011 | 2012 | 2013 | 2014 | 2015 |
|---|---|---|---|---|---|---|---|---|---|---|---|---|---|
| **National Accounts** | | | | | | | *Millions of Ringgit* | | | | | | |
| Househ.Cons.Expend.,incl.NPISHs.... | 96f | 208,571 | 240,187 | 264,584 | 300,418 | 344,215 | 348,168 | 395,245 | 437,340 | 482,238 | 527,749 | 579,985 | 626,239 |
| Government Consumption Expend... | 91f | 59,635 | 62,368 | 66,647 | 76,959 | 88,581 | 93,017 | 103,346 | 120,993 | 134,442 | 139,707 | 147,385 | 151,989 |
| Gross Fixed Capital Formation.......... | 93e | 99,336 | 121,237 | 131,024 | 149,064 | 158,381 | 156,660 | 184,292 | 202,251 | 246,343 | 269,699 | 287,417 | 302,948 |
| Changes in Inventories.................... | 93i | 9,930 | 505 | 4,467 | 6,689 | 6,837 | −29,517 | 7,813 | 9,164 | 3,741 | −5,500 | −10,942 | −12,601 |
| Exports of Goods and Services......... | 90c | 546,925 | 613,694 | 669,505 | 706,382 | 766,096 | 651,671 | 714,075 | 777,302 | 770,202 | 770,368 | 816,483 | 820,459 |
| Imports of Goods and Services (-)..... | 98c | 450,350 | 494,414 | 539,444 | 574,172 | 594,160 | 507,142 | 583,337 | 635,316 | 665,714 | 683,408 | 713,863 | 731,895 |
| Gross Domestic Product (GDP)......... | 99b | 474,048 | 543,578 | 596,783 | 665,340 | 769,949 | 712,857 | 821,434 | 911,733 | 971,252 | 1,018,614 | 1,106,466 | 1,157,139 |
| Net Primary Income from Abroad..... | 98.n | −24,402 | −23,942 | −17,294 | −13,984 | −23,034 | −14,215 | −26,131 | −21,600 | −35,841 | −33,975 | −36,624 | −32,011 |
| Gross National Income (GNI)............ | 99a | 449,646 | 519,635 | 579,489 | 651,355 | 746,915 | 698,642 | 795,303 | 839,052 | 871,804 | 916,722 | 972,593 | 1,038,527 |
| GDP Volume 2000 Prices................ | 99b.p | 426,508 | 449,250 | 475,526 | 506,341 | 530,683 | 522,001 | 559,554 | 588,297 | . . . . | . . . . | . . . . | . . . . |
| GDP Volume 2005 Prices................ | 99b.p | . . . . | 543,578 | 573,935 | 610,087 | 639,565 | 629,885 | 676,653 | 711,760 | 751,934 | 787,611 | 835,041 | . . . . |
| GDP Volume 2010 Prices................ | 99b.p | . . . . | . . . . | . . . . | . . . . | . . . . | . . . . | 821,434 | 864,920 | 912,261 | 955,080 | 1,012,506 | 1,062,805 |
| GDP Volume (2010=100)................ | 99bvp | 76.3 | † 80.3 | 84.8 | 90.2 | 94.5 | 93.1 | † 100.0 | 105.3 | 111.1 | 116.3 | 123.3 | 129.4 |
| GDP Deflator (2010=100)............... | 99bip | 75.7 | 82.4 | 85.7 | 89.8 | 99.2 | 93.2 | 100.0 | 105.4 | 106.5 | 106.7 | 109.3 | 108.9 |
| | | | | | | | *Millions: Midyear Estimates* | | | | | | |
| Population.................................. | 99z | 25.33 | 25.80 | 26.26 | 26.73 | 27.20 | 27.66 | 28.12 | 28.57 | 29.02 | 29.47 | 29.90 | 30.33 |

# Maldives 556

|  | | 2004 | 2005 | 2006 | 2007 | 2008 | 2009 | 2010 | 2011 | 2012 | 2013 | 2014 | 2015 |
|---|---|---|---|---|---|---|---|---|---|---|---|---|---|
| **Exchange Rates** | | | | | | *Rufiyaa per SDR: End of Period* | | | | | | | |
| Market Rate | aa | 19.879 | 18.295 | 19.256 | 20.227 | 19.715 | 20.066 | 19.712 | 23.659 | 23.615 | 23.731 | 22.312 | 21.354 |
| | | | | | | *Rufiyaa per US Dollar: End of Period (ae) Period Average (rf)* | | | | | | | |
| Market Rate | ae | 12.800 | 12.800 | 12.800 | 12.800 | 12.800 | 12.800 | 12.800 | 15.410 | 15.365 | 15.410 | 15.400 | 15.410 |
| Market Rate | rf | 12.800 | 12.800 | 12.800 | 12.800 | 12.800 | 12.800 | 12.800 | 14.602 | 15.365 | 15.367 | 15.380 | 15.366 |
| **Fund Position** | | | | | | *Millions of SDRs: End of Period* | | | | | | | |
| Quota | 2f.s | 8.20 | 8.20 | 8.20 | 8.20 | 8.20 | 8.20 | 8.20 | 10.00 | 10.00 | 10.00 | 10.00 | 10.00 |
| SDR Holdings | 1b.s | .32 | .32 | .33 | .36 | .40 | 7.77 | 7.63 | 6.97 | 6.89 | 6.82 | 6.77 | 6.46 |
| Reserve Position in the Fund | 1c.s | 1.55 | 1.55 | 1.55 | 1.55 | 1.55 | 1.55 | 1.55 | 2.00 | 2.00 | 2.00 | 2.00 | 2.00 |
| Total Fund Cred.&Loans Outstg | 2tl | — | 4.10 | 4.10 | 4.10 | 2.56 | 5.64 | 10.25 | 10.25 | 10.25 | 6.66 | 2.56 | 1.74 |
| SDR Allocations | 1bd | .28 | .28 | .28 | .28 | .28 | 7.69 | 7.69 | 7.69 | 7.69 | 7.69 | 7.69 | 7.69 |
| **International Liquidity** | | | | | | *Millions of US Dollars Unless Otherwise Indicated: End of Period* | | | | | | | |
| Total Reserves minus Gold | 1l.d | 206.51 | 189.03 | 234.39 | 311.43 | 243.59 | 275.59 | 364.32 | 348.65 | 318.27 | 381.89 | 627.41 | 575.76 |
| SDR Holdings | 1b.d | .50 | .46 | .50 | .57 | .61 | 12.18 | 11.75 | 10.70 | 10.59 | 10.50 | 9.80 | 8.95 |
| Reserve Position in the Fund | 1c.d | 2.41 | 2.22 | 2.34 | 2.46 | 2.39 | 2.44 | 2.39 | 3.08 | 3.08 | 3.09 | 2.90 | 2.78 |
| Foreign Exchange | 1d.d | 203.59 | 186.35 | 231.55 | 308.40 | 240.58 | 260.98 | 350.18 | 334.87 | 304.60 | 368.30 | 614.70 | 564.03 |
| Gold (Million Fine Troy Ounces) | 1ad | — | — | — | — | — | — | — | — | — | — | — | — |
| Gold (National Valuation) | 1and | — | — | — | — | — | — | — | — | — | — | — | — |
| Central Bank: Other Assets | 3..d | .79 | .85 | .85 | .79 | .77 | .70 | .70 | .60 | .61 | .61 | .61 | .59 |
| Central Bank: Other Liabs | 4..d | .86 | .93 | 5.96 | .94 | .87 | .81 | 5.47 | 1.36 | 1.61 | .76 | 7.41 | 17.52 |
| Other Depository Corps.: Assets | 7a.d | 76.80 | 44.59 | 65.51 | † 81.21 | 58.20 | 69.41 | 80.79 | 113.93 | 174.74 | 306.80 | 299.22 | 331.88 |
| Other Depository Corps.: Liabs | 7b.d | 18.60 | 85.03 | 210.98 | † 422.42 | 429.62 | 413.97 | 345.01 | 234.14 | 108.53 | 79.32 | 76.42 | 73.62 |
| Other Financial Corps.: Assets | 7e.d | — | — | — | 8.73 | 10.57 | 14.74 | 7.03 | 5.45 | 7.58 | 12.09 | 15.41 | 18.20 |
| Other Financial Corps.: Liabs | 7f.d | 4.02 | 4.34 | 8.26 | 15.56 | 20.79 | 22.49 | 20.72 | 21.37 | 18.81 | 20.27 | 22.29 | 24.71 |
| **Central Bank** | | | | | | *Millions of Rufiyaa: End of Period* | | | | | | | |
| Net Foreign Assets | 11n | 2,599.60 | 2,304.15 | 2,814.01 | 3,857.06 | 3,022.04 | 3,071.70 | 4,066.66 | 4,724.85 | 4,241.07 | 5,332.59 | 9,132.60 | 8,227.25 |
| Claims on Nonresidents | 11 | 2,616.17 | 2,396.18 | 2,974.69 | 3,957.68 | 3,089.30 | 3,349.54 | 4,490.28 | 5,170.31 | 4,689.53 | 5,684.87 | 9,475.48 | 8,698.66 |
| Liabilities to Nonresidents | 16c | 16.57 | 92.03 | 160.68 | 100.62 | 67.26 | 277.84 | 423.62 | 445.46 | 448.47 | 352.28 | 342.88 | 471.42 |
| Claims on Other Depository Corps | 12e | | | | | | | | | | | | .44 |
| Net Claims on Central Government | 12an | 836.14 | 1,280.00 | 967.00 | 906.13 | 2,640.62 | 3,419.22 | 2,724.99 | 3,527.38 | 4,685.55 | 5,962.09 | 5,324.23 | 5,455.31 |
| Claims on Central Government | 12a | 1,324.08 | 1,951.27 | 1,722.93 | 1,830.69 | 3,365.02 | 4,213.04 | 3,921.49 | 3,920.16 | 5,005.91 | 6,259.21 | 6,440.47 | 6,372.98 |
| Liabilities to Central Government | 16d | 487.94 | 671.27 | 755.93 | 924.56 | 724.40 | 793.83 | 1,196.49 | 392.78 | 320.36 | 297.12 | 1,116.24 | 917.67 |
| Claims on Other Sectors | 12s | 5.55 | 4.35 | 4.42 | 12.27 | 9.70 | 4.84 | 5.95 | 4.66 | 6.87 | 7.05 | 6.52 | 91.52 |
| Claims on Other Financial Corps | 12g | — | — | — | — | — | — | — | — | — | — | — | — |
| Claims on State & Local Govts | 12b | — | — | — | — | — | — | — | — | — | — | — | — |
| Claims on Public Nonfin. Corps | 12c | 1.48 | | | | .10 | | | | | | | 84.76 |
| Claims on Private Sector | 12d | 4.07 | 4.35 | 4.42 | 12.27 | 9.60 | 4.84 | 5.95 | 4.66 | 6.87 | 7.05 | 6.52 | 6.77 |
| Monetary Base | 14 | 2,947.98 | 2,978.15 | 3,423.55 | 4,374.15 | 5,382.38 | 6,143.92 | 6,064.30 | 7,551.31 | 8,181.86 | 9,628.72 | 12,502.31 | 10,274.07 |
| Currency in Circulation | 14a | 828.03 | 947.19 | 1,160.71 | 1,322.28 | 1,762.19 | 1,799.72 | 1,871.14 | 2,196.67 | 2,475.54 | 3,252.43 | 3,099.43 | 3,220.69 |
| Liabs. to Other Depository Corps | 14c | 1,815.98 | 1,867.62 | 2,209.84 | 2,990.64 | 3,609.65 | 4,308.55 | 4,182.63 | 5,294.19 | 5,705.67 | 6,374.74 | 9,401.82 | 7,052.29 |
| Liabilities to Other Sectors | 14d | 303.98 | 163.33 | 53.00 | 61.22 | 10.54 | 35.65 | 10.54 | 60.45 | .64 | 1.55 | 1.05 | 1.09 |
| Other Liabs. to Other Dep. Corps | 14n | 174.07 | 221.12 | 4.15 | 7.81 | 6.32 | 15.71 | 496.67 | 85.35 | 197.35 | 997.89 | 1,701.42 | 3,364.74 |
| Dep. & Sec. Excl. f/Monetary Base | 14o | .29 | .14 | .10 | .06 | .08 | .06 | 10.07 | 10.07 | 10.00 | 10.00 | 10.00 | 9.40 |
| Deposits Included in Broad Money | 15 | — | — | — | — | — | — | — | — | — | — | — | — |
| Sec.Ot.th.Shares Incl.in Brd. Money | 16a | — | — | — | — | — | — | — | — | — | — | — | — |
| Deposits Excl. from Broad Money | 16b | .29 | .14 | .10 | .06 | .08 | .06 | 10.07 | 10.07 | 10.00 | 10.00 | 10.00 | 9.40 |
| Sec.Ot.th.Shares Excl.f/Brd.Money | 16s | — | — | — | — | — | — | — | — | — | — | — | — |
| Loans | 16l | — | — | — | — | — | — | — | — | — | — | — | — |
| Financial Derivatives | 16m | — | — | — | — | — | — | — | — | — | — | — | — |
| Shares and Other Equity | 17a | 144.18 | 154.17 | 336.22 | 197.45 | 205.73 | 432.66 | 349.77 | 752.13 | 628.62 | 659.40 | 177.95 | 319.40 |
| Other Items (Net) | 17r | 174.76 | 234.92 | 21.41 | 195.99 | 77.85 | −96.60 | −123.20 | −141.97 | −84.35 | 5.72 | 71.67 | −193.10 |
| Memo Item: | | | | | | | | | | | | | |
| Total Assets | 10ra | 4,081.89 | 4,584.40 | 4,948.71 | 6,071.92 | 6,764.29 | 7,987.38 | 8,962.48 | 9,551.22 | 10,199.88 | 12,448.50 | 16,406.86 | 15,796.20 |
| **Other Depository Corporations** | | | | | | *Millions of Rufiyaa: End of Period* | | | | | | | |
| Net Foreign Assets | 21n | 745.00 | −517.68 | −1,861.94 | † −4,367.50 | −4,754.16 | −4,410.36 | −3,382.02 | −1,852.48 | 1,017.26 | 3,505.41 | 3,431.07 | 3,979.86 |
| Claims on Nonresidents | 21 | 983.09 | 570.70 | 838.56 | † 1,039.46 | 744.94 | 888.40 | 1,034.14 | 1,755.62 | 2,684.83 | 4,727.79 | 4,607.98 | 5,114.34 |
| Liabilities to Nonresidents | 26c | 238.09 | 1,088.38 | 2,700.51 | † 5,406.96 | 5,499.10 | 5,298.75 | 4,416.16 | 3,608.10 | 1,667.57 | 1,222.38 | 1,176.91 | 1,134.49 |
| Claims on Central Bank | 20 | 2,057.04 | 2,153.26 | 2,423.63 | † 3,240.62 | 3,848.25 | 4,638.57 | 4,979.59 | 5,696.43 | 6,251.39 | 7,810.54 | 12,033.88 | 10,809.89 |
| Currency | 20a | 65.14 | 63.59 | 92.59 | † 180.33 | 251.98 | 258.32 | 300.09 | 339.12 | 358.75 | 450.54 | 416.72 | 464.36 |
| Reserve Deposits and Securities | 20b | 1,820.19 | 1,871.11 | 2,331.05 | † 3,060.29 | 3,596.27 | 4,370.24 | 4,587.47 | 5,357.31 | 5,892.64 | 6,457.80 | 11,617.16 | 10,345.53 |
| Other Claims | 20n | 171.72 | 218.56 | — | † — | — | 10.01 | 92.03 | — | 902.20 | — | — | — |
| Net Claims on Central Government | 22an | −403.60 | −550.31 | −414.12 | † −689.77 | −1,744.31 | 643.49 | 2,655.73 | 3,303.50 | 2,964.01 | 2,676.14 | 3,941.15 | 5,907.03 |
| Claims on Central Government | 22a | 21.33 | 12.80 | 330.37 | † 566.01 | 799.08 | 3,351.67 | 4,665.40 | 5,192.32 | 4,735.46 | 4,475.02 | 5,965.16 | 7,843.14 |
| Liabilities to Central Government | 26d | 424.93 | 563.11 | 744.49 | † 1,255.77 | 2,543.39 | 2,708.18 | 2,009.67 | 1,888.81 | 1,771.46 | 1,798.88 | 2,024.01 | 1,936.11 |
| Claims on Other Sectors | 22s | 3,780.54 | 6,124.29 | 8,946.20 | † 13,519.78 | 17,684.09 | 17,119.89 | 16,794.54 | 17,852.82 | 16,237.16 | 16,314.04 | 16,712.54 | 18,620.66 |
| Claims on Other Financial Corps | 22g | 6.43 | 6.43 | 6.43 | † 17.54 | 97.82 | 172.02 | 144.52 | 98.79 | 161.03 | 109.23 | 288.35 | 303.03 |
| Claims on State & Local Govts | 22b | — | — | — | † — | — | — | — | — | — | — | — | — |
| Claims on Public Nonfin. Corps | 22c | 248.51 | 487.92 | 572.50 | † 1,005.39 | 1,377.32 | 1,398.85 | 1,465.00 | 1,668.15 | 1,577.55 | 1,574.43 | 1,333.90 | 1,406.62 |
| Claims on Private Sector | 22d | 3,525.60 | 5,629.94 | 8,367.27 | † 12,496.84 | 16,208.95 | 15,549.01 | 15,185.02 | 16,085.88 | 14,498.58 | 14,630.38 | 15,090.30 | 16,911.01 |
| Liabilities to Central Bank | 26g | — | — | — | † — | | | | | | | | |
| Transf.Dep.Included in Broad Money | 24 | 3,947.08 | 4,693.96 | 5,453.15 | † 7,080.96 | 8,290.98 | 9,923.00 | 10,942.49 | 13,111.12 | 13,677.82 | 16,684.20 | 19,410.04 | 22,872.07 |
| Other Dep.Included in Broad Money | 25 | 1,076.86 | 881.47 | 1,307.13 | † 1,654.68 | 2,298.54 | 2,355.22 | 3,359.89 | 4,033.12 | 4,206.35 | 4,189.08 | 5,067.44 | 5,244.96 |
| Sec.Ot.th.Shares Incl.in Brd. Money | 26a | — | 114.85 | 127.25 | † — | | | | | | | | |
| Deposits Excl. from Broad Money | 26b | 97.90 | 175.38 | 190.31 | † 241.13 | 181.45 | 218.47 | 292.57 | 326.80 | 275.43 | 370.33 | 375.99 | 349.40 |
| Sec.Ot.th.Shares Excl.f/Brd.Money | 26s | — | — | — | † — | | | | | | | | |
| Loans | 26l | — | — | — | † — | | | | | | | | |
| Financial Derivatives | 26m | — | — | — | † — | | | | | | | | |
| Insurance Technical Reserves | 26r | — | — | — | † — | | | | | | | | |
| Shares and Other Equity | 27a | 871.54 | 1,098.87 | 1,666.25 | † 2,448.17 | 3,772.06 | 4,249.84 | 4,761.53 | 4,908.78 | 5,733.64 | 7,194.72 | 8,549.56 | 9,355.19 |
| Other Items (Net) | 27r | 185.59 | 245.05 | 349.69 | † 278.19 | 490.83 | 1,245.07 | 1,691.36 | 2,620.46 | 2,576.57 | 1,867.80 | 2,715.62 | 1,495.82 |
| Memo Item: | | | | | | | | | | | | | |
| Total Assets | 20ra | 7,054.11 | 9,168.34 | 12,857.37 | † 18,743.29 | 23,446.22 | 26,388.36 | 27,885.22 | 31,318.01 | 30,947.40 | 34,984.55 | 41,193.49 | 44,200.12 |

# Maldives 556

|  |  | 2004 | 2005 | 2006 | 2007 | 2008 | 2009 | 2010 | 2011 | 2012 | 2013 | 2014 | 2015 |
|---|---|---|---|---|---|---|---|---|---|---|---|---|---|
| **Depository Corporations** | | | | | | *Millions of Rufiyaa: End of Period* | | | | | | | |
| Net Foreign Assets | 31n | 3,344.60 | 1,786.48 | 952.06 | † −510.44 | −1,732.12 | −1,338.66 | 684.64 | 2,872.37 | 5,258.33 | 8,838.00 | 12,563.67 | 12,207.10 |
| Claims on Nonresidents | 31 | 3,599.26 | 2,966.88 | 3,813.25 | † 4,997.14 | 3,834.25 | 4,237.93 | 5,524.42 | 6,925.94 | 7,374.36 | 10,412.66 | 14,083.46 | 13,813.00 |
| Liabilities to Nonresidents | 36c | 254.66 | 1,180.41 | 2,861.19 | † 5,507.57 | 5,566.37 | 5,576.59 | 4,839.78 | 4,053.56 | 2,116.03 | 1,574.66 | 1,519.79 | 1,605.90 |
| Domestic Claims | 32 | 4,218.62 | 6,858.33 | 9,503.51 | † 13,748.41 | 18,590.09 | 21,187.44 | 22,181.21 | 24,688.36 | 23,893.58 | 24,959.32 | 25,984.44 | 30,074.52 |
| Net Claims on Central Government | 32an | 432.53 | 729.69 | 552.88 | † 216.36 | 896.31 | 4,062.71 | 5,380.72 | 6,830.88 | 7,649.55 | 8,638.23 | 9,265.38 | 11,362.34 |
| Claims on Central Government | 32a | 1,345.41 | 1,964.07 | 2,053.31 | † 2,396.70 | 4,164.10 | 7,564.71 | 8,586.89 | 9,112.47 | 9,741.37 | 10,734.23 | 12,405.63 | 14,216.12 |
| Liabilities to Central Government | 36d | 912.87 | 1,234.38 | 1,500.42 | † 2,180.34 | 3,267.79 | 3,502.00 | 3,206.16 | 2,281.59 | 2,091.82 | 2,095.99 | 3,140.25 | 2,853.78 |
| Claims on Other Sectors | 32s | 3,786.09 | 6,128.64 | 8,950.62 | † 13,532.05 | 17,693.78 | 17,124.73 | 16,800.49 | 17,857.48 | 16,244.03 | 16,321.09 | 16,719.06 | 18,712.18 |
| Claims on Other Financial Corps | 32g | 6.43 | 6.43 | 6.43 | † 17.54 | 97.82 | 172.02 | 144.52 | 98.79 | 161.03 | 109.23 | 288.35 | 303.03 |
| Claims on State & Local Govts | 32b | — | — | — | † — | — | — | — | — | — | — | — | — |
| Claims on Public Nonfin. Corps | 32c | 250.00 | 487.92 | 572.50 | † 1,005.39 | 1,377.42 | 1,398.85 | 1,465.00 | 1,668.15 | 1,577.55 | 1,574.43 | 1,333.90 | 1,491.38 |
| Claims on Private Sector | 32d | 3,529.67 | 5,634.29 | 8,371.70 | † 12,509.11 | 16,218.55 | 15,553.85 | 15,190.97 | 16,090.54 | 14,505.45 | 14,637.43 | 15,096.82 | 16,917.78 |
| Broad Money Liabilities | 35l | 6,090.81 | 6,737.21 | 8,008.65 | † 9,938.82 | 12,110.27 | 13,855.28 | 15,883.97 | 19,062.24 | 20,001.61 | 23,676.73 | 27,161.24 | 30,874.44 |
| Currency Outside Depository Corps | 34a | 762.90 | 883.60 | 1,068.13 | † 1,141.95 | 1,510.22 | 1,541.40 | 1,571.05 | 1,857.55 | 2,116.80 | 2,801.89 | 2,682.71 | 2,756.33 |
| Transferable Deposits | 34 | 4,046.40 | 4,762.44 | 5,506.15 | † 7,142.18 | 8,301.52 | 9,958.35 | 10,952.28 | 13,170.82 | 13,678.47 | 16,685.76 | 19,411.09 | 22,873.16 |
| Other Deposits | 35 | 1,076.86 | 881.47 | 1,307.13 | † 1,654.68 | 2,298.54 | 2,355.52 | 3,360.64 | 4,033.87 | 4,206.35 | 4,189.08 | 5,067.44 | 5,244.96 |
| Securities Other than Shares | 36a | 204.66 | 209.71 | 127.25 | † — | — | — | — | — | — | — | — | — |
| Deposits Excl. from Broad Money | 36b | 98.20 | 175.52 | 190.41 | † 241.19 | 181.53 | 218.53 | 302.64 | 336.87 | 285.43 | 380.33 | 385.99 | 358.80 |
| Sec.Ot.th.Shares Excl.f/Brd.Money | 36s | — | — | — | † — | — | — | — | — | — | — | — | — |
| Loans | 36l | — | — | — | † — | — | — | — | — | — | — | — | — |
| Financial Derivatives | 36m | — | — | — | † — | — | — | — | — | — | — | — | — |
| Insurance Technical Reserves | 36r | — | — | — | † — | — | — | — | — | — | — | — | — |
| Shares and Other Equity | 37a | 1,015.72 | 1,253.04 | 2,002.48 | † 2,645.62 | 3,977.79 | 4,682.50 | 5,111.29 | 5,660.90 | 6,362.26 | 7,854.12 | 8,727.50 | 9,674.59 |
| Other Items (Net) | 37r | 358.49 | 479.03 | 254.03 | † 412.34 | 588.38 | 1,092.48 | 1,567.95 | 2,500.72 | 2,502.61 | 1,886.16 | 2,273.38 | 1,373.79 |
| Broad Money Liabs., Seasonally Adj. | 35l.b | 6,165.58 | 6,819.92 | 8,108.05 | † 10,151.00 | 12,366.06 | 14,145.40 | 16,210.40 | 19,459.30 | 20,404.53 | 24,142.70 | 27,662.57 | 31,438.52 |
| **Other Financial Corporations** | | | | | | *Millions of Rufiyaa: End of Period* | | | | | | | |
| Net Foreign Assets | 41n | −51.40 | −55.56 | −105.72 | −87.40 | −130.86 | −99.21 | −175.15 | −245.30 | −172.56 | −126.11 | −105.93 | −100.43 |
| Claims on Nonresidents | 41 | — | — | — | 111.74 | 135.25 | 188.63 | 90.03 | 83.98 | 116.42 | 186.30 | 237.36 | 280.42 |
| Liabilities to Nonresidents | 46c | 51.40 | 55.56 | 105.72 | 199.14 | 266.11 | 287.84 | 265.18 | 329.28 | 288.99 | 312.42 | 343.30 | 380.85 |
| Claims on Depository Corporations | 40 | 38.77 | 3.62 | 3.87 | 114.18 | 323.01 | 424.34 | 329.76 | 410.09 | 412.58 | 509.99 | 466.04 | 583.82 |
| Net Claims on Central Government | 42an | — | — | — | −151.14 | −258.81 | −101.08 | 2,783.28 | 2,903.64 | 3,779.78 | 4,625.97 | 6,081.31 | 7,260.89 |
| Claims on Central Government | 42a | — | — | — | 38.99 | 12.04 | 27.56 | 2,840.10 | 3,037.94 | 3,933.40 | 4,779.55 | 6,195.58 | 7,432.90 |
| Liabilities to Central Government | 46d | — | — | — | 190.13 | 270.85 | 128.65 | 56.82 | 134.31 | 153.62 | 153.58 | 114.27 | 172.01 |
| Claims on Other Sectors | 42s | 94.91 | 149.77 | 224.96 | 555.88 | 574.73 | 596.74 | 648.70 | 1,153.62 | 1,127.48 | 1,227.89 | 1,523.50 | 1,728.29 |
| Claims on State & Local Govts | 42b | — | — | — | — | — | — | — | — | — | — | — | — |
| Claims on Public Nonfin. Corps | 42c | — | — | — | — | 5.82 | 5.65 | 42.44 | 56.05 | 59.37 | 59.95 | 107.88 | 78.90 |
| Claims on Private Sector | 42d | 94.91 | 149.77 | 224.96 | 555.88 | 568.91 | 591.09 | 606.26 | 1,097.57 | 1,068.11 | 1,167.93 | 1,415.62 | 1,649.39 |
| Deposits | 46b | 8.74 | 14.81 | 25.92 | 43.73 | 52.46 | 60.28 | 134.79 | 63.83 | 59.79 | 58.24 | 56.16 | 70.76 |
| Securities Other than Shares | 46s | — | — | — | — | — | — | .54 | .28 | 20.28 | .28 | 3.79 | 3.75 |
| Loans | 46l | — | — | — | 29.48 | 103.52 | 35.87 | 14.54 | 78.18 | 85.11 | 167.96 | 248.32 | 290.85 |
| Financial Derivatives | 46m | — | — | — | — | — | — | — | — | — | — | — | — |
| Insurance Technical Reserves | 46r | — | — | — | 146.54 | 130.49 | 218.27 | 2,825.11 | 3,571.36 | 4,384.22 | 5,320.72 | 6,822.16 | 8,168.08 |
| Shares and Other Equity | 47a | 71.81 | 74.82 | 80.29 | 173.53 | 192.50 | 371.07 | 403.69 | 441.87 | 518.15 | 622.05 | 773.03 | 842.04 |
| Other Items (Net) | 47r | 1.73 | 8.20 | 16.90 | 38.25 | 29.11 | 135.30 | 207.90 | 66.52 | 79.73 | 68.48 | 61.46 | 97.09 |
| Memo Item: | | | | | | | | | | | | | |
| Total Assets | 40ra | 133.98 | 154.37 | 230.19 | 833.05 | 1,063.47 | 1,251.75 | 3,928.44 | 4,755.31 | 5,744.33 | 6,883.38 | 8,624.29 | 10,209.82 |
| **Financial Corporations** | | | | | | *Millions of Rufiyaa: End of Period* | | | | | | | |
| Net Foreign Assets | 51n | 3,293.20 | 1,730.92 | 846.34 | † −597.84 | −1,862.98 | −1,437.86 | 509.48 | 2,627.07 | 5,085.77 | 8,711.89 | 12,457.73 | 12,106.67 |
| Claims on Nonresidents | 51 | 3,599.26 | 2,966.88 | 3,813.25 | † 5,108.87 | 3,969.49 | 4,426.57 | 5,614.45 | 7,009.91 | 7,490.79 | 10,598.96 | 14,320.82 | 14,093.42 |
| Liabilities to Nonresidents | 56c | 306.06 | 1,235.96 | 2,966.91 | † 5,706.71 | 5,832.47 | 5,864.43 | 5,104.96 | 4,382.84 | 2,405.02 | 1,887.07 | 1,863.09 | 1,986.75 |
| Domestic Claims | 52 | 4,307.11 | 7,001.68 | 9,722.04 | † 14,135.61 | 18,808.21 | 21,511.07 | 25,468.67 | 28,646.83 | 28,639.81 | 30,703.95 | 33,300.91 | 38,760.66 |
| Net Claims on Central Government | 52an | 432.53 | 729.69 | 552.88 | † 65.23 | 637.50 | 3,961.62 | 8,164.00 | 9,734.52 | 11,429.33 | 13,264.20 | 15,346.70 | 18,623.22 |
| Claims on Central Government | 52a | 1,345.41 | 1,964.07 | 2,053.31 | † 2,435.69 | 4,176.14 | 7,592.28 | 11,426.98 | 12,150.42 | 13,674.77 | 15,513.77 | 18,601.21 | 21,649.01 |
| Liabilities to Central Government | 56d | 912.87 | 1,234.38 | 1,500.42 | † 2,370.47 | 3,538.63 | 3,630.65 | 3,262.98 | 2,415.90 | 2,245.44 | 2,249.58 | 3,254.51 | 3,025.79 |
| Claims on Other Sectors | 52s | 3,874.57 | 6,271.99 | 9,169.15 | † 14,070.38 | 18,170.70 | 17,549.45 | 17,304.67 | 18,912.31 | 17,210.48 | 17,439.75 | 17,954.21 | 20,137.44 |
| Claims on State & Local Govts | 52b | — | — | — | † — | — | — | — | — | — | — | — | — |
| Claims on Public Nonfin. Corps | 52c | 250.00 | 487.92 | 572.50 | † 1,005.39 | 1,383.25 | 1,404.51 | 1,507.44 | 1,724.20 | 1,636.92 | 1,634.38 | 1,441.78 | 1,570.27 |
| Claims on Private Sector | 52d | 3,624.58 | 5,784.06 | 8,596.65 | † 13,064.99 | 16,787.46 | 16,144.94 | 15,797.23 | 17,188.11 | 15,573.56 | 15,805.37 | 16,512.43 | 18,567.17 |
| Currency Outside Financial Corps | 54a | 762.90 | 883.60 | 1,068.13 | † 1,141.94 | 1,510.20 | 1,538.97 | 1,569.96 | 1,857.54 | 2,115.82 | 2,800.88 | 2,681.54 | 2,755.26 |
| Deposits | 55l | 5,230.19 | 5,834.23 | 7,029.60 | † 9,056.63 | 10,702.86 | 12,177.63 | 14,479.92 | 17,451.27 | 18,004.15 | 21,015.86 | 24,598.65 | 28,005.77 |
| Securities Other than Shares | 56a | 204.66 | 209.71 | 127.25 | † — | — | — | .54 | .28 | 20.28 | .28 | 3.79 | 3.75 |
| Loans | 56l | — | — | — | † — | — | — | — | — | — | — | — | — |
| Financial Derivatives | 56m | — | — | — | † — | — | — | — | — | — | — | — | — |
| Insurance Technical Reserves | 56r | — | — | — | † 146.54 | 130.49 | 218.27 | 2,825.11 | 3,571.36 | 4,380.41 | 5,314.70 | 6,816.74 | 8,163.35 |
| Shares and Other Equity | 57a | 1,087.53 | 1,327.86 | 2,082.76 | † 2,819.15 | 4,170.29 | 5,053.56 | 5,514.98 | 6,102.77 | 6,880.40 | 8,476.16 | 9,500.53 | 10,516.63 |
| Other Items (Net) | 57r | 315.03 | 477.19 | 260.64 | † 373.51 | 431.39 | 1,084.76 | 1,587.63 | 2,290.67 | 2,324.51 | 1,807.96 | 2,157.39 | 1,422.58 |
| **Monetary Aggregates** | | | | | | *Millions of Rufiyaa: End of Period* | | | | | | | |
| Broad Money | 59m | 6,090.81 | 6,737.21 | 8,008.65 | 9,938.82 | 12,110.27 | 13,855.28 | 15,883.97 | 19,062.24 | 20,001.61 | 23,676.73 | 27,161.24 | 30,874.44 |
| o/w:Currency Issued by Cent.Govt | 59m.a | — | — | — | — | — | — | — | — | — | — | — | — |
| o/w: Dep.in Nonfin. Corporations | 59m.b | — | — | — | — | — | — | — | — | — | — | — | — |
| o/w:Secs. Issued by Central Govt | 59m.c | — | — | — | — | — | — | — | — | — | — | — | — |
| Money (National Definitions) | | | | | | | | | | | | | |
| Reserve Money | 19mb | 2,947.98 | 2,978.15 | 3,423.55 | 4,374.15 | 5,382.38 | 6,143.92 | 6,064.30 | 7,551.31 | 8,181.86 | 9,629.07 | 12,502.31 | 10,274.07 |
| Narrow Money | 59mak | 2,477.26 | 3,033.65 | 3,707.60 | 4,448.82 | 6,097.64 | 7,456.61 | 7,538.72 | 8,192.37 | 8,428.29 | 10,415.84 | 11,196.71 | 13,338.74 |
| Quasi Money | 59mal | 3,613.55 | 3,703.56 | 4,301.06 | 5,490.00 | 6,012.64 | 6,398.67 | 8,345.25 | 10,869.87 | 11,573.32 | 13,260.89 | 15,964.53 | 17,535.71 |
| Broad Money | 59mea | 6,090.81 | 6,737.21 | 8,008.65 | 9,938.82 | 12,110.27 | 13,855.28 | 15,883.97 | 19,062.24 | 20,001.61 | 23,676.73 | 27,161.24 | 30,874.44 |

# Maldives 556

| | | 2004 | 2005 | 2006 | 2007 | 2008 | 2009 | 2010 | 2011 | 2012 | 2013 | 2014 | 2015 |
|---|---|---|---|---|---|---|---|---|---|---|---|---|---|
| **Interest Rates** | | | | | | | *Percent Per Annum* | | | | | | | |
| Discount Rate (End of Period).......... | 60.a | 18.00 | 18.00 | † 12.00 | 13.00 | 13.00 | 13.00 | † 16.00 | 16.00 | 16.00 | 12.00 | 10.00 | 10.00 |
| Reverse Repurchase Rate (EOP)........ | 60.d | .... | .... | .... | .... | .... | 4.68 | 4.46 | 6.96 | 7.00 | 7.00 | 7.00 | 7.00 |
| Overnight Deposit Rate (EOP)......... | 60.r | .... | .... | .... | .... | .... | .... | 1.50 | .25 | .25 | 3.00 | 1.50 | 1.50 |
| Treasury Bill Rate............................ | 60c | .... | .... | .... | 5.50 | 6.00 | 6.00 | 4.90 | 5.44 | 7.26 | 8.94 | 8.18 | 6.83 |
| Savings Rate................................... | 60k | † 3.00 | 3.00 | 3.00 | 3.00 | 3.00 | 3.00 | † 2.25 | 2.25 | 2.25 | 2.25 | 2.25 | 2.23 |
| Savings Rate (Fgn. Currency)............ | 60k.f | 3.00 | 3.00 | 3.00 | 3.00 | 3.00 | 3.00 | † 2.40 | 2.27 | 2.24 | 2.22 | 2.28 | 2.29 |
| Deposit Rate.................................. | 60l | 6.50 | 6.50 | 6.50 | 6.50 | 6.50 | 6.50 | † 4.05 | 4.17 | 3.73 | 3.81 | 4.14 | 4.12 |
| Deposit Rate (Fgn. Currency)........... | 60l.f | 6.50 | 6.50 | 6.50 | 6.50 | 6.50 | 6.50 | † 3.94 | 3.92 | 4.04 | 3.76 | 3.23 | 3.00 |
| Lending Rate.................................. | 60p | † 13.00 | 13.00 | 13.00 | 13.00 | 13.00 | 13.00 | † 10.38 | 10.20 | 10.48 | 11.14 | 11.42 | 11.10 |
| Lending Rate (Fgn. Currency).......... | 60p.f | 13.25 | 13.00 | 13.00 | 13.00 | 13.00 | 13.00 | † 8.37 | 8.30 | 8.67 | 8.60 | 8.50 | 8.73 |
| Government Bond Yield................... | 61 | .... | .... | .... | .... | .... | 8.00 | 8.00 | 8.00 | 8.00 | † 7.73 | † 2.40 | 2.40 |
| **Prices, Production, Labor** | | | | | | *Index Numbers (2010=100): Period Averages* | | | | | | | | |
| Share Prices.................................... | 62 | 81.13 | 123.19 | 88.96 | 120.58 | 160.48 | 125.66 | 100.00 | 77.15 | 71.85 | 68.03 | 64.77 | 70.54 |
| Share Prices (End of Month)............. | 62.ep | 82.61 | 121.66 | 86.80 | 123.30 | 158.65 | 125.15 | 100.00 | 76.43 | 71.45 | 67.43 | 64.24 | 70.33 |
| Consumer Prices.............................. | 64 | .... | 72.3 | 74.8 | 80.4 | 90.2 | 93.8 | 100.0 | 112.8 | † 126.5 | 129.4 | 132.2 | 133.4 |
| Total Fish Catch............................... | 66al | 129.5 | 152.2 | 150.7 | 118.0 | 108.5 | 95.5 | 100.0 | 98.9 | 98.2 | 106.3 | 105.3 | .... |
| Tourist Bed Night Index.................. | 66.t | 85.4 | 55.1 | 80.6 | 88.4 | 91.0 | 86.0 | 100.0 | 109.1 | 107.8 | 117.9 | 121.8 | 116.5 |
| **Intl. Transactions & Positions** | | | | | | *Millions of US Dollars* | | | | | | | | |
| Exports........................................... | 70..d | 122.4 | 103.8 | 135.1 | 107.8 | 125.9 | 76.4 | 73.9 | 127.4 | 161.6 | 166.5 | 144.8 | 144.1 |
| Imports, c.i.f.................................. | 71..d | 639.3 | 742.0 | 922.9 | 1,092.0 | 1,382.1 | 962.5 | 1,090.9 | 1,465.3 | 1,554.3 | 1,733.4 | 1,992.5 | 1,896.3 |
| Imports, f.o.b................................ | 71.vd | 562.6 | 682.6 | 849.2 | 999.1 | 1,271.8 | 877.7 | 999.3 | 1,353.4 | 1,436.4 | 1,602.1 | 1,847.3 | .... |
| **Balance of Payments** | | | | | | *Millions of US Dollars* | | | | | | | | |
| A. Current Account*...................... | 109bx | −122.3 | −273.0 | −302.0 | −269.0 | −611.7 | −220.8 | −196.1 | † −383.4 | −184.5 | −127.4 | −117.8 | −295.5 |
| Goods, credit (exports)................... | 1a9cx | 181.0 | 161.6 | 225.2 | 227.0 | 331.4 | 169.0 | 197.5 | † 346.4 | 314.4 | 331.0 | 300.9 | 239.7 |
| Goods, debit (imports).................... | 1a9dx | 564.8 | 655.5 | 815.3 | 1,304.8 | 1,649.0 | 1,081.7 | 1,241.8 | † 1,716.8 | 1,575.8 | 1,703.0 | 1,960.9 | 1,894.5 |
| Balance on goods....................... | 1a9bx | −383.8 | −493.8 | −590.1 | −1,077.8 | −1,317.6 | −912.7 | −1,044.3 | † −1,370.5 | −1,261.4 | −1,372.0 | −1,660.0 | −1,654.8 |
| Services, credit (exports)................. | 1b9cx | 507.7 | 322.9 | 551.9 | 1,576.9 | 1,638.4 | 1,543.2 | 1,809.9 | † 2,104.5 | 2,178.9 | 2,592.1 | 3,015.2 | 2,901.3 |
| Services, debit (imports)................. | 1b9dx | 157.4 | 213.1 | 231.2 | 330.9 | 427.9 | 398.3 | 451.4 | † 581.0 | 570.6 | 696.6 | 793.1 | 829.3 |
| Balance on Goods & Services....... | 1z9bx | −33.6 | −384.0 | −269.4 | 168.2 | −107.2 | 232.2 | 314.2 | † 153.0 | 346.8 | 523.5 | 562.1 | 417.2 |
| Primary income: credit................... | 1c9cx | 9.8 | 10.9 | 15.6 | 26.7 | 14.0 | 5.8 | 4.0 | † 3.6 | 4.2 | 4.2 | 5.6 | 10.1 |
| Primary income: debit.................... | 1c9dx | 44.9 | 41.8 | 56.3 | 307.3 | 303.8 | 278.2 | 315.3 | † 298.2 | 276.3 | 367.9 | 360.9 | 357.4 |
| Balance on gds, serv. & prim. inc. | 1y9bx | −68.8 | −415.0 | −310.1 | −112.4 | −397.0 | −40.2 | 3.0 | † −141.6 | 74.7 | 159.8 | 206.8 | 69.9 |
| Secondary income: credit............... | 1d9ca | 7.6 | 211.5 | 91.3 | 47.9 | 19.8 | 24.5 | 15.4 | † 17.9 | 19.9 | 2.6 | 4.2 | 24.1 |
| Secondary income: debit............... | 1d9da | 61.1 | 69.5 | 83.2 | 204.4 | 234.6 | 205.1 | 214.5 | † 259.7 | 279.1 | 289.8 | 328.8 | 389.5 |
| B. Capital Account*...................... | 209ba | — | — | — | 46.1 | 51.2 | 29.3 | 9.3 | † 28.5 | 17.4 | 7.9 | 6.6 | 23.9 |
| Capital account: credit................... | 209ca | — | — | — | 46.1 | 51.2 | 29.3 | 9.3 | † 28.5 | 17.4 | 7.9 | 6.6 | 23.9 |
| Capital account: debit................... | 209da | — | — | — | — | — | — | — | .... | .... | .... | .... | .... |
| Balance on current & capital acct. | 129ba | −122.3 | −273.0 | −302.0 | −222.9 | −560.5 | −191.5 | −186.8 | † −355.0 | −167.1 | −119.5 | −111.2 | −271.6 |
| C. Financial Account* .................. | 309na | −119.9 | −222.6 | −238.9 | −220.3 | −181.2 | −173.1 | −153.4 | † −416.4 | −187.7 | −67.4 | −543.9 | −363.7 |
| Direct investment: assets............... | 3a9aa | — | — | — | — | — | — | — | .... | .... | .... | .... | .... |
| Equity & investment fund shares.. | 3aaaa | — | — | — | — | — | — | — | .... | .... | .... | .... | .... |
| Debt instruments........................ | 3abaa | — | — | — | — | — | — | — | .... | .... | .... | .... | .... |
| Direct investment: liabilities .......... | 3a9la | 52.9 | 53.0 | 63.8 | 132.4 | 181.3 | 158.0 | 216.5 | † 423.5 | 228.0 | 360.8 | 333.4 | 323.9 |
| Equity & investment fund shares . | 3aala | 52.9 | 53.0 | 63.8 | 132.4 | 181.3 | 158.0 | 216.5 | † 423.5 | 228.0 | 360.8 | 333.4 | 323.9 |
| Debt instruments........................ | 3abla | — | — | — | — | — | — | — | .... | .... | .... | .... | .... |
| Portfolio investment: assets .......... | 3b9aa | — | — | — | — | — | — | — | † — | — | — | 15.3 | 4.9 |
| Equity & investment fund shares | 3baaa | — | — | — | — | — | — | — | † — | — | — | .... | .... |
| Debt securities ........................... | 3bbaa | — | — | — | — | — | — | — | .... | — | .... | 15.3 | 4.9 |
| Portfolio investment: liabilities....... | 3b9la | — | — | — | 3.3 | 11.4 | −12.0 | −12.2 | † .1 | 53.1 | −53.3 | −2.0 | .... |
| Equity & investment fund shares . | 3bala | — | — | — | −.5 | 13.9 | −14.5 | −10.4 | † 2.3 | −2.0 | .2 | −1.2 | .... |
| Debt securities............................ | 3bbla | .... | .... | .... | 3.8 | −2.6 | 2.4 | −1.8 | † −2.2 | 55.1 | −53.5 | −.8 | .... |
| Fin. der.& empl.stk.ops.(ESOs): net. | 3c9na | .... | .... | .... | .... | .... | .... | .... | .... | .... | .... | .... | .... |
| Fin. der. & ESOs.: assets............... | 3c9aa | .... | .... | .... | .... | .... | .... | .... | .... | .... | .... | .... | .... |
| Fin. der. & ESOs.: liabilities.......... | 3c9la | .... | .... | .... | .... | .... | .... | .... | .... | .... | .... | .... | .... |
| Other investment: assets............... | 3d9aa | 15.5 | −32.2 | 20.9 | 152.0 | 117.3 | 143.7 | 165.6 | † 47.8 | 69.2 | 164.7 | −43.9 | 34.6 |
| Other equity............................... | 3daaa | .... | .... | .... | .... | .... | .... | .... | .... | .... | .... | .... | .... |
| Debt instruments........................ | 3dzaa | 15.5 | −32.2 | 20.9 | 152.0 | 117.3 | 143.7 | 165.6 | † 47.8 | 69.2 | 164.7 | −43.9 | 34.6 |
| Other investment: liabilities........... | 3d9la | 82.4 | 137.4 | 196.0 | 236.6 | 105.8 | 170.9 | 114.7 | † 40.6 | −24.2 | −75.4 | 183.9 | 79.3 |
| Other equity............................... | 3dala | .... | .... | .... | .... | .... | .... | .... | .... | .... | .... | .... | .... |
| Debt instruments........................ | 3dzla | 82.4 | 137.4 | 196.0 | 236.6 | 105.8 | 170.9 | 114.7 | † 40.6 | −24.2 | −75.4 | 183.9 | 79.3 |
| Curr.+ cap.− finan. acct. balance... | 4y9na | −2.5 | −50.4 | −63.1 | −2.6 | −379.3 | −18.4 | −33.4 | † 61.5 | 20.6 | −52.1 | 432.7 | 92.1 |
| D. Net Errors and Omissions............. | 409na | 46.5 | 27.1 | 108.1 | 79.3 | 314.0 | 33.8 | 115.7 | † −76.6 | −51.0 | 121.4 | −179.3 | −141.3 |
| E. Reserves and Related Items.......... | 4z9na | 44.1 | −23.3 | 45.0 | 76.7 | −65.3 | 15.4 | 82.3 | † −15.2 | −30.4 | 69.2 | 253.4 | −49.1 |
| Reserve assets............................... | 3e9aa | 44.1 | −17.1 | 45.0 | 76.7 | −67.7 | 20.3 | 89.4 | † −15.2 | −30.4 | 63.8 | 247.2 | −50.2 |
| Credit and loans from the IMF........ | 3dcla | — | 6.3 | — | — | −2.4 | 4.9 | 7.0 | † — | .... | −5.5 | −6.2 | −1.1 |
| Exceptional financing..................... | 409la | — | — | — | — | — | — | — | .... | .... | .... | .... | .... |

*Excludes components in group E

# Maldives 556

| | | 2004 | 2005 | 2006 | 2007 | 2008 | 2009 | 2010 | 2011 | 2012 | 2013 | 2014 | 2015 |
|---|---|---|---|---|---|---|---|---|---|---|---|---|---|
| **International Investment Position** | | | | | | | *Millions of US Dollars* | | | | | | | |
| Assets............................ | 809aa | 284.5 | 234.2 | 300.3 | 390.4 | 299.5 | 331.1 | 431.6 | 449.4 | .... | .... | .... | .... |
| Direct investment.......................... | 8a9aa | .... | .... | .... | .... | .... | .... | .... | .... | .... | .... | .... | .... |
| Equity & investment fund shares.. | 8aaaa | .... | .... | .... | .... | .... | .... | .... | .... | .... | .... | .... | .... |
| Debt instruments...................... | 8abaa | .... | .... | .... | .... | .... | .... | .... | .... | .... | .... | .... | .... |
| Portfolio investment...................... | 8b9aa | .... | .... | .... | .... | .... | .... | .... | .... | .... | .... | .... | .... |
| Equity & investment fund shares.. | 8baaa | .... | .... | .... | .... | .... | .... | .... | .... | .... | .... | .... | .... |
| Debt securities............................ | 8bbaa | .... | .... | .... | .... | .... | .... | .... | .... | .... | .... | .... | .... |
| Fin. der.(oth.than reserves) & ESOs | 8c9aa | .... | .... | .... | .... | .... | .... | .... | .... | .... | .... | .... | .... |
| Other investment.......................... | 8d9aa | 79.4 | 47.1 | 68.1 | 81.2 | 58.2 | 69.4 | 80.8 | 113.9 | .... | .... | .... | .... |
| Other equity.......................... | 8daaa | .... | .... | .... | .... | .... | .... | .... | .... | .... | .... | .... | .... |
| Debt instruments...................... | 8dzaa | 79.4 | 47.1 | 68.1 | 81.2 | 58.2 | 69.4 | 80.8 | 113.9 | .... | .... | .... | .... |
| Reserve assets.......................... | 8e9aa | 205.2 | 187.1 | 232.2 | 309.2 | 241.3 | 261.7 | 350.8 | 335.5 | .... | .... | .... | .... |
| Liabilities.............................. | 809la | 333.1 | 410.5 | 588.6 | 864.6 | 916.5 | 982.8 | 1,005.6 | 946.4 | .... | .... | .... | .... |
| Direct investment.......................... | 8a9la | .... | .... | .... | .... | .... | .... | .... | .... | .... | .... | .... | .... |
| Equity & investment fund shares.. | 8aala | .... | .... | .... | .... | .... | .... | .... | .... | .... | .... | .... | .... |
| Debt instruments...................... | 8abla | .... | .... | .... | .... | .... | .... | .... | .... | .... | .... | .... | .... |
| Portfolio investment...................... | 8b9la | .... | .... | .... | 15.7 | 27.1 | 15.1 | 2.9 | .... | .... | .... | .... | .... |
| Equity & investment fund shares.. | 8bala | .... | .... | .... | 11.7 | 25.6 | 11.1 | .7 | .... | .... | .... | .... | .... |
| Debt securities............................ | 8bbla | .... | .... | .... | 4.1 | 1.5 | 3.9 | 2.2 | .... | .... | .... | .... | .... |
| Fin. der.(oth.than reserves) & ESOs | 8c9la | .... | .... | .... | .... | .... | .... | .... | .... | .... | .... | .... | .... |
| Other investment.......................... | 8d9la | 333.1 | 410.5 | 588.6 | 848.9 | 889.4 | 967.7 | 1,002.7 | 946.4 | .... | .... | .... | .... |
| Other equity.......................... | 8dala | .... | .... | .... | .... | .... | .... | .... | .... | .... | .... | .... | .... |
| Debt instruments...................... | 8dzla | 333.1 | 410.5 | 588.6 | 848.9 | 889.4 | 967.7 | 1,002.7 | 946.4 | .... | .... | .... | .... |
| **Government Finance** | | | | | | | | | | | | | | |
| **Cash Flow Statement** | | | | | | | | | | | | | | |
| **General Government** | | | | | | | *Millions of Rufiyaa: Fiscal Year Ends December 31* | | | | | | | |
| Cash Receipts:Operating Activities... | c1 | 3,404.0 | 4,577.9 | 6,104.7 | 7,534.7 | 7,414.2 | 5,720.9 | 6,497.6 | 9,370.1 | .... | .... | 14,750.7 | .... |
| Taxes............................ | c11 | 1,647.2 | 1,722.8 | 2,370.4 | 2,905.1 | 3,366.8 | 2,732.0 | 2,931.1 | 4,893.0 | .... | .... | 11,068.4 | .... |
| Social Contributions...................... | c12 | — | | | | | | | — | .... | .... | — | .... |
| Grants.................................... | c13 | 72.9 | 824.6 | 867.4 | 1,044.0 | 517.0 | 421.5 | 154.5 | 732.5 | .... | .... | 163.8 | .... |
| Other Receipts.............................. | c14 | 1,683.9 | 2,030.5 | 2,866.9 | 3,585.6 | 3,530.4 | 2,567.4 | 3,412.0 | 3,744.7 | .... | .... | 3,518.6 | .... |
| Cash Payments:Operating Activities. | c2 | 2,788.1 | 4,643.3 | 5,607.8 | 6,560.1 | 7,463.2 | 8,764.9 | 8,428.1 | 9,075.7 | .... | .... | 14,252.2 | .... |
| Compensation of Employees.......... | c21 | 718.7 | 974.3 | 1,085.1 | 1,208.5 | 2,589.9 | 2,944.8 | 2,486.5 | 5,725.6 | .... | .... | 5,842.2 | .... |
| Purchases of Goods & Services....... | c22 | 1,882.1 | 3,286.6 | 4,174.1 | 4,949.0 | 4,115.1 | 4,780.6 | 4,627.0 | 1,627.4 | .... | .... | 2,851.1 | .... |
| Interest.................................. | c24 | 138.6 | 154.9 | 198.8 | 234.3 | 280.0 | 617.9 | 675.8 | 725.8 | .... | .... | 978.3 | .... |
| Subsidies.................................. | c25 | 48.7 | 227.5 | 149.8 | 168.3 | 479.2 | 421.6 | 638.8 | 748.9 | .... | .... | 1,677.8 | .... |
| Grants.................................... | c26 | — | — | — | — | — | — | — | — | .... | .... | .1 | .... |
| Social Benefits.............................. | c27 | — | — | — | — | — | — | — | 248.0 | .... | .... | 2,358.0 | .... |
| Other Payments.......................... | c28 | — | — | — | — | — | — | — | — | .... | .... | 544.5 | .... |
| Net Cash Inflow:Operating Act.[1-2] | ccio | 615.9 | −65.4 | 496.9 | 974.6 | −49.0 | −3,044.0 | −1,930.5 | 294.4 | .... | .... | 498.5 | .... |
| Net Cash Outflow:Invest. in NFA.... | c31 | 970.3 | 1,097.1 | 1,408.9 | 1,728.8 | 2,836.9 | 2,325.4 | 2,518.9 | 3,053.5 | .... | .... | .... | .... |
| Purchases of Nonfinancial Assets.... | c31.1 | 991.0 | 1,132.1 | 1,458.4 | 1,765.3 | 2,879.2 | 2,339.3 | 2,568.3 | 3,588.0 | .... | .... | .... | .... |
| Sales of Nonfinancial Assets.......... | c31.2 | 20.7 | 35.0 | 49.5 | 36.5 | 42.3 | 13.9 | 49.4 | 534.5 | .... | .... | .... | .... |
| Cash Surplus/Deficit [1-2-31=1-2M] | ccsd | −354.4 | −1,162.5 | −912.1 | −754.1 | −2,885.9 | −5,369.4 | −4,449.4 | −2,759.1 | .... | .... | .... | .... |
| Net Acq. Fin. Assets, excl. Cash....... | c32x | −196.5 | −117.8 | −108.8 | −42.2 | −166.4 | −150.8 | −181.3 | −717.4 | .... | .... | .... | .... |
| Domestic.............................. | c321x | −196.5 | −118.6 | −108.8 | −42.2 | −166.4 | −150.8 | −181.3 | −717.4 | .... | .... | .... | .... |
| Foreign.................................. | c322x | — | .8 | | | | | | | .... | .... | .... | .... |
| Net Incurrence of Liabilities.............. | c33 | 206.0 | 1,102.9 | 851.6 | 766.1 | 2,750.0 | 5,216.0 | 4,315.7 | 2,360.1 | .... | .... | .... | .... |
| Domestic.............................. | c331 | −197.7 | 867.9 | 313.1 | 68.8 | 2,002.3 | 4,209.8 | 3,087.5 | 1,392.1 | .... | .... | .... | .... |
| Foreign.................................. | c332 | 403.7 | 235.0 | 538.5 | 697.3 | 747.7 | 1,006.2 | 1,228.2 | 968.0 | .... | .... | .... | .... |
| Net Cash Inflow, Fin.Act.[-32x+33].. | cnfb | 402.5 | 1,220.7 | 960.4 | 808.3 | 2,916.4 | 5,366.8 | 4,497.0 | 3,077.5 | .... | .... | .... | .... |
| Net Change in Stock of Cash........ | cncb | 48.1 | 58.2 | 48.3 | 54.2 | 30.5 | −2.6 | 47.6 | 318.4 | .... | .... | .... | .... |
| Stat. Discrep. [32X-33+NCB-CSD].... | ccsdz | — | — | — | — | — | — | — | — | .... | .... | .... | .... |
| Memo Item:Cash Expenditure[2+31] | c2m | 3,779.1 | 5,740.4 | 7,066.2 | 8,325.3 | 10,342.4 | 11,104.3 | 10,996.4 | 12,663.7 | .... | .... | .... | .... |
| Memo Item: Gross Debt.................. | c63 | 4,282.8 | 5,052.1 | 5,956.2 | 6,979.5 | 8,822.9 | 13,867.2 | 18,182.8 | 23,212.1 | .... | .... | .... | .... |
| **National Accounts** | | | | | | | *Millions of Rufiyaa* | | | | | | | |
| Househ.Cons.Expend.,incl.NPISHs.... | 96f | 2,724 | .... | .... | .... | .... | .... | .... | .... | .... | .... | .... | .... |
| Government Consumption Expend... | 91f | 2,433 | .... | .... | .... | .... | .... | .... | .... | .... | .... | .... | .... |
| Gross Fixed Capital Formation......... | 93e | 3,573 | .... | .... | .... | .... | .... | .... | .... | .... | .... | .... | .... |
| Exports of Goods and Services......... | 90c | 9,183 | .... | .... | .... | .... | .... | .... | .... | .... | .... | .... | .... |
| Imports of Goods and Services (-).... | 98c | 8,539 | .... | .... | .... | .... | .... | .... | .... | .... | .... | .... | .... |
| Gross Domestic Product (GDP)......... | 99b | 15,389 | 14,334 | 18,876 | 22,349 | 27,008 | 27,511 | 29,740 | 35,768 | 38,693 | .... | 47,122 | .... |
| GDP Volume 1995 Prices................ | 99b.p | .... | .... | .... | .... | .... | .... | .... | .... | .... | .... | .... | .... |
| GDP Volume 2003 Prices................. | 99b.p | 15,113 | 13,885 | 16,647 | 18,340 | 20,664 | 19,564 | 20,966 | 22,792 | 23,361 | .... | 26,044 | .... |
| GDP Volume (2010=100)................ | 99bvp | 72.1 | 66.2 | 79.4 | 87.5 | 98.6 | 93.3 | 100.0 | 108.7 | 111.4 | .... | 124.2 | .... |
| GDP Deflator (2010=100)............... | 99bip | 71.8 | 72.8 | 79.9 | 85.9 | 92.1 | 99.1 | 100.0 | 110.6 | 116.8 | .... | 127.6 | .... |
| | | | | | | | *Millions: Midyear Estimates* | | | | | | | |
| **Population................................** | 99z | .30 | .30 | .31 | .32 | .32 | .33 | .33 | .34 | .34 | .35 | .36 | .36 |

# Mali 678

| | | 2004 | 2005 | 2006 | 2007 | 2008 | 2009 | 2010 | 2011 | 2012 | 2013 | 2014 | 2015 |
|---|---|---|---|---|---|---|---|---|---|---|---|---|---|
| **Exchange Rates** | | | | | | *CFA Francs per SDR: End of Period* | | | | | | | |
| Official Rate | aa | 747.90 | 794.73 | 749.30 | 704.15 | 725.98 | 713.83 | 756.02 | 778.32 | 764.10 | 732.49 | 782.77 | 834.92 |
| | | | | | | *CFA Francs per US Dollar: End of Period (ae) Period Average (rf)* | | | | | | | |
| Official Rate | ae | 481.58 | 556.04 | 498.07 | 445.59 | 471.34 | 455.34 | 490.91 | 506.96 | 497.16 | 475.64 | 540.28 | 602.51 |
| Official Rate | rf | 528.28 | 527.47 | 522.89 | 479.27 | 447.81 | 472.19 | 495.28 | 471.87 | 510.53 | 494.04 | 494.41 | 591.45 |
| **Fund Position** | | | | | | *Millions of SDRs: End of Period* | | | | | | | |
| Quota | 2f.s | 93.30 | 93.30 | 93.30 | 93.30 | 93.30 | 93.30 | 93.30 | 93.30 | 93.30 | 93.30 | 93.30 | 93.30 |
| SDR Holdings | 1b.s | .40 | .19 | .03 | .05 | .05 | 73.38 | 73.44 | 73.39 | 73.38 | 73.37 | 73.35 | 68.55 |
| Reserve Position in the Fund | 1c.s | 8.97 | 9.14 | 9.34 | 9.58 | 9.69 | 9.89 | 10.00 | 10.00 | 10.00 | 10.00 | 10.00 | 10.00 |
| Total Fund Cred.&Loans Outstg. | 2tl | 93.24 | 76.40 | 5.33 | 8.00 | 25.99 | 27.99 | 31.86 | 60.32 | 65.13 | 90.23 | 93.03 | 95.36 |
| SDR Allocations | 1bd | 15.91 | 15.91 | 15.91 | 15.91 | 15.91 | 89.36 | 89.36 | 89.36 | 89.36 | 89.36 | 89.36 | 89.36 |
| **International Liquidity** | | | | | | *Millions of US Dollars Unless Otherwise Indicated: End of Period* | | | | | | | |
| Total Reserves minus Gold | 1l.d | 851.3 | 854.3 | 969.5 | 1,087.1 | 1,071.5 | 1,604.5 | 1,344.4 | 1,378.6 | 1,341.4 | 1,305.7 | 860.8 | 624.0 |
| SDR Holdings | 1b.d | .6 | .3 | .1 | .1 | .1 | 115.0 | 113.1 | 112.7 | 112.8 | 113.0 | 106.3 | 95.0 |
| Reserve Position in the Fund | 1c.d | 13.9 | 13.1 | 14.1 | 15.1 | 14.9 | 15.5 | 15.4 | 15.4 | 15.4 | 15.4 | 14.5 | 13.9 |
| Foreign Exchange | 1d.d | 836.8 | 840.9 | 955.4 | 1,071.9 | 1,056.5 | 1,473.9 | 1,215.9 | 1,250.6 | 1,213.2 | 1,177.3 | 740.1 | 515.1 |
| Gold (Million Fine Troy Ounces) | 1ad | — | — | — | — | — | — | — | — | — | — | — | — |
| Gold (National Valuation) | 1and | — | — | — | — | — | — | — | — | — | — | — | .... |
| Monetary Authorities: Other Liabs. | 4..d | 8.6 | 7.4 | 10.6 | 10.0 | 23.3 | 13.8 | 35.3 | 5.3 | 12.6 | 12.6 | 18.7 | 13.3 |
| Deposit Money Banks: Assets | 7a.d | 278.9 | 245.5 | 376.4 | 445.0 | 404.7 | 640.1 | 859.9 | 771.8 | 870.8 | 1,183.9 | 1,349.6 | 1,311.6 |
| Deposit Money Banks: Liabs. | 7b.d | 178.8 | 198.5 | 247.8 | 297.2 | 342.4 | 425.6 | 516.4 | 556.8 | 559.8 | 586.1 | 791.4 | 779.1 |
| **Monetary Authorities** | | | | | | *Billions of CFA Francs: End of Period* | | | | | | | |
| Foreign Assets | 11 | 410.0 | 475.0 | 482.9 | 484.4 | 505.1 | 730.6 | 660.0 | 698.9 | 666.9 | 621.0 | 465.1 | 376.0 |
| Claims on Central Government | 12a | 99.1 | 83.6 | 19.5 | 19.1 | 29.3 | 77.7 | 78.2 | 99.8 | 99.3 | 110.9 | 106.5 | 101.8 |
| Claims on Deposit Money Banks | 12e | — | — | — | 7.0 | 22.3 | 16.2 | 67.4 | 74.9 | 115.7 | 261.0 | 458.8 | 578.6 |
| Claims on Other Financial Insts. | 12f | — | — | — | — | — | — | — | — | — | — | — | — |
| Reserve Money | 14 | 402.7 | 462.3 | 449.5 | 467.5 | 492.3 | 542.1 | 545.1 | 643.5 | 733.6 | 742.5 | 709.9 | 759.2 |
| of which: Currency Outside DMBs. | 14a | 275.4 | 344.9 | 343.7 | 323.9 | 318.3 | 304.6 | 312.3 | 415.4 | 514.3 | 510.0 | 438.3 | 415.2 |
| Foreign Liabilities | 16c | 85.8 | 77.5 | 21.2 | 21.3 | 41.4 | 90.0 | 109.0 | 119.2 | 124.3 | 137.5 | 152.9 | 162.3 |
| Central Government Deposits | 16d | 15.7 | 21.2 | 30.0 | 19.3 | 22.6 | 190.2 | 152.2 | 111.0 | 23.4 | 110.9 | 171.7 | 136.6 |
| Other Items (Net) | 17r | 4.9 | −2.4 | 1.7 | 2.5 | .4 | 2.1 | −.8 | −.1 | .5 | 2.1 | −4.1 | −1.7 |
| **Deposit Money Banks** | | | | | | *Billions of CFA Francs: End of Period* | | | | | | | |
| Reserves | 20 | 125.0 | 109.8 | 89.5 | 138.8 | 179.2 | 215.6 | 232.3 | 225.2 | 216.1 | 210.6 | 255.6 | 317.7 |
| Foreign Assets | 21 | 134.3 | 136.5 | 187.4 | 198.3 | 190.7 | 291.5 | 422.1 | 391.3 | 432.9 | 563.1 | 729.2 | 790.3 |
| Claims on Central Government | 22a | 15.7 | 43.6 | 30.0 | 67.1 | 63.4 | 92.0 | 93.4 | 115.0 | 111.7 | 171.9 | 329.0 | 432.8 |
| Claims on Private Sector | 22d | 515.4 | 481.4 | 574.9 | 617.9 | 671.2 | 740.7 | 841.4 | 1,049.3 | 1,099.2 | 1,232.2 | 1,458.2 | 1,747.5 |
| Claims on Other Financial Insts. | 22f | — | — | — | — | — | — | — | — | — | — | — | — |
| Demand Deposits | 24 | 294.1 | 297.5 | 356.4 | 375.4 | 416.2 | 495.5 | 610.7 | 677.2 | 769.5 | 808.0 | 972.0 | 1,134.0 |
| Time Deposits | 25 | 197.1 | 197.6 | 208.9 | 288.9 | 264.4 | 344.4 | 361.8 | 392.2 | 428.9 | 497.2 | 556.0 | 688.3 |
| Foreign Liabilities | 26c | 69.1 | 94.8 | 106.3 | 114.6 | 130.0 | 162.6 | 212.3 | 260.2 | 262.2 | 238.4 | 378.7 | 412.5 |
| Long-Term Foreign Liabilities | 26cl | 17.0 | 15.5 | 17.1 | 17.9 | 31.4 | 31.2 | 41.2 | 22.1 | 16.1 | 40.4 | 48.8 | 56.9 |
| Central Government Deposits | 26d | 158.6 | 133.6 | 147.3 | 190.1 | 225.0 | 267.2 | 288.6 | 307.0 | 241.8 | 276.7 | 349.4 | 445.2 |
| Credit from Monetary Authorities | 26g | — | — | — | 7.1 | 22.3 | 14.9 | 39.9 | 41.2 | 78.2 | 238.3 | 398.8 | 566.6 |
| Capital Accounts | 27a | 84.8 | 87.3 | 91.0 | 108.5 | 124.5 | 153.7 | 170.0 | 193.8 | 200.3 | 216.1 | 242.6 | 302.8 |
| Other Items (Net) | 27r | −30.2 | −55.0 | −45.2 | −80.3 | −109.5 | −129.8 | −135.4 | −112.9 | −136.9 | −137.4 | −174.5 | −318.3 |
| Treasury Claims: Private Sector | 22d.i | .1 | .8 | .4 | .5 | .1 | .1 | .3 | — | — | — | — | — |
| Post Office: Checking Deposits | 24..i | — | — | — | — | — | — | — | — | — | — | — | — |
| **Monetary Survey** | | | | | | *Billions of CFA Francs: End of Period* | | | | | | | |
| Foreign Assets (Net) | 31n | 389.4 | 439.2 | 542.8 | 546.8 | 524.4 | 769.4 | 760.9 | 710.8 | 713.3 | 808.2 | 662.6 | 591.4 |
| Domestic Credit | 32 | 455.8 | 453.8 | 447.1 | 494.8 | 516.2 | 453.0 | 572.1 | 846.1 | 1,045.0 | 1,127.3 | 1,372.6 | 1,700.2 |
| Claims on Central Govt. (Net) | 32an | −59.7 | −28.4 | −128.2 | −123.5 | −155.0 | −287.7 | −269.6 | −203.2 | −54.2 | −104.9 | −85.6 | −47.3 |
| Claims on Private Sector | 32d | 515.5 | 482.2 | 575.2 | 618.3 | 671.2 | 740.7 | 841.7 | 1,049.3 | 1,099.2 | 1,232.2 | 1,458.2 | 1,747.5 |
| Claims on Other Financial Insts. | 32f | — | — | — | — | — | — | — | — | — | — | — | — |
| Money | 34 | 569.7 | 642.7 | 700.5 | 699.7 | 734.9 | 800.5 | 923.1 | 1,092.9 | 1,284.2 | 1,318.4 | 1,410.6 | 1,550.0 |
| Quasi-Money | 35 | 197.1 | 197.6 | 208.9 | 288.9 | 264.4 | 344.4 | 361.8 | 392.2 | 428.9 | 497.2 | 556.0 | 688.3 |
| Long-Term Foreign Liabilities | 36cl | 17.0 | 15.5 | 17.1 | 17.9 | 31.4 | 31.2 | 41.2 | 22.1 | 16.1 | 40.4 | 48.8 | 56.9 |
| Other Items (Net) | 37r | 61.5 | 37.2 | 63.4 | 35.2 | 9.9 | 46.4 | 6.7 | 49.7 | 29.2 | 79.6 | 19.8 | −3.6 |
| Money plus Quasi-Money | 35l | 766.8 | 840.3 | 909.3 | 988.5 | 999.3 | 1,144.8 | 1,285.0 | 1,485.1 | 1,713.1 | 1,815.5 | 1,966.6 | 2,238.3 |
| **Interest Rates** | | | | | | *Percent Per Annum* | | | | | | | |
| Repurchase Agreement Rate | 60.q | 4.00 | 4.00 | 4.25 | 4.25 | 4.75 | 4.25 | 4.25 | 4.25 | 4.00 | 3.50 | 3.50 | 3.50 |
| Deposit Rate | 60l | 3.50 | 3.50 | 3.50 | 3.50 | 3.50 | 3.50 | 3.50 | 3.50 | 3.50 | 3.50 | 3.50 | 3.50 |
| **Prices** | | | | | | *Index Numbers (2010=100): Period Averages* | | | | | | | |
| Consumer Prices | 64 | 80.7 | 85.9 | 87.2 | 88.4 | †96.5 | 98.9 | 100.0 | 102.9 | 108.4 | 107.8 | 108.7 | 110.3 |
| **Intl. Transactions & Positions** | | | | | | *Billions of CFA Francs* | | | | | | | |
| Exports | 70 | 515.83 | 580.70 | 810.48 | 745.86 | 939.10 | 841.30 | 989.20 | 1,128.30 | 1,104.60 | .... | .... | .... |
| Imports, c.i.f. | 71 | 720.58 | 814.20 | 951.54 | 1,047.12 | 1,495.19 | 1,174.00 | 1,693.10 | 1,597.00 | 1,500.00 | .... | .... | .... |

# Mali 678

| Balance of Payments | | 2004 | 2005 | 2006 | 2007 | 2008 | 2009 | 2010 | 2011 | 2012 | 2013 | 2014 | 2015 |
|---|---|---|---|---|---|---|---|---|---|---|---|---|---|
| | | | | | | | *Millions of US Dollars* | | | | | | |
| A. Current Account* | 109bx | −409.0 | † −437.7 | −218.6 | −581.1 | −1,063.4 | −654.8 | −1,190.0 | −656.4 | −272.7 | −374.7 | .... | .... |
| Goods, credit (exports) | 1a9cx | 976.4 | † 1,100.9 | 1,550.2 | 1,555.7 | 2,095.7 | 1,772.2 | 2,052.6 | 2,389.8 | 3,001.1 | 2,873.3 | .... | .... |
| Goods, debit (imports) | 1a9dx | 1,090.9 | † 1,243.5 | 1,473.2 | 1,844.5 | 2,730.5 | 1,982.3 | 2,717.2 | 2,722.6 | 2,889.5 | 3,121.9 | .... | .... |
| Balance on goods | 1a9bx | −114.4 | † −142.7 | 77.1 | −288.8 | −634.9 | −210.1 | −664.6 | −332.8 | 111.7 | −248.6 | .... | .... |
| Services, credit (exports) | 1b9cx | 241.1 | † 274.3 | 313.4 | 377.2 | 455.8 | 355.8 | 383.7 | 410.9 | 345.0 | 428.6 | .... | .... |
| Services, debit (imports) | 1b9dx | 533.8 | † 590.0 | 676.6 | 778.1 | 1,026.6 | 829.6 | 1,027.6 | 1,128.4 | 1,064.3 | 2,157.4 | .... | .... |
| Balance on Goods & Services | 1z9bx | −407.1 | † −458.3 | −286.2 | −689.7 | −1,205.7 | −683.9 | −1,308.5 | −1,050.3 | −607.6 | −1,977.4 | .... | .... |
| Primary income: credit | 1c9cx | 24.0 | † 67.7 | 69.0 | 71.4 | 101.6 | 81.6 | 71.8 | 58.4 | 81.1 | 82.2 | .... | .... |
| Primary income: debit | 1c9dx | 218.8 | † 274.7 | 326.5 | 362.8 | 414.3 | 539.0 | 490.7 | 520.2 | 541.1 | 514.8 | .... | .... |
| Balance on gds, serv. & prim. inc. | 1y9bx | −601.9 | † −665.3 | −543.7 | −981.1 | −1,518.3 | −1,141.2 | −1,727.5 | −1,512.1 | −1,067.6 | −2,410.0 | .... | .... |
| Secondary income: credit | 1d9ca | 251.3 | † 286.0 | 380.9 | 482.8 | 554.0 | 648.3 | 700.8 | 986.4 | 907.4 | 2,178.2 | .... | .... |
| Secondary income: debit | 1d9da | 58.3 | † 58.5 | 55.8 | 82.9 | 99.2 | 161.9 | 163.3 | 130.7 | 112.5 | 142.9 | .... | .... |
| B. Capital Account* | 209ba | 151.4 | † 148.9 | 140.6 | 301.8 | 328.8 | 384.0 | 229.6 | 361.8 | 91.7 | 210.2 | .... | .... |
| Capital account: credit | 209ca | 151.5 | † 149.5 | 141.2 | 302.4 | 329.6 | 384.8 | 230.5 | 361.8 | 96.1 | 211.8 | .... | .... |
| Capital account: debit | 209da | — | † .6 | .6 | .6 | .8 | .8 | .9 | .... | 4.4 | 1.6 | .... | .... |
| Balance on current & capital acct. | 129ba | −257.5 | † −288.8 | −78.0 | −279.4 | −734.6 | −270.8 | −960.4 | −294.6 | −180.9 | −164.5 | .... | .... |
| C. Financial Account* | 309na | −99.9 | † −333.4 | 1,922.1 | −229.5 | −623.8 | −892.4 | −752.3 | −359.8 | −109.8 | 14.4 | .... | .... |
| Direct investment: assets | 3a9aa | −15.4 | † −64.6 | 78.0 | 140.6 | 86.7 | −102.8 | −26.9 | 4.4 | 16.0 | 2.9 | .... | .... |
| Equity & investment fund shares | 3aaaa | −24.2 | † 76.9 | 79.9 | 151.9 | 168.5 | 272.6 | 13.0 | 4.4 | 16.0 | 2.9 | .... | .... |
| Debt instruments | 3abaa | 8.8 | † −141.6 | −2.0 | −11.3 | −81.8 | −375.3 | −39.9 | .... | .... | .... | .... | .... |
| Direct investment: liabilities | 3a9la | 84.8 | † 160.2 | 148.2 | 206.1 | 266.4 | 646.6 | 371.6 | 556.1 | 397.9 | 307.9 | .... | .... |
| Equity & investment fund shares | 3aala | 66.0 | † 160.4 | 146.6 | 209.3 | 268.4 | 645.0 | 373.2 | 392.9 | 188.5 | 94.7 | .... | .... |
| Debt instruments | 3abla | 18.9 | † −.2 | 1.6 | −3.3 | −1.9 | 1.6 | −1.6 | 163.2 | 209.3 | 213.2 | .... | .... |
| Portfolio investment: assets | 3b9aa | 3.2 | † 18.0 | 6.9 | 31.1 | 117.9 | 60.3 | 462.2 | 7.7 | 53.9 | 118.3 | .... | .... |
| Equity & investment fund shares | 3baaa | 5.1 | .... | .3 | .... | 2.2 | 6.3 | −.2 | −1.2 | .1 | .8 | .... | .... |
| Debt securities | 3bbaa | −1.9 | † 18.0 | 6.6 | 31.1 | 115.7 | 54.0 | 462.4 | 8.9 | 53.7 | 117.5 | .... | .... |
| Portfolio investment: liabilities | 3b9la | .6 | † 2.9 | −4.2 | −15.5 | 22.6 | 21.3 | 7.1 | 62.6 | 12.6 | 10.4 | .... | .... |
| Equity & investment fund shares | 3bala | −.7 | † 8.9 | 2.8 | −6.4 | −3.0 | −3.0 | 1.2 | 1.6 | −3.9 | −.7 | .... | .... |
| Debt securities | 3bbla | 1.3 | † −6.0 | −6.9 | −9.1 | 25.6 | 24.3 | 6.0 | 61.0 | 16.6 | 11.2 | .... | .... |
| Fin. der.& empl.stk.ops.(ESOs): net | 3c9na | .4 | † .1 | — | .1 | −3.6 | 1.6 | 3.9 | .... | .... | .... | .... | .... |
| Fin. der. & ESOs: assets | 3c9aa | .4 | † .1 | — | .1 | −3.6 | 1.6 | 3.9 | .... | .... | .... | .... | .... |
| Fin. der. & ESOs: liabilities | 3c9la | — | .... | .... | .... | .... | .... | .... | .... | .... | .... | .... | .... |
| Other investment: assets | 3d9aa | 130.9 | † 109.2 | 209.3 | 68.4 | −205.5 | 370.7 | −304.9 | 468.1 | 218.8 | 311.4 | .... | .... |
| Other equity | 3daaa | .... | .... | .... | .... | .... | .... | .... | .... | .... | .... | .... | .... |
| Debt instruments | 3dzaa | 130.9 | † 109.2 | 209.3 | 68.4 | −205.5 | 370.7 | −304.9 | 468.1 | 218.8 | 311.4 | .... | .... |
| Other investment: liabilities | 3d9la | 133.5 | † 232.9 | −1,771.9 | 279.1 | 330.4 | 554.3 | 507.9 | 221.2 | −12.1 | 99.9 | .... | .... |
| Other equity | 3dala | .... | .... | .... | .... | .... | .... | .... | .... | .... | .... | .... | .... |
| Debt instruments | 3dzla | 133.5 | † 232.9 | −1,771.9 | 279.1 | 330.4 | 554.3 | 507.9 | 221.2 | −12.1 | 99.9 | .... | .... |
| Curr.+ cap.− finan. acct. balance | 4y9na | −157.7 | † 44.6 | −2,000.1 | −49.9 | −110.8 | 621.6 | −208.1 | 65.2 | −71.1 | −178.9 | .... | .... |
| D. Net Errors and Omissions | 409na | −26.3 | † −29.1 | −34.9 | 30.2 | 31.1 | −175.3 | 31.2 | −60.7 | −9.5 | −34.0 | .... | .... |
| E. Reserves and Related Items | 4z9na | −184.0 | † 15.5 | −2,035.0 | −19.7 | −79.7 | 446.3 | −176.9 | 4.5 | −80.6 | −212.9 | .... | .... |
| Reserve assets | 3e9aa | −159.9 | † 122.7 | 14.9 | 4.6 | 46.3 | 481.5 | −143.5 | 78.5 | −60.4 | −92.6 | .... | .... |
| Credit and loans from the IMF | 3dcla | −30.1 | † −24.8 | −102.8 | 4.1 | 28.6 | 3.1 | 5.9 | 45.1 | 7.4 | 38.3 | .... | .... |
| Exceptional financing | 409la | 54.2 | † 132.0 | 2,152.7 | 20.1 | 97.4 | 32.1 | 27.6 | 28.9 | 12.8 | 82.0 | .... | .... |

*Excludes components in group E

| International Investment Position | | 2004 | 2005 | 2006 | 2007 | 2008 | 2009 | 2010 | 2011 | 2012 | 2013 | 2014 | 2015 |
|---|---|---|---|---|---|---|---|---|---|---|---|---|---|
| | | | | | | | *Millions of US Dollars* | | | | | | |
| Assets | 809aa | 1,409.7 | † 1,347.7 | 1,596.0 | 1,728.7 | 1,673.0 | 2,364.6 | 2,214.6 | 2,736.2 | 2,454.1 | 2,725.4 | .... | .... |
| Direct investment | 8a9aa | 10.2 | † 7.9 | 7.5 | 12.1 | 10.9 | 10.6 | 6.1 | 38.9 | 57.4 | 39.0 | .... | .... |
| Equity & investment fund shares | 8aaaa | 7.5 | † 6.6 | 7.5 | 10.3 | 11.4 | 17.3 | 10.8 | 38.8 | 57.3 | 39.0 | .... | .... |
| Debt instruments | 8abaa | 2.7 | † 1.3 | .... | 1.9 | −.4 | −6.7 | −4.7 | .... | .... | .... | .... | .... |
| Portfolio investment | 8b9aa | 96.8 | † 65.7 | 120.7 | 76.4 | 221.1 | 285.5 | 731.1 | 429.2 | 325.1 | 414.8 | .... | .... |
| Equity & investment fund shares | 8baaa | 6.4 | † 6.8 | 3.4 | 1.1 | 1.3 | 2.9 | 2.4 | 40.1 | 4.0 | 6.4 | .... | .... |
| Debt securities | 8bbaa | 90.4 | † 59.0 | 117.3 | 75.3 | 219.8 | 282.6 | 728.7 | 389.1 | 321.1 | 408.3 | .... | .... |
| Fin. der.(oth.than reserves) & ESOs | 8c9aa | .5 | † .4 | .4 | .5 | .3 | .3 | 4.3 | .8 | .8 | .... | .... | .... |
| Other investment | 8d9aa | 450.9 | † 419.2 | 498.7 | 552.8 | 368.7 | 463.3 | 122.1 | 888.8 | 729.5 | 971.3 | .... | .... |
| Other equity | 8daaa | .... | .... | .... | .... | .... | .... | .... | .... | .... | .... | .... | .... |
| Debt instruments | 8dzaa | 450.9 | † 419.2 | 498.7 | 552.8 | 368.7 | 463.3 | 122.1 | 888.8 | 729.5 | 971.3 | .... | .... |
| Reserve assets | 8e9aa | 851.3 | † 854.5 | 968.8 | 1,086.8 | 1,071.9 | 1,604.9 | 1,350.9 | 1,378.6 | 1,341.4 | 1,300.3 | .... | .... |
| Liabilities | 809la | 4,981.4 | † 4,463.5 | 2,915.2 | 3,228.6 | 3,448.9 | 4,300.6 | 4,928.2 | 5,084.6 | 6,305.6 | 6,525.0 | .... | .... |
| Direct investment | 8a9la | 756.4 | † 871.6 | 969.3 | 966.7 | 977.6 | 1,882.8 | 2,144.7 | 1,751.7 | 2,336.6 | 2,223.7 | .... | .... |
| Equity & investment fund shares | 8aala | 682.9 | † 654.6 | 680.5 | 655.1 | 608.5 | 574.1 | 890.7 | 1,036.4 | 1,295.5 | 1,382.6 | .... | .... |
| Debt instruments | 8abla | 73.5 | † 217.0 | 288.8 | 311.6 | 369.1 | 1,308.7 | 1,254.0 | 715.3 | 1,041.0 | 841.1 | .... | .... |
| Portfolio investment | 8b9la | 16.4 | † 33.5 | 38.1 | 72.1 | 77.4 | 92.1 | 96.6 | 282.1 | 272.4 | 267.3 | .... | .... |
| Equity & investment fund shares | 8bala | 16.2 | † 22.4 | 28.7 | 24.1 | 19.8 | 17.3 | 17.3 | 11.5 | 10.1 | 15.5 | .... | .... |
| Debt securities | 8bbla | .2 | † 11.0 | 9.4 | 48.0 | 57.6 | 74.7 | 79.3 | 270.6 | 262.3 | 251.9 | .... | .... |
| Fin. der.(oth.than reserves) & ESOs | 8c9la | .... | .... | .... | .... | 3.2 | 3.3 | −.9 | .... | .... | .... | .... | .... |
| Other investment | 8d9la | 4,208.7 | † 3,558.4 | 1,907.7 | 2,189.8 | 2,390.7 | 2,322.4 | 2,687.9 | 3,050.8 | 3,696.5 | 4,033.9 | .... | .... |
| Other equity | 8dala | .... | .... | .... | .... | .... | .... | .... | .... | .... | .... | .... | .... |
| Debt instruments | 8dzla | 4,208.7 | † 3,558.4 | 1,907.7 | 2,189.8 | 2,390.7 | 2,322.4 | 2,687.9 | 3,050.8 | 3,696.5 | 4,033.9 | .... | .... |

# Mali   678

| | | 2004 | 2005 | 2006 | 2007 | 2008 | 2009 | 2010 | 2011 | 2012 | 2013 | 2014 | 2015 |
|---|---|---|---|---|---|---|---|---|---|---|---|---|---|
| **Government Finance** | | | | | | | | | | | | | |
| **Operations Statement** | | | | | | | | | | | | | |
| **Budgetary Central Government** | | | | | *Billions of CFA Francs: Fiscal Year Ends December 31* | | | | | | | |
| Revenue............................. | a1 | 556.6 | 618.0 | 1,789.5 | † 742.8 | 752.4 | 909.6 | 937.6 | 1,012.1 | 895.8 | 1,178.6 | .... | .... |
| Taxes................................. | a11 | 393.7 | 438.1 | 480.4 | † 487.2 | 519.4 | 624.3 | 681.9 | 768.3 | 825.3 | 852.4 | .... | .... |
| Social Contributions..................... | a12 | — | — | — | † — | — | — | — | — | — | — | .... | .... |
| Grants.............................. | a13 | 103.3 | 115.0 | 1,276.5 | † 172.9 | 145.1 | 184.6 | 131.2 | 207.6 | 19.5 | 215.3 | .... | .... |
| Other Revenue............................. | a14 | 59.6 | 64.8 | 32.6 | † 82.7 | 87.9 | 100.7 | 124.5 | 36.3 | 51.0 | 110.8 | .... | .... |
| Expense............................. | a2 | 392.9 | 422.7 | 481.1 | † 497.5 | 537.7 | 620.6 | 675.9 | 749.7 | 761.6 | 866.9 | .... | .... |
| Compensation of Employees............. | a21 | 121.7 | 137.8 | 159.6 | † 162.8 | 186.0 | 213.7 | 231.8 | 276.3 | 306.9 | 307.0 | .... | .... |
| Use of Goods & Services............. | a22 | 136.5 | 140.9 | 154.1 | † 161.3 | 177.0 | 190.2 | 213.1 | 232.0 | 207.8 | 239.5 | .... | .... |
| Consumption of Fixed Capital........ | a23 | .... | .... | .... | .... | .... | .... | .... | .... | .... | .... | .... | .... |
| Interest........................... | a24 | 17.6 | 18.7 | 15.2 | † 13.9 | 14.1 | 15.5 | 19.1 | 30.6 | 26.9 | 38.6 | .... | .... |
| Subsidies................................. | a25 | .... | .... | — | † — | — | — | 13.5 | 38.5 | 49.9 | 87.0 | .... | .... |
| Grants.............................. | a26 | .... | .... | 38.2 | † 84.7 | 75.0 | 92.8 | 96.3 | 107.4 | 88.3 | 110.6 | .... | .... |
| Social Benefits............................. | a27 | .... | .... | 52.3 | † — | — | — | — | — | — | — | .... | .... |
| Other Expense............................. | a28 | .... | .... | 61.7 | † 74.8 | 85.6 | 108.5 | 102.1 | 65.0 | 81.8 | 84.1 | .... | .... |
| Gross Operating Balance [1-2+23]... | agob | 163.7 | 195.2 | 1,308.4 | † 245.3 | 214.7 | 289.0 | 261.6 | 262.4 | 134.2 | 311.7 | .... | .... |
| Net Operating Balance [1-2]............ | anob | .... | .... | .... | .... | .... | .... | .... | 262.4 | | | .... | .... |
| Net Acq. of Nonfinancial Assets....... | a31 | 240.8 | 265.0 | 324.9 | † 395.6 | 309.9 | 376.2 | 378.1 | 437.9 | 134.2 | 388.9 | .... | .... |
| Aquisition of Nonfin. Assets........... | a31.1 | .... | .... | .... | .... | .... | 376.2 | .... | .... | .... | .... | .... | .... |
| Disposal of Nonfin. Assets............ | a31.2 | .... | .... | .... | .... | .... | .... | .... | .... | .... | .... | .... | .... |
| Net Lending/Borrowing [1-2-31]...... | anlb | −77.1 | −69.8 | 983.5 | † −150.3 | −95.2 | −87.2 | −116.5 | −175.4 | — | −77.2 | .... | .... |
| Net Acq. of Financial Assets............. | a32 | −6.0 | 13.0 | .... | † −48.3 | −31.5 | −104.5 | 19.7 | −2.0 | −129.3 | 77.3 | .... | .... |
| By instrument | | | | | | | | | | | | | |
| Monetary Gold & SDRs................. | a3201 | — | — | — | † — | — | | | | | | .... | .... |
| Currency & Deposits..................... | a3202 | .... | .... | .... | .... | .... | 56.1 | 4.8 | −23.8 | −152.7 | 118.2 | .... | .... |
| Securities other than Shares........... | a3203 | .... | .... | .... | .... | .... | | | | | | .... | .... |
| Loans.............................. | a3204 | −9.0 | 22.7 | .... | .... | .... | 19.0 | 14.7 | −3.2 | −2.8 | −6.2 | .... | .... |
| Shares & Other Equity.................. | a3205 | .... | .... | .... | .... | .... | −179.7 | .2 | — | — | — | .... | .... |
| Insurance Technical Reserves......... | a3206 | — | — | .... | .... | .... | — | — | — | — | — | .... | .... |
| Financial Derivatives..................... | a3207 | — | — | .... | .... | .... | — | — | — | — | — | .... | .... |
| Other Accounts Receivable............. | a3208 | — | — | .... | .... | .... | — | — | 25.0 | 26.2 | −34.7 | .... | .... |
| By debtor | | | | | | | | | | | | | |
| Domestic......................................... | a321 | −6.0 | 13.0 | .... | .... | .... | −104.5 | 19.7 | −2.0 | −129.3 | 77.3 | .... | .... |
| Foreign............................................ | a322 | — | — | .... | .... | .... | | | | | | .... | .... |
| Net Incurrence of Liabilities.............. | a33 | 70.8 | 81.9 | .... | † 102.0 | 63.7 | −56.4 | 137.3 | 173.4 | −129.4 | 154.5 | .... | .... |
| By instrument | | | | | | | | | | | | | |
| Special Drawing Rights (SDRs)....... | a3301 | — | | .... | † — | | | | — | — | — | .... | .... |
| Currency & Deposits..................... | a3302 | −12.2 | — | .... | .... | .... | — | — | 5.5 | −79.5 | 42.3 | .... | .... |
| Securities other than Shares........... | a3303 | — | — | .... | .... | .... | — | — | — | — | — | .... | .... |
| Loans.............................. | a3304 | 47.4 | 93.6 | .... | .... | .... | −32.2 | 147.9 | 188.7 | 5.6 | 152.3 | .... | .... |
| Shares & Other Equity.................. | a3305 | — | — | .... | .... | .... | — | — | — | — | — | .... | .... |
| Insurance Technical Reserves......... | a3306 | — | — | .... | .... | .... | — | — | — | — | — | .... | .... |
| Financial Derivatives..................... | a3307 | — | — | .... | .... | .... | — | — | — | — | — | .... | .... |
| Other Accounts Payable................. | a3308 | 35.6 | −11.7 | .... | .... | .... | −24.2 | −10.6 | −20.8 | −55.6 | −40.2 | .... | .... |
| By creditor | | | | | | | | | | | | | |
| Domestic......................................... | a331 | −3.7 | −26.9 | .... | .... | .... | −167.0 | 19.9 | 43.5 | −134.6 | 84.2 | .... | .... |
| Foreign............................................ | a332 | 74.5 | 108.8 | −1,042.0 | .... | .... | 110.5 | 117.4 | 130.0 | 5.2 | 70.2 | .... | .... |
| Stat. Discrepancy [32-33-NLB]........ | anlbz | .3 | .8 | .... | .... | † — | 39.1 | −1.1 | — | .1 | | .... | .... |
| Memo Item: Expenditure [2+31]...... | a2m | 633.7 | 687.7 | 806.0 | † 893.1 | 847.6 | 996.8 | 1,054.1 | 1,187.6 | 895.8 | 1,255.8 | .... | .... |
| **National Accounts** | | | | | *Billions of CFA Francs* | | | | | | | | |
| Househ.Cons.Expend.,incl.NPISHs..... | 96f | 1,796.7 | 1,994.6 | 2,091.1 | 2,215.1 | 2,495.0 | 2,632.8 | 2,831.1 | 3,612.0 | 3,994.3 | 4,248.3 | 4,844.3 | .... |
| Government Consumption Expend... | 91f | 472.6 | 490.4 | 553.5 | 596.8 | 687.7 | 733.9 | 788.3 | 707.5 | 620.4 | 747.7 | 867.5 | .... |
| Gross Fixed Capital Formation.......... | 93e | 446.6 | 446.7 | 528.6 | 664.4 | 715.8 | 868.3 | 985.9 | 1,170.1 | 944.6 | 1,357.0 | 1,474.7 | .... |
| Changes in Inventories..................... | 93i | 131.2 | 190.4 | 123.3 | 74.0 | 74.7 | 30.9 | 155.0 | 30.2 | 30.2 | 30.2 | 30.2 | .... |
| Exports of Goods and Services......... | 90c | 643.2 | 724.3 | 958.0 | 995.9 | 896.3 | 914.2 | 1,104.7 | 1,322.4 | 1,708.3 | 1,631.2 | 1,539.5 | .... |
| Imports of Goods and Services (-)..... | 98c | 858.3 | 952.5 | 1,053.0 | 1,121.6 | 956.8 | 947.2 | 1,209.4 | 1,818.0 | 2,018.5 | 2,608.3 | 2,831.0 | .... |
| Gross Domestic Product (GDP)........ | 99b | 2,632.1 | 2,893.9 | 3,201.5 | 3,424.5 | 3,912.8 | 4,232.9 | 4,655.7 | 5,024.2 | 5,279.3 | 5,406.2 | 5,925.2 | .... |
| GDP Volume 2008 Prices.................. | 99b.p | 3,198.9 | 3,395.2 | 3,575.1 | 3,727.1 | 3,912.8 | 4,087.4 | 4,325.1 | 4,443.2 | 4,444.0 | 4,519.2 | 4,845.9 | .... |
| GDP Volume (2010=100)................ | 99bvp | 74.0 | 78.5 | 82.7 | 86.2 | 90.5 | 94.5 | 100.0 | 102.7 | 102.8 | 104.5 | 112.0 | .... |
| GDP Deflator (2010=100)............... | 99bip | 76.4 | 79.2 | 83.2 | 85.4 | 92.9 | 96.2 | 100.0 | 105.0 | 110.4 | 111.1 | 113.6 | .... |
| | | | | | *Millions: Midyear Estimates* | | | | | | | | |
| Population................................ | 99z | 12.47 | 12.88 | 13.31 | 13.76 | 14.22 | 14.69 | 15.17 | 15.64 | 16.11 | 16.59 | 17.09 | 17.60 |

| | | 2004 | 2005 | 2006 | 2007 | 2008 | 2009 | 2010 | 2011 | 2012 | 2013 | 2014 | 2015 |
|---|---|---|---|---|---|---|---|---|---|---|---|---|---|
| **Exchange Rates** | | \multicolumn{12}{c}{*SDRs per Liri through 2007; Euros per SDR Thereafter: End of Period*} |
| Market Rate | ac | 2.0214 | 1.9290 | 2.0406 | 2.1700 | 1.1068 | 1.0882 | 1.1525 | 1.1865 | 1.1649 | 1.1167 | 1.1933 | 1.2728 |
| | | \multicolumn{12}{c}{*US Dollars per Liri through 2007; Euros per US Dollar Thereafter: End of Period (ae) Period Average (rf)*} |
| Market Rate | ae | .3185 | .3627 | .3257 | .2916 | .7185 | .6942 | .7484 | .7729 | .7579 | .7251 | .8237 | .9185 |
| Market Rate | rf | .3447 | .3458 | .3409 | .3117 | .6827 | .7198 | .7550 | .7194 | .7783 | .7532 | .7537 | .9017 |
| | | \multicolumn{12}{c}{*Index Numbers (2010=100): Period Averages*} |
| Official Rate (2005=100) | ahx | 100.3 | 100.0 | 101.3 | 111.0 | . . . . | . . . . | . . . . | . . . . | . . . . | . . . . | . . . . | . . . . |
| Nominal Effective Exchange Rate | nec | 98.2 | 97.5 | 97.7 | 100.7 | 98.8 | 104.4 | 100.0 | 100.6 | 96.8 | 99.5 | 100.1 | 95.1 |
| CPI-Based Real Effect. Ex. Rate | rec | 98.9 | 98.4 | 98.8 | 99.6 | 98.0 | 104.8 | 100.0 | 99.7 | 96.5 | 98.1 | 97.9 | 93.2 |
| **Fund Position** | | \multicolumn{12}{c}{*Millions of SDRs: End of Period*} |
| Quota | 2f.s | 102.00 | 102.00 | 102.00 | 102.00 | 102.00 | 102.00 | 102.00 | 102.00 | 102.00 | 102.00 | 102.00 | 102.00 |
| SDR Holdings | 1b.s | 30.77 | 32.10 | 34.04 | 37.85 | 11.68 | 95.98 | 95.85 | 90.70 | 91.04 | 89.47 | 84.51 | 87.51 |
| Reserve Position in the Fund | 1c.s | 40.26 | 40.26 | 40.26 | 40.26 | 40.26 | 33.13 | 30.97 | 45.82 | 47.86 | 51.60 | 45.10 | 30.73 |
| Total Fund Cred. & Loans Outstg. | 2tl | — | — | — | — | — | — | — | — | — | — | — | — |
| SDR Allocations | 1bd | 11.29 | 11.29 | 11.29 | 11.29 | 11.29 | 95.40 | 95.40 | 95.40 | 95.40 | 95.40 | 95.40 | 95.40 |
| **International Liquidity** | | \multicolumn{12}{c}{*Millions of US Dollars Unless Otherwise Indicated: End of Period*} |
| Total Res.Min.Gold (Eurosys.Def) | 1l.d | 2,732.0 | 2,576.4 | 2,976.8 | 3,785.4 | † 368.3 | 532.1 | 535.8 | 499.8 | 688.5 | 584.9 | 615.6 | 568.5 |
| SDR Holdings | 1b.d | 47.8 | 45.9 | 51.2 | 59.8 | 18.0 | 150.5 | 147.6 | 139.2 | 139.9 | 137.8 | 122.4 | 121.3 |
| Reserve Position in the Fund | 1c.d | 62.5 | 57.5 | 60.6 | 63.6 | 62.0 | 51.9 | 47.7 | 70.4 | 73.6 | 79.5 | 65.3 | 42.6 |
| Foreign Exchange | 1d.d | 2,621.7 | 2,473.0 | 2,865.0 | 3,662.0 | † 288.3 | 329.7 | 340.5 | 290.2 | 474.8 | 367.6 | 427.9 | 404.7 |
| o/w:Fin.Deriv.Rel.to Reserves | 1ddd | . . . . | . . . . | . . . . | . . . . | 15.2 | −10.1 | 1.5 | −2.9 | 9.1 | 5.9 | −16.4 | −7.5 |
| Other Reserve Assets | 1e.d | . . . . | . . . . | . . . . | . . . . | — | — | — | — | — | — | — | — |
| Gold (Million Fine Troy Ounces) | 1ad | .004 | .004 | .006 | .016 | .006 | .006 | .003 | .010 | .010 | .010 | .003 | .003 |
| Gold (Eurosystem Valuation) | 1and | 1.9 | 2.3 | 4.1 | 13.0 | † 5.1 | 6.5 | 4.4 | 15.7 | 16.6 | 12.0 | 3.6 | 3.2 |
| Memo:Euro Cl. on Non-EA Res. | 1dgd | . . . . | . . . . | . . . . | . . . . | 403.5 | 176.8 | 181.1 | 276.4 | 554.7 | 875.7 | 1,022.7 | 1,058.2 |
| Non-Euro Cl. on EA Res. | 1dhd | . . . . | . . . . | . . . . | . . . . | 635.4 | 341.5 | 339.6 | 357.7 | 303.8 | 191.8 | 122.4 | 171.6 |
| Central Bank: Other Assets | 3..d | . . . . | −44 | −72 | −81 | 1,719 | 1,724 | 2,248 | 2,745 | 2,812 | 3,522 | 3,546 | 3,305 |
| Central Bank: Other Liabs | 4..d | . . . . | 114 | 143 | 162 | 129 | 275 | 276 | 258 | 259 | 250 | 235 | 233 |
| Other Depository Corps.: Assets | 7a.d | . . . . | 15,390 | 21,048 | 32,337 | 35,451 | 34,050 | 38,273 | 36,136 | 40,660 | 40,437 | 38,863 | 27,766 |
| Other Depository Corps.: Liabs | 7b.d | . . . . | 11,770 | 15,876 | 23,908 | 24,566 | 25,294 | 28,192 | 26,863 | 28,724 | 29,428 | 26,188 | 18,840 |
| **Central Bank** | | \multicolumn{12}{c}{*Millions of Euros: End of Period*} |
| Euro Area Wide Residency Criterion | | | | | | | | | | | | | |
| Net Foreign Assets | 11n.u | . . . . | 726 | 879 | 1,077 | 448 | 310 | 324 | 407 | 739 | 1,134 | 1,498 | 1,655 |
| Claims on Nonresidents | 11..u | . . . . | 822 | 988 | 1,186 | 541 | 501 | 531 | 607 | 935 | 1,315 | 1,691 | 1,870 |
| Liabilities to Nonresidents | 16c.u | . . . . | 97 | 108 | 110 | 93 | 191 | 207 | 200 | 196 | 181 | 193 | 214 |
| Claims on Other Depository Corps. | 12e.u | . . . . | 1,094 | 940 | 1,045 | 1,307 | 1,742 | 1,610 | 1,219 | 1,102 | 832 | 1,095 | 755 |
| Net Claims on Central Government | 12anu | . . . . | −222 | 2 | 63 | 261 | 355 | 735 | 864 | 875 | 843 | 934 | 1,299 |
| Claims on Central Govt | 12a.u | . . . . | 123 | 251 | 450 | 651 | 795 | 1,219 | 1,395 | 1,205 | 1,172 | 1,267 | 1,626 |
| Liabs. to Central Govt | 16d.u | . . . . | 345 | 249 | 387 | 390 | 440 | 483 | 531 | 330 | 328 | 333 | 327 |
| Claims on Other Sectors | 12s.u | . . . . | 137 | 107 | 54 | 44 | 56 | 75 | 133 | 149 | 172 | 157 | 132 |
| Claims on Other Financial Corps. | 12g.u | . . . . | 68 | 53 | 25 | 26 | 26 | 21 | 55 | 61 | 88 | 92 | 56 |
| Claims on State & Local Govts. | 12b.u | . . . . | 46 | 36 | 19 | 13 | 20 | 20 | 35 | 45 | 42 | 36 | 60 |
| Claims on Public Nonfin. Corps. | 12c.u | . . . . | — | — | — | — | — | — | — | — | — | — | — |
| Claims on Private Sector | 12d.u | . . . . | 23 | 17 | 11 | 5 | 10 | 34 | 43 | 43 | 42 | 28 | 16 |
| Monetary Base | 14..u | . . . . | 1,638 | 1,840 | 2,154 | 1,235 | 1,324 | 1,267 | 1,913 | 2,399 | 2,074 | 1,482 | 2,619 |
| Currency in Circulation | 14a.u | . . . . | 1,211 | 1,174 | 677 | 741 | 710 | 742 | 783 | 807 | 858 | 924 | 989 |
| Liabs. to Other Depository Corps. | 14c.u | . . . . | 425 | 661 | 1,442 | 483 | 603 | 511 | 1,116 | 1,569 | 1,188 | 553 | 1,612 |
| Liabs. to Other Sectors | 14d.u | . . . . | 2 | 5 | 35 | 10 | 11 | 14 | 14 | 23 | 28 | 5 | 18 |
| Other Liabs. to Other Dep. Corps. | 14n.u | . . . . | — | — | — | — | — | — | — | — | — | — | — |
| Dep. & Sec. Excl. f/Monetary Base | 14o.u | . . . . | — | — | — | — | — | — | — | — | — | — | — |
| Deposits Included in Broad Money. | 15..u | . . . . | — | — | — | — | — | — | — | — | — | — | — |
| Sec.Ot.th.Shares Inc.in.Brd.Money. | 16a.u | . . . . | — | — | — | — | — | — | — | — | — | — | — |
| Deposits Excl. from Broad Money | 16b.u | . . . . | — | — | — | — | — | — | — | — | — | — | — |
| Sec.Oh.th.Shares Excl. f/Brd.Money | 16s.u | . . . . | — | — | — | — | — | — | — | — | — | — | — |
| Loans | 16l.u | . . . . | — | — | — | — | — | — | — | — | — | — | — |
| Financial Derivatives | 16m.u | . . . . | — | — | — | — | — | — | — | — | — | — | — |
| Shares and Other Equity | 17a.u | . . . . | 226 | 214 | 213 | 294 | 326 | 337 | 347 | 400 | 414 | 449 | 497 |
| Other Items (Net) | 17r.u | . . . . | −130 | −126 | −129 | 531 | 814 | 1,141 | 362 | 66 | 494 | 1,753 | 723 |
| Memorandum Items | | | | | | | | | | | | | |
| National Residency Criterion | | | | | | | | | | | | | |
| Net Foreign Assets | 11n | . . . . | 2,051 | 2,100 | 2,416 | 743 | 565 | 654 | 1,889 | 2,268 | 2,135 | 1,307 | 2,425 |
| Claims on Nonresidents | 11 | . . . . | 2,148 | 2,209 | 2,525 | 1,503 | 1,571 | 2,087 | 2,518 | 2,665 | 2,989 | 3,431 | 3,561 |
| Liabilities to Nonresidents | 16c | . . . . | 97 | 108 | 110 | 761 | 1,005 | 1,432 | 628 | 397 | 854 | 2,124 | 1,136 |
| Claims on Other Depository Corps. | 12e | . . . . | 1 | — | 1 | 763 | 1,304 | 1,104 | 522 | 454 | 200 | 412 | 115 |
| Net Claims on Central Government | 12an | . . . . | −323 | −179 | −184 | −118 | −225 | −209 | −187 | −28 | 3 | 65 | 409 |
| Claims on Central Government | 12a | . . . . | 21 | 71 | 204 | 271 | 215 | 275 | 344 | 302 | 332 | 398 | 736 |
| Liabilities to Central Government | 16d | . . . . | 345 | 249 | 387 | 390 | 440 | 483 | 531 | 330 | 328 | 333 | 327 |
| Claims on Other Sectors | 12s | . . . . | 5 | 5 | 6 | 5 | 5 | 6 | 6 | 6 | 7 | 7 | 7 |
| Claims on Other Fin. Corps. | 12g | . . . . | — | — | — | — | — | — | — | — | — | — | — |
| Claims on State & Local Govts. | 12b | . . . . | — | — | — | — | — | — | — | — | — | — | — |
| Claims on Private Sector | 12d | . . . . | 5 | 5 | 6 | 5 | 5 | 6 | 6 | 6 | 7 | 7 | 7 |
| Liabs.to ODCs, Inc.in Mon.Base | 14c | . . . . | 425 | 661 | 1,441 | 483 | 603 | 511 | 1,116 | 1,569 | 1,188 | 553 | 1,612 |
| Liabs.to Ot.Sectors, Inc.in Mon.Base | 14d | . . . . | 2 | 5 | 35 | 10 | 11 | 14 | 14 | 23 | 28 | 5 | 18 |
| Liabs.to ODCs,Excl.f/Mon.Base | 14n | . . . . | — | — | — | — | — | — | — | — | — | — | — |
| Net Claims on Eurosystem | 12e.s | . . . . | . . . . | . . . . | . . . . | −656 | −803 | −1,176 | −378 | −150 | −621 | −1,893 | −884 |

# Malta 181

| Other Depository Corporations | | 2004 | 2005 | 2006 | 2007 | 2008 | 2009 | 2010 | 2011 | 2012 | 2013 | 2014 | 2015 |
|---|---|---|---|---|---|---|---|---|---|---|---|---|---|
| Euro Area Wide Residency Criterion | | | | | | *Millions of Euros: End of Period* | | | | | | | |
| Net Foreign Assets | 21n.u | .... | 3,068 | 3,927 | 5,726 | 7,821 | 6,078 | 7,545 | 7,167 | 9,046 | 7,983 | 10,440 | 8,199 |
| Claims on Nonresidents | 21..u | .... | 13,046 | 15,982 | 21,967 | 25,473 | 23,636 | 28,643 | 27,928 | 30,817 | 29,321 | 32,010 | 25,504 |
| Liabilities to Nonresidents | 26c.u | .... | 9,977 | 12,055 | 16,241 | 17,652 | 17,558 | 21,098 | 20,762 | 21,771 | 21,339 | 21,570 | 17,305 |
| Claims on Eurosystem | 20..u | .... | 53 | 66 | 76 | 81 | 208 | 600 | 1,180 | 1,644 | 1,260 | 642 | 1,629 |
| Currency | 20a.u | .... | 53 | 66 | 76 | 72 | 70 | 68 | 73 | 81 | 80 | 85 | 96 |
| Reserve Deposits and Securities | 20b.u | .... | — | — | — | 9 | 138 | 532 | 1,107 | 1,563 | 1,180 | 557 | 1,533 |
| Other Claims | 20n.u | .... | — | — | — | — | — | — | — | — | — | — | — |
| Net Claims on Central Government | 22anu | .... | 1,453 | 1,119 | 1,256 | 1,284 | 2,102 | 2,181 | 2,779 | 1,997 | 2,182 | 2,234 | 2,222 |
| Claims on Central Government | 22a.u | .... | 1,553 | 1,321 | 1,367 | 1,367 | 2,204 | 2,373 | 2,973 | 2,170 | 2,345 | 2,404 | 2,434 |
| Liabilities to Central Government | 26d.u | .... | 101 | 203 | 112 | 83 | 102 | 192 | 194 | 174 | 163 | 170 | 212 |
| Claims on Other Sectors | 22s.u | .... | 8,007 | 7,424 | 8,334 | 10,366 | 10,324 | 11,025 | 11,887 | 12,391 | 11,095 | 12,311 | 12,962 |
| Claims on Other Financial Corps | 22g.u | .... | 2,093 | 550 | 789 | 1,622 | 975 | 1,309 | 1,914 | 2,580 | 1,260 | 1,718 | 2,627 |
| Claims on State & Local Govts | 22b.u | .... | 15 | 5 | 5 | 49 | 146 | 274 | 191 | 128 | 215 | 294 | 486 |
| Claims on Public Nonfin. Corps | 22c.u | .... | — | — | — | — | — | — | — | — | — | — | — |
| Claims on Private Sector | 22d.u | .... | 5,899 | 6,868 | 7,539 | 8,695 | 9,202 | 9,443 | 9,781 | 9,683 | 9,620 | 10,299 | 9,849 |
| Liabilities to Eurosystem | 26g.u | .... | 801 | 623 | 368 | 1,038 | 1,588 | 1,485 | 1,037 | 1,037 | 771 | 1,065 | 713 |
| Transf.Dep.Included in Broad Money | 24..u | .... | 2,795 | 2,826 | 3,128 | 3,170 | 3,714 | 4,319 | 4,713 | 5,212 | 5,944 | 8,669 | 10,908 |
| Other.Dep.Included in Broad Money. | 25..u | .... | 3,456 | 3,780 | 4,739 | 5,126 | 4,603 | 4,355 | 4,231 | 4,499 | 4,911 | 4,957 | 4,064 |
| Sec.Ot.th.Shares Inc.in.Brd. Money | 26a.u | .... | −115 | −113 | −121 | −144 | −115 | −2 | −2 | −13 | −50 | −60 | 20 |
| Deposits Excl. from Broad Money | 26b.u | .... | 731 | 698 | 654 | 559 | 741 | 945 | 1,889 | 2,059 | 2,360 | 2,577 | 2,304 |
| Sec.Ot.th.Shares Excl.f/Brd. Money | 26s.u | .... | −2,468 | −2,711 | −2,576 | −2,115 | −2,082 | −1,673 | −1,715 | −1,607 | −1,364 | −1,676 | −969 |
| Loans | 26l.u | .... | — | — | — | — | — | — | — | — | — | — | — |
| Financial Derivatives | 26m.u | .... | 1,517 | 51 | 80 | 320 | 175 | 308 | 386 | 459 | 362 | 425 | 463 |
| Insurance Technical Reserves | 26r.u | .... | — | — | — | — | — | — | — | — | — | — | — |
| Shares and Other Equity | 27a.u | .... | 2,360 | 3,083 | 3,360 | 3,339 | 4,120 | 9,854 | 9,816 | 10,369 | 7,139 | 4,985 | 4,080 |
| Other Items (Net) | 27r.u | .... | 3,511 | 4,306 | 5,759 | 8,259 | 5,967 | 1,759 | 2,657 | 3,063 | 2,448 | 4,056 | 3,394 |
| Memorandum Items | | | | | | | | | | | | | |
| Total Assets | 20ra | .... | 27,195 | 30,033 | 37,807 | 42,477 | 41,501 | 50,162 | 51,347 | 53,527 | 50,336 | 53,262 | 47,388 |
| National Residency Criterion | | | | | | | | | | | | | |
| Net Foreign Assets | 21n | .... | 1,966 | 2,451 | 3,013 | 4,696 | 4,424 | 10,279 | 9,232 | 9,791 | 7,370 | 8,256 | 6,276 |
| Claims on Nonresidents | 21 | .... | 17,518 | 21,194 | 27,344 | 31,627 | 29,822 | 38,011 | 38,039 | 39,593 | 36,552 | 39,388 | 31,759 |
| Liabilities to Nonresidents | 26c | .... | 15,552 | 18,743 | 24,331 | 26,931 | 25,398 | 27,732 | 28,808 | 29,802 | 29,182 | 31,133 | 25,482 |
| Net Claims on Central Government | 22an | .... | 1,355 | 1,029 | 1,208 | 1,262 | 1,609 | 1,622 | 1,813 | 1,808 | 1,981 | 1,926 | 1,968 |
| Claims on Central Government | 22a | .... | 1,455 | 1,231 | 1,319 | 1,345 | 1,710 | 1,813 | 2,007 | 1,982 | 2,143 | 2,097 | 2,180 |
| Liabilities to Central Government | 26d | .... | 100 | 202 | 111 | 83 | 102 | 192 | 194 | 173 | 162 | 170 | 212 |
| Claims on Other Sectors | 22s | .... | 6,634 | 5,885 | 6,506 | 7,548 | 7,936 | 8,411 | 8,861 | 9,013 | 9,013 | 9,602 | 10,216 |
| Claims on Other Fin. Corps | 22g | .... | 1,613 | 137 | 232 | 415 | 295 | 522 | 640 | 893 | 897 | 1,099 | 1,605 |
| Claims on State & Local Govts | 22b | .... | 2 | 2 | 2 | 2 | 2 | 3 | 3 | 3 | 3 | 3 | 3 |
| Claims on Private Sector | 22d | .... | 5,020 | 5,746 | 6,272 | 7,131 | 7,638 | 7,886 | 8,218 | 8,117 | 8,113 | 8,500 | 8,608 |
| Transf.Dep.Included in Broad Money | 24 | .... | 2,749 | 2,776 | 3,086 | 3,110 | 3,628 | 4,219 | 4,589 | 5,043 | 5,768 | 8,412 | 10,493 |
| Other.Dep.Included in Broad Money. | 25 | .... | 3,201 | 3,600 | 4,567 | 4,962 | 4,486 | 4,206 | 4,008 | 4,021 | 4,084 | 4,228 | 3,717 |
| Sec.Ot.th.Shares Inc.in.Brd. Money | 26a | .... | — | — | — | — | — | — | — | — | — | — | — |
| Deposits Excl. from Broad Money | 26b | .... | 665 | 636 | 584 | 532 | 713 | 924 | 1,320 | 1,392 | 1,542 | 1,499 | 1,637 |
| Sec.Ot.th.Shares Excl.f/Brd. Money | 26s | .... | 94 | 83 | 139 | 166 | 242 | 297 | 344 | 393 | 342 | 363 | 433 |

| | | 2004 | 2005 | 2006 | 2007 | 2008 | 2009 | 2010 | 2011 | 2012 | 2013 | 2014 | 2015 |
|---|---|---|---|---|---|---|---|---|---|---|---|---|---|
| **Depository Corporations** | | | | | | *Millions of Euros: End of Period* | | | | | | | |
| Euro Area Wide Residency Criterion | | | | | | | | | | | | | |
| Net Foreign Assets | 31n.u | .... | 3,794 | 4,806 | 6,803 | 8,269 | 6,388 | 7,869 | 7,573 | 9,786 | 9,117 | 11,938 | 9,854 |
| Claims on Nonresidents | 31..u | .... | 13,868 | 16,969 | 23,153 | 26,014 | 24,137 | 29,174 | 28,535 | 31,752 | 30,637 | 33,701 | 27,374 |
| Liabilities to Nonresidents | 36c.u | .... | 10,074 | 12,163 | 16,350 | 17,745 | 17,749 | 21,305 | 20,961 | 21,967 | 21,520 | 21,763 | 17,519 |
| Domestic Claims | 32..u | .... | 9,374 | 8,651 | 9,707 | 11,955 | 12,837 | 14,017 | 15,663 | 15,411 | 14,292 | 15,635 | 16,615 |
| Net Claims on Central Government | 32anu | .... | 1,231 | 1,120 | 1,319 | 1,545 | 2,457 | 2,916 | 3,643 | 2,872 | 3,026 | 3,168 | 3,520 |
| Claims on Central Government | 32a.u | .... | 1,676 | 1,573 | 1,818 | 2,018 | 2,999 | 3,592 | 4,368 | 3,376 | 3,517 | 3,671 | 4,059 |
| Liabilities to Central Government | 36d.u | .... | 445 | 452 | 499 | 473 | 542 | 676 | 725 | 504 | 491 | 503 | 539 |
| Claims on Other Sectors | 32s.u | .... | 8,143 | 7,531 | 8,388 | 10,410 | 10,380 | 11,101 | 12,020 | 12,539 | 11,267 | 12,467 | 13,094 |
| Claims on Other Financial Corps | 32g.u | .... | 2,161 | 603 | 814 | 1,648 | 1,000 | 1,329 | 1,969 | 2,641 | 1,348 | 1,810 | 2,683 |
| Claims on State & Local Govts | 32b.u | .... | 61 | 41 | 24 | 62 | 166 | 294 | 226 | 173 | 257 | 331 | 547 |
| Claims on Public Nonfin. Corps | 32c.u | .... | — | — | — | — | — | — | — | — | — | — | — |
| Claims on Private Sector | 32d.u | .... | 5,922 | 6,886 | 7,550 | 8,700 | 9,213 | 9,477 | 9,824 | 9,725 | 9,662 | 10,327 | 9,865 |
| Broad Money Liabilities | 35l.u | .... | 7,296 | 7,608 | 8,389 | 8,837 | 8,854 | 9,363 | 9,668 | 10,449 | 11,613 | 14,413 | 15,911 |
| Currency Outside Depository Corps | 34a.u | .... | 1,158 | 1,108 | 602 | 669 | 640 | 674 | 711 | 726 | 779 | 839 | 893 |
| Transferable Deposits | 34..u | .... | 2,797 | 2,831 | 3,150 | 3,180 | 3,720 | 4,325 | 4,715 | 5,217 | 5,947 | 8,674 | 10,926 |
| Other Deposits | 35..u | .... | 3,456 | 3,782 | 4,758 | 5,132 | 4,610 | 4,366 | 4,244 | 4,518 | 4,937 | 4,960 | 4,072 |
| Securities Other than Shares | 36a.u | .... | −115 | −113 | −121 | −144 | −115 | −2 | −2 | −13 | −50 | −60 | 20 |
| Deposits Excl. from Broad Money | 36b.u | .... | 731 | 698 | 654 | 559 | 741 | 945 | 1,889 | 2,059 | 2,360 | 2,577 | 2,304 |
| Sec.Oth.th.Shares Excl.f/Brd. Money | 36s.u | .... | −2,468 | −2,711 | −2,576 | −2,115 | −2,082 | −1,673 | −1,715 | −1,607 | −1,364 | −1,676 | −969 |
| Loans | 36l.u | .... | — | — | — | — | — | — | — | — | — | — | — |
| Financial Derivatives | 36m.u | .... | 1,517 | 51 | 80 | 320 | 175 | 308 | 386 | 459 | 362 | 425 | 463 |
| Insurance Technical Reserves | 36r.u | .... | — | — | — | — | — | — | — | — | — | — | — |
| Shares and Other Equity | 37a.u | .... | 2,586 | 3,297 | 3,574 | 3,634 | 4,446 | 10,191 | 10,163 | 10,769 | 7,553 | 5,434 | 4,577 |
| Other Items (Net) | 37r.u | .... | 3,513 | 4,524 | 6,395 | 8,995 | 7,092 | 2,754 | 2,846 | 3,071 | 2,889 | 5,775 | 4,154 |
| Broad Money Liabs., Seasonally Adj. | 35lub | .... | 7,314 | 7,627 | 8,406 | 8,852 | 8,856 | 9,351 | 9,633 | 10,395 | 11,531 | 14,299 | 15,776 |
| Memorandum Items | | | | | | | | | | | | | |
| National Residency Criterion | | | | | | | | | | | | | |
| Net Foreign Assets | 31n | .... | 4,017 | 4,552 | 5,428 | 5,438 | 4,990 | 10,934 | 11,121 | 12,059 | 9,505 | 9,563 | 8,701 |
| Claims on Nonresidents | 31 | .... | 19,666 | 23,403 | 29,869 | 33,130 | 31,393 | 40,098 | 40,557 | 42,258 | 39,541 | 42,819 | 35,320 |
| Liabilities to Nonresidents | 36c | .... | 15,648 | 18,851 | 24,441 | 27,692 | 26,403 | 29,164 | 29,436 | 30,199 | 30,037 | 33,256 | 26,619 |
| Domestic Claims | 32 | .... | 7,671 | 6,741 | 7,535 | 8,697 | 9,325 | 9,829 | 10,493 | 10,799 | 11,003 | 11,600 | 12,600 |
| Net Claims on Central Government | 32an | .... | 1,031 | 850 | 1,024 | 1,144 | 1,383 | 1,413 | 1,626 | 1,780 | 1,984 | 1,991 | 2,377 |
| Claims on Central Government | 32a | .... | 1,476 | 1,302 | 1,523 | 1,616 | 1,925 | 2,088 | 2,350 | 2,284 | 2,475 | 2,495 | 2,916 |
| Liabilities to Central Government | 36d | .... | 445 | 452 | 499 | 472 | 542 | 675 | 725 | 504 | 491 | 504 | 539 |
| Claims on Other Sectors | 32s | .... | 6,640 | 5,891 | 6,511 | 7,553 | 7,942 | 8,417 | 8,867 | 9,019 | 9,019 | 9,609 | 10,223 |
| Claims on Other Financial Corps | 32g | .... | 1,613 | 137 | 232 | 415 | 295 | 522 | 640 | 893 | 897 | 1,099 | 1,605 |
| Claims on State & Local Govts | 32b | .... | 2 | 2 | 2 | 2 | 2 | 3 | 3 | 3 | 3 | 3 | 3 |
| Claims on Private Sector | 32d | .... | 5,025 | 5,752 | 6,277 | 7,136 | 7,644 | 7,892 | 8,224 | 8,123 | 8,120 | 8,507 | 8,615 |
| Transf.Dep.Included in Broad Money | 34 | .... | 2,750 | 2,779 | 3,101 | 3,114 | 3,633 | 4,223 | 4,590 | 5,046 | 5,770 | 8,415 | 10,503 |
| Other Dep.Included in Broad Money | 35 | .... | 3,201 | 3,602 | 4,586 | 4,968 | 4,492 | 4,216 | 4,021 | 4,040 | 4,110 | 4,231 | 3,725 |
| Sec.Ot.th.Shares Inc.in.Brd. Money | 36a | .... | — | — | — | — | — | — | — | — | — | — | — |
| Deposits Excl. from Broad Money | 36b | .... | 665 | 636 | 584 | 532 | 713 | 924 | 1,320 | 1,392 | 1,542 | 1,499 | 1,637 |
| Sec.Ot.th.Shares Excl./f.Brd. Money | 36s | .... | 94 | 83 | 139 | 166 | 242 | 297 | 344 | 393 | 342 | 363 | 433 |
| **Monetary Aggregates** | | | | | | *Millions of Liri: End of Period* | | | | | | | |
| Money (National Definitions) | | | | | | | | | | | | | |
| M1 | 59ma | 1,581 | 1,670 | 1,657 | 1,586 | .... | .... | .... | .... | .... | .... | .... | .... |
| M2 | 59mb | 2,918 | 3,042 | 3,199 | 3,553 | .... | .... | .... | .... | .... | .... | .... | .... |
| M3 | 59mc | 2,918 | 3,042 | 3,199 | 3,553 | .... | .... | .... | .... | .... | .... | .... | .... |
| **Interest Rates** | | | | | | *Percent Per Annum* | | | | | | | |
| Discount Rate (End of Period) | 60.a | 3.00 | 3.25 | 3.75 | 4.00 | .... | .... | .... | .... | .... | .... | .... | .... |
| Treasury Bill Rate | 60c | 2.94 | 3.18 | 3.49 | 4.25 | 4.44 | 1.78 | .82 | 1.23 | .99 | .58 | .... | .... |
| Deposit Rate | 60l | 2.63 | 2.71 | 3.03 | .... | .... | .... | .... | .... | .... | .... | .... | .... |
| Households: Stocks, up to 2 years | 60lhs | .... | .... | .... | .... | 4.06 | 2.91 | 2.10 | 2.05 | 2.08 | 2.08 | 1.93 | 1.38 |
| New Business, up to 1 year | 60lhn | .... | .... | .... | .... | 3.83 | 2.03 | 1.83 | 1.90 | 1.99 | 1.93 | 1.56 | 1.00 |
| Corporations: Stocks, up to 2 years | 60lcs | .... | .... | .... | .... | 4.24 | 2.46 | 1.94 | 1.90 | 1.85 | 1.84 | 1.61 | 1.52 |
| New Business, up to 1 year | 60lcn | .... | .... | .... | .... | 4.23 | 1.83 | 1.73 | 1.79 | 1.88 | 1.95 | 1.24 | .83 |
| Lending Rates | | | | | | | | | | | | | |
| Households: Stocks, up to 1 year | 60phs | .... | .... | .... | .... | 7.51 | 6.20 | 6.35 | 6.27 | 6.24 | 6.24 | 6.27 | 6.38 |
| New Bus., Floating & up to 1 year | 60pns | .... | .... | .... | .... | 6.89 | 5.75 | 5.81 | 5.52 | 5.74 | 5.33 | 4.97 | 5.15 |
| House Purch., Stocks,Over 5 years | 60phm | .... | .... | .... | .... | 5.10 | 3.53 | 3.46 | 3.42 | 3.39 | 3.36 | 3.28 | 3.18 |
| Corporations: Stocks, up to 1 year | 60pcs | .... | .... | .... | .... | 5.98 | 4.81 | 4.71 | 4.52 | 4.43 | 4.66 | 4.25 | 3.99 |
| New Bus., Over € 1 mil.,up to 1 yr | 60pcn | .... | .... | .... | .... | 5.81 | 4.43 | 4.47 | 4.31 | 4.11 | 4.05 | 3.77 | 3.55 |
| Government Bond Yield | 61 | 4.69 | 4.56 | 4.32 | 4.72 | 4.81 | 4.54 | 4.19 | 4.49 | 4.13 | 3.36 | 2.61 | 1.49 |
| **Prices, Production, Labor** | | | | | | *Index Numbers (2010=100): Period Averages* | | | | | | | |
| Consumer Prices | 64 | 86.3 | 88.9 | † 91.4 | 92.6 | 96.5 | 98.5 | 100.0 | 102.7 | 105.2 | 106.7 | 107.0 | 108.2 |
| Harmonized CPI | 64h | 86.8 | 89.0 | 91.3 | 91.9 | 96.2 | 98.0 | 100.0 | 102.5 | 105.8 | 106.9 | 107.7 | 108.9 |
| Industrial Production | 66 | 103.2 | 97.5 | 104.6 | 112.0 | 107.2 | 92.2 | 100.0 | 100.0 | 106.1 | 100.0 | 94.4 | 100.2 |
| | | | | | | *Number in Thousands: Period Averages* | | | | | | | |
| Labor Force | 67d | † 158 | 160 | 161 | 166 | 168 | 170 | 173 | 176 | 179 | 185 | 189 | 193 |
| Employment | 67e | † 146 | 149 | 151 | 155 | 159 | 160 | 163 | 167 | 170 | 176 | 182 | 186 |
| Unemployment | 67c | † 12 | 11 | 11 | 11 | 10 | 12 | 12 | 11 | 12 | 12 | 11 | 11 |
| Unemployment Rate (%) | 67r | † 7.2 | 6.9 | 6.8 | 6.5 | 6.0 | 6.9 | 6.9 | 6.4 | 6.3 | 6.4 | 5.8 | 5.4 |
| **Intl. Transactions & Positions** | | | | | | *Millions of Liri through 2007; Millions of Euros Beginning 2008* | | | | | | | |
| Exports | 70 | 905.40 | 821.99 | 920.43 | 927.90 | 2,455.78 | 2,087.44 | 2,809.34 | 3,819.02 | 4,438.61 | 3,904.29 | 3,632.70 | 3,470.50 |
| Imports, c.i.f. | 71 | 1,315.36 | 1,318.19 | 1,387.48 | 1,400.10 | 3,897.19 | 3,475.24 | 4,330.27 | 5,339.39 | 6,187.15 | 5,641.02 | 6,124.80 | 5,803.10 |

# Malta 181

| | | 2004 | 2005 | 2006 | 2007 | 2008 | 2009 | 2010 | 2011 | 2012 | 2013 | 2014 | 2015 |
|---|---|---|---|---|---|---|---|---|---|---|---|---|---|
| **Balance of Payments** | | | | | | | *Millions of US Dollars* | | | | | | |
| A. Current Account* | 109bx | † −231.0 | −418.3 | −530.5 | −159.3 | −77.7 | −557.6 | −419.9 | −230.5 | 112.7 | 359.0 | 369.4 | 959.4 |
| Goods, credit (exports) | 1a9cx | † 2,718.9 | 2,545.7 | 3,237.0 | 3,697.1 | 3,652.9 | 2,794.6 | 3,346.6 | 3,951.1 | 4,118.6 | 3,817.7 | 3,480.3 | 2,956.0 |
| Goods, debit (imports) | 1a9dx | † 3,569.5 | 3,692.6 | 4,434.5 | 4,975.2 | 5,485.7 | 4,357.8 | 5,002.5 | 5,635.4 | 5,527.5 | 5,284.0 | 4,963.6 | 4,602.6 |
| Balance on goods | 1a9bx | † −850.7 | −1,147.0 | −1,197.5 | −1,278.1 | −1,832.7 | −1,563.1 | −1,655.9 | −1,684.4 | −1,408.9 | −1,466.4 | −1,483.3 | −1,646.6 |
| Services, credit (exports) | 1b9cx | † 3,526.4 | 4,153.8 | 5,154.4 | 6,627.5 | 9,824.0 | 9,868.6 | 10,048.1 | 11,255.7 | 11,027.6 | 11,823.7 | 12,233.9 | 10,657.4 |
| Services, debit (imports) | 1b9dx | † 2,834.6 | 3,264.8 | 4,231.5 | 5,225.1 | 7,913.2 | 8,410.4 | 8,455.2 | 9,326.6 | 9,195.1 | 9,672.0 | 9,903.4 | 8,337.4 |
| Balance on Goods & Services | 1z9bx | † −158.9 | −257.9 | −274.7 | 124.4 | 78.1 | −105.0 | −62.9 | 244.8 | 423.6 | 685.3 | 847.3 | 673.4 |
| Primary income: credit | 1c9cx | † 1,414.2 | 2,983.9 | 5,440.5 | 11,234.5 | 14,792.8 | 10,730.5 | 8,895.4 | 13,845.1 | 12,861.1 | 13,267.0 | 13,305.2 | 10,813.2 |
| Primary income: debit | 1c9dx | † 1,428.2 | 3,187.8 | 5,684.8 | 11,482.1 | 15,018.8 | 11,312.1 | 9,353.7 | 14,441.6 | 13,312.4 | 13,778.1 | 14,043.6 | 10,775.9 |
| Balance on gds, serv. & prim. inc. | 1y9bx | † −173.0 | −461.8 | −519.0 | −123.3 | −148.0 | −686.6 | −521.2 | −351.8 | −27.7 | 174.2 | 108.8 | 710.6 |
| Secondary income: credit | 1d9ca | † 373.2 | 342.9 | 523.5 | 882.9 | 1,348.3 | 1,958.1 | 1,681.6 | 1,223.4 | 1,188.5 | 1,206.4 | 1,262.6 | 1,077.3 |
| Secondary income: debit | 1d9da | † 431.3 | 299.4 | 535.0 | 918.9 | 1,278.0 | 1,829.1 | 1,580.3 | 1,102.1 | 1,048.1 | 1,021.6 | 1,002.1 | 828.5 |
| B. Capital Account* | 209bx | † 86.5 | 197.2 | 195.7 | 99.0 | 33.8 | 104.4 | 170.8 | 112.6 | 173.0 | 175.7 | 189.1 | 175.5 |
| Capital account: credit | 209ca | † 87.2 | 205.5 | 199.7 | 104.5 | 46.9 | 113.2 | 198.7 | 136.3 | 180.4 | 178.0 | 192.2 | 178.1 |
| Capital account: debit | 209da | † .7 | 8.3 | 4.0 | 5.5 | 13.1 | 8.8 | 27.9 | 23.7 | 7.4 | 2.3 | 3.1 | 2.6 |
| Balance on current & capital acct. | 129ba | † −144.5 | −221.1 | −334.7 | −60.3 | −43.9 | −453.2 | −249.2 | −117.9 | 285.7 | 534.7 | 558.4 | 1,134.8 |
| C. Financial Account* | 309na | † 233.8 | −355.6 | −500.7 | −938.2 | −228.4 | −121.5 | −91.0 | −24.6 | 1,008.5 | −284.7 | 575.4 | 1,095.5 |
| Direct investment: assets | 3a9aa | † 5,310.3 | 10,975.9 | 14,854.3 | 14,642.0 | 16,161.7 | −6,096.3 | 3,330.4 | −4,563.6 | −8,232.1 | −8,750.8 | −8,907.0 | −7,109.0 |
| Equity & investment fund shares | 3aaaa | † 1,192.2 | 3,385.5 | 3,795.7 | 14,869.4 | 4,819.8 | 1,170.8 | −895.2 | 5,189.2 | 833.7 | 949.0 | 496.0 | 955.2 |
| Debt instruments | 3abaa | † 4,118.1 | 7,590.5 | 11,058.6 | −227.4 | 11,341.9 | −7,267.1 | 4,225.6 | −9,752.7 | −9,065.8 | −9,699.8 | −9,403.0 | −8,064.2 |
| Direct investment: liabilities | 3a9la | † 7,463.3 | 21,812.5 | 25,024.1 | 35,597.5 | 14,837.4 | 1,444.1 | 9,246.7 | 7,845.0 | 3,280.9 | 388.1 | 9.3 | 2,188.6 |
| Equity & investment fund shares | 3aala | † 3,806.1 | 17,923.4 | 18,551.3 | 33,867.6 | 13,862.7 | −4,759.0 | 1,093.5 | 5,041.2 | 817.5 | −2,641.7 | −3,053.9 | −363.8 |
| Debt instruments | 3abla | † 3,657.1 | 3,889.2 | 6,472.9 | 1,729.9 | 974.8 | 6,203.2 | 8,153.3 | 2,803.9 | 2,463.3 | 3,029.7 | 3,063.1 | 2,552.5 |
| Portfolio investment: assets | 3b9aa | † 3,786.3 | 16,726.1 | 8,973.9 | 18,003.6 | 2,442.5 | 10,608.0 | 6,161.4 | 16,259.3 | 11,444.0 | 10,827.2 | 17,176.7 | 3,995.8 |
| Equity & investment fund shares | 3baaa | † 1,662.2 | 14,251.8 | 6,561.4 | 18,704.0 | 2,310.1 | 7,514.1 | 1,290.5 | 11,542.3 | 8,781.3 | 8,595.2 | 10,242.6 | 7,940.1 |
| Debt securities | 3bbaa | † 2,124.1 | 2,474.3 | 2,412.5 | −700.4 | 132.5 | 3,093.9 | 4,870.9 | 4,717.0 | 2,662.7 | 2,232.0 | 6,934.1 | −3,944.3 |
| Portfolio investment: liabilities | 3b9la | † 409.2 | 1,846.6 | 1,067.7 | 2,565.6 | −1,822.4 | 1,674.6 | −259.0 | 174.8 | −516.9 | −900.7 | −123.2 | −1,275.2 |
| Equity & investment fund shares | 3bala | † 412.3 | 1,846.0 | 1,077.1 | 2,565.1 | −2,063.3 | 1,711.6 | −236.9 | 167.2 | −527.4 | −982.4 | −303.5 | −1,422.1 |
| Debt securities | 3bbla | † −3.1 | .6 | −9.4 | .4 | 240.8 | −37.0 | −22.1 | 7.6 | 10.5 | 81.7 | 180.3 | 146.9 |
| Fin. der.& empl.stk.ops.(ESOs): net | 3c9na | † 107.2 | 462.5 | 228.5 | 443.2 | −57.3 | 1,019.6 | −349.1 | −349.2 | −561.8 | −134.6 | −1,155.5 | −919.8 |
| Fin. der. & ESOs.: assets | 3c9aa | † 128.2 | 466.6 | 274.0 | 620.0 | 688.7 | 1,204.6 | 252.9 | 91.7 | 155.2 | 247.8 | 221.7 | 291.9 |
| Fin. der. & ESOs.: liabilities | 3c9la | † 21.0 | 4.1 | 45.5 | 176.8 | 746.1 | 185.0 | 602.0 | 440.9 | 717.0 | 382.4 | 1,377.1 | 1,211.8 |
| Other investment: assets | 3d9aa | † 5,616.5 | 162.4 | 5,193.9 | 19,690.3 | 9,200.3 | −1,688.2 | −550.3 | 2,767.4 | 2,851.3 | 2,015.0 | −2,539.6 | −2,348.5 |
| Other equity | 3daaa | .... | .... | .... | .... | .... | .... | .... | .... | .... | .... | .... | .... |
| Debt instruments | 3dzaa | † 5,616.5 | 162.4 | 5,193.9 | 19,690.3 | 9,200.3 | −1,688.2 | −550.3 | 2,767.4 | 2,851.3 | 2,015.0 | −2,539.6 | −2,348.5 |
| Other investment: liabilities | 3d9la | † 6,714.0 | 5,023.5 | 3,659.5 | 15,554.2 | 14,960.7 | 845.9 | −304.4 | 6,118.7 | 1,728.9 | 4,754.0 | 4,113.1 | −8,390.6 |
| Other equity | 3dala | .... | .... | .... | .... | .... | .... | .... | .... | .... | .... | .... | .... |
| Debt instruments | 3dzla | † 6,714.0 | 5,023.5 | 3,659.5 | 15,554.2 | 14,960.7 | 845.9 | −304.4 | 6,118.7 | 1,728.9 | 4,754.0 | 4,113.1 | −8,390.6 |
| Curr.+ cap.− finan. acct. balance | 4y9na | † −378.3 | 134.5 | 166.0 | 878.0 | 184.5 | −331.7 | −158.2 | −93.3 | −722.8 | 819.4 | −16.9 | 39.3 |
| D. Net Errors and Omissions | 409na | † 170.5 | 82.4 | −51.7 | −382.7 | −334.4 | 330.4 | 188.5 | 17.2 | 882.9 | −869.5 | 64.9 | −121.6 |
| E. Reserves and Related Items | 4z9na | † −207.9 | 216.8 | 114.3 | 495.2 | −149.9 | −1.3 | 30.3 | −76.1 | 160.1 | −50.1 | 48.0 | −82.3 |
| Reserve assets | 3e9aa | † −207.9 | 216.8 | 114.3 | 495.2 | −149.9 | −1.3 | 30.3 | −76.1 | 160.1 | −50.1 | 48.0 | −82.3 |
| Credit and loans from the IMF | 3dcla | † — | — | — | — | — | — | — | — | — | — | — | — |
| Exceptional financing | 409la | .... | .... | .... | .... | .... | .... | .... | .... | .... | .... | .... | .... |

*Excludes components in group E

| **International Investment Position** | | | | | | | *Millions of US Dollars* | | | | | | |
|---|---|---|---|---|---|---|---|---|---|---|---|---|---|
| Assets | 809aa | 23,486.9 | 27,449.1 | 36,060.4 | 50,451.1 | † 207,058.6 | 222,114.2 | 231,954.7 | 249,015.5 | 269,336.2 | 287,165.3 | 267,493.3 | .... |
| Direct investment | 8a9aa | 1,791.1 | 1,636.2 | 1,902.9 | 2,077.2 | † 66,802.7 | 64,091.2 | 71,483.0 | 70,001.5 | 70,332.5 | 71,743.9 | 61,617.3 | .... |
| Equity & investment fund shares | 8aaaa | 921.2 | 854.5 | 1,022.0 | 1,053.6 | † 10,805.3 | 10,172.0 | 10,333.5 | 7,872.4 | 7,803.1 | 7,903.2 | 6,220.6 | .... |
| Debt instruments | 8abaa | 869.8 | 781.7 | 880.9 | 1,023.6 | † 55,997.4 | 53,919.2 | 61,149.5 | 62,129.1 | 62,529.4 | 63,840.7 | 55,396.7 | .... |
| Portfolio investment | 8b9aa | 9,731.3 | 11,860.6 | 14,975.6 | 15,743.7 | † 63,624.9 | 77,156.7 | 78,542.4 | 89,440.8 | 104,608.0 | 116,785.1 | 120,222.5 | .... |
| Equity & investment fund shares | 8baaa | 605.5 | 775.4 | 1,059.9 | 1,319.4 | † 50,428.7 | 59,914.7 | 56,771.3 | 65,617.3 | 75,908.0 | 88,374.8 | 86,353.5 | .... |
| Debt securities | 8bbaa | 9,125.9 | 11,085.2 | 13,915.7 | 14,424.3 | † 13,196.2 | 17,242.1 | 21,771.1 | 23,823.5 | 28,700.0 | 28,410.3 | 33,869.0 | .... |
| Fin. der.(oth.than reserves) & ESOs | 8c9aa | 14.6 | 49.9 | 45.3 | 157.2 | † 1,570.3 | 2,414.3 | 2,685.4 | 2,476.1 | 2,633.7 | 2,450.9 | 2,297.3 | .... |
| Other investment | 8d9aa | 9,187.7 | 11,320.3 | 16,186.1 | 28,703.0 | † 74,687.4 | 77,913.4 | 78,703.6 | 86,584.8 | 91,057.9 | 95,585.2 | 82,736.8 | .... |
| Other equity | 8daaa | .... | .... | .... | .... | .... | .... | .... | .... | .... | .... | .... | .... |
| Debt instruments | 8dzaa | 9,187.7 | 11,320.3 | 16,186.1 | 28,703.0 | † 74,687.4 | 77,913.4 | 78,703.6 | 86,584.8 | 91,057.9 | 95,585.2 | 82,736.8 | .... |
| Reserve assets | 8e9aa | 2,762.3 | 2,582.1 | 2,950.4 | 3,770.0 | † 373.4 | 538.6 | 540.2 | 512.2 | 704.1 | 600.2 | 619.4 | .... |
| Liabilities | 809la | 21,033.7 | 25,366.2 | 34,206.0 | 48,832.7 | † 206,994.5 | 221,137.6 | 231,000.8 | 248,388.7 | 267,312.8 | 284,767.5 | 264,014.8 | .... |
| Direct investment | 8a9la | 4,731.3 | 4,945.2 | 7,286.8 | 8,994.9 | † 139,852.5 | 150,175.9 | 163,920.1 | 179,043.3 | 193,781.8 | 208,020.0 | 189,481.7 | .... |
| Equity & investment fund shares | 8aala | 4,294.3 | 4,338.6 | 6,056.3 | 7,581.6 | † 115,671.1 | 118,713.9 | 126,408.1 | 140,223.7 | 151,570.4 | 161,108.6 | 145,828.6 | .... |
| Debt instruments | 8abla | 437.0 | 606.6 | 1,230.5 | 1,413.3 | † 24,181.4 | 31,462.0 | 37,512.0 | 38,819.5 | 42,211.3 | 46,911.4 | 43,653.1 | .... |
| Portfolio investment | 8b9la | 483.0 | 487.2 | 537.5 | 598.9 | † 5,529.7 | 7,468.6 | 6,777.6 | 6,307.6 | 7,155.5 | 6,166.6 | 5,980.5 | .... |
| Equity & investment fund shares | 8bala | 160.8 | 214.3 | 245.4 | 262.4 | † 4,982.9 | 6,953.5 | 6,335.2 | 5,881.6 | 6,708.9 | 5,637.1 | 5,350.1 | .... |
| Debt securities | 8bbla | 322.2 | 272.9 | 292.1 | 336.5 | † 546.8 | 515.1 | 442.5 | 426.0 | 446.7 | 529.5 | · 630.4 | .... |
| Fin. der.(oth.than reserves) & ESOs | 8c9la | 51.9 | 52.1 | 65.0 | 116.4 | † 452.0 | 372.1 | 724.7 | 786.5 | 774.6 | 645.6 | 642.9 | .... |
| Other investment | 8d9la | 15,767.5 | 19,881.7 | 26,316.6 | 39,122.4 | † 61,160.2 | 63,121.0 | 59,578.3 | 62,251.3 | 65,600.9 | 69,935.3 | 67,909.7 | .... |
| Other equity | 8dala | .... | .... | .... | .... | .... | .... | .... | .... | .... | .... | .... | .... |
| Debt instruments | 8dzla | 15,767.5 | 19,881.7 | 26,316.6 | 39,122.4 | † 61,160.2 | 63,121.0 | 59,578.3 | 62,251.3 | 65,600.9 | 69,935.3 | 67,909.7 | .... |

| | | 2004 | 2005 | 2006 | 2007 | 2008 | 2009 | 2010 | 2011 | 2012 | 2013 | 2014 | 2015 |
|---|---|---|---|---|---|---|---|---|---|---|---|---|---|
| **Government Finance Operations Statement General Government** | | *Millions of Euros: Fiscal Year Ends December 31; Data Reported through Eurostat* | | | | | | | | | | | |
| Revenue.......................... | a1 | 1,837.5 | 2,037.0 | 2,139.1 | 2,241.9 | 2,354.6 | 2,368.6 | 2,499.7 | 2,643.8 | 2,806.7 | 3,011.6 | 3,330.3 | 3,683.1 |
| Taxes.............. | a11 | 1,156.7 | 1,303.3 | 1,392.7 | 1,555.9 | 1,603.0 | 1,629.5 | 1,678.7 | 1,786.1 | 1,889.1 | 2,037.1 | 2,265.0 | 2,441.7 |
| Social Contributions............. | a12 | 360.3 | 380.2 | 389.8 | 398.3 | 432.0 | 434.9 | 456.5 | 486.7 | 504.4 | 524.8 | 560.3 | 596.3 |
| Grants........................... | a13 | .... | .... | .... | .... | .... | .... | .... | .... | .... | .... | .... | .... |
| Other Revenue..................... | a14 | .... | .... | .... | .... | .... | .... | .... | .... | .... | .... | .... | .... |
| Expense................. | a2 | 2,001.3 | 2,078.4 | 2,186.1 | 2,299.2 | 2,598.7 | 2,573.2 | 2,707.8 | 2,784.6 | 2,986.5 | 3,156.5 | 3,371.4 | 3,593.8 |
| Compensation of Employees........... | a21 | 666.0 | 676.3 | 686.5 | 715.8 | 846.2 | 838.3 | 855.1 | 882.1 | 922.4 | 976.1 | 1,048.6 | 1,116.4 |
| Use of Goods & Services.... | a22 | 257.8 | 247.5 | 296.4 | 306.7 | 391.5 | 365.0 | 403.1 | 430.3 | 483.2 | 471.8 | 524.8 | 596.5 |
| Consumption of Fixed Capital........ | a23 | 106.3 | 102.7 | 112.8 | 118.0 | 126.9 | 136.1 | 144.2 | 151.5 | 161.0 | 168.9 | 171.2 | 177.1 |
| Interest.............. | a24 | 180.1 | 194.2 | 199.3 | 200.3 | 205.0 | 200.8 | 203.2 | 216.9 | 215.1 | 219.1 | 230.8 | 227.6 |
| Subsidies.................. | a25 | 69.8 | 85.2 | 93.8 | 97.9 | 115.1 | 50.0 | 52.8 | 51.0 | 76.9 | 80.3 | 105.0 | 110.6 |
| Grants............................ | a26 | .... | .... | .... | .... | .... | .... | .... | .... | .... | .... | .... | .... |
| Social Benefits..................... | a27 | 599.2 | 642.2 | 665.4 | 717.5 | 755.7 | 807.3 | 842.4 | 878.9 | 924.9 | 964.2 | 1,004.1 | 1,033.2 |
| Other Expense.................. | a28 | .... | .... | .... | .... | .... | .... | .... | .... | .... | .... | .... | .... |
| Gross Operating Balance [1-2+23]... | agob | −57.4 | 61.2 | 65.8 | 60.6 | −117.2 | −68.5 | −63.9 | 10.6 | −18.8 | 24.0 | 130.1 | 266.4 |
| Net Operating Balance [1-2]........ | anob | −163.8 | −41.5 | −47.0 | −57.4 | −244.1 | −204.6 | −208.1 | −140.8 | −179.8 | −144.9 | −41.1 | 89.3 |
| Net Acq. of Nonfinancial Assets....... | a31 | 49.0 | 97.4 | 93.8 | 72.4 | 10.6 | −3.2 | 2.3 | 36.0 | 76.3 | 53.0 | 122.3 | 218.3 |
| Aquisition of Nonfin. Assets.......... | a31.1 | .... | .... | .... | .... | .... | .... | .... | .... | .... | .... | .... | .... |
| Disposal of Nonfin. Assets........... | a31.2 | .... | .... | .... | .... | .... | .... | .... | .... | .... | .... | .... | .... |
| Net Lending/Borrowing [1-2-31]...... | anlb | −212.8 | −138.9 | −140.8 | −129.8 | −254.7 | −201.5 | −210.5 | −176.9 | −256.1 | −197.9 | −163.4 | −129.0 |
| Net Acq. of Financial Assets......... | a32 | 9.0 | 42.5 | −160.3 | 98.0 | 29.4 | 170.4 | 135.1 | 252.5 | 108.3 | 160.3 | 108.5 | 3.4 |
| By instrument | | | | | | | | | | | | | |
| Monetary Gold & SDRs................. | a3201 | — | — | — | — | — | — | — | — | — | — | — | — |
| Currency & Deposits..................... | a3202 | 25.6 | 86.6 | 69.6 | 83.3 | −16.3 | 141.9 | 44.0 | 64.5 | −227.3 | −19.2 | 74.6 | −27.2 |
| Securities other than Shares........... | a3203 | — | — | — | — | — | — | — | — | — | — | — | — |
| Loans.............. | a3204 | −5.5 | .1 | −2.8 | 1.1 | 5.3 | −3.3 | 33.5 | 84.8 | 120.2 | 36.2 | 11.4 | −52.1 |
| Shares & Other Equity.................. | a3205 | −9.4 | −55.4 | −220.0 | −48.3 | −5.4 | −1.0 | −.9 | 11.6 | 39.8 | 26.4 | 15.1 | −8.1 |
| Insurance Technical Reserves......... | a3206 | — | — | — | — | — | — | — | — | — | — | — | — |
| Financial Derivatives................... | a3207 | — | — | — | — | — | — | — | — | — | — | — | — |
| Other Accounts Receivable............. | a3208 | −1.7 | 11.2 | −7.0 | 61.9 | 45.8 | 32.8 | 58.5 | 91.5 | 175.6 | 116.9 | 7.5 | 90.8 |
| By debtor | | | | | | | | | | | | | |
| Domestic.......................... | a321 | .... | .... | .... | .... | .... | .... | .... | .... | .... | .... | .... | .... |
| Foreign............................ | a322 | .... | .... | .... | .... | .... | .... | .... | .... | .... | .... | .... | .... |
| Net Incurrence of Liabilities.............. | a33 | 222.3 | 166.5 | −39.1 | 211.9 | 282.3 | 369.1 | 334.6 | 429.3 | 367.6 | 348.2 | 263.1 | 133.6 |
| By instrument | | | | | | | | | | | | | |
| Special Drawing Rights (SDRs)....... | a3301 | — | — | — | — | — | — | — | — | — | — | — | — |
| Currency & Deposits............. | a3302 | — | — | — | 8.3 | 22.9 | 6.0 | 3.8 | 4.9 | 4.6 | 4.8 | 5.1 | 7.5 |
| Securities other than Shares........... | a3303 | 284.0 | 153.5 | −66.9 | 122.9 | 214.3 | 371.7 | 291.4 | 313.0 | 176.1 | 334.4 | 159.2 | 212.0 |
| Loans.............. | a3304 | −73.9 | −43.4 | −37.6 | 12.3 | −15.8 | −53.8 | −9.2 | 14.4 | 85.1 | 30.9 | 16.5 | −16.4 |
| Shares & Other Equity.............. | a3305 | — | — | — | — | — | — | — | — | — | — | — | — |
| Insurance Technical Reserves......... | a3306 | — | — | — | — | — | — | — | — | — | — | — | — |
| Financial Derivatives................... | a3307 | — | — | — | — | — | — | — | — | — | — | — | — |
| Other Accounts Payable............... | a3308 | 12.2 | 56.4 | 65.4 | 68.3 | 61.0 | 45.3 | 48.6 | 97.0 | 101.7 | −22.0 | 82.4 | −69.5 |
| By creditor | | | | | | | | | | | | | |
| Domestic.................... | a331 | .... | .... | .... | .... | .... | .... | .... | .... | .... | .... | .... | .... |
| Foreign..................... | a332 | .... | .... | .... | .... | .... | .... | .... | .... | .... | .... | .... | .... |
| Stat. Discrepancy [32-33-NLB]........ | anlbz | −.5 | 14.8 | 19.6 | 15.8 | 1.8 | 2.7 | 10.9 | .1 | −3.1 | 10.1 | 8.8 | −1.2 |
| Memo Item: Expenditure [2+31]...... | a2m | 2,050.3 | 2,175.8 | 2,279.9 | 2,371.6 | 2,609.2 | 2,570.0 | 2,710.2 | 2,820.6 | 3,062.8 | 3,209.5 | 3,493.8 | 3,812.1 |
| **Balance Sheet** | | | | | | | | | | | | | |
| Net Worth.................... | a6 | .... | .... | .... | .... | .... | .... | .... | .... | .... | .... | .... | .... |
| Nonfinancial Assets................ | a61 | .... | .... | .... | .... | .... | .... | .... | .... | .... | .... | .... | .... |
| Financial Assets.................... | a62 | 1,538.2 | 1,777.4 | 1,520.8 | 1,680.2 | 1,606.8 | 1,806.2 | 1,975.5 | 2,200.5 | 2,507.7 | 2,711.0 | 2,695.7 | 2,749.5 |
| By instrument | | | | | | | | | | | | | |
| Monetary Gold & SDRs................. | a6201 | — | — | — | — | — | — | — | — | — | — | — | — |
| Currency & Deposits..................... | a6202 | 319.6 | 406.3 | 441.2 | 518.7 | 498.0 | 604.8 | 608.5 | 670.2 | 431.3 | 408.8 | 486.3 | 427.4 |
| Securities other than Shares........... | a6203 | — | — | — | — | — | — | — | — | — | — | — | — |
| Loans..................... | a6204 | 31.7 | 17.9 | 15.1 | 16.1 | 21.5 | 18.2 | 51.7 | 136.6 | 256.8 | 292.9 | 304.4 | 254.2 |
| Shares and Other Equity................ | a6205 | 1,035.5 | 1,138.3 | 866.8 | 848.0 | 753.0 | 812.4 | 871.9 | 856.5 | 1,113.4 | 1,186.1 | 1,074.5 | 1,146.4 |
| Insurance Technical Reserves......... | a6206 | — | — | — | — | — | — | — | — | — | — | — | — |
| Financial Derivatives................... | a6207 | — | 9.7 | — | — | 2.1 | — | — | — | — | — | — | — |
| Other Accounts Receivable............. | a6208 | 151.5 | 205.1 | 197.8 | 297.4 | 332.3 | 370.8 | 443.3 | 537.3 | 706.2 | 823.2 | 830.6 | 921.4 |
| By debtor | | | | | | | | | | | | | |
| Domestic........................... | a621 | .... | .... | .... | .... | .... | .... | .... | .... | .... | .... | .... | .... |
| Foreign............................ | a622 | .... | .... | .... | .... | .... | .... | .... | .... | .... | .... | .... | .... |
| Liabilities................... | a63 | 4,046.6 | 4,318.1 | 4,172.7 | 4,264.0 | 4,734.9 | 5,072.9 | 5,381.9 | 5,797.6 | 6,038.4 | 6,452.8 | 7,157.4 | 7,424.1 |
| By instrument | | | | | | | | | | | | | |
| Special Drawing Rights (SDRs)....... | a6301 | — | — | — | — | — | — | — | — | — | — | — | — |
| Currency & Deposits................ | a6302 | — | — | — | 8.3 | 31.2 | 37.2 | 41.0 | 45.8 | 50.4 | 55.3 | 60.4 | 67.9 |
| Securities other than Shares........... | a6303 | 3,204.1 | 3,420.1 | 3,296.7 | 3,308.6 | 3,662.9 | 3,994.2 | 4,307.5 | 4,621.3 | 4,887.3 | 5,291.7 | 5,889.5 | 6,265.5 |
| Loans.......................... | a6304 | 567.7 | 555.2 | 492.1 | 479.9 | 497.0 | 436.7 | 443.0 | 462.3 | 347.1 | 378.0 | 394.5 | 378.1 |
| Shares and Other Equity............... | a6305 | — | — | — | — | — | — | — | — | — | — | — | — |
| Insurance Technical Reserves......... | a6306 | — | — | — | — | — | — | — | — | — | — | — | — |
| Financial Derivatives................... | a6307 | 18.4 | .9 | 11.9 | 31.2 | — | 50.7 | 30.9 | 14.1 | — | — | — | — |
| Other Accounts Payable................ | a6308 | 256.4 | 341.9 | 371.9 | 435.9 | 543.8 | 554.1 | 559.6 | 654.1 | 753.5 | 727.8 | 813.0 | 712.6 |
| By creditor | | | | | | | | | | | | | |
| Domestic.................... | a631 | .... | .... | .... | .... | .... | .... | .... | .... | .... | .... | .... | .... |
| Foreign..................... | a632 | .... | .... | .... | .... | .... | .... | .... | .... | .... | .... | .... | .... |
| Net Financial Worth [62-63]......... | a6m2 | −2,508.4 | −2,540.7 | −2,651.9 | −2,583.7 | −3,128.0 | −3,266.7 | −3,406.4 | −3,597.1 | −3,530.7 | −3,741.8 | −4,461.7 | −4,674.6 |
| Memo Item: Debt at Market Value... | a6m3 | 4,028.2 | 4,317.2 | 4,160.8 | 4,232.8 | 4,734.9 | 5,022.2 | 5,351.0 | 5,783.5 | 6,038.4 | 6,452.8 | 7,157.4 | 7,424.1 |
| Memo Item: Debt at Face Value........ | a6m35 | 3,748.7 | 3,952.0 | 3,852.2 | 4,028.0 | 4,389.3 | 4,715.9 | 5,022.9 | 5,463.5 | 5,626.0 | 5,973.0 | 6,234.8 | 6,333.2 |
| Memo Item: Maastricht Debt.......... | a6m36 | 3,492.3 | 3,610.1 | 3,480.3 | 3,592.1 | 3,845.5 | 4,161.9 | 4,463.3 | 4,809.4 | 4,872.5 | 5,245.2 | 5,421.9 | 5,620.7 |
| Memo Item: Debt at Nominal Value. | a6m4 | .... | .... | .... | .... | .... | .... | .... | .... | .... | .... | .... | .... |

| | | 2004 | 2005 | 2006 | 2007 | 2008 | 2009 | 2010 | 2011 | 2012 | 2013 | 2014 | 2015 |
|---|---|---|---|---|---|---|---|---|---|---|---|---|---|
| **National Accounts** | | | | | | *Millions of Liri through 2007; Millions of Euros Beginning 2008* | | | | | | | |
| Househ.Cons.Expend.,incl.NPISHs.... | 96f | 1,276.9 | 1,333.2 | 3,419.1 | 3,485.0 | † 3,605.5 | 3,742.3 | 3,814.9 | 4,025.8 | 4,129.6 | 4,254.3 | 4,397.7 | 4,615.6 |
| Government Consumption Expend... | 91f | 400.9 | 405.7 | 1,002.8 | 1,032.7 | † 1,209.4 | 1,213.9 | 1,286.4 | 1,343.8 | 1,446.4 | 1,478.6 | 1,606.2 | 1,711.9 |
| Gross Fixed Capital Formation......... | 93e | 363.0 | 400.7 | 1,183.3 | 1,288.2 | † 1,203.1 | 1,114.8 | 1,411.6 | 1,202.9 | 1,316.7 | 1,360.4 | 1,530.6 | 1,806.7 |
| Changes in Inventories.................... | 93i | −30.7 | 30.3 | −37.1 | −80.8 | † 126.0 | 159.9 | 146.6 | 132.1 | −54.9 | 2.9 | −131.2 | −53.1 |
| Exports of Goods and Services......... | 90c | 1,527.1 | 1,588.6 | 6,649.5 | 7,458.0 | † 9,099.7 | 9,068.9 | 10,114.1 | 10,988.8 | 11,857.0 | 11,776.3 | 11,826.0 | 12,465.3 |
| Imports of Goods and Services (-)..... | 98c | 1,601.6 | 1,697.8 | 6,831.2 | 7,425.6 | † 9,114.9 | 9,161.2 | 10,174.2 | 10,800.4 | 11,491.8 | 11,364.2 | 11,317.2 | 11,795.3 |
| Gross Domestic Product (GDP)......... | 99b | 1,935.6 | 2,060.6 | 5,386.1 | 5,757.5 | † 6,128.7 | 6,138.6 | 6,599.5 | 6,892.9 | 7,203.1 | 7,508.3 | 7,912.1 | 8,751.1 |
| Net Primary Income from Abroad..... | 98.n | −23.3 | −93.6 | −96.7 | −62.6 | † −197.0 | −444.5 | −426.8 | −339.4 | −424.3 | −448.0 | . . . . | . . . . |
| Gross National Income (GNI)........... | 99a | 1,912.3 | 1,967.0 | 2,090.8 | 2,262.0 | † 5,766.5 | 5,511.6 | 6,022.0 | 6,354.4 | 6,456.1 | 6,738.4 | . . . . | . . . . |
| Consumption of Fixed Capital.......... | 99cf | 288.5 | 289.8 | 302.4 | 311.5 | † 801.6 | 837.4 | 876.4 | 942.0 | 984.1 | 994.6 | . . . . | . . . . |
| GDP Volume 2000 Prices................. | 99b.p | 1,726.4 | 1,781.8 | 1,842.3 | 1,912.2 | † 4,722.0 | 4,598.4 | 4,731.3 | 5,005.1 | 5,037.5 | 5,156.1 | | . . . . |
| GDP Volume 2010 Prices................. | 99b.p | . . . . | . . . . | 2,610.4 | 2,714.6 | 2,805.3 | 2,736.2 | 2,833.2 | 2,892.6 | 2,964.0 | 3,031.6 | 3,138.7 | 3,393.5 |
| GDP Volume 2010 Ref., Chained..... | 99b.p | . . . . | . . . . | 6,080.6 | 6,322.9 | † 6,534.6 | 6,373.7 | 6,599.5 | 6,737.9 | 6,904.2 | 7,061.7 | 7,311.2 | 7,904.8 |
| GDP Volume (2010=100)................. | 99bvp | 86.3 | 89.1 | † 92.1 | 95.8 | 99.0 | 96.6 | 100.0 | 102.1 | 104.6 | 107.0 | 110.8 | 119.8 |
| GDP Deflator (2010=100)............... | 99bip | 79.1 | 81.6 | 88.6 | 91.1 | 93.8 | 96.3 | 100.0 | 102.3 | 104.3 | 106.3 | 108.2 | 110.7 |
| | | | | | | *Millions: Midyear Estimates* | | | | | | | |
| Population............................... | 99z | .39 | .40 | .40 | .40 | .41 | .41 | .41 | .41 | .42 | .42 | .42 | .42 |

# Marshall Islands, Republic of   867

| | | 2004 | 2005 | 2006 | 2007 | 2008 | 2009 | 2010 | 2011 | 2012 | 2013 | 2014 | 2015 |
|---|---|---|---|---|---|---|---|---|---|---|---|---|---|
| **Exchange Rates** | | | | | | *End of Period (sa) Period Averages (sb)* | | | | | | | |
| US Dollar/SDR Rate......................... | sa | 1.5530 | 1.4293 | 1.5044 | 1.5803 | 1.5403 | 1.5677 | 1.5400 | 1.5353 | 1.5369 | 1.5400 | 1.4488 | 1.3857 |
| US Dollar/SDR Rate......................... | sb | 1.4810 | 1.4773 | 1.4712 | 1.5306 | 1.5801 | 1.5420 | 1.5257 | 1.5787 | 1.5317 | 1.5196 | 1.5190 | 1.3991 |
| **Fund Position** | | | | | | *Millions of SDRs: End of Period* | | | | | | | |
| Quota.......................................... | 2f.s | 3.50 | 3.50 | 3.50 | 3.50 | 3.50 | 3.50 | 3.50 | 3.50 | 3.50 | 3.50 | 3.50 | 3.50 |
| SDR Holdings................................ | 1b.s | — | — | — | — | — | 3.33 | 3.33 | 3.33 | 3.34 | 3.36 | 3.36 | 3.36 |
| Reserve Position in the Fund............ | 1c.s | — | — | — | — | — | — | — | — | — | — | — | — |
| Total Fund Cred. & Loans Outstg..... | 2tl | — | — | — | — | — | — | — | — | — | — | — | — |
| SDR Allocations............................. | 1bd | — | — | — | — | — | 3.33 | 3.33 | 3.33 | 3.33 | 3.33 | 3.33 | 3.33 |
| **Balance of Payments** | | | | | | *Millions of US Dollars* | | | | | | | |
| A. Current Account*....................... | 109bx | .... | † −2.54 | −6.18 | −8.22 | −5.52 | −26.40 | −14.34 | −5.78 | −19.61 | −28.92 | −4.88 | .... |
| Goods, credit (exports)................. | 1a9cx | .... | † 23.46 | 17.90 | 18.33 | 20.23 | 20.79 | 45.57 | 66.48 | 106.79 | 101.75 | 75.83 | .... |
| Goods, debit (imports)................. | 1a9dx | .... | † 85.13 | 81.97 | 87.93 | 90.01 | 94.31 | 110.32 | 118.67 | 125.31 | 135.84 | 121.13 | .... |
| Balance on goods....................... | 1a9bx | .... | † −61.66 | −64.06 | −69.60 | −69.78 | −73.52 | −64.74 | −52.20 | −18.52 | −34.09 | −45.29 | .... |
| Services, credit (exports)............... | 1b9cx | .... | † 9.82 | 9.75 | 9.40 | 9.53 | 10.15 | 9.39 | 10.75 | 9.91 | 11.03 | 12.89 | .... |
| Services, debit (imports)............... | 1b9dx | .... | † 49.70 | 47.21 | 52.77 | 49.16 | 63.63 | 54.25 | 58.40 | 60.86 | 66.86 | 60.37 | .... |
| Balance on Goods & Services....... | 1z9bx | .... | † −101.54 | −101.52 | −112.97 | −109.41 | −127.00 | −109.60 | −99.85 | −69.46 | −89.92 | −92.77 | .... |
| Primary income: credit.................. | 1c9cx | .... | † 52.10 | 55.67 | 56.53 | 54.77 | 52.89 | 50.19 | 56.12 | 56.31 | 58.68 | 62.78 | .... |
| Primary income: debit.................. | 1c9dx | .... | † 10.54 | 14.40 | 13.71 | 12.93 | 12.32 | 14.66 | 20.38 | 60.39 | 54.03 | 28.80 | .... |
| Balance on gds, serv. & prim. inc. | 1y9bx | .... | † −59.97 | −60.25 | −70.14 | −67.57 | −86.43 | −74.06 | −64.10 | −73.54 | −85.27 | −58.79 | .... |
| Secondary income: credit............. | 1d9ca | .... | † 61.01 | 57.78 | 65.80 | 66.16 | 64.46 | 65.45 | 64.56 | 67.00 | 71.62 | 71.70 | .... |
| Secondary income: debit.............. | 1d9da | .... | † 3.58 | 3.71 | 3.88 | 4.11 | 4.43 | 5.73 | 6.25 | 13.07 | 15.27 | 17.79 | .... |
| B. Capital Account*....................... | 209ba | .... | † 6.08 | 22.34 | 23.24 | 19.67 | 23.81 | 18.87 | 15.76 | 9.14 | 12.91 | 8.82 | .... |
| Capital account: credit................. | 209ca | .... | † 8.58 | 24.84 | 23.24 | 19.67 | 23.81 | 18.87 | 15.76 | 9.14 | 12.91 | 8.82 | .... |
| Capital account: debit.................. | 209da | .... | † 2.50 | 2.50 | .... | .... | .... | .... | .... | .... | .... | .... | .... |
| Balance on current & capital acct. | 129ba | .... | † 3.54 | 16.16 | 15.02 | 14.16 | −2.59 | 4.53 | 9.98 | −10.47 | −16.01 | 3.94 | .... |
| C. Financial Account*  ................... | 309na | .... | † −3.91 | −27.65 | .10 | −22.47 | −35.95 | 18.85 | −21.34 | −28.86 | −34.39 | −14.04 | .... |
| Direct investment: assets............. | 3a9aa | .... | .... | 2.94 | .... | .... | .... | .... | .... | .... | .... | .... | .... |
| Equity & investment fund shares.. | 3aaaa | .... | .... | 2.94 | .... | .... | .... | .... | .... | .... | .... | .... | .... |
| Debt instruments...................... | 3abaa | .... | .... | .... | .... | .... | .... | .... | .... | .... | .... | .... | .... |
| Direct investment: liabilities .......... | 3a9la | .... | † 3.28 | 1.88 | 6.99 | 5.69 | 14.65 | −9.36 | −4.38 | 21.37 | 32.55 | 9.05 | .... |
| Equity & investment fund shares . | 3aala | .... | † 3.28 | 1.88 | 6.99 | 5.69 | 14.65 | 2.24 | 7.24 | 33.00 | 24.70 | 9.05 | .... |
| Debt instruments...................... | 3abla | .... | .... | .... | .... | .... | .... | −11.60 | −11.62 | −11.62 | 7.84 | .... | .... |
| Portfolio investment: assets .......... | 3b9aa | .... | † −6.32 | −22.73 | .49 | −18.25 | −11.17 | −.61 | −10.07 | −3.13 | −3.66 | −6.01 | .... |
| Equity & investment fund shares.. | 3baaa | .... | † −6.32 | −22.73 | .49 | −18.25 | −11.17 | −.59 | −10.05 | −3.16 | −3.69 | −6.10 | .... |
| Debt securities......................... | 3bbaa | .... | .... | .... | .... | .... | .... | −.02 | −.02 | .03 | .03 | .09 | .... |
| Portfolio investment: liabilities....... | 3b9la | .... | † −.28 | −.12 | −1.48 | −.61 | .80 | .... | .... | .... | .... | .... | .... |
| Equity & investment fund shares . | 3bala | .... | † −.28 | −.12 | −1.48 | −.61 | .80 | .... | .... | .... | .... | .... | .... |
| Debt securities......................... | 3bbla | .... | .... | .... | .... | .... | .... | .... | .... | .... | .... | .... | .... |
| Fin. der.& empl.stk.ops.(ESOs): net. | 3c9na | .... | .... | .... | .... | .... | .... | .... | .... | .... | .... | .... | .... |
| Fin. der. & ESOs.: assets............. | 3c9aa | .... | .... | .... | .... | .... | .... | .... | .... | .... | .... | .... | .... |
| Fin. der. & ESOs.: liabilities.......... | 3c9la | .... | .... | .... | .... | .... | .... | .... | .... | .... | .... | .... | .... |
| Other investment: assets............... | 3d9aa | .... | † 2.62 | 3.98 | 3.17 | −3.64 | 6.50 | 6.88 | .14 | −8.88 | 2.76 | −2.71 | .... |
| Other equity.............................. | 3daaa | .... | .... | .... | .... | .... | .... | .23 | .12 | .... | .... | .... | .... |
| Debt instruments...................... | 3dzaa | .... | † 2.62 | 3.98 | 3.17 | −3.64 | 6.50 | 6.65 | .02 | −8.88 | 2.76 | −2.71 | .... |
| Other investment: liabilities........... | 3d9la | .... | † −2.80 | 10.08 | −1.95 | −4.51 | 15.83 | −3.22 | 15.78 | −4.52 | .94 | −3.73 | .... |
| Other equity.............................. | 3dala | .... | .... | .... | .... | .... | .... | .... | .... | .... | .... | .... | .... |
| Debt instruments...................... | 3dzla | .... | † −2.80 | 10.08 | −1.95 | −4.51 | 15.83 | −3.22 | 15.78 | −4.52 | .94 | −3.73 | .... |
| Curr.+ cap.− finan. acct. balance... | 4y9na | .... | † 7.45 | 43.80 | 14.92 | 36.63 | 33.36 | −14.32 | 31.32 | 18.39 | 18.38 | 17.97 | .... |
| D. Net Errors and Omissions............ | 409na | .... | † −7.45 | −43.80 | −14.92 | −36.63 | −28.15 | 14.32 | −31.32 | −18.38 | −18.34 | −17.97 | .... |
| E. Reserves and Related Items.......... | 4z9na | .... | † — | — | — | — | 5.20 | — | — | .02 | .04 | — | .... |
| Reserve assets............................. | 3e9aa | .... | † — | — | — | — | 5.20 | — | — | .02 | .04 | — | .... |
| Credit and loans from the IMF....... | 3dcla | .... | † — | — | — | — | — | — | — | — | — | — | .... |
| Exceptional financing................... | 409la | .... | .... | .... | .... | .... | .... | .... | .... | .... | .... | .... | .... |
| *Excludes components in group E | | | | | | | | | | | | | |
| **International Investment Position** | | | | | | *Millions of US Dollars* | | | | | | | |
| Assets.......................................... | 809aa | .... | .... | .... | .... | .... | .... | † 388.65 | 371.85 | 385.17 | 397.17 | 399.08 | .... |
| Direct investment......................... | 8a9aa | .... | .... | .... | .... | .... | .... | .... | .... | .... | .... | .... | .... |
| Equity & investment fund shares.. | 8aaaa | .... | .... | .... | .... | .... | .... | .... | .... | .... | .... | .... | .... |
| Debt instruments...................... | 8abaa | .... | .... | .... | .... | .... | .... | .... | .... | .... | .... | .... | .... |
| Portfolio investment..................... | 8b9aa | .... | .... | .... | .... | .... | .... | † 270.05 | 253.38 | 267.60 | 270.97 | 273.11 | .... |
| Equity & investment fund shares.. | 8baaa | .... | .... | .... | .... | .... | .... | † 269.47 | 252.83 | 267.02 | 270.38 | 272.44 | .... |
| Debt securities......................... | 8bbaa | .... | .... | .... | .... | .... | .... | † .58 | .55 | .59 | .59 | .67 | .... |
| Fin. der.(oth.than reserves) & ESOs | 8c9aa | .... | .... | .... | .... | .... | .... | .... | .... | .... | .... | .... | .... |
| Other investment......................... | 8d9aa | .... | .... | .... | .... | .... | .... | † 113.48 | 113.36 | 112.43 | 121.02 | 121.09 | .... |
| Other equity.............................. | 8daaa | .... | .... | .... | .... | .... | .... | † 39.97 | 39.83 | 47.78 | 53.60 | 56.39 | .... |
| Debt instruments...................... | 8dzaa | .... | .... | .... | .... | .... | .... | † 73.52 | 73.53 | 64.65 | 67.41 | 64.71 | .... |
| Reserve assets............................. | 8e9aa | .... | .... | .... | .... | .... | .... | † 5.13 | 5.11 | 5.13 | 5.18 | 4.87 | .... |
| Liabilities...................................... | 809la | .... | .... | .... | .... | .... | .... | † 228.65 | 238.00 | 296.48 | 327.77 | 337.55 | .... |
| Direct investment......................... | 8a9la | .... | .... | .... | .... | .... | .... | † 119.66 | 121.49 | 184.29 | 214.20 | 227.95 | .... |
| Equity & investment fund shares.. | 8aala | .... | .... | .... | .... | .... | .... | † 87.21 | 100.67 | 175.08 | 197.14 | 210.90 | .... |
| Debt instruments...................... | 8abla | .... | .... | .... | .... | .... | .... | † 32.45 | 20.83 | 9.21 | 17.05 | 17.05 | .... |
| Portfolio investment..................... | 8b9la | .... | .... | .... | .... | .... | .... | .... | .... | .... | .... | .... | .... |
| Equity & investment fund shares.. | 8bala | .... | .... | .... | .... | .... | .... | .... | .... | .... | .... | .... | .... |
| Debt securities......................... | 8bbla | .... | .... | .... | .... | .... | .... | .... | .... | .... | .... | .... | .... |
| Fin. der.(oth.than reserves) & ESOs | 8c9la | .... | .... | .... | .... | .... | .... | .... | .... | .... | .... | .... | .... |
| Other investment......................... | 8d9la | .... | .... | .... | .... | .... | .... | † 108.99 | 116.51 | 112.19 | 113.57 | 109.61 | .... |
| Other equity.............................. | 8dala | .... | .... | .... | .... | .... | .... | .... | .... | .... | .... | .... | .... |
| Debt instruments...................... | 8dzla | .... | .... | .... | .... | .... | .... | † 108.99 | 116.51 | 112.19 | 113.57 | 109.61 | .... |

# Marshall Islands, Republic of   867

|  |  | 2004 | 2005 | 2006 | 2007 | 2008 | 2009 | 2010 | 2011 | 2012 | 2013 | 2014 | 2015 |
|---|---|---|---|---|---|---|---|---|---|---|---|---|---|
| **Government Finance Operations Statement** | | | | | | | | | | | | | |
| **Budgetary Central Government** | | | | | | *Thousands of US Dollars: Fiscal Year Ends September 30* | | | | | | | |
| Revenue | a1 | .... | .... | .... | .... | 99,648 | 97,651 | 101,038 | 100,020 | 94,782 | 102,919 | 98,638 | .... |
| Taxes | a11 | .... | .... | .... | .... | 26,159 | 24,329 | 25,243 | 25,259 | 25,229 | 26,385 | 24,500 | .... |
| Social Contributions | a12 | .... | .... | .... | .... | | | | | | | | .... |
| Grants | a13 | .... | .... | .... | .... | 67,804 | 66,906 | 68,186 | 65,471 | 59,192 | 62,138 | 59,027 | .... |
| Other Revenue | a14 | .... | .... | .... | .... | 5,684 | 6,417 | 7,608 | 9,290 | 10,360 | 14,396 | 15,111 | .... |
| Expense | a2 | .... | .... | .... | .... | 85,846 | 84,637 | 84,298 | 88,970 | 94,004 | 98,926 | 91,805 | .... |
| Compensation of Employees | a21 | .... | .... | .... | .... | 36,651 | 36,984 | 37,621 | 37,717 | 38,584 | 40,466 | 40,443 | .... |
| Use of Goods & Services | a22 | .... | .... | .... | .... | 25,002 | 24,347 | 24,280 | 26,811 | 28,096 | 28,490 | 26,089 | .... |
| Consumption of Fixed Capital | a23 | .... | .... | .... | .... | 5,456 | 5,502 | 5,404 | 5,730 | 5,144 | 4,583 | 4,938 | .... |
| Interest | a24 | .... | .... | .... | .... | 1,319 | 897 | 893 | 1,423 | 1,432 | 1,173 | 439 | .... |
| Subsidies | a25 | .... | .... | .... | .... | 6,900 | 8,477 | 6,641 | 6,133 | 8,794 | 9,734 | 6,180 | .... |
| Grants | a26 | .... | .... | .... | .... | 3,891 | 5,363 | 4,006 | 6,185 | 4,981 | 4,653 | 5,960 | .... |
| Social Benefits | a27 | .... | .... | .... | .... | — | — | — | — | — | — | — | .... |
| Other Expense | a28 | .... | .... | .... | .... | 6,627 | 3,068 | 5,453 | 4,972 | 6,973 | 9,827 | 7,756 | .... |
| Gross Operating Balance [1-2+23] | agob | .... | .... | .... | .... | 19,258 | 18,516 | 22,144 | 16,781 | 5,922 | 8,576 | 11,771 | .... |
| Net Operating Balance [1-2] | anob | .... | .... | .... | .... | 13,801 | 13,014 | 16,740 | 11,051 | 778 | 3,993 | 6,833 | .... |
| Net Acq. of Nonfinancial Assets | a31 | .... | .... | .... | .... | 8,399 | 10,727 | 11,082 | 7,375 | 2,155 | 2,587 | 1,209 | .... |
| Aquisition of Nonfin. Assets | a31.1 | .... | .... | .... | .... | .... | .... | .... | .... | .... | .... | .... | .... |
| Disposal of Nonfin. Assets | a31.2 | .... | .... | .... | .... | .... | .... | .... | .... | .... | .... | .... | .... |
| Net Lending/Borrowing [1-2-31] | anlb | .... | .... | .... | .... | 5,402 | 2,287 | 5,658 | 3,676 | −1,378 | 1,406 | 5,624 | .... |
| Net Acq. of Financial Assets | a32 | .... | .... | .... | .... | 7,033 | 6,123 | 7,590 | −9,975 | −4,211 | 1,250 | 3,879 | .... |
| By instrument | | | | | | | | | | | | | |
| Monetary Gold & SDRs | a3201 | .... | .... | .... | .... | — | — | — | — | — | — | — | .... |
| Currency & Deposits | a3202 | .... | .... | .... | .... | 4,254 | 5,885 | 6,384 | −25,006 | −6,242 | −1,058 | 4,278 | .... |
| Securities other than Shares | a3203 | .... | .... | .... | .... | — | — | — | — | — | — | — | .... |
| Loans | a3204 | .... | .... | .... | .... | — | — | — | — | — | — | — | .... |
| Shares & Other Equity | a3205 | .... | .... | .... | .... | — | — | — | 248 | 250 | −69 | 75 | .... |
| Insurance Technical Reserves | a3206 | .... | .... | .... | .... | — | — | — | — | — | — | — | .... |
| Financial Derivatives | a3207 | .... | .... | .... | .... | — | — | — | — | — | — | — | .... |
| Other Accounts Receivable | a3208 | .... | .... | .... | .... | 2,779 | 238 | 1,206 | 14,783 | 1,781 | 2,377 | −474 | .... |
| By debtor | | | | | | | | | | | | | |
| Domestic | a321 | .... | .... | .... | .... | 3,925 | −122 | −739 | 13,594 | −741 | 1,051 | −474 | .... |
| Foreign | a322 | .... | .... | .... | .... | 3,108 | 6,245 | 8,328 | −23,569 | −3,470 | 199 | 4,353 | .... |
| Net Incurrence of Liabilities | a33 | .... | .... | .... | .... | 1,631 | 3,836 | 1,932 | −13,651 | −2,833 | −156 | −1,745 | .... |
| By instrument | | | | | | | | | | | | | |
| Special Drawing Rights (SDRs) | a3301 | .... | .... | .... | .... | — | — | — | — | — | — | — | .... |
| Currency & Deposits | a3302 | .... | .... | .... | .... | — | — | — | — | — | — | — | .... |
| Securities other than Shares | a3303 | .... | .... | .... | .... | — | — | — | — | — | — | — | .... |
| Loans | a3304 | .... | .... | .... | .... | −766 | −1,893 | −2,649 | 7,778 | −2,306 | 2,545 | −2,798 | .... |
| Shares & Other Equity | a3305 | .... | .... | .... | .... | — | — | — | — | — | — | — | .... |
| Insurance Technical Reserves | a3306 | .... | .... | .... | .... | — | — | — | — | — | — | — | .... |
| Financial Derivatives | a3307 | .... | .... | .... | .... | — | — | — | — | — | — | — | .... |
| Other Accounts Payable | a3308 | .... | .... | .... | .... | 2,397 | 5,729 | 4,581 | −21,428 | −527 | −2,701 | 1,053 | .... |
| By creditor | | | | | | | | | | | | | |
| Domestic | a331 | .... | .... | .... | .... | 2,259 | 6,560 | 4,891 | −21,895 | −488 | −2,058 | 1,053 | .... |
| Foreign | a332 | .... | .... | .... | .... | −628 | −2,724 | −2,959 | 8,244 | −2,345 | 1,902 | −2,798 | .... |
| Stat. Discrepancy [32-33-NLB] | anlbz | .... | .... | .... | .... | | | | | | | | .... |
| Memo Item: Expenditure [2+31] | a2m | .... | .... | .... | .... | 94,246 | 95,364 | 95,380 | 96,345 | 96,159 | 101,513 | 93,014 | .... |
| **Balance Sheet** | | | | | | | | | | | | | |
| Net Worth | a6 | .... | .... | .... | .... | 34,149 | 36,651 | 46,478 | 48,620 | 47,708 | 61,625 | 57,621 | .... |
| Nonfinancial Assets | a61 | .... | .... | .... | .... | 85,095 | 86,436 | 89,722 | 88,382 | 88,735 | 91,466 | 99,239 | .... |
| Financial Assets | a62 | .... | .... | .... | .... | 44,765 | 48,597 | 62,048 | 52,073 | 47,862 | 49,112 | 34,666 | .... |
| By instrument | | | | | | | | | | | | | |
| Monetary Gold & SDRs | a6201 | .... | .... | .... | .... | — | — | — | — | — | — | — | .... |
| Currency & Deposits | a6202 | .... | .... | .... | .... | 28,232 | 33,501 | 38,638 | 13,632 | 7,390 | 6,332 | 9,150 | .... |
| Securities other than Shares | a6203 | .... | .... | .... | .... | — | — | — | — | — | — | — | .... |
| Loans | a6204 | .... | .... | .... | .... | — | — | — | — | — | — | — | .... |
| Shares and Other Equity | a6205 | .... | .... | .... | .... | 319 | 319 | 319 | 567 | 817 | 748 | 1,495 | .... |
| Insurance Technical Reserves | a6206 | .... | .... | .... | .... | — | — | — | — | — | — | — | .... |
| Financial Derivatives | a6207 | .... | .... | .... | .... | — | — | — | — | — | — | — | .... |
| Other Accounts Receivable | a6208 | .... | .... | .... | .... | 16,214 | 14,777 | 23,091 | 37,874 | 39,655 | 42,032 | 24,021 | .... |
| By debtor | | | | | | | | | | | | | |
| Domestic | a621 | .... | .... | .... | .... | 16,214 | 14,777 | 18,899 | 32,493 | 31,752 | 32,803 | 22,865 | .... |
| Foreign | a622 | .... | .... | .... | .... | 28,551 | 33,820 | 43,148 | 19,579 | 16,110 | 16,308 | 11,801 | .... |
| Liabilities | a63 | .... | .... | .... | .... | 95,711 | 98,382 | 105,291 | 91,834 | 88,889 | 78,952 | 76,284 | .... |
| By instrument | | | | | | | | | | | | | |
| Special Drawing Rights (SDRs) | a6301 | .... | .... | .... | .... | — | — | — | — | — | — | — | .... |
| Currency & Deposits | a6302 | .... | .... | .... | .... | — | — | — | — | — | — | — | .... |
| Securities other than Shares | a6303 | .... | .... | .... | .... | — | — | — | — | — | — | — | .... |
| Loans | a6304 | .... | .... | .... | .... | 60,933 | 59,040 | 54,484 | 62,158 | 59,809 | 64,714 | 59,497 | .... |
| Shares and Other Equity | a6305 | .... | .... | .... | .... | — | — | — | — | — | — | — | .... |
| Insurance Technical Reserves | a6306 | .... | .... | .... | .... | — | — | — | — | — | — | — | .... |
| Financial Derivatives | a6307 | .... | .... | .... | .... | — | — | — | — | — | — | — | .... |
| Other Accounts Payable | a6308 | .... | .... | .... | .... | 34,777 | 39,342 | 50,807 | 29,677 | 29,080 | 14,238 | 16,787 | .... |
| By creditor | | | | | | | | | | | | | |
| Domestic | a631 | .... | .... | .... | .... | 33,254 | 38,650 | 50,425 | 28,829 | 28,271 | 14,072 | 16,787 | .... |
| Foreign | a632 | .... | .... | .... | .... | 62,456 | 59,732 | 54,865 | 63,005 | 60,618 | 64,880 | 59,497 | .... |
| Net Financial Worth [62-63] | a6m2 | .... | .... | .... | .... | −50,946 | −49,785 | −43,243 | −39,762 | −41,027 | −29,841 | −41,618 | .... |
| Memo Item: Debt at Market Value | a6m3 | .... | .... | .... | .... | 95,711 | 98,382 | 105,291 | 91,834 | 88,889 | 78,952 | 76,284 | .... |
| Memo Item: Debt at Face Value | a6m35 | .... | .... | .... | .... | .... | .... | .... | .... | .... | .... | .... | .... |
| Memo Item: Debt at Nominal Value | a6m4 | .... | .... | .... | .... | .... | .... | .... | .... | .... | .... | .... | .... |

# Mauritania   682

| | | 2004 | 2005 | 2006 | 2007 | 2008 | 2009 | 2010 | 2011 | 2012 | 2013 | 2014 | 2015 |
|---|---|---|---|---|---|---|---|---|---|---|---|---|---|
| **Exchange Rates** | | *Ouguiyas per SDR: End of Period* | | | | | | | | | | | |
| Official Rate | aa | 399.419 | 386.775 | 407.106 | 399.614 | 402.781 | 410.719 | 434.288 | 442.925 | 465.741 | 460.460 | 452.956 | 469.693 |
| | | *Ouguiyas per US Dollar End of Period (ae) Period Average (rf)* | | | | | | | | | | | |
| Official Rate | ae | 257.190 | 270.610 | 270.610 | 252.880 | 261.500 | 261.990 | 282.000 | 288.500 | 303.035 | 299.000 | 312.640 | 338.950 |
| Official Rate | rf | .... | 265.528 | 268.600 | 258.587 | 238.203 | 262.366 | 275.894 | 281.118 | 296.620 | 300.682 | 302.725 | 324.672 |
| **Fund Position** | | *Millions of SDRs: End of Period* | | | | | | | | | | | |
| Quota | 2f.s | 64.40 | 64.40 | 64.40 | 64.40 | 64.40 | 64.40 | 64.40 | 64.40 | 64.40 | 64.40 | 64.40 | 64.40 |
| SDR Holdings | 1b.s | .02 | .10 | .03 | .04 | .09 | .12 | .05 | .99 | 2.27 | 1.45 | .93 | .84 |
| Reserve Position in the Fund | 1c.s | — | — | — | — | — | — | — | — | — | — | .03 | .03 |
| Total Fund Cred.&Loans Outstg. | 2tl | 58.17 | 48.51 | — | 8.38 | 10.31 | 10.31 | 32.39 | 54.47 | 75.91 | 85.08 | 83.01 | 79.85 |
| SDR Allocations | 1bd | 9.72 | 9.72 | 9.72 | 9.72 | 9.72 | 61.67 | 61.67 | 61.67 | 61.67 | 61.67 | 61.67 | 61.67 |
| **International Liquidity** | | *Millions of US Dollars Unless Otherwise Indicated: End of Period* | | | | | | | | | | | |
| Total Reserves minus Gold | 1l.d | 33.7 | 64.5 | 187.2 | 197.8 | 188.6 | 225.4 | 271.7 | 484.7 | 949.5 | .... | .... | .... |
| SDR Holdings | 1b.d | — | .1 | — | .1 | .1 | .2 | .1 | 1.5 | 3.5 | 2.2 | 1.4 | 1.2 |
| Reserve Position in the Fund | 1c.d | — | — | — | — | — | — | — | — | — | | | |
| Foreign Exchange | 1d.d | 33.7 | 64.3 | 187.1 | 197.8 | 188.5 | 225.2 | 271.6 | 483.2 | 946.0 | .... | .... | .... |
| Gold (Million Fine Troy Ounces) | 1ad | .012 | .012 | .012 | .012 | .012 | .012 | .012 | .012 | .012 | | | |
| Gold (National Valuation) | 1and | 5.0 | 5.6 | 5.8 | 9.5 | 9.9 | 12.6 | 16.1 | 18.0 | 19.0 | .... | .... | .... |
| Monetary Authorities: Other Liabs. | 4..d | 130.6 | 77.2 | 175.2 | 131.8 | 109.5 | 119.8 | 96.4 | 90.3 | 41.4 | .... | .... | .... |
| Deposit Money Banks: Assets | 7a.d | .... | 61.1 | 111.3 | 101.1 | 70.5 | 127.0 | 109.9 | 133.9 | 102.5 | .... | .... | .... |
| Deposit Money Banks: Liabs. | 7b.d | .... | 179.6 | 125.6 | 102.7 | 145.3 | 145.9 | 123.7 | 121.2 | 174.8 | .... | .... | .... |
| **Monetary Authorities** | | *Millions of Ouguiyas: End of Period* | | | | | | | | | | | |
| Foreign Assets | 11 | † 9,952 | 18,951 | 52,232 | 52,422 | 50,986 | 62,383 | 81,184 | 145,139 | 291,812 | .... | .... | .... |
| Claims on Central Government | 12a | .... | † 134,575 | 130,971 | 132,187 | 129,480 | 146,493 | 155,391 | 162,075 | 158,953 | .... | .... | .... |
| Claims on Nonfin.Pub.Enterprises | 12c | .... | | | | | | | | | .... | .... | .... |
| Claims on Private Sector | 12d | .... | † 3,528 | 1,966 | 2,356 | 14,771 | 14,835 | 14,524 | 14,770 | 15,518 | .... | .... | .... |
| Claims on Deposit Money Banks | 12e | .... | † — | 300 | 3,645 | 3,293 | 2,693 | 5,693 | 5,693 | — | .... | .... | .... |
| Claims on Nonbank Financial Insts. | 12g | .... | — | — | — | — | — | — | — | — | .... | .... | .... |
| Reserve Money | 14 | .... | † 68,046 | 83,973 | 95,924 | 110,560 | 127,457 | 128,119 | 179,275 | 213,956 | .... | .... | .... |
| of which: Currency Outside DMBs | 14a | .... | † 49,109 | 66,430 | 68,924 | 69,989 | 82,226 | 86,703 | 100,932 | 115,293 | .... | .... | .... |
| Restricted Deposits | 16b | .... | 105 | 63 | 34 | 50 | 30 | 54 | 82 | 245 | .... | .... | .... |
| Foreign Liabilities | 16c | † 23,597 | 604 | 535 | 491 | 298 | 213 | 187 | 208 | 102 | .... | .... | .... |
| Long-Term Foreign Liabilities | 16cl | 37,095 | 42,800 | 50,840 | 40,083 | 36,397 | 60,728 | 67,833 | 77,296 | 76,528 | .... | .... | .... |
| Central Government Deposits | 16d | .... | † 21,964 | 45,629 | 44,486 | 33,923 | 22,035 | 33,055 | 16,624 | 108,026 | .... | .... | .... |
| Capital Accounts | 17a | .... | † 3,171 | 7,473 | 3,839 | 337 | −1,547 | 5,268 | 3,266 | 21,539 | .... | .... | .... |
| Other Items (Net) | 17r | † 20,593 | 20,392 | −3,011 | 5,814 | 16,948 | 17,581 | 22,395 | 50,804 | 45,855 | .... | .... | .... |
| **Deposit Money Banks** | | *Millions of Ouguiyas: End of Period* | | | | | | | | | | | |
| Reserves | 20 | .... | † 18,269 | 17,146 | 28,292 | 40,596 | 44,293 | 38,422 | 79,518 | 88,379 | .... | .... | .... |
| Foreign Assets | 21 | .... | † 16,535 | 30,111 | 25,555 | 18,448 | 33,275 | 30,998 | 38,641 | 31,072 | .... | .... | .... |
| Claims on Central Government | 22a | .... | † 47,356 | 27,512 | 35,383 | 46,564 | 48,676 | 59,732 | 42,533 | 51,303 | .... | .... | .... |
| Claims on Nonfin.Pub.Enterprises | 22c | .... | | | | | | | | | .... | .... | .... |
| Claims on Private Sector | 22d | .... | † 139,968 | 151,926 | 180,826 | 223,450 | 232,279 | 269,288 | 300,781 | 343,019 | .... | .... | .... |
| Claims on Nonbank Financial Insts. | 22g | .... | — | — | — | — | — | — | — | — | .... | .... | .... |
| Demand Deposits | 24 | .... | † 79,173 | 82,311 | 102,133 | 133,068 | 148,967 | 172,001 | 222,926 | 246,525 | .... | .... | .... |
| Time Deposits | 25 | .... | † 25,527 | 29,177 | 40,501 | 37,576 | 45,924 | 48,810 | 50,329 | 51,620 | .... | .... | .... |
| Foreign Liabilities | 26c | .... | † 48,602 | 34,002 | 25,965 | 37,998 | 38,233 | 34,881 | 34,980 | 52,966 | .... | .... | .... |
| Long-Term Foreign Liabilities | 26cl | .... | † — | — | — | — | — | — | — | — | .... | .... | .... |
| Central Government Deposits | 26d | .... | † 315 | 671 | 1,223 | 426 | 217 | 20 | 749 | 1,913 | .... | .... | .... |
| Central Govt. Lending Funds | 26f | .... | † — | — | — | — | — | — | — | — | .... | .... | .... |
| Credit from Monetary Authorities | 26g | .... | † — | 300 | 3,645 | 3,293 | 2,693 | 2,693 | 2,693 | 1,293 | .... | .... | .... |
| Capital Accounts | 27a | .... | † 72,538 | 88,809 | 100,374 | 110,178 | 123,623 | 145,758 | 173,061 | 186,188 | .... | .... | .... |
| Other Items (Net) | 27r | .... | † −4,027 | −8,575 | −3,785 | 6,519 | −1,134 | −5,723 | −23,265 | −26,732 | .... | .... | .... |
| **Monetary Survey** | | *Millions of Ouguiyas: End of Period* | | | | | | | | | | | |
| Foreign Assets (Net) | 31n | .... | † −56,520 | −3,034 | 11,438 | −5,258 | −3,516 | 9,281 | 71,296 | 193,288 | .... | .... | .... |
| Domestic Credit | 32 | .... | † 303,148 | 266,075 | 305,043 | 379,916 | 420,031 | 465,860 | 502,786 | 458,854 | .... | .... | .... |
| Claims on Central Govt. (Net) | 32an | .... | † 159,652 | 112,183 | 121,861 | 141,695 | 172,917 | 182,047 | 187,235 | 100,317 | .... | .... | .... |
| Claims on Nonfin.Pub.Enterprises | 32c | .... | | | | | | | | | .... | .... | .... |
| Claims on Private Sector | 32d | .... | † 143,496 | 153,892 | 183,182 | 238,221 | 247,114 | 283,812 | 315,551 | 358,537 | .... | .... | .... |
| Claims on Nonbank Financial Insts. | 32g | .... | — | — | — | — | — | — | — | — | .... | .... | .... |
| Money | 34 | .... | † 128,282 | 148,741 | 171,057 | 203,057 | 232,111 | 259,969 | 325,221 | 363,488 | .... | .... | .... |
| Quasi-Money | 35 | .... | † 25,527 | 29,177 | 40,501 | 37,576 | 45,924 | 48,810 | 50,329 | 51,620 | .... | .... | .... |
| Restricted Deposits | 36b | .... | 105 | 63 | 34 | 50 | 30 | 54 | 82 | 245 | .... | .... | .... |
| Central Government Lending Funds | 36f | .... | † — | — | — | — | — | — | — | — | .... | .... | .... |
| Other Items (Net) | 37r | .... | † 92,742 | 85,093 | 104,950 | 133,957 | 138,543 | 166,427 | 198,328 | 236,759 | .... | .... | .... |
| Money plus Quasi-Money | 35l | .... | † 153,809 | 177,918 | 211,558 | 240,633 | 278,035 | 308,779 | 375,550 | 415,108 | .... | .... | .... |
| **Interest Rates** | | *Percent Per Annum* | | | | | | | | | | | |
| Discount Rate (End of Period) | 60.a | 11.00 | 14.00 | 14.00 | 12.00 | 12.00 | 9.00 | 9.00 | 9.00 | 9.00 | .... | 9.00 | .... |
| Treasury Bill Rate | 60c | 7.22 | 11.84 | 11.50 | 10.43 | 11.09 | 8.66 | 8.55 | 2.68 | 3.33 | .... | 3.45 | .... |
| Deposit Rate | 60l | 8.00 | 8.00 | 8.00 | 8.00 | 8.00 | 8.00 | 8.00 | 8.00 | 5.81 | .... | .... | .... |
| Lending Rate | 60p | 21.00 | 23.08 | 24.00 | 23.50 | 20.33 | 19.50 | 17.00 | 17.00 | 17.00 | .... | .... | .... |
| **Prices** | | *Index Numbers (2010=100): Period Averages* | | | | | | | | | | | |
| Consumer Prices | 64 | 67.1 | 75.2 | 79.9 | 85.7 | 92.0 | 94.1 | 100.0 | 105.6 | 110.9 | 115.4 | 119.5 | 120.1 |

# Mauritania   682

| | | 2004 | 2005 | 2006 | 2007 | 2008 | 2009 | 2010 | 2011 | 2012 | 2013 | 2014 | 2015 |
|---|---|---|---|---|---|---|---|---|---|---|---|---|---|
| **Balance of Payments** | | | | | | *Millions of US Dollars* | | | | | | | |
| A. Current Account*...................... | 109bx | .... | .... | .... | .... | .... | .... | .... | .... | −1,498.0 | −1,348.7 | −1,537.1 | −1,065.7 |
| Goods, credit (exports)................. | 1a9cx | .... | .... | .... | .... | .... | .... | .... | .... | 2,641.0 | 2,651.5 | 1,938.1 | 1,388.6 |
| Goods, debit (imports).................. | 1a9dx | .... | .... | .... | .... | .... | .... | .... | .... | 3,128.8 | 3,044.3 | 2,650.4 | 1,948.0 |
| Balance on goods..................... | 1a9bx | .... | .... | .... | .... | .... | .... | .... | .... | −487.9 | −392.9 | −712.3 | −559.4 |
| Services, credit (exports)............... | 1b9cx | .... | .... | .... | .... | .... | .... | .... | .... | 145.2 | 186.2 | 278.8 | 246.2 |
| Services, debit (imports)............... | 1b9dx | .... | .... | .... | .... | .... | .... | .... | .... | 1,016.7 | 999.4 | 900.3 | 640.7 |
| Balance on Goods & Services....... | 1z9bx | .... | .... | .... | .... | .... | .... | .... | .... | −1,359.4 | −1,206.0 | −1,333.9 | −954.0 |
| Primary income: credit................... | 1c9cx | .... | .... | .... | .... | .... | .... | .... | .... | 125.1 | 119.8 | 18.4 | 77.4 |
| Primary income: debit................... | 1c9dx | .... | .... | .... | .... | .... | .... | .... | .... | 302.8 | 316.3 | 271.5 | 257.4 |
| Balance on gds, serv. & prim. inc. | 1y9bx | .... | .... | .... | .... | .... | .... | .... | .... | −1,537.1 | −1,402.5 | −1,587.0 | −1,134.1 |
| Secondary income: credit.............. | 1d9ca | .... | .... | .... | .... | .... | .... | .... | .... | 61.2 | 71.8 | 64.2 | 90.8 |
| Secondary income: debit.............. | 1d9da | .... | .... | .... | .... | .... | .... | .... | .... | 22.0 | 18.0 | 14.4 | 22.4 |
| B. Capital Account*...................... | 209ba | .... | .... | .... | .... | .... | .... | .... | .... | 40.7 | 4.9 | 16.0 | 31.2 |
| Capital account: credit.................. | 209ca | .... | .... | .... | .... | .... | .... | .... | .... | 40.7 | 4.9 | 16.0 | 31.2 |
| Capital account: debit................... | 209da | .... | .... | .... | .... | .... | .... | .... | .... | — | — | — | — |
| Balance on current & capital acct. | 129ba | .... | .... | .... | .... | .... | .... | .... | .... | −1,457.2 | −1,343.8 | −1,521.1 | −1,034.4 |
| C. Financial Account* ................... | 309na | .... | .... | .... | .... | .... | .... | .... | .... | −1,806.8 | −1,587.8 | −1,194.3 | −1,246.4 |
| Direct investment: assets.............. | 3a9aa | .... | .... | .... | .... | .... | .... | .... | .... | | | | |
| Equity & investment fund shares.. | 3aaaa | .... | .... | .... | .... | .... | .... | .... | .... | — | — | — | — |
| Debt instruments........................ | 3abaa | .... | .... | .... | .... | .... | .... | .... | .... | | | | |
| Direct investment: liabilities .......... | 3a9la | .... | .... | .... | .... | .... | .... | .... | .... | 1,386.1 | 1,126.0 | 502.6 | 501.7 |
| Equity & investment fund shares . | 3aala | .... | .... | .... | .... | .... | .... | .... | .... | 1,386.1 | 1,126.0 | 502.6 | 501.7 |
| Debt instruments........................ | 3abla | .... | .... | .... | .... | .... | .... | .... | .... | — | — | — | — |
| Portfolio investment: assets .......... | 3b9aa | .... | .... | .... | .... | .... | .... | .... | .... | — | — | — | — |
| Equity & investment fund shares | 3baaa | .... | .... | .... | .... | .... | .... | .... | .... | — | — | — | — |
| Debt securities ........................... | 3bbaa | .... | .... | .... | .... | .... | .... | .... | .... | — | — | — | — |
| Portfolio investment: liabilities....... | 3b9la | .... | .... | .... | .... | .... | .... | .... | .... | — | — | — | — |
| Equity & investment fund shares . | 3bala | .... | .... | .... | .... | .... | .... | .... | .... | — | — | — | — |
| Debt securities........................... | 3bbla | .... | .... | .... | .... | .... | .... | .... | .... | — | — | — | — |
| Fin. der.& empl.stk.ops.(ESOs): net. | 3c9na | .... | .... | .... | .... | .... | .... | .... | .... | — | — | — | — |
| Fin. der. & ESOs.: assets.............. | 3c9aa | .... | .... | .... | .... | .... | .... | .... | .... | — | — | — | — |
| Fin. der. & ESOs.: liabilities.......... | 3c9la | .... | .... | .... | .... | .... | .... | .... | .... | | | | |
| Other investment: assets............... | 3d9aa | .... | .... | .... | .... | .... | .... | .... | .... | 71.3 | −306.7 | −686.4 | −426.6 |
| Other equity........................... | 3daaa | .... | .... | .... | .... | .... | .... | .... | .... | .... | .... | .... | .... |
| Debt instruments....................... | 3dzaa | .... | .... | .... | .... | .... | .... | .... | .... | 71.3 | −306.7 | −686.4 | −426.6 |
| Other investment: liabilities........... | 3d9la | .... | .... | .... | .... | .... | .... | .... | .... | 492.0 | 155.0 | 5.3 | 318.0 |
| Other equity........................... | 3dala | .... | .... | .... | .... | .... | .... | .... | .... | .... | .... | .... | .... |
| Debt instruments....................... | 3dzla | .... | .... | .... | .... | .... | .... | .... | .... | 492.0 | 155.0 | 5.3 | 318.0 |
| Curr.+ cap.− finan. acct. balance... | 4y9na | .... | .... | .... | .... | .... | .... | .... | .... | 349.5 | 244.0 | −326.7 | 212.0 |
| D. Net Errors and Omissions............ | 409na | .... | .... | .... | .... | .... | .... | .... | .... | −139.2 | −306.7 | −59.0 | −133.8 |
| E. Reserves and Related Items........ | 4z9na | .... | .... | .... | .... | .... | .... | .... | .... | 210.3 | −62.7 | −385.8 | 78.2 |
| Reserve assets............................ | 3e9aa | .... | .... | .... | .... | .... | .... | .... | .... | 428.2 | 49.1 | −314.3 | 189.4 |
| Credit and loans from the IMF....... | 3dcla | .... | .... | .... | .... | .... | .... | .... | .... | 32.6 | 13.9 | −3.1 | −4.4 |
| Exceptional financing.................... | 409la | .... | .... | .... | .... | .... | .... | .... | .... | 185.3 | 97.9 | 74.6 | 115.6 |

*Excludes components in group E

| | | 2004 | 2005 | 2006 | 2007 | 2008 | 2009 | 2010 | 2011 | 2012 | 2013 | 2014 | 2015 |
|---|---|---|---|---|---|---|---|---|---|---|---|---|---|
| **National Accounts** | | | | | | *Millions of Ouguiyas* | | | | | | | |
| Househ.Cons.Expend.,incl.NPISHs.... | 96f | 326,141 | 377,491 | 429,777 | 489,130 | 537,778 | 562,649 | 612,545 | .... | .... | .... | .... | .... |
| Government Consumption Expend... | 91f | 129,215 | 146,207 | 176,403 | 218,377 | 193,135 | 192,747 | 219,815 | .... | .... | .... | .... | .... |
| Gross Fixed Capital Formation......... | 93e | 215,907 | 341,973 | 223,556 | 239,208 | 201,429 | 222,365 | 373,113 | .... | .... | .... | .... | .... |
| Changes in Inventories.................... | 93i | 13,606 | 14,565 | 28,177 | 36,405 | 106,831 | −66,717 | −214,159 | .... | .... | .... | .... | .... |
| Exports of Goods and Services......... | 90c | 124,621 | 178,210 | 381,412 | 389,503 | 456,705 | 388,746 | 531,912 | .... | .... | .... | .... | .... |
| Imports of Goods and Services (-)..... | 98c | 323,628 | 478,414 | 422,588 | 504,610 | 655,709 | 543,903 | 652,575 | .... | .... | .... | .... | .... |
| Gross Domestic Product (GDP)......... | 99b | 485,861 | 580,032 | 816,737 | 868,013 | 840,170 | 755,887 | 870,651 | .... | .... | .... | .... | .... |
| GDP Volume 2004 Prices................. | 99b.p | 485,861 | 529,442 | 629,343 | 639,502 | .... | .... | .... | .... | .... | .... | .... | .... |
| GDP Volume (2005=100)............... | 99bvp | 91.8 | 100.0 | 118.9 | 120.8 | .... | .... | .... | .... | .... | .... | .... | .... |
| GDP Deflator (2005=100)............... | 99bip | 91.3 | 100.0 | 118.5 | 123.9 | .... | .... | .... | .... | .... | .... | .... | .... |
| | | | | | | *Millions: Midyear Estimates* | | | | | | | |
| Population................................ | 99z | 3.06 | 3.15 | 3.24 | 3.33 | 3.41 | 3.50 | 3.59 | 3.68 | 3.78 | 3.87 | 3.97 | 4.07 |

| | | 2004 | 2005 | 2006 | 2007 | 2008 | 2009 | 2010 | 2011 | 2012 | 2013 | 2014 | 2015 |
|---|---|---|---|---|---|---|---|---|---|---|---|---|---|
| **Exchange Rates** | | | | | | *Rupees per SDR: End of Period* | | | | | | | |
| Market Rate | aa | 43.802 | 43.831 | 51.656 | 44.589 | 48.912 | 47.486 | 46.803 | 45.024 | 46.914 | 46.322 | 45.968 | 49.732 |
| | | | | | | *Rupees per US Dollar: End of Period (ae) Period Average (rf)* | | | | | | | |
| Market Rate | ae | 28.204 | 30.667 | 34.337 | 28.216 | 31.756 | 30.291 | 30.391 | 29.326 | 30.525 | 30.079 | 31.728 | 35.889 |
| Market Rate | rf | 27.499 | 29.496 | 31.708 | 31.314 | 28.453 | 31.960 | 30.784 | 28.706 | 30.050 | 30.701 | 30.622 | 35.057 |
| **Fund Position** | | | | | | *Millions of SDRs: End of Period* | | | | | | | |
| Quota | 2f.s | 101.60 | 101.60 | 101.60 | 101.60 | 101.60 | 101.60 | 101.60 | 101.60 | 101.60 | 101.60 | 101.60 | 101.60 |
| SDR Holdings | 1b.s | 17.53 | 17.97 | 18.31 | 18.54 | 18.82 | 99.94 | 99.81 | 99.91 | 99.95 | 99.97 | 100.00 | 100.01 |
| Reserve Position in the Fund | 1c.s | 21.88 | 17.51 | 10.50 | 7.04 | 13.15 | 13.15 | 22.05 | 31.54 | 33.65 | 37.74 | 38.47 | 32.17 |
| Total Fund Cred.&Loans Outstg. | 2tl | — | — | — | — | — | — | — | — | — | — | — | — |
| SDR Allocations | 1bd | 15.74 | 15.74 | 15.74 | 15.74 | 15.74 | 96.81 | 96.81 | 96.81 | 96.81 | 96.81 | 96.81 | 96.81 |
| **International Liquidity** | | | | | | *Millions of US Dollars Unless Otherwise Indicated: End of Period* | | | | | | | |
| Total Reserves minus Gold | 1l.d | 1,605.9 | 1,339.9 | 1,269.6 | 1,780.3 | 1,742.7 | 2,178.8 | 2,441.8 | 2,582.7 | 2,836.7 | 3,340.2 | 3,614.7 | 3,957.0 |
| SDR Holdings | 1b.d | 27.2 | 25.7 | 27.5 | 29.3 | 29.0 | 156.7 | 153.7 | 153.4 | 153.6 | 154.0 | 144.9 | 138.6 |
| Reserve Position in the Fund | 1c.d | 34.0 | 25.0 | 15.8 | 11.1 | 20.3 | 20.6 | 34.0 | 48.4 | 51.7 | 58.1 | 55.7 | 44.6 |
| Foreign Exchange | 1d.d | 1,544.7 | 1,289.2 | 1,226.3 | 1,739.9 | 1,693.4 | 2,001.5 | 2,254.2 | 2,380.9 | 2,631.4 | 3,128.1 | 3,414.1 | 3,773.8 |
| Gold (Million Fine Troy Ounces) | 1ad | .062 | .062 | .062 | .062 | .061 | .126 | .126 | .126 | .130 | .125 | .254 | .286 |
| Gold (National Valuation) | 1and | 23.9 | 25.9 | 31.3 | 41.5 | 42.7 | 124.9 | 159.6 | 196.0 | 209.6 | 150.8 | 304.4 | 303.4 |
| Central Bank: Other Assets | 3..d | — | — | — | — | — | — | — | .2 | 1.4 | 3.8 | 2.8 | 3.6 |
| Central Bank: Other Liabs. | 4..d | 7.0 | 4.5 | 3.5 | 7.4 | 1.1 | 2.1 | 3.9 | 4.6 | 3.3 | 3.0 | 5.3 | 9.4 |
| Other Depository Corps.: Assets | 7a.d | 7,403.8 | 8,621.7 | 12,030.4 | 16,814.7 | 15,809.5 | 17,598.9 | 23,092.8 | 26,705.1 | 26,304.4 | 25,681.2 | 24,662.5 | 21,677.4 |
| Other Depository Corps.: Liabs. | 7b.d | 4,878.0 | 5,202.4 | 6,364.6 | 9,191.1 | 8,594.1 | 8,765.6 | 12,625.3 | 16,794.0 | 16,156.5 | 15,946.9 | 14,101.3 | 11,158.6 |
| **Central Bank** | | | | | | *Millions of Rupees: End of Period* | | | | | | | |
| Net Foreign Assets | 11n | 44,814.2 | 40,977.5 | 44,007.2 | 50,880.9 | 56,015.0 | 69,091.0 | 77,907.3 | 80,100.9 | 91,559.8 | 103,497.9 | 122,735.5 | 151,519.5 |
| Claims on Nonresidents | 11 | 45,010.6 | 41,116.6 | 44,127.6 | 51,089.3 | 56,050.7 | 69,154.2 | 78,027.0 | 80,237.1 | 91,662.0 | 103,588.6 | 122,902.9 | 151,856.3 |
| Liabilities to Nonresidents | 16c | 196.4 | 139.1 | 120.4 | 208.4 | 35.6 | 63.2 | 119.7 | 136.2 | 102.2 | 90.7 | 167.4 | 336.8 |
| Claims on Other Depository Corps. | 12e | 1,937.0 | 2,032.1 | 1,568.8 | 1,082.6 | 1,013.4 | 1,427.4 | 992.1 | 1,138.7 | 1,804.6 | 2,715.7 | 2,467.9 | 1,056.7 |
| Net Claims on Central Government | 12an | −63.1 | 1,741.0 | 6,116.1 | −270.2 | −3,797.5 | −14,288.1 | −9,687.7 | −7,837.3 | −11,467.0 | −10,932.7 | −20,743.4 | −28,634.9 |
| Claims on Central Government | 12a | 1,881.5 | 3,714.4 | 6,974.4 | 1,308.7 | 1,552.9 | 543.2 | 5,382.4 | 9,153.1 | 5,183.1 | 6,797.8 | 4,203.0 | 2,951.4 |
| Liabilities to Central Government | 16d | 1,944.6 | 1,973.5 | 858.3 | 1,578.9 | 5,350.2 | 14,831.3 | 15,070.0 | 16,990.4 | 16,650.1 | 17,730.5 | 24,946.4 | 31,586.3 |
| Claims on Other Sectors | 12s | 425.9 | 459.9 | 262.0 | 260.1 | 177.1 | 161.7 | 289.1 | 187.7 | 184.5 | 172.7 | 152.2 | 3,668.5 |
| Claims on Other Financial Corps. | 12g | 309.4 | 277.2 | 71.4 | 76.2 | 75.0 | 70.7 | 50.5 | 30.3 | 15.2 | — | — | 3,500.0 |
| Claims on State & Local Govts. | 12b | — | — | — | — | — | — | — | — | — | — | — | — |
| Claims on Public Nonfin. Corps. | 12c | — | — | — | — | — | — | .8 | .8 | .8 | .8 | .8 | 4.8 |
| Claims on Private Sector | 12d | 116.5 | 182.8 | 190.6 | 183.9 | 102.1 | 91.0 | 237.8 | 156.5 | 168.5 | 171.9 | 151.4 | 163.7 |
| Monetary Base | 14 | 22,434.7 | 23,514.0 | 25,321.9 | 28,079.1 | 30,640.3 | 35,931.5 | 44,935.5 | 48,280.9 | 52,622.9 | 62,350.0 | 67,933.6 | 73,569.0 |
| Currency in Circulation | 14a | 14,222.3 | 15,144.0 | 16,350.6 | 17,698.0 | 19,943.5 | 21,068.8 | 22,591.8 | 24,469.8 | 26,961.3 | 30,127.7 | 32,530.9 | 33,337.4 |
| Liabs. to Other Depository Corps. | 14c | 4,492.1 | 6,544.2 | 8,102.2 | 9,857.7 | 10,393.0 | 14,726.8 | 22,187.6 | 23,666.4 | 25,515.1 | 31,894.8 | 35,269.7 | 39,962.3 |
| Liabilities to Other Sectors | 14d | 3,720.3 | 1,825.7 | 869.0 | 523.4 | 303.8 | 135.9 | 156.2 | 144.7 | 146.5 | 327.6 | 133.0 | 269.3 |
| Other Liabs. to Other Dep. Corps. | 14n | 6,956.5 | 3,493.1 | 829.5 | 4,088.6 | 2,696.9 | 2.4 | 3,601.3 | 5,539.8 | 3,916.3 | 10,796.4 | 17,351.4 | 26,747.8 |
| Dep. & Sec. Excl. f/Monetary Base | 14o | 64.5 | 62.7 | 63.4 | 63.4 | 63.9 | 62.0 | 539.4 | 1,042.4 | 928.8 | 1,887.1 | 2,036.8 | 3,082.8 |
| Deposits Included in Broad Money. | 15 | — | — | — | — | — | — | — | — | — | — | — | — |
| Sec.Ot.th.Shares Incl.in Brd. Money. | 16a | — | — | — | — | — | — | 477.4 | 973.9 | 860.3 | 1,818.7 | 1,977.8 | 3,023.8 |
| Deposits Excl. from Broad Money. | 16b | 63.3 | 61.8 | 62.4 | 62.4 | 62.9 | 61.0 | 61.0 | 67.5 | 67.5 | 67.5 | 58.1 | 58.1 |
| Sec.Ot.th.Shares Excl.f/Brd.Money. | 16s | 1.2 | 1.0 | 1.0 | 1.0 | 1.0 | 1.0 | 1.0 | .9 | .9 | .9 | .9 | .9 |
| Loans | 16l | — | — | — | — | — | — | — | — | — | — | — | — |
| Financial Derivatives | 16m | — | — | — | — | — | — | — | — | — | — | — | — |
| Shares and Other Equity | 17a | 17,855.5 | 18,830.5 | 26,696.0 | 20,729.8 | 20,942.3 | 21,854.8 | 21,361.0 | 19,543.0 | 25,383.9 | 20,881.1 | 17,271.9 | 24,330.7 |
| Other Items (Net) | 17r | −197.1 | −689.9 | −956.7 | −1,007.3 | −935.2 | −1,458.7 | −936.4 | −816.0 | −770.0 | −461.2 | 18.5 | −120.4 |
| Memo Item: | | | | | | | | | | | | | |
| Total Assets | 10ra | 49,819.7 | 48,467.4 | 54,700.6 | 55,711.9 | 60,820.1 | 73,243.4 | 86,612.2 | 92,681.0 | 100,930.6 | 115,230.1 | 131,563.5 | 161,362.6 |
| **Other Depository Corporations** | | | | | | *Millions of Rupees: End of Period* | | | | | | | |
| Net Foreign Assets | 21n | 71,237.7 | 104,858.0 | 194,545.7 | 215,109.2 | 229,127.3 | 267,565.4 | 318,118.5 | 290,654.2 | 309,761.1 | 292,802.0 | 335,087.7 | 377,506.1 |
| Claims on Nonresidents | 21 | 208,818.4 | 264,399.3 | 413,085.6 | 474,446.1 | 502,038.5 | 533,079.2 | 701,810.0 | 783,159.2 | 802,935.7 | 772,471.3 | 782,494.5 | 777,975.2 |
| Liabilities to Nonresidents | 26c | 137,580.7 | 159,541.3 | 218,539.8 | 259,336.9 | 272,911.2 | 265,513.8 | 383,691.5 | 492,505.0 | 493,174.6 | 479,669.3 | 447,406.8 | 400,469.1 |
| Claims on Central Bank | 20 | 14,734.1 | 13,491.4 | 12,207.8 | 17,423.9 | 16,856.1 | 18,626.4 | 29,434.8 | 33,371.3 | 34,037.2 | 49,632.3 | 58,250.5 | 72,682.4 |
| Currency | 20a | 3,570.8 | 3,479.9 | 3,322.3 | 3,437.8 | 3,787.4 | 3,916.3 | 3,616.8 | 4,162.0 | 4,791.6 | 6,811.0 | 7,139.8 | 5,699.8 |
| Reserve Deposits and Securities | 20b | 4,494.1 | 6,542.0 | 8,087.6 | 9,859.7 | 10,395.2 | 14,710.1 | 22,158.7 | 23,667.5 | 25,339.9 | 32,104.8 | 35,352.2 | 47,600.8 |
| Other Claims | 20n | 6,669.2 | 3,469.4 | 797.9 | 4,126.5 | 2,673.5 | — | 3,659.4 | 5,541.8 | 3,905.7 | 10,716.6 | 15,758.6 | 19,381.7 |
| Net Claims on Central Government | 22an | 42,755.6 | 43,509.7 | 40,065.1 | 45,794.5 | 50,764.3 | 44,480.0 | 39,530.6 | 38,010.7 | 38,215.2 | 45,691.7 | 65,514.9 | 70,615.3 |
| Claims on Central Government | 22a | 43,202.4 | 44,754.3 | 42,233.9 | 47,698.8 | 51,617.3 | 61,031.3 | 57,799.4 | 51,334.6 | 56,068.2 | 58,807.7 | 73,828.3 | 80,508.4 |
| Liabilities to Central Government | 26d | 446.8 | 1,244.6 | 2,168.9 | 1,904.3 | 853.0 | 16,551.3 | 18,268.9 | 13,323.9 | 17,852.9 | 13,116.0 | 8,313.4 | 9,893.0 |
| Claims on Other Sectors | 22s | 136,411.2 | 152,981.9 | 171,564.1 | 196,405.6 | 248,953.9 | 251,160.0 | 278,722.8 | 310,940.9 | 364,089.2 | 413,242.8 | 401,882.4 | 431,003.6 |
| Claims on Other Financial Corps. | 22g | 2,375.3 | 3,853.0 | 8,087.2 | 6,207.9 | 6,319.4 | 6,270.8 | 6,967.1 | 8,736.6 | 9,452.1 | 9,604.2 | 7,496.2 | 7,227.0 |
| Claims on State & Local Govts. | 22b | 65.5 | 59.1 | 121.4 | 55.8 | 45.3 | 4.5 | 6.2 | 3.5 | 1.5 | — | — | — |
| Claims on Public Nonfin. Corps. | 22c | 5,808.8 | 9,728.5 | 10,461.5 | 7,220.3 | 10,177.1 | 11,346.2 | 9,130.3 | 7,071.6 | 8,201.1 | 7,928.4 | 7,294.6 | 2,917.0 |
| Claims on Private Sector | 22d | 128,161.7 | 139,340.8 | 152,894.0 | 182,921.7 | 232,412.1 | 233,538.5 | 262,619.3 | 295,129.2 | 346,434.5 | 395,710.3 | 387,091.5 | 420,859.5 |
| Liabilities to Central Bank | 26g | 1,961.5 | 2,029.2 | 1,571.0 | 1,055.9 | 1,065.1 | 1,451.1 | 1,003.2 | 1,145.4 | 1,721.8 | 2,626.8 | 2,237.1 | 1,015.1 |
| Transf.Dep.Included in Broad Money | 24 | 34,647.7 | 34,194.0 | 39,250.4 | 49,645.5 | 59,359.7 | 68,788.2 | 66,798.1 | 69,409.1 | 74,618.5 | 80,380.3 | 92,691.4 | 107,961.5 |
| Other Dep.Included in Broad Money. | 25 | 128,575.9 | 140,831.6 | 153,271.8 | 173,610.8 | 197,105.0 | 193,977.7 | 212,932.7 | 227,713.2 | 246,708.2 | 258,515.2 | 275,983.1 | 297,602.4 |
| Sec.Ot.th.Shares Incl.in Brd. Money. | 26a | 166.1 | 924.2 | 1,101.5 | 1,278.6 | 1,389.2 | 772.2 | 892.0 | 987.9 | 1,114.0 | 1,250.3 | 1,380.1 | 1,504.1 |
| Deposits Excl. from Broad Money. | 26b | 53,013.4 | 83,299.0 | 160,496.6 | 180,469.1 | 195,631.6 | 227,511.7 | 285,066.2 | 258,918.4 | 269,984.2 | 273,154.7 | 313,532.9 | 346,961.8 |
| Sec.Ot.th.Shares Excl.f/Brd.Money. | 26s | 896.6 | 774.5 | 847.9 | 596.1 | 782.9 | 736.0 | 975.5 | 1,019.3 | 878.8 | 4,573.5 | 5,416.7 | 2,667.9 |
| Loans | 26l | 643.4 | 501.0 | 742.1 | 306.5 | 779.0 | 841.9 | 1,197.8 | 1,762.6 | 2,023.4 | 4,047.4 | 4,642.4 | 4,243.4 |
| Financial Derivatives | 26m | 4,254.1 | 5,077.7 | 5,280.8 | 7,325.9 | 10,681.8 | 8,830.8 | 9,501.2 | 17,280.5 | 33,923.0 | 48,880.6 | 24,875.9 | 26,324.6 |
| Insurance Technical Reserves | 26r | — | — | — | — | — | — | — | — | — | — | — | — |
| Shares and Other Equity | 27a | 37,991.8 | 42,617.3 | 48,476.3 | 51,923.8 | 67,572.6 | 72,014.3 | 85,038.9 | 92,655.6 | 109,157.3 | 116,443.7 | 125,985.9 | 146,278.9 |
| Other Items (Net) | 27r | 2,988.2 | 4,592.5 | 7,344.2 | 8,521.2 | 11,334.7 | 6,907.9 | 2,401.1 | 2,085.2 | 5,973.5 | 11,496.4 | 13,990.0 | 17,247.8 |
| Memo Item: | | | | | | | | | | | | | |
| Total Assets | 20ra | 423,418.7 | 496,790.4 | 661,145.9 | 758,266.4 | 847,548.1 | 894,608.7 | 1,106,725.2 | 1,221,711.2 | 1,298,120.8 | 1,337,575.2 | 1,362,220.9 | 1,411,260.1 |

| | | 2004 | 2005 | 2006 | 2007 | 2008 | 2009 | 2010 | 2011 | 2012 | 2013 | 2014 | 2015 |
|---|---|---|---|---|---|---|---|---|---|---|---|---|---|
| **Depository Corporations** | | | | | | | *Millions of Rupees: End of Period* | | | | | | | |
| Net Foreign Assets | 31n | 116,052.0 | 145,835.5 | 238,552.9 | 265,990.1 | 285,142.3 | 336,656.3 | 396,025.7 | 370,755.1 | 401,320.9 | 396,299.9 | 457,823.2 | 529,025.5 |
| Claims on Nonresidents | 31 | 253,829.0 | 305,515.9 | 457,213.2 | 525,535.5 | 558,089.1 | 602,233.3 | 779,836.9 | 863,396.3 | 894,597.7 | 876,059.8 | 905,397.4 | 929,831.5 |
| Liabilities to Nonresidents | 36c | 137,777.1 | 159,680.4 | 218,660.2 | 259,545.3 | 272,946.8 | 265,577.0 | 383,811.2 | 492,641.2 | 493,276.8 | 479,760.0 | 447,574.2 | 400,806.0 |
| Domestic Claims | 32 | 179,529.6 | 198,692.5 | 218,007.3 | 242,190.1 | 296,098.0 | 281,513.6 | 308,854.8 | 341,302.0 | 391,021.9 | 448,174.6 | 446,806.1 | 476,652.6 |
| Net Claims on Central Government | 32an | 42,692.5 | 45,250.6 | 46,181.1 | 45,524.4 | 46,967.0 | 30,191.9 | 29,842.9 | 30,173.4 | 26,748.3 | 34,759.0 | 44,771.5 | 41,980.5 |
| Claims on Central Government | 32a | 45,083.9 | 48,468.7 | 49,208.3 | 49,007.6 | 53,170.3 | 61,574.5 | 63,181.8 | 60,487.7 | 61,251.3 | 65,605.5 | 78,031.4 | 83,459.8 |
| Liabilities to Central Government | 36d | 2,391.3 | 3,218.1 | 3,027.2 | 3,483.2 | 6,203.3 | 31,382.6 | 33,338.9 | 30,314.2 | 34,503.0 | 30,846.5 | 33,259.9 | 41,479.3 |
| Claims on Other Sectors | 32s | 136,837.1 | 153,441.9 | 171,826.1 | 196,665.7 | 249,131.0 | 251,321.7 | 279,011.9 | 311,128.6 | 364,273.6 | 413,415.5 | 402,034.6 | 434,672.1 |
| Claims on Other Financial Corps. | 32g | 2,684.7 | 4,130.8 | 8,158.5 | 6,284.1 | 6,394.4 | 6,341.5 | 7,017.6 | 8,767.0 | 9,467.3 | 9,604.2 | 7,496.2 | 10,727.0 |
| Claims on State & Local Govts. | 32b | 65.5 | 59.1 | 121.4 | 55.8 | 45.3 | 4.5 | 6.2 | 3.5 | 1.5 | — | — | — |
| Claims on Public Nonfin. Corps. | 32c | 5,808.8 | 9,728.5 | 10,461.5 | 7,220.3 | 10,177.1 | 11,346.2 | 9,131.1 | 7,072.4 | 8,201.9 | 7,929.2 | 7,295.4 | 2,921.8 |
| Claims on Private Sector | 32d | 128,278.2 | 139,523.5 | 153,084.7 | 183,105.6 | 232,514.2 | 233,629.5 | 262,857.1 | 295,285.7 | 346,603.0 | 395,882.1 | 387,243.0 | 421,023.3 |
| Broad Money Liabilities | 35l | 177,761.4 | 189,439.7 | 207,521.0 | 239,318.4 | 274,313.7 | 280,826.5 | 300,231.4 | 319,536.7 | 345,617.2 | 365,608.7 | 397,556.5 | 437,998.6 |
| Currency Outside Depository Corps | 34a | 10,651.5 | 11,664.1 | 13,028.3 | 14,260.2 | 16,156.1 | 17,152.6 | 18,975.0 | 20,307.8 | 22,169.7 | 23,316.7 | 25,391.2 | 27,637.6 |
| Transferable Deposits | 34 | 34,738.1 | 34,521.4 | 39,648.2 | 50,051.1 | 59,434.2 | 68,848.9 | 66,822.6 | 69,425.5 | 74,630.8 | 80,391.4 | 92,719.2 | 107,987.4 |
| Other Deposits | 35 | 128,841.1 | 141,134.8 | 153,493.2 | 173,660.6 | 197,188.4 | 194,052.9 | 213,064.4 | 227,841.5 | 246,842.4 | 258,831.7 | 276,088.2 | 297,845.8 |
| Securities Other than Shares | 36a | 3,530.8 | 2,119.4 | 1,351.3 | 1,346.5 | 1,535.0 | 772.2 | 1,369.4 | 1,961.8 | 1,974.3 | 3,069.0 | 3,358.0 | 4,527.8 |
| Deposits Excl. from Broad Money | 36b | 53,076.6 | 83,360.7 | 160,559.0 | 180,531.5 | 195,694.6 | 227,572.7 | 285,127.2 | 258,985.9 | 270,051.7 | 273,223.3 | 313,590.9 | 347,019.8 |
| Sec.Ot.th.Shares Excl.f/Brd.Money | 36s | 897.8 | 775.4 | 848.9 | 597.1 | 783.8 | 737.0 | 976.5 | 1,020.2 | 879.7 | 4,574.4 | 5,417.6 | 2,668.8 |
| Loans | 36l | 643.4 | 501.0 | 742.1 | 306.5 | 779.0 | 841.9 | 1,197.8 | 1,762.6 | 2,023.4 | 4,047.4 | 4,642.4 | 4,243.4 |
| Financial Derivatives | 36m | 4,254.1 | 5,077.7 | 5,280.8 | 7,325.9 | 10,681.8 | 8,830.8 | 9,501.2 | 17,280.5 | 33,923.0 | 48,880.6 | 24,875.9 | 26,324.6 |
| Insurance Technical Reserves | 36r | — | — | — | — | — | — | — | — | — | — | — | — |
| Shares and Other Equity | 37a | 55,847.3 | 61,447.9 | 75,172.3 | 72,653.6 | 88,515.0 | 93,869.1 | 106,399.9 | 112,198.6 | 134,541.2 | 137,324.9 | 143,257.8 | 170,609.6 |
| Other Items (Net) | 37r | 3,100.9 | 3,925.6 | 6,436.0 | 7,447.2 | 10,472.4 | 5,491.9 | 1,446.6 | 1,272.7 | 5,306.6 | 10,816.2 | 15,288.1 | 16,813.3 |
| Broad Money Liabs., Seasonally Adj. | 35l.b | 176,085.0 | 187,403.4 | 204,943.5 | 235,791.1 | 269,786.8 | 275,866.4 | 299,867.6 | 314,140.1 | 340,310.5 | 360,564.7 | 392,505.2 | 432,588.2 |
| **Monetary Aggregates** | | | | | | | *Millions of Rupees: End of Period* | | | | | | | |
| Broad Money | 59m | 177,761.4 | 189,439.7 | 207,521.0 | 239,318.4 | 274,313.7 | 280,826.5 | 300,231.4 | 319,536.7 | 345,617.2 | 365,608.7 | 397,556.5 | 437,998.6 |
| o/w:Currency Issued by Cent.Govt | 59m.a | — | — | — | — | — | — | — | — | — | — | — | — |
| o/w: Dep.in Nonfin. Corporations | 59m.b | — | — | — | — | — | — | — | — | — | — | — | — |
| o/w:Secs. Issued by Central Govt. | 59m.c | — | — | — | — | — | — | — | — | — | — | — | — |
| Money (National Definitions) | | | | | | | | | | | | | | |
| Monetary Base | 19ma | .... | .... | .... | .... | 30,494.7 | 35,933.9 | 44,935.5 | 48,280.9 | 52,622.9 | 62,350.0 | 67,933.6 | 73,569.0 |
| Reserve Money | 19mb | 24,621.8 | 25,049.0 | 25,818.2 | 32,078.9 | .... | .... | .... | .... | .... | .... | .... | .... |
| M1 | 59ma | 23,617.2 | 25,958.1 | 28,164.3 | 35,050.6 | .... | .... | .... | .... | .... | .... | .... | .... |
| Narrow Money | 59mak | .... | .... | .... | .... | 53,186.5 | 60,903.6 | 61,975.1 | 66,353.9 | 72,590.3 | 77,054.8 | 83,579.3 | 91,398.2 |
| M2 | 59mb | 148,631.6 | 169,718.2 | 186,704.1 | 215,967.9 | .... | .... | .... | .... | .... | .... | .... | .... |
| Broad Money | 59mea | 177,761.4 | 189,439.7 | 207,521.0 | 239,318.4 | 274,313.7 | 296,480.4 | 300,231.4 | 319,536.7 | 345,617.2 | 365,608.7 | 397,556.5 | 437,998.6 |
| **Interest Rates** | | | | | | | *Percent Per Annum* | | | | | | | |
| Central Bank Policy Rate (EOP) | 60 | .... | .... | 8.50 | 9.25 | 6.75 | 5.75 | 4.75 | 5.40 | 4.90 | 4.65 | 4.65 | 4.40 |
| Money Market Rate | 60b | 1.33 | 2.45 | 5.59 | 8.52 | 7.52 | 4.63 | 3.07 | 2.33 | 1.82 | 1.85 | 1.65 | 1.36 |
| Treasury Bill Rate | 60c | 5.61 | 6.44 | 8.47 | 10.95 | 8.31 | 5.25 | 3.83 | 3.96 | 3.63 | 2.86 | 2.37 | 2.14 |
| Savings Rate | 60k | 3.88 | 4.73 | 6.28 | 7.60 | 6.58 | 4.17 | 3.70 | 3.29 | 3.08 | 2.79 | 2.42 | 2.00 |
| Deposit Rate | 60l | 8.15 | 7.25 | 9.55 | 11.77 | 10.11 | 8.45 | 8.35 | 7.11 | 6.23 | 6.81 | 6.78 | 6.09 |
| Lending Rate | 60p | 21.00 | 21.04 | 21.08 | 21.87 | 11.54 | 9.25 | 8.88 | 8.92 | 8.67 | 8.50 | 8.50 | 8.50 |
| Government Bond Yield | 61 | 7.61 | 8.39 | 9.86 | 10.15 | 10.12 | 8.90 | 6.93 | 6.74 | 6.08 | 4.46 | 5.07 | 4.49 |
| **Prices and Labor** | | | | | | | *Index Numbers (2010=100): Period Averages* | | | | | | | |
| Share Prices | 62 | 37.1 | 43.7 | 53.4 | 85.1 | 98.0 | 79.1 | 100.0 | 114.9 | 101.6 | 111.2 | 121.1 | 112.2 |
| SEM-7 | 62b | 39.0 | 46.9 | 58.2 | 101.4 | 120.9 | 88.0 | 100.0 | 107.4 | 96.8 | 109.0 | 115.9 | 106.4 |
| Consumer Prices | 64 | † 69.4 | 72.9 | 79.4 | 86.4 | 94.8 | 97.2 | 100.0 | 106.5 | † 110.6 | 114.6 | 118.2 | 119.8 |
| | | | | | | *Number in Thousands: Period Averages* | | | | | | | | |
| Labor Force | 67d | 532 | 542 | 546 | 547 | 540 | 541 | 552 | 549 | 558 | 570 | 574 | 585 |
| Employment | 67e | 487 | 491 | 496 | 501 | 494 | 501 | 510 | 506 | 514 | 524 | 530 | 538 |
| Unemployment | 67c | 40 | 34 | 23 | 24 | 38 | 40 | 42 | 43 | 44 | 46 | 44 | 46 |
| Unemployment Rate (%) | 67r | 8.4 | 9.5 | 9.2 | 8.4 | 7.2 | 7.4 | 7.6 | 7.8 | 7.9 | 8.0 | 7.7 | 8.0 |
| **Intl. Transactions & Positions** | | | | | | | *Millions of Rupees* | | | | | | | |
| Exports | 70 | 54,905 | 63,219 | 74,037 | 69,708 | 67,970 | 61,681 | 69,550 | 73,586 | 79,658 | 88,148 | 94,323 | 94,108 |
| Imports, c.i.f. | 71 | 76,387 | 93,282 | 115,502 | 121,037 | 132,165 | 118,444 | 134,882 | 147,815 | 160,996 | 165,661 | 172,023 | 168,077 |
| | | | | | | | *2010=100* | | | | | | | |
| Volume of Exports | 72 | 88.1 | 95.6 | 105.6 | † 94.7 | 94.9 | 86.5 | 100.0 | 103.6 | 104.9 | 94.8 | 107.0 | 104.5 |
| Volume of Imports | 73 | 88.5 | 93.4 | 96.8 | † 99.2 | 98.9 | 93.9 | 100.0 | 103.0 | 105.8 | 99.2 | 107.1 | 117.4 |
| Export Prices | 76 | 90.1 | 95.3 | 101.4 | † 106.8 | 103.7 | 103.6 | 100.0 | 103.8 | 110.9 | 106.7 | 102.2 | 103.4 |
| Import Prices | 76.x | 65.4 | 75.8 | 85.4 | † 90.4 | 99.1 | 93.4 | 100.0 | 106.3 | 112.7 | 90.4 | 87.1 | 77.7 |

# Mauritius 684

## Balance of Payments

*Millions of US Dollars*

| | Code | 2004 | 2005 | 2006 | 2007 | 2008 | 2009 | 2010 | 2011 | 2012 | 2013 | 2014 | 2015 |
|---|---|---|---|---|---|---|---|---|---|---|---|---|---|
| A. Current Account* | 109bx | −111.8 | −324.0 | −604.4 | −433.9 | −975.8 | −655.0 | −1,005.8 | −1,560.3 | −827.5 | † −750.3 | −714.3 | −565.6 |
| Goods, credit (exports) | 1a9cx | 1,993.1 | 2,138.4 | 2,328.8 | 2,237.9 | 2,383.9 | 1,938.5 | 2,261.5 | 2,565.0 | 2,649.1 | † 2,868.8 | 3,093.9 | 2,685.0 |
| Goods, debit (imports) | 1a9dx | 2,572.6 | 2,935.2 | 3,408.8 | 3,655.7 | 4,386.0 | 3,503.9 | 4,156.7 | 4,917.4 | 5,104.8 | † 5,139.0 | 5,353.9 | 4,525.6 |
| Balance on goods | 1a9bx | −579.5 | −796.8 | −1,080.0 | −1,417.8 | −2,002.1 | −1,565.4 | −1,895.2 | −2,352.4 | −2,455.7 | † −2,270.3 | −2,260.0 | −1,840.6 |
| Services, credit (exports) | 1b9cx | 1,455.6 | 1,618.1 | 1,671.3 | 2,205.2 | 2,543.9 | 2,239.0 | 2,695.1 | 3,261.0 | 3,407.9 | † 2,776.7 | 3,190.1 | 2,843.3 |
| Services, debit (imports) | 1b9dx | 1,023.3 | 1,197.7 | 1,316.9 | 1,569.4 | 1,919.9 | 1,607.3 | 1,978.9 | 2,470.1 | 2,443.4 | † 2,210.7 | 2,497.6 | 2,241.5 |
| Balance on Goods & Services | 1z9bx | −147.2 | −376.5 | −725.5 | −782.0 | −1,378.1 | −933.7 | −1,179.0 | −1,561.5 | −1,491.1 | † −1,704.2 | −1,567.6 | −1,238.8 |
| Primary income: credit | 1c9cx | 51.7 | 142.9 | 373.9 | 816.4 | 819.9 | 457.6 | 5,231.9 | 1,157.0 | 1,990.7 | † 6,622.4 | 6,791.3 | 6,245.2 |
| Primary income: debit | 1c9dx | 65.7 | 151.3 | 323.8 | 593.3 | 641.7 | 402.6 | 5,242.0 | 1,276.1 | 1,469.0 | † 5,576.4 | 5,727.0 | 5,346.2 |
| Balance on gds, serv. & prim. inc. | 1y9bx | −161.1 | −385.0 | −675.5 | −558.9 | −1,200.0 | −878.7 | −1,189.1 | −1,680.6 | −969.5 | † −658.2 | −503.3 | −339.8 |
| Secondary income: credit | 1d9ca | 168.1 | 162.3 | 179.3 | 250.1 | 411.2 | 413.1 | 404.4 | 402.8 | 384.0 | † 315.6 | 351.9 | 274.1 |
| Secondary income: debit | 1d9da | 118.7 | 101.3 | 108.2 | 125.2 | 187.0 | 189.4 | 221.1 | 282.5 | 242.0 | † 407.7 | 562.8 | 499.9 |
| B. Capital Account* | 209ba | — | — | — | — | — | — | — | — | — | .... | .... | .... |
| Capital account: credit | 209ca | — | — | — | — | — | — | — | — | — | .... | .... | .... |
| Capital account: debit | 209da | — | — | — | — | — | — | — | — | — | .... | .... | .... |
| Balance on current & capital acct. | 129ba | −111.8 | −324.0 | −604.4 | −433.9 | −975.8 | −655.0 | −1,005.8 | −1,560.3 | −827.5 | † −750.3 | −714.3 | −565.6 |
| C. Financial Account* | 309na | −8.1 | −142.1 | −172.8 | −494.9 | −943.2 | −753.7 | −1,065.0 | −1,557.4 | −1,394.8 | † −1,061.3 | −1,367.0 | −1,081.1 |
| Direct investment: assets | 3a9aa | 31.8 | 47.0 | 9.6 | 59.6 | 52.4 | 37.8 | 20,405.4 | 60,991.7 | 21,493.1 | † −6,712.6 | 3,969.4 | 6,591.6 |
| Equity & investment fund shares | 3aaaa | 31.8 | 47.0 | 9.6 | 59.6 | 52.4 | 37.8 | 18,657.6 | 54,892.6 | 19,343.7 | † −5,370.1 | 3,175.6 | 5,273.2 |
| Debt instruments | 3abaa | .... | .... | .... | .... | .... | .... | 1,747.8 | 6,099.2 | 2,149.3 | † −1,342.5 | 793.9 | 1,318.3 |
| Direct investment: liabilities | 3a9la | 13.9 | 41.8 | 106.8 | 340.8 | 377.7 | 256.7 | 34,248.7 | 60,002.9 | 27,163.2 | † −5,508.8 | 4,502.3 | 6,948.1 |
| Equity & investment fund shares | 3aala | 13.9 | 41.8 | 106.8 | 340.8 | 377.7 | 256.7 | 31,224.0 | 54,002.7 | 24,446.9 | † −4,407.0 | 3,601.8 | 5,558.5 |
| Debt instruments | 3abla | .... | .... | .... | .... | .... | .... | 3,024.6 | 6,000.3 | 2,716.3 | † −1,101.8 | 900.5 | 1,389.7 |
| Portfolio investment: assets | 3b9aa | 52.4 | 41.6 | 110.5 | 95.3 | 92.9 | 261.1 | 17,589.4 | −3,823.7 | 268.1 | † 1,167.1 | 1,830.2 | 719.7 |
| Equity & investment fund shares | 3baaa | 52.4 | 41.6 | 110.5 | 95.3 | 92.9 | 261.1 | 16,409.7 | −5,737.7 | −1,656.8 | † 1,465.2 | 1,160.4 | 720.5 |
| Debt securities | 3bbaa | .... | .... | .... | .... | .... | .... | 1,179.7 | 1,914.0 | 1,924.9 | † −298.1 | 669.8 | −.8 |
| Portfolio investment: liabilities | 3b9la | 15.3 | 25.4 | 80.6 | 153.7 | −76.8 | 204.8 | 7,767.2 | 5,429.9 | 2,233.2 | † 698.2 | 938.4 | 434.1 |
| Equity & investment fund shares | 3bala | 19.3 | 35.6 | 35.1 | 49.8 | 33.9 | 206.0 | 7,820.7 | 5,915.6 | 521.7 | † 882.2 | 801.0 | 285.2 |
| Debt securities | 3bbla | −3.9 | −10.2 | 45.5 | 104.0 | −110.6 | −1.3 | −53.6 | −485.7 | 1,711.5 | † −184.0 | 137.4 | 148.9 |
| Fin. der.& empl.stk.ops.(ESOs): net. | 3c9na | — | — | .... | .... | .... | .... | −544.5 | −675.6 | −114.4 | † 3,317.9 | 883.6 | −3,445.9 |
| Fin. der. & ESOs.: assets | 3c9aa | .... | .... | .... | .... | .... | .... | 1,110.2 | 757.7 | −1,662.2 | † −17,291.9 | −17,570.8 | −4,796.2 |
| Fin. der. & ESOs.: liabilities | 3c9la | — | .... | .... | .... | .... | .... | 1,654.7 | 1,433.3 | −1,547.7 | † −20,609.8 | −18,454.5 | −1,350.3 |
| Other investment: assets | 3d9aa | 49.4 | 230.9 | 371.0 | 2,972.8 | −631.8 | 357.7 | 4,527.4 | −3,183.1 | 7,286.6 | † −1,223.6 | 245.6 | −596.1 |
| Other equity | 3daaa | .... | .... | .... | .... | .... | .... | .... | .... | .... | .... | | |
| Debt instruments | 3dzaa | 49.4 | 230.9 | 371.0 | 2,972.8 | −631.8 | 357.7 | 4,527.4 | −3,183.1 | 7,286.6 | † −1,223.6 | 245.6 | −596.1 |
| Other investment: liabilities | 3d9la | 112.4 | 394.3 | 476.5 | 3,128.2 | 155.7 | 948.9 | 1,026.9 | −10,566.0 | 931.8 | † 2,420.6 | 2,855.2 | −3,031.9 |
| Other equity | 3dala | .... | .... | .... | .... | .... | .... | .... | .... | .... | .... | | |
| Debt instruments | 3dzla | 112.4 | 394.3 | 476.5 | 3,128.2 | 155.7 | 948.9 | 1,026.9 | −10,566.0 | 931.8 | † 2,420.6 | 2,855.2 | −3,031.9 |
| Curr.+ cap.− finan. acct. balance | 4y9na | −103.7 | −181.9 | −431.6 | 61.0 | −32.6 | 98.8 | 59.2 | −2.9 | 567.3 | † 311.0 | 652.7 | 515.5 |
| D. Net Errors and Omissions | 409na | 76.2 | 16.9 | 291.5 | 375.0 | 210.5 | 285.9 | 149.8 | 198.0 | −375.8 | † 230.0 | 103.2 | 51.8 |
| E. Reserves and Related Items | 4z9na | −27.5 | −165.0 | −140.1 | 436.0 | 177.9 | 384.7 | 209.0 | 195.1 | 191.5 | † 541.0 | 755.8 | 567.3 |
| Reserve assets | 3e9aa | −27.5 | −165.0 | −140.1 | 436.0 | 177.9 | 384.7 | 209.0 | 195.1 | 191.5 | † 541.0 | 755.8 | 567.3 |
| Credit and loans from the IMF | 3dcla | — | — | — | — | — | — | — | — | — | † — | | |
| Exceptional financing | 409la | .... | — | — | — | — | — | — | — | — | .... | .... | .... |

*Excludes components in group E

## International Investment Position

*Millions of US Dollars*

| | Code | 2004 | 2005 | 2006 | 2007 | 2008 | 2009 | 2010 | 2011 | 2012 | 2013 | 2014 | 2015 |
|---|---|---|---|---|---|---|---|---|---|---|---|---|---|
| Assets | 809aa | 2,184.3 | 2,139.0 | 2,484.7 | 12,615.0 | 11,713.2 | 323,961.1 | 450,351.2 | 436,508.6 | 451,408.5 | 406,338.9 | 441,366.1 | .... |
| Direct investment | 8a9aa | .... | .... | .... | .... | .... | 166,987.2 | 226,652.9 | 277,874.7 | 292,780.1 | 232,898.2 | 229,933.4 | .... |
| Equity & investment fund shares | 8aaaa | .... | .... | .... | .... | .... | 130,391.3 | 153,133.1 | 180,667.9 | 191,268.8 | 189,360.4 | 186,541.0 | .... |
| Debt instruments | 8abaa | .... | .... | .... | .... | .... | 36,596.0 | 73,519.9 | 97,206.8 | 101,511.3 | 43,537.8 | 43,392.3 | .... |
| Portfolio investment | 8b9aa | .... | .... | .... | 1,417.3 | 1,435.6 | 129,717.1 | 176,953.7 | 103,959.6 | 101,357.3 | 92,516.0 | 120,838.5 | .... |
| Equity & investment fund shares | 8baaa | .... | .... | .... | 430.3 | 350.6 | 84,344.2 | 127,325.4 | 97,110.5 | 91,594.0 | 87,283.0 | 114,655.8 | .... |
| Debt securities | 8bbaa | .... | .... | .... | 987.0 | 1,084.9 | 45,372.9 | 49,628.4 | 6,849.1 | 9,763.2 | 5,233.0 | 6,182.7 | .... |
| Fin. der.(oth.than reserves) & ESOs | 8c9aa | .... | .... | .... | 729.8 | 1,223.4 | 3,019.2 | 6,449.3 | 9,343.4 | 8,096.4 | 34,374.9 | 38,771.9 | .... |
| Other investment | 8d9aa | 554.4 | 773.2 | 1,183.8 | 8,646.8 | 7,271.4 | 21,934.6 | 37,693.8 | 42,552.3 | 46,128.4 | 43,058.9 | 47,903.3 | .... |
| Other equity | 8daaa | .... | .... | .... | .... | .... | .... | .... | .... | .... | .... | .... | .... |
| Debt instruments | 8dzaa | 554.4 | 773.2 | 1,183.8 | 8,646.8 | 7,271.4 | 21,934.6 | 37,693.8 | 42,552.3 | 46,128.4 | 43,058.9 | 47,903.3 | .... |
| Reserve assets | 8e9aa | 1,629.9 | 1,365.8 | 1,300.9 | 1,821.2 | 1,782.8 | 2,303.0 | 2,601.4 | 2,778.7 | 3,046.3 | 3,491.0 | 3,919.0 | .... |
| Liabilities | 809la | 1,287.3 | 1,256.1 | 1,157.9 | 10,947.9 | 9,795.1 | 238,977.7 | 320,176.8 | 397,942.9 | 413,043.8 | 393,018.6 | 427,919.4 | .... |
| Direct investment | 8a9la | .... | .... | .... | .... | .... | 179,037.5 | 185,269.3 | 299,703.4 | 312,568.3 | 265,890.0 | 297,248.3 | .... |
| Equity & investment fund shares | 8aala | .... | .... | .... | .... | .... | 80,751.2 | 98,821.4 | 126,523.7 | 131,668.6 | 148,118.8 | 162,517.2 | .... |
| Debt instruments | 8abla | .... | .... | .... | .... | .... | 98,286.3 | 86,447.9 | 173,179.6 | 180,899.7 | 117,771.2 | 134,731.1 | .... |
| Portfolio investment | 8b9la | 62.5 | 82.1 | 149.9 | 1,518.6 | 488.4 | 42,526.8 | 60,747.3 | 33,992.4 | 37,696.1 | 33,367.5 | 35,677.0 | .... |
| Equity & investment fund shares | 8bala | 49.9 | 80.3 | 104.0 | 773.0 | 426.4 | 10,063.8 | 22,339.9 | 16,762.0 | 18,692.3 | 21,350.6 | 18,006.2 | .... |
| Debt securities | 8bbla | 12.7 | 1.8 | 45.9 | 745.6 | 62.0 | 32,463.0 | 38,407.4 | 17,230.4 | 19,003.8 | 12,016.9 | 17,670.8 | .... |
| Fin. der.(oth.than reserves) & ESOs | 8c9la | .... | .... | .... | 830.5 | 1,238.9 | 2,998.7 | 6,430.7 | 9,342.4 | 8,059.5 | 30,848.5 | 32,857.8 | .... |
| Other investment | 8d9la | 1,224.8 | 1,174.0 | 1,008.0 | 8,598.7 | 8,067.8 | 14,414.7 | 67,729.5 | 54,904.7 | 54,719.8 | 62,912.6 | 62,136.3 | .... |
| Other equity | 8dala | .... | .... | .... | .... | .... | .... | .... | .... | .... | .... | .... | .... |
| Debt instruments | 8dzla | 1,224.8 | 1,174.0 | 1,008.0 | 8,598.7 | 8,067.8 | 14,414.7 | 67,729.5 | 54,904.7 | 54,719.8 | 62,912.6 | 62,136.3 | .... |

# Mauritius  684

| | | 2004 | 2005 | 2006 | 2007 | 2008 | 2009 | 2010 | 2011 | 2012 | 2013 | 2014 | 2015 |
|---|---|---|---|---|---|---|---|---|---|---|---|---|---|
| **Government Finance** | | | | | | | | | | | | | |
| **Operations Statement** | | | | | | | | | | | | | |
| **Budgetary Central Government** | | | | | | *Millions of Rupees: Fiscal Year Ends December 31* | | | | | | | |
| Revenue | a1 | .... | .... | .... | .... | .... | 60,344.2 | 65,479.5 | 69,223.1 | 73,791.0 | 78,224.2 | 79,674.1 | 84,159.5 |
| Taxes | a11 | .... | .... | .... | .... | .... | 51,858.4 | 55,209.1 | 59,180.3 | 64,919.2 | 67,990.4 | 71,727.4 | 75,497.5 |
| Social Contributions | a12 | .... | .... | .... | .... | .... | 975.5 | 1,008.2 | 1,020.4 | 1,051.1 | 1,268.6 | 1,284.3 | 1,323.7 |
| Grants | a13 | .... | .... | .... | .... | .... | 3,432.9 | 1,991.0 | 2,344.4 | 2,395.1 | 1,402.7 | 406.3 | 1,829.2 |
| Other Revenue | a14 | .... | .... | .... | .... | .... | 4,077.4 | 7,271.1 | 6,678.0 | 5,425.6 | 7,562.5 | 6,256.1 | 5,509.1 |
| Expense | a2 | .... | .... | .... | .... | .... | 70,120.7 | 66,983.1 | 70,937.5 | 70,429.0 | 79,886.4 | 82,697.3 | 89,684.4 |
| Compensation of Employees | a21 | .... | .... | .... | .... | .... | 16,692.3 | 17,541.0 | 18,001.3 | 18,683.8 | 22,698.0 | 24,025.1 | 24,963.1 |
| Use of Goods & Services | a22 | .... | .... | .... | .... | .... | 5,773.6 | 6,149.6 | 6,194.6 | 6,515.8 | 7,086.5 | 7,546.2 | 7,571.1 |
| Consumption of Fixed Capital | a23 | .... | .... | .... | .... | .... | .... | .... | .... | .... | .... | .... | .... |
| Interest | a24 | .... | .... | .... | .... | .... | 10,734.2 | 10,261.9 | 9,629.2 | 10,303.0 | 9,629.4 | 10,117.6 | 9,845.4 |
| Subsidies | a25 | .... | .... | .... | .... | .... | 940.0 | 979.1 | 1,141.9 | 1,146.6 | 1,471.0 | 1,577.5 | 1,568.6 |
| Grants | a26 | .... | .... | .... | .... | .... | 20,133.2 | 15,428.7 | 19,284.2 | 16,007.4 | 18,460.8 | 18,079.9 | 18,856.1 |
| Social Benefits | a27 | .... | .... | .... | .... | .... | 12,190.4 | 13,539.8 | 14,364.4 | 15,399.8 | 17,504.8 | 19,249.5 | 24,152.6 |
| Other Expense | a28 | .... | .... | .... | .... | .... | 3,657.0 | 3,083.0 | 2,321.8 | 2,372.6 | 3,035.8 | 2,101.5 | 2,727.4 |
| Gross Operating Balance [1-2+23] | agob | .... | .... | .... | .... | .... | −9,776.5 | −1,503.6 | −1,714.3 | 3,362.0 | −1,662.2 | −3,023.2 | −5,524.9 |
| Net Operating Balance [1-2] | anob | .... | .... | .... | .... | .... | .... | .... | .... | .... | .... | .... | .... |
| Net Acq. of Nonfinancial Assets | a31 | .... | .... | .... | .... | .... | 8,799.9 | 8,076.1 | 8,632.5 | 9,616.0 | 11,161.1 | 9,527.8 | 5,889.9 |
| Aquisition of Nonfin. Assets | a31.1 | .... | .... | .... | .... | .... | .... | .... | .... | .... | .... | .... | .... |
| Disposal of Nonfin. Assets | a31.2 | .... | .... | .... | .... | .... | .... | .... | .... | .... | .... | .... | .... |
| Net Lending/Borrowing [1-2-31] | anlb | .... | .... | .... | .... | .... | −18,576.4 | −9,579.8 | −10,346.8 | −6,254.0 | −12,823.3 | −12,551.0 | −11,414.9 |
| Net Acq. of Financial Assets | a32 | .... | .... | .... | .... | .... | 1,366.9 | 558.3 | 2,992.0 | 1,397.1 | 5,265.0 | 996.2 | 1,689.0 |
| Monetary Gold & SDRs | a3201 | .... | .... | .... | .... | .... | — | 430.4 | 433.1 | 95.5 | 190.9 | — | −308.8 |
| Currency & Deposits | a3202 | .... | .... | .... | .... | .... | 990.1 | .... | .... | .... | .... | .... | .... |
| Securities other than Shares | a3203 | .... | .... | .... | .... | .... | — | .... | .... | .... | .... | .... | .... |
| Loans | a3204 | .... | .... | .... | .... | .... | 263.4 | .... | .... | .... | .... | .... | .... |
| Shares & Other Equity | a3205 | .... | .... | .... | .... | .... | 1,161.3 | .... | .... | .... | .... | .... | .... |
| Insurance Technical Reserves | a3206 | .... | .... | .... | .... | .... | — | .... | .... | .... | .... | .... | .... |
| Financial Derivatives | a3207 | .... | .... | .... | .... | .... | — | .... | .... | .... | .... | .... | .... |
| Other Accounts Receivable | a3208 | .... | .... | .... | .... | .... | — | .... | .... | .... | .... | .... | .... |
| Domestic | a321 | .... | .... | .... | .... | .... | 1,366.9 | 21.9 | 2,458.2 | 1,032.1 | 4,967.5 | 851.2 | 1,784.1 |
| Foreign | a322 | .... | .... | .... | .... | .... | — | 106.0 | 100.7 | 269.5 | 297.5 | 111.0 | 213.8 |
| Net Incurrence of Liabilities | a33 | .... | .... | .... | .... | .... | 19,943.3 | 10,138.1 | 13,338.8 | 7,651.1 | 18,088.2 | 13,547.2 | 13,103.8 |
| Special Drawing Rights (SDRs) | a3301 | .... | .... | .... | .... | .... | — | .... | .... | .... | .... | .... | .... |
| Currency & Deposits | a3302 | .... | .... | .... | .... | .... | 90.9 | .... | .... | .... | .... | .... | .... |
| Securities other than Shares | a3303 | .... | .... | .... | .... | .... | 6,223.1 | .... | .... | .... | .... | .... | .... |
| Loans | a3304 | .... | .... | .... | .... | .... | 4,600.7 | .... | .... | .... | .... | .... | .... |
| Shares & Other Equity | a3305 | .... | .... | .... | .... | .... | — | .... | .... | .... | .... | .... | .... |
| Insurance Technical Reserves | a3306 | .... | .... | .... | .... | .... | — | .... | .... | .... | .... | .... | .... |
| Financial Derivatives | a3307 | .... | .... | .... | .... | .... | — | .... | .... | .... | .... | .... | .... |
| Other Accounts Payable | a3308 | .... | .... | .... | .... | .... | 219.1 | .... | .... | .... | .... | .... | .... |
| Domestic | a331 | .... | .... | .... | .... | .... | 14,897.0 | 4,702.1 | 7,774.6 | 4,669.5 | 7,283.1 | 9,314.0 | 15,402.6 |
| Foreign | a332 | .... | .... | .... | .... | .... | 5,046.3 | 5,436.0 | 5,564.2 | 2,981.5 | 10,805.1 | 4,233.5 | −2,298.8 |
| Stat. Discrepancy [32-33-NLB] | anlbz | .... | .... | .... | .... | .... | — | −.1 | — | — | .1 | — | — |
| Memo Item: Expenditure [2+31] | a2m | .... | .... | .... | .... | .... | 78,920.6 | 75,059.3 | 79,570.0 | 80,045.0 | 91,047.5 | 92,225.1 | 95,574.3 |
| **National Accounts** | | | | | | *Millions of Rupees* | | | | | | | |
| Househ.Cons.Expend.,incl.NPISHs | 96f | 114,383 | 130,161 | 148,766 | 169,522 | 200,760 | 208,879 | 220,305 | 237,166 | 254,468 | 270,260 | 285,740 | 299,289 |
| Government Consumption Expend | 91f | 25,693 | 27,795 | 30,124 | 31,492 | 34,789 | 39,751 | 41,625 | 43,705 | 45,917 | 52,748 | 56,104 | 58,183 |
| Gross Fixed Capital Formation | 93e | 39,271 | 41,111 | 51,695 | 61,240 | 67,529 | 74,430 | 74,397 | 77,565 | 79,185 | 77,617 | 73,991 | 71,305 |
| Changes in Inventories | 93i | 4,858 | 2,274 | 5,299 | 4,453 | 7,353 | −14,292 | −3,413 | 6,287 | 5,965 | 4,647 | 14,433 | 14,239 |
| Exports of Goods and Services | 90c | 96,466 | 112,969 | 128,994 | 141,187 | 145,204 | 138,243 | 157,036 | 172,564 | 187,689 | 198,892 | 199,354 | 200,968 |
| Imports of Goods and Services (-) | 98c | 99,763 | 122,916 | 151,434 | 163,896 | 181,319 | 164,655 | 190,779 | 214,328 | 229,251 | 243,568 | 243,551 | 240,448 |
| Gross Domestic Product (GDP) | 99b | 180,908 | 191,394 | 213,444 | 243,998 | 274,316 | 282,355 | 299,171 | 322,958 | 343,973 | 366,228 | 387,068 | 403,536 |
| Net Primary Income from Abroad | 98.n | −868 | −1,180 | −861 | 5,579 | 2,073 | −1,333 | 3,603 | 2,382 | 3,668 | 262 | −9,087 | −3,930 |
| Gross National Income (GNI) | 99a | 180,041 | 190,214 | 212,583 | 249,577 | 276,389 | 281,022 | 302,774 | 325,340 | 347,641 | 366,490 | 377,981 | 399,606 |
| GDP Volume 1999 Prices | 99b.p | 137,241 | 139,234 | 145,519 | 155,130 | 163,677 | 169,098 | 176,174 | 183,243 | .... | .... | .... | .... |
| GDP Volume 2006 Prices | 99b.p | | | | 226,122 | 238,589 | 245,969 | 256,070 | 266,086 | 274,672 | 283,080 | 293,323 | 303,608 |
| GDP Volume (2010=100) | 99bvp | 78.1 | 79.3 | 82.8 | † 88.3 | 93.2 | 96.1 | 100.0 | 103.9 | 107.3 | 110.5 | 114.5 | 118.6 |
| GDP Deflator (2010=100) | 99bip | 77.4 | 80.7 | 86.1 | 92.4 | 98.4 | 98.3 | 100.0 | 103.9 | 107.2 | 110.7 | 112.9 | 113.8 |
| | | | | | | *Millions: Midyear Estimates* | | | | | | | |
| **Population** | 99z | 1.22 | 1.22 | 1.23 | 1.23 | 1.24 | 1.24 | 1.25 | 1.25 | 1.26 | 1.26 | 1.27 | 1.27 |

| | | 2004 | 2005 | 2006 | 2007 | 2008 | 2009 | 2010 | 2011 | 2012 | 2013 | 2014 | 2015 |
|---|---|---|---|---|---|---|---|---|---|---|---|---|---|
| **Exchange Rates** | | | | | | | | *Pesos per SDR: End of Period* | | | | | |
| Market Rate.............aa=......... | wa | 17.494 | 15.404 | 16.369 | 17.171 | 20.853 | 20.472 | 19.030 | 21.479 | 19.995 | 20.138 | 21.324 | 23.844 |
| | | | | | | *Pesos per US Dollar: End of Period (we) Period Average (wf)* | | | | | | | |
| Market Rate.............ae=......... | we | 11.265 | 10.778 | 10.881 | 10.866 | 13.538 | 13.059 | 12.357 | 13.990 | 13.010 | 13.077 | 14.718 | 17.207 |
| Market Rate.............rf=......... | wf | 11.286 | 10.898 | 10.899 | 10.928 | 11.130 | 13.513 | 12.636 | 12.423 | 13.169 | 12.772 | 13.292 | 15.848 |
| | | | | | | *Index Numbers (2010=100): Period Averages* | | | | | | | |
| Nominal Effective Exchange Rate..... | nec | 116.74 | 120.54 | 119.72 | 117.00 | 113.69 | 94.25 | 100.00 | 100.13 | 95.37 | 99.03 | 95.79 | 84.29 |
| CPI-Based Real Effect. Ex. Rate........ | rec | 103.36 | 107.85 | 108.08 | 106.91 | 105.16 | 92.07 | 100.00 | 100.40 | 97.54 | 103.52 | 102.45 | 92.14 |
| **Fund Position** | | | | | | *Millions of SDRs: End of Period* | | | | | | | |
| Quota......... | 2f.s | 2,585.80 | 2,585.80 | 2,585.80 | 3,152.80 | 3,152.80 | 3,152.80 | 3,152.80 | 3,625.70 | 3,625.70 | 3,625.70 | 3,625.70 | 3,625.70 |
| SDR Holdings......... | 1b.s | 299.23 | 311.57 | 320.62 | 294.84 | 337.10 | 2,886.66 | 2,808.20 | 2,660.24 | 2,689.74 | 2,669.17 | 2,528.29 | 2,554.71 |
| Reserve Position in the Fund........... | 1c.s | 578.31 | 415.76 | 226.31 | 211.31 | 397.86 | 613.06 | 686.06 | 1,577.28 | 1,826.05 | 1,758.72 | 1,432.98 | 1,114.98 |
| Total Fund Cred.&Loans Outstg....... | 2tl | — | — | — | — | — | — | — | — | — | — | — | — |
| SDR Allocations........ | 1bd | 290.02 | 290.02 | 290.02 | 290.02 | 290.02 | 2,851.20 | 2,851.20 | 2,851.20 | 2,851.20 | 2,851.20 | 2,851.20 | 2,851.20 |
| **International Liquidity** | | | | | | *Millions of US Dollars Unless Otherwise Indicated: End of Period* | | | | | | | |
| Total Reserves minus Gold.............. | 1l.d | 64,141 | 74,054 | 76,271 | 87,109 | 95,126 | 99,589 | 120,265 | 143,991 | 160,413 | 175,432 | 190,923 | 173,458 |
| SDR Holdings......... | 1b.d | 465 | 445 | 482 | 466 | 519 | 4,525 | 4,325 | 4,084 | 4,134 | 4,111 | 3,663 | 3,540 |
| Reserve Position in the Fund......... | 1c.d | 898 | 594 | 340 | 334 | 613 | 961 | 1,057 | 2,422 | 2,806 | 2,708 | 2,076 | 1,545 |
| Foreign Exchange......... | 1d.d | 62,778 | 73,015 | 75,448 | 86,309 | 93,994 | 94,103 | 114,884 | 137,485 | 153,473 | 168,613 | 185,184 | 168,373 |
| Gold (Million Fine Troy Ounces)........ | 1ad | .139 | .108 | .093 | .119 | .200 | .275 | .227 | 3.408 | 4.004 | 3.958 | 3.946 | 3.905 |
| Gold (National Valuation)................. | 1and | 61 | 56 | 59 | 99 | 172 | 302 | 322 | 5,217 | 6,636 | 4,768 | 4,758 | 4,139 |
| Central Bank: Other Assets.............. | 3..d | 773 | 772 | 772 | 773 | 773 | 776 | 773 | 772 | 773 | 773 | 772 | 772 |
| Central Bank: Other Liabs............... | 4..d | 156 | 313 | 149 | 132 | 113 | 3,324 | 78 | 135 | 124 | 91 | 77 | 66 |
| Other Depository Corps.: Assets....... | 7a.d | 14,486 | 20,817 | 20,647 | 24,992 | 28,522 | 24,309 | 45,205 | 42,924 | 43,550 | 51,692 | 43,223 | 40,559 |
| Other Depository Corps.: Liabs......... | 7b.d | 29,721 | 28,423 | 23,985 | 24,134 | 24,318 | 25,330 | 54,081 | 50,126 | 46,057 | 60,143 | 43,974 | 40,217 |
| Other Financial Corps.: Assets.......... | 7e.d | — | — | — | — | — | — | — | — | — | — | — | — |
| Other Financial Corps.: Liabs............ | 7f.d | — | — | — | — | — | — | — | — | — | — | 44 | 39 |
| **Central Bank** | | | | | | *Millions of Pesos: End of Period* | | | | | | | |
| Net Foreign Assets......... | 11n | 717,677 | 788,599 | 827,279 | 953,965 | 1,321,208 | 1,213,485 | 1,443,563 | 2,036,298 | 2,129,276 | 2,322,347 | 2,846,756 | 3,018,991 |
| Claims on Nonresidents................. | 11 | 724,435 | 796,331 | 833,601 | 960,413 | 1,328,947 | 1,315,325 | 1,498,748 | 2,099,233 | 2,187,699 | 2,380,983 | 2,908,779 | 3,088,271 |
| Liabilities to Nonresidents.............. | 16c | 6,758 | 7,732 | 6,323 | 6,448 | 7,738 | 101,839 | 55,185 | 62,935 | 58,424 | 58,637 | 62,023 | 69,280 |
| Claims on Other Depository Corps.... | 12e | 105,243 | 124,445 | 201,420 | 203,266 | 171,413 | 262,609 | 27,351 | 68,672 | 84,486 | 192,849 | 222,738 | 604,421 |
| Net Claims on Central Government.. | 12an | −124,958 | −195,724 | −335,042 | −475,250 | −568,972 | −620,883 | −577,460 | −909,365 | −1,141,642 | −1,439,365 | −1,550,953 | −1,536,383 |
| Claims on Central Government...... | 12a | — | — | — | — | — | — | — | — | — | — | — | — |
| Liabilities to Central Government... | 16d | 124,958 | 195,724 | 335,042 | 475,250 | 568,972 | 620,883 | 577,460 | 909,365 | 1,141,642 | 1,439,365 | 1,550,953 | 1,536,383 |
| Claims on Other Sectors................. | 12s | 81,901 | 81,106 | 81,129 | 74,783 | 158,199 | 131,756 | 89,945 | 68,333 | 49,854 | 30,788 | 17,307 | — |
| Claims on Other Financial Corps...... | 12g | 81,901 | 81,106 | 81,129 | 74,783 | 158,199 | 131,756 | 89,945 | 68,333 | 49,854 | 30,788 | 17,307 | — |
| Claims on State & Local Govts...... | 12b | — | — | — | — | — | — | — | — | — | — | — | — |
| Claims on Public Nonfin. Corps...... | 12c | — | — | — | — | — | — | — | — | — | — | — | — |
| Claims on Private Sector............... | 12d | — | — | — | — | — | — | — | — | — | — | — | — |
| Monetary Base......... | 14 | 340,178 | 380,034 | 449,821 | 494,743 | 577,543 | 632,032 | 693,423 | 763,492 | 846,019 | 917,876 | 1,062,893 | 1,241,685 |
| Currency in Circulation........ | 14a | 340,178 | 380,034 | 449,821 | 494,743 | 577,542 | 631,938 | 693,423 | 763,491 | 845,396 | 917,875 | 1,062,892 | 1,239,327 |
| Liabs. to Other Depository Corps... | 14c | — | — | — | — | 1 | 95 | — | 1 | 624 | 1 | 1 | 2,358 |
| Liabilities to Other Sectors............ | 14d | — | — | — | — | — | — | — | — | — | — | — | — |
| Other Liabs. to Other Dep. Corps..... | 14n | 307,877 | 350,353 | 314,039 | 290,918 | 338,164 | 310,288 | 292,330 | 281,147 | 282,411 | 283,749 | 323,971 | 354,417 |
| Dep. & Sec. Excl. f/Monetary Base..... | 14o | 174,335 | 174,732 | 107,930 | 37,885 | 33,592 | 64,825 | 74,144 | 71,319 | 23,293 | 13,003 | 12,227 | 6,174 |
| Deposits Included in Broad Money. | 15 | — | — | — | — | — | — | — | — | — | — | — | — |
| Sec.Ot.th.Shares Incl.in Brd. Money | 16a | 154,880 | 168,583 | 73,315 | 4,034 | 1,018 | 1,013 | 1,023 | — | — | — | — | — |
| Deposits Excl. from Broad Money... | 16b | 19,455 | 6,149 | 34,615 | 33,850 | 32,574 | 63,812 | 73,122 | 71,319 | 23,293 | 13,003 | 12,227 | 6,174 |
| Sec.Ot.th.Shares Excl.f/Brd.Money.. | 16s | — | — | — | — | — | — | — | — | — | — | — | — |
| Loans......... | 16l | — | — | — | — | — | — | — | — | — | — | — | — |
| Financial Derivatives......... | 16m | — | — | — | — | — | — | — | — | — | — | — | — |
| Shares and Other Equity......... | 17a | −19,631 | −90,688 | −90,848 | −70,916 | 101,818 | −58,851 | −92,242 | 115,791 | −78,712 | −175,200 | 71,698 | 418,683 |
| Other Items (Net)......... | 17r | −22,897 | −16,004 | −6,157 | 4,134 | 30,731 | 38,672 | 15,744 | 32,189 | 48,963 | 67,191 | 65,058 | 66,070 |
| Memo Item: | | | | | | | | | | | | | |
| Total Assets......... | 10ra | 998,434 | 1,085,510 | 1,218,286 | 1,312,319 | 1,726,063 | 1,769,076 | 1,667,687 | 2,282,134 | 2,333,657 | 2,605,620 | 3,151,428 | 3,698,213 |

# Mexico   273

| | | 2004 | 2005 | 2006 | 2007 | 2008 | 2009 | 2010 | 2011 | 2012 | 2013 | 2014 | 2015 |
|---|---|---|---|---|---|---|---|---|---|---|---|---|---|
| **Other Depository Corporations** | | | | | | | *Millions of Pesos: End of Period* | | | | | | |
| Net Foreign Assets........................... | 21n | −169,859 | −80,888 | −36,088 | 9,363 | 58,158 | −13,341 | −109,623 | −100,454 | −32,501 | −110,573 | −11,072 | 5,895 |
| Claims on Nonresidents................. | 21 | 161,514 | 221,377 | 223,225 | 272,804 | 394,531 | 317,625 | 558,261 | 598,690 | 564,660 | 676,359 | 637,170 | 699,592 |
| Liabilities to Nonresidents.............. | 26c | 331,373 | 302,265 | 259,312 | 263,441 | 336,373 | 330,966 | 667,884 | 699,144 | 597,161 | 786,932 | 648,242 | 693,697 |
| Claims on Central Bank................... | 20 | 406,561 | 501,727 | 424,435 | 357,634 | 425,603 | 406,559 | 388,949 | 380,447 | 395,875 | 414,834 | 456,944 | 508,544 |
| Currency......................................... | 20a | 39,196 | 44,130 | 60,562 | 64,890 | 83,198 | 95,114 | 94,353 | 97,973 | 111,945 | 125,614 | 134,845 | 152,068 |
| Reserve Deposits and Securities..... | 20b | 231,938 | 281,299 | 280,826 | 282,350 | 339,454 | 311,031 | 293,354 | 282,473 | 283,929 | 289,216 | 269,405 | 301,792 |
| Other Claims.................................... | 20n | 135,427 | 176,298 | 83,047 | 10,394 | 2,951 | 413 | 1,242 | 1 | 1 | 4 | 52,694 | 54,684 |
| Net Claims on Central Government.. | 22an | 865,645 | 844,236 | 1,065,255 | 1,249,545 | 1,383,183 | 1,568,044 | 1,553,608 | 1,744,030 | 1,840,778 | 2,066,391 | 2,146,205 | 2,128,825 |
| Claims on Central Government....... | 22a | 919,479 | 933,920 | 1,166,834 | 1,395,878 | 1,545,357 | 1,736,284 | 1,742,622 | 1,903,044 | 2,031,759 | 2,256,114 | 2,364,323 | 2,369,404 |
| Liabilities to Central Government.... | 26d | 53,834 | 89,684 | 101,579 | 146,332 | 162,174 | 168,239 | 189,013 | 159,015 | 190,981 | 189,723 | 218,118 | 240,580 |
| Claims on Other Sectors.................. | 22s | 2,027,241 | 2,232,008 | 2,604,680 | 2,946,301 | 2,913,128 | 3,201,863 | 3,558,067 | 4,126,647 | 4,511,811 | 5,075,787 | 5,466,533 | 6,272,000 |
| Claims on Other Financial Corps.. | 22g | 748,855 | 750,296 | 720,386 | 745,148 | 646,433 | 635,698 | 697,385 | 793,479 | 776,288 | 808,361 | 849,396 | 991,032 |
| Claims on State & Local Govts....... | 22b | 100,315 | 111,312 | 105,327 | 107,959 | 131,084 | 232,802 | 270,671 | 308,908 | 373,788 | 427,083 | 452,138 | 477,366 |
| Claims on Public Nonfin. Corps...... | 22c | 48,557 | 39,625 | 39,282 | 41,087 | 46,367 | 138,663 | 139,595 | 177,693 | 204,831 | 220,483 | 326,757 | 367,528 |
| Claims on Private Sector................ | 22d | 1,129,514 | 1,330,775 | 1,739,685 | 2,052,106 | 2,089,245 | 2,194,699 | 2,450,415 | 2,846,566 | 3,156,904 | 3,619,861 | 3,838,242 | 4,436,073 |
| Liabilities to Central Bank............. | 26g | 106,709 | 124,968 | 202,526 | 190,677 | 172,113 | 263,020 | 27,464 | 69,145 | 84,460 | 197,541 | 223,186 | 608,420 |
| Transf.Dep.Included in Broad Money | 24 | 583,195 | 690,275 | 790,369 | 903,916 | 987,210 | 1,079,230 | 1,261,669 | 1,452,518 | 1,560,182 | 1,734,497 | 1,944,619 | 2,156,843 |
| Other Dep.Included in Broad Money. | 25 | 1,241,377 | 1,311,714 | 1,418,172 | 1,621,493 | 1,765,066 | 1,999,716 | 2,217,835 | 2,372,440 | 2,655,909 | 2,832,151 | 3,141,477 | 3,479,049 |
| Sec.Ot.th.Shares Incl.in Brd.Money.. | 26a | 32,598 | 37,131 | 42,725 | 29,937 | 7,606 | 13,500 | 14,158 | 11,791 | 6,732 | 7,724 | 6,823 | 39,066 |
| Deposits Excl. from Broad Money..... | 26b | — | — | — | — | — | — | — | — | — | — | — | — |
| Sec.Ot.th.Shares Excl.f/Brd.Money.... | 26s | 533 | — | — | — | — | — | — | — | — | — | — | — |
| Loans............................................... | 26l | 658,420 | 676,301 | 816,607 | 844,436 | 924,427 | 762,434 | 732,746 | 903,010 | 916,014 | 1,084,781 | 1,081,605 | 1,004,292 |
| Financial Derivatives......................... | 26m | — | — | — | — | — | — | — | — | — | — | — | — |
| Insurance Technical Reserves.......... | 26r | — | — | — | — | — | — | — | — | — | — | — | — |
| Shares and Other Equity.................. | 27a | 299,763 | 360,093 | 453,533 | 511,248 | 570,767 | 664,774 | 724,814 | 791,573 | 825,910 | 885,145 | 996,400 | 1,105,664 |
| Other Items (Net)............................. | 27r | 206,993 | 296,600 | 334,352 | 461,136 | 352,884 | 380,452 | 412,315 | 550,191 | 666,756 | 704,603 | 664,500 | 521,929 |
| Memo Item: | | | | | | | | | | | | | |
| Total Assets..................................... | 20ra | 4,510,936 | 4,957,510 | 5,397,082 | 6,089,963 | 6,736,840 | 7,005,644 | 8,001,543 | 8,887,018 | 9,520,686 | 10,450,722 | 11,101,232 | 12,257,154 |
| **Depository Corporations** | | | | | | | *Millions of Pesos: End of Period* | | | | | | |
| Net Foreign Assets........................... | 31n | 547,818 | 707,711 | 791,191 | 963,328 | 1,379,366 | 1,200,145 | 1,333,940 | 1,935,844 | 2,096,775 | 2,211,774 | 2,835,684 | 3,024,887 |
| Claims on Nonresidents................. | 31 | 885,949 | 1,017,708 | 1,056,826 | 1,233,218 | 1,723,477 | 1,632,950 | 2,057,009 | 2,697,923 | 2,752,359 | 3,057,343 | 3,545,949 | 3,787,864 |
| Liabilities to Nonresidents.............. | 36c | 338,131 | 309,997 | 265,635 | 269,890 | 344,111 | 432,805 | 723,069 | 762,079 | 655,584 | 845,568 | 710,265 | 762,977 |
| Domestic Claims.............................. | 32 | 2,849,829 | 2,961,626 | 3,416,021 | 3,795,379 | 3,885,538 | 4,280,781 | 4,624,160 | 5,029,644 | 5,260,802 | 5,733,601 | 6,079,092 | 6,864,442 |
| Net Claims on Central Government | 32an | 740,687 | 648,512 | 730,213 | 774,295 | 814,210 | 947,162 | 976,148 | 834,664 | 699,136 | 627,026 | 595,252 | 592,442 |
| Claims on Central Government.... | 32a | 919,479 | 933,920 | 1,166,834 | 1,395,878 | 1,545,357 | 1,736,284 | 1,742,622 | 1,903,044 | 2,031,759 | 2,256,114 | 2,364,323 | 2,369,404 |
| Liabilities to Central Government. | 36d | 178,792 | 285,408 | 436,621 | 621,582 | 731,146 | 789,122 | 766,473 | 1,068,380 | 1,332,622 | 1,629,088 | 1,769,071 | 1,776,962 |
| Claims on Other Sectors.. | 32s | 2,109,142 | 2,313,114 | 2,685,809 | 3,021,084 | 3,071,327 | 3,333,619 | 3,648,011 | 4,194,980 | 4,561,665 | 5,106,576 | 5,483,840 | 6,272,000 |
| Claims on Other Financial Corps.. | 32g | 830,756 | 831,403 | 801,515 | 819,931 | 804,632 | 767,454 | 787,329 | 861,812 | 826,142 | 839,149 | 866,704 | 991,032 |
| Claims on State & Local Govts..... | 32b | 100,315 | 111,312 | 105,327 | 107,959 | 131,084 | 232,802 | 270,671 | 308,908 | 373,788 | 427,083 | 452,138 | 477,366 |
| Claims on Public Nonfin. Corps.... | 32c | 48,557 | 39,625 | 39,282 | 41,087 | 46,367 | 138,663 | 139,595 | 177,693 | 204,831 | 220,483 | 326,757 | 367,528 |
| Claims on Private Sector.............. | 32d | 1,129,514 | 1,330,775 | 1,739,685 | 2,052,106 | 2,089,245 | 2,194,699 | 2,450,415 | 2,846,566 | 3,156,904 | 3,619,861 | 3,838,242 | 4,436,073 |
| Broad Money Liabilities.................. | 35l | 2,313,032 | 2,543,606 | 2,713,840 | 2,989,234 | 3,255,244 | 3,630,283 | 4,093,755 | 4,502,267 | 4,956,274 | 5,366,633 | 6,020,966 | 6,762,217 |
| Currency Outside Depository Corps | 34a | 300,982 | 335,904 | 389,259 | 429,854 | 494,345 | 536,824 | 599,070 | 665,518 | 733,450 | 792,261 | 928,047 | 1,087,259 |
| Transferable Deposits................... | 34 | 583,195 | 690,275 | 790,369 | 903,916 | 987,210 | 1,079,230 | 1,261,669 | 1,452,518 | 1,560,182 | 1,734,497 | 1,944,619 | 2,156,843 |
| Other Deposits............................... | 35 | 1,241,377 | 1,311,714 | 1,418,172 | 1,621,493 | 1,765,066 | 1,999,716 | 2,217,835 | 2,372,440 | 2,655,909 | 2,832,151 | 3,141,477 | 3,479,049 |
| Securities Other than Shares........ | 36a | 187,478 | 205,714 | 116,040 | 33,971 | 8,624 | 14,513 | 15,181 | 11,791 | 6,732 | 7,724 | 6,823 | 39,066 |
| Deposits Excl. from Broad Money..... | 36b | 19,455 | 6,149 | 34,615 | 33,850 | 32,574 | 63,812 | 73,122 | 71,319 | 23,293 | 13,003 | 12,227 | 6,174 |
| Sec.Ot.th.Shares Excl.f/Brd.Money.... | 36s | 533 | — | — | — | — | — | — | — | — | — | — | — |
| Loans............................................... | 36l | 658,420 | 676,301 | 816,607 | 844,436 | 924,427 | 762,434 | 732,746 | 903,010 | 916,014 | 1,084,781 | 1,081,605 | 1,004,292 |
| Financial Derivatives......................... | 36m | — | — | — | — | — | — | — | — | — | — | — | — |
| Insurance Technical Reserves.......... | 36r | — | — | — | — | — | — | — | — | — | — | — | — |
| Shares and Other Equity.................. | 37a | 280,132 | 269,405 | 362,685 | 440,332 | 672,585 | 605,923 | 632,572 | 907,365 | 747,198 | 709,945 | 1,068,098 | 1,524,348 |
| Other Items (Net)............................. | 37r | 126,075 | 173,876 | 279,466 | 450,855 | 380,074 | 418,473 | 425,905 | 581,528 | 714,797 | 771,015 | 731,880 | 592,299 |
| Broad Money Liabs., Seasonally Adj. | 35l.b | 2,254,078 | 2,471,521 | 2,630,173 | 2,891,340 | 3,147,013 | 3,511,575 | 3,969,338 | 4,380,174 | 4,842,822 | 5,262,977 | 5,921,320 | 6,657,858 |
| **Other Financial Corporations** | | | | | | | *Millions of Pesos: End of Period* | | | | | | |
| Net Foreign Assets........................... | 41n | — | — | — | — | — | — | — | — | — | — | −646 | −679 |
| Claims on Nonresidents................. | 41 | — | — | — | — | — | — | — | — | — | — | — | — |
| Liabilities to Nonresidents.............. | 46c | — | — | — | — | — | — | — | — | — | — | 646 | 679 |
| Claims on Depository Corporations.. | 40 | 170,931 | 166,130 | 182,531 | 155,413 | 229,152 | 325,213 | 257,681 | 258,629 | 322,343 | 385,870 | 363,009 | 412,631 |
| Net Claims on Central Government.. | 42an | 530,671 | 634,221 | 703,300 | 826,665 | 991,046 | 1,139,095 | 1,282,314 | 1,465,541 | 1,711,279 | 1,771,282 | 1,929,961 | 2,226,628 |
| Claims on Central Government...... | 42a | 530,790 | 634,310 | 703,362 | 826,705 | 991,067 | 1,139,136 | 1,282,314 | 1,465,541 | 1,711,279 | 1,771,282 | 1,929,961 | 2,226,628 |
| Liabilities to Central Government... | 46d | 119 | 89 | 62 | 40 | 21 | 41 | | | | | | |
| Claims on Other Sectors................. | 42s | 175,357 | 200,811 | 301,332 | 410,429 | 464,976 | 559,488 | 779,212 | 894,458 | 1,144,451 | 1,309,137 | 1,502,325 | 1,721,275 |
| Claims on State & Local Govts....... | 42b | 340 | 288 | 265 | 243 | 293 | 319 | | | | | | |
| Claims on Public Nonfin. Corps...... | 42c | — | — | — | — | — | — | 69 | 106 | 58 | 403 | 27 | 29 |
| Claims on Private Sector................ | 42d | 175,017 | 200,523 | 301,067 | 410,186 | 464,683 | 559,169 | 779,143 | 894,352 | 1,144,393 | 1,308,734 | 1,502,298 | 1,721,246 |
| Deposits........................................... | 46b | — | — | — | — | | | | | | | | |
| Securities Other than Shares............ | 46s | — | — | — | — | | | | | | | | |
| Loans............................................... | 46l | 107,425 | 100,533 | 98,254 | 83,139 | 131,248 | 256,639 | 211,146 | 239,298 | 340,606 | 362,898 | 328,741 | 448,119 |
| Financial Derivatives......................... | 46m | 224 | 582 | 73 | 3,349 | 2,231 | 5,046 | 30,691 | 17,734 | 31,232 | 59,429 | 17,302 | 38,784 |
| Insurance Technical Reserves.......... | 46r | 215,869 | 257,613 | 289,431 | 333,997 | 412,655 | 450,616 | 498,985 | 575,047 | 642,288 | 717,491 | 820,987 | 929,082 |
| Shares and Other Equity.................. | 47a | 606,907 | 712,475 | 862,426 | 997,691 | 1,130,158 | 1,354,755 | 1,628,566 | 1,830,186 | 2,187,683 | 2,331,417 | 2,671,080 | 2,876,264 |
| Other Items (Net)............................. | 47r | −53,466 | −70,041 | −63,021 | −25,669 | 8,882 | −43,260 | −50,181 | −43,637 | −23,736 | −4,946 | −43,461 | 67,606 |
| Memo Item: | | | | | | | | | | | | | |
| Total Assets..................................... | 40ra | 1,001,932 | 1,159,159 | 1,347,905 | 1,558,395 | 1,881,868 | 2,265,443 | 2,570,771 | 2,900,054 | 3,459,081 | 3,757,079 | 4,124,313 | 4,646,414 |

|  |  | 2004 | 2005 | 2006 | 2007 | 2008 | 2009 | 2010 | 2011 | 2012 | 2013 | 2014 | 2015 |
|---|---|---|---|---|---|---|---|---|---|---|---|---|---|
| **Financial Corporations** | | | | | | *Millions of Pesos: End of Period* | | | | | | | |
| Net Foreign Assets | 51n | 547,818 | 707,711 | 791,191 | 963,328 | 1,379,366 | 1,200,145 | 1,333,940 | 1,935,844 | 2,096,775 | 2,211,774 | 2,835,038 | 3,024,208 |
| Claims on Nonresidents | 51 | 885,949 | 1,017,708 | 1,056,826 | 1,233,218 | 1,723,477 | 1,632,950 | 2,057,009 | 2,697,923 | 2,752,359 | 3,057,343 | 3,545,949 | 3,787,864 |
| Liabilities to Nonresidents | 56c | 338,131 | 309,997 | 265,635 | 269,890 | 344,111 | 432,805 | 723,069 | 762,079 | 655,584 | 845,568 | 710,911 | 763,655 |
| Domestic Claims | 52 | 2,725,101 | 2,965,255 | 3,619,138 | 4,212,542 | 4,536,928 | 5,211,909 | 5,898,356 | 6,527,831 | 7,290,389 | 7,974,871 | 8,644,674 | 9,821,312 |
| Net Claims on Central Government | 52an | 1,271,358 | 1,282,733 | 1,433,513 | 1,600,960 | 1,805,256 | 2,086,257 | 2,258,462 | 2,300,205 | 2,410,415 | 2,398,308 | 2,525,213 | 2,819,070 |
| Claims on Central Government | 52a | 1,450,269 | 1,568,230 | 1,870,196 | 2,222,583 | 2,536,424 | 2,875,420 | 3,024,936 | 3,368,585 | 3,743,038 | 4,027,396 | 4,294,284 | 4,596,032 |
| Liabilities to Central Government | 56d | 178,911 | 285,497 | 436,683 | 621,622 | 731,167 | 789,163 | 766,473 | 1,068,380 | 1,332,622 | 1,629,088 | 1,769,071 | 1,776,962 |
| Claims on Other Sectors | 52s | 1,453,743 | 1,682,522 | 2,185,626 | 2,611,582 | 2,731,672 | 3,125,653 | 3,639,894 | 4,227,626 | 4,879,974 | 5,576,564 | 6,119,461 | 7,002,243 |
| Claims on State & Local Govts | 52b | 100,655 | 111,600 | 105,592 | 108,202 | 131,377 | 233,121 | 270,671 | 308,908 | 373,788 | 427,083 | 452,138 | 477,366 |
| Claims on Public Nonfin. Corps | 52c | 48,557 | 39,625 | 39,282 | 41,087 | 46,367 | 138,663 | 139,664 | 177,799 | 204,889 | 220,886 | 326,784 | 367,558 |
| Claims on Private Sector | 52d | 1,304,531 | 1,531,298 | 2,040,752 | 2,462,292 | 2,553,928 | 2,753,868 | 3,229,558 | 3,740,918 | 4,301,297 | 4,928,595 | 5,340,540 | 6,157,319 |
| Currency Outside Financial Corps | 54a | 300,807 | 335,852 | 389,193 | 429,754 | 493,916 | 536,254 | 598,666 | 665,161 | 733,093 | 791,947 | 927,727 | 1,087,043 |
| Deposits | 55l | 1,814,082 | 2,006,191 | 2,232,494 | 2,552,862 | 2,782,637 | 3,137,767 | 3,547,319 | 3,877,827 | 4,220,082 | 4,577,921 | 5,090,290 | 5,618,560 |
| Securities Other than Shares | 56a | 140,403 | 160,030 | 91,363 | 32,808 | 8,445 | 14,472 | 15,149 | 11,040 | 6,161 | 7,724 | 6,823 | 39,066 |
| Loans | 56l | 508,628 | 471,993 | 624,993 | 639,517 | 632,988 | 527,783 | 486,451 | 561,731 | 538,720 | 711,626 | 684,581 | 588,014 |
| Financial Derivatives | 56m | — | — | — | — | — | — | — | — | — | — | — | — |
| Insurance Technical Reserves | 56r | 215,869 | 257,613 | 289,431 | 333,997 | 412,655 | 450,616 | 498,985 | 575,047 | 642,288 | 717,491 | 820,987 | 929,082 |
| Shares and Other Equity | 57a | 887,039 | 981,880 | 1,225,111 | 1,438,023 | 1,802,743 | 1,960,678 | 2,261,138 | 2,737,551 | 2,934,881 | 3,041,362 | 3,739,178 | 4,400,612 |
| Other Items (Net) | 57r | −593,910 | −540,592 | −442,256 | −251,091 | −217,088 | −215,516 | −175,411 | 35,319 | 311,938 | 338,575 | 210,126 | 183,144 |
| **Monetary Aggregates** | | | | | | *Millions of Pesos: End of Period* | | | | | | | |
| Broad Money | 59m | 3,041,492 | 3,382,264 | 3,926,708 | 4,315,747 | 4,846,539 | 5,414,353 | 5,960,458 | 6,628,801 | 7,285,215 | 7,895,720 | 8,910,625 | 9,648,480 |
| o/w:Currency Issued by Cent.Govt | 59m.a | — | — | — | — | — | — | — | — | — | — | — | — |
| o/w: Dep.in Nonfin. Corporations | 59m.b | — | — | — | — | — | — | — | — | — | — | — | — |
| o/w:Secs. Issued by Central Govt | 59m.c | 728,460 | 838,658 | 1,212,869 | 1,326,513 | 1,591,294 | 1,784,071 | 1,866,703 | 2,126,534 | 2,328,941 | 2,529,088 | 2,889,660 | 2,886,264 |
| Money (National Definitions) | | | | | | | | | | | | | |
| Base Money | 19ma | 340,178 | 380,034 | 449,821 | 494,744 | 577,543 | 632,032 | 693,423 | 763,492 | 846,019 | 917,876 | 1,062,893 | 1,241,685 |
| M1 | 59ma | 946,567 | 1,068,500 | 1,218,520 | 1,350,053 | 1,482,920 | 1,614,643 | 1,833,318 | 2,083,179 | 2,280,049 | 2,513,758 | 2,879,196 | 3,351,971 |
| M2 | 59mb | 3,800,700 | 4,366,056 | 4,972,338 | 5,384,859 | 6,269,942 | 6,672,271 | 7,207,837 | 8,065,740 | 8,740,157 | 9,507,203 | 10,539,707 | 11,301,886 |
| M3 | 59mc | 3,889,855 | 4,503,844 | 5,149,697 | 5,647,690 | 6,596,618 | 7,052,965 | 7,952,034 | 9,227,071 | 10,573,933 | 11,566,141 | 12,989,421 | 13,726,003 |
| M4 | 59md | 3,928,827 | 4,545,899 | 5,201,449 | 5,719,994 | 6,680,585 | 7,126,818 | 8,037,240 | 9,330,572 | 10,684,893 | 11,658,630 | 13,107,550 | 13,858,258 |
| M4A | 59mda | 4,245,474 | 4,875,358 | 5,511,495 | 6,129,485 | 7,157,420 | 7,592,803 | 8,504,128 | 9,835,480 | 11,263,202 | 12,246,936 | 13,698,828 | 14,568,170 |
| M4 National Currency | 59mdb | 3,769,482 | 4,360,578 | 5,003,490 | 5,501,514 | 6,426,214 | 6,861,044 | 7,754,313 | 9,016,741 | 10,327,290 | 11,279,088 | 12,609,846 | 13,194,231 |
| M4 Foreign Currency | 59mdd | 159,345 | 185,321 | 197,959 | 218,481 | 254,372 | 265,774 | 282,927 | 313,831 | 357,604 | 379,542 | 497,703 | 664,028 |
| **Interest Rates** | | | | | | *Percent Per Annum* | | | | | | | |
| Central Bank Policy Rate (EOP) | 60 | .... | .... | .... | .... | 8.25 | 4.50 | 4.50 | 4.50 | 4.50 | 3.50 | 3.00 | 3.25 |
| Money Market Rate | 60b | 7.15 | 9.59 | 7.51 | 7.66 | 8.28 | 5.93 | 4.91 | 4.82 | 4.79 | 4.28 | 3.52 | 3.32 |
| Treasury Bill Rate | 60c | 6.82 | 9.20 | 7.19 | 7.19 | 7.68 | 5.43 | 4.40 | 4.24 | 4.24 | 3.75 | 3.00 | 2.98 |
| Savings Rate | 60k | 1.42 | .93 | .93 | 1.11 | 1.12 | 1.12 | 1.02 | .66 | 1.55 | 2.29 | 2.02 | 1.78 |
| Deposit Rate | 60l | 2.70 | 3.46 | 3.30 | 3.21 | 3.04 | 2.01 | 1.21 | .96 | 1.08 | 1.33 | .84 | .59 |
| Average Cost of Funds | 60n | 5.41 | 7.64 | 6.06 | 5.99 | 6.73 | 5.07 | 4.17 | 4.18 | 4.20 | 3.86 | 3.23 | 3.03 |
| Lending Rate | 60p | 7.44 | 9.70 | 7.51 | 7.56 | 8.71 | 7.07 | 5.29 | 4.92 | 4.73 | 4.25 | 3.55 | 3.42 |
| Government Bond Yield | 61 | 9.54 | 9.42 | 8.39 | 7.79 | 8.31 | 7.96 | 7.11 | 6.65 | 5.60 | 5.68 | 6.01 | 5.99 |
| **Prices, Production, Labor** | | | | | | *Index Numbers (2010=100): Period Averages* | | | | | | | |
| Share Prices | 62 | 31.6 | 42.9 | 62.4 | 89.2 | 80.4 | 76.0 | 100.0 | 108.0 | 119.4 | 126.0 | 127.9 | 131.9 |
| Share Prices (End of Month) | 62.ep | 32.1 | 43.4 | 63.3 | 89.3 | 80.7 | 76.0 | 100.0 | 109.2 | 120.3 | 126.4 | 128.1 | 131.5 |
| Producer Prices | 63 | † 74.3 | 77.8 | 82.1 | 85.8 | 91.9 | 96.0 | 100.0 | 105.2 | 110.1 | 111.6 | 114.6 | 117.9 |
| Consumer Prices | 64 | † 77.4 | 80.5 | 83.4 | 86.7 | 91.2 | 96.0 | 100.0 | 103.4 | 107.7 | 111.8 | 116.2 | 119.4 |
| Wages, Monthly | 65 | 82.8 | 85.8 | 93.3 | 100.6 | 101.5 | 100.7 | 100.0 | 100.2 | 100.3 | 100.5 | 100.9 | 101.6 |
| Industrial Production | 66 | 94.4 | 96.7 | 100.9 | 102.4 | 101.9 | 95.6 | 100.0 | 103.4 | 106.3 | 105.8 | 108.7 | 109.7 |
| Manufacturing Production | 66ey | 93.7 | 96.3 | 100.6 | 101.5 | 100.5 | 92.1 | 100.0 | 104.6 | 108.9 | 110.2 | 114.8 | 118.0 |
| Mining Production | 66zx | 109.6 | 109.6 | 108.9 | 107.3 | 103.3 | 99.1 | 100.0 | 99.6 | 100.5 | 100.4 | 98.8 | 93.1 |
| Crude Petroleum Production | 66aa | 117.6 | 116.6 | 115.8 | 112.2 | 105.9 | 100.7 | 100.0 | 98.3 | 97.8 | 96.7 | 94.4 | 89.0 |
| | | | | | | *Number in Thousands: Period Averages* | | | | | | | |
| Labor Force | 67d | 41,962 | 43,632 | 44,983 | 45,905 | 46,769 | 48,018 | 48,718 | 49,722 | † 51,229 | 51,787 | 51,924 | 52,905 |
| Employment | 67e | 40,320 | 42,079 | 43,378 | 44,231 | 44,944 | 45,435 | 46,122 | 47,139 | † 48,707 | 49,227 | 49,415 | 50,611 |
| Unemployment | 67c | 1,643 | 1,552 | 1,604 | 1,673 | 1,826 | 2,583 | 2,596 | 2,583 | † 2,522 | 2,560 | 2,509 | 2,294 |
| Unemployment Rate (%) | 67r | 3.9 | 3.6 | 3.6 | 3.6 | 3.9 | 5.4 | 5.3 | 5.2 | † 4.9 | 4.9 | 4.8 | 4.3 |
| **Intl. Transactions & Positions** | | | | | | *Millions of US Dollars* | | | | | | | |
| Excluding Maquiladoras | | | | | | | | | | | | | |
| Exports | 70n.d | 101,252 | 125,217 | 138,520 | .... | .... | .... | .... | .... | .... | .... | .... | .... |
| Imports, f.o.b. | 71nvd | 128,723 | 146,285 | 168,627 | .... | .... | .... | .... | .... | .... | .... | .... | .... |
| Including Maquiladoras | | | | | | | | | | | | | |
| Exports | 70..d | 189,084 | 213,891 | 250,441 | 272,055 | 291,827 | 229,683 | 298,138 | 349,569 | 370,889 | 380,107 | 397,658 | 380,763 |
| Imports, f.o.b. | 71.vd | 197,347 | 221,415 | 256,130 | 283,264 | 310,561 | 234,385 | 301,482 | 350,856 | 370,746 | 381,202 | 399,977 | 395,232 |
| | | | | | | *2010=100* | | | | | | | |
| Export Prices | 76 | 77.6 | 84.0 | 90.3 | 94.9 | 104.3 | 89.1 | 100.0 | 114.6 | 111.6 | 111.2 | 106.3 | .... |
| Import Prices | 76.x | 79.4 | 83.4 | 87.2 | 91.9 | 99.7 | 95.9 | 100.0 | 107.3 | 108.4 | 108.2 | 108.9 | .... |

# Mexico 273

## Balance of Payments

*Millions of US Dollars*

| | | 2004 | 2005 | 2006 | 2007 | 2008 | 2009 | 2010 | 2011 | 2012 | 2013 | 2014 | 2015 |
|---|---|---|---|---|---|---|---|---|---|---|---|---|---|
| A. Current Account* | 109bx | −7,017.2 | −9,052.0 | −7,474.6 | −14,499.1 | −20,262.4 | −8,536.3 | −5,207.7 | −13,370.1 | −16,698.1 | −30,409.3 | −24,665.4 | −31,725.1 |
| Goods, credit (exports) | 1a9cx | 188,294.1 | 214,632.9 | 250,319.0 | 272,293.0 | 291,886.3 | 229,975.0 | 298,859.8 | 350,004.0 | 371,441.8 | 380,729.0 | 397,866.5 | 381,198.4 |
| Goods, debit (imports) | 1a9dx | 197,137.4 | 222,295.4 | 256,631.3 | 282,604.4 | 309,501.3 | 234,900.6 | 301,802.7 | 351,209.1 | 371,150.6 | 381,638.2 | 400,439.6 | 395,573.4 |
| Balance on goods | 1a9bx | −8,843.3 | −7,662.5 | −6,312.2 | −10,311.4 | −17,615.0 | −4,925.6 | −2,942.9 | −1,205.1 | 291.2 | −909.2 | −2,573.1 | −14,375.0 |
| Services, credit (exports) | 1b9cx | 13,705.9 | 15,735.9 | 15,908.4 | 17,243.9 | 17,672.6 | 14,824.3 | 15,234.5 | 15,581.9 | 16,145.5 | 20,193.8 | 21,085.9 | 22,609.4 |
| Services, debit (imports) | 1b9dx | 20,546.8 | 22,804.2 | 23,641.1 | 24,904.4 | 25,649.0 | 25,042.6 | 25,791.9 | 30,374.9 | 30,150.1 | 31,177.1 | 33,537.3 | 32,057.4 |
| Balance on Goods & Services | 1z9bx | −15,684.2 | −14,730.8 | −14,044.9 | −17,971.9 | −25,591.4 | −15,143.8 | −13,500.3 | −15,998.0 | −13,713.4 | −11,892.6 | −15,024.5 | −23,823.1 |
| Primary income: credit | 1c9cx | 5,705.5 | 4,818.5 | 5,578.1 | 7,664.2 | 8,529.6 | 6,797.2 | 10,811.9 | 10,568.6 | 13,154.1 | 11,320.0 | 11,318.8 | 8,167.6 |
| Primary income: debit | 1c9dx | 15,785.6 | 21,262.0 | 24,942.0 | 30,581.9 | 28,655.3 | 21,768.7 | 24,042.8 | 30,901.2 | 38,697.7 | 51,490.0 | 43,874.9 | 40,377.1 |
| Balance on gds, serv. & prim. inc. | 1y9bx | −25,764.3 | −31,174.3 | −33,408.7 | −40,889.6 | −45,717.0 | −30,115.3 | −26,731.2 | −36,330.6 | −39,256.9 | −52,062.6 | −47,580.6 | −56,032.5 |
| Secondary income: credit | 1d9ca | 18,827.1 | 22,179.0 | 26,021.8 | 26,498.3 | 25,582.9 | 21,639.4 | 21,609.4 | 23,138.7 | 22,768.3 | 22,648.6 | 24,025.8 | 25,212.7 |
| Secondary income: debit | 1d9da | 80.0 | 56.6 | 87.7 | 107.7 | 128.2 | 60.4 | 85.9 | 178.2 | 209.4 | 995.3 | 1,110.7 | 905.2 |
| B. Capital Account* | 209ba | — | — | — | — | — | — | — | — | — | — | — | — |
| Capital account: credit | 209ca | — | — | — | — | — | — | — | — | — | — | — | — |
| Capital account: debit | 209da | — | — | — | — | — | — | — | — | — | — | — | — |
| Balance on current & capital acct. | 129ba | −7,017.2 | −9,052.0 | −7,474.6 | −14,499.1 | −20,262.4 | −8,536.3 | −5,207.7 | −13,370.1 | −16,698.1 | −30,409.3 | −24,665.4 | −31,725.1 |
| C. Financial Account* | 309na | −16,743.3 | −15,104.7 | −10,058.0 | −24,584.0 | −34,031.6 | −16,697.6 | −48,333.4 | −52,680.9 | −55,036.3 | −67,895.7 | −58,834.5 | −31,520.6 |
| Direct investment: assets | 3a9aa | 4,431.9 | 6,474.0 | 5,758.5 | 8,256.3 | 1,157.1 | 9,603.7 | 15,049.5 | 12,636.2 | 22,470.0 | 13,138.4 | 7,462.8 | 12,126.1 |
| Equity & investment fund shares | 3aaaa | 3,776.5 | 4,701.6 | 5,451.6 | 4,736.0 | 1,637.6 | 8,503.6 | 13,439.9 | 7,479.0 | 9,549.5 | 8,385.4 | 10,871.6 | 10,718.5 |
| Debt instruments | 3abaa | 655.4 | 1,772.4 | 306.8 | 3,520.4 | −480.5 | 1,100.0 | 1,609.6 | 5,157.3 | 12,920.5 | 4,753.0 | −3,408.8 | 1,407.7 |
| Direct investment: liabilities | 3a9la | 24,913.5 | 25,971.1 | 21,110.0 | 32,407.3 | 29,078.4 | 17,899.6 | 26,431.3 | 23,649.2 | 20,436.9 | 45,854.6 | 25,675.4 | 30,284.6 |
| Equity & investment fund shares | 3aala | 17,428.3 | 18,575.1 | 14,949.0 | 26,545.2 | 21,833.1 | 16,520.9 | 20,529.0 | 18,849.4 | 14,125.1 | 38,400.7 | 19,239.5 | 20,664.8 |
| Debt instruments | 3abla | 7,485.2 | 7,395.9 | 6,161.0 | 5,862.1 | 7,245.3 | 1,378.7 | 5,902.2 | 4,799.8 | 6,311.7 | 7,453.8 | 6,435.9 | 9,619.8 |
| Portfolio investment: assets | 3b9aa | 1,754.0 | 20,547.7 | 1,728.9 | 14,739.3 | −14,182.8 | 34,540.5 | 5,356.9 | −6,048.6 | 8,610.5 | 1,616.8 | 63.0 | −1,589.0 |
| Equity & investment fund shares | 3baaa | .... | .... | .... | .... | .... | .... | .... | .... | .... | .... | .... | .... |
| Debt securities | 3bbaa | 1,754.0 | 20,547.7 | 1,728.9 | 14,739.3 | −14,182.8 | 34,540.5 | 5,356.9 | −6,048.6 | 8,610.5 | 1,616.8 | 63.0 | −1,589.0 |
| Portfolio investment: liabilities | 3b9la | 5,006.3 | 7,060.4 | 122.3 | 13,265.5 | 4,577.2 | 15,287.8 | 38,059.7 | 42,512.3 | 81,841.9 | 51,118.7 | 47,078.8 | 20,376.8 |
| Equity & investment fund shares | 3bala | −2,522.2 | 3,352.9 | 2,805.2 | −482.1 | −3,503.3 | 4,155.3 | 373.1 | −6,565.9 | 9,876.7 | −942.8 | 4,833.4 | 3,601.1 |
| Debt securities | 3bbla | 7,528.5 | 3,707.5 | −2,682.9 | 13,747.6 | 8,080.5 | 11,132.5 | 37,686.6 | 49,078.2 | 71,965.2 | 52,061.5 | 42,245.3 | 16,775.7 |
| Fin. der.& empl.stk.ops.(ESOs): net. | 3c9na | | | | | 1,522.0 | −4,271.2 | 545.9 | 725.1 | −116.8 | 469.5 | 671.1 | −6,006.6 |
| Fin. der. & ESOs: assets | 3c9aa | — | — | — | — | | | | | | | | |
| Fin. der. & ESOs: liabilities | 3c9la | | | | | −1,522.0 | 4,271.2 | −545.9 | −725.1 | 116.8 | −469.5 | −671.1 | 6,006.6 |
| Other investment: assets | 3d9aa | 5,278.6 | −5,824.6 | 4,110.0 | 18,808.6 | 18,704.9 | −20,977.0 | 27,005.3 | 3,673.5 | 6,274.0 | 27,278.8 | 20,910.3 | 12,852.6 |
| Other equity | 3daaa | .... | .... | .... | .... | .... | .... | .... | .... | .... | .... | .... | .... |
| Debt instruments | 3dzaa | 5,278.6 | −5,824.6 | 4,110.0 | 18,808.6 | 18,704.9 | −20,977.0 | 27,005.3 | 3,673.5 | 6,274.0 | 27,278.8 | 20,910.3 | 12,852.6 |
| Other investment: liabilities | 3d9la | −1,712.0 | 3,270.3 | 423.2 | 20,715.5 | 7,577.1 | 2,406.1 | 31,800.1 | −2,494.4 | −10,004.7 | 13,425.9 | 15,187.5 | −1,757.6 |
| Other equity | 3dala | .... | .... | .... | .... | .... | .... | .... | .... | .... | .... | .... | .... |
| Debt instruments | 3dzla | −1,712.0 | 3,270.3 | 423.2 | 20,715.5 | 7,577.1 | 2,406.1 | 31,800.1 | −2,494.4 | −10,004.7 | 13,425.9 | 15,187.5 | −1,757.6 |
| Curr.+ cap.− finan. acct. balance | 4y9na | 9,726.1 | 6,052.8 | 2,583.5 | 10,085.0 | 13,769.2 | 8,161.3 | 43,125.6 | 39,310.8 | 38,338.3 | 37,486.3 | 34,169.1 | −204.4 |
| D. Net Errors and Omissions | 409na | −4,631.2 | 3,942.8 | −436.7 | 717.7 | −5,686.4 | −3,689.0 | −22,427.3 | −11,089.1 | −20,821.9 | −19,708.4 | −17,447.2 | −15,212.2 |
| E. Reserves and Related Items | 4z9na | 5,094.8 | 9,995.6 | 2,146.8 | 10,802.6 | 8,082.8 | 4,472.3 | 20,698.3 | 28,221.7 | 17,516.4 | 17,778.0 | 16,721.9 | −15,416.7 |
| Reserve assets | 3e9aa | 5,110.3 | 10,010.7 | 2,161.5 | 10,817.0 | 8,096.8 | 4,486.1 | 20,711.7 | 28,234.8 | 17,516.4 | 17,778.0 | 16,721.9 | −15,416.7 |
| Credit and loans from the IMF | 3dc1a | — | — | — | — | — | — | — | — | — | — | — | — |
| Exceptional financing | 409la | 15.5 | 15.1 | 14.8 | 14.4 | 14.1 | 13.7 | 13.4 | 13.1 | — | — | — | — |

*Excludes components in group E

## International Investment Position

*Millions of US Dollars*

| | | 2004 | 2005 | 2006 | 2007 | 2008 | 2009 | 2010 | 2011 | 2012 | 2013 | 2014 | 2015 |
|---|---|---|---|---|---|---|---|---|---|---|---|---|---|
| Assets | 809aa | 187,781.1 | 223,338.9 | 238,507.8 | 297,244.1 | 300,736.5 | 313,899.4 | 400,433.5 | 419,879.5 | 486,301.3 | 519,538.2 | 560,204.1 | 552,242.1 |
| Direct investment | 8a9aa | 42,926.6 | 53,854.7 | 60,964.2 | 75,269.8 | 66,148.1 | 88,078.4 | 121,556.8 | 114,755.4 | 148,450.2 | 139,641.7 | 143,852.0 | 142,917.0 |
| Equity & investment fund shares | 8aaaa | .... | .... | .... | .... | .... | .... | .... | 110,683.5 | 138,724.2 | 127,954.6 | 136,138.3 | 133,795.7 |
| Debt instruments | 8abaa | .... | .... | .... | .... | .... | .... | .... | 4,071.8 | 9,726.0 | 11,687.0 | 7,713.7 | 9,121.4 |
| Portfolio investment | 8b9aa | 17,029.5 | 37,577.1 | 39,306.0 | 54,045.3 | 39,862.5 | 47,481.4 | 52,838.3 | 46,789.6 | 55,400.1 | 57,016.9 | 57,079.9 | 55,413.2 |
| Equity & investment fund shares | 8baaa | .... | .... | .... | .... | .... | .... | .... | .... | .... | .... | .... | .... |
| Debt securities | 8bbaa | 17,029.5 | 37,577.1 | 39,306.0 | 54,045.3 | 39,862.5 | 47,481.4 | 52,838.3 | 46,789.6 | 55,400.1 | 57,016.9 | 57,079.9 | 55,413.2 |
| Fin. der.(oth.than reserves) & ESOs | 8c9aa | .... | .... | .... | .... | .... | .... | .... | .... | .... | .... | .... | .... |
| Other investment | 8d9aa | 63,627.0 | 57,802.4 | 61,912.3 | 80,721.0 | 99,425.9 | 78,448.9 | 105,454.2 | 109,127.7 | 115,401.7 | 142,680.5 | 163,590.8 | 176,315.6 |
| Other equity | 8daaa | .... | .... | .... | .... | .... | .... | .... | .... | .... | .... | .... | .... |
| Debt instruments | 8dzaa | 63,627.0 | 57,802.4 | 61,912.3 | 80,721.0 | 99,425.9 | 78,448.9 | 105,454.2 | 109,127.7 | 115,401.7 | 142,680.5 | 163,590.8 | 176,315.6 |
| Reserve assets | 8e9aa | 64,198.0 | 74,104.6 | 76,325.2 | 87,208.0 | 95,300.1 | 99,890.8 | 120,584.3 | 149,206.7 | 167,049.2 | 180,199.0 | 195,681.3 | 177,596.3 |
| Liabilities | 809la | 438,468.4 | 523,336.1 | 606,734.4 | 679,865.8 | 641,179.8 | 653,771.9 | 804,617.3 | 785,525.0 | 932,295.3 | 1,010,066.0 | 1,024,691.4 | 961,879.5 |
| Direct investment | 8a9la | 190,735.9 | 233,479.4 | 267,126.5 | 298,051.0 | 250,162.8 | 305,831.9 | 363,791.2 | 338,995.4 | 376,348.3 | 394,726.6 | 389,671.5 | 356,896.4 |
| Equity & investment fund shares | 8aala | .... | .... | .... | .... | .... | 298,316.3 | 357,099.9 | 330,433.9 | 349,541.7 | 358,104.3 | 342,694.7 | 300,299.8 |
| Debt instruments | 8abla | .... | .... | .... | .... | .... | 7,515.6 | 6,691.3 | 8,561.4 | 26,806.6 | 36,622.3 | 46,976.8 | 56,596.6 |
| Portfolio investment | 8b9la | 168,882.4 | 207,935.7 | 255,312.9 | 273,405.2 | 271,949.5 | 238,643.3 | 304,385.9 | 311,190.0 | 430,349.4 | 475,952.2 | 481,014.4 | 455,852.1 |
| Equity & investment fund shares | 8bala | 73,966.6 | 106,555.0 | 154,239.1 | 154,444.6 | 148,697.2 | 134,384.0 | 161,334.0 | 129,323.2 | 171,554.9 | 168,242.7 | 153,096.6 | 134,145.8 |
| Debt securities | 8bbla | 94,915.8 | 101,380.7 | 101,073.9 | 118,960.6 | 123,252.3 | 104,259.3 | 143,051.9 | 181,866.7 | 258,794.5 | 307,709.5 | 327,917.8 | 321,706.2 |
| Fin. der.(oth.than reserves) & ESOs | 8c9la | .... | .... | .... | .... | .... | .... | .... | .... | .... | .... | .... | .... |
| Other investment | 8d9la | 78,850.1 | 81,921.0 | 84,294.9 | 108,409.6 | 119,067.5 | 109,296.7 | 136,440.2 | 135,339.7 | 125,597.6 | 139,387.2 | 154,005.5 | 149,131.1 |
| Other equity | 8dala | .... | .... | .... | .... | .... | .... | .... | .... | .... | .... | .... | .... |
| Debt instruments | 8dzla | 78,850.1 | 81,921.0 | 84,294.9 | 108,409.6 | 119,067.5 | 109,296.7 | 136,440.2 | 135,339.7 | 125,597.6 | 139,387.2 | 154,005.5 | 149,131.1 |

| | | 2004 | 2005 | 2006 | 2007 | 2008 | 2009 | 2010 | 2011 | 2012 | 2013 | 2014 | 2015 |
|---|---|---|---|---|---|---|---|---|---|---|---|---|---|
| **Government Finance** | | | | | | | | | | | | | |
| **Cash Flow Statement** | | | | | | | | | | | | | |
| **Central Government** | | | | | *Billions of Pesos: Fiscal Year Ends December 31* | | | | | | | | |
| Cash Receipts:Operating Activities... | c1 | 1,171.0 | 1,299.2 | 1,387.7 | 1,543.4 | 1,791.7 | 1,723.8 | 1,826.5 | 2,079.2 | 2,215.6 | .... | .... | .... |
| Taxes.......................................... | c11 | .... | .... | .... | .... | .... | .... | .... | .... | .... | .... | .... | .... |
| Social Contributions...................... | c12 | .... | .... | .... | .... | .... | .... | .... | .... | .... | .... | .... | .... |
| Grants......................................... | c13 | .... | .... | .... | .... | .... | .... | .... | .... | .... | .... | .... | .... |
| Other Receipts............................. | c14 | .... | .... | .... | .... | .... | .... | .... | .... | .... | .... | .... | .... |
| Cash Payments:Operating Activities. | c2 | 1,249.0 | 1,361.8 | 1,538.6 | 1,721.2 | 1,954.4 | 1,956.8 | 2,142.7 | 2,410.8 | 2,585.7 | .... | .... | .... |
| Compensation of Employees.......... | c21 | .... | .... | .... | .... | .... | .... | .... | .... | .... | .... | .... | .... |
| Purchases of Goods & Services....... | c22 | .... | .... | .... | .... | .... | .... | .... | .... | .... | .... | .... | .... |
| Interest........................................ | c24 | .... | .... | .... | .... | .... | .... | .... | .... | .... | .... | .... | .... |
| Subsidies..................................... | c25 | .... | .... | .... | .... | .... | .... | .... | .... | .... | .... | .... | .... |
| Grants......................................... | c26 | .... | .... | .... | .... | .... | .... | .... | .... | .... | .... | .... | .... |
| Social Benefits............................. | c27 | .... | .... | .... | .... | .... | .... | .... | .... | .... | .... | .... | .... |
| Other Payments........................... | c28 | .... | .... | .... | .... | .... | .... | .... | .... | .... | .... | .... | .... |
| Net Cash Inflow:Operating Act.[1-2] | ccio | .... | .... | .... | .... | .... | .... | .... | .... | .... | .... | .... | .... |
| Net Cash Outflow:Invest. in NFA...... | c31 | .... | .... | .... | .... | .... | .... | .... | .... | .... | .... | .... | .... |
| Purchases of Nonfinancial Assets... | c31.1 | .... | .... | .... | .... | .... | .... | .... | .... | .... | .... | .... | .... |
| Sales of Nonfinancial Assets.......... | c31.2 | .... | .... | .... | .... | .... | .... | .... | .... | .... | .... | .... | .... |
| Cash Surplus/Deficit [1-2-31=1-2M] | ccsd | −78.0 | −62.6 | −150.9 | −177.7 | −162.8 | −233.0 | −316.3 | −331.6 | −370.1 | .... | .... | .... |
| Net Acq. Fin. Assets, excl. Cash....... | c32x | .... | .... | .... | .... | .... | .... | .... | .... | .... | .... | .... | .... |
| Domestic..................................... | c321x | .... | .... | .... | .... | .... | .... | .... | .... | .... | .... | .... | .... |
| Foreign....................................... | c322x | .... | .... | .... | .... | .... | .... | .... | .... | .... | .... | .... | .... |
| Net Incurrence of Liabilities.............. | c33 | 78.0 | 62.6 | 150.9 | 177.7 | 162.8 | 233.0 | 316.3 | 331.6 | 370.1 | .... | .... | .... |
| Domestic..................................... | c331 | 65.8 | 80.5 | 349.0 | 199.1 | 163.0 | 144.6 | 211.0 | 280.2 | 293.6 | .... | .... | .... |
| Foreign....................................... | c332 | 12.2 | −17.9 | −198.1 | −21.4 | −.3 | 88.4 | 105.3 | 51.4 | 76.5 | .... | .... | .... |
| Net Cash Inflow, Fin.Act.[-32x+33].. | cnfb | .... | .... | .... | .... | .... | .... | .... | .... | .... | .... | .... | .... |
| Net Change in Stock of Cash........... | cncb | .... | .... | .... | .... | .... | .... | .... | .... | .... | .... | .... | .... |
| Stat. Discrep. [32X-33+NCB-CSD].... | ccsdz | .... | .... | .... | .... | .... | .... | .... | .... | .... | .... | .... | .... |
| Memo Item:Cash Expenditure[2+31] | c2m | .... | .... | .... | .... | .... | .... | .... | .... | .... | .... | .... | .... |
| Memo Item: Gross Debt................. | c63 | 1,776.0 | 1,871.3 | 2,129.1 | 2,497.8 | 3,172.2 | 3,961.0 | 4,252.8 | 4,826.5 | 5,211.0 | .... | .... | .... |
| **National Accounts** | | | | | | *Billions of Pesos* | | | | | | | |
| Househ.Cons.Expend.,incl.NPISHs.... | 96fac | 5,840.60 | 6,385.90 | 6,975.50 | 7,549.54 | 8,198.84 | 8,063.91 | 8,899.92 | 9,642.53 | 10,510.02 | 11,041.49 | 11,730.13 | 12,571.21 |
| Government Consumption Expend... | 91fac | 928.27 | 1,009.65 | 1,106.40 | 1,204.72 | 1,333.81 | 1,449.59 | 1,548.45 | 1,683.83 | 1,849.07 | 1,963.37 | 2,100.84 | 2,222.41 |
| Gross Fixed Capital Formation.......... | 93eac | 1,841.41 | 2,009.64 | 2,315.71 | 2,539.11 | 2,830.42 | 2,724.72 | 2,806.75 | 3,163.35 | 3,489.18 | 3,401.08 | 3,621.64 | 4,024.59 |
| Changes in Inventories.................... | 93iac | 130.51 | 95.79 | 157.47 | 128.34 | 164.70 | 45.61 | 122.74 | 75.49 | 112.99 | 90.65 | 95.25 | 96.16 |
| Exports of Goods and Services......... | 90cac | 2,280.56 | 2,508.35 | 2,903.85 | 3,163.33 | 3,419.44 | 3,299.27 | 3,967.57 | 4,548.97 | 5,101.40 | 5,121.62 | 5,574.63 | 6,408.36 |
| Imports of Goods and Services (-)..... | 98cac | 2,433.48 | 2,644.40 | 3,035.67 | 3,343.91 | 3,698.25 | 3,477.52 | 4,127.39 | 4,730.53 | 5,276.17 | 5,264.59 | 5,759.17 | 6,793.82 |
| Gross Domestic Product (GDP)........ | 99bac | 8,690.25 | 9,424.60 | 10,520.79 | 11,399.47 | 12,256.86 | 12,072.54 | 13,266.86 | 14,527.34 | 15,599.27 | 16,077.06 | 17,209.66 | 18,135.71 |
| GDP Volume 2003 Prices................ | 99bar | 7,863.29 | 8,120.84 | 8,531.66 | 8,818.62 | 8,926.01 | 8,390.68 | 8,837.36 | 9,183.59 | 9,530.07 | .... | .... | .... |
| GDP Volume 2008 Prices................ | 99bar | 10,824.20 | 11,157.11 | 11,712.33 | 12,090.03 | 12,256.86 | 11,675.44 | 12,282.46 | 12,763.88 | 13,279.40 | 13,464.63 | 13,765.00 | 14,120.02 |
| GDP Volume (2010=100)............... | 99bvr | 88.1 | 90.8 | 95.4 | 98.4 | 99.8 | 95.1 | 100.0 | 103.9 | 108.1 | 109.6 | 112.1 | 115.0 |
| GDP Deflator (2010=100)............... | 99bir | 74.3 | 78.2 | 83.2 | 87.3 | 92.6 | 95.7 | 100.0 | 105.4 | 108.8 | 110.5 | 115.7 | 118.9 |
| | | | | | | *Millions: Midyear Estimates* | | | | | | | |
| **Population**................................ | 99z | 108.26 | 109.75 | 111.38 | 113.14 | 114.97 | 116.82 | 118.62 | 120.37 | 122.07 | 123.74 | 125.39 | 127.02 |

# Micronesia, Federated States of   868

| | | 2004 | 2005 | 2006 | 2007 | 2008 | 2009 | 2010 | 2011 | 2012 | 2013 | 2014 | 2015 |
|---|---|---|---|---|---|---|---|---|---|---|---|---|---|
| **Exchange Rates** | | *US Dollars per SDR: End of Period* | | | | | | | | | | | |
| Market Rate............................. | aa | 1.5530 | 1.4293 | 1.5044 | 1.5803 | 1.5403 | 1.5677 | 1.5400 | 1.5353 | 1.5369 | 1.5400 | 1.4488 | 1.3857 |
| **Fund Position** | | *Millions of SDRs: End of Period* | | | | | | | | | | | |
| Quota................................ | 2f.s | 5.10 | 5.10 | 5.10 | 5.10 | 5.10 | 5.10 | 5.10 | 5.10 | 5.10 | 5.10 | 5.10 | 5.10 |
| SDR Holdings.............................. | 1b.s | 1.22 | 1.25 | 1.29 | 1.35 | 1.39 | 6.20 | 6.20 | 6.21 | 6.23 | 6.23 | 6.23 | 6.23 |
| Reserve Position in the Fund............ | 1c.s | — | — | — | — | — | — | — | — | — | — | — | — |
| Total Fund Cred.&Loans Outstg........ | 2tl | — | — | — | — | — | — | — | — | — | — | — | — |
| SDR Allocations........................ | 1bd | — | — | — | — | — | 4.81 | 4.81 | 4.81 | 4.81 | 4.81 | 4.81 | 4.81 |
| **International Liquidity** | | *Millions of US Dollars Unless Otherwise Indicated: End of Period* | | | | | | | | | | | |
| Total Reserves minus Gold.............. | 1l.d | 54.839 | 49.953 | 46.623 | 48.479 | 39.986 | 55.719 | 55.764 | 75.062 | 76.796 | 84.343 | 114.125 | 135.115 |
| SDR Holdings............................ | 1b.d | 1.890 | 1.783 | 1.943 | 2.127 | 2.135 | 9.721 | 9.555 | 9.535 | 9.571 | 9.591 | 9.025 | 8.633 |
| Reserve Position in the Fund.......... | 1c.d | .001 | .001 | .001 | .001 | .001 | .001 | .001 | .001 | .001 | .001 | .001 | .001 |
| Foreign Exchange...................... | 1d.d | 52.948 | 48.170 | 44.679 | 46.352 | 37.850 | 45.997 | 46.208 | 65.527 | 67.225 | 74.751 | 105.099 | 126.481 |
| Gold (Million Fine Troy Ounces)........ | 1ad | — | — | — | — | — | — | — | — | — | — | — | — |
| Gold (National Valuation)............... | 1and | — | — | — | — | — | — | — | — | — | — | — | — |
| Monetary Authorities:Other Assets... | 3..d | 43.751 | 49.020 | 53.927 | 59.345 | 42.211 | 53.220 | 21.867 | — | — | — | — | — |
| Monetary Authorities: Other Liabs.... | 4..d | — | — | — | — | — | — | — | — | — | — | — | — |
| Banking Institutions: Assets.............. | 7a.d | 115.506 | 106.676 | 103.325 | 110.230 | 111.978 | 126.571 | 137.355 | 152.160 | 174.328 | 203.526 | 226.574 | 214.323 |
| Banking Institutions: Liabs.............. | 7b.d | 1.663 | 2.076 | 1.359 | 1.405 | 3.556 | 3.374 | 3.599 | 3.208 | 2.520 | 2.159 | 2.973 | 5.451 |
| **Monetary Authorities** | | *Millions of US Dollars: End of Period* | | | | | | | | | | | |
| Foreign Assets........................ | 11 | 98.590 | 98.973 | 100.550 | 107.824 | 82.197 | 108.939 | 77.631 | 75.062 | 76.796 | 84.343 | 114.125 | 135.115 |
| Foreign Liabilities.................... | 16c | — | — | — | — | — | 7.535 | 7.403 | 7.380 | 7.388 | 7.402 | 6.964 | 6.661 |
| Central Government Deposits........... | 16d | 98.590 | 98.974 | 100.550 | 107.824 | 82.197 | 108.939 | 77.631 | 75.062 | 76.796 | 84.343 | 114.125 | 135.115 |
| Other Items (Net)........................... | 17r | — | — | — | — | — | −7.536 | −7.403 | −7.379 | −7.388 | −7.402 | −6.964 | −6.661 |
| **Banking Institutions** | | *Millions of US Dollars: End of Period* | | | | | | | | | | | |
| Foreign Assets........................ | 21 | 115.506 | 106.676 | 103.325 | 110.230 | 111.978 | 126.571 | 137.355 | 152.160 | 174.328 | 203.526 | 226.574 | 214.323 |
| Claims on Central Government........ | 22a | — | — | — | — | — | — | — | — | — | — | — | — |
| Claims on State & Local Govts......... | 22b | — | — | — | .345 | — | — | — | — | — | — | — | — |
| Claims on Nonfin.Pub.Enterprises..... | 22c | — | — | — | 1.021 | 10.171 | 5.578 | 4.427 | 3.287 | 2.331 | .704 | .048 | .808 |
| Claims on Private Sector................. | 22d | 43.176 | 49.466 | 52.422 | 53.918 | 52.280 | 59.104 | 61.137 | 60.699 | 63.274 | 62.338 | 67.582 | 72.255 |
| Demand Deposits...................... | 24 | 23.578 | 25.007 | 20.225 | 22.449 | 21.205 | 29.021 | 26.988 | 27.224 | 37.384 | 33.743 | 45.743 | 44.072 |
| Time, Savings,& Fgn.Currency Dep... | 25 | 74.030 | 74.175 | 70.570 | 72.492 | 76.799 | 84.941 | 86.901 | 91.159 | 97.423 | 112.032 | 148.643 | 134.201 |
| Foreign Liabilities.......................... | 26c | 1.663 | 2.076 | 1.359 | 1.405 | 3.556 | 3.374 | 3.599 | 3.208 | 2.520 | 2.159 | 2.973 | 5.451 |
| Central Government Deposits.......... | 26d | 16.660 | 11.837 | 19.621 | 23.458 | 24.005 | 21.422 | 31.653 | 45.693 | 51.083 | 64.606 | 36.802 | 40.966 |
| Liabs. to Nonbank Financial Insts..... | 26j | 2.353 | 3.479 | 3.480 | 1.692 | 3.569 | 4.197 | 7.805 | 5.732 | 6.815 | 7.541 | 9.008 | 9.621 |
| Capital Accounts......................... | 27a | 44.370 | 43.895 | 49.152 | 52.211 | 49.609 | 52.304 | 54.386 | 56.219 | 59.197 | 63.016 | 66.826 | 69.092 |
| Other Items (Net)........................ | 27r | −3.972 | −4.327 | −8.660 | −8.193 | −4.314 | −4.006 | −8.410 | −13.089 | −13.761 | −16.056 | −15.791 | −16.017 |
| **Banking Survey** | | *Millions of US Dollars: End of Period* | | | | | | | | | | | |
| Foreign Assets (Net)...................... | 31n | 212.433 | 203.573 | 202.516 | 216.649 | 190.619 | 224.600 | 203.984 | 216.635 | 241.217 | 278.308 | 330.762 | 337.326 |
| Domestic Credit............................ | 32 | −72.074 | −61.345 | −67.749 | −75.998 | −43.751 | −65.679 | −43.720 | −56.769 | −62.274 | −85.907 | −83.297 | −103.018 |
| Claims on Central Govt. (Net)........ | 32an | −115.250 | −110.811 | −120.171 | −131.282 | −106.202 | −130.361 | −109.284 | −120.755 | −127.879 | −148.949 | −150.927 | −176.081 |
| Claims on Local Government.......... | 32b | — | — | — | .345 | — | — | — | — | — | — | — | — |
| Claims on Nonfin.Pub.Enterprises.. | 32c | — | — | — | 1.021 | 10.171 | 5.578 | 4.427 | 3.287 | 2.331 | .704 | .048 | .808 |
| Claims on Private Sector............... | 32d | 43.176 | 49.466 | 52.422 | 53.918 | 52.280 | 59.104 | 61.137 | 60.699 | 63.274 | 62.338 | 67.582 | 72.255 |
| Money..................................... | 34 | 23.578 | 25.007 | 20.225 | 22.449 | 21.205 | 29.021 | 26.988 | 27.224 | 37.384 | 33.743 | 45.743 | 44.072 |
| Quasi-Money.............................. | 35 | 74.030 | 74.175 | 70.570 | 72.492 | 76.799 | 84.941 | 86.901 | 91.159 | 97.423 | 112.032 | 148.643 | 134.201 |
| Liabs. to Nonbank Financial Insts..... | 36j | 2.353 | 3.479 | 3.480 | 1.692 | 3.569 | 4.197 | 7.805 | 5.732 | 6.815 | 7.541 | 9.008 | 9.621 |
| Capital Accounts........................... | 37a | 44.370 | 43.895 | 49.152 | 52.211 | 49.609 | 52.304 | 54.386 | 56.219 | 59.197 | 63.016 | 66.826 | 69.092 |
| Other Items (Net)........................ | 37r | −3.972 | −4.327 | −8.660 | −8.193 | −4.314 | −11.542 | −15.813 | −20.468 | −21.149 | −23.458 | −22.755 | −22.678 |
| Money plus Quasi-Money................ | 35l | 97.608 | 99.182 | 90.795 | 94.941 | 98.004 | 113.962 | 113.889 | 118.383 | 134.807 | 145.775 | 194.386 | 178.273 |
| **Interest Rates** | | *Percent Per Annum* | | | | | | | | | | | |
| Savings Rate................................ | 60k | .88 | .95 | 1.50 | 1.88 | 1.27 | 1.38 | 1.16 | .97 | .79 | .64 | .50 | .23 |
| Deposit Rate................................ | 60l | 1.02 | 1.62 | 2.04 | 2.54 | 2.47 | 1.29 | .91 | .59 | .42 | .53 | .54 | 56 |
| Lending Rate................................ | 60p | 15.38 | 16.38 | 15.62 | 14.03 | 14.38 | 15.38 | 15.13 | 14.35 | 14.32 | 14.83 | 15.83 | 15.93 |

# Micronesia, Federated States of   868

| | | 2004 | 2005 | 2006 | 2007 | 2008 | 2009 | 2010 | 2011 | 2012 | 2013 | 2014 | 2015 |
|---|---|---|---|---|---|---|---|---|---|---|---|---|---|
| **Balance of Payments** | | | | | | | *Millions of US Dollars* | | | | | | |
| A. Current Account*...................... | 109bx | .... | .... | .... | .... | .... | † −38.3 | −24.6 | −44.2 | −23.8 | −2.2 | 22.4 | .... |
| Goods, credit (exports).................. | 1a9cx | .... | .... | .... | .... | .... | † 45.0 | 57.0 | 58.7 | 84.0 | 92.5 | 88.1 | .... |
| Goods, debit (imports).................. | 1a9dx | .... | .... | .... | .... | .... | † 153.4 | 160.0 | 174.4 | 183.2 | 178.9 | 154.4 | .... |
| Balance on goods................ | 1a9bx | .... | .... | .... | .... | .... | † −108.4 | −103.0 | −115.8 | −99.2 | −86.4 | −66.4 | .... |
| Services: credit (exports)............. | 1b9cx | .... | .... | .... | .... | .... | † 32.0 | 35.5 | 32.4 | 33.9 | 34.1 | 38.1 | .... |
| Services, debit (imports)............. | 1b9dx | .... | .... | .... | .... | .... | † 86.6 | 80.3 | 78.8 | 80.9 | 80.4 | 76.8 | .... |
| Balance on Goods & Services...... | 1z9bx | .... | .... | .... | .... | .... | † −163.0 | −148.0 | −162.2 | −146.1 | −132.7 | −105.1 | .... |
| Primary income: credit............... | 1c9cx | .... | .... | .... | .... | .... | † 26.5 | 23.5 | 23.7 | 31.4 | 39.9 | 54.6 | .... |
| Primary income: debit................ | 1c9dx | .... | .... | .... | .... | .... | † 10.1 | 12.4 | 13.4 | 15.1 | 13.2 | 28.0 | .... |
| Balance on gds, serv. & prim. inc. | 1y9bx | .... | .... | .... | .... | .... | † −146.6 | −136.9 | −151.8 | −129.8 | −106.0 | −78.4 | .... |
| Secondary income: credit........... | 1d9ca | .... | .... | .... | .... | .... | † 122.2 | 126.9 | 122.4 | 121.3 | 118.7 | 117.0 | .... |
| Secondary income: debit.............. | 1d9da | .... | .... | .... | .... | .... | † 13.8 | 14.5 | 14.7 | 15.3 | 14.8 | 16.2 | .... |
| B. Capital Account*..................... | 209ba | .... | .... | .... | .... | .... | † 54.9 | 64.2 | 62.0 | 68.3 | 42.2 | 21.2 | .... |
| Capital account: credit.................. | 209ca | .... | .... | .... | .... | .... | † 54.9 | 64.2 | 62.0 | 68.3 | 42.2 | 21.2 | .... |
| Capital account: debit.................. | 209da | .... | .... | .... | .... | .... | .... | .... | .... | .... | .... | .... | .... |
| Balance on current & capital acct. | 129ba | .... | .... | .... | .... | .... | † 16.6 | 39.6 | 17.8 | 44.5 | 40.0 | 43.6 | .... |
| C. Financial Account*................... | 309na | .... | .... | .... | .... | .... | † −6.9 | 24.3 | −19.4 | 34.3 | 14.7 | 27.6 | .... |
| Direct investment: assets.............. | 3a9aa | .... | .... | .... | .... | .... | .... | .... | .... | .... | .... | −.5 | .... |
| Equity & investment fund shares.. | 3aaaa | .... | .... | .... | .... | .... | .... | .... | .... | .... | .... | −.5 | .... |
| Debt instruments...................... | 3abaa | .... | .... | .... | .... | .... | .... | .... | .... | .... | .... | .... | .... |
| Direct investment: liabilities ......... | 3a9la | .... | .... | .... | .... | .... | † — | — | — | — | — | 20.2 | .... |
| Equity & investment fund shares . | 3aala | .... | .... | .... | .... | .... | † — | — | — | — | — | 20.2 | .... |
| Debt instruments....................... | 3abla | .... | .... | .... | .... | .... | .... | .... | .... | .... | .... | .... | .... |
| Portfolio investment: assets ......... | 3b9aa | .... | .... | .... | .... | .... | † −6.4 | −.5 | −29.2 | −3.3 | 4.4 | 6.2 | .... |
| Equity & investment fund shares | 3baaa | .... | .... | .... | .... | .... | † −4.7 | 4.8 | −26.5 | −5.8 | 2.0 | 3.0 | .... |
| Debt securities ..................... | 3bbaa | .... | .... | .... | .... | .... | † −1.7 | −5.3 | −2.7 | 2.5 | 2.4 | 3.2 | .... |
| Portfolio investment: liabilities....... | 3b9la | .... | .... | .... | .... | .... | .... | .... | .... | .... | .... | .... | .... |
| Equity & investment fund shares . | 3bala | .... | .... | .... | .... | .... | .... | .... | .... | .... | .... | .... | .... |
| Debt securities..................... | 3bbla | .... | .... | .... | .... | .... | .... | .... | .... | .... | .... | .... | .... |
| Fin. der.& empl.stk.ops.(ESOs): net. | 3c9na | .... | .... | .... | .... | .... | .... | .... | .... | .... | .... | .... | .... |
| Fin. der. & ESOs.: assets.............. | 3c9aa | .... | .... | .... | .... | .... | .... | .... | .... | .... | .... | .... | .... |
| Fin. der. & ESOs.: liabilities.......... | 3c9la | .... | .... | .... | .... | .... | .... | .... | .... | .... | .... | .... | .... |
| Other investment: assets................ | 3d9aa | .... | .... | .... | .... | .... | † 17.7 | 24.1 | 12.4 | 37.3 | 9.6 | 45.7 | .... |
| Other equity........................ | 3daaa | .... | .... | .... | .... | .... | .... | .... | .... | .... | .... | .... | .... |
| Debt instruments...................... | 3dzaa | .... | .... | .... | .... | .... | † 17.7 | 24.1 | 12.4 | 37.3 | 9.6 | 45.7 | .... |
| Other investment: liabilities............ | 3d9la | .... | .... | .... | .... | .... | † 18.2 | −.7 | 2.6 | −.4 | −.6 | 3.6 | .... |
| Other equity........................ | 3dala | .... | .... | .... | .... | .... | .... | .... | .... | .... | .... | .... | .... |
| Debt instruments...................... | 3dzla | .... | .... | .... | .... | .... | † 18.2 | −.7 | 2.6 | −.4 | −.6 | 3.6 | .... |
| Curr.+ cap.− finan. acct. balance.. | 4y9na | .... | .... | .... | .... | .... | † 23.5 | 15.4 | 37.2 | 10.1 | 25.3 | 16.0 | .... |
| D. Net Errors and Omissions........... | 409na | .... | .... | .... | .... | .... | † −15.3 | −10.7 | −12.1 | −5.1 | −24.0 | −5.5 | .... |
| E. Reserves and Related Items.......... | 4z9na | .... | .... | .... | .... | .... | † 8.2 | 4.7 | 25.1 | 5.0 | 1.4 | 10.5 | .... |
| Reserve assets........................... | 3e9aa | .... | .... | .... | .... | .... | † 8.2 | 4.7 | 25.1 | 5.0 | 1.4 | 10.5 | .... |
| Credit and loans from the IMF....... | 3dcla | .... | .... | .... | .... | .... | † — | — | — | — | .... | .... | .... |
| Exceptional financing................... | 409la | .... | .... | .... | .... | .... | .... | .... | .... | .... | .... | .... | .... |
| *Excludes components in group E | | | | | | | | | | | | | |
| | | | | | | | | | | | | | |
| **International Investment Position** | | | | | | | *Millions of US Dollars* | | | | | | |
| Assets................................... | 809aa | .... | .... | .... | .... | .... | † 296.5 | 328.2 | 329.1 | 371.6 | 550.0 | 614.9 | .... |
| Direct investment........................... | 8a9aa | .... | .... | .... | .... | .... | .... | .... | .... | .... | 4.9 | 4.8 | .... |
| Equity & investment fund shares.. | 8aaaa | .... | .... | .... | .... | .... | .... | .... | .... | .... | 4.9 | 4.8 | .... |
| Debt instruments...................... | 8abaa | .... | .... | .... | .... | .... | .... | .... | .... | .... | .... | .... | .... |
| Portfolio investment................... | 8b9aa | .... | .... | .... | .... | .... | † 124.6 | 128.8 | 97.1 | 102.5 | 147.5 | 154.5 | .... |
| Equity & investment fund shares.. | 8baaa | .... | .... | .... | .... | .... | † 91.7 | 101.1 | 72.2 | 76.5 | 103.9 | 107.7 | .... |
| Debt securities..................... | 8bbaa | .... | .... | .... | .... | .... | † 32.8 | 27.6 | 24.9 | 25.9 | 43.6 | 46.8 | .... |
| Fin. der.(oth.than reserves) & ESOs | 8c9aa | .... | .... | .... | .... | .... | .... | .... | .... | .... | .... | .... | .... |
| Other investment...................... | 8d9aa | .... | .... | .... | .... | .... | † 118.9 | 143.0 | 155.4 | 192.7 | 314.3 | 362.1 | .... |
| Other equity........................ | 8daaa | .... | .... | .... | .... | .... | † 30.3 | 30.3 | 30.3 | 30.3 | 44.3 | 47.5 | .... |
| Debt instruments...................... | 8dzaa | .... | .... | .... | .... | .... | † 88.7 | 112.7 | 125.1 | 162.4 | 270.0 | 314.6 | .... |
| Reserve assets........................... | 8e9aa | .... | .... | .... | .... | .... | † 53.0 | 56.4 | 76.7 | 76.5 | 83.2 | 93.5 | .... |
| Liabilities................................... | 809la | .... | .... | .... | .... | .... | † 102.5 | 101.9 | 103.3 | 102.3 | 311.5 | 353.9 | .... |
| Direct investment........................... | 8a9la | .... | .... | .... | .... | .... | † 6.6 | 6.9 | 5.7 | 5.1 | 195.5 | 235.3 | .... |
| Equity & investment fund shares.. | 8aala | .... | .... | .... | .... | .... | † 6.6 | 6.9 | 5.7 | 5.1 | 195.5 | 235.3 | .... |
| Debt instruments...................... | 8abla | .... | .... | .... | .... | .... | .... | .... | .... | .... | .... | .... | .... |
| Portfolio investment................... | 8b9la | .... | .... | .... | .... | .... | .... | .... | .... | .... | .... | .... | .... |
| Equity & investment fund shares.. | 8bala | .... | .... | .... | .... | .... | .... | .... | .... | .... | .... | .... | .... |
| Debt securities..................... | 8bbla | .... | .... | .... | .... | .... | .... | .... | .... | .... | .... | .... | .... |
| Fin. der.(oth.than reserves) & ESOs | 8c9la | .... | .... | .... | .... | .... | .... | .... | .... | .... | .... | .... | .... |
| Other investment...................... | 8d9la | .... | .... | .... | .... | .... | † 95.9 | 95.0 | 97.6 | 97.2 | 115.9 | 118.6 | .... |
| Other equity........................ | 8dala | .... | .... | .... | .... | .... | .... | .... | .... | .... | .... | .... | .... |
| Debt instruments...................... | 8dzla | .... | .... | .... | .... | .... | † 95.9 | 95.0 | 97.6 | 97.2 | 115.9 | 118.6 | .... |

# Micronesia, Federated States of  868

| | | 2004 | 2005 | 2006 | 2007 | 2008 | 2009 | 2010 | 2011 | 2012 | 2013 | 2014 | 2015 |
|---|---|---|---|---|---|---|---|---|---|---|---|---|---|
| **Government Finance** | | | | | | | | | | | | | |
| **Operations Statement** | | | | | | | | | | | | | |
| **Budgetary Central Government** | | | | | | *Thousands of US Dollars: Fiscal Year Ends December 31* | | | | | | | |
| Revenue | a1 | .... | .... | .... | .... | 61,814 | 89,227 | 104,236 | 102,637 | 118,943 | 100,255 | 114,061 | .... |
| Taxes | a11 | .... | .... | .... | .... | 11,284 | 12,321 | 13,841 | 15,453 | 16,008 | 17,341 | 40,050 | .... |
| Social Contributions | a12 | .... | .... | .... | .... | — | — | — | — | — | — | — | .... |
| Grants | a13 | .... | .... | .... | .... | 27,641 | 53,377 | 68,033 | 65,188 | 71,475 | 43,828 | 22,465 | .... |
| Other Revenue | a14 | .... | .... | .... | .... | 22,889 | 23,529 | 22,362 | 21,995 | 31,459 | 39,087 | 51,546 | .... |
| Expense | a2 | .... | .... | .... | .... | 47,933 | 46,684 | 49,815 | 48,816 | 57,085 | 57,721 | 57,789 | .... |
| Compensation of Employees | a21 | .... | .... | .... | .... | 14,718 | 16,951 | 18,022 | 17,853 | 18,340 | 17,908 | 16,972 | .... |
| Use of Goods & Services | a22 | .... | .... | .... | .... | 26,316 | 22,492 | 22,403 | 21,281 | 24,119 | 20,688 | 24,513 | .... |
| Consumption of Fixed Capital | a23 | .... | .... | .... | .... | 3,126 | 3,585 | 3,661 | 5,232 | 7,587 | 9,043 | 9,420 | .... |
| Interest | a24 | .... | .... | .... | .... | 539 | 549 | 604 | 637 | 564 | 733 | 788 | .... |
| Subsidies | a25 | .... | .... | .... | .... | 216 | 408 | 324 | 319 | 302 | 305 | 347 | .... |
| Grants | a26 | .... | .... | .... | .... | 620 | 545 | 2,866 | 1,318 | 1,239 | 1,039 | 1,746 | .... |
| Social Benefits | a27 | .... | .... | .... | .... | — | — | — | — | — | — | — | .... |
| Other Expense | a28 | .... | .... | .... | .... | 2,397 | 2,154 | 1,935 | 2,175 | 4,935 | 8,004 | 4,004 | .... |
| Gross Operating Balance [1-2+23] | agob | .... | .... | .... | .... | 17,007 | 46,128 | 58,082 | 59,053 | 69,444 | 51,578 | 65,692 | .... |
| Net Operating Balance [1-2] | anob | .... | .... | .... | .... | 13,881 | 42,544 | 54,421 | 53,821 | 61,857 | 42,535 | 56,272 | .... |
| Net Acq. of Nonfinancial Assets | a31 | .... | .... | .... | .... | 12,244 | 37,425 | 51,525 | 52,613 | 53,886 | 31,341 | 13,348 | .... |
| Aquisition of Nonfin. Assets | a31.1 | .... | .... | .... | .... | .... | .... | .... | .... | .... | .... | .... | |
| Disposal of Nonfin. Assets | a31.2 | .... | .... | .... | .... | .... | .... | .... | .... | .... | .... | .... | |
| Net Lending/Borrowing [1-2-31] | anlb | .... | .... | .... | .... | 1,637 | 5,118 | 2,896 | 1,208 | 7,971 | 11,194 | 42,924 | .... |
| Net Acq. of Financial Assets | a32 | .... | .... | .... | .... | 9,720 | 6,951 | 2,201 | 8,357 | 16,246 | 5,952 | 34,110 | .... |
| By instrument | | | | | | | | | | | | | |
| Monetary Gold & SDRs | a3201 | .... | .... | .... | .... | .... | .... | .... | .... | .... | .... | .... | |
| Currency & Deposits | a3202 | .... | .... | .... | .... | −315 | 3,226 | 56 | 1,304 | 10,073 | 5,153 | 32,605 | .... |
| Securities other than Shares | a3203 | .... | .... | .... | .... | 2,495 | −895 | −1,159 | −109 | −3,524 | −1,532 | −6,094 | .... |
| Loans | a3204 | .... | .... | .... | .... | 794 | −1,788 | −187 | 1,686 | 779 | −2,703 | 1,822 | .... |
| Shares & Other Equity | a3205 | .... | .... | .... | .... | −1,006 | 1,773 | 1,632 | −3,114 | 5,054 | 2,243 | 12,519 | .... |
| Insurance Technical Reserves | a3206 | .... | .... | .... | .... | — | — | — | — | — | — | — | .... |
| Financial Derivatives | a3207 | .... | .... | .... | .... | — | — | — | — | — | — | — | |
| Other Accounts Receivable | a3208 | .... | .... | .... | .... | 7,752 | 4,636 | 1,859 | 8,589 | 3,864 | 2,791 | −6,742 | .... |
| By debtor | | | | | | | | | | | | | |
| Domestic | a321 | .... | .... | .... | .... | 4,534 | −2,415 | 1,596 | 7,721 | 9,686 | 6,787 | 34,383 | .... |
| Foreign | a322 | .... | .... | .... | .... | 5,186 | 9,366 | 605 | 636 | 6,560 | −835 | −273 | .... |
| Net Incurrence of Liabilities | a33 | .... | .... | .... | .... | 8,083 | 1,833 | −695 | 7,149 | 8,275 | −5,241 | −8,813 | .... |
| By instrument | | | | | | | | | | | | | |
| Special Drawing Rights (SDRs) | a3301 | .... | .... | .... | .... | — | — | — | — | — | — | — | .... |
| Currency & Deposits | a3302 | .... | .... | .... | .... | — | — | — | — | — | — | — | .... |
| Securities other than Shares | a3303 | .... | .... | .... | .... | — | — | — | — | — | — | — | |
| Loans | a3304 | .... | .... | .... | .... | 2,859 | 118 | −363 | 3,968 | 1,682 | 927 | −383 | |
| Shares & Other Equity | a3305 | .... | .... | .... | .... | — | — | — | — | — | — | — | |
| Insurance Technical Reserves | a3306 | .... | .... | .... | .... | — | — | — | — | — | — | — | |
| Financial Derivatives | a3307 | .... | .... | .... | .... | — | — | — | — | — | — | — | .... |
| Other Accounts Payable | a3308 | .... | .... | .... | .... | 5,224 | 1,715 | −333 | 3,181 | 6,592 | −6,168 | −8,431 | |
| By creditor | | | | | | | | | | | | | |
| Domestic | a331 | .... | .... | .... | .... | 3,682 | −13 | 1,288 | 3,386 | 6,910 | −6,168 | −8,431 | .... |
| Foreign | a332 | .... | .... | .... | .... | 4,401 | 1,846 | −1,983 | 3,763 | 1,364 | 927 | −383 | .... |
| Stat. Discrepancy [32-33-NLB] | anlbz | .... | .... | .... | .... | — | — | — | — | — | — | — | |
| Memo Item: Expenditure [2+31] | a2m | .... | .... | .... | .... | 60,177 | 84,109 | 101,340 | 101,429 | 110,971 | 89,062 | 71,137 | |
| **Balance Sheet** | | | | | | | | | | | | | |
| Net Worth | a6 | .... | .... | .... | .... | 71,023 | 109,518 | 154,113 | 205,686 | 267,493 | 274,016 | 298,811 | .... |
| Nonfinancial Assets | a61 | .... | .... | .... | .... | 53,443 | 85,303 | 126,277 | 175,391 | 224,648 | 227,100 | 202,866 | .... |
| Financial Assets | a62 | .... | .... | .... | .... | 87,601 | 95,523 | 99,562 | 108,749 | 131,580 | 130,417 | 170,622 | .... |
| By instrument | | | | | | | | | | | | | |
| Monetary Gold & SDRs | a6201 | .... | .... | .... | .... | .... | .... | .... | .... | .... | .... | .... | .... |
| Currency & Deposits | a6202 | .... | .... | .... | .... | 6,943 | 10,169 | 10,226 | 16,148 | 26,221 | 31,374 | 63,979 | .... |
| Securities other than Shares | a6203 | .... | .... | .... | .... | — | — | — | — | — | — | — | |
| Loans | a6204 | .... | .... | .... | .... | 39,748 | 37,960 | 39,705 | 41,392 | 42,185 | 39,468 | 41,290 | .... |
| Shares and Other Equity | a6205 | .... | .... | .... | .... | 26,442 | 28,215 | 29,847 | 26,734 | 31,787 | 34,030 | 46,549 | .... |
| Insurance Technical Reserves | a6206 | .... | .... | .... | .... | — | — | — | — | — | — | — | .... |
| Financial Derivatives | a6207 | .... | .... | .... | .... | — | — | — | — | — | — | — | |
| Other Accounts Receivable | a6208 | .... | .... | .... | .... | 14,467 | 19,179 | 19,783 | 24,476 | 31,386 | 25,545 | 18,803 | .... |
| By debtor | | | | | | | | | | | | | |
| Domestic | a621 | .... | .... | .... | .... | 51,229 | 48,891 | 51,164 | 54,988 | 67,736 | 65,876 | 100,259 | .... |
| Foreign | a622 | .... | .... | .... | .... | 36,372 | 46,632 | 48,398 | 53,761 | 63,844 | 64,541 | 70,362 | .... |
| Liabilities | a63 | .... | .... | .... | .... | 70,020 | 71,309 | 71,726 | 78,454 | 88,734 | 83,500 | 74,677 | .... |
| By instrument | | | | | | | | | | | | | |
| Special Drawing Rights (SDRs) | a6301 | .... | .... | .... | .... | — | — | — | — | — | — | — | .... |
| Currency & Deposits | a6302 | .... | .... | .... | .... | — | — | — | — | — | — | — | .... |
| Securities other than Shares | a6303 | .... | .... | .... | .... | — | — | — | — | — | — | — | |
| Loans | a6304 | .... | .... | .... | .... | 50,012 | 49,585 | 49,109 | 53,066 | 56,330 | 57,257 | 56,993 | .... |
| Shares and Other Equity | a6305 | .... | .... | .... | .... | — | — | — | — | — | — | — | .... |
| Insurance Technical Reserves | a6306 | .... | .... | .... | .... | — | — | — | — | — | — | — | |
| Financial Derivatives | a6307 | .... | .... | .... | .... | — | — | — | — | — | — | — | |
| Other Accounts Payable | a6308 | .... | .... | .... | .... | 20,009 | 21,724 | 22,618 | 25,388 | 32,404 | 26,243 | 17,684 | .... |
| By creditor | | | | | | | | | | | | | |
| Domestic | a631 | .... | .... | .... | .... | 18,467 | 18,454 | 20,968 | 23,944 | 31,277 | 25,117 | 16,557 | |
| Foreign | a632 | .... | .... | .... | .... | 51,554 | 52,855 | 50,758 | 54,510 | 57,457 | 58,384 | 58,119 | |
| Net Financial Worth [62-63] | a6m2 | .... | .... | .... | .... | 17,580 | 24,214 | 27,836 | 30,295 | 42,846 | 46,917 | 95,945 | .... |
| Memo Item: Debt at Market Value | a6m3 | .... | .... | .... | .... | .... | .... | .... | .... | .... | .... | .... | .... |
| Memo Item: Debt at Face Value | a6m35 | .... | .... | .... | .... | .... | .... | .... | .... | .... | .... | .... | .... |
| Memo Item: Debt at Nominal Value | a6m4 | .... | .... | .... | .... | .... | .... | .... | .... | .... | .... | .... | .... |

# Micronesia, Federated States of   868

| | | 2004 | 2005 | 2006 | 2007 | 2008 | 2009 | 2010 | 2011 | 2012 | 2013 | 2014 | 2015 |
|---|---|---|---|---|---|---|---|---|---|---|---|---|---|
| | | | | | | *Millions: Midyear Estimates* | | | | | | | |
| Population............................. | 99z | .11 | .11 | .11 | .11 | .10 | .10 | .10 | .10 | .10 | .10 | .10 | .10 |

# Moldova 921

| | | 2004 | 2005 | 2006 | 2007 | 2008 | 2009 | 2010 | 2011 | 2012 | 2013 | 2014 | 2015 |
|---|---|---|---|---|---|---|---|---|---|---|---|---|---|
| **Exchange Rates** | | | | | | *Lei per SDR: End of Period* | | | | | | | |
| Official Rate.............................. | aa | 19.352 | 18.340 | 19.414 | 17.887 | 16.019 | 19.285 | 18.717 | 17.986 | 18.540 | 20.108 | 22.623 | 27.241 |
| | | | | | | *Lei per US Dollar: End of Period (ae) Period Average (rf)* | | | | | | | |
| Official Rate.............................. | ae | 12.461 | 12.832 | 12.905 | 11.319 | 10.400 | 12.302 | 12.154 | 11.715 | 12.063 | 13.057 | 15.615 | 19.659 |
| Official Rate.............................. | rf | 12.330 | 12.600 | 13.131 | 12.140 | 10.392 | 11.110 | 12.369 | 11.739 | 12.111 | 12.587 | 14.036 | 18.818 |
| | | | | | | *Index Numbers (2010=100): Period Averages* | | | | | | | |
| Nominal Effective Exchange Rate..... | nec | 100.98 | 96.87 | 92.08 | 92.77 | 104.74 | 110.28 | 100.00 | 103.10 | 106.38 | 102.06 | 97.23 | 90.31 |
| CPI-Based Real Effect. Ex. Rate........ | rec | 76.98 | 78.73 | 81.05 | 87.73 | 104.60 | 106.51 | 100.00 | 105.85 | 110.21 | 107.67 | 104.39 | 100.78 |
| **Fund Position** | | | | | | *Millions of SDRs: End of Period* | | | | | | | |
| Quota.......................................... | 2f.s | 123.20 | 123.20 | 123.20 | 123.20 | 123.20 | 123.20 | 123.20 | 123.20 | 123.20 | 123.20 | 123.20 | 123.20 |
| SDR Holdings.............................. | 1b.s | .05 | .01 | .12 | .10 | .10 | 2.28 | .23 | .58 | 1.03 | 4.16 | .82 | 12.75 |
| Reserve Position in the Fund............ | 1c.s | .01 | .01 | .01 | .01 | .01 | .01 | .01 | .01 | .01 | .01 | .01 | .01 |
| Total Fund Cred.&Loans Outstg....... | 2tl | 81.37 | 66.78 | 93.77 | 100.96 | 108.80 | 98.16 | 212.62 | 308.70 | 398.17 | 384.01 | 364.74 | 335.64 |
| SDR Allocations............................ | 1bd | — | — | — | — | — | 117.71 | 117.71 | 117.71 | 117.71 | 117.71 | 117.71 | 117.71 |
| **International Liquidity** | | | | | | *Millions of US Dollars Unless Otherwise Indicated: End of Period* | | | | | | | |
| Total Reserves minus Gold.............. | 1l.d | 470.26 | 597.45 | 775.48 | 1,333.68 | 1,672.41 | 1,480.27 | 1,717.69 | 1,964.98 | 2,511.05 | 2,817.77 | 2,153.80 | 1,754.25 |
| SDR Holdings............................... | 1b.d | .07 | .01 | .19 | .15 | .15 | 3.57 | .35 | .89 | 1.59 | 6.41 | 1.19 | 17.67 |
| Reserve Position in the Fund.......... | 1c.d | .01 | .01 | .01 | .01 | .01 | .01 | .01 | .01 | .01 | .01 | .01 | .01 |
| Foreign Exchange........................ | 1d.d | 470.18 | 597.43 | 775.28 | 1,333.53 | 1,672.25 | 1,476.68 | 1,717.33 | 1,964.08 | 2,509.45 | 2,811.35 | 2,152.60 | 1,736.57 |
| Gold (Million Fine Troy Ounces)........ | 1ad | — | — | — | — | — | — | — | — | .002 | .002 | .002 | .002 |
| Gold (National Valuation)................ | 1and | — | — | — | — | — | — | — | .35 | 3.95 | 2.86 | 2.83 | 2.55 |
| Central Bank: Other Assets.............. | 3..d | 1.02 | † .86 | — | .37 | — | — | .03 | .28 | .16 | .02 | 1.88 | .08 |
| Central Bank: Other Liabs............... | 4..d | 1.54 | † 1.07 | 3.16 | 3.58 | .65 | 1.47 | 1.75 | 3.66 | 1.40 | 4.60 | 3.78 | 1.94 |
| Other Depository Corps.: Assets....... | 7a.d | 98.98 | † 153.96 | 249.57 | 209.63 | 248.10 | 438.40 | 381.48 | 302.94 | 396.98 | 861.48 | 1,771.67 | 1,543.10 |
| Other Depository Corps.: Liabs......... | 7b.d | 68.98 | † 83.72 | 146.84 | 346.49 | 547.11 | 444.89 | 402.13 | 533.11 | 525.51 | 777.10 | 705.80 | 475.41 |
| Other Financial Corps.: Assets.......... | 7e.d | .... | .... | .... | .... | .... | .... | | .61 | 5.44 | 8.08 | 10.34 | 21.10 | 17.57 |
| Other Financial Corps.: Liabs............ | 7f.d | .... | .... | .... | .... | .... | .... | 49.24 | 42.81 | 37.98 | 57.73 | 69.77 | 64.42 |
| **Central Bank** | | | | | | *Millions of Lei: End of Period* | | | | | | | |
| Net Foreign Assets......................... | 11n | 4,517.89 | † 6,438.74 | 8,143.80 | 13,254.18 | 15,643.75 | 16,298.61 | 16,875.93 | 17,432.54 | 22,942.08 | 29,066.69 | 25,395.26 | 25,355.97 |
| Claims on Nonresidents................ | 11 | 6,111.68 | † 7,677.29 | 10,005.13 | 15,100.48 | 17,393.40 | 18,209.83 | 20,876.89 | 23,027.83 | 30,341.30 | 36,848.28 | 33,705.95 | 34,537.38 |
| Liabilities to Nonresidents............. | 16c | 1,593.79 | † 1,238.55 | 1,861.33 | 1,846.30 | 1,749.65 | 1,911.23 | 4,000.95 | 5,595.29 | 7,399.22 | 7,781.59 | 8,310.69 | 9,181.41 |
| Claims on Other Depository Corps.... | 12e | 62.28 | † 51.69 | 40.67 | 33.46 | 26.39 | 1,865.37 | 979.35 | 394.10 | 290.10 | 262.36 | 7,647.45 | 14,013.11 |
| Net Claims on Central Government.. | 12an | 2,696.14 | † 2,290.86 | 1,682.56 | −92.36 | −479.27 | −582.62 | −1,067.00 | 322.85 | 192.46 | 476.21 | −1,158.96 | −1,162.93 |
| Claims on Central Government...... | 12a | 2,740.99 | † 2,625.86 | 2,516.40 | 2,381.10 | 2,304.22 | 2,227.59 | 2,232.45 | 2,245.61 | 2,075.42 | 2,079.36 | 2,075.12 | 2,118.56 |
| Liabilities to Central Government... | 16d | 44.85 | † 335.00 | 833.83 | 2,473.45 | 2,783.49 | 2,810.21 | 3,299.45 | 1,922.77 | 1,882.97 | 1,603.15 | 3,234.07 | 3,281.49 |
| Claims on Other Sectors................... | 12s | 5.78 | † 4.72 | 5.36 | 5.38 | 5.67 | 7.33 | 12.85 | 14.19 | 15.74 | 19.11 | 23.57 | 25.95 |
| Claims on Other Financial Corps.... | 12g | — | † — | — | — | — | — | — | — | — | — | — | — |
| Claims on State & Local Govts....... | 12b | — | † — | — | — | — | — | — | — | — | — | — | — |
| Claims on Public Nonfin. Corps...... | 12c | — | † — | — | — | — | — | — | — | — | — | — | — |
| Claims on Private Sector................ | 12d | 5.78 | † 4.72 | 5.36 | 5.38 | 5.67 | 7.33 | 12.85 | 14.19 | 15.74 | 19.11 | 23.57 | 25.95 |
| Monetary Base............................... | 14 | 5,319.06 | † 7,517.28 | 7,389.45 | 11,771.75 | 14,781.64 | 12,934.34 | 14,085.93 | 17,153.97 | 20,531.14 | 26,077.68 | 27,722.15 | 29,689.13 |
| Currency in Circulation.................. | 14a | 4,094.33 | † 5,148.89 | 5,817.19 | 7,603.35 | 8,732.08 | 9,882.54 | 11,105.96 | 12,016.67 | 14,554.21 | 19,040.70 | 19,217.00 | 17,044.07 |
| Liabs. to Other Depository Corps.... | 14c | 1,219.81 | † 2,367.26 | 1,571.76 | 4,168.26 | 6,045.95 | 3,048.83 | 2,979.58 | 5,136.61 | 5,971.47 | 7,024.59 | 8,504.40 | 12,644.20 |
| Liabilities to Other Sectors............ | 14d | 4.92 | † 1.14 | .50 | .15 | 3.61 | 2.97 | .38 | .68 | 5.46 | 12.38 | .75 | .86 |
| Other Liabs. to Other Dep. Corps..... | 14n | 1,227.86 | † 745.10 | 1,211.06 | 836.31 | 1,117.65 | 3,108.48 | 3,676.17 | 2,927.68 | 3,787.86 | 2,739.17 | 273.14 | 787.93 |
| Dep. & Sec. Excl. f/Monetary Base.... | 14o | 4.33 | † — | — | — | — | — | — | — | .22 | — | — | — |
| Deposits Included in Broad Money. | 15 | — | † — | — | — | — | — | — | — | .22 | — | — | — |
| Sec.Ot.th.Shares Incl.in Brd. Money | 16a | — | † — | — | — | — | — | — | — | — | — | — | — |
| Deposits Excl. from Broad Money... | 16b | 4.33 | † — | — | — | — | — | — | — | — | — | — | — |
| Sec.Ot.th.Shares Excl.f/Brd.Money.. | 16s | — | † — | — | — | — | — | — | — | — | — | — | — |
| Loans.......................................... | 16l | — | † — | — | — | — | — | — | — | — | — | — | — |
| Financial Derivatives...................... | 16m | — | † — | — | — | — | — | — | — | — | — | — | — |
| Shares and Other Equity.................. | 17a | 555.83 | † 522.11 | 999.98 | 628.45 | −668.85 | 1,236.18 | 521.89 | −220.24 | 780.68 | 2,813.77 | 6,093.54 | 10,289.04 |
| Other Items (Net)............................ | 17r | 175.02 | † 1.51 | 271.90 | −35.86 | −33.90 | 309.70 | −1,482.85 | −1,697.73 | −1,659.53 | −1,806.26 | −2,181.51 | −2,534.00 |
| Memo Item: | | | | | | | | | | | | | |
| Total Assets................................... | 10ra | 11,351.25 | † 10,615.28 | 12,714.83 | 17,668.20 | 19,877.61 | 22,459.39 | 24,251.55 | 25,837.58 | 32,889.05 | 39,393.72 | 43,638.91 | 50,933.96 |

# Moldova 921

|  |  | 2004 | 2005 | 2006 | 2007 | 2008 | 2009 | 2010 | 2011 | 2012 | 2013 | 2014 | 2015 |
|---|---|---|---|---|---|---|---|---|---|---|---|---|---|
| **Other Depository Corporations** |  | \multicolumn{12}{c}{*Millions of Lei: End of Period*} |
| Net Foreign Assets | 21n | 373.82 | † 901.26 | 1,325.73 | −1,549.19 | −3,109.74 | −79.84 | −250.87 | −2,696.47 | −1,550.40 | 1,101.79 | 16,643.86 | 20,989.22 |
| Claims on Nonresidents | 21 | 1,233.37 | † 1,975.58 | 3,220.76 | 2,372.79 | 2,580.34 | 5,393.02 | 4,636.52 | 3,549.10 | 4,788.99 | 11,248.36 | 27,665.06 | 30,335.00 |
| Liabilities to Nonresidents | 26c | 859.55 | † 1,074.32 | 1,895.02 | 3,921.98 | 5,690.08 | 5,472.85 | 4,887.39 | 6,245.58 | 6,339.39 | 10,146.56 | 11,021.19 | 9,345.78 |
| Claims on Central Bank | 20 | 2,842.09 | † 3,672.33 | 3,408.76 | 5,789.01 | 8,282.12 | 7,851.28 | 8,238.14 | 9,204.20 | 11,017.40 | 11,140.87 | 10,416.99 | 14,705.55 |
| Currency | 20a | 394.42 | † 577.67 | 671.38 | 938.41 | 1,153.42 | 1,033.57 | 1,005.28 | 1,158.78 | 1,320.71 | 1,498.24 | 1,708.30 | 1,534.69 |
| Reserve Deposits and Securities | 20b | 2,447.67 | † 2,948.64 | 1,740.45 | 3,735.28 | 5,866.95 | 3,134.89 | 2,869.54 | 5,136.43 | 5,971.38 | 7,034.81 | 8,504.30 | 12,775.09 |
| Other Claims | 20n | — | † 146.02 | 996.94 | 1,115.32 | 1,261.74 | 3,682.82 | 4,363.31 | 2,908.98 | 3,725.31 | 2,607.82 | 204.39 | 395.77 |
| Net Claims on Central Government | 22an | 71.45 | † −644.49 | −192.82 | 585.21 | 318.37 | 1,677.45 | 859.76 | 1,179.72 | 913.50 | 815.11 | 922.41 | 1,041.54 |
| Claims on Central Government | 22a | 788.23 | † 1,103.66 | 1,268.10 | 1,387.78 | 1,267.09 | 2,878.36 | 2,551.45 | 3,313.49 | 4,090.50 | 4,321.74 | 4,501.38 | 4,287.48 |
| Liabilities to Central Government | 26d | 716.78 | † 1,748.16 | 1,460.92 | 802.57 | 948.72 | 1,200.90 | 1,691.69 | 2,133.77 | 3,177.00 | 3,506.63 | 3,578.97 | 3,245.95 |
| Claims on Other Sectors | 22s | 7,478.64 | † 10,217.78 | 13,949.31 | 20,964.61 | 25,173.03 | 23,903.75 | 27,075.37 | 31,127.16 | 36,168.41 | 43,086.37 | 41,486.36 | 42,962.94 |
| Claims on Other Financial Corps. | 22g | 51.24 | † 709.83 | 1,016.84 | 687.44 | 1,834.42 | 1,815.13 | 2,387.06 | 2,509.18 | 1,007.87 | 1,138.71 | 1,394.32 | 1,541.17 |
| Claims on State & Local Govts. | 22b | 79.33 | † 133.33 | 186.86 | 86.23 | 56.12 | 26.97 | 21.43 | 15.14 | 48.44 | 222.75 | 241.30 | 395.62 |
| Claims on Public Nonfin. Corps. | 22c | 553.21 | † 488.36 | 450.26 | 504.56 | 349.57 | 312.58 | 614.74 | 819.28 | 1,514.91 | 1,646.41 | 1,615.99 | 1,807.25 |
| Claims on Private Sector | 22d | 6,794.87 | † 8,886.25 | 12,295.35 | 19,686.39 | 22,932.92 | 21,749.08 | 24,052.14 | 27,783.56 | 33,597.20 | 40,078.50 | 38,234.77 | 39,218.89 |
| Liabilities to Central Bank | 26g | 63.29 | † 51.69 | 40.68 | 39.26 | 27.52 | 1,950.16 | 1,063.87 | 394.44 | 298.25 | 262.37 | 7,647.21 | 14,013.11 |
| Transf.Dep.Included in Broad Money | 24 | 3,059.23 | † 4,334.27 | 5,301.66 | 6,488.24 | 5,978.05 | 7,154.24 | 8,533.23 | 9,957.48 | 10,715.88 | 13,472.65 | 14,527.60 | 15,615.71 |
| Other Dep.Included in Broad Money. | 25 | 5,008.47 | † 6,920.13 | 9,095.11 | 14,173.59 | 18,103.58 | 16,676.94 | 18,501.16 | 20,257.54 | 25,671.01 | 31,755.01 | 33,935.93 | 32,880.28 |
| Sec.Ot.th.Shares Incl.in Brd. Money. | 26a | .46 | † .07 | 15.02 | 17.32 | 16.86 | 1.34 | 1.28 | .52 | .12 | — | — | — |
| Deposits Excl. from Broad Money | 26b | 568.96 | † 422.24 | 432.34 | 28.46 | 33.69 | 282.53 | 269.03 | 325.08 | 396.32 | 381.17 | 425.05 | 643.34 |
| Sec.Ot.th.Shares Excl.f/Brd.Money. | 26s | — | † — | — | — | — | — | — | — | — | — | — | — |
| Loans | 26l | — | † 1.91 | 5.05 | 62.00 | 11.92 | 17.59 | 59.28 | 79.64 | 112.16 | 125.25 | 95.79 | 331.65 |
| Financial Derivatives | 26m | — | † — | — | — | — | — | — | — | — | — | — | — |
| Insurance Technical Reserves | 26r | — | † — | — | — | — | — | — | — | — | — | — | — |
| Shares and Other Equity | 27a | 3,020.87 | † 3,019.40 | 3,933.69 | 5,524.30 | 7,036.30 | 7,107.24 | 7,464.85 | 8,138.86 | 10,211.47 | 11,533.86 | 12,448.61 | 13,267.00 |
| Other Items (Net) | 27r | −955.27 | † −602.83 | −332.57 | −543.54 | −544.15 | 162.61 | 29.70 | −338.95 | −856.30 | −1,386.16 | 389.43 | 2,948.16 |
| Memo Item: |  |  |  |  |  |  |  |  |  |  |  |  |  |
| Total Assets | 20ra | 17,316.72 | † 18,940.51 | 24,023.53 | 33,575.82 | 41,196.95 | 43,818.31 | 46,726.66 | 51,837.64 | 62,618.88 | 83,843.51 | 103,618.94 | 127,581.14 |
| **Depository Corporations** |  | \multicolumn{12}{c}{*Millions of Lei: End of Period*} |
| Net Foreign Assets | 31n | 4,891.71 | † 7,340.01 | 9,469.53 | 11,704.99 | 12,534.01 | 16,218.77 | 16,625.06 | 14,736.06 | 21,391.67 | 30,168.48 | 42,039.13 | 46,345.19 |
| Claims on Nonresidents | 31 | 7,345.06 | † 9,652.87 | 13,225.89 | 17,473.27 | 19,973.74 | 23,602.85 | 25,513.40 | 26,576.93 | 35,130.29 | 48,096.64 | 61,371.01 | 64,872.38 |
| Liabilities to Nonresidents | 36c | 2,453.34 | † 2,312.87 | 3,756.36 | 5,768.28 | 7,439.73 | 7,384.08 | 8,888.35 | 11,840.87 | 13,738.62 | 17,928.16 | 19,331.88 | 18,527.19 |
| Domestic Claims | 32 | 10,252.02 | † 11,868.86 | 15,444.41 | 21,462.84 | 25,017.81 | 25,005.91 | 26,880.99 | 32,643.92 | 37,290.11 | 44,396.80 | 41,273.39 | 42,867.50 |
| Net Claims on Central Government | 32an | 2,767.60 | † 1,646.37 | 1,489.74 | 492.85 | −160.90 | 1,094.83 | −207.23 | 1,502.57 | 1,105.96 | 1,291.31 | −236.55 | −121.39 |
| Claims on Central Government | 32a | 3,529.22 | † 3,729.52 | 3,784.50 | 3,768.87 | 3,571.31 | 5,105.94 | 4,783.91 | 5,559.11 | 6,165.92 | 6,401.10 | 6,576.50 | 6,406.04 |
| Liabilities to Central Government. | 36d | 761.63 | † 2,083.16 | 2,294.75 | 3,276.02 | 3,732.21 | 4,011.11 | 4,991.14 | 4,056.54 | 5,059.97 | 5,109.78 | 6,813.05 | 6,527.44 |
| Claims on Other Sectors | 32s | 7,484.42 | † 10,222.50 | 13,954.67 | 20,969.99 | 25,178.71 | 23,911.08 | 27,088.22 | 31,141.35 | 36,184.15 | 43,105.48 | 41,509.94 | 42,988.89 |
| Claims on Other Financial Corps. | 32g | 51.24 | † 709.83 | 1,016.84 | 687.44 | 1,834.42 | 1,815.13 | 2,387.06 | 2,509.18 | 1,007.87 | 1,138.71 | 1,394.32 | 1,541.17 |
| Claims on State & Local Govts. | 32b | 79.33 | † 133.33 | 186.86 | 86.23 | 56.12 | 26.97 | 21.43 | 15.14 | 48.44 | 222.75 | 241.30 | 395.62 |
| Claims on Public Nonfin. Corps. | 32c | 553.21 | † 488.36 | 450.26 | 504.56 | 349.57 | 312.58 | 614.74 | 819.28 | 1,514.91 | 1,646.41 | 1,615.99 | 1,807.25 |
| Claims on Private Sector | 32d | 6,800.65 | † 8,890.97 | 12,300.72 | 19,691.77 | 22,938.59 | 21,756.41 | 24,064.98 | 27,797.75 | 33,612.94 | 40,097.61 | 38,258.34 | 39,244.84 |
| Broad Money Liabilities | 35l | 11,772.99 | † 15,826.82 | 19,558.10 | 27,344.24 | 31,680.77 | 32,684.46 | 37,136.74 | 41,074.11 | 49,626.19 | 62,782.50 | 65,972.99 | 64,006.24 |
| Currency Outside Depository Corps | 34a | 3,699.91 | † 4,571.22 | 5,145.81 | 6,664.94 | 7,578.66 | 8,848.98 | 10,100.68 | 10,857.89 | 13,233.51 | 17,542.46 | 17,508.70 | 15,509.38 |
| Transferable Deposits | 34 | 3,064.15 | † 4,335.40 | 5,302.16 | 6,488.39 | 5,981.66 | 7,157.21 | 8,533.62 | 9,958.16 | 10,721.34 | 13,485.03 | 14,528.36 | 15,616.57 |
| Other Deposits | 35 | 5,008.47 | † 6,920.13 | 9,095.11 | 14,173.59 | 18,103.58 | 16,676.94 | 18,501.16 | 20,257.54 | 25,671.23 | 31,755.01 | 33,935.93 | 32,880.28 |
| Securities Other than Shares | 36a | .46 | † .07 | 15.02 | 17.32 | 16.86 | 1.34 | 1.28 | .52 | .12 | — | — | — |
| Deposits Excl. from Broad Money | 36b | 573.29 | † 422.24 | 432.34 | 28.46 | 33.69 | 282.53 | 269.03 | 325.08 | 396.32 | 381.17 | 425.05 | 643.34 |
| Sec.Ot.th.Shares Excl.f/Brd.Money. | 36s | — | † — | — | — | — | — | — | — | — | — | — | — |
| Loans | 36l | — | † 1.91 | 5.05 | 62.00 | 11.92 | 17.59 | 59.28 | 79.64 | 112.16 | 125.25 | 95.79 | 331.65 |
| Financial Derivatives | 36m | — | † — | — | — | — | — | — | — | — | — | — | — |
| Insurance Technical Reserves | 36r | — | † — | — | — | — | — | — | — | — | — | — | — |
| Shares and Other Equity | 37a | 3,576.69 | † 3,541.52 | 4,933.67 | 6,152.75 | 6,367.45 | 8,343.42 | 7,986.74 | 7,918.62 | 10,992.16 | 14,347.63 | 18,542.16 | 23,556.04 |
| Other Items (Net) | 37r | −779.24 | † −583.61 | −15.22 | −419.62 | −542.01 | −103.31 | −1,945.73 | −2,017.46 | −2,445.05 | −3,071.27 | −1,723.46 | 675.42 |
| Broad Money Liabs., Seasonally Adj. | 35l.b | 11,373.67 | † 15,374.86 | 18,996.09 | 26,572.33 | 30,836.36 | 31,860.46 | 36,256.96 | 40,154.40 | 48,597.19 | 61,520.47 | 64,665.02 | 62,724.39 |
| **Other Financial Corporations** |  | \multicolumn{12}{c}{*Millions of Lei: End of Period*} |
| Net Foreign Assets | 41n | .... | .... | .... | .... | .... | .... | −591.0 | −437.7 | −360.7 | −618.8 | −759.9 | −921.0 |
| Claims on Nonresidents | 41 | .... | .... | .... | .... | .... | .... | 7.4 | 63.8 | 97.5 | 135.0 | 329.5 | 345.4 |
| Liabilities to Nonresidents | 46c | .... | .... | .... | .... | .... | .... | 598.4 | 501.5 | 458.1 | 753.8 | 1,089.4 | 1,266.4 |
| Claims on Depository Corporations | 40 | .... | .... | .... | .... | .... | .... | 859.6 | 711.1 | 826.0 | 1,011.7 | 1,129.8 | 1,226.7 |
| Net Claims on Central Government | 42an | .... | .... | .... | .... | .... | .... | 242.7 | 227.6 | 124.6 | 172.4 | 370.0 | 667.2 |
| Claims on Central Government | 42a | .... | .... | .... | .... | .... | .... | 243.7 | 228.7 | 128.0 | 180.9 | 378.3 | 669.2 |
| Liabilities to Central Government | 46d | .... | .... | .... | .... | .... | .... | 1.0 | 1.1 | 3.4 | 8.5 | 8.3 | 2.0 |
| Claims on Other Sectors | 42s | .... | .... | .... | .... | .... | .... | 1,383.7 | 1,762.8 | 1,936.5 | 2,617.6 | 3,242.0 | 3,217.3 |
| Claims on State & Local Govts. | 42b | .... | .... | .... | .... | .... | .... | — | — | — | — | — | .1 |
| Claims on Public Nonfin. Corps. | 42c | .... | .... | .... | .... | .... | .... | — | — | — | .1 | 58.5 | 65.2 |
| Claims on Private Sector | 42d | .... | .... | .... | .... | .... | .... | 1,383.7 | 1,762.8 | 1,936.5 | 2,617.6 | 3,183.5 | 3,152.0 |
| Deposits | 46b | .... | .... | .... | .... | .... | .... | 1.1 | — | — | .2 | .1 | — |
| Securities Other than Shares | 46s | .... | .... | .... | .... | .... | .... | — | — | — | — | — | — |
| Loans | 46l | .... | .... | .... | .... | .... | .... | 243.8 | 269.1 | 310.8 | 372.1 | 763.8 | 767.4 |
| Financial Derivatives | 46m | .... | .... | .... | .... | .... | .... | — | — | — | — | .6 | — |
| Insurance Technical Reserves | 46r | .... | .... | .... | .... | .... | .... | 678.3 | 860.3 | 947.1 | 1,184.7 | 1,117.3 | 1,388.5 |
| Shares and Other Equity | 47a | .... | .... | .... | .... | .... | .... | 1,740.6 | 1,971.5 | 1,986.7 | 2,128.9 | 2,358.2 | 2,305.3 |
| Other Items (Net) | 47r | .... | .... | .... | .... | .... | .... | −768.7 | −837.1 | −718.1 | −503.1 | −258.1 | −226.4 |
| Memo Item: |  |  |  |  |  |  |  |  |  |  |  |  |  |
| Total Assets | 40ra | .... | .... | .... | .... | .... | .... | 3,724.51 | 4,027.41 | 4,166.02 | 5,238.24 | 6,210.69 | 6,517.42 |

# Moldova 921

| | | 2004 | 2005 | 2006 | 2007 | 2008 | 2009 | 2010 | 2011 | 2012 | 2013 | 2014 | 2015 |
|---|---|---|---|---|---|---|---|---|---|---|---|---|---|
| **Financial Corporations** | | | | | | *Millions of Lei: End of Period* | | | | | | | |
| Net Foreign Assets............................ | 51n | .... | .... | .... | .... | .... | .... | 16,034.0 | 14,298.3 | 21,031.0 | 29,549.7 | 41,279.2 | 45,424.2 |
| Claims on Nonresidents................ | 51 | .... | .... | .... | .... | .... | .... | 25,520.8 | 26,640.7 | 35,227.8 | 48,231.7 | 61,700.5 | 65,217.7 |
| Liabilities to Nonresidents.............. | 56c | .... | .... | .... | .... | .... | .... | 9,486.8 | 12,342.4 | 14,196.7 | 18,682.0 | 20,421.3 | 19,793.5 |
| Domestic Claims............................. | 52 | .... | .... | .... | .... | .... | .... | 26,120.3 | 32,125.2 | 38,343.4 | 46,048.1 | 43,491.1 | 45,210.8 |
| Net Claims on Central Government | 52an | .... | .... | .... | .... | .... | .... | 35.5 | 1,730.1 | 1,230.5 | 1,463.7 | 133.5 | 545.8 |
| Claims on Central Government. .. | 52a | .... | .... | .... | .... | .... | .... | 5,027.6 | 5,787.8 | 6,293.9 | 6,581.9 | 6,954.8 | 7,075.3 |
| Liabilities to Central Government. | 56d | .... | .... | .... | .... | .... | .... | 4,992.2 | 4,057.7 | 5,063.4 | 5,118.3 | 6,821.4 | 6,529.5 |
| Claims on Other Sectors................. | 52s | .... | .... | .... | .... | .... | .... | 26,084.9 | 30,395.0 | 37,112.8 | 44,584.4 | 43,357.6 | 44,665.0 |
| Claims on State & Local Govts..... | 52b | .... | .... | .... | .... | .... | .... | 21.4 | 15.1 | 48.4 | 222.7 | 241.3 | 395.7 |
| Claims on Pub. Nonfin. Corps...... | 52c | .... | .... | .... | .... | .... | .... | 614.8 | 819.3 | 1,514.9 | 1,646.5 | 1,674.4 | 1,872.4 |
| Claims on Private Sector.............. | 52d | .... | .... | .... | .... | .... | .... | 25,448.7 | 29,560.6 | 35,549.4 | 42,715.2 | 41,441.9 | 42,396.8 |
| Currency Outside Fin. Corporations.. | 54a | .... | .... | .... | .... | .... | .... | 10,075.1 | 10,828.3 | 13,213.8 | 17,521.9 | 17,473.8 | 15,476.4 |
| Deposits...................................... | 55l | .... | .... | .... | .... | .... | .... | 25,845.3 | 29,383.2 | 35,625.8 | 44,257.5 | 47,321.1 | 47,630.3 |
| Securities Other than Shares............ | 56a | .... | .... | .... | .... | .... | .... | 1.3 | .5 | .1 | — | — | — |
| Loans........................................... | 56l | .... | .... | .... | .... | .... | .... | 57.5 | 56.2 | 68.0 | 87.1 | 162.9 | 558.0 |
| Financial Derivatives......................... | 56m | .... | .... | .... | .... | .... | .... | — | — | — | — | .6 | — |
| Insurance Technical Reserves........... | 56r | .... | .... | .... | .... | .... | .... | 678.3 | 860.3 | 947.1 | 1,184.7 | 1,020.5 | 1,262.7 |
| Shares and Other Equity.................. | 57a | .... | .... | .... | .... | .... | .... | 9,727.3 | 9,890.1 | 12,978.9 | 16,476.5 | 20,900.3 | 25,861.4 |
| Other Items (Net)........................... | 57r | .... | .... | .... | .... | .... | .... | −4,230.4 | −4,595.1 | −3,459.2 | −3,929.9 | −2,115.0 | −109.0 |
| **Monetary Aggregates** | | | | | | | *Millions of Lei: End of Period* | | | | | | |
| Broad Money................................ | 59m | .... | 15,826.82 | 19,558.10 | 27,344.24 | 31,680.77 | 32,684.46 | 37,136.74 | 41,074.11 | 49,626.19 | 62,782.50 | 65,972.99 | 64,006.24 |
| o/w:Currency Issued by Cent.Govt | 59m.a | .... | — | — | — | — | — | — | — | — | — | — | — |
| o/w: Dep.in Nonfin. Corporations. | 59m.b | .... | — | — | — | — | — | — | — | — | — | — | — |
| o/w:Secs. Issued by Central Govt.. | 59m.c | .... | — | — | — | — | — | — | — | — | — | — | — |
| Money (National Definitions) | | | | | | | | | | | | | |
| Monetary Base.......................... | 19ma | 5,313.10 | 7,002.90 | 6,512.32 | 9,537.17 | 11,633.59 | 10,456.28 | 12,114.95 | 14,345.15 | 17,633.53 | 23,254.15 | 21,781.21 | 25,283.53 |
| Broad Monetary Base.................. | 19md | .... | 7,517.28 | 7,389.45 | 11,771.75 | 14,781.64 | 12,934.34 | 14,085.93 | 17,153.97 | 20,531.14 | 26,077.68 | 27,722.15 | 29,689.13 |
| M1.......................................... | 59ma | 5,564.20 | 7,333.20 | 8,268.25 | 10,923.55 | 11,609.20 | 13,206.78 | 15,720.17 | 17,385.57 | 20,607.27 | 27,119.78 | 26,513.18 | 23,561.73 |
| M2.......................................... | 59mb | 8,137.00 | 11,125.60 | 12,485.21 | 18,396.74 | 21,774.06 | 20,942.03 | 24,770.73 | 28,265.39 | 34,914.60 | 45,117.14 | 43,219.94 | 39,260.78 |
| M2, Seasonally Adjusted............. | 59mbc | 7,926.00 | 10,914.60 | 12,246.08 | 18,121.20 | 21,230.86 | 20,398.76 | 24,226.16 | 27,715.84 | 33,013.70 | 35,219.48 | 42,544.75 | 38,576.01 |
| M3.......................................... | 59mc | 11,772.99 | 15,826.82 | 19,558.10 | 27,344.24 | 31,680.77 | 32,684.46 | 37,136.74 | 41,074.11 | 49,626.19 | 62,782.50 | 65,972.99 | 64,006.24 |
| M3, Seasonally Adjusted............. | 59mcc | 11,491.20 | 15,468.40 | 19,280.78 | 27,047.30 | 31,134.95 | 32,138.65 | 36,495.61 | 40,405.59 | 47,156.62 | 50,062.61 | 65,257.16 | 63,320.72 |
| **Interest Rates** | | | | | | | *Percent Per Annum* | | | | | | |
| Central Bank Policy Rate (EOP)........ | 60 | 14.50 | 12.50 | 14.50 | 16.00 | 14.00 | 5.00 | 7.00 | 9.50 | 4.50 | 3.50 | 6.50 | 19.50 |
| Overnight Deposit Rate (EOP).......... | 60.r | .... | 2.00 | 2.00 | 2.00 | 2.00 | 2.00 | 5.00 | 6.50 | 1.50 | .50 | 3.50 | 16.50 |
| Central Bank Bill Rate.................... | 60a | .... | .... | 8.35 | 14.16 | 16.97 | 5.00 | 6.63 | 8.64 | 5.06 | 3.75 | 3.75 | 16.00 |
| Money Market Rate........................ | 60b | † 13.21 | 6.26 | 9.38 | 12.35 | 16.01 | 10.93 | 5.58 | 8.44 | 5.43 | 6.95 | 8.74 | .... |
| Money Market Rate (Fgn. Cur.)........ | 60b.f | .78 | 2.49 | 4.13 | 3.96 | 2.57 | .87 | .37 | .50 | .... | .... | .... | .... |
| Treasury Bill Rate........................... | 60c | 12.29 | 3.75 | 7.43 | 13.52 | 18.89 | 11.82 | 7.13 | 11.71 | 6.26 | 5.57 | 6.76 | 20.58 |
| Deposit Rate................................. | 60l | 15.12 | 13.22 | 11.88 | 15.01 | 17.93 | 14.94 | 7.67 | 7.57 | 7.63 | 7.23 | 5.72 | 11.97 |
| Deposit Rate (Fgn. Currency)........... | 60l.f | 4.97 | 5.16 | 5.16 | 5.98 | 9.38 | 7.57 | 3.41 | 3.68 | 4.30 | 4.39 | 4.17 | 2.48 |
| Lending Rate................................. | 60p | 20.94 | 19.26 | 18.13 | 18.83 | 21.06 | 20.54 | 16.36 | 14.44 | 13.42 | 12.29 | 11.01 | 14.15 |
| Lending Rate (Fgn. Currency).......... | 60p.f | 11.40 | 11.10 | 11.06 | 10.91 | 12.11 | 12.62 | 10.00 | 8.87 | 8.25 | 7.67 | 7.87 | 7.03 |
| Government Bond Yield................... | 61 | .... | .... | 9.53 | 14.71 | .... | .... | .... | 7.90 | 12.41 | 7.16 | 6.19 | 20.30 |
| **Prices and Labor** | | | | | | | *Index Numbers (2010=100): Period Averages* | | | | | | |
| Consumer Prices............................ | 64 | 58.4 | 65.2 | 73.6 | 82.6 | 93.2 | 93.2 | 100.0 | 107.6 | 112.6 | 117.8 | 123.8 | 135.8 |
| | | | | | | | *Number in Thousands: Period Averages* | | | | | | |
| Labor Force................................... | 67d | 1,433 | 1,422 | 1,357 | 1,314 | 1,303 | 1,265 | 1,241 | 1,258 | 1,215 | 1,236 | 1,252 | .... |
| Employment.................................. | 67e | 1,316 | 1,319 | 1,257 | 1,247 | 1,251 | 1,184 | 1,150 | 1,173 | 1,147 | 1,173 | 1,203 | .... |
| Unemployment.............................. | 67c | 116 | 104 | 100 | 67 | 52 | 81 | 92 | 84 | 68 | 63 | 49 | .... |
| Unemployment Rate (%)................. | 67r | 8.1 | 7.3 | 7.4 | 5.1 | 4.0 | 6.4 | 7.4 | 6.7 | 5.6 | 5.1 | 3.9 | .... |
| **Intl. Transactions & Positions** | | | | | | | *Millions of US Dollars* | | | | | | |
| Exports......................................... | 70..d | 980 | 1,091 | 1,050 | 1,340 | 1,591 | 1,283 | 1,542 | 2,217 | 2,162 | 2,399 | 2,340 | 1,967 |
| Imports, c.i.f................................. | 71..d | 1,773 | 2,292 | 2,693 | 3,690 | 4,899 | 3,278 | 3,855 | 5,191 | 5,213 | 5,493 | 5,317 | 3,987 |

# Moldova 921

## Balance of Payments

*Millions of US Dollars*

| | | 2004 | 2005 | 2006 | 2007 | 2008 | 2009 | 2010 | 2011 | 2012 | 2013 | 2014 | 2015 |
|---|---|---|---|---|---|---|---|---|---|---|---|---|---|
| A. Current Account* | 109bx | −47.1 | −247.7 | −391.1 | −723.3 | −1,037.5 | −516.0 | −545.4 | † −930.5 | −700.2 | −561.4 | −675.6 | −464.2 |
| Goods, credit (exports) | 1a9cx | 794.4 | 886.1 | 787.0 | 1,026.0 | 1,179.7 | 929.8 | 1,175.0 | † 1,742.5 | 1,687.5 | 1,897.5 | 1,805.5 | 1,507.0 |
| Goods, debit (imports) | 1a9dx | 1,592.9 | 2,118.8 | 2,434.0 | 3,409.0 | 4,529.7 | 2,986.7 | 3,491.7 | † 4,727.1 | 4,755.4 | 5,036.6 | 4,857.7 | 3,595.1 |
| Balance on goods | 1a9bx | −798.6 | −1,232.7 | −1,647.1 | −2,383.0 | −3,350.0 | −2,056.9 | −2,316.7 | † −2,984.6 | −3,067.9 | −3,139.1 | −3,052.2 | −2,088.1 |
| Services, credit (exports) | 1b9cx | 379.8 | 446.1 | 535.1 | 719.5 | 970.0 | 785.7 | 783.2 | † 998.1 | 1,021.2 | 1,138.0 | 1,127.6 | 974.8 |
| Services, debit (imports) | 1b9dx | 356.4 | 425.7 | 491.3 | 656.3 | 839.2 | 717.4 | 709.4 | † 839.1 | 912.2 | 991.4 | 1,007.2 | 830.9 |
| Balance on Goods & Services | 1z9bx | −775.1 | −1,212.2 | −1,603.2 | −2,319.8 | −3,219.2 | −1,988.5 | −2,242.9 | † −2,825.5 | −2,958.9 | −2,992.5 | −2,931.8 | −1,944.2 |
| Primary income: credit | 1c9cx | 490.0 | 539.3 | 605.9 | 710.1 | 906.2 | 592.1 | 767.0 | † 933.4 | 1,047.0 | 1,161.1 | 1,118.5 | 812.5 |
| Primary income: debit | 1c9dx | 133.0 | 128.4 | 203.4 | 293.7 | 301.4 | 270.8 | 262.3 | † 355.8 | 230.7 | 289.4 | 291.6 | 409.9 |
| Balance on gds, serv. & prim. inc. | 1y9bx | −418.1 | −801.4 | −1,200.7 | −1,903.4 | −2,614.4 | −1,667.3 | −1,738.2 | † −2,248.0 | −2,142.6 | −2,120.9 | −2,104.9 | −1,541.5 |
| Secondary income: credit | 1d9ca | 406.8 | 596.8 | 859.6 | 1,245.1 | 1,688.4 | 1,254.6 | 1,284.8 | † 1,430.5 | 1,560.2 | 1,686.9 | 1,575.6 | 1,217.9 |
| Secondary income: debit | 1d9da | 35.8 | 43.2 | 50.0 | 65.1 | 111.5 | 103.4 | 92.0 | † 113.0 | 117.8 | 127.4 | 146.3 | 140.7 |
| B. Capital Account* | 209ba | 3.3 | — | .2 | −.1 | −.7 | .1 | .7 | † 32.0 | 21.2 | 58.0 | 94.5 | 22.8 |
| Capital account: credit | 209ca | 3.3 | — | .2 | — | .1 | .1 | 1.3 | † 84.7 | 76.0 | 110.4 | 175.4 | 97.3 |
| Capital account: debit | 209da | .1 | — | — | .1 | .8 | — | .6 | † 52.7 | 54.8 | 52.4 | 80.9 | 74.5 |
| Balance on current & capital acct. | 129ba | −43.8 | −247.7 | −391.0 | −723.4 | −1,038.2 | −516.0 | −544.7 | † −898.5 | −679.0 | −503.4 | −581.0 | −441.4 |
| C. Financial Account* | 309na | −113.0 | −200.5 | −359.5 | −1,013.4 | −1,286.3 | −78.0 | −399.0 | † −860.5 | −810.5 | −655.7 | −20.3 | −192.4 |
| Direct investment: assets | 3a9aa | 3.2 | −.2 | −.7 | 12.1 | 31.2 | −3.4 | 7.6 | † 33.8 | 29.6 | 41.6 | 35.5 | 5.6 |
| Equity & investment fund shares | 3aaaa | .2 | −.2 | .8 | 12.6 | 16.1 | 8.2 | 3.4 | † 20.2 | 18.4 | 26.4 | 38.4 | 14.5 |
| Debt instruments | 3abaa | 3.0 | .1 | −1.6 | −.5 | 15.1 | −11.6 | 4.2 | † 13.6 | 11.2 | 15.2 | −2.9 | −8.9 |
| Direct investment: liabilities | 3a9la | 87.7 | 190.7 | 258.7 | 536.0 | 726.6 | 135.2 | 212.0 | † 347.9 | 282.6 | 290.5 | 349.9 | 271.0 |
| Equity & investment fund shares | 3aala | 88.9 | 107.0 | 160.6 | 340.2 | 540.4 | 150.0 | 171.5 | † 230.6 | 133.5 | 179.5 | 198.7 | 233.4 |
| Debt instruments | 3abla | −1.2 | 83.7 | 98.1 | 195.8 | 186.2 | −14.9 | 40.5 | † 117.3 | 149.0 | 110.9 | 151.3 | 37.5 |
| Portfolio investment: assets | 3b9aa | 1.5 | 1.2 | .2 | .1 | .2 | .3 | 4.8 | † 5.2 | −7.0 | .4 | −3.4 | .1 |
| Equity & investment fund shares | 3baaa | .2 | — | .2 | .1 | .2 | .3 | .5 | † −.1 | .2 | .1 | −.7 | — |
| Debt securities | 3bbaa | 1.3 | 1.2 | — | — | — | — | 4.4 | † 5.3 | −7.2 | .3 | −2.7 | .1 |
| Portfolio investment: liabilities | 3b9la | −8.3 | −5.8 | −4.6 | −4.4 | 6.4 | −5.6 | 5.8 | † 5.1 | 14.4 | 10.2 | 10.3 | 3.6 |
| Equity & investment fund shares | 3bala | −.8 | .6 | 1.8 | 1.7 | 11.4 | 2.4 | 5.8 | † 5.1 | 14.4 | 10.1 | 10.3 | 3.6 |
| Debt securities | 3bbla | −7.5 | −6.4 | −6.4 | −6.2 | −4.9 | −8.0 | | † .1 | | .1 | .... | .... |
| Fin. der.& empl.stk.ops.(ESOs): net | 3c9na | −.6 | 1.6 | −.2 | .5 | −.9 | −.3 | .6 | † −.2 | .2 | −.1 | −.6 | −.5 |
| Fin. der. & ESOs.: assets | 3c9aa | .5 | 1.7 | .1 | .5 | .1 | .1 | .6 | † — | .2 | .1 | .1 | — |
| Fin. der. & ESOs.: liabilities | 3c9la | 1.0 | .1 | .3 | .1 | 1.0 | .4 | — | † .2 | — | .2 | .7 | .5 |
| Other investment: assets | 3d9aa | 31.6 | 78.2 | 49.4 | −35.3 | −52.1 | 210.6 | −75.5 | † −108.6 | −225.2 | 121.6 | 338.5 | 41.5 |
| Other equity | 3daaa | .... | .... | .... | .... | .... | .... | .... | .... | .... | .... | .... | .... |
| Debt instruments | 3dzaa | 31.6 | 78.2 | 49.4 | −35.3 | −52.1 | 210.6 | −75.5 | † −108.6 | −225.2 | 121.6 | 338.5 | 41.5 |
| Other investment: liabilities | 3d9la | 69.3 | 96.3 | 154.0 | 459.1 | 531.6 | 155.5 | 118.7 | † 437.5 | 311.2 | 518.6 | 30.0 | −35.5 |
| Other equity | 3dala | .... | .... | .... | .... | .... | .... | .... | .... | .... | .... | .... | .... |
| Debt instruments | 3dzla | 69.3 | 96.3 | 154.0 | 459.1 | 531.6 | 155.5 | 118.7 | † 437.5 | 311.2 | 518.6 | 30.0 | −35.5 |
| Curr.+ cap.− finan. acct. balance | 4y9na | 69.1 | −47.3 | −31.5 | 289.9 | 248.1 | −437.9 | −145.7 | † −38.0 | 131.5 | 152.3 | −560.7 | −249.0 |
| D. Net Errors and Omissions | 409nm | 79.1 | 161.5 | 59.0 | 100.0 | 48.1 | 44.0 | 34.6 | † 72.4 | 127.7 | 86.4 | −93.9 | −31.9 |
| E. Reserves and Related Items | 4z9na | 148.2 | 114.2 | 27.5 | 389.9 | 296.2 | −393.9 | −111.1 | † 34.3 | 259.2 | 238.7 | −654.5 | −281.0 |
| Reserve assets | 3e9aa | 148.0 | 128.6 | 140.7 | 528.9 | 452.0 | −202.1 | 294.4 | † 275.0 | 498.7 | 282.0 | −538.5 | −306.7 |
| Credit and loans from the IMF | 3dcla | −21.6 | −21.7 | 41.1 | 11.2 | 13.5 | −16.3 | 174.6 | † 153.5 | 138.4 | −21.6 | −29.2 | −40.8 |
| Exceptional financing | 409la | 21.4 | 36.1 | 72.1 | 127.8 | 142.3 | 208.1 | 230.8 | † 87.2 | 101.1 | 64.9 | 145.3 | 15.0 |

*Excludes components in group E

## International Investment Position

*Millions of US Dollars*

| | | 2004 | 2005 | 2006 | 2007 | 2008 | 2009 | 2010 | 2011 | 2012 | 2013 | 2014 | 2015 |
|---|---|---|---|---|---|---|---|---|---|---|---|---|---|
| Assets | 809aa | 1,008.5 | 1,201.4 | 1,458.6 | 2,055.0 | 2,383.9 | 2,504.9 | 2,756.5 | 3,030.0 | 3,582.6 | 4,081.5 | 3,750.3 | 3,361.8 |
| Direct investment | 8a9aa | 28.7 | 29.9 | 29.2 | 41.3 | 72.5 | 70.1 | 77.7 | 111.5 | 141.1 | 182.7 | 218.2 | 223.8 |
| Equity & investment fund shares | 8aaaa | 23.5 | 24.6 | 25.5 | 38.1 | 54.2 | 62.4 | 65.8 | 86.0 | 104.4 | 130.8 | 169.2 | 183.8 |
| Debt instruments | 8abaa | 5.2 | 5.3 | 3.7 | 3.2 | 18.3 | 7.7 | 11.9 | 25.5 | 36.7 | 51.9 | 48.9 | 40.0 |
| Portfolio investment | 8b9aa | 2.7 | 3.4 | 1.2 | 1.3 | 1.2 | 1.5 | 6.4 | 12.2 | 5.2 | 7.2 | 3.8 | 4.3 |
| Equity & investment fund shares | 8baaa | .7 | .7 | .9 | .9 | 1.1 | 1.4 | 1.9 | 2.4 | 2.6 | 2.7 | 2.0 | 2.3 |
| Debt securities | 8bbaa | 2.1 | 2.7 | .4 | .4 | .1 | .1 | 4.5 | 9.8 | 2.6 | 4.5 | 1.8 | 2.0 |
| Fin. der.(oth.than reserves) & ESOs | 8c9aa | .4 | 2.1 | 2.2 | 2.8 | 2.8 | 2.9 | 3.5 | 3.5 | 3.8 | 3.9 | 4.0 | 4.0 |
| Other investment | 8d9aa | 506.5 | 568.6 | 650.7 | 675.9 | 634.9 | 950.1 | 951.3 | 937.5 | 917.7 | 1,067.1 | 1,367.7 | 1,372.9 |
| Other equity | 8daaa | .... | .... | .... | .... | .... | .... | .... | .... | .... | .... | .... | .... |
| Debt instruments | 8dzaa | 506.5 | 568.6 | 650.7 | 675.9 | 634.9 | 950.1 | 951.3 | 937.5 | 917.7 | 1,067.1 | 1,367.7 | 1,372.9 |
| Reserve assets | 8e9aa | 470.3 | 597.4 | 775.3 | 1,333.7 | 1,672.4 | 1,480.3 | 1,717.7 | 1,965.3 | 2,515.0 | 2,820.6 | 2,156.6 | 1,756.8 |
| Liabilities | 809la | 2,583.7 | 2,885.2 | 3,465.3 | 4,686.1 | 6,018.3 | 6,381.2 | 6,944.1 | 7,857.2 | 8,665.6 | 9,427.6 | 9,349.0 | 9,074.7 |
| Direct investment | 8a9la | 848.7 | 1,025.0 | 1,283.1 | 1,876.3 | 2,611.2 | 2,778.7 | 2,974.3 | 3,284.1 | 3,499.5 | 3,666.6 | 3,652.4 | 3,566.1 |
| Equity & investment fund shares | 8aala | 680.7 | 785.4 | 943.1 | 1,325.5 | 1,885.2 | 2,000.7 | 2,174.6 | 2,420.7 | 2,557.9 | 2,639.5 | 2,661.2 | 2,615.4 |
| Debt instruments | 8abla | 168.0 | 239.6 | 340.0 | 550.8 | 726.0 | 778.0 | 799.7 | 863.5 | 941.6 | 1,027.0 | 991.2 | 950.8 |
| Portfolio investment | 8b9la | 51.5 | 46.1 | 51.1 | 53.9 | 56.9 | 49.3 | 55.5 | 72.6 | 87.1 | 110.3 | 113.3 | 116.9 |
| Equity & investment fund shares | 8bala | 19.7 | 20.7 | 32.0 | 41.0 | 48.9 | 49.3 | 55.5 | 72.6 | 87.1 | 110.2 | 113.2 | 116.8 |
| Debt securities | 8bbla | 31.8 | 25.4 | 19.0 | 12.9 | 8.0 | .... | .... | — | — | .1 | .1 | .1 |
| Fin. der.(oth.than reserves) & ESOs | 8c9la | 1.1 | 1.2 | 1.5 | 1.5 | 2.5 | 3.0 | 3.0 | 3.1 | 3.1 | 3.4 | 4.1 | 4.6 |
| Other investment | 8d9la | 1,682.5 | 1,813.0 | 2,129.6 | 2,754.4 | 3,347.7 | 3,550.3 | 3,911.4 | 4,497.3 | 5,075.8 | 5,647.4 | 5,579.2 | 5,387.1 |
| Other equity | 8dala | .... | .... | .... | .... | .... | .... | .... | .... | .... | .... | .... | .... |
| Debt instruments | 8dzla | 1,682.5 | 1,813.0 | 2,129.6 | 2,754.4 | 3,347.7 | 3,550.3 | 3,911.4 | 4,497.3 | 5,075.8 | 5,647.4 | 5,579.2 | 5,387.1 |

# Moldova 921

| | | 2004 | 2005 | 2006 | 2007 | 2008 | 2009 | 2010 | 2011 | 2012 | 2013 | 2014 | 2015 |
|---|---|---|---|---|---|---|---|---|---|---|---|---|---|
| **Government Finance** | | | | | | | | | | | | | |
| **Cash Flow Statement** | | | | | | | | | | | | | |
| **Budgetary Central Government** | | | | *Millions of Lei: Fiscal Year Ends December 31* | | | | | | | | | |
| Cash Receipts:Operating Activities... | c1 | 5,625.2 | 7,941.0 | 9,823.2 | 14,058.6 | 15,977.5 | 13,833.0 | 17,167.7 | 18,639.0 | 20,090.6 | 22,436.7 | 27,717.7 | .... |
| Taxes............................... | c11 | 5,239.6 | 6,960.1 | 8,556.6 | 10,900.4 | 12,865.0 | 10,687.2 | 13,079.9 | 15,053.3 | 16,450.0 | 18,491.3 | 22,208.0 | .... |
| Social Contributions...................... | c12 | — | — | — | — | — | — | — | — | — | — | — | .... |
| Grants............................... | c13 | 152.1 | 524.0 | 454.9 | 966.9 | 1,028.6 | 1,159.3 | 1,937.5 | 1,565.4 | 1,512.7 | 2,198.3 | 3,883.0 | .... |
| Other Receipts.............................. | c14 | 233.5 | 456.9 | 811.7 | 2,191.3 | 2,083.9 | 1,986.5 | 2,150.3 | 2,020.3 | 2,127.9 | 1,747.1 | 1,626.7 | .... |
| Cash Payments:Operating Activities. | c2 | 5,526.2 | 7,030.5 | 9,120.5 | 12,163.9 | 14,118.0 | 15,734.7 | 17,499.7 | 18,702.2 | 20,298.0 | 22,475.4 | 27,944.6 | .... |
| Compensation of Employees.......... | c21 | 1,005.0 | 1,175.3 | 1,768.1 | 2,634.4 | 2,944.3 | 3,468.9 | 3,458.8 | 3,501.7 | 3,943.5 | 3,875.4 | 4,252.9 | .... |
| Purchases of Goods & Services....... | c22 | 474.1 | 644.0 | 871.1 | 1,255.1 | 1,445.0 | 1,333.9 | 1,665.6 | 2,011.0 | 2,314.0 | 3,234.9 | 3,344.7 | .... |
| Interest................................. | c24 | 772.7 | 470.5 | 428.6 | 609.8 | 721.6 | 834.2 | 547.6 | 662.4 | 666.4 | 492.6 | 591.8 | .... |
| Subsidies............................. | c25 | 281.0 | 291.6 | 1,091.0 | 1,262.2 | 1,432.3 | 842.0 | 650.7 | 694.2 | 734.1 | 785.6 | 1,014.6 | .... |
| Grants................................. | c26 | 2,014.6 | 3,028.9 | 3,779.8 | 4,596.6 | 5,634.1 | 7,041.1 | 9,023.7 | 8,855.7 | 8,888.6 | 9,428.5 | 12,967.1 | .... |
| Social Benefits........................... | c27 | 245.4 | 359.1 | 351.1 | 668.4 | 801.4 | 905.6 | 816.1 | 1,007.7 | 1,006.8 | 1,114.7 | 1,170.8 | .... |
| Other Payments.......................... | c28 | 733.4 | 1,061.1 | 830.8 | 1,137.4 | 1,139.3 | 1,309.0 | 1,337.2 | 1,969.5 | 2,744.6 | 3,543.7 | 4,602.7 | .... |
| Net Cash Inflow:Operating Act.[1-2] | ccio | 99.0 | 910.5 | 702.7 | 1,894.7 | 1,859.5 | −1,901.7 | −332.0 | −63.2 | −207.4 | −38.7 | −226.9 | .... |
| Net Cash Outflow:Invest. in NFA...... | c31 | 311.7 | 506.2 | 688.3 | 2,129.1 | 2,279.3 | 1,457.1 | 1,352.4 | 1,311.5 | 1,482.8 | 1,518.1 | 1,545.1 | .... |
| Purchases of Nonfinancial Assets... | c31.1 | 326.7 | 509.5 | 688.3 | 2,140.9 | 2,292.1 | 1,485.7 | 1,381.1 | 1,341.1 | 1,497.9 | .... | .... | .... |
| Sales of Nonfinancial Assets.......... | c31.2 | 15.0 | 3.3 | — | 11.8 | 12.8 | 28.6 | 28.7 | 29.6 | 15.1 | .... | .... | .... |
| Cash Surplus/Deficit [1-2-31=1-2M] | ccsd | −212.7 | 404.3 | 14.4 | −234.4 | −419.8 | −3,358.8 | −1,684.4 | −1,374.7 | −1,690.2 | −1,556.8 | −1,772.0 | .... |
| Net Acq. Fin. Assets, excl. Cash....... | c32x | −56.2 | −70.3 | −218.4 | −235.6 | −867.5 | −60.4 | −152.0 | −145.4 | −237.4 | .... | .... | .... |
| Domestic.................................... | c321x | −56.2 | −70.3 | −218.4 | −235.6 | −867.5 | −60.4 | −152.0 | −145.4 | −237.4 | .... | .... | .... |
| Foreign...................................... | c322x | — | — | — | — | — | — | — | — | — | .... | .... | .... |
| Net Incurrence of Liabilities.............. | c33 | 177.0 | 10.2 | −238.6 | 181.5 | −320.4 | 3,576.8 | 2,334.6 | 426.1 | 1,522.8 | 1,242.1 | 1,925.0 | .... |
| Domestic.................................... | c331 | 778.5 | 63.6 | −8.2 | 74.6 | −335.4 | 1,608.8 | 274.6 | 24.8 | 358.9 | 654.1 | 497.6 | .... |
| Foreign...................................... | c332 | −601.5 | −53.4 | −230.4 | 106.9 | 15.0 | 1,968.0 | 2,060.0 | 401.3 | 1,163.9 | 588.0 | 1,427.4 | .... |
| Net Cash Inflow, Fin.Act.[-32x+33].. | cnfb | 233.2 | 80.5 | −20.2 | 417.1 | 547.1 | 3,637.2 | 2,486.6 | 571.5 | 1,760.2 | 1,427.0 | 2,258.2 | .... |
| Net Change in Stock of Cash........... | cncb | 20.5 | 484.8 | −5.8 | 182.7 | 127.3 | 278.4 | 802.2 | −803.2 | 70.0 | −129.8 | 486.2 | .... |
| Stat. Discrep. [32X-33+NCB-CSD].... | ccsdz | | | | | | | | | | | | .... |
| Memo Item:Cash Expenditure[2+31] | c2m | 5,781.7 | 7,534.6 | 9,808.8 | 14,293.0 | 16,397.3 | 17,191.8 | 18,852.1 | 20,013.7 | 21,780.8 | 23,993.5 | 29,489.7 | .... |
| Memo Item: Gross Debt.................. | c63 | 16,642.0 | 12,208.7 | 13,058.9 | 12,416.9 | 11,604.4 | 16,698.1 | 18,922.4 | 19,524.1 | 21,462.2 | 23,808.5 | 27,799.6 | .... |
| **National Accounts** | | | | | *Millions of Lei* | | | | | | | | |
| Househ.Cons.Expend.,incl.NPISHs.... | 96f | 28,524 | 35,179 | 42,028 | 49,960 | 58,607 | 54,214 | 67,310 | 79,507 | 85,224 | 94,629 | 103,927 | 108,603 |
| Government Consumption Expend... | 91f | 4,774 | 6,189 | 8,945 | 10,658 | 12,845 | 14,360 | 15,931 | 16,584 | 17,838 | 18,540 | 20,372 | 22,627 |
| Gross Fixed Capital Formation.......... | 93e | 6,787 | 9,258 | 12,691 | 18,222 | 21,391 | 13,655 | 16,263 | 19,179 | 20,864 | 23,062 | 27,707 | 29,492 |
| Changes in Inventories.................... | 93i | 1,657 | 2,349 | 1,965 | 2,138 | 3,292 | 330 | 648 | 725 | −3 | 1,722 | 1,495 | −1,952 |
| Exports (Net)................................ | 90n | −9,709 | −15,323 | −20,874 | −27,548 | −33,213 | −22,129 | −28,265 | −33,646 | −35,696 | −37,442 | −41,451 | −36,919 |
| Gross Domestic Product (GDP)......... | 99b | 32,032 | 37,652 | 44,754 | 53,430 | 62,922 | 60,430 | 71,885 | 82,349 | 88,228 | 100,510 | 112,050 | 121,851 |
| Net Primary Income from Abroad..... | 98.n | 4,382 | 5,088 | 5,272 | 4,980 | 6,176 | 3,404 | 5,999 | 6,630 | 10,201 | 10,888 | 11,668 | .... |
| Gross National Income (GNI)........... | 99a | 36,414 | 42,740 | 50,026 | 58,410 | 69,098 | 63,834 | 77,884 | 88,979 | 98,428 | 111,398 | 123,717 | .... |
| Net Current Transf.from Abroad....... | 98t | 4,496 | 7,192 | 10,279 | 13,819 | 16,382 | 13,041 | 15,672 | 17,125 | 18,784 | 20,350 | 21,564 | .... |
| Gross Nat'l Disposable Inc.(GNDI).... | 99i | 40,910 | 49,932 | 60,305 | 72,229 | 85,479 | 76,874 | 93,556 | 106,104 | 117,212 | 131,749 | 145,282 | .... |
| Gross Saving................................. | 99s | 7,612 | 8,564 | 9,333 | 11,611 | 14,028 | 8,300 | 10,316 | 10,013 | 14,150 | 18,580 | 20,983 | .... |
| | | | | | | *Millions: Midyear Estimates* | | | | | | | |
| **Population...............................** | 99z | 4.17 | 4.16 | 4.14 | 4.13 | 4.11 | 4.10 | 4.08 | 4.08 | 4.07 | 4.07 | 4.07 | 4.07 |

| | | 2004 | 2005 | 2006 | 2007 | 2008 | 2009 | 2010 | 2011 | 2012 | 2013 | 2014 | 2015 |
|---|---|---|---|---|---|---|---|---|---|---|---|---|---|
| **Exchange Rates** | | *Togrogs per SDR: End of Period* | | | | | | | | | | | |
| Market Rate | aa | 1,877.6 | 1,745.1 | 1,752.6 | 1,848.8 | 1,952.3 | 2,261.9 | 1,935.0 | 2,143.8 | 2,139.5 | 2,547.3 | 2,731.9 | 2,765.9 |
| | | *Togrogs per US Dollar: End of Period (ae) Period Average (rf)* | | | | | | | | | | | |
| Market Rate | ae | 1,209.0 | 1,221.0 | 1,165.0 | 1,170.0 | 1,267.5 | 1,442.8 | 1,256.5 | 1,396.4 | 1,392.1 | 1,654.1 | 1,885.6 | 1,996.0 |
| Market Rate | rf | 1,185.3 | 1,205.2 | 1,179.7 | 1,170.4 | 1,165.8 | 1,437.8 | 1,357.1 | 1,265.5 | 1,357.6 | 1,523.9 | 1,817.9 | 1,970.3 |
| **Fund Position** | | *Millions of SDRs: End of Period* | | | | | | | | | | | |
| Quota | 2f.s | 51.10 | 51.10 | 51.10 | 51.10 | 51.10 | 51.10 | 51.10 | 51.10 | 51.10 | 51.10 | 51.10 | 51.10 |
| SDR Holdings | 1b.s | .03 | .01 | — | .01 | .04 | 48.75 | 47.23 | 45.46 | 44.11 | 43.22 | 42.93 | 42.91 |
| Reserve Position in the Fund | 1c.s | .12 | .14 | .14 | .14 | .14 | .14 | .14 | .14 | .14 | .14 | .14 | .14 |
| Total Fund Cred.&Loans Outstg | 2tl | 28.50 | 24.49 | 20.45 | 16.14 | 12.96 | 116.04 | 128.34 | 125.90 | 103.19 | 42.16 | 1.92 | — |
| SDR Allocations | 1bd | — | — | — | — | — | 48.76 | 48.76 | 48.76 | 48.76 | 48.76 | 48.76 | 48.76 |
| **International Liquidity** | | *Millions of US Dollars Unless Otherwise Indicated: End of Period* | | | | | | | | | | | |
| Total Reserves Minus Gold | 1l.d | 193.74 | 333.15 | 583.40 | 801.75 | 561.48 | 1,294.47 | 2,196.70 | 2,275.16 | 3,930.30 | 2,095.81 | 1,540.36 | 1,246.50 |
| SDR Holdings | 1b.d | .04 | .02 | .01 | .02 | .06 | 76.42 | 72.73 | 69.80 | 67.79 | 66.55 | 62.20 | 59.47 |
| Reserve Position in the Fund | 1c.d | .19 | .19 | .20 | .21 | .21 | .21 | .21 | .21 | .21 | .21 | .20 | .19 |
| Foreign Exchange | 1d.d | 193.50 | 332.94 | 583.18 | 801.51 | 561.21 | 1,217.84 | 2,123.76 | 2,205.16 | 3,862.30 | 2,029.05 | 1,477.96 | 1,186.85 |
| Gold (Million Fine Troy Ounces) | 1ad | .03 | — | .21 | .24 | .11 | .03 | .06 | .11 | .12 | .13 | .09 | .07 |
| Gold (National Valuation) | 1and | 14.08 | — | 134.64 | 198.86 | 95.91 | 32.83 | 91.56 | 175.86 | 195.32 | 152.01 | 109.81 | 76.70 |
| Central Bank: Other Assets | 3..d | .91 | 6.57 | 1.80 | 2.13 | 2.30 | 1.68 | .33 | .45 | .25 | .56 | .18 | .25 |
| Central Bank: Other Liabs | 4..d | .01 | 2.61 | 4.39 | 14.98 | 13.72 | 13.12 | 13.36 | 11.30 | 347.56 | 1,000.10 | 1,522.62 | 1,908.38 |
| Other Depository Corps.: Assets | 7a.d | 149.32 | 229.38 | 402.32 | 393.94 | 238.50 | 289.79 | 522.68 | 509.99 | 590.09 | 540.02 | 508.72 | 611.11 |
| Other Depository Corps.: Liabs | 7b.d | 44.42 | 44.91 | 65.24 | 178.66 | 335.66 | 292.82 | 355.35 | 493.36 | 978.18 | 1,083.47 | 1,479.30 | 1,936.44 |
| **Central Bank** | | *Millions of Togrogs: End of Period* | | | | | | | | | | | |
| Net Foreign Assets | 11n | 198,807 | 368,884 | 797,654 | 1,125,797 | 793,479 | 1,525,808 | 2,516,092 | 3,032,688 | 4,934,675 | 1,833,187 | 102,392 | −1,302,372 |
| Claims on Nonresidents | 11 | 252,328 | 414,804 | 838,604 | 1,173,177 | 836,167 | 1,917,504 | 2,875,553 | 3,422,895 | 5,743,616 | 3,719,049 | 3,111,885 | 2,641,583 |
| Liabilities to Nonresidents | 16c | 53,520 | 45,920 | 40,951 | 47,380 | 42,688 | 391,696 | 359,461 | 390,207 | 808,941 | 1,885,861 | 3,009,493 | 3,943,955 |
| Claims on Other Depository Corps | 12e | 22,332 | 17,610 | 18,191 | 18,550 | 243,077 | 198,448 | 131,316 | 341,506 | 400,643 | 4,297,025 | 2,607,816 | 1,686,407 |
| Net Claims on Central Government | 12an | 29,896 | 34,704 | −353,435 | −579,529 | −189,278 | −272,801 | −497,529 | −713,537 | −2,780,067 | −1,692,784 | −577,460 | −480,333 |
| Claims on Central Government | 12a | 105,300 | 142,275 | 70,459 | 33,206 | 25,563 | 432,755 | 311,387 | 436,310 | 165,614 | — | 204,828 | 206,718 |
| Liabilities to Central Government | 16d | 75,404 | 107,571 | 423,894 | 612,735 | 214,841 | 705,556 | 808,916 | 1,149,847 | 2,945,682 | 1,692,784 | 782,288 | 687,051 |
| Claims on Other Sectors | 12s | — | — | — | — | — | — | — | — | — | 204,912 | 1,491,238 | 2,511,248 |
| Claims on Other Financial Corps | 12g | — | — | — | — | — | — | — | — | — | 204,912 | 1,130,335 | 2,158,774 |
| Claims on State & Local Govts | 12b | — | — | — | — | — | — | — | — | — | — | — | — |
| Claims on Public Nonfin. Corps | 12c | — | — | — | — | — | — | — | — | — | — | — | — |
| Claims on Private Sector | 12d | — | — | — | — | — | — | — | — | — | — | 360,903 | 352,475 |
| Monetary Base | 14 | 234,858 | 281,188 | 381,792 | 535,048 | 633,682 | 913,416 | 1,160,377 | 1,661,597 | 2,168,392 | 3,337,855 | 3,504,986 | 2,521,797 |
| Currency in Circulation | 14a | 168,474 | 191,640 | 245,059 | 364,021 | 407,156 | 371,778 | 519,647 | 713,305 | 828,393 | 841,077 | 809,617 | 706,605 |
| Liabs. to Other Depository Corps | 14c | 66,384 | 89,548 | 136,733 | 171,026 | 226,526 | 541,638 | 640,730 | 948,292 | 1,339,999 | 2,496,778 | 2,695,369 | 1,815,192 |
| Liabilities to Other Sectors | 14d | — | — | — | — | — | — | — | — | — | — | — | — |
| Other Liabs. to Other Dep. Corps | 14n | 68,551 | 125,697 | 87,978 | 103,425 | 119,786 | 392,512 | 1,100,997 | 882,113 | 752,151 | 1,627,017 | 863,172 | 1,028,597 |
| Dep. & Sec. Excl. f/Monetary Base | 14o | — | — | — | — | — | — | — | 70,770 | 38,702 | 10,814 | 115,895 | 10,419 |
| Deposits Included in Broad Money | 15 | — | — | — | — | — | — | — | — | — | — | — | — |
| Sec.Ot.th.Shares Incl.in Brd. Money | 16a | — | — | — | — | — | — | — | — | — | — | — | — |
| Deposits Excl. from Broad Money | 16b | — | — | — | — | — | — | — | 70,770 | 38,702 | 10,814 | 115,895 | 10,419 |
| Sec.Ot.th.Shares Excl.f/Brd.Money | 16s | — | — | — | — | — | — | — | — | — | — | — | — |
| Loans | 16l | — | — | — | — | — | — | — | — | — | — | — | — |
| Financial Derivatives | 16m | — | — | — | — | — | — | — | — | — | — | — | — |
| Shares and Other Equity | 17a | 31,985 | 46,115 | 36,789 | 86,000 | 92,447 | 125,598 | −139,166 | 42,334 | −138,689 | −510,976 | −917,909 | −1,357,544 |
| Other Items (Net) | 17r | −84,359 | −31,802 | −44,149 | −159,655 | 1,364 | 19,930 | 27,672 | 3,844 | −265,306 | 177,630 | 57,843 | 211,681 |
| Memo Item: | | | | | | | | | | | | | |
| Total Assets | 10ra | 564,417 | 701,086 | 1,082,261 | 1,515,070 | 1,284,837 | 2,984,889 | 3,766,746 | 4,670,738 | 6,679,645 | 8,482,602 | 7,863,576 | 7,663,180 |
| **Other Depository Corporations** | | *Millions of Togrogs: End of Period* | | | | | | | | | | | |
| Net Foreign Assets | 21n | 126,830 | 225,236 | 392,696 | 251,872 | −123,155 | −4,381 | 210,239 | 23,229 | −540,264 | −898,922 | −1,830,134 | −2,645,319 |
| Claims on Nonresidents | 21 | 180,531 | 280,068 | 468,699 | 460,909 | 302,299 | 418,114 | 656,727 | 712,141 | 821,458 | 893,248 | 959,240 | 1,219,770 |
| Liabilities to Nonresidents | 26c | 53,701 | 54,832 | 76,002 | 209,037 | 425,454 | 422,494 | 446,488 | 688,911 | 1,361,721 | 1,792,170 | 2,789,375 | 3,865,089 |
| Claims on Central Bank | 20 | 157,037 | 251,711 | 278,344 | 354,511 | 424,230 | 1,020,641 | 1,873,292 | 2,097,032 | 2,552,654 | 4,896,510 | 4,227,035 | 3,316,767 |
| Currency | 20a | 24,961 | 39,271 | 59,932 | 80,696 | 78,432 | 86,784 | 131,444 | 195,810 | 224,509 | 258,930 | 310,359 | 247,938 |
| Reserve Deposits and Securities | 20b | 63,525 | 86,762 | 135,806 | 171,017 | 226,076 | 541,642 | 640,851 | 951,294 | 1,341,991 | 2,513,166 | 2,704,760 | 1,819,186 |
| Other Claims | 20n | 68,551 | 125,678 | 82,606 | 102,798 | 119,723 | 392,215 | 1,100,997 | 949,928 | 986,155 | 2,124,414 | 1,211,916 | 1,249,643 |
| Net Claims on Central Government | 22an | −7,252 | −96,897 | −92,919 | −113,026 | −383,589 | −444,090 | −337,339 | −656,223 | −266,107 | 636,818 | 575,860 | 1,156,901 |
| Claims on Central Government | 22a | 31,226 | 3,167 | 4,898 | 24,102 | 2,504 | 9,186 | 79,025 | 275,270 | 667,374 | 1,822,988 | 2,140,845 | 2,610,765 |
| Liabilities to Central Government | 26d | 38,478 | 100,064 | 97,817 | 137,128 | 386,093 | 453,276 | 416,364 | 931,493 | 933,481 | 1,186,170 | 1,564,985 | 1,453,864 |
| Claims on Other Sectors | 22s | 616,932 | 872,599 | 1,251,394 | 2,091,048 | 2,654,592 | 2,681,159 | 3,363,819 | 5,843,544 | 7,347,547 | 12,018,456 | 13,191,547 | 12,875,425 |
| Claims on Other Financial Corps | 22g | 462 | 502 | 1,600 | 2,916 | 3,994 | 4,721 | 14,321 | 17,641 | 9,883 | 129,902 | 160,602 | 319,856 |
| Claims on State & Local Govts | 22b | — | — | — | — | — | — | — | — | — | — | — | — |
| Claims on Public Nonfin. Corps | 22c | 13,126 | 34,169 | 36,732 | 27,332 | 34,795 | 20,429 | 17,074 | 100,646 | 41,960 | 80,546 | 128,551 | 223,268 |
| Claims on Private Sector | 22d | 603,345 | 837,928 | 1,213,062 | 2,060,800 | 2,615,804 | 2,656,009 | 3,332,424 | 5,725,256 | 7,295,704 | 11,808,007 | 12,902,394 | 12,332,300 |
| Liabilities to Central Bank | 26g | 23,838 | 18,150 | 19,092 | 18,936 | 241,176 | 198,432 | 131,326 | 413,291 | 634,740 | 4,775,157 | 2,898,527 | 1,767,186 |
| Transf.Dep.Included in Broad Money | 24 | 186,109 | 316,061 | 355,962 | 628,009 | 601,736 | 738,245 | 1,535,555 | 2,004,421 | 2,090,631 | 2,485,408 | 2,756,510 | 2,208,517 |
| Other Dep.Included in Broad Money | 25 | 516,825 | 663,360 | 978,829 | 1,479,926 | 1,292,521 | 1,810,362 | 2,728,573 | 3,837,067 | 4,787,388 | 6,189,692 | 7,191,523 | 7,215,222 |
| Sec.Ot.th.Shares Incl.in Brd. Money | 26a | 585 | 8,369 | 16,673 | 9,989 | 47,021 | 46,432 | 27,651 | 53,277 | 135,369 | 203,706 | 188,531 | 167,823 |
| Deposits Excl. from Broad Money | 26b | 5,273 | 3,025 | 7,242 | 13,197 | 7,692 | 7,649 | 5,880 | — | — | — | — | — |
| Sec.Ot.th.Shares Excl.f/Brd.Money | 26s | 60 | 181 | 150 | 14,068 | 15,210 | 24,528 | 21,360 | 24,436 | 33,410 | 54,585 | 74,411 | 92,799 |
| Loans | 26l | — | — | — | — | — | — | — | 2,198 | 51,647 | 349,309 | 418,736 | 671,202 |
| Financial Derivatives | 26m | 39,186 | 63,596 | 151,363 | 97,183 | 2,196 | — | — | 4,049 | 119,787 | 638,698 | 193,140 | 156,971 |
| Insurance Technical Reserves | 26r | — | — | — | — | — | — | — | — | — | — | — | — |
| Shares and Other Equity | 27a | 167,101 | 207,076 | 294,780 | 376,386 | 340,566 | 230,212 | 393,541 | 688,911 | 1,000,874 | 1,341,458 | 2,153,087 | 2,482,757 |
| Other Items (Net) | 27r | −45,430 | −27,169 | 5,424 | −53,289 | 23,962 | 197,468 | 266,125 | 279,931 | 239,984 | 614,849 | 289,843 | −58,704 |
| Memo Item: | | | | | | | | | | | | | |
| Total Assets | 20ra | 1,152,647 | 1,639,442 | 2,378,287 | 3,452,568 | 3,870,248 | 4,846,784 | 6,689,860 | 9,810,812 | 12,409,677 | 21,539,673 | 23,196,564 | 22,351,699 |

# Mongolia 948

| | | 2004 | 2005 | 2006 | 2007 | 2008 | 2009 | 2010 | 2011 | 2012 | 2013 | 2014 | 2015 |
|---|---|---|---|---|---|---|---|---|---|---|---|---|---|
| **Depository Corporations** | | | | | | *Millions of Togrogs: End of Period* | | | | | | | | |
| Net Foreign Assets............................ | 31n | 325,637 | 594,120 | 1,190,350 | 1,377,669 | 670,324 | 1,521,427 | 2,726,331 | 3,055,917 | 4,394,412 | 934,265 | −1,727,742 | −3,947,691 |
| Claims on Nonresidents................ | 31 | 432,858 | 694,872 | 1,307,303 | 1,634,086 | 1,138,466 | 2,335,617 | 3,532,280 | 4,135,036 | 6,565,073 | 4,612,296 | 4,071,126 | 3,861,353 |
| Liabilities to Nonresidents............. | 36c | 107,221 | 100,752 | 116,953 | 256,418 | 468,142 | 814,190 | 805,949 | 1,079,118 | 2,170,662 | 3,678,031 | 5,798,868 | 7,809,044 |
| Domestic Claims............................... | 32 | 639,576 | 810,406 | 805,039 | 1,398,493 | 2,081,726 | 1,964,268 | 2,528,952 | 4,473,784 | 4,301,372 | 11,167,402 | 14,681,185 | 16,063,241 |
| Net Claims on Central Government | 32an | 22,643 | −62,193 | −446,354 | −692,555 | −572,866 | −716,891 | −834,867 | −1,369,760 | −3,046,174 | −1,055,965 | −1,600 | 676,568 |
| Claims on Central Government.... | 32a | 136,526 | 145,442 | 75,357 | 57,308 | 28,067 | 441,941 | 390,412 | 711,580 | 832,988 | 1,822,988 | 2,345,673 | 2,817,483 |
| Liabilities to Central Government. | 36d | 113,882 | 207,635 | 521,711 | 749,863 | 600,934 | 1,158,832 | 1,225,280 | 2,081,340 | 3,879,163 | 2,878,954 | 2,347,273 | 2,140,915 |
| Claims on Other Sectors................ | 32s | 616,932 | 872,599 | 1,251,394 | 2,091,048 | 2,654,592 | 2,681,159 | 3,363,819 | 5,843,544 | 7,347,547 | 12,223,368 | 14,682,785 | 15,386,673 |
| Claims on Other Financial Corps.. | 32g | 462 | 502 | 1,600 | 2,916 | 3,994 | 4,721 | 14,321 | 17,641 | 9,883 | 334,814 | 1,290,937 | 2,478,630 |
| Claims on State & Local Govts..... | 32b | — | — | — | — | — | — | — | — | — | — | — | — |
| Claims on Public Nonfin. Corps.... | 32c | 13,126 | 34,169 | 36,732 | 27,332 | 34,795 | 20,429 | 17,074 | 100,646 | 41,960 | 80,546 | 128,551 | 223,268 |
| Claims on Private Sector.............. | 32d | 603,345 | 837,928 | 1,213,062 | 2,060,800 | 2,615,804 | 2,656,009 | 3,332,424 | 5,725,256 | 7,295,704 | 11,808,007 | 13,263,297 | 12,684,775 |
| Broad Money Liabilities.................... | 35l | 847,032 | 1,140,159 | 1,536,590 | 2,401,250 | 2,270,001 | 2,880,034 | 4,679,981 | 6,412,259 | 7,617,272 | 9,460,953 | 10,635,822 | 10,050,229 |
| Currency Outside Depository Corps | 34a | 143,513 | 152,370 | 185,127 | 283,325 | 328,724 | 284,994 | 388,203 | 517,494 | 603,884 | 582,147 | 499,258 | 458,667 |
| Transferable Deposits................... | 34 | 186,109 | 316,061 | 355,962 | 628,009 | 601,736 | 738,245 | 1,535,555 | 2,004,421 | 2,090,631 | 2,485,408 | 2,756,510 | 2,208,517 |
| Other Deposits............................... | 35 | 516,825 | 663,360 | 978,829 | 1,479,926 | 1,292,521 | 1,810,362 | 2,728,573 | 3,837,067 | 4,787,388 | 6,189,692 | 7,191,523 | 7,215,222 |
| Securities Other than Shares.......... | 36a | 585 | 8,369 | 16,673 | 9,989 | 47,021 | 46,432 | 27,651 | 53,277 | 135,369 | 203,706 | 188,531 | 167,823 |
| Deposits Excl. from Broad Money..... | 36b | 5,273 | 3,025 | 7,242 | 13,197 | 7,692 | 7,649 | 5,880 | 70,770 | 38,702 | 10,814 | 115,895 | 10,419 |
| Sec.Ot.th.Shares Excl.f/Brd.Money.... | 36s | 60 | 181 | 150 | 14,068 | 15,210 | 24,528 | 21,360 | 24,436 | 33,410 | 54,585 | 74,411 | 92,799 |
| Loans............................................. | 36l | — | — | — | — | — | — | — | 2,198 | 51,647 | 349,309 | 418,736 | 671,202 |
| Financial Derivatives...................... | 36m | 39,186 | 63,596 | 151,363 | 97,183 | 2,196 | — | — | 4,049 | 119,787 | 638,698 | 193,140 | 156,971 |
| Insurance Technical Reserves.............. | 36r | — | — | — | — | — | — | — | — | — | — | — | — |
| Shares and Other Equity.................. | 37a | 199,086 | 253,191 | 331,569 | 462,386 | 433,013 | 355,810 | 254,375 | 731,245 | 862,185 | 830,482 | 1,235,177 | 1,125,213 |
| Other Items (Net)............................ | 37r | −125,424 | −55,626 | −31,525 | −211,922 | 23,938 | 217,674 | 293,686 | 284,743 | −27,219 | 756,826 | 280,263 | 8,715 |
| Broad Money Liabs., Seasonally Adj. | 35l.b | 852,688 | 1,149,865 | 1,548,019 | 2,410,941 | 2,263,691 | 2,848,832 | 4,588,326 | 6,232,775 | 7,359,643 | 9,110,412 | 10,237,808 | 9,673,993 |
| **Monetary Aggregates** | | | | | | *Millions of Togrogs: End of Period* | | | | | | | | |
| Broad Money................................ | 59m | 847,032 | 1,140,159 | 1,536,590 | 2,401,250 | 2,270,001 | 2,880,034 | 4,679,981 | 6,412,259 | 7,617,272 | 9,460,953 | 10,635,822 | 10,050,229 |
| o/w:Currency Issued by Cent.Govt | 59m.a | — | — | — | — | — | — | — | — | — | — | — | — |
| o/w: Dep.in Nonfin. Corporations. | 59m.b | — | — | — | — | — | — | — | — | — | — | — | — |
| o/w:Secs. Issued by Central Govt.. | 59m.c | — | — | — | — | — | — | — | — | — | — | — | — |
| Money (National Definitions) | | | | | | | | | | | | | |
| M1.............................................. | 59ma | 221,328 | 269,124 | 331,903 | 590,472 | 647,335 | 651,247 | 1,157,618 | 1,741,076 | 1,835,413 | 2,083,310 | 1,816,687 | 1,685,443 |
| M2.............................................. | 59mb | 847,032 | 1,140,139 | 1,536,493 | 2,401,250 | 2,270,001 | 2,880,034 | 4,679,981 | 6,412,259 | 7,617,272 | 9,460,953 | 10,635,822 | 10,050,229 |
| **Interest Rates** | | | | | | *Percent per Annum* | | | | | | | | |
| Central Bank Policy Rate (EOP)........ | 60 | .... | .... | .... | 8.40 | 9.75 | 10.00 | 11.00 | 12.25 | 13.25 | 10.50 | 12.00 | 13.00 |
| Central Bank Bill Rate..................... | 60aa | 15.75 | 4.75 | 6.42 | 9.85 | 14.78 | 10.82 | 10.99 | 14.25 | 15.47 | 11.61 | 11.18 | 12.96 |
| Treasury Bill Rate............................ | 60c | 10.39 | 13.73 | 6.73 | 6.82 | .... | .... | .... | .... | .... | .... | .... | .... |
| Deposit Rate................................... | 60l | 14.15 | 13.00 | 13.01 | 13.46 | † 11.39 | 13.28 | 11.86 | 10.47 | 11.27 | 12.05 | 12.31 | 12.98 |
| Deposit Rate (Fgn. Currency)............ | 60l.f | 6.27 | 5.73 | 6.26 | 6.36 | † 7.28 | 6.73 | 5.44 | 4.70 | 5.54 | 5.77 | 5.56 | 6.31 |
| Lending Rate................................... | 60p | 31.47 | 30.57 | 26.93 | 21.83 | 20.58 | 21.67 | 20.07 | 16.61 | 18.11 | 18.48 | 19.03 | 19.56 |
| Lending Rate (Fgn. Currency)........... | 60p.f | 19.28 | 16.54 | 16.01 | 14.22 | 15.40 | 17.06 | 14.42 | 12.65 | 13.34 | 12.84 | 12.43 | 12.32 |
| **Prices and Production** | | | | | | *Index Numbers (2010=100): Period Averages* | | | | | | | | |
| Consumer Prices............................. | 64 | 52.9 | 59.6 | † 62.6 | 68.3 | 85.4 | 90.8 | 100.0 | † 109.5 | 125.9 | 136.7 | 154.5 | 163.5 |
| **Intl. Transactions & Positions** | | | | | | *Millions of US Dollars* | | | | | | | | |
| Exports......................................... | 70..d | 869.7 | 1,064.9 | 1,542.8 | 1,889.0 | 2,539.3 | 1,902.6 | 2,899.2 | 4,780.4 | 4,384.6 | 4,272.7 | 5,774.6 | 4,669.5 |
| Imports, c.i.f................................... | 71..d | 1,021.1 | 1,184.3 | 1,485.6 | 2,117.3 | 3,615.8 | 2,131.3 | 3,277.9 | 6,526.9 | 6,738.9 | 6,354.7 | 5,236.6 | 3,797.2 |

# Mongolia 948

## Balance of Payments

*Millions of US Dollars*

| | | 2004 | 2005 | 2006 | 2007 | 2008 | 2009 | 2010 | 2011 | 2012 | 2013 | 2014 | 2015 |
|---|---|---|---|---|---|---|---|---|---|---|---|---|---|
| A. Current Account* | 109bx | −24.6 | −4.5 | 109.0 | 171.8 | −690.1 | −342.6 | −886.8 | −2,758.6 | −3,362.3 | −3,192.0 | −1,405.0 | .... |
| Goods, credit (exports) | 1a9cx | 872.1 | 1,068.6 | 1,545.2 | 1,950.7 | 2,508.6 | 1,880.9 | 2,907.9 | 4,816.4 | 4,381.5 | 4,267.7 | 5,773.8 | .... |
| Goods, debit (imports) | 1a9dx | 901.0 | 1,097.4 | 1,356.7 | 2,003.1 | 3,138.0 | 2,059.1 | 3,079.9 | 5,806.6 | 5,933.4 | 5,574.0 | 4,745.6 | .... |
| Balance on goods | 1a9bx | −28.9 | −28.8 | 188.5 | −52.4 | −629.5 | −178.2 | −172.0 | −990.1 | −1,552.0 | −1,306.3 | 1,028.2 | .... |
| Services, credit (exports) | 1b9cx | 338.4 | 414.5 | 485.8 | 581.8 | 519.9 | 417.2 | 485.9 | 621.3 | 963.4 | 710.6 | 575.5 | .... |
| Services, debit (imports) | 1b9dx | 503.7 | 475.9 | 523.2 | 472.4 | 628.5 | 571.8 | 788.7 | 1,784.6 | 2,065.0 | 2,039.0 | 2,163.0 | .... |
| Balance on Goods & Services | 1z9bx | −194.2 | −90.2 | 151.0 | 57.0 | −738.0 | −332.8 | −474.9 | −2,153.4 | −2,653.6 | −2,634.7 | −559.3 | .... |
| Primary income: credit | 1c9cx | 16.5 | 10.7 | 17.4 | 53.5 | 16.5 | 24.3 | 28.9 | 43.7 | 57.2 | 51.9 | 57.1 | .... |
| Primary income: debit | 1c9dx | 27.7 | 61.4 | 161.9 | 151.0 | 189.3 | 219.8 | 627.8 | 887.1 | 1,005.3 | 750.9 | 1,045.6 | .... |
| Balance on gds, serv. & prim. inc. | 1y9bx | −205.3 | −140.9 | 6.5 | −40.5 | −910.8 | −528.2 | −1,073.8 | −2,996.8 | −3,601.7 | −3,333.8 | −1,547.9 | .... |
| Secondary income: credit | 1d9ca | 230.9 | 177.6 | 179.8 | 303.8 | 378.4 | 260.3 | 309.4 | 452.4 | 501.8 | 343.9 | 327.4 | .... |
| Secondary income: debit | 1d9da | 50.2 | 41.2 | 77.4 | 91.5 | 157.7 | 74.6 | 122.4 | 214.3 | 262.4 | 202.1 | 184.4 | .... |
| B. Capital Account* | 209ba | — | .... | .... | — | 83.3 | 160.5 | 141.7 | 113.9 | 120.4 | 125.8 | 100.0 | .... |
| Capital account: credit | 209ca | — | .... | .... | — | 83.8 | 160.5 | 142.4 | 116.9 | 122.6 | 129.1 | 101.2 | .... |
| Capital account: debit | 209da | — | .... | .... | — | .5 | — | .7 | 3.1 | 2.2 | 3.4 | 1.2 | .... |
| Balance on current & capital acct. | 129ba | −24.6 | −4.5 | 109.0 | 171.8 | −606.8 | −182.1 | −745.0 | −2,644.8 | −3,241.9 | −3,066.3 | −1,305.0 | .... |
| C. Financial Account* | 309na | 23.2 | −45.6 | −181.4 | −276.0 | −1,147.6 | −608.5 | −1,592.3 | −2,748.7 | −4,809.0 | −1,323.6 | −963.1 | .... |
| Direct investment: assets | 3a9aa | — | .... | .... | 12.8 | 6.2 | 53.8 | 61.7 | 94.5 | 44.0 | 41.5 | 107.9 | .... |
| Equity & investment fund shares | 3aaaa | .... | .... | .... | 1.1 | 6.4 | −.4 | 46.1 | 60.9 | 43.2 | 36.5 | 104.4 | .... |
| Debt instruments | 3abaa | .... | .... | .... | 11.7 | −.2 | 54.2 | 15.6 | 33.6 | .8 | 5.0 | 3.6 | .... |
| Direct investment: liabilities | 3a9la | 92.9 | 184.6 | 344.0 | 372.8 | 844.7 | 623.6 | 1,692.2 | 4,712.8 | 4,451.8 | 2,150.9 | 383.9 | .... |
| Equity & investment fund shares | 3aala | 92.9 | 184.6 | 344.0 | 322.8 | 828.5 | 488.0 | 1,331.8 | 1,499.4 | 1,487.5 | 376.8 | 30.9 | .... |
| Debt instruments | 3abla | .... | .... | .... | 49.9 | 16.2 | 135.6 | 360.4 | 3,213.4 | 2,964.3 | 1,774.1 | 353.0 | .... |
| Portfolio investment: assets | 3b9aa | 2.5 | .... | .... | 1.2 | 51.2 | 138.8 | −143.2 | −20.9 | 33.9 | 11.9 | 40.5 | .... |
| Equity & investment fund shares | 3baaa | 2.5 | .... | .... | .3 | 25.1 | 6.4 | 12.9 | 20.0 | 33.5 | 7.9 | 38.2 | .... |
| Debt securities | 3bbaa | .... | .... | .... | .9 | 26.1 | 132.4 | −156.2 | −40.9 | .3 | 4.0 | 2.2 | .... |
| Portfolio investment: liabilities | 3b9la | −50.0 | .... | .... | 76.0 | 14.8 | 56.7 | 751.0 | 56.0 | 2,359.3 | −144.2 | 318.4 | .... |
| Equity & investment fund shares | 3bala | .... | .... | .... | .8 | 13.4 | 3.6 | 680.3 | 9.3 | 15.3 | 3.1 | −1.3 | .... |
| Debt securities | 3bbla | −50.0 | .... | .... | 75.2 | 1.3 | 53.1 | 70.7 | 46.8 | 2,344.0 | −147.3 | 319.7 | .... |
| Fin. der.& empl.stk.ops.(ESOs): net | 3c9na | .... | .... | .... | — | — | — | — | — | — | — | −1.1 | .... |
| Fin. der. & ESOs.: assets | 3c9aa | .... | .... | .... | .... | — | — | — | — | — | — | 3.3 | .... |
| Fin. der. & ESOs.: liabilities | 3c9la | .... | .... | .... | .... | — | — | — | — | — | — | 4.4 | .... |
| Other investment: assets | 3d9aa | 132.2 | 124.8 | 223.4 | 207.8 | −64.5 | 144.8 | 1,040.2 | 2,383.8 | 2,483.6 | 1,460.3 | 886.8 | .... |
| Other equity | 3daaa | .... | .... | .... | .... | .... | .... | .... | .... | .... | .... | .... | .... |
| Debt instruments | 3dzaa | 132.2 | 124.8 | 223.4 | 207.8 | −64.5 | 144.8 | 1,040.2 | 2,383.8 | 2,483.6 | 1,460.3 | 886.8 | .... |
| Other investment: liabilities | 3d9la | 68.6 | −14.2 | 60.8 | 49.0 | 281.2 | 265.6 | 107.8 | 437.1 | 559.4 | 830.6 | 1,294.9 | .... |
| Other equity | 3dala | .... | .... | .... | .... | .... | .... | .... | .... | .... | .... | .... | .... |
| Debt instruments | 3dzla | 68.6 | −14.2 | 60.8 | 49.0 | 281.2 | 265.6 | 107.8 | 437.1 | 559.4 | 830.6 | 1,294.9 | .... |
| Curr.+ cap.− finan. acct. balance | 4y9na | −47.7 | 41.1 | 290.4 | 447.8 | 540.8 | 426.4 | 847.2 | 103.9 | 1,567.2 | −1,742.6 | −341.8 | .... |
| D. Net Errors and Omissions | 409na | 1.4 | −75.5 | −7.9 | −158.7 | −773.9 | 128.4 | 27.6 | −76.1 | 137.2 | −124.2 | −129.1 | .... |
| E. Reserves and Related Items | 4z9na | −46.3 | −34.4 | 282.5 | 289.1 | −233.1 | 554.7 | 874.8 | 27.9 | 1,704.4 | −1,866.8 | −471.0 | .... |
| Reserve assets | 3e9aa | 34.4 | 48.5 | 389.2 | 282.6 | −237.7 | 712.5 | 893.6 | 24.0 | 1,669.6 | −1,959.6 | −532.5 | .... |
| Credit and loans from the IMF | 3dcla | −7.2 | −5.9 | −5.9 | −6.6 | −5.1 | 157.8 | 18.7 | −3.9 | −34.7 | −92.8 | −61.5 | .... |
| Exceptional financing | 409la | 88.0 | 88.8 | 112.6 | — | .4 | — | — | — | — | — | — | .... |

*Excludes components in group E

## International Investment Position

*Millions of US Dollars*

| | | 2004 | 2005 | 2006 | 2007 | 2008 | 2009 | 2010 | 2011 | 2012 | 2013 | 2014 | 2015 |
|---|---|---|---|---|---|---|---|---|---|---|---|---|---|
| Assets | 809aa | .... | .... | .... | .... | .... | .... | 6,549.4 | 5,420.5 | 6,379.9 | 4,004.9 | 3,437.6 | .... |
| Direct investment | 8a9aa | .... | .... | .... | .... | .... | .... | 2,901.4 | 1,857.1 | 1,191.4 | 257.7 | 354.8 | .... |
| Equity & investment fund shares | 8aaaa | .... | .... | .... | .... | .... | .... | 2,899.5 | 1,857.1 | 1,190.6 | 252.0 | 347.5 | .... |
| Debt instruments | 8abaa | .... | .... | .... | .... | .... | .... | 1.9 | .... | .8 | 5.7 | 7.3 | .... |
| Portfolio investment | 8b9aa | .... | .... | .... | .... | .... | .... | 45.4 | 24.9 | 105.6 | 387.3 | 280.4 | .... |
| Equity & investment fund shares | 8baaa | .... | .... | .... | .... | .... | .... | .4 | 20.6 | 100.9 | 378.8 | 205.0 | .... |
| Debt securities | 8bbaa | .... | .... | .... | .... | .... | .... | 45.1 | 4.3 | 4.7 | 8.5 | 75.4 | .... |
| Fin. der.(oth.than reserves) & ESOs | 8c9aa | .... | .... | .... | .... | .... | .... | — | 1.5 | .... | .... | 8.6 | .... |
| Other investment | 8d9aa | .... | .... | .... | .... | .... | .... | 1,314.2 | 1,086.2 | 957.0 | 1,112.0 | 1,143.6 | .... |
| Other equity | 8daaa | .... | .... | .... | .... | .... | .... | .... | .... | .... | .... | .... | .... |
| Debt instruments | 8dzaa | .... | .... | .... | .... | .... | .... | 1,314.2 | 1,086.2 | 957.0 | 1,112.0 | 1,143.6 | .... |
| Reserve assets | 8e9aa | .... | .... | .... | .... | .... | .... | 2,288.3 | 2,450.8 | 4,125.9 | 2,247.8 | 1,650.2 | .... |
| Liabilities | 809la | .... | .... | .... | .... | .... | .... | 8,227.4 | 13,649.1 | 20,755.4 | 24,509.8 | 27,129.4 | .... |
| Direct investment | 8a9la | .... | .... | .... | .... | .... | .... | 4,949.5 | 9,675.1 | 13,458.2 | 15,729.2 | 16,692.8 | .... |
| Equity & investment fund shares | 8aala | .... | .... | .... | .... | .... | .... | 2,234.2 | 3,924.7 | 5,100.9 | 5,388.2 | 6,078.1 | .... |
| Debt instruments | 8abla | .... | .... | .... | .... | .... | .... | 2,715.3 | 5,750.4 | 8,357.4 | 10,341.0 | 10,614.7 | .... |
| Portfolio investment | 8b9la | .... | .... | .... | .... | .... | .... | 275.2 | 337.3 | 2,689.4 | 2,470.2 | 2,913.4 | .... |
| Equity & investment fund shares | 8bala | .... | .... | .... | .... | .... | .... | 65.2 | 94.6 | 112.9 | 34.8 | 94.1 | .... |
| Debt securities | 8bbla | .... | .... | .... | .... | .... | .... | 210.1 | 242.8 | 2,576.5 | 2,435.4 | 2,819.2 | .... |
| Fin. der.(oth.than reserves) & ESOs | 8c9la | .... | .... | .... | .... | .... | .... | — | 1.5 | .... | .... | 12.0 | .... |
| Other investment | 8d9la | .... | .... | .... | .... | .... | .... | 3,002.6 | 3,635.3 | 4,607.8 | 6,310.4 | 7,511.2 | .... |
| Other equity | 8dala | .... | .... | .... | .... | .... | .... | .... | .... | .... | .... | .... | .... |
| Debt instruments | 8dzla | .... | .... | .... | .... | .... | .... | 3,002.6 | 3,635.3 | 4,607.8 | 6,310.4 | 7,511.2 | .... |

# Mongolia   948

| | | 2004 | 2005 | 2006 | 2007 | 2008 | 2009 | 2010 | 2011 | 2012 | 2013 | 2014 | 2015 |
|---|---|---|---|---|---|---|---|---|---|---|---|---|---|
| **Government Finance** | | | | | | | | | | | | | |
| **Cash Flow Statement** | | | | | | | | | | | | | |
| **General Government** | | | | | | *Billions of Togrogs: Fiscal Year Ends December 31* | | | | | | |
| Cash Receipts:Operating Activities... | c1 | 692.0 | 832.2 | 1,358.8 | 1,848.7 | 2,153.0 | 1,990.0 | 3,065.3 | 4,142.8 | 4,849.4 | 5,875.8 | 6,197.9 | 5,919.1 |
| Taxes.............................. | c11 | 499.2 | 596.6 | 1,016.2 | 1,342.3 | 1,666.8 | 1,181.0 | 2,113.1 | 2,727.0 | 2,983.8 | 3,624.9 | 3,548.4 | 3,342.7 |
| Social Contributions...................... | c12 | 79.6 | 93.5 | 111.9 | 158.4 | 223.3 | 257.3 | 321.7 | 450.4 | 688.0 | 861.0 | 971.4 | 1,038.8 |
| Grants................................. | c13 | 6.1 | 3.1 | 4.7 | 5.0 | 15.9 | 24.5 | 34.6 | 1.5 | 24.7 | — | 118.2 | 39.2 |
| Other Receipts............................. | c14 | 107.1 | 139.1 | 226.0 | 342.9 | 247.2 | 527.2 | 596.0 | 963.8 | 1,152.9 | 1,389.9 | 1,559.9 | 1,498.4 |
| Cash Payments:Operating Activities. | c2 | 525.8 | 589.0 | 804.8 | 1,202.1 | 1,749.6 | 1,792.1 | 2,254.2 | 3,234.4 | 4,452.1 | 4,690.6 | 5,226.6 | 5,907.6 |
| Compensation of Employees.......... | c21 | 129.4 | 142.8 | 196.6 | 292.5 | 543.1 | 578.9 | 650.6 | 801.2 | 1,196.9 | 1,531.3 | 1,566.9 | 1,937.5 |
| Purchases of Goods & Services....... | c22 | 215.7 | 232.4 | 318.4 | 383.5 | 487.6 | 390.7 | 518.9 | 726.9 | 875.9 | 993.6 | 1,030.7 | 1,115.4 |
| Interest................................. | c24 | 22.1 | 20.7 | 18.1 | 18.3 | 19.8 | 29.0 | 41.9 | 37.3 | 126.4 | 270.5 | 500.4 | 731.1 |
| Subsidies................................. | c25 | 11.3 | 8.7 | 12.3 | 15.5 | 71.0 | 31.0 | 68.2 | 96.9 | 83.6 | 157.2 | 143.2 | 138.1 |
| Grants................................. | c26 | — | — | — | — | — | 1.7 | 1.8 | 3.0 | 2.1 | 26.0 | 40.3 | 3.2 |
| Social Benefits.......................... | c27 | 147.3 | 184.4 | 259.5 | 492.4 | 628.1 | 616.2 | 816.8 | 1,401.9 | 1,850.2 | 1,516.8 | 1,748.7 | 1,978.3 |
| Other Payments............................. | c28 | — | — | — | — | — | 144.7 | 156.0 | 167.3 | 316.9 | 195.2 | 196.3 | 4.0 |
| Net Cash Inflow:Operating Act.[1-2] | ccio | 166.2 | 243.2 | 554.0 | 646.6 | 403.5 | 198.0 | 811.2 | 908.4 | 397.3 | 1,185.2 | 971.3 | 11.5 |
| Net Cash Outflow:Invest. in NFA...... | c31 | 104.7 | 84.2 | 174.0 | 446.2 | 620.5 | 455.0 | 559.3 | 1,050.4 | 1,445.3 | 1,445.6 | 1,738.2 | 1,337.3 |
| Purchases of Nonfinancial Assets... | c31.1 | 105.5 | 85.3 | 175.7 | 448.8 | 624.9 | 457.9 | 567.2 | 1,067.2 | 1,460.7 | 1,447.3 | 1,739.9 | 1,338.0 |
| Sales of Nonfinancial Assets........... | c31.2 | .8 | 1.1 | 1.6 | 2.5 | 4.4 | 3.0 | 8.0 | 16.8 | 15.4 | 1.7 | 1.7 | .7 |
| Cash Surplus/Deficit [1-2-31=1-2M] | ccsd | 61.5 | 159.0 | 379.9 | 200.3 | −217.0 | −257.0 | 251.9 | −142.0 | −1,048.0 | −260.5 | −766.9 | −1,325.8 |
| Net Acq. Fin. Assets, excl. Cash...... | c32x | 86.0 | 98.6 | 79.0 | 100.7 | 19.9 | 62.2 | 251.8 | 489.0 | 87.8 | 168.1 | 41.4 | −5.1 |
| Domestic................................. | c321x | 86.0 | 98.6 | 79.0 | 100.7 | 19.9 | 62.2 | 251.8 | 489.0 | 87.8 | 168.1 | 41.4 | −5.1 |
| Foreign................................. | c322x | — | — | — | — | — | — | — | — | — | — | — | — |
| Net Incurrence of Liabilities.............. | c33 | 27.1 | — | −87.2 | 79.9 | 324.6 | 828.3 | 23.3 | 816.0 | 2,736.1 | 697.8 | 659.5 | 1,046.5 |
| Domestic................................. | c331 | −56.7 | — | −155.9 | — | 281.6 | 385.0 | 97.4 | 774.9 | 480.5 | 882.8 | 441.4 | 558.5 |
| Foreign................................. | c332 | 83.8 | — | 68.7 | 79.9 | 43.0 | 443.3 | −74.1 | 41.1 | 2,255.7 | −185.1 | 218.1 | 487.9 |
| Net Cash Inflow, Fin.Act.[-32x+33].. | cnfb | −58.9 | −98.6 | −166.2 | −20.9 | 304.7 | 766.1 | −228.5 | 327.0 | 2,648.3 | 529.7 | 618.1 | 1,051.5 |
| Net Change in Stock of Cash........... | cncb | .... | .... | 213.7 | 179.5 | 87.7 | 509.1 | 23.4 | 185.0 | 1,600.3 | 269.2 | −148.8 | −274.3 |
| Stat. Discrep. [32X-33+NCB-CSD].... | ccsdz | .... | .... | — | — | — | — | — | — | — | — | | |
| Memo Item:Cash Expenditure[2+31] | c2m | 630.5 | 673.1 | 978.9 | 1,648.3 | 2,370.0 | 2,247.0 | 2,813.4 | 4,284.8 | 5,897.4 | 6,136.3 | 6,964.7 | 7,244.9 |
| Memo Item: Gross Debt.................. | c63 | .... | .... | .... | .... | .... | .... | .... | .... | .... | .... | .... | .... |
| **National Accounts** | | | | | | *Millions of Togrogs* | | | | | | |
| Househ.Cons.Expend.,incl.NPISHs.... | 96f | 1,559,875 | 1,702,808 | 1,949,408 | 2,458,606 | 3,686,403 | 3,851,266 | 4,572,651 | 5,583,511 | 7,499,769 | 10,508,495 | .... | .... |
| Government Consumption Expend... | 91f | 312,843 | 344,488 | 426,293 | 598,566 | 959,880 | 930,206 | 1,098,117 | 1,370,048 | 1,883,665 | 2,665,864 | .... | .... |
| Gross Fixed Capital Formation.......... | 93e | 656,855 | 849,709 | 1,341,268 | 1,740,220 | 2,374,102 | 1,903,969 | 2,738,308 | 5,472,654 | 7,206,640 | 7,634,503 | .... | .... |
| Changes in Inventories.................... | 93i | 79,429 | 291,687 | 104,029 | 178,257 | 481,906 | 361,296 | 694,363 | 1,458,141 | 1,646,439 | 2,420,568 | .... | .... |
| Exports of Goods and Services......... | 90c | 1,435,295 | 1,787,415 | 2,394,112 | 2,954,878 | 3,541,124 | 3,313,640 | 4,602,725 | 6,912,279 | 7,102,502 | 7,651,259 | .... | .... |
| Imports of Goods and Services (-)..... | 98c | 1,665,597 | 1,934,701 | 2,154,209 | 2,888,039 | 4,404,096 | 3,791,973 | 5,246,600 | 9,628,492 | 10,717,953 | 11,554,517 | .... | .... |
| Gross Domestic Product (GDP)........ | 99b | 2,378,699 | 3,041,406 | 4,060,901 | 5,042,489 | 6,639,320 | 6,568,403 | 8,459,564 | 11,168,141 | 14,621,061 | 19,326,172 | .... | .... |
| Net Primary Income from Abroad..... | 98.n | −13,106 | −62,420 | −50,331 | −114,163 | −201,986 | −281,572 | −760,081 | −917,799 | −921,656 | .... | .... | .... |
| Gross National Income (GNI)........... | 99a | 2,348,051 | 2,978,985 | 3,977,227 | 4,842,484 | 6,353,583 | 6,309,065 | 7,654,423 | 10,020,494 | 13,022,583 | | .... | .... |
| GDP Volume 2005 Prices................. | 99b.p | 2,835,713 | 3,041,406 | 3,301,636 | 3,639,988 | 3,963,960 | 3,913,673 | 4,162,785 | 4,891,840 | 5,492,723 | 6,144,175 | .... | .... |
| GDP Volume (2010=100)................. | 99bvp | 68.1 | 73.1 | 79.3 | 87.4 | 95.2 | 94.0 | 100.0 | 117.5 | 131.9 | 147.6 | .... | .... |
| GDP Deflator (2010=100)............... | 99bip | 41.3 | 49.2 | 60.5 | 68.2 | 82.4 | 82.6 | 100.0 | 112.3 | 131.0 | 154.8 | .... | .... |
| | | | | | | *Millions: Midyear Estimates* | | | | | | | |
| Population.............................. | 99z | 2.50 | 2.53 | 2.56 | 2.59 | 2.63 | 2.67 | 2.71 | 2.76 | 2.81 | 2.86 | 2.91 | 2.96 |

| | | 2004 | 2005 | 2006 | 2007 | 2008 | 2009 | 2010 | 2011 | 2012 | 2013 | 2014 | 2015 |
|---|---|---|---|---|---|---|---|---|---|---|---|---|---|
| **Exchange Rates** | | *Euros per SDR: End of Period* | | | | | | | | | | | |
| Market Rate................................. | aa | 1.1402 | 1.2116 | 1.1423 | 1.0735 | 1.1068 | 1.0882 | 1.1525 | 1.1865 | 1.1649 | 1.1167 | 1.1933 | 1.2728 |
| | | *Euros per US Dollar: End of Period (ae) Period Average (rf)* | | | | | | | | | | | |
| Market Rate................................. | ae | .7342 | .8477 | .7593 | .6793 | .7185 | .6942 | .7484 | .7729 | .7579 | .7251 | .8237 | .9185 |
| Market Rate................................. | rf | .8054 | .8041 | .7971 | .7306 | .6827 | .7198 | .7550 | .7194 | .7783 | .7532 | .7537 | .9017 |
| **Fund Position** | | *Millions of SDRs: End of Period* | | | | | | | | | | | |
| Quota................................. | 2f.s | — | — | — | 27.50 | 27.50 | 27.50 | 27.50 | 27.50 | 27.50 | 27.50 | 27.50 | 27.50 |
| SDR Holdings................................. | 1b.s | — | — | — | .12 | .29 | 26.15 | 26.16 | 26.19 | 26.23 | 26.34 | 26.35 | 26.35 |
| Reserve Position in the Fund............. | 1c.s | — | — | — | 6.60 | 6.60 | 6.60 | 6.60 | 6.60 | 6.60 | 6.60 | 6.60 | 6.60 |
| Total Fund Cred.&Loans Outstg........ | 2tl | — | — | — | — | — | — | — | — | — | — | — | — |
| SDR Allocations................................. | 1bd | — | — | — | — | — | 25.82 | 25.82 | 25.82 | 25.82 | 25.82 | 25.82 | 25.82 |
| **International Liquidity** | | *Millions of US Dollars Unless Otherwise Indicated: End of Period* | | | | | | | | | | | |
| Total Reserves minus Gold.............. | 1l.d | 81.80 | 203.99 | 432.67 | 688.84 | 435.67 | 572.61 | 556.16 | 392.69 | 458.67 | 583.98 | 661.40 | 733.51 |
| SDR Holdings................................. | 1b.d | — | — | — | .20 | .45 | 40.99 | 40.29 | 40.20 | 40.32 | 40.56 | 38.17 | 36.51 |
| Reserve Position in the Fund.......... | 1c.d | — | — | — | 10.43 | 10.17 | 10.35 | 10.17 | 10.13 | 10.15 | 10.17 | 9.56 | 9.15 |
| Foreign Exchange............................ | 1d.d | 81.80 | 203.99 | 432.67 | 678.21 | 425.05 | 521.27 | 505.70 | 342.36 | 408.20 | 533.25 | 613.66 | 687.86 |
| Gold (Million Fine Troy Ounces)....... | 1ad | — | — | .04 | — | — | — | — | — | — | — | — | — |
| Gold (National Valuation)................ | 1and | — | — | 24.46 | — | — | — | — | — | — | — | — | — |
| Monetary Authorities: Other Liabs.... | 4..d | — | — | — | — | — | 40.48 | 39.77 | 39.64 | 39.69 | 39.77 | 37.41 | 35.79 |
| Banking Institutions: Assets............. | 7a.d | 84.41 | 195.75 | 374.94 | 503.50 | 347.94 | 472.23 | 533.36 | 589.84 | 716.55 | 773.40 | 744.16 | 642.93 |
| Banking Institutions: Liabs............... | 7b.d | 109.82 | 145.92 | 415.46 | 1,176.09 | 1,497.95 | 1,749.95 | 1,497.57 | 1,244.80 | 1,039.80 | 922.97 | 996.63 | 808.13 |
| **Monetary Authorities** | | *Thousands of Euros: End of Period* | | | | | | | | | | | |
| Foreign Assets................................. | 11 | 60,054 | 172,918 | 310,306 | 467,929 | 313,049 | 397,482 | 416,221 | 303,497 | 347,890 | 423,671 | 544,762 | 673,820 |
| Claims on Central Government........ | 12a | 9,693 | 12,860 | 1,543 | 150 | 218 | 487 | 550 | 653 | 702 | 801 | 791 | 786 |
| Claims on Other General Govt......... | 12b | 44 | 45 | 34 | 608 | 380 | 395 | — | 2 | 1 | 8 | 47 | 75 |
| Claims on Private Sector................. | 12d | 197 | 195 | 499 | 457 | 2,304 | 3,043 | 3,442 | 3,334 | 3,242 | 3,192 | 3,204 | 3,130 |
| Claims on Banking Institutions......... | 12e | 1,010 | 2,108 | 646 | 490 | 583 | 777 | 718 | 698 | 540 | 612 | 446 | 465 |
| Claims on Nonbank Financial Insts... | 12g | 107 | 95 | 91 | 92 | 100 | 99 | 104 | 122 | 115 | 116 | 198 | 201 |
| Bankers Deposits............................ | 14c | 40,942 | 101,301 | 233,942 | 342,546 | 262,512 | 238,312 | 276,233 | 206,430 | 236,408 | 318,531 | 415,548 | 524,333 |
| Demand Deposits............................ | 14d | 203 | 1,281 | 2,646 | 180 | 178 | 126 | 177 | 172 | 2,854 | 3,815 | 183 | 4,499 |
| Time, Savings,& Fgn.Currency Dep... | 15 | — | — | — | 5,969 | 11,594 | 12,857 | 18,493 | 21,374 | 27,852 | 34,880 | 45,651 | 50,356 |
| Restricted Deposits......................... | 16b | 1,013 | 1,104 | 221 | 48 | 13 | 1 | — | 1 | 2 | 1 | 1 | 1 |
| Foreign Liabilities........................... | 16c | — | — | — | — | — | 28,100 | 29,761 | 30,639 | 30,079 | 28,835 | 30,814 | 32,928 |
| Central Government Deposits.......... | 16d | 7,519 | 52,067 | 58,563 | 97,502 | 11,452 | 96,649 | 71,279 | 18,976 | 24,753 | 12,753 | 26,011 | 31,180 |
| Capital Accounts............................ | 17a | 33,875 | 34,391 | 39,364 | 44,453 | 51,441 | 46,476 | 47,230 | 60,683 | 60,130 | 58,808 | 59,776 | 61,245 |
| Other Items (Net)............................ | 17r | −12,447 | −1,924 | −21,618 | −20,971 | −20,556 | −20,237 | −22,139 | −29,969 | −29,588 | −29,224 | −28,537 | −26,068 |
| **Banking Institutions** | | *Thousands of Euros: End of Period* | | | | | | | | | | | |
| Reserves................................. | 20 | 41,572 | 101,295 | 233,777 | 342,438 | 262,165 | 238,299 | 276,160 | 206,074 | 236,234 | 318,350 | 415,105 | 524,145 |
| Foreign Assets................................. | 21 | 61,974 | 165,934 | 284,689 | 342,028 | 250,010 | 327,802 | 399,159 | 455,862 | 543,091 | 560,804 | 612,933 | 591,491 |
| Claims on Central Government........ | 22a | 28,379 | 22,968 | 19,176 | 9,362 | 6,328 | 48,515 | 57,313 | 122,207 | 133,092 | 203,017 | 213,504 | 327,161 |
| Claims on Other General Govt......... | 22b | 9,191 | 15,512 | 27,004 | 24,560 | 24,018 | 56,400 | 34,128 | 59,573 | 45,329 | 44,063 | 36,515 | 56,937 |
| Claims on Nonfin.Pub.Enterprises.... | 22c | 18,379 | 27,109 | 33,335 | 32,287 | 37,599 | 44,967 | 60,077 | 55,297 | 57,055 | 55,453 | 49,335 | 50,738 |
| Claims on Private Sector................. | 22d | 244,059 | 325,641 | 779,642 | 2,150,896 | 2,682,780 | 2,278,516 | 2,073,852 | 1,801,897 | 1,748,482 | 1,780,562 | 1,773,691 | 1,816,864 |
| Claims on Nonbank Financial Insts... | 22g | 4,823 | 760 | 9,073 | 32,429 | 42,709 | 27,830 | 29,480 | 25,362 | 18,373 | 9,620 | 15,520 | 18,928 |
| Demand Deposits............................ | 24 | 124,374 | 214,925 | 490,438 | 791,196 | 576,480 | 534,199 | 586,056 | 578,728 | 610,435 | 696,037 | 770,604 | 980,559 |
| Time, Savings,& Fgn.Currency Dep... | 25 | 98,267 | 192,445 | 402,502 | 983,480 | 1,012,500 | 909,730 | 899,287 | 931,704 | 1,012,034 | 1,000,359 | 1,092,445 | 1,104,008 |
| Foreign Liabilities........................... | 26c | 80,629 | 123,689 | 315,459 | 798,923 | 1,257,419 | 1,039,548 | 931,595 | 803,618 | 699,540 | 722,668 | 686,507 | 743,478 |
| Central Government Deposits.......... | 26d | 23,387 | 34,675 | 41,111 | 57,382 | 69,988 | 92,854 | 81,418 | 52,268 | 58,083 | 54,441 | 66,317 | 87,479 |
| Credit from Monetary Authorities..... | 26g | 1,387 | 1,010 | 662 | 552 | 435 | 344 | 214 | 107 | 22 | — | — | — |
| Bonds................................. | 26n | — | — | — | 1,881 | 1,891 | 1,898 | 2,485 | 2,491 | 2,496 | — | — | — |
| Capital Accounts............................ | 27a | 90,765 | 106,958 | 148,763 | 236,941 | 279,376 | 331,734 | 310,906 | 317,920 | 288,685 | 389,393 | 440,514 | 465,179 |
| Other Items (Net)............................ | 27r | −10,434 | −14,482 | −12,236 | 63,644 | 107,507 | 112,023 | 118,208 | 39,438 | 110,360 | 108,969 | 60,219 | 5,560 |
| **Banking Survey** | | *Thousands of Euros: End of Period* | | | | | | | | | | | |
| Foreign Assets (Net)........................ | 31n | 41,399 | 215,163 | 279,536 | 11,034 | −694,360 | −342,364 | −145,976 | −74,898 | 161,362 | 232,972 | 440,374 | 488,905 |
| Domestic Credit............................ | 32 | 283,966 | 318,443 | 770,723 | 2,095,957 | 2,714,997 | 2,270,750 | 2,106,248 | 1,997,203 | 1,923,556 | 2,029,637 | 2,000,476 | 2,156,160 |
| Claims on Central Govt. (Net)........ | 32an | 7,166 | −50,914 | −78,955 | −145,372 | −74,893 | −140,501 | −94,835 | 51,616 | 50,959 | 136,623 | 121,966 | 209,288 |
| Claims on Other General Govt......... | 32b | 9,235 | 15,557 | 27,038 | 25,168 | 24,398 | 56,795 | 34,128 | 59,575 | 45,330 | 44,071 | 36,562 | 57,012 |
| Claims on Nonfin.Pub.Enterprises... | 32c | 18,379 | 27,109 | 33,335 | 32,287 | 37,599 | 44,967 | 60,077 | 55,297 | 57,055 | 55,453 | 49,335 | 50,738 |
| Claims on Private Sector............... | 32d | 244,256 | 325,836 | 780,141 | 2,151,353 | 2,685,084 | 2,281,559 | 2,077,294 | 1,805,231 | 1,751,724 | 1,783,754 | 1,776,895 | 1,819,994 |
| Claims on Nonbank Financial Insts. | 32g | 4,930 | 855 | 9,164 | 32,521 | 42,809 | 27,929 | 29,584 | 25,484 | 18,488 | 9,736 | 15,718 | 19,129 |
| Deposit Money................................. | 34 | 124,577 | 216,206 | 493,084 | 791,376 | 576,658 | 534,325 | 586,233 | 578,900 | 613,289 | 699,852 | 770,787 | 985,058 |
| Quasi-Money................................. | 35 | 98,267 | 192,445 | 402,502 | 989,449 | 1,024,094 | 922,587 | 917,780 | 953,078 | 1,039,886 | 1,035,239 | 1,138,096 | 1,154,364 |
| Restricted Deposits......................... | 36b | 1,013 | 1,104 | 221 | 48 | 13 | 1 | — | 1 | 2 | 1 | 1 | 1 |
| Bonds................................. | 36n | — | — | — | 1,881 | 1,891 | 1,898 | 2,485 | 2,491 | 2,496 | — | — | — |
| Capital Accounts............................ | 37a | 124,640 | 141,349 | 188,127 | 281,394 | 330,817 | 378,210 | 358,136 | 378,603 | 348,815 | 448,201 | 500,290 | 526,424 |
| Other Items (Net)............................ | 37r | −23,134 | −17,498 | −33,673 | 42,842 | 87,150 | 91,366 | 95,638 | 9,234 | 80,428 | 79,314 | 31,680 | −20,784 |
| Deposit Money plus Quasi-Money.... | 35l | 222,844 | 408,651 | 895,586 | 1,780,825 | 1,600,752 | 1,456,912 | 1,504,013 | 1,531,977 | 1,653,175 | 1,735,090 | 1,908,882 | 2,139,422 |
| **Interest Rates** | | *Percent Per Annum* | | | | | | | | | | | |
| Treasury Bill Rate............................ | 60c | 10.39 | 6.03 | 1.28 | .52 | .49 | 3.18 | 3.20 | 2.66 | 4.73 | 3.25 | 1.35 | .64 |
| Deposit Rate................................. | 60l | 4.87 | 4.84 | 5.06 | 5.08 | † 3.82 | 3.81 | 3.70 | 3.13 | 3.26 | 2.91 | 2.14 | 1.46 |
| Lending Rate................................. | 60p | .... | .... | 11.15 | 9.20 | 9.24 | 9.36 | 9.53 | 9.69 | 9.56 | 9.39 | 9.41 | 8.93 |

# Montenegro 943

| | | 2004 | 2005 | 2006 | 2007 | 2008 | 2009 | 2010 | 2011 | 2012 | 2013 | 2014 | 2015 |
|---|---|---|---|---|---|---|---|---|---|---|---|---|---|
| **Prices, Production, Tourism, & Labor** | | | | | | *Index Numbers (2010=100): Period Averages* | | | | | | | |
| Share Prices (End of Month)............. | 62.ep | 13.0 | 43.0 | 105.0 | 261.1 | 136.6 | 96.9 | 100.0 | 83.1 | 65.2 | 67.9 | 76.8 | 86.0 |
| Producer Prices............................ | 63 | .... | 81.2 | 84.3 | 91.6 | 106.3 | 100.5 | 100.0 | 103.7 | 105.7 | 107.6 | .... | .... |
| Consumer Prices........................... | 64 | .... | 82.2 | 84.6 | 88.3 | 96.0 | 99.3 | † 100.0 | 103.5 | 107.7 | 110.1 | 109.3 | 111.0 |
| Wages: Monthly Earnings............... | 65 | .... | 45.7 | 60.8 | 69.4 | 85.2 | 90.1 | 100.0 | 101.0 | 101.8 | 101.6 | 101.3 | 101.5 |
| Industrial Production...................... | 66 | .... | 126.9 | 128.1 | 128.1 | 125.6 | 85.1 | 100.0 | 89.7 | 83.5 | 92.3 | 81.8 | 88.2 |
| Number of Tourists........................ | 66t | .... | 65.0 | 75.5 | 89.7 | 94.1 | 95.6 | 100.0 | 108.7 | 114.0 | 118.1 | 120.1 | 135.6 |
| | | | | | | *Number in Thousands: Period Averages* | | | | | | | |
| Labor Force................................. | 67d | .... | 198 | 194 | 191 | 196 | 203 | 193 | 194 | 204 | 204 | .... | .... |
| Employment................................ | 67e | .... | 145 | 151 | 157 | 167 | 174 | 161 | 163 | 167 | 171 | 174 | .... |
| Unemployment............................. | 67c | .... | 54 | 42 | 34 | 29 | 29 | 32 | 31 | 30 | 32 | 33 | .... |
| Unemployment Rate (%)................. | 67r | .... | 27.4 | 22.3 | 18.0 | 15.1 | 14.0 | 16.5 | 15.9 | .... | .... | .... | .... |
| **Intl. Transactions & Positions** | | | | | | *Millions of Euros* | | | | | | | |
| Exports...................................... | 70 | .... | 369.3 | 441.1 | 454.7 | 416.2 | 277.0 | 330.4 | 454.4 | 366.8 | 375.6 | 338.0 | 317.1 |
| Imports, c.i.f................................. | 71 | .... | 1,042.8 | 1,457.4 | 2,073.1 | 2,529.7 | 1,654.2 | 1,657.3 | 1,823.3 | 1,799.6 | 1,773.3 | 1,783.6 | 1,840.4 |
| **Balance of Payments** | | | | | | *Millions of US Dollars* | | | | | | | |
| A. Current Account*....................... | 109bx | .... | .... | .... | −1,464.4 | −2,257.5 | −1,150.3 | −952.4 | −791.2 | −769.2 | † −649.0 | −698.7 | −531.6 |
| Goods, credit (exports)................... | 1a9cx | .... | .... | .... | 648.4 | 623.1 | 383.5 | 449.1 | 653.9 | 498.6 | † 525.3 | 473.1 | 360.4 |
| Goods, debit (imports)................... | 1a9dx | .... | .... | .... | 2,776.9 | 3,639.5 | 2,246.6 | 2,128.4 | 2,471.7 | 2,273.9 | † 2,289.5 | 2,300.8 | 1,981.4 |
| Balance on goods........................ | 1a9bx | .... | .... | .... | −2,128.5 | −3,016.4 | −1,863.2 | −1,679.4 | −1,817.8 | −1,775.3 | † −1,764.3 | −1,827.7 | −1,621.0 |
| Services, credit (exports)............... | 1b9cx | .... | .... | .... | 933.3 | 1,192.8 | 1,053.0 | 1,053.4 | 1,275.9 | 1,211.1 | † 1,317.3 | 1,368.5 | 1,346.6 |
| Services, debit (imports)............... | 1b9dx | .... | .... | .... | 393.7 | 609.0 | 467.0 | 450.7 | 447.6 | 448.9 | † 453.2 | 450.6 | 470.1 |
| Balance on Goods & Services....... | 1z9bx | .... | .... | .... | −1,588.9 | −2,432.6 | −1,277.1 | −1,076.6 | −989.4 | −1,013.1 | † −900.1 | −909.7 | −744.4 |
| Primary income: credit................... | 1c9cx | .... | .... | .... | 144.9 | 247.7 | 226.7 | 219.9 | 268.2 | 264.9 | † 282.4 | 300.1 | 274.7 |
| Primary income: debit................... | 1c9dx | .... | .... | .... | 102.2 | 179.8 | 219.5 | 247.3 | 232.9 | 195.2 | † 194.9 | 240.6 | 171.3 |
| Balance on gds, serv. & prim. inc. | 1y9bx | .... | .... | .... | −1,546.2 | −2,364.7 | −1,270.0 | −1,104.0 | −954.1 | −943.4 | † −812.7 | −850.2 | −641.0 |
| Secondary income: credit............... | 1d9ca | .... | .... | .... | 138.6 | 160.6 | 164.5 | 194.0 | 216.6 | 230.9 | † 249.5 | 243.9 | 190.5 |
| Secondary income: debit............... | 1d9da | .... | .... | .... | 56.8 | 53.4 | 44.8 | 42.3 | 53.6 | 56.8 | † 85.8 | 92.4 | 81.0 |
| B. Capital Account*....................... | 209ba | .... | .... | .... | −1.9 | −.4 | 2.7 | −.7 | −4.0 | 9.7 | † 3.5 | — | −.2 |
| Capital account: credit................... | 209ca | .... | .... | .... | 1.2 | — | 3.0 | .1 | .6 | 11.1 | † 3.7 | — | — |
| Capital account: debit................... | 209da | .... | .... | .... | 3.1 | .4 | .3 | .8 | 4.6 | 1.4 | † .3 | — | .2 |
| Balance on current & capital acct. | 129ba | .... | .... | .... | −1,466.3 | −2,257.9 | −1,147.6 | −953.1 | −795.2 | −759.6 | † −645.6 | −698.7 | −531.7 |
| C. Financial Account* | 309na | .... | .... | .... | −1,882.5 | −1,946.9 | −1,018.2 | −709.5 | −404.7 | −496.1 | † −420.4 | −320.1 | −279.2 |
| Direct investment: assets............... | 3a9aa | .... | .... | .... | 159.3 | 110.3 | 45.8 | 27.1 | 18.0 | 27.9 | † 17.6 | 27.9 | 12.4 |
| Equity & investment fund shares.. | 3aaaa | .... | .... | .... | 159.3 | 110.3 | 45.8 | 13.7 | 34.2 | 4.4 | † 4.9 | 10.6 | 12.2 |
| Debt instruments....................... | 3abaa | .... | .... | .... | — | — | — | 13.4 | −16.2 | 23.5 | † 12.8 | 17.3 | .2 |
| Direct investment: liabilities .......... | 3a9la | .... | .... | .... | 937.5 | 975.1 | 1,549.3 | 758.4 | 556.3 | 618.4 | † 446.5 | 496.8 | 699.7 |
| Equity & investment fund shares . | 3aala | .... | .... | .... | 723.6 | 623.2 | 1,359.1 | 565.6 | 437.6 | 534.9 | † 330.2 | 271.9 | 465.3 |
| Debt instruments....................... | 3abla | .... | .... | .... | 214.0 | 351.9 | 190.2 | 192.8 | 118.6 | 83.5 | † 116.3 | 224.9 | 234.5 |
| Portfolio investment: assets .......... | 3b9aa | .... | .... | .... | 11.7 | 16.1 | 52.5 | 4.1 | 19.8 | 26.1 | † 50.3 | 87.1 | −15.3 |
| Equity & investment fund shares | 3baaa | .... | .... | .... | 19.0 | 12.6 | 48.1 | −1.5 | 4.2 | 1.5 | † 10.7 | 48.9 | 24.2 |
| Debt securities.......................... | 3bbaa | .... | .... | .... | −7.3 | 3.5 | 4.4 | 5.6 | 15.6 | 24.5 | † 39.6 | 38.2 | −39.5 |
| Portfolio investment: liabilities....... | 3b9la | .... | .... | .... | 3.5 | −6.4 | −5.1 | 250.8 | 234.6 | −5.9 | † 108.4 | 207.6 | 116.9 |
| Equity & investment fund shares . | 3bala | .... | .... | .... | 3.5 | −6.2 | −5.1 | −7.8 | −15.1 | −.3 | † 14.2 | 16.2 | 10.4 |
| Debt securities........................... | 3bbla | .... | .... | .... | — | −.2 | — | 258.7 | 249.6 | −5.6 | † 94.2 | 191.4 | 106.5 |
| Fin. der.& empl.stk.ops.(ESOs): net. | 3c9na | .... | .... | .... | .... | .... | .... | .... | .... | .... | .... | .... | .... |
| Fin. der. & ESOs.: assets............... | 3c9aa | .... | .... | .... | .... | .... | .... | .... | .... | .... | .... | .... | .... |
| Fin. der. & ESOs.: liabilities.......... | 3c9la | .... | .... | .... | .... | .... | .... | .... | .... | .... | .... | .... | .... |
| Other investment: assets............... | 3d9aa | .... | .... | .... | 188.5 | 76.0 | 290.2 | 247.0 | 322.1 | 294.0 | † 111.6 | 245.6 | 541.2 |
| Other equity............................... | 3daaa | .... | .... | .... | .... | .... | .... | .... | .... | .... | .... | .... | .... |
| Debt instruments....................... | 3dzaa | .... | .... | .... | 188.5 | 76.0 | 290.2 | 247.0 | 322.1 | 294.0 | † 111.6 | 245.6 | 541.2 |
| Other investment: liabilities............ | 3d9la | .... | .... | .... | 1,300.9 | 1,180.5 | −137.4 | −21.5 | −26.3 | 231.6 | † 45.0 | −23.7 | .8 |
| Other equity............................... | 3dala | .... | .... | .... | .... | .... | .... | .... | .... | .... | .... | .... | .... |
| Debt instruments....................... | 3dzla | .... | .... | .... | 1,300.9 | 1,180.5 | −137.4 | −21.5 | −26.3 | 231.6 | † 45.0 | −23.7 | .8 |
| Curr.+ cap.− finan. acct. balance... | 4y9na | .... | .... | .... | 416.2 | −311.0 | −129.4 | −243.5 | −390.5 | −263.5 | † −225.2 | −378.6 | −252.6 |
| D. Net Errors and Omissions............ | 409na | .... | .... | .... | −248.5 | 123.4 | 257.3 | 256.9 | 241.2 | 316.2 | † 330.5 | 539.7 | 399.3 |
| E. Reserves and Related Items......... | 4z9na | .... | .... | .... | 167.7 | −187.6 | 127.9 | 13.4 | −149.4 | 52.7 | † 105.3 | 161.1 | 146.7 |
| Reserve assets........................... | 3e9aa | .... | .... | .... | 167.7 | −187.6 | 127.9 | 13.4 | −149.4 | 52.7 | † 105.3 | 161.1 | 146.7 |
| Credit and loans from the IMF........ | 3dcla | .... | .... | .... | — | — | — | — | — | — | † — | — | — |
| Exceptional financing..................... | 409la | .... | .... | .... | .... | .... | .... | .... | .... | .... | .... | .... | .... |

*Excludes components in group E

| **National Accounts** | | | | | | *Millions of Euros* | | | | | | | |
|---|---|---|---|---|---|---|---|---|---|---|---|---|---|
| Houseь.Cons.Expend.,incl.NPISHs.... | 96f | 1,221.1 | 1,267.9 | 1,660.9 | 2,369.0 | 2,814.8 | 2,503.7 | 2,557.2 | 2,663.1 | 2,632.4 | 2,723.7 | 2,774.8 | .... |
| Government Consumption Expend... | 91f | 439.2 | 543.4 | 580.0 | 539.3 | 698.1 | 661.4 | 690.4 | 687.7 | 671.1 | 654.9 | 669.9 | .... |
| Gross Fixed Capital Formation......... | 93e | 286.1 | 326.3 | 469.8 | 867.1 | 118.0 | 797.6 | 676.3 | 637.0 | 628.4 | 678.1 | 657.1 | .... |
| Changes in Inventories.................... | 93i | −8.4 | −4.6 | 77.0 | 39.0 | 74.7 | 10.8 | 4.0 | −5.9 | 26.6 | −18.8 | 42.1 | .... |
| Exports of Goods and Services......... | 90c | 701.7 | 790.4 | 1,061.0 | 1,189.9 | 1,218.2 | 9,575.0 | 1,157.7 | 1,382.6 | 1,389.4 | 1,390.1 | 1,388.1 | .... |
| Imports of Goods and Services (-)..... | 98c | 969.9 | 1,108.5 | 1,699.8 | 2,323.9 | 2,900.4 | 1,950.1 | 1,960.6 | 2,099.6 | 2,166.4 | 2,065.5 | 2,074.2 | .... |
| Gross Domestic Product (GDP)......... | 99b | 1,669.8 | 1,814.9 | 2,148.9 | 2,680.4 | 3,085.6 | 2,980.9 | 3,125.1 | 3,264.8 | 3,181.5 | 3,362.5 | 3,457.9 | .... |
| | | | | | | *Millions: Midyear Estimates* | | | | | | | |
| Population................................... | 99z | .62 | .62 | .62 | .62 | .62 | .62 | .62 | .62 | .62 | .62 | .63 | .63 |

| | | 2004 | 2005 | 2006 | 2007 | 2008 | 2009 | 2010 | 2011 | 2012 | 2013 | 2014 | 2015 |
|---|---|---|---|---|---|---|---|---|---|---|---|---|---|
| **Exchange Rates** | | | | | | *E. Caribbean Dollars per SDR: End of Period* | | | | | | | |
| Official Rate | aa | 4.1931 | 3.8590 | 4.0619 | 4.2667 | 4.1587 | 4.2328 | 4.1581 | 4.1452 | 4.1497 | 4.1580 | 3.9118 | 3.7415 |
| | | | | | | *E. Caribbean Dollars per US Dollar: End of Period (ae) Period Average (rf)* | | | | | | | |
| Official Rate | ae | 2.7000 | 2.7000 | 2.7000 | 2.7000 | 2.7000 | 2.7000 | 2.7000 | 2.7000 | 2.7000 | 2.7000 | 2.7000 | 2.7000 |
| Official Rate | rf | 2.7000 | 2.7000 | 2.7000 | 2.7000 | 2.7000 | 2.7000 | 2.7000 | 2.7000 | 2.7000 | 2.7000 | 2.7000 | 2.7000 |
| **International Liquidity** | | | | | | *Millions of US Dollars: End of Period* | | | | | | | |
| Total Reserves minus Gold | 1l.d | 14.10 | 13.95 | 14.56 | 14.50 | 11.67 | 14.30 | 16.82 | 24.81 | 32.08 | 40.51 | 45.10 | 51.47 |
| Foreign Exchange | 1d.d | 14.10 | 13.95 | 14.56 | 14.50 | 11.67 | 14.30 | 16.82 | 24.81 | 32.08 | 40.51 | 45.10 | 51.47 |
| Central Bank: Other Assets | 3..d | — | — | — | — | — | — | — | — | — | — | — | — |
| Central Bank: Other Liabs. | 4..d | — | — | — | — | — | — | — | — | — | — | — | — |
| Other Depository Corps.: Assets | 7a.d | 61.75 | 59.80 | 71.83 | 90.24 | 101.23 | 109.08 | 103.04 | 117.05 | 92.49 | 82.57 | 88.07 | 97.88 |
| Other Depository Corps.: Liabs. | 7b.d | 11.73 | 13.51 | 25.16 | 42.08 | 51.67 | 55.64 | 51.58 | 56.87 | 21.29 | 23.05 | 26.46 | 30.64 |
| **Central Bank** | | | | | | *Millions of E. Caribbean Dollars: End of Period* | | | | | | | |
| Net Foreign Assets | 11n | 38.07 | 37.74 | 41.09 | 40.84 | 33.30 | 40.57 | 47.82 | 69.48 | 86.63 | 109.38 | 121.77 | 138.96 |
| Claims on Nonresidents | 11 | 38.07 | 37.74 | 41.09 | 40.84 | 33.30 | 40.57 | 47.82 | 69.48 | 86.63 | 109.38 | 121.77 | 138.96 |
| Liabilities to Nonresidents | 16c | — | — | — | — | — | — | — | — | — | — | — | — |
| Claims on Other Depository Corps. | 12e | .02 | .01 | .02 | .02 | — | .01 | .02 | .02 | .01 | .02 | .03 | .04 |
| Net Claims on Central Government | 12an | −2.42 | −2.74 | −2.78 | −3.44 | −4.74 | −5.54 | −5.81 | −5.83 | −5.82 | −5.92 | −19.82 | −5.79 |
| Claims on Central Government | 12a | .93 | .83 | .97 | .86 | .11 | — | — | — | — | — | — | — |
| Liabilities to Central Government | 16d | 3.35 | 3.56 | 3.76 | 4.29 | 4.85 | 5.54 | 5.81 | 5.83 | 5.82 | 5.92 | 19.82 | 5.79 |
| Claims on Other Sectors | 12s | — | — | — | — | — | — | — | — | — | — | — | — |
| Claims on Other Financial Corps. | 12g | — | — | — | — | — | — | — | — | — | — | — | — |
| Claims on State & Local Govts. | 12b | — | — | — | — | — | — | — | — | — | — | — | — |
| Claims on Public Nonfin. Corps. | 12c | — | — | — | — | — | — | — | — | — | — | — | — |
| Claims on Private Sector | 12d | — | — | — | — | — | — | — | — | — | — | — | — |
| Monetary Base | 14 | 35.66 | 35.01 | 36.63 | 35.78 | 26.87 | 33.23 | 39.67 | 61.19 | 78.13 | 100.22 | 98.52 | 127.34 |
| Currency in Circulation | 14a | 15.32 | 16.07 | 16.67 | 17.43 | 14.22 | 17.80 | 18.80 | 26.33 | 29.43 | 22.80 | 22.16 | 24.75 |
| Liabs. to Other Depository Corps. | 14c | 20.35 | 18.94 | 19.96 | 18.35 | 12.64 | 15.43 | 20.87 | 34.86 | 48.70 | 77.42 | 76.36 | 102.59 |
| Liabilities to Other Sectors | 14d | — | — | — | — | — | — | — | — | — | — | — | — |
| Other Liabs. to Other Dep. Corps. | 14n | — | — | 1.70 | 1.65 | 1.70 | 1.81 | 2.35 | 2.48 | 2.69 | 3.26 | 3.45 | 5.87 |
| Dep. & Sec. Excl. f/Monetary Base | 14o | — | — | — | — | — | — | — | — | — | — | — | — |
| Deposits Included in Broad Money | 15 | — | — | — | — | — | — | — | — | — | — | — | — |
| Sec.Ot.th.Shares Incl.in Brd. Money | 16a | — | — | — | — | — | — | — | — | — | — | — | — |
| Deposits Excl. from Broad Money | 16b | — | — | — | — | — | — | — | — | — | — | — | — |
| Sec.Ot.th.Shares Excl.f/Brd.Money | 16s | — | — | — | — | — | — | — | — | — | — | — | — |
| Loans | 16l | — | — | — | — | — | — | — | — | — | — | — | — |
| Financial Derivatives | 16m | — | — | — | — | — | — | — | — | — | — | — | — |
| Shares and Other Equity | 17a | — | — | — | — | — | — | — | — | — | — | — | — |
| Other Items (Net) | 17r | — | — | — | — | — | — | — | — | — | — | — | — |
| Memo Item: | | | | | | | | | | | | | |
| Total Assets | 10ra | 39.01 | 38.57 | 42.08 | 41.72 | 33.42 | 40.58 | 47.84 | 69.50 | 86.64 | 109.40 | 121.79 | 139.00 |
| **Other Depository Corporations** | | | | | | *Millions of E. Caribbean Dollars: End of Period* | | | | | | | |
| Net Foreign Assets | 21n | 135.06 | 124.98 | 126.00 | 130.04 | 133.80 | 144.27 | 138.92 | 162.50 | 192.24 | 160.70 | 166.33 | 181.55 |
| Claims on Nonresidents | 21 | 166.73 | 161.45 | 193.95 | 243.64 | 273.32 | 294.51 | 278.20 | 316.05 | 249.72 | 222.93 | 237.78 | 264.27 |
| Liabilities to Nonresidents | 26c | 31.67 | 36.47 | 67.94 | 113.60 | 139.52 | 150.23 | 139.27 | 153.55 | 57.48 | 62.24 | 71.45 | 82.72 |
| Claims on Central Bank | 20 | 34.87 | 32.20 | 30.74 | 28.68 | 18.12 | 22.53 | 27.49 | 43.39 | 55.21 | 81.60 | 80.32 | 110.20 |
| Currency | 20a | 2.35 | 3.78 | 2.49 | 2.36 | 2.66 | 2.93 | 2.83 | 4.70 | 3.73 | 4.42 | 3.80 | 4.56 |
| Reserve Deposits and Securities | 20b | 32.51 | 28.42 | 28.25 | 26.33 | 15.46 | 19.59 | 24.67 | 38.69 | 51.47 | 77.19 | 76.51 | 105.64 |
| Other Claims | 20n | — | — | — | — | — | — | — | — | — | — | — | — |
| Net Claims on Central Government | 22an | −38.00 | −27.74 | −20.80 | −22.08 | −14.67 | −15.65 | −21.77 | −48.79 | −58.49 | −50.71 | −32.94 | −76.96 |
| Claims on Central Government | 22a | .97 | .77 | .75 | .72 | 1.76 | .48 | .42 | .22 | .13 | .07 | — | — |
| Liabilities to Central Government | 26d | 38.97 | 28.51 | 21.54 | 22.80 | 16.43 | 16.13 | 22.19 | 49.00 | 58.62 | 50.78 | 32.94 | 76.96 |
| Claims on Other Sectors | 22s | 24.52 | 28.35 | 33.64 | 40.46 | 46.22 | 53.19 | 61.76 | 68.36 | 75.14 | 66.86 | 67.13 | 70.76 |
| Claims on Other Financial Corps. | 22g | .81 | — | 1.26 | .70 | .10 | — | — | — | — | — | — | — |
| Claims on State & Local Govts. | 22b | — | — | — | — | — | — | — | — | — | — | — | — |
| Claims on Public Nonfin. Corps. | 22c | — | .28 | — | — | .04 | — | — | — | — | — | — | — |
| Claims on Private Sector | 22d | 23.71 | 28.07 | 32.38 | 39.77 | 46.09 | 53.19 | 61.76 | 68.36 | 75.14 | 66.86 | 67.13 | 70.76 |
| Liabilities to Central Bank | 26g | .37 | — | — | — | — | .02 | .02 | .02 | .01 | .02 | .03 | .04 |
| Transf.Dep.Included in Broad Money | 24 | 36.57 | 32.75 | 35.17 | 42.76 | 41.29 | 41.83 | 33.35 | 33.60 | 35.77 | 50.29 | 39.45 | 44.91 |
| Other Dep.Included in Broad Money | 25 | 94.64 | 105.04 | 110.64 | 109.00 | 114.89 | 131.29 | 140.39 | 156.17 | 187.25 | 166.60 | 202.54 | 198.65 |
| Sec.Ot.th.Shares Incl.in Brd. Money | 26a | — | — | — | — | — | — | — | — | — | — | — | — |
| Deposits Excl. from Broad Money | 26b | — | — | — | — | — | — | — | — | — | — | — | — |
| Sec.Ot.th.Shares Excl.f/Brd.Money | 26s | 1.00 | 1.00 | 1.00 | 1.00 | 1.00 | .91 | .91 | — | — | — | — | — |
| Loans | 26l | — | — | — | — | — | — | — | — | — | — | — | — |
| Financial Derivatives | 26m | — | — | — | — | — | — | — | — | — | — | — | — |
| Insurance Technical Reserves | 26r | — | — | — | — | — | — | — | — | — | — | — | — |
| Shares and Other Equity | 27a | 18.44 | 20.85 | 22.99 | 26.55 | 28.66 | 30.56 | 24.32 | 14.03 | 21.22 | 24.19 | 23.15 | 24.94 |
| Other Items (Net) | 27r | 5.42 | −1.85 | −.22 | −2.21 | −2.38 | −.27 | 7.43 | 21.64 | 19.84 | 17.36 | 15.67 | 17.03 |
| Memo Item: | | | | | | | | | | | | | |
| Total Assets | 20ra | 239.21 | 239.34 | 275.11 | 332.52 | 356.17 | 386.75 | 388.04 | 446.66 | 395.70 | 387.02 | 405.26 | 464.02 |

| | | 2004 | 2005 | 2006 | 2007 | 2008 | 2009 | 2010 | 2011 | 2012 | 2013 | 2014 | 2015 |
|---|---|---|---|---|---|---|---|---|---|---|---|---|---|
| **Depository Corporations** | | *Millions of E. Caribbean Dollars: End of Period* | | | | | | | | | | | |
| Net Foreign Assets........................... | 31n | 173.13 | 162.72 | 167.09 | 170.88 | 167.10 | 184.85 | 186.74 | 231.97 | 278.87 | 270.08 | 288.10 | 320.51 |
| Claims on Nonresidents................ | 31 | 204.80 | 199.19 | 235.04 | 284.48 | 306.62 | 335.08 | 326.01 | 385.52 | 336.35 | 332.32 | 359.55 | 403.23 |
| Liabilities to Nonresidents............. | 36c | 31.67 | 36.47 | 67.94 | 113.60 | 139.52 | 150.23 | 139.27 | 153.55 | 57.48 | 62.24 | 71.45 | 82.72 |
| Domestic Claims........................... | 32 | −15.90 | −2.13 | 10.06 | 14.95 | 26.81 | 32.00 | 34.18 | 13.74 | 10.83 | 10.23 | 14.37 | −11.98 |
| Net Claims on Central Government | 32an | −40.42 | −30.48 | −23.58 | −25.52 | −19.40 | −21.19 | −27.58 | −54.62 | −64.31 | −56.63 | −52.76 | −82.75 |
| Claims on Central Government.... | 32a | 1.90 | 1.59 | 1.72 | 1.57 | 1.88 | .48 | .42 | .22 | .13 | .07 | — | — |
| Liabilities to Central Government. | 36d | 42.32 | 32.07 | 25.30 | 27.09 | 21.28 | 21.67 | 28.00 | 54.84 | 64.44 | 56.70 | 52.76 | 82.75 |
| Claims on Other Sectors................ | 32s | 24.52 | 28.35 | 33.64 | 40.46 | 46.22 | 53.19 | 61.76 | 68.36 | 75.14 | 66.86 | 67.13 | 70.76 |
| Claims on Other Financial Corps.. | 32g | .81 | — | 1.26 | .70 | .10 | — | — | — | — | — | — | — |
| Claims on State & Local Govts..... | 32b | — | — | — | — | — | — | — | — | — | — | — | — |
| Claims on Public Nonfin. Corps.... | 32c | — | .28 | — | — | .04 | — | — | — | — | — | — | — |
| Claims on Private Sector.............. | 32d | 23.71 | 28.07 | 32.38 | 39.77 | 46.09 | 53.19 | 61.76 | 68.36 | 75.14 | 66.86 | 67.13 | 70.76 |
| Broad Money Liabilities.................. | 35l | 144.17 | 150.08 | 159.99 | 166.83 | 167.75 | 187.99 | 189.71 | 211.40 | 248.71 | 235.27 | 260.34 | 263.76 |
| Currency Outside Depository Corps | 34a | 12.96 | 12.29 | 14.18 | 15.07 | 11.57 | 14.86 | 15.97 | 21.63 | 25.69 | 18.39 | 18.36 | 20.20 |
| Transferable Deposits................... | 34 | 36.57 | 32.76 | 35.17 | 42.76 | 41.30 | 41.83 | 33.35 | 33.60 | 35.77 | 50.29 | 39.45 | 44.91 |
| Other Deposits............................. | 35 | 94.64 | 105.04 | 110.64 | 109.00 | 114.89 | 131.29 | 140.39 | 156.17 | 187.25 | 166.60 | 202.54 | 198.65 |
| Securities Other than Shares......... | 36a | — | — | — | — | — | — | — | — | — | — | — | — |
| Deposits Excl. from Broad Money..... | 36b | — | — | — | — | — | — | — | — | — | — | — | — |
| Sec.Ot.th.Shares Excl.f/Brd.Money.... | 36s | 1.00 | 1.00 | 1.00 | 1.00 | 1.00 | .91 | .91 | — | — | — | — | — |
| Loans......................................... | 36l | — | — | — | — | — | — | — | — | — | — | — | — |
| Financial Derivatives..................... | 36m | — | — | — | — | — | — | — | — | — | — | — | — |
| Insurance Technical Reserves........... | 36r | — | — | — | — | — | — | — | — | — | — | — | — |
| Shares and Other Equity................. | 37a | 18.44 | 20.85 | 22.99 | 26.55 | 28.66 | 30.56 | 24.32 | 14.03 | 21.22 | 24.19 | 23.15 | 24.94 |
| Other Items (Net)......................... | 37r | −6.39 | −11.34 | −6.83 | −8.56 | −3.50 | −2.61 | 5.99 | 20.29 | 19.76 | 20.85 | 18.97 | 19.84 |
| Broad Money Liabs., Seasonally Adj. | 35l.b | 142.84 | 148.40 | 157.90 | 164.60 | 165.67 | 186.28 | 188.90 | 211.56 | 250.00 | 237.23 | 263.09 | 266.81 |
| **Monetary Aggregates** | | *Millions of E. Caribbean Dollars: End of Period* | | | | | | | | | | | |
| Broad Money............................... | 59m | 144.17 | 150.08 | 159.99 | 166.83 | 167.75 | 187.99 | 189.71 | 211.40 | 248.71 | 235.27 | 260.34 | 263.76 |
| o/w:Currency Issued by Cent.Govt | 59m.a | — | — | — | — | — | — | — | — | — | — | — | — |
| o/w: Dep.in Nonfin. Corporations. | 59m.b | — | — | — | — | — | — | — | — | — | — | — | — |
| o/w:Secs. Issued by Central Govt.. | 59m.c | — | — | — | — | — | — | — | — | — | — | — | — |
| Money (National Definitions) | | | | | | | | | | | | | |
| M1............................................. | 59ma | 36.05 | 31.96 | 32.70 | 36.59 | 39.17 | 38.15 | 35.43 | 41.17 | 47.37 | 53.62 | 45.07 | 47.64 |
| M2............................................. | 59mb | 119.51 | 123.65 | 134.86 | 144.62 | 152.84 | 165.77 | 170.55 | 192.56 | 220.84 | 215.33 | 239.20 | 244.86 |
| **Interest Rates** | | *Percent Per Annum* | | | | | | | | | | | |
| Discount Rate (End of Period).......... | 60.a | 6.50 | 6.50 | 6.50 | 6.50 | 6.50 | 6.50 | 6.50 | 6.50 | 6.50 | 6.50 | 6.50 | 6.50 |
| Money Market Rate........................ | 60b | 4.67 | 4.01 | 4.76 | 5.24 | 4.92 | 6.03 | 6.36 | 5.68 | 5.19 | 6.23 | 6.19 | 6.44 |
| Savings Rate................................. | 60k | 3.38 | 3.42 | 3.43 | 3.47 | 3.47 | 3.43 | 3.37 | 3.29 | 3.07 | 3.06 | 3.05 | 2.21 |
| Deposit Rate................................. | 60l | 2.29 | 2.52 | 2.67 | 2.55 | 2.52 | 2.69 | 2.60 | 2.42 | 2.37 | 2.04 | 1.93 | 1.36 |
| Deposit Rate (Fgn. Currency)........... | 60l.f | 2.05 | 1.95 | 2.26 | 2.15 | 2.25 | 2.28 | 1.61 | 1.39 | .97 | 1.00 | .86 | .32 |
| Lending Rate................................. | 60p | 10.95 | 10.56 | 10.48 | 10.40 | 9.89 | 9.04 | 8.73 | 8.56 | 8.16 | 8.00 | 8.02 | 7.82 |
| **Prices** | | *Index Numbers (2010=100): Period Averages* | | | | | | | | | | | |
| Consumer Prices............................ | 64 | 84.5 | 86.8 | 88.4 | 90.8 | 95.3 | 97.9 | 100.0 | 103.7 | 108.6 | 109.6 | † 109.2 | 108.0 |

## Balance of Payments

| | | 2004 | 2005 | 2006 | 2007 | 2008 | 2009 | 2010 | 2011 | 2012 | 2013 | 2014 | 2015 |
|---|---|---|---|---|---|---|---|---|---|---|---|---|---|
| | | | | | | | *Millions of US Dollars* | | | | | | |
| A. Current Account* | 109bx | −11.1 | −15.8 | −7.5 | −10.4 | −19.7 | −12.7 | −19.5 | −10.1 | −13.6 | −27.5 | .... | .... |
| Goods, credit (exports) | 1a9cx | 4.8 | 1.9 | 1.8 | 3.1 | 4.1 | 3.2 | 1.0 | 2.5 | 1.9 | 6.1 | .... | .... |
| Goods, debit (imports) | 1a9dx | 25.3 | 26.2 | 26.6 | 26.1 | 33.5 | 26.1 | 25.8 | 29.7 | 32.8 | 35.5 | .... | .... |
| Balance on goods | 1a9bx | −20.5 | −24.3 | −24.8 | −23.0 | −29.5 | −22.8 | −24.9 | −27.3 | −31.0 | −29.3 | .... | .... |
| Services, credit (exports) | 1b9cx | 14.9 | 14.8 | 14.8 | 14.7 | 13.9 | 11.8 | 11.3 | 12.0 | 13.3 | 13.9 | .... | .... |
| Services, debit (imports) | 1b9dx | 25.3 | 25.7 | 17.3 | 19.0 | 23.4 | 17.6 | 16.8 | 17.9 | 18.2 | 18.7 | .... | .... |
| Balance on Goods & Services | 1z9bx | −30.9 | −35.3 | −27.3 | −27.3 | −38.9 | −28.6 | −30.4 | −33.2 | −35.8 | −34.1 | .... | .... |
| Primary income: credit | 1c9cx | 1.2 | 2.1 | 2.5 | 2.1 | 1.1 | 1.0 | .5 | .4 | .4 | .4 | .... | .... |
| Primary income: debit | 1c9dx | 4.7 | 4.9 | 4.4 | 5.8 | 5.6 | 4.7 | 4.3 | 3.9 | 3.4 | 3.4 | .... | .... |
| Balance on gds, serv. & prim. inc. | 1y9bx | −34.3 | −38.1 | −29.3 | −31.0 | −43.4 | −32.2 | −34.2 | −36.8 | −38.8 | −37.1 | .... | .... |
| Secondary income: credit | 1d9ca | 28.3 | 28.0 | 25.4 | 25.3 | 27.9 | 24.2 | 19.0 | 30.8 | 30.4 | 14.9 | .... | .... |
| Secondary income: debit | 1d9da | 5.1 | 5.8 | 3.7 | 4.7 | 4.2 | 4.7 | 4.2 | 4.1 | 5.3 | 5.3 | .... | .... |
| B. Capital Account* | 209ba | 13.5 | 7.2 | 5.6 | 7.0 | 9.8 | 21.0 | 13.0 | 9.2 | 19.9 | 30.0 | .... | .... |
| Capital account: credit | 209ca | 13.5 | 7.2 | 5.6 | 7.0 | 9.8 | 21.0 | 13.0 | 9.2 | 19.9 | 30.0 | .... | .... |
| Capital account: debit | 209da | — | — | — | — | — | — | — | — | — | — | .... | .... |
| Balance on current & capital acct. | 129ba | 2.4 | −8.6 | −2.0 | −3.4 | −9.9 | 8.3 | −6.4 | −.8 | 6.3 | 2.5 | .... | .... |
| C. Financial Account* | 309na | 1.7 | −10.1 | −4.3 | −5.2 | −9.0 | 1.4 | −8.8 | −9.5 | −.3 | −7.5 | .... | .... |
| Direct investment: assets | 3a9aa | — | — | — | — | — | — | — | — | — | — | .... | .... |
| Equity & investment fund shares | 3aaaa | .... | .... | .... | .... | .... | .... | .... | .... | .... | .... | .... | .... |
| Debt instruments | 3abaa | .... | .... | .... | .... | .... | .... | .... | .... | .... | .... | .... | .... |
| Direct investment: liabilities | 3a9la | 2.3 | 5.4 | 4.0 | 6.9 | 12.7 | 2.6 | 3.6 | 2.5 | 2.6 | 2.2 | .... | .... |
| Equity & investment fund shares | 3aala | .8 | .8 | .8 | .9 | .8 | .8 | .8 | .7 | .7 | .7 | .... | .... |
| Debt instruments | 3abla | 1.6 | 4.6 | 3.2 | 6.0 | 11.9 | 1.8 | 2.7 | 1.8 | 1.9 | 1.5 | .... | .... |
| Portfolio investment: assets | 3b9aa | — | — | — | — | — | — | — | — | — | — | .... | .... |
| Equity & investment fund shares | 3baaa | .... | .... | .... | .... | .... | .... | .... | .... | .... | .... | .... | .... |
| Debt securities | 3bbaa | .... | .... | .... | .... | .... | .... | .... | .... | .... | .... | .... | .... |
| Portfolio investment: liabilities | 3b9la | — | −.1 | .1 | .1 | −.5 | .5 | .4 | .2 | .1 | .1 | .... | .... |
| Equity & investment fund shares | 3bala | .... | .... | .... | .... | .... | .... | .... | .... | .... | .... | .... | .... |
| Debt securities | 3bbla | .... | .... | .... | .... | .... | .... | .... | .... | .... | .... | .... | .... |
| Fin. der.& empl.stk.ops.(ESOs): net. | 3c9na | .... | .... | .... | .... | .... | .... | .... | .... | .... | .... | .... | .... |
| Fin. der. & ESOs.: assets | 3c9aa | .... | .... | .... | .... | .... | .... | .... | .... | .... | .... | .... | .... |
| Fin. der. & ESOs.: liabilities | 3c9la | .... | .... | .... | .... | .... | .... | .... | .... | .... | .... | .... | .... |
| Other investment: assets | 3d9aa | 5.5 | 3.7 | 3.3 | 4.6 | 3.8 | 8.1 | .4 | 10.2 | 13.5 | 9.8 | .... | .... |
| Other equity | 3daaa | .... | .... | .... | .... | .... | .... | .... | .... | .... | .... | .... | .... |
| Debt instruments | 3dzaa | 5.5 | 3.7 | 3.3 | 4.6 | 3.8 | 8.1 | .4 | 10.2 | 13.5 | 9.8 | .... | .... |
| Other investment: liabilities | 3d9la | 1.4 | 8.4 | 3.5 | 2.8 | .6 | 3.7 | 5.3 | 17.0 | 11.1 | 14.9 | .... | .... |
| Other equity | 3dala | .... | .... | .... | .... | .... | .... | .... | .... | .... | .... | .... | .... |
| Debt instruments | 3dzla | 1.4 | 8.4 | 3.5 | 2.8 | .6 | 3.7 | 5.3 | 17.0 | 11.1 | 14.9 | .... | .... |
| Curr.+ cap.− finan. acct. balance | 4y9na | .7 | 1.5 | 2.3 | 1.8 | −.9 | 6.9 | 2.4 | 8.6 | 6.6 | 10.0 | .... | .... |
| D. Net Errors and Omissions | 409na | −2.2 | −1.6 | −1.7 | −1.9 | −1.9 | −4.2 | .3 | −.6 | −.3 | −1.6 | .... | .... |
| E. Reserves and Related Items | 4z9na | −1.5 | −.1 | .6 | −.1 | −2.8 | 2.7 | 2.7 | 8.0 | 6.4 | 8.4 | .... | .... |
| Reserve assets | 3e9aa | −1.5 | −.1 | .6 | −.1 | −2.8 | 2.7 | 2.7 | 8.0 | 6.4 | 8.4 | .... | .... |
| Credit and loans from the IMF | 3dcla | .... | .... | .... | .... | .... | .... | .... | .... | .... | .... | .... | .... |
| Exceptional financing | 409la | .... | .... | .... | .... | .... | .... | .... | .... | .... | .... | .... | .... |

*Excludes components in group E

## Government Finance
## Cash Flow Statement
## Budgetary Central Government

| | | 2004 | 2005 | 2006 | 2007 | 2008 | 2009 | 2010 | 2011 | 2012 | 2013 | 2014 | 2015 |
|---|---|---|---|---|---|---|---|---|---|---|---|---|---|
| | | | | | | *Millions of E. Caribbean Dollars: Fiscal Year Ends December 31* | | | | | | | | |
| Cash Receipts:Operating Activities | c1 | 124.70 | 86.00 | 98.10 | 111.70 | 108.24 | 149.57 | 126.80 | 140.87 | 190.58 | 98.39 | 151.34 | .... |
| Taxes | c11 | 30.60 | 32.50 | 31.80 | 31.60 | 33.99 | 36.85 | 35.63 | 36.14 | 36.70 | 37.79 | 39.15 | .... |
| Social Contributions | c12 | — | — | — | — | — | — | — | — | — | — | — | .... |
| Grants | c13 | 92.30 | 51.40 | 63.60 | 76.00 | 68.59 | 107.85 | 86.49 | 99.72 | 148.41 | 55.37 | 106.40 | .... |
| Other Receipts | c14 | 1.80 | 2.10 | 2.70 | 4.20 | 5.66 | 4.87 | 4.68 | 5.01 | 5.47 | 5.23 | 5.79 | .... |
| Cash Payments:Operating Activities. | c2 | 89.80 | 78.70 | 83.40 | 92.30 | 95.05 | 98.98 | 92.04 | 112.98 | 98.04 | 113.76 | 119.06 | .... |
| Compensation of Employees | c21 | 25.90 | 30.30 | 35.50 | 37.90 | 39.61 | 42.27 | 42.51 | 42.81 | 42.21 | 43.21 | 41.33 | .... |
| Purchases of Goods & Services | c22 | 29.80 | 24.60 | 25.70 | 30.80 | 30.68 | 23.49 | 19.61 | 21.45 | 23.39 | 24.66 | 38.04 | .... |
| Interest | c24 | .20 | .10 | .10 | .10 | .09 | .03 | .12 | .03 | .04 | .04 | .04 | .... |
| Subsidies | c25 | 21.80 | 16.10 | 11.50 | 11.40 | 11.84 | 15.86 | 17.64 | 19.33 | 16.67 | 32.42 | 25.51 | .... |
| Grants | c26 | — | — | — | — | — | — | — | — | — | — | — | .... |
| Social Benefits | c27 | 12.10 | 7.60 | 10.70 | 12.10 | 12.83 | 17.33 | 12.16 | 29.36 | 15.73 | 13.43 | 14.14 | .... |
| Other Payments | c28 | — | — | — | — | — | — | — | — | — | — | — | .... |
| Net Cash Inflow:Operating Act.[1-2] | ccio | 35.00 | 7.30 | 14.70 | 19.40 | 13.19 | 50.59 | 34.76 | 27.89 | 92.54 | −15.37 | 32.28 | .... |
| Net Cash Outflow:Invest. in NFA | c31 | 33.00 | 25.40 | 18.60 | 26.60 | 35.73 | 37.80 | 30.96 | 30.60 | 54.38 | 66.72 | 33.69 | .... |
| Purchases of Nonfinancial Assets | c31.1 | 33.00 | 25.40 | 18.60 | 26.60 | 35.73 | 37.80 | 30.96 | 30.60 | 54.38 | 66.72 | 33.69 | .... |
| Sales of Nonfinancial Assets | c31.2 | — | — | — | — | — | — | — | — | — | — | — | .... |
| Cash Surplus/Deficit [1-2-31=1-2M] | ccsd | 2.00 | −18.00 | −4.00 | −7.20 | −22.54 | 12.79 | 3.80 | −2.71 | 38.16 | −82.09 | −1.41 | .... |
| Net Acq. Fin. Assets, excl. Cash | c32x | — | — | — | — | — | — | — | — | — | — | — | .... |
| Domestic | c321x | — | — | — | — | — | — | — | — | — | — | — | .... |
| Foreign | c322x | — | — | — | — | — | — | — | — | — | — | — | .... |
| Net Incurrence of Liabilities | c33 | −6.20 | 9.90 | 6.80 | −2.10 | 6.75 | −13.15 | −13.57 | 1.94 | −44.36 | 20.38 | 11.96 | .... |
| Domestic | c331 | −6.10 | 10.00 | 6.90 | −1.90 | 6.87 | −13.06 | −13.45 | 2.06 | −44.24 | 20.32 | 11.84 | .... |
| Foreign | c332 | −.10 | −.10 | −.10 | −.10 | −.12 | −.09 | −.12 | −.12 | −.12 | .06 | .12 | .... |
| Net Cash Inflow, Fin.Act.[-32x+33] | cnfb | −6.20 | 9.90 | 6.80 | −2.10 | 6.75 | −13.15 | −13.57 | 1.94 | −44.36 | 20.38 | 11.96 | .... |
| Net Change in Stock of Cash | cncb | −4.20 | −8.20 | 2.80 | −9.20 | −15.79 | −.36 | −9.77 | −.77 | −6.20 | −61.71 | 10.55 | .... |
| Stat. Discrep. [32X-33+NCB-CSD] | ccsdz | .10 | — | −.10 | .10 | — | — | — | — | — | — | — | .... |
| Memo Item:Cash Expenditure[2+31] | c2m | 122.80 | 104.10 | 102.00 | 118.90 | 130.78 | 136.78 | 123.00 | 143.58 | 152.42 | 180.48 | 152.75 | .... |
| Memo Item: Gross Debt | c63 | .... | .... | .... | .... | .... | .... | .... | .... | .... | .... | .... | .... |

# Montserrat   351

| | | 2004 | 2005 | 2006 | 2007 | 2008 | 2009 | 2010 | 2011 | 2012 | 2013 | 2014 | 2015 |
|---|---|---|---|---|---|---|---|---|---|---|---|---|---|
| **National Accounts** | | | | | | | *Millions of E. Caribbean Dollars* | | | | | | |
| Househ.Cons.Expend.,incl.NPISHs.... | 96f | 90.2 | 121.0 | 108.9 | 106.0 | 140.2 | 118.5 | 123.0 | 143.0 | 145.2 | 161.5 | 164.9 | .... |
| Government Consumption Expend... | 91f | 63.3 | 63.6 | 71.8 | 79.7 | 82.2 | 82.0 | 72.9 | 81.9 | 84.3 | 85.7 | 92.6 | .... |
| Gross Fixed Capital Formation......... | 93e | 48.9 | 42.5 | 32.5 | 34.0 | 37.7 | 37.2 | 36.1 | 36.8 | 38.1 | 42.6 | 38.2 | .... |
| Exports of Goods and Services......... | 90c | 53.1 | 45.0 | 44.7 | 48.1 | 48.5 | 40.6 | 33.1 | 39.0 | 40.9 | 51.5 | 50.8 | .... |
| Imports of Goods and Services (-)..... | 98c | 136.5 | 140.2 | 118.5 | 121.8 | 153.6 | 117.9 | 115.2 | 128.7 | 137.7 | 178.6 | 176.2 | .... |
| Gross Domestic Product (GDP)........ | 99b | 119.0 | 132.0 | 139.3 | 146.0 | 155.0 | 160.4 | 149.9 | 172.0 | 170.8 | 162.6 | 170.3 | .... |
| GDP Volume 1990 Prices................ | 99b.p | 71.1 | 71.4 | 67.2 | 68.2 | 72.7 | 75.3 | .... | .... | .... | .... | .... | .... |
| GDP Volume (2005=100)................ | 99bvp | 99.6 | 100.0 | 94.1 | 95.4 | 101.8 | 105.5 | .... | .... | .... | .... | .... | .... |
| GDP Deflator (2005=100).............. | 99bip | 90.6 | 100.0 | 112.2 | 115.9 | 115.4 | 115.2 | .... | .... | .... | .... | .... | .... |
| | | | | | | | *Millions: Midyear Estimates* | | | | | | |
| Population............................... | 99z | .0046 | .0048 | .0048 | .0049 | .0049 | .0049 | .0050 | .0050 | .0050 | .0051 | .0051 | .0051 |

| | | 2004 | 2005 | 2006 | 2007 | 2008 | 2009 | 2010 | 2011 | 2012 | 2013 | 2014 | 2015 |
|---|---|---|---|---|---|---|---|---|---|---|---|---|---|
| **Exchange Rates** | | \multicolumn{12}{c}{*Dirhams per SDR: End of Period*} | | | | | | | | | | | |
| Official Rate | aa | 12.762 | 13.220 | 12.722 | 12.189 | 12.473 | 12.322 | 12.870 | 13.168 | 12.962 | 12.552 | 13.101 | 13.727 |
| | | \multicolumn{12}{c}{*Dirhams per US Dollar: End of Period (ae) Period Average (rf)*} | | | | | | | | | | | |
| Official Rate | ae | 8.218 | 9.249 | 8.457 | 7.713 | 8.098 | 7.860 | 8.357 | 8.577 | 8.434 | 8.151 | 9.043 | 9.906 |
| Official Rate | rf | 8.868 | 8.865 | 8.796 | 8.192 | 7.750 | 8.057 | 8.090 | 8.628 | 8.406 | 8.406 | 9.764 |
| | | \multicolumn{12}{c}{*Index Numbers (2010=100): Period Averages*} | | | | | | | | | | | |
| Official Rate | ahx | 94.9 | 94.9 | 95.6 | 102.7 | 108.8 | 104.5 | 100.0 | 104.0 | 97.5 | 100.0 | 100.1 | 86.1 |
| Nominal Effective Exchange Rate | nec | 101.4 | 100.2 | 100.2 | 100.1 | 100.9 | 102.7 | 100.0 | 100.1 | 99.5 | 101.5 | 102.7 | 102.5 |
| CPI-Based Real Effect. Ex. Rate | rec | 104.7 | 102.1 | 102.6 | 101.7 | 102.2 | 104.3 | 100.0 | 97.7 | 95.8 | 97.5 | 97.6 | 97.9 |
| **Fund Position** | | \multicolumn{12}{c}{*Millions of SDRs: End of Period*} | | | | | | | | | | | |
| Quota | 2f.s | 588.20 | 588.20 | 588.20 | 588.20 | 588.20 | 588.20 | 588.20 | 588.20 | 588.20 | 588.20 | 588.20 | 588.20 |
| SDR Holdings | 1b.s | 77.41 | 55.09 | 34.98 | 20.22 | 12.51 | 486.90 | 482.18 | 401.44 | 283.01 | 245.37 | 558.41 | 550.47 |
| Reserve Position in the Fund | 1c.s | 70.44 | 70.44 | 70.45 | 70.45 | 70.45 | 70.45 | 70.45 | 70.45 | 70.45 | 70.45 | 70.46 | 70.46 |
| Total Fund Cred.&Loans Outstg. | 2tl | — | — | — | — | — | — | — | — | — | — | — | — |
| SDR Allocations | 1bd | 85.69 | 85.69 | 85.69 | 85.69 | 85.69 | 561.42 | 561.42 | 561.42 | 561.42 | 561.42 | 561.42 | 561.42 |
| **International Liquidity** | | \multicolumn{12}{c}{*Millions of US Dollars Unless Otherwise Indicated: End of Period*} | | | | | | | | | | | |
| Total Reserves minus Gold | 1l.d | 16,337 | 16,187 | 20,341 | 24,123 | 22,104 | 22,797 | 22,960 | 19,333 | 16,211 | 18,197 | 19,672 | 22,254 |
| SDR Holdings | 1b.d | 120 | 79 | 53 | 32 | 19 | 763 | 743 | 616 | 435 | 378 | 809 | 763 |
| Reserve Position in the Fund | 1c.d | 109 | 101 | 106 | 111 | 109 | 110 | 108 | 108 | 108 | 108 | 102 | 98 |
| Foreign Exchange | 1d.d | 16,107 | 16,008 | 20,182 | 23,980 | 21,976 | 21,924 | 22,109 | 18,608 | 15,668 | 17,711 | 18,761 | 21,393 |
| Gold (Million Fine Troy Ounces) | 1ad | .708 | .708 | .708 | .708 | .708 | .709 | .709 | .709 | .709 | .709 | .709 | .709 |
| Gold (National Valuation) | 1and | 239 | 280 | 450 | 593 | 613 | 783 | 1,000 | 1,116 | 1,179 | 852 | 851 | 754 |
| Central Bank: Other Assets | 3..d | 47 | 61 | 70 | 73 | 71 | 74 | 39 | 39 | 555 | 536 | 174 | 117 |
| Central Bank: Other Liabs | 4..d | 140 | 184 | 207 | 261 | 264 | 331 | 330 | 380 | 379 | 823 | 413 | 339 |
| Other Depository Corps.: Assets | 7a.d | 2,396 | 3,031 | 3,621 | 4,188 | 3,563 | 3,638 | 2,599 | 3,051 | 3,330 | 3,441 | 3,462 | 3,847 |
| Other Depository Corps.: Liabs | 7b.d | 1,391 | 1,300 | 1,519 | 1,604 | 1,664 | 1,563 | 2,022 | 2,851 | 3,012 | 3,666 | 3,577 | 3,007 |
| **Central Bank** | | \multicolumn{12}{c}{*Millions of Dirhams: End of Period*} | | | | | | | | | | | |
| Net Foreign Assets | 11n | 134,900 | 149,981 | 173,766 | 188,142 | 181,715 | 176,397 | 187,672 | 166,737 | 140,873 | 145,871 | 176,053 | 218,005 |
| Claims on Nonresidents | 11 | 137,142 | 152,818 | 176,610 | 191,200 | 184,925 | 185,915 | 197,654 | 177,385 | 151,344 | 159,625 | 187,147 | 229,071 |
| Liabilities to Nonresidents | 16c | 2,242 | 2,837 | 2,844 | 3,058 | 3,211 | 9,518 | 9,982 | 10,648 | 10,471 | 13,754 | 11,094 | 11,066 |
| Claims on Other Depository Corps. | 12e | 992 | 1,008 | 729 | 5,511 | 16,711 | 18,261 | 7,804 | 40,309 | 70,366 | 72,077 | 43,327 | 23,250 |
| Net Claims on Central Government | 12an | 2,896 | 48 | −646 | 4,336 | 6,438 | 3,332 | 3,524 | 2,216 | 456 | 807 | −111 | −1,190 |
| Claims on Central Government | 12a | 18,444 | 13,997 | 13,988 | 13,787 | 11,521 | 8,379 | 7,486 | 5,577 | 4,907 | 5,394 | 4,527 | 4,763 |
| Liabilities to Central Government | 16d | 15,548 | 13,949 | 14,634 | 9,451 | 5,083 | 5,047 | 3,962 | 3,361 | 4,451 | 4,587 | 4,638 | 5,953 |
| Claims on Other Sectors | 12s | 637 | 538 | 592 | 624 | 654 | 708 | 969 | 1,058 | 810 | 896 | 808 | 943 |
| Claims on Other Financial Corps. | 12g | 6 | 6 | 6 | 6 | 6 | 6 | 26 | 26 | 25 | 25 | 25 | 55 |
| Claims on State & Local Govts. | 12b | — | — | — | — | — | — | — | — | — | — | — | — |
| Claims on Public Nonfin. Corps. | 12c | 2 | 1 | 1 | 1 | — | — | — | — | — | — | — | — |
| Claims on Private Sector | 12d | 630 | 531 | 585 | 617 | 648 | 703 | 943 | 1,033 | 785 | 871 | 784 | 888 |
| Monetary Base | 14 | 123,873 | 140,818 | 160,195 | 182,334 | 191,260 | 183,915 | 183,120 | 193,881 | 195,240 | 205,098 | 205,289 | 226,210 |
| Currency in Circulation | 14a | 83,289 | 93,505 | 114,234 | 125,534 | 134,772 | 143,139 | 152,059 | 166,253 | 172,493 | 182,080 | 191,458 | 205,884 |
| Liabs. to Other Depository Corps. | 14c | 39,486 | 45,424 | 44,831 | 55,531 | 54,956 | 38,922 | 28,717 | 25,143 | 20,532 | 20,595 | 10,372 | 14,189 |
| Liabilities to Other Sectors | 14d | 1,098 | 1,889 | 1,131 | 1,269 | 1,533 | 1,853 | 2,343 | 2,485 | 2,214 | 2,423 | 3,460 | 6,136 |
| Other Liabs. to Other Dep. Corps. | 14n | 5,678 | 1,121 | 4,000 | — | — | — | — | — | 28 | 12 | 4 | — |
| Dep. & Sec. Excl. f/Monetary Base | 14o | 29 | 33 | 3 | 4 | 7 | 5 | 6 | 8 | 5 | 5 | 10 | 6 |
| Deposits Included in Broad Money | 15 | — | — | — | — | — | — | — | — | — | — | — | — |
| Sec.Ot.th.Shares Incl.in Brd. Money | 16a | — | — | — | — | — | — | — | — | — | — | — | — |
| Deposits Excl. from Broad Money | 16b | 29 | 33 | 3 | 4 | 7 | 5 | 6 | 8 | 5 | 5 | 10 | 6 |
| Sec.Ot.th.Shares Excl.f/Brd.Money | 16s | — | — | — | — | — | — | — | — | — | — | — | — |
| Loans | 16l | — | — | — | — | — | — | — | 1 | 1 | 1 | 1 | 1 |
| Financial Derivatives | 16m | — | — | — | — | — | — | — | — | — | — | — | — |
| Shares and Other Equity | 17a | 14,535 | 10,085 | 12,350 | 14,715 | 15,691 | 16,064 | 16,950 | 17,651 | 18,446 | 16,294 | 15,920 | 15,249 |
| Other Items (Net) | 17r | −4,690 | −482 | −2,108 | 1,559 | −1,442 | −1,284 | −108 | −1,222 | −1,213 | −1,759 | −1,147 | −458 |
| Memo Item: | | | | | | | | | | | | | |
| Total Assets | 10ra | 160,082 | 171,146 | 195,331 | 214,508 | 220,109 | 219,945 | 217,635 | 228,250 | 233,009 | 243,278 | 240,864 | 262,294 |

# Morocco   686

| | | 2004 | 2005 | 2006 | 2007 | 2008 | 2009 | 2010 | 2011 | 2012 | 2013 | 2014 | 2015 |
|---|---|---|---|---|---|---|---|---|---|---|---|---|---|
| **Other Depository Corporations** | | | | | | *Millions of Dirhams: End of Period* | | | | | | | |
| Net Foreign Assets.......................... | 21n | 8,263 | 16,016 | 17,771 | 19,927 | 15,384 | 16,316 | 4,819 | 1,719 | 2,684 | −1,836 | −1,040 | 8,320 |
| Claims on Nonresidents................. | 21 | 19,693 | 28,038 | 30,618 | 32,299 | 28,856 | 28,598 | 21,720 | 26,172 | 28,085 | 28,047 | 31,302 | 38,109 |
| Liabilities to Nonresidents.............. | 26c | 11,430 | 12,022 | 12,847 | 12,372 | 13,472 | 12,282 | 16,901 | 24,453 | 25,401 | 29,883 | 32,342 | 29,789 |
| Claims on Central Bank................... | 20 | 47,753 | 48,987 | 53,206 | 65,932 | 61,097 | 42,829 | 36,582 | 33,187 | 27,354 | 29,061 | 20,802 | 26,131 |
| Currency............................... | 20a | 3,046 | 3,599 | 5,057 | 5,488 | 6,681 | 6,475 | 7,399 | 7,965 | 8,852 | 10,698 | 12,047 | 13,250 |
| Reserve Deposits and Securities..... | 20b | 44,707 | 45,388 | 48,150 | 60,444 | 54,416 | 36,354 | 29,183 | 25,221 | 18,502 | 18,363 | 8,755 | 12,882 |
| Other Claims............................. | 20n | — | — | — | — | — | — | — | — | — | — | — | — |
| Net Claims on Central Government.. | 22an | 76,490 | 87,117 | 90,301 | 90,456 | 90,368 | 84,465 | 77,694 | 99,927 | 124,946 | 148,474 | 143,831 | 149,164 |
| Claims on Central Government... | 22a | 82,084 | 93,378 | 99,155 | 99,714 | 100,280 | 95,283 | 92,006 | 111,517 | 136,888 | 164,102 | 156,893 | 165,334 |
| Liabilities to Central Government... | 26d | 5,594 | 6,261 | 8,854 | 9,258 | 9,912 | 10,818 | 14,312 | 11,590 | 11,943 | 15,628 | 13,062 | 16,169 |
| Claims on Other Sectors................ | 22s | 261,823 | 295,221 | 358,261 | 461,800 | 576,646 | 643,448 | 714,279 | 788,768 | 829,154 | 858,203 | 895,178 | 903,231 |
| Claims on Other Financial Corps..... | 22g | 38,039 | 41,650 | 62,895 | 86,228 | 113,835 | 128,495 | 150,885 | 170,443 | 174,567 | 195,612 | 206,140 | 211,704 |
| Claims on State & Local Govts.... | 22b | 4,765 | 4,382 | 4,718 | 5,889 | 7,227 | 8,610 | 9,758 | 10,441 | 11,568 | 12,313 | 13,257 | 14,135 |
| Claims on Public Nonfin. Corps...... | 22c | 4,488 | 6,352 | 10,527 | 10,567 | 21,082 | 33,267 | 29,956 | 31,155 | 36,399 | 38,719 | 41,683 | 42,542 |
| Claims on Private Sector................ | 22d | 214,531 | 242,837 | 280,121 | 359,115 | 434,503 | 473,076 | 523,680 | 576,728 | 606,620 | 611,558 | 634,098 | 634,850 |
| Liabilities to Central Bank............... | 26g | 1,721 | 1,977 | 1,601 | 7,681 | 16,921 | 19,744 | 10,141 | 34,450 | 68,415 | 76,511 | 43,407 | 23,409 |
| Transf.Dep.Included in Broad Money | 24 | 180,433 | 207,502 | 242,861 | 305,097 | 320,030 | 336,695 | 361,180 | 390,625 | 408,823 | 424,467 | 449,978 | 481,298 |
| Other Dep.Included in Broad Money. | 25 | 142,130 | 166,668 | 199,440 | 226,892 | 287,343 | 298,490 | 319,021 | 329,717 | 338,961 | 352,981 | 384,996 | 397,226 |
| Sec.Ot.th.Shares Incl.in Brd. Money.. | 26a | 276 | 502 | 1,916 | 5,614 | 6,046 | 12,473 | 15,533 | 23,064 | 29,640 | 29,293 | 23,191 | 18,477 |
| Deposits Excl. from Broad Money..... | 26b | 3,036 | 3,557 | 4,159 | 4,783 | 5,239 | 5,708 | 5,843 | 6,901 | 7,465 | 7,081 | 7,569 | 6,667 |
| Sec.Ot.th.Shares Excl.f/Brd.Money.... | 26s | 7,283 | 775 | 5,445 | 6,623 | 22,595 | 22,022 | 15,148 | 25,345 | 24,456 | 21,016 | 24,265 | 27,339 |
| Loans.......................................... | 26l | — | 8 | 84 | 2,973 | 4,099 | 6,727 | 10,065 | 7,585 | 7,733 | 8,284 | 9,265 | 7,231 |
| Financial Derivatives........................ | 26m | 5 | 5 | 6 | 9 | 10 | 10 | 45 | 51 | 40 | 8 | 59 | 27 |
| Insurance Technical Reserves........... | 26r | 2 | 30 | 47 | 59 | 129 | 169 | 198 | 243 | 272 | 285 | 256 | 234 |
| Shares and Other Equity.................. | 27a | 37,074 | 38,986 | 47,137 | 57,041 | 66,266 | 73,212 | 82,390 | 86,532 | 95,939 | 104,516 | 108,126 | 112,446 |
| Other Items (Net)............................. | 27r | 22,370 | 27,331 | 16,843 | 21,343 | 14,816 | 11,808 | 13,811 | 19,088 | 2,393 | 9,460 | 7,659 | 12,493 |
| Memo Item: | | | | | | | | | | | | | |
| Total Assets.................................. | 20ra | 442,487 | 507,702 | 591,284 | 720,313 | 828,100 | 888,566 | 958,969 | 1,048,351 | 1,129,595 | 1,169,574 | 1,213,186 | 1,253,039 |
| **Depository Corporations** | | | | | | *Millions of Dirhams: End of Period* | | | | | | | |
| Net Foreign Assets.......................... | 31n | 143,163 | 165,997 | 191,537 | 208,069 | 197,099 | 192,714 | 192,491 | 168,456 | 143,557 | 144,036 | 175,013 | 226,325 |
| Claims on Nonresidents................. | 31 | 156,836 | 180,856 | 207,228 | 223,499 | 213,782 | 214,513 | 219,374 | 203,558 | 179,429 | 187,673 | 218,449 | 267,180 |
| Liabilities to Nonresidents.............. | 36c | 13,672 | 14,859 | 15,691 | 15,430 | 16,682 | 21,800 | 26,883 | 35,102 | 35,872 | 43,637 | 43,436 | 40,855 |
| Domestic Claims............................. | 32 | 341,846 | 382,925 | 448,508 | 557,214 | 674,106 | 731,954 | 796,465 | 891,970 | 955,366 | 1,008,380 | 1,039,707 | 1,052,148 |
| Net Claims on Central Government | 32an | 79,386 | 87,166 | 89,655 | 94,791 | 96,806 | 87,797 | 81,218 | 102,143 | 125,402 | 149,281 | 143,720 | 147,974 |
| Claims on Central Government.... | 32a | 100,528 | 107,375 | 113,144 | 113,501 | 111,801 | 103,662 | 99,491 | 117,094 | 141,795 | 169,496 | 161,420 | 170,096 |
| Liabilities to Central Government. | 36d | 21,142 | 20,210 | 23,489 | 18,709 | 14,995 | 15,865 | 18,274 | 14,951 | 16,394 | 20,215 | 17,700 | 22,122 |
| Claims on Other Sectors................ | 32s | 262,460 | 295,759 | 358,853 | 462,423 | 577,300 | 644,157 | 715,247 | 789,826 | 829,964 | 859,099 | 895,987 | 904,174 |
| Claims on Other Financial Corps.... | 32g | 38,045 | 41,656 | 62,901 | 86,233 | 113,840 | 128,501 | 150,911 | 170,468 | 174,592 | 195,637 | 206,165 | 211,759 |
| Claims on State & Local Govts.... | 32b | 4,765 | 4,382 | 4,718 | 5,889 | 7,227 | 8,610 | 9,758 | 10,441 | 11,568 | 12,313 | 13,257 | 14,135 |
| Claims on Public Nonfin. Corps.... | 32c | 4,490 | 6,353 | 10,528 | 10,569 | 21,082 | 33,267 | 29,956 | 31,155 | 36,399 | 38,719 | 41,683 | 42,542 |
| Claims on Private Sector.............. | 32d | 215,161 | 243,368 | 280,706 | 359,732 | 435,151 | 473,778 | 524,623 | 577,761 | 607,405 | 612,429 | 634,881 | 635,738 |
| Broad Money Liabilities................... | 35l | 404,181 | 466,468 | 554,525 | 658,917 | 743,044 | 786,175 | 842,738 | 904,178 | 943,278 | 980,546 | 1,041,035 | 1,095,772 |
| Currency Outside Depository Corps | 34a | 80,243 | 89,906 | 109,177 | 120,045 | 128,091 | 136,664 | 144,660 | 158,288 | 163,641 | 171,382 | 179,411 | 192,634 |
| Transferable Deposits.................... | 34 | 181,530 | 209,390 | 243,990 | 306,366 | 321,563 | 338,548 | 363,523 | 393,110 | 410,899 | 426,872 | 453,291 | 487,329 |
| Other Deposits............................. | 35 | 142,131 | 166,670 | 199,442 | 226,892 | 287,344 | 298,490 | 319,022 | 329,717 | 339,099 | 353,000 | 385,142 | 397,332 |
| Securities Other than Shares.......... | 36a | 276 | 502 | 1,916 | 5,614 | 6,046 | 12,473 | 15,533 | 23,064 | 29,640 | 29,293 | 23,191 | 18,477 |
| Deposits Excl. from Broad Money..... | 36b | 3,065 | 3,590 | 4,162 | 4,787 | 5,246 | 5,713 | 5,849 | 6,910 | 7,470 | 7,086 | 7,579 | 6,673 |
| Sec.Ot.th.Shares Excl.f/Brd.Money.... | 36s | 7,283 | 775 | 5,445 | 6,623 | 22,595 | 22,022 | 15,148 | 25,345 | 24,456 | 21,016 | 24,265 | 27,339 |
| Loans.......................................... | 36l | — | 8 | 84 | 2,974 | 4,099 | 6,728 | 10,065 | 7,586 | 7,734 | 8,285 | 9,267 | 7,232 |
| Financial Derivatives........................ | 36m | 5 | 5 | 6 | 9 | 10 | 10 | 45 | 51 | 40 | 8 | 59 | 27 |
| Insurance Technical Reserves........... | 36r | 2 | 30 | 47 | 59 | 129 | 169 | 198 | 243 | 272 | 285 | 256 | 234 |
| Shares and Other Equity.................. | 37a | 51,609 | 49,072 | 59,487 | 71,756 | 81,958 | 89,276 | 99,340 | 104,183 | 114,385 | 120,810 | 124,046 | 127,695 |
| Other Items (Net)........................... | 37r | 18,865 | 28,974 | 16,289 | 20,159 | 14,124 | 14,575 | 15,574 | 11,929 | 1,288 | 14,380 | 8,213 | 13,501 |
| Broad Money Liabs., Seasonally Adj. | 35l.b | 400,823 | 462,146 | 548,821 | 651,233 | 733,557 | 775,168 | 829,899 | 889,113 | 926,247 | 961,763 | 1,020,549 | 1,073,943 |
| **Monetary Aggregates** | | | | | | *Millions of Dirhams: End of Period* | | | | | | | |
| Broad Money................................. | 59m | 445,883 | 508,563 | 600,555 | 705,935 | 799,905 | 855,955 | 891,866 | 949,287 | 992,176 | 1,023,166 | 1,090,867 | 1,148,039 |
| o/w:Currency Issued by Cent.Govt | 59m.a | 29,431 | 27,897 | 30,826 | 29,922 | 37,378 | 48,529 | 49,128 | 45,109 | 48,898 | 42,620 | 49,832 | 52,267 |
| o/w: Dep.in Nonfin. Corporations. | 59m.b | 12,271 | 14,198 | 15,204 | 17,097 | 19,483 | 21,251 | — | — | — | — | — | — |
| o/w:Secs. Issued by Central Govt.. | 59m.c | — | — | — | — | — | — | — | — | — | — | — | — |
| Money (National Definitions) | | | | | | | | | | | | | |
| M1................................................ | 59ma | 292,295 | 328,900 | 385,213 | 457,175 | 488,877 | 525,380 | 549,478 | 586,777 | 612,163 | 628,941 | 660,584 | 706,901 |
| M2................................................ | 59mb | 345,509 | 388,329 | 450,659 | 529,596 | 568,746 | 612,715 | 643,504 | 689,692 | 723,519 | 749,263 | 790,616 | 845,301 |
| M3................................................ | 59mc | 445,883 | 508,563 | 600,555 | 705,935 | 799,905 | 855,955 | 891,866 | 949,287 | 992,176 | 1,023,166 | 1,090,867 | 1,148,039 |
| **Interest Rates** | | | | | | *Percent Per Annum* | | | | | | | |
| Discount Rate (End of Period)......... | 60.a | 3.25 | 3.25 | 3.25 | 3.25 | 3.32 | 3.31 | 3.25 | 3.25 | 3.04 | 3.00 | 2.92 | 2.50 |
| Money Market Rate........................ | 60b | 2.39 | 2.78 | 2.58 | 3.31 | 3.37 | 3.26 | 3.29 | 3.29 | 3.19 | 3.06 | 2.94 | 2.51 |
| Deposit Rate.................................. | 60l | 3.61 | 3.52 | 3.67 | 3.67 | 3.91 | 3.81 | 3.69 | 3.76 | 3.83 | 3.91 | 3.89 | 3.80 |
| Lending Rate................................. | 60p | 11.50 | 11.50 | .... | .... | .... | .... | .... | .... | .... | .... | .... | .... |
| Govt.Bond Yield: Long-Term............ | 61 | 5.67 | 5.35 | 4.04 | 3.65 | .... | .... | 4.34 | 4.36 | 4.57 | .... | 4.30 | 4.01 |
| Govt.Bond Yield: Med.-Term........... | 61a | 4.26 | 3.97 | 3.59 | 3.52 | 3.85 | 3.79 | 3.90 | 3.86 | 4.22 | .... | 3.92 | 3.13 |
| **Prices, Production, Labor** | | | | | | *Index Numbers (2010=100): Period Averages* | | | | | | | |
| Share Prices (End of Month)............. | 62.ep | 36.9 | 41.3 | 65.7 | 101.1 | 113.2 | 91.3 | 100.0 | 98.8 | 85.9 | 75.5 | 81.1 | 81.3 |
| Wholesale Prices (2000=100).......... | 63 | .... | .... | .... | .... | .... | .... | .... | .... | .... | .... | .... | .... |
| Producer Prices: Manufacturing....... | 63ey | 79.8 | 87.0 | 92.2 | 93.8 | 110.7 | 94.0 | 100.0 | † 114.8 | 118.2 | 115.9 | 112.7 | 107.5 |
| Consumer Prices............................ | 64 | 88.8 | 89.7 | 92.6 | † 94.5 | 98.0 | 99.0 | 100.0 | 100.9 | 102.2 | 104.1 | 104.6 | 106.2 |
| | | | | | | *Number in Thousands: Period Averages* | | | | | | | |
| Labor Force................................... | 67d | 11,070 | 11,124 | 11,559 | 11,421 | 11,487 | 11,505 | 11,493 | 11,556 | 11,566 | 11,720 | 11,846 | 11,852 |
| Employment................................... | 67e | 9,826 | 9,877 | 10,476 | 10,332 | 10,411 | 10,475 | 10,453 | 10,534 | 10,520 | 10,640 | 10,697 | 10,731 |
| Unemployment.............................. | 67c | 1,243 | 1,247 | 1,083 | 1,089 | 1,075 | 1,031 | 1,040 | 1,023 | 1,046 | 1,080 | 1,149 | 1,150 |
| Unemployment Rate (%)................. | 67r | 11.2 | 11.2 | 9.4 | 9.5 | 9.4 | 9.0 | 9.1 | 8.8 | 9.0 | 9.2 | 9.7 | 9.7 |

| | | 2004 | 2005 | 2006 | 2007 | 2008 | 2009 | 2010 | 2011 | 2012 | 2013 | 2014 | 2015 |
|---|---|---|---|---|---|---|---|---|---|---|---|---|---|
| **Intl. Transactions & Positions** | | | | | | | *Millions of Dirhams* | | | | | | |
| Exports...... | 70 | 87,897 | 99,264 | 111,979 | 125,517 | 155,740 | 113,020 | 149,583 | 174,994 | 184,885 | 185,387 | 200,013 | .... |
| Imports, c.i.f...... | 71 | 157,921 | 184,380 | 210,554 | 261,288 | 326,042 | 263,982 | 297,963 | 357,770 | 386,949 | 383,720 | 386,118 | .... |
| Imports, f.o.b...... | 71.v | 144,882 | 165,383 | .... | .... | .... | .... | .... | .... | .... | .... | .... | .... |
| | | | | | | | *2010=100* | | | | | | |
| Volume of Exports...... | 72 | 89.1 | 100.0 | 108.2 | 111.3 | .... | .... | .... | .... | 125.9 | .... | .... | .... |
| Volume of Imports...... | 73 | 90.8 | 100.0 | 110.4 | 125.6 | .... | .... | .... | .... | 162.9 | .... | .... | .... |
| Unit Value of Exports...... | 74 | 99.3 | 100.0 | 104.3 | 107.7 | .... | .... | .... | .... | 141.1 | .... | .... | .... |
| Unit Value of Imports...... | 75 | 94.3 | 100.0 | 103.3 | 108.9 | .... | .... | .... | .... | 123.6 | .... | .... | .... |
| **Balance of Payments** | | | | | | | *Millions of US Dollars* | | | | | | |
| A. Current Account* ...... | 109bx | 921.6 | 948.7 | 1,315.3 | −224.3 | −5,658.8 | −5,361.5 | −4,209.3 | −8,336.9 | −9,842.9 | −8,692.4 | † −6,267.2 | −1,923.3 |
| Goods, credit (exports)...... | 1a9cx | 6,483.5 | 7,328.1 | 8,038.4 | 9,884.7 | 15,252.2 | 9,166.1 | 12,309.4 | 15,945.7 | 16,992.0 | 18,261.8 | † 19,996.2 | 18,483.6 |
| Goods, debit (imports)...... | 1a9dx | 14,274.6 | 16,697.9 | 19,383.0 | 25,954.0 | 36,650.6 | 28,027.4 | 29,627.3 | 37,333.0 | 38,877.0 | 39,853.6 | † 40,682.7 | 32,738.2 |
| Balance on goods...... | 1a9bx | −7,791.0 | −9,369.9 | −11,344.6 | −16,069.3 | −21,398.3 | −18,861.3 | −17,317.9 | −21,387.3 | −21,885.0 | −21,591.9 | † −20,686.4 | −14,254.6 |
| Services, credit (exports)...... | 1b9cx | 8,014.8 | 9,264.1 | 11,376.7 | 14,064.8 | 15,301.7 | 14,832.7 | 14,736.1 | 15,899.1 | 15,346.6 | 14,352.6 | † 15,831.3 | 14,269.8 |
| Services, debit (imports)...... | 1b9dx | 3,451.4 | 3,845.4 | 4,472.9 | 5,416.1 | 6,678.1 | 6,898.4 | 7,371.5 | 8,574.4 | 8,136.4 | 7,571.2 | † 8,785.0 | 7,913.5 |
| Balance on Goods & Services...... | 1z9bx | −3,227.6 | −3,951.2 | −4,440.7 | −7,420.6 | −12,774.7 | −10,926.9 | −9,953.3 | −14,062.6 | −14,674.8 | −14,810.4 | † −13,640.2 | −7,898.4 |
| Primary income: credit...... | 1c9cx | 505.0 | 688.6 | 750.1 | 960.8 | 1,059.1 | 925.3 | 868.0 | 804.3 | 615.8 | 471.4 | † 587.5 | 522.1 |
| Primary income: debit...... | 1c9dx | 1,175.7 | 1,072.2 | 1,226.9 | 1,365.4 | 1,581.0 | 2,420.5 | 2,110.2 | 2,856.2 | 2,899.2 | 2,242.6 | † 3,239.4 | 2,402.8 |
| Balance on gds, serv. & prim. inc. | 1y9bx | −3,898.2 | −4,334.8 | −4,917.5 | −7,825.2 | −13,296.7 | −12,422.2 | −11,195.5 | −16,114.5 | −16,958.2 | −16,581.6 | † −16,292.1 | −9,779.0 |
| Secondary income: credit...... | 1d9ca | 4,974.4 | 5,441.1 | 6,409.6 | 7,785.6 | 7,849.2 | 7,278.4 | 7,240.3 | 8,071.3 | 7,405.2 | 8,302.7 | † 10,600.8 | 8,285.5 |
| Secondary income: debit...... | 1d9da | 154.5 | 157.6 | 176.8 | 184.6 | 211.3 | 217.8 | 254.0 | 293.7 | 290.0 | 413.4 | † 575.8 | 429.8 |
| B. Capital Account* ...... | 209ba | — | — | — | — | — | — | — | — | — | — | † 1.8 | .6 |
| Capital account: credit...... | 209ca | — | — | — | — | — | — | — | — | — | — | † 1.8 | .6 |
| Capital account: debit...... | 209da | — | — | — | — | — | — | — | — | — | — | .... | .... |
| Balance on current & capital acct. | 129ba | 921.6 | 948.7 | 1,315.3 | −224.3 | −5,658.8 | −5,361.5 | −4,209.3 | −8,336.9 | −9,842.9 | −8,692.4 | † −6,265.4 | −1,922.7 |
| C. Financial Account* ...... | 309na | −101.7 | 88.4 | 184.9 | 717.7 | −371.3 | −1,481.2 | −1,363.6 | −2,294.8 | −1,884.3 | −3,055.5 | † −8,833.1 | −5,616.9 |
| Direct investment: assets...... | 3a9aa | 30.9 | 74.1 | 450.9 | 632.0 | 315.9 | 479.0 | 580.0 | 248.0 | 359.6 | 444.7 | † 431.2 | 652.3 |
| Equity & investment fund shares... | 3aaaa | 30.9 | 74.1 | 450.9 | 632.0 | 315.9 | 479.0 | 580.0 | 248.0 | 359.6 | 444.7 | † 367.4 | 691.3 |
| Debt instruments...... | 3abaa | | | | | | | | | | | † 63.9 | −39.0 |
| Direct investment: liabilities...... | 3a9la | 787.1 | 1,619.8 | 2,366.0 | 2,806.6 | 2,466.3 | 1,970.3 | 1,240.6 | 2,521.4 | 2,842.0 | 3,360.9 | † 3,525.6 | 3,160.0 |
| Equity & investment fund shares . | 3aala | 657.5 | 898.9 | 2,589.7 | 2,539.4 | 2,422.7 | 2,456.1 | 1,369.4 | 2,076.0 | 2,091.9 | 3,213.1 | † 3,134.2 | 2,151.2 |
| Debt instruments...... | 3abla | 129.5 | 720.8 | −223.7 | 267.3 | 43.6 | −485.8 | −128.7 | 445.4 | 750.1 | 147.9 | † 391.5 | 1,008.8 |
| Portfolio investment: assets...... | 3b9aa | — | 3.8 | −2.9 | 16.2 | 257.4 | 12.2 | 22.0 | 399.6 | −102.6 | −178.2 | † 1.5 | −150.0 |
| Equity & investment fund shares | 3baaa | — | 3.8 | −2.9 | 16.2 | 257.4 | 12.2 | 22.0 | 399.6 | −102.6 | −178.2 | .... | .... |
| Debt securities...... | 3bbaa | | | | | | | | | | | .... | .... |
| Portfolio investment: liabilities...... | 3b9la | 596.8 | 63.7 | −297.8 | −63.9 | 148.3 | −4.4 | 131.9 | 166.1 | −108.3 | 43.1 | † 3,117.0 | 1,165.7 |
| Equity & investment fund shares . | 3bala | 596.8 | 63.7 | −297.8 | −63.9 | 148.3 | −4.4 | 131.9 | 166.1 | −108.3 | 43.1 | .... | .... |
| Debt securities...... | 3bbla | | | | | | | | | | | .... | .... |
| Fin. der.& empl.stk.ops.(ESOs): net. | 3c9na | — | — | — | — | — | — | — | — | — | — | † −18.3 | −55.4 |
| Fin. der. & ESOs.: assets...... | 3c9aa | — | — | — | — | — | — | .... | .... | .... | .... | † −246.6 | −249.8 |
| Fin. der. & ESOs.: liabilities...... | 3c9la | — | — | — | — | — | — | .... | .... | .... | .... | † −228.2 | −194.3 |
| Other investment: assets...... | 3d9aa | 454.4 | 891.2 | 762.2 | 1,617.1 | 413.2 | 56.2 | −880.0 | 536.3 | 237.0 | 447.4 | † 862.1 | −15.4 |
| Other equity...... | 3daaa | .... | .... | .... | .... | .... | .... | .... | .... | .... | .... | † 20.7 | 29.7 |
| Debt instruments...... | 3dzaa | 454.4 | 891.2 | 762.2 | 1,617.1 | 413.2 | 56.2 | −880.0 | 536.3 | 237.0 | 447.4 | † 841.4 | −45.0 |
| Other investment: liabilities...... | 3d9la | −796.9 | −802.6 | −1,042.9 | −1,195.0 | −1,256.8 | 62.7 | −286.9 | 791.3 | −355.4 | 365.4 | † 3,467.1 | 1,722.7 |
| Other equity...... | 3dala | .... | .... | .... | .... | .... | .... | .... | .... | .... | .... | † — | — |
| Debt instruments...... | 3dzla | −796.9 | −802.6 | −1,042.9 | −1,195.0 | −1,256.8 | 62.7 | −286.9 | 791.3 | −355.4 | 365.4 | † 3,467.1 | 1,722.7 |
| Curr.+ cap.− finan. acct. balance... | 4y9na | 1,023.4 | 860.3 | 1,130.4 | −942.0 | −5,287.5 | −3,880.3 | −2,845.7 | −6,042.1 | −7,958.6 | −5,636.9 | † 2,567.8 | 3,694.2 |
| D. Net Errors and Omissions...... | 409na | −290.0 | −411.6 | −502.4 | 101.8 | −416.4 | −523.4 | −166.7 | −370.5 | −409.6 | 378.5 | † 1,158.2 | 612.4 |
| E. Reserves and Related Items...... | 4z9na | 733.3 | 448.7 | 628.0 | −840.1 | −5,704.0 | −4,403.7 | −3,012.4 | −6,412.6 | −8,368.2 | −5,258.3 | † 3,725.9 | 4,306.6 |
| Reserve assets...... | 3e9aa | 1,901.4 | 2,352.3 | 2,710.7 | 2,033.7 | −1,305.5 | −147.9 | 1,211.4 | −2,760.3 | −3,652.3 | 1,344.0 | † 3,725.9 | 4,306.6 |
| Credit and loans from the IMF...... | 3dcla | — | — | — | — | — | — | — | — | — | — | † — | |
| Exceptional financing...... | 409la | 1,168.1 | 1,903.6 | 2,082.7 | 2,873.8 | 4,398.5 | 4,255.9 | 4,223.8 | 3,652.3 | 4,715.9 | 6,602.3 | .... | .... |
| *Excludes components in group E | | | | | | | | | | | | | |
| **International Investment Position** | | | | | | | *Millions of US Dollars* | | | | | | |
| Assets...... | 809aa | 20,675.3 | 21,271.2 | 26,781.9 | 32,678.8 | 30,370.4 | 30,750.2 | 29,829.1 | 27,510.3 | 23,974.2 | † 27,113.6 | 31,467.2 | 34,297.1 |
| Direct investment...... | 8a9aa | 675.5 | 665.6 | 1,053.6 | 1,337.1 | 1,699.1 | 1,861.4 | 1,914.0 | 2,018.6 | 2,175.3 | † 2,554.7 | 4,187.0 | 4,554.8 |
| Equity & investment fund shares... | 8aaaa | 490.1 | 534.7 | 983.9 | 1,245.6 | 1,551.8 | 1,799.3 | 1,853.5 | 1,893.5 | 2,014.3 | † 2,173.5 | 3,807.8 | 4,156.0 |
| Debt instruments...... | 8abaa | 185.4 | 130.9 | 69.7 | 91.5 | 147.3 | 62.0 | 60.5 | 125.1 | 161.0 | † 381.2 | 379.2 | 398.8 |
| Portfolio investment...... | 8b9aa | 156.2 | 175.5 | 178.5 | 915.8 | 1,022.2 | 724.1 | 961.6 | 796.8 | 817.2 | † 759.6 | 1,207.2 | 965.4 |
| Equity & investment fund shares... | 8baaa | 156.2 | 175.5 | 170.6 | 907.0 | 946.2 | 707.3 | 948.8 | 729.9 | 778.0 | † 749.2 | 1,196.8 | 963.7 |
| Debt securities...... | 8bbaa | .... | .... | 7.9 | 8.8 | 76.0 | 16.8 | 12.7 | 66.9 | 39.2 | † 10.4 | 10.4 | 1.7 |
| Fin. der.(oth.than reserves) & ESOs | 8c9aa | .... | .... | .... | .... | .... | .... | .... | .... | .... | † 10.6 | 98.0 | 115.9 |
| Other investment...... | 8d9aa | 3,202.4 | 3,969.2 | 4,735.5 | 5,710.2 | 4,885.1 | 4,585.2 | 3,341.1 | 4,052.9 | 3,446.8 | † 4,533.1 | 5,569.7 | 5,652.8 |
| Other equity...... | 8daaa | .... | .... | .... | .... | .... | .... | .... | .... | .... | † 95.4 | 109.3 | 129.8 |
| Debt instruments...... | 8dzaa | 3,202.4 | 3,969.2 | 4,735.5 | 5,710.2 | 4,885.1 | 4,585.2 | 3,341.1 | 4,052.9 | 3,446.8 | † 4,437.7 | 5,460.4 | 5,523.0 |
| Reserve assets...... | 8e9aa | 16,641.2 | 16,460.8 | 20,814.3 | 24,715.6 | 22,764.0 | 23,579.4 | 23,612.5 | 20,642.0 | 17,534.9 | † 19,255.5 | 20,405.3 | 23,008.3 |
| Liabilities...... | 809la | 38,924.2 | 38,452.5 | 49,106.3 | 61,739.8 | 63,459.9 | 71,557.4 | 76,412.9 | 78,660.4 | 82,889.4 | † 97,677.6 | 99,063.0 | 94,654.6 |
| Direct investment...... | 8a9la | 19,883.1 | 20,751.5 | 29,938.7 | 38,613.3 | 39,388.3 | 42,581.1 | 45,081.6 | 44,515.9 | 45,620.3 | † 51,816.0 | 51,192.0 | 48,695.9 |
| Equity & investment fund shares... | 8aala | 18,675.5 | 19,016.9 | 28,213.5 | 36,530.9 | 37,347.8 | 40,749.6 | 43,428.1 | 42,493.5 | 42,797.6 | † 48,729.9 | 48,049.4 | 44,829.2 |
| Debt instruments...... | 8abla | 1,207.6 | 1,734.6 | 1,725.2 | 2,082.4 | 2,040.5 | 1,831.5 | 1,653.5 | 2,022.4 | 2,822.7 | † 3,086.0 | 3,142.6 | 3,866.7 |
| Portfolio investment...... | 8b9la | 1,719.6 | 2,037.5 | 2,110.3 | 3,277.1 | 3,210.0 | 3,663.9 | 3,576.3 | 3,245.8 | 3,003.7 | † 7,768.1 | 10,594.1 | 10,373.2 |
| Equity & investment fund shares... | 8bala | 1,678.7 | 2,017.0 | 2,107.9 | 3,270.9 | 3,210.0 | 3,663.9 | 3,576.3 | 3,245.8 | 3,003.7 | † 3,377.5 | 3,127.7 | 2,594.3 |
| Debt securities...... | 8bbla | 40.9 | 20.5 | 2.4 | 6.2 | .... | .... | .... | .... | .... | † 4,390.6 | 7,466.4 | 7,778.9 |
| Fin. der.(oth.than reserves) & ESOs | 8c9la | .... | .... | .... | .... | .... | .... | .... | .... | .... | † 57.6 | 134.3 | 50.7 |
| Other investment...... | 8d9la | 17,321.4 | 15,663.5 | 17,057.3 | 19,849.5 | 20,861.6 | 25,312.4 | 27,755.0 | 30,898.7 | 34,265.4 | † 38,035.9 | 37,142.6 | 35,534.8 |
| Other equity...... | 8dala | .... | .... | .... | .... | .... | .... | .... | .... | .... | .... | .... | — |
| Debt instruments...... | 8dzla | 17,321.4 | 15,663.5 | 17,057.3 | 19,849.5 | 20,861.6 | 25,312.4 | 27,755.0 | 30,898.7 | 34,265.4 | † 38,035.9 | 37,142.6 | 35,534.8 |

# Morocco  686

| | | 2004 | 2005 | 2006 | 2007 | 2008 | 2009 | 2010 | 2011 | 2012 | 2013 | 2014 | 2015 |
|---|---|---|---|---|---|---|---|---|---|---|---|---|---|
| **Government Finance** | | | | | | | | | | | | | |
| **Operations Statement** | | | | | | | | | | | | | |
| **Budgetary Central Government** | | | | | | *Billions of Dirhams: Fiscal Year Ends December 31* | | | | | | | |
| Revenue........................... | a1 | 121.11 | 138.65 | 157.98 | 184.40 | 224.09 | 215.43 | 208.66 | 222.99 | 237.74 | 250.02 | 259.35 | 260.39 |
| Taxes............................. | a11 | 100.35 | 115.91 | 129.51 | 154.79 | 189.88 | 171.94 | 179.08 | 191.05 | 202.67 | 200.68 | 203.83 | 209.56 |
| Social Contributions...................... | a12 | — | — | — | — | — | — | — | — | — | — | — | — |
| Grants............................ | a13 | 1.30 | 1.80 | 2.46 | 2.40 | 2.40 | 2.80 | — | 1.31 | .46 | 6.11 | 13.84 | 4.97 |
| Other Revenue........................... | a14 | 19.46 | 20.94 | 26.01 | 27.20 | 31.81 | 40.68 | 29.58 | 30.63 | 34.61 | 43.23 | 41.68 | 45.86 |
| Expense.......................... | a2 | 125.28 | 155.40 | 153.14 | 166.19 | 192.66 | 196.56 | 211.74 | 240.33 | 252.53 | 250.01 | 254.54 | 248.62 |
| Compensation of Employees.......... | a21 | 62.15 | 68.88 | 73.83 | 76.75 | 83.22 | 92.92 | 88.60 | 98.04 | 108.90 | 112.76 | 117.31 | 118.20 |
| Use of Goods & Services................ | a22 | 13.21 | 23.56 | 14.48 | 13.89 | 17.63 | 17.40 | 25.07 | 22.74 | 21.06 | 21.53 | 23.65 | 25.14 |
| Consumption of Fixed Capital........ | a23 | .... | .... | .... | .... | .... | .... | .... | .... | .... | .... | .... | .... |
| Interest........................... | a24 | 17.59 | 17.44 | 18.57 | 19.24 | 18.23 | 17.33 | 17.57 | 18.23 | 20.10 | 22.50 | 24.78 | 27.29 |
| Subsidies........................... | a25 | 12.15 | — | — | — | — | — | — | — | 54.87 | 41.60 | 32.65 | 13.98 |
| Grants............................ | a26 | 19.26 | 37.75 | 31.90 | 38.45 | 52.78 | 43.50 | 50.86 | 76.45 | 35.52 | 37.77 | 41.38 | 47.26 |
| Social Benefits........................ | a27 | — | — | — | — | — | — | — | — | — | — | — | — |
| Other Expense...................... | a28 | .92 | 7.77 | 14.36 | 17.86 | 20.80 | 25.42 | 29.65 | 24.87 | 12.09 | 13.85 | 14.77 | 16.75 |
| Gross Operating Balance [1-2+23]... | agob | −4.17 | −16.75 | 4.84 | 18.21 | 31.43 | 18.86 | −3.08 | −17.34 | −14.79 | .01 | 4.81 | 11.77 |
| Net Operating Balance [1-2]............ | anob | .... | .... | .... | .... | .... | .... | .... | .... | .... | .... | .... | .... |
| Net Acq. of Nonfinancial Assets....... | a31 | 14.79 | 15.88 | 16.60 | 19.03 | 26.57 | 32.03 | 32.12 | 37.10 | 46.06 | 45.70 | 49.67 | 54.51 |
| Aquisition of Nonfin. Assets........... | a31.1 | .... | .... | .... | .... | .... | .... | .... | .... | .... | .... | .... | .... |
| Disposal of Nonfin. Assets............ | a31.2 | .... | .... | .... | .... | .... | .... | .... | .... | .... | .... | .... | .... |
| Net Lending/Borrowing [1-2-31]...... | anlb | −18.96 | −32.63 | −11.76 | −.81 | 4.85 | −13.16 | −35.21 | −54.44 | −60.85 | −45.69 | −44.87 | −42.75 |
| Net Acq. of Financial Assets............ | a32 | −14.08 | −11.58 | −6.04 | −.94 | .58 | 2.29 | −1.80 | −5.38 | −6.45 | .... | .... | .... |
| By instrument | | | | | | | | | | | | | |
| Monetary Gold & SDRs................ | a3201 | — | — | — | — | — | — | — | — | — | .... | .... | .... |
| Currency & Deposits.................... | a3202 | .... | .83 | .15 | .41 | 1.20 | 2.35 | −1.77 | −.06 | −3.16 | .... | .... | .... |
| Securities other than Shares........... | a3203 | — | — | — | — | — | — | — | — | — | .... | .... | .... |
| Loans.............................. | a3204 | .... | −.15 | −.50 | −.43 | −.87 | −.32 | — | — | — | .... | .... | .... |
| Shares & Other Equity................ | a3205 | .... | −13.55 | −3.96 | −4.79 | .25 | .26 | −.04 | −5.32 | −3.29 | .... | .... | .... |
| Insurance Technical Reserves........ | a3206 | — | — | — | — | — | — | — | — | — | .... | .... | .... |
| Financial Derivatives.................... | a3207 | — | — | — | — | — | — | — | — | — | .... | .... | .... |
| Other Accounts Receivable............ | a3208 | .... | 1.31 | −1.74 | 3.86 | — | — | .01 | .01 | — | .... | .... | .... |
| By debtor | | | | | | | | | | | | | |
| Domestic.................................. | a321 | −14.08 | −11.58 | −6.04 | −4.80 | .58 | 2.29 | −1.80 | −5.38 | −6.45 | .... | .... | .... |
| Foreign................................... | a322 | — | — | — | — | — | — | — | — | — | .... | .... | .... |
| Net Incurrence of Liabilities.............. | a33 | 4.88 | 21.05 | 5.72 | −.12 | −4.27 | 15.45 | 33.40 | 49.06 | 54.40 | .... | .... | .... |
| By instrument | | | | | | | | | | | | | |
| Special Drawing Rights (SDRs)........ | a3301 | — | — | — | — | — | — | — | — | — | .... | .... | .... |
| Currency & Deposits.................... | a3302 | .... | −4.30 | 2.04 | .80 | 3.28 | −1.81 | −14.24 | −3.91 | −4.82 | .... | .... | .... |
| Securities other than Shares........... | a3303 | .... | 34.62 | 7.29 | −1.94 | −7.58 | 9.31 | 24.85 | 37.37 | 45.58 | .... | .... | .... |
| Loans.............................. | a3304 | .... | −1.46 | −2.36 | .77 | 2.01 | 10.02 | 15.91 | 5.75 | 15.25 | .... | .... | .... |
| Shares & Other Equity.................. | a3305 | — | — | — | — | — | — | — | — | — | .... | .... | .... |
| Insurance Technical Reserves........ | a3306 | — | — | — | — | — | — | — | — | — | .... | .... | .... |
| Financial Derivatives.................... | a3307 | — | — | — | — | — | — | — | — | — | .... | .... | .... |
| Other Accounts Payable................ | a3308 | .... | −7.81 | −1.26 | .24 | −1.99 | −2.07 | 6.89 | 9.85 | −1.61 | .... | .... | .... |
| By creditor | | | | | | | | | | | | | |
| Domestic.................................. | a331 | 12.59 | 22.51 | 8.08 | −.90 | −6.29 | 5.43 | 17.50 | 43.31 | 39.15 | .... | .... | .... |
| Foreign................................... | a332 | −7.72 | −1.46 | −2.36 | .77 | 2.01 | 10.02 | 15.91 | 5.75 | 15.25 | .... | .... | .... |
| Stat. Discrepancy [32-33-NLB]........ | anlbz | — | — | — | — | — | — | — | — | — | — | .... | .... |
| Memo Item: Expenditure [2+31]...... | a2m | 140.07 | 171.28 | 169.74 | 185.21 | 219.23 | 228.59 | 243.86 | 277.43 | 298.59 | 295.71 | 304.21 | 303.13 |
| **National Accounts** | | | | | | *Billions of Dirhams* | | | | | | | |
| Househ.Cons.Expend.,incl.NPISHs.... | 96f | 298.97 | 316.40 | 345.59 | 375.21 | 418.22 | 438.78 | 461.04 | 488.35 | 512.21 | 540.10 | 557.52 | .... |
| Government Consumption Expend... | 91f | 94.68 | 102.50 | 107.72 | 113.41 | 120.21 | 136.52 | 140.82 | 153.36 | 168.19 | 178.31 | 183.85 | .... |
| Gross Fixed Capital Formation.......... | 93e | 144.31 | 157.44 | 176.11 | 208.22 | 246.76 | 236.99 | 240.54 | 258.29 | 276.39 | 273.39 | 272.09 | .... |
| Changes in Inventories.................... | 93i | 19.25 | 9.91 | 10.46 | 11.20 | 33.50 | 25.33 | 26.82 | 35.11 | 20.53 | 39.45 | 25.59 | .... |
| Exports of Goods and Services.......... | 90c | 148.62 | 170.88 | 197.76 | 223.86 | 256.26 | 209.60 | 252.91 | 284.57 | 296.16 | 294.32 | 316.86 | .... |
| Imports of Goods and Services (-).... | 98c | 177.08 | 204.46 | 233.89 | 284.37 | 357.98 | 298.73 | 337.50 | 399.60 | 425.60 | 424.21 | 431.14 | .... |
| Gross Domestic Product (GDP)........ | 99b | 528.76 | 552.67 | 603.74 | 647.53 | 716.96 | 748.48 | 784.62 | 820.08 | 847.88 | 901.37 | 924.77 | .... |
| Net Primary Income from Abroad..... | 98.n | −5.07 | −2.43 | −3.33 | −2.32 | −1.52 | −10.33 | −10.81 | −13.83 | −17.12 | −12.24 | −20.89 | .... |
| Gross National Income (GNI)........... | 99a | 523.69 | 550.24 | 600.40 | 645.22 | 715.44 | 738.16 | 773.82 | 806.24 | 830.76 | 889.12 | 903.88 | .... |
| GDP Volume 1998 Prices................. | 99b.p | 486.05 | 500.53 | 539.36 | 554.00 | 584.85 | 612.74 | 635.06 | 666.73 | 684.52 | 714.51 | .... | .... |
| GDP Volume 2007 Prices................. | 99b.p | 562.87 | 581.40 | 625.44 | 647.53 | 685.89 | 714.99 | 742.27 | 781.21 | 804.73 | 842.75 | 863.12 | .... |
| GDP Volume (2010=100)................ | 99bvp | 75.8 | 78.3 | 84.3 | 87.2 | 92.4 | 96.3 | 100.0 | 105.2 | 108.4 | 113.5 | 116.3 | .... |
| GDP Deflator (2010=100)............... | 99bip | 88.9 | 89.9 | 91.3 | 94.6 | 98.9 | 99.0 | 100.0 | 99.3 | 99.7 | 101.2 | 101.4 | .... |
| | | | | | | *Millions: Midyear Estimates* | | | | | | | |
| **Population............................** | 99z | 30.09 | 30.39 | 30.69 | 31.01 | 31.35 | 31.71 | 32.11 | 32.53 | 32.98 | 33.45 | 33.92 | 34.38 |

# Mozambique 688

| | | 2004 | 2005 | 2006 | 2007 | 2008 | 2009 | 2010 | 2011 | 2012 | 2013 | 2014 | 2015 |
|---|---|---|---|---|---|---|---|---|---|---|---|---|---|
| **Exchange Rates** | | | | | *Meticais Novos per SDR: End of Period* | | | | | | | | |
| Market Rate | aa | 29.35 | 34.56 | 39.07 | 37.64 | 39.28 | 45.76 | 50.17 | 41.93 | 45.72 | 46.32 | 48.68 | 63.61 |
| | | | | | *Meticais Novos per US Dollar: End of Period (ae) Period Average (rf)* | | | | | | | | |
| Market Rate | ae | 18.90 | 24.18 | 25.97 | 23.82 | 25.50 | 29.19 | 32.58 | 27.31 | 29.75 | 30.08 | 33.60 | 45.90 |
| Market Rate | rf | 22.58 | 23.06 | 25.40 | 25.84 | 24.30 | 27.52 | 33.96 | 29.07 | 28.37 | 30.10 | 31.35 | 39.98 |
| **Fund Position** | | | | | *Millions of SDRs: End of Period* | | | | | | | | |
| Quota | 2f.s | 113.60 | 113.60 | 113.60 | 113.60 | 113.60 | 113.60 | 113.60 | 113.60 | 113.60 | 113.60 | 113.60 | 113.60 |
| SDR Holdings | 1b.s | .05 | .16 | .15 | .11 | .07 | 108.66 | 108.48 | 107.51 | 106.04 | 104.09 | 101.97 | 78.88 |
| Reserve Position in the Fund | 1c.s | .01 | .01 | .01 | .01 | .01 | .01 | .01 | .01 | .01 | .01 | .03 | .03 |
| Total Fund Cred.&Loans Outstg | 2tl | 127.04 | 109.80 | 6.48 | 9.74 | 9.74 | 109.14 | 123.18 | 122.21 | 120.75 | 118.80 | 116.69 | 178.80 |
| SDR Allocations | 1bd | — | — | — | — | — | 108.84 | 108.84 | 108.84 | 108.84 | 108.84 | 108.84 | 108.84 |
| **International Liquidity** | | | | | *Millions of US Dollars Unless Otherwise Indicated: End of Period* | | | | | | | | |
| Total Reserves minus Gold | 1l.d | 1,130.96 | 1,053.82 | 1,155.73 | 1,444.69 | 1,577.73 | 2,099.27 | 2,159.39 | 2,468.77 | 2,770.24 | 3,142.33 | 3,009.98 | 2,411.42 |
| SDR Holdings | 1b.d | .08 | .23 | .23 | .18 | .10 | 170.34 | 167.07 | 165.05 | 162.98 | 160.30 | 147.74 | 109.30 |
| Reserve Position in the Fund | 1c.d | .01 | .01 | .01 | .01 | .01 | .01 | .01 | .01 | .01 | .01 | .04 | .04 |
| Foreign Exchange | 1d.d | 1,130.86 | 1,053.58 | 1,155.49 | 1,444.50 | 1,577.62 | 1,928.91 | 1,992.32 | 2,303.71 | 2,607.25 | 2,982.02 | 2,862.20 | 2,302.08 |
| Gold (Million Fine Troy Ounces) | 1ad | .065 | .095 | .095 | .095 | .095 | .075 | .075 | .080 | .115 | .175 | .175 | .160 |
| Gold (National Valuation) | 1and | 28.95 | 49.00 | 60.51 | 79.22 | 82.68 | 83.03 | 106.25 | 125.26 | 191.29 | 209.91 | 209.81 | 170.22 |
| Central Bank: Other Assets | 3..d | 62.49 | 46.44 | 38.78 | 18.61 | 5.40 | 42.58 | 7.09 | 21.26 | 31.51 | 34.78 | 10.33 | 4.02 |
| Central Bank: Other Liabs | 4..d | 5.18 | .04 | 2.79 | 7.26 | 9.07 | 12.54 | 4.78 | 12.15 | 19.62 | 26.65 | 31.83 | 78.04 |
| Other Depository Corps.: Assets | 7a.d | 332.49 | 417.21 | 563.58 | 854.14 | 735.93 | 761.48 | 1,010.44 | 960.31 | 1,212.86 | 1,139.11 | 1,056.42 | 1,087.82 |
| Other Depository Corps.: Liabs | 7b.d | 89.99 | 99.52 | 66.70 | 126.42 | 143.86 | 278.51 | 311.61 | 369.70 | 498.56 | 664.48 | 661.32 | 574.60 |
| **Central Bank** | | | | | *Millions of Meticais Novos: End of Period* | | | | | | | | |
| Net Foreign Assets | 11n | 21,534.0 | 26,401.4 | 34,703.1 | 36,948.2 | 41,859.5 | 49,638.8 | 57,107.5 | 56,869.4 | 73,083.1 | 85,683.1 | 91,486.0 | 91,740.9 |
| Claims on Nonresidents | 11 | 25,360.7 | 30,197.6 | 35,028.7 | 37,487.8 | 42,473.3 | 59,979.8 | 68,904.4 | 66,888.3 | 84,164.3 | 97,029.7 | 103,533.9 | 113,618.2 |
| Liabilities to Nonresidents | 16c | 3,826.7 | 3,796.2 | 325.6 | 539.6 | 613.8 | 10,341.0 | 11,796.9 | 10,019.0 | 11,081.2 | 11,346.6 | 12,048.0 | 21,877.2 |
| Claims on Other Depository Corps. | 12e | 426.8 | 773.4 | 560.9 | 289.4 | 192.5 | 2,349.1 | 510.6 | 358.1 | 493.8 | 74.6 | 77.5 | 1,738.2 |
| Net Claims on Central Government | 12an | −7,626.3 | −14,916.5 | −17,223.1 | −18,951.8 | −23,751.4 | −25,154.8 | −20,611.7 | −26,756.7 | −27,543.6 | −45,685.2 | −50,966.7 | −31,567.7 |
| Claims on Central Government | 12a | 3,455.3 | 1,682.1 | 3,182.1 | 4,502.3 | 4,755.2 | 4,789.6 | 4,518.6 | 4,519.1 | 4,523.2 | 5,510.1 | 9,216.5 | 6,658.1 |
| Liabilities to Central Government | 16d | 11,081.6 | 16,598.6 | 20,405.2 | 23,454.1 | 28,506.6 | 29,944.4 | 25,130.3 | 31,275.8 | 32,066.8 | 51,195.3 | 60,183.3 | 38,225.8 |
| Claims on Other Sectors | 12s | 50.4 | 73.4 | 291.4 | 307.9 | 390.8 | 424.3 | 510.8 | 930.3 | 1,341.2 | 1,332.1 | 1,680.6 | 1,696.7 |
| Claims on Other Financial Corps. | 12g | — | — | — | — | — | — | — | — | — | — | — | — |
| Claims on State & Local Govts. | 12b | .2 | .2 | .2 | — | — | — | — | — | — | — | — | — |
| Claims on Public Nonfin. Corps. | 12c | — | — | — | — | — | — | — | — | — | — | — | — |
| Claims on Private Sector | 12d | 50.1 | 73.2 | 291.2 | 307.9 | 390.8 | 424.3 | 510.7 | 930.3 | 1,341.2 | 1,332.1 | 1,680.6 | 1,696.7 |
| Monetary Base | 14 | 10,433.4 | 12,184.8 | 14,735.9 | 17,821.9 | 19,220.4 | 24,463.9 | 31,618.3 | 34,311.1 | 41,086.0 | 47,537.8 | 57,283.2 | 73,907.7 |
| Currency in Circulation | 14a | 6,202.7 | 7,335.8 | 8,789.3 | 10,942.2 | 11,995.9 | 16,117.4 | 20,446.6 | 21,898.7 | 26,242.2 | 30,351.1 | 36,316.0 | 39,334.5 |
| Liabs. to Other Depository Corps. | 14c | 4,230.8 | 4,849.0 | 5,946.6 | 6,879.8 | 7,224.5 | 8,346.6 | 11,171.7 | 12,412.4 | 14,843.8 | 17,186.7 | 20,967.3 | 34,573.3 |
| Liabilities to Other Sectors | 14d | — | — | — | — | — | — | — | — | — | — | — | — |
| Other Liabs. to Other Dep. Corps. | 14n | 4,331.0 | 300.1 | — | 197.2 | 1,392.1 | 46.9 | 74.4 | 4,199.2 | 13,173.7 | 10,082.7 | 4,435.8 | 8,998.1 |
| Dep. & Sec. Excl. f/Monetary Base | 14o | 307.5 | 476.7 | 476.9 | 600.8 | 670.3 | 608.1 | 736.5 | 1,050.8 | 1,095.3 | 1,316.6 | 1,610.0 | 1,940.9 |
| Deposits Included in Broad Money | 15 | 307.5 | 476.7 | 476.9 | 600.8 | 670.3 | 608.1 | 736.5 | 1,050.8 | 1,095.3 | 1,316.6 | 1,610.0 | 1,940.9 |
| Sec.Ot.th.Shares Incl.in Brd. Money | 16a | — | — | — | — | — | — | — | — | — | — | — | — |
| Deposits Excl. from Broad Money | 16b | — | — | — | — | — | — | — | — | — | — | — | — |
| Sec.Ot.th.Shares Excl.f/Brd.Money. | 16s | — | — | — | — | — | — | — | — | — | — | — | — |
| Loans | 16l | — | — | — | — | — | — | — | — | — | — | — | — |
| Financial Derivatives | 16m | — | — | — | — | — | — | — | — | — | — | — | — |
| Shares and Other Equity | 17a | −4,830.2 | −1,852.0 | 2,863.9 | 3,007.9 | 1,853.6 | 4,145.5 | 7,295.7 | −5,449.4 | −4,982.9 | −15,138.3 | −13,236.6 | −2,434.5 |
| Other Items (Net) | 17r | 4,143.1 | 1,222.2 | 255.7 | −3,034.0 | −4,445.0 | −2,007.1 | −2,207.6 | −2,710.7 | −2,997.6 | −2,394.3 | −7,815.1 | −18,804.0 |
| Memo Item: | | | | | | | | | | | | | |
| Total Assets | 10ra | 30,884.2 | 34,902.3 | 42,378.0 | 47,606.1 | 53,665.4 | 70,921.2 | 78,300.0 | 340,498.7 | 420,906.8 | 500,516.8 | 570,678.9 | 634,046.9 |
| **Other Depository Corporations** | | | | | *Millions of Meticais Novos: End of Period* | | | | | | | | |
| Net Foreign Assets | 21n | 4,583.1 | 7,682.6 | 12,903.9 | 17,334.4 | 15,097.8 | 14,097.8 | 22,767.8 | 16,129.6 | 21,250.4 | 14,276.6 | 13,275.2 | 23,556.8 |
| Claims on Nonresidents | 21 | 6,283.9 | 10,089.3 | 14,636.2 | 20,345.7 | 18,766.2 | 22,227.5 | 32,920.1 | 26,226.2 | 36,082.5 | 34,264.3 | 35,495.6 | 49,931.0 |
| Liabilities to Nonresidents | 26c | 1,700.8 | 2,406.8 | 1,732.3 | 3,011.3 | 3,668.5 | 8,129.7 | 10,152.3 | 10,096.6 | 14,832.1 | 19,987.7 | 22,220.3 | 26,374.2 |
| Claims on Central Bank | 20 | 9,631.1 | 6,353.1 | 7,757.0 | 8,843.9 | 11,331.4 | 11,896.2 | 14,450.3 | 20,874.7 | 34,589.9 | 34,436.5 | 35,537.2 | 52,166.5 |
| Currency | 20a | 977.9 | 1,225.6 | 1,637.3 | 1,991.8 | 2,409.2 | 3,063.8 | 3,053.0 | 4,423.1 | 6,580.4 | 7,639.9 | 8,979.2 | 9,311.1 |
| Reserve Deposits and Securities | 20b | 4,316.8 | 4,789.4 | 6,049.7 | 6,759.4 | 7,817.5 | 8,616.1 | 11,219.3 | 12,423.2 | 15,655.0 | 16,674.8 | 23,270.3 | 39,327.4 |
| Other Claims | 20n | 4,336.4 | 338.1 | 70.0 | 92.7 | 1,104.6 | 216.3 | 178.0 | 4,028.4 | 12,354.5 | 10,121.9 | 3,287.8 | 3,528.0 |
| Net Claims on Central Government | 22an | 4,503.3 | 7,535.3 | 5,291.2 | 8,968.4 | 12,228.6 | 13,824.4 | 8,409.6 | 21,106.5 | 27,481.2 | 31,659.2 | 42,071.4 | 54,857.4 |
| Claims on Central Government | 22a | 8,708.9 | 13,030.9 | 11,958.1 | 16,038.0 | 20,253.8 | 24,084.9 | 18,441.0 | 33,159.8 | 40,958.2 | 51,889.3 | 64,786.8 | 78,514.2 |
| Liabilities to Central Government | 26d | 4,205.7 | 5,495.6 | 6,666.9 | 7,069.6 | 8,025.3 | 10,260.5 | 10,031.4 | 12,053.4 | 13,477.1 | 20,230.1 | 22,715.3 | 23,656.7 |
| Claims on Other Sectors | 22s | 13,547.9 | 19,903.5 | 26,198.2 | 30,569.9 | 44,652.3 | 71,016.8 | 91,861.4 | 97,321.3 | 116,489.0 | 150,331.2 | 192,989.2 | 230,431.0 |
| Claims on Other Financial Corps. | 22g | — | — | — | — | 40.9 | 43.6 | 246.7 | 237.1 | 518.4 | 359.7 | 1,045.7 | 1,332.1 |
| Claims on State & Local Govts. | 22b | — | — | — | — | — | .3 | — | 30.0 | .2 | 4.8 | 4.7 | 584.4 |
| Claims on Public Nonfin. Corps. | 22c | 1,419.2 | 2,011.7 | 2,591.5 | 2,822.9 | 1,007.0 | 5,415.7 | 8,224.2 | 9,086.6 | 11,100.6 | 15,336.1 | 23,455.5 | 22,482.7 |
| Claims on Private Sector | 22d | 12,128.7 | 17,891.8 | 23,606.6 | 27,747.0 | 43,604.4 | 65,557.1 | 83,390.5 | 87,967.6 | 104,869.9 | 134,630.5 | 168,483.4 | 206,031.7 |
| Liabilities to Central Bank | 26g | 82.9 | 514.7 | 179.8 | 98.1 | 55.3 | 2,669.6 | 445.6 | 46.6 | 55.3 | 21.2 | 738.3 | 1,359.7 |
| Transf.Dep.Included in Broad Money | 24 | 19,388.6 | 25,418.7 | 30,408.4 | 36,813.3 | 43,610.6 | 60,239.5 | 73,008.0 | 79,052.0 | 108,439.1 | 121,993.1 | 152,655.1 | 186,429.7 |
| Other Dep.Included in Broad Money | 25 | 9,198.5 | 10,399.5 | 13,437.4 | 18,620.3 | 26,652.4 | 33,173.7 | 42,273.7 | 46,223.3 | 56,816.9 | 70,404.0 | 82,868.0 | 115,070.7 |
| Sec.Ot.th.Shares Incl.in Brd. Money | 26a | 361.1 | 1,379.7 | 2,530.0 | 2,114.7 | 203.8 | — | — | — | — | — | — | — |
| Deposits Excl. from Broad Money | 26b | — | — | — | — | — | — | — | — | — | — | — | — |
| Sec.Ot.th.Shares Excl.f/Brd.Money. | 26s | 2.4 | 2.0 | 2.8 | 2.6 | 715.1 | 808.8 | 1,914.1 | 3,070.3 | 3,706.9 | 3,873.4 | 4,227.2 | 4,813.6 |
| Loans | 26l | — | — | — | — | 40.9 | 33.0 | 45.7 | 54.4 | 84.0 | 103.8 | 426.6 | 753.5 |
| Financial Derivatives | 26m | — | — | — | — | — | — | — | — | — | — | — | — |
| Insurance Technical Reserves | 26r | — | — | — | — | — | — | — | — | — | — | — | — |
| Shares and Other Equity | 27a | 3,690.7 | 4,389.9 | 6,498.9 | 8,514.4 | 11,039.1 | 14,076.6 | 19,262.9 | 27,936.5 | 34,237.9 | 38,296.7 | 48,799.3 | 63,176.7 |
| Other Items (Net) | 27r | −458.9 | −629.9 | −907.0 | −446.8 | 993.0 | −166.0 | 539.1 | −951.0 | −3,529.5 | −3,988.7 | −5,841.3 | −10,591.3 |
| Memo Item: | | | | | | | | | | | | | |
| Total Assets | 20ra | 44,149.0 | 56,138.7 | 68,308.9 | 84,523.7 | 103,947.7 | 139,485.8 | 181,895.2 | 204,950.2 | 263,993.5 | 307,163.9 | 381,306.8 | 473,315.5 |

# Mozambique  688

| | | 2004 | 2005 | 2006 | 2007 | 2008 | 2009 | 2010 | 2011 | 2012 | 2013 | 2014 | 2015 |
|---|---|---|---|---|---|---|---|---|---|---|---|---|---|
| **Depository Corporations** | | Millions of Meticais Novos: End of Period | | | | | | | | | | | |
| Net Foreign Assets | 31n | 26,117.1 | 34,084.0 | 47,607.0 | 54,282.6 | 56,957.3 | 63,736.5 | 79,875.4 | 72,998.9 | 94,333.5 | 99,959.7 | 104,761.2 | 115,297.7 |
| Claims on Nonresidents | 31 | 31,644.6 | 40,286.9 | 49,664.9 | 57,833.5 | 61,239.5 | 82,207.3 | 101,824.6 | 93,114.5 | 120,246.8 | 131,294.0 | 139,029.5 | 163,549.2 |
| Liabilities to Nonresidents | 36c | 5,527.5 | 6,203.0 | 2,057.9 | 3,550.9 | 4,282.3 | 18,470.8 | 21,949.2 | 20,115.6 | 25,913.3 | 31,334.3 | 34,268.3 | 48,251.4 |
| Domestic Claims | 32 | 10,475.2 | 12,595.7 | 14,557.7 | 20,894.5 | 33,520.2 | 60,110.7 | 80,170.1 | 92,601.3 | 117,767.8 | 137,637.3 | 185,774.5 | 255,417.5 |
| Net Claims on Central Government | 32an | −3,123.1 | −7,381.2 | −11,931.9 | −9,983.3 | −11,522.9 | −11,330.4 | −12,202.1 | −5,650.3 | −62.5 | −14,026.0 | −8,895.3 | 23,289.8 |
| Claims on Central Government | 32a | 12,164.2 | 14,713.0 | 15,140.2 | 20,540.4 | 25,009.0 | 28,874.5 | 22,959.6 | 37,678.9 | 45,481.4 | 57,399.4 | 74,003.3 | 85,172.3 |
| Liabilities to Central Government | 36d | 15,287.3 | 22,094.2 | 27,072.1 | 30,523.7 | 36,531.9 | 40,204.9 | 35,161.7 | 43,329.1 | 45,543.9 | 71,425.5 | 82,898.6 | 61,882.5 |
| Claims on Other Sectors | 32s | 13,598.3 | 19,976.9 | 26,489.6 | 30,877.8 | 45,043.1 | 71,441.1 | 92,372.2 | 98,251.6 | 117,830.2 | 151,663.3 | 194,669.8 | 232,127.7 |
| Claims on Other Financial Corps. | 32g | — | — | — | — | 40.9 | 43.6 | 246.7 | 237.1 | 518.4 | 359.7 | 1,045.7 | 1,332.1 |
| Claims on State & Local Govts. | 32b | .2 | .2 | .2 | — | — | .3 | — | 30.0 | .2 | 4.8 | 4.7 | 584.4 |
| Claims on Public Nonfin. Corps. | 32c | 1,419.2 | 2,011.7 | 2,591.5 | 2,822.9 | 1,007.0 | 5,415.7 | 8,224.2 | 9,086.6 | 11,100.6 | 15,336.1 | 23,455.5 | 22,482.7 |
| Claims on Private Sector | 32d | 12,178.8 | 17,965.0 | 23,897.9 | 28,054.9 | 43,995.2 | 65,981.4 | 83,901.2 | 88,897.9 | 106,211.0 | 135,962.6 | 170,164.0 | 207,728.4 |
| Broad Money Liabilities | 35l | 34,480.5 | 43,784.7 | 54,004.8 | 67,099.4 | 80,723.7 | 107,075.0 | 133,411.8 | 143,801.7 | 186,013.0 | 216,424.9 | 264,469.8 | 333,464.6 |
| Currency Outside Depository Corps | 34a | 5,224.8 | 6,110.2 | 7,152.0 | 8,950.4 | 9,586.7 | 13,053.6 | 17,393.6 | 17,475.6 | 19,661.8 | 22,711.3 | 27,336.8 | 30,023.4 |
| Transferable Deposits | 34 | 19,696.1 | 25,895.4 | 30,885.3 | 37,414.0 | 44,280.8 | 60,847.7 | 73,744.5 | 80,102.8 | 109,534.3 | 123,309.7 | 154,265.1 | 188,370.6 |
| Other Deposits | 35 | 9,198.5 | 10,399.5 | 13,437.4 | 18,620.3 | 26,652.4 | 33,173.7 | 42,273.7 | 46,223.3 | 56,816.9 | 70,404.0 | 82,868.0 | 115,070.7 |
| Securities Other than Shares | 36a | 361.1 | 1,379.7 | 2,530.0 | 2,114.7 | 203.8 | — | — | — | — | — | — | — |
| Deposits Excl. from Broad Money | 36b | — | — | — | — | — | — | — | — | — | — | — | — |
| Sec.Ot.th.Shares Excl.f/Brd.Money | 36s | 2.4 | 2.0 | 2.8 | 2.6 | 715.1 | 808.8 | 1,914.1 | 3,070.3 | 3,706.9 | 3,873.4 | 4,227.2 | 4,813.6 |
| Loans | 36l | — | — | — | — | 40.9 | 33.0 | 45.7 | 54.4 | 84.0 | 103.8 | 426.6 | 753.5 |
| Financial Derivatives | 36m | — | — | — | — | — | — | — | — | — | — | — | — |
| Insurance Technical Reserves | 36r | — | — | — | — | — | — | — | — | — | — | — | — |
| Shares and Other Equity | 37a | −1,139.5 | 2,537.9 | 9,362.7 | 11,522.3 | 12,892.7 | 18,222.1 | 26,558.6 | 22,487.1 | 29,255.0 | 23,158.5 | 35,562.6 | 60,742.2 |
| Other Items (Net) | 37r | 3,249.0 | 355.2 | −1,205.6 | −3,447.2 | −3,894.8 | −2,291.6 | −1,884.8 | −3,813.3 | −6,957.6 | −5,963.6 | −14,150.5 | −29,057.8 |
| Broad Money Liabs., Seasonally Adj. | 35l.b | 33,782.9 | 42,735.1 | 52,512.6 | 65,085.6 | 78,136.2 | 103,509.6 | 128,904.6 | 138,785.3 | 179,235.7 | 208,165.9 | 254,187.7 | 320,434.1 |
| **Monetary Aggregates** | | Millions of Meticais Novos: End of Period | | | | | | | | | | | |
| Broad Money | 59m | 34,480.5 | 43,784.7 | 54,004.8 | 67,099.4 | 80,723.7 | 107,075.0 | 133,411.8 | 143,801.7 | 186,013.0 | 216,424.9 | 264,469.8 | 333,464.6 |
| o/w:Currency Issued by Cent.Govt | 59m.a | — | — | — | — | — | — | — | — | — | — | — | — |
| o/w: Dep.in Nonfin. Corporations | 59m.b | — | — | — | — | — | — | — | — | — | — | — | — |
| o/w:Secs. Issued by Central Govt. | 59m.c | — | — | — | — | — | — | — | — | — | — | — | — |
| Money (National Definitions) | | | | | | | | | | | | | |
| Base Money | 19ma | 10,433.4 | 12,184.8 | 14,736.0 | 17,821.9 | 19,220.4 | 24,463.9 | 31,618.3 | 34,311.1 | 41,086.0 | 47,537.8 | 57,283.2 | 73,907.7 |
| M1 | 59ma | 24,479.8 | 32,287.3 | 38,389.7 | 45,838.0 | 53,867.5 | 73,901.3 | 89,193.3 | 97,578.4 | 129,196.1 | 146,021.0 | 181,601.8 | 218,393.9 |
| M2 | 59mb | 34,480.5 | 43,784.7 | 54,004.8 | 67,099.4 | 80,723.7 | 107,075.0 | 133,411.8 | 143,801.7 | 186,013.0 | 216,424.9 | 264,469.8 | 333,464.6 |
| **Interest Rates** | | Percent Per Annum | | | | | | | | | | | |
| Discount Rate (End of Period) | 60.a | 9.95 | 9.95 | 9.95 | 9.95 | 9.95 | 9.95 | 9.95 | 9.95 | 9.95 | 9.95 | 9.95 | 9.95 |
| Money Market Rate | 60b | 9.87 | 6.35 | 15.25 | 15.15 | 12.84 | 8.66 | 10.24 | 14.06 | 5.79 | 3.24 | 3.18 | 3.66 |
| Treasury Bill Rate | 60c | 12.37 | 9.10 | 15.05 | 15.16 | 13.76 | 10.59 | 11.99 | 15.24 | 5.27 | 4.13 | 5.33 | .... |
| Deposit Rate | 60l | 9.90 | 7.80 | 10.37 | 11.85 | 10.98 | 9.52 | 9.68 | 12.98 | 11.43 | 8.80 | 8.58 | 8.53 |
| Lending Rate | 60p | 22.08 | 19.47 | 18.56 | 19.52 | 18.31 | 15.68 | 16.26 | 19.10 | 16.81 | 15.32 | 14.80 | 14.87 |
| **Prices** | | Index Numbers (2010=100): Period Averages | | | | | | | | | | | |
| Consumer Prices | 64 | 59.3 | †63.6 | 72.0 | 77.9 | 85.9 | 88.7 | †100.0 | 110.4 | 113.3 | 118.1 | 121.2 | 125.5 |
| **Intl. Transactions & Positions** | | Millions of US Dollars | | | | | | | | | | | |
| Exports | 70..d | 1,504 | 1,745 | 2,381 | 2,412 | 2,653 | 2,147 | 2,333 | 3,604 | 3,856 | 4,024 | 5,072 | 4,195 |
| Imports, c.i.f | 71..d | 2,035 | 2,408 | 2,869 | 3,050 | 4,008 | 3,764 | 3,864 | 6,312 | 8,688 | 10,099 | 11,611 | 8,293 |

# Mozambique 688

## Balance of Payments

| | | 2004 | 2005 | 2006 | 2007 | 2008 | 2009 | 2010 | 2011 | 2012 | 2013 | 2014 | 2015 |
|---|---|---|---|---|---|---|---|---|---|---|---|---|---|
| | | | | | | | *Millions of US Dollars* | | | | | | |
| A. Current Account* | 109bx | .... | −760.6 | −755.4 | −786.2 | −1,147.2 | −1,226.2 | −1,679.4 | −3,328.9 | −6,790.0 | −6,253.4 | −5,797.1 | −6,155.4 |
| Goods, credit (exports) | 1a9cx | .... | 1,745.3 | 2,381.1 | 2,412.1 | 2,653.3 | 2,147.2 | 2,333.3 | 3,118.3 | 3,855.5 | 4,122.6 | 3,916.4 | 3,413.3 |
| Goods, debit (imports) | 1a9dx | .... | 2,242.3 | 2,648.8 | 2,811.1 | 3,643.4 | 3,422.0 | 3,512.4 | 5,367.6 | 7,903.1 | 8,479.5 | 7,951.7 | 7,576.6 |
| Balance on goods | 1a9bx | .... | −497.1 | −267.7 | −399.0 | −990.2 | −1,274.8 | −1,179.2 | −2,249.3 | −4,047.5 | −4,356.9 | −4,035.3 | −4,163.3 |
| Services, credit (exports) | 1b9cx | .... | 342.0 | 395.6 | 458.7 | 555.3 | 611.7 | 244.9 | 366.0 | 792.1 | 645.5 | 724.9 | 722.6 |
| Services, debit (imports) | 1b9dx | .... | 648.6 | 749.6 | 856.5 | 965.3 | 1,044.3 | 1,213.7 | 2,250.6 | 4,497.8 | 3,904.3 | 3,657.1 | 3,344.7 |
| Balance on Goods & Services | 1z9bx | .... | −803.7 | −621.7 | −796.8 | −1,400.2 | −1,707.4 | −2,148.0 | −4,133.9 | −7,753.2 | −7,615.7 | −6,967.5 | −6,785.4 |
| Primary income: credit | 1c9cx | .... | 98.9 | 159.8 | 193.6 | 156.5 | 150.3 | 134.8 | 184.0 | 133.1 | 134.3 | 128.0 | 112.5 |
| Primary income: debit | 1c9dx | .... | 458.8 | 794.3 | 785.2 | 798.3 | 432.1 | 494.0 | 383.1 | 208.5 | 192.9 | 329.9 | 336.2 |
| Balance on gds, serv. & prim. inc. | 1y9bx | .... | −1,163.5 | −1,256.1 | −1,388.4 | −2,042.1 | −1,989.3 | −2,507.3 | −4,333.0 | −7,828.7 | −7,674.3 | −7,169.5 | −7,009.1 |
| Secondary income: credit | 1d9ca | .... | 480.7 | 574.5 | 667.6 | 1,019.9 | 931.7 | 861.6 | 1,041.7 | 1,109.2 | 1,506.0 | 1,497.1 | 991.0 |
| Secondary income: debit | 1d9da | .... | 77.8 | 73.8 | 65.4 | 125.1 | 168.6 | 33.7 | 37.5 | 70.5 | 85.2 | 124.8 | 137.3 |
| B. Capital Account* | 209ba | .... | 187.9 | 524.5 | 415.1 | 419.9 | 422.3 | 354.9 | 445.6 | 489.6 | 422.8 | 374.9 | 287.8 |
| Capital account: credit | 209ca | .... | 191.8 | 526.8 | 416.1 | 427.9 | 428.9 | 354.9 | 445.6 | 489.6 | 422.8 | 374.9 | 287.8 |
| Capital account: debit | 209da | .... | 3.9 | 2.3 | 1.0 | 8.0 | 6.6 | | | | | | |
| Balance on current & capital acct. | 129ba | .... | −572.7 | −230.9 | −371.1 | −727.3 | −803.9 | −1,324.5 | −2,883.2 | −6,300.4 | −5,830.7 | −5,422.3 | −5,867.6 |
| C. Financial Account* | 309na | .... | −427.2 | 1,323.1 | −458.1 | −872.0 | −1,231.3 | −1,470.8 | −3,136.3 | −6,645.7 | −6,204.4 | −5,338.8 | −5,199.2 |
| Direct investment: assets | 3a9aa | .... | 14.6 | 138.1 | 17.4 | 49.8 | 34.5 | 237.9 | 83.6 | 8.9 | 522.3 | 97.0 | 1.5 |
| Equity & investment fund shares.. | 3aaaa | .... | .... | −.4 | .8 | .... | — | −.6 | −1.0 | .... | .... | .... | .... |
| Debt instruments | 3abaa | .... | 14.6 | 138.5 | 16.6 | 49.8 | 34.5 | 238.5 | 84.6 | 8.9 | 522.3 | 97.0 | 1.5 |
| Direct investment: liabilities | 3a9la | .... | 122.4 | 251.1 | 416.7 | 641.4 | 930.1 | 1,258.5 | 3,663.9 | 5,635.1 | 6,697.4 | 4,998.8 | 3,712.3 |
| Equity & investment fund shares . | 3aala | .... | 59.8 | 189.0 | 192.2 | 254.3 | 242.4 | 410.1 | 1,402.0 | 216.0 | 959.0 | 553.2 | 1,128.1 |
| Debt instruments | 3abla | .... | 62.6 | 62.2 | 224.5 | 387.1 | 687.7 | 848.3 | 2,261.9 | 5,419.1 | 5,738.4 | 4,445.6 | 2,584.2 |
| Portfolio investment: assets | 3b9aa | .... | 88.8 | 124.2 | 1.4 | 10.0 | −3.4 | .3 | 33.7 | 22.0 | 56.5 | −6.5 | −17.5 |
| Equity & investment fund shares | 3baaa | .... | .1 | .2 | 1.4 | .4 | .4 | .1 | 1.7 | 41.9 | 1.9 | 5.8 | −3.6 |
| Debt securities | 3bbaa | .... | 88.7 | 124.0 | .... | 9.6 | −3.8 | .2 | 32.0 | −19.9 | 54.6 | −12.3 | −13.9 |
| Portfolio investment: liabilities | 3b9la | .... | .3 | .4 | .2 | .5 | — | .8 | .... | .... | 798.2 | 9.6 | −82.7 |
| Equity & investment fund shares . | 3bala | .... | .3 | .4 | .3 | .4 | — | | .... | .... | .... | .... | .... |
| Debt securities | 3bbla | .... | .... | .... | — | .1 | — | .8 | .... | .... | 798.2 | 9.6 | −82.7 |
| Fin. der.& empl.stk.ops.(ESOs): net. | 3c9na | .... | .... | .... | 16.0 | .... | .... | .... | .... | .... | .... | .... | .... |
| Fin. der. & ESOs.: assets | 3c9aa | .... | .... | .... | 16.0 | .... | .... | .... | .... | .... | .... | .... | .... |
| Fin. der. & ESOs.: liabilities | 3c9la | .... | .... | .... | .... | .... | .... | .... | .... | .... | .... | .... | .... |
| Other investment: assets | 3d9aa | .... | −253.5 | −205.2 | 385.1 | −92.0 | −200.7 | −48.0 | 567.7 | −27.8 | 1,856.6 | 1,553.9 | −100.3 |
| Other equity | 3daaa | .... | .... | .... | .... | .... | .... | .... | .... | .... | .... | .... | .... |
| Debt instruments | 3dzaa | .... | −253.5 | −205.2 | 385.1 | −92.0 | −200.7 | −48.0 | 567.7 | −27.8 | 1,856.6 | 1,553.9 | −100.3 |
| Other investment: liabilities | 3d9la | .... | 154.3 | −1,517.5 | 461.1 | 197.8 | 131.7 | 401.6 | 157.4 | 1,013.6 | 1,144.1 | 1,974.9 | 1,453.3 |
| Other equity | 3dala | .... | .... | .... | .... | .... | .... | .... | .... | .... | .... | .... | .... |
| Debt instruments | 3dzla | .... | 154.3 | −1,517.5 | 461.1 | 197.8 | 131.7 | 401.6 | 157.4 | 1,013.6 | 1,144.1 | 1,974.9 | 1,453.3 |
| Curr.+ cap.− finan. acct. balance.. | 4y9na | .... | −145.5 | −1,554.0 | 87.0 | 144.7 | 427.5 | 146.2 | 253.1 | 345.3 | 373.7 | −83.4 | −668.4 |
| D. Net Errors and Omissions | 409na | .... | 24.4 | 3.4 | 28.3 | −66.9 | −217.7 | 54.8 | −9.4 | 32.1 | 22.4 | −23.9 | −13.0 |
| E. Reserves and Related Items | 4z9na | .... | −121.1 | −1,550.6 | 115.3 | 77.8 | 209.8 | 201.1 | 243.7 | 377.4 | 396.1 | −107.3 | −681.4 |
| Reserve assets | 3e9aa | .... | −54.3 | 121.3 | 263.4 | 97.3 | 366.4 | 232.0 | 242.4 | 375.2 | 393.1 | −110.6 | −595.8 |
| Credit and loans from the IMF | 3dcla | .... | −25.3 | −149.4 | 4.9 | — | 154.7 | 20.6 | −1.5 | −2.2 | −3.0 | −3.2 | 85.6 |
| Exceptional financing | 409la | .... | 92.1 | 1,821.4 | 143.1 | 19.5 | 1.9 | 10.4 | .3 | .... | .... | .... | .... |

*Excludes components in group E

## International Investment Position

| | | 2004 | 2005 | 2006 | 2007 | 2008 | 2009 | 2010 | 2011 | 2012 | 2013 | 2014 | 2015 |
|---|---|---|---|---|---|---|---|---|---|---|---|---|---|
| | | | | | | | *Millions of US Dollars* | | | | | | |
| Assets | 809aa | .... | 2,248.4 | † 2,445.6 | 3,311.5 | 3,484.4 | 3,530.1 | 3,854.5 | 4,736.7 | 6,020.6 | 8,409.3 | 9,908.3 | 9,190.2 |
| Direct investment | 8a9aa | .... | 6.3 | † 153.5 | 17.9 | 5.0 | 124.0 | 80.7 | 90.3 | 97.2 | 100.6 | 170.5 | 172.1 |
| Equity & investment fund shares.. | 8aaaa | .... | .... | † .4 | .... | .... | .... | .... | .... | .... | .... | .... | .... |
| Debt instruments | 8abaa | .... | 6.3 | † 153.5 | 17.9 | 5.0 | 124.0 | 80.7 | 90.3 | 97.2 | 100.6 | 170.5 | 172.1 |
| Portfolio investment | 8b9aa | .... | 157.2 | † 68.5 | 203.1 | 213.0 | 7.0 | 7.3 | 41.0 | 21.0 | 73.5 | 68.5 | 51.0 |
| Equity & investment fund shares.. | 8baaa | .... | 7.2 | † — | 1.7 | 2.1 | 2.1 | 2.2 | 3.9 | 2.8 | 3.9 | 11.2 | 7.7 |
| Debt securities | 8bbaa | .... | 150.1 | † 68.5 | 201.4 | 211.0 | 4.9 | 5.1 | 37.1 | 18.2 | 69.5 | 57.3 | 43.3 |
| Fin. der.(oth.than reserves) & ESOs | 8c9aa | .... | .... | .... | 16.0 | 16.0 | 16.0 | 16.0 | 16.0 | 16.0 | 16.0 | 16.0 | 16.0 |
| Other investment | 8d9aa | .... | 982.6 | † 1,360.3 | 1,587.6 | 1,666.0 | 1,431.9 | 1,570.3 | 2,167.3 | 3,088.8 | 5,028.3 | 6,582.2 | 6,481.9 |
| Other equity | 8daaa | .... | .... | .... | .... | .... | .... | .... | .... | .... | .... | .... | .... |
| Debt instruments | 8dzaa | .... | 982.6 | † 1,360.3 | 1,587.6 | 1,666.0 | 1,431.9 | 1,570.3 | 2,167.3 | 3,088.8 | 5,028.3 | 6,582.2 | 6,481.9 |
| Reserve assets | 8e9aa | .... | 1,102.3 | † 863.2 | 1,487.0 | 1,584.3 | 1,951.2 | 2,180.2 | 2,422.2 | 2,797.5 | 3,190.9 | 3,071.0 | 2,469.3 |
| Liabilities | 809la | .... | 12,061.9 | † 14,610.5 | 11,587.5 | 12,267.3 | 13,580.7 | 14,737.5 | 18,426.2 | 25,024.4 | 33,379.4 | 40,381.2 | 45,536.0 |
| Direct investment | 8a9la | .... | 2,658.7 | † 2,541.6 | 3,230.6 | 3,665.9 | 3,905.4 | 4,719.3 | 8,313.5 | 13,907.3 | 20,266.4 | 25,238.2 | 28,950.5 |
| Equity & investment fund shares.. | 8aala | .... | 2,440.7 | † 2,380.9 | 2,720.6 | 2,851.2 | 2,010.1 | 2,389.7 | 3,791.7 | 3,988.5 | 4,462.1 | 5,015.3 | 6,143.4 |
| Debt instruments | 8abla | .... | 218.0 | † 160.7 | 510.0 | 814.7 | 1,895.3 | 2,329.6 | 4,521.8 | 9,918.8 | 15,804.3 | 20,222.9 | 22,807.1 |
| Portfolio investment | 8b9la | .... | .3 | † — | 3.4 | 4.0 | 1.5 | 2.3 | 1.5 | 1.9 | 800.2 | 809.8 | 727.1 |
| Equity & investment fund shares.. | 8bala | .... | .3 | † — | 1.0 | 1.4 | 1.3 | 1.3 | 1.3 | 1.8 | 1.8 | 1.8 | 1.8 |
| Debt securities | 8bbla | .... | .... | .... | 2.4 | 2.7 | .1 | 1.0 | .1 | .1 | 798.4 | 808.0 | 725.3 |
| Fin. der.(oth.than reserves) & ESOs | 8c9la | .... | .... | .... | .... | .... | .... | .... | .... | .... | .... | .... | .... |
| Other investment | 8d9la | .... | 9,402.9 | † 12,068.9 | 8,353.6 | 8,597.3 | 9,673.8 | 10,015.9 | 10,111.2 | 11,115.2 | 12,312.8 | 14,333.3 | 15,858.4 |
| Other equity | 8dala | .... | .... | .... | .... | .... | .... | .... | .... | .... | .... | .... | .... |
| Debt instruments | 8dzla | .... | 9,402.9 | † 12,068.9 | 8,353.6 | 8,597.3 | 9,673.8 | 10,015.9 | 10,111.2 | 11,115.2 | 12,312.8 | 14,333.3 | 15,858.4 |

| | | 2004 | 2005 | 2006 | 2007 | 2008 | 2009 | 2010 | 2011 | 2012 | 2013 | 2014 | 2015 |
|---|---|---|---|---|---|---|---|---|---|---|---|---|---|
| **Government Finance** | | | | | | | | | | | | | |
| **Cash Flow Statement** | | | | | | | | | | | | | |
| **Budgetary Central Government** | | | | | | *Millions of Meticais: Fiscal Year Ends December 31* | | | | | | | |
| Cash Receipts:Operating Activities... | c1 | .... | .... | .... | .... | .... | .... | 89,016 | 106,839 | 124,454 | 154,285 | .... | .... |
| Taxes........................................ | c11 | .... | .... | .... | .... | .... | .... | 55,600 | 71,389 | 88,206 | 111,523 | .... | .... |
| Social Contributions...................... | c12 | .... | .... | .... | .... | .... | .... | 1,161 | 1,421 | 1,687 | 2,108 | .... | .... |
| Grants........................................ | c13 | .... | .... | .... | .... | .... | .... | 27,318 | 27,399 | 27,332 | 30,299 | .... | .... |
| Other Receipts............................. | c14 | .... | .... | .... | .... | .... | .... | 4,936 | 6,631 | 7,229 | 10,355 | .... | .... |
| Cash Payments:Operating Activities. | c2 | .... | .... | .... | .... | .... | .... | 76,038 | 90,492 | 105,321 | 77,178 | .... | .... |
| Compensation of Employees.......... | c21 | .... | .... | .... | .... | .... | .... | 32,504 | 39,033 | 44,373 | 48,096 | .... | .... |
| Purchases of Goods & Services....... | c22 | .... | .... | .... | .... | .... | .... | 22,367 | 25,205 | 30,521 | | .... | .... |
| Interest...................................... | c24 | .... | .... | .... | .... | .... | .... | 2,673 | 3,501 | 4,125 | 6,207 | .... | .... |
| Subsidies................................... | c25 | .... | .... | .... | .... | .... | .... | 5,259 | 5,238 | 5,240 | | .... | .... |
| Grants........................................ | c26 | .... | .... | .... | .... | .... | .... | 1,441 | 2,040 | 2,489 | 5,935 | .... | .... |
| Social Benefits............................. | c27 | .... | .... | .... | .... | .... | .... | 7,540 | 8,396 | 11,051 | 16,771 | .... | .... |
| Other Payments............................ | c28 | .... | .... | .... | .... | .... | .... | 4,255 | 7,079 | 7,521 | 169 | .... | .... |
| Net Cash Inflow:Operating Act.[1-2] | ccio | .... | .... | .... | .... | .... | .... | 12,978 | 16,347 | 19,133 | 77,107 | .... | .... |
| Net Cash Outflow:Invest. in NFA...... | c31 | .... | .... | .... | .... | .... | .... | 25,130 | 29,850 | 30,586 | 50,888 | .... | .... |
| Purchases of Nonfinancial Assets... | c31.1 | .... | .... | .... | .... | .... | .... | 25,437 | 30,036 | 30,748 | 51,069 | .... | .... |
| Sales of Nonfinancial Assets.......... | c31.2 | .... | .... | .... | .... | .... | .... | 306 | 186 | 162 | 181 | .... | .... |
| Cash Surplus/Deficit [1-2-31=1-2M] | ccsd | .... | .... | .... | .... | .... | .... | −12,152 | −13,502 | −11,453 | 26,219 | .... | .... |
| Net Acq. Fin. Assets, excl. Cash....... | c32x | .... | .... | .... | .... | .... | .... | 2,090 | 3,871 | 4,827 | 9,994 | .... | .... |
| Domestic...................................... | c321x | .... | .... | .... | .... | .... | .... | 2,090 | 3,871 | 4,827 | 9,994 | .... | .... |
| Foreign....................................... | c322x | .... | .... | .... | .... | .... | .... | — | — | — | — | .... | .... |
| Net Incurrence of Liabilities.............. | c33 | .... | .... | .... | .... | .... | .... | 20,310 | 17,174 | 15,425 | 34,689 | .... | .... |
| Domestic...................................... | c331 | .... | .... | .... | .... | .... | .... | 6,834 | 3,583 | 1,408 | 5,990 | .... | .... |
| Foreign....................................... | c332 | .... | .... | .... | .... | .... | .... | 13,476 | 13,591 | 14,017 | 28,699 | .... | .... |
| Net Cash Inflow, Fin.Act.[-32x+33].. | cnfb | .... | .... | .... | .... | .... | .... | 18,220 | 13,302 | 10,598 | 24,695 | .... | .... |
| Net Change in Stock of Cash........... | cncb | .... | .... | .... | .... | .... | .... | 5,769 | −200 | −736 | 50,914 | .... | .... |
| Stat. Discrep. [32X-33+NCB-CSD].... | ccsdz | .... | .... | .... | .... | .... | .... | −298 | — | 119 | — | .... | .... |
| Memo Item:Cash Expenditure[2+31] | c2m | .... | .... | .... | .... | .... | .... | 101,168 | 120,342 | 135,907 | 128,066 | .... | .... |
| Memo Item: Gross Debt.................. | c63 | .... | .... | .... | .... | .... | .... | .... | .... | .... | .... | .... | .... |
| **National Accounts** | | | | | | *Millions of Meticais Novos:* | | | | | | | |
| Househ.Cons.Expend.,incl.NPISHs.... | 96f | 109,881 | 126,354 | 143,382 | 186,767 | 211,290 | 235,826 | 268,348 | 289,576 | 337,190 | 363,123 | 389,891 | .... |
| Government Consumption Expend... | 91f | 17,729 | 19,663 | 22,228 | 40,614 | 47,328 | 54,299 | 64,131 | 76,137 | 90,282 | 115,101 | 136,058 | .... |
| Gross Fixed Capital Formation.......... | 93e | 23,997 | 28,361 | 31,819 | 27,276 | 42,386 | 42,340 | 61,599 | 82,232 | 152,145 | 189,791 | 225,911 | .... |
| Changes in Inventories................... | 93i | −392 | −1,544 | −1,187 | 9,346 | 5,803 | 1,759 | 1,491 | 15,738 | 53,076 | 72,875 | 19,535 | .... |
| Exports of Goods and Services......... | 90c | 38,341 | 46,213 | 54,861 | 74,638 | 81,948 | 89,990 | 108,659 | 127,587 | 140,228 | 146,451 | 162,981 | .... |
| Imports of Goods and Services (-)..... | 98c | 60,888 | 67,340 | 70,861 | 96,603 | 109,424 | 123,944 | 159,389 | 209,578 | 339,800 | 405,108 | 403,077 | .... |
| Gross Domestic Product (GDP)......... | 99b | 128,668 | 151,707 | 180,242 | 242,038 | 279,331 | 300,270 | 344,839 | 381,692 | 433,122 | 482,233 | 531,299 | .... |
| GDP Volume 2009 Prices................. | 99b.p | .... | .... | .... | 264,172 | 282,337 | 300,270 | 320,351 | 343,153 | 367,854 | 394,123 | 423,423 | .... |
| GDP Volume (2010=100)................ | 99bvp | 65.3 | 70.7 | 76.9 | † 82.5 | 88.1 | 93.7 | 100.0 | 107.1 | 114.8 | 123.0 | 132.2 | .... |
| GDP Deflator (2010=100)............... | 99bip | 57.2 | 62.2 | 68.0 | 85.1 | 91.9 | 92.9 | 100.0 | 103.3 | 109.4 | 113.7 | 116.6 | .... |
| | | | | | | *Millions: Midyear Estimates* | | | | | | | |
| Population............................... | 99z | 20.52 | 21.13 | 21.74 | 22.36 | 22.99 | 23.65 | 24.32 | 25.02 | 25.73 | 26.47 | 27.22 | 27.98 |

# Myanmar 518

| | | 2004 | 2005 | 2006 | 2007 | 2008 | 2009 | 2010 | 2011 | 2012 | 2013 | 2014 | 2015 |
|---|---|---|---|---|---|---|---|---|---|---|---|---|---|
| **Exchange Rates** | | | | | | *Kyats per SDR: End of Period* | | | | | | | |
| Official Rate | aa | 8.51 | 8.51 | 8.51 | 8.51 | 8.51 | 8.51 | 8.51 | 8.51 | 1,314.07 | 1,521.52 | 1,494.45 | 1,806.99 |
| | | | | | | *Kyats per US Dollar: End of Period (ae) Period Average (rf)* | | | | | | | |
| Official Rate | ae | 5.55 | 5.99 | 5.72 | 5.44 | 5.55 | 5.50 | 5.58 | 5.62 | 855.00 | 988.00 | 1,031.50 | 1,304.00 |
| Official Rate | rf | 5.81 | 5.82 | 5.84 | 5.62 | 5.44 | 5.58 | 5.63 | 5.44 | 640.65 | 933.57 | 984.35 | 1,162.62 |
| **Fund Position** | | | | | | *Millions of SDRs: End of Period* | | | | | | | |
| Quota | 2f.s | 258.40 | 258.40 | 258.40 | 258.40 | 258.40 | 258.40 | 258.40 | 258.40 | 258.40 | 258.40 | 258.40 | 258.40 |
| SDR Holdings | 1b.s | .03 | .16 | .14 | .25 | .05 | 72.27 | 1.68 | .62 | .31 | 1.13 | 1.90 | 1.77 |
| Reserve Position in the Fund | 1c.s | — | — | — | — | — | — | — | — | — | — | — | — |
| Total Fund Cred.&Loans Outstg | 2tl | — | — | — | — | — | — | — | — | — | — | — | — |
| SDR Allocations | 1bd | 43.47 | 43.47 | 43.47 | 43.47 | 43.47 | 245.76 | 245.76 | 245.76 | 245.76 | 245.76 | 245.76 | 245.76 |
| **International Liquidity** | | | | | | *Millions of US Dollars Unless Otherwise Indicated: End of Period* | | | | | | | |
| Total Reserves minus Gold | 1l.d | 672.1 | 770.7 | 1,235.6 | 3,088.9 | 3,717.5 | 5,251.7 | 5,716.9 | 7,003.9 | 6,964.0 | .... | .... | .... |
| SDR Holdings | 1b.d | — | .2 | .2 | .4 | .1 | 113.3 | 2.6 | 1.0 | .5 | 1.7 | 2.8 | 2.5 |
| Reserve Position in the Fund | 1c.d | — | — | — | — | — | — | — | — | — | | | |
| Foreign Exchange | 1d.d | 672.1 | 770.5 | 1,235.4 | 3,088.5 | 3,717.4 | 5,138.4 | 5,714.3 | 7,003.0 | 6,963.5 | .... | .... | .... |
| Gold (Million Fine Troy Ounces) | 1ad | .231 | .231 | .231 | .234 | .234 | .234 | .234 | .234 | .234 | .... | .... | .... |
| Gold (National Valuation) | 1and | 12.6 | 11.6 | 12.2 | 12.9 | 12.6 | 12.8 | 12.6 | 12.6 | 12.6 | .... | .... | .... |
| Central Bank: Other Assets | 3..d | | | | | | | | | | | | 7.36 |
| Central Bank: Other Liabs | 4..d | 268.68 | 575.50 | 590.55 | 540.47 | 540.55 | 481.07 | 533.94 | 452.87 | 722.61 | 468.35 | 326.44 | 393.23 |
| Other Depository Corps.: Assets | 7a.d | 503.04 | 852.84 | 1,543.56 | 2,658.87 | 3,557.90 | 4,457.20 | 4,873.78 | 8,428.55 | 5,947.85 | 5,765.25 | 6,236.31 | 6,284.15 |
| Other Depository Corps.: Liabs | 7b.d | 2,164.02 | 2,143.61 | 2,342.22 | 2,611.14 | 2,713.78 | 3,100.94 | 3,266.50 | 3,774.58 | 881.30 | 1,164.32 | 2,986.15 | 2,725.97 |
| **Central Bank** | | | | | | *Billions of Kyats: End of Period* | | | | | | | |
| Net Foreign Assets | 11n | −.80 | −2.62 | −2.56 | −2.09 | −2.23 | −1.77 | −2.16 | −1.58 | 1,203.54 | 3,074.35 | 4,126.56 | 5,313.25 |
| Claims on Nonresidents | 11 | 1.04 | 1.18 | 1.15 | 1.19 | 1.12 | 2.93 | 2.88 | 3.08 | 2,144.31 | 3,910.15 | 4,826.80 | 6,273.78 |
| Liabilities to Nonresidents | 16c | 1.84 | 3.80 | 3.71 | 3.28 | 3.36 | 4.70 | 5.04 | 4.66 | 940.77 | 835.81 | 700.24 | 960.52 |
| Claims on Other Depository Corps. | 12e | 55.28 | 11.17 | 7.21 | 10.90 | 23.93 | 12.54 | 20.88 | 42.44 | 677.36 | 909.48 | 819.79 | 673.14 |
| Net Claims on Central Government | 12an | 1,686.34 | 2,165.15 | 2,762.63 | 3,534.69 | 3,880.77 | 4,892.47 | 6,021.41 | 6,983.14 | 6,759.25 | 7,162.66 | 7,157.17 | 10,061.90 |
| Claims on Central Government | 12a | 1,686.34 | 2,165.15 | 2,762.63 | 3,534.69 | 3,880.77 | 4,892.47 | 6,021.41 | 6,983.14 | 6,759.25 | 7,163.34 | 7,167.06 | 10,322.20 |
| Liabilities to Central Government | 16d | — | — | — | — | — | — | — | — | — | .68 | 9.89 | 260.29 |
| Claims on Other Sectors | 12s | — | — | — | — | — | — | — | — | — | — | — | — |
| Claims on Other Financial Corps. | 12g | — | — | — | — | — | — | — | — | — | — | — | — |
| Claims on State & Local Govts | 12b | — | — | — | — | — | — | — | — | — | — | — | — |
| Claims on Public Nonfin. Corps. | 12c | — | — | — | — | — | — | — | — | — | — | — | — |
| Claims on Private Sector | 12d | — | — | — | — | — | — | — | — | — | — | — | — |
| Monetary Base | 14 | 1,666.06 | 2,074.45 | 2,655.17 | 3,393.76 | 3,708.08 | 4,665.75 | 5,700.62 | 6,671.84 | 8,366.59 | 10,050.01 | 10,471.95 | 13,180.21 |
| Currency in Circulation | 14a | 1,457.42 | 1,834.04 | 2,278.13 | 2,852.87 | 3,137.67 | 3,812.74 | 4,712.31 | 5,600.84 | 6,652.06 | 7,988.11 | 9,054.10 | 11,173.81 |
| Liabs. to Other Depository Corps. | 14c | 208.64 | 240.41 | 377.04 | 540.89 | 570.42 | 853.01 | 988.32 | 1,071.00 | 1,714.53 | 2,061.88 | 1,417.81 | 2,006.35 |
| Liabilities to Other Sectors | 14d | — | — | — | — | — | — | — | — | — | .02 | .05 | .05 |
| Other Liabs. to Other Dep. Corps. | 14n | 21.15 | 21.15 | 21.15 | 21.15 | 21.15 | 21.15 | 21.15 | — | 43.73 | 50.00 | 180.10 | 280.00 |
| Dep. & Sec. Excl. f/Monetary Base | 14o | — | — | — | — | — | — | — | — | — | — | — | — |
| Deposits Included in Broad Money | 15 | — | — | — | — | — | — | — | — | — | — | — | — |
| Sec.Ot.th.Shares Incl.in Brd. Money | 16a | — | — | — | — | — | — | — | — | — | — | — | — |
| Deposits Excl. from Broad Money | 16b | — | — | — | — | — | — | — | — | — | — | — | — |
| Sec.Ot.th.Shares Excl.f/Brd.Money | 16s | — | — | — | — | — | — | — | — | — | — | — | — |
| Loans | 16l | — | — | — | — | — | — | — | — | — | — | — | — |
| Financial Derivatives | 16m | — | — | — | — | — | — | — | — | — | — | — | — |
| Shares and Other Equity | 17a | 59.00 | 86.09 | 99.85 | 139.16 | 185.35 | 228.76 | 308.86 | 379.92 | 969.03 | 1,498.69 | 1,903.28 | 2,682.61 |
| Other Items (Net) | 17r | −5.38 | −7.98 | −8.90 | −10.56 | −12.12 | −12.41 | 9.50 | −27.76 | −739.21 | −452.22 | −451.81 | −94.53 |
| Memo Item: | | | | | | | | | | | | | |
| Total Assets | 10ra | 1,760.28 | 2,209.99 | 2,810.19 | 3,574.09 | 3,941.96 | 4,923.74 | 6,068.14 | 7,071.19 | 10,014.73 | 12,082.47 | 12,924.72 | 17,398.14 |
| **Other Depository Corporations** | | | | | | *Billions of Kyats: End of Period* | | | | | | | |
| Net Foreign Assets | 21n | −9.10 | −7.68 | −4.52 | .26 | 4.66 | 7.36 | 8.88 | 26.13 | 4,331.90 | 4,541.12 | 3,334.67 | 4,657.66 |
| Claims on Nonresidents | 21 | 2.76 | 5.08 | 8.73 | 14.32 | 19.65 | 24.19 | 26.93 | 47.33 | 5,085.41 | 5,690.31 | 6,398.46 | 8,225.96 |
| Liabilities to Nonresidents | 26c | 11.86 | 12.76 | 13.25 | 14.06 | 14.99 | 16.83 | 18.05 | 21.20 | 753.51 | 1,149.18 | 3,063.79 | 3,568.30 |
| Claims on Central Bank | 20 | 395.97 | 304.13 | 419.30 | 778.00 | 810.57 | 950.05 | 1,188.89 | 1,430.47 | 2,249.56 | 2,831.62 | 3,977.24 | 4,981.92 |
| Currency | 20a | 109.84 | 90.35 | 125.19 | 156.21 | 215.02 | 244.18 | 433.38 | 468.23 | 795.30 | 1,038.93 | 1,431.32 | 1,780.80 |
| Reserve Deposits and Securities | 20b | 264.98 | 192.67 | 272.96 | 600.64 | 574.41 | 684.72 | 734.37 | 962.23 | 1,232.25 | 759.17 | 552.08 | 3,041.91 |
| Other Claims | 20n | 21.15 | 21.11 | 21.15 | 21.15 | 21.15 | 21.15 | 21.15 | — | 222.01 | 1,033.52 | 1,993.84 | 159.21 |
| Net Claims on Central Government | 22an | 80.52 | 87.53 | 174.06 | 371.78 | 604.22 | 1,095.86 | 2,105.65 | 2,671.37 | −2,335.70 | −353.40 | −831.30 | −1,115.03 |
| Claims on Central Government | 22a | 119.23 | 82.84 | 117.39 | 183.80 | 506.34 | 988.60 | 1,716.78 | 2,103.32 | 2,312.91 | 3,097.57 | 12,964.90 | 13,587.30 |
| Liabilities to Central Government | 26d | 38.71 | −4.68 | −56.67 | −187.98 | −97.87 | −107.27 | −388.87 | −568.05 | 4,648.61 | 3,450.97 | 13,796.20 | 14,702.33 |
| Claims on Other Sectors | 22s | 462.16 | 581.01 | 661.85 | 807.06 | 922.77 | 1,184.12 | 1,903.15 | 3,131.69 | 7,118.14 | 8,685.08 | 12,559.41 | 15,235.90 |
| Claims on Other Financial Corps. | 22g | 2.27 | 4.55 | 4.06 | 3.75 | 5.50 | 2.27 | 2.08 | 2.20 | 1.70 | .01 | .01 | 21.29 |
| Claims on State & Local Govts | 22b | — | — | — | — | — | — | — | — | — | 240.00 | 1,031.18 | 1,178.43 |
| Claims on Public Nonfin. Corps. | 22c | 29.53 | 4.26 | 4.38 | 4.34 | 4.87 | 4.99 | 4.94 | 5.21 | 2,344.07 | 997.23 | 1,388.30 | 886.74 |
| Claims on Private Sector | 22d | 430.36 | 572.20 | 653.41 | 798.97 | 912.40 | 1,176.86 | 1,896.14 | 3,124.28 | 4,772.37 | 7,447.84 | 10,139.92 | 13,149.43 |
| Liabilities to Central Bank | 26g | 48.22 | 7.75 | 1.92 | 4.20 | 17.10 | 5.85 | 16.07 | 50.40 | 146.10 | 138.19 | 1,712.65 | — |
| Transf.Dep.Included in Broad Money | 24 | 124.17 | 188.04 | 292.65 | 484.45 | 462.74 | 630.61 | 1,269.95 | 1,556.02 | 1,774.66 | 2,636.03 | 3,295.26 | 5,003.30 |
| Other Dep.Included in Broad Money | 25 | 610.11 | 718.65 | 928.64 | 1,202.73 | 1,651.31 | 2,380.64 | 3,827.33 | 5,542.64 | 8,471.04 | 11,920.16 | 14,886.29 | 19,317.61 |
| Sec.Ot.th.Shares Incl.in Brd. Money | 26a | — | — | — | — | — | — | — | — | — | — | — | — |
| Deposits Excl. from Broad Money | 26b | .02 | .02 | .02 | .02 | .02 | .02 | .02 | .02 | .02 | .03 | .06 | .01 |
| Sec.Ot.th.Shares Excl.f/Brd.Money | 26s | — | — | — | — | — | — | — | — | — | — | — | — |
| Loans | 26l | — | — | — | — | — | — | — | — | — | — | — | 39.47 |
| Financial Derivatives | 26m | — | — | — | — | — | — | — | — | — | — | — | — |
| Insurance Technical Reserves | 26r | — | — | — | — | — | — | — | — | — | — | — | — |
| Shares and Other Equity | 27a | 77.40 | 71.41 | 80.17 | 86.89 | 103.65 | 123.98 | 214.44 | 333.81 | 2,345.21 | 2,720.00 | 1,260.71 | 2,786.07 |
| Other Items (Net) | 27r | 69.63 | −20.89 | −52.71 | 178.80 | 107.40 | 96.29 | −121.24 | −223.22 | −1,373.13 | −1,709.99 | −2,114.93 | −3,386.02 |
| Memo Item: | | | | | | | | | | | | | |
| Total Assets | 20ra | 1,200.12 | 1,158.37 | 1,517.54 | 1,920.46 | 2,601.70 | 3,589.89 | 5,708.52 | 7,910.99 | 19,741.20 | 25,490.98 | 42,837.13 | 52,997.66 |

| | | 2004 | 2005 | 2006 | 2007 | 2008 | 2009 | 2010 | 2011 | 2012 | 2013 | 2014 | 2015 |
|---|---|---|---|---|---|---|---|---|---|---|---|---|---|
| **Depository Corporations** | | | | | | *Billions of Kyats: End of Period* | | | | | | | |
| Net Foreign Assets.......................... | 31n | −9.90 | −10.30 | −7.08 | −1.83 | 2.43 | 5.59 | 6.72 | 24.55 | 5,535.44 | 7,615.47 | 7,461.23 | 9,970.91 |
| Claims on Nonresidents................ | 31 | 3.80 | 6.25 | 9.88 | 15.51 | 20.78 | 27.12 | 29.80 | 50.41 | 7,229.72 | 9,600.46 | 11,225.25 | 14,499.73 |
| Liabilities to Nonresidents............. | 36c | 13.70 | 16.56 | 16.96 | 17.34 | 18.35 | 21.53 | 23.09 | 25.86 | 1,694.28 | 1,984.99 | 3,764.03 | 4,528.82 |
| Domestic Claims............................. | 32 | 2,229.02 | 2,833.69 | 3,598.53 | 4,713.53 | 5,407.75 | 7,172.45 | 10,030.21 | 12,786.20 | 11,541.69 | 15,494.34 | 18,885.28 | 24,182.77 |
| Net Claims on Central Government | 32an | 1,766.86 | 2,252.68 | 2,936.69 | 3,906.47 | 4,484.98 | 5,988.33 | 8,127.06 | 9,654.51 | 4,423.55 | 6,809.26 | 6,325.87 | 8,946.87 |
| Claims on Central Government.... | 32a | 1,805.57 | 2,248.00 | 2,880.02 | 3,718.48 | 4,387.11 | 5,881.06 | 7,738.19 | 9,086.46 | 9,072.15 | 10,260.91 | 20,131.96 | 23,909.49 |
| Liabilities to Central Government. | 36d | 38.71 | −4.68 | −56.67 | −187.98 | −97.87 | −107.27 | −388.87 | −568.05 | 4,648.61 | 3,451.65 | 13,806.09 | 14,962.62 |
| Claims on Other Sectors................. | 32s | 462.16 | 581.01 | 661.85 | 807.06 | 922.77 | 1,184.12 | 1,903.15 | 3,131.69 | 7,118.14 | 8,685.08 | 12,559.41 | 15,235.90 |
| Claims on Other Financial Corps.. | 32g | 2.27 | 4.55 | 4.06 | 3.75 | 5.50 | 2.27 | 2.08 | 2.20 | 1.70 | .01 | .01 | 21.29 |
| Claims on State & Local Govts..... | 32b | — | — | — | — | — | — | — | — | — | 240.00 | 1,031.18 | 1,178.43 |
| Claims on Public Nonfin. Corps.... | 32c | 29.53 | 4.26 | 4.38 | 4.34 | 4.87 | 4.99 | 4.94 | 5.21 | 2,344.07 | 997.23 | 1,388.30 | 886.74 |
| Claims on Private Sector.............. | 32d | 430.36 | 572.20 | 653.41 | 798.97 | 912.40 | 1,176.86 | 1,896.14 | 3,124.28 | 4,772.37 | 7,447.84 | 10,139.92 | 13,149.43 |
| Broad Money Liabilities................... | 35l | 2,081.86 | 2,650.39 | 3,374.24 | 4,383.84 | 5,036.70 | 6,579.81 | 9,376.21 | 12,231.26 | 16,102.45 | 21,505.38 | 25,804.37 | 33,713.97 |
| Currency Outside Depository Corps | 34a | 1,347.58 | 1,743.69 | 2,152.94 | 2,696.66 | 2,922.65 | 3,568.55 | 4,278.93 | 5,132.60 | 5,856.76 | 6,949.18 | 7,622.78 | 9,393.01 |
| Transferable Deposits................... | 34 | 124.17 | 188.04 | 292.65 | 484.45 | 462.74 | 630.61 | 1,269.95 | 1,556.02 | 1,774.66 | 2,636.04 | 3,295.30 | 5,003.35 |
| Other Deposits.............................. | 35 | 610.11 | 718.65 | 928.64 | 1,202.73 | 1,651.31 | 2,380.64 | 3,827.33 | 5,542.64 | 8,471.04 | 11,920.16 | 14,886.29 | 19,317.61 |
| Securities Other than Shares.......... | 36a | — | — | — | — | — | — | — | — | — | — | — | — |
| Deposits Excl. from Broad Money..... | 36b | .02 | .02 | .02 | .02 | .02 | .02 | .02 | .02 | .02 | .03 | .06 | .01 |
| Sec.Ot.th.Shares Excl.f/Brd.Money.... | 36s | — | — | — | — | — | — | — | — | — | — | — | 39.47 |
| Loans.............................................. | 36l | — | — | — | — | — | — | — | — | — | — | — | — |
| Financial Derivatives....................... | 36m | — | — | — | — | — | — | — | — | — | — | — | — |
| Insurance Technical Reserves.......... | 36r | — | — | — | — | — | — | — | — | — | — | — | — |
| Shares and Other Equity.................. | 37a | 136.40 | 157.50 | 180.02 | 226.05 | 289.00 | 352.74 | 523.30 | 713.73 | 3,314.24 | 4,218.69 | 3,163.99 | 5,468.68 |
| Other Items (Net)............................ | 37r | .84 | 15.48 | 37.18 | 101.78 | 84.47 | 245.48 | 137.40 | −134.25 | −2,339.59 | −2,614.30 | −2,621.90 | −5,068.45 |
| Broad Money Liabs., Seasonally Adj. | 35l.b | 2,084.14 | 2,654.63 | 3,376.38 | 4,375.33 | 5,009.66 | 6,523.61 | 9,270.10 | 12,068.09 | 18,683.21 | 21,387.04 | . . . . | . . . . |
| **Monetary Aggregates** | | | | | | *Billions of Kyats: End of Period* | | | | | | | |
| Broad Money................................... | 59m | 2,081.86 | 2,650.39 | 3,374.24 | 4,383.84 | 5,036.70 | 6,579.81 | 9,376.21 | 12,231.26 | 16,102.45 | 21,505.38 | 25,804.37 | 33,713.97 |
| o/w:Currency Issued by Cent.Govt | 59m.a | — | — | — | — | — | — | — | — | — | — | — | — |
| o/w: Dep.in Nonfin. Corporations. | 59m.b | — | — | — | — | — | — | — | — | — | — | — | — |
| o/w:Secs. Issued by Central Govt.. | 59m.c | — | — | — | — | — | — | — | — | — | — | — | — |
| Money (National Definitions) | | | | | | | | | | | | | |
| Reserve Money.............................. | 19mb | 1,666.06 | 2,074.45 | 2,655.17 | 3,393.76 | 3,708.08 | 4,665.75 | 5,700.62 | 6,671.84 | 8,366.59 | 10,050.01 | 10,472.00 | 13,180.20 |
| Broad Money............................... | 59mea | 2,081.86 | 2,650.39 | 3,374.24 | 4,383.84 | 5,036.70 | 6,579.81 | 9,376.21 | 12,231.26 | 16,102.45 | 21,505.38 | 26,382.00 | 31,393.80 |
| **Interest Rates** | | | | | | *Percent Per Annum* | | | | | | | |
| Discount Rate (End of Period).......... | 60.a | 10.00 | 10.00 | 12.00 | 12.00 | 12.00 | 12.00 | 12.00 | 12.00 | 10.00 | 10.00 | 10.00 | 10.00 |
| Deposit Rate.................................... | 60l | 9.50 | 9.50 | 11.38 | 12.00 | 12.00 | 12.00 | 12.00 | 11.33 | 8.00 | 8.00 | 8.00 | 8.00 |
| Lending Rate.................................... | 60p | 15.00 | 15.00 | 16.08 | 17.00 | 17.00 | 17.00 | 17.00 | 16.33 | 13.00 | 13.00 | 13.00 | 13.00 |
| Government Bond Yield................... | 61 | 9.00 | 9.00 | 12.00 | 12.00 | 12.00 | 12.00 | 12.00 | 12.00 | 9.00 | 9.00 | 9.00 | 9.00 |
| **Prices and Labor** | | | | | | *Index Numbers (2010=100): Period Averages* | | | | | | | |
| Consumer Prices............................. | 64 | 40.7 | 44.5 | 53.4 | 72.2 | †91.5 | 92.8 | 100.0 | 105.0 | 106.6 | 112.4 | 118.6 | 131.4 |
| | | | | | | *Number in Thousands: Period Averages* | | | | | | | |
| Unemployment................................ | 67c | 291 | . . . . | . . . . | . . . . | . . . . | . . . . | . . . . | . . . . | . . . . | . . . . | . . . . | . . . . |
| **Intl. Transactions & Positions** | | | | | | *Millions of US Dollars* | | | | | | | |
| Exports............................................ | 70..d | 2,355.48 | 3,776.45 | 4,539.12 | 6,252.69 | 6,882.19 | 6,661.54 | 8,661.08 | 9,238.04 | 8,876.91 | 11,232.80 | 11,299.20 | 5,950.00 |
| Imports, c.i.f.................................... | 71..d | 2,173.93 | 1,908.13 | 2,538.21 | 3,246.61 | 4,256.23 | 4,347.62 | 4,759.66 | 9,018.97 | 9,151.13 | 12,042.50 | 16,226.70 | 15,920.00 |

| | | 2004 | 2005 | 2006 | 2007 | 2008 | 2009 | 2010 | 2011 | 2012 | 2013 | 2014 | 2015 |
|---|---|---|---|---|---|---|---|---|---|---|---|---|---|
| **Balance of Payments** | | | | | | | | *Millions of US Dollars* | | | | | |
| A. Current Account* | 109bx | 110.3 | 581.8 | 793.9 | 1,380.7 | 1,247.0 | 986.0 | 1,574.2 | −1,561.1 | −1,259.6 | † −388.6 | −1,640.7 | −4,618.9 |
| Goods, credit (exports) | 1a9cx | 2,669.4 | 3,502.3 | 4,221.7 | 5,402.5 | 5,905.4 | 5,903.4 | 7,334.7 | 7,699.0 | 8,220.3 | † 9,403.8 | 9,082.6 | 9,136.1 |
| Goods, debit (imports) | 1a9dx | 1,750.0 | 1,518.4 | 2,069.6 | 2,653.7 | 2,965.4 | 3,315.3 | 3,857.5 | 7,491.0 | 7,628.6 | † 9,517.8 | 12,087.8 | 14,235.3 |
| Balance on goods | 1a9bx | 919.4 | 1,984.0 | 2,152.1 | 2,748.8 | 2,939.9 | 2,588.1 | 3,477.2 | 208.0 | 591.7 | † −114.0 | −3,005.2 | −5,099.2 |
| Services, credit (exports) | 1b9cx | 250.9 | 280.8 | 313.6 | 334.8 | 356.7 | 349.2 | 369.2 | 758.5 | 1,231.3 | † 2,745.8 | 4,211.7 | 3,933.6 |
| Services, debit (imports) | 1b9dx | 454.9 | 497.1 | 557.1 | 653.1 | 617.2 | 617.2 | 789.0 | 1,090.2 | 1,459.3 | † 2,187.3 | 2,603.2 | 2,312.5 |
| Balance on Goods & Services | 1z9bx | 715.4 | 1,767.7 | 1,908.6 | 2,430.6 | 2,679.4 | 2,320.1 | 3,057.5 | −123.7 | 363.7 | † 444.5 | −1,395.8 | −3,478.0 |
| Primary income: credit | 1c9cx | 39.9 | 55.0 | 96.8 | 174.1 | 176.9 | 94.7 | 147.5 | 200.5 | 293.3 | † 237.0 | 165.5 | 260.0 |
| Primary income: debit | 1c9dx | 777.7 | 1,413.1 | 1,332.6 | 1,428.4 | 1,917.2 | 1,861.9 | 1,869.5 | 2,032.5 | 2,466.6 | † 2,220.3 | 2,918.2 | 4,025.4 |
| Balance on gds, serv. & prim. inc. | 1y9bx | −22.3 | 409.6 | 672.8 | 1,176.3 | 939.1 | 552.9 | 1,335.5 | −1,955.7 | −1,809.7 | † −1,538.9 | −4,148.5 | −7,243.5 |
| Secondary income: credit | 1d9ca | 158.9 | 195.8 | 159.8 | 231.6 | 360.5 | 496.6 | 345.7 | 498.6 | 664.4 | † 1,569.6 | 3,281.2 | 3,419.4 |
| Secondary income: debit | 1d9da | 26.4 | 23.6 | 38.7 | 27.2 | 52.6 | 63.4 | 107.1 | 103.9 | 114.3 | † 419.4 | 773.4 | 794.8 |
| B. Capital Account* | 209ba | .... | .... | .... | .... | .... | .... | .... | .... | −3.5 | † 6,466.6 | −.8 | −6.0 |
| Capital account: credit | 209ca | .... | .... | .... | .... | .... | .... | .... | .... | — | † 6,471.5 | .... | — |
| Capital account: debit | 209da | .... | .... | .... | .... | .... | .... | .... | .... | 3.5 | † 4.8 | .8 | 6.0 |
| Balance on current & capital acct. | 129ba | 110.3 | 581.8 | 793.9 | 1,380.7 | 1,247.0 | 986.0 | 1,574.2 | −1,561.1 | −1,263.1 | † 6,078.1 | −1,641.5 | −4,624.9 |
| C. Financial Account* | 309na | −123.9 | −164.5 | −250.4 | −643.3 | −993.3 | −1,538.5 | −1,117.3 | −2,969.2 | −2,315.1 | † 947.9 | −1,563.8 | −3,644.7 |
| Direct investment: assets | 3a9aa | .... | .... | .... | .... | .... | .... | .... | .... | .... | .... | .... | .... |
| Equity & investment fund shares.. | 3aaaa | .... | .... | .... | .... | .... | .... | .... | .... | .... | .... | .... | .... |
| Debt instruments | 3abaa | .... | .... | .... | .... | .... | .... | .... | .... | .... | .... | .... | .... |
| Direct investment: liabilities | 3a9la | 211.4 | 234.9 | 275.8 | 709.9 | 863.9 | 1,079.0 | 901.1 | 2,519.8 | 1,333.9 | † 2,254.6 | 1,398.2 | 3,137.3 |
| Equity & investment fund shares . | 3aala | 211.4 | 234.9 | 275.8 | 709.9 | 863.9 | 1,079.0 | 901.1 | 2,519.8 | 1,333.9 | † 2,254.6 | 1,398.2 | 3,137.3 |
| Debt instruments | 3abla | .... | .... | .... | .... | .... | .... | .... | .... | .... | .... | .... | .... |
| Portfolio investment: assets | 3b9aa | .... | .... | .... | .... | .... | .... | .... | .... | .... | .... | .... | .... |
| Equity & investment fund shares | 3baaa | .... | .... | .... | .... | .... | .... | .... | .... | .... | .... | .... | .... |
| Debt securities | 3bbaa | .... | .... | .... | .... | .... | .... | .... | .... | .... | .... | .... | .... |
| Portfolio investment: liabilities | 3b9la | .... | .... | .... | .... | .... | .... | .... | .... | .... | .... | .... | .... |
| Equity & investment fund shares . | 3bala | .... | .... | .... | .... | .... | .... | .... | .... | .... | .... | .... | .... |
| Debt securities | 3bbla | .... | .... | .... | .... | .... | .... | .... | .... | .... | .... | .... | .... |
| Fin. der.& empl.stk.ops.(ESOs): net. | 3c9na | .... | .... | .... | .... | .... | .... | .... | .... | .... | .... | .... | .... |
| Fin. der. & ESOs.: assets | 3c9aa | .... | .... | .... | .... | .... | .... | .... | .... | .... | .... | .... | .... |
| Fin. der. & ESOs.: liabilities | 3c9la | .... | .... | .... | .... | .... | .... | .... | .... | .... | .... | .... | .... |
| Other investment: assets | 3d9aa | .... | .... | .... | .... | .... | .... | .... | .... | .... | .... | .... | .... |
| Other equity | 3daaa | .... | .... | .... | .... | .... | .... | .... | .... | .... | .... | .... | .... |
| Debt instruments | 3dzaa | .... | .... | .... | .... | .... | .... | .... | .... | .... | .... | .... | .... |
| Other investment: liabilities | 3d9la | −87.4 | −70.4 | −25.4 | −66.6 | 129.4 | 459.5 | 216.2 | 449.4 | 981.3 | † −3,202.5 | 165.6 | 507.5 |
| Other equity | 3dala | .... | .... | .... | .... | .... | .... | .... | .... | .... | .... | .... | .... |
| Debt instruments | 3dzla | −87.4 | −70.4 | −25.4 | −66.6 | 129.4 | 459.5 | 216.2 | 449.4 | 981.3 | † −3,202.5 | 165.6 | 507.5 |
| Curr.+ cap.− finan. acct. balance | 4y9na | 234.2 | 746.3 | 1,044.3 | 2,024.0 | 2,240.3 | 2,524.5 | 2,691.5 | 1,408.0 | 1,052.0 | † 5,130.2 | −77.7 | −980.1 |
| D. Net Errors and Omissions | 409na | −141.1 | −604.2 | −625.7 | −335.7 | −1,361.9 | −1,324.6 | −2,132.9 | −137.4 | 5,864.3 | † −2,513.5 | 1,188.7 | 3,140.5 |
| E. Reserves and Related Items | 4z9na | 93.1 | 142.1 | 418.6 | 1,688.3 | 878.5 | 1,199.9 | 558.5 | 1,270.7 | 6,916.3 | † 2,616.7 | 1,111.0 | 2,160.4 |
| Reserve assets | 3e9aa | 93.1 | 142.1 | 418.6 | 1,688.3 | 878.5 | 1,199.9 | 558.5 | 1,270.7 | 6,916.3 | † 2,616.7 | 1,111.0 | 2,160.4 |
| Credit and loans from the IMF. | 3dcla | — | — | — | — | — | — | — | — | — | † — | — | — |
| Exceptional financing | 409la | — | .... | .... | .... | .... | .... | .... | .... | .... | .... | .... | .... |
| *Excludes components in group E | | | | | | | | | | | | | |
| | | | | | | | | | | | | | |
| **International Investment Position** | | | | | | | | *Millions of US Dollars* | | | | | |
| Assets | 809aa | 782.1 | 885.2 | 1,375.5 | 3,239.3 | 4,051.1 | 5,330.0 | 5,905.4 | 7,126.5 | 7,319.6 | † 8,827.9 | 9,520.8 | 9,422.1 |
| Direct investment | 8a9aa | .... | .... | .... | .... | .... | .... | .... | .... | .... | .... | .... | .... |
| Equity & investment fund shares.. | 8aaaa | .... | .... | .... | .... | .... | .... | .... | .... | .... | .... | .... | .... |
| Debt instruments | 8abaa | .... | .... | .... | .... | .... | .... | .... | .... | .... | .... | .... | .... |
| Portfolio investment | 8b9aa | .... | .... | .... | .... | .... | .... | .... | .... | .... | .... | .... | .... |
| Equity & investment fund shares.. | 8baaa | .... | .... | .... | .... | .... | .... | .... | .... | .... | .... | .... | .... |
| Debt securities | 8bbaa | .... | .... | .... | .... | .... | .... | .... | .... | .... | .... | .... | .... |
| Fin. der.(oth.than reserves) & ESOs | 8c9aa | .... | .... | .... | .... | .... | .... | .... | .... | .... | .... | .... | .... |
| Other investment | 8d9aa | .... | .... | .... | .... | .... | .... | .... | .... | .... | .... | .... | .... |
| Other equity | 8daaa | .... | .... | .... | .... | .... | .... | .... | .... | .... | .... | .... | .... |
| Debt instruments | 8dzaa | .... | .... | .... | .... | .... | .... | .... | .... | .... | .... | .... | .... |
| Reserve assets | 8e9aa | 782.1 | 885.2 | 1,375.5 | 3,239.3 | 4,051.1 | 5,330.0 | 5,905.4 | 7,126.5 | 7,319.6 | † 8,827.9 | 9,520.8 | 9,422.1 |
| Liabilities | 809la | 10,614.7 | 10,081.6 | 10,817.9 | 11,864.6 | 12,606.5 | 14,416.9 | 15,476.6 | 19,085.4 | 10,815.0 | † 13,337.9 | 13,883.9 | 16,291.3 |
| Direct investment | 8a9la | 4,751.1 | 4,686.0 | 5,191.2 | 6,087.9 | 6,809.3 | 7,957.5 | 8,751.5 | 11,713.4 | 1,128.0 | † 3,166.8 | 4,365.6 | 6,821.9 |
| Equity & investment fund shares.. | 8aala | 4,751.1 | 4,686.0 | 5,191.2 | 6,087.9 | 6,809.3 | 7,957.5 | 8,751.5 | 11,713.4 | 1,128.0 | † 3,166.8 | 4,365.6 | 6,821.9 |
| Debt instruments | 8abla | .... | .... | .... | .... | .... | .... | .... | .... | .... | .... | .... | .... |
| Portfolio investment | 8b9la | .... | .... | .... | .... | .... | .... | .... | .... | .... | .... | .... | .... |
| Equity & investment fund shares.. | 8bala | .... | .... | .... | .... | .... | .... | .... | .... | .... | .... | .... | .... |
| Debt securities | 8bbla | .... | .... | .... | .... | .... | .... | .... | .... | .... | .... | .... | .... |
| Fin. der.(oth.than reserves) & ESOs | 8c9la | .... | .... | .... | .... | .... | .... | .... | .... | .... | .... | .... | .... |
| Other investment | 8d9la | 5,863.6 | 5,395.6 | 5,626.7 | 5,776.7 | 5,797.3 | 6,459.4 | 6,725.1 | 7,372.1 | 9,687.0 | † 10,171.0 | 9,518.2 | 9,469.4 |
| Other equity | 8dala | .... | .... | .... | .... | .... | .... | .... | .... | .... | .... | .... | .... |
| Debt instruments | 8dzla | 5,863.6 | 5,395.6 | 5,626.7 | 5,776.7 | 5,797.3 | 6,459.4 | 6,725.1 | 7,372.1 | 9,687.0 | † 10,171.0 | 9,518.2 | 9,469.4 |

# Myanmar 518

| | | 2004 | 2005 | 2006 | 2007 | 2008 | 2009 | 2010 | 2011 | 2012 | 2013 | 2014 | 2015 |
|---|---|---|---|---|---|---|---|---|---|---|---|---|---|
| **National Accounts** | | *Millions of Kyats: Fiscal Year Begins April 1* | | | | | | | | | | | |
| Househ.Cons.Expend.,incl.NPISHs.... | 96f | 7,965,511 | .... | .... | .... | .... | .... | .... | .... | .... | .... | .... | .... |
| Gross Fixed Capital Formation.......... | 93e | 1,069,021 | .... | .... | .... | .... | .... | .... | .... | .... | .... | .... | .... |
| Changes in Inventories................... | 93i | 39,689 | .... | .... | .... | .... | .... | .... | .... | .... | .... | .... | .... |
| Exports of Goods and Services......... | 90c | 16,046 | .... | .... | .... | .... | .... | .... | .... | .... | .... | .... | .... |
| Imports of Goods and Services (-)..... | 98c | 11,339 | .... | .... | .... | .... | .... | .... | .... | .... | .... | .... | .... |
| Gross Domestic Product (GDP)......... | 99b | 9,022,227 | .... | .... | .... | .... | .... | .... | .... | .... | .... | .... | .... |
| Net Primary Income from Abroad..... | 98.n | −91 | .... | .... | .... | .... | .... | .... | .... | .... | .... | .... | .... |
| Gross National Income (GNI)............ | 99a | 9,078,831 | .... | .... | .... | .... | .... | .... | .... | .... | .... | .... | .... |
| GDP Volume 2000/01 Prices............ | 99b.p | 4,116,635 | 4,675,220 | .... | .... | .... | .... | .... | .... | .... | .... | .... | .... |
| GDP Volume (2000=100)................ | 99bvp | 161.3 | 183.1 | .... | .... | .... | .... | .... | .... | .... | .... | .... | .... |
| GDP Deflator (2000=100)............... | 99bip | .... | .... | .... | .... | .... | .... | .... | .... | .... | .... | .... | .... |
| | | *Millions: Midyear Estimates* | | | | | | | | | | | |
| Population.................................. | 99z | 49.58 | 49.98 | 50.36 | 50.70 | 51.03 | 51.37 | 51.73 | 52.13 | 52.54 | 52.98 | 53.44 | 53.90 |

| | | 2004 | 2005 | 2006 | 2007 | 2008 | 2009 | 2010 | 2011 | 2012 | 2013 | 2014 | 2015 |
|---|---|---|---|---|---|---|---|---|---|---|---|---|---|
| **Exchange Rates** | | | | | | *Namibia Dollars per SDR: End of Period* | | | | | | | |
| Market Rate | aa | 8.743 | 9.040 | 10.486 | 10.762 | 14.332 | 11.570 | 10.213 | 12.502 | 13.066 | 16.154 | 16.779 | 21.541 |
| | | | | | | *Namibia Dollars per US Dollar: End of Period (ae) Period Average (rf)* | | | | | | | |
| Market Rate | ae | 5.6300 | 6.3250 | 6.9700 | 6.8100 | 9.3050 | 7.3800 | 6.6316 | 8.1429 | 8.5012 | 10.4899 | 11.5810 | 15.5450 |
| Market Rate | rf | 6.4597 | 6.3593 | 6.7715 | 7.0454 | 8.2612 | 8.4737 | 7.3212 | 7.2611 | 8.2100 | 9.6551 | 10.8527 | 12.7589 |
| **Fund Position** | | | | | | *Millions of SDRs: End of Period* | | | | | | | |
| Quota | 2f.s | 136.50 | 136.50 | 136.50 | 136.50 | 136.50 | 136.50 | 136.50 | 136.50 | 136.50 | 136.50 | 136.50 | 136.50 |
| SDR Holdings | 1b.s | .02 | .02 | .02 | .02 | .02 | 130.41 | 130.41 | 5.27 | 5.11 | 5.02 | 4.90 | 4.84 |
| Reserve Position in the Fund | 1c.s | .06 | .07 | .08 | .08 | .08 | .08 | .08 | .08 | .08 | .08 | .08 | .08 |
| Total Fund Cred.&Loans Outstg | 2tl | — | — | — | — | — | — | — | — | — | — | — | — |
| SDR Allocations | 1bd | — | — | — | — | — | 130.39 | 130.39 | 130.39 | 130.39 | 130.39 | 130.39 | 130.39 |
| **International Liquidity** | | | | | | *Millions of US Dollars Unless Otherwise Indicated: End of Period* | | | | | | | |
| Total Reserves minus Gold | 1l.d | 345.06 | 312.10 | 449.58 | 896.02 | 1,292.93 | 2,050.93 | 1,695.69 | 1,786.69 | 1,745.87 | 1,511.16 | 1,177.20 | 1,688.18 |
| SDR Holdings | 1b.d | .03 | .03 | .03 | .03 | .03 | 204.44 | 200.83 | 8.09 | 7.86 | 7.73 | 7.10 | 6.70 |
| Reserve Position in the Fund | 1c.d | .09 | .10 | .11 | .12 | .12 | .12 | .12 | .12 | .12 | .12 | .11 | .11 |
| Foreign Exchange | 1d.d | 344.94 | 311.98 | 449.44 | 895.87 | 1,292.79 | 1,846.37 | 1,494.74 | 1,778.48 | 1,737.89 | 1,503.31 | 1,169.99 | 1,681.37 |
| Gold (Million Fine Troy Ounces) | 1ad | — | — | — | — | — | — | — | — | — | — | — | — |
| Gold (National Valuation) | 1and | — | — | — | — | — | — | — | — | — | — | — | — |
| Central Bank: Other Assets | 3..d | 16.73 | 20.10 | 52.86 | 26.77 | 15.58 | 23.29 | 25.46 | 19.75 | 22.40 | 20.74 | 19.02 | 174.95 |
| Central Bank: Other Liabs | 4..d | 1.50 | 2.39 | 58.72 | 8.33 | .09 | −.20 | .05 | .16 | .04 | .03 | — | — |
| Other Depository Corps.: Assets | 7a.d | 147.61 | 45.16 | 393.44 | 250.87 | 194.44 | 1,678.92 | 1,719.91 | 1,356.27 | 1,174.70 | 1,199.83 | 833.53 | 629.53 |
| Other Depository Corps.: Liabs | 7b.d | 411.32 | 383.54 | 152.37 | 145.47 | 116.35 | 55.50 | 134.16 | 110.46 | 288.08 | 300.66 | 226.41 | 273.72 |
| **Central Bank** | | | | | | *Millions of Namibia Dollars: End of Period* | | | | | | | |
| Net Foreign Assets | 11n | 1,977.8 | 1,983.6 | 3,165.1 | 6,744.8 | 12,932.4 | 12,619.4 | 9,118.7 | 13,027.2 | 13,364.4 | 13,900.1 | 11,690.2 | 24,545.0 |
| Claims on Nonresidents | 11 | 1,986.2 | 1,998.7 | 3,574.4 | 6,801.5 | 12,933.2 | 14,126.5 | 10,450.6 | 14,658.6 | 15,068.4 | 16,006.8 | 14,124.9 | 27,355.5 |
| Liabilities to Nonresidents | 16c | 8.4 | 15.1 | 409.3 | 56.7 | .8 | 1,507.1 | 1,331.9 | 1,631.4 | 1,703.9 | 2,106.7 | 2,434.7 | 2,810.5 |
| Claims on Other Depository Corps | 12e | 238.7 | 515.2 | 1,333.0 | 1,215.9 | 162.4 | 36.7 | 39.2 | 41.9 | 44.3 | 46.6 | 407.4 | 835.8 |
| Net Claims on Central Government | 12an | −889.7 | −608.1 | −2,093.3 | −4,595.1 | −6,719.5 | −6,994.3 | −3,482.7 | −5,915.8 | −6,617.2 | −5,329.1 | −945.8 | −10,323.1 |
| Claims on Central Government | 12a | — | — | — | — | — | — | — | — | — | — | — | — |
| Liabilities to Central Government | 16d | 889.7 | 608.1 | 2,093.3 | 4,595.1 | 6,719.5 | 6,994.3 | 3,482.7 | 5,915.8 | 6,617.2 | 5,329.1 | 945.8 | 10,323.1 |
| Claims on Other Sectors | 12s | 13.6 | 13.4 | 15.8 | 17.4 | 24.9 | 23.1 | 23.2 | 26.4 | 39.3 | 39.8 | 39.2 | 41.4 |
| Claims on Other Financial Corps | 12g | — | — | — | — | — | — | — | — | 3.7 | — | — | — |
| Claims on State & Local Govts | 12b | — | — | — | — | — | — | — | — | — | — | — | — |
| Claims on Public Nonfin. Corps | 12c | — | — | — | — | — | — | — | — | — | — | — | — |
| Claims on Private Sector | 12d | 13.6 | 13.4 | 15.8 | 17.4 | 24.9 | 23.1 | 23.2 | 26.4 | 35.6 | 39.8 | 39.2 | 41.4 |
| Monetary Base | 14 | 1,238.6 | 1,372.6 | 1,532.4 | 1,647.7 | 2,351.0 | 2,555.7 | 3,242.3 | 5,507.8 | 4,983.2 | 4,942.3 | 6,707.3 | 6,372.3 |
| Currency in Circulation | 14a | 945.8 | 1,026.8 | 1,151.4 | 1,323.7 | 1,656.6 | 1,704.9 | 1,908.6 | 2,397.5 | 2,772.5 | 3,373.4 | 4,118.0 | 4,495.0 |
| Liabs. to Other Depository Corps | 14c | 292.9 | 345.7 | 381.0 | 323.9 | 694.4 | 850.7 | 1,333.7 | 3,110.3 | 2,210.7 | 1,569.0 | 2,589.3 | 1,877.4 |
| Liabilities to Other Sectors | 14d | — | — | — | — | — | — | — | — | — | — | — | — |
| Other Liabs. to Other Dep. Corps | 14n | — | — | — | 627.7 | 749.8 | 1,506.9 | 1,638.9 | .5 | 10.9 | 268.3 | 2.4 | 14.5 |
| Dep. & Sec. Excl. f/Monetary Base | 14o | — | — | — | — | — | — | — | — | — | — | — | 2,910.8 |
| Deposits Included in Broad Money | 15 | — | — | — | — | — | — | — | — | — | — | — | — |
| Sec.Ot.th.Shares Incl.in Brd. Money | 16a | — | — | — | — | — | — | — | — | — | — | — | — |
| Deposits Excl. from Broad Money | 16b | — | — | — | — | — | — | — | — | — | — | — | — |
| Sec.Ot.th.Shares Excl.f/Brd.Money | 16s | — | — | — | — | — | — | — | — | — | — | — | 2,910.8 |
| Loans | 16l | — | — | — | — | — | — | — | — | — | — | — | — |
| Financial Derivatives | 16m | — | — | — | — | — | — | — | — | — | — | — | — |
| Shares and Other Equity | 17a | 611.2 | 666.1 | 997.9 | 1,272.4 | 3,436.9 | 1,720.1 | 1,029.4 | 1,929.6 | 2,231.1 | 3,838.3 | 5,073.3 | 6,122.6 |
| Other Items (Net) | 17r | −509.4 | −134.6 | −109.7 | −164.9 | −137.4 | −97.8 | −212.2 | −258.1 | −394.2 | −391.5 | −592.0 | −321.1 |
| Memo Item: | | | | | | | | | | | | | |
| Total Assets | 10ra | 2,771.4 | 2,683.9 | 5,062.1 | 8,234.5 | 13,402.6 | 14,520.3 | 10,912.6 | 15,186.8 | 15,783.1 | 16,736.6 | 15,205.6 | 28,893.9 |
| **Other Depository Corporations** | | | | | | *Millions of Namibia Dollars: End of Period* | | | | | | | |
| Net Foreign Assets | 21n | −1,484.7 | −2,140.3 | 1,680.2 | 717.8 | 726.7 | 11,980.8 | 10,516.0 | 10,144.5 | 7,537.3 | 9,432.3 | 7,825.7 | 5,536.3 |
| Claims on Nonresidents | 21 | 831.0 | 285.6 | 2,742.2 | 1,708.4 | 1,809.3 | 12,390.4 | 11,405.7 | 11,044.0 | 9,986.3 | 12,586.2 | 10,744.2 | 9,795.4 |
| Liabilities to Nonresidents | 26c | 2,315.7 | 2,425.9 | 1,062.0 | 990.7 | 1,082.6 | 409.6 | 889.7 | 899.5 | 2,449.0 | 3,153.9 | 2,918.4 | 4,259.1 |
| Claims on Central Bank | 20 | 585.1 | 672.4 | 747.0 | 961.6 | 1,972.2 | 3,041.8 | 3,490.8 | 4,421.0 | 3,936.2 | 3,684.2 | 5,209.9 | 4,778.6 |
| Currency | 20a | 313.1 | 346.8 | 388.1 | 503.4 | 516.5 | 548.7 | 617.0 | 700.5 | 1,087.6 | 1,236.2 | 1,574.0 | 1,453.4 |
| Reserve Deposits and Securities | 20b | 272.0 | 325.6 | 358.9 | 338.2 | 651.1 | 632.4 | 1,315.7 | 3,099.3 | 2,113.2 | 1,433.7 | 2,524.0 | 1,863.9 |
| Other Claims | 20n | — | — | — | 120.0 | 804.6 | 1,860.8 | 1,558.1 | 621.2 | 735.5 | 1,014.2 | 1,111.8 | 1,461.3 |
| Net Claims on Central Government | 22an | 1,761.5 | 2,013.8 | 2,206.6 | 2,331.3 | 2,026.6 | 1,766.8 | 1,761.4 | 5,361.9 | 5,311.5 | 5,598.5 | 4,948.1 | 8,714.7 |
| Claims on Central Government | 22a | 2,180.3 | 2,586.1 | 2,767.3 | 2,981.3 | 2,631.7 | 2,814.0 | 3,080.0 | 6,969.0 | 6,825.2 | 7,340.6 | 7,134.1 | 10,170.4 |
| Liabilities to Central Government | 26d | 418.9 | 572.2 | 560.7 | 650.1 | 605.1 | 1,047.1 | 1,318.6 | 1,607.1 | 1,513.7 | 1,742.1 | 2,186.0 | 1,455.7 |
| Claims on Other Sectors | 22s | 20,284.6 | 24,251.0 | 28,268.4 | 32,338.6 | 36,586.8 | 39,708.5 | 44,435.8 | 46,892.8 | 54,426.0 | 62,557.2 | 73,023.9 | 84,882.2 |
| Claims on Other Financial Corps | 22g | 11.7 | 30.1 | 1,831.2 | 2,321.6 | 2,576.9 | 2,365.5 | 3,070.5 | 1,399.1 | 1,395.7 | 1,706.9 | 1,820.1 | 3,347.8 |
| Claims on State & Local Govts | 22b | 20.3 | 22.4 | 48.2 | 45.0 | 82.3 | 86.2 | 116.5 | 175.9 | 66.0 | 163.6 | 184.9 | 206.0 |
| Claims on Public Nonfin. Corps | 22c | 347.6 | 289.5 | 180.0 | 230.9 | 655.1 | 689.0 | 682.6 | 903.0 | 1,029.8 | 1,240.2 | 1,776.0 | 2,507.3 |
| Claims on Private Sector | 22d | 19,905.1 | 23,908.9 | 26,209.0 | 29,741.1 | 33,272.5 | 36,567.7 | 40,566.2 | 44,414.8 | 51,934.4 | 59,446.6 | 69,242.9 | 78,821.1 |
| Liabilities to Central Bank | 26g | 302.7 | 408.8 | 1,548.2 | 867.2 | 158.0 | 33.6 | 36.7 | 40.6 | 44.1 | 47.4 | 49.0 | 594.4 |
| Transf.Dep.Included in Broad Money | 24 | 8,929.8 | 8,728.6 | 12,915.6 | 13,815.7 | 16,857.8 | 19,391.1 | 21,769.5 | 24,621.7 | 23,263.9 | 31,743.1 | 34,171.8 | 37,099.9 |
| Other Dep.Included in Broad Money | 25 | 6,259.1 | 7,961.4 | 8,833.3 | 10,166.1 | 11,239.1 | 27,180.2 | 28,505.9 | 31,391.2 | 36,381.3 | 35,077.7 | 37,650.3 | 41,803.4 |
| Sec.Ot.th.Shares Incl.in Brd. Money | 26a | — | — | 5.9 | 6.0 | 3.9 | 3.9 | — | — | — | — | — | — |
| Deposits Excl. from Broad Money | 26b | 190.6 | 314.6 | 1,090.9 | 1,410.8 | 741.5 | 1,055.6 | 406.9 | 642.0 | 954.4 | 1,088.6 | 1,360.4 | 2,148.3 |
| Sec.Ot.th.Shares Excl.f/Brd.Money | 26s | — | 408.4 | 4,076.9 | 4,986.0 | 6,491.6 | 10,553.0 | 10,798.9 | 11,906.4 | 13,352.6 | 16,352.8 | 17,360.7 | 21,284.5 |
| Loans | 26l | 1,773.1 | 2,819.1 | 5.3 | 7.1 | 6.9 | 34.7 | 32.3 | 27.7 | 50.2 | 52.3 | 37.9 | 16.0 |
| Financial Derivatives | 26m | — | — | — | — | — | — | — | 103.8 | 42.9 | 48.7 | 89.5 | 88.7 |
| Insurance Technical Reserves | 26r | — | — | — | — | — | — | — | — | — | — | — | — |
| Shares and Other Equity | 27a | 3,976.5 | 4,174.4 | 4,355.3 | 4,800.6 | 5,965.2 | 6,469.4 | 7,308.7 | 7,925.1 | 8,893.8 | 10,612.2 | 12,129.3 | 13,964.8 |
| Other Items (Net) | 27r | −285.3 | −18.4 | 70.8 | 289.6 | −151.8 | −8,223.5 | −8,655.0 | −9,838.2 | −11,772.1 | −13,750.6 | −11,841.1 | −13,088.3 |
| Memo Item: | | | | | | | | | | | | | |
| Total Assets | 20ra | 26,834.1 | 31,354.4 | 37,204.9 | 40,714.0 | 46,465.7 | 71,347.8 | 76,092.7 | 84,446.3 | 93,802.1 | 104,583.3 | 113,865.7 | 130,336.9 |

# Namibia 728

2016, International Monetary Fund : *International Financial Statistics Yearbook*

| | | 2004 | 2005 | 2006 | 2007 | 2008 | 2009 | 2010 | 2011 | 2012 | 2013 | 2014 | 2015 |
|---|---|---|---|---|---|---|---|---|---|---|---|---|---|
| **Depository Corporations** | | *Millions of Namibia Dollars: End of Period* | | | | | | | | | | | |
| Net Foreign Assets.................... | 31n | 493.1 | −156.7 | 4,845.3 | 7,462.6 | 13,659.1 | 24,600.2 | 19,634.7 | 23,171.7 | 20,901.7 | 23,332.4 | 19,516.0 | 30,081.3 |
| Claims on Nonresidents................ | 31 | 2,817.3 | 2,284.3 | 6,316.6 | 8,509.9 | 14,742.5 | 26,516.9 | 21,856.3 | 25,702.6 | 25,054.7 | 28,593.0 | 24,869.1 | 37,150.9 |
| Liabilities to Nonresidents............. | 36c | 2,324.2 | 2,441.0 | 1,471.3 | 1,047.4 | 1,083.4 | 1,916.7 | 2,221.6 | 2,530.9 | 4,152.9 | 5,260.6 | 5,353.1 | 7,069.7 |
| Domestic Claims............................ | 32 | 21,170.0 | 25,670.1 | 28,397.5 | 30,092.1 | 31,918.8 | 34,504.1 | 42,737.6 | 46,365.4 | 53,159.7 | 62,866.5 | 77,065.3 | 83,315.2 |
| Net Claims on Central Government | 32an | 871.7 | 1,405.7 | 113.3 | −2,263.9 | −4,692.9 | −5,227.5 | −1,721.3 | −553.9 | −1,305.6 | 269.4 | 4,002.3 | −1,608.4 |
| Claims on Central Government.... | 32a | 2,180.3 | 2,586.1 | 2,767.3 | 2,981.3 | 2,631.7 | 2,814.0 | 3,080.0 | 6,969.0 | 6,825.2 | 7,340.6 | 7,134.1 | 10,170.4 |
| Liabilities to Central Government. | 36d | 1,308.6 | 1,180.3 | 2,654.0 | 5,245.2 | 7,324.6 | 8,041.4 | 4,801.3 | 7,522.9 | 8,130.9 | 7,071.2 | 3,131.8 | 11,778.8 |
| Claims on Other Sectors................ | 32s | 20,298.2 | 24,264.4 | 28,284.2 | 32,355.9 | 36,611.7 | 39,731.5 | 44,458.9 | 46,919.3 | 54,465.3 | 62,597.1 | 73,063.1 | 84,923.5 |
| Claims on Other Financial Corps.. | 32g | 11.7 | 30.1 | 1,831.2 | 2,321.6 | 2,576.9 | 2,365.5 | 3,070.5 | 1,399.1 | 1,399.4 | 1,706.9 | 1,820.1 | 3,347.8 |
| Claims on State & Local Govts..... | 32b | 20.3 | 22.4 | 48.2 | 45.0 | 82.3 | 86.2 | 116.5 | 175.9 | 66.0 | 163.6 | 184.9 | 206.0 |
| Claims on Public Nonfin. Corps.... | 32c | 347.6 | 289.5 | 180.0 | 230.9 | 655.1 | 689.0 | 682.6 | 903.0 | 1,029.8 | 1,240.2 | 1,776.0 | 2,507.3 |
| Claims on Private Sector............. | 32d | 19,918.7 | 23,922.4 | 26,224.8 | 29,758.5 | 33,297.4 | 36,590.8 | 40,589.3 | 44,441.2 | 51,970.0 | 59,486.4 | 69,282.0 | 78,862.5 |
| Broad Money Liabilities.................... | 35l | 15,821.6 | 17,370.2 | 22,518.2 | 24,808.2 | 29,240.9 | 47,731.4 | 51,567.0 | 57,709.9 | 61,330.1 | 68,957.8 | 74,366.0 | 81,944.9 |
| Currency Outside Depository Corps | 34a | 632.7 | 680.0 | 763.4 | 820.3 | 1,140.1 | 1,156.3 | 1,291.6 | 1,697.0 | 1,685.0 | 2,137.1 | 2,543.9 | 3,041.6 |
| Transferable Deposits................... | 34 | 8,929.8 | 8,728.8 | 12,915.6 | 13,815.7 | 16,857.8 | 19,391.1 | 21,769.5 | 24,621.7 | 23,263.9 | 31,743.1 | 34,171.8 | 37,099.9 |
| Other Deposits............................. | 35 | 6,259.1 | 7,961.4 | 8,833.3 | 10,166.1 | 11,239.1 | 27,180.2 | 28,505.9 | 31,391.2 | 36,381.3 | 35,077.7 | 37,650.3 | 41,803.4 |
| Securities Other than Shares.......... | 36a | — | — | 5.9 | 6.0 | 3.9 | 3.9 | — | — | — | — | — | — |
| Deposits Excl. from Broad Money..... | 36b | 190.6 | 314.6 | 1,090.9 | 1,410.8 | 741.5 | 1,055.6 | 406.9 | 642.0 | 954.4 | 1,088.6 | 1,360.4 | 2,148.3 |
| Sec.Ot.th.Shares Excl.f/Brd.Money.... | 36s | — | 408.4 | 4,076.9 | 4,986.0 | 6,491.6 | 10,553.0 | 10,798.9 | 11,906.4 | 13,352.6 | 16,352.8 | 17,360.7 | 24,195.3 |
| Loans......................................... | 36l | 1,773.1 | 2,819.1 | 5.3 | 7.1 | 6.9 | 34.7 | 32.3 | 27.7 | 50.2 | 52.3 | 37.9 | 16.0 |
| Financial Derivatives.................... | 36m | — | — | — | — | — | — | — | 103.8 | 42.9 | 48.7 | 89.5 | 88.7 |
| Insurance Technical Reserves.......... | 36r | — | — | — | — | — | — | — | — | — | — | — | — |
| Shares and Other Equity................. | 37a | 4,587.7 | 4,840.4 | 5,353.2 | 6,073.0 | 9,402.2 | 8,189.5 | 8,338.1 | 9,854.6 | 11,124.9 | 14,450.5 | 17,202.6 | 20,087.3 |
| Other Items (Net)......................... | 37r | −709.9 | −239.2 | 198.4 | 269.5 | −305.1 | −8,459.9 | −8,771.0 | −10,707.3 | −12,793.6 | −14,751.9 | −13,835.7 | −15,084.2 |
| Broad Money Liabs., Seasonally Adj. | 35l.b | 16,157.0 | 17,734.6 | 22,951.3 | 25,173.5 | 29,486.4 | 47,754.2 | 51,239.7 | 57,166.4 | 60,845.9 | 68,688.5 | 74,347.4 | 82,106.2 |
| **Monetary Aggregates** | | *Millions of Namibia Dollars: End of Period* | | | | | | | | | | | |
| Broad Money................................ | 59m | 15,821.6 | 17,370.2 | 22,518.2 | 24,808.2 | 29,240.9 | 47,731.4 | 51,567.0 | 57,709.9 | 61,330.1 | 68,957.8 | 74,366.0 | 81,944.9 |
| o/w:Currency Issued by Cent.Govt | 59m.a | — | — | — | — | — | — | — | — | — | — | — | — |
| o/w: Dep.in Nonfin. Corporations. | 59m.b | — | — | — | — | — | — | — | — | — | — | — | — |
| o/w:Secs. Issued by Central Govt.. | 59m.c | — | — | — | — | — | — | — | — | — | — | — | — |
| Money (National Definitions) | | | | | | | | | | | | | |
| M1.......................................... | 59ma | 9,562.5 | 9,408.9 | 13,679.0 | 14,636.1 | 17,997.9 | 20,547.3 | 23,061.1 | 26,318.7 | 24,948.9 | 33,880.1 | 36,715.7 | 40,141.5 |
| M2.......................................... | 59mb | 15,821.6 | 17,370.2 | 22,518.2 | 24,808.2 | 29,240.9 | 47,731.4 | 51,567.0 | 57,709.9 | 61,330.1 | 68,957.8 | 74,366.0 | 81,944.9 |
| **Interest Rates** | | *Percent Per Annum* | | | | | | | | | | | |
| Overdraft Rate............................. | 60.i | 7.50 | 7.00 | 9.00 | 10.50 | 10.00 | 7.00 | 6.00 | 6.00 | 5.50 | 5.50 | 6.00 | 6.50 |
| Money Market Rate........................ | 60b | 6.93 | 6.93 | 7.12 | 8.61 | 9.37 | 7.75 | .... | .... | .... | .... | .... | .... |
| Treasury Bill Rate......................... | 60c | 7.78 | 7.09 | 7.26 | 8.59 | 9.64 | 8.19 | 6.46 | 5.62 | 5.54 | 5.42 | 5.81 | .... |
| Deposit Rate................................ | 60l | 6.35 | 6.24 | 6.30 | 7.55 | 8.38 | 6.24 | 5.00 | 4.28 | 4.21 | 3.98 | 4.25 | 4.71 |
| Lending Rate................................ | 60p | 11.39 | 10.61 | 11.18 | 12.88 | 13.74 | 11.12 | 9.72 | 8.73 | 8.65 | 8.29 | 8.70 | 9.32 |
| Government Bond Yield................... | 61 | 12.11 | 10.89 | 9.61 | 10.02 | 10.02 | 10.02 | .... | .... | .... | .... | .... | .... |
| **Prices** | | *Index Numbers (2010=100): Period Averages* | | | | | | | | | | | |
| Consumer Prices............................ | 64 | 69.8 | 71.4 | 74.9 | 79.9 | 87.1 | 95.4 | 100.0 | 105.0 | 112.1 | 118.3 | 124.7 | 128.9 |
| **Intl. Transactions & Positions** | | *Millions of Namibia Dollars* | | | | | | | | | | | |
| Exports........................................ | 70 | 16,664 | 17,677 | 24,854 | 31,378 | 44,163 | 42,616 | 38,775 | 38,985 | 45,019 | 55,416 | .... | .... |
| Imports, c.i.f................................ | 71 | 16,311 | 17,491 | 22,286 | 31,853 | 43,165 | 52,832 | 47,642 | 48,218 | 60,013 | 73,399 | .... | .... |

# Namibia 728

|  |  | 2004 | 2005 | 2006 | 2007 | 2008 | 2009 | 2010 | 2011 | 2012 | 2013 | 2014 | 2015 |
|---|---|---|---|---|---|---|---|---|---|---|---|---|---|
| **Balance of Payments** |  |  |  |  |  | *Millions of US Dollars* |  |  |  |  |  |  |  |
| A. Current Account* | 109bx | 384.5 | 266.8 | 1,016.5 | 694.4 | 77.0 | −339.7 | −716.6 | −642.4 | −908.8 | −660.3 | −1,139.9 | −1,631.1 |
| Goods, credit (exports) | 1a9cx | 1,827.5 | 2,069.9 | 2,646.6 | 2,922.1 | 3,140.4 | 3,146.4 | 4,025.5 | 4,406.5 | 4,388.8 | 4,628.9 | 4,612.1 | 4,015.1 |
| Goods, debit (imports) | 1a9dx | 2,110.3 | 2,326.2 | 2,544.2 | 3,101.6 | 3,833.3 | 4,396.6 | 5,143.7 | 5,503.0 | 6,523.4 | 6,616.5 | 7,190.6 | 6,913.5 |
| Balance on goods | 1a9bx | −282.8 | −256.3 | 102.4 | −179.5 | −692.8 | −1,250.2 | −1,118.2 | −1,096.5 | −2,134.6 | −1,987.6 | −2,578.5 | −2,898.4 |
| Services, credit (exports) | 1b9cx | 475.4 | 412.6 | 525.7 | 598.6 | 554.7 | 653.8 | 682.7 | 741.9 | 1,075.9 | 927.1 | 1,043.7 | 951.7 |
| Services, debit (imports) | 1b9dx | 420.2 | 368.8 | 429.0 | 512.3 | 585.3 | 576.4 | 730.7 | 782.9 | 725.7 | 933.6 | 1,126.9 | 975.2 |
| Balance on Goods & Services | 1z9bx | −227.7 | −212.4 | 199.1 | −93.2 | −723.4 | −1,172.8 | −1,166.1 | −1,137.5 | −1,784.4 | −1,993.5 | −2,661.7 | −2,921.9 |
| Primary income: credit | 1c9cx | 217.0 | 225.4 | 256.0 | 277.3 | 324.3 | 265.0 | 295.6 | 318.1 | 299.2 | 316.2 | 329.0 | 304.9 |
| Primary income: debit | 1c9dx | 212.1 | 352.6 | 318.9 | 435.6 | 474.2 | 419.7 | 733.2 | 709.8 | 828.3 | 416.2 | 353.1 | 336.9 |
| Balance on gds, serv. & prim. inc. | 1y9bx | −222.8 | −339.6 | 136.2 | −251.5 | −873.3 | −1,327.5 | −1,603.7 | −1,529.1 | −2,313.5 | −2,093.5 | −2,685.9 | −2,953.9 |
| Secondary income: credit | 1d9ca | 642.1 | 651.1 | 925.6 | 998.3 | 1,009.3 | 1,063.9 | 974.7 | 966.2 | 1,510.1 | 1,537.6 | 1,638.7 | 1,415.3 |
| Secondary income: debit | 1d9da | 34.9 | 44.7 | 45.4 | 52.3 | 59.0 | 76.0 | 87.5 | 79.4 | 105.5 | 104.4 | 92.7 | 92.4 |
| B. Capital Account* | 209ba | 77.0 | 79.7 | 83.4 | 83.4 | 77.2 | 66.8 | 112.6 | 186.8 | 148.8 | 129.2 | 137.7 | 137.6 |
| Capital account: credit | 209ca | 77.0 | 79.7 | 83.4 | 83.4 | 77.2 | 74.7 | 121.6 | 196.5 | 157.5 | 136.6 | 144.3 | 143.2 |
| Capital account: debit | 209da | — | — | — | — | — | 7.9 | 9.1 | 9.7 | 8.7 | 7.4 | 6.6 | 5.6 |
| Balance on current & capital acct. | 129ba | 461.5 | 346.4 | 1,099.9 | 777.8 | 154.2 | −272.9 | −604.1 | −455.6 | −760.0 | −531.1 | −1,002.2 | −1,493.5 |
| C. Financial Account* | 309na | 779.0 | 874.8 | 1,525.3 | 1,467.0 | 901.1 | 767.2 | 63.6 | −802.8 | −179.4 | 1,781.7 | −73.3 | −719.3 |
| Direct investment: assets | 3a9aa | −22.5 | −10.3 | 206.2 | −48.7 | 7.2 | −12.9 | −26.1 | −123.6 | −45.6 | 25.7 | −90.1 | 127.3 |
| Equity & investment fund shares | 3aaaa | −3.5 | .5 | −6.6 | 2.3 | 2.3 | −1.4 | 4.3 | .7 | −13.5 | −9.0 | −31.0 | 28.9 |
| Debt instruments | 3abaa | −19.1 | −10.9 | 212.9 | −51.0 | 4.8 | −11.4 | −30.4 | −124.3 | −32.1 | 34.7 | −59.1 | 98.4 |
| Direct investment: liabilities | 3a9la | 88.4 | 168.0 | 187.9 | 118.5 | 409.9 | 463.9 | 755.7 | 712.3 | 595.2 | −558.3 | 382.4 | 258.1 |
| Equity & investment fund shares | 3aala | 68.2 | 204.5 | 154.4 | 184.1 | 134.1 | 139.5 | 448.8 | 316.1 | 404.7 | 194.4 | 96.8 | 43.3 |
| Debt instruments | 3abla | 20.2 | −36.4 | 33.5 | −65.7 | 275.8 | 324.4 | 306.9 | 396.2 | 190.5 | −752.7 | 285.6 | 214.8 |
| Portfolio investment: assets | 3b9aa | 825.5 | 1,052.8 | 1,133.0 | 1,482.9 | 1,027.2 | 900.3 | 641.9 | 513.3 | 709.6 | 398.2 | 290.9 | −317.9 |
| Equity & investment fund shares | 3baaa | 500.4 | 754.2 | 785.7 | 1,210.6 | 756.3 | 530.8 | 381.7 | 305.0 | 222.1 | 163.2 | 167.7 | −242.7 |
| Debt securities | 3bbaa | 325.0 | 298.7 | 347.3 | 272.3 | 271.0 | 369.5 | 260.2 | 208.3 | 487.5 | 235.0 | 123.2 | −75.2 |
| Portfolio investment: liabilities | 3b9la | 4.5 | 5.1 | 4.7 | 4.5 | 3.9 | 4.0 | 4.3 | 484.2 | 101.6 | 12.4 | 15.0 | 856.8 |
| Equity & investment fund shares | 3bala | 4.5 | 5.1 | 4.7 | 4.5 | 3.9 | 3.7 | 4.3 | 4.3 | 3.8 | 12.4 | 15.0 | 2.3 |
| Debt securities | 3bbla | — | — | — | — | — | .3 | — | 479.9 | 97.8 | — | — | 854.5 |
| Fin. der.& empl.stk.ops.(ESOs): net. | 3c9na | — | — | — | — | — | −.1 | — | −5.5 | −3.9 | −1.3 | −.7 | −18.9 |
| Fin. der. & ESOs.: assets | 3c9aa | .... | .... | .... | .... | — | −.1 | — | .3 | — | 1.9 | 1.6 | 4.9 |
| Fin. der. & ESOs.: liabilities | 3c9la | .... | .... | .... | .... | — | — | — | 5.8 | 3.9 | 3.2 | 2.3 | 23.8 |
| Other investment: assets | 3d9aa | −44.6 | −43.2 | 353.7 | −136.2 | 111.0 | 177.5 | −1.8 | 113.1 | −283.6 | 337.6 | −28.0 | 172.9 |
| Other equity | 3daaa | .... | .... | .... | .... | .... | .... | .... | .... | .... | .... | .... | .... |
| Debt instruments | 3dzaa | −44.6 | −43.2 | 353.7 | −136.2 | 111.0 | 177.5 | −1.8 | 113.1 | −283.6 | 337.6 | −28.0 | 172.9 |
| Other investment: liabilities | 3d9la | −113.6 | −48.6 | −25.0 | −292.0 | −169.5 | −170.3 | −209.6 | 103.6 | −140.9 | −475.6 | −152.1 | −432.2 |
| Other equity | 3dala | .... | .... | .... | .... | .... | .... | .... | .... | .... | .... | .... | .... |
| Debt instruments | 3dzla | −113.6 | −48.6 | −25.0 | −292.0 | −169.5 | −170.3 | −209.6 | 103.6 | −140.9 | −475.6 | −152.1 | −432.2 |
| Curr.+ cap.− finan. acct. balance. | 4y9na | −317.5 | −528.4 | −425.4 | −689.1 | −746.9 | −1,040.1 | −667.7 | 347.2 | −580.6 | −2,312.8 | −928.9 | −774.2 |
| D. Net Errors and Omissions | 409na | 115.4 | 127.9 | 122.0 | 484.4 | 634.0 | 362.0 | −355.5 | −583.6 | −500.4 | −245.9 | −326.4 | −263.8 |
| E. Reserves and Related Items | 4z9na | −202.1 | −400.5 | −303.5 | −204.7 | −112.9 | −678.1 | −1,023.1 | −236.3 | −1,081.0 | −2,558.7 | −1,255.3 | −1,038.0 |
| Reserve assets | 3e9aa | −14.2 | 1.1 | 164.2 | 566.6 | 753.3 | 134.9 | −522.7 | 325.4 | 6.9 | 64.8 | −150.4 | 707.3 |
| Credit and loans from the IMF | 3dcla | — | — | — | — | — | — | — | — | — | — | — | — |
| Exceptional financing | 409la | 187.9 | 401.6 | 467.6 | 771.4 | 866.2 | 813.0 | 500.4 | 561.7 | 1,087.9 | 2,623.5 | 1,104.9 | 1,745.3 |

*Excludes components in group E

| **International Investment Position** |  |  |  |  |  | *Millions of US Dollars* |  |  |  |  |  |  |  |
|---|---|---|---|---|---|---|---|---|---|---|---|---|---|
| Assets | 809aa | 3,720.8 | 4,717.9 | 5,966.2 | 8,433.8 | 6,843.5 | 11,407.5 | 11,644.8 | 10,498.5 | 11,314.8 | 10,678.7 | 9,829.6 | 8,891.1 |
| Direct investment | 8a9aa | 57.2 | 25.7 | 7.3 | 15.6 | 11.4 | 68.4 | 50.5 | 42.9 | 37.2 | 31.8 | 101.7 | 207.0 |
| Equity & investment fund shares | 8aaaa | 33.1 | 21.6 | 5.4 | 12.7 | 8.1 | 24.8 | 32.3 | 22.6 | 24.0 | 24.6 | 31.6 | 64.4 |
| Debt instruments | 8abaa | 24.2 | 4.1 | 1.9 | 2.9 | 3.2 | 43.6 | 18.2 | 20.3 | 13.2 | 7.1 | 70.1 | 142.6 |
| Portfolio investment | 8b9aa | 3,025.6 | 4,095.0 | 4,493.4 | 6,022.8 | 4,260.1 | 5,756.1 | 5,058.7 | 4,603.3 | 5,758.5 | 5,174.7 | 5,226.2 | 3,937.0 |
| Equity & investment fund shares | 8aaaa | 1,706.4 | 2,977.2 | 3,304.3 | 3,643.4 | 2,182.9 | 3,366.5 | 2,334.0 | 2,862.6 | 3,326.5 | 2,908.9 | 2,986.1 | 2,349.0 |
| Debt securities | 8bbaa | 1,319.2 | 1,117.8 | 1,189.0 | 2,379.5 | 2,077.2 | 2,389.6 | 2,724.7 | 1,740.7 | 2,432.0 | 2,265.8 | 2,240.1 | 1,587.9 |
| Fin. der.(oth.than reserves) & ESOs | 8c9aa | .... | .... | .... | .... | .... | .... | .... | .... | .... | .... | .... | .... |
| Other investment | 8d9aa | 309.8 | 302.9 | 1,043.7 | 1,440.7 | 1,205.7 | 3,692.1 | 4,985.2 | 4,084.3 | 3,787.8 | 3,905.8 | 3,335.3 | 3,223.6 |
| Other equity | 8daaa | .... | .... | .... | .... | .... | .... | .... | .... | .... | .... | .... | .... |
| Debt instruments | 8dzaa | 309.8 | 302.9 | 1,043.7 | 1,440.7 | 1,205.7 | 3,692.1 | 4,985.2 | 4,084.3 | 3,787.8 | 3,905.8 | 3,335.3 | 3,223.6 |
| Reserve assets | 8e9aa | 328.2 | 294.4 | 421.8 | 954.6 | 1,366.4 | 1,890.8 | 1,550.4 | 1,767.9 | 1,731.2 | 1,566.5 | 1,166.3 | 1,523.5 |
| Liabilities | 809la | 5,231.7 | 4,123.9 | 4,641.2 | 5,126.5 | 4,451.1 | 5,727.9 | 7,267.1 | 7,418.7 | 6,166.9 | 7,598.5 | 7,860.1 | 8,426.2 |
| Direct investment | 8a9la | 4,120.4 | 2,453.4 | 2,785.7 | 3,854.4 | 3,542.6 | 4,293.2 | 5,333.9 | 5,153.4 | 3,600.3 | 4,023.9 | 3,731.8 | 3,707.3 |
| Equity & investment fund shares | 8aala | 3,368.4 | 2,260.0 | 2,381.6 | 2,851.3 | 2,438.8 | 3,031.7 | 3,546.4 | 2,261.2 | 1,332.2 | 2,415.7 | 2,161.3 | 2,404.6 |
| Debt instruments | 8abla | 752.1 | 193.5 | 404.1 | 1,003.1 | 1,103.9 | 1,261.5 | 1,787.5 | 2,892.2 | 2,268.1 | 1,608.2 | 1,570.5 | 1,302.7 |
| Portfolio investment | 8b9la | 68.7 | 92.4 | 83.8 | 85.8 | 62.8 | 79.1 | 88.1 | 512.5 | 609.8 | 588.5 | 581.0 | 1,411.6 |
| Equity & investment fund shares | 8bala | 6.9 | 15.6 | 14.1 | 14.4 | 10.5 | 13.3 | 14.8 | 12.0 | 11.5 | 9.3 | 8.5 | 6.4 |
| Debt securities | 8bbla | 61.8 | 76.9 | 69.7 | 71.4 | 52.2 | 65.9 | 73.3 | 500.4 | 598.3 | 579.1 | 572.6 | 1,405.2 |
| Fin. der.(oth.than reserves) & ESOs | 8c9la | .... | .... | .... | .... | .... | .... | .... | .... | .... | .... | .... | .... |
| Other investment | 8d9la | 1,042.6 | 1,578.0 | 1,771.7 | 1,186.3 | 845.7 | 1,355.6 | 1,845.1 | 1,752.8 | 1,956.8 | 2,986.1 | 3,547.2 | 3,307.3 |
| Other equity | 8dala | .... | .... | .... | .... | .... | .... | .... | .... | .... | .... | .... | .... |
| Debt instruments | 8dzla | 1,042.6 | 1,578.0 | 1,771.7 | 1,186.3 | 845.7 | 1,355.6 | 1,845.1 | 1,752.8 | 1,956.8 | 2,986.1 | 3,547.2 | 3,307.3 |

# Namibia 728

| | | 2004 | 2005 | 2006 | 2007 | 2008 | 2009 | 2010 | 2011 | 2012 | 2013 | 2014 | 2015 |
|---|---|---|---|---|---|---|---|---|---|---|---|---|---|
| **Government Finance** | | | | | | | | | | | | | |
| **Cash Flow Statement** | | | | | | | | | | | | | |
| **Budgetary Central Government** | | *Millions of Namibia Dollars: Fiscal Year Ends March 31* | | | | | | | | | | | |
| Cash Receipts:Operating Activities... | c1 | 11,331.5 | 13,070.0 | 17,566.9 | 18,355.7 | 23,398.5 | 24,046.6 | 19,660.6 | 23,560.1 | .... | .... | .... | .... |
| Taxes.......................... | c11 | 10,365.4 | 11,895.5 | 15,746.6 | 16,969.4 | 21,223.6 | 22,272.7 | 17,936.1 | 20,825.9 | .... | .... | .... | .... |
| Social Contributions...................... | c12 | 69.0 | 76.9 | 74.7 | 81.4 | — | — | — | — | .... | .... | .... | .... |
| Grants............................. | c13 | 70.5 | 39.8 | 50.5 | 204.9 | 82.9 | 200.8 | 23.5 | 178.7 | .... | .... | .... | .... |
| Other Receipts............................. | c14 | 826.7 | 1,057.8 | 1,695.2 | 1,100.0 | 2,091.9 | 1,573.1 | 1,700.9 | 2,555.5 | .... | .... | .... | .... |
| Cash Payments:Operating Activities. | c2 | 11,286.7 | 11,836.1 | 13,110.2 | 14,941.2 | 18,020.9 | 20,928.0 | 23,607.2 | 31,551.6 | .... | .... | .... | .... |
| Compensation of Employees.......... | c21 | 5,445.8 | 5,888.8 | 6,213.7 | 6,725.0 | 7,559.3 | 9,045.0 | 10,801.5 | 12,689.7 | .... | .... | .... | .... |
| Purchases of Goods & Services....... | c22 | 1,871.6 | 1,928.3 | 2,165.7 | 2,997.3 | 3,886.7 | 4,647.5 | 4,322.0 | 5,820.3 | .... | .... | .... | .... |
| Interest.......................... | c24 | 997.2 | 1,160.2 | 1,261.7 | 1,154.1 | 1,110.3 | 1,196.4 | 965.5 | 1,130.3 | .... | .... | .... | .... |
| Subsidies.......................... | c25 | 469.2 | 258.0 | 263.0 | 664.9 | 218.3 | 351.1 | 252.1 | 283.1 | .... | .... | .... | .... |
| Grants.......................... | c26 | 940.7 | 970.5 | 1,040.0 | 1,326.3 | 2,388.1 | 2,694.0 | 4,217.9 | 7,486.4 | .... | .... | .... | .... |
| Social Benefits............................. | c27 | — | — | — | — | 2,602.8 | 2,764.5 | 3,016.0 | 3,882.3 | .... | .... | .... | .... |
| Other Payments........................... | c28 | 1,562.2 | 1,630.3 | 2,166.1 | 2,073.5 | 255.5 | 229.6 | 32.2 | 259.5 | .... | .... | .... | .... |
| Net Cash Inflow:Operating Act.[1-2] | ccio | 44.9 | 1,233.9 | 4,456.8 | 3,414.5 | 5,377.6 | 3,118.6 | −3,946.7 | −15,128.5 | .... | .... | .... | .... |
| Net Cash Outflow:Invest. in NFA...... | c31 | 1,146.6 | 1,256.4 | 1,662.4 | 2,197.6 | 1,474.0 | 2,089.7 | 2,046.9 | 2,711.5 | .... | .... | .... | .... |
| Purchases of Nonfinancial Assets... | c31.1 | 1,202.8 | 1,261.6 | 1,671.5 | 2,205.6 | 1,474.0 | 2,089.7 | 2,046.9 | 2,711.5 | .... | .... | .... | .... |
| Sales of Nonfinancial Assets.......... | c31.2 | 56.2 | 5.3 | 9.1 | 8.0 | — | — | — | — | .... | .... | .... | .... |
| Cash Surplus/Deficit [1-2-31=1-2M] | ccsd | −1,101.7 | −22.5 | 2,794.3 | 1,216.9 | 3,903.6 | 1,028.8 | −5,993.6 | −17,840.1 | .... | .... | .... | .... |
| Net Acq. Fin. Assets, excl. Cash....... | c32x | −36.8 | 59.1 | 480.1 | 656.8 | 1,136.0 | 674.7 | 577.3 | 1,248.2 | .... | .... | .... | .... |
| Domestic.......................... | c321x | −36.8 | 59.1 | 480.1 | 656.8 | 1,136.0 | 674.7 | 577.3 | 1,248.2 | .... | .... | .... | .... |
| Foreign.......................... | c322x | — | — | — | — | — | — | — | — | .... | .... | .... | .... |
| Net Incurrence of Liabilities.............. | c33 | 852.6 | 575.7 | −423.5 | −553.7 | 1,355.4 | −1,010.2 | 5,624.4 | 8,376.3 | .... | .... | .... | .... |
| Domestic.......................... | c331 | 906.8 | 696.7 | −327.9 | −479.3 | 979.7 | −977.9 | 4,538.7 | 7,824.1 | .... | .... | .... | .... |
| Foreign.......................... | c332 | −54.2 | −121.0 | −95.7 | −74.4 | 375.7 | −32.3 | 1,085.7 | 552.2 | .... | .... | .... | .... |
| Net Cash Inflow, Fin.Act.[-32x+33].. | cnfb | 889.4 | 516.6 | −903.7 | −1,210.5 | 219.4 | −1,684.9 | 5,047.1 | 7,128.2 | .... | .... | .... | .... |
| Net Change in Stock of Cash.......... | cncb | −212.3 | 494.2 | 1,890.7 | 6.3 | 4,123.0 | −656.1 | −946.5 | −10,711.9 | .... | .... | .... | .... |
| Stat. Discrep. [32X-33+NCB-CSD].... | ccsdz | — | — | — | — | — | — | — | — | .... | .... | .... | .... |
| Memo Item:Cash Expenditure[2+31] | c2m | 12,433.2 | 13,092.5 | 14,772.6 | 17,138.8 | 19,494.9 | 23,017.7 | 25,654.1 | 34,263.2 | .... | .... | .... | .... |
| Memo Item: Gross Debt.................. | c63 | .... | .... | .... | .... | 12,170.9 | 17,944.2 | 26,543.6 | 32,020.5 | .... | .... | .... | .... |
| **National Accounts** | | *Millions of Namibia Dollars* | | | | | | | | | | | |
| Househ.Cons.Expend.,incl.NPISHs.... | 96f | 25,916 | 26,734 | 30,340 | 35,169 | 43,537 | † 52,399 | 52,155 | 59,829 | 69,247 | 83,740 | 99,758 | .... |
| Government Consumption Expend... | 91f | 8,693 | 8,905 | 10,526 | 14,695 | 15,282 | † 17,945 | 21,107 | 20,895 | 26,710 | 33,809 | 39,476 | .... |
| Gross Fixed Capital Formation.......... | 93e | 7,922 | 8,594 | 11,686 | 13,554 | 17,751 | † 21,025 | 20,884 | 20,453 | 27,636 | 32,601 | 40,827 | .... |
| Changes in Inventories.................... | 93i | 216 | 498 | 342 | 1,450 | 2,103 | † −529 | −958 | −291 | 1,043 | −1,576 | −20 | .... |
| Exports of Goods and Services......... | 90c | 16,991 | 18,678 | 24,566 | 31,089 | 38,108 | † 39,372 | 39,447 | 41,023 | 46,536 | 54,887 | 57,730 | .... |
| Imports of Goods and Services (-)..... | 98c | 17,959 | 18,615 | 22,454 | 34,374 | 46,871 | † 55,005 | 50,102 | 51,789 | 64,277 | 78,601 | 92,052 | .... |
| Gross Domestic Product (GDP)......... | 99b | 42,678 | 46,177 | 54,028 | 61,583 | 69,910 | † 75,208 | 82,534 | 90,120 | 106,895 | 124,863 | 145,744 | .... |
| Statistical Discrepancy..................... | 99bs | 899 | 1,382 | −979 | — | — | — | — | 1 | — | 2 | 25 | .... |
| | | *Millions: Midyear Estimates* | | | | | | | | | | | |
| **Population...............................** | 99z | 2.00 | 2.03 | 2.05 | 2.08 | 2.12 | 2.15 | 2.19 | 2.24 | 2.29 | 2.35 | 2.40 | 2.46 |

|  |  | 2004 | 2005 | 2006 | 2007 | 2008 | 2009 | 2010 | 2011 | 2012 | 2013 | 2014 | 2015 |
|---|---|---|---|---|---|---|---|---|---|---|---|---|---|
| **Exchange Rates** |  | | | | | | *Rupees per SDR: End of Period* | | | | | | |
| Market Rate | aa | 111.506 | 105.837 | 106.963 | 100.425 | 119.602 | 116.699 | 110.343 | 131.281 | 134.895 | 152.629 | 143.968 | 148.273 |
|  |  | | | | | *Rupees per US Dollar: End of Period (ae) Period Average (rf)* | | | | | | | |
| Market Rate | ae | 71.800 | 74.050 | 71.100 | 63.550 | 77.650 | 74.440 | 71.650 | 85.510 | 87.770 | 99.110 | 99.370 | 107.000 |
| Market Rate | rf | 73.674 | 71.368 | 72.756 | 66.415 | 69.762 | 77.573 | 73.262 | 74.020 | 85.197 | 92.993 | 97.554 | 102.405 |
| **Fund Position** |  | | | | | *Millions of SDRs: End of Period* | | | | | | | |
| Quota | 2f.s | 71.30 | 71.30 | 71.30 | 71.30 | 71.30 | 71.30 | 71.30 | 71.30 | 71.30 | 71.30 | 71.30 | 71.30 |
| SDR Holdings | 1b.s | 6.23 | 6.15 | 6.00 | 5.73 | 5.41 | 63.71 | 60.84 | 57.96 | 51.17 | 41.17 | 32.59 | 22.59 |
| Reserve Position in the Fund | 1c.s | — | — | — | — | — | — | .02 | .02 | .02 | .02 | .02 | .02 |
| Total Fund Cred.&Loans Outstg | 2tl | 14.26 | 14.26 | 28.52 | 49.90 | 49.90 | 48.47 | 74.14 | 71.29 | 64.52 | 54.54 | 45.98 | 71.65 |
| SDR Allocations | 1bd | 8.10 | 8.10 | 8.10 | 8.10 | 8.10 | 68.10 | 68.10 | 68.10 | 68.10 | 68.10 | 68.10 | 68.10 |
| **International Liquidity** |  | | | | *Millions of US Dollars Unless Otherwise Indicated: Data as of Middle of Month* | | | | | | | | |
| Total Reserves minus Gold | 1l.d | 1,462.2 | 1,499.0 | 1,935.5 | 2,014.0 | 2,457.9 | 2,768.6 | 2,936.9 | 3,630.8 | 4,306.6 | 5,293.5 | 6,027.1 | 7,936.8 |
| SDR Holdings | 1b.d | 9.7 | 8.8 | 9.0 | 9.1 | 8.3 | 99.9 | 93.7 | 89.0 | 78.6 | 63.4 | 47.2 | 31.3 |
| Reserve Position in the Fund | 1c.d | — | — | — | — | — | — | — | — | — | — | — | — |
| Foreign Exchange | 1d.d | 1,452.5 | 1,490.2 | 1,926.5 | 2,005.0 | 2,449.6 | 2,668.7 | 2,843.2 | 3,541.8 | 4,227.9 | 5,230.0 | 5,979.9 | 7,905.5 |
| Gold (Million Fine Troy Ounces) | 1ad | .153 | .129 | — | — | — | .047 | .047 | .047 | .067 | .117 | .157 | .197 |
| Gold (National Valuation) | 1and | 6.5 | 5.4 | — | — | — | 2.0 | 2.0 | 2.0 | 2.8 | 4.9 | 6.6 | 8.3 |
| Central Bank: Other Assets | 3..d | — | — | — | — | — | — | — | — | — | — | — | — |
| Central Bank: Other Liabs | 4..d | † 4.6 | 1.2 | .1 | 1.0 | — | — | .7 | — | 2.1 | .2 | .2 | .4 |
| Other Depository Corps.: Assets | 7a.d | 322.2 | 386.5 | 466.5 | 581.3 | 702.8 | 744.8 | 831.4 | 754.7 | 926.1 | 1,041.5 | 986.4 | 1,294.3 |
| Other Depository Corps.: Liabs | 7b.d | 112.8 | 88.3 | 86.2 | 81.3 | 181.3 | 139.3 | 236.6 | 288.2 | 604.1 | 530.8 | 350.3 | 415.2 |
| **Central Bank** |  | | | | *Millions of Rupees: Data as of Middle of Month* | | | | | | | | |
| Net Foreign Assets | 11n | † 103,827 | 109,951 | 135,089 | 124,128 | 187,020 | 195,804 | 198,890 | 298,581 | 366,018 | 520,146 | 601,440 | 851,063 |
| Claims on Nonresidents | 11 | † 106,648 | 112,403 | 139,010 | 130,015 | 193,961 | 209,411 | 214,637 | 316,884 | 383,850 | 538,889 | 617,881 | 871,827 |
| Liabilities to Nonresidents | 16c | † 2,821 | 2,452 | 3,921 | 5,888 | 6,941 | 13,607 | 15,748 | 18,303 | 17,832 | 18,743 | 16,441 | 20,764 |
| Claims on Other Depository Corps | 12e | † 5,111 | 4,668 | 6,880 | 4,820 | 5,798 | 16,802 | 15,322 | 14,049 | 16,383 | 20,646 | 19,216 | 20,121 |
| Net Claims on Central Government | 12an | † 8,568 | 14,955 | 3,676 | 19,694 | 12,027 | 24,830 | 29,805 | 30,902 | −3,415 | −28,328 | −54,767 | −65,873 |
| Claims on Central Government | 12a | † 11,326 | 16,023 | 14,000 | 24,161 | 20,603 | 25,774 | 31,623 | 31,356 | 24,201 | 25,250 | 22,665 | 16,426 |
| Liabilities to Central Government | 16d | † 2,758 | 1,068 | 10,324 | 4,467 | 8,575 | 944 | 1,818 | 453 | 27,617 | 53,577 | 77,432 | 82,299 |
| Claims on Other Sectors | 12s | † 3,349 | 3,515 | 3,986 | 4,159 | 4,119 | 4,353 | 4,939 | 6,884 | 6,607 | 5,897 | 6,540 | 8,098 |
| Claims on Other Financial Corps | 12g | † 424 | 493 | 463 | 437 | 399 | 354 | 427 | 661 | 253 | 487 | 1,018 | 2,661 |
| Claims on State & Local Govts | 12b | † — | — | — | — | — | — | — | — | — | — | — | — |
| Claims on Public Nonfin. Corps | 12c | † 9 | 9 | 9 | 9 | 11 | 11 | 11 | — | — | 11 | 11 | 11 |
| Claims on Private Sector | 12d | † 2,916 | 3,013 | 3,514 | 3,714 | 3,709 | 3,988 | 4,501 | 6,222 | 6,354 | 5,399 | 5,511 | 5,426 |
| Monetary Base | 14 | † 87,814 | 95,835 | 109,556 | 121,844 | 158,712 | 191,596 | 203,972 | 271,221 | 289,819 | 381,846 | 402,530 | 526,394 |
| Currency in Circulation | 14a | † 69,638 | 76,290 | 84,512 | 95,499 | 121,431 | 150,616 | 158,850 | 177,136 | 207,651 | 252,087 | 279,381 | 352,713 |
| Liabs. to Other Depository Corps | 14c | † 15,273 | 16,815 | 20,665 | 22,188 | 31,302 | 34,077 | 37,960 | 88,195 | 74,059 | 119,932 | 114,560 | 109,538 |
| Liabilities to Other Sectors | 14d | † 2,903 | 2,731 | 4,380 | 4,157 | 5,980 | 6,903 | 7,163 | 5,889 | 8,109 | 9,827 | 8,589 | 64,143 |
| Other Liabs. to Other Dep. Corps | 14n | † — | — | — | — | 2 | 1 | 1 | — | — | — | — | — |
| Dep. & Sec. Excl. f/Monetary Base | 14o | † — | — | — | — | — | — | — | — | — | — | — | — |
| Deposits Included in Broad Money | 15 | † — | — | — | — | — | — | — | — | — | — | — | — |
| Sec.Ot.th.Shares Incl.in Brd. Money | 16a | † — | — | — | — | — | — | — | — | — | — | — | — |
| Deposits Excl. from Broad Money | 16b | † — | — | — | — | — | — | — | — | — | — | — | — |
| Sec.Ot.th.Shares Excl.f/Brd.Money | 16s | † — | — | — | — | — | — | — | — | — | — | — | — |
| Loans | 16l | † — | — | — | — | — | — | — | — | — | — | — | — |
| Financial Derivatives | 16m | † — | — | — | — | — | — | — | — | — | — | — | — |
| Shares and Other Equity | 17a | † 26,574 | 29,277 | 29,778 | 23,016 | 40,640 | 43,568 | 40,499 | 75,093 | 79,650 | 100,548 | 106,385 | 129,278 |
| Other Items (Net) | 17r | † 6,468 | 7,977 | 10,297 | 7,942 | 9,610 | 6,623 | 4,484 | 4,102 | 16,123 | 35,968 | 63,514 | 157,738 |
| Memo Item: |  | | | | | | | | | | | | |
| Total Assets | 10ra | † 136,391 | 145,728 | 173,337 | 170,475 | 233,765 | 266,887 | 282,596 | 384,000 | 445,365 | 611,280 | 677,691 | 931,225 |
| **Other Depository Corporations** |  | | | | *Millions of Rupees: Data as of Middle of Month* | | | | | | | | |
| Net Foreign Assets | 21n | 15,036 | 22,079 | 27,037 | 31,774 | 40,489 | 45,074 | 42,619 | 39,896 | 27,883 | 50,619 | 63,206 | 94,069 |
| Claims on Nonresidents | 21 | 23,133 | 28,619 | 33,166 | 36,942 | 54,569 | 55,445 | 59,570 | 64,538 | 80,206 | 103,223 | 98,018 | 138,492 |
| Liabilities to Nonresidents | 26c | 8,097 | 6,540 | 6,129 | 5,168 | 14,080 | 10,371 | 16,951 | 24,641 | 52,323 | 52,605 | 34,812 | 44,423 |
| Claims on Central Bank | 20 | 18,322 | 22,304 | 28,374 | 38,973 | 60,543 | 69,488 | 77,777 | 119,576 | 113,958 | 161,685 | 154,932 | 188,129 |
| Currency | 20a | 4,979 | 5,605 | 6,198 | 9,512 | 15,326 | 21,642 | 21,458 | 21,854 | 28,161 | 32,236 | 36,964 | 46,302 |
| Reserve Deposits and Securities | 20b | 13,343 | 16,699 | 22,176 | 29,461 | 44,931 | 47,845 | 56,070 | 97,721 | 85,798 | 129,449 | 117,969 | 141,827 |
| Other Claims | 20n | — | — | — | — | 285 | 1 | 249 | — | — | — | — | — |
| Net Claims on Central Government | 22an | 50,644 | 47,832 | 61,578 | 63,017 | 81,848 | 58,919 | 103,642 | 134,802 | 158,005 | 185,230 | 183,385 | 227,185 |
| Claims on Central Government | 22a | 51,811 | 53,565 | 66,892 | 63,725 | 86,512 | 79,912 | 106,409 | 136,206 | 158,036 | 185,421 | 183,412 | 227,186 |
| Liabilities to Central Government | 26d | 1,166 | 5,734 | 5,314 | 708 | 4,664 | 20,993 | 2,767 | 1,404 | 31 | 190 | 27 | — |
| Claims on Other Sectors | 22s | 162,384 | 182,578 | 222,376 | 277,191 | 429,025 | 594,477 | 665,002 | 739,595 | 881,499 | 1,006,885 | 1,252,813 | 1,427,261 |
| Claims on Other Financial Corps | 22g | 14,541 | 12,083 | 5,945 | 6,513 | 8,052 | 10,475 | 12,587 | 15,818 | 20,496 | 22,468 | 35,032 | 47,613 |
| Claims on State & Local Govts | 22b | 1 | — | — | 7 | 2 | 447 | 441 | 536 | 347 | 81 | 65 | 2 |
| Claims on Public Nonfin. Corps | 22c | 5,314 | 4,192 | 3,107 | 3,040 | 3,371 | 2,699 | 5,340 | 5,599 | 9,724 | 6,077 | 7,237 | 5,822 |
| Claims on Private Sector | 22d | 142,528 | 166,302 | 213,324 | 267,631 | 417,600 | 580,856 | 646,634 | 717,641 | 850,932 | 978,260 | 1,210,480 | 1,373,825 |
| Liabilities to Central Bank | 26g | 1,495 | 3,792 | 3,618 | 1,943 | 2,225 | 10,601 | 6,351 | 4,006 | 674 | 1,479 | 1,091 | 2,483 |
| Transf.Dep.Included in Broad Money | 24 | 28,251 | 30,661 | 36,161 | 43,381 | 48,933 | 66,856 | 66,504 | 69,399 | 65,737 | 90,901 | 101,461 | 135,570 |
| Other Dep.Included in Broad Money | 25 | 195,279 | 215,378 | 254,859 | 309,432 | 453,989 | 594,438 | 662,555 | 806,149 | 937,402 | 1,128,050 | 1,329,975 | 1,587,424 |
| Sec.Ot.th.Shares Incl.in Brd. Money | 26a | — | — | — | — | — | — | — | — | — | — | — | — |
| Deposits Excl. from Broad Money | 26b | — | — | — | — | — | — | — | — | — | — | — | — |
| Sec.Ot.th.Shares Excl.f/Brd.Money | 26s | — | — | — | — | 147 | — | 3,511 | 5,589 | 6,790 | 8,763 | 10,450 | 11,232 |
| Loans | 26l | 901 | 1,253 | 4,012 | 4,220 | 7,388 | 5,665 | 3,375 | 310 | 4,925 | 1,553 | 1,362 | 1,038 |
| Financial Derivatives | 26m | — | — | — | — | — | — | — | — | — | — | — | — |
| Insurance Technical Reserves | 26r | — | — | — | — | — | — | — | — | — | — | — | — |
| Shares and Other Equity | 27a | −18,911 | −12,145 | −7,601 | −1,219 | 32,479 | 66,081 | 101,930 | 115,768 | 133,935 | 156,484 | 174,714 | 207,612 |
| Other Items (Net) | 27r | 39,371 | 35,854 | 48,317 | 53,198 | 66,744 | 24,318 | 44,815 | 32,650 | 31,883 | 17,190 | 35,283 | −8,715 |
| Memo Item: |  | | | | | | | | | | | | |
| Total Assets | 20ra | 313,192 | 350,780 | 412,773 | 496,853 | 741,313 | 936,914 | 1,055,650 | 1,221,470 | 1,424,786 | 1,686,908 | 1,946,535 | 2,291,974 |

# Nepal 558

|  |  | 2004 | 2005 | 2006 | 2007 | 2008 | 2009 | 2010 | 2011 | 2012 | 2013 | 2014 | 2015 |
|---|---|---|---|---|---|---|---|---|---|---|---|---|---|
| **Depository Corporations** | | | | | *Millions of Rupees: Data as of Middle of Month* | | | | | | | | |
| Net Foreign Assets........................... | 31n | † 118,862 | 132,030 | 162,127 | 155,902 | 227,510 | 240,877 | 241,508 | 338,477 | 393,901 | 570,765 | 664,646 | 945,132 |
| Claims on Nonresidents................ | 31 | † 129,781 | 141,023 | 172,176 | 166,957 | 248,530 | 264,855 | 274,207 | 381,421 | 464,056 | 642,112 | 715,899 | 1,010,319 |
| Liabilities to Nonresidents............. | 36c | † 10,919 | 8,993 | 10,050 | 11,055 | 21,021 | 23,978 | 32,699 | 42,944 | 70,155 | 71,347 | 51,253 | 65,187 |
| Domestic Claims................................ | 32 | † 224,946 | 248,879 | 291,615 | 364,062 | 527,020 | 682,579 | 803,389 | 912,183 | 1,042,696 | 1,169,685 | 1,387,972 | 1,596,672 |
| Net Claims on Central Government | 32an | † 59,213 | 62,787 | 65,254 | 82,712 | 93,875 | 83,749 | 133,448 | 165,705 | 154,589 | 156,903 | 128,618 | 161,312 |
| Claims on Central Government.... | 32a | † 63,137 | 69,588 | 80,892 | 87,887 | 107,115 | 105,686 | 138,032 | 167,562 | 182,237 | 210,671 | 206,077 | 243,611 |
| Liabilities to Central Government. | 36d | † 3,924 | 6,801 | 15,638 | 5,175 | 13,240 | 21,937 | 4,585 | 1,857 | 27,647 | 53,768 | 77,459 | 82,299 |
| Claims on Other Sectors................ | 32s | † 165,733 | 186,092 | 226,362 | 281,350 | 433,145 | 598,830 | 669,942 | 746,478 | 888,106 | 1,012,782 | 1,259,354 | 1,435,360 |
| Claims on Other Financial Corps.. | 32g | † 14,965 | 12,576 | 6,408 | 6,950 | 8,451 | 10,829 | 13,014 | 16,480 | 20,750 | 22,955 | 36,050 | 50,274 |
| Claims on State & Local Govts..... | 32b | † 1 | — | — | 7 | 2 | 447 | 441 | 536 | 347 | 81 | 65 | 2 |
| Claims on Public Nonfin. Corps.... | 32c | † 5,322 | 4,201 | 3,116 | 3,048 | 3,382 | 2,710 | 5,351 | 5,599 | 9,724 | 6,088 | 7,248 | 5,833 |
| Claims on Private Sector.............. | 32d | † 145,445 | 169,315 | 216,838 | 271,345 | 421,309 | 584,844 | 651,135 | 723,864 | 857,286 | 983,658 | 1,215,991 | 1,379,251 |
| Broad Money Liabilities.................. | 35l | † 291,091 | 319,454 | 373,713 | 442,957 | 615,007 | 797,171 | 873,613 | 1,036,719 | 1,190,739 | 1,448,629 | 1,682,443 | 2,093,549 |
| Currency Outside Depository Corps | 34a | † 64,659 | 70,684 | 78,314 | 85,987 | 106,105 | 128,974 | 137,392 | 155,282 | 179,491 | 219,852 | 242,418 | 306,411 |
| Transferable Deposits................... | 34 | † 31,154 | 33,392 | 40,540 | 47,538 | 53,207 | 72,075 | 70,107 | 75,288 | 73,846 | 100,728 | 110,051 | 199,713 |
| Other Deposits.............................. | 35 | † 195,279 | 215,378 | 254,859 | 309,432 | 455,695 | 596,122 | 666,115 | 806,149 | 937,402 | 1,128,050 | 1,329,975 | 1,587,424 |
| Securities Other than Shares.......... | 36a | † — | — | — | — | — | — | — | — | — | — | — | — |
| Deposits Excl. from Broad Money..... | 36b | † — | — | — | — | — | — | — | — | — | — | — | — |
| Sec.Ot.th.Shares Excl.f/Brd.Money.... | 36s | † — | — | — | — | 147 | — | 3,511 | 5,589 | 6,790 | 8,763 | 10,450 | 11,232 |
| Loans....................................... | 36l | † 901 | 1,253 | 4,012 | 4,220 | 7,388 | 5,665 | 3,375 | 310 | 4,925 | 1,553 | 1,362 | 1,038 |
| Financial Derivatives..................... | 36m | † — | — | — | — | — | — | — | — | — | — | — | — |
| Insurance Technical Reserves........... | 36r | † — | — | — | — | — | — | — | — | — | — | — | — |
| Shares and Other Equity.................. | 37a | † 7,663 | 17,131 | 22,176 | 21,796 | 73,119 | 109,648 | 142,429 | 190,860 | 213,585 | 257,032 | 281,099 | 336,889 |
| Other Items (Net)........................... | 37r | † 44,153 | 43,071 | 53,841 | 50,990 | 58,869 | 10,972 | 21,970 | 17,182 | 20,558 | 24,473 | 77,263 | 99,096 |
| Broad Money Liabs., Seasonally Adj. | 35l.b | † 293,206 | 321,769 | 376,339 | 445,982 | 618,269 | 800,353 | 875,304 | 1,036,940 | 1,188,228 | 1,443,845 | 1,675,383 | 2,084,223 |
| **Monetary Aggregates** | | | | | *Millions of Rupees: Data as of Middle of Month* | | | | | | | | |
| Broad Money................................. | 59m | 291,091 | 319,454 | 373,713 | 442,957 | 615,007 | 797,171 | 873,613 | 1,036,719 | 1,190,739 | 1,448,629 | 1,682,443 | 2,093,549 |
| o/w:Currency Issued by Cent.Govt | 59m.a | — | — | — | — | — | — | — | — | — | — | — | — |
| o/w: Dep.in Nonfin. Corporations. | 59m.b | — | — | — | — | — | — | — | — | — | — | — | — |
| o/w:Secs. Issued by Central Govt.. | 59m.c | — | — | — | — | — | — | — | — | — | — | — | — |
| Money (National Definitions) | | | | | | | | | | | | | |
| Reserve Money................................ | 19mb | 87,814 | 95,835 | 109,556 | 121,844 | 157,006 | 189,914 | 200,759 | 273,027 | 292,186 | 380,294 | 402,530 | 526,394 |
| M1................................................ | 59ma | 93,080 | 102,233 | 116,162 | 132,833 | 161,647 | 202,443 | 210,841 | 232,820 | 272,466 | 332,150 | 354,489 | 509,543 |
| M2................................................ | 59mb | 284,176 | 314,509 | 360,659 | 433,037 | 540,240 | 669,497 | 719,252 | 865,928 | 1,027,515 | 1,242,124 | 1,625,296 | 2,031,571 |
| Broad Money................................ | 59mea | 291,091 | 319,454 | 373,713 | 442,957 | 615,007 | 797,171 | 873,613 | 1,036,719 | 1,190,739 | 1,448,629 | 1,682,443 | 2,093,549 |
| **Interest Rates** | | | | | *Percent Per Annum: Data as of Middle of Month* | | | | | | | | |
| Central Bank Policy Rate (EOP)........ | 60 | 5.50 | 6.00 | 6.25 | 6.25 | 6.50 | 6.50 | 7.00 | 7.00 | 8.00 | 8.00 | 8.00 | 7.00 |
| Discount Rate................................ | 60.a | 1.50 | 1.50 | 1.50 | 1.50 | 1.50 | 1.50 | 1.50 | 1.50 | 1.50 | 1.00 | 1.00 | 1.00 |
| Treasury Bill Rate........................... | 60c | 2.40 | 2.20 | 1.98 | 3.59 | 4.72 | 6.35 | 6.82 | .80 | .74 | .08 | .13 | .48 |
| Deposit Rate.................................. | 60l | 2.65 | 2.25 | 2.25 | 2.25 | 2.40 | 2.50 | 3.63 | .... | .... | .... | .... | .... |
| Lending Rate.................................. | 60p | 8.50 | 8.13 | 8.00 | 8.00 | 8.00 | 8.00 | 8.00 | .... | .... | .... | .... | .... |
| Government Bond Yield.................. | 61 | 6.63 | 6.50 | 6.13 | 6.00 | 6.00 | 6.00 | 6.00 | 6.00 | 6.00 | 6.00 | 6.00 | 6.00 |
| **Prices** | | | | | *Index Numbers (2010=100): Period Averages* | | | | | | | | |
| Consumer Prices............................. | 64 | 62.0 | † 66.3 | 70.9 | 74.9 | 82.3 | 91.5 | 100.0 | 109.3 | 119.6 | 130.4 | † 141.3 | 152.5 |
| **Intl. Transactions & Positions** | | | | | *Millions of US Dollars* | | | | | | | | |
| Exports........................................ | 70..d | 772 | 823 | 828 | 894 | 850 | 873 | 830 | 869 | 872 | 827 | 943 | 720 |
| Imports, c.i.f.................................. | 71..d | 1,939 | 2,094 | 2,389 | 2,931 | 3,181 | 3,667 | 5,110 | 5,352 | 5,419 | 5,987 | 7,323 | 6,380 |

# Nepal 558

## Balance of Payments

| | | 2004 | 2005 | 2006 | 2007 | 2008 | 2009 | 2010 | 2011 | 2012 | 2013 | 2014 | 2015 |
|---|---|---|---|---|---|---|---|---|---|---|---|---|---|
| | | | | | | | *Millions of US Dollars* | | | | | | |
| A. Current Account* | 109bx | −45.0 | 153.1 | 150.1 | 5.7 | 733.3 | 21.4 | −127.6 | 288.6 | 576.9 | 1,160.2 | 496.2 | 2,446.6 |
| Goods, credit (exports) | 1a9cx | 773.1 | 902.9 | 848.8 | 924.9 | 986.6 | 837.1 | 900.6 | 999.0 | 1,004.3 | 998.0 | 1,022.3 | 813.2 |
| Goods, debit (imports) | 1a9dx | 1,908.0 | 2,276.5 | 2,441.0 | 2,932.6 | 3,519.3 | 4,259.4 | 5,009.2 | 5,665.1 | 5,951.2 | 6,543.0 | 7,580.5 | 6,510.7 |
| Balance on goods | 1a9bx | −1,134.9 | −1,373.6 | −1,592.2 | −2,007.6 | −2,532.8 | −3,422.3 | −4,108.6 | −4,666.1 | −4,946.9 | −5,544.9 | −6,558.2 | −5,697.6 |
| Services, credit (exports) | 1b9cx | 460.9 | 380.3 | 385.7 | 511.3 | 723.7 | 704.8 | 670.9 | 863.5 | 924.9 | 1,189.6 | 1,388.5 | 1,430.5 |
| Services, debit (imports) | 1b9dx | 385.0 | 434.7 | 492.8 | 722.6 | 851.7 | 841.7 | 869.7 | 782.2 | 896.3 | 984.6 | 1,197.1 | 1,200.8 |
| Balance on Goods & Services | 1z9bx | −1,059.1 | −1,428.0 | −1,699.4 | −2,218.9 | −2,660.9 | −3,559.2 | −4,307.3 | −4,584.8 | −4,918.2 | −5,340.0 | −6,366.8 | −5,467.9 |
| Primary income: credit | 1c9cx | 63.0 | 139.9 | 158.2 | 224.3 | 235.6 | 210.2 | 209.6 | 287.7 | 247.5 | 328.2 | 391.8 | 437.5 |
| Primary income: debit | 1c9dx | 78.0 | 91.6 | 96.1 | 87.6 | 84.6 | 52.3 | 116.1 | 140.3 | 121.9 | 90.6 | 66.0 | 87.0 |
| Balance on gds, serv. & prim. inc. | 1y9bx | −1,074.1 | −1,379.7 | −1,637.3 | −2,082.2 | −2,509.8 | −3,401.3 | −4,213.9 | −4,437.4 | −4,792.7 | −5,102.4 | −6,041.0 | −5,117.4 |
| Secondary income: credit | 1d9ca | 1,091.8 | 1,593.3 | 1,856.2 | 2,129.4 | 3,294.4 | 3,532.1 | 4,139.5 | 4,778.1 | 5,447.7 | 6,317.0 | 6,569.9 | 7,590.8 |
| Secondary income: debit | 1d9da | 62.8 | 60.5 | 68.9 | 41.5 | 51.2 | 109.4 | 53.3 | 52.1 | 78.0 | 54.5 | 32.7 | 26.7 |
| B. Capital Account* | 209ba | 15.7 | 40.3 | 46.3 | 75.4 | 113.6 | 132.0 | 185.1 | 189.5 | 201.6 | 166.9 | 141.2 | 161.6 |
| Capital account: credit | 209ca | 15.7 | 40.5 | 46.4 | 75.5 | 115.0 | 132.6 | 186.1 | 190.3 | 202.5 | 166.9 | 141.2 | 161.6 |
| Capital account: debit | 209da | — | .2 | .1 | .1 | 1.4 | .6 | 1.0 | .7 | .9 | — | — | — |
| Balance on current & capital acct. | 129ca | −29.4 | 193.4 | 196.4 | 81.0 | 846.9 | 153.4 | 57.5 | 478.2 | 778.5 | 1,327.1 | 637.5 | 2,608.3 |
| C. Financial Account* | 309na | 488.5 | 161.5 | −2.8 | 132.1 | −91.7 | 157.8 | −284.8 | −242.9 | 117.8 | −66.8 | −35.4 | 326.0 |
| Direct investment: assets | 3a9aa | .... | .... | .... | .... | .... | .... | — | — | — | — | — | — |
| Equity & investment fund shares | 3aaaa | .... | .... | .... | .... | .... | .... | — | — | — | — | — | — |
| Debt instruments | 3abaa | .... | .... | .... | .... | .... | .... | — | — | — | — | — | — |
| Direct investment: liabilities | 3a9la | −.4 | 2.5 | −6.6 | 5.7 | 1.0 | 38.3 | 87.7 | 94.0 | 92.0 | 74.2 | 30.4 | 18.6 |
| Equity & investment fund shares | 3aala | −.4 | 2.5 | −6.6 | 5.3 | −5.3 | — | — | 94.0 | 92.0 | 74.2 | 30.4 | 18.6 |
| Debt instruments | 3abla | .... | .... | .... | .5 | 6.3 | 38.3 | 87.7 | — | — | — | — | — |
| Portfolio investment: assets | 3b9aa | .... | .... | .... | .... | .... | .... | .... | .... | .... | .... | .... | .... |
| Equity & investment fund shares | 3baaa | .... | .... | .... | .... | .... | .... | .... | .... | .... | .... | .... | .... |
| Debt securities | 3bbaa | .... | .... | .... | .... | .... | .... | .... | .... | .... | .... | .... | .... |
| Portfolio investment: liabilities | 3b9la | .... | .... | .... | .... | .... | .... | .... | .... | .... | .... | .... | .... |
| Equity & investment fund shares | 3bala | .... | .... | .... | .... | .... | .... | .... | .... | .... | .... | .... | .... |
| Debt securities | 3bbla | .... | .... | .... | .... | .... | .... | .... | .... | .... | .... | .... | .... |
| Fin. der.& empl.stk.ops.(ESOs): net. | 3c9na | .... | .... | .... | .... | .... | .... | .... | .... | .... | .... | .... | .... |
| Fin. der. & ESOs.: assets | 3c9aa | .... | .... | .... | .... | .... | .... | .... | .... | .... | .... | .... | .... |
| Fin. der. & ESOs.: liabilities | 3c9la | .... | .... | .... | .... | .... | .... | .... | .... | .... | .... | .... | .... |
| Other investment: assets | 3d9aa | 348.0 | 242.4 | 250.9 | 161.0 | 386.7 | 306.0 | 354.8 | 300.1 | 504.2 | 402.8 | 373.2 | 594.4 |
| Other equity | 3daaa | .... | .... | .... | .... | .... | .... | .... | .... | .... | .... | .... | .... |
| Debt instruments | 3dzaa | 348.0 | 242.4 | 250.9 | 161.0 | 386.7 | 306.0 | 354.8 | 300.1 | 504.2 | 402.8 | 373.2 | 594.4 |
| Other investment: liabilities | 3d9la | −140.0 | 78.5 | 260.3 | 23.1 | 477.3 | 110.0 | 551.9 | 448.9 | 294.4 | 395.3 | 378.2 | 249.7 |
| Other equity | 3dala | .... | .... | .... | .... | .... | .... | .... | .... | .... | .... | .... | .... |
| Debt instruments | 3dzla | −140.0 | 78.5 | 260.3 | 23.1 | 477.3 | 110.0 | 551.9 | 448.9 | 294.4 | 395.3 | 378.2 | 249.7 |
| Curr.+ cap.– finan. acct. balance | 4y9na | −517.8 | 31.9 | 199.2 | −51.0 | 938.6 | −4.4 | 342.3 | 721.0 | 660.7 | 1,393.9 | 672.8 | 2,282.3 |
| D. Net Errors and Omissions | 409na | 415.9 | 139.0 | 108.5 | 19.1 | −107.5 | 7.2 | −180.1 | 278.6 | 56.5 | 63.1 | 173.6 | 46.8 |
| E. Reserves and Related Items | 4z9na | −101.9 | 170.9 | 307.7 | −32.0 | 831.2 | 2.8 | 162.3 | 999.6 | 717.2 | 1,457.0 | 846.4 | 2,329.0 |
| Reserve assets | 3e9aa | 178.0 | 170.9 | 329.0 | 1.1 | 831.2 | .6 | 199.8 | 995.1 | 706.8 | 1,441.9 | 833.6 | 2,365.1 |
| Credit and loans from the IMF | 3dcla | 10.0 | — | 21.2 | 33.1 | — | −2.2 | 37.5 | −4.5 | −10.4 | −15.1 | −12.9 | 36.1 |
| Exceptional financing | 409la | 270.0 | — | — | — | — | — | — | — | — | — | — | — |

*Excludes components in group E

## International Investment Position

| | | 2004 | 2005 | 2006 | 2007 | 2008 | 2009 | 2010 | 2011 | 2012 | 2013 | 2014 | 2015 |
|---|---|---|---|---|---|---|---|---|---|---|---|---|---|
| | | | | | | | *Millions of US Dollars* | | | | | | |
| Assets | 809aa | .... | .... | .... | .... | .... | .... | .... | .... | † 5,368.1 | 6,574.6 | .... | .... |
| Direct investment | 8a9aa | .... | .... | .... | .... | .... | .... | .... | .... | .... | .... | .... | .... |
| Equity & investment fund shares | 8aaaa | .... | .... | .... | .... | .... | .... | .... | .... | .... | .... | .... | .... |
| Debt instruments | 8abaa | .... | .... | .... | .... | .... | .... | .... | .... | .... | .... | .... | .... |
| Portfolio investment | 8b9aa | .... | .... | .... | .... | .... | .... | .... | .... | † 4.9 | 4.8 | .... | .... |
| Equity & investment fund shares | 8baaa | .... | .... | .... | .... | .... | .... | .... | .... | † .5 | .5 | .... | .... |
| Debt securities | 8bbaa | .... | .... | .... | .... | .... | .... | .... | .... | † 4.3 | 4.3 | .... | .... |
| Fin. der.(oth.than reserves) & ESOs | 8c9aa | .... | .... | .... | .... | .... | .... | .... | .... | .... | .... | .... | .... |
| Other investment | 8d9aa | .... | .... | .... | .... | .... | .... | .... | .... | † 975.5 | 1,073.9 | .... | .... |
| Other equity | 8daaa | .... | .... | .... | .... | .... | .... | .... | .... | † 18.7 | 28.5 | .... | .... |
| Debt instruments | 8dzaa | .... | .... | .... | .... | .... | .... | .... | .... | † 956.8 | 1,045.4 | .... | .... |
| Reserve assets | 8e9aa | .... | .... | .... | .... | .... | .... | .... | .... | † 4,387.7 | 5,495.9 | .... | .... |
| Liabilities | 809la | .... | .... | .... | .... | .... | .... | .... | .... | † 4,913.5 | 4,837.6 | .... | .... |
| Direct investment | 8a9la | .... | .... | .... | .... | .... | .... | .... | .... | † 563.5 | 545.4 | .... | .... |
| Equity & investment fund shares | 8aala | .... | .... | .... | .... | .... | .... | .... | .... | † 552.7 | 535.2 | .... | .... |
| Debt instruments | 8abla | .... | .... | .... | .... | .... | .... | .... | .... | † 10.8 | 10.2 | .... | .... |
| Portfolio investment | 8b9la | .... | .... | .... | .... | .... | .... | .... | .... | † .8 | .8 | .... | .... |
| Equity & investment fund shares | 8bala | .... | .... | .... | .... | .... | .... | .... | .... | † .8 | .8 | .... | .... |
| Debt securities | 8bbla | .... | .... | .... | .... | .... | .... | .... | .... | .... | .... | .... | .... |
| Fin. der.(oth.than reserves) & ESOs | 8c9la | .... | .... | .... | .... | .... | .... | .... | .... | .... | .... | .... | .... |
| Other investment | 8d9la | .... | .... | .... | .... | .... | .... | .... | .... | † 4,349.2 | 4,291.5 | .... | .... |
| Other equity | 8dala | .... | .... | .... | .... | .... | .... | .... | .... | .... | .... | .... | .... |
| Debt instruments | 8dzla | .... | .... | .... | .... | .... | .... | .... | .... | † 4,349.2 | 4,291.5 | .... | .... |

# Nepal 558

| | | 2004 | 2005 | 2006 | 2007 | 2008 | 2009 | 2010 | 2011 | 2012 | 2013 | 2014 | 2015 |
|---|---|---|---|---|---|---|---|---|---|---|---|---|---|
| **Government Finance** | | | | | | | | | | | | | |
| **Cash Flow Statement** | | | | | | | | | | | | | |
| **Budgetary Central Government** | | | | | | *Millions of Rupees: Fiscal Year Ends July 15* | | | | | | | |
| Cash Receipts:Operating Activities... | c1 | 71,064 | 82,456 | 84,100 | 102,188 | 120,650 | 166,024 | 216,250 | 252,910 | 285,065 | 330,916 | 404,631 | .... |
| Taxes............................. | c11 | 48,173 | 54,105 | 57,427 | 71,127 | 85,155 | 117,051 | 159,786 | 181,255 | 211,723 | 259,215 | 312,440 | .... |
| Social Contributions................. | c12 | — | — | — | — | — | — | — | — | — | — | — | .... |
| Grants............................. | c13 | 11,283 | 14,391 | 13,827 | 15,801 | 20,321 | 26,383 | 38,546 | 49,327 | 40,810 | 35,230 | 42,206 | .... |
| Other Receipts..................... | c14 | 11,608 | 13,960 | 12,846 | 15,260 | 15,174 | 22,590 | 17,918 | 22,328 | 32,533 | 36,471 | 49,986 | .... |
| Cash Payments:Operating Activities. | c2 | 78,346 | 88,782 | 94,881 | 116,234 | .... | .... | 186,493 | 217,323 | 243,348 | 247,374 | 303,244 | .... |
| Compensation of Employees.......... | c21 | .... | .... | .... | .... | .... | .... | 51,561 | 59,472 | 65,966 | 66,046 | 84,357 | .... |
| Purchases of Goods & Services....... | c22 | .... | .... | .... | .... | .... | .... | 19,380 | 27,133 | 23,751 | 23,285 | 29,950 | .... |
| Interest............................ | c24 | 6,544 | 6,218 | 6,159 | 6,164 | 6,374 | 8,154 | 9,981 | 12,519 | 15,161 | 13,737 | 12,038 | .... |
| Subsidies........................... | c25 | .... | .... | .... | .... | .... | .... | 4,101 | 5,445 | 4,640 | 4,227 | 1,146 | .... |
| Grants............................. | c26 | .... | .... | .... | .... | .... | .... | 81,875 | 90,074 | 103,664 | 102,173 | 133,392 | .... |
| Social Benefits...................... | c27 | .... | .... | .... | .... | .... | .... | 18,210 | 20,819 | 28,169 | 35,630 | 39,028 | .... |
| Other Payments..................... | c28 | .... | .... | .... | .... | .... | .... | 1,384 | 1,861 | 1,997 | 2,275 | 3,333 | .... |
| Net Cash Inflow:Operating Act.[1-2] | ccio | −7,282 | −6,325 | −10,781 | −15,655 | .... | .... | 29,757 | 35,587 | 41,718 | 83,542 | 101,388 | .... |
| Net Cash Outflow:Invest. in NFA...... | c31 | .... | −564 | −250 | −74 | .... | .... | 46,138 | 49,264 | 51,272 | 54,264 | 66,485 | .... |
| Purchases of Nonfinancial Assets... | c31.1 | .... | — | — | — | .... | .... | 46,322 | 49,492 | 51,391 | 53,570 | .... | .... |
| Sales of Nonfinancial Assets.......... | c31.2 | 453 | 564 | 250 | 72 | 4,423 | 112 | 183 | 228 | 119 | 132 | .... | .... |
| Cash Surplus/Deficit [1-2-31=1-2M] | ccsd | −6,829 | −5,761 | −10,531 | −14,345 | −12,800 | −30,267 | −16,381 | −13,677 | −9,554 | 29,278 | 34,903 | .... |
| Net Acq. Fin. Assets, excl. Cash...... | c32x | −1,796 | −1,248 | −16 | −1,006 | 4,220 | −20,715 | 12,196 | 1,613 | 24,157 | 22,602 | .... | .... |
| Domestic.......................... | c321x | −1,796 | −1,248 | −16 | −1,006 | 4,220 | −20,715 | 11,644 | 1,613 | 24,157 | 22,602 | .... | .... |
| Foreign........................... | c322x | — | — | — | — | — | — | 552 | — | — | — | .... | .... |
| Net Incurrence of Liabilities............. | c33 | 2,442 | 4,671 | 5,784 | 11,194 | 13,089 | 30,970 | 22,705 | 23,656 | −9,076 | −35,130 | −3,895 | .... |
| Domestic.......................... | c331 | 579 | 1,358 | 4,557 | 8,679 | 11,979 | 31,122 | 22,225 | 22,906 | −6,627 | −20,940 | −5,170 | .... |
| Foreign........................... | c332 | 1,863 | 3,313 | 1,227 | 2,515 | 1,111 | −151 | 480 | 750 | −2,449 | −14,190 | 1,274 | .... |
| Net Cash Inflow, Fin.Act.[-32x+33].. | cnfb | 4,238 | 5,919 | 5,800 | 12,200 | 8,869 | 51,686 | 10,509 | 22,043 | −33,234 | −56,584 | −26,844 | .... |
| Net Change in Stock of Cash........... | cncb | −2,591 | 158 | −4,731 | −2,146 | −3,930 | 21,419 | −60 | 682 | −42,788 | −27,305 | 8,059 | .... |
| Stat. Discrep. [32X-33+NCB-CSD]... | ccsdz | — | — | — | — | — | — | 5,812 | −7,685 | — | — | — | .... |
| Memo Item:Cash Expenditure[2+31] | c2m | .... | .... | .... | .... | .... | .... | .... | 266,587 | 294,620 | 301,638 | 369,728 | .... |
| Memo Item: Gross Debt................. | c63 | .... | .... | .... | .... | .... | .... | .... | .... | .... | .... | .... | .... |
| **National Accounts** | | | | | | *Millions of Rupees: Fiscal Year Ends July 15* | | | | | | | |
| Househ.Cons.Expend.,incl.NPISHs.... | 96f | 427,288 | 468,849 | 558,222 | 612,635 | 680,474 | 825,204 | 978,711 | 1,089,958 | 1,249,969 | 1,408,729 | 1,614,463 | .... |
| Government Consumption Expend... | 91f | 46,397 | 52,453 | 56,794 | 66,949 | 80,663 | 106,527 | 119,189 | 130,917 | 164,370 | 168,192 | 220,658 | .... |
| Gross Fixed Capital Formation......... | 93e | 109,181 | 117,539 | 135,532 | 153,337 | 178,446 | 211,039 | 264,888 | 292,730 | 317,185 | 382,153 | 456,129 | .... |
| Changes in Inventories................... | 93i | 22,489 | 38,368 | 40,101 | 55,442 | 68,826 | 101,990 | 191,602 | 226,537 | 209,704 | 242,492 | 269,436 | .... |
| Exports of Goods and Services......... | 90c | 89,544 | 85,958 | 87,952 | 93,567 | 104,207 | 122,737 | 114,298 | 121,714 | 153,863 | 181,181 | 226,021 | .... |
| Imports of Goods and Services (-)..... | 98c | 158,151 | 173,754 | 204,828 | 230,893 | 271,291 | 342,536 | 434,198 | 450,059 | 512,948 | 634,899 | 800,552 | .... |
| Gross Domestic Product (GDP)........ | 99b | 536,749 | 589,412 | 654,084 | 727,827 | 815,658 | 988,272 | 1,192,774 | 1,366,954 | 1,527,344 | 1,692,643 | 1,928,517 | .... |
| GDP Volume 2000/2001 Prices........ | 99b.p | 481,004 | 497,739 | 514,486 | 532,038 | 564,517 | 590,107 | 618,529 | 639,694 | 670,279 | 697,954 | 735,508 | .... |
| GDP Volume (2010=100)............... | 99bvp | 77.8 | 80.5 | 83.2 | 86.0 | 91.3 | 95.4 | 100.0 | 103.4 | 108.4 | 112.8 | 118.9 | .... |
| GDP Deflator (2010=100)............... | 99bip | 57.9 | 61.4 | 65.9 | 70.9 | 74.9 | 86.8 | 100.0 | 110.8 | 118.2 | 125.8 | 136.0 | .... |
| | | | | | | *Millions: Midyear Estimates* | | | | | | | |
| Population............................... | 99z | 25.20 | 25.51 | 25.79 | 26.06 | 26.33 | 26.59 | 26.88 | 27.18 | 27.50 | 27.83 | 28.17 | 28.51 |

# Netherlands 138

| | | 2004 | 2005 | 2006 | 2007 | 2008 | 2009 | 2010 | 2011 | 2012 | 2013 | 2014 | 2015 |
|---|---|---|---|---|---|---|---|---|---|---|---|---|---|
| **Exchange Rates** | | | | | | *Euros per SDR: End of Period* | | | | | | | |
| Market Rate.................................. | aa | 1.1402 | 1.2116 | 1.1423 | 1.0735 | 1.1068 | 1.0882 | 1.1525 | 1.1865 | 1.1649 | 1.1167 | 1.1933 | 1.2728 |
| | | | | | *Euros per US Dollar: End of Period (ae) Period Average (rf)* | | | | | | | | |
| Market Rate.................................. | ae | .7342 | .8477 | .7593 | .6793 | .7185 | .6942 | .7484 | .7729 | .7579 | .7251 | .8237 | .9185 |
| Market Rate.................................. | rf | .8054 | .8041 | .7971 | .7306 | .6827 | .7198 | .7550 | .7194 | .7783 | .7532 | .7537 | .9017 |
| | | | | | *Index Numbers (2010=100): Period Averages* | | | | | | | | |
| Nominal Effective Exchange Rate..... | nec | 98.2 | 97.8 | 97.9 | 99.6 | 102.0 | 103.1 | 100.0 | 100.3 | 97.5 | 99.6 | 99.9 | 95.8 |
| CPI-Based Real Effect. Ex. Rate........ | rec | 101.8 | 101.0 | 99.9 | 100.6 | 101.8 | 103.8 | 100.0 | 99.6 | 96.9 | 99.9 | 99.9 | 95.8 |
| ULC-Based Real Effect. Ex. Rate....... | rel | 102.6 | 100.9 | 100.4 | 101.0 | 105.3 | 103.8 | 100.0 | 99.9 | 98.1 | 100.0 | 99.9 | 95.2 |
| **Fund Position** | | | | | | *Millions of SDRs: End of Period* | | | | | | | |
| Quota.......................................... | 2f.s | 5,162.40 | 5,162.40 | 5,162.40 | 5,162.40 | 5,162.40 | 5,162.40 | 5,162.40 | 5,162.40 | 5,162.40 | 5,162.40 | 5,162.40 | 5,162.40 |
| SDR Holdings............................... | 1b.s | 500.82 | 500.95 | 521.56 | 620.81 | 662.70 | 4,886.30 | 4,871.11 | 4,739.35 | 4,660.58 | 4,560.07 | 4,569.88 | 4,716.10 |
| Reserve Position in the Fund........... | 1c.s | 1,717.59 | 833.83 | 459.18 | 341.71 | 705.55 | 1,018.66 | 1,342.65 | 2,493.67 | 2,657.34 | 2,520.15 | 2,022.97 | 1,421.75 |
| Total Fund Cred. & Loans Outstg...... | 2tl | — | — | — | — | — | — | — | — | — | — | — | — |
| SDR Allocations............................. | 1bd | 530.34 | 530.34 | 530.34 | 530.34 | 530.34 | 4,836.63 | 4,836.63 | 4,836.63 | 4,836.63 | 4,836.63 | 4,836.63 | 4,836.63 |
| **International Liquidity** | | | | | | *Millions of US Dollars Unless Otherwise Indicated: End of Period* | | | | | | | |
| Total Res.Min.Gold (Eurosys.Def)..... | 1l.d | 10,655 | 8,986 | 10,802 | 10,270 | 11,476 | 17,871 | 18,471 | 20,264 | 22,050 | 22,591 | 19,307 | 17,341 |
| SDR Holdings............................... | 1b.d | 778 | 716 | 785 | 981 | 1,021 | 7,660 | 7,502 | 7,276 | 7,163 | 7,023 | 6,621 | 6,535 |
| Reserve Position in the Fund......... | 1c.d | 2,667 | 1,192 | 691 | 540 | 1,087 | 1,597 | 2,068 | 3,828 | 4,084 | 3,881 | 2,931 | 1,970 |
| Foreign Exchange......................... | 1d.d | 7,210 | 7,078 | 9,327 | 8,749 | 9,369 | 8,613 | 8,902 | 9,160 | 10,803 | 11,688 | 9,755 | 8,836 |
| o/w:Fin.Deriv.Rel.to Reserves...... | 1ddd | 324.18 | −121.51 | 119.85 | 288.53 | 44.53 | −74.91 | 45.43 | −428.28 | 389.22 | 248.24 | −291.38 | −95.81 |
| Other Reserve Assets..................... | 1e.d | | | | | | | | | | | | |
| Gold (Million Fine Troy Ounces)...... | 1ad | 25.00 | 22.34 | 20.61 | 19.98 | 19.69 | 19.69 | 19.69 | 19.69 | 19.69 | 19.69 | 19.69 | 19.69 |
| Gold (Eurosystem Valuation)............ | 1and | 10,948 | 11,462 | 13,100 | 16,713 | 17,033 | 21,739 | 27,769 | 31,003 | 32,766 | 23,659 | 23,614 | 20,864 |
| Memo:Euro Cl. on Non-EA Res........ | 1dgd | 392 | 225 | 633 | 935 | 136 | 137 | 37 | 164 | 244 | 335 | 301 | 391 |
| Non-Euro Cl. on EA Res.............. | 1dhd | 1,975 | 1,305 | 1,200 | 3,641 | 20,644 | 1,855 | 914 | 242 | 282 | 120 | 215 | 221 |
| Central Bank: Other Assets.............. | 3..d | 17,333 | 15,998 | 32,194 | 26,783 | 29,803 | 55,950 | 87,831 | 242,623 | 203,193 | 107,373 | 57,639 | 91,168 |
| Central Bank: Other Liabs............... | 4..d | 829 | 898 | 4,629 | 6,969 | 9,476 | 10,778 | 13,946 | 15,531 | 15,182 | 9,895 | 7,720 | 11,125 |
| Other Depository Corps.: Assets....... | 7a.d | 376,874 | 413,180 | 576,253 | 749,832 | 579,505 | 523,118 | 560,426 | 516,327 | 514,748 | 519,409 | 561,650 | 536,837 |
| Other Depository Corps.: Liabs........ | 7b.d | 410,096 | 446,079 | 589,229 | 755,012 | 683,384 | 701,461 | 684,555 | 699,989 | 604,912 | 537,348 | 518,959 | 528,148 |
| **Central Bank** | | | | | | *Millions of Euros: End of Period* | | | | | | | |
| *Euro Area Wide Residency Criterion* | | | | | | | | | | | | | |
| Net Foreign Assets......................... | 11n.u | 16,274 | 17,867 | 15,330 | 14,603 | 15,006 | 21,451 | 25,371 | 28,886 | 30,846 | 26,933 | 30,436 | 26,561 |
| Claims on Nonresidents................ | 11..u | 16,976 | 18,961 | 20,141 | 19,903 | 21,815 | 28,932 | 35,809 | 40,889 | 42,353 | 34,423 | 36,794 | 36,779 |
| Liabilities to Nonresidents............ | 16c.u | 703 | 1,095 | 4,811 | 5,300 | 6,809 | 7,481 | 10,437 | 12,003 | 11,507 | 7,490 | 6,359 | 10,218 |
| Claims on Other Depository Corps.... | 12e.u | 23,474 | 27,419 | 17,470 | 56,169 | 58,389 | 48,185 | 13,715 | 13,842 | 29,338 | 12,934 | 15,233 | 24,692 |
| Net Claims on Central Government.. | 12anu | 6,577 | 7,474 | 7,600 | 10,854 | 14,959 | 15,129 | 16,605 | 27,360 | 26,638 | 25,815 | 23,305 | 44,430 |
| Claims on Central Govt................ | 12a.u | 6,612 | 7,493 | 7,611 | 10,858 | 14,983 | 15,155 | 16,704 | 27,365 | 26,644 | 25,862 | 23,497 | 44,515 |
| Liabs. to Central Govt.................. | 16d.u | 35 | 19 | 11 | 4 | 24 | 26 | 99 | 5 | 6 | 47 | 192 | 85 |
| Claims on Other Sectors.............. | 12s.u | 477 | 345 | 313 | 206 | 186 | 202 | 368 | 1,230 | 1,281 | 1,329 | 1,569 | 928 |
| Claims on Other Financial Corps.... | 12g.u | 477 | 345 | 313 | 206 | 186 | 202 | 323 | 1,195 | 1,250 | 1,302 | 1,547 | 912 |
| Claims on State & Local Govts....... | 12b.u | — | — | — | — | — | — | — | — | — | — | — | — |
| Claims on Public Nonfin. Corps...... | 12c.u | — | — | — | — | — | — | — | — | — | — | — | — |
| Claims on Private Sector.............. | 12d.u | — | — | — | — | — | — | 45 | 35 | 31 | 27 | 22 | 16 |
| Monetary Base.............................. | 14..u | 38,012 | 46,004 | 46,595 | 57,012 | 69,222 | 100,873 | 94,642 | 222,650 | 206,456 | 125,509 | 105,675 | 172,945 |
| Currency in Circulation................. | 14a.u | 26,422 | 29,691 | 32,911 | 35,457 | 39,799 | 42,905 | 44,587 | 46,976 | 48,291 | 50,653 | 54,061 | 57,270 |
| Liabs. to Other Depository Corps... | 14c.u | 11,588 | 16,311 | 13,682 | 21,552 | 29,417 | 57,966 | 50,050 | 175,672 | 158,162 | 74,855 | 51,613 | 115,218 |
| Liabs. to Other Sectors................. | 14d.u | 2 | 2 | 2 | 3 | 6 | 2 | 5 | 2 | 3 | 1 | 1 | 457 |
| Other Liabs. to Other Dep. Corps..... | 14n.u | — | — | — | — | — | — | — | — | — | — | — | — |
| Dep. & Sec. Excl. f/Monetary Base.... | 14o.u | — | — | — | — | — | — | — | — | — | — | — | — |
| Deposits Included in Broad Money. | 15..u | — | — | — | — | — | — | — | — | — | — | — | — |
| Sec.Ot.th.Shares Inc.in.Brd.Money.. | 16a.u | — | — | — | — | — | — | — | — | — | — | — | — |
| Deposits Excl. from Broad Money... | 16b.u | — | — | — | — | — | — | — | — | — | — | — | — |
| Sec.Oh.th.Shares Excl. f/Brd.Money | 16s.u | — | — | — | — | — | — | — | — | — | — | — | — |
| Loans........................................... | 16l.u | — | — | — | — | — | — | — | — | — | — | — | — |
| Financial Derivatives..................... | 16m.u | — | — | — | — | — | — | — | — | — | — | — | — |
| Shares and Other Equity................. | 17a.u | 12,428 | 15,537 | 16,272 | 18,747 | 20,740 | 23,702 | 29,165 | 32,041 | 34,245 | 25,859 | 27,936 | 27,407 |
| Other Items (Net)........................... | 17r.u | −3,638 | −8,435 | −22,155 | 6,073 | −1,421 | −39,609 | −67,748 | −183,372 | −152,601 | −84,355 | −63,065 | −103,739 |
| *Memorandum Items* | | | | | | | | | | | | | |
| *National Residency Criterion* | | | | | | | | | | | | | |
| Net Foreign Assets......................... | 11n | 24,274 | 28,808 | 37,772 | 9,260 | 16,289 | 58,837 | 89,880 | 215,102 | 184,012 | 103,824 | 75,364 | 108,613 |
| Claims on Nonresidents................ | 11 | 28,585 | 30,894 | 42,594 | 36,524 | 41,900 | 66,333 | 100,338 | 227,135 | 195,550 | 111,393 | 82,827 | 118,832 |
| Liabilities to Nonresidents............ | 16c | 4,312 | 2,087 | 4,822 | 27,264 | 25,611 | 7,496 | 10,457 | 12,033 | 11,538 | 7,569 | 7,464 | 10,219 |
| Claims on Other Depository Corps.... | 12e | 20,311 | 25,082 | 14,577 | 51,796 | 54,171 | 42,773 | 7,866 | 8,996 | 25,505 | 9,762 | 12,497 | 19,901 |
| Net Claims on Central Government.. | 12an | 795 | 442 | 503 | 1,054 | 1,520 | 1,068 | 1,045 | 1,776 | 1,063 | 1,203 | 3,087 | 25,276 |
| Claims on Central Government...... | 12a | 830 | 461 | 514 | 1,058 | 1,544 | 1,094 | 1,144 | 1,781 | 1,069 | 1,250 | 3,279 | 25,361 |
| Liabilities to Central Government... | 16d | 35 | 19 | 11 | 4 | 24 | 26 | 99 | 5 | 6 | 47 | 192 | 85 |
| Claims on Other Sectors.............. | 12s | 36 | 4 | 4 | 1 | 1 | — | 45 | 494 | 561 | 557 | 473 | 107 |
| Claims on Other Fin. Corps........... | 12g | 36 | 4 | 4 | 1 | 1 | — | — | 459 | 530 | 530 | 451 | 91 |
| Claims on State & Local Govts....... | 12b | — | — | — | — | — | — | — | — | — | — | — | — |
| Claims on Private Sector.............. | 12d | — | — | — | — | — | — | 45 | 35 | 31 | 27 | 22 | 16 |
| Liabs.to ODCs, Inc.in Mon.Base...... | 14c | 11,573 | 16,295 | 13,671 | 21,537 | 29,401 | 57,951 | 50,030 | 175,642 | 158,132 | 74,776 | 50,508 | 115,217 |
| Liabs.to Ot.Sectors, Inc.in Mon.Base | 14d | 2 | 2 | 2 | 3 | 6 | 2 | 5 | 2 | 2 | 1 | 1 | 457 |
| Liabs.to ODCs,Excl.f/Mon.Base........ | 14n | — | — | — | — | — | — | — | — | — | — | — | — |
| Net Claims on Eurosystem.............. | 12e.s | −1,141 | 1,477 | 12,384 | −19,471 | −16,308 | 17,995 | 43,133 | 155,482 | 123,538 | 48,883 | 22,465 | 57,769 |

# Netherlands 138

Millions of Euros: End of Period

| | | 2004 | 2005 | 2006 | 2007 | 2008 | 2009 | 2010 | 2011 | 2012 | 2013 | 2014 | 2015 |
|---|---|---|---|---|---|---|---|---|---|---|---|---|---|
| **Other Depository Corporations** | | | | | | | | | | | | | |
| Euro Area Wide Residency Criterion | | | | | | | | | | | | | |
| Net Foreign Assets | 21n.u | −24,390 | −27,888 | −9,853 | −3,519 | −74,642 | −123,798 | −92,897 | −141,945 | −68,337 | −13,008 | 35,163 | 7,981 |
| Claims on Nonresidents | 21..u | 276,686 | 350,242 | 437,550 | 509,362 | 416,401 | 363,125 | 419,418 | 399,047 | 390,138 | 376,629 | 462,606 | 493,099 |
| Liabilities to Nonresidents | 26c.u | 301,076 | 378,130 | 447,403 | 512,881 | 491,043 | 486,923 | 512,315 | 540,992 | 458,475 | 389,637 | 427,443 | 485,118 |
| Claims on Eurosystem | 20..u | 13,137 | 17,730 | 15,225 | 22,193 | 23,760 | 64,380 | 51,817 | 180,183 | 164,232 | 77,185 | 52,869 | 118,075 |
| Currency | 20a.u | 1,922 | 2,049 | 2,215 | 2,077 | 2,508 | 2,096 | 1,818 | 1,773 | 1,778 | 1,731 | 1,555 | 1,649 |
| Reserve Deposits and Securities | 20b.u | 11,215 | 15,681 | 13,010 | 20,116 | 21,252 | 62,284 | 49,999 | 178,410 | 162,454 | 75,454 | 51,314 | 116,426 |
| Other Claims | 20n.u | — | — | — | — | — | — | — | — | — | — | — | — |
| Net Claims on Central Government | 22anu | 82,002 | 91,595 | 76,906 | 62,868 | 20,331 | 68,043 | 91,796 | 73,892 | 89,641 | 91,379 | 98,369 | 91,995 |
| Claims on Central Government | 22a.u | 83,366 | 93,344 | 80,653 | 67,122 | 67,112 | 78,557 | 99,229 | 83,169 | 97,063 | 97,826 | 104,165 | 97,349 |
| Liabilities to Central Government | 26d.u | 1,364 | 1,749 | 3,747 | 4,254 | 46,781 | 10,514 | 7,433 | 9,277 | 7,422 | 6,447 | 5,796 | 5,354 |
| Claims on Other Sectors | 22s.u | 867,805 | 944,816 | 996,503 | 1,187,362 | 1,278,385 | 1,362,801 | 1,444,653 | 1,506,321 | 1,571,616 | 1,441,874 | 1,618,501 | 1,586,381 |
| Claims on Other Financial Corps | 22g.u | 203,139 | 234,085 | 272,301 | 416,449 | 475,876 | 544,348 | 624,482 | 663,745 | 700,386 | 571,380 | 726,932 | 690,561 |
| Claims on State & Local Govts | 22b.u | 51,808 | 51,381 | 50,262 | 49,337 | 48,212 | 48,317 | 53,090 | 52,657 | 52,189 | 52,647 | 55,633 | 55,242 |
| Claims on Public Nonfin. Corps | 22c.u | — | — | — | — | — | — | — | — | — | — | — | — |
| Claims on Private Sector | 22d.u | 612,858 | 659,350 | 673,940 | 721,576 | 754,297 | 770,136 | 767,081 | 789,919 | 819,041 | 817,847 | 835,936 | 840,578 |
| Liabilities to Eurosystem | 26g.u | 24,089 | 26,400 | 15,829 | 55,211 | 43,497 | 38,107 | 14,627 | 15,553 | 29,264 | 12,751 | 15,483 | 24,549 |
| Transf.Dep.Included in Broad Money | 24..u | 162,249 | 184,710 | 206,242 | 201,702 | 200,572 | 231,731 | 262,287 | 272,426 | 274,567 | 278,344 | 358,321 | 372,183 |
| Other.Dep.Included in Broad Money. | 25..u | 292,104 | 336,782 | 378,653 | 393,731 | 430,455 | 410,709 | 400,458 | 417,412 | 428,254 | 417,314 | 409,291 | 401,220 |
| Sec.Ot.th.Shares Inc.in.Brd. Money | 26a.u | 22,655 | 13,109 | 8,921 | 12,719 | 23,852 | 44,861 | 43,757 | 53,208 | 50,459 | 32,364 | 29,268 | 20,430 |
| Deposits Excl. from Broad Money | 26b.u | 70,895 | 80,102 | 82,874 | 149,734 | 161,244 | 171,959 | 157,316 | 167,577 | 186,422 | 190,030 | 218,914 | 226,629 |
| Sec.Ot.th.Shares Excl.f/Brd. Money | 26s.u | 231,717 | 277,938 | 294,030 | 307,513 | 292,186 | 328,467 | 382,747 | 405,065 | 422,170 | 394,846 | 390,256 | 396,650 |
| Loans | 26l.u | — | — | — | — | — | — | — | — | — | — | — | — |
| Financial Derivatives | 26m.u | — | — | — | — | — | — | 141,403 | 185,305 | 252,415 | 155,773 | 257,879 | 221,343 |
| Insurance Technical Reserves | 26r.u | | | | | | | | | | | | |
| Shares and Other Equity | 27a.u | 64,753 | 72,507 | 75,348 | 109,693 | 92,604 | 100,030 | 99,605 | 108,703 | 117,155 | 112,292 | 130,936 | 121,768 |
| Other Items (Net) | 27r.u | 70,096 | 34,709 | 16,886 | 38,598 | 3,419 | 45,563 | −6,831 | −3,376 | −6,419 | 4,151 | −2,141 | 22,529 |
| Memorandum Items | | | | | | | | | | | | | |
| Total Assets | 20ra | 1,677,579 | 1,697,777 | 1,843,177 | 2,168,280 | 2,231,515 | 2,217,007 | 2,260,807 | 2,401,717 | 2,451,454 | 2,204,893 | 2,455,930 | 2,501,649 |
| National Residency Criterion | | | | | | | | | | | | | |
| Net Foreign Assets | 21n | 39,940 | 68,297 | 76,622 | 71,504 | 51,511 | −1,884 | 11,492 | −80,292 | −35,191 | 39,632 | 117,398 | 89,091 |
| Claims on Nonresidents | 21 | 502,250 | 597,157 | 715,927 | 830,295 | 708,403 | 646,255 | 703,000 | 668,913 | 645,457 | 648,476 | 770,963 | 829,583 |
| Liabilities to Nonresidents | 26c | 462,310 | 528,860 | 639,305 | 758,791 | 656,892 | 648,139 | 691,508 | 749,205 | 680,648 | 608,844 | 653,565 | 740,492 |
| Net Claims on Central Government | 22an | 19,894 | 21,408 | 18,412 | 15,469 | −24,596 | 9,837 | 28,874 | 31,097 | 46,642 | 46,811 | 48,516 | 48,259 |
| Claims on Central Government | 22a | 21,052 | 23,005 | 19,649 | 17,710 | 21,877 | 20,178 | 35,889 | 36,510 | 52,393 | 52,407 | 52,951 | 53,058 |
| Liabilities to Central Government | 26d | 1,158 | 1,597 | 1,237 | 2,241 | 46,473 | 10,341 | 7,015 | 5,413 | 5,751 | 5,596 | 4,435 | 4,799 |
| Claims on Other Sectors | 22s | 813,007 | 885,016 | 941,070 | 1,113,184 | 1,188,220 | 1,268,835 | 1,348,422 | 1,407,013 | 1,461,521 | 1,317,988 | 1,475,470 | 1,413,513 |
| Claims on Other Fin. Corps | 22g | 178,101 | 206,314 | 239,619 | 373,323 | 430,422 | 495,078 | 576,388 | 616,578 | 651,707 | 517,539 | 659,383 | 610,410 |
| Claims on State & Local Govts | 22b | 37,801 | 37,684 | 37,888 | 37,884 | 39,945 | 41,237 | 45,495 | 45,453 | 47,220 | 48,547 | 50,254 | 48,855 |
| Claims on Private Sector | 22d | 597,105 | 641,018 | 663,563 | 701,977 | 717,853 | 732,520 | 726,539 | 744,982 | 762,594 | 751,902 | 765,833 | 754,248 |
| Transf.Dep.Included in Broad Money | 24 | 158,479 | 180,124 | 190,584 | 184,171 | 183,625 | 209,521 | 236,856 | 238,221 | 228,151 | 227,563 | 302,401 | 298,490 |
| Other.Dep.Included in Broad Money. | 25 | 276,488 | 324,064 | 361,943 | 374,617 | 414,522 | 392,089 | 378,327 | 394,282 | 404,213 | 393,545 | 395,966 | 389,375 |
| Sec.Ot.th.Shares Inc.in.Brd. Money | 26a | 15,955 | 9,870 | 9,068 | 9,626 | 10,966 | 24,609 | 24,971 | 29,044 | 23,870 | 17,886 | 17,344 | 10,474 |
| Deposits Excl. from Broad Money | 26b | 65,131 | 75,490 | 70,751 | 136,546 | 157,039 | 168,624 | 153,719 | 163,009 | 181,797 | 182,521 | 203,066 | 209,232 |
| Sec.Ot.th.Shares Excl.f/Brd. Money | 26s | 247,685 | 298,213 | 320,324 | 333,812 | 313,354 | 350,231 | 400,180 | 420,478 | 437,728 | 409,831 | 405,038 | 413,091 |

| | | 2004 | 2005 | 2006 | 2007 | 2008 | 2009 | 2010 | 2011 | 2012 | 2013 | 2014 | 2015 |
|---|---|---|---|---|---|---|---|---|---|---|---|---|---|
| **Depository Corporations** | | *Millions of Euros: End of Period* | | | | | | | | | | | |
| Euro Area Wide Residency Criterion | | | | | | | | | | | | | |
| Net Foreign Assets | 31n.u | −8,117 | −10,021 | 5,478 | 11,084 | −59,636 | −102,347 | −67,525 | −113,058 | −37,491 | 13,926 | 65,598 | 34,542 |
| Claims on Nonresidents | 31..u | 293,662 | 369,203 | 457,691 | 529,265 | 438,216 | 392,057 | 455,227 | 439,936 | 432,491 | 411,052 | 499,400 | 529,878 |
| Liabilities to Nonresidents | 36c.u | 301,779 | 379,224 | 452,213 | 518,181 | 497,852 | 494,404 | 522,752 | 552,994 | 469,982 | 397,127 | 433,802 | 495,336 |
| Domestic Claims | 32..u | 956,861 | 1,044,230 | 1,081,322 | 1,261,290 | 1,313,861 | 1,446,175 | 1,553,422 | 1,608,803 | 1,689,176 | 1,560,397 | 1,741,744 | 1,723,734 |
| Net Claims on Central Government | 32anu | 88,579 | 99,069 | 84,506 | 73,722 | 35,290 | 83,172 | 108,401 | 101,252 | 116,279 | 117,194 | 121,674 | 136,425 |
| Claims on Central Government | 32a.u | 89,978 | 100,837 | 88,264 | 77,980 | 82,095 | 93,712 | 115,933 | 110,534 | 123,707 | 123,688 | 127,662 | 141,864 |
| Liabilities to Central Government | 36d.u | 1,399 | 1,768 | 3,758 | 4,258 | 46,805 | 10,540 | 7,532 | 9,282 | 7,428 | 6,494 | 5,988 | 5,439 |
| Claims on Other Sectors | 32s.u | 868,282 | 945,161 | 996,816 | 1,187,568 | 1,278,571 | 1,363,003 | 1,445,021 | 1,507,551 | 1,572,897 | 1,443,203 | 1,620,070 | 1,587,309 |
| Claims on Other Financial Corps | 32g.u | 203,616 | 234,430 | 272,614 | 416,655 | 476,062 | 544,550 | 624,805 | 664,940 | 701,636 | 572,682 | 728,479 | 691,473 |
| Claims on State & Local Govts | 32b.u | 51,808 | 51,381 | 50,262 | 49,337 | 48,212 | 48,317 | 53,090 | 52,657 | 52,189 | 52,647 | 55,633 | 55,242 |
| Claims on Public Nonfin. Corps | 32c.u | — | — | — | — | — | — | — | — | — | — | — | — |
| Claims on Private Sector | 32d.u | 612,858 | 659,350 | 673,940 | 721,576 | 754,297 | 770,136 | 767,126 | 789,954 | 819,072 | 817,874 | 835,958 | 840,594 |
| Broad Money Liabilities | 35l.u | 501,510 | 562,245 | 624,514 | 641,535 | 692,176 | 728,112 | 749,276 | 788,251 | 799,796 | 776,945 | 849,387 | 849,911 |
| Currency Outside Depository Corps | 34a.u | 24,500 | 27,642 | 30,696 | 33,380 | 37,291 | 40,809 | 42,769 | 45,203 | 46,513 | 48,922 | 52,506 | 55,621 |
| Transferable Deposits | 34..u | 162,251 | 184,712 | 206,244 | 201,705 | 200,578 | 231,733 | 262,292 | 272,428 | 274,570 | 278,345 | 358,322 | 372,640 |
| Other Deposits | 35..u | 292,104 | 336,782 | 378,653 | 393,731 | 430,455 | 410,709 | 400,458 | 417,412 | 428,254 | 417,314 | 409,291 | 401,220 |
| Securities Other than Shares | 36a.u | 22,655 | 13,109 | 8,921 | 12,719 | 23,852 | 44,861 | 43,757 | 53,208 | 50,459 | 32,364 | 29,268 | 20,430 |
| Deposits Excl. from Broad Money | 36b.u | 70,895 | 80,102 | 82,874 | 149,734 | 161,244 | 171,959 | 157,316 | 167,577 | 186,422 | 190,030 | 218,914 | 226,629 |
| Sec.Oth.th.Shares Excl.f/Brd. Money. | 36s.u | 231,717 | 277,938 | 294,030 | 307,513 | 292,186 | 328,467 | 382,747 | 405,065 | 422,170 | 394,846 | 390,256 | 396,650 |
| Loans | 36l.u | — | — | — | — | — | — | — | — | — | — | — | — |
| Financial Derivatives | 36m.u | — | — | — | — | — | — | 141,403 | 185,305 | 252,415 | 155,773 | 257,879 | 221,343 |
| Insurance Technical Reserves | 36r.u | — | — | — | — | — | — | — | — | — | — | — | — |
| Shares and Other Equity | 37a.u | 77,181 | 88,044 | 91,620 | 128,440 | 113,344 | 123,732 | 128,770 | 140,744 | 151,400 | 138,151 | 158,872 | 149,175 |
| Other Items (Net) | 37r.u | 67,446 | 25,885 | −6,238 | 45,149 | −4,729 | −8,442 | −73,616 | −187,775 | −163,386 | −80,986 | −64,657 | −82,561 |
| Broad Money Liabs., Seasonally Adj. | 35lub | 501,998 | 561,439 | 623,874 | 641,970 | 694,518 | 732,158 | 754,874 | 794,908 | 807,284 | 785,100 | 859,364 | 860,394 |
| Memorandum Items | | | | | | | | | | | | | |
| National Residency Criterion | | | | | | | | | | | | | |
| Net Foreign Assets | 31n | 64,214 | 97,105 | 114,395 | 80,764 | 67,801 | 56,952 | 101,372 | 134,810 | 148,822 | 143,456 | 192,761 | 197,705 |
| Claims on Nonresidents | 31 | 530,835 | 628,051 | 758,521 | 866,819 | 750,303 | 712,588 | 803,338 | 896,048 | 841,007 | 759,869 | 853,790 | 948,415 |
| Liabilities to Nonresidents | 36c | 466,621 | 530,947 | 644,126 | 786,055 | 682,503 | 655,636 | 701,965 | 761,238 | 692,186 | 616,413 | 661,029 | 750,711 |
| Domestic Claims | 32 | 833,732 | 906,870 | 959,989 | 1,129,708 | 1,165,145 | 1,279,740 | 1,378,386 | 1,440,380 | 1,509,787 | 1,366,559 | 1,527,546 | 1,487,155 |
| Net Claims on Central Government | 32an | 20,689 | 21,850 | 18,915 | 16,523 | −23,076 | 10,905 | 29,919 | 32,873 | 47,705 | 48,014 | 51,603 | 73,535 |
| Claims on Central Government | 32a | 21,882 | 23,466 | 20,163 | 18,768 | 23,421 | 21,272 | 37,033 | 38,291 | 53,462 | 53,657 | 56,230 | 78,419 |
| Liabilities to Central Government. | 36d | 1,193 | 1,616 | 1,248 | 2,245 | 46,497 | 10,367 | 7,114 | 5,418 | 5,757 | 5,643 | 4,627 | 4,884 |
| Claims on Other Sectors | 32s | 813,043 | 885,020 | 941,074 | 1,113,185 | 1,188,221 | 1,268,835 | 1,348,467 | 1,407,507 | 1,462,082 | 1,318,545 | 1,475,943 | 1,413,620 |
| Claims on Other Financial Corps | 32g | 178,137 | 206,318 | 239,623 | 373,324 | 430,423 | 495,078 | 576,388 | 617,037 | 652,237 | 518,069 | 659,834 | 610,501 |
| Claims on State & Local Govts | 32b | 37,801 | 37,684 | 37,888 | 37,884 | 39,945 | 41,237 | 45,495 | 45,453 | 47,220 | 48,547 | 50,254 | 48,855 |
| Claims on Private Sector | 32d | 597,105 | 641,018 | 663,563 | 701,977 | 717,853 | 732,520 | 726,584 | 745,017 | 762,625 | 751,929 | 765,855 | 754,264 |
| Transf.Dep.Included in Broad Money | 34 | 158,481 | 180,126 | 190,586 | 184,174 | 183,631 | 209,523 | 236,861 | 238,223 | 228,153 | 227,564 | 302,402 | 298,947 |
| Other Dep.Included in Broad Money. | 35 | 276,488 | 324,064 | 361,943 | 374,617 | 414,522 | 392,089 | 378,327 | 394,282 | 404,213 | 393,545 | 395,966 | 389,375 |
| Sec.Ot.th.Shares Inc.in.Brd. Money | 36a | 15,955 | 9,870 | 9,068 | 9,626 | 10,966 | 24,609 | 24,971 | 29,044 | 23,870 | 17,886 | 17,344 | 10,474 |
| Deposits Excl. from Broad Money | 36b | 65,131 | 75,490 | 70,751 | 136,546 | 157,039 | 168,624 | 153,719 | 163,009 | 181,797 | 182,521 | 203,066 | 209,232 |
| Sec.Ot.th.Shares Excl./f.Brd. Money.. | 36s | 247,685 | 298,213 | 320,324 | 333,812 | 313,354 | 350,231 | 400,180 | 420,478 | 437,728 | 409,831 | 405,038 | 413,091 |
| **Interest Rates** | | *Percent Per Annum* | | | | | | | | | | | |
| Deposit Rate | | | | | | | | | | | | | |
| Households: Stocks, up to 2 years | 60lhs | 2.81 | 3.18 | 3.22 | 3.86 | 4.42 | 4.63 | 3.28 | 2.81 | 3.04 | 2.45 | 2.17 | 1.83 |
| New Business, up to 1 year | 60lhn | 2.31 | 2.34 | 2.98 | 3.90 | 4.37 | 2.60 | 2.37 | 2.61 | 2.74 | 2.07 | 1.85 | 1.74 |
| Corporations: Stocks, up to 2 years | 60lcs | 2.28 | 2.20 | 2.88 | 3.91 | 4.44 | 2.76 | .95 | 1.44 | 1.37 | .56 | .40 | .27 |
| New Business, up to 1 year | 60lcn | 2.07 | 2.11 | 2.88 | 3.97 | 4.19 | .89 | .56 | 1.14 | .43 | .18 | .16 | .05 |
| Lending Rate | | | | | | | | | | | | | |
| Households: Stocks, up to 1 year | 60phs | 6.46 | 6.26 | 6.51 | 7.36 | 7.74 | 6.98 | 6.43 | 6.44 | 6.53 | 6.23 | 6.01 | 5.87 |
| New Bus., Floating & up to 1 year | 60pns | 7.80 | 7.30 | 7.94 | 8.71 | 9.66 | 10.01 | 5.75 | 3.21 | .... | .... | .... | .... |
| House Purch., Stocks,Over 5 years | 60phm | 5.12 | 4.83 | 4.70 | 4.82 | 4.90 | 4.80 | 4.76 | 4.77 | 4.71 | 4.57 | 4.37 | 4.11 |
| House Purch., New Bus., 5-10 yrs | 60phn | 4.80 | 4.11 | 4.44 | 4.91 | 5.27 | 5.37 | 4.86 | 4.92 | 4.73 | 4.37 | 3.74 | 2.97 |
| Corporations: Stocks, up to 1 year | 60pcs | 4.27 | 4.16 | 4.72 | 5.48 | 5.76 | 3.37 | 3.01 | 3.19 | 2.65 | 2.31 | 2.27 | 1.85 |
| New Bus., Over € 1 mil.,up to 1 yr | 60pcn | 2.78 | 2.94 | 3.77 | 4.78 | 4.96 | 2.03 | 1.84 | 2.50 | 1.87 | 1.77 | 1.74 | 1.29 |
| Government Bond Yield | 61 | 4.09 | 3.37 | 3.78 | 4.29 | 4.23 | 3.69 | 2.99 | 2.99 | 1.93 | 1.96 | 1.45 | .69 |
| **Prices, Production, Labor** | | *Index Numbers (2010=100): Period Averages* | | | | | | | | | | | |
| Share Prices | 62 | 101.4 | 114.9 | 138.3 | 156.1 | 117.2 | 81.4 | 100.0 | 97.9 | 96.0 | 109.1 | 121.2 | 139.5 |
| Share Prices: Manuf.: (2000=100) | 62a | .... | .... | .... | .... | .... | .... | .... | .... | .... | .... | .... | .... |
| Prices: Final Products | 63 | 82.3 | 87.7 | 92.2 | 96.5 | 103.1 | 92.1 | 100.0 | 110.2 | 113.7 | 112.2 | 109.9 | 102.8 |
| Consumer Prices | 64 | 91.1 | 92.6 | 93.7 | 95.2 | 97.6 | 98.7 | † 100.0 | 102.3 | 104.9 | 107.5 | 108.5 | 109.2 |
| Harmonized CPI | 64h | 91.6 | 93.0 | 94.5 | 96.0 | 98.1 | 99.1 | 100.0 | 102.5 | 105.4 | 108.1 | 108.4 | 108.6 |
| Wages: Hourly Rates | 65 | 88.7 | 89.5 | 91.1 | 92.6 | 96.0 | 98.8 | † 100.0 | 101.1 | 102.9 | 104.5 | 106.1 | 107.8 |
| Industrial Production | 66 | 93.4 | 93.7 | 95.6 | 99.5 | 100.2 | 93.0 | 100.0 | 99.5 | 99.0 | 99.5 | 96.7 | 93.8 |
| | | *Number in Thousands: Period Averages* | | | | | | | | | | | |
| Labor Force | 67d | 8,572 | 8,414 | 8,484 | 8,622 | 8,704 | 8,742 | 8,614 | 8,582 | 8,684 | 8,743 | 8,677 | 8,719 |
| Employment | 67e | 8,098 | 8,014 | 8,152 | 8,345 | 8,468 | 8,443 | 8,227 | 8,152 | 8,175 | 8,104 | 8,029 | 8,116 |
| Unemployment | 67c | 466 | 489 | 419 | 355 | 318 | 381 | 435 | 434 | 516 | 647 | 660 | 614 |
| Unemployment Rate (%) | 67r | 5.7 | 5.9 | 5.0 | 4.2 | 3.7 | 4.4 | 5.0 | 5.0 | 5.8 | 7.2 | 7.4 | 6.9 |
| **Intl. Transactions & Positions** | | *Millions of Euros* | | | | | | | | | | | |
| Exports | 70 | 255,660 | 281,300 | 318,094 | 344,310 | 370,488 | 309,369 | 371,552 | 409,358 | 431,403 | 427,447 | 432,306 | 424,746 |
| Imports, c.i.f. | 71 | 228,247 | 249,845 | 285,370 | 306,827 | 335,929 | 274,026 | 331,914 | 364,921 | 389,449 | 386,353 | 382,416 | 377,993 |
| | | *2010=100* | | | | | | | | | | | |
| Volume of Exports | 72 | 76.4 | 81.0 | 89.0 | 95.5 | 97.3 | 88.8 | 100.0 | 104.8 | † 108.1 | 109.9 | 113.3 | 117.2 |
| Volume of Imports | 73 | 77.7 | 82.4 | 90.8 | 96.2 | 99.4 | 88.6 | 100.0 | 104.8 | † 109.0 | 110.0 | 114.0 | 119.4 |
| Unit Value of Exports | 74 | 90.0 | 93.4 | 96.5 | 97.9 | 102.5 | 93.8 | 100.0 | 105.1 | † 107.4 | 106.6 | 104.2 | 100.1 |
| Unit Value of Imports | 75 | 89.3 | 92.1 | 95.5 | 97.1 | 101.9 | 93.2 | 100.0 | 105.0 | † 107.8 | 106.2 | 102.8 | 97.5 |

## Balance of Payments

*Millions of US Dollars*

| | | 2004 | 2005 | 2006 | 2007 | 2008 | 2009 | 2010 | 2011 | 2012 | 2013 | 2014 | 2015 |
|---|---|---|---|---|---|---|---|---|---|---|---|---|---|
| A. Current Account* | 109bx | †44,275.2 | 41,598.6 | 57,168.3 | 50,056.6 | 38,952.8 | 50,014.7 | 61,820.4 | 81,315.6 | 89,545.6 | 87,349.3 | 83,532.2 | 68,773.2 |
| Goods, credit (exports) | 1a9cx | †322,807.0 | 353,773.2 | 401,410.2 | 473,875.8 | 537,949.6 | 423,126.1 | 477,769.6 | 554,541.7 | 546,888.4 | 569,575.9 | 574,672.7 | 476,524.6 |
| Goods, debit (imports) | 1a9dx | †266,078.1 | 290,578.9 | 332,832.3 | 393,146.4 | 450,112.3 | 348,152.0 | 397,724.9 | 464,347.9 | 455,418.8 | 467,330.6 | 469,423.0 | 389,567.1 |
| Balance on goods | 1a9bx | †56,728.9 | 63,194.4 | 68,577.9 | 80,729.4 | 87,837.3 | 74,974.2 | 80,046.1 | 90,195.1 | 91,469.6 | 102,245.3 | 105,249.7 | 86,957.5 |
| Services, credit (exports) | 1b9cx | †87,198.3 | 92,595.5 | 97,611.2 | 118,984.9 | 135,395.4 | 127,174.7 | 124,743.5 | 137,124.1 | 132,600.1 | 144,742.7 | 154,954.7 | 146,383.6 |
| Services, debit (imports) | 1b9dx | †96,733.2 | 101,351.7 | 107,943.4 | 128,362.2 | 145,322.1 | 137,620.5 | 134,468.2 | 151,150.6 | 144,307.7 | 152,030.5 | 159,978.6 | 148,823.3 |
| Balance on Goods & Services | 1z9bx | †47,194.0 | 54,438.2 | 58,245.7 | 71,352.1 | 77,910.5 | 64,528.4 | 70,320.0 | 76,167.3 | 79,762.0 | 94,957.5 | 100,225.8 | 84,517.8 |
| Primary income: credit | 1c9cx | †160,881.2 | 194,791.8 | 238,743.8 | 338,035.4 | 305,061.8 | 250,816.6 | 292,009.5 | 334,608.7 | 298,081.9 | 303,513.9 | 329,706.1 | 246,524.2 |
| Primary income: debit | 1c9dx | †153,073.7 | 195,092.1 | 224,012.6 | 340,061.9 | 328,762.7 | 254,248.3 | 288,614.4 | 317,552.5 | 276,906.9 | 293,510.9 | 329,038.7 | 247,408.4 |
| Balance on gds, serv. & prim. inc. | 1y9bx | †55,001.4 | 54,138.0 | 72,976.9 | 69,325.6 | 54,209.6 | 61,096.7 | 73,715.1 | 93,223.4 | 100,936.9 | 104,960.5 | 100,893.3 | 83,633.6 |
| Secondary income: credit | 1d9ca | †10,605.5 | 11,841.9 | 12,348.7 | 13,083.4 | 16,257.5 | 14,514.5 | 16,470.9 | 18,372.8 | 17,571.3 | 13,427.7 | 14,436.0 | 11,543.1 |
| Secondary income: debit | 1d9da | †21,331.7 | 24,381.3 | 28,157.3 | 32,352.5 | 31,514.3 | 25,596.5 | 28,365.6 | 30,280.7 | 28,962.6 | 31,038.9 | 31,797.1 | 26,403.5 |
| B. Capital Account* | 209ba | †180.9 | 84.3 | −2,108.1 | −15,583.8 | −1,383.6 | 665.0 | −4,121.5 | 522.2 | −11,874.4 | 1,140.2 | −386.6 | −38,907.0 |
| Capital account: credit | 209ca | †1,597.0 | 1,828.1 | 2,130.2 | 1,498.7 | 4,135.4 | 4,166.9 | 2,268.9 | 3,961.2 | 3,019.1 | 5,539.6 | 1,274.5 | 3,459.2 |
| Capital account: debit | 209da | †1,416.1 | 1,743.8 | 4,238.4 | 17,082.5 | 5,519.0 | 3,501.9 | 6,390.3 | 3,439.0 | 14,893.4 | 4,399.4 | 1,661.1 | 42,366.3 |
| Balance on current & capital acct. | 129bx | †44,456.1 | 41,682.8 | 55,060.2 | 34,472.7 | 37,569.2 | 50,679.7 | 57,699.0 | 81,837.8 | 77,671.3 | 88,489.5 | 83,145.7 | 29,866.1 |
| C. Financial Account* | 309na | †49,634.5 | 34,148.5 | 52,132.3 | 33,328.5 | 33,082.3 | 57,210.6 | 50,863.1 | 66,987.4 | 57,282.3 | 86,769.1 | 66,842.7 | 36,059.5 |
| Direct investment: assets | 3a9aa | †151,363.1 | 266,635.6 | 523,275.9 | 596,514.3 | 272,347.5 | 140,300.8 | 191,499.5 | 371,406.9 | 238,025.3 | 410,649.1 | 63,549.3 | 56,005.1 |
| Equity & investment fund shares | 3aaaa | †140,756.5 | 180,068.8 | 393,764.5 | 251,490.0 | 207,647.4 | 216,731.5 | 118,532.2 | 308,027.8 | 95,020.8 | 278,944.3 | 19,889.6 | −20,606.7 |
| Debt instruments | 3abaa | †10,606.6 | 86,568.1 | 129,515.3 | 345,025.7 | 64,701.7 | −76,430.8 | 72,967.3 | 63,376.3 | 143,003.2 | 131,706.1 | 43,658.5 | 76,611.8 |
| Direct investment: liabilities | 3a9la | †139,818.5 | 209,981.0 | 375,135.9 | 734,010.3 | 195,192.2 | 95,931.3 | 115,729.8 | 331,838.5 | 239,754.9 | 363,760.2 | 94,377.4 | 68,733.1 |
| Equity & investment fund shares | 3aala | †81,402.8 | 72,553.0 | 357,436.9 | 436,494.2 | 167,404.8 | 177,717.9 | 85,640.4 | 312,102.9 | 226,385.7 | 256,789.0 | 29,008.0 | −32,936.2 |
| Debt instruments | 3abla | †58,414.4 | 137,426.8 | 17,697.8 | 297,514.8 | 27,783.1 | −81,785.2 | 30,090.7 | 19,735.6 | 13,369.2 | 106,972.6 | 65,369.4 | 101,668.2 |
| Portfolio investment: assets | 3b9aa | †112,302.0 | 101,265.8 | 44,000.3 | 57,573.5 | 1,363.9 | 82,050.6 | −3,432.5 | 18,771.9 | 77,896.8 | 33,722.2 | 77,575.2 | −6,528.5 |
| Equity & investment fund shares | 3baaa | †33,879.5 | 15,259.6 | 10,419.9 | 32,062.8 | 26,937.5 | 36,561.1 | 4,975.7 | 21,269.9 | 29,487.2 | 9,631.0 | 35,093.6 | −43,283.4 |
| Debt securities | 3bbaa | †78,422.5 | 86,005.0 | 33,581.6 | 25,512.0 | −25,573.6 | 45,488.1 | −8,408.2 | −2,499.5 | 48,409.7 | 24,089.8 | 42,481.6 | 36,753.7 |
| Portfolio investment: liabilities | 3b9la | †73,642.0 | 153,936.2 | 132,374.6 | −57,659.3 | 93,456.9 | 73,659.9 | 48,134.7 | 20,334.8 | 3,538.7 | 20,391.4 | −7,207.5 | −46,128.0 |
| Equity & investment fund shares | 3bala | †4,165.5 | 83,331.9 | 39,088.5 | −141,098.5 | −14,047.7 | 21,929.9 | 15,334.4 | 7,662.7 | 4,190.8 | 14,645.7 | 3,853.2 | 26,904.2 |
| Debt securities | 3bbla | †69,477.8 | 70,603.0 | 93,286.1 | 83,440.6 | 107,504.7 | 51,731.3 | 32,801.7 | 12,673.5 | −652.1 | 5,745.7 | −11,060.8 | −73,031.1 |
| Fin. der.& empl.stk.ops.(ESOs): net | 3c9na | †1,521.7 | 5,161.7 | 11,508.6 | 25,191.9 | 10,408.9 | −38,673.2 | 11,551.9 | 8,841.3 | −10,535.9 | −11,070.0 | 1,078.5 | 4,183.0 |
| Fin. der. & ESOs.: assets | 3c9aa | .... | .... | .... | .... | .... | .... | .... | .... | .... | .... | .... | .... |
| Fin. der. & ESOs.: liabilities | 3c9la | .... | .... | .... | .... | .... | .... | .... | .... | .... | .... | .... | .... |
| Other investment: assets | 3d9aa | †81,233.6 | 67,955.9 | 245,252.9 | 270,294.3 | −71,151.0 | −74,625.6 | 64,481.2 | 135,570.7 | −65,705.0 | −45,589.3 | 58,839.5 | 36,214.3 |
| Other equity | 3daaa | †21.2 | 23.9 | — | −39.8 | 52.0 | 177.2 | 214.1 | 98.8 | 2,476.5 | 3,079.7 | 1,702.0 | — |
| Debt instruments | 3dzaa | †81,212.4 | 67,932.0 | 245,252.9 | 270,334.1 | −71,203.0 | −74,802.8 | 64,267.1 | 135,471.9 | −68,181.5 | −48,669.0 | 57,137.5 | 36,214.3 |
| Other investment: liabilities | 3d9la | †83,324.0 | 42,954.6 | 264,395.1 | 239,897.4 | −108,760.7 | −117,750.8 | 49,377.8 | 115,428.7 | −60,897.3 | −83,206.1 | 47,028.6 | 31,206.0 |
| Other equity | 3dala | †— | | | | | | | | | | | |
| Debt instruments | 3dzla | †83,324.0 | 42,954.6 | 264,395.1 | 239,897.4 | −108,760.7 | −117,750.8 | 49,377.8 | 115,428.7 | −60,897.3 | −83,206.1 | 47,028.6 | 31,206.0 |
| Curr.+ cap.− finan. acct. balance | 4y9na | †−5,178.4 | 7,534.3 | 2,927.9 | 1,144.3 | 4,486.9 | −6,530.9 | 6,835.8 | 14,850.4 | 20,388.9 | 1,720.4 | 16,303.0 | −6,193.4 |
| D. Net Errors and Omissions | 409na | †4,266.9 | −9,324.0 | −2,151.3 | −2,559.0 | −3,644.3 | 13,480.1 | −6,342.5 | −11,587.2 | −17,622.9 | −1,846.9 | −17,899.9 | 5,727.9 |
| E. Reserves and Related Items | 4z9na | †−914.0 | −1,789.7 | 776.5 | −1,409.2 | 844.2 | 6,956.1 | 492.0 | 3,265.9 | 2,767.4 | −129.2 | −1,595.9 | −463.3 |
| Reserve assets | 3e9aa | †−914.0 | −1,789.7 | 776.5 | −1,409.2 | 844.2 | 6,956.1 | 492.0 | 3,265.9 | 2,767.4 | −129.2 | −1,595.9 | −463.3 |
| Credit and loans from the IMF | 3dcla | †— | | | | | | | | | | | |
| Exceptional financing | 409la | .... | .... | .... | .... | .... | .... | .... | .... | .... | .... | .... | .... |

*Excludes components in group E

## International Investment Position

*Millions of US Dollars*

| | | 2004 | 2005 | 2006 | 2007 | 2008 | 2009 | 2010 | 2011 | 2012 | 2013 | 2014 | 2015 |
|---|---|---|---|---|---|---|---|---|---|---|---|---|---|
| Assets | 809aa | 4,505,516.7 | 4,529,949.1 | 5,883,180.3 | 7,554,658.5 | 7,081,725.7 | 7,550,200.3 | 7,568,034.6 | 8,035,754.7 | 8,652,314.3 | 9,204,531.6 | 8,842,027.3 | 8,112,945.0 |
| Direct investment | 8a9aa | 2,526,605.6 | 2,479,729.4 | 3,308,012.9 | 4,281,296.7 | 4,227,997.1 | 4,520,667.6 | 4,526,181.1 | 4,835,207.3 | 5,183,718.1 | 5,772,394.1 | 5,225,168.3 | 4,802,532.2 |
| Equity & investment fund shares | 8aaaa | 1,546,714.9 | 1,523,500.0 | 2,124,812.2 | 2,633,229.2 | 2,658,425.3 | 2,969,085.2 | 2,991,598.1 | 3,273,605.8 | 3,435,720.2 | 3,858,244.6 | 3,523,119.1 | 3,160,554.9 |
| Debt instruments | 8abaa | 979,892.0 | 956,229.4 | 1,183,200.7 | 1,648,067.5 | 1,569,571.8 | 1,551,583.8 | 1,534,582.9 | 1,561,601.4 | 1,747,997.9 | 1,914,149.4 | 1,702,049.2 | 1,641,977.3 |
| Portfolio investment | 8b9aa | 1,103,426.3 | 1,161,434.7 | 1,332,927.8 | 1,567,396.4 | 1,232,035.8 | 1,503,585.9 | 1,490,640.7 | 1,437,498.3 | 1,666,639.7 | 1,794,382.9 | 1,851,734.4 | 1,703,572.7 |
| Equity & investment fund shares | 8baaa | 447,177.4 | 479,218.9 | 566,162.5 | 667,373.6 | 428,919.2 | 588,087.5 | 648,722.4 | 613,953.0 | 721,198.6 | 832,503.4 | 880,708.1 | 803,089.4 |
| Debt securities | 8bbaa | 656,248.9 | 682,215.8 | 766,766.6 | 900,024.3 | 803,116.7 | 915,498.4 | 841,918.2 | 823,545.4 | 945,441.1 | 961,878.1 | 971,026.3 | 900,483.4 |
| Fin. der.(oth.than reserves) & ESOs | 8c9aa | 97,416.0 | 87,953.7 | 116,733.6 | 234,501.1 | 327,795.5 | 262,928.2 | 293,640.6 | 413,474.8 | 482,352.8 | 335,689.5 | 541,907.5 | 413,928.1 |
| Other investment | 8d9aa | 756,465.4 | 780,373.9 | 1,101,603.3 | 1,444,480.5 | 1,265,387.9 | 1,223,407.9 | 1,211,334.8 | 1,298,308.3 | 1,264,787.4 | 1,255,816.7 | 1,180,298.2 | 1,154,653.4 |
| Other equity | 8daaa | 1,452.0 | 1,334.2 | 1,489.5 | 1,576.6 | 1,510.0 | 1,610.6 | 1,540.6 | 1,577.3 | 4,127.1 | 7,502.3 | 8,112.6 | 7,274.7 |
| Debt instruments | 8dzaa | 755,013.4 | 779,039.7 | 1,100,113.8 | 1,442,903.8 | 1,263,877.9 | 1,221,797.4 | 1,209,794.1 | 1,296,731.1 | 1,260,660.3 | 1,248,314.4 | 1,172,185.6 | 1,147,378.8 |
| Reserve assets | 8e9aa | 21,603.4 | 20,457.4 | 23,902.6 | 26,983.9 | 28,509.4 | 39,610.6 | 46,240.1 | 51,267.3 | 54,816.3 | 46,249.9 | 42,921.3 | 38,259.6 |
| Liabilities | 809la | 4,509,149.9 | 4,564,301.2 | 5,900,238.8 | 7,692,313.3 | 7,156,589.0 | 7,542,235.8 | 7,478,546.3 | 7,871,271.0 | 8,389,449.8 | 8,911,633.8 | 8,406,537.2 | 7,621,097.3 |
| Direct investment | 8a9la | 2,037,471.4 | 1,995,751.6 | 2,597,163.5 | 3,692,468.4 | 3,600,986.2 | 3,754,591.1 | 3,683,895.4 | 3,976,082.2 | 4,298,519.4 | 4,822,417.6 | 4,438,115.8 | 4,079,102.0 |
| Equity & investment fund shares | 8aala | 1,230,269.2 | 1,166,890.8 | 1,691,848.5 | 2,387,974.4 | 2,340,310.6 | 2,547,874.0 | 2,494,758.9 | 2,801,883.5 | 3,060,763.9 | 3,386,613.1 | 3,104,163.5 | 2,737,253.1 |
| Debt instruments | 8abla | 807,202.3 | 828,860.8 | 905,313.7 | 1,304,494.1 | 1,260,677.0 | 1,206,717.1 | 1,189,136.5 | 1,174,197.4 | 1,237,755.5 | 1,435,803.1 | 1,333,952.3 | 1,341,850.0 |
| Portfolio investment | 8b9la | 1,509,732.6 | 1,624,372.6 | 1,989,511.6 | 2,209,782.6 | 1,919,023.5 | 2,227,205.1 | 2,251,529.1 | 2,244,904.9 | 2,404,500.9 | 2,526,382.9 | 2,365,344.8 | 2,071,013.3 |
| Equity & investment fund shares | 8bala | 380,574.8 | 548,091.0 | 700,123.8 | 685,184.5 | 359,648.7 | 472,610.4 | 507,373.8 | 475,536.7 | 522,035.1 | 614,277.3 | 595,507.6 | 548,747.3 |
| Debt securities | 8bbla | 1,129,157.7 | 1,076,281.6 | 1,289,387.8 | 1,524,598.0 | 1,559,374.8 | 1,754,594.6 | 1,744,155.2 | 1,769,368.1 | 1,882,464.5 | 1,912,105.6 | 1,769,837.3 | 1,522,266.1 |
| Fin. der.(oth.than reserves) & ESOs | 8c9la | 109,758.0 | 102,777.8 | 115,755.1 | 197,944.5 | 274,344.4 | 243,870.5 | 260,437.4 | 324,034.0 | 395,149.7 | 289,907.5 | 417,276.5 | 331,956.6 |
| Other investment | 8d9la | 852,189.2 | 841,399.2 | 1,197,809.9 | 1,592,119.3 | 1,362,234.9 | 1,316,569.1 | 1,282,684.4 | 1,326,251.2 | 1,291,279.6 | 1,272,927.1 | 1,185,801.3 | 1,139,025.4 |
| Other equity | 8dala | — | — | — | — | — | — | — | — | — | — | — | — |
| Debt instruments | 8dzla | 852,189.2 | 841,399.2 | 1,197,809.9 | 1,592,119.3 | 1,362,234.9 | 1,316,569.1 | 1,282,684.4 | 1,326,251.2 | 1,291,279.6 | 1,272,927.1 | 1,185,801.3 | 1,139,025.4 |

# Netherlands  138

| | | 2004 | 2005 | 2006 | 2007 | 2008 | 2009 | 2010 | 2011 | 2012 | 2013 | 2014 | 2015 |
|---|---|---|---|---|---|---|---|---|---|---|---|---|---|
| **Government Finance Operations Statement** | | | | | | | | | | | | | |
| **General Government** | | | | | *Millions of Euros: Fiscal Year Ends December 31; Data Reported through Eurostat* | | | | | | | |
| Revenue | a1 | 219,611 | 229,470 | 250,495 | 261,648 | 279,849 | 263,942 | 272,585 | 274,438 | 278,801 | 286,536 | 290,909 | 291,987 |
| Taxes | a11 | 114,265 | 124,654 | 133,147 | 141,857 | 144,346 | 137,654 | 143,212 | 139,852 | 135,482 | 139,107 | 147,694 | 155,691 |
| Social Contributions | a12 | 72,740 | 70,844 | 79,127 | 80,581 | 89,593 | 82,463 | 86,277 | 92,026 | 98,213 | 100,737 | 101,761 | 99,722 |
| Grants | a13 | .... | .... | .... | .... | .... | .... | .... | .... | .... | .... | .... | .... |
| Other Revenue | a14 | .... | .... | .... | .... | .... | .... | .... | .... | .... | .... | .... | .... |
| Expense | a2 | 225,949 | 229,409 | 246,782 | 257,051 | 273,970 | 290,727 | 299,280 | 298,876 | 302,075 | 304,907 | 306,432 | 304,924 |
| Compensation of Employees | a21 | 48,700 | 49,463 | 50,498 | 52,561 | 55,456 | 58,579 | 60,116 | 59,718 | 60,113 | 60,242 | 60,786 | 59,957 |
| Use of Goods & Services | a22 | 32,343 | 33,823 | 36,040 | 38,107 | 41,314 | 44,228 | 43,908 | 42,804 | 42,608 | 41,594 | 41,650 | 40,394 |
| Consumption of Fixed Capital | a23 | 15,984 | 16,628 | 17,424 | 18,330 | 19,205 | 19,721 | 20,588 | 21,023 | 21,438 | 21,753 | 21,902 | 21,962 |
| Interest | a24 | 12,138 | 11,800 | 11,623 | 11,998 | 12,995 | 12,494 | 11,162 | 11,295 | 10,606 | 9,907 | 9,551 | 8,211 |
| Subsidies | a25 | 7,174 | 6,827 | 6,938 | 7,974 | 8,305 | 10,110 | 10,398 | 9,674 | 8,929 | 8,200 | 8,102 | 7,883 |
| Grants | a26 | .... | .... | .... | .... | .... | .... | .... | .... | .... | .... | .... | .... |
| Social Benefits | a27 | 95,930 | 97,348 | 109,511 | 113,394 | 119,860 | 128,656 | 134,095 | 137,578 | 141,486 | 145,648 | 146,714 | 149,548 |
| Other Expense | a28 | .... | .... | .... | .... | .... | .... | .... | .... | .... | .... | .... | .... |
| Gross Operating Balance [1-2+23] | agob | 9,646 | 16,689 | 21,137 | 22,927 | 25,084 | −7,064 | −6,107 | −3,415 | −1,836 | 3,382 | 6,379 | 9,025 |
| Net Operating Balance [1-2] | anob | −6,338 | 61 | 3,713 | 4,597 | 5,879 | −26,785 | −26,695 | −24,438 | −23,274 | −18,371 | −15,523 | −12,937 |
| Net Acq. of Nonfinancial Assets | a31 | 2,688 | 1,458 | 2,494 | 3,299 | 4,449 | 6,753 | 4,827 | 3,134 | 1,790 | −2,834 | 95 | −504 |
| Aquisition of Nonfin. Assets | a31.1 | .... | .... | .... | .... | .... | .... | .... | .... | .... | .... | .... | .... |
| Disposal of Nonfin. Assets | a31.2 | .... | .... | .... | .... | .... | .... | .... | .... | .... | .... | .... | .... |
| Net Lending/Borrowing [1-2-31] | anlb | −9,026 | −1,397 | 1,219 | 1,298 | 1,430 | −33,538 | −31,522 | −27,572 | −25,064 | −15,537 | −15,618 | −12,433 |
| Net Acq. of Financial Assets | a32 | −2,141 | 6,044 | −6,590 | 6,535 | 85,054 | −27,338 | −3,998 | −9,463 | 7,643 | −5,345 | −4,990 | −20,133 |
| **By instrument** | | | | | | | | | | | | | |
| Monetary Gold & SDRs | a3201 | — | — | — | — | — | — | — | — | — | — | — | — |
| Currency & Deposits | a3202 | 237 | 4,865 | −5,015 | 4,623 | 238 | −1,071 | −3,840 | 39 | 754 | −3,798 | 430 | −2,084 |
| Securities other than Shares | a3203 | −286 | 80 | −29 | 393 | 34 | 22,619 | −1,662 | −1,323 | −2,294 | −6,429 | −4,571 | −870 |
| Loans | a3204 | −608 | 2,511 | −397 | 2,863 | 44,842 | −27,906 | −1,043 | 959 | 8,868 | 3,371 | 198 | −4,513 |
| Shares & Other Equity | a3205 | −563 | −70 | −4,220 | −1,632 | 37,020 | −25,387 | −1,554 | −6,899 | 731 | 1,006 | −1,455 | −4,297 |
| Insurance Technical Reserves | a3206 | — | — | — | — | — | — | — | — | — | — | — | — |
| Financial Derivatives | a3207 | −95 | −90 | −127 | −111 | −1,393 | 932 | 194 | 511 | 214 | 1,536 | −1,037 | −6,024 |
| Other Accounts Receivable | a3208 | −826 | −1,252 | 3,198 | 399 | 4,313 | 3,475 | 3,907 | −2,750 | −630 | −1,031 | 1,445 | −2,345 |
| **By debtor** | | | | | | | | | | | | | |
| Domestic | a321 | .... | .... | .... | .... | .... | .... | .... | .... | .... | .... | .... | .... |
| Foreign | a322 | .... | .... | .... | .... | .... | .... | .... | .... | .... | .... | .... | .... |
| Net Incurrence of Liabilities | a33 | 6,948 | 6,721 | −5,794 | 4,446 | 82,480 | 6,247 | 27,517 | 19,087 | 33,186 | 9,917 | 10,864 | −8,459 |
| **By instrument** | | | | | | | | | | | | | |
| Special Drawing Rights (SDRs) | a3301 | — | — | — | — | — | — | — | — | — | — | — | — |
| Currency & Deposits | a3302 | 25 | 1,424 | −500 | −19 | −247 | −565 | −108 | 155 | 27 | −90 | 71 | 157 |
| Securities other than Shares | a3303 | 11,590 | 4,666 | −10,047 | −3,126 | 73,825 | −11,512 | 26,279 | 15,702 | 23,929 | 16,511 | 9,696 | −9,665 |
| Loans | a3304 | −1,641 | 414 | 145 | 5,152 | 13,306 | 17,274 | −2,001 | 5,751 | 10,954 | −6,765 | 166 | −1,981 |
| Shares & Other Equity | a3305 | — | — | — | — | — | — | — | — | — | — | — | — |
| Insurance Technical Reserves | a3306 | — | — | — | — | — | — | — | — | — | — | — | — |
| Financial Derivatives | a3307 | — | — | — | — | — | — | — | — | — | — | — | — |
| Other Accounts Payable | a3308 | −3,026 | 217 | 4,608 | 2,439 | −4,404 | 1,050 | 3,347 | −2,521 | −1,724 | 261 | 931 | 3,030 |
| **By creditor** | | | | | | | | | | | | | |
| Domestic | a331 | .... | .... | .... | .... | .... | .... | .... | .... | .... | .... | .... | .... |
| Foreign | a332 | .... | .... | .... | .... | .... | .... | .... | .... | .... | .... | .... | .... |
| Stat. Discrepancy [32-33-NLB] | anlbz | −63 | 720 | −2,015 | 791 | 1,144 | −47 | 7 | −978 | −479 | 275 | −236 | 759 |
| Memo Item: Expenditure [2+31] | a2m | 228,637 | 230,867 | 249,276 | 260,350 | 278,419 | 297,480 | 304,107 | 302,010 | 303,865 | 302,073 | 306,527 | 304,420 |
| **Balance Sheet** | | | | | | | | | | | | | |
| Net Worth | a6 | .... | .... | .... | .... | .... | .... | .... | .... | .... | .... | .... | .... |
| Nonfinancial Assets | a61 | .... | .... | .... | .... | .... | .... | .... | .... | .... | .... | .... | .... |
| Financial Assets | a62 | 132,399 | 147,926 | 137,790 | 151,326 | 244,806 | 224,269 | 225,321 | 224,276 | 245,913 | 239,410 | 250,050 | 239,274 |
| **By instrument** | | | | | | | | | | | | | |
| Monetary Gold & SDRs | a6201 | — | — | — | — | — | — | — | — | — | — | — | — |
| Currency & Deposits | a6202 | 15,602 | 20,677 | 14,233 | 18,625 | 19,136 | 18,108 | 14,304 | 14,287 | 14,809 | 10,958 | 11,452 | 9,429 |
| Securities other than Shares | a6203 | 2,498 | 2,540 | 2,341 | 2,753 | 2,122 | 23,965 | 23,493 | 22,425 | 20,027 | 13,255 | 9,031 | 8,367 |
| Loans | a6204 | 27,794 | 30,306 | 29,828 | 32,694 | 77,539 | 49,635 | 48,403 | 49,384 | 58,133 | 68,207 | 68,493 | 63,327 |
| Shares and Other Equity | a6205 | 47,949 | 56,933 | 53,820 | 60,532 | 102,279 | 87,121 | 87,761 | 82,572 | 94,450 | 92,302 | 90,801 | 95,834 |
| Insurance Technical Reserves | a6206 | — | — | — | — | — | — | — | — | — | — | — | — |
| Financial Derivatives | a6207 | 619 | 803 | 315 | −973 | 1,651 | −225 | 1,830 | 9,232 | 12,849 | 9,741 | 23,828 | 18,040 |
| Other Accounts Receivable | a6208 | 37,937 | 36,667 | 37,253 | 37,695 | 42,079 | 45,665 | 49,530 | 46,376 | 45,645 | 44,947 | 46,445 | 44,277 |
| **By debtor** | | | | | | | | | | | | | |
| Domestic | a621 | .... | .... | .... | .... | .... | .... | .... | .... | .... | .... | .... | .... |
| Foreign | a622 | .... | .... | .... | .... | .... | .... | .... | .... | .... | .... | .... | .... |
| Liabilities | a63 | 303,830 | 311,285 | 295,217 | 295,350 | 389,729 | 393,326 | 426,972 | 460,346 | 499,042 | 496,962 | 537,120 | 524,726 |
| **By instrument** | | | | | | | | | | | | | |
| Special Drawing Rights (SDRs) | a6301 | — | — | — | — | — | — | — | — | — | — | — | — |
| Currency & Deposits | a6302 | 978 | 2,402 | 1,902 | 1,883 | 1,636 | 1,071 | 963 | 1,118 | 1,145 | 1,055 | 1,126 | 1,283 |
| Securities other than Shares | a6303 | 234,188 | 239,537 | 221,132 | 213,893 | 299,342 | 287,054 | 317,993 | 347,693 | 377,652 | 376,994 | 415,844 | 402,007 |
| Loans | a6304 | 44,120 | 44,691 | 44,425 | 49,326 | 62,804 | 78,033 | 77,354 | 83,372 | 93,814 | 91,936 | 92,242 | 90,345 |
| Shares and Other Equity | a6305 | — | — | — | — | — | — | — | — | — | — | — | — |
| Insurance Technical Reserves | a6306 | — | — | — | — | — | — | — | — | — | — | — | — |
| Financial Derivatives | a6307 | — | — | — | — | — | — | — | — | — | — | — | — |
| Other Accounts Payable | a6308 | 24,544 | 24,655 | 27,758 | 30,248 | 25,947 | 27,168 | 30,662 | 28,163 | 26,431 | 26,977 | 27,908 | 31,091 |
| **By creditor** | | | | | | | | | | | | | |
| Domestic | a631 | .... | .... | .... | .... | .... | .... | .... | .... | .... | .... | .... | .... |
| Foreign | a632 | .... | .... | .... | .... | .... | .... | .... | .... | .... | .... | .... | .... |
| Net Financial Worth [62-63] | a6m2 | −171,431 | −163,359 | −157,427 | −144,024 | −144,923 | −169,057 | −201,651 | −236,070 | −253,129 | −257,552 | −287,070 | −285,452 |
| Memo Item: Debt at Market Value | a6m3 | 303,830 | 311,285 | 295,217 | 295,350 | 389,729 | 393,326 | 426,972 | 460,346 | 499,042 | 496,962 | 537,120 | 524,726 |
| Memo Item: Debt at Face Value | a6m35 | 284,491 | 291,693 | 285,360 | 290,132 | 374,078 | 376,032 | 403,289 | 424,584 | 455,022 | 469,174 | 479,964 | 472,755 |
| Memo Item: Maastricht Debt | a6m36 | 259,947 | 267,038 | 257,602 | 259,884 | 348,131 | 348,864 | 372,627 | 396,421 | 428,591 | 442,197 | 452,056 | 441,664 |
| Memo Item: Debt at Nominal Value. | a6m4 | .... | .... | .... | .... | .... | .... | .... | .... | .... | .... | .... | .... |

|  |  | 2004 | 2005 | 2006 | 2007 | 2008 | 2009 | 2010 | 2011 | 2012 | 2013 | 2014 | 2015 |
|---|---|---|---|---|---|---|---|---|---|---|---|---|---|
| **National Accounts** | | | | | | | *Billions of Euros:* | | | | | | |
| Househ.Cons.Expend.,incl.NPISHs.... | 96f.c | 256.4 | 262.5 | 268.5 | 279.9 | 288.5 | 279.6 | 282.5 | 288.9 | 289.8 | 292.2 | 296.1 | 301.8 |
| Government Consumption Expend... | 91f.c | 117.7 | 121.7 | 135.5 | 142.8 | 152.7 | 163.4 | 167.2 | 167.2 | 169.9 | 170.1 | 171.2 | 170.6 |
| Gross Fixed Capital Formation......... | 93e.c | 107.5 | 112.4 | 123.2 | 133.7 | 142.4 | 131.6 | 124.6 | 130.4 | 121.9 | 116.6 | 120.4 | 132.3 |
| Changes in Inventories................... | 93i.c | .9 | 1.7 | 1.4 | 2.7 | .4 | −2.2 | 4.3 | 1.5 | 1.7 | .5 | −.5 | −4.1 |
| Exports of Goods and Services.......... | 90c.c | 332.9 | 363.5 | 401.3 | 431.0 | 457.9 | 390.0 | 454.4 | 497.3 | 528.6 | 537.8 | 549.4 | 556.6 |
| Imports of Goods and Services (-)..... | 98c.c | 291.4 | 316.1 | 350.7 | 376.9 | 402.8 | 344.7 | 401.6 | 442.4 | 466.7 | 466.3 | 473.8 | 478.8 |
| Gross Domestic Product (GDP)......... | 99b.c | 523.9 | 545.6 | 579.2 | 613.3 | 639.2 | 617.5 | 631.5 | 642.9 | 645.2 | 650.9 | 662.8 | 678.1 |
| Net Primary Income from Abroad..... | 98.nc | −19.6 | −29.7 | −24.5 | −32.0 | −57.3 | −58.2 | −53.7 | −42.0 | −40.2 | −50.9 | . . . . | . . . . |
| Gross National Income (GNI)........... | 99a.c | 504.3 | 515.9 | 554.7 | 581.3 | 581.9 | 559.4 | 577.8 | 601.0 | 605.0 | 599.9 | . . . . | . . . . |
| Net Current Transf.from Abroad....... | 98t.c | −7.5 | −8.2 | −8.0 | −8.8 | −9.0 | −8.3 | −8.9 | −9.2 | −10.1 | −11.1 | . . . . | . . . . |
| Gross Nat'l Disposable Inc.(GNDI).... | 99i.c | 496.8 | 507.7 | 546.7 | 572.5 | 572.9 | 551.1 | 568.9 | 591.8 | 594.9 | . . . . | . . . . | . . . . |
| Consumption of Fixed Capital.......... | 99cfc | 73.5 | 75.7 | 78.6 | 82.1 | 85.4 | 88.0 | 89.7 | 88.9 | 89.0 | 89.8 | . . . . | . . . . |
| GDP Volume 2010 Ref., Chained..... | 99b.r | 580.3 | 592.8 | 613.7 | 636.3 | 647.2 | 622.8 | 631.5 | 642.0 | 635.2 | 632.1 | 638.5 | 651.0 |
| GDP Volume (2010=100)............... | 99bvr | 91.9 | 93.9 | 97.2 | 100.8 | 102.5 | 98.6 | 100.0 | 101.7 | 100.6 | 100.1 | 101.1 | 103.1 |
| GDP Deflator (2010=100)............... | 99bir | 90.3 | 92.0 | 94.4 | 96.4 | 98.8 | 99.2 | 100.0 | 100.1 | 101.6 | 103.0 | 103.8 | 104.2 |
| | | | | | | | *Millions: Midyear Estimates* | | | | | | |
| **Population................................** | **99z** | 16.25 | 16.33 | 16.40 | 16.46 | 16.52 | 16.58 | 16.63 | 16.69 | 16.75 | 16.81 | 16.87 | 16.92 |

| | | 2004 | 2005 | 2006 | 2007 | 2008 | 2009 | 2010 | 2011 | 2012 | 2013 | 2014 | 2015 |
|---|---|---|---|---|---|---|---|---|---|---|---|---|---|
| **Exchange Rates** | | | | | | *Guilders per SDR: End of Period* | | | | | | | |
| Official Rate............... | aa | 2.780 | 2.558 | 2.693 | 2.829 | 2.757 | 2.806 | .... | .... | .... | .... | .... | .... |
| | | | | *Guilders per US Dollar: End of Period (ae)  Period Average (rf)* | | | | | | | | | |
| Official Rate................... | ae | 1.790 | 1.790 | 1.790 | 1.790 | 1.790 | 1.790 | .... | .... | .... | .... | .... | .... |
| Official Rate................... | rf | 1.790 | 1.790 | 1.790 | 1.790 | 1.790 | 1.790 | .... | .... | .... | .... | .... | .... |
| | | | | *Index Numbers (2010=100): Period Averages* | | | | | | | | | |
| Official Rate (2005=100)............. | ahx | 100.0 | 100.0 | 100.0 | 100.0 | 100.0 | 100.0 | .... | .... | .... | .... | .... | .... |
| Nominal Effective Exchange Rate..... | nec | 98.3 | 99.0 | 98.2 | 96.5 | 95.6 | 99.5 | .... | .... | .... | .... | .... | .... |
| CPI-Based Real Effect. Ex. Rate........ | rec | 102.9 | 100.6 | 99.0 | 96.4 | 96.1 | 100.1 | .... | .... | .... | .... | .... | .... |
| **International Liquidity** | | | | *Millions of US Dollars Unless Otherwise Indicated: End of Period* | | | | | | | | | |
| Total Reserves minus Gold.............. | 1l.d | 415 | 545 | 495 | 661 | 819 | 867 | .... | .... | .... | .... | .... | .... |
| Foreign Exchange........................... | 1d.d | 415 | 545 | 495 | 661 | 819 | 867 | .... | .... | .... | .... | .... | .... |
| Gold (Million Fine Troy Ounces)........ | 1ad | .421 | .421 | .421 | .421 | .421 | .421 | .... | .... | .... | .... | .... | .... |
| Gold (National Valuation)................ | 1and | 152 | 152 | 204 | 244 | 304 | 356 | .... | .... | .... | .... | .... | .... |
| Monetary Authorities: Other Liabs..... | 4..d | — | 2 | 236 | 371 | 358 | 445 | .... | .... | .... | .... | .... | .... |
| Deposit Money Banks: Assets.......... | 7a.d | 760 | 813 | 1,167 | 1,164 | 1,654 | 1,985 | .... | .... | .... | .... | .... | .... |
| Deposit Money Banks: Liabs............ | 7b.d | 510 | 532 | 877 | 884 | 1,253 | 1,402 | .... | .... | .... | .... | .... | .... |
| OBU: Assets.................................... | 7k.d | 42,134 | 34,174 | 31,298 | .... | .... | .... | .... | .... | .... | .... | .... | .... |
| Liabilities.................... | 7m.d | 38,275 | 30,902 | 27,927 | .... | .... | .... | .... | .... | .... | .... | .... | .... |
| **Monetary Authorities** | | | | | | *Millions of Guilders End of Period* | | | | | | | |
| Foreign Assets.............................. | 11 | 1,015.7 | 1,153.1 | 1,674.0 | 2,285.1 | 2,451.2 | 2,984.9 | .... | .... | .... | .... | .... | .... |
| Claims on Central Government........ | 12a | 185.6 | 168.2 | 200.5 | 165.1 | 147.1 | 254.0 | .... | .... | .... | .... | .... | .... |
| Reserve Money......................... | 14 | 954.2 | 1,062.0 | 1,196.9 | 1,420.1 | 1,558.1 | 1,889.0 | .... | .... | .... | .... | .... | .... |
| of which: Currency Outside DMBs.. | 14a | 231.3 | 221.7 | 263.7 | 304.4 | 294.6 | 334.1 | .... | .... | .... | .... | .... | .... |
| Time Deposits................................ | 15 | — | — | — | — | — | 81.9 | .... | .... | .... | .... | .... | .... |
| Foreign Liabilities......................... | 16c | .4 | 2.9 | 422.1 | 664.5 | 640.2 | 796.0 | .... | .... | .... | .... | .... | .... |
| Central Government Deposits.......... | 16d | 107.3 | 102.9 | 11.4 | 10.6 | 69.4 | 155.2 | .... | .... | .... | .... | .... | .... |
| Capital Accounts........................... | 17a | 274.7 | 274.7 | 369.8 | 442.8 | 442.3 | 687.9 | .... | .... | .... | .... | .... | .... |
| Other Items (Net)........................... | 17r | −135.3 | −121.2 | −125.7 | −87.8 | −111.7 | −371.1 | .... | .... | .... | .... | .... | .... |
| **Deposit Money Banks** | | | | | | *Millions of Guilders: End of Period* | | | | | | | |
| Reserves......................... | 20 | 644.5 | 674.5 | 737.2 | 826.1 | 896.1 | 1,236.8 | .... | .... | .... | .... | .... | .... |
| Foreign Assets.............................. | 21 | 1,359.6 | 1,455.1 | 2,089.7 | 2,083.8 | 2,960.5 | 3,553.8 | .... | .... | .... | .... | .... | .... |
| Claims on Local Government........... | 22b | 288.7 | 300.9 | 211.1 | 272.9 | 260.5 | 201.4 | .... | .... | .... | .... | .... | .... |
| Claims on Private Sector................. | 22d | 3,059.7 | 3,098.9 | 4,058.3 | 4,532.9 | 4,693.7 | 5,370.1 | .... | .... | .... | .... | .... | .... |
| Demand Deposits.......................... | 24 | 1,096.8 | 1,185.7 | 1,270.0 | 1,433.8 | 1,583.4 | 2,106.0 | .... | .... | .... | .... | .... | .... |
| Time and Savings Deposits............. | 25a | 2,434.6 | 2,448.7 | 2,675.7 | 2,949.0 | 3,028.5 | 3,519.9 | .... | .... | .... | .... | .... | .... |
| Foreign Currency Deposits.............. | 25b | 753.1 | 813.5 | 1,080.1 | 1,184.7 | 1,287.7 | 1,354.3 | .... | .... | .... | .... | .... | .... |
| Foreign Liabilities........................... | 26c | 913.3 | 953.1 | 1,569.2 | 1,582.8 | 2,242.6 | 2,510.4 | .... | .... | .... | .... | .... | .... |
| Central Government Deposits.......... | 26d | 45.8 | 35.4 | 76.2 | 127.9 | 94.3 | 183.1 | .... | .... | .... | .... | .... | .... |
| Capital Accounts........................... | 27a | 481.8 | 499.4 | 670.6 | 756.0 | 929.4 | 1,122.8 | .... | .... | .... | .... | .... | .... |
| Other Items (Net)........................... | 27r | −372.9 | −406.4 | −245.5 | −318.5 | −354.7 | −434.4 | .... | .... | .... | .... | .... | .... |
| **Girosystem Curacao** | | | | | | | | | | | | | |
| Private Sector Deposits................. | 24..i | — | — | — | — | — | — | .... | .... | .... | .... | .... | .... |
| Central Government Deposits......... | 26d.i | — | — | — | — | — | — | .... | .... | .... | .... | .... | .... |
| **Monetary Survey** | | | | | | *Millions of Guilders End of Period* | | | | | | | |
| Foreign Assets (Net)........................ | 31n | 1,461.6 | 1,652.2 | 1,772.4 | 2,121.6 | 2,528.9 | 3,232.3 | .... | .... | .... | .... | .... | .... |
| Domestic Credit............................. | 32 | 3,765.3 | 3,836.1 | 4,688.4 | 5,239.3 | 5,353.2 | 6,112.2 | .... | .... | .... | .... | .... | .... |
| Claims on Central Govt. (Net)........ | 32an | 363.9 | 387.3 | 358.5 | 394.9 | 360.4 | 238.2 | .... | .... | .... | .... | .... | .... |
| Claims on Local Government.......... | 32b | 341.7 | 349.9 | 271.6 | 311.5 | 299.1 | 240.0 | .... | .... | .... | .... | .... | .... |
| Claims on Private Sector................ | 32d | 3,059.7 | 3,098.9 | 4,058.3 | 4,532.9 | 4,693.7 | 5,634.0 | .... | .... | .... | .... | .... | .... |
| Money............................................ | 34 | 1,406.5 | 1,573.2 | 1,729.7 | 2,027.8 | 2,245.0 | 2,758.2 | .... | .... | .... | .... | .... | .... |
| Quasi-Money................................. | 35 | 3,187.7 | 3,262.2 | 3,755.8 | 4,133.7 | 4,316.2 | 4,956.1 | .... | .... | .... | .... | .... | .... |
| Other Items (Net)........................... | 37r | 632.7 | 652.9 | 975.3 | 1,199.4 | 1,320.9 | 1,630.2 | .... | .... | .... | .... | .... | .... |
| Money plus Quasi-Money.................. | 35l | 4,594.2 | 4,835.4 | 5,485.5 | 6,161.5 | 6,561.2 | 7,714.3 | .... | .... | .... | .... | .... | .... |
| **Interest Rates** | | | | | | *Percent Per Annum* | | | | | | | |
| Treasury Bill Rate........................... | 60c | 3.86 | 3.52 | 5.39 | 6.04 | 4.40 | 1.35 | .... | .... | .... | .... | .... | .... |
| Deposit Rate.................................. | 60l | 2.92 | 2.78 | 2.78 | 2.73 | 2.29 | 2.16 | .... | .... | .... | .... | .... | .... |
| Lending Rate.................................. | 60p | 10.56 | 9.60 | 9.28 | 9.36 | 8.41 | 7.51 | .... | .... | .... | .... | .... | .... |
| Government Bond Yield.................. | 61 | 7.09 | 6.46 | 6.75 | 7.32 | 5.66 | 4.82 | .... | .... | .... | .... | .... | .... |
| **Prices and Labor** | | | | | | *Index Numbers (2005=100): Period Averages* | | | | | | | |
| Consumer Prices.............................. | 64 | 96.1 | 100.0 | † 103.1 | 106.3 | 113.6 | 115.6 | .... | .... | .... | .... | .... | .... |
| | | | | *Number in Thousands: Period Averages* | | | | | | | | | |
| Labor Force.................................... | 67d | 61 | 63 | 61 | 62 | 63 | 63 | .... | .... | .... | .... | .... | .... |
| Employment................................... | 67e | 51 | 51 | 52 | 54 | 57 | 57 | .... | .... | .... | .... | .... | .... |
| Unemployment.............................. | 67c | 10 | 11 | 9 | 8 | 6 | 6 | .... | .... | .... | .... | .... | .... |
| Unemployment Rate (%)................. | 67r | 16.1 | 18.2 | 14.6 | 12.4 | 10.3 | 9.7 | .... | .... | .... | .... | .... | .... |
| **Intl. Transactions & Positions** | | | | | | *Millions of Guilders* | | | | | | | |
| Exports.......................................... | 70 | 933 | 1,088 | 1,243 | 1,211 | 1,948 | 1,450 | .... | .... | .... | .... | .... | .... |
| Imports, c.i.f.................................... | 71 | 3,084 | 3,491 | 3,955 | 4,562 | 5,512 | 4,666 | .... | .... | .... | .... | .... | .... |

# Netherlands Antilles   353

| | | 2004 | 2005 | 2006 | 2007 | 2008 | 2009 | 2010 | 2011 | 2012 | 2013 | 2014 | 2015 |
|---|---|---|---|---|---|---|---|---|---|---|---|---|---|
| **Balance of Payments** | | | | | | | *Millions of US Dollars* | | | | | | |
| A. Current Account* | 109bx | −88.1 | −105.8 | −202.0 | −563.1 | −845.8 | −793.5 | .... | .... | .... | .... | .... | .... |
| Goods, credit (exports) | 1a9cx | 461.9 | 553.9 | 630.2 | 605.3 | 1,011.4 | 745.8 | .... | .... | .... | .... | .... | .... |
| Goods, debit (imports) | 1a9dx | 1,705.6 | 1,940.7 | 2,204.3 | 2,535.0 | 3,069.0 | 2,599.0 | .... | .... | .... | .... | .... | .... |
| Balance on goods | 1a9bx | −1,243.7 | −1,386.8 | −1,574.1 | −1,929.8 | −2,057.5 | −1,853.1 | .... | .... | .... | .... | .... | .... |
| Services: credit (exports) | 1b9cx | 1,838.0 | 1,911.5 | 2,043.8 | 2,148.5 | 2,109.9 | 2,089.7 | .... | .... | .... | .... | .... | .... |
| Services, debit (imports) | 1b9dx | 720.5 | 725.8 | 751.5 | 789.9 | 859.6 | 927.7 | .... | .... | .... | .... | .... | .... |
| Balance on Goods & Services | 1z9bx | −126.3 | −201.1 | −281.8 | −571.2 | −807.3 | −691.1 | .... | .... | .... | .... | .... | .... |
| Primary income: credit | 1c9cx | 88.5 | 106.2 | 137.0 | 170.2 | 139.6 | 109.6 | .... | .... | .... | .... | .... | .... |
| Primary income: debit | 1c9dx | 105.0 | 121.3 | 138.1 | 167.3 | 181.0 | 206.1 | .... | .... | .... | .... | .... | .... |
| Balance on gds, serv. & prim. inc. | 1y9bx | −142.8 | −216.1 | −282.9 | −568.3 | −848.7 | −787.7 | .... | .... | .... | .... | .... | .... |
| Secondary income: credit | 1d9ca | 323.2 | 415.1 | 386.9 | 332.0 | 400.5 | 409.0 | .... | .... | .... | .... | .... | .... |
| Secondary income: debit | 1d9da | 268.5 | 304.7 | 305.9 | 326.8 | 397.7 | 414.8 | .... | .... | .... | .... | .... | .... |
| B. Capital Account* | 209ba | 79.6 | 96.1 | 101.2 | 123.8 | 133.7 | 111.7 | .... | .... | .... | .... | .... | .... |
| Capital account: credit | 209ca | 79.7 | 96.1 | 101.3 | 123.8 | 133.7 | 111.7 | .... | .... | .... | .... | .... | .... |
| Capital account: debit | 209da | .1 | — | .1 | — | — | — | .... | .... | .... | .... | .... | .... |
| Balance on current & capital acct. | 129ba | −8.5 | −9.7 | −100.8 | −439.3 | −712.1 | −681.8 | .... | .... | .... | .... | .... | .... |
| C. Financial Account* | 309na | 11.2 | −26.8 | −81.7 | −492.3 | −832.0 | −430.8 | .... | .... | .... | .... | .... | .... |
| Direct investment: assets | 3a9aa | 22.1 | 65.9 | 56.0 | −4.2 | 15.1 | 7.3 | .... | .... | .... | .... | .... | .... |
| Equity & investment fund shares | 3aaaa | 7.1 | 71.4 | 43.9 | 8.8 | 16.0 | 8.0 | .... | .... | .... | .... | .... | .... |
| Debt instruments | 3abaa | 15.0 | −5.5 | 12.2 | −13.1 | −.9 | −.7 | .... | .... | .... | .... | .... | .... |
| Direct investment: liabilities | 3a9la | 21.7 | 42.4 | −22.5 | 233.3 | 266.0 | 116.9 | .... | .... | .... | .... | .... | .... |
| Equity & investment fund shares | 3aala | 53.0 | 121.7 | −7.9 | 202.8 | 225.1 | 49.4 | .... | .... | .... | .... | .... | .... |
| Debt instruments | 3abla | −31.3 | −79.3 | −14.5 | 30.5 | 40.8 | 67.5 | .... | .... | .... | .... | .... | .... |
| Portfolio investment: assets | 3b9aa | 94.1 | 25.8 | −67.3 | 67.9 | 47.4 | 39.4 | .... | .... | .... | .... | .... | .... |
| Equity & investment fund shares | 3baaa | 13.6 | 2.3 | 12.5 | 71.6 | −5.9 | −5.2 | .... | .... | .... | .... | .... | .... |
| Debt securities | 3bbaa | 80.6 | 23.5 | −79.8 | −3.7 | 53.4 | 44.6 | .... | .... | .... | .... | .... | .... |
| Portfolio investment: liabilities | 3b9la | 93.3 | 1.6 | −8.9 | −11.2 | −23.1 | −66.2 | .... | .... | .... | .... | .... | .... |
| Equity & investment fund shares | 3bala | — | — | — | — | — | — | .... | .... | .... | .... | .... | .... |
| Debt securities | 3bbla | 93.3 | 1.6 | −8.9 | −11.2 | −23.1 | −66.2 | .... | .... | .... | .... | .... | .... |
| Fin. der.& empl.stk.ops.(ESOs): net. | 3c9na | — | −.4 | 1.6 | 4.2 | .2 | −.2 | .... | .... | .... | .... | .... | .... |
| Fin. der. & ESOs.: assets | 3c9aa | — | −.4 | 1.6 | 4.2 | .2 | −.2 | .... | .... | .... | .... | .... | .... |
| Fin. der. & ESOs.: liabilities | 3c9la | — | — | — | — | — | — | .... | .... | .... | .... | .... | .... |
| Other investment: assets | 3d9aa | 4.7 | −40.5 | −135.2 | −377.1 | −680.7 | −470.7 | .... | .... | .... | .... | .... | .... |
| Other equity | 3daaa | .... | .... | .... | .... | .... | .... | .... | .... | .... | .... | .... | .... |
| Debt instruments | 3dzaa | 4.7 | −40.5 | −135.2 | −377.1 | −680.7 | −470.7 | .... | .... | .... | .... | .... | .... |
| Other investment: liabilities | 3d9la | −5.3 | 33.7 | −31.8 | −39.0 | −29.0 | −44.2 | .... | .... | .... | .... | .... | .... |
| Other equity | 3dala | .... | .... | .... | .... | .... | .... | .... | .... | .... | .... | .... | .... |
| Debt instruments | 3dzla | −5.3 | 33.7 | −31.8 | −39.0 | −29.0 | −44.2 | .... | .... | .... | .... | .... | .... |
| Curr.+ cap.− finan. acct. balance | 4y9na | −19.7 | 17.0 | −19.1 | 53.0 | 119.9 | −251.0 | .... | .... | .... | .... | .... | .... |
| D. Net Errors and Omissions | 409na | 27.3 | 31.2 | 34.7 | 76.2 | 60.1 | 75.1 | .... | .... | .... | .... | .... | .... |
| E. Reserves and Related Items | 4z9na | 7.6 | 48.3 | 15.6 | 129.2 | 179.9 | −175.9 | .... | .... | .... | .... | .... | .... |
| Reserve assets | 3e9aa | 36.9 | 74.0 | 47.1 | 155.0 | 207.6 | 301.2 | .... | .... | .... | .... | .... | .... |
| Credit and loans from the IMF | 3dcla | .... | .... | .... | .... | .... | .... | .... | .... | .... | .... | .... | .... |
| Exceptional financing | 409la | 29.3 | 25.7 | 31.5 | 25.8 | 27.6 | 477.0 | .... | .... | .... | .... | .... | .... |
| *Excludes components in group E | | | | | | | | | | | | | |
| | | | | | | | *Millions: Midyear Estimates* | | | | | | |
| **Population** | 99z | .01 | .01 | .02 | .02 | .02 | .02 | .02 | .02 | .02 | .02 | .02 | .02 |

# New Zealand 196

|  |  | 2004 | 2005 | 2006 | 2007 | 2008 | 2009 | 2010 | 2011 | 2012 | 2013 | 2014 | 2015 |
|---|---|---|---|---|---|---|---|---|---|---|---|---|---|
| **Exchange Rates** | | *New Zealand Dollars per SDR: End of Period* | | | | | | | | | | | |
| Market Rate | aa | 2.1618 | 2.0975 | 2.1312 | 2.0417 | 2.6625 | 2.1722 | 1.9985 | 1.9905 | 1.8737 | 1.8776 | 1.8506 | 2.0236 |
| | | *New Zealand Dollars per US Dollar: End of Period (ae) Period Average (rf)* | | | | | | | | | | | |
| Market Rate | ae | 1.3920 | 1.4676 | 1.4166 | 1.2920 | 1.7286 | 1.3856 | 1.2977 | 1.2965 | 1.2191 | 1.2192 | 1.2773 | 1.4603 |
| Market Rate | rf | 1.5087 | 1.4203 | 1.5421 | 1.3607 | 1.4227 | 1.6009 | 1.3878 | 1.2658 | 1.2343 | 1.2194 | 1.2054 | 1.4340 |
| | | *Index Numbers (2010=100): Period Averages* | | | | | | | | | | | |
| Market Rate | ahx | 92.1 | 97.7 | 90.0 | 102.1 | 99.1 | 87.9 | 100.0 | 109.7 | 112.4 | 113.8 | 115.2 | 97.1 |
| Nominal Effective Exchange Rate | nec | 103.6 | 108.4 | 99.5 | 106.1 | 98.8 | 91.5 | 100.0 | 103.1 | 107.9 | 112.3 | 116.6 | 111.2 |
| CPI-Based Real Effect. Ex. Rate | rec | 99.8 | 105.3 | 97.6 | 104.0 | 97.0 | 91.3 | 100.0 | 104.1 | 107.8 | 111.4 | 115.0 | 109.0 |
| ULC-Based Real Effect. Ex. Rate | rel | 94.2 | 103.5 | 99.6 | 106.5 | 99.0 | 88.8 | 100.0 | 102.0 | 102.6 | 107.1 | 112.4 | 109.0 |
| **Fund Position** | | *Millions of SDRs: End of Period* | | | | | | | | | | | |
| Quota | 2f.s | 894.60 | 894.60 | 894.60 | 894.60 | 894.60 | 894.60 | 894.60 | 894.60 | 894.60 | 894.60 | 894.60 | 894.60 |
| SDR Holdings | 1b.s | 21.99 | 24.08 | 22.14 | 17.98 | 14.57 | 854.66 | 854.93 | 828.26 | 818.36 | 846.05 | 875.54 | 872.47 |
| Reserve Position in the Fund | 1c.s | 305.45 | 115.26 | 79.18 | 59.88 | 113.74 | 173.84 | 177.26 | 324.82 | 355.83 | 393.22 | 360.50 | 278.91 |
| Total Fund Cred.&Loans Outstg | 2tl | — | — | — | — | — | — | — | — | — | — | — | — |
| SDR Allocations | 1bd | 141.32 | 141.32 | 141.32 | 141.32 | 141.32 | 853.76 | 853.76 | 853.76 | 853.76 | 853.76 | 853.76 | 853.76 |
| **International Liquidity** | | *Millions of US Dollars Unless Otherwise Indicated: End of Period* | | | | | | | | | | | |
| Total Reserves minus Gold | 1l.d | 6,947 | 8,893 | 14,068 | 17,247 | 11,052 | 15,594 | 16,723 | 17,012 | 17,583 | 16,318 | 15,861 | 14,700 |
| SDR Holdings | 1b.d | 34 | 34 | 33 | 28 | 22 | 1,340 | 1,317 | 1,272 | 1,258 | 1,303 | 1,268 | 1,209 |
| Reserve Position in the Fund | 1c.d | 474 | 165 | 119 | 95 | 175 | 273 | 273 | 499 | 547 | 606 | 522 | 386 |
| Foreign Exchange | 1d.d | 6,439 | 8,694 | 13,916 | 17,124 | 10,855 | 13,982 | 15,133 | 15,242 | 15,778 | 14,409 | 14,070 | 13,104 |
| Monetary Authorities | 1dad | 3,395 | 4,627 | 10,259 | 12,852 | 8,560 | 11,665 | 12,975 | 13,611 | 12,597 | 13,334 | 12,627 | 12,362 |
| Government | 1dbd | 3,044 | 4,067 | 3,657 | 4,272 | 2,294 | 2,317 | 2,158 | 1,631 | 3,182 | 1,075 | 1,443 | 742 |
| Gold (Million Fine Troy Ounces) | 1ad | — | — | — | — | — | — | — | — | — | — | — | — |
| Gold (National Valuation) | 1and | — | — | — | — | — | — | — | — | — | — | — | — |
| Monetary Authorities: Other Liabs | 4..d | 1,279 | 1,333 | 741 | 798 | 1,157 | 768 | 1,365 | .... | .... | .... | .... | .... |
| Banking Institutions: Assets | 7a.d | 16,101 | 8,260 | 9,842 | 11,944 | 9,105 | 10,807 | 9,463 | .... | .... | .... | .... | .... |
| Banking Institutions: Liabs | 7b.d | 51,438 | 52,134 | 67,652 | 82,686 | 69,155 | 89,113 | 92,159 | .... | .... | .... | .... | .... |
| **Monetary Authorities** | | *Millions of New Zealand Dollars: End of Period* | | | | | | | | | | | |
| Foreign Assets | 11 | 11,900 | 14,872 | 20,883 | 23,662 | 21,359 | 23,106 | 23,970 | .... | .... | .... | .... | .... |
| Claims on Central Government | 12a | 4,714 | 4,974 | 5,029 | 4,529 | 5,196 | 5,234 | 5,412 | .... | .... | .... | .... | .... |
| Claims on Banking Institutions | 12e | 363 | 518 | 222 | 626 | 4,906 | 2,827 | — | .... | .... | .... | .... | .... |
| Reserve Money | 14 | 3,745 | 4,241 | 12,843 | 12,231 | 13,379 | 13,552 | 12,379 | .... | .... | .... | .... | .... |
| of which: Currency Outside DMBs | 14a | 2,737 | 3,020 | 3,061 | 3,191 | 3,526 | 3,580 | 3,720 | .... | .... | .... | .... | .... |
| Other Liabs. to Banking Insts | 14n | — | 544 | 763 | 333 | 218 | 133 | 385 | .... | .... | .... | .... | .... |
| Liabs. of Central Bank: Securities | 16ac | — | — | — | — | 3,690 | 1,079 | — | .... | .... | .... | .... | .... |
| Foreign Liabilities | 16c | 2,086 | 2,252 | 1,351 | 1,320 | 2,377 | 2,919 | 3,478 | .... | .... | .... | .... | .... |
| Central Government Deposits | 16d | 9,622 | 11,442 | 9,485 | 13,240 | 8,223 | 10,899 | 10,595 | .... | .... | .... | .... | .... |
| Capital Accounts | 17a | 1,552 | 1,709 | 1,591 | 1,670 | 3,570 | 2,574 | 2,533 | .... | .... | .... | .... | .... |
| Other Items (Net) | 17r | −26 | 175 | 100 | 22 | 3 | 12 | 13 | .... | .... | .... | .... | .... |
| **Banking Institutions** | | *Millions of New Zealand Dollars: End of Period* | | | | | | | | | | | |
| Reserves | 20 | 1,009 | 974 | 9,050 | 8,570 | 9,311 | 9,408 | 8,474 | .... | .... | .... | .... | .... |
| Claims on Mon.Author.:Securities | 20c | — | — | — | — | 3,690 | 1,079 | — | .... | .... | .... | .... | .... |
| Other Claims on Central Bank | 20n | — | 245 | 763 | 333 | 218 | 133 | 385 | .... | .... | .... | .... | .... |
| Foreign Assets | 21 | 22,413 | 12,123 | 13,943 | 15,431 | 15,740 | 14,974 | 12,281 | .... | .... | .... | .... | .... |
| Claims on Central Government | 22a | 5,656 | 5,228 | 2,444 | 2,239 | 3,008 | 10,306 | 13,867 | .... | .... | .... | .... | .... |
| Claims on State & Local Govts | 22b | 1,308 | 1,396 | 1,396 | 1,698 | 2,361 | 2,706 | 2,889 | .... | .... | .... | .... | .... |
| Claims on Private Sector | 22d | 170,977 | 196,534 | 222,497 | 251,511 | 273,822 | 276,063 | 289,538 | .... | .... | .... | .... | .... |
| Claims on Nonbank Financial Insts | 22g | 8,449 | 9,538 | 9,465 | 11,443 | 8,718 | 6,474 | 6,183 | .... | .... | .... | .... | .... |
| Demand Deposits | 24 | 34,393 | 33,031 | 32,751 | 31,423 | 31,361 | 31,316 | 32,760 | .... | .... | .... | .... | .... |
| Time and Savings Deposits | 25 | 80,036 | 92,232 | 106,925 | 124,026 | 140,173 | 139,057 | 152,014 | .... | .... | .... | .... | .... |
| Restricted Deposits | 26b | 5,620 | 7,769 | 8,011 | 9,876 | 9,130 | 7,568 | 7,240 | .... | .... | .... | .... | .... |
| Foreign Liabilities | 26c | 71,600 | 76,509 | 95,839 | 106,830 | 119,541 | 123,477 | 119,593 | .... | .... | .... | .... | .... |
| Central Government Deposits | 26d | 534 | 353 | 498 | 355 | 369 | 360 | 757 | .... | .... | .... | .... | .... |
| Liabilities to Central Bank | 26g | 363 | 518 | 222 | 626 | 4,906 | 2,827 | — | .... | .... | .... | .... | .... |
| Capital Accounts | 27a | 18,396 | 19,063 | 20,355 | 20,719 | 22,707 | 20,846 | 22,911 | .... | .... | .... | .... | .... |
| Other Items (Net) | 27r | −1,130 | −3,437 | −5,042 | −2,630 | −11,319 | −4,308 | −1,660 | .... | .... | .... | .... | .... |
| **Banking Survey** | | *Millions of New Zealand Dollars: End of Period* | | | | | | | | | | | |
| Foreign Assets (Net) | 31n | −39,373 | −51,767 | −62,364 | −69,056 | −84,820 | −88,315 | −86,820 | .... | .... | .... | .... | .... |
| Domestic Credit | 32 | 180,949 | 205,875 | 230,848 | 257,825 | 284,513 | 289,524 | 306,536 | .... | .... | .... | .... | .... |
| Claims on Central Govt. (Net) | 32an | 215 | −1,593 | −2,510 | −6,828 | −388 | 4,281 | 7,927 | .... | .... | .... | .... | .... |
| Claims on State & Local Govts | 32b | 1,308 | 1,396 | 1,396 | 1,698 | 2,361 | 2,706 | 2,889 | .... | .... | .... | .... | .... |
| Claims on Private Sector | 32d | 170,977 | 196,534 | 222,497 | 251,511 | 273,822 | 276,063 | 289,538 | .... | .... | .... | .... | .... |
| Claims on Nonbank Financial Insts | 32g | 8,449 | 9,538 | 9,465 | 11,443 | 8,718 | 6,474 | 6,183 | .... | .... | .... | .... | .... |
| Money | 34 | 37,130 | 36,051 | 35,812 | 34,614 | 34,888 | 34,896 | 36,480 | .... | .... | .... | .... | .... |
| Quasi-Money | 35 | 80,036 | 92,232 | 106,925 | 124,026 | 140,173 | 139,057 | 152,014 | .... | .... | .... | .... | .... |
| Liabilities of Central Bank: Securities | 36ac | — | — | — | — | — | — | — | .... | .... | .... | .... | .... |
| Restricted Deposits | 36b | 5,620 | 7,769 | 8,011 | 9,876 | 9,130 | 7,568 | 7,240 | .... | .... | .... | .... | .... |
| Capital Accounts | 37a | 19,948 | 20,772 | 21,946 | 22,389 | 26,277 | 23,420 | 25,444 | .... | .... | .... | .... | .... |
| Other Items (Net) | 37r | −1,158 | −2,717 | −4,210 | −2,137 | −10,775 | −3,732 | −1,462 | .... | .... | .... | .... | .... |
| Money plus Quasi-Money | 35l | 117,166 | 128,283 | 142,737 | 158,641 | 175,061 | 173,953 | 188,494 | .... | .... | .... | .... | .... |
| **Money (National Definitions)** | | *Millions of New Zealand Dollars: End of Period* | | | | | | | | | | | |
| M1 | 59ma | 22,834 | 22,427 | 23,265 | 23,537 | 24,239 | 24,551 | 31,521 | 34,044 | 36,420 | 39,881 | 42,359 | 46,111 |
| M2 | 59mb | 54,708 | 61,101 | 71,151 | 69,226 | 74,284 | 74,194 | 79,543 | 91,666 | 103,080 | 119,170 | 131,463 | 150,158 |
| M3R | 59mca | 117,167 | 128,209 | 142,738 | 158,641 | 175,035 | 173,952 | 190,084 | 203,173 | 219,416 | 235,341 | 250,399 | 272,618 |
| M3 Broad Money | 59mcb | 148,395 | 159,281 | 185,715 | 199,481 | 212,502 | 210,210 | 224,755 | 239,293 | 253,611 | 268,384 | 283,086 | 305,985 |

| | | 2004 | 2005 | 2006 | 2007 | 2008 | 2009 | 2010 | 2011 | 2012 | 2013 | 2014 | 2015 |
|---|---|---|---|---|---|---|---|---|---|---|---|---|---|
| **Interest Rates** | | | | | | | *Percent Per Annum* | | | | | | |
| Central Bank Policy Rate (EOP)........ | 60 | 6.50 | 7.25 | 7.25 | 8.25 | 5.00 | 2.50 | 3.00 | 2.50 | 2.50 | 2.50 | 3.50 | 2.50 |
| Money Market Rate........................ | 60b | 5.77 | 6.76 | 7.30 | 7.93 | 7.55 | 2.82 | 2.61 | 2.50 | 2.46 | 2.47 | 3.09 | 3.08 |
| Treasury Bill Rate........................... | 60c | 5.85 | 6.52 | 7.05 | 7.55 | 7.01 | 2.83 | 2.78 | 2.55 | 2.46 | 2.39 | 3.24 | 2.99 |
| Deposit Rate................................. | 60l | 5.77 | 6.68 | 6.92 | 7.78 | 7.55 | 4.04 | 4.58 | 4.27 | 4.11 | 3.83 | 4.01 | 3.73 |
| Lending Rate................................. | 60p | 7.10 | 7.76 | 8.19 | 8.61 | 8.94 | 6.66 | 6.26 | 6.11 | 5.82 | 5.53 | 5.80 | 5.76 |
| Government Bond Yield.................. | 61 | 5.98 | 5.98 | 6.01 | 6.81 | 6.17 | 4.66 | 4.86 | 4.02 | 3.11 | 3.52 | 4.02 | 3.01 |
| **Prices, Production, Labor** | | | | | | | *Index Numbers (2010=100): Period Averages* | | | | | | |
| Share Prices................................. | 62 | 84.6 | 101.0 | 113.6 | 130.9 | 103.9 | 91.1 | 100.0 | 106.2 | 113.5 | 142.5 | 162.6 | 183.3 |
| Input Prices: All Industry................ | 63 | 78.2 | 82.4 | 86.6 | 89.7 | 98.7 | 96.3 | 100.0 | 104.0 | 104.4 | 106.8 | 105.0 | 103.6 |
| Consumer Prices........................... | 64 | 84.4 | 87.0 | 89.9 | 92.1 | 95.7 | 97.7 | 100.0 | 104.4 | 105.4 | 106.7 | 107.7 | 108.1 |
| Labor Cost Index........................... | 65a | 84.7 | 87.3 | 90.1 | 93.0 | 96.4 | 98.3 | 100.0 | 102.0 | 103.9 | 105.6 | 107.4 | 109.1 |
| Manufacturing Production.............. | 66ey | 102.7 | 102.8 | 101.7 | 105.2 | 103.5 | 96.5 | 100.0 | 97.6 | 97.6 | 98.6 | 101.1 | 98.3 |
| Manufacturing Employment........... | 67ey | 115.7 | 111.5 | 110.7 | 108.9 | 106.9 | 99.8 | 100.0 | 101.0 | 96.4 | 98.0 | 100.1 | 102.3 |
| | | | | | | | *Number in Thousands: Period Averages* | | | | | | |
| Labor Force.................................. | 67d | 2,115 | 2,167 | 2,223 | 2,256 | 2,295 | 2,173 | 2,207 | 2,376 | 2,344 | 2,396 | 2,464 | 2,513 |
| Employment................................. | 67e | 2,042 | 2,099 | 2,145 | 2,173 | 2,192 | 2,164 | 2,185 | 2,220 | 2,195 | 2,248 | 2,324 | 2,369 |
| Unemployment............................. | 67c | 98 | 83 | 75 | 56 | 60 | 108 | 142 | 188 | 222 | 253 | 270 | 281 |
| Unemployment Rate (%)................ | 67r | 4.0 | 3.9 | 3.8 | 3.7 | 4.5 | 6.4 | 6.7 | 6.6 | 6.7 | 6.2 | 5.7 | 5.8 |
| **Intl. Transactions & Positions** | | | | | | | *Millions of New Zealand Dollars* | | | | | | |
| Exports........................ | 70 | 31,088.0 | 31,098.0 | 35,303.0 | 38,126.0 | 43,353.0 | 39,556.0 | 44,764.0 | 47,468.0 | 46,160.0 | 50,028.0 | 48,915.0 | 48,839.0 |
| Butter........................ | 70fl | 910.0 | 925.0 | 1,121.0 | 1,390.0 | 1,681.0 | 1,625.0 | 2,252.0 | 2,458.0 | 1,911.0 | 2,497.0 | 2,396.0 | 2,368.7 |
| Imports, c.i.f.................. | 71 | 35,446.0 | 38,160.0 | 41,082.0 | 42,653.0 | 48,037.0 | 39,719.0 | 44,024.0 | 47,201.0 | 46,681.0 | 49,230.0 | 51,287.0 | 52,604.0 |
| Imports, f.o.b................. | 71.v | 33,139.0 | 35,715.0 | 38,554.0 | 40,157.0 | 45,177.0 | 37,640.0 | 41,619.0 | 44,820.0 | 44,327.0 | 46,742.0 | 48,754.0 | 49,979.4 |
| | | | | | | | *2010=100* | | | | | | |
| Volume of Exports......................... | 72 | 86.8 | 85.9 | 88.7 | 94.4 | 90.8 | 98.4 | 100.0 | 102.4 | 109.8 | 109.8 | 112.3 | 115.8 |
| Butter........................ | 72fl | 79.5 | 80.6 | 107.4 | 91.0 | 87.0 | 114.6 | 100.0 | 111.8 | 119.7 | 121.7 | 127.7 | 126.9 |
| Volume of Imports......................... | 73 | 87.2 | 92.3 | 93.0 | 101.6 | 99.9 | 90.2 | 100.0 | 106.2 | 107.3 | 119.0 | 130.7 | 134.0 |
| Butter (Unit Value)........................ | 74fl | 53.1 | 54.4 | 48.6 | 65.6 | 88.2 | 63.7 | 100.0 | 94.4 | 67.8 | 89.5 | 80.3 | 79.2 |
| Export Price Index......................... | 76 | 79.5 | 80.3 | 87.6 | 90.2 | 106.0 | 89.4 | 100.0 | 103.7 | 94.4 | 102.5 | 97.4 | 94.2 |
| Import Price Index......................... | 76.x | 91.3 | 93.0 | 99.6 | 95.0 | 108.7 | 100.2 | 100.0 | 101.3 | 99.2 | 94.4 | 89.7 | 89.2 |
| **Balance of Payments** | | | | | | | *Millions of US Dollars* | | | | | | |
| A. Current Account*...................... | 109bx | −4,685.9 | −8,025.1 | −7,879.7 | −9,323.4 | −10,263.7 | −3,009.5 | −3,430.1 | −4,796.5 | −6,868.5 | −5,782.0 | −6,137.0 | −5,068.9 |
| Goods, credit (exports)............. | 1a9cx | 20,526.4 | 22,014.8 | 22,494.7 | 27,241.4 | 31,087.6 | 25,225.6 | 31,727.0 | 38,119.8 | 37,648.3 | 39,728.6 | 41,961.5 | 34,412.6 |
| Goods, debit (imports)............. | 1a9dx | 22,190.0 | 25,056.9 | 25,006.5 | 29,489.0 | 33,228.8 | 24,269.9 | 29,725.1 | 35,906.8 | 37,594.8 | 38,673.9 | 41,000.2 | 35,795.8 |
| Balance on goods.................. | 1a9bx | −1,663.0 | −3,042.8 | −2,512.4 | −2,248.4 | −2,141.7 | 956.3 | 2,002.6 | 2,213.8 | 54.3 | 1,054.7 | 961.3 | −1,382.5 |
| Services, credit (exports)............... | 1b9cx | 9,595.9 | 10,151.9 | 9,836.6 | 11,604.4 | 11,815.5 | 10,192.2 | 11,568.3 | 13,239.6 | 13,140.2 | 13,488.0 | 14,394.4 | 14,299.6 |
| Services, debit (imports)................ | 1b9dx | 7,316.5 | 8,392.9 | 8,082.4 | 9,617.1 | 10,477.9 | 8,705.7 | 10,248.0 | 12,148.7 | 12,408.1 | 12,649.3 | 13,191.9 | 11,679.6 |
| Balance on Goods & Services..... | 1z9bx | 615.7 | −1,283.1 | −757.5 | −260.3 | −803.6 | 2,442.3 | 3,322.2 | 3,303.9 | 785.6 | 1,893.3 | 2,163.7 | 1,236.7 |
| Primary income: credit.............. | 1c9cx | 3,440.3 | 3,847.5 | 3,804.7 | 5,227.0 | 4,514.8 | 3,291.2 | 4,177.1 | 4,852.2 | 5,443.4 | 5,788.9 | 6,250.8 | 5,505.7 |
| Primary income: debit................ | 1c9dx | 8,838.4 | 10,796.0 | 11,315.8 | 14,679.2 | 14,636.0 | 9,016.5 | 10,967.2 | 12,798.0 | 12,737.5 | 13,113.0 | 14,221.0 | 11,602.3 |
| Balance on gds, serv. & prim. inc. | 1y9bx | −4,782.4 | −8,231.6 | −8,268.6 | −9,712.5 | −10,924.8 | −3,282.9 | −3,467.8 | −4,641.9 | −6,508.6 | −5,430.8 | −5,806.5 | −4,859.8 |
| Secondary income: credit............. | 1d9ca | 906.5 | 1,250.5 | 1,299.4 | 1,436.4 | 1,710.8 | 1,201.7 | 1,008.8 | 1,038.2 | 1,025.1 | 1,027.3 | 1,397.6 | 1,436.0 |
| Secondary income: debit.............. | 1d9da | 810.0 | 1,044.0 | 910.6 | 1,047.2 | 1,049.7 | 928.3 | 971.0 | 1,192.8 | 1,385.0 | 1,378.5 | 1,728.2 | 1,645.0 |
| B. Capital Account*....................... | 209ba | 3.8 | −.7 | −.7 | .8 | 118.7 | 522.9 | 4,353.8 | 10,828.3 | −6.4 | 2.5 | 33.2 | 226.4 |
| Capital account: credit................. | 209ca | 4.4 | .7 | — | 2.3 | 125.7 | 536.3 | 4,381.5 | 10,874.8 | 21.9 | 14.0 | 41.4 | 247.4 |
| Capital account: debit................. | 209da | .6 | 1.4 | .7 | 1.5 | 7.0 | 13.5 | 27.7 | 46.5 | 28.3 | 11.6 | 8.2 | 20.9 |
| Balance on current & capital acct. | 129ba | −4,682.1 | −8,025.8 | −7,880.4 | −9,322.6 | −10,144.9 | −2,486.6 | 923.7 | 6,031.8 | −6,874.9 | −5,779.5 | −6,103.7 | −4,842.4 |
| C. Financial Account* | 309na | −9,212.6 | −11,367.5 | −13,157.8 | −10,557.4 | −2,532.3 | −5,374.0 | −98.8 | 163.0 | −6,392.2 | 1,279.4 | −3,060.5 | 2,489.2 |
| Direct investment: assets............. | 3a9aa | 853.7 | −640.9 | −399.9 | 3,990.6 | 839.3 | −2,072.6 | 1,033.3 | −280.0 | −112.3 | −1,420.0 | 1,008.8 | 282.0 |
| Equity & investment fund shares.. | 3a9aa | −53.1 | −1,107.3 | 558.5 | 3,227.6 | 1,313.1 | 19.8 | 436.3 | −242.0 | −150.9 | 921.4 | 47.3 | 176.2 |
| Debt instruments................... | 3abaa | 908.1 | 466.5 | −957.7 | 764.5 | −473.8 | −2,092.3 | 595.6 | −37.2 | 40.1 | −2,340.5 | 961.5 | 105.2 |
| Direct investment: liabilities ......... | 3a9la | 2,319.8 | 1,906.7 | 2,912.6 | 4,335.5 | 2,592.0 | −52.4 | 286.3 | 1,370.0 | 3,737.4 | −99.4 | 3,245.4 | −660.0 |
| Equity & investment fund shares . | 3aala | −7.5 | −419.4 | 2,047.7 | 2,172.6 | −226.8 | 653.3 | 2,100.1 | 3,914.8 | 4,781.0 | 1,299.9 | 4,532.1 | 1,977.1 |
| Debt instruments................... | 3abla | 2,328.6 | 2,328.2 | 866.2 | 2,162.9 | 2,819.3 | −705.6 | −1,813.1 | −2,545.7 | −1,042.8 | −1,400.2 | −1,286.8 | −2,637.0 |
| Portfolio investment: assets......... | 3b9aa | 1,447.9 | 464.0 | 753.6 | 3,007.0 | −1,802.2 | 4,141.9 | 2,183.1 | 1,111.1 | 3,490.1 | 6,831.3 | 10,177.2 | 3,652.4 |
| Equity & investment fund shares | 3baaa | 1,230.4 | 1,048.5 | 592.6 | 2,375.3 | −2,541.0 | 2,279.2 | 1,857.8 | −439.9 | 388.5 | 4,320.7 | 3,760.6 | 1,250.4 |
| Debt securities ........................ | 3bbaa | 218.2 | −585.2 | 161.6 | 630.2 | 738.8 | 1,863.4 | 325.2 | 1,550.9 | 3,101.5 | 2,509.7 | 6,415.7 | 2,401.3 |
| Portfolio investment: liabilities....... | 3b9la | 8,457.1 | 536.1 | 462.9 | 12,268.7 | −5,654.8 | 5,908.9 | 4,835.8 | 4,292.3 | 9,377.6 | 5,215.9 | 8,685.3 | 4,708.3 |
| Equity & investment fund shares . | 3bala | 98.7 | −97.8 | −397.3 | 229.1 | 170.0 | 966.6 | −292.9 | 1,570.3 | 441.7 | 3,506.5 | 2,247.4 | 2,460.3 |
| Debt securities........................ | 3bbla | 8,358.4 | 633.2 | 859.6 | 12,038.9 | −5,825.6 | 4,942.3 | 5,128.0 | 2,722.0 | 8,936.8 | 1,711.1 | 6,438.0 | 2,248.7 |
| Fin. der.& empl.stk.ops.(ESOs): net | 3c9na | −2.1 | 14.4 | 11.7 | −11.2 | 178.9 | −571.0 | −67.1 | −62.0 | 569.0 | −895.0 | −164.1 | 1,168.6 |
| Fin. der. & ESOs.: assets............ | 3c9aa | −2.8 | 13.0 | 2.8 | 34.8 | 454.4 | −880.0 | 53.4 | 115.6 | 250.3 | −540.6 | −1,921.0 | −4,389.3 |
| Fin. der. & ESOs.: liabilities........ | 3c9la | −.7 | −1.4 | −8.9 | 45.9 | 275.5 | −309.0 | 120.5 | 177.6 | −318.7 | 354.3 | −1,756.9 | −5,557.8 |
| Other investment: assets............. | 3d9aa | −968.6 | −5,262.9 | 227.4 | 875.5 | −3,032.9 | 620.7 | 2,188.4 | 2,824.8 | −3,833.0 | −2,728.6 | −2,740.0 | 745.4 |
| Other equity.......................... | 3daaa | . . . . | . . . . | . . . . | . . . . | . . . . | . . . . | . . . . | . . . . | . . . . | . . . . | . . . . | . . . . |
| Debt instruments................... | 3dzaa | −968.6 | −5,262.9 | 227.4 | 875.5 | −3,032.9 | 620.7 | 2,188.4 | 2,824.8 | −3,833.0 | −2,728.6 | −2,740.0 | 745.4 |
| Other investment: liabilities............ | 3d9la | −234.0 | 3,498.9 | 10,374.6 | 1,815.2 | 1,778.3 | 1,636.4 | 314.2 | −2,231.4 | −6,609.1 | −4,608.3 | −587.2 | −688.6 |
| Other equity.......................... | 3dala | . . . . | | | | | | | | | | | |
| Debt instruments................... | 3dzla | −234.0 | 3,498.9 | 10,374.6 | 1,815.2 | 1,778.3 | 1,636.4 | 314.2 | −2,231.4 | −6,609.1 | −4,608.3 | −587.2 | −688.6 |
| Curr.+ cap.− finan. acct. balance... | 4y9na | 4,530.5 | 3,341.7 | 5,277.4 | 1,234.8 | −7,612.6 | 2,887.4 | 1,022.5 | 5,868.8 | −482.7 | −7,058.9 | −3,043.3 | −7,331.6 |
| D. Net Errors and Omissions.......... | 409na | −3,902.9 | −925.0 | −1,020.5 | 1,853.2 | 2,613.3 | 764.0 | −177.0 | −5,453.3 | 996.8 | 6,218.4 | 2,902.9 | 6,806.6 |
| E. Reserves and Related Items......... | 4z9na | 629.5 | 2,417.4 | 4,255.5 | 3,087.4 | −4,997.7 | 3,651.4 | 846.9 | 413.9 | 514.9 | −842.2 | −139.6 | −520.9 |
| Reserve assets............................. | 3e9aa | 629.5 | 2,417.4 | 4,255.5 | 3,087.4 | −4,997.7 | 3,651.4 | 846.9 | 413.9 | 514.9 | −842.2 | −139.6 | −520.9 |
| Credit and loans from the IMF....... | 3dcla | — | — | — | — | — | — | — | — | — | — | — | — |
| Exceptional financing................... | 409la | . . . . | . . . . | . . . . | . . . . | . . . . | . . . . | . . . . | . . . . | . . . . | . . . . | . . . . | . . . . |

*Excludes components in group E

| | | 2004 | 2005 | 2006 | 2007 | 2008 | 2009 | 2010 | 2011 | 2012 | 2013 | 2014 | 2015 |
|---|---|---|---|---|---|---|---|---|---|---|---|---|---|
| **International Investment Position** | | | | | | | *Millions of US Dollars* | | | | | | |
| Assets............................ | 809aa | 81,064.7 | 75,965.6 | 91,648.6 | 116,310.1 | 89,645.1 | 108,521.4 | 129,025.0 | 135,616.5 | 145,326.8 | 146,100.9 | 155,059.1 | 153,950.2 |
| Direct investment.......................... | 8a9aa | 25,266.1 | 22,122.3 | 23,081.6 | 27,911.2 | 23,411.9 | 24,961.4 | 29,049.3 | 27,997.4 | 29,758.7 | 27,429.9 | 27,914.3 | 24,915.8 |
| Equity & investment fund shares.. | 8aaaa | 12,044.7 | 10,243.5 | 10,963.3 | 12,924.3 | 12,038.0 | 12,724.3 | 14,625.2 | 14,316.1 | 14,712.0 | 14,798.9 | 15,088.8 | 13,762.4 |
| Debt instruments.................. | 8abaa | 13,220.7 | 11,878.2 | 12,118.2 | 14,987.7 | 11,373.9 | 12,237.1 | 14,424.9 | 13,681.3 | 15,046.7 | 12,630.3 | 12,825.5 | 11,153.3 |
| Portfolio investment..................... | 8b9aa | 28,749.6 | 30,778.2 | 36,033.4 | 45,056.9 | 26,823.9 | 40,198.7 | 47,248.6 | 46,268.7 | 55,725.3 | 65,342.1 | 77,372.4 | 75,749.2 |
| Equity & investment fund shares.. | 8baaa | 22,488.1 | 25,298.3 | 30,079.8 | 36,525.8 | 19,279.1 | 29,674.1 | 35,093.9 | 32,019.0 | 37,550.2 | 44,371.2 | 47,999.6 | 46,530.8 |
| Debt securities.......................... | 8bbaa | 6,261.6 | 5,479.8 | 5,953.6 | 8,531.0 | 7,544.8 | 10,524.6 | 12,155.4 | 14,249.8 | 18,175.1 | 20,970.9 | 29,372.8 | 29,219.0 |
| Fin. der.(oth.than reserves) & ESOs | 8c9aa | 4,252.2 | 2,955.2 | 4,598.2 | 7,912.6 | 15,485.9 | 10,632.1 | 13,477.0 | 17,258.6 | 15,729.9 | 11,135.0 | 12,461.4 | 17,500.1 |
| Other investment......................... | 8d9aa | 15,849.3 | 11,213.8 | 13,866.7 | 18,182.0 | 12,871.0 | 17,134.6 | 22,526.9 | 27,079.6 | 26,530.2 | 25,875.7 | 21,451.5 | 21,085.7 |
| Other equity............................. | 8daaa | .... | .... | .... | .... | .... | .... | .... | .... | .... | .... | .... | .... |
| Debt instruments...................... | 8dzaa | 15,849.3 | 11,213.8 | 13,866.7 | 18,182.0 | 12,871.0 | 17,134.6 | 22,526.9 | 27,079.6 | 26,530.2 | 25,875.7 | 21,451.5 | 21,085.7 |
| Reserve assets............................ | 8e9aa | 6,947.4 | 8,895.8 | 14,068.5 | 17,246.5 | 11,052.2 | 15,594.0 | 16,722.8 | 17,012.2 | 17,583.3 | 16,318.0 | 15,860.1 | 14,699.4 |
| Liabilities........................ | 809la | 160,930.9 | 157,986.0 | 183,608.8 | 221,322.2 | 179,448.4 | 219,537.5 | 240,504.3 | 248,177.3 | 268,849.2 | 266,036.8 | 275,480.6 | 257,466.3 |
| Direct investment.......................... | 8a9la | 55,604.9 | 54,437.7 | 60,432.8 | 71,882.9 | 53,655.3 | 67,618.2 | 72,071.1 | 73,433.2 | 81,699.4 | 83,897.4 | 85,567.8 | 73,709.8 |
| Equity & investment fund shares.. | 8aala | 29,491.8 | 27,878.1 | 31,873.5 | 36,306.0 | 24,003.1 | 30,918.3 | 34,327.9 | 37,582.4 | 43,502.0 | 46,260.1 | 50,117.3 | 45,450.2 |
| Debt instruments.................. | 8abla | 26,113.1 | 26,559.6 | 28,559.3 | 35,576.9 | 29,651.6 | 36,699.9 | 37,743.2 | 35,850.8 | 38,197.4 | 37,637.3 | 35,450.5 | 28,259.6 |
| Portfolio investment..................... | 8b9la | 58,116.4 | 54,077.9 | 56,918.1 | 72,171.6 | 52,819.9 | 66,483.0 | 75,083.4 | 78,684.2 | 93,604.5 | 97,445.5 | 112,022.8 | 107,384.2 |
| Equity & investment fund shares.. | 8bala | 12,077.7 | 11,489.1 | 11,818.2 | 12,533.4 | 5,738.1 | 9,232.7 | 9,229.5 | 8,864.6 | 11,778.8 | 16,542.6 | 21,781.1 | 22,966.1 |
| Debt securities.......................... | 8bbla | 46,038.7 | 42,588.9 | 45,100.0 | 59,638.2 | 47,081.8 | 57,250.3 | 65,853.2 | 69,820.4 | 81,825.7 | 80,902.9 | 90,241.8 | 84,418.0 |
| Fin. der.(oth.than reserves) & ESOs | 8c9la | 5,520.2 | 3,708.9 | 5,592.1 | 7,712.9 | 14,585.1 | 12,274.0 | 13,904.7 | 17,614.9 | 15,231.2 | 12,112.7 | 14,528.3 | 19,716.8 |
| Other investment......................... | 8d9la | 41,688.8 | 45,761.5 | 60,665.0 | 69,554.7 | 58,388.6 | 73,161.6 | 79,445.8 | 78,445.1 | 78,314.2 | 72,581.1 | 63,361.7 | 56,655.6 |
| Other equity............................. | 8dala | .... | .... | .... | .... | .... | .... | .... | .... | .... | .... | .... | .... |
| Debt instruments...................... | 8dzla | 41,688.8 | 45,761.5 | 60,665.0 | 69,554.7 | 58,388.6 | 73,161.6 | 79,445.8 | 78,445.1 | 78,314.2 | 72,581.1 | 63,361.7 | 56,655.6 |

| | | 2004 | 2005 | 2006 | 2007 | 2008 | 2009 | 2010 | 2011 | 2012 | 2013 | 2014 | 2015 |
|---|---|---|---|---|---|---|---|---|---|---|---|---|---|
| **Government Finance** | | | | | | | | | | | | | |
| **Operations Statement** | | | | | | | | | | | | | |
| **General Government** | | | | | | *Millions of New Zealand Dollars: Fiscal Year Ends June 30* | | | | | | | |
| Revenue | a1 | 57,857.7 | 63,860.3 | 68,622.2 | 71,088.9 | .... | 98,001.4 | 97,685.5 | 103,796.9 | 104,774.6 | .... | .... | .... |
| Taxes | a11 | 48,028.9 | 52,384.6 | 58,061.3 | 59,540.1 | .... | 63,744.2 | 60,436.3 | 63,158.5 | 66,608.1 | .... | .... | .... |
| Social Contributions | a12 | 112.8 | 106.7 | 109.0 | 101.0 | .... | 2,278.5 | 2,522.6 | 2,745.5 | 2,820.9 | .... | .... | .... |
| Grants | a13 | — | | | — | .... | 19,830.7 | 21,134.7 | 20,997.2 | 21,443.1 | .... | .... | .... |
| Other Revenue | a14 | 9,716.1 | 11,369.0 | 10,451.9 | 11,447.8 | .... | 12,148.1 | 13,591.9 | 16,895.8 | 13,902.4 | .... | .... | .... |
| Expense | a2 | 50,805.6 | 54,511.5 | 58,261.1 | 63,088.2 | .... | 93,884.1 | 99,033.6 | 117,325.7 | 104,467.0 | .... | .... | .... |
| Compensation of Employees | a21 | 12,968.1 | 14,034.5 | 15,133.6 | 15,899.3 | .... | 18,966.5 | 20,007.2 | 20,539.5 | 21,152.2 | .... | .... | .... |
| Use of Goods & Services | a22 | 14,481.1 | 16,279.3 | 18,217.3 | 20,201.8 | .... | 11,244.1 | 11,482.1 | 12,011.3 | 12,827.0 | .... | .... | .... |
| Consumption of Fixed Capital | a23 | 2,767.5 | 2,957.7 | 2,946.8 | 3,156.7 | .... | 3,872.5 | 4,170.9 | 4,516.3 | 4,313.7 | .... | .... | .... |
| Interest | a24 | 2,660.4 | 2,815.6 | 2,639.8 | 2,495.2 | .... | 2,629.5 | 2,899.8 | 4,165.5 | 4,046.7 | .... | .... | .... |
| Subsidies | a25 | 380.4 | 416.9 | 482.1 | 498.1 | .... | 967.7 | 675.6 | 1,077.4 | 1,015.5 | .... | .... | .... |
| Grants | a26 | 263.6 | 329.0 | 1,102.3 | 1,222.9 | .... | 22,578.6 | 23,320.1 | 23,336.0 | 23,064.6 | .... | .... | .... |
| Social Benefits | a27 | 16,245.0 | 16,633.2 | 16,359.0 | 17,811.0 | .... | 28,873.4 | 30,854.9 | 32,347.1 | 32,084.1 | .... | .... | .... |
| Other Expense | a28 | 1,039.5 | 1,045.3 | 1,380.3 | 1,803.3 | .... | 4,751.8 | 5,622.9 | 19,332.6 | 5,963.3 | .... | .... | .... |
| Gross Operating Balance [1-2+23] | agob | 9,819.6 | 12,306.5 | 13,307.8 | 11,157.3 | .... | 7,989.8 | 2,822.8 | –9,012.6 | 4,621.3 | .... | .... | .... |
| Net Operating Balance [1-2] | anob | 7,052.1 | 9,348.8 | 10,361.1 | 8,000.7 | .... | 4,117.3 | –1,348.1 | –13,528.9 | 307.6 | .... | .... | .... |
| Net Acq. of Nonfinancial Assets | a31 | 1,818.8 | 2,328.8 | 2,919.0 | 2,245.9 | .... | 3,154.1 | 3,719.8 | 3,752.0 | 1,825.0 | .... | .... | .... |
| Aquisition of Nonfin. Assets | a31.1 | .... | .... | .... | .... | .... | .... | .... | .... | .... | .... | .... | .... |
| Disposal of Nonfin. Assets | a31.2 | .... | .... | .... | .... | .... | .... | .... | .... | .... | .... | .... | .... |
| Net Lending/Borrowing [1-2-31] | anlb | 5,233.3 | 7,020.0 | 7,442.1 | 5,754.8 | .... | 963.2 | –5,067.8 | –17,280.9 | –1,517.4 | .... | .... | .... |
| Net Acq. of Financial Assets | a32 | .... | .... | .... | .... | .... | .... | .... | .... | .... | .... | .... | .... |
| By instrument | | | | | | | | | | | | | |
| Monetary Gold & SDRs | a3201 | — | — | — | — | .... | .... | .... | .... | .... | .... | .... | .... |
| Currency & Deposits | a3202 | –1,413.9 | –15.4 | 1,625.7 | 727.6 | .... | .... | .... | .... | .... | .... | .... | .... |
| Securities other than Shares | a3203 | .... | .... | .... | .... | .... | .... | .... | .... | .... | .... | .... | .... |
| Loans | a3204 | .... | .... | .... | .... | .... | .... | .... | .... | .... | .... | .... | .... |
| Shares & Other Equity | a3205 | .... | .... | .... | .... | .... | .... | .... | .... | .... | .... | .... | .... |
| Insurance Technical Reserves | a3206 | .... | .... | .... | .... | .... | .... | .... | .... | .... | .... | .... | .... |
| Financial Derivatives | a3207 | .... | .... | .... | .... | .... | .... | .... | .... | .... | .... | .... | .... |
| Other Accounts Receivable | a3208 | .... | .... | .... | .... | .... | .... | .... | .... | .... | .... | .... | .... |
| By debtor | | | | | | | | | | | | | |
| Domestic | a321 | .... | .... | .... | .... | .... | .... | .... | .... | .... | .... | .... | .... |
| Foreign | a322 | .... | .... | .... | .... | .... | .... | .... | .... | .... | .... | .... | .... |
| Net Incurrence of Liabilities | a33 | .... | .... | .... | .... | .... | .... | .... | .... | .... | .... | .... | .... |
| By instrument | | | | | | | | | | | | | |
| Special Drawing Rights (SDRs) | a3301 | .... | .... | .... | .... | .... | .... | .... | .... | .... | .... | .... | .... |
| Currency & Deposits | a3302 | .... | .... | .... | .... | .... | .... | .... | .... | .... | .... | .... | .... |
| Securities other than Shares | a3303 | .... | .... | .... | .... | .... | .... | .... | .... | .... | .... | .... | .... |
| Loans | a3304 | .... | .... | .... | .... | .... | .... | .... | .... | .... | .... | .... | .... |
| Shares & Other Equity | a3305 | .... | .... | .... | .... | .... | .... | .... | .... | .... | .... | .... | .... |
| Insurance Technical Reserves | a3306 | .... | .... | .... | .... | .... | .... | .... | .... | .... | .... | .... | .... |
| Financial Derivatives | a3307 | .... | .... | .... | .... | .... | .... | .... | .... | .... | .... | .... | .... |
| Other Accounts Payable | a3308 | .... | .... | .... | .... | .... | .... | .... | .... | .... | .... | .... | .... |
| By creditor | | | | | | | | | | | | | |
| Domestic | a331 | .... | .... | .... | .... | .... | .... | .... | .... | .... | .... | .... | .... |
| Foreign | a332 | .... | .... | .... | .... | .... | .... | .... | .... | .... | .... | .... | .... |
| Stat. Discrepancy [32-33-NLB] | anlbz | .... | .... | .... | .... | .... | .... | .... | .... | .... | .... | .... | .... |
| Memo Item: Expenditure [2+31] | a2m | 52,624.4 | 56,840.3 | 61,180.1 | 65,334.1 | .... | 97,038.2 | 102,753.3 | 121,077.8 | 106,292.0 | .... | .... | .... |
| **Balance Sheet** | | | | | | | *Millions of New Zealand Dollars: Fiscal Year Ends June 30* | | | | | | | |
| Net Worth | a6 | 92,162.9 | 114,026.0 | 132,379.2 | 151,174.8 | .... | 186,609.5 | 182,208.7 | 172,362.5 | 154,850.5 | .... | .... | .... |
| Nonfinancial Assets | a61 | 107,037.5 | 120,785.8 | 130,917.8 | 142,456.6 | .... | 160,608.8 | 164,276.9 | 166,958.1 | 170,481.9 | .... | .... | .... |
| Financial Assets | a62 | 56,177.6 | 69,319.0 | 79,735.7 | 82,821.9 | .... | 125,174.6 | 127,628.9 | 149,412.5 | 142,455.1 | .... | .... | .... |
| By instrument | | | | | | | | | | | | | |
| Monetary Gold & SDRs | a6201 | — | — | — | — | .... | — | — | — | — | .... | .... | .... |
| Currency & Deposits | a6202 | 4,983.1 | 4,872.7 | 5,634.0 | 6,332.3 | .... | 14,017.6 | 13,261.3 | 19,344.4 | 15,551.6 | .... | .... | .... |
| Securities other than Shares | a6203 | 13,255.8 | 18,150.8 | 24,213.5 | 21,928.2 | .... | 9,268.0 | 10,479.4 | 11,156.2 | 13,918.1 | .... | .... | .... |
| Loans | a6204 | 6,858.7 | 7,503.6 | 6,113.8 | 7,474.6 | .... | 16,580.9 | 18,578.0 | 19,625.9 | 20,843.4 | .... | .... | .... |
| Shares and Other Equity | a6205 | 20,657.9 | 28,016.6 | 29,876.0 | 34,161.7 | .... | 65,355.0 | 67,243.6 | 73,498.6 | 67,040.6 | .... | .... | .... |
| Insurance Technical Reserves | a6206 | .... | .... | .... | .... | .... | .... | .... | .... | .... | .... | .... | .... |
| Financial Derivatives | a6207 | — | — | — | 66.3 | .... | — | — | — | — | .... | .... | .... |
| Other Accounts Receivable | a6208 | 10,422.1 | 10,775.3 | 13,898.4 | 12,858.9 | .... | 19,953.1 | 18,066.5 | 25,787.3 | 25,101.4 | .... | .... | .... |
| By debtor | | | | | | | | | | | | | |
| Domestic | a621 | 42,155.8 | 48,954.0 | .... | .... | .... | .... | .... | .... | .... | .... | .... | .... |
| Foreign | a622 | 14,021.8 | 20,365.1 | .... | .... | .... | .... | .... | .... | .... | .... | .... | .... |
| Liabilities | a63 | 71,052.2 | 76,078.9 | 78,274.4 | 74,103.6 | .... | 99,173.9 | 109,697.0 | 144,008.2 | 158,086.5 | .... | .... | .... |
| By instrument | | | | | | | | | | | | | |
| Special Drawing Rights (SDRs) | a6301 | | | | | .... | | | | | .... | .... | .... |
| Currency & Deposits | a6302 | 209.4 | 302.3 | 153.7 | 61.7 | .... | 30.7 | 26.6 | 3.2 | 6.1 | .... | .... | .... |
| Securities other than Shares | a6303 | 33,721.9 | 32,467.6 | — | — | .... | 32,724.5 | 39,055.5 | 56,449.6 | 64,728.1 | .... | .... | .... |
| Loans | a6304 | 2,026.7 | 2,430.6 | 35,055.2 | 30,697.8 | .... | 12,837.0 | 16,304.9 | 17,561.9 | 18,291.6 | .... | .... | .... |
| Shares and Other Equity | a6305 | — | — | — | — | .... | — | — | — | — | .... | .... | .... |
| Insurance Technical Reserves | a6306 | 22,887.9 | 26,336.9 | 27,946.0 | 28,048.0 | .... | — | — | — | — | .... | .... | .... |
| Financial Derivatives | a6307 | — | — | — | — | .... | — | — | — | — | .... | .... | .... |
| Other Accounts Payable | a6308 | 12,206.4 | 14,541.6 | 15,119.5 | 15,296.2 | .... | 53,581.6 | 54,310.0 | 69,993.6 | 75,060.7 | .... | .... | .... |
| By creditor | | | | | | | | | | | | | |
| Domestic | a631 | 65,086.7 | 66,259.4 | .... | .... | .... | .... | .... | .... | .... | .... | .... | .... |
| Foreign | a632 | 5,965.5 | 9,819.4 | .... | .... | .... | .... | .... | .... | .... | .... | .... | .... |
| Net Financial Worth [62-63] | a6m2 | –14,874.6 | –6,759.8 | 1,461.3 | 8,718.2 | .... | 26,000.7 | 17,931.8 | 5,404.3 | –15,631.4 | .... | .... | .... |
| Memo Item: Debt at Market Value | a6m3 | 71,052.2 | 76,078.9 | 78,274.4 | 74,103.6 | .... | 99,173.9 | 109,697.0 | 144,008.2 | 158,086.5 | .... | .... | .... |
| Memo Item: Debt at Face Value | a6m35 | .... | .... | .... | .... | .... | .... | .... | .... | .... | .... | .... | .... |
| Memo Item: Debt at Nominal Value | a6m4 | .... | .... | .... | .... | .... | .... | .... | .... | .... | .... | .... | .... |

|  |  | 2004 | 2005 | 2006 | 2007 | 2008 | 2009 | 2010 | 2011 | 2012 | 2013 | 2014 | 2015 |
|---|---|---|---|---|---|---|---|---|---|---|---|---|---|
| **National Accounts** |  | *Millions of New Zealand Dollars; Fiscal Year Begins April 1* | | | | | | | | | | | |
| Househ.Cons.Expend.,incl.NPISHs.... | **96f.c** | 88,793 | 94,792 | 100,507 | 106,174 | 109,860 | 113,390 | 118,143 | 124,940 | 128,792 | 133,732 | 138,232 | 142,784 |
| Government Consumption Expend... | **91f.c** | 26,246 | 29,085 | 31,401 | 34,196 | 37,231 | 38,164 | 39,768 | 41,406 | 41,877 | 43,533 | 44,978 | 46,480 |
| Gross Fixed Capital Formation.......... | **93e.c** | 37,431 | 40,320 | 41,132 | 44,639 | 42,952 | 39,037 | 39,992 | 42,326 | 45,010 | 48,508 | 54,091 | 57,614 |
| Changes in Inventories.................... | **93i.c** | 1,644 | 1,100 | −265 | 1,611 | 51 | −851 | 862 | 1,268 | 803 | 1,679 | 536 | 222 |
| Exports of Goods and Services......... | **90c.c** | 45,662 | 46,087 | 50,928 | 54,645 | 60,759 | 55,832 | 61,559 | 64,749 | 62,765 | 66,998 | 67,482 | 69,804 |
| Imports of Goods and Services (-)..... | **98c.c** | 45,218 | 48,447 | 51,592 | 54,419 | 61,235 | 51,320 | 56,891 | 61,448 | 61,252 | 63,323 | 65,778 | 68,257 |
| Gross Domestic Product (GDP)......... | **99b.c** | 154,558 | 162,936 | 172,112 | 186,846 | 189,617 | 194,251 | 203,434 | 213,241 | 217,995 | 231,128 | 239,541 | 248,647 |
| Net Primary Income from Abroad..... | **98.nc** | −8,706 | −10,526 | −11,550 | −13,315 | −13,742 | −7,964 | −10,108 | −9,656 | −9,020 | −7,771 | −7,752 | −3,945 |
| Gross National Income (GNI)............ | **99a.c** | 145,852 | 152,410 | 160,562 | 173,531 | 175,875 | 186,287 | 193,326 | 203,585 | 208,975 | 223,357 | 231,789 | 244,702 |
| Consumption of Fixed Capital.......... | **99cfc** | 21,091 | 22,661 | 24,759 | 26,103 | 28,589 | 29,995 | 29,977 | 30,280 | 31,034 | 31,945 | 33,467 | .... |
| GDP Volume 2009/10 Prices............ | **99b.r** | 176,029 | 181,892 | 186,599 | 193,572 | 190,580 | 194,251 | 196,106 | 201,381 | 206,892 | 210,159 | 216,832 | 223,446 |
| GDP Volume (2010=100)................ | **99bvr** | 89.8 | 92.8 | 95.2 | 98.7 | 97.2 | 99.1 | 100.0 | 102.7 | 105.5 | 107.2 | 110.6 | 113.9 |
| GDP Deflator (2010=100).............. | **99bir** | 84.6 | 86.4 | 88.9 | 93.0 | 95.9 | 96.4 | 100.0 | 102.1 | 101.6 | 106.0 | 106.5 | 107.3 |
|  |  | *Millions: Midyear Estimates* | | | | | | | | | | | |
| **Population**................................. | **99z** | 4.08 | 4.13 | 4.19 | 4.24 | 4.29 | 4.33 | 4.37 | 4.40 | 4.44 | 4.47 | 4.50 | 4.53 |

# Nicaragua 278

| | | 2004 | 2005 | 2006 | 2007 | 2008 | 2009 | 2010 | 2011 | 2012 | 2013 | 2014 | 2015 |
|---|---|---|---|---|---|---|---|---|---|---|---|---|---|
| **Exchange Rates** | | | | | | *Córdobas per SDR: End of Period* | | | | | | | |
| Principal Rate.................................. | aa | 25.36 | 24.51 | 27.08 | 29.87 | 30.57 | 32.67 | 33.70 | 35.28 | 37.08 | 39.01 | 38.54 | 38.70 |
| | | | | | | *Córdobas per US Dollar: End of Period (ae) Period Average (rf)* | | | | | | | |
| Principal Rate.................................. | ae | 16.33 | 17.15 | 18.00 | 18.90 | 19.85 | 20.84 | 21.88 | 22.98 | 24.13 | 25.33 | 26.60 | 27.93 |
| Principal Rate.................................. | rf | 15.94 | 16.73 | 17.57 | 18.45 | 19.37 | 20.34 | 21.36 | 22.42 | 23.55 | 24.72 | 25.96 | 27.26 |
| | | | | | | *Index Numbers (2010=100): Period Averages* | | | | | | | |
| Principal Rate.................................. | ahx | 134.00 | 127.63 | 121.55 | 115.76 | 110.24 | 105.00 | 100.00 | 95.24 | 90.70 | 86.38 | 82.27 | 78.35 |
| Nominal Effective Exchange Rate..... | nec | 137.36 | 129.86 | 123.58 | 114.99 | 107.72 | 107.44 | 100.00 | 92.63 | 90.20 | 86.50 | 83.98 | 85.87 |
| CPI-Based Real Effect. Ex. Rate........ | rec | 96.74 | 95.82 | 96.31 | 94.24 | 97.77 | 107.10 | 100.00 | 95.95 | 97.98 | 98.31 | 98.87 | 103.94 |
| **Fund Position** | | | | | | *Millions of SDRs: End of Period* | | | | | | | |
| Quota........................................... | 2f.s | 130.00 | 130.00 | 130.00 | 130.00 | 130.00 | 130.00 | 130.00 | 130.00 | 130.00 | 130.00 | 130.00 | 130.00 |
| SDR Holdings................................ | 1b.s | .32 | .22 | .26 | .08 | .09 | 104.92 | 104.86 | 114.49 | 106.11 | 95.36 | 118.92 | 99.73 |
| Reserve Position in the Fund............ | 1c.s | — | — | — | — | — | — | — | — | — | — | — | — |
| Total Fund Cred.&Loans Outstg....... | 2tl | 159.51 | 140.48 | 41.78 | 53.68 | 72.08 | 95.88 | 108.68 | 118.39 | 110.03 | 99.30 | 84.88 | 65.70 |
| SDR Allocations............................. | 1bd | 19.48 | 19.48 | 19.48 | 19.48 | 19.48 | 124.54 | 124.54 | 124.54 | 124.54 | 124.54 | 124.54 | 124.54 |
| **International Liquidity** | | | | | | *Millions of US Dollars Unless Otherwise Indicated: End of Period* | | | | | | | |
| Total Reserves minus Gold.............. | 1l.d | 668.20 | 727.81 | 921.89 | 1,103.32 | 1,140.84 | 1,573.08 | 1,798.98 | 1,892.25 | 1,887.21 | 1,992.96 | 2,276.18 | 2,492.26 |
| SDR Holdings.......................... | 1b.d | .50 | .31 | .39 | .12 | .14 | 164.48 | 161.48 | 175.77 | 163.09 | 146.86 | 172.29 | 138.20 |
| Reserve Position in the Fund......... | 1c.d | — | — | — | — | — | — | — | — | — | — | — | — |
| Foreign Exchange..................... | 1d.d | 667.70 | 727.50 | 921.50 | 1,103.20 | 1,140.70 | 1,408.60 | 1,637.50 | 1,716.48 | 1,724.13 | 1,846.10 | 2,103.89 | 2,354.06 |
| Gold (Million Fine Troy Ounces)........ | 1ad | — | — | — | — | — | — | — | — | — | — | — | — |
| Gold (National Valuation)................ | 1and | — | — | — | — | — | — | — | — | — | — | — | — |
| Central Bank: Other Assets.............. | 3..d | 210.42 | 196.97 | 207.98 | 218.35 | 211.98 | 219.62 | 215.34 | 218.13 | 217.96 | 240.70 | 228.64 | 244.32 |
| Central Bank: Other Liabs................ | 4..d | 1,704.12 | 1,738.53 | 1,797.31 | 1,824.62 | 1,846.32 | 1,706.82 | 1,709.53 | 1,707.69 | 1,714.71 | 1,743.25 | 1,622.72 | 1,387.68 |
| Other Depository Corps.: Assets....... | 7a.d | 117.73 | 141.28 | 125.22 | 130.14 | 176.60 | 413.25 | 662.30 | 730.35 | 564.79 | 545.38 | 635.87 | 445.85 |
| Other Depository Corps.: Liabs......... | 7b.d | 110.47 | 202.56 | 361.70 | 409.61 | 462.65 | 486.68 | 407.88 | 311.30 | 326.87 | 360.44 | 492.18 | 708.99 |
| Other Financial Corps.: Assets.......... | 7e.d | — | — | 1.45 | .87 | 15.05 | 14.07 | 12.73 | 7.71 | 8.50 | 9.18 | 9.70 | 7.95 |
| Other Financial Corps.: Liabs............ | 7f.d | 10.60 | 19.75 | 31.12 | 168.18 | 192.06 | 175.88 | 150.44 | 139.28 | 112.79 | 152.35 | 169.03 | 178.63 |
| **Central Bank** | | | | | | *Millions of Córdobas: End of Period* | | | | | | | |
| Net Foreign Assets.......................... | 11n | −17,982.2 | −17,837.0 | −14,755.1 | −13,037.6 | −14,151.5 | −7,180.6 | −3,205.0 | −1,600.4 | −1,914.7 | 676.2 | 11,961.6 | 26,411.3 |
| Claims on Nonresidents................. | 11 | 14,383.6 | 15,890.9 | 19,260.7 | 23,638.8 | 25,293.7 | 35,591.9 | 42,063.3 | 46,206.2 | 48,151.1 | 53,568.0 | 63,193.7 | 72,529.5 |
| Liabilities to Nonresidents............. | 16c | 32,365.8 | 33,727.9 | 34,015.8 | 36,676.3 | 39,445.2 | 42,772.5 | 45,268.4 | 47,806.6 | 50,065.9 | 52,891.8 | 51,232.2 | 46,118.2 |
| Claims on Other Depository Corps.... | 12e | .3 | .6 | | | | | | | | | | |
| Net Claims on Central Government.. | 12an | 40,124.1 | 40,527.3 | 38,593.7 | 37,853.4 | 40,109.4 | 42,435.2 | 42,715.6 | 43,203.8 | 42,034.0 | 44,326.0 | 39,272.2 | 37,165.1 |
| Claims on Central Government...... | 12a | 46,378.5 | 47,983.6 | 46,824.4 | 48,842.6 | 50,544.6 | 53,411.8 | 53,139.2 | 54,857.0 | 56,086.3 | 57,506.9 | 55,284.3 | 55,494.4 |
| Liabilities to Central Government... | 16d | 6,254.4 | 7,456.3 | 8,230.7 | 10,989.2 | 10,435.2 | 10,976.6 | 10,423.7 | 11,653.2 | 14,052.3 | 13,180.9 | 16,012.1 | 18,329.3 |
| Claims on Other Sectors.................. | 12s | 317.0 | 334.2 | 348.8 | 351.7 | 360.7 | 367.6 | 367.7 | 359.6 | 361.6 | 373.2 | 477.5 | 455.2 |
| Claims on Other Financial Corps..... | 12g | .9 | .9 | .9 | .9 | .9 | .9 | .8 | .8 | .8 | .8 | .8 | .8 |
| Claims on State & Local Govts........ | 12b | | | | | | | | | | | | |
| Claims on Public Nonfin. Corps...... | 12c | 260.0 | 260.0 | 260.0 | 260.0 | 260.0 | 260.0 | 260.0 | 260.1 | 260.0 | 260.1 | 369.3 | 369.3 |
| Claims on Private Sector................ | 12d | 56.1 | 73.3 | 87.8 | 90.7 | 99.7 | 106.7 | 106.9 | 98.7 | 100.7 | 112.4 | 107.4 | 85.0 |
| Monetary Base............................... | 14 | 15,721.5 | 16,305.2 | 18,100.2 | 18,728.2 | 20,835.9 | 27,460.9 | 34,313.7 | 36,492.7 | 35,948.1 | 41,303.7 | 48,596.1 | 55,788.9 |
| Currency in Circulation.................. | 14a | 3,416.6 | 4,240.5 | 5,024.1 | 6,610.8 | 6,853.9 | 7,619.3 | 9,931.4 | 11,418.5 | 13,232.8 | 14,410.5 | 16,876.1 | 18,776.3 |
| Liabs. to Other Depository Corps..... | 14c | 12,303.8 | 12,061.8 | 13,074.3 | 12,115.0 | 13,981.7 | 19,841.1 | 24,382.1 | 25,074.0 | 22,714.9 | 26,892.9 | 31,719.8 | 37,012.4 |
| Liabilities to Other Sectors............. | 14d | 1.1 | 2.9 | 1.8 | 2.4 | .4 | .5 | .2 | .2 | .4 | .2 | .2 | .3 |
| Other Liabs. to Other Dep. Corps..... | 14n | 740.4 | 934.5 | 13.3 | 14.5 | 9.5 | 11.1 | .1 | .3 | .4 | .2 | .1 | 1.1 |
| Dep. & Sec. Excl. f/Monetary Base.... | 14o | 88.3 | .1 | .6 | 34.0 | 234.4 | .8 | .7 | 1.0 | 1.0 | 1.1 | 1.5 | 1.1 |
| Deposits Included in Broad Money. | 15 | — | — | — | — | — | — | — | — | — | — | — | — |
| Sec.Ot.th.Shares Incl.in Brd. Money | 16a | — | — | — | — | — | — | — | — | — | — | — | — |
| Deposits Excl. from Broad Money... | 16b | .1 | .1 | .6 | .6 | 1.0 | .8 | .7 | 1.0 | 1.0 | 1.1 | 1.5 | 1.1 |
| Sec.Ot.th.Shares Excl.f/Brd.Money.. | 16s | 88.2 | — | — | 33.4 | 233.4 | — | — | — | — | — | — | — |
| Loans......................................... | 16l | — | — | — | — | — | — | — | — | — | — | — | — |
| Financial Derivatives....................... | 16m | — | — | — | — | — | — | — | — | — | — | — | — |
| Shares and Other Equity.................. | 17a | 31.7 | 31.7 | 31.7 | 31.7 | −1,404.1 | 1,308.9 | −1,388.2 | −1,460.8 | −2,366.5 | −2,867.0 | −5,295.6 | −556.6 |
| Other Items (Net)............................ | 17r | 5,877.3 | 5,753.6 | 6,041.6 | 6,359.2 | 6,642.9 | 6,840.6 | 6,951.9 | 6,929.9 | 6,897.8 | 6,937.5 | 8,409.3 | 8,797.0 |
| Memo Item: | | | | | | | | | | | | | |
| Total Assets.................................. | 10ra | 61,381.6 | 64,541.1 | 66,774.3 | 73,189.6 | 76,390.7 | 89,577.5 | 95,789.1 | 101,827.5 | 104,976.6 | 111,844.1 | 119,336.9 | 128,857.3 |

# Nicaragua 278

| | | 2004 | 2005 | 2006 | 2007 | 2008 | 2009 | 2010 | 2011 | 2012 | 2013 | 2014 | 2015 |
|---|---|---|---|---|---|---|---|---|---|---|---|---|---|
| **Other Depository Corporations** | | | | | | *Millions of Córdobas: End of Period* | | | | | | | |
| Net Foreign Assets.......................... | 21n | 118.5 | −1,050.7 | −4,257.4 | −5,282.7 | −5,677.6 | −1,530.4 | 5,567.3 | 9,628.4 | 5,740.0 | 4,685.1 | 3,822.0 | −7,349.1 |
| Claims on Nonresidents................. | 21 | 1,922.4 | 2,422.3 | 2,254.2 | 2,460.1 | 3,505.1 | 8,612.3 | 14,492.7 | 16,781.1 | 13,625.8 | 13,815.5 | 16,913.2 | 12,451.9 |
| Liabilities to Nonresidents............. | 26c | 1,803.9 | 3,472.9 | 6,511.6 | 7,742.8 | 9,182.7 | 10,142.7 | 8,925.4 | 7,152.7 | 7,885.8 | 9,130.5 | 13,091.2 | 19,801.0 |
| Claims on Central Bank.................. | 20 | 12,575.8 | 12,361.1 | 13,677.8 | 13,155.3 | 15,075.0 | 20,998.2 | 24,613.8 | 26,703.0 | 24,635.5 | 28,406.3 | 34,854.7 | 41,434.3 |
| Currency............................ | 20a | 313.3 | 432.5 | 622.8 | 1,073.6 | 1,355.1 | 1,461.6 | 1,706.6 | 1,732.1 | 2,358.4 | 2,887.4 | 3,557.5 | 4,078.6 |
| Reserve Deposits and Securities..... | 20b | 5,849.6 | 6,461.6 | 8,928.7 | 8,567.7 | 9,836.0 | 14,168.3 | 16,658.4 | 18,869.9 | 16,272.8 | 18,651.2 | 23,498.3 | 29,324.5 |
| Other Claims.............................. | 20n | 6,412.9 | 5,467.0 | 4,126.3 | 3,514.0 | 3,883.9 | 5,368.4 | 6,248.8 | 6,101.1 | 6,004.3 | 6,867.7 | 7,798.9 | 8,031.2 |
| Net Claims on Central Government.. | 22an | 1,128.4 | 157.5 | −1,277.0 | −2,268.4 | −2,596.3 | −1,700.8 | 45.2 | −333.7 | 971.0 | 649.5 | −150.9 | −242.7 |
| Claims on Central Government...... | 22a | 4,654.6 | 5,274.9 | 5,159.9 | 5,273.6 | 4,178.6 | 4,194.5 | 6,572.8 | 7,672.2 | 7,004.2 | 8,239.8 | 7,518.8 | 7,651.3 |
| Liabilities to Central Government... | 26d | 3,526.2 | 5,117.4 | 6,437.0 | 7,542.1 | 6,774.9 | 5,895.2 | 6,527.6 | 8,005.9 | 6,033.2 | 7,590.3 | 7,669.7 | 7,894.0 |
| Claims on Other Sectors.................. | 22s | 18,873.7 | 24,614.0 | 32,102.2 | 42,188.7 | 46,944.6 | 43,532.7 | 46,032.5 | 53,179.8 | 66,783.1 | 80,722.5 | 97,284.7 | 121,163.3 |
| Claims on Other Financial Corps.... | 22g | 198.7 | 177.3 | 177.7 | 189.7 | 21.7 | .6 | 106.6 | 60.3 | 25.4 | 1.9 | 1.8 | 978.4 |
| Claims on State & Local Govts....... | 22b | — | 7.7 | 51.9 | 34.9 | 10.2 | 86.1 | 124.2 | 113.8 | 37.3 | 564.9 | 716.0 | 714.0 |
| Claims on Public Nonfin. Corps..... | 22c | 599.2 | 576.0 | 513.9 | 712.2 | 578.3 | 603.1 | 413.1 | 513.7 | 401.5 | 408.8 | 434.3 | 681.4 |
| Claims on Private Sector.............. | 22d | 18,075.7 | 23,853.0 | 31,358.7 | 41,252.1 | 46,334.4 | 42,842.9 | 45,388.6 | 52,492.0 | 66,318.8 | 79,746.8 | 96,132.6 | 118,789.5 |
| Liabilities to Central Bank............... | 26g | 290.3 | 332.8 | 142.6 | 591.6 | 582.9 | 686.0 | 769.3 | 923.0 | 660.8 | 697.5 | 786.4 | 930.2 |
| Transf.Dep.Included in Broad Money | 24 | 3,972.5 | 4,876.9 | 5,751.5 | 7,839.9 | 10,710.7 | 13,966.9 | 18,674.3 | 17,622.0 | 22,001.5 | 27,818.9 | 31,066.4 | 39,177.5 |
| Other Dep.Included in Broad Money. | 25 | 23,311.4 | 24,672.3 | 26,014.5 | 29,473.3 | 29,784.0 | 32,463.8 | 37,087.5 | 44,754.4 | 50,279.9 | 59,047.6 | 69,187.0 | 81,232.2 |
| Sec.Ot.th.Shares Incl.in Brd. Money.. | 26a | | | | | | | | | | | | |
| Deposits Excl. from Broad Money..... | 26b | 432.2 | 518.3 | 531.2 | 643.5 | 1,126.1 | 2,051.7 | 3,495.3 | 3,974.8 | 4,538.1 | 5,482.4 | 5,745.9 | 7,418.4 |
| Sec.Ot.th.Shares Excl.f/Brd.Money.... | 26s | — | — | — | — | — | — | — | — | — | — | — | — |
| Loans............................................ | 26l | 1,347.4 | 1,508.8 | 1,725.0 | 1,869.5 | 2,109.1 | 1,973.1 | 1,074.1 | 736.0 | 631.8 | 495.2 | 537.6 | 452.8 |
| Financial Derivatives...................... | 26m | — | — | — | — | — | — | — | — | — | — | — | 431.0 |
| Insurance Technical Reserves........... | 26r | — | — | — | — | — | — | — | — | — | — | — | — |
| Shares and Other Equity.................. | 27a | 3,555.0 | 4,191.0 | 5,345.6 | 6,375.3 | 7,598.9 | 8,040.7 | 8,641.7 | 9,685.4 | 11,754.9 | 13,953.8 | 16,989.1 | 20,515.7 |
| Other Items (Net)............................ | 27r | −212.5 | −18.2 | 735.1 | 999.7 | 1,833.9 | 2,117.6 | 6,516.7 | 11,482.0 | 8,262.7 | 6,967.9 | 11,498.2 | 4,848.2 |
| Memo Item: | | | | | | | | | | | | | |
| Total Assets.................................... | 20ra | 40,809.7 | 47,645.4 | 56,320.5 | 67,328.4 | 75,232.0 | 84,119.3 | 98,169.2 | 111,663.4 | 118,198.4 | 137,936.0 | 164,366.2 | 192,437.1 |
| **Depository Corporations** | | | | | | *Millions of Córdobas: End of Period* | | | | | | | |
| Net Foreign Assets.......................... | 31n | −17,863.7 | −18,887.7 | −19,012.4 | −18,320.3 | −19,829.1 | −8,711.0 | 2,362.3 | 8,028.0 | 3,825.2 | 5,361.2 | 15,783.6 | 19,062.3 |
| Claims on Nonresidents................ | 31 | 16,306.0 | 18,313.1 | 21,514.9 | 26,098.9 | 28,798.9 | 44,204.2 | 56,556.0 | 62,987.3 | 61,776.9 | 67,383.5 | 80,107.0 | 84,981.5 |
| Liabilities to Nonresidents............. | 36c | 34,169.8 | 37,200.9 | 40,527.4 | 44,419.2 | 48,628.0 | 52,915.2 | 54,193.7 | 54,959.3 | 57,951.7 | 62,022.3 | 64,323.3 | 65,919.2 |
| Domestic Claims............................ | 32 | 60,443.2 | 65,633.0 | 69,767.5 | 78,125.4 | 84,818.3 | 84,634.8 | 89,161.1 | 96,409.5 | 110,149.7 | 126,071.2 | 136,883.6 | 158,540.9 |
| Net Claims on Central Government | 32an | 41,252.4 | 40,684.8 | 37,316.6 | 35,585.0 | 37,513.1 | 40,734.4 | 42,760.8 | 42,870.1 | 43,005.0 | 44,975.5 | 39,121.3 | 36,922.4 |
| Claims on Central Government...... | 32a | 51,033.0 | 53,258.5 | 51,984.3 | 54,116.3 | 54,723.2 | 57,606.3 | 59,712.1 | 62,529.2 | 63,090.5 | 65,746.6 | 62,803.1 | 63,145.7 |
| Liabilities to Central Government. | 36d | 9,780.6 | 12,573.7 | 14,667.7 | 18,531.3 | 17,210.1 | 16,871.8 | 16,951.3 | 19,659.1 | 20,085.5 | 20,771.1 | 23,681.8 | 26,223.3 |
| Claims on Other Sectors................ | 32s | 19,190.7 | 24,948.2 | 32,450.9 | 42,540.4 | 47,305.2 | 43,900.3 | 46,400.3 | 53,539.4 | 67,144.7 | 81,095.7 | 97,762.2 | 121,618.5 |
| Claims on Other Financial Corps.. | 32g | 199.6 | 178.2 | 178.6 | 190.5 | 22.6 | 1.5 | 107.4 | 61.0 | 26.2 | 2.7 | 2.6 | 979.2 |
| Claims on State & Local Govts....... | 32b | — | 7.7 | 51.9 | 34.9 | 10.2 | 86.1 | 124.2 | 113.8 | 37.3 | 564.9 | 716.0 | 714.0 |
| Claims on Public Nonfin. Corps..... | 32c | 859.2 | 836.1 | 773.9 | 972.2 | 838.3 | 863.1 | 673.2 | 773.8 | 661.5 | 668.9 | 803.6 | 1,050.7 |
| Claims on Private Sector............. | 32d | 18,131.9 | 23,926.3 | 31,446.5 | 41,342.8 | 46,434.1 | 42,949.6 | 45,495.5 | 52,590.8 | 66,419.6 | 79,859.2 | 96,240.0 | 118,874.6 |
| Broad Money Liabilities................... | 35l | 30,388.3 | 33,360.1 | 36,169.1 | 42,852.8 | 45,993.9 | 52,589.0 | 63,986.8 | 72,062.9 | 83,156.2 | 98,389.8 | 113,572.1 | 135,107.6 |
| Currency Outside Depository Corps | 34a | 3,103.3 | 3,808.0 | 4,401.3 | 5,537.2 | 5,498.8 | 6,157.7 | 8,224.8 | 9,686.4 | 10,874.4 | 11,523.1 | 13,318.5 | 14,697.6 |
| Transferable Deposits.................... | 34 | 3,973.5 | 4,879.4 | 5,753.3 | 7,842.3 | 10,711.1 | 13,967.4 | 18,674.5 | 17,622.2 | 22,001.9 | 27,819.1 | 31,066.6 | 39,177.8 |
| Other Deposits............................ | 35 | 23,311.4 | 24,672.3 | 26,014.5 | 29,473.3 | 29,784.0 | 32,463.8 | 37,087.5 | 44,754.4 | 50,279.9 | 59,047.6 | 69,187.0 | 81,232.2 |
| Securities Other than Shares........... | 36a | | | | | | | | | | | | |
| Deposits Excl. from Broad Money..... | 36b | 432.3 | 518.3 | 531.8 | 644.1 | 1,127.1 | 2,052.5 | 3,496.0 | 3,975.8 | 4,539.1 | 5,483.5 | 5,747.3 | 7,419.5 |
| Sec.Ot.th.Shares Excl.f/Brd.Money... | 36s | 88.2 | | | 33.4 | 233.4 | | | | | | | |
| Loans............................................ | 36l | 1,347.4 | 1,508.8 | 1,725.0 | 1,869.5 | 2,109.1 | 1,973.1 | 1,074.1 | 736.0 | 631.8 | 495.2 | 537.6 | 452.8 |
| Financial Derivatives...................... | 36m | — | — | — | — | — | — | — | — | — | — | — | 431.0 |
| Insurance Technical Reserves........... | 36r | | | | | | | | | | | | |
| Shares and Other Equity.................. | 37a | 3,586.7 | 4,222.7 | 5,377.4 | 6,407.1 | 6,194.8 | 9,349.6 | 7,253.5 | 8,224.6 | 9,388.5 | 11,086.8 | 11,693.5 | 19,959.0 |
| Other Items (Net)............................ | 37r | 6,736.5 | 7,135.3 | 6,951.8 | 7,998.2 | 9,330.9 | 9,959.7 | 15,712.9 | 19,438.3 | 16,259.4 | 15,977.2 | 21,116.6 | 14,233.2 |
| Broad Money Liabs., Seasonally Adj. | 35l.b | 30,669.0 | 33,604.0 | 36,326.6 | 42,921.9 | 45,917.9 | 52,449.9 | 63,800.7 | 71,935.3 | 83,002.3 | 98,202.6 | 113,241.2 | 134,633.5 |
| **Other Financial Corporations** | | | | | | *Millions of Córdobas: End of Period* | | | | | | | |
| Net Foreign Assets.......................... | 41n | −173.1 | −338.5 | −534.2 | −3,162.7 | −3,513.4 | −3,372.2 | −3,013.4 | −3,023.0 | −2,515.9 | −3,626.7 | −4,237.8 | −4,747.3 |
| Claims on Nonresidents................ | 41 | | | 26.0 | 16.4 | 298.7 | 293.1 | 278.6 | 177.1 | 205.2 | 232.6 | 258.0 | 221.0 |
| Liabilities to Nonresidents............. | 46c | 173.1 | 338.6 | 560.3 | 3,179.0 | 3,812.1 | 3,665.4 | 3,292.0 | 3,200.2 | 2,721.0 | 3,859.3 | 4,495.8 | 4,968.3 |
| Claims on Depository Corporations.. | 40 | 1,389.6 | 1,635.8 | 1,935.5 | 2,745.0 | 4,092.5 | 4,673.9 | 4,902.0 | 5,414.7 | 6,468.1 | 7,653.3 | 7,930.0 | 8,670.8 |
| Net Claims on Central Government.. | 42an | −245.6 | −258.5 | −271.3 | −284.5 | 266.4 | 369.9 | 338.7 | 320.2 | −930.6 | −941.9 | −445.0 | −73.2 |
| Claims on Central Government...... | 42a | | | | | 635.4 | 764.2 | 737.7 | 719.7 | 594.6 | 901.2 | 1,200.7 | 1,556.2 |
| Liabilities to Central Government... | 46d | 245.6 | 258.5 | 271.3 | 284.5 | 369.0 | 394.4 | 399.0 | 399.4 | 1,525.2 | 1,843.0 | 1,645.6 | 1,629.5 |
| Claims on Other Sectors.................. | 42s | — | — | — | 3,799.6 | 5,235.3 | 5,095.3 | 4,616.6 | 4,839.9 | 4,818.5 | 6,682.7 | 8,189.0 | 9,325.0 |
| Claims on State & Local Govts....... | 42b | — | — | — | — | — | — | — | — | — | — | — | — |
| Claims on Public Nonfin. Corps..... | 42c | — | — | — | — | — | — | — | — | — | — | — | — |
| Claims on Private Sector.............. | 42d | — | — | — | 3,799.6 | 5,235.3 | 5,095.3 | 4,616.6 | 4,839.9 | 4,818.5 | 6,682.7 | 8,189.0 | 9,325.0 |
| Deposits......................................... | 46b | — | — | — | — | 36.2 | 30.4 | 30.6 | 46.4 | 53.1 | 93.6 | 130.7 | 227.7 |
| Securities Other than Shares............ | 46s | — | — | — | — | — | — | — | — | — | — | — | — |
| Loans............................................ | 46l | — | — | — | — | — | 9.0 | 17.9 | 15.2 | 1.4 | 130.5 | 19.8 | — |
| Financial Derivatives...................... | 46m | — | — | — | — | — | — | — | — | — | — | — | — |
| Insurance Technical Reserves........... | 46r | — | — | — | — | 1,640.1 | 1,698.2 | 1,949.9 | 2,217.5 | 2,599.3 | 3,042.5 | 3,520.6 | 3,988.8 |
| Shares and Other Equity.................. | 47a | 960.1 | 1,026.6 | 1,110.3 | 2,280.0 | 3,142.0 | 3,454.1 | 3,844.0 | 4,342.3 | 4,656.3 | 5,655.9 | 6,762.7 | 7,715.3 |
| Other Items (Net)............................ | 47r | 10.8 | 12.2 | 19.7 | 817.5 | 1,262.6 | 1,575.2 | 1,001.4 | 930.3 | 530.1 | 844.9 | 1,002.4 | 1,243.6 |
| Memo Item: | | | | | | | | | | | | | |
| Total Assets.................................... | 40ra | 1,488.6 | 1,733.8 | 2,041.7 | 6,964.7 | 10,999.4 | 11,740.0 | 11,718.8 | 12,246.8 | 13,288.4 | 16,612.9 | 18,832.1 | 21,147.1 |

# Nicaragua   278

| | | 2004 | 2005 | 2006 | 2007 | 2008 | 2009 | 2010 | 2011 | 2012 | 2013 | 2014 | 2015 |
|---|---|---|---|---|---|---|---|---|---|---|---|---|---|
| **Financial Corporations** | | *Millions of Córdobas: End of Period* | | | | | | | | | | | |
| Net Foreign Assets............................ | 51n | −18,036.8 | −19,226.3 | −19,546.7 | −21,482.9 | −23,342.5 | −12,083.2 | −651.1 | 5,005.0 | 1,309.4 | 1,734.5 | 11,545.8 | 14,315.0 |
| Claims on Nonresidents................ | 51 | 16,306.1 | 18,313.2 | 21,541.0 | 26,115.3 | 29,097.6 | 44,497.3 | 56,834.6 | 63,164.5 | 61,982.1 | 67,616.1 | 80,365.0 | 85,202.5 |
| Liabilities to Nonresidents.............. | 56c | 34,342.9 | 37,539.4 | 41,087.6 | 47,598.2 | 52,440.1 | 56,580.5 | 57,485.7 | 58,159.4 | 60,672.7 | 65,881.6 | 68,819.2 | 70,887.4 |
| Domestic Claims............................. | 52 | 59,998.0 | 65,196.3 | 69,317.6 | 81,450.0 | 90,297.5 | 90,098.4 | 94,009.0 | 101,508.6 | 114,011.4 | 131,809.3 | 144,625.0 | 166,813.4 |
| Net Claims on Central Government | 52an | 41,006.9 | 40,426.3 | 37,045.3 | 35,300.5 | 37,779.5 | 41,104.3 | 43,099.5 | 43,190.3 | 42,074.4 | 44,033.6 | 38,676.4 | 36,849.1 |
| Claims on Central Government.... | 52a | 51,033.0 | 53,258.5 | 51,984.3 | 54,116.3 | 55,358.6 | 58,370.5 | 60,449.7 | 63,248.8 | 63,685.1 | 66,647.8 | 64,003.8 | 64,701.9 |
| Liabilities to Central Government. | 56d | 10,026.2 | 12,832.2 | 14,939.0 | 18,815.8 | 17,579.1 | 17,266.2 | 17,350.3 | 20,058.5 | 21,610.7 | 22,614.2 | 25,327.4 | 27,852.8 |
| Claims on Other Sectors................ | 52s | 18,991.1 | 24,770.1 | 32,272.3 | 46,149.5 | 52,517.9 | 48,994.1 | 50,909.5 | 58,318.3 | 71,937.0 | 87,775.7 | 105,948.6 | 129,964.3 |
| Claims on State & Local Govts..... | 52b | — | 7.7 | 51.9 | 34.9 | 10.2 | 86.1 | 124.2 | 113.8 | 37.3 | 564.9 | 716.0 | 714.0 |
| Claims on Pub. Nonfin. Corps...... | 52c | 859.2 | 836.1 | 773.9 | 972.2 | 838.3 | 863.1 | 673.2 | 773.8 | 661.5 | 668.9 | 803.6 | 1,050.7 |
| Claims on Private Sector................ | 52d | 18,131.9 | 23,926.3 | 31,446.5 | 45,142.4 | 51,669.4 | 48,044.9 | 50,112.1 | 57,430.7 | 71,238.1 | 86,541.9 | 104,429.0 | 128,199.6 |
| Currency Outside Fin. Corporations.. | 54a | 3,103.3 | 3,808.0 | 4,401.3 | 5,442.2 | 5,434.4 | 6,093.2 | 8,171.3 | 9,633.9 | 10,819.9 | 11,404.1 | 13,197.4 | 14,599.6 |
| Deposits........................................... | 55l | 27,285.0 | 29,552.1 | 31,767.8 | 37,315.6 | 40,531.3 | 46,461.7 | 55,792.6 | 62,423.0 | 72,334.9 | 86,960.3 | 100,384.3 | 120,637.6 |
| Securities Other than Shares............ | 56a | 88.2 | — | — | — | — | — | — | — | — | — | — | — |
| Loans............................................... | 56l | — | — | — | — | — | — | — | — | — | — | — | — |
| Financial Derivatives........................ | 56m | — | — | — | — | — | — | — | — | — | — | — | 431.0 |
| Insurance Technical Reserves........... | 56r | — | — | — | — | 1,640.1 | 1,698.2 | 1,949.9 | 2,217.5 | 2,599.3 | 3,042.5 | 3,520.6 | 3,988.8 |
| Shares and Other Equity.................. | 57a | 4,546.8 | 5,249.2 | 6,487.6 | 8,687.0 | 9,336.8 | 12,803.7 | 11,097.5 | 12,566.9 | 14,044.7 | 16,742.7 | 18,456.2 | 27,674.3 |
| Other Items (Net)............................. | 57r | 6,937.9 | 7,360.7 | 7,114.2 | 8,522.2 | 10,012.3 | 10,958.5 | 16,346.7 | 19,672.3 | 15,522.0 | 15,394.3 | 20,612.4 | 13,797.1 |
| **Monetary Aggregates** | | *Millions of Córdobas: End of Period* | | | | | | | | | | | |
| Broad Money.................................... | 59m | 30,388.3 | 33,360.1 | 36,169.1 | 42,852.8 | 45,993.9 | 52,589.0 | 63,986.8 | 72,062.9 | 83,156.2 | 98,389.8 | 113,572.1 | 135,107.6 |
| o/w:Currency Issued by Cent.Govt | 59m.a | — | — | — | — | — | — | — | — | — | — | — | — |
| o/w: Dep.in Nonfin. Corporations. | 59m.b | — | — | — | — | — | — | — | — | — | — | — | — |
| o/w:Secs. Issued by Central Govt.. | 59m.c | — | — | — | — | — | — | — | — | — | — | — | — |
| Money (National Definitions) | | | | | | | | | | | | | |
| Base Money.................................. | 19ma | 5,345.5 | 6,338.1 | 8,121.8 | 9,847.8 | 10,369.5 | 12,425.7 | 14,549.8 | 18,278.0 | 19,174.4 | 20,466.9 | 23,502.5 | 29,661.4 |
| M1................................................ | 59ma | 5,656.2 | 6,827.9 | 8,019.5 | 9,910.5 | 10,192.6 | 11,295.9 | 14,522.9 | 16,306.1 | 19,020.1 | 21,449.8 | 25,102.7 | 30,524.9 |
| M1A.............................................. | 59maa | 6,074.5 | 7,668.3 | 8,832.7 | 10,972.0 | 11,980.9 | 13,610.9 | 15,968.3 | 18,523.4 | 21,133.8 | 23,758.7 | 27,789.6 | 34,085.4 |
| M2................................................ | 59mb | 10,236.9 | 11,003.5 | 12,632.5 | 14,962.7 | 14,688.3 | 16,080.1 | 20,864.2 | 25,282.1 | 27,397.1 | 31,169.7 | 36,055.2 | 42,445.9 |
| M2A.............................................. | 59mba | 12,766.2 | 15,033.6 | 17,743.0 | 20,722.7 | 20,811.6 | 21,597.6 | 26,946.1 | 33,627.7 | 33,091.7 | 37,363.9 | 41,908.8 | 49,418.6 |
| M3................................................ | 59mc | 30,598.4 | 33,656.5 | 36,660.1 | 43,274.3 | 46,250.3 | 53,855.3 | 69,339.7 | 78,826.8 | 87,845.0 | 99,316.5 | 118,182.4 | 135,352.2 |
| M3A.............................................. | 59mca | 34,259.2 | 39,019.3 | 43,177.2 | 50,792.9 | 54,202.5 | 62,616.5 | 78,614.6 | 90,670.0 | 97,397.9 | 110,101.1 | 130,651.0 | 148,315.4 |
| **Interest Rates** | | *Percent Per Annum* | | | | | | | | | | | |
| Savings Rate.................................... | 60k | 3.43 | 3.34 | 3.22 | 3.03 | 2.90 | 2.77 | 1.96 | 1.14 | 1.15 | 1.05 | 1.07 | 1.10 |
| Savings Rate (Fgn. Currency)............ | 60k.f | 2.65 | 2.53 | 2.36 | 2.24 | 2.07 | 1.91 | 1.47 | 1.08 | 1.01 | .85 | .79 | .98 |
| Deposit Rate.................................... | 60l | 4.72 | 4.03 | 4.87 | 6.08 | 6.57 | 6.01 | 2.99 | 1.85 | 1.00 | 1.01 | 1.05 | 1.05 |
| Deposit Rate (Fgn. Currency)............ | 60l.f | 3.91 | 3.39 | 4.21 | 5.27 | 5.77 | 4.82 | 2.47 | 1.67 | .84 | 1.05 | 1.24 | .93 |
| Lending Rate.................................... | 60p | 13.49 | 12.10 | 11.58 | 13.04 | 13.17 | 14.04 | 13.32 | 10.54 | 11.99 | 14.98 | 13.54 | 12.05 |
| Lending Rate (Fgn. Currency).......... | 60p.f | 10.94 | 10.32 | 10.45 | 10.96 | 11.00 | 12.83 | 10.77 | 9.41 | 8.65 | 8.63 | 8.72 | 8.71 |
| **Prices, Production, Labor** | | *Index Numbers (2010=100): Period Averages* | | | | | | | | | | | |
| Consumer Prices.............................. | 64 | 57.4 | 62.9 | 68.7 | 76.3 | 91.5 | 94.8 | 100.0 | 108.1 | 115.9 | 124.1 | 131.6 | 136.9 |
| Industrial Production........................ | 66 | 83.4 | 84.8 | 88.8 | 94.0 | 91.4 | 92.8 | 100.0 | 106.1 | 109.2 | 109.1 | .... | .... |
| | | *Number in Thousands: Period Averages* | | | | | | | | | | | |
| Labor Force...................................... | 67d | .... | .... | .... | 2,273 | 2,308 | 2,283 | 2,812 | 2,997 | .... | .... | .... | .... |
| Employment..................................... | 67e | .... | .... | .... | 2,138 | 2,168 | 2,097 | 2,592 | 2,807 | .... | .... | .... | .... |
| Unemployment................................ | 67c | .... | .... | .... | 135 | 140 | 186 | 220 | 190 | .... | .... | .... | .... |
| Unemployment Rate (%)................. | 67r | .... | .... | .... | 5.9 | 6.1 | 8.2 | 7.9 | 6.3 | .... | .... | .... | .... |
| **Intl. Transactions & Positions** | | *Millions of US Dollars* | | | | | | | | | | | |
| Exports............................................ | 70..d | 755.6 | 857.9 | 1,027.4 | 1,193.8 | 1,472.7 | 1,392.9 | 1,845.2 | 2,294.2 | 2,643.5 | 2,407.8 | 2,625.8 | 2,422.8 |
| Imports, c.i.f.................................... | 71..d | 2,212.3 | 2,595.1 | 3,000.3 | 3,579.2 | 4,299.5 | 3,438.3 | 4,228.9 | 5,180.4 | 5,847.4 | 5,646.9 | 5,873.5 | 5,899.1 |
| Imports, f.o.b................................... | 71.vd | 2,022.0 | 2,378.1 | 2,751.9 | 3,266.8 | 3,907.1 | 3,224.5 | 3,923.2 | 4,841.1 | 5,415.2 | 5,194.9 | 5,450.9 | 5,429.8 |

| Balance of Payments | | 2004 | 2005 | 2006 | 2007 | 2008 | 2009 | 2010 | 2011 | 2012 | 2013 | 2014 | 2015 |
|---|---|---|---|---|---|---|---|---|---|---|---|---|---|
| | | | | | | *Millions of US Dollars* | | | | | | | |
| A. Current Account* | 109bx | −687.4 | † −783.6 | −842.3 | −1,168.4 | −1,508.0 | −728.6 | −790.5 | −1,177.7 | −1,098.3 | −1,180.1 | −913.4 | −1,045.2 |
| Goods, credit (exports) | 1a9cx | 772.3 | † 880.4 | 1,515.3 | 1,753.9 | 1,957.7 | 1,927.2 | 2,425.0 | 3,036.4 | 3,491.1 | 3,325.9 | 3,621.8 | 3,341.4 |
| Goods, debit (imports) | 1a9dx | 2,027.7 | † 2,404.6 | 3,145.0 | 3,759.4 | 4,417.2 | 3,679.2 | 4,350.1 | 5,462.6 | 5,938.1 | 5,801.5 | 6,023.5 | 6,082.6 |
| Balance on goods | 1a9bx | −1,255.4 | † −1,524.2 | −1,629.7 | −2,005.5 | −2,459.5 | −1,752.0 | −1,925.1 | −2,426.2 | −2,447.0 | −2,475.6 | −2,401.7 | −2,741.2 |
| Services, credit (exports) | 1b9cx | 452.8 | † 530.7 | 538.7 | 665.6 | 877.9 | 894.0 | 935.3 | 1,133.5 | 1,244.1 | 1,325.0 | 1,388.4 | 1,437.1 |
| Services, debit (imports) | 1b9dx | 409.0 | † 448.2 | 535.7 | 691.3 | 838.1 | 731.9 | 712.7 | 842.4 | 898.6 | 1,071.0 | 1,036.0 | 947.9 |
| Balance on Goods & Services | 1z9bx | −1,211.6 | † −1,441.7 | −1,626.7 | −2,031.2 | −2,419.7 | −1,589.8 | −1,702.5 | −2,135.1 | −2,101.5 | −2,221.6 | −2,049.3 | −2,252.0 |
| Primary income: credit | 1c9cx | 9.4 | † 22.7 | 42.6 | 49.6 | 40.4 | 17.3 | 18.2 | 21.6 | 25.2 | 22.9 | 20.6 | 23.5 |
| Primary income: debit | 1c9dx | 240.2 | † 222.0 | 261.5 | 261.4 | 263.9 | 274.5 | 266.8 | 293.8 | 331.8 | 350.4 | 334.6 | 365.1 |
| Balance on gds, serv. & prim. inc. | 1y9bx | −1,442.4 | † −1,641.0 | −1,845.6 | −2,243.0 | −2,643.2 | −1,847.0 | −1,951.0 | −2,407.3 | −2,408.1 | −2,549.1 | −2,363.3 | −2,593.6 |
| Secondary income: credit | 1d9ca | 755.0 | † 857.4 | 1,010.4 | 1,080.2 | 1,145.7 | 1,127.9 | 1,170.9 | 1,240.0 | 1,320.5 | 1,380.1 | 1,460.7 | 1,559.9 |
| Secondary income: debit | 1d9da | — | .... | 7.1 | 5.6 | 10.5 | 9.5 | 10.3 | 10.4 | 10.7 | 11.1 | 10.8 | 11.5 |
| B. Capital Account* | 209ba | 294.2 | † 479.1 | 1,590.2 | 2,930.4 | 404.0 | 532.8 | 264.1 | 251.5 | 238.8 | 228.6 | 298.3 | 363.2 |
| Capital account: credit | 209ca | 294.2 | † 479.1 | 1,590.2 | 2,930.4 | 404.0 | 532.8 | 264.1 | 251.5 | 238.8 | 228.6 | 298.3 | 363.2 |
| Capital account: debit | 209da | — | .... | .... | .... | .... | .... | .... | .... | .... | .... | .... | .... |
| Balance on current & capital acct. | 129ba | −393.2 | † −304.5 | 747.9 | 1,762.0 | −1,104.0 | −195.8 | −526.4 | −926.2 | −859.5 | −951.5 | −615.1 | −682.0 |
| C. Financial Account* | 309na | −363.8 | † −403.1 | 320.4 | 1,420.3 | −1,044.6 | −647.1 | −550.4 | −1,514.8 | −1,820.8 | −1,392.6 | −1,316.7 | −1,291.5 |
| Direct investment: assets | 3a9aa | — | .... | 21.0 | 15.3 | 18.9 | −29.1 | 16.4 | 7.7 | 64.7 | 116.0 | 79.9 | 50.5 |
| Equity & investment fund shares.. | 3aaaa | — | .... | 21.0 | 15.3 | 18.9 | −29.1 | 16.4 | 7.7 | 64.7 | 116.0 | 79.9 | 50.5 |
| Debt instruments | 3abaa | — | .... | .... | .... | .... | .... | .... | .... | .... | .... | .... | .... |
| Direct investment: liabilities | 3a9la | 250.0 | † 241.1 | 286.8 | 381.7 | 627.3 | 433.9 | 489.9 | 936.3 | 767.7 | 815.5 | 883.5 | 835.0 |
| Equity & investment fund shares . | 3aala | 250.0 | † 241.1 | 286.8 | 381.7 | 627.3 | 433.9 | 489.9 | 936.3 | 767.7 | 815.5 | 883.5 | 835.0 |
| Debt instruments | 3abla | | | .... | .... | .... | .... | .... | .... | .... | .... | .... | .... |
| Portfolio investment: assets | 3b9aa | — | .... | — | — | 2.5 | 8.4 | 66.2 | 206.3 | −63.6 | −129.9 | −33.7 | 3.2 |
| Equity & investment fund shares | 3baaa | — | .... | .... | .... | .... | .... | .... | .... | .... | .... | .... | .... |
| Debt securities | 3bbaa | — | .... | — | — | 2.5 | 8.4 | 66.2 | 206.3 | −63.6 | −129.9 | −33.7 | 3.2 |
| Portfolio investment: liabilities | 3b9la | — | .... | — | — | — | −20.8 | −20.0 | −12.9 | −6.4 | −3.2 | 30.4 | −3.9 |
| Equity & investment fund shares . | 3bala | — | .... | — | — | — | — | — | — | −.3 | — | — | .... |
| Debt securities | 3bbla | — | .... | — | — | — | −20.8 | −20.0 | −12.9 | −6.1 | −3.2 | 30.4 | −3.9 |
| Fin. der.& empl.stk.ops.(ESOs): net. | 3c9na | | .... | .... | .... | .... | .... | .... | .... | .... | .... | .... | .... |
| Fin. der. & ESOs.: assets | 3c9aa | — | .... | .... | .... | .... | .... | .... | .... | .... | .... | .... | .... |
| Fin. der. & ESOs.: liabilities | 3c9la | — | .... | .... | .... | .... | .... | .... | .... | .... | .... | .... | .... |
| Other investment: assets | 3d9aa | −275.2 | † 180.4 | 79.5 | 88.3 | 257.9 | 275.0 | 349.0 | −268.6 | −105.7 | 160.3 | 91.2 | −122.6 |
| Other equity | 3daaa | | .... | .... | .... | .... | .... | .... | .... | .... | .... | .... | .... |
| Debt instruments | 3dzaa | −275.2 | † 180.4 | 79.5 | 88.3 | 257.9 | 275.0 | 349.0 | −268.6 | −105.7 | 160.3 | 91.2 | −122.6 |
| Other investment: liabilities | 3d9la | −161.4 | † 342.4 | −506.7 | −1,698.4 | 696.6 | 488.3 | 512.1 | 536.8 | 954.9 | 726.7 | 540.2 | 391.5 |
| Other equity | 3dala | | .... | .... | .... | .... | .... | .... | .... | .... | .... | .... | .... |
| Debt instruments | 3dzla | −161.4 | † 342.4 | −506.7 | −1,698.4 | 696.6 | 488.3 | 512.1 | 536.8 | 954.9 | 726.7 | 540.2 | 391.5 |
| Curr.+ cap.− finan. acct. balance | 4y9na | −29.4 | † 98.6 | 427.5 | 341.7 | −59.4 | 451.3 | 24.0 | 588.6 | 961.3 | 441.1 | 701.6 | 609.5 |
| D. Net Errors and Omissions | 409na | −405.4 | † −64.7 | −107.2 | −193.1 | 62.3 | −66.5 | 178.0 | −516.0 | −963.8 | −329.4 | −388.2 | −378.4 |
| E. Reserves and Related Items | 4z9na | −434.8 | † 34.0 | 320.3 | 148.6 | 2.9 | 384.7 | 202.0 | 72.6 | −2.5 | 111.7 | 313.4 | 231.2 |
| Reserve assets | 3e9aa | 159.9 | † 5.5 | 178.8 | 167.1 | 31.5 | 422.8 | 221.7 | 88.0 | −15.3 | 95.4 | 291.5 | 204.4 |
| Credit and loans from the IMF | 3dcla | 23.9 | † −28.4 | −141.5 | 18.5 | 28.6 | 38.1 | 19.7 | 15.4 | −12.8 | −16.3 | −21.9 | −26.8 |
| Exceptional financing | 409la | 570.9 | .... | .... | .... | .... | .... | .... | .... | .... | .... | .... | .... |

*Excludes components in group E

| International Investment Position | | | | | | *Millions of US Dollars* | | | | | | | |
|---|---|---|---|---|---|---|---|---|---|---|---|---|---|
| Assets | 809aa | 990.7 | † 1,286.6 | 1,626.5 | 1,912.1 | 2,223.7 | 2,878.9 | 3,524.2 | 3,546.6 | 3,430.3 | 3,671.5 | 4,074.7 | 4,213.5 |
| Direct investment | 8a9aa | .... | † 112.7 | 184.7 | 200.3 | 220.1 | 164.0 | 180.7 | 181.8 | 246.9 | 362.9 | 442.8 | 494.4 |
| Equity & investment fund shares.. | 8aaaa | .... | † 112.7 | 184.7 | 200.3 | 220.1 | 164.0 | 180.7 | 181.8 | 246.9 | 362.9 | 442.8 | 494.4 |
| Debt instruments | 8abaa | .... | .... | .... | .... | .... | .... | .... | .... | .... | .... | .... | .... |
| Portfolio investment | 8b9aa | .... | .... | — | — | 2.5 | 10.9 | 77.2 | 283.5 | 219.9 | 90.0 | 56.3 | 59.5 |
| Equity & investment fund shares.. | 8baaa | .... | .... | .... | .... | .... | .... | .... | .... | .... | .... | .... | .... |
| Debt securities | 8bbaa | .... | .... | — | — | 2.5 | 10.9 | 77.2 | 283.5 | 219.9 | 90.0 | 56.3 | 59.5 |
| Fin. der.(oth.than reserves) & ESOs | 8c9aa | .... | .... | .... | .... | .... | .... | .... | .... | .... | .... | .... | .... |
| Other investment | 8d9aa | 322.5 | † 500.1 | 582.2 | 679.7 | 938.8 | 1,215.9 | 1,559.4 | 1,288.5 | 1,185.6 | 1,344.6 | 1,428.4 | 1,306.9 |
| Other equity | 8daaa | .... | .... | .... | .... | .... | .... | .... | .... | .... | .... | .... | .... |
| Debt instruments | 8dzaa | 322.5 | † 500.1 | 582.2 | 679.7 | 938.8 | 1,215.9 | 1,559.4 | 1,288.5 | 1,185.6 | 1,344.6 | 1,428.4 | 1,306.9 |
| Reserve assets | 8e9aa | 668.2 | † 673.8 | 859.6 | 1,032.1 | 1,062.3 | 1,488.1 | 1,706.9 | 1,792.9 | 1,777.9 | 1,874.0 | 2,147.2 | 2,352.7 |
| Liabilities | 809la | 9,003.1 | † 9,204.1 | 8,017.2 | 7,656.1 | 8,805.6 | 10,552.2 | 11,616.4 | 13,222.5 | 14,966.0 | 16,524.7 | 17,899.2 | 19,062.8 |
| Direct investment | 8a9la | 2,219.9 | † 2,461.0 | 2,747.8 | 3,129.5 | 3,756.8 | 4,190.7 | 4,680.6 | 5,616.9 | 6,384.6 | 7,200.1 | 8,083.6 | 8,918.6 |
| Equity & investment fund shares.. | 8aala | 2,219.9 | † 2,461.0 | 2,747.8 | 3,129.5 | 3,756.8 | 4,190.7 | 4,680.6 | 5,616.9 | 6,384.6 | 7,200.1 | 8,083.6 | 8,918.6 |
| Debt instruments | 8abla | .... | .... | .... | .... | .... | .... | .... | .... | .... | .... | .... | .... |
| Portfolio investment | 8b9la | .... | .... | 108.8 | 108.8 | 108.8 | 88.0 | 68.1 | 56.7 | 50.5 | 49.0 | 79.8 | 74.8 |
| Equity & investment fund shares.. | 8bala | .... | .... | — | — | — | — | — | 1.5 | 1.3 | 2.1 | 2.5 | 1.4 |
| Debt securities | 8bbla | .... | .... | 108.8 | 108.8 | 108.8 | 88.0 | 68.1 | 55.2 | 49.2 | 46.9 | 77.3 | 73.4 |
| Fin. der.(oth.than reserves) & ESOs | 8c9la | .... | .... | .... | .... | .... | .... | .... | .... | .... | .... | .... | .... |
| Other investment | 8d9la | 6,783.2 | † 6,743.1 | 5,160.6 | 4,417.8 | 4,940.0 | 6,273.5 | 6,867.7 | 7,548.9 | 8,530.9 | 9,275.6 | 9,735.8 | 10,069.4 |
| Other equity | 8dala | .... | .... | .... | .... | .... | .... | .... | .... | .... | .... | .... | .... |
| Debt instruments | 8dzla | 6,783.2 | † 6,743.1 | 5,160.6 | 4,417.8 | 4,940.0 | 6,273.5 | 6,867.7 | 7,548.9 | 8,530.9 | 9,275.6 | 9,735.8 | 10,069.4 |

# Nicaragua   278

| | | 2004 | 2005 | 2006 | 2007 | 2008 | 2009 | 2010 | 2011 | 2012 | 2013 | 2014 | 2015 |
|---|---|---|---|---|---|---|---|---|---|---|---|---|---|
| **Government Finance** | | | | | | | | | | | | | |
| **Cash Flow Statement** | | | | | | | | | | | | | |
| **Budgetary Central Government** | | | | | | *Millions of Córdobas: Fiscal Year Ends December 31* | | | | | | | |
| Cash Receipts:Operating Activities... | c1 | 14,604.4 | 17,431.2 | 21,205.8 | 24,490.9 | 27,041.9 | 26,938.7 | 30,409.0 | 37,695.8 | 43,748.2 | 46,701.0 | 53,731.0 | .... |
| Taxes............................................ | c11 | 11,252.5 | 13,645.5 | 16,262.2 | 18,984.2 | 21,730.3 | 22,175.2 | 25,585.7 | 31,824.6 | 37,221.7 | 40,785.0 | 47,235.7 | .... |
| Social Contributions........................ | c12 | — | — | — | — | — | — | — | — | — | — | — | .... |
| Grants.......................................... | c13 | 2,373.6 | 2,723.1 | 3,692.2 | 3,912.1 | 3,573.9 | 3,079.5 | 2,833.9 | 3,151.2 | 3,026.0 | 2,667.4 | 3,046.3 | .... |
| Other Receipts.............................. | c14 | 978.3 | 1,062.6 | 1,251.4 | 1,594.6 | 1,737.8 | 1,684.1 | 1,989.3 | 2,720.0 | 3,500.4 | 3,248.6 | 3,449.0 | .... |
| Cash Payments:Operating Activities. | c2 | 11,931.6 | 14,510.3 | 17,918.4 | 20,124.0 | 25,031.8 | 26,158.3 | 28,045.3 | 32,822.7 | 37,766.7 | 40,975.7 | 47,579.8 | .... |
| Compensation of Employees.......... | c21 | 4,178.0 | 4,998.9 | 6,117.4 | 7,247.3 | 9,050.6 | 10,177.9 | 10,661.2 | 11,957.1 | 13,629.8 | 15,203.8 | 18,305.2 | .... |
| Purchases of Goods & Services....... | c22 | 1,468.3 | 1,796.3 | 2,600.8 | 2,526.5 | 3,947.6 | 3,313.1 | 3,590.3 | 5,537.6 | 6,099.4 | 6,349.5 | 7,432.7 | .... |
| Interest....................................... | c24 | 1,478.1 | 1,561.4 | 1,684.4 | 1,579.8 | 1,447.4 | 1,711.3 | 1,990.6 | 2,261.9 | 2,466.3 | 2,519.6 | 2,639.1 | .... |
| Subsidies...................................... | c25 | | | | | | 114.4 | 127.5 | 105.1 | 44.7 | 144.3 | 230.9 | .... |
| Grants.......................................... | c26 | 4,202.1 | 5,109.3 | 5,904.1 | 7,075.2 | 8,027.5 | 8,097.9 | 8,980.9 | 10,339.6 | 11,620.1 | 12,847.8 | 14,287.6 | .... |
| Social Benefits.............................. | c27 | 227.4 | 278.9 | 422.0 | 528.7 | 903.8 | 1,324.0 | 1,291.3 | 822.0 | 1,079.5 | 963.9 | 1,103.8 | .... |
| Other Payments............................ | c28 | 377.8 | 765.4 | 1,189.7 | 1,166.5 | 1,654.9 | 1,419.6 | 1,403.4 | 1,799.3 | 2,827.0 | 2,946.9 | 3,580.5 | .... |
| Net Cash Inflow:Operating Act.[1-2] | ccio | 2,672.8 | 2,920.9 | 3,287.4 | 4,366.9 | 2,010.1 | 780.5 | 2,363.7 | 4,873.0 | 5,981.5 | 5,725.2 | 6,151.1 | .... |
| Net Cash Outflow:Invest. in NFA...... | c31 | 4,252.6 | 4,415.0 | 3,224.5 | 3,926.2 | 3,448.1 | 3,634.4 | 3,715.0 | 3,867.5 | 4,718.7 | 5,548.7 | 7,104.3 | .... |
| Purchases of Nonfinancial Assets... | c31.1 | 4,267.7 | 4,415.0 | 3,224.5 | 3,926.2 | 3,448.1 | 3,634.4 | 3,715.0 | 3,867.5 | 4,718.7 | .... | .... | .... |
| Sales of Nonfinancial Assets........... | c31.2 | 15.1 | — | — | — | — | — | — | — | — | .... | .... | .... |
| Cash Surplus/Deficit [1-2-31=1-2M] | ccsd | −1,579.7 | −1,494.1 | 62.9 | 440.7 | −1,438.0 | −2,854.0 | −1,351.3 | 1,005.6 | 1,262.7 | 176.5 | −953.2 | .... |
| Net Acq. Fin. Assets, excl. Cash....... | c32x | .... | .... | .... | .... | .... | .... | .... | .... | .... | .... | .... | .... |
| Domestic....................................... | c321x | .... | .... | .... | .... | .... | .... | .... | .... | .... | .... | .... | .... |
| Foreign......................................... | c322x | .... | .... | .... | .... | .... | .... | .... | .... | .... | .... | .... | .... |
| Net Incurrence of Liabilities.............. | c33 | .... | .... | .... | .... | .... | .... | .... | .... | .... | .... | .... | .... |
| Domestic....................................... | c331 | .... | .... | .... | .... | .... | .... | .... | .... | .... | .... | .... | .... |
| Foreign......................................... | c332 | .... | .... | .... | .... | .... | .... | .... | .... | .... | .... | .... | .... |
| Net Cash Inflow, Fin.Act.[-32x+33].. | cnfb | .... | .... | .... | .... | .... | .... | .... | .... | .... | .... | .... | .... |
| Net Change in Stock of Cash........... | cncb | .... | .... | .... | .... | .... | .... | .... | .... | .... | .... | .... | .... |
| Stat. Discrep. [32X-33+NCB-CSD].... | ccsdz | .... | .... | .... | .... | .... | .... | .... | .... | .... | .... | .... | .... |
| Memo Item:Cash Expenditure[2+31] | c2m | 16,184.2 | 18,925.3 | 21,142.9 | 24,050.2 | 28,479.9 | 29,792.7 | 31,760.3 | 36,690.2 | 42,485.4 | 46,524.4 | 54,684.1 | .... |
| Memo Item: Gross Debt.................. | c63 | .... | .... | .... | .... | .... | .... | .... | .... | .... | .... | .... | .... |
| **National Accounts** | | | | | | *Millions of Córdobas* | | | | | | | |
| Househ.Cons.Expend.,incl.NPISHs.... | 96f | 57,843.6 | 65,917.7 | 103,659.5 | 119,905.3 | 142,155.5 | 147,681.3 | 162,616.3 | 182,612.2 | 208,480.1 | 229,111.5 | 256,129.8 | .... |
| Government Consumption Expend... | 91f | 12,845.2 | 15,274.4 | 11,064.9 | 10,572.1 | 12,538.0 | 12,835.0 | 14,547.5 | 16,331.0 | 17,459.2 | 18,692.1 | 20,453.5 | .... |
| Gross Fixed Capital Formation......... | 93e | 18,897.9 | 23,193.7 | 28,016.6 | 34,097.7 | 41,245.6 | 33,286.1 | 39,998.2 | 54,212.5 | 68,867.3 | 77,545.3 | 83,217.7 | .... |
| Changes in Inventories.................... | 93i | 1,040.0 | 1,330.5 | 3,538.1 | 6,746.5 | 9,848.5 | 4,162.7 | 5,897.9 | 13,503.2 | 1,745.2 | −730.7 | −1,376.9 | .... |
| Exports of Goods and Services......... | 90c | 19,492.5 | 23,613.6 | 32,239.8 | 39,927.4 | 51,536.3 | 52,662.0 | 71,777.9 | 93,457.7 | 111,235.1 | 113,852.1 | 129,725.9 | .... |
| Imports of Goods and Services (-)..... | 98c | 38,963.7 | 47,805.5 | 59,283.7 | 73,658.2 | 92,829.5 | 80,167.1 | 108,154.7 | 141,353.6 | 161,480.4 | 170,209.9 | 181,688.5 | .... |
| Gross Domestic Product (GDP)........ | 99b | 71,155.6 | 81,524.4 | 119,235.2 | 137,590.8 | 164,494.3 | 170,459.9 | 186,683.0 | 218,762.9 | 246,306.5 | 268,260.5 | 306,461.5 | .... |
| Net Primary Income from Abroad..... | 98.n | −3,061.6 | −2,510.0 | −4,635.1 | −4,120.5 | −4,332.2 | −5,187.3 | −5,175.3 | −5,695.9 | −6,858.9 | .... | .... | .... |
| Gross National Income (GNI)........... | 99a | 68,094.0 | 79,014.4 | 114,600.1 | 133,258.8 | 155,570.1 | 160,760.4 | 178,205.6 | 210,388.2 | 240,562.1 | .... | .... | .... |
| GDP Volume 1994 Prices................. | 99b.p | 30,325.2 | 31,623.9 | 32,936.9 | 34,136.9 | 35,078.8 | 34,563.4 | 36,112.0 | 37,792.8 | .... | .... | .... | .... |
| GDP Volume 2006 Ref., Chained..... | 99b.p | .... | .... | 119,235.2 | 125,231.5 | 130,235.0 | 127,397.7 | 132,012.9 | 139,206.0 | 146,451.3 | .... | .... | .... |
| GDP Volume (2010=100)................. | 99bvp | 83.2 | 86.7 | † 90.3 | 94.9 | 98.7 | 96.5 | 100.0 | 105.4 | 110.9 | .... | .... | .... |
| GDP Deflator (2010=100)................. | 99bip | 45.8 | 50.4 | 70.7 | 77.7 | 89.3 | 94.6 | 100.0 | 111.1 | 118.9 | .... | .... | .... |
| | | | | | | *Millions: Midyear Estimates* | | | | | | | |
| Population................................. | 99z | 5.31 | 5.38 | 5.45 | 5.52 | 5.59 | 5.67 | 5.74 | 5.81 | 5.88 | 5.95 | 6.01 | 6.08 |

|  |  | 2004 | 2005 | 2006 | 2007 | 2008 | 2009 | 2010 | 2011 | 2012 | 2013 | 2014 | 2015 |
|---|---|---|---|---|---|---|---|---|---|---|---|---|---|
| **Exchange Rates** | | | | | | *CFA Francs per SDR: End of Period* | | | | | | | |
| Official Rate | aa | 747.90 | 794.73 | 749.30 | 704.15 | 725.98 | 713.83 | 756.02 | 778.32 | 764.10 | 732.49 | 782.77 | 834.92 |
| | | | | | | *CFA Francs per US Dollar: End of Period (ae) Period Average (rf)* | | | | | | | |
| Official Rate | ae | 481.58 | 556.04 | 498.07 | 445.59 | 471.34 | 455.34 | 490.91 | 506.96 | 497.16 | 475.64 | 540.28 | 602.51 |
| Official Rate | rf | 528.28 | 527.47 | 522.89 | 479.27 | 447.81 | 472.19 | 495.28 | 471.87 | 510.53 | 494.04 | 494.41 | 591.45 |
| **Fund Position** | | | | | | *Millions of SDRs: End of Period* | | | | | | | |
| Quota | 2f.s | 65.80 | 65.80 | 65.80 | 65.80 | 65.80 | 65.80 | 65.80 | 65.80 | 65.80 | 65.80 | 65.80 | 65.80 |
| SDR Holdings | 1b.s | .60 | .21 | .08 | .04 | .96 | 54.29 | 54.28 | 54.27 | 54.26 | 54.26 | 54.25 | 47.46 |
| Reserve Position in the Fund | 1c.s | 8.56 | 8.61 | 8.61 | 8.61 | 8.61 | 8.64 | 8.64 | 8.64 | 8.64 | 8.64 | 8.64 | 8.64 |
| Total Fund Cred.&Loans Outstg | 2tl | 87.21 | 89.30 | 17.63 | 25.38 | 32.90 | 36.19 | 39.39 | 36.45 | 43.52 | 49.30 | 76.23 | 107.77 |
| SDR Allocations | 1bd | 9.41 | 9.41 | 9.41 | 9.41 | 9.41 | 62.94 | 62.94 | 62.94 | 62.94 | 62.94 | 62.94 | 62.94 |
| **International Liquidity** | | | | | | *Millions of US Dollars Unless Otherwise Indicated: End of Period* | | | | | | | |
| Total Reserves minus Gold | 1l.d | 249.8 | 250.7 | 370.9 | 593.0 | 705.2 | 655.5 | 760.3 | 673.0 | 1,014.5 | 1,166.6 | 1,281.5 | 1,039.0 |
| SDR Holdings | 1b.d | .9 | .3 | .1 | .1 | 1.5 | 85.1 | 83.6 | 83.3 | 83.4 | 83.6 | 78.6 | 65.8 |
| Reserve Position in the Fund | 1c.d | 13.3 | 12.3 | 13.0 | 13.6 | 13.3 | 13.5 | 13.3 | 13.3 | 13.3 | 13.3 | 12.5 | 12.0 |
| Foreign Exchange | 1d.d | 235.6 | 238.1 | 357.8 | 579.3 | 690.5 | 556.9 | 663.4 | 576.5 | 917.8 | 1,069.8 | 1,190.4 | 961.2 |
| Gold (Million Fine Troy Ounces) | 1ad | — | — | — | — | — | — | — | — | — | — | — | .... |
| Gold (National Valuation) | 1and | — | — | — | — | — | — | — | — | — | — | — | .... |
| Monetary Authorities: Other Liabs | 4..d | 4.7 | 5.1 | 4.0 | 8.7 | 14.3 | 4.5 | 8.2 | 4.5 | 5.9 | 11.0 | 17.1 | 15.1 |
| Deposit Money Banks: Assets | 7a.d | 80.9 | 86.1 | 89.2 | 134.7 | 149.6 | 148.3 | 247.0 | 255.1 | 316.5 | 531.9 | 541.8 | 461.3 |
| Deposit Money Banks: Liabs | 7b.d | 41.6 | 64.7 | 100.9 | 154.9 | 175.7 | 215.1 | 246.3 | 258.4 | 293.2 | 389.5 | 284.5 | 288.8 |
| **Monetary Authorities** | | | | | | *Billions of CFA Francs: End of Period* | | | | | | | |
| Foreign Assets | 11 | 120.3 | 139.4 | 184.7 | 264.2 | 332.4 | 298.5 | 373.2 | 341.2 | 504.4 | 554.9 | 692.4 | 626.0 |
| Claims on Central Government | 12a | 107.6 | 107.8 | 49.0 | 53.3 | 58.1 | 93.3 | 91.5 | 91.4 | 92.6 | 89.8 | 102.5 | 121.5 |
| Claims on Deposit Money Banks | 12e | 1.2 | 1.1 | 1.1 | .2 | 2.5 | 12.7 | 11.1 | 33.3 | 38.2 | 51.3 | 114.5 | 152.4 |
| Claims on Other Financial Insts | 12f | — | — | — | — | — | — | — | — | — | — | — | — |
| Reserve Money | 14 | 129.8 | 138.3 | 163.6 | 205.5 | 202.4 | 260.5 | 339.4 | 348.8 | 465.4 | 489.9 | 651.7 | 656.1 |
| of which: Currency Outside DMBs | 14a | 97.7 | 108.3 | 132.9 | 133.3 | 147.7 | 187.9 | 234.9 | 269.6 | 345.2 | 398.1 | 502.6 | 535.3 |
| Foreign Liabilities | 16c | 74.5 | 81.3 | 22.2 | 28.4 | 37.5 | 72.8 | 81.4 | 79.6 | 84.3 | 87.4 | 118.2 | 151.6 |
| Central Government Deposits | 16d | 22.0 | 32.5 | 48.4 | 84.0 | 154.2 | 74.3 | 55.5 | 41.1 | 84.9 | 117.1 | 142.3 | 92.2 |
| Other Items (Net) | 17r | 2.8 | −3.8 | .6 | −.1 | −1.1 | −3.1 | −.5 | −3.6 | .5 | 1.6 | −2.8 | −.1 |
| **Deposit Money Banks** | | | | | | *Billions of CFA Francs: End of Period* | | | | | | | |
| Reserves | 20 | 31.0 | 28.3 | 29.1 | 78.0 | 51.4 | 73.0 | 105.3 | 80.0 | 126.9 | 91.4 | 143.6 | 108.6 |
| Foreign Assets | 21 | 39.0 | 47.9 | 44.5 | 60.0 | 70.5 | 67.5 | 121.2 | 129.3 | 157.3 | 253.0 | 292.7 | 278.0 |
| Claims on Central Government | 22a | 10.3 | 12.1 | 17.3 | 16.4 | 23.7 | 20.8 | 29.0 | 37.6 | 36.1 | 40.7 | 81.6 | 136.5 |
| Claims on Private Sector | 22d | 101.1 | 121.2 | 159.6 | 191.9 | 262.6 | 310.9 | 347.1 | 402.6 | 500.0 | 519.8 | 573.6 | 649.1 |
| Claims on Other Financial Insts | 22f | — | — | — | — | — | — | — | — | — | — | — | — |
| Demand Deposits | 24 | 81.8 | 81.4 | 93.6 | 134.5 | 141.8 | 166.6 | 214.1 | 204.7 | 289.5 | 306.3 | 389.4 | 368.9 |
| Time Deposits | 25 | 50.3 | 56.2 | 60.0 | 86.3 | 106.9 | 116.2 | 124.2 | 132.6 | 162.0 | 173.2 | 210.0 | 241.4 |
| Foreign Liabilities | 26c | 17.4 | 30.3 | 37.3 | 40.2 | 44.6 | 54.8 | 70.2 | 74.6 | 90.1 | 105.4 | 71.9 | 103.3 |
| Long-Term Foreign Liabilities | 26cl | 2.6 | 5.6 | 13.0 | 28.8 | 38.2 | 43.1 | 50.8 | 56.5 | 55.7 | 79.9 | 81.9 | 70.7 |
| Central Government Deposits | 26d | 13.8 | 19.2 | 27.6 | 37.0 | 43.9 | 41.1 | 62.3 | 73.8 | 92.2 | 102.1 | 118.7 | 126.8 |
| Credit from Monetary Authorities | 26g | 1.2 | 1.1 | 1.1 | .2 | 2.5 | 12.7 | 11.1 | 33.3 | 38.2 | 51.3 | 114.5 | 152.4 |
| Capital Accounts | 27a | 26.0 | 30.4 | 34.0 | 36.8 | 47.1 | 59.2 | 75.9 | 95.1 | 118.0 | 128.5 | 147.7 | 159.8 |
| Other Items (Net) | 27r | −11.8 | −14.8 | −16.2 | −17.5 | −16.7 | −21.5 | −5.7 | −21.1 | −25.2 | −41.8 | −42.6 | −51.2 |
| Treasury Claims: Private Sector | 22d.i | — | — | — | — | — | — | — | — | — | — | — | — |
| Post Office: Checking Deposits | 24..i | 3.2 | 2.5 | 1.8 | 1.4 | 1.5 | 1.7 | 1.4 | 1.8 | 3.3 | 2.2 | 1.8 | 1.9 |
| **Monetary Survey** | | | | | | *Billions of CFA Francs: End of Period* | | | | | | | |
| Foreign Assets (Net) | 31n | 67.3 | 75.7 | 169.7 | 255.7 | 320.8 | 238.4 | 342.9 | 316.3 | 487.3 | 615.1 | 795.0 | 649.0 |
| Domestic Credit | 32 | 186.4 | 191.9 | 151.7 | 142.1 | 147.8 | 311.3 | 351.2 | 418.4 | 454.9 | 433.3 | 498.5 | 689.9 |
| Claims on Central Govt. (Net) | 32an | 85.3 | 70.6 | −7.9 | −49.8 | −114.8 | .4 | 4.1 | 15.8 | −45.1 | −86.4 | −75.1 | 40.8 |
| Claims on Private Sector | 32d | 101.1 | 121.2 | 159.6 | 191.9 | 262.6 | 310.9 | 347.1 | 402.6 | 500.0 | 519.8 | 573.6 | 649.1 |
| Claims on Other Financial Insts | 32f | — | — | — | — | — | — | — | — | — | — | — | — |
| Money | 34 | 182.8 | 192.3 | 228.8 | 269.3 | 291.2 | 356.4 | 450.5 | 476.4 | 638.4 | 707.0 | 895.5 | 908.5 |
| Quasi-Money | 35 | 50.3 | 56.2 | 60.0 | 86.3 | 106.9 | 116.2 | 124.2 | 132.6 | 162.0 | 173.2 | 210.0 | 241.4 |
| Long-Term Foreign Liabilities | 36cl | 2.6 | 5.6 | 13.0 | 28.8 | 38.2 | 43.1 | 50.8 | 56.5 | 55.7 | 79.9 | 81.9 | 70.7 |
| Other Items (Net) | 37r | 18.0 | 13.4 | 19.6 | 13.3 | 32.3 | 34.0 | 68.7 | 69.3 | 86.2 | 88.3 | 106.2 | 118.3 |
| Money plus Quasi-Money | 35l | 233.1 | 248.5 | 288.8 | 355.7 | 398.1 | 472.5 | 574.7 | 609.0 | 800.3 | 880.2 | 1,105.5 | 1,149.9 |
| **Interest Rates** | | | | | | *Percent Per Annum* | | | | | | | |
| Repurchase Agreement Rate | 60.q | 4.00 | 4.00 | 4.25 | 4.25 | 4.75 | 4.25 | 4.25 | 4.25 | 4.00 | 3.50 | 3.50 | 3.50 |
| Deposit Rate | 60l | 3.50 | 3.50 | 3.50 | 3.50 | 3.50 | 3.50 | 3.50 | 3.50 | 3.50 | 3.50 | 3.50 | 3.50 |
| **Prices** | | | | | | *Index Numbers (2010=100): Period Averages* | | | | | | | |
| Consumer Prices | 64 | 82.1 | 88.5 | 88.6 | 88.6 | † 98.6 | 99.2 | 100.0 | 102.9 | 103.4 | 105.8 | 104.8 | 105.9 |
| **Intl. Transactions & Positions** | | | | | | *Millions of CFA Francs* | | | | | | | |
| Exports | 70 | 230,860 | 257,932 | 265,600 | 317,891 | 407,503 | 278,900 | 318,700 | 428,000 | .... | .... | .... | .... |
| Imports, c.i.f. | 71 | 396,214 | 497,402 | 496,223 | 550,541 | 759,672 | 704,900 | 1,081,200 | 854,400 | .... | .... | .... | .... |

# Niger   692

## Balance of Payments

| | | 2004 | 2005 | 2006 | 2007 | 2008 | 2009 | 2010 | 2011 | 2012 | 2013 | 2014 | 2015 |
|---|---|---|---|---|---|---|---|---|---|---|---|---|---|
| | | | | | | | *Millions of US Dollars* | | | | | | |
| A. Current Account* | 109bx | −230.9 | −311.5 | −313.7 | −351.3 | −651.4 | −1,320.1 | −1,136.0 | † −1,431.1 | −1,021.7 | −1,150.3 | . . . . | . . . . |
| Goods, credit (exports) | 1a9cx | 436.7 | 477.6 | 508.0 | 662.5 | 912.2 | 996.9 | 1,151.0 | † 1,270.4 | 1,442.4 | 1,588.1 | . . . . | . . . . |
| Goods, debit (imports) | 1a9dx | 588.9 | 768.5 | 747.5 | 913.9 | 1,349.3 | 1,793.2 | 1,962.5 | † 2,192.4 | 1,903.0 | 2,017.8 | . . . . | . . . . |
| Balance on goods | 1a9bx | −152.3 | −291.0 | −239.6 | −251.4 | −437.1 | −796.4 | −811.5 | † −922.0 | −460.6 | −429.7 | . . . . | . . . . |
| Services, credit (exports) | 1b9cx | 93.4 | 87.5 | 90.6 | 84.6 | 131.0 | 99.9 | 119.0 | † 69.3 | 75.4 | 147.5 | . . . . | . . . . |
| Services, debit (imports) | 1b9dx | 263.0 | 280.3 | 329.3 | 369.3 | 601.4 | 735.7 | 844.7 | † 870.4 | 829.8 | 978.9 | . . . . | . . . . |
| Balance on Goods & Services | 1z9bx | −321.8 | −483.7 | −478.3 | −536.1 | −907.5 | −1,432.1 | −1,537.2 | † −1,723.1 | −1,215.0 | −1,261.0 | . . . . | . . . . |
| Primary income: credit | 1c9cx | 26.5 | 37.1 | 42.0 | 59.2 | 81.3 | 88.9 | 61.7 | † 93.7 | 147.0 | 83.9 | . . . . | . . . . |
| Primary income: debit | 1c9dx | 39.4 | 46.6 | 40.8 | 59.6 | 55.6 | 127.7 | 108.9 | † 144.8 | 282.3 | 268.6 | . . . . | . . . . |
| Balance on gds, serv. & prim. inc. | 1y9bx | −334.7 | −493.2 | −477.1 | −536.5 | −881.8 | −1,470.9 | −1,584.4 | † −1,774.1 | −1,350.4 | −1,445.7 | . . . . | . . . . |
| Secondary income: credit | 1d9ca | 128.6 | 217.1 | 199.5 | 207.9 | 253.9 | 170.2 | 506.7 | † 472.3 | 391.6 | 382.3 | . . . . | . . . . |
| Secondary income: debit | 1d9da | 24.7 | 35.4 | 36.1 | 22.6 | 23.6 | 19.3 | 58.3 | † 129.2 | 62.9 | 86.9 | . . . . | . . . . |
| B. Capital Account* | 209ba | 249.2 | 49.4 | 220.2 | 268.8 | 532.1 | 247.1 | 195.8 | † 145.2 | 272.9 | 570.9 | . . . . | . . . . |
| Capital account: credit | 209ca | 384.5 | 188.3 | 220.2 | 268.8 | 532.1 | 247.2 | 195.9 | † 152.3 | 286.0 | 667.3 | . . . . | . . . . |
| Capital account: debit | 209da | 135.3 | 138.9 | — | — | — | .1 | .1 | † 7.1 | 13.1 | 96.3 | . . . . | . . . . |
| Balance on current & capital acct. | 129ba | 18.4 | −262.1 | −93.6 | −82.4 | −119.4 | −1,072.9 | −940.2 | † −1,285.8 | −748.8 | −579.3 | . . . . | . . . . |
| C. Financial Account* | 309na | 166.2 | −174.0 | −37.0 | −95.7 | −287.6 | −886.8 | −1,031.1 | † −1,234.0 | −1,081.7 | −689.3 | . . . . | . . . . |
| Direct investment: assets | 3a9aa | 11.1 | 15.0 | −11.2 | −22.0 | −34.1 | −94.6 | −204.2 | † 9.3 | 2.3 | 100.7 | . . . . | . . . . |
| Equity & investment fund shares.. | 3aaaa | 8.2 | 14.6 | −12.8 | −31.0 | −29.3 | −133.5 | −180.6 | † 9.3 | 2.3 | 26.4 | . . . . | . . . . |
| Debt instruments | 3abaa | 2.9 | .4 | 1.5 | 9.0 | −4.8 | 38.9 | −23.6 | † — | — | 74.3 | . . . . | . . . . |
| Direct investment: liabilities | 3a9la | 24.4 | 49.7 | 40.3 | 98.9 | 281.9 | 631.3 | 795.9 | † 1,065.8 | 851.0 | 719.1 | . . . . | . . . . |
| Equity & investment fund shares . | 3aala | 25.8 | 22.7 | 4.0 | 12.5 | −47.8 | −6.4 | .2 | † 1,061.7 | 526.1 | 446.5 | . . . . | . . . . |
| Debt instruments | 3abla | −1.4 | 27.1 | 36.3 | 86.4 | 329.8 | 637.6 | 795.7 | † 4.0 | 325.0 | 272.7 | . . . . | . . . . |
| Portfolio investment: assets | 3b9aa | .2 | .8 | −.2 | — | 20.7 | 29.7 | 9.7 | † 10.5 | .9 | 23.1 | . . . . | . . . . |
| Equity & investment fund shares | 3baaa | .3 | .7 | −.4 | −.2 | −4.1 | −2.2 | 5.0 | † — | — | — | . . . . | . . . . |
| Debt securities | 3bbaa | −.1 | .1 | .2 | .2 | 24.8 | 31.8 | 4.7 | † 10.5 | .9 | 23.1 | . . . . | . . . . |
| Portfolio investment: liabilities | 3b9la | 5.0 | 42.5 | −4.1 | −8.2 | −9.5 | 10.2 | 32.7 | † 27.0 | 33.2 | 4.1 | . . . . | . . . . |
| Equity & investment fund shares . | 3bala | 3.8 | .6 | — | −.5 | 1.5 | 9.5 | 6.5 | † −3.8 | 20.3 | — | . . . . | . . . . |
| Debt securities | 3bbla | 1.1 | 41.9 | −4.1 | −7.7 | −10.9 | .8 | 26.2 | † 30.8 | 13.0 | 4.1 | . . . . | . . . . |
| Fin. der.& empl.stk.ops.(ESOs): net. | 3c9na | −1.1 | — | — | −1.8 | 2.3 | — | — | † −.2 | — | — | . . . . | . . . . |
| Fin. der. & ESOs.: assets | 3c9aa | . . . . | — | — | — | .3 | — | — | † −.2 | — | — | . . . . | . . . . |
| Fin. der. & ESOs.: liabilities | 3c9la | 1.1 | — | — | 1.8 | −2.0 | — | — | † — | — | — | . . . . | . . . . |
| Other investment: assets | 3d9aa | 72.8 | 19.4 | 30.1 | 44.4 | −67.3 | −112.4 | 169.2 | † 127.8 | 113.8 | 211.7 | . . . . | . . . . |
| Other equity | 3daaa | . . . . | . . . . | . . . . | . . . . | | | . . . . | † — | — | — | . . . . | . . . . |
| Debt instruments | 3dzaa | 72.8 | 19.4 | 30.1 | 44.4 | −67.3 | −112.4 | 169.2 | † 127.8 | 113.8 | 211.7 | . . . . | . . . . |
| Other investment: liabilities | 3d9la | −112.6 | 117.0 | 19.4 | 25.5 | −63.3 | 68.0 | 177.2 | † 288.6 | 314.5 | 301.7 | . . . . | . . . . |
| Other equity | 3dala | . . . . | . . . . | . . . . | . . . . | | | . . . . | † — | — | — | . . . . | . . . . |
| Debt instruments | 3dzla | −112.6 | 117.0 | 19.4 | 25.5 | −63.3 | 68.0 | 177.2 | † 288.6 | 314.5 | 301.7 | . . . . | . . . . |
| Curr.+ cap.− finan. acct. balance.. | 4y9na | −147.8 | −88.1 | −56.6 | 13.3 | 168.2 | −186.1 | 90.9 | † −51.8 | 332.9 | 110.0 | . . . . | . . . . |
| D. Net Errors and Omissions | 409na | 109.2 | 120.9 | 1,501.1 | −16.3 | −66.4 | 323.7 | 14.9 | † −14.4 | −22.5 | −12.3 | . . . . | . . . . |
| E. Reserves and Related Items | 4z9na | −38.7 | 32.8 | 1,444.5 | −3.0 | 101.8 | 137.5 | 105.8 | † −66.2 | 310.4 | 97.7 | . . . . | . . . . |
| Reserve assets | 3e9aa | −40.6 | 35.4 | 87.5 | 166.7 | 151.8 | 251.9 | 145.6 | † −70.8 | 321.4 | 106.3 | . . . . | . . . . |
| Credit and loans from the IMF | 3dcla | −1.9 | 2.6 | −103.5 | 11.7 | 11.9 | 5.0 | 4.9 | † −4.6 | 11.0 | 8.6 | . . . . | . . . . |
| Exceptional financing | 409la | . . . . | — | −1,253.5 | 158.0 | 38.1 | 109.4 | 34.8 | . . . . | . . . . | . . . . | . . . . | . . . . |

*Excludes components in group E

## International Investment Position

| | | 2004 | 2005 | 2006 | 2007 | 2008 | 2009 | 2010 | 2011 | 2012 | 2013 | 2014 | 2015 |
|---|---|---|---|---|---|---|---|---|---|---|---|---|---|
| | | | | | | | *Millions of US Dollars* | | | | | | |
| Assets | 809aa | 411.9 | 374.2 | 542.4 | 778.8 | 964.0 | 925.4 | 1,133.5 | † 1,488.4 | 1,564.4 | 2,093.6 | . . . . | . . . . |
| Direct investment | 8a9aa | 8.2 | 13.3 | 12.4 | 5.0 | 12.9 | 74.8 | 11.7 | † 48.0 | 306.5 | 422.6 | . . . . | . . . . |
| Equity & investment fund shares.. | 8aaaa | 9.5 | 7.6 | 9.2 | .6 | 12.4 | 45.8 | 10.4 | † 27.4 | 172.7 | 205.6 | . . . . | . . . . |
| Debt instruments | 8abaa | −1.3 | 5.7 | 3.2 | 4.5 | .5 | 29.0 | 1.3 | † 20.6 | 133.7 | 217.0 | . . . . | . . . . |
| Portfolio investment | 8b9aa | 3.0 | 15.3 | 31.2 | 19.1 | 37.7 | 39.5 | 46.4 | † 128.8 | 65.6 | 94.3 | . . . . | . . . . |
| Equity & investment fund shares.. | 8baaa | 2.2 | 2.4 | 11.9 | 11.3 | 1.8 | 19.3 | 13.5 | † 1.7 | .1 | .1 | . . . . | . . . . |
| Debt securities | 8bbaa | .8 | 12.9 | 19.3 | 7.8 | 35.9 | 20.1 | 33.0 | † 127.0 | 65.5 | 94.2 | . . . . | . . . . |
| Fin. der.(oth.than reserves) & ESOs | 8c9aa | . . . . | 1.1 | . . . . | — | .3 | . . . . | — | † .2 | — | — | . . . . | . . . . |
| Other investment | 8d9aa | 150.8 | 93.8 | 127.8 | 161.6 | 207.8 | 155.6 | 315.0 | † 638.4 | 177.8 | 410.1 | . . . . | . . . . |
| Other equity | 8daaa | . . . . | . . . . | | | | | | | | | | |
| Debt instruments | 8dzaa | 150.8 | 93.8 | 127.8 | 161.6 | 207.8 | 155.6 | 315.0 | † 638.4 | 177.8 | 410.1 | . . . . | . . . . |
| Reserve assets | 8e9aa | 249.8 | 250.7 | 370.9 | 593.0 | 705.2 | 655.5 | 760.3 | † 673.0 | 1,014.5 | 1,166.6 | . . . . | . . . . |
| Liabilities | 809la | 2,242.0 | 2,086.9 | 910.3 | 1,264.1 | 1,783.1 | 2,777.5 | 3,824.8 | † 1,558.0 | 5,355.0 | 7,133.5 | . . . . | . . . . |
| Direct investment | 8a9la | 115.5 | 100.0 | 161.1 | 276.6 | 623.8 | 1,404.3 | 2,251.2 | † 652.1 | 1,010.0 | 1,797.0 | . . . . | . . . . |
| Equity & investment fund shares.. | 8aala | 110.7 | 76.3 | 103.8 | 126.8 | 192.6 | 262.0 | 635.0 | † 578.2 | 703.8 | 1,192.7 | . . . . | . . . . |
| Debt instruments | 8abla | 4.8 | 23.7 | 57.3 | 149.9 | 431.2 | 1,142.3 | 1,616.2 | † 73.8 | 306.2 | 604.4 | . . . . | . . . . |
| Portfolio investment | 8b9la | 5.3 | 24.9 | 18.7 | .7 | 1.6 | 12.2 | 136.4 | † 26.6 | 202.3 | 216.4 | . . . . | . . . . |
| Equity & investment fund shares.. | 8bala | 5.3 | 5.1 | 5.1 | .7 | 1.6 | 11.3 | 57.5 | † 16.5 | 4.0 | 4.2 | . . . . | . . . . |
| Debt securities | 8bbla | | 19.8 | 13.6 | . . . . | | .9 | 78.9 | † 10.1 | 198.2 | 212.2 | . . . . | . . . . |
| Fin. der.(oth.than reserves) & ESOs | 8c9la | . . . . | . . . . | . . . . | 2.0 | . . . . | 4.7 | . . . . | . . . . | — | — | . . . . | . . . . |
| Other investment | 8d9la | 2,121.2 | 1,962.0 | 730.5 | 984.9 | 1,157.7 | 1,356.3 | 1,437.2 | † 879.4 | 4,142.7 | 5,120.0 | . . . . | . . . . |
| Other equity | 8dala | . . . . | . . . . | . . . . | . . . . | . . . . | . . . . | . . . . | | | | | |
| Debt instruments | 8dzla | 2,121.2 | 1,962.0 | 730.5 | 984.9 | 1,157.7 | 1,356.3 | 1,437.2 | † 879.4 | 4,142.7 | 5,120.0 | . . . . | . . . . |

# Niger   692

| | | 2004 | 2005 | 2006 | 2007 | 2008 | 2009 | 2010 | 2011 | 2012 | 2013 | 2014 | 2015 |
|---|---|---|---|---|---|---|---|---|---|---|---|---|---|
| **Government Finance** | | | | | | | | | | | | | |
| **Operations Statement** | | | | | | | | | | | | | |
| **Budgetary Central Government** | | | | | *Billions of CFA Francs: Fiscal Year Ends December 31* | | | | | | | |
| Revenue | a1 | .... | 322,987 | 1,130,257 | 396,056 | † 591,934 | .... | .... | .... | .... | .... | .... | .... |
| Taxes | a11 | .... | 181,239 | 203,954 | 233,186 | † 283,404 | .... | .... | .... | .... | .... | .... | .... |
| Social Contributions | a12 | .... | — | — | | † — | .... | .... | .... | .... | .... | .... | .... |
| Grants | a13 | .... | 134,019 | 882,948 | 118,539 | † 142,012 | .... | .... | .... | .... | .... | .... | .... |
| Other Revenue | a14 | .... | 7,729 | 43,355 | 44,331 | † 166,518 | .... | .... | .... | .... | .... | .... | .... |
| Expense | a2 | .... | 163,683 | 176,931 | 239,471 | † 292,714 | .... | .... | .... | .... | .... | .... | .... |
| Compensation of Employees | a21 | .... | 63,042 | 67,965 | 72,233 | † 83,830 | .... | .... | .... | .... | .... | .... | .... |
| Use of Goods & Services | a22 | .... | 47,914 | 57,374 | 70,884 | † 77,040 | .... | .... | .... | .... | .... | .... | .... |
| Consumption of Fixed Capital | a23 | .... | .... | .... | .... | .... | .... | .... | .... | .... | .... | .... | .... |
| Interest | a24 | .... | 10,410 | 10,728 | 7,134 | † 5,960 | .... | .... | .... | .... | .... | .... | .... |
| Subsidies | a25 | .... | 1,365 | 1,958 | 2,080 | † — | .... | .... | .... | .... | .... | .... | .... |
| Grants | a26 | .... | 5,395 | 9,393 | 20,142 | † 52,156 | .... | .... | .... | .... | .... | .... | .... |
| Social Benefits | a27 | .... | — | — | — | † — | .... | .... | .... | .... | .... | .... | .... |
| Other Expense | a28 | .... | 35,558 | 29,512 | 66,997 | † 73,728 | .... | .... | .... | .... | .... | .... | .... |
| Gross Operating Balance [1-2+23] | agob | .... | 159,304 | 953,326 | 156,585 | † 299,220 | .... | .... | .... | .... | .... | .... | .... |
| Net Operating Balance [1-2] | anob | .... | .... | .... | .... | .... | .... | .... | .... | .... | .... | .... | .... |
| Net Acq. of Nonfinancial Assets | a31 | .... | 193,046 | 182,652 | 175,615 | † 256,150 | .... | .... | .... | .... | .... | .... | .... |
| Aquisition of Nonfin. Assets | a31.1 | .... | .... | .... | .... | .... | .... | .... | .... | .... | .... | .... | .... |
| Disposal of Nonfin. Assets | a31.2 | .... | .... | .... | .... | .... | .... | .... | .... | .... | .... | .... | .... |
| Net Lending/Borrowing [1-2-31] | anlb | .... | −33,742 | 770,674 | −19,030 | † 43,070 | .... | .... | .... | .... | .... | .... | .... |
| Net Acq. of Financial Assets | a32 | .... | 1,300 | 14,000 | −9,400 | .... | .... | .... | .... | .... | .... | .... | .... |
| By instrument | | | | | | | | | | | | | |
| Monetary Gold & SDRs | a3201 | .... | — | — | — | .... | .... | .... | .... | .... | .... | .... | .... |
| Currency & Deposits | a3202 | .... | 1,300 | 14,000 | −9,400 | .... | .... | .... | .... | .... | .... | .... | .... |
| Securities other than Shares | a3203 | .... | — | — | — | .... | .... | .... | .... | .... | .... | .... | .... |
| Loans | a3204 | .... | — | — | — | .... | .... | .... | .... | .... | .... | .... | .... |
| Shares & Other Equity | a3205 | .... | — | — | — | .... | .... | .... | .... | .... | .... | .... | .... |
| Insurance Technical Reserves | a3206 | .... | — | — | — | .... | .... | .... | .... | .... | .... | .... | .... |
| Financial Derivatives | a3207 | .... | — | — | — | .... | .... | .... | .... | .... | .... | .... | .... |
| Other Accounts Receivable | a3208 | .... | — | — | — | .... | .... | .... | .... | .... | .... | .... | .... |
| By debtor | | | | | | | | | | | | | |
| Domestic | a321 | .... | 1,300 | 14,000 | −9,400 | .... | .... | .... | .... | .... | .... | .... | .... |
| Foreign | a322 | .... | — | — | .... | .... | .... | .... | .... | .... | .... | .... | .... |
| Net Incurrence of Liabilities | a33 | .... | 35,059 | −756,689 | 9,620 | † −27,600 | .... | .... | .... | .... | .... | .... | .... |
| By instrument | | | | | | | | | | | | | |
| Special Drawing Rights (SDRs) | a3301 | .... | .... | .... | .... | .... | .... | .... | .... | .... | .... | .... | .... |
| Currency & Deposits | a3302 | .... | — | — | — | .... | .... | .... | .... | .... | .... | .... | .... |
| Securities other than Shares | a3303 | .... | 11,500 | −6,210 | 285 | .... | .... | .... | .... | .... | .... | .... | .... |
| Loans | a3304 | .... | 31,194 | −753,994 | 17,514 | .... | .... | .... | .... | .... | .... | .... | .... |
| Shares & Other Equity | a3305 | .... | 154 | — | — | .... | .... | .... | .... | .... | .... | .... | .... |
| Insurance Technical Reserves | a3306 | .... | — | — | — | .... | .... | .... | .... | .... | .... | .... | .... |
| Financial Derivatives | a3307 | .... | 425 | — | — | .... | .... | .... | .... | .... | .... | .... | .... |
| Other Accounts Payable | a3308 | .... | −8,188 | 3,500 | −8,200 | .... | .... | .... | .... | .... | .... | .... | .... |
| By creditor | | | | | | | | | | | | | |
| Domestic | a331 | .... | −10,915 | −81,358 | −39,469 | † — | .... | .... | .... | .... | .... | .... | .... |
| Foreign | a332 | .... | 46,000 | −675,331 | 49,089 | † −27,600 | .... | .... | .... | .... | .... | .... | .... |
| Stat. Discrepancy [32-33-NLB] | anlbz | .... | — | — | — | † −15,000 | .... | .... | .... | .... | .... | .... | .... |
| Memo Item: Expenditure [2+31] | a2m | .... | 356,729 | 359,583 | 415,086 | † 548,864 | .... | .... | .... | .... | .... | .... | .... |
| **National Accounts** | | | | | *Billions of CFA Francs* | | | | | | | | |
| Househ.Cons.Expend.,incl.NPISHs | 96f | 1,223.5 | 1,320.0 | 1,403.5 | 1,532.6 | 1,714.6 | 1,926.4 | 2,076.0 | 2,239.7 | 2,413.8 | 2,543.8 | 2,668.2 | 2,820.2 |
| Government Consumption Expend | 91f | 263.3 | 280.2 | 286.2 | 321.9 | 363.1 | 413.0 | 386.4 | 436.5 | 468.5 | 497.9 | 610.3 | 704.6 |
| Gross Fixed Capital Formation | 93e | 258.1 | 384.6 | 430.2 | 468.0 | 746.5 | 883.8 | 1,101.6 | 1,159.1 | 1,257.7 | 1,363.5 | 1,538.3 | 1,637.4 |
| Changes in Inventories | 93i | −34.8 | 25.8 | 19.5 | 3.0 | 30.0 | 1.5 | 29.9 | 2.1 | 24.5 | 5.9 | 2.6 | 3.0 |
| Exports of Goods and Services | 90c | 282.8 | 333.1 | 344.7 | 358.5 | 429.0 | 517.9 | 628.7 | 632.1 | 774.9 | 857.5 | 855.3 | 725.7 |
| Imports of Goods and Services (-) | 98c | 450.1 | 553.2 | 563.1 | 615.4 | 863.5 | 1,194.1 | 1,390.4 | 1,445.2 | 1,395.2 | 1,480.5 | 1,598.1 | 1,666.2 |
| Gross Domestic Product (GDP) | 99b | 1,530.4 | 1,777.0 | 1,906.8 | 2,053.0 | 2,419.7 | 2,548.4 | 2,832.3 | 3,024.3 | 3,544.2 | 3,788.3 | 4,076.6 | 4,224.7 |
| GDP Volume 2008 Prices | 99b.p | 1,884.4 | 2,023.8 | 2,141.2 | 2,207.6 | 2,419.7 | 2,402.6 | 2,603.7 | 2,663.0 | 2,978.5 | 3,115.0 | 3,330.0 | .... |
| GDP Volume (2010=100) | 99bvp | 72.4 | 77.7 | 82.2 | 84.8 | 92.9 | 92.3 | 100.0 | 102.3 | 114.4 | 119.6 | 127.9 | .... |
| GDP Deflator (2010=100) | 99bip | 74.7 | 80.7 | 81.9 | 85.5 | 91.9 | 97.5 | 100.0 | 104.4 | 109.4 | 111.8 | 112.5 | .... |
| | | | | | | *Millions: Midyear Estimates* | | | | | | | |
| Population | 99z | 13.00 | 13.49 | 14.00 | 14.53 | 15.09 | 15.67 | 16.29 | 16.95 | 17.64 | 18.36 | 19.11 | 19.90 |

# Nigeria 694

| | | 2004 | 2005 | 2006 | 2007 | 2008 | 2009 | 2010 | 2011 | 2012 | 2013 | 2014 | 2015 |
|---|---|---|---|---|---|---|---|---|---|---|---|---|---|
| **Exchange Rates** | | | | | | *Naira per SDR: End of Period* | | | | | | | |
| Principal Rate.................... | aa | 205.541 | 184.376 | 192.969 | 186.419 | 204.182 | 234.497 | 232.024 | 242.983 | 241.800 | 242.176 | 245.834 | 272.989 |
| | | | | | | *Naira per US Dollar: End of Period (ae) Period Average (rf)* | | | | | | | |
| Principal Rate.................... | ae | 132.350 | 129.000 | 128.270 | 117.968 | 132.563 | 149.581 | 150.662 | 158.267 | 157.328 | 157.257 | 169.680 | 197.000 |
| Principal Rate.................... | rf | 132.888 | 131.274 | 128.652 | 125.808 | 118.546 | 148.902 | 150.298 | 153.862 | 157.311 | 157.311 | 158.553 | 192.441 |
| | | | | | | *Index Numbers (2010=100): Period Averages* | | | | | | | |
| Principal Rate.................... | ahx | 113.1 | 114.5 | 117.8 | 119.5 | 126.8 | 101.0 | 100.0 | 97.7 | 95.4 | 95.5 | 94.8 | 78.3 |
| Nominal Effective Exchange Rate..... | nec | 118.8 | 118.3 | 120.2 | 115.5 | 120.1 | 101.8 | 100.0 | 94.1 | 95.9 | 96.7 | 98.0 | 91.2 |
| CPI-Based Real Effect. Ex. Rate........ | rec | 74.9 | 85.5 | 91.5 | 89.6 | 99.1 | 92.1 | 100.0 | 100.3 | 111.4 | 118.8 | 127.1 | 126.1 |
| **Fund Position** | | | | | | *Millions of SDRs: End of Period* | | | | | | | |
| Quota................................ | 2f.s | 1,753.20 | 1,753.20 | 1,753.20 | 1,753.20 | 1,753.20 | 1,753.20 | 1,753.20 | 1,753.20 | 1,753.20 | 1,753.20 | 1,753.20 | 1,753.20 |
| SDR Holdings......................... | 1b.s | .27 | .29 | .28 | .55 | .77 | 1,518.15 | 1,675.21 | 1,675.19 | 1,675.17 | 1,675.16 | 1,675.15 | 1,675.12 |
| Reserve Position in the Fund........... | 1c.s | .14 | .14 | .14 | .14 | .14 | .14 | .14 | .14 | .14 | .14 | .14 | .14 |
| Total Fund Cred.&Loans Outstg....... | 2tl | — | — | — | — | — | — | — | — | — | — | — | — |
| SDR Allocations........................ | 1bd | 157.16 | 157.16 | 157.16 | 157.16 | 157.16 | 1,675.38 | 1,675.38 | 1,675.38 | 1,675.38 | 1,675.38 | 1,675.38 | 1,675.38 |
| **International Liquidity** | | | | | *Millions of US Dollars Unless Otherwise Indicated: End of Period* | | | | | | | | |
| Total Reserves minus Gold.............. | 1l.d | 16,956 | 28,280 | 42,299 | 51,334 | 53,002 | 44,763 | 34,919 | 35,212 | 46,405 | 45,427 | 36,669 | 30,606 |
| SDR Holdings...................... | 1b.d | — | — | — | 1 | 1 | 2,380 | 2,580 | 2,572 | 2,575 | 2,580 | 2,427 | 2,321 |
| Reserve Position in the Fund.......... | 1c.d | — | — | — | — | — | — | — | — | — | — | — | — |
| Foreign Exchange.................. | 1d.d | 16,955 | 28,279 | 42,298 | 51,333 | 53,000 | 42,382 | 32,339 | 32,640 | 43,830 | 42,847 | 34,242 | 28,285 |
| Gold (Million Fine Troy Ounces)....... | 1ad | .687 | .687 | .687 | .687 | .687 | .687 | .687 | .687 | .687 | .687 | .687 | .687 |
| Gold (National Valuation)................ | 1and | .14 | .15 | .15 | .16 | .14 | .13 | .13 | .12 | .12 | .12 | .11 | .10 |
| Central Bank: Other Assets............. | 3..d | 134 | 122 | — | † 5,217 | 2,936 | 4,667 | 3,506 | 5,364 | 4,345 | 3,557 | 3,745 | 5,349 |
| Central Bank: Other Liabs.............. | 4..d | 2,239 | 1,422 | — | † 191 | 14 | 9 | 1 | — | 1 | 34 | 3 | 238 |
| Other Depository Corps.: Assets....... | 7a.d | 3,637 | 3,591 | 4,975 | † 7,891 | 11,472 | 8,462 | 8,739 | 11,049 | 13,066 | 13,556 | 12,618 | .... |
| Other Depository Corps.: Liabs......... | 7b.d | 143 | 180 | 284 | † 2,046 | 1,747 | 1,327 | 1,103 | 3,636 | 2,372 | 3,409 | 7,514 | .... |
| **Central Bank** | | | | | | *Billions of Naira: End of Period* | | | | | | | |
| Net Foreign Assets.......................... | 11n | 2,150.0 | 3,425.4 | 5,587.0 | † 6,620.9 | 7,308.1 | 6,220.6 | 5,044.7 | 5,485.8 | 7,055.2 | 6,686.9 | 5,888.4 | 5,163.7 |
| Claims on Nonresidents................ | 11 | 2,478.6 | 3,637.9 | 5,617.3 | † 6,672.7 | 7,342.1 | 6,614.8 | 5,433.6 | 5,887.7 | 7,455.1 | 7,092.7 | 6,295.5 | 5,667.8 |
| Liabilities to Nonresidents.............. | 16c | 328.7 | 212.4 | 30.3 | † 51.9 | 34.0 | 394.2 | 388.9 | 401.8 | 399.9 | 405.8 | 407.1 | 504.2 |
| Claims on Other Depository Corps.... | 12e | 92.0 | 92.7 | 130.2 | † 895.6 | 1,378.4 | 915.8 | 1,444.5 | 4,986.5 | 6,291.8 | 892.9 | 830.5 | 1,105.9 |
| Net Claims on Central Government.. | 12an | −764.2 | −1,349.1 | −2,796.0 | † −3,165.3 | −4,107.4 | −3,353.3 | −2,375.0 | −3,625.0 | −4,245.8 | −1,793.3 | −1,639.6 | −1,391.9 |
| Claims on Central Government...... | 12a | 441.6 | 337.0 | 652.5 | † 1,122.0 | 718.0 | 407.1 | 695.1 | 681.2 | 731.6 | 692.0 | 925.7 | 2,726.1 |
| Liabilities to Central Government... | 16d | 1,205.8 | 1,686.2 | 3,448.5 | † 4,287.3 | 4,825.4 | 3,760.4 | 3,070.1 | 4,306.3 | 4,977.4 | 2,485.3 | 2,565.3 | 4,118.0 |
| Claims on Other Sectors................ | 12s | 15.2 | 16.0 | 16.1 | † 237.8 | 293.7 | 472.9 | 443.3 | 4,399.3 | 4,665.4 | 4,569.8 | 4,862.5 | 5,030.5 |
| Claims on Other Financial Corps.... | 12g | 11.3 | 11.3 | — | † 54.1 | 228.1 | 450.0 | 375.0 | 4,368.4 | 4,630.8 | 4,539.1 | 4,787.2 | 4,981.2 |
| Claims on State & Local Govts....... | 12b | — | — | — | † — | — | — | — | — | — | — | — | — |
| Claims on Public Nonfin. Corps...... | 12c | 1.9 | 2.4 | 13.2 | † 41.9 | 41.6 | 13.3 | 52.2 | 23.6 | 23.6 | 23.6 | 25.6 | 25.6 |
| Claims on Private Sector............... | 12d | 1.9 | 2.3 | 2.8 | † 141.8 | 23.9 | 9.6 | 17.1 | 7.3 | 11.0 | 7.1 | 49.7 | 23.6 |
| Monetary Base.............................. | 14 | 732.7 | 766.0 | 993.0 | † 1,196.7 | 1,584.3 | 1,696.9 | 1,939.4 | 2,906.0 | 3,705.1 | 5,185.9 | 5,930.9 | 5,815.0 |
| Currency in Circulation.................. | 14a | 545.8 | 642.4 | 779.3 | † 955.9 | 1,155.6 | 1,181.5 | 1,378.2 | 1,566.0 | 1,631.7 | 1,776.4 | 1,798.0 | 1,857.9 |
| Liabs. to Other Depository Corps.... | 14c | 186.5 | 116.5 | 195.6 | † 240.8 | 428.7 | 515.3 | 561.2 | 1,339.9 | 2,073.3 | 3,409.5 | 4,133.0 | 3,957.0 |
| Liabilities to Other Sectors............. | 14d | .4 | 7.1 | 18.1 | † — | — | — | — | — | — | — | — | — |
| Other Liabs. to Other Dep. Corps..... | 14n | — | — | — | † 2,118.0 | 1,812.2 | 125.1 | 673.3 | 5,447.5 | 7,820.0 | 3,872.9 | 2,811.4 | 2,315.1 |
| Dep. & Sec. Excl. f/Monetary Base.. | 14o | 143.1 | 24.7 | 113.7 | † 743.0 | 900.0 | 1,342.9 | 1,048.3 | 1,951.0 | 1,313.7 | 935.3 | 798.5 | 1,428.6 |
| Deposits Included in Broad Money. | 15 | — | — | — | † 26.3 | 390.8 | 726.2 | 548.7 | 507.0 | 546.8 | 326.6 | 135.7 | 351.4 |
| Sec.Ot.th.Shares Incl.in Brd.Money | 16a | — | — | — | † — | — | — | — | 2.7 | 4.0 | 3.3 | 3.9 | 2.4 |
| Deposits Excl. from Broad Money... | 16b | 143.1 | 24.7 | 113.7 | † 716.7 | 509.1 | 616.7 | 496.9 | 1,330.3 | 638.9 | 523.8 | 587.1 | 942.4 |
| Sec.Ot.th.Shares Excl.f/Brd.Money.. | 16s | — | — | — | † — | — | — | — | 109.7 | 124.8 | 80.0 | 71.9 | 132.4 |
| Loans........................................ | 16l | — | — | — | † — | — | — | — | — | — | — | — | — |
| Financial Derivatives...................... | 16m | — | — | — | † — | — | — | — | — | — | — | — | — |
| Shares and Other Equity.................. | 17a | 513.0 | 754.6 | 1,518.0 | † 328.6 | 508.3 | 584.2 | 193.2 | 281.5 | 282.0 | 386.3 | 449.9 | 519.4 |
| Other Items (Net)........................... | 17r | 104.1 | 639.8 | 312.6 | † 202.6 | 67.9 | 507.0 | 704.5 | 660.5 | 645.8 | −24.3 | −49.0 | −170.0 |
| Memo Item: | | | | | | | | | | | | | |
| Total Assets.................................. | 10ra | 3,399,611 | 4,559,966 | 9,258,849 | † 9,694,103 | 10,320,452 | 9,056,658 | 8,721,049 | 16,750,588 | 20,042,179 | 14,136,474 | 13,859,225 | 15,632,772 |

| | | 2004 | 2005 | 2006 | 2007 | 2008 | 2009 | 2010 | 2011 | 2012 | 2013 | 2014 | 2015 |
|---|---|---|---|---|---|---|---|---|---|---|---|---|---|
| **Other Depository Corporations** | | | | | | *Billions of Naira: End of Period* | | | | | | | |
| Net Foreign Assets | 21n | 462.4 | 440.0 | 601.7 | † 689.6 | 1,289.1 | 1,067.3 | 1,150.4 | 1,157.9 | 1,660.5 | 1,575.3 | 855.0 | .... |
| Claims on Nonresidents | 21 | 481.3 | 463.2 | 638.1 | † 930.9 | 1,520.7 | 1,265.8 | 1,316.6 | 1,725.9 | 2,028.8 | 2,104.6 | 2,113.5 | .... |
| Liabilities to Nonresidents | 26c | 18.9 | 23.3 | 36.4 | † 241.3 | 231.6 | 198.5 | 166.2 | 568.0 | 368.3 | 529.3 | 1,258.5 | .... |
| Claims on Central Bank | 20 | 364.2 | 515.2 | 471.6 | † 1,390.7 | 1,330.7 | 668.3 | 792.5 | 1,820.9 | 1,909.6 | 4,163.2 | 5,544.1 | .... |
| Currency | 20a | 87.2 | 79.2 | 88.4 | † 222.9 | 262.7 | 254.3 | 295.8 | 320.9 | 330.2 | 328.8 | 430.0 | .... |
| Reserve Deposits and Securities | 20b | 277.0 | 436.1 | 383.2 | † 423.6 | 644.6 | 359.6 | 286.8 | 966.0 | 1,579.0 | 3,292.7 | 4,102.4 | .... |
| Other Claims | 20n | — | — | — | † 744.1 | 423.4 | 54.4 | 209.9 | 534.0 | .4 | 541.7 | 1,011.8 | .... |
| Net Claims on Central Government | 22an | 491.8 | 511.8 | 984.0 | † 1,309.6 | 1,025.1 | 1,509.0 | 2,821.9 | 4,374.7 | 5,005.9 | 3,631.7 | 2,342.3 | .... |
| Claims on Central Government | 22a | 609.1 | 630.8 | 1,145.8 | † 1,489.8 | 1,297.1 | 1,868.7 | 3,233.1 | 4,888.8 | 5,661.7 | 4,590.7 | 3,433.6 | .... |
| Liabilities to Central Government | 26d | 117.2 | 119.1 | 161.8 | † 180.2 | 272.0 | 359.7 | 411.3 | 514.1 | 655.8 | 959.0 | 1,091.4 | .... |
| Claims on Other Sectors | 22s | 1,623.1 | 2,088.6 | 2,714.5 | † 5,638.5 | 9,338.3 | 10,735.3 | 9,535.7 | 8,963.3 | 9,677.3 | 11,294.5 | 14,082.4 | .... |
| Claims on Other Financial Corps | 22g | 66.8 | 86.0 | 188.5 | † 390.1 | 874.8 | 729.5 | 609.0 | 496.8 | 439.2 | 298.7 | 279.3 | .... |
| Claims on State & Local Govts | 22b | 24.6 | 54.5 | 62.2 | † 87.8 | 149.8 | 310.3 | 369.8 | 513.2 | 665.9 | 778.1 | 731.8 | .... |
| Claims on Public Nonfin. Corps | 22c | — | — | — | † 15.2 | 12.8 | 17.8 | 19.8 | 11.5 | 13.7 | 22.4 | 12.5 | .... |
| Claims on Private Sector | 22d | 1,531.7 | 1,948.1 | 2,463.7 | † 5,145.5 | 8,300.9 | 9,677.7 | 8,537.1 | 7,941.8 | 8,558.6 | 10,195.4 | 13,058.8 | .... |
| Liabilities to Central Bank | 26g | 62.1 | 42.7 | 16.6 | † 49.7 | 132.2 | 409.2 | 418.7 | 295.0 | 228.0 | 262.2 | 224.6 | .... |
| Transf.Dep.Included in Broad Money | 24 | 739.2 | 953.2 | 1,114.2 | † 2,429.7 | 3,783.5 | 3,557.2 | 4,087.8 | 4,896.8 | 5,520.5 | 5,925.7 | 5,349.6 | .... |
| Other Dep.Included in Broad Money | 25 | 932.9 | 1,089.5 | 1,739.6 | † 2,686.8 | 4,247.8 | 5,708.0 | 5,941.4 | 6,526.2 | 8,019.1 | 9,602.4 | 11,312.7 | .... |
| Sec.Ot.th.Shares Incl.in Brd. Money | 26a | | | | † — | | | | | | | | .... |
| Deposits Excl. from Broad Money | 26b | — | — | — | † 103.8 | 437.7 | 388.0 | 227.0 | 198.7 | 141.4 | 14.2 | 30.8 | .... |
| Sec.Ot.th.Shares Excl.f/Brd.Money | 26s | 39.4 | 65.4 | 94.1 | † 126.0 | 143.7 | 482.3 | 482.4 | 304.0 | 262.8 | 470.7 | 974.5 | .... |
| Loans | 26l | 10.3 | 23.0 | 45.6 | † — | — | — | — | — | — | — | — | .... |
| Financial Derivatives | 26m | — | — | — | † — | — | — | — | — | — | — | — | .... |
| Insurance Technical Reserves | 26r | | | | † — | | | | | | | | .... |
| Shares and Other Equity | 27a | 348.4 | 591.7 | 953.0 | † 1,916.8 | 3,150.9 | 742.1 | 979.0 | 2,478.3 | 2,824.8 | 3,126.4 | 3,567.8 | .... |
| Other Items (Net) | 27r | 809.2 | 790.0 | 808.7 | † 1,715.5 | 1,087.3 | 2,693.1 | 2,164.3 | 1,617.8 | 1,256.8 | 1,263.1 | 1,363.8 | .... |
| Memo Item: | | | | | | | | | | | | | |
| Total Assets | 20ra | 3,753,278 | 4,515,118 | 6,400,784 | † 10,847,120 | 15,836,640 | 17,292,319 | 17,308,324 | 19,362,939 | 21,235,293 | 24,415,728 | 27,508,454 | .... |
| **Depository Corporations** | | | | | | *Billions of Naira: End of Period* | | | | | | | |
| Net Foreign Assets | 31n | 2,612.4 | 3,865.4 | 6,188.7 | † 7,310.4 | 8,597.2 | 7,287.9 | 6,195.1 | 6,643.7 | 8,715.6 | 8,262.2 | 6,743.4 | .... |
| Claims on Nonresidents | 31 | 2,959.9 | 4,101.1 | 6,255.4 | † 7,603.6 | 8,862.8 | 7,880.6 | 6,750.2 | 7,613.6 | 9,483.9 | 9,197.2 | 8,409.1 | .... |
| Liabilities to Nonresidents | 36c | 347.5 | 235.7 | 66.7 | † 293.2 | 265.6 | 592.7 | 555.1 | 969.8 | 768.2 | 935.1 | 1,665.6 | .... |
| Domestic Claims | 32 | 1,366.0 | 1,267.3 | 918.5 | † 4,020.6 | 6,549.6 | 9,363.9 | 10,426.9 | 14,112.2 | 15,102.8 | 17,702.7 | 19,647.6 | .... |
| Net Claims on Central Government | 32an | −272.4 | −837.4 | −1,812.0 | † −1,855.7 | −3,082.4 | −1,844.3 | 446.9 | 749.6 | 760.1 | 1,838.3 | 702.7 | .... |
| Claims on Central Government | 32a | 1,050.7 | 967.9 | 1,798.3 | † 2,611.8 | 2,015.0 | 2,275.8 | 3,928.2 | 5,570.0 | 6,393.3 | 5,282.7 | 4,359.4 | .... |
| Liabilities to Central Government | 36d | 1,323.0 | 1,805.2 | 3,610.3 | † 4,467.5 | 5,097.4 | 4,120.0 | 3,481.3 | 4,820.4 | 5,633.2 | 3,444.3 | 3,656.7 | .... |
| Claims on Other Sectors | 32s | 1,638.3 | 2,104.7 | 2,730.6 | † 5,876.3 | 9,632.0 | 11,208.2 | 9,980.1 | 13,362.6 | 14,342.7 | 15,864.4 | 18,944.9 | .... |
| Claims on Other Financial Corps | 32g | 78.2 | 97.3 | 188.5 | † 444.2 | 1,103.0 | 1,179.5 | 984.0 | 4,865.2 | 5,070.0 | 4,837.8 | 5,066.5 | .... |
| Claims on State & Local Govts | 32b | 24.6 | 54.5 | 62.2 | † 87.8 | 149.8 | 310.3 | 369.8 | 513.2 | 665.9 | 778.1 | 731.8 | .... |
| Claims on Public Nonfin. Corps | 32c | 1.9 | 2.4 | 13.2 | † 57.1 | 54.5 | 31.1 | 72.0 | 35.0 | 37.2 | 45.9 | 38.1 | .... |
| Claims on Private Sector | 32d | 1,533.6 | 1,950.4 | 2,466.6 | † 5,287.3 | 8,324.8 | 9,687.3 | 8,554.2 | 7,949.1 | 8,569.6 | 10,202.5 | 13,108.6 | .... |
| Broad Money Liabilities | 35l | 2,131.2 | 2,612.9 | 3,562.7 | † 5,875.8 | 9,315.1 | 10,918.7 | 11,662.9 | 13,179.0 | 15,391.2 | 17,307.4 | 18,170.0 | .... |
| Currency Outside Depository Corps | 34a | 458.6 | 563.2 | 690.8 | † 732.9 | 892.9 | 927.2 | 1,082.4 | 1,245.1 | 1,301.5 | 1,447.6 | 1,368.0 | .... |
| Transferable Deposits | 34 | 739.6 | 960.2 | 1,132.2 | † 2,456.0 | 4,174.4 | 4,283.4 | 4,636.4 | 5,403.2 | 6,065.2 | 6,251.3 | 5,484.6 | .... |
| Other Deposits | 35 | 933.0 | 1,089.5 | 1,739.6 | † 2,686.8 | 4,247.8 | 5,708.0 | 5,941.4 | 6,526.7 | 8,021.2 | 9,603.5 | 11,313.5 | .... |
| Securities Other than Shares | 36a | | | | † — | — | — | 2.7 | 4.0 | 3.3 | 5.0 | 3.9 | .... |
| Deposits Excl. from Broad Money | 36b | 143.1 | 24.7 | 113.7 | † 820.5 | 946.9 | 1,004.7 | 723.8 | 1,529.0 | 780.3 | 537.9 | 617.9 | .... |
| Sec.Ot.th.Shares Excl.f/Brd.Money | 36s | 39.4 | 65.4 | 94.1 | † 126.0 | 143.7 | 482.3 | 482.4 | 413.7 | 387.5 | 550.7 | 1,046.3 | .... |
| Loans | 36l | 10.3 | 23.0 | 45.6 | † — | — | — | — | — | — | — | — | .... |
| Financial Derivatives | 36m | — | — | — | † — | — | — | — | — | — | — | — | .... |
| Insurance Technical Reserves | 36r | | | | † — | | | | | | | | .... |
| Shares and Other Equity | 37a | 861.4 | 1,346.4 | 2,471.0 | † 2,245.4 | 3,659.2 | 1,326.3 | 1,172.2 | 2,759.8 | 3,106.8 | 3,512.7 | 4,017.7 | .... |
| Other Items (Net) | 37r | 792.9 | 1,060.2 | 820.1 | † 2,263.3 | 1,081.9 | 2,919.9 | 2,580.8 | 2,874.3 | 4,152.6 | 4,056.2 | 2,539.2 | .... |
| Broad Money Liabs., Seasonally Adj. | 35l.b | 2,244.0 | 2,761.4 | 3,772.9 | † 5,630.2 | 8,946.4 | 10,528.1 | 11,301.9 | 12,844.7 | 15,062.6 | 16,976.0 | 17,830.4 | .... |
| **Monetary Aggregates** | | | | | | *Billions of Naira: End of Period* | | | | | | | |
| Broad Money | 59m | .... | .... | .... | 5,875.8 | 9,315.1 | 10,918.7 | 11,662.9 | 13,179.0 | 15,391.2 | 17,307.4 | 18,173.8 | .... |
| o/w:Currency Issued by Cent.Govt | 59m.a | .... | .... | .... | — | — | — | — | — | — | — | — | — |
| o/w: Dep.in Nonfin. Corporations | 59m.b | .... | .... | .... | — | — | — | — | — | — | — | — | — |
| o/w:Secs. Issued by Central Govt | 59m.c | .... | .... | .... | — | — | — | — | — | — | — | 3.9 | — |
| Money (National Definitions) | | | | | | | | | | | | | |
| M1 | 59ma | 1,330.7 | 1,537.0 | 1,935.0 | 3,188.9 | 5,067.3 | 5,210.7 | 5,718.8 | 6,648.4 | 7,366.8 | 7,698.9 | 6,852.6 | .... |
| Quasi Money | 59mal | 933.0 | 1,089.5 | 1,739.6 | 2,686.8 | 4,247.8 | 5,708.0 | 5,941.4 | 6,526.7 | 8,021.2 | 9,603.5 | 11,313.5 | .... |
| M2 | 59mb | 2,263.6 | 2,437.9 | 3,674.6 | 5,875.8 | 9,315.1 | 10,918.7 | 11,660.2 | 13,175.0 | 15,388.0 | 17,302.3 | 18,166.1 | .... |
| **Interest Rates** | | | | | | *Percent Per Annum* | | | | | | | |
| Discount Rate (End of Period) | 60.a | 15.00 | 13.00 | 10.00 | 9.50 | 9.75 | 6.00 | 6.25 | 12.00 | 12.00 | 12.00 | 13.00 | 11.00 |
| Treasury Bill Rate | 60c | 14.34 | 7.63 | 9.99 | 6.85 | 8.20 | 3.79 | 3.85 | 9.70 | 13.64 | 10.85 | 10.50 | 9.40 |
| Deposit Rate | 60l | 13.70 | 10.53 | 9.74 | 10.29 | 11.97 | 13.30 | 6.52 | 5.70 | 8.41 | 7.95 | 9.34 | 9.15 |
| Lending Rate | 60p | 19.18 | 17.95 | 16.90 | 16.94 | 15.48 | 18.36 | 17.59 | 16.02 | 16.79 | 16.72 | 16.55 | 16.85 |
| **Prices and Production** | | | | | | *Index Numbers (2010=100): Period Averages* | | | | | | | |
| Consumer Prices | 64 | 52.6 | 61.9 | 67.0 | 70.7 | 78.8 | † 87.9 | 100.0 | 110.8 | 124.4 | 134.9 | 145.8 | 158.9 |
| Industrial Production | 66 | 95.7 | 100.0 | 100.3 | 100.1 | 97.8 | .... | .... | .... | .... | .... | .... | .... |
| Crude Petroleum Production | 66aa | 104.1 | 100.0 | 93.5 | 90.6 | .... | .... | .... | .... | .... | .... | .... | .... |
| Manufacturing Prod. (2005=100) | 66ey | 99.7 | 100.0 | 99.8 | 100.0 | 101.6 | .... | .... | .... | .... | .... | .... | .... |
| **Intl. Transactions & Positions** | | | | | | *Millions of US Dollars* | | | | | | | |
| Exports | 70..d | 31,148 | 55,144 | 57,444 | 65,133 | 80,615 | 56,742 | 84,000 | 114,500 | 114,000 | .... | .... | .... |
| Crude Petroleum | 70aad | 28,428 | 39,703 | 43,273 | 55,817 | 74,305 | .... | .... | .... | .... | .... | .... | .... |
| Imports, c.i.f | 71..d | 14,164 | 21,314 | 26,760 | 37,576 | 42,378 | 33,906 | 44,235 | 64,410 | 35,703 | 44,598 | .... | .... |
| Volume of Exports | | | | | | *2010=100* | | | | | | | |
| Crude Petroleum | 72aa | 102.4 | 100.0 | 88.6 | 85.8 | .... | .... | .... | .... | .... | .... | .... | .... |

# Nigeria 694

| | | 2004 | 2005 | 2006 | 2007 | 2008 | 2009 | 2010 | 2011 | 2012 | 2013 | 2014 | 2015 |
|---|---|---|---|---|---|---|---|---|---|---|---|---|---|
| **Balance of Payments** | | | | | | | | *Millions of US Dollars* | | | | | |
| A. Current Account* | 109bx | 16,840.3 | 36,529.0 | 36,518.0 | 27,643.4 | 29,154.2 | 13,867.6 | 13,111.2 | 10,668.4 | 17,374.3 | 19,049.0 | 1,268.3 | .... |
| Goods, credit (exports) | 1a9cx | 34,766.2 | 55,201.5 | 56,934.9 | 66,039.6 | 85,772.0 | 56,167.4 | 79,618.5 | 99,051.5 | 96,123.9 | 97,023.1 | 81,917.9 | .... |
| Goods, debit (imports) | 1a9dx | 15,008.8 | 26,003.1 | 21,988.0 | 28,291.2 | 39,844.1 | 30,779.3 | 49,520.3 | 66,223.2 | 56,933.4 | 54,851.2 | 61,095.4 | .... |
| Balance on goods | 1a9bx | 19,757.5 | 29,198.4 | 34,947.0 | 37,748.4 | 45,927.9 | 25,388.1 | 30,098.1 | 32,828.3 | 39,190.4 | 42,171.9 | 20,822.5 | .... |
| Services, credit (exports) | 1b9cx | 3,336.0 | 1,792.6 | 2,298.7 | 1,442.9 | 2,263.7 | 2,217.9 | 3,080.5 | 3,386.6 | 2,400.3 | 2,396.2 | 1,975.2 | .... |
| Services, debit (imports) | 1b9dx | 5,973.2 | 6,623.5 | 13,923.9 | 18,345.2 | 24,376.7 | 18,696.8 | 21,332.4 | 24,571.0 | 23,941.1 | 21,802.9 | 24,259.6 | .... |
| Balance on Goods & Services | 1z9bx | 17,120.2 | 24,367.5 | 23,321.8 | 20,846.1 | 23,814.9 | 8,909.2 | 11,846.2 | 11,643.9 | 17,649.6 | 22,765.1 | −1,461.8 | .... |
| Primary income: credit | 1c9cx | 157.4 | 155.1 | 1,875.2 | 2,563.7 | 2,351.9 | 935.3 | 997.7 | 897.5 | 956.5 | 880.8 | 1,619.8 | .... |
| Primary income: debit | 1c9dx | 2,689.2 | 3,146.1 | 6,476.8 | 14,311.4 | 17,410.9 | 15,338.7 | 20,437.7 | 23,679.7 | 23,042.0 | 26,401.5 | 20,630.3 | .... |
| Balance on gds, serv. & prim. inc. | 1y9bx | 14,588.4 | 21,376.5 | 18,720.1 | 9,098.5 | 8,755.9 | −5,494.2 | −7,593.7 | −11,138.3 | −4,435.8 | −2,755.5 | −20,472.3 | .... |
| Secondary income: credit | 1d9ca | 2,272.7 | 15,283.9 | 17,975.0 | 18,695.0 | 20,929.1 | 19,825.5 | 21,183.0 | 22,278.6 | 22,292.6 | 22,527.3 | 22,616.2 | .... |
| Secondary income: debit | 1d9da | 20.9 | 131.4 | 177.1 | 150.1 | 530.7 | 463.7 | 478.0 | 471.9 | 482.4 | 722.8 | 875.6 | .... |
| B. Capital Account* | 209ba | .3 | 7,335.6 | 10,555.6 | — | — | — | — | — | — | — | — | .... |
| Capital account: credit | 209ca | .3 | 7,335.6 | 10,555.6 | — | — | — | — | — | — | — | — | .... |
| Capital account: debit | 209da | — | — | — | — | — | — | — | — | — | — | — | .... |
| Balance on current & capital acct. | 129ba | 16,840.6 | 43,864.6 | 47,073.7 | 27,643.4 | 29,154.2 | 13,867.6 | 13,111.2 | 10,668.4 | 17,374.3 | 19,049.0 | 1,268.3 | .... |
| C. Financial Account* | 309na | 13,060.5 | 15,184.3 | 16,027.8 | 4,286.0 | 6,714.9 | −1,995.7 | 7,890.4 | 5,097.7 | 1,278.1 | −6,705.8 | −4,638.6 | .... |
| Direct investment: assets | 3a9aa | — | 14.6 | 319.6 | 867.5 | 1,051.6 | 1,525.1 | 911.7 | 816.8 | 1,530.1 | 1,227.4 | 1,601.2 | .... |
| Equity & investment fund shares | 3aaaa | — | 14.6 | 319.6 | 867.5 | 1,051.6 | 1,525.1 | 911.7 | 816.8 | 1,530.1 | 1,227.4 | 1,601.2 | .... |
| Debt instruments | 3abaa | .... | | | | | | | | | | | .... |
| Direct investment: liabilities | 3a9la | 1,874.0 | 4,982.5 | 4,854.4 | 6,035.0 | 8,196.6 | 8,554.8 | 6,026.2 | 8,841.1 | 7,069.9 | 5,562.9 | 4,655.8 | .... |
| Equity & investment fund shares | 3aala | 1,615.5 | 4,982.5 | 4,854.4 | 5,997.3 | 8,133.4 | 8,534.4 | 5,966.4 | 8,588.8 | 7,002.6 | 5,534.3 | 4,642.9 | .... |
| Debt instruments | 3abla | 258.5 | .... | — | 37.7 | 63.2 | 20.5 | 59.9 | 252.3 | 67.3 | 28.6 | 12.9 | .... |
| Portfolio investment: assets | 3b9aa | −177.8 | 1,371.9 | 1,512.5 | 1,843.3 | 4,728.7 | 821.7 | 1,116.8 | 1,609.5 | 2,069.4 | 3,220.2 | 3,421.2 | .... |
| Equity & investment fund shares | 3baaa | | 1,240.2 | 1,364.4 | 1,706.1 | 4,041.0 | 753.2 | 1,023.7 | 1,475.4 | 1,896.9 | 2,576.2 | 2,737.0 | .... |
| Debt securities | 3bbaa | −177.8 | 131.7 | 148.2 | 137.2 | 687.7 | 68.5 | 93.1 | 134.1 | 172.4 | 644.0 | 684.2 | .... |
| Portfolio investment: liabilities | 3b9la | — | 883.9 | 2,800.6 | 2,642.8 | 1,325.9 | 476.4 | 3,703.2 | 5,149.8 | 17,061.9 | 13,541.2 | 5,249.9 | .... |
| Equity & investment fund shares | 3bala | .... | 750.8 | 1,769.2 | 1,447.1 | −953.7 | 487.3 | 2,153.3 | 2,570.8 | 9,959.1 | 5,532.1 | 1,036.5 | .... |
| Debt securities | 3bbla | — | 133.1 | 1,031.4 | 1,195.8 | 2,279.6 | −10.9 | 1,549.9 | 2,579.0 | 7,102.8 | 8,009.1 | 4,213.4 | .... |
| Fin. der.& empl.stk.ops.(ESOs): net | 3c9na | .... | | | | | | | | | | | .... |
| Fin. der. & ESOs.: assets | 3c9aa | .... | .... | .... | .... | .... | .... | .... | .... | .... | .... | .... | .... |
| Fin. der. & ESOs.: liabilities | 3c9la | .... | .... | .... | .... | .... | .... | .... | .... | .... | .... | .... | .... |
| Other investment: assets | 3d9aa | 7,300.8 | 1,487.0 | 6,199.0 | 13,227.7 | 10,763.5 | 6,487.9 | 13,449.1 | 17,392.6 | 22,618.6 | 10,274.2 | 10,819.8 | .... |
| Other equity | 3daaa | .... | | | | | | | | | | | .... |
| Debt instruments | 3dzaa | 7,300.8 | 1,487.0 | 6,199.0 | 13,227.7 | 10,763.5 | 6,487.9 | 13,449.1 | 17,392.6 | 22,618.6 | 10,274.2 | 10,819.8 | .... |
| Other investment: liabilities | 3d9la | −7,811.6 | −18,177.3 | −15,651.6 | 2,974.7 | 306.5 | 1,799.1 | −2,142.3 | 730.2 | 808.3 | 2,323.6 | 10,575.1 | .... |
| Other equity | 3dala | | | | | | | | | | | | .... |
| Debt instruments | 3dzla | −7,811.6 | −18,177.3 | −15,651.6 | 2,974.7 | 306.5 | 1,799.1 | −2,142.3 | 730.2 | 808.3 | 2,323.6 | 10,575.1 | .... |
| Curr.+ cap.− finan. acct. balance | 4y9na | 3,780.0 | 28,680.3 | 31,045.9 | 23,357.4 | 22,439.4 | 15,863.3 | 5,220.8 | 5,570.7 | 16,096.3 | 25,754.8 | 5,906.9 | .... |
| D. Net Errors and Omissions | 409na | 4,711.2 | −17,344.5 | −17,151.3 | −14,398.8 | −20,782.2 | −26,378.0 | −14,913.7 | −5,264.9 | −4,998.5 | −26,734.9 | −14,291.0 | .... |
| E. Reserves and Related Items | 4z9na | 8,491.3 | 11,335.8 | 13,894.7 | 8,958.6 | 1,657.1 | −10,514.7 | −9,692.9 | 305.9 | 11,097.8 | −980.1 | −8,384.1 | .... |
| Reserve assets | 3e9aa | 9,530.9 | 11,335.8 | 13,894.7 | 8,958.6 | 1,657.1 | −10,514.7 | −9,692.9 | 305.9 | 11,097.8 | −980.1 | −8,384.1 | .... |
| Credit and loans from the IMF | 3dcla | — | — | — | — | — | — | — | — | — | — | — | .... |
| Exceptional financing | 409la | 1,039.7 | — | — | — | — | — | — | — | — | — | — | .... |

*Excludes components in group E

| **International Investment Position** | | | | | | | | *Millions of US Dollars* | | | | | |
|---|---|---|---|---|---|---|---|---|---|---|---|---|---|
| Assets | 809aa | .... | 41,832.3 | 60,495.4 | 75,506.8 | 91,380.5 | 80,763.7 | 84,379.6 | 99,070.8 | 120,816.6 | 124,376.6 | 119,786.7 | .... |
| Direct investment | 8a9aa | .... | 305.0 | 624.5 | 1,506.4 | 2,564.6 | 4,118.3 | 5,041.0 | 5,864.7 | 7,347.0 | 8,574.4 | 10,258.9 | .... |
| Equity & investment fund shares | 8aaaa | .... | 305.0 | 624.5 | 1,506.4 | 2,564.6 | 4,118.3 | 5,041.0 | 5,864.7 | 7,347.0 | 8,574.4 | 10,258.9 | .... |
| Debt instruments | 8abaa | .... | | | | | | | | | | | .... |
| Portfolio investment | 8b9aa | .... | 2,851.4 | 4,349.2 | 6,208.4 | 10,966.9 | 11,797.8 | 12,928.0 | 14,551.3 | 16,502.1 | 19,722.2 | 23,333.0 | .... |
| Equity & investment fund shares | 8baaa | .... | 2,572.1 | 3,923.2 | 5,644.0 | 9,710.4 | 10,472.0 | 11,508.0 | 12,996.1 | 14,787.1 | 17,363.1 | 20,264.8 | .... |
| Debt securities | 8bbaa | .... | 279.3 | 426.0 | 564.5 | 1,256.5 | 1,325.8 | 1,419.9 | 1,555.2 | 1,715.0 | 2,359.0 | 3,068.2 | .... |
| Fin. der.(oth.than reserves) & ESOs | 8c9aa | .... | | | | | | | | | | | .... |
| Other investment | 8d9aa | .... | 10,318.1 | 13,223.4 | 16,457.6 | 24,849.4 | 22,508.4 | 34,071.5 | 46,014.3 | 53,471.9 | 53,559.7 | 51,952.3 | .... |
| Other equity | 8daaa | .... | | | | | | | | | | | .... |
| Debt instruments | 8dzaa | .... | 10,318.1 | 13,223.4 | 16,457.6 | 24,849.4 | 22,508.4 | 34,071.5 | 46,014.3 | 53,471.9 | 53,559.7 | 51,952.3 | .... |
| Reserve assets | 8e9aa | .... | 28,357.7 | 42,298.3 | 51,334.3 | 52,999.6 | 42,339.2 | 32,339.2 | 32,640.5 | 43,495.6 | 42,520.3 | 34,242.4 | .... |
| Liabilities | 809la | .... | 64,221.3 | 55,202.5 | 66,968.0 | 76,850.6 | 88,655.0 | 96,286.8 | 111,125.9 | 139,050.3 | 162,307.5 | 182,671.8 | .... |
| Direct investment | 8a9la | .... | 26,608.5 | 31,242.8 | 37,330.2 | 45,577.3 | 54,227.3 | 60,326.0 | 69,242.9 | 75,748.7 | 81,310.9 | 86,671.2 | .... |
| Equity & investment fund shares | 8aala | .... | 25,278.0 | 29,925.6 | 35,974.9 | 44,158.5 | 52,787.8 | 58,825.8 | 67,488.2 | 73,941.0 | 79,474.7 | 84,806.9 | .... |
| Debt instruments | 8abla | .... | 1,330.4 | 1,317.3 | 1,355.3 | 1,418.9 | 1,439.6 | 1,500.2 | 1,754.7 | 1,807.7 | 1,836.3 | 1,864.3 | .... |
| Portfolio investment | 8b9la | .... | 6,946.4 | 9,703.2 | 12,368.9 | 13,702.7 | 14,368.8 | 18,116.6 | 23,310.0 | 40,181.1 | 53,721.9 | 59,455.0 | .... |
| Equity & investment fund shares | 8bala | .... | 3,585.5 | 5,335.0 | 6,794.6 | 5,834.6 | 6,327.3 | 8,506.5 | 11,099.1 | 20,967.2 | 26,499.1 | 27,761.3 | .... |
| Debt securities | 8bbla | .... | 3,360.9 | 4,368.2 | 5,574.3 | 7,868.2 | 8,041.5 | 9,610.0 | 12,210.9 | 19,213.9 | 27,222.8 | 31,693.7 | .... |
| Fin. der.(oth.than reserves) & ESOs | 8c9la | .... | | | | | | | | | | | .... |
| Other investment | 8d9la | .... | 30,666.5 | 14,256.5 | 17,269.0 | 17,570.5 | 20,058.8 | 17,844.2 | 18,573.0 | 23,120.4 | 27,274.7 | 36,545.6 | .... |
| Other equity | 8dala | .... | | | | | | | | | | | .... |
| Debt instruments | 8dzla | .... | 30,666.5 | 14,256.5 | 17,269.0 | 17,570.5 | 20,058.8 | 17,844.2 | 18,573.0 | 23,120.4 | 27,274.7 | 36,545.6 | .... |

# Nigeria 694

| | | 2004 | 2005 | 2006 | 2007 | 2008 | 2009 | 2010 | 2011 | 2012 | 2013 | 2014 | 2015 |
|---|---|---|---|---|---|---|---|---|---|---|---|---|---|
| **Government Finance** | | | | | | | | | | | | | |
| **Cash Flow Statement** | | | | | | | | | | | | | |
| **Budgetary Central Government** | | | | | | *Billions of Naira: Fiscal Year Ends December 31* | | | | | | | |
| Cash Receipts:Operating Activities... | c1 | 1,331.6 | 1,758.3 | 1,937.1 | 2,333.7 | 3,193.5 | 2,642.9 | 3,089.2 | 3,553.5 | 3,629.7 | 4,031.8 | .... | .... |
| Taxes........................................ | c11 | 105.7 | 423.6 | 450.6 | 832.8 | 1,346.5 | 1,289.3 | 1,258.3 | 1,149.6 | 1,130.2 | 1,201.0 | .... | .... |
| Social Contributions...................... | c12 | — | — | — | — | — | — | — | — | — | — | .... | .... |
| Grants........................................ | c13 | — | — | — | — | — | — | — | — | — | — | .... | .... |
| Other Receipts............................. | c14 | 1,225.9 | 1,334.7 | 1,486.5 | 1,500.9 | 1,847.0 | 1,353.6 | 1,830.9 | 2,403.9 | 2,499.5 | 2,830.8 | .... | .... |
| Cash Payments:Operating Activities. | c2 | 1,153.0 | 1,400.3 | 1,485.6 | 1,691.6 | 2,280.0 | 2,300.1 | 3,310.8 | 3,793.7 | 3,730.5 | 4,076.8 | .... | .... |
| Compensation of Employees.......... | c21 | 370.4 | 443.3 | 527.9 | 761.2 | 942.8 | 952.6 | 1,380.5 | 1,722.4 | 1,663.5 | 1,721.3 | .... | .... |
| Purchases of Goods & Services....... | c22 | 128.1 | 203.2 | 258.6 | 368.1 | 457.4 | 564.2 | 982.3 | 673.3 | 589.6 | 525.8 | .... | .... |
| Interest...................................... | c24 | 382.5 | 394.0 | 249.3 | 213.7 | 381.2 | 251.7 | 415.7 | 527.2 | 679.3 | 828.1 | .... | .... |
| Subsidies.................................... | c25 | — | — | — | — | — | 3.6 | 19.3 | 263.4 | 246.5 | 183.4 | .... | .... |
| Grants........................................ | c26 | 42.2 | 78.9 | 95.4 | 102.3 | 162.6 | 168.6 | 182.0 | 215.7 | 158.9 | 204.4 | .... | .... |
| Social Benefits............................. | c27 | 229.8 | 280.9 | 354.4 | 246.3 | 336.0 | 359.4 | 331.0 | 391.7 | 392.7 | 613.8 | .... | .... |
| Other Payments........................... | c28 | — | — | — | — | — | — | — | — | — | — | .... | .... |
| Net Cash Inflow:Operating Act.[1-2] | ccio | 178.6 | 358.0 | 451.5 | 642.1 | 913.5 | 342.8 | −221.6 | −240.2 | −100.8 | −45.0 | .... | .... |
| Net Cash Outflow:Invest. in NFA...... | c31 | 351.3 | 519.5 | 552.4 | 759.3 | 960.9 | 1,152.8 | 883.9 | 918.5 | 874.7 | 1,108.4 | .... | .... |
| Purchases of Nonfinancial Assets... | c31.1 | 351.3 | 519.5 | 552.4 | 759.3 | 960.9 | 1,152.8 | 883.9 | 918.5 | 874.7 | .... | .... | .... |
| Sales of Nonfinancial Assets.......... | c31.2 | — | — | — | — | — | — | — | — | — | .... | .... | .... |
| Cash Surplus/Deficit [1-2-31=1-2M] | ccsd | −172.7 | −161.5 | −100.9 | −117.2 | −47.4 | −810.0 | −1,105.5 | −1,158.7 | −975.5 | −1,153.4 | .... | .... |
| Net Acq. Fin. Assets, excl. Cash...... | c32x | — | — | — | −12.3 | — | −7.0 | −6.4 | −3.0 | −7.5 | .... | .... | .... |
| Domestic.................................... | c321x | — | — | — | −12.3 | — | −7.0 | −6.4 | −3.0 | −7.5 | .... | .... | .... |
| Foreign...................................... | c322x | — | — | — | — | — | — | — | — | — | .... | .... | .... |
| Net Incurrence of Liabilities............. | c33 | 46.5 | 161.4 | 100.8 | 117.2 | 150.7 | 607.4 | 1,185.5 | 928.6 | 975.7 | 1,153.5 | .... | .... |
| Domestic.................................... | c331 | 46.5 | 161.4 | 100.8 | 117.2 | 150.7 | 577.6 | 1,110.5 | 855.3 | 975.7 | 1,153.5 | .... | .... |
| Foreign...................................... | c332 | — | — | — | — | — | 29.8 | 75.0 | 73.3 | — | — | .... | .... |
| Net Cash Inflow, Fin.Act.[-32x+33].. | cnfb | 46.5 | 161.4 | 100.8 | 129.5 | 150.7 | 614.4 | 1,191.9 | 931.6 | 983.2 | 1,153.5 | .... | .... |
| Net Change in Stock of Cash........... | cncb | −126.2 | −.1 | −.1 | 12.3 | 103.3 | −195.6 | 86.4 | −227.1 | 7.7 | .1 | .... | .... |
| Stat. Discrep. [32X-33+NCB-CSD].... | ccsdz | — | — | — | — | — | — | — | — | — | — | .... | .... |
| Memo Item:Cash Expenditure[2+31] | c2m | 1,504.3 | 1,919.8 | 2,038.0 | 2,450.9 | 3,240.9 | 3,452.9 | 4,194.7 | 4,712.2 | 4,605.2 | 5,185.2 | .... | .... |
| Memo Item: Gross Debt.................. | c63 | 6,260.6 | 4,221.0 | 2,204.8 | 2,597.7 | 2,843.6 | 3,818.4 | 5,241.6 | 6,519.6 | 7,564.4 | 8,506.3 | .... | .... |
| **National Accounts** | | | | | | *Billions of Naira* | | | | | | | |
| Househ.Cons.Expend.,incl.NPISHs.... | 96f | 8,638 | 11,075 | 11,290 | 15,683 | 15,756 | 18,860 | † 36,677 | 41,687 | 42,394 | 59,048 | 63,861 | .... |
| Government Consumption Expend... | 91f | 786 | 1,003 | 1,283 | 2,609 | 3,134 | 3,213 | † 4,832 | 5,412 | 5,953 | 5,796 | 6,639 | .... |
| Gross Fixed Capital Formation.......... | 93e | 1,382 | .... | .... | .... | .... | .... | † 9,183 | 9,897 | 10,282 | 11,478 | 13,594 | .... |
| Changes in Inventories.................... | 93i | 1 | 1 | 1 | 2 | 2 | 2 | † 408 | 432 | 541 | 596 | 648 | .... |
| Exports of Goods and Services......... | 90c | 3,521 | 4,665 | 8,599 | 7,063 | 9,837 | 7,766 | † 14,014 | 19,961 | 22,824 | 14,622 | 16,617 | .... |
| Imports of Goods and Services (-)..... | 98c | 2,135 | 2,813 | 4,011 | 6,350 | 6,115 | 7,664 | † 9,645 | 13,676 | 9,395 | 10,530 | 11,222 | .... |
| Gross Domestic Product (GDP)......... | 99b | 11,411 | 14,572 | 18,565 | 20,657 | 24,296 | 24,794 | † 55,469 | 63,713 | 72,600 | 81,010 | 90,137 | .... |
| Net Primary Income from Abroad..... | 98.n | −461 | .... | .... | .... | .... | .... | .... | .... | .... | .... | .... | .... |
| Gross National Income (GNI)........... | 99a | 8,092 | .... | .... | .... | .... | .... | .... | .... | .... | .... | .... | .... |
| Consumption of Fixed Capital.......... | 99cf | 47 | .... | .... | .... | .... | .... | † 2,451 | 3,054 | 3,779 | 3,715 | 4,195 | .... |
| GDP, Production Based................... | 99bp | .... | .... | .... | .... | .... | .... | † 33,985 | 37,303 | .... | .... | .... | .... |
| GDP at Fact.Cost,Vol.'84 Prices....... | 99bap | .... | .... | .... | .... | .... | .... | .... | .... | .... | .... | .... | .... |
| GDP Volume 2010 Prices................ | 99b.p | .... | .... | .... | .... | .... | .... | † 55,469 | 58,180 | 60,670 | 63,943 | .... | .... |
| GDP Volume (2010=100)................ | 99bvp | .... | .... | .... | .... | 86.7 | 92.7 | † 100.0 | 104.9 | 109.4 | 115.3 | .... | .... |
| GDP Deflator (2010=100)............... | 99bip | .... | .... | .... | .... | 50.5 | 48.2 | † 100.0 | 109.5 | 119.7 | 126.7 | .... | .... |
| | | | | | | *Millions: Midyear Estimates* | | | | | | | |
| **Population................................** | 99z | 136.03 | 139.61 | 143.32 | 147.15 | 151.12 | 155.21 | 159.42 | 163.77 | 168.24 | 172.82 | 177.48 | 182.20 |

|  |  | 2004 | 2005 | 2006 | 2007 | 2008 | 2009 | 2010 | 2011 | 2012 | 2013 | 2014 | 2015 |
|---|---|---|---|---|---|---|---|---|---|---|---|---|---|
| **Exchange Rates** | | | | | | *Kroner per SDR: End of Period* | | | | | | | |
| Official Rate | aa | 9.380 | 9.676 | 9.418 | 8.549 | 10.782 | 9.061 | 9.025 | 9.196 | 8.561 | 9.363 | 10.765 | 12.208 |
|  | | | | | *Kroner per US Dollar: End of Period (ae) Period Average (rf)* | | | | | | | | |
| Official Rate | ae | 6.040 | 6.770 | 6.260 | 5.410 | 7.000 | 5.780 | 5.860 | 5.990 | 5.570 | 6.080 | 7.430 | 8.810 |
| Official Rate | rf | 6.741 | 6.443 | 6.413 | 5.862 | 5.640 | 6.288 | 6.044 | 5.605 | 5.818 | 5.875 | 6.302 | 8.064 |
|  | | | | *Kroner per Euro: End of Period (ea)  Period Average (eb)* | | | | | | | | | |
| Euro Rate | ea | 8.240 | 7.990 | 8.240 | 7.960 | 9.860 | 8.310 | 7.810 | 7.750 | 7.340 | 8.380 | 9.040 | 9.620 |
| Euro Rate | eb | 8.371 | 8.013 | 8.048 | 8.018 | 8.223 | 8.729 | 8.008 | 7.793 | 7.476 | 7.804 | 8.354 | 8.941 |
|  | | | | | *Index Numbers (2010=100): Period Averages* | | | | | | | | |
| Official Rate | ahx | 89.7 | 93.7 | 94.2 | 103.3 | 108.5 | 96.5 | 100.0 | 107.8 | 103.8 | 102.9 | 96.1 | 75.0 |
| Nominal Effective Exchange Rate | nec | 94.6 | 98.6 | 98.1 | 100.4 | 100.3 | 95.8 | 100.0 | 102.3 | 103.4 | 101.2 | 95.3 | 86.1 |
| CPI-Based Real Effect. Ex. Rate | rec | 93.7 | 97.3 | 97.2 | 97.7 | 97.8 | 95.2 | 100.0 | 100.6 | 100.3 | 98.9 | 94.0 | 86.3 |
| ULC-Based Real Effect. Ex. Rate | rel | 78.5 | 83.9 | 90.8 | 96.9 | 97.5 | 92.8 | 100.0 | 107.1 | 110.4 | 109.7 | 105.0 | 96.6 |
| **Fund Position** | | | | | | *Millions of SDRs: End of Period* | | | | | | | |
| Quota | 2f.s | 1,671.70 | 1,671.70 | 1,671.70 | 1,671.70 | 1,671.70 | 1,671.70 | 1,671.70 | 1,883.70 | 1,883.70 | 1,883.70 | 1,883.70 | 1,883.70 |
| SDR Holdings | 1b.s | 232.31 | 214.85 | 301.22 | 232.57 | 283.48 | 1,600.22 | 1,594.47 | 1,523.46 | 1,501.57 | 1,486.66 | 1,481.75 | 1,506.17 |
| Reserve Position in the Fund | 1c.s | 559.24 | 210.92 | 137.61 | 112.64 | 194.19 | 403.19 | 391.00 | 941.69 | 1,007.95 | 912.91 | 733.64 | 569.30 |
| Total Fund Cred. & Loans Outstg. | 2tl | — | — | — | — | — | — | — | — | — | — | — | — |
| SDR Allocations | 1bd | 167.77 | 167.77 | 167.77 | 167.77 | 167.77 | 1,563.07 | 1,563.07 | 1,563.07 | 1,563.07 | 1,563.07 | 1,563.07 | 1,563.07 |
| **International Liquidity** | | | | *Millions of US Dollars Unless Otherwise Indicated: End of Period* | | | | | | | | | |
| Total Reserves minus Gold | 1l.d | 44,307.5 | 46,985.9 | 56,841.6 | 60,839.6 | 50,949.8 | 48,859.3 | 52,797.9 | 49,397.1 | 51,856.4 | 58,283.1 | 64,800.7 | 57,455.9 |
| SDR Holdings | 1b.d | 360.8 | 307.1 | 453.2 | 367.5 | 436.6 | 2,508.7 | 2,455.5 | 2,338.9 | 2,307.8 | 2,289.5 | 2,146.8 | 2,087.1 |
| Reserve Position in the Fund | 1c.d | 868.5 | 301.5 | 207.0 | 178.0 | 299.1 | 632.1 | 602.2 | 1,445.7 | 1,549.1 | 1,405.9 | 1,062.9 | 788.9 |
| Foreign Exchange | 1d.d | 43,078.2 | 46,377.4 | 56,181.4 | 60,294.1 | 50,214.1 | 45,718.6 | 49,740.2 | 45,612.4 | 47,999.5 | 54,587.8 | 61,591.1 | 54,579.9 |
| Gold (Million Fine Troy Ounces) | 1ad | — | — | — | — | — | — | — | — | — | — | — | — |
| Gold (National Valuation) | 1and | — | — | — | — | — | — | — | — | — | — | — | — |
| Monetary Authorities: Other Liabs. | 4..d | 51 | 56 | 14 | 16 | 7,982 | 43 | .... | .... | .... | .... | .... | .... |
| Deposit Money Banks: Assets | 7a.d | 25,182.4 | 34,060.9 | 63,105.3 | .... | .... | .... | .... | .... | .... | .... | .... | .... |
| Deposit Money Banks: Liabs | 7b.d | 76,042.3 | 93,243.4 | 140,232.3 | .... | .... | .... | .... | .... | .... | .... | .... | .... |
| Other Banking Insts.: Liabilities | 7f.d | 33,134.5 | 34,014.5 | 44,157.4 | .... | .... | .... | .... | .... | .... | .... | .... | .... |
| **Monetary Authorities** | | | | | | *Billions of Kroner: End of Period* | | | | | | | |
| Foreign Assets | 11 | 268.19 | 316.03 | 350.29 | 327.47 | 413.48 | 280.74 | .... | .... | .... | .... | .... | .... |
| Claims on Central Government | 12a | — | — | — | — | — | — | .... | .... | .... | .... | .... | .... |
| Claims on Local Government | 12b | — | — | — | — | — | — | .... | .... | .... | .... | .... | .... |
| Claims on Nonfin.Pub.Enterprises | 12c | — | — | — | — | — | — | .... | .... | .... | .... | .... | .... |
| Claims on Private Sector | 12d | .49 | .48 | .47 | .44 | .49 | .48 | .... | .... | .... | .... | .... | .... |
| Claims on Deposit Money Banks | 12e | .71 | 24.92 | 55.12 | 75.02 | 136.60 | 74.65 | .... | .... | .... | .... | .... | .... |
| Claims on Other Financial Insts. | 12g | .02 | .02 | — | — | — | — | .... | .... | .... | .... | .... | .... |
| Reserve Money | 14 | 84.66 | 94.56 | 78.79 | 109.08 | 155.95 | 134.56 | .... | .... | .... | .... | .... | .... |
| of which: Currency Outside DMBs | 14a | 43.34 | 46.57 | 48.25 | .... | .... | .... | .... | .... | .... | .... | .... | .... |
| Foreign Liabilities | 16c | 1.88 | 2.00 | 1.67 | 1.52 | 57.68 | 14.41 | .... | .... | .... | .... | .... | .... |
| Central Government Deposits | 16d | 88.88 | 109.65 | 159.73 | 148.51 | 147.42 | 138.08 | .... | .... | .... | .... | .... | .... |
| Capital Accounts | 17a | 47.30 | 68.62 | 74.12 | 56.55 | 59.89 | 48.93 | .... | .... | .... | .... | .... | .... |
| Other Items (Net) | 17r | 46.68 | 66.62 | 91.59 | 87.29 | 129.63 | 19.89 | .... | .... | .... | .... | .... | .... |
| **Deposit Money Banks** | | | | | | *Billions of Kroner: End of Period* | | | | | | | |
| Reserves | 20 | 47.70 | 53.37 | 30.45 | .... | .... | .... | .... | .... | .... | .... | .... | .... |
| Foreign Assets | 21 | 152.10 | 230.59 | 395.04 | .... | .... | .... | .... | .... | .... | .... | .... | .... |
| Claims on Central Government | 22a | 13.94 | 21.37 | 28.67 | .... | .... | .... | .... | .... | .... | .... | .... | .... |
| Claims on Local Government | 22b | 6.45 | 5.62 | 6.39 | .... | .... | .... | .... | .... | .... | .... | .... | .... |
| Claims on Nonfin.Pub.Enterprises | 22c | 24.40 | 25.16 | 29.32 | .... | .... | .... | .... | .... | .... | .... | .... | .... |
| Claims on Private Sector | 22d | 1,354.10 | 1,583.47 | 1,879.21 | .... | .... | .... | .... | .... | .... | .... | .... | .... |
| Claims on Other Financial Insts. | 22f | 103.59 | 113.86 | 127.16 | .... | .... | .... | .... | .... | .... | .... | .... | .... |
| Demand Deposits | 24 | 700.07 | 791.12 | 923.21 | .... | .... | .... | .... | .... | .... | .... | .... | .... |
| Time, Savings,& Fgn.Currency Dep. | 25 | 198.55 | 210.10 | 248.62 | .... | .... | .... | .... | .... | .... | .... | .... | .... |
| Foreign Liabilities | 26c | 459.30 | 631.26 | 877.85 | .... | .... | .... | .... | .... | .... | .... | .... | .... |
| Central Government Deposits | 26d | 7.36 | 10.92 | 15.16 | .... | .... | .... | .... | .... | .... | .... | .... | .... |
| Credit from Bank of Norway | 26g | 5.27 | 27.21 | 57.76 | .... | .... | .... | .... | .... | .... | .... | .... | .... |
| Capital Accounts | 27a | † 27.16 | 27.00 | 28.28 | .... | .... | .... | .... | .... | .... | .... | .... | .... |
| Other Items (Net) | 27r | 304.57 | 335.83 | 345.36 | .... | .... | .... | .... | .... | .... | .... | .... | .... |
| **Monetary Survey** | | | | | | *Billions of Kroner: End of Period* | | | | | | | |
| Foreign Assets (Net) | 31n | −40.89 | −86.64 | −134.19 | .... | .... | .... | .... | .... | .... | .... | .... | .... |
| Domestic Credit | 32 | 1,406.75 | 1,629.41 | 1,896.34 | .... | .... | .... | .... | .... | .... | .... | .... | .... |
| Claims on Central Govt. (Net) | 32an | −82.31 | −99.20 | −146.21 | .... | .... | .... | .... | .... | .... | .... | .... | .... |
| Claims on Local Government | 32b | 6.45 | 5.62 | 6.39 | .... | .... | .... | .... | .... | .... | .... | .... | .... |
| Claims on Nonfin.Pub.Enterprises | 32c | 24.40 | 25.16 | 29.32 | .... | .... | .... | .... | .... | .... | .... | .... | .... |
| Claims on Private Sector | 32d | 1,354.60 | 1,583.95 | 1,879.68 | .... | .... | .... | .... | .... | .... | .... | .... | .... |
| Claims on Other Financial Insts. | 32f | 103.60 | 113.87 | 127.16 | .... | .... | .... | .... | .... | .... | .... | .... | .... |
| Money | 34 | 743.44 | 839.01 | 971.48 | .... | .... | .... | .... | .... | .... | .... | .... | .... |
| Quasi-Money | 35 | 198.55 | 210.10 | 248.62 | .... | .... | .... | .... | .... | .... | .... | .... | .... |
| Capital Accounts | 37a | † 74.46 | 95.62 | 102.40 | .... | .... | .... | .... | .... | .... | .... | .... | .... |
| Other Items (Net) | 37r | 349.40 | 398.04 | 439.66 | .... | .... | .... | .... | .... | .... | .... | .... | .... |
| Money plus Quasi-Money | 35l | 941.99 | 1,049.11 | 1,220.10 | .... | .... | .... | .... | .... | .... | .... | .... | .... |

| | | 2004 | 2005 | 2006 | 2007 | 2008 | 2009 | 2010 | 2011 | 2012 | 2013 | 2014 | 2015 |
|---|---|---|---|---|---|---|---|---|---|---|---|---|---|
| **Other Banking Institutions** | | | | | | | | | | | | | |
| State Lending Institutions | | | | | *Billions of Kroner: End of Period* | | | | | | | | |
| Claims on State & Local Govts......... | 42b | 19.65 | 19.55 | 19.57 | .... | .... | .... | .... | .... | .... | .... | .... | .... |
| Claims on Private Sector.................. | 42d | 167.20 | 171.56 | 174.92 | .... | .... | .... | .... | .... | .... | .... | .... | .... |
| Bonds (Net)..................................... | 46ab | .02 | .01 | — | .... | .... | .... | .... | .... | .... | .... | .... | .... |
| Foreign Liabilities............................ | 46c | — | — | — | .... | .... | .... | .... | .... | .... | .... | .... | .... |
| Central Govt. Lending Funds............ | 46f | 187.92 | 191.79 | 195.78 | .... | .... | .... | .... | .... | .... | .... | .... | .... |
| Capital Accounts.............................. | 47a | 3.70 | 4.28 | 3.01 | .... | .... | .... | .... | .... | .... | .... | .... | .... |
| Other Items (Net)............................ | 47r | −4.79 | −4.96 | −4.30 | .... | .... | .... | .... | .... | .... | .... | .... | .... |
| Mortgage Institutions | | | | | *Billions of Kroner: End of Period* | | | | | | | | |
| Foreign Assets................................. | 41..l | 59.86 | 88.67 | 107.80 | .... | .... | .... | .... | .... | .... | .... | .... | .... |
| Claims on Central Government........ | 42a.l | .46 | .38 | .14 | .... | .... | .... | .... | .... | .... | .... | .... | .... |
| Claims on State & Local Govts......... | 42b.l | 99.72 | 113.76 | 126.99 | .... | .... | .... | .... | .... | .... | .... | .... | .... |
| Claims on Nonfin.Pub.Enterprises.... | 42c.l | 9.60 | 10.50 | 15.66 | .... | .... | .... | .... | .... | .... | .... | .... | .... |
| Claims on Private Sector.................. | 42d.l | 129.75 | 115.65 | 113.38 | .... | .... | .... | .... | .... | .... | .... | .... | .... |
| Credit Market Instruments............... | 46aal | 3.25 | 3.75 | 4.00 | .... | .... | .... | .... | .... | .... | .... | .... | .... |
| Bonds (net)..................................... | 46abl | 50.83 | 51.25 | 73.51 | .... | .... | .... | .... | .... | .... | .... | .... | .... |
| Foreign Liabilities............................ | 46c.l | 200.13 | 230.28 | 276.43 | .... | .... | .... | .... | .... | .... | .... | .... | .... |
| Capital Accounts.............................. | 47a.l | 12.14 | 12.27 | 12.24 | .... | .... | .... | .... | .... | .... | .... | .... | .... |
| Other Items (Net)............................ | 47r.l | 33.04 | 31.42 | −2.20 | .... | .... | .... | .... | .... | .... | .... | .... | .... |
| **Nonbank Financial Institutions** | | | | | *Billions of Kroner: End of Period* | | | | | | | | |
| Claims on Central Government........ | 42a.s | 62.43 | 60.13 | 59.66 | .... | .... | .... | .... | .... | .... | .... | .... | .... |
| Claims on Local Government............ | 42b.s | 44.32 | 46.40 | 46.19 | .... | .... | .... | .... | .... | .... | .... | .... | .... |
| Claims on Private Sector.................. | 42d.s | 149.64 | 160.74 | 179.70 | .... | .... | .... | .... | .... | .... | .... | .... | .... |
| Claims on Other Financial Insts........ | 42f.s | 66.11 | 77.06 | 62.69 | .... | .... | .... | .... | .... | .... | .... | .... | .... |
| Incr.in Total Assets(Within Per.)....... | 49z.s | 23.47 | 19.44 | 3.39 | .... | .... | .... | .... | .... | .... | .... | .... | .... |
| **Money (National Definitions)** | | | | | *Billions of Kroner: End of Period* | | | | | | | | |
| Broad Money (M2), Unadjusted....... | 59mb | .... | .... | .... | .... | 1,374.1 | 1,416.1 | 1,507.0 | 1,593.1 | 1,671.8 | 1,793.7 | 1,908.0 | 1,926.1 |
| Broad Money (M2), Seasonally Adj... | 59mbc | .... | .... | .... | .... | .... | .... | .... | .... | .... | .... | .... | .... |
| **Interest Rates** | | | | | *Percent Per Annum* | | | | | | | | |
| Central Bank Policy Rate (EOP)........ | 60 | 3.75 | 4.25 | 5.50 | 6.25 | 4.00 | 1.75 | 2.00 | 1.75 | 1.50 | 1.50 | 1.25 | .75 |
| Avg.Cost for Centr.Bank Funding..... | 60.d | 2.22 | 3.16 | 3.18 | .... | 5.09 | .... | .... | .... | .... | .... | .... | .... |
| Deposit Rate.................................... | 60l | 1.48 | 1.83 | 2.83 | 4.86 | 5.50 | 2.28 | .... | .... | .... | .... | .... | .... |
| Lending Rate.................................... | 60p | 4.04 | 4.04 | 4.70 | 6.65 | 7.28 | 4.28 | .... | .... | .... | .... | .... | .... |
| Three Month Interbank Rate............ | 60zb | 2.01 | 2.21 | 3.10 | 4.96 | 6.22 | 2.46 | 2.50 | 2.87 | 2.24 | 1.75 | 1.70 | 1.29 |
| Government Bond Yield.................... | 61 | 3.60 | 3.28 | 3.93 | 4.78 | 4.35 | 3.32 | 2.77 | 2.56 | 1.57 | 1.92 | 1.76 | .97 |
| **Prices, Production, Labor** | | | | | *Index Numbers (2010=100): Period Averages* | | | | | | | | |
| Share Prices.................................... | 62 | 50.6 | 74.0 | 104.5 | 130.1 | 105.0 | 79.0 | 100.0 | 109.9 | 112.8 | 129.2 | 153.0 | 156.9 |
| Producer Prices............................... | 63 | 52.7 | 61.4 | 69.3 | 69.3 | 85.2 | 84.5 | 100.0 | 116.3 | 119.5 | 120.3 | 118.6 | 108.9 |
| Consumer Prices.............................. | 64 | 88.0 | 89.4 | 91.4 | 92.1 | 95.6 | 97.7 | 100.0 | 101.3 | 102.0 | 104.2 | 106.3 | 108.6 |
| Wages: Monthly Earnings................. | 65 | 76.2 | 79.1 | 82.4 | 87.6 | 92.5 | 96.5 | 100.0 | 104.5 | 109.1 | 113.1 | 116.1 | 119.3 |
| Industrial Production....................... | 66 | 113.5 | 113.5 | 111.0 | 109.7 | 110.2 | 105.9 | 100.0 | 95.0 | 96.7 | 94.1 | 96.1 | 97.5 |
| Crude Petrol. Prod. (2000=100)..... | 66aa | 90.0 | .... | .... | .... | .... | .... | .... | .... | .... | .... | .... | .... |
| | | | | | | *Number in Thousands: Period Averages* | | | | | | | |
| Labor Force..................................... | 67d | 2,369 | 2,391 | 2,437 | 2,497 | 2,579 | 2,581 | 2,594 | 2,622 | 2,671 | 2,697 | 2,723 | 2,760 |
| Employment.................................... | 67e | 2,276 | 2,291 | 2,361 | 2,443 | 2,513 | 2,510 | 2,506 | 2,544 | 2,592 | 2,609 | 2,627 | 2,641 |
| Unemployment................................ | 67c | 102 | 109 | 84 | 63 | 66 | 82 | 93 | 87 | 85 | 95 | 96 | 121 |
| Unemployment Rate (%)................. | 67r | 4.3 | 4.5 | 3.4 | 2.5 | 2.5 | 3.2 | 3.6 | 3.3 | 3.2 | 3.5 | 3.5 | 4.4 |
| **Intl. Transactions & Positions** | | | | | *Millions of Kroner* | | | | | | | | |
| Exports........................................... | 70 | 554,896 | 668,759 | 782,943 | 795,365 | 953,153 | 731,306 | 788,120 | 898,593 | 935,720 | 899,351 | 894,513 | 832,344 |
| Imports, c.i.f.................................... | 71 | 326,102 | 357,658 | 411,756 | 468,919 | 504,480 | 430,362 | 467,285 | 508,628 | 507,649 | 528,783 | 553,738 | 609,693 |
| | | | | | | *2010=100* | | | | | | | |
| Volume of Exports.......................... | 72 | 107.0 | 106.1 | 104.3 | 105.4 | 105.8 | 102.2 | 100.0 | 96.9 | 97.8 | 93.5 | 95.4 | 98.4 |
| Volume of Imports.......................... | 73 | 79.5 | 87.0 | 96.1 | 105.1 | 106.1 | 93.3 | 100.0 | 105.2 | 106.4 | 107.7 | 108.7 | 109.7 |
| Unit Value of Exports...................... | 74 | 65.7 | 79.7 | 95.3 | 95.4 | 114.2 | 90.2 | 100.0 | 118.0 | 121.5 | 123.9 | 120.3 | 108.7 |
| Unit Value of Imports...................... | 75 | 89.7 | 89.8 | 93.8 | 97.6 | 101.7 | 100.8 | 100.0 | 104.0 | 104.4 | 106.8 | 112.6 | 119.2 |

# Norway   142

## Balance of Payments

*Millions of US Dollars*

| | | 2004 | 2005 | 2006 | 2007 | 2008 | 2009 | 2010 | 2011 | 2012 | 2013 | 2014 | 2015 |
|---|---|---|---|---|---|---|---|---|---|---|---|---|---|
| A. Current Account* | 109bx | 33,000.0 | 49,967.5 | 55,913.1 | 49,732.4 | 72,915.1 | 45,169.0 | 50,258.1 | 66,453.6 | † 63,501.1 | 53,449.8 | 59,761.6 | 35,343.6 |
| Goods, credit (exports) | 1a9cx | 82,830.2 | 103,384.1 | 121,656.7 | 135,860.2 | 171,688.0 | 116,811.3 | 129,118.9 | 164,773.2 | † 159,825.0 | 155,303.3 | 143,739.4 | 103,385.6 |
| Goods, debit (imports) | 1a9dx | 48,574.0 | 54,743.3 | 63,580.2 | 78,372.5 | 86,849.9 | 68,125.6 | 75,038.2 | 91,010.2 | † 87,798.7 | 91,599.7 | 90,887.3 | 75,437.0 |
| Balance on goods | 1a9bx | 34,256.2 | 48,640.7 | 58,076.5 | 57,487.7 | 84,838.1 | 48,685.7 | 54,080.8 | 73,763.1 | † 72,026.3 | 63,703.6 | 52,852.0 | 27,948.6 |
| Services, credit (exports) | 1b9cx | 25,596.4 | 29,834.2 | 32,009.8 | 37,824.2 | 42,627.8 | 35,397.1 | 41,452.7 | 40,942.0 | † 46,429.8 | 48,631.8 | 49,358.1 | 40,452.3 |
| Services, debit (imports) | 1b9dx | 24,764.6 | 29,128.4 | 31,673.5 | 41,260.6 | 47,695.4 | 37,073.0 | 45,072.6 | 47,757.8 | † 52,456.4 | 56,350.1 | 56,170.8 | 45,851.3 |
| Balance on Goods & Services | 1z9bx | 35,088.0 | 49,346.6 | 58,412.7 | 54,051.3 | 79,770.5 | 47,009.8 | 50,460.9 | 66,947.3 | † 65,999.7 | 55,985.3 | 46,039.3 | 22,549.7 |
| Primary income: credit | 1c9cx | 17,117.3 | 26,123.8 | 30,935.7 | 42,549.4 | 43,883.7 | 27,291.9 | 34,999.0 | 39,278.7 | † 42,549.7 | 41,751.7 | 49,914.1 | 42,218.9 |
| Primary income: debit | 1c9dx | 16,570.4 | 22,871.0 | 30,455.6 | 43,260.9 | 47,162.6 | 24,549.7 | 30,140.6 | 34,041.8 | † 38,289.6 | 36,372.2 | 28,558.1 | 22,523.5 |
| Balance on gds, serv. & prim. inc. | 1y9bx | 35,634.9 | 52,599.4 | 58,892.8 | 53,339.7 | 76,491.5 | 49,752.0 | 55,319.3 | 72,184.3 | † 70,259.9 | 61,364.8 | 67,395.3 | 42,245.0 |
| Secondary income: credit | 1d9ca | 2,553.1 | 3,457.9 | 2,655.3 | 3,228.2 | 3,560.1 | 3,229.1 | 3,361.6 | 3,746.9 | † 4,315.7 | 4,603.7 | 5,090.4 | 4,027.6 |
| Secondary income: debit | 1d9da | 5,188.0 | 6,089.7 | 5,635.0 | 6,835.5 | 7,136.6 | 7,812.0 | 8,422.8 | 9,477.6 | † 11,074.5 | 12,518.8 | 12,724.1 | 10,929.1 |
| B. Capital Account* | 209ba | −154.4 | −279.5 | −133.2 | −158.0 | −207.1 | −122.7 | −163.7 | −298.0 | † −224.8 | −242.6 | −183.9 | −113.5 |
| Capital account: credit | 209ca | 105.4 | 10.8 | 12.5 | 5.3 | 3.3 | 50.7 | 49.5 | 12.7 | † .5 | .2 | | |
| Capital account: debit | 209da | 259.7 | 290.3 | 145.7 | 163.3 | 210.4 | 173.4 | 213.2 | 310.7 | † 225.3 | 242.8 | 183.9 | 113.5 |
| Balance on current & capital acct. | 129ba | 32,845.6 | 49,688.0 | 55,779.9 | 49,574.3 | 72,707.9 | 45,046.3 | 50,094.4 | 66,155.6 | † 63,276.4 | 53,207.2 | 59,577.7 | 35,230.1 |
| C. Financial Account* | 309na | 22,299.8 | 45,214.0 | 35,850.2 | 16,762.5 | 73,929.4 | 49,140.7 | 39,185.6 | 82,910.8 | † 42,162.9 | 44,004.3 | 60,736.9 | 38,018.5 |
| Direct investment: assets | 3a9aa | 7,624.8 | 31,735.0 | 18,521.6 | 22,925.0 | 36,326.1 | 9,968.1 | 29,942.0 | 12,996.2 | † 26,639.6 | 8,254.6 | 25,231.2 | 13,596.1 |
| Equity & investment fund shares | 3aaaa | 5,456.0 | 21,133.8 | 19,526.9 | 15,657.0 | 21,371.4 | 7,894.2 | 25,734.6 | 11,594.6 | † 25,667.9 | 12,123.6 | 18,652.3 | 21,851.6 |
| Debt instruments | 3abaa | 2,168.8 | 10,601.2 | −1,005.3 | 7,268.0 | 14,954.6 | 2,073.9 | 4,207.4 | 1,401.6 | † 971.7 | −3,868.9 | 6,578.9 | −8,255.5 |
| Direct investment: liabilities | 3a9la | 4,918.5 | 10,058.8 | 11,877.9 | 24,806.1 | 20,578.2 | 8,635.8 | 21,634.3 | 10,296.3 | † 27,654.3 | 1,314.4 | 7,828.6 | −9,923.1 |
| Equity & investment fund shares | 3aala | −1,290.4 | 4,844.5 | 6,145.6 | 4,414.1 | 1,068.4 | 1,132.4 | 7,863.9 | 11,229.0 | † 7,858.4 | 8,859.4 | 7,078.8 | 4,985.0 |
| Debt instruments | 3abla | 6,208.9 | 5,214.3 | 5,732.4 | 20,392.0 | 19,509.9 | 7,503.4 | 13,770.4 | −932.7 | † 19,795.9 | −7,545.1 | 749.8 | −14,908.1 |
| Portfolio investment: assets | 3b9aa | 38,030.5 | 38,073.1 | 113,049.3 | 68,048.8 | 133,545.4 | 4,312.9 | 50,833.1 | 62,307.1 | † 74,488.6 | 70,022.8 | 47,426.9 | 37,126.8 |
| Equity & investment fund shares | 3baaa | 7,269.9 | 18,255.2 | 18,987.0 | 51,820.4 | 91,467.4 | 59,462.9 | 17,875.3 | 49,399.0 | † 39,276.7 | 5,002.8 | 19,350.0 | 9,222.0 |
| Debt securities | 3bbaa | 30,760.6 | 19,817.9 | 94,062.3 | 16,228.3 | 42,078.1 | −55,150.0 | 32,957.7 | 12,908.1 | † 35,211.9 | 65,020.0 | 28,076.9 | 27,904.8 |
| Portfolio investment: liabilities | 3b9la | 9,352.9 | 30,061.8 | 36,063.0 | 47,751.8 | 21,133.6 | 6,746.7 | 36,212.0 | 20,163.0 | † 22,916.9 | 18,196.9 | 22,326.0 | −1,346.5 |
| Equity & investment fund shares | 3bala | 4,493.3 | 9,381.5 | 4,774.9 | 9,750.6 | −12,097.0 | 3,343.4 | 2,561.3 | 1,852.4 | † 428.8 | 2,627.3 | −264.6 | 160.8 |
| Debt securities | 3bbla | 4,859.6 | 20,680.3 | 31,288.1 | 38,001.1 | 33,230.6 | 3,403.3 | 33,650.6 | 18,310.5 | † 22,488.2 | 15,569.5 | 22,590.6 | −1,507.4 |
| Fin. der.& empl.stk.ops.(ESOs): net | 3c9na | −143.7 | — | — | — | — | — | — | — | | .... | .... | .... |
| Fin. der. & ESOs.: assets | 3c9aa | 636.5 | — | — | — | — | — | — | — | | .... | .... | .... |
| Fin. der. & ESOs.: liabilities | 3c9la | 780.2 | — | — | — | — | — | — | — | | .... | .... | .... |
| Other investment: assets | 3d9aa | 16,517.2 | 36,731.9 | 28,890.7 | 44,822.6 | −24,054.1 | −44,328.4 | 21,617.0 | 24,832.4 | † −8,104.6 | 6,059.8 | 22,516.5 | −10,916.3 |
| Other equity | 3daaa | .... | .... | .... | .... | .... | .... | .... | .... | | .... | .... | .... |
| Debt instruments | 3dzaa | 16,517.2 | 36,731.9 | 28,890.7 | 44,822.6 | −24,054.1 | −44,328.4 | 21,617.0 | 24,832.4 | † −8,104.6 | 6,059.8 | 22,516.5 | −10,916.3 |
| Other investment: liabilities | 3d9la | 25,457.5 | 21,205.5 | 76,670.5 | 46,476.0 | 30,176.3 | −94,570.6 | 5,360.4 | −13,234.5 | † 289.5 | 20,821.7 | 4,283.1 | 13,057.7 |
| Other equity | 3dala | .... | .... | .... | .... | .... | .... | .... | .... | | .... | .... | .... |
| Debt instruments | 3dzla | 25,457.5 | 21,205.5 | 76,670.5 | 46,476.0 | 30,176.3 | −94,570.6 | 5,360.4 | −13,234.5 | † 289.5 | 20,821.7 | 4,283.1 | 13,057.7 |
| Curr.+ cap.− finan. acct. balance | 4y9na | 10,545.8 | 4,474.0 | 19,929.6 | 32,811.9 | −1,221.4 | −4,094.5 | 10,908.8 | −16,755.3 | † 21,113.5 | 9,202.8 | −1,159.3 | −2,788.4 |
| D. Net Errors and Omissions | 409na | −5,318.7 | −92.2 | −14,397.3 | −32,019.7 | 3,171.2 | −5,058.2 | −7,146.5 | 13,646.1 | † −20,578.1 | −6,006.3 | 8,338.4 | −2,185.5 |
| E. Reserves and Related Items | 4z9na | 5,227.0 | 4,381.8 | 5,532.3 | 792.2 | 1,949.8 | −9,152.6 | 3,762.3 | −3,109.2 | † 535.4 | 3,196.6 | 7,179.1 | −4,973.9 |
| Reserve assets | 3e9aa | 5,227.0 | 4,381.8 | 5,532.3 | 792.2 | 1,949.8 | −9,152.6 | 3,762.3 | −3,109.2 | † 535.4 | 3,196.6 | 7,179.1 | −4,973.9 |
| Credit and loans from the IMF | 3dcla | | | | | | | | | † — | | | |
| Exceptional financing | 409la | .... | .... | .... | .... | .... | .... | .... | .... | † | .... | .... | .... |

*Excludes components in group E

## International Investment Position

*Millions of US Dollars*

| | | 2004 | 2005 | 2006 | 2007 | 2008 | 2009 | 2010 | 2011 | 2012 | 2013 | 2014 | 2015 |
|---|---|---|---|---|---|---|---|---|---|---|---|---|---|
| Assets | 809aa | 499,303.0 | 579,126.6 | 807,226.3 | 1,041,883.6 | 951,685.5 | 1,091,007.9 | 1,215,306.7 | 1,258,163.0 | † 1,442,074.5 | 1,586,921.3 | 1,572,471.1 | 1,473,949.6 |
| Direct investment | 8a9aa | 88,914.9 | 106,443.6 | 130,916.5 | 184,319.6 | 180,176.6 | 211,519.4 | 227,448.8 | 246,955.1 | † 277,565.4 | 264,366.3 | 225,866.1 | 202,290.7 |
| Equity & investment fund shares | 8aaaa | .... | 73,723.5 | 96,670.9 | 139,355.1 | 128,070.6 | 152,905.5 | 167,785.8 | 179,405.3 | † 205,202.7 | 197,013.8 | 160,457.6 | 151,650.1 |
| Debt instruments | 8abaa | .... | 32,720.1 | 34,245.5 | 44,964.5 | 52,106.0 | 58,613.8 | 59,663.0 | 67,549.7 | † 72,362.7 | 67,352.5 | 65,408.5 | 50,640.6 |
| Portfolio investment | 8b9aa | 251,966.7 | 280,637.4 | 434,332.7 | 545,818.3 | 523,336.7 | 650,082.9 | 731,840.3 | 741,564.3 | † 896,963.9 | 1,048,030.3 | 1,063,796.0 | 1,028,652.1 |
| Equity & investment fund shares | 8baaa | 99,439.7 | 125,958.6 | 174,889.9 | 248,248.1 | 203,333.0 | 353,413.7 | 408,184.6 | 400,423.7 | † 501,411.0 | 609,261.2 | 619,200.8 | 602,137.6 |
| Debt securities | 8bbaa | 152,527.0 | 154,678.7 | 259,442.8 | 297,570.2 | 320,003.7 | 296,669.2 | 323,655.6 | 341,140.6 | † 395,553.0 | 438,769.1 | 444,595.2 | 426,514.5 |
| Fin. der.(oth.than reserves) & ESOs | 8c9aa | .... | .... | .... | .... | .... | .... | .... | .... | | .... | .... | .... |
| Other investment | 8d9aa | 113,606.1 | 144,983.5 | 185,483.2 | 250,606.1 | 188,679.0 | 180,515.6 | 200,456.0 | 216,858.4 | † 215,547.2 | 216,147.5 | 217,396.2 | 185,295.0 |
| Other equity | 8daaa | .... | .... | .... | .... | .... | .... | .... | .... | † 262.3 | 240.3 | 196.6 | 165.8 |
| Debt instruments | 8dzaa | 113,606.1 | 144,983.5 | 185,483.2 | 250,606.1 | 188,679.0 | 180,515.6 | 200,456.0 | 216,858.4 | † 215,284.9 | 215,907.2 | 217,199.6 | 185,129.2 |
| Reserve assets | 8e9aa | 44,815.2 | 47,062.2 | 56,493.9 | 61,139.6 | 59,493.2 | 48,890.0 | 55,561.6 | 52,785.2 | † 51,998.1 | 58,377.3 | 65,412.8 | 57,711.8 |
| Liabilities | 809la | 374,222.3 | 413,513.6 | 603,778.4 | 815,990.6 | 732,794.0 | 767,168.7 | 830,734.6 | 830,648.5 | † 946,983.5 | 953,815.7 | 864,155.6 | 765,742.8 |
| Direct investment | 8a9la | 85,027.8 | 92,067.1 | 110,013.4 | 161,563.6 | 153,679.4 | 190,962.3 | 213,951.7 | 222,194.2 | † 272,165.2 | 259,317.1 | 229,475.6 | 189,316.7 |
| Equity & investment fund shares | 8aala | .... | 47,321.4 | 59,060.9 | 84,083.0 | 68,976.0 | 84,116.6 | 93,130.2 | 101,491.5 | † 121,308.1 | 121,920.4 | 107,265.1 | 93,952.3 |
| Debt instruments | 8abla | .... | 44,745.6 | 50,952.6 | 77,480.6 | 84,703.4 | 106,845.7 | 120,821.5 | 120,702.7 | † 150,857.1 | 137,396.7 | 122,210.5 | 95,364.4 |
| Portfolio investment | 8b9la | 131,046.7 | 158,209.7 | 238,509.4 | 323,425.9 | 246,316.3 | 299,344.5 | 335,666.6 | 341,141.4 | † 395,559.8 | 405,778.3 | 376,151.8 | 334,943.5 |
| Equity & investment fund shares | 8bala | 40,549.3 | 58,822.0 | 100,857.2 | 132,994.5 | 40,754.6 | 76,559.5 | 87,419.6 | 75,580.8 | † 90,672.0 | 101,628.3 | 85,940.0 | 75,235.5 |
| Debt securities | 8bbla | 90,497.4 | 99,387.7 | 137,652.2 | 190,431.4 | 205,561.7 | 222,784.9 | 248,246.9 | 265,560.6 | † 304,887.8 | 304,150.0 | 290,211.8 | 259,707.9 |
| Fin. der.(oth.than reserves) & ESOs | 8c9la | .... | .... | .... | .... | .... | .... | .... | .... | | .... | .... | .... |
| Other investment | 8d9la | 158,147.8 | 163,236.8 | 255,255.6 | 331,001.2 | 332,798.3 | 276,862.0 | 281,116.4 | 267,312.9 | † 279,258.5 | 288,720.3 | 258,528.1 | 241,482.7 |
| Other equity | 8dala | .... | .... | .... | .... | .... | .... | .... | .... | | .... | .... | .... |
| Debt instruments | 8dzla | 158,147.8 | 163,236.8 | 255,255.6 | 331,001.2 | 332,798.3 | 276,862.0 | 281,116.4 | 267,312.9 | † 279,258.5 | 288,720.3 | 258,528.1 | 241,482.7 |
| Monetary Gold & SDRs | a3201 | .... | — | — | — | — | — | — | — | | .... | .... | .... |

# Norway 142

| | | 2004 | 2005 | 2006 | 2007 | 2008 | 2009 | 2010 | 2011 | 2012 | 2013 | 2014 | 2015 |
|---|---|---|---|---|---|---|---|---|---|---|---|---|---|
| **Government Finance** | | | | | | | | | | | | | |
| **Cash Flow Statement** | | | | | | | | | | | | | |
| **Budgetary Central Government** | | | | | | *Millions of Kroner: Fiscal Year Ends December 31* | | | | | | | |
| Cash Receipts:Operating Activities... | c1 | 725,246 | 842,597 | 973,794 | 1,015,197 | 1,161,727 | 1,026,001 | 1,041,402 | 1,194,524 | 1,259,791 | 1,258,148 | .... | .... |
| Taxes............................. | c11 | 449,979 | 530,196 | 609,718 | 639,241 | 719,982 | 635,239 | 649,970 | 745,503 | 787,964 | 785,712 | .... | .... |
| Social Contributions...................... | c12 | 148,675 | 157,610 | 169,973 | 184,096 | 204,850 | 217,879 | 221,156 | 239,799 | 250,617 | 267,972 | .... | .... |
| Grants.................................. | c13 | 1,688 | 1,999 | 6,340 | 2,094 | 1,757 | 1,325 | 1,824 | 1,100 | 1,347 | 1,265 | .... | .... |
| Other Receipts............................ | c14 | 124,904 | 152,792 | 187,763 | 189,766 | 235,138 | 171,558 | 168,452 | 208,122 | 219,863 | 203,199 | .... | .... |
| Cash Payments:Operating Activities. | c2 | 707,781 | 821,772 | 941,604 | 995,010 | 1,137,295 | 973,997 | 1,003,607 | 1,163,576 | 1,215,280 | 1,212,731 | .... | .... |
| Compensation of Employees........ | c21 | 45,282 | 47,435 | 50,244 | 54,058 | 58,469 | 62,173 | 64,748 | 70,524 | 76,679 | 78,786 | .... | .... |
| Purchases of Goods & Services....... | c22 | 46,546 | 46,150 | 47,772 | 50,151 | 55,455 | 60,150 | 61,662 | 60,354 | 57,331 | 60,190 | .... | .... |
| Interest................................. | c24 | 16,790 | 15,780 | 24,285 | .... | 17,525 | 21,134 | 21,525 | 18,514 | 15,085 | 15,042 | .... | .... |
| Subsidies................................ | c25 | 22,688 | 22,815 | 25,090 | 32,616 | 27,600 | 30,272 | 30,565 | 30,495 | 32,033 | 33,943 | .... | .... |
| Grants.................................. | c26 | 310,597 | 418,824 | 517,131 | 552,612 | 669,601 | 463,194 | 470,247 | 610,755 | 640,104 | 608,288 | .... | .... |
| Social Benefits........................... | c27 | 255,246 | 259,255 | 264,278 | 275,642 | 294,314 | 322,082 | 339,145 | 356,245 | 375,964 | 395,943 | .... | .... |
| Other Payments........................ | c28 | 10,632 | 11,513 | 12,804 | .... | 14,331 | 14,992 | 15,715 | 16,689 | 18,084 | 20,539 | .... | .... |
| Net Cash Inflow:Operating Act.[1-2] | ccio | 17,465 | 20,825 | 32,190 | 20,187 | 24,432 | 52,004 | 37,795 | 30,948 | 44,511 | 45,417 | .... | .... |
| Net Cash Outflow:Invest. in NFA...... | c31 | 11,089 | 11,398 | 12,389 | 15,670 | 18,923 | 19,739 | 19,428 | 17,539 | 20,492 | 32,677 | .... | .... |
| Purchases of Nonfinancial Assets... | c31.1 | 12,186 | 12,583 | 13,131 | 16,572 | 19,705 | 22,380 | 21,001 | 20,150 | .... | 33,585 | .... | .... |
| Sales of Nonfinancial Assets.......... | c31.2 | 1,097 | 1,185 | 742 | 902 | 782 | 2,641 | 1,573 | 2,611 | .... | 908 | .... | .... |
| Cash Surplus/Deficit [1-2-31=1-2M] | ccsd | 6,376 | 9,427 | 19,801 | 4,517 | 5,509 | 32,265 | 18,367 | 13,409 | 24,019 | 12,740 | .... | .... |
| Net Acq. Fin. Assets, excl. Cash.... | c32x | 156,648 | 109,283 | 140,827 | 152,758 | 109,618 | 290,359 | 144,648 | 179,252 | 161,474 | 269,003 | .... | .... |
| Domestic................................. | c321x | 153,615 | 109,254 | 140,827 | 152,758 | 109,618 | 290,359 | 144,648 | 179,252 | 161,474 | 269,003 | .... | .... |
| Foreign.................................. | c322x | 3,033 | 29 | — | — | — | — | — | — | — | — | .... | .... |
| Net Incurrence of Liabilities.............. | c33 | 111,203 | 90,501 | 88,919 | 88,074 | 65,316 | 86,378 | 92,212 | 104,282 | 181,145 | 120,679 | .... | .... |
| Domestic................................. | c331 | 111,203 | 90,501 | 88,916 | 88,074 | 65,316 | 86,378 | 92,212 | 104,282 | 181,145 | 120,679 | .... | .... |
| Foreign.................................. | c332 | — | — | 3 | — | — | — | — | — | — | — | .... | .... |
| Net Cash Inflow, Fin.Act.[-32x+33].. | cnfb | −45,445 | −18,782 | −51,908 | −64,684 | −44,302 | −203,981 | −52,436 | −74,970 | 19,671 | −148,324 | .... | .... |
| Net Change in Stock of Cash........... | cncb | −39,069 | −9,354 | −32,106 | −60,167 | −39,184 | .... | .... | .... | .... | .... | .... | .... |
| Stat. Discrep. [32X-33+NCB-CSD].... | ccsdz | — | 1 | 1 | — | −391 | .... | .... | .... | .... | .... | .... | .... |
| Memo Item:Cash Expenditure[2+31] | c2m | 718,870 | 833,170 | 953,993 | 1,010,680 | 1,156,218 | 993,736 | 1,023,035 | 1,181,115 | 1,235,772 | 1,245,408 | .... | .... |
| Memo Item: Gross Debt.................. | c63 | .... | .... | .... | .... | .... | .... | .... | .... | .... | .... | .... | .... |
| **National Accounts** | | | | | | *Billions of Kroner* | | | | | | | |
| Househ.Cons.Expend.,incl.NPISHs..... | 96f | 790.39 | 834.62 | 892.01 | 952.06 | 1,002.65 | 1,027.71 | 1,089.95 | 1,130.18 | 1,176.58 | 1,233.19 | 1,288.88 | 1,335.59 |
| Government Consumption Expend... | 91f | 371.57 | 385.70 | 411.78 | 444.30 | 488.44 | 530.68 | 558.47 | 592.08 | 620.75 | 656.63 | 690.32 | 727.26 |
| Gross Fixed Capital Formation.......... | 93e | 319.52 | 376.11 | 433.10 | 513.77 | 542.28 | 515.58 | 481.99 | 539.30 | 602.99 | 681.90 | 747.71 | 728.75 |
| Changes in Inventories................... | 93i | 36.45 | 44.25 | 68.61 | 81.09 | 84.80 | 14.89 | 110.21 | 114.13 | 121.03 | 123.19 | 147.62 | 168.45 |
| Exports of Goods and Services......... | 90c | 732.66 | 863.71 | 989.47 | 1,017.59 | 1,197.09 | 953.87 | 1,029.97 | 1,153.62 | 1,189.65 | 1,153.13 | 1,207.56 | 1,162.77 |
| Imports of Goods and Services (-)..... | 98c | 497.78 | 545.48 | 614.17 | 702.37 | 755.34 | 660.41 | 726.32 | 778.52 | 802.08 | 844.43 | 932.40 | 981.98 |
| Gross Domestic Product (GDP)........ | 99b | 1,752.81 | 1,958.91 | 2,180.80 | 2,306.45 | 2,559.91 | 2,382.33 | 2,544.27 | 2,750.78 | 2,908.93 | 3,003.61 | 3,149.68 | 3,140.84 |
| Net Primary Income from Abroad..... | 98.n | 3.36 | 21.77 | 1.57 | −7.27 | −11.81 | 13.47 | 29.96 | 15.38 | 57.39 | 48.74 | 52.27 | 122.91 |
| Gross National Income (GNI)........... | 99a | 1,756.17 | 1,980.68 | 2,182.37 | 2,299.18 | 2,548.10 | 2,395.80 | 2,574.22 | 2,766.16 | 2,966.32 | 3,052.35 | 3,201.95 | 3,263.75 |
| Net Current Transf.from Abroad....... | 98t | −14.27 | 4.62 | −17.55 | −27.79 | −33.46 | −14.18 | −.47 | −13.39 | 27.82 | 12.54 | 1.14 | 63.92 |
| Gross Nat'l Disposable Inc.(GNDI).... | 99i | 1,507.76 | 1,718.34 | 1,897.99 | 1,985.41 | 2,201.37 | 2,017.98 | 2,180.23 | 2,355.30 | 2,532.88 | 2,585.30 | 2,646.57 | 2,659.47 |
| Gross Saving............................... | 99s | 576.58 | 743.20 | 859.45 | 882.30 | 1,035.37 | 809.76 | 895.37 | 1,015.14 | 1,139.41 | 1,126.33 | 1,171.61 | 1,141.91 |
| Consumption of Fixed Capital.......... | 99cf | 230.79 | 245.18 | 265.26 | 293.25 | 325.08 | 350.17 | 363.57 | 382.10 | 403.87 | 430.85 | 504.25 | 545.29 |
| GDP Volume 2012 Ref., Chained.... | 99b.p | 2,659.82 | 2,729.63 | 2,795.01 | 2,876.89 | 2,887.95 | 2,841.09 | 2,858.19 | 2,885.88 | 2,965.21 | 2,987.21 | 3,053.19 | 3,188.29 |
| GDP Volume (2010=100)............... | 99bvp | 93.1 | 95.5 | 97.8 | 100.7 | 101.0 | 99.4 | 100.0 | 101.0 | 103.7 | 104.5 | 106.8 | 111.5 |
| GDP Deflator (2010=100)............... | 99bip | 74.0 | 80.6 | 87.7 | 90.1 | 99.6 | 94.2 | 100.0 | 107.1 | 110.2 | 113.0 | 115.9 | 110.7 |
| | | | | | | *Millions: Midyear Estimates* | | | | | | | |
| Population............................. | 99z | 4.59 | 4.62 | 4.67 | 4.72 | 4.77 | 4.83 | 4.89 | 4.95 | 5.02 | 5.08 | 5.15 | 5.21 |

# Oman 449

| | | 2004 | 2005 | 2006 | 2007 | 2008 | 2009 | 2010 | 2011 | 2012 | 2013 | 2014 | 2015 |
|---|---|---|---|---|---|---|---|---|---|---|---|---|---|
| **Exchange Rates** | | | | | | *Rials Omani per SDR: End of Period* | | | | | | | |
| Official Rate................... | aa | .5971 | .5496 | .5784 | .6076 | .5922 | .6028 | .5921 | .5903 | .5909 | .5921 | .5571 | .5328 |
| | | | | | | *Rials Omani per US Dollar: End of Period (ae) Period Average (rf)* | | | | | | | |
| Official Rate................... | ae | .3845 | .3845 | .3845 | .3845 | .3845 | .3845 | .3845 | .3845 | .3845 | .3845 | .3845 | .3845 |
| Official Rate................... | rf | .3845 | .3845 | .3845 | .3845 | .3845 | .3845 | .3845 | .3845 | .3845 | .3845 | .3845 | .3845 |
| | | | | | | *Index Numbers (2010=100): Period Averages* | | | | | | | |
| Official Rate................... | ahx | 100.0 | 100.0 | 100.0 | 100.0 | 100.0 | 100.0 | 100.0 | 100.0 | 100.0 | 100.0 | 100.0 | 100.0 |
| Nominal Effective Exchange Rate..... | nec | 106.2 | 105.8 | 106.0 | 102.0 | 99.2 | 101.7 | 100.0 | 96.5 | 99.5 | 103.9 | 106.6 | 116.2 |
| **Fund Position** | | | | | | *Millions of SDRs: End of Period* | | | | | | | |
| Quota................................ | 2f.s | 194.00 | 194.00 | 194.00 | 194.00 | 194.00 | 194.00 | 194.00 | 237.00 | 237.00 | 237.00 | 237.00 | 237.00 |
| SDR Holdings..................... | 1b.s | 8.98 | 10.32 | 11.10 | 11.84 | 12.83 | 185.50 | 185.61 | 175.09 | 175.87 | 175.23 | 175.30 | 175.33 |
| Reserve Position in the Fund.......... | 1c.s | 63.68 | 24.24 | 18.07 | 12.43 | 13.63 | 35.63 | 43.63 | 73.78 | 75.08 | 83.08 | 84.08 | 78.92 |
| Total Fund Cred. & Loans Outstg...... | 2tl | — | — | — | — | — | — | — | — | — | — | — | — |
| SDR Allocations..................... | 1bd | 6.26 | 6.26 | 6.26 | 6.26 | 6.26 | 178.82 | 178.82 | 178.82 | 178.82 | 178.82 | 178.82 | 178.82 |
| **International Liquidity** | | | | | | *Millions of US Dollars Unless Otherwise Indicated: End of Period* | | | | | | | |
| Total Reserves minus Gold............... | 1l.d | 3,597.3 | 4,358.1 | 5,014.0 | 9,523.5 | 11,581.9 | 12,202.9 | 13,024.4 | 14,365.3 | 14,400.1 | 15,950.3 | 16,323.7 | 17,543.3 |
| SDR Holdings..................... | 1b.d | 13.9 | 14.8 | 16.7 | 18.7 | 19.8 | 290.8 | 285.8 | 268.8 | 270.3 | 269.8 | 254.0 | 243.0 |
| Reserve Position in the Fund.......... | 1c.d | 98.9 | 34.6 | 27.2 | 19.6 | 21.0 | 55.9 | 67.2 | 113.3 | 115.4 | 128.0 | 121.8 | 109.4 |
| Foreign Exchange........................ | 1d.d | 3,484.5 | 4,308.7 | 4,970.2 | 9,485.1 | 11,541.1 | 11,856.3 | 12,671.3 | 13,983.2 | 14,014.4 | 15,552.5 | 15,947.9 | 17,191.0 |
| Gold (Million Fine Troy Ounces)........ | 1ad | .001 | .001 | .001 | .001 | .001 | .001 | .001 | .001 | .001 | .001 | .001 | .001 |
| Gold (National Valuation)............... | 1and | .3 | .3 | .4 | .5 | .5 | .7 | .9 | 1.0 | 1.0 | .7 | .8 | .7 |
| Central Bank: Other Assets............. | 3..d | . . . . | . . . . | . . . . | . . . . | . . . . | . . . . | . . . . | . . . . | . . . . | . . . . | . . . . | . . . . |
| Central Bank: Other Liabs............... | 4..d | 3.0 | 3.1 | 2.0 | † 2.1 | 3.1 | 3.4 | 2.4 | 4.1 | 1.2 | 2.3 | 1.2 | 1.8 |
| Other Depository Corps.: Assets....... | 7a.d | 1,877.0 | 2,449.6 | 4,074.3 | † 4,212.2 | 5,605.7 | 4,500.3 | 4,156.9 | 6,022.8 | 7,127.1 | 6,681.5 | 7,156.6 | 7,581.2 |
| Other Depository Corps.: Liabs......... | 7b.d | 953.6 | 685.1 | 1,572.3 | † 3,622.2 | 5,706.1 | 5,050.6 | 3,512.8 | 4,422.2 | 5,481.5 | 4,866.3 | 5,792.3 | 12,108.8 |
| **Central Bank** | | | | | | *Millions of Rials Omani: End of Period* | | | | | | | |
| Net Foreign Assets..................... | 11n | 1,378.8 | 1,671.2 | 1,923.7 | † 3,700.7 | 4,428.2 | 4,612.1 | 4,927.7 | 5,439.8 | 5,422.4 | 6,046.3 | 6,196.9 | 6,670.0 |
| Claims on Nonresidents............... | 11 | 1,383.7 | 1,675.8 | 1,928.1 | † 3,705.3 | 4,433.0 | 4,721.2 | 5,034.5 | 5,547.0 | 5,528.5 | 6,153.2 | 6,297.1 | 6,765.9 |
| Liabilities to Nonresidents............. | 16c | 4.9 | 4.6 | 4.4 | † 4.6 | 4.9 | 109.1 | 106.8 | 107.2 | 106.1 | 106.9 | 100.2 | 96.0 |
| Claims on Other Depository Corps.... | 12e | .1 | 15.5 | 55.6 | † .5 | 54.3 | 42.2 | .6 | .3 | 27.7 | .1 | .4 | .3 |
| Net Claims on Central Government.. | 12an | −82.4 | −167.5 | −204.2 | † −398.4 | −870.4 | −679.9 | −651.1 | −939.9 | −720.6 | −873.0 | −339.2 | 184.3 |
| Claims on Central Government...... | 12a | 3.6 | .8 | .3 | † .3 | 5.1 | 148.4 | 143.7 | — | 86.2 | — | 173.2 | 658.2 |
| Liabilities to Central Government... | 16d | 85.9 | 168.3 | 204.5 | † 398.7 | 875.5 | 828.3 | 794.8 | 939.9 | 806.8 | 873.0 | 512.5 | 473.9 |
| Claims on Other Sectors............... | 12s | — | — | — | † 13.6 | 12.0 | 12.3 | 4.0 | 4.4 | 5.1 | 6.4 | 7.2 | 9.0 |
| Claims on Other Financial Corps.... | 12g | — | — | — | † 9.8 | 8.4 | 8.5 | .1 | — | — | — | — | .5 |
| Claims on State & Local Govts....... | 12b | — | — | — | † — | — | — | — | — | — | — | — | — |
| Claims on Public Nonfin. Corps...... | 12c | — | — | — | † — | — | — | — | — | — | — | — | — |
| Claims on Private Sector............... | 12d | — | — | — | † 3.8 | 3.6 | 3.8 | 3.9 | 4.4 | 5.1 | 6.4 | 7.2 | 8.4 |
| Monetary Base........................ | 14 | 503.1 | 525.7 | 726.8 | † 1,235.1 | 2,061.3 | 1,405.9 | 2,237.5 | 1,826.8 | 2,493.6 | 2,652.4 | 3,302.3 | 5,612.5 |
| Currency in Circulation.................. | 14a | 382.2 | 459.5 | 560.6 | † 663.1 | 780.6 | 773.3 | 913.4 | 1,037.3 | 1,178.8 | 1,342.7 | 1,593.7 | 1,788.2 |
| Liabs. to Other Depository Corps.... | 14c | 121.0 | 66.3 | 166.1 | † 572.1 | 1,280.7 | 632.6 | 1,324.2 | 789.4 | 1,314.8 | 1,309.7 | 1,708.6 | 3,824.4 |
| Liabilities to Other Sectors............. | 14d | — | — | — | † — | — | — | — | — | — | — | — | — |
| Other Liabs. to Other Dep. Corps..... | 14n | 59.0 | 273.7 | 249.0 | † 1,085.2 | 391.1 | 1,389.9 | 804.0 | 1,372.1 | 909.5 | 1,247.1 | 1,323.2 | .1 |
| Dep. & Sec. Excl. f/Monetary Base..... | 14o | — | — | — | † — | — | — | — | — | — | — | — | — |
| Deposits Included in Broad Money. | 15 | — | — | — | † — | — | — | — | — | — | — | — | — |
| Sec.Ot.th.Shares Incl.in Brd. Money. | 16a | — | — | — | † — | — | — | — | — | — | — | — | — |
| Deposits Excl. from Broad Money... | 16b | — | — | — | † — | — | — | — | — | — | — | — | — |
| Sec.Ot.th.Shares Excl.f/Brd.Money.. | 16s | — | — | — | † — | — | — | — | — | — | — | — | — |
| Loans.................................. | 16l | — | — | — | † — | — | — | — | — | — | — | — | — |
| Financial Derivatives....................... | 16m | — | — | — | † — | — | — | — | — | — | — | — | — |
| Shares and Other Equity................. | 17a | 404.8 | 446.9 | 446.7 | † 975.5 | 1,156.4 | 1,174.4 | 1,241.0 | 1,324.3 | 1,356.6 | 1,332.9 | 1,298.8 | 1,304.8 |
| Other Items (Net)........................... | 17r | 329.6 | 272.8 | 352.6 | † 20.5 | 15.3 | 16.5 | −1.4 | −18.4 | −25.2 | −52.5 | −59.0 | −53.9 |
| Memo Item: | | | | | | | | | | | | | |
| Total Assets..................................... | 10ra | . . . . | . . . . | . . . . | † 3,854.0 | 4,650.7 | 5,063.0 | 5,320.5 | 5,708.0 | 5,813.7 | 6,348.8 | 6,671.7 | 7,630.5 |

# Oman 449

| | | 2004 | 2005 | 2006 | 2007 | 2008 | 2009 | 2010 | 2011 | 2012 | 2013 | 2014 | 2015 |
|---|---|---|---|---|---|---|---|---|---|---|---|---|---|
| **Other Depository Corporations** | | | | | | *Millions of Rials Omani: End of Period* | | | | | | | |
| Net Foreign Assets..................... | 21n | 355.1 | 678.5 | 962.0 | † 226.8 | −38.6 | −211.6 | 248.0 | 615.4 | 632.8 | 698.8 | 525.2 | −1,740.9 |
| Claims on Nonresidents................ | 21 | 721.7 | 941.9 | 1,566.6 | † 1,619.6 | 2,155.4 | 1,730.4 | 1,600.4 | 2,315.8 | 2,740.4 | 2,572.4 | 2,755.3 | 2,915.0 |
| Liabilities to Nonresidents............. | 26c | 366.7 | 263.4 | 604.5 | † 1,392.7 | 2,194.0 | 1,942.0 | 1,352.4 | 1,700.3 | 2,107.6 | 1,873.5 | 2,230.1 | 4,655.8 |
| Claims on Central Bank.................. | 20 | 224.1 | 410.9 | 494.9 | † 1,745.0 | 1,815.0 | 2,164.9 | 2,316.1 | 2,345.9 | 2,469.2 | 2,775.9 | 3,292.9 | 4,199.4 |
| Currency............................. | 20a | 53.1 | 76.2 | 89.7 | † 99.7 | 152.1 | 149.1 | 211.4 | 194.3 | 252.9 | 297.7 | 395.7 | 392.8 |
| Reserve Deposits and Securities..... | 20b | 111.9 | 60.9 | 156.2 | † 562.2 | 1,272.9 | 625.9 | 1,300.7 | 779.6 | 1,306.8 | 1,231.2 | 1,574.2 | 3,806.5 |
| Other Claims......................... | 20n | 59.0 | 273.7 | 249.0 | † 1,083.1 | 390.0 | 1,389.9 | 804.0 | 1,372.0 | 909.5 | 1,247.0 | 1,323.0 | — |
| Net Claims on Central Government.. | 22an | −1.5 | −289.5 | −447.8 | † −761.2 | −1,535.1 | −1,617.1 | −1,967.1 | −2,939.8 | −3,425.5 | −3,890.5 | −4,309.7 | −3,407.9 |
| Claims on Central Government...... | 22a | 439.9 | 254.1 | 228.6 | † 151.5 | 161.5 | 216.0 | 334.1 | 433.3 | 529.5 | 613.8 | 661.8 | 1,971.2 |
| Liabilities to Central Government... | 26d | 441.4 | 543.5 | 676.5 | † 912.7 | 1,696.6 | 1,833.1 | 2,301.2 | 3,373.1 | 3,955.1 | 4,504.3 | 4,971.5 | 5,379.1 |
| Claims on Other Sectors................ | 22s | 3,346.1 | 3,774.8 | 4,593.1 | † 6,418.8 | 9,169.0 | 9,720.6 | 10,995.4 | 12,789.5 | 14,761.3 | 15,830.7 | 17,594.8 | 20,557.4 |
| Claims on Other Financial Corps.... | 22g | — | — | — | † 305.0 | 478.2 | 458.8 | 513.0 | 564.8 | 677.3 | 1,012.2 | 973.6 | 978.2 |
| Claims on State & Local Govts....... | 22b | — | — | — | † — | | | | | | | | |
| Claims on Public Nonfin. Corps...... | 22c | 87.3 | 111.8 | 195.8 | † 364.8 | 469.1 | 577.6 | 937.2 | 1,471.3 | 1,714.2 | 1,750.0 | 2,016.1 | 1,982.3 |
| Claims on Private Sector............... | 22d | 3,258.8 | 3,663.0 | 4,397.3 | † 5,749.0 | 8,221.7 | 8,684.3 | 9,545.2 | 10,753.5 | 12,369.7 | 13,068.5 | 14,605.1 | 17,597.0 |
| Liabilities to Central Bank............... | 26g | .2 | 15.7 | 55.7 | † .4 | 52.9 | 39.2 | .6 | .4 | 27.8 | .2 | .6 | .5 |
| Transf.Dep.Included in Broad Money | 24 | 582.7 | 750.4 | 756.9 | † 1,635.6 | 1,660.8 | 2,073.1 | 2,596.1 | 2,600.2 | 3,042.4 | 3,415.9 | 4,120.9 | 4,732.4 |
| Other Dep.Included in Broad Money. | 25 | 2,032.6 | 2,436.6 | 3,220.5 | † 3,912.3 | 5,243.9 | 5,192.6 | 5,369.5 | 6,342.2 | 6,913.0 | 7,366.0 | 7,933.0 | 9,018.7 |
| Sec.Ot.th.Shares Incl.in Brd. Money.. | 26a | — | — | — | † — | — | — | 117.2 | 69.4 | 30.7 | 11.0 | 10.0 | — |
| Deposits Excl. from Broad Money..... | 26b | — | — | — | † 44.2 | 17.4 | 14.5 | — | — | — | — | .3 | — |
| Sec.Ot.th.Shares Excl.f/Brd.Money.... | 26s | — | — | — | † 150.7 | 164.4 | 238.4 | 388.6 | 415.0 | 517.4 | 390.5 | 492.4 | 403.2 |
| Loans..................................... | 26l | — | — | — | † — | — | — | — | — | — | — | — | — |
| Financial Derivatives................... | 26m | — | — | — | † — | — | — | 11.5 | 5.2 | .1 | 2.6 | 1.3 | .6 |
| Insurance Technical Reserves.......... | 26r | — | — | — | † — | | | | | | | | |
| Shares and Other Equity............... | 27a | 587.3 | 659.6 | 742.5 | † 1,551.9 | 1,954.2 | 2,109.6 | 2,545.3 | 2,934.3 | 3,279.9 | 3,645.6 | 3,895.6 | 4,711.6 |
| Other Items (Net)........................ | 27r | 721.0 | 712.4 | 826.5 | † 334.3 | 316.8 | 389.4 | 563.5 | 444.5 | 626.5 | 583.2 | 649.1 | 740.9 |
| Memo Item: | | | | | | | | | | | | | |
| Total Assets............................... | 20ra | .... | .... | .... | † 10,307.1 | 13,778.4 | 14,173.8 | 15,796.9 | 18,559.5 | 21,137.3 | 22,551.1 | 25,027.3 | 30,482.7 |
| **Depository Corporations** | | | | | | *Millions of Rials Omani: End of Period* | | | | | | | |
| Net Foreign Assets....................... | 31n | 1,733.9 | 2,349.7 | 2,885.7 | † 3,927.5 | 4,389.6 | 4,400.5 | 5,175.6 | 6,055.3 | 6,055.1 | 6,745.2 | 6,722.2 | 4,929.1 |
| Claims on Nonresidents................. | 31 | 2,105.4 | 2,617.7 | 3,494.6 | † 5,324.8 | 6,588.5 | 6,451.6 | 6,634.9 | 7,862.8 | 8,268.9 | 8,725.6 | 9,052.4 | 9,680.9 |
| Liabilities to Nonresidents............. | 36c | 371.5 | 268.0 | 608.9 | † 1,397.3 | 2,198.9 | 2,051.1 | 1,459.2 | 1,807.5 | 2,213.8 | 1,980.4 | 2,330.3 | 4,751.8 |
| Domestic Claims.......................... | 32 | 3,262.2 | 3,317.8 | 3,941.0 | † 5,272.7 | 6,775.5 | 7,436.0 | 8,381.2 | 8,914.2 | 10,620.2 | 11,073.6 | 12,953.0 | 17,342.8 |
| Net Claims on Central Government | 32an | −83.9 | −457.0 | −652.1 | † −1,159.6 | −2,405.5 | −2,297.0 | −2,618.2 | −3,879.7 | −4,146.1 | −4,763.5 | −4,648.9 | −3,223.6 |
| Claims on Central Government.... | 32a | 443.4 | 254.8 | 228.9 | † 151.8 | 166.6 | 364.4 | 477.8 | 433.3 | 615.7 | 613.8 | 835.0 | 2,629.4 |
| Liabilities to Central Government. | 36d | 527.3 | 711.8 | 881.0 | † 1,311.4 | 2,572.1 | 2,661.4 | 3,096.0 | 4,313.0 | 4,761.8 | 5,377.3 | 5,484.0 | 5,853.0 |
| Claims on Other Sectors................ | 32s | 3,346.1 | 3,774.8 | 4,593.1 | † 6,432.3 | 9,181.0 | 9,733.0 | 10,999.4 | 12,794.0 | 14,766.4 | 15,837.1 | 17,602.0 | 20,566.4 |
| Claims on Other Financial Corps.. | 32g | — | — | — | † 314.8 | 486.6 | 467.3 | 513.1 | 564.8 | 677.3 | 1,012.2 | 973.6 | 978.7 |
| Claims on State & Local Govts.... | 32b | — | — | — | † — | | | | | | | | |
| Claims on Public Nonfin. Corps.... | 32c | 87.3 | 111.8 | 195.8 | † 364.8 | 469.1 | 577.6 | 937.2 | 1,471.3 | 1,714.2 | 1,750.0 | 2,016.1 | 1,982.3 |
| Claims on Private Sector............. | 32d | 3,258.8 | 3,663.0 | 4,397.3 | † 5,752.8 | 8,225.3 | 8,688.1 | 9,549.2 | 10,757.9 | 12,374.8 | 13,074.9 | 14,612.3 | 17,605.4 |
| Broad Money Liabilities.................. | 35l | 2,944.3 | 3,570.2 | 4,448.3 | † 6,111.3 | 7,533.2 | 7,889.9 | 8,784.8 | 9,854.9 | 10,912.0 | 11,837.9 | 13,262.0 | 15,146.5 |
| Currency Outside Depository Corps | 34a | 329.0 | 383.2 | 470.9 | † 563.4 | 628.6 | 624.2 | 702.0 | 843.1 | 926.0 | 1,045.0 | 1,198.0 | 1,395.3 |
| Transferable Deposits................ | 34 | 582.7 | 750.4 | 756.9 | † 1,635.6 | 1,660.8 | 2,073.1 | 2,596.1 | 2,600.2 | 3,042.4 | 3,415.9 | 4,120.9 | 4,732.4 |
| Other Deposits........................ | 35 | 2,032.6 | 2,436.6 | 3,220.5 | † 3,912.3 | 5,243.9 | 5,192.6 | 5,369.5 | 6,342.2 | 6,913.0 | 7,366.0 | 7,933.0 | 9,018.7 |
| Securities Other than Shares......... | 36a | — | — | — | † — | — | — | 117.2 | 69.4 | 30.7 | 11.0 | 10.0 | — |
| Deposits Excl. from Broad Money..... | 36b | — | — | — | † 44.2 | 17.4 | 14.5 | — | — | — | — | .3 | — |
| Sec.Ot.th.Shares Excl.f/Brd.Money.... | 36s | — | — | — | † 150.7 | 164.4 | 238.4 | 388.6 | 415.0 | 517.4 | 390.5 | 492.4 | 403.2 |
| Loans..................................... | 36l | — | — | — | † — | — | — | — | — | — | — | — | — |
| Financial Derivatives................... | 36m | — | — | — | † — | — | — | 11.5 | 5.2 | .1 | 2.6 | 1.3 | .6 |
| Insurance Technical Reserves.......... | 36r | — | — | — | † — | | | | | | | | |
| Shares and Other Equity............... | 37a | 992.1 | 1,106.4 | 1,189.2 | † 2,527.4 | 3,110.5 | 3,284.0 | 3,786.2 | 4,258.5 | 4,636.4 | 4,978.5 | 5,194.4 | 6,016.4 |
| Other Items (Net)........................ | 37r | 1,059.8 | 990.8 | 1,189.2 | † 366.7 | 339.5 | 409.6 | 585.7 | 435.9 | 609.4 | 609.3 | 724.8 | 705.2 |
| Broad Money Liabs., Seasonally Adj. | 35l.b | 2,961.2 | 3,590.7 | 4,474.2 | † 6,088.5 | 7,504.2 | 7,865.8 | 8,772.2 | 9,862.9 | 10,939.8 | 11,885.4 | 13,328.4 | 15,232.5 |
| **Monetary Aggregates** | | | | | | *Millions of Rials Omani: End of Period* | | | | | | | |
| Broad Money............................. | 59m | .... | .... | .... | 6,111.3 | 7,533.2 | 7,889.9 | 8,784.8 | 9,854.9 | 10,912.0 | 11,837.9 | 13,262.0 | 15,146.5 |
| o/w:Currency Issued by Cent.Govt | 59m.a | .... | .... | .... | — | — | — | — | — | — | — | — | — |
| o/w: Dep.in Nonfin. Corporations. | 59m.b | .... | .... | .... | — | — | — | — | — | — | — | — | — |
| o/w: Secs. Issued by Central Govt. | 59m.c | .... | .... | .... | — | — | — | — | — | — | — | — | — |
| Money (National Definitions) | | | | | | | | | | | | | |
| Reserve Money........................ | 19mb | 503.2 | 525.7 | 726.7 | 1,234.9 | 2,061.2 | 1,405.7 | 2,237.4 | 1,826.5 | 2,493.5 | 2,652.2 | 3,302.1 | 5,612.4 |
| M1......................................... | 59ma | 907.4 | 1,128.1 | 1,229.6 | 1,916.9 | 1,993.0 | 2,364.8 | 2,875.9 | 3,064.9 | 3,492.3 | 3,951.2 | 4,808.0 | 5,369.4 |
| M2......................................... | 59mb | 2,944.3 | 3,573.1 | 4,461.3 | 6,111.3 | 7,533.2 | 7,889.9 | 8,784.8 | 9,854.9 | 10,912.0 | 11,837.9 | 13,766.9 | 15,146.5 |
| **Interest Rates** | | | | | | *Percent Per Annum* | | | | | | | |
| Discount Rate (End of Period)........... | 60.a | 7.50 | 7.50 | 7.50 | 7.50 | 7.50 | 7.50 | 7.50 | 7.50 | 7.50 | 7.50 | 7.50 | 7.50 |
| Central Bank Bill Rate.................... | 60ae | .59 | 2.29 | 3.65 | 3.18 | .84 | .06 | .06 | .12 | .08 | .13 | .13 | .07 |
| Money Market Rate....................... | 60b | .66 | 2.25 | 3.40 | 1.47 | .29 | .08 | .10 | .11 | .17 | .12 | .13 | .19 |
| Deposit Rate.............................. | 60l | 2.32 | 3.30 | 4.00 | 4.14 | 4.48 | 4.14 | 3.37 | 2.80 | 2.62 | 2.39 | 2.02 | 1.93 |
| Deposit Rate (Foreign Currency)....... | 60l.f | 2.41 | 4.08 | 5.13 | 4.54 | 3.17 | 1.18 | 1.05 | 1.55 | 1.50 | 1.32 | 1.37 | 1.38 |
| Lending Rate............................. | 60p | 7.57 | 7.07 | 7.40 | 7.29 | 7.10 | 7.44 | 6.84 | 6.19 | 5.65 | 5.41 | 5.08 | 4.76 |
| Lending Rate (Foreign Currency)...... | 60p.f | 2.43 | 4.72 | 6.02 | 5.95 | 3.21 | 2.87 | 2.38 | 2.38 | 2.39 | 2.30 | 2.38 | 2.59 |
| **Prices and Production** | | | | | | *Index Numbers (2010=100): Period Averages* | | | | | | | |
| Consumer Prices.......................... | 64 | 74.7 | 76.1 | 78.5 | 83.2 | 93.2 | 96.9 | 100.0 | 104.1 | 107.1 | † 108.4 | 109.5 | 109.6 |
| Crude Petroleum Production............ | 66aa | 96.2 | 95.4 | 90.8 | 87.4 | 93.4 | 100.7 | 100.0 | 108.9 | 104.5 | 103.9 | 105.4 | 109.0 |
| **Intl. Transactions & Positions** | | | | | | *Millions of Rials Omani* | | | | | | | |
| Exports...................................... | 70 | 5,129.8 | 7,187.0 | 8,299.5 | 9,280.2 | 14,503.0 | 10,786.5 | 14,073.2 | 18,106.8 | 20,445.4 | 21,696.9 | 20,314.8 | 13,355.2 |
| Crude Petroleum......................... | 70aa | 3,489.5 | 5,070.9 | 5,524.8 | 5,553.4 | 8,415.9 | 5,314.5 | 8,007.7 | 10,659.6 | 11,794.9 | 12,337.5 | 11,591.6 | 6,642.6 |
| Imports, c.i.f............................... | 71 | 3,408.7 | 3,394.0 | 4,196.9 | 6,143.4 | 8,814.5 | 6,869.1 | 7,603.3 | 9,081.8 | 11,322.5 | 13,201.0 | 11,316.6 | 11,153.3 |
| Volume of Exports | | | | | | *2010=100* | | | | | | | |
| Crude Petroleum......................... | 72aa | 98.1 | 97.6 | 86.8 | 82.6 | 80.7 | 90.4 | 100.0 | 99.2 | 103.5 | 113.2 | 108.7 | 114.7 |
| Unit Value of Imports..................... | 75 | 95.1 | 100.0 | .... | .... | .... | .... | .... | .... | .... | .... | .... | .... |
| Export Prices | | | | | | *2010=100: Index of Prices in US Dollars* | | | | | | | |
| Crude Petroleum......................... | 76aad | 44.9 | 65.6 | 80.5 | 85.0 | 131.9 | 73.8 | 100.0 | 134.3 | 143.0 | 137.7 | 134.7 | 73.7 |

# Oman   449

| | | 2004 | 2005 | 2006 | 2007 | 2008 | 2009 | 2010 | 2011 | 2012 | 2013 | 2014 | 2015 |
|---|---|---|---|---|---|---|---|---|---|---|---|---|---|
| **Balance of Payments** | | | | | | *Millions of US Dollars* | | | | | | | |
| A. Current Account* | 109bx | 876.6 | 5,177.5 | 5,664.4 | 2,462.2 | 5,019.0 | −501.1 | 4,884.3 | 8,847.9 | 7,739.9 | 5,245.8 | 4,055.7 | .... |
| Goods, credit (exports) | 1a9cx | 13,381.0 | 18,691.8 | 21,586.5 | 24,691.8 | 37,719.1 | 27,651.5 | 36,600.8 | 47,092.3 | 52,137.8 | 56,429.1 | 53,219.8 | .... |
| Goods, debit (imports) | 1a9dx | 7,872.6 | 8,028.6 | 9,881.1 | 14,343.3 | 20,707.2 | 16,051.8 | 17,875.2 | 21,498.0 | 25,628.1 | 32,044.2 | 27,888.2 | .... |
| Balance on goods | 1a9bx | 5,508.5 | 10,663.2 | 11,705.5 | 10,348.5 | 17,012.0 | 11,599.7 | 18,725.6 | 25,594.3 | 26,509.8 | 24,384.9 | 25,331.6 | .... |
| Services, credit (exports) | 1b9cx | 736.0 | 938.9 | 1,310.8 | 1,682.7 | 1,825.7 | 1,620.3 | 1,807.5 | 2,330.3 | 2,689.2 | 2,931.1 | 3,065.8 | .... |
| Services, debit (imports) | 1b9dx | 3,152.3 | 3,145.5 | 3,896.3 | 5,094.9 | 5,877.8 | 5,483.5 | 6,364.1 | 7,724.3 | 8,767.2 | 9,807.5 | 10,228.1 | .... |
| Balance on Goods & Services | 129bx | 3,092.2 | 8,456.6 | 9,119.8 | 6,936.3 | 12,959.9 | 7,736.5 | 14,169.1 | 20,200.3 | 20,431.7 | 17,508.5 | 18,169.3 | .... |
| Primary income: credit | 1c9cx | 762.0 | 765.1 | 1,742.0 | 2,161.5 | 1,096.7 | 749.4 | 772.4 | 733.4 | 717.8 | 1,922.0 | 1,214.6 | .... |
| Primary income: debit | 1c9dx | 1,151.9 | 1,786.7 | 2,409.4 | 2,965.9 | 3,857.0 | 3,671.0 | 4,353.7 | 4,871.3 | 5,323.8 | 5,079.3 | 5,027.3 | .... |
| Balance on gds, serv. & prim. inc. | 1y9bx | 2,702.3 | 7,435.0 | 8,452.4 | 6,131.9 | 10,199.7 | 4,814.9 | 10,587.8 | 16,062.4 | 15,825.7 | 14,351.1 | 14,356.6 | .... |
| Secondary income: credit | 1d9ca | — | — | — | — | — | — | — | — | — | — | — | .... |
| Secondary income: debit | 1d9da | 1,825.7 | 2,257.5 | 2,788.0 | 3,669.7 | 5,180.8 | 5,316.0 | 5,703.5 | 7,214.6 | 8,085.8 | 9,105.3 | 10,300.9 | .... |
| B. Capital Account* | 209ba | 20.8 | −15.6 | −96.2 | 827.0 | −52.0 | 54.6 | −65.0 | −145.6 | −85.8 | −111.8 | −130.0 | .... |
| Capital account: credit | 209ca | 20.8 | — | — | 860.9 | — | 54.6 | — | — | — | — | — | .... |
| Capital account: debit | 209da | — | 15.6 | 96.2 | 33.8 | 52.0 | — | 65.0 | 145.6 | 85.8 | 111.8 | 130.0 | .... |
| Balance on current & capital acct. | 129ba | 897.4 | 5,161.9 | 5,568.2 | 3,289.2 | 4,967.0 | −446.4 | 4,819.2 | 8,702.2 | 7,654.1 | 5,133.9 | 3,925.6 | .... |
| C. Financial Account* | 309na | −360.2 | 1,501.4 | 3,351.6 | −2,752.7 | 3,762.8 | −2,629.9 | 4,215.9 | 5,987.0 | 6,184.7 | −6,033.8 | 1,922.0 | .... |
| Direct investment: assets | 3a9aa | 41.6 | 233.6 | 274.6 | −37.2 | 584.4 | 109.2 | 1,498.0 | 1,222.4 | 884.3 | 10.4 | 1,669.7 | .... |
| Equity & investment fund shares | 3aaaa | 41.6 | 233.6 | 274.6 | −37.2 | 584.4 | 109.2 | 1,498.0 | 1,222.4 | 884.3 | 10.4 | 1,669.7 | .... |
| Debt instruments | 3abaa | .... | .... | .... | .... | .... | .... | .... | .... | .... | .... | .... | .... |
| Direct investment: liabilities | 3a9la | 111.1 | 1,538.4 | 1,596.1 | 3,332.1 | 2,951.9 | 1,485.8 | 1,243.2 | 1,752.9 | 850.5 | 876.5 | 738.6 | .... |
| Equity & investment fund shares | 3aala | 111.1 | 1,538.4 | 1,596.1 | 3,332.1 | 2,951.9 | 1,485.8 | 1,243.2 | 1,752.9 | 850.5 | 876.5 | 738.6 | .... |
| Debt instruments | 3abla | .... | .... | .... | .... | .... | .... | .... | .... | .... | .... | .... | .... |
| Portfolio investment: assets | 3b9aa | 174.0 | 437.5 | 1,019.8 | 122.8 | 149.5 | 143.8 | 1,063.7 | 91.0 | 1,474.6 | 1,001.3 | 1,305.6 | .... |
| Equity & investment fund shares | 3baaa | 174.0 | 437.5 | 1,019.8 | 122.8 | 149.5 | 143.8 | 1,063.7 | 91.0 | 1,474.6 | 1,001.3 | 1,305.6 | .... |
| Debt securities | 3bbaa | .... | .... | .... | .... | .... | .... | .... | .... | .... | .... | .... | .... |
| Portfolio investment: liabilities | 3b9la | 161.8 | 565.4 | 1,180.8 | 1,604.7 | −1,523.3 | 246.3 | 1,308.2 | −410.9 | 1,771.1 | 1,360.2 | 910.3 | .... |
| Equity & investment fund shares | 3bala | 31.7 | 573.2 | 1,180.8 | 1,629.4 | −1,460.1 | 332.9 | 1,308.2 | −410.9 | 1,771.1 | 1,360.2 | 910.3 | .... |
| Debt securities | 3bbla | 130.0 | −7.8 | — | −24.7 | −63.2 | −86.6 | .... | .... | .... | .... | — | .... |
| Fin. der.& empl.stk.ops.(ESOs): net. | 3c9na | .... | .... | .... | .... | .... | .... | .... | .... | .... | .... | .... | .... |
| Fin. der. & ESOs.: assets | 3c9aa | .... | .... | .... | .... | .... | .... | .... | .... | .... | .... | .... | .... |
| Fin. der. & ESOs.: liabilities | 3c9la | .... | .... | .... | .... | .... | .... | .... | .... | .... | .... | .... | .... |
| Other investment: assets | 3d9aa | 977.1 | 3,225.7 | 6,937.6 | 4,959.7 | 7,659.8 | −2,165.4 | 2,858.3 | 7,326.4 | 7,027.3 | −6,426.5 | −36.4 | .... |
| Other equity | 3daaa | .... | .... | .... | .... | .... | .... | .... | .... | .... | .... | .... | .... |
| Debt instruments | 3dzaa | 977.1 | 3,225.7 | 6,937.6 | 4,959.7 | 7,659.8 | −2,165.4 | 2,858.3 | 7,326.4 | 7,027.3 | −6,426.5 | −36.4 | .... |
| Other investment: liabilities | 3d9la | 1,280.1 | 291.5 | 2,103.5 | 2,861.1 | 3,202.3 | −1,014.5 | −1,347.2 | 1,310.8 | 580.0 | −1,617.7 | −632.0 | .... |
| Other equity | 3dala | .... | .... | .... | .... | .... | .... | .... | .... | .... | .... | .... | .... |
| Debt instruments | 3dzla | 1,280.1 | 291.5 | 2,103.5 | 2,861.1 | 3,202.3 | −1,014.5 | −1,347.2 | 1,310.8 | 580.0 | −1,617.7 | −632.0 | .... |
| Curr.+ cap.− finan. acct. balance. | 4y9na | 1,257.6 | 3,660.5 | 2,216.5 | 6,041.9 | 1,204.2 | 2,183.5 | 603.4 | 2,715.2 | 1,469.4 | 11,167.8 | 2,003.6 | .... |
| D. Net Errors and Omissions | 409na | −396.1 | −851.5 | −10.8 | 208.6 | 622.8 | −1,133.7 | 907.1 | −1,191.6 | −433.7 | 1,132.0 | −886.3 | .... |
| E. Reserves and Related Items | 4z9na | 861.4 | 2,809.0 | 2,205.8 | 6,250.5 | 1,827.0 | 1,049.8 | 1,510.5 | 1,523.6 | 1,035.7 | 12,299.8 | 1,117.4 | .... |
| Reserve assets | 3e9aa | 861.4 | 2,809.0 | 2,205.8 | 6,250.5 | 1,827.0 | 1,049.8 | 1,510.5 | 1,523.6 | 1,035.7 | 12,299.8 | 1,117.4 | .... |
| Credit and loans from the IMF | 3dcla | — | — | — | — | — | — | — | — | — | — | — | .... |
| Exceptional financing | 409la | — | — | — | — | — | .... | .... | .... | .... | — | — | .... |
| *Excludes components in group E | | | | | | | | | | | | | |

**Government Finance**
**Cash Flow Statement**

| Budgetary Central Government | | | | | | *Millions of Rials: Fiscal Year Ends December 31* | | | | | | | |
|---|---|---|---|---|---|---|---|---|---|---|---|---|---|
| Cash Receipts:Operating Activities | c1 | 4,014.5 | 4,443.8 | 4,912.8 | 5,838.6 | 7,536.5 | 6,807.0 | 9,051.1 | 12,536.1 | 14,766.1 | 14,994.5 | .... | .... |
| Taxes | c11 | 185.4 | 238.7 | 278.2 | 437.6 | 565.7 | 630.3 | 573.2 | 593.6 | 767.0 | 766.0 | .... | .... |
| Social Contributions | c12 | — | — | — | — | — | — | — | — | — | — | .... | .... |
| Grants | c13 | 8.3 | — | — | 4.6 | −20.3 | 54.2 | 9.3 | 13.5 | 5.9 | 5.8 | .... | .... |
| Other Receipts | c14 | 3,820.8 | 4,205.1 | 4,634.6 | 5,396.4 | 6,991.1 | 6,122.5 | 8,468.6 | 11,929.0 | 13,993.2 | 14,222.7 | .... | .... |
| Cash Payments:Operating Activities. | c2 | 2,857.3 | 3,291.4 | 3,773.5 | 4,183.1 | 4,183.1 | 4,769.8 | 5,046.5 | 7,319.3 | 10,096.1 | 10,467.8 | .... | .... |
| Compensation of Employees | c21 | 805.6 | 938.1 | 1,227.5 | 1,347.9 | 1,347.9 | 1,506.5 | 1,722.7 | 1,935.4 | 2,307.6 | 2,472.1 | .... | .... |
| Purchases of Goods & Services | c22 | 1,765.9 | 1,972.5 | 2,184.8 | 2,474.5 | 2,474.5 | 2,841.0 | 2,843.1 | 3,463.6 | 5,885.4 | 5,734.0 | .... | .... |
| Interest | c24 | 74.4 | 66.8 | 55.6 | 77.7 | 77.7 | 45.0 | 37.4 | 38.1 | 45.3 | 53.6 | .... | .... |
| Subsidies | c25 | 160.2 | 263.7 | 268.8 | 283.0 | 283.0 | 345.3 | 409.3 | 1,813.0 | 1,819.2 | 2,158.9 | .... | .... |
| Grants | c26 | — | 5.6 | 36.8 | — | — | 32.0 | 34.0 | 69.2 | 38.6 | 49.2 | .... | .... |
| Social Benefits | c27 | — | — | — | — | — | — | — | — | — | — | .... | .... |
| Other Payments | c28 | 51.2 | 44.7 | — | — | — | — | — | — | — | — | .... | .... |
| Net Cash Inflow:Operating Act.[1-2] | ccio | 1,157.2 | 1,152.4 | 1,139.3 | 1,655.5 | 3,353.4 | 2,037.2 | 4,004.6 | 5,216.8 | 4,670.0 | 4,526.7 | .... | .... |
| Net Cash Outflow:Invest. in NFA | c31 | 936.4 | 886.8 | 1,150.5 | 1,631.1 | 2,212.6 | 2,666.9 | 2,571.8 | 2,942.8 | 2,874.5 | 3,109.8 | .... | .... |
| Purchases of Nonfinancial Assets | c31.1 | 952.6 | 921.8 | 1,199.5 | 1,697.3 | 2,280.9 | 2,690.9 | 2,596.8 | 2,959.5 | 2,886.5 | .... | .... | .... |
| Sales of Nonfinancial Assets | c31.2 | 16.2 | 35.0 | 49.0 | 66.2 | 68.3 | 24.0 | 25.0 | 16.7 | 12.0 | .... | .... | .... |
| Cash Surplus/Deficit [1-2-31=1-2M] | ccsd | 220.8 | 265.6 | −11.2 | 24.4 | 1,140.8 | −629.7 | 1,432.8 | 2,274.0 | 1,795.5 | 1,416.9 | .... | .... |
| Net Acq. Fin. Assets, excl. Cash | c32x | −17.8 | −31.7 | −18.1 | −20.4 | −13.6 | −10.0 | −22.4 | −39.3 | −12.8 | .... | .... | .... |
| Domestic | c321x | −17.8 | −31.7 | −18.1 | −20.4 | −13.6 | −10.0 | −22.4 | −39.3 | −12.8 | .... | .... | .... |
| Foreign | c322x | — | — | — | — | — | — | — | — | — | .... | .... | .... |
| Net Incurrence of Liabilities | c33 | 3.6 | −159.1 | 115.5 | −126.8 | −36.0 | 40.0 | 131.3 | 111.1 | 113.3 | 126.0 | .... | .... |
| Domestic | c331 | 88.5 | −8.0 | −80.0 | −130.0 | −80.0 | −100.0 | 78.0 | 150.0 | 150.0 | 200.0 | .... | .... |
| Foreign | c332 | −84.9 | −151.1 | 195.5 | 3.2 | 44.0 | 140.0 | 53.3 | −38.9 | −36.7 | −74.0 | .... | .... |
| Net Cash Inflow, Fin.Act.[-32x+33] | cnfb | 21.4 | −127.4 | 133.6 | −106.4 | −22.4 | 50.0 | −202.3 | −377.9 | −542.6 | −304.7 | .... | .... |
| Net Change in Stock of Cash | cncb | 242.2 | 138.3 | 122.5 | −82.0 | 22.1 | −619.0 | 1,230.5 | 1,896.1 | 1,254.7 | 1,113.3 | .... | .... |
| Stat. Discrep. [32X-33+NCB-CSD] | ccsdz | — | .1 | .1 | — | −1,096.3 | −39.3 | — | — | 1.8 | 1.1 | .... | .... |
| Memo Item:Cash Expenditure[2+31] | c2m | 3,793.7 | 4,178.2 | 4,924.0 | 5,814.2 | 6,395.7 | 7,436.7 | 7,618.3 | 10,262.1 | 12,970.6 | 13,577.6 | .... | .... |
| Memo Item: Gross Debt | c63 | 1,319.1 | 1,018.0 | 1,127.6 | 1,000.9 | 964.8 | 1,044.8 | 1,136.2 | 1,247.2 | 1,360.5 | 1,486.5 | .... | .... |

# Oman 449

| | | 2004 | 2005 | 2006 | 2007 | 2008 | 2009 | 2010 | 2011 | 2012 | 2013 | 2014 | 2015 |
|---|---|---|---|---|---|---|---|---|---|---|---|---|---|
| **National Accounts** | | | | | | | *Millions of Rials Omani* | | | | | | |
| Househ.Cons.Expend.,incl.NPISHs.... | 96f | 3,519 | 3,634 | 4,240 | 4,942 | 6,559 | 6,761 | 7,200 | 7,364 | 8,410 | 9,091 | 9,662 | .... |
| Government Consumption Expend... | 91f | 2,135 | 2,485 | 2,666 | 3,044 | 3,316 | 3,601 | 4,092 | 4,714 | 5,762 | 6,465 | 7,854 | .... |
| Gross Fixed Capital Formation.......... | 93e | 2,426 | 2,751 | 3,427 | 4,928 | 6,890 | .... | .... | .... | .... | .... | .... | .... |
| Changes in Inventories.................... | 93i | 216 | −239 | 283 | 189 | 225 | .... | .... | .... | .... | .... | .... | .... |
| Exports of Goods and Services......... | 90c | 4,892 | 6,965 | 8,038 | 9,140 | 13,695 | 9,421 | 12,882 | 19,046 | 18,594 | 19,283 | 18,699 | .... |
| Imports of Goods and Services (-)..... | 98c | 3,701 | 3,712 | 4,531 | 6,471 | 8,707 | 6,447 | 7,370 | 11,241 | 13,225 | 16,091 | 14,656 | .... |
| Gross Domestic Product (GDP)........ | 99b | 9,487 | 11,883 | 14,310 | 16,182 | 23,418 | 18,604 | 22,548 | 26,122 | 29,353p | 30,061p | 31,451 | .... |
| Net Primary Income from Abroad..... | 98.n | −150 | −393 | −1,368 | −1,767 | −3,114 | −3,231 | 3,637 | −4,434 | −4,957 | −4,785 | −5,506 | .... |
| Gross Nat'l Disposable Inc. (GNDI)... | 99i | 8,597 | 10,575 | 14,054 | 15,873 | 22,357 | 17,481 | 21,171 | 24,531 | 27,637 | 28,815 | .... | .... |
| Gross National Income (GNI)........... | 99a | 9,337 | 11,490 | 12,777 | 14,334 | 20,256 | 15,298 | 19,313 | 21,688 | 24,396 | 25,276 | 25,945 | .... |
| GDP Volume 2010 Prices................ | 99b.p | .... | .... | 17,940 | 18,739 | 20,275 | 21,514 | 22,548 | 22,302 | 23,881p | 24,815p | 25,533 | .... |
| GDP Volume (2010=100)............... | 99bvp | 72.5 | 75.4 | † 79.6 | 83.1 | 89.9 | 95.4 | 100.0 | 98.9 | 105.9 | 110.1 | 113.2 | .... |
| GDP Deflator (2010=100)............... | 99bip | 58.0 | 69.9 | 79.8 | 86.4 | 115.5 | 86.5 | 100.0 | 117.1 | 122.9 | 121.1 | 123.2 | .... |
| | | | | | | | *Millions: Midyear Estimates* | | | | | | |
| Population................................. | 99z | 2.45 | 2.51 | 2.55 | 2.59 | 2.65 | 2.76 | 2.94 | 3.21 | 3.55 | 3.91 | 4.24 | 4.49 |

2016, International Monetary Fund : *International Financial Statistics Yearbook*

# Pakistan 564

| | | 2004 | 2005 | 2006 | 2007 | 2008 | 2009 | 2010 | 2011 | 2012 | 2013 | 2014 | 2015 |
|---|---|---|---|---|---|---|---|---|---|---|---|---|---|
| **Exchange Rates** | | | | | | | *Rupees per SDR: End of Period (aa)* | | | | | | |
| Market Rate.................................. | aa | 91.820 | 85.513 | 91.645 | 96.744 | 121.832 | 132.099 | 131.997 | 138.125 | 149.290 | 162.744 | 145.545 | 145.315 |
| | | | | | | *Rupees per US Dollar: End of Period (ae) Period Average (rf)* | | | | | | | |
| Market Rate.................................. | ae | 59.124 | 59.830 | 60.918 | 61.221 | 79.098 | 84.263 | 85.711 | 89.968 | 97.136 | 105.678 | 100.459 | 104.866 |
| Market Rate.................................. | rf | 58.258 | 59.514 | 60.271 | 60.739 | 70.408 | 81.713 | 85.194 | 86.343 | 93.395 | 101.629 | 101.100 | 102.769 |
| | | | | | | *Index Numbers (2010=100): Period Averages* | | | | | | | |
| Nominal Effective Exchange Rate..... | nec | 157.5 | 152.6 | 149.6 | 141.7 | 119.3 | 105.8 | 100.0 | 95.0 | 90.1 | 83.8 | 85.4 | 92.1 |
| CPI-Based Real Effect. Ex. Rate........ | rec | 93.7 | 96.7 | 99.4 | 98.1 | 94.5 | 95.1 | 100.0 | 102.8 | 104.4 | 102.3 | 109.7 | 119.8 |
| **Fund Position** | | | | | | | *Millions of SDRs: End of Period* | | | | | | |
| Quota......................................... | 2f.s | 1,033.70 | 1,033.70 | 1,033.70 | 1,033.70 | 1,033.70 | 1,033.70 | 1,033.70 | 1,033.70 | 1,033.70 | 1,033.70 | 1,033.70 | 1,033.70 |
| SDR Holdings................................ | 1b.s | 157.76 | 151.02 | 143.28 | 136.06 | 118.55 | 880.60 | 798.90 | 686.22 | 599.26 | 552.11 | 520.16 | 485.52 |
| Reserve Position in the Fund............ | 1c.s | — | — | — | — | .12 | .12 | .12 | .12 | .12 | .12 | .12 | .12 |
| Total Fund Cred.&Loans Outstg........ | 2tl | 1,207.93 | 1,044.03 | 972.00 | 874.12 | 2,825.36 | 4,780.94 | 5,672.34 | 5,500.05 | 4,010.87 | 2,331.27 | 2,463.04 | 3,600.00 |
| SDR Allocations............................. | 1bd | 169.99 | 169.99 | 169.99 | 169.99 | 169.99 | 988.56 | 988.56 | 988.56 | 988.56 | 988.56 | 988.56 | 988.56 |
| **International Liquidity** | | | | | | *Millions of US Dollars Unless Otherwise Indicated: Last Thursday of Period* | | | | | | | |
| Total Reserves minus Gold.............. | 1l.d | 9,799 | 10,033 | 11,543 | 14,044 | 7,194 | 11,318 | 14,346 | 14,528 | 10,242 | 5,156 | 11,807 | 17,830 |
| SDR Holdings................................ | 1b.d | 245 | 216 | 216 | 215 | 183 | 1,381 | 1,230 | 1,054 | 921 | 850 | 754 | 673 |
| Reserve Position in the Fund.......... | 1c.d | — | — | — | — | — | — | — | — | — | — | — | — |
| Foreign Exchange.......................... | 1d.d | 9,554 | 9,817 | 11,328 | 13,829 | 7,011 | 9,938 | 13,115 | 13,474 | 9,320 | 4,306 | 11,053 | 17,157 |
| Gold (Million Fine Troy Ounces)....... | 1ad | 2.099 | 2.099 | 2.100 | 2.104 | 2.104 | 2.104 | 2.070 | 2.071 | 2.072 | 2.072 | 2.073 | 2.074 |
| Gold (National Valuation)................ | 1and | 817 | 915 | 1,273 | 1,645 | 1,709 | 2,452 | 2,864 | 3,566 | 3,555 | 2,666 | 2,486 | 2,215 |
| Central Bank: Other Assets............. | 3..d | 15 | 69 | †49 | 43 | †164 | 109 | 123 | 134 | 148 | 123 | 130 | 127 |
| Central Bank: Other Liabs............... | 4..d | 708 | 703 | †700 | 707 | †1,300 | 1,308 | 1,222 | 1,135 | 1,049 | 2,066 | 1,942 | 2,500 |
| Other Depository Corps.: Assets....... | 7a.d | 3,175 | 2,167 | †2,957 | 3,246 | †3,782 | 4,017 | 4,160 | 3,898 | 4,662 | 4,275 | 4,270 | 4,570 |
| Other Depository Corps.: Liabs......... | 7b.d | 646 | 525 | †515 | 752 | †660 | 913 | 1,004 | 1,497 | 1,794 | 1,930 | 2,434 | 3,215 |
| **Central Bank** | | | | | | | *Millions of Rupees: End of Period* | | | | | | |
| Net Foreign Assets......................... | 11n | 464,257 | 508,749 | †626,928 | 813,829 | †304,161 | 415,472 | 564,225 | 599,639 | 480,717 | 28,829 | 757,013 | 1,119,215 |
| Claims on Nonresidents................ | 11 | 632,633 | 654,600 | †774,256 | 958,109 | †771,926 | 1,287,848 | 1,548,187 | 1,598,032 | 1,328,985 | 787,507 | 1,464,099 | 2,048,163 |
| Liabilities to Nonresidents.............. | 16c | 168,376 | 145,850 | †147,329 | 144,280 | †467,765 | 872,377 | 983,961 | 998,392 | 848,269 | 758,678 | 707,086 | 928,948 |
| Claims on Other Depository Corps.... | 12e | 207,726 | 214,573 | †286,353 | 283,615 | †313,842 | 469,775 | 390,131 | 539,397 | 926,351 | 648,578 | 908,258 | 1,573,550 |
| Net Claims on Central Government.. | 12an | 328,515 | 426,383 | †497,663 | 545,483 | †1,325,686 | 1,134,468 | 1,364,584 | 1,452,557 | 1,599,991 | 2,881,953 | 2,364,190 | 1,961,345 |
| Claims on Central Government...... | 12a | 355,400 | 535,481 | †568,249 | 600,468 | †1,423,986 | 1,305,568 | 1,544,277 | 1,543,809 | 1,688,998 | 2,965,421 | 2,723,542 | 2,317,538 |
| Liabilities to Central Government... | 16d | 26,885 | 109,098 | †70,586 | 54,985 | †98,299 | 171,100 | 179,693 | 91,252 | 89,007 | 83,468 | 359,352 | 356,193 |
| Claims on Other Sectors................ | 12s | 26,016 | 29,918 | †31,766 | 41,867 | †50,195 | 140,699 | 72,149 | 34,698 | 33,724 | 34,019 | 37,000 | 33,943 |
| Claims on Other Financial Corps..... | 12g | 18,774 | 15,415 | †17,819 | 17,280 | †15,393 | 14,437 | 14,538 | 14,427 | 14,008 | 11,763 | 11,762 | 11,816 |
| Claims on State & Local Govts....... | 12b | 7,242 | 14,503 | †6,560 | 14,753 | †20,800 | 112,798 | 39,115 | 3,087 | — | — | — | — |
| Claims on Public Nonfin. Corps...... | 12c | — | — | †— | | †7 | 7 | 6 | 7 | 7 | 8 | 9 | 11 |
| Claims on Private Sector............... | 12d | — | — | †7,387 | 9,834 | †13,996 | 13,458 | 18,490 | 17,178 | 19,709 | 22,248 | 25,230 | 22,116 |
| Monetary Base.............................. | 14 | 892,793 | 980,694 | †1,186,963 | 1,362,666 | †1,447,895 | 1,650,643 | 1,924,904 | 2,068,948 | 2,415,684 | 2,708,666 | 2,763,509 | 3,455,644 |
| Currency in Circulation.................. | 14a | 690,946 | 769,617 | †917,809 | 1,070,960 | †1,205,289 | 1,368,144 | 1,595,122 | 1,694,829 | 1,958,437 | 2,212,092 | 2,431,975 | 3,034,996 |
| Liabs. to Other Depository Corps.... | 14c | 196,348 | 207,750 | †264,356 | 286,560 | †240,010 | 280,177 | 325,362 | 369,236 | 452,293 | 491,968 | 327,156 | 416,608 |
| Liabilities to Other Sectors............. | 14d | 5,499 | 3,327 | †4,798 | 5,146 | †2,595 | 2,322 | 4,420 | 4,882 | 4,954 | 4,606 | 4,379 | 4,040 |
| Other Liabs. to Other Dep. Corps..... | 14n | — | — | †1,829 | 1,220 | †3,091 | 1,225 | 1,935 | 1,813 | 1,379 | 760 | 95,371 | 96,760 |
| Dep. & Sec. Excl. f/Monetary Base..... | 14o | 67,601 | 81,155 | †73,800 | 67,272 | †100,824 | 84,177 | 74,982 | 87,807 | 118,051 | 181,527 | 300,102 | 395,853 |
| Deposits Included in Broad Money. | 15 | — | — | †— | — | †— | — | — | — | — | — | — | — |
| Sec.Ot.th.Shares Incl.in Brd. Money | 16a | — | — | †— | — | †— | — | — | — | — | — | — | — |
| Deposits Excl. from Broad Money... | 16b | 67,601 | 81,155 | †73,800 | 67,272 | †100,824 | 84,177 | 74,982 | 87,807 | 118,051 | 181,527 | 300,102 | 395,853 |
| Sec.Ot.th.Shares Excl.f/Brd.Money.. | 16s | — | — | †— | — | †— | — | — | — | — | — | — | — |
| Loans......................................... | 16l | — | — | †— | — | †— | — | — | — | — | — | — | — |
| Financial Derivatives...................... | 16m | — | — | †— | — | †— | — | — | — | — | — | — | — |
| Shares and Other Equity................. | 17a | 62,021 | 78,461 | †120,363 | 181,139 | †440,307 | 521,823 | 530,147 | 618,511 | 641,342 | 774,310 | 849,280 | 639,220 |
| Other Items (Net)........................... | 17r | 4,099 | 39,313 | †59,755 | 72,497 | †1,768 | −97,454 | −140,878 | −150,787 | −135,674 | −71,884 | 58,200 | 100,575 |
| Memo Item: | | | | | | | | | | | | | |
| Total Assets.................................. | 10ra | 1,353,440 | 1,558,789 | †1,788,955 | 2,021,450 | †2,710,684 | 3,365,268 | 3,717,198 | 3,888,743 | 4,163,065 | 4,633,645 | 5,312,772 | 6,153,885 |

| | | 2004 | 2005 | 2006 | 2007 | 2008 | 2009 | 2010 | 2011 | 2012 | 2013 | 2014 | 2015 |
|---|---|---|---|---|---|---|---|---|---|---|---|---|---|
| **Other Depository Corporations** | | | | | | *Millions of Rupees: End of Period* | | | | | | | |
| Net Foreign Assets | 21n | 149,488 | 98,213 | † 148,766 | 152,692 | † 246,959 | 261,570 | 270,499 | 215,992 | 278,634 | 247,789 | 186,972 | 142,131 |
| Claims on Nonresidents | 21 | 187,711 | 129,635 | † 180,110 | 198,717 | † 299,132 | 338,466 | 356,551 | 350,664 | 452,855 | 451,768 | 434,850 | 479,246 |
| Liabilities to Nonresidents | 26c | 38,223 | 31,422 | † 31,344 | 46,025 | † 52,173 | 76,896 | 86,051 | 134,672 | 174,221 | 203,980 | 247,878 | 337,115 |
| Claims on Central Bank | 20 | 270,921 | 298,125 | † 306,682 | 345,691 | † 323,191 | 367,640 | 413,607 | 482,432 | 586,761 | 627,328 | 466,218 | 661,595 |
| Currency | 20a | 38,836 | 42,265 | † 48,029 | 68,015 | † 77,698 | 75,953 | 86,136 | 109,109 | 131,695 | 133,505 | 139,064 | 163,803 |
| Reserve Deposits and Securities | 20b | 232,085 | 255,860 | † 258,653 | 277,676 | † 245,162 | 291,589 | 326,874 | 370,914 | 454,189 | 492,433 | 319,257 | 418,995 |
| Other Claims | 20n | — | — | † — | — | † 331 | 98 | 596 | 2,410 | 876 | 1,390 | 7,897 | 78,796 |
| Net Claims on Central Government | 22an | 413,596 | 439,077 | † 446,209 | 693,465 | † 632,003 | 1,165,799 | 1,514,309 | 2,528,291 | 3,447,768 | 3,683,703 | 4,604,617 | 6,061,137 |
| Claims on Central Government | 22a | 526,753 | 587,225 | † 626,982 | 965,029 | † 882,393 | 1,464,440 | 1,854,818 | 2,894,594 | 3,871,102 | 4,100,562 | 5,138,037 | 6,701,490 |
| Liabilities to Central Government | 26d | 113,157 | 148,148 | † 180,773 | 271,564 | † 250,390 | 298,641 | 340,509 | 366,302 | 423,333 | 416,859 | 533,420 | 640,353 |
| Claims on Other Sectors | 22s | 1,658,371 | 2,125,906 | † 2,491,280 | 2,920,021 | † 3,442,314 | 3,722,863 | 3,915,539 | 3,789,956 | 4,112,684 | 4,414,428 | 4,990,640 | 5,314,241 |
| Claims on Other Financial Corps. | 22g | — | 104,131 | † 121,183 | 155,659 | † 106,488 | 116,434 | 99,258 | 118,048 | 139,959 | 122,015 | 114,961 | 101,210 |
| Claims on State & Local Govts. | 22b | 21,707 | 34,983 | † 35,320 | 24,937 | † 22,851 | 148,447 | 216,737 | 191,984 | 189,118 | 184,574 | 257,971 | 322,609 |
| Claims on Public Nonfin. Corps. | 22c | 15,780 | 124,893 | † 136,126 | 176,606 | † 270,336 | 472,099 | 434,576 | 184,253 | 407,976 | 522,993 | 640,489 | 683,580 |
| Claims on Private Sector | 22d | 1,620,884 | 1,861,899 | † 2,198,651 | 2,562,819 | † 3,042,638 | 2,985,883 | 3,164,968 | 3,295,671 | 3,375,631 | 3,584,845 | 3,977,219 | 4,206,841 |
| Liabilities to Central Bank | 26g | 176,354 | 192,709 | † 255,829 | 241,778 | † 304,278 | 472,566 | 393,106 | 548,011 | 936,066 | 449,022 | 692,200 | 1,435,750 |
| Transf.Dep.Included in Broad Money | 24 | 1,026,569 | 1,739,235 | † 1,975,397 | 2,390,315 | † 2,190,510 | 2,566,330 | 3,039,686 | 3,482,818 | 4,223,493 | 5,020,442 | 5,710,365 | 6,493,037 |
| Other Dep.Included in Broad Money. | 25 | 1,043,698 | 727,102 | † 810,751 | 984,293 | † 1,309,780 | 1,454,904 | 1,562,996 | 1,778,923 | 1,964,013 | 2,096,704 | 2,167,333 | 2,133,599 |
| Sec.Ot.th.Shares Incl.in Brd. Money. | 26a | — | — | † — | — | † 1,816 | 233 | 111 | 59 | 83 | 10 | 10 | 10 |
| Deposits Excl. from Broad Money | 26b | 83,595 | 92,604 | † 126,269 | 152,434 | † 189,982 | 232,786 | 253,368 | 262,469 | 281,057 | 339,100 | 360,259 | 454,360 |
| Sec.Ot.th.Shares Excl.f/Brd.Money. | 26s | — | — | † — | — | † 14,334 | 19,252 | 16,949 | 18,228 | 14,714 | 13,145 | 11,783 | 14,256 |
| Loans | 26l | — | 1,540 | † 5,203 | 7,231 | † 2,570 | 6,113 | 7,945 | 8,830 | 5,288 | 9,864 | 12,099 | 6,665 |
| Financial Derivatives | 26m | — | — | † — | — | † 21 | 25,265 | 21,648 | 28,080 | 13,445 | 5,358 | 10,331 | 1,041 |
| Insurance Technical Reserves | 26r | — | — | † — | — | † — | | | | | | | |
| Shares and Other Equity | 27a | — | 509,073 | † 386,954 | 513,773 | † 696,259 | 781,911 | 804,174 | 910,541 | 979,999 | 1,034,728 | 1,273,773 | 1,556,289 |
| Other Items (Net) | 27r | 162,160 | −300,942 | † −167,466 | −177,955 | † −65,082 | −41,487 | 13,971 | −21,285 | 7,689 | 4,874 | 10,293 | 84,096 |
| Memo Item: | | | | | | | | | | | | | |
| Total Assets | 20ra | 2,676,503 | 4,089,784 | † 4,513,538 | 5,486,264 | † 5,783,548 | 6,889,834 | 7,589,799 | 8,693,635 | 10,282,889 | 10,977,618 | 12,671,706 | 14,808,738 |
| **Depository Corporations** | | | | | | *Millions of Rupees: End of Period* | | | | | | | |
| Net Foreign Assets | 31n | 613,745 | 606,962 | † 775,694 | 966,521 | † 551,120 | 677,042 | 834,725 | 815,631 | 759,350 | 276,618 | 943,985 | 1,261,346 |
| Claims on Nonresidents | 31 | 820,344 | 784,235 | † 954,366 | 1,156,826 | † 1,071,057 | 1,626,314 | 1,904,737 | 1,948,695 | 1,781,840 | 1,239,276 | 1,898,949 | 2,527,409 |
| Liabilities to Nonresidents | 36c | 206,599 | 177,272 | † 178,673 | 190,305 | † 519,938 | 949,273 | 1,070,013 | 1,133,064 | 1,022,490 | 962,658 | 954,964 | 1,266,062 |
| Domestic Claims | 32 | 2,426,498 | 3,021,284 | † 3,466,918 | 4,200,836 | † 5,450,199 | 6,163,829 | 6,866,580 | 7,805,503 | 9,194,167 | 11,014,103 | 11,996,447 | 13,370,665 |
| Net Claims on Central Government | 32an | 742,111 | 865,460 | † 943,872 | 1,238,948 | † 1,957,690 | 2,300,267 | 2,878,893 | 3,980,848 | 5,047,759 | 6,565,656 | 6,968,807 | 8,022,482 |
| Claims on Central Government | 32a | 882,153 | 1,122,706 | † 1,195,231 | 1,565,497 | † 2,306,379 | 2,770,008 | 3,399,094 | 4,438,402 | 5,560,100 | 7,065,983 | 7,861,579 | 9,019,028 |
| Liabilities to Central Government. | 36d | 140,042 | 257,246 | † 251,359 | 326,549 | † 348,689 | 469,742 | 520,202 | 457,554 | 512,340 | 500,327 | 892,772 | 996,546 |
| Claims on Other Sectors | 32s | 1,684,387 | 2,155,824 | † 2,523,046 | 2,961,888 | † 3,492,509 | 3,863,563 | 3,987,688 | 3,824,655 | 4,146,408 | 4,448,447 | 5,027,640 | 5,348,183 |
| Claims on Other Financial Corps. | 32g | 18,774 | 119,546 | † 139,002 | 172,939 | † 121,881 | 130,871 | 113,796 | 132,475 | 153,967 | 133,778 | 126,723 | 113,026 |
| Claims on State & Local Govts. | 32b | 28,949 | 49,486 | † 41,880 | 39,690 | † 43,651 | 261,244 | 255,851 | 195,071 | 189,118 | 184,574 | 257,971 | 322,609 |
| Claims on Public Nonfin. Corps. | 32c | 15,780 | 124,893 | † 136,126 | 176,606 | † 270,343 | 472,106 | 434,582 | 184,260 | 407,983 | 523,001 | 640,498 | 683,592 |
| Claims on Private Sector | 32d | 1,620,884 | 1,861,899 | † 2,206,038 | 2,572,653 | † 3,056,634 | 2,999,341 | 3,183,458 | 3,312,849 | 3,395,339 | 3,607,093 | 4,002,449 | 4,228,956 |
| Broad Money Liabilities | 35l | 2,727,876 | 3,197,016 | † 3,660,726 | 4,382,699 | † 4,632,293 | 5,315,979 | 6,116,199 | 6,852,402 | 8,019,284 | 9,200,350 | 10,174,998 | 11,501,879 |
| Currency Outside Depository Corps | 34a | 652,110 | 727,352 | † 869,780 | 1,002,945 | † 1,127,591 | 1,292,190 | 1,508,986 | 1,585,720 | 1,826,742 | 2,078,587 | 2,292,911 | 2,871,192 |
| Transferable Deposits | 34 | 1,032,068 | 1,742,562 | † 1,980,195 | 2,395,461 | † 2,191,921 | 2,566,930 | 3,040,414 | 3,482,924 | 4,223,926 | 5,020,982 | 5,710,750 | 6,493,374 |
| Other Deposits | 35 | 1,043,698 | 727,102 | † 810,751 | 984,293 | † 1,310,964 | 1,456,625 | 1,566,688 | 1,783,699 | 1,968,534 | 2,100,771 | 2,171,327 | 2,137,303 |
| Securities Other than Shares | 36a | — | — | † — | — | † 1,816 | 233 | 111 | 59 | 83 | 10 | 10 | 10 |
| Deposits Excl. from Broad Money | 36b | 151,196 | 173,759 | † 200,069 | 219,706 | † 290,806 | 316,962 | 328,350 | 350,276 | 399,108 | 520,627 | 660,361 | 850,213 |
| Sec.Ot.th.Shares Excl.f/Brd.Money. | 36s | — | — | † — | — | † 14,334 | 19,252 | 16,949 | 18,228 | 14,714 | 13,145 | 11,783 | 14,256 |
| Loans | 36l | — | 1,540 | † 5,203 | 7,231 | † 2,570 | 6,113 | 7,945 | 8,830 | 5,288 | 9,864 | 12,099 | 6,665 |
| Financial Derivatives | 36m | — | — | † — | — | † 21 | 25,265 | 21,648 | 28,080 | 13,445 | 5,358 | 10,331 | 1,041 |
| Insurance Technical Reserves | 36r | — | — | † — | — | † — | | | | | | | |
| Shares and Other Equity | 37a | 62,021 | 587,534 | † 507,317 | 694,912 | † 1,136,566 | 1,303,734 | 1,334,321 | 1,529,052 | 1,621,342 | 1,809,038 | 2,123,053 | 2,195,509 |
| Other Items (Net) | 37r | 99,150 | −331,603 | † −130,703 | −137,191 | † −75,271 | −146,435 | −124,107 | −165,733 | −119,663 | −267,661 | −52,192 | 62,447 |
| Broad Money Liabs., Seasonally Adj. | 35l.b | 2,671,582 | 3,130,367 | † 3,582,797 | 4,289,669 | † 4,542,279 | 5,214,326 | 6,000,698 | 6,724,377 | 7,870,672 | 9,031,872 | 10,002,398 | .... |
| **Monetary Aggregates** | | | | | | *Millions of Rupees: End of Period* | | | | | | | |
| Broad Money | 59m | .... | .... | 4,631,578 | 5,439,249 | 5,794,144 | 6,814,496 | 7,807,083 | 8,790,980 | 10,306,617 | 11,676,559 | 13,028,161 | 14,637,381 |
| o/w:Currency Issued by Cent.Govt | 59m.a | 3,177 | 4,658 | 4,817 | 5,241 | 5,494 | 5,747 | 5,698 | 6,308 | 7,027 | 8,166 | 7,401 | 7,559 |
| o/w: Dep.in Nonfin. Corporations. | 59m.b | 53,901 | 39,257 | 966,035 | 1,051,309 | 1,156,357 | 1,492,770 | 1,681,536 | 1,928,645 | 2,276,654 | 2,467,844 | 2,845,563 | 3,127,744 |
| o/w:Secs. Issued by Central Govt.. | 59m.c | — | — | — | — | — | — | 3,650 | 3,625 | 3,652 | 199 | 199 | 199 |
| Money (National Definitions) | | | | | | | | | | | | | |
| Reserve Money | 19mb | 895,963 | 985,352 | 1,186,963 | 1,362,666 | 1,447,894 | 1,650,643 | 1,924,904 | 2,068,827 | 2,415,684 | 2,708,666 | 2,763,509 | 3,455,644 |
| M1 | 59ma | 2,385,053 | 2,474,573 | 2,849,975 | 3,398,406 | 3,319,513 | 3,859,121 | 4,549,400 | 5,068,644 | 6,050,668 | 7,099,569 | 8,003,661 | 9,364,567 |
| M2 | 59mb | 2,725,436 | 3,201,675 | 3,665,543 | 4,387,940 | 4,637,786 | 5,321,727 | 6,121,897 | 6,858,709 | 8,026,312 | 9,208,515 | 10,182,399 | 11,508,975 |
| M3 | 59mc | .... | .... | 4,631,578 | 5,439,249 | 5,794,144 | 6,814,496 | 7,807,083 | 8,790,980 | 10,306,617 | 11,676,559 | 13,028,161 | 14,637,381 |
| **Interest Rates** | | | | | | *Percent Per Annum* | | | | | | | |
| Discount Rate (End of Period) | 60.a | 7.50 | 9.00 | 9.50 | 10.00 | 15.00 | 12.50 | 14.00 | 12.00 | 9.50 | 10.00 | 9.50 | 6.50 |
| Money Market Rate | 60b | 2.70 | 6.83 | 8.89 | 9.30 | 12.33 | 11.96 | 11.69 | 12.47 | 10.45 | 8.81 | 9.24 | 6.98 |
| Treasury Bill Rate | 60c | 2.49 | 7.18 | 8.54 | 8.99 | 11.37 | 12.52 | 12.55 | 13.12 | 11.00 | 9.32 | 9.89 | 7.12 |
| Government Bond Yield | 61 | 4.63 | 6.19 | 8.47 | 9.50 | 11.66 | 12.73 | 13.05 | 13.36 | 11.73 | 10.49 | 11.87 | 7.72 |
| **Prices, Production, Labor** | | | | | | *Index Numbers (2010=100): Period Averages* | | | | | | | |
| Share Prices (End of Month) | 62.ep | 51.94 | 76.50 | 103.65 | 125.47 | 111.09 | 75.58 | 100.00 | 115.22 | 142.01 | 206.98 | 284.45 | 326.06 |
| Wholesale Prices | 63 | 48.0 | 52.2 | 56.7 | 61.3 | 76.8 | 82.4 | † 100.0 | 118.8 | 127.3 | 137.2 | 143.7 | 140.1 |
| Consumer Prices | 64 | 50.7 | 55.3 | 59.7 | 64.2 | 77.3 | 87.8 | † 100.0 | 111.9 | 122.8 | 132.2 | 141.7 | 145.3 |
| Manufacturing Production | 66ey | 77.6 | 88.6 | 98.6 | 103.7 | 103.6 | 98.0 | 100.0 | 102.7 | 104.4 | 107.7 | 112.0 | 118.8 |
| | | | | | | *Number in Thousands: Period Averages* | | | | | | | |
| Labor Force | 67d | 45,508 | 46,482 | 50,055 | 50,330 | 51,780 | 53,720 | 56,330 | 57,240 | .... | 59,740 | .... | .... |
| Employment | 67e | 42,009 | 42,916 | 46,952 | 47,650 | 49,090 | 50,790 | 53,210 | 53,840 | .... | 56,010 | .... | .... |
| Unemployment | 67c | 3,499 | 3,566 | 3,103 | 2,680 | 2,690 | 2,930 | 3,120 | 3,400 | .... | 3,730 | .... | .... |
| Unemployment Rate (%) | 67r | 7.7 | 7.7 | 6.2 | 5.3 | 5.2 | 5.5 | 5.6 | 6.0 | .... | 6.2 | .... | .... |

# Pakistan   564

| | | 2004 | 2005 | 2006 | 2007 | 2008 | 2009 | 2010 | 2011 | 2012 | 2013 | 2014 | 2015 |
|---|---|---|---|---|---|---|---|---|---|---|---|---|---|
| **Intl. Transactions & Positions** | | | | | | | *Millions of Rupees* | | | | | | |
| Exports | 70 | 779,286 | 955,464 | 1,020,483 | 1,083,395 | 1,423,451 | 1,433,554 | 1,824,376 | 2,188,534 | 2,293,566 | 2,553,395 | 2,498,595 | 2,268,535 |
| Imports, c.i.f. | 71 | 1,045,981 | 1,509,814 | 1,797,826 | 1,979,325 | 2,947,053 | 2,587,779 | 3,218,900 | 3,797,902 | 4,119,732 | 4,531,895 | 4,796,973 | 4,502,945 |
| | | | | | | | *2010=100* | | | | | | |
| Volume of Exports | 72 | 78.9 | 96.7 | 97.5 | 94.8 | 101.6 | 96.3 | 100.0 | 96.5 | 101.1 | 118.5 | 114.8 | 100.4 |
| Volume of Imports | 73 | 81.9 | 95.4 | 88.7 | 97.9 | 106.5 | 103.0 | 100.0 | 92.9 | 90.8 | 88.7 | 103.2 | 114.4 |
| Unit Value of Exports | 74 | 53.7 | 55.1 | 57.2 | 59.5 | 77.7 | 84.5 | 100.0 | 119.9 | 130.3 | 138.5 | 142.0 | 137.3 |
| Unit Value of Imports | 75 | 41.1 | 47.4 | 52.8 | 58.7 | 87.3 | 84.3 | 100.0 | 125.5 | 142.0 | 158.0 | 156.3 | 147.5 |
| **Balance of Payments** | | | | | | | *Millions of US Dollars* | | | | | | |
| A. Current Account* | 109bx | −817.0 | † −3,606.2 | −6,747.0 | −8,301.0 | −15,654.5 | −3,993.4 | −1,354.0 | −2,207.0 | −2,342.0 | −4,416.0 | −3,616.0 | −1,602.8 |
| Goods, credit (exports) | 1a9cx | 13,281.0 | † 15,441.0 | 17,065.0 | 18,218.0 | 21,223.5 | 18,356.0 | 21,481.0 | 26,328.0 | 24,792.0 | 25,115.0 | 24,777.0 | 22,730.0 |
| Goods, debit (imports) | 1a9dx | 16,643.0 | † 21,683.2 | 26,597.0 | 28,639.0 | 38,132.0 | 28,536.0 | 32,843.0 | 38,995.0 | 40,385.0 | 41,214.0 | 42,654.0 | 39,292.0 |
| Balance on goods | 1a9bx | −3,362.0 | † −6,242.2 | −9,532.0 | −10,421.0 | −16,908.5 | −10,180.0 | −11,362.0 | −12,667.0 | −15,593.0 | −16,099.0 | −17,877.0 | −16,562.0 |
| Services, credit (exports) | 1b9cx | 2,746.0 | † 3,664.0 | 3,475.0 | 3,728.0 | 4,249.0 | 3,957.0 | 6,575.0 | 5,105.0 | 6,582.0 | 4,928.0 | 5,823.0 | 5,781.0 |
| Services, debit (imports) | 1b9dx | 5,364.0 | † 7,592.0 | 8,501.0 | 8,947.0 | 9,797.0 | 6,615.4 | 7,173.0 | 8,156.0 | 8,517.0 | 7,953.0 | 8,465.0 | 8,238.0 |
| Balance on Goods & Services | 1z9bx | −5,980.0 | † −10,170.2 | −14,558.0 | −15,640.0 | −22,456.5 | −12,838.4 | −11,960.0 | −15,718.0 | −17,528.0 | −19,124.0 | −20,519.0 | −19,019.0 |
| Primary income: credit | 1c9cx | 221.0 | † 658.0 | 869.0 | 1,359.0 | 1,310.0 | 607.0 | 681.0 | 846.0 | 589.0 | 501.0 | 507.0 | 660.0 |
| Primary income: debit | 1c9dx | 2,584.1 | † 3,173.0 | 3,999.0 | 5,104.0 | 5,644.0 | 4,221.0 | 3,868.0 | 3,938.0 | 3,974.0 | 4,464.0 | 4,812.0 | 5,346.9 |
| Balance on gds, serv. & prim. inc. | 1y9bx | −8,343.0 | † −12,685.2 | −17,688.0 | −19,385.0 | −26,790.5 | −16,452.4 | −15,147.0 | −18,810.0 | −20,913.0 | −23,087.0 | −24,824.0 | −23,705.9 |
| Secondary income: credit | 1d9ca | 7,666.0 | † 9,169.0 | 11,030.0 | 11,215.0 | 11,252.0 | 12,552.0 | 13,930.0 | 16,775.0 | 18,688.0 | 18,747.0 | 21,476.0 | 22,286.1 |
| Secondary income: debit | 1d9da | 140.0 | † 90.0 | 89.0 | 131.0 | 116.0 | 93.0 | 137.0 | 172.0 | 117.0 | 76.0 | 268.0 | 183.0 |
| B. Capital Account* | 209ba | 591.0 | † 202.0 | 345.0 | 176.0 | 146.0 | 484.0 | 109.0 | 216.0 | 191.0 | 329.0 | 1,961.0 | 307.0 |
| Capital account: credit | 209ca | 596.0 | † 214.0 | 351.0 | 182.0 | 151.0 | 490.0 | 109.0 | 218.0 | 192.0 | 331.0 | 1,961.0 | 313.0 |
| Capital account: debit | 209da | 5.0 | † 12.0 | 6.0 | 6.0 | 5.0 | 6.0 | .... | 2.0 | 1.0 | 2.0 | — | 6.0 |
| Balance on current & capital acct. | 129ba | −226.0 | † −3,404.2 | −6,402.0 | −8,125.0 | −15,508.5 | −3,509.4 | −1,245.0 | −1,991.0 | −2,151.0 | −4,087.0 | −1,655.0 | −1,295.8 |
| C. Financial Account* | 309na | 1,810.0 | † −3,811.0 | −7,282.0 | −10,656.0 | −6,571.0 | −6,836.1 | −3,127.0 | −1,398.0 | −537.0 | −2,049.0 | −8,777.0 | −5,691.7 |
| Direct investment: assets | 3a9aa | 56.0 | † 45.0 | 109.0 | 98.0 | 49.0 | 71.0 | 47.0 | 62.0 | 77.0 | 212.0 | 122.0 | 23.0 |
| Equity & investment fund shares | 3aaaa | — | † 13.0 | 109.0 | 98.0 | 49.0 | 71.0 | 47.0 | 62.0 | 77.0 | 212.0 | 122.0 | 23.0 |
| Debt instruments | 3abaa | 56.0 | † 32.0 | .... | .... | .... | .... | .... | .... | .... | .... | .... | .... |
| Direct investment: liabilities | 3a9la | 1,118.0 | † 2,201.0 | 4,273.0 | 5,590.0 | 5,438.0 | 2,338.0 | 2,022.0 | 1,326.0 | 859.0 | 1,333.0 | 1,867.0 | 979.0 |
| Equity & investment fund shares . | 3aala | 1,115.0 | † 2,201.0 | 4,273.0 | 5,590.0 | 5,438.0 | 2,338.0 | 2,022.0 | 1,380.0 | 1,140.0 | 1,536.0 | 1,899.0 | 884.0 |
| Debt instruments | 3abla | 3.0 | .... | .... | .... | .... | .... | .... | −54.0 | −281.0 | −203.0 | −32.0 | 95.0 |
| Portfolio investment: assets | 3b9aa | −9.0 | † −19.0 | 4.0 | −5.0 | 26.0 | 26.0 | −6.0 | 1.0 | 57.0 | 50.0 | −51.0 | 26.0 |
| Equity & investment fund shares | 3baaa | −9.0 | † −13.0 | 16.0 | 15.0 | 19.0 | 35.0 | −10.0 | 10.0 | 103.0 | 92.0 | .... | .... |
| Debt securities | 3bbaa | — | † −6.0 | −12.0 | −20.0 | 7.0 | −9.0 | 4.0 | −9.0 | −46.0 | −42.0 | −51.0 | 26.0 |
| Portfolio investment: liabilities | 3b9la | 392.0 | † 1,061.0 | 1,973.0 | 2,081.0 | −243.0 | −582.0 | −114.0 | −37.0 | 174.0 | 77.0 | 3,785.0 | 935.0 |
| Equity & investment fund shares . | 3bala | 49.0 | † 451.0 | 1,152.0 | 1,276.0 | −270.0 | −37.0 | 511.0 | 25.0 | 178.0 | 111.0 | 765.0 | 524.0 |
| Debt securities | 3bbla | 343.0 | † 610.0 | 821.0 | 805.0 | 27.0 | −545.0 | −625.0 | −62.0 | −4.0 | −34.0 | 3,020.0 | 411.0 |
| Fin. der.& empl.stk.ops.(ESOs): net | 3c9na | .... | .... | .... | .... | .... | .... | .... | .... | .... | 2.0 | — | −2.0 |
| Fin. der. & ESOs.: assets | 3c9aa | .... | .... | .... | .... | .... | .... | .... | .... | .... | 2.0 | — | −2.0 |
| Fin. der. & ESOs.: liabilities | 3c9la | .... | .... | .... | .... | .... | .... | .... | .... | .... | .... | .... | .... |
| Other investment: assets | 3d9aa | 1,339.0 | † 141.0 | 396.0 | −284.0 | 494.0 | 3.0 | 283.0 | 719.0 | 819.0 | −790.0 | −360.0 | 142.0 |
| Other equity | 3daaa | .... | .... | .... | .... | .... | .... | .... | .... | .... | .... | — | 33.0 |
| Debt instruments | 3dzaa | 1,339.0 | † 141.0 | 396.0 | −284.0 | 494.0 | 3.0 | 283.0 | 719.0 | 819.0 | −790.0 | −360.0 | 109.0 |
| Other investment: liabilities | 3d9la | −1,934.0 | † 716.0 | 1,545.0 | 2,794.0 | 1,945.0 | 5,180.1 | 1,543.0 | 891.0 | 457.0 | 113.0 | 2,836.0 | 3,966.7 |
| Other equity | 3dala | .... | .... | .... | .... | .... | .... | .... | .... | .... | .... | .... | .... |
| Debt instruments | 3dzla | −1,934.0 | † 716.0 | 1,545.0 | 2,794.0 | 1,945.0 | 5,180.1 | 1,543.0 | 891.0 | 457.0 | 113.0 | 2,836.0 | 3,966.7 |
| Curr.+ cap.− finan. acct. balance | 4y9na | −2,036.0 | † 406.8 | 880.0 | 2,531.0 | −8,937.5 | 3,326.6 | 1,882.0 | −593.0 | −1,614.0 | −2,038.0 | 7,122.0 | 4,395.9 |
| D. Net Errors and Omissions | 409na | 676.4 | † −147.2 | 549.6 | 30.8 | −67.2 | −1,664.3 | −1,188.2 | 317.2 | −403.1 | −517.9 | −23.3 | −545.0 |
| E. Reserves and Related Items | 4z9na | −1,359.6 | † 259.6 | 1,429.6 | 2,561.8 | −9,004.7 | 1,662.3 | 693.8 | −275.8 | −2,017.1 | −2,555.9 | 7,098.7 | 3,850.9 |
| Reserve assets | 3e9aa | −1,728.5 | † −38.9 | 1,423.5 | 2,410.9 | −6,122.3 | 5,017.1 | 2,319.3 | −547.5 | −4,296.2 | −5,101.7 | 7,268.5 | 5,434.5 |
| Credit and loans from the IMF | 3dcla | −313.9 | † −243.5 | −106.1 | −150.9 | 2,882.4 | 3,031.8 | 1,325.5 | −271.6 | −2,279.1 | −2,545.7 | 169.8 | 1,583.7 |
| Exceptional financing | 409la | −55.0 | † −55.0 | 100.0 | — | — | 323.0 | 300.0 | .... | .... | .... | .... | .... |
| *Excludes components in group E | | | | | | | | | | | | | |
| **International Investment Position** | | | | | | | *Millions of US Dollars* | | | | | | |
| Assets | 809aa | 17,071.0 | 17,680.9 | 19,734.6 | 22,701.0 | 16,772.8 | 23,426.8 | 26,222.7 | 26,650.2 | 23,711.4 | 17,231.9 | † 24,049.1 | 29,485.5 |
| Direct investment | 8a9aa | 702.0 | 870.0 | 1,010.0 | 1,249.0 | 1,269.0 | 1,897.1 | 1,424.5 | 1,474.5 | 1,605.4 | 1,670.2 | † 1,752.6 | 1,975.1 |
| Equity & investment fund shares.. | 8aaaa | 702.0 | 870.0 | 1,010.0 | 1,249.0 | 1,269.0 | 1,797.5 | 1,341.3 | 1,401.5 | 1,546.1 | 1,613.7 | † 1,696.1 | 1,918.6 |
| Debt instruments | 8abaa | .... | .... | .... | .... | .... | 99.6 | 83.2 | 73.0 | 59.3 | 56.5 | † 56.5 | 56.5 |
| Portfolio investment | 8b9aa | 158.0 | 452.0 | 311.0 | 330.0 | 111.0 | 153.0 | 177.9 | 196.0 | 378.6 | 491.4 | † 381.2 | 404.2 |
| Equity & investment fund shares.. | 8baaa | 155.0 | 447.0 | 307.0 | 316.0 | 97.0 | 120.0 | 120.3 | 104.0 | 157.5 | 205.8 | † 206.0 | 206.4 |
| Debt securities | 8bbaa | 3.0 | 5.0 | 4.0 | 14.0 | 14.0 | 33.0 | 57.6 | 92.0 | 221.1 | 285.6 | † 175.2 | 197.9 |
| Fin. der.(oth.than reserves) & ESOs | 8c9aa | .... | .... | .... | .... | .... | 27.0 | 20.9 | 25.0 | 21.7 | 21.3 | † 84.8 | 18.8 |
| Other investment | 8d9aa | 5,492.0 | 5,336.0 | 5,752.0 | 5,651.0 | 6,255.0 | 6,204.0 | 6,648.8 | 7,332.0 | 8,180.5 | 7,702.2 | † 7,405.4 | 7,665.6 |
| Other equity | 8daaa | .... | .... | .... | .... | .... | .... | .... | .... | .... | .... | .... | .... |
| Debt instruments | 8dzaa | 5,492.0 | 5,336.0 | 5,752.0 | 5,651.0 | 6,255.0 | 6,204.0 | 6,648.8 | 7,332.0 | 8,180.5 | 7,702.2 | † 7,405.4 | 7,665.6 |
| Reserve assets | 8e9aa | 10,719.0 | 11,022.9 | 12,661.6 | 15,471.0 | 9,137.8 | 15,145.7 | 17,950.6 | 17,622.7 | 13,525.2 | 7,346.8 | † 14,425.0 | 19,421.7 |
| Liabilities | 809la | 45,136.9 | 47,111.2 | 55,453.0 | 73,742.0 | 87,223.6 | 79,359.9 | 85,384.2 | 86,469.8 | 87,473.1 | 88,019.5 | † 98,434.2 | 101,812.2 |
| Direct investment | 8a9la | 7,606.0 | 10,209.0 | 13,682.0 | 25,621.0 | 31,059.0 | 17,720.1 | 19,890.8 | 20,988.0 | 23,180.6 | 25,147.2 | † 30,791.1 | 30,018.3 |
| Equity & investment fund shares.. | 8aala | 6,628.0 | 9,109.0 | 12,241.0 | 23,065.0 | 28,503.0 | 15,870.1 | 18,196.2 | 18,132.0 | 20,245.9 | 22,405.1 | † 28,074.4 | 27,281.0 |
| Debt instruments | 8abla | 978.0 | 1,100.0 | 1,441.0 | 2,556.0 | 2,556.0 | 1,850.0 | 1,694.6 | 2,856.0 | 2,934.7 | 2,742.1 | † 2,716.7 | 2,737.3 |
| Portfolio investment | 8b9la | 1,162.0 | 2,173.0 | 4,064.0 | 6,767.0 | 6,784.0 | 3,548.0 | 4,487.9 | 4,216.0 | 5,233.8 | 6,719.4 | † 11,070.6 | 11,106.4 |
| Equity & investment fund shares.. | 8bala | 495.0 | 1,064.0 | 1,960.0 | 3,859.0 | 3,859.0 | 1,258.0 | 2,750.9 | 2,534.0 | 3,560.1 | 5,078.6 | † 6,403.7 | 6,040.4 |
| Debt securities | 8bbla | 667.0 | 1,109.0 | 2,104.0 | 2,908.0 | 2,925.0 | 2,290.0 | 1,737.0 | 1,682.0 | 1,673.7 | 1,640.8 | † 4,666.9 | 5,066.0 |
| Fin. der.(oth.than reserves) & ESOs | 8c9la | .... | .... | .... | .... | .... | 57.0 | 51.0 | 41.0 | 9.3 | 8.5 | † 16.0 | 4.4 |
| Other investment | 8d9la | 36,368.9 | 34,729.2 | 37,707.0 | 41,354.0 | 49,380.6 | 58,034.8 | 60,954.5 | 61,224.8 | 59,049.4 | 56,144.3 | † 56,556.4 | 60,683.1 |
| Other equity | 8dala | .... | .... | .... | .... | .... | .... | .... | .... | .... | .... | .... | .... |
| Debt instruments | 8dzla | 36,368.9 | 34,729.2 | 37,707.0 | 41,354.0 | 49,380.6 | 58,034.8 | 60,954.5 | 61,224.8 | 59,049.4 | 56,144.3 | † 56,556.4 | 60,683.1 |

# Pakistan  564

| | | 2004 | 2005 | 2006 | 2007 | 2008 | 2009 | 2010 | 2011 | 2012 | 2013 | 2014 | 2015 |
|---|---|---|---|---|---|---|---|---|---|---|---|---|---|
| **Government Finance** | | | | | | | | | | | | | |
| **Cash Flow Statement** | | | | | | | | | | | | | |
| **Budgetary Central Government** | | | | | | *Billions of Rupees: Fiscal Year Ends June 30* | | | | | | | |
| Cash Receipts:Operating Activities... | c1 | 795.5 | 863.4 | 1,066.2 | 1,280.9 | 1,408.4 | 1,803.2 | 2,179.7 | 2,271.0 | 2,582.4 | 3,345.9 | 3,635.9 | .... |
| Taxes................................................ | c11 | 580.1 | 624.3 | 718.7 | 853.3 | 1,009.9 | 1,180.5 | 1,483.0 | 1,679.4 | 2,024.6 | 2,503.6 | 2,514.0 | .... |
| Social Contributions...................... | c12 | — | — | — | — | — | — | — | — | — | — | — | .... |
| Grants............................................. | c13 | 34.5 | 18.6 | 44.8 | 25.9 | 33.0 | 19.6 | 127.8 | 35.1 | 45.6 | 112.0 | 38.8 | .... |
| Other Receipts................................ | c14 | 180.9 | 220.6 | 302.7 | 401.7 | 365.4 | 603.1 | 568.9 | 556.5 | 512.2 | 730.3 | 1,083.2 | .... |
| Cash Payments:Operating Activities. | c2 | 814.2 | 950.5 | 1,162.3 | 1,415.6 | 1,908.7 | 2,137.4 | 2,601.8 | 3,219.2 | 3,768.6 | 3,990.7 | 4,533.4 | .... |
| Compensation of Employees.......... | c21 | 37.3 | 42.2 | 50.5 | 60.7 | 67.9 | 75.4 | 92.1 | 123.1 | 134.3 | 155.0 | 451.6 | .... |
| Purchases of Goods & Services....... | c22 | 251.8 | 345.7 | 424.9 | 440.7 | 397.9 | 465.2 | 584.9 | 635.0 | 755.3 | 884.2 | 434.6 | .... |
| Interest............................................ | c24 | 317.7 | 274.7 | 361.6 | 373.6 | 489.7 | 751.6 | 814.6 | 855.5 | 980.7 | 1,141.7 | 1,450.9 | .... |
| Subsidies......................................... | c25 | 43.5 | 51.4 | 64.3 | 107.1 | 395.0 | 220.4 | 229.0 | 395.8 | 512.3 | 208.6 | 323.0 | .... |
| Grants............................................. | c26 | 163.8 | 236.5 | 261.0 | 327.1 | 126.7 | 166.9 | 341.1 | 300.0 | 251.4 | 312.3 | 335.9 | .... |
| Social Benefits................................ | c27 | — | — | — | — | — | 72.1 | 92.2 | 102.9 | 149.0 | 144.1 | 187.7 | .... |
| Other Payments.............................. | c28 | — | — | — | 106.3 | 431.4 | 385.9 | 447.9 | 807.0 | 985.6 | 1,144.7 | 1,349.7 | .... |
| Net Cash Inflow:Operating Act.[1-2] | ccio | −18.7 | −87.1 | −96.1 | −134.7 | −500.3 | −334.2 | −422.1 | −948.2 | −1,186.2 | −644.8 | −897.5 | .... |
| Net Cash Outflow:Invest. in NFA...... | c31 | 91.4 | 121.1 | 226.3 | 227.3 | 261.4 | 271.4 | 319.7 | 220.7 | 418.9 | 526.7 | 755.5 | .... |
| Purchases of Nonfinancial Assets... | c31.1 | 91.4 | 121.1 | 226.3 | 227.3 | 261.4 | 271.4 | 319.7 | 220.7 | 418.9 | 526.7 | 755.5 | .... |
| Sales of Nonfinancial Assets.......... | c31.2 | — | — | — | — | — | — | — | — | — | — | — | .... |
| Cash Surplus/Deficit [1-2-31=1-2M] | ccsd | −110.1 | −208.2 | −322.4 | −362.0 | −761.7 | −605.6 | −741.8 | −1,168.9 | −1,605.0 | −1,171.5 | −1,652.9 | .... |
| Net Acq. Fin. Assets, excl. Cash....... | c32x | .... | .... | .... | .... | .... | .... | .... | .... | .... | .... | ..... | .... |
| Domestic......................................... | c321x | .... | .... | .... | .... | .... | .... | .... | .... | .... | .... | ..... | .... |
| Foreign............................................ | c322x | .... | .... | .... | .... | .... | .... | .... | .... | .... | .... | ..... | .... |
| Net Incurrence of Liabilities.............. | c33 | .... | .... | .... | .... | .... | .... | .... | .... | .... | .... | ..... | .... |
| Domestic......................................... | c331 | .... | .... | .... | .... | .... | .... | .... | .... | .... | — | — | .... |
| Foreign............................................ | c332 | .... | .... | .... | .... | .... | .... | .... | .... | .... | — | — | .... |
| Net Cash Inflow, Fin.Act.[-32x+33]... | cnfb | .... | .... | .... | .... | .... | .... | .... | .... | .... | .... | ..... | .... |
| Net Change in Stock of Cash........... | cncb | .... | .... | .... | .... | .... | .... | .... | .... | .... | .... | ..... | .... |
| Stat. Discrep. [32X-33+NCB-CSD].... | ccsdz | .... | .... | .... | .... | .... | .... | .... | .... | .... | .... | ..... | .... |
| Memo Item:Cash Expenditure[2+31] | c2m | 905.5 | 1,071.6 | 1,388.6 | 1,642.8 | 2,170.1 | 2,408.8 | 2,921.5 | 3,439.9 | 4,187.4 | 4,517.4 | 5,288.9 | .... |
| Memo Item: Gross Debt.................. | c63 | .... | .... | .... | .... | .... | .... | .... | .... | .... | .... | ..... | .... |
| **National Accounts** | | | | | | *Billions of Rupees: Fiscal Year Ends June 30* | | | | | | | |
| Househ.Cons.Expend.,incl.NPISHs..... | 96f | 4,184.72 | 5,001.50 | 5,720.20 | 6,543.84 | 7,835.31 | 10,455.75 | 11,851.32 | 14,831.29 | 16,527.83 | 18,085.28 | 20,219.32 | 21,688.18 |
| Government Consumption Expend... | 91f | 462.46 | 509.86 | 824.30 | 796.20 | 1,278.43 | 1,388.46 | 1,533.71 | 1,779.42 | 2,102.63 | 2,463.12 | 2,708.92 | 3,242.66 |
| Gross Fixed Capital Formation.......... | 93e | 844.85 | 1,134.94 | 1,565.84 | 1,814.62 | 2,094.74 | 2,105.29 | 2,111.79 | 2,288.33 | 2,701.46 | 2,990.13 | 3,355.00 | 3,701.63 |
| Changes in Inventories.................... | 93i | 90.25 | 105.30 | 121.97 | 138.77 | 163.89 | 211.20 | 237.87 | 292.42 | 320.74 | 358.06 | 401.09 | 438.14 |
| Exports of Goods and Services........ | 90c | 883.70 | 1,019.78 | 1,161.26 | 1,230.66 | 1,316.44 | 1,636.20 | 2,009.46 | 2,552.61 | 2,485.10 | 2,972.18 | 3,077.63 | 2,997.46 |
| Imports of Goods and Services (-).... | 98c | 825.40 | 1,271.60 | 1,770.39 | 1,851.09 | 2,446.01 | 2,597.19 | 2,877.16 | 3,467.63 | 4,091.26 | 4,489.77 | 4,693.89 | 4,684.33 |
| Gross Domestic Product (GDP)......... | 99b | 5,640.59 | 6,499.78 | 7,623.21 | 8,673.01 | 10,242.80 | 13,199.71 | 14,867.00 | 18,276.44 | 20,046.50 | 22,379.00 | 25,068.06 | 27,383.72 |
| Net Primary Income from Abroad..... | 98.n | 124.48 | 134.47 | 149.90 | 157.63 | 208.92 | 346.28 | 566.25 | 820.23 | 1,035.71 | 1,161.61 | 1,428.92 | 1,677.69 |
| Gross National Income (GNI)........... | 99a | 5,765.06 | 6,634.24 | 7,773.10 | 8,830.64 | 10,451.72 | 13,545.99 | 15,433.24 | 19,096.67 | 21,082.21 | 23,540.60 | 26,496.98 | 29,061.41 |
| Consumption of Fixed Capital......... | 99cf | 428.30 | 487.45 | 560.95 | 625.34 | 712.23 | 902.33 | 966.08 | 1,039.28 | 1,126.94 | 1,207.21 | 1,302.71 | 1,408.96 |
| GDP Volume 2000 Prices................. | 99b.p | 4,534.12 | 4,881.80 | 5,183.37 | 5,477.95 | 5,565.38 | 5,765.47 | 5,969.96 | 6,146.42 | 6,403.67 | .... | .... | .... |
| GDP Volume 2005/2006 Prices........ | 99b.p | .... | .... | 8,216.16 | 8,613.23 | 8,759.78 | 9,007.83 | 9,152.55 | 9,404.10 | 9,733.91 | 10,159.01 | 10,640.38 | 11,229.66 |
| GDP Volume (2010=100)............... | 99bvp | 78.5 | 84.5 | † 89.8 | 94.1 | 95.7 | 98.4 | 100.0 | 102.7 | 106.4 | 111.0 | 116.3 | 122.7 |
| GDP Deflator (2010=100).............. | 99bip | 48.3 | 51.7 | 57.1 | 62.0 | 72.0 | 90.2 | 100.0 | 119.6 | 126.8 | 135.6 | 145.0 | 150.1 |
| | | | | | | *Millions: Midyear Estimates* | | | | | | | |
| Population................................ | 99z | 150.27 | 153.36 | 156.52 | 159.77 | 163.10 | 166.52 | 170.04 | 173.67 | 177.39 | 181.19 | 185.04 | 188.92 |

# Palau 565

| | | 2004 | 2005 | 2006 | 2007 | 2008 | 2009 | 2010 | 2011 | 2012 | 2013 | 2014 | 2015 |
|---|---|---|---|---|---|---|---|---|---|---|---|---|---|
| **Exchange Rates** | | | | | *End of Period (sa) Period Averages (sb)* | | | | | | | | |
| US Dollar/SDR Rate......................... | sa | 1.5530 | 1.4293 | 1.5044 | 1.5803 | 1.5403 | 1.5677 | 1.5400 | 1.5353 | 1.5369 | 1.5400 | 1.4488 | 1.3857 |
| US Dollar/SDR Rate......................... | sb | 1.4810 | 1.4773 | 1.4712 | 1.5306 | 1.5801 | 1.5420 | 1.5257 | 1.5787 | 1.5317 | 1.5196 | 1.5190 | 1.3991 |
| **Fund Position** | | | | | *Millions of SDRs: End of Period* | | | | | | | | |
| Quota......................................... | 2f.s | 3.10 | 3.10 | 3.10 | 3.10 | 3.10 | 3.10 | 3.10 | 3.10 | 3.10 | 3.10 | 3.10 | 3.10 |
| SDR Holdings................................. | 1b.s | — | — | — | — | — | 2.96 | 2.96 | 2.96 | 2.97 | 2.99 | 2.99 | 2.99 |
| Reserve Position in the Fund............ | 1c.s | .12 | .12 | .12 | .12 | — | — | — | — | — | — | — | — |
| Total Fund Cred. & Loans Outstg...... | 2tl | — | — | — | — | — | — | — | — | — | — | — | — |
| SDR Allocations.............................. | 1bd | — | — | — | — | — | 2.96 | 2.96 | 2.96 | 2.96 | 2.96 | 2.96 | 2.96 |
| **Balance of Payments** | | | | | *Millions of US Dollars* | | | | | | | | |
| A. Current Account*...................... | 109bx | .... | † −39.58 | −48.79 | −36.19 | −34.22 | −6.14 | −18.68 | −25.34 | −34.48 | −29.21 | −48.39 | .... |
| Goods, credit (exports)................... | 1a9cx | .... | † 10.98 | 9.66 | 9.49 | 12.00 | 8.13 | 11.65 | 12.84 | 15.02 | 14.38 | 19.08 | .... |
| Goods, debit (imports)................... | 1a9dx | .... | † 108.08 | 115.28 | 108.53 | 120.31 | 94.03 | 102.75 | 125.06 | 138.94 | 146.51 | 177.73 | .... |
| Balance on goods...................... | 1a9bx | .... | † −97.10 | −105.62 | −99.04 | −108.31 | −85.90 | −91.10 | −112.22 | −123.92 | −132.13 | −158.65 | .... |
| Services, credit (exports)................. | 1b9cx | .... | † 71.72 | 70.50 | 78.20 | 87.57 | 84.40 | 84.01 | 101.90 | 116.61 | 124.85 | 139.25 | .... |
| Services, debit (imports)................. | 1b9dx | .... | † 30.92 | 33.30 | 35.93 | 40.21 | 36.43 | 42.96 | 39.02 | 45.12 | 42.98 | 44.04 | .... |
| Balance on Goods & Services....... | 1z9bx | .... | † −56.30 | −68.41 | −56.76 | −60.95 | −37.93 | −50.05 | −49.34 | −52.43 | −50.26 | −63.44 | .... |
| Primary income: credit.................. | 1c9cx | .... | † 6.38 | 7.30 | 8.69 | 11.50 | 10.49 | 10.97 | 13.27 | 11.45 | 16.02 | 14.50 | .... |
| Primary income: debit................... | 1c9dx | .... | † 11.02 | 8.50 | 11.36 | 9.58 | 1.26 | 6.14 | 15.64 | 19.77 | 20.92 | 25.16 | .... |
| Balance on gds, serv. & prim. inc. | 1y9bx | .... | † −60.94 | −69.61 | −59.43 | −59.03 | −28.70 | −45.22 | −51.72 | −60.75 | −55.16 | −74.11 | .... |
| Secondary income: credit.............. | 1d9ca | .... | † 36.66 | 36.34 | 38.06 | 38.81 | 35.58 | 39.47 | 39.92 | 40.41 | 40.64 | 40.46 | .... |
| Secondary income: debit............... | 1d9da | .... | † 15.30 | 15.52 | 14.82 | 14.00 | 13.02 | 12.93 | 13.54 | 14.14 | 14.68 | 14.75 | .... |
| B. Capital Account*...................... | 209ba | .... | † 50.97 | 48.95 | 42.81 | 31.57 | 17.80 | 29.81 | 20.23 | 26.46 | 23.89 | 21.05 | .... |
| Capital account: credit.................. | 209ca | .... | † 50.97 | 48.95 | 42.81 | 31.57 | 17.80 | 29.81 | 20.23 | 26.46 | 23.89 | 21.05 | .... |
| Capital account: debit................... | 209da | .... | .... | .... | .... | .... | .... | .... | .... | .... | .... | .... | .... |
| Balance on current & capital acct. | 129ba | .... | † 11.39 | .16 | 6.62 | −2.65 | 11.65 | 11.14 | −5.12 | −8.02 | −5.32 | −27.34 | .... |
| C. Financial Account* .................... | 309na | .... | † 6.68 | −11.12 | −.52 | −6.76 | 2.49 | 5.90 | 3.29 | 3.16 | −1.69 | −15.02 | .... |
| Direct investment: assets.............. | 3a9aa | .... | .... | .... | .... | .... | .... | .... | .... | .... | .... | .... | .... |
| Equity & investment fund shares.. | 3aaaa | .... | .... | .... | .... | .... | .... | .... | .... | .... | .... | .... | .... |
| Debt instruments........................ | 3abaa | .... | .... | .... | .... | .... | .... | .... | .... | .... | .... | .... | .... |
| Direct investment: liabilities .......... | 3a9la | .... | † 3.97 | 33.28 | 4.38 | 4.74 | 2.79 | 2.69 | 8.33 | 21.64 | 18.04 | 39.86 | .... |
| Equity & investment fund shares . | 3aala | .... | † 5.02 | 32.79 | 4.16 | 5.12 | 3.06 | 2.74 | 8.43 | 22.26 | 17.46 | 39.24 | .... |
| Debt instruments........................ | 3abla | .... | † −1.05 | .49 | .22 | −.37 | −.27 | −.05 | −.11 | −.62 | .58 | .62 | .... |
| Portfolio investment: assets .......... | 3b9aa | .... | † 4.74 | .38 | 5.32 | −7.25 | 3.16 | −.63 | −1.93 | 6.22 | 10.23 | −6.97 | .... |
| Equity & investment fund shares.. | 3baaa | .... | .... | .... | .... | .... | .... | .... | .... | .... | .... | .... | .... |
| Debt securities .......................... | 3bbaa | .... | † 4.74 | .38 | 5.32 | −7.25 | 3.16 | −.63 | −1.93 | 6.22 | 10.23 | −6.97 | .... |
| Portfolio investment: liabilities....... | 3b9la | .... | .... | .... | .... | .... | .... | .... | .... | .... | .... | .... | .... |
| Equity & investment fund shares . | 3bala | .... | .... | .... | .... | .... | .... | .... | .... | .... | .... | .... | .... |
| Debt securities........................... | 3bbla | .... | .... | .... | .... | .... | .... | .... | .... | .... | .... | .... | .... |
| Fin. der.& empl.stk.ops.(ESOs): net. | 3c9na | .... | .... | .... | .... | .... | .... | .... | .... | .... | .... | .... | .... |
| Fin. der. & ESOs.: assets.............. | 3c9aa | .... | .... | .... | .... | .... | .... | .... | .... | .... | .... | .... | .... |
| Fin. der. & ESOs.: liabilities.......... | 3c9la | .... | .... | .... | .... | .... | .... | .... | .... | .... | .... | .... | .... |
| Other investment: assets............... | 3d9aa | .... | † 5.51 | 20.11 | 10.05 | 2.96 | 10.29 | 2.95 | 9.36 | 23.39 | 2.06 | 33.75 | .... |
| Other equity............................... | 3daaa | .... | .... | .... | .... | .... | .... | .... | .... | .... | .... | .... | .... |
| Debt instruments........................ | 3dzaa | .... | † 5.51 | 20.11 | 10.05 | 2.96 | 10.29 | 2.95 | 9.36 | 23.39 | 2.06 | 33.75 | .... |
| Other investment: liabilities............ | 3d9la | .... | † −.40 | −1.67 | 11.51 | −2.27 | 8.18 | −6.26 | −4.19 | 4.81 | −4.06 | 1.94 | .... |
| Other equity............................... | 3dala | .... | .... | .... | .... | .... | .... | .... | .... | .... | .... | .... | .... |
| Debt instruments........................ | 3dzla | .... | † −.40 | −1.67 | 11.51 | −2.27 | 8.18 | −6.26 | −4.19 | 4.81 | −4.06 | 1.94 | .... |
| Curr.+ cap.– finan. acct. balance... | 4y9na | .... | † 4.71 | 11.29 | 7.13 | 4.11 | 9.17 | 5.24 | −8.41 | −11.19 | −3.64 | −12.32 | .... |
| D. Net Errors and Omissions............ | 409na | .... | † −4.71 | −11.29 | −7.13 | −4.29 | −4.61 | −5.24 | 8.41 | 11.20 | 3.67 | 12.32 | .... |
| E. Reserves and Related Items.......... | 4z9na | .... | † — | — | — | −.19 | 4.56 | — | — | .01 | .03 | — | .... |
| Reserve assets............................ | 3e9aa | .... | .... | .... | .... | −.19 | 4.56 | — | — | .01 | .03 | — | .... |
| Credit and loans from the IMF........ | 3dcla | .... | † — | — | — | — | — | — | — | — | — | — | .... |
| Exceptional financing.................... | 409la | .... | .... | .... | .... | .... | .... | .... | .... | .... | .... | .... | .... |
| *Excludes components in group E | | | | | | | | | | | | | |
| **International Investment Position** | | | | | *Millions of US Dollars* | | | | | | | | |
| Assets............................................ | 809aa | .... | † 293.3 | 317.7 | 365.0 | 305.6 | 334.9 | 344.6 | 338.0 | 408.6 | 435.1 | 477.8 | .... |
| Direct investment.......................... | 8a9aa | .... | .... | .... | .... | .... | .... | .... | .... | .... | .... | .... | .... |
| Equity & investment fund shares.. | 8aaaa | .... | .... | .... | .... | .... | .... | .... | .... | .... | .... | .... | .... |
| Debt instruments........................ | 8abaa | .... | .... | .... | .... | .... | .... | .... | .... | .... | .... | .... | .... |
| Portfolio investment...................... | 8b9aa | .... | † 264.8 | 268.9 | 306.4 | 244.0 | 257.8 | 264.7 | 248.7 | 295.9 | 320.3 | 329.5 | .... |
| Equity & investment fund shares.. | 8baaa | .... | .... | .... | .... | .... | .... | .... | .... | .... | .... | .... | .... |
| Debt securities........................... | 8bbaa | .... | † 264.8 | 268.9 | 306.4 | 244.0 | 257.8 | 264.7 | 248.7 | 295.9 | 320.3 | 329.5 | .... |
| Fin. der.(oth.than reserves) & ESOs | 8c9aa | .... | .... | .... | .... | .... | .... | .... | .... | .... | .... | .... | .... |
| Other investment.......................... | 8d9aa | .... | † 28.5 | 48.8 | 58.6 | 61.6 | 72.4 | 75.4 | 84.7 | 108.1 | 110.2 | 143.9 | .... |
| Other equity............................... | 8daaa | .... | .... | .... | .... | .... | .... | .... | .... | .... | .... | .... | .... |
| Debt instruments........................ | 8dzaa | .... | † 28.5 | 48.8 | 58.6 | 61.6 | 72.4 | 75.4 | 84.7 | 108.1 | 110.2 | 143.9 | .... |
| Reserve assets.............................. | 8e9aa | .... | .... | .... | .... | 4.6 | 4.6 | 4.5 | 4.6 | 4.6 | 4.3 | .... |
| Liabilities....................................... | 809la | .... | † 249.6 | 281.2 | 297.1 | 299.6 | 315.0 | 311.3 | 315.4 | 341.9 | 356.5 | 394.7 | .... |
| Direct investment.......................... | 8a9la | .... | † 190.0 | 223.3 | 227.7 | 232.4 | 235.2 | 237.9 | 246.2 | 267.9 | 286.5 | 323.1 | .... |
| Equity & investment fund shares.. | 8aala | .... | † 187.8 | 220.6 | 224.8 | 229.9 | 232.9 | 235.7 | 244.1 | 266.4 | 283.8 | 323.1 | .... |
| Debt instruments........................ | 8abla | .... | † 2.2 | 2.7 | 2.9 | 2.6 | 2.3 | 2.2 | 2.1 | 1.5 | 2.7 | .... |
| Portfolio investment...................... | 8b9la | .... | .... | .... | .... | .... | .... | .... | .... | .... | .... | .... | .... |
| Equity & investment fund shares.. | 8bala | .... | .... | .... | .... | .... | .... | .... | .... | .... | .... | .... | .... |
| Debt securities............................ | 8bbla | .... | .... | .... | .... | .... | .... | .... | .... | .... | .... | .... | .... |
| Fin. der.(oth.than reserves) & ESOs | 8c9la | .... | .... | .... | .... | .... | .... | .... | .... | .... | .... | .... | .... |
| Other investment.......................... | 8d9la | .... | † 59.6 | 57.9 | 69.4 | 67.1 | 79.8 | 73.4 | 69.2 | 74.0 | 70.0 | 71.6 | .... |
| Other equity............................... | 8dala | .... | .... | .... | .... | .... | .... | .... | .... | .... | .... | .... | .... |
| Debt instruments........................ | 8dzla | .... | † 59.6 | 57.9 | 69.4 | 67.1 | 79.8 | 73.4 | 69.2 | 74.0 | 70.0 | 71.6 | .... |

| | | 2004 | 2005 | 2006 | 2007 | 2008 | 2009 | 2010 | 2011 | 2012 | 2013 | 2014 | 2015 |
|---|---|---|---|---|---|---|---|---|---|---|---|---|---|
| **Exchange Rates** | | | | | | *Balboas per SDR: End of Period* | | | | | | | |
| Official Rate | aa | 1.5530 | 1.4293 | 1.5044 | 1.5803 | 1.5403 | 1.5677 | 1.5400 | 1.5353 | 1.5369 | 1.5400 | 1.4488 | 1.3857 |
| | | | | | | *Balboas per US Dollar: End of Period* | | | | | | | |
| Official Rate | ae | 1.0000 | 1.0000 | 1.0000 | 1.0000 | 1.0000 | 1.0000 | 1.0000 | 1.0000 | 1.0000 | 1.0000 | 1.0000 | 1.0000 |
| **Fund Position** | | | | | | *Millions of SDRs: End of Period* | | | | | | | |
| Quota | 2f.s | 206.60 | 206.60 | 206.60 | 206.60 | 206.60 | 206.60 | 206.60 | 206.60 | 206.60 | 206.60 | 206.60 | 206.60 |
| SDR Holdings | 1b.s | .56 | .76 | .85 | .56 | .50 | 171.07 | 171.00 | 170.90 | 170.87 | 170.85 | 170.83 | 170.81 |
| Reserve Position in the Fund | 1c.s | 11.86 | 11.86 | 11.86 | 11.86 | 11.86 | 11.86 | 11.86 | 11.86 | 11.86 | 11.86 | 11.86 | 11.86 |
| Total Fund Cred.&Loans Outstg | 2tl | 23.33 | 16.67 | 10.00 | 3.33 | — | — | — | — | — | — | — | — |
| SDR Allocations | 1bd | 26.32 | 26.32 | 26.32 | 26.32 | 26.32 | 197.01 | 197.01 | 197.01 | 197.01 | 197.01 | 197.01 | 197.01 |
| **International Liquidity** | | | | | | *Millions of US Dollars Unless Otherwise Indicated: End of Period* | | | | | | | |
| Total Reserves minus Gold | 1l.d | 630.6 | 1,210.5 | 1,335.0 | 1,935.1 | 2,423.8 | 3,028.3 | 2,714.5 | 2,303.7 | 2,466.3 | 2,848.0 | 4,032.2 | 3,378.1 |
| SDR Holdings | 1b.d | .9 | 1.1 | 1.3 | .9 | .8 | 268.2 | 263.3 | 262.4 | 262.6 | 263.1 | 247.5 | 236.7 |
| Reserve Position in the Fund | 1c.d | 18.4 | 17.0 | 17.8 | 18.7 | 18.3 | 18.6 | 18.3 | 18.2 | 18.2 | 18.3 | 17.2 | 16.4 |
| Foreign Exchange | 1d.d | 611.4 | 1,192.5 | 1,315.9 | 1,915.4 | 2,404.7 | 2,741.5 | 2,432.9 | 2,023.1 | 2,185.4 | 2,566.6 | 3,767.5 | 3,125.0 |
| Gold (National Valuation) | 1and | — | — | — | — | — | — | — | — | — | — | — | — |
| Central Bank: Other Assets | 3..d | — | .4 | .4 | .4 | .3 | .5 | 62.2 | 20.0 | 25.4 | 24.0 | 89.3 | 188.2 |
| Central Bank: Other Liabs | 4..d | 90.7 | 79.3 | 80.7 | 19.9 | 85.5 | 78.3 | 78.1 | 78.3 | 82.5 | 79.3 | 65.6 | 47.1 |
| Other Depository Corps.: Assets | 7a.d | 11,706.9 | 11,926.4 | 14,151.5 | 17,246.9 | 20,778.2 | 21,598.0 | 22,871.0 | 25,961.7 | 27,548.2 | 26,122.9 | 33,231.6 | 36,264.1 |
| Other Depository Corps.: Liabs | 7b.d | 9,692.1 | 10,496.5 | 11,858.6 | 14,257.6 | 17,637.1 | 16,584.1 | 17,429.2 | 21,595.2 | 24,045.3 | 24,067.6 | 30,881.3 | 35,392.0 |
| **Central Bank** | | | | | | *Millions of Balboas: End of Period* | | | | | | | |
| Net Foreign Assets | 11n | 531.2 | 1,105.2 | 1,243.6 | 2,027.3 | 2,511.7 | 2,835.6 | 2,523.6 | 2,153.4 | 2,361.4 | 2,697.6 | 3,996.9 | 4,031.9 |
| Claims on Nonresidents | 11 | 699.1 | 1,245.9 | 1,379.0 | 2,094.1 | 2,637.7 | 3,222.7 | 2,905.1 | 2,534.2 | 2,746.7 | 3,080.3 | 4,348.0 | 4,351.9 |
| Liabilities to Nonresidents | 16c | 167.8 | 140.8 | 135.4 | 66.8 | 126.0 | 387.1 | 381.5 | 380.8 | 385.3 | 382.6 | 351.0 | 320.1 |
| Claims on Other Depository Corps. | 12e | 59.5 | 102.4 | 164.1 | 208.9 | 298.8 | 230.9 | 215.0 | 521.7 | 529.1 | 650.5 | 467.9 | 595.5 |
| Net Claims on Central Government | 12an | −395.0 | −821.8 | −844.4 | −1,835.0 | −2,456.2 | −2,632.1 | −2,403.4 | −2,345.0 | −2,835.3 | −3,991.9 | −5,105.2 | −4,910.8 |
| Claims on Central Government | 12a | 1,206.9 | 1,223.2 | 1,296.8 | 1,214.0 | 1,203.8 | 1,318.6 | 1,428.8 | 1,988.1 | 2,278.2 | 2,226.7 | 1,976.3 | 2,422.5 |
| Liabilities to Central Government | 16d | 1,601.9 | 2,045.0 | 2,141.2 | 3,049.0 | 3,660.0 | 3,950.7 | 3,832.2 | 4,333.2 | 5,113.4 | 6,218.6 | 7,081.5 | 7,333.3 |
| Claims on Other Sectors | 12s | 1,349.4 | 1,233.4 | 1,202.9 | 1,428.1 | 1,618.9 | 1,731.5 | 2,017.0 | 2,300.3 | 2,592.1 | 3,061.0 | 3,160.1 | 3,214.5 |
| Claims on Other Financial Corps. | 12g | 21.0 | 106.9 | 49.4 | 65.2 | 140.6 | 126.5 | 8.4 | 92.7 | 86.1 | 110.6 | 79.1 | 19.7 |
| Claims on State & Local Govts. | 12b | — | — | — | — | — | — | — | — | — | .1 | .1 | 54.9 |
| Claims on Public Nonfin. Corps. | 12c | — | — | — | — | — | — | — | — | — | — | — | — |
| Claims on Private Sector | 12d | 1,328.4 | 1,126.5 | 1,153.5 | 1,362.9 | 1,478.3 | 1,605.0 | 2,008.5 | 2,207.6 | 2,506.0 | 2,950.4 | 3,080.9 | 3,139.8 |
| Monetary Base | 14 | 791.7 | 811.1 | 840.1 | 1,007.4 | 1,024.5 | 1,261.0 | 1,179.1 | 1,223.4 | 1,250.7 | 1,184.7 | 1,343.0 | 1,520.8 |
| Currency in Circulation | 14a | 154.3 | 161.2 | 176.7 | 196.7 | 218.9 | 239.9 | 268.5 | 333.2 | 397.4 | 360.7 | 495.4 | 625.5 |
| Liabs. to Other Depository Corps. | 14c | — | — | — | — | — | — | — | — | — | — | — | — |
| Liabilities to Other Sectors | 14d | 637.4 | 649.9 | 663.4 | 810.7 | 805.6 | 1,021.1 | 910.6 | 890.2 | 853.3 | 824.0 | 847.5 | 895.4 |
| Other Liabs. to Other Dep. Corps. | 14n | 204.6 | 240.6 | 276.1 | 327.6 | 381.8 | 409.1 | 511.7 | 706.4 | 612.1 | 710.2 | 629.5 | 685.0 |
| Dep. & Sec. Excl. f/Monetary Base | 14o | — | — | — | .1 | .1 | .1 | .1 | — | — | — | — | — |
| Deposits Included in Broad Money | 15 | — | — | — | — | — | — | — | — | — | — | — | — |
| Sec.Ot.th.Shares Incl.in Brd. Money | 16a | — | — | — | — | — | — | — | — | — | — | — | — |
| Deposits Excl. from Broad Money | 16b | — | — | — | — | — | — | — | — | — | — | — | — |
| Sec.Ot.th.Shares Excl.f/Brd.Money | 16s | — | — | — | .1 | .1 | .1 | .1 | — | — | — | — | — |
| Loans | 16l | — | — | — | — | — | — | — | — | — | — | — | — |
| Financial Derivatives | 16m | — | — | — | — | — | — | — | — | — | — | — | — |
| Shares and Other Equity | 17a | 500.0 | 525.8 | 534.9 | 512.3 | 508.3 | 521.8 | 533.0 | 679.4 | 644.8 | 592.8 | 656.6 | 692.0 |
| Other Items (Net) | 17r | 48.8 | 41.7 | 115.1 | −18.1 | 58.5 | −26.1 | 128.4 | 21.2 | 139.7 | −70.4 | −109.4 | 33.2 |
| Memo Item: | | | | | | | | | | | | | |
| Total Assets | 10ra | 3,448.2 | 3,956.2 | 4,213.2 | 5,215.9 | 5,979.8 | 6,536.2 | 6,556.1 | 7,470.5 | 8,269.6 | 9,178.3 | 10,152.9 | 10,588.2 |
| **Other Depository Corporations** | | | | | | *Millions of Balboas: End of Period* | | | | | | | |
| Net Foreign Assets | 21n | 2,014.9 | 1,429.9 | 2,292.9 | 2,989.3 | 3,141.2 | 5,013.9 | 5,441.9 | 4,366.5 | 3,502.8 | 2,055.4 | 2,350.3 | 872.0 |
| Claims on Nonresidents | 21 | 11,706.9 | 11,926.4 | 14,151.5 | 17,246.9 | 20,778.2 | 21,598.0 | 22,871.0 | 25,961.7 | 27,548.2 | 26,122.9 | 33,231.6 | 36,264.1 |
| Liabilities to Nonresidents | 26c | 9,692.1 | 10,496.5 | 11,858.6 | 14,257.6 | 17,637.1 | 16,584.1 | 17,429.2 | 21,595.2 | 24,045.3 | 24,067.6 | 30,881.3 | 35,392.0 |
| Claims on Central Bank | 20 | 353.7 | 394.3 | 443.8 | 515.0 | 587.8 | 631.4 | 766.0 | 982.0 | 985.6 | 1,050.7 | 1,105.3 | 1,288.3 |
| Currency | 20a | 154.3 | 161.2 | 176.7 | 196.7 | 218.9 | 239.9 | 268.5 | 333.2 | 397.4 | 360.7 | 495.4 | 625.5 |
| Reserve Deposits and Securities | 20b | 199.3 | 233.1 | 267.1 | 318.3 | 368.9 | 391.4 | 497.5 | 648.8 | 585.7 | 690.0 | 609.9 | 662.8 |
| Other Claims | 20n | — | — | — | — | — | — | — | — | 2.4 | — | — | — |
| Net Claims on Central Government | 22an | 392.1 | 252.9 | 293.1 | 278.7 | 379.5 | 437.6 | 560.6 | 985.8 | 1,318.0 | 1,447.4 | 1,399.3 | 1,100.4 |
| Claims on Central Government | 22a | 584.9 | 497.2 | 593.4 | 644.9 | 864.7 | 957.3 | 1,138.3 | 1,551.5 | 1,929.1 | 2,093.4 | 2,170.5 | 2,396.8 |
| Liabilities to Central Government | 26d | 192.9 | 244.3 | 300.3 | 366.2 | 485.3 | 519.7 | 577.7 | 565.6 | 611.1 | 646.0 | 771.2 | 1,296.4 |
| Claims on Other Sectors | 22s | 11,462.0 | 13,303.0 | 14,877.8 | 17,513.6 | 20,258.5 | 20,633.0 | 23,321.0 | 27,160.6 | 31,195.8 | 28,314.0 | 39,212.9 | 43,576.4 |
| Claims on Other Financial Corps. | 22g | 722.1 | 957.2 | 889.2 | 934.2 | 1,013.9 | 1,031.3 | 911.2 | 1,069.0 | 1,092.8 | 1,078.8 | 1,321.4 | 1,338.5 |
| Claims on State & Local Govts. | 22b | .9 | .1 | .1 | 19.9 | 2.0 | 18.4 | 11.1 | 138.3 | 122.5 | 26.6 | 148.7 | 125.0 |
| Claims on Public Nonfin. Corps. | 22c | — | — | — | — | — | — | — | — | — | — | — | — |
| Claims on Private Sector | 22d | 10,738.9 | 12,345.8 | 13,988.5 | 16,559.5 | 19,242.6 | 19,583.3 | 22,398.8 | 25,953.3 | 29,980.4 | 27,208.5 | 37,742.9 | 42,112.8 |
| Liabilities to Central Bank | 26g | 59.5 | 271.6 | 178.1 | 303.6 | 549.6 | 457.7 | 213.1 | 693.6 | 674.0 | 838.9 | 595.0 | 606.3 |
| Transf.Dep.Included in Broad Money | 24 | 1,539.6 | 1,810.8 | 2,519.2 | 2,933.8 | 3,633.5 | 4,260.8 | 5,076.2 | 6,058.6 | 6,899.5 | 6,194.1 | 8,141.7 | 8,030.1 |
| Other Dep.Included in Broad Money | 25 | 8,931.3 | 9,599.3 | 11,564.1 | 13,361.6 | 15,161.7 | 16,500.4 | 18,207.3 | 19,300.6 | 21,388.4 | 18,725.6 | 25,587.7 | 27,206.0 |
| Sec.Ot.th.Shares Incl.in Brd. Money | 26a | 119.8 | 146.1 | 200.7 | 224.5 | 179.4 | 29.9 | 40.1 | 27.0 | 78.6 | 64.3 | 76.4 | 59.6 |
| Deposits Excl. from Broad Money | 26b | — | — | — | — | — | — | — | — | — | — | — | — |
| Sec.Ot.th.Shares Excl.f/Brd.Money | 26s | 275.4 | 221.2 | 221.6 | 220.9 | 168.3 | 120.2 | 256.0 | 236.0 | 290.6 | 353.6 | 387.2 | 530.9 |
| Loans | 26l | .7 | .7 | 3.4 | 2.6 | 3.9 | 3.4 | 4.4 | 3.0 | — | .1 | 3.6 | 18.2 |
| Financial Derivatives | 26m | — | — | — | — | — | — | — | — | — | — | — | — |
| Insurance Technical Reserves | 26r | — | — | — | — | — | — | — | — | — | — | — | — |
| Shares and Other Equity | 27a | 3,443.9 | 3,676.8 | 4,068.2 | 5,741.1 | 6,599.7 | 5,763.5 | 6,638.5 | 7,148.7 | 7,129.5 | 6,390.9 | 8,417.1 | 9,178.7 |
| Other Items (Net) | 27r | −147.8 | −346.3 | −847.6 | −1,491.6 | −1,929.0 | −419.9 | −346.2 | 27.5 | 541.6 | 299.9 | 859.2 | 1,207.3 |
| Memo Item: | | | | | | | | | | | | | |
| Total Assets | 20ra | 26,633.7 | 29,086.2 | 34,629.3 | 41,678.0 | 48,753.5 | 48,411.3 | 52,332.2 | 60,224.2 | 66,248.4 | 62,272.2 | 81,694.3 | 89,793.3 |

|  | | 2004 | 2005 | 2006 | 2007 | 2008 | 2009 | 2010 | 2011 | 2012 | 2013 | 2014 | 2015 |
|---|---|---|---|---|---|---|---|---|---|---|---|---|---|
| **Depository Corporations** | | | | | | *Millions of Balboas: End of Period* | | | | | | | |
| Net Foreign Assets.......................... | **31n** | 2,546.1 | 2,535.1 | 3,536.4 | 5,016.6 | 5,652.8 | 7,849.6 | 7,965.5 | 6,520.0 | 5,864.2 | 4,753.0 | 6,347.2 | 4,903.9 |
| Claims on Nonresidents................ | **31** | 12,406.0 | 13,172.4 | 15,530.4 | 19,341.0 | 23,415.9 | 24,820.7 | 25,776.1 | 28,495.9 | 30,294.9 | 29,203.2 | 37,579.5 | 40,616.0 |
| Liabilities to Nonresidents............. | **36c** | 9,859.9 | 10,637.3 | 11,994.0 | 14,324.3 | 17,763.1 | 16,971.2 | 17,810.7 | 21,975.9 | 24,430.7 | 24,450.2 | 31,232.3 | 35,712.1 |
| Domestic Claims............................. | **32** | 12,808.5 | 13,967.5 | 15,529.4 | 17,385.5 | 19,800.7 | 20,170.0 | 23,495.1 | 28,101.7 | 32,270.6 | 28,830.5 | 38,667.1 | 42,980.5 |
| Net Claims on Central Government | **32an** | −2.9 | −568.9 | −551.3 | −1,556.3 | −2,076.7 | −2,194.5 | −1,842.9 | −1,359.2 | −1,517.3 | −2,544.5 | −3,705.9 | −3,810.4 |
| Claims on Central Government.... | **32a** | 1,791.8 | 1,720.4 | 1,890.2 | 1,859.0 | 2,068.6 | 2,275.9 | 2,567.0 | 3,539.6 | 4,207.2 | 4,320.2 | 4,146.8 | 4,819.3 |
| Liabilities to Central Government. | **36d** | 1,794.8 | 2,289.3 | 2,441.5 | 3,415.3 | 4,145.3 | 4,470.3 | 4,409.9 | 4,898.8 | 5,724.5 | 6,864.7 | 7,852.7 | 8,629.7 |
| Claims on Other Sectors................ | **32s** | 12,811.4 | 14,536.3 | 16,080.7 | 18,941.8 | 21,877.4 | 22,364.5 | 25,338.0 | 29,460.9 | 33,787.9 | 31,375.0 | 42,373.0 | 46,790.9 |
| Claims on Other Financial Corps.. | **32g** | 743.1 | 1,064.0 | 938.6 | 999.5 | 1,154.5 | 1,157.8 | 919.6 | 1,161.7 | 1,178.9 | 1,189.4 | 1,400.5 | 1,358.2 |
| Claims on State & Local Govts..... | **32b** | .9 | .1 | .1 | 19.9 | 2.0 | 18.4 | 11.1 | 138.3 | 122.5 | 26.7 | 148.8 | 180.0 |
| Claims on Public Nonfin. Corps.... | **32c** | — | — | — | — | — | — | — | — | — | — | — | — |
| Claims on Private Sector.............. | **32d** | 12,067.4 | 13,472.3 | 15,142.0 | 17,922.4 | 20,720.9 | 21,188.3 | 24,407.3 | 28,160.9 | 32,486.4 | 30,158.9 | 40,823.7 | 45,252.7 |
| Broad Money Liabilities................... | **35l** | 11,228.1 | 12,206.1 | 14,947.3 | 17,330.7 | 19,780.2 | 21,812.1 | 24,234.2 | 26,276.5 | 29,219.9 | 25,808.0 | 34,653.3 | 36,191.1 |
| Currency Outside Depository Corps | **34a** | — | — | — | — | — | — | — | — | — | — | — | — |
| Transferable Deposits................... | **34** | 1,633.1 | 1,906.3 | 2,610.3 | 3,054.2 | 3,763.6 | 4,403.5 | 5,230.4 | 6,229.3 | 7,069.2 | 6,346.5 | 8,316.5 | 8,214.7 |
| Other Deposits............................ | **35** | 9,475.3 | 10,153.7 | 12,136.3 | 14,052.0 | 15,837.2 | 17,378.7 | 18,963.7 | 20,020.2 | 22,072.0 | 19,397.2 | 26,260.3 | 27,916.8 |
| Securities Other than Shares.......... | **36a** | 119.8 | 146.1 | 200.7 | 224.5 | 179.4 | 29.9 | 40.1 | 27.0 | 78.6 | 64.3 | 76.4 | 59.6 |
| Deposits Excl. from Broad Money..... | **36b** | — | — | — | — | — | — | — | — | — | — | — | — |
| Sec.Ot.th.Shares Excl.f/Brd.Money.... | **36s** | 275.4 | 221.2 | 221.6 | 221.0 | 168.3 | 120.2 | 256.1 | 236.0 | 290.6 | 353.6 | 387.2 | 530.9 |
| Loans........................................... | **36l** | .7 | .7 | 3.4 | 2.6 | 3.9 | 3.4 | 4.4 | 3.0 | — | .1 | 3.6 | 18.2 |
| Financial Derivatives...................... | **36m** | — | — | — | — | — | — | — | — | — | — | — | — |
| Insurance Technical Reserves.......... | **36r** | — | — | — | — | — | — | — | — | — | — | — | — |
| Shares and Other Equity................. | **37a** | 3,943.9 | 4,202.6 | 4,603.1 | 6,253.5 | 7,108.0 | 6,285.3 | 7,171.5 | 7,828.1 | 7,774.3 | 6,983.7 | 9,073.7 | 9,870.7 |
| Other Items (Net)........................... | **37r** | −93.7 | −128.0 | −709.5 | −1,405.7 | −1,606.9 | −201.5 | −205.7 | 278.1 | 850.0 | 438.1 | 896.5 | 1,273.4 |
| Broad Money Liabs., Seasonally Adj. | **35l.b** | 11,041.1 | 11,999.8 | 14,703.9 | 17,060.9 | 19,519.9 | 21,592.5 | 24,089.4 | 26,214.0 | 29,274.1 | 25,941.0 | 34,918.9 | 36,499.3 |
| **Interest Rates** | | | | | | *Percent Per Annum* | | | | | | | |
| Money Market Rate........................ | **60b** | 1.90 | 3.13 | 5.06 | 5.05 | 2.57 | .42 | .28 | .30 | .25 | .81 | .90 | .25 |
| Savings Rate.................................. | **60k** | 1.36 | 1.66 | 2.11 | 2.19 | 1.64 | 1.52 | 1.19 | .98 | .78 | .78 | .80 | .79 |
| Deposit Rate.................................. | **60l** | 2.23 | 2.70 | 3.83 | 4.76 | 3.53 | 3.49 | 3.04 | 2.32 | 2.14 | 2.12 | 2.16 | 2.14 |
| Lending Rate.................................. | **60p** | 8.82 | 8.67 | 8.39 | 8.25 | 8.16 | 8.25 | 7.74 | 6.91 | 6.91 | 6.59 | 6.83 | 7.46 |
| **Prices, Production and Labor** | | | | | | *Index Numbers (2010=100): Period Averages* | | | | | | | |
| Wholesale Prices............................ | **63** | 75.5 | 79.8 | 84.6 | 89.1 | 103.2 | 96.3 | 100.0 | 111.9 | 117.1 | 117.3 | 115.4 | 108.8 |
| Consumer Prices............................. | **64** | 79.1 | 81.6 | 83.3 | 86.8 | 94.4 | 96.6 | 100.0 | 105.9 | 111.9 | † 116.4 | 119.5 | 119.6 |
| Manufacturing Production (1995).... | **66ey** | . . . . | . . . . | . . . . | . . . . | . . . . | . . . . | . . . . | . . . . | . . . . | . . . . | . . . . | . . . . |
| | | | | | | *Number in Thousands: Period Averages* | | | | | | | |
| Labor Force.................................... | **67d** | 1,295 | 1,325 | 1,332 | . . . . | 1,485 | 1,541 | . . . . | 1,560 | 1,681 | 1,704 | 1,776 | . . . . |
| Employment................................... | **67e** | 1,135 | 1,188 | 1,211 | . . . . | 1,396 | 1,442 | . . . . | 1,481 | 1,608 | 1,630 | 1,695 | . . . . |
| Unemployment............................... | **67c** | 160 | 137 | 121 | . . . . | 89 | 99 | . . . . | 78 | 73 | 74 | 81 | . . . . |
| Unemployment Rate (%)................. | **67r** | 12.3 | 10.3 | 9.1 | . . . . | 6.0 | 6.4 | . . . . | 5.0 | 4.4 | 4.3 | 4.6 | . . . . |
| **Intl. Transactions & Positions** | | | | | | *Millions of Balboas* | | | | | | | |
| Exports........................................... | **70** | 943.7 | 1,018.3 | 1,093.2 | 1,163.6 | 1,246.9 | 947.7 | 832.0 | . . . . | . . . . | . . . . | . . . . | . . . . |
| Imports, c.i.f................................... | **71** | 3,594.2 | 4,180.0 | 4,831.0 | 6,872.1 | 9,050.2 | 7,800.6 | 9,145.4 | 11,339.7 | 12,494.3 | 13,035.4 | . . . . | . . . . |
| Imports, f.o.b.................................. | **71.v** | 3,270.9 | 3,787.9 | 4,391.9 | 6,185.2 | 8,158.0 | 7,082.7 | 8,274.9 | . . . . | . . . . | . . . . | . . . . | . . . . |
| | | | | | | *2010=100* | | | | | | | |
| Volume of Exports.......................... | **72** | 58.3 | 64.1 | 68.1 | 69.4 | 54.7 | 44.8 | 43.9 | . . . . | . . . . | . . . . | . . . . | . . . . |

| | | 2004 | 2005 | 2006 | 2007 | 2008 | 2009 | 2010 | 2011 | 2012 | 2013 | 2014 | 2015 |
|---|---|---|---|---|---|---|---|---|---|---|---|---|---|
| **Balance of Payments** | | | | | | | *Millions of US Dollars* | | | | | | |
| A. Current Account* | 109bx | −1,003.2 | −1,064.1 | −462.7 | −1,537.2 | −2,640.9 | −212.2 | −3,112.9 | −4,522.6 | −4,176.8 | −4,400.9 | −4,794.4 | −3,377.1 |
| Goods, credit (exports) | 1a9cx | 6,096.1 | 7,388.6 | 8,464.6 | 10,351.1 | 13,886.0 | 13,162.8 | 14,146.0 | 19,076.2 | 21,078.8 | 19,599.1 | 17,224.4 | 15,919.0 |
| Goods, debit (imports) | 1a9dx | 7,615.7 | 8,932.1 | 10,189.3 | 13,488.0 | 18,043.8 | 15,357.2 | 18,709.5 | 25,661.5 | 28,130.1 | 26,585.4 | 25,698.4 | 22,483.7 |
| Balance on goods | 1a9bx | −1,519.6 | −1,543.5 | −1,724.7 | −3,136.9 | −4,157.8 | −2,194.4 | −4,563.5 | −6,585.3 | −7,051.3 | −6,986.3 | −8,474.0 | −6,564.7 |
| Services, credit (exports) | 1b9cx | 2,734.9 | 3,175.4 | 3,979.0 | 4,352.2 | 5,165.2 | 5,494.8 | 6,412.0 | 8,108.5 | 9,346.9 | 10,162.4 | 10,826.4 | 11,294.2 |
| Services, debit (imports) | 1b9dx | 1,415.2 | 1,770.8 | 1,696.1 | 2,134.1 | 2,673.5 | 2,190.9 | 2,787.8 | 4,302.5 | 4,292.9 | 4,932.8 | 4,629.4 | 4,439.5 |
| Balance on Goods & Services | 1z9bx | −199.9 | −138.9 | 558.2 | −918.8 | −1,666.1 | 1,109.5 | −939.3 | −2,779.3 | −1,997.3 | −1,756.7 | −2,277.0 | 290.0 |
| Primary income: credit | 1c9cx | 790.9 | 1,013.5 | 1,360.3 | 1,873.5 | 1,875.5 | 1,458.8 | 1,435.1 | 1,793.0 | 1,929.6 | 2,171.7 | 2,170.3 | 2,088.1 |
| Primary income: debit | 1c9dx | 1,811.3 | 2,180.4 | 2,661.3 | 3,127.8 | 3,382.6 | 2,906.8 | 3,746.4 | 3,707.0 | 4,197.1 | 4,878.4 | 4,807.9 | 5,687.5 |
| Balance on gds, serv. & prim. inc. | 1y9bx | −1,220.3 | −1,305.8 | −742.8 | −2,173.1 | −3,173.2 | −338.5 | −3,250.6 | −4,693.3 | −4,264.8 | −4,463.4 | −4,914.6 | −3,309.4 |
| Secondary income: credit | 1d9ca | 297.6 | 338.2 | 531.8 | 1,061.9 | 1,111.4 | 749.0 | 791.2 | 796.2 | 844.7 | 843.5 | 1,110.6 | 954.5 |
| Secondary income: debit | 1d9da | 80.5 | 96.5 | 251.7 | 426.0 | 579.1 | 622.7 | 653.5 | 625.5 | 756.7 | 781.0 | 990.4 | 1,022.2 |
| B. Capital Account* | 209ba | — | 15.8 | 15.2 | 43.7 | 56.9 | 30.0 | 42.5 | 22.1 | 16.5 | 28.2 | 24.2 | 26.9 |
| Capital account: credit | 209ca | — | 15.8 | 15.2 | 43.7 | 56.9 | 30.0 | 42.5 | 22.1 | 16.5 | 28.2 | 24.2 | 26.9 |
| Capital account: debit | 209da | — | — | — | — | — | — | — | — | — | — | — | — |
| Balance on current & capital acct. | 129ba | −1,003.2 | −1,048.3 | −447.5 | −1,493.5 | −2,584.0 | −182.2 | −3,070.4 | −4,500.5 | −4,160.3 | −4,372.7 | −4,770.2 | −3,350.2 |
| C. Financial Account* | 309na | −496.7 | −1,785.1 | 202.6 | −2,078.2 | −2,386.1 | −312.1 | −1,527.7 | −3,121.3 | −2,735.6 | −4,368.3 | −5,699.3 | −3,713.2 |
| Direct investment: assets | 3a9aa | 258.8 | 186.8 | 397.0 | 325.4 | 243.3 | −173.8 | 142.6 | 1,418.6 | −103.0 | 659.9 | 780.9 | 1,249.4 |
| Equity & investment fund shares | 3aaaa | — | — | — | — | — | — | 316.8 | 175.7 | −274.4 | 330.9 | 329.1 | 527.9 |
| Debt instruments | 3abaa | 258.8 | 186.8 | 397.0 | 325.4 | 243.3 | −173.8 | −174.2 | 1,242.9 | 171.4 | 329.0 | 451.8 | 721.5 |
| Direct investment: liabilities | 3a9la | 1,277.9 | 1,104.4 | 2,944.3 | 2,224.0 | 2,390.0 | 1,085.5 | 2,549.1 | 4,395.6 | 3,381.9 | 4,272.2 | 4,761.2 | 5,760.1 |
| Equity & investment fund shares | 3aala | 984.9 | 469.6 | 2,260.2 | 1,556.6 | 2,035.8 | 1,154.7 | 1,967.1 | 1,928.9 | 2,403.9 | 3,393.5 | 3,980.4 | 4,087.5 |
| Debt instruments | 3abla | 293.0 | 634.8 | 684.1 | 667.4 | 354.2 | −69.2 | 582.0 | 2,466.7 | 978.0 | 878.7 | 780.8 | 1,672.6 |
| Portfolio investment: assets | 3b9aa | 650.9 | 1,102.8 | 1,049.1 | 1,005.7 | 519.3 | 915.1 | 898.1 | 759.6 | 18.1 | 656.8 | 1,124.4 | 2,731.2 |
| Equity & investment fund shares | 3baaa | −6.8 | 16.9 | 142.8 | −125.4 | 16.7 | 40.1 | 66.5 | 53.8 | 145.2 | 165.8 | 111.1 | 254.6 |
| Debt securities | 3bbaa | 657.7 | 1,085.9 | 906.3 | 1,131.1 | 502.6 | 875.0 | 831.6 | 705.8 | −127.1 | 491.0 | 1,013.3 | 2,476.6 |
| Portfolio investment: liabilities | 3b9la | 775.9 | 319.5 | 247.9 | 450.0 | −62.3 | 1,323.0 | — | 168.4 | −492.5 | 666.4 | 1,250.0 | 871.2 |
| Equity & investment fund shares | 3bala | — | — | — | — | — | — | — | — | — | — | — | — |
| Debt securities | 3bbla | 775.9 | 319.5 | 247.9 | 450.0 | −62.3 | 1,323.0 | — | 168.4 | −492.5 | 666.4 | 1,250.0 | 871.2 |
| Fin. der.& empl.stk.ops.(ESOs): net. | 3c9na | — | — | — | — | — | 56.7 | −45.1 | −69.6 | 70.6 | −12.5 | −46.4 | 1.9 |
| Fin. der. & ESOs.: assets | 3c9aa | — | — | — | — | — | 56.7 | −42.4 | −10.1 | 91.9 | −63.4 | 89.5 | −90.7 |
| Fin. der. & ESOs.: liabilities | 3c9la | — | — | — | — | — | — | 2.7 | 59.5 | 21.3 | −50.9 | 135.9 | −92.6 |
| Other investment: assets | 3d9aa | 1,542.8 | 334.4 | 4,340.1 | 5,682.7 | 2,881.6 | 1,593.8 | 3,869.8 | 3,881.2 | 3,582.3 | 2,987.7 | 5,215.5 | 4,779.0 |
| Other equity | 3daaa | .... | .... | .... | .... | .... | .... | .... | .... | .... | .... | .... | .... |
| Debt instruments | 3dzaa | 1,542.8 | 334.4 | 4,340.1 | 5,682.7 | 2,881.6 | 1,593.8 | 3,869.8 | 3,881.2 | 3,582.3 | 2,987.7 | 5,215.5 | 4,779.0 |
| Other investment: liabilities | 3d9la | 895.4 | 1,985.2 | 2,391.4 | 6,418.0 | 3,702.6 | 295.4 | 3,844.0 | 4,547.1 | 3,414.2 | 3,721.6 | 6,762.5 | 5,843.4 |
| Other equity | 3dala | .... | .... | .... | .... | .... | .... | .... | .... | .... | .... | .... | .... |
| Debt instruments | 3dzla | 895.4 | 1,985.2 | 2,391.4 | 6,418.0 | 3,702.6 | 295.4 | 3,844.0 | 4,547.1 | 3,414.2 | 3,721.6 | 6,762.5 | 5,843.4 |
| Curr.+ cap.− finan. acct. balance | 4y9na | −506.5 | 736.8 | −650.1 | 584.7 | −197.9 | 129.9 | −1,542.7 | −1,379.2 | −1,424.7 | −4.4 | 929.1 | 363.0 |
| D. Net Errors and Omissions | 409na | 110.4 | −239.8 | 300.2 | 42.3 | 759.9 | 440.5 | 266.9 | −363.6 | 467.2 | −105.5 | −532.1 | −1,347.3 |
| E. Reserves and Related Items | 4z9na | −396.1 | 497.0 | −349.9 | 627.0 | 562.0 | 570.4 | −1,275.8 | −1,742.8 | −957.5 | −109.9 | 397.0 | −984.3 |
| Reserve assets | 3e9aa | −397.0 | 487.3 | −359.8 | 616.7 | 556.7 | 570.4 | 312.4 | −253.4 | 37.0 | 400.9 | 1,221.7 | −77.5 |
| Credit and loans from the IMF | 3dcla | −10.0 | −9.7 | −9.9 | −10.3 | −5.3 | — | — | — | — | — | — | — |
| Exceptional financing | 409la | 9.1 | — | — | — | — | — | 1,588.2 | 1,489.4 | 994.5 | 510.8 | 824.7 | 906.8 |

*Excludes components in group E

| | | 2004 | 2005 | 2006 | 2007 | 2008 | 2009 | 2010 | 2011 | 2012 | 2013 | 2014 | 2015 |
|---|---|---|---|---|---|---|---|---|---|---|---|---|---|
| **International Investment Position** | | | | | | | *Millions of US Dollars* | | | | | | |
| Assets | 809aa | 23,813.2 | 26,521.9 | 31,075.5 | 39,048.8 | 43,701.6 | 45,161.5 | 50,547.4 | 55,098.1 | 58,799.8 | 62,322.1 | 71,416.2 | 79,935.3 |
| Direct investment | 8a9aa | 1,468.2 | 1,655.0 | 2,052.0 | 2,377.4 | 2,620.7 | 5,503.7 | 5,646.2 | 6,846.1 | 6,743.1 | 7,403.0 | 8,505.5 | 9,754.9 |
| Equity & investment fund shares | 8aaaa | .... | .... | .... | .... | .... | 3,056.8 | 3,373.5 | 3,549.2 | 3,274.8 | 3,605.7 | 4,256.4 | 4,784.3 |
| Debt instruments | 8abaa | 1,468.2 | 1,655.0 | 2,052.0 | 2,377.4 | 2,620.7 | 2,446.9 | 2,272.7 | 3,296.9 | 3,468.3 | 3,797.3 | 4,249.1 | 4,970.6 |
| Portfolio investment | 8b9aa | 4,206.1 | 5,241.7 | 6,290.8 | 7,631.6 | 8,454.8 | 5,940.4 | 7,071.1 | 7,558.0 | 8,528.5 | 9,140.2 | 10,197.3 | 12,867.9 |
| Equity & investment fund shares | 8baaa | 38.1 | 50.0 | 192.8 | 67.4 | 95.4 | 133.9 | 200.3 | 255.8 | 441.1 | 606.9 | 611.7 | 869.9 |
| Debt securities | 8bbaa | 4,168.0 | 5,191.7 | 6,098.0 | 7,564.2 | 8,359.4 | 5,806.5 | 6,870.8 | 7,302.2 | 8,087.4 | 8,533.3 | 9,585.6 | 11,998.0 |
| Fin. der.(oth.than reserves) & ESOs | 8c9aa | .... | .... | .... | .... | .... | 56.7 | 14.3 | 4.2 | 96.8 | 33.2 | 122.6 | 31.8 |
| Other investment | 8d9aa | 16,228.6 | 16,550.9 | 20,012.8 | 25,695.3 | 28,745.0 | 29,999.6 | 33,840.4 | 36,870.1 | 40,805.3 | 42,718.2 | 48,358.3 | 53,137.2 |
| Other equity | 8daaa | .... | .... | .... | .... | .... | .... | .... | .... | .... | .... | .... | .... |
| Debt instruments | 8dzaa | 16,228.6 | 16,550.9 | 20,012.8 | 25,695.3 | 28,745.0 | 29,999.6 | 33,840.4 | 36,870.1 | 40,805.3 | 42,718.2 | 48,358.3 | 53,137.2 |
| Reserve assets | 8e9aa | 1,910.4 | 3,074.3 | 2,719.9 | 3,344.5 | 3,881.1 | 3,661.2 | 3,975.4 | 3,819.7 | 2,626.1 | 3,027.6 | 4,232.6 | 4,143.5 |
| Liabilities | 809la | 34,021.6 | 37,143.0 | 42,725.4 | 51,825.4 | 57,834.6 | 59,470.6 | 67,211.1 | 78,381.3 | 85,252.6 | 94,011.3 | 106,756.2 | 119,482.2 |
| Direct investment | 8a9la | 10,717.7 | 11,822.1 | 14,766.4 | 16,990.4 | 19,380.4 | 20,465.9 | 23,015.0 | 27,109.3 | 30,491.2 | 34,763.4 | 39,524.6 | 45,284.7 |
| Equity & investment fund shares | 8aala | 8,101.4 | 8,571.0 | 10,831.2 | 12,387.8 | 14,423.6 | 15,578.3 | 17,545.4 | 19,478.1 | 21,882.0 | 25,275.5 | 29,255.9 | 33,343.4 |
| Debt instruments | 8abla | 2,616.3 | 3,251.1 | 3,935.2 | 4,602.6 | 4,956.8 | 4,887.6 | 5,469.6 | 7,631.2 | 8,609.2 | 9,487.9 | 10,268.7 | 11,941.3 |
| Portfolio investment | 8b9la | 5,702.8 | 5,919.8 | 6,160.7 | 6,610.7 | 6,548.4 | 8,790.7 | 10,477.2 | 12,259.0 | 12,149.3 | 12,926.0 | 14,216.9 | 15,816.9 |
| Equity & investment fund shares | 8bala | .... | .... | .... | .... | .... | .... | .... | .... | .... | .... | .... | .... |
| Debt securities | 8bbla | 5,702.8 | 5,919.8 | 6,160.7 | 6,610.7 | 6,548.4 | 8,790.7 | 10,477.2 | 12,259.0 | 12,149.3 | 12,926.0 | 14,216.9 | 15,816.9 |
| Fin. der.(oth.than reserves) & ESOs | 8c9la | .... | .... | .... | .... | .... | .... | 2.7 | 62.1 | 91.1 | 40.5 | 176.3 | 83.9 |
| Other investment | 8d9la | 17,601.1 | 19,401.1 | 21,798.3 | 28,224.3 | 31,905.8 | 30,214.0 | 33,716.2 | 38,950.9 | 42,521.0 | 46,281.4 | 52,838.4 | 58,296.7 |
| Other equity | 8dala | .... | .... | .... | .... | .... | .... | .... | .... | .... | .... | .... | .... |
| Debt instruments | 8dzla | 17,601.1 | 19,401.1 | 21,798.3 | 28,224.3 | 31,905.8 | 30,214.0 | 33,716.2 | 38,950.9 | 42,521.0 | 46,281.4 | 52,838.4 | 58,296.7 |

| | | 2004 | 2005 | 2006 | 2007 | 2008 | 2009 | 2010 | 2011 | 2012 | 2013 | 2014 | 2015 |
|---|---|---|---|---|---|---|---|---|---|---|---|---|---|
| **National Accounts** | | | | | | | *Millions of Balboas* | | | | | | |
| Househ.Cons.Expend.,incl.NPISHs.... | 96f | 9,072.9 | 9,597.2 | 10,445.6 | 12,239.2 | 14,346.0 | 15,469.2 | 17,268.4 | 19,198.7 | 21,566.5 | 23,308.0 | 25,005.2 | .... |
| Government Consumption Expend... | 91f | 1,929.7 | 2,033.8 | 2,116.3 | 2,510.7 | 2,881.3 | 3,015.7 | 3,576.5 | 3,943.2 | 4,253.1 | 4,640.5 | 4,886.4 | .... |
| Gross Fixed Capital Formation......... | 93e | 2,351.0 | 2,601.3 | 3,134.9 | 5,935.1 | 7,659.6 | 7,568.2 | 8,728.1 | 11,652.1 | 14,938.9 | 18,751.0 | 21,310.1 | .... |
| Changes in Inventories.................... | 93i | 300.9 | 237.7 | 200.0 | 1,708.7 | 2,547.5 | 523.0 | 2,029.2 | 3,298.8 | 2,814.3 | 1,811.2 | 1,820.3 | .... |
| Exports of Goods and Services......... | 90c | 9,586.5 | 11,674.2 | 13,146.6 | 14,540.2 | 17,802.3 | 17,839.0 | 19,165.1 | 25,056.6 | 28,230.8 | 27,124.6 | 26,338.0 | .... |
| Imports of Goods and Services (-)..... | 98c | 9,061.7 | 10,679.5 | 11,906.4 | 15,975.9 | 20,714.4 | 17,821.6 | 21,850.2 | 28,775.6 | 31,848.9 | 30,779.1 | 30,194.3 | .... |
| Gross Domestic Product (GDP)......... | 99b | 14,179.3 | 15,464.7 | 17,137.0 | 20,958.0 | 24,522.2 | 26,593.5 | 28,917.2 | 34,373.8 | 39,954.8 | 44,856.2 | 49,165.8 | .... |
| Net Primary Income from Abroad..... | 98.n | −1,268.9 | −1,436.5 | −1,546.0 | −1,741.2 | −2,035.6 | −1,821.6 | −2,226.6 | −2,401.3 | −3,016.2 | .... | .... | .... |
| Gross National Income (GNI)............ | 99a | 12,910.4 | 14,028.2 | 15,591.0 | 18,052.5 | 20,966.0 | 22,341.3 | 24,826.4 | 28,918.9 | 32,922.0 | .... | .... | .... |
| Consumption of Fixed Capital.......... | 99cf | 1,039.6 | 1,060.4 | 1,254.0 | 1,369.7 | 1,362.8 | 1,350.3 | 1,518.0 | 1,708.8 | 1,913.4 | .... | .... | .... |
| GDP Volume 2007 Ref., Chained..... | 99b.p | .... | .... | .... | 20,958.0 | 22,762.8 | 23,126.7 | 24,460.5 | 27,348.8 | 29,873.0 | 31,851.9 | 33,780.0 | .... |
| GDP Volume 1996 Prices................. | 99b.p | 13,099.2 | 14,041.2 | 15,238.6 | 17,084.4 | 18,812.9 | 19,538.4 | 20,994.4 | 23,274.5 | 25,787.1 | .... | .... | .... |
| GDP Volume (2010=100)................ | 99bvp | 65.7 | 70.4 | 76.4 | † 85.7 | 93.1 | 94.5 | 100.0 | 111.8 | 122.1 | 130.2 | 138.1 | .... |
| GDP Deflator (2010=100)............... | 99bip | 74.6 | 75.9 | 77.5 | 84.6 | 91.1 | 97.3 | 100.0 | 106.3 | 113.1 | 119.1 | 123.1 | .... |
| | | | | | | | *Millions: Midyear Estimates* | | | | | | |
| Population................................ | 99z | 3.26 | 3.32 | 3.38 | 3.44 | 3.50 | 3.56 | 3.62 | 3.68 | 3.74 | 3.81 | 3.87 | 3.93 |

| | | 2004 | 2005 | 2006 | 2007 | 2008 | 2009 | 2010 | 2011 | 2012 | 2013 | 2014 | 2015 |
|---|---|---|---|---|---|---|---|---|---|---|---|---|---|
| **Exchange Rates** | | | | | | *Kina per SDR: End of Period* | | | | | | | |
| Market Rate.................................. | aa | 4.8532 | 4.4250 | 4.5588 | 4.4830 | 4.1239 | 4.2370 | 4.0688 | 3.2910 | 3.2322 | 3.7288 | 3.7582 | 4.1676 |
| | | | | | *Kina per US Dollar: End of Period (ae) Period Average (rf)* | | | | | | | | |
| Market Rate.................................. | ae | 3.1250 | 3.0960 | 3.0303 | 2.8369 | 2.6774 | 2.7027 | 2.6420 | 2.1436 | 2.1030 | 2.4213 | 2.5940 | 3.0075 |
| Market Rate.................................. | rf | 3.2225 | 3.1019 | 3.0567 | 2.9653 | 2.7001 | 2.7551 | 2.7193 | 2.3710 | 2.0836 | 2.2445 | 2.4614 | 2.7684 |
| | | | | | *Index Numbers (2010=100): Period Averages* | | | | | | | | |
| Market Rate.................................. | ahx | 84.4 | 87.6 | 88.9 | 91.7 | 100.8 | 98.7 | 100.0 | 115.2 | 130.5 | 121.4 | 110.5 | 98.4 |
| Nominal Effective Exchange Rate..... | nec | 97.9 | 99.3 | 100.0 | 96.4 | 103.5 | 106.2 | 100.0 | 107.8 | 124.6 | 120.6 | 114.2 | 116.4 |
| CPI-Based Real Effect. Ex. Rate........ | rec | 88.1 | 88.4 | 88.4 | 83.8 | 95.2 | 102.9 | 100.0 | 108.7 | 128.1 | 127.0 | 123.5 | 131.0 |
| **Fund Position** | | | | | | *Millions of SDRs: End of Period* | | | | | | | |
| Quota........................................... | 2f.s | 131.60 | 131.60 | 131.60 | 131.60 | 131.60 | 131.60 | 131.60 | 131.60 | 131.60 | 131.60 | 131.60 | 131.60 |
| SDR Holdings................................. | 1b.s | .47 | .02 | .04 | .06 | .07 | 116.22 | 10.06 | 9.56 | 9.42 | 9.33 | 9.22 | 9.16 |
| Reserve Position in the Fund............ | 1c.s | .43 | .44 | .44 | .44 | .44 | .44 | .44 | .44 | .44 | .44 | .45 | .45 |
| Total Fund Cred.&Loans Outstg........ | 2tl | 41.38 | — | — | — | — | — | — | — | — | — | — | — |
| SDR Allocations.............................. | 1bd | 9.30 | 9.30 | 9.30 | 9.30 | 9.30 | 125.49 | 125.49 | 125.49 | 125.49 | 125.49 | 125.49 | 125.49 |
| **International Liquidity** | | | | | *Millions of US Dollars Unless Otherwise Indicated: Approximately End of Period* | | | | | | | | |
| Total Reserves minus Gold.............. | 1l.d | 632.56 | 718.10 | 1,400.68 | 2,053.71 | 1,953.40 | 2,560.61 | 3,032.64 | 4,256.35 | 3,930.35 | 2,774.72 | 2,253.53 | 1,691.79 |
| SDR Holdings................................. | 1b.d | .73 | .03 | .06 | .09 | .11 | 182.19 | 15.50 | 14.68 | 14.47 | 14.37 | 13.36 | 12.69 |
| Reserve Position in the Fund.......... | 1c.d | .66 | .63 | .66 | .69 | .67 | .69 | .67 | .67 | .67 | .67 | .65 | .62 |
| Foreign Exchange.......................... | 1d.d | 631.17 | 717.45 | 1,399.96 | 2,052.92 | 1,952.62 | 2,377.73 | 3,016.46 | 4,241.00 | 3,915.20 | 2,759.67 | 2,239.51 | 1,678.47 |
| Gold (Million Fine Troy Ounces)........ | 1ad | .063 | .063 | .063 | .063 | .063 | .063 | .063 | .063 | .063 | .063 | .063 | .063 |
| Gold (National Valuation)................ | 1and | 27.55 | 30.65 | 26.76 | 32.84 | 33.73 | 46.40 | 59.54 | 66.24 | 70.97 | 50.80 | 51.70 | 45.89 |
| Central Bank: Other Assets.............. | 3..d | — | .04 | .05 | .05 | .04 | .05 | .05 | .16 | .17 | .17 | .15 | .14 |
| Central Bank: Other Liabs............... | 4..d | .41 | .36 | 2.09 | 3.92 | 1.49 | 1.73 | 2.70 | 2.86 | 2.91 | 4.74 | 2.81 | 2.83 |
| Other Depository Corps.: Assets...... | 7a.d | 115.92 | 212.58 | 141.81 | 458.49 | † 264.58 | 578.08 | 578.97 | 655.31 | 793.00 | 1,127.20 | 613.08 | 553.78 |
| Other Depository Corps.: Liabs....... | 7b.d | 21.80 | 31.00 | 33.20 | 47.85 | † 46.70 | 71.16 | 80.87 | 62.78 | 93.12 | 339.89 | 102.47 | 161.34 |
| Other Financial Corps.: Assets.......... | 7e.d | .... | .... | .... | .... | .... | 269.81 | 403.68 | 411.90 | 455.17 | 488.32 | 523.70 | 494.74 |
| Other Financial Corps.: Liabs........... | 7f.d | .... | .... | .... | .... | .... | — | 1.88 | 6.36 | 7.16 | 4.51 | 3.30 | 4.39 |
| **Central Bank** | | | | | | *Millions of Kina : End of Period* | | | | | | | |
| Net Foreign Assets.......................... | 11n | 1,823.59 | 2,325.81 | 4,276.90 | 5,866.57 | 5,566.28 | 6,554.13 | 7,651.83 | 8,847.25 | 8,003.56 | 6,362.85 | 5,501.23 | 4,694.95 |
| Claims on Nonresidents................. | 11 | 2,072.30 | 2,368.05 | 4,325.64 | 5,919.40 | 5,608.45 | 7,090.53 | 8,169.57 | 9,266.39 | 8,415.31 | 6,842.27 | 5,980.18 | 5,226.47 |
| Liabilities to Nonresidents.............. | 16c | 248.71 | 42.24 | 48.74 | 52.82 | 42.17 | 536.40 | 517.74 | 419.13 | 411.75 | 479.42 | 478.94 | 531.53 |
| Claims on Other Depository Corps.... | 12e | 24.15 | 23.85 | 25.72 | 24.05 | 24.01 | 4.84 | 2.59 | 68.01 | 21.93 | 35.95 | 40.17 | 310.28 |
| Net Claims on Central Government.. | 12an | −26.33 | −538.18 | −659.03 | −1,134.11 | −1,826.95 | −260.54 | −652.26 | −1,501.49 | −486.72 | −155.82 | 1,301.33 | 897.36 |
| Claims on Central Government...... | 12a | 78.54 | 108.29 | 143.96 | 202.82 | 107.50 | 332.64 | 366.53 | 431.25 | 498.58 | 862.79 | 2,353.30 | 1,688.41 |
| Liabilities to Central Government... | 16d | 104.87 | 646.47 | 802.99 | 1,336.93 | 1,934.45 | 593.18 | 1,018.79 | 1,932.74 | 985.30 | 1,018.60 | 1,051.97 | 791.06 |
| Claims on Other Sectors.................. | 12s | 35.90 | 38.15 | 58.80 | 33.68 | 55.41 | 35.32 | 10.84 | 10.50 | 26.87 | 20.52 | 20.08 | 21.26 |
| Claims on Other Financial Corps..... | 12g | 1.05 | 1.26 | .92 | .56 | .30 | .35 | .05 | .19 | .04 | — | — | — |
| Claims on State & Local Govts........ | 12b | — | — | — | — | — | — | — | — | — | — | — | — |
| Claims on Public Nonfin. Corps...... | 12c | 26.22 | 26.22 | 26.22 | 26.22 | 26.22 | — | — | — | — | — | — | — |
| Claims on Private Sector................ | 12d | 8.63 | 10.67 | 31.66 | 6.90 | 28.89 | 34.97 | 10.79 | 10.30 | 26.82 | 20.52 | 20.08 | 21.26 |
| Monetary Base.............................. | 14 | 870.76 | 935.39 | 1,138.20 | 1,841.61 | 1,620.09 | 1,813.55 | 2,015.65 | 3,258.72 | 3,833.68 | 3,853.00 | 5,282.92 | 5,171.04 |
| Currency in Circulation.................. | 14a | 531.04 | 605.87 | 692.87 | 822.51 | 850.41 | 1,002.34 | 1,192.71 | 1,532.45 | 1,679.33 | 1,749.23 | 1,851.56 | 1,891.26 |
| Liabs. to Other Depository Corps.... | 14c | 332.03 | 321.54 | 442.50 | 1,016.40 | 766.97 | 808.49 | 810.23 | 1,723.56 | 2,141.63 | 2,101.06 | 3,431.36 | 3,279.78 |
| Liabilities to Other Sectors............. | 14d | 7.70 | 7.97 | 2.83 | 2.71 | 2.71 | 2.72 | 12.72 | 2.72 | 12.72 | 2.72 | — | — |
| Other Liabs. to Other Dep. Corps...... | 14n | 270.28 | 344.23 | 1,846.78 | 2,199.40 | 2,137.89 | 4,119.25 | 4,596.67 | 5,689.55 | 5,153.37 | 3,260.93 | 2,333.88 | 1,699.18 |
| Dep. & Sec. Excl. f/Monetary Base..... | 14o | 2.77 | 2.42 | 2.47 | 3.16 | 4.15 | 4.82 | 4.86 | 7.10 | 6.67 | 6.24 | 7.23 | 7.05 |
| Deposits Included in Broad Money. | 15 | 2.57 | 2.21 | 2.30 | 3.06 | 4.05 | 4.72 | 4.76 | 6.98 | 6.54 | 6.10 | 7.12 | 6.91 |
| Sec.Ot.th.Shares Incl.in Brd. Money | 16a | — | — | — | — | — | — | — | — | — | — | — | — |
| Deposits Excl. from Broad Money.... | 16b | .10 | .11 | .11 | .05 | .05 | .05 | .05 | .05 | .05 | .05 | — | — |
| Sec.Ot.th.Shares Excl.f/Brd.Money.. | 16s | .11 | .10 | .05 | .05 | .05 | .05 | .06 | .08 | .09 | .10 | .11 | .14 |
| Loans........................................... | 16l | — | — | — | — | — | — | — | — | — | — | — | — |
| Financial Derivatives...................... | 16m | — | — | — | — | — | — | — | — | — | — | — | — |
| Shares and Other Equity................. | 17a | 688.48 | 584.66 | 736.24 | 770.72 | 90.83 | 474.18 | 481.77 | −1,395.58 | −1,331.64 | −679.21 | −503.16 | −233.09 |
| Other Items (Net)............................ | 17r | 25.03 | −17.07 | −21.29 | −24.70 | −34.21 | −78.04 | −85.95 | −135.52 | −96.44 | −177.46 | −258.04 | −720.33 |
| Memo Item: | | | | | | | | | | | | | |
| Total Assets.................................. | 10ra | 2,243.52 | 2,574.36 | 4,598.53 | 6,228.82 | 5,867.30 | 7,564.67 | 8,670.44 | 9,948.21 | 9,150.47 | 8,001.46 | 8,727.18 | 8,328.58 |

| | | 2004 | 2005 | 2006 | 2007 | 2008 | 2009 | 2010 | 2011 | 2012 | 2013 | 2014 | 2015 |
|---|---|---|---|---|---|---|---|---|---|---|---|---|---|
| **Other Depository Corporations** | | | | | | *Millions of Kina : End of Period* | | | | | | | |
| Net Foreign Assets.......................... | 21n | 295.86 | 561.72 | 329.11 | 1,164.95 | † 581.03 | 1,370.06 | 1,315.99 | 1,270.15 | 1,471.89 | 1,906.31 | 1,324.53 | 1,181.25 |
| Claims on Nonresidents................. | 21 | 364.40 | 657.63 | 429.73 | 1,300.69 | † 705.55 | 1,562.37 | 1,529.65 | 1,404.73 | 1,667.72 | 2,729.29 | 1,590.35 | 1,666.87 |
| Liabilities to Nonresidents.............. | 26c | 68.54 | 95.91 | 100.62 | 135.74 | † 124.52 | 192.32 | 213.66 | 134.57 | 195.83 | 822.97 | 265.82 | 485.62 |
| Claims on Central Bank................... | 20 | 729.36 | 823.45 | 2,460.35 | 3,429.57 | † 3,173.53 | 5,125.09 | 5,622.53 | 7,768.22 | 7,906.79 | 5,686.55 | 6,307.62 | 5,435.99 |
| Currency....................................... | 20a | 131.49 | 160.40 | 173.05 | 214.98 | † 174.48 | 213.39 | 237.80 | 344.12 | 465.34 | 448.94 | 459.56 | 447.92 |
| Reserve Deposits and Securities..... | 20b | 332.33 | 323.40 | 442.84 | 1,016.77 | † 767.67 | 809.31 | 810.69 | 1,724.17 | 2,141.95 | 2,098.36 | 3,388.62 | 3,278.10 |
| Other Claims............................... | 20n | 265.53 | 339.65 | 1,844.46 | 2,197.82 | † 2,231.38 | 4,102.39 | 4,574.04 | 5,699.94 | 5,299.51 | 3,139.25 | 2,459.44 | 1,709.97 |
| Net Claims on Central Government.. | 22an | 1,319.78 | 1,652.27 | 1,621.43 | 1,305.26 | † 1,426.98 | 834.61 | 450.32 | 424.82 | 783.70 | 2,911.29 | 2,862.48 | 4,446.46 |
| Claims on Central Government....... | 22a | 1,594.45 | 2,013.66 | 2,248.88 | 2,323.80 | † 3,124.16 | 2,806.88 | 2,693.91 | 3,317.52 | 3,564.98 | 5,844.79 | 6,148.85 | 7,145.02 |
| Liabilities to Central Government.... | 26d | 274.67 | 361.39 | 627.45 | 1,018.55 | † 1,697.18 | 1,972.27 | 2,243.59 | 2,892.70 | 2,781.28 | 2,933.49 | 3,286.37 | 2,698.56 |
| Claims on Other Sectors................. | 22s | 1,763.00 | 2,202.93 | 2,977.69 | 4,015.64 | † 5,224.71 | 6,055.91 | 7,183.97 | 7,696.52 | 8,806.72 | 10,086.21 | 11,704.02 | 13,033.45 |
| Claims on Other Financial Corps..... | 22g | — | — | — | — | † 63.09 | 50.88 | 43.39 | 28.69 | 33.16 | 69.34 | 84.31 | 108.71 |
| Claims on State & Local Govts...... | 22b | 3.67 | 1.84 | 3.37 | 1.14 | † 3.56 | 4.27 | .33 | .30 | .06 | .10 | .06 | — |
| Claims on Public Nonfin. Corps...... | 22c | 44.32 | 79.00 | 57.04 | 60.23 | † 58.58 | 133.99 | 180.17 | 155.59 | 365.99 | 123.79 | 1,375.86 | 2,334.07 |
| Claims on Private Sector............... | 22d | 1,715.01 | 2,122.09 | 2,917.28 | 3,954.27 | † 5,099.48 | 5,866.78 | 6,960.09 | 7,511.94 | 8,407.52 | 9,892.99 | 10,243.78 | 10,590.67 |
| Liabilities to Central Bank............... | 26g | 23.68 | 23.42 | 23.59 | 23.59 | † 23.69 | 23.99 | 4.85 | 5.28 | 5.10 | 6.17 | 7.91 | 179.84 |
| Transf.Dep.Included in Broad Money | 24 | 1,823.86 | 2,563.41 | 3,267.32 | 4,312.65 | † 4,840.67 | 5,440.44 | 6,675.21 | 8,427.70 | 9,920.57 | 10,743.10 | 12,047.33 | 13,401.07 |
| Other Dep.Included in Broad Money. | 25 | 1,681.14 | 2,050.22 | 3,247.93 | 4,068.97 | † 4,177.03 | 5,533.08 | 5,319.41 | 5,605.69 | 5,750.57 | 5,989.26 | 5,208.26 | 5,305.12 |
| Sec.Ot.th.Shares Incl.in Brd. Money.. | 26a | — | — | — | — | † — | 52.66 | 66.91 | 61.98 | 62.44 | 62.41 | 61.57 | 62.16 |
| Deposits Excl. from Broad Money..... | 26b | — | — | — | — | † 14.38 | 13.29 | 17.10 | 8.45 | 6.00 | 3.23 | 35.44 | .14 |
| Sec.Ot.th.Shares Excl.f/Brd.Money.... | 26s | 10.00 | — | — | — | † — | — | — | 5.06 | 5.10 | 5.09 | 5.02 | 5.07 |
| Loans.......................................... | 26l | — | .19 | — | — | † 4.89 | 5.03 | 23.00 | 17.00 | 10.34 | 2.67 | — | — |
| Financial Derivatives........................ | 26m | — | — | — | — | † — | — | — | — | — | — | — | — |
| Insurance Technical Reserves........... | 26r | — | — | — | — | † — | — | — | — | — | — | — | .02 |
| Shares and Other Equity.................. | 27a | 784.83 | 943.91 | 1,182.20 | 1,729.90 | † 2,145.20 | 2,585.39 | 3,072.66 | 3,550.98 | 4,223.94 | 5,015.69 | 5,565.56 | 5,766.55 |
| Other Items (Net)............................. | 27r | −215.50 | −340.78 | −332.45 | −219.69 | † −799.62 | −268.20 | −606.33 | −522.42 | −1,014.94 | −1,237.24 | −732.44 | −622.84 |
| Memo Item: | | | | | | | | | | | | | |
| Total Assets.................................... | 20ra | 4,960.35 | 6,351.12 | 8,872.40 | 11,821.48 | † 14,350.69 | 17,057.40 | 18,703.04 | 22,213.64 | 24,717.94 | 27,279.30 | 28,341.94 | 30,036.46 |
| **Depository Corporations** | | | | | | *Millions of Kina : End of Period* | | | | | | | |
| Net Foreign Assets.......................... | 31n | 2,119.45 | 2,887.53 | 4,606.01 | 7,031.52 | † 6,147.31 | 7,924.19 | 8,967.82 | 10,117.41 | 9,475.45 | 8,269.17 | 6,825.76 | 5,876.19 |
| Claims on Nonresidents................. | 31 | 2,436.70 | 3,025.68 | 4,755.37 | 7,220.09 | † 6,314.00 | 8,652.90 | 9,699.22 | 10,671.11 | 10,083.03 | 9,571.56 | 7,570.53 | 6,893.34 |
| Liabilities to Nonresidents.............. | 36c | 317.25 | 138.15 | 149.35 | 188.57 | † 166.69 | 728.71 | 731.39 | 553.71 | 607.58 | 1,302.39 | 744.76 | 1,017.15 |
| Domestic Claims............................. | 32 | 3,092.35 | 3,355.17 | 3,998.90 | 4,220.46 | † 4,880.15 | 6,665.30 | 6,992.87 | 6,630.34 | 9,130.57 | 12,862.21 | 15,887.91 | 18,398.52 |
| Net Claims on Central Government.. | 32an | 1,293.45 | 1,114.09 | 962.41 | 171.14 | † −399.97 | 574.07 | −201.94 | −1,076.68 | 296.98 | 2,755.47 | 4,163.81 | 5,343.81 |
| Claims on Central Government.... | 32a | 1,672.98 | 2,121.95 | 2,392.84 | 2,526.62 | † 3,231.65 | 3,139.52 | 3,060.44 | 3,748.76 | 4,063.56 | 6,707.57 | 8,502.15 | 8,833.43 |
| Liabilities to Central Government. | 36d | 379.53 | 1,007.86 | 1,430.44 | 2,355.48 | † 3,631.62 | 2,565.45 | 3,262.38 | 4,825.44 | 3,766.58 | 3,952.10 | 4,338.34 | 3,489.62 |
| Claims on Other Sectors................ | 32s | 1,798.90 | 2,241.08 | 3,036.49 | 4,049.32 | † 5,280.12 | 6,091.24 | 7,194.81 | 7,707.01 | 8,833.59 | 10,106.73 | 11,724.10 | 13,054.71 |
| Claims on Other Financial Corps.. | 32g | 1.05 | 1.26 | .92 | .56 | † 63.39 | 51.23 | 43.44 | 28.88 | 33.20 | 69.34 | 84.32 | 108.71 |
| Claims on State & Local Govts..... | 32b | 3.67 | 1.84 | 3.37 | 1.14 | † 3.56 | 4.27 | .33 | .30 | .06 | .10 | .06 | — |
| Claims on Public Nonfin. Corps..... | 32c | 70.54 | 105.22 | 83.26 | 86.45 | † 84.80 | 133.99 | 180.17 | 155.59 | 365.99 | 123.79 | 1,375.86 | 2,334.07 |
| Claims on Private Sector.............. | 32d | 1,723.63 | 2,132.76 | 2,948.94 | 3,961.17 | † 5,128.37 | 5,901.75 | 6,970.87 | 7,522.24 | 8,434.34 | 9,913.51 | 10,263.86 | 10,611.92 |
| Broad Money Liabilities.................... | 35l | 3,914.80 | 5,069.28 | 7,040.20 | 8,994.90 | † 9,700.39 | 11,822.57 | 13,033.92 | 15,293.39 | 16,966.83 | 18,103.86 | 18,716.28 | 20,218.60 |
| Currency Outside Depository Corps | 34a | 399.54 | 445.47 | 519.82 | 607.52 | † 675.93 | 788.95 | 954.91 | 1,188.33 | 1,213.99 | 1,300.29 | 1,392.00 | 1,443.34 |
| Transferable Deposits.................... | 34 | 1,832.24 | 2,571.88 | 3,270.53 | 4,315.77 | † 4,843.68 | 5,443.73 | 6,688.71 | 8,431.35 | 9,934.49 | 10,746.39 | 12,047.82 | 13,401.56 |
| Other Deposits............................. | 35 | 1,683.02 | 2,051.93 | 3,249.85 | 4,071.60 | † 4,180.78 | 5,537.23 | 5,323.39 | 5,611.73 | 5,755.91 | 5,994.78 | 5,214.88 | 5,311.55 |
| Securities Other than Shares.......... | 36a | — | — | — | — | † — | 52.66 | 66.91 | 61.98 | 62.44 | 62.41 | 61.57 | 62.16 |
| Deposits Excl. from Broad Money..... | 36b | .10 | .11 | .11 | .05 | † 14.42 | 13.34 | 17.15 | 8.50 | 6.04 | 3.27 | 35.44 | .14 |
| Sec.Ot.th.Shares Excl.f/Brd.Money..... | 36s | 10.11 | .10 | .05 | .05 | † .05 | .05 | .06 | 5.14 | 5.18 | 5.19 | 5.13 | 5.21 |
| Loans.......................................... | 36l | — | .19 | — | — | † 4.89 | 5.03 | 23.00 | 17.00 | 10.34 | 2.67 | — | — |
| Financial Derivatives........................ | 36m | — | — | — | — | † — | — | — | — | — | — | — | — |
| Insurance Technical Reserves........... | 36r | — | — | — | — | † — | — | — | — | — | — | — | .02 |
| Shares and Other Equity.................. | 37a | 1,473.30 | 1,528.56 | 1,918.44 | 2,500.62 | † 2,236.04 | 3,059.57 | 3,554.43 | 2,155.39 | 2,892.30 | 4,336.48 | 5,062.40 | 5,533.46 |
| Other Items (Net)............................. | 37r | −186.51 | −355.54 | −353.88 | −243.64 | † −928.33 | −311.06 | −667.86 | −731.67 | −1,274.67 | −1,320.10 | −1,105.57 | −1,482.72 |
| Broad Money Liabs., Seasonally Adj. | 35l.b | 3,815.61 | 4,938.76 | 6,880.57 | 8,820.93 | † 9,663.17 | 11,765.05 | 12,947.35 | 15,152.73 | 16,779.03 | 17,863.10 | 18,442.46 | 19,910.04 |
| **Other Financial Corporations** | | | | | | *Millions of Kina: End of Period* | | | | | | | |
| Net Foreign Assets.......................... | 41n | .... | .... | .... | .... | .... | 729.22 | 1,061.55 | 869.32 | 942.19 | 1,171.47 | 1,349.94 | 1,474.74 |
| Claims on Nonresidents................. | 41 | .... | .... | .... | .... | .... | 729.22 | 1,066.51 | 882.97 | 957.25 | 1,182.38 | 1,358.50 | 1,487.94 |
| Liabilities to Nonresidents.............. | 46c | .... | .... | .... | .... | .... | — | 4.97 | 13.64 | 15.06 | 10.91 | 8.55 | 13.21 |
| Claims on Depository Corporations.. | 40 | .... | .... | .... | .... | .... | 1,800.16 | 1,750.22 | 2,156.71 | 2,403.11 | 2,811.78 | 2,416.53 | 2,347.88 |
| Net Claims on Central Government.. | 42an | .... | .... | .... | .... | .... | 749.97 | 928.94 | 1,226.98 | 1,629.99 | 1,892.62 | 2,593.70 | 3,056.95 |
| Claims on Central Government.... | 42a | .... | .... | .... | .... | .... | 768.80 | 965.86 | 1,275.61 | 1,728.48 | 1,960.09 | 2,641.84 | 3,156.91 |
| Liabilities to Central Government.... | 46d | .... | .... | .... | .... | .... | 18.83 | 36.92 | 48.62 | 98.50 | 67.47 | 48.14 | 99.96 |
| Claims on Other Sectors................. | 42s | .... | .... | .... | .... | .... | 1,139.01 | 1,306.22 | 1,458.12 | 1,777.98 | 2,186.99 | 2,846.89 | 3,031.95 |
| Claims on State & Local Govts....... | 42b | .... | .... | .... | .... | .... | .07 | — | — | — | — | — | — |
| Claims on Public Nonfin. Corps...... | 42c | .... | .... | .... | .... | .... | 65.96 | 103.69 | 54.27 | 70.50 | 122.65 | 184.55 | 80.35 |
| Claims on Private Sector............... | 42d | .... | .... | .... | .... | .... | 1,072.99 | 1,202.53 | 1,403.85 | 1,707.48 | 2,064.35 | 2,662.34 | 2,951.59 |
| Deposits........................................ | 46b | .... | .... | .... | .... | .... | 11.18 | 13.19 | 8.23 | 10.25 | 11.04 | 12.74 | 18.35 |
| Securities Other than Shares............ | 46s | .... | .... | .... | .... | .... | — | — | — | — | — | — | — |
| Loans............................................ | 46l | .... | .... | .... | .... | .... | .01 | — | 2.87 | 3.14 | 2.67 | 2.46 | 2.24 |
| Financial Derivatives........................ | 46m | .... | .... | .... | .... | .... | — | — | — | — | — | — | — |
| Insurance Technical Reserves........... | 46r | .... | .... | .... | .... | .... | 4,586.04 | 5,283.20 | 6,277.10 | 6,578.21 | 7,553.05 | 8,611.10 | 9,369.85 |
| Shares and Other Equity.................. | 47a | .... | .... | .... | .... | .... | 1,020.54 | 1,109.55 | 924.67 | 1,809.17 | 2,179.41 | 2,339.45 | 2,426.81 |
| Other Items (Net)............................. | 47r | .... | .... | .... | .... | .... | −1,199.41 | −1,359.01 | −1,501.72 | −1,647.49 | −1,683.31 | −1,758.68 | −1,905.74 |
| Memo Item: | | | | | | | | | | | | | |
| Total Assets.................................... | 40ra | .... | .... | .... | .... | .... | 5,765.12 | 6,565.24 | 7,503.59 | 8,777.81 | 10,189.55 | 11,415.79 | 12,246.23 |

# Papua New Guinea   853

|  |  | 2004 | 2005 | 2006 | 2007 | 2008 | 2009 | 2010 | 2011 | 2012 | 2013 | 2014 | 2015 |
|---|---|---|---|---|---|---|---|---|---|---|---|---|---|
| **Financial Corporations** |  | *Millions of Kina: End of Period* | | | | | | | | | | | |
| Net Foreign Assets.................... | 51n | .... | .... | .... | .... | .... | 8,653.41 | 10,029.37 | 10,986.73 | 10,417.64 | 9,440.63 | 8,175.71 | 7,350.93 |
| Claims on Nonresidents............... | 51 | .... | .... | .... | .... | .... | 9,382.12 | 10,765.73 | 11,554.08 | 11,040.27 | 10,753.94 | 8,929.02 | 8,381.29 |
| Liabilities to Nonresidents............. | 56c | .... | .... | .... | .... | .... | 728.71 | 736.36 | 567.35 | 622.64 | 1,313.30 | 753.31 | 1,030.36 |
| Domestic Claims........................... | 52 | .... | .... | .... | .... | .... | 8,503.06 | 9,184.58 | 9,286.56 | 12,505.35 | 16,872.48 | 21,244.19 | 24,378.70 |
| Net Claims on Central Government | 52an | .... | .... | .... | .... | .... | 1,324.04 | 726.99 | 150.31 | 1,926.97 | 4,648.10 | 6,757.51 | 8,400.76 |
| Claims on Central Government.... | 52a | .... | .... | .... | .... | .... | 3,908.32 | 4,026.30 | 5,024.37 | 5,792.05 | 8,667.66 | 11,143.99 | 11,990.34 |
| Liabilities to Central Government. | 56d | .... | .... | .... | .... | .... | 2,584.28 | 3,299.30 | 4,874.06 | 3,865.07 | 4,019.57 | 4,386.48 | 3,589.58 |
| Claims on Other Sectors............... | 52s | .... | .... | .... | .... | .... | 7,179.02 | 8,457.59 | 9,136.25 | 10,578.37 | 12,224.39 | 14,486.68 | 15,977.94 |
| Claims on State & Local Govts..... | 52b | .... | .... | .... | .... | .... | 4.33 | .33 | .30 | .06 | .10 | .06 | — |
| Claims on Public Nonfin. Corps.... | 52c | .... | .... | .... | .... | .... | 199.95 | 283.86 | 209.86 | 436.49 | 246.44 | 1,560.42 | 2,414.42 |
| Claims on Private Sector.............. | 52d | .... | .... | .... | .... | .... | 6,974.74 | 8,173.40 | 8,926.09 | 10,141.83 | 11,977.85 | 12,926.20 | 13,563.52 |
| Currency Outside Financial Corps..... | 54a | .... | .... | .... | .... | .... | 788.92 | 954.89 | 1,188.30 | 1,213.95 | 1,300.17 | 1,391.91 | 1,443.22 |
| Deposits........................................ | 55l | .... | .... | .... | .... | .... | 9,674.56 | 10,673.43 | 12,711.67 | 14,055.86 | 14,882.07 | 15,732.75 | 17,197.38 |
| Securities Other than Shares............ | 56a | .... | .... | .... | .... | .... | 39.22 | 61.87 | 62.01 | 62.48 | 62.45 | 61.63 | 62.25 |
| Loans........................................... | 56l | .... | .... | .... | .... | .... | — | 18.00 | 12.00 | 5.58 | 2.67 | — | — |
| Financial Derivatives...................... | 56m | .... | .... | .... | .... | .... | — | — | — | — | — | — | — |
| Insurance Technical Reserves........... | 56r | .... | .... | .... | .... | .... | 4,586.04 | 5,283.20 | 6,277.10 | 6,578.21 | 7,553.05 | 8,611.10 | 9,369.87 |
| Shares and Other Equity.................. | 57a | .... | .... | .... | .... | .... | 4,080.11 | 4,663.97 | 3,080.07 | 4,701.47 | 6,515.89 | 7,401.85 | 7,960.28 |
| Other Items (Net)............................ | 57r | .... | .... | .... | .... | .... | −2,012.37 | −2,441.41 | −3,057.86 | −3,694.56 | −4,003.20 | −3,779.34 | −4,303.36 |
| **Monetary Aggregates** |  | *Millions of Kina : End of Period* | | | | | | | | | | | |
| Broad Money................................ | 59m | 3,914.80 | 5,069.28 | 7,040.20 | 8,994.90 | 9,700.39 | 11,822.57 | 13,033.92 | 15,293.39 | 16,966.83 | 18,103.86 | 18,716.28 | 20,218.60 |
| o/w:Currency Issued by Cent.Govt | 59m.a | — | — | — | — | — | — | — | — | — | — | — | — |
| o/w: Dep.in Nonfin. Corporations | 59m.b | — | — | — | — | — | — | — | — | — | — | — | — |
| o/w:Secs. Issued by Central Govt.. | 59m.c | — | — | — | — | — | — | — | — | — | — | — | — |
| **Money (National Definitions)** |  |  |  |  |  |  |  |  |  |  |  |  |  |
| Reserve Money.......................... | 19mb | 870.76 | 935.39 | 1,138.20 | 1,841.61 | 1,620.09 | 1,813.55 | 2,015.65 | 3,258.72 | 3,833.68 | 3,853.00 | 5,282.92 | 5,171.04 |
| M1*.......................................... | 59maa | 2,231.78 | 3,017.35 | 3,790.35 | 4,923.30 | 5,519.61 | 6,232.68 | 7,643.62 | 9,619.68 | 11,148.48 | 12,046.68 | 13,439.83 | 14,844.90 |
| M3*.......................................... | 59mca | 3,914.80 | 5,069.28 | 7,040.20 | 8,994.90 | 9,700.39 | 11,822.57 | 13,033.92 | 15,293.39 | 16,966.83 | 18,103.86 | 18,716.28 | 20,218.60 |
| **Interest Rates** |  | *Percent Per Annum* | | | | | | | | | | | |
| Central Bank Policy Rate (EOP)........ | 60 | 7.00 | 6.00 | 6.00 | 6.00 | 8.00 | 7.00 | 7.00 | 7.75 | 6.75 | 6.25 | 6.25 | 6.25 |
| Discount Rate (End of Period).......... | 60.a | 12.67 | 9.67 | 8.13 | 7.38 | 7.00 | 6.92 | 6.00 | 6.35 | 6.42 | 23.56 | 36.50 | 36.50 |
| Repo Rate.................................... | 60.q | 12.67 | 9.67 | 8.13 | 7.38 | 7.50 | 8.92 | 8.00 | 8.35 | 8.42 | 6.17 | 5.25 | 5.25 |
| Reverse Repo Rate......................... | 60.c | 7.17 | 3.67 | 3.88 | 4.63 | 5.50 | 6.92 | 6.00 | 6.35 | 6.42 | 6.50 | 7.25 | 7.25 |
| Central Bank Bill Rate................... | 60ae | .... | 2.99 | 3.56 | 4.40 | 5.69 | 6.42 | 3.45 | 2.79 | 2.15 | 1.77 | 1.90 | 1.49 |
| Money Market Rate........................ | 60b | 7.79 | 4.36 | 3.29 | 3.00 | 5.50 | 7.67 | 7.00 | 6.98 | 7.67 | 6.75 | 6.75 | 6.75 |
| Treasury Bill Rate.......................... | 60c | 8.85 | 3.81 | 4.01 | 4.67 | 6.19 | 7.08 | 4.64 | 4.14 | 2.74 | 2.15 | 3.97 | 5.27 |
| Savings Rate................................. | 60k | 1.63 | 1.64 | 1.63 | .83 | .83 | .87 | .90 | .86 | .93 | .83 | .83 | .83 |
| Deposit Rate................................. | 60l | 1.73 | .85 | .98 | 1.06 | 1.31 | 2.32 | 1.38 | .92 | .49 | .33 | .33 | .43 |
| Lending Rate................................. | 60p | 13.25 | 11.47 | 10.57 | 9.78 | 9.20 | 10.09 | 10.45 | 10.81 | 10.82 | 10.13 | 9.38 | 8.73 |
| Government Bond Yield................... | 61 | .... | 8.00 | 8.17 | 8.42 | 9.24 | 11.66 | 10.86 | 8.95 | 9.06 | 8.13 | 10.15 | 10.79 |
| **Prices and Labor** |  | *Index Numbers (2010=100): Period Averages* | | | | | | | | | | | |
| Share Prices.................................. | 62 | 30.23 | 46.09 | 62.74 | 72.43 | 86.76 | 79.22 | 100.00 | 103.22 | 74.34 | 62.97 | 55.21 | 51.72 |
| Consumer Prices............................ | 64 | 75.76 | 77.11 | 78.93 | 79.65 | 88.22 | 94.33 | † 100.00 | 104.44 | 109.18 | 114.60 | 120.56 | 127.81 |
| Total Employment.......................... | 67 | 79.52 | 87.79 | 94.71 | 98.88 | 97.70 | 98.88 | 100.00 | 106.75 | 113.02 | 118.04 | 116.63 | 114.05 |
| **Intl. Transactions & Positions** |  | *Millions of Kina* | | | | | | | | | | | |
| Exports........................................ | 70 | 8,223.50 | 10,154.17 | 12,733.87 | 13,881.26 | 15,426.16 | 12,106.71 | 15,601.80 | 16,376.10 | 13,181.40 | 13,337.20 | 21,625.70 | 23,125.60 |
| Imports, c.i.f................................. | 71 | 5,413.87 | 5,362.62 | 6,996.61 | 8,747.77 | .... | .... | .... | .... | .... | .... | .... | .... |
| Imports, f.o.b................................. | 71.v | 5,413.87 | 5,362.62 | 6,908.22 | 8,866.38 | 9,612.31 | 8,816.46 | 9,576.20 | 10,101.00 | 9,912.00 | 12,141.80 | 9,844.80 | 6,245.20 |
|  |  | *2010=100* | | | | | | | | | | | |
| Volume of Exports......................... | 72 | 97.05 | 103.99 | 89.99 | 91.87 | 98.05 | 99.40 | 100.00 | 100.60 | 86.45 | 89.08 | 96.74 | 91.32 |
| Unit Value of Exports...................... | 74 | 51.30 | 61.40 | 95.65 | 101.78 | 112.23 | 77.34 | 100.00 | 113.83 | 98.42 | 97.54 | 95.34 | 80.79 |

# Papua New Guinea   853

| | | 2004 | 2005 | 2006 | 2007 | 2008 | 2009 | 2010 | 2011 | 2012 | 2013 | 2014 | 2015 |
|---|---|---|---|---|---|---|---|---|---|---|---|---|---|
| **Balance of Payments** | | | | | | *Millions of US Dollars* | | | | | | | |
| A. Current Account* | 109bx | 85.6 | 539.4 | 332.7 | 56.3 | 707.9 | −851.8 | −913.6 | −702.0 | −2,832.9 | −3,972.5 | 1,932.2 | .... |
| Goods, credit (exports) | 1a9cx | 2,618.1 | 3,317.6 | 4,204.3 | 4,747.8 | 5,805.5 | 4,391.9 | 5,744.7 | 6,915.2 | 6,332.2 | 5,951.4 | 8,758.1 | .... |
| Goods, debit (imports) | 1a9dx | 1,459.3 | 1,525.3 | 1,990.5 | 2,629.3 | 3,140.2 | 2,870.7 | 3,528.9 | 4,240.5 | 4,766.6 | 5,418.5 | 4,007.8 | .... |
| Balance on goods | 1a9bx | 1,158.8 | 1,792.4 | 2,213.8 | 2,118.5 | 2,665.4 | 1,521.2 | 2,215.8 | 2,674.7 | 1,565.6 | 532.9 | 4,750.3 | .... |
| Services, credit (exports) | 1b9cx | 211.1 | 304.9 | 322.5 | 352.6 | 368.7 | 185.4 | 310.4 | 424.4 | 479.0 | 417.6 | 209.4 | .... |
| Services, debit (imports) | 1b9dx | 1,105.3 | 1,277.9 | 1,595.8 | 1,945.4 | 1,843.4 | 1,840.0 | 2,756.7 | 2,964.9 | 3,732.8 | 3,887.6 | 2,286.1 | .... |
| Balance on Goods & Services | 1z9bx | 264.5 | 819.4 | 940.5 | 525.8 | 1,190.7 | −133.4 | −230.5 | 134.2 | −1,688.2 | −2,937.1 | 2,673.7 | .... |
| Primary income: credit | 1c9cx | 19.8 | 26.1 | 70.3 | 104.4 | 85.1 | 46.3 | 41.6 | 40.0 | 44.8 | 38.5 | 16.3 | .... |
| Primary income: debit | 1c9dx | 456.0 | 564.6 | 875.8 | 824.0 | 729.2 | 671.1 | 634.0 | 590.7 | 774.3 | 683.8 | 418.0 | .... |
| Balance on gds, serv. & prim. inc. | 1y9bx | −171.6 | 280.9 | 135.1 | −193.8 | 546.6 | −758.1 | −822.9 | −416.5 | −2,417.7 | −3,582.5 | 2,271.9 | .... |
| Secondary income: credit | 1d9ca | 334.5 | 352.1 | 327.0 | 411.0 | 392.2 | 112.7 | 157.8 | 47.0 | 19.1 | 13.7 | 4.9 | .... |
| Secondary income: debit | 1d9da | 77.3 | 93.6 | 129.4 | 160.9 | 230.9 | 206.5 | 248.4 | 332.6 | 434.3 | 403.8 | 344.6 | .... |
| B. Capital Account* | 209ba | — | 32.6 | 44.2 | 38.3 | 18.6 | 26.7 | 37.2 | 31.1 | 25.1 | 24.1 | 9.7 | .... |
| Capital account: credit | 209ca | — | 32.6 | 44.2 | 38.3 | 18.6 | 26.7 | 37.2 | 31.1 | 25.1 | 24.1 | 9.7 | .... |
| Capital account: debit | 209da | — | — | — | — | — | — | — | — | — | — | — | .... |
| Balance on current & capital acct. | 129ba | 85.6 | 572.0 | 376.9 | 94.6 | 726.5 | −825.1 | −876.4 | −670.9 | −2,807.9 | −3,948.5 | 1,941.9 | .... |
| C. Financial Account* | 309na | 280.4 | 605.8 | −175.8 | −305.1 | 1,059.2 | −1,156.4 | −1,037.3 | −633.9 | −1,882.2 | −2,742.4 | 2,762.1 | .... |
| Direct investment: assets | 3a9aa | — | — | — | — | — | — | — | — | — | — | — | .... |
| Equity & investment fund shares | 3aaaa | — | — | — | — | — | — | — | — | — | — | — | .... |
| Debt instruments | 3abaa | .... | .... | .... | .... | .... | .... | .... | .... | .... | .... | .... | .... |
| Direct investment: liabilities | 3a9la | 29.9 | 31.8 | 11.8 | 94.6 | −30.6 | 418.8 | 28.7 | −309.8 | −63.8 | 18.2 | −30.4 | .... |
| Equity & investment fund shares | 3aala | 30.6 | 31.2 | 11.2 | 95.6 | −25.5 | 419.4 | 28.4 | −308.9 | −63.8 | 18.2 | −30.4 | .... |
| Debt instruments | 3abla | −.7 | .6 | .6 | −1.0 | −5.1 | −.6 | .3 | −1.0 | — | — | — | .... |
| Portfolio investment: assets | 3b9aa | 104.0 | −23.1 | −125.1 | −408.0 | −349.0 | −150.4 | 104.4 | −430.0 | −664.6 | 110.3 | −379.4 | .... |
| Equity & investment fund shares | 3baaa | 16.0 | 15.3 | −382.9 | −96.4 | −176.4 | −4.9 | 12.4 | 19.5 | 15.4 | 27.4 | 29.0 | .... |
| Debt securities | 3bbaa | 88.0 | −38.5 | 257.8 | −311.6 | −172.7 | −145.5 | 91.9 | −449.5 | −680.0 | 82.9 | −408.5 | .... |
| Portfolio investment: liabilities | 3b9la | — | −1.8 | — | — | — | — | — | −.1 | — | — | −5.8 | .... |
| Equity & investment fund shares | 3bala | .... | .... | .... | .... | .... | .... | .... | .... | .... | .... | −5.6 | .... |
| Debt securities | 3bbla | — | −1.8 | — | — | — | — | — | −.1 | — | — | −.2 | .... |
| Fin. der.& empl.stk.ops.(ESOs): net | 3c9na | 9.4 | 1.9 | 11.2 | 92.6 | 131.6 | −21.1 | 7.5 | 33.1 | 16.5 | 5.4 | — | .... |
| Fin. der. & ESOs.: assets | 3c9aa | 9.4 | 1.9 | 11.2 | 92.6 | 131.6 | −21.1 | 7.5 | 33.1 | 16.5 | 5.4 | — | .... |
| Fin. der. & ESOs.: liabilities | 3c9la | .... | .... | .... | .... | .... | .... | .... | .... | .... | .... | .... | .... |
| Other investment: assets | 3d9aa | 38.1 | 679.6 | −250.6 | −8.9 | 954.9 | −447.2 | −1,182.0 | −568.8 | −1,607.0 | −247.0 | 2,816.1 | .... |
| Other equity | 3daaa | .... | .... | .... | .... | .... | .... | .... | .... | .... | .... | .... | .... |
| Debt instruments | 3dzaa | 38.1 | 679.6 | −250.6 | −8.9 | 954.9 | −447.2 | −1,182.0 | −568.8 | −1,607.0 | −247.0 | 2,816.1 | .... |
| Other investment: liabilities | 3d9la | −158.9 | 22.5 | −200.4 | −113.7 | −291.2 | 118.8 | −61.6 | −21.9 | −309.1 | 2,592.9 | −289.2 | .... |
| Other equity | 3dala | .... | .... | .... | .... | .... | .... | .... | .... | .... | .... | .... | .... |
| Debt instruments | 3dzla | −158.9 | 22.5 | −200.4 | −113.7 | −291.2 | 118.8 | −61.6 | −21.9 | −309.1 | 2,592.9 | −289.2 | .... |
| Curr.+ cap.− finan. acct. balance | 4y9na | −194.9 | −33.8 | 552.7 | 399.8 | −332.7 | 331.2 | 160.9 | −37.0 | −925.7 | −1,206.1 | −820.1 | .... |
| D. Net Errors and Omissions | 409na | 306.4 | 3.5 | −15.1 | 9.7 | −73.2 | −162.6 | −75.9 | −971.7 | 799.2 | 1,386.5 | 715.4 | .... |
| E. Reserves and Related Items | 4z9na | 111.5 | −30.4 | 537.6 | 409.4 | −406.0 | 168.6 | 85.0 | −1,008.7 | −126.5 | 180.5 | −104.7 | .... |
| Reserve assets | 3e9aa | 102.3 | 95.4 | 640.5 | 537.5 | −221.8 | 629.3 | 406.9 | −467.1 | 407.7 | 702.9 | 349.9 | .... |
| Credit and loans from the IMF | 3dcla | −60.0 | −62.2 | — | — | — | — | — | — | — | — | — | .... |
| Exceptional financing | 409la | 50.8 | 187.9 | 102.8 | 128.1 | 184.1 | 460.7 | 321.9 | 541.6 | 534.2 | 522.4 | 454.7 | .... |

*Excludes components in group E

| | | 2004 | 2005 | 2006 | 2007 | 2008 | 2009 | 2010 | 2011 | 2012 | 2013 | 2014 | 2015 |
|---|---|---|---|---|---|---|---|---|---|---|---|---|---|
| **National Accounts** | | | | | | *Millions of Kina* | | | | | | | |
| Househ.Cons.Expend.,incl.NPISHs | 96f | 6,891 | .... | .... | .... | .... | .... | .... | .... | .... | .... | | |
| Government Consumption Expend | 91f | 1,938 | .... | .... | .... | .... | .... | .... | .... | .... | .... | | |
| Gross Fixed Capital Formation | 93e | 2,294 | .... | .... | .... | .... | .... | .... | .... | .... | .... | | |
| Changes in Inventories | 93i | 236 | .... | .... | .... | .... | .... | .... | .... | .... | .... | | |
| Exports of Goods and Services | 90c | 9,130 | .... | .... | .... | .... | .... | .... | .... | .... | .... | | |
| Imports of Goods and Services (-) | 98c | 7,455 | .... | .... | .... | .... | .... | .... | .... | .... | .... | | |
| Gross Domestic Product (GDP) | 99b | 13,861 | .... | .... | .... | .... | .... | .... | .... | .... | .... | | |
| Net Primary Income from Abroad | 98.n | −435 | .... | .... | .... | .... | .... | .... | .... | .... | .... | | |
| Gross National Income (GNI) | 99a | 12,600 | .... | .... | .... | .... | .... | .... | .... | .... | .... | | |
| Consumption of Fixed Capital | 99cf | 827 | .... | .... | .... | .... | .... | .... | .... | .... | .... | | |
| GDP Volume 1998 Prices | 99b.p | 8,183 | .... | .... | .... | .... | .... | .... | .... | .... | .... | | |
| GDP Volume (2000=100) | 99bvp | 105.6 | .... | .... | .... | .... | .... | .... | .... | .... | .... | | |
| GDP Deflator (2000=100) | 99bip | 134.8 | .... | .... | .... | .... | .... | .... | .... | .... | .... | | |
| | | | | | | *Millions: Midyear Estimates* | | | | | | | |
| Population | 99z | 5.94 | 6.09 | 6.24 | 6.39 | 6.54 | 6.69 | 6.85 | 7.00 | 7.15 | 7.31 | 7.46 | 7.62 |

| | | 2004 | 2005 | 2006 | 2007 | 2008 | 2009 | 2010 | 2011 | 2012 | 2013 | 2014 | 2015 |
|---|---|---|---|---|---|---|---|---|---|---|---|---|---|
| **Exchange Rates** | | | | | | *Guaranies per SDR: End of Period* | | | | | | | |
| Market Rate.............aa=........ | wa | 9,706.3 | 8,747.1 | 7,807.8 | 7,703.7 | 7,616.6 | 7,227.1 | 7,043.7 | 6,816.5 | 6,591.5 | 6,967.0 | 6,702.6 | 8,046.8 |
| | | | | | *Guaranies per US Dollar: End of Period (we) Period Average (wf)* | | | | | | | | |
| Market Rate.............ae=........ | we | 6,250.0 | 6,120.0 | 5,190.0 | 4,875.0 | 4,945.0 | 4,610.0 | 4,573.8 | 4,439.9 | 4,288.8 | 4,524.0 | 4,626.3 | 5,806.9 |
| Market Rate.............rf=........ | wf | 5,974.6 | 6,178.0 | 5,635.5 | 5,032.7 | 4,363.2 | 4,965.4 | 4,735.5 | 4,191.4 | 4,424.9 | 4,320.7 | 4,462.2 | 5,204.9 |
| | | | | | *Index Numbers (2010=100): Period Averages* | | | | | | | | |
| Market Rate................................... | ahx | 79.3 | 76.6 | 84.2 | 94.1 | 109.2 | 95.4 | 100.0 | 113.4 | 107.1 | 109.8 | 106.2 | 91.4 |
| Nominal Effective Exchange Rate..... | nec | 92.8 | 85.1 | 91.1 | 97.0 | 107.3 | 98.4 | 100.0 | 109.5 | 109.1 | 117.1 | 120.5 | 119.2 |
| CPI-Based Real Effect. Ex. Rate........ | rec | 80.0 | 74.9 | 84.6 | 93.1 | 107.1 | 98.2 | 100.0 | 111.8 | 110.1 | 115.8 | 119.4 | 117.2 |
| **Fund Position** | | | | | | *Millions of SDRs: End of Period* | | | | | | | |
| Quota.......................................... | 2f.s | 99.90 | 99.90 | 99.90 | 99.90 | 99.90 | 99.90 | 99.90 | 99.90 | 99.90 | 99.90 | 99.90 | 99.90 |
| SDR Holdings............................... | 1b.s | 86.04 | 88.21 | 91.61 | 27.62 | 28.69 | 110.35 | 110.44 | 110.58 | 110.61 | 110.64 | 110.67 | 110.68 |
| Reserve Position in the Fund............ | 1c.s | 21.48 | 21.48 | 21.48 | 21.48 | 21.48 | 21.48 | 21.48 | 21.48 | 21.48 | 21.48 | 21.48 | 21.48 |
| Total Fund Cred.&Loans Outstg....... | 2tl | — | — | — | — | — | — | — | — | — | — | — | — |
| SDR Allocations............................ | 1bd | 13.70 | 13.70 | 13.70 | 13.70 | 13.70 | 95.19 | 95.19 | 95.19 | 95.19 | 95.19 | 95.19 | 95.19 |
| **International Liquidity** | | | | | *Millions of US Dollars Unless Otherwise Indicated: End of Period* | | | | | | | | |
| Total Reserves minus Gold.............. | 1l.d | 1,168.05 | 1,297.09 | 1,702.15 | 2,461.47 | 2,844.56 | 3,838.64 | 4,136.81 | 4,950.06 | 4,556.61 | 5,555.58 | 6,668.90 | 5,659.14 |
| SDR Holdings........................... | 1b.d | 133.62 | 126.08 | 137.82 | 43.65 | 44.19 | 173.00 | 170.08 | 169.76 | 170.00 | 170.38 | 160.33 | 153.37 |
| Reserve Position in the Fund.......... | 1c.d | 33.35 | 30.69 | 32.31 | 33.94 | 33.08 | 33.67 | 33.07 | 32.97 | 33.01 | 33.07 | 31.11 | 29.76 |
| Foreign Exchange........................ | 1d.d | 1,001.07 | 1,140.32 | 1,532.02 | 2,383.89 | 2,767.29 | 3,631.97 | 3,933.66 | 4,747.33 | 4,353.60 | 5,352.13 | 6,477.45 | 5,476.01 |
| of which: US Dollars.................. | 1dxd | 749.50 | 905.76 | 1,421.86 | 2,111.66 | 2,479.14 | 3,289.54 | 3,256.22 | 3,520.41 | 3,479.54 | 4,499.23 | 5,604.00 | 5,010.75 |
| Gold (Million Fine Troy Ounces)....... | 1ad | — | — | — | — | .021 | .021 | .021 | .021 | .263 | .263 | .263 | .263 |
| Gold (National Valuation)............... | 1and | — | — | — | — | 18.40 | 23.18 | 29.93 | 32.48 | 437.55 | 317.77 | 317.17 | 279.55 |
| Central Bank: Other Assets.............. | 3..d | 9.28 | 8.23 | 7.27 | 6.54 | 5.24 | 62.86 | 78.97 | 95.64 | 115.06 | 135.31 | 161.50 | 526.79 |
| Central Bank: Other Liabs............... | 4..d | 62.62 | 69.25 | 71.10 | 58.19 | 23.61 | 21.54 | 10.34 | 6.13 | .85 | 1.58 | .05 | 91.68 |
| Other Depository Corps.: Assets....... | 7a.d | 383.43 | 343.92 | 348.17 | 374.54 | 671.48 | 746.78 | 901.75 | 825.52 | 925.19 | 883.13 | 929.46 | 1,159.45 |
| Other Depository Corps.: Liabs......... | 7b.d | 54.42 | 63.82 | 82.24 | 215.05 | 374.15 | 467.41 | 751.70 | 942.27 | 1,278.66 | 1,673.74 | 2,099.82 | 2,184.24 |
| **Central Bank** | | | | | | *Billions of Guaranies: End of Period* | | | | | | | |
| Net Foreign Assets.......................... | 11n | 6,851.30 | 7,455.60 | 8,442.60 | 11,703.34 | 13,980.12 | 17,007.90 | 18,335.37 | 21,678.34 | 20,534.94 | 26,320.25 | 31,360.23 | 35,342.14 |
| Claims on Nonresidents................ | 11 | 7,374.78 | 7,997.46 | 8,916.72 | 12,090.53 | 14,200.51 | 17,793.45 | 19,050.70 | 22,360.23 | 21,156.51 | 26,999.64 | 31,998.90 | 36,640.54 |
| Liabilities to Nonresidents............. | 16c | 523.48 | 541.87 | 474.12 | 387.19 | 220.38 | 785.55 | 715.33 | 681.89 | 621.56 | 679.39 | 638.66 | 1,298.40 |
| Claims on Other Depository Corps.... | 12e | 1,441.82 | 1,413.80 | 1,387.50 | 1,371.53 | 1,367.27 | 1,361.93 | 1,358.98 | 1,418.94 | 1,090.97 | 1,360.07 | 1,090.09 | 1,152.57 |
| Net Claims on Central Government.. | 12an | 1,088.03 | 1,244.99 | 663.64 | −122.84 | −1,350.00 | −2,047.68 | −3,567.05 | −3,773.71 | −1,243.86 | −5,818.11 | −8,281.70 | −7,117.76 |
| Claims on Central Government...... | 12a | 2,276.89 | 2,343.80 | 2,130.87 | 2,121.69 | 2,235.74 | 2,219.75 | 2,301.04 | 2,382.09 | 3,927.46 | 138.59 | 107.47 | 148.39 |
| Liabilities to Central Government.... | 16d | 1,188.86 | 1,098.80 | 1,467.23 | 2,244.53 | 3,585.74 | 4,267.43 | 5,868.09 | 6,155.81 | 5,171.32 | 5,956.70 | 8,389.17 | 7,266.15 |
| Claims on Other Sectors.................. | 12s | 701.67 | 690.78 | 694.06 | 741.61 | 801.10 | 767.45 | 768.18 | 797.13 | 62.72 | 88.14 | 101.39 | 57.79 |
| Claims on Other Financial Corps.... | 12g | 140.58 | 150.09 | 159.29 | 166.41 | 175.00 | 182.93 | 191.95 | 201.77 | 7.77 | 8.13 | 7.72 | 6.28 |
| Claims on State & Local Govts....... | 12b | 1.41 | 1.46 | 1.51 | 1.56 | 1.61 | 1.66 | 1.71 | 1.75 | — | — | — | — |
| Claims on Public Nonfin. Corps...... | 12c | 506.15 | 485.86 | 478.29 | 490.24 | 495.37 | 491.74 | 486.64 | 488.43 | — | — | — | — |
| Claims on Private Sector............... | 12d | 53.53 | 53.36 | 54.98 | 83.40 | 129.12 | 91.13 | 87.88 | 105.17 | 54.95 | 80.00 | 93.67 | 51.51 |
| Monetary Base............................... | 14 | 5,774.63 | 5,995.78 | 6,471.63 | 8,638.28 | 9,886.10 | 12,887.61 | 13,342.42 | 15,884.96 | 17,472.05 | 18,520.47 | 21,747.34 | 24,816.95 |
| Currency in Circulation................. | 14a | 2,487.57 | 2,924.90 | 3,371.32 | 4,326.10 | 4,973.92 | 5,537.80 | 6,563.53 | 7,324.27 | 8,606.19 | 9,743.95 | 10,615.18 | 10,920.03 |
| Liabs. to Other Depository Corps.... | 14c | 3,278.68 | 3,053.46 | 2,954.01 | 4,130.00 | 4,872.67 | 7,347.24 | 6,775.81 | 8,556.58 | 8,860.51 | 8,769.10 | 11,117.87 | 13,882.22 |
| Liabilities to Other Sectors........... | 14d | 8.38 | 17.42 | 146.29 | 182.18 | 39.50 | 2.57 | 3.08 | 4.12 | 5.35 | 7.43 | 14.29 | 14.70 |
| Other Liabs. to Other Dep. Corps..... | 14n | 1,558.62 | 2,300.02 | 3,228.77 | 3,912.27 | 3,290.71 | 3,419.39 | 3,145.13 | 4,167.97 | 3,613.77 | 7,624.44 | 6,884.73 | 5,328.55 |
| Dep. & Sec. Excl. f/Monetary Base.... | 14o | 162.31 | 143.34 | 163.96 | 125.60 | 46.26 | 310.47 | 153.46 | 309.36 | 184.45 | 381.43 | 879.04 | 777.04 |
| Deposits Included in Broad Money. | 15 | 50.49 | 77.56 | 107.03 | 92.27 | 17.60 | 177.49 | 130.48 | 94.61 | 114.18 | 79.93 | 254.12 | 194.49 |
| Sec.Ot.th.Shares Incl.in Brd. Money | 16a | — | — | — | — | — | — | — | — | — | — | — | — |
| Deposits Excl. from Broad Money... | 16b | 111.82 | 65.78 | 56.93 | 33.33 | 28.66 | 132.98 | 22.98 | 214.75 | 70.27 | 301.50 | 624.92 | 582.56 |
| Sec.Ot.th.Shares Excl.f/Brd.Money.. | 16s | — | — | — | — | — | — | — | — | — | — | — | — |
| Loans........................................... | 16l | 13.84 | 1.52 | 2.87 | 2.90 | 5.67 | 6.37 | 12.40 | 1.59 | 1.18 | — | — | — |
| Financial Derivatives...................... | 16m | | | | | | | | | | | | |
| Shares and Other Equity................. | 17a | 1,588.00 | 1,201.94 | 61.57 | −338.75 | −70.00 | −1,149.75 | −1,410.22 | −1,975.86 | −2,234.55 | −6,065.88 | −6,856.63 | −3,507.98 |
| Other Items (Net)............................ | 17r | 985.42 | 1,162.58 | 1,259.01 | 1,353.36 | 1,639.76 | 1,615.52 | 1,652.28 | 1,732.67 | 1,407.87 | 1,489.88 | 1,615.53 | 2,020.17 |
| Memo Item: | | | | | | | | | | | | | |
| Total Assets................................. | 10ra | 12,310.63 | 12,994.09 | 13,730.17 | 16,920.57 | 19,223.77 | 22,763.26 | 24,111.46 | 27,625.04 | 26,912.80 | 29,262.87 | 33,978.98 | 38,668.58 |

Paraguay 288

| | | 2004 | 2005 | 2006 | 2007 | 2008 | 2009 | 2010 | 2011 | 2012 | 2013 | 2014 | 2015 |
|---|---|---|---|---|---|---|---|---|---|---|---|---|---|
| **Other Depository Corporations** | | | | | | | *Billions of Guaranies: End of Period* | | | | | | |
| Net Foreign Assets | 21n | 2,053.01 | 1,708.58 | 1,374.87 | 773.54 | 1,465.82 | 1,285.08 | 683.90 | –522.80 | –1,493.03 | –3,624.97 | –5,417.59 | –5,950.90 |
| Claims on Nonresidents | 21 | 2,392.62 | 2,097.89 | 1,800.04 | 1,816.54 | 3,310.40 | 3,435.18 | 4,110.15 | 3,696.70 | 3,908.02 | 4,049.14 | 4,302.49 | 6,732.80 |
| Liabilities to Nonresidents | 26c | 339.61 | 389.31 | 425.16 | 1,043.00 | 1,844.58 | 2,150.11 | 3,426.25 | 4,219.50 | 5,401.05 | 7,674.10 | 9,720.08 | 12,683.70 |
| Claims on Central Bank | 20 | 4,798.59 | 5,472.28 | 6,293.28 | 8,262.80 | 8,912.01 | 11,394.12 | 10,667.28 | 14,010.08 | 14,588.20 | 19,350.20 | 20,922.73 | 21,817.71 |
| Currency | 20a | 367.82 | 383.96 | 384.17 | 521.93 | 1,036.38 | 1,193.20 | 1,368.26 | 1,562.54 | 2,177.18 | 2,616.29 | 2,771.08 | 2,428.83 |
| Reserve Deposits and Securities | 20b | 3,220.27 | 3,000.34 | 2,957.78 | 4,148.41 | 4,856.90 | 7,147.18 | 6,417.56 | 8,336.59 | 8,745.77 | 9,260.45 | 11,233.21 | 14,039.82 |
| Other Claims | 20n | 1,210.50 | 2,087.98 | 2,951.33 | 3,592.46 | 3,018.73 | 3,053.73 | 2,881.45 | 4,110.95 | 3,665.24 | 7,473.46 | 6,918.45 | 5,349.06 |
| Net Claims on Central Government | 22an | –528.26 | –863.46 | –657.23 | –924.70 | –1,144.47 | –1,292.75 | –1,820.67 | –3,526.69 | –3,825.31 | –4,043.23 | –4,634.62 | –5,515.83 |
| Claims on Central Government | 22a | 599.79 | 475.29 | 729.30 | 956.65 | 1,019.66 | 1,697.03 | 1,685.22 | 1,012.77 | 1,355.38 | 1,961.97 | 2,521.35 | 2,718.07 |
| Liabilities to Central Government | 26d | 1,128.05 | 1,338.75 | 1,386.53 | 1,881.35 | 2,164.14 | 2,989.78 | 3,505.90 | 4,539.45 | 5,180.69 | 6,005.20 | 7,155.97 | 8,233.90 |
| Claims on Other Sectors | 22s | 7,024.46 | 8,108.06 | 8,796.56 | 12,288.31 | 20,086.50 | 23,977.52 | 32,814.75 | 41,071.10 | 46,809.35 | 57,641.61 | 69,014.74 | 82,574.07 |
| Claims on Other Financial Corps. | 22g | 1.23 | .46 | .51 | .85 | 6.22 | 26.99 | 21.00 | 80.64 | 198.86 | 161.30 | 25.30 | 35.22 |
| Claims on State & Local Govts. | 22b | 5.85 | 14.31 | 20.28 | 43.32 | 60.82 | 75.97 | 60.88 | 95.85 | 108.47 | 101.47 | 95.39 | 107.19 |
| Claims on Public Nonfin. Corps. | 22c | — | .02 | — | .01 | — | 3.62 | — | 36.28 | 112.77 | 270.94 | 272.66 | 361.06 |
| Claims on Private Sector | 22d | 7,017.38 | 8,093.26 | 8,775.77 | 12,244.13 | 20,019.47 | 23,870.94 | 32,732.87 | 40,858.34 | 46,389.25 | 57,107.90 | 68,621.38 | 82,070.61 |
| Liabilities to Central Bank | 26g | 41.55 | 39.83 | 29.33 | 24.97 | 23.06 | 27.24 | 29.49 | 31.81 | 35.21 | 52.73 | 90.55 | 100.99 |
| Transf.Dep.Included in Broad Money | 24 | 4,042.85 | 4,813.76 | 5,297.58 | 7,611.05 | 8,981.35 | 12,055.31 | 14,236.17 | 15,363.43 | 16,988.15 | 20,717.11 | 23,244.12 | 26,077.83 |
| Other Dep.Included in Broad Money | 25 | 4,219.18 | 4,019.00 | 3,926.96 | 4,451.77 | 7,919.07 | 9,012.27 | 10,415.62 | 11,811.16 | 12,839.90 | 15,692.88 | 18,525.28 | 21,125.69 |
| Sec.Ot.th.Shares Incl.in Brd. Money | 26a | 2,044.40 | 2,398.72 | 2,887.52 | 3,805.95 | 5,951.05 | 6,888.16 | 8,676.49 | 11,843.76 | 13,779.20 | 17,031.99 | 19,873.34 | 23,316.31 |
| Deposits Excl. from Broad Money | 26b | 134.88 | 107.28 | 167.49 | 288.73 | 333.70 | 428.83 | 343.52 | 422.67 | 392.90 | 937.91 | 1,050.39 | 1,163.03 |
| Sec.Ot.th.Shares Excl.f/Brd.Money | 26s | 224.29 | 126.21 | 44.86 | 116.95 | 186.11 | 287.92 | 517.28 | 996.87 | 1,014.53 | 1,311.31 | 1,948.08 | 2,904.46 |
| Loans | 26l | 5.97 | 21.81 | 382.01 | 326.51 | 597.62 | 508.28 | 622.21 | 629.91 | 805.92 | 1,025.32 | 1,416.89 | 2,383.98 |
| Financial Derivatives | 26m | 1.35 | — | — | 5.13 | 2.48 | 236.20 | 238.60 | 523.69 | 596.08 | 880.93 | 1,025.90 | 1,219.27 |
| Insurance Technical Reserves | 26r | — | — | — | — | — | — | — | — | — | — | — | — |
| Shares and Other Equity | 27a | 1,698.28 | 1,961.70 | 2,372.20 | 2,823.80 | 4,704.52 | 5,324.69 | 6,557.57 | 7,805.57 | 9,386.39 | 10,780.47 | 12,751.56 | 14,104.23 |
| Other Items (Net) | 27r | 935.08 | 937.14 | 699.53 | 945.08 | 620.91 | 595.07 | 708.30 | 1,602.84 | 240.93 | 892.95 | –40.85 | 529.27 |
| Memo Item: | | | | | | | | | | | | | |
| Total Assets | 20ra | 15,816.15 | 17,036.65 | 18,753.88 | 24,796.53 | 36,603.23 | 44,317.28 | 53,480.39 | 64,823.47 | 72,474.18 | 90,723.59 | 106,579.46 | 123,739.37 |
| **Depository Corporations** | | | | | | | *Billions of Guaranies: End of Period* | | | | | | |
| Net Foreign Assets | 31n | 8,904.31 | 9,164.17 | 9,817.48 | 12,476.89 | 15,445.94 | 18,292.98 | 19,019.27 | 21,155.54 | 19,041.91 | 22,695.28 | 25,942.64 | 29,391.24 |
| Claims on Nonresidents | 31 | 9,767.40 | 10,095.35 | 10,716.76 | 13,907.07 | 17,510.90 | 21,228.64 | 23,160.85 | 26,056.93 | 25,064.52 | 31,048.77 | 36,301.38 | 43,373.33 |
| Liabilities to Nonresidents | 36c | 863.09 | 931.18 | 899.28 | 1,430.18 | 2,064.96 | 2,935.65 | 4,141.58 | 4,901.38 | 6,022.61 | 8,353.49 | 10,358.74 | 13,982.09 |
| Domestic Claims | 32 | 8,285.90 | 9,180.37 | 9,497.03 | 11,982.38 | 18,393.13 | 21,404.54 | 28,195.22 | 34,567.83 | 41,802.91 | 47,868.41 | 56,199.80 | 69,998.27 |
| Net Claims on Central Government | 32an | 559.77 | 381.53 | 6.41 | –1,047.54 | –2,494.47 | –3,340.43 | –5,387.72 | –7,300.40 | –5,069.17 | –9,861.34 | –12,916.32 | –12,633.59 |
| Claims on Central Government | 32a | 2,876.68 | 2,819.09 | 2,860.16 | 3,078.34 | 3,255.41 | 3,916.78 | 3,986.27 | 3,394.86 | 5,282.84 | 2,100.56 | 2,628.82 | 2,866.46 |
| Liabilities to Central Government | 36d | 2,316.91 | 2,437.55 | 2,853.76 | 4,125.88 | 5,749.88 | 7,257.21 | 9,373.99 | 10,695.26 | 10,352.01 | 11,961.89 | 15,545.14 | 15,500.05 |
| Claims on Other Sectors | 32s | 7,726.13 | 8,798.84 | 9,490.62 | 13,029.92 | 20,887.60 | 24,744.97 | 33,582.94 | 41,868.23 | 46,872.08 | 57,729.75 | 69,116.12 | 82,631.86 |
| Claims on Other Financial Corps. | 32g | 141.81 | 150.56 | 159.79 | 167.26 | 181.21 | 209.92 | 212.95 | 282.41 | 206.63 | 169.43 | 33.02 | 41.49 |
| Claims on State & Local Govts. | 32b | 7.26 | 15.77 | 21.79 | 44.88 | 62.42 | 77.63 | 62.59 | 97.61 | 108.47 | 101.47 | 95.39 | 107.19 |
| Claims on Public Nonfin. Corps. | 32c | 506.15 | 485.88 | 478.29 | 490.25 | 495.37 | 495.36 | 486.64 | 524.70 | 112.77 | 270.94 | 272.66 | 361.06 |
| Claims on Private Sector | 32d | 7,070.91 | 8,146.63 | 8,830.75 | 12,327.52 | 20,148.59 | 23,962.06 | 32,820.75 | 40,963.51 | 46,444.20 | 57,187.90 | 68,715.05 | 82,122.12 |
| Broad Money Liabilities | 35l | 12,485.04 | 13,867.41 | 15,352.53 | 19,947.40 | 26,846.10 | 32,480.39 | 38,657.12 | 44,878.79 | 50,155.80 | 60,657.00 | 69,755.26 | 79,220.22 |
| Currency Outside Depository Corps | 34a | 2,119.75 | 2,540.94 | 2,987.15 | 3,804.17 | 3,937.54 | 4,344.60 | 5,195.27 | 5,761.73 | 6,429.01 | 7,127.66 | 7,844.10 | 8,491.20 |
| Transferable Deposits | 34 | 4,095.42 | 4,903.04 | 5,541.69 | 7,851.48 | 9,026.60 | 12,102.11 | 14,249.69 | 15,364.78 | 16,998.88 | 20,717.12 | 23,244.13 | 26,077.83 |
| Other Deposits | 35 | 4,225.48 | 4,024.70 | 3,936.17 | 4,485.80 | 7,930.91 | 9,145.53 | 10,535.67 | 11,908.53 | 12,948.70 | 15,780.24 | 18,793.69 | 21,334.87 |
| Securities Other than Shares | 36a | 2,044.40 | 2,398.72 | 2,887.52 | 3,805.95 | 5,951.05 | 6,888.16 | 8,676.49 | 11,843.76 | 13,779.20 | 17,031.99 | 19,873.34 | 23,316.31 |
| Deposits Excl. from Broad Money | 36b | 246.70 | 173.05 | 224.43 | 322.06 | 362.36 | 561.80 | 366.50 | 637.42 | 463.17 | 1,239.42 | 1,675.31 | 1,745.58 |
| Sec.Ot.th.Shares Excl.f/Brd.Money | 36s | 224.29 | 126.21 | 44.86 | 116.95 | 186.11 | 287.92 | 517.28 | 996.87 | 1,014.53 | 1,311.31 | 1,948.08 | 2,904.46 |
| Loans | 36l | 19.81 | 23.33 | 384.88 | 329.41 | 603.28 | 514.65 | 634.61 | 631.51 | 807.10 | 1,025.32 | 1,416.89 | 2,383.98 |
| Financial Derivatives | 36m | 1.35 | — | — | 5.13 | 2.48 | 236.20 | 238.60 | 523.69 | 596.08 | 880.93 | 1,025.90 | 1,219.27 |
| Insurance Technical Reserves | 36r | — | — | — | — | — | — | — | — | — | — | — | — |
| Shares and Other Equity | 37a | 3,286.27 | 3,163.64 | 2,433.77 | 2,485.05 | 4,634.52 | 4,174.94 | 5,147.36 | 5,829.72 | 7,151.84 | 4,714.59 | 5,894.93 | 10,596.24 |
| Other Items (Net) | 37r | 926.76 | 990.91 | 874.04 | 1,253.27 | 1,204.21 | 1,441.62 | 1,653.03 | 2,225.39 | 656.30 | 735.12 | 426.07 | 1,319.75 |
| Broad Money Liabs., Seasonally Adj. | 35l.b | 12,143.60 | 13,506.64 | 14,981.48 | 19,491.35 | 26,262.70 | 31,809.73 | 37,896.98 | 44,044.75 | 49,243.76 | 59,580.31 | 68,544.74 | 77,877.69 |
| **Monetary Aggregates** | | | | | | | *Billions of Guaranies: End of Period* | | | | | | |
| Broad Money | 59m | 12,485.04 | 13,867.41 | 15,352.53 | 19,947.40 | 26,846.10 | 32,480.39 | 38,657.12 | 44,878.79 | 50,155.80 | 60,657.00 | 69,755.26 | 79,220.22 |
| o/w:Currency Issued by Cent.Govt | 59m.a | — | — | — | — | — | — | — | — | — | — | — | — |
| o/w: Dep.in Nonfin. Corporations | 59m.b | — | — | — | — | — | — | — | — | — | — | — | — |
| o/w:Secs. Issued by Central Govt. | 59m.c | — | — | — | — | — | — | — | — | — | — | — | — |
| Money (National Definitions) | | | | | | | | | | | | | |
| Base Money | 19ma | 4,060.38 | 4,240.52 | 4,789.62 | 6,476.44 | 7,616.94 | 10,160.30 | 10,273.55 | 11,598.79 | 13,591.72 | 13,164.10 | 14,589.64 | 15,006.67 |
| M1 | 59ma | 4,705.78 | 5,674.71 | 6,628.53 | 9,179.82 | 9,810.24 | 12,714.16 | 14,412.88 | 16,170.40 | 17,736.13 | 20,359.53 | 22,233.81 | 23,061.71 |
| M2 | 59mb | 6,299.83 | 7,328.80 | 8,493.42 | 11,837.44 | 16,893.19 | 21,250.41 | 24,764.59 | 29,079.13 | 32,753.04 | 38,661.87 | 42,286.52 | 44,722.79 |
| M3 | 59mc | 11,733.89 | 12,708.50 | 14,032.98 | 18,432.77 | 25,835.28 | 31,195.62 | 38,083.12 | 43,356.42 | 48,674.52 | 59,212.27 | 67,695.57 | 77,273.74 |
| M4 | 59md | 11,742.09 | 12,711.05 | 14,032.98 | 18,432.77 | 25,944.23 | 31,362.63 | 38,435.28 | 44,272.43 | 49,637.39 | 60,299.40 | 68,909.76 | 79,189.26 |
| M5 | 59me | 11,742.09 | 12,711.05 | 14,032.98 | 18,432.77 | 25,944.23 | 31,362.63 | 38,435.28 | 44,272.43 | 49,637.39 | 60,299.40 | 68,909.76 | 79,189.26 |
| **Interest Rates** | | | | | | | *Percent Per Annum* | | | | | | |
| Central Bank Policy Rate (EOP) | 60 | .... | .... | .... | .... | .... | .... | .... | 7.25 | 5.50 | 6.00 | 6.75 | 5.75 |
| Discount Rate (End of Period) | 60.a | 20.00 | 20.00 | 20.00 | 20.00 | 20.00 | 20.00 | 20.00 | 20.00 | 20.00 | 20.00 | 20.00 | 20.00 |
| Money Market Rate | 60b | 1.33 | 2.29 | 8.33 | 3.93 | 4.50 | 8.94 | 1.85 | 7.70 | 6.63 | 6.25 | 6.28 | 6.30 |
| Savings Rate | 60k | 1.33 | .20 | .19 | .35 | .56 | .81 | .62 | .64 | .72 | .79 | .81 | .82 |
| Savings Rate (Fgn. Currency) | 60k.f | .15 | .11 | .11 | .15 | .16 | .22 | .20 | .19 | .17 | .22 | .22 | .20 |
| Deposit Rate | 60l | 5.11 | 1.66 | 6.72 | 5.00 | 3.08 | 1.46 | 1.21 | 4.03 | 3.92 | 4.24 | 4.31 | 3.51 |
| Deposit Rate (Fgn. Currency) | 60l.f | .68 | 1.18 | 1.81 | 1.67 | 1.25 | 1.34 | 1.25 | 1.39 | 1.37 | 2.24 | 1.63 | 1.47 |
| Lending Rate | 60p | 33.54 | 29.91 | 30.14 | 25.02 | 25.81 | 28.26 | 26.04 | † 17.40 | 17.16 | 19.27 | 21.19 | 19.74 |
| Lending Rate (Fgn. Currency) | 60p.f | 8.08 | 9.13 | 9.13 | 8.75 | 10.28 | 11.48 | 9.28 | † 7.98 | 9.30 | 8.48 | 8.18 | 8.71 |
| **Prices and Labor** | | | | | | | *Index Numbers (2010=100): Period Averages* | | | | | | |
| Producer Prices | 63 | 68.9 | 75.0 | 80.4 | 83.3 | 94.2 | 93.9 | † 100.0 | 112.6 | 116.3 | 116.9 | 120.2 | 122.6 |
| Consumer Prices | 64 | 66.8 | 71.4 | 78.2 | 84.6 | 93.1 | 95.6 | 100.0 | 108.3 | 112.2 | 115.2 | 121.0 | 124.8 |
| | | | | | | | *Number in Thousands: Period Averages* | | | | | | |
| Employment | 67e | .... | .... | .... | .... | .... | .... | 1,110 | 1,150 | 1,175 | 1,248 | 1,273 | .... |
| Unemployment | 67c | .... | .... | .... | .... | .... | .... | 87 | 88 | 103 | 110 | 111 | .... |
| Unemployment Rate (%) | 67r | .... | .... | .... | .... | .... | .... | 7.2 | 7.1 | 8.1 | 8.1 | 8.0 | .... |

# Paraguay   288

| | | 2004 | 2005 | 2006 | 2007 | 2008 | 2009 | 2010 | 2011 | 2012 | 2013 | 2014 | 2015 |
|---|---|---|---|---|---|---|---|---|---|---|---|---|---|
| **Intl. Transactions & Positions** | | | | | | | *Millions of U.S. Dollars* | | | | | | |
| Exports | 70..d | 2,874.5 | 3,152.6 | 3,472.4 | 4,723.6 | 6,407.1 | 5,079.6 | 6,516.6 | 7,776.4 | 7,282.8 | 9,456.3 | 9,635.9 | 8,356.5 |
| Imports, c.i.f. | 71..d | 3,097.0 | 3,790.0 | 6,090.0 | 5,859.4 | 9,033.2 | 6,939.9 | 10,040.3 | 12,316.8 | 11,502.1 | 12,142.0 | 12,168.6 | 10,215.0 |
| Imports, f.o.b. | 71.vd | 2,657.7 | 3,251.4 | 5,250.2 | 6,286.9 | 8,303.7 | 6,481.3 | 9,400.3 | 11,502.2 | 10,706.8 | 11,302.1 | 11,299.4 | 9,459.8 |
| **Balance of Payments** | | | | | | | *Millions of US Dollars* | | | | | | |
| A. Current Account* | 109bx | −9.8 | −67.5 | 167.1 | 779.0 | 183.1 | 481.5 | −57.3 | 109.0 | −501.4 | 477.4 | −116.7 | .... |
| Goods, credit (exports) | 1a9cx | 4,163.7 | 4,827.7 | 5,949.9 | 7,297.4 | 9,651.0 | 7,693.0 | 10,366.6 | 12,499.6 | 11,514.8 | 13,444.3 | 12,879.4 | .... |
| Goods, debit (imports) | 1a9dx | 3,016.9 | 3,682.1 | 4,852.7 | 5,937.5 | 8,644.4 | 6,603.1 | 9,544.6 | 11,722.8 | 11,014.0 | 11,861.0 | 11,940.7 | .... |
| Balance on goods | 1a9bx | 1,146.8 | 1,145.6 | 1,097.3 | 1,359.9 | 1,006.6 | 1,089.9 | 822.0 | 776.9 | 500.8 | 1,583.3 | 938.7 | .... |
| Services, credit (exports) | 1b9cx | 233.0 | 281.4 | 349.1 | 504.2 | 487.0 | 614.8 | 722.7 | 800.4 | 827.1 | 928.4 | 990.3 | .... |
| Services, debit (imports) | 1b9dx | 301.7 | 344.1 | 384.5 | 464.0 | 598.5 | 541.2 | 747.4 | 903.7 | 927.3 | 1,068.7 | 1,114.7 | .... |
| Balance on Goods & Services | 1z9bx | 1,078.1 | 1,082.9 | 1,061.9 | 1,400.1 | 895.2 | 1,163.4 | 797.3 | 673.6 | 400.6 | 1,443.0 | 814.3 | .... |
| Primary income: credit | 1c9cx | 34.4 | 72.7 | 144.0 | 168.4 | 139.5 | 78.2 | 45.4 | 35.9 | 42.1 | 40.0 | 38.5 | .... |
| Primary income: debit | 1c9dx | 1,316.5 | 1,446.9 | 1,464.8 | 1,162.8 | 1,265.7 | 1,279.0 | 1,457.4 | 1,314.1 | 1,702.8 | 1,725.5 | 1,575.6 | .... |
| Balance on gds, serv. & prim. inc. | 1y9bx | −204.0 | −291.3 | −258.9 | 405.7 | −231.1 | −37.4 | −614.8 | −604.6 | −1,260.1 | −242.5 | −722.9 | .... |
| Secondary income: credit | 1d9ca | 195.7 | 225.3 | 430.0 | 374.8 | 415.6 | 520.3 | 558.9 | 715.0 | 760.1 | 721.3 | 609.6 | .... |
| Secondary income: debit | 1d9da | 1.5 | 1.5 | 4.0 | 1.5 | 1.4 | 1.4 | 1.4 | 1.4 | 1.4 | 1.4 | 3.4 | .... |
| B. Capital Account* | 209ba | 16.0 | 20.0 | 30.0 | 28.0 | 33.0 | 47.0 | 40.0 | 40.0 | 51.0 | 61.2 | 141.0 | .... |
| Capital account: credit | 209ca | 16.0 | 20.0 | 30.0 | 28.0 | 33.0 | 47.0 | 40.0 | 40.0 | 51.0 | 61.2 | 141.0 | .... |
| Capital account: debit | 209da | — | — | — | — | — | — | — | — | — | — | — | .... |
| Balance on current & capital acct. | 129ba | 6.2 | −47.5 | 197.1 | 807.0 | 216.1 | 528.5 | −17.3 | 149.0 | −450.4 | 538.6 | 24.3 | .... |
| C. Financial Account* | 309na | −119.7 | −565.3 | −181.2 | −421.2 | −218.7 | −27.1 | −155.0 | −426.6 | −872.7 | 47.3 | −1,699.8 | .... |
| Direct investment: assets | 3a9aa | 66.3 | −28.2 | 73.6 | −97.3 | 52.2 | −45.6 | 128.2 | −109.2 | 7.7 | 2.3 | 99.5 | .... |
| Equity & investment fund shares | 3aaaa | — | | | | | | | | | | — | .... |
| Debt instruments | 3abaa | 66.3 | −28.2 | 73.6 | −97.3 | 52.2 | −45.6 | 128.2 | −109.2 | 7.7 | 2.3 | 99.5 | .... |
| Direct investment: liabilities | 3a9la | 94.0 | 7.3 | 187.8 | 105.0 | 260.9 | 49.1 | 344.1 | 447.8 | 745.4 | 74.0 | 523.3 | .... |
| Equity & investment fund shares | 3aala | 85.9 | 32.1 | 106.1 | 73.8 | 77.1 | 196.9 | 86.7 | 276.6 | 676.6 | 393.5 | 483.9 | .... |
| Debt instruments | 3abla | 8.1 | −24.8 | 81.7 | 31.2 | 183.8 | −147.8 | 257.4 | 171.2 | 68.8 | −319.5 | 39.4 | .... |
| Portfolio investment: assets | 3b9aa | — | — | — | — | — | — | — | | | | — | .... |
| Equity & investment fund shares | 3baaa | — | — | — | — | — | — | — | | | | — | .... |
| Debt securities | 3bbaa | — | — | — | — | — | — | — | | | | — | .... |
| Portfolio investment: liabilities | 3b9la | −.1 | — | — | — | — | — | — | 100.0 | 500.0 | 500.0 | 1,300.0 | .... |
| Equity & investment fund shares | 3bala | — | — | — | — | — | — | — | — | — | — | — | .... |
| Debt securities | 3bbla | −.1 | — | — | — | — | — | — | 100.0 | 500.0 | 500.0 | 1,300.0 | .... |
| Fin. der.& empl.stk.ops.(ESOs): net | 3c9na | — | | | | | | | | | | — | .... |
| Fin. der. & ESOs.: assets | 3c9aa | — | .... | .... | .... | .... | .... | .... | .... | .... | .... | — | .... |
| Fin. der. & ESOs.: liabilities | 3c9la | — | .... | .... | .... | .... | .... | .... | .... | .... | .... | — | .... |
| Other investment: assets | 3d9aa | 74.7 | −298.8 | −36.4 | −513.9 | 91.5 | −330.3 | 23.3 | −248.5 | 126.7 | 64.7 | −307.4 | .... |
| Other equity | 3daaa | .... | .... | .... | .... | .... | .... | .... | .... | .... | .... | .... | .... |
| Debt instruments | 3dzaa | 74.7 | −298.8 | −36.4 | −513.9 | 91.5 | −330.3 | 23.3 | −248.5 | 126.7 | 64.7 | −307.4 | .... |
| Other investment: liabilities | 3d9la | 166.8 | 230.9 | 30.6 | −295.1 | 101.5 | −397.9 | −37.5 | −478.9 | −238.3 | −554.4 | −331.3 | .... |
| Other equity | 3dala | .... | .... | .... | .... | .... | .... | .... | .... | .... | .... | .... | .... |
| Debt instruments | 3dzla | 166.8 | 230.9 | 30.6 | −295.1 | 101.5 | −397.9 | −37.5 | −478.9 | −238.3 | −554.4 | −331.3 | .... |
| Curr.+ cap.− finan. acct. balance | 4y9na | 125.9 | 517.8 | 378.3 | 1,228.1 | 434.8 | 555.7 | 137.7 | 575.6 | 422.3 | 491.2 | 1,724.1 | .... |
| D. Net Errors and Omissions | 409na | 147.3 | −354.6 | 4.4 | −603.1 | −38.5 | 371.7 | 181.7 | 206.4 | −446.4 | 544.5 | −586.0 | .... |
| E. Reserves and Related Items | 4z9na | 273.2 | 163.2 | 382.7 | 625.0 | 396.4 | 927.3 | 319.4 | 782.0 | −24.1 | 1,035.7 | 1,138.1 | .... |
| Reserve assets | 3e9aa | 181.2 | 149.2 | 386.8 | 629.5 | 396.0 | 927.2 | 319.3 | 784.3 | −24.5 | 1,035.7 | 1,131.1 | .... |
| Credit and loans from the IMF | 3dcla | — | — | — | — | — | — | — | — | — | — | — | .... |
| Exceptional financing | 409la | −92.0 | −14.0 | 4.1 | 4.5 | −.4 | −.1 | −.1 | 2.3 | −.4 | — | −7.0 | .... |
| *Excludes components in group E | | | | | | | | | | | | | |
| **International Investment Position** | | | | | | | *Millions of US Dollars* | | | | | | |
| Assets | 809aa | 2,853.3 | 3,537.3 | 4,657.0 | 4,810.4 | 5,400.7 | 7,485.9 | 8,793.0 | 9,046.7 | 9,197.5 | 10,141.9 | 10,956.1 | .... |
| Direct investment | 8a9aa | 136.2 | 108.0 | 195.1 | 97.8 | 150.0 | 104.4 | 232.6 | 123.4 | 131.5 | 133.8 | 233.3 | .... |
| Equity & investment fund shares | 8aaaa | .... | .... | .... | .... | .... | .... | .... | .... | .... | .... | .... | .... |
| Debt instruments | 8abaa | 136.2 | 108.0 | 195.1 | 97.8 | 150.0 | 104.4 | 232.6 | 123.4 | 131.5 | 133.8 | 233.3 | .... |
| Portfolio investment | 8b9aa | 4.0 | 4.0 | 4.0 | 4.0 | 4.0 | 4.0 | 4.0 | 3.8 | 3.8 | 3.8 | 3.8 | .... |
| Equity & investment fund shares | 8baaa | 4.0 | 4.0 | 4.0 | 4.0 | 4.0 | 4.0 | 4.0 | 3.8 | 3.8 | 3.8 | 3.8 | .... |
| Debt securities | 8bbaa | .... | .... | .... | .... | .... | .... | .... | .... | .... | .... | .... | .... |
| Fin. der.(oth.than reserves) & ESOs | 8c9aa | .... | .... | .... | .... | .... | .... | .... | .... | .... | .... | .... | .... |
| Other investment | 8d9aa | 1,525.2 | 2,108.2 | 2,733.6 | 2,243.6 | 2,383.5 | 3,517.1 | 4,379.8 | 3,936.5 | 4,068.8 | 4,133.4 | 3,828.1 | .... |
| Other equity | 8daaa | .... | .... | .... | .... | .... | .... | .... | .... | .... | .... | .... | .... |
| Debt instruments | 8dzaa | 1,525.2 | 2,108.2 | 2,733.6 | 2,243.6 | 2,383.5 | 3,517.1 | 4,379.8 | 3,936.5 | 4,068.8 | 4,133.4 | 3,828.1 | .... |
| Reserve assets | 8e9aa | 1,187.9 | 1,317.1 | 1,724.4 | 2,465.1 | 2,863.2 | 3,860.4 | 4,176.7 | 4,983.0 | 4,993.5 | 5,870.9 | 6,890.9 | .... |
| Liabilities | 809la | 16,758.2 | 16,957.5 | 17,627.3 | 17,711.9 | 18,252.0 | 18,096.9 | 18,664.7 | 18,945.6 | 20,628.5 | 20,303.8 | 21,907.8 | .... |
| Direct investment | 8a9la | 1,149.2 | 1,235.1 | 1,811.0 | 2,124.9 | 2,519.5 | 2,759.7 | 3,329.0 | 4,000.6 | 5,419.5 | 5,210.8 | 5,802.9 | .... |
| Equity & investment fund shares | 8aala | 897.8 | 1,007.0 | 1,501.2 | 1,783.9 | 1,994.7 | 2,382.7 | 2,694.6 | 3,195.0 | 4,525.3 | 4,636.1 | 5,188.8 | .... |
| Debt instruments | 8abla | 251.4 | 228.1 | 309.8 | 341.0 | 524.8 | 377.0 | 634.4 | 805.6 | 894.2 | 574.7 | 614.1 | .... |
| Portfolio investment | 8b9la | .... | .1 | .2 | .2 | .2 | .2 | .2 | 100.0 | 600.0 | 1,100.0 | 2,400.0 | .... |
| Equity & investment fund shares | 8bala | .... | .... | .... | .... | .... | .... | .... | .... | .... | .... | .... | .... |
| Debt securities | 8bbla | .... | .1 | .2 | .2 | .2 | .2 | .2 | 100.0 | 600.0 | 1,100.0 | 2,400.0 | .... |
| Fin. der.(oth.than reserves) & ESOs | 8c9la | .... | .... | .... | .... | .... | .... | .... | .... | .... | .... | .... | .... |
| Other investment | 8d9la | 15,609.0 | 15,722.3 | 15,816.1 | 15,586.8 | 15,732.4 | 15,337.0 | 15,335.5 | 14,844.9 | 14,609.1 | 13,992.9 | 13,704.9 | .... |
| Other equity | 8dala | .... | .... | .... | .... | .... | .... | .... | .... | .... | .... | .... | .... |
| Debt instruments | 8dzla | 15,609.0 | 15,722.3 | 15,816.1 | 15,586.8 | 15,732.4 | 15,337.0 | 15,335.5 | 14,844.9 | 14,609.1 | 13,992.9 | 13,704.9 | .... |

| | | 2004 | 2005 | 2006 | 2007 | 2008 | 2009 | 2010 | 2011 | 2012 | 2013 | 2014 | 2015 |
|---|---|---|---|---|---|---|---|---|---|---|---|---|---|
| **Government Finance** | | | | | | | | | | | | | |
| **Cash Flow Statement** | | | | | | | | | | | | | |
| **Budgetary Central Government** | | | | | *Billions of Guaranies: Fiscal Year Ends December 31* | | | | | | | |
| Cash Receipts:Operating Activities... | c1 | 7,648.5 | 8,430.0 | 9,556.5 | 10,812.4 | 12,719.1 | 13,877.9 | 16,242.2 | 18,969.3 | 20,636.9 | 20,941.9 | 24,146.5 | . . . . |
| Taxes............................ | c11 | 4,929.2 | 5,470.5 | 6,294.6 | 7,018.7 | 8,656.0 | 9,206.8 | 11,405.6 | 13,210.8 | 13,870.7 | 14,887.7 | 17,485.0 | . . . . |
| Social Contributions..................... | c12 | 439.7 | 541.3 | 559.8 | 752.1 | 906.7 | 1,019.4 | 1,140.7 | 1,329.9 | 1,693.1 | 1,607.1 | 2,312.9 | . . . . |
| Grants............................. | c13 | 222.6 | 106.4 | 119.6 | 317.6 | 385.1 | 435.5 | 561.4 | 900.6 | 765.3 | 550.7 | 530.4 | . . . . |
| Other Receipts........................... | c14 | 2,057.0 | 2,311.8 | 2,582.5 | 2,724.0 | 2,771.4 | 3,216.3 | 3,134.5 | 3,532.0 | 4,307.8 | 3,896.5 | 3,818.3 | . . . . |
| Cash Payments:Operating Activities. | c2 | 5,702.6 | 7,157.4 | 8,175.6 | 8,975.2 | 10,005.1 | 12,057.1 | 13,076.6 | 15,716.9 | 19,823.0 | 20,372.8 | 21,930.6 | . . . . |
| Compensation of Employees.......... | c21 | 2,983.5 | 3,334.1 | 3,919.4 | 4,456.1 | 5,262.9 | 6,078.7 | 6,950.6 | 8,046.9 | 10,435.6 | 10,996.3 | 12,131.2 | . . . . |
| Purchases of Goods & Services....... | c22 | 465.6 | 924.8 | 961.5 | 762.0 | 758.8 | 1,068.4 | 1,338.6 | 1,705.8 | 1,826.8 | 1,677.2 | 2,042.4 | . . . . |
| Interest.......................... | c24 | 474.2 | 539.7 | 516.3 | 512.6 | 445.1 | 434.5 | 346.3 | 284.1 | 259.2 | 416.0 | 526.7 | . . . . |
| Subsidies.......................... | c25 | — | — | — | — | — | — | — | — | — | 45.1 | 45.1 | . . . . |
| Grants.............................. | c26 | 612.8 | 937.1 | 985.5 | 1,218.2 | 1,338.0 | 1,787.1 | 1,750.1 | 2,534.6 | 3,490.4 | 3,393.6 | 3,233.6 | . . . . |
| Social Benefits......................... | c27 | 1,008.0 | 1,145.4 | 1,310.5 | 1,442.6 | 1,448.0 | 1,662.4 | 1,827.6 | 1,965.2 | 2,409.8 | 2,942.7 | 2,998.6 | . . . . |
| Other Payments............................ | c28 | 158.6 | 276.2 | 482.4 | 583.8 | 752.3 | 1,026.0 | 863.3 | 1,180.2 | 1,401.3 | 901.8 | 952.9 | . . . . |
| Net Cash Inflow:Operating Act.[1-2] | ccio | 2,014.9 | 1,272.6 | 1,380.9 | 1,837.2 | 2,714.0 | 1,820.9 | 3,165.7 | 3,252.4 | 813.9 | 569.1 | 2,216.0 | . . . . |
| Net Cash Outflow:Invest. in NFA...... | c31 | 1,316.6 | 942.3 | 1,044.4 | 1,136.8 | 921.7 | 1,727.5 | 1,940.1 | 2,201.8 | 2,617.5 | 2,923.1 | 3,293.6 | . . . . |
| Purchases of Nonfinancial Assets... | c31.1 | 1,318.3 | 944.3 | 1,048.5 | 1,137.7 | 924.8 | 1,729.8 | 1,944.9 | 2,203.8 | 2,620.8 | . . . . | . . . . | . . . . |
| Sales of Nonfinancial Assets.......... | c31.2 | 1.8 | 2.0 | 4.2 | .9 | 3.1 | 2.3 | 4.8 | 2.0 | 3.2 | . . . . | . . . . | . . . . |
| Cash Surplus/Deficit [1-2-31=1-2M] | ccsd | 698.3 | 330.4 | 336.5 | 700.4 | 1,792.3 | 93.4 | 1,225.6 | 1,050.6 | −1,803.6 | −2,354.0 | −1,077.6 | . . . . |
| Net Acq. Fin. Assets, excl. Cash....... | c32x | −29.2 | −54.7 | 72.1 | 107.6 | −38.2 | 49.2 | 77.3 | 273.2 | 152.0 | . . . . | . . . . | . . . . |
| Domestic......................... | c321x | −31.3 | −60.0 | 72.1 | 107.6 | −38.2 | 49.2 | 77.3 | 273.2 | 152.0 | . . . . | . . . . | . . . . |
| Foreign........................... | c322x | 2.1 | 5.3 | — | — | — | — | — | — | — | . . . . | . . . . | . . . . |
| Net Incurrence of Liabilities.............. | c33 | −614.5 | −272.4 | 257.8 | 281.3 | −798.6 | 958.4 | 329.5 | −375.9 | 904.2 | 3,271.6 | 5,057.3 | . . . . |
| Domestic......................... | c331 | −533.8 | 37.2 | 409.3 | 492.8 | −438.5 | 892.3 | 57.3 | −459.5 | 954.7 | 1,126.7 | 823.7 | . . . . |
| Foreign........................... | c332 | −80.6 | −309.6 | −151.5 | −211.5 | −360.1 | 66.0 | 272.2 | 83.6 | −50.4 | 2,144.9 | 4,233.6 | . . . . |
| Net Cash Inflow, Fin.Act.[-32x+33].. | cnfb | −585.2 | −217.7 | 185.7 | 173.7 | −760.4 | 909.2 | 252.2 | −649.1 | 752.2 | 2,920.4 | 3,454.9 | . . . . |
| Net Change in Stock of Cash........... | cncb | 113.1 | 129.4 | 384.9 | 73.3 | 1,031.9 | 1,010.1 | 1,613.5 | 332.3 | −1,027.6 | 798.2 | 2,415.4 | . . . . |
| Stat. Discrep. [32X-33+NCB-CSD].... | ccsdz | — | 16.7 | −137.3 | −800.8 | — | 7.5 | 135.8 | −69.2 | 23.8 | 231.8 | 38.0 | . . . . |
| Memo Item:Cash Expenditure[2+31] | c2m | 7,019.2 | 8,099.7 | 9,220.0 | 10,112.0 | 10,926.8 | 13,784.6 | 15,016.6 | 17,918.6 | 22,440.5 | 23,295.9 | 25,224.1 | . . . . |
| Memo Item: Gross Debt.................. | c63 | . . . . | . . . . | . . . . | . . . . | . . . . | . . . . | . . . . | . . . . | . . . . | . . . . | . . . . | . . . . |
| **National Accounts** | | | | | *Billions of Guaranies* | | | | | | | | |
| Houseэ.Cons.Expend.,incl.NPISHs.... | 96f | 29,877.1 | 33,700.2 | 38,422.9 | 45,582.2 | 56,864.1 | 54,592.8 | 66,661.8 | 79,714.3 | 82,422.4 | 82,005.0 | 94,342.6 | . . . . |
| Government Consumption Expend... | 91f | 4,090.3 | 5,010.0 | 5,861.1 | 6,399.2 | 7,178.3 | 8,641.8 | 9,916.6 | 11,156.2 | 13,860.1 | 14,833.1 | 16,619.8 | . . . . |
| Gross Fixed Capital Formation.......... | 93e | 7,749.3 | 8,963.9 | 9,971.1 | 10,562.8 | 12,936.1 | 10,684.8 | 15,049.5 | 17,231.6 | 16,312.2 | 18,611.5 | 21,865.0 | . . . . |
| Changes in Inventories.................... | 93i | 234.6 | 218.9 | 312.1 | 388.6 | 307.8 | 226.7 | 355.0 | 401.1 | 394.4 | 629.2 | 746.7 | . . . . |
| Exports of Goods and Services......... | 90c | 25,802.9 | 30,931.1 | 34,976.3 | 39,087.0 | 43,802.2 | 40,479.9 | 51,863.0 | 53,148.4 | 54,280.3 | 64,106.2 | 62,473.2 | . . . . |
| Imports of Goods and Services (-)..... | 98c | 19,755.2 | 24,861.7 | 29,547.0 | 32,593.5 | 40,353.9 | 35,508.9 | 48,911.6 | 52,857.0 | 53,827.8 | 55,419.2 | 57,787.4 | . . . . |
| Gross Domestic Product (GDP)........ | 99b | 47,999.0 | 53,962.3 | 59,996.5 | 69,426.3 | 80,734.8 | 79,117.2 | 94,934.3 | 108,794.6 | 113,441.7 | 124,765.8 | 138,259.9 | . . . . |
| Net Primary Income from Abroad..... | 98.n | . . . . | . . . . | . . . . | . . . . | . . . . | . . . . | . . . . | . . . . | . . . . | . . . . | . . . . | . . . . |
| Gross National Income (GNI)........... | 99a | . . . . | . . . . | . . . . | . . . . | . . . . | . . . . | . . . . | . . . . | . . . . | . . . . | . . . . | . . . . |
| Consumption of Fixed Capital.......... | 99cf | 7,749.3 | 8,963.9 | 9,971.1 | 10,562.8 | 12,936.1 | 10,684.8 | 15,049.5 | 17,231.6 | 16,484.1 | . . . . | . . . . | . . . . |
| GDP Volume 1994 Prices................. | 99b.p | 17,596.5 | 17,971.9 | 18,835.9 | 19,857.1 | 21,119.8 | 20,282.3 | 22,937.8 | 23,933.5 | 23,643.7 | 27,031.7 | 28,174.2 | . . . . |
| GDP Volume (2010=100)................ | 99bvp | 76.7 | 78.4 | 82.1 | 86.6 | 92.1 | 88.4 | 100.0 | 104.3 | 103.1 | 117.8 | 122.8 | . . . . |
| GDP Deflator (2010=100)................ | 99bip | 65.9 | 72.5 | 77.0 | 84.5 | 92.4 | 94.3 | 100.0 | 109.8 | 115.9 | 111.5 | 118.6 | . . . . |
| | | | | | *Millions: Midyear Estimates* | | | | | | | | |
| Population................................ | 99z | 5.70 | 5.80 | 5.88 | 5.97 | 6.05 | 6.13 | 6.21 | 6.29 | 6.38 | 6.47 | 6.55 | 6.64 |

| | | 2004 | 2005 | 2006 | 2007 | 2008 | 2009 | 2010 | 2011 | 2012 | 2013 | 2014 | 2015 |
|---|---|---|---|---|---|---|---|---|---|---|---|---|---|
| **Exchange Rates** | | | | | | *Nuevos Soles per SDR: End of Period* | | | | | | | |
| Market Rate.................................... | aa | 5.0962 | 4.9024 | 4.8073 | 4.7344 | 4.8357 | 4.5298 | 4.3252 | 4.1391 | 3.9191 | 4.3043 | 4.3247 | 4.7260 |
| | | | | | | *Nuevos Soles per US Dollar: End of Period (ae) Period Average (rf)* | | | | | | | |
| Market Rate.................................... | ae | 3.2815 | 3.4300 | 3.1955 | 2.9960 | 3.1395 | 2.8895 | 2.8085 | 2.6960 | 2.5500 | 2.7950 | 2.9850 | 3.4105 |
| Market Rate.................................... | rf | 3.4132 | 3.2958 | 3.2740 | 3.1280 | 2.9244 | 3.0115 | 2.8251 | 2.7541 | 2.6376 | 2.7019 | 2.8390 | 3.1844 |
| **Fund Position** | | | | | | *Millions of SDRs: End of Period* | | | | | | | |
| Quota........................................... | 2f.s | 638.40 | 638.40 | 638.40 | 638.40 | 638.40 | 638.40 | 638.40 | 638.40 | 638.40 | 638.40 | 638.40 | 638.40 |
| SDR Holdings............................... | 1b.s | .23 | .34 | .61 | 2.35 | 5.82 | 524.09 | 524.16 | 524.37 | 526.34 | 531.11 | 531.21 | 531.25 |
| Reserve Position in the Fund............ | 1c.s | — | — | — | — | — | 122.00 | 122.00 | 198.50 | 210.50 | 232.50 | 240.10 | 200.15 |
| Total Fund Cred.&Loans Outstg....... | 2tl | 66.88 | 40.13 | 13.38 | — | — | — | — | — | — | — | — | — |
| SDR Allocations............................. | 1bd | 91.32 | 91.32 | 91.32 | 91.32 | 91.32 | 609.89 | 609.89 | 609.89 | 609.89 | 609.89 | 609.89 | 609.89 |
| **International Liquidity** | | | | | | *Millions of US Dollars Unless Otherwise Indicated: End of Period* | | | | | | | |
| Total Reserves minus Gold.............. | 1l.d | 12,176.4 | 13,599.4 | 16,733.3 | 26,856.5 | 30,271.5 | 32,012.6 | 42,647.9 | 47,206.3 | 62,300.3 | 64,423.2 | 61,185.3 | 60,413.1 |
| SDR Holdings............................ | 1b.d | .4 | .5 | .9 | 3.7 | 9.0 | 821.6 | 807.2 | 805.0 | 808.9 | 817.9 | 769.6 | 736.2 |
| Reserve Position in the Fund......... | 1c.d | — | — | — | — | — | 191.3 | 187.9 | 304.8 | 323.5 | 358.1 | 347.9 | 277.3 |
| Foreign Exchange....................... | 1d.d | 12,176.1 | 13,598.9 | 16,732.4 | 26,852.7 | 30,262.5 | 30,999.8 | 41,652.8 | 46,096.5 | 61,167.8 | 63,247.3 | 60,067.8 | 59,399.6 |
| Gold (Million Fine Troy Ounces)....... | 1ad | 1.115 | 1.115 | 1.115 | 1.115 | 1.115 | 1.115 | 1.115 | 1.115 | 1.115 | 1.115 | 1.115 | 1.115 |
| Gold (National Valuation)................ | 1and | 488.7 | 575.9 | 705.9 | 927.8 | 982.6 | 1,217.7 | 1,564.9 | 1,722.3 | 1,866.5 | 1,339.0 | 1,319.7 | 1,180.7 |
| Monetary Authorities: Other Liabs..... | 4..d | 984.2 | 919.3 | 971.3 | 1,917.8 | 1,682.4 | 890.1 | 794.5 | 671.0 | 657.9 | 620.7 | 580.1 | 607.5 |
| Deposit Money Banks: Assets.......... | 7a.d | 1,023.1 | 1,288.4 | 1,604.5 | 1,379.0 | 2,139.3 | 2,464.8 | 2,588.5 | 2,980.9 | 3,264.5 | 3,624.2 | 4,093.8 | 3,523.4 |
| Deposit Money Banks: Liabs............ | 7b.d | 830.2 | 1,162.1 | 1,003.7 | 4,616.1 | 5,507.8 | 5,156.1 | 7,925.3 | 10,196.5 | 15,099.0 | 14,324.5 | 15,028.9 | 14,392.4 |
| Other Banking Insts.: Assets........... | 7e.d | — | — | — | — | — | — | — | — | .... | .... | .... | .... |
| Other Banking Insts.: Liabs.............. | 7f.d | — | — | — | — | — | — | — | — | .... | .... | .... | .... |
| **Monetary Authorities** | | | | | | *Millions of Nuevos Soles: End of Period* | | | | | | | |
| Foreign Assets............................. | 11 | 44,751 | 51,617 | 58,591 | 86,332 | 101,242 | 98,835 | 126,897 | 134,610 | 165,877 | 185,784 | 187,596 | 211,977 |
| Claims on Central Government........ | 12a | 39 | — | — | — | — | — | — | — | 817 | 1,569 | 1,998 | 2,813 |
| Claims on Private Sector................ | 12d | — | — | — | — | — | — | — | — | — | — | 521 | 388 |
| Claims on Deposit Money Banks...... | 12e | — | 2,850 | — | — | 5,412 | — | — | — | — | 950 | 9,379 | 29,717 |
| Claims on Other Banking Insts......... | 12f | — | — | — | — | — | — | — | — | — | — | — | — |
| Reserve Money............................. | 14 | 26,218 | 34,157 | 35,147 | 44,792 | 55,022 | 50,015 | 86,743 | 77,442 | 97,132 | 104,775 | 107,658 | 134,052 |
| of which: Currency Outside DMBs.. | 14a | 8,036 | 10,116 | 11,796 | 14,985 | 17,507 | 19,497 | 24,450 | 27,643 | 32,677 | 35,705 | 39,785 | 41,358 |
| Time, Savings,& Fgn.Currency Dep... | 15 | 192 | 195 | 246 | 195 | 91 | 257 | 354 | 370 | 431 | 831 | 1,857 | 2,285 |
| Liabs. of Central Bank: Securities..... | 16ac | 8,100 | 8,728 | 7,980 | 18,337 | 16,132 | 13,680 | 3,687 | 12,858 | 19,676 | 21,253 | 17,978 | 22,790 |
| Restricted Deposits........................ | 16b | — | 1 | 1 | 1 | 1 | 1 | 1 | 1 | 1 | 1 | 1 | 1 |
| Foreign Liabilities.......................... | 16c | 4,034 | 3,798 | 3,612 | 6,186 | 5,724 | 5,336 | 4,872 | 4,340 | 4,068 | 4,368 | 4,362 | 4,954 |
| Central Government Deposits.......... | 16d | 4,835 | 5,295 | 9,004 | 14,317 | 22,073 | 24,674 | 28,083 | 40,506 | 52,560 | 57,322 | 64,231 | 70,070 |
| Capital Accounts........................... | 17a | 592 | 598 | 1,317 | 2,429 | 3,697 | 4,167 | 3,609 | 3,078 | 1,851 | −450 | −592 | 738 |
| Other Items (Net).......................... | 17r | 819 | 1,696 | 1,285 | 74 | 3,914 | 706 | −452 | −3,985 | −9,024 | 205 | 3,999 | 10,006 |
| **Deposit Money Banks** | | | | | | *Millions of Nuevos Soles: End of Period* | | | | | | | |
| Reserves..................................... | 20 | 12,432 | 19,425 | 19,243 | 26,395 | 34,813 | 29,640 | 58,883 | 47,408 | 61,990 | 66,776 | 70,277 | 95,543 |
| Claims on Mon.Author.:Securities.... | 20c | 5,101 | 6,808 | 6,531 | 15,212 | 14,575 | 11,921 | 3,278 | 10,020 | 11,532 | 13,809 | 10,918 | 17,164 |
| Foreign Assets............................. | 21 | 3,356 | 4,419 | 5,134 | 4,137 | 6,717 | 7,123 | 7,274 | 8,048 | 8,324 | 10,148 | 12,200 | 12,015 |
| Claims on Central Government........ | 22a | 6,144 | 6,554 | 5,938 | 6,422 | 6,780 | 10,013 | 7,544 | 8,148 | 7,038 | 9,749 | 12,472 | 15,592 |
| Claims on State & Local Govts......... | 22b | 313 | 182 | 99 | 153 | 234 | 314 | 262 | 294 | 279 | 380 | 254 | 410 |
| Claims on Official Entities................ | 22bx | 332 | 406 | 265 | 278 | 1,045 | 1,076 | 1,172 | 1,312 | 1,357 | 2,469 | 3,626 | 4,304 |
| Claims on Private Sector................. | 22d | 40,824 | 47,809 | 50,777 | 67,701 | 90,613 | 91,768 | 104,896 | 127,594 | 143,382 | 171,752 | 194,417 | 225,842 |
| Claims on Other Banking Insts......... | 22f | — | — | — | — | — | — | — | — | — | — | — | — |
| Demand Deposits.......................... | 24 | 9,728 | 11,400 | 16,588 | 25,164 | 27,556 | 29,713 | 32,829 | 37,541 | 45,752 | 50,239 | 55,585 | 58,488 |
| Time, Savings,& Fgn.Currency Dep... | 25 | 39,789 | 48,023 | 50,588 | 59,664 | 79,225 | 80,110 | 97,671 | 105,708 | 114,524 | 143,587 | 150,195 | 178,221 |
| Bonds.......................................... | 26ab | 466 | 511 | 874 | 1,771 | 2,219 | 2,548 | 2,682 | 3,156 | 4,309 | 4,084 | 4,967 | 5,186 |
| Foreign Liabilities.......................... | 26c | 2,723 | 3,986 | 3,212 | 13,848 | 17,294 | 14,901 | 22,270 | 27,531 | 38,503 | 40,109 | 44,786 | 49,078 |
| Central Government Deposits.......... | 26d | 4,711 | 6,277 | 4,799 | 7,046 | 7,479 | 7,224 | 7,979 | 7,476 | 6,865 | 8,628 | 6,616 | 9,795 |
| Credit from Monetary Authorities..... | 26g | — | 2,850 | — | — | 5,412 | — | — | — | — | 950 | 9,379 | 29,717 |
| Capital Accounts........................... | 27a | 21,468 | 22,097 | 22,201 | 24,515 | 28,955 | 31,364 | 34,756 | 37,123 | 40,814 | 44,983 | 50,381 | 59,209 |
| Other Items (Net).......................... | 27r | −10,384 | −9,540 | −10,275 | −11,710 | −13,364 | −14,004 | −14,879 | −15,708 | −16,863 | −17,497 | −17,745 | −18,824 |
| **Monetary Survey** | | | | | | *Millions of Nuevos Soles: End of Period* | | | | | | | |
| Foreign Assets (Net)....................... | 31n | 41,350 | 48,253 | 56,902 | 70,434 | 84,941 | 85,721 | 107,029 | 110,788 | 131,631 | 151,455 | 150,647 | 169,960 |
| Domestic Credit............................. | 32 | 38,105 | 43,379 | 43,276 | 53,192 | 69,119 | 71,274 | 77,811 | 89,366 | 93,448 | 119,969 | 142,441 | 169,484 |
| Claims on Central Govt. (Net)......... | 32an | −3,363 | −5,018 | −7,865 | −14,941 | −22,772 | −21,884 | −28,518 | −39,834 | −51,569 | −54,632 | −56,377 | −61,460 |
| Claims on State & Local Govts....... | 32b | 313 | 182 | 99 | 153 | 234 | 314 | 262 | 294 | 279 | 380 | 254 | 410 |
| Claims on Official Entities............. | 32bx | 332 | 406 | 265 | 278 | 1,045 | 1,076 | 1,172 | 1,312 | 1,357 | 2,469 | 3,626 | 4,304 |
| Claims on Private Sector............... | 32d | 40,824 | 47,809 | 50,777 | 67,701 | 90,613 | 91,768 | 104,896 | 127,594 | 143,382 | 171,752 | 194,938 | 226,230 |
| Claims on Other Banking Insts....... | 32f | — | — | — | — | — | — | — | — | — | — | — | — |
| Money......................................... | 34 | 23,514 | 26,132 | 32,492 | 43,561 | 47,765 | 50,088 | 60,690 | 67,811 | 82,850 | 91,053 | 97,465 | 100,914 |
| Quasi-Money................................. | 35 | 39,981 | 48,217 | 50,834 | 59,859 | 79,316 | 80,367 | 98,025 | 106,078 | 114,955 | 144,418 | 152,052 | 180,506 |
| Bonds.......................................... | 36ab | 466 | 511 | 874 | 1,771 | 2,219 | 2,548 | 2,682 | 3,156 | 4,309 | 4,084 | 4,967 | 5,186 |
| Liabs. of Central Bank:Securities...... | 36ac | 2,999 | 1,920 | 1,449 | 3,126 | 1,557 | 1,759 | 409 | 2,837 | 8,144 | 7,444 | 7,060 | 5,626 |
| Restricted Deposits........................ | 36b | — | 1 | 1 | 1 | 1 | 1 | 1 | 1 | 1 | 1 | 1 | 1 |
| Capital Accounts........................... | 37a | 22,060 | 22,695 | 23,518 | 26,944 | 32,653 | 35,531 | 38,364 | 40,200 | 42,664 | 44,533 | 49,789 | 59,947 |
| Other Items (Net)........................... | 37r | −9,565 | −7,844 | −8,990 | −11,636 | −9,450 | −13,299 | −15,331 | −19,929 | −27,843 | −20,109 | −18,246 | −12,735 |
| Money plus Quasi-Money................. | 35l | 63,494 | 74,349 | 83,326 | 103,420 | 127,081 | 130,455 | 158,714 | 173,889 | 197,805 | 235,471 | 249,517 | 281,420 |

# Peru   293

| | | 2004 | 2005 | 2006 | 2007 | 2008 | 2009 | 2010 | 2011 | 2012 | 2013 | 2014 | 2015 |
|---|---|---|---|---|---|---|---|---|---|---|---|---|---|
| **Other Banking Institutions** | | | | | | *Millions of Nuevos Soles: End of Period* | | | | | | | | |
| Reserves............................... | 40 | — | — | — | — | — | — | — | — | .... | .... | .... | .... |
| Claims on Mon.Author.:Securities.... | 40c | — | — | — | — | — | — | — | — | .... | .... | .... | .... |
| Foreign Assets................................. | 41 | — | — | — | — | — | — | — | — | .... | .... | .... | .... |
| Claims on Central Government........ | 42a | — | — | — | — | — | — | — | — | .... | .... | .... | .... |
| Claims on Official Entities............... | 42bx | — | — | — | — | — | — | — | — | .... | .... | .... | .... |
| Claims on Private Sector.................. | 42d | 709 | 752 | 761 | 765 | 838 | 817 | 831 | 810 | .... | .... | .... | .... |
| Claims on Deposit Money Banks...... | 42e | 18 | 2 | 108 | 81 | 52 | 26 | 20 | 27 | .... | .... | .... | .... |
| Demand Deposits........................... | 44 | — | — | 22 | 20 | 31 | 21 | 35 | 16 | .... | .... | .... | .... |
| Time, Savings,& Fgn.Currency Dep... | 45 | 27 | 28 | 27 | 27 | 27 | 26 | 26 | 26 | .... | .... | .... | .... |
| Bonds........................................... | 46ab | — | — | — | — | — | — | — | — | .... | .... | .... | .... |
| Foreign Liabilities........................... | 46c | — | — | — | — | — | — | — | — | .... | .... | .... | .... |
| Central Government Deposits.......... | 46d | — | — | — | — | — | — | — | — | .... | .... | .... | .... |
| Credit from Monetary Authorities..... | 46g | — | — | — | — | — | — | — | — | .... | .... | .... | .... |
| Credit from Deposit Money Banks.... | 46h | — | — | — | 15 | 7 | 5 | 4 | 4 | .... | .... | .... | .... |
| Capital Accounts............................. | 47a | 1,101 | 1,139 | 1,235 | 1,211 | 1,243 | 1,201 | 1,195 | 1,186 | .... | .... | .... | .... |
| Other Items (Net)............................ | 47r | −401 | −413 | −415 | −425 | −416 | −411 | −409 | −395 | .... | .... | .... | .... |
| **Banking Survey** | | | | | | *Millions of Nuevos Soles: End of Period* | | | | | | | | |
| Foreign Assets (Net)........................ | 51n | 41,350 | 48,253 | 56,902 | 70,434 | 84,941 | 85,721 | 107,029 | 110,788 | .... | .... | .... | .... |
| Domestic Credit............................... | 52 | 38,814 | 44,131 | 44,037 | 53,957 | 69,958 | 72,091 | 78,642 | 90,176 | .... | .... | .... | .... |
| Claims on Central Govt. (Net)........ | 52an | −3,363 | −5,018 | −7,865 | −14,941 | −22,772 | −21,884 | −28,518 | −39,834 | .... | .... | .... | .... |
| Claims on State & Local Govts....... | 52b | 313 | 182 | 99 | 153 | 234 | 314 | 262 | 294 | .... | .... | .... | .... |
| Claims on Official Entities.............. | 52bx | 332 | 406 | 265 | 278 | 1,045 | 1,076 | 1,172 | 1,312 | .... | .... | .... | .... |
| Claims on Private Sector................ | 52d | 41,532 | 48,561 | 51,538 | 68,467 | 91,451 | 92,585 | 105,727 | 128,404 | .... | .... | .... | .... |
| Liquid Liabilities............................. | 55l | 63,522 | 74,377 | 83,374 | 103,466 | 127,139 | 130,503 | 158,775 | 173,931 | .... | .... | .... | .... |
| Bonds........................................... | 56ab | 466 | 511 | 874 | 1,771 | 2,219 | 2,548 | 2,682 | 3,156 | .... | .... | .... | .... |
| Liabs. of Central Bank:Securities...... | 56ac | 2,999 | 1,920 | 1,449 | 3,126 | 1,557 | 1,759 | 409 | 2,837 | .... | .... | .... | .... |
| Restricted Deposits........................ | 56b | — | 1 | 1 | 1 | 1 | 1 | 1 | 1 | 1 | 1 | 1 | 1 |
| Capital Accounts............................. | 57a | 23,161 | 23,835 | 24,754 | 28,155 | 33,896 | 36,732 | 39,559 | 41,386 | .... | .... | .... | .... |
| Other Items (Net)............................ | 57r | −9,984 | −8,259 | −9,513 | −12,127 | −9,912 | −13,731 | −15,756 | −20,347 | .... | .... | .... | .... |
| **Money (National Definitions)** | | | | | | *Millions of Nuevos Soles: End of Period* | | | | | | | | |
| Monetary Base............................... | 19ma | 9,327 | 11,724 | 13,864 | 17,779 | 22,311 | 23,548 | 34,208 | 39,967 | 52,735 | 51,937 | 53,865 | 51,291 |
| Money............................................ | 59maj | 12,420 | 15,489 | 18,975 | 24,476 | 28,930 | 33,147 | 42,651 | 48,817 | 57,247 | 62,229 | 68,382 | 71,324 |
| Quasi-Money in National Currency... | 59mal | 9,027 | 12,775 | 14,364 | 20,390 | 28,153 | 32,178 | 42,715 | 50,202 | 65,488 | 74,747 | 83,167 | 84,846 |
| Quasi-Money in Foreign Currency..... | 59mam | 28,197 | 32,840 | 34,776 | 38,952 | 48,165 | 47,097 | 51,467 | 57,943 | 54,357 | 67,163 | 72,080 | 93,231 |
| Liquidity in National Currency.......... | 59mfa | 21,446 | 28,264 | 33,340 | 44,866 | 57,083 | 65,324 | 85,366 | 99,019 | 122,734 | 136,976 | 151,549 | 156,170 |
| Liquidity........................................ | 59mf | 49,643 | 61,104 | 68,116 | 83,818 | 105,249 | 112,422 | 136,832 | 156,962 | 177,091 | 204,139 | 223,629 | 249,401 |
| **Interest Rates** | | | | | | *Percent Per Annum* | | | | | | | | |
| Central Bank Policy Rate (EOP)........ | 60 | 3.00 | 3.25 | 4.50 | 5.00 | 6.50 | 1.25 | 3.00 | 4.25 | 4.25 | 4.00 | 3.50 | 3.75 |
| Discount Rate (End of Period).......... | 60.a | 3.75 | 4.00 | 5.25 | 5.75 | 7.25 | 2.05 | 3.80 | 5.05 | 5.05 | 4.80 | 4.30 | 4.30 |
| Discount Rate (Fgn.Cur.) (EOP)........ | 60.af | .... | 5.36 | 6.35 | 6.00 | 2.01 | 1.23 | 1.26 | 1.28 | 1.21 | 1.17 | 1.16 | 1.36 |
| Money Market Rate.......................... | 60b | 3.00 | 3.34 | 4.51 | 4.99 | 6.54 | 1.24 | 2.98 | 4.24 | 4.24 | 4.09 | 3.80 | 3.77 |
| Money Market Rate (Fgn. Cur.)......... | 60b.f | 2.19 | 4.19 | 5.37 | 5.92 | 1.02 | .21 | 1.14 | .28 | 1.16 | .15 | .16 | .18 |
| Savings Rate................................... | 60k | 1.27 | 1.20 | 1.27 | 1.46 | 1.45 | 1.06 | .58 | .56 | .58 | .53 | .48 | .53 |
| Savings Rate (Fgn. Currency)............ | 60k.f | .60 | .56 | .71 | .81 | .82 | .43 | .35 | .30 | .28 | .25 | .21 | .17 |
| Deposit Rate................................... | 60l | 2.42 | 2.59 | 3.21 | 3.23 | 3.51 | 2.83 | 1.54 | 2.33 | 2.46 | 2.32 | 2.31 | 2.29 |
| Deposit Rate (Fgn. Currency)............ | 60l.f | 1.24 | 1.82 | 2.16 | 2.50 | 1.92 | .91 | .76 | .66 | .89 | .41 | .36 | .33 |
| Lending Rate.................................. | 60p | 24.67 | 25.53 | 23.93 | 22.86 | 23.67 | 21.04 | 18.98 | 18.68 | 19.24 | 18.14 | 15.74 | 16.11 |
| Lending Rate (Fgn. Currency)........... | 60p.f | 9.19 | 10.41 | 10.80 | 10.45 | 10.54 | 8.63 | 8.54 | 7.76 | 8.15 | 8.01 | 7.55 | 7.88 |
| **Prices, Production, Labor** | | | | | | *Index Numbers (2010=100): Period Averages* | | | | | | | | |
| Share Prices (End of Month)............. | 62.ep | 18.6 | 26.5 | 52.7 | 117.1 | 81.0 | 73.0 | 100.0 | 124.7 | 128.5 | 103.6 | 95.1 | 71.6 |
| Wholesale Prices............................. | 63 | 84.8 | † 86.8 | 89.6 | 91.8 | 100.0 | 98.2 | 100.0 | 106.3 | 108.2 | 108.6 | 110.6 | 112.6 |
| Consumer Prices............................. | 64 | 85.7 | 87.1 | 88.9 | 90.5 | † 95.7 | 98.5 | 100.0 | 103.4 | 107.1 | 110.2 | 113.7 | 117.8 |
| Manufacturing Production................ | 66ey | 69.5 | 74.6 | 80.2 | † 89.1 | 96.8 | 90.3 | 100.0 | 108.6 | 110.1 | 116.4 | .... | .... |
| Industrial Employment.................... | 67 | 100.3 | 105.9 | 112.9 | 123.9 | 101.1 | 94.6 | 100.0 | 106.0 | 105.9 | 106.3 | | |
| | | | | | | *Number in Thousands: Period Averages* | | | | | | | | |
| Labor Force.................................... | 67d | 4,104 | 4,120 | 4,219 | 4,384 | 4,413 | 4,517 | 4,707 | 4,786 | 4,816 | 4,890 | 4,938 | 5,007 |
| Employment................................... | 67e | 3,717 | 3,725 | 3,862 | 4,015 | 4,044 | 4,138 | 4,335 | 4,415 | 4,489 | 4,599 | 4,618 | 4,685 |
| Unemployment............................... | 67c | 390 | 393 | 360 | 368 | 370 | 379 | 375 | 368 | 329 | 289 | 294 | 322 |
| Unemployment Rate (%)................. | 67r | 9.4 | 9.6 | 8.5 | 8.4 | 8.4 | 8.4 | 7.9 | 7.8 | 6.8 | 5.9 | 6.0 | 6.4 |
| **Intl. Transactions & Positions** | | | | | | *Millions of US Dollars* | | | | | | | | |
| Exports.......................................... | 70..d | 12,809.2 | 17,367.7 | 23,830.1 | 27,881.6 | 31,529.4 | 26,884.8 | 35,564.8 | 46,117.5 | 45,599.8 | 41,484.0 | 37,869.8 | 33,970.0 |
| Imports, c.i.f................................... | 71..d | 11,774.9 | 14,500.7 | 17,876.2 | 23,496.2 | 29,889.4 | 20,944.4 | 30,104.5 | 37,558.4 | 41,093.0 | 41,517.0 | 42,679.6 | .... |
| Imports, f.o.b................................. | 71.vd | 9,812.4 | 12,084.0 | 14,896.8 | 19,580.2 | 28,372.6 | 21,006.2 | 28,817.5 | 37,112.2 | 41,089.4 | 42,199.4 | 40,766.3 | .... |
| | | | | | | *2010=100* | | | | | | | | |
| Volume of Exports.......................... | 72 | 80.2 | 90.9 | 86.2 | 94.7 | 102.5 | 102.3 | 100.0 | 99.9 | 108.8 | 106.7 | 108.1 | .... |
| | | | | | | *2010=100: Indexes of Unit Values in US Dollars* | | | | | | | | |
| Unit Value of Exports/Export Prices.. | 74..d | 39.9 | 52.0 | 85.4 | 94.0 | 88.4 | 68.6 | 100.0 | 120.2 | 109.5 | 105.1 | 96.6 | .... |

| | | 2004 | 2005 | 2006 | 2007 | 2008 | 2009 | 2010 | 2011 | 2012 | 2013 | 2014 | 2015 |
|---|---|---|---|---|---|---|---|---|---|---|---|---|---|
| **Balance of Payments** | | | | | | | *Millions of US Dollars* | | | | | | |
| A. Current Account* | 109bx | 19.3 | 1,147.6 | 2,872.5 | 1,460.3 | −5,317.6 | −722.9 | −3,782.1 | −3,176.6 | −5,236.9 | −8,473.9 | −8,031.0 | −8,429.9 |
| Goods, credit (exports) | 1a9cx | 12,806.7 | 17,365.6 | 23,830.0 | 28,093.4 | 31,018.4 | 26,961.5 | 35,564.8 | 46,376.0 | 47,410.6 | 42,860.0 | 39,532.6 | 34,156.9 |
| Goods, debit (imports) | 1a9dx | 9,582.5 | 11,782.2 | 14,468.1 | 19,257.9 | 28,078.2 | 20,808.1 | 28,390.3 | 36,448.8 | 40,396.3 | 41,595.1 | 40,478.4 | 36,994.7 |
| Balance on goods | 1a9bx | 3,224.2 | 5,583.4 | 9,361.9 | 8,835.5 | 2,940.2 | 6,153.4 | 7,174.6 | 9,927.2 | 7,014.3 | 1,264.8 | −945.8 | −2,837.8 |
| Services, credit (exports) | 1b9cx | 1,782.0 | 2,015.8 | 2,295.4 | 2,830.6 | 3,288.3 | 3,439.1 | 3,273.1 | 3,565.3 | 4,181.0 | 5,165.4 | 5,547.6 | 5,861.8 |
| Services, debit (imports) | 1b9dx | 2,733.7 | 3,147.4 | 3,408.4 | 4,354.5 | 5,714.8 | 4,817.7 | 6,043.6 | 6,512.4 | 7,339.6 | 7,619.1 | 7,678.5 | 7,962.6 |
| Balance on Goods & Services | 1z9bx | 2,272.6 | 4,451.8 | 8,248.9 | 7,311.5 | 513.7 | 4,774.8 | 4,404.0 | 6,980.0 | 3,855.7 | −1,188.8 | −3,076.7 | −4,938.6 |
| Primary income: credit | 1c9cx | 331.6 | 624.9 | 1,050.0 | 1,586.6 | 1,837.0 | 1,400.0 | 1,148.5 | 1,111.2 | 1,151.7 | 1,222.2 | 1,211.6 | 1,011.0 |
| Primary income: debit | 1c9dx | 4,017.5 | 5,701.1 | 8,611.6 | 9,945.4 | 10,611.2 | 9,785.1 | 12,360.6 | 14,468.5 | 13,550.9 | 11,853.2 | 10,540.1 | 7,833.5 |
| Balance on gds, serv. & prim. inc. | 1y9bx | −1,413.3 | −624.3 | 687.3 | −1,047.3 | −8,260.6 | −3,610.3 | −6,808.1 | −6,377.3 | −8,543.4 | −11,819.9 | −12,405.2 | −11,761.1 |
| Secondary income: credit | 1d9ca | 1,438.8 | 1,781.5 | 2,194.7 | 2,517.4 | 2,949.8 | 2,894.4 | 3,033.1 | 3,211.6 | 3,313.8 | 3,353.6 | 4,382.3 | 3,339.6 |
| Secondary income: debit | 1d9da | 6.2 | 9.5 | 9.5 | 9.7 | 6.9 | 7.0 | 7.0 | 10.8 | 7.3 | 7.7 | 8.1 | 8.5 |
| B. Capital Account* | 209ba | 27.4 | 6.3 | 6.1 | 3.0 | 11.9 | 7.6 | 7.3 | 7.6 | 8.8 | 12.4 | 12.4 | 5.9 |
| Capital account: credit | 209ca | 27.4 | 6.3 | 6.1 | 3.0 | 11.9 | 7.6 | 7.3 | 7.6 | 8.8 | 12.4 | 12.4 | 5.9 |
| Capital account: debit | 209da | — | — | — | — | — | — | — | — | — | — | — | — |
| Balance on current & capital acct. | 129ba | 46.7 | 1,153.9 | 2,878.6 | 1,463.4 | −5,305.7 | −715.3 | −3,774.8 | −3,169.0 | −5,228.1 | −8,461.6 | −8,018.6 | −8,424.0 |
| C. Financial Account* | 309na | −2,285.9 | −23.8 | −844.0 | −9,136.2 | −9,017.1 | −4,113.5 | −13,391.1 | −8,738.5 | −20,196.0 | −10,168.3 | −5,648.4 | −9,330.6 |
| Direct investment: assets | 3a9aa | — | — | — | 65.6 | 735.8 | 410.7 | 265.9 | 147.2 | 77.7 | 137.1 | 96.0 | 126.8 |
| Equity & investment fund shares | 3aaaa | — | — | — | 65.6 | 735.8 | 410.7 | 265.9 | 147.2 | 77.7 | 137.1 | 96.0 | 126.8 |
| Debt instruments | 3abaa | — | — | — | | | | | | | | | |
| Direct investment: liabilities | 3a9la | 1,599.0 | 2,578.7 | 3,466.5 | 5,491.0 | 6,923.7 | 6,430.7 | 8,454.6 | 7,664.9 | 11,917.9 | 9,297.8 | 7,884.5 | 6,861.2 |
| Equity & investment fund shares | 3aala | 1,599.0 | 2,578.7 | 3,226.9 | 4,567.4 | 6,267.4 | 7,212.9 | 7,762.1 | 5,548.4 | 12,426.3 | 6,223.2 | 5,464.2 | 6,007.2 |
| Debt instruments | 3abla | — | — | 239.6 | 923.5 | 656.3 | −782.2 | 692.5 | 2,116.6 | −508.4 | 3,074.6 | 2,420.4 | 854.0 |
| Portfolio investment: assets | 3b9aa | 424.8 | 817.0 | 1,991.9 | 390.3 | −461.5 | 3,057.6 | 1,144.7 | 1,736.6 | 2,768.4 | 1,159.9 | 4,664.1 | −94.6 |
| Equity & investment fund shares | 3baaa | 425.8 | 817.7 | 1,992.7 | 391.1 | −460.8 | 3,058.3 | 1,145.5 | 1,742.1 | 2,769.0 | 1,159.9 | 4,664.1 | −94.6 |
| Debt securities | 3bbaa | −1.0 | −.7 | −.8 | −.7 | −.7 | −.7 | −.8 | −5.6 | −.6 | — | — | — |
| Portfolio investment: liabilities | 3b9la | 1,244.4 | 2,578.7 | 380.3 | 4,029.6 | −1.0 | 757.6 | 6,357.8 | 1,054.4 | 4,971.2 | 6,330.9 | 3,639.6 | 3,043.5 |
| Equity & investment fund shares | 3bala | −46.9 | 769.1 | −45.0 | 69.7 | 84.7 | 46.7 | 86.6 | 147.1 | −142.4 | 584.8 | −79.5 | −59.7 |
| Debt securities | 3bbla | 1,291.4 | 1,809.6 | 425.3 | 3,959.9 | −85.8 | 710.8 | 6,271.2 | 907.3 | 5,113.7 | 5,746.2 | 3,719.1 | 3,103.2 |
| Fin. der.& empl.stk.ops.(ESOs): net. | 3c9na | .... | .... | .... | .... | .... | .... | .... | .... | .... | .... | .... | .... |
| Fin. der. & ESOs.: assets | 3c9aa | .... | .... | .... | .... | .... | .... | .... | .... | .... | .... | .... | .... |
| Fin. der. & ESOs.: liabilities | 3c9la | .... | .... | .... | .... | .... | .... | .... | .... | .... | .... | .... | .... |
| Other investment: assets | 3d9aa | −13.7 | 1,083.8 | 508.5 | 443.3 | −859.6 | −116.0 | 1,948.7 | 1,243.6 | −297.1 | 829.5 | 1,769.1 | 1,994.6 |
| Other equity | 3daaa | .... | .... | .... | .... | .... | .... | .... | .... | .... | .... | .... | .... |
| Debt instruments | 3dzaa | −13.7 | 1,083.8 | 508.5 | 443.3 | −859.6 | −116.0 | 1,948.7 | 1,243.6 | −297.1 | 829.5 | 1,769.1 | 1,994.6 |
| Other investment: liabilities | 3d9la | −146.4 | −3,232.9 | −502.4 | 514.9 | 1,509.1 | 277.6 | 1,938.0 | 3,146.5 | 5,856.0 | −3,333.8 | 653.4 | 1,452.7 |
| Other equity | 3dala | .... | .... | .... | .... | .... | .... | .... | .... | .... | .... | .... | .... |
| Debt instruments | 3dzla | −146.4 | −3,232.9 | −502.4 | 514.9 | 1,509.1 | 277.6 | 1,938.0 | 3,146.5 | 5,856.0 | −3,333.8 | 653.4 | 1,452.7 |
| Curr.+ cap.− finan. acct. balance | 4y9na | 2,332.6 | 1,177.6 | 3,722.6 | 10,599.6 | 3,711.4 | 3,398.2 | 9,616.3 | 5,569.6 | 14,968.0 | 1,706.7 | −2,370.2 | 906.6 |
| D. Net Errors and Omissions | 409na | 123.0 | 233.6 | −501.1 | −256.1 | −254.6 | −1,496.1 | 1,353.9 | −885.5 | 180.6 | −57.1 | −937.3 | −1,675.8 |
| E. Reserves and Related Items | 4z9na | 2,455.7 | 1,411.3 | 3,221.5 | 10,343.5 | 3,456.7 | 1,902.2 | 10,970.2 | 4,684.0 | 15,148.6 | 1,649.6 | −3,307.5 | −769.2 |
| Reserve assets | 3e9aa | 2,442.4 | 1,471.6 | 3,209.1 | 10,390.2 | 3,513.2 | 1,938.3 | 10,989.2 | 4,716.8 | 15,185.7 | 1,658.7 | −3,286.7 | −769.2 |
| Credit and loans from the IMF | 3dcla | −39.6 | −39.9 | −39.1 | −20.0 | — | — | — | — | — | — | — | |
| Exceptional financing | 409la | 26.3 | 100.2 | 26.7 | 66.8 | 56.5 | 36.1 | 19.0 | 32.8 | 37.1 | 9.1 | 20.8 | — |

*Excludes components in group E

| **International Investment Position** | | | | | | | *Millions of US Dollars* | | | | | | |
|---|---|---|---|---|---|---|---|---|---|---|---|---|---|
| Assets | 809aa | 21,204.4 | 24,962.4 | 32,747.0 | 47,615.4 | 48,252.7 | 55,644.5 | 72,093.8 | 79,977.4 | 100,212.3 | 102,081.9 | 103,320.2 | 102,669.8 |
| Direct investment | 8a9aa | 873.8 | 1,047.4 | 1,475.5 | 2,284.2 | 1,694.1 | 2,282.2 | 3,318.8 | 3,098.8 | 3,986.2 | 3,657.2 | 4,127.4 | 2,815.0 |
| Equity & investment fund shares | 8aaaa | 873.8 | 1,047.4 | 1,475.5 | 2,284.2 | 1,694.1 | 2,282.2 | 3,318.8 | 3,098.8 | 3,986.2 | 3,657.2 | 4,127.4 | 2,815.0 |
| Debt instruments | 8abaa | .... | .... | .... | .... | .... | .... | .... | .... | .... | .... | .... | .... |
| Portfolio investment | 8b9aa | 5,237.9 | 6,643.4 | 9,636.8 | 12,119.6 | 10,323.2 | 14,580.7 | 17,199.8 | 19,374.3 | 23,476.3 | 24,384.7 | 28,253.6 | 28,637.1 |
| Equity & investment fund shares | 8baaa | 4,346.1 | 5,575.6 | 8,380.2 | 10,738.9 | 9,006.1 | 13,173.9 | 15,860.1 | 18,018.2 | 22,010.9 | 22,777.3 | 26,120.2 | 25,580.7 |
| Debt securities | 8bbaa | 891.9 | 1,067.8 | 1,256.6 | 1,380.7 | 1,317.2 | 1,406.8 | 1,339.7 | 1,356.1 | 1,465.4 | 1,607.4 | 2,133.4 | 3,056.4 |
| Fin. der.(oth.than reserves) & ESOs | 8c9aa | .... | .... | .... | .... | .... | .... | .... | .... | .... | .... | .... | .... |
| Other investment | 8d9aa | 2,453.3 | 3,160.7 | 4,314.8 | 5,501.3 | 5,012.4 | 5,612.6 | 7,435.0 | 8,651.9 | 8,710.6 | 8,339.4 | 8,595.5 | 9,691.8 |
| Other equity | 8daaa | .... | .... | .... | .... | .... | .... | .... | .... | .... | .... | .... | .... |
| Debt instruments | 8dzaa | 2,453.3 | 3,160.7 | 4,314.8 | 5,501.3 | 5,012.4 | 5,612.6 | 7,435.0 | 8,651.9 | 8,710.6 | 8,339.4 | 8,595.5 | 9,691.8 |
| Reserve assets | 8e9aa | 12,639.4 | 14,110.8 | 17,320.0 | 27,710.4 | 31,223.0 | 33,168.9 | 44,140.3 | 48,852.4 | 64,039.3 | 65,700.6 | 62,343.7 | 61,525.9 |
| Liabilities | 809la | 48,624.5 | 51,380.9 | 58,562.1 | 78,923.7 | 78,638.7 | 90,268.4 | 115,849.2 | 121,507.5 | 147,021.1 | 155,647.0 | 164,320.7 | 168,143.7 |
| Direct investment | 8a9la | 13,310.5 | 15,889.2 | 20,484.4 | 26,807.7 | 32,340.3 | 34,521.2 | 42,975.9 | 50,640.8 | 62,558.7 | 71,856.5 | 79,706.7 | 86,114.4 |
| Equity & investment fund shares | 8aala | 13,310.5 | 15,889.2 | 20,484.4 | 26,807.7 | 32,340.3 | 34,521.2 | 42,975.9 | 50,640.8 | 62,558.7 | 71,856.5 | 79,706.7 | 86,114.4 |
| Debt instruments | 8abla | .... | .... | .... | .... | .... | .... | .... | .... | .... | .... | .... | .... |
| Portfolio investment | 8b9la | 10,963.2 | 15,316.2 | 17,851.2 | 28,780.8 | 19,451.0 | 28,693.5 | 41,324.9 | 36,075.7 | 44,058.9 | 46,514.1 | 46,163.2 | 41,596.1 |
| Equity & investment fund shares | 8bala | 3,928.4 | 6,704.6 | 9,042.8 | 19,077.4 | 11,319.5 | 19,633.7 | 28,260.3 | 21,840.4 | 24,149.4 | 22,020.9 | 19,219.4 | 12,940.4 |
| Debt securities | 8bbla | 7,034.8 | 8,611.6 | 8,808.4 | 9,703.5 | 8,131.5 | 9,059.8 | 13,064.6 | 14,235.4 | 19,909.5 | 24,493.2 | 26,943.8 | 28,655.8 |
| Fin. der.(oth.than reserves) & ESOs | 8c9la | .... | .... | .... | .... | .... | .... | .... | .... | .... | .... | .... | .... |
| Other investment | 8d9la | 24,350.9 | 20,175.6 | 20,226.5 | 23,335.2 | 26,847.3 | 27,053.7 | 31,548.5 | 34,791.0 | 40,403.5 | 37,276.5 | 38,450.8 | 40,433.1 |
| Other equity | 8dala | .... | .... | .... | .... | .... | .... | .... | .... | .... | .... | .... | .... |
| Debt instruments | 8dzla | 24,350.9 | 20,175.6 | 20,226.5 | 23,335.2 | 26,847.3 | 27,053.7 | 31,548.5 | 34,791.0 | 40,403.5 | 37,276.5 | 38,450.8 | 40,433.1 |

# Peru 293

| | | 2004 | 2005 | 2006 | 2007 | 2008 | 2009 | 2010 | 2011 | 2012 | 2013 | 2014 | 2015 |
|---|---|---|---|---|---|---|---|---|---|---|---|---|---|
| **Government Finance** | | | | | | | | | | | | | |
| **Cash Flow Statement** | | | | | | | | | | | | | |
| **Budgetary Central Government** | | | | | | *Millions of Nuevos Soles: Fiscal Year Ends December 31* | | | | | | | |
| Cash Receipts:Operating Activities... | c1 | 35,900.0 | 41,776.0 | 53,033.0 | 61,663.0 | 68,245.2 | 61,255.4 | 76,011.7 | 89,049.6 | 98,135.0 | 104,705.0 | 110,356.2 | .... |
| Taxes............................... | c11 | 31,144.0 | 35,368.0 | 45,485.0 | 52,454.0 | 58,241.6 | 52,613.5 | 64,462.2 | 75,540.7 | 84,078.8 | 89,322.6 | 95,310.5 | .... |
| Social Contributions..................... | c12 | — | — | — | — | — | — | — | — | — | — | — | .... |
| Grants................................ | c13 | 254.0 | 271.0 | 248.0 | 282.0 | 301.8 | 580.1 | 555.7 | 833.0 | 602.9 | 479.0 | 524.0 | .... |
| Other Receipts............................. | c14 | 4,502.0 | 6,138.0 | 7,299.0 | 8,927.0 | 9,701.9 | 8,061.8 | 10,993.9 | 12,675.9 | 13,453.3 | 14,903.4 | 14,521.8 | .... |
| Cash Payments:Operating Activities. | c2 | 35,789.0 | 40,351.0 | 45,126.0 | 51,968.0 | 56,954.3 | 60,508.9 | 66,320.7 | 74,524.0 | 81,559.1 | 92,077.0 | 102,927.5 | .... |
| Compensation of Employees........... | c21 | 7,092.0 | 7,598.0 | 8,198.0 | 8,358.0 | 9,199.1 | 10,109.3 | 10,781.4 | 11,936.0 | 13,606.2 | 15,968.7 | 18,749.6 | .... |
| Purchases of Goods & Services....... | c22 | 7,032.0 | 7,787.0 | 8,614.0 | 9,252.0 | 9,274.8 | 11,345.8 | 13,046.0 | 13,783.3 | 15,544.4 | 17,529.2 | 19,679.8 | .... |
| Interest............................... | c24 | 4,383.0 | 4,796.0 | 5,414.0 | 5,527.0 | 5,129.1 | 4,867.5 | 4,766.2 | 5,039.1 | 5,233.1 | 5,723.8 | 5,778.5 | .... |
| Subsidies............................ | c25 | — | — | — | — | — | — | — | — | — | — | — | .... |
| Grants................................ | c26 | 10,989.0 | 15,923.0 | 19,018.0 | 24,359.0 | 25,772.0 | 24,249.2 | 27,280.3 | 32,206.8 | 37,153.8 | 40,292.7 | 45,512.4 | .... |
| Social Benefits............................. | c27 | 2,465.0 | 2,627.0 | 2,667.0 | 2,701.0 | 2,719.2 | 2,777.0 | 2,878.9 | 3,215.5 | 3,110.7 | 3,303.3 | 4,355.1 | .... |
| Other Payments............................ | c28 | 3,829.0 | 1,621.0 | 1,215.0 | 1,771.0 | 4,860.2 | 7,160.0 | 7,567.8 | 8,343.2 | 6,910.9 | 9,259.3 | 8,852.1 | .... |
| Net Cash Inflow:Operating Act.[1-2] | ccio | 110.0 | 1,425.0 | 7,907.0 | 9,695.0 | 11,290.9 | 746.5 | 9,691.1 | 14,525.6 | 16,575.9 | 12,628.0 | 7,428.7 | .... |
| Net Cash Outflow:Invest. in NFA..... | c31 | 2,679.5 | 3,315.7 | 3,001.6 | 3,422.5 | 3,987.2 | 5,854.9 | 8,131.5 | 9,182.6 | 8,153.8 | 8,536.2 | 11,124.0 | .... |
| Purchases of Nonfinancial Assets... | c31.1 | 3,068.8 | 3,500.7 | 3,305.9 | 3,871.6 | 4,143.6 | 5,956.5 | 8,550.3 | 9,317.7 | 8,179.7 | 9,273.7 | .... | .... |
| Sales of Nonfinancial Assets.......... | c31.2 | 389.3 | 185.0 | 304.3 | 449.1 | 156.4 | 101.6 | 418.8 | 135.2 | 25.9 | 737.4 | .... | .... |
| Cash Surplus/Deficit [1-2-31=1-2M] | ccsd | −2,569.3 | −1,890.7 | 4,905.3 | 6,272.4 | 7,303.7 | −5,108.4 | 1,559.6 | 5,343.0 | 8,422.1 | 4,091.8 | −3,698.3 | .... |
| Net Acq. Fin. Assets, excl. Cash....... | c32x | 4,913.9 | 1,943.3 | 65.7 | 234.2 | −97.0 | −165.4 | −86.3 | −102.5 | −49.2 | −12.4 | | .... |
| Domestic....................................... | c321x | −114.1 | −117.4 | −114.3 | −106.0 | −97.0 | −55.2 | −32.8 | −12.4 | −.3 | — | .... | .... |
| Foreign...................................... | c322x | — | — | — | — | — | −110.2 | −53.5 | −90.1 | −48.9 | −12.4 | .... | .... |
| Net Incurrence of Liabilities.............. | c33 | 4,913.9 | 1,943.3 | 65.7 | 234.2 | −3,545.7 | 3,070.6 | −4,802.3 | 1,119.5 | 2,429.8 | −6,004.6 | −5,371.8 | .... |
| Domestic....................................... | c331 | 1,090.7 | 5,072.2 | 1,915.9 | 7,029.7 | 364.2 | −1,047.9 | −1,694.1 | 616.3 | 2,937.6 | −797.5 | −3,866.6 | .... |
| Foreign...................................... | c332 | 3,823.2 | −3,128.9 | −1,850.2 | −6,795.5 | −3,909.9 | 4,118.5 | −3,108.2 | 503.1 | −507.8 | −5,207.1 | −1,505.2 | .... |
| Net Cash Inflow, Fin.Act.[-32x+33].. | cnfb | 5,028.0 | 2,060.7 | 180.0 | 340.2 | −3,448.7 | 3,236.0 | −4,716.0 | 1,221.9 | 2,479.0 | −5,992.2 | −5,342.5 | .... |
| Net Change in Stock of Cash........... | cncb | 2,458.7 | 170.0 | 5,085.3 | 6,612.6 | 3,855.0 | −1,872.4 | −3,156.4 | 6,565.0 | 10,901.1 | −1,900.4 | −9,040.8 | .... |
| Stat. Discrep. [32X-33+NCB-CSD]... | ccsdz | — | — | — | — | — | — | — | — | — | — | — | .... |
| Memo Item:Cash Expenditure[2+31] | c2m | 38,469.0 | 43,667.0 | 48,127.0 | 55,390.0 | 60,498.6 | 66,363.7 | 74,452.2 | 83,706.6 | 89,712.9 | 100,613.2 | 114,054.5 | .... |
| Memo Item: Gross Debt.................. | c63 | .... | .... | 85,521.0 | 82,260.0 | 82,669.9 | 87,410.8 | 90,737.1 | 90,340.9 | 88,908.2 | 92,694.3 | 103,311.9 | .... |
| **National Accounts** | | | | | | *Millions of Nuevos Soles* | | | | | | | |
| Househ.Cons.Expend.,incl.NPISHs.... | 96f | 154,995 | 162,815 | 174,582 | 192,316 | 220,107 | 232,368 | 256,465 | 281,718 | 310,040 | 335,904 | 363,071 | .... |
| Government Consumption Expend... | 91f | 25,657 | 28,697 | 31,688 | 33,424 | 36,755 | 42,117 | 44,531 | 48,111 | 55,002 | 61,210 | 68,008 | .... |
| Gross Fixed Capital Formation......... | 93e | 37,963 | 42,939 | 52,520 | 64,948 | 85,119 | 85,192 | 105,204 | 112,656 | 131,172 | 145,523 | 149,129 | .... |
| Changes in Inventories.................... | 93i | 412 | −2,866 | 2,702 | 6,240 | 12,588 | −9,054 | 453 | 8,253 | 4,588 | 9,215 | 3,668 | .... |
| Exports of Goods and Services......... | 90c | 51,041 | 65,647 | 86,234 | 97,501 | 100,996 | 91,943 | 111,470 | 139,337 | 135,189 | 129,781 | 128,848 | .... |
| Imports of Goods and Services (-)..... | 98c | 42,384 | 50,151 | 60,013 | 74,736 | 99,857 | 77,510 | 98,429 | 120,219 | 127,800 | 134,726 | 137,608 | .... |
| Gross Domestic Product (GDP)......... | 99b | 227,684 | 247,081 | 287,713 | 319,693 | 355,708 | 365,056 | 419,694 | 469,855 | 508,191 | 546,908 | 575,117 | .... |
| GDP Volume 1994 Prices................ | 99b.p | 139,463 | 148,458 | 160,383 | 174,328 | 191,479 | 193,155 | 210,143 | 224,670 | 238,588 | | | .... |
| GDP Volume 2007 Prices................ | 99b.p | 257,770 | 273,971 | 294,598 | 319,693 | 348,923 | 352,584 | 382,380 | 407,052 | 431,273 | 456,214 | 466,879 | .... |
| GDP Volume (2010=100)............... | 99bvp | † 67.4 | 71.6 | 77.0 | 83.6 | 91.3 | 92.2 | 100.0 | 106.5 | 112.8 | 119.3 | 122.1 | .... |
| GDP Deflator (2010=100)............... | 99bip | 80.5 | 82.2 | 89.0 | 91.1 | 92.9 | 94.3 | 100.0 | 105.2 | 107.4 | 109.2 | 112.2 | .... |
| | | | | | | *Millions: Midyear Estimates* | | | | | | | |
| **Population**.............................. | 99z | 27.27 | 27.61 | 27.95 | 28.29 | 28.64 | 29.00 | 29.37 | 29.76 | 30.16 | 30.57 | 30.97 | 31.38 |

|  |  | 2004 | 2005 | 2006 | 2007 | 2008 | 2009 | 2010 | 2011 | 2012 | 2013 | 2014 | 2015 |
|---|---|---|---|---|---|---|---|---|---|---|---|---|---|
| **Exchange Rates** | | | | | | *Pesos per SDR: End of Period* | | | | | | | |
| Market Rate................................. | aa | 87.383 | 75.847 | 73.914 | 65.424 | 73.140 | 72.672 | 67.584 | 67.441 | 63.309 | 68.398 | 64.642 | 65.359 |
| | | | | | | *Pesos per US Dollar: End of Period (ae) Period Average (rf)* | | | | | | | |
| Market Rate................................. | ae | 56.267 | 53.067 | 49.132 | 41.401 | 47.485 | 46.356 | 43.885 | 43.928 | 41.192 | 44.414 | 44.617 | 47.166 |
| Market Rate................................. | rf | 56.040 | 55.085 | 51.314 | 46.148 | 44.323 | 47.680 | 45.110 | 43.313 | 42.229 | 42.446 | 44.395 | 45.503 |
| | | | | | | *Index Numbers (2010=100): Period Averages* | | | | | | | |
| Market Rate................................. | ahx | 80.5 | 81.9 | 87.9 | 97.9 | 102.1 | 94.6 | 100.0 | 104.1 | 106.8 | 106.3 | 101.6 | 99.1 |
| Nominal Effective Exchange Rate..... | nec | 90.2 | 90.9 | 97.0 | 104.6 | 103.7 | 97.5 | 100.0 | 99.0 | 102.6 | 105.4 | 102.7 | 108.8 |
| CPI-Based Real Effect. Ex. Rate........ | rec | 75.1 | 79.0 | 87.3 | 94.5 | 97.3 | 95.7 | 100.0 | 100.7 | 105.6 | 109.8 | 109.4 | 116.6 |
| **Fund Position** | | | | | | *Millions of SDRs: End of Period* | | | | | | | |
| Quota........................................ | 2f.s | 879.90 | 879.90 | 879.90 | 879.90 | 879.90 | 879.90 | 879.90 | 1,019.30 | 1,019.30 | 1,019.30 | 1,019.30 | 1,019.30 |
| SDR Holdings.............................. | 1b.s | .65 | .59 | 1.55 | .47 | 6.91 | 727.93 | 727.78 | 728.13 | 838.26 | 845.98 | 846.30 | 846.43 |
| Reserve Position in the Fund........... | 1c.s | 87.43 | 87.49 | 87.55 | 87.60 | 87.66 | 87.71 | 162.79 | 307.51 | 347.76 | 385.70 | 393.85 | 316.54 |
| Total Fund Cred.&Loans Outstg....... | 2tl | 486.93 | 272.06 | — | — | — | — | — | — | — | — | — | — |
| SDR Allocations............................ | 1bd | 116.60 | 116.60 | 116.60 | 116.60 | 116.60 | 837.96 | 837.96 | 837.96 | 837.96 | 837.96 | 837.96 | 837.96 |
| **International Liquidity** | | | | | | *Millions of US Dollars Unless Otherwise Indicated: End of Period* | | | | | | | |
| Total Reserves minus Gold.............. | 1l.d | 13,116 | 15,926 | 20,025 | 30,211 | 33,193 | 38,783 | 55,363 | 67,290 | 73,478 | 75,689 | 72,057 | 73,964 |
| SDR Holdings.............................. | 1b.d | 1 | 1 | 2 | 1 | 11 | 1,141 | 1,121 | 1,118 | 1,288 | 1,303 | 1,226 | 1,173 |
| Reserve Position in the Fund......... | 1c.d | 136 | 125 | 132 | 138 | 135 | 138 | 251 | 472 | 534 | 594 | 571 | 439 |
| Foreign Exchange........................ | 1d.d | 12,980 | 15,800 | 19,891 | 30,071 | 33,047 | 37,504 | 53,991 | 65,700 | 71,656 | 73,792 | 70,260 | 72,352 |
| Gold (Million Fine Troy Ounces)....... | 1ad | 7.119 | 4.968 | 4.621 | 4.233 | 4.949 | 4.987 | 4.954 | 5.117 | 6.196 | 6.221 | 6.279 | 6.299 |
| Gold (National Valuation)............... | 1and | 3,112 | 2,568 | 2,941 | 3,541 | 4,358 | 5,460 | 7,010 | 8,013 | 10,353 | 7,498 | 7,484 | 6,703 |
| Central Bank: Other Assets.............. | 3..d | 74 | 64 | 67 | 83 | 69 | 70 | 69 | 70 | 204 | 596 | 645 | 772 |
| Central Bank: Other Liabs............... | 4..d | 3,226 | 2,177 | 1,064 | 813 | 2,187 | 572 | 497 | 455 | 408 | 420 | 419 | 418 |
| Other Depository Corps.: Assets....... | 7a.d | 9,894 | 13,294 | † 15,397 | 16,511 | 15,927 | 16,871 | 16,094 | 13,537 | 14,174 | 15,672 | 23,055 | 21,707 |
| Other Depository Corps.: Liabs......... | 7b.d | 6,533 | 8,375 | † 8,541 | 9,334 | 8,603 | 7,038 | 11,359 | 13,338 | 17,423 | 17,221 | 17,727 | 16,705 |
| **Central Bank** | | | | | | *Billions of Pesos: End of Period* | | | | | | | |
| Net Foreign Assets.......................... | 11n | 684.20 | 839.76 | 1,068.83 | 1,359.81 | 1,680.07 | 1,969.72 | 2,657.28 | 3,233.79 | 3,382.38 | 3,643.85 | 3,514.33 | 3,762.87 |
| Claims on Nonresidents................ | 11 | 918.47 | 984.75 | 1,129.72 | 1,401.10 | 1,792.45 | 2,057.11 | 2,735.73 | 3,310.29 | 3,452.24 | 3,719.82 | 3,587.21 | 3,837.34 |
| Liabilities to Nonresidents............ | 16c | 234.27 | 145.00 | 60.88 | 41.30 | 112.38 | 87.40 | 78.44 | 76.50 | 69.85 | 75.97 | 72.87 | 74.47 |
| Claims on Other Depository Corps.... | 12e | 35.78 | 25.57 | 24.29 | 21.36 | 53.28 | 71.54 | 33.61 | 32.06 | 32.77 | 11.05 | 7.77 | 6.93 |
| Net Claims on Central Government.. | 12an | 81.61 | 27.37 | 132.09 | 176.01 | 204.83 | 139.17 | 162.25 | 237.67 | −59.86 | −114.98 | −107.08 | −109.82 |
| Claims on Central Government...... | 12a | 142.68 | 115.21 | 240.63 | 343.39 | 346.75 | 282.93 | 272.39 | 297.77 | 281.01 | 297.31 | 308.12 | 317.02 |
| Liabilities to Central Government... | 16d | 61.07 | 87.84 | 108.55 | 167.38 | 141.92 | 143.76 | 110.14 | 60.10 | 340.86 | 412.29 | 415.20 | 426.85 |
| Claims on Other Sectors.................. | 12s | 85.34 | 80.30 | 90.06 | 79.19 | 82.70 | 84.33 | 85.73 | 80.43 | 81.81 | 79.97 | 73.40 | 74.59 |
| Claims on Other Financial Corps.... | 12g | 85.33 | 80.28 | 90.05 | 79.18 | 82.69 | 84.32 | 85.72 | 80.42 | 81.80 | 79.96 | 73.39 | 74.56 |
| Claims on State & Local Govts....... | 12b | — | — | — | — | — | — | — | — | — | — | — | — |
| Claims on Public Nonfin. Corps...... | 12c | .01 | .01 | .01 | .01 | .01 | .01 | .01 | .01 | .01 | .01 | .01 | .03 |
| Claims on Private Sector............... | 12d | — | — | — | — | — | — | — | — | — | — | — | — |
| Monetary Base............................... | 14 | 427.80 | 467.59 | 719.03 | 848.78 | 961.47 | 1,047.93 | 1,120.55 | 1,323.00 | 1,475.63 | 1,926.20 | 2,323.91 | 2,467.06 |
| Currency in Circulation................. | 14a | 322.47 | 336.56 | 384.49 | 433.85 | 545.09 | 582.53 | 601.27 | 648.91 | 692.66 | 797.45 | 929.50 | 1,005.19 |
| Liabs. to Other Depository Corps.... | 14c | 95.49 | 120.54 | 331.94 | 412.38 | 414.38 | 464.96 | 518.75 | 673.51 | 782.65 | 1,128.30 | 1,386.75 | 1,456.21 |
| Liabilities to Other Sectors............ | 14d | 9.85 | 10.49 | 2.60 | 2.55 | 1.99 | .43 | .52 | .58 | .33 | .45 | 7.66 | 5.65 |
| Other Liabs. to Other Dep. Corps..... | 14n | 143.25 | 216.72 | 337.96 | 419.81 | 428.30 | 358.08 | 740.18 | 642.20 | 624.89 | 1,294.73 | 803.31 | 767.49 |
| Dep. & Sec. Excl. f/Monetary Base.... | 14o | 5.46 | 1.60 | 1.75 | 314.71 | 251.63 | 520.52 | 831.87 | 1,321.02 | 1,323.17 | 379.38 | 353.02 | 383.86 |
| Deposits Included in Broad Money. | 15 | 5.35 | 1.51 | 1.71 | 22.73 | 14.41 | 31.77 | 33.58 | 2.14 | 20.54 | 4.83 | .77 | 2.70 |
| Sec.Ot.th.Shares Incl.in Brd. Money | 16a | — | — | — | — | — | — | — | — | — | — | — | — |
| Deposits Excl. from Broad Money... | 16b | .11 | .09 | .04 | 291.98 | 237.22 | 488.76 | 798.29 | 1,318.88 | 1,302.63 | 374.55 | 352.26 | 381.16 |
| Sec.Ot.th.Shares Excl.f/Brd.Money.. | 16s | — | — | — | — | — | — | — | — | — | — | — | — |
| Loans........................................ | 16l | — | — | — | — | — | — | — | — | — | — | — | — |
| Financial Derivatives..................... | 16m | — | — | — | — | — | — | — | — | — | — | — | — |
| Shares and Other Equity.................. | 17a | 314.02 | 312.85 | 277.72 | 77.15 | 388.09 | 323.24 | 233.20 | 287.25 | 1.76 | 3.82 | 5.39 | 112.42 |
| Other Items (Net).......................... | 17r | −3.62 | −25.78 | −21.19 | −24.08 | −8.61 | 14.99 | 13.08 | 10.48 | 11.66 | 15.76 | 2.80 | 3.73 |
| Memo Item: | | | | | | | | | | | | | |
| Total Assets................................... | 10ra | 1,278.06 | 1,310.71 | 1,590.62 | 1,952.53 | 2,364.86 | 2,586.59 | 3,213.77 | 3,806.19 | 3,930.33 | 4,189.21 | 4,066.70 | 4,330.62 |

# Philippines 566

| | | 2004 | 2005 | 2006 | 2007 | 2008 | 2009 | 2010 | 2011 | 2012 | 2013 | 2014 | 2015 |
|---|---|---|---|---|---|---|---|---|---|---|---|---|---|
| **Other Depository Corporations** | | | | | | *Billions of Pesos: End of Period* | | | | | | | |
| Net Foreign Assets | 21n | 189.09 | 261.04 | † 336.80 | 297.13 | 347.79 | 455.82 | 207.80 | 8.75 | −133.83 | −68.80 | 237.73 | 235.94 |
| Claims on Nonresidents | 21 | 556.70 | 705.46 | † 756.46 | 683.59 | 756.28 | 782.06 | 706.36 | 594.67 | 583.83 | 696.05 | 1,028.65 | 1,023.85 |
| Liabilities to Nonresidents | 26c | 367.61 | 444.42 | † 419.66 | 386.46 | 408.49 | 326.24 | 498.56 | 585.92 | 717.66 | 764.84 | 790.92 | 787.91 |
| Claims on Central Bank | 20 | 210.14 | 302.02 | † 696.94 | 847.03 | 836.10 | 917.18 | 1,369.99 | 1,432.00 | 1,541.37 | 2,580.06 | 2,409.11 | 2,441.04 |
| Currency | 20a | 69.76 | 69.72 | † 79.07 | 89.06 | 112.12 | 121.04 | 122.85 | 133.98 | 133.87 | 157.11 | 215.35 | 213.76 |
| Reserve Deposits and Securities | 20b | 100.46 | 122.95 | † 382.04 | 498.62 | 490.70 | 539.00 | 958.25 | 999.85 | 1,125.80 | 2,125.23 | 1,888.80 | 1,912.46 |
| Other Claims | 20n | 39.93 | 109.35 | † 235.83 | 259.35 | 233.28 | 257.14 | 288.89 | 298.17 | 281.70 | 297.72 | 304.97 | 314.81 |
| Net Claims on Central Government | 22an | 751.40 | 695.60 | † 635.02 | 617.51 | 692.65 | 842.52 | 966.16 | 923.89 | 1,012.78 | 1,065.83 | 1,242.82 | 1,371.52 |
| Claims on Central Government | 22a | 802.68 | 764.62 | † 740.95 | 767.11 | 881.53 | 1,083.61 | 1,175.34 | 1,135.31 | 1,262.30 | 1,341.52 | 1,571.26 | 1,675.55 |
| Liabilities to Central Government | 26d | 51.28 | 69.02 | † 105.93 | 149.59 | 188.88 | 241.09 | 209.18 | 211.42 | 249.53 | 275.70 | 328.44 | 304.03 |
| Claims on Other Sectors | 22s | 1,845.72 | 1,879.29 | † 2,168.56 | 2,459.63 | 2,682.85 | 2,843.91 | 3,218.45 | 3,804.42 | 4,340.71 | 4,957.88 | 5,847.94 | 6,524.75 |
| Claims on Other Financial Corps | 22g | — | — | † 176.44 | 258.64 | 223.47 | 291.75 | 311.83 | 348.06 | 460.33 | 479.10 | 557.45 | 605.93 |
| Claims on State & Local Govts | 22b | 24.42 | 26.23 | † 33.27 | 37.94 | 50.20 | 57.89 | 68.63 | 72.40 | 71.21 | 74.71 | 71.50 | 76.63 |
| Claims on Public Nonfin. Corps | 22c | 170.41 | 202.34 | † 159.41 | 173.52 | 165.11 | 153.62 | 174.89 | 290.08 | 280.25 | 266.41 | 269.25 | 277.94 |
| Claims on Private Sector | 22d | 1,650.90 | 1,650.72 | † 1,799.44 | 1,989.52 | 2,244.08 | 2,340.65 | 2,663.10 | 3,093.88 | 3,528.92 | 4,137.66 | 4,949.75 | 5,564.25 |
| Liabilities to Central Bank | 26g | 10.32 | 9.98 | † 40.54 | 29.14 | 42.28 | 58.94 | 27.67 | 21.73 | 22.90 | 6.22 | 4.35 | 3.82 |
| Transf.Dep.Included in Broad Money | 24 | 311.37 | 348.67 | † 493.12 | 593.38 | 648.41 | 773.29 | 898.21 | 1,009.72 | 1,085.07 | 1,441.00 | 1,639.20 | 1,917.03 |
| Other Dep.Included in Broad Money | 25 | 2,291.15 | 2,441.22 | † 2,982.86 | 3,186.48 | 3,379.65 | 3,604.04 | 3,915.58 | 4,074.06 | 4,343.62 | 5,736.12 | 6,380.74 | 6,809.25 |
| Sec.Ot.th.Shares Incl.in Brd. Money | 26a | 13.86 | 12.91 | † 18.68 | 19.88 | 111.09 | 113.87 | 201.78 | 220.02 | 219.32 | 231.47 | 313.43 | 362.66 |
| Deposits Excl. from Broad Money | 26b | 5.46 | 1.33 | † — | — | — | — | — | — | — | — | — | — |
| Sec.Ot.th.Shares Excl.f/Brd.Money | 26s | — | — | † 7.35 | 22.39 | 13.96 | 6.33 | 6.49 | 6.53 | 6.20 | — | — | — |
| Loans | 26l | 10.37 | 8.52 | † 10.01 | 4.23 | — | .30 | 5.65 | .19 | .19 | .64 | .60 | 1.98 |
| Financial Derivatives | 26m | — | — | † — | — | 7.73 | 8.60 | 12.69 | 10.88 | 17.79 | 12.95 | 11.15 | 12.67 |
| Insurance Technical Reserves | 26r | — | — | † — | — | — | — | — | — | — | — | — | — |
| Shares and Other Equity | 27a | 601.41 | 582.62 | † 589.81 | 651.26 | 624.00 | 720.78 | 847.55 | 971.51 | 1,111.85 | 1,200.07 | 1,457.15 | 1,570.79 |
| Other Items (Net) | 27r | −247.58 | −267.31 | † −305.05 | −285.48 | −267.72 | −226.72 | −153.22 | −145.57 | −45.91 | −93.51 | −69.03 | −104.96 |
| Memo Item: | | | | | | | | | | | | | |
| Total Assets | 20ra | 4,120.41 | 4,396.06 | † 5,162.25 | 5,595.00 | 6,093.91 | 6,590.39 | 7,420.64 | 7,886.07 | 8,651.59 | 10,609.76 | 11,959.84 | 12,810.02 |
| **Depository Corporations** | | | | | | *Billions of Pesos: End of Period* | | | | | | | |
| Net Foreign Assets | 31n | 873.29 | 1,100.80 | † 1,405.63 | 1,656.94 | 2,027.86 | 2,425.53 | 2,865.08 | 3,242.54 | 3,248.55 | 3,575.05 | 3,752.06 | 3,998.80 |
| Claims on Nonresidents | 31 | 1,475.16 | 1,690.22 | † 1,886.18 | 2,084.69 | 2,548.73 | 2,839.17 | 3,442.09 | 3,904.96 | 4,036.06 | 4,415.87 | 4,615.86 | 4,861.19 |
| Liabilities to Nonresidents | 36c | 601.88 | 589.42 | † 480.55 | 427.75 | 520.87 | 413.64 | 577.01 | 662.42 | 787.52 | 840.81 | 863.79 | 862.38 |
| Domestic Claims | 32 | 2,764.07 | 2,682.55 | † 3,025.72 | 3,332.34 | 3,663.04 | 3,909.93 | 4,432.59 | 5,046.41 | 5,375.44 | 5,988.69 | 7,057.08 | 7,861.03 |
| Net Claims on Central Government | 32an | 833.00 | 722.96 | † 767.11 | 793.53 | 897.48 | 981.70 | 1,128.41 | 1,161.55 | 952.92 | 950.85 | 1,135.74 | 1,261.69 |
| Claims on Central Government | 32a | 945.36 | 879.83 | † 981.58 | 1,110.50 | 1,228.28 | 1,366.54 | 1,447.73 | 1,433.08 | 1,543.31 | 1,638.83 | 1,879.37 | 1,992.57 |
| Liabilities to Central Government | 36d | 112.36 | 156.87 | † 214.47 | 316.97 | 330.80 | 384.85 | 319.32 | 271.53 | 590.39 | 687.99 | 743.64 | 730.88 |
| Claims on Other Sectors | 32s | 1,931.06 | 1,959.58 | † 2,258.62 | 2,538.81 | 2,765.56 | 2,928.24 | 3,304.18 | 3,884.85 | 4,422.52 | 5,037.84 | 5,921.34 | 6,599.33 |
| Claims on Other Financial Corps | 32g | 85.33 | 80.28 | † 266.49 | 337.82 | 306.16 | 376.07 | 397.55 | 428.48 | 542.13 | 559.06 | 630.84 | 680.48 |
| Claims on State & Local Govts | 32b | 24.42 | 26.23 | † 33.27 | 37.94 | 50.20 | 57.89 | 68.63 | 72.40 | 71.21 | 74.71 | 71.50 | 76.63 |
| Claims on Public Nonfin. Corps | 32c | 170.42 | 202.35 | † 159.42 | 173.53 | 165.12 | 153.63 | 174.90 | 290.09 | 280.26 | 266.42 | 269.26 | 277.97 |
| Claims on Private Sector | 32d | 1,650.90 | 1,650.72 | † 1,799.45 | 1,989.52 | 2,244.08 | 2,340.65 | 2,663.10 | 3,093.88 | 3,528.92 | 4,137.66 | 4,949.75 | 5,564.25 |
| Broad Money Liabilities | 35l | 2,884.28 | 3,081.63 | † 3,804.39 | 4,169.82 | 4,588.51 | 4,984.89 | 5,528.09 | 5,821.45 | 6,227.66 | 8,054.21 | 9,055.95 | 9,888.72 |
| Currency Outside Depository Corps | 34a | 252.70 | 266.83 | † 305.42 | 344.80 | 432.98 | 461.49 | 478.43 | 514.93 | 558.78 | 640.34 | 714.15 | 791.43 |
| Transferable Deposits | 34 | 323.28 | 359.91 | † 496.46 | 596.44 | 651.32 | 773.88 | 899.32 | 1,010.44 | 1,085.52 | 1,441.57 | 1,647.02 | 1,922.78 |
| Other Deposits | 35 | 2,294.44 | 2,441.98 | † 2,983.83 | 3,208.70 | 3,393.13 | 3,635.64 | 3,948.57 | 4,076.06 | 4,364.04 | 5,740.82 | 6,381.34 | 6,811.85 |
| Securities Other than Shares | 36a | 13.86 | 12.91 | † 18.68 | 19.88 | 111.09 | 113.87 | 201.78 | 220.02 | 219.32 | 231.47 | 313.43 | 362.66 |
| Deposits Excl. from Broad Money | 36b | 5.57 | 1.42 | † .04 | 291.98 | 237.22 | 488.76 | 798.29 | 1,318.88 | 1,302.63 | 374.55 | 352.26 | 381.16 |
| Sec.Ot.th.Shares Excl.f/Brd.Money | 36s | — | — | † 7.35 | 22.39 | 13.96 | 6.33 | 6.49 | 6.53 | 6.20 | — | — | — |
| Loans | 36l | 10.37 | 8.52 | † 10.01 | 4.23 | — | .30 | 5.65 | .19 | .19 | .64 | .60 | 1.98 |
| Financial Derivatives | 36m | — | — | † — | — | 7.73 | 8.60 | 12.69 | 10.88 | 17.79 | 12.95 | 11.15 | 12.67 |
| Insurance Technical Reserves | 36r | — | — | † — | — | — | — | — | — | — | — | — | — |
| Shares and Other Equity | 37a | 915.44 | 895.47 | † 867.53 | 728.41 | 1,012.09 | 1,044.02 | 1,080.75 | 1,258.76 | 1,113.61 | 1,203.89 | 1,462.54 | 1,683.22 |
| Other Items (Net) | 37r | −178.30 | −203.70 | † −257.96 | −227.57 | −168.63 | −197.43 | −134.29 | −127.74 | −44.08 | −82.50 | −73.35 | −107.91 |
| Broad Money Liabs., Seasonally Adj. | 35l.b | 2,826.98 | 3,019.02 | † 3,689.13 | 4,039.95 | 4,436.69 | 4,807.36 | 5,318.71 | 5,592.07 | 5,980.55 | 7,737.59 | 8,710.32 | 9,517.74 |
| **Monetary Aggregates** | | | | | | *Billions of Pesos: End of Period* | | | | | | | |
| Broad Money | 59m | .... | .... | 3,804.39 | 4,169.82 | 4,588.51 | 4,984.89 | 5,528.09 | 5,821.45 | 6,227.66 | 8,054.21 | 9,055.95 | 9,888.72 |
| o/w:Currency Issued by Cent.Govt | 59m.a | .... | .... | — | — | — | — | — | — | — | — | — | — |
| o/w: Dep.in Nonfin. Corporations | 59m.b | .... | .... | — | — | — | — | — | — | — | — | — | — |
| o/w:Secs. Issued by Central Govt | 59m.c | .... | .... | — | — | — | — | — | — | — | — | — | — |
| Money (National Definitions) | | | | | | | | | | | | | |
| Reserve Money | 19mb | 410.54 | 446.81 | 694.11 | 825.37 | 940.23 | 1,046.81 | 1,119.67 | 1,322.79 | 1,475.33 | 1,926.20 | 2,323.91 | 2,467.06 |
| Narrow Money | 59mak | 556.42 | 605.35 | 752.97 | 861.98 | 1,070.83 | 1,216.92 | 1,345.93 | 1,492.40 | 1,603.48 | 2,045.19 | 2,319.20 | 2,667.61 |
| Quasi-Money | 59mal | 1,326.26 | 1,446.16 | 1,748.74 | 1,902.90 | 2,541.08 | 2,672.65 | 2,960.29 | 3,093.93 | 3,482.20 | 4,648.38 | 5,076.47 | 5,399.66 |
| M3 | 59mc | 1,883.76 | 2,052.55 | 2,510.73 | 2,773.16 | 3,668.43 | 3,973.97 | 4,396.81 | 4,674.26 | 5,171.69 | 6,925.04 | 7,709.11 | 8,429.93 |
| M4 | 59md | 2,649.30 | 2,814.33 | 3,328.60 | 3,463.68 | 4,610.40 | 4,999.90 | 5,446.78 | 5,680.35 | 6,162.89 | 8,054.21 | 9,055.95 | 9,888.72 |
| **Interest Rates** | | | | | | *Percent Per Annum* | | | | | | | |
| Central Bank Policy Rate | 60 | 6.843 | 7.140 | 7.591 | 6.830 | 5.555 | .... | 4.103 | 4.599 | 3.598 | 3.521 | 3.688 | 4.000 |
| Discount Rate | 60.a | 6.640 | 6.626 | 5.399 | 3.732 | 4.796 | 3.923 | 3.875 | 4.355 | 3.902 | 3.506 | 3.724 | 4.079 |
| Money Market Rate | 60b | 7.047 | 7.314 | 7.841 | 7.023 | 5.480 | 4.538 | 4.196 | 4.556 | 4.035 | 2.381 | 2.234 | 2.526 |
| Treasury Bill Rate | 60c | 7.320 | 6.132 | 5.294 | 3.377 | 5.165 | 4.163 | 3.515 | 1.340 | 1.500 | .288 | 1.217 | 1.745 |
| Savings Rate | 60k | 4.265 | 3.760 | 3.562 | 2.196 | 2.221 | 2.068 | 1.599 | 1.620 | 1.341 | .841 | .629 | .709 |
| Savings Rate (Fgn. Currency) | 60k.f | .837 | .940 | 1.081 | 1.097 | .854 | .517 | .390 | .356 | .307 | .241 | .220 | .192 |
| Deposit Rate | 60l | 6.178 | 5.556 | 5.294 | 3.696 | 4.490 | 2.741 | 3.220 | 3.388 | 3.156 | 1.662 | 1.229 | 1.592 |
| Deposit Rate (Fgn. Currency) | 60l.f | 1.916 | 2.407 | 3.211 | 3.262 | 2.189 | 1.433 | 1.081 | .937 | .937 | .796 | .720 | .689 |
| Lending Rate | 60p | 10.079 | 10.185 | 9.779 | 8.691 | 8.751 | 8.566 | 7.673 | 6.663 | 5.680 | 5.767 | 5.526 | 5.578 |
| Government Bond Yield | 61 | 10.270 | 8.660 | 7.384 | 5.340 | .... | .... | .... | .... | .... | .... | .... | .... |

# Philippines 566

| | | 2004 | 2005 | 2006 | 2007 | 2008 | 2009 | 2010 | 2011 | 2012 | 2013 | 2014 | 2015 |
|---|---|---|---|---|---|---|---|---|---|---|---|---|---|
| **Prices, Production, Labor** | | | | | | | | | | | | | |
| | | | | | | | | | | | | | |

**Prices, Production, Labor** — *Index Numbers (2010=100): Period Averages*

| | | 2004 | 2005 | 2006 | 2007 | 2008 | 2009 | 2010 | 2011 | 2012 | 2013 | 2014 | 2015 |
|---|---|---|---|---|---|---|---|---|---|---|---|---|---|
| Share Prices | 62 | 45.0 | 52.8 | 64.9 | 95.8 | 72.5 | 69.9 | 100.0 | 132.8 | 152.3 | 176.7 | 179.8 | 189.6 |
| Share Prices (End of Month) | 62.ep | 44.8 | 52.0 | 65.0 | 94.7 | 70.4 | 69.7 | 100.0 | 130.4 | 151.3 | 173.8 | 177.8 | 185.7 |
| Producer Prices | 63 | 85.1 | 92.9 | 101.6 | 102.5 | 106.7 | 105.2 | 100.0 | 100.9 | 100.4 | 92.8 | 91.9 | 85.8 |
| Consumer Prices | 64 | 73.9 | 78.7 | 83.0 | 85.4 | 92.4 | 96.3 | 100.0 | 104.6 | 108.0 | 111.2 | 115.8 | 117.4 |
| Manufacturing Production | 66ey | 87.1 | 96.1 | 97.6 | 94.3 | 98.5 | 85.5 | 100.0 | 102.1 | 109.3 | 115.2 | 122.4 | 117.0 |

*Number in Thousands: Period Averages*

| | | 2004 | 2005 | 2006 | 2007 | 2008 | 2009 | 2010 | 2011 | 2012 | 2013 | 2014 | 2015 |
|---|---|---|---|---|---|---|---|---|---|---|---|---|---|
| Labor Force | 67d | 35,862 | 35,382 | 35,464 | 36,213 | 36,804 | 37,892 | 38,894 | 40,006 | 40,426 | 41,023 | 41,379 | 41,343 |
| Employment | 67e | 31,613 | 32,313 | 32,636 | 33,560 | 34,089 | 35,061 | 36,035 | 37,192 | 37,600 | 38,118 | 38,651 | 38,741 |
| Unemployment | 67c | 4,249 | 3,068 | 2,829 | 2,653 | 2,716 | 2,831 | 2,859 | 2,814 | 2,826 | 2,905 | 2,728 | 2,602 |
| Unemployment Rate (%) | 67r | 11.8 | 8.7 | 8.0 | 7.3 | 7.4 | 7.5 | 7.4 | 7.0 | 7.0 | 7.1 | 6.6 | 6.3 |

**Intl. Transactions & Positions** — *Millions of Pesos*

| | | 2004 | 2005 | 2006 | 2007 | 2008 | 2009 | 2010 | 2011 | 2012 | 2013 | 2014 | 2015 |
|---|---|---|---|---|---|---|---|---|---|---|---|---|---|
| Exports | 70 | 2,223,719 | 2,272,552 | 2,432,760 | 2,328,879 | 2,182,680 | 1,830,976 | 2,322,985 | 2,092,234 | 2,200,131 | 2,406,612 | 2,757,001 | 2,668,677 |
| Sugar | 70i | 3,733 | 3,598 | 2,593 | 3,198 | 2,828 | 1,883 | 1,336 | 15,222 | 4,594 | 11,583 | 4,756 | 990 |
| Coconut Oil | 70ai | 32,379 | 36,258 | 29,699 | 33,263 | 45,924 | 28,179 | 56,974 | 61,591 | 43,749 | 38,668 | 53,185 | 51,327 |
| Imports, c.i.f. | 71 | 2,373,188 | 2,587,381 | 2,773,800 | 2,652,969 | 2,668,514 | 2,185,443 | 2,637,537 | 2,776,233 | 2,780,231 | 2,790,400 | 3,050,158 | 3,192,126 |
| Imports, f.o.b. | 71.v | 2,468,053 | 2,611,989 | 2,656,695 | 2,561,975 | 2,523,756 | 2,052,774 | 2,477,983 | 2,620,220 | 2,623,603 | 2,649,097 | 2,903,389 | 3,034,459 |

*2010=100*

| | | 2004 | 2005 | 2006 | 2007 | 2008 | 2009 | 2010 | 2011 | 2012 | 2013 | 2014 | 2015 |
|---|---|---|---|---|---|---|---|---|---|---|---|---|---|
| Volume of Exports (2005=100) | 72 | 105.7 | 100.0 | 119.3 | .... | .... | .... | .... | .... | .... | .... | .... | .... |
| Sugar | 72i | 376.3 | 363.9 | 212.6 | 342.3 | 330.3 | 204.0 | 100.0 | 945.3 | 329.8 | 476.8 | 337.8 | 63.3 |
| Coconut Oil | 72ai | 71.4 | 85.8 | 79.4 | 66.2 | 63.3 | 61.8 | 100.0 | 61.4 | 65.6 | 48.4 | 65.3 | 61.7 |
| Volume of Imports (2005=100) | 73 | 112.1 | 100.0 | 102.6 | .... | .... | .... | .... | .... | .... | .... | .... | .... |
| Export Prices (2005=100) | 76 | 91.0 | 100.0 | 97.4 | .... | .... | .... | .... | .... | .... | .... | .... | .... |
| Sugar (Wholesale Price) | 76i | 74.3 | 74.0 | 91.3 | 69.9 | 64.1 | 69.1 | 100.0 | 120.5 | 104.2 | 181.8 | 105.4 | 117.1 |
| Coconut Oil (W'sale price) | 76ai | 79.5 | 72.1 | 65.5 | 88.3 | 126.8 | 80.1 | 100.0 | 176.0 | 117.1 | 262.3 | 162.1 | 139.6 |
| Import Prices (2005=100) | 76.x | 87.6 | 100.0 | 112.3 | .... | .... | .... | .... | .... | .... | .... | .... | .... |

**Balance of Payments** — *Millions of US Dollars*

| | | 2004 | 2005 | 2006 | 2007 | 2008 | 2009 | 2010 | 2011 | 2012 | 2013 | 2014 | 2015 |
|---|---|---|---|---|---|---|---|---|---|---|---|---|---|
| A. Current Account* | 109bx | 1,625.0 | † 1,990.4 | 6,962.9 | 8,071.9 | 144.0 | 8,448.2 | 7,179.2 | 5,642.7 | 6,949.5 | 11,383.5 | 10,755.9 | 8,396.0 |
| Goods, credit (exports) | 1a9cx | 25,819.0 | † 25,161.8 | 30,734.4 | 32,802.6 | 34,678.8 | 29,142.9 | 36,771.7 | 38,276.5 | 46,384.3 | 44,512.4 | 49,823.7 | 43,276.0 |
| Goods, debit (imports) | 1a9dx | 34,158.0 | † 37,307.4 | 42,193.6 | 46,768.8 | 53,324.4 | 43,003.0 | 53,630.9 | 58,704.5 | 65,310.4 | 62,174.4 | 67,154.1 | 64,974.5 |
| Balance on goods | 1a9bx | -8,339.0 | † -12,145.6 | -11,459.2 | -13,966.2 | -18,645.6 | -13,860.1 | -16,859.2 | -20,428.0 | -18,926.1 | -17,662.0 | -17,330.4 | -21,698.5 |
| Services, credit (exports) | 1b9cx | 6,743.0 | † 8,610.9 | 11,064.2 | 13,501.7 | 13,054.8 | 14,084.1 | 17,782.2 | 18,878.2 | 20,439.2 | 23,335.2 | 25,498.1 | 28,167.4 |
| Services, debit (imports) | 1b9dx | 5,865.0 | † 6,463.3 | 6,587.5 | 7,543.7 | 11,084.3 | 9,186.2 | 12,017.2 | 12,316.2 | 14,260.5 | 16,320.4 | 20,921.6 | 23,923.8 |
| Balance on Goods & Services | 129bx | -7,461.0 | † -9,998.1 | -6,982.4 | -8,008.1 | -16,675.1 | -8,962.2 | -11,094.1 | -13,866.0 | -12,747.4 | -10,647.2 | -12,753.9 | -17,454.9 |
| Primary income: credit | 1c9cx | 3,725.0 | † 4,741.1 | 6,075.9 | 7,392.4 | 7,004.5 | 6,404.9 | 6,687.5 | 7,637.0 | 8,257.0 | 8,358.3 | 8,779.0 | 9,496.2 |
| Primary income: debit | 1c9dx | 3,799.0 | † 4,387.1 | 5,374.3 | 5,758.0 | 5,904.5 | 5,564.2 | 6,010.1 | 6,695.2 | 8,059.7 | 7,401.0 | 8,051.5 | 7,165.4 |
| Balance on gds, serv. & prim. inc. | 1y9bx | -7,535.0 | † -9,644.0 | -6,280.8 | -6,373.7 | -15,575.1 | -8,121.5 | -10,416.7 | -12,924.3 | -12,550.2 | -9,689.9 | -12,026.5 | -15,124.1 |
| Secondary income: credit | 1d9ca | 9,420.0 | † 11,815.9 | 13,482.1 | 14,632.7 | 16,036.6 | 16,970.9 | 17,969.9 | 19,044.2 | 20,057.0 | 21,679.7 | 23,445.7 | 24,347.1 |
| Secondary income: debit | 1d9da | 260.0 | † 181.5 | 238.5 | 187.0 | 317.5 | 401.2 | 374.1 | 477.2 | 557.3 | 606.3 | 663.3 | 827.0 |
| B. Capital Account* | 209ba | 31.0 | † 79.3 | 103.1 | 36.4 | 110.1 | 89.9 | 88.5 | 159.9 | 94.8 | 133.8 | 107.9 | 81.7 |
| Capital account: credit | 209ca | 43.0 | † 81.3 | 127.1 | 81.4 | 127.1 | 97.9 | 98.5 | 188.9 | 110.8 | 151.4 | 120.5 | 96.9 |
| Capital account: debit | 209da | 12.0 | † 2.0 | 24.0 | 45.0 | 17.0 | 8.0 | 10.0 | 29.0 | 16.0 | 17.6 | 12.7 | 15.2 |
| Balance on current & capital acct. | 129ba | 1,656.0 | † 2,069.7 | 7,066.0 | 8,108.4 | 254.1 | 8,538.1 | 7,267.7 | 5,802.6 | 7,044.3 | 11,517.3 | 10,863.8 | 8,477.7 |
| C. Financial Account* | 309na | 1,671.0 | † 2,582.5 | 214.7 | -320.1 | 1,362.0 | 1,113.9 | -13,774.8 | -5,317.6 | -6,747.0 | 2,230.2 | 9,631.2 | 2,522.8 |
| Direct investment: assets | 3a9aa | 483.0 | † 794.1 | 1,068.3 | 5,372.7 | 1,970.0 | 1,897.1 | 2,712.2 | 2,349.6 | 4,173.2 | 3,646.9 | 6,753.9 | 5,601.9 |
| Equity & investment fund shares | 3aaaa | 579.0 | † 192.7 | 102.7 | 3,469.5 | 325.2 | 359.2 | 615.4 | 229.8 | 1,190.7 | 978.1 | 2,764.4 | 1,616.1 |
| Debt instruments | 3abaa | -96.0 | † 601.4 | 965.6 | 1,903.1 | 1,644.8 | 1,538.0 | 2,096.8 | 2,119.8 | 2,982.5 | 2,668.8 | 3,989.5 | 3,985.9 |
| Direct investment: liabilities | 3a9la | 592.0 | † 1,664.0 | 2,707.4 | 2,918.7 | 1,340.0 | 2,064.6 | 1,070.4 | 2,007.2 | 3,215.4 | 3,737.4 | 5,739.6 | 5,724.2 |
| Equity & investment fund shares | 3aala | 891.0 | † 1,321.0 | 1,809.4 | 2,568.7 | 1,288.0 | 1,885.6 | -213.6 | 1,530.6 | 2,824.4 | 1,083.8 | 2,476.1 | 2,587.7 |
| Debt instruments | 3abla | -299.0 | † 343.0 | 898.0 | 350.0 | 52.0 | 179.0 | 1,284.0 | 476.5 | 391.0 | 2,653.5 | 3,263.4 | 3,136.5 |
| Portfolio investment: assets | 3b9aa | 910.0 | † 1,643.8 | 559.2 | 141.1 | -1,604.9 | 234.2 | 1,468.2 | -563.2 | 964.0 | -637.8 | 2,704.9 | 2,615.5 |
| Equity & investment fund shares | 3baaa | 18.0 | † -55.2 | 5.4 | 92.0 | -126.0 | -22.7 | 3.0 | 19.5 | 20.2 | 68.4 | 234.5 | 283.4 |
| Debt securities | 3bbaa | 892.0 | † 1,699.0 | 553.8 | 49.2 | -1,478.9 | 256.9 | 1,465.2 | -582.6 | 943.9 | -706.2 | 2,470.4 | 2,332.1 |
| Portfolio investment: liabilities | 3b9la | 288.0 | † 2,766.6 | 5,112.4 | 1,849.6 | -3,192.0 | 2,288.2 | 8,643.5 | 3,100.1 | 4,169.1 | 363.4 | -3.4 | -2,141.3 |
| Equity & investment fund shares | 3bala | 518.0 | † 420.2 | 1,347.6 | 1,137.0 | -461.9 | 308.1 | 832.6 | 1,039.8 | 1,752.5 | -34.1 | 1,195.5 | -755.8 |
| Debt securities | 3bbla | -230.0 | † 2,346.4 | 3,764.7 | 712.5 | -2,730.1 | 1,980.1 | 7,811.0 | 2,060.3 | 2,416.5 | 397.4 | -1,198.9 | -1,385.4 |
| Fin. der.& empl.stk.ops.(ESOs): net. | 3c9na | 27.0 | † 43.0 | 138.0 | 288.0 | 113.7 | -30.2 | 193.6 | -1,004.7 | -13.7 | -88.0 | 4.0 | -32.6 |
| Fin. der. & ESOs.: assets | 3c9aa | -58.0 | † -98.0 | -159.0 | -170.0 | -539.8 | -400.9 | -427.8 | -1,541.7 | -277.2 | -312.4 | -292.9 | -465.4 |
| Fin. der. & ESOs.: liabilities | 3c9la | -85.0 | † -141.0 | -297.0 | -458.0 | -653.6 | -370.7 | -621.4 | -537.0 | -263.5 | -224.5 | -296.9 | -432.8 |
| Other investment: assets | 3d9aa | 859.0 | † 4,043.2 | 3,946.1 | 3,216.0 | -4,423.6 | 890.2 | -2,807.2 | 348.3 | -1,014.3 | 3,639.9 | 5,838.3 | -1,076.5 |
| Other equity | 3daaa | .... | .... | .... | .... | .... | .... | .... | .... | .... | .... | .... | .... |
| Debt instruments | 3dzaa | 859.0 | † 4,043.2 | 3,946.1 | 3,216.0 | -4,423.6 | 890.2 | -2,807.2 | 348.3 | -1,014.3 | 3,639.9 | 5,838.3 | -1,076.5 |
| Other investment: liabilities | 3d9la | -272.0 | † -489.0 | -2,322.8 | 4,569.6 | -3,454.7 | -2,475.4 | 5,627.7 | 1,340.5 | 3,471.8 | 230.2 | -66.2 | 1,002.5 |
| Other equity | 3dala | .... | .... | .... | .... | .... | .... | .... | .... | .... | .... | .... | .... |
| Debt instruments | 3dzla | -272.0 | † -489.0 | -2,322.8 | 4,569.6 | -3,454.7 | -2,475.4 | 5,627.7 | 1,340.5 | 3,471.8 | 230.2 | -66.2 | 1,002.5 |
| Curr.+ cap.– finan. acct. balance | 4y9na | -15.0 | † -512.8 | 6,851.3 | 8,428.5 | -1,107.9 | 7,424.1 | 21,042.4 | 11,120.2 | 13,791.3 | 9,287.2 | 1,232.6 | 5,954.9 |
| D. Net Errors and Omissions | 409na | -287.9 | † 2,174.6 | 1,609.7 | 277.5 | 1,204.4 | -3,012.9 | -3,514.8 | 281.0 | -4,555.2 | -4,202.1 | -4,090.7 | -3,339.2 |
| E. Reserves and Related Items | 4z9na | -302.9 | † 1,661.8 | 5,241.8 | 8,706.0 | 96.5 | 4,411.2 | 17,527.6 | 11,401.2 | 9,236.1 | 5,085.1 | -2,858.1 | 2,615.7 |
| Reserve assets | 3e9aa | -1,636.8 | † 1,622.1 | 2,935.3 | 8,549.0 | 1,596.5 | 4,911.2 | 15,242.6 | 11,401.2 | 9,236.1 | 5,085.1 | -2,858.1 | 2,615.7 |
| Credit and loans from the IMF | 3dcla | -471.9 | † -320.7 | -404.4 | — | — | — | — | — | — | — | | |
| Exceptional financing | 409la | -862.0 | † 281.0 | -1,902.0 | -157.0 | 1,500.0 | 500.0 | -2,285.0 | .... | .... | .... | — | — |

*Excludes components in group E

# Philippines 566

| | | 2004 | 2005 | 2006 | 2007 | 2008 | 2009 | 2010 | 2011 | 2012 | 2013 | 2014 | 2015 |
|---|---|---|---|---|---|---|---|---|---|---|---|---|---|
| **International Investment Position** | | | | | | *Millions of US Dollars* | | | | | | | |
| Assets............. | 809aa | 34,516.8 | 41,135.9 | 52,051.1 | 69,344.2 | 71,005.7 | 80,026.5 | 102,307.9 | † 115,970.5 | 129,204.3 | 136,117.5 | 147,988.7 | 155,103.1 |
| Direct investment............. | 8a9aa | 2,536.0 | 2,535.0 | 4,200.9 | 7,230.5 | 9,750.1 | 12,188.9 | 17,653.7 | † 18,503.6 | 24,401.3 | 29,010.2 | 35,791.3 | 41,100.0 |
| Equity & investment fund shares.. | 8aaaa | 1,839.0 | 2,028.0 | 2,650.2 | 3,871.7 | 4,542.4 | 5,517.5 | 8,657.5 | † 7,151.2 | 10,679.6 | 12,662.3 | 15,536.2 | 16,857.2 |
| Debt instruments............. | 8abaa | 697.0 | 507.0 | 1,550.7 | 3,358.8 | 5,207.7 | 6,671.4 | 8,996.2 | † 11,352.3 | 13,721.7 | 16,347.9 | 20,255.2 | 24,242.8 |
| Portfolio investment............. | 8b9aa | 5,022.0 | 5,303.0 | 7,854.4 | 7,995.5 | 6,383.4 | 6,622.9 | 8,089.0 | † 7,525.6 | 8,490.3 | 7,850.6 | 10,552.6 | 12,900.1 |
| Equity & investment fund shares.. | 8baaa | 185.0 | 190.0 | 98.1 | 190.1 | 63.4 | 40.8 | 43.7 | † 63.1 | 83.6 | 151.3 | 387.3 | 535.3 |
| Debt securities............. | 8bbaa | 4,837.0 | 5,113.0 | 7,756.3 | 7,805.5 | 6,320.0 | 6,582.1 | 8,045.3 | † 7,462.6 | 8,406.7 | 7,699.3 | 10,165.3 | 12,364.8 |
| Fin. der.(oth.than reserves) & ESOs | 8c9aa | .... | .... | .... | .... | 1,429.4 | 129.7 | 150.8 | † 282.8 | 275.5 | 303.7 | 685.1 | 299.4 |
| Other investment............. | 8d9aa | 10,730.0 | 14,804.0 | 17,029.0 | 20,366.5 | 15,892.0 | 16,842.5 | 14,042.0 | † 14,356.1 | 12,205.9 | 15,765.9 | 21,419.0 | 20,136.7 |
| Other equity............. | 8daaa | .... | .... | 67.4 | 82.9 | 69.0 | 70.3 | 69.0 | † 68.8 | 68.9 | 69.0 | 64.9 | 62.1 |
| Debt instruments............. | 8dzaa | 10,730.0 | 14,804.0 | 16,961.7 | 20,283.7 | 15,823.0 | 16,772.2 | 13,973.0 | † 14,287.3 | 12,137.0 | 15,696.9 | 21,354.1 | 20,074.6 |
| Reserve assets............. | 8e9aa | 16,228.8 | 18,493.9 | 22,966.7 | 33,751.6 | 37,550.8 | 44,242.6 | 62,372.3 | † 75,302.4 | 83,831.4 | 83,187.0 | 79,540.6 | 80,666.9 |
| Liabilities............. | 809la | 74,727.3 | 81,033.5 | 98,224.5 | 116,603.8 | 102,563.3 | 109,166.1 | 131,620.2 | † 139,024.1 | 169,841.7 | 172,074.7 | 188,885.3 | 184,092.4 |
| Direct investment............. | 8a9la | 13,434.0 | 15,485.0 | 23,748.7 | 26,965.9 | 27,852.6 | 29,800.5 | 30,716.0 | † 33,684.0 | 45,054.7 | 47,276.1 | 56,646.3 | 59,302.6 |
| Equity & investment fund shares.. | 8aala | 8,920.0 | 10,226.0 | 18,455.2 | 21,319.8 | 22,450.6 | 24,323.9 | 24,039.1 | † 26,937.5 | 37,981.2 | 36,964.5 | 43,062.6 | 42,544.5 |
| Debt instruments............. | 8abla | 4,514.0 | 5,259.0 | 5,293.5 | 5,646.2 | 5,402.0 | 5,476.6 | 6,676.9 | † 6,746.5 | 7,073.5 | 10,311.6 | 13,583.7 | 16,758.1 |
| Portfolio investment............. | 8b9la | 21,303.0 | 26,877.0 | 36,318.3 | 46,293.5 | 30,662.3 | 37,864.8 | 52,749.2 | † 55,331.3 | 71,635.8 | 73,269.9 | 81,579.3 | 72,666.3 |
| Equity & investment fund shares.. | 8bala | 4,293.0 | 7,299.0 | 15,232.4 | 24,741.9 | 11,284.2 | 16,092.4 | 25,438.8 | † 25,871.5 | 38,930.7 | 41,159.4 | 51,225.3 | 44,417.6 |
| Debt securities............. | 8bbla | 17,010.0 | 19,578.0 | 21,085.9 | 21,551.6 | 19,378.1 | 21,772.5 | 27,310.4 | † 29,459.8 | 32,705.1 | 32,110.6 | 30,354.0 | 28,248.7 |
| Fin. der.(oth.than reserves) & ESOs | 8c9la | .... | .... | .... | .... | 353.4 | 239.7 | 316.5 | † 285.5 | 367.6 | 276.4 | 674.1 | 266.0 |
| Other investment............. | 8d9la | 39,990.3 | 38,671.5 | 38,157.5 | 43,344.4 | 43,695.0 | 41,261.1 | 47,838.4 | † 49,723.2 | 52,783.5 | 51,252.3 | 49,985.6 | 51,857.5 |
| Other equity............. | 8dala | | | | | | | | | | | | |
| Debt instruments............. | 8dzla | 39,990.3 | 38,671.5 | 38,157.5 | 43,344.4 | 43,695.0 | 41,261.1 | 47,838.4 | † 49,723.2 | 52,783.5 | 51,252.3 | 49,985.6 | 51,857.5 |
| **Government Finance** | | | | | | | | | | | | | |
| **Cash Flow Statement** | | | | | | | | | | | | | |
| **Budgetary Central Government** | | | | | | *Billions of Pesos: Fiscal Year Ends December 31* | | | | | | | |
| Cash Receipts:Operating Activities... | c1 | 708.90 | 815.63 | 975.40 | 1,047.50 | 1,172.75 | 1,123.13 | 1,207.95 | 1,359.52 | 1,526.79 | 1,715.91 | 1,906.75 | .... |
| Taxes............. | c11 | 604.96 | 705.62 | 859.86 | 932.94 | 1,049.18 | 981.63 | 1,093.64 | 1,202.06 | 1,360.85 | 1,535.87 | 1,720.21 | .... |
| Social Contributions............. | c12 | | | | | | | | | | | | .... |
| Grants............. | c13 | .07 | .09 | .18 | .15 | .13 | .19 | .41 | .26 | .10 | .13 | .23 | .... |
| Other Receipts............. | c14 | 103.87 | 109.92 | 115.36 | 114.42 | 123.44 | 141.31 | 113.90 | 157.21 | 165.84 | 179.90 | 186.30 | .... |
| Cash Payments:Operating Activities. | c2 | 905.59 | 976.80 | 1,053.93 | 1,145.03 | 1,265.58 | 1,425.34 | 1,519.47 | 1,530.75 | 1,732.85 | 1,853.38 | 1,693.32 | .... |
| Compensation of Employees............. | c21 | 283.07 | 296.36 | 322.27 | 350.29 | 627.49 | 741.22 | 791.74 | 779.66 | 966.05 | 1,045.05 | 603.70 | .... |
| Purchases of Goods & Services....... | c22 | 177.62 | 175.19 | 199.20 | 209.43 | .... | .... | .... | .... | .... | .... | .... | .... |
| Interest............. | c24 | 278.43 | 315.57 | 323.30 | 277.30 | 282.86 | 288.89 | 302.84 | 283.04 | 316.51 | 324.77 | 324.03 | .... |
| Subsidies............. | c25 | 14.24 | 12.24 | 13.81 | 27.34 | 21.12 | 17.44 | 21.01 | 53.70 | 41.74 | 66.33 | 80.44 | .... |
| Grants............. | c26 | 145.28 | 157.00 | 174.71 | 193.71 | 223.00 | 264.65 | 279.55 | 315.11 | 298.32 | 319.05 | 345.90 | .... |
| Social Benefits............. | c27 | — | — | — | — | .... | .... | .... | .... | .... | .... | .... | .... |
| Other Payments............. | c28 | 6.95 | 20.45 | 20.64 | 86.96 | .... | .... | .... | .... | .... | .... | .... | .... |
| Net Cash Inflow:Operating Act.[1-2] | ccio | −196.69 | −161.17 | −78.53 | −97.52 | −92.83 | −302.21 | −311.52 | −171.23 | −206.06 | −137.47 | 213.43 | .... |
| Net Cash Outflow:Invest. in NFA...... | c31 | .... | .... | .... | .... | .... | .... | .... | .... | .... | .... | .... | .... |
| Purchases of Nonfinancial Assets... | c31.1 | .... | .... | .... | .... | .... | .... | .... | .... | .... | .... | .... | .... |
| Sales of Nonfinancial Assets.......... | c31.2 | .42 | 2.43 | .... | .... | .... | .... | .... | .... | .... | .... | .... | .... |
| Cash Surplus/Deficit [1-2-31=1-2M] | ccsd | −196.26 | −158.74 | −78.53 | −97.52 | .... | .... | .... | .... | .... | .... | .... | .... |
| Net Acq. Fin. Assets, excl. Cash....... | c32x | 99.61 | 1.44 | 31.45 | −67.56 | −12.92 | 5.60 | 11.13 | 32.59 | 97.08 | 27.72 | 11.37 | .... |
| Domestic............. | c321x | 99.61 | 1.44 | 31.45 | −67.56 | −12.92 | 5.60 | 11.13 | 32.59 | 97.08 | 27.72 | 11.37 | .... |
| Foreign............. | c322x | — | — | — | — | .... | .... | .... | .... | .... | .... | .... | .... |
| Net Incurrence of Liabilities............. | c33 | 276.46 | 182.51 | 116.04 | 136.91 | 127.39 | 241.78 | 359.82 | 124.48 | 594.92 | 231.12 | 127.82 | .... |
| Domestic............. | c331 | 190.71 | 78.16 | −6.36 | 76.50 | 114.47 | 89.28 | 226.77 | 71.04 | 489.14 | 313.21 | 114.99 | .... |
| Foreign............. | c332 | 85.75 | 104.35 | 122.40 | 60.42 | 12.92 | 152.50 | 133.05 | 53.45 | 105.79 | −82.09 | 12.84 | .... |
| Net Cash Inflow, Fin.Act.[-32x+33].. | cnfb | 176.85 | 181.07 | 84.59 | 204.47 | 140.30 | 236.18 | 348.69 | 91.89 | 497.84 | 203.40 | 116.45 | .... |
| Net Change in Stock of Cash........... | cncb | −19.41 | 22.33 | 6.06 | 106.95 | 34.56 | −66.03 | 37.17 | −79.34 | 291.78 | 65.93 | 53.88 | .... |
| Stat. Discrep. [32X-33+NCB-CSD].... | ccsdz | | | | | .... | .... | .... | .... | .... | .... | .... | .... |
| Memo Item:Cash Expenditure[2+31] | c2m | 905.59 | 976.80 | 1,053.93 | 1,145.03 | .... | .... | .... | .... | .... | .... | .... | .... |
| Memo Item: Gross Debt................. | c63 | 3,786.30 | .... | .... | .... | .... | .... | .... | .... | .... | .... | .... | .... |
| **National Accounts** | | | | | | *Billions of Pesos* | | | | | | | |
| Househ.Cons.Expend.,incl.NPISHs.... | 96f | 3,814.9 | 4,259.1 | 4,678.0 | 5,064.5 | 5,739.6 | 5,993.4 | 6,442.0 | 7,132.6 | 7,837.9 | 8,463.8 | 9,167.6 | 9,822.5 |
| Government Consumption Expend... | 91f | 480.4 | 513.3 | 575.7 | 640.0 | 681.9 | 791.4 | 875.3 | 941.8 | 1,145.1 | 1,250.8 | 1,334.0 | 1,458.4 |
| Gross Fixed Capital Formation......... | 93e | 1,041.6 | 1,129.9 | 1,261.9 | 1,371.6 | 1,518.2 | 1,526.1 | 1,847.7 | 1,819.3 | 2,068.9 | 2,380.3 | 2,610.2 | 2,852.0 |
| Changes in Inventories.................... | 93i | 65.0 | 93.6 | −132.6 | −176.6 | −29.0 | −194.4 | 1.6 | 167.7 | −146.4 | −70.8 | −14.5 | −117.1 |
| Exports of Goods and Services.......... | 90c | 2,487.1 | 2,619.5 | 2,921.0 | 2,981.8 | 2,849.9 | 2,587.0 | 3,133.5 | 3,109.7 | 3,254.8 | 3,232.8 | 3,647.5 | 3,751.3 |
| Imports of Goods and Services (-)..... | 98c | 2,768.6 | 2,937.8 | 3,032.9 | 2,988.6 | 3,039.7 | 2,677.4 | 3,296.7 | 3,462.7 | 3,599.3 | 3,718.6 | 4,099.4 | 4,459.7 |
| Gross Domestic Product (GDP)......... | 99b | 5,120.4 | 5,677.7 | 6,271.2 | 6,892.7 | 7,720.9 | 8,026.1 | 9,003.5 | 9,708.3 | 10,561.1 | 11,538.4 | 12,645.3 | 13,307.3 |
| Net Primary Income from Abroad..... | 98.n | 1,184.7 | 1,472.6 | 1,611.9 | 1,741.4 | 2,055.3 | 2,626.3 | 1,849.0 | 1,921.0 | 2,166.2 | 2,480.6 | 2,660.9 | 2,789.6 |
| Gross National Income (GNI)........... | 99a | 6,305.1 | 7,150.3 | 7,883.1 | 8,634.1 | 9,776.2 | 10,652.5 | 10,852.4 | 11,629.3 | 12,727.2 | 14,019.0 | 15,306.2 | 16,096.9 |
| GDP Volume 2000 Prices............. | 99b.p | 4,276.9 | 4,481.3 | 4,716.2 | 5,028.3 | 5,237.1 | 5,297.2 | 5,701.5 | 5,910.2 | 6,305.2 | 6,750.6 | 7,170.4 | 7,593.8 |
| GDP Volume (2010=100)................. | 99bvp | 75.0 | 78.6 | 82.7 | 88.2 | 91.9 | 92.9 | 100.0 | 103.7 | 110.6 | 118.4 | 125.8 | 133.2 |
| GDP Deflator (2010=100)............... | 99bip | 75.8 | 80.2 | 84.2 | 86.8 | 93.4 | 95.9 | 100.0 | 104.0 | 106.1 | 108.2 | 111.7 | 111.0 |
| | | | | | | *Millions: Midyear Estimates* | | | | | | | |
| Population............. | 99z | 84.60 | 86.14 | 87.59 | 88.97 | 90.30 | 91.64 | 93.04 | 94.50 | 96.02 | 97.57 | 99.14 | 100.70 |

# Poland 964

| | | 2004 | 2005 | 2006 | 2007 | 2008 | 2009 | 2010 | 2011 | 2012 | 2013 | 2014 | 2015 |
|---|---|---|---|---|---|---|---|---|---|---|---|---|---|
| **Exchange Rates** | | | | | | *Zlotys per SDR: End of Period* | | | | | | | |
| Market Rate................................. | aa | 4.6441 | 4.6613 | 4.3786 | 3.8479 | 4.5620 | 4.4684 | 4.5648 | 5.2466 | 4.7638 | 4.6385 | 5.0813 | 5.4059 |
| | | | | | *Zlotys per US Dollar: End of Period (ae) Period Average (rf)* | | | | | | | | |
| Market Rate................................. | ae | 2.9904 | 3.2613 | 2.9105 | 2.4350 | 2.9618 | 2.8503 | 2.9641 | 3.4174 | 3.0996 | 3.0120 | 3.5072 | 3.9011 |
| Market Rate................................. | rf | 3.6576 | 3.2355 | 3.1032 | 2.7680 | 2.4092 | 3.1201 | 3.0153 | 2.9628 | 3.2565 | 3.1606 | 3.1545 | 3.7695 |
| | | | | | *Index Numbers (2010=100): Period Averages* | | | | | | | | |
| Market Rate................................. | ahx | 82.6 | 93.0 | 97.0 | 109.0 | 126.5 | 97.1 | 100.0 | 102.0 | 92.4 | 95.2 | 95.5 | 79.8 |
| Nominal Effective Exchange Rate..... | nec | 87.1 | 97.3 | 100.6 | 104.7 | 114.6 | 94.6 | 100.0 | 97.4 | 93.9 | 95.2 | 97.1 | 95.9 |
| CPI-Based Real Effect. Ex. Rate........ | rec | 85.6 | 95.5 | 97.5 | 101.0 | 110.7 | 94.1 | 100.0 | 98.6 | 96.0 | 96.7 | 97.3 | 94.0 |
| **Fund Position** | | | | | | *Millions of SDRs: End of Period* | | | | | | | |
| Quota.......................................... | 2f.s | 1,369.00 | 1,369.00 | 1,369.00 | 1,369.00 | 1,369.00 | 1,369.00 | 1,369.00 | 1,688.40 | 1,688.40 | 1,688.40 | 1,688.40 | 1,688.40 |
| SDR Holdings.............................. | 1b.s | 45.17 | 54.43 | 59.24 | 63.75 | 70.59 | 1,339.25 | 1,302.91 | 1,170.83 | 1,126.09 | 1,063.10 | 987.22 | 946.67 |
| Reserve Position in the Fund............ | 1c.s | 451.33 | 209.17 | 116.28 | 92.23 | 172.62 | 274.45 | 323.30 | 756.10 | 877.44 | 819.37 | 667.49 | 477.55 |
| Total Fund Cred.&Loans Outstg....... | 2tl | — | — | — | — | — | — | — | — | — | — | — | — |
| SDR Allocations............................. | 1bd | | | | | | 1,304.64 | 1,304.64 | 1,304.64 | 1,304.64 | 1,304.64 | 1,304.64 | 1,304.64 |
| **International Liquidity** | | | | | *Millions of US Dollars Unless Otherwise Indicated: End of Period* | | | | | | | | |
| Total Reserves minus Gold.............. | 1l.d | 35,323.9 | 40,863.7 | 46,371.1 | 62,966.8 | 59,305.6 | 75,923.3 | 88,821.8 | 92,646.5 | 103,396.2 | 102,235.9 | 96,461.5 | 91,394.8 |
| SDR Holdings........................ | 1b.d | 70.1 | 77.8 | 89.1 | 100.7 | 108.7 | 2,099.5 | 2,006.5 | 1,797.5 | 1,730.7 | 1,637.2 | 1,430.3 | 1,311.8 |
| Reserve Position in the Fund.......... | 1c.d | 700.9 | 299.0 | 174.9 | 145.8 | 265.9 | 430.3 | 497.9 | 1,160.8 | 1,348.6 | 1,261.8 | 967.1 | 661.8 |
| Foreign Exchange........................ | 1d.d | 34,552.8 | 40,486.9 | 46,107.0 | 62,720.3 | 58,931.0 | 73,393.6 | 86,317.4 | 89,688.1 | 100,316.9 | 99,336.9 | 94,064.2 | 89,421.2 |
| Gold (Million Fine Troy Ounces)....... | 1ad | 3.308 | 3.308 | 3.308 | 3.308 | 3.309 | 3.309 | 3.309 | 3.309 | 3.309 | 3.309 | 3.309 | 3.309 |
| Gold (National Valuation)................ | 1and | 1,448.8 | 1,697.2 | 2,103.1 | 2,767.4 | 2,862.1 | 3,652.9 | 4,666.4 | 5,209.9 | 5,506.0 | 3,975.7 | 3,968.6 | 3,515.3 |
| Central Bank: Other Assets............. | 3..d | 8,298.2 | 11,118.6 | 10,073.5 | 19,193.8 | 5,884.9 | 8,753.1 | 11,570.5 | 11,345.2 | 10,978.5 | 13,045.5 | 14,532.7 | 12,713.3 |
| Central Bank: Other Liabs.............. | 4..d | 1,611.8 | 3,661.4 | 3,195.3 | 10,387.7 | 4,248.1 | 5,212.4 | 6,509.9 | 4,753.0 | 5,342.0 | 7,448.9 | 5,755.0 | 5,704.8 |
| Other Depository Corps.: Assets....... | 7a.d | 24,956.5 | 25,511.0 | 29,537.5 | 29,932.2 | 20,389.6 | 13,144.9 | 13,827.5 | 15,071.7 | 16,487.0 | 16,144.8 | 16,050.7 | 14,456.9 |
| Other Depository Corps.: Liabs......... | 7b.d | 13,725.3 | 12,654.2 | 19,683.9 | 37,928.1 | 58,549.5 | 60,681.3 | 66,383.4 | 64,476.5 | 62,649.1 | 64,941.2 | 58,344.3 | 52,803.6 |
| **Central Bank** | | | | | | *Millions of Zlotys: End of Period* | | | | | | | |
| Net Foreign Assets........................ | 11n | † 109,944 | 132,795 | 132,287 | 135,213 | 171,753 | 206,282 | 251,982 | 311,465 | 314,909 | 291,549 | 325,556 | 341,089 |
| Claims on Nonresidents................. | 11 | † 114,764 | 144,736 | 141,587 | 160,507 | 184,335 | 226,969 | 277,233 | 334,553 | 337,683 | 320,037 | 352,369 | 370,397 |
| Liabilities to Nonresidents............. | 16c | † 4,820 | 11,941 | 9,300 | 25,294 | 12,582 | 20,687 | 25,251 | 23,088 | 22,773 | 28,488 | 26,813 | 29,308 |
| Claims on Other Depository Corps.... | 12e | † 3,276 | 3,239 | 5,448 | 3,401 | 19,054 | 15,630 | 729 | 356 | | | | 181 |
| Net Claims on Central Government.. | 12an | † −13,713 | −16,320 | −16,718 | −26,444 | −21,330 | −22,739 | −12,196 | −19,500 | −16,759 | −6,859 | −19,871 | −13,134 |
| Claims on Central Government...... | 12a | † 129 | 138 | 31 | — | — | — | — | — | — | — | — | — |
| Liabilities to Central Government... | 16d | † 13,842 | 16,458 | 16,749 | 26,444 | 21,330 | 22,739 | 12,196 | 19,500 | 16,759 | 6,859 | 19,871 | 13,134 |
| Claims on Other Sectors............... | 12s | † 109 | 107 | 79 | 79 | 77 | 80 | 79 | 80 | 78 | 78 | 76 | 149 |
| Claims on Other Financial Corps.... | 12g | † 52 | 52 | 52 | 52 | 53 | 53 | 52 | 52 | 52 | 52 | 52 | 127 |
| Claims on State & Local Govts....... | 12b | † — | — | — | — | — | — | — | — | — | — | | |
| Claims on Public Nonfin. Corps...... | 12c | † — | — | — | — | — | — | — | — | — | — | | |
| Claims on Private Sector............... | 12d | † 57 | 55 | 27 | 27 | 24 | 27 | 27 | 28 | 26 | 26 | 24 | 22 |
| Monetary Base............................. | 14 | † 70,365 | 74,528 | 91,761 | 107,056 | 133,598 | 139,302 | 141,983 | 139,415 | 171,068 | 166,636 | 193,226 | 215,036 |
| Currency in Circulation.................. | 14a | † 55,925 | 62,597 | 75,073 | 85,671 | 101,774 | 99,954 | 102,663 | 111,845 | 113,415 | 125,884 | 142,661 | 162,952 |
| Liabs. to Other Depository Corps.... | 14c | † 13,300 | 10,679 | 14,612 | 17,533 | 25,314 | 37,865 | 37,610 | 26,723 | 56,585 | 39,662 | 49,308 | 50,300 |
| Liabilities to Other Sectors........... | 14d | † 1,140 | 1,252 | 2,076 | 3,852 | 6,510 | 1,483 | 1,710 | 847 | 1,068 | 1,090 | 1,257 | 1,784 |
| Other Liabs. to Other Dep. Corps..... | 14n | † 13,556 | 30,816 | 26,216 | 15,585 | 18,029 | 40,984 | 74,640 | 93,431 | 99,842 | 117,341 | 84,661 | 74,121 |
| Dep. & Sec. Excl. f/Monetary Base..... | 14o | † — | — | — | — | — | — | — | — | — | — | — | — |
| Deposits Included in Broad Money. | 15 | † — | — | — | — | — | — | — | — | — | — | — | — |
| Sec.Ot.th.Shares Incl.in Brd. Money | 16a | † — | — | — | — | — | — | — | — | — | — | — | — |
| Deposits Excl. from Broad Money. | 16b | † — | — | — | — | — | — | — | — | — | — | — | — |
| Sec.Ot.th.Shares Excl.f/Brd.Money.. | 16s | † — | — | — | — | — | — | — | — | — | — | — | — |
| Loans.......................................... | 16l | † — | — | — | — | — | — | — | — | — | — | — | — |
| Financial Derivatives....................... | 16m | † — | | | | | | | | | | | |
| Shares and Other Equity................. | 17a | † 2,944 | 3,245 | 3,450 | 3,626 | 24,581 | 26,173 | 30,614 | 67,179 | 34,665 | 8,250 | 36,131 | 48,830 |
| Other Items (Net)............................ | 17r | † 12,751 | 11,234 | −331 | −14,017 | 13,072 | −173 | 8,358 | 44,329 | 12,008 | −8,053 | −8,258 | −9,701 |
| **Other Depository Corporations** | | | | | | *Millions of Zlotys: End of Period* | | | | | | | |
| Net Foreign Assets........................ | 21n | † 33,586 | 41,930 | 28,679 | −19,470 | −113,022 | −135,493 | −155,781 | −168,836 | −143,084 | −146,975 | −148,332 | −149,594 |
| Claims on Nonresidents................. | 21 | † 74,630 | 83,199 | 85,969 | 72,885 | 60,390 | 37,467 | 40,986 | 51,506 | 51,103 | 48,628 | 56,293 | 56,398 |
| Liabilities to Nonresidents............. | 26c | † 41,044 | 41,269 | 57,290 | 92,355 | 173,412 | 172,960 | 196,767 | 220,342 | 194,187 | 195,603 | 204,625 | 205,992 |
| Claims on Central Bank.................. | 20 | † 32,006 | 46,977 | 47,166 | 41,651 | 54,326 | 89,043 | 122,158 | 130,167 | 167,176 | 168,403 | 146,136 | 138,255 |
| Currency........................................ | 20a | † 5,149 | 5,442 | 6,305 | 8,511 | 10,962 | 10,176 | 9,956 | 9,997 | 10,944 | 11,481 | 12,631 | 13,265 |
| Reserve Deposits and Securities..... | 20b | † 13,301 | 10,719 | 14,645 | 17,555 | 25,335 | 37,883 | 37,562 | 26,739 | 56,390 | 39,581 | 48,844 | 50,869 |
| Other Claims................................. | 20n | † 13,556 | 30,816 | 26,216 | 15,585 | 18,029 | 40,984 | 74,640 | 93,431 | 99,842 | 117,341 | 84,661 | 74,121 |
| Net Claims on Central Government.. | 22an | † 82,880 | 80,976 | 89,505 | 88,344 | 132,196 | 138,103 | 136,549 | 141,060 | 124,688 | 152,170 | 188,309 | 214,437 |
| Claims on Central Government...... | 22a | † 95,519 | 94,357 | 104,347 | 106,758 | 153,334 | 164,349 | 169,228 | 167,532 | 160,908 | 182,792 | 224,413 | 239,781 |
| Liabilities to Central Government... | 26d | † 12,639 | 13,381 | 14,842 | 18,414 | 21,138 | 26,246 | 32,679 | 26,472 | 36,221 | 30,622 | 36,104 | 25,344 |
| Claims on Other Sectors............... | 22s | † 294,425 | 315,812 | 385,627 | 505,729 | 705,842 | 729,610 | 789,430 | 911,105 | 935,916 | 968,470 | 1,051,870 | 1,114,901 |
| Claims on Other Financial Corps.... | 22g | † 31,091 | 28,477 | 31,935 | 46,500 | 77,511 | 51,467 | 44,776 | 55,752 | 67,388 | 70,970 | 100,569 | 97,058 |
| Claims on State & Local Govts....... | 22b | † 18,187 | 18,793 | 19,909 | 18,487 | 20,496 | 32,785 | 40,116 | 50,208 | 52,159 | 51,385 | 53,263 | 53,030 |
| Claims on Public Nonfin. Corps...... | 22c | † — | — | — | — | — | — | — | — | — | — | — | — |
| Claims on Private Sector............... | 22d | † 245,147 | 268,542 | 333,783 | 440,742 | 607,835 | 645,358 | 704,538 | 805,145 | 816,369 | 846,115 | 898,038 | 964,813 |
| Liabilities to Central Bank............... | 26g | † 3,522 | 2,563 | 4,956 | 3,041 | 18,043 | 14,397 | 733 | 361 | 4 | 5 | 6 | 186 |
| Transf.Dep.Included in Broad Money | 24 | † 124,109 | 162,234 | 204,985 | 254,253 | 252,622 | 297,082 | 354,775 | 365,358 | 381,277 | 440,345 | 474,997 | 540,623 |
| Other Dep.Included in Broad Money. | 25 | † 192,259 | 204,283 | 216,547 | 222,602 | 314,490 | 330,044 | 332,406 | 405,595 | 428,571 | 416,786 | 448,621 | 460,837 |
| Sec.Ot.th.Shares Incl.in Brd. Money.. | 26a | † 2,986 | 2,197 | 2,932 | 3,757 | 1,796 | 1,843 | 2,050 | 7,850 | 8,025 | 6,279 | 4,113 | 2,465 |
| Deposits Excl. from Broad Money... | 26b | † 17,611 | 10,260 | 7,764 | 7,050 | 8,896 | 8,870 | 9,073 | 9,044 | 10,843 | 17,154 | 20,511 | 21,993 |
| Sec.Ot.th.Shares Excl.f/Brd.Money..... | 26s | † 2,504 | 7,139 | 11,712 | 8,621 | 10,495 | 16,776 | 22,653 | 30,734 | 35,870 | 40,874 | 40,422 | 43,201 |
| Loans.......................................... | 26l | † — | | | | | | | | | | | |
| Financial Derivatives....................... | 26m | † 15,535 | 11,614 | 11,832 | 21,836 | 61,431 | 18,931 | 26,354 | 28,742 | 29,463 | 23,231 | 40,564 | 32,517 |
| Insurance Technical Reserves.......... | 26r | † — | | | | | | | | | | | |
| Shares and Other Equity................. | 27a | † 47,939 | 52,401 | 57,569 | 63,712 | 89,205 | 104,397 | 117,449 | 131,571 | 149,983 | 157,260 | 170,297 | 176,266 |
| Other Items (Net)............................ | 27r | † 36,432 | 33,122 | 32,680 | 31,384 | 22,367 | 28,922 | 26,862 | 34,243 | 40,656 | 40,137 | 40,347 | 39,907 |
| Memo Item: | | | | | | | | | | | | | |
| Total Assets................................. | 20ra | 578,246 | 630,684 | 726,888 | 840,651 | 1,090,668 | 1,124,708 | 1,238,140 | 1,380,642 | 1,442,302 | 1,501,046 | 1,620,113 | 1,680,736 |

# Poland 964

| | | 2004 | 2005 | 2006 | 2007 | 2008 | 2009 | 2010 | 2011 | 2012 | 2013 | 2014 | 2015 |
|---|---|---|---|---|---|---|---|---|---|---|---|---|---|
| **Depository Corporations** | | | | | | | *Millions of Zlotys: End of Period* | | | | | | |
| Net Foreign Assets | 31n | † 143,530 | 174,725 | 160,966 | 115,743 | 58,731 | 70,789 | 96,201 | 142,629 | 171,825 | 144,574 | 177,224 | 191,495 |
| Claims on Nonresidents | 31 | † 189,394 | 227,935 | 227,556 | 233,392 | 244,725 | 264,436 | 318,219 | 386,059 | 388,786 | 368,665 | 408,662 | 426,795 |
| Liabilities to Nonresidents | 36c | † 45,864 | 53,210 | 66,590 | 117,649 | 185,994 | 193,647 | 222,018 | 243,430 | 216,960 | 224,091 | 231,438 | 235,300 |
| Domestic Claims | 32 | † 363,701 | 380,575 | 458,493 | 567,708 | 816,785 | 845,054 | 913,862 | 1,032,745 | 1,043,922 | 1,113,859 | 1,220,384 | 1,316,353 |
| Net Claims on Central Government | 32an | † 69,167 | 64,656 | 72,787 | 61,900 | 110,866 | 115,364 | 124,353 | 121,560 | 107,928 | 145,311 | 168,438 | 201,303 |
| Claims on Central Government | 32a | † 95,648 | 94,495 | 104,378 | 106,758 | 153,334 | 164,349 | 169,228 | 167,532 | 160,908 | 182,792 | 224,413 | 239,781 |
| Liabilities to Central Government | 36d | † 26,481 | 29,839 | 31,591 | 44,858 | 42,468 | 48,985 | 44,875 | 45,972 | 52,980 | 37,481 | 55,975 | 38,478 |
| Claims on Other Sectors | 32s | † 294,534 | 315,919 | 385,706 | 505,808 | 705,919 | 729,690 | 789,509 | 911,185 | 935,994 | 968,548 | 1,051,946 | 1,115,050 |
| Claims on Other Financial Corps | 32g | † 31,143 | 28,529 | 31,987 | 46,552 | 77,564 | 51,520 | 44,828 | 55,804 | 67,440 | 71,022 | 100,621 | 97,185 |
| Claims on State & Local Govts | 32b | † 18,187 | 18,793 | 19,909 | 18,487 | 20,496 | 32,785 | 40,116 | 50,208 | 52,159 | 51,385 | 53,263 | 53,030 |
| Claims on Public Nonfin. Corps | 32c | † — | — | — | — | — | — | — | — | — | — | — | — |
| Claims on Private Sector | 32d | † 245,204 | 268,597 | 333,810 | 440,769 | 607,859 | 645,385 | 704,565 | 805,173 | 816,395 | 846,141 | 898,062 | 964,835 |
| Broad Money Liabilities | 35l | † 371,270 | 427,121 | 495,308 | 561,624 | 666,230 | 720,230 | 783,648 | 881,498 | 921,412 | 978,903 | 1,059,018 | 1,155,396 |
| Currency Outside Depository Corps | 34a | † 50,776 | 57,155 | 68,768 | 77,160 | 90,812 | 89,778 | 92,707 | 101,848 | 102,471 | 114,403 | 130,030 | 149,687 |
| Transferable Deposits | 34 | † 124,944 | 163,486 | 207,061 | 258,105 | 259,132 | 298,565 | 356,485 | 366,205 | 382,344 | 441,435 | 476,254 | 542,407 |
| Other Deposits | 35 | † 192,564 | 204,283 | 216,547 | 222,602 | 314,490 | 330,044 | 332,406 | 405,595 | 428,572 | 416,786 | 448,621 | 460,837 |
| Securities Other than Shares | 36a | † 2,986 | 2,197 | 2,932 | 3,757 | 1,796 | 1,843 | 2,050 | 7,850 | 8,025 | 6,279 | 4,113 | 2,465 |
| Deposits Excl. from Broad Money | 36b | † 17,611 | 10,260 | 7,764 | 7,050 | 8,896 | 8,870 | 9,073 | 9,044 | 10,843 | 17,154 | 20,511 | 21,993 |
| Sec.Ot.th.Shares Excl.f/Brd.Money | 36s | † 2,504 | 7,139 | 11,712 | 8,621 | 10,495 | 16,776 | 22,653 | 30,734 | 35,870 | 40,874 | 40,422 | 43,201 |
| Loans | 36l | † — | — | — | — | — | — | — | — | — | — | — | — |
| Financial Derivatives | 36m | † 15,535 | 11,614 | 11,832 | 21,836 | 61,431 | 18,931 | 26,354 | 28,742 | 29,463 | 23,231 | 40,564 | 32,517 |
| Insurance Technical Reserves | 36r | † — | — | — | — | — | — | — | — | — | — | — | — |
| Shares and Other Equity | 37a | † 50,883 | 55,646 | 61,019 | 67,338 | 113,786 | 130,570 | 148,063 | 198,750 | 184,648 | 165,510 | 206,428 | 225,096 |
| Other Items (Net) | 37r | † 49,428 | 43,640 | 31,824 | 16,985 | 34,407 | 27,498 | 35,272 | 78,561 | 52,863 | 32,170 | 32,559 | 29,642 |
| Broad Money Liabs., Seasonally Adj. | 35l.b | † 370,145 | 425,578 | 492,624 | 557,037 | 658,430 | 709,749 | 770,486 | 865,929 | 905,389 | 963,163 | 1,043,175 | 1,138,676 |
| **Monetary Aggregates** | | | | | | | *Millions of Zlotys: End of Period* | | | | | | |
| Broad Money | 59m | 371,270 | 427,121 | 495,308 | 561,624 | 666,230 | 720,230 | 783,648 | 881,498 | 921,412 | 978,903 | 1,059,018 | 1,155,396 |
| o/w:Currency Issued by Cent.Govt | 59m.a | — | — | — | — | — | — | — | — | — | — | — | — |
| o/w: Dep.in Nonfin. Corporations | 59m.b | — | — | — | — | — | — | — | — | — | — | — | — |
| o/w:Secs. Issued by Central Govt | 59m.c | — | — | — | — | — | — | — | — | — | — | — | — |
| Money (National Definitions) | | | | | | | | | | | | | |
| M0 | 19mc | 69,173 | 70,505 | 86,826 | 102,669 | 126,350 | 137,507 | 139,727 | 138,129 | 167,205 | 164,010 | 191,620 | 212,177 |
| M1 | 59ma | 181,976 | 220,639 | 275,831 | 335,278 | 349,719 | 388,851 | 449,192 | 467,975 | 484,819 | 555,851 | 606,293 | 692,094 |
| M2 | 59mb | 368,714 | 415,164 | 481,210 | 549,415 | 660,313 | 715,274 | 774,658 | 863,769 | 900,336 | 960,361 | 1,044,571 | 1,145,667 |
| M3 | 59mc | † 377,534 | 427,125 | 495,309 | 561,654 | 666,305 | 720,327 | 783,649 | 881,503 | 921,412 | 978,924 | 1,059,186 | 1,155,401 |
| **Interest Rates** | | | | | | | *Percent Per Annum* | | | | | | |
| Repurchase Agreement Rate (EOP) | 60.q | 6.50 | 4.50 | 4.00 | 5.00 | 5.00 | 3.50 | 3.50 | 4.50 | 4.25 | 2.50 | 2.00 | 1.50 |
| Refinancing Rate | 60a | 9.00 | 7.00 | 6.50 | 7.50 | 7.50 | 6.00 | 6.00 | 7.00 | 6.75 | 5.00 | 4.00 | 3.50 |
| Money Market Rate | 60b | 5.67 | 5.34 | 4.10 | 4.42 | 5.75 | 3.18 | 3.08 | 4.10 | 4.66 | 3.01 | 2.48 | 1.66 |
| Treasury Bill Rate | 60c | 6.60 | 4.90 | 4.19 | 4.70 | 6.27 | 4.56 | 3.93 | 4.46 | .... | .... | .... | .... |
| Deposit Rate | 60l | 3.75 | 2.79 | 2.20 | .... | .... | .... | .... | .... | .... | .... | .... | .... |
| Households: Stocks, up to 2 years | 60lhs | 3.46 | 3.86 | 2.81 | 3.07 | 4.38 | 5.53 | 4.39 | 4.12 | 4.65 | 3.60 | 2.46 | 1.96 |
| New Business, 6 months to 1 year | 60lhn | 4.76 | 3.97 | 3.30 | 3.55 | 5.12 | 4.96 | 4.28 | 4.28 | 4.53 | 2.94 | 2.59 | 1.98 |
| Corporations: Stocks, up to 2 years | 60lcs | 4.88 | 4.70 | 3.71 | 3.94 | 5.31 | 4.34 | 3.69 | 4.32 | 4.96 | 3.15 | 2.53 | 1.79 |
| New Business, 6 months to 1 year | 60lcn | 5.29 | 4.51 | 3.72 | 4.05 | 5.55 | 5.00 | 4.39 | 4.89 | 5.20 | 3.25 | 2.80 | 1.89 |
| Repos, Stocks | 60lcr | .... | 5.01 | 3.95 | 4.26 | 5.79 | 3.74 | 3.25 | .... | .... | .... | .... | .... |
| Deposit Rate (Euros) | 60l.f | 1.47 | 1.70 | 2.42 | 3.45 | 3.61 | .82 | .45 | .90 | .46 | .29 | .27 | .20 |
| Lending Rate | 60p | 7.56 | 6.83 | 5.48 | .... | .... | .... | .... | .... | .... | .... | .... | .... |
| Households: Stocks, up to 1 year | 60phs | 14.56 | 9.25 | 7.31 | 8.96 | 10.45 | 11.74 | 12.38 | 12.09 | 11.91 | 12.98 | 12.61 | 9.06 |
| New Bus., Fixed & 3 mo. to 1 year | 60pns | .... | 9.65 | 10.03 | 10.05 | 11.29 | 11.70 | 12.09 | 12.05 | 14.27 | 9.52 | 7.14 | 4.35 |
| House Purch., Stocks, 5-10 years | 60phm | .... | 7.28 | 6.01 | 5.90 | 7.17 | 6.56 | 6.08 | 6.32 | 6.88 | 5.25 | 4.49 | 3.68 |
| House Purch., New.Bus., 5-10 yrs | 60phn | 7.45 | 7.46 | 7.62 | 7.66 | 8.23 | 7.99 | 6.71 | 6.60 | 6.97 | 5.48 | 5.13 | 4.39 |
| Corporations: Stocks, up to 1 year | 60pcs | 7.44 | 7.06 | 5.91 | 6.06 | 7.50 | 6.52 | 6.19 | 6.19 | 6.36 | 5.08 | 4.65 | 3.79 |
| New Bus.,> PLN 4 mil.,3 mo.-1 yr | 60pcn | .... | 6.18 | 5.05 | 5.61 | 7.57 | 6.84 | 6.97 | 7.60 | 7.23 | 5.27 | 4.12 | 3.46 |
| Lending Rate (Euros) | 60p.f | 3.82 | 3.87 | 4.51 | 5.72 | 5.99 | 3.99 | 3.56 | 3.70 | 3.52 | 2.81 | 2.68 | .... |
| Government Bond Yield | 61 | 6.90 | 5.22 | 5.23 | 5.48 | 6.07 | 6.12 | 5.78 | 5.96 | 5.00 | 4.03 | 3.52 | 2.70 |
| **Prices, Production, Labor** | | | | | | | *Index Numbers (2010=100): Period Averages* | | | | | | |
| Share Prices | 62 | 56.4 | 69.1 | 100.9 | 137.7 | 95.2 | 74.9 | 100.0 | 104.4 | 97.4 | 113.1 | 122.2 | 121.8 |
| Share Prices (End of Month) | 62.ep | 56.7 | 69.9 | 101.6 | 138.7 | 93.5 | 75.4 | 100.0 | 104.5 | 97.9 | 112.9 | 122.1 | 121.2 |
| WIG-20 | 62a | 70.2 | 86.7 | 120.4 | 143.8 | 103.2 | 78.2 | 100.0 | 103.1 | 92.0 | 97.4 | 97.1 | 89.8 |
| WIG-20 (End of Month) | 62aep | 70.6 | 87.9 | 120.6 | 144.0 | 104.6 | 78.5 | 100.0 | 103.5 | 92.5 | 96.8 | 97.1 | 89.1 |
| Producer Prices: Industry | 63 | 87.6 | 88.3 | 90.3 | 92.3 | † 94.7 | 97.9 | † 100.0 | 107.5 | 111.0 | 109.5 | 107.9 | 105.6 |
| Consumer Prices | 64 | 85.0 | 86.8 | 87.8 | 89.9 | 93.8 | 97.4 | † 100.0 | 104.3 | 108.0 | 109.1 | 109.2 | 108.1 |
| Harmonized CPI | 64h | 84.7 | 86.5 | 87.6 | 89.9 | 93.7 | 97.4 | 100.0 | 103.9 | 107.7 | 108.6 | 108.7 | 107.9 |
| Wages: Average Earnings | 65 | 70.1 | 72.3 | 76.1 | 82.7 | 90.8 | 95.2 | † 100.0 | 105.5 | 110.0 | 113.4 | 117.3 | 120.3 |
| Industrial Production | 66 | 71.8 | 74.4 | 83.3 | 91.1 | 93.6 | 90.0 | 100.0 | 106.7 | 108.0 | 110.9 | 114.6 | 119.9 |
| Industrial Employment | 67 | 97.2 | 98.3 | 100.6 | 104.1 | 106.3 | 100.3 | † 100.0 | 102.2 | 101.5 | 100.6 | 101.6 | 103.1 |
| | | | | | | *Number in Thousands: Period Averages* | | | | | | | |
| Labor Force | 67d | 16,907 | 16,873 | 16,679 | 16,610 | 16,765 | 17,039 | 16,879 | 16,968 | 17,086 | 17,101 | 17,153 | 17,110 |
| Employment | 67e | 13,682 | 13,834 | 14,339 | 14,997 | 15,558 | 15,629 | 15,233 | 15,313 | 15,340 | 15,313 | 15,591 | 15,810 |
| Unemployment | 67c | 3,209 | 3,019 | 2,311 | 1,579 | 1,165 | 1,360 | 1,650 | 1,659 | 1,749 | 1,793 | 1,567 | 1,304 |
| Unemployment Rate (%) | 67r | 19.1 | 17.9 | 13.9 | 9.6 | 7.1 | 8.1 | 9.7 | 9.7 | 10.1 | 10.3 | 9.0 | 7.5 |
| **Intl. Transactions & Positions** | | | | | | | *Millions of Zlotys* | | | | | | |
| Exports | 70 | 272,106 | 288,682 | 343,779 | 382,200 | 399,353 | 423,241 | 481,058 | 553,430 | 597,096 | 638,600 | 682,360 | 747,248 |
| Imports, c.i.f. | 71 | 324,663 | 326,120 | 394,030 | 446,895 | 485,833 | 463,383 | 536,221 | 611,004 | 638,288 | 648,195 | 692,573 | 731,720 |
| | | | | | | | *2010=100* | | | | | | |
| Volume of Exports | 72 | 63.9 | 70.6 | 82.1 | 89.9 | 96.4 | 88.2 | 100.0 | † 107.8 | 103.0 | 118.6 | 125.1 | 135.4 |
| Volume of Imports | 73 | 66.8 | 70.3 | 82.1 | 94.6 | 103.0 | 88.1 | 100.0 | † 105.4 | 97.7 | 106.6 | 115.7 | 122.1 |
| Export Prices | 76 | 104.2 | 100.0 | 102.1 | 105.2 | 103.5 | 117.5 | .... | .... | .... | .... | .... | .... |
| Import Prices | 76.x | 104.4 | 100.0 | 102.3 | 103.3 | 103.3 | 117.1 | .... | .... | .... | .... | .... | .... |

# Poland 964

## Balance of Payments

*Millions of US Dollars*

| | Code | 2004 | 2005 | 2006 | 2007 | 2008 | 2009 | 2010 | 2011 | 2012 | 2013 | 2014 | 2015 |
|---|---|---|---|---|---|---|---|---|---|---|---|---|---|
| A. Current Account* | 109bx | † −13,851.0 | −7,981.0 | −13,893.0 | −27,429.0 | −35,829.0 | −17,867.0 | −25,875.0 | −27,355.0 | −18,605.0 | −6,749.0 | −11,124.0 | −1,136.8 |
| Goods, credit (exports) | 1a9cx | † 72,783.0 | 87,736.0 | 108,168.0 | 134,719.0 | 166,450.0 | 133,285.0 | 156,542.0 | 184,425.0 | 181,259.0 | 198,108.0 | 210,627.0 | 190,727.0 |
| Goods, debit (imports) | 1a9dx | † 81,002.0 | 93,279.0 | 118,113.0 | 157,446.0 | 200,879.0 | 144,100.0 | 171,037.0 | 202,980.0 | 191,755.0 | 198,560.0 | 214,920.0 | 188,351.0 |
| Balance on goods | 1a9bx | † −8,219.0 | −5,543.0 | −9,945.0 | −22,727.0 | −34,429.0 | −10,815.0 | −14,495.0 | −18,555.0 | −10,496.0 | −452.0 | −4,293.0 | 2,376.0 |
| Services, credit (exports) | 1b9cx | † 15,183.0 | 18,164.0 | 22,574.0 | 31,791.0 | 38,295.0 | 31,430.0 | 35,400.0 | 40,926.0 | 41,024.0 | 44,625.0 | 48,112.0 | 43,503.0 |
| Services, debit (imports) | 1b9dx | † 13,469.0 | 15,712.0 | 20,023.0 | 24,427.0 | 30,939.0 | 24,435.0 | 31,039.0 | 33,705.0 | 33,309.0 | 34,484.0 | 36,708.0 | 32,602.0 |
| Balance on Goods & Services | 1z9bx | † −6,505.0 | −3,091.0 | −7,394.0 | −15,363.0 | −27,073.0 | −3,820.0 | −10,134.0 | −11,334.0 | −2,781.0 | 9,689.0 | 7,111.0 | 13,277.0 |
| Primary income: credit | 1c9cx | † 5,733.0 | 8,967.0 | 11,804.0 | 13,682.0 | 14,248.0 | 10,710.0 | 12,777.0 | 14,288.0 | 14,969.0 | 15,263.0 | 15,190.0 | 12,308.0 |
| Primary income: debit | 1c9dx | † 13,791.0 | 14,066.0 | 19,014.0 | 26,815.0 | 24,410.0 | 23,368.0 | 28,400.0 | 31,425.0 | 30,593.0 | 31,161.0 | 32,851.0 | 25,741.8 |
| Balance on gds, serv. & prim. inc. | 1y9bx | † −14,563.0 | −8,190.0 | −14,604.0 | −28,496.0 | −37,235.0 | −16,478.0 | −25,757.0 | −28,471.0 | −18,405.0 | −6,209.0 | −10,550.0 | −156.8 |
| Secondary income: credit | 1d9ca | † 3,962.0 | 4,883.0 | 6,042.0 | 7,599.0 | 9,276.0 | 7,275.0 | 6,836.0 | 8,442.0 | 7,818.0 | 8,028.0 | 7,884.0 | 6,419.0 |
| Secondary income: debit | 1d9da | † 3,250.0 | 4,674.0 | 5,331.0 | 6,532.0 | 7,870.0 | 8,664.0 | 6,954.0 | 7,326.0 | 8,018.0 | 8,568.0 | 8,458.0 | 7,399.0 |
| B. Capital Account* | 209ba | † 1,180.0 | 996.0 | 2,106.0 | 4,772.0 | 6,115.0 | 7,040.0 | 8,612.0 | 10,020.0 | 10,958.0 | 11,962.3 | 13,305.0 | 11,327.0 |
| Capital account: credit | 209ca | † 1,326.0 | 1,186.0 | 2,573.0 | 5,411.0 | 7,089.0 | 7,438.0 | 9,217.0 | 11,798.0 | 11,618.0 | 12,618.0 | 14,340.0 | 12,012.0 |
| Capital account: debit | 209da | † 146.0 | 190.0 | 467.0 | 639.0 | 974.0 | 398.0 | 605.0 | 1,778.0 | 660.0 | 655.7 | 1,035.0 | 685.0 |
| Balance on current & capital acct. | 129ba | † −12,671.0 | −6,985.0 | −11,787.0 | −22,657.0 | −29,714.0 | −10,827.0 | −17,263.0 | −17,335.0 | −7,647.0 | 5,213.3 | 2,181.0 | 10,190.2 |
| C. Financial Account* | 309na | † −7,974.0 | −15,171.0 | −13,174.0 | −38,047.0 | −39,125.0 | −34,825.6 | −46,129.0 | −33,604.0 | −22,662.0 | −6,963.0 | −4,915.0 | 7,352.0 |
| Direct investment: assets | 3a9aa | † 2,139.0 | 4,134.0 | 10,803.0 | 7,586.0 | 4,666.0 | 5,931.0 | 9,516.0 | 4,815.0 | 1,327.0 | −3,411.0 | 6,191.0 | 2,904.0 |
| Equity & investment fund shares.. | 3aaaa | † 586.0 | 2,790.0 | 8,430.0 | 4,045.0 | 3,079.0 | 3,560.0 | 764.0 | 6,310.0 | −68.0 | −351.0 | 4,204.0 | 1,910.0 |
| Debt instruments | 3abaa | † 1,553.0 | 1,344.0 | 2,373.0 | 3,541.0 | 1,587.0 | 2,371.0 | 8,752.0 | −1,495.0 | 1,395.0 | −3,060.0 | 1,987.0 | 994.0 |
| Direct investment: liabilities | 3a9la | † 13,868.0 | 11,041.0 | 21,473.0 | 25,031.0 | 14,574.0 | 14,025.0 | 18,395.0 | 18,485.0 | 7,358.0 | 795.0 | 17,275.0 | 6,281.0 |
| Equity & investment fund shares . | 3aala | † 13,530.0 | 7,896.0 | 13,136.0 | 17,065.0 | 8,759.0 | 10,291.0 | 13,071.0 | 11,060.0 | 2,654.0 | −2,636.0 | 10,337.0 | 5,638.0 |
| Debt instruments | 3abla | † 338.0 | 3,145.0 | 8,337.0 | 7,966.0 | 5,815.0 | 3,734.0 | 5,324.0 | 7,425.0 | 4,704.0 | 3,431.0 | 6,938.0 | 643.0 |
| Portfolio investment: assets | 3b9aa | † 1,331.0 | 2,509.0 | 4,651.0 | 6,341.0 | −2,360.0 | 1,447.0 | −142.0 | −845.0 | 445.0 | 2,162.0 | 5,823.0 | 10,997.0 |
| Equity & investment fund shares | 3baaa | † 55.0 | 574.0 | 2,994.0 | 5,880.0 | −1,459.0 | 1,860.0 | 649.0 | −681.0 | 567.0 | 1,185.0 | 2,595.0 | 9,962.0 |
| Debt securities | 3bbaa | † 1,276.0 | 1,935.0 | 1,657.0 | 461.0 | −901.0 | −413.0 | −791.0 | −164.0 | −122.0 | 977.0 | 3,228.0 | 1,035.0 |
| Portfolio investment: liabilities | 3b9la | † 10,573.0 | 15,092.0 | 1,707.0 | 117.0 | −4,720.0 | 16,202.0 | 28,921.0 | 16,539.0 | 20,100.0 | 2,399.0 | 3,940.0 | 7,689.0 |
| Equity & investment fund shares . | 3bala | † 1,660.0 | 1,331.0 | −2,129.0 | −470.0 | 566.0 | 1,580.0 | 7,395.0 | 3,078.0 | 3,613.0 | 2,648.0 | 3,290.0 | 4,031.0 |
| Debt securities | 3bbla | † 8,913.0 | 13,761.0 | 3,836.0 | 587.0 | −5,286.0 | 14,622.0 | 21,526.0 | 13,461.0 | 16,487.0 | −249.0 | 650.0 | 3,658.0 |
| Fin. der.& empl.stk.ops.(ESOs): net. | 3c9na | † −201.0 | −194.0 | 688.0 | 2,048.0 | 993.0 | 1,697.0 | 603.0 | 168.0 | −2,732.0 | −710.0 | −59.0 | −906.0 |
| Fin. der. & ESOs.: assets | 3c9aa | .... | .... | .... | .... | .... | .... | .... | .... | .... | .... | .... | .... |
| Fin. der. & ESOs.: liabilities | 3c9la | .... | .... | .... | .... | .... | .... | .... | .... | .... | .... | .... | .... |
| Other investment: assets | 3d9aa | † 12,026.0 | 2,779.0 | 4,003.0 | 1,784.0 | −5,278.0 | −5,192.0 | 4,112.0 | 3,758.0 | 2,125.0 | 1,559.0 | 4,478.0 | 5,116.0 |
| Other equity | 3daaa | † 31.0 | 84.0 | 91.0 | 199.0 | 210.0 | 84.0 | 119.0 | 64.0 | 249.0 | 631.0 | 184.0 | 277.0 |
| Debt instruments | 3dzaa | † 11,995.0 | 2,695.0 | 3,912.0 | 1,585.0 | −5,488.0 | −5,276.0 | 3,993.0 | 3,694.0 | 1,876.0 | 928.0 | 4,294.0 | 4,839.0 |
| Other investment: liabilities | 3d9la | † −1,172.0 | −1,734.0 | 10,139.0 | 30,658.0 | 27,292.0 | 8,481.6 | 12,902.0 | 6,476.0 | −3,631.0 | 3,369.0 | 133.0 | −3,211.0 |
| Other equity | 3dala | .... | .... | .... | .... | .... | .... | 57.0 | −54.0 | 61.0 | 5.0 | −4.0 | 5.0 |
| Debt instruments | 3dzla | † −1,172.0 | −1,734.0 | 10,139.0 | 30,658.0 | 27,292.0 | 8,481.6 | 12,845.0 | 6,530.0 | −3,692.0 | 3,364.0 | 137.0 | −3,216.0 |
| Curr.+ cap.− finan. acct. balance. | 4y9na | † −4,697.0 | 8,186.0 | 1,387.0 | 15,390.0 | 9,411.0 | 23,998.6 | 28,866.0 | 16,269.0 | 15,015.0 | 12,176.3 | 7,096.0 | 2,838.2 |
| D. Net Errors and Omissions | 409na | † 5,494.6 | −43.2 | 1,104.8 | −2,348.5 | −11,367.6 | −9,239.4 | −13,756.6 | −10,155.1 | −3,827.2 | −11,230.5 | −6,725.5 | −1,740.1 |
| E. Reserves and Related Items | 4z9na | † 797.6 | 8,142.8 | 2,491.8 | 13,041.5 | −1,956.6 | 14,759.2 | 15,109.4 | 6,113.9 | 11,187.8 | 945.8 | 370.5 | 1,098.1 |
| Reserve assets | 3e9aa | † 797.6 | 8,142.8 | 2,491.8 | 13,041.5 | −1,956.6 | 14,759.2 | 15,109.4 | 6,113.9 | 11,187.8 | 945.8 | 370.5 | 1,098.1 |
| Credit and loans from the IMF | 3dcla | † — | — | — | — | — | — | — | — | — | — | — | — |
| Exceptional financing | 409la | .... | .... | .... | .... | .... | .... | .... | .... | .... | .... | .... | .... |

*Excludes components in group E

## International Investment Position

*Millions of US Dollars*

| | Code | 2004 | 2005 | 2006 | 2007 | 2008 | 2009 | 2010 | 2011 | 2012 | 2013 | 2014 | 2015 |
|---|---|---|---|---|---|---|---|---|---|---|---|---|---|
| Assets | 809aa | † 86,126.1 | 98,602.8 | 126,746.1 | 168,538.5 | 147,821.6 | 169,069.8 | 206,115.4 | 212,634.4 | 236,811.3 | 236,714.0 | 230,472.4 | 230,448.6 |
| Direct investment | 8a9aa | † 8,323.0 | 11,506.0 | 21,779.0 | 31,432.0 | 33,464.0 | 40,436.0 | 62,836.0 | 65,744.0 | 72,026.0 | 70,857.0 | 65,853.0 | 63,160.0 |
| Equity & investment fund shares.. | 8aaaa | † 2,341.0 | 4,698.0 | 11,834.0 | 16,731.0 | 18,339.0 | 22,418.0 | 23,411.0 | 28,910.0 | 31,811.0 | 33,055.0 | 31,036.0 | 30,341.0 |
| Debt instruments | 8abaa | † 5,982.0 | 6,808.0 | 9,945.0 | 14,701.0 | 15,125.0 | 18,018.0 | 39,425.0 | 36,834.0 | 40,215.0 | 37,802.0 | 34,817.0 | 32,819.0 |
| Portfolio investment | 8b9aa | † 6,711.0 | 8,780.0 | 13,841.0 | 21,983.0 | 10,588.0 | 14,073.0 | 14,695.0 | 10,701.0 | 13,019.0 | 16,086.0 | 20,334.0 | 30,879.0 |
| Equity & investment fund shares.. | 8baaa | † 744.0 | 1,681.0 | 5,214.0 | 12,038.0 | 4,225.0 | 8,759.0 | 10,795.0 | 7,072.0 | 9,185.0 | 11,122.0 | 12,416.0 | 22,800.0 |
| Debt securities | 8bbaa | † 5,967.0 | 7,099.0 | 8,627.0 | 9,945.0 | 6,363.0 | 5,314.0 | 3,900.0 | 3,629.0 | 3,834.0 | 4,964.0 | 7,918.0 | 8,079.0 |
| Fin. der.(oth.than reserves) & ESOs | 8c9aa | † 303.0 | 499.0 | 551.0 | 1,283.0 | 2,365.0 | 981.0 | 3,698.0 | 5,766.0 | 6,109.0 | 5,608.0 | 7,870.0 | 4,674.0 |
| Other investment | 8d9aa | † 34,005.0 | 35,246.0 | 42,092.0 | 48,095.0 | 39,227.0 | 33,992.0 | 31,388.0 | 32,556.0 | 36,745.0 | 37,940.0 | 35,975.0 | 36,815.0 |
| Other equity | 8daaa | † 362.0 | 423.0 | 582.0 | 925.0 | 962.0 | 1,119.0 | 656.0 | 643.0 | 981.0 | 1,723.0 | 1,082.0 | 1,295.0 |
| Debt instruments | 8dzaa | † 33,643.0 | 34,823.0 | 41,510.0 | 47,170.0 | 38,265.0 | 32,873.0 | 30,732.0 | 31,913.0 | 35,764.0 | 36,217.0 | 34,893.0 | 35,520.0 |
| Reserve assets | 8e9aa | † 36,784.1 | 42,571.8 | 48,483.1 | 65,745.5 | 62,177.6 | 79,587.8 | 93,498.4 | 97,867.4 | 108,912.3 | 106,223.0 | 100,440.4 | 94,920.6 |
| Liabilities | 809la | † 213,596.0 | 225,460.0 | 291,939.0 | 408,592.0 | 389,154.0 | 445,106.3 | 523,450.2 | 498,771.0 | 580,145.1 | 613,851.1 | 565,236.2 | 514,366.9 |
| Direct investment | 8a9la | † 91,300.0 | 95,689.0 | 132,703.0 | 187,426.0 | 172,259.0 | 194,493.0 | 236,223.0 | 216,453.0 | 250,727.0 | 271,688.0 | 249,517.0 | 221,610.0 |
| Equity & investment fund shares.. | 8aala | † 69,283.0 | 73,116.0 | 98,573.0 | 140,469.0 | 123,631.0 | 140,446.0 | 164,348.0 | 141,736.0 | 167,210.0 | 181,372.0 | 163,547.0 | 142,383.0 |
| Debt instruments | 8abla | † 22,017.0 | 22,573.0 | 34,130.0 | 46,957.0 | 48,628.0 | 54,047.0 | 71,875.0 | 74,717.0 | 83,517.0 | 90,316.0 | 85,970.0 | 79,227.0 |
| Portfolio investment | 8b9la | † 56,628.0 | 71,383.0 | 84,786.0 | 104,867.0 | 77,831.0 | 102,099.0 | 131,710.0 | 126,613.0 | 171,155.0 | 175,851.0 | 162,196.0 | 152,938.0 |
| Equity & investment fund shares.. | 8bala | † 13,714.0 | 18,739.0 | 22,753.0 | 32,929.0 | 16,026.0 | 22,788.0 | 33,314.0 | 25,324.0 | 37,027.0 | 42,208.0 | 38,368.0 | 36,916.0 |
| Debt securities | 8bbla | † 42,914.0 | 52,644.0 | 62,033.0 | 71,938.0 | 61,805.0 | 79,311.0 | 98,396.0 | 101,289.0 | 134,128.0 | 133,643.0 | 123,828.0 | 116,022.0 |
| Fin. der.(oth.than reserves) & ESOs | 8c9la | † 417.0 | 524.0 | 618.0 | 1,590.0 | 4,481.0 | 1,384.0 | 6,084.0 | 7,179.0 | 7,081.0 | 6,077.0 | 8,522.0 | 6,526.0 |
| Other investment | 8d9la | † 65,251.0 | 57,864.0 | 73,832.0 | 114,709.0 | 134,583.0 | 147,130.3 | 149,433.2 | 148,526.0 | 151,182.1 | 160,235.1 | 145,001.2 | 133,292.9 |
| Other equity | 8dala | † — | — | — | — | — | — | 394.0 | 213.0 | 90.0 | 93.0 | 77.0 | 97.0 |
| Debt instruments | 8dzla | † 65,251.0 | 57,864.0 | 73,832.0 | 114,709.0 | 134,583.0 | 147,130.3 | 149,039.2 | 148,313.0 | 151,092.1 | 160,142.1 | 144,924.2 | 133,195.9 |

# Poland 964

| | | 2004 | 2005 | 2006 | 2007 | 2008 | 2009 | 2010 | 2011 | 2012 | 2013 | 2014 | 2015 |
|---|---|---|---|---|---|---|---|---|---|---|---|---|---|
| **Government Finance** | | | | | | | | | | | | | |
| **Operations Statement** | | | | | | | | | | | | | |
| **General Government** | | *Millions of Zlotys: Fiscal Year Ends December 31; Data Reported through Eurostat* | | | | | | | | | | | |
| Revenue | a1 | 358,687 | 399,446 | 438,670 | 490,013 | 522,010 | 517,084 | 550,428 | 607,107 | 633,303 | 635,456 | 668,224 | 695,708 |
| Taxes | a11 | 184,548 | 205,058 | 230,151 | 269,806 | 293,033 | 274,776 | 292,751 | 319,888 | 323,267 | 323,858 | 340,173 | 354,518 |
| Social Contributions | a12 | 122,344 | 130,236 | 138,954 | 151,179 | 155,929 | 164,888 | 169,722 | 188,919 | 210,557 | 219,599 | 227,548 | 242,773 |
| Grants | a13 | .... | .... | .... | .... | .... | .... | .... | .... | .... | .... | .... | .... |
| Other Revenue | a14 | .... | .... | .... | .... | .... | .... | .... | .... | .... | .... | .... | .... |
| Expense | a2 | 401,018 | 428,556 | 459,410 | 485,475 | 535,772 | 577,509 | 610,188 | 628,259 | 656,618 | 676,680 | 693,521 | 707,252 |
| Compensation of Employees | a21 | 102,052 | 108,305 | 114,246 | 124,154 | 139,140 | 150,615 | 158,905 | 164,877 | 167,905 | 171,693 | 178,611 | 182,352 |
| Use of Goods & Services | a22 | 60,717 | 61,303 | 66,760 | 72,614 | 81,120 | 81,928 | 92,809 | 91,462 | 95,123 | 98,434 | 105,329 | 103,663 |
| Consumption of Fixed Capital | a23 | 23,108 | 24,394 | 25,836 | 27,659 | 28,605 | 30,871 | 32,497 | 34,046 | 35,797 | 36,923 | 39,316 | 40,024 |
| Interest | a24 | 25,269 | 24,392 | 25,330 | 25,861 | 27,190 | 33,641 | 35,978 | 39,594 | 43,226 | 41,360 | 33,469 | 31,921 |
| Subsidies | a25 | 8,109 | 7,608 | 9,167 | 10,934 | 12,897 | 12,044 | 12,794 | 11,580 | 11,204 | 10,850 | 10,907 | 8,693 |
| Grants | a26 | .... | .... | .... | .... | .... | .... | .... | .... | .... | .... | .... | .... |
| Social Benefits | a27 | 166,865 | 171,940 | 182,576 | 189,078 | 203,891 | 225,338 | 237,873 | 243,582 | 256,933 | 270,367 | 278,841 | 291,175 |
| Other Expense | a28 | | | | | | | | | | | | |
| Gross Operating Balance [1-2+23] | agob | −19,223 | −4,716 | 5,095 | 32,197 | 14,843 | −29,554 | −27,263 | 12,894 | 12,483 | −4,302 | 14,019 | 28,480 |
| Net Operating Balance [1-2] | anob | −42,331 | −29,110 | −20,740 | 4,538 | −13,762 | −60,425 | −59,760 | −21,152 | −23,314 | −41,225 | −25,297 | −11,544 |
| Net Acq. of Nonfinancial Assets | a31 | 4,732 | 10,130 | 17,317 | 26,544 | 32,539 | 39,096 | 49,010 | 54,843 | 36,846 | 25,472 | 31,660 | 35,122 |
| Aquisition of Nonfin. Assets | a31.1 | .... | .... | .... | .... | .... | .... | .... | .... | .... | .... | .... | .... |
| Disposal of Nonfin. Assets | a31.2 | .... | .... | .... | .... | .... | .... | .... | .... | .... | .... | .... | .... |
| Net Lending/Borrowing [1-2-31] | anlb | −47,063 | −39,241 | −38,057 | −22,005 | −46,300 | −99,521 | −108,770 | −75,995 | −60,160 | −66,696 | −56,957 | −46,666 |
| Net Acq. of Financial Assets | a32 | −4,230 | 8,269 | 11,900 | 16,272 | 4,155 | −16,121 | −15,626 | −21,138 | −2,428 | −17,025 | 16,814 | 2,976 |
| **By instrument** | | | | | | | | | | | | | |
| Monetary Gold & SDRs | a3201 | — | — | — | — | — | — | — | — | — | — | — | — |
| Currency & Deposits | a3202 | 505 | 7,180 | 6,912 | 11,414 | 6,170 | 955 | −3,567 | −9,877 | 12,494 | −17,230 | 10,797 | −16,556 |
| Securities other than Shares | a3203 | 62 | 222 | 712 | 183 | −56 | −117 | 795 | 358 | 257 | 2,296 | −2,564 | 190 |
| Loans | a3204 | 521 | 180 | −685 | 4,089 | −1,254 | −276 | 2,855 | 1,293 | −204 | −12 | 2,942 | −284 |
| Shares & Other Equity | a3205 | −10,767 | −2,516 | 754 | −1,744 | −2,229 | −5,787 | −23,526 | −20,251 | −16,947 | −9,442 | 3,474 | −121 |
| Insurance Technical Reserves | a3206 | −85 | 507 | −88 | 100 | 16 | 109 | 281 | — | 19 | 44 | 34 | −238 |
| Financial Derivatives | a3207 | — | 6 | 6 | −24 | −35 | −3 | −110 | −225 | 35 | −16 | 97 | 35 |
| Other Accounts Receivable | a3208 | 5,534 | 2,690 | 4,289 | 2,254 | 1,543 | −11,002 | 7,646 | 7,564 | 1,918 | 7,335 | 2,034 | 19,950 |
| **By debtor** | | | | | | | | | | | | | |
| Domestic | a321 | .... | .... | .... | .... | .... | .... | .... | .... | .... | .... | .... | .... |
| Foreign | a322 | .... | .... | .... | .... | .... | .... | .... | .... | .... | .... | .... | .... |
| Net Incurrence of Liabilities | a33 | 43,030 | 47,450 | 50,473 | 38,330 | 50,278 | 82,456 | 93,337 | 53,649 | 57,255 | 48,959 | 73,213 | 48,922 |
| **By instrument** | | | | | | | | | | | | | |
| Special Drawing Rights (SDRs) | a3301 | — | — | — | — | — | — | — | — | — | — | — | — |
| Currency & Deposits | a3302 | −8 | −34 | −2 | −4 | 1 | −1 | — | — | — | — | 391 | 3,851 |
| Securities other than Shares | a3303 | 55,924 | 68,422 | 46,720 | 41,571 | 36,067 | 58,331 | 68,105 | 30,082 | 39,484 | 34,559 | −101,276 | 30,869 |
| Loans | a3304 | −11,514 | −23,512 | −514 | −8,506 | 6,899 | 25,034 | 22,049 | 21,355 | 12,511 | 12,339 | 15,631 | 11,242 |
| Shares & Other Equity | a3305 | — | — | — | — | — | — | — | — | — | — | — | — |
| Insurance Technical Reserves | a3306 | 1 | 2 | 3 | 8 | 9 | −11 | −6 | −3 | 8 | 34 | 45 | 99 |
| Financial Derivatives | a3307 | — | — | — | — | −35 | 1 | −16 | −55 | −19 | −5 | — | — |
| Other Accounts Payable | a3308 | −1,373 | 2,572 | 4,266 | 5,261 | 7,337 | −898 | 3,205 | 2,270 | 5,271 | 2,032 | 158,422 | 2,861 |
| **By creditor** | | | | | | | | | | | | | |
| Domestic | a331 | .... | .... | .... | .... | .... | .... | .... | .... | .... | .... | .... | .... |
| Foreign | a332 | .... | .... | .... | .... | .... | .... | .... | .... | .... | .... | .... | .... |
| Stat. Discrepancy [32-33-NLB] | anlbz | −197 | 60 | −516 | −53 | 177 | 944 | −193 | 1,208 | 477 | 712 | 558 | 720 |
| Memo Item: Expenditure [2+31] | a2m | 405,750 | 438,686 | 476,727 | 512,018 | 568,311 | 616,605 | 659,198 | 683,102 | 693,463 | 702,152 | 725,181 | 742,374 |
| **Balance Sheet** | | | | | | | | | | | | | |
| Net Worth | a6 | .... | .... | .... | .... | .... | .... | .... | .... | .... | .... | .... | .... |
| Nonfinancial Assets | a61 | .... | .... | .... | .... | .... | .... | .... | .... | .... | .... | .... | .... |
| Financial Assets | a62 | 292,830 | 317,859 | 357,623 | 419,369 | 484,336 | 493,792 | 492,613 | 479,454 | 473,272 | 452,276 | 479,805 | 487,594 |
| **By instrument** | | | | | | | | | | | | | |
| Monetary Gold & SDRs | a6201 | — | — | — | — | — | — | — | — | — | — | — | — |
| Currency & Deposits | a6202 | 40,658 | 48,607 | 51,693 | 75,596 | 81,920 | 76,463 | 65,992 | 68,532 | 74,960 | 57,350 | 76,728 | 61,868 |
| Securities other than Shares | a6203 | 1,740 | 2,487 | 1,990 | 2,103 | 1,949 | 2,310 | 3,912 | 3,439 | 2,601 | 4,941 | 2,378 | 2,627 |
| Loans | a6204 | 10,915 | 10,705 | 9,780 | 10,325 | 10,183 | 11,577 | 13,520 | 16,886 | 15,248 | 15,663 | 19,314 | 19,238 |
| Shares and Other Equity | a6205 | 159,138 | 181,568 | 212,534 | 244,669 | 301,136 | 313,627 | 308,058 | 288,166 | 271,677 | 262,260 | 266,422 | 266,180 |
| Insurance Technical Reserves | a6206 | 366 | 873 | 785 | 885 | 901 | 1,010 | 1,291 | 1,291 | 1,310 | 1,354 | 1,388 | 1,150 |
| Financial Derivatives | a6207 | 70 | 76 | 82 | 58 | 23 | 33 | 4,261 | 4,060 | 4,096 | 4,088 | 4,185 | 4,220 |
| Other Accounts Receivable | a6208 | 79,943 | 73,543 | 80,759 | 85,733 | 88,224 | 88,772 | 95,579 | 97,080 | 103,380 | 106,620 | 109,390 | 132,311 |
| **By debtor** | | | | | | | | | | | | | |
| Domestic | a621 | .... | .... | .... | .... | .... | .... | .... | .... | .... | .... | .... | .... |
| Foreign | a622 | .... | .... | .... | .... | .... | .... | .... | .... | .... | .... | .... | .... |
| Liabilities | a63 | 498,685 | 535,961 | 581,430 | 604,723 | 689,310 | 778,079 | 876,679 | 957,896 | 989,560 | 1,036,678 | 1,137,252 | 1,188,796 |
| **By instrument** | | | | | | | | | | | | | |
| Special Drawing Rights (SDRs) | a6301 | — | — | — | — | — | — | — | — | — | — | — | — |
| Currency & Deposits | a6302 | 40 | 6 | 4 | — | — | — | — | — | — | — | 391 | 4,242 |
| Securities other than Shares | a6303 | 325,722 | 392,087 | 440,935 | 466,360 | 530,146 | 586,813 | 658,575 | 711,032 | 733,561 | 766,182 | 682,390 | 712,642 |
| Loans | a6304 | 99,027 | 75,052 | 69,527 | 60,543 | 67,789 | 92,772 | 115,006 | 143,991 | 150,447 | 163,497 | 187,341 | 200,006 |
| Shares and Other Equity | a6305 | — | — | — | — | — | — | — | — | — | — | — | — |
| Insurance Technical Reserves | a6306 | 1 | — | 6 | 14 | 23 | 12 | 6 | 3 | 10 | 44 | 89 | 189 |
| Financial Derivatives | a6307 | — | — | — | — | — | — | — | — | — | — | — | — |
| Other Accounts Payable | a6308 | 73,895 | 68,816 | 70,958 | 77,806 | 91,352 | 98,482 | 103,092 | 102,870 | 105,542 | 106,955 | 267,041 | 271,717 |
| **By creditor** | | | | | | | | | | | | | |
| Domestic | a631 | .... | .... | .... | .... | .... | .... | .... | .... | .... | .... | .... | .... |
| Foreign | a632 | .... | .... | .... | .... | .... | .... | .... | .... | .... | .... | .... | .... |
| Net Financial Worth [62-63] | a6m2 | −205,855 | −218,102 | −223,807 | −185,354 | −204,974 | −284,287 | −384,066 | −478,442 | −516,288 | −584,402 | −657,447 | −701,202 |
| Memo Item: Debt at Market Value | a6m3 | 498,685 | 535,961 | 581,430 | 604,723 | 689,310 | 778,079 | 876,679 | 957,896 | 989,560 | 1,036,678 | 1,137,252 | 1,188,796 |
| Memo Item: Debt at Face Value | a6m35 | 494,177 | 528,801 | 573,219 | 602,206 | 686,752 | 776,810 | 873,697 | 954,562 | 984,874 | 1,033,987 | 1,134,962 | 1,189,489 |
| Memo Item: Maastricht Debt | a6m36 | 420,282 | 459,985 | 502,261 | 524,400 | 595,380 | 678,328 | 770,605 | 851,692 | 879,332 | 927,032 | 867,921 | 917,772 |
| Memo Item: Debt at Nominal Value | a6m4 | .... | .... | .... | .... | .... | .... | .... | .... | .... | .... | .... | .... |

# Poland   964

| | | 2004 | 2005 | 2006 | 2007 | 2008 | 2009 | 2010 | 2011 | 2012 | 2013 | 2014 | 2015 |
|---|---|---|---|---|---|---|---|---|---|---|---|---|---|
| **National Accounts** | | | | | | | *Millions of Zlotys* | | | | | | |
| Househ.Cons.Expend.,incl.NPISHs.... | 96f | 598,127 | 624,132 | 663,611 | 713,249 | 785,150 | 821,435 | 868,751 | 933,174 | 971,404 | 1,012,294 | 1,038,156 | 1,051,367 |
| Government Consumption Expend... | 91f | 162,656 | 177,786 | 193,708 | 211,028 | 236,179 | 248,892 | 268,427 | 274,758 | 284,374 | 292,905 | 309,399 | 324,033 |
| Gross Fixed Capital Formation.......... | 93e | 167,158 | 179,180 | 208,308 | 253,729 | 283,906 | 284,649 | 281,320 | 308,693 | 305,406 | 299,608 | 337,784 | 360,611 |
| Changes in Inventories.................... | 93i | 18,384 | 10,264 | 14,854 | 33,929 | 20,943 | −11,081 | 16,129 | 28,384 | 20,282 | 5,253 | 11,703 | 4,143 |
| Exports of Goods and Services......... | 90c | 346,631 | 364,658 | 427,776 | 479,606 | 508,888 | 530,278 | 598,370 | 688,738 | 744,748 | 779,865 | 805,562 | 880,137 |
| Imports of Goods and Services (-)..... | 98c | 368,366 | 371,946 | 446,928 | 513,426 | 559,522 | 529,269 | 615,470 | 706,326 | 739,948 | 740,766 | 779,184 | 830,184 |
| Gross Domestic Product (GDP)......... | 99b | 924,538 | 983,302 | 1,060,031 | 1,176,737 | 1,275,509 | 1,344,505 | 1,416,585 | 1,528,127 | 1,595,225 | 1,631,764 | 1,724,723 | 1,790,107 |
| GDP Volume 2005 Ref., Chained..... | 99b.p | 948,977 | 983,302 | 1,044,537 | 1,115,412 | 1,172,594 | 1,191,687 | 1,237,862 | 1,299,172 | 1,322,051 | 1,344,902 | 1,391,225 | . . . . |
| GDP Volume 2010 Ref., Chained..... | 99b.p | . . . . | . . . . | . . . . | . . . . | . . . . | . . . . | . . . . | 1,505,801 | 1,532,319 | 1,558,804 | 1,612,495 | . . . . |
| GDP Volume (2010=100)............... | 99bvp | 76.7 | 79.4 | 84.4 | 90.1 | 94.7 | 96.3 | 100.0 | † 105.0 | 106.8 | 108.6 | 112.4 | . . . . |
| GDP Deflator (2010=100)............... | 99bip | 85.1 | 87.4 | 88.7 | 92.2 | 95.1 | 98.6 | 100.0 | 102.8 | 105.4 | 106.0 | 108.3 | . . . . |
| | | | | | | | *Millions: Midyear Estimates* | | | | | | |
| **Population................................** | 99z | 38.45 | 38.46 | 38.48 | 38.50 | 38.53 | 38.55 | 38.57 | 38.59 | 38.61 | 38.62 | 38.62 | 38.61 |

# Portugal 182

| | | 2004 | 2005 | 2006 | 2007 | 2008 | 2009 | 2010 | 2011 | 2012 | 2013 | 2014 | 2015 |
|---|---|---|---|---|---|---|---|---|---|---|---|---|---|
| **Exchange Rates** | | | | | | *Euros per SDR: End of Period* | | | | | | | |
| Market Rate................................ | aa | 1.1402 | 1.2116 | 1.1423 | 1.0735 | 1.1068 | 1.0882 | 1.1525 | 1.1865 | 1.1649 | 1.1167 | 1.1933 | 1.2728 |
| | | | | | | *Euros per US Dollar: End of Period (ae) Period Average (rf)* | | | | | | | |
| Market Rate................................ | ae | .7342 | .8477 | .7593 | .6793 | .7185 | .6942 | .7484 | .7729 | .7579 | .7251 | .8237 | .9185 |
| Market Rate................................ | rf | .8054 | .8041 | .7971 | .7306 | .6827 | .7198 | .7550 | .7194 | .7783 | .7532 | .7537 | .9017 |
| | | | | | | *Index Numbers (2010=100): Period Averages* | | | | | | | |
| Nominal Effective Exchange Rate..... | nec | 98.4 | 98.4 | 98.5 | 99.6 | 101.4 | 101.7 | 100.0 | 100.2 | 98.4 | 99.8 | 99.8 | 97.0 |
| CPI-Based Real Effect. Ex. Rate........ | rec | 100.1 | 100.1 | 100.5 | 101.9 | 102.7 | 102.2 | 100.0 | 100.9 | 99.5 | 99.6 | 98.5 | 95.9 |
| **Fund Position** | | | | | | *Millions of SDRs: End of Period* | | | | | | | |
| Quota....................................... | 2f.s | 867.40 | 867.40 | 867.40 | 867.40 | 867.40 | 867.40 | 867.40 | 1,029.70 | 1,029.70 | 1,029.70 | 1,029.70 | 1,029.70 |
| SDR Holdings................................ | 1b.s | 66.25 | 71.98 | 75.31 | 77.89 | 79.53 | 833.29 | 833.28 | 792.57 | 793.29 | 792.64 | 792.79 | 793.03 |
| Reserve Position in the Fund............ | 1c.s | 283.34 | 141.61 | 76.44 | 57.17 | 107.07 | 215.07 | 231.10 | 271.72 | 271.76 | 271.80 | 241.85 | 207.89 |
| Total Fund Cred.&Loans Outstg........ | 2tl | — | — | — | — | — | 806.48 | 806.48 | 11,503.00 | 18,402.00 | 21,379.00 | 22,942.00 | 16,362.83 |
| SDR Allocations............................ | 1bd | 53.32 | 53.32 | 53.32 | 53.32 | 53.32 | 806.48 | 806.48 | 806.48 | 806.48 | 806.48 | 806.48 | 806.48 |
| **International Liquidity** | | | | | | *Millions of US Dollars Unless Otherwise Indicated: End of Period* | | | | | | | |
| Total Res.Min.Gold (Eurosys.Def)..... | 1l.d | 5,174 | 3,479 | 2,064 | 1,258 | 1,309 | 2,455 | 3,652 | 1,975 | 2,196 | 2,778 | 4,869 | 6,367 |
| SDR Holdings............................. | 1b.d | 103 | 103 | 113 | 123 | 123 | 1,306 | 1,283 | 1,217 | 1,219 | 1,221 | 1,149 | 1,099 |
| Reserve Position in the Fund......... | 1c.d | 440 | 202 | 115 | 90 | 165 | 337 | 356 | 417 | 418 | 419 | 350 | 288 |
| Foreign Exchange........................ | 1d.d | 4,631 | 3,173 | 1,835 | 1,044 | 1,022 | 811 | 2,013 | 341 | 559 | 1,138 | 3,370 | 4,980 |
| o/w:Fin.Deriv.Rel.to Reserves.... | 1ddd | 31.15 | 14.53 | 14.96 | 15.69 | 7.70 | — | −.87 | .13 | .04 | .12 | −.11 | −.28 |
| Other Reserve Assets.................... | 1e.d | — | | | | | | | | | | | |
| Gold (Million Fine Troy Ounces)....... | 1ad | 14.86 | 13.42 | 12.30 | 12.30 | 12.30 | 12.30 | 12.30 | 12.30 | 12.30 | 12.30 | 12.30 | 12.30 |
| Gold (Eurosystem Valuation)............ | 1and | 6,510 | 6,885 | 7,819 | 10,288 | 10,639 | 13,577 | 17,343 | 19,362 | 20,462 | 14,775 | 14,748 | 13,030 |
| Memo:Euro Cl. on Non-EA Res.......... | 1dgd | .... | .... | .... | .... | .... | .... | .... | .... | .... | .... | .... | .... |
| Non-Euro Cl. on EA Res............ | 1dhd | 1,021 | 615 | 1,048 | 960 | 10 | 5 | 479 | 413 | 478 | 224 | 122 | 50 |
| Central Bank: Other Assets............. | 3..d | 16,352 | 16,033 | 19,169 | 22,456 | 21,091 | 23,237 | 28,394 | 28,715 | 27,485 | 26,848 | 28,114 | 24,502 |
| Central Bank: Other Liabs................ | 4..d | 654 | 579 | 178 | 96 | 86 | 1,269 | 1,242 | 1,238 | 1,239 | 1,242 | 1,168 | 1,118 |
| Other Depository Corps.: Assets....... | 7a.d | 37,669 | 36,831 | 46,102 | 49,348 | 44,227 | 53,488 | 53,031 | 54,738 | 58,562 | 44,069 | 37,326 | 24,769 |
| Other Depository Corps.: Liabs......... | 7b.d | 94,381 | 86,556 | 120,585 | 135,582 | 111,728 | 118,972 | 104,500 | 89,649 | 81,647 | 64,303 | 51,547 | 38,212 |
| **Central Bank** | | | | | | *Millions of Euros: End of Period* | | | | | | | |
| Euro Area Wide Residency Criterion | | | | | | | | | | | | | |
| Net Foreign Assets.......................... | 11n.u | 8,538 | 9,475 | 9,940 | 12,216 | 9,409 | 12,036 | 16,725 | 16,306 | 16,825 | 12,418 | 15,576 | 17,232 |
| Claims on Nonresidents............... | 11..u | 9,305 | 10,188 | 10,076 | 12,281 | 9,472 | 12,918 | 17,655 | 17,263 | 17,765 | 13,319 | 16,539 | 18,259 |
| Liabilities to Nonresidents.............. | 16c.u | 767 | 713 | 136 | 65 | 63 | 882 | 930 | 957 | 939 | 901 | 962 | 1,027 |
| Claims on Other Depository Corps..... | 12e.u | 3,724 | 6,251 | 2,156 | 4,135 | 11,902 | 18,142 | 44,276 | 49,386 | 56,876 | 51,491 | 34,181 | 30,969 |
| Net Claims on Central Government.. | 12anu | 9,713 | 10,523 | 9,143 | 8,230 | 11,596 | 11,666 | 17,030 | 14,600 | 12,177 | 8,758 | 13,057 | 24,347 |
| Claims on Central Govt................ | 12a.u | 9,713 | 10,523 | 9,143 | 8,230 | 11,596 | 11,668 | 17,031 | 19,343 | 17,400 | 16,387 | 21,046 | 30,916 |
| Liabs. to Central Govt................. | 16d.u | — | — | — | — | — | 2 | 1 | 4,743 | 5,223 | 7,629 | 7,989 | 6,569 |
| Claims on Other Sectors................ | 12s.u | 239 | 169 | 169 | 171 | 156 | 183 | 227 | 218 | 223 | 215 | 227 | 170 |
| Claims on Other Financial Corps.... | 12g.u | 111 | 38 | 38 | 38 | 38 | 48 | 63 | 50 | 67 | 66 | 66 | 12 |
| Claims on State & Local Govts...... | 12b.u | — | — | — | — | — | — | — | — | — | — | — | — |
| Claims on Public Nonfin. Corps...... | 12c.u | — | — | — | — | — | — | — | — | — | — | — | — |
| Claims on Private Sector............... | 12d.u | 128 | 131 | 131 | 133 | 118 | 135 | 164 | 168 | 156 | 149 | 161 | 158 |
| Monetary Base............................. | 14..u | 18,196 | 18,085 | 19,796 | 25,095 | 23,151 | 27,901 | 24,835 | 26,819 | 29,953 | 31,087 | 27,467 | 33,064 |
| Currency in Circulation............... | 14a.u | 11,801 | 13,268 | 14,721 | 15,828 | 17,749 | 19,130 | 19,914 | 21,002 | 21,557 | 22,869 | 23,878 | 25,291 |
| Liabs. to Other Depository Corps.... | 14c.u | 6,394 | 4,816 | 5,074 | 9,266 | 5,402 | 8,771 | 4,921 | 5,691 | 8,136 | 8,218 | 3,589 | 7,726 |
| Liabs. to Other Sectors.................. | 14d.u | 1 | 1 | 1 | 1 | — | — | — | 126 | 260 | — | — | 47 |
| Other Liabs. to Other Dep. Corps..... | 14n.u | — | — | — | — | — | — | — | — | — | — | — | — |
| Dep. & Sec. Excl. f/Monetary Base..... | 14o.u | — | — | — | — | — | — | — | — | — | — | — | — |
| Deposits Included in Broad Money. | 15..u | — | — | — | — | — | — | — | — | — | — | — | — |
| Sec.Ot.th.Shares Inc.in.Brd.Money. | 16a.u | — | — | — | — | — | — | — | — | — | — | — | — |
| Deposits Excl. from Broad Money... | 16b.u | — | — | — | — | — | — | — | — | — | — | — | — |
| Sec.Oh.th.Shares Excl. f/Brd.Money | 16s.u | — | — | — | — | — | — | — | — | — | — | — | — |
| Loans....................................... | 16l.u | — | — | — | — | — | — | — | — | — | — | — | — |
| Financial Derivatives...................... | 16m.u | — | — | — | — | — | — | — | — | — | — | — | — |
| Shares and Other Equity.................. | 17a.u | 4,113 | 5,711 | 6,283 | 7,427 | 8,523 | 10,463 | 14,235 | 16,318 | 17,462 | 12,702 | 14,917 | 15,010 |
| Other Items (Net)........................... | 17r.u | −96 | 2,623 | −4,671 | −7,772 | 1,388 | 3,661 | 39,188 | 37,370 | 38,682 | 29,093 | 20,656 | 24,644 |
| Memorandum Items | | | | | | | | | | | | | |
| National Residency Criterion | | | | | | | | | | | | | |
| Net Foreign Assets.......................... | 11n | 11,969 | 9,582 | 15,297 | 16,827 | 4,724 | 2,941 | −23,880 | −23,197 | −28,961 | −28,270 | −16,240 | −22,392 |
| Claims on Nonresidents................ | 11 | 20,583 | 22,377 | 22,059 | 23,098 | 23,740 | 27,259 | 36,962 | 38,683 | 38,005 | 32,196 | 39,314 | 40,322 |
| Liabilities to Nonresidents............ | 16c | 8,614 | 12,795 | 6,762 | 6,271 | 19,016 | 24,318 | 60,842 | 61,880 | 66,965 | 60,466 | 55,553 | 62,714 |
| Claims on Other Depository Corps.... | 12e | 3,141 | 5,567 | 298 | 2,535 | 10,217 | 16,502 | 41,936 | 46,927 | 53,724 | 48,810 | 32,503 | 29,616 |
| Net Claims on Central Government.. | 12an | — | — | — | — | — | −2 | 1,137 | −3,301 | −3,850 | −6,374 | −6,983 | 4,669 |
| Claims on Central Government...... | 12a | — | — | — | — | — | — | 1,138 | 1,442 | 1,373 | 1,255 | 1,006 | 11,238 |
| Liabilities to Central Government... | 16d | — | — | — | — | — | 2 | 1 | 4,743 | 5,223 | 7,629 | 7,989 | 6,569 |
| Claims on Other Sectors................ | 12s | 239 | 169 | 169 | 171 | 156 | 158 | 161 | 166 | 170 | 173 | 180 | 148 |
| Claims on Other Fin. Corps............ | 12g | 111 | 38 | 38 | 38 | 38 | 38 | 38 | 38 | 38 | 38 | 38 | 1 |
| Claims on State & Local Govts....... | 12b | — | — | — | — | — | — | — | — | — | — | — | — |
| Claims on Private Sector............... | 12d | 128 | 131 | 131 | 133 | 118 | 120 | 123 | 128 | 132 | 135 | 142 | 147 |
| Liabs. to ODCs, Inc.in Mon.Base....... | 14c | 6,252 | 4,665 | 5,049 | 9,266 | 5,402 | 8,771 | 4,921 | 5,691 | 8,136 | 8,218 | 3,589 | 7,726 |
| Liabs.to Ot.Sectors, Inc.in Mon.Base | 14d | 1 | 1 | 1 | 1 | — | — | — | 126 | 260 | — | — | 47 |
| Liabs.to ODCs,Excl.f/Mon.Base........ | 14n | — | — | — | — | — | — | — | — | — | — | — | — |
| Net Claims on Eurosystem.............. | 12e.s | −6,623 | −10,849 | −5,519 | −5,118 | −17,865 | −22,314 | −58,760 | −59,742 | −64,816 | −58,330 | −53,377 | −60,473 |

# Portugal 182

Millions of Euros: End of Period

| | | 2004 | 2005 | 2006 | 2007 | 2008 | 2009 | 2010 | 2011 | 2012 | 2013 | 2014 | 2015 |
|---|---|---|---|---|---|---|---|---|---|---|---|---|---|
| **Other Depository Corporations** | | | | | | | | | | | | | |
| Euro Area Wide Residency Criterion | | | | | | | | | | | | | |
| Net Foreign Assets | 21n.u | −41,636 | −42,150 | −56,555 | −58,579 | −48,503 | −45,456 | −38,519 | −26,981 | −17,497 | −14,672 | −11,713 | −12,348 |
| Claims on Nonresidents | 21..u | 27,655 | 31,221 | 35,005 | 33,522 | 31,779 | 37,129 | 39,688 | 42,305 | 44,385 | 31,955 | 30,744 | 22,751 |
| Liabilities to Nonresidents | 26c.u | 69,291 | 73,371 | 91,560 | 92,101 | 80,282 | 82,585 | 78,207 | 69,286 | 61,882 | 46,627 | 42,457 | 35,099 |
| Claims on Eurosystem | 20..u | 7,739 | 6,050 | 6,687 | 10,999 | 7,118 | 10,629 | 6,611 | 7,297 | 9,741 | 9,840 | 5,083 | 9,339 |
| Currency | 20a.u | 1,487 | 1,385 | 1,638 | 1,733 | 1,716 | 1,786 | 1,690 | 1,606 | 1,605 | 1,622 | 1,504 | 1,627 |
| Reserve Deposits and Securities | 20b.u | 6,252 | 4,665 | 5,049 | 9,266 | 5,402 | 8,843 | 4,921 | 5,691 | 8,136 | 8,218 | 3,579 | 7,712 |
| Other Claims | 20n.u | — | — | — | — | — | — | — | — | — | — | — | — |
| Net Claims on Central Government | 22anu | 2,806 | 1,860 | 1,906 | 2,325 | 2,456 | 12,863 | 27,812 | 19,959 | 25,935 | 29,799 | 31,811 | 35,652 |
| Claims on Central Government | 22a.u | 6,399 | 6,479 | 6,576 | 5,937 | 6,109 | 15,741 | 31,402 | 28,882 | 36,829 | 39,023 | 40,933 | 42,321 |
| Liabilities to Central Government | 26d.u | 3,593 | 4,619 | 4,670 | 3,612 | 3,653 | 2,878 | 3,590 | 8,923 | 10,894 | 9,224 | 9,122 | 6,669 |
| Claims on Other Sectors | 22s.u | 223,098 | 241,559 | 264,828 | 301,788 | 347,160 | 370,140 | 387,604 | 377,587 | 340,343 | 322,431 | 300,452 | 285,207 |
| Claims on Other Financial Corps. | 22g.u | 30,945 | 36,145 | 33,068 | 41,281 | 63,347 | 76,502 | 95,537 | 90,897 | 73,660 | 70,210 | 65,874 | 60,634 |
| Claims on State & Local Govts. | 22b.u | 4,133 | 4,515 | 4,665 | 4,609 | 5,468 | 5,955 | 6,595 | 6,775 | 6,085 | 5,871 | 6,611 | 6,463 |
| Claims on Public Nonfin. Corps. | 22c.u | | | | | | | | | | | | |
| Claims on Private Sector | 22d.u | 188,020 | 200,899 | 227,095 | 255,898 | 278,345 | 287,683 | 285,472 | 279,915 | 260,598 | 246,350 | 227,967 | 218,110 |
| Liabilities to Eurosystem | 26g.u | 3,184 | 5,805 | 1,397 | 3,486 | 12,023 | 18,030 | 44,076 | 49,212 | 56,459 | 51,235 | 33,920 | 30,744 |
| Transf.Dep.Included in Broad Money | 24..u | 49,739 | 56,134 | 57,831 | 56,148 | 53,930 | 54,131 | 53,014 | 49,228 | 46,457 | 49,603 | 54,697 | 65,985 |
| Other.Dep.Included in Broad Money. | 25..u | 80,752 | 82,831 | 85,362 | 97,464 | 112,302 | 102,866 | 105,105 | 106,110 | 94,297 | 93,859 | 89,671 | 84,130 |
| Sec.Ot.th.Shares Inc.in.Brd. Money... | 26a.u | 380 | 367 | −297 | 734 | 8,469 | 11,848 | 3,515 | 1,067 | 3,230 | 1,478 | 280 | −171 |
| Deposits Excl. from Broad Money | 26b.u | 6,676 | 12,680 | 18,785 | 22,429 | 30,770 | 52,666 | 68,092 | 77,534 | 71,090 | 71,960 | 69,573 | 67,471 |
| Sec.Ot.th.Shares Excl.f/Brd. Money... | 26s.u | 19,722 | 13,133 | 13,396 | 27,571 | 33,543 | 50,166 | 51,706 | 46,538 | 36,557 | 31,450 | 24,769 | 19,124 |
| Loans | 26l.u | — | — | — | — | — | — | — | — | — | — | — | — |
| Financial Derivatives | 26m.u | 2,486 | 3,050 | 4,440 | 5,670 | 8,031 | 7,815 | 9,378 | 11,834 | 11,233 | 7,978 | 9,214 | 7,276 |
| Insurance Technical Reserves | 26r.u | — | — | — | — | — | — | — | — | — | — | — | — |
| Shares and Other Equity | 27a.u | 21,437 | 20,807 | 24,346 | 25,197 | 23,385 | 27,770 | 28,155 | 23,571 | 28,504 | 25,818 | 25,142 | 24,666 |
| Other Items (Net) | 27r.u | 7,666 | 12,516 | 11,599 | 17,836 | 25,816 | 22,889 | 20,548 | 12,768 | 10,701 | 14,019 | 19,613 | 20,651 |
| Memorandum Items | | | | | | | | | | | | | |
| Total Assets | 20ra | 346,448 | 361,287 | 397,878 | 439,843 | 482,142 | 520,158 | 558,839 | 573,312 | 557,077 | 515,121 | 467,196 | 447,464 |
| National Residency Criterion | | | | | | | | | | | | | |
| Net Foreign Assets | 21n | −45,090 | −47,938 | −65,655 | −69,997 | −54,053 | −37,601 | −18,212 | −9,110 | −1,710 | 982 | 3,161 | 4,361 |
| Claims on Nonresidents | 21 | 73,918 | 80,367 | 84,963 | 93,539 | 100,050 | 111,926 | 114,117 | 96,585 | 88,379 | 71,565 | 70,851 | 63,369 |
| Liabilities to Nonresidents | 26c | 119,008 | 128,305 | 150,618 | 163,536 | 154,103 | 149,527 | 132,329 | 105,695 | 90,089 | 70,583 | 67,690 | 59,008 |
| Net Claims on Central Government | 22an | 782 | 498 | 741 | 659 | 1,441 | 7,989 | 23,752 | 16,745 | 22,006 | 23,714 | 24,004 | 24,966 |
| Claims on Central Government | 22a | 4,355 | 4,774 | 5,411 | 4,270 | 4,743 | 10,792 | 27,341 | 25,667 | 32,899 | 32,936 | 33,124 | 31,633 |
| Liabilities to Central Government | 26d | 3,573 | 4,276 | 4,670 | 3,611 | 3,302 | 2,803 | 3,589 | 8,922 | 10,893 | 9,222 | 9,120 | 6,667 |
| Claims on Other Sectors | 22s | 209,497 | 224,577 | 253,434 | 285,118 | 312,757 | 329,193 | 345,498 | 347,155 | 320,572 | 303,537 | 283,390 | 269,847 |
| Claims on Other Fin. Corps. | 22g | 20,981 | 22,363 | 27,115 | 31,068 | 36,127 | 42,967 | 59,645 | 65,468 | 57,429 | 53,963 | 52,424 | 48,325 |
| Claims on State & Local Govts. | 22b | 4,133 | 4,514 | 4,637 | 4,583 | 5,441 | 5,923 | 6,493 | 6,649 | 5,868 | 5,756 | 6,486 | 6,315 |
| Claims on Private Sector | 22d | 184,383 | 197,700 | 221,682 | 249,467 | 271,189 | 280,303 | 279,360 | 275,038 | 257,275 | 243,818 | 224,480 | 215,207 |
| Transf.Dep.Included in Broad Money | 24 | 49,138 | 55,120 | 56,589 | 54,525 | 52,090 | 53,294 | 51,706 | 47,982 | 45,575 | 48,648 | 53,198 | 63,941 |
| Other.Dep.Included in Broad Money. | 25 | 70,355 | 73,797 | 77,665 | 86,973 | 105,474 | 93,733 | 100,386 | 103,432 | 91,874 | 91,270 | 88,295 | 82,911 |
| Sec.Ot.th.Shares Inc.in.Brd. Money... | 26a | 636 | 670 | 170 | 235 | 868 | 3,019 | 1,506 | 1,045 | 3,590 | 1,458 | 281 | −5 |
| Deposits Excl. from Broad Money | 26b | 5,899 | 10,510 | 16,264 | 20,819 | 29,337 | 50,903 | 66,557 | 76,906 | 70,358 | 71,117 | 68,766 | 66,628 |
| Sec.Ot.th.Shares Excl.f/Brd. Money... | 26s | 20,679 | 14,739 | 16,403 | 30,593 | 37,363 | 54,644 | 57,320 | 50,824 | 41,300 | 35,234 | 27,327 | 21,078 |

2016, International Monetary Fund : *International Financial Statistics Yearbook*

# Portugal 182

| | | 2004 | 2005 | 2006 | 2007 | 2008 | 2009 | 2010 | 2011 | 2012 | 2013 | 2014 | 2015 |
|---|---|---|---|---|---|---|---|---|---|---|---|---|---|
| **Depository Corporations** | | | | | | *Millions of Euros: End of Period* | | | | | | | |
| Euro Area Wide Residency Criterion | | | | | | | | | | | | | |
| Net Foreign Assets | **31n.u** | −33,098 | −32,675 | −46,615 | −46,363 | −39,094 | −33,420 | −21,794 | −10,675 | −672 | −2,254 | 3,863 | 4,884 |
| Claims on Nonresidents | **31..u** | 36,960 | 41,409 | 45,081 | 45,803 | 41,251 | 50,047 | 57,343 | 59,568 | 62,150 | 45,274 | 47,283 | 41,010 |
| Liabilities to Nonresidents | **36c.u** | 70,058 | 74,084 | 91,696 | 92,166 | 80,345 | 83,467 | 79,137 | 70,243 | 62,821 | 47,528 | 43,419 | 36,126 |
| Domestic Claims | **32..u** | 235,856 | 254,111 | 276,046 | 312,514 | 361,368 | 394,852 | 432,673 | 412,364 | 378,678 | 361,203 | 345,547 | 345,376 |
| Net Claims on Central Government | **32anu** | 12,519 | 12,383 | 11,049 | 10,555 | 14,052 | 24,529 | 44,842 | 34,559 | 38,112 | 38,557 | 44,868 | 59,999 |
| Claims on Central Government | **32a.u** | 16,112 | 17,002 | 15,719 | 14,167 | 17,705 | 27,409 | 48,433 | 48,225 | 54,229 | 55,410 | 61,979 | 73,237 |
| Liabilities to Central Government | **36d.u** | 3,593 | 4,619 | 4,670 | 3,612 | 3,653 | 2,880 | 3,591 | 13,666 | 16,117 | 16,853 | 17,111 | 13,238 |
| Claims on Other Sectors | **32s.u** | 223,337 | 241,728 | 264,997 | 301,959 | 347,316 | 370,323 | 387,831 | 377,805 | 340,566 | 322,646 | 300,679 | 285,377 |
| Claims on Other Financial Corps. | **32g.u** | 31,056 | 36,183 | 33,106 | 41,319 | 63,385 | 76,550 | 95,600 | 90,947 | 73,727 | 70,276 | 65,940 | 60,646 |
| Claims on State & Local Govts. | **32b.u** | 4,133 | 4,515 | 4,665 | 4,609 | 5,468 | 5,955 | 6,595 | 6,775 | 6,085 | 5,871 | 6,611 | 6,463 |
| Claims on Public Nonfin. Corps. | **32c.u** | — | — | — | — | — | — | — | — | — | — | — | — |
| Claims on Private Sector | **32d.u** | 188,148 | 201,030 | 227,226 | 256,031 | 278,463 | 287,818 | 285,636 | 280,083 | 260,754 | 246,499 | 228,128 | 218,268 |
| Broad Money Liabilities | **35l.u** | 141,186 | 151,216 | 155,980 | 168,442 | 190,734 | 186,189 | 179,858 | 175,927 | 164,196 | 166,187 | 167,022 | 173,655 |
| Currency Outside Depository Corps | **34a.u** | 10,314 | 11,883 | 13,083 | 14,095 | 16,033 | 17,344 | 18,224 | 19,396 | 19,952 | 21,247 | 22,374 | 23,664 |
| Transferable Deposits | **34..u** | 49,740 | 56,135 | 57,832 | 56,149 | 53,930 | 54,131 | 53,014 | 49,354 | 46,717 | 49,603 | 54,697 | 66,032 |
| Other Deposits | **35..u** | 80,752 | 82,831 | 85,362 | 97,464 | 112,302 | 102,866 | 105,105 | 106,110 | 94,297 | 93,859 | 89,671 | 84,130 |
| Securities Other than Shares | **36a.u** | 380 | 367 | −297 | 734 | 8,469 | 11,848 | 3,515 | 1,067 | 3,230 | 1,478 | 280 | −171 |
| Deposits Excl. from Broad Money | **36b.u** | 6,676 | 12,680 | 18,785 | 22,429 | 30,770 | 52,666 | 68,092 | 77,534 | 71,090 | 71,960 | 69,573 | 67,471 |
| Sec.Oth.th.Shares Excl.f/Brd. Money. | **36s.u** | 19,722 | 13,133 | 13,396 | 27,571 | 33,543 | 50,166 | 51,706 | 46,538 | 36,557 | 31,450 | 24,769 | 19,124 |
| Loans | **36l.u** | — | — | — | — | — | — | — | — | — | — | — | — |
| Financial Derivatives | **36m.u** | 2,486 | 3,050 | 4,440 | 5,670 | 8,031 | 7,815 | 9,378 | 11,834 | 11,233 | 7,978 | 9,214 | 7,276 |
| Insurance Technical Reserves | **36r.u** | — | — | — | — | — | — | — | — | — | — | — | — |
| Shares and Other Equity | **37a.u** | 25,550 | 26,518 | 30,629 | 32,624 | 31,908 | 38,233 | 42,390 | 39,889 | 45,966 | 38,520 | 40,059 | 39,676 |
| Other Items (Net) | **37r.u** | 7,172 | 14,844 | 6,194 | 9,415 | 27,325 | 26,366 | 59,536 | 49,964 | 48,966 | 42,856 | 40,018 | 45,084 |
| Broad Money Liabs., Seasonally Adj. | **35lub** | 139,736 | 149,265 | 153,767 | 166,076 | 188,213 | 184,011 | 177,978 | 174,320 | 162,881 | 165,093 | 166,063 | 172,699 |
| Memorandum Items | | | | | | | | | | | | | |
| National Residency Criterion | | | | | | | | | | | | | |
| Net Foreign Assets | **31n** | −33,121 | −38,356 | −50,358 | −53,170 | −49,329 | −34,660 | −42,092 | −32,307 | −30,671 | −27,288 | −13,079 | −18,031 |
| Claims on Nonresidents | **31** | 94,501 | 102,744 | 107,022 | 116,637 | 123,790 | 139,185 | 151,079 | 135,268 | 126,384 | 103,761 | 110,165 | 103,691 |
| Liabilities to Nonresidents | **36c** | 127,622 | 141,100 | 157,380 | 169,807 | 173,119 | 173,845 | 193,171 | 167,575 | 157,054 | 131,049 | 123,243 | 121,722 |
| Domestic Claims | **32** | 210,518 | 225,244 | 254,344 | 285,948 | 314,354 | 337,338 | 370,548 | 360,765 | 338,898 | 321,050 | 300,591 | 299,630 |
| Net Claims on Central Government | **32an** | 782 | 498 | 741 | 659 | 1,441 | 7,987 | 24,889 | 13,444 | 18,156 | 17,340 | 17,021 | 29,635 |
| Claims on Central Government | **32a** | 4,355 | 4,774 | 5,411 | 4,270 | 4,743 | 10,792 | 28,479 | 27,109 | 34,272 | 34,191 | 34,130 | 42,871 |
| Liabilities to Central Government | **36d** | 3,573 | 4,276 | 4,670 | 3,611 | 3,302 | 2,805 | 3,590 | 13,665 | 16,116 | 16,851 | 17,109 | 13,236 |
| Claims on Other Sectors | **32s** | 209,736 | 224,746 | 253,603 | 285,289 | 312,913 | 329,351 | 345,659 | 347,321 | 320,742 | 303,710 | 283,570 | 269,995 |
| Claims on Other Financial Corps. | **32g** | 21,092 | 22,401 | 27,153 | 31,106 | 36,165 | 43,005 | 59,683 | 65,506 | 57,467 | 54,001 | 52,462 | 48,326 |
| Claims on State & Local Govts. | **32b** | 4,133 | 4,514 | 4,637 | 4,583 | 5,441 | 5,923 | 6,493 | 6,649 | 5,868 | 5,756 | 6,486 | 6,315 |
| Claims on Private Sector | **32d** | 184,511 | 197,831 | 221,813 | 249,600 | 271,307 | 280,423 | 279,483 | 275,166 | 257,407 | 243,953 | 224,622 | 215,354 |
| Transf.Dep.Included in Broad Money | **34** | 49,139 | 55,121 | 56,590 | 54,526 | 52,090 | 53,294 | 51,706 | 48,108 | 45,835 | 48,648 | 53,198 | 63,988 |
| Other Dep. Included in Broad Money | **35** | 70,355 | 73,797 | 77,665 | 86,973 | 105,474 | 93,733 | 100,386 | 103,432 | 91,874 | 91,270 | 88,295 | 82,911 |
| Sec.Oth.th.Shares Inc.in.Brd. Money | **36a** | 636 | 670 | 170 | 235 | 868 | 3,019 | 1,506 | 1,045 | 3,590 | 1,458 | 281 | −5 |
| Deposits Excl. from Broad Money | **36b** | 5,899 | 10,510 | 16,264 | 20,819 | 29,337 | 50,903 | 66,557 | 76,906 | 70,358 | 71,117 | 68,766 | 66,628 |
| Sec.Oth.th.Shares Excl./f.Brd. Money | **36s** | 20,679 | 14,739 | 16,403 | 30,593 | 37,363 | 54,644 | 57,320 | 50,824 | 41,300 | 35,234 | 27,327 | 21,078 |
| **Interest Rates** | | | | | | *Percent Per Annum* | | | | | | | |
| Deposit Rate | | | | | | | | | | | | | |
| Households: Stocks, up to 2 years | **60lhs** | 1.97 | 1.94 | 2.13 | 2.80 | 3.58 | 2.57 | 1.48 | 2.82 | 3.31 | 2.49 | 1.94 | 1.10 |
| New Business, up to 1 year | **60lhn** | 1.82 | 1.87 | 2.50 | 3.67 | 4.21 | 1.99 | 1.71 | 3.52 | 3.01 | 2.13 | 1.59 | .77 |
| Corporations: Stocks, up to 2 years | **60lcs** | 2.16 | 2.18 | 2.87 | 4.06 | 4.61 | 2.13 | 1.89 | 3.84 | 2.90 | 2.28 | 1.60 | .89 |
| New Business, up to 1 year | **60lcn** | 2.06 | 2.13 | 2.89 | 4.04 | 4.41 | 1.44 | 1.55 | 3.62 | 1.76 | 1.55 | .94 | .45 |
| Lending Rate | | | | | | | | | | | | | |
| Households: Stocks, up to 1 year | **60phs** | 9.15 | 9.05 | 9.46 | 10.15 | 10.94 | 10.22 | 10.32 | 11.77 | 13.54 | 13.85 | 13.60 | 13.25 |
| New Bus., Floating & up to 1 year | **60pns** | 7.65 | 7.57 | 7.64 | 7.92 | 8.35 | 6.12 | 6.26 | 7.80 | 8.14 | 8.41 | 7.78 | 6.60 |
| House Purch., Stocks,Over 5 years | **60phm** | 3.76 | 3.68 | 4.26 | 5.14 | 5.69 | 3.30 | 1.94 | 2.47 | 2.13 | 1.48 | 1.50 | 1.30 |
| Corporations: Stocks, up to 1 year | **60pcs** | 4.58 | 4.57 | 5.23 | 6.13 | 6.75 | 4.69 | 4.23 | 5.71 | 6.37 | 5.91 | 5.30 | 4.49 |
| New Bus., Over € 1 mil.,up to 1 yr | **60pcn** | 3.51 | 3.73 | 4.34 | 5.25 | 5.94 | 3.84 | 3.73 | 5.33 | 5.47 | 4.99 | 4.34 | 3.31 |
| Government Bond Yield | **61** | 4.14 | 3.44 | 3.92 | 4.42 | 4.52 | 4.21 | 5.40 | 10.24 | 10.55 | 6.29 | 3.75 | 2.42 |
| **Prices, Production, Labor** | | | | | | *Index Numbers (2010=100): Period Averages* | | | | | | | |
| Share Prices (End of Month) | **62.ep** | 97.9 | 104.4 | 132.5 | 167.2 | 118.5 | 97.7 | 100.0 | 90.8 | 68.7 | 80.3 | 84.0 | 73.5 |
| Producer Prices | **63** | 85.9 | 88.7 | 92.6 | 95.3 | 100.2 | 96.4 | † 100.0 | 105.8 | 109.1 | 109.3 | 107.9 | 104.7 |
| Consumer Prices | **64** | 89.7 | 91.8 | 94.3 | † 96.9 | † 99.4 | 98.6 | 100.0 | 103.7 | 106.5 | 106.8 | 106.5 | 107.0 |
| Harmonized CPI | **64h** | 89.9 | 91.9 | 94.7 | 97.0 | 99.5 | 98.6 | 100.0 | 103.6 | 106.4 | 106.9 | 106.7 | 107.3 |
| Wages | **65ey** | 86.6 | 88.0 | 88.7 | 93.3 | 96.0 | 100.0 | 100.0 | † 97.1 | 88.4 | 86.6 | 85.9 | 88.5 |
| Industrial Production | **66** | 112.5 | 108.6 | 111.9 | 111.8 | 107.3 | 98.4 | 100.0 | 99.1 | 93.0 | 93.4 | 94.9 | 96.6 |
| | | | | | | *Number in Thousands: Period Averages* | | | | | | | |
| Labor Force | **67d** | 5,477 | 5,136 | 5,171 | 5,196 | 5,203 | 5,162 | 5,166 | 5,138 | 5,087 | 5,010 | 4,976 | 4,950 |
| Employment | **67e** | 5,054 | 4,723 | 4,751 | 4,756 | 4,786 | 4,645 | 4,577 | 4,453 | 4,256 | 4,158 | 4,255 | 4,309 |
| Unemployment | **67c** | 413 | 470 | 478 | 494 | 475 | 574 | 646 | 689 | 835 | 855 | 729 | 647 |
| Unemployment Rate (%) | **67r** | 7.8 | 8.8 | 8.9 | 9.1 | 8.8 | 10.7 | 12.0 | 12.9 | 15.8 | 16.4 | 14.1 | 12.6 |
| **Intl. Transactions & Positions** | | | | | | *Millions of Euros* | | | | | | | |
| Exports | **70** | 26,586.3 | 25,873.7 | 34,136.5 | 36,655.0 | 38,950.3 | 31,768.2 | 36,762.2 | 42,828.0 | 45,324.0 | 47,337.2 | 48,221.9 | 49,951.8 |
| Imports, c.i.f. | **71** | 39,597.0 | 42,939.2 | 52,231.7 | 55,626.5 | 64,193.9 | 51,367.9 | 57,053.1 | 59,229.3 | 56,234.3 | 56,523.4 | 58,538.3 | 59,936.8 |
| | | | | | | *2010=100* | | | | | | | |
| Volume of Exports | **72** | 112.0 | 101.4 | 109.5 | 107.2 | 101.5 | 87.6 | 100.0 | . . . . | . . . . | . . . . | . . . . | . . . . |
| Volume of Imports | **73** | 107.4 | 94.0 | 95.1 | 103.9 | 96.4 | 83.3 | 100.0 | . . . . | . . . . | . . . . | . . . . | . . . . |
| Export Prices | **76** | 95.6 | 96.6 | 99.1 | 97.2 | 97.0 | 90.4 | 100.0 | . . . . | . . . . | . . . . | . . . . | . . . . |
| Import Prices | **76.x** | 97.4 | 98.5 | 99.1 | 95.9 | 99.6 | 85.6 | 100.0 | . . . . | . . . . | . . . . | . . . . | . . . . |

Portugal 182

| | | 2004 | 2005 | 2006 | 2007 | 2008 | 2009 | 2010 | 2011 | 2012 | 2013 | 2014 | 2015 |
|---|---|---|---|---|---|---|---|---|---|---|---|---|---|
| **Balance of Payments** | | | | | | | *Millions of US Dollars* | | | | | | |
| A. Current Account* | **109bx** | –15,814.2 | –19,536.9 | –22,217.0 | –23,524.9 | –31,944.3 | –25,452.4 | –24,199.2 | –14,781.2 | –4,191.4 | 3,311.4 | 209.9 | 900.7 |
| Goods, credit (exports) | **1a9cx** | 37,243.8 | 38,022.1 | 44,296.5 | 52,089.7 | 56,907.8 | 43,841.1 | 48,942.4 | 58,839.3 | 56,962.7 | 61,723.7 | 62,719.3 | 54,329.8 |
| Goods, debit (imports) | **1a9dx** | 58,395.8 | 61,062.5 | 68,427.8 | 79,618.8 | 92,148.2 | 69,146.6 | 74,463.2 | 79,000.5 | 68,955.9 | 72,438.8 | 75,291.6 | 64,486.1 |
| Balance on goods | **1a9bx** | –21,150.8 | –23,039.1 | –24,130.1 | –27,529.0 | –35,242.0 | –25,304.2 | –25,524.8 | –20,161.2 | –11,994.5 | –10,715.1 | –12,572.3 | –10,154.1 |
| Services, credit (exports) | **1b9cx** | 14,709.1 | 15,101.7 | 18,372.1 | 23,215.5 | 26,025.3 | 22,595.4 | 22,753.5 | 26,894.4 | 25,715.5 | 29,369.7 | 31,195.2 | 27,798.3 |
| Services, debit (imports) | **1b9dx** | 8,931.6 | 9,487.3 | 11,220.5 | 13,449.4 | 15,426.6 | 13,750.8 | 14,247.2 | 15,719.4 | 13,582.2 | 14,515.5 | 16,003.8 | 14,187.7 |
| Balance on Goods & Services | **1z9bx** | –15,374.4 | –17,426.1 | –16,979.8 | –17,763.0 | –24,641.7 | –16,460.9 | –17,014.6 | –8,986.1 | 140.1 | 4,139.1 | 2,619.2 | 3,454.2 |
| Primary income: credit | **1c9cx** | 9,825.3 | 11,155.5 | 15,084.3 | 19,241.2 | 20,639.1 | 14,341.2 | 17,951.9 | 17,010.3 | 11,525.0 | 11,730.8 | 11,330.5 | 8,799.4 |
| Primary income: debit | **1c9dx** | 11,721.7 | 13,960.4 | 21,215.2 | 26,491.6 | 29,406.0 | 23,602.9 | 25,459.7 | 23,625.6 | 17,141.4 | 14,594.6 | 15,394.5 | 13,069.6 |
| Balance on gds, serv. & prim. inc. | **1y9bx** | –17,270.8 | –20,231.0 | –23,110.7 | –25,013.4 | –33,408.6 | –25,722.7 | –24,522.3 | –15,601.4 | –5,476.2 | 1,275.4 | –1,444.9 | –816.0 |
| Secondary income: credit | **1d9ca** | 5,096.6 | 5,025.6 | 5,714.6 | 6,574.9 | 7,204.7 | 6,227.0 | 6,365.9 | 7,191.7 | 7,039.6 | 8,220.0 | 7,704.6 | 6,408.6 |
| Secondary income: debit | **1d9da** | 3,640.0 | 4,331.5 | 4,820.9 | 5,086.4 | 5,740.4 | 5,956.7 | 6,042.7 | 6,371.6 | 5,754.9 | 6,184.0 | 6,049.8 | 4,691.8 |
| B. Capital Account* | **209ba** | 3,287.9 | 2,782.4 | 2,477.3 | 2,733.9 | 3,082.7 | 2,849.7 | 3,316.8 | 3,643.5 | 4,505.3 | 3,716.0 | 3,390.4 | 2,492.8 |
| Capital account: credit | **209ca** | 3,463.4 | 2,977.9 | 2,830.6 | 3,057.1 | 3,517.1 | 3,265.3 | 3,754.3 | 4,107.2 | 4,998.2 | 4,258.0 | 3,724.1 | 3,159.0 |
| Capital account: debit | **209da** | 175.5 | 195.5 | 353.3 | 323.3 | 434.4 | 415.5 | 437.6 | 463.6 | 492.8 | 542.0 | 333.6 | 666.3 |
| Balance on current & capital acct. | **129ba** | –12,526.3 | –16,754.6 | –19,739.7 | –20,791.0 | –28,861.6 | –22,602.7 | –20,882.4 | –11,137.7 | 313.9 | 7,027.4 | 3,600.4 | 3,393.5 |
| C. Financial Account* | **309na** | –10,691.2 | –15,564.3 | –17,126.8 | –20,298.1 | –28,305.0 | –23,849.2 | –21,653.3 | 8,991.6 | 10,756.0 | 11,420.5 | 4,212.6 | –7,426.2 |
| Direct investment: assets | **3a9aa** | 8,211.4 | 2,621.6 | 8,772.7 | 8,479.7 | 5,448.4 | 3,556.3 | –3,676.8 | 15,637.3 | 4,915.1 | 6,868.1 | 9,503.3 | 790.9 |
| Equity & investment fund shares | **3aaaa** | 6,933.1 | 1,117.4 | 6,501.1 | 2,476.8 | 3,195.5 | 258.2 | –7,965.0 | 8,500.5 | 5,106.8 | 3,861.2 | 4,104.5 | 847.0 |
| Debt instruments | **3abaa** | 1,278.4 | 1,503.0 | 2,269.1 | 6,001.6 | 2,252.9 | 3,295.3 | 4,288.1 | 7,135.5 | –189.1 | 3,006.9 | 5,402.7 | –56.1 |
| Direct investment: liabilities | **3a9la** | 2,497.0 | 4,428.9 | 13,198.6 | 6,026.2 | 7,821.4 | 5,578.9 | 8,455.8 | 9,817.7 | 21,990.7 | 11,624.2 | 13,116.2 | –1,315.6 |
| Equity & investment fund shares | **3aala** | 5,964.5 | 3,613.1 | 9,802.9 | 3,301.7 | 4,232.3 | 2,534.8 | 4,656.1 | 6,151.4 | 9,802.2 | 1,672.1 | 7,001.7 | 1,840.4 |
| Debt instruments | **3abla** | –3,466.3 | 815.8 | 3,395.6 | 2,723.1 | 3,587.6 | 3,042.7 | 3,799.6 | 3,667.6 | 12,187.3 | 9,953.4 | 6,115.7 | –3,153.8 |
| Portfolio investment: assets | **3b9aa** | 13,598.5 | 19,660.0 | 7,990.6 | 10,731.9 | 17,148.8 | 22,418.0 | 3,866.0 | –33,489.5 | –13,146.6 | –160.6 | 10,115.6 | 348.1 |
| Equity & investment fund shares | **3baaa** | 1,708.8 | 1,844.4 | 4,105.2 | 2,192.9 | –578.9 | 1,555.0 | –90.7 | –5,406.3 | –588.3 | 3,430.2 | 5,338.6 | 2,358.7 |
| Debt securities | **3bbaa** | 11,889.6 | 17,814.3 | 3,886.6 | 8,539.1 | 17,727.7 | 20,863.0 | 3,955.3 | –28,083.2 | –12,559.6 | –3,592.1 | 4,778.4 | –2,010.6 |
| Portfolio investment: liabilities | **3b9la** | 14,825.3 | 19,263.3 | 12,956.8 | 24,668.6 | 40,787.9 | 42,656.7 | –10,658.5 | –39,870.6 | –51,620.9 | –5,131.3 | 12,392.7 | 3,103.8 |
| Equity & investment fund shares | **3bala** | 7,233.1 | 5,594.0 | 3,828.1 | 292.7 | 8,678.5 | 3,406.0 | –1,612.2 | –9,508.9 | –10,203.2 | –72.0 | 2,342.7 | –1,918.1 |
| Debt securities | **3bbla** | 7,592.3 | 13,670.4 | 9,128.7 | 24,375.9 | 32,109.4 | 39,250.5 | –9,046.3 | –30,361.7 | –41,416.4 | –5,059.4 | 10,048.7 | 5,023.0 |
| Fin. der.& empl.stk.ops.(ESOs): net | **3c9na** | 89.6 | 210.2 | 263.0 | –234.3 | –215.6 | –209.6 | –503.5 | –578.4 | –92.7 | 1,342.4 | 2,604.3 | 348.6 |
| Fin. der. & ESOs.: assets | **3c9aa** | 89.6 | 210.2 | 263.0 | –234.3 | –215.6 | –209.6 | –503.5 | –578.4 | –92.7 | 1,342.4 | 2,604.3 | 348.6 |
| Fin. der. & ESOs.: liabilities | **3c9la** | — | — | — | — | — | — | — | — | — | — | — | — |
| Other investment: assets | **3d9aa** | 1,371.6 | 2,006.4 | 18,704.9 | 16,549.7 | –10,173.1 | 5,017.3 | 10,403.6 | –1,410.0 | 3,059.3 | –13,965.3 | 6,394.2 | –10,452.0 |
| Other equity | **3daaa** | 4.0 | — | 3.8 | 1.3 | 14.1 | 25.3 | 172.1 | 76.1 | 1,205.8 | 1,162.0 | 563.6 | — |
| Debt instruments | **3dzaa** | 1,367.7 | 2,006.4 | 18,701.1 | 16,548.4 | –10,187.2 | 4,992.0 | 10,231.5 | –1,486.1 | 1,853.5 | –15,127.3 | 5,830.6 | –10,452.0 |
| Other investment: liabilities | **3d9la** | 16,638.9 | 16,371.5 | 26,699.0 | 25,127.4 | –8,094.2 | 6,394.2 | 33,946.5 | 1,219.4 | 13,609.2 | –23,827.4 | –1,099.9 | –3,326.4 |
| Other equity | **3dala** | — | — | — | — | — | — | — | — | — | — | 51.8 | 96.9 |
| Debt instruments | **3dzla** | 16,638.9 | 16,371.5 | 26,699.0 | 25,127.4 | –8,094.2 | 6,394.2 | 33,946.5 | 1,219.4 | 13,609.2 | –23,827.4 | –1,151.7 | –3,423.3 |
| Curr.+ cap.– finan. acct. balance | **4y9na** | –1,835.1 | –1,190.2 | –2,612.9 | –492.9 | –556.6 | 1,246.5 | 770.9 | –20,129.3 | –10,442.1 | –4,393.1 | –612.2 | 10,819.7 |
| D. Net Errors and Omissions | **409na** | –25.8 | –552.3 | 255.2 | –473.4 | 676.7 | –152.0 | 503.5 | 238.7 | 67.3 | 403.4 | 425.1 | –39.0 |
| E. Reserves and Related Items | **4z9na** | –1,862.1 | –1,742.6 | –2,356.5 | –964.9 | 117.3 | 1,095.7 | 1,270.5 | –19,890.6 | –10,373.5 | –3,985.7 | –185.8 | 10,786.3 |
| Reserve assets | **3e9aa** | –1,862.1 | –1,742.6 | –2,356.5 | –964.9 | 117.3 | 1,095.7 | 1,270.5 | –1,717.7 | 218.6 | 564.1 | 2,227.3 | 1,644.9 |
| Credit and loans from the IMF | **3dcla** | — | — | — | — | — | — | — | 18,172.9 | 10,592.1 | 4,549.8 | 2,413.0 | –9,141.4 |
| Exceptional financing | **409la** | .... | .... | .... | .... | .... | .... | .... | .... | .... | .... | .... | .... |

*Excludes components in group E

| | | 2004 | 2005 | 2006 | 2007 | 2008 | 2009 | 2010 | 2011 | 2012 | 2013 | 2014 | 2015 |
|---|---|---|---|---|---|---|---|---|---|---|---|---|---|
| **International Investment Position** | | | | | | | *Millions of US Dollars* | | | | | | |
| Assets | **809aa** | 319,574.0 | 313,151.1 | 382,727.2 | 462,042.1 | 422,665.6 | 478,680.9 | 465,209.7 | 409,977.2 | 419,459.2 | 424,667.1 | 402,773.6 | 357,952.6 |
| Direct investment | **8a9aa** | 52,247.4 | 49,548.6 | 63,493.9 | 79,748.1 | 75,746.1 | 84,112.3 | 82,821.7 | 82,484.8 | 90,518.8 | 99,102.1 | 95,581.2 | 87,444.4 |
| Equity & investment fund shares | **8aaaa** | 40,658.7 | 38,299.0 | 48,918.6 | 59,777.6 | 56,699.2 | 62,850.5 | 59,189.7 | 55,971.5 | 68,730.2 | 74,297.6 | 71,549.3 | 65,941.5 |
| Debt instruments | **8abaa** | 11,590.1 | 11,249.6 | 14,575.2 | 19,970.5 | 19,046.8 | 21,260.4 | 23,632.0 | 26,513.3 | 21,789.9 | 24,804.5 | 24,031.9 | 21,501.8 |
| Portfolio investment | **8b9aa** | 124,949.5 | 134,737.1 | 160,336.8 | 190,591.3 | 176,346.5 | 210,683.4 | 194,814.0 | 147,798.3 | 144,594.4 | 152,067.8 | 144,545.9 | 129,510.7 |
| Equity & investment fund shares | **8baaa** | 16,555.0 | 27,494.1 | 39,544.2 | 50,953.8 | 32,396.0 | 38,462.6 | 36,391.4 | 27,733.5 | 28,962.1 | 35,278.8 | 36,257.9 | 35,751.8 |
| Debt securities | **8bbaa** | 108,393.2 | 107,243.0 | 120,792.6 | 139,639.0 | 143,950.5 | 172,220.8 | 158,422.5 | 120,064.9 | 115,632.2 | 116,789.1 | 108,288.0 | 93,758.8 |
| Fin. der.(oth.than reserves) & ESOs | **8c9aa** | –835.0 | –75.5 | 238.4 | 120.7 | 226.8 | –639.6 | –1,511.2 | –3,105.4 | –4,805.3 | –4,278.0 | –2,193.9 | 104.5 |
| Other investment | **8d9aa** | 131,527.1 | 118,576.4 | 148,774.9 | 180,034.9 | 158,397.7 | 168,538.7 | 168,088.6 | 161,463.2 | 166,491.1 | 160,216.9 | 145,222.1 | 121,493.5 |
| Other equity | **8daaa** | 3,786.6 | 3,401.1 | 3,694.2 | 4,023.2 | 3,867.5 | 4,017.8 | 3,968.5 | 3,907.6 | 5,152.3 | 6,699.7 | 7,022.4 | 6,390.7 |
| Debt instruments | **8dzaa** | 127,740.5 | 115,175.3 | 145,080.7 | 176,011.6 | 154,530.2 | 164,520.8 | 164,120.1 | 157,555.6 | 161,338.9 | 153,517.3 | 138,199.8 | 115,102.8 |
| Reserve assets | **8e9aa** | 11,684.9 | 10,364.6 | 9,883.2 | 11,545.6 | 11,948.5 | 15,984.7 | 20,995.4 | 21,336.2 | 22,657.6 | 17,552.7 | 19,618.2 | 19,396.3 |
| Liabilities | **809la** | 458,108.0 | 444,064.6 | 556,431.1 | 691,413.3 | 659,482.1 | 751,399.1 | 716,060.9 | 639,408.8 | 678,427.9 | 697,947.2 | 643,522.2 | 571,432.1 |
| Direct investment | **8a9la** | 80,310.8 | 75,317.9 | 101,027.1 | 131,704.4 | 118,487.9 | 135,423.6 | 135,529.4 | 124,791.5 | 148,164.7 | 163,677.1 | 153,731.8 | 138,099.4 |
| Equity & investment fund shares | **8aala** | 68,468.7 | 64,905.9 | 85,793.3 | 111,467.4 | 96,504.7 | 109,688.7 | 107,939.6 | 94,952.9 | 106,947.9 | 115,757.5 | 109,175.5 | 101,068.4 |
| Debt instruments | **8abla** | 11,842.1 | 10,412.0 | 15,233.7 | 20,237.0 | 21,983.3 | 25,734.9 | 27,589.9 | 29,838.6 | 41,216.7 | 47,919.6 | 44,556.3 | 37,031.0 |
| Portfolio investment | **8b9la** | 156,523.0 | 159,339.7 | 193,729.4 | 244,140.4 | 250,917.9 | 311,682.5 | 261,188.4 | 185,603.5 | 168,483.4 | 177,418.5 | 169,589.1 | 154,988.4 |
| Equity & investment fund shares | **8bala** | 47,721.2 | 48,506.9 | 64,123.4 | 75,979.5 | 58,448.6 | 71,724.6 | 63,008.5 | 45,818.3 | 43,406.9 | 49,167.7 | 38,232.0 | 34,830.8 |
| Debt securities | **8bbla** | 108,801.8 | 110,832.8 | 129,607.3 | 168,160.9 | 192,470.7 | 239,957.9 | 198,179.8 | 139,785.2 | 125,076.5 | 128,250.8 | 131,358.3 | 120,157.6 |
| Fin. der.(oth.than reserves) & ESOs | **8c9la** | — | — | — | — | — | — | — | — | .... | .... | .... | .... |
| Other investment | **8d9la** | 221,274.2 | 209,406.9 | 261,674.6 | 315,568.5 | 290,076.2 | 304,293.1 | 319,343.1 | 329,013.9 | 361,777.2 | 356,851.6 | 320,203.7 | 278,343.2 |
| Other equity | **8dala** | — | — | — | — | — | — | — | — | — | — | 46.1 | 137.2 |
| Debt instruments | **8dzla** | 221,274.2 | 209,406.9 | 261,674.6 | 315,568.5 | 290,076.2 | 304,293.1 | 319,343.1 | 329,013.9 | 361,777.2 | 356,851.6 | 320,157.6 | 278,206.0 |

# Portugal 182

| | | 2004 | 2005 | 2006 | 2007 | 2008 | 2009 | 2010 | 2011 | 2012 | 2013 | 2014 | 2015 |
|---|---|---|---|---|---|---|---|---|---|---|---|---|---|
| **Government Finance Operations Statement General Government** | | | | | *Millions of Euros: Fiscal Year Ends December 31; Data Reported through Eurostat* | | | | | | | | |
| Revenue | a1 | 60,750 | 64,227 | 68,019 | 72,780 | 74,357 | 70,913 | 73,137 | 75,106 | 72,190 | 76,787 | 77,231 | 78,671 |
| Taxes | a11 | 33,436 | 35,739 | 38,478 | 41,365 | 41,606 | 37,331 | 39,074 | 41,115 | 38,739 | 42,733 | 43,567 | 45,530 |
| Social Contributions | a12 | 17,278 | 18,398 | 19,193 | 19,866 | 20,699 | 21,190 | 21,362 | 21,201 | 19,142 | 20,449 | 20,371 | 20,718 |
| Grants | a13 | .... | .... | .... | .... | .... | .... | .... | .... | .... | .... | .... | .... |
| Other Revenue | a14 | .... | .... | .... | .... | .... | .... | .... | .... | .... | .... | .... | .... |
| Expense | a2 | 67,050 | 71,602 | 73,694 | 76,904 | 80,691 | 85,375 | 88,612 | 87,156 | 83,067 | 86,276 | 91,195 | 87,824 |
| Compensation of Employees | a21 | 21,746 | 23,044 | 22,916 | 23,007 | 23,491 | 24,608 | 24,611 | 22,614 | 19,688 | 21,317 | 20,495 | 20,264 |
| Use of Goods & Services | a22 | 7,402 | 8,070 | 8,434 | 9,493 | 9,920 | 10,834 | 10,627 | 10,645 | 9,685 | 9,611 | 10,079 | 10,601 |
| Consumption of Fixed Capital | a23 | 3,752 | 3,979 | 4,216 | 4,425 | 4,674 | 4,710 | 4,989 | 5,161 | 5,187 | 5,092 | 5,097 | 5,216 |
| Interest | a24 | 3,894 | 4,046 | 4,599 | 5,174 | 5,556 | 5,218 | 5,268 | 7,604 | 8,214 | 8,258 | 8,502 | 8,192 |
| Subsidies | a25 | 1,360 | 1,438 | 1,435 | 1,337 | 1,154 | 1,258 | 1,295 | 1,168 | 1,018 | 1,031 | 1,210 | 1,172 |
| Grants | a26 | .... | .... | .... | .... | .... | .... | .... | .... | .... | .... | .... | .... |
| Social Benefits | a27 | 23,919 | 25,780 | 27,053 | 28,342 | 29,946 | 32,917 | 33,452 | 33,325 | 33,010 | 34,785 | 34,106 | 34,517 |
| Other Expense | a28 | .... | .... | .... | .... | .... | .... | .... | .... | .... | .... | .... | .... |
| Gross Operating Balance [1-2+23] | agob | −2,547 | −3,396 | −1,459 | 301 | −1,660 | −9,752 | −10,486 | −6,889 | −5,690 | −4,397 | −8,868 | −3,937 |
| Net Operating Balance [1-2] | anob | −6,300 | −7,375 | −5,675 | −4,124 | −6,334 | −14,462 | −15,475 | −12,049 | −10,878 | −9,489 | −13,964 | −9,153 |
| Net Acq. of Nonfinancial Assets | a31 | 3,139 | 2,452 | 1,519 | 1,155 | 401 | 2,741 | 4,625 | 957 | −1,348 | −1,244 | −1,518 | −1,260 |
| Aquisition of Nonfin. Assets | a31.1 | .... | .... | .... | .... | .... | .... | .... | .... | .... | .... | .... | .... |
| Disposal of Nonfin. Assets | a31.2 | .... | .... | .... | .... | .... | .... | .... | .... | .... | .... | .... | .... |
| Net Lending/Borrowing [1-2-31] | anlb | −9,439 | −9,827 | −7,195 | −5,279 | −6,736 | −17,204 | −20,100 | −13,006 | −9,529 | −8,245 | −12,446 | −7,893 |
| Net Acq. of Financial Assets | a32 | 1,784 | 859 | 488 | −1,064 | 979 | 2,091 | 5,658 | 14,238 | 1,705 | −1,963 | −6,751 | −4,383 |
| By instrument | | | | | | | | | | | | | |
| Monetary Gold & SDRs | a3201 | — | — | — | — | — | — | — | — | — | — | −4 | — |
| Currency & Deposits | a3202 | −224 | 1,009 | 1,285 | −786 | 50 | −491 | 483 | 10,129 | 1,539 | 1,211 | −4,698 | −3,012 |
| Securities other than Shares | a3203 | −305 | 408 | 183 | 108 | −590 | 552 | 30 | 283 | 6,150 | −273 | −961 | −961 |
| Loans | a3204 | 133 | 295 | 63 | −1,885 | 50 | 33 | 1,256 | 841 | 1,191 | −17 | −276 | 139 |
| Shares & Other Equity | a3205 | 547 | −569 | −1,505 | 1,096 | 2,153 | 1,135 | 2,106 | −437 | −3,837 | −1,088 | −2,074 | −193 |
| Insurance Technical Reserves | a3206 | 2 | 3 | 2 | 1 | — | — | −2 | 1 | −1 | — | 1 | −1 |
| Financial Derivatives | a3207 | 20 | 29 | 118 | −219 | −333 | −93 | −428 | −217 | −188 | −23 | 112 | −290 |
| Other Accounts Receivable | a3208 | 1,611 | −315 | 342 | 623 | −350 | 954 | 2,211 | 3,637 | −3,149 | −1,773 | 189 | −66 |
| By debtor | | | | | | | | | | | | | |
| Domestic | a321 | .... | .... | .... | .... | .... | .... | .... | .... | .... | .... | .... | .... |
| Foreign | a322 | .... | .... | .... | .... | .... | .... | .... | .... | .... | .... | .... | .... |
| Net Incurrence of Liabilities | a33 | 11,222 | 10,686 | 7,683 | 4,216 | 7,714 | 19,295 | 25,757 | 27,244 | 11,234 | 6,282 | 5,695 | 3,510 |
| By instrument | | | | | | | | | | | | | |
| Special Drawing Rights (SDRs) | a3301 | — | — | — | — | — | — | — | — | — | — | — | — |
| Currency & Deposits | a3302 | −142 | 538 | 2,052 | 930 | −1,094 | −368 | −527 | −2,979 | −1,356 | 1,223 | 4,919 | 3,969 |
| Securities other than Shares | a3303 | 5,393 | 12,602 | 5,319 | 3,674 | 10,803 | 17,256 | 19,167 | −11,092 | −7,921 | −2,828 | −1,810 | 11,228 |
| Loans | a3304 | 3,415 | −277 | 57 | 1,268 | −678 | 2,489 | 3,639 | 35,812 | 24,624 | 8,985 | 3,565 | −9,538 |
| Shares & Other Equity | a3305 | — | — | — | — | — | — | — | — | 351 | −340 | 12 | −200 |
| Insurance Technical Reserves | a3306 | — | — | — | — | — | — | — | — | — | — | — | −24 |
| Financial Derivatives | a3307 | — | −5 | 5 | −24 | 26 | 16 | 8 | 34 | 32 | 18 | −6 | — |
| Other Accounts Payable | a3308 | 2,557 | −2,172 | 250 | −1,633 | −1,342 | −98 | 3,470 | 5,468 | −4,496 | −776 | −984 | −1,924 |
| By creditor | | | | | | | | | | | | | |
| Domestic | a331 | .... | .... | .... | .... | .... | .... | .... | .... | .... | .... | .... | .... |
| Foreign | a332 | .... | .... | .... | .... | .... | .... | .... | .... | .... | .... | .... | .... |
| Stat. Discrepancy [32-33-NLB] | anlbz | — | — | — | — | — | — | 1 | — | — | — | — | — |
| Memo Item: Expenditure [2+31] | a2m | 70,189 | 74,054 | 75,214 | 78,060 | 81,093 | 88,116 | 93,237 | 88,112 | 81,719 | 85,032 | 89,677 | 86,564 |
| **Balance Sheet** | | | | | | | | | | | | | |
| Net Worth | a6 | .... | .... | .... | .... | .... | .... | .... | .... | .... | .... | .... | .... |
| Nonfinancial Assets | a61 | .... | .... | .... | .... | .... | .... | .... | .... | .... | .... | .... | .... |
| Financial Assets | a62 | 34,595 | 38,133 | 41,079 | 40,516 | 41,445 | 45,277 | 59,510 | 73,500 | 81,331 | 74,751 | 76,132 | 74,477 |
| By instrument | | | | | | | | | | | | | |
| Monetary Gold & SDRs | a6201 | — | — | — | — | — | — | — | — | — | — | — | — |
| Currency & Deposits | a6202 | 6,521 | 7,531 | 8,791 | 7,988 | 8,071 | 7,583 | 8,239 | 18,604 | 20,145 | 21,347 | 21,271 | 18,285 |
| Securities other than Shares | a6203 | 2,424 | 2,549 | 2,844 | 2,969 | 2,401 | 2,693 | 2,658 | 3,005 | 9,478 | 9,047 | 4,586 | 3,524 |
| Loans | a6204 | 3,911 | 4,597 | 4,567 | 2,895 | 2,998 | 2,998 | 4,313 | 5,386 | 6,569 | 6,720 | 6,582 | 6,860 |
| Shares and Other Equity | a6205 | 14,061 | 16,138 | 16,986 | 18,149 | 19,753 | 22,804 | 32,732 | 30,987 | 32,828 | 27,524 | 32,066 | 32,994 |
| Insurance Technical Reserves | a6206 | 15 | 17 | 19 | 20 | 20 | 21 | 19 | 19 | 19 | 19 | 19 | 18 |
| Financial Derivatives | a6207 | −262 | −309 | −59 | −57 | −69 | −47 | 112 | 408 | 397 | −27 | 1,295 | 2,539 |
| Other Accounts Receivable | a6208 | 7,925 | 7,609 | 7,929 | 8,552 | 8,270 | 9,224 | 11,436 | 15,090 | 11,895 | 10,123 | 10,312 | 10,255 |
| By debtor | | | | | | | | | | | | | |
| Domestic | a621 | .... | .... | .... | .... | .... | .... | .... | .... | .... | .... | .... | .... |
| Foreign | a622 | .... | .... | .... | .... | .... | .... | .... | .... | .... | .... | .... | .... |
| Liabilities | a63 | 116,795 | 126,880 | 132,016 | 137,018 | 148,039 | 168,645 | 187,292 | 190,900 | 233,822 | 242,841 | 264,371 | 269,627 |
| By instrument | | | | | | | | | | | | | |
| Special Drawing Rights (SDRs) | a6301 | — | — | — | — | — | — | — | — | — | — | — | — |
| Currency & Deposits | a6302 | 16,606 | 17,030 | 19,082 | 20,012 | 18,918 | 18,550 | 18,023 | 15,044 | 13,688 | 14,748 | 19,350 | 23,319 |
| Securities other than Shares | a6303 | 73,463 | 85,455 | 87,945 | 89,908 | 103,196 | 120,032 | 127,424 | 92,119 | 111,471 | 112,067 | 123,528 | 135,187 |
| Loans | a6304 | 16,013 | 15,797 | 16,042 | 17,534 | 16,724 | 19,828 | 26,510 | 62,718 | 87,196 | 95,571 | 100,912 | 93,313 |
| Shares and Other Equity | a6305 | — | — | — | — | — | — | — | — | 1,962 | 1,620 | 1,573 | 1,360 |
| Insurance Technical Reserves | a6306 | — | — | — | — | — | — | — | — | — | — | — | — |
| Financial Derivatives | a6307 | — | −5 | — | −24 | 2 | 18 | 38 | 913 | 1,200 | 1,017 | 1,537 | 1,311 |
| Other Accounts Payable | a6308 | 10,713 | 8,603 | 8,947 | 9,587 | 9,200 | 10,217 | 15,298 | 20,106 | 18,306 | 17,818 | 17,471 | 15,137 |
| By creditor | | | | | | | | | | | | | |
| Domestic | a631 | .... | .... | .... | .... | .... | .... | .... | .... | .... | .... | .... | .... |
| Foreign | a632 | .... | .... | .... | .... | .... | .... | .... | .... | .... | .... | .... | .... |
| Net Financial Worth [62-63] | a6m2 | −82,200 | −88,746 | −90,937 | −96,502 | −106,595 | −123,368 | −127,783 | −117,400 | −152,491 | −168,090 | −188,240 | −195,150 |
| Memo Item: Debt at Market Value | a6m3 | 116,795 | 126,885 | 132,016 | 137,041 | 148,038 | 168,627 | 187,254 | 189,988 | 230,661 | 240,204 | 261,261 | 266,956 |
| Memo Item: Debt at Face Value | a6m35 | 105,167 | 115,522 | 123,950 | 129,675 | 137,391 | 156,909 | 188,360 | 216,338 | 230,835 | 237,467 | 243,238 | 246,482 |
| Memo Item: Maastricht Debt | a6m36 | 94,454 | 106,919 | 115,002 | 120,088 | 128,191 | 146,691 | 173,062 | 196,231 | 212,529 | 219,649 | 225,767 | 231,345 |
| Memo Item: Debt at Nominal Value | a6m4 | .... | .... | .... | .... | .... | .... | .... | .... | .... | .... | .... | .... |

| National Accounts | | 2004 | 2005 | 2006 | 2007 | 2008 | 2009 | 2010 | 2011 | 2012 | 2013 | 2014 | 2015 |
|---|---|---|---|---|---|---|---|---|---|---|---|---|---|
| | | *Billions of Euros: Quarterly Data Seasonally Adjusted* | | | | | | | | | | | |
| Househ.Cons.Expend.,incl.NPISHs.... | 96f.c | 97 | 102 | 107 | 114 | 118 | 114 | 118 | 116 | 112 | 111 | 114 | 118 |
| Government Consumption Expend... | 91f.c | 31 | 33 | 34 | 35 | 36 | 38 | 37 | 35 | 31 | 33 | 32 | 33 |
| Gross Fixed Capital Formation.......... | 93e.c | 36 | 37 | 37 | 39 | 41 | 37 | 37 | 32 | 27 | 25 | 26 | 27 |
| Changes in Inventories.................... | 93i.c | 1 | 1 | 1 | 1 | 1 | −1 | 1 | — | — | — | — | — |
| Exports of Goods and Services......... | 90c.c | 42 | 42 | 50 | 54 | 56 | 48 | 54 | 60 | 64 | 67 | 69 | 72 |
| Imports of Goods and Services (-)..... | 98c.c | 54 | 57 | 63 | 68 | 73 | 60 | 67 | 68 | 64 | 66 | 69 | 71 |
| Gross Domestic Product (GDP)......... | 99b.c | 152 | 159 | 166 | 175 | 179 | 175 | 180 | 176 | 168 | 170 | 173 | 179 |
| Net Primary Income from Abroad..... | 98.nc | −2 | −2 | −5 | −6 | −7 | −6 | −6 | −4 | −4 | −2 | −2 | .... |
| Gross National Income (GNI)........... | 99a.c | 150 | 156 | 161 | 170 | 172 | 169 | 174 | 173 | 164 | 168 | 171 | .... |
| Net Current Transf.from Abroad....... | 98t.c | 2 | 1 | 2 | 2 | 2 | 1 | 1 | 1 | 2 | 2 | .... | .... |
| Gross Nat'l Disposable Inc.(GNDI).... | 99i.c | 149 | 153 | 158 | 166 | 168 | 163 | 168 | 166 | 162 | .... | .... | .... |
| Gross Saving................................. | 99s.c | 23 | 20 | 20 | 21 | 18 | 16 | 17 | 19 | 24 | .... | .... | .... |
| Consumption of Fixed Capital......... | 99cfc | 25 | 26 | 27 | 28 | 30 | 30 | 30 | 31 | 31 | 31 | .... | .... |
| GDP Volume 2010 Ref., Chained..... | 99b.r | 173 | 175 | 177 | 182 | 182 | 177 | 180 | 177 | 170 | 168 | 169 | 172 |
| GDP Volume (2010=100)............... | 99bvr | 96.2 | 97.0 | 98.5 | 100.9 | 101.1 | 98.1 | 100.0 | 98.2 | 94.2 | 93.2 | 94.0 | 95.4 |
| GDP Deflator (2010=100)............... | 99bir | 88.0 | 90.9 | 93.8 | 96.6 | 98.3 | 99.4 | 100.0 | 99.7 | 99.3 | 101.6 | 102.6 | 104.5 |
| | | *Millions: Midyear Estimates* | | | | | | | | | | | |
| **Population................................** | 99z | 10.44 | 10.48 | 10.52 | 10.55 | 10.58 | 10.59 | 10.58 | 10.56 | 10.52 | 10.46 | 10.40 | 10.35 |

# Qatar 453

| | | 2004 | 2005 | 2006 | 2007 | 2008 | 2009 | 2010 | 2011 | 2012 | 2013 | 2014 | 2015 |
|---|---|---|---|---|---|---|---|---|---|---|---|---|---|
| **Exchange Rates** | | | | | | *Riyals per SDR: End of Period* | | | | | | | |
| Official Rate | aa | 5.6530 | 5.2025 | 5.4760 | 5.7521 | 5.6066 | 5.7064 | 5.6057 | 5.5884 | 5.5944 | 5.6056 | 5.2737 | 5.0441 |
| | | | | | | *Riyals per US Dollar: End of Period (ae) Period Average (rf)* | | | | | | | |
| Official Rate | ae | 3.6400 | 3.6400 | 3.6400 | 3.6400 | 3.6400 | 3.6400 | 3.6400 | 3.6400 | 3.6400 | 3.6400 | 3.6400 | 3.6400 |
| Official Rate | rf | 3.6400 | 3.6400 | 3.6400 | 3.6400 | 3.6400 | 3.6400 | 3.6400 | 3.6400 | 3.6400 | 3.6400 | 3.6400 | 3.6400 |
| | | | | | | *Index Numbers (2010=100): Period Averages* | | | | | | | |
| Official Rate | ahx | 100.0 | 100.0 | 100.0 | 100.0 | 100.0 | 100.0 | 100.0 | 100.0 | 100.0 | 100.0 | 100.0 | 100.0 |
| Nominal Effective Exchange Rate | nec | 106.5 | 105.7 | 105.3 | 100.4 | 97.3 | 100.8 | 100.0 | 96.1 | 99.3 | 100.7 | 101.8 | 112.2 |
| **Fund Position** | | | | | | *Millions of SDRs: End of Period* | | | | | | | |
| Quota | 2f.s | 263.80 | 263.80 | 263.80 | 263.80 | 263.80 | 263.80 | 263.80 | 302.60 | 302.60 | 302.60 | 302.60 | 302.60 |
| SDR Holdings | 1b.s | 23.45 | 25.41 | 26.83 | 28.07 | 29.33 | 268.16 | 268.32 | 268.70 | 268.83 | 271.14 | 271.24 | 271.29 |
| Reserve Position in the Fund | 1c.s | 86.36 | 34.66 | 23.43 | 17.12 | 33.32 | 51.32 | 62.32 | 94.22 | 98.42 | 105.42 | 103.00 | 96.62 |
| Total Fund Cred. & Loans Outstg. | 2tl | — | — | — | — | — | — | — | — | — | — | — | — |
| SDR Allocations | 1bd | 12.82 | 12.82 | 12.82 | 12.82 | 12.82 | 251.40 | 251.40 | 251.40 | 251.40 | 251.40 | 251.40 | 251.40 |
| **International Liquidity** | | | | | | *Millions of US Dollars Unless Otherwise Indicated: End of Period* | | | | | | | |
| Total Reserves minus Gold | 1l.d | 3,395.9 | 4,542.4 | 5,382.7 | 9,416.4 | 9,649.5 | 18,369.7 | 30,620.8 | 16,198.5 | 32,521.0 | 41,601.5 | 42,734.1 | 36,500.3 |
| SDR Holdings | 1b.d | 36.4 | 36.3 | 40.4 | 44.4 | 45.2 | 420.4 | 413.2 | 412.5 | 413.2 | 417.5 | 393.0 | 375.9 |
| Reserve Position in the Fund | 1c.d | 134.1 | 49.5 | 35.2 | 27.0 | 51.3 | 80.4 | 96.0 | 144.6 | 151.3 | 162.3 | 149.2 | 133.9 |
| Foreign Exchange | 1d.d | 3,225.4 | 4,456.5 | 5,307.1 | 9,345.0 | 9,553.0 | 17,868.9 | 30,111.6 | 15,641.3 | 31,956.5 | 41,021.6 | 42,191.9 | 35,990.5 |
| Gold (Million Fine Troy Ounces) | 1ad | .042 | .019 | .019 | .399 | .399 | .399 | .399 | .399 | .399 | .399 | .399 | .399 |
| Gold (National Valuation) | 1and | 18.3 | 9.9 | 12.2 | 335.2 | 348.1 | 436.0 | 566.5 | 626.1 | 668.3 | 601.4 | 590.7 | 757.7 |
| Central Bank: Other Assets | 3..d | 47.5 | 43.8 | 46.0 | 88.0 | 85.9 | 87.4 | 95.9 | 95.7 | 95.7 | 99.7 | 94.7 | 110.3 |
| Central Bank: Other Liabs | 4..d | 1.2 | 16.4 | 4.8 | 205.8 | 4.1 | 3.8 | 7.8 | 13.8 | 6.8 | 12.0 | 8.7 | 12.7 |
| Other Depository Corps.: Assets | 7a.d | 7,401.7 | 11,162.3 | 17,663.5 | 23,836.5 | 26,257.7 | 23,515.8 | 24,092.7 | 31,953.9 | † 35,124.4 | 44,696.6 | 53,849.4 | 61,116.6 |
| Other Depository Corps.: Liabs | 7b.d | 2,449.8 | 3,065.2 | 7,096.4 | 17,779.4 | 24,497.3 | 30,273.1 | 38,271.8 | 44,376.9 | † 61,237.1 | 56,667.0 | 61,854.1 | 84,739.2 |
| **Central Bank** | | | | | | *Millions of Riyals: End of Period* | | | | | | | |
| Net Foreign Assets | 11n | 12,440 | 16,672 | 19,790 | 34,862 | 36,131 | 67,323 | 112,433 | 60,134 | 119,726 | 152,528 | 156,014 | 134,707 |
| Claims on Nonresidents | 11 | 12,517 | 16,798 | 19,878 | 35,685 | 36,218 | 68,771 | 113,871 | 61,590 | 121,157 | 153,981 | 157,372 | 136,021 |
| Liabilities to Nonresidents | 16c | 77 | 126 | 88 | 823 | 87 | 1,449 | 1,438 | 1,455 | 1,431 | 1,453 | 1,358 | 1,314 |
| Claims on Other Depository Corps. | 12e | 367 | 357 | 227 | 8,547 | 8,215 | 2,528 | 3,240 | 5,050 | 40,297 | 59,207 | 55,866 | 57,476 |
| Net Claims on Central Government | 12an | −172 | −265 | −423 | −439 | −1,019 | −472 | −672 | −13,914 | −16,983 | −60,449 | −28,586 | −7,889 |
| Claims on Central Government | 12a | — | — | — | — | — | — | — | — | — | — | — | — |
| Liabilities to Central Government | 16d | 172 | 265 | 423 | 439 | 1,019 | 472 | 672 | 13,914 | 16,983 | 60,449 | 28,586 | 7,889 |
| Claims on Other Sectors | 12s | 9 | 9 | 8 | 9 | 9 | 20 | 23 | 27 | 29 | 60 | 79 | 250 |
| Claims on Other Financial Corps. | 12g | 2 | 2 | 2 | 2 | 2 | 12 | — | — | — | — | — | — |
| Claims on State & Local Govts | 12b | — | — | — | — | — | — | — | — | — | — | — | — |
| Claims on Public Nonfin. Corps. | 12c | — | — | — | — | — | — | — | — | — | — | — | — |
| Claims on Private Sector | 12d | 7 | 7 | 7 | 7 | 7 | 8 | 23 | 27 | 29 | 60 | 79 | 250 |
| Monetary Base | 14 | 6,018 | 8,251 | 10,147 | 30,634 | 23,619 | 45,903 | 91,809 | 31,186 | 45,555 | 44,039 | 54,209 | 48,662 |
| Currency in Circulation | 14a | 3,123 | 3,531 | 5,070 | 5,625 | 6,913 | 7,191 | 7,974 | 9,092 | 10,976 | 12,340 | 14,076 | 14,985 |
| Liabs. to Other Depository Corps. | 14c | 2,895 | 4,720 | 5,078 | 25,010 | 16,706 | 38,712 | 83,834 | 22,093 | 34,579 | 31,698 | 40,133 | 33,677 |
| Liabilities to Other Sectors | 14d | — | — | — | — | — | — | — | — | — | — | — | — |
| Other Liabs. to Other Dep. Corps. | 14n | — | — | — | — | 4,961 | 6,207 | 4,137 | 150 | 7 | 3 | 7 | — |
| Dep. & Sec. Excl. f/Monetary Base | 14o | — | — | — | — | — | — | — | — | — | — | — | — |
| Deposits Included in Broad Money | 15 | — | — | — | — | — | — | — | — | — | — | — | — |
| Sec.Ot.th.Shares Incl.in Brd. Money | 16a | — | — | — | — | — | — | — | — | — | — | — | — |
| Deposits Excl. from Broad Money | 16b | — | — | — | — | — | — | — | — | — | — | — | — |
| Sec.Ot.th.Shares Excl.f/Brd.Money | 16s | — | — | — | — | — | — | — | — | — | — | — | — |
| Loans | 16l | — | — | — | — | — | — | — | — | — | — | — | — |
| Financial Derivatives | 16m | — | — | — | — | — | — | — | — | — | — | — | — |
| Shares and Other Equity | 17a | 6,497 | 8,499 | 9,514 | 12,394 | 14,355 | 16,820 | 18,715 | 19,667 | 96,220 | 106,032 | 129,191 | 135,764 |
| Other Items (Net) | 17r | 129 | 23 | −59 | −50 | 402 | 469 | 363 | 295 | 1,288 | 1,272 | −34 | 117 |
| Memo Item: | | | | | | | | | | | | | |
| Total Assets | 10ra | 12,867 | 17,254 | 20,207 | 44,348 | 44,459 | 71,280 | 117,038 | 66,471 | 161,237 | 213,156 | 213,730 | 194,175 |

| | | 2004 | 2005 | 2006 | 2007 | 2008 | 2009 | 2010 | 2011 | 2012 | 2013 | 2014 | 2015 |
|---|---|---|---|---|---|---|---|---|---|---|---|---|---|
| **Other Depository Corporations** | | | | | | *Millions of Riyals: End of Period* | | | | | | | |
| Net Foreign Assets | 21n | 18,025 | 29,473 | 38,464 | 22,048 | 6,408 | −24,596 | −51,612 | −45,220 | † −95,050 | −43,572 | −29,137 | −85,986 |
| Claims on Nonresidents | 21 | 26,942 | 40,631 | 64,295 | 86,765 | 95,578 | 85,598 | 87,697 | 116,312 | † 127,853 | 162,696 | 196,012 | 222,464 |
| Liabilities to Nonresidents | 26c | 8,917 | 11,157 | 25,831 | 64,717 | 89,170 | 110,194 | 139,309 | 161,532 | † 222,903 | 206,268 | 225,149 | 308,451 |
| Claims on Central Bank | 20 | 3,397 | 5,182 | 6,140 | 26,097 | 23,032 | 46,017 | 89,478 | 24,028 | † 37,094 | 34,524 | 43,616 | 37,433 |
| Currency | 20a | 529 | 665 | 1,111 | 1,137 | 1,545 | 1,538 | 1,879 | 2,079 | † 2,814 | 3,136 | 3,754 | 3,952 |
| Reserve Deposits and Securities | 20b | 2,868 | 4,516 | 5,029 | 24,960 | 16,562 | 38,361 | 83,579 | 21,802 | † 33,203 | 30,663 | 37,250 | 33,181 |
| Other Claims | 20n | — | — | — | — | 4,925 | 6,117 | 4,020 | 146 | † 1,077 | 725 | 2,612 | 300 |
| Net Claims on Central Government | 22an | 11,218 | 8,023 | 4,148 | 229 | −1,244 | 47,327 | 56,518 | 104,951 | † 119,847 | 113,491 | 107,440 | 140,121 |
| Claims on Central Government | 22a | 18,845 | 16,618 | 17,238 | 13,822 | 18,169 | 62,738 | 75,004 | 145,776 | † 164,291 | 181,785 | 166,693 | 193,399 |
| Liabilities to Central Government | 26d | 7,627 | 8,595 | 13,090 | 13,593 | 19,413 | 15,412 | 18,486 | 40,825 | † 44,445 | 68,294 | 59,252 | 53,278 |
| Claims on Other Sectors | 22s | 38,215 | 61,388 | 88,742 | 147,381 | 218,572 | 223,897 | 270,324 | 351,124 | † 439,854 | 491,146 | 535,933 | 597,783 |
| Claims on Other Financial Corps | 22g | | | | | | | | | † 15,505 | 13,904 | 17,218 | 16,831 |
| Claims on State & Local Govts | 22b | — | — | — | — | — | — | — | — | † — | | | |
| Claims on Public Nonfin. Corps | 22c | 4,741 | 6,735 | 8,974 | 26,752 | 47,383 | 39,735 | 66,755 | 108,379 | † 171,878 | 187,916 | 172,765 | 164,128 |
| Claims on Private Sector | 22d | 33,474 | 54,653 | 79,768 | 120,629 | 171,188 | 184,162 | 203,569 | 242,745 | † 252,472 | 289,326 | 345,950 | 416,823 |
| Liabilities to Central Bank | 26g | 339 | 423 | 298 | 1,316 | 6,782 | 2,719 | 3,413 | 4,910 | † 2,170 | 4,600 | 6,675 | 7,042 |
| Transf.Dep.Included in Broad Money | 24 | 17,227 | 29,557 | 39,288 | 48,013 | 61,938 | 65,740 | 81,484 | 106,305 | † 110,415 | 127,951 | 144,978 | 141,285 |
| Other Dep.Included in Broad Money | 25 | 35,410 | 46,479 | 66,926 | 101,235 | 116,699 | 143,689 | 177,137 | 196,648 | † 262,476 | 318,559 | 348,724 | 369,065 |
| Sec.Ot.th.Shares Incl.in Brd. Money | 26a | — | — | — | — | — | — | — | — | † — | | | |
| Deposits Excl. from Broad Money | 26b | 232 | 397 | 454 | 764 | 1,381 | 1,882 | 1,048 | 1,097 | † 1,255 | 2,124 | 2,090 | 2,275 |
| Sec.Ot.th.Shares Excl.f/Brd.Money | 26s | — | — | — | — | — | — | — | — | † 1,114 | 5,290 | 7,416 | 12,104 |
| Loans | 26l | — | — | — | 36 | 77 | 300 | 115 | 7,541 | † — | — | 25 | 120 |
| Financial Derivatives | 26m | — | — | — | — | — | — | — | — | † 742 | 753 | 930 | 1,134 |
| Insurance Technical Reserves | 26r | — | — | — | — | — | — | — | — | † — | | | |
| Shares and Other Equity | 27a | 13,235 | 19,000 | 25,274 | 37,921 | 48,711 | 59,973 | 69,599 | 94,452 | † 119,404 | 128,723 | 136,538 | 141,924 |
| Other Items (Net) | 27r | 4,412 | 8,211 | 5,254 | 6,469 | 11,178 | 18,342 | 31,912 | 23,931 | † 4,168 | 7,588 | 10,475 | 14,401 |
| Memo Item: | | | | | | | | | | | | | |
| Total Assets | 20ra | 92,026 | 130,301 | 189,482 | 294,336 | 401,915 | 467,899 | 567,482 | 694,301 | † 819,463 | 913,356 | 1,008,425 | 1,116,826 |
| **Depository Corporations** | | | | | | *Millions of Riyals: End of Period* | | | | | | | |
| Net Foreign Assets | 31n | 30,465 | 46,145 | 58,255 | 56,910 | 42,538 | 42,726 | 60,821 | 14,915 | † 24,676 | 108,956 | 126,877 | 48,721 |
| Claims on Nonresidents | 31 | 39,459 | 57,429 | 84,173 | 122,450 | 131,796 | 154,369 | 201,568 | 177,902 | † 249,010 | 316,677 | 353,383 | 358,485 |
| Liabilities to Nonresidents | 36c | 8,994 | 11,284 | 25,918 | 65,540 | 89,257 | 111,643 | 140,747 | 162,987 | † 224,334 | 207,721 | 226,506 | 309,765 |
| Domestic Claims | 32 | 49,270 | 69,155 | 92,475 | 147,179 | 216,318 | 270,772 | 326,193 | 442,189 | † 542,747 | 544,247 | 614,866 | 730,264 |
| Net Claims on Central Government | 32an | 11,046 | 7,758 | 3,724 | −210 | −2,263 | 46,855 | 55,846 | 91,037 | † 102,863 | 53,041 | 78,854 | 132,232 |
| Claims on Central Government | 32a | 18,845 | 16,618 | 17,238 | 13,822 | 18,169 | 62,738 | 75,004 | 145,776 | † 164,291 | 181,785 | 166,693 | 193,399 |
| Liabilities to Central Government | 36d | 7,799 | 8,860 | 13,513 | 14,032 | 20,432 | 15,883 | 19,157 | 54,739 | † 61,428 | 128,743 | 87,838 | 61,167 |
| Claims on Other Sectors | 32s | 38,224 | 61,397 | 88,750 | 147,390 | 218,581 | 223,917 | 270,347 | 351,152 | † 439,884 | 491,206 | 536,012 | 598,033 |
| Claims on Other Financial Corps | 32g | 2 | 2 | 2 | 2 | 2 | 12 | — | — | † 15,505 | 13,904 | 17,218 | 16,831 |
| Claims on State & Local Govts | 32b | — | — | — | — | — | — | — | — | † — | | | |
| Claims on Public Nonfin. Corps | 32c | 4,741 | 6,735 | 8,974 | 26,752 | 47,383 | 39,735 | 66,755 | 108,379 | † 171,878 | 187,916 | 172,765 | 164,128 |
| Claims on Private Sector | 32d | 33,481 | 54,660 | 79,774 | 120,636 | 171,195 | 184,170 | 203,592 | 242,773 | † 252,501 | 289,386 | 346,029 | 417,073 |
| Broad Money Liabilities | 35l | 55,231 | 78,901 | 110,173 | 153,735 | 184,005 | 215,082 | 264,716 | 309,966 | † 381,053 | 455,715 | 504,025 | 521,383 |
| Currency Outside Depository Corps | 34a | 2,594 | 2,866 | 3,959 | 4,487 | 5,368 | 5,653 | 6,095 | 7,013 | † 8,161 | 9,205 | 10,322 | 11,033 |
| Transferable Deposits | 34 | 17,227 | 29,557 | 39,288 | 48,013 | 61,938 | 65,740 | 81,484 | 106,305 | † 110,415 | 127,951 | 144,978 | 141,285 |
| Other Deposits | 35 | 35,410 | 46,479 | 66,926 | 101,235 | 116,699 | 143,689 | 177,137 | 196,648 | † 262,476 | 318,559 | 348,724 | 369,065 |
| Securities Other than Shares | 36a | — | — | — | — | — | — | — | — | † — | | | |
| Deposits Excl. from Broad Money | 36b | 232 | 397 | 454 | 764 | 1,381 | 1,882 | 1,048 | 1,097 | † 1,255 | 2,124 | 2,090 | 2,275 |
| Sec.Ot.th.Shares Excl.f/Brd.Money | 36s | — | — | — | — | — | — | — | — | † 1,114 | 5,290 | 7,416 | 12,104 |
| Loans | 36l | — | — | — | 36 | 77 | 300 | 115 | 7,541 | † — | — | 25 | 120 |
| Financial Derivatives | 36m | — | — | — | — | — | — | — | — | † 742 | 753 | 930 | 1,134 |
| Insurance Technical Reserves | 36r | — | — | — | — | — | — | — | — | † — | | | |
| Shares and Other Equity | 37a | 19,732 | 27,498 | 34,788 | 50,315 | 63,066 | 76,793 | 88,314 | 114,119 | † 215,624 | 234,756 | 265,729 | 277,689 |
| Other Items (Net) | 37r | 4,540 | 8,504 | 5,315 | −762 | 10,327 | 19,441 | 32,822 | 24,381 | † −32,365 | −45,434 | −38,471 | −35,720 |
| Broad Money Liabs., Seasonally Adj. | 35l.b | 55,055 | 78,774 | 110,444 | 154,762 | 185,884 | 218,030 | 269,222 | 316,186 | † 386,691 | 461,203 | 508,700 | 525,894 |
| **Monetary Aggregates** | | | | | | *Millions of Riyals: End of Period* | | | | | | | |
| Broad Money | 59m | 55,231 | 78,901 | 110,173 | 153,735 | 184,005 | 215,082 | 264,716 | 309,966 | 381,053 | 455,715 | 504,025 | 521,383 |
| o/w:Currency Issued by Cent.Govt | 59m.a | — | — | — | — | — | — | — | — | — | — | — | — |
| o/w: Dep.in Nonfin. Corporations | 59m.b | — | — | — | — | — | — | — | — | — | — | — | — |
| o/w:Secs. Issued by Central Govt | 59m.c | — | — | — | — | — | — | — | — | — | — | — | — |
| Money (National Definitions) | | | | | | | | | | | | | |
| Reserve Money | 19mb | 6,019 | 8,258 | 10,154 | 30,652 | 23,623 | 45,903 | 91,809 | 31,186 | 45,555 | 44,039 | 54,209 | 48,662 |
| M1 | 59ma | 14,598 | 22,362 | 27,883 | 40,737 | 50,870 | 53,116 | 68,337 | 81,847 | 90,939 | 105,931 | 124,256 | 126,925 |
| Quasi-Money | 59mal | 30,267 | 41,909 | 60,775 | 112,999 | 133,136 | 161,966 | 196,379 | 228,119 | 290,114 | 349,784 | 379,769 | 394,458 |
| M2 | 59mb | 44,865 | 64,271 | 88,659 | 153,735 | 184,005 | 215,082 | 264,716 | 309,966 | 381,053 | 455,715 | 504,025 | 521,383 |
| M3 | 59mc | 63,027 | 87,759 | 123,683 | 167,764 | 204,434 | 230,961 | 283,870 | 361,974 | 442,481 | 576,814 | 597,910 | 573,679 |
| **Interest Rates** | | | | | | *Percent Per Annum* | | | | | | | |
| Central Bank Policy Rate (EOP) | 60 | 2.60 | 4.50 | 5.50 | 5.50 | 5.50 | 5.50 | 5.50 | 4.50 | 4.50 | 4.50 | 4.50 | 4.50 |
| Money Market Rate | 60b | 2.09 | 3.13 | 4.77 | 4.38 | 1.06 | 2.09 | 1.70 | .46 | .76 | .77 | .64 | .89 |
| Reverse Repo Rate (End of Period) | 60.c | 3.15 | 5.10 | 5.55 | 5.55 | 5.55 | 5.55 | 5.55 | 4.50 | 4.50 | 4.50 | 4.50 | 4.50 |
| Deposit Facility Rate (End of Period) | 60.r | 2.50 | 4.40 | 5.15 | 4.00 | 2.00 | 2.00 | 1.50 | .75 | .75 | .75 | .75 | .75 |
| Savings Rate | 60k | .83 | .97 | 1.42 | 1.48 | 1.40 | 1.64 | 1.75 | 1.33 | 1.12 | .89 | .78 | .64 |
| Deposit Rate | 60l | 3.20 | 3.19 | 4.23 | 4.43 | 2.97 | 4.24 | 2.90 | 1.75 | 1.67 | 1.42 | 1.35 | 1.61 |
| Lending Rate | 60p | 6.99 | 6.65 | 7.18 | 7.43 | 6.84 | 7.04 | 7.27 | 5.49 | 5.38 | 5.11 | 4.96 | 4.44 |
| **Prices and Production** | | | | | | *Index Numbers (2010=100): Period Averages* | | | | | | | |
| Share Prices (End of Month) | 62.ep | 74.3 | 142.2 | 107.9 | 103.2 | 130.6 | 85.9 | 100.0 | 114.5 | 114.9 | 126.9 | 170.4 | 156.9 |
| Consumer Prices | 64 | 67.6 | 73.6 | 82.3 | 93.6 | † 107.7 | † 102.5 | 100.0 | 101.9 | 103.8 | † 107.1 | 110.4 | 112.4 |
| Crude Petroleum | 66aa | 106.5 | 113.4 | 113.4 | 111.2 | 114.6 | 110.0 | 100.0 | 100.8 | 101.0 | 99.5 | 97.4 | 90.4 |
| **Intl. Transactions & Positions** | | | | | | *Millions of Riyals* | | | | | | | |
| Exports | 70 | 68,013 | 93,774 | 123,948 | 161,821 | 244,998 | 174,746 | 272,271 | 416,592 | 484,065 | 498,153 | 477,790 | 283,530 |
| Imports, c.i.f. | 71 | 21,857 | 36,621 | 59,846 | 85,284 | 101,556 | 90,716 | 84,593 | 81,293 | 91,813 | 98,418 | 110,916 | 118,698 |

# Qatar 453

| | | 2004 | 2005 | 2006 | 2007 | 2008 | 2009 | 2010 | 2011 | 2012 | 2013 | 2014 | 2015 |
|---|---|---|---|---|---|---|---|---|---|---|---|---|---|
| **Balance of Payments** | | | | | | *Millions of US Dollars* | | | | | | | |
| A. Current Account*......................... | 109bx | .... | .... | .... | .... | .... | .... | .... | 52,123.6 | 62,000.2 | 60,461.0 | 49,409.9 | 13,750.8 |
| Goods, credit (exports)................. | 1a9cx | .... | .... | .... | .... | .... | .... | .... | 114,444.2 | 132,953.8 | 133,336.0 | 126,702.5 | 77,294.2 |
| Goods, debit (imports)................... | 1a9dx | .... | .... | .... | .... | .... | .... | .... | 26,925.9 | 30,787.2 | 31,474.7 | 31,145.3 | 28,496.2 |
| Balance on goods................... | 1a9bx | .... | .... | .... | .... | .... | .... | .... | 87,518.4 | 102,166.7 | 101,861.3 | 95,557.1 | 48,798.1 |
| Services, credit (exports)............... | 1b9cx | .... | .... | .... | .... | .... | .... | .... | 7,393.7 | 9,922.3 | 11,174.5 | 13,526.4 | 14,997.0 |
| Services, debit (imports)................ | 1b9dx | .... | .... | .... | .... | .... | .... | .... | 16,866.8 | 23,906.3 | 27,478.6 | 32,859.1 | 30,775.3 |
| Balance on Goods & Services....... | 1z9bx | .... | .... | .... | .... | .... | .... | .... | 78,045.3 | 88,182.6 | 85,557.1 | 76,224.5 | 33,019.8 |
| Primary income: credit.................. | 1c9cx | .... | .... | .... | .... | .... | .... | .... | 6,166.3 | 6,518.1 | 6,391.2 | 7,396.4 | 7,793.4 |
| Primary income: debit.................... | 1c9dx | .... | .... | .... | .... | .... | .... | .... | 19,437.3 | 18,642.9 | 16,754.9 | 16,697.0 | 11,358.8 |
| Balance on gds, serv. & prim. inc. | 1y9bx | .... | .... | .... | .... | .... | .... | .... | 64,774.3 | 76,057.9 | 75,193.4 | 66,923.9 | 29,454.4 |
| Secondary income: credit.............. | 1d9ca | .... | .... | .... | .... | .... | .... | .... | 1,785.2 | 1,970.3 | 1,116.5 | 704.9 | 625.8 |
| Secondary income: debit.............. | 1d9da | .... | .... | .... | .... | .... | .... | .... | 14,435.8 | 16,028.0 | 15,848.9 | 18,219.0 | 16,329.4 |
| B. Capital Account*........................ | 209ba | .... | .... | .... | .... | .... | .... | .... | −993.4 | −3,506.9 | −1,960.7 | −2,722.3 | −737.1 |
| Capital account: credit.................. | 209ca | .... | .... | .... | .... | .... | .... | .... | — | — | — | — | — |
| Capital account: debit................... | 209da | .... | .... | .... | .... | .... | .... | .... | 993.4 | 3,506.9 | 1,960.7 | 2,722.3 | 737.1 |
| Balance on current & capital acct. | 129ba | .... | .... | .... | .... | .... | .... | .... | 51,130.2 | 58,493.3 | 58,500.3 | 46,687.6 | 13,013.7 |
| C. Financial Account* ..................... | 309na | .... | .... | .... | .... | .... | .... | .... | 62,142.4 | 38,289.0 | 47,366.3 | 43,647.3 | 18,936.0 |
| Direct investment: assets.............. | 3a9aa | .... | .... | .... | .... | .... | .... | .... | 10,108.5 | 1,840.1 | 8,021.4 | 6,748.4 | 4,023.4 |
| Equity & investment fund shares.. | 3aaaa | .... | .... | .... | .... | .... | .... | .... | .... | .... | .... | .... | .... |
| Debt instruments....................... | 3abaa | .... | .... | .... | .... | .... | .... | .... | .... | .... | .... | .... | .... |
| Direct investment: liabilities .......... | 3a9la | .... | .... | .... | .... | .... | .... | .... | 938.5 | 395.9 | −840.4 | 1,040.4 | 1,070.9 |
| Equity & investment fund shares . | 3aala | .... | .... | .... | .... | .... | .... | .... | .... | .... | .... | .... | .... |
| Debt instruments....................... | 3abla | .... | .... | .... | .... | .... | .... | .... | .... | .... | .... | .... | .... |
| Portfolio investment: assets .......... | 3b9aa | .... | .... | .... | .... | .... | .... | .... | 17,278.1 | 7,609.3 | 16,436.3 | 16,694.8 | 11,604.9 |
| Equity & investment fund shares | 3baaa | .... | .... | .... | .... | .... | .... | .... | 16,620.3 | 7,303.0 | 13,169.8 | 16,306.9 | 10,559.1 |
| Debt securities ........................... | 3bbaa | .... | .... | .... | .... | .... | .... | .... | 657.8 | 306.3 | 3,266.5 | 387.9 | 1,045.9 |
| Portfolio investment: liabilities....... | 3b9la | .... | .... | .... | .... | .... | .... | .... | −1,750.2 | 10,408.7 | −1,873.9 | −3,238.2 | −4,943.4 |
| Equity & investment fund shares . | 3bala | .... | .... | .... | .... | .... | .... | .... | −903.0 | −925.4 | 615.9 | 2,482.4 | 115.9 |
| Debt securities........................... | 3bbla | .... | .... | .... | .... | .... | .... | .... | −847.3 | 11,334.1 | −2,489.8 | −5,720.6 | −5,059.3 |
| Fin. der.& empl.stk.ops.(ESOs): net. | 3c9na | .... | .... | .... | .... | .... | .... | .... | −1,584.3 | 1,542.6 | −742.3 | −318.1 | 89.6 |
| Fin. der. & ESOs.: assets.............. | 3c9aa | .... | .... | .... | .... | .... | .... | .... | −1,583.0 | 1,510.7 | −437.9 | −142.6 | 13.5 |
| Fin. der. & ESOs.: liabilities.......... | 3c9la | .... | .... | .... | .... | .... | .... | .... | 1.4 | −31.9 | 304.4 | 175.5 | −76.1 |
| Other investment: assets................ | 3d9aa | .... | .... | .... | .... | .... | .... | .... | 41,338.3 | 36,926.9 | 11,004.5 | 22,488.7 | 18,990.4 |
| Other equity......................... | 3daaa | .... | .... | .... | .... | .... | .... | .... | .... | .... | .... | .... | .... |
| Debt instruments....................... | 3dzaa | .... | .... | .... | .... | .... | .... | .... | 41,338.3 | 36,926.9 | 11,004.5 | 22,488.7 | 18,990.4 |
| Other investment: liabilities............ | 3d9la | .... | .... | .... | .... | .... | .... | .... | 5,809.9 | −1,174.6 | −9,932.1 | 4,164.3 | 19,644.8 |
| Other equity........................ | 3dala | .... | .... | .... | .... | .... | .... | .... | .... | .... | .... | .... | .... |
| Debt instruments....................... | 3dzla | .... | .... | .... | .... | .... | .... | .... | 5,809.9 | −1,174.6 | −9,932.1 | 4,164.3 | 19,644.8 |
| Curr.+ cap.− finan. acct. balance... | 4y9na | .... | .... | .... | .... | .... | .... | .... | −11,012.2 | 20,204.4 | 11,133.9 | 3,040.4 | −5,922.3 |
| D. Net Errors and Omissions............ | 409na | .... | .... | .... | .... | .... | .... | .... | −3,331.5 | −4,124.9 | −2,069.7 | −1,746.8 | 419.2 |
| E. Reserves and Related Items.......... | 4z9na | .... | .... | .... | .... | .... | .... | .... | −14,343.7 | 16,079.5 | 9,064.3 | 1,293.5 | −5,503.0 |
| Reserve assets............................ | 3e9aa | .... | .... | .... | .... | .... | .... | .... | −14,343.7 | 16,079.5 | 9,064.3 | 1,293.5 | −5,503.0 |
| Credit and loans from the IMF....... | 3dcla | .... | .... | .... | .... | .... | .... | .... | .... | .... | .... | .... | .... |
| Exceptional financing................... | 409la | .... | .... | .... | .... | .... | .... | .... | .... | .... | .... | .... | .... |
| *Excludes components in group E | | | | | | | | | | | | | |

## Government Finance
### Cash Flow Statement
#### Budgetary Central Government

| | | 2004 | 2005 | 2006 | 2007 | 2008 | 2009 | 2010 | 2011 | 2012 | 2013 | 2014 | 2015 |
|---|---|---|---|---|---|---|---|---|---|---|---|---|---|
| | | | | | | | *Millions of Riyals: Fiscal Year Ends March 31* | | | | | | |
| Cash Receipts:Operating Activities... | c1 | 54,346.1 | 64,909.3 | 86,063.0 | 117,864.0 | 140,947.0 | 169,078.0 | 155,875.4 | .... | .... | .... | .... | .... |
| Taxes........................................ | c11 | 29,464.8 | 32,975.8 | 44,436.1 | 59,786.6 | 66,811.0 | 70,928.3 | 66,745.3 | .... | .... | .... | .... | .... |
| Social Contributions...................... | c12 | — | — | — | — | — | — | — | .... | .... | .... | .... | .... |
| Grants....................................... | c13 | | | | | | | | .... | .... | .... | .... | .... |
| Other Receipts.............................. | c14 | 24,881.3 | 31,933.5 | 41,355.2 | 57,747.6 | 73,974.7 | 98,149.7 | 89,130.1 | .... | .... | .... | .... | .... |
| Cash Payments:Operating Activities. | c2 | 27,108.8 | 32,145.3 | 67,146.8 | 85,593.2 | 98,856.8 | 69,019.3 | 85,271.7 | .... | .... | .... | .... | .... |
| Compensation of Employees.......... | c21 | 8,662.9 | 7,233.5 | 14,020.4 | 16,740.1 | 19,390.1 | 22,383.8 | 24,057.8 | .... | .... | .... | .... | .... |
| Purchases of Goods & Services....... | c22 | 8,248.2 | 12,222.6 | 17,953.0 | 11,309.4 | 17,446.0 | 17,317.2 | 23,877.9 | .... | .... | .... | .... | .... |
| Interest..................................... | c24 | 1,879.6 | 1,898.3 | 2,006.2 | 1,855.2 | 2,100.1 | 3,598.9 | 5,548.2 | .... | .... | .... | .... | .... |
| Subsidies................................... | c25 | 2,571.7 | 3,866.3 | 4,144.8 | 5,547.6 | 6,152.4 | 10,678.5 | 9,289.3 | .... | .... | .... | .... | .... |
| Grants....................................... | c26 | 418.3 | 575.1 | 2,098.8 | 1,601.4 | 1,261.8 | 724.1 | 1,255.1 | .... | .... | .... | .... | .... |
| Social Benefits............................ | c27 | 1,115.6 | 1,069.4 | 1,545.0 | 1,771.2 | 2,539.4 | 3,136.5 | 2,887.9 | .... | .... | .... | .... | .... |
| Other Payments............................ | c28 | 4,212.5 | 5,279.9 | 7,352.0 | 7,781.2 | 10,955.8 | 11,180.2 | 18,355.4 | .... | .... | .... | .... | .... |
| Net Cash Inflow:Operating Act.[1-2] | ccio | 27,237.3 | 32,764.0 | 36,671.2 | 70,928.2 | 80,940.2 | 100,058.7 | 70,603.7 | .... | .... | .... | .... | .... |
| Net Cash Outflow:Invest. in NFA...... | c31 | 8,275.5 | 17,846.6 | 17,755.4 | 39,312.0 | 39,243.0 | 45,539.2 | 57,196.2 | .... | .... | .... | .... | .... |
| Purchases of Nonfinancial Assets... | c31.1 | 8,993.3 | 18,622.8 | 18,027.2 | 39,643.6 | 39,449.4 | 45,555.4 | 57,227.2 | .... | .... | .... | .... | .... |
| Sales of Nonfinancial Assets.......... | c31.2 | 717.8 | 776.2 | 271.9 | 331.6 | 206.4 | 16.2 | 31.1 | .... | .... | .... | .... | .... |
| Cash Surplus/Deficit [1-2-31=1-2M] | ccsd | 18,961.9 | 14,917.4 | 18,916.2 | 32,270.8 | 42,090.2 | 54,519.5 | 13,407.5 | .... | .... | .... | .... | .... |
| Net Acq. Fin. Assets, excl. Cash....... | c32x | .... | .... | .... | .... | .... | .... | .... | .... | .... | .... | .... | .... |
| Domestic................................... | c321x | .... | .... | .... | .... | .... | .... | .... | .... | .... | .... | .... | .... |
| Foreign..................................... | c322x | .... | .... | .... | .... | .... | .... | .... | .... | .... | .... | .... | .... |
| Net Incurrence of Liabilities.............. | c33 | .... | .... | .... | .... | .... | .... | .... | .... | .... | .... | .... | .... |
| Domestic................................... | c331 | .... | .... | .... | .... | .... | .... | .... | .... | .... | .... | .... | .... |
| Foreign..................................... | c332 | .... | .... | .... | .... | .... | .... | .... | .... | .... | .... | .... | .... |
| Net Cash Inflow, Fin.Act.[-32x+33].. | cnfb | .... | .... | .... | .... | .... | .... | .... | .... | .... | .... | .... | .... |
| Net Change in Stock of Cash........... | cncb | .... | .... | .... | .... | .... | .... | .... | .... | .... | .... | .... | .... |
| Stat. Discrep. [32X-33+NCB-CSD].... | ccsdz | .... | .... | .... | .... | .... | .... | .... | .... | .... | .... | .... | .... |
| Memo Item:Cash Expenditure[2+31] | c2m | 36,102.1 | 50,768.1 | 67,147.3 | 86,249.6 | 99,295.0 | 114,574.7 | 142,498.9 | .... | .... | .... | .... | .... |
| Memo Item: Gross Debt.................. | c63 | .... | .... | .... | .... | .... | .... | .... | .... | .... | .... | .... | .... |

# Qatar 453

| | | 2004 | 2005 | 2006 | 2007 | 2008 | 2009 | 2010 | 2011 | 2012 | 2013 | 2014 | 2015 |
|---|---|---|---|---|---|---|---|---|---|---|---|---|---|
| **National Accounts** | | | | | | | *Millions of Riyals* | | | | | | |
| Househ.Cons.Expend.,incl.NPISHs.... | **96f** | 20,166 | 25,890 | 36,186 | 49,729 | 64,676 | 68,623 | 73,646 | 79,906 | 87,682 | 98,874 | 109,376 | .... |
| Government Consumption Expend... | **91f** | 15,094 | 23,172 | 32,616 | 35,990 | 42,696 | 55,652 | 63,689 | 77,007 | 89,527 | 98,260 | 108,199 | .... |
| Gross Fixed Capital Formation.......... | **93e** | 36,399 | 55,610 | 92,830 | 133,518 | 172,524 | 152,946 | 143,011 | 177,621 | 194,347 | 218,724 | 257,732 | .... |
| Changes in Inventories.................... | **93i** | — | — | — | — | — | — | — | — | — | — | — | .... |
| Exports of Goods and Services.......... | **90c** | 74,122 | 105,497 | 139,211 | 174,896 | 257,466 | 182,034 | 283,270 | 442,960 | 520,182 | 538,508 | 528,682 | .... |
| Imports of Goods and Services (-)..... | **98c** | 30,269 | 48,077 | 79,233 | 103,981 | 117,779 | 103,269 | 108,171 | 159,405 | 199,084 | 214,590 | 232,976 | .... |
| Gross Domestic Product (GDP)......... | **99b** | 115,512 | 162,091 | 221,610 | 290,152 | 419,583 | 355,986 | 455,445 | 618,089 | 692,655 | 739,776 | 771,013 | .... |
| GDP Volume 2004 Prices................. | **99b.p** | 115,512 | 124,167 | 156,662 | 184,838 | 217,486 | 243,492 | 284,226 | 324,356 | 340,912 | 362,181 | 384,467 | .... |
| GDP Deflator (2010=100)............... | **99bip** | 62.4 | 81.5 | 88.3 | 98.0 | 120.4 | 91.2 | 100.0 | 118.9 | 126.8 | 127.5 | 125.1 | .... |
| GDP Volume (2010=100)................ | **99bvp** | 40.6 | 43.7 | 55.1 | 65.0 | 76.5 | 85.7 | 100.0 | 114.1 | 119.9 | 127.4 | 135.3 | .... |
| | | | | | | | *Millions: Midyear Estimates* | | | | | | |
| Population................................ | **99z** | .73 | .84 | .99 | 1.18 | 1.39 | 1.59 | 1.77 | 1.91 | 2.02 | 2.10 | 2.17 | 2.24 |

# Romania 968

2016, International Monetary Fund : *International Financial Statistics Yearbook*

|  |  | 2004 | 2005 | 2006 | 2007 | 2008 | 2009 | 2010 | 2011 | 2012 | 2013 | 2014 | 2015 |
|---|---|---|---|---|---|---|---|---|---|---|---|---|---|
| **Exchange Rates** | | | | | | | *Lei per SDR: End of Period* | | | | | | |
| Market Rate | aa | 4.514 | 4.442 | 3.863 | 3.882 | 4.365 | 4.603 | 4.935 | 5.127 | 5.160 | 5.013 | 5.341 | 5.748 |
| | | | | | | | *Lei per US Dollar: End of Period (ae) Period Average (rf)* | | | | | | |
| Market Rate | ae | 2.907 | 3.108 | 2.568 | 2.456 | 2.834 | 2.936 | 3.205 | 3.339 | 3.358 | 3.255 | 3.687 | 4.148 |
| Market Rate | rf | 3.264 | 2.914 | 2.809 | 2.438 | 2.519 | 3.049 | 3.178 | 3.049 | 3.468 | 3.328 | 3.349 | 4.006 |
| | | | | | | | *Index Numbers (2010=100): Period Averages* | | | | | | |
| Nominal Effective Exchange Rate | nec | 103.1 | 114.1 | 117.8 | 125.5 | 115.1 | 101.7 | 100.0 | 100.2 | 93.8 | 96.2 | 96.7 | 94.5 |
| CPI-Based Real Effect. Ex. Rate | rec | 81.5 | 96.1 | 103.0 | 111.7 | 106.1 | 98.1 | 100.0 | 102.9 | 96.7 | 101.2 | 101.5 | 97.7 |
| **Fund Position** | | | | | | | *Millions of SDRs: End of Period* | | | | | | |
| Quota | 2f.s | 1,030.20 | 1,030.20 | 1,030.20 | 1,030.20 | 1,030.20 | 1,030.20 | 1,030.20 | 1,030.20 | 1,030.20 | 1,030.20 | 1,030.20 | 1,030.20 |
| SDR Holdings | 1b.s | .36 | .38 | .25 | .32 | 78.86 | 900.87 | 686.86 | 384.37 | 98.02 | 24.93 | 13.44 | 8.58 |
| Reserve Position in the Fund | 1c.s | — | — | — | — | — | — | — | — | — | — | — | — |
| Total Fund Cred.&Loans Outstg. | 2tl | 285.35 | 182.56 | 68.89 | 75.95 | — | 6,088.00 | 9,800.00 | 10,569.00 | 9,261.75 | 5,210.00 | 1,328.88 | 96.13 |
| SDR Allocations | 1bd | 75.95 | 75.95 | 75.95 | 75.95 | 75.95 | 984.77 | 984.77 | 984.77 | 984.77 | 984.77 | 984.77 | 984.77 |
| **International Liquidity** | | | | | | | *Millions of US Dollars Unless Otherwise Indicated: End of Period* | | | | | | |
| Total Reserves minus Gold | 1l.d | 14,616 | 19,872 | 28,066 | 37,194 | 36,868 | 40,757 | 43,361 | 42,939 | 41,162 | 44,811 | 39,165 | 35,167 |
| SDR Holdings | 1b.d | 1 | 1 | — | 1 | 121 | 1,412 | 1,058 | 590 | 151 | 38 | 19 | 12 |
| Reserve Position in the Fund | 1c.d | — | — | — | — | — | — | — | — | — | — | — | — |
| Foreign Exchange | 1d.d | 14,616 | 19,872 | 28,066 | 37,194 | 36,747 | 39,344 | 42,303 | 42,349 | 41,012 | 44,773 | 39,145 | 35,155 |
| Gold (Million Fine Troy Ounces) | 1ad | 3.377 | 3.371 | 3.366 | 3.334 | 3.334 | 3.335 | 3.335 | 3.335 | 3.335 | 3.335 | 3.335 | 3.334 |
| Gold (National Valuation) | 1and | 1,480 | 1,728 | 2,140 | 2,762 | 2,882 | 3,680 | 4,704 | 5,250 | 5,549 | 4,009 | 3,999 | 3,542 |
| Central Bank: Other Assets | 3..d | 84 | 25 | 27 | 43 | 42 | 42 | 41 | 40 | 39 | 41 | 39 | 36 |
| Central Bank: Other Liabs | 4..d | 266 | 943 | — | 1,889 | 2,028 | 9,923 | 13,874 | 14,894 | 12,675 | 8,062 | 3,232 | 1,766 |
| Other Depository Corps.: Assets | 7a.d | 1,805 | 1,454 | 1,805 | 2,467 | 2,435 | 4,344 | 3,996 | 2,971 | 3,284 | 3,695 | 5,143 | 4,854 |
| Other Depository Corps.: Liabs | 7b.d | 4,981 | 8,149 | 16,418 | 29,861 | 36,788 | 32,693 | 32,258 | 31,198 | 27,059 | 25,688 | 19,461 | 15,543 |
| Other Financial Corps.: Assets | 7e.d | .... | .... | .... | .... | 163 | 218 | 481 | 531 | 1,035 | 2,494 | 2,150 | 2,983 |
| Other Financial Corps.: Liabs | 7f.d | .... | .... | .... | .... | 11,348 | 9,619 | 7,069 | 5,720 | 4,826 | 4,806 | 3,861 | 5,944 |
| **Central Bank** | | | | | | | *Billions of Lei: End of Period* | | | | | | |
| Net Foreign Assets | 11n | 36.79 | 54.43 | 76.32 | 92.47 | 105.82 | 68.21 | 56.04 | 50.63 | 57.71 | 100.92 | 134.47 | 146.51 |
| Claims on Nonresidents | 11 | 39.19 | 58.51 | 76.87 | 97.41 | 111.90 | 129.98 | 153.58 | 159.62 | 156.30 | 158.22 | 158.74 | 160.05 |
| Liabilities to Nonresidents | 16c | 2.40 | 4.08 | .56 | 4.94 | 6.07 | 61.77 | 97.54 | 108.99 | 98.59 | 57.30 | 24.27 | 13.54 |
| Claims on Other Depository Corps. | 12e | 7.84 | 8.16 | — | .01 | 1.39 | 9.45 | 3.28 | 6.84 | 12.63 | .21 | .70 | .59 |
| Net Claims on Central Government | 12an | — | — | −9.56 | −8.50 | −1.43 | −13.63 | −12.80 | −13.56 | −24.97 | −31.20 | −41.76 | −37.68 |
| Claims on Central Government | 12a | — | — | — | — | — | — | — | — | — | — | — | — |
| Liabilities to Central Government | 16d | — | — | 9.56 | 8.50 | 1.43 | 13.63 | 12.80 | 13.56 | 24.97 | 31.20 | 41.76 | 37.68 |
| Claims on Other Sectors | 12s | — | — | — | — | — | — | — | — | — | — | — | — |
| Claims on Other Financial Corps. | 12g | — | — | — | — | — | — | — | — | — | — | — | — |
| Claims on State & Local Govts. | 12b | — | — | — | — | — | — | — | — | — | — | — | — |
| Claims on Public Nonfin. Corps. | 12c | — | — | — | — | — | — | — | — | — | — | — | — |
| Claims on Private Sector | 12d | — | — | — | — | — | — | — | — | — | — | — | — |
| Monetary Base | 14 | 13.70 | 22.21 | 34.58 | 48.87 | 50.47 | 51.66 | 55.10 | 61.57 | 57.31 | 68.67 | 68.35 | 74.00 |
| Currency in Circulation | 14a | 8.25 | 12.73 | 17.36 | 25.44 | 29.05 | 27.50 | 29.94 | 34.23 | 36.01 | 40.32 | 46.34 | 53.59 |
| Liabs. to Other Depository Corps. | 14c | 5.46 | 9.48 | 17.22 | 23.43 | 21.42 | 24.16 | 25.17 | 27.34 | 21.30 | 28.35 | 22.02 | 20.41 |
| Liabilities to Other Sectors | 14d | — | — | — | — | — | — | — | — | — | — | — | — |
| Other Liabs. to Other Dep. Corps. | 14n | 14.60 | 33.00 | 37.78 | 41.17 | 52.50 | 33.29 | 29.42 | 26.20 | 27.04 | 24.46 | 24.75 | 28.05 |
| Dep. & Sec. Excl. f/Monetary Base | 14o | 16.43 | 10.75 | — | — | — | — | — | — | — | — | — | — |
| Deposits Included in Broad Money | 15 | 16.35 | 10.67 | — | — | — | — | — | — | — | — | — | — |
| Sec.Ot.th.Shares Incl.in Brd. Money | 16a | — | — | — | — | — | — | — | — | — | — | — | — |
| Deposits Excl. from Broad Money | 16b | .08 | .08 | — | — | — | — | — | — | — | — | — | — |
| Sec.Ot.th.Shares Excl.f/Brd.Money | 16s | — | — | — | — | — | — | — | — | — | — | — | — |
| Loans | 16l | — | — | — | — | — | — | — | — | — | — | — | — |
| Financial Derivatives | 16m | — | — | — | — | — | — | — | — | — | — | — | — |
| Shares and Other Equity | 17a | .03 | −3.03 | −6.59 | .24 | 9.58 | 13.72 | 17.31 | 18.36 | 18.00 | 12.14 | 15.52 | 16.12 |
| Other Items (Net) | 17r | −.14 | −.35 | .98 | −6.30 | −6.75 | −34.64 | −55.30 | −62.22 | −56.98 | −35.33 | −15.20 | −8.74 |
| Memo Item: | | | | | | | | | | | | | |
| Total Assets | 10ra | 52.90 | 72.52 | 82.26 | 103.90 | 120.22 | 146.41 | 164.41 | 174.99 | 176.74 | 167.87 | 167.70 | 168.96 |

# Romania 968

| | | 2004 | 2005 | 2006 | 2007 | 2008 | 2009 | 2010 | 2011 | 2012 | 2013 | 2014 | 2015 |
|---|---|---|---|---|---|---|---|---|---|---|---|---|---|
| **Other Depository Corporations** | | | | | | *Billions of Lei: End of Period* | | | | | | | |
| Net Foreign Assets | 21n | −9.23 | −20.80 | −37.52 | −67.39 | −97.22 | −83.35 | −90.44 | −94.28 | −82.47 | −71.59 | −52.79 | −44.34 |
| Claims on Nonresidents | 21 | 5.25 | 4.52 | 4.64 | 6.07 | 6.89 | 12.77 | 12.79 | 9.92 | 11.39 | 12.03 | 18.96 | 20.13 |
| Liabilities to Nonresidents | 26c | 14.48 | 25.32 | 42.15 | 73.46 | 104.11 | 96.12 | 103.23 | 104.20 | 93.86 | 83.62 | 71.75 | 64.47 |
| Claims on Central Bank | 20 | 31.55 | 50.33 | 57.22 | 68.55 | 77.65 | 60.98 | 57.74 | 57.30 | 52.53 | 58.36 | 53.34 | 55.47 |
| Currency | 20a | .78 | 1.35 | 2.23 | 4.00 | 3.73 | 3.53 | 3.14 | 3.62 | 4.54 | 5.53 | 6.47 | 7.11 |
| Reserve Deposits and Securities | 20b | 26.07 | 32.72 | 53.29 | 64.54 | 73.92 | 57.45 | 54.59 | 53.68 | 48.00 | 52.83 | 46.86 | 48.36 |
| Other Claims | 20n | 4.70 | 16.27 | 1.70 | — | — | — | — | — | — | — | — | — |
| Net Claims on Central Government | 22an | −.11 | −.83 | −1.72 | 1.04 | 4.22 | 34.99 | 49.43 | 57.23 | 65.38 | 66.60 | 71.40 | 74.23 |
| Claims on Central Government | 22a | 2.22 | 2.55 | 2.45 | 6.81 | 13.08 | 41.43 | 54.87 | 61.98 | 69.66 | 70.87 | 75.99 | 79.52 |
| Liabilities to Central Government | 26d | 2.34 | 3.38 | 4.18 | 5.77 | 8.86 | 6.44 | 5.44 | 4.76 | 4.28 | 4.27 | 4.60 | 5.28 |
| Claims on Other Sectors | 22s | 41.76 | 60.67 | 94.15 | 152.02 | 203.38 | 206.62 | 217.59 | 232.61 | 237.22 | 230.15 | 223.71 | 230.85 |
| Claims on Other Financial Corps | 22g | .07 | .06 | 3.92 | 4.53 | 5.31 | 4.74 | 4.17 | 4.96 | 4.63 | 4.95 | 6.22 | 7.65 |
| Claims on State & Local Govts | 22b | — | — | 1.09 | 2.76 | 4.19 | 5.39 | 6.50 | 7.83 | 9.20 | 9.37 | 9.55 | 10.12 |
| Claims on Public Nonfin. Corps | 22c | 3.07 | 3.07 | — | — | — | — | — | — | — | — | — | — |
| Claims on Private Sector | 22d | 38.62 | 57.54 | 89.14 | 144.73 | 193.88 | 196.48 | 206.92 | 219.82 | 223.39 | 215.83 | 207.93 | 213.08 |
| Liabilities to Central Bank | 26g | — | — | — | — | 1.38 | 8.94 | 3.27 | 6.22 | 12.32 | 1.00 | — | — |
| Transf.Dep.Included in Broad Money | 24 | 14.43 | 20.65 | 33.60 | 57.50 | 67.30 | 55.40 | 54.80 | 55.23 | 57.54 | 65.53 | 78.69 | 103.07 |
| Other Dep.Included in Broad Money | 25 | 39.70 | 50.96 | 61.72 | 69.10 | 81.12 | 108.65 | 117.98 | 126.22 | 132.81 | 140.94 | 142.99 | 136.58 |
| Sec.Oth.Shares Incl.in Brd.Money | 26a | 2.86 | 3.34 | .27 | .12 | .35 | 1.80 | 3.18 | 3.81 | .17 | .23 | .12 | .13 |
| Deposits Excl. from Broad Money | 26b | — | 1.30 | 2.34 | 3.97 | 4.40 | 4.76 | 5.57 | 6.08 | 7.90 | 10.23 | 12.86 | 15.11 |
| Sec.Oth.Shares Excl.f/Brd.Money | 26s | — | — | .24 | .31 | .31 | .07 | .20 | .45 | — | — | — | — |
| Loans | 26l | — | — | .11 | .04 | .19 | — | .12 | .48 | .02 | .06 | .13 | — |
| Financial Derivatives | 26m | — | — | — | — | — | — | — | — | — | — | — | — |
| Insurance Technical Reserves | 26r | — | — | — | — | — | — | — | — | — | — | — | — |
| Shares and Other Equity | 27a | 10.95 | 15.87 | 18.08 | 21.49 | 28.17 | 28.31 | 30.11 | 31.28 | 39.32 | 39.24 | 35.45 | 39.22 |
| Other Items (Net) | 27r | −3.98 | −2.75 | −4.22 | 1.68 | 4.81 | 11.31 | 19.08 | 23.11 | 22.58 | 26.28 | 25.40 | 22.11 |
| Memo Item: | | | | | | | | | | | | | |
| Total Assets | 20ra | 91.38 | 130.27 | 175.46 | 259.59 | 339.83 | 366.67 | 388.41 | 396.41 | 404.83 | 408.54 | 405.40 | 417.14 |
| **Depository Corporations** | | | | | | *Billions of Lei: End of Period* | | | | | | | |
| Net Foreign Assets | 31n | 27.56 | 33.62 | 38.80 | 25.08 | 8.60 | −15.14 | −34.40 | −43.65 | −24.76 | 29.33 | 81.68 | 102.18 |
| Claims on Nonresidents | 31 | 44.44 | 63.03 | 81.51 | 103.48 | 118.79 | 142.75 | 166.37 | 169.54 | 167.69 | 170.25 | 177.70 | 180.18 |
| Liabilities to Nonresidents | 36c | 16.88 | 29.40 | 42.71 | 78.40 | 110.18 | 157.89 | 200.77 | 213.19 | 192.45 | 140.91 | 96.02 | 78.01 |
| Domestic Claims | 32 | 41.65 | 59.84 | 82.86 | 144.56 | 206.17 | 227.98 | 254.22 | 276.27 | 277.63 | 265.55 | 253.35 | 267.41 |
| Net Claims on Central Government | 32an | −.11 | −.83 | −11.29 | −7.46 | 2.79 | 21.36 | 36.64 | 43.66 | 40.41 | 35.40 | 29.64 | 36.56 |
| Claims on Central Government | 32a | 2.22 | 2.55 | 2.45 | 6.81 | 13.08 | 41.43 | 54.87 | 61.98 | 69.66 | 70.87 | 75.99 | 79.52 |
| Liabilities to Central Government | 36d | 2.34 | 3.38 | 13.74 | 14.27 | 10.29 | 20.06 | 18.23 | 18.32 | 29.25 | 35.47 | 46.35 | 42.96 |
| Claims on Other Sectors | 32s | 41.76 | 60.67 | 94.15 | 152.02 | 203.38 | 206.62 | 217.59 | 232.61 | 237.23 | 230.15 | 223.72 | 230.85 |
| Claims on Other Financial Corps | 32g | .07 | .06 | 3.92 | 4.53 | 5.31 | 4.74 | 4.17 | 4.96 | 4.63 | 4.96 | 6.23 | 7.65 |
| Claims on State & Local Govts | 32b | — | — | 1.09 | 2.76 | 4.19 | 5.39 | 6.50 | 7.83 | 9.20 | 9.37 | 9.55 | 10.12 |
| Claims on Public Nonfin. Corps | 32c | 3.07 | 3.07 | — | — | — | — | — | — | — | — | — | — |
| Claims on Private Sector | 32d | 38.62 | 57.54 | 89.14 | 144.73 | 193.88 | 196.49 | 206.92 | 219.82 | 223.39 | 215.83 | 207.93 | 213.08 |
| Broad Money Liabilities | 35l | 80.81 | 97.01 | 110.71 | 148.17 | 174.09 | 189.81 | 202.75 | 215.87 | 222.00 | 241.49 | 261.67 | 286.25 |
| Currency Outside Depository Corps | 34a | 7.46 | 11.39 | 15.13 | 21.44 | 25.32 | 23.97 | 26.79 | 30.61 | 31.48 | 34.79 | 39.87 | 46.48 |
| Transferable Deposits | 34 | 19.57 | 24.59 | 33.60 | 57.50 | 67.30 | 55.40 | 54.80 | 55.23 | 57.54 | 65.53 | 78.69 | 103.07 |
| Other Deposits | 35 | 50.91 | 57.69 | 61.72 | 69.10 | 81.12 | 108.65 | 117.98 | 126.22 | 132.81 | 140.94 | 142.99 | 136.58 |
| Securities Other than Shares | 36a | 2.86 | 3.34 | .27 | .12 | .35 | 1.80 | 3.18 | 3.81 | .17 | .23 | .12 | .13 |
| Deposits Excl. from Broad Money | 36b | .08 | 1.38 | 2.34 | 3.97 | 4.40 | 4.76 | 5.57 | 6.08 | 7.90 | 10.23 | 12.86 | 15.11 |
| Sec.Oth.Shares Excl.f/Brd.Money | 36s | — | — | .24 | .31 | .31 | .07 | .20 | .45 | — | — | — | — |
| Loans | 36l | — | — | .11 | .04 | .19 | — | .12 | .48 | .02 | .06 | .13 | — |
| Financial Derivatives | 36m | — | — | — | — | — | — | — | — | — | — | — | — |
| Insurance Technical Reserves | 36r | — | — | — | — | — | — | — | — | — | — | — | — |
| Shares and Other Equity | 37a | 10.98 | 12.83 | 11.49 | 21.73 | 37.75 | 42.04 | 47.42 | 49.64 | 57.32 | 51.38 | 50.97 | 55.34 |
| Other Items (Net) | 37r | −22.67 | −17.76 | −3.23 | −4.57 | −1.96 | −23.84 | −36.24 | −39.88 | −34.37 | −8.28 | 9.40 | 12.88 |
| Broad Money Liabs., Seasonally Adj. | 35l.b | 78.29 | 94.58 | 108.30 | 145.14 | 170.52 | 185.99 | 198.90 | 212.14 | 218.31 | 237.42 | 257.13 | 281.13 |
| **Other Financial Corporations** | | | | | | *Billions of Lei: End of Period* | | | | | | | |
| Net Foreign Assets | 41n | .... | .... | .... | .... | −31.65 | −27.64 | −21.08 | −17.33 | −13.15 | −7.53 | −6.31 | −12.28 |
| Claims on Nonresidents | 41 | .... | .... | .... | .... | .46 | .64 | 1.54 | 1.77 | 3.59 | 8.12 | 7.93 | 12.37 |
| Liabilities to Nonresidents | 46c | .... | .... | .... | .... | 32.11 | 28.28 | 22.62 | 19.11 | 16.74 | 15.64 | 14.24 | 24.65 |
| Claims on Depository Corporations | 40 | .... | .... | .... | .... | 3.50 | 10.29 | 8.79 | 7.72 | 10.41 | 15.26 | 15.95 | 18.84 |
| Net Claims on Central Government | 42an | .... | .... | .... | .... | −.09 | .46 | 1.52 | 1.71 | 4.58 | 21.41 | 28.83 | 33.02 |
| Claims on Central Government | 42a | .... | .... | .... | .... | .13 | .79 | 1.98 | 2.50 | 5.51 | 22.41 | 29.91 | 34.88 |
| Liabilities to Central Government | 46d | .... | .... | .... | .... | .22 | .34 | .46 | .79 | .93 | 1.00 | 1.08 | 1.86 |
| Claims on Other Sectors | 42s | .... | .... | .... | .... | 37.92 | 35.02 | 30.37 | 28.26 | 41.26 | 46.01 | 44.91 | 43.23 |
| Claims on State & Local Govts | 42b | .... | .... | .... | .... | .17 | .24 | .28 | .34 | .47 | .45 | .38 | .65 |
| Claims on Public Nonfin. Corps | 42c | .... | .... | .... | .... | — | — | — | — | — | — | — | — |
| Claims on Private Sector | 42d | .... | .... | .... | .... | 37.74 | 34.79 | 30.09 | 27.92 | 40.80 | 45.56 | 44.53 | 42.58 |
| Deposits | 46b | .... | .... | .... | .... | — | — | — | — | — | — | — | — |
| Securities Other than Shares | 46s | .... | .... | .... | .... | .01 | .01 | — | — | — | — | — | .01 |
| Loans | 46l | .... | .... | .... | .... | 5.32 | 3.76 | 2.54 | 2.33 | 1.30 | 3.73 | .35 | 5.18 |
| Financial Derivatives | 46m | .... | .... | .... | .... | .01 | .01 | .01 | .01 | .01 | .02 | .05 | .08 |
| Insurance Technical Reserves | 46r | .... | .... | .... | .... | — | — | — | — | — | 25.62 | 31.92 | 37.29 |
| Shares and Other Equity | 47a | .... | .... | .... | .... | 4.49 | 15.57 | 17.18 | 18.29 | 40.56 | 49.28 | 51.49 | 44.10 |
| Other Items (Net) | 47r | .... | .... | .... | .... | −.16 | −1.23 | −.15 | −.26 | 1.24 | −3.49 | −4.34 | −3.80 |
| Memo Item: | | | | | | | | | | | | | |
| Total Assets | 40ra | .... | .... | .... | .... | 44.50 | 50.28 | 46.06 | 43.60 | 65.00 | 105.21 | 109.57 | 118.58 |

# Romania 968

| | | 2004 | 2005 | 2006 | 2007 | 2008 | 2009 | 2010 | 2011 | 2012 | 2013 | 2014 | 2015 |
|---|---|---|---|---|---|---|---|---|---|---|---|---|---|
| **Monetary Aggregates** | | | | | | *Billions of Lei: End of Period* | | | | | | | |
| Broad Money | 59m | 80.81 | 97.01 | 110.71 | 148.17 | 174.09 | 189.81 | 202.75 | 215.87 | 222.00 | 241.55 | 261.67 | 286.25 |
| o/w:Currency Issued by Cent.Govt | 59m.a | — | — | — | — | — | — | — | — | — | — | — | — |
| o/w: Dep.in Nonfin. Corporations. | 59m.b | — | — | — | — | — | — | — | — | — | .06 | — | — |
| o/w:Secs. Issued by Central Govt.. | 59m.c | — | — | — | — | — | — | — | — | — | — | — | — |
| Money (National Definitions) | | | | | | | | | | | | | |
| M1 | 59ma | 15.29 | 24.55 | 35.37 | 79.91 | 92.55 | 79.36 | 81.59 | 85.83 | 89.02 | 100.31 | 118.58 | 149.60 |
| M2 | 59mb | 64.46 | 86.33 | 111.71 | 148.04 | 173.63 | 188.01 | 199.57 | 212.06 | 221.83 | 241.25 | 261.57 | 286.17 |
| M3 | 59mc | .... | .... | .... | 148.17 | 174.09 | 189.81 | 202.75 | 215.87 | 222.00 | 241.55 | 261.83 | 286.25 |
| **Interest Rates** | | | | | | *Percent Per Annum* | | | | | | | |
| Discount Rate (End of Period) | 60.a | 20.27 | 9.59 | 8.56 | 7.46 | 9.75 | 9.33 | 6.67 | 6.21 | 5.31 | 4.81 | 3.31 | 1.92 |
| Money Market Rate | 60b | 20.01 | 8.99 | 8.34 | 7.55 | 11.37 | 10.92 | 5.44 | 4.80 | 4.55 | 3.58 | 1.85 | .69 |
| Treasury Bill Rate | 60c | .... | .... | .... | 7.11 | 10.42 | 10.90 | 7.21 | 7.32 | 6.27 | 4.89 | 3.86 | 2.46 |
| Deposit Rate | 60l | 11.54 | 6.42 | 4.77 | 6.70 | 9.51 | 11.99 | 7.31 | 6.30 | 5.51 | 4.55 | 3.02 | 1.89 |
| Lending Rate | 60p | 25.61 | 19.60 | 13.98 | 13.35 | 14.99 | 17.28 | 14.07 | 12.13 | 11.33 | 10.52 | 8.47 | 6.77 |
| Government Bond Yield | 61 | .... | .... | 7.23 | 7.14 | 7.70 | 9.69 | 7.34 | 6.65 | 5.69 | 4.25 | 2.21 | 1.27 |
| **Prices, Production, Labor** | | | | | *Index Numbers (2010=100): Period Averages* | | | | | | | | |
| Producer Prices | 63 | 66.1 | † 73.1 | 78.0 | 82.9 | 93.5 | 95.8 | 100.0 | 107.1 | 112.9 | 115.3 | 115.1 | 112.6 |
| Consumer Prices | 64 | † 68.0 | 74.1 | 79.0 | 82.8 | 89.3 | 94.3 | † 100.0 | 105.8 | 109.3 | 113.7 | 114.9 | † 114.2 |
| Harmonized CPI | 64h | 67.8 | 74.0 | 78.9 | 82.7 | 89.3 | 94.3 | 100.0 | 105.8 | 109.4 | 112.9 | 114.5 | 114.0 |
| Wages: Average Earnings | 65 | 42.4 | 52.5 | 61.3 | 74.2 | 91.1 | 98.2 | 100.0 | 104.9 | 110.0 | 115.4 | 121.3 | 131.4 |
| Industrial Production | 66 | 79.6 | † 81.3 | 89.3 | 98.3 | 100.9 | 95.4 | 100.0 | 107.6 | 110.7 | 118.8 | 127.6 | 131.6 |
| | | | | | *Number in Thousands: Period Averages* | | | | | | | | |
| Employment | 67e | 9,142 | 8,651 | 8,838 | 8,842 | 8,882 | 8,805 | 8,307 | 8,140 | 8,222 | 8,179 | 8,255 | 8,235 |
| Unemployment | 67c | 793 | 701 | 719 | 634 | 549 | 624 | 652 | 659 | 627 | 653 | 629 | 624 |
| Unemployment Rate (%) | 67r | 8.0 | 7.1 | 7.2 | 6.4 | 5.6 | 6.5 | 7.0 | 7.2 | 6.8 | 7.1 | 6.8 | 6.8 |
| **Intl. Transactions & Positions** | | | | | | *Millions of US Dollars* | | | | | | | |
| Exports | 70..d | 23,485.2 | 27,729.6 | 32,336.0 | 40,041.7 | 49,538.9 | 40,620.9 | 49,356.6 | 62,659.1 | 57,904.4 | 65,881.4 | 69,890.8 | 60,605.0 |
| Imports, c.i.f. | 71..d | 32,663.7 | 40,462.9 | 51,106.1 | 69,601.7 | 82,965.0 | 54,256.2 | 61,884.9 | 76,251.1 | 70,259.7 | 73,452.2 | 77,882.2 | 69,857.7 |
| Imports, f.o.b. | 71.vd | 30,149.3 | 37,348.1 | 47,171.9 | 64,353.6 | 76,578.3 | 50,079.6 | 57,121.0 | 70,381.3 | 67,363.1 | 70,424.0 | 74,671.5 | 66,977.6 |
| **Balance of Payments** | | | | | | *Millions of US Dollars* | | | | | | | |
| A. Current Account* | 109bx | −6,382.0 | † −8,540.6 | −12,909.8 | −23,925.5 | −24,986.5 | −8,234.5 | −8,478.8 | −9,275.9 | −8,199.2 | −2,076.6 | −950.8 | −2,007.8 |
| Goods, credit (exports) | 1a9cx | 22,478.0 | † 14,451.9 | 18,002.8 | 30,070.1 | 39,933.5 | 33,710.9 | 43,347.3 | 55,793.8 | 51,267.9 | 58,315.0 | 62,158.8 | 54,516.8 |
| Goods, debit (imports) | 1a9dx | 30,138.0 | † 28,695.1 | 38,246.7 | 58,964.7 | 72,323.0 | 46,302.1 | 56,086.7 | 68,870.8 | 63,157.0 | 66,047.9 | 70,498.9 | 63,122.3 |
| Balance on goods | 1a9bx | −7,660.0 | † −14,243.2 | −20,244.0 | −28,895.1 | −32,389.4 | −12,590.9 | −12,739.1 | −13,077.7 | −11,889.7 | −7,732.6 | −8,340.4 | −8,605.5 |
| Services, credit (exports) | 1b9cx | 3,742.0 | † 9,668.1 | 12,268.2 | 13,092.4 | 16,356.3 | 11,798.5 | 10,380.5 | 12,085.2 | 12,692.0 | 17,852.8 | 20,025.8 | 18,612.1 |
| Services, debit (imports) | 1b9dx | 3,012.0 | † 5,498.0 | 7,057.9 | 9,008.9 | 12,069.3 | 10,497.0 | 8,396.6 | 9,794.9 | 9,508.5 | 11,606.9 | 12,242.0 | 10,920.6 |
| Balance on Goods & Services | 1z9bx | −6,930.0 | † −10,073.2 | −15,033.6 | −24,811.6 | −28,102.4 | −11,289.7 | −10,755.1 | −10,787.1 | −8,706.0 | −1,487.1 | −555.6 | −914.3 |
| Primary income: credit | 1c9cx | 433.0 | † 1,440.0 | 2,143.6 | 2,996.4 | 3,749.6 | 2,325.6 | 1,914.2 | 2,712.3 | 2,785.6 | 3,297.9 | 2,973.8 | 2,689.1 |
| Primary income: debit | 1c9dx | 3,582.0 | † 4,354.3 | 6,126.6 | 8,709.9 | 8,733.3 | 4,533.1 | 3,818.7 | 5,098.3 | 5,761.0 | 7,477.2 | 5,596.9 | 6,901.9 |
| Balance on gds, serv. & prim. inc. | 1y9bx | −10,079.0 | † −12,987.4 | −19,016.7 | −30,525.1 | −33,086.2 | −13,497.2 | −12,659.6 | −13,173.1 | −11,681.3 | −5,666.4 | −3,178.7 | −5,127.0 |
| Secondary income: credit | 1d9ca | 4,188.0 | † 5,052.0 | 6,973.6 | 9,848.6 | 12,287.4 | 8,472.5 | 7,062.6 | 6,858.9 | 6,192.9 | 7,113.6 | 6,042.9 | 6,311.4 |
| Secondary income: debit | 1d9da | 491.0 | † 605.2 | 866.8 | 3,249.0 | 4,187.7 | 3,209.7 | 2,881.7 | 2,961.8 | 2,710.8 | 3,523.9 | 3,814.9 | 3,192.1 |
| B. Capital Account* | 209ba | 644.0 | † 714.1 | −68.3 | 1,080.0 | 814.8 | 867.9 | 258.3 | 990.8 | 2,422.5 | 4,047.6 | 5,205.7 | 4,345.6 |
| Capital account: credit | 209ca | 668.0 | † 805.9 | 882.3 | 1,632.8 | 1,350.9 | 1,343.3 | 691.5 | 1,628.5 | 2,881.5 | 4,213.8 | 5,328.4 | 4,461.2 |
| Capital account: debit | 209da | 24.0 | † 91.8 | 950.7 | 552.9 | 536.0 | 475.4 | 433.1 | 637.7 | 459.0 | 166.2 | 122.6 | 115.6 |
| Balance on current & capital acct. | 129ba | −5,738.0 | † −7,826.4 | −12,978.2 | −22,845.5 | −24,171.6 | −7,366.5 | −8,220.4 | −8,285.1 | −5,776.7 | 1,971.0 | 4,254.9 | 2,337.8 |
| C. Financial Account* | 309na | −10,761.0 | † −14,161.6 | −18,664.5 | −29,218.5 | −26,109.0 | −1,747.1 | −6,391.8 | −6,781.0 | −4,478.0 | −6,754.5 | 3.2 | 2,273.9 |
| Direct investment: assets | 3a9aa | 70.0 | † 330.4 | 501.6 | 666.1 | 313.0 | 13.5 | 235.6 | 56.8 | −207.4 | −60.5 | 269.2 | 812.8 |
| Equity & investment fund shares.. | 3aaaa | 70.0 | † −69.5 | 242.0 | 32.7 | 50.2 | −167.6 | −68.5 | 56.1 | −112.0 | 170.2 | −270.0 | 144.9 |
| Debt instruments | 3abaa | — | † 400.2 | 259.2 | 633.8 | 263.1 | 181.1 | 303.8 | .8 | −95.7 | −230.4 | 539.2 | 667.9 |
| Direct investment: liabilities | 3a9la | 6,443.0 | † 6,498.7 | 11,006.6 | 10,103.1 | 13,667.8 | 4,637.1 | 3,213.7 | 2,370.1 | 3,047.6 | 3,854.8 | 3,869.2 | 3,890.5 |
| Equity & investment fund shares . | 3aala | 5,573.0 | † 4,795.5 | 8,693.1 | 4,850.0 | 7,459.4 | 2,345.5 | 2,396.8 | 2,019.6 | 1,074.4 | 3,235.8 | 3,754.3 | 3,649.6 |
| Debt instruments | 3abla | 870.0 | † 1,703.5 | 2,313.5 | 5,253.1 | 6,208.5 | 2,292.5 | 816.6 | 350.5 | 1,973.5 | 618.7 | 115.2 | 240.9 |
| Portfolio investment: assets | 3b9aa | 559.0 | † 154.5 | 827.4 | −142.5 | 312.8 | 194.6 | 513.2 | 57.8 | 601.4 | 296.3 | 129.7 | 280.0 |
| Equity & investment fund shares | 3baaa | 559.0 | † 133.0 | 389.9 | 236.9 | 274.3 | −205.1 | 230.7 | 210.3 | 242.4 | −60.9 | −2.7 | 137.1 |
| Debt securities | 3bbaa | — | † 21.6 | 437.5 | −379.3 | 38.1 | 399.7 | 283.7 | −151.1 | 359.0 | 357.3 | 133.0 | 143.4 |
| Portfolio investment: liabilities | 3b9la | 28.0 | † 1,117.3 | 578.4 | 476.4 | −392.9 | 955.9 | 1,772.9 | 2,522.6 | 5,215.6 | 7,476.3 | 3,901.4 | −639.6 |
| Equity & investment fund shares . | 3bala | 111.0 | † 232.2 | 302.6 | 742.1 | 21.1 | 6.8 | 3.4 | −38.3 | 408.3 | 1,054.1 | 534.8 | −559.8 |
| Debt securities | 3bbla | −83.0 | † 885.4 | 275.8 | −265.3 | −414.1 | 949.1 | 1,768.8 | 2,560.9 | 4,807.0 | 6,421.9 | 3,366.6 | −80.1 |
| Fin. der.& empl.stk.ops.(ESOs): net. | 3c9na | — | † 27.0 | 108.7 | 415.3 | 406.2 | 62.3 | −25.6 | 100.8 | 226.4 | −46.7 | −28.3 | −40.9 |
| Fin. der. & ESOs.: assets | 3c9aa | — | .... | .... | .... | .... | .... | .... | .... | .... | .... | .... | .... |
| Fin. der. & ESOs.: liabilities | 3c9la | — | .... | .... | .... | .... | .... | .... | .... | .... | .... | .... | .... |
| Other investment: assets | 3d9aa | 212.0 | † 1,202.9 | 1,083.6 | 759.3 | 1,286.0 | 2,905.0 | −46.9 | −915.5 | 69.6 | 98.9 | 1,592.8 | 575.4 |
| Other equity | 3daaa | — | † — | — | — | — | — | — | — | — | 76.4 | 6.6 | 11.8 |
| Debt instruments | 3dzaa | 212.0 | † 1,202.9 | 1,083.6 | 759.3 | 1,286.0 | 2,905.0 | −46.9 | −915.5 | 69.6 | 22.5 | 1,586.2 | 563.7 |
| Other investment: liabilities | 3d9la | 5,131.0 | † 8,261.2 | 9,600.1 | 20,338.0 | 15,152.1 | −671.1 | 2,082.1 | 1,188.3 | −3,095.3 | −4,287.7 | −5,810.1 | −3,896.9 |
| Other equity | 3dala | .... | † — | | | | | | | | | | |
| Debt instruments | 3dzla | 5,131.0 | † 8,261.2 | 9,600.1 | 20,338.0 | 15,152.1 | −671.1 | 2,082.1 | 1,188.3 | −3,095.3 | −4,287.7 | −5,810.1 | −3,896.9 |
| Curr.+ cap.− finan. acct. balance... | 4y9na | 5,023.0 | † 6,335.2 | 5,686.3 | 6,372.9 | 1,937.4 | −5,619.5 | −1,828.6 | −1,504.1 | −1,298.7 | 8,725.5 | 4,251.7 | 64.0 |
| D. Net Errors and Omissions | 409na | 1,166.1 | † 468.7 | 1,082.0 | −195.1 | −1,988.1 | 952.2 | 672.7 | 1,706.3 | 1,529.3 | 99.8 | −292.9 | 831.1 |
| E. Reserves and Related Items | 4z9na | 6,189.1 | † 6,803.8 | 6,767.9 | 6,179.0 | −50.7 | −4,667.3 | −1,155.8 | 201.9 | 229.7 | 8,825.3 | 3,959.7 | 894.6 |
| Reserve assets | 3e9aa | 6,018.2 | † 6,652.2 | 6,601.6 | 6,074.1 | −50.7 | 4,689.0 | 4,519.0 | 1,391.2 | −1,762.6 | 2,669.1 | −1,971.5 | −834.9 |
| Credit and loans from the IMF | 3dcla | −170.9 | † −151.7 | −166.3 | −104.8 | — | 9,356.3 | 5,674.8 | 1,189.3 | −1,992.3 | −6,156.2 | −5,931.2 | −1,729.5 |
| Exceptional financing | 409la | — | .... | .... | .... | — | .... | .... | .... | .... | .... | — | — |

*Excludes components in group E

# Romania 968

| | | 2004 | 2005 | 2006 | 2007 | 2008 | 2009 | 2010 | 2011 | 2012 | 2013 | 2014 | 2015 |
|---|---|---|---|---|---|---|---|---|---|---|---|---|---|
| **International Investment Position** | | | | | | | *Millions of US Dollars* | | | | | | |
| Assets.......................... | 809aa | 24,188.7 | † 30,902.1 | 42,813.9 | 55,160.9 | 55,869.8 | 64,049.1 | 68,903.3 | 69,094.0 | 68,449.1 | 71,944.0 | 67,431.0 | 62,919.5 |
| Direct investment.......................... | 8a9aa | 323.9 | † 646.1 | 1,455.4 | 2,202.0 | 2,446.9 | 2,474.4 | 2,553.6 | 2,554.7 | 2,219.2 | 2,340.3 | 3,139.9 | 3,618.1 |
| Equity & investment fund shares.. | 8aaaa | 243.2 | † 150.3 | 517.6 | 588.7 | 643.6 | 446.9 | 510.2 | 482.4 | 455.4 | 596.9 | 130.5 | 254.6 |
| Debt instruments.......................... | 8abaa | 80.8 | † 495.8 | 937.8 | 1,613.3 | 1,803.3 | 2,027.5 | 2,043.7 | 2,072.0 | 1,763.8 | 1,743.4 | 3,009.1 | 3,363.6 |
| Portfolio investment.......................... | 8b9aa | 605.7 | † 724.0 | 1,663.4 | 1,704.9 | 1,519.7 | 1,719.6 | 2,114.5 | 2,081.9 | 2,709.5 | 3,234.9 | 2,961.4 | 2,960.0 |
| Equity & investment fund shares.. | 8baaa | 29.5 | † 174.1 | 593.9 | 917.2 | 780.8 | 582.4 | 779.8 | 939.4 | 1,200.0 | 1,189.2 | 1,008.2 | 1,080.6 |
| Debt securities.......................... | 8bbaa | 576.2 | † 550.2 | 1,069.5 | 787.7 | 738.8 | 1,137.2 | 1,334.4 | 1,142.5 | 1,509.5 | 2,045.4 | 1,953.2 | 1,879.4 |
| Fin. der.(oth.than reserves) & ESOs | 8c9aa | .... | † — | — | — | — | — | −12.2 | .3 | .6 | 1.5 | 12.5 | 11.1 |
| Other investment.......................... | 8d9aa | 6,975.9 | † 7,928.4 | 9,488.2 | 11,297.4 | 12,152.6 | 15,417.7 | 16,181.6 | 16,268.4 | 16,808.3 | 17,547.8 | 18,152.9 | 17,621.3 |
| Other equity.......................... | 8daaa | 805.9 | † 808.0 | 837.7 | 894.4 | 916.3 | 949.6 | 993.9 | 1,071.2 | 1,076.4 | 1,237.1 | 1,189.9 | 1,159.7 |
| Debt instruments.......................... | 8dzaa | 6,170.0 | † 7,120.5 | 8,650.5 | 10,403.0 | 11,236.3 | 14,468.2 | 15,187.7 | 15,197.2 | 15,731.9 | 16,310.7 | 16,962.9 | 16,461.7 |
| Reserve assets.......................... | 8e9aa | 16,283.2 | † 21,603.6 | 30,206.8 | 39,956.9 | 39,750.3 | 44,437.7 | 48,065.7 | 48,188.7 | 46,711.5 | 48,819.7 | 43,164.7 | 38,708.8 |
| Liabilities.......................... | 809la | 46,760.7 | † 58,401.8 | 91,518.7 | 134,973.9 | 153,018.0 | 172,684.4 | 176,535.2 | 181,868.4 | 189,967.2 | 194,486.0 | 171,347.6 | 150,790.9 |
| Direct investment.......................... | 8a9la | 20,573.4 | † 25,905.8 | 45,106.7 | 62,486.6 | 66,406.0 | 70,708.1 | 68,971.8 | 70,032.9 | 76,586.4 | 84,096.6 | 76,002.8 | 72,211.8 |
| Equity & investment fund shares.. | 8aala | 16,384.0 | † 20,692.8 | 35,584.6 | 46,297.4 | 49,060.8 | 51,267.0 | 47,510.1 | 47,867.5 | 51,796.0 | 56,092.9 | 52,596.6 | 49,899.5 |
| Debt instruments.......................... | 8abla | 4,189.4 | † 5,213.0 | 9,522.5 | 16,189.1 | 17,345.3 | 19,441.1 | 21,461.7 | 22,165.4 | 24,790.5 | 28,003.7 | 23,405.9 | 22,312.1 |
| Portfolio investment.......................... | 8b9la | 4,831.7 | † 5,252.3 | 6,291.5 | 7,247.2 | 6,210.6 | 7,083.5 | 7,775.3 | 9,729.0 | 15,977.7 | 23,101.6 | 25,707.4 | 22,680.0 |
| Equity & investment fund shares.. | 8bala | 877.4 | † 984.3 | 1,525.2 | 2,350.2 | 2,060.5 | 1,997.9 | 1,835.5 | 1,732.4 | 3,158.6 | 3,285.3 | 3,561.1 | 2,672.6 |
| Debt securities.......................... | 8bbla | 3,954.3 | † 4,267.6 | 4,766.3 | 4,897.0 | 4,150.0 | 5,085.7 | 5,939.5 | 7,996.6 | 12,819.4 | 19,816.3 | 22,146.3 | 20,007.5 |
| Fin. der.(oth.than reserves) & ESOs | 8c9la | .... | † — | — | — | — | — | −.6 | 1.2 | 1.8 | 2.2 | 6.5 | 5.3 |
| Other investment.......................... | 8d9la | 21,355.7 | † 27,243.8 | 40,120.1 | 65,240.1 | 80,401.7 | 94,892.7 | 99,788.2 | 102,106.2 | 97,403.1 | 87,285.6 | 69,631.2 | 55,893.8 |
| Other equity.......................... | 8dala | .... | † — | — | — | — | — | — | 905.9 | — | — | — | — |
| Debt instruments.......................... | 8dzla | 21,355.7 | † 27,243.8 | 40,120.1 | 65,240.1 | 80,401.7 | 94,892.7 | 99,788.2 | 101,200.3 | 97,403.1 | 87,285.6 | 69,631.2 | 55,893.8 |

# Romania 968

| | | 2004 | 2005 | 2006 | 2007 | 2008 | 2009 | 2010 | 2011 | 2012 | 2013 | 2014 | 2015 |
|---|---|---|---|---|---|---|---|---|---|---|---|---|---|
| **Government Finance Operations Statement** | | | | | | | | | | | | | |
| **General Government** | | | | | *Millions of Lei: Fiscal Year Ends December 31; Data Reported through Eurostat* | | | | | | | |
| Revenue | a1 | 79,988 | 93,725 | 114,791 | 147,866 | 174,259 | 160,748 | 174,533 | 190,540 | 199,003 | 211,251 | 223,443 | 247,941 |
| Taxes | a11 | 44,905 | 52,625 | 64,877 | 79,777 | 95,501 | 85,952 | 93,460 | 107,286 | 113,398 | 119,470 | 126,918 | 141,920 |
| Social Contributions | a12 | 23,888 | 29,650 | 35,604 | 43,639 | 51,988 | 51,261 | 49,552 | 50,808 | 52,585 | 55,279 | 57,379 | 58,074 |
| Grants | a13 | .... | .... | .... | .... | .... | .... | .... | .... | .... | .... | .... | .... |
| Other Revenue | a14 | .... | .... | .... | .... | .... | .... | .... | .... | .... | .... | .... | .... |
| Expense | a2 | 81,619 | 94,718 | 111,742 | 141,888 | 179,240 | 190,284 | 192,949 | 204,125 | 205,150 | 208,489 | 214,869 | 228,024 |
| Compensation of Employees | a21 | 20,127 | 25,261 | 31,940 | 40,436 | 54,126 | 54,819 | 50,637 | 44,105 | 46,329 | 51,653 | 51,393 | 54,323 |
| Use of Goods & Services | a22 | 13,826 | 18,629 | 20,923 | 27,093 | 33,867 | 32,107 | 28,863 | 32,373 | 35,479 | 36,279 | 37,783 | 40,203 |
| Consumption of Fixed Capital | a23 | 5,776 | 6,877 | 7,564 | 8,884 | 11,152 | 11,917 | 12,124 | 13,692 | 13,295 | 12,897 | 11,333 | 11,359 |
| Interest | a24 | 3,568 | 3,567 | 2,877 | 2,963 | 3,667 | 7,671 | 8,007 | 9,080 | 10,427 | 11,141 | 11,096 | 11,732 |
| Subsidies | a25 | 4,972 | 4,953 | 6,801 | 6,403 | 5,720 | 5,583 | 5,366 | 4,807 | 3,886 | 3,450 | 3,188 | 3,477 |
| Grants | a26 | .... | .... | .... | .... | .... | .... | .... | .... | .... | .... | .... | .... |
| Social Benefits | a27 | 24,084 | 28,663 | 33,203 | 41,899 | 57,880 | 67,177 | 73,346 | 74,274 | 72,274 | 74,460 | 76,684 | 81,782 |
| Other Expense | a28 | .... | .... | .... | .... | .... | .... | .... | .... | .... | .... | .... | .... |
| Gross Operating Balance [1-2+23] | agob | 4,144 | 5,884 | 10,612 | 14,861 | 6,171 | −17,620 | −6,292 | 106 | 7,149 | 15,659 | 19,907 | 31,276 |
| Net Operating Balance [1-2] | anob | −1,632 | −993 | 3,048 | 5,977 | −4,981 | −29,537 | −18,416 | −13,586 | −6,147 | 2,762 | 8,574 | 19,917 |
| Net Acq. of Nonfinancial Assets | a31 | 1,087 | 1,378 | 10,423 | 17,758 | 24,101 | 18,769 | 18,315 | 16,992 | 15,824 | 16,199 | 14,376 | 25,205 |
| Aquisition of Nonfin. Assets | a31.1 | .... | .... | .... | .... | .... | .... | .... | .... | .... | .... | .... | .... |
| Disposal of Nonfin. Assets | a31.2 | .... | .... | .... | .... | .... | .... | .... | .... | .... | .... | .... | .... |
| Net Lending/Borrowing [1-2-31] | anlb | −2,718 | −2,371 | −7,375 | −11,781 | −29,082 | −48,305 | −36,731 | −30,577 | −21,971 | −13,438 | −5,802 | −5,288 |
| Net Acq. of Financial Assets | a32 | 4,200 | 1,711 | −1,773 | 5,411 | −7,124 | 5,839 | −602 | 10,334 | 9,828 | 4,069 | 15,648 | 3,867 |
| By instrument | | | | | | | | | | | | | |
| Monetary Gold & SDRs | a3201 | — | — | — | — | — | — | — | — | — | — | — | — |
| Currency & Deposits | a3202 | 4,400 | 1,049 | 5,843 | −572 | −6,078 | 8,588 | −2,328 | 5,752 | 10,637 | 5,870 | 11,125 | −3,785 |
| Securities other than Shares | a3203 | — | — | — | — | — | — | — | — | — | — | — | — |
| Loans | a3204 | 919 | −65 | −22 | −198 | −32 | 133 | 513 | 258 | 115 | 80 | 63 | −1 |
| Shares & Other Equity | a3205 | −2,983 | −1,010 | −7,827 | 327 | −298 | −2,189 | −584 | 497 | −1,752 | −2,015 | −298 | −243 |
| Insurance Technical Reserves | a3206 | — | — | — | — | — | — | — | — | — | 18 | 5 | 100 |
| Financial Derivatives | a3207 | — | — | — | — | — | — | — | — | — | — | — | — |
| Other Accounts Receivable | a3208 | 1,863 | 1,737 | 233 | 5,855 | −717 | −693 | 1,797 | 3,827 | 828 | 115 | 4,753 | 7,795 |
| By debtor | | | | | | | | | | | | | |
| Domestic | a321 | .... | .... | .... | .... | .... | .... | .... | .... | .... | .... | .... | .... |
| Foreign | a322 | .... | .... | .... | .... | .... | .... | .... | .... | .... | .... | .... | .... |
| Net Incurrence of Liabilities | a33 | 7,124 | 4,925 | 5,769 | 17,962 | 22,267 | 52,169 | 35,806 | 40,967 | 31,809 | 18,117 | 21,035 | 9,538 |
| By instrument | | | | | | | | | | | | | |
| Special Drawing Rights (SDRs) | a3301 | — | — | — | — | — | — | — | — | — | — | — | — |
| Currency & Deposits | a3302 | 62 | 1,598 | 1,075 | 684 | −1,634 | −708 | 2,319 | 1,720 | −1,410 | −765 | 2,533 | 1,999 |
| Securities other than Shares | a3303 | 1,457 | −3,249 | −1,120 | 5,362 | 8,634 | 31,885 | 21,427 | 23,849 | 31,015 | 22,744 | 28,622 | 13,451 |
| Loans | a3304 | 3,977 | 2,197 | 1,417 | 3,483 | 2,572 | 16,703 | 16,146 | 6,988 | −2,580 | −2,003 | −5,195 | −5,968 |
| Shares & Other Equity | a3305 | — | — | 139 | 1,542 | 2,390 | 263 | 1,041 | 1,618 | 3 | — | — | — |
| Insurance Technical Reserves | a3306 | — | — | — | — | — | 22 | 39 | 28 | 39 | 36 | 38 | 57 |
| Financial Derivatives | a3307 | 113 | 246 | 1,308 | −708 | 1,250 | 72 | −1,105 | −1,108 | −3 | — | — | — |
| Other Accounts Payable | a3308 | 1,515 | 4,132 | 2,950 | 7,600 | 9,055 | 3,932 | −4,063 | 7,871 | 4,745 | −1,895 | −4,963 | — |
| By creditor | | | | | | | | | | | | | |
| Domestic | a331 | .... | .... | .... | .... | .... | .... | .... | .... | .... | .... | .... | .... |
| Foreign | a332 | .... | .... | .... | .... | .... | .... | .... | .... | .... | .... | .... | .... |
| Stat. Discrepancy [32-33-NLB] | anlbz | −206 | −843 | −167 | −771 | −309 | 1,975 | 323 | −55 | −11 | −610 | 415 | −383 |
| Memo Item: Expenditure [2+31] | a2m | 82,706 | 96,096 | 122,165 | 159,646 | 203,341 | 209,053 | 211,264 | 221,117 | 220,974 | 224,689 | 229,245 | 253,229 |
| **Balance Sheet** | | | | | | | | | | | | | |
| Net Worth | a6 | .... | .... | .... | .... | .... | .... | .... | .... | .... | .... | .... | .... |
| Nonfinancial Assets | a61 | .... | .... | .... | .... | .... | .... | .... | .... | .... | .... | .... | .... |
| Financial Assets | a62 | 102,056 | 103,128 | 88,513 | 123,368 | 178,975 | 191,547 | 159,092 | 153,768 | 170,070 | 167,113 | 189,550 | 195,623 |
| By instrument | | | | | | | | | | | | | |
| Monetary Gold & SDRs | a6201 | — | — | — | — | — | — | — | — | — | — | — | — |
| Currency & Deposits | a6202 | 7,878 | 8,824 | 14,971 | 16,169 | 12,076 | 21,151 | 19,850 | 19,658 | 30,863 | 37,201 | 48,371 | 45,140 |
| Securities other than Shares | a6203 | — | — | — | — | — | — | — | — | — | — | — | — |
| Loans | a6204 | 5,581 | 5,516 | 5,494 | 5,337 | 5,419 | 6,271 | 6,345 | 6,633 | 6,666 | 6,403 | 6,463 | 6,571 |
| Shares and Other Equity | a6205 | 59,154 | 56,732 | 34,818 | 61,503 | 120,404 | 125,161 | 90,891 | 81,654 | 84,091 | 75,289 | 81,340 | 83,303 |
| Insurance Technical Reserves | a6206 | — | — | — | — | — | — | — | — | — | 18 | 23 | 123 |
| Financial Derivatives | a6207 | — | — | — | — | — | — | — | — | — | — | — | — |
| Other Accounts Receivable | a6208 | 29,443 | 32,055 | 33,230 | 40,359 | 41,077 | 38,964 | 42,005 | 45,824 | 48,450 | 48,203 | 53,353 | 60,487 |
| By debtor | | | | | | | | | | | | | |
| Domestic | a621 | .... | .... | .... | .... | .... | .... | .... | .... | .... | .... | .... | .... |
| Foreign | a622 | .... | .... | .... | .... | .... | .... | .... | .... | .... | .... | .... | .... |
| Liabilities | a63 | 53,732 | 58,126 | 54,476 | 75,345 | 103,996 | 163,483 | 200,773 | 240,733 | 276,534 | 297,973 | 323,391 | 331,882 |
| By instrument | | | | | | | | | | | | | |
| Special Drawing Rights (SDRs) | a6301 | — | — | — | — | — | — | — | — | — | — | — | — |
| Currency & Deposits | a6302 | 1,342 | 2,940 | 4,016 | 4,700 | 3,066 | 2,358 | 4,677 | 6,398 | 4,987 | 4,222 | 6,755 | 8,754 |
| Securities other than Shares | a6303 | 17,856 | 14,341 | 12,600 | 18,243 | 27,665 | 62,882 | 84,731 | 110,589 | 145,165 | 167,839 | 202,936 | 215,222 |
| Loans | a6304 | 27,132 | 28,677 | 26,764 | 30,769 | 37,838 | 56,680 | 73,833 | 81,542 | 81,906 | 80,990 | 75,526 | 69,725 |
| Shares and Other Equity | a6305 | — | — | 1,139 | 1,745 | 4,212 | 5,654 | 7,930 | 5,583 | 2 | — | — | — |
| Insurance Technical Reserves | a6306 | — | — | — | — | — | 22 | 61 | 89 | 128 | 164 | 202 | 259 |
| Financial Derivatives | a6307 | 113 | 359 | 1,667 | 959 | 2,209 | 2,282 | 1,177 | 69 | — | — | — | — |
| Other Accounts Payable | a6308 | 7,290 | 11,810 | 8,290 | 18,931 | 29,006 | 33,606 | 28,365 | 36,463 | 44,345 | 44,757 | 37,972 | 37,922 |
| By creditor | | | | | | | | | | | | | |
| Domestic | a631 | .... | .... | .... | .... | .... | .... | .... | .... | .... | .... | .... | .... |
| Foreign | a632 | .... | .... | .... | .... | .... | .... | .... | .... | .... | .... | .... | .... |
| Net Financial Worth [62-63] | a6m2 | 48,324 | 45,002 | 34,037 | 48,023 | 74,979 | 28,064 | −41,681 | −86,965 | −106,464 | −130,860 | −133,840 | −136,258 |
| Memo Item: Debt at Market Value | a6m3 | 53,620 | 57,767 | 51,669 | 72,642 | 97,575 | 155,547 | 191,666 | 235,080 | 276,532 | 297,973 | 323,391 | 331,882 |
| Memo Item: Debt at Face Value | a6m35 | 53,647 | 57,436 | 50,874 | 72,191 | 98,026 | 152,097 | 188,052 | 229,679 | 267,219 | 287,090 | 303,795 | 311,816 |
| Memo Item: Maastricht Debt | a6m36 | 46,357 | 45,626 | 42,583 | 53,261 | 69,020 | 118,491 | 159,687 | 193,217 | 222,873 | 242,332 | 265,823 | 273,895 |
| Memo Item: Debt at Nominal Value. | a6m4 | .... | .... | .... | .... | .... | .... | .... | .... | .... | .... | .... | .... |

# Romania   968

| National Accounts | | | | | | | *Millions of Lei* | | | | | | | |
|---|---|---|---|---|---|---|---|---|---|---|---|---|---|---|
| Househ.Cons.Expend.,incl.NPISHs.... | 96f | 170,773 | 200,872 | 237,455 | 278,359 | 333,794 | 311,372 | 334,357 | 353,465 | 372,897 | 394,473 | 418,090 | 443,156 |
| Government Consumption Expend... | 91f | 40,281 | 50,166 | 57,413 | 66,579 | 87,124 | 92,904 | 85,444 | 83,891 | 89,039 | 93,567 | 94,492 | .... |
| Gross Fixed Capital Formation......... | 93e | 53,850 | 68,527 | 88,272 | 125,645 | 164,279 | 122,442 | 129,422 | 145,193 | 154,280 | 148,208 | 146,559 | 161,338 |
| Changes in Inventories.................... | 93i | 4,701 | −1,240 | 2,916 | 3,213 | −3,383 | 4,696 | 4,477 | 4,428 | −1,795 | −4,125 | 6,912 | 13,736 |
| Exports of Goods and Services......... | 90c | 88,646 | 95,596 | 111,250 | 121,896 | 156,629 | 153,356 | 185,500 | 222,945 | 238,470 | 264,949 | 274,184 | 290,622 |
| Imports of Goods and Services (-)..... | 98c | 110,884 | 124,966 | 152,656 | 179,685 | 223,744 | 183,629 | 215,506 | 252,574 | 266,142 | 268,491 | 273,600 | 294,898 |
| Gross Domestic Product (GDP).......... | 99b | 247,368 | 288,955 | 344,651 | 416,007 | 514,700 | 501,139 | 523,693 | 557,348 | 586,750 | 628,581 | 666,637 | 710,267 |
| GDP Volume 2010 Prices................ | 99b.p | 443,699 | 462,252 | 499,484 | 533,647 | 579,503 | 538,371 | 533,881 | 539,684 | 543,012 | 561,375 | 576,937 | 600,509 |
| GDP Volume (2010=100)............... | 99bvp | 83.1 | 86.6 | 93.6 | 100.0 | 108.5 | 100.8 | 100.0 | 101.1 | 101.7 | 105.1 | 108.1 | 112.5 |
| GDP Deflator (2010=100)............... | 99bip | 56.8 | 63.7 | 70.3 | 79.5 | 90.5 | 94.9 | 100.0 | 105.3 | 110.2 | 114.2 | 117.8 | 120.6 |
| | | | | | | | *Millions: Midyear Estimates* | | | | | | | |
| Population............................... | 99z | 21.58 | 21.41 | 21.21 | 20.98 | 20.74 | 20.51 | 20.30 | 20.11 | 19.94 | 19.79 | 19.65 | 19.51 |

# Russian Federation  922

| | | 2004 | 2005 | 2006 | 2007 | 2008 | 2009 | 2010 | 2011 | 2012 | 2013 | 2014 | 2015 |
|---|---|---|---|---|---|---|---|---|---|---|---|---|---|
| **Exchange Rates** | | | | | *Rubles per SDR: End of Period* | | | | | | | | |
| Official Rate...................... | aa | 43.094 | 41.138 | 39.613 | 38.789 | 45.254 | 47.414 | 46.935 | 49.430 | 46.680 | 50.403 | 81.508 | 100.996 |
| | | | | *Rubles per US Dollar: End of Period (ae) Period Average (rf)* | | | | | | | | | |
| Official Rate...................... | ae | 27.749 | 28.783 | 26.331 | 24.546 | 29.380 | 30.244 | 30.477 | 32.196 | 30.373 | 32.729 | 56.258 | 72.883 |
| Official Rate...................... | rf | 28.814 | 28.284 | 27.191 | 25.581 | 24.853 | 31.740 | 30.368 | 29.382 | 30.840 | 31.837 | 38.378 | 60.938 |
| | | | | *Index Numbers (2010=100): Period Averages* | | | | | | | | | |
| Nominal Effective Exchange Rate..... | nec | 108.5 | 109.2 | 112.6 | 113.0 | 111.8 | 95.2 | 100.0 | 101.8 | 103.0 | 100.8 | 88.2 | 65.2 |
| CPI-Based Real Effect. Ex. Rate........ | rec | 72.5 | 79.4 | 87.3 | 92.0 | 98.3 | 91.7 | 100.0 | 104.9 | 106.5 | 108.4 | 99.2 | 81.9 |
| **Fund Position** | | | | | *Millions of SDRs: End of Period* | | | | | | | | |
| Quota............................. | 2f.s | 5,945.40 | 5,945.40 | 5,945.40 | 5,945.40 | 5,945.40 | 5,945.40 | 5,945.40 | 5,945.40 | 5,945.40 | 5,945.40 | 5,945.40 | 5,945.40 |
| SDR Holdings..................... | 1b.s | .55 | 3.95 | 4.75 | .49 | .51 | 5,675.19 | 5,677.78 | 5,683.80 | 5,686.85 | 5,688.86 | 5,691.27 | 5,692.06 |
| Reserve Position in the Fund........... | 1c.s | 1.83 | 137.04 | 188.33 | 236.64 | 683.92 | 1,229.23 | 1,229.45 | 2,644.72 | 3,075.11 | 2,853.88 | 2,345.04 | 1,847.51 |
| Total Fund Cred.&Loans Outstg....... | 2tl | 2,293.77 | — | — | — | — | — | — | — | — | — | — | — |
| SDR Allocations.................... | 1bd | — | — | — | — | — | 5,671.80 | 5,671.80 | 5,671.80 | 5,671.80 | 5,671.80 | 5,671.80 | 5,671.80 |
| **International Liquidity** | | | | *Millions of US Dollars Unless Otherwise Indicated: End of Period* | | | | | | | | | |
| Total Reserves minus Gold.............. | 1l.d | 120,808.8 | 175,891.4 | 295,567.6 | 466,750.4 | 411,749.6 | 416,648.9 | 443,585.8 | 453,948.2 | 486,576.8 | 469,602.7 | 339,370.0 | 319,835.2 |
| SDR Holdings................... | 1b.d | .9 | 5.6 | 7.1 | .8 | .8 | 8,896.9 | 8,744.0 | 8,726.2 | 8,740.2 | 8,760.8 | 8,245.6 | 7,887.7 |
| Reserve Position in the Fund.......... | 1c.d | 2.8 | 195.9 | 283.3 | 373.9 | 1,053.4 | 1,927.0 | 1,893.4 | 4,060.4 | 4,726.2 | 4,395.0 | 3,397.5 | 2,560.1 |
| Foreign Exchange........................ | 1d.d | 120,805.1 | 175,689.9 | 295,277.1 | 466,375.7 | 410,695.4 | 405,824.9 | 432,948.5 | 441,161.7 | 473,110.4 | 456,446.9 | 327,726.9 | 309,387.4 |
| Gold (Million Fine Troy Ounces)....... | 1ad | 12.441 | 12.438 | 12.908 | 14.479 | 16.705 | 20.867 | 25.355 | 28.388 | 30.793 | 33.283 | 38.844 | 45.479 |
| Gold (National Valuation)............... | 1and | 3,732.4 | † 6,349.0 | 8,164.4 | 12,011.9 | 14,533.4 | 22,797.7 | 35,788.1 | 44,696.7 | 51,039.3 | 39,989.9 | 46,089.0 | 48,562.6 |
| Central Bank: Other Liabs............... | 4..d | 4,182.3 | 10,381.3 | 3,007.9 | 48.9 | 44.2 | 2,409.7 | 29.3 | 26.2 | 3,043.5 | 1,876.7 | 25.0 | 2,153.8 |
| Other Depository Corps.: Assets....... | 7a.d | 25,521.9 | 38,019.6 | 62,553.4 | 93,525.7 | 159,351.1 | 160,367.9 | 169,328.2 | 210,497.5 | 239,323.5 | 267,947.3 | 243,590.3 | 224,401.7 |
| Other Depository Corps.: Liabs....... | 7b.d | 34,221.4 | 52,254.0 | 105,305.1 | 168,506.7 | 170,583.1 | 129,985.3 | 146,550.3 | 161,156.2 | 199,218.4 | 213,891.6 | 172,232.1 | 131,840.6 |
| Other Financial Corps.: Assets.......... | 7e.d | .... | 1,125.7 | 1,477.3 | 1,218.1 | 1,313.8 | 1,587.1 | 2,054.0 | 3,230.2 | 3,957.5 | 5,417.2 | 5,181.4 | .... |
| Other Financial Corps.: Liabs........... | 7f.d | .... | 788.7 | 854.5 | 880.0 | 633.1 | 760.5 | 849.8 | 1,292.1 | 1,303.8 | 1,158.0 | 1,494.9 | .... |
| **Central Bank** | | | | | *Billions of Rubles: End of Period* | | | | | | | | |
| Net Foreign Assets.......................... | 11n | 3,395.6 | 5,256.0 | 8,007.7 | 11,753.3 | 12,527.8 | 13,023.8 | 14,347.1 | 15,803.4 | 16,096.2 | 16,410.8 | 21,236.5 | 26,397.3 |
| Claims on Nonresidents................. | 11 | 3,610.5 | 5,554.8 | 8,086.9 | 11,754.5 | 12,529.1 | 13,365.6 | 14,614.2 | 16,084.6 | 16,453.4 | 16,758.1 | 21,700.2 | 27,127.1 |
| Liabilities to Nonresidents............. | 16c | 214.9 | 298.8 | 79.2 | 1.2 | 1.3 | 341.8 | 267.1 | 281.2 | 357.2 | 347.3 | 463.7 | 729.8 |
| Claims on Other Depository Corps.... | 12e | 182.8 | 32.5 | 47.8 | 134.4 | 3,951.9 | 1,990.3 | 666.8 | 1,561.6 | 3,067.7 | 4,815.4 | 9,840.3 | 6,109.3 |
| Net Claims on Central Government.. | 12an | −621.6 | −1,870.3 | −3,441.1 | −5,687.0 | −7,784.8 | −5,658.2 | −4,072.6 | −5,406.3 | −6,499.7 | −7,251.1 | −10,480.4 | −9,165.3 |
| Claims on Central Government....... | 12a | 426.7 | 276.1 | 247.1 | 354.5 | 354.7 | 358.6 | 347.7 | 333.3 | 370.7 | 364.6 | 368.4 | 517.7 |
| Liabilities to Central Government... | 16d | 1,048.3 | 2,146.4 | 3,688.2 | 6,041.5 | 8,139.5 | 6,016.8 | 4,420.3 | 5,739.6 | 6,870.4 | 7,615.7 | 10,848.8 | 9,683.0 |
| Claims on Other Sectors.................. | 12s | 1.2 | 1.2 | 1.2 | .9 | 116.3 | 169.0 | 115.5 | 355.6 | 348.7 | 313.5 | 654.5 | 1,146.3 |
| Claims on Other Financial Corps.... | 12g | .3 | .3 | .3 | .3 | 115.0 | 167.6 | 113.8 | 354.0 | 346.9 | 311.8 | 653.1 | 1,144.6 |
| Claims on State & Local Govts....... | 12b | — | — | — | — | — | — | — | — | — | — | — | — |
| Claims on Public Nonfin. Corps...... | 12c | — | — | — | — | — | — | — | — | — | — | — | — |
| Claims on Private Sector................ | 12d | .9 | .9 | .9 | .6 | 1.3 | 1.4 | 1.7 | 1.6 | 1.8 | 1.7 | 1.4 | 1.7 |
| Monetary Base............................. | 14 | 2,380.3 | 2,914.3 | 4,122.4 | 5,513.4 | 5,578.7 | 6,467.3 | 8,190.4 | 8,644.1 | 9,852.8 | 10,503.9 | 11,331.9 | 11,043.8 |
| Currency in Circulation................. | 14a | 1,669.9 | 2,195.4 | 3,062.1 | 4,118.6 | 4,372.1 | 4,622.9 | 5,785.2 | 6,895.8 | 7,667.7 | 8,307.5 | 8,840.5 | 8,522.2 |
| Liabs. to Other Depository Corps.... | 14c | 710.4 | 718.9 | 1,060.3 | 1,394.8 | 1,206.6 | 1,844.4 | 2,405.2 | 1,748.3 | 2,185.1 | 2,196.4 | 2,491.4 | 2,521.6 |
| Liabilities to Other Sectors............. | 14d | — | — | — | — | — | — | — | — | — | — | — | — |
| Other Liabs. to Other Dep. Corps..... | 14n | — | — | — | .1 | 816.0 | 170.7 | .7 | .1 | — | — | 378.2 | 6.8 |
| Dep. & Sec. Excl. f/Monetary Base.... | 14o | 35.7 | 43.0 | 58.5 | 75.9 | 270.4 | 161.2 | 142.8 | 141.3 | 42.1 | 108.6 | 54.3 | 75.5 |
| Deposits Included in Broad Money. | 15 | 35.7 | 43.0 | 58.5 | 75.9 | 270.4 | 161.2 | 142.8 | 141.3 | 42.1 | 108.6 | 54.3 | 75.5 |
| Sec.Ot.th.Shares Incl.in Brd. Money | 16a | — | — | — | — | — | — | — | — | — | — | — | — |
| Deposits Excl. from Broad Money... | 16b | — | — | — | — | — | — | — | — | — | — | — | — |
| Sec.Ot.th.Shares Excl.f/Brd.Money.. | 16s | — | — | — | — | — | — | — | — | — | — | — | — |
| Loans.................................... | 16l | — | — | — | — | — | — | — | — | — | — | — | — |
| Financial Derivatives....................... | 16m | — | — | — | — | — | — | — | — | — | — | — | — |
| Shares and Other Equity.................. | 17a | 188.0 | 210.4 | 84.2 | 462.1 | 1,902.4 | 2,099.1 | 2,358.9 | 3,235.4 | 2,724.5 | 3,151.9 | 9,054.1 | 9,072.2 |
| Other Items (Net)............................ | 17r | 355.1 | 251.8 | 350.5 | 150.4 | 243.7 | 626.5 | 364.1 | 293.3 | 393.6 | 524.2 | 432.3 | 4,289.3 |
| Memo Item: | | | | | | | | | | | | | |
| Total Assets..................... | 10ra | 4,328.1 | 5,994.0 | 8,505.1 | 12,470.8 | 17,303.2 | 16,134.8 | 16,072.9 | 18,642.9 | 20,539.1 | 22,549.0 | 32,862.6 | 35,342.4 |

# Russian Federation  922

| | | 2004 | 2005 | 2006 | 2007 | 2008 | 2009 | 2010 | 2011 | 2012 | 2013 | 2014 | 2015 |
|---|---|---|---|---|---|---|---|---|---|---|---|---|---|
| **Other Depository Corporations** | | *Billions of Rubles: End of Period* | | | | | | | | | | | |
| Net Foreign Assets | 21n | −241.4 | −409.7 | −1,125.7 | −1,840.5 | −330.0 | 918.9 | 694.2 | 1,588.6 | 1,218.1 | 1,769.2 | 4,014.5 | 6,746.1 |
| Claims on Nonresidents | 21 | 708.2 | 1,094.3 | 1,647.1 | 2,295.7 | 4,681.8 | 4,850.2 | 5,160.6 | 6,777.2 | 7,268.9 | 8,769.7 | 13,704.0 | 16,355.0 |
| Liabilities to Nonresidents | 26c | 949.6 | 1,504.0 | 2,772.8 | 4,136.2 | 5,011.8 | 3,931.3 | 4,466.4 | 5,188.6 | 6,050.8 | 7,000.5 | 9,689.5 | 9,608.9 |
| Claims on Central Bank | 20 | 847.2 | 906.0 | 1,339.6 | 1,817.8 | 2,593.3 | 2,599.2 | 3,127.5 | 2,705.6 | 3,423.0 | 3,516.4 | 4,538.6 | 3,812.0 |
| Currency | 20a | 135.2 | 186.1 | 276.9 | 416.3 | 577.3 | 584.9 | 722.4 | 957.3 | 1,237.6 | 1,321.9 | 1,669.1 | 1,283.0 |
| Reserve Deposits and Securities | 20b | 712.0 | 719.9 | 1,062.7 | 1,401.5 | 2,016.0 | 2,014.3 | 2,405.1 | 1,748.3 | 2,185.4 | 2,194.5 | 2,869.5 | 2,529.0 |
| Other Claims | 20n | — | — | — | — | — | — | — | — | — | — | — | — |
| Net Claims on Central Government | 22an | 615.3 | 478.8 | 476.2 | 560.4 | −82.3 | 484.2 | 753.9 | 941.1 | 1,298.2 | 2,244.4 | 2,140.8 | 3,363.1 |
| Claims on Central Government | 22a | 762.9 | 672.2 | 780.5 | 868.8 | 887.9 | 1,380.2 | 1,959.1 | 2,688.7 | 2,859.0 | 3,524.3 | 3,831.6 | 5,045.3 |
| Liabilities to Central Government | 26d | 147.6 | 193.4 | 304.3 | 308.4 | 970.2 | 896.0 | 1,205.2 | 1,747.6 | 1,560.8 | 1,279.9 | 1,690.8 | 1,682.2 |
| Claims on Other Sectors | 22s | 4,373.8 | 5,888.2 | 8,759.2 | 13,077.5 | 17,829.1 | 18,246.9 | 20,671.4 | 26,265.2 | 31,432.3 | 36,927.4 | 45,085.3 | 48,666.8 |
| Claims on Other Financial Corps | 22g | 67.4 | 93.2 | 209.5 | 226.7 | 383.4 | 396.8 | 535.2 | 823.5 | 1,142.0 | 1,435.0 | 2,197.4 | 2,545.3 |
| Claims on State & Local Govts | 22b | — | — | — | — | — | — | — | — | — | — | — | — |
| Claims on Public Nonfin. Corps | 22c | 166.9 | 194.1 | 221.9 | 289.3 | 294.8 | 287.0 | 299.3 | 376.6 | 385.2 | 442.9 | 538.4 | 578.2 |
| Claims on Private Sector | 22d | 4,139.5 | 5,600.9 | 8,327.8 | 12,561.5 | 17,150.9 | 17,563.1 | 19,836.9 | 25,065.1 | 29,905.1 | 35,049.5 | 42,349.5 | 45,543.3 |
| Liabilities to Central Bank | 26g | 181.1 | 29.0 | 44.3 | 50.7 | 3,867.9 | 1,906.4 | 583.5 | 1,477.7 | 3,006.2 | 4,744.6 | 9,543.3 | 5,816.7 |
| Transf.Dep.Included in Broad Money | 24 | 1,261.0 | 1,786.4 | 2,720.5 | 3,792.1 | 3,688.2 | 4,172.1 | 5,663.1 | 6,799.3 | 7,281.4 | 8,442.4 | 8,164.5 | 9,260.5 |
| Other Dep.Included in Broad Money | 25 | 2,457.3 | 3,374.7 | 4,562.6 | 6,665.9 | 8,523.3 | 10,724.5 | 12,922.5 | 15,875.5 | 18,472.8 | 21,735.3 | 27,641.9 | 34,947.8 |
| Sec.Ot.th.Shares Incl.in Brd. Money | 26a | — | — | — | — | — | — | — | — | — | — | — | — |
| Deposits Excl. from Broad Money | 26b | 35.8 | 30.8 | 21.4 | 40.5 | 307.0 | 336.4 | 289.0 | 533.3 | 573.1 | 853.8 | 1,989.3 | 2,595.5 |
| Sec.Ot.th.Shares Excl.f/Brd.Money | 26s | 482.9 | 527.4 | 723.7 | 701.4 | 657.2 | 617.9 | 643.1 | 806.5 | 1,120.0 | 1,411.2 | 1,610.1 | 1,869.9 |
| Loans | 26l | — | — | — | — | — | — | — | — | — | — | — | — |
| Financial Derivatives | 26m | — | — | — | — | — | — | — | — | — | — | — | — |
| Insurance Technical Reserves | 26r | — | — | — | — | — | — | — | — | — | — | — | — |
| Shares and Other Equity | 27a | 839.9 | 1,163.4 | 1,574.6 | 2,739.9 | 3,255.8 | 4,120.3 | 4,609.8 | 5,186.3 | 6,028.5 | 6,764.3 | 6,600.7 | 6,842.6 |
| Other Items (Net) | 27r | 337.0 | −48.3 | −197.8 | −375.3 | −289.4 | 371.6 | 535.9 | 821.9 | 889.5 | 505.6 | 229.3 | 1,255.0 |
| Memo Item: | | | | | | | | | | | | | |
| Total Assets | 20ra | .... | .... | .... | .... | .... | .... | 33,181.4 | 41,044.7 | 48,166.7 | 56,790.6 | 75,436.2 | 82,260.8 |
| **Depository Corporations** | | *Billions of Rubles: End of Period* | | | | | | | | | | | |
| Net Foreign Assets | 31n | 3,154.2 | 4,846.3 | 6,882.0 | 9,912.8 | 12,197.8 | 13,942.7 | 15,041.3 | 17,392.0 | 17,314.3 | 18,180.0 | 25,251.0 | 33,143.4 |
| Claims on Nonresidents | 31 | 4,318.7 | 6,649.1 | 9,734.0 | 14,050.2 | 17,210.9 | 18,215.8 | 19,774.8 | 22,861.8 | 23,722.3 | 25,527.8 | 35,404.2 | 43,482.1 |
| Liabilities to Nonresidents | 36c | 1,164.5 | 1,802.8 | 2,852.0 | 4,137.4 | 5,013.1 | 4,273.1 | 4,733.5 | 5,469.8 | 6,408.0 | 7,347.8 | 10,153.2 | 10,338.7 |
| Domestic Claims | 32 | 4,368.7 | 4,497.9 | 5,795.5 | 7,951.8 | 10,078.3 | 13,241.9 | 17,468.2 | 22,155.6 | 26,579.5 | 32,234.2 | 37,400.2 | 44,010.9 |
| Net Claims on Central Government | 32an | −6.3 | −1,391.5 | −2,964.9 | −5,126.6 | −7,867.1 | −5,174.0 | −3,318.7 | −4,465.2 | −5,201.5 | −5,006.7 | −8,339.6 | −5,802.2 |
| Claims on Central Government | 32a | 1,189.6 | 948.3 | 1,027.6 | 1,223.3 | 1,242.6 | 1,738.8 | 2,306.8 | 3,022.0 | 3,229.7 | 3,888.9 | 4,200.0 | 5,563.0 |
| Liabilities to Central Government | 36d | 1,195.9 | 2,339.8 | 3,992.5 | 6,349.9 | 9,109.7 | 6,912.8 | 5,625.5 | 7,487.2 | 8,431.2 | 8,895.6 | 12,539.6 | 11,365.2 |
| Claims on Other Sectors | 32s | 4,375.0 | 5,889.4 | 8,760.4 | 13,078.4 | 17,945.4 | 18,415.9 | 20,786.9 | 26,620.8 | 31,781.0 | 37,240.9 | 45,739.8 | 49,813.1 |
| Claims on Other Financial Corps | 32g | 67.7 | 93.5 | 209.8 | 227.0 | 498.4 | 564.4 | 649.0 | 1,177.5 | 1,488.9 | 1,746.8 | 2,850.5 | 3,689.9 |
| Claims on State & Local Govts | 32b | — | — | — | — | — | — | — | — | — | — | — | — |
| Claims on Public Nonfin. Corps | 32c | 166.9 | 194.1 | 221.9 | 289.3 | 294.8 | 287.0 | 299.3 | 376.6 | 385.2 | 442.9 | 538.4 | 578.2 |
| Claims on Private Sector | 32d | 4,140.4 | 5,601.8 | 8,328.7 | 12,562.1 | 17,152.2 | 17,564.5 | 19,838.6 | 25,066.7 | 29,906.9 | 35,051.2 | 42,350.9 | 45,545.0 |
| Broad Money Liabilities | 35l | 5,288.7 | 7,213.4 | 10,126.8 | 14,236.2 | 16,276.7 | 19,095.8 | 23,791.2 | 28,754.6 | 32,226.4 | 37,271.9 | 43,032.1 | 51,523.1 |
| Currency Outside Depository Corps | 34a | 1,534.7 | 2,009.3 | 2,785.2 | 3,702.3 | 3,794.8 | 4,038.0 | 5,062.8 | 5,938.5 | 6,430.1 | 6,985.6 | 7,171.4 | 7,239.2 |
| Transferable Deposits | 34 | 1,296.7 | 1,829.4 | 2,779.0 | 3,868.0 | 3,858.6 | 4,287.6 | 5,797.1 | 6,918.9 | 7,323.5 | 8,551.0 | 8,217.3 | 9,336.1 |
| Other Deposits | 35 | 2,457.3 | 3,374.7 | 4,562.6 | 6,665.9 | 8,623.3 | 10,770.2 | 12,931.3 | 15,897.2 | 18,472.8 | 21,735.3 | 27,643.4 | 34,947.8 |
| Securities Other than Shares | 36a | — | — | — | — | — | — | — | — | — | — | — | — |
| Deposits Excl. from Broad Money | 36b | 35.8 | 30.8 | 21.4 | 40.5 | 307.0 | 336.4 | 289.0 | 533.3 | 573.1 | 853.8 | 1,989.3 | 2,595.5 |
| Sec.Ot.th.Shares Excl.f/Brd.Money | 36s | 482.9 | 527.4 | 723.7 | 701.4 | 657.2 | 617.9 | 643.1 | 806.5 | 1,120.0 | 1,411.2 | 1,610.1 | 1,869.9 |
| Loans | 36l | — | — | — | — | — | — | — | — | — | — | — | — |
| Financial Derivatives | 36m | — | — | — | — | — | — | — | — | — | — | — | — |
| Insurance Technical Reserves | 36r | — | — | — | — | — | — | — | — | — | — | — | — |
| Shares and Other Equity | 37a | 1,027.9 | 1,373.8 | 1,658.8 | 3,202.0 | 5,158.2 | 6,219.4 | 6,968.7 | 8,421.7 | 8,753.0 | 9,916.2 | 15,654.8 | 15,914.8 |
| Other Items (Net) | 37r | 688.8 | 199.0 | 146.8 | −315.2 | −123.1 | 915.0 | 817.5 | 1,031.4 | 1,221.3 | 960.9 | 364.7 | 5,251.1 |
| Broad Money Liabs., Seasonally Adj. | 35l.b | 5,095.6 | 6,943.2 | 9,738.5 | 13,677.4 | 15,623.7 | 18,313.2 | 22,798.1 | 27,533.2 | 30,844.0 | 35,662.1 | 41,173.7 | 49,302.5 |
| **Other Financial Corporations** | | *Billions of Rubles: End of Period* | | | | | | | | | | | |
| Net Foreign Assets | 41n | .... | 9.7 | 16.4 | 8.3 | 20.0 | 25.0 | 36.7 | 62.4 | 80.6 | 139.4 | 207.4 | .... |
| Claims on Nonresidents | 41 | .... | 32.4 | 38.9 | 29.9 | 38.6 | 48.0 | 62.6 | 104.0 | 120.2 | 177.3 | 291.5 | .... |
| Liabilities to Nonresidents | 46c | .... | 22.7 | 22.5 | 21.6 | 18.6 | 23.0 | 25.9 | 41.6 | 39.6 | 37.9 | 84.1 | .... |
| Claims on Depository Corporations | 40 | .... | 243.6 | 333.0 | 466.7 | 491.7 | 551.7 | 601.9 | 757.9 | 1,462.3 | 1,791.1 | 2,465.8 | .... |
| Net Claims on Central Government | 42an | .... | 33.5 | 52.9 | 51.9 | 43.8 | 63.5 | 77.1 | 69.3 | 257.1 | 314.9 | 1,251.7 | .... |
| Claims on Central Government | 42a | .... | 40.3 | 59.9 | 57.7 | 50.4 | 71.1 | 82.1 | 122.0 | 277.2 | 361.4 | 1,306.7 | .... |
| Liabilities to Central Government | 46d | .... | 6.8 | 7.0 | 5.8 | 6.6 | 7.6 | 5.0 | 52.7 | 20.1 | 46.5 | 55.0 | .... |
| Claims on Other Sectors | 42s | .... | 342.6 | 415.3 | 341.1 | 261.4 | 346.0 | 445.2 | 497.8 | 636.9 | 998.4 | 964.3 | .... |
| Claims on State & Local Govts | 42b | .... | — | — | — | — | — | — | — | — | — | — | .... |
| Claims on Public Nonfin. Corps | 42c | .... | — | — | — | — | — | — | — | — | — | — | .... |
| Claims on Private Sector | 42d | .... | 342.6 | 415.3 | 341.1 | 261.4 | 346.0 | 445.2 | 497.8 | 636.9 | 998.4 | 964.3 | .... |
| Deposits | 46b | .... | | | | | | | | | | | |
| Securities Other than Shares | 46s | .... | 2.1 | 2.1 | 5.6 | 5.9 | 4.5 | 18.3 | .6 | 13.6 | 16.5 | 11.2 | .... |
| Loans | 46l | .... | 5.8 | 6.1 | 8.8 | 11.8 | 22.3 | 24.5 | 25.5 | 352.4 | 316.8 | 657.7 | .... |
| Financial Derivatives | 46m | .... | | | | | | | | | | | .... |
| Insurance Technical Reserves | 46r | .... | 409.7 | 565.9 | 755.6 | 871.6 | 984.6 | 1,164.9 | 1,501.8 | 2,114.4 | 2,729.4 | 2,889.1 | .... |
| Shares and Other Equity | 47a | .... | 266.8 | 319.1 | 306.4 | 287.7 | 345.6 | 359.9 | 384.0 | 615.8 | 658.1 | 1,684.6 | .... |
| Other Items (Net) | 47r | .... | −55.0 | −75.7 | −208.4 | −360.1 | −370.8 | −406.7 | −524.7 | −659.3 | −477.0 | −353.4 | .... |

# Russian Federation   922

| | | 2004 | 2005 | 2006 | 2007 | 2008 | 2009 | 2010 | 2011 | 2012 | 2013 | 2014 | 2015 |
|---|---|---|---|---|---|---|---|---|---|---|---|---|---|
| **Monetary Aggregates** | | *Billions of Rubles: End of Period* | | | | | | | | | | | |
| Broad Money | 59m | 5,298.7 | 7,221.1 | 10,126.8 | 14,236.1 | 16,276.7 | 19,095.8 | 23,791.2 | 28,754.6 | 32,226.4 | 37,271.9 | 43,032.1 | 51,523.0 |
| o/w:Currency Issued by Cent.Govt | 59m.a | — | — | — | — | — | — | — | — | — | — | — | — |
| o/w: Dep.in Nonfin. Corporations. | 59m.b | — | — | — | — | — | — | — | — | — | — | — | — |
| o/w:Secs. Issued by Central Govt.. | 59m.c | — | — | — | — | — | — | — | — | — | — | — | — |
| Money (National Definitions) | | | | | | | | | | | | | |
| Broad Monetary Base | 19maa | 2,380.3 | 2,914.2 | 4,122.4 | 5,513.3 | 5,578.7 | 6,467.3 | 8,190.3 | 8,644.1 | 9,852.8 | 10,503.9 | 11,332.0 | 11,043.8 |
| M0 | 19mc | 1,534.8 | 2,009.2 | 2,785.2 | 3,702.2 | 3,794.8 | 4,038.1 | 5,062.7 | 5,938.6 | 6,430.1 | 6,985.6 | 7,171.5 | 7,239.1 |
| M1 | 59ma | .... | .... | .... | 7,570.2 | 7,653.4 | 8,325.6 | 10,859.9 | 12,857.4 | 13,753.6 | 15,536.6 | 15,388.8 | 16,575.2 |
| M2 | 59mb | 4,363.3 | 6,044.7 | 8,970.7 | 12,869.0 | 12,975.9 | 15,267.6 | 20,011.9 | 24,483.1 | 27,405.4 | 31,404.7 | 32,110.5 | 35,809.2 |
| Broad Money Liabilities | 59mca | 5,298.6 | 7,222.8 | 10,126.6 | 14,236.1 | 16,276.7 | 19,095.8 | 23,791.2 | 28,754.6 | 32,226.4 | 37,271.9 | 43,032.1 | 51,523.0 |
| **Interest Rates** | | *Percent Per Annum* | | | | | | | | | | | |
| Central Bank Policy Rate (EOP) | 60 | .... | .... | .... | .... | .... | .... | .... | 5.25 | 5.50 | 5.50 | 17.00 | 11.00 |
| Refinancing Rate (End of Period) | 60.b | 13.00 | 12.00 | 11.00 | 10.00 | 13.00 | 8.75 | 7.75 | 8.00 | 8.25 | 8.25 | 8.25 | 8.25 |
| Money Market Rate | 60b | 3.33 | 2.68 | 3.43 | 4.43 | 5.48 | 7.78 | 3.07 | 3.93 | 5.50 | 6.10 | 8.52 | 12.82 |
| Deposit Rate | 60l | 3.79 | 3.99 | 4.08 | 5.14 | 5.76 | 8.58 | 6.01 | 4.44 | 5.53 | 5.59 | 6.04 | 9.20 |
| Lending Rate | 60p | 11.44 | 10.68 | 10.43 | 10.03 | 12.23 | 15.31 | 10.82 | 8.46 | 9.10 | 9.47 | 11.14 | 15.72 |
| Government Bond Yield | 61 | .... | 7.84 | 6.74 | 6.52 | 7.53 | 10.06 | 7.57 | 7.71 | .... | .... | .... | .... |
| **Prices, Production, Labor** | | *Index Numbers (2010=100): Period Averages* | | | | | | | | | | | |
| Share Prices | 62 | 40.39 | 50.41 | 96.83 | 121.52 | 99.67 | 71.77 | 100.00 | 112.13 | 102.81 | 101.90 | 101.13 | 119.16 |
| Russian Trading System | 62a | 41.40 | 52.75 | 101.96 | 131.19 | 112.32 | 66.06 | 100.00 | 116.32 | 98.27 | 94.66 | 79.04 | 57.98 |
| | | *Percent Change over Previous Period Unless Otherwise Indicated* | | | | | | | | | | | |
| Producer Prices | 63.xx | 23.36 | 20.57 | 12.40 | 14.10 | 21.40 | −7.19 | 12.22 | 17.72 | 6.79 | 3.31 | 6.07 | 12.39 |
| Consumer Prices (2010=100) | 64 | 54.5 | 61.4 | 67.4 | 73.5 | 83.8 | 93.6 | 100.0 | 108.4 | 113.9 | 121.7 | 131.2 | 151.5 |
| Wages | 65.xx | 13.2 | 22.0 | 18.4 | 24.6 | 23.4 | 6.1 | 14.4 | 13.7 | 12.1 | 9.8 | 9.1 | 7.8 |
| | | *Index Numbers (2010=100): Period Averages* | | | | | | | | | | | |
| Industrial Production | 66 | 87.1 | 91.5 | 97.2 | 103.8 | 104.4 | 93.2 | 100.0 | 105.0 | 108.5 | 109.0 | 110.8 | 107.2 |
| Industrial Employment | 67 | 111.9 | 116.1 | 114.6 | 114.5 | 113.0 | 103.1 | 100.0 | 99.9 | 98.5 | 97.6 | 95.2 | 93.6 |
| | | *Number in Thousands: Period Averages* | | | | | | | | | | | |
| Labor Force | 67d | 72,950 | 73,432 | 74,146 | 75,133 | † 75,725 | 75,708 | 75,442 | 75,742 | 75,683 | 75,533 | 75,433 | 76,583 |
| Employment | 67e | 67,212 | 68,169 | 68,855 | 70,550 | † 70,908 | 69,375 | 69,792 | 70,725 | 71,542 | 71,392 | 71,542 | 72,317 |
| Unemployment | 67c | 5,927 | 5,600 | 5,332 | 4,600 | † 4,808 | 6,358 | 5,617 | 5,025 | 4,133 | 4,142 | 3,892 | 4,267 |
| Unemployment Rate (%) | 67r | 8.1 | 7.6 | 7.2 | 6.1 | † 6.2 | 8.4 | 7.5 | 6.6 | 5.5 | 5.5 | 5.2 | 5.6 |
| **Intl. Transactions & Positions** | | *Millions of US Dollars* | | | | | | | | | | | |
| Exports | 70..d | 183,207 | 243,799 | 297,481 | 346,530 | 466,298 | 297,155 | 392,674 | 515,409 | 527,434 | 523,275 | 497,763 | 340,349 |
| Imports, c.i.f. | 71..d | 107,120 | 137,977 | 179,506 | 245,392 | 317,540 | 202,316 | 270,248 | 350,411 | 369,348 | 375,471 | 338,829 | 213,495 |
| Imports, f.o.b. | 71.vd | 97,382 | 125,434 | 163,187 | 223,084 | 288,673 | 183,924 | 245,680 | 318,555 | 335,771 | 341,337 | 308,026 | 194,086 |
| **Balance of Payments** | | *Millions of US Dollars* | | | | | | | | | | | |
| A. Current Account* | 109bx | 58,559.9 | 84,388.7 | 92,315.6 | 72,193.0 | 103,935.4 | 50,383.7 | 67,452.2 | 97,273.9 | 71,282.2 | 33,428.2 | 58,319.2 | 69,564.2 |
| Goods, credit (exports) | 1a9cx | 177,860.6 | 240,024.1 | 297,481.4 | 346,530.5 | 466,298.0 | 297,154.6 | 392,674.2 | 515,409.1 | 527,434.0 | 521,835.5 | 497,762.7 | 341,467.2 |
| Goods, debit (imports) | 1a9dx | 94,244.4 | 123,839.0 | 163,187.3 | 223,083.5 | 288,672.6 | 183,924.1 | 245,679.7 | 318,554.8 | 335,771.2 | 341,269.2 | 308,025.6 | 192,954.5 |
| Balance on goods | 1a9bx | 83,616.2 | 116,185.1 | 134,294.1 | 123,447.0 | 177,625.4 | 113,230.5 | 146,994.5 | 196,854.3 | 191,662.8 | 180,566.3 | 189,737.0 | 148,512.7 |
| Services, credit (exports) | 1b9cx | 22,969.3 | 28,845.4 | 35,718.5 | 43,860.1 | 57,136.0 | 45,796.5 | 49,159.0 | 58,039.1 | 62,340.0 | 70,122.5 | 65,744.5 | 51,790.7 |
| Services, debit (imports) | 1b9dx | 34,253.1 | 40,470.9 | 46,273.1 | 60,577.9 | 77,555.5 | 63,396.8 | 75,278.7 | 91,495.3 | 108,926.5 | 128,381.9 | 121,022.2 | 88,401.6 |
| Balance on Goods & Services | 1z9bx | 72,332.4 | 104,559.6 | 123,739.6 | 106,729.1 | 157,205.9 | 95,630.3 | 120,874.8 | 163,398.1 | 145,076.2 | 122,306.9 | 134,459.3 | 111,901.8 |
| Primary income: credit | 1c9cx | 11,997.9 | 17,481.1 | 29,770.4 | 45,583.9 | 61,819.8 | 33,399.5 | 38,063.7 | 42,687.0 | 47,758.5 | 42,176.6 | 47,172.7 | 37,180.6 |
| Primary income: debit | 1c9dx | 24,769.0 | 36,007.4 | 58,573.7 | 74,412.4 | 108,302.3 | 73,138.9 | 85,168.2 | 103,086.5 | 115,419.3 | 121,780.9 | 115,134.9 | 73,893.9 |
| Balance on gds, serv. & prim. inc. | 1y9bx | 59,561.2 | 86,033.2 | 94,936.2 | 77,900.6 | 110,723.4 | 55,890.8 | 73,770.2 | 102,998.6 | 77,415.4 | 42,702.6 | 66,497.2 | 75,188.5 |
| Secondary income: credit | 1d9ca | 3,315.5 | 3,883.8 | 5,318.5 | 6,220.5 | 7,345.4 | 6,369.1 | 7,258.4 | 13,768.3 | 16,458.6 | 17,332.3 | 17,643.1 | 10,118.3 |
| Secondary income: debit | 1d9da | 4,316.9 | 5,528.3 | 7,939.1 | 11,928.1 | 14,133.4 | 11,876.3 | 13,576.5 | 19,493.0 | 22,591.8 | 26,606.7 | 25,821.1 | 15,742.6 |
| B. Capital Account* | 209ba | −1,002.5 | −12,387.4 | 290.7 | −10,640.7 | −103.8 | −12,466.2 | −41.1 | 129.7 | −5,217.7 | −394.9 | −42,005.1 | −333.1 |
| Capital account: credit | 209ca | 501.4 | 99.0 | 370.8 | 188.4 | 260.4 | 496.7 | 370.3 | 479.0 | 622.3 | 530.0 | 547.7 | 325.7 |
| Capital account: debit | 209da | 1,503.9 | 12,486.4 | 80.1 | 10,829.2 | 364.2 | 12,962.9 | 411.4 | 349.3 | 5,840.0 | 925.0 | 42,552.7 | 658.8 |
| Balance on current & capital acct. | 129ba | 57,557.4 | 72,001.3 | 92,606.2 | 61,552.3 | 103,831.6 | 37,917.5 | 67,411.1 | 97,403.6 | 66,064.5 | 33,033.3 | 16,314.1 | 69,231.1 |
| C. Financial Account* | 309na | 5,177.5 | 2,047.5 | −3,611.7 | −97,107.8 | 139,617.0 | 28,157.2 | 21,528.7 | 76,118.1 | 25,674.9 | 46,212.9 | 131,820.8 | 72,554.1 |
| Direct investment: assets | 3a9aa | 13,782.0 | 17,879.7 | 29,993.2 | 44,801.2 | 55,662.6 | 43,280.5 | 52,616.3 | 66,850.8 | 48,822.4 | 86,506.5 | 57,082.2 | 21,571.8 |
| Equity & investment fund shares.. | 3aaaa | 11,651.3 | 15,927.2 | 28,222.8 | 33,389.2 | 54,067.2 | 34,307.8 | 34,940.6 | 39,069.5 | 46,743.6 | 90,915.3 | 37,117.2 | 13,901.2 |
| Debt instruments | 3abaa | 2,130.7 | 1,952.5 | 1,770.4 | 11,412.1 | 1,595.4 | 8,972.7 | 17,675.6 | 27,781.3 | 2,078.8 | −4,408.7 | 19,965.0 | 7,670.6 |
| Direct investment: liabilities | 3a9la | 15,403.0 | 15,508.1 | 37,594.8 | 55,873.7 | 74,782.9 | 36,583.1 | 43,167.8 | 55,083.6 | 50,587.6 | 69,218.9 | 22,031.3 | 4,838.6 |
| Equity & investment fund shares . | 3aala | 13,976.2 | 13,031.7 | 29,601.9 | 49,660.7 | 68,841.9 | 23,161.4 | 28,683.8 | 33,157.4 | 23,510.0 | 32,357.5 | 23,098.9 | 10,140.7 |
| Debt instruments | 3abla | 1,426.8 | 2,476.4 | 7,992.9 | 6,212.9 | 5,941.1 | 13,421.7 | 14,484.0 | 21,926.2 | 27,077.5 | 36,861.4 | −1,067.6 | −5,302.1 |
| Portfolio investment: assets | 3b9aa | 3,819.8 | 10,666.5 | −6,276.1 | 10,536.4 | 7,774.4 | 10,598.9 | 3,443.5 | 9,837.3 | 2,280.8 | 11,759.1 | 16,740.1 | 13,968.1 |
| Equity & investment fund shares | 3baaa | 25.3 | 733.3 | −121.1 | 3,474.4 | 129.5 | 741.1 | 890.5 | 743.4 | 769.0 | −918.9 | 1,019.5 | −648.1 |
| Debt securities | 3bbaa | 3,794.5 | 9,933.2 | −6,155.1 | 7,062.0 | 7,644.9 | 9,857.7 | 2,553.0 | 9,093.9 | 1,511.8 | 12,678.0 | 15,720.6 | 14,616.2 |
| Portfolio investment: liabilities | 3b9la | 4,428.6 | −776.1 | 10,209.6 | 15,392.9 | −27,916.4 | 8,716.5 | 1,948.3 | −5,440.1 | 19,311.8 | 747.6 | −23,203.3 | −12,672.5 |
| Equity & investment fund shares . | 3bala | 255.7 | −163.3 | 7,234.5 | 18,399.2 | −15,383.1 | 3,762.7 | −4,885.3 | −9,795.7 | 1,162.4 | −7,625.0 | −12,966.3 | −5,542.8 |
| Debt securities | 3bbla | 4,172.8 | −612.8 | 2,975.2 | −3,006.3 | −12,533.3 | 4,953.7 | 6,833.6 | 4,355.6 | 18,149.4 | 8,372.6 | −10,237.0 | −7,129.7 |
| Fin. der.& empl.stk.ops.(ESOs): net | 3c9na | 99.6 | 233.0 | 99.4 | −331.7 | 1,370.0 | 3,243.8 | 1,841.5 | 1,394.0 | 1,356.2 | 346.0 | 5,312.5 | 7,431.8 |
| Fin. der. & ESOs.: assets | 3c9aa | −757.6 | −858.4 | −1,242.4 | −2,761.6 | −9,116.8 | −9,890.0 | −8,840.1 | −16,438.3 | −16,695.6 | −8,488.4 | −16,568.9 | −21,222.1 |
| Fin. der. & ESOs.: liabilities | 3c9la | −857.2 | −1,091.3 | −1,341.8 | −2,429.9 | −10,486.7 | −13,133.8 | −10,681.6 | −17,832.3 | −18,051.8 | −8,834.3 | −21,881.3 | −28,653.9 |
| Other investment: assets | 3d9aa | 26,714.1 | 34,005.4 | 50,995.1 | 59,930.1 | 185,775.3 | −9,250.3 | 19,235.2 | 83,370.5 | 83,703.6 | 80,824.5 | 24,781.4 | −15,141.5 |
| Other equity | 3daaa | 245.6 | 34.8 | 225.1 | 66.0 | 665.6 | 38.1 | 310.7 | 1,254.7 | 199.3 | 706.0 | 214.2 | 1,011.6 |
| Debt instruments | 3dzaa | 26,468.5 | 33,970.6 | 50,770.0 | 59,864.1 | 185,109.7 | −9,288.4 | 18,924.4 | 82,115.8 | 83,504.3 | 80,118.5 | 24,567.2 | −16,153.1 |
| Other investment: liabilities | 3d9la | 19,406.5 | 46,005.0 | 30,618.8 | 140,777.2 | 64,098.8 | −25,583.8 | 10,491.6 | 35,691.0 | 40,588.7 | 63,256.7 | −26,732.7 | −36,890.1 |
| Other equity | 3dala | | | | | | | | | 14.9 | −2.8 | −1.9 | 25.2 |
| Debt instruments | 3dzla | 19,406.5 | 46,005.0 | 30,618.8 | 140,777.2 | 64,098.8 | −25,583.8 | 10,491.6 | 35,691.0 | 40,573.7 | 63,259.5 | −26,730.8 | −36,915.3 |
| Curr.+ cap.− finan. acct. balance.. | 4y9na | 52,379.9 | 69,953.8 | 96,217.9 | 158,660.0 | −35,785.4 | 9,760.3 | 45,882.4 | 21,285.6 | 40,389.6 | −13,179.6 | −115,506.7 | −3,323.1 |
| D. Net Errors and Omissions | 409na | −5,489.7 | −4,986.1 | 11,247.6 | −9,732.3 | −3,133.4 | −6,397.2 | −9,133.2 | −8,647.4 | −10,370.0 | −8,898.5 | 7,960.8 | 5,025.1 |
| E. Reserves and Related Items | 4z9na | 46,890.2 | 64,967.7 | 107,465.6 | 148,927.7 | −38,918.8 | 3,363.1 | 36,749.2 | 12,638.2 | 30,019.6 | −22,078.1 | −107,545.9 | 1,702.0 |
| Reserve assets | 3e9aa | 45,235.6 | 61,461.3 | 107,465.6 | 148,927.7 | −38,918.8 | 3,363.1 | 36,749.2 | 12,638.2 | 30,019.6 | −22,078.1 | −107,545.9 | 1,702.0 |
| Credit and loans from the IMF | 3dcla | −1,654.6 | −3,506.4 | — | — | — | — | — | — | — | — | — | — |
| Exceptional financing | 409la | .... | .... | .... | .... | .... | .... | .... | .... | .... | .... | .... | .... |

*Excludes components in group E

# Russian Federation   922

| International Investment Position | | 2004 | 2005 | 2006 | 2007 | 2008 | 2009 | 2010 | 2011 | 2012 | 2013 | 2014 | 2015 |
|---|---|---|---|---|---|---|---|---|---|---|---|---|---|
| | | | | | | | *Millions of US Dollars* | | | | | | |
| Assets | 809aa | † 411,655.5 | 515,912.7 | 754,952.5 | 1,093,383.8 | 1,006,156.4 | 1,087,569.1 | 1,171,104.7 | 1,244,677.9 | 1,380,697.9 | 1,474,595.8 | 1,249,211.8 | 1,145,787.8 |
| Direct investment | 8a9aa | † 107,087.1 | 140,775.2 | 234,631.6 | 365,797.4 | 198,437.0 | 298,357.0 | 361,120.7 | 361,750.0 | 409,567.1 | 479,501.1 | 384,688.7 | 336,276.4 |
| Equity & investment fund shares | 8aaaa | † 100,729.2 | 139,045.7 | 231,122.8 | 350,854.2 | 182,061.4 | 272,608.6 | 314,334.1 | 287,228.6 | 327,503.5 | 400,396.8 | 296,932.6 | 247,832.7 |
| Debt instruments | 8abaa | † 6,357.9 | 1,729.5 | 3,508.8 | 14,943.2 | 16,375.7 | 25,748.5 | 46,786.5 | 74,521.5 | 82,063.6 | 79,104.3 | 87,756.0 | 88,443.7 |
| Portfolio investment | 8b9aa | † 7,920.0 | 17,774.7 | 12,248.1 | 19,935.5 | 24,221.4 | 38,155.8 | 36,656.3 | 42,434.9 | 48,299.8 | 53,743.4 | 56,629.4 | 70,727.0 |
| Equity & investment fund shares | 8baaa | † 127.1 | 333.7 | 489.7 | 4,123.9 | 2,855.4 | 2,532.1 | 3,985.3 | 4,518.5 | 5,271.4 | 3,232.0 | 4,432.9 | 3,256.9 |
| Debt securities | 8bbaa | † 7,792.9 | 17,441.0 | 11,758.4 | 15,811.6 | 21,366.0 | 35,623.7 | 32,671.0 | 37,916.4 | 43,028.4 | 50,511.5 | 52,196.6 | 67,470.1 |
| Fin. der.(oth.than reserves) & ESOs | 8c9aa | † 153.2 | 50.9 | 222.1 | 1,423.4 | 5,302.0 | 2,240.2 | 1,639.3 | 5,674.9 | 5,553.5 | 5,931.9 | 17,564.8 | 11,145.7 |
| Other investment | 8d9aa | † 171,954.0 | 175,071.5 | 204,118.9 | 227,465.2 | 351,913.0 | 309,369.6 | 292,314.5 | 336,173.1 | 379,661.4 | 425,826.8 | 404,870.0 | 359,240.9 |
| Other equity | 8daaa | † 619.5 | 622.0 | 856.0 | 941.0 | 1,596.3 | 1,642.4 | 1,945.8 | 3,198.4 | 3,425.5 | 4,200.8 | 4,370.7 | 5,349.4 |
| Debt instruments | 8dzaa | † 171,334.4 | 174,449.5 | 203,262.9 | 226,524.2 | 350,316.7 | 307,727.2 | 290,368.6 | 332,974.7 | 376,235.9 | 421,626.0 | 400,499.3 | 353,891.5 |
| Reserve assets | 8e9aa | † 124,541.2 | 182,240.3 | 303,731.9 | 478,762.4 | 426,283.0 | 439,446.6 | 479,373.9 | 498,644.9 | 537,616.1 | 509,592.6 | 385,458.9 | 368,397.8 |
| Liabilities | 809la | † 416,452.7 | 547,794.2 | 769,807.2 | 1,242,051.5 | 755,887.7 | 984,794.9 | 1,152,738.7 | 1,095,447.1 | 1,238,366.6 | 1,342,860.2 | 958,898.1 | 831,920.4 |
| Direct investment | 8a9la | † 121,513.6 | 180,171.0 | 265,652.7 | 490,595.1 | 214,049.0 | 377,447.1 | 488,992.9 | 454,949.2 | 514,925.6 | 565,654.2 | 365,439.0 | 342,942.9 |
| Equity & investment fund shares | 8aala | † 111,269.1 | 167,740.1 | 244,386.4 | 464,243.9 | 183,335.0 | 331,680.5 | 425,800.7 | 370,561.9 | 394,699.9 | 409,855.9 | 230,091.6 | 204,783.9 |
| Debt instruments | 8abla | † 10,244.6 | 12,430.9 | 21,266.3 | 26,351.3 | 30,714.0 | 45,766.6 | 63,192.2 | 84,387.3 | 120,225.7 | 155,798.3 | 135,347.4 | 138,159.0 |
| Portfolio investment | 8b9la | † 130,698.9 | 166,178.9 | 265,341.5 | 366,660.2 | 111,805.7 | 217,125.2 | 277,038.7 | 225,062.1 | 270,724.5 | 273,736.5 | 156,424.3 | 140,454.2 |
| Equity & investment fund shares | 8bala | † 89,202.7 | 118,160.9 | 207,480.4 | 308,005.3 | 83,786.8 | 177,783.1 | 231,385.7 | 176,020.2 | 194,461.2 | 195,094.1 | 111,198.9 | 101,854.8 |
| Debt securities | 8bbla | † 41,496.1 | 48,018.0 | 57,861.1 | 58,654.9 | 28,019.0 | 39,342.0 | 45,653.0 | 49,042.0 | 76,263.3 | 78,642.4 | 45,225.4 | 38,599.4 |
| Fin. der.(oth.than reserves) & ESOs | 8c9la | † 188.6 | 52.1 | 177.7 | 874.9 | 10,396.2 | 5,204.8 | 2,840.3 | 5,905.1 | 4,284.9 | 4,354.5 | 21,529.8 | 9,244.9 |
| Other investment | 8d9la | † 164,051.6 | 201,392.2 | 238,635.3 | 383,921.2 | 419,636.8 | 385,017.8 | 383,866.8 | 409,530.7 | 448,431.7 | 499,115.0 | 415,505.0 | 339,278.4 |
| Other equity | 8dala | .... | .... | .... | .... | .... | .... | .... | 1.1 | — | .8 | 2.1 | 22.2 |
| Debt instruments | 8dzla | † 164,051.6 | 201,392.2 | 238,635.3 | 383,921.2 | 419,636.8 | 385,017.8 | 383,866.8 | 409,529.6 | 448,431.6 | 499,114.1 | 415,503.0 | 339,256.2 |

# Russian Federation   922

| | | 2004 | 2005 | 2006 | 2007 | 2008 | 2009 | 2010 | 2011 | 2012 | 2013 | 2014 | 2015 |
|---|---|---|---|---|---|---|---|---|---|---|---|---|---|
| **Government Finance** | | | | | | | | | | | | | |
| **Operations Statement** | | | | | | | | | | | | | |
| **General Government** | | | | | *Billions of Rubles: Fiscal Year Ends December 31;* | | | | | | | |
| Revenue.......................................... | a1 | 6,772.8 | 9,690.9 | 12,952.7 | 15,798.3 | 20,097.4 | 16,340.2 | 18,864.9 | 25,389.7 | 27,796.6 | 28,752.2 | 31,045.5 | .... |
| Taxes........................................ | a11 | 3,966.5 | 5,795.8 | 6,120.4 | 8,973.3 | 10,704.0 | 8,785.2 | 10,550.4 | 13,410.2 | 15,183.9 | 15,323.9 | 16,742.6 | .... |
| Social Contributions...................... | a12 | 1,263.9 | 1,189.9 | 1,562.4 | 2,008.6 | 2,218.1 | 2,354.8 | 2,508.8 | 3,493.5 | 3,993.0 | 4,601.9 | 5,222.0 | .... |
| Grants...................................... | a13 | — | 63.0 | −26.7 | .7 | .4 | | .6 | | | | .1 | .... |
| Other Revenue............................. | a14 | 1,542.3 | 2,642.2 | 5,296.6 | 4,815.7 | 7,174.9 | 5,200.2 | 5,805.1 | 8,486.0 | 8,619.7 | 8,826.4 | 9,080.8 | .... |
| Expense......................................... | a2 | 5,365.9 | 7,784.2 | 9,323.8 | 11,720.1 | 13,708.2 | 16,802.5 | 18,156.4 | 20,570.9 | 23,854.6 | 26,364.8 | 30,373.0 | .... |
| Compensation of Employees.......... | a21 | 1,313.5 | 3,287.9 | 2,288.9 | 2,853.5 | 3,648.2 | 4,250.8 | 4,403.1 | 5,065.8 | 5,964.6 | 6,929.0 | 7,513.0 | .... |
| Use of Goods & Services.............. | a22 | 1,320.5 | 1,379.5 | 1,757.0 | 2,273.1 | 2,848.5 | 2,852.1 | 3,171.2 | 3,470.1 | 4,088.5 | 4,299.4 | 4,592.9 | .... |
| Consumption of Fixed Capital....... | a23 | .... | 666.7 | 535.0 | 1,051.1 | 837.2 | 1,404.9 | 1,292.1 | 1,629.7 | 1,642.2 | 1,334.7 | 1,318.7 | .... |
| Interest..................................... | a24 | 211.5 | 238.9 | 191.8 | 166.5 | 232.2 | 244.6 | 256.5 | 318.0 | 396.6 | 467.8 | 551.5 | .... |
| Subsidies.................................. | a25 | 560.8 | 2,078.5 | 1,552.7 | 1,548.7 | 1,705.2 | 2,667.9 | 2,061.9 | 2,206.2 | 2,770.9 | 3,074.8 | 4,293.4 | .... |
| Grants...................................... | a26 | — | | 58.7 | 21.6 | 38.7 | 42.5 | 47.1 | 90.1 | 69.3 | 93.8 | 1,733.3 | .... |
| Social Benefits............................. | a27 | 1,530.7 | 2,116.4 | 2,568.2 | 3,188.9 | 4,010.8 | 4,939.6 | 6,466.1 | 7,136.4 | 8,174.6 | 9,344.2 | 9,958.8 | .... |
| Other Expense.............................. | a28 | 33.8 | −1,983.7 | 371.5 | 616.7 | 387.4 | 400.1 | 458.4 | 654.6 | 747.9 | 821.1 | 411.4 | .... |
| Gross Operating Balance [1-2+23]... | agob | 1,802.1 | 2,573.4 | 4,163.9 | 5,129.3 | 7,226.4 | 942.6 | 2,000.6 | 6,448.5 | 5,584.2 | 3,722.1 | 1,991.3 | .... |
| Net Operating Balance [1-2]............ | anob | .... | 1,906.8 | 3,628.9 | 4,078.2 | 6,389.2 | −462.3 | 708.5 | 4,818.8 | 3,942.0 | 2,387.4 | 672.5 | .... |
| Net Acq. of Nonfinancial Assets..... | a31 | 420.6 | 501.4 | 1,199.1 | 1,709.5 | 4,147.0 | 1,340.2 | 1,378.8 | 2,946.4 | 2,052.6 | 1,872.4 | 1,351.6 | .... |
| Aquisition of Nonfin. Assets.......... | a31.1 | .... | .... | .... | .... | .... | .... | .... | .... | .... | .... | .... | .... |
| Disposal of Nonfin. Assets............. | a31.2 | .... | .... | .... | .... | .... | .... | .... | .... | .... | .... | .... | .... |
| Net Lending/Borrowing [1-2-31]...... | anlb | 986.3 | 1,405.4 | 2,429.8 | 2,368.7 | 2,242.2 | −1,802.5 | −670.3 | 1,872.4 | 1,889.4 | 515.0 | −679.1 | .... |
| Net Acq. of Financial Assets............. | a32 | 828.1 | 806.5 | 1,726.6 | 2,287.5 | 2,614.7 | −1,307.2 | 79.5 | 2,851.0 | 2,667.7 | 1,887.2 | 812.3 | .... |
| By instrument | | | | | | | | | | | | | |
| Monetary Gold & SDRs................. | a3201 | — | — | — | — | — | — | — | — | — | — | — | .... |
| Currency & Deposits...................... | a3202 | 926.1 | 1,418.6 | 1,722.6 | 2,053.6 | 1,880.1 | −1,450.7 | −923.4 | 1,667.2 | 1,031.7 | −18.7 | 49.1 | .... |
| Securities other than Shares........... | a3203 | — | 14.9 | | 60.6 | 187.2 | −34.6 | −16.9 | −184.9 | −28.1 | 101.4 | 25.4 | .... |
| Loans........................................ | a3204 | 4.3 | 9.8 | .2 | −326.3 | 372.8 | −214.0 | −41.5 | 103.3 | 65.6 | 143.4 | −1,341.3 | .... |
| Shares & Other Equity................... | a3205 | −102.4 | −56.8 | 54.0 | 176.9 | 290.0 | 217.5 | 404.5 | 1,322.5 | 1,012.4 | 545.8 | 703.0 | .... |
| Insurance Technical Reserves......... | a3206 | — | — | — | — | — | — | — | — | — | — | — | .... |
| Financial Derivatives..................... | a3207 | — | — | — | — | — | — | — | — | — | — | — | .... |
| Other Accounts Receivable............. | a3208 | — | .... | .... | 322.7 | −115.4 | 174.6 | 656.8 | −57.1 | 586.1 | 1,115.3 | 1,376.1 | .... |
| By debtor | | | | | | | | | | | | | |
| Domestic................................... | a321 | 824.5 | 806.5 | 1,726.6 | 2,287.5 | 2,614.7 | −1,307.2 | 79.5 | 2,851.0 | 2,667.7 | 1,887.2 | 812.3 | .... |
| Foreign..................................... | a322 | 3.6 | | | | | | | | | | | .... |
| Net Incurrence of Liabilities.............. | a33 | −158.2 | −835.3 | −669.4 | −81.2 | 372.5 | 495.3 | 749.8 | 978.6 | 778.3 | 1,372.2 | 1,491.4 | .... |
| By instrument | | | | | | | | | | | | | |
| Special Drawing Rights (SDRs)....... | a3301 | — | — | — | — | — | — | — | — | — | — | — | .... |
| Currency & Deposits..................... | a3302 | — | — | — | — | — | — | — | — | — | — | — | .... |
| Securities other than Shares........... | a3303 | 190.9 | — | — | — | 320.6 | — | — | — | 650.4 | 638.8 | 934.8 | .... |
| Loans........................................ | a3304 | −217.4 | −821.8 | −586.8 | −18.3 | 94.2 | 542.5 | 683.0 | 1,010.2 | 169.9 | 448.9 | 285.0 | .... |
| Shares & Other Equity................... | a3305 | — | — | — | — | — | — | — | — | — | — | — | .... |
| Insurance Technical Reserves......... | a3306 | — | — | — | — | — | — | — | — | — | — | — | .... |
| Financial Derivatives..................... | a3307 | — | — | — | — | — | — | — | — | — | — | — | .... |
| Other Accounts Payable................. | a3308 | −131.7 | .... | .... | −62.9 | −42.3 | −47.2 | 66.8 | −31.6 | −42.0 | 284.5 | 271.5 | .... |
| By creditor | | | | | | | | | | | | | |
| Domestic................................... | a331 | 62.3 | 135.5 | 204.4 | 192.1 | 284.3 | 555.2 | 674.0 | 1,062.9 | 702.5 | 1,114.0 | 555.6 | .... |
| Foreign..................................... | a332 | −220.5 | −970.8 | −873.8 | −273.3 | 88.2 | −59.9 | 75.8 | −84.3 | 75.8 | 258.2 | 935.8 | .... |
| Stat. Discrepancy [32-33-NLB]........ | anlbz | — | 236.5 | −33.9 | — | | | | | | | | .... |
| Memo Item: Expenditure [2+31]...... | a2m | 5,786.5 | 8,285.6 | 10,522.9 | 13,429.6 | 17,855.2 | 18,142.7 | 19,535.2 | 23,517.3 | 25,907.2 | 28,237.2 | 31,724.6 | .... |
| **Balance Sheet** | | | | | | | | | | | | | |
| Net Worth.................................... | a6 | .... | 9,943.1 | 13,936.9 | 20,900.9 | 28,431.3 | 31,926.1 | 32,333.6 | 37,804.5 | 41,604.5 | 46,588.2 | 73,020.0 | .... |
| Nonfinancial Assets........................ | a61 | .... | 8,084.6 | 9,541.1 | 14,029.0 | 18,450.1 | 20,030.2 | 21,397.7 | 24,794.2 | 27,166.8 | 30,872.4 | 54,521.0 | .... |
| Financial Assets............................. | a62 | .... | 5,558.8 | 7,386.4 | 9,797.3 | 13,336.9 | 16,148.0 | 16,048.2 | 19,133.7 | 21,403.3 | 23,931.7 | 29,209.7 | .... |
| By instrument | | | | | | | | | | | | | |
| Monetary Gold & SDRs................. | a6201 | .... | — | — | — | — | — | — | — | — | — | — | .... |
| Currency & Deposits...................... | a6202 | .... | 2,542.2 | 4,117.6 | 6,171.6 | 9,168.9 | 7,645.9 | 6,831.0 | 9,035.2 | 9,967.8 | 8,855.1 | 12,397.1 | .... |
| Securities other than Shares........... | a6203 | .... | 140.0 | 133.5 | 193.7 | 380.9 | 400.4 | 383.5 | 197.3 | 159.6 | 261.0 | 357.9 | .... |
| Loans........................................ | a6204 | .... | 2,453.1 | 2,340.4 | 2,029.9 | 2,399.3 | 2,158.2 | 2,148.4 | 2,251.3 | 2,323.1 | 2,476.7 | 2,250.3 | .... |
| Shares and Other Equity................. | a6205 | .... | 149.5 | 283.1 | 463.5 | 751.3 | 4,708.8 | 5,012.8 | 6,612.6 | 9,814.5 | 7,530.7 | 7,840.6 | .... |
| Insurance Technical Reserves......... | a6206 | .... | — | — | — | — | — | — | — | — | — | — | .... |
| Financial Derivatives..................... | a6207 | .... | — | — | — | — | — | — | — | — | — | — | .... |
| Other Accounts Receivable............. | a6208 | .... | 274.0 | 511.8 | 938.6 | 636.5 | 1,234.7 | 1,672.5 | 1,037.3 | −861.7 | 4,808.2 | 6,363.7 | .... |
| By debtor | | | | | | | | | | | | | |
| Domestic................................... | a621 | .... | 3,478.9 | 5,454.8 | 9,797.3 | 13,336.9 | 16,148.0 | 16,048.2 | 19,133.7 | 21,403.3 | 23,931.7 | 29,209.7 | .... |
| Foreign..................................... | a622 | .... | 2,079.9 | 1,931.6 | — | — | — | — | — | — | — | — | .... |
| Liabilities...................................... | a63 | .... | 3,700.3 | 2,990.6 | 2,925.4 | 3,355.7 | 4,252.1 | 5,112.3 | 6,123.4 | 6,965.6 | 8,215.9 | 10,710.7 | .... |
| By instrument | | | | | | | | | | | | | |
| Special Drawing Rights (SDRs)....... | a6301 | .... | — | — | — | — | — | — | — | — | — | — | .... |
| Currency & Deposits..................... | a6302 | .... | — | — | — | — | — | — | — | — | 1.1 | — | .... |
| Securities other than Shares........... | a6303 | .... | | | | | | | | 5,491.7 | 6,219.4 | 8,189.2 | .... |
| Loans........................................ | a6304 | .... | 3,308.7 | 2,733.0 | 2,729.6 | 3,141.0 | 3,656.6 | 4,407.7 | 5,439.4 | 848.2 | 1,124.0 | 1,364.1 | .... |
| Shares and Other Equity................. | a6305 | .... | | | | | | | | 47.3 | | | .... |
| Insurance Technical Reserves......... | a6306 | .... | — | — | — | — | — | — | — | — | — | — | .... |
| Financial Derivatives..................... | a6307 | .... | 391.6 | 257.6 | — | — | — | — | — | — | — | — | .... |
| Other Accounts Payable................. | a6308 | .... | — | — | 195.8 | 214.7 | 595.5 | 704.6 | 684.0 | 578.4 | 871.4 | 1,157.4 | .... |
| By creditor | | | | | | | | | | | | | |
| Domestic................................... | a631 | .... | 1,437.3 | 1,600.7 | 1,838.5 | 2,166.1 | 3,078.0 | 3,860.5 | 6,029.6 | 5,753.1 | 6,742.9 | 8,293.6 | .... |
| Foreign..................................... | a632 | .... | 2,263.0 | 1,389.9 | 1,086.9 | 1,189.6 | 1,174.1 | 1,251.8 | 93.8 | 1,212.5 | 1,473.0 | 2,417.1 | .... |
| Net Financial Worth [62-63]............ | a6m2 | .... | 1,858.5 | 4,395.8 | 6,871.9 | 9,981.2 | 11,895.9 | 10,935.9 | 13,010.3 | 14,437.7 | 15,715.8 | 18,498.9 | .... |
| Memo Item: Debt at Market Value... | a6m3 | .... | .... | .... | .... | .... | .... | .... | .... | .... | .... | .... | .... |
| Memo Item: Debt at Face Value....... | a6m35 | .... | 3,308.7 | 2,733.0 | 2,925.4 | 3,355.7 | 4,252.1 | 5,112.3 | 6,123.4 | 6,965.6 | .... | .... | .... |
| Memo Item: Debt at Nominal Value. | a6m4 | .... | .... | .... | .... | .... | .... | .... | .... | .... | .... | .... | .... |

# Russian Federation 922

688

| National Accounts | | 2004 | 2005 | 2006 | 2007 | 2008 | 2009 | 2010 | 2011 | 2012 | 2013 | 2014 | 2015 |
|---|---|---|---|---|---|---|---|---|---|---|---|---|---|
| | | | | | | | *Billions of Rubles* | | | | | | |
| Househ.Cons.Expend.,incl.NPISHs.... | 96f | 8,588 | 10,792 | 13,129 | 16,218 | 20,184 | 21,203 | 23,843 | 27,427 | 31,275 | 34,937 | 38,319 | 43,664 |
| Government Consumption Expend... | 91f | 2,890 | 3,646 | 4,680 | 5,751 | 7,360 | 8,067 | 8,671 | 10,103 | 11,675 | 13,020 | 13,932 | 15,403 |
| Gross Fixed Capital Formation.......... | 93e | 3,131 | 3,837 | 4,981 | 6,980 | 9,201 | 8,536 | 10,014 | 11,950 | 13,639 | 14,460 | 14,706 | 17,668 |
| Changes in Inventories.................... | 93i | 428 | 502 | 718 | 1,054 | 1,325 | −1,191 | 458 | 2,032 | 1,820 | 644 | −186 | −906 |
| Exports of Goods and Services.......... | 90c | 5,860 | 7,607 | 9,079 | 10,029 | 12,924 | 10,842 | 13,529 | 16,941 | 18,365 | 18,945 | 21,437 | 23,863 |
| Imports of Goods and Services (-)..... | 98c | 3,774 | 4,648 | 5,653 | 7,162 | 9,111 | 7,954 | 9,790 | 12,164 | 13,853 | 15,023 | 16,331 | 17,135 |
| Statistical Discrepancy..................... | 99bs | −96 | −126 | −17 | 378 | −605 | −695 | −418 | −321 | −745 | −794 | −471 | −1,752 |
| Gross Domestic Product (GDP)........ | 99b | 17,123 | 21,736 | 26,934 | 32,869 | 41,882 | 39,502 | 46,727 | 56,288 | 62,922 | 66,984 | 71,877 | 82,556 |
| GDP, Production Based.................. | 99bp | 17,027 | 21,610 | 26,917 | 33,248 | 41,277 | 38,807 | 46,309 | 55,967 | 62,176 | 66,190 | 71,406 | 80,804 |
| GDP Volume 2008 Prices................. | 99b.p | 31,408 | 33,410 | 36,135 | 39,219 | 41,277 | 38,049 | 39,762 | 41,468 | 42,896 | 43,448 | 43,723 | .... |
| GDP Volume (2010=100).............. | 99bvp | 79.0 | 84.0 | 90.9 | 98.6 | 103.8 | 95.7 | 100.0 | 104.3 | 107.9 | 109.3 | 110.0 | .... |
| GDP Deflator (2010=100)............... | 99bip | 46.4 | 55.4 | 63.4 | 71.3 | 86.3 | 88.3 | 100.0 | 115.5 | 124.8 | 131.2 | 139.9 | .... |
| | | | | | | | *Millions: Midyear Estimates* | | | | | | |
| Population............................... | 99z | 144.04 | 143.62 | 143.34 | 143.18 | 143.12 | 143.13 | 143.16 | 143.21 | 143.29 | 143.37 | 143.43 | 143.46 |

# Rwanda 714

| | | 2004 | 2005 | 2006 | 2007 | 2008 | 2009 | 2010 | 2011 | 2012 | 2013 | 2014 | 2015 |
|---|---|---|---|---|---|---|---|---|---|---|---|---|---|
| **Exchange Rates** | | | | | *Francs per SDR: End of Period* | | | | | | | | |
| Official Rate | aa | 880.34 | 791.41 | 825.39 | 860.00 | 860.85 | 895.53 | 915.47 | 927.52 | 970.42 | 1,031.92 | 1,006.02 | 1,035.70 |
| | | | | | *Francs per US Dollar: End of Period (ae) Period Average (rf)* | | | | | | | | |
| Official Rate | ae | 566.86 | 553.72 | 548.65 | 544.22 | 558.90 | 571.24 | 594.45 | 604.14 | 631.41 | 670.08 | 694.37 | 747.41 |
| Official Rate | rf | 577.45 | 557.82 | 551.71 | 546.96 | 546.85 | 568.28 | 583.13 | 600.31 | 614.30 | 646.64 | 681.86 | 720.98 |
| **Fund Position** | | | | | *Millions of SDRs: End of Period* | | | | | | | | |
| Quota | 2f.s | 80.10 | 80.10 | 80.10 | 80.10 | 80.10 | 80.10 | 80.10 | 80.10 | 80.10 | 80.10 | 80.10 | 80.10 |
| SDR Holdings | 1b.s | 19.45 | 18.13 | 15.19 | 15.23 | 20.40 | 83.51 | 83.47 | 83.10 | 82.42 | 81.28 | 79.46 | 77.58 |
| Reserve Position in the Fund | 1c.s | — | — | — | — | — | — | — | — | — | — | — | — |
| Total Fund Cred.&Loans Outstg | 2tl | 59.41 | 53.89 | 2.85 | 5.13 | 7.41 | 9.72 | 9.67 | 9.27 | 8.58 | 7.44 | 5.62 | 3.73 |
| SDR Allocations | 1bd | 13.70 | 13.70 | 13.70 | 13.70 | 13.70 | 76.82 | 76.82 | 76.82 | 76.82 | 76.82 | 76.82 | 76.82 |
| **International Liquidity** | | | | | *Millions of US Dollars Unless Otherwise Indicated: End of Period* | | | | | | | | |
| Total Reserves minus Gold | 1l.d | 314.64 | 405.76 | 439.67 | 552.79 | 596.28 | 742.74 | 812.75 | 1,050.04 | 847.80 | 1,070.50 | 1,065.97 | 1,029.82 |
| SDR Holdings | 1b.d | 30.20 | 25.91 | 22.85 | 24.06 | 31.42 | 130.92 | 128.55 | 127.58 | 126.68 | 125.18 | 115.13 | 107.50 |
| Reserve Position in the Fund | 1c.d | — | — | — | — | — | — | — | — | — | — | — | — |
| Foreign Exchange | 1d.d | 284.44 | 379.85 | 416.82 | 528.73 | 564.86 | 611.82 | 684.21 | 922.46 | 721.12 | 945.32 | 950.84 | 922.32 |
| Monetary Authorities: Other Liabs | 4..d | 2.76 | 1.29 | 25.34 | .... | .... | .... | .... | .... | .... | .... | .... | .... |
| Deposit Money Banks: Assets | 7a.d | 107.18 | 94.97 | .... | .... | .... | .... | .... | .... | .... | .... | .... | .... |
| Deposit Money Banks: Liabs | 7b.d | 22.45 | 21.32 | .... | .... | .... | .... | .... | .... | .... | .... | .... | .... |
| Other Banking Insts.: Liabilities | 7f.d | .... | .... | .... | .... | .... | .... | .... | .... | .... | .... | .... | .... |
| **Monetary Authorities** | | | | | *Millions of Francs: End of Period* | | | | | | | | |
| Foreign Assets | 11 | 178,311 | 224,675 | 241,225 | .... | .... | .... | .... | .... | .... | .... | .... | .... |
| Claims on Central Government | 12a | 42,126 | 42,126 | 41,793 | .... | .... | .... | .... | .... | .... | .... | .... | .... |
| Claims on Official Entities | 12bx | 116 | 61 | 24 | .... | .... | .... | .... | .... | .... | .... | .... | .... |
| Claims on Private Sector | 12d | 2,756 | 3,024 | 3,232 | .... | .... | .... | .... | .... | .... | .... | .... | .... |
| Claims on Deposit Money Banks | 12e | 1,578 | 1,380 | 1,189 | .... | .... | .... | .... | .... | .... | .... | .... | .... |
| Claims on Other Financial Insts | 12f | 551 | 424 | 278 | .... | .... | .... | .... | .... | .... | .... | .... | .... |
| Reserve Money | 14 | 63,973 | 101,976 | 128,660 | .... | .... | .... | .... | .... | .... | .... | .... | .... |
| of which: Currency Outside DMBs | 14a | 36,512 | 46,277 | 52,620 | .... | .... | .... | .... | .... | .... | .... | .... | .... |
| Time Deposits | 15 | 1,595 | 1,688 | 1,594 | .... | .... | .... | .... | .... | .... | .... | .... | .... |
| Foreign Liabilities | 16c | 65,923 | 54,200 | 27,566 | .... | .... | .... | .... | .... | .... | .... | .... | .... |
| Central Government Deposits | 16d | 76,596 | 103,290 | 115,003 | .... | .... | .... | .... | .... | .... | .... | .... | .... |
| Counterpart Funds | 16e | 864 | 1,033 | 1,149 | .... | .... | .... | .... | .... | .... | .... | .... | .... |
| Capital Accounts | 17a | 15,886 | 15,342 | 19,089 | .... | .... | .... | .... | .... | .... | .... | .... | .... |
| Other Items (Net) | 17r | 602 | −5,839 | −5,319 | .... | .... | .... | .... | .... | .... | .... | .... | .... |
| **Deposit Money Banks** | | | | | *Millions of Francs: End of Period* | | | | | | | | |
| Reserves | 20 | 28,907 | 36,753 | .... | .... | .... | .... | .... | .... | .... | .... | .... | .... |
| Foreign Assets | 21 | 60,759 | 52,584 | .... | .... | .... | .... | .... | .... | .... | .... | .... | .... |
| Claims on Central Government | 22a | 21,015 | 22,475 | .... | .... | .... | .... | .... | .... | .... | .... | .... | .... |
| Claims on Official Entities | 22bx | 4,941 | 2,381 | .... | .... | .... | .... | .... | .... | .... | .... | .... | .... |
| Claims on Private Sector | 22d | 127,568 | 158,328 | .... | .... | .... | .... | .... | .... | .... | .... | .... | .... |
| Demand Deposits | 24 | 62,604 | 82,524 | .... | .... | .... | .... | .... | .... | .... | .... | .... | .... |
| Time and Savings Deposits | 25 | 113,026 | 122,063 | .... | .... | .... | .... | .... | .... | .... | .... | .... | .... |
| Foreign Liabilities | 26c | 12,724 | 11,805 | .... | .... | .... | .... | .... | .... | .... | .... | .... | .... |
| Central Government Deposits | 26d | 9,341 | 11,157 | .... | .... | .... | .... | .... | .... | .... | .... | .... | .... |
| Credit from Monetary Authorities | 26g | 1,624 | 2,059 | .... | .... | .... | .... | .... | .... | .... | .... | .... | .... |
| Capital Accounts | 27a | 60,937 | 65,203 | .... | .... | .... | .... | .... | .... | .... | .... | .... | .... |
| Other Items (Net) | 27r | −17,064 | −22,290 | .... | .... | .... | .... | .... | .... | .... | .... | .... | .... |
| **Monetary Survey** | | | | | *Millions of Francs: End of Period* | | | | | | | | |
| Foreign Assets (Net) | 31n | 160,423 | 211,253 | .... | .... | .... | .... | .... | .... | .... | .... | .... | .... |
| Domestic Credit | 32 | 113,785 | 115,815 | .... | .... | .... | .... | .... | .... | .... | .... | .... | .... |
| Claims on Central Govt. (Net) | 32an | −22,796 | −49,847 | .... | .... | .... | .... | .... | .... | .... | .... | .... | .... |
| Claims on Official Entities | 32bx | 5,058 | 2,442 | .... | .... | .... | .... | .... | .... | .... | .... | .... | .... |
| Claims on Private Sector | 32d | 130,323 | 161,352 | .... | .... | .... | .... | .... | .... | .... | .... | .... | .... |
| Claims on Other Financial Insts | 32f | 1,200 | 1,868 | .... | .... | .... | .... | .... | .... | .... | .... | .... | .... |
| Money | 34 | 99,941 | 129,326 | .... | .... | .... | .... | .... | .... | .... | .... | .... | .... |
| Quasi-Money | 35 | 114,621 | 123,751 | .... | .... | .... | .... | .... | .... | .... | .... | .... | .... |
| Other Items (Net) | 37r | 59,648 | 73,991 | .... | .... | .... | .... | .... | .... | .... | .... | .... | .... |
| Money plus Quasi-Money | 35l | 214,562 | 253,077 | .... | .... | .... | .... | .... | .... | .... | .... | .... | .... |
| **Interest Rates** | | | | | *Percent Per Annum* | | | | | | | | |
| Discount Rate (End of Period) | 60.a | 14.50 | 12.50 | 12.50 | 12.50 | 6.56 | 6.27 | 5.47 | 6.53 | 7.46 | 3.99 | 2.77 | 2.36 |
| Interbank Market Rate | 60b | 11.02 | 8.28 | 8.26 | 7.21 | 7.14 | 8.81 | 6.89 | 7.05 | 9.22 | 8.73 | 5.59 | 3.63 |
| Treasury Bill Rate | 60c | 12.52 | 8.35 | 9.86 | † 7.24 | .... | .... | 7.44 | 6.70 | 9.82 | 9.54 | 4.93 | 3.77 |
| Deposit Rate | 60l | 9.39 | 8.01 | 8.29 | 6.77 | 6.72 | 8.54 | 7.10 | 7.96 | 10.04 | 8.58 | 7.76 | 7.59 |
| Lending Rate | 60p | 16.48 | 16.08 | 16.07 | 16.11 | 16.51 | 15.77 | 16.94 | 16.73 | 16.49 | 16.93 | 17.66 | 17.03 |
| **Prices** | | | | | *Index Numbers (2010=100): Period Averages* | | | | | | | | |
| Consumer Prices | 64 | 59.2 | 64.6 | 70.3 | 76.7 | 88.5 | 97.7 | 100.0 | 105.7 | 112.3 | 117.1 | 119.1 | 122.1 |
| **Intl. Transactions & Positions** | | | | | *Millions of US Dollars* | | | | | | | | |
| Exports | 70..d | 98.16 | 124.78 | 147.35 | 176.79 | 267.59 | 192.63 | 255.00 | 464.24 | 508.77 | 605.75 | 651.80 | .... |
| Imports, c.i.f. | 71..d | 284.18 | 430.48 | 548.16 | 737.36 | 1,135.99 | 1,226.98 | 1,400.00 | 1,775.80 | 1,653.65 | 1,654.72 | 1,718.41 | .... |

# Rwanda 714

| Balance of Payments | | 2004 | 2005 | 2006 | 2007 | 2008 | 2009 | 2010 | 2011 | 2012 | 2013 | 2014 | 2015 |
|---|---|---|---|---|---|---|---|---|---|---|---|---|---|
| | | | | | | | *Millions of US Dollars* | | | | | | |
| A. Current Account*........................ | 109bx | −207.2 | −97.5 | −138.9 | −85.3 | −242.3 | −378.6 | −411.9 | −459.9 | −820.8 | † −814.8 | −1,046.6 | −1,098.7 |
| Goods, credit (exports).................. | 1a9cx | 98.1 | 125.0 | 163.1 | 182.0 | 259.6 | 230.4 | 297.3 | 469.0 | 590.7 | † 703.0 | 723.1 | 683.7 |
| Goods, debit (imports).................. | 1a9dx | 285.3 | 363.9 | 450.9 | 583.0 | 890.0 | 999.2 | 1,084.0 | 1,566.0 | 1,967.0 | † 1,899.7 | 1,990.2 | 1,917.4 |
| Balance on goods...................... | 1a9bx | −187.2 | −238.9 | −287.7 | −401.0 | −630.4 | −768.9 | −786.7 | −1,097.0 | −1,376.2 | † −1,196.7 | −1,267.1 | −1,233.8 |
| Services, credit (exports)............... | 1b9cx | 102.7 | 119.7 | 208.0 | 242.8 | 432.6 | 357.0 | 325.2 | 443.7 | 425.4 | † 581.1 | 516.9 | 720.3 |
| Services, debit (imports)............... | 1b9dx | 239.8 | 286.2 | 356.0 | 371.1 | 528.0 | 534.0 | 565.3 | 635.4 | 518.6 | † 883.1 | 663.1 | 915.1 |
| Balance on Goods & Services....... | 1z9bx | −324.4 | −405.4 | −435.8 | −529.4 | −725.8 | −945.9 | −1,026.8 | −1,288.6 | −1,469.5 | † −1,498.7 | −1,413.3 | −1,428.5 |
| Primary income: credit.................. | 1c9cx | 5.6 | 15.4 | 26.6 | 48.0 | 28.3 | 14.9 | 16.1 | 20.1 | 10.7 | † 15.0 | 16.2 | 11.5 |
| Primary income: debit.................. | 1c9dx | 39.2 | 42.7 | 55.3 | 65.2 | 63.3 | 51.7 | 58.6 | 71.9 | 84.5 | † 132.0 | 172.2 | 204.0 |
| Balance on gds, serv. & prim. inc. | 1y9bx | −358.0 | −432.6 | −464.4 | −546.6 | −760.9 | −982.7 | −1,069.3 | −1,340.4 | −1,543.3 | † −1,615.7 | −1,569.2 | −1,621.0 |
| Secondary income: credit............. | 1d9ca | 169.2 | 352.6 | 349.0 | 497.6 | 558.6 | 654.6 | 713.8 | 955.1 | 801.0 | † 877.2 | 606.8 | 601.3 |
| Secondary income: debit............... | 1d9da | 18.3 | 17.5 | 23.5 | 36.2 | 40.0 | 50.6 | 56.5 | 74.5 | 78.5 | † 76.4 | 84.2 | 79.0 |
| B. Capital Account*........................ | 209ba | 61.3 | 93.5 | 1,400.1 | 92.0 | 210.1 | 200.0 | 285.6 | 196.7 | 171.2 | † 234.5 | 337.1 | 299.9 |
| Capital account: credit.................. | 209ca | 61.3 | 93.5 | 1,400.1 | 92.0 | 210.1 | 200.0 | 285.6 | 196.7 | 171.2 | † 234.5 | 337.1 | 299.9 |
| Capital account: debit................... | 209da | .... | .... | .... | .... | .... | .... | .... | .... | .... | .... | .... | .... |
| Balance on current & capital acct. | 129ba | −145.9 | −4.1 | 1,261.2 | 6.8 | −32.2 | −178.6 | −126.3 | −263.2 | −649.6 | † −580.3 | −709.6 | −798.8 |
| C. Financial Account* ................... | 309na | −74.4 | −82.5 | 1,184.1 | −104.7 | −106.1 | −325.4 | −213.7 | −485.8 | −411.2 | † −751.3 | −591.3 | −795.1 |
| Direct investment: assets.............. | 3a9aa | .... | .... | .... | .... | .... | .... | .... | .... | .... | .... | 3.8 | 3.4 |
| Equity & investment fund shares.. | 3aaaa | .... | .... | .... | .... | .... | .... | .... | .... | .... | .... | 1.7 | 1.6 |
| Debt instruments........................ | 3abaa | .... | .... | .... | .... | .... | .... | .... | .... | .... | .... | 2.0 | 1.8 |
| Direct investment: liabilities .......... | 3a9la | 7.7 | 10.5 | 30.6 | 82.3 | 103.3 | 118.7 | 42.3 | 106.2 | 159.8 | † 257.6 | 291.7 | 323.2 |
| Equity & investment fund shares . | 3aala | 7.7 | 10.5 | 30.6 | 82.3 | 103.3 | 118.7 | 42.3 | 106.2 | 159.8 | † 113.2 | 124.1 | 151.1 |
| Debt instruments........................ | 3abla | .... | .... | .... | .... | .... | .... | .... | .... | .... | † 144.4 | 167.6 | 172.1 |
| Portfolio investment: assets .......... | 3b9aa | .... | .... | .... | .... | 18.8 | .... | .... | .... | .... | .... | 3.5 | .... |
| Equity & investment fund shares | 3baaa | .... | .... | .... | .... | .... | .... | .... | .... | .... | .... | 3.5 | .... |
| Debt securities.......................... | 3bbaa | .... | .... | .... | .... | 18.8 | .... | .... | .... | .... | .... | .... | .... |
| Portfolio investment: liabilities....... | 3b9la | .... | .... | .... | .... | .... | .... | 21.4 | 31.3 | 6.8 | † 1.7 | 1.4 | 6.8 |
| Equity & investment fund shares . | 3bala | .... | .... | .... | .... | .... | .... | 21.4 | 31.3 | 6.8 | † 1.7 | 1.4 | 1.4 |
| Debt securities.......................... | 3bbla | .... | .... | .... | .... | .... | .... | .... | .... | .... | .... | .... | 5.4 |
| Fin. der.& empl.stk.ops.(ESOs): net. | 3c9na | .... | .... | .... | .... | .... | .... | .... | .... | .... | .... | .... | .... |
| Fin. der. & ESOs.: assets.............. | 3c9aa | .... | .... | .... | .... | .... | .... | .... | .... | .... | .... | .... | .... |
| Fin. der. & ESOs.: liabilities.......... | 3c9la | .... | .... | .... | .... | .... | .... | .... | .... | .... | .... | .... | .... |
| Other investment: assets.............. | 3d9aa | 7.9 | −14.4 | 34.6 | 9.4 | 15.6 | 9.5 | 28.5 | 2.5 | −5.1 | † 17.2 | −1.6 | −73.0 |
| Other equity............................. | 3daaa | .... | .... | .... | .... | .... | .... | .... | .... | .... | .... | .... | .... |
| Debt instruments........................ | 3dzaa | 7.9 | −14.4 | 34.6 | 9.4 | 15.6 | 9.5 | 28.5 | 2.5 | −5.1 | † 17.2 | −1.6 | −73.0 |
| Other investment: liabilities........... | 3d9la | 74.7 | 57.6 | −1,180.2 | 31.8 | 37.1 | 216.2 | 178.5 | 350.8 | 239.6 | † 509.1 | 304.0 | 395.5 |
| Other equity............................. | 3dala | .... | .... | .... | .... | .... | .... | .... | .... | .... | .... | .... | .... |
| Debt instruments........................ | 3dzla | 74.7 | 57.6 | −1,180.2 | 31.8 | 37.1 | 216.2 | 178.5 | 350.8 | 239.6 | † 509.1 | 304.0 | 395.5 |
| Curr.+ cap.− finan. acct. balance... | 4y9na | −71.5 | 78.4 | 77.1 | 111.4 | 73.8 | 146.7 | 87.4 | 222.6 | −238.4 | † 170.9 | −118.2 | −3.7 |
| D. Net Errors and Omissions............ | 409na | 14.3 | 9.3 | 76.5 | −.8 | −11.1 | −93.2 | −15.3 | 11.7 | 25.9 | † 57.6 | 27.8 | −24.8 |
| E. Reserves and Related Items......... | 4z9na | −57.1 | 87.7 | 153.6 | 110.6 | 62.7 | 53.5 | 72.1 | 234.4 | −212.4 | † 228.5 | −90.4 | −28.5 |
| Reserve assets.......................... | 3e9aa | 102.3 | 111.6 | 79.8 | 114.1 | 66.4 | 57.1 | 72.0 | 233.7 | −213.5 | † 226.8 | −93.2 | −31.2 |
| Credit and loans from the IMF....... | 3dcla | −3.6 | −8.1 | −73.8 | 3.4 | 3.7 | 3.6 | −.1 | −.6 | −1.0 | † −1.7 | −2.8 | −2.6 |
| Exceptional financing.................... | 409la | 163.1 | 32.0 | .... | .... | .... | .... | .... | .... | .... | .... | .... | .... |

*Excludes components in group E

| International Investment Position | | 2004 | 2005 | 2006 | 2007 | 2008 | 2009 | 2010 | 2011 | 2012 | 2013 | 2014 | 2015 |
|---|---|---|---|---|---|---|---|---|---|---|---|---|---|
| | | | | | | | *Millions of US Dollars* | | | | | | |
| Assets............................................ | 809aa | 243.7 | 106.9 | 567.5 | 676.6 | 878.7 | 1,173.6 | 1,250.8 | 1,632.4 | 1,439.4 | † 1,778.0 | 1,883.3 | 1,876.9 |
| Direct investment........................ | 8a9aa | .... | .... | .... | 12.9 | 13.0 | 13.0 | 12.9 | 12.9 | 12.9 | † 12.9 | 16.7 | 25.6 |
| Equity & investment fund shares.. | 8aaaa | .... | .... | .... | 12.9 | 13.0 | 13.0 | 12.9 | 12.9 | 12.9 | † 12.9 | 14.7 | 22.0 |
| Debt instruments........................ | 8abaa | .... | .... | .... | .... | .... | .... | .... | .... | .... | .... | 2.0 | 3.6 |
| Portfolio investment..................... | 8b9aa | .... | .... | .... | .... | 18.8 | 18.8 | 18.8 | 18.8 | 18.8 | † 18.8 | 22.3 | 31.2 |
| Equity & investment fund shares.. | 8baaa | .... | .... | .... | .... | 18.8 | 18.8 | 18.8 | 18.8 | 18.8 | † 18.8 | 22.3 | 31.2 |
| Debt securities.......................... | 8bbaa | .... | .... | .... | .... | .... | .... | .... | .... | .... | .... | .... | .... |
| Fin. der.(oth.than reserves) & ESOs | 8c9aa | .... | .... | .... | .... | .... | .... | .... | .... | .... | .... | .... | .... |
| Other investment........................ | 8d9aa | 107.1 | 94.8 | 127.8 | 115.0 | 246.8 | 249.3 | 258.5 | 254.2 | 274.5 | † 334.2 | 423.8 | 422.4 |
| Other equity............................. | 8daaa | .... | .... | .... | .... | .... | .... | .... | .... | .... | .... | .... | .... |
| Debt instruments........................ | 8dzaa | 107.1 | 94.8 | 127.8 | 115.0 | 246.8 | 249.3 | 258.5 | 254.2 | 274.5 | † 334.2 | 423.8 | 422.4 |
| Reserve assets.......................... | 8e9aa | 136.6 | 12.1 | 439.7 | 548.7 | 600.1 | 892.6 | 960.6 | 1,346.5 | 1,133.2 | † 1,412.0 | 1,420.5 | 1,397.8 |
| Liabilities....................................... | 809la | 1,840.4 | 1,731.8 | 485.0 | 589.2 | 1,071.7 | 1,422.8 | 1,667.9 | 2,352.3 | 2,759.8 | † 3,161.4 | 3,946.1 | 4,393.7 |
| Direct investment........................ | 8a9la | 69.3 | 77.3 | 88.2 | 170.4 | 273.7 | 392.4 | 434.7 | 583.3 | 743.1 | † 853.9 | 1,152.4 | 1,484.2 |
| Equity & investment fund shares.. | 8aala | 69.3 | 77.3 | 88.2 | 170.4 | 273.7 | 392.4 | 434.7 | 583.3 | 743.1 | † 853.9 | 886.0 | 965.8 |
| Debt instruments........................ | 8abla | .... | .... | .... | .... | .... | .... | .... | .... | .... | .... | 266.4 | 518.5 |
| Portfolio investment..................... | 8b9la | .... | .... | .... | .... | .... | .... | 21.4 | 74.1 | 80.9 | † 80.9 | 95.0 | 103.3 |
| Equity & investment fund shares.. | 8bala | .... | .... | .... | .... | .... | .... | 21.4 | 74.1 | 80.9 | † 80.9 | 95.0 | 97.9 |
| Debt securities.......................... | 8bbla | .... | .... | .... | .... | .... | .... | .... | .... | .... | .... | .... | 5.4 |
| Fin. der.(oth.than reserves) & ESOs | 8c9la | .... | .... | .... | .... | .... | .... | .... | .... | .... | .... | .... | .... |
| Other investment........................ | 8d9la | 1,771.1 | 1,654.5 | 396.8 | 418.9 | 798.0 | 1,030.4 | 1,211.8 | 1,695.0 | 1,935.9 | † 2,226.6 | 2,698.8 | 2,806.2 |
| Other equity............................. | 8dala | .... | .... | .... | .... | .... | .... | .... | .... | .... | .... | .... | .... |
| Debt instruments........................ | 8dzla | 1,771.1 | 1,654.5 | 396.8 | 418.9 | 798.0 | 1,030.4 | 1,211.8 | 1,695.0 | 1,935.9 | † 2,226.6 | 2,698.8 | 2,806.2 |

# Rwanda 714

| | | 2004 | 2005 | 2006 | 2007 | 2008 | 2009 | 2010 | 2011 | 2012 | 2013 | 2014 | 2015 |
|---|---|---|---|---|---|---|---|---|---|---|---|---|---|
| **Government Finance** | | | | | | | | | | | | | |
| **Cash Flow Statement** | | | | | | | | | | | | | |
| **Budgetary Central Government** | | | | | | *Millions of Francs: Fiscal Year Ends December 31* | | | | | | | |
| Cash Receipts:Operating Activities... | c1 | .... | .... | .... | .... | .... | 726,758 | 829,753 | 982,475 | 1,002,300 | 1,101,322 | 1,338,763 | 1,414,536 |
| Taxes.............................. | c11 | .... | .... | .... | .... | .... | 362,817 | 415,691 | 505,030 | 606,200 | 651,922 | 763,425 | 894,552 |
| Social Contributions...................... | c12 | .... | .... | .... | .... | .... | — | — | — | — | — | — | — |
| Grants........................... | c13 | .... | .... | .... | .... | .... | 347,397 | 395,939 | 440,774 | 345,300 | 364,900 | 474,289 | 417,123 |
| Other Receipts............................. | c14 | .... | .... | .... | .... | .... | 16,544 | 18,123 | 36,671 | 50,800 | 84,500 | 101,049 | 102,861 |
| Cash Payments:Operating Activities. | c2 | .... | .... | .... | .... | .... | 424,373 | 502,796 | 569,382 | 641,700 | 633,900 | 779,934 | 794,400 |
| Compensation of Employees.......... | c21 | .... | .... | .... | .... | .... | 97,402 | 116,113 | 130,385 | 158,700 | 168,900 | 187,872 | 207,000 |
| Purchases of Goods & Services....... | c22 | .... | .... | .... | .... | .... | 104,806 | 127,002 | 137,781 | 146,300 | 123,100 | 142,516 | 151,155 |
| Interest................................. | c24 | .... | .... | .... | .... | .... | 11,412 | 15,283 | 17,350 | 19,100 | 30,700 | 43,661 | 42,947 |
| Subsidies............................... | c25 | .... | .... | .... | .... | .... | — | — | — | — | — | — | — |
| Grants............................. | c26 | .... | .... | .... | .... | .... | — | — | — | — | .... | .... | .... |
| Social Benefits......................... | c27 | .... | .... | .... | .... | .... | 162,440 | 182,169 | 220,302 | 317,600 | .... | .... | .... |
| Other Payments........................ | c28 | .... | .... | .... | .... | .... | 48,312 | 62,230 | 63,563 | | .... | .... | .... |
| Net Cash Inflow:Operating Act.[1-2] | ccio | .... | .... | .... | .... | .... | 302,386 | 326,957 | 413,093 | 360,600 | 467,422 | 558,829 | 620,136 |
| Net Cash Outflow:Invest. in NFA...... | c31 | .... | .... | .... | .... | .... | 291,882 | 364,666 | 440,963 | 536,300 | 564,500 | 712,452 | 786,957 |
| Purchases of Nonfinancial Assets... | c31.1 | .... | .... | .... | .... | .... | 291,882 | 364,666 | 440,963 | 536,300 | .... | .... | .... |
| Sales of Nonfinancial Assets.......... | c31.2 | .... | .... | .... | .... | .... | | | | | .... | .... | .... |
| Cash Surplus/Deficit [1-2-31=1-2M] | ccsd | .... | .... | .... | .... | .... | 10,504 | −37,709 | −27,869 | −175,700 | −97,078 | −153,623 | −166,821 |
| Net Acq. Fin. Assets, excl. Cash...... | c32x | .... | .... | .... | .... | .... | 34,683 | 28,306 | −23,153 | 25,800 | 137,200 | 50,220 | 118,820 |
| Domestic........................... | c321x | .... | .... | .... | .... | .... | 34,683 | 28,306 | −23,153 | 25,800 | 137,200 | 50,220 | 118,820 |
| Foreign.............................. | c322x | .... | .... | .... | .... | .... | | | | | .... | .... | .... |
| Net Incurrence of Liabilities.............. | c33 | .... | .... | .... | .... | .... | 4,857 | 26,491 | 92,804 | 54,949 | 353,800 | 58,253 | 184,458 |
| Domestic........................... | c331 | .... | .... | .... | .... | .... | −29,544 | −25,109 | −32,012 | — | 15,200 | −46,904 | −13,000 |
| Foreign.............................. | c332 | .... | .... | .... | .... | .... | 34,401 | 51,600 | 124,815 | 54,949 | 338,600 | 105,157 | 197,458 |
| Net Cash Inflow, Fin.Act.[-32x+33].. | cnfb | .... | .... | .... | .... | .... | −29,825 | −1,815 | 115,957 | 29,149 | 216,600 | 8,034 | 65,638 |
| Net Change in Stock of Cash........... | cncb | .... | .... | .... | .... | .... | −19,322 | −39,523 | 88,088 | −146,551 | 119,522 | −145,589 | −101,183 |
| Stat. Discrep. [32X-33+NCB-CSD].... | ccsdz | .... | .... | .... | .... | .... | | | | | | | |
| Memo Item:Cash Expenditure[2+31] | c2m | .... | .... | .... | .... | .... | 716,255 | 867,462 | 1,010,344 | 1,178,000 | 1,198,400 | 1,492,386 | 1,581,357 |
| Memo Item: Gross Debt................... | c63 | .... | .... | .... | .... | .... | .... | .... | .... | .... | .... | .... | .... |
| **National Accounts** | | | | | | *Billions of Francs* | | | | | | | |
| Househ.Cons.Expend.,incl.NPISHs.... | 96f | 968.3 | 1,149.3 | 1,452.0 | 1,738.0 | 2,225.0 | 2,508.0 | 2,779.0 | 3,205.0 | 3,573.0 | 3,889.0 | 4,279.0 | .... |
| Government Consumption Expend... | 91f | 221.4 | 261.7 | 314.0 | 349.0 | 414.0 | 457.0 | 479.0 | 634.0 | 645.0 | 791.0 | 763.0 | .... |
| Gross Fixed Capital Formation.......... | 93e | 181.1 | 227.4 | 318.0 | 473.0 | 717.0 | 681.0 | 817.0 | 957.0 | 1,205.0 | 1,298.0 | 1,425.0 | .... |
| Changes in Inventories.................... | 93i | — | — | 13.0 | 16.0 | 20.0 | 22.0 | 19.0 | 38.0 | 49.0 | 47.0 | 39.0 | .... |
| Exports of Goods and Services......... | 90c | 134.2 | 164.5 | 264.0 | 332.0 | 344.0 | 374.0 | 457.0 | 560.0 | 650.0 | 730.0 | 836.0 | .... |
| Imports of Goods and Services (-)..... | 98c | 298.7 | 363.0 | 457.0 | 623.0 | 838.0 | 884.0 | 1,027.0 | 1,266.0 | 1,441.0 | 1,618.0 | 1,763.0 | .... |
| Gross Domestic Product (GDP)........ | 99b | 1,206.3 | 1,439.9 | 1,904.0 | 2,284.0 | 2,882.0 | 3,157.0 | 3,523.0 | 4,128.0 | 4,681.0 | 5,137.0 | 5,580.0 | .... |
| Net Primary Income from Abroad..... | 98.n | −19.0 | −15.0 | −16.0 | −9.0 | −19.0 | −21.0 | −27.0 | −33.0 | — | .... | .... | .... |
| Gross National Income (GNI)........... | 99a | 1,186.9 | 1,424.8 | 1,700.5 | 2,035.2 | 2,557.4 | 2,964.1 | 3,253.1 | 3,783.3 | 4,318.0 | .... | .... | .... |
| Net Current Transf.from Abroad....... | 98t | 160.2 | 177.1 | 138.6 | 198.3 | 243.9 | 297.9 | 330.4 | 448.6 | 331.4 | .... | .... | .... |
| Gross Nat'l Disposable Inc.(GNDI).... | 99i | 1,347.2 | 1,601.8 | 1,839.1 | 2,233.5 | 2,801.3 | 3,262.0 | 3,583.5 | 4,232.0 | 4,649.4 | .... | .... | .... |
| Gross Saving................................ | 99s | 157.5 | 190.8 | 153.1 | 263.4 | 403.8 | 342.1 | 317.8 | 572.7 | 424.7 | .... | .... | .... |
| GDP Volume 2006 Prices................. | 99b.p | 1,437.0 | 1,575.0 | 1,716.4 | 1,847.4 | 2,053.6 | 2,181.9 | 2,339.4 | 2,532.1 | 2,734.2 | .... | .... | .... |
| GDP Volume (2010=100)................ | 99bvp | 61.4 | 67.3 | 73.4 | 79.0 | 87.8 | 93.3 | 100.0 | 108.2 | 116.9 | .... | .... | .... |
| GDP Deflator (2010=100)............... | 99bip | 55.7 | 60.7 | 73.7 | 82.1 | 93.2 | 96.1 | 100.0 | 108.3 | 113.7 | .... | .... | .... |
| | | | | | | *Millions: Midyear Estimates* | | | | | | | |
| Population............................... | 99z | 8.83 | 9.01 | 9.23 | 9.48 | 9.75 | 10.02 | 10.29 | 10.56 | 10.82 | 11.08 | 11.34 | 11.61 |

| | | 2004 | 2005 | 2006 | 2007 | 2008 | 2009 | 2010 | 2011 | 2012 | 2013 | 2014 | 2015 |
|---|---|---|---|---|---|---|---|---|---|---|---|---|---|
| **Exchange Rates** | | — *E. Caribbean Dollars per SDR: End of Period* | | | | | | | | | | | |
| Official Rate | aa | 4.1931 | 3.8590 | 4.0619 | 4.2667 | 4.1587 | 4.2328 | 4.1581 | 4.1452 | 4.1497 | 4.1580 | 3.9118 | 3.7415 |
| | | *E. Caribbean Dollars per US Dollar: End of Period (ae) Period Average (rf)* | | | | | | | | | | | |
| Official Rate | ae | 2.7000 | 2.7000 | 2.7000 | 2.7000 | 2.7000 | 2.7000 | 2.7000 | 2.7000 | 2.7000 | 2.7000 | 2.7000 | 2.7000 |
| Official Rate | rf | 2.7000 | 2.7000 | 2.7000 | 2.7000 | 2.7000 | 2.7000 | 2.7000 | 2.7000 | 2.7000 | 2.7000 | 2.7000 | 2.7000 |
| | | *Index Numbers (2010=100): Period Averages* | | | | | | | | | | | |
| Nominal Effective Exchange Rate | nec | 96.7 | 95.2 | 94.6 | 93.4 | 93.0 | 100.3 | 100.0 | 98.8 | 99.6 | 100.3 | 107.0 | 121.7 |
| CPI-Based Real Effect. Ex. Rate | rec | 97.0 | 95.3 | 98.9 | 97.7 | 95.7 | 102.9 | 100.0 | 101.7 | 101.9 | 102.0 | 106.2 | 109.7 |
| **Fund Position** | | *Millions of SDRs: End of Period* | | | | | | | | | | | |
| Quota | 2f.s | 8.90 | 8.90 | 8.90 | 8.90 | 8.90 | 8.90 | 8.90 | 8.90 | 8.90 | 8.90 | 8.90 | 8.90 |
| SDR Holdings | 1b.s | — | — | — | — | — | 8.51 | 8.49 | 8.21 | 7.62 | 6.84 | 6.02 | 5.66 |
| Reserve Position in the Fund | 1c.s | .08 | .08 | .08 | .08 | .08 | .08 | .08 | .08 | .08 | .08 | .08 | .08 |
| Total Fund Cred.&Loans Outstg | 2tl | — | — | — | — | — | 2.23 | 2.23 | 24.38 | 44.77 | 47.93 | 33.52 | 6.41 |
| SDR Allocations | 1bd | — | — | — | — | — | 8.50 | 8.50 | 8.50 | 8.50 | 8.50 | 8.50 | 8.50 |
| **International Liquidity** | | *Millions of US Dollars Unless Otherwise Indicated: End of Period* | | | | | | | | | | | |
| Total Reserves minus Gold | 1l.d | 78.47 | 71.61 | 88.70 | 95.79 | 110.41 | 136.41 | 168.86 | 244.26 | 263.49 | 301.95 | 327.25 | 288.39 |
| SDR Holdings | 1b.d | — | — | — | — | .01 | 13.35 | 13.07 | 12.60 | 11.72 | 10.53 | 8.72 | 7.84 |
| Reserve Position in the Fund | 1c.d | .13 | .12 | .12 | .13 | .13 | .13 | .13 | .13 | .13 | .13 | .12 | .11 |
| Foreign Exchange | 1d.d | 78.34 | 71.49 | 88.57 | 95.66 | 110.28 | 122.93 | 155.66 | 231.54 | 251.64 | 291.30 | 318.41 | 280.44 |
| Central Bank: Other Assets | 3..d | — | — | — | — | — | — | — | — | — | — | — | — |
| Central Bank: Other Liabs | 4..d | — | — | — | — | — | — | — | — | — | — | — | — |
| Other Depository Corps.: Assets | 7a.d | 244.92 | 314.48 | 339.76 | 406.81 | 483.79 | 621.53 | 668.53 | 705.75 | 815.71 | 967.04 | 1,174.07 | 1,184.49 |
| Other Depository Corps.: Liabs | 7b.d | 216.93 | 246.52 | 258.72 | 295.96 | 317.53 | 519.52 | 586.78 | 596.22 | 557.15 | 537.66 | 616.97 | 647.86 |
| **Central Bank** | | *Millions of E. Caribbean Dollars: End of Period* | | | | | | | | | | | |
| Net Foreign Assets | 11n | 205.53 | 186.63 | 230.89 | 251.12 | 290.37 | 314.30 | 402.34 | 514.78 | 477.56 | 568.68 | 708.45 | 712.48 |
| Claims on Nonresidents | 11 | 205.53 | 186.63 | 230.89 | 251.12 | 290.37 | 359.71 | 446.95 | 651.07 | 698.63 | 803.31 | 872.84 | 768.30 |
| Liabilities to Nonresidents | 16c | — | — | — | — | — | 45.41 | 44.61 | 136.29 | 221.07 | 234.63 | 164.40 | 55.82 |
| Claims on Other Depository Corps | 12e | 7.76 | 8.36 | 10.63 | 10.10 | 9.96 | 11.11 | 13.02 | 12.88 | 13.22 | 13.99 | 12.18 | 11.52 |
| Net Claims on Central Government | 12an | .37 | .23 | 1.30 | .58 | −23.46 | 12.87 | .13 | −47.91 | −121.83 | −129.83 | −110.01 | −34.58 |
| Claims on Central Government | 12a | 7.25 | 7.25 | 7.94 | 9.20 | 9.04 | 26.19 | 24.53 | 26.82 | 3.83 | 3.83 | 3.83 | 3.83 |
| Liabilities to Central Government | 16d | 6.88 | 7.02 | 6.64 | 8.61 | 32.50 | 13.32 | 24.40 | 74.73 | 125.66 | 133.66 | 113.84 | 38.41 |
| Claims on Other Sectors | 12s | — | — | — | — | — | — | — | — | — | — | — | — |
| Claims on Other Financial Corps | 12g | — | — | — | — | — | — | — | — | — | — | — | — |
| Claims on State & Local Govts | 12b | — | — | — | — | — | — | — | — | — | — | — | — |
| Claims on Public Nonfin. Corps | 12c | — | — | — | — | — | — | — | — | — | — | — | — |
| Claims on Private Sector | 12d | — | — | — | — | — | — | — | — | — | — | — | — |
| Monetary Base | 14 | 211.94 | 193.47 | 240.68 | 259.41 | 274.40 | 344.78 | 420.51 | 577.24 | 553.47 | 647.42 | 707.95 | 685.88 |
| Currency in Circulation | 14a | 60.61 | 65.78 | 78.26 | 83.57 | 96.10 | 102.21 | 124.74 | 125.49 | 135.31 | 162.77 | 186.10 | 195.50 |
| Liabs. to Other Depository Corps | 14c | 151.14 | 127.68 | 162.41 | 175.81 | 178.19 | 242.47 | 295.24 | 451.73 | 418.11 | 484.59 | 521.80 | 490.34 |
| Liabilities to Other Sectors | 14d | .19 | .01 | .02 | .03 | .11 | .09 | .53 | .02 | .05 | .06 | .05 | .05 |
| Other Liabs. to Other Dep. Corps | 14n | 1.28 | 1.33 | 1.70 | 1.94 | 2.00 | 2.42 | 3.85 | 4.34 | 4.47 | 11.17 | 43.08 | 37.78 |
| Dep. & Sec. Excl. f/Monetary Base | 14o | — | — | — | — | — | — | — | — | — | — | — | — |
| Deposits Included in Broad Money | 15 | — | — | — | — | — | — | — | — | — | — | — | — |
| Sec.Ot.th.Shares Incl.in Brd. Money | 16a | — | — | — | — | — | — | — | — | — | — | — | — |
| Deposits Excl. from Broad Money | 16b | — | — | — | — | — | — | — | — | — | — | — | — |
| Sec.Ot.th.Shares Excl.f/Brd.Money | 16s | — | — | — | — | — | — | — | — | — | — | — | — |
| Loans | 16l | — | — | — | — | — | — | — | — | — | — | — | — |
| Financial Derivatives | 16m | — | — | — | — | — | — | — | — | — | — | — | — |
| Shares and Other Equity | 17a | — | — | — | — | — | — | — | — | — | — | — | — |
| Other Items (Net) | 17r | .44 | .42 | .44 | .46 | .47 | −8.92 | −8.88 | −101.82 | −188.99 | −205.75 | −140.41 | −34.23 |
| Memo Item: | | | | | | | | | | | | | |
| Total Assets | 10ra | 220.19 | 201.92 | 249.12 | 270.06 | 309.01 | 360.62 | 448.86 | 656.41 | 683.70 | 792.36 | 864.98 | 762.18 |
| **Other Depository Corporations** | | *Millions of E. Caribbean Dollars: End of Period* | | | | | | | | | | | |
| Net Foreign Assets | 21n | 75.58 | 183.50 | 218.80 | 299.28 | 448.91 | 275.43 | 220.71 | 295.73 | 698.13 | 1,159.34 | 1,504.17 | 1,448.91 |
| Claims on Nonresidents | 21 | 661.28 | 849.10 | 917.34 | 1,098.38 | 1,306.23 | 1,678.14 | 1,805.02 | 1,905.52 | 2,202.43 | 2,611.01 | 3,169.98 | 3,198.12 |
| Liabilities to Nonresidents | 26c | 585.70 | 665.61 | 698.54 | 799.10 | 857.32 | 1,402.71 | 1,584.32 | 1,609.78 | 1,504.30 | 1,451.67 | 1,665.81 | 1,749.22 |
| Claims on Central Bank | 20 | 164.92 | 144.23 | 183.37 | 205.62 | 201.83 | 264.86 | 305.65 | 477.87 | 439.76 | 523.18 | 578.65 | 550.58 |
| Currency | 20a | 15.99 | 15.89 | 23.16 | 27.38 | 25.98 | 23.88 | 23.68 | 23.50 | 27.71 | 29.67 | 31.46 | 27.24 |
| Reserve Deposits and Securities | 20b | 148.93 | 128.34 | 160.21 | 178.24 | 175.86 | 240.98 | 281.97 | 454.37 | 412.06 | 493.51 | 547.19 | 523.34 |
| Other Claims | 20n | — | — | — | — | — | — | — | — | — | — | — | — |
| Net Claims on Central Government | 22an | 215.81 | 296.29 | 396.07 | 411.50 | 286.41 | 641.14 | 682.06 | 574.45 | 504.94 | −265.12 | 397.92 | 368.41 |
| Claims on Central Government | 22a | 268.10 | 350.42 | 455.32 | 486.93 | 430.38 | 832.04 | 875.87 | 800.54 | 717.57 | 145.22 | 941.97 | 944.10 |
| Liabilities to Central Government | 26d | 52.28 | 54.13 | 59.25 | 75.43 | 143.97 | 190.90 | 193.81 | 226.09 | 212.64 | 410.33 | 544.05 | 575.69 |
| Claims on Other Sectors | 22s | 1,243.49 | 1,366.42 | 1,526.29 | 1,700.29 | 1,872.14 | 1,607.11 | 1,708.19 | 1,795.66 | 1,803.02 | 1,757.83 | 1,578.90 | 1,632.50 |
| Claims on Other Financial Corps | 22g | 74.42 | 86.93 | 100.98 | 108.99 | 41.32 | 46.48 | 47.35 | 48.33 | 49.18 | 46.88 | 16.20 | 15.22 |
| Claims on State & Local Govts | 22b | 53.21 | 56.53 | 61.03 | 95.18 | 116.15 | 134.57 | 175.18 | 201.82 | 198.22 | 205.74 | 179.47 | 188.10 |
| Claims on Public Nonfin. Corps | 22c | 367.36 | 418.35 | 464.77 | 477.38 | 558.08 | 195.88 | 219.59 | 226.41 | 237.98 | 198.05 | 37.18 | 36.68 |
| Claims on Private Sector | 22d | 748.51 | 804.61 | 899.51 | 1,018.74 | 1,156.59 | 1,230.17 | 1,266.08 | 1,319.10 | 1,317.65 | 1,307.16 | 1,346.05 | 1,392.49 |
| Liabilities to Central Bank | 26g | 6.72 | .40 | .87 | .85 | .33 | .09 | .18 | 5.62 | 11.28 | 11.11 | 5.22 | 4.85 |
| Transf.Dep.Included in Broad Money | 24 | 503.35 | 509.00 | 641.38 | 692.17 | 656.15 | 605.80 | 642.62 | 755.21 | 975.10 | 1,067.92 | 1,332.53 | 1,330.24 |
| Other Dep.Included in Broad Money | 25 | 1,012.16 | 1,107.82 | 1,212.10 | 1,373.69 | 1,400.64 | 1,546.39 | 1,629.51 | 1,745.86 | 1,832.02 | 2,035.36 | 2,095.26 | 2,257.92 |
| Sec.Ot.th.Shares Incl.in Brd. Money | 26a | — | — | — | — | — | — | — | — | — | — | — | — |
| Deposits Excl. from Broad Money | 26b | — | — | — | — | — | — | — | — | — | — | — | — |
| Sec.Ot.th.Shares Excl.f/Brd.Money | 26s | — | — | — | — | — | — | — | — | — | — | — | — |
| Loans | 26l | — | — | — | — | — | — | — | — | — | — | — | — |
| Financial Derivatives | 26m | — | — | — | — | — | — | — | — | — | — | — | — |
| Insurance Technical Reserves | 26r | — | — | — | — | — | — | — | — | — | — | — | — |
| Shares and Other Equity | 27a | 224.59 | 290.18 | 316.38 | 422.42 | 564.96 | 538.46 | 583.07 | 546.04 | 541.70 | 527.89 | 524.91 | 512.85 |
| Other Items (Net) | 27r | −47.01 | 83.03 | 153.81 | 127.56 | 187.22 | 97.81 | 61.24 | 90.99 | 85.76 | −467.06 | 101.72 | −105.45 |
| Memo Item: | | | | | | | | | | | | | |
| Total Assets | 20ra | 2,605.11 | 2,932.08 | 3,282.37 | 3,746.91 | 4,026.76 | 4,645.77 | 5,134.54 | 5,446.77 | 5,643.72 | 6,154.48 | 6,892.62 | 7,183.64 |

| | | 2004 | 2005 | 2006 | 2007 | 2008 | 2009 | 2010 | 2011 | 2012 | 2013 | 2014 | 2015 |
|---|---|---|---|---|---|---|---|---|---|---|---|---|---|
| **Depository Corporations** | | | | | | *Millions of E. Caribbean Dollars: End of Period* | | | | | | | |
| Net Foreign Assets | 31n | 281.11 | 370.12 | 449.69 | 550.40 | 739.29 | 589.73 | 623.04 | 810.51 | 1,175.69 | 1,728.02 | 2,212.62 | 2,161.38 |
| Claims on Nonresidents | 31 | 866.80 | 1,035.73 | 1,148.23 | 1,349.51 | 1,596.61 | 2,037.84 | 2,251.97 | 2,556.58 | 2,901.06 | 3,414.32 | 4,042.82 | 3,966.42 |
| Liabilities to Nonresidents | 36c | 585.70 | 665.61 | 698.54 | 799.10 | 857.32 | 1,448.12 | 1,628.93 | 1,746.07 | 1,725.37 | 1,686.30 | 1,830.20 | 1,805.03 |
| Domestic Claims | 32 | 1,459.68 | 1,662.94 | 1,923.66 | 2,112.37 | 2,135.09 | 2,261.13 | 2,390.38 | 2,322.20 | 2,186.13 | 1,362.88 | 1,866.81 | 1,966.33 |
| Net Claims on Central Government | 32an | 216.18 | 296.52 | 397.37 | 412.08 | 262.95 | 654.02 | 682.19 | 526.54 | 383.11 | −394.94 | 287.91 | 333.84 |
| Claims on Central Government | 32a | 275.35 | 357.67 | 463.26 | 496.12 | 439.42 | 858.23 | 900.40 | 827.36 | 721.40 | 149.05 | 945.80 | 947.94 |
| Liabilities to Central Government | 36d | 59.16 | 61.15 | 65.89 | 84.04 | 176.47 | 204.21 | 218.20 | 300.82 | 338.30 | 544.00 | 657.89 | 614.10 |
| Claims on Other Sectors | 32s | 1,243.49 | 1,366.42 | 1,526.29 | 1,700.29 | 1,872.14 | 1,607.11 | 1,708.19 | 1,795.66 | 1,803.02 | 1,757.83 | 1,578.90 | 1,632.50 |
| Claims on Other Financial Corps | 32g | 74.42 | 86.93 | 100.98 | 108.99 | 41.32 | 46.48 | 47.35 | 48.33 | 49.18 | 46.88 | 16.20 | 15.22 |
| Claims on State & Local Govts | 32b | 53.21 | 56.53 | 61.03 | 95.18 | 116.15 | 134.57 | 175.18 | 201.82 | 198.22 | 205.74 | 179.47 | 188.10 |
| Claims on Public Nonfin. Corps | 32c | 367.36 | 418.35 | 464.77 | 477.38 | 558.08 | 195.88 | 219.59 | 226.41 | 237.98 | 198.05 | 37.18 | 36.68 |
| Claims on Private Sector | 32d | 748.51 | 804.61 | 899.51 | 1,018.74 | 1,156.59 | 1,230.17 | 1,266.08 | 1,319.10 | 1,317.65 | 1,307.16 | 1,346.05 | 1,392.49 |
| Broad Money Liabilities | 35l | 1,560.31 | 1,666.72 | 1,908.59 | 2,122.08 | 2,127.02 | 2,230.62 | 2,373.71 | 2,603.08 | 2,914.77 | 3,236.44 | 3,582.47 | 3,756.46 |
| Currency Outside Depository Corps | 34a | 44.61 | 49.88 | 55.10 | 56.19 | 70.12 | 78.33 | 101.05 | 101.99 | 107.60 | 133.10 | 154.64 | 168.26 |
| Transferable Deposits | 34 | 503.54 | 509.01 | 641.39 | 692.19 | 656.26 | 605.90 | 643.15 | 755.23 | 975.14 | 1,067.98 | 1,332.58 | 1,330.29 |
| Other Deposits | 35 | 1,012.16 | 1,107.82 | 1,212.10 | 1,373.69 | 1,400.64 | 1,546.39 | 1,629.51 | 1,745.86 | 1,832.02 | 2,035.36 | 2,095.26 | 2,257.92 |
| Securities Other than Shares | 36a | — | — | — | — | — | — | — | — | — | — | — | — |
| Deposits Excl. from Broad Money | 36b | — | — | — | — | — | — | — | — | — | — | — | — |
| Sec.Ot.th.Shares Excl.f/Brd.Money | 36s | — | — | — | — | — | — | — | — | — | — | — | — |
| Loans | 36l | — | — | — | — | — | — | — | — | — | — | — | — |
| Financial Derivatives | 36m | — | — | — | — | — | — | — | — | — | — | — | — |
| Insurance Technical Reserves | 36r | — | — | — | — | — | — | — | — | — | — | — | — |
| Shares and Other Equity | 37a | 224.59 | 290.18 | 316.38 | 422.42 | 564.96 | 538.46 | 583.07 | 546.04 | 541.70 | 527.89 | 524.91 | 512.85 |
| Other Items (Net) | 37r | −44.12 | 76.16 | 148.37 | 118.28 | 182.40 | 81.78 | 56.65 | −16.40 | −94.65 | −673.43 | −27.96 | −141.59 |
| Broad Money Liabs., Seasonally Adj. | 35l.b | 1,585.14 | 1,695.01 | 1,941.42 | 2,156.68 | 2,156.03 | 2,251.78 | 2,385.06 | 2,599.66 | 2,895.17 | 3,199.39 | 3,533.13 | 3,700.38 |
| **Monetary Aggregates** | | | | | | *Millions of E. Caribbean Dollars: End of Period* | | | | | | | |
| Broad Money | 59m | 1,560.31 | 1,666.72 | 1,908.59 | 2,122.08 | 2,127.02 | 2,230.62 | 2,373.71 | 2,603.08 | 2,914.77 | 3,236.44 | 3,582.47 | 3,756.46 |
| o/w:Currency Issued by Cent.Govt | 59m.a | — | — | — | — | — | — | — | — | — | — | — | — |
| o/w: Dep.in Nonfin. Corporations | 59m.b | — | — | — | — | — | — | — | — | — | — | — | — |
| o/w:Secs. Issued by Central Govt | 59m.c | — | — | — | — | — | — | — | — | — | — | — | — |
| Money (National Definitions) | | | | | | | | | | | | | |
| M1 | 59ma | 166.38 | 163.69 | 184.49 | 205.10 | 251.71 | 255.24 | 357.33 | 480.18 | 541.16 | 521.09 | 582.11 | 624.28 |
| M2 | 59mb | 1,098.69 | 1,150.84 | 1,298.33 | 1,443.55 | 1,650.51 | 1,759.29 | 1,911.01 | 2,103.09 | 2,346.69 | 2,588.54 | 2,955.13 | 3,028.02 |
| **Interest Rates** | | | | | | *Percent Per Annum* | | | | | | | |
| Discount Rate (End of Period) | 60.a | 6.50 | 6.50 | 6.50 | 6.50 | 6.50 | 6.50 | 6.50 | 6.50 | 6.50 | 6.50 | 6.50 | 6.50 |
| Money Market Rate | 60b | 4.67 | 4.01 | 4.76 | 5.24 | 4.92 | 6.03 | 6.37 | 5.68 | 5.04 | 6.28 | 6.19 | 6.44 |
| Treasury Bill Rate | 60c | 7.00 | 7.00 | 7.00 | 7.00 | 7.00 | 6.85 | 6.75 | 6.75 | 6.75 | . . . . | . . . . | . . . . |
| Savings Rate | 60k | 3.58 | 3.58 | 3.59 | 3.62 | 3.58 | 3.52 | 3.54 | 3.52 | 3.35 | 3.34 | 3.30 | 2.69 |
| Savings Rate (Fgn. Currency) | 60k.f | 1.05 | 1.60 | 2.14 | 2.21 | 2.31 | 1.77 | 1.19 | 1.04 | 1.64 | 1.50 | .92 | .63 |
| Deposit Rate | 60l | 4.54 | 4.51 | 4.56 | 4.60 | 4.55 | 4.59 | 4.59 | 4.47 | 4.27 | 3.74 | 3.18 | 2.72 |
| Deposit Rate (Fgn. Currency) | 60l.f | .51 | .92 | 1.09 | 1.08 | .95 | .78 | .53 | .37 | 1.25 | 1.34 | 1.03 | .51 |
| Lending Rate | 60p | 10.25 | 10.03 | 9.30 | 9.28 | 8.70 | 8.75 | 8.62 | 9.45 | 8.73 | 8.78 | 9.28 | 9.30 |
| Lending Rate (Fgn. Currency) | 60p.f | 5.21 | 6.83 | 8.39 | 8.89 | 7.50 | 6.50 | 6.40 | 6.31 | 6.54 | 6.38 | 5.72 | 5.68 |
| **Prices** | | | | | | *Index Numbers (2010=100): Period Averages* | | | | | | | |
| Consumer Prices | 64 | 79.0 | 81.7 | 88.6 | 92.6 | 97.5 | 99.5 | † 100.0 | 105.8 | 106.7 | 107.9 | 108.1 | 105.7 |
| **Intl. Transactions & Positions** | | | | | | *Millions of E. Caribbean Dollars* | | | | | | | |
| Exports | 70 | 101 | 81 | 96 | 86 | 116 | 115 | 122 | 92 | 134 | 136 | 144 | 158 |
| Imports, c.i.f | 71 | 493 | 568 | 674 | 735 | 877 | 816 | 616 | 669 | 609 | 672 | 725 | 1,009 |

| | | 2004 | 2005 | 2006 | 2007 | 2008 | 2009 | 2010 | 2011 | 2012 | 2013 | 2014 | 2015 |
|---|---|---|---|---|---|---|---|---|---|---|---|---|---|
| **Balance of Payments** | | | | | | | *Millions of US Dollars* | | | | | | |
| A. Current Account* | 109bx | −68.4 | −64.7 | −85.1 | −113.0 | −203.3 | −180.1 | −138.6 | −102.2 | −84.7 | −62.7 | .... | .... |
| Goods, credit (exports) | 1a9cx | 58.8 | 63.4 | 58.2 | 57.5 | 68.9 | 37.4 | 57.9 | 67.7 | 62.8 | 58.1 | .... | .... |
| Goods, debit (imports) | 1a9dx | 160.8 | 185.2 | 219.6 | 243.0 | 311.9 | 265.7 | 252.7 | 246.4 | 227.7 | 251.3 | .... | .... |
| Balance on goods | 1a9bx | −102.1 | −121.8 | −161.4 | −185.4 | −243.0 | −228.3 | −194.8 | −178.6 | −164.9 | −193.2 | .... | .... |
| Services, credit (exports) | 1b9cx | 135.2 | 163.2 | 177.5 | 175.5 | 165.8 | 137.3 | 150.2 | 174.8 | 194.4 | 236.2 | .... | .... |
| Services, debit (imports) | 1b9dx | 80.8 | 94.9 | 101.1 | 103.4 | 125.1 | 100.5 | 111.4 | 115.3 | 119.6 | 126.1 | .... | .... |
| Balance on Goods & Services | 1z9bx | −47.7 | −53.5 | −85.0 | −113.3 | −202.3 | −191.4 | −155.9 | −119.1 | −90.1 | −83.1 | .... | .... |
| Primary income: credit | 1c9cx | 7.6 | 10.7 | 13.3 | 14.7 | 10.0 | 10.5 | 7.7 | 6.4 | 5.3 | 5.3 | .... | .... |
| Primary income: debit | 1c9dx | 46.5 | 45.8 | 45.6 | 45.7 | 44.2 | 44.4 | 36.9 | 36.0 | 29.1 | 19.9 | .... | .... |
| Balance on gds, serv. & prim. inc. | 1y9bx | −86.6 | −88.6 | −117.3 | −144.2 | −236.5 | −225.3 | −185.1 | −148.8 | −113.9 | −97.7 | .... | .... |
| Secondary income: credit | 1d9ca | 31.1 | 36.8 | 44.9 | 43.9 | 51.1 | 60.8 | 64.1 | 67.9 | 59.8 | 67.0 | .... | .... |
| Secondary income: debit | 1d9da | 12.9 | 12.9 | 12.7 | 12.7 | 18.0 | 15.6 | 17.5 | 21.3 | 30.7 | 32.0 | .... | .... |
| B. Capital Account* | 209ba | 2.7 | 11.7 | 10.0 | 16.4 | 29.8 | 21.4 | 55.6 | 81.6 | 164.0 | 128.5 | .... | .... |
| Capital account: credit | 209ca | 2.7 | 11.7 | 10.0 | 16.4 | 29.8 | 21.4 | 55.6 | 81.6 | 164.0 | 128.5 | .... | .... |
| Capital account: debit | 209da | — | — | — | — | — | — | — | — | — | — | .... | .... |
| Balance on current & capital acct. | 129ba | −65.7 | −53.0 | −75.1 | −96.6 | −173.5 | −158.7 | −82.9 | −20.6 | 79.3 | 65.8 | .... | .... |
| C. Financial Account* | 309na | −84.9 | −28.9 | −89.6 | −110.4 | −187.3 | −212.6 | −142.2 | −67.8 | 110.3 | 62.2 | .... | .... |
| Direct investment: assets | 3a9aa | — | — | — | — | — | — | — | — | — | — | .... | .... |
| Equity & investment fund shares.. | 3aaaa | .... | .... | .... | .... | .... | .... | .... | .... | .... | .... | .... | .... |
| Debt instruments | 3abaa | .... | .... | .... | .... | .... | .... | .... | .... | .... | .... | .... | .... |
| Direct investment: liabilities | 3a9la | 55.8 | 93.0 | 110.4 | 134.5 | 177.9 | 130.8 | 116.3 | 109.6 | 92.4 | 110.8 | .... | .... |
| Equity & investment fund shares . | 3aala | 19.1 | 41.4 | 21.2 | 43.0 | 80.6 | 51.5 | 42.0 | 33.1 | 15.0 | 13.6 | .... | .... |
| Debt instruments | 3abla | 36.7 | 51.6 | 89.2 | 91.4 | 97.3 | 79.3 | 74.3 | 76.5 | 77.5 | 97.2 | .... | .... |
| Portfolio investment: assets | 3b9aa | .4 | — | 1.8 | — | — | .1 | 3.3 | 3.4 | 5.9 | — | .... | .... |
| Equity & investment fund shares | 3baaa | .... | .... | .... | .... | .... | .... | .... | .... | .... | .... | .... | .... |
| Debt securities | 3bbaa | .... | .... | .... | .... | .... | .... | .... | .... | .... | .... | .... | .... |
| Portfolio investment: liabilities | 3b9la | −9.5 | −15.0 | −19.2 | −13.0 | 10.5 | −11.1 | −13.9 | −12.1 | 16.1 | — | .... | .... |
| Equity & investment fund shares . | 3bala | .... | .... | .... | .... | .... | .... | .... | .... | .... | .... | .... | .... |
| Debt securities | 3bbla | .... | .... | .... | .... | .... | .... | .... | .... | .... | .... | .... | .... |
| Fin. der.& empl.stk.ops.(ESOs): net. | 3c9na | .... | .... | .... | .... | .... | .... | .... | .... | .... | .... | .... | .... |
| Fin. der. & ESOs.: assets | 3c9aa | .... | .... | .... | .... | .... | .... | .... | .... | .... | .... | .... | .... |
| Fin. der. & ESOs.: liabilities | 3c9la | .... | .... | .... | .... | .... | .... | .... | .... | .... | .... | .... | .... |
| Other investment: assets | 3d9aa | 23.2 | 46.0 | 18.9 | 42.5 | 63.4 | 14.4 | 9.4 | 35.6 | 207.7 | 186.2 | .... | .... |
| Other equity | 3daaa | .... | .... | .... | .... | .... | .... | .... | .... | .... | .... | .... | .... |
| Debt instruments | 3dzaa | 23.2 | 46.0 | 18.9 | 42.5 | 63.4 | 14.4 | 9.4 | 35.6 | 207.7 | 186.2 | .... | .... |
| Other investment: liabilities | 3d9la | 62.1 | −3.1 | 19.0 | 31.4 | 62.3 | 107.4 | 52.5 | 9.2 | −5.3 | 13.2 | .... | .... |
| Other equity | 3dala | .... | .... | .... | .... | .... | .... | .... | .... | .... | .... | .... | .... |
| Debt instruments | 3dzla | 62.1 | −3.1 | 19.0 | 31.4 | 62.3 | 107.4 | 52.5 | 9.2 | −5.3 | 13.2 | .... | .... |
| Curr.+ cap.− finan. acct. balance... | 4y9na | 19.2 | −24.1 | 14.5 | 13.8 | 13.8 | 53.9 | 59.3 | 47.3 | −31.1 | 3.5 | .... | .... |
| D. Net Errors and Omissions | 409na | −5.6 | 17.4 | 2.7 | −6.6 | .8 | −31.2 | −26.0 | −6.9 | 17.4 | 30.2 | .... | .... |
| E. Reserves and Related Items | 4z9na | 13.6 | −6.7 | 17.1 | 7.2 | 14.6 | 22.7 | 33.3 | 40.3 | −13.7 | 33.7 | .... | .... |
| Reserve assets | 3e9aa | 13.6 | −6.7 | 17.1 | 7.2 | 14.6 | 26.1 | 33.3 | 75.7 | 17.6 | 38.5 | .... | .... |
| Credit and loans from the IMF | 3dcla | — | — | — | — | — | 3.4 | — | 35.3 | 31.3 | 4.7 | .... | .... |
| Exceptional financing | 409la | .... | .... | .... | .... | .... | .... | .... | .... | .... | .... | .... | .... |
| *Excludes components in group E | | | | | | | | | | | | | |

**Government Finance**
**Cash Flow Statement**

| **Budgetary Central Government** | | | | | | *Millions of E. Caribbean Dollars: Fiscal Year Ends December 31* | | | | | | | | |
|---|---|---|---|---|---|---|---|---|---|---|---|---|---|
| Cash Receipts:Operating Activities... | c1 | 369.40 | 466.00 | 518.50 | 544.50 | 571.11 | 579.15 | 561.76 | 730.50 | 830.91 | 896.42 | 944.10 | .... |
| Taxes | c11 | 281.90 | 344.10 | 374.10 | 399.60 | 420.74 | 380.66 | 342.96 | 408.22 | 399.00 | 429.38 | 478.56 | .... |
| Social Contributions | c12 | — | — | — | — | — | — | — | — | — | — | — | .... |
| Grants | c13 | 4.10 | 32.20 | 27.00 | 28.40 | 28.25 | 58.11 | 53.95 | 80.39 | 186.30 | 109.93 | 57.98 | .... |
| Other Receipts | c14 | 83.50 | 89.60 | 117.40 | 116.60 | 122.12 | 140.38 | 164.85 | 241.89 | 245.61 | 357.11 | 407.56 | .... |
| Cash Payments:Operating Activities. | c2 | 381.50 | 439.80 | 478.20 | 500.10 | 536.12 | 521.67 | 524.93 | 641.91 | 546.47 | 539.22 | 623.23 | .... |
| Compensation of Employees | c21 | 159.70 | 163.10 | 169.50 | 189.70 | 212.11 | 219.89 | 223.50 | 221.99 | 222.26 | 237.44 | 257.09 | .... |
| Purchases of Goods & Services | c22 | 95.80 | 114.70 | 129.40 | 140.40 | 136.52 | 130.28 | 118.15 | 210.24 | 129.21 | 137.25 | 162.68 | .... |
| Interest | c24 | 81.60 | 95.80 | 109.20 | 115.90 | 128.85 | 117.29 | 125.76 | 113.48 | 116.66 | 82.08 | 77.78 | .... |
| Subsidies | c25 | 23.10 | 45.20 | 47.40 | 30.50 | 37.60 | 32.97 | 35.46 | 72.07 | 52.44 | 52.78 | 94.47 | .... |
| Grants | c26 | — | — | — | — | — | — | — | — | — | — | — | .... |
| Social Benefits | c27 | 21.20 | 21.10 | 22.70 | 23.60 | 21.04 | 21.24 | 22.06 | 24.13 | 25.90 | 29.67 | 31.21 | .... |
| Other Payments | c28 | — | — | — | — | — | — | — | — | — | — | — | .... |
| Net Cash Inflow:Operating Act.[1-2] | ccio | −12.00 | 26.10 | 40.30 | 44.40 | 34.99 | 57.48 | 36.83 | 88.59 | 284.44 | 357.20 | 320.87 | .... |
| Net Cash Outflow:Invest. in NFA | c31 | 62.10 | 74.80 | 65.40 | 64.20 | 21.83 | 44.53 | 105.57 | 74.77 | 62.09 | 67.55 | 91.23 | .... |
| Purchases of Nonfinancial Assets... | c31.1 | 66.70 | 78.80 | 71.00 | 100.70 | 83.83 | 70.99 | 118.42 | 84.43 | 72.19 | 92.70 | 125.68 | .... |
| Sales of Nonfinancial Assets | c31.2 | 4.60 | 4.00 | 5.60 | 36.40 | 62.00 | 26.46 | 12.85 | 9.66 | 10.10 | 25.15 | 34.45 | .... |
| Cash Surplus/Deficit [1-2-31=1-2M] | ccsd | −74.10 | −48.70 | −25.10 | −19.80 | 13.16 | 12.95 | −68.74 | 13.82 | 222.35 | 289.65 | 229.64 | .... |
| Net Acq. Fin. Assets, excl. Cash | c32x | 11.30 | — | 6.00 | 13.10 | 15.36 | 3.58 | 5.73 | −.58 | .08 | 1.10 | .75 | .... |
| By debtor | | | | | | | | | | | | | |
| Domestic | c321x | 11.30 | — | 6.00 | 13.10 | 15.36 | 3.58 | 5.73 | −.58 | .08 | 1.10 | .75 | .... |
| Foreign | c322x | — | — | — | — | — | — | — | — | — | — | — | .... |
| Net Incurrence of Liabilities | c33 | 51.30 | 41.80 | 27.30 | −3.80 | 31.74 | −71.66 | 41.75 | −110.94 | −277.19 | −755.63 | 8.23 | .... |
| By creditor | | | | | | | | | | | | | |
| Domestic | c331 | 86.50 | 88.70 | 70.80 | 42.30 | −90.34 | −12.20 | 68.02 | −124.11 | −266.92 | −769.20 | 90.14 | .... |
| Foreign | c332 | −35.20 | −46.90 | −43.50 | −46.00 | 122.08 | −59.46 | −26.27 | 13.17 | −10.27 | 13.57 | −81.91 | .... |
| Net Cash Inflow, Fin.Act.[-32x+33].. | cnfb | 40.00 | 41.80 | 21.30 | −16.90 | 16.38 | −75.24 | 36.02 | −110.36 | −277.27 | −756.73 | 7.48 | .... |
| Net Change in Stock of Cash | cncb | −34.20 | −6.90 | −3.80 | −36.70 | 29.54 | −62.29 | −32.72 | −96.54 | −54.92 | −467.08 | 237.12 | .... |
| Stat. Discrep. [32X-33+NCB-CSD].... | ccsdz | — | −.10 | — | — | — | — | — | — | — | — | — | .... |
| Memo Item:Cash Expenditure[2+31] | c2m | 443.60 | 514.60 | 543.60 | 564.30 | 557.95 | 566.20 | 630.50 | 716.68 | 608.56 | 606.77 | 714.46 | .... |
| Memo Item: Gross Debt | c63 | .... | .... | .... | .... | .... | .... | .... | .... | 2,158.60 | 1,585.10 | 1,482.43 | .... |

| National Accounts | | 2004 | 2005 | 2006 | 2007 | 2008 | 2009 | 2010 | 2011 | 2012 | 2013 | 2014 | 2015 |
|---|---|---|---|---|---|---|---|---|---|---|---|---|---|
| | | | | | | *Millions of E. Caribbean Dollars* | | | | | | | |
| Househ.Cons.Expend.,incl.NPISHs.... | 96f | 676.3 | 730.9 | 953.4 | 1,025.7 | 1,382.4 | 1,303.6 | 1,314.7 | 1,401.7 | 1,308.5 | 1,244.9 | 1,357.8 | .... |
| Government Consumption Expend... | 91f | 234.9 | 260.7 | 267.0 | 296.5 | 338.4 | 349.3 | 335.1 | 337.0 | 379.4 | 441.2 | 468.7 | .... |
| Gross Fixed Capital Formation......... | 93e | 570.7 | 619.4 | 726.4 | 831.0 | 807.0 | 776.3 | 638.7 | 569.3 | 524.5 | 597.1 | 651.8 | .... |
| Exports of Goods and Services......... | 90c | 523.7 | 612.0 | 636.4 | 629.2 | 635.7 | 476.8 | 572.9 | 668.3 | 713.9 | 833.0 | 886.0 | .... |
| Imports of Goods and Services (-)..... | 98c | 652.5 | 756.4 | 865.9 | 935.1 | 1,179.9 | 991.9 | 991.8 | 1,010.6 | 950.1 | 1,025.9 | 1,113.3 | .... |
| Gross Domestic Product (GDP)......... | 99b | 1,353.1 | 1,466.6 | 1,717.4 | 1,847.2 | 1,983.6 | 1,914.0 | 1,869.6 | 1,965.7 | 1,976.2 | 2,090.3 | 2,251.0 | .... |
| Net Primary Income from Abroad..... | 98.n | −105.0 | −94.9 | −87.3 | −83.6 | −92.2 | −91.5 | −78.7 | −80.0 | −64.1 | −60.9 | −74.8 | .... |
| Gross National Income (GNI)............ | 99a | 1,248.1 | 1,371.7 | 1,630.1 | 1,763.7 | 1,891.4 | 1,822.5 | 1,791.0 | 1,885.7 | 1,912.1 | 2,029.5 | 2,176.2 | .... |
| Net Current Transf.from Abroad....... | 98t | 49.2 | 64.5 | 87.0 | 84.3 | 89.4 | 121.9 | 125.6 | 125.8 | 122.7 | 121.7 | 120.5 | .... |
| Gross Nat'l Disposable Inc.(GNDI).... | 99i | 1,297.3 | 1,436.2 | 1,717.1 | 1,847.9 | 1,980.8 | 1,944.4 | 1,916.6 | 2,011.5 | 2,034.8 | 2,151.2 | 2,296.7 | .... |
| Gross Saving................................... | 99s | 386.1 | 444.6 | 496.6 | 525.8 | 260.0 | 291.5 | 266.8 | 272.8 | 346.9 | 465.0 | 470.2 | .... |
| GDP Volume 1990 Prices................. | 99b.p | 718.7 | 759.0 | 800.8 | 817.0 | 851.9 | 786.2 | .... | .... | .... | .... | .... | .... |
| GDP Volume 2006 Prices................. | 99b.p | 1,275.7 | 1,393.6 | 1,441.8 | 1,513.8 | 1,575.0 | 1,486.9 | 1,446.9 | .... | .... | .... | .... | .... |
| GDP Volume (2010=100)................ | 99bvp | 88.2 | 96.3 | 99.6 | 104.6 | 108.9 | 102.8 | 100.0 | .... | .... | .... | .... | .... |
| GDP Deflator (2010=100)............... | 99bip | 82.1 | 81.4 | 92.2 | 94.4 | 97.5 | 99.6 | 100.0 | .... | .... | .... | .... | .... |
| | | | | | | *Millions: Midyear Estimates* | | | | | | | |
| Population................................. | 99z | .05 | .05 | .05 | .05 | .05 | .05 | .05 | .05 | .05 | .05 | .05 | .06 |

# St. Lucia  362

|  |  | 2004 | 2005 | 2006 | 2007 | 2008 | 2009 | 2010 | 2011 | 2012 | 2013 | 2014 | 2015 |
|---|---|---|---|---|---|---|---|---|---|---|---|---|---|
| **Exchange Rates** | | | | | | | *E.Caribbean Dollars per SDR: End of Period* | | | | | | |
| Official Rate | aa | 4.1931 | 3.8590 | 4.0619 | 4.2667 | 4.1587 | 4.2328 | 4.1581 | 4.1452 | 4.1497 | 4.1580 | 3.9118 | 3.7415 |
| | | | | | | *E.Caribbean Dollars per US Dollar: End of Period (ae) Period Average (rf)* | | | | | | | |
| Official Rate | ae | 2.7000 | 2.7000 | 2.7000 | 2.7000 | 2.7000 | 2.7000 | 2.7000 | 2.7000 | 2.7000 | 2.7000 | 2.7000 | 2.7000 |
| Official Rate | rf | 2.7000 | 2.7000 | 2.7000 | 2.7000 | 2.7000 | 2.7000 | 2.7000 | 2.7000 | 2.7000 | 2.7000 | 2.7000 | 2.7000 |
| | | | | | | *Index Numbers (2010=100): Period Averages* | | | | | | | |
| Official Rate | ahx | 100.0 | 100.0 | 100.0 | 100.0 | 100.0 | 100.0 | 100.0 | 100.0 | 100.0 | 100.0 | 100.0 | 100.0 |
| Nominal Effective Exchange Rate | nec | 103.5 | 102.6 | 102.2 | 99.2 | 97.3 | 100.3 | 100.0 | 97.6 | 99.6 | 100.8 | 101.5 | 108.6 |
| CPI-Based Real Effect. Ex. Rate | rec | 102.7 | 102.2 | 102.1 | 98.8 | 97.8 | 99.8 | 100.0 | 96.8 | 100.1 | 100.8 | 103.2 | 108.1 |
| **Fund Position** | | | | | | | *Millions of SDRs: End of Period* | | | | | | |
| Quota | 2f.s | 15.30 | 15.30 | 15.30 | 15.30 | 15.30 | 15.30 | 15.30 | 15.30 | 15.30 | 15.30 | 15.30 | 15.30 |
| SDR Holdings | 1b.s | 1.50 | 1.52 | 1.55 | 1.59 | 1.61 | 15.43 | 15.53 | 15.41 | 15.44 | 15.42 | 15.41 | 14.02 |
| Reserve Position in the Fund | 1c.s | .01 | .01 | .01 | .01 | .01 | .01 | .01 | .01 | .01 | .01 | .01 | .01 |
| Total Fund Cred.&Loans Outstg. | 2tl | — | — | — | — | — | — | 6.89 | 12.25 | 12.25 | 12.25 | 11.68 | 9.53 |
| SDR Allocations | 1bd | .74 | .74 | .74 | .74 | .74 | 14.57 | 14.57 | 14.57 | 14.57 | 14.57 | 14.57 | 14.57 |
| **International Liquidity** | | | | | | | *Millions of US Dollars Unless Otherwise Indicated: End of Period* | | | | | | |
| Total Reserves minus Gold | 1l.d | 132.54 | 116.39 | 134.54 | 153.72 | 142.77 | 174.80 | 206.26 | 213.43 | 231.97 | 192.22 | 257.66 | 317.54 |
| SDR Holdings | 1b.d | 2.34 | 2.18 | 2.33 | 2.51 | 2.48 | 24.19 | 23.92 | 23.66 | 23.73 | 23.75 | 22.32 | 19.43 |
| Reserve Position in the Fund | 1c.d | .01 | .01 | .01 | .01 | .01 | .01 | .01 | .01 | .01 | .01 | .01 | .01 |
| Foreign Exchange | 1d.d | 130.19 | 114.20 | 132.19 | 151.20 | 140.28 | 150.60 | 182.33 | 189.77 | 208.23 | 168.46 | 235.33 | 298.10 |
| Central Bank: Other Assets | 3..d | — | — | — | — | — | — | — | — | — | — | — | — |
| Central Bank: Other Liabs. | 4..d | — | — | — | — | — | — | — | — | — | — | — | — |
| Other Depository Corps.: Assets | 7a.d | 178.83 | 235.36 | 301.92 | 396.53 | 260.62 | 299.76 | 310.02 | 304.77 | 323.21 | 335.86 | 364.89 | 454.15 |
| Other Depository Corps.: Liabs. | 7b.d | 178.38 | 259.55 | 390.55 | 565.39 | 602.14 | 636.87 | 604.88 | 677.75 | 745.09 | 743.64 | 713.24 | 652.85 |
| **Central Bank** | | | | | | | *Millions of E.Caribbean Dollars: End of Period* | | | | | | |
| Net Foreign Assets | 11n | 358.72 | 313.76 | 363.15 | 415.05 | 385.92 | 414.71 | 472.06 | 470.99 | 515.46 | 407.93 | 593.46 | 767.62 |
| Claims on Nonresidents | 11 | 361.83 | 316.62 | 366.17 | 418.22 | 389.00 | 476.37 | 561.27 | 582.15 | 626.75 | 519.44 | 696.11 | 857.79 |
| Liabilities to Nonresidents | 16c | 3.11 | 2.86 | 3.01 | 3.16 | 3.08 | 61.66 | 89.22 | 111.16 | 111.28 | 111.50 | 102.66 | 90.17 |
| Claims on Other Depository Corps. | 12e | .05 | .04 | .05 | .02 | .02 | .01 | .04 | .03 | .04 | .05 | .14 | .15 |
| Net Claims on Central Government | 12an | −15.74 | −10.31 | −19.82 | −43.28 | 5.87 | −3.75 | −49.84 | −52.53 | −30.84 | 34.90 | .80 | −25.89 |
| Claims on Central Government | 12a | 9.30 | 9.31 | 6.97 | 11.16 | 7.01 | 2.50 | 1.57 | 1.98 | 2.12 | 37.09 | 52.19 | — |
| Liabilities to Central Government | 16d | 25.05 | 19.62 | 26.79 | 54.44 | 1.13 | 6.25 | 51.41 | 54.51 | 32.96 | 2.19 | 51.39 | 25.89 |
| Claims on Other Sectors | 12s | — | — | — | — | — | — | — | — | — | — | — | — |
| Claims on Other Financial Corps. | 12g | — | — | — | — | — | — | — | — | — | — | — | — |
| Claims on State & Local Govts | 12b | — | — | — | — | — | — | — | — | — | — | — | — |
| Claims on Public Nonfin. Corps. | 12c | — | — | — | — | — | — | — | — | — | — | — | — |
| Claims on Private Sector | 12d | — | — | — | — | — | — | — | — | — | — | — | — |
| Monetary Base | 14 | 337.82 | 298.35 | 337.16 | 365.07 | 384.71 | 403.42 | 442.49 | 459.87 | 525.65 | 483.64 | 629.50 | 733.78 |
| Currency in Circulation | 14a | 140.47 | 161.72 | 179.27 | 187.13 | 211.85 | 198.14 | 212.17 | 237.64 | 246.66 | 239.33 | 231.99 | 229.71 |
| Liabs. to Other Depository Corps. | 14c | 197.35 | 136.62 | 157.89 | 177.94 | 172.86 | 205.28 | 230.32 | 222.22 | 278.99 | 244.31 | 397.51 | 504.07 |
| Liabilities to Other Sectors | 14d | — | — | — | — | — | — | — | — | — | — | — | — |
| Other Liabs. to Other Dep. Corps. | 14n | 1.54 | 1.67 | 2.47 | 2.65 | 3.02 | 3.44 | 3.95 | 5.44 | 5.78 | 6.17 | 6.82 | 45.35 |
| Dep. & Sec. Excl. f/Monetary Base. | 14o | — | — | — | — | — | — | — | — | — | — | — | — |
| Deposits Included in Broad Money. | 15 | — | — | — | — | — | — | — | — | — | — | — | — |
| Sec.Ot.th.Shares Incl.in Brd. Money | 16a | — | — | — | — | — | — | — | — | — | — | — | — |
| Deposits Excl. from Broad Money | 16b | — | — | — | — | — | — | — | — | — | — | — | — |
| Sec.Ot.th.Shares Excl.f/Brd.Money. | 16s | — | — | — | — | — | — | — | — | — | — | — | — |
| Loans | 16l | — | — | — | — | — | — | — | — | — | — | — | — |
| Financial Derivatives | 16m | — | — | — | — | — | — | — | — | — | — | — | — |
| Shares and Other Equity | 17a | — | — | — | — | — | — | — | — | — | — | — | — |
| Other Items (Net) | 17r | 3.66 | 3.48 | 3.75 | 4.07 | 4.08 | 4.11 | −24.18 | −46.83 | −46.76 | −46.92 | −41.93 | −37.25 |
| Memo Item: | | | | | | | | | | | | | |
| Total Assets | 10ra | 364.85 | 320.07 | 366.85 | 422.59 | 389.30 | 413.55 | 498.28 | 520.26 | 564.82 | 492.43 | 688.14 | 805.46 |
| **Other Depository Corporations** | | | | | | | *Millions of E.Caribbean Dollars: End of Period* | | | | | | |
| Net Foreign Assets | 21n | 1.20 | −65.30 | −239.31 | −455.91 | −922.10 | −910.21 | −796.14 | −1,007.06 | −1,139.07 | −1,101.00 | −940.56 | −536.49 |
| Claims on Nonresidents | 21 | 482.83 | 635.48 | 815.17 | 1,070.64 | 703.68 | 809.35 | 837.05 | 822.87 | 872.68 | 906.82 | 985.20 | 1,226.21 |
| Liabilities to Nonresidents | 26c | 481.63 | 700.78 | 1,054.48 | 1,526.55 | 1,625.78 | 1,719.56 | 1,633.19 | 1,829.93 | 2,011.75 | 2,007.83 | 1,925.76 | 1,762.70 |
| Claims on Central Bank | 20 | 240.56 | 198.63 | 204.39 | 207.33 | 258.93 | 263.93 | 290.63 | 299.50 | 355.84 | 321.03 | 528.21 | 622.04 |
| Currency | 20a | 41.31 | 55.34 | 52.69 | 59.09 | 69.28 | 55.67 | 60.64 | 72.40 | 83.65 | 79.36 | 77.10 | 75.86 |
| Reserve Deposits and Securities | 20b | 199.25 | 143.29 | 151.70 | 148.24 | 189.65 | 208.26 | 229.99 | 227.10 | 272.19 | 241.67 | 451.11 | 546.17 |
| Other Claims | 20n | — | — | — | — | — | — | — | — | — | — | — | — |
| Net Claims on Central Government | 22an | −114.27 | −68.68 | −7.12 | 86.66 | 90.21 | 59.05 | 4.11 | 51.76 | 196.79 | 276.48 | 263.30 | 264.04 |
| Claims on Central Government | 22a | 177.86 | 269.86 | 283.50 | 338.96 | 330.21 | 284.69 | 267.74 | 286.92 | 403.66 | 382.60 | 338.05 | 351.86 |
| Liabilities to Central Government | 26d | 292.13 | 338.54 | 290.62 | 252.30 | 240.00 | 225.64 | 263.63 | 235.16 | 206.86 | 106.12 | 74.76 | 87.82 |
| Claims on Other Sectors | 22s | 1,781.02 | 2,074.01 | 2,540.25 | 3,241.74 | 3,624.08 | 3,715.62 | 3,809.17 | 3,895.00 | 4,149.69 | 4,127.66 | 3,837.33 | 3,538.17 |
| Claims on Other Financial Corps. | 22g | 30.83 | 36.76 | 37.17 | 38.10 | 57.94 | 41.25 | 30.45 | 22.48 | 37.01 | 28.10 | 19.17 | 14.93 |
| Claims on State & Local Govts | 22b | .25 | .02 | .10 | .42 | 1.00 | .09 | 1.62 | 4.71 | 2.29 | 1.63 | 1.39 | 1.12 |
| Claims on Public Nonfin. Corps. | 22c | 99.50 | 119.97 | 116.15 | 112.42 | 115.28 | 135.65 | 139.67 | 134.14 | 103.99 | 90.60 | 68.90 | 61.49 |
| Claims on Private Sector | 22d | 1,650.45 | 1,917.27 | 2,386.83 | 3,090.80 | 3,449.87 | 3,538.63 | 3,637.44 | 3,733.67 | 4,006.39 | 4,007.33 | 3,747.87 | 3,460.62 |
| Liabilities to Central Bank | 26g | — | 10.16 | 5.76 | 17.24 | 16.64 | 10.69 | 1.04 | 1.08 | .46 | 4.86 | 2.39 | 1.34 |
| Transf.Dep.Included in Broad Money | 24 | 469.25 | 573.04 | 719.38 | 700.16 | 680.43 | 664.20 | 658.32 | 674.67 | 734.39 | 738.49 | 889.94 | 1,019.96 |
| Other Dep.Included in Broad Money. | 25 | 1,315.84 | 1,439.54 | 1,642.38 | 1,832.95 | 2,042.79 | 2,145.88 | 2,196.48 | 2,262.69 | 2,306.95 | 2,401.72 | 2,348.79 | 2,403.68 |
| Sec.Ot.th.Shares Incl.in Brd. Money. | 26a | — | — | — | — | — | — | — | — | — | — | — | — |
| Deposits Excl. from Broad Money. | 26b | — | — | — | — | — | — | — | — | — | — | — | — |
| Sec.Ot.th.Shares Excl.f/Brd.Money. | 26s | — | — | — | — | — | — | — | — | — | — | — | — |
| Loans | 26l | — | — | — | — | — | — | — | — | — | — | — | — |
| Financial Derivatives | 26m | — | — | — | — | — | — | — | — | — | — | — | — |
| Insurance Technical Reserves | 26r | — | — | — | — | — | — | — | — | — | — | — | — |
| Shares and Other Equity | 27a | 225.71 | 244.48 | 311.05 | 421.77 | 442.85 | 451.39 | 455.09 | 390.47 | 408.39 | 221.85 | 182.84 | 162.91 |
| Other Items (Net) | 27r | −102.29 | −128.56 | −180.35 | 107.70 | −131.59 | −143.77 | −3.16 | −89.71 | 113.06 | 257.25 | 264.31 | 299.87 |
| Memo Item: | | | | | | | | | | | | | |
| Total Assets | 20ra | 3,096.10 | 3,605.75 | 4,291.60 | 5,405.73 | 5,526.12 | 5,646.83 | 5,751.88 | 5,941.75 | 6,214.63 | 6,146.87 | 6,081.85 | 6,192.32 |

# St. Lucia 362

| | | 2004 | 2005 | 2006 | 2007 | 2008 | 2009 | 2010 | 2011 | 2012 | 2013 | 2014 | 2015 |
|---|---|---|---|---|---|---|---|---|---|---|---|---|---|
| **Depository Corporations** | | *Millions of E.Caribbean Dollars: End of Period* | | | | | | | | | | | |
| Net Foreign Assets.................... | 31n | 359.92 | 248.46 | 123.85 | −40.86 | −536.18 | −495.50 | −324.08 | −536.07 | −623.60 | −693.07 | −347.11 | 231.13 |
| Claims on Nonresidents................ | 31 | 844.66 | 952.10 | 1,181.34 | 1,488.86 | 1,092.68 | 1,285.72 | 1,398.33 | 1,405.02 | 1,499.42 | 1,426.26 | 1,681.31 | 2,084.00 |
| Liabilities to Nonresidents............ | 36c | 484.74 | 703.64 | 1,057.49 | 1,529.72 | 1,628.87 | 1,781.21 | 1,722.41 | 1,941.09 | 2,123.03 | 2,119.33 | 2,028.42 | 1,852.86 |
| Domestic Claims........................... | 32 | 1,651.01 | 1,995.03 | 2,513.31 | 3,285.12 | 3,720.16 | 3,770.92 | 3,763.44 | 3,894.23 | 4,315.65 | 4,439.04 | 4,101.42 | 3,776.32 |
| Net Claims on Central Government | 32an | −130.01 | −78.98 | −26.94 | 43.38 | 96.08 | 55.30 | −45.73 | −.78 | 165.96 | 311.38 | 264.10 | 238.15 |
| Claims on Central Government.... | 32a | 187.17 | 279.18 | 290.47 | 350.11 | 337.22 | 287.19 | 269.31 | 288.90 | 405.78 | 419.69 | 390.24 | 351.86 |
| Liabilities to Central Government. | 36d | 317.18 | 358.16 | 317.41 | 306.74 | 241.14 | 231.89 | 315.05 | 289.68 | 239.82 | 108.31 | 126.14 | 113.71 |
| Claims on Other Sectors................ | 32s | 1,781.02 | 2,074.01 | 2,540.25 | 3,241.74 | 3,624.08 | 3,715.62 | 3,809.17 | 3,895.00 | 4,149.69 | 4,127.66 | 3,837.33 | 3,538.17 |
| Claims on Other Financial Corps.. | 32g | 30.83 | 36.76 | 37.17 | 38.10 | 57.94 | 41.25 | 30.45 | 22.48 | 37.01 | 28.10 | 19.17 | 14.93 |
| Claims on State & Local Govts..... | 32b | .25 | .02 | .10 | .42 | 1.00 | .09 | 1.62 | 4.71 | 2.29 | 1.63 | 1.39 | 1.12 |
| Claims on Public Nonfin. Corps.... | 32c | 99.50 | 119.97 | 116.15 | 112.42 | 115.28 | 135.65 | 139.67 | 134.14 | 103.99 | 90.60 | 68.90 | 61.49 |
| Claims on Private Sector.............. | 32d | 1,650.45 | 1,917.27 | 2,386.83 | 3,090.80 | 3,449.87 | 3,538.63 | 3,637.44 | 3,733.67 | 4,006.39 | 4,007.33 | 3,747.87 | 3,460.62 |
| Broad Money Liabilities................... | 35l | 1,884.26 | 2,118.97 | 2,488.34 | 2,661.16 | 2,865.78 | 2,952.55 | 3,006.33 | 3,102.61 | 3,204.35 | 3,300.17 | 3,393.62 | 3,577.49 |
| Currency Outside Depository Corps | 34a | 99.16 | 106.38 | 126.58 | 128.05 | 142.57 | 142.46 | 151.53 | 165.24 | 163.01 | 159.97 | 154.89 | 153.85 |
| Transferable Deposits................... | 34 | 469.26 | 573.05 | 719.38 | 700.17 | 680.43 | 664.21 | 658.32 | 674.67 | 734.39 | 738.49 | 889.94 | 1,019.96 |
| Other Deposits........................... | 35 | 1,315.84 | 1,439.54 | 1,642.38 | 1,832.95 | 2,042.79 | 2,145.88 | 2,196.48 | 2,262.69 | 2,306.95 | 2,401.72 | 2,348.79 | 2,403.68 |
| Securities Other than Shares.......... | 36a | — | — | — | — | — | — | — | — | — | — | — | — |
| Deposits Excl. from Broad Money..... | 36b | — | — | — | — | — | — | — | — | — | — | — | — |
| Sec.Ot.th.Shares Excl.f/Brd.Money.... | 36s | — | — | — | — | — | — | — | — | — | — | — | — |
| Loans............................................ | 36l | — | — | — | — | — | — | — | — | — | — | — | — |
| Financial Derivatives..................... | 36m | — | — | — | — | — | — | — | — | — | — | — | — |
| Insurance Technical Reserves.......... | 36r | — | — | — | — | — | — | — | — | — | — | — | — |
| Shares and Other Equity................. | 37a | 225.71 | 244.48 | 311.05 | 421.77 | 442.85 | 451.39 | 455.09 | 390.47 | 408.39 | 221.85 | 182.84 | 162.91 |
| Other Items (Net)........................... | 37r | −99.04 | −119.96 | −162.23 | 161.33 | −124.65 | −128.52 | −22.06 | −134.93 | 79.30 | 223.95 | 177.86 | 267.05 |
| Broad Money Liabs., Seasonally Adj. | 35l.b | 1,897.09 | 2,132.57 | 2,500.79 | 2,672.92 | 2,878.49 | 2,971.61 | 3,031.94 | 3,135.76 | 3,243.85 | 3,346.47 | 3,444.56 | 3,632.68 |
| **Monetary Aggregates** | | *Millions of E.Caribbean Dollars: End of Period* | | | | | | | | | | | |
| Broad Money............................... | 59m | 1,884.26 | 2,118.97 | 2,488.34 | 2,661.16 | 2,865.78 | 2,952.55 | 3,006.33 | 3,102.61 | 3,204.35 | 3,300.17 | 3,393.62 | 3,577.49 |
| o/w:Currency Issued by Cent.Govt | 59m.a | — | — | — | — | — | — | — | — | — | — | — | — |
| o/w: Dep.in Nonfin. Corporations. | 59m.b | — | — | — | — | — | — | — | — | — | — | — | — |
| o/w:Secs. Issued by Central Govt.. | 59m.c | — | — | — | — | — | — | — | — | — | — | — | — |
| Money (National Definitions) | | | | | | | | | | | | | |
| M1.................................................... | 59ma | 481.29 | 547.32 | 560.67 | 638.97 | 661.41 | 659.58 | 644.53 | 675.03 | 701.03 | 695.44 | 748.57 | 769.09 |
| M2.................................................... | 59mb | 1,509.13 | 1,711.78 | 2,056.20 | 2,183.21 | 2,466.58 | 2,510.80 | 2,559.19 | 2,729.77 | 2,798.49 | 2,853.20 | 2,887.94 | 3,054.70 |
| **Interest Rates** | | *Percent Per Annum* | | | | | | | | | | | |
| Discount Rate (End of Period).......... | 60.a | 6.50 | 6.50 | 6.50 | 6.50 | 6.50 | 6.50 | 6.50 | 6.50 | 6.50 | 6.50 | 6.50 | 6.50 |
| Money Market Rate........................ | 60b | 4.67 | 4.01 | 4.76 | 5.24 | 4.92 | 6.03 | 6.36 | 5.68 | 5.04 | 6.28 | 6.19 | 6.44 |
| Treasury Bill Rate........................... | 60c | † 5.50 | 4.48 | 5.17 | † 5.65 | 5.60 | 5.20 | 4.50 | 4.45 | 5.10 | 6.00 | 6.00 | 6.00 |
| Savings Rate.................................. | 60k | 3.51 | 3.36 | 3.36 | 3.36 | 3.37 | 3.34 | 3.38 | 3.40 | 3.27 | 3.26 | 3.22 | 2.75 |
| Deposit Rate.................................. | 60l | 3.05 | 2.83 | 2.95 | 3.10 | 3.26 | 3.25 | 3.32 | 3.49 | 3.06 | 2.93 | 2.80 | 2.27 |
| Deposit Rate (Fgn. Currency)............ | 60l.f | .67 | .76 | .96 | 1.69 | 1.91 | 1.37 | 1.69 | 1.31 | 1.71 | 1.55 | 1.11 | .70 |
| Lending Rate.................................. | 60p | 11.07 | 10.61 | 10.78 | 10.12 | 10.08 | 10.58 | 10.62 | 10.00 | 9.50 | 9.08 | 9.00 | 8.86 |
| Lending Rate (Fgn. Currency).......... | 60p.f | 7.11 | 7.15 | 8.39 | 8.34 | 5.81 | 5.17 | 5.21 | 5.37 | 4.90 | 5.30 | 5.31 | 5.50 |
| **Prices and Labor** | | *Index Numbers (2010=100): Period Averages* | | | | | | | | | | | |
| Consumer Prices............................ | 64 | 83.8 | 87.1 | 89.2 | † 91.9 | 98.5 | 96.9 | 100.0 | 102.8 | 107.1 | 108.6 | 112.5 | 111.4 |
| | | *Number in Thousands: Period Averages* | | | | | | | | | | | |
| Labor Force.................................... | 67d | 78.8 | .... | .... | .... | .... | .... | .... | .... | .... | .... | .... | .... |
| Employment.................................. | 67e | 62.3 | .... | .... | .... | .... | .... | .... | .... | .... | .... | .... | .... |
| Unemployment.............................. | 67c | 16.5 | .... | .... | .... | .... | .... | .... | .... | .... | .... | .... | .... |
| Unemployment Rate (%)................. | 67r | 21.0 | .... | .... | .... | .... | .... | .... | .... | .... | .... | .... | .... |
| **Intl. Transactions & Positions** | | *Millions of E. Caribbean Dollars* | | | | | | | | | | | |
| Exports........................................... | 70 | 338.31 | 239.10 | 264.85 | 287.78 | 391.70 | 439.28 | 616.36 | 690.61 | 421.19 | 461.15 | 454.90 | 486.84 |
| Imports, c.i.f.................................. | 71 | 1,179.90 | 1,293.30 | 1,598.40 | 1,714.50 | 1,775.09 | 1,454.18 | 1,623.07 | 1,808.76 | 1,843.53 | 1,613.68 | 1,502.35 | 1,538.94 |
| | | *2002=100* | | | | | | | | | | | |
| Export Prices.................................. | 76 | .... | .... | .... | .... | .... | .... | .... | .... | .... | .... | .... | .... |
| Import Prices.................................. | 76.x | .... | .... | .... | .... | .... | .... | .... | .... | .... | .... | .... | .... |

|  |  | 2004 | 2005 | 2006 | 2007 | 2008 | 2009 | 2010 | 2011 | 2012 | 2013 | 2014 | 2015 |
|---|---|---|---|---|---|---|---|---|---|---|---|---|---|
| **Balance of Payments** |  |  |  |  | | *Millions of US Dollars* | | | | | | | |
| A. Current Account*........................ | 109bx | −91.1 | −129.5 | −309.0 | −344.7 | −339.9 | −136.7 | −202.8 | −242.7 | −182.9 | −100.3 | .... | .... |
| Goods, credit (exports)................. | 1a9cx | 96.3 | 88.8 | 96.6 | 101.2 | 172.5 | 191.3 | 238.9 | 192.3 | 212.4 | 205.3 | .... | .... |
| Goods, debit (imports)................. | 1a9dx | 348.0 | 418.1 | 521.0 | 541.7 | 604.8 | 458.0 | 583.0 | 613.2 | 566.4 | 496.7 | .... | .... |
| Balance on goods................. | 1a9bx | −251.7 | −329.4 | −424.3 | −440.5 | −432.4 | −266.6 | −344.1 | −421.0 | −353.9 | −291.3 | .... | .... |
| Services, credit (exports).............. | 1b9cx | 367.9 | 436.1 | 343.6 | 355.9 | 363.6 | 352.6 | 370.0 | 380.6 | 391.6 | 409.0 | .... | .... |
| Services, debit (imports)................ | 1b9dx | 152.3 | 176.7 | 185.7 | 205.7 | 215.5 | 190.0 | 204.4 | 203.0 | 190.1 | 187.4 | .... | .... |
| Balance on Goods & Services...... | 1z9bx | −36.1 | −69.9 | −266.5 | −290.3 | −284.2 | −104.0 | −178.6 | −243.4 | −152.4 | −69.8 | .... | .... |
| Primary income: credit.................. | 1c9cx | 6.2 | 8.1 | 11.6 | 12.4 | 8.2 | 16.5 | 17.7 | 16.2 | 17.6 | 17.3 | .... | .... |
| Primary income: debit.................. | 1c9dx | 75.2 | 80.6 | 66.1 | 80.4 | 80.1 | 61.7 | 57.3 | 36.1 | 55.3 | 55.2 | .... | .... |
| Balance on gds, serv. & prim. inc. | 1y9bx | −105.1 | −142.4 | −321.0 | −358.2 | −356.1 | −149.2 | −218.1 | −263.2 | −190.1 | −107.6 | .... | .... |
| Secondary income: credit.............. | 1d9ca | 29.9 | 29.7 | 31.4 | 35.3 | 36.8 | 32.1 | 40.8 | 34.2 | 32.3 | 32.7 | .... | .... |
| Secondary income: debit............... | 1d9da | 16.0 | 16.7 | 19.4 | 21.7 | 20.6 | 19.6 | 25.4 | 13.6 | 25.2 | 25.5 | .... | .... |
| B. Capital Account*....................... | 209ba | 2.2 | 4.1 | 10.0 | 7.2 | 9.5 | 24.5 | 42.4 | 32.5 | 31.4 | 26.7 | .... | .... |
| Capital account: credit.................. | 209ca | 2.2 | 4.1 | 10.0 | 7.2 | 9.5 | 24.5 | 42.4 | 32.5 | 31.4 | 26.7 | .... | .... |
| Capital account: debit.................. | 209da |  |  |  |  |  |  |  |  |  |  | .... | .... |
| Balance on current & capital acct. | 129ba | −88.9 | −125.4 | −299.0 | −337.4 | −330.4 | −112.3 | −160.3 | −210.2 | −151.6 | −73.7 | .... | .... |
| C. Financial Account* ................... | 309na | −106.3 | −122.6 | −309.5 | −355.9 | −327.9 | −181.2 | −157.0 | −201.8 | −159.9 | −56.5 | .... | .... |
| Direct investment: assets.............. | 3a9aa | — | — | — | — | — | — | — | 15.6 | — | — | .... | .... |
| Equity & investment fund shares.. | 3aaaa | .... | .... | .... | .... | .... | .... | .... | .... | .... | | .... | .... |
| Debt instruments....................... | 3abaa | .... | .... | .... | .... | .... | .... | .... | .... | .... | | .... | .... |
| Direct investment: liabilities ......... | 3a9la | 76.5 | 78.2 | 233.9 | 271.9 | 161.2 | 146.4 | 121.3 | 96.4 | 75.8 | 83.5 | .... | .... |
| Equity & investment fund shares . | 3aala | 67.5 | 75.3 | 179.2 | 194.6 | 108.5 | 72.6 | 67.9 | 44.8 | 45.2 | 52.4 | .... | .... |
| Debt instruments....................... | 3abla | 9.0 | 3.0 | 54.7 | 77.3 | 52.7 | 73.8 | 53.4 | 51.6 | 30.5 | 31.1 | .... | .... |
| Portfolio investment: assets.......... | 3b9aa | −.9 | −.2 | 7.8 | 4.7 | −5.7 | 21.5 | 1.1 | −1.7 | .6 | −36.1 | .... | .... |
| Equity & investment fund shares | 3baaa | .... | .... | .... | .... | .... | .... | .... | .... | .... | | .... | .... |
| Debt securities .......................... | 3bbaa | .... | .... | .... | .... | .... | .... | .... | .... | .... | | .... | .... |
| Portfolio investment: liabilities....... | 3b9la | 15.4 | 23.9 | 4.8 | 5.2 | −15.3 | −7.6 | 31.7 | 32.1 | 52.8 | 58.0 | .... | .... |
| Equity & investment fund shares . | 3bala | .... | .... | .... | .... | .... | .... | .... | .... | .... | | .... | .... |
| Debt securities.......................... | 3bbla | .... | .... | .... | .... | .... | .... | .... | .... | .... | | .... | .... |
| Fin. der.& empl.stk.ops.(ESOs): net. | 3c9na | .... | .... | .... | .... | .... | .... | .... | .... | .... | | .... | .... |
| Fin. der. & ESOs.: assets.............. | 3c9aa | .... | .... | .... | .... | .... | .... | .... | .... | .... | | .... | .... |
| Fin. der. & ESOs.: liabilities.......... | 3c9la | .... | .... | .... | .... | .... | .... | .... | .... | .... | | .... | .... |
| Other investment: assets............... | 3d9aa | 31.2 | 49.7 | 25.7 | 41.1 | 31.1 | 50.1 | 88.8 | 67.5 | 82.3 | 200.9 | .... | .... |
| Other equity............................ | 3daaa | .... | .... | .... | .... | .... | .... | .... | .... | .... | | .... | .... |
| Debt instruments....................... | 3dzaa | 31.2 | 49.7 | 25.7 | 41.1 | 31.1 | 50.1 | 88.8 | 67.5 | 82.3 | 200.9 | .... | .... |
| Other investment: liabilities........... | 3d9la | 44.6 | 70.1 | 104.2 | 124.6 | 207.3 | 114.1 | 93.8 | 154.7 | 114.3 | 79.8 | .... | .... |
| Other equity............................ | 3dala | .... | .... | .... | .... | .... | .... | .... | .... | .... | | .... | .... |
| Debt instruments....................... | 3dzla | 44.6 | 70.1 | 104.2 | 124.6 | 207.3 | 114.1 | 93.8 | 154.7 | 114.3 | 79.8 | .... | .... |
| Curr.+ cap.− finan. acct. balance... | 4y9na | 17.4 | −2.8 | 10.5 | 18.5 | −2.5 | 69.0 | −3.4 | −8.3 | 8.3 | −17.1 | .... | .... |
| D. Net Errors and Omissions............ | 409nan | 7.6 | −13.8 | 3.0 | .1 | −8.4 | −36.7 | 24.5 | 7.8 | 8.1 | −22.7 | .... | .... |
| E. Reserves and Related Items.......... | 4z9na | 25.0 | −16.6 | 13.5 | 18.6 | −10.9 | 32.3 | 21.1 | −.5 | 16.5 | −39.8 | .... | .... |
| Reserve assets............................ | 3e9aa | 25.0 | −16.6 | 13.5 | 18.6 | −10.9 | 32.3 | 31.9 | 7.8 | 16.5 | −39.8 | .... | .... |
| Credit and loans from the IMF....... | 3dcla | — | — | — | — | — | — | 10.8 | 8.3 | — | — | .... | .... |
| Exceptional financing.................... | 409la | .... | .... | .... | .... | .... | .... | .... | .... | .... | | .... | .... |

*Excludes components in group E

**Government Finance**
**Cash Flow Statement**
**Budgetary Central Government**

|  |  | 2004 | 2005 | 2006 | 2007 | 2008 | 2009 | 2010 | 2011 | 2012 | 2013 | 2014 | 2015 |
|---|---|---|---|---|---|---|---|---|---|---|---|---|---|
|  |  |  | | | | *Millions of E. Caribbean Dollars: Fiscal Year Ends December 31* | | | | | | | |
| Cash Receipts:Operating Activities... | c1 | 543.94 | 581.07 | 651.04 | 712.67 | 801.94 | 789.60 | 838.04 | 838.50 | 833.45 | 882.75 | 930.43 | .... |
| Taxes...................................... | c11 | 495.71 | 540.83 | 603.82 | 659.05 | 725.32 | 724.04 | 728.46 | 763.41 | 740.22 | 814.26 | 855.50 | .... |
| Social Contributions..................... | c12 | — | — | — | — | — | — | — | — | — | — | — | .... |
| Grants..................................... | c13 | 6.02 | 4.20 | 3.27 | 9.27 | 20.68 | 25.91 | 59.21 | 28.28 | 23.09 | 17.33 | 29.05 | .... |
| Other Receipts............................. | c14 | 42.21 | 36.04 | 43.94 | 44.35 | 55.93 | 39.65 | 50.37 | 46.81 | 70.14 | 51.16 | 45.88 | .... |
| Cash Payments:Operating Activities. | c2 | 490.39 | 480.16 | 484.78 | 482.38 | 627.39 | 653.47 | 721.47 | 758.62 | 822.77 | 847.95 | 858.68 | .... |
| Compensation of Employees.......... | c21 | 227.06 | 222.68 | 255.06 | 252.38 | 288.26 | 307.83 | 336.38 | 344.64 | 358.66 | 372.93 | 378.98 | .... |
| Purchases of Goods & Services....... | c22 | 95.51 | 91.01 | 104.25 | 103.47 | 133.08 | 127.85 | 147.38 | 145.75 | 157.72 | 168.13 | 160.70 | .... |
| Interest.................................... | c24 | 61.89 | 70.00 | 79.13 | 81.07 | 78.39 | 89.84 | 92.82 | 107.29 | 123.19 | 134.81 | 142.78 | .... |
| Subsidies.................................. | c25 | 70.65 | 54.05 | 4.93 | 4.43 | 120.99 | 120.99 | 136.30 | 122.67 | 120.91 | 108.00 | 105.50 | .... |
| Grants..................................... | c26 | — | — | — | — | — | — | — | — | — | — | — | .... |
| Social Benefits............................ | c27 | 35.27 | 42.42 | 41.40 | 41.04 | 6.67 | 6.96 | 8.59 | 38.27 | 62.29 | 64.08 | 70.72 | .... |
| Other Payments........................... | c28 | — | — | — | — | — | — | — | — | — | — | — | .... |
| Net Cash Inflow:Operating Act.[1-2] | ccio | 53.55 | 100.91 | 166.26 | 230.29 | 174.55 | 136.13 | 116.57 | 79.88 | 10.68 | 34.80 | 71.75 | .... |
| Net Cash Outflow:Invest. in NFA...... | c31 | 153.94 | 234.11 | 250.39 | 216.28 | 173.19 | 200.13 | 139.33 | 264.09 | 241.23 | 275.82 | 209.73 | .... |
| Purchases of Nonfinancial Assets... | c31.1 | 154.81 | 234.11 | 251.32 | 216.31 | 179.91 | 200.23 | 147.97 | 264.61 | 241.53 | 276.24 | 209.91 | .... |
| Sales of Nonfinancial Assets.......... | c31.2 | .87 | — | .93 | .04 | 6.72 | .10 | 8.64 | .52 | .30 | .42 | .18 | .... |
| Cash Surplus/Deficit [1-2-31=1-2M] | ccsd | −100.39 | −133.21 | −84.13 | 14.01 | 1.36 | −64.00 | −22.76 | −184.21 | −230.55 | −241.02 | −137.98 | .... |
| Net Acq. Fin. Assets, excl. Cash...... | c32x | — | — | — | — | — | — | — | — | — | — | — | .... |
| Domestic................................... | c321x | — | — | — | — | — | — | — | — | — | — | — | .... |
| Foreign.................................... | c322x | — | — | — | — | — | — | — | — | — | — | — | .... |
| Net Incurrence of Liabilities............. | c33 | 23.01 | 139.42 | 151.00 | 112.02 | 47.35 | 18.77 | −23.77 | 160.23 | 212.15 | 112.40 | 54.19 | .... |
| Domestic................................... | c331 | −25.87 | 39.49 | 58.75 | 49.26 | 51.95 | −21.37 | −99.66 | 51.06 | 163.36 | 145.62 | −50.83 | .... |
| Foreign.................................... | c332 | 48.88 | 99.93 | 92.25 | 62.76 | −4.60 | 40.14 | 75.89 | 109.17 | 48.79 | −33.22 | 105.02 | .... |
| Net Cash Inflow, Fin.Act.[-32x+33].. | cnfb | 23.01 | 139.42 | 151.00 | 112.02 | 47.35 | 18.77 | −23.77 | 160.23 | 212.15 | 112.40 | 54.19 | .... |
| Net Change in Stock of Cash........... | cncb | −77.38 | 6.21 | 66.87 | 126.03 | 48.71 | −45.23 | −46.53 | −23.98 | −18.40 | −128.62 | −83.79 | .... |
| Stat. Discrep. [32X-33+NCB-CSD].... | ccsdz |  |  |  |  |  |  |  |  |  |  |  | .... |
| Memo Item:Cash Expenditure[2+31] | c2m | 644.32 | 714.28 | 735.17 | 698.66 | 800.58 | 853.60 | 860.80 | 1,022.71 | 1,064.00 | 1,123.77 | 1,068.41 | .... |
| Memo Item: Gross Debt.................. | c63 | 1,428.00 | 1,595.40 | 1,616.20 | 1,634.10 | 1,835.40 | .... | .... | .... | 2,389.18 | 2,558.69 | 2,728.52 | .... |

# St. Lucia   362

| | | 2004 | 2005 | 2006 | 2007 | 2008 | 2009 | 2010 | 2011 | 2012 | 2013 | 2014 | 2015 |
|---|---|---|---|---|---|---|---|---|---|---|---|---|---|
| **National Accounts** | | | | | | *Millions of E. Caribbean Dollars* | | | | | | | |
| Househ.Cons.Expend.,incl.NPISHs.... | 96f | 1,581.8 | 1,672.7 | 2,129.0 | 2,596.2 | 2,490.1 | 2,098.3 | 2,424.8 | 2,673.3 | 2,465.9 | 2,637.3 | 2,747.5 | .... |
| Government Consumption Expend... | 91f | 314.0 | 313.5 | 363.4 | 372.7 | 413.9 | 438.9 | 476.0 | 484.7 | 512.9 | 534.4 | 552.7 | .... |
| Gross Fixed Capital Formation.......... | 93e | 591.7 | 728.4 | 1,088.1 | 902.2 | 1,026.1 | 920.5 | 940.9 | 980.8 | 937.5 | 841.9 | 667.2 | .... |
| Exports of Goods and Services......... | 90c | 1,253.4 | 1,417.3 | 1,188.6 | 1,234.2 | 1,447.4 | 1,468.7 | 1,643.9 | 1,546.7 | 1,630.2 | 1,580.6 | 1,662.3 | .... |
| Imports of Goods and Services (-)..... | 98c | 1,350.8 | 1,606.1 | 1,908.1 | 2,017.9 | 2,214.8 | 1,749.5 | 2,126.1 | 2,203.8 | 2,029.3 | 1,987.7 | 1,943.0 | .... |
| Gross Domestic Product (GDP)........ | 99b | 2,390.2 | 2,525.8 | 2,861.1 | 3,087.4 | 3,162.7 | 3,176.8 | 3,359.6 | 3,481.7 | 3,517.2 | 3,606.6 | 3,686.7 | .... |
| Net Primary Income from Abroad..... | 98.n | −186.3 | −195.8 | −147.1 | −183.5 | −194.1 | −121.9 | −106.8 | −53.6 | −95.3 | −68.7 | −56.9 | .... |
| Gross National Income (GNI)........... | 99a | 2,203.9 | 2,330.0 | 2,713.9 | 2,903.9 | 2,968.6 | 3,054.9 | 3,252.8 | 3,428.2 | 3,421.9 | 3,537.9 | 3,629.8 | .... |
| Net Current Transf.from Abroad....... | 98t | 37.6 | 35.0 | 32.4 | 36.6 | 43.8 | 33.6 | 41.5 | 55.5 | 17.1 | 12.8 | 12.2 | .... |
| Gross Nat'l Disposable Inc.(GNDI).... | 99i | 2,241.4 | 2,365.0 | 2,746.3 | 2,940.5 | 3,012.5 | 3,088.5 | 3,294.3 | 3,483.6 | 3,439.0 | 3,550.6 | 3,642.0 | .... |
| Gross Saving.................................. | 99s | 345.6 | 378.8 | 253.8 | −70.0 | 108.5 | 551.3 | 393.5 | 325.6 | 460.2 | 378.9 | 341.8 | .... |
| GDP Volume 1990 Prices................. | 99b.p | 1,538.2 | 1,604.9 | 1,699.4 | 1,736.0 | 1,730.6 | 1,683.5 | 1,690.7 | .... | .... | .... | .... | .... |
| GDP Volume (2010=100)............... | 99bvp | 86.4 | 84.1 | 90.4 | 91.7 | 97.0 | 95.8 | 100.0 | .... | .... | .... | .... | .... |
| GDP Deflator (2010=100)............... | 99bip | 82.4 | 89.4 | 94.2 | 100.2 | 97.0 | 98.7 | 100.0 | .... | .... | .... | .... | .... |
| | | | | | | *Millions: Midyear Estimates* | | | | | | | |
| Population................................ | 99z | .16 | .17 | .17 | .17 | .17 | .18 | .18 | .18 | .18 | .18 | .18 | .18 |

| | | 2004 | 2005 | 2006 | 2007 | 2008 | 2009 | 2010 | 2011 | 2012 | 2013 | 2014 | 2015 |
|---|---|---|---|---|---|---|---|---|---|---|---|---|---|
| **Exchange Rates** | | | | | | *E. Caribbean Dollars per SDR: End of Period* | | | | | | | |
| Official Rate | aa | 4.1931 | 3.8590 | 4.0619 | 4.2667 | 4.1587 | 4.2328 | 4.1581 | 4.1452 | 4.1497 | 4.1580 | 3.9118 | 3.7415 |
| | | | | | *E.Caribbean Dollars per US Dollar: End of Period (ae) Period Average (rf)* | | | | | | | | |
| Official Rate | ae | 2.7000 | 2.7000 | 2.7000 | 2.7000 | 2.7000 | 2.7000 | 2.7000 | 2.7000 | 2.7000 | 2.7000 | 2.7000 | 2.7000 |
| Official Rate | rf | 2.7000 | 2.7000 | 2.7000 | 2.7000 | 2.7000 | 2.7000 | 2.7000 | 2.7000 | 2.7000 | 2.7000 | 2.7000 | 2.7000 |
| | | | | | *Index Numbers (2010=100): Period Averages* | | | | | | | | |
| Official Rate | ahx | 100.0 | 100.0 | 100.0 | 100.0 | 100.0 | 100.0 | 100.0 | 100.0 | 100.0 | 100.0 | 100.0 | 100.0 |
| Nominal Effective Exchange Rate | nec | 101.7 | 103.3 | 102.6 | 96.1 | 91.6 | 99.2 | 100.0 | 96.9 | 103.7 | 103.3 | 104.7 | 120.4 |
| CPI-Based Real Effect. Ex. Rate | rec | 99.2 | 101.0 | 99.9 | 96.4 | 95.9 | 102.0 | 100.0 | 95.9 | 101.7 | 99.6 | 99.6 | 111.3 |
| **Fund Position** | | | | | | *Millions of SDRs: End of Period* | | | | | | | |
| Quota | 2f.s | 8.30 | 8.30 | 8.30 | 8.30 | 8.30 | 8.30 | 8.30 | 8.30 | 8.30 | 8.30 | 8.30 | 8.30 |
| SDR Holdings | 1b.s | — | — | — | — | — | 7.55 | .74 | .71 | .73 | .78 | .39 | .42 |
| Reserve Position in the Fund | 1c.s | .50 | .50 | .50 | .50 | .50 | .50 | .50 | .50 | .50 | .50 | .50 | .50 |
| Total Fund Cred.&Loans Outstg | 2tl | — | — | — | — | 3.74 | 7.47 | 3.74 | 7.06 | 7.06 | 7.06 | 10.83 | 10.08 |
| SDR Allocations | 1bd | .35 | .35 | .35 | .35 | .35 | 7.91 | 7.91 | 7.91 | 7.91 | 7.91 | 7.91 | 7.91 |
| **International Liquidity** | | | | | *Millions of US Dollars Unless Otherwise Indicated: End of Period* | | | | | | | | |
| Total Reserves minus Gold | 1l.d | 74.98 | 69.51 | 78.69 | 86.98 | 83.69 | 87.82 | 112.70 | 89.63 | 111.02 | 135.10 | 157.37 | 166.01 |
| SDR Holdings | 1b.d | — | — | — | .01 | — | 11.84 | 1.14 | 1.09 | 1.12 | 1.21 | .56 | .58 |
| Reserve Position in the Fund | 1c.d | .78 | .71 | .75 | .79 | .77 | .78 | .77 | .77 | .77 | .77 | .72 | .69 |
| Foreign Exchange | 1d.d | 74.20 | 68.80 | 77.94 | 86.18 | 82.92 | 75.20 | 110.79 | 87.76 | 109.13 | 133.12 | 156.08 | 164.74 |
| Central Bank: Other Assets | 3..d | — | — | — | — | — | — | — | — | — | — | — | — |
| Central Bank: Other Liabs | 4..d | — | — | — | — | — | — | — | — | — | — | — | — |
| Other Depository Corps.: Assets | 7a.d | 162.39 | 184.72 | 189.83 | 210.26 | 217.98 | 194.63 | 196.47 | 182.49 | 155.59 | 166.92 | 154.04 | 159.87 |
| Other Depository Corps.: Liabs | 7b.d | 78.50 | 94.30 | 109.10 | 165.90 | 158.33 | 136.05 | 131.54 | 124.64 | 113.32 | 117.42 | 121.90 | 127.60 |
| **Central Bank** | | | | | | *Millions of E. Caribbean Dollars: End of Period* | | | | | | | |
| Net Foreign Assets | 11n | 201.08 | 186.49 | 211.23 | 233.71 | 209.49 | 172.62 | 256.81 | 181.19 | 237.75 | 302.62 | 351.68 | 399.03 |
| Claims on Nonresidents | 11 | 202.57 | 187.85 | 212.67 | 235.21 | 226.50 | 237.72 | 305.24 | 243.23 | 299.85 | 364.86 | 425.00 | 466.37 |
| Liabilities to Nonresidents | 16c | 1.48 | 1.36 | 1.44 | 1.51 | 17.00 | 65.11 | 48.43 | 62.04 | 62.11 | 62.23 | 73.32 | 67.33 |
| Claims on Other Depository Corps. | 12e | .01 | — | .05 | .01 | .02 | .01 | .02 | .01 | .02 | .04 | .08 | .10 |
| Net Claims on Central Government | 12an | −30.50 | −12.65 | −15.46 | −1.29 | 3.44 | −18.43 | −17.10 | 4.62 | −17.64 | −10.83 | −8.65 | −1.93 |
| Claims on Central Government | 12a | 10.38 | 9.48 | 7.18 | 5.18 | 6.08 | 5.26 | 3.30 | 10.95 | 11.03 | 16.04 | 21.27 | 24.35 |
| Liabilities to Central Government | 16d | 40.88 | 22.13 | 22.64 | 6.47 | 2.64 | 23.69 | 20.40 | 6.34 | 28.68 | 26.87 | 29.92 | 26.27 |
| Claims on Other Sectors | 12s | — | — | — | — | — | — | — | — | — | — | — | — |
| Claims on Other Financial Corps | 12g | — | — | — | — | — | — | — | — | — | — | — | — |
| Claims on State & Local Govts | 12b | — | — | — | — | — | — | — | — | — | — | — | — |
| Claims on Public Nonfin. Corps | 12c | — | — | — | — | — | — | — | — | — | — | — | — |
| Claims on Private Sector | 12d | — | — | — | — | — | — | — | — | — | — | — | — |
| Monetary Base | 14 | 169.73 | 172.99 | 194.91 | 231.42 | 227.34 | 184.61 | 282.06 | 241.60 | 275.55 | 346.73 | 408.10 | 439.75 |
| Currency in Circulation | 14a | 88.65 | 103.98 | 101.40 | 121.35 | 115.49 | 89.66 | 74.90 | 74.82 | 80.53 | 76.98 | 81.52 | 91.22 |
| Liabs. to Other Depository Corps | 14c | 81.08 | 69.00 | 93.51 | 109.94 | 111.72 | 94.94 | 207.02 | 166.44 | 195.02 | 269.44 | 326.57 | 348.52 |
| Liabilities to Other Sectors | 14d | .01 | .01 | — | .14 | .14 | .01 | .14 | .33 | — | .31 | — | .01 |
| Other Liabs. to Other Dep. Corps | 14n | .15 | .19 | .23 | .26 | .43 | .52 | .84 | 1.15 | 1.49 | 1.89 | 4.76 | 21.27 |
| Dep. & Sec. Excl. f/Monetary Base | 14o | — | — | — | — | — | — | — | — | — | — | — | — |
| Deposits Included in Broad Money | 15 | — | — | — | — | — | — | — | — | — | — | — | — |
| Sec.Ot.th.Shares Incl.in Brd. Money | 16a | — | — | — | — | — | — | — | — | — | — | — | — |
| Deposits Excl. from Broad Money | 16b | — | — | — | — | — | — | — | — | — | — | — | — |
| Sec.Ot.th.Shares Excl.f/Brd.Money | 16s | — | — | — | — | — | — | — | — | — | — | — | — |
| Loans | 16l | — | — | — | — | — | — | — | — | — | — | — | — |
| Financial Derivatives | 16m | — | — | — | — | — | — | — | — | — | — | — | — |
| Shares and Other Equity | 17a | — | — | — | — | — | — | — | — | — | — | — | — |
| Other Items (Net) | 17r | .70 | .65 | .69 | .73 | −14.82 | −30.94 | −43.16 | −56.92 | −56.91 | −56.80 | −69.75 | −63.81 |
| Memo Item: | | | | | | | | | | | | | |
| Total Assets | 10ra | 210.85 | 195.40 | 217.86 | 238.25 | 230.51 | 208.92 | 303.39 | 249.17 | 305.81 | 375.60 | 442.87 | 487.39 |
| **Other Depository Corporations** | | | | | | *Millions of E. Caribbean Dollars: End of Period* | | | | | | | |
| Net Foreign Assets | 21n | 226.49 | 244.11 | 217.96 | 119.78 | 161.06 | 158.16 | 175.33 | 156.19 | 114.12 | 133.66 | 86.80 | 87.13 |
| Claims on Nonresidents | 21 | 438.45 | 498.74 | 512.54 | 567.70 | 588.55 | 525.50 | 530.48 | 492.71 | 420.10 | 450.68 | 415.92 | 431.66 |
| Liabilities to Nonresidents | 26c | 211.96 | 254.62 | 294.58 | 447.92 | 427.49 | 367.33 | 355.15 | 336.52 | 305.98 | 317.03 | 329.12 | 344.52 |
| Claims on Central Bank | 20 | 106.08 | 98.50 | 108.16 | 147.61 | 152.04 | 123.41 | 231.97 | 176.75 | 229.85 | 297.33 | 379.42 | 411.24 |
| Currency | 20a | 24.26 | 29.54 | 20.90 | 31.53 | 34.95 | 26.16 | 24.29 | 28.31 | 36.66 | 28.84 | 27.91 | 26.60 |
| Reserve Deposits and Securities | 20b | 81.82 | 68.95 | 87.26 | 116.07 | 117.09 | 97.26 | 207.68 | 148.44 | 193.19 | 268.49 | 351.51 | 384.64 |
| Other Claims | 20n | — | — | — | — | — | — | — | — | — | — | — | — |
| Net Claims on Central Government | 22an | 24.07 | 87.18 | 57.35 | 89.09 | 101.86 | 146.04 | 39.42 | 39.88 | 67.20 | 75.53 | 97.77 | 113.80 |
| Claims on Central Government | 22a | 126.25 | 211.80 | 187.78 | 235.07 | 228.96 | 251.89 | 158.72 | 146.95 | 180.14 | 153.68 | 161.47 | 158.64 |
| Liabilities to Central Government | 26d | 102.19 | 124.62 | 130.43 | 145.98 | 127.10 | 105.85 | 119.29 | 107.07 | 112.94 | 78.15 | 63.71 | 44.83 |
| Claims on Other Sectors | 22s | 742.97 | 739.30 | 859.06 | 959.19 | 1,021.79 | 1,015.73 | 987.60 | 1,006.60 | 1,043.48 | 1,054.37 | 1,050.28 | 1,073.31 |
| Claims on Other Financial Corps | 22g | 33.84 | 14.21 | 13.15 | 7.75 | 8.45 | 6.47 | 6.66 | 27.86 | 16.60 | 16.43 | 16.06 | 15.49 |
| Claims on State & Local Govts | 22b | 15.82 | — | 26.90 | — | 3.00 | — | — | — | — | — | — | — |
| Claims on Public Nonfin. Corps | 22c | 50.16 | 46.87 | 43.91 | 59.98 | 92.35 | 72.88 | 27.60 | 11.36 | 11.84 | 10.53 | 9.03 | 7.42 |
| Claims on Private Sector | 22d | 643.16 | 678.23 | 775.10 | 891.46 | 917.99 | 936.38 | 953.34 | 967.39 | 1,015.05 | 1,027.41 | 1,025.20 | 1,050.40 |
| Liabilities to Central Bank | 26g | 1.71 | — | .27 | .01 | .02 | 3.88 | 1.04 | 3.41 | 3.02 | 8.06 | 5.82 | 4.91 |
| Transf.Dep.Included in Broad Money | 24 | 291.44 | 314.95 | 345.60 | 379.26 | 380.44 | 349.36 | 369.31 | 370.61 | 375.96 | 422.71 | 476.09 | 489.16 |
| Other Dep.Included in Broad Money | 25 | 644.36 | 650.73 | 663.57 | 707.36 | 763.36 | 786.96 | 811.88 | 841.12 | 900.30 | 938.02 | 1,002.08 | 1,041.79 |
| Sec.Ot.th.Shares Incl.in Brd. Money | 26a | — | — | — | — | — | — | — | — | — | — | — | — |
| Deposits Excl. from Broad Money | 26b | — | — | — | — | — | — | — | — | — | — | — | — |
| Sec.Ot.th.Shares Excl.f/Brd.Money | 26s | — | — | — | — | — | — | — | — | — | — | — | — |
| Loans | 26l | — | — | — | — | — | — | — | — | — | — | — | — |
| Financial Derivatives | 26m | — | — | — | — | — | — | — | — | — | — | — | — |
| Insurance Technical Reserves | 26r | — | — | — | — | — | — | — | — | — | — | — | — |
| Shares and Other Equity | 27a | 120.09 | 195.86 | 218.48 | 228.55 | 242.78 | 249.92 | 245.86 | 210.08 | 219.33 | 211.56 | 157.76 | 160.89 |
| Other Items (Net) | 27r | 42.01 | 7.54 | 14.62 | .48 | 50.14 | 53.22 | 6.22 | −45.79 | −43.96 | −19.46 | −27.48 | −11.28 |
| Memo Item: | | | | | | | | | | | | | |
| Total Assets | 20ra | 1,483.92 | 1,627.78 | 1,755.41 | 2,002.85 | 2,108.93 | 2,019.14 | 2,031.47 | 2,004.16 | 2,074.17 | 2,159.97 | 2,231.96 | 2,299.01 |

| | | 2004 | 2005 | 2006 | 2007 | 2008 | 2009 | 2010 | 2011 | 2012 | 2013 | 2014 | 2015 |
|---|---|---|---|---|---|---|---|---|---|---|---|---|---|
| **Depository Corporations** | | *Millions of E. Caribbean Dollars: End of Period* | | | | | | | | | | | |
| Net Foreign Assets.................. | 31n | 427.58 | 430.60 | 429.19 | 353.48 | 370.56 | 330.78 | 432.13 | 337.38 | 351.87 | 436.28 | 438.48 | 486.17 |
| Claims on Nonresidents................ | 31 | 641.02 | 686.59 | 725.21 | 802.91 | 815.05 | 763.22 | 835.72 | 735.95 | 719.95 | 815.54 | 840.92 | 898.02 |
| Liabilities to Nonresidents............. | 36c | 213.44 | 255.99 | 296.02 | 449.43 | 444.49 | 432.44 | 403.58 | 398.56 | 368.08 | 379.26 | 402.44 | 411.86 |
| Domestic Claims........................... | 32 | 736.53 | 813.83 | 900.95 | 1,046.99 | 1,127.09 | 1,143.33 | 1,009.93 | 1,051.10 | 1,093.04 | 1,119.07 | 1,139.39 | 1,185.19 |
| Net Claims on Central Government | 32an | −6.44 | 74.53 | 41.89 | 87.80 | 105.30 | 127.60 | 22.33 | 44.49 | 49.56 | 64.70 | 89.11 | 111.88 |
| Claims on Central Government..... | 32a | 136.63 | 221.28 | 194.96 | 240.26 | 235.04 | 257.14 | 162.02 | 157.90 | 191.18 | 169.72 | 182.74 | 182.98 |
| Liabilities to Central Government. | 36d | 143.07 | 146.75 | 153.07 | 152.46 | 129.74 | 129.54 | 139.69 | 113.40 | 141.62 | 105.02 | 93.63 | 71.11 |
| Claims on Other Sectors................ | 32s | 742.97 | 739.30 | 859.06 | 959.19 | 1,021.79 | 1,015.73 | 987.60 | 1,006.60 | 1,043.48 | 1,054.37 | 1,050.28 | 1,073.31 |
| Claims on Other Financial Corps.. | 32g | 33.84 | 14.21 | 13.15 | 7.75 | 8.45 | 6.47 | 6.66 | 27.86 | 16.60 | 16.43 | 16.06 | 15.49 |
| Claims on State & Local Govts..... | 32b | 15.82 | — | 26.90 | — | 3.00 | — | — | — | — | — | — | — |
| Claims on Public Nonfin. Corps.... | 32c | 50.16 | 46.87 | 43.91 | 59.98 | 92.35 | 72.88 | 27.60 | 11.36 | 11.84 | 10.53 | 9.03 | 7.42 |
| Claims on Private Sector............. | 32d | 643.16 | 678.23 | 775.10 | 891.46 | 917.99 | 936.38 | 953.34 | 967.39 | 1,015.05 | 1,027.41 | 1,025.20 | 1,050.40 |
| Broad Money Liabilities.................. | 35l | 1,000.19 | 1,040.13 | 1,089.66 | 1,176.57 | 1,224.48 | 1,199.83 | 1,231.94 | 1,258.57 | 1,320.13 | 1,409.19 | 1,531.78 | 1,595.58 |
| Currency Outside Depository Corps | 34a | 64.39 | 74.44 | 80.50 | 89.82 | 80.54 | 63.50 | 50.61 | 46.51 | 43.87 | 48.14 | 53.61 | 64.62 |
| Transferable Deposits................... | 34 | 291.44 | 314.96 | 345.60 | 379.40 | 380.58 | 349.37 | 369.45 | 370.94 | 375.96 | 423.02 | 476.09 | 489.17 |
| Other Deposits............................ | 35 | 644.36 | 650.73 | 663.57 | 707.36 | 763.36 | 786.96 | 811.88 | 841.12 | 900.30 | 938.02 | 1,002.08 | 1,041.79 |
| Securities Other than Shares......... | 36a | — | — | — | — | — | — | — | — | — | — | — | — |
| Deposits Excl. from Broad Money..... | 36b | — | — | — | — | — | — | — | — | — | — | — | — |
| Sec.Ot.th.Shares Excl.f/Brd.Money.... | 36s | — | — | — | — | — | — | — | — | — | — | — | — |
| Loans.......................................... | 36l | — | — | — | — | — | — | — | — | — | — | — | — |
| Financial Derivatives.................... | 36m | — | — | — | — | — | — | — | — | — | — | — | — |
| Insurance Technical Reserves.......... | 36r | — | — | — | — | — | — | — | — | — | — | — | — |
| Shares and Other Equity................ | 37a | 120.09 | 195.86 | 218.48 | 228.55 | 242.78 | 249.92 | 245.86 | 210.08 | 219.33 | 211.56 | 157.76 | 160.89 |
| Other Items (Net)......................... | 37r | 43.83 | 8.44 | 22.00 | −4.65 | 30.38 | 24.36 | −35.75 | −80.17 | −94.56 | −65.39 | −111.67 | −85.12 |
| Broad Money Liabs., Seasonally Adj. | 35l.b | 995.99 | 1,036.41 | 1,087.68 | 1,177.18 | 1,228.43 | 1,204.63 | 1,237.22 | 1,262.03 | 1,322.59 | 1,409.03 | 1,530.52 | 1,593.47 |
| **Monetary Aggregates** | | *Millions of E. Caribbean Dollars: End of Period* | | | | | | | | | | | |
| Broad Money.......................... | 59m | 1,000.19 | 1,040.13 | 1,089.66 | 1,176.57 | 1,224.48 | 1,199.83 | 1,231.94 | 1,258.57 | 1,320.13 | 1,409.19 | 1,531.78 | 1,595.58 |
| o/w:Currency Issued by Cent.Govt | 59m.a | — | — | — | — | — | — | — | — | — | — | — | — |
| o/w: Dep.in Nonfin. Corporations. | 59m.b | — | — | — | — | — | — | — | — | — | — | — | — |
| o/w:Secs. Issued by Central Govt.. | 59m.c | — | — | — | — | — | — | — | — | — | — | — | — |
| Money (National Definitions) | | | | | | | | | | | | | |
| M1.......................................... | 59ma | 287.04 | 327.71 | 344.31 | 371.67 | 374.57 | 359.13 | 345.66 | 331.45 | 360.94 | 374.21 | 426.30 | 437.83 |
| M2.......................................... | 59mb | 821.49 | 874.08 | 939.76 | 1,006.34 | 1,071.19 | 1,085.77 | 1,114.00 | 1,110.14 | 1,183.95 | 1,285.03 | 1,408.62 | 1,475.78 |
| **Interest Rates** | | *Percent Per Annum* | | | | | | | | | | | |
| Discount Rate (End of Period).......... | 60.a | 6.50 | 6.50 | 6.50 | 6.50 | 6.50 | 6.50 | 6.50 | 6.50 | 6.50 | 6.50 | 6.50 | 6.50 |
| Money Market Rate...................... | 60b | 4.67 | 4.01 | 4.76 | 5.24 | 4.92 | 6.03 | 6.36 | 5.68 | 5.19 | 6.28 | 6.19 | 6.44 |
| Treasury Bill Rate......................... | 60c | 4.60 | 4.85 | 5.62 | 5.75 | 5.56 | 5.67 | 4.92 | 4.16 | 3.96 | 3.43 | 2.85 | 5.82 |
| Savings Rate................................ | 60k | 3.40 | 3.30 | 3.37 | 3.29 | 3.20 | 3.30 | 3.32 | 3.42 | 3.25 | 3.16 | 3.18 | 2.47 |
| Deposit Rate................................ | 60l | 3.30 | 2.89 | 2.92 | 2.82 | 2.79 | 2.94 | 2.86 | 2.99 | 2.88 | 2.73 | 2.64 | 2.12 |
| Deposit Rate (Fgn. Currency)........... | 60l.f | .96 | 1.77 | .23 | 1.38 | 1.69 | 2.20 | 1.42 | 1.05 | 1.23 | 1.15 | 1.15 | 1.13 |
| Lending Rate................................ | 60p | 9.69 | 9.58 | 9.73 | 9.61 | 9.52 | 9.19 | 9.17 | 9.14 | 9.41 | 9.44 | 9.15 | 9.30 |
| Lending Rate (Fgn. Currency).......... | 60p.f | 6.94 | 7.97 | 10.22 | 8.80 | 7.85 | 5.33 | 5.27 | 4.56 | 6.71 | 7.82 | 7.81 | 7.06 |
| **Prices** | | *Index Numbers (2010=100): Period Averages* | | | | | | | | | | | |
| Consumer Prices............................ | 64 | 78.0 | 80.9 | 83.4 | 89.2 | 98.1 | 98.5 | † 100.0 | 103.2 | 105.9 | 106.7 | 106.9 | 105.1 |
| **Intl. Transactions & Positions** | | *Millions of E. Caribbean Dollars* | | | | | | | | | | | |
| Exports........................................ | 70 | 98.9 | 107.7 | 102.9 | 128.8 | 141.0 | 134.7 | 118.8 | 105.3 | 117.5 | 129.8 | 130.0 | 123.6 |
| Imports, c.i.f................................. | 71 | 608.5 | 649.4 | 727.0 | 882.4 | 1,007.4 | 900.8 | 932.8 | 896.2 | 964.4 | 1,020.9 | 977.4 | 901.0 |

| Balance of Payments | | 2004 | 2005 | 2006 | 2007 | 2008 | 2009 | 2010 | 2011 | 2012 | 2013 | 2014 | 2015 |
|---|---|---|---|---|---|---|---|---|---|---|---|---|---|
| | | | | | | *Millions of US Dollars* | | | | | | | |
| A. Current Account* | 109bx | −103.2 | −102.2 | −119.4 | −191.7 | −230.3 | −197.3 | −208.3 | −198.9 | −192.9 | −210.3 | .... | .... |
| Goods, credit (exports) | 1a9cx | 39.3 | 42.6 | 41.2 | 51.3 | 57.2 | 53.4 | 45.0 | 43.4 | 47.8 | 53.4 | .... | .... |
| Goods, debit (imports) | 1a9dx | 199.0 | 212.4 | 237.7 | 287.9 | 328.7 | 293.8 | 297.7 | 292.3 | 315.0 | 333.5 | .... | .... |
| Balance on goods | 1a9bx | −159.7 | −169.8 | −196.5 | −236.6 | −271.5 | −240.5 | −252.7 | −248.9 | −267.2 | −280.1 | .... | .... |
| Services, credit (exports) | 1b9cx | 145.2 | 158.0 | 170.8 | 160.9 | 153.0 | 139.0 | 138.2 | 139.4 | 140.5 | 140.7 | ..... | .... |
| Services, debit (imports) | 1b9dx | 73.2 | 78.8 | 88.2 | 114.2 | 102.1 | 94.2 | 91.5 | 84.3 | 87.1 | 91.4 | .... | .... |
| Balance on Goods & Services | 1z9bx | −87.7 | −90.6 | −113.9 | −189.9 | −220.6 | −195.7 | −206.0 | −193.8 | −213.8 | −230.8 | .... | .... |
| Primary income: credit | 1c9cx | 4.9 | 8.4 | 13.6 | 13.4 | 10.1 | 13.7 | 12.7 | 9.5 | 14.1 | 14.6 | .... | .... |
| Primary income: debit | 1c9dx | 34.5 | 38.0 | 39.3 | 35.4 | 33.0 | 26.7 | 24.9 | 22.5 | 18.0 | 18.3 | .... | .... |
| Balance on gds, serv. & prim. inc. | 1y9bx | −117.3 | −120.3 | −139.6 | −211.9 | −243.5 | −208.7 | −218.3 | −206.8 | −217.6 | −234.5 | .... | .... |
| Secondary income: credit | 1d9ca | 25.1 | 26.4 | 32.2 | 35.4 | 27.9 | 25.8 | 27.9 | 26.3 | 38.2 | 38.3 | .... | .... |
| Secondary income: debit | 1d9da | 11.0 | 8.3 | 12.1 | 15.3 | 14.7 | 14.4 | 18.0 | 18.4 | 13.4 | 14.0 | .... | .... |
| B. Capital Account* | 209ba | 16.2 | 11.6 | 5.6 | 71.1 | 46.3 | 51.9 | 52.5 | 37.2 | 32.6 | 11.4 | .... | .... |
| Capital account: credit | 209ca | 16.2 | 11.6 | 5.6 | 71.1 | 46.3 | 51.9 | 52.5 | 37.2 | 32.6 | 11.4 | .... | .... |
| Capital account: debit | 209da | — | — | — | — | — | — | — | — | — | — | .... | .... |
| Balance on current & capital acct. | 129ba | −86.9 | −90.6 | −113.8 | −120.7 | −184.0 | −145.5 | −155.9 | −161.6 | −160.3 | −198.9 | .... | .... |
| C. Financial Account* | 309na | −126.3 | −108.1 | −139.7 | −116.8 | −156.5 | −155.6 | −179.4 | −133.5 | −186.6 | −210.3 | .... | .... |
| Direct investment: assets | 3a9aa | — | — | — | — | — | — | — | — | — | — | .... | .... |
| Equity & investment fund shares | 3aaaa | — | — | — | — | — | — | — | — | — | — | .... | .... |
| Debt instruments | 3abaa | .... | .... | .... | .... | .... | .... | .... | .... | .... | .... | .... | .... |
| Direct investment: liabilities | 3a9la | 65.7 | 40.1 | 109.1 | 119.4 | 159.2 | 110.2 | 97.2 | 85.6 | 115.4 | 126.7 | .... | .... |
| Equity & investment fund shares | 3aala | 49.3 | 23.7 | 62.2 | 66.7 | 75.2 | 60.2 | 63.1 | 74.6 | 88.3 | 89.5 | .... | .... |
| Debt instruments | 3abla | 16.4 | 16.4 | 46.9 | 52.7 | 84.1 | 50.0 | 34.1 | 11.0 | 27.1 | 37.2 | .... | .... |
| Portfolio investment: assets | 3b9aa | 10.2 | 2.2 | 1.7 | .6 | 2.1 | .8 | 1.8 | .8 | −2.7 | 2.0 | .... | .... |
| Equity & investment fund shares | 3baaa | .... | .... | .... | .... | .... | .... | .... | .... | .... | .... | .... | .... |
| Debt securities | 3bbaa | .... | .... | .... | .... | .... | .... | .... | .... | .... | .... | .... | .... |
| Portfolio investment: liabilities | 3b9la | 43.4 | −6.0 | 14.2 | −2.8 | −1.0 | 19.0 | 1.3 | −2.4 | 2.8 | 16.7 | .... | .... |
| Equity & investment fund shares | 3bala | .... | .... | .... | .... | .... | .... | .... | .... | .... | .... | .... | .... |
| Debt securities | 3bbla | .... | .... | .... | .... | .... | .... | .... | .... | .... | .... | .... | .... |
| Fin. der.& empl.stk.ops.(ESOs): net. | 3c9na | .... | .... | .... | .... | .... | .... | .... | .... | .... | .... | .... | .... |
| Fin. der. & ESOs.: assets | 3c9aa | .... | .... | .... | .... | .... | .... | .... | .... | .... | .... | .... | .... |
| Fin. der. & ESOs.: liabilities | 3c9la | .... | .... | .... | .... | .... | .... | .... | .... | .... | .... | .... | .... |
| Other investment: assets | 3d9aa | 66.5 | 54.5 | 35.1 | 81.4 | 65.2 | 59.8 | 63.3 | 80.5 | 50.3 | 74.3 | .... | .... |
| Other equity | 3daaa | .... | .... | .... | .... | .... | .... | .... | .... | .... | .... | .... | .... |
| Debt instruments | 3dzaa | 66.5 | 54.5 | 35.1 | 81.4 | 65.2 | 59.8 | 63.3 | 80.5 | 50.3 | 74.3 | .... | .... |
| Other investment: liabilities | 3d9la | 93.9 | 130.7 | 53.2 | 82.2 | 65.6 | 87.0 | 146.1 | 131.5 | 116.0 | 143.1 | .... | .... |
| Other equity | 3dala | .... | .... | .... | .... | .... | .... | .... | .... | .... | .... | .... | .... |
| Debt instruments | 3dzla | 93.9 | 130.7 | 53.2 | 82.2 | 65.6 | 87.0 | 146.1 | 131.5 | 116.0 | 143.1 | .... | .... |
| Curr.+ cap.− finan. acct. balance | 4y9na | 39.3 | 17.5 | 25.9 | −3.9 | −27.4 | 10.2 | 23.6 | −28.2 | 26.3 | 11.4 | .... | .... |
| D. Net Errors and Omissions | 409nan | −13.9 | −20.4 | −13.8 | 2.1 | 18.1 | −11.8 | 7.7 | −.2 | −5.4 | 12.6 | .... | .... |
| E. Reserves and Related Items | 4z9na | 25.4 | −2.9 | 12.1 | −1.8 | −9.3 | −1.6 | 31.2 | −28.3 | 21.0 | 24.1 | .... | .... |
| Reserve assets | 3e9aa | 25.4 | −2.9 | 12.1 | −1.8 | −3.3 | 4.1 | 25.4 | −23.1 | 21.0 | 24.1 | .... | .... |
| Credit and loans from the IMF | 3dcla | — | — | — | — | 6.1 | 5.7 | −5.8 | 5.3 | — | — | .... | .... |
| Exceptional financing | 409la | .... | .... | .... | .... | .... | .... | .... | .... | .... | .... | .... | .... |

*Excludes components in group E

## Government Finance
## Cash Flow Statement
### Budgetary Central Government

| | | 2004 | 2005 | 2006 | 2007 | 2008 | 2009 | 2010 | 2011 | 2012 | 2013 | 2014 | 2015 |
|---|---|---|---|---|---|---|---|---|---|---|---|---|---|
| | | | | | | *Millions of E. Caribbean Dollars: Fiscal Year Ends December 31* | | | | | | | |
| Cash Receipts:Operating Activities | c1 | 343.6 | 346.1 | 399.9 | 463.6 | 534.7 | 543.4 | 498.0 | 498.7 | 499.2 | 473.5 | 555.7 | .... |
| Taxes | c11 | 290.9 | 305.3 | 362.8 | 402.6 | 448.0 | 432.6 | 421.5 | 412.1 | 430.6 | 417.0 | 471.0 | .... |
| Social Contributions | c12 | — | — | — | — | — | — | — | — | — | — | — | .... |
| Grants | c13 | 18.7 | 12.0 | 5.5 | 30.0 | 52.5 | 58.3 | 14.2 | 36.2 | 26.6 | 17.4 | 20.7 | .... |
| Other Receipts | c14 | 34.0 | 28.8 | 31.6 | 30.9 | 41.6 | 34.7 | 61.0 | 50.3 | 42.0 | 39.1 | 64.0 | .... |
| Cash Payments:Operating Activities. | c2 | 288.1 | 327.1 | 356.4 | 378.8 | 433.2 | 465.5 | 480.3 | 505.0 | 488.9 | 500.9 | 508.9 | .... |
| Compensation of Employees | c21 | 144.8 | 159.1 | 171.3 | 189.0 | 206.9 | 212.0 | 221.8 | 231.2 | 242.9 | 250.8 | 247.9 | .... |
| Purchases of Goods & Services | c22 | 66.6 | 70.3 | 77.7 | 74.7 | 91.0 | 85.6 | 66.2 | 75.3 | 70.5 | 65.2 | 74.5 | .... |
| Interest | c24 | 27.6 | 38.0 | 43.2 | 45.3 | 49.3 | 48.2 | 51.8 | 46.0 | 44.4 | 47.3 | 45.7 | .... |
| Subsidies | c25 | 29.3 | 35.5 | 36.1 | 40.7 | 49.3 | 78.5 | 95.2 | 107.5 | 81.6 | 83.2 | 82.2 | .... |
| Grants | c26 | — | — | — | — | — | — | — | — | — | — | — | .... |
| Social Benefits | c27 | 19.8 | 24.2 | 28.1 | 29.2 | 36.9 | 41.2 | 45.3 | 45.0 | 49.6 | 54.4 | 58.6 | .... |
| Other Payments | c28 | — | — | — | — | — | — | — | — | — | — | — | .... |
| Net Cash Inflow:Operating Act.[1-2] | ccio | 55.5 | 19.0 | 43.5 | 84.8 | 103.0 | 55.5 | 5.6 | −6.3 | 10.3 | −27.4 | 46.8 | .... |
| Net Cash Outflow:Invest. in NFA | c31 | 75.0 | 92.8 | 100.2 | 130.6 | 119.6 | 104.6 | 72.8 | 52.7 | 48.8 | 95.0 | 124.5 | .... |
| Purchases of Nonfinancial Assets | c31.1 | 78.9 | 96.7 | 103.6 | 131.5 | 131.0 | 106.0 | 73.8 | 63.0 | 54.2 | 123.9 | 125.2 | .... |
| Sales of Nonfinancial Assets | c31.2 | 3.9 | 3.9 | 3.4 | .9 | 15.7 | 1.5 | 1.0 | 10.4 | 5.4 | 29.0 | .7 | .... |
| Cash Surplus/Deficit [1-2-31=1-2M] | ccsd | −19.5 | −73.8 | −56.7 | −45.8 | −16.6 | −49.0 | −67.2 | −59.0 | −38.5 | −122.4 | −77.7 | .... |
| Net Acq. Fin. Assets, excl. Cash | c32x | −3.8 | −4.5 | −2.3 | — | — | — | — | — | — | — | — | .... |
| By debtor | | | | | | | | | | | | | |
| Domestic | c321x | −3.8 | −4.5 | −2.3 | — | — | — | — | — | — | — | — | .... |
| Foreign | c322x | — | — | — | — | — | — | — | — | — | — | — | .... |
| Net Incurrence of Liabilities | c33 | 170.2 | 231.4 | 54.9 | 39.2 | 33.7 | 29.2 | 34.7 | 64.1 | 40.2 | 85.8 | 123.9 | .... |
| By creditor | | | | | | | | | | | | | |
| Domestic | c331 | −38.0 | 65.3 | −5.7 | 19.0 | 20.5 | 19.3 | −105.3 | 35.0 | 41.6 | 24.2 | 27.1 | .... |
| Foreign | c332 | 208.2 | 166.1 | 60.6 | 20.1 | 13.1 | 9.9 | 140.0 | 29.1 | −1.4 | 61.7 | 96.8 | .... |
| Net Cash Inflow, Fin.Act.[-32x+33] | cnfb | 174.0 | 235.9 | 57.2 | 39.2 | 33.7 | 29.2 | 34.7 | 64.1 | 40.2 | 85.8 | 123.9 | .... |
| Net Change in Stock of Cash | cncb | 154.5 | 162.0 | .6 | −6.6 | 17.1 | −19.8 | −32.5 | 5.2 | 1.7 | −36.6 | 46.2 | .... |
| Stat. Discrep. [32X-33+NCB-CSD] | ccsdz | — | −.1 | .1 | — | — | — | — | — | — | — | .2 | — |
| Memo Item:Cash Expenditure[2+31] | c2m | 363.1 | 420.0 | 456.5 | 509.4 | 552.8 | 570.0 | 553.1 | 557.7 | 537.7 | 595.9 | 633.4 | .... |
| Memo Item: Gross Debt | c63 | .... | .... | .... | .... | .... | .... | .... | .... | 1,145.1 | 1,237.6 | 1,350.8 | .... |

# St. Vincent and the Grenadines   364

| | | 2004 | 2005 | 2006 | 2007 | 2008 | 2009 | 2010 | 2011 | 2012 | 2013 | 2014 | 2015 |
|---|---|---|---|---|---|---|---|---|---|---|---|---|---|
| **National Accounts** | | | | | | | *Millions of E. Caribbean Dollars* | | | | | | |
| Househ.Cons.Expend.,incl.NPISHs.... | 96f | 1,050.4 | 1,124.7 | 1,238.6 | 1,559.2 | 1,604.1 | 1,597.8 | 1,647.1 | 1,596.7 | 1,663.7 | 1,739.5 | 1,815.7 | .... |
| Government Consumption Expend... | 91f | 221.1 | 234.1 | 248.2 | 290.6 | 317.2 | 314.4 | 284.8 | 314.3 | 337.2 | 356.3 | 372.5 | .... |
| Gross Fixed Capital Formation.......... | 93e | 374.6 | 372.9 | 469.6 | 509.9 | 552.1 | 438.6 | 464.0 | 440.4 | 443.1 | 481.8 | 417.7 | .... |
| Exports of Goods and Services........ | 90c | 498.2 | 541.5 | 572.4 | 573.0 | 567.5 | 519.2 | 494.6 | 493.5 | 514.8 | 501.1 | 508.7 | .... |
| Imports of Goods and Services (-)..... | 98c | 734.9 | 786.2 | 879.8 | 1,085.7 | 1,163.2 | 1,047.7 | 1,050.8 | 1,016.9 | 1,083.8 | 1,137.7 | 1,147.1 | .... |
| Gross Domestic Product (GDP)......... | 99b | 1,409.3 | 1,487.0 | 1,649.1 | 1,846.9 | 1,877.7 | 1,822.3 | 1,839.7 | 1,828.0 | 1,875.0 | 1,941.0 | 1,967.5 | .... |
| Net Primary Income from Abroad..... | 98.n | −79.9 | −79.9 | −69.4 | −59.4 | −61.7 | −35.1 | −33.2 | −34.9 | −10.3 | .3 | −1.0 | .... |
| Gross National Income (GNI)............ | 99a | 1,329.5 | 1,407.0 | 1,579.7 | 1,787.5 | 1,816.0 | 1,787.2 | 1,806.6 | 1,793.1 | 1,864.7 | 1,941.3 | 1,966.5 | .... |
| Net Current Transf.from Abroad....... | 98t | 38.1 | 48.7 | 54.5 | 54.4 | 35.5 | 30.8 | 26.9 | 21.3 | 63.7 | 37.3 | 36.6 | .... |
| Gross Nat'l Disposable Inc.(GNDI).... | 99i | 1,367.6 | 1,455.8 | 1,634.2 | 1,841.9 | 1,851.5 | 1,818.0 | 1,833.4 | 1,814.4 | 1,928.4 | 1,978.5 | 2,003.1 | .... |
| Gross Saving................................... | 99s | 96.1 | 96.9 | 147.2 | −7.8 | −69.8 | −94.2 | −98.5 | −96.6 | −72.4 | −117.3 | −185.1 | .... |
| GDP Volume 1990 Prices................. | 99b.p | 848.6 | 866.6 | 949.2 | 1,030.5 | 1,043.9 | 1,014.7 | 975.5 | .... | .... | .... | .... | .... |
| GDP Volume (2010=100)................ | 99bvp | 88.3 | 90.4 | 97.4 | 100.8 | 102.5 | 101.3 | 100.0 | .... | .... | .... | .... | .... |
| GDP Deflator (2010=100)............... | 99bip | 86.8 | 89.4 | 92.1 | 99.6 | 99.6 | 97.8 | 100.0 | .... | .... | .... | .... | .... |
| | | | | | | | *Millions: Midyear Estimates* | | | | | | |
| Population................................ | 99z | .11 | .11 | .11 | .11 | .11 | .11 | .11 | .11 | .11 | .11 | .11 | .11 |

# Samoa 862

| | | 2004 | 2005 | 2006 | 2007 | 2008 | 2009 | 2010 | 2011 | 2012 | 2013 | 2014 | 2015 |
|---|---|---|---|---|---|---|---|---|---|---|---|---|---|
| **Exchange Rates** | | | | | | *Tala per SDR: End of Period* | | | | | | | |
| Official Rate.................... | aa | 4.1513 | 3.9504 | 4.0397 | 4.0426 | 4.4736 | 3.9095 | 3.5982 | 3.6158 | 3.5057 | 3.6099 | 3.5106 | 3.5984 |
| | | | | *Tala per US Dollar: End of Period (ae) Period Average (rf)* | | | | | | | | | |
| Official Rate.................... | ae | 2.6731 | 2.7640 | 2.6853 | 2.5582 | 2.9044 | 2.4938 | 2.3364 | 2.3552 | 2.2810 | 2.3441 | 2.4231 | 2.5967 |
| Official Rate.................... | rf | 2.7807 | 2.7103 | 2.7793 | 2.6166 | 2.6442 | 2.7308 | 2.4847 | 2.3175 | 2.2923 | 2.3109 | 2.3318 | 2.5609 |
| | | | | *Index Numbers (2010=100): Period Averages* | | | | | | | | | |
| Official Rate.................... | ahx | 89.3 | 91.6 | 89.4 | 94.9 | 94.3 | 91.5 | 100.0 | 107.2 | 108.3 | 107.5 | 106.5 | 97.0 |
| Nominal Effective Exchange Rate..... | nec | 101.2 | 101.7 | 100.8 | 99.1 | 96.6 | 99.5 | 100.0 | 99.1 | 100.9 | 104.0 | 106.5 | 111.6 |
| CPI-Based Real Effect. Ex. Rate........ | rec | 88.5 | 88.3 | 88.0 | 89.2 | 93.3 | 101.0 | 100.0 | 100.9 | 102.9 | 104.7 | 104.7 | 109.4 |
| **Fund Position** | | | | | | *Millions of SDRs: End of Period* | | | | | | | |
| Quota................................... | 2f.s | 11.60 | 11.60 | 11.60 | 11.60 | 11.60 | 11.60 | 11.60 | 11.60 | 11.60 | 11.60 | 11.60 | 11.60 |
| SDR Holdings..................... | 1b.s | 2.43 | 2.46 | 2.52 | 2.58 | 2.64 | 12.60 | 12.60 | 12.61 | 12.65 | 12.65 | 12.65 | 11.49 |
| Reserve Position in the Fund........... | 1c.s | .69 | .69 | .69 | .69 | .69 | .69 | .69 | .69 | .69 | .69 | .69 | .69 |
| Total Fund Cred.&Loans Outstg....... | 2tl | — | — | — | — | — | — | 5.80 | 5.80 | 5.80 | 11.60 | 11.60 | 10.44 |
| SDR Allocations................... | 1bd | 1.14 | 1.14 | 1.14 | 1.14 | 1.14 | 11.09 | 11.09 | 11.09 | 11.09 | 11.09 | 11.09 | 11.09 |
| **International Liquidity** | | | | | *Millions of US Dollars Unless Otherwise Indicated: End of Period* | | | | | | | | |
| Total Reserves minus Gold............... | 1l.d | 86.13 | 81.77 | 80.74 | 95.35 | 87.08 | 165.85 | 209.44 | 166.79 | 168.67 | 170.71 | 140.65 | 139.36 |
| SDR Holdings..................... | 1b.d | 3.77 | 3.52 | 3.78 | 4.08 | 4.07 | 19.75 | 19.41 | 19.36 | 19.43 | 19.48 | 18.32 | 15.92 |
| Reserve Position in the Fund.......... | 1c.d | 1.08 | .99 | 1.04 | 1.10 | 1.07 | 1.09 | 1.07 | 1.06 | 1.07 | 1.07 | 1.00 | .96 |
| Foreign Exchange...................... | 1d.d | 81.29 | 77.26 | 75.91 | 90.18 | 81.94 | 145.01 | 188.97 | 146.37 | 148.17 | 150.16 | 121.32 | 122.47 |
| Central Bank: Other Assets............... | 3..d | — | — | † — | — | — | — | — | — | — | — | — | 4.44 |
| Central Bank: Other Liabs............... | 4..d | .09 | 1.08 | † .65 | .73 | .69 | .02 | .42 | .38 | .32 | .13 | .17 | .11 |
| Other Depository Corps.: Assets....... | 7a.d | 14.55 | 14.86 | † 15.46 | 25.52 | 22.60 | 30.13 | 21.50 | 31.26 | 26.56 | 32.18 | 44.22 | 43.73 |
| Other Depository Corps.: Liabs........ | 7b.d | 12.13 | 9.91 | † 9.38 | 23.64 | 27.66 | 37.84 | 38.91 | 43.08 | 48.56 | 35.73 | 72.51 | 69.02 |
| Other Financial Corps.: Assets........ | 7e.d | .... | .... | .... | 2.33 | 1.93 | 2.65 | 11.70 | 13.20 | 22.92 | 14.22 | 17.19 | 16.37 |
| Other Financial Corps.: Liabs........... | 7f.d | .... | .... | .... | 17.34 | 16.56 | 19.36 | 19.76 | 17.32 | 15.83 | 15.86 | 12.23 | 7.97 |
| **Central Bank** | | | | | | *Millions of Tala: End of Period* | | | | | | | |
| Net Foreign Assets....................... | 11n | 167.98 | 164.98 | † 153.02 | 175.95 | 173.53 | 271.82 | 355.48 | 231.50 | 224.94 | 176.53 | 158.45 | 225.23 |
| Claims on Nonresidents.............. | 11 | 168.21 | 167.96 | † 154.77 | 177.80 | 175.53 | 271.86 | 356.46 | 253.41 | 245.99 | 254.07 | 199.53 | 303.00 |
| Liabilities to Nonresidents.............. | 16c | .23 | 2.98 | † 1.75 | 1.86 | 2.00 | .04 | .98 | 21.91 | 21.05 | 77.54 | 41.08 | 77.76 |
| Claims on Other Depository Corps.... | 12e | .88 | 2.99 | † 1.56 | .89 | 2.22 | 4.43 | 2.28 | 5.49 | 5.33 | 2.03 | 8.58 | 33.07 |
| Net Claims on Central Government.. | 12an | −29.29 | −45.23 | † −54.20 | −35.84 | −31.39 | −45.79 | −84.21 | −83.05 | −73.92 | −78.08 | −31.05 | −68.63 |
| Claims on Central Government...... | 12a | — | — | † .03 | .15 | .48 | 6.73 | .01 | .01 | .01 | .01 | 37.00 | 34.04 |
| Liabilities to Central Government... | 16d | 29.29 | 45.23 | † 54.22 | 35.99 | 31.87 | 52.51 | 84.22 | 83.05 | 73.93 | 78.09 | 68.05 | 102.67 |
| Claims on Other Sectors................. | 12s | 2.52 | 1.11 | † 8.20 | 9.28 | 12.81 | 16.42 | 15.44 | 35.08 | 40.13 | 79.40 | 102.97 | 109.30 |
| Claims on Other Financial Corps.... | 12g | — | — | † .14 | .20 | .16 | 5.00 | 5.09 | 20.16 | 21.37 | 60.37 | 83.17 | 102.57 |
| Claims on State & Local Govts....... | 12b | — | — | † — | — | — | — | — | — | — | — | — | — |
| Claims on Public Nonfin. Corps....... | 12c | — | — | † — | — | — | — | — | — | — | — | — | — |
| Claims on Private Sector............... | 12d | 2.52 | 1.11 | † 8.06 | 9.08 | 12.65 | 11.42 | 10.35 | 14.92 | 18.76 | 19.03 | 19.80 | 6.73 |
| Monetary Base............................... | 14 | 94.71 | 97.96 | † 95.80 | 120.84 | 132.79 | 208.94 | 236.32 | 162.01 | 168.07 | 204.37 | 228.38 | 260.17 |
| Currency in Circulation.................. | 14a | 49.48 | 62.95 | † 67.91 | 70.88 | 67.85 | 70.01 | 77.07 | 86.13 | 93.01 | 95.55 | 88.52 | 85.95 |
| Liabs. to Other Depository Corps.... | 14c | 45.23 | 35.01 | † 27.90 | 49.95 | 64.94 | 138.93 | 159.25 | 75.88 | 75.05 | 108.82 | 139.87 | 174.22 |
| Liabilities to Other Sectors............. | 14d | — | — | † — | — | — | — | — | — | — | — | — | — |
| Other Liabs. to Other Dep. Corps..... | 14n | 41.19 | 21.86 | † .99 | 13.96 | 19.93 | 27.49 | 24.49 | 9.50 | 8.50 | 7.00 | 7.00 | 13.00 |
| Dep. & Sec. Excl. f/Monetary Base..... | 14o | — | — | † — | — | .93 | .94 | .95 | .95 | .95 | .95 | .95 | .95 |
| Deposits Included in Broad Money. | 15 | — | — | † — | — | — | — | — | — | — | — | — | — |
| Sec.Ot.th.Shares Incl.in Brd. Money. | 16a | — | — | † — | — | — | — | — | — | — | — | — | — |
| Deposits Excl. from Broad Money... | 16b | — | — | † — | — | .93 | .94 | .95 | .95 | .95 | .95 | .95 | .95 |
| Sec.Ot.th.Shares Excl.f/Brd.Money.. | 16s | — | — | † — | — | — | — | — | — | — | — | — | — |
| Loans.................................. | 16l | — | — | † — | — | — | — | — | — | — | — | — | — |
| Financial Derivatives...................... | 16m | — | — | † — | — | — | — | — | — | — | — | — | — |
| Shares and Other Equity.................. | 17a | 29.11 | 26.40 | † 31.26 | 34.27 | 21.47 | 27.60 | 44.29 | 32.46 | 35.36 | 18.89 | 21.72 | 37.53 |
| Other Items (Net)........................... | 17r | −22.92 | −22.37 | † −19.48 | −18.78 | −17.94 | −18.09 | −17.08 | −15.91 | −16.41 | −51.33 | −19.10 | −12.69 |
| Memo Item: | | | | | | | | | | | | | |
| Total Assets..................................... | 10ra | 196.10 | 196.83 | † 196.56 | 220.48 | 224.06 | 333.18 | 408.08 | 328.75 | 327.50 | 371.33 | 388.38 | 559.64 |

# Samoa 862

|  |  | 2004 | 2005 | 2006 | 2007 | 2008 | 2009 | 2010 | 2011 | 2012 | 2013 | 2014 | 2015 |
|---|---|---|---|---|---|---|---|---|---|---|---|---|---|
| **Other Depository Corporations** |  | *Millions of Tala: End of Period* |  |  |  |  |  |  |  |  |  |  |  |
| Net Foreign Assets | 21n | 6.48 | 13.66 | † 16.33 | 5.06 | −14.65 | −19.20 | −40.75 | −27.88 | −50.15 | −8.29 | −68.47 | −65.75 |
| Claims on Nonresidents | 21 | 38.90 | 41.06 | † 41.51 | 68.65 | 65.55 | 75.01 | 50.30 | 73.78 | 60.57 | 75.31 | 107.00 | 113.69 |
| Liabilities to Nonresidents | 26c | 32.42 | 27.40 | † 25.18 | 63.59 | 80.20 | 94.22 | 91.05 | 101.66 | 110.72 | 83.60 | 175.47 | 179.44 |
| Claims on Central Bank | 20 | 96.96 | 71.32 | † 44.46 | 79.80 | 100.47 | 181.19 | 202.36 | 107.48 | 112.60 | 148.15 | 177.26 | 216.20 |
| Currency | 20a | 10.54 | 14.45 | † 15.57 | 15.93 | 15.61 | 14.80 | 18.62 | 22.10 | 29.04 | 32.33 | 30.39 | 28.99 |
| Reserve Deposits and Securities | 20b | 45.23 | 35.01 | † 27.91 | 49.95 | 64.94 | 138.93 | 159.25 | 75.88 | 75.05 | 108.82 | 139.87 | 174.22 |
| Other Claims | 20n | 41.19 | 21.86 | † .98 | 13.92 | 19.93 | 27.46 | 24.49 | 9.50 | 8.50 | 7.00 | 7.00 | 13.00 |
| Net Claims on Central Government | 22an | −14.09 | −9.35 | † 1.63 | 8.11 | −6.30 | −21.64 | −23.33 | −22.43 | −31.61 | −24.89 | −29.50 | −31.60 |
| Claims on Central Government | 22a | 3.25 | 10.33 | † 34.56 | 33.17 | 36.79 | 33.60 | 33.84 | 36.28 | 28.86 | 35.49 | 17.03 | 18.79 |
| Liabilities to Central Government | 26d | 17.34 | 19.68 | † 32.93 | 25.06 | 43.09 | 55.24 | 57.17 | 58.70 | 60.46 | 60.39 | 46.53 | 50.39 |
| Claims on Other Sectors | 22s | 366.83 | 454.81 | † 565.70 | 619.44 | 692.74 | 710.66 | 740.40 | 786.54 | 777.63 | 771.85 | 881.01 | 927.64 |
| Claims on Other Financial Corps | 22g | — | — | † 20.96 | 28.94 | 28.34 | 30.03 | 28.46 | 26.21 | 13.29 | 12.81 | 13.84 | 8.79 |
| Claims on State & Local Govts | 22b | — | — | † — |  |  |  |  |  |  |  |  |  |
| Claims on Public Nonfin. Corps | 22c | 10.61 | 15.86 | † 6.99 | 25.98 | 45.68 | 59.29 | 57.09 | 59.50 | 50.44 | 34.96 | 37.23 | 39.20 |
| Claims on Private Sector | 22d | 356.22 | 438.95 | † 537.75 | 564.52 | 618.72 | 621.33 | 654.85 | 700.83 | 713.91 | 724.08 | 829.94 | 879.66 |
| Liabilities to Central Bank | 26g | 2.99 | 3.18 | † 1.56 | 1.12 | 2.61 | 4.90 | 2.48 | 5.70 | 5.48 | 2.27 | 8.91 | 33.48 |
| Transf.Dep.Included in Broad Money | 24 | 95.75 | 129.15 | † 135.31 | 137.35 | 136.53 | 168.63 | 206.18 | 189.56 | 182.29 | 222.34 | 290.43 | 316.90 |
| Other Dep.Included in Broad Money | 25 | 283.83 | 306.36 | † 362.92 | 418.86 | 467.43 | 490.90 | 495.94 | 460.34 | 455.93 | 461.52 | 470.37 | 494.55 |
| Sec.Ot.th.Shares Incl.in Brd. Money | 26a | — | — | † — | — | — | — | — | — | — | — | — | — |
| Deposits Excl. from Broad Money | 26b | — | — | † — | — | — | — | — | — | — | — | — | — |
| Sec.Ot.th.Shares Excl.f/Brd.Money | 26s | — | — | † — | — | — | — | — | — | — | — | — | — |
| Loans | 26l | — | — | † — | — | — | — | — | — | — | — | — | — |
| Financial Derivatives | 26m | — | — | † — | — | — | — | — | — | — | — | — | — |
| Insurance Technical Reserves | 26r | — | — | † — | — | — | — | — | — | — | — | — | — |
| Shares and Other Equity | 27a | 50.29 | 43.23 | † 127.30 | 146.15 | 169.56 | 184.32 | 178.50 | 192.23 | 189.83 | 199.47 | 207.95 | 214.13 |
| Other Items (Net) | 27r | 23.32 | 48.52 | † 1.03 | 8.93 | −3.87 | 2.25 | −4.42 | −4.11 | −25.06 | 1.22 | −17.36 | −12.57 |
| Memo Item: |  |  |  |  |  |  |  |  |  |  |  |  |  |
| Total Assets | 20ra | 572.45 | 635.96 | † 749.61 | 871.22 | 973.07 | 1,083.56 | 1,108.17 | 1,094.85 | 1,098.37 | 1,150.84 | 1,315.23 | 1,407.83 |
| **Depository Corporations** |  | *Millions of Tala: End of Period* |  |  |  |  |  |  |  |  |  |  |  |
| Net Foreign Assets | 31n | 174.46 | 178.64 | † 169.35 | 181.00 | 158.88 | 252.61 | 314.73 | 203.62 | 174.78 | 168.24 | 89.99 | 159.49 |
| Claims on Nonresidents | 31 | 207.11 | 209.02 | † 196.28 | 246.45 | 241.09 | 346.87 | 406.76 | 327.19 | 306.56 | 329.38 | 306.53 | 416.69 |
| Liabilities to Nonresidents | 36c | 32.65 | 30.38 | † 26.93 | 65.45 | 82.21 | 94.26 | 92.03 | 123.57 | 131.77 | 161.14 | 216.55 | 257.21 |
| Domestic Claims | 32 | 325.97 | 401.34 | † 521.33 | 600.99 | 667.86 | 659.65 | 648.30 | 716.14 | 712.23 | 748.27 | 923.44 | 936.70 |
| Net Claims on Central Government | 32an | −43.38 | −54.58 | † −52.57 | −27.73 | −37.69 | −67.43 | −107.54 | −105.47 | −105.53 | −102.98 | −60.55 | −100.24 |
| Claims on Central Government | 32a | 3.25 | 10.33 | † 34.59 | 33.32 | 37.27 | 40.32 | 33.85 | 36.28 | 28.87 | 35.50 | 54.03 | 52.83 |
| Liabilities to Central Government | 36d | 46.63 | 64.91 | † 87.15 | 61.05 | 74.96 | 107.75 | 141.39 | 141.76 | 134.39 | 138.48 | 114.58 | 153.06 |
| Claims on Other Sectors | 32s | 369.35 | 455.92 | † 573.90 | 628.72 | 705.55 | 727.08 | 755.84 | 821.62 | 817.76 | 851.25 | 983.99 | 1,036.93 |
| Claims on Other Financial Corps | 32g | — | — | † 21.10 | 29.14 | 28.50 | 35.03 | 33.56 | 46.37 | 34.66 | 73.18 | 97.02 | 111.35 |
| Claims on State & Local Govts | 32b | — | — | † — |  |  |  |  |  |  |  |  |  |
| Claims on Public Nonfin. Corps | 32c | 10.61 | 15.86 | † 6.99 | 25.98 | 45.68 | 59.29 | 57.09 | 59.50 | 50.44 | 34.96 | 37.23 | 39.20 |
| Claims on Private Sector | 32d | 358.74 | 440.06 | † 545.81 | 573.60 | 631.37 | 632.75 | 665.20 | 715.74 | 732.66 | 743.11 | 849.75 | 886.38 |
| Broad Money Liabilities | 35l | 418.52 | 484.01 | † 550.57 | 611.17 | 656.21 | 714.74 | 760.58 | 713.92 | 702.19 | 747.08 | 818.92 | 868.41 |
| Currency Outside Depository Corps | 34a | 38.94 | 48.50 | † 52.34 | 54.95 | 52.25 | 55.21 | 58.45 | 64.04 | 63.97 | 63.22 | 58.12 | 56.97 |
| Transferable Deposits | 34 | 95.75 | 129.15 | † 135.31 | 137.35 | 136.53 | 168.63 | 206.18 | 189.55 | 182.29 | 222.33 | 290.43 | 316.90 |
| Other Deposits | 35 | 283.83 | 306.36 | † 362.92 | 418.86 | 467.43 | 490.90 | 495.94 | 460.34 | 455.93 | 461.52 | 470.37 | 494.55 |
| Securities Other than Shares | 36a | — | — | † — | — | — | — | — | — | — | — | — | — |
| Deposits Excl. from Broad Money | 36b | — | — | † — | — | .93 | .94 | .95 | .95 | .95 | .95 | .95 | .95 |
| Sec.Ot.th.Shares Excl.f/Brd.Money | 36s | — | — | † — | — | — | — | — | — | — | — | — | — |
| Loans | 36l | — | — | † — | — | — | — | — | — | — | — | — | — |
| Financial Derivatives | 36m | — | — | † — | — | — | — | — | — | — | — | — | — |
| Insurance Technical Reserves | 36r | — | — | † — | — | — | — | — | — | — | — | — | — |
| Shares and Other Equity | 37a | 79.40 | 69.63 | † 158.56 | 180.42 | 191.02 | 211.92 | 222.79 | 224.69 | 225.19 | 218.35 | 229.67 | 251.66 |
| Other Items (Net) | 37r | 2.51 | 26.34 | † −18.44 | −9.59 | −21.42 | −15.33 | −21.29 | −19.81 | −41.32 | −49.87 | −36.12 | −24.84 |
| Broad Money Liabs., Seasonally Adj. | 35l.b | 405.13 | 469.28 | † 541.11 | 601.38 | 647.12 | 706.85 | 753.57 | 708.13 | 696.40 | 740.89 | 817.59 | 866.61 |
| **Other Financial Corporations** |  | *Millions of Tala: End of Period* |  |  |  |  |  |  |  |  |  |  |  |
| Net Foreign Assets | 41n | .... | .... | .... | −38.39 | −42.43 | −41.60 | −18.85 | −9.73 | 16.17 | −3.84 | 12.01 | 21.83 |
| Claims on Nonresidents | 41 | .... | .... | .... | 5.95 | 5.60 | 6.60 | 27.39 | 31.15 | 52.26 | 33.27 | 41.60 | 42.51 |
| Liabilities to Nonresidents | 46c | .... | .... | .... | 44.35 | 48.02 | 48.20 | 46.23 | 40.87 | 36.10 | 37.11 | 29.59 | 20.68 |
| Claims on Depository Corporations | 40 | .... | .... | .... | 68.73 | 79.57 | 90.77 | 102.76 | 101.70 | 76.42 | 85.78 | 88.59 | 115.47 |
| Net Claims on Central Government | 42an | .... | .... | .... | 1.03 | .77 | .66 | 1.52 | 4.35 | 2.48 | 11.19 | 22.29 | 21.89 |
| Claims on Central Government | 42a | .... | .... | .... | 1.03 | .77 | .66 | 1.52 | 4.35 | 2.50 | 21.73 | 32.83 | 36.48 |
| Liabilities to Central Government | 46d | .... | .... | .... | — | — | — | — | — | .01 | 10.53 | 10.53 | 14.59 |
| Claims on Other Sectors | 42s | .... | .... | .... | 346.12 | 368.52 | 370.82 | 426.10 | 433.32 | 448.02 | 549.39 | 596.81 | 636.09 |
| Claims on State & Local Govts | 42b | .... | .... | .... | — | — | — | — | — | — | — | — | — |
| Claims on Public Nonfin. Corps | 42c | .... | .... | .... | 22.87 | 20.37 | 17.11 | 13.99 | 8.31 | 6.28 | 43.46 | 49.22 | 46.17 |
| Claims on Private Sector | 42d | .... | .... | .... | 323.26 | 348.15 | 353.71 | 412.11 | 425.01 | 441.74 | 505.92 | 547.60 | 589.93 |
| Deposits | 46b | .... | .... | .... | — | — | — | — | — | — | — | — | — |
| Securities Other than Shares | 46s | .... | .... | .... | — | — | — | — | — | — | — | — | — |
| Loans | 46l | .... | .... | .... | 20.90 | 20.49 | 24.95 | 5.54 | 20.89 | 22.78 | 91.35 | 115.46 | 139.36 |
| Financial Derivatives | 46m | .... | .... | .... | — | — | — | — | — | — | — | — | — |
| Insurance Technical Reserves | 46r | .... | .... | .... | 336.29 | 363.65 | 382.67 | 450.66 | 477.41 | 507.68 | 504.60 | 537.63 | 568.98 |
| Shares and Other Equity | 47a | .... | .... | .... | 112.48 | 122.21 | 120.20 | 151.79 | 146.11 | 142.88 | 178.72 | 189.89 | 201.10 |
| Other Items (Net) | 47r | .... | .... | .... | −92.18 | −99.91 | −107.17 | −96.46 | −114.77 | −130.25 | −132.14 | −123.26 | −114.16 |
| Memo Item: |  |  |  |  |  |  |  |  |  |  |  |  |  |
| Total Assets | 40ra | .... | .... | .... | 563.01 | 602.61 | 622.56 | 731.26 | 764.90 | 796.72 | 918.65 | 985.73 | 1,061.53 |

# Samoa  862

| | | 2004 | 2005 | 2006 | 2007 | 2008 | 2009 | 2010 | 2011 | 2012 | 2013 | 2014 | 2015 |
|---|---|---|---|---|---|---|---|---|---|---|---|---|---|
| **Financial Corporations** | | | | | *Millions of Tala: End of Period* | | | | | | | | |
| Net Foreign Assets............................ | 51n | .... | .... | .... | 142.61 | 116.46 | 211.01 | 295.88 | 193.89 | 190.95 | 164.40 | 102.00 | 181.31 |
| Claims on Nonresidents................ | 51 | .... | .... | .... | 252.40 | 246.68 | 353.47 | 434.15 | 358.33 | 358.82 | 362.65 | 348.14 | 459.20 |
| Liabilities to Nonresidents.............. | 56c | .... | .... | .... | 109.79 | 130.23 | 142.46 | 138.27 | 164.44 | 167.87 | 198.26 | 246.14 | 277.89 |
| Domestic Claims............................ | 52 | .... | .... | .... | 919.00 | 1,008.66 | 996.09 | 1,042.36 | 1,107.44 | 1,128.08 | 1,235.68 | 1,445.53 | 1,483.32 |
| Net Claims on Central Government | 52an | .... | .... | .... | −26.70 | −36.92 | −66.77 | −106.02 | −101.12 | −103.04 | −91.78 | −38.26 | −78.35 |
| Claims on Central Government.... | 52a | .... | .... | .... | 34.35 | 38.04 | 40.98 | 35.37 | 40.64 | 31.36 | 57.23 | 86.86 | 89.30 |
| Liabilities to Central Government. | 56d | .... | .... | .... | 61.05 | 74.96 | 107.75 | 141.39 | 141.76 | 134.40 | 149.01 | 125.11 | 167.65 |
| Claims on Other Sectors................ | 52s | .... | .... | .... | 945.71 | 1,045.58 | 1,062.87 | 1,148.38 | 1,208.56 | 1,231.12 | 1,327.46 | 1,483.79 | 1,561.67 |
| Claims on State & Local Govts..... | 52b | .... | .... | .... | — | — | — | — | — | — | — | — | — |
| Claims on Pub. Nonfin. Corps...... | 52c | .... | .... | .... | 48.85 | 66.05 | 76.41 | 71.08 | 67.82 | 56.72 | 78.42 | 86.44 | 85.36 |
| Claims on Private Sector.............. | 52d | .... | .... | .... | 896.86 | 979.52 | 986.46 | 1,077.31 | 1,140.75 | 1,174.40 | 1,249.03 | 1,397.34 | 1,476.31 |
| Currency Outside Fin. Corporations.. | 54a | .... | .... | .... | 54.95 | 52.25 | 55.21 | 58.45 | 64.04 | 63.97 | 62.91 | 58.12 | 56.97 |
| Deposits.......................................... | 55l | .... | .... | .... | 486.04 | 533.02 | 563.19 | 627.57 | 565.82 | 568.32 | 608.06 | 652.94 | 689.17 |
| Securities Other than Shares............ | 56a | .... | .... | .... | — | — | — | — | — | — | — | — | — |
| Loans.............................................. | 56l | .... | .... | .... | — | — | — | — | — | — | 26.00 | 26.00 | 32.00 |
| Financial Derivatives........................ | 56m | .... | .... | .... | | | | | | | | | |
| Insurance Technical Reserves........... | 56r | .... | .... | .... | 336.29 | 363.65 | 382.67 | 450.66 | 477.41 | 507.68 | 504.60 | 537.63 | 568.98 |
| Shares and Other Equity.................. | 57a | .... | .... | .... | 292.90 | 313.24 | 332.12 | 374.58 | 370.80 | 368.06 | 397.07 | 419.56 | 452.76 |
| Other Items (Net)............................ | 57r | .... | .... | .... | −108.57 | −137.03 | −126.08 | −173.02 | −176.74 | −189.00 | −198.56 | −146.72 | −135.24 |
| **Monetary Aggregates** | | | | | *Millions of Tala: End of Period* | | | | | | | | |
| Broad Money.................................. | 59m | .... | .... | 550.57 | 611.17 | 656.21 | 714.74 | 760.58 | 713.92 | 702.19 | 747.08 | 818.92 | 868.41 |
| o/w:Currency Issued by Cent.Govt | 59m.a | .... | .... | — | — | — | — | — | — | — | — | — | — |
| o/w: Dep.in Nonfin. Corporations. | 59m.b | .... | .... | — | — | — | — | — | — | — | — | — | — |
| o/w:Secs. Issued by Central Govt.. | 59m.c | .... | .... | — | — | — | — | — | — | — | — | — | — |
| Money (National Definitions) | | | | | | | | | | | | | |
| M1.................................................. | 59ma | 124.93 | 160.74 | 170.13 | 179.22 | 174.38 | 200.60 | 246.99 | 223.56 | 222.87 | 244.05 | 275.80 | 302.60 |
| Quasi-Money.................................. | 59mal | 293.59 | 323.27 | 380.43 | 431.95 | 481.83 | 514.13 | 513.59 | 490.37 | 479.32 | 503.03 | 543.12 | 565.81 |
| M2.................................................. | 59mb | 418.52 | 484.01 | 550.56 | 611.17 | 656.21 | 714.74 | 760.58 | 713.93 | 702.19 | 747.08 | 818.93 | 868.41 |
| **Interest Rates** | | | | | *Percent Per Annum* | | | | | | | | |
| Central Bank Bill Rate.................... | 60aa | 3.56 | 2.14 | 5.25 | 4.75 | 3.87 | .27 | .17 | .15 | .21 | .26 | .14 | .15 |
| Savings Rate.................................... | 60k | 2.50 | 2.50 | 2.50 | 2.50 | 2.50 | 1.88 | .... | .... | .... | .... | .... | .... |
| Deposit Rate.................................... | 60l | 4.39 | 4.35 | 4.87 | 6.44 | 6.06 | 4.81 | 2.70 | 2.29 | 2.47 | 2.88 | 3.02 | 2.48 |
| Lending Rate................................... | 60p | 11.23 | 11.43 | 11.72 | 12.65 | 12.66 | 12.08 | 10.72 | 9.96 | 9.86 | 10.20 | 9.98 | 9.39 |
| Government Bond Yield.................... | 61 | 13.50 | 13.50 | 13.50 | .... | .... | .... | .... | .... | .... | .... | .... | .... |
| **Prices and Production** | | | | | *Index Numbers (2010=100): Period Averages* | | | | | | | | |
| Consumer Prices............................ | 64 | 75.0 | 76.4 | 79.2 | 83.7 | 93.3 | 99.2 | 100.0 | 105.2 | 107.4 | 108.0 | 107.6 | 108.3 |
| **Intl. Transactions & Positions** | | | | | *Thousands of Tala* | | | | | | | | |
| Exports............................................ | 70 | 29,870 | 32,303 | 29,640 | 40,282 | 29,526 | 31,337 | 33,526 | 39,254 | 78,239 | 55,396 | .... | .... |
| Imports, c.i.f.................................... | 71 | 431,628 | 507,710 | 607,809 | 593,639 | 659,181 | 550,338 | 690,111 | 739,048 | 706,694 | 752,718 | .... | .... |

# Samoa 862

| Balance of Payments | | 2004 | 2005 | 2006 | 2007 | 2008 | 2009 | 2010 | 2011 | 2012 | 2013 | 2014 | 2015 |
|---|---|---|---|---|---|---|---|---|---|---|---|---|---|
| | | | | | | *Millions of US Dollars* | | | | | | | |
| A. Current Account* | 109bx | −26.2 | † −47.5 | −76.7 | −45.8 | −54.2 | −11.2 | −43.7 | −83.6 | .8 | −37.1 | −48.6 | . . . . |
| Goods, credit (exports) | 1a9cx | 11.9 | † 12.0 | 10.3 | 13.9 | 11.3 | 11.6 | 23.1 | 24.6 | 31.2 | 23.9 | 27.5 | . . . . |
| Goods, debit (imports) | 1a9dx | 155.4 | † 187.2 | 218.9 | 227.1 | 249.0 | 207.9 | 280.0 | 347.2 | 308.4 | 325.4 | 341.3 | . . . . |
| Balance on goods | 1a9bx | −143.5 | † −175.2 | −208.5 | −213.2 | −237.7 | −196.3 | −256.9 | −322.5 | −277.3 | −301.4 | −313.8 | . . . . |
| Services, credit (exports) | 1b9cx | 94.8 | † 129.7 | 138.7 | 167.9 | 168.9 | 162.1 | 171.8 | 181.3 | 199.9 | 206.2 | 196.3 | . . . . |
| Services, debit (imports) | 1b9dx | 42.0 | † 68.9 | 70.6 | 71.1 | 73.6 | 79.7 | 82.2 | 78.8 | 89.6 | 89.0 | 74.8 | . . . . |
| Balance on Goods & Services | 1z9bx | −90.6 | † −114.3 | −140.4 | −116.4 | −142.4 | −113.9 | −167.2 | −220.0 | −167.1 | −184.2 | −192.4 | . . . . |
| Primary income: credit | 1c9cx | 4.4 | † 5.6 | 5.1 | 6.7 | 13.3 | 7.8 | 6.8 | 5.8 | 7.0 | 19.1 | 18.2 | . . . . |
| Primary income: debit | 1c9dx | 22.2 | † 44.3 | 39.3 | 46.2 | 54.4 | 32.4 | 30.6 | 37.5 | 25.7 | 49.8 | 39.3 | . . . . |
| Balance on gds, serv. & prim. inc. | 1y9bx | −108.4 | † −153.1 | −174.6 | −155.9 | −183.5 | −138.5 | −191.0 | −251.7 | −185.8 | −214.9 | −213.4 | . . . . |
| Secondary income: credit | 1d9ca | 95.8 | † 111.9 | 112.1 | 120.4 | 138.0 | 135.4 | 157.1 | 182.1 | 198.5 | 190.4 | 175.2 | . . . . |
| Secondary income: debit | 1d9da | 13.6 | † 6.3 | 14.1 | 10.3 | 8.8 | 8.1 | 9.8 | 14.0 | 12.0 | 12.6 | 10.4 | . . . . |
| B. Capital Account* | 209ba | 38.8 | † 35.1 | 41.8 | 33.4 | 37.2 | 48.3 | 31.2 | 54.6 | 15.4 | 37.4 | 39.3 | . . . . |
| Capital account: credit | 209ca | 42.0 | † 36.5 | 43.0 | 33.5 | 39.4 | 51.8 | 33.1 | 60.1 | 15.7 | 38.0 | 40.4 | . . . . |
| Capital account: debit | 209da | 3.2 | † 1.4 | 1.3 | .1 | 2.2 | 3.5 | 1.9 | 5.5 | .3 | .7 | 1.1 | . . . . |
| Balance on current & capital acct. | 129ba | 12.6 | † −12.4 | −34.9 | −12.4 | −17.1 | 37.1 | −12.4 | −29.0 | 16.2 | .3 | −9.4 | . . . . |
| C. Financial Account* | 309na | 2.2 | † −7.6 | −13.5 | −13.9 | −42.6 | −12.3 | −45.7 | −22.6 | 9.5 | −29.5 | −23.5 | . . . . |
| Direct investment: assets | 3a9aa | .6 | . . . . | . . . . | . . . . | . . . . | 1.0 | . . . . | .6 | 10.0 | .1 | 4.3 | . . . . |
| Equity & investment fund shares | 3aaaa | .6 | . . . . | . . . . | . . . . | . . . . | 1.0 | . . . . | .6 | 10.0 | .1 | 4.3 | . . . . |
| Debt instruments | 3abaa | . . . . | . . . . | . . . . | . . . . | . . . . | . . . . | . . . . | . . . . | . . . . | . . . . | . . . . | . . . . |
| Direct investment: liabilities | 3a9la | 2.5 | † 3.8 | 21.9 | 6.8 | 45.9 | 9.9 | −1.3 | 9.0 | 13.9 | 24.2 | 22.8 | . . . . |
| Equity & investment fund shares | 3aala | 3.8 | † 3.8 | 21.9 | 6.8 | 45.9 | 9.9 | −1.3 | 9.0 | 13.9 | 24.2 | 22.6 | . . . . |
| Debt instruments | 3abla | −1.3 | . . . . | . . . . | . . . . | . . . . | . . . . | . . . . | . . . . | . . . . | — | .3 | . . . . |
| Portfolio investment: assets | 3b9aa | — | † 2.8 | .4 | .1 | −1.1 | 1.6 | 1.7 | .4 | 9.9 | 1.7 | 5.0 | . . . . |
| Equity & investment fund shares | 3baaa | . . . . | † 2.8 | .4 | .1 | −1.1 | 1.6 | 1.7 | .4 | 9.9 | 1.7 | — | . . . . |
| Debt securities | 3bbaa | . . . . | . . . . | . . . . | . . . . | . . . . | . . . . | . . . . | . . . . | . . . . | . . . . | 5.0 | . . . . |
| Portfolio investment: liabilities | 3b9la | .4 | . . . . | . . . . | . . . . | . . . . | . . . . | . . . . | . . . . | . . . . | . . . . | — | . . . . |
| Equity & investment fund shares | 3bala | . . . . | . . . . | . . . . | . . . . | . . . . | . . . . | . . . . | . . . . | . . . . | . . . . | . . . . | . . . . |
| Debt securities | 3bbla | . . . . | . . . . | . . . . | . . . . | . . . . | . . . . | . . . . | . . . . | . . . . | . . . . | . . . . | . . . . |
| Fin. der. & empl.stk.ops.(ESOs): net. | 3c9na | . . . . | . . . . | . . . . | . . . . | . . . . | . . . . | . . . . | . . . . | . . . . | . . . . | . . . . | . . . . |
| Fin. der. & ESOs.: assets | 3c9aa | . . . . | . . . . | . . . . | . . . . | . . . . | . . . . | . . . . | . . . . | . . . . | . . . . | . . . . | . . . . |
| Fin. der. & ESOs.: liabilities | 3c9la | . . . . | . . . . | . . . . | . . . . | . . . . | . . . . | . . . . | . . . . | . . . . | . . . . | . . . . | . . . . |
| Other investment: assets | 3d9aa | 9.4 | † −2.8 | −2.6 | 7.5 | 51.6 | 11.1 | 24.4 | 26.4 | 10.1 | 10.3 | 53.9 | . . . . |
| Other equity | 3daaa | . . . . | . . . . | . . . . | . . . . | . . . . | . . . . | . . . . | . . . . | . . . . | . . . . | . . . . | . . . . |
| Debt instruments | 3dzaa | 9.4 | † −2.8 | −2.6 | 7.5 | 51.6 | 11.1 | 24.4 | 26.4 | 10.1 | 10.3 | 53.9 | . . . . |
| Other investment: liabilities | 3d9la | 4.9 | † 3.9 | −10.7 | 14.7 | 47.2 | 16.1 | 73.1 | 41.1 | 6.6 | 17.4 | 63.9 | . . . . |
| Other equity | 3dala | . . . . | . . . . | . . . . | . . . . | . . . . | . . . . | . . . . | . . . . | . . . . | . . . . | . . . . | . . . . |
| Debt instruments | 3dzla | 4.9 | † 3.9 | −10.7 | 14.7 | 47.2 | 16.1 | 73.1 | 41.1 | 6.6 | 17.4 | 63.9 | . . . . |
| Curr.+ cap.– finan. acct. balance | 4y9na | 10.4 | † −4.8 | −21.4 | 1.6 | 25.6 | 49.4 | 33.2 | −6.4 | 6.7 | 29.7 | 14.1 | . . . . |
| D. Net Errors and Omissions | 409na | −2.6 | † 3.9 | 6.2 | −2.1 | −22.7 | −1.2 | −8.9 | −35.4 | −6.7 | −50.7 | −39.3 | . . . . |
| E. Reserves and Related Items | 4z9na | 7.8 | † −1.0 | −15.2 | −.5 | 2.9 | 48.2 | 24.3 | −41.8 | — | −21.0 | −25.1 | . . . . |
| Reserve assets | 3e9aa | 7.8 | † −1.0 | −15.2 | −.5 | 2.9 | 48.2 | 33.4 | −41.8 | — | −12.3 | −25.1 | . . . . |
| Credit and loans from the IMF | 3dcla | — | † — | — | — | — | — | 9.1 | — | — | 8.7 | — | . . . . |
| Exceptional financing | 409la | . . . . | . . . . | . . . . | . . . . | . . . . | . . . . | . . . . | . . . . | . . . . | . . . . | . . . . | . . . . |

*Excludes components in group E

| National Accounts | | 2004 | 2005 | 2006 | 2007 | 2008 | 2009 | 2010 | 2011 | 2012 | 2013 | 2014 | 2015 |
|---|---|---|---|---|---|---|---|---|---|---|---|---|---|
| | | | | | | *Millions of Tala* | | | | | | | |
| Gross Domestic Product (GDP) | 99b | 1,010.5 | . . . . | . . . . | . . . . | . . . . | . . . . | . . . . | . . . . | . . . . | . . . . | . . . . | . . . . |
| GDP Volume 1994 Prices | 99b.p | 708.4 | . . . . | . . . . | . . . . | . . . . | . . . . | . . . . | . . . . | . . . . | . . . . | . . . . | . . . . |
| GDP Volume (2000=100) | 99bvp | 109.8 | . . . . | . . . . | . . . . | . . . . | . . . . | . . . . | . . . . | . . . . | . . . . | . . . . | . . . . |
| GDP Deflator (2000=100) | 99bip | 121.3 | . . . . | . . . . | . . . . | . . . . | . . . . | . . . . | . . . . | . . . . | . . . . | . . . . | . . . . |
| | | | | | | *Millions: Midyear Estimates* | | | | | | | |
| Population | 99z | .18 | .18 | .18 | .18 | .18 | .18 | .19 | .19 | .19 | .19 | .19 | .19 |

# San Marino   135

| | | 2004 | 2005 | 2006 | 2007 | 2008 | 2009 | 2010 | 2011 | 2012 | 2013 | 2014 | 2015 |
|---|---|---|---|---|---|---|---|---|---|---|---|---|---|
| **Exchange Rates** | | *Lire per SDR through 1998, Euros per SDR Thereafter: End of Period* | | | | | | | | | | | |
| Market Rate | aa | 1.1402 | 1.2116 | 1.1423 | 1.0735 | 1.1068 | 1.0882 | 1.1525 | 1.1865 | 1.1649 | 1.1167 | 1.1933 | 1.2728 |
| | | *Euros per US Dollar: End of Period (ae) Period Average (rf)* | | | | | | | | | | | |
| Market Rate | ae | .7342 | .8477 | .7593 | .6793 | .7185 | .6942 | .7484 | .7729 | .7579 | .7251 | .8237 | .9185 |
| Market Rate | rf | .8054 | .8041 | .7971 | .7306 | .6827 | .7198 | .7550 | .7194 | .7783 | .7532 | .7537 | .9017 |
| **Fund Position** | | *Millions of SDRs: End of Period* | | | | | | | | | | | |
| Quota | 2f.s | 17.00 | 17.00 | 17.00 | 17.00 | 17.00 | 17.00 | 17.00 | 22.40 | 22.40 | 22.40 | 22.40 | 22.40 |
| SDR Holdings | 1b.s | .56 | .66 | .80 | .97 | 1.13 | 16.69 | 16.70 | 15.37 | 15.37 | 15.46 | 15.46 | 15.47 |
| Reserve Position in the Fund | 1c.s | 4.10 | 4.10 | 4.10 | 4.10 | 4.10 | 4.10 | 4.10 | 5.45 | 5.45 | 5.45 | 5.45 | 5.45 |
| Total Fund Cred.&Loans Outstg. | 2tl | — | — | — | — | — | — | — | — | — | — | — | — |
| SDR Allocations | 1bd | — | — | — | — | — | 15.53 | 15.53 | 15.53 | 15.53 | 15.53 | 15.53 | 15.53 |
| **International Liquidity** | | *Millions of US Dollars Unless Otherwise Indicated: End of Period* | | | | | | | | | | | |
| Total Reserves Minus Gold | 1l.d | 355.58 | 347.77 | 479.13 | 647.81 | 706.80 | 790.27 | 449.16 | 341.86 | 384.95 | 539.29 | 392.04 | .... |
| SDR Holdings | 1b.d | .87 | .94 | 1.20 | 1.54 | 1.74 | 26.16 | 25.72 | 23.60 | 23.63 | 23.81 | 22.40 | 21.43 |
| Reserve Position in the Fund | 1c.d | 6.37 | 5.86 | 6.17 | 6.48 | 6.32 | 6.43 | 6.32 | 8.37 | 8.38 | 8.40 | 7.90 | 7.55 |
| Foreign Exchange | 1d.d | 348.34 | 340.97 | 471.77 | 639.79 | 698.74 | 757.69 | 417.13 | 309.90 | 352.94 | 507.09 | 361.74 | .... |
| Monetary Authorities: Other Liabs. | 4..d | .75 | .07 | .04 | — | — | .30 | .22 | .18 | — | .06 | .02 | .... |
| Deposit Money Banks: Assets | 7a.d | 6,037.44 | 5,937.54 | 6,609.78 | 8,691.17 | 8,421.70 | 5,162.52 | 3,788.78 | 3,374.97 | 2,015.80 | 2,350.20 | 2,314.71 | .... |
| Deposit Money Banks: Liabs. | 7b.d | 5,153.35 | 4,996.87 | 6,329.67 | 8,287.69 | 8,366.33 | 5,702.30 | 3,665.66 | 2,805.39 | 2,871.09 | 2,779.76 | 2,593.12 | .... |
| **Monetary Authorities** | | *Millions of Lire through 1998; Thousands of Euros Beginning 1999: End of Period* | | | | | | | | | | | |
| Foreign Assets | 11 | 261,051 | 294,792 | 363,807 | 440,055 | 507,865 | 548,573 | 336,148 | 264,209 | 291,762 | 391,044 | 322,910 | .... |
| Claims on General Government | 12a | 13,958 | 13,673 | 11,827 | 20,447 | 17,338 | 16,727 | 14,298 | 11,469 | 38,666 | 65,541 | 60,824 | .... |
| Claims on Other Resident Sectors | 12d | 2,807 | 600 | 764 | 825 | 1,016 | 897 | 1,050 | 1,520 | 1,825 | 1,307 | 1,179 | .... |
| Claims on Deposit Money Banks | 12e | — | — | — | — | — | 101,353 | 271,960 | 193,377 | 45,534 | 5,286 | 2,256 | .... |
| Bankers Deposits | 14c | 22,556 | 19,291 | 34,135 | 27,988 | 74,997 | 192,711 | 156,934 | 114,682 | 100,574 | 181,512 | 142,875 | .... |
| Demand Deposits | 14d | 56,223 | 29,373 | 24,428 | 62,930 | 48,816 | 59,178 | 97,468 | 53,469 | 53,580 | 65,322 | 50,707 | .... |
| Time, Savings,& Fgn.Currency Dep. | 15 | 65 | 33,907 | 40,219 | 60,019 | 2,763 | 1,077 | 501 | 221 | — | — | — | .... |
| Foreign Liabilities | 16c | 554 | 58 | 31 | — | 2 | 17,111 | 18,069 | 18,570 | 18,098 | 17,392 | 18,553 | .... |
| General Government Deposits | 16d | 154,532 | 182,073 | 235,355 | 264,258 | 352,256 | 333,053 | 303,484 | 230,548 | 146,784 | 138,361 | 116,046 | .... |
| Capital Accounts | 17a | 44,879 | 46,412 | 48,610 | 52,027 | 53,813 | 67,367 | 75,276 | 76,418 | 81,827 | 82,522 | 81,966 | .... |
| Other Items (Net) | 17r | −994 | −2,050 | −6,381 | −5,895 | −6,429 | −2,947 | −28,277 | −23,333 | −23,075 | −21,931 | −22,977 | .... |
| **Deposit Money Banks** | | *Millions of Lire through 1998; Thousands of Euros Beginning 1999: End of Period* | | | | | | | | | | | |
| Claims on Monetary Authorities | 20 | 22,534 | 19,193 | 33,969 | 27,988 | 74,470 | 192,711 | 156,934 | 114,682 | 100,574 | 181,512 | 142,875 | .... |
| Foreign Assets | 21 | 4,432,450 | 5,033,096 | 5,018,818 | 5,903,926 | 6,051,373 | 3,583,587 | 2,835,486 | 2,608,368 | 1,527,818 | 1,704,153 | 1,906,525 | .... |
| Claims on Other Resident Sectors | 22d | 2,596,601 | 2,914,905 | 3,886,793 | 4,394,781 | 4,931,523 | 4,601,086 | 4,369,297 | 3,510,916 | 3,911,483 | 3,569,835 | 3,443,544 | .... |
| Claims on Nonbank Financial Insts. | 22g | 522,739 | 583,555 | 821,958 | 955,740 | 1,072,581 | 1,072,193 | 927,501 | 725,909 | 799,695 | 690,732 | 625,910 | .... |
| Demand Deposits | 24 | 693,647 | 830,778 | 907,389 | 1,015,105 | 1,114,754 | 1,536,146 | 1,363,345 | 1,113,960 | 1,109,946 | 1,133,627 | 1,220,756 | .... |
| Time, Savings,& Fgn.Currency Dep. | 25 | 2,157,768 | 2,382,061 | 2,685,736 | 3,056,973 | 3,201,861 | 2,211,946 | 2,114,826 | 2,067,602 | 1,928,340 | 2,000,093 | 1,942,497 | .... |
| Foreign Liabilities | 26c | 3,783,388 | 4,235,715 | 4,806,128 | 5,629,839 | 6,011,587 | 3,958,282 | 2,743,349 | 2,168,169 | 2,176,059 | 2,015,632 | 2,135,289 | .... |
| Credit from Monetary Authorities | 26g | — | — | — | — | — | 101,353 | 271,960 | 193,377 | 45,534 | 5,286 | 2,256 | .... |
| Capital Accounts | 27a | 909,090 | 989,445 | 982,419 | 1,032,727 | 1,047,856 | 1,078,861 | 1,022,244 | 712,641 | 508,604 | 517,056 | 462,758 | .... |
| Other Items (Net) | 27r | 30,431 | 112,750 | 379,866 | 547,791 | 753,889 | 562,989 | 773,494 | 704,126 | 571,091 | 474,537 | 354,748 | .... |
| **Monetary Survey** | | *Millions of Lire through 1998; Thousands of Euros Beginning 1999: End of Period* | | | | | | | | | | | |
| Foreign Assets (Net) | 31n | 909,559 | 1,092,115 | 576,466 | 714,142 | 547,648 | 156,767 | 410,216 | 685,838 | −374,577 | 62,173 | 75,043 | .... |
| Domestic Credit | 32 | 2,981,573 | 3,330,659 | 4,485,987 | 5,107,535 | 5,670,202 | 5,357,850 | 5,008,661 | 4,019,266 | 4,604,889 | 4,189,053 | 4,015,411 | .... |
| Claims on General Govt. (Net) | 32an | −140,574 | −168,401 | −223,528 | −243,811 | −334,918 | −316,326 | −289,186 | −219,079 | −108,118 | −72,820 | −55,222 | .... |
| Claims on Other Resident Sectors | 32d | 2,599,408 | 2,915,505 | 3,887,557 | 4,395,606 | 4,932,539 | 4,601,983 | 4,370,347 | 3,512,436 | 3,913,312 | 3,571,142 | 3,444,723 | .... |
| Claims on Nonbank Financial Insts. | 32g | 522,739 | 583,555 | 821,958 | 955,740 | 1,072,581 | 1,072,193 | 927,501 | 725,909 | 799,695 | 690,732 | 625,910 | .... |
| Deposit Money | 34 | 749,870 | 860,151 | 931,817 | 1,078,035 | 1,163,570 | 1,595,324 | 1,460,813 | 1,167,429 | 1,163,526 | 1,198,950 | 1,271,463 | .... |
| Quasi-Money | 35 | 2,157,833 | 2,415,968 | 2,725,955 | 3,116,992 | 3,204,624 | 2,213,023 | 2,115,327 | 2,067,823 | 1,928,340 | 2,000,093 | 1,942,497 | .... |
| Capital Accounts | 37a | 953,969 | 1,035,857 | 1,031,029 | 1,084,754 | 1,101,669 | 1,146,228 | 1,097,520 | 789,059 | 590,431 | 599,578 | 544,724 | .... |
| Other Items (Net) | 37r | 29,460 | 110,798 | 373,652 | 541,896 | 747,987 | 560,041 | 745,217 | 680,793 | 548,016 | 452,606 | 331,771 | .... |
| Money, Seasonally Adjusted | 34..b | 743,891 | 849,457 | 914,650 | 1,052,895 | 1,136,424 | 1,563,599 | 1,438,259 | 1,152,343 | 1,151,888 | 1,187,050 | 1,256,591 | .... |
| Money plus Quasi-Money | 35l | 2,907,703 | 3,276,120 | 3,657,772 | 4,195,027 | 4,368,194 | 3,808,348 | 3,576,140 | 3,235,251 | 3,091,866 | 3,199,042 | 3,213,960 | .... |
| **Interest Rates** | | *Percent Per Annum* | | | | | | | | | | | |
| Deposit Rate | 60l | 1.44 | 1.35 | 2.13 | 2.63 | 2.23 | .96 | .71 | 1.08 | .... | .... | .... | .... |
| Lending Rate | 60p | 7.14 | 7.18 | 6.71 | 7.58 | 7.89 | 5.74 | 5.38 | 5.92 | .... | .... | .... | .... |
| **Prices, Tourism, Labor** | | *Index Numbers (2010=100): Period Averages* | | | | | | | | | | | |
| Consumer Prices | 64 | 85.9 | 87.4 | 89.2 | 91.5 | 95.4 | 97.5 | 100.0 | † 102.0 | 104.9 | 106.6 | 107.8 | 107.9 |
| Tourist Arrivals (2000=100) | 66ta | 107.6 | 106.6 | 108.1 | 109.5 | 106.8 | 104.0 | 100.0 | 103.1 | 94.6 | 96.4 | .... | .... |
| | | *Number in Thousands: Period Averages* | | | | | | | | | | | |
| Labor Force | 67d | .... | .... | .... | .... | .... | .... | 23 | 22 | 22 | 22 | 22 | .... |
| Employment | 67e | .... | .... | .... | .... | .... | .... | 22 | 21 | 21 | 21 | 20 | .... |
| Unemployment | 67c | .... | .... | .... | .... | .... | .... | 1 | 1 | 1 | 1 | 1 | .... |
| Unemployment Rate (%) | 67r | .... | .... | .... | .... | .... | .... | 3.2 | 3.8 | 5.2 | 6.4 | 6.6 | .... |
| **National Accounts** | | *Billions of Lire through 1998; Millions of Euros Beginning 1999* | | | | | | | | | | | |
| Househ.Cons.Expend.,incl.NPISHs. | 96f | .... | .... | .... | † 544.10 | 538.61 | 539.50 | 500.26 | 507.05 | 479.55 | .... | .... | .... |
| Government Consumption Expend. | 91f | .... | .... | .... | † 221.16 | 241.60 | 253.82 | 253.29 | 253.32 | 265.53 | .... | .... | .... |
| Changes in Inventories | 93i | .... | .... | .... | † 57.19 | 20.26 | −36.65 | −18.49 | −22.51 | −28.31 | .... | .... | .... |
| Exports of Goods and Services | 90c | .... | .... | .... | † 3,799.65 | 3,952.47 | 3,296.06 | 2,907.46 | 2,580.14 | 2,245.41 | .... | .... | .... |
| Imports of Goods and Services (-) | 98c | .... | .... | .... | † 3,348.10 | 3,515.55 | 2,887.74 | 2,520.28 | 2,238.97 | 1,974.16 | .... | .... | .... |
| Gross Domestic Product (GDP) | 99b | .... | .... | .... | † 1,796.09 | 1,777.51 | 1,602.22 | 1,471.99 | 1,396.22 | 1,256.69 | 1,414.20 | .... | .... |
| GDP Volume 1995 Prices | 99b.p | .... | .... | .... | .... | .... | .... | .... | .... | .... | .... | .... | .... |
| GDP Volume (2010=100) | 99bvp | .... | .... | .... | 128.3 | 124.9 | 108.4 | 100.0 | 93.9 | 82.4 | .... | .... | .... |
| GDP Deflator (2010=100) | 99bip | .... | .... | .... | 95.1 | 96.7 | 100.4 | 100.0 | 101.0 | 103.6 | .... | .... | .... |
| | | *Millions: Midyear Estimates* | | | | | | | | | | | |
| Population | 99z | .029 | .029 | .030 | .030 | .030 | .030 | .031 | .031 | .031 | .031 | .032 | .032 |

# São Tomé and Príncipe   716

| | | 2004 | 2005 | 2006 | 2007 | 2008 | 2009 | 2010 | 2011 | 2012 | 2013 | 2014 | 2015 |
|---|---|---|---|---|---|---|---|---|---|---|---|---|---|
| **Exchange Rates** | | | | | *Dobras per SDR: End of Period* | | | | | | | | |
| Market Rate............... | aa | 15,692 | 17,051 | 19,668 | 22,696 | 23,455 | 26,360 | 28,237 | 29,070 | 28,539 | 27,358 | 29,236 | 31,184 |
| | | | | | *Dobras per US Dollar: End of Period (ae) Period Average (rf)* | | | | | | | | |
| Market Rate............... | ae | 10,104 | 11,930 | 13,074 | 14,362 | 15,228 | 16,814 | 18,336 | 18,935 | 18,569 | 17,765 | 20,180 | 22,504 |
| Market Rate............... | rf | 9,902 | 10,558 | 12,449 | 13,537 | 14,695 | 16,208 | 18,499 | 17,623 | 19,068 | 18,450 | 18,466 | 22,091 |
| **Fund Position** | | | | | | *Millions of SDRs: End of Period* | | | | | | | |
| Quota....................... | 2f.s | 7.40 | 7.40 | 7.40 | 7.40 | 7.40 | 7.40 | 7.40 | 7.40 | 7.40 | 7.40 | 7.40 | 7.40 |
| SDR Holdings............... | 1b.s | — | .03 | .04 | .01 | .02 | 6.48 | 3.78 | 3.77 | .46 | .33 | .46 | .31 |
| Reserve Position in the Fund......... | 1c.s | — | — | — | — | — | — | — | — | — | — | — | — |
| Total Fund Cred.&Loans Outstg....... | 2tl | 1.90 | 2.23 | 2.70 | 1.62 | 2.47 | 2.84 | 3.21 | 3.21 | 3.58 | 3.92 | 3.21 | 3.14 |
| SDR Allocations............... | 1bd | .62 | .62 | .62 | .62 | .62 | 7.10 | 7.10 | 7.10 | 7.10 | 7.10 | 7.10 | 7.10 |
| **International Liquidity** | | | | *Millions of US Dollars Unless Otherwise Indicated: End of Period* | | | | | | | | | |
| Total Reserves minus Gold............... | 1l.d | 19.50 | 26.70 | 34.18 | 39.33 | 61.29 | 66.66 | 48.17 | 52.31 | 51.63 | 63.82 | 63.43 | 72.61 |
| SDR Holdings............... | 1b.d | — | .04 | .07 | .01 | .03 | 10.16 | 5.82 | 5.78 | .71 | .50 | .67 | .43 |
| Reserve Position in the Fund......... | 1c.d | — | — | — | — | — | — | — | — | — | — | — | — |
| Foreign Exchange............... | 1d.d | 19.50 | 26.66 | 34.12 | 39.32 | 61.26 | 56.50 | 42.35 | 46.52 | 50.92 | 63.32 | 62.75 | 72.18 |
| Central Bank: Other Assets............... | 3..d | 4.89 | 4.88 | † 10.96 | 11.94 | 12.80 | 22.88 | 13.93 | 12.45 | 13.40 | 14.42 | 15.53 | 16.91 |
| Central Bank: Other Liabs............... | 4..d | 2.76 | 1.53 | † .99 | 2.72 | 2.28 | 10.59 | .99 | 10.15 | 1.00 | 1.00 | 1.00 | 1.00 |
| Other Depository Corps.: Assets....... | 7a.d | 9.15 | 20.68 | † 21.68 | 29.17 | 34.84 | 30.82 | † 32.92 | 30.04 | 52.54 | 52.29 | 67.49 | 77.45 |
| Other Depository Corps.: Liabs......... | 7b.d | .28 | 1.65 | † 12.85 | 17.16 | 20.49 | 27.83 | † 13.19 | 10.48 | 29.63 | 32.28 | 29.96 | 45.50 |
| **Central Bank** | | | | | *Millions of Dobras: End of Period* | | | | | | | | |
| Net Foreign Assets........................... | 11n | 179,022 | 586,120 | † 621,984 | 856,945 | 1,199,228 | 1,228,330 | 997,538 | 890,893 | 1,061,627 | 1,291,744 | 1,473,735 | 1,902,646 |
| Claims on Nonresidents................. | 11 | 246,516 | 652,922 | † 700,165 | 946,983 | 1,306,363 | 1,668,317 | 1,311,028 | 1,384,648 | 1,385,184 | 1,611,180 | 1,794,730 | 2,243,171 |
| Liabilities to Nonresidents............... | 16c | 67,494 | 66,802 | † 78,181 | 90,038 | 107,135 | 439,987 | 313,490 | 493,755 | 323,557 | 319,437 | 320,995 | 340,524 |
| Claims on Other Depository Corps.... | 12e | 5,152 | 5,181 | † 2,488 | 884 | 603 | 666 | 8,921 | 760 | 41,110 | 72,110 | 106,090 | 128,409 |
| Net Claims on Central Government.... | 12an | 40,795 | −256,879 | † −108,309 | −162,512 | −406,390 | −232,120 | −22,827 | 34,614 | −29,919 | −100,589 | −83,930 | −133,166 |
| Claims on Central Government...... | 12a | 81,777 | 78,824 | † 105,626 | 111,729 | 125,741 | 157,335 | 258,051 | 262,271 | 233,160 | 244,102 | 255,244 | 246,614 |
| Liabilities to Central Government... | 16d | 40,983 | 335,704 | † 213,935 | 274,241 | 532,132 | 389,456 | 280,878 | 227,657 | 263,079 | 344,691 | 339,174 | 379,780 |
| Claims on Other Sectors................. | 12s | 7,043 | 8,061 | † 9,888 | 9,799 | 13,000 | 20,293 | 28,290 | 34,519 | 44,842 | 82,570 | 95,225 | 114,579 |
| Claims on Other Financial Corps.... | 12g | — | — | † — | — | — | — | — | 930 | 2,309 | 24,133 | 27,090 | 30,258 |
| Claims on State & Local Govts....... | 12b | — | — | † — | — | — | — | — | — | — | — | — | — |
| Claims on Public Nonfin. Corps...... | 12c | — | — | † — | — | — | — | — | — | — | — | — | — |
| Claims on Private Sector............... | 12d | 7,043 | 8,061 | † 9,888 | 9,799 | 13,000 | 20,293 | 28,290 | 33,589 | 42,534 | 58,437 | 68,135 | 84,321 |
| Monetary Base............................. | 14 | 119,250 | 210,635 | † 303,032 | 417,119 | 495,795 | 606,231 | 558,054 | 554,049 | 712,469 | 921,725 | 1,135,763 | 1,561,846 |
| Currency in Circulation................. | 14a | 67,155 | 81,103 | † 102,704 | 126,239 | 140,505 | 167,437 | 190,714 | 203,577 | 217,071 | 226,476 | 266,970 | 315,296 |
| Liabs. to Other Depository Corps.... | 14c | 52,095 | 129,532 | † 200,328 | 290,880 | 355,290 | 438,794 | 367,340 | 350,472 | 495,399 | 695,250 | 868,794 | 1,246,550 |
| Liabilities to Other Sectors............. | 14d | — | — | † — | — | — | — | — | — | — | — | — | — |
| Other Liabs. to Other Dep. Corps.... | 14n | — | — | † — | — | — | — | 22,923 | — | 34,118 | 113,959 | 66,064 | 56 |
| Dep. & Sec. Excl. f/Monetary Base.... | 14o | 127 | 934 | † 16,742 | 1,366 | 2,487 | 2,929 | 2,737 | 4,228 | 4,366 | 6,953 | 8,322 | 11,691 |
| Deposits Included in Broad Money. | 15 | 127 | 934 | † 16,742 | 1,366 | 2,487 | 2,929 | 2,737 | 4,228 | 4,366 | 6,953 | 8,322 | 11,691 |
| Sec.Ot.th.Shares Incl.in Brd. Money | 16a | — | — | † — | — | — | — | — | — | — | — | — | — |
| Deposits Excl. from Broad Money... | 16b | — | — | † — | — | — | — | — | — | — | — | — | — |
| Sec.Ot.th.Shares Excl.f/Brd.Money.. | 16s | — | — | † — | — | — | — | — | — | — | — | — | — |
| Loans........................................ | 16l | — | — | † — | — | — | — | — | — | — | — | — | — |
| Financial Derivatives..................... | 16m | — | — | † — | — | — | — | — | — | — | — | — | — |
| Shares and Other Equity.................. | 17a | 109,702 | 139,538 | † 206,680 | 264,746 | 294,467 | 383,329 | 418,884 | 400,124 | 395,303 | 359,942 | 468,398 | 574,136 |
| Other Items (Net)........................... | 17r | 2,933 | −8,624 | † −403 | 21,886 | 13,692 | 24,680 | 9,324 | 2,385 | −28,595 | −56,745 | −87,427 | −135,262 |
| Memo Item: | | | | | | | | | | | | | |
| Total Assets.................................. | 10ra | 346,716 | 750,015 | † 932,624 | 1,235,497 | 1,641,140 | 2,024,493 | 1,854,691 | 1,939,178 | 2,022,121 | 2,321,560 | 2,576,689 | 3,113,278 |
| **Other Depository Corporations** | | | | | *Millions of Dobras: End of Period* | | | | | | | | |
| Net Foreign Assets........................... | 21n | 89,656 | 227,100 | † 115,529 | 172,555 | 218,603 | 50,301 | † 366,604 | 371,820 | 425,851 | 355,818 | 756,051 | 624,101 |
| Claims on Nonresidents................. | 21 | 92,458 | 246,763 | † 283,468 | 418,948 | 530,551 | 518,278 | † 611,811 | 571,046 | 976,464 | 929,570 | 1,359,713 | 1,512,753 |
| Liabilities to Nonresidents............... | 26c | 2,802 | 19,663 | † 167,939 | 246,393 | 311,948 | 467,978 | † 245,207 | 199,226 | 550,613 | 573,752 | 603,662 | 888,651 |
| Claims on Central Bank................... | 20 | 62,968 | 157,110 | † 195,294 | 306,538 | 362,389 | 474,022 | † 423,503 | 359,126 | 533,233 | 892,257 | 963,812 | 1,281,016 |
| Currency................................... | 20a | 7,152 | 8,586 | † 10,390 | 16,940 | 20,170 | 18,374 | † 27,239 | 26,194 | 41,349 | 39,524 | 44,499 | 68,349 |
| Reserve Deposits and Securities...... | 20b | 55,752 | 148,523 | † 184,904 | 289,597 | 342,219 | 455,648 | † 396,263 | 332,932 | 491,884 | 852,733 | 919,314 | 1,212,667 |
| Other Claims............................. | 20n | 64 | — | † — | — | — | — | † — | — | — | — | — | — |
| Net Claims on Central Government.. | 22an | −6,846 | −6,464 | † −15,084 | −15,544 | −43,604 | −48,004 | † −37,617 | −56,686 | −93,518 | −149,588 | −168,189 | −190,099 |
| Claims on Central Government...... | 22a | — | — | † 239 | 583 | 884 | 616 | † 2,600 | 5,172 | 2,561 | 2,213 | 2,673 | 8,578 |
| Liabilities to Central Government... | 26d | 6,846 | 6,464 | † 15,324 | 16,128 | 44,488 | 48,620 | † 40,217 | 61,858 | 96,079 | 151,801 | 170,862 | 198,677 |
| Claims on Other Sectors................. | 22s | 169,059 | 312,185 | † 466,585 | 628,250 | 770,617 | 1,069,404 | † 1,497,657 | 1,715,244 | 1,843,865 | 1,818,935 | 1,786,991 | 1,838,784 |
| Claims on Other Financial Corps.... | 22g | — | — | † — | — | — | — | † 3,724 | 4,212 | 4,427 | 1,329 | 4,084 | 4,557 |
| Claims on State & Local Govts....... | 22b | — | — | † — | — | — | — | † — | — | — | — | 4 | −5 |
| Claims on Public Nonfin. Corps...... | 22c | — | — | † 12,230 | 16,352 | 20,314 | 26,246 | † 77,909 | 77,169 | 61,172 | 86,292 | 86,503 | 24,945 |
| Claims on Private Sector............... | 22d | 169,059 | 312,185 | † 454,355 | 611,898 | 750,303 | 1,043,158 | † 1,416,023 | 1,633,862 | 1,778,265 | 1,731,315 | 1,696,400 | 1,809,287 |
| Liabilities to Central Bank............... | 26g | 3,991 | — | † 518 | 569 | 603 | 666 | † 8,921 | — | 41,110 | 72,102 | 63,590 | 85,909 |
| Transf.Dep.Included in Broad Money | 24 | 207,813 | 271,005 | † 360,763 | 504,736 | 717,265 | 718,057 | † 922,493 | 955,111 | 1,037,609 | 1,404,299 | 1,584,749 | 1,934,650 |
| Other Dep.Included in Broad Money. | 25 | 30,286 | 89,054 | † 100,034 | 149,799 | 207,216 | 263,235 | † 328,636 | 429,398 | 635,904 | 549,129 | 692,461 | 646,631 |
| Sec.Ot.th.Shares Incl.in Brd. Money. | 26a | — | — | † — | — | — | — | † — | — | — | — | — | — |
| Deposits Excl. from Broad Money..... | 26b | — | — | † 144,300 | 179,723 | 182,775 | 204,920 | † 96,017 | 100,152 | 95,930 | 69,529 | 100,346 | 21,015 |
| Sec.Ot.th.Shares Excl.f/Brd.Money... | 26s | — | — | † — | — | — | — | † — | — | — | — | — | — |
| Loans........................................ | 26l | — | — | † 2,224 | 1,422 | — | — | † 30 | 8 | 23 | 23 | 23 | 147 |
| Financial Derivatives..................... | 26m | — | — | † — | — | — | — | † — | — | — | — | — | — |
| Insurance Technical Reserves.......... | 26r | — | — | † — | — | — | — | † — | — | — | — | — | — |
| Shares and Other Equity.................. | 27a | 107,128 | 158,796 | † 174,244 | 359,045 | 464,819 | 460,564 | † 946,109 | 1,010,255 | 1,061,228 | 968,786 | 1,054,347 | 823,742 |
| Other Items (Net)........................... | 27r | −34,381 | 171,075 | † −19,758 | −103,494 | −264,674 | −101,719 | † −52,060 | −105,421 | −162,375 | −146,447 | −156,851 | 41,709 |
| Memo Item: | | | | | | | | | | | | | |
| Total Assets.................................. | 20ra | 429,312 | 832,106 | † 1,098,462 | 1,545,754 | 2,061,523 | 2,445,553 | † 2,960,663 | 3,228,360 | 4,046,277 | 4,571,765 | 5,111,333 | 5,618,775 |

| | | 2004 | 2005 | 2006 | 2007 | 2008 | 2009 | 2010 | 2011 | 2012 | 2013 | 2014 | 2015 |
|---|---|---|---|---|---|---|---|---|---|---|---|---|---|
| **Depository Corporations** | | | | | | | *Millions of Dobras: End of Period* | | | | | | | |
| Net Foreign Assets.......................... | 31n | 268,678 | 813,220 | † 737,513 | 1,029,500 | 1,417,830 | 1,278,631 | † 1,364,142 | 1,262,714 | 1,487,478 | 1,647,562 | 2,229,786 | 2,526,748 |
| Claims on Nonresidents................ | 31 | 338,974 | 899,685 | † 983,633 | 1,365,931 | 1,836,913 | 2,186,596 | † 1,922,839 | 1,955,694 | 2,361,648 | 2,540,750 | 3,154,442 | 3,755,923 |
| Liabilities to Nonresidents............. | 36c | 70,295 | 86,465 | † 246,120 | 336,431 | 419,083 | 907,965 | † 558,697 | 692,980 | 874,170 | 893,188 | 924,657 | 1,229,176 |
| Domestic Claims........................... | 32 | 210,051 | 56,902 | † 353,080 | 459,993 | 333,622 | 809,573 | † 1,465,504 | 1,727,691 | 1,765,270 | 1,651,328 | 1,630,097 | 1,630,098 |
| Net Claims on Central Government | 32an | 33,948 | −263,344 | † −123,394 | −178,056 | −449,995 | −280,124 | † −60,444 | −22,072 | −123,437 | −250,177 | −252,119 | −323,265 |
| Claims on Central Government.... | 32a | 81,777 | 78,824 | † 105,866 | 112,312 | 126,625 | 157,951 | † 260,651 | 267,443 | 235,721 | 246,315 | 257,917 | 255,192 |
| Liabilities to Central Government. | 36d | 47,829 | 342,168 | † 229,259 | 290,368 | 576,620 | 438,076 | † 321,094 | 289,515 | 359,158 | 496,492 | 510,035 | 578,457 |
| Claims on Other Sectors............ | 32s | 176,103 | 320,246 | † 476,473 | 638,049 | 783,617 | 1,089,697 | † 1,525,947 | 1,749,763 | 1,888,707 | 1,901,505 | 1,882,216 | 1,953,363 |
| Claims on Other Financial Corps.. | 32g | — | — | † — | — | — | — | † 3,724 | 5,142 | 6,736 | 25,461 | 31,174 | 34,815 |
| Claims on State & Local Govts..... | 32b | — | — | † — | — | — | — | † — | — | — | — | 4 | −5 |
| Claims on Public Nonfin. Corps.... | 32c | — | — | † 12,230 | 16,352 | 20,314 | 26,246 | † 77,909 | 77,169 | 61,172 | 86,292 | 86,503 | 24,945 |
| Claims on Private Sector.............. | 32d | 176,103 | 320,246 | † 464,243 | 621,697 | 763,303 | 1,063,451 | † 1,444,314 | 1,667,451 | 1,820,799 | 1,789,752 | 1,764,535 | 1,893,607 |
| Broad Money Liabilities.................. | 35l | 298,229 | 433,508 | † 569,852 | 765,200 | 1,047,304 | 1,133,284 | † 1,417,341 | 1,566,120 | 1,853,600 | 2,147,333 | 2,508,002 | 2,839,920 |
| Currency Outside Depository Corps | 34a | 60,003 | 72,516 | † 92,313 | 109,299 | 120,336 | 149,063 | † 163,474 | 177,383 | 175,722 | 186,952 | 222,471 | 246,948 |
| Transferable Deposits................... | 34 | 207,813 | 271,005 | † 360,763 | 504,736 | 717,265 | 718,057 | † 922,493 | 955,111 | 1,037,609 | 1,404,299 | 1,584,749 | 1,934,650 |
| Other Deposits........................... | 35 | 30,413 | 89,987 | † 116,776 | 151,165 | 209,703 | 266,164 | † 331,373 | 433,626 | 640,270 | 556,082 | 700,783 | 658,323 |
| Securities Other than Shares.......... | 36a | — | — | † — | — | — | — | † — | — | — | — | — | — |
| Deposits Excl. from Broad Money..... | 36b | — | — | † 144,300 | 179,723 | 182,775 | 204,920 | † 96,017 | 100,152 | 95,930 | 69,529 | 100,346 | 21,015 |
| Sec.Ot.th.Shares Excl.f/Brd.Money.... | 36s | — | — | † — | — | — | — | † — | — | — | — | — | — |
| Loans....................................... | 36l | — | — | † 2,224 | 1,422 | — | — | † 30 | 8 | 23 | 23 | 23 | 147 |
| Financial Derivatives..................... | 36m | — | — | † — | — | — | — | † — | — | — | — | — | — |
| Insurance Technical Reserves.......... | 36r | — | — | † — | — | — | — | † — | — | — | — | — | — |
| Shares and Other Equity................. | 37a | 216,830 | 298,334 | † 380,924 | 623,791 | 759,286 | 843,893 | † 1,364,993 | 1,410,379 | 1,456,531 | 1,328,728 | 1,522,745 | 1,397,878 |
| Other Items (Net)......................... | 37r | −36,330 | 138,280 | † −6,707 | −80,642 | −237,912 | −93,892 | † −48,736 | −86,255 | −153,337 | −246,724 | −271,233 | −102,114 |
| Broad Money Liabs., Seasonally Adj. | 35l.b | 290,183 | 422,591 | † 534,134 | 717,237 | 981,658 | 1,062,249 | † 1,379,263 | 1,523,035 | 1,799,997 | 2,081,857 | 2,429,346 | 2,750,742 |
| **Monetary Aggregates** | | | | | | | *Millions of Dobras: End of Period* | | | | | | | |
| Broad Money................................ | 59m | 298,229 | 433,508 | 569,852 | 765,200 | 1,047,304 | 1,133,284 | 1,417,341 | 1,566,120 | 1,853,600 | 2,147,333 | 2,508,002 | 2,839,920 |
| o/w:Currency Issued by Cent.Govt | 59m.a | .... | .... | — | — | — | — | — | — | — | — | — | — |
| o/w: Dep.in Nonfin. Corporations. | 59m.b | .... | .... | — | — | — | — | — | — | — | — | — | — |
| o/w:Secs. Issued by Central Govt.. | 59m.c | .... | .... | — | — | — | — | — | — | — | — | — | — |
| Money (National Definitions) | | | | | | | | | | | | | | |
| Base Money................................. | 19ma | 119,250 | 210,635 | 303,032 | 417,119 | 495,795 | 606,231 | 558,054 | 554,049 | 712,469 | 921,725 | 1,135,763 | 1,561,846 |
| M1............................................ | 59ma | 161,233 | 180,353 | 224,073 | 285,418 | 429,001 | 436,593 | 562,354 | 670,250 | 733,589 | 1,058,941 | 1,106,347 | 1,431,010 |
| M2............................................ | 59mb | 177,866 | 199,531 | 261,577 | 329,980 | 536,448 | 555,630 | 587,801 | 722,764 | 917,460 | 1,362,223 | 1,570,946 | 1,905,855 |
| M3............................................ | 59mc | 298,229 | 433,508 | 569,852 | 765,200 | 1,047,304 | 1,133,284 | 1,417,341 | 1,566,120 | 1,853,600 | 2,147,333 | 2,508,002 | 2,839,920 |
| **Interest Rates** | | | | | | | *Percent Per Annum* | | | | | | | |
| Central Bank Policy Rate (EOP)........ | 60 | 14.50 | 18.20 | 28.00 | 28.00 | 28.00 | 16.00 | 15.00 | 15.00 | 14.00 | 14.00 | 12.00 | 10.00 |
| Deposit Rate................................. | 60l | 11.49 | † 12.14 | 10.75 | 12.75 | 12.75 | 11.92 | 11.12 | 12.36 | 12.89 | † 9.38 | 3.38 | .... |
| Lending Rate................................ | 60p | 29.77 | 31.20 | 29.30 | 32.40 | 32.40 | 31.11 | 28.87 | 26.95 | 26.17 | † 23.28 | 15.90 | .... |
| **Prices** | | | | | | | *Index Numbers (2010=100): Period Averages* | | | | | | | |
| Consumer Prices............................ | 64 | 33.4 | 39.2 | 48.2 | 57.2 | 75.4 | 88.2 | 100.0 | 114.3 | 126.5 | 136.7 | 146.3 | † 154.0 |

# São Tomé and Príncipe   716

|  | | 2004 | 2005 | 2006 | 2007 | 2008 | 2009 | 2010 | 2011 | 2012 | 2013 | 2014 | 2015 |
|---|---|---|---|---|---|---|---|---|---|---|---|---|---|
| **Balance of Payments** | | | | | | | *Millions of US Dollars* | | | | | | |
| A. Current Account* | 109bx | −37.0 | −36.2 | −57.7 | −64.3 | −93.5 | −78.8 | −87.6 | −105.8 | −98.9 | −74.7 | −103.7 | −78.6 |
| Goods, credit (exports) | 1a9cx | 5.4 | 6.8 | 7.7 | 6.8 | 7.8 | 9.2 | 10.9 | 10.9 | 15.1 | 12.9 | 17.2 | 11.3 |
| Goods, debit (imports) | 1a9dx | 38.4 | 41.6 | 59.2 | 64.9 | 92.2 | 83.8 | 96.2 | 115.7 | 119.1 | 128.6 | 144.6 | 118.9 |
| Balance on goods | 1a9bx | −32.9 | −34.8 | −51.5 | −58.1 | −84.3 | −74.6 | −85.3 | −104.7 | −104.0 | −115.8 | −127.4 | −107.6 |
| Services, credit (exports) | 1b9cx | 9.6 | 9.2 | 8.4 | 6.7 | 9.7 | 10.4 | 13.4 | 18.4 | 17.9 | 36.2 | 69.9 | 68.5 |
| Services, debit (imports) | 1b9dx | 15.5 | 11.1 | 17.8 | 18.7 | 21.4 | 19.0 | 24.3 | 31.4 | 24.6 | 48.1 | 84.4 | 66.9 |
| Balance on Goods & Services | 1z9bx | −38.8 | −36.7 | −60.9 | −70.0 | −96.1 | −83.1 | −96.2 | −117.7 | −110.8 | −127.6 | −141.9 | −106.0 |
| Primary income: credit | 1c9cx | 1.2 | 2.0 | 6.2 | 6.8 | 1.9 | 1.6 | 1.9 | 1.9 | 1.0 | 5.4 | 12.5 | 6.9 |
| Primary income: debit | 1c9dx | 3.7 | 4.9 | 3.1 | 2.3 | 2.0 | 1.9 | 2.3 | 2.3 | 3.2 | 3.4 | 5.8 | 4.1 |
| Balance on gds, serv. & prim. inc. | 1y9bx | −41.3 | −39.6 | −57.9 | −65.6 | −96.2 | −83.4 | −96.6 | −118.2 | −113.0 | −125.6 | −135.2 | −103.1 |
| Secondary income: credit | 1d9ca | 8.3 | 7.5 | 5.3 | 6.5 | 8.8 | 11.3 | 15.3 | 16.8 | 16.9 | 53.1 | 34.0 | 26.9 |
| Secondary income: debit | 1d9da | 4.1 | 4.0 | 5.1 | 5.3 | 6.1 | 6.6 | 6.3 | 4.4 | 2.8 | 2.2 | 2.6 | 2.4 |
| B. Capital Account* | 209ba | 18.0 | 65.6 | 23.5 | 62.4 | 47.5 | 39.9 | 41.6 | 46.5 | 38.7 | 27.5 | 28.8 | 27.3 |
| Capital account: credit | 209ca | 18.0 | 65.6 | 23.5 | 62.4 | 47.5 | 39.9 | 41.6 | 46.5 | 38.7 | 27.5 | 28.8 | 27.3 |
| Capital account: debit | 209da | — | — | — | — | — | — | — | — | — | .... | .... | .... |
| Balance on current & capital acct. | 129ba | −19.0 | 29.4 | −34.1 | −1.9 | −46.0 | −38.9 | −45.9 | −59.3 | −60.2 | −47.2 | −74.9 | −51.3 |
| C. Financial Account* | 309na | −10.7 | 4.3 | −43.9 | 140.3 | −92.2 | −58.0 | −74.5 | −60.7 | −65.1 | −9.5 | 17.3 | 10.5 |
| Direct investment: assets | 3a9aa | — | 14.6 | 3.1 | 3.1 | .1 | .2 | .1 | .3 | .4 | .9 | 3.9 | 2.7 |
| Equity & investment fund shares | 3aaaa | — | 11.4 | 3.1 | — | — | — | — | — | — | .3 | .3 | .2 |
| Debt instruments | 3abaa | — | 3.1 | 3.1 | 3.1 | .1 | .2 | .1 | .3 | .4 | .6 | 3.6 | 2.5 |
| Direct investment: liabilities | 3a9la | 3.5 | 15.7 | 38.0 | 36.0 | 79.1 | 15.5 | 50.6 | 32.2 | 22.5 | 5.8 | 27.1 | 28.5 |
| Equity & investment fund shares | 3aala | 3.5 | 15.7 | 38.0 | 36.0 | 79.1 | 15.5 | 50.6 | 32.2 | 22.5 | 2.5 | 17.1 | 25.3 |
| Debt instruments | 3abla | | | | | | | | | | 3.3 | 10.0 | 3.2 |
| Portfolio investment: assets | 3b9aa | — | — | — | — | — | 1.5 | — | — | — | −.3 | 1.3 | .3 |
| Equity & investment fund shares | 3baaa | — | — | — | — | — | — | — | — | — | .... | .... | .... |
| Debt securities | 3bbaa | — | — | — | — | — | 1.5 | — | — | — | −.3 | 1.3 | .3 |
| Portfolio investment: liabilities | 3b9la | — | — | — | — | — | — | — | — | — | .1 | 1.4 | — |
| Equity & investment fund shares | 3bala | — | — | — | — | — | — | — | — | — | — | .... | −.1 |
| Debt instruments | 3bbla | — | — | — | — | — | — | — | — | — | .1 | 1.4 | .1 |
| Fin. der.& empl.stk.ops.(ESOs): net. | 3c9na | — | — | — | — | — | — | — | — | — | .... | .... | .... |
| Fin. der. & ESOs.: assets | 3c9aa | — | — | — | — | — | — | — | — | — | .... | .... | .... |
| Fin. der. & ESOs.: liabilities | 3c9la | — | — | — | — | — | — | — | — | — | .... | .... | .... |
| Other investment: assets | 3d9aa | 2.8 | 3.4 | −9.3 | −7.9 | −32.1 | −10.0 | −11.2 | −6.8 | −28.5 | 6.9 | 15.5 | 41.1 |
| Other equity | 3daaa | .... | .... | .... | .... | .... | .... | .... | .... | .... | .... | .... | .... |
| Debt instruments | 3dzaa | 2.8 | 3.4 | −9.3 | −7.9 | −32.1 | −10.0 | −11.2 | −6.8 | −28.5 | 6.9 | 15.5 | 41.1 |
| Other investment: liabilities | 3d9la | 10.0 | −2.0 | −.3 | −181.1 | −19.0 | 34.1 | 12.8 | 22.1 | 14.6 | 11.1 | −25.0 | 5.1 |
| Other equity | 3dala | .... | .... | .... | .... | .... | .... | .... | .... | .... | .... | .... | .... |
| Debt instruments | 3dzla | 10.0 | −2.0 | −.3 | −181.1 | −19.0 | 34.1 | 12.8 | 22.1 | 14.6 | 11.1 | −25.0 | 5.1 |
| Curr.+ cap.− finan. acct. balance | 4y9na | −8.3 | 25.1 | 9.8 | −142.2 | 46.1 | 19.1 | 28.6 | 1.4 | 5.0 | −37.7 | −92.2 | −61.8 |
| D. Net Errors and Omissions | 409na | .6 | 5.4 | −9.6 | −12.4 | −33.2 | −10.2 | −15.3 | −6.7 | −15.7 | 43.3 | 90.2 | 65.9 |
| E. Reserves and Related Items | 4z9na | −7.6 | 30.5 | .1 | −154.6 | 12.9 | 8.9 | 13.3 | −5.3 | −10.7 | 5.5 | −2.0 | 4.2 |
| Reserve assets | 3e9aa | −4.0 | 37.2 | .8 | 9.9 | 22.6 | 11.6 | 18.3 | −5.0 | −9.5 | 12.1 | 2.6 | 9.8 |
| Credit and loans from the IMF | 3dcla | — | .5 | .7 | −1.7 | 1.4 | .5 | .6 | — | .6 | .5 | −1.1 | −.1 |
| Exceptional financing | 409la | 3.6 | 6.2 | — | 166.2 | 8.3 | 2.1 | 4.5 | .3 | .6 | 6.1 | 5.6 | 5.8 |

*Excludes components in group E

| **International Investment Position** | | | | | | | *Millions of US Dollars* | | | | | | |
|---|---|---|---|---|---|---|---|---|---|---|---|---|---|
| Assets | 809aa | .... | .... | .... | .... | .... | .... | .... | .... | .... | .... | † 159.3 | 164.9 |
| Direct investment | 8a9aa | .... | .... | .... | .... | .... | .... | .... | .... | .... | .... | † 3.4 | 2.5 |
| Equity & investment fund shares | 8aaaa | .... | .... | .... | .... | .... | .... | .... | .... | .... | .... | † 2.5 | 2.5 |
| Debt instruments | 8abaa | .... | .... | .... | .... | .... | .... | .... | .... | .... | .... | † .9 | — |
| Portfolio investment | 8b9aa | .... | .... | .... | .... | .... | .... | .... | .... | .... | .... | † .6 | — |
| Equity & investment fund shares | 8baaa | .... | .... | .... | .... | .... | .... | .... | .... | .... | .... | .... | — |
| Debt securities | 8bbaa | .... | .... | .... | .... | .... | .... | .... | .... | .... | .... | † .6 | — |
| Fin. der.(oth.than reserves) & ESOs | 8c9aa | .... | .... | .... | .... | .... | .... | .... | .... | .... | .... | .... | — |
| Other investment | 8d9aa | .... | .... | .... | .... | .... | .... | .... | .... | .... | .... | † 90.2 | 87.7 |
| Other equity | 8daaa | .... | .... | .... | .... | .... | .... | .... | .... | .... | .... | .... | .... |
| Debt instruments | 8dzaa | .... | .... | .... | .... | .... | .... | .... | .... | .... | .... | † 90.2 | 87.7 |
| Reserve assets | 8e9aa | .... | .... | .... | .... | .... | .... | .... | .... | .... | .... | † 65.2 | 74.7 |
| Liabilities | 809la | .... | .... | .... | .... | .... | .... | .... | .... | .... | .... | † 745.9 | 736.0 |
| Direct investment | 8a9la | .... | .... | .... | .... | .... | .... | .... | .... | .... | .... | † 393.8 | 369.3 |
| Equity & investment fund shares | 8aala | .... | .... | .... | .... | .... | .... | .... | .... | .... | .... | † 78.5 | 78.4 |
| Debt instruments | 8abla | .... | .... | .... | .... | .... | .... | .... | .... | .... | .... | † 315.3 | 290.9 |
| Portfolio investment | 8b9la | .... | .... | .... | .... | .... | .... | .... | .... | .... | .... | † 4.5 | 1.9 |
| Equity & investment fund shares | 8bala | .... | .... | .... | .... | .... | .... | .... | .... | .... | .... | † 1.6 | 1.9 |
| Debt securities | 8bbla | .... | .... | .... | .... | .... | .... | .... | .... | .... | .... | † 2.9 | — |
| Fin. der.(oth.than reserves) & ESOs | 8c9la | .... | .... | .... | .... | .... | .... | .... | .... | .... | .... | .... | — |
| Other investment | 8d9la | .... | .... | .... | .... | .... | .... | .... | .... | .... | .... | † 347.6 | 364.8 |
| Other equity | 8dala | .... | .... | .... | .... | .... | .... | .... | .... | .... | .... | .... | .... |
| Debt instruments | 8dzla | .... | .... | .... | .... | .... | .... | .... | .... | .... | .... | † 347.6 | 364.8 |

| | | 2004 | 2005 | 2006 | 2007 | 2008 | 2009 | 2010 | 2011 | 2012 | 2013 | 2014 | 2015 |
|---|---|---|---|---|---|---|---|---|---|---|---|---|---|
| **Government Finance** | | | | | | | | | | | | | |
| **Operations Statement** | | | | | | | | | | | | | |
| **Budgetary Central Government** | | | | | *Millions of Dobras: Fiscal Year Ends December 31* | | | | | | | | |
| Revenue............................ | a1 | 381,230 | 982,707 | 570,157 | 3,263,229 | 1,224,923 | 994,860 | 1,458,724 | 1,764,511 | 1,612,067 | .... | .... | .... |
| Taxes.............................. | a11 | 147,328 | 180,012 | 266,617 | 319,777 | 411,008 | 461,570 | 646,952 | 726,009 | 703,734 | .... | .... | .... |
| Taxes on Inc.,Profits,& Cap.Gains. | a111 | 44,486 | 56,909 | 72,401 | 82,374 | 109,377 | 144,308 | 168,095 | 225,588 | 206,588 | .... | .... | .... |
| Individuals................... | a1111 | 23,922 | 48,373 | 44,118 | 47,587 | 68,048 | 87,005 | 106,221 | 130,089 | 149,929 | .... | .... | .... |
| Corporations & Oth. Enterprises. | a1112 | 20,564 | 8,536 | 28,283 | 34,788 | 41,328 | 57,304 | 61,874 | 95,498 | 56,659 | .... | .... | .... |
| Unallocable...................... | a1113 | — | — | — | — | — | — | — | — | — | .... | .... | .... |
| Taxes on Payroll and Workforce... | a112 | — | — | — | — | — | — | — | — | — | .... | .... | .... |
| Taxes on Property............... | a113 | — | — | — | 5,329 | 3,378 | — | 13,170 | 9,268 | 15,837 | .... | .... | .... |
| Taxes on Goods and Services....... | a114 | 7,172 | 9,524 | 30,507 | 37,105 | 47,569 | 79,503 | 62,723 | 55,605 | 53,847 | .... | .... | .... |
| Taxes on Intl.Trade & Trans........ | a115 | 82,047 | 96,307 | 137,549 | 156,791 | 214,591 | 164,628 | 311,583 | 299,506 | 334,043 | .... | .... | .... |
| Other Taxes..................... | a116 | 13,624 | 17,272 | 26,159 | 38,177 | 36,094 | 73,131 | 91,380 | 136,042 | 93,419 | .... | .... | .... |
| Social Contributions...................... | a12 | | | | | | | | | | .... | .... | .... |
| Grants............................ | a13 | 216,267 | 214,022 | 264,221 | 2,478,752 | 780,448 | 465,994 | 751,783 | 977,282 | 841,351 | .... | .... | .... |
| From Foreign Governments.......... | a131 | 123,545 | 109,989 | 174,929 | 128,254 | 6,200 | 3,896 | 520,106 | 484,787 | 178,132 | .... | .... | .... |
| From International Organizations. | a132 | 92,722 | 104,033 | 89,292 | 2,350,497 | 774,248 | 462,098 | 231,677 | 492,495 | 663,219 | .... | .... | .... |
| From other General Govt. Units.... | a133 | — | — | — | — | — | — | — | — | — | .... | .... | .... |
| Other Revenue............................ | a14 | 17,635 | 588,673 | 39,319 | 464,701 | 33,467 | 67,296 | 59,989 | 61,220 | 66,983 | .... | .... | .... |
| Property Income....................... | a141 | 11,023 | 575,040 | 23,531 | 456,849 | 25,018 | 43,384 | 41,106 | 39,218 | 36,600 | .... | .... | .... |
| Misc. and Unidentified Revenue... | a145 | 6,612 | 13,633 | 15,788 | 7,852 | 8,449 | 23,912 | 18,883 | 22,002 | 30,383 | .... | .... | .... |
| Expense.......................... | a2 | 292,345 | 314,423 | 441,769 | 508,435 | 569,445 | 648,777 | 766,694 | 850,538 | 875,136 | .... | .... | .... |
| Compensation of Employees.......... | a21 | 75,743 | 103,203 | 133,334 | 174,344 | 219,099 | 252,090 | 338,383 | 369,185 | 419,418 | .... | .... | .... |
| Wages and Salaries.................... | a211 | 73,444 | 100,044 | 129,551 | 169,829 | 213,829 | 245,174 | 328,268 | 359,630 | 408,993 | .... | .... | .... |
| Social Contributions................... | a212 | 2,299 | 3,159 | 3,783 | 4,515 | 5,270 | 6,915 | 10,115 | 9,554 | 10,425 | .... | .... | .... |
| Use of Goods and Services............. | a22 | 95,764 | 66,200 | 90,696 | 111,536 | 164,260 | 194,846 | 190,862 | 233,682 | 197,632 | .... | .... | .... |
| Consumption of Fixed Capital....... | a23 | .... | .... | .... | .... | .... | .... | .... | .... | .... | .... | .... | .... |
| Interest............................ | a24 | 30,139 | 33,730 | 55,686 | 26,019 | 23,483 | 23,010 | 16,225 | 23,824 | 29,500 | .... | .... | .... |
| To Nonresidents................. | a241 | 26,450 | 32,269 | 48,689 | 24,421 | 23,237 | 22,460 | 16,225 | 23,824 | 23,699 | .... | .... | .... |
| To Residents other than Gen.Govt | a242 | 3,689 | 1,461 | 6,997 | 1,598 | 246 | 550 | — | — | 5,801 | .... | .... | .... |
| To other General Govt. Units....... | a243 | — | — | — | — | — | — | — | — | — | .... | .... | .... |
| Subsidies............................... | a25 | — | — | 59 | — | — | — | — | — | — | .... | .... | .... |
| Grants.............................. | a26 | 40,214 | 58,510 | 73,263 | 93,906 | 60,553 | 94,340 | 123,916 | 123,993 | 149,724 | .... | .... | .... |
| To Foreign Governments............. | a261 | — | — | — | — | — | — | — | — | — | .... | .... | .... |
| To International Organizations..... | a262 | 26,006 | 32,919 | 38,204 | 42,281 | 1,390 | 2,436 | 999 | 5,442 | 7,773 | .... | .... | .... |
| To other General Govt. Units....... | a263 | 14,208 | 25,591 | 35,059 | 51,625 | 59,163 | 91,905 | 122,917 | 118,550 | 141,952 | .... | .... | .... |
| Social Benefits........................ | a27 | — | — | — | — | — | 2,309 | 12,938 | 14,928 | 13,426 | .... | .... | .... |
| Social Security Benefits............... | a271 | — | — | — | — | — | 2,309 | 12,938 | 14,928 | 13,426 | .... | .... | .... |
| Social Assistance Benefits........... | a272 | — | — | — | — | — | — | — | — | — | .... | .... | .... |
| Employer Social Benefits............. | a273 | — | — | — | — | — | — | — | — | — | .... | .... | .... |
| Other Expense........................ | a28 | 50,485 | 52,780 | 88,730 | 102,630 | 102,051 | 82,182 | 84,370 | 84,926 | 65,435 | .... | .... | .... |
| Gross Operating Balance................. | agob | 88,885 | 668,285 | 128,388 | 2,754,795 | 655,478 | 346,083 | 692,031 | 913,973 | 736,931 | .... | .... | .... |
| Net Operating Balance.................... | anob | .... | .... | .... | .... | .... | .... | .... | .... | .... | .... | .... | .... |
| Net Acq. of Nonfinancial Assets..... | a31 | 341,980 | 423,633 | 307,391 | 225,837 | 218,999 | 907,356 | 1,080,887 | 1,466,277 | 1,350,373 | .... | .... | .... |
| Acquisition of nonfinancial Assets.... | a31.1 | .... | .... | .... | .... | .... | .... | .... | .... | .... | .... | .... | .... |
| Net Lending/Borrowing [1-2-31]...... | anlb | −253,095 | 244,652 | −179,003 | 2,528,958 | 436,479 | −561,273 | −388,856 | −552,305 | −613,442 | .... | .... | .... |
| Net Acq. of Financial Assets............. | a32 | .... | .... | .... | .... | .... | .... | .... | 44,371 | −33,707 | .... | .... | .... |
| Net Incurrence of Liabilities............. | a33 | .... | .... | .... | .... | .... | .... | .... | 507,933 | 644,683 | .... | .... | .... |
| Memo Item: Expenditure [2+31]...... | a2m | 634,325 | 738,056 | 749,160 | 734,272 | 788,444 | 1,556,133 | 1,847,580 | 2,316,815 | 2,225,510 | .... | .... | .... |
| | | | | | | *Millions: Midyear Estimates* | | | | | | | |
| **Population................................** | 99z | .15 | .15 | .16 | .16 | .16 | .17 | .17 | .17 | .18 | .18 | .19 | .19 |

| | | 2004 | 2005 | 2006 | 2007 | 2008 | 2009 | 2010 | 2011 | 2012 | 2013 | 2014 | 2015 |
|---|---|---|---|---|---|---|---|---|---|---|---|---|---|
| **Exchange Rates** | | | | | | *Riyals per SDR: End of Period* | | | | | | | |
| Official Rate | aa | 5.8238 | 5.3526 | 5.6340 | 5.9259 | 5.7760 | 5.8788 | 5.7751 | 5.7573 | 5.7635 | 5.7750 | 5.4330 | 5.1965 |
| | | | | | | *Riyals per US Dollar: End of Period (ae) Period Average (rf)* | | | | | | | |
| Official Rate | ae | 3.7500 | 3.7450 | 3.7450 | 3.7500 | 3.7500 | 3.7500 | 3.7500 | 3.7500 | 3.7500 | 3.7500 | 3.7500 | 3.7500 |
| Official Rate | rf | 3.7500 | 3.7471 | 3.7450 | 3.7475 | 3.7500 | 3.7500 | 3.7500 | 3.7500 | 3.7500 | 3.7500 | 3.7500 | |
| | | | | | | *Index Numbers (2010=100): Period Averages* | | | | | | | |
| Official Rate | ahx | 100.0 | 100.1 | 100.1 | 100.1 | 100.0 | 100.0 | 100.0 | 100.0 | 100.0 | 100.0 | 100.0 | 100.1 |
| Nominal Effective Exchange Rate | nec | 107.5 | 106.5 | 105.9 | 101.1 | 97.7 | 101.3 | 100.0 | 96.3 | 99.6 | 102.1 | 104.1 | 114.8 |
| CPI-Based Real Effect. Ex. Rate | rec | 103.5 | 100.5 | 98.9 | 96.0 | 93.6 | 100.2 | 100.0 | 96.6 | 99.6 | 102.4 | 105.4 | 118.6 |
| **Fund Position** | | | | | | *Millions of SDRs: End of Period* | | | | | | | |
| Quota | 2f.s | 6,985.50 | 6,985.50 | 6,985.50 | 6,985.50 | 6,985.50 | 6,985.50 | 6,985.50 | 6,985.50 | 6,985.50 | 6,985.50 | 6,985.50 | 6,985.50 |
| SDR Holdings | 1b.s | 334.08 | 384.64 | 425.25 | 456.32 | 477.25 | 6,970.97 | 6,912.76 | 6,704.62 | 6,415.21 | 6,263.61 | 6,266.26 | 6,498.00 |
| Reserve Position in the Fund | 1c.s | 2,253.06 | 1,333.75 | 606.32 | 462.67 | 898.72 | 1,286.61 | 1,286.61 | 3,167.01 | 3,662.86 | 3,351.31 | 2,706.29 | 2,161.11 |
| Total Fund Cred. & Loans Outstg | 2tl | — | — | — | — | — | — | — | — | — | — | — | — |
| SDR Allocations | 1bd | 195.53 | 195.53 | 195.53 | 195.53 | 195.53 | 6,682.50 | 6,682.50 | 6,682.50 | 6,682.50 | 6,682.50 | 6,682.50 | 6,682.50 |
| **International Liquidity** | | | | | | *Millions of US Dollars Unless Otherwise Indicated: Approximately End of Period* | | | | | | | |
| Total Reserves minus Gold | 1l.d | 27,291 | † 155,029 | 226,035 | 305,455 | 442,249 | 409,694 | 444,722 | 540,677 | 656,464 | 725,292 | 731,920 | 615,985 |
| SDR Holdings | 1b.d | 519 | 550 | 640 | 721 | 735 | 10,928 | 10,646 | 10,293 | 9,860 | 9,646 | 9,079 | 9,004 |
| Reserve Position in the Fund | 1c.d | 3,499 | 1,906 | 912 | 731 | 1,384 | 2,017 | 1,981 | 4,862 | 5,630 | 5,161 | 3,921 | 2,995 |
| Foreign Exchange | 1d.d | 23,273 | † 152,573 | 224,483 | 304,003 | 440,130 | 396,748 | 432,094 | 525,521 | 640,975 | 710,485 | 718,921 | 603,986 |
| Gold (Million Fine Troy Ounces) | 1ad | 4.596 | 4.596 | 4.596 | 4.596 | 10.382 | 10.382 | 10.382 | 10.382 | 10.382 | 10.382 | 10.382 | 10.382 |
| Gold (National Valuation) | 1and | 250 | 230 | 242 | 254 | † 415 | 415 | 415 | 415 | 415 | 433 | 433 | 433 |
| Deposit Money Banks: Assets | 7a.d | 24,746 | 24,392 | 34,630 | 39,350 | 41,002 | 56,223 | 51,469 | 55,532 | 56,609 | 56,020 | 66,950 | 84,129 |
| Deposit Money Banks: Liabs | 7b.d | 12,199 | 17,367 | 15,807 | 28,061 | 30,201 | 26,589 | 25,255 | 20,120 | 21,172 | 19,841 | 24,607 | 24,312 |
| Other Banking Insts.: Assets | 7e.d | 1,045 | 1,101 | 1,178 | 1,287 | 2,066 | 2,080 | 2,080 | 2,269 | 4,602 | 3,617 | 3,580 | 3,782 |
| **Monetary Authorities** | | | | | | *Billions of Riyals: Approximately End of Period* | | | | | | | |
| Foreign Assets | 11 | 329.14 | 573.68 | 843.33 | 1,143.40 | 1,654.80 | 1,530.34 | 1,701.75 | 2,049.46 | 2,469.64 | 2,730.32 | 2,759.73 | 2,339.59 |
| Reserve Money | 14 | 83.71 | 92.76 | 110.58 | 118.49 | 146.93 | 164.95 | 180.29 | 219.10 | 269.35 | 271.20 | 303.16 | 327.62 |
| of which: Currency Outside DMBs | 14a | 60.13 | 64.29 | 69.32 | 72.19 | 83.01 | 88.40 | 95.52 | 119.93 | 163.22 | 143.17 | 153.78 | 168.53 |
| Central Government Deposits | 16d | 98.20 | 240.65 | 333.53 | 508.48 | 1,047.74 | 908.13 | 992.56 | 1,171.25 | 1,500.07 | 1,616.63 | 1,529.99 | 1,129.93 |
| Other Items (Net) | 17r | 147.24 | 240.27 | 399.22 | 516.44 | 460.13 | 457.26 | 528.90 | 659.11 | 700.21 | 842.49 | 926.57 | 882.04 |
| Memo Item: | | | | | | | | | | | | | |
| Total Assets | 10ra | 351.15 | 595.27 | 858.56 | 1,170.28 | 1,687.69 | 1,556.45 | 1,728.94 | 2,080.84 | 2,474.31 | 2,760.12 | 2,811.59 | 2,390.05 |
| **Deposit Money Banks** | | | | | | *Billions of Riyals: Approximately End of Period* | | | | | | | |
| Reserves | 20 | 32.04 | 32.65 | 52.06 | 108.61 | 97.28 | 160.12 | 159.31 | 179.17 | 217.45 | 200.37 | 213.07 | 146.24 |
| Foreign Assets | 21 | 92.80 | 91.35 | 129.69 | 147.56 | 153.76 | 210.83 | 193.01 | 208.24 | 212.28 | 210.07 | 251.06 | 315.48 |
| Claims on Central Government | 22a | 146.66 | 127.81 | 123.25 | 144.18 | 209.92 | 154.19 | 182.05 | 177.80 | 181.18 | 228.74 | 279.13 | 222.43 |
| Claims on Public Enterprises | 22c | 29.14 | 31.67 | 34.96 | 37.43 | 32.07 | 28.14 | 32.28 | 31.83 | 35.78 | 41.68 | 44.72 | 38.56 |
| Claims on Private Sector | 22d | 313.93 | 435.93 | 476.02 | 577.88 | 734.56 | 734.24 | 775.76 | 858.37 | 1,002.93 | 1,126.10 | 1,256.21 | 1,371.93 |
| Demand Deposits | 24 | 203.81 | 220.28 | 243.62 | 311.92 | 343.01 | 433.48 | 530.39 | 641.51 | 754.35 | 857.66 | 989.72 | 976.96 |
| Quasi-Monetary Deposits | 25a | 153.73 | 185.08 | 245.59 | 307.69 | 397.65 | 354.90 | 341.55 | 338.98 | 362.32 | 390.12 | 444.38 | 487.88 |
| Foreign Currency Deposits | 25b | 67.57 | 79.84 | 103.10 | 103.09 | 113.99 | 162.24 | 125.29 | 137.25 | 161.86 | 171.22 | 158.98 | 164.24 |
| Foreign Liabilities | 26c | 45.75 | 65.04 | 59.20 | 105.23 | 113.25 | 99.71 | 94.71 | 75.45 | 79.40 | 74.41 | 92.28 | 91.17 |
| Credit from Monetary Authorities | 26g | 7.41 | 5.47 | 4.62 | 4.15 | 15.79 | .76 | .85 | .71 | 1.01 | 1.42 | 1.06 | 5.46 |
| Capital Accounts | 27a | 68.81 | 92.22 | 114.61 | 135.75 | 161.75 | 190.49 | 204.14 | 221.06 | 243.00 | 261.55 | 288.27 | 313.65 |
| Other Items (Net) | 27r | 67.48 | 71.46 | 45.25 | 47.29 | 82.15 | 45.93 | 45.47 | 40.46 | 47.69 | 50.59 | 69.50 | 55.53 |
| Memo Item: | | | | | | | | | | | | | |
| Total Assets | 20ra | 655.38 | 759.08 | 861.09 | 1,075.22 | 1,302.27 | 1,370.26 | 1,415.27 | 1,544.43 | 1,734.14 | 1,893.28 | 2,132.58 | 2,208.77 |
| **Monetary Survey** | | | | | | *Billions of Riyals: Approximately End of Period* | | | | | | | |
| Foreign Assets (Net) | 31n | 375.06 | 598.94 | 912.72 | 1,184.58 | 1,694.18 | 1,602.18 | 1,761.47 | 2,143.78 | 2,564.01 | 2,827.40 | 2,882.21 | 2,529.18 |
| Domestic Credit | 32 | 391.52 | 354.76 | 300.70 | 251.02 | −71.20 | 8.43 | −2.47 | −103.25 | −280.18 | −220.12 | 50.07 | 502.99 |
| Claims on Central Govt. (Net) | 32an | 48.46 | −112.84 | −210.28 | −364.30 | −837.82 | −753.94 | −810.51 | −993.45 | −1,318.89 | −1,387.89 | −1,250.87 | −907.50 |
| Claims on Public Enterprises | 32c | 29.14 | 31.67 | 34.96 | 37.43 | 32.07 | 28.14 | 32.28 | 31.83 | 35.78 | 41.68 | 44.72 | 38.56 |
| Claims on Private Sector | 32d | 313.93 | 435.93 | 476.02 | 577.88 | 734.56 | 734.24 | 775.76 | 858.37 | 1,002.93 | 1,126.10 | 1,256.21 | 1,371.93 |
| Money | 34 | 263.94 | 284.57 | 312.94 | 384.11 | 426.02 | 521.87 | 625.91 | 761.44 | 917.57 | 1,000.83 | 1,143.50 | 1,145.49 |
| Quasi-Money | 35 | 221.30 | 264.92 | 348.69 | 410.78 | 511.63 | 517.14 | 466.85 | 476.23 | 524.18 | 561.34 | 603.36 | 652.12 |
| Other Items (Net) | 37r | 281.34 | 404.21 | 551.79 | 640.16 | 685.32 | 571.59 | 666.24 | 802.86 | 842.08 | 1,045.12 | 1,185.41 | 1,234.81 |
| Money plus Quasi-Money | 35l | 485.24 | 549.49 | 661.63 | 794.90 | 937.66 | 1,039.02 | 1,092.76 | 1,237.66 | 1,441.75 | 1,562.16 | 1,746.86 | 1,797.61 |
| **Other Banking Institutions** | | | | | | *Billions of Riyals: Approximately End of Period* | | | | | | | |
| Cash | 40 | 23.15 | 28.79 | 30.46 | 56.16 | 43.60 | 28.07 | 40.68 | 57.03 | 80.31 | 82.45 | 69.28 | 37.06 |
| Foreign Assets | 41 | 3.92 | 4.13 | 4.41 | 4.83 | 7.75 | 7.80 | 8.51 | 15.87 | 17.26 | 13.56 | 13.42 | 14.18 |
| Claims on Private Sector | 42d | 211.45 | 189.58 | 186.37 | 201.37 | 239.06 | 280.18 | 293.74 | 345.38 | 361.13 | 384.57 | 426.81 | 500.94 |
| Capital Accounts | 47a | 202.45 | 184.71 | 199.75 | 316.83 | 335.90 | 347.77 | 369.05 | 525.60 | 553.20 | 571.93 | 614.33 | 634.17 |
| Other Items (Net) | 47r | 36.07 | 37.80 | 21.49 | −54.48 | −45.49 | −31.72 | −26.12 | −107.32 | −94.50 | −91.34 | −104.81 | −81.98 |
| **Money (National Definitions)** | | | | | | | | | | | | | |
| Monetary Base | 19ma | 92.17 | 96.93 | 121.39 | 180.81 | 180.18 | 248.51 | 254.83 | 299.10 | 350.60 | 343.53 | 366.85 | 301.50 |
| M1 | 59ma | 271.30 | 283.54 | 312.74 | 383.56 | 425.49 | 521.56 | 625.59 | 760.99 | 887.12 | 1,000.45 | 1,142.95 | 1,145.56 |
| M2 | 59mb | 407.98 | 448.81 | 538.77 | 666.62 | 793.12 | 844.94 | 923.87 | 1,066.43 | 1,221.54 | 1,345.48 | 1,541.69 | 1,580.06 |
| M3 | 59mc | 496.10 | 553.68 | 660.58 | 789.76 | 929.13 | 1,028.94 | 1,080.37 | 1,223.56 | 1,393.75 | 1,545.15 | 1,729.36 | 1,774.10 |
| **Interest Rates** | | | | | | *Percent per Annum* | | | | | | | |
| Central Bank Policy Rate (EOP) | 60 | 2.250 | 4.250 | 4.700 | 4.000 | 1.500 | .250 | .250 | .250 | .250 | .250 | .250 | .500 |
| Central Bank Repo Rate | 60.q | 2.500 | 4.750 | 5.200 | 5.500 | 2.500 | 2.000 | 2.000 | 2.000 | 2.000 | 2.000 | 2.000 | 2.000 |
| Money Market Rate | 60b | .... | .... | .... | .... | .... | .... | .738 | .694 | .916 | .953 | .936 | .879 |
| Money Market Rate (Fgn. Currency) | 60b.f | .... | .... | .... | .... | .... | .... | .356 | .327 | .364 | .266 | .232 | .315 |
| Treasury Bill Rate | 60c | .... | .... | .... | .... | .... | .... | .383 | .332 | .386 | .490 | .516 | .466 |
| **Prices, Production, Labor** | | | | | | *Index Numbers (2010=100): Period Averages* | | | | | | | |
| Share Prices (End of Month) | 62.ep | 97.1 | 203.9 | 198.5 | 127.4 | 128.0 | 83.8 | 100.0 | 99.3 | 109.4 | 119.9 | 150.6 | 131.6 |
| Wholesale Prices | 63 | 82.5 | 84.8 | 85.8 | 90.7 | 98.8 | 95.8 | 100.0 | 104.2 | 106.5 | 108.1 | 108.7 | 107.6 |
| Consumer Prices | 64 | 76.7 | 77.2 | 78.9 | 82.2 | 90.4 | 94.9 | 100.0 | † 105.8 | 108.9 | 112.7 | 115.7 | 118.2 |
| Crude Petroleum Production | 66aa | 111.3 | 115.1 | 111.9 | 105.2 | 110.8 | 98.9 | 100.0 | 112.5 | 118.7 | 117.0 | 118.9 | 126.7 |
| | | | | | | *Number in Thousands: Period Averages* | | | | | | | |
| Employment | 67e | 6,718 | 7,121 | 7,523 | 7,755 | 7,987 | 8,148 | 8,835 | 9,936 | 10,263 | 10,682 | 10,984 | .... |

# Saudi Arabia 456

| | | 2004 | 2005 | 2006 | 2007 | 2008 | 2009 | 2010 | 2011 | 2012 | 2013 | 2014 | 2015 |
|---|---|---|---|---|---|---|---|---|---|---|---|---|---|
| **Intl. Transactions & Positions** | | | | | | | *Billions of Riyals* | | | | | | | |
| Exports | 70 | 472.49 | 677.14 | 791.34 | 874.40 | 1,175.35 | 721.11 | 941.80 | 1,367.62 | 1,456.39 | 1,409.52 | 1,283.62 | 758.39 |
| Petroleum | 70a | 415.86 | 606.22 | 704.87 | 770.59 | 1,053.73 | 2,293.09 | 3,026.91 | 4,466.44 | 4,745.81 | 4,526.55 | .... | .... |
| Crude Petroleum | 70aa | 348.67 | 514.22 | 606.70 | 668.12 | 926.61 | 1,999.41 | 2,663.91 | 4,007.47 | 4,294.75 | 4,134.29 | .... | .... |
| Refined Petroleum | 70ab | 67.19 | 91.99 | 98.17 | 102.47 | 127.12 | 293.67 | 363.00 | 458.97 | 451.07 | 392.26 | .... | .... |
| Imports, c.i.f. | 71 | 167.79 | 222.79 | 261.40 | 338.09 | 431.75 | 358.29 | 400.74 | 493.45 | 583.47 | 630.58 | 651.88 | 655.03 |
| Volume of Exports | | | | | | | *2010=100* | | | | | | | |
| Petroleum | 72a | 107.1 | 113.0 | 109.2 | 106.6 | 110.3 | 95.7 | 100.0 | 107.0 | 112.3 | 110.3 | .... | .... |
| Crude Petroleum | 72aa | 102.5 | 108.5 | 105.8 | 104.8 | 110.2 | 94.3 | 100.0 | 108.6 | 114.8 | 113.9 | .... | .... |
| Refined Petroleum | 72ab | 140.3 | 145.7 | 134.4 | 119.8 | 111.3 | 106.1 | 100.0 | 94.9 | 93.8 | 83.5 | .... | .... |
| Export Prices | | | | | | | *2010=100: Index of Prices in US Dollars* | | | | | | | |
| Crude Petroleum | 76aad | 43.2 | 62.1 | 74.8 | 85.6 | 120.0 | 76.1 | 100.0 | 138.9 | 132.2 | 134.3 | 124.3 | 63.4 |
| **Balance of Payments** | | | | | | | *Millions of US Dollars* | | | | | | | |
| A. Current Account* | 109bx | 51,926.0 | † 90,060.3 | 99,066.1 | 93,379.5 | 132,322.2 | 20,954.6 | 66,751.0 | 158,545.2 | 164,763.7 | 135,442.4 | 73,758.2 | −53,477.9 |
| Goods, credit (exports) | 1a9cx | 125,997.6 | † 180,712.3 | 211,305.4 | 233,310.8 | 313,480.5 | 192,307.2 | 251,142.7 | 364,735.5 | 388,369.6 | 375,901.1 | 342,456.9 | 202,268.5 |
| Goods, debit (imports) | 1a9dx | 41,050.4 | † 54,595.4 | 63,914.4 | 82,594.7 | 101,453.6 | 87,077.6 | 97,431.1 | 119,960.7 | 141,799.2 | 153,343.6 | 158,462.0 | 154,990.9 |
| Balance on goods | 1a9bx | 84,947.2 | † 126,116.9 | 147,391.0 | 150,716.1 | 212,026.9 | 105,229.6 | 153,711.5 | 244,774.8 | 246,570.4 | 222,557.4 | 183,994.9 | 47,277.6 |
| Services, credit (exports) | 1b9cx | 5,851.7 | † 11,409.9 | 14,201.5 | 16,403.7 | 9,373.1 | 9,749.3 | 10,688.5 | 11,488.7 | 11,049.9 | 11,844.7 | 12,516.3 | 14,473.9 |
| Services, debit (imports) | 1b9dx | 25,695.7 | † 33,120.5 | 49,580.7 | 63,093.9 | 75,231.0 | 74,991.4 | 76,772.1 | 78,016.6 | 73,407.0 | 76,651.7 | 100,544.9 | 90,200.0 |
| Balance on Goods & Services | 1z9bx | 65,103.3 | † 104,406.3 | 112,011.8 | 104,025.9 | 146,169.0 | 39,987.6 | 87,628.0 | 178,246.9 | 184,213.3 | 157,750.4 | 95,966.2 | −28,448.6 |
| Primary income: credit | 1c9cx | 4,277.9 | † 5,057.7 | 10,481.4 | 15,137.7 | 21,498.2 | 19,752.0 | 18,171.5 | 19,765.7 | 23,647.5 | 25,170.5 | 27,110.7 | 23,960.0 |
| Primary income: debit | 1c9dx | 3,800.1 | † 4,625.8 | 6,646.5 | 8,741.3 | 12,333.3 | 11,112.5 | 11,127.6 | 10,081.6 | 12,658.9 | 11,609.1 | 10,584.8 | 8,296.6 |
| Balance on gds, serv. & prim. inc. | 1y9bx | 65,581.0 | † 104,838.2 | 115,846.8 | 110,422.3 | 155,333.9 | 48,627.2 | 94,671.9 | 187,931.0 | 195,201.9 | 171,311.7 | 112,492.2 | −12,785.2 |
| Secondary income: credit | 1d9ca | — | † — | | | | | — | 34.7 | 70.8 | 93.3 | — | — |
| Secondary income: debit | 1d9da | 13,655.1 | † 14,777.9 | 16,780.6 | 17,042.8 | 23,011.7 | 27,672.6 | 27,920.9 | 29,420.5 | 30,509.1 | 35,962.6 | 38,734.0 | 40,692.8 |
| B. Capital Account* | 209ba | — | .... | .... | .... | .... | .... | .... | .... | −271.2 | −335.2 | −328.8 | −461.9 |
| Capital account: credit | 209ca | — | .... | .... | .... | .... | .... | .... | .... | .... | .... | .... | .... |
| Capital account: debit | 209da | — | .... | .... | .... | .... | .... | .... | .... | 271.2 | 335.2 | 328.8 | 461.9 |
| Balance on current & capital acct. | 129ba | 51,926.0 | † 90,060.3 | 99,066.1 | 93,379.5 | 132,322.2 | 20,954.6 | 66,751.0 | 158,545.2 | 164,492.5 | 135,107.2 | 73,429.4 | −53,939.8 |
| C. Financial Account* | 309na | 47,428.2 | † −8,361.4 | 7,497.2 | −2,116.0 | −34,728.5 | −7,243.8 | −2,657.0 | 14,412.7 | 6,369.3 | 57,382.2 | 57,357.5 | 42,025.4 |
| Direct investment: assets | 3a9aa | — | † −350.1 | −38.6 | −134.8 | 3,497.6 | 2,177.3 | 3,906.8 | 3,429.9 | 4,401.5 | 4,943.3 | 5,396.0 | 5,520.3 |
| Equity & investment fund shares | 3aaaa | | | | | | | .... | .... | .... | .... | .... | .... |
| Debt instruments | 3abaa | | | | | | | .... | .... | .... | .... | .... | .... |
| Direct investment: liabilities | 3a9la | −334.3 | † 12,106.7 | 18,317.6 | 24,333.8 | 39,455.9 | 36,457.7 | 29,232.7 | 16,308.3 | 12,182.4 | 8,864.7 | 8,011.8 | 8,141.0 |
| Equity & investment fund shares . | 3aala | — | .... | .... | .... | .... | .... | .... | .... | .... | .... | .... | .... |
| Debt instruments | 3abla | −334.3 | .... | .... | .... | .... | .... | .... | .... | .... | .... | .... | .... |
| Portfolio investment: assets | 3b9aa | 26,654.3 | † −350.4 | 11,948.8 | 5,479.6 | 3,847.5 | 20,133.5 | 16,656.9 | 15,423.9 | 4,093.4 | 8,387.8 | 26,982.7 | 10,316.4 |
| Equity & investment fund shares | 3baaa | | † — | — | — | 6,902.9 | 7,692.2 | 17,769.5 | 10,353.0 | 4,588.3 | 7,898.0 | 17,533.6 | 7,097.9 |
| Debt securities | 3bbaa | 26,654.3 | † — | — | — | −3,055.2 | 12,441.3 | −1,112.5 | 5,070.9 | −494.9 | 489.9 | 9,449.1 | 3,218.5 |
| Portfolio investment: liabilities | 3b9la | | † — | — | — | 2,217.0 | −5.2 | 1,502.7 | −623.7 | 909.1 | 1,781.7 | 202.5 | 347.2 |
| Equity & investment fund shares . | 3bala | — | .... | .... | .... | .... | .... | .... | .... | .... | .... | .... | .... |
| Debt securities | 3bbla | — | .... | .... | .... | .... | .... | .... | .... | .... | .... | .... | .... |
| Fin. der.& empl.stk.ops.(ESOs): net. | 3c9na | .... | .... | .... | .... | .... | .... | .... | .... | .... | .... | .... | .... |
| Fin. der. & ESOs.: assets | 3c9aa | .... | .... | .... | .... | .... | .... | .... | .... | .... | .... | .... | .... |
| Fin. der. & ESOs.: liabilities | 3c9la | .... | .... | .... | .... | .... | .... | .... | .... | .... | .... | .... | .... |
| Other investment: assets | 3d9aa | 21,955.4 | † 4,424.5 | 13,976.0 | 16,849.3 | 2,562.0 | 9,542.4 | 6,523.2 | 7,249.5 | 10,285.0 | 52,336.7 | 39,201.5 | 38,570.8 |
| Other equity | 3daaa | | | | | | | .... | .... | .... | .... | .... | .... |
| Debt instruments | 3dzaa | 21,955.4 | † 4,424.5 | 13,976.0 | 16,849.3 | 2,562.0 | 9,542.4 | 6,523.2 | 7,249.5 | 10,285.0 | 52,336.7 | 39,201.5 | 38,570.8 |
| Other investment: liabilities | 3d9la | 1,515.8 | † −21.3 | 71.3 | −23.7 | 2,962.7 | 2,644.5 | −991.4 | −3,993.9 | −680.8 | −2,360.8 | 6,008.4 | 3,893.9 |
| Other equity | 3dala | | | | | | | .... | .... | .... | .... | .... | .... |
| Debt instruments | 3dzla | 1,515.8 | † −21.3 | 71.3 | −23.7 | 2,962.7 | 2,644.5 | −991.4 | −3,993.9 | −680.8 | −2,360.8 | 6,008.4 | 3,893.9 |
| Curr.+ cap.− finan. acct. balance. | 4y9na | 4,497.8 | † 98,421.7 | 91,568.9 | 95,495.5 | 167,050.7 | 28,198.4 | 69,408.0 | 144,132.6 | 158,123.2 | 77,725.0 | 16,072.0 | −95,965.2 |
| D. Net Errors and Omissions | 409na | — | † −34,453.2 | −20,658.7 | −15,701.9 | −30,007.6 | −60,836.6 | −34,152.7 | −48,075.2 | −42,350.0 | −8,598.2 | −8,594.9 | −19,403.6 |
| E. Reserves and Related Items | 4z9na | 4,497.8 | † 63,968.6 | 70,910.1 | 79,793.6 | 137,043.1 | −32,638.2 | 35,255.4 | 96,057.3 | 115,773.3 | 69,126.8 | 7,477.0 | −115,368.9 |
| Reserve assets | 3e9aa | 4,497.8 | † 63,968.6 | 70,910.1 | 79,793.6 | 137,043.1 | −32,638.2 | 35,255.4 | 96,057.3 | 115,773.3 | 69,126.8 | 7,477.0 | −115,368.9 |
| Credit and loans from the IMF | 3dcla | — | † — | | | | | | | | | | |
| Exceptional financing | 409la | .... | | .... | .... | .... | .... | .... | .... | .... | .... | .... | .... |
| *Excludes components in group E | | | | | | | | | | | | | |
| **International Investment Position** | | | | | | | *Millions of US Dollars* | | | | | | | |
| Assets | 809aa | .... | .... | .... | † 495,395.4 | 630,816.4 | 635,977.5 | 707,596.0 | 823,874.7 | 935,900.2 | 1,027,912.1 | 1,069,292.0 | 992,752.6 |
| Direct investment | 8a9aa | .... | .... | .... | † 17,047.5 | 20,444.0 | 22,621.2 | 26,528.0 | 29,957.9 | 34,359.5 | 39,302.8 | 44,698.8 | 63,250.9 |
| Equity & investment fund shares.. | 8aaaa | .... | .... | .... | † 17,047.5 | 20,444.0 | 22,621.2 | 26,528.0 | 29,957.9 | 34,359.5 | .... | .... | .... |
| Debt instruments | 8abaa | .... | .... | .... | .... | .... | .... | .... | .... | .... | .... | .... | .... |
| Portfolio investment | 8b9aa | .... | .... | .... | † 104,947.0 | 98,592.5 | 121,536.9 | 146,168.1 | 158,197.3 | 167,531.6 | 178,178.5 | 198,990.5 | 202,429.4 |
| Equity & investment fund shares.. | 8baaa | .... | .... | .... | † 52,659.3 | 50,196.7 | 58,807.7 | 78,576.4 | 81,504.0 | 92,177.6 | 98,958.2 | 111,026.2 | 108,709.7 |
| Debt securities | 8bbaa | .... | .... | .... | † 52,287.7 | 48,395.8 | 62,729.1 | 67,591.7 | 76,693.3 | 75,354.0 | 79,220.3 | 87,964.3 | 93,719.7 |
| Fin. der.(oth.than reserves) & ESOs | 8c9aa | .... | .... | .... | .... | .... | .... | .... | .... | .... | .... | .... | .... |
| Other investment | 8d9aa | .... | .... | .... | † 67,761.8 | 69,115.5 | 81,710.9 | 89,763.3 | 91,704.6 | 77,435.1 | 84,706.0 | 93,249.4 | 110,654.3 |
| Other equity | 8daaa | .... | .... | .... | .... | .... | .... | .... | .... | .... | .... | .... | .... |
| Debt instruments | 8dzaa | .... | .... | .... | † 67,761.8 | 69,115.5 | 81,710.9 | 89,763.3 | 91,704.6 | 77,435.1 | 84,706.0 | 93,249.4 | 110,654.3 |
| Reserve assets | 8e9aa | .... | .... | .... | † 305,639.2 | 442,664.4 | 410,108.5 | 445,136.6 | 544,014.8 | 656,574.0 | 725,724.8 | 732,353.4 | 616,418.0 |
| Liabilities | 809la | .... | .... | .... | † 115,584.5 | 159,849.1 | 201,397.8 | 228,932.3 | 238,603.2 | 251,143.3 | 264,745.3 | 277,714.8 | 289,448.8 |
| Direct investment | 8a9la | .... | .... | .... | † 73,479.7 | 112,935.5 | 148,088.8 | 176,377.9 | 186,758.1 | 199,032.1 | 207,897.0 | 215,908.7 | 224,049.8 |
| Equity & investment fund shares.. | 8aala | .... | .... | .... | .... | .... | .... | .... | .... | .... | .... | .... | .... |
| Debt instruments | 8abla | .... | .... | .... | .... | .... | .... | .... | .... | .... | .... | .... | .... |
| Portfolio investment | 8b9la | .... | .... | .... | .... | 3,199.5 | 3,908.5 | 3,617.6 | 6,329.9 | 10,171.7 | 17,200.9 | 16,718.4 | 16,914.9 |
| Equity & investment fund shares.. | 8bala | .... | .... | .... | .... | .... | .... | .... | .... | 9,053.1 | 15,088.5 | 14,665.2 | 14,837.6 |
| Debt securities | 8bbla | .... | .... | .... | .... | .... | .... | .... | .... | 1,118.7 | 2,112.4 | 2,053.1 | 2,077.3 |
| Fin. der.(oth.than reserves) & ESOs | 8c9la | .... | .... | .... | .... | .... | .... | .... | .... | .... | .... | .... | .... |
| Other investment | 8d9la | .... | .... | .... | † 42,104.8 | 43,714.1 | 49,400.5 | 48,936.8 | 45,515.2 | 41,939.4 | 39,647.4 | 45,087.7 | 48,484.2 |
| Other equity | 8dala | .... | .... | .... | .... | .... | .... | .... | .... | .... | .... | .... | .... |
| Debt instruments | 8dzla | .... | .... | .... | † 42,104.8 | 43,714.1 | 49,400.5 | 48,936.8 | 45,515.2 | 41,939.4 | 39,647.4 | 45,087.7 | 48,484.2 |

# Saudi Arabia   456

| | | 2004 | 2005 | 2006 | 2007 | 2008 | 2009 | 2010 | 2011 | 2012 | 2013 | 2014 | 2015 |
|---|---|---|---|---|---|---|---|---|---|---|---|---|---|
| **National Accounts** | | | | | | | *Billions of Riyals* | | | | | | | |
| Househ.Cons.Expend.,incl.NPISHs.... | 96f | 294.85 | 324.15 | 367.36 | 434.19 | 523.95 | 591.81 | 639.42 | 681.76 | 785.40 | 838.74 | 909.86 | 988.81 |
| Government Consumption Expend... | 91f | 221.80 | 262.65 | 311.08 | 322.09 | 345.10 | 357.02 | 400.17 | 488.06 | 551.18 | 628.52 | 739.16 | 716.14 |
| Gross Fixed Capital Formation......... | 93e | 185.87 | 237.69 | 288.68 | 368.69 | 444.50 | 414.45 | 483.92 | 568.79 | 614.91 | 662.46 | 714.25 | 697.53 |
| Changes in Inventories.................... | 93i | 6.87 | 10.62 | 24.89 | 43.98 | 87.56 | 95.88 | 123.43 | 103.61 | 110.04 | 70.01 | 91.76 | 141.84 |
| Exports of Goods and Services......... | 90c | 494.70 | 702.16 | 844.52 | 934.32 | 1,210.70 | 757.71 | 981.87 | 1,410.84 | 1,497.82 | 1,453.67 | 1,329.53 | 817.59 |
| Imports of Goods and Services (-)..... | 98c | 233.81 | 306.50 | 425.04 | 544.43 | 662.57 | 607.76 | 653.26 | 742.41 | 807.02 | 862.13 | 957.69 | 939.40 |
| Gross Domestic Product (GDP)......... | 99b | 970.28 | 1,230.77 | 1,411.49 | 1,558.83 | 1,949.24 | 1,609.12 | 1,975.54 | 2,510.65 | 2,752.33 | 2,791.26 | 2,826.87 | 2,422.51 |
| Net Primary Income from Abroad..... | 98.n | 8.00 | 1.62 | 14.36 | 23.97 | 34.37 | 32.40 | 26.42 | 36.32 | 41.21 | 40.37 | 61.84 | .... |
| Gross National Income (GNI)............ | 99a | 978.29 | 1,232.39 | 1,425.85 | 1,582.80 | 1,983.61 | 1,641.52 | 2,001.96 | 2,546.97 | 2,793.54 | 2,831.63 | 2,888.71 | 2,422.51 |
| GDP Volume 1999 Prices................ | 99b.p | 749.52 | 803.91 | 848.74 | 899.60 | 975.41 | 993.25 | 1,067.10 | 1,158.55 | 1,225.89 | 1,274.31 | .... | .... |
| GDP Volume 2010 Prices................ | 99b.p | .... | .... | .... | .... | .... | .... | 1,975.54 | 2,172.29 | 2,289.25 | 2,350.37 | 2,435.90 | 2,520.80 |
| GDP Volume (2010=100)............... | 99bvp | 70.2 | 75.3 | 79.5 | 84.3 | 91.4 | 93.1 | † 100.0 | 110.0 | 115.9 | 119.0 | 123.3 | 127.6 |
| GDP Deflator (2010=100).............. | 99bip | 69.9 | 82.7 | 89.8 | 93.6 | 107.9 | 87.5 | 100.0 | 115.6 | 120.2 | 118.8 | 116.1 | 96.1 |
| | | | | | | | *Millions: Midyear Estimates* | | | | | | | |
| **Population**............................... | 99z | 24.06 | 24.75 | 25.42 | 26.08 | 26.74 | 27.41 | 28.09 | 28.79 | 29.50 | 30.20 | 30.89 | 31.54 |

# Senegal 722

| | | 2004 | 2005 | 2006 | 2007 | 2008 | 2009 | 2010 | 2011 | 2012 | 2013 | 2014 | 2015 |
|---|---|---|---|---|---|---|---|---|---|---|---|---|---|
| **Exchange Rates** | | | | | | *CFA Francs per SDR: End of Period* | | | | | | | |
| Official Rate | aa | 747.90 | 794.73 | 749.30 | 704.15 | 725.98 | 713.83 | 756.02 | 778.32 | 764.10 | 732.49 | 782.77 | 834.92 |
| | | | | | | *CFA Francs per US Dollar: End of Period (ae) Period Average (rf)* | | | | | | | |
| Official Rate | ae | 481.58 | 556.04 | 498.07 | 445.59 | 471.34 | 455.34 | 490.91 | 506.96 | 497.16 | 475.64 | 540.28 | 602.51 |
| Official Rate | rf | 528.28 | 527.47 | 522.89 | 479.27 | 447.81 | 472.19 | 495.28 | 471.87 | 510.53 | 494.04 | 494.41 | 591.45 |
| **Fund Position** | | | | | | *Millions of SDRs: End of Period* | | | | | | | |
| Quota | 2f.s | 161.80 | 161.80 | 161.80 | 161.80 | 161.80 | 161.80 | 161.80 | 161.80 | 161.80 | 161.80 | 161.80 | 161.80 |
| SDR Holdings | 1b.s | 4.71 | .96 | .04 | .07 | .11 | 130.39 | 130.32 | 130.21 | 130.18 | 130.16 | 130.13 | 107.70 |
| Reserve Position in the Fund | 1c.s | 1.53 | 1.57 | 1.60 | 1.64 | 1.68 | 1.71 | 1.79 | 1.82 | 1.88 | 1.88 | 1.88 | 1.88 |
| Total Fund Cred.&Loans Outstg. | 2tl | 131.47 | 103.79 | 17.33 | 17.33 | 41.60 | 106.32 | 138.33 | 136.25 | 132.79 | 129.32 | 117.77 | 93.61 |
| SDR Allocations | 1bd | 24.46 | 24.46 | 24.46 | 24.46 | 24.46 | 154.80 | 154.80 | 154.80 | 154.80 | 154.80 | 154.80 | 154.80 |
| **International Liquidity** | | | | | | *Millions of US Dollars Unless Otherwise Indicated: End of Period* | | | | | | | |
| Total Reserves minus Gold | 1l.d | 1,367.6 | 1,186.0 | 1,334.2 | 1,660.0 | 1,602.2 | 2,123.2 | 2,047.5 | 1,945.7 | 2,081.6 | 2,253.1 | 2,038.1 | 2,011.8 |
| SDR Holdings | 1b.d | 7.3 | 1.4 | .1 | .1 | .2 | 204.4 | 200.7 | 199.9 | 200.1 | 200.4 | 188.5 | 149.2 |
| Reserve Position in the Fund | 1c.d | 2.4 | 2.2 | 2.4 | 2.6 | 2.6 | 2.7 | 2.8 | 2.8 | 2.9 | 2.9 | 2.7 | 2.6 |
| Foreign Exchange | 1d.d | 1,357.9 | 1,182.4 | 1,331.8 | 1,657.3 | 1,599.4 | 1,916.1 | 1,844.0 | 1,742.9 | 1,878.7 | 2,049.8 | 1,846.9 | 1,859.9 |
| Gold (Million Fine Troy Ounces) | 1ad | — | — | — | — | — | — | — | — | — | — | — | .... |
| Gold (National Valuation) | 1and | — | — | — | — | — | — | — | — | — | — | — | .... |
| Monetary Authorities: Other Liabs. | 4..d | 131.8 | 137.3 | 118.5 | 137.0 | 126.7 | 111.7 | 100.9 | 86.3 | 77.9 | 200.5 | 58.2 | 72.1 |
| Deposit Money Banks: Assets | 7a.d | 616.6 | 535.8 | 732.7 | 837.8 | 697.7 | 781.6 | 870.7 | 902.7 | 901.2 | 980.8 | 1,181.1 | 1,333.9 |
| Deposit Money Banks: Liabs | 7b.d | 203.1 | 224.3 | 310.6 | 373.5 | 466.1 | 489.0 | 354.6 | 629.1 | 692.2 | 782.7 | 752.8 | 886.3 |
| **Monetary Authorities** | | | | | | *Billions of CFA Francs: End of Period* | | | | | | | |
| Foreign Assets | 11 | 658.6 | 659.5 | 664.5 | 739.7 | 755.2 | 966.8 | 1,005.1 | 986.4 | 1,034.9 | 1,071.7 | 1,101.2 | 1,212.1 |
| Claims on Central Government | 12a | 226.1 | 203.3 | 113.2 | 104.3 | 116.9 | 233.0 | 250.0 | 243.8 | 223.4 | 200.7 | 176.9 | 144.6 |
| Claims on Deposit Money Banks | 12e | — | — | 21.6 | 46.7 | 107.2 | 34.6 | 60.3 | 120.5 | 123.7 | 276.4 | 343.4 | 437.9 |
| Claims on Other Financial Insts. | 12f | | | | | | | | | | | | |
| Reserve Money | 14 | 578.5 | 568.4 | 635.8 | 745.7 | 745.4 | 873.3 | 996.5 | 950.5 | 861.3 | 1,061.9 | 1,132.7 | 1,445.8 |
| of which: Currency Outside DMBs | 14a | 344.3 | 389.3 | 453.4 | 483.6 | 474.3 | 494.8 | 561.8 | 589.4 | 586.7 | 619.9 | 684.5 | 806.8 |
| Foreign Liabilities | 16c | 180.1 | 178.3 | 90.3 | 90.5 | 107.7 | 237.2 | 271.2 | 270.3 | 258.5 | 303.5 | 244.8 | 250.8 |
| Central Government Deposits | 16d | 118.1 | 119.9 | 68.2 | 49.9 | 130.6 | 119.9 | 47.6 | 137.9 | 259.8 | 179.3 | 251.8 | 98.5 |
| Other Items (Net) | 17r | 8.1 | −3.8 | 5.1 | 4.6 | −4.4 | 4.0 | .2 | −8.0 | 2.4 | 4.1 | −7.8 | −.6 |
| **Deposit Money Banks** | | | | | | *Billions of CFA Francs: End of Period* | | | | | | | |
| Reserves | 20 | 233.8 | 178.6 | 181.8 | 253.1 | 258.4 | 377.6 | 433.6 | 359.7 | 273.8 | 440.2 | 445.9 | 621.8 |
| Foreign Assets | 21 | 297.0 | 297.9 | 364.9 | 373.3 | 328.9 | 355.9 | 427.4 | 457.6 | 448.0 | 466.5 | 638.1 | 803.7 |
| Claims on Central Government | 22a | 71.3 | 69.1 | 145.9 | 234.4 | 214.2 | 267.0 | 290.3 | 323.3 | 375.1 | 349.2 | 424.2 | 577.4 |
| Claims on Private Sector | 22d | 853.9 | 1,064.0 | 1,106.2 | 1,225.0 | 1,434.5 | 1,488.4 | 1,638.8 | 1,950.0 | 2,140.8 | 2,412.4 | 2,562.1 | 2,729.5 |
| Claims on Other Financial Insts. | 22f | — | — | — | — | — | — | — | — | — | — | — | — |
| Demand Deposits | 24 | 548.9 | 585.4 | 633.8 | 759.7 | 763.4 | 856.6 | 980.3 | 1,051.0 | 1,182.2 | 1,357.2 | 1,429.3 | 1,737.0 |
| Time Deposits | 25 | 536.8 | 580.4 | 644.2 | 703.5 | 753.5 | 867.5 | 991.2 | 1,062.7 | 1,118.4 | 1,139.9 | 1,358.8 | 1,376.9 |
| Foreign Liabilities | 26c | 72.3 | 95.2 | 97.7 | 130.3 | 201.3 | 189.0 | 132.8 | 269.8 | 296.4 | 324.5 | 385.0 | 503.5 |
| Long-Term Foreign Liabilities | 26cl | 25.5 | 29.6 | 57.0 | 36.2 | 18.4 | 33.7 | 41.3 | 49.1 | 47.7 | 47.8 | 21.7 | 30.5 |
| Central Government Deposits | 26d | 165.1 | 191.7 | 191.5 | 213.1 | 181.1 | 276.3 | 290.2 | 264.8 | 245.5 | 225.6 | 281.8 | 428.1 |
| Credit from Monetary Authorities | 26g | — | — | 21.6 | 46.7 | 107.2 | 34.6 | 60.3 | 120.5 | 123.7 | 276.4 | 343.4 | 437.9 |
| Capital Accounts | 27a | 139.5 | 166.0 | 202.6 | 231.2 | 274.4 | 300.7 | 358.0 | 387.3 | 411.4 | 446.0 | 509.8 | 567.1 |
| Other Items (Net) | 27r | −32.1 | −38.5 | −49.5 | −34.8 | −63.3 | −69.5 | −63.9 | −114.4 | −187.7 | −149.0 | −259.4 | −348.7 |
| Treasury Claims: Private Sector | 22d.i | 3.0 | 3.0 | 5.1 | 5.2 | 5.0 | 3.6 | 8.2 | 3.0 | — | 1.9 | 5.6 | 5.6 |
| Post Office: Checking Deposits | 24..i | 12.8 | 6.5 | 16.8 | 22.7 | 13.9 | 14.6 | 6.1 | 7.9 | 7.9 | 7.9 | 7.9 | 7.9 |
| **Monetary Survey** | | | | | | *Billions of CFA Francs: End of Period* | | | | | | | |
| Foreign Assets (Net) | 31n | 703.2 | 683.9 | 841.4 | 892.3 | 775.1 | 896.4 | 1,028.6 | 903.9 | 928.1 | 910.2 | 1,109.5 | 1,261.5 |
| Domestic Credit | 32 | 881.0 | 1,031.3 | 1,122.4 | 1,323.4 | 1,467.7 | 1,606.8 | 1,847.3 | 2,122.3 | 2,241.9 | 2,565.4 | 2,637.6 | 2,932.7 |
| Claims on Central Govt. (Net) | 32an | 24.1 | −35.6 | 11.1 | 93.2 | 28.2 | 114.8 | 200.3 | 169.3 | 101.1 | 151.1 | 69.8 | 197.6 |
| Claims on Private Sector | 32d | 856.9 | 1,067.0 | 1,111.3 | 1,230.3 | 1,439.6 | 1,492.0 | 1,647.0 | 1,953.0 | 2,140.8 | 2,414.3 | 2,567.7 | 2,735.1 |
| Claims on Other Financial Insts. | 32f | — | — | — | — | — | — | — | — | — | — | — | — |
| Money | 34 | 906.4 | 981.7 | 1,104.5 | 1,266.6 | 1,252.7 | 1,366.9 | 1,549.2 | 1,649.7 | 1,778.1 | 1,986.8 | 2,123.9 | 2,569.0 |
| Quasi-Money | 35 | 536.8 | 580.4 | 644.2 | 703.5 | 753.5 | 867.5 | 991.2 | 1,062.7 | 1,118.4 | 1,139.9 | 1,358.8 | 1,376.9 |
| Long-Term Foreign Liabilities | 36cl | 25.5 | 29.6 | 57.0 | 36.2 | 18.4 | 33.7 | 41.3 | 49.1 | 47.7 | 47.8 | 21.7 | 30.5 |
| Other Items (Net) | 37r | 115.5 | 123.6 | 158.2 | 209.4 | 218.2 | 235.2 | 294.3 | 264.8 | 225.8 | 301.1 | 242.6 | 217.8 |
| Money plus Quasi-Money | 35l | 1,443.2 | 1,562.1 | 1,748.7 | 1,970.1 | 2,006.2 | 2,234.4 | 2,540.3 | 2,712.3 | 2,896.5 | 3,126.7 | 3,482.7 | 3,945.9 |
| **Interest Rates** | | | | | | *Percent Per Annum* | | | | | | | |
| Repurchase Agreement Rate | 60.q | 4.00 | 4.00 | 4.25 | 4.25 | 4.75 | 4.25 | 4.25 | 4.25 | 4.00 | 3.50 | 3.50 | 3.50 |
| Deposit Rate | 60l | 3.50 | 3.50 | 3.50 | 3.50 | 3.50 | 3.50 | 3.50 | 3.50 | 3.50 | 3.50 | 3.50 | 3.50 |
| **Prices and Production** | | | | | | *Index Numbers (2010=100): Period Averages* | | | | | | | |
| Producer Prices | 63 | .... | .... | .... | .... | 94.1 | 94.2 | 100.0 | 107.6 | 112.5 | 109.5 | 108.4 | .... |
| Consumer Prices | 64 | 86.9 | 88.4 | 90.3 | 95.5 | † 101.1 | 98.8 | 100.0 | 103.4 | 104.9 | 105.6 | 104.5 | 104.6 |
| Industrial Production | 66 | 95.0 | 96.7 | 91.2 | † 99.6 | 90.3 | 96.9 | 100.0 | 106.7 | 105.9 | 99.1 | 99.1 | .... |
| **Intl. Transactions & Positions** | | | | | | *Billions of CFA Francs* | | | | | | | |
| Exports | 70 | 522.41 | 562.57 | 530.76 | 554.22 | 890.91 | 864.51 | 1,020.27 | 1,146.42 | 1,216.27 | 1,207.15 | 1,292.78 | 1,358.66 |
| Imports, c.i.f. | 71 | 1,505.00 | 1,686.34 | 1,795.60 | 2,036.88 | 2,534.38 | 2,141.97 | 2,202.04 | 2,544.28 | 3,005.46 | 2,994.55 | 2,998.02 | 3,054.73 |

# Senegal 722

| | | 2004 | 2005 | 2006 | 2007 | 2008 | 2009 | 2010 | 2011 | 2012 | 2013 | 2014 | 2015 |
|---|---|---|---|---|---|---|---|---|---|---|---|---|---|
| **Balance of Payments** | | | | | | | *Millions of US Dollars* | | | | | | |
| A. Current Account* | 109bx | −510.4 | † −675.9 | −861.2 | −1,310.8 | −1,883.8 | −853.8 | −589.0 | −1,151.2 | .... | .... | .... | .... |
| Goods, credit (exports) | 1a9cx | 1,517.6 | † 1,592.9 | 1,599.8 | 1,681.5 | 2,208.4 | 2,096.9 | 2,164.2 | 2,621.0 | .... | .... | .... | .... |
| Goods, debit (imports) | 1a9dx | 2,487.9 | † 2,884.4 | 3,192.6 | 4,153.7 | 5,595.3 | 4,122.9 | 4,082.3 | 5,129.4 | .... | .... | .... | .... |
| Balance on goods | 1a9bx | −970.3 | † −1,291.5 | −1,592.8 | −2,472.2 | −3,387.0 | −2,026.0 | −1,918.1 | −2,508.4 | .... | .... | .... | .... |
| Services, credit (exports) | 1b9cx | 661.1 | † 761.8 | 801.0 | 1,192.4 | 1,285.6 | 1,017.7 | 1,048.3 | 1,166.7 | .... | .... | .... | .... |
| Services, debit (imports) | 1b9dx | 702.6 | † 810.4 | 842.6 | 1,246.6 | 1,419.0 | 1,149.0 | 1,118.9 | 1,291.0 | .... | .... | .... | .... |
| Balance on Goods & Services | 1z9bx | −1,011.7 | † −1,340.1 | −1,634.4 | −2,526.4 | −3,520.4 | −2,157.2 | −1,988.8 | −2,632.6 | .... | .... | .... | .... |
| Primary income: credit | 1c9cx | 156.8 | † 206.9 | 175.3 | 201.6 | 290.6 | 171.3 | 205.5 | 267.5 | .... | .... | .... | .... |
| Primary income: debit | 1c9dx | 287.5 | † 296.5 | 238.8 | 275.4 | 338.5 | 341.0 | 355.5 | 548.9 | .... | .... | .... | .... |
| Balance on gds, serv. & prim. inc. | 1y9bx | −1,142.4 | † −1,429.6 | −1,697.8 | −2,600.3 | −3,568.3 | −2,327.0 | −2,138.7 | −2,914.1 | .... | .... | .... | .... |
| Secondary income: credit | 1d9ca | 715.1 | † 859.2 | 973.7 | 1,557.5 | 1,985.9 | 1,756.8 | 1,873.7 | 2,065.9 | .... | .... | .... | .... |
| Secondary income: debit | 1d9da | 83.1 | † 105.4 | 137.0 | 268.0 | 301.3 | 283.6 | 324.0 | 303.0 | .... | .... | .... | .... |
| B. Capital Account* | 209ba | 750.0 | † 199.5 | 158.9 | 332.7 | 239.5 | 305.1 | 301.9 | 253.2 | .... | .... | .... | .... |
| Capital account: credit | 209ca | 750.4 | † 200.3 | 162.5 | 384.4 | 240.8 | 307.3 | 306.1 | 256.9 | .... | .... | .... | .... |
| Capital account: debit | 209da | .4 | † .8 | 3.6 | 51.8 | 1.3 | 2.2 | 4.2 | 3.7 | .... | .... | .... | .... |
| Balance on current & capital acct. | 129ba | 239.6 | † −476.4 | −702.3 | −978.1 | −1,644.3 | −548.7 | −287.2 | −898.0 | .... | .... | .... | .... |
| C. Financial Account* | 309na | 53.7 | † −117.9 | 1,580.6 | −835.5 | −1,091.2 | −473.2 | 224.2 | −857.9 | .... | .... | .... | .... |
| Direct investment: assets | 3a9aa | 73.4 | † 115.6 | 79.2 | 78.3 | 182.5 | 87.2 | 2.2 | 47.5 | .... | .... | .... | .... |
| Equity & investment fund shares.. | 3aaaa | 68.7 | † 114.1 | 59.4 | 97.2 | 127.6 | 40.8 | 51.6 | 41.0 | .... | .... | .... | .... |
| Debt instruments | 3abaa | 4.7 | † 1.5 | 19.8 | −19.0 | 55.0 | 46.4 | −49.4 | 6.5 | .... | .... | .... | .... |
| Direct investment: liabilities | 3a9la | 137.3 | † 167.9 | 289.6 | 351.0 | 453.9 | 330.1 | 266.1 | 338.2 | .... | .... | .... | .... |
| Equity & investment fund shares . | 3aala | 141.6 | † 152.5 | 324.6 | 341.1 | 442.4 | 244.3 | 266.5 | 296.1 | .... | .... | .... | .... |
| Debt instruments | 3abla | −4.2 | † 15.4 | −35.0 | 9.9 | 11.5 | 85.9 | −.4 | 42.1 | .... | .... | .... | .... |
| Portfolio investment: assets | 3b9aa | 47.5 | † 48.9 | 53.3 | −6.5 | −51.6 | 91.3 | 125.4 | −103.4 | .... | .... | .... | .... |
| Equity & investment fund shares | 3baaa | −22.8 | † −4.3 | −1.8 | −10.0 | — | 1.7 | −.5 | .5 | .... | .... | .... | .... |
| Debt securities | 3bbaa | 70.3 | † 53.2 | 55.1 | 3.5 | −51.5 | 89.5 | 125.9 | −103.9 | .... | .... | .... | .... |
| Portfolio investment: liabilities | 3b9la | .8 | † −8.5 | −13.7 | 24.7 | 20.9 | −1.6 | 43.5 | 777.0 | .... | .... | .... | .... |
| Equity & investment fund shares . | 3bala | −27.7 | † −6.1 | −.4 | 8.0 | −92.6 | −1.6 | 23.3 | 14.2 | .... | .... | .... | .... |
| Debt securities | 3bbla | 28.5 | † −2.4 | −13.3 | 16.7 | 113.5 | — | 20.1 | 762.8 | .... | .... | .... | .... |
| Fin. der.& empl.stk.ops.(ESOs): net. | 3c9na | — | † .1 | .... | −25.5 | — | — | −.2 | .... | .... | .... | .... | .... |
| Fin. der. & ESOs: assets | 3c9aa | −.7 | † — | .1 | — | −.2 | — | −.1 | .... | .... | .... | .... | .... |
| Fin. der. & ESOs: liabilities | 3c9la | −.8 | † −.1 | .1 | 25.6 | −.2 | .... | .1 | .... | .... | .... | .... | .... |
| Other investment: assets | 3d9aa | −6.0 | † −79.2 | 34.3 | −84.4 | −147.7 | 128.2 | 188.0 | 915.7 | .... | .... | .... | .... |
| Other equity | 3daaa | .... | .... | .... | .... | .... | .... | .... | .... | .... | .... | .... | .... |
| Debt instruments | 3dzaa | −6.0 | † −79.2 | 34.3 | −84.4 | −147.7 | 128.2 | 188.0 | 915.7 | .... | .... | .... | .... |
| Other investment: liabilities | 3d9la | −76.9 | † 43.9 | −1,689.7 | 421.7 | 599.7 | 451.4 | −218.3 | 602.4 | .... | .... | .... | .... |
| Other equity | 3dala | .... | .... | .... | .... | .... | .... | .... | .... | .... | .... | .... | .... |
| Debt instruments | 3dzla | −76.9 | † 43.9 | −1,689.7 | 421.7 | 599.7 | 451.4 | −218.3 | 602.4 | .... | .... | .... | .... |
| Curr.+ cap.− finan. acct. balance... | 4y9na | 185.9 | † −358.4 | −2,282.8 | −142.6 | −553.1 | −75.5 | −511.3 | −40.1 | .... | .... | .... | .... |
| D. Net Errors and Omissions | 409na | 13.2 | † −3.1 | 28.3 | 11.8 | −13.5 | −171.3 | −18.0 | −7.3 | .... | .... | .... | .... |
| E. Reserves and Related Items | 4z9na | 199.1 | † −361.6 | −2,254.6 | −130.8 | −566.5 | −246.8 | −529.4 | −47.4 | .... | .... | .... | .... |
| Reserve assets | 3e9aa | 155.0 | † 4.5 | 9.9 | 157.0 | 34.5 | 454.7 | 66.2 | −46.2 | .... | .... | .... | .... |
| Credit and loans from the IMF | 3dcla | −44.4 | † −40.6 | −125.1 | — | 36.9 | 101.2 | 47.0 | −3.3 | .... | .... | .... | .... |
| Exceptional financing | 409la | .3 | † 406.1 | 2,389.5 | 287.7 | 564.1 | 600.3 | 548.6 | 4.5 | .... | .... | .... | .... |

*Excludes components in group E

| **International Investment Position** | | | | | | | *Millions of US Dollars* | | | | | | |
|---|---|---|---|---|---|---|---|---|---|---|---|---|---|
| Assets | 809aa | 2,803.7 | † 2,014.6 | 2,608.9 | 3,017.8 | 2,761.7 | 3,630.1 | 3,765.9 | 4,408.7 | .... | .... | .... | .... |
| Direct investment | 8a9aa | 78.5 | † 58.3 | 81.2 | 131.6 | 193.4 | 280.3 | 262.5 | 296.1 | .... | .... | .... | .... |
| Equity & investment fund shares.. | 8aaaa | 61.9 | † 52.2 | 63.7 | 122.7 | 207.6 | 245.9 | 280.0 | 307.0 | .... | .... | .... | .... |
| Debt instruments | 8abaa | 16.6 | † 6.1 | 17.4 | 9.0 | −14.2 | 34.4 | −17.5 | −10.9 | .... | .... | .... | .... |
| Portfolio investment | 8b9aa | 331.5 | † 260.0 | 329.0 | 359.0 | 290.5 | 394.0 | 492.0 | 380.3 | .... | .... | .... | .... |
| Equity & investment fund shares.. | 8baaa | 20.0 | † 14.5 | 14.9 | 10.6 | 9.8 | 11.9 | 10.6 | 10.8 | .... | .... | .... | .... |
| Debt securities | 8bbaa | 311.5 | † 245.5 | 314.1 | 348.5 | 280.7 | 382.1 | 481.4 | 369.5 | .... | .... | .... | .... |
| Fin. der.(oth.than reserves) & ESOs | 8c9aa | .1 | † .1 | .2 | .2 | .1 | .1 | — | .... | .... | .... | .... | .... |
| Other investment | 8d9aa | 1,026.1 | † 506.9 | 864.3 | 866.9 | 675.7 | 832.6 | 963.7 | 1,786.6 | .... | .... | .... | .... |
| Other equity | 8daaa | .... | .... | .... | .... | .... | .... | .... | .... | .... | .... | .... | .... |
| Debt instruments | 8dzaa | 1,026.1 | † 506.9 | 864.3 | 866.9 | 675.7 | 832.6 | 963.7 | 1,786.6 | .... | .... | .... | .... |
| Reserve assets | 8e9aa | 1,367.6 | † 1,189.3 | 1,334.2 | 1,660.1 | 1,602.2 | 2,123.2 | 2,047.7 | 1,945.7 | .... | .... | .... | .... |
| Liabilities | 809la | 6,641.7 | † 5,651.6 | 4,435.1 | 6,034.0 | 7,243.7 | 8,812.0 | 8,876.7 | 10,190.2 | .... | .... | .... | .... |
| Direct investment | 8a9la | 441.2 | † 358.2 | 477.1 | 838.6 | 1,170.5 | 1,543.2 | 1,699.3 | 1,946.5 | .... | .... | .... | .... |
| Equity & investment fund shares.. | 8aala | 362.5 | † 272.6 | 440.7 | 784.9 | 1,109.9 | 1,390.6 | 1,558.4 | 1,764.0 | .... | .... | .... | .... |
| Debt instruments | 8abla | 78.7 | † 85.6 | 36.4 | 53.7 | 60.7 | 152.6 | 141.0 | 182.5 | .... | .... | .... | .... |
| Portfolio investment | 8b9la | 189.0 | † 267.8 | 294.9 | 370.4 | 378.7 | 629.6 | 791.6 | 1,489.8 | .... | .... | .... | .... |
| Equity & investment fund shares.. | 8bala | 113.6 | † 91.8 | 102.1 | 121.1 | 26.5 | 25.8 | 47.2 | 59.0 | .... | .... | .... | .... |
| Debt securities | 8bbla | 75.5 | † 176.0 | 192.8 | 249.3 | 352.3 | 603.9 | 744.4 | 1,430.8 | .... | .... | .... | .... |
| Fin. der.(oth.than reserves) & ESOs | 8c9la | .1 | † — | .1 | .2 | | | — | | .... | .... | .... | .... |
| Other investment | 8d9la | 6,011.3 | † 5,025.6 | 3,663.0 | 4,824.8 | 5,694.4 | 6,639.2 | 6,385.7 | 6,753.9 | .... | .... | .... | .... |
| Other equity | 8dala | .... | .... | .... | .... | .... | .... | .... | .... | .... | .... | .... | .... |
| Debt instruments | 8dzla | 6,011.3 | † 5,025.6 | 3,663.0 | 4,824.8 | 5,694.4 | 6,639.2 | 6,385.7 | 6,753.9 | .... | .... | .... | .... |

| | | 2004 | 2005 | 2006 | 2007 | 2008 | 2009 | 2010 | 2011 | 2012 | 2013 | 2014 | 2015 |
|---|---|---|---|---|---|---|---|---|---|---|---|---|---|
| **National Accounts** | | | | | | | *Billions of CFA Francs* | | | | | | |
| Househ.Cons.Expend.,incl.NPISHs.... | 96f | 3,290.2 | 3,565.0 | 3,871.5 | 4,270.6 | 4,890.0 | 4,844.3 | 4,977.5 | 5,234.7 | 5,562.6 | 5,722.1 | 5,986.5 | .... |
| Government Consumption Expend... | 91f | 571.1 | 610.6 | 668.1 | 767.1 | 806.4 | 870.7 | 944.2 | 1,052.5 | 1,108.2 | 1,133.1 | 1,200.3 | .... |
| Gross Fixed Capital Formation.......... | 93e | 944.1 | 1,071.4 | 1,279.7 | 1,414.1 | 1,607.6 | 1,388.0 | 1,414.5 | 1,660.0 | 1,714.2 | 1,884.0 | 2,039.7 | .... |
| Changes in Inventories.................... | 93i | −26.6 | 53.2 | −70.9 | 168.0 | 267.1 | −34.4 | 54.0 | 77.8 | 402.7 | 174.5 | 26.7 | .... |
| Exports of Goods and Services......... | 90c | 1,151.5 | 1,240.8 | 1,254.0 | 1,376.2 | 1,566.3 | 1,471.8 | 1,592.7 | 1,787.3 | 2,025.4 | 2,079.1 | 2,076.0 | .... |
| Imports of Goods and Services (-)..... | 98c | 1,687.3 | 1,948.4 | 2,109.0 | 2,587.6 | 3,142.9 | 2,490.3 | 2,577.7 | 3,029.6 | 3,549.3 | 3,606.0 | 3,587.5 | .... |
| Gross Domestic Product (GDP)......... | 99b | 4,242.8 | 4,592.7 | 4,893.6 | 5,408.3 | 5,994.5 | 6,050.1 | 6,405.1 | 6,782.8 | 7,263.8 | 7,386.7 | 7,741.6 | .... |
| Net Primary Income from Abroad..... | 98.n | 214.2 | 369.3 | 291.4 | 518.7 | 704.5 | 589.9 | 536.9 | −190.4 | .... | .... | .... | .... |
| Gross National Income (GNI)........... | 99a | 4,457.0 | 4,962.0 | 5,185.0 | 5,927.0 | 6,699.0 | 6,640.0 | 6,942.0 | 6,592.4 | .... | .... | .... | .... |
| GDP Volume 2008 Prices................ | 99b.p | 5,071.7 | 5,360.1 | 5,494.1 | 5,763.3 | 5,994.5 | 6,139.7 | 6,396.3 | 6,509.0 | 6,793.0 | 7,039.0 | 7,371.6 | .... |
| GDP Volume (2010=100)............... | 99bvp | 79.3 | 83.8 | 85.9 | 90.1 | 93.7 | 96.0 | 100.0 | 101.8 | 106.2 | 110.0 | 115.2 | .... |
| GDP Deflator (2010=100)............... | 99bip | 83.5 | 85.6 | 88.9 | 93.7 | 99.9 | 98.4 | 100.0 | 104.1 | 106.8 | 104.8 | 104.9 | .... |
| | | | | | | | *Millions: Midyear Estimates* | | | | | | |
| **Population**............................... | 99z | 10.97 | 11.27 | 11.58 | 11.90 | 12.23 | 12.58 | 12.96 | 13.36 | 13.78 | 14.22 | 14.67 | 15.13 |

# Serbia, Republic of   942

|  |  | 2004 | 2005 | 2006 | 2007 | 2008 | 2009 | 2010 | 2011 | 2012 | 2013 | 2014 | 2015 |
|---|---|---|---|---|---|---|---|---|---|---|---|---|---|
| **Exchange Rates** | | | | | | | *Dinars per SDR: End of Period* | | | | | | |
| Official Rate | aa | 89.97 | 103.22 | 90.23 | 84.90 | 96.88 | 104.61 | 122.09 | 124.15 | 132.45 | 128.02 | 144.10 | 154.16 |
| | | | | | | *Dinars per US Dollar: End of Period (ae) Period Average (rf)* | | | | | | | |
| Official Rate | ae | 57.94 | 72.22 | 59.98 | 53.73 | 62.90 | 66.73 | 79.28 | 80.87 | 86.18 | 83.13 | 99.46 | 111.25 |
| Official Rate | rf | 58.38 | 66.71 | 67.15 | 58.45 | 55.72 | 67.58 | 77.73 | 73.33 | 87.97 | 85.16 | 88.41 | 108.81 |
| **Fund Position** | | | | | | | *Millions of SDRs: End of Period* | | | | | | |
| Quota | 2f.s | 467.70 | 467.70 | 467.70 | 467.70 | 467.70 | 467.70 | 467.70 | 467.70 | 467.70 | 467.70 | 467.70 | 467.70 |
| SDR Holdings | 1b.s | .03 | 21.16 | 5.87 | .51 | 1.40 | 12.30 | 1.92 | 1.67 | 178.78 | 119.79 | 44.23 | 11.80 |
| Reserve Position in the Fund | 1c.s | — | — | — | — | — | — | — | — | — | — | — | — |
| Total Fund Cred.&Loans Outstg. | 2tl | 620.96 | 606.25 | 162.50 | — | — | 1,021.15 | 1,321.04 | 1,367.74 | 1,192.36 | 624.32 | 127.51 | 11.68 |
| SDR Allocations | 1bd | 56.66 | 56.66 | 56.66 | 56.66 | 56.66 | 445.04 | 445.04 | 445.04 | 445.04 | 445.04 | 445.04 | 445.04 |
| **International Liquidity** | | | | | *Millions of US Dollars Unless Otherwise Indicated: End of Period* | | | | | | | | |
| Total Reserves minus Gold | 1l.d | 4,095.9 | 5,627.9 | 11,647.7 | 13,892.6 | 11,122.9 | 14,769.2 | 12,714.6 | 14,877.2 | 13,584.8 | 14,802.9 | 11,371.9 | 10,727.1 |
| SDR Holdings | 1b.d | .1 | 30.2 | 8.8 | .8 | 2.2 | 19.3 | 3.0 | 2.6 | 274.8 | 184.5 | 64.1 | 16.3 |
| Reserve Position in the Fund | 1c.d | — | — | — | — | — | — | — | — | — | — | — | — |
| Foreign Exchange | 1d.d | 4,095.8 | 5,597.7 | 11,638.9 | 13,891.8 | 11,120.7 | 14,749.9 | 12,711.7 | 14,874.6 | 13,310.1 | 14,618.4 | 11,307.8 | 10,710.7 |
| Gold (Million Fine Troy Ounces) | 1ad | .3408 | .4180 | .3794 | .3858 | .4083 | .4218 | .4218 | .4610 | .4917 | .5221 | .5639 | .5829 |
| Gold (National Valuation) | 1and | 148.8 | 147.0 | 235.9 | 323.2 | 354.1 | 465.7 | 594.9 | 725.9 | 817.4 | 627.6 | 676.2 | 619.1 |
| Central Bank: Other Assets | 3..d | 24.09 | 20.37 | 14.06 | 6.11 | 6.50 | 93.43 | 99.45 | 99.51 | 107.07 | 97.32 | 100.52 | 92.29 |
| Central Bank: Other Liabs | 4..d | 231.10 | 267.18 | 684.12 | 256.94 | 218.32 | 121.74 | 109.57 | 102.47 | 87.29 | 80.34 | 81.27 | 53.52 |
| Other Depository Corps.: Assets | 7a.d | 1,121.55 | 928.27 | 931.79 | 2,068.80 | 1,906.31 | 2,424.23 | 2,829.52 | 1,563.45 | 1,964.87 | 1,633.27 | 2,679.66 | 1,865.45 |
| Other Depository Corps.: Liabs | 7b.d | 1,436.52 | 2,646.45 | 5,131.12 | 5,579.51 | 5,557.40 | 7,486.25 | 7,690.65 | 6,772.75 | 6,740.98 | 5,931.80 | 4,138.15 | 3,465.09 |
| **Central Bank** | | | | | | | *Millions of Dinars: End of Period* | | | | | | |
| Net Foreign Assets | 11n | 171,875 | 334,519 | 652,621 | 745,041 | 704,334 | 861,342 | 838,747 | 1,036,432 | 1,025,969 | 1,147,222 | 1,117,765 | 1,196,140 |
| Claims on Nonresidents | 11 | 246,233 | 422,241 | 713,426 | 763,656 | 723,556 | 1,022,842 | 1,063,062 | 1,269,777 | 1,250,357 | 1,290,797 | 1,208,356 | 1,272,499 |
| Liabilities to Nonresidents | 16c | 74,358 | 87,722 | 60,805 | 18,616 | 19,222 | 161,500 | 224,314 | 233,345 | 224,388 | 143,575 | 90,590 | 76,359 |
| Claims on Other Depository Corps. | 12e | 1,748 | 954 | 489 | 595 | 2,241 | 387 | 404 | 350 | 654 | 120 | 625 | 711 |
| Net Claims on Central Government | 12an | −10,548 | −43,014 | −106,670 | −100,387 | −49,514 | −100,939 | −106,392 | −147,501 | −159,625 | −236,121 | −256,415 | −227,644 |
| Claims on Central Government | 12a | 22,408 | 16,511 | 16,450 | 10,811 | 10,913 | 11,300 | 1,319 | 1,275 | 1,227 | 1,166 | 1,223 | 1,181 |
| Liabilities to Central Government | 16d | 32,956 | 59,524 | 123,120 | 111,198 | 60,427 | 112,239 | 107,711 | 148,776 | 160,852 | 237,287 | 257,638 | 228,824 |
| Claims on Other Sectors | 12s | 7,815 | 8,919 | 14,835 | 6,950 | 7,660 | 7,342 | 8,922 | 8,051 | 8,028 | 7,370 | 4,912 | 3,526 |
| Claims on Other Financial Corps. | 12g | 7,346 | 8,249 | 13,482 | 5,264 | 5,731 | 4,879 | 5,519 | 5,565 | 5,391 | 5,245 | 2,562 | 1,213 |
| Claims on State & Local Govts. | 12b | — | — | — | — | — | — | — | 1 | 1 | 1 | 13 | 11 |
| Claims on Public Nonfin. Corps. | 12c | 218 | 187 | 230 | 230 | — | — | — | — | — | — | 1,183 | 1,154 |
| Claims on Private Sector | 12d | 251 | 483 | 1,123 | 1,456 | 1,928 | 2,463 | 3,403 | 2,485 | 2,636 | 2,124 | 1,155 | 1,149 |
| Monetary Base | 14 | 148,866 | 249,118 | 400,068 | 440,709 | 517,646 | 539,172 | 542,227 | 614,980 | 632,159 | 650,929 | 626,414 | 679,356 |
| Currency in Circulation | 14a | 49,446 | 60,703 | 78,667 | 92,614 | 108,818 | 112,925 | 109,627 | 132,401 | 136,107 | 148,791 | 158,485 | 171,432 |
| Liabs. to Other Depository Corps. | 14c | 93,376 | 181,117 | 308,820 | 336,614 | 394,458 | 413,133 | 418,713 | 467,068 | 478,365 | 470,777 | 422,381 | 446,704 |
| Liabilities to Other Sectors | 14d | 6,045 | 7,298 | 12,581 | 11,481 | 14,370 | 13,114 | 13,888 | 15,511 | 17,688 | 31,361 | 45,549 | 61,220 |
| Other Liabs. to Other Dep. Corps. | 14n | 1,754 | 16,837 | 149,740 | 217,690 | 90,423 | 151,680 | 46,908 | 120,595 | 39,841 | 110,032 | 7,514 | 30,643 |
| Dep. & Sec. Excl. f/Monetary Base | 14o | 502 | 562 | 629 | 713 | 418 | 448 | 708 | 427 | 2,026 | 776 | 2,875 | 2,764 |
| Deposits Included in Broad Money. | 15 | — | — | — | — | — | — | — | — | — | — | — | — |
| Sec.Ot.th.Shares Incl.in Brd.Money | 16a | — | — | — | — | — | — | — | — | — | — | — | — |
| Deposits Excl. from Broad Money. | 16b | 502 | 562 | 629 | 713 | 418 | 448 | 708 | 427 | 2,026 | 776 | 2,875 | 2,764 |
| Sec.Ot.th.Shares Excl.f/Brd.Money. | 16s | — | — | — | — | — | — | — | — | — | — | — | — |
| Loans | 16l | — | — | — | — | 58 | 22 | 15 | 15 | 15 | 15 | 11 | 11 |
| Financial Derivatives | 16m | — | — | — | — | — | — | — | — | — | — | — | — |
| Shares and Other Equity | 17a | 28,481 | 35,601 | 2,342 | 1,904 | 59,313 | 123,187 | 202,334 | 208,575 | 264,199 | 216,899 | 306,793 | 341,107 |
| Other Items (Net) | 17r | −8,714 | −740 | 8,495 | −8,817 | −3,139 | −46,378 | −50,511 | −47,260 | −63,214 | −60,060 | −76,720 | −81,147 |
| Memo Item: | | | | | | | | | | | | | |
| Total Assets | 10ra | 360,472.1 | 535,472.9 | 817,980.5 | 855,460.7 | 822,582.5 | 1,136,014.5 | 1,187,781.7 | 1,391,206.7 | 1,379,881.6 | 1,410,066.9 | 1,362,234.5 | 1,431,752.4 |
| **Other Depository Corporations** | | | | | | | *Millions of Dinars: End of Period* | | | | | | |
| Net Foreign Assets | 21n | −18,248 | −124,085 | −251,858 | −188,619 | −229,653 | −337,781 | −385,390 | −421,257 | −411,605 | −357,329 | −145,067 | −177,955 |
| Claims on Nonresidents | 21 | 64,978 | 67,039 | 55,885 | 111,150 | 119,907 | 161,765 | 224,324 | 126,430 | 169,333 | 135,771 | 266,530 | 207,525 |
| Liabilities to Nonresidents | 26c | 83,225 | 191,124 | 307,742 | 299,769 | 349,560 | 499,546 | 609,715 | 547,687 | 580,937 | 493,100 | 411,597 | 385,480 |
| Claims on Central Bank | 20 | 99,461 | 205,632 | 468,312 | 569,419 | 507,614 | 582,991 | 484,417 | 605,947 | 544,111 | 607,963 | 458,847 | 509,094 |
| Currency | 20a | 4,281 | 7,053 | 10,206 | 15,614 | 18,743 | 17,406 | 17,877 | 18,211 | 25,560 | 26,352 | 28,017 | 31,614 |
| Reserve Deposits and Securities | 20b | 92,757 | 181,082 | 306,574 | 335,102 | 394,014 | 412,818 | 418,823 | 466,802 | 478,336 | 471,164 | 422,396 | 446,282 |
| Other Claims | 20n | 2,424 | 17,496 | 151,532 | 218,703 | 94,857 | 152,768 | 47,717 | 120,934 | 40,215 | 110,447 | 8,435 | 31,197 |
| Net Claims on Central Government | 22an | 16,500 | 15,181 | 2,460 | −11,842 | −3,421 | 96,521 | 172,036 | 177,039 | 254,723 | 285,012 | 379,084 | 451,003 |
| Claims on Central Government | 22a | 21,594 | 23,595 | 18,446 | 8,393 | 9,455 | 107,824 | 192,664 | 198,081 | 290,360 | 336,021 | 457,026 | 538,476 |
| Liabilities to Central Government | 26d | 5,094 | 8,413 | 15,986 | 20,235 | 12,876 | 11,304 | 20,628 | 21,042 | 35,636 | 51,009 | 77,941 | 87,473 |
| Claims on Other Sectors | 22s | 334,850 | 509,379 | 594,336 | 827,297 | 1,117,196 | 1,298,737 | 1,647,983 | 1,780,252 | 1,950,055 | 1,863,546 | 1,920,672 | 1,976,766 |
| Claims on Other Financial Corps. | 22g | 870 | 619 | 918 | 1,395 | 13,802 | 13,897 | 29,915 | 38,193 | 40,210 | 44,564 | 21,026 | 23,557 |
| Claims on State & Local Govts. | 22b | 1,269 | 2,208 | 5,033 | 7,008 | 9,244 | 11,533 | 18,106 | 25,713 | 31,731 | 34,360 | 35,233 | 32,182 |
| Claims on Public Nonfin. Corps. | 22c | 15,948 | 19,171 | 16,866 | 17,820 | 25,278 | 50,317 | 69,521 | 98,087 | 106,214 | 97,962 | 168,274 | 168,351 |
| Claims on Private Sector | 22d | 316,764 | 487,380 | 571,518 | 801,074 | 1,068,872 | 1,222,991 | 1,530,441 | 1,618,258 | 1,771,901 | 1,686,659 | 1,696,139 | 1,752,676 |
| Liabilities to Central Bank | 26g | 1,755 | 735 | 443 | 2,076 | 5,615 | 919 | 850 | 425 | 667 | 188 | 960 | 400 |
| Transf.Dep.Included in Broad Money | 24 | 109,184 | 150,091 | 197,331 | 262,912 | 247,062 | 277,475 | 292,085 | 341,246 | 379,207 | 450,672 | 558,174 | 705,593 |
| Other Dep.Included in Broad Money. | 25 | 162,483 | 247,987 | 358,244 | 553,298 | 640,643 | 819,461 | 963,054 | 1,029,497 | 1,134,362 | 1,112,410 | 1,131,252 | 1,092,938 |
| Sec.Ot.th.Shares Incl.in Brd.Money.. | 26a | — | — | — | — | — | — | — | — | — | — | — | — |
| Deposits Excl. from Broad Money.... | 26b | 1,103 | 2,708 | 2,365 | 2,541 | 1,426 | 2,091 | 51,211 | 53,243 | 42,875 | 51,703 | 58,572 | 61,329 |
| Sec.Ot.th.Shares Excl.f/Brd.Money.... | 26s | 4 | 23 | 21 | — | — | — | — | — | — | — | — | — |
| Loans | 26l | — | — | — | — | 10,129 | 11,700 | 12,167 | 26,013 | 30,565 | 27,949 | 32,763 | 31,370 |
| Financial Derivatives | 26m | — | — | — | — | 17 | 768 | 108 | 2,380 | 133 | 169 | 107 | 50 |
| Insurance Technical Reserves | 26r | — | — | — | — | — | — | — | — | — | — | — | — |
| Shares and Other Equity | 27a | 109,173 | 140,322 | 234,800 | 349,541 | 432,356 | 459,708 | 519,692 | 569,964 | 611,491 | 613,424 | 620,126 | 610,402 |
| Other Items (Net) | 27r | 48,861 | 64,242 | 20,047 | 25,887 | 54,488 | 68,346 | 79,878 | 119,213 | 137,984 | 142,678 | 211,582 | 256,826 |
| Memo Item: | | | | | | | | | | | | | |
| Total Assets | 20ra | 614,972.0 | 914,191.4 | 1,274,287.0 | 1,678,368.7 | 1,916,650.0 | 2,336,046.0 | 2,741,266.6 | 2,901,919.8 | 3,158,571.1 | 3,148,832.9 | 3,306,185.0 | 3,427,140.6 |

# Serbia, Republic of   942

| | | 2004 | 2005 | 2006 | 2007 | 2008 | 2009 | 2010 | 2011 | 2012 | 2013 | 2014 | 2015 |
|---|---|---|---|---|---|---|---|---|---|---|---|---|---|
| **Depository Corporations** | | | | | | *Millions of Dinars: End of Period* | | | | | | | |
| Net Foreign Assets | 31n | 153,627 | 210,434 | 400,763 | 556,421 | 474,681 | 523,561 | 453,357 | 615,175 | 614,364 | 789,894 | 972,698 | 1,018,185 |
| Claims on Nonresidents | 31 | 311,211 | 489,279 | 769,311 | 874,806 | 843,463 | 1,184,608 | 1,287,386 | 1,396,207 | 1,419,690 | 1,426,568 | 1,474,886 | 1,480,024 |
| Liabilities to Nonresidents | 36c | 157,583 | 278,845 | 368,547 | 318,384 | 368,782 | 661,046 | 834,029 | 781,032 | 805,326 | 636,675 | 502,188 | 461,840 |
| Domestic Claims | 32 | 348,617 | 490,465 | 504,960 | 722,018 | 1,071,921 | 1,301,660 | 1,722,549 | 1,817,840 | 2,053,181 | 1,919,806 | 2,048,253 | 2,203,651 |
| Net Claims on Central Government | 32an | 5,952 | −27,832 | −104,210 | −112,229 | −52,936 | −4,419 | 65,644 | 29,538 | 95,099 | 48,891 | 122,669 | 223,360 |
| Claims on Central Government | 32a | 44,001 | 40,105 | 34,896 | 19,203 | 20,368 | 119,124 | 193,983 | 199,356 | 291,586 | 337,186 | 458,249 | 539,657 |
| Liabilities to Central Government | 36d | 38,049 | 67,938 | 139,107 | 131,432 | 73,303 | 123,543 | 128,339 | 169,818 | 196,488 | 288,296 | 335,580 | 316,297 |
| Claims on Other Sectors | 32s | 342,665 | 518,298 | 609,171 | 834,247 | 1,124,856 | 1,306,079 | 1,656,905 | 1,788,302 | 1,958,083 | 1,870,915 | 1,925,584 | 1,980,291 |
| Claims on Other Financial Corps | 32g | 8,216 | 8,868 | 14,400 | 6,659 | 19,533 | 18,776 | 35,433 | 43,758 | 45,601 | 49,809 | 23,588 | 24,770 |
| Claims on State & Local Govts | 32b | 1,269 | 2,208 | 5,033 | 7,008 | 9,244 | 11,533 | 18,106 | 25,714 | 31,731 | 34,361 | 35,246 | 32,193 |
| Claims on Public Nonfin. Corps | 32c | 16,166 | 19,358 | 17,097 | 18,050 | 25,278 | 50,317 | 69,522 | 98,088 | 106,214 | 97,962 | 169,456 | 169,505 |
| Claims on Private Sector | 32d | 317,015 | 487,863 | 572,641 | 802,530 | 1,070,801 | 1,225,453 | 1,533,844 | 1,620,743 | 1,774,537 | 1,688,783 | 1,697,294 | 1,753,825 |
| Broad Money Liabilities | 35l | 322,877 | 459,026 | 636,616 | 904,691 | 992,150 | 1,205,570 | 1,360,777 | 1,500,444 | 1,641,804 | 1,716,882 | 1,865,443 | 1,999,567 |
| Currency Outside Depository Corps | 34a | 45,165 | 53,650 | 68,461 | 77,000 | 90,075 | 95,519 | 91,750 | 114,190 | 110,547 | 122,439 | 130,468 | 139,818 |
| Transferable Deposits | 34 | 115,210 | 157,223 | 207,756 | 273,569 | 258,824 | 289,720 | 304,786 | 353,425 | 396,530 | 481,552 | 601,824 | 745,971 |
| Other Deposits | 35 | 162,502 | 247,997 | 358,253 | 553,303 | 643,251 | 820,330 | 964,241 | 1,032,829 | 1,134,727 | 1,112,891 | 1,133,151 | 1,113,779 |
| Securities Other than Shares | 36a | — | 157 | 2,147 | 819 | — | — | — | — | — | — | — | — |
| Deposits Excl. from Broad Money | 36b | 1,605 | 3,270 | 2,994 | 3,253 | 1,844 | 2,540 | 51,920 | 53,671 | 44,900 | 52,480 | 61,447 | 64,093 |
| Sec.Ot.th.Shares Excl.f/Brd.Money | 36s | 4 | 23 | 21 | — | — | — | — | — | — | — | — | — |
| Loans | 36l | — | — | — | — | 10,187 | 11,722 | 12,182 | 26,028 | 30,580 | 27,964 | 32,773 | 31,381 |
| Financial Derivatives | 36m | — | — | — | — | 17 | 768 | 108 | 2,380 | 133 | 169 | 107 | 50 |
| Insurance Technical Reserves | 36r | — | — | — | — | — | — | — | — | — | — | — | — |
| Shares and Other Equity | 37a | 137,655 | 175,924 | 237,142 | 351,445 | 491,669 | 582,895 | 722,026 | 778,539 | 875,690 | 830,322 | 926,919 | 951,508 |
| Other Items (Net) | 37r | 40,103 | 62,657 | 28,950 | 19,050 | 50,734 | 21,727 | 28,893 | 71,954 | 74,438 | 81,883 | 134,262 | 175,236 |
| Broad Money Liabs., Seasonally Adj. | 35l.b | 314,322 | 448,274 | 623,508 | 887,641 | 973,625 | 1,182,533 | 1,333,575 | 1,470,177 | 1,608,942 | 1,683,980 | 1,829,856 | 1,961,926 |
| **Monetary Aggregates** | | | | | | *Millions of Dinars: End of Period* | | | | | | | |
| Broad Money | 59m | 322,877 | 459,026 | 636,616 | 904,691 | 992,150 | 1,205,570 | 1,360,777 | 1,500,444 | 1,641,804 | 1,716,882 | 1,865,443 | 1,999,567 |
| o/w:Currency Issued by Cent.Govt | 59m.a | — | — | — | — | — | — | — | — | — | — | — | — |
| o/w: Dep.in Nonfin. Corporations | 59m.b | — | — | — | — | — | — | — | — | — | — | — | — |
| o/w:Secs. Issued by Central Govt | 59m.c | — | — | — | — | — | — | — | — | — | — | — | — |
| Money (National Definitions) | | | | | | | | | | | | | |
| M1 | 59ma | 111,258 | 144,949 | 200,090 | 248,873 | 240,970 | 258,442 | 253,330 | 293,694 | 308,687 | 388,265 | 430,915 | 504,515 |
| M2 | 59mb | 146,209 | 192,180 | 278,966 | 390,485 | 395,088 | 436,784 | 410,172 | 487,734 | 480,571 | 547,566 | 614,259 | 702,589 |
| M3 | 59mc | 322,877 | 458,869 | 634,469 | 903,872 | 992,150 | 1,205,570 | 1,360,777 | 1,500,444 | 1,641,676 | 1,716,882 | 1,865,443 | 1,999,568 |
| **Interest Rates** | | | | | | *Percent Per Annum* | | | | | | | |
| Repurchase Agreement Rate | 60.q | 16.30 | 19.16 | 15.35 | 9.57 | 17.75 | 9.92 | 11.17 | 9.82 | 9.90 | 8.00 | 5.98 | 2.52 |
| Money Market Rate | 60b | 12.86 | 20.51 | 16.51 | 10.31 | 15.55 | 11.01 | 13.10 | 11.04 | 11.89 | 9.11 | 8.59 | 3.86 |
| Treasury Bill Rate | 60c | 21.17 | 14.58 | 10.24 | 4.42 | 9.61 | 10.34 | 14.16 | 11.51 | 12.32 | 9.04 | 7.67 | 3.89 |
| Deposit Rate | | | | | | | | | | | | | |
| Households | | | | | | | | | | | | | |
| Households (RSD) | 60lh | .... | .... | .... | .... | .... | .... | 10.64 | 9.67 | 9.92 | 8.33 | 6.51 | 4.17 |
| Indexed to FX & FX Deposits | 60lhi | .... | .... | .... | .... | .... | .... | 4.51 | 4.55 | 4.03 | 2.77 | 1.68 | 1.06 |
| Nonfinancial Corporations | | | | | | | | | | | | | |
| Nonfinancial Corporations (RSD) | 60lc | .... | .... | .... | .... | .... | .... | 11.36 | 9.76 | 10.60 | 7.88 | 6.83 | 2.98 |
| Indexed to FX & FX Deposits | 60lci | .... | .... | .... | .... | .... | .... | 3.82 | 3.39 | 2.76 | 1.80 | 1.19 | .60 |
| Lending Rate | | | | | | | | | | | | | |
| Households | | | | | | | | | | | | | |
| Households (RSD) | 60ph | .... | .... | .... | .... | .... | .... | 21.71 | 19.67 | 21.51 | 19.67 | 16.87 | 12.05 |
| Indexed to FX & FX Loans | 60phi | .... | .... | .... | .... | .... | .... | 8.02 | 6.47 | 7.79 | 7.65 | 6.85 | 5.79 |
| Nonfinancial Corporations | | | | | | | | | | | | | |
| Nonfinancial Corporations (RSD) | 60pc | .... | .... | .... | .... | .... | .... | 16.50 | 16.17 | 17.01 | 14.22 | 10.89 | 6.24 |
| Indexed FX & FX Loans | 60pci | .... | .... | .... | .... | .... | .... | 8.81 | 8.13 | 8.25 | 6.48 | 4.91 | 4.24 |
| **Prices and Production** | | | | | | *Index Numbers (2010=100): Period Averages* | | | | | | | |
| Share Prices | 62 | 171.8 | 207.8 | 186.8 | 394.1 | 220.3 | 90.1 | 100.0 | 101.7 | 71.8 | 80.9 | 92.6 | 99.4 |
| Consumer Prices | 64 | 56.2 | 65.2 | 72.9 | † 77.5 | 87.1 | 94.2 | 100.0 | 111.1 | 119.3 | 128.5 | 131.1 | 133.0 |
| Industrial Production | 66 | 102.1 | 102.8 | 107.0 | 111.5 | 113.1 | 98.8 | 100.0 | 102.5 | 100.3 | 105.7 | 98.8 | 107.1 |
| **International Transactions** | | | | | | *Millions of US Dollars* | | | | | | | |
| Exports | 70..d | 3,534.68 | 4,140.35 | 7,177.56 | 9,385.97 | 9,327.03 | 12,117.55 | 9,497.33 | 11,021.37 | 11,559.17 | 11,862.10 | 14,843.30 | 13,354.80 |
| Imports, c.i.f. | 71..d | 10,753.14 | 9,694.91 | 14,726.11 | 19,557.66 | 19,477.25 | 18,919.67 | 16,197.56 | 18,622.37 | 19,217.58 | 16,692.33 | 20,608.60 | 18,172.80 |

# Serbia, Republic of  942

| | | 2004 | 2005 | 2006 | 2007 | 2008 | 2009 | 2010 | 2011 | 2012 | 2013 | 2014 | 2015 |
|---|---|---|---|---|---|---|---|---|---|---|---|---|---|
| **Balance of Payments** | | | | | | *Millions of US Dollars* | | | | | | | |
| A. Current Account* | 109bx | .... | .... | .... | † −7,524.8 | −10,535.2 | −2,799.6 | −2,691.9 | −5,087.1 | −4,729.9 | −2,794.6 | −2,634.6 | −1,751.1 |
| Goods, credit (exports) | 1a9cx | .... | .... | .... | † 7,986.9 | 10,089.8 | 7,748.1 | 9,074.7 | 11,303.1 | 10,761.1 | 13,975.8 | 14,137.2 | 12,596.9 |
| Goods, debit (imports) | 1a9dx | .... | .... | .... | † 17,780.2 | 22,588.1 | 14,795.0 | 15,328.6 | 18,930.7 | 18,016.6 | 19,503.8 | 19,584.9 | 17,026.1 |
| Balance on goods | 1a9bx | .... | .... | .... | † −9,793.3 | −12,498.3 | −7,046.9 | −6,253.9 | −7,627.6 | −7,255.4 | −5,528.0 | −5,447.7 | −4,429.2 |
| Services, credit (exports) | 1b9cx | .... | .... | .... | † 3,159.2 | 4,029.3 | 3,493.8 | 3,519.7 | 4,210.6 | 3,971.9 | 4,549.7 | 5,042.8 | 4,740.1 |
| Services, debit (imports) | 1b9dx | .... | .... | .... | † 3,496.4 | 4,323.1 | 3,475.0 | 3,533.6 | 4,000.0 | 3,827.5 | 4,131.4 | 4,433.3 | 3,936.4 |
| Balance on Goods & Services | 1z9bx | .... | .... | .... | † −10,130.5 | −12,792.2 | −7,028.1 | −6,267.8 | −7,417.0 | −7,111.0 | −5,109.7 | −4,838.2 | −3,625.6 |
| Primary income: credit | 1c9cx | .... | .... | .... | † 705.9 | 835.8 | 671.4 | 572.7 | 703.5 | 853.7 | 806.6 | 851.8 | 756.8 |
| Primary income: debit | 1c9dx | .... | .... | .... | † 2,054.4 | 2,295.3 | 1,352.1 | 1,439.8 | 2,629.3 | 2,259.4 | 2,694.7 | 2,636.4 | 2,595.0 |
| Balance on gds, serv. & prim. inc. | 1y9bx | .... | .... | .... | † −11,478.9 | −14,251.7 | −7,708.9 | −7,134.9 | −9,342.8 | −8,516.7 | −6,997.8 | −6,622.9 | −5,463.7 |
| Secondary income: credit | 1d9ca | .... | .... | .... | † 4,252.1 | 4,115.6 | 5,255.2 | 4,802.2 | 4,748.5 | 4,228.0 | 4,697.4 | 4,513.2 | 4,207.0 |
| Secondary income: debit | 1d9da | .... | .... | .... | † 298.0 | 399.1 | 346.0 | 359.3 | 492.8 | 441.2 | 494.2 | 524.9 | 494.4 |
| B. Capital Account* | 209ba | .... | .... | .... | † −408.8 | 9.6 | .4 | −.5 | −3.8 | −10.6 | 20.1 | 8.8 | −19.2 |
| Capital account: credit | 209ca | .... | .... | .... | † 18.3 | 12.9 | 4.6 | 2.0 | 2.9 | .5 | 25.3 | 16.5 | 8.3 |
| Capital account: debit | 209da | .... | .... | .... | † 427.1 | 3.4 | 4.2 | 2.5 | 6.6 | 11.1 | 5.2 | 7.7 | 27.6 |
| Balance on current & capital acct. | 129ba | .... | .... | .... | † −7,933.6 | −10,525.6 | −2,799.2 | −2,692.4 | −5,090.9 | −4,740.5 | −2,774.5 | −2,625.8 | −1,770.4 |
| C. Financial Account* | 942na | .... | .... | .... | .... | .... | .... | .... | .... | .... | .... | .... | .... |
| Direct investment: assets | 3a9aa | .... | .... | .... | † 940.8 | 328.3 | 46.9 | 192.6 | 309.7 | 327.3 | 331.9 | 350.7 | 344.5 |
| Equity & investment fund shares | 3aaaa | .... | .... | .... | † 940.3 | 295.4 | 34.3 | 181.3 | 276.6 | 204.2 | 191.9 | 303.9 | 300.7 |
| Debt instruments | 3abaa | .... | .... | .... | † .4 | 32.9 | 12.6 | 11.3 | 33.1 | 123.1 | 140.0 | 46.8 | 43.8 |
| Direct investment: liabilities | 3a9la | .... | .... | .... | † 4,423.9 | 4,055.6 | 2,928.9 | 1,693.3 | 4,929.9 | 1,276.1 | 2,059.7 | 1,999.5 | 2,345.2 |
| Equity & investment fund shares | 3aala | .... | .... | .... | † 2,830.9 | 2,761.8 | 1,592.3 | 1,040.3 | 3,505.0 | 209.9 | 1,474.6 | 1,878.5 | 2,108.1 |
| Debt instruments | 3abla | .... | .... | .... | † 1,593.0 | 1,293.8 | 1,336.5 | 653.0 | 1,424.9 | 1,066.2 | 585.1 | 121.0 | 237.1 |
| Portfolio investment: assets | 3b9aa | .... | .... | .... | † 4.8 | 40.8 | 8.2 | 34.7 | −66.4 | 27.5 | 36.2 | 92.7 | 85.0 |
| Equity & investment fund shares | 3baaa | .... | .... | .... | † 13.2 | 41.1 | 9.3 | −16.8 | −2.6 | −3.6 | 15.8 | 4.7 | −1.6 |
| Debt securities | 3bbaa | .... | .... | .... | † −8.4 | −.3 | −1.1 | 51.5 | −63.9 | 31.1 | 20.4 | 87.9 | 86.6 |
| Portfolio investment: liabilities | 3b9la | .... | .... | .... | † 922.6 | −91.8 | −56.8 | 129.3 | 2,179.1 | 2,204.6 | 2,567.6 | 582.4 | −225.9 |
| Equity & investment fund shares | 3bala | .... | .... | .... | † 764.2 | −54.7 | 23.0 | 84.4 | 69.3 | −23.9 | −40.8 | −21.6 | −90.2 |
| Debt securities | 3bbla | .... | .... | .... | † 158.4 | −37.1 | −79.9 | 44.8 | 2,109.7 | 2,228.4 | 2,608.4 | 604.0 | −135.7 |
| Fin. der.& empl.stk.ops.(ESOs): net | 3c9na | .... | .... | .... | † — | .2 | 1.5 | 36.0 | −35.0 | 2.3 | −.9 | −7.7 | 2.1 |
| Fin. der. & ESOs.: assets | 3c9aa | .... | .... | .... | † — | .3 | −2.7 | −2.0 | −36.8 | −3.9 | −8.4 | −7.4 | 2.1 |
| Fin. der. & ESOs.: liabilities | 3c9la | .... | .... | .... | † — | .1 | −4.2 | −38.0 | −1.8 | −6.1 | −7.5 | .3 | — |
| Other investment: assets | 3d9aa | .... | .... | .... | † 1,366.0 | 1,236.5 | −518.3 | 521.8 | −976.7 | 819.0 | 341.5 | 1,757.2 | 345.6 |
| Other equity | 3daaa | .... | .... | .... | .... | .... | .... | .... | .... | .... | .... | .... | — |
| Debt instruments | 3dzaa | .... | .... | .... | † 1,366.0 | 1,236.5 | −518.3 | 521.8 | −976.7 | 819.0 | 341.5 | 1,757.2 | 345.6 |
| Other investment: liabilities | 3d9la | .... | .... | .... | † 5,587.6 | 5,136.3 | 1,665.8 | −635.1 | −799.4 | 826.9 | 88.2 | 279.4 | 343.1 |
| Other equity | 3dala | .... | .... | .... | .... | .... | .... | .... | .... | .... | .... | .... | .... |
| Debt instruments | 3dzla | .... | .... | .... | † 5,587.6 | 5,136.3 | 1,665.8 | −635.1 | −799.4 | 826.9 | 88.2 | 279.4 | 343.1 |
| Curr.+ cap.− finan. acct. balance | 4y9na | .... | .... | .... | † 689.0 | −3,031.3 | 2,200.2 | −2,290.0 | 1,987.1 | −1,609.0 | 1,232.4 | −1,957.3 | −85.3 |
| D. Net Errors and Omissions | 409na | .... | .... | .... | † 592.3 | 791.3 | −372.2 | 614.4 | 442.7 | 425.8 | 605.4 | 360.2 | 431.6 |
| E. Reserves and Related Items | 4z9na | .... | .... | .... | † 1,281.4 | −2,240.0 | 1,828.0 | −1,675.6 | 2,429.8 | −1,183.2 | 1,837.8 | −1,597.1 | 346.3 |
| Reserve assets | 3e9aa | .... | .... | .... | † 1,036.5 | −2,240.0 | 3,400.5 | −1,221.6 | 2,504.5 | −1,450.0 | 974.6 | −2,354.7 | 184.2 |
| Credit and loans from the IMF | 3dc1a | .... | .... | .... | † −244.9 | — | 1,572.5 | 454.0 | 74.7 | −266.8 | −863.2 | −757.6 | −162.1 |
| Exceptional financing | 409la | .... | .... | .... | .... | .... | .... | .... | .... | .... | .... | .... | .... |
| *Excludes components in group E | | | | | | | | | | | | | |
| | | | | | | | | | | | | | |
| **International Investment Position** | | | | | | *Millions of US Dollars* | | | | | | | |
| Assets | 809aa | .... | .... | .... | .... | 19,892.8 | 23,486.4 | 21,670.2 | 23,030.5 | 22,739.7 | † 24,878.7 | 22,471.1 | 21,095.3 |
| Direct investment | 8a9aa | .... | .... | .... | .... | 1,747.3 | 1,878.6 | 1,951.5 | 2,090.7 | 2,204.7 | † 2,866.3 | 2,848.8 | 2,884.0 |
| Equity & investment fund shares | 8aaaa | .... | .... | .... | .... | 1,663.7 | 1,777.8 | 1,847.5 | 1,978.4 | 2,079.7 | † 2,514.4 | 2,496.3 | 2,526.1 |
| Debt instruments | 8abaa | .... | .... | .... | .... | 83.6 | 100.8 | 104.0 | 112.2 | 125.1 | † 352.0 | 352.4 | 357.9 |
| Portfolio investment | 8b9aa | .... | .... | .... | .... | 12.7 | 12.1 | 68.3 | 9.7 | 43.4 | † 77.3 | 171.8 | 216.8 |
| Equity & investment fund shares | 8baaa | .... | .... | .... | .... | .... | .... | .... | .... | .... | † 65.6 | 64.2 | 30.1 |
| Debt securities | 8bbaa | .... | .... | .... | .... | 12.7 | 12.1 | 68.3 | 9.7 | 43.4 | † 11.6 | 107.6 | 186.7 |
| Fin. der.(oth.than reserves) & ESOs | 8c9aa | .... | .... | .... | .... | .... | .... | .... | .... | .... | .... | .... | 3.5 |
| Other investment | 8d9aa | .... | .... | .... | .... | 6,638.0 | 6,360.7 | 6,340.8 | 5,327.5 | 6,089.2 | † 6,504.6 | 7,402.2 | 6,717.7 |
| Other equity | 8daaa | .... | .... | .... | .... | .... | .... | .... | .... | .... | .... | .... | .... |
| Debt instruments | 8dzaa | .... | .... | .... | .... | 6,638.0 | 6,360.7 | 6,340.8 | 5,327.5 | 6,089.2 | † 6,504.6 | 7,402.2 | 6,717.7 |
| Reserve assets | 8e9aa | .... | .... | .... | .... | 11,494.8 | 15,235.0 | 13,309.6 | 15,602.7 | 14,402.3 | † 15,430.5 | 12,048.3 | 11,273.3 |
| Liabilities | 809la | .... | .... | .... | .... | 50,960.1 | 53,507.3 | 53,382.1 | 56,230.8 | 59,419.1 | † 68,428.0 | 62,635.7 | 58,730.7 |
| Direct investment | 8a9la | .... | .... | .... | .... | 19,568.1 | 20,817.6 | 22,207.5 | 24,676.5 | 25,454.8 | † 31,542.0 | 29,568.2 | 28,781.6 |
| Equity & investment fund shares | 8aala | .... | .... | .... | .... | 15,836.2 | 15,890.7 | 17,115.0 | 18,881.5 | 18,180.8 | † 23,318.9 | 22,312.2 | 21,993.9 |
| Debt instruments | 8abla | .... | .... | .... | .... | 3,732.0 | 4,926.9 | 5,092.5 | 5,795.1 | 7,274.1 | † 8,223.1 | 7,255.9 | 6,787.6 |
| Portfolio investment | 8b9la | .... | .... | .... | .... | 1,529.0 | 1,508.3 | 1,333.9 | 3,263.8 | 5,323.2 | † 8,842.2 | 9,000.0 | 8,204.6 |
| Equity & investment fund shares | 8bala | .... | .... | .... | .... | .1 | 3.0 | 11.2 | 45.4 | 66.9 | † 821.8 | 705.2 | 438.5 |
| Debt securities | 8bbla | .... | .... | .... | .... | 1,528.9 | 1,505.3 | 1,322.7 | 3,218.4 | 5,256.2 | † 8,020.4 | 8,294.8 | 7,766.1 |
| Fin. der.(oth.than reserves) & ESOs | 8c9la | .... | .... | .... | .... | .... | .... | .... | .... | .... | .... | .... | — |
| Other investment | 8d9la | .... | .... | .... | .... | 29,862.9 | 31,181.3 | 29,840.7 | 28,290.4 | 28,641.1 | † 28,043.8 | 24,067.5 | 21,744.5 |
| Other equity | 8dala | .... | .... | .... | .... | .... | .... | .... | .... | .... | .... | .... | .... |
| Debt instruments | 8dzla | .... | .... | .... | .... | 29,862.9 | 31,181.3 | 29,840.7 | 28,290.4 | 28,641.1 | † 28,043.8 | 24,067.5 | 21,744.5 |

# Serbia, Republic of  942

2016, International Monetary Fund : *International Financial Statistics Yearbook*

|  |  | 2004 | 2005 | 2006 | 2007 | 2008 | 2009 | 2010 | 2011 | 2012 | 2013 | 2014 | 2015 |
|---|---|---|---|---|---|---|---|---|---|---|---|---|---|
| **Government Finance** | | | | | | | | | | | | | |
| **Cash Flow Statement** | | | | | | | | | | | | | |
| **Budgetary Central Government** | | | | *Millions of Serbian Dinars: Fiscal Year Ends December 31* | | | | | | | | |
| Cash Receipts:Operating Activities... | c1 | .... | .... | .... | 574,491 | 653,029 | 654,610 | 710,387 | 743,014 | 781,192 | .... | .... | .... |
| Taxes................................ | c11 | .... | .... | .... | 516,326 | 587,929 | 580,600 | 625,431 | 654,277 | 690,661 | .... | .... | .... |
| Social Contributions...................... | c12 | .... | .... | .... | — | — | — | — | — | — | .... | .... | .... |
| Grants.............................. | c13 | .... | .... | .... | 746 | 745 | 5,956 | 6,670 | 1,941 | 2,388 | .... | .... | .... |
| Other Receipts.............................. | c14 | .... | .... | .... | 57,419 | 64,355 | 68,054 | 78,286 | 86,795 | 88,143 | .... | .... | .... |
| Cash Payments:Operating Activities. | c2 | .... | .... | .... | 538,587 | 640,967 | 699,039 | 780,882 | 848,742 | 946,028 | .... | .... | .... |
| Compensation of Employees.......... | c21 | .... | .... | .... | 152,732 | 180,382 | 184,157 | 192,383 | 215,077 | 238,672 | .... | .... | .... |
| Purchases of Goods & Services....... | c22 | .... | .... | .... | 46,205 | 50,801 | 50,161 | 60,050 | 64,658 | 68,657 | .... | .... | .... |
| Interest.............................. | c24 | .... | .... | .... | 14,807 | 13,880 | 20,016 | 30,133 | 40,337 | 63,146 | .... | .... | .... |
| Subsidies.............................. | c25 | .... | .... | .... | 36,253 | 49,375 | 40,875 | 74,848 | 80,927 | 93,495 | .... | .... | .... |
| Grants.............................. | c26 | .... | .... | .... | 184,755 | 236,945 | 297,442 | 303,914 | 320,749 | 369,296 | .... | .... | .... |
| Social Benefits.............................. | c27 | .... | .... | .... | 92,610 | 97,870 | 96,681 | 108,135 | 110,213 | 92,362 | .... | .... | .... |
| Other Payments.......................... | c28 | .... | .... | .... | 11,227 | 11,713 | 9,708 | 11,419 | 16,782 | 20,401 | .... | .... | .... |
| Net Cash Inflow:Operating Act.[1-2] | ccio | .... | .... | .... | 35,903 | 12,062 | −44,429 | −70,495 | −105,729 | −164,836 | .... | .... | .... |
| Net Cash Outflow:Invest. in NFA...... | c31 | .... | .... | .... | 60,941 | 42,663 | 32,350 | 37,521 | 38,700 | 48,202 | .... | .... | .... |
| Purchases of Nonfinancial Assets... | c31.1 | .... | .... | .... | 65,906 | 44,040 | 33,736 | 39,359 | 40,480 | 55,348 | .... | .... | .... |
| Sales of Nonfinancial Assets.......... | c31.2 | .... | .... | .... | 4,965 | 1,377 | 1,385 | 1,838 | 1,780 | 7,145 | .... | .... | .... |
| Cash Surplus/Deficit [1-2-31=1-2M] | ccsd | .... | .... | .... | −25,038 | −30,602 | −76,780 | −108,016 | −144,428 | −213,038 | .... | .... | .... |
| Net Acq. Fin. Assets, excl. Cash...... | c32x | .... | .... | .... | −26,178 | −8,263 | 2,623 | −4,699 | −794 | 8,945 | .... | .... | .... |
| Domestic................................ | c321x | .... | .... | .... | −26,299 | −8,570 | 2,608 | −4,699 | −794 | 8,945 | .... | .... | .... |
| Foreign.............................. | c322x | .... | .... | .... | 121 | 307 | 15 | — | — | — | .... | .... | .... |
| Net Incurrence of Liabilities.............. | c33 | .... | .... | .... | −32,719 | −27,080 | 113,298 | 92,956 | 178,959 | 242,469 | .... | .... | .... |
| Domestic.............................. | c331 | .... | .... | .... | −30,212 | −20,795 | 81,309 | 69,322 | 67,039 | 108,057 | .... | .... | .... |
| Foreign.............................. | c332 | .... | .... | .... | −2,508 | −6,285 | 31,990 | 23,635 | 111,920 | 134,412 | .... | .... | .... |
| Net Cash Inflow, Fin.Act.[-32x+33].. | cnfb | .... | .... | .... | −6,541 | −18,817 | 110,676 | 97,655 | 179,752 | 233,524 | .... | .... | .... |
| Net Change in Stock of Cash........... | cncb | .... | .... | .... | −31,579 | −49,418 | 33,896 | −10,361 | 35,324 | 20,486 | .... | .... | .... |
| Stat. Discrep. [32X-33+NCB-CSD]... | ccsdz | .... | .... | .... | — | — | — | — | — | — | .... | .... | .... |
| Memo Item:Cash Expenditure[2+31] | c2m | .... | .... | .... | 599,529 | 683,631 | 731,389 | 818,403 | 887,442 | 994,230 | .... | .... | .... |
| Memo Item: Gross Debt.................. | c63 | .... | .... | .... | 691,120 | 756,166 | 867,243 | 1,115,356 | 1,322,699 | 1,681,621 | .... | .... | .... |
| **National Accounts** | | | | | *Millions of Dinars* | | | | | | | | |
| Househ.Cons.Expend.,incl.NPISHs.... | 96f | 1,099,331 | 1,326,110 | 1,561,640 | 1,766,522 | 2,065,006 | 2,236,373 | 2,393,552 | 2,627,585 | 2,763,136 | 2,918,779 | 2,955,818 | 2,981,896 |
| Gross Fixed Capital Formation......... | 93e | 298,239 | 351,667 | 457,446 | 594,704 | 684,243 | 566,157 | 570,055 | 626,667 | 758,695 | 668,358 | 652,002 | 721,023 |
| Changes in Inventories.................... | 93i | 135,195 | 82,161 | 57,146 | 90,917 | 148,589 | −6,971 | −3,563 | 58,352 | −5,628 | 15,821 | 31,747 | −15,873 |
| Exports of Goods and Services......... | 90c | 351,532 | 475,337 | 622,031 | 667,986 | 799,235 | 773,198 | 1,010,110 | 1,157,758 | 1,323,598 | 1,597,092 | 1,695,334 | 1,894,742 |
| Imports of Goods and Services (-)..... | 98c | 734,916 | 825,582 | 1,039,917 | 1,240,257 | 1,486,066 | 1,231,074 | 1,469,852 | 1,682,434 | 1,921,030 | 2,012,214 | 2,119,288 | 2,282,052 |
| Gross Domestic Product (GDP)........ | 99b | 1,451,448 | 1,751,371 | 2,055,198 | 2,355,066 | 2,744,913 | 2,880,059 | 3,067,210 | 3,407,563 | 3,584,236 | 3,876,403 | 3,908,470 | 3,973,034 |
| Gross National Income (GNI)........... | 99a | 1,368,101 | 1,709,083 | 1,991,077 | 2,276,745 | 2,665,045 | 2,835,229 | 2,999,633 | 3,268,316 | 3,460,113 | 3,715,739 | 3,749,899 | .... |
| GDP Volume 2010 Ref., Chained..... | 99b.p | 2,547,973 | 2,689,142 | 2,821,027 | 2,987,150 | 3,147,461 | 3,049,387 | 3,067,210 | 3,110,196 | 3,078,619 | 3,157,793 | 3,099,964 | 3,122,949 |
| GDP Volume (2010=100)............... | 99bvp | 83.1 | 87.7 | 92.0 | 97.4 | 102.6 | 99.4 | 100.0 | 101.4 | 100.4 | 103.0 | 101.1 | 101.8 |
| GDP Deflator (2010=100)............... | 99bip | 57.0 | 65.1 | 72.9 | 78.8 | 87.2 | 94.4 | 100.0 | 109.6 | 116.4 | 122.8 | 126.1 | 127.2 |
| | | | | | | *Millions: Midyear Estimates* | | | | | | | |
| Population................................ | 99z | 9.23 | 9.19 | 9.15 | 9.13 | 9.11 | 9.09 | 9.06 | 9.02 | 8.98 | 8.94 | 8.89 | 8.85 |

# Seychelles 718

| | | 2004 | 2005 | 2006 | 2007 | 2008 | 2009 | 2010 | 2011 | 2012 | 2013 | 2014 | 2015 |
|---|---|---|---|---|---|---|---|---|---|---|---|---|---|
| **Exchange Rates** | | | | | | *Rupees per SDR: End of Period* | | | | | | | |
| Official Rate.................................. | aa | 8.513 | 7.860 | 8.715 | 12.625 | 25.480 | 17.491 | 18.709 | 21.071 | 19.983 | 18.597 | 20.340 | 18.229 |
| | | | | | | *Rupees per US Dollar: End of Period (ae) Period Average (rf)* | | | | | | | |
| Official Rate.................................. | ae | 5.500 | 5.500 | 5.796 | 7.998 | † 16.573 | 11.255 | 12.148 | 13.724 | 13.002 | 12.076 | 14.039 | 13.155 |
| Official Rate.................................. | rf | 5.500 | 5.500 | 5.520 | 6.701 | 9.457 | 13.610 | 12.068 | 12.381 | 13.704 | 12.058 | 12.747 | 13.314 |
| **Fund Position** | | | | | | *Millions of SDRs: End of Period* | | | | | | | |
| Quota.......................................... | 2f.s | 8.80 | 8.80 | 8.80 | 8.80 | 8.80 | 8.80 | 8.80 | 10.90 | 10.90 | 10.90 | 10.90 | 10.90 |
| SDR Holdings................................ | 1b.s | — | — | — | .01 | — | 7.84 | 7.63 | 6.77 | 6.44 | 6.13 | 5.80 | 5.48 |
| Reserve Position in the Fund............ | 1c.s | — | — | — | — | — | — | — | .53 | .53 | .53 | .53 | .53 |
| Total Fund Cred.&Loans Outstg....... | 2tl | — | — | — | — | 6.16 | 11.88 | 20.24 | 23.76 | 27.17 | 28.27 | 29.16 | 30.59 |
| SDR Allocations............................ | 1bd | .41 | .41 | .41 | .41 | .41 | 8.28 | 8.28 | 8.28 | 8.28 | 8.28 | 8.28 | 8.28 |
| **International Liquidity** | | | | | *Millions of US Dollars Unless Otherwise Indicated: End of Period* | | | | | | | | |
| Total Reserves minus Gold.............. | 1l.d | 34.59 | 56.24 | 112.92 | 40.77 | 63.83 | 190.55 | 255.58 | 279.12 | 308.09 | 425.90 | 465.01 | 536.15 |
| SDR Holdings................................ | 1b.d | — | — | — | .02 | — | 12.29 | 11.75 | 10.39 | 9.90 | 9.44 | 8.41 | 7.59 |
| Reserve Position in the Fund......... | 1c.d | .01 | — | — | .01 | .01 | .01 | .01 | .81 | .81 | .81 | .77 | .73 |
| Foreign Exchange....................... | 1d.d | 34.58 | 56.24 | 112.92 | 40.75 | 63.82 | 178.25 | 243.83 | 267.91 | 297.38 | 415.65 | 455.84 | 527.83 |
| Central Bank: Other Assets............ | 3..d | — | — | — | — | — | — | — | — | — | — | — | — |
| Central Bank: Other Liabs.............. | 4..d | 89.83 | 71.71 | — | .01 | .01 | .01 | .01 | .81 | .80 | .81 | .76 | .73 |
| Other Depository Corps.: Assets...... | 7a.d | 57.73 | 72.27 | 172.30 | 276.03 | 336.03 | 363.18 | 363.38 | 394.02 | 453.64 | 634.76 | 562.97 | 318.98 |
| Other Depository Corps.: Liabs....... | 7b.d | 77.05 | 106.44 | 192.92 | 263.02 | 272.37 | 283.26 | 286.39 | 310.41 | 313.81 | 413.92 | 299.57 | 104.06 |
| Other Financial Corps.: Assets....... | 7e.d | — | — | — | — | — | — | — | — | — | — | — | — |
| Other Financial Corps.: Liabs.......... | 7f.d | 24.61 | 25.31 | 11.81 | 9.75 | 6.09 | 14.55 | 10.99 | .40 | .43 | 1.19 | 1.20 | 1.70 |
| **Central Bank** | | | | | | *Millions of Rupees: End of Period* | | | | | | | |
| Net Foreign Assets......................... | 11n | −309.7 | −88.9 | 649.7 | 317.4 | 1,039.4 | 1,851.2 | 2,553.6 | 3,114.9 | 3,254.0 | 4,414.4 | 5,726.1 | 6,344.0 |
| Claims on Nonresidents................ | 11 | 187.8 | 308.7 | 653.3 | 322.5 | 1,207.1 | 2,207.0 | 3,087.3 | 3,801.1 | 3,972.9 | 5,104.0 | 6,498.4 | 7,062.2 |
| Liabilities to Nonresidents............. | 16c | 497.5 | 397.6 | 3.6 | 5.2 | 167.7 | 355.8 | 533.7 | 686.2 | 718.9 | 689.5 | 772.2 | 718.3 |
| Claims on Other Depository Corps.... | 12e | 120.0 | — | — | — | 40.3 | — | — | — | — | — | — | — |
| Net Claims on Central Government.. | 12an | 1,277.7 | 1,228.1 | 818.6 | 1,102.6 | 947.7 | 703.3 | 766.8 | 835.2 | −358.6 | −414.5 | −1,490.8 | −1,979.0 |
| Claims on Central Government...... | 12a | 1,400.6 | 1,340.8 | 1,111.1 | 1,139.0 | 1,138.7 | 998.1 | 1,185.1 | 1,185.1 | 1,185.1 | 1,185.1 | 1,185.1 | 1,185.1 |
| Liabilities to Central Government... | 16d | 122.9 | 112.7 | 292.4 | 36.4 | 191.0 | 294.8 | 418.2 | 349.8 | 1,543.6 | 1,599.5 | 2,675.9 | 3,164.1 |
| Claims on Other Sectors................. | 12s | 3.6 | 4.4 | — | — | — | — | — | — | — | — | — | — |
| Claims on Other Financial Corps.... | 12g | — | — | — | — | — | — | — | — | — | — | — | — |
| Claims on State & Local Govts....... | 12b | — | — | — | — | — | — | — | — | — | — | — | — |
| Claims on Public Nonfin. Corps...... | 12c | — | — | — | — | — | — | — | — | — | — | — | — |
| Claims on Private Sector............... | 12d | 3.6 | 4.4 | — | — | — | — | — | — | — | — | — | — |
| Monetary Base............................. | 14 | 1,055.1 | 1,091.4 | 1,448.1 | 1,113.1 | 1,119.9 | 1,295.9 | 1,746.2 | 1,698.7 | 1,816.4 | 2,096.0 | 2,387.6 | 2,614.0 |
| Currency in Circulation................. | 14a | 314.5 | 344.8 | 417.2 | 450.6 | 477.6 | 555.0 | 653.9 | 707.8 | 739.7 | 899.6 | 1,017.6 | 1,096.9 |
| Liabs. to Other Depository Corps.... | 14c | 151.2 | 248.2 | 647.0 | 570.5 | 637.5 | 740.9 | 1,092.3 | 990.9 | 1,076.7 | 1,196.4 | 1,370.0 | 1,517.1 |
| Liabilities to Other Sectors............ | 14d | 589.5 | 498.4 | 383.9 | 92.0 | 4.8 | — | — | — | — | — | — | — |
| Other Liabs. to Other Dep. Corps..... | 14n | — | — | — | — | 62.3 | 1,266.1 | 1,135.3 | 1,512.0 | 636.0 | 1,570.1 | 884.8 | 1,180.0 |
| Dep. & Sec. Excl. f/Monetary Base.... | 14o | — | — | — | — | 186.2 | 113.9 | 151.4 | 206.2 | 118.6 | 97.9 | 99.5 | 141.9 |
| Deposits Included in Broad Money. | 15 | — | — | — | — | — | — | — | — | — | — | — | — |
| Sec.Ot.th.Shares Incl.in Brd. Money. | 16a | — | — | — | — | — | — | — | — | — | — | — | — |
| Deposits Excl. from Broad Money... | 16b | — | — | — | — | 186.2 | 113.9 | 151.4 | 206.2 | 118.6 | 97.9 | 99.5 | 141.9 |
| Sec.Ot.th.Shares Excl.f/Brd.Money.. | 16s | — | — | — | — | — | — | — | — | — | — | — | — |
| Loans.......................................... | 16l | — | — | — | — | — | — | — | — | — | — | — | — |
| Financial Derivatives...................... | 16m | — | — | — | — | — | — | — | — | — | — | — | — |
| Shares and Other Equity.................. | 17a | 52.7 | 83.6 | 89.0 | 327.6 | 244.2 | 70.4 | 416.9 | 679.4 | 506.0 | 416.3 | 1,003.2 | 636.5 |
| Other Items (Net)........................... | 17r | −16.1 | −31.3 | −68.8 | −20.7 | 414.8 | −191.8 | −129.4 | −146.1 | −181.7 | −180.3 | −139.7 | −207.4 |
| Memo Item: | | | | | | | | | | | | | |
| Total Assets................................... | 10ra | 1,736.3 | 1,697.7 | 1,845.7 | 1,510.6 | 2,469.6 | 3,415.1 | 4,419.5 | 5,150.1 | 5,384.5 | 6,503.8 | 7,860.6 | 8,478.6 |
| **Other Depository Corporations** | | | | | | *Millions of Rupees: End of Period* | | | | | | | |
| Net Foreign Assets......................... | 21n | −106.3 | −188.0 | −119.5 | 104.0 | 1,055.0 | 899.5 | 935.3 | 1,147.5 | 1,818.0 | 2,666.9 | 3,697.9 | 2,827.3 |
| Claims on Nonresidents................ | 21 | 317.5 | 397.5 | 998.5 | 2,207.1 | 5,569.1 | 4,087.4 | 4,414.5 | 5,407.7 | 5,898.1 | 7,665.3 | 7,903.5 | 4,196.1 |
| Liabilities to Nonresidents............. | 26c | 423.8 | 585.4 | 1,118.1 | 2,103.7 | 4,514.1 | 3,188.0 | 3,479.1 | 4,260.2 | 4,080.1 | 4,998.4 | 4,205.6 | 1,368.8 |
| Claims on Central Bank.................. | 20 | 169.9 | 267.4 | 671.4 | 613.3 | 684.7 | 626.0 | 973.5 | 753.0 | 834.9 | 968.1 | 951.8 | 1,008.8 |
| Currency..................................... | 20a | 18.7 | 19.2 | 24.4 | 42.8 | 47.1 | 54.7 | 73.8 | 84.3 | 108.2 | 143.0 | 142.9 | 162.8 |
| Reserve Deposits and Securities..... | 20b | 151.2 | 248.2 | 647.0 | 570.5 | 637.5 | 571.2 | 899.6 | 668.7 | 726.6 | 825.1 | 809.0 | 846.0 |
| Other Claims................................ | 20n | — | — | — | — | — | — | — | — | — | — | — | — |
| Net Claims on Central Government.. | 22an | 2,470.6 | 2,408.3 | 2,409.8 | 2,075.6 | 1,982.9 | 1,531.9 | 1,792.6 | 1,544.5 | 2,118.9 | 2,725.8 | 2,904.8 | 3,281.6 |
| Claims on Central Government...... | 22a | 2,746.1 | 2,638.0 | 2,630.8 | 2,315.8 | 2,307.3 | 1,785.5 | 2,094.4 | 1,834.9 | 2,391.0 | 3,020.5 | 3,202.2 | 3,424.1 |
| Liabilities to Central Government... | 26d | 275.5 | 229.8 | 221.0 | 240.2 | 324.4 | 253.6 | 301.8 | 290.5 | 272.1 | 294.7 | 297.4 | 142.5 |
| Claims on Other Sectors................. | 22s | 1,348.6 | 1,550.4 | 1,570.1 | 2,103.4 | 3,106.7 | 2,730.4 | 3,247.7 | 3,416.1 | 3,546.0 | 3,712.7 | 4,584.8 | 5,164.7 |
| Claims on Other Financial Corps.... | 22g | 138.5 | 221.5 | 115.4 | 173.5 | 239.6 | 190.1 | 163.2 | 214.2 | 187.9 | 222.2 | 200.6 | 303.7 |
| Claims on State & Local Govts....... | 22b | — | — | — | — | — | — | — | — | — | — | — | — |
| Claims on Public Nonfin. Corps...... | 22c | 45.3 | 75.8 | 177.6 | 212.5 | 317.3 | 225.1 | 223.2 | 266.3 | 243.9 | 78.3 | 96.8 | 276.2 |
| Claims on Private Sector............... | 22d | 1,164.8 | 1,253.1 | 1,277.2 | 1,717.4 | 2,549.9 | 2,315.2 | 2,861.4 | 2,935.5 | 3,114.3 | 3,412.1 | 4,287.4 | 4,584.7 |
| Liabilities to Central Bank.............. | 26g | 120.0 | — | — | — | 40.3 | — | — | — | — | — | — | — |
| Transf.Dep.Included in Broad Money | 24 | 1,930.7 | 2,140.2 | 2,260.1 | 2,858.8 | 4,294.5 | 4,283.6 | 4,774.6 | 5,707.8 | 5,586.0 | 7,185.2 | 9,350.9 | 10,055.2 |
| Other Dep.Included in Broad Money. | 25 | 1,996.3 | 1,927.5 | 2,003.1 | 1,279.5 | 1,206.5 | 1,617.0 | 1,920.5 | 1,264.4 | 1,204.4 | 1,398.4 | 1,528.9 | 1,117.0 |
| Sec.Ot.th.Shares Incl.in Brd. Money.. | 26a | — | — | — | — | — | — | — | — | — | — | — | — |
| Deposits Excl. from Broad Money..... | 26b | 45.7 | 49.1 | 124.7 | 140.4 | 162.8 | 139.1 | 312.7 | 480.7 | 636.6 | 954.6 | 814.8 | 1,064.9 |
| Sec.Ot.th.Shares Excl.f/Brd.Money.... | 26s | — | — | — | — | — | — | — | — | — | — | — | — |
| Loans.......................................... | 26l | — | — | — | — | — | — | — | — | — | — | — | — |
| Financial Derivatives...................... | 26m | — | — | — | — | — | — | — | — | — | — | — | — |
| Insurance Technical Reserves........... | 26r | — | — | — | — | — | — | — | — | — | — | — | — |
| Shares and Other Equity.................. | 27a | 273.0 | 285.9 | 331.6 | 371.1 | 537.7 | 804.7 | 894.8 | 918.9 | 1,104.0 | 1,376.2 | 1,265.8 | 1,325.9 |
| Other Items (Net)........................... | 27r | −482.8 | −364.6 | −187.6 | 246.4 | 587.6 | −1,056.8 | −953.5 | −1,510.8 | −213.2 | −841.0 | −821.1 | −1,280.7 |
| Memo Item: | | | | | | | | | | | | | |
| Total Assets................................... | 20ra | 5,416.7 | 5,633.5 | 6,563.3 | 7,713.4 | 12,519.7 | 11,539.0 | 12,791.2 | 14,245.2 | 14,835.7 | 18,818.6 | 19,833.3 | 16,925.6 |

| | | 2004 | 2005 | 2006 | 2007 | 2008 | 2009 | 2010 | 2011 | 2012 | 2013 | 2014 | 2015 |
|---|---|---|---|---|---|---|---|---|---|---|---|---|---|
| **Depository Corporations** | | | | | | *Millions of Rupees: End of Period* | | | | | | | |
| Net Foreign Assets | 31n | −416.0 | −276.9 | 530.2 | 421.4 | 2,094.5 | 2,750.7 | 3,488.9 | 4,262.4 | 5,072.0 | 7,081.3 | 9,424.1 | 9,171.3 |
| Claims on Nonresidents | 31 | 505.3 | 706.2 | 1,651.8 | 2,530.2 | 6,776.3 | 6,294.4 | 7,501.8 | 9,208.8 | 9,870.9 | 12,769.2 | 14,401.9 | 11,258.4 |
| Liabilities to Nonresidents | 36c | 921.3 | 983.0 | 1,121.6 | 2,108.9 | 4,681.8 | 3,543.8 | 4,012.8 | 4,946.4 | 4,799.0 | 5,687.9 | 4,977.8 | 2,087.1 |
| Domestic Claims | 32 | 5,100.6 | 5,191.2 | 4,798.6 | 5,281.6 | 6,037.4 | 4,965.5 | 5,807.1 | 5,795.8 | 5,306.4 | 6,024.0 | 5,998.8 | 6,467.3 |
| Net Claims on Central Government | 32an | 3,748.4 | 3,636.4 | 3,228.5 | 3,178.2 | 2,930.6 | 2,235.2 | 2,559.4 | 2,379.7 | 1,760.3 | 2,311.3 | 1,414.0 | 1,302.6 |
| Claims on Central Government | 32a | 4,146.7 | 3,978.8 | 3,741.8 | 3,454.8 | 3,446.0 | 2,783.6 | 3,279.5 | 3,020.0 | 3,576.1 | 4,205.5 | 4,387.2 | 4,609.1 |
| Liabilities to Central Government | 36d | 398.4 | 342.4 | 513.4 | 276.6 | 515.4 | 548.4 | 720.0 | 640.3 | 1,815.7 | 1,894.2 | 2,973.3 | 3,306.5 |
| Claims on Other Sectors | 32s | 1,352.2 | 1,554.8 | 1,570.1 | 2,103.4 | 3,106.7 | 2,730.4 | 3,247.7 | 3,416.1 | 3,546.0 | 3,712.7 | 4,584.8 | 5,164.7 |
| Claims on Other Financial Corps | 32g | 138.5 | 221.5 | 115.4 | 173.5 | 239.6 | 190.1 | 163.2 | 214.2 | 187.9 | 222.2 | 200.6 | 303.7 |
| Claims on State & Local Govts | 32b | — | — | — | — | — | — | — | — | — | — | — | — |
| Claims on Public Nonfin. Corps | 32c | 45.3 | 75.8 | 177.6 | 212.5 | 317.3 | 225.1 | 223.2 | 266.3 | 243.9 | 78.3 | 96.8 | 276.2 |
| Claims on Private Sector | 32d | 1,168.4 | 1,257.5 | 1,277.2 | 1,717.4 | 2,549.9 | 2,315.2 | 2,861.4 | 2,935.5 | 3,114.3 | 3,412.1 | 4,287.4 | 4,584.7 |
| Broad Money Liabilities | 35l | 4,812.2 | 4,891.7 | 5,039.9 | 4,638.1 | 5,936.2 | 6,400.9 | 7,275.1 | 7,595.7 | 7,421.8 | 9,340.2 | 11,754.6 | 12,106.3 |
| Currency Outside Depository Corps | 34a | 295.8 | 325.7 | 392.8 | 407.8 | 430.4 | 500.3 | 580.0 | 623.5 | 631.5 | 756.6 | 874.7 | 934.1 |
| Transferable Deposits | 34 | 1,930.7 | 2,140.2 | 2,260.1 | 2,858.8 | 4,294.5 | 4,283.6 | 4,774.6 | 5,707.8 | 5,586.0 | 7,185.2 | 9,350.9 | 10,055.2 |
| Other Deposits | 35 | 2,585.7 | 2,425.9 | 2,387.0 | 1,371.5 | 1,211.3 | 1,617.0 | 1,920.5 | 1,264.4 | 1,204.4 | 1,398.4 | 1,528.9 | 1,117.0 |
| Securities Other than Shares | 36a | — | — | — | — | — | — | — | — | — | — | — | — |
| Deposits Excl. from Broad Money | 36b | 45.7 | 49.1 | 124.7 | 140.4 | 349.0 | 252.9 | 464.2 | 686.9 | 755.2 | 1,052.5 | 914.4 | 1,206.8 |
| Sec.Ot.th.Shares Excl.f/Brd.Money | 36s | — | — | — | — | — | — | — | — | — | — | — | — |
| Loans | 36l | — | — | — | — | — | — | — | — | — | — | — | — |
| Financial Derivatives | 36m | — | — | — | — | — | — | — | — | — | — | — | — |
| Insurance Technical Reserves | 36r | — | — | — | — | — | — | — | — | — | — | — | — |
| Shares and Other Equity | 37a | 325.6 | 369.4 | 420.6 | 698.7 | 781.8 | 875.1 | 1,311.8 | 1,598.3 | 1,610.1 | 1,792.5 | 2,269.0 | 1,962.5 |
| Other Items (Net) | 37r | −498.9 | −395.9 | −256.5 | 225.7 | 1,064.7 | 187.2 | 245.1 | 177.3 | 591.2 | 920.0 | 484.9 | 363.0 |
| Broad Money Liabs., Seasonally Adj. | 35l.b | 4,826.3 | 4,883.4 | 4,997.9 | 4,574.0 | 5,831.4 | 6,293.2 | 7,179.4 | 7,549.0 | 7,417.8 | 9,373.7 | 11,812.8 | 12,173.3 |
| **Other Financial Corporations** | | | | | | *Millions of Rupees: End of Period* | | | | | | | |
| Net Foreign Assets | 41n | −135.3 | −139.2 | −68.4 | −78.0 | −101.0 | −163.8 | −133.5 | −5.5 | −5.5 | −14.4 | −16.9 | −22.3 |
| Claims on Nonresidents | 41 | — | — | — | — | — | — | — | — | — | — | — | — |
| Liabilities to Nonresidents | 46c | 135.3 | 139.2 | 68.4 | 78.0 | 101.0 | 163.8 | 133.5 | 5.5 | 5.5 | 14.4 | 16.9 | 22.3 |
| Claims on Depository Corporations | 40 | 17.4 | 21.4 | 24.2 | 62.3 | 69.8 | 47.3 | 52.1 | 38.9 | 50.0 | 119.7 | 97.6 | 126.7 |
| Net Claims on Central Government | 42an | 2.5 | 1.1 | .6 | .2 | 1.4 | 1.2 | 1.2 | −47.3 | −94.2 | −93.3 | −73.9 | −89.7 |
| Claims on Central Government | 42a | 2.5 | 1.1 | .6 | .2 | 1.4 | 1.2 | 1.2 | 49.1 | 2.3 | 1.9 | 18.7 | — |
| Liabilities to Central Government | 46d | — | — | — | — | — | — | — | 96.4 | 96.4 | 95.2 | 92.7 | 89.7 |
| Claims on Other Sectors | 42s | 288.4 | 303.4 | 304.1 | 269.8 | 279.6 | 298.5 | 386.3 | 469.9 | 467.9 | 391.4 | 419.1 | 553.6 |
| Claims on State & Local Govts | 42b | — | — | — | — | — | — | — | — | — | — | — | — |
| Claims on Public Nonfin. Corps | 42c | 2.0 | 2.0 | 2.0 | 2.0 | — | — | — | — | — | — | — | — |
| Claims on Private Sector | 42d | 286.4 | 301.4 | 302.1 | 267.8 | 279.6 | 298.5 | 386.3 | 469.9 | 467.9 | 391.4 | 419.1 | 553.6 |
| Deposits | 46b | — | — | 75.2 | 64.2 | 54.6 | 45.2 | 10.7 | 6.0 | — | — | — | — |
| Securities Other than Shares | 46s | — | — | — | — | — | — | — | — | — | — | — | — |
| Loans | 46l | — | — | — | — | — | — | — | — | — | 36.1 | 28.9 | 152.2 |
| Financial Derivatives | 46m | — | — | — | — | — | — | — | — | — | — | — | — |
| Insurance Technical Reserves | 46r | — | — | — | — | — | — | — | — | — | — | — | — |
| Shares and Other Equity | 47a | 140.3 | 139.8 | 144.9 | 149.8 | 55.7 | 59.1 | 114.8 | 214.8 | 253.0 | 261.7 | 281.5 | 308.5 |
| Other Items (Net) | 47r | 32.6 | 46.9 | 40.3 | 40.3 | 139.5 | 78.9 | 180.7 | 235.1 | 165.2 | 105.6 | 115.4 | 107.5 |
| Memo Item: | | | | | | | | | | | | | |
| Total Assets | 40ra | 318.3 | 335.4 | 338.5 | 344.2 | 363.9 | 359.7 | 453.0 | 573.0 | 548.4 | 542.0 | 577.8 | 714.3 |
| **Monetary Aggregates** | | | | | | *Millions of Rupees: End of Period* | | | | | | | |
| Broad Money | 59m | 4,812.2 | 4,891.7 | 5,039.9 | 4,638.1 | 5,936.2 | 6,400.9 | 7,275.1 | 7,595.7 | 7,421.8 | 9,340.2 | 11,754.6 | 12,106.3 |
| o/w:Currency Issued by Cent.Govt | 59m.a | — | — | — | — | — | — | — | — | — | — | — | — |
| o/w: Dep.in Nonfin. Corporations | 59m.b | — | — | — | — | — | — | — | — | — | — | — | — |
| o/w:Secs. Issued by Central Govt | 59m.c | — | — | — | — | — | — | — | — | — | — | — | — |
| Money (National Definitions) | | | | | | | | | | | | | |
| M1 | 59ma | 1,203.5 | 1,374.2 | 1,392.0 | 1,602.0 | † 2,868.1 | 3,273.7 | 3,886.3 | 4,149.2 | 3,920.2 | 5,207.1 | 5,716.9 | 6,481.8 |
| M2 | 59mb | 4,222.8 | 4,393.3 | 4,656.0 | 4,546.1 | † 4,018.6 | 4,791.0 | 5,567.4 | 5,189.6 | 4,981.3 | 6,392.1 | 6,861.6 | 7,426.9 |
| M2(p) | 59mba | 4,812.2 | 4,891.7 | 5,039.9 | 4,638.1 | † 4,023.4 | 4,791.0 | 5,567.4 | 5,189.6 | 4,981.3 | 6,392.1 | 6,861.6 | 7,426.9 |
| **Interest Rates** | | | | | | *Percent Per Annum* | | | | | | | |
| Discount Rate (End of Period) | 60.a | 3.51 | 3.87 | 4.44 | 5.13 | .... | .... | .... | .... | .... | .... | .... | .... |
| Treasury Bill Rate | 60c | 3.17 | 3.34 | 3.70 | 3.92 | 7.07 | 12.97 | 3.04 | 4.23 | 10.74 | 3.93 | 3.64 | 9.08 |
| Savings Rate | 60k | 2.88 | 2.98 | 2.73 | 2.68 | 4.52 | 6.67 | 1.76 | 1.13 | 1.47 | 1.72 | 1.74 | 2.53 |
| Deposit Rate | 60l | 3.55 | 3.72 | 2.46 | 3.07 | 3.97 | 9.77 | 2.86 | 2.08 | 3.30 | 3.43 | 2.33 | 3.16 |
| Lending Rate | 60p | 9.99 | 9.77 | 10.05 | 10.89 | 11.81 | 15.35 | 12.70 | 11.19 | 12.19 | 12.29 | 11.65 | 12.36 |
| Government Bond Yield | 61 | 6.58 | 6.00 | 6.89 | 7.14 | 7.32 | 8.75 | 8.06 | 9.00 | .... | .... | 5.50 | 5.50 |
| **Prices and Labor** | | | | | | *Index Numbers (2010=100): Period Averages* | | | | | | | |
| Consumer Prices | 64 | 53.6 | 54.1 | † 53.9 | † 56.8 | 77.8 | 102.5 | 100.0 | 102.6 | 109.9 | 114.6 | 116.2 | 120.9 |
| Employment (2005=100) | 67 | 94.9 | 100.0 | .... | .... | .... | .... | .... | .... | .... | .... | .... | .... |
| | | | | | | *Number in Thousands: Period Averages* | | | | | | | |
| Employment | 67e | 33 | 35 | 38 | 40 | 41 | .... | .... | .... | .... | .... | .... | .... |
| **Intl. Transactions & Positions** | | | | | | *Millions of Rupees* | | | | | | | |
| Exports | 70 | 1,599.35 | 1,868.48 | 2,097.12 | 2,413.37 | 4,069.60 | 5,381.20 | 4,827.79 | 5,983.14 | 6,802.50 | 6,972.63 | 6,867.25 | .... |
| Imports, c.i.f. | 71 | 2,731.49 | 3,711.93 | 4,180.84 | 5,757.36 | 9,959.28 | 10,792.12 | 11,955.60 | 12,999.36 | 14,705.67 | 13,229.22 | 14,603.92 | .... |

# Seychelles  718

**Balance of Payments** — *Millions of US Dollars*

| Item | Code | 2004 | 2005 | 2006 | 2007 | 2008 | 2009 | 2010 | 2011 | 2012 | 2013 | 2014 | 2015 |
|---|---|---|---|---|---|---|---|---|---|---|---|---|---|
| A. Current Account* | 109bx | −63.7 | −188.2 | −145.2 | † −194.0 | −262.9 | −189.5 | −214.4 | −301.3 | −161.3 | −158.6 | −310.3 | −244.0 |
| Goods, credit (exports) | 1a9cx | 300.4 | 350.1 | 419.2 | † 397.6 | 437.6 | 431.8 | 400.2 | 476.9 | 559.1 | 629.2 | 538.9 | 449.4 |
| Goods, debit (imports) | 1a9dx | 451.4 | 644.6 | 701.8 | † 701.9 | 841.1 | 750.7 | 781.2 | 915.0 | 1,028.6 | 1,074.6 | 1,080.6 | 922.4 |
| Balance on goods | 1a9bx | −151.0 | −294.5 | −282.6 | † −304.3 | −403.5 | −318.9 | −381.0 | −438.1 | −469.5 | −445.4 | −541.7 | −473.0 |
| Services, credit (exports) | 1b9cx | 327.3 | 369.6 | 431.2 | † 456.2 | 464.5 | 418.0 | 440.5 | 465.6 | 673.7 | 826.7 | 833.9 | 847.7 |
| Services, debit (imports) | 1b9dx | 220.7 | 240.3 | 282.7 | † 246.8 | 243.3 | 240.9 | 266.5 | 265.9 | 386.5 | 472.3 | 503.4 | 498.5 |
| Balance on Goods & Services | 1z9bx | −44.4 | −165.2 | −134.1 | † −94.9 | −182.3 | −141.7 | −207.0 | −238.5 | −182.3 | −91.0 | −211.2 | −123.8 |
| Primary income: credit | 1c9cx | 9.4 | 9.8 | 10.3 | † 3.6 | 4.9 | 3.6 | 9.6 | 10.0 | 120.4 | 35.1 | 12.6 | 15.4 |
| Primary income: debit | 1c9dx | 43.1 | 49.9 | 53.9 | † 74.4 | 80.0 | 58.4 | 21.7 | 79.4 | 124.2 | 117.6 | 114.5 | 116.8 |
| Balance on gds, serv. & prim. inc. | 1y9bx | −78.1 | −205.3 | −177.8 | † −165.8 | −257.4 | −196.5 | −219.1 | −307.9 | −186.1 | −173.4 | −313.1 | −225.2 |
| Secondary income: credit | 1d9ca | 17.3 | 21.4 | 42.7 | † 18.7 | 38.0 | 60.5 | 42.9 | 53.8 | 72.0 | 64.4 | 52.3 | 35.1 |
| Secondary income: debit | 1d9da | 2.9 | 4.3 | 10.1 | † 46.9 | 43.5 | 53.5 | 38.2 | 47.2 | 47.2 | 49.6 | 49.5 | 53.9 |
| B. Capital Account* | 209ba | 1.0 | 29.9 | 13.2 | † 8.2 | 5.0 | 52.5 | 275.1 | 60.6 | 64.2 | 70.5 | 39.1 | 33.9 |
| Capital account: credit | 209ca | 1.0 | 29.9 | 13.2 | † 8.2 | 5.0 | 52.5 | 275.1 | 60.6 | 64.2 | 70.5 | 39.1 | 33.9 |
| Capital account: debit | 209da | — | .... | .... | .... | .... | .... | .... | .... | .... | .... | .... | .... |
| Balance on current & capital acct. | 129ba | −62.7 | −158.3 | −131.9 | † −185.8 | −257.9 | −137.0 | 60.7 | −240.6 | −97.2 | −88.1 | −271.2 | −210.1 |
| C. Financial Account* | 309na | 30.5 | −129.2 | −223.6 | † −217.7 | 130.6 | −93.0 | −164.0 | −173.3 | −228.2 | −133.9 | −236.1 | −288.6 |
| Direct investment: assets | 3a9aa | 7.6 | 2.5 | 2.7 | † 17.8 | 13.0 | 5.3 | 6.2 | 7.9 | 187.6 | −68.0 | −76.8 | −87.1 |
| Equity & investment fund shares | 3aaaa | 7.6 | 2.5 | 2.7 | † 17.8 | 13.0 | 5.3 | 6.2 | 7.9 | 33.1 | 4.4 | −4.1 | −4.5 |
| Debt instruments | 3abaa | .... | .... | .... | .... | .... | .... | .... | .... | 154.6 | −72.4 | −72.8 | −82.5 |
| Direct investment: liabilities | 3a9la | 38.0 | 80.7 | 140.6 | † 175.9 | 179.8 | 168.3 | 159.8 | 143.2 | 613.2 | 57.3 | 108.3 | 105.9 |
| Equity & investment fund shares | 3aala | 38.0 | 80.4 | 139.7 | † 126.5 | 130.4 | 118.4 | 118.9 | 89.6 | 114.7 | 158.8 | 170.9 | 128.8 |
| Debt instruments | 3abla | — | .4 | .9 | † 49.4 | 49.5 | 49.8 | 40.9 | 53.6 | 498.5 | −101.5 | −62.6 | −22.9 |
| Portfolio investment: assets | 3b9aa | — | — | — | † 14.4 | .1 | 5.7 | −27.1 | 34.6 | 68.3 | 39.1 | −8.0 | −43.9 |
| Equity & investment fund shares | 3baaa | .... | .... | .... | .... | .... | 6.0 | .... | 6.2 | 2.1 | 18.4 | 18.4 | 19.3 |
| Debt securities | 3bbaa | — | — | — | † 14.4 | .1 | −.3 | −27.1 | 28.3 | 66.1 | 20.8 | −26.4 | −63.2 |
| Portfolio investment: liabilities | 3b9la | 1.1 | 1.1 | 198.2 | † 132.7 | −310.0 | .... | −17.6 | −13.3 | 12.0 | 21.3 | −20.9 | −8.0 |
| Equity & investment fund shares | 3bala | .... | .... | .... | .... | .... | .... | .... | .... | 8.4 | 19.3 | −21.0 | −11.1 |
| Debt securities | 3bbla | 1.1 | 1.1 | 198.2 | † 132.7 | −310.0 | .... | −17.6 | −13.3 | 3.6 | 2.0 | .1 | 3.1 |
| Fin. der.& empl.stk.ops.(ESOs): net | 3c9na | .... | .... | .... | .... | .... | .... | .... | .... | .... | .... | .... | .... |
| Fin. der. & ESOs.: assets | 3c9aa | .... | .... | .... | .... | .... | .... | .... | .... | .... | .... | .... | .... |
| Fin. der. & ESOs.: liabilities | 3c9la | .... | .... | .... | .... | .... | .... | .... | .... | .... | .... | .... | .... |
| Other investment: assets | 3d9aa | 12.2 | 9.6 | 8.7 | † 53.9 | 10.8 | −5.4 | −8.5 | 3.9 | 318.3 | −57.0 | −46.3 | −187.4 |
| Other equity | 3daaa | .... | .... | .... | .... | .... | .... | .... | .... | .... | .... | .... | .... |
| Debt instruments | 3dzaa | 12.2 | 9.6 | 8.7 | † 53.9 | 10.8 | −5.4 | −8.5 | 3.9 | 318.3 | −57.0 | −46.3 | −187.4 |
| Other investment: liabilities | 3d9la | −49.7 | 59.6 | −103.7 | † −4.8 | 23.4 | −69.6 | −7.8 | 89.7 | 177.3 | −30.5 | 17.6 | −127.6 |
| Other equity | 3dala | .... | .... | .... | .... | .... | .... | .... | .... | .... | .... | .... | .... |
| Debt instruments | 3dzla | −49.7 | 59.6 | −103.7 | † −4.8 | 23.4 | −69.6 | −7.8 | 89.7 | 177.3 | −30.5 | 17.6 | −127.6 |
| Curr.+ cap.− finan. acct. balance | 4y9na | −93.2 | −29.1 | 91.6 | † 31.9 | −388.5 | −44.0 | 224.7 | −67.4 | 131.1 | 45.8 | −35.1 | 78.5 |
| D. Net Errors and Omissions | 409na | .7 | −.3 | 1.6 | † 29.3 | 78.9 | 141.2 | 77.6 | 89.8 | −109.4 | 48.9 | 76.3 | −8.0 |
| E. Reserves and Related Items | 4z9na | −92.5 | −29.4 | 93.2 | † 61.2 | −309.6 | 97.2 | 302.3 | 22.4 | 21.7 | 94.7 | 41.2 | 70.6 |
| Reserve assets | 3e9aa | −33.0 | 22.0 | 62.0 | † −45.1 | 46.8 | 132.8 | 81.1 | 36.0 | 27.9 | 96.4 | 42.5 | 72.6 |
| Credit and loans from the IMF | 3dcla | — | — | — | † — | 9.1 | 9.0 | 12.8 | 5.6 | 5.2 | 1.7 | 1.3 | 2.0 |
| Exceptional financing | 409la | 59.6 | 51.3 | −31.3 | † −106.3 | 347.3 | 26.6 | −234.0 | 7.9 | 1.1 | .... | .... | .... |

*Excludes components in group E

**International Investment Position** — *Millions of US Dollars*

| Item | Code | 2004 | 2005 | 2006 | 2007 | 2008 | 2009 | 2010 | 2011 | 2012 | 2013 | 2014 | 2015 |
|---|---|---|---|---|---|---|---|---|---|---|---|---|---|
| Assets | 809aa | .... | .... | .... | .... | .... | .... | .... | .... | 5,097.1 | 4,038.5 | 3,956.0 | 3,759.2 |
| Direct investment | 8a9aa | .... | .... | .... | .... | .... | .... | .... | .... | 2,211.7 | 1,171.2 | 1,061.9 | 956.3 |
| Equity & investment fund shares | 8aaaa | .... | .... | .... | .... | .... | .... | .... | .... | 221.5 | 209.4 | 200.1 | 189.2 |
| Debt instruments | 8abaa | .... | .... | .... | .... | .... | .... | .... | .... | 1,990.2 | 961.8 | 861.9 | 767.1 |
| Portfolio investment | 8b9aa | .... | .... | .... | .... | .... | .... | .... | .... | 1,231.6 | 1,181.7 | 1,181.1 | 1,145.0 |
| Equity & investment fund shares | 8baaa | .... | .... | .... | .... | .... | .... | .... | .... | 996.9 | 1,015.3 | 1,033.7 | 1,053.0 |
| Debt securities | 8bbaa | .... | .... | .... | .... | .... | .... | .... | .... | 234.7 | 166.3 | 147.4 | 91.9 |
| Fin. der.(oth.than reserves) & ESOs | 8c9aa | .... | .... | .... | .... | .... | .... | .... | .... | .... | .... | .... | .... |
| Other investment | 8d9aa | .... | .... | .... | .... | .... | .... | .... | .... | 1,345.5 | 1,306.4 | 1,249.6 | 1,122.5 |
| Other equity | 8daaa | .... | .... | .... | .... | .... | .... | .... | .... | .... | .... | .... | .... |
| Debt instruments | 8dzaa | .... | .... | .... | .... | .... | .... | .... | .... | 1,345.5 | 1,306.4 | 1,249.6 | 1,122.5 |
| Reserve assets | 8e9aa | .... | .... | .... | .... | .... | .... | .... | .... | 308.3 | 379.2 | 463.3 | 535.5 |
| Liabilities | 809la | .... | .... | .... | .... | .... | .... | .... | .... | 4,705.4 | 4,410.0 | 4,162.1 | 4,008.5 |
| Direct investment | 8a9la | .... | .... | .... | .... | .... | .... | .... | .... | 2,973.4 | 2,780.7 | 2,536.8 | 2,542.8 |
| Equity & investment fund shares | 8aala | .... | .... | .... | .... | .... | .... | .... | .... | 825.1 | 739.0 | 721.3 | 706.4 |
| Debt instruments | 8abla | .... | .... | .... | .... | .... | .... | .... | .... | 2,148.3 | 2,041.7 | 1,815.6 | 1,836.4 |
| Portfolio investment | 8b9la | .... | .... | .... | .... | .... | .... | .... | .... | 223.6 | 244.9 | 224.0 | 216.0 |
| Equity & investment fund shares | 8bala | .... | .... | .... | .... | .... | .... | .... | .... | 49.7 | 69.0 | 48.0 | 36.9 |
| Debt securities | 8bbla | .... | .... | .... | .... | .... | .... | .... | .... | 173.9 | 175.9 | 176.0 | 179.1 |
| Fin. der.(oth.than reserves) & ESOs | 8c9la | .... | .... | .... | .... | .... | .... | .... | .... | .... | .... | .... | .... |
| Other investment | 8d9la | .... | .... | .... | .... | .... | .... | .... | .... | 1,508.4 | 1,384.4 | 1,401.3 | 1,249.7 |
| Other equity | 8dala | .... | .... | .... | .... | .... | .... | .... | .... | .... | .... | .... | .... |
| Debt instruments | 8dzla | .... | .... | .... | .... | .... | .... | .... | .... | 1,508.4 | 1,384.4 | 1,401.3 | 1,249.7 |

# Seychelles 718

| | | 2004 | 2005 | 2006 | 2007 | 2008 | 2009 | 2010 | 2011 | 2012 | 2013 | 2014 | 2015 |
|---|---|---|---|---|---|---|---|---|---|---|---|---|---|
| **Government Finance** | | | | | | | | | | | | | |
| **Cash Flow Statement** | | | | | | | | | | | | | |
| **General Government** | | | | | | *Millions of Rupees: Fiscal Year Ends December 31* | | | | | | | |
| Cash Receipts:Operating Activities... | c1 | .... | .... | .... | .... | .... | .... | .... | .... | † 6,071.3 | 6,163.2 | 6,484.2 | .... |
| Taxes.............................. | c11 | .... | .... | .... | .... | .... | .... | .... | .... | † 4,685.9 | 4,676.0 | 5,291.5 | .... |
| Social Contributions...................... | c12 | .... | .... | .... | .... | .... | .... | .... | .... | † — | | | .... |
| Grants................................ | c13 | .... | .... | .... | .... | .... | .... | .... | .... | † 628.0 | 690.8 | 540.5 | .... |
| Other Receipts.............................. | c14 | .... | .... | .... | .... | .... | .... | .... | .... | † 757.4 | 796.4 | 652.3 | .... |
| Cash Payments:Operating Activities. | c2 | .... | .... | .... | .... | .... | .... | .... | .... | † 4,369.4 | 4,778.1 | 4,984.1 | .... |
| Compensation of Employees........... | c21 | .... | .... | .... | .... | .... | .... | .... | .... | † 1,053.2 | 1,129.4 | 1,229.8 | .... |
| Purchases of Goods & Services....... | c22 | .... | .... | .... | .... | .... | .... | .... | .... | † 1,290.2 | 1,218.5 | 1,265.9 | .... |
| Interest.................................... | c24 | .... | .... | .... | .... | .... | .... | .... | .... | † 598.7 | 789.8 | 394.0 | .... |
| Subsidies.................................. | c25 | .... | .... | .... | .... | .... | .... | .... | .... | † 164.6 | 90.7 | 90.2 | .... |
| Grants..................................... | c26 | .... | .... | .... | .... | .... | .... | .... | .... | † 348.2 | 572.1 | 985.5 | .... |
| Social Benefits............................. | c27 | .... | .... | .... | .... | .... | .... | .... | .... | † 594.7 | 755.5 | 861.5 | .... |
| Other Payments............................. | c28 | .... | .... | .... | .... | .... | .... | .... | .... | † 319.8 | 222.0 | 157.3 | .... |
| Net Cash Inflow:Operating Act.[1-2] | ccio | .... | .... | .... | .... | .... | .... | .... | .... | † 1,701.8 | 1,385.1 | 1,500.2 | .... |
| Net Cash Outflow:Invest. in NFA...... | c31 | .... | .... | .... | .... | .... | .... | .... | .... | † 1,130.7 | 1,327.8 | 876.9 | .... |
| Purchases of Nonfinancial Assets... | c31.1 | .... | .... | .... | .... | .... | .... | .... | .... | † 1,214.0 | 1,379.0 | 916.2 | .... |
| Sales of Nonfinancial Assets........... | c31.2 | .... | .... | .... | .... | .... | .... | .... | .... | † 83.3 | 51.2 | 39.3 | .... |
| Cash Surplus/Deficit [1-2-31=1-2M] | ccsd | .... | .... | .... | .... | .... | .... | .... | .... | † 571.2 | 57.3 | 623.2 | .... |
| Net Acq. Fin. Assets, excl. Cash...... | c32x | .... | .... | .... | .... | .... | .... | .... | .... | † −36.9 | 5.9 | 42.0 | .... |
| Domestic........................................ | c321x | .... | .... | .... | .... | .... | .... | .... | .... | † −36.9 | 5.9 | 42.0 | .... |
| Foreign.......................................... | c322x | .... | .... | .... | .... | .... | .... | .... | .... | † — | — | — | .... |
| Net Incurrence of Liabilities.............. | c33 | .... | .... | .... | .... | .... | .... | .... | .... | † −403.6 | −13.9 | −1,019.0 | .... |
| Domestic........................................ | c331 | .... | .... | .... | .... | .... | .... | .... | .... | † −314.3 | −126.0 | −1,084.4 | .... |
| Foreign.......................................... | c332 | .... | .... | .... | .... | .... | .... | .... | .... | † −89.4 | 112.1 | 65.4 | .... |
| Net Cash Inflow, Fin.Act.[-32x+33].. | cnfb | .... | .... | .... | .... | .... | .... | .... | .... | † −366.7 | −19.8 | −1,061.0 | .... |
| Net Change in Stock of Cash........... | cncb | .... | .... | .... | .... | .... | .... | .... | .... | † 204.5 | 37.5 | −437.8 | .... |
| Stat. Discrep. [32X-33+NCB-CSD].... | ccsdz | .... | .... | .... | .... | .... | .... | .... | .... | † — | — | — | .... |
| Memo Item:Cash Expenditure[2+31] | c2m | .... | .... | .... | .... | .... | .... | .... | .... | † 5,500.1 | 6,105.9 | 5,861.0 | .... |
| Memo Item: Gross Debt.................. | c63 | | | | | | | | | .... | .... | .... | .... |
| **National Accounts** | | | | | | *Millions of Rupees* | | | | | | | |
| Househ.Cons.Expend.,incl.NPISHs.... | 96f | 2,414.2 | 2,521.9 | .... | .... | .... | .... | .... | .... | .... | .... | .... | .... |
| Government Consumption Expend... | 91f | 1,018.5 | 883.1 | .... | .... | .... | .... | .... | .... | .... | .... | .... | .... |
| Exports of Goods and Services.......... | 90c | 3,456.9 | 3,718.3 | .... | .... | .... | .... | .... | .... | .... | .... | .... | .... |
| Imports of Goods and Services (-)..... | 98c | 4,558.6 | 3,730.4 | .... | .... | .... | .... | .... | .... | .... | .... | .... | .... |
| Gross Domestic Product (GDP)........ | 99b | 4,616.3 | 5,055.1 | 5,610.3 | 6,926.5 | 9,147.2 | 11,533.4 | 11,705.4 | 13,195.9 | 15,543.6 | 17,014.7 | 19,257.6 | .... |
| | | | | | | *Millions: Midyear Estimates* | | | | | | | |
| **Population.................................** | 99z | .09 | .09 | .09 | .09 | .09 | .09 | .09 | .09 | .09 | .10 | .10 | .10 |

# Sierra Leone 724

| | | 2004 | 2005 | 2006 | 2007 | 2008 | 2009 | 2010 | 2011 | 2012 | 2013 | 2014 | 2015 |
|---|---|---|---|---|---|---|---|---|---|---|---|---|---|
| **Exchange Rates** | | | | | | | *Leones per SDR: End of Period* | | | | | | | |
| Market Rate | aa | 4,321.9 | 4,191.4 | 4,474.0 | 4,705.4 | 4,685.9 | 6,044.5 | 6,465.1 | 6,721.0 | 6,661.2 | 6,708.8 | 7,176.4 | 7,814.3 |
| | | | | | | *Leones per US Dollar: End of Period (ae) Period Average (rf)* | | | | | | | | |
| Market Rate | ae | 2,860.5 | 2,932.5 | 2,973.9 | 2,977.6 | 3,042.2 | 3,855.7 | 4,198.0 | 4,377.7 | 4,334.1 | 4,356.4 | 4,953.3 | 5,639.1 |
| Market Rate | rf | 2,701.3 | 2,889.6 | 2,961.9 | 2,985.2 | 2,981.5 | 3,385.7 | 3,978.1 | 4,349.2 | 4,344.0 | 4,332.5 | 4,524.2 | 5,080.7 |
| | | | | | | *Index Numbers (2010=100): Period Averages* | | | | | | | | |
| Market Rate | ahx | 147.3 | 137.6 | 134.2 | 133.2 | 133.3 | 118.2 | 100.0 | 91.4 | 91.5 | 91.8 | 88.0 | 78.4 |
| Nominal Effective Exchange Rate | nec | 156.9 | 144.4 | 139.8 | 130.4 | 126.6 | 119.1 | 100.0 | 87.8 | 92.4 | 93.2 | 90.3 | 91.4 |
| CPI-Based Real Effect. Ex. Rate | rec | 91.1 | 91.7 | 94.7 | 95.6 | 102.1 | 103.5 | 100.0 | 100.6 | 117.3 | 126.9 | 130.7 | 142.4 |
| **Fund Position** | | | | | | | *Millions of SDRs: End of Period* | | | | | | | |
| Quota | 2f.s | 103.70 | 103.70 | 103.70 | 103.70 | 103.70 | 103.70 | 103.70 | 103.70 | 103.70 | 103.70 | 103.70 | 103.70 |
| SDR Holdings | 1b.s | 32.82 | 22.93 | 19.44 | 19.41 | 19.73 | 120.94 | 119.59 | 116.40 | 111.80 | 107.19 | 107.96 | 107.52 |
| Reserve Position in the Fund | 1c.s | .02 | .02 | .02 | .02 | .02 | .02 | .02 | .02 | .02 | .02 | .02 | .02 |
| Total Fund Cred.&Loans Outstg. | 2tl | 126.05 | 134.39 | 23.11 | 23.11 | 34.51 | 46.70 | 73.36 | 78.97 | 78.79 | 83.06 | 109.75 | 182.64 |
| SDR Allocations | 1bd | 17.46 | 17.46 | 17.46 | 17.46 | 17.46 | 99.51 | 99.51 | 99.51 | 99.51 | 99.51 | 99.51 | 99.51 |
| **International Liquidity** | | | | | | *Millions of US Dollars Unless Otherwise Indicated: End of Period* | | | | | | | | |
| Total Reserves minus Gold | 1l.d | 125.1 | 170.5 | 183.9 | 216.6 | 220.2 | 405.0 | 409.0 | 439.1 | 478.0 | 532.5 | 600.8 | 620.5 |
| SDR Holdings | 1b.d | 51.0 | 32.8 | 29.2 | 30.7 | 30.4 | 189.6 | 184.2 | 178.7 | 171.8 | 165.1 | 156.4 | 149.0 |
| Reserve Position in the Fund | 1c.d | — | — | — | — | — | — | — | — | — | — | — | — |
| Foreign Exchange | 1d.d | 74.1 | 137.7 | 154.7 | 185.8 | 189.7 | 215.3 | 224.8 | 260.4 | 306.1 | 367.4 | 444.3 | 471.5 |
| Central Bank: Other Assets | 3..d | 4.1 | 3.5 | 19.5 | 4.1 | 4.6 | 5.0 | 4.7 | 3.7 | 6.1 | 6.5 | 7.1 | 7.1 |
| Central Bank: Other Liabs. | 4..d | 13.4 | 10.4 | 25.8 | 10.0 | 11.3 | 16.3 | 17.3 | 16.2 | 10.1 | 12.7 | 15.6 | 13.0 |
| Other Depository Corps.: Assets | 7a.d | 35.0 | 51.0 | 69.5 | † 103.5 | 117.3 | 136.9 | 168.1 | 217.5 | 276.0 | 305.4 | 265.1 | 242.1 |
| Other Depository Corps.: Liabs. | 7b.d | — | — | — | † 20.2 | 16.9 | 17.6 | 34.5 | 18.9 | 40.3 | 60.3 | 21.6 | 8.0 |
| **Central Bank** | | | | | | | *Millions of Leones: End of Period* | | | | | | | |
| Net Foreign Assets | 11n | −305,358 | −156,398 | 349,006 | 427,068 | 372,673 | 372,238 | 278,681 | 400,805 | 607,199 | 815,116 | 1,189,595 | 1,027,234 |
| Claims on Nonresidents | 11 | 370,568 | 510,633 | 607,155 | 647,524 | 650,657 | 1,318,857 | 1,468,962 | 1,671,393 | 1,838,578 | 2,095,121 | 2,768,528 | 3,305,440 |
| Liabilities to Nonresidents | 16c | 675,926 | 667,031 | 258,149 | 220,456 | 277,984 | 946,619 | 1,190,281 | 1,270,587 | 1,231,379 | 1,280,005 | 1,578,933 | 2,278,206 |
| Claims on Other Depository Corps. | 12e | 3,154 | 3,346 | 3,128 | 1,885 | 1,530 | 6,000 | 21,731 | 5,898 | 13,539 | 9,407 | 4,229 | 5,663 |
| Net Claims on Central Government | 12an | 585,365 | 513,862 | 546,256 | 39,648 | 129,155 | 253,619 | 554,087 | 593,311 | 487,507 | 425,209 | 606,052 | 977,000 |
| Claims on Central Government | 12a | 1,245,240 | 1,369,570 | 654,587 | 752,450 | 616,140 | 776,717 | 1,153,824 | 755,587 | 575,850 | 562,060 | 1,008,184 | 1,129,659 |
| Liabilities to Central Government | 16d | 659,875 | 855,708 | 108,331 | 712,802 | 486,985 | 523,098 | 599,737 | 162,276 | 88,343 | 136,852 | 402,132 | 152,659 |
| Claims on Other Sectors | 12s | 2,817 | 10,647 | 7,658 | 7,853 | 8,865 | 11,747 | 11,561 | 11,948 | 13,396 | 18,021 | 11,378 | 28,583 |
| Claims on Other Financial Corps. | 12g | 259 | 5,135 | 5,135 | 5,137 | 6,135 | 6,280 | 6,194 | 6,245 | 6,308 | 6,394 | 1,000 | 1,000 |
| Claims on State & Local Govts. | 12b | — | — | — | — | — | — | — | — | — | — | — | — |
| Claims on Public Nonfin. Corps. | 12c | — | — | — | — | — | — | — | — | — | — | — | — |
| Claims on Private Sector | 12d | 2,558 | 5,513 | 2,523 | 2,715 | 2,731 | 5,467 | 5,368 | 5,703 | 7,088 | 11,627 | 10,378 | 27,583 |
| Monetary Base | 14 | 234,712 | 290,617 | 321,643 | 383,671 | 443,282 | 537,219 | 724,111 | 815,403 | 995,475 | 1,164,662 | 1,524,179 | 1,687,802 |
| Currency in Circulation | 14a | 221,425 | 255,078 | 294,682 | 333,324 | 383,299 | 486,438 | 631,512 | 707,501 | 902,941 | 907,433 | 1,136,945 | 1,356,504 |
| Liabs. to Other Depository Corps. | 14c | 10,237 | 31,234 | 23,053 | 41,831 | 54,744 | 48,543 | 90,547 | 105,860 | 90,635 | 251,138 | 384,169 | 330,939 |
| Liabilities to Other Sectors | 14d | 3,051 | 4,305 | 3,908 | 8,516 | 5,239 | 2,239 | 2,052 | 2,041 | 1,899 | 6,090 | 3,064 | 359 |
| Other Liabs. to Other Dep. Corps. | 14n | — | — | — | — | — | — | — | — | — | — | — | — |
| Dep. & Sec. Excl. f/Monetary Base | 14o | 3,944 | 11,055 | 10,423 | 10,150 | 12,514 | 13,365 | 18,032 | 17,922 | 12,767 | 19,748 | 18,781 | 12,680 |
| Deposits Included in Broad Money | 15 | 1,062 | 794 | 750 | 390 | 401 | 1,105 | 1,909 | 503 | 691 | 2,246 | 649 | 707 |
| Sec.Ot.th.Shares Incl.in Brd. Money | 16a | — | — | — | — | — | — | — | — | — | — | — | — |
| Deposits Excl. from Broad Money | 16b | 2,882 | 10,261 | 9,673 | 9,760 | 12,113 | 12,261 | 16,123 | 17,419 | 12,077 | 17,501 | 18,131 | 11,973 |
| Sec.Ot.th.Shares Excl.f/Brd.Money | 16s | — | — | — | — | — | — | — | — | — | — | — | — |
| Loans | 16l | 1,226 | 750 | 39 | 92 | — | — | — | — | — | — | — | — |
| Financial Derivatives | 16m | — | — | — | — | — | — | — | — | — | — | — | — |
| Shares and Other Equity | 17a | −107,735 | −154,218 | −5,825 | −81,630 | −91,078 | −49,269 | 243,360 | 225,550 | 179,548 | 197,230 | 414,775 | 541,711 |
| Other Items (Net) | 17r | 153,830 | 223,255 | 579,766 | 164,172 | 147,506 | 142,289 | −119,443 | −46,913 | −66,149 | −113,886 | −146,479 | −203,712 |
| Memo Item: | | | | | | | | | | | | | | |
| Total Assets | 10ra | 2,145,832 | 2,375,418 | 1,791,606 | 1,992,965 | 1,859,894 | 2,571,087 | 3,426,520 | 3,274,584 | 3,262,682 | 3,527,793 | 4,704,814 | 5,435,307 |
| **Other Depository Corporations** | | | | | | | *Millions of Leones: End of Period* | | | | | | | |
| Net Foreign Assets | 21n | 100,047 | 149,532 | 206,817 | † 247,851 | 305,441 | 460,168 | 560,814 | 869,580 | 1,021,500 | 1,067,847 | 1,206,189 | 1,319,876 |
| Claims on Nonresidents | 21 | 100,047 | 149,532 | 206,817 | † 307,853 | 356,975 | 527,946 | 705,643 | 952,158 | 1,196,017 | 1,330,350 | 1,313,064 | 1,365,209 |
| Liabilities to Nonresidents | 26c | — | — | — | † 60,002 | 51,534 | 67,778 | 144,830 | 82,578 | 174,517 | 262,503 | 106,876 | 45,332 |
| Claims on Central Bank | 20 | 27,999 | 56,276 | 39,860 | † 56,368 | 93,262 | 170,251 | 169,300 | 183,203 | 241,978 | 351,290 | 498,812 | 501,685 |
| Currency | 20a | 16,692 | 23,804 | 19,277 | † 26,396 | 42,945 | 70,743 | 74,252 | 65,670 | 101,868 | 131,030 | 139,402 | 180,220 |
| Reserve Deposits and Securities | 20b | 11,307 | 32,472 | 20,583 | † 29,972 | 50,317 | 99,508 | 95,048 | 117,532 | 140,110 | 220,259 | 359,410 | 321,465 |
| Other Claims | 20n | — | — | — | † — | — | — | — | — | — | — | — | — |
| Net Claims on Central Government | 22an | 131,828 | 171,210 | 213,351 | † 216,376 | 316,887 | 195,236 | 337,260 | 418,784 | 654,357 | 863,951 | 1,252,148 | 1,551,729 |
| Claims on Central Government | 22a | 151,374 | 205,695 | 234,439 | † 264,617 | 403,021 | 376,158 | 467,696 | 547,658 | 794,124 | 1,151,851 | 1,561,309 | 1,896,117 |
| Liabilities to Central Government | 26d | 19,547 | 34,485 | 21,088 | † 48,241 | 86,134 | 180,923 | 130,436 | 128,874 | 139,767 | 287,899 | 309,161 | 344,387 |
| Claims on Other Sectors | 22s | 152,349 | 175,038 | 205,752 | † 290,897 | 440,816 | 734,541 | 874,853 | 1,068,021 | 1,157,807 | 1,294,755 | 1,361,459 | 1,357,528 |
| Claims on Other Financial Corps. | 22g | 15,547 | 16,649 | 14,114 | † 1,901 | 2,657 | 3,752 | 6,537 | 14,882 | 15,701 | 15,079 | 16,542 | 16,542 |
| Claims on State & Local Govts. | 22b | — | — | — | † 1,724 | 7,169 | 13,479 | 17,291 | 24,199 | 49,280 | 73,234 | 86,895 | 81,199 |
| Claims on Public Nonfin. Corps. | 22c | 3,440 | 4,338 | 5,228 | † 11,174 | 17,277 | 39,483 | 54,012 | 53,494 | 72,812 | 201,378 | 199,229 | 181,798 |
| Claims on Private Sector | 22d | 133,362 | 154,052 | 186,409 | † 276,098 | 413,712 | 677,828 | 797,013 | 975,445 | 1,020,015 | 1,005,064 | 1,058,793 | 1,077,989 |
| Liabilities to Central Bank | 26g | — | — | — | † 892 | — | — | 9,810 | — | — | — | — | 3,000 |
| Transf.Dep.Included in Broad Money | 24 | 127,416 | 176,649 | 195,870 | † 403,692 | 514,966 | 742,434 | 930,593 | 1,223,037 | 1,401,939 | 1,606,295 | 2,011,181 | 2,335,797 |
| Other Dep.Included in Broad Money | 25 | 204,148 | 295,700 | 386,302 | † 290,231 | 416,776 | 557,463 | 642,327 | 899,033 | 1,169,037 | 1,343,891 | 1,556,236 | 1,588,179 |
| Sec.Ot.th.Shares Incl.in Brd. Money | 26a | — | — | — | † — | — | — | — | — | — | — | — | — |
| Deposits Excl. from Broad Money | 26b | 160 | 259 | 183 | † — | 76 | 8,249 | 2,457 | 1,063 | 727 | 545 | 639 | 656 |
| Sec.Ot.th.Shares Excl.f/Brd.Money | 26s | — | — | — | † — | — | — | — | — | — | — | — | — |
| Loans | 26l | — | — | — | † 2,000 | — | 25,085 | 11,860 | — | — | — | — | 500 |
| Financial Derivatives | 26m | — | — | — | † — | — | — | — | — | — | — | — | — |
| Insurance Technical Reserves | 26r | — | — | — | † — | — | — | — | — | — | — | — | — |
| Shares and Other Equity | 27a | 102,086 | 123,817 | 137,352 | † 197,509 | 263,757 | 352,239 | 404,155 | 458,488 | 543,609 | 597,767 | 591,027 | 663,758 |
| Other Items (Net) | 27r | −21,587 | −44,368 | −53,928 | † −82,832 | −39,170 | −125,274 | −58,975 | −42,033 | −39,671 | 29,346 | 159,527 | 138,928 |
| Memo Item: | | | | | | | | | | | | | | |
| Total Assets | 20ra | 500,455 | 699,186 | 828,754 | † 1,125,500 | 1,599,364 | 2,151,125 | 2,552,957 | 3,136,979 | 3,792,211 | 4,533,754 | 5,134,113 | 5,601,548 |

# Sierra Leone 724

| | | 2004 | 2005 | 2006 | 2007 | 2008 | 2009 | 2010 | 2011 | 2012 | 2013 | 2014 | 2015 |
|---|---|---|---|---|---|---|---|---|---|---|---|---|---|
| **Depository Corporations** | | | | | | *Millions of Leones: End of Period* | | | | | | | |
| Net Foreign Assets.................... | 31n | −205,311 | −6,866 | 555,823 | † 674,919 | 678,114 | 832,407 | 839,494 | 1,270,385 | 1,628,700 | 1,882,963 | 2,395,784 | 2,347,110 |
| Claims on Nonresidents................ | 31 | 470,615 | 660,165 | 813,972 | † 955,377 | 1,007,631 | 1,846,803 | 2,174,605 | 2,623,551 | 3,034,595 | 3,425,471 | 4,081,592 | 4,670,649 |
| Liabilities to Nonresidents............ | 36c | 675,926 | 667,031 | 258,149 | † 280,458 | 329,517 | 1,014,396 | 1,335,111 | 1,353,166 | 1,405,895 | 1,542,508 | 1,685,808 | 2,323,539 |
| Domestic Claims........................ | 32 | 872,359 | 870,758 | 973,016 | † 554,774 | 895,723 | 1,195,143 | 1,777,761 | 2,092,063 | 2,313,066 | 2,601,936 | 3,231,038 | 3,914,841 |
| Net Claims on Central Government | 32an | 717,193 | 685,073 | 759,607 | † 256,024 | 446,042 | 448,855 | 891,347 | 1,012,095 | 1,141,863 | 1,289,160 | 1,858,200 | 2,528,729 |
| Claims on Central Government.... | 32a | 1,396,615 | 1,575,265 | 889,026 | † 1,017,067 | 1,019,161 | 1,152,876 | 1,621,520 | 1,303,245 | 1,369,974 | 1,713,911 | 2,569,493 | 3,025,776 |
| Liabilities to Central Government. | 36d | 679,422 | 890,193 | 129,419 | † 761,044 | 573,119 | 704,021 | 730,173 | 291,150 | 228,110 | 424,751 | 711,293 | 497,046 |
| Claims on Other Sectors............. | 32s | 155,166 | 185,686 | 213,410 | † 298,750 | 449,681 | 746,288 | 886,414 | 1,079,968 | 1,171,203 | 1,312,776 | 1,372,838 | 1,386,111 |
| Claims on Other Financial Corps.. | 32g | 15,807 | 21,783 | 19,249 | † 7,038 | 8,792 | 10,032 | 12,730 | 21,127 | 22,009 | 21,473 | 17,542 | 17,542 |
| Claims on State & Local Govts..... | 32b | — | — | — | † 1,724 | 7,169 | 13,479 | 17,291 | 24,199 | 49,280 | 73,234 | 86,895 | 81,199 |
| Claims on Public Nonfin. Corps.... | 32c | 3,440 | 4,338 | 5,228 | † 11,174 | 17,277 | 39,483 | 54,012 | 53,494 | 72,812 | 201,378 | 199,229 | 181,798 |
| Claims on Private Sector............. | 32d | 135,919 | 159,565 | 188,933 | † 278,814 | 416,443 | 683,295 | 802,381 | 981,148 | 1,027,103 | 1,016,691 | 1,069,171 | 1,105,572 |
| Broad Money Liabilities................... | 35l | 540,409 | 708,722 | 862,235 | † 1,009,757 | 1,277,737 | 1,718,934 | 2,134,141 | 2,766,444 | 3,374,638 | 3,734,925 | 4,568,673 | 5,101,326 |
| Currency Outside Depository Corps | 34a | 204,732 | 231,274 | 275,405 | † 306,928 | 340,354 | 415,695 | 557,260 | 641,831 | 801,073 | 776,403 | 997,543 | 1,176,284 |
| Transferable Deposits................... | 34 | 128,620 | 177,443 | 196,620 | † 404,082 | 515,368 | 743,538 | 932,502 | 1,223,540 | 1,402,630 | 1,611,090 | 2,012,230 | 2,336,504 |
| Other Deposits.......................... | 35 | 207,057 | 300,005 | 390,210 | † 298,746 | 422,015 | 559,702 | 644,379 | 901,074 | 1,170,936 | 1,347,432 | 1,558,900 | 1,588,538 |
| Securities Other than Shares.......... | 36a | — | — | — | † — | — | — | — | — | — | — | — | — |
| Deposits Excl. from Broad Money..... | 36b | 3,042 | 10,520 | 9,857 | † 9,760 | 12,189 | 20,510 | 18,579 | 18,482 | 12,804 | 18,046 | 18,770 | 12,629 |
| Sec.Ot.th.Shares Excl.f/Brd.Money.... | 36s | — | — | — | † — | — | — | — | — | — | — | — | — |
| Loans............................................ | 36l | 1,226 | 750 | 39 | † 2,092 | — | 25,085 | 11,860 | — | — | — | — | 500 |
| Financial Derivatives...................... | 36m | — | — | — | † — | — | — | — | — | — | — | — | — |
| Insurance Technical Reserves.......... | 36r | — | — | — | † — | — | — | — | — | — | — | — | — |
| Shares and Other Equity................. | 37a | −5,649 | −30,401 | 131,528 | † 115,879 | 172,679 | 302,970 | 647,514 | 684,038 | 723,157 | 794,996 | 1,005,801 | 1,205,469 |
| Other Items (Net)........................ | 37r | 128,020 | 174,302 | 525,181 | † 92,205 | 111,233 | −39,950 | −194,839 | −106,516 | −168,833 | −63,068 | 33,577 | −57,973 |
| Broad Money Liabs., Seasonally Adj. | 35l.b | 550,259 | 692,991 | 843,426 | † 976,651 | 1,235,334 | 1,661,052 | 2,060,632 | 2,669,502 | 3,257,309 | 3,608,909 | 4,418,959 | 4,935,012 |
| **Monetary Aggregates** | | | | | | *Millions of Leones: End of Period* | | | | | | | |
| Broad Money.............................. | 59m | 540,409 | 708,722 | 862,235 | 1,009,757 | 1,277,737 | 1,718,934 | 2,134,141 | 2,766,444 | 3,374,638 | 3,734,925 | 4,568,673 | 5,101,326 |
| o/w:Currency Issued by Cent.Govt | 59m.a | — | — | — | — | — | — | — | — | — | — | — | — |
| o/w: Dep.in Nonfin. Corporations. | 59m.b | — | — | — | — | — | — | — | — | — | — | — | — |
| o/w:Secs. Issued by Central Govt.. | 59m.c | — | — | — | — | — | — | — | — | — | — | — | — |
| Money (National Definitions) | | | | | | | | | | | | | |
| Reserve Money........................... | 19mb | 234,712 | 290,617 | 321,643 | 383,671 | 443,282 | 537,219 | 724,111 | 815,403 | 995,475 | 1,164,662 | 1,524,179 | 1,687,802 |
| M0................................................ | 19mc | 204,732 | 231,274 | 275,405 | 306,928 | 340,354 | 415,695 | 557,260 | 641,831 | 801,073 | 776,403 | 997,543 | 1,176,284 |
| M1................................................ | 59ma | 336,261 | 413,022 | 475,933 | 543,532 | 655,410 | 827,011 | 1,026,378 | 1,233,910 | 1,481,192 | 1,614,486 | 2,140,329 | 2,584,969 |
| M2................................................ | 59mb | 540,409 | 708,722 | 862,235 | 1,009,757 | 1,277,737 | 1,718,934 | 2,134,141 | 2,766,444 | 3,374,638 | 3,734,925 | 4,568,673 | 5,101,326 |
| **Interest Rates** | | | | | | *Percent Per Annum* | | | | | | | |
| Central Bank Policy Rate (EOP)........ | 60 | .... | .... | .... | .... | .... | .... | .... | 20.00 | 20.00 | 10.00 | 10.00 | 9.50 |
| Repurchase Agreement Rate (EOP)... | 60.q | .... | .... | .... | .... | .... | .... | .... | 22.00 | 22.00 | 10.50 | .... | .... |
| Treasury Bill Rate........................... | 60c | 26.14 | 22.98 | 17.71 | 18.41 | 15.48 | 10.47 | 17.21 | 24.45 | 22.40 | 8.05 | 2.37 | 2.06 |
| Savings Rate................................ | 60k | 8.14 | 7.63 | 7.63 | 7.25 | 6.65 | 6.32 | 6.19 | 6.42 | 6.42 | 4.73 | 3.23 | 2.54 |
| Deposit Rate.................................. | 60l | 11.17 | 11.80 | 11.14 | 10.79 | 10.59 | 9.72 | 9.47 | 10.31 | 10.39 | 8.91 | 6.61 | 4.49 |
| Lending Rate.................................. | 60p | 22.08 | 24.58 | 24.00 | 25.00 | 24.50 | 22.17 | 21.25 | 21.00 | 21.00 | 20.56 | 19.41 | 18.73 |
| **Prices** | | | | | | *Index Numbers (2010=100): Period Averages* | | | | | | | |
| Consumer Prices............................ | 64 | .... | .... | 61.2 | 68.3 | 78.5 | † 85.7 | 100.0 | 116.2 | 131.1 | 144.6 | 155.2 | 167.6 |
| **Intl. Transactions & Positions** | | | | | | *Millions of Leones* | | | | | | | |
| Exports........................................... | 70 | 377,546 | 458,055 | 676,225 | 729,894 | 641,797 | 788,564 | 1,357,289 | 1,521,014 | 4,871,105 | 8,276,288 | 6,921,722 | .... |
| Imports, c.i.f.................................... | 71 | 606,711 | 985,482 | 1,169,256 | 1,332,783 | 1,590,338 | 1,764,303 | 3,083,669 | 7,471,822 | 6,964,739 | 7,003,118 | 7,046,331 | .... |

# Sierra Leone   724

| | | 2004 | 2005 | 2006 | 2007 | 2008 | 2009 | 2010 | 2011 | 2012 | 2013 | 2014 | 2015 |
|---|---|---|---|---|---|---|---|---|---|---|---|---|---|
| **Balance of Payments** | | | | | | | *Millions of US Dollars* | | | | | | |
| A. Current Account* | 109bx | −140.7 | −170.6 | −139.0 | −216.9 | −300.0 | −424.2 | −745.9 | −1,997.8 | −1,286.3 | −775.3 | −1,317.1 | .... |
| Goods, credit (exports) | 1a9cx | 146.1 | 183.6 | 262.5 | 287.2 | 271.5 | 267.7 | 360.2 | 381.5 | 1,053.5 | 1,536.1 | 1,281.7 | .... |
| Goods, debit (imports) | 1a9dx | 274.3 | 361.7 | 351.2 | 395.4 | 471.2 | 617.5 | 880.7 | 2,056.0 | 1,970.5 | 1,571.1 | 1,634.9 | .... |
| Balance on goods | 1a9bx | −128.2 | −178.0 | −88.7 | −108.3 | −199.7 | −349.9 | −520.6 | −1,674.5 | −917.0 | −34.9 | −353.2 | .... |
| Services, credit (exports) | 1b9cx | 61.5 | 78.2 | 40.0 | 43.4 | 59.0 | 100.7 | 56.7 | 156.7 | 177.8 | 221.2 | 204.6 | .... |
| Services, debit (imports) | 1b9dx | 84.4 | 91.4 | 84.0 | 94.3 | 121.0 | 132.1 | 251.6 | 427.7 | 525.5 | 689.1 | 1,207.8 | .... |
| Balance on Goods & Services | 1z9bx | −151.1 | −191.3 | −132.7 | −159.2 | −261.7 | −381.3 | −715.5 | −1,945.5 | −1,264.7 | −502.8 | −1,356.4 | .... |
| Primary income: credit | 1c9cx | 4.1 | 5.4 | 12.3 | 43.3 | 17.7 | 11.3 | 9.7 | 9.4 | 11.3 | 11.1 | 7.3 | .... |
| Primary income: debit | 1c9dx | 71.1 | 56.3 | 52.0 | 147.6 | 92.4 | 46.9 | 58.8 | 227.5 | 193.1 | 447.3 | 388.3 | .... |
| Balance on gds, serv. & prim. inc. | 1y9bx | −218.1 | −242.2 | −172.3 | −263.5 | −336.5 | −417.0 | −764.6 | −2,163.5 | −1,446.5 | −939.0 | −1,737.4 | .... |
| Secondary income: credit | 1d9ca | 80.3 | 73.6 | 38.2 | 49.4 | 43.9 | 58.7 | 68.8 | 187.9 | 182.8 | 176.1 | 432.7 | .... |
| Secondary income: debit | 1d9da | 2.8 | 2.0 | 4.9 | 2.8 | 7.4 | 65.9 | 50.1 | 22.2 | 22.6 | 12.4 | 12.3 | .... |
| B. Capital Account* | 209ba | 18.4 | 36.8 | 224.1 | 239.5 | 56.5 | 134.1 | 78.8 | 133.6 | 100.2 | 93.3 | 162.6 | .... |
| Capital account: credit | 209ca | 18.4 | 36.8 | 224.1 | 239.5 | 56.5 | 134.1 | 78.8 | 133.6 | 100.2 | 93.3 | 162.6 | .... |
| Capital account: debit | 209da | — | — | — | — | — | — | — | — | — | — | — | .... |
| Balance on current & capital acct. | 129bx | −122.3 | −133.8 | 85.1 | 22.6 | −243.5 | −290.1 | −667.0 | −1,864.2 | −1,186.2 | −682.0 | −1,154.4 | .... |
| C. Financial Account* | 309na | −76.2 | −62.8 | −34.6 | −90.7 | −95.4 | −384.6 | −324.8 | −1,673.1 | −1,042.2 | −752.5 | −623.6 | .... |
| Direct investment: assets | 3a9aa | — | — | .1 | −1.1 | −4.5 | −.4 | — | — | — | — | — | .... |
| Equity & investment fund shares.. | 3aaaa | — | — | — | — | — | — | — | — | — | — | — | .... |
| Debt instruments | 3abaa | — | — | .1 | −1.1 | −4.5 | −.4 | — | — | — | — | — | .... |
| Direct investment: liabilities | 3a9la | 61.2 | 90.7 | 58.9 | 95.5 | 53.1 | 110.4 | 238.4 | 950.5 | 722.4 | 429.7 | 403.9 | .... |
| Equity & investment fund shares . | 3aala | 33.8 | 53.3 | 67.0 | −11.8 | 73.8 | 84.6 | 225.3 | 769.9 | 552.9 | 421.9 | 389.3 | .... |
| Debt instruments | 3abla | 27.4 | 37.5 | −8.2 | 107.3 | −20.7 | 25.9 | 13.1 | 180.6 | 169.6 | 7.8 | 14.6 | .... |
| Portfolio investment: assets | 3b9aa | — | — | — | — | — | 26.0 | −16.3 | −12.7 | −8.6 | −3.3 | −1.2 | .... |
| Equity & investment fund shares | 3baaa | — | — | — | — | — | — | — | — | — | — | — | .... |
| Debt securities | 3bbaa | — | — | — | — | — | 26.0 | −16.3 | −12.7 | −8.6 | −3.3 | −1.2 | .... |
| Portfolio investment: liabilities | 3b9la | — | — | — | — | 1.6 | 5.6 | 2.0 | 47.2 | — | — | — | .... |
| Equity & investment fund shares . | 3bala | — | — | — | — | — | 5.6 | .1 | .1 | — | — | — | .... |
| Debt securities | 3bbla | — | — | — | — | 1.6 | — | 1.9 | 47.1 | — | — | — | .... |
| Fin. der.& empl.stk.ops.(ESOs): net. | 3c9na | — | — | — | — | — | — | — | — | — | — | — | .... |
| Fin. der. & ESOs.: assets | 3c9aa | — | — | — | — | — | — | — | — | — | — | — | .... |
| Fin. der. & ESOs.: liabilities | 3c9la | — | — | — | — | — | — | — | — | — | — | — | .... |
| Other investment: assets | 3d9aa | −10.1 | 1.9 | 8.0 | 6.1 | 2.8 | −21.7 | 5.5 | −276.3 | −16.3 | −100.0 | .7 | .... |
| Other equity | 3daaa | .... | .... | .... | .... | .... | .... | .... | .... | .... | .... | .... | .... |
| Debt instruments | 3dzaa | −10.1 | 1.9 | 8.0 | 6.1 | 2.8 | −21.7 | 5.5 | −276.3 | −16.3 | −100.0 | .7 | .... |
| Other investment: liabilities | 3d9la | 5.0 | −26.1 | −16.1 | .2 | 39.0 | 272.3 | 73.6 | 386.4 | 294.9 | 219.6 | 219.1 | .... |
| Other equity | 3dala | .... | .... | .... | .... | .... | .... | .... | .... | .... | .... | .... | .... |
| Debt instruments | 3dzla | 5.0 | −26.1 | −16.1 | .2 | 39.0 | 272.3 | 73.6 | 386.4 | 294.9 | 219.6 | 219.1 | .... |
| Curr.+ cap.− finan. acct. balance... | 4y9na | −46.1 | −71.1 | 119.7 | 113.3 | −148.1 | 94.4 | −342.3 | −191.0 | −144.0 | 70.5 | −530.9 | .... |
| D. Net Errors and Omissions | 409na | −53.6 | −58.5 | −59.4 | −143.2 | −16.7 | −190.6 | 23.0 | 49.2 | 9.7 | −139.6 | 26.1 | .... |
| E. Reserves and Related Items | 4z9na | −99.7 | −129.6 | 60.4 | −29.9 | −164.8 | −96.1 | −319.2 | −141.9 | −134.3 | −69.0 | −504.8 | .... |
| Reserve assets | 3e9aa | 45.2 | 56.4 | 11.4 | 33.9 | 9.5 | 110.5 | 19.9 | 35.4 | 40.5 | 43.3 | 88.0 | .... |
| Credit and loans from the IMF | 3dcla | 18.5 | 12.3 | −167.8 | — | 17.8 | 18.8 | 40.7 | 8.6 | −.2 | 6.6 | 40.1 | .... |
| Exceptional financing | 409la | 126.3 | 173.7 | 118.8 | 63.8 | 156.5 | 187.8 | 298.4 | 168.7 | 175.0 | 105.7 | 552.8 | .... |

*Excludes components in group E

| | | 2004 | 2005 | 2006 | 2007 | 2008 | 2009 | 2010 | 2011 | 2012 | 2013 | 2014 | 2015 |
|---|---|---|---|---|---|---|---|---|---|---|---|---|---|
| **International Investment Position** | | | | | | | *Millions of US Dollars* | | | | | | |
| Assets | 809aa | 131.2 | 188.5 | 256.3 | 376.4 | 367.1 | 525.7 | 612.1 | 817.1 | 903.9 | 982.6 | 1,023.4 | .... |
| Direct investment | 8a9aa | .... | .... | .... | .... | .... | .... | .... | .... | .... | .... | .... | .... |
| Equity & investment fund shares.. | 8aaaa | .... | .... | .... | .... | .... | .... | .... | .... | .... | .... | .... | .... |
| Debt instruments | 8abaa | .... | .... | .... | .... | .... | .... | .... | .... | .... | .... | .... | .... |
| Portfolio investment | 8b9aa | .... | .... | .... | .... | .... | .... | 27.2 | 39.9 | 38.7 | 26.6 | 27.6 | .... |
| Equity & investment fund shares.. | 8baaa | .... | .... | .... | .... | .... | .... | .... | .... | .... | .... | .... | .... |
| Debt securities | 8bbaa | .... | .... | .... | .... | .... | .... | 27.2 | 39.9 | 38.7 | 26.6 | 27.6 | .... |
| Fin. der.(oth.than reserves) & ESOs | 8c9aa | .... | .... | .... | .... | .... | .... | .... | .... | .... | .... | .... | .... |
| Other investment | 8d9aa | 25.0 | 34.0 | 83.3 | 162.5 | 158.5 | 201.8 | 244.4 | 402.9 | 448.6 | 482.3 | 447.3 | .... |
| Other equity | 8daaa | .... | .... | .... | .... | .... | .... | .... | .... | .... | .... | .... | .... |
| Debt instruments | 8dzaa | 25.0 | 34.0 | 83.3 | 162.5 | 158.5 | 201.8 | 244.4 | 402.9 | 448.6 | 482.3 | 447.3 | .... |
| Reserve assets | 8e9aa | 106.2 | 154.6 | 173.0 | 213.9 | 208.7 | 323.9 | 340.5 | 374.3 | 416.6 | 473.6 | 548.4 | .... |
| Liabilities | 809la | 2,125.3 | 2,058.1 | 2,131.6 | 1,102.9 | 1,085.8 | 1,109.3 | 1,423.9 | 2,705.8 | 3,176.7 | 2,686.4 | 2,753.4 | .... |
| Direct investment | 8a9la | 355.7 | 299.9 | 453.0 | 612.1 | 490.9 | 272.9 | 482.2 | 1,310.7 | 1,884.8 | 1,361.1 | 1,094.7 | .... |
| Equity & investment fund shares.. | 8aala | 167.4 | 52.6 | 118.4 | 74.0 | 175.8 | 173.2 | 320.7 | 949.4 | 1,565.7 | 1,142.1 | 905.1 | .... |
| Debt instruments | 8abla | 188.3 | 247.3 | 334.6 | 538.1 | 315.1 | 99.7 | 161.5 | 361.2 | 319.1 | 219.0 | 189.6 | .... |
| Portfolio investment | 8b9la | .... | .... | .... | .... | 1.6 | 17.5 | 2.2 | 238.1 | .... | .... | .... | .... |
| Equity & investment fund shares.. | 8bala | .... | .... | .... | .... | .... | .... | .2 | .8 | .... | .... | .... | .... |
| Debt securities | 8bbla | .... | .... | .... | .... | 1.6 | 17.5 | 2.0 | 237.4 | .... | .... | .... | .... |
| Fin. der.(oth.than reserves) & ESOs | 8c9la | .... | .... | .... | .... | .... | .... | .... | .... | .... | .... | .... | .... |
| Other investment | 8d9la | 1,769.6 | 1,758.2 | 1,678.7 | 490.8 | 593.4 | 819.0 | 939.5 | 1,157.0 | 1,291.9 | 1,325.3 | 1,658.7 | .... |
| Other equity | 8dala | .... | .... | .... | .... | .... | .... | .... | .... | .... | .... | .... | .... |
| Debt instruments | 8dzla | 1,769.6 | 1,758.2 | 1,678.7 | 490.8 | 593.4 | 819.0 | 939.5 | 1,157.0 | 1,291.9 | 1,325.3 | 1,658.7 | .... |

# Sierra Leone   724

| | | 2004 | 2005 | 2006 | 2007 | 2008 | 2009 | 2010 | 2011 | 2012 | 2013 | 2014 | 2015 |
|---|---|---|---|---|---|---|---|---|---|---|---|---|---|
| **Government Finance** | | | | | | | | | | | | | |
| **Cash Flow Statement** | | | | | | | | | | | | | |
| **Budgetary Central Government** | | *Billions of Leones: Fiscal Year Ends December 31* | | | | | | | | | | | |
| Cash Receipts:Operating Activities... | c1 | 616.34 | 763.38 | 841.99 | 776.20 | 926.10 | 1,250.40 | 1,551.58 | 2,170.76 | 2,506.07 | 2,827.61 | 3,185.68 | .... |
| Taxes.................... | c11 | 319.27 | 385.58 | 470.89 | 507.50 | 613.50 | 698.90 | 931.29 | 1,191.24 | 1,571.22 | 1,943.99 | 1,950.20 | .... |
| Social Contributions...................... | c12 | — | — | — | — | — | — | — | — | — | — | — | .... |
| Grants............................... | c13 | 259.38 | 351.90 | 346.55 | 239.30 | 264.60 | 500.30 | 543.95 | 708.66 | 632.56 | 547.60 | 959.48 | .... |
| Other Receipts.............................. | c14 | 37.70 | 25.90 | 24.55 | 29.40 | 48.00 | 51.20 | 76.34 | 270.86 | 302.29 | 336.02 | 276.00 | .... |
| Cash Payments:Operating Activities. | c2 | 688.09 | 822.90 | 917.33 | 824.80 | 1,184.70 | 1,452.20 | 1,401.51 | 1,672.64 | 2,185.94 | 2,209.57 | 2,670.52 | .... |
| Compensation of Employees.......... | c21 | 178.75 | 229.90 | 274.68 | 295.90 | 332.70 | 401.50 | 541.08 | 681.88 | 948.39 | 1,066.25 | 1,442.72 | .... |
| Purchases of Goods & Services....... | c22 | 191.17 | 210.40 | 210.70 | 171.00 | 261.30 | 352.20 | 535.97 | 465.54 | 540.53 | 538.04 | 635.55 | .... |
| Interest............................... | c24 | 129.56 | 125.60 | 119.95 | 112.10 | 119.50 | 103.20 | 159.18 | 250.22 | 290.83 | 301.16 | 221.36 | .... |
| Subsidies.............................. | c25 | — | — | — | — | — | — | — | 95.44 | — | — | — | .... |
| Grants............................... | c26 | 65.33 | 157.40 | 219.10 | 138.70 | 277.00 | 328.80 | 159.55 | 136.75 | 228.66 | 294.07 | 296.87 | .... |
| Social Benefits.......................... | c27 | — | — | — | — | — | — | .44 | — | — | — | 58.07 | .... |
| Other Payments.......................... | c28 | 123.28 | 99.60 | 92.90 | 107.10 | 194.20 | 266.50 | 5.29 | 42.81 | 177.53 | 10.06 | 15.96 | .... |
| Net Cash Inflow:Operating Act.[1-2] | ccio | −71.75 | −59.50 | −75.50 | −48.60 | −258.60 | −201.80 | 150.07 | 498.12 | 320.13 | 618.04 | 515.16 | .... |
| Net Cash Outflow:Invest. in NFA...... | c31 | .... | .... | .... | .... | .... | .... | 787.29 | 1,149.13 | 1,262.94 | 1,146.53 | 1,204.79 | .... |
| Purchases of Nonfinancial Assets... | c31.1 | .... | .... | .... | .... | .... | .... | .... | .... | .... | .... | .... | .... |
| Sales of Nonfinancial Assets.......... | c31.2 | .... | .... | .... | .... | .... | .... | .... | .... | .... | .... | .... | .... |
| Cash Surplus/Deficit [1-2-31=1-2M] | ccsd | .... | .... | .... | .... | .... | .... | −637.21 | −651.01 | −942.81 | −528.49 | −689.63 | .... |
| Net Acq. Fin. Assets, excl. Cash........ | c32x | .... | .... | .... | .... | .... | .... | .... | .... | .... | .... | .... | .... |
| Domestic........................... | c321x | .... | .... | .... | .... | .... | .... | .... | .... | .... | .... | .... | .... |
| Foreign............................. | c322x | .... | .... | .... | .... | .... | .... | .... | .... | .... | .... | .... | .... |
| Net Incurrence of Liabilities.............. | c33 | .... | .... | .... | .... | .... | .... | 607.89 | 425.35 | 870.50 | 525.36 | 866.63 | .... |
| Domestic........................... | c331 | .... | .... | .... | .... | .... | .... | 446.16 | 120.72 | 347.22 | 231.25 | 600.88 | .... |
| Foreign............................. | c332 | .... | .... | .... | .... | .... | .... | 161.73 | 304.63 | 523.28 | 294.11 | 265.75 | .... |
| Net Cash Inflow, Fin.Act.[-32x+33].. | cnfb | .... | .... | .... | .... | .... | .... | 607.89 | .... | .... | .... | .... | .... |
| Net Change in Stock of Cash........... | cncb | .... | .... | .... | .... | .... | .... | .... | .... | .... | .... | .... | .... |
| Stat. Discrep. [32X-33+NCB-CSD]... | ccsdz | .... | .... | .... | .... | .... | .... | .... | .... | .... | .... | .... | .... |
| Memo Item:Cash Expenditure[2+31] | c2m | .... | .... | .... | .... | .... | .... | 2,188.80 | 2,821.77 | 3,448.88 | 3,356.10 | 3,875.31 | .... |
| Memo Item: Gross Debt................... | c63 | .... | .... | .... | .... | .... | .... | .... | .... | .... | .... | .... | .... |
| **National Accounts** | | *Millions of Leones: Fiscal Year Ends December 31* | | | | | | | | | | | |
| Househ.Cons.Expend.,incl.NPISHs.... | 96f | 3,549,838 | 4,252,880 | 4,832,485 | 5,770,674 | 6,819,562 | 7,701,895 | 7,815,188 | 11,161,180 | 13,414,128 | 16,957,725 | 15,680,490 | .... |
| Government Consumption Expend... | 91f | 405,514 | 471,496 | 563,878 | 557,136 | 721,134 | 873,436 | 1,066,555 | 1,289,136 | 1,693,056 | 1,855,847 | 2,146,741 | .... |
| Gross Fixed Capital Formation.......... | 93e | 386,063 | 516,789 | 552,922 | 580,756 | 646,774 | 783,487 | 3,150,100 | 5,315,874 | 4,082,899 | 2,968,030 | 3,017,591 | .... |
| Changes in Inventories.................... | 93i | 16,888 | 19,637 | 22,979 | 25,567 | 29,383 | 30,684 | 38,276 | 49,952 | 517,693 | −255,246 | 411,774 | .... |
| Exports of Goods and Services......... | 90c | 644,487 | 838,103 | 941,684 | 1,005,419 | 1,009,892 | 1,121,567 | 1,722,427 | 2,081,748 | 5,394,184 | 9,515,288 | 15,452,990 | .... |
| Imports of Goods and Services (-)..... | 98c | 1,139,343 | 1,397,379 | 1,398,530 | 1,591,020 | 1,919,379 | 2,320,999 | 3,536,401 | 7,144,955 | 8,641,304 | 9,754,969 | 12,978,090 | .... |
| Gross Domestic Product (GDP)........ | 99b | 3,863,447 | 4,701,526 | 5,515,418 | 6,348,533 | 7,307,366 | 8,190,069 | 10,256,144 | 12,752,935 | 16,460,656 | 21,286,675 | 23,731,496 | .... |
| GDP Volume 2006 Prices................. | 99b.p | 5,219,572 | 5,310,625 | 5,405,634 | 5,814,812 | 6,354,178 | 6,796,181 | 6,912,753 | 7,324,821 | 8,438,400 | 10,137,732 | 10,803,992 | .... |
| GDP Volume (2010=100)............... | 99bvp | 75.5 | 76.8 | 78.2 | 84.1 | 91.9 | 98.3 | 100.0 | 106.0 | 122.1 | 146.7 | 156.3 | .... |
| GDP Deflator (2010=100)............... | 99bip | 49.9 | 59.7 | 68.8 | 73.6 | 77.5 | 81.2 | 100.0 | 117.3 | 131.5 | 141.5 | 148.0 | .... |
| | | *Millions: Midyear Estimates* | | | | | | | | | | | |
| Population.............................. | 99z | 4.87 | 5.07 | 5.24 | 5.39 | 5.52 | 5.65 | 5.78 | 5.91 | 6.04 | 6.18 | 6.32 | 6.45 |

# Singapore 576

|  |  | 2004 | 2005 | 2006 | 2007 | 2008 | 2009 | 2010 | 2011 | 2012 | 2013 | 2014 | 2015 |
|---|---|---|---|---|---|---|---|---|---|---|---|---|---|
| **Exchange Rates** |  | | | | | *Singapore Dollars per SDR: End of Period* | | | | | | | |
| Market Rate | aa | 2.5373 | 2.3786 | 2.3071 | 2.2775 | 2.2168 | 2.2001 | 1.9828 | 1.9969 | 1.8804 | 1.9486 | 1.9143 | 1.9593 |
|  |  | | | | *Singapore Dollars per US Dollar: End of Period (ae) Period Average (rf)* | | | | | | | | |
| Market Rate | ae | 1.6338 | 1.6642 | 1.5336 | 1.4412 | 1.4392 | 1.4034 | 1.2875 | 1.3007 | 1.2235 | 1.2653 | 1.3213 | 1.4139 |
| Market Rate | rf | 1.6902 | 1.6644 | 1.5889 | 1.5071 | 1.4149 | 1.4545 | 1.3635 | 1.2578 | 1.2497 | 1.2513 | 1.2671 | 1.3748 |
|  |  | | | | *Index Numbers (2010=100): Period Averages* | | | | | | | | |
| Market Rate | ahx | 80.6 | 81.9 | 85.8 | 90.4 | 96.4 | 93.8 | 100.0 | 108.4 | 109.0 | 108.9 | 107.5 | 99.1 |
| Nominal Effective Exchange Rate | nec | 88.7 | 89.4 | 92.4 | 93.8 | 97.1 | 97.0 | 100.0 | 103.7 | 106.2 | 109.0 | 110.0 | 109.6 |
| CPI-Based Real Effect. Ex. Rate | rec | 91.3 | 89.9 | 91.2 | 91.7 | 96.7 | 96.7 | 100.0 | 105.5 | 110.4 | 113.4 | 112.9 | 110.6 |
| ULC-Based Real Effect. Ex. Rate | rel | 74.8 | 76.1 | 81.0 | 85.1 | 91.1 | 88.8 | 100.0 | 108.1 | 116.5 | 122.6 | 127.1 | 132.2 |
| **Fund Position** |  | | | | | *Millions of SDRs: End of Period* | | | | | | | |
| Quota | 2f.s | 862.50 | 862.50 | 862.50 | 862.50 | 862.50 | 862.50 | 862.50 | 1,408.00 | 1,408.00 | 1,408.00 | 1,408.00 | 1,408.00 |
| SDR Holdings | 1b.s | 188.86 | 199.57 | 210.34 | 221.75 | 240.25 | 980.38 | 991.84 | 867.78 | 872.74 | 873.27 | 873.98 | 874.26 |
| Reserve Position in the Fund | 1c.s | 283.42 | 121.84 | 86.45 | 56.72 | 112.99 | 166.93 | 193.08 | 542.53 | 593.41 | 672.37 | 562.37 | 433.95 |
| Total Fund Cred.&Loans Outstg. | 2tl | — | — | — | — | — | — | — | — | — | — | — | — |
| SDR Allocations | 1bd | 16.48 | 16.48 | 16.48 | 16.48 | 16.48 | 744.21 | 744.21 | 744.21 | 744.21 | 744.21 | 744.21 | 744.21 |
| **International Liquidity** |  | | | | *Millions of US Dollars Unless Otherwise Indicated: End of Period* | | | | | | | | |
| Total Reserves minus Gold | 1l.d | 112,367 | 115,960 | 136,049 | 162,746 | 173,981 | 187,592 | 225,503 | 237,527 | 259,094 | 272,864 | 256,643 | 247,534 |
| SDR Holdings | 1b.d | 293 | 285 | 316 | 350 | 370 | 1,537 | 1,527 | 1,332 | 1,341 | 1,345 | 1,266 | 1,211 |
| Reserve Position in the Fund | 1c.d | 440 | 174 | 130 | 90 | 174 | 262 | 297 | 833 | 912 | 1,035 | 815 | 601 |
| Foreign Exchange | 1d.d | 111,634 | 115,501 | 135,602 | 162,306 | 173,437 | 185,793 | 223,678 | 235,362 | 256,841 | 270,484 | 254,562 | 245,721 |
| Gold (Million Fine Troy Ounces) | 1ad | 4 | 4 | 4 | 4 | 4 | 4 | 4 | 4 | 4 | 4 | 4 | 4 |
| Gold (National Valuation) | 1and | 212 | 212 | 212 | 212 | 212 | 212 | 212 | 212 | 212 | 212 | 212 | 212 |
| Monetary Authorities: Other Liabs. | 4..d | 273 | 456 | 512 | 564 | 472 | 1,558 | 1,334 | 1,189 | 1,145 | 2,848 | 1,294 | 3,255 |
| Deposit Money Banks: Assets | 7a.d | 61,848 | 70,717 | 109,779 | 128,498 | 154,708 | 174,941 | 190,933 | 207,590 | 228,369 | 228,823 | 251,859 | 225,887 |
| Deposit Money Banks: Liabs. | 7b.d | 67,003 | 69,434 | 98,802 | 125,853 | 143,883 | 148,628 | 173,813 | 211,917 | 237,500 | 268,345 | 291,293 | 260,437 |
| Other Banking Insts.: Assets | 7e.d | 17 | 31 | 24 | 45 | 36 | 52 | 52 | 44 | 25 | 22 | 19 | 17 |
| Other Banking Insts.: Liabs | 7f.d | 1 | 5 | 9 | 10 | 10 | 10 | 10 | 10 | 12 | 27 | 49 | 47 |
| ACU: Foreign Assets | 7k.d | 403,436 | 440,483 | 478,485 | 610,489 | 594,291 | 557,721 | 623,496 | 674,892 | 716,944 | 796,137 | 782,162 | 735,104 |
| Foreign Liabilities | 7m.d | 464,025 | 490,509 | 534,585 | 711,837 | 668,403 | 642,616 | 725,180 | 764,713 | 826,571 | 896,521 | 893,865 | 845,844 |
| **Monetary Authorities** |  | | | | | *Millions of Singapore Dollars: End of Period* | | | | | | | |
| Foreign Assets | 11 | 183,844 | 193,601 | 209,747 | 235,692 | 251,318 | 264,533 | 289,377 | 308,531 | 316,869 | 344,737 | 345,214 | 357,118 |
| Claims on Central Government | 12a | 7,039 | 7,010 | 6,608 | 6,502 | 6,860 | 7,382 | 7,481 | 6,814 | 7,006 | 6,998 | 7,000 | 7,915 |
| Reserve Money | 14 | 21,835 | 23,396 | 25,757 | 28,061 | 34,123 | 36,344 | 40,530 | 45,432 | 48,709 | 63,994 | 55,207 | 60,736 |
| of which: Currency Outside DMBs | 14a | 13,694 | 14,585 | 15,285 | 16,669 | 18,997 | 20,217 | 22,300 | 24,690 | 26,361 | 28,852 | 31,507 | 34,042 |
| Foreign Liabilities | 16c | 487 | 798 | 823 | 850 | 716 | 3,823 | 3,193 | 3,033 | 2,801 | 5,054 | 3,135 | 6,061 |
| Central Government Deposits | 16d | 98,497 | 107,772 | 108,712 | 108,948 | 132,711 | 117,078 | 130,490 | 144,113 | 158,185 | 141,508 | 113,568 | 127,754 |
| Other Items (Net) | 17r | 70,064 | 68,646 | 81,064 | 104,334 | 90,628 | 114,670 | 122,644 | 122,767 | 114,180 | 141,180 | 180,304 | 170,483 |
| **Deposit Money Banks** |  | | | | | *Millions of Singapore Dollars: End of Period* | | | | | | | |
| Reserves | 20 | 8,173 | 8,813 | 10,463 | 11,298 | 15,202 | 16,022 | 18,095 | 20,606 | 22,255 | 34,910 | 23,224 | 26,608 |
| Foreign Assets | 21 | 101,048 | 117,688 | 168,357 | 185,191 | 222,656 | 245,512 | 245,826 | 270,012 | 279,410 | 289,530 | 332,781 | 319,381 |
| Claims on Central Government | 22a | 45,058 | 43,750 | 50,738 | 59,934 | 66,696 | 81,319 | 84,853 | 91,414 | 98,415 | 98,214 | 106,234 | 108,845 |
| Claims on Private Sector | 22d | 186,128 | 189,798 | 199,051 | 232,752 | 268,091 | 273,531 | 310,168 | 367,895 | 416,613 | 477,493 | 512,789 | 522,189 |
| Demand Deposits | 24 | 30,468 | 31,501 | 36,958 | 47,270 | 56,706 | 73,256 | 90,188 | 105,902 | 114,348 | 125,746 | 128,711 | 126,404 |
| Time and Savings Deposits | 25 | 162,816 | 173,712 | 210,127 | 233,620 | 257,707 | 277,736 | 290,609 | 312,766 | 334,683 | 341,311 | 352,213 | 359,794 |
| Foreign Liabilities | 26c | 109,470 | 115,552 | 151,523 | 181,379 | 207,077 | 208,584 | 223,784 | 275,641 | 290,581 | 339,537 | 384,885 | 368,232 |
| Central Government Deposits | 26d | 1,847 | 3,080 | 3,122 | 4,164 | 2,099 | 3,324 | 11,698 | 16,130 | 19,937 | 21,272 | 19,864 | 24,013 |
| Other Items (Net) | 27r | 35,806 | 36,204 | 26,879 | 22,742 | 49,055 | 53,484 | 42,663 | 39,488 | 57,145 | 72,281 | 89,356 | 98,580 |
| **Monetary Survey** |  | | | | | *Millions of Singapore Dollars: End of Period* | | | | | | | |
| Foreign Assets (Net) | 31n | 174,935 | 194,940 | 225,758 | 238,654 | 266,181 | 297,638 | 308,225 | 299,869 | 302,897 | 289,677 | 289,975 | 302,206 |
| Domestic Credit | 32 | 137,881 | 129,707 | 144,564 | 186,076 | 206,837 | 241,830 | 260,314 | 305,880 | 343,912 | 419,925 | 492,591 | 487,182 |
| Claims on Central Govt. (Net) | 32an | −48,247 | −60,092 | −54,487 | −46,676 | −61,254 | −31,701 | −49,855 | −62,015 | −72,701 | −57,568 | −20,198 | −35,007 |
| Claims on Private Sector | 32d | 186,129 | 189,799 | 199,051 | 232,752 | 268,091 | 273,531 | 310,168 | 367,895 | 416,613 | 477,493 | 512,789 | 522,189 |
| Money | 34 | 44,162 | 46,086 | 52,243 | 63,939 | 75,703 | 93,473 | 112,488 | 130,592 | 140,709 | 154,598 | 160,218 | 160,446 |
| Quasi-Money | 35 | 162,816 | 173,712 | 210,127 | 233,620 | 257,707 | 277,736 | 290,609 | 312,766 | 334,683 | 341,311 | 352,213 | 359,794 |
| Other Items (Net) | 37r | 105,838 | 104,849 | 107,952 | 127,171 | 139,606 | 168,259 | 165,442 | 162,390 | 171,418 | 213,693 | 270,137 | 269,148 |
| Money plus Quasi-Money | 35l | 206,978 | 219,798 | 262,370 | 297,559 | 333,410 | 371,209 | 403,097 | 443,358 | 475,392 | 495,909 | 512,431 | 520,240 |
| **Other Banking Institutions** |  | | | | | *Millions of Singapore Dollars: End of Period* | | | | | | | |
| Finance Companies |  | | | | | | | | | | | | |
| Cash | 40 | 622 | 651 | 969 | 1,160 | 1,270 | 2,011 | 2,091 | 1,422 | 2,139 | 1,708 | 1,864 | 2,293 |
| Foreign Assets | 41 | 28 | 51 | 37 | 65 | 51 | 73 | 67 | 57 | 30 | 27 | 25 | 24 |
| Claims on Private Sector | 42d | 6,854 | 7,825 | 7,966 | 10,130 | 9,713 | 8,069 | 8,026 | 9,445 | 11,304 | 11,641 | 12,372 | 13,238 |
| Time and Savings Deposits | 45 | 5,666 | 6,356 | 7,136 | 10,073 | 9,961 | 9,098 | 8,878 | 9,467 | 12,333 | 12,361 | 13,231 | 14,601 |
| Foreign Liabilities | 46c | 2 | 9 | 14 | 15 | 15 | 14 | 13 | 14 | 15 | 35 | 65 | 67 |
| Capital Accounts | 47a | 1,444 | 1,658 | 1,693 | 1,683 | 1,713 | 1,825 | 1,926 | 1,999 | 2,105 | 2,110 | 2,214 | 2,242 |
| Other Items (Net) | 47r | 392 | 502 | 128 | −416 | −655 | −783 | −634 | −555 | −979 | −1,129 | −1,249 | −1,354 |
| **Nonbank Financial Institutions** |  | | | | | *Millions of Singapore Dollars: End of Period* | | | | | | | |
| Cash | 40..s | 4,375 | 4,533 | 5,021 | 4,413 | 6,139 | 4,909 | 5,372 | 8,154 | 6,766 | 5,804 | 5,128 | 5,531 |
| Foreign Assets | 41..s | 17,779 | .... | .... | .... | .... | .... | .... | .... | .... | .... | .... | .... |
| Claims on Central Government | 42a.s | 13,068 | .... | .... | .... | .... | .... | .... | .... | .... | .... | .... | .... |
| Claims on Private Sector | 42d.s | 33,888 | .... | .... | .... | .... | .... | .... | .... | .... | .... | .... | .... |
| Fixed Assets | 42h.s | 2,172 | 2,081 | 2,366 | 3,451 | 3,169 | 2,819 | 3,043 | 3,204 | 3,281 | 3,400 | 3,458 | 3,485 |
| Incr.in Total Assets(Within Per.) | 49z.s | 23,909 | 29,550 | 29,265 | 36,254 | 8,741 | 16,289 | 9,970 | 26,638 | 23,660 | 18,762 | 33,305 | 27,657 |
| **Money (National Definitions)** |  | | | | | *Millions of Singapore Dollars: End of Period* | | | | | | | |
| M1 | 59ma | 44,162 | 46,086 | 52,243 | 63,939 | 75,704 | 93,472 | 112,487 | 130,592 | 140,709 | 154,607 | 160,218 | 160,446 |
| M2 | 59mb | 206,978 | 219,798 | 262,370 | 297,559 | 333,411 | 371,208 | 403,096 | 443,358 | 475,393 | 495,917 | 512,431 | 520,240 |
| M3 | 59mc | 212,183 | 225,700 | 268,749 | 306,755 | 342,388 | 378,526 | 410,109 | 451,666 | 485,915 | 506,909 | 524,166 | 532,945 |

# Singapore 576

| | | 2004 | 2005 | 2006 | 2007 | 2008 | 2009 | 2010 | 2011 | 2012 | 2013 | 2014 | 2015 |
|---|---|---|---|---|---|---|---|---|---|---|---|---|---|
| **Interest Rates** | | | | | | | *Percent Per Annum* | | | | | | | |
| Central Bank Policy Rate (EOP) | 60 | 1.46 | 3.19 | 3.32 | .98 | .44 | .31 | .20 | .18 | .18 | .21 | . . . . | . . . . |
| Money Market Rate | 60b | 1.05 | 2.30 | † 3.32 | 2.25 | .80 | .27 | .14 | .09 | .09 | .05 | .14 | .50 |
| Money Market Rate (Fgn. Currency) | 60b.f | 1.68 | 3.65 | 5.23 | 5.26 | 2.80 | .66 | .35 | .35 | .42 | .27 | . . . . | . . . . |
| Treasury Bill Rate | 60c | .96 | 2.06 | 2.96 | 2.35 | .91 | .34 | .34 | .29 | .27 | . . . . | . . . . | . . . . |
| Savings Rate | 60k | .23 | .24 | .26 | .25 | .23 | .18 | .14 | .12 | .11 | .10 | .11 | .12 |
| Deposit Rate | 60l | .40 | .44 | .57 | .53 | .42 | .29 | .21 | .17 | .14 | .14 | .14 | .17 |
| Lending Rate | 60p | 5.30 | 5.30 | 5.31 | 5.33 | 5.38 | 5.38 | 5.38 | 5.38 | 5.38 | 5.38 | 5.35 | 5.35 |
| Government Bond Yield | 61 | 3.23 | 2.92 | 3.36 | 2.88 | 2.78 | 2.37 | 2.37 | 2.09 | 1.46 | 2.06 | 2.36 | 2.44 |
| **Prices, Production, Labor** | | | | | | | *Index Numbers (2010=100): Period Averages* | | | | | | | |
| Share Prices | 62 | 64.18 | 74.92 | 85.81 | 115.49 | 90.36 | 76.72 | 100.00 | 100.33 | 101.02 | 108.68 | 109.94 | 107.21 |
| Share Prices (End of Month) | 62.ep | 64.68 | 75.17 | 87.09 | 116.58 | 89.17 | 78.48 | 100.00 | 100.76 | 101.35 | 109.04 | 110.30 | 107.42 |
| Wholesale Prices | 63 | 89.3 | † 75.9 | 102.9 | 103.1 | 110.9 | 95.5 | 100.0 | 108.4 | † 109.0 | 106.0 | 102.5 | 86.8 |
| Consumer Prices | 64 | † 87.6 | 88.0 | 88.9 | 90.8 | † 96.7 | 97.3 | 100.0 | 105.3 | † 110.0 | 112.6 | 113.8 | 113.2 |
| Manufacturing Production | 66ey | 64.8 | 70.9 | 79.3 | † 84.0 | 80.4 | 77.1 | 100.0 | † 107.6 | 107.9 | 109.8 | 112.7 | † 106.9 |
| | | | | | | | *Number in Thousands: Period Averages* | | | | | | | |
| Labor Force | 67d | 2,252 | 2,348 | 2,496 | 2,697 | 2,957 | 3,045 | 3,128 | 3,239 | 3,364 | 3,498 | 3,631 | 3,691 |
| Employment | 67e | 2,172 | 2,271 | 2,427 | 2,639 | 2,891 | 2,958 | 3,063 | 3,178 | 3,304 | 3,438 | 3,570 | 3,629 |
| Unemployment | 67c | 80 | 77 | 70 | 59 | 66 | 87 | 65 | 61 | 60 | 60 | 61 | 62 |
| Unemployment Rate (%) | 67r | 3.6 | 4.1 | 2.8 | 2.2 | 2.2 | 2.9 | 2.1 | 1.9 | 1.8 | 1.7 | 2.7 | 1.7 |
| **Intl. Transactions & Positions** | | | | | | | *Millions of Singapore Dollars* | | | | | | | |
| Exports | 70 | 335,615 | 382,532 | 431,559 | 450,587 | 476,762 | 391,118 | 478,841 | 514,741 | 510,329 | 513,391 | 513,248 | 476,285 |
| Imports, c.i.f. | 71 | 276,894 | 333,191 | 378,924 | 395,980 | 450,893 | 356,299 | 423,222 | 459,655 | 474,554 | 466,762 | 463,779 | 407,768 |
| | | | | | | | *2010=100* | | | | | | | |
| Volume of Exports | 72 | 66.1 | 73.8 | 81.6 | 88.4 | 92.3 | 82.8 | 100.0 | 104.9 | 105.2 | 108.8 | 111.4 | 110.9 |
| Volume of Imports | 73 | 66.3 | 75.9 | 83.9 | 89.3 | 98.7 | 84.8 | 100.0 | 103.6 | 107.3 | 108.6 | 111.0 | 111.8 |
| Export Prices (Survey) | 76 | 106.1 | † 108.3 | 110.5 | 106.5 | 107.8 | 98.7 | 100.0 | † 102.4 | 101.3 | 98.6 | 96.3 | 89.7 |
| Import Prices (Survey) | 76.x | 98.6 | † 103.7 | 106.7 | 104.7 | 107.9 | 99.3 | 100.0 | † 104.8 | 104.5 | 101.6 | 98.7 | 86.2 |
| **Balance of Payments** | | | | | | | *Millions of US Dollars* | | | | | | | |
| A. Current Account* | 109bx | 20,790.1 | 28,133.2 | 37,182.0 | 46,982.0 | 28,016.2 | 32,659.4 | 56,291.6 | 62,796.2 | 52,346.7 | 53,770.9 | 53,515.7 | 57,921.9 |
| Goods, credit (exports) | 1a9cx | 206,576.2 | 241,638.3 | 280,864.1 | 312,281.3 | 352,974.0 | 287,361.8 | 370,257.2 | 434,093.2 | 437,436.7 | 437,357.5 | 437,792.1 | 377,050.0 |
| Goods, debit (imports) | 1a9dx | 166,273.7 | 193,894.6 | 229,571.1 | 254,531.7 | 311,326.3 | 239,782.0 | 307,417.7 | 360,048.6 | 367,073.5 | 361,713.5 | 358,165.3 | 294,525.6 |
| Balance on goods | 1a9bx | 40,302.5 | 47,743.7 | 51,293.0 | 57,749.6 | 41,647.7 | 47,579.8 | 62,839.5 | 74,044.6 | 70,363.2 | 75,644.1 | 79,626.8 | 82,524.5 |
| Services, credit (exports) | 1b9cx | 40,450.4 | 46,427.3 | 59,215.3 | 74,214.2 | 89,674.9 | 81,828.0 | 100,831.6 | 118,924.8 | 127,764.2 | 140,256.6 | 150,750.3 | 139,610.7 |
| Services, debit (imports) | 1b9dx | 50,631.0 | 56,164.3 | 66,392.7 | 76,481.5 | 91,182.1 | 84,135.3 | 101,212.1 | 118,212.9 | 129,753.2 | 146,489.0 | 155,481.2 | 143,469.2 |
| Balance on Goods & Services | 1z9bx | 30,122.0 | 38,006.7 | 44,115.7 | 55,482.3 | 40,140.5 | 45,272.5 | 62,459.0 | 74,756.6 | 68,374.2 | 69,411.7 | 74,895.9 | 78,666.0 |
| Primary income: credit | 1c9cx | 21,334.3 | 29,202.9 | 40,975.6 | 58,374.2 | 47,945.4 | 50,200.9 | 62,620.3 | 65,677.6 | 64,540.6 | 66,887.2 | 63,329.5 | 58,837.9 |
| Primary income: debit | 1c9dx | 29,375.4 | 37,628.2 | 46,223.7 | 64,051.7 | 56,615.9 | 59,117.3 | 63,965.7 | 71,671.5 | 73,738.6 | 76,004.8 | 78,461.9 | 72,639.2 |
| Balance on gds, serv. & prim. inc. | 1y9bx | 22,080.9 | 29,581.4 | 38,867.6 | 49,804.8 | 31,470.0 | 36,356.1 | 61,113.6 | 68,762.6 | 59,176.1 | 60,294.1 | 59,763.5 | 64,864.7 |
| Secondary income: credit | 1d9ca | 1,923.8 | 2,007.8 | 1,999.7 | 2,331.4 | 2,981.9 | 2,989.7 | 3,973.1 | 5,073.6 | 7,732.7 | 8,442.5 | 7,450.9 | 6,773.7 |
| Secondary income: debit | 1d9da | 3,214.5 | 3,455.9 | 3,685.3 | 5,154.2 | 6,435.7 | 6,686.4 | 8,795.0 | 11,040.0 | 14,562.2 | 14,965.7 | 13,698.6 | 13,716.5 |
| B. Capital Account* | 209ba | . . . . | . . . . | . . . . | . . . . | . . . . | . . . . | . . . . | . . . . | . . . . | . . . . | . . . . | . . . . |
| Capital account: credit | 209ca | . . . . | . . . . | . . . . | . . . . | . . . . | . . . . | . . . . | . . . . | . . . . | . . . . | . . . . | . . . . |
| Capital account: debit | 209da | . . . . | . . . . | . . . . | . . . . | . . . . | . . . . | . . . . | . . . . | . . . . | . . . . | . . . . | . . . . |
| Balance on current & capital acct. | 129ba | 20,790.1 | 28,133.2 | 37,182.0 | 46,982.0 | 28,016.2 | 32,659.4 | 56,291.6 | 62,796.2 | 52,346.7 | 53,770.9 | 53,515.7 | 57,921.9 |
| C. Financial Account* | 309na | 8,557.4 | 16,836.7 | 19,220.6 | 28,471.6 | 15,772.8 | 23,460.7 | 17,604.8 | 46,153.0 | 23,101.7 | 37,326.5 | 46,230.9 | 56,045.2 |
| Direct investment: assets | 3a9aa | 13,138.6 | 12,552.5 | 20,063.1 | 40,882.2 | 7,964.4 | 32,039.6 | 35,407.2 | 31,459.3 | 18,340.6 | 39,591.9 | 39,131.3 | 35,485.2 |
| Equity & investment fund shares | 3aaaa | 7,203.8 | 9,751.8 | 12,011.8 | 26,630.5 | 8,229.1 | 28,133.9 | 31,322.4 | 24,380.3 | 17,115.2 | 33,613.0 | 36,704.1 | 31,649.1 |
| Debt instruments | 3abaa | 5,934.8 | 2,800.7 | 8,051.3 | 14,251.8 | −264.7 | 3,905.7 | 4,084.8 | 7,079.1 | 1,225.4 | 5,979.0 | 2,427.2 | 3,836.1 |
| Direct investment: liabilities | 3a9la | 24,390.3 | 18,090.3 | 36,923.9 | 47,733.2 | 12,200.7 | 23,821.2 | 55,075.9 | 48,329.2 | 57,149.9 | 66,066.9 | 68,495.6 | 65,262.6 |
| Equity & investment fund shares | 3aala | 20,561.7 | 16,175.5 | 37,329.6 | 34,392.6 | 7,661.2 | 22,848.2 | 46,680.0 | 40,361.3 | 46,181.8 | 59,427.3 | 59,042.9 | 67,895.4 |
| Debt instruments | 3abla | 3,828.6 | 1,914.8 | −405.7 | 13,340.6 | 4,539.5 | 973.0 | 8,395.8 | 7,967.9 | 10,968.1 | 6,639.6 | 9,452.7 | −2,632.8 |
| Portfolio investment: assets | 3b9aa | 20,753.0 | 7,282.2 | 27,925.5 | 65,922.7 | −26,221.7 | 28,334.7 | 37,439.9 | 6,520.2 | 83,332.5 | 61,051.1 | 56,542.3 | 47,913.4 |
| Equity & investment fund shares | 3baaa | 13,145.3 | 8,156.1 | 8,771.0 | 36,081.0 | −1,662.8 | 9,492.3 | 21,093.7 | 2,674.0 | 40,497.9 | 33,709.4 | 30,140.2 | 46,427.7 |
| Debt securities | 3bbaa | 7,607.7 | −873.9 | 19,154.4 | 29,841.6 | −24,558.9 | 18,842.4 | 16,346.1 | 3,846.2 | 42,834.6 | 27,341.6 | 26,402.1 | 1,485.7 |
| Portfolio investment: liabilities | 3b9la | 2,956.3 | 6,355.5 | 11,740.3 | 18,473.3 | −14,643.3 | 1,183.1 | 8,004.9 | −6,335.9 | 5,120.3 | −1,426.3 | 3,180.0 | −6,868.1 |
| Equity & investment fund shares | 3bala | 2,326.8 | 4,905.5 | 10,062.6 | 18,062.7 | −11,657.5 | 962.0 | 5,290.4 | −5,730.8 | 3,514.3 | −7,446.1 | −739.8 | −3,030.9 |
| Debt securities | 3bbla | 629.4 | 1,450.0 | 1,677.7 | 410.6 | −2,986.7 | 221.0 | 2,714.5 | −605.0 | 1,606.0 | 6,019.8 | 3,919.8 | −3,837.2 |
| Fin. der.& empl.stk.ops.(ESOs): net. | 3c9na | . . . . | . . . . | 5,792.3 | 640.6 | −3,980.5 | 14,108.0 | −3,596.3 | 17,078.3 | −17,407.4 | −13,243.8 | −11,963.8 | −19,875.2 |
| Fin. der. & ESOs.: assets | 3c9aa | . . . . | . . . . | 9,759.7 | 4,922.8 | 27,654.0 | −19,251.6 | 4,575.3 | 35,094.2 | −40,275.8 | −10,691.4 | −6,421.7 | −17,199.9 |
| Fin. der. & ESOs.: liabilities | 3c9la | . . . . | . . . . | 3,967.4 | 4,282.2 | 31,634.6 | −33,359.6 | 8,171.6 | 18,015.8 | −22,868.4 | 2,552.5 | 5,542.1 | 2,675.2 |
| Other investment: assets | 3d9aa | 48,199.9 | 64,981.5 | 32,601.1 | 153,847.0 | 32,650.8 | −67,712.1 | 69,891.6 | 77,640.0 | 20,487.1 | 108,053.5 | 82,012.9 | 46,673.3 |
| Other equity | 3daaa | . . . . | . . . . | . . . . | . . . . | . . . . | . . . . | . . . . | . . . . | . . . . | . . . . | . . . . | . . . . |
| Debt instruments | 3dzaa | 48,199.9 | 64,981.5 | 32,601.1 | 153,847.0 | 32,650.8 | −67,712.1 | 69,891.6 | 77,640.0 | 20,487.1 | 108,053.5 | 82,012.9 | 46,673.3 |
| Other investment: liabilities | 3d9la | 46,187.4 | 43,533.7 | 18,497.2 | 166,614.4 | −2,916.3 | −41,694.8 | 58,456.8 | 44,551.5 | 19,380.9 | 93,485.6 | 47,816.2 | −4,243.2 |
| Other equity | 3dala | . . . . | . . . . | . . . . | . . . . | . . . . | . . . . | . . . . | . . . . | . . . . | . . . . | . . . . | . . . . |
| Debt instruments | 3dzla | 46,187.4 | 43,533.7 | 18,497.2 | 166,614.4 | −2,916.3 | −41,694.8 | 58,456.8 | 44,551.5 | 19,380.9 | 93,485.6 | 47,816.2 | −4,243.2 |
| Curr.+ cap.− finan. acct. balance | 4y9na | 12,232.7 | 11,296.6 | 17,961.4 | 18,510.4 | 12,243.4 | 9,198.7 | 38,686.8 | 16,643.3 | 29,245.0 | 16,444.4 | 7,284.8 | 1,876.7 |
| D. Net Errors and Omissions | 409na | −120.0 | 986.9 | −957.0 | 937.9 | 854.0 | 2,115.2 | 3,666.2 | 599.7 | −3,022.6 | 1,652.3 | −465.9 | −824.9 |
| E. Reserves and Related Items | 4z9na | 12,112.8 | 12,283.4 | 17,004.4 | 19,448.3 | 13,097.4 | 11,314.0 | 42,353.0 | 17,242.9 | 26,222.4 | 18,096.7 | 6,818.9 | 1,051.8 |
| Reserve assets | 3e9aa | 12,112.8 | 12,283.4 | 17,004.4 | 19,448.3 | 13,097.4 | 11,314.0 | 42,353.0 | 17,242.9 | 26,222.4 | 18,096.7 | 6,818.9 | 1,051.8 |
| Credit and loans from the IMF | 3dcla | — | — | — | — | — | — | — | — | — | — | — | — |
| Exceptional financing | 409la | . . . . | . . . . | . . . . | . . . . | . . . . | . . . . | . . . . | . . . . | . . . . | . . . . | . . . . | . . . . |

*Excludes components in group E

# Singapore 576

## International Investment Position

*Millions of US Dollars*

| | | 2004 | 2005 | 2006 | 2007 | 2008 | 2009 | 2010 | 2011 | 2012 | 2013 | 2014 | 2015 |
|---|---|---|---|---|---|---|---|---|---|---|---|---|---|
| Assets | 809aa | 1,074,922.0 | 1,217,801.8 | 1,508,345.0 | 1,929,121.8 | 1,841,176.3 | 1,930,749.0 | 2,330,870.1 | 2,447,798.8 | 2,739,887.9 | 2,920,147.9 | 2,990,797.9 | 2,935,406.2 |
| Direct investment | 8a9aa | 171,654.1 | 191,211.2 | 270,521.1 | 346,292.3 | 318,154.0 | 381,178.4 | 466,129.1 | 499,651.5 | 567,186.5 | 612,821.1 | 626,589.4 | 625,259.1 |
| Equity & investment fund shares.. | 8aaaa | 116,337.5 | 128,556.5 | 168,867.0 | 226,192.6 | 205,060.2 | 252,767.8 | 320,697.6 | 335,746.9 | 397,046.8 | 423,366.0 | 456,914.6 | 451,701.6 |
| Debt instruments | 8abaa | 55,316.6 | 62,654.6 | 101,654.1 | 120,099.7 | 113,093.8 | 128,410.6 | 145,431.5 | 163,904.6 | 170,139.8 | 189,455.1 | 169,674.8 | 173,557.5 |
| Portfolio investment | 8b9aa | 257,736.6 | 283,148.6 | 377,821.7 | 508,767.7 | 369,630.6 | 465,272.5 | 588,935.8 | 610,643.3 | 804,039.6 | 914,532.8 | 964,528.2 | 961,638.4 |
| Equity & investment fund shares.. | 8baaa | 106,901.8 | 128,680.3 | 178,104.1 | 258,696.9 | 179,752.2 | 208,609.2 | 296,060.8 | 306,998.2 | 428,147.4 | 470,465.3 | 485,797.9 | 484,569.4 |
| Debt securities | 8bbaa | 150,834.8 | 154,468.3 | 199,717.7 | 250,070.8 | 189,878.3 | 256,663.3 | 292,875.0 | 303,645.2 | 375,892.3 | 444,067.4 | 478,730.3 | 477,069.0 |
| Fin. der.(oth.than reserves) & ESOs | 8c9aa | .... | 39,782.0 | 56,470.9 | 73,027.5 | 122,287.0 | 85,712.4 | 107,430.4 | 142,074.3 | 92,730.1 | 87,847.2 | 106,757.8 | 113,976.0 |
| Other investment | 8d9aa | 533,238.5 | 587,800.7 | 667,255.9 | 838,291.1 | 857,156.7 | 810,502.9 | 943,944.4 | 958,324.1 | 1,017,048.0 | 1,032,498.2 | 1,035,268.5 | 986,289.7 |
| Other equity | 8daaa | .... | .... | .... | .... | .... | .... | .... | .... | .... | .... | .... | .... |
| Debt instruments | 8dzaa | 533,238.5 | 587,800.7 | 667,255.9 | 838,291.1 | 857,156.7 | 810,502.9 | 943,944.4 | 958,324.1 | 1,017,048.0 | 1,032,498.2 | 1,035,268.5 | 986,289.7 |
| Reserve assets | 8e9aa | 112,292.8 | 115,859.3 | 136,275.3 | 162,743.3 | 173,948.0 | 188,082.8 | 224,430.4 | 237,105.6 | 258,883.7 | 272,448.6 | 257,653.9 | 248,243.0 |
| Liabilities | 809la | 821,546.4 | 924,297.0 | 1,116,662.1 | 1,510,765.5 | 1,500,542.8 | 1,486,519.8 | 1,818,582.3 | 1,914,731.9 | 2,153,798.6 | 2,315,140.4 | 2,413,186.2 | 2,338,437.9 |
| Direct investment | 8a9la | 215,969.5 | 237,009.4 | 313,183.8 | 420,877.0 | 458,864.0 | 506,178.6 | 632,759.5 | 682,360.5 | 820,090.1 | 885,144.7 | 962,670.6 | 978,410.8 |
| Equity & investment fund shares.. | 8aala | 184,623.6 | 202,108.8 | 263,852.5 | 355,664.3 | 366,655.7 | 419,080.5 | 525,262.4 | 552,536.9 | 681,663.4 | 737,222.7 | 801,636.6 | 827,513.8 |
| Debt instruments | 8abla | 31,345.9 | 34,900.7 | 49,331.3 | 65,212.7 | 92,208.2 | 87,098.1 | 107,497.1 | 129,823.6 | 138,426.6 | 147,922.0 | 161,034.1 | 150,897.0 |
| Portfolio investment | 8b9la | 72,207.4 | 84,807.6 | 126,441.8 | 179,068.9 | 83,199.8 | 113,355.2 | 159,111.2 | 127,802.8 | 165,073.3 | 195,547.1 | 206,369.5 | 171,192.2 |
| Equity & investment fund shares.. | 8bala | 59,885.5 | 72,668.7 | 112,737.6 | 164,742.0 | 71,649.5 | 101,100.1 | 142,098.3 | 112,276.7 | 142,775.4 | 163,519.6 | 171,177.9 | 141,070.5 |
| Debt securities | 8bbla | 12,321.9 | 12,138.9 | 13,704.2 | 14,326.9 | 11,550.2 | 12,255.1 | 17,013.0 | 15,526.1 | 22,297.9 | 32,027.5 | 35,191.6 | 30,121.6 |
| Fin. der.(oth.than reserves) & ESOs | 8c9la | .... | 35,601.1 | 45,351.7 | 67,648.6 | 117,278.6 | 65,001.9 | 92,148.2 | 100,008.5 | 85,433.1 | 83,629.0 | 99,710.3 | 112,177.2 |
| Other investment | 8d9la | 533,369.7 | 566,878.7 | 631,684.6 | 843,171.1 | 841,199.9 | 801,957.8 | 934,561.5 | 1,004,560.1 | 1,083,202.2 | 1,150,822.2 | 1,144,432.6 | 1,076,657.7 |
| Other equity | 8dala | | | | | | | | | | | | |
| Debt instruments | 8dzla | 533,369.7 | 566,878.7 | 631,684.6 | 843,171.1 | 841,199.9 | 801,957.8 | 934,561.5 | 1,004,560.1 | 1,083,202.2 | 1,150,822.2 | 1,144,432.6 | 1,076,657.7 |

## Government Finance
## Cash Flow Statement
### Budgetary Central Government

*Millions of Singapore Dollars: Fiscal Year Begins April 1*

| | | 2004 | 2005 | 2006 | 2007 | 2008 | 2009 | 2010 | 2011 | 2012 | 2013 | 2014 | 2015 |
|---|---|---|---|---|---|---|---|---|---|---|---|---|---|
| Cash Receipts:Operating Activities... | c1 | 37,480.6 | 43,177.7 | 47,848.9 | 65,736.3 | 64,306.4 | 49,245.9 | 68,902.9 | 66,767.1 | 80,365.8 | 67,602.9 | 69,972.8 | 72,761.9 |
| Taxes | c11 | .... | .... | .... | .... | .... | .... | .... | .... | .... | .... | .... | .... |
| Social Contributions | c12 | .... | .... | .... | .... | .... | .... | .... | .... | .... | .... | .... | .... |
| Grants | c13 | .... | .... | .... | .... | .... | .... | .... | .... | .... | .... | .... | .... |
| Other Receipts | c14 | .... | .... | .... | .... | .... | .... | .... | .... | .... | .... | .... | .... |
| Cash Payments:Operating Activities. | c2 | 25,819.9 | 26,321.0 | 30,928.1 | 32,840.8 | 49,451.6 | 53,214.8 | 49,668.1 | .... | 46,259.7 | 52,163.4 | 56,519.2 | 71,586.9 |
| Compensation of Employees | c21 | .... | .... | .... | .... | .... | .... | .... | .... | .... | .... | .... | .... |
| Purchases of Goods & Services | c22 | .... | .... | .... | .... | .... | .... | .... | .... | .... | .... | .... | .... |
| Interest | c24 | .... | .... | .... | .... | .... | .... | .... | .... | .... | .... | .... | .... |
| Subsidies | c25 | .... | .... | .... | .... | .... | .... | .... | .... | .... | .... | .... | .... |
| Grants | c26 | .... | .... | .... | .... | .... | .... | .... | .... | .... | .... | .... | .... |
| Social Benefits | c27 | .... | .... | .... | .... | .... | .... | .... | .... | .... | .... | .... | .... |
| Other Payments | c28 | .... | .... | .... | .... | .... | .... | .... | .... | .... | .... | .... | .... |
| Net Cash Inflow:Operating Act.[1-2] | ccio | .... | .... | .... | .... | .... | .... | .... | .... | .... | .... | 13,453.6 | 1,175.0 |
| Net Cash Outflow:Invest. in NFA | c31 | .... | .... | .... | .... | .... | .... | .... | .... | .... | .... | −8,904.4 | −9,020.2 |
| Purchases of Nonfinancial Assets... | c31.1 | .... | .... | .... | .... | .... | .... | .... | .... | .... | .... | 6,021.6 | 6,521.7 |
| Sales of Nonfinancial Assets | c31.2 | .... | .... | .... | .... | .... | .... | .... | .... | .... | .... | 14,926.0 | 15,541.8 |
| Cash Surplus/Deficit [1-2-31=1-2M] | ccsd | 11,660.7 | 16,856.7 | 16,920.8 | 32,895.5 | 14,854.8 | −4,240.3 | 18,449.6 | 19,910.9 | 31,115.5 | 24,155.7 | 22,358.0 | 10,195.1 |
| Net Acq. Fin. Assets, excl. Cash | c32x | .... | .... | .... | .... | .... | .... | −3,839.8 | −2,242.7 | −2,990.6 | 415.5 | −802.0 | 2,545.3 |
| Domestic | c321x | .... | .... | .... | .... | .... | .... | .... | .... | .... | .... | −802.0 | 2,545.3 |
| Foreign | c322x | .... | .... | .... | .... | .... | .... | .... | .... | .... | .... | — | — |
| Net Incurrence of Liabilities | c33 | 16,090.7 | 12,141.1 | 8,947.1 | 32,403.6 | 20,422.3 | 38,282.9 | 31,330.7 | 39,472.7 | 32,556.7 | −12,599.0 | 14,651.7 | 40,114.8 |
| Domestic | c331 | .... | .... | .... | .... | .... | .... | .... | .... | .... | .... | 14,651.7 | 40,114.8 |
| Foreign | c332 | .... | .... | .... | .... | .... | .... | .... | .... | .... | .... | .... | .... |
| Net Cash Inflow, Fin.Act.[-32x+33].. | cnfb | .... | .... | .... | .... | .... | .... | 35,170.5 | 41,715.4 | 35,547.3 | −13,014.5 | 15,453.7 | 37,569.4 |
| Net Change in Stock of Cash | cncb | 27,751.4 | 28,997.8 | 25,867.9 | 65,299.1 | 35,277.1 | 42,633.6 | −53,620.1 | −61,626.3 | −66,662.8 | .... | .... | .... |
| Stat. Discrep. [32X-33+NCB-CSD].... | ccsdz | .... | .... | — | — | — | 8,319.6 | −107,240.2 | −123,252.6 | −133,325.6 | | | |
| Memo Item:Cash Expenditure[2+31] | c2m | .... | .... | .... | .... | .... | .... | 50,453.3 | 46,856.2 | 49,250.3 | .... | .... | .... |
| Memo Item: Gross Debt | c63 | 197,892.0 | 202,016.0 | 211,055.7 | 243,920.1 | 264,210.4 | 300,468.4 | 331,163.0 | 367,172.3 | 395,466.3 | .... | .... | .... |

## National Accounts

*Millions of Singapore Dollars*

| | | 2004 | 2005 | 2006 | 2007 | 2008 | 2009 | 2010 | 2011 | 2012 | 2013 | 2014 | 2015 |
|---|---|---|---|---|---|---|---|---|---|---|---|---|---|
| Househ.Cons.Expend.,incl.NPISHs | 96f | 80,373 | 82,999 | 87,071 | 96,481 | 104,602 | 104,884 | 114,519 | 123,941 | 132,268 | 138,620 | 143,375 | .... |
| Government Consumption Expend... | 91f | 20,283 | 21,597 | 24,185 | 25,800 | 28,689 | 28,791 | 32,838 | 33,486 | 33,583 | 38,223 | 39,132 | .... |
| Gross Fixed Capital Formation | 93e | 47,329 | 48,936 | 54,154 | 66,406 | 77,073 | 81,917 | 84,225 | 88,314 | 96,833 | 99,984 | 98,957 | .... |
| Changes in Inventories | 93i | −2,737 | −3,623 | −1,732 | −3,693 | 5,712 | −4,493 | 5,616 | 6,085 | 11,833 | 9,676 | 8,855 | .... |
| Exports (Net) | 90n | 50,913 | 63,258 | 70,097 | 83,618 | 56,793 | 65,850 | 85,163 | 91,429 | 82,065 | 87,816 | 95,331 | .... |
| Gross Domestic Product (GDP) | 99b | 193,002 | 212,074 | 234,835 | 271,250 | 271,980 | 279,858 | 322,361 | 346,354 | 362,333 | 378,200 | 390,089 | .... |
| Net Primary Income from Abroad | 98.n | −13,591 | −14,023 | −8,339 | −8,557 | −12,268 | −12,969 | −1,835 | −7,901 | −10,567 | −11,582 | −11,759 | .... |
| Gross National Income (GNI) | 99a | 179,410 | 198,051 | 226,496 | 262,693 | 259,713 | 266,889 | 320,527 | 338,453 | 351,766 | 366,618 | 378,330 | .... |
| GDP Volume 2010 Prices | 99b.p | 216,554 | 232,773 | 253,397 | 276,485 | 281,427 | 279,729 | 322,361 | 342,372 | 354,061 | 369,793 | 380,585 | .... |
| GDP Volume (2010=100) | 99bvp | 67.2 | 72.2 | 78.6 | 85.8 | 87.3 | 86.8 | 100.0 | 106.2 | 109.8 | 114.7 | 118.1 | .... |
| GDP Deflator (2010=100) | 99bip | 89.1 | 91.1 | 92.7 | 98.1 | 96.6 | 100.0 | 100.0 | 101.2 | 102.3 | 102.3 | 102.5 | .... |

*Millions: Midyear Estimates*

| | | 2004 | 2005 | 2006 | 2007 | 2008 | 2009 | 2010 | 2011 | 2012 | 2013 | 2014 | 2015 |
|---|---|---|---|---|---|---|---|---|---|---|---|---|---|
| Population | 99z | 4.38 | 4.50 | 4.61 | 4.73 | 4.85 | 4.97 | 5.08 | 5.19 | 5.30 | 5.41 | 5.51 | 5.60 |

# Sint Maarten   352

| | | 2004 | 2005 | 2006 | 2007 | 2008 | 2009 | 2010 | 2011 | 2012 | 2013 | 2014 | 2015 |
|---|---|---|---|---|---|---|---|---|---|---|---|---|---|
| **Exchange Rates** | | | | | | *Guilders per SDR: End of Period* | | | | | | | |
| Official Rate | aa | 2.780 | 2.558 | 2.693 | 2.829 | 2.757 | 2.806 | 2.757 | 2.748 | 2.751 | 2.757 | 2.593 | 2.480 |
| | | | | *Guilders per US Dollar: End of Period (ae)  Period Average (rf)* | | | | | | | | | |
| Official Rate | ae | 1.790 | 1.790 | 1.790 | 1.790 | 1.790 | 1.790 | 1.790 | 1.790 | 1.790 | 1.790 | 1.790 | 1.790 |
| Official Rate | rf | 1.790 | 1.790 | 1.790 | 1.790 | 1.790 | 1.790 | 1.790 | 1.790 | 1.790 | 1.790 | 1.790 | 1.790 |
| **Prices** | | | | | *Index Numbers (2010=100): Period Averages* | | | | | | | | |
| Consumer Prices | 64 | .... | 89.284 | 89.552 | 93.522 | 93.131 | 98.679 | 100.000 | 105.134 | 108.966 | 111.918 | 113.260 | .... |
| **Balance of Payments** | | | | | | *Millions of US Dollars* | | | | | | | |
| A. Current Account* | 109bx | .... | .... | .... | .... | .... | .... | .... | −4.5 | 95.9 | 4.0 | −110.3 | 23.3 |
| Goods, credit (exports) | 1a9cx | .... | .... | .... | .... | .... | .... | .... | 126.8 | 130.5 | 164.3 | 132.2 | 128.9 |
| Goods, debit (imports) | 1a9dx | .... | .... | .... | .... | .... | .... | .... | 733.0 | 767.8 | 924.2 | 1,011.8 | 887.9 |
| Balance on goods | 1a9bx | .... | .... | .... | .... | .... | .... | .... | −606.2 | −637.3 | −759.9 | −879.6 | −759.1 |
| Services, credit (exports) | 1b9cx | .... | .... | .... | .... | .... | .... | .... | 899.9 | 1,039.8 | 1,063.2 | 1,116.2 | 1,125.8 |
| Services, debit (imports) | 1b9dx | .... | .... | .... | .... | .... | .... | .... | 238.1 | 261.4 | 263.6 | 291.9 | 279.2 |
| Balance on Goods & Services | 1z9bx | .... | .... | .... | .... | .... | .... | .... | 55.6 | 141.1 | 39.7 | −55.4 | 87.5 |
| Primary income: credit | 1c9cx | .... | .... | .... | .... | .... | .... | .... | 31.9 | 41.4 | 59.2 | 53.0 | 62.1 |
| Primary income: debit | 1c9dx | .... | .... | .... | .... | .... | .... | .... | 50.3 | 50.5 | 55.5 | 68.1 | 71.5 |
| Balance on gds, serv. & prim. inc. | 1y9bx | .... | .... | .... | .... | .... | .... | .... | 37.2 | 132.0 | 43.3 | −70.6 | 78.1 |
| Secondary income: credit | 1d9ca | .... | .... | .... | .... | .... | .... | .... | 68.7 | 76.2 | 84.6 | 78.6 | 67.2 |
| Secondary income: debit | 1d9da | .... | .... | .... | .... | .... | .... | .... | 110.4 | 112.4 | 123.9 | 118.4 | 121.9 |
| B. Capital Account* | 209ba | .... | .... | .... | .... | .... | .... | .... | 15.4 | 11.9 | 7.1 | 3.7 | .2 |
| Capital account: credit | 209ca | .... | .... | .... | .... | .... | .... | .... | 15.4 | 12.0 | 7.1 | 3.9 | .2 |
| Capital account: debit | 209da | .... | .... | .... | .... | .... | .... | .... | — | .1 | — | .2 | .1 |
| Balance on current & capital acct. | 129ba | .... | .... | .... | .... | .... | .... | .... | 10.8 | 107.8 | 11.0 | −106.6 | 23.4 |
| C. Financial Account* | 309na | .... | .... | .... | .... | .... | .... | .... | 33.6 | 244.0 | 87.3 | −141.0 | 36.8 |
| Direct investment: assets | 3a9aa | .... | .... | .... | .... | .... | .... | .... | 1.2 | −2.7 | 3.4 | 1.2 | .1 |
| Equity & investment fund shares | 3aaaa | .... | .... | .... | .... | .... | .... | .... | 2.4 | 1.4 | 1.5 | 1.7 | .7 |
| Debt instruments | 3abaa | .... | .... | .... | .... | .... | .... | .... | −1.2 | −4.1 | 2.0 | −.5 | −.6 |
| Direct investment: liabilities | 3a9la | .... | .... | .... | .... | .... | .... | .... | −48.5 | 13.5 | 47.4 | 47.7 | 27.8 |
| Equity & investment fund shares | 3aala | .... | .... | .... | .... | .... | .... | .... | −48.3 | 9.1 | 17.4 | 2.3 | −9.6 |
| Debt instruments | 3abla | .... | .... | .... | .... | .... | .... | .... | −.2 | 4.4 | 30.0 | 45.4 | 37.4 |
| Portfolio investment: assets | 3b9aa | .... | .... | .... | .... | .... | .... | .... | 26.6 | 64.2 | 42.8 | −12.1 | −5.5 |
| Equity & investment fund shares | 3baaa | .... | .... | .... | .... | .... | .... | .... | 22.0 | 63.2 | 34.7 | .5 | 1.0 |
| Debt securities | 3bbaa | .... | .... | .... | .... | .... | .... | .... | 4.6 | 1.0 | 8.1 | −12.7 | −6.4 |
| Portfolio investment: liabilities | 3b9la | .... | .... | .... | .... | .... | .... | .... | −26.9 | −19.5 | −12.2 | 85.3 | −15.4 |
| Equity & investment fund shares | 3bala | .... | .... | .... | .... | .... | .... | .... | .... | .... | .... | .... | .... |
| Debt securities | 3bbla | .... | .... | .... | .... | .... | .... | .... | −26.9 | −19.5 | −12.2 | 85.3 | −15.4 |
| Fin. der.& empl.stk.ops.(ESOs): net. | 3c9na | .... | .... | .... | .... | .... | .... | .... | — | .4 | — | .6 | — |
| Fin. der. & ESOs.: assets | 3c9aa | .... | .... | .... | .... | .... | .... | .... | — | .4 | — | .6 | — |
| Fin. der. & ESOs.: liabilities | 3c9la | .... | .... | .... | .... | .... | .... | .... | .... | .... | .... | .... | .... |
| Other investment: assets | 3d9aa | .... | .... | .... | .... | .... | .... | .... | −109.1 | 20.9 | 106.3 | 59.3 | 53.6 |
| Other equity | 3daaa | .... | .... | .... | .... | .... | .... | .... | .... | .... | .... | .... | .... |
| Debt instruments | 3dzaa | .... | .... | .... | .... | .... | .... | .... | −109.1 | 20.9 | 106.3 | 59.3 | 53.6 |
| Other investment: liabilities | 3d9la | .... | .... | .... | .... | .... | .... | .... | −39.6 | −155.2 | 30.1 | 56.9 | −1.0 |
| Other equity | 3dala | .... | .... | .... | .... | .... | .... | .... | .... | .... | .... | .... | .... |
| Debt instruments | 3dzla | .... | .... | .... | .... | .... | .... | .... | −39.6 | −155.2 | 30.1 | 56.9 | −1.0 |
| Curr.+ cap.– finan. acct. balance | 4y9na | .... | .... | .... | .... | .... | .... | .... | −22.8 | −136.2 | −76.2 | 34.4 | −13.3 |
| D. Net Errors and Omissions | 409na | .... | .... | .... | .... | .... | .... | .... | 20.4 | 49.8 | 55.1 | 29.2 | 16.8 |
| E. Reserves and Related Items | 4z9na | .... | .... | .... | .... | .... | .... | .... | −2.4 | −86.4 | −21.1 | 63.6 | 3.4 |
| Reserve assets | 3e9aa | .... | .... | .... | .... | .... | .... | .... | 7.0 | −40.3 | −7.0 | 66.8 | 4.0 |
| Credit and loans from the IMF | 3dcla | .... | .... | .... | .... | .... | .... | .... | .... | .... | .... | .... | .... |
| Exceptional financing | 409la | .... | .... | .... | .... | .... | .... | .... | 9.4 | 46.1 | 14.2 | 3.2 | .6 |

*Excludes components in group E

| | | | | | | *Millions: Midyear Estimates* | | | | | | | |
|---|---|---|---|---|---|---|---|---|---|---|---|---|---|
| **Population** | 99z | .03 | .03 | .03 | .03 | .03 | .03 | .03 | .03 | .04 | .04 | .04 | .04 |

# Slovak Republic   936

| | | 2004 | 2005 | 2006 | 2007 | 2008 | 2009 | 2010 | 2011 | 2012 | 2013 | 2014 | 2015 |
|---|---|---|---|---|---|---|---|---|---|---|---|---|---|
| **Exchange Rates** | | | | | *Koruny per SDR through 2008; Euros per SDR Thereafter: End of Period* | | | | | | | | |
| Market Rate | aa | 44.255 | 45.662 | 39.484 | 36.140 | 32.939 | 1.0882 | 1.1525 | 1.1865 | 1.1649 | 1.1167 | 1.1933 | 1.2728 |
| | | | | *Koruny per US Dollar through 2008; Euros per US Dollar Thereafter: End of Period (ae) Period Average (rf)* | | | | | | | | | |
| Market Rate | ae | 28.496 | 31.948 | 26.246 | 22.870 | 21.385 | .6942 | .7484 | .7729 | .7579 | .7251 | .8237 | .9185 |
| Market Rate | rf | 32.257 | 31.018 | 29.697 | 24.694 | 21.361 | .7198 | .7550 | .7194 | .7783 | .7532 | .7537 | .9017 |
| | | | | | *Index Numbers (2010=100): Period Averages* | | | | | | | | |
| Nominal Effective Exchange Rate | nec | 76.00 | 77.64 | 80.53 | 89.30 | 97.06 | 102.70 | 100.00 | 100.21 | 98.75 | 100.47 | 101.50 | 99.11 |
| CPI-Based Real Effect. Ex. Rate | rec | 73.65 | 75.62 | 80.15 | 88.88 | 97.25 | 103.73 | 100.00 | 101.18 | 100.72 | 102.16 | 101.94 | 98.53 |
| **Fund Position** | | | | | | *Millions of SDRs: End of Period* | | | | | | | |
| Quota | 2f.s | 357.50 | 357.50 | 357.50 | 357.50 | 357.50 | 357.50 | 357.50 | 427.50 | 427.50 | 427.50 | 427.50 | 427.50 |
| SDR Holdings | 1b.s | .88 | .90 | .93 | .97 | 1.00 | 341.62 | 341.79 | 324.81 | 326.40 | 354.73 | 323.05 | 322.72 |
| Reserve Position in the Fund | 1c.s | — | — | — | 3.00 | 31.00 | 67.78 | 91.44 | 184.64 | 194.94 | 208.64 | 187.54 | 124.92 |
| Total Fund Cred.&Loans Outstg. | 2tl | — | — | — | — | — | — | — | — | — | — | — | — |
| SDR Allocations | 1bd | — | — | — | — | — | 340.48 | 340.48 | 340.48 | 340.48 | 340.48 | 340.48 | 340.48 |
| **International Liquidity** | | | | | *Millions of US Dollars Unless Otherwise Indicated: End of Period* | | | | | | | | |
| Total Res. Min. Gold (Eurosys.Def) | 1l.d | 14,417 | 14,901 | 12,647 | 18,032 | 17,854 | † 692 | 719 | 853 | 818 | 922 | 1,392 | 1,812 |
| SDR Holdings | 1b.d | 1 | 1 | 1 | 2 | 2 | 536 | 526 | 499 | 502 | 546 | 468 | 447 |
| Reserve Position in the Fund | 1c.d | — | — | — | 5 | 48 | 106 | 141 | 283 | 300 | 321 | 272 | 173 |
| Foreign Exchange | 1d.d | 14,416 | 14,899 | 12,645 | 18,026 | 17,805 | † 50 | 52 | 71 | 17 | 54 | 652 | 1,192 |
| o/w:Fin. Deriv. Rel to Reserves | 1ddd | .... | .... | .... | | | — | — | — | — | — | — | — |
| Other Reserve Assets | 1e.d | .... | .... | .... | .... | .... | — | — | — | — | — | — | — |
| Gold (Million Fine Troy Ounces) | 1ad | 1.129 | 1.129 | 1.129 | 1.129 | 1.129 | 1.022 | 1.022 | 1.022 | 1.022 | 1.022 | 1.019 | 1.019 |
| Gold (Eurosystem Valuation) | 1and | 494 | 579 | 717 | 944 | 976 | † 1,128 | 1,441 | 1,609 | 1,701 | 1,228 | 1,222 | 1,080 |
| Memo:Euro Cl. On Non-EA Res | 1dgd | .... | .... | .... | .... | .... | | | | | | | |
| Non-Euro Cl. on EA Res | 1dhd | .... | .... | .... | .... | .... | 155.6 | 153.7 | 340.3 | 162.3 | 51.3 | 123.1 | 201.2 |
| Central Bank: Other Assets | 3..d | .... | .... | 1,789 | 2,147 | 54 | 19,420 | 19,785 | 21,490 | 18,685 | 19,461 | 16,871 | 9,924 |
| Central Bank: Other Liabs | 4..d | .... | .... | 193 | 103 | 112 | 1,067 | 921 | 2,697 | 5,422 | 4,902 | 4,225 | 2,473 |
| Other Depository Corps.: Assets | 7a.d | .... | .... | 2,141 | 3,453 | 3,043 | 4,937 | 4,393 | 3,752 | 4,833 | 5,087 | 5,853 | 6,033 |
| Other Depository Corps.: Liabs | 7b.d | .... | .... | 3,253 | 3,599 | 4,606 | 2,384 | 2,655 | 2,911 | 2,362 | 2,778 | 3,484 | 3,158 |
| **Central Bank** | | | | | | *Millions of Euros: End of Period* | | | | | | | |
| Euro Area Wide Residency Criterion | | | | | | | | | | | | | |
| Net Foreign Assets | 11n.u | .... | .... | 4,872 | 4,488 | 2,100 | 3,159 | 4,119 | 3,210 | 737 | 1,099 | 3,175 | 3,374 |
| Claims on Nonresidents | 11..u | .... | .... | 5,125 | 4,576 | 2,382 | 3,956 | 4,860 | 5,358 | 4,910 | 4,716 | 6,910 | 6,113 |
| Liabilities to Nonresidents | 16c.u | .... | .... | 253 | 88 | 282 | 798 | 740 | 2,147 | 4,173 | 3,616 | 3,735 | 2,739 |
| Claims on Other Depository Corps. | 12e.u | .... | .... | 2,886 | 3,890 | 5,184 | 9,909 | 8,771 | 9,653 | 8,998 | 6,195 | 5,577 | 4,555 |
| Net Claims on Central Government | 12anu | .... | .... | 3,670 | 6,014 | 6,031 | 1,390 | 2,441 | 3,420 | 228 | −860 | 202 | 4,878 |
| Claims on Central Govt | 12a.u | .... | .... | 3,671 | 6,019 | 6,031 | 1,390 | 2,441 | 3,420 | 2,834 | 1,891 | 1,203 | 4,912 |
| Liabs. to Central Govt | 16d.u | .... | .... | 1 | 5 | — | — | — | 1 | 2,607 | 2,751 | 1,001 | 34 |
| Claims on Other Sectors | 12s.u | .... | .... | 23 | 41 | 46 | 1,220 | 1,060 | 1,199 | 240 | 220 | 306 | 401 |
| Claims on Other Financial Corps. | 12g.u | .... | .... | 11 | 28 | 32 | 773 | 839 | 978 | 184 | 168 | 167 | 70 |
| Claims on State & Local Govts | 12b.u | .... | .... | — | — | — | — | — | — | 42 | 38 | 103 | 229 |
| Claims on Public Nonfin. Corps. | 12c.u | .... | .... | — | — | — | — | — | — | — | — | — | — |
| Claims on Private Sector | 12d.u | .... | .... | 12 | 14 | 14 | 447 | 221 | 221 | 14 | 13 | 37 | 102 |
| Monetary Base | 14..u | .... | .... | 13,614 | 16,076 | 17,399 | 8,963 | 9,844 | 9,688 | 15,190 | 13,430 | 16,495 | 18,663 |
| Currency in Circulation | 14a.u | .... | .... | 4,764 | 5,150 | 2,556 | 7,597 | 7,896 | 8,326 | 8,444 | 8,834 | 10,465 | 11,090 |
| Liabs. to Other Depository Corps. | 14c.u | .... | .... | 8,828 | 10,902 | 14,818 | 1,315 | 1,854 | 1,219 | 6,578 | 4,420 | 5,823 | 7,355 |
| Liabs. to Other Sectors | 14d.u | .... | .... | 23 | 23 | 26 | 50 | 94 | 142 | 167 | 177 | 207 | 217 |
| Other Liabs. to Other Dep. Corps | 14n.u | .... | .... | 1,243 | 2,248 | 1,002 | — | — | — | — | — | — | — |
| Dep. & Sec. Excl. f/Monetary Base | 14o.u | .... | .... | 4 | 10 | 15 | 16 | 18 | 17 | 16 | 18 | 20 | 20 |
| Deposits Included in Broad Money. | 15..u | .... | .... | — | — | — | — | — | — | — | — | — | — |
| Sec.Ot.th.Shares Inc.in.Brd.Money | 16a.u | .... | .... | — | — | — | — | — | — | — | — | — | — |
| Deposits Excl. from Broad Money | 16b.u | .... | .... | 4 | 10 | 15 | 16 | 18 | 17 | 16 | 18 | 20 | 20 |
| Sec.Oh.th.Shares Excl. f/Brd.Money | 16s.u | .... | .... | — | — | — | — | — | — | — | — | — | — |
| Loans | 16l.u | .... | .... | — | — | — | — | — | — | — | — | — | — |
| Financial Derivatives | 16m.u | .... | .... | — | — | — | — | — | — | — | — | — | — |
| Shares and Other Equity | 17a.u | .... | .... | −3,132 | −3,653 | −4,729 | −4,356 | −4,625 | −4,481 | −3,836 | −3,969 | −3,935 | −4,016 |
| Other Items (Net) | 17r.u | .... | .... | −278 | −247 | −326 | 11,055 | 11,154 | 12,258 | −1,167 | −2,825 | −3,320 | −1,463 |
| Memorandum Items | | | | | | | | | | | | | |
| National Residency Criterion | | | | | | | | | | | | | |
| Net Foreign Assets | 11n | .... | .... | 11,237 | 14,251 | 13,199 | −694 | 1,230 | 2,166 | 6,007 | 8,916 | 7,242 | 3,172 |
| Claims on Nonresidents | 11 | .... | .... | 11,584 | 14,422 | 13,559 | 14,742 | 16,420 | 18,508 | 16,067 | 15,667 | 16,049 | 11,772 |
| Liabilities to Nonresidents | 16c | .... | .... | 347 | 171 | 360 | 15,435 | 15,191 | 16,342 | 10,061 | 6,751 | 8,806 | 8,600 |
| Claims on Other Depository Corps. | 12e | .... | .... | 109 | 91 | 70 | 2,119 | 1,054 | 1,462 | 1,980 | 362 | 624 | 963 |
| Net Claims on Central Government | 12an | .... | .... | −1 | −5 | — | — | 42 | 44 | −2,398 | −2,688 | −1,001 | 4,107 |
| Claims on Central Government | 12a | .... | .... | — | — | — | — | 42 | 44 | 208 | 63 | — | 4,141 |
| Liabilities to Central Government | 16d | .... | .... | 1 | 5 | — | — | — | 1 | 2,607 | 2,751 | 1,001 | 34 |
| Claims on Other Sectors | 12s | .... | .... | 12 | 14 | 14 | 14 | 15 | 15 | 14 | 13 | 12 | 12 |
| Claims on Other Fin. Corps | 12g | .... | .... | — | — | — | — | — | — | — | — | — | — |
| Claims on State & Local Govts | 12b | .... | .... | — | — | — | — | — | — | — | — | — | — |
| Claims on Private Sector | 12d | .... | .... | 12 | 14 | 14 | 14 | 15 | 15 | 14 | 13 | 12 | 12 |
| Liabs.to ODCs, Inc.in Mon.Base | 14c | .... | .... | 8,734 | 10,819 | 14,739 | 1,198 | 715 | 646 | 691 | 1,285 | 752 | 1,496 |
| Liabs.to Ot.Sectors, Inc.in Mon.Base | 14d | .... | .... | 23 | 23 | 26 | 50 | 94 | 142 | 167 | 177 | 207 | 217 |
| Liabs.to ODCs,Excl.f/Mon.Base | 14n | .... | .... | 1,243 | 2,248 | 1,002 | — | — | — | — | — | — | — |
| Net Claims on Eurosystem | 12e.s | .... | .... | — | — | — | −14,081 | −12,860 | −13,160 | 1,361 | 3,160 | 2,797 | 1,017 |

| Other Depository Corporations | | 2004 | 2005 | 2006 | 2007 | 2008 | 2009 | 2010 | 2011 | 2012 | 2013 | 2014 | 2015 |
|---|---|---|---|---|---|---|---|---|---|---|---|---|---|
| Euro Area Wide Residency Criterion | | | | *Millions of Euros: End of Period* | | | | | | | | | |
| Net Foreign Assets | 21n.u | .... | .... | −844 | −99 | −1,124 | 1,772 | 1,301 | 650 | 1,873 | 1,674 | 1,951 | 2,641 |
| Claims on Nonresidents | 21..u | .... | .... | 1,626 | 2,346 | 2,186 | 3,427 | 3,288 | 2,899 | 3,663 | 3,689 | 4,821 | 5,542 |
| Liabilities to Nonresidents | 26c.u | .... | .... | 2,470 | 2,445 | 3,310 | 1,655 | 1,987 | 2,250 | 1,790 | 2,014 | 2,870 | 2,901 |
| Claims on Eurosystem | 20..u | .... | .... | 10,464 | 13,610 | 16,870 | 1,812 | 1,288 | 1,306 | 1,367 | 1,960 | 1,533 | 2,339 |
| Currency | 20a.u | .... | .... | 486 | 530 | 1,129 | 614 | 572 | 660 | 676 | 675 | 781 | 843 |
| Reserve Deposits and Securities | 20b.u | .... | .... | 8,736 | 10,833 | 14,739 | 1,198 | 716 | 646 | 691 | 1,285 | 752 | 1,496 |
| Other Claims | 20n.u | .... | .... | 1,243 | 2,248 | 1,002 | — | — | — | — | — | — | — |
| Net Claims on Central Government | 22anu | .... | .... | 5,597 | 5,022 | 5,383 | 10,270 | 11,318 | 11,364 | 11,744 | 10,999 | 10,613 | 10,402 |
| Claims on Central Government | 22a.u | .... | .... | 7,954 | 8,068 | 8,325 | 11,550 | 12,595 | 11,724 | 12,100 | 11,369 | 11,002 | 11,414 |
| Liabilities to Central Government | 26d.u | .... | .... | 2,356 | 3,046 | 2,941 | 1,280 | 1,278 | 360 | 356 | 370 | 389 | 1,012 |
| Claims on Other Sectors | 22s.u | .... | .... | 23,246 | 28,015 | 32,452 | 32,431 | 34,003 | 36,726 | 37,509 | 39,570 | 42,047 | 45,769 |
| Claims on Other Financial Corps | 22g.u | .... | .... | 3,481 | 3,404 | 3,203 | 2,194 | 1,727 | 1,957 | 1,759 | 1,844 | 1,834 | 1,781 |
| Claims on State & Local Govts | 22b.u | .... | .... | 556 | 639 | 727 | 854 | 1,086 | 1,075 | 1,008 | 946 | 970 | 976 |
| Claims on Public Nonfin. Corps | 22c.u | .... | .... | | | | | | | | | | |
| Claims on Private Sector | 22d.u | .... | .... | 19,209 | 23,971 | 28,521 | 29,383 | 31,190 | 33,694 | 34,741 | 36,779 | 39,243 | 43,012 |
| Liabilities to Eurosystem | 26g.u | .... | .... | 3,362 | 3,852 | 5,083 | 9,825 | 8,719 | 9,512 | 8,793 | 6,029 | 5,367 | 4,390 |
| Transf.Dep.Included in Broad Money | 24..u | .... | .... | 13,297 | 15,363 | 16,665 | 16,833 | 18,487 | 18,298 | 19,794 | 22,021 | 23,900 | 28,032 |
| Other.Dep.Included in Broad Money. | 25..u | .... | .... | 13,228 | 14,906 | 18,383 | 14,963 | 13,921 | 13,639 | 14,642 | 14,621 | 13,697 | 13,830 |
| Sec.Ot.th.Shares Inc.in.Brd. Money. | 26a.u | .... | .... | −1,518 | −2,694 | −1,548 | −673 | 94 | 170 | 164 | 99 | −51 | −9 |
| Deposits Excl. from Broad Money | 26b.u | .... | .... | 3,019 | 3,216 | 3,387 | 4,623 | 5,770 | 6,586 | 6,342 | 5,998 | 6,025 | 5,731 |
| Sec.Ot.th.Shares Excl.f/Brd. Money | 26s.u | .... | .... | −1,736 | −2,084 | −2,593 | −4,751 | −5,308 | −5,301 | −3,988 | −2,656 | −1,558 | −262 |
| Loans | 26l.u | .... | .... | — | — | — | — | — | — | — | — | — | — |
| Financial Derivatives | 26m.u | .... | .... | 1,013 | 684 | 918 | 520 | 503 | 545 | 455 | 346 | 488 | 412 |
| Insurance Technical Reserves | 26r.u | .... | .... | — | — | — | — | — | — | — | — | — | — |
| Shares and Other Equity | 27a.u | .... | .... | 3,819 | 4,208 | 5,104 | 5,077 | 5,363 | 5,992 | 6,730 | 7,118 | 7,404 | 7,519 |
| Other Items (Net) | 27r.u | .... | .... | 3,981 | 9,099 | 8,182 | −132 | 362 | 603 | −440 | 628 | 874 | 1,502 |
| Memorandum Items | | | | | | | | | | | | | |
| Total Assets | 20ra | .... | .... | 49,151 | 58,054 | 65,509 | 56,233 | 58,132 | 58,024 | 59,716 | 61,032 | 64,239 | 69,102 |
| National Residency Criterion | | | | | | | | | | | | | |
| Net Foreign Assets | 21n | .... | .... | −2,817 | −5,629 | −7,530 | 2,869 | 2,553 | 2,191 | 3,570 | 3,151 | 3,622 | 3,579 |
| Claims on Nonresidents | 21 | .... | .... | 3,356 | 4,415 | 4,552 | 6,931 | 7,484 | 6,527 | 6,430 | 6,856 | 8,291 | 8,541 |
| Liabilities to Nonresidents | 26c | .... | .... | 6,173 | 10,045 | 12,081 | 4,062 | 4,930 | 4,336 | 2,860 | 3,706 | 4,670 | 4,962 |
| Net Claims on Central Government | 22an | .... | .... | 5,546 | 5,001 | 5,370 | 10,093 | 10,425 | 10,585 | 11,536 | 10,540 | 10,151 | 9,421 |
| Claims on Central Government | 22a | .... | .... | 7,901 | 8,046 | 8,310 | 11,372 | 11,701 | 10,945 | 11,891 | 10,909 | 10,539 | 10,433 |
| Liabilities to Central Government | 26d | .... | .... | 2,356 | 3,045 | 2,940 | 1,279 | 1,277 | 359 | 355 | 369 | 388 | 1,012 |
| Claims on Other Sectors | 22s | .... | .... | 22,797 | 27,328 | 31,694 | 31,700 | 33,160 | 35,872 | 36,622 | 38,134 | 40,444 | 44,565 |
| Claims on Other Fin. Corps | 22g | .... | .... | 3,228 | 3,094 | 3,080 | 2,087 | 1,613 | 1,864 | 1,603 | 1,607 | 1,587 | 1,537 |
| Claims on State & Local Govts | 22b | .... | .... | 556 | 639 | 727 | 854 | 1,086 | 1,069 | 1,003 | 946 | 970 | 976 |
| Claims on Private Sector | 22d | .... | .... | 19,013 | 23,594 | 27,887 | 28,759 | 30,461 | 32,939 | 34,017 | 35,580 | 37,887 | 42,052 |
| Transf.Dep.Included in Broad Money | 24 | .... | .... | 13,196 | 15,155 | 16,511 | 16,695 | 18,361 | 18,162 | 19,628 | 21,742 | 23,645 | 27,724 |
| Other.Dep.Included in Broad Money. | 25 | .... | .... | 13,198 | 14,737 | 17,904 | 14,594 | 13,354 | 13,515 | 14,581 | 14,474 | 13,652 | 13,629 |
| Sec.Ot.th.Shares Inc.in.Brd. Money. | 26a | .... | .... | 179 | 295 | 674 | 663 | 120 | 178 | 199 | 154 | 84 | 126 |
| Deposits Excl. from Broad Money | 26b | .... | .... | 3,018 | 3,216 | 3,357 | 4,590 | 5,702 | 6,552 | 6,301 | 5,935 | 5,954 | 5,654 |
| Sec.Ot.th.Shares Excl.f/Brd. Money | 26s | .... | .... | 1,048 | 1,485 | 1,662 | 1,972 | 2,589 | 2,902 | 2,901 | 3,134 | 3,262 | 3,205 |

# Slovak Republic   936

| | | 2004 | 2005 | 2006 | 2007 | 2008 | 2009 | 2010 | 2011 | 2012 | 2013 | 2014 | 2015 |
|---|---|---|---|---|---|---|---|---|---|---|---|---|---|
| **Depository Corporations** | | | | | *Millions of Euros: End of Period* | | | | | | | | |
| Euro Area Wide Residency Criterion | | | | | | | | | | | | | |
| Net Foreign Assets | 31n.u | .... | .... | 4,028 | 4,389 | 977 | 4,931 | 5,420 | 3,860 | 2,610 | 2,773 | 5,127 | 6,014 |
| Claims on Nonresidents | 31..u | .... | .... | 6,751 | 6,922 | 4,568 | 7,384 | 8,147 | 8,257 | 8,573 | 8,404 | 11,731 | 11,655 |
| Liabilities to Nonresidents | 36c.u | .... | .... | 2,723 | 2,533 | 3,591 | 2,452 | 2,727 | 4,397 | 5,963 | 5,631 | 6,605 | 5,640 |
| Domestic Claims | 32..u | .... | .... | 32,537 | 39,092 | 43,911 | 45,311 | 48,821 | 52,709 | 49,720 | 49,929 | 53,167 | 61,449 |
| Net Claims on Central Government | 32anu | .... | .... | 9,268 | 11,036 | 11,414 | 11,659 | 13,758 | 14,783 | 11,972 | 10,139 | 10,814 | 15,280 |
| Claims on Central Government | 32a.u | .... | .... | 11,624 | 14,087 | 14,356 | 12,940 | 15,036 | 15,144 | 14,935 | 13,260 | 12,204 | 16,326 |
| Liabilities to Central Government | 36d.u | .... | .... | 2,357 | 3,051 | 2,942 | 1,280 | 1,278 | 361 | 2,963 | 3,120 | 1,390 | 1,046 |
| Claims on Other Sectors | 32s.u | .... | .... | 23,269 | 28,056 | 32,497 | 33,651 | 35,063 | 37,926 | 37,748 | 39,790 | 42,353 | 46,169 |
| Claims on Other Financial Corps | 32g.u | .... | .... | 3,493 | 3,432 | 3,235 | 2,967 | 2,566 | 2,935 | 1,943 | 2,013 | 2,000 | 1,850 |
| Claims on State & Local Govts | 32b.u | .... | .... | 556 | 639 | 727 | 854 | 1,086 | 1,075 | 1,050 | 984 | 1,074 | 1,205 |
| Claims on Public Nonfin. Corps | 32c.u | .... | .... | — | — | — | — | — | — | — | — | — | — |
| Claims on Private Sector | 32d.u | .... | .... | 19,221 | 23,985 | 28,535 | 29,830 | 31,411 | 33,915 | 34,756 | 36,793 | 39,279 | 43,114 |
| Broad Money Liabilities | 35l.u | .... | .... | 29,308 | 32,218 | 34,952 | 38,158 | 39,919 | 39,917 | 42,536 | 45,076 | 47,437 | 52,317 |
| Currency Outside Depository Corps | 34a.u | .... | .... | 4,278 | 4,620 | 1,427 | 6,984 | 7,324 | 7,667 | 7,768 | 8,159 | 9,684 | 10,247 |
| Transferable Deposits | 34..u | .... | .... | 13,305 | 15,373 | 16,676 | 16,847 | 18,498 | 18,310 | 19,806 | 22,037 | 23,914 | 28,047 |
| Other Deposits | 35..u | .... | .... | 13,243 | 14,919 | 18,397 | 15,000 | 14,003 | 13,770 | 14,798 | 14,782 | 13,890 | 14,032 |
| Securities Other than Shares | 36a.u | .... | .... | −1,518 | −2,694 | −1,548 | −673 | 94 | 170 | 164 | 99 | −51 | −9 |
| Deposits Excl. from Broad Money | 36b.u | .... | .... | 3,023 | 3,226 | 3,402 | 4,639 | 5,788 | 6,603 | 6,358 | 6,016 | 6,045 | 5,751 |
| Sec.Oth.th.Shares Excl.f/Brd. Money | 36s.u | .... | .... | −1,736 | −2,084 | −2,593 | −4,751 | −5,308 | −5,301 | −3,988 | −2,656 | −1,558 | −262 |
| Loans | 36l.u | .... | .... | — | — | — | — | — | — | — | — | — | — |
| Financial Derivatives | 36m.u | .... | .... | 1,013 | 684 | 918 | 520 | 503 | 545 | 455 | 346 | 488 | 412 |
| Insurance Technical Reserves | 36r.u | .... | .... | — | — | — | — | — | — | — | — | — | — |
| Shares and Other Equity | 37a.u | .... | .... | 687 | 555 | 375 | 721 | 738 | 1,511 | 2,894 | 3,149 | 3,469 | 3,503 |
| Other Items (Net) | 37r.u | .... | .... | 4,270 | 8,883 | 7,834 | 10,955 | 12,602 | 13,294 | 4,075 | 771 | 2,415 | 5,734 |
| Broad Money Liabs., Seasonally Adj. | 35lub | .... | .... | 29,000 | 31,880 | 34,582 | 37,772 | 39,544 | 39,588 | 42,213 | 44,722 | 47,043 | 51,868 |
| Memorandum Items | | | | | | | | | | | | | |
| National Residency Criterion | | | | | | | | | | | | | |
| Net Foreign Assets | 31n | .... | .... | 8,420 | 8,622 | 5,669 | 2,175 | 3,783 | 4,357 | 9,577 | 12,067 | 10,864 | 6,751 |
| Claims on Nonresidents | 31 | .... | .... | 14,940 | 18,838 | 18,111 | 21,673 | 23,904 | 25,035 | 22,497 | 22,524 | 24,340 | 20,313 |
| Liabilities to Nonresidents | 36c | .... | .... | 6,520 | 10,216 | 12,442 | 19,498 | 20,121 | 20,678 | 12,921 | 10,457 | 13,476 | 13,562 |
| Domestic Claims | 32 | .... | .... | 28,354 | 32,338 | 37,077 | 41,808 | 43,641 | 46,516 | 45,775 | 45,999 | 49,606 | 58,105 |
| Net Claims on Central Government | 32an | .... | .... | 5,545 | 4,997 | 5,369 | 10,093 | 10,466 | 10,629 | 9,138 | 7,852 | 9,150 | 13,528 |
| Claims on Central Government | 32a | .... | .... | 7,901 | 8,046 | 8,310 | 11,372 | 11,743 | 10,989 | 12,100 | 10,972 | 10,539 | 14,574 |
| Liabilities to Central Government | 36d | .... | .... | 2,356 | 3,050 | 2,941 | 1,279 | 1,277 | 360 | 2,962 | 3,120 | 1,389 | 1,046 |
| Claims on Other Sectors | 32s | .... | .... | 22,809 | 27,342 | 31,708 | 31,714 | 33,175 | 35,887 | 36,637 | 38,147 | 40,456 | 44,577 |
| Claims on Other Financial Corps | 32g | .... | .... | 3,228 | 3,094 | 3,080 | 2,087 | 1,613 | 1,864 | 1,603 | 1,607 | 1,587 | 1,537 |
| Claims on State & Local Govts | 32b | .... | .... | 556 | 639 | 727 | 854 | 1,086 | 1,069 | 1,003 | 946 | 970 | 976 |
| Claims on Private Sector | 32d | .... | .... | 19,024 | 23,608 | 27,901 | 28,773 | 30,476 | 32,954 | 34,031 | 35,594 | 37,899 | 42,064 |
| Transf.Dep.Included in Broad Money | 34 | .... | .... | 13,205 | 15,166 | 16,522 | 16,708 | 18,372 | 18,173 | 19,640 | 21,758 | 23,658 | 27,739 |
| Other Dep. Included in Broad Money | 35 | .... | .... | 13,212 | 14,750 | 17,919 | 14,631 | 13,436 | 13,646 | 14,737 | 14,635 | 13,846 | 13,832 |
| Sec.Ot.th.Shares Inc.in.Brd. Money | 36a | .... | .... | 179 | 295 | 674 | 663 | 120 | 178 | 199 | 154 | 84 | 126 |
| Deposits Excl. from Broad Money | 36b | .... | .... | 3,023 | 3,226 | 3,372 | 4,606 | 5,720 | 6,569 | 6,317 | 5,953 | 5,974 | 5,674 |
| Sec.Ot.th.Shares Excl./f.Brd. Money | 36s | .... | .... | 1,048 | 1,485 | 1,662 | 1,972 | 2,589 | 2,902 | 2,901 | 3,134 | 3,262 | 3,205 |
| **Monetary Aggregates** | | | | | *Millions of Koruny: End of Period* | | | | | | | | |
| Money (National Definitions) | | | | | | | | | | | | | |
| M1 | 59ma | 404,722 | 485,826 | 546,063 | 622,617 | 575,890 | .... | .... | .... | .... | .... | .... | .... |
| M2 | 59mb | 731,665 | 784,960 | 908,142 | 1,015,058 | 1,071,029 | .... | .... | .... | .... | .... | .... | .... |
| M3 | 59mc | 771,242 | 831,400 | 958,483 | 1,082,390 | 1,135,674 | .... | .... | .... | .... | .... | .... | .... |
| **Interest Rates** | | | | | *Percent Per Annum* | | | | | | | | |
| Central Bank Policy Rate (EOP) | 60 | 4.00 | 3.00 | 4.75 | 4.25 | .... | .... | .... | .... | .... | .... | .... | .... |
| Money Market Rate | 60b | 3.82 | 3.02 | 4.83 | 4.25 | 3.73 | .... | .... | .... | .... | .... | .... | .... |
| Deposit Rate | | | | | | | | | | | | | |
| Households: Stocks, up to 2 years | 60lhs | .... | .... | .... | .... | .... | 2.20 | 1.60 | 1.77 | 2.16 | 1.87 | 1.35 | 1.12 |
| New Business, up to 1 year | 60lhn | .... | .... | .... | .... | .... | 1.49 | 1.75 | 1.97 | 2.09 | 1.57 | 1.53 | 1.69 |
| Corporations: Stocks, up to 2 years | 60lcs | .... | .... | .... | .... | .... | 1.18 | .83 | 1.39 | 1.11 | .69 | .61 | .46 |
| New Business, up to 1 year | 60lcn | .... | .... | .... | .... | .... | .76 | .57 | 1.17 | .63 | .43 | .39 | .24 |
| Lending Rate | | | | | | | | | | | | | |
| Households: Stocks, up to 1 year | 60phs | .... | .... | .... | .... | .... | 13.59 | 14.05 | 13.60 | 13.11 | 13.09 | 13.05 | 13.49 |
| New Bus., Floating & up to 1 year | 60pns | .... | .... | .... | .... | .... | 8.14 | 7.61 | 13.58 | 13.52 | 12.48 | 10.82 | 8.50 |
| House Purch., Stocks, Over 5 years | 60phm | .... | .... | .... | .... | .... | 6.06 | 5.65 | 5.32 | 5.13 | 4.85 | 4.33 | 3.76 |
| House Purch., New Bus., 5-10 yrs | 60phn | .... | .... | .... | .... | .... | 7.90 | 6.57 | 5.67 | 6.97 | 6.46 | 6.04 | 4.93 |
| Corporations: Stocks, up to 1 year | 60pcs | .... | .... | .... | .... | .... | 3.57 | 3.41 | 3.80 | 3.22 | 3.34 | 3.11 | 2.91 |
| New Bus., Over € 1 mil.,up to 1 yr | 60pcn | .... | .... | .... | .... | .... | 2.70 | 3.10 | 3.18 | 2.42 | 2.13 | 2.13 | 1.99 |
| Government Bond Yield | 61 | 5.03 | 3.52 | 4.41 | 4.49 | 4.72 | 4.71 | 3.87 | 4.42 | 4.55 | 3.19 | 2.07 | .89 |
| **Prices, Production, Labor** | | | | | *Index Numbers (2010=100): Period Averages* | | | | | | | | |
| Share Prices | 62 | 94.2 | 193.3 | 178.6 | 186.9 | 190.9 | 140.8 | 100.0 | 101.0 | 87.1 | 84.5 | 93.5 | 114.9 |
| Producer Prices | 63 | 85.9 | 90.0 | † 97.5 | 99.5 | 105.6 | 102.8 | 100.0 | † 102.7 | 104.8 | 103.8 | 100.2 | 97.2 |
| Consumer Prices | 64 | 84.5 | 86.8 | 90.7 | 93.2 | 97.5 | 99.1 | 100.0 | 103.9 | 107.7 | 109.2 | 109.1 | 108.7 |
| Harmonized CPI | 64h | 86.7 | 89.1 | 92.9 | 94.7 | 98.4 | 99.3 | 100.0 | 104.1 | 108.0 | 109.6 | 109.4 | 109.1 |
| Wages | 65 | 68.3 | 74.5 | 80.9 | 86.9 | 94.0 | 96.8 | 100.0 | 102.2 | 104.7 | 107.1 | 111.6 | 114.8 |
| Industrial Production | 66 | 71.6 | 69.9 | 78.5 | 91.1 | 95.5 | 83.2 | 100.0 | 106.3 | 116.8 | 123.3 | 127.1 | 135.2 |
| Employment | 67 | 100.9 | 103.0 | 106.9 | 103.3 | 106.0 | 101.1 | 100.0 | 101.9 | 108.2 | 108.2 | 109.8 | 112.6 |
| | | | | | | *Number in Thousands: Period Averages* | | | | | | | | |
| Labor Force | 67d | 2,648 | 2,637 | 2,651 | 2,646 | 2,679 | 2,680 | 2,696 | 2,668 | 2,695 | 2,704 | 2,707 | 2,719 |
| Employment | 67e | 2,180 | 2,207 | 2,295 | 2,350 | 2,424 | 2,357 | 2,307 | 2,303 | 2,318 | 2,318 | 2,349 | 2,405 |
| Unemployment | 67c | 480 | 427 | 353 | 294 | 254 | 321 | 387 | 363 | 378 | 386 | 359 | 314 |
| Unemployment Rate (%) | 67r | 18.4 | 16.4 | 13.5 | 11.2 | 9.6 | 12.1 | 14.5 | 13.7 | 14.0 | 14.2 | 13.2 | 11.5 |
| **Intl. Transactions & Positions** | | | | | *Millions of Koruny through 2008; Millions of Euros Beginning 2009* | | | | | | | | |
| Exports | 70 | 889,705 | 994,571 | 1,239,359 | 1,419,849 | 1,509,107 | † 39,721 | 48,272 | 56,783 | 62,144 | 64,172 | 64,678 | 67,999 |
| Imports, c.i.f. | 71 | 981,075 | 1,124,439 | 1,397,535 | 1,525,556 | 1,573,011 | † 40,714 | 49,868 | 58,556 | 61,518 | 62,937 | 62,885 | 67,523 |
| Imports, f.o.b. | 71.v | 934,357 | 1,070,894 | 1,330,986 | 1,452,910 | 1,498,106 | † 38,775 | 47,494 | 55,768 | 58,588 | 59,940 | 59,890 | 64,307 |

# Slovak Republic   936

## Balance of Payments

*Millions of US Dollars*

| | | 2004 | 2005 | 2006 | 2007 | 2008 | 2009 | 2010 | 2011 | 2012 | 2013 | 2014 | 2015 |
|---|---|---|---|---|---|---|---|---|---|---|---|---|---|
| A. Current Account* | 109bx | † −4,355.1 | −5,125.2 | −5,450.0 | −4,634.5 | −6,271.1 | −3,018.1 | −4,210.5 | −4,906.6 | 889.7 | 1,886.9 | 175.5 | −1,118.7 |
| Goods, credit (exports) | 1a9cx | † 33,631.4 | 38,676.1 | 49,945.3 | 63,370.4 | 71,349.1 | 53,581.3 | 61,630.7 | 76,017.5 | 77,311.7 | 82,565.1 | 83,115.3 | 73,073.1 |
| Goods, debit (imports) | 1a9dx | † 36,267.5 | 42,145.6 | 53,520.1 | 64,839.5 | 73,087.4 | 53,199.2 | 61,736.2 | 76,100.0 | 74,083.5 | 78,541.7 | 79,278.5 | 71,026.5 |
| Balance on goods | 1a9bx | † −2,636.1 | −3,469.5 | −3,574.8 | −1,469.1 | −1,738.4 | 382.1 | −105.5 | −82.6 | 3,228.1 | 4,023.5 | 3,836.8 | 2,046.6 |
| Services, credit (exports) | 1b9cx | † 5,843.4 | 6,401.9 | 7,390.2 | 8,688.6 | 9,494.4 | 6,609.4 | 6,413.5 | 7,271.5 | 7,771.6 | 9,154.4 | 9,067.1 | 8,040.4 |
| Services, debit (imports) | 1b9dx | † 4,942.7 | 5,585.6 | 6,148.0 | 7,835.5 | 9,993.4 | 7,854.7 | 7,279.1 | 7,651.8 | 7,232.3 | 8,613.9 | 8,947.2 | 7,937.4 |
| Balance on Goods & Services | 1z9bx | † −1,735.4 | −2,653.2 | −2,332.6 | −616.1 | −2,237.3 | −863.1 | −971.1 | −463.0 | 3,767.4 | 4,563.9 | 3,956.7 | 2,149.6 |
| Primary income: credit | 1c9cx | † 1,740.2 | 2,501.1 | 3,069.7 | 3,162.9 | 3,962.4 | 3,765.7 | 3,665.5 | 4,529.1 | 4,276.1 | 4,329.6 | 4,303.3 | 4,220.2 |
| Primary income: debit | 1c9dx | † 4,256.6 | 4,708.4 | 5,801.2 | 6,518.0 | 6,885.5 | 4,558.9 | 6,164.2 | 7,879.4 | 5,824.0 | 5,252.6 | 6,493.2 | 6,250.9 |
| Balance on gds, serv. & prim. inc. | 1y9bx | † −4,251.8 | −4,860.5 | −5,064.1 | −3,971.3 | −5,160.4 | −1,656.3 | −3,469.8 | −3,813.3 | 2,219.5 | 3,640.9 | 1,766.8 | 118.8 |
| Secondary income: credit | 1d9ca | † 756.9 | 1,296.8 | 1,455.7 | 1,863.9 | 2,501.2 | 1,190.0 | 1,096.4 | 764.0 | 518.6 | 528.7 | 641.5 | 609.8 |
| Secondary income: debit | 1d9da | † 860.2 | 1,561.5 | 1,841.7 | 2,527.2 | 3,612.0 | 2,551.8 | 1,837.1 | 1,857.3 | 1,848.4 | 2,282.6 | 2,232.7 | 1,847.4 |
| B. Capital Account* | 209ba | † 182.3 | −12.6 | −33.9 | 640.0 | 1,136.8 | 655.4 | 1,392.3 | 1,242.6 | 1,814.5 | 1,422.3 | 937.0 | 3,078.5 |
| Capital account: credit | 209ca | † 205.1 | 18.8 | 41.6 | 764.5 | 1,190.6 | 703.1 | 1,435.8 | 1,282.7 | 1,855.8 | 1,730.1 | 1,006.5 | 3,280.2 |
| Capital account: debit | 209da | † 22.8 | 31.4 | 75.5 | 124.5 | 53.8 | 47.7 | 43.4 | 40.1 | 41.2 | 307.9 | 69.5 | 201.7 |
| Balance on current & capital acct. | 129ba | † −4,172.7 | −5,137.8 | −5,483.9 | −3,994.5 | −5,134.4 | −2,362.7 | −2,818.2 | −3,663.9 | 2,704.2 | 3,309.2 | 1,112.5 | 1,959.7 |
| C. Financial Account* | 309na | † −4,795.5 | −6,035.0 | −4,316.4 | −6,072.4 | −7,431.2 | −3,140.4 | −3,177.1 | −4,730.4 | 429.5 | −1,711.5 | −2,706.3 | −1,250.2 |
| Direct investment: assets | 3a9aa | † 4.4 | 1,015.4 | 497.5 | 1,643.8 | 522.5 | 2,490.8 | 1,240.6 | 2,695.1 | −1,232.9 | 1,276.4 | 351.0 | 1,157.8 |
| Equity & investment fund shares | 3aaaa | † 214.4 | 142.0 | 593.6 | 576.2 | 606.3 | 718.6 | 856.7 | −217.2 | 50.6 | −105.9 | −296.4 | −100.6 |
| Debt instruments | 3abaa | † −209.9 | 873.4 | −96.1 | 1,067.5 | −83.8 | 1,772.2 | 383.8 | 2,912.2 | −1,283.5 | 1,382.3 | 647.4 | 1,258.4 |
| Direct investment: liabilities | 3a9la | † 4,060.9 | 3,924.7 | 5,696.4 | 5,059.5 | 4,641.9 | 1,519.1 | 2,117.5 | 5,426.6 | 1,776.8 | 1,003.8 | 85.1 | 2,149.7 |
| Equity & investment fund shares | 3aala | † 3,699.6 | 2,016.3 | 4,059.9 | 2,582.2 | 2,132.6 | 2,010.6 | 1,920.8 | 3,590.1 | 830.6 | 617.8 | 383.6 | 1,167.2 |
| Debt instruments | 3abla | † 361.3 | 1,908.4 | 1,636.5 | 2,477.3 | 2,509.3 | −491.5 | 196.7 | 1,836.5 | 946.2 | 386.0 | −298.5 | 982.4 |
| Portfolio investment: assets | 3b9aa | † 2,042.3 | 3,833.2 | −2,064.0 | 2,846.2 | 1,476.6 | 3,890.8 | 3,587.4 | 2,321.1 | −4,814.8 | −325.4 | 938.2 | −1,532.5 |
| Equity & investment fund shares | 3baaa | † 51.8 | −131.8 | 386.6 | 303.0 | −487.1 | −32.3 | 266.2 | −186.3 | 624.6 | 35.4 | −9.3 | 139.9 |
| Debt securities | 3bbaa | † 1,990.4 | 3,965.0 | −2,450.6 | 2,543.2 | 1,963.7 | 3,923.1 | 3,321.2 | 2,507.4 | −5,439.3 | −360.8 | 947.6 | −1,672.4 |
| Portfolio investment: liabilities | 3b9la | † 2,233.1 | −321.8 | 2,165.2 | 381.3 | 1,875.3 | 1,513.5 | 5,266.8 | 2,147.4 | 5,792.7 | 9,185.9 | 4,404.5 | −2,633.1 |
| Equity & investment fund shares | 3bala | † −125.4 | 176.1 | 43.7 | 257.9 | 104.1 | 183.0 | −9.2 | 94.4 | .2 | 85.6 | 17.7 | 67.9 |
| Debt securities | 3bbla | † 2,358.5 | −497.9 | 2,121.5 | 123.4 | 1,771.2 | 1,330.5 | 5,275.9 | 2,052.9 | 5,792.5 | 9,100.2 | 4,386.7 | −2,701.0 |
| Fin. der.& empl.stk.ops.(ESOs): net. | 3c9na | † −23.1 | 44.5 | 203.0 | −60.3 | 220.3 | −354.8 | 380.2 | 476.6 | 39.5 | 424.7 | 483.6 | 272.2 |
| Fin. der. & ESOs.: assets | 3c9aa | . . . . | . . . . | . . . . | . . . . | . . . . | . . . . | . . . . | . . . . | . . . . | . . . . | . . . . | . . . . |
| Fin. der. & ESOs.: liabilities | 3c9la | . . . . | . . . . | . . . . | . . . . | . . . . | . . . . | . . . . | . . . . | . . . . | . . . . | . . . . | . . . . |
| Other investment: assets | 3d9aa | † 821.9 | −416.5 | 1,134.4 | 2,000.3 | −57.5 | −529.7 | −1,050.1 | −2,097.1 | 5,497.9 | 6,419.4 | 4,082.2 | −1,783.7 |
| Other equity | 3daaa | . . . . | . . . . | . . . . | . . . . | . . . . | . . . . | . . . . | . . . . | 368.3 | 359.3 | 286.1 | 3.3 |
| Debt instruments | 3dzaa | † 821.9 | −416.5 | 1,134.4 | 2,000.3 | −57.5 | −529.7 | −1,050.1 | −2,097.1 | 5,129.6 | 6,060.2 | 3,796.1 | −1,787.0 |
| Other investment: liabilities | 3d9la | † 1,347.1 | 6,908.7 | −3,774.4 | 7,061.5 | 3,075.9 | 5,604.9 | −49.0 | 552.0 | −8,509.1 | −683.0 | 4,071.8 | −152.7 |
| Other equity | 3dala | . . . . | . . . . | . . . . | . . . . | . . . . | . . . . | . . . . | . . . . | . . . . | . . . . | . . . . | . . . . |
| Debt instruments | 3dzla | † 1,347.1 | 6,908.7 | −3,774.4 | 7,061.5 | 3,075.9 | 5,604.9 | −49.0 | 552.0 | −8,509.1 | −683.0 | 4,071.8 | −152.7 |
| Curr.+ cap.− finan. acct. balance | 4y9na | † 622.8 | 897.1 | −1,167.5 | 2,077.9 | 2,296.8 | 777.8 | 359.0 | 1,066.5 | 2,274.7 | 5,020.7 | 3,818.8 | 3,209.9 |
| D. Net Errors and Omissions | 409na | † 64.4 | 397.2 | 316.2 | 183.4 | −3,483.4 | −949.0 | −322.3 | −947.3 | −2,296.1 | −4,924.4 | −3,266.5 | −2,873.8 |
| E. Reserves and Related Items | 4z9na | † 687.2 | 1,294.3 | −851.4 | 2,261.3 | −1,186.7 | −171.3 | 36.7 | 119.2 | −21.4 | 96.4 | 552.3 | 336.1 |
| Reserve assets | 3e9aa | † 687.2 | 1,294.3 | −851.4 | 2,261.3 | −1,186.7 | −171.3 | 36.7 | 119.2 | −21.4 | 96.4 | 552.3 | 336.1 |
| Credit and loans from the IMF | 3dcla | † — | — | — | — | — | — | — | — | — | — | — | — |
| Exceptional financing | 409la | . . . . | . . . . | . . . . | . . . . | . . . . | . . . . | . . . . | . . . . | . . . . | . . . . | . . . . | . . . . |

*Excludes components in group E

## International Investment Position

*Millions of US Dollars*

| | | 2004 | 2005 | 2006 | 2007 | 2008 | 2009 | 2010 | 2011 | 2012 | 2013 | 2014 | 2015 |
|---|---|---|---|---|---|---|---|---|---|---|---|---|---|
| Assets | 809aa | † 34,096.2 | 34,948.7 | 33,996.0 | 45,826.6 | 43,132.4 | 57,255.0 | 58,012.1 | 58,514.5 | 59,839.1 | 68,982.1 | 64,991.4 | 56,554.3 |
| Direct investment | 8a9aa | † 4,066.3 | 4,219.0 | 5,365.3 | 7,499.6 | 8,085.4 | 9,961.3 | 9,598.3 | 12,195.3 | 11,681.4 | 13,061.2 | 10,438.0 | 10,707.7 |
| Equity & investment fund shares | 8aaaa | † 1,264.2 | 926.3 | 1,615.5 | 2,072.8 | 2,855.2 | 2,884.2 | 3,218.8 | 2,901.5 | 3,962.3 | 4,609.3 | 2,470.0 | 2,151.3 |
| Debt instruments | 8abaa | † 2,802.1 | 3,292.7 | 3,749.8 | 5,426.8 | 5,230.2 | 7,077.1 | 6,379.5 | 9,293.8 | 7,719.1 | 8,451.9 | 7,967.9 | 8,556.4 |
| Portfolio investment | 8b9aa | † 13,945.9 | 15,369.3 | 13,325.0 | 20,979.2 | 21,044.1 | 27,602.0 | 29,663.8 | 30,056.0 | 27,267.6 | 28,150.1 | 25,682.9 | 21,166.8 |
| Equity & investment fund shares | 8baaa | † 708.8 | 513.8 | 1,008.5 | 1,462.9 | 797.5 | 1,140.5 | 1,398.9 | 1,255.7 | 2,073.3 | 2,415.8 | 2,205.7 | 2,141.6 |
| Debt securities | 8bbaa | † 13,237.1 | 14,855.5 | 12,316.4 | 19,516.3 | 20,246.6 | 26,461.5 | 28,264.9 | 28,800.3 | 25,194.3 | 25,734.3 | 23,477.3 | 19,025.3 |
| Fin. der.(oth.than reserves) & ESOs | 8c9aa | † 301.1 | 368.4 | 935.2 | 696.4 | 1,088.1 | 455.7 | 648.5 | 688.5 | 558.8 | 314.9 | 384.4 | 317.6 |
| Other investment | 8d9aa | † 9,070.6 | 7,948.7 | 8,508.1 | 11,024.3 | 9,730.6 | 17,415.6 | 15,939.6 | 13,156.1 | 17,823.4 | 25,304.3 | 25,873.8 | 21,470.7 |
| Other equity | 8daaa | . . . . | . . . . | . . . . | . . . . | . . . . | 83.6 | 120.1 | 132.6 | 499.6 | 889.2 | 1,044.8 | 885.9 |
| Debt instruments | 8dzaa | † 9,070.6 | 7,948.7 | 8,508.1 | 11,024.3 | 9,730.6 | 17,332.1 | 15,819.5 | 13,023.5 | 17,323.8 | 24,415.1 | 24,829.0 | 20,584.8 |
| Reserve assets | 8e9aa | † 6,712.2 | 7,043.2 | 5,862.4 | 5,627.1 | 3,184.3 | 1,820.4 | 2,161.9 | 2,418.5 | 2,507.9 | 2,151.7 | 2,612.3 | 2,891.4 |
| Liabilities | 809la | † 58,524.5 | 63,191.3 | 72,880.7 | 92,519.1 | 96,497.8 | 118,559.7 | 113,951.9 | 117,402.9 | 119,117.2 | 133,697.6 | 128,357.6 | 115,558.9 |
| Direct investment | 8a9la | † 31,167.3 | 33,066.8 | 42,412.2 | 53,131.7 | 55,561.5 | 59,346.6 | 56,469.9 | 60,154.0 | 62,040.5 | 66,252.7 | 59,938.6 | 56,307.9 |
| Equity & investment fund shares | 8aala | † 25,813.3 | 26,257.6 | 33,081.5 | 39,912.4 | 41,112.2 | 43,884.0 | 42,482.4 | 44,020.9 | 45,033.2 | 48,612.9 | 44,945.3 | 41,381.9 |
| Debt instruments | 8abla | † 5,354.0 | 6,809.2 | 9,330.7 | 13,219.3 | 14,449.3 | 15,462.6 | 13,987.5 | 16,133.1 | 17,007.3 | 17,639.9 | 14,993.3 | 14,926.0 |
| Portfolio investment | 8b9la | † 8,686.5 | 7,239.8 | 10,007.1 | 11,001.4 | 11,765.3 | 14,791.5 | 15,336.8 | 16,042.8 | 23,912.3 | 33,686.9 | 35,743.8 | 29,852.9 |
| Equity & investment fund shares | 8bala | † 593.2 | 673.2 | 761.9 | 763.8 | 832.7 | 1,871.5 | 335.4 | 528.4 | 429.2 | 314.4 | 372.7 | 408.9 |
| Debt securities | 8bbla | † 8,093.3 | 6,566.5 | 9,245.2 | 10,237.6 | 10,932.6 | 12,920.0 | 15,001.4 | 15,514.4 | 23,483.1 | 33,372.4 | 35,371.1 | 29,444.0 |
| Fin. der.(oth.than reserves) & ESOs | 8c9la | † 397.6 | 412.9 | 771.1 | 604.9 | 828.4 | 595.9 | 1,338.6 | 1,285.0 | 1,243.1 | 838.2 | 753.0 | 515.2 |
| Other investment | 8d9la | † 18,273.1 | 22,471.7 | 19,690.3 | 27,781.0 | 28,342.5 | 43,825.7 | 40,806.7 | 39,921.0 | 31,921.3 | 32,919.7 | 31,922.2 | 28,882.7 |
| Other equity | 8dala | . . . . | . . . . | . . . . | . . . . | . . . . | . . . . | . . . . | . . . . | . . . . | . . . . | . . . . | . . . . |
| Debt instruments | 8dzla | † 18,273.1 | 22,471.7 | 19,690.3 | 27,781.0 | 28,342.5 | 43,825.7 | 40,806.7 | 39,921.0 | 31,921.3 | 32,919.7 | 31,922.2 | 28,882.7 |

# Slovak Republic   936

2016, International Monetary Fund : *International Financial Statistics Yearbook*

|  |  | 2004 | 2005 | 2006 | 2007 | 2008 | 2009 | 2010 | 2011 | 2012 | 2013 | 2014 | 2015 |
|---|---|---|---|---|---|---|---|---|---|---|---|---|---|
| **Government Finance Operations Statement General Government** | | *Millions of Euros: Fiscal Year Ends December 31; Data Reported through Eurostat* | | | | | | | | | | | |
| Revenue | a1 | 16,370 | 18,462 | 19,642 | 21,517 | 23,447 | 23,020 | 23,250 | 25,640 | 26,229 | 28,497 | 29,646 | 33,304 |
| Taxes | a11 | 8,556 | 9,418 | 9,825 | 10,967 | 11,680 | 10,369 | 10,591 | 11,431 | 11,391 | 12,347 | 13,252 | 14,145 |
| Social Contributions | a12 | 6,007 | 6,319 | 6,555 | 7,292 | 8,018 | 7,978 | 8,260 | 8,661 | 9,049 | 9,942 | 10,291 | 10,954 |
| Grants | a13 | .... | .... | .... | .... | .... | .... | .... | .... | .... | .... | .... | .... |
| Other Revenue | a14 | .... | .... | .... | .... | .... | .... | .... | .... | .... | .... | .... | .... |
| Expense | a2 | 17,870 | 19,994 | 21,558 | 22,785 | 25,021 | 27,805 | 28,098 | 28,489 | 29,498 | 30,680 | 31,766 | 33,698 |
| Compensation of Employees | a21 | 3,642 | 3,941 | 4,346 | 4,523 | 5,058 | 5,410 | 5,643 | 5,775 | 5,966 | 6,329 | 6,670 | 7,025 |
| Use of Goods & Services | a22 | 2,364 | 2,392 | 3,160 | 3,067 | 3,129 | 3,686 | 3,682 | 3,801 | 3,971 | 4,036 | 4,164 | 4,580 |
| Consumption of Fixed Capital | a23 | 1,793 | 1,842 | 1,933 | 2,001 | 2,142 | 2,239 | 2,304 | 2,485 | 2,577 | 2,644 | 2,793 | 3,014 |
| Interest | a24 | 984 | 846 | 804 | 857 | 851 | 911 | 875 | 1,076 | 1,280 | 1,384 | 1,441 | 1,393 |
| Subsidies | a25 | 843 | 620 | 697 | 708 | 1,086 | 1,005 | 851 | 566 | 491 | 574 | 520 | 464 |
| Grants | a26 | .... | .... | .... | .... | .... | .... | .... | .... | .... | .... | .... | .... |
| Social Benefits | a27 | 7,118 | 8,513 | 9,222 | 10,136 | 11,021 | 12,196 | 13,082 | 13,053 | 13,581 | 13,936 | 14,355 | 14,796 |
| Other Expense | a28 | .... | .... | .... | .... | .... | .... | .... | .... | .... | .... | .... | .... |
| Gross Operating Balance [1-2+23] | agob | 293 | 309 | 17 | 734 | 568 | −2,546 | −2,544 | −364 | −693 | 461 | 673 | 2,619 |
| Net Operating Balance [1-2] | anob | −1,501 | −1,533 | −1,916 | −1,267 | −1,574 | −4,786 | −4,848 | −2,848 | −3,269 | −2,183 | −2,120 | −394 |
| Net Acq. of Nonfinancial Assets | a31 | −436 | −92 | 82 | −62 | 25 | 237 | 184 | 36 | −149 | −191 | −84 | 1,924 |
| Aquisition of Nonfin. Assets | a31.1 | .... | .... | .... | .... | .... | .... | .... | .... | .... | .... | .... | .... |
| Disposal of Nonfin. Assets | a31.2 | .... | .... | .... | .... | .... | .... | .... | .... | .... | .... | .... | .... |
| Net Lending/Borrowing [1-2-31] | anlb | −1,064 | −1,440 | −1,998 | −1,205 | −1,599 | −5,022 | −5,032 | −2,885 | −3,120 | −1,991 | −2,036 | −2,318 |
| Net Acq. of Financial Assets | a32 | 696 | −3,285 | −1,337 | 529 | −257 | −949 | −44 | −282 | 4,129 | 1,437 | −1,403 | −919 |
| By instrument | | | | | | | | | | | | | |
| Monetary Gold & SDRs | a3201 | — | — | — | — | — | — | — | — | — | — | — | — |
| Currency & Deposits | a3202 | 263 | −2,417 | 50 | 950 | 64 | −1,135 | −254 | −937 | 2,848 | 406 | −2,207 | 540 |
| Securities other than Shares | a3203 | 123 | −135 | −37 | −8 | 1 | 12 | −4 | −4 | −5 | 1 | −10 | −37 |
| Loans | a3204 | −34 | −505 | −117 | −110 | 29 | 83 | 45 | 262 | 1,420 | 580 | 112 | −45 |
| Shares & Other Equity | a3205 | −145 | −318 | −1,031 | −232 | −146 | 133 | −140 | −231 | 185 | −28 | −171 | −1,031 |
| Insurance Technical Reserves | a3206 | — | — | — | — | — | — | — | — | — | — | — | — |
| Financial Derivatives | a3207 | — | — | −40 | — | — | — | — | — | — | — | — | — |
| Other Accounts Receivable | a3208 | 489 | 90 | −162 | −71 | −206 | −42 | 309 | 628 | −319 | 477 | 873 | −346 |
| By debtor | | | | | | | | | | | | | |
| Domestic | a321 | .... | .... | .... | .... | .... | .... | .... | .... | .... | .... | .... | .... |
| Foreign | a322 | .... | .... | .... | .... | .... | .... | .... | .... | .... | .... | .... | .... |
| Net Incurrence of Liabilities | a33 | 1,750 | −1,912 | 605 | 1,672 | 1,341 | 4,042 | 5,007 | 2,610 | 7,283 | 3,398 | 624 | 1,352 |
| By instrument | | | | | | | | | | | | | |
| Special Drawing Rights (SDRs) | a3301 | — | — | — | — | — | — | — | — | — | — | — | — |
| Currency & Deposits | a3302 | 1 | 39 | 69 | 48 | −9 | −24 | −12 | 30 | −9 | 17 | −5 | 315 |
| Securities other than Shares | a3303 | 1,331 | −493 | 992 | 1,216 | 867 | 3,779 | 4,551 | 2,196 | 5,981 | 1,788 | 886 | 274 |
| Loans | a3304 | 289 | −1,527 | −411 | 8 | 50 | −47 | −39 | 522 | 1,406 | 1,081 | −529 | 103 |
| Shares & Other Equity | a3305 | — | — | — | — | — | — | — | — | 3 | — | — | — |
| Insurance Technical Reserves | a3306 | 7 | 2 | 1 | −3 | 10 | −3 | 9 | −3 | — | 6 | −2 | −1 |
| Financial Derivatives | a3307 | — | — | — | — | — | — | — | — | — | — | — | — |
| Other Accounts Payable | a3308 | 122 | 67 | −46 | 403 | 424 | 338 | 499 | −136 | −98 | 506 | 273 | 660 |
| By creditor | | | | | | | | | | | | | |
| Domestic | a331 | .... | .... | .... | .... | .... | .... | .... | .... | .... | .... | .... | .... |
| Foreign | a332 | .... | .... | .... | .... | .... | .... | .... | .... | .... | .... | .... | .... |
| Stat. Discrepancy [32-33-NLB] | anlbz | 11 | 67 | 56 | 62 | 1 | 31 | −19 | −7 | −34 | 31 | 10 | 47 |
| Memo Item: Expenditure [2+31] | a2m | 17,434 | 19,902 | 21,640 | 22,723 | 25,047 | 28,042 | 28,282 | 28,525 | 29,349 | 30,489 | 31,682 | 35,622 |
| **Balance Sheet** | | | | | | | | | | | | | |
| Net Worth | a6 | .... | .... | .... | .... | .... | .... | .... | .... | .... | .... | .... | .... |
| Nonfinancial Assets | a61 | .... | .... | .... | .... | .... | .... | .... | .... | .... | .... | .... | .... |
| Financial Assets | a62 | 18,574 | 14,375 | 12,362 | 13,576 | 12,830 | 12,939 | 13,120 | 12,083 | 19,460 | 20,886 | 18,845 | 18,512 |
| By instrument | | | | | | | | | | | | | |
| Monetary Gold & SDRs | a6201 | — | — | — | — | — | — | — | — | — | — | — | — |
| Currency & Deposits | a6202 | 5,307 | 2,938 | 2,716 | 3,973 | 3,816 | 2,621 | 2,384 | 1,479 | 4,353 | 4,763 | 2,636 | 3,147 |
| Securities other than Shares | a6203 | 233 | 172 | 134 | 295 | 297 | 366 | 209 | 209 | 206 | 20 | 50 | 20 |
| Loans | a6204 | 3,288 | 1,679 | 1,396 | 1,285 | 1,315 | 1,168 | 1,281 | 1,478 | 2,860 | 3,297 | 3,572 | 3,581 |
| Shares and Other Equity | a6205 | 5,626 | 6,202 | 5,483 | 5,180 | 5,034 | 6,268 | 6,323 | 5,307 | 8,386 | 8,531 | 8,403 | 7,933 |
| Insurance Technical Reserves | a6206 | — | — | — | — | — | — | — | — | — | — | — | — |
| Financial Derivatives | a6207 | — | 25 | 9 | 9 | 9 | — | — | — | — | — | — | 1 |
| Other Accounts Receivable | a6208 | 4,120 | 3,359 | 2,623 | 2,834 | 2,360 | 2,517 | 2,921 | 3,611 | 3,655 | 4,275 | 4,184 | 3,830 |
| By debtor | | | | | | | | | | | | | |
| Domestic | a621 | .... | .... | .... | .... | .... | .... | .... | .... | .... | .... | .... | .... |
| Foreign | a622 | .... | .... | .... | .... | .... | .... | .... | .... | .... | .... | .... | .... |
| Liabilities | a63 | 20,800 | 19,172 | 20,182 | 21,696 | 22,870 | 26,825 | 31,584 | 34,773 | 42,276 | 45,274 | 45,910 | 46,655 |
| By instrument | | | | | | | | | | | | | |
| Special Drawing Rights (SDRs) | a6301 | — | — | — | — | — | — | — | — | — | — | — | — |
| Currency & Deposits | a6302 | — | — | 69 | 117 | 108 | 83 | 71 | 101 | 93 | 110 | 105 | 421 |
| Securities other than Shares | a6303 | 14,313 | 13,727 | 15,241 | 16,391 | 17,156 | 20,857 | 25,479 | 27,672 | 33,486 | 34,997 | 36,161 | 35,952 |
| Loans | a6304 | 4,238 | 3,270 | 2,676 | 2,556 | 2,525 | 2,502 | 2,497 | 3,346 | 5,041 | 6,155 | 5,452 | 5,688 |
| Shares and Other Equity | a6305 | — | — | — | — | — | — | — | — | — | — | — | — |
| Insurance Technical Reserves | a6306 | 14 | 20 | 21 | 18 | 28 | 24 | 33 | 30 | 31 | 37 | 35 | 34 |
| Financial Derivatives | a6307 | — | — | — | — | — | — | — | — | — | — | — | — |
| Other Accounts Payable | a6308 | 2,236 | 2,155 | 2,175 | 2,615 | 3,054 | 3,358 | 3,503 | 3,624 | 3,625 | 3,975 | 4,156 | 4,559 |
| By creditor | | | | | | | | | | | | | |
| Domestic | a631 | .... | .... | .... | .... | .... | .... | .... | .... | .... | .... | .... | .... |
| Foreign | a632 | .... | .... | .... | .... | .... | .... | .... | .... | .... | .... | .... | .... |
| Net Financial Worth [62-63] | a6m2 | −2,226 | −4,798 | −7,820 | −8,120 | −10,040 | −13,886 | −18,464 | −22,690 | −22,816 | −24,388 | −27,065 | −28,143 |
| Memo Item: Debt at Market Value | a6m3 | 20,800 | 19,172 | 20,182 | 21,696 | 22,870 | 26,825 | 31,584 | 34,773 | 42,276 | 45,274 | 45,910 | 46,655 |
| Memo Item: Debt at Face Value | a6m35 | 20,971 | 19,204 | 19,437 | 21,416 | 22,330 | 26,338 | 31,007 | 34,104 | 41,551 | 44,575 | 44,881 | 45,865 |
| Memo Item: Maastricht Debt | a6m36 | 18,735 | 17,049 | 17,262 | 18,801 | 19,276 | 22,980 | 27,504 | 30,480 | 37,926 | 40,600 | 40,725 | 41,306 |
| Memo Item: Debt at Nominal Value | a6m4 | .... | .... | .... | .... | .... | .... | .... | .... | .... | .... | .... | .... |

# Slovak Republic 936

International Financial Statistics Yearbook

| | | 2004 | 2005 | 2006 | 2007 | 2008 | 2009 | 2010 | 2011 | 2012 | 2013 | 2014 | 2015 |
|---|---|---|---|---|---|---|---|---|---|---|---|---|---|
| **National Accounts** | | | | | | *Millions of Koruny through 2008; Billions of Euros Beginning 2009* | | | | | | | |
| Househ.Cons.Expend.,incl.NPISHs.... | 96f | 792,019 | 861,164 | 956,745 | 1,055,076 | 1,168,563 | † 38.5 | 39.1 | 40.4 | 41.6 | 41.8 | 42.7 | 43.7 |
| Government Consumption Expend... | 91f | 256,725 | 275,541 | 313,464 | 318,679 | 351,760 | † 12.7 | 13.0 | 13.1 | 13.0 | 13.4 | 14.2 | 14.9 |
| Gross Fixed Capital Formation......... | 93e | 346,907 | 415,317 | 462,115 | 509,033 | 527,163 | † 13.9 | 14.9 | 16.9 | 15.4 | 15.3 | 15.8 | 18.0 |
| Changes in Inventories.................... | 93i | 33,374 | 35,958 | 26,863 | 32,021 | 64,171 | † −.4 | 1.3 | .7 | −.3 | .2 | .1 | −.1 |
| Exports of Goods and Services......... | 90c | 954,316 | 1,094,234 | 1,373,619 | 1,581,874 | 1,651,640 | † 43.3 | 51.6 | 60.1 | 66.5 | 69.3 | 69.4 | 73.2 |
| Imports of Goods and Services (-)..... | 98c | 992,326 | 1,163,918 | 1,441,056 | 1,603,137 | 1,710,036 | † 44.2 | 52.6 | 60.7 | 63.8 | 66.1 | 66.6 | 71.3 |
| Gross Domestic Product (GDP)........ | 99b | 1,391,011 | 1,518,296 | 1,691,753 | 1,893,546 | 2,053,259 | † 63.8 | 67.4 | 70.4 | 72.4 | 73.8 | 75.6 | 78.1 |
| GDP Volume 2000 Ref.,Chained...... | 99b.p | 1,117,840 | 1,192,345 | 1,293,734 | 1,430,599 | 1,518,875 | .... | .... | .... | .... | .... | .... | .... |
| GDP Volume 2010 Ref., Chained...... | 99b.p | .... | .... | .... | .... | .... | † 64.1 | 67.4 | 69.3 | 70.4 | 71.4 | 73.2 | 75.8 |
| GDP Volume (2010=100)............... | 99bvp | 73.8 | 78.7 | 85.4 | 94.4 | 100.2 | † 95.2 | 100.0 | 102.8 | 104.4 | 105.9 | 108.6 | 112.5 |
| GDP Deflator (2010=100)............... | 99bip | 92.9 | 95.1 | 97.6 | 98.8 | 100.9 | 99.5 | 100.0 | 101.6 | 102.9 | 103.5 | 103.3 | 103.0 |
| | | | | | | *Millions: Midyear Estimates* | | | | | | | |
| Population............................... | 99z | 5.38 | 5.39 | 5.39 | 5.39 | 5.40 | 5.40 | 5.41 | 5.41 | 5.42 | 5.42 | 5.42 | 5.43 |

# Slovenia 961

|  |  | 2004 | 2005 | 2006 | 2007 | 2008 | 2009 | 2010 | 2011 | 2012 | 2013 | 2014 | 2015 |
|---|---|---|---|---|---|---|---|---|---|---|---|---|---|
| **Exchange Rates** |  | | *Tolars per SDR through 2006; Euros per SDR Thereafter: End of Period* | | | | | | | | | | |
| Market Rate | aa | 273.71 | 289.33 | 273.70 | 1.0735 | 1.1068 | 1.0882 | 1.1525 | 1.1865 | 1.1649 | 1.1167 | 1.1933 | 1.2728 |
|  |  | | *Tolars per US Dollar through 2006; Euros per US Dollar Thereafter: End of Period (ae) Period Average (rf)* | | | | | | | | | | |
| Market Rate | ae | 176.24 | 202.43 | 181.93 | .6793 | .7185 | .6942 | .7484 | .7729 | .7579 | .7251 | .8237 | .9185 |
| Market Rate | rf | 192.38 | 192.71 | 191.03 | .7306 | .6827 | .7198 | .7550 | .7194 | .7783 | .7532 | .7537 | .9017 |
| **Fund Position** |  | | *Millions of SDRs: End of Period* | | | | | | | | | | |
| Quota | 2f.s | 231.70 | 231.70 | 231.70 | 231.70 | 231.70 | 231.70 | 231.70 | 275.00 | 275.00 | 275.00 | 275.00 | 275.00 |
| SDR Holdings | 1b.s | 7.18 | 8.13 | 8.25 | 7.97 | 7.66 | 198.13 | 198.18 | 208.64 | 207.57 | 196.71 | 207.01 | 207.10 |
| Reserve Position in the Fund | 1c.s | 77.26 | 36.12 | 24.36 | 15.93 | 30.09 | 42.09 | 74.29 | 118.45 | 124.95 | 133.03 | 121.33 | 81.38 |
| Total Fund Cred.&Loans Outstg | 2tl | — | — | — | — | — | — | — | — | — | — | — | — |
| SDR Allocations | 1bd | 25.43 | 25.43 | 25.43 | 25.43 | 25.43 | 215.88 | 215.88 | 215.88 | 215.88 | 215.88 | 215.88 | 215.88 |
| **International Liquidity** |  | | *Millions of US Dollars Unless Otherwise Indicated: End of Period* | | | | | | | | | | |
| Total Res.Min.Gold (Eurosys.Def) | 1l.d | 8,793.39 | 8,076.37 | 7,036.13 | † 979.80 | 868.06 | 966.15 | 926.93 | 830.73 | 782.19 | 799.30 | 893.36 | 748.09 |
| SDR Holdings | 1b.d | 11.15 | 11.63 | 12.41 | 12.59 | 11.80 | 310.61 | 305.20 | 320.32 | 319.02 | 302.93 | 299.92 | 286.98 |
| Reserve Position in the Fund | 1c.d | 119.98 | 51.62 | 36.64 | 25.17 | 46.35 | 65.99 | 114.41 | 181.85 | 192.04 | 204.87 | 175.78 | 112.78 |
| Foreign Exchange | 1d.d | 8,662.27 | 8,013.12 | 6,987.08 | † 942.04 | 809.91 | 589.55 | 507.31 | 328.56 | 271.13 | 291.50 | 417.65 | 348.34 |
| o/w:Fin.Deriv.Rel.to Reserves | 1ddd | .... | .... | .... | — | — | −6.9 | .4 | −1.7 | .8 | 2.0 | — | — |
| Other Reserve Assets | 1e.d | .... | .... | .... | — | — | — | — | — | — | — | — | — |
| Gold (Million Fine Troy Ounces) | 1ad | .2428 | .1625 | .1625 | .1026 | .1030 | .1030 | .1023 | .1020 | .1020 | .1020 | .1020 | .1020 |
| Gold (Eurosystem Valuation) | 1and | 105.80 | 83.35 | 103.30 | † 85.74 | 89.10 | 113.71 | 144.32 | 160.60 | 169.73 | 122.55 | 122.32 | 108.07 |
| Memo:Euro Cl. on Non-EA Res | 1dgd | .... | .... | .... | 1,593.9 | 1,586.5 | 1,262.4 | 1,025.6 | 1,016.9 | 1,031.6 | 1,081.2 | 1,240.9 | 1,152.6 |
| Non-Euro Cl. on EA Res | 1dhd | .... | .... | .... | 727.8 | 365.8 | 355.6 | 346.6 | 318.1 | 358.7 | 292.7 | 161.5 | 228.4 |
| Central Bank: Other Assets | 3..d | −72 | −96 | −49 | 7,165 | 6,489 | 5,983 | 5,747 | 6,289 | 6,354 | 5,657 | 7,820 | 5,034 |
| Central Bank: Other Liabs | 4..d | 48.85 | 46.47 | 58.79 | 142.62 | 85.74 | 361.73 | 377.05 | 358.36 | 347.19 | 352.98 | 325.19 | 316.45 |
| Other Depository Corps.: Assets | 7a.d | 1,193.80 | 1,819.75 | 3,069.56 | 6,115.82 | 6,220.54 | 6,328.04 | 5,657.39 | 5,217.28 | 5,195.90 | 5,080.51 | 4,293.66 | 3,727.48 |
| Other Depository Corps.: Liabs | 7b.d | 1,538 | 1,944 | 2,113 | 4,537 | 3,617 | 3,225 | 3,140 | 2,649 | 2,825 | 2,673 | 2,259 | 1,986 |
| **Central Bank** |  | | *Millions of Euros: End of Period* | | | | | | | | | | |
| Euro Area Wide Residency Criterion |  | | | | | | | | | | | | |
| Net Foreign Assets | 11n.u | 2,015 | 2,423 | 1,902 | 1,700 | 1,783 | 1,400 | 1,338 | 1,295 | 1,260 | 1,215 | 1,610 | 1,575 |
| Claims on Nonresidents | 11..u | 2,051 | 2,462 | 1,947 | 1,797 | 1,844 | 1,651 | 1,620 | 1,572 | 1,523 | 1,471 | 1,878 | 1,865 |
| Liabilities to Nonresidents | 16c.u | 36 | 39 | 45 | 97 | 62 | 251 | 282 | 277 | 263 | 256 | 268 | 291 |
| Claims on Other Depository Corps | 12e.u | 2,602 | 2,595 | 1,946 | 2,635 | 3,182 | 3,883 | 2,573 | 3,515 | 5,532 | 5,137 | 3,024 | 3,069 |
| Net Claims on Central Government | 12anu | 441 | 869 | 639 | 308 | 676 | 709 | 980 | 1,120 | 855 | −428 | −1,737 | 1,301 |
| Claims on Central Govt | 12a.u | 1,169 | 1,148 | 1,044 | 760 | 1,010 | 1,039 | 1,317 | 2,053 | 1,935 | 1,332 | 1,047 | 3,037 |
| Liabs. to Central Govt | 16d.u | 727 | 279 | 405 | 452 | 334 | 329 | 337 | 933 | 1,080 | 1,759 | 2,784 | 1,736 |
| Claims on Other Sectors | 12s.u | 770 | 705 | 521 | 438 | 428 | 486 | 256 | 251 | 562 | 557 | 102 | 225 |
| Claims on Other Financial Corps | 12g.u | 466 | 338 | 81 | 72 | 109 | — | 9 | — | 99 | 61 | 11 | 87 |
| Claims on State & Local Govts | 12b.u | 289 | 363 | 439 | 365 | 317 | 485 | 246 | 249 | 461 | 494 | 89 | 41 |
| Claims on Public Nonfin. Corps | 12c.u | — | — | — | — | — | — | — | — | — | — | — | — |
| Claims on Private Sector | 12d.u | 14 | 4 | 1 | 1 | 1 | 1 | 1 | 2 | 2 | 2 | 2 | 97 |
| Monetary Base | 14..u | 2,163 | 2,220 | 2,505 | 3,354 | 4,291 | 4,805 | 4,605 | 5,059 | 5,364 | 6,338 | 6,269 | 6,652 |
| Currency in Circulation | 14a.u | 824 | 907 | 719 | 2,943 | 3,254 | 3,534 | 3,683 | 3,891 | 3,994 | 4,187 | 4,670 | 4,955 |
| Liabs. to Other Depository Corps | 14c.u | 1,300 | 1,288 | 1,759 | 358 | 994 | 1,234 | 896 | 1,141 | 1,338 | 2,108 | 1,526 | 1,634 |
| Liabs. to Other Sectors | 14d.u | 39 | 25 | 27 | 53 | 43 | 37 | 25 | 27 | 31 | 43 | 73 | 63 |
| Other Liabs. to Other Dep. Corps | 14n.u | 2,989 | 3,544 | 1,815 | — | — | — | — | — | — | — | — | — |
| Dep. & Sec. Excl. f/Monetary Base | 14o.u | 1 | — | 2 | 4 | 4 | 2 | 1 | 2 | 2 | 1 | — | — |
| Deposits Included in Broad Money | 15..u | — | — | — | — | — | — | — | — | — | — | — | — |
| Sec.Ot.th.Shares Inc.in.Brd.Money | 16a.u | — | — | — | — | — | — | — | — | — | — | — | — |
| Deposits Excl. from Broad Money | 16b.u | 1 | — | 2 | 4 | 4 | 2 | 1 | 2 | 2 | 1 | — | — |
| Sec.Oh.th.Shares Excl. f/Brd.Money | 16s.u | — | — | — | — | — | — | — | — | — | — | — | — |
| Loans | 16l.u | — | — | — | — | — | — | — | — | — | — | — | — |
| Financial Derivatives | 16m.u | — | — | — | — | — | — | — | — | — | — | — | — |
| Shares and Other Equity | 17a.u | 724 | 861 | 782 | 848 | 915 | 1,010 | 1,109 | 1,137 | 1,180 | 1,339 | 1,440 | 1,472 |
| Other Items (Net) | 17r.u | −49 | −33 | −95 | 875 | 860 | 662 | −568 | −16 | 1,663 | −1,196 | −4,709 | −1,954 |
| Memorandum Items |  | | | | | | | | | | | | |
| National Residency Criterion |  | | | | | | | | | | | | |
| Net Foreign Assets | 11n | 6,445 | 6,796 | 5,339 | 2,003 | 1,719 | 1,307 | 2,728 | 2,616 | 836 | 3,476 | 7,010 | 5,121 |
| Claims on Nonresidents | 11 | 6,481 | 6,836 | 5,384 | 5,591 | 5,350 | 4,902 | 5,103 | 5,627 | 5,538 | 4,770 | 7,278 | 5,411 |
| Liabilities to Nonresidents | 16c | 36 | 39 | 45 | 3,588 | 3,631 | 3,596 | 2,375 | 3,010 | 4,702 | 1,295 | 268 | 291 |
| Claims on Other Depository Corps | 12e | — | — | 5 | 156 | 1,230 | 2,185 | 715 | 1,852 | 3,982 | 3,682 | 1,098 | 944 |
| Net Claims on Central Government | 12an | −619 | −206 | −335 | −385 | −266 | −169 | −199 | −831 | −859 | −1,526 | −2,525 | 543 |
| Claims on Central Government | 12a | 108 | 73 | 69 | 67 | 68 | 160 | 138 | 102 | 221 | 233 | 260 | 2,279 |
| Liabilities to Central Government | 16d | 727 | 279 | 405 | 452 | 334 | 329 | 337 | 933 | 1,080 | 1,759 | 2,784 | 1,736 |
| Claims on Other Sectors | 12s | 1 | 1 | 1 | 1 | 1 | 1 | 1 | 1 | 2 | 2 | 2 | 2 |
| Claims on Other Fin. Corps | 12g | — | — | — | — | — | — | — | — | — | — | — | — |
| Claims on State & Local Govts | 12b | — | — | — | — | — | — | — | — | — | — | — | — |
| Claims on Private Sector | 12d | 1 | 1 | 1 | 1 | 1 | 1 | 1 | 1 | 2 | 2 | 2 | 2 |
| Liabs.to ODCs, Inc.in Mon.Base | 14c | 1,300 | 1,288 | 1,759 | 358 | 994 | 1,234 | 896 | 1,141 | 1,338 | 2,108 | 1,526 | 1,634 |
| Liabs.to Ot.Sectors, Inc.in Mon.Base | 14d | 39 | 25 | 27 | 53 | 43 | 37 | 25 | 27 | 31 | 43 | 73 | 63 |
| Liabs.to ODCs,Excl.f/Mon.Base | 14n | 2,989 | 3,544 | 1,815 | — | — | — | — | — | — | — | — | — |
| Net Claims on Eurosystem | 12e.s | .... | .... | .... | −3,306 | −3,385 | −3,154 | −1,902 | −2,543 | −4,248 | −849 | 2,668 | 523 |

# Slovenia 961

|  |  | 2004 | 2005 | 2006 | 2007 | 2008 | 2009 | 2010 | 2011 | 2012 | 2013 | 2014 | 2015 |
|---|---|---|---|---|---|---|---|---|---|---|---|---|---|
| **Other Depository Corporations** | | | | | | | *Millions of Euros: End of Period* | | | | | | |
| Euro Area Wide Residency Criterion | | | | | | | | | | | | | |
| Net Foreign Assets.......................... | **21n.u** | −253 | −105 | 726 | 1,072 | 1,871 | 2,154 | 1,884 | 1,985 | 1,797 | 1,745 | 1,676 | 1,600 |
| Claims on Nonresidents................ | **21..u** | 876 | 1,543 | 2,331 | 4,154 | 4,470 | 4,393 | 4,234 | 4,032 | 3,938 | 3,684 | 3,537 | 3,424 |
| Liabilities to Nonresidents............. | **26c.u** | 1,129 | 1,648 | 1,605 | 3,082 | 2,599 | 2,239 | 2,350 | 2,047 | 2,141 | 1,938 | 1,861 | 1,824 |
| Claims on Eurosystem...................... | **20..u** | 6,686 | 5,850 | 4,214 | 597 | 1,243 | 1,466 | 1,108 | 1,366 | 1,581 | 2,374 | 1,801 | 1,911 |
| Currency.................................. | **20a.u** | 161 | 168 | 219 | 245 | 259 | 246 | 234 | 240 | 261 | 282 | 292 | 294 |
| Reserve Deposits and Securities..... | **20b.u** | 3,536 | 2,138 | 2,180 | 352 | 984 | 1,220 | 873 | 1,126 | 1,320 | 2,093 | 1,509 | 1,617 |
| Other Claims.............................. | **20n.u** | 2,989 | 3,544 | 1,815 | — | — | — | — | — | — | — | — | — |
| Net Claims on Central Government.. | **22anu** | 2,390 | 2,979 | 3,311 | 3,540 | 2,836 | 1,823 | 2,311 | 2,574 | 3,347 | 6,244 | 6,748 | 6,873 |
| Claims on Central Government...... | **22a.u** | 2,736 | 3,521 | 4,078 | 4,593 | 4,270 | 5,360 | 5,017 | 5,437 | 5,912 | 7,532 | 8,658 | 8,518 |
| Liabilities to Central Government... | **26d.u** | 345 | 542 | 766 | 1,053 | 1,434 | 3,537 | 2,706 | 2,864 | 2,566 | 1,288 | 1,910 | 1,645 |
| Claims on Other Sectors.................. | **22s.u** | 13,687 | 16,540 | 20,885 | 27,712 | 32,616 | 33,810 | 34,645 | 33,897 | 32,165 | 26,774 | 23,233 | 21,915 |
| Claims on Other Financial Corps.... | **22g.u** | 695 | 983 | 1,628 | 2,446 | 3,172 | 3,009 | 2,889 | 2,678 | 2,562 | 2,145 | 1,835 | 1,770 |
| Claims on State & Local Govts....... | **22b.u** | 454 | 107 | 104 | 129 | 227 | 376 | 554 | 611 | 646 | 609 | 704 | 635 |
| Claims on Public Nonfin. Corps...... | **22c.u** | | | | | | | | | | | | |
| Claims on Private Sector.............. | **22d.u** | 12,538 | 15,450 | 19,154 | 25,138 | 29,218 | 30,425 | 31,201 | 30,608 | 28,957 | 24,020 | 20,694 | 19,511 |
| Liabilities to Eurosystem.................. | **26g.u** | 2,145 | 1,928 | 1,254 | 1,474 | 2,473 | 3,806 | 2,399 | 3,087 | 5,391 | 5,027 | 2,684 | 2,852 |
| Transf.Dep.Included in Broad Money | **24..u** | 5,028 | 6,266 | 7,111 | 7,095 | 6,843 | 7,381 | 8,395 | 8,519 | 8,886 | 8,884 | 10,509 | 13,155 |
| Other.Dep.Included in Broad Money. | **25..u** | 7,860 | 7,599 | 8,156 | 10,303 | 11,472 | 11,012 | 10,687 | 11,046 | 10,487 | 10,231 | 9,858 | 8,253 |
| Sec.Ot.th.Shares Inc.in.Brd. Money... | **26a.u** | −823 | −2,728 | −1,428 | −857 | −293 | −265 | −123 | 47 | −38 | −36 | −151 | −222 |
| Deposits Excl. from Broad Money..... | **26b.u** | 1,860 | 1,644 | 1,528 | 857 | 835 | 1,609 | 1,736 | 1,792 | 1,517 | 1,716 | 1,803 | 1,789 |
| Sec.Ot.th.Shares Excl.f/Brd. Money... | **26s.u** | −1,290 | −1,074 | −538 | −422 | −695 | 561 | 1,321 | 1,378 | 2 | −369 | −548 | −1,548 |
| Loans.......................................... | **26l.u** | — | — | — | — | — | — | — | — | — | — | — | — |
| Financial Derivatives...................... | **26m.u** | 20 | 15 | 63 | 147 | 271 | 246 | 339 | 314 | 289 | 163 | 186 | 181 |
| Insurance Technical Reserves........... | **26r.u** | — | — | — | — | — | — | — | — | — | — | — | — |
| Shares and Other Equity.................. | **27a.u** | 1,902 | 2,170 | 2,855 | 3,571 | 4,011 | 4,310 | 4,141 | 3,951 | 3,742 | 3,670 | 4,194 | 4,394 |
| Other Items (Net)........................... | **27r.u** | 5,808 | 9,445 | 10,136 | 10,753 | 13,650 | 10,592 | 11,053 | 9,690 | 8,615 | 7,851 | 4,920 | 3,447 |
| Memorandum Items | | | | | | | | | | | | | |
| Total Assets.................................. | **20ra** | 24,463 | 30,136 | 34,841 | 43,491 | 49,008 | 53,402 | 53,018 | 52,423 | 50,787 | 46,315 | 43,578 | 41,603 |
| National Residency Criterion | | | | | | | | | | | | | |
| Net Foreign Assets.......................... | **21n** | −2,509 | −4,738 | −5,766 | −6,092 | −8,232 | −4,661 | −5,343 | −3,772 | −2,407 | 181 | 2,676 | 3,734 |
| Claims on Nonresidents................ | **21** | 2,095 | 3,504 | 4,877 | 9,734 | 9,279 | 9,705 | 7,890 | 7,215 | 6,560 | 6,832 | 8,278 | 8,267 |
| Liabilities to Nonresidents............. | **26c** | 4,604 | 8,242 | 10,643 | 15,827 | 17,510 | 14,366 | 13,234 | 10,987 | 8,967 | 6,651 | 5,602 | 4,533 |
| Net Claims on Central Government.. | **22an** | 2,390 | 2,716 | 2,475 | 1,315 | 729 | −39 | 714 | 1,436 | 2,492 | 5,275 | 5,331 | 5,466 |
| Claims on Central Government...... | **22a** | 2,736 | 3,258 | 3,241 | 2,367 | 2,162 | 3,497 | 3,419 | 4,299 | 5,057 | 6,563 | 7,240 | 7,111 |
| Liabilities to Central Government... | **26d** | 345 | 542 | 766 | 1,052 | 1,434 | 3,537 | 2,705 | 2,863 | 2,565 | 1,288 | 1,909 | 1,645 |
| Claims on Other Sectors.................. | **22s** | 13,471 | 16,298 | 20,582 | 27,457 | 32,302 | 33,440 | 34,279 | 33,477 | 31,766 | 26,296 | 22,815 | 21,509 |
| Claims on Other Fin. Corps........... | **22g** | 692 | 979 | 1,593 | 2,416 | 3,115 | 2,946 | 2,824 | 2,564 | 2,419 | 1,896 | 1,615 | 1,530 |
| Claims on State & Local Govts....... | **22b** | 454 | 97 | 104 | 118 | 212 | 376 | 526 | 584 | 610 | 581 | 685 | 622 |
| Claims on Private Sector............... | **22d** | 12,325 | 15,222 | 18,884 | 24,923 | 28,976 | 30,117 | 30,929 | 30,330 | 28,737 | 23,819 | 20,514 | 19,357 |
| Transf.Dep.Included in Broad Money | **24** | 4,982 | 6,224 | 7,071 | 7,057 | 6,799 | 7,338 | 8,351 | 8,467 | 8,829 | 8,832 | 10,442 | 13,058 |
| Other.Dep.Included in Broad Money. | **25** | 7,798 | 7,561 | 8,118 | 9,989 | 11,340 | 10,905 | 10,514 | 10,863 | 10,198 | 10,049 | 9,779 | 8,208 |
| Sec.Ot.th.Shares Inc.in.Brd. Money... | **26a** | 2,316 | 879 | 423 | 65 | 61 | 74 | 22 | 176 | 66 | 49 | 5 | 19 |
| Deposits Excl. from Broad Money..... | **26b** | 1,595 | 1,640 | 1,522 | 847 | 796 | 1,523 | 1,652 | 1,726 | 1,462 | 1,289 | 1,428 | 1,484 |
| Sec.Ot.th.Shares Excl.f/Brd. Money... | **26s** | 852 | 1,024 | 1,094 | 1,077 | 976 | 2,716 | 3,561 | 3,146 | 1,629 | 1,164 | 1,255 | 816 |

# Slovenia 961

| | | 2004 | 2005 | 2006 | 2007 | 2008 | 2009 | 2010 | 2011 | 2012 | 2013 | 2014 | 2015 |
|---|---|---|---|---|---|---|---|---|---|---|---|---|---|
| **Depository Corporations** | | | | | | | *Millions of Euros: End of Period* | | | | | | |
| Euro Area Wide Residency Criterion | | | | | | | | | | | | | |
| Net Foreign Assets | 31n.u | 1,762 | 2,318 | 2,628 | 2,773 | 3,654 | 3,554 | 3,222 | 3,280 | 3,057 | 2,961 | 3,286 | 3,174 |
| Claims on Nonresidents | 31..u | 2,928 | 4,005 | 4,278 | 5,952 | 6,314 | 6,044 | 5,854 | 5,604 | 5,461 | 5,155 | 5,415 | 5,289 |
| Liabilities to Nonresidents | 36c.u | 1,165 | 1,687 | 1,649 | 3,179 | 2,660 | 2,490 | 2,632 | 2,324 | 2,404 | 2,194 | 2,129 | 2,115 |
| Domestic Claims | 32..u | 17,288 | 21,094 | 25,357 | 31,999 | 36,556 | 36,828 | 38,192 | 37,843 | 36,929 | 33,148 | 28,346 | 30,315 |
| Net Claims on Central Government | 32anu | 2,831 | 3,848 | 3,951 | 3,849 | 3,512 | 2,532 | 3,291 | 3,694 | 4,201 | 5,816 | 5,010 | 8,175 |
| Claims on Central Government | 32a.u | 3,904 | 4,668 | 5,122 | 5,353 | 5,280 | 6,398 | 6,334 | 7,491 | 7,848 | 8,864 | 9,705 | 11,556 |
| Liabilities to Central Government | 36d.u | 1,073 | 820 | 1,171 | 1,504 | 1,768 | 3,866 | 3,043 | 3,796 | 3,646 | 3,047 | 4,694 | 3,381 |
| Claims on Other Sectors | 32s.u | 14,457 | 17,245 | 21,406 | 28,150 | 33,044 | 34,297 | 34,901 | 34,148 | 32,728 | 27,332 | 23,335 | 22,140 |
| Claims on Other Financial Corps | 32g.u | 1,161 | 1,321 | 1,708 | 2,519 | 3,281 | 3,009 | 2,898 | 2,678 | 2,661 | 2,207 | 1,846 | 1,857 |
| Claims on State & Local Govts | 32b.u | 743 | 470 | 543 | 493 | 544 | 861 | 800 | 861 | 1,107 | 1,103 | 793 | 675 |
| Claims on Public Nonfin. Corps | 32c.u | — | — | — | — | — | — | — | — | — | — | — | — |
| Claims on Private Sector | 32d.u | 12,553 | 15,454 | 19,155 | 25,139 | 29,219 | 30,427 | 31,203 | 30,609 | 28,959 | 24,022 | 20,696 | 19,608 |
| Broad Money Liabilities | 35l.u | 12,767 | 11,900 | 14,366 | 19,292 | 21,060 | 21,453 | 22,433 | 23,290 | 23,100 | 23,027 | 24,666 | 25,910 |
| Currency Outside Depository Corps | 34a.u | 663 | 738 | 500 | 2,698 | 2,995 | 3,288 | 3,449 | 3,651 | 3,734 | 3,905 | 4,378 | 4,661 |
| Transferable Deposits | 34..u | 5,067 | 6,289 | 7,138 | 7,149 | 6,886 | 7,419 | 8,420 | 8,546 | 8,918 | 8,928 | 10,580 | 13,217 |
| Other Deposits | 35..u | 7,860 | 7,601 | 8,156 | 10,303 | 11,472 | 11,012 | 10,687 | 11,046 | 10,487 | 10,231 | 9,859 | 8,254 |
| Securities Other than Shares | 36a.u | −823 | −2,728 | −1,428 | −857 | −293 | −265 | −123 | 47 | −38 | −36 | −151 | −222 |
| Deposits Excl. from Broad Money | 36b.u | 1,862 | 1,644 | 1,530 | 861 | 839 | 1,611 | 1,738 | 1,793 | 1,519 | 1,717 | 1,803 | 1,789 |
| Sec.Oth.th.Shares Excl.f/Brd. Money | 36s.u | −1,290 | −1,074 | −538 | −422 | −695 | 561 | 1,321 | 1,378 | 2 | −369 | −548 | −1,548 |
| Loans | 36l.u | — | — | — | — | — | — | — | — | — | — | — | — |
| Financial Derivatives | 36m.u | 20 | 15 | 63 | 147 | 271 | 246 | 339 | 314 | 289 | 163 | 186 | 181 |
| Insurance Technical Reserves | 36r.u | — | — | — | — | — | — | — | — | — | — | — | — |
| Shares and Other Equity | 37a.u | 2,625 | 3,031 | 3,637 | 4,419 | 4,925 | 5,320 | 5,249 | 5,088 | 4,921 | 5,009 | 5,634 | 5,866 |
| Other Items (Net) | 37r.u | 3,066 | 7,896 | 8,928 | 10,474 | 13,809 | 11,191 | 10,333 | 9,261 | 10,154 | 6,561 | −113 | 1,293 |
| Broad Money Liabs., Seasonally Adj. | 35lub | 12,650 | 11,787 | 14,228 | 19,116 | 20,891 | 21,320 | 22,346 | 23,254 | 23,106 | 23,053 | 24,701 | 25,947 |
| Memorandum Items | | | | | | | | | | | | | |
| National Residency Criterion | | | | | | | | | | | | | |
| Net Foreign Assets | 31n | 3,936 | 2,058 | −426 | −4,089 | −6,513 | −3,354 | −2,616 | −1,156 | −1,571 | 3,656 | 9,686 | 8,855 |
| Claims on Nonresidents | 31 | 8,576 | 10,339 | 10,261 | 15,325 | 14,629 | 14,607 | 12,993 | 12,842 | 12,097 | 11,602 | 15,556 | 13,678 |
| Liabilities to Nonresidents | 36c | 4,640 | 8,281 | 10,688 | 19,414 | 21,142 | 17,961 | 15,609 | 13,998 | 13,669 | 7,946 | 5,870 | 4,824 |
| Domestic Claims | 32 | 15,243 | 18,809 | 22,723 | 28,388 | 32,766 | 33,233 | 34,795 | 34,084 | 33,400 | 30,047 | 25,623 | 27,520 |
| Net Claims on Central Government | 32an | 1,771 | 2,510 | 2,140 | 930 | 463 | −208 | 515 | 605 | 1,632 | 3,749 | 2,807 | 6,009 |
| Claims on Central Government | 32a | 2,844 | 3,331 | 3,310 | 2,434 | 2,230 | 3,658 | 3,557 | 4,401 | 5,278 | 6,796 | 7,500 | 9,390 |
| Liabilities to Central Government | 36d | 1,073 | 820 | 1,170 | 1,504 | 1,767 | 3,866 | 3,042 | 3,796 | 3,646 | 3,047 | 4,693 | 3,381 |
| Claims on Other Sectors | 32s | 13,472 | 16,299 | 20,583 | 27,458 | 32,303 | 33,441 | 34,280 | 33,479 | 31,767 | 26,298 | 22,817 | 21,511 |
| Claims on Other Financial Corps | 32g | 692 | 979 | 1,593 | 2,416 | 3,115 | 2,946 | 2,824 | 2,564 | 2,419 | 1,896 | 1,615 | 1,530 |
| Claims on State & Local Govts | 32b | 454 | 97 | 104 | 118 | 212 | 376 | 526 | 584 | 610 | 581 | 685 | 622 |
| Claims on Private Sector | 32d | 12,326 | 15,223 | 18,885 | 24,924 | 28,976 | 30,118 | 30,930 | 30,331 | 28,739 | 23,821 | 20,516 | 19,359 |
| Transf.Dep.Included in Broad Money | 34 | 5,021 | 6,247 | 7,098 | 7,110 | 6,842 | 7,375 | 8,376 | 8,494 | 8,861 | 8,875 | 10,513 | 13,120 |
| Other Dep.Included in Broad Money | 35 | 7,798 | 7,563 | 8,118 | 9,989 | 11,340 | 10,905 | 10,514 | 10,863 | 10,198 | 10,049 | 9,781 | 8,209 |
| Sec.Ot.th.Shares Inc.in.Brd. Money | 36a | 2,316 | 879 | 423 | 65 | 61 | 74 | 22 | 176 | 66 | 49 | 5 | 19 |
| Deposits Excl. from Broad Money | 36b | 1,596 | 1,640 | 1,525 | 851 | 800 | 1,525 | 1,654 | 1,728 | 1,464 | 1,290 | 1,428 | 1,484 |
| Sec.Ot.th.Shares Excl./f.Brd. Money | 36s | 852 | 1,024 | 1,094 | 1,077 | 976 | 2,716 | 3,561 | 3,146 | 1,629 | 1,164 | 1,255 | 816 |
| **Monetary Aggregates** | | | | | | | *Millions of Tolars: End of Period* | | | | | | |
| Money (National Definitions) | | | | | | | | | | | | | |
| M1 | 59ma | † 1,370.42 | 1,682.48 | 1,834.11 | .... | .... | .... | .... | .... | .... | .... | .... | .... |
| M2 | 59mb | † 3,239.95 | 3,493.23 | 3,778.03 | .... | .... | .... | .... | .... | .... | .... | .... | .... |
| M3 | 59mc | † 3,980.22 | 3,502.77 | 3,786.15 | .... | .... | .... | .... | .... | .... | .... | .... | .... |
| **Interest Rates** | | | | | | | *Percent Per Annum* | | | | | | |
| Discount Rate (End of Period) | 60.a | 5.00 | 5.00 | 4.50 | .... | .... | .... | .... | .... | .... | .... | .... | .... |
| Money Market Rate | 60b | 4.40 | 3.73 | 3.38 | 4.08 | 4.27 | .90 | .57 | 1.18 | .33 | .13 | .13 | −.07 |
| Treasury Bill Rate | 60c | 4.17 | 3.66 | 3.30 | 3.90 | 3.88 | 1.14 | .55 | 1.09 | 1.10 | .... | .... | .... |
| Deposit Rate | | | | | | | | | | | | | |
| Households: Stocks, up to 2 years | 60lhs | .... | .... | 2.17 | 3.29 | 4.35 | 3.48 | 2.62 | 2.90 | 3.29 | 3.08 | 1.99 | 1.01 |
| New Business, up to 1 year | 60lhn | .... | .... | 2.17 | 3.36 | 4.31 | 2.52 | 1.82 | 2.15 | 2.31 | 1.86 | .98 | .37 |
| Corporations: Stocks, up to 2 years | 60lcs | .... | .... | 2.54 | 3.93 | 4.69 | 2.93 | 2.16 | 2.48 | 2.87 | 2.36 | 1.25 | .56 |
| New Business, up to 1 year | 60lcn | .... | .... | 2.27 | 3.89 | 4.31 | 1.91 | 1.38 | 1.95 | 2.11 | 1.58 | .63 | .19 |
| Lending Rate | | | | | | | | | | | | | |
| Households: Stocks, up to 1 year | 60phs | .... | .... | 4.70 | 8.10 | 8.32 | 7.61 | 7.02 | 7.15 | 7.30 | 7.12 | 6.83 | 6.56 |
| New Bus., Floating & up to 1 year | 60pns | 5.12 | 5.56 | 6.30 | 6.82 | 7.41 | 5.47 | 4.71 | 5.09 | 5.02 | 5.04 | 5.01 | 4.37 |
| House Purch., Stocks,Over 5 years | 60phm | .... | .... | 5.51 | 6.71 | 7.42 | 4.64 | 3.53 | 3.91 | 3.47 | 2.78 | 2.82 | 2.61 |
| House Purch., New Bus., 5-10 yrs | 60phn | 4.82 | .... | 5.19 | 5.80 | 6.77 | 6.43 | 5.53 | 5.45 | 5.48 | 5.40 | 5.06 | 3.54 |
| Corporations: Stocks, up to 1 year | 60pcs | .... | .... | 4.05 | 5.33 | 6.23 | 5.64 | 5.58 | 5.64 | 5.49 | 5.51 | 5.25 | 3.95 |
| New Bus., Over € 1 mil.,up to 1 yr | 60pcn | 3.09 | 3.25 | 4.08 | 5.22 | 6.24 | 5.29 | 4.89 | 5.01 | 4.67 | 4.54 | 4.12 | 2.91 |
| Government Bond Yield | 61 | 4.68 | 3.81 | 3.85 | 4.53 | 4.61 | 4.38 | 3.83 | 4.97 | 5.81 | 5.81 | 3.27 | 1.71 |
| **Prices and Labor** | | | | | | | *Index Numbers (2010=100): Period Averages* | | | | | | |
| Share Prices (End of Month) | 62.ep | 97.0 | 100.7 | 135.7 | 248.5 | 184.1 | 109.5 | 100.0 | 81.1 | 64.1 | 70.7 | 88.1 | 83.6 |
| Producer Prices | 63 | 84.0 | 86.3 | 88.4 | 93.2 | 98.4 | 98.0 | 100.0 | 103.8 | 104.8 | 105.1 | 104.0 | 103.5 |
| Consumer Prices | 64 | 84.7 | 86.8 | 88.9 | 92.2 | 97.4 | 98.2 | 100.0 | 101.8 | 104.5 | 106.3 | † 106.5 | 106.0 |
| Harmonized CPI | 64h | 84.4 | 86.5 | 88.7 | 92.0 | 97.1 | 97.9 | 100.0 | 102.1 | 105.0 | 107.0 | 107.4 | 106.6 |
| Wages | 65 | 74.7 | 77.4 | 81.1 | 85.9 | 93.1 | 96.3 | 100.0 | 102.0 | 102.0 | 101.9 | 103.0 | 103.8 |
| Industrial Production | 66 | 94.0 | † 97.3 | 102.8 | 110.2 | 112.9 | 93.3 | 100.0 | 101.3 | 100.2 | 99.2 | 101.4 | .... |
| Employment | 67 | 100.4 | 98.2 | 99.4 | 101.6 | 103.5 | 101.4 | 100.0 | 97.2 | 96.3 | 94.3 | 94.7 | 95.7 |
| | | | | | | | *Number in Thousands: Period Averages* | | | | | | |
| Labor Force | 67d | 1,006 | 991 | 998 | 1,007 | 1,021 | 1,016 | 1,017 | 998 | 996 | 990 | 991 | 992 |
| Employment | 67e | 946 | 925 | 937 | 957 | 975 | 955 | 942 | 915 | 907 | 888 | 892 | 901 |
| Unemployment | 67c | 63 | 66 | 61 | 50 | 46 | 61 | 76 | 83 | 90 | 102 | 98 | 90 |
| Unemployment Rate (%) | 67r | 6.3 | 6.5 | 6.0 | 4.9 | 4.4 | 5.9 | 7.3 | 8.2 | 8.9 | 10.1 | 9.7 | 9.0 |
| **Intl. Transactions & Positions** | | | | | | | *Millions of US Dollars* | | | | | | |
| Exports | 70..d | 15,879 | 17,896 | 21,293 | 26,857 | 29,600 | 22,646 | 24,716 | 29,242 | 27,080 | 28,629 | 30,522 | 26,616 |
| Imports, c.i.f. | 71..d | 17,571 | 19,626 | 23,032 | 29,499 | 33,991 | 24,085 | 26,304 | 31,405 | 28,392 | 29,380 | 30,052 | 25,769 |

# Slovenia   961

| | | 2004 | 2005 | 2006 | 2007 | 2008 | 2009 | 2010 | 2011 | 2012 | 2013 | 2014 | 2015 |
|---|---|---|---|---|---|---|---|---|---|---|---|---|---|
| **Balance of Payments** | | | | | | | *Millions of US Dollars* | | | | | | |
| A. Current Account* | 109bx | −892.5 | −680.5 | −696.0 | −2,015.3 | † −2,946.0 | −277.3 | −54.8 | 97.4 | 1,191.2 | 2,683.7 | 3,451.3 | 3,133.3 |
| Goods, credit (exports) | 1a9cx | 16,006.5 | 18,074.6 | 21,765.4 | 27,571.8 | † 29,554.4 | 22,698.0 | 24,684.4 | 29,279.5 | 27,323.1 | 28,809.1 | 30,516.1 | 26,687.9 |
| Goods, debit (imports) | 1a9dx | 17,255.9 | 19,322.8 | 22,771.7 | 29,330.6 | † 32,650.9 | 23,312.1 | 25,685.2 | 30,627.2 | 27,433.6 | 27,875.1 | 28,911.5 | 24,882.7 |
| Balance on goods | 1a9bx | −1,249.4 | −1,248.2 | −1,006.3 | −1,758.8 | † −3,096.5 | −614.2 | −1,000.7 | −1,347.7 | −110.5 | 934.0 | 1,604.6 | 1,805.2 |
| Services, credit (exports) | 1b9cx | 3,459.9 | 3,976.0 | 4,356.6 | 5,457.7 | † 7,444.7 | 6,149.9 | 6,158.6 | 6,830.6 | 6,552.0 | 7,057.7 | 7,370.3 | 6,621.5 |
| Services, debit (imports) | 1b9dx | 2,616.5 | 2,925.4 | 3,266.6 | 4,297.0 | † 5,360.1 | 4,602.7 | 4,557.1 | 4,871.9 | 4,615.6 | 4,723.0 | 5,064.9 | 4,344.3 |
| Balance on Goods & Services | 1z9bx | −406.0 | −197.6 | 83.8 | −598.1 | † −1,011.9 | 933.0 | 600.7 | 611.0 | 1,825.8 | 3,268.7 | 3,910.0 | 4,082.4 |
| Primary income: credit | 1c9cx | 667.4 | 780.6 | 1,097.5 | 1,609.4 | † 2,281.6 | 1,308.9 | 1,187.1 | 1,834.4 | 1,490.7 | 1,431.9 | 1,866.2 | 1,672.2 |
| Primary income: debit | 1c9dx | 1,060.2 | 1,143.4 | 1,656.4 | 2,693.3 | † 3,797.4 | 2,043.9 | 1,669.4 | 2,227.6 | 1,834.0 | 1,657.5 | 1,976.8 | 2,083.7 |
| Balance on gds, serv. & prim. inc. | 1y9bx | −798.8 | −560.4 | −475.2 | −1,682.0 | † −2,527.7 | 198.0 | 118.4 | 217.8 | 1,482.5 | 3,043.0 | 3,799.3 | 3,670.8 |
| Secondary income: credit | 1d9ca | 698.4 | 877.6 | 988.2 | 1,295.3 | † 875.9 | 956.2 | 1,149.5 | 1,377.1 | 1,196.6 | 1,233.4 | 1,242.3 | 927.2 |
| Secondary income: debit | 1d9da | 792.1 | 997.7 | 1,209.0 | 1,628.6 | † 1,294.2 | 1,431.4 | 1,322.8 | 1,497.5 | 1,487.9 | 1,592.8 | 1,590.3 | 1,464.7 |
| B. Capital Account* | 209ba | −125.8 | −137.2 | −170.8 | −72.0 | † −39.4 | 8.4 | 71.6 | −114.8 | 52.1 | 96.0 | −223.5 | 26.2 |
| Capital account: credit | 209ca | 186.3 | 208.4 | 259.5 | 440.8 | † 420.5 | 434.0 | 576.1 | 425.6 | 554.4 | 627.9 | 799.9 | 745.5 |
| Capital account: debit | 209da | 312.1 | 345.6 | 430.2 | 512.8 | † 460.0 | 425.7 | 504.5 | 540.4 | 502.2 | 531.9 | 1,023.4 | 719.3 |
| Balance on current & capital acct. | 129ba | −1,018.3 | −817.7 | −866.7 | −2,087.3 | † −2,985.4 | −268.9 | 16.7 | −17.4 | 1,243.4 | 2,779.7 | 3,227.8 | 3,159.4 |
| C. Financial Account* | 309na | −701.8 | −843.6 | 77.0 | −2,564.3 | † −4,890.7 | −1,887.3 | −1,879.4 | −936.2 | −154.4 | 1,781.0 | 2,980.7 | 2,243.4 |
| Direct investment: assets | 3a9aa | 481.6 | 1,059.3 | 906.1 | 2,216.2 | † 1,331.8 | 339.5 | 199.8 | −14.1 | −566.3 | 32.0 | 200.3 | −7.7 |
| Equity & investment fund shares | 3aaaa | 490.2 | 607.8 | 655.8 | 1,128.6 | † 1,061.2 | 280.4 | −243.7 | 86.3 | −53.3 | −101.7 | −75.5 | −136.3 |
| Debt instruments | 3abaa | −8.6 | 451.5 | 250.3 | 1,087.5 | † 270.6 | 59.1 | 443.5 | −100.5 | −513.1 | 133.7 | 275.8 | 128.6 |
| Direct investment: liabilities | 3a9la | 763.1 | 970.8 | 691.6 | 1,884.9 | † 1,081.1 | −346.3 | 319.1 | 875.5 | 33.5 | 104.0 | 1,030.1 | 1,049.7 |
| Equity & investment fund shares | 3aala | 744.2 | 613.8 | 563.2 | 698.5 | † 558.3 | 180.6 | 268.3 | −23.2 | −6.8 | −74.2 | 1,042.6 | 1,463.6 |
| Debt instruments | 3abla | 18.9 | 357.0 | 128.4 | 1,186.4 | † 522.8 | −526.9 | 50.8 | 898.8 | 40.4 | 178.2 | −12.5 | −414.0 |
| Portfolio investment: assets | 3b9aa | 809.4 | 2,100.0 | 2,677.4 | 4,467.7 | † 357.7 | −34.1 | 514.5 | −28.2 | −181.5 | −631.2 | 515.3 | 2,205.5 |
| Equity & investment fund shares | 3baaa | 270.6 | 1,022.3 | 928.7 | 1,226.8 | † −150.8 | 94.0 | 260.6 | −172.1 | 58.6 | 79.7 | 168.6 | 129.8 |
| Debt securities | 3bbaa | 538.8 | 1,077.7 | 1,748.7 | 3,240.8 | † 508.5 | −128.2 | 254.0 | 143.9 | −240.1 | −710.8 | 346.7 | 2,075.7 |
| Portfolio investment: liabilities | 3b9la | 37.0 | 102.1 | 850.4 | 1,379.0 | † 951.1 | 6,406.6 | 3,165.5 | 2,450.9 | −434.5 | 4,664.6 | 5,987.8 | −952.7 |
| Equity & investment fund shares | 3bala | −13.1 | 97.8 | 196.7 | 274.5 | † −270.8 | 23.3 | 170.0 | 228.0 | 148.2 | 150.6 | 122.7 | 57.9 |
| Debt securities | 3bbla | 50.1 | 4.3 | 653.7 | 1,104.5 | † 1,221.9 | 6,383.3 | 2,995.6 | 2,223.0 | −582.7 | 4,514.0 | 5,865.1 | −1,010.6 |
| Fin. der.& empl.stk.ops.(ESOs): net. | 3c9na | −6.9 | 13.4 | 15.6 | 19.5 | † −68.1 | −21.4 | 152.5 | 214.5 | 114.6 | 43.5 | −5.0 | 31.8 |
| Fin. der. & ESOs.: assets | 3c9aa | −6.9 | 13.4 | 15.6 | 45.6 | .... | .... | .... | .... | .... | .... | .... | .... |
| Fin. der. & ESOs.: liabilities | 3c9la | | | | 26.1 | .... | .... | .... | .... | .... | .... | .... | .... |
| Other investment: assets | 3d9aa | 1,607.6 | 1,898.7 | 2,432.3 | 6,333.0 | † −115.1 | −574.6 | −2,442.9 | 597.9 | 637.0 | 954.9 | 6,472.2 | −786.4 |
| Other equity | 3daaa | .... | .... | .... | .... | † 39.4 | 23.9 | 13.9 | 14.0 | 200.5 | 202.3 | 112.2 | 5.6 |
| Debt instruments | 3dzaa | 1,607.6 | 1,898.7 | 2,432.3 | 6,333.0 | † −154.4 | −598.5 | −2,456.8 | 583.9 | 436.5 | 752.6 | 6,360.0 | −792.0 |
| Other investment: liabilities | 3d9la | 2,793.4 | 4,842.1 | 4,412.3 | 12,336.7 | † 4,364.9 | −4,463.5 | −3,181.2 | −1,620.3 | 559.1 | −6,150.3 | −2,815.8 | −897.2 |
| Other equity | 3dala | .... | .... | .... | .... | † −19.3 | 7.7 | −.7 | −2.4 | .2 | −39.7 | 4.2 | −.1 |
| Debt instruments | 3dzla | 2,793.4 | 4,842.1 | 4,412.3 | 12,336.7 | † 4,384.2 | −4,471.2 | −3,180.4 | −1,617.9 | 558.9 | −6,110.6 | −2,820.0 | −897.1 |
| Curr.+ cap.– finan. acct. balance | 4y9na | −316.5 | 25.9 | −943.7 | 477.0 | † 1,905.3 | 1,618.4 | 1,896.2 | 918.8 | 1,397.8 | 998.7 | 247.1 | 916.0 |
| D. Net Errors and Omissions | 409na | 20.0 | 180.5 | −712.5 | −675.8 | † −1,938.9 | −1,542.7 | −1,927.3 | −1,023.0 | −1,439.6 | −993.2 | −122.7 | −1,039.0 |
| E. Reserves and Related Items | 4z9na | −296.5 | 206.4 | −1,656.2 | −198.8 | † −33.6 | 75.7 | −31.1 | −104.3 | −41.9 | 5.5 | 124.4 | −123.0 |
| Reserve assets | 3e9aa | −296.5 | 206.4 | −1,656.2 | −198.8 | † −33.6 | 75.7 | −31.1 | −104.3 | −41.9 | 5.5 | 124.4 | −123.0 |
| Credit and loans from the IMF | 3dcla | — | — | — | — | † — | | | | | | | |
| Exceptional financing | 409la | .... | .... | — | — | .... | .... | .... | .... | .... | .... | .... | .... |
| *Excludes components in group E | | | | | | | | | | | | | |

| | | 2004 | 2005 | 2006 | 2007 | 2008 | 2009 | 2010 | 2011 | 2012 | 2013 | 2014 | 2015 |
|---|---|---|---|---|---|---|---|---|---|---|---|---|---|
| **International Investment Position** | | | | | | | *Millions of US Dollars* | | | | | | |
| Assets | 809aa | 581.2 | 27,428.0 | 33,850.2 | 52,172.3 | † 47,097.6 | 49,374.3 | 44,988.6 | 43,459.7 | 44,261.0 | 46,020.9 | 47,802.5 | 43,887.4 |
| Direct investment | 8a9aa | 3,606.2 | 4,337.7 | 5,310.3 | 9,508.4 | † 9,711.3 | 11,154.6 | 10,535.9 | 10,021.3 | 9,497.0 | 9,395.8 | 8,427.1 | 7,364.4 |
| Equity & investment fund shares | 8aaaa | 2,066.5 | 2,759.0 | 3,498.9 | 5,694.9 | † 6,400.4 | 6,831.3 | 5,927.4 | 5,581.9 | 5,520.4 | 5,233.7 | 4,548.0 | 3,777.3 |
| Debt instruments | 8abaa | 1,539.7 | 1,578.8 | 1,811.5 | 3,813.5 | † 3,310.9 | 4,323.2 | 4,608.6 | 4,439.4 | 3,976.7 | 4,162.1 | 3,880.3 | 3,587.1 |
| Portfolio investment | 8b9aa | 1,729.6 | 3,253.5 | 6,759.5 | 18,471.7 | † 14,750.6 | 16,214.0 | 15,757.8 | 14,737.5 | 15,345.9 | 15,702.4 | 15,024.5 | 15,715.8 |
| Equity & investment fund shares | 8baaa | 642.1 | 1,465.5 | 2,974.3 | 5,391.2 | † 2,386.8 | 3,283.1 | 3,589.0 | 2,990.2 | 3,340.7 | 3,799.4 | 3,876.6 | 3,766.1 |
| Debt securities | 8bbaa | 1,087.5 | 1,787.9 | 3,785.2 | 13,080.5 | † 12,365.3 | 12,930.8 | 12,168.8 | 11,747.3 | 12,003.9 | 11,903.0 | 11,147.9 | 11,949.7 |
| Fin. der.(oth.than reserves) & ESOs | 8c9aa | 2.0 | 17.1 | 35.2 | 194.0 | † 115.5 | 129.1 | 163.0 | 243.3 | 199.2 | 122.7 | 100.8 | 70.7 |
| Other investment | 8d9aa | 9,916.4 | 11,686.1 | 14,609.0 | 22,932.7 | † 21,563.0 | 20,797.9 | 17,461.5 | 17,466.4 | 18,267.1 | 19,878.3 | 23,231.8 | 19,880.1 |
| Other equity | 8daaa | .... | .... | .... | .... | † 222.7 | 311.2 | 298.0 | 286.0 | 488.2 | 730.9 | 763.7 | 695.5 |
| Debt instruments | 8dzaa | 9,916.4 | 11,686.1 | 14,609.0 | 22,932.7 | † 21,340.3 | 20,486.8 | 17,163.5 | 17,180.4 | 17,778.9 | 19,147.4 | 22,468.1 | 19,184.6 |
| Reserve assets | 8e9aa | 8,899.1 | 8,133.7 | 7,136.2 | 1,065.5 | † 957.2 | 1,078.2 | 1,070.3 | 991.3 | 951.7 | 921.5 | 1,016.0 | 856.5 |
| Liabilities | 809la | 620.3 | 31,193.2 | 40,875.8 | 63,330.6 | † 67,881.8 | 72,089.0 | 67,834.6 | 65,036.8 | 67,968.2 | 68,862.7 | 67,543.6 | 60,039.4 |
| Direct investment | 8a9la | 8,170.7 | 8,283.8 | 9,748.7 | 15,851.4 | † 13,208.6 | 13,580.5 | 13,056.0 | 13,685.6 | 14,166.4 | 14,523.3 | 14,273.0 | 13,738.4 |
| Equity & investment fund shares | 8aala | 6,630.3 | 6,615.1 | 8,274.9 | 9,975.0 | † 10,524.0 | 10,842.0 | 10,180.5 | 9,862.1 | 10,049.9 | 10,056.4 | 9,842.7 | 9,982.8 |
| Debt instruments | 8abla | 1,540.4 | 1,668.7 | 1,473.8 | 5,876.4 | † 2,684.6 | 2,738.6 | 2,875.5 | 3,823.5 | 4,116.5 | 4,468.3 | 4,430.3 | 3,755.6 |
| Portfolio investment | 8b9la | 3,156.0 | 2,829.2 | 4,131.9 | 6,697.4 | † 6,362.9 | 13,443.7 | 15,680.3 | 15,337.9 | 16,193.0 | 22,191.1 | 27,773.8 | 24,090.1 |
| Equity & investment fund shares | 8bala | 287.1 | 362.1 | 865.6 | 1,999.6 | † 807.2 | 894.6 | 928.7 | 876.0 | 972.4 | 1,118.5 | 1,226.2 | 1,112.4 |
| Debt securities | 8bbla | 2,868.9 | 2,467.1 | 3,266.3 | 4,697.7 | † 5,555.7 | 12,549.1 | 14,750.3 | 14,461.9 | 15,220.6 | 21,072.6 | 26,546.3 | 22,977.7 |
| Fin. der.(oth.than reserves) & ESOs | 8c9la | .... | .... | .... | 112.4 | † 317.3 | 293.9 | 418.2 | 357.1 | 354.9 | 206.9 | 212.5 | 178.5 |
| Other investment | 8d9la | 16,501.8 | 20,080.3 | 26,995.2 | 40,669.4 | † 47,994.4 | 44,769.4 | 38,681.4 | 35,656.2 | 37,253.9 | 31,941.4 | 25,284.4 | 22,032.4 |
| Other equity | 8dala | .... | .... | .... | .... | † 26.4 | 31.7 | 25.4 | 25.9 | 27.7 | 31.7 | 31.6 | 29.8 |
| Debt instruments | 8dzla | 16,501.8 | 20,080.3 | 26,995.2 | 40,669.4 | † 47,967.9 | 44,737.7 | 38,656.0 | 35,630.3 | 37,226.2 | 31,909.7 | 25,252.8 | 22,002.6 |

# Slovenia 961

| | | 2004 | 2005 | 2006 | 2007 | 2008 | 2009 | 2010 | 2011 | 2012 | 2013 | 2014 | 2015 |
|---|---|---|---|---|---|---|---|---|---|---|---|---|---|
| **Government Finance** | | | | | | | | | | | | | |
| **Operations Statement** | | | | | | | | | | | | | |
| **General Government** | | | | | | *Millions of Euros; Data Reported through Eurostat: Fiscal Year Ends December 31* | | | | | | | |
| Revenue | a1 | 11,998 | 12,737 | 13,573 | 14,799 | 16,112 | 15,311 | 15,813 | 15,991 | 16,002 | 16,247 | 16,766 | 17,384 |
| Taxes | a11 | 6,503 | 6,996 | 7,516 | 8,246 | 8,618 | 7,850 | 8,024 | 8,072 | 7,939 | 7,969 | 8,286 | 8,539 |
| Social Contributions | a12 | 3,925 | 4,165 | 4,428 | 4,814 | 5,326 | 5,388 | 5,497 | 5,523 | 5,481 | 5,366 | 5,464 | 5,702 |
| Grants | a13 | .... | .... | .... | .... | .... | .... | .... | .... | .... | .... | .... | .... |
| Other Revenue | a14 | .... | .... | .... | .... | .... | .... | .... | .... | .... | .... | .... | .... |
| Expense | a2 | 12,069 | 12,693 | 13,334 | 13,952 | 15,625 | 16,451 | 17,043 | 17,884 | 17,034 | 21,065 | 17,929 | 17,698 |
| Compensation of Employees | a21 | 3,139 | 3,305 | 3,480 | 3,641 | 4,112 | 4,400 | 4,561 | 4,670 | 4,546 | 4,328 | 4,255 | 4,269 |
| Use of Goods & Services | a22 | 1,624 | 1,718 | 1,863 | 1,948 | 2,266 | 2,341 | 2,457 | 2,631 | 2,488 | 2,471 | 2,486 | 2,524 |
| Consumption of Fixed Capital | a23 | 597 | 635 | 686 | 740 | 811 | 875 | 929 | 983 | 1,034 | 1,088 | 1,153 | 1,175 |
| Interest | a24 | 459 | 447 | 432 | 437 | 416 | 474 | 591 | 698 | 730 | 920 | 1,181 | 1,145 |
| Subsidies | a25 | 462 | 435 | 491 | 550 | 593 | 665 | 648 | 377 | 329 | 380 | 329 | 309 |
| Grants | a26 | — | — | — | — | — | — | — | — | — | — | — | — |
| Social Benefits | a27 | 4,847 | 5,089 | 5,369 | 5,624 | 6,203 | 6,631 | 6,861 | 7,135 | 6,921 | 6,927 | 6,892 | 6,941 |
| Other Expense | a28 | .... | .... | .... | .... | .... | .... | .... | .... | .... | .... | .... | .... |
| Gross Operating Balance [1-2+23] | agob | 526 | 679 | 925 | 1,587 | 1,298 | −265 | −301 | −911 | 2 | −3,731 | −10 | 861 |
| Net Operating Balance [1-2] | anob | −71 | 44 | 239 | 847 | 486 | −1,140 | −1,230 | −1,894 | −1,032 | −4,819 | −1,163 | −314 |
| Net Acq. of Nonfinancial Assets | a31 | 473 | 434 | 619 | 878 | 1,024 | 987 | 814 | 563 | 442 | 576 | 692 | 817 |
| Aquisition of Nonfin. Assets | a31.1 | .... | .... | .... | .... | .... | .... | .... | .... | .... | .... | .... | .... |
| Disposal of Nonfin. Assets | a31.2 | .... | .... | .... | .... | .... | .... | .... | .... | .... | .... | .... | .... |
| Net Lending/Borrowing [1-2-31] | anlb | −544 | −390 | −380 | −31 | −537 | −2,127 | −2,044 | −2,456 | −1,474 | −5,395 | −1,855 | −1,131 |
| Net Acq. of Financial Assets | a32 | 152 | −118 | 567 | 75 | 156 | 2,261 | −695 | 806 | 729 | 975 | 3,013 | 655 |
| By instrument | | | | | | | | | | | | | |
| Monetary Gold & SDRs | a3201 | — | — | — | — | — | — | — | — | — | — | — | — |
| Currency & Deposits | a3202 | 12 | −157 | 351 | 412 | 244 | 2,062 | −989 | 747 | −70 | −281 | 2,180 | 1,140 |
| Securities other than Shares | a3203 | −19 | 14 | −14 | 97 | −34 | −44 | 34 | −92 | 2 | −3 | −38 | 34 |
| Loans | a3204 | −13 | 8 | 12 | 8 | — | 1 | 100 | 263 | 981 | 852 | 819 | −749 |
| Shares & Other Equity | a3205 | −78 | −87 | −98 | −806 | −8 | 154 | −1 | 80 | 64 | 218 | −29 | 74 |
| Insurance Technical Reserves | a3206 | 2 | −2 | 15 | 3 | — | −1 | −1 | — | — | — | 2 | — |
| Financial Derivatives | a3207 | 1 | — | 4 | 6 | −4 | −3 | — | −1 | −1 | −1 | −1 | — |
| Other Accounts Receivable | a3208 | 247 | 107 | 297 | 355 | −41 | 92 | 162 | −192 | −246 | 190 | 79 | 156 |
| By debtor | | | | | | | | | | | | | |
| Domestic | a321 | .... | .... | .... | .... | .... | .... | .... | .... | .... | .... | .... | .... |
| Foreign | a322 | .... | .... | .... | .... | .... | .... | .... | .... | .... | .... | .... | .... |
| Net Incurrence of Liabilities | a33 | 692 | 250 | 930 | 125 | 622 | 4,353 | 1,381 | 3,261 | 2,228 | 6,386 | 4,913 | 1,789 |
| By instrument | | | | | | | | | | | | | |
| Special Drawing Rights (SDRs) | a3301 | — | — | — | — | — | — | — | — | — | — | — | — |
| Currency & Deposits | a3302 | 4 | 3 | −5 | 119 | 1 | 6 | 7 | 9 | −9 | 22 | −8 | 5 |
| Securities other than Shares | a3303 | 597 | 178 | 678 | −194 | 379 | 4,126 | 875 | 3,038 | 1,121 | 5,762 | 4,393 | 1,007 |
| Loans | a3304 | −34 | 107 | −118 | −145 | 44 | 212 | 442 | 122 | 1,092 | 332 | 381 | 872 |
| Shares & Other Equity | a3305 | — | — | — | — | — | — | — | — | — | — | — | 110 |
| Insurance Technical Reserves | a3306 | — | — | — | — | — | — | — | — | — | — | — | — |
| Financial Derivatives | a3307 | −5 | — | — | — | — | — | — | — | — | −1 | −2 | −2 |
| Other Accounts Payable | a3308 | 130 | −38 | 375 | 345 | 197 | 10 | 57 | 91 | 22 | 270 | 149 | −204 |
| By creditor | | | | | | | | | | | | | |
| Domestic | a331 | .... | .... | .... | .... | .... | .... | .... | .... | .... | .... | .... | .... |
| Foreign | a332 | .... | .... | .... | .... | .... | .... | .... | .... | .... | .... | .... | .... |
| Stat. Discrepancy [32-33-NLB] | anlbz | 4 | 21 | 17 | −18 | 72 | 34 | −32 | 2 | −25 | −16 | −44 | −3 |
| Memo Item: Expenditure [2+31] | a2m | 12,542 | 13,127 | 13,953 | 14,830 | 16,649 | 17,438 | 17,857 | 18,447 | 17,476 | 21,642 | 18,621 | 18,516 |
| **Balance Sheet** | | | | | | | | | | | | | |
| Net Worth | a6 | .... | .... | .... | .... | .... | .... | .... | .... | .... | .... | .... | .... |
| Nonfinancial Assets | a61 | .... | .... | .... | .... | .... | .... | .... | .... | .... | .... | .... | .... |
| Financial Assets | a62 | 12,183 | 12,316 | 13,733 | 16,660 | 13,485 | 16,150 | 17,237 | 17,733 | 18,709 | 23,598 | 28,963 | 28,357 |
| By instrument | | | | | | | | | | | | | |
| Monetary Gold & SDRs | a6201 | — | — | — | — | — | — | — | — | — | — | — | — |
| Currency & Deposits | a6202 | 1,395 | 1,258 | 1,592 | 1,978 | 2,280 | 4,336 | 3,510 | 4,372 | 4,285 | 4,000 | 6,197 | 7,356 |
| Securities other than Shares | a6203 | 234 | 250 | 244 | 350 | 304 | 269 | 316 | 217 | 222 | 203 | 172 | 201 |
| Loans | a6204 | 352 | 376 | 360 | 363 | 448 | 280 | 382 | 674 | 1,657 | 4,831 | 6,704 | 4,596 |
| Shares and Other Equity | a6205 | 7,678 | 7,815 | 9,263 | 11,319 | 7,811 | 8,561 | 10,274 | 9,935 | 10,276 | 12,099 | 13,321 | 13,458 |
| Insurance Technical Reserves | a6206 | 3 | 1 | 16 | 16 | 14 | 10 | 9 | 9 | 2 | 2 | 12 | 23 |
| Financial Derivatives | a6207 | 1 | 1 | 4 | 10 | 7 | 5 | 5 | 4 | 2 | 1 | — | — |
| Other Accounts Receivable | a6208 | 2,521 | 2,616 | 2,254 | 2,624 | 2,621 | 2,689 | 2,739 | 2,523 | 2,266 | 2,462 | 2,557 | 2,723 |
| By debtor | | | | | | | | | | | | | |
| Domestic | a621 | .... | .... | .... | .... | .... | .... | .... | .... | .... | .... | .... | .... |
| Foreign | a622 | .... | .... | .... | .... | .... | .... | .... | .... | .... | .... | .... | .... |
| Liabilities | a63 | 9,484 | 9,755 | 10,499 | 10,237 | 10,760 | 15,369 | 16,968 | 18,620 | 21,851 | 28,596 | 36,322 | 38,048 |
| By instrument | | | | | | | | | | | | | |
| Special Drawing Rights (SDRs) | a6301 | — | — | — | — | — | — | — | — | — | — | — | — |
| Currency & Deposits | a6302 | 12 | 14 | 55 | 165 | 82 | 88 | 145 | 157 | 148 | 170 | 163 | 169 |
| Securities other than Shares | a6303 | 6,806 | 6,922 | 7,406 | 7,191 | 7,603 | 11,946 | 12,979 | 14,211 | 16,321 | 22,441 | 29,631 | 30,586 |
| Loans | a6304 | 1,028 | 1,144 | 975 | 836 | 838 | 1,045 | 1,620 | 1,909 | 3,006 | 3,339 | 3,722 | 4,588 |
| Shares and Other Equity | a6305 | — | 1 | 1 | — | 1 | — | 1 | 41 | 44 | 45 | 43 | 149 |
| Insurance Technical Reserves | a6306 | — | — | — | — | — | — | — | — | — | — | — | — |
| Financial Derivatives | a6307 | — | — | — | — | — | — | — | — | — | 7 | 4 | 5 | 3 |
| Other Accounts Payable | a6308 | 1,638 | 1,674 | 2,062 | 2,044 | 2,235 | 2,290 | 2,224 | 2,302 | 2,325 | 2,597 | 2,757 | 2,553 |
| By creditor | | | | | | | | | | | | | |
| Domestic | a631 | .... | .... | .... | .... | .... | .... | .... | .... | .... | .... | .... | .... |
| Foreign | a632 | .... | .... | .... | .... | .... | .... | .... | .... | .... | .... | .... | .... |
| Net Financial Worth [62-63] | a6m2 | 2,699 | 2,561 | 3,233 | 6,423 | 2,726 | 781 | 268 | −886 | −3,142 | −4,998 | −7,358 | −9,691 |
| Memo Item: Debt at Market Value | a6m3 | 9,484 | 9,754 | 10,498 | 10,237 | 10,758 | 15,369 | 16,967 | 18,579 | 21,800 | 28,547 | 36,273 | 37,896 |
| Memo Item: Debt at Face Value | a6m35 | 9,067 | 9,357 | 10,266 | 10,070 | 10,510 | 14,817 | 16,131 | 19,505 | 21,729 | 28,102 | 32,956 | 34,623 |
| Memo Item: Maastricht Debt | a6m36 | 7,429 | 7,683 | 8,204 | 8,025 | 8,275 | 12,527 | 13,907 | 17,204 | 19,404 | 25,505 | 30,199 | 32,070 |
| Memo Item: Debt at Nominal Value | a6m4 | .... | .... | .... | .... | .... | .... | .... | .... | .... | .... | .... | .... |

# Slovenia 961

| National Accounts | | 2004 | 2005 | 2006 | 2007 | 2008 | 2009 | 2010 | 2011 | 2012 | 2013 | 2014 | 2015 |
|---|---|---|---|---|---|---|---|---|---|---|---|---|---|
| | | *Billions of Tolars through 2006; Millions of Euros Beginning 2007* | | | | | | | | | | | |
| Househ.Cons.Expend.,incl.NPISHs.... | 96f | 3,592.6 | 3,752.5 | 3,889.1 | † 17,973.2 | 19,433.3 | 19,779.4 | 20,316.5 | 20,667.8 | 20,422.7 | 19,741.1 | 19,876.6 | 19,998.7 |
| Government Consumption Expend... | 91f | 1,237.7 | 1,308.3 | 1,394.4 | † 6,078.9 | 6,841.0 | 7,254.5 | 7,353.3 | 7,537.4 | 7,295.4 | 7,111.0 | 7,116.5 | 7,149.7 |
| Gross Fixed Capital Formation......... | 93e | 1,735.0 | 1,866.4 | 2,104.0 | † 10,107.9 | 11,230.0 | 8,806.1 | 7,726.6 | 7,450.7 | 6,933.9 | 7,069.0 | 7,323.9 | 7,469.1 |
| Changes in Inventories.................... | 93i | 162.0 | 121.3 | 178.0 | † 1,448.8 | 1,178.1 | −349.6 | 335.9 | 563.2 | −185.4 | −119.6 | 49.9 | 314.8 |
| Exports of Goods and Services.......... | 90c | 3,645.1 | 4,172.9 | 4,892.2 | † 23,762.1 | 25,089.1 | 20,702.5 | 23,306.0 | 25,965.4 | 26,380.5 | 27,004.9 | 28,546.9 | 30,000.4 |
| Imports of Goods and Services (-)..... | 98c | 3,740.9 | 4,217.6 | 4,895.8 | † 24,218.3 | 25,820.3 | 20,026.6 | 22,785.8 | 25,288.1 | 24,858.8 | 24,898.9 | 25,610.6 | 26,389.5 |
| Gross Domestic Product (GDP)......... | 99b | 6,631.5 | 7,003.9 | 7,561.9 | † 35,152.6 | 37,951.2 | 36,166.2 | 36,252.4 | 36,896.3 | 35,988.3 | 35,907.5 | 37,303.2 | 38,543.2 |
| Net Primary Income from Abroad..... | 98.n | −61.3 | −33.4 | −59.0 | † −636.8 | −917.4 | −493.5 | −337.5 | −293.3 | −255.3 | −201.0 | −58.2 | −310.1 |
| Gross National Income (GNI)............ | 99a | 6,570.2 | 6,970.5 | 7,502.9 | † 34,515.8 | 37,033.8 | 35,672.7 | 35,914.9 | 36,603.0 | 35,733.0 | 35,706.4 | 37,245.0 | 38,233.2 |
| Net Current Transf.from Abroad....... | 98t | — | −.1 | −.2 | † −307.4 | −352.1 | −322.5 | −391.3 | −431.8 | −509.1 | −521.3 | −452.8 | −593.2 |
| Gross Nat'l Disposable Inc.(GNDI).... | 99i | 6,535.3 | 6,909.2 | 7,437.5 | † 34,208.3 | 36,681.7 | 35,350.2 | 35,523.7 | 36,171.1 | 35,223.9 | 35,185.1 | 36,792.2 | 37,640.0 |
| Gross Saving................................. | 99s | 6.7 | 7.3 | 8.2 | † 10,156.3 | 10,407.4 | 8,316.3 | 7,853.9 | 7,966.0 | 7,505.9 | 8,333.0 | 9,799.1 | 10,491.6 |
| GDP Volume 2000 Prices................. | 99b.p | 5,109.9 | 5,314.7 | 5,625.6 | † 25,108.9 | .... | .... | .... | .... | .... | .... | .... | .... |
| GDP Volume 2005 Ref., Chained..... | 99b.p | .... | .... | .... | † 33,023.2 | 34,113.0 | 31,453.1 | 31,842.4 | 32,049.2 | 31,178.0 | 30,848.2 | 31,788.6 | 32,703.8 |
| GDP Volume (2010=100)............... | 99bvp | 88.1 | 91.6 | 97.0 | † 103.7 | 107.1 | 98.8 | 100.0 | 100.6 | 97.9 | 96.9 | 99.8 | 102.7 |
| GDP Deflator (2010=100)............... | 99bip | 86.7 | 88.0 | 89.8 | 93.5 | 97.7 | 101.0 | 100.0 | 101.1 | 101.4 | 102.2 | 103.1 | 103.5 |
| | | *Millions: Midyear Estimates* | | | | | | | | | | | |
| Population............................... | 99z | 1.99 | 2.00 | 2.01 | 2.02 | 2.03 | 2.04 | 2.05 | 2.06 | 2.06 | 2.06 | 2.07 | 2.07 |

# Solomon Islands   813

| | | 2004 | 2005 | 2006 | 2007 | 2008 | 2009 | 2010 | 2011 | 2012 | 2013 | 2014 | 2015 |
|---|---|---|---|---|---|---|---|---|---|---|---|---|---|
| **Exchange Rates** | | | | | *Solomon Islands Dollars per SDR: End of Period* | | | | | | | | |
| Official Rate........................... | aa | 11.6592 | 10.8278 | 11.4577 | 12.1092 | 12.3222 | 12.6427 | 12.4196 | 11.2971 | 11.2843 | 11.3319 | 10.6609 | 11.1752 |
| | | | | *Solomon Islands Dollars per US Dollar: End of Period (ae) Period Average (rf)* | | | | | | | | | |
| Official Rate........................... | ae | 7.5075 | 7.5758 | 7.6161 | 7.6628 | 8.0000 | 8.0645 | 8.0645 | 7.3584 | 7.3421 | 7.3584 | 7.3584 | 8.0645 |
| Official Rate........................... | rf | 7.4847 | 7.5299 | 7.6095 | 7.6520 | 7.7479 | 8.0550 | 8.0645 | 7.6413 | 7.3552 | 7.3021 | 7.3753 | 7.9147 |
| | | | | *Index Numbers (2010=100): Period Averages* | | | | | | | | | |
| Official Rate........................... | ahx | 107.7 | 107.1 | 106.0 | 105.4 | 104.1 | 100.1 | 100.0 | 105.7 | 109.6 | 110.4 | 109.4 | 101.9 |
| Nominal Effective Exchange Rate..... | nec | 122.6 | 119.6 | 117.8 | 110.1 | 105.2 | 106.2 | 100.0 | 99.1 | 104.4 | 108.7 | 111.8 | 119.7 |
| CPI-Based Real Effect. Ex. Rate........ | rec | 87.2 | 89.2 | 95.3 | 93.4 | 100.6 | 107.6 | 100.0 | 103.1 | 112.6 | 121.1 | 128.1 | 134.5 |
| **Fund Position** | | | | | *Millions of SDRs: End of Period* | | | | | | | | |
| Quota............................. | 2f.s | 10.40 | 10.40 | 10.40 | 10.40 | 10.40 | 10.40 | 10.40 | 10.40 | 10.40 | 10.40 | 10.40 | 10.40 |
| SDR Holdings...................... | 1b.s | — | — | .01 | — | .01 | 9.26 | 9.26 | 9.26 | 9.40 | 9.40 | 8.51 | 8.58 |
| Reserve Position in the Fund............ | 1c.s | .55 | .55 | .55 | .55 | .55 | .55 | .55 | .55 | .55 | .55 | .55 | .55 |
| Total Fund Cred.&Loans Outstg........ | 2tl | — | — | — | — | — | — | 6.24 | 12.48 | 12.63 | 12.78 | 12.03 | 10.10 |
| SDR Allocations....................... | 1bd | .65 | .65 | .65 | .65 | .65 | 9.91 | 9.91 | 9.91 | 9.91 | 9.91 | 9.91 | 9.91 |
| **International Liquidity** | | | | | *Millions of US Dollars Unless Otherwise Indicated: End of Period* | | | | | | | | |
| Total Reserves minus Gold.............. | 1l.d | 79.81 | 94.83 | 104.08 | 120.53 | 88.83 | 145.99 | 265.83 | 412.27 | 469.49 | 491.52 | 466.91 | 494.08 |
| SDR Holdings......................... | 1b.d | — | — | .01 | — | .01 | 14.52 | 14.26 | 14.21 | 14.45 | 14.48 | 12.33 | 11.89 |
| Reserve Position in the Fund.......... | 1c.d | .85 | .79 | .83 | .87 | .85 | .86 | .85 | .84 | .85 | .85 | .80 | .76 |
| Foreign Exchange...................... | 1d.d | 78.96 | 94.04 | 103.24 | 119.66 | 87.97 | 130.61 | 250.73 | 397.22 | 454.20 | 476.19 | 453.78 | 481.43 |
| Gold (Million Fine Troy Ounces)....... | 1ad | .... | .... | .... | .... | .... | .... | .... | .... | .02 | .02 | .02 | .02 |
| Gold (National Valuation)................ | 1and | .... | .... | .... | .... | .... | .... | .... | .... | 30.00 | 40.00 | 40.00 | 40.00 |
| Central Bank: Other Assets........ | 3..d | — | — | † — | — | — | — | — | — | — | — | — | — |
| Central Bank: Other Liabs............... | 4..d | 1.15 | .50 | † .04 | .07 | .06 | .07 | .15 | .31 | .12 | .06 | .23 | .81 |
| Other Depository Corps.: Assets....... | 7a.d | 9.58 | 9.98 | 10.41 | 8.19 | 17.75 | 22.77 | † 17.43 | 22.72 | † 16.64 | 31.32 | 47.78 | 34.82 |
| Other Depository Corps.: Liabs....... | 7b.d | 8.82 | .64 | .65 | 1.04 | .78 | .27 | † 11.05 | 10.84 | † 14.98 | 13.29 | 10.15 | 13.87 |
| Other Financial Corps.: Assets....... | 7e.d | — | — | .82 | 18.77 | 25.03 | 26.47 | 27.11 | 36.07 | † 38.43 | 37.74 | 36.23 | 35.08 |
| Other Financial Corps.: Liabs............ | 7f.d | 4.13 | 4.34 | 4.33 | 4.39 | 4.35 | 4.45 | 2.01 | 1.52 | † 2.14 | 2.16 | 2.03 | 2.50 |
| **Central Bank** | | | | | *Millions of Solomon Islands Dollars: End of Period* | | | | | | | | |
| Net Foreign Assets........................... | 11n | 582.97 | 707.51 | † 786.70 | 915.13 | 707.71 | 1,051.48 | 1,942.06 | 2,778.46 | 3,412.60 | 3,651.16 | 3,539.68 | 3,959.87 |
| Claims on Nonresidents............. | 11 | 599.22 | 718.38 | † 794.49 | 923.61 | 716.35 | 1,177.30 | 2,143.81 | 3,033.63 | 3,667.81 | 3,908.64 | 3,784.14 | 4,190.00 |
| Liabilities to Nonresidents............... | 16c | 16.25 | 10.87 | † 7.80 | 8.47 | 8.64 | 125.82 | 201.76 | 255.17 | 255.21 | 257.48 | 244.46 | 230.14 |
| Claims on Other Depository Corps.... | 12e | — | — | † 20.36 | 2.91 | 33.27 | 29.37 | 46.34 | 46.19 | 45.31 | 97.90 | 36.93 | .70 |
| Net Claims on Central Government.. | 12an | −20.54 | −100.52 | † −88.35 | −148.15 | −51.91 | −77.35 | −361.05 | −837.79 | −945.62 | −1,164.57 | −1,279.65 | −1,109.56 |
| Claims on Central Government....... | 12a | 185.58 | 196.90 | † 162.04 | 149.82 | 138.35 | 124.07 | 117.46 | 103.33 | 82.25 | 74.67 | 69.02 | 5.07 |
| Liabilities to Central Government.... | 16d | 206.12 | 297.42 | † 250.39 | 297.98 | 190.26 | 201.43 | 478.51 | 941.12 | 1,027.87 | 1,239.24 | 1,348.67 | 1,114.63 |
| Claims on Other Sectors.................. | 12s | 3.67 | 2.10 | † 15.55 | 15.92 | 16.03 | 16.53 | 15.80 | 17.17 | 17.65 | 19.03 | 18.51 | 19.07 |
| Claims on Other Financial Corps..... | 12g | — | — | † 12.15 | 12.15 | 12.15 | 12.15 | 12.15 | 12.15 | 12.15 | 12.15 | 12.15 | 12.15 |
| Claims on State & Local Govts........ | 12b | — | — | † .01 | — | — | — | — | — | — | — | — | — |
| Claims on Public Nonfin. Corps...... | 12c | .67 | — | † — | — | — | — | — | — | — | — | — | — |
| Claims on Private Sector............... | 12d | 3.00 | 2.10 | † 3.39 | 3.77 | 3.88 | 4.38 | 3.65 | 5.02 | 5.50 | 6.88 | 6.36 | 6.92 |
| Monetary Base............................ | 14 | 376.70 | 452.46 | † 481.22 | 451.70 | 440.64 | 717.19 | 1,263.29 | 1,659.49 | 2,054.42 | 2,033.55 | 1,827.58 | 2,257.16 |
| Currency in Circulation................... | 14a | 130.93 | 156.66 | † 187.20 | 244.55 | 272.54 | 326.06 | 436.41 | 526.45 | 599.21 | 602.52 | 658.26 | 739.82 |
| Liabs. to Other Depository Corps.... | 14c | 244.56 | 294.66 | † 288.14 | 200.75 | 165.91 | 389.34 | 822.37 | 1,125.91 | 1,446.50 | 1,423.68 | 1,164.86 | 1,510.97 |
| Liabilities to Other Sectors............. | 14d | 1.20 | 1.14 | † 5.88 | 6.41 | 2.19 | 1.78 | 4.50 | 7.13 | 8.71 | 7.35 | 4.47 | 6.37 |
| Other Liabs. to Other Dep. Corps...... | 14n | — | — | † .68 | .93 | .81 | .82 | 1.26 | 201.21 | 357.31 | 602.14 | 612.16 | 712.44 |
| Dep. & Sec. Excl. f/Monetary Base.... | 14o | — | — | † 4.28 | 4.76 | 25.60 | 25.12 | 57.36 | 67.12 | 12.68 | 16.31 | 16.48 | 16.60 |
| Deposits Included in Broad Money. | 15 | — | — | † 3.98 | 4.41 | 4.97 | 4.68 | .32 | 24.54 | .32 | 3.83 | 3.93 | 4.06 |
| Sec.Ot.th.Shares Incl.in Brd. Money. | 16a | — | — | † — | — | — | — | — | — | — | — | — | — |
| Deposits Excl. from Broad Money... | 16b | — | — | † .31 | .35 | .37 | .35 | .26 | .26 | .29 | .45 | .46 | .51 |
| Sec.Ot.th.Shares Excl.f/Brd.Money.. | 16s | — | — | † — | — | 20.27 | 20.09 | 56.79 | 42.32 | 12.07 | 12.03 | 12.09 | 12.03 |
| Loans...................................... | 16l | — | — | † — | — | — | — | — | — | — | — | — | — |
| Financial Derivatives........................ | 16m | — | — | † — | — | — | — | — | — | — | — | — | — |
| Shares and Other Equity................. | 17a | 16.46 | 158.78 | † 275.17 | 354.98 | 274.83 | 317.31 | 384.02 | 152.56 | 228.02 | 80.29 | −5.49 | 19.79 |
| Other Items (Net)........................... | 17r | 172.94 | −2.14 | † −27.09 | −26.56 | −36.76 | −40.41 | −62.79 | −76.33 | −122.49 | −128.75 | −135.27 | −135.93 |
| Memo Item: | | | | | | | | | | | | | |
| Total Assets................................... | 10ra | 799.25 | 930.81 | † 1,046.29 | 1,150.16 | 972.47 | 1,414.77 | 2,412.73 | 3,313.90 | 3,977.83 | 4,277.12 | 4,202.72 | 4,508.68 |

# Solomon Islands 813

| | | 2004 | 2005 | 2006 | 2007 | 2008 | 2009 | 2010 | 2011 | 2012 | 2013 | 2014 | 2015 |
|---|---|---|---|---|---|---|---|---|---|---|---|---|---|
| **Other Depository Corporations** | | | | | | *Millions of Solomon Islands Dollars: End of Period* | | | | | | | |
| Net Foreign Assets.................... | 21n | 5.68 | 70.73 | 74.46 | 54.79 | 136.86 | 181.45 | † 51.47 | 87.41 | † 12.17 | 132.68 | 287.27 | 168.95 |
| Claims on Nonresidents................ | 21 | 71.86 | 75.60 | 79.44 | 62.76 | 143.17 | 183.59 | † 140.54 | 167.19 | † 122.18 | 230.49 | 364.73 | 280.79 |
| Liabilities to Nonresidents.............. | 26c | 66.18 | 4.87 | 4.98 | 7.97 | 6.32 | 2.14 | † 89.07 | 79.78 | † 110.01 | 97.82 | 77.46 | 111.85 |
| Claims on Central Bank.................. | 20 | 259.09 | 309.74 | 314.63 | 232.99 | 189.18 | 411.00 | † 847.88 | 1,370.51 | † 1,870.27 | 2,097.29 | 1,859.34 | 2,308.35 |
| Currency................................. | 20a | 14.53 | 15.08 | 25.82 | 31.31 | 22.47 | 20.84 | † 24.58 | 45.29 | † 66.38 | 71.38 | 83.26 | 84.67 |
| Reserve Deposits and Securities..... | 20b | 244.56 | 294.66 | 288.81 | 200.75 | 165.91 | 389.34 | † 822.28 | 1,125.91 | † 1,446.45 | 1,423.68 | 1,163.80 | 1,511.18 |
| Other Claims.............................. | 20n | — | — | .01 | .93 | .81 | .82 | † 1.01 | 199.32 | † 357.44 | 602.23 | 612.27 | 712.50 |
| Net Claims on Central Government.. | 22an | 102.37 | 123.18 | 75.79 | 93.99 | 89.81 | 50.97 | † 53.11 | −27.81 | † −97.12 | −163.65 | −146.16 | −242.58 |
| Claims on Central Government...... | 22a | 145.88 | 141.79 | 133.34 | 130.56 | 116.10 | 125.36 | † 120.70 | 101.38 | † 65.45 | 48.10 | 44.31 | 14.85 |
| Liabilities to Central Government.... | 26d | 43.52 | 18.61 | 57.55 | 36.57 | 26.29 | 74.39 | † 67.59 | 129.19 | † 162.57 | 211.75 | 190.47 | 257.43 |
| Claims on Other Sectors.................. | 22s | 259.62 | 413.11 | 656.20 | 1,007.16 | 1,273.27 | 1,220.29 | † 1,162.82 | 1,216.54 | † 1,302.62 | 1,489.21 | 1,738.99 | 2,016.40 |
| Claims on Other Financial Corps.... | 22g | .01 | — | 1.04 | 1.08 | 1.00 | .77 | † .08 | .09 | † .75 | .36 | 1.45 | .70 |
| Claims on State & Local Govts....... | 22b | .43 | — | .01 | .01 | .10 | .05 | † — | — | † .44 | — | .01 | — |
| Claims on Public Nonfin. Corps...... | 22c | — | — | — | — | — | — | † — | — | † 35.78 | 32.28 | 40.75 | 35.09 |
| Claims on Private Sector............... | 22d | 259.19 | 413.11 | 655.15 | 1,006.08 | 1,272.17 | 1,219.47 | † 1,162.73 | 1,216.45 | † 1,265.66 | 1,456.58 | 1,696.79 | 1,980.62 |
| Liabilities to Central Bank.............. | 26g | — | — | 20.36 | 2.91 | 33.27 | 29.37 | † 46.34 | 46.19 | † 45.21 | 97.92 | 37.86 | .70 |
| Transf.Dep.Included in Broad Money | 24 | 251.11 | 445.69 | 604.09 | 750.69 | 738.17 | 815.87 | † 887.15 | 1,360.01 | † 1,853.94 | 2,156.15 | 2,069.62 | 2,606.37 |
| Other Dep.Included in Broad Money. | 25 | 276.70 | 354.67 | 416.95 | 476.26 | 571.76 | 703.20 | † 770.81 | 737.06 | † 667.87 | 744.69 | 981.57 | 908.21 |
| Sec.Ot.th.Shares Incl.in Brd. Money.. | 26a | — | — | — | — | — | — | † — | — | † — | — | — | — |
| Deposits Excl. from Broad Money..... | 26b | — | — | — | — | — | — | † — | — | † .11 | .10 | — | — |
| Sec.Ot.th.Shares Excl.f/Brd.Money.... | 26s | — | — | — | — | — | — | † — | — | † — | — | — | — |
| Loans....................................... | 26l | — | — | — | — | — | — | † — | — | † — | — | — | — |
| Financial Derivatives.................... | 26m | — | — | — | — | — | — | † — | — | † — | — | — | — |
| Insurance Technical Reserves........... | 26r | — | — | — | — | — | — | † — | — | † — | — | — | — |
| Shares and Other Equity.................. | 27a | 122.49 | 161.64 | 192.67 | 208.48 | 339.59 | 327.23 | † 490.88 | 596.50 | † 611.69 | 666.75 | 733.96 | 794.02 |
| Other Items (Net)............................ | 27r | −23.55 | −45.23 | −112.97 | −49.41 | 6.32 | −11.96 | † −79.90 | −93.11 | † −90.88 | −110.09 | −83.59 | −58.19 |
| Memo Item: | | | | | | | | | | | | | |
| Total Assets................................. | 20ra | 806.16 | 1,025.36 | 1,324.97 | 1,570.38 | 1,902.25 | 2,091.80 | † 2,434.15 | 3,111.78 | † 3,603.90 | 4,178.26 | 4,310.97 | 5,257.13 |
| **Depository Corporations** | | | | | | *Millions of Solomon Islands Dollars: End of Period* | | | | | | | |
| Net Foreign Assets.................... | 31n | 588.65 | 778.24 | † 861.16 | 969.92 | 844.57 | 1,232.93 | † 1,993.53 | 2,865.87 | † 3,424.77 | 3,783.84 | 3,826.94 | 4,128.81 |
| Claims on Nonresidents................ | 31 | 671.08 | 793.98 | † 873.93 | 986.36 | 859.52 | 1,360.90 | † 2,284.36 | 3,200.82 | † 3,789.99 | 4,139.13 | 4,148.86 | 4,470.79 |
| Liabilities to Nonresidents.............. | 36c | 82.43 | 15.74 | † 12.78 | 16.44 | 14.95 | 127.97 | † 290.83 | 334.95 | † 365.21 | 355.30 | 321.92 | 341.98 |
| Domestic Claims........................ | 32 | 345.12 | 437.88 | † 659.20 | 968.93 | 1,327.21 | 1,210.43 | † 870.68 | 368.12 | † 277.54 | 180.02 | 331.69 | 683.33 |
| Net Claims on Central Government | 32an | 81.83 | 22.67 | † −12.56 | −54.16 | 37.91 | −26.39 | † −307.93 | −865.60 | † −1,042.73 | −1,328.22 | −1,425.81 | −1,352.15 |
| Claims on Central Government...... | 32a | 331.46 | 338.69 | † 295.38 | 280.38 | 254.45 | 249.43 | † 238.16 | 204.71 | † 147.70 | 122.77 | 113.33 | 19.92 |
| Liabilities to Central Government. | 36d | 249.64 | 316.03 | † 307.94 | 334.54 | 216.54 | 275.82 | † 546.09 | 1,070.31 | † 1,190.44 | 1,450.99 | 1,539.14 | 1,372.07 |
| Claims on Other Sectors.................. | 32s | 263.29 | 415.22 | † 671.76 | 1,023.08 | 1,289.30 | 1,236.82 | † 1,178.61 | 1,233.72 | † 1,320.27 | 1,508.24 | 1,757.50 | 2,035.48 |
| Claims on Other Financial Corps.. | 32g | .01 | — | † 13.19 | 13.23 | 13.15 | 12.92 | † 12.23 | 12.24 | † 12.90 | 12.51 | 13.60 | 12.85 |
| Claims on State & Local Govts....... | 32b | .43 | — | † .03 | .01 | .10 | .05 | † — | — | † .45 | — | .01 | — |
| Claims on Public Nonfin. Corps..... | 32c | .67 | — | † — | — | — | — | † — | — | † 35.78 | 32.28 | 40.75 | 35.09 |
| Claims on Private Sector............. | 32d | 262.18 | 415.22 | † 658.54 | 1,009.85 | 1,276.06 | 1,223.85 | † 1,166.38 | 1,221.47 | † 1,271.15 | 1,463.45 | 1,703.15 | 1,987.54 |
| Broad Money Liabilities.................. | 35l | 645.42 | 943.08 | † 1,192.28 | 1,451.00 | 1,567.16 | 1,830.75 | † 2,074.62 | 2,609.90 | † 3,063.68 | 3,443.15 | 3,634.59 | 4,180.16 |
| Currency Outside Depository Corps | 34a | 116.41 | 141.58 | † 161.38 | 213.24 | 250.08 | 305.22 | † 411.83 | 481.16 | † 532.83 | 531.13 | 575.00 | 655.15 |
| Transferable Deposits.................. | 34 | 252.32 | 446.83 | † 613.95 | 761.51 | 745.32 | 822.33 | † 891.97 | 1,391.68 | † 1,862.97 | 2,167.33 | 2,078.02 | 2,616.80 |
| Other Deposits........................... | 35 | 276.70 | 354.67 | † 416.95 | 476.26 | 571.76 | 703.20 | † 770.81 | 737.06 | † 667.87 | 744.69 | 981.57 | 908.21 |
| Securities Other than Shares.......... | 36a | — | — | † — | — | — | — | † — | — | † — | — | — | — |
| Deposits Excl. from Broad Money..... | 36b | — | — | † .31 | .35 | .37 | .35 | † .26 | .26 | † .39 | .55 | .46 | .51 |
| Sec.Ot.th.Shares Excl.f/Brd.Money..... | 36s | — | — | † — | — | 20.27 | 20.09 | † 56.79 | 42.32 | † 12.07 | 12.03 | 12.09 | 12.03 |
| Loans....................................... | 36l | — | — | † — | — | — | — | † — | — | † — | — | — | — |
| Financial Derivatives.................... | 36m | — | — | † — | — | — | — | † — | — | † — | — | — | — |
| Insurance Technical Reserves........... | 36r | — | — | † — | — | — | — | † — | — | † — | — | — | — |
| Shares and Other Equity.................. | 37a | 138.95 | 320.41 | † 467.84 | 563.46 | 614.42 | 644.54 | † 874.90 | 749.06 | † 839.72 | 747.04 | 728.47 | 813.81 |
| Other Items (Net)............................ | 37r | 149.39 | −47.37 | † −140.07 | −75.96 | −30.44 | −52.37 | † −142.35 | −167.55 | † −213.55 | −238.92 | −216.98 | −194.38 |
| Broad Money Liabs., Seasonally Adj. | 35l.b | 627.50 | 919.98 | † 1,167.59 | 1,427.70 | 1,547.23 | 1,812.59 | † 2,054.30 | 2,584.85 | † 3,032.63 | 3,410.67 | 3,598.42 | 4,137.82 |
| **Other Financial Corporations** | | | | | | *Millions of Solomon Islands Dollars: End of Period* | | | | | | | |
| Net Foreign Assets.................... | 41n | −31.02 | −32.89 | −26.70 | 110.17 | 166.82 | 177.58 | 202.37 | 254.26 | † 266.44 | 261.81 | 261.03 | 262.74 |
| Claims on Nonresidents................ | 41 | — | — | 6.25 | 143.79 | 201.89 | 213.49 | 218.61 | 265.45 | † 282.14 | 277.73 | 276.55 | 282.90 |
| Liabilities to Nonresidents.............. | 46c | 31.02 | 32.89 | 32.96 | 33.63 | 35.06 | 35.91 | 16.24 | 11.19 | † 15.70 | 15.93 | 15.52 | 20.16 |
| Claims on Depository Corporations.. | 40 | 165.36 | 152.44 | 228.73 | 226.61 | 250.05 | 369.59 | 429.37 | 537.60 | † 640.06 | 607.49 | 636.28 | 819.15 |
| Net Claims on Central Government.. | 42an | 53.44 | 121.74 | 121.37 | 122.56 | 114.34 | 100.99 | 103.17 | 100.18 | † 80.95 | 75.53 | 71.61 | 33.57 |
| Claims on Central Government...... | 42a | 54.94 | 123.27 | 121.49 | 122.56 | 114.34 | 100.99 | 103.17 | 100.18 | † 80.95 | 75.53 | 71.61 | 33.63 |
| Liabilities to Central Government.... | 46d | 1.50 | 1.53 | .12 | — | — | — | — | — | † — | — | — | .07 |
| Claims on Other Sectors.................. | 42s | 375.43 | 357.32 | 321.85 | 333.36 | 348.79 | 422.72 | 509.82 | 501.69 | † 541.81 | 1,382.99 | 1,505.47 | 1,523.80 |
| Claims on State & Local Govts....... | 42b | 19.43 | 18.07 | — | — | — | — | — | — | † — | — | — | — |
| Claims on Public Nonfin. Corps..... | 42c | 115.32 | 113.45 | 109.88 | 105.28 | 106.45 | 104.24 | 188.80 | 191.53 | † 93.84 | 93.84 | 93.84 | 93.84 |
| Claims on Private Sector............... | 42d | 240.69 | 225.80 | 211.97 | 228.09 | 242.34 | 318.48 | 321.02 | 310.16 | † 447.97 | 1,289.15 | 1,411.62 | 1,429.95 |
| Deposits..................................... | 46b | 15.56 | 4.63 | .29 | .24 | .23 | .22 | .22 | .22 | † .65 | .22 | .22 | .22 |
| Securities Other than Shares........... | 46s | — | — | — | — | — | — | — | — | † — | — | — | — |
| Loans....................................... | 46l | — | .54 | .54 | .54 | .54 | .63 | .62 | .96 | † .78 | 2.84 | 6.65 | 2.66 |
| Financial Derivatives.................... | 46m | — | — | — | — | — | — | — | — | † — | — | — | — |
| Insurance Technical Reserves........... | 46r | 410.13 | 459.18 | 525.01 | 668.84 | 844.25 | 956.50 | 1,074.13 | 1,251.77 | † 1,457.55 | 1,819.51 | 2,151.62 | 2,384.55 |
| Shares and Other Equity.................. | 47a | 65.75 | 64.90 | 104.33 | 142.79 | 50.29 | 234.60 | 275.98 | 316.74 | † 344.17 | 882.40 | 754.87 | 647.39 |
| Other Items (Net)............................ | 47r | 71.77 | 69.36 | 15.07 | −19.71 | −15.31 | −121.07 | −106.22 | −175.96 | † −273.91 | −377.15 | −438.97 | −395.56 |
| Memo Item: | | | | | | | | | | | | | |
| Total Assets................................. | 40ra | 693.77 | 725.16 | 772.36 | 918.60 | 1,008.01 | 1,312.67 | 1,449.05 | 1,671.35 | † 1,930.98 | 2,839.13 | 3,066.56 | 3,198.58 |

# Solomon Islands   813

| | | 2004 | 2005 | 2006 | 2007 | 2008 | 2009 | 2010 | 2011 | 2012 | 2013 | 2014 | 2015 |
|---|---|---|---|---|---|---|---|---|---|---|---|---|---|
| **Financial Corporations** | | *Millions of Solomon Islands Dollars: End of Period* | | | | | | | | | | | |
| Net Foreign Assets | 51n | 557.63 | 745.35 | † 834.46 | 1,080.09 | 1,011.39 | 1,410.51 | † 2,195.89 | 3,120.13 | † 3,691.21 | 4,045.65 | 4,087.97 | 4,391.55 |
|   Claims on Nonresidents | 51 | 671.08 | 793.98 | † 880.19 | 1,130.16 | 1,061.41 | 1,574.38 | † 2,502.97 | 3,466.27 | † 4,072.13 | 4,416.87 | 4,425.41 | 4,753.69 |
|   Liabilities to Nonresidents | 56c | 113.45 | 48.63 | † 45.73 | 50.07 | 50.02 | 163.88 | † 307.07 | 346.14 | † 380.91 | 371.22 | 337.44 | 362.14 |
| Domestic Claims | 52 | 773.98 | 916.94 | † 1,089.23 | 1,411.62 | 1,777.19 | 1,721.22 | † 1,471.44 | 957.75 | † 887.40 | 1,626.03 | 1,895.17 | 2,227.85 |
|   Net Claims on Central Government | 52an | 135.26 | 144.41 | † 108.82 | 68.40 | 152.25 | 74.60 | † −204.77 | −765.42 | † −961.79 | −1,252.69 | −1,354.20 | −1,318.58 |
|     Claims on Central Government | 52a | 386.40 | 461.97 | † 416.88 | 402.94 | 368.79 | 350.42 | † 341.33 | 304.89 | † 228.65 | 198.30 | 184.94 | 53.55 |
|     Liabilities to Central Government | 56d | 251.14 | 317.56 | † 308.06 | 334.54 | 216.54 | 275.82 | † 546.09 | 1,070.31 | † 1,190.44 | 1,450.99 | 1,539.14 | 1,372.13 |
|   Claims on Other Sectors | 52s | 638.72 | 772.54 | † 980.41 | 1,343.22 | 1,624.94 | 1,646.62 | † 1,676.20 | 1,723.16 | † 1,849.19 | 2,878.72 | 3,249.37 | 3,546.43 |
|     Claims on State & Local Govts | 52b | 19.85 | 18.07 | † .03 | .01 | .10 | .05 | † — | — | † .45 | — | .01 | — |
|     Claims on Public Nonfin. Corps | 52c | 115.99 | 113.45 | † 109.88 | 105.28 | 106.45 | 104.24 | † 188.80 | 191.53 | † 129.62 | 126.12 | 134.59 | 128.93 |
|     Claims on Private Sector | 52d | 502.88 | 641.01 | † 870.50 | 1,237.94 | 1,518.40 | 1,542.33 | † 1,487.40 | 1,531.63 | † 1,719.12 | 2,752.60 | 3,114.77 | 3,417.50 |
| Currency Outside Financial Corps | 54a | 115.99 | 141.39 | † 160.65 | 210.74 | 248.98 | 300.69 | † 398.15 | 480.26 | † 530.99 | 530.12 | 573.89 | 654.25 |
| Deposits | 55l | 452.32 | 664.20 | † 833.90 | 1,040.10 | 1,076.52 | 1,111.74 | † 1,302.35 | 1,634.31 | † 1,915.34 | 2,330.19 | 2,440.99 | 2,714.56 |
| Securities Other than Shares | 56a | — | — | † — | — | 1.17 | 1.75 | † 5.47 | .85 | † — | — | — | — |
| Loans | 56l | — | .54 | † .54 | .54 | .54 | .63 | † .62 | .62 | † .62 | .75 | .54 | .54 |
| Financial Derivatives | 56m | — | — | † — | — | — | — | † — | — | † — | — | — | — |
| Insurance Technical Reserves | 56r | 410.13 | 459.18 | † 525.01 | 668.84 | 844.25 | 956.50 | † 1,074.13 | 1,251.77 | † 1,457.55 | 1,819.51 | 2,151.62 | 2,384.55 |
| Shares and Other Equity | 57a | 204.70 | 385.32 | † 572.17 | 706.25 | 664.72 | 879.14 | † 1,150.88 | 1,065.80 | † 1,183.89 | 1,629.44 | 1,483.33 | 1,461.20 |
| Other Items (Net) | 57r | 148.47 | 11.66 | † −168.57 | −134.76 | −47.59 | −118.70 | † −264.26 | −355.73 | † −509.78 | −638.32 | −667.25 | −595.70 |
| **Monetary Aggregates** | | *Millions of Solomon Islands Dollars: End of Period* | | | | | | | | | | | |
| Broad Money | 59m | 645.42 | 943.08 | 1,192.28 | 1,451.00 | 1,567.16 | 1,830.75 | 2,074.62 | 2,609.90 | 3,063.68 | 3,443.15 | 3,634.59 | 4,180.16 |
|   o/w:Currency Issued by Cent.Govt | 59m.a | — | — | — | — | — | — | — | — | — | — | — | — |
|   o/w: Dep.in Nonfin. Corporations | 59m.b | — | — | — | — | — | — | — | — | — | — | — | — |
|   o/w:Secs. Issued by Central Govt | 59m.c | — | — | — | — | — | — | — | — | — | — | — | — |
| Money (National Definitions) | | | | | | | | | | | | | |
|   M1 | 59ma | 368.72 | 588.41 | 775.33 | 974.75 | 995.40 | 1,127.55 | 1,303.81 | 1,872.84 | 2,396.01 | 2,698.46 | 2,653.02 | 3,271.96 |
|   M2 | 59mb | 471.13 | 705.14 | 902.91 | 1,129.97 | 1,149.89 | 1,260.20 | 1,564.75 | 1,983.27 | 2,484.47 | 2,836.33 | 2,799.69 | 3,447.01 |
|   M3 | 59mc | 645.42 | 943.08 | 1,192.28 | 1,451.00 | 1,567.16 | 1,830.75 | 2,074.62 | 2,609.90 | 3,063.68 | 3,443.15 | 3,634.59 | 4,180.16 |
| **Interest Rates** | | *Percent Per Annum* | | | | | | | | | | | |
| Treasury Bill Rate | 60c | 6.00 | 4.53 | † 3.41 | 3.17 | 3.20 | 4.00 | 3.71 | 2.53 | 1.42 | .40 | .23 | .47 |
| Savings Rate | 60k | .86 | .90 | .87 | .86 | .79 | .86 | .29 | .29 | .31 | .32 | .32 | .29 |
| Deposit Rate | 60l | 1.10 | .76 | .69 | .68 | .95 | 4.15 | 3.29 | 2.00 | .86 | .29 | .25 | .31 |
| Lending Rate | 60p | 14.29 | 14.12 | 13.92 | 14.12 | 14.44 | 15.26 | 14.43 | 13.17 | 11.28 | 10.77 | 10.91 | 10.48 |
| Government Bond Yield | 61 | 4.60 | † 2.99 | 3.24 | 3.24 | 3.24 | 3.24 | 3.24 | 3.24 | 3.24 | 3.24 | 3.24 | 3.24 |
| **Prices, Production, Labor** | | *Index Numbers (2010=100): Period Averages* | | | | | | | | | | | |
| Consumer Prices | 64 | 61.3 | 65.8 | † 73.2 | 78.8 | 92.4 | 99.0 | 100.0 | 107.3 | 113.7 | 119.8 | 126.0 | 125.3 |
| Copra Production | 66ag | 86.0 | 103.1 | 83.6 | 85.9 | 153.5 | 86.5 | 100.0 | 139.0 | 104.8 | 54.8 | 75.2 | .... |
| Fish Catch | 66al | 654.3 | 572.8 | 710.7 | 509.0 | 609.4 | 463.4 | 100.0 | 56.4 | 176.3 | 149.3 | 65.6 | .... |
| | | *Number in Thousands: Period Averages* | | | | | | | | | | | |
| Labor Force | 67d | .... | .... | .... | .... | .... | .... | .... | .... | .... | .... | .... | .... |
| Employment | 67e | 52 | 57 | .... | .... | .... | 81 | .... | .... | .... | .... | .... | .... |
| Unemployment | 67c | .... | .... | .... | .... | .... | 4 | .... | .... | .... | .... | .... | .... |
| Unemployment Rate | 67r | .... | .... | .... | .... | .... | 2.0 | .... | .... | .... | .... | .... | .... |
| **Intl. Transactions & Positions** | | *Millions of Solomon Islands Dollars* | | | | | | | | | | | |
| Exports | 70 | 727.70 | 753.13 | 901.79 | 1,211.80 | 1,640.57 | 1,286.72 | 1,753.78 | 3,115.70 | 3,590.64 | 3,553.57 | 3,377.79 | 3,176.07 |
| Imports, c.i.f. | 71 | 908.74 | 1,393.70 | 1,650.14 | 2,190.20 | 2,382.29 | 2,099.66 | 3,212.43 | 3,615.30 | 3,656.46 | 3,922.39 | 3,683.77 | 3,698.81 |

| | | 2004 | 2005 | 2006 | 2007 | 2008 | 2009 | 2010 | 2011 | 2012 | 2013 | 2014 | 2015 |
|---|---|---|---|---|---|---|---|---|---|---|---|---|---|
| **Balance of Payments** | | | | | | | *Millions of US Dollars* | | | | | | |
| A. Current Account* | 109bx | −18.9 | −90.2 | † −42.2 | −80.2 | −79.5 | −59.5 | −143.9 | −18.8 | 26.4 | −38.5 | −50.3 | −17.5 |
| Goods, credit (exports) | 1a9cx | 85.6 | 104.8 | † 114.0 | 164.5 | 209.8 | 164.9 | 224.0 | 419.7 | 499.7 | 447.8 | 455.2 | 419.9 |
| Goods, debit (imports) | 1a9dx | 121.4 | 185.1 | † 195.4 | 261.1 | 278.6 | 239.0 | 360.3 | 423.0 | 434.1 | 464.6 | 460.1 | 425.7 |
| Balance on goods | 1a9bx | −35.8 | −80.3 | † −81.4 | −96.7 | −68.8 | −74.1 | −136.4 | −3.4 | 65.6 | −16.8 | −4.9 | −5.8 |
| Services, credit (exports) | 1b9cx | 30.8 | 41.4 | † 48.6 | 54.2 | 49.6 | 59.3 | 91.9 | 117.5 | 119.1 | 125.7 | 111.8 | 101.2 |
| Services, debit (imports) | 1b9dx | 41.3 | 58.0 | † 68.0 | 96.6 | 114.2 | 105.0 | 187.5 | 187.1 | 203.3 | 248.0 | 223.6 | 177.0 |
| Balance on Goods & Services | 1z9bx | −46.3 | −96.9 | † −100.8 | −139.1 | −133.3 | −119.8 | −232.0 | −72.9 | −18.6 | −139.0 | −116.7 | −81.7 |
| Primary income: credit | 1c9cx | 10.5 | 8.7 | † 12.6 | 14.3 | 20.4 | 13.2 | 19.1 | 28.9 | 33.5 | 31.3 | 45.6 | 51.6 |
| Primary income: debit | 1c9dx | 8.3 | 7.1 | † 26.4 | 47.9 | 76.4 | 69.1 | 63.0 | 102.7 | 90.6 | 27.5 | 59.8 | 69.8 |
| Balance on gds, serv. & prim. inc. | 1y9bx | −44.1 | −95.3 | † −114.7 | −172.7 | −189.3 | −175.7 | −275.9 | −146.7 | −75.8 | −135.2 | −130.8 | −99.9 |
| Secondary income: credit | 1d9ca | 50.0 | 41.1 | † 82.8 | 101.5 | 122.8 | 151.3 | 191.3 | 190.7 | 149.8 | 140.7 | 128.3 | 142.5 |
| Secondary income: debit | 1d9da | 24.9 | 36.0 | † 10.3 | 8.9 | 13.0 | 35.1 | 59.4 | 62.7 | 47.6 | 44.0 | 47.8 | 60.1 |
| B. Capital Account* | 209ba | 1.6 | 27.7 | † 19.5 | 25.6 | 14.5 | 26.8 | 50.3 | 71.2 | 98.2 | 86.7 | 70.6 | 55.2 |
| Capital account: credit | 209ca | 1.6 | 19.7 | † 19.5 | 25.6 | 14.7 | 26.8 | 50.3 | 71.2 | 98.2 | 86.7 | 70.6 | 55.2 |
| Capital account: debit | 209da | — | −8.0 | .... | .... | .2 | .... | .... | .... | .... | .... | .... | .... |
| Balance on current & capital acct. | 129ba | −17.3 | −62.5 | † −22.6 | −54.6 | −65.0 | −32.6 | −93.6 | 52.5 | 124.6 | 48.1 | 20.3 | 37.8 |
| C. Financial Account* | 309na | 19.1 | 9.4 | † −54.1 | −49.8 | −45.3 | −69.4 | −209.3 | −74.9 | 9.8 | −9.5 | 8.7 | −20.3 |
| Direct investment: assets | 3a9aa | −8.7 | −16.5 | † 4.7 | 12.2 | 3.8 | 3.0 | 2.3 | 3.7 | 2.5 | 3.0 | .7 | 4.7 |
| Equity & investment fund shares.. | 3aaaa | −8.7 | −16.5 | † 4.7 | 12.2 | 3.8 | 3.0 | 2.3 | 3.7 | 2.5 | 1.7 | 1.5 | 1.5 |
| Debt instruments | 3abaa | — | — | .... | .... | .... | .... | .... | .... | .... | 1.4 | −.8 | 3.2 |
| Direct investment: liabilities | 3a9la | −2.7 | .5 | † 44.3 | 86.0 | 75.2 | 48.6 | 165.9 | 120.1 | 23.9 | 53.4 | 21.0 | 21.9 |
| Equity & investment fund shares . | 3aala | 1.7 | .3 | † 29.1 | 63.3 | 57.7 | 35.0 | 77.6 | 60.6 | 29.5 | −31.0 | 1.2 | 1.7 |
| Debt instruments | 3abla | −4.4 | .2 | † 15.2 | 22.7 | 17.5 | 13.6 | 88.3 | 59.5 | −5.6 | 84.5 | 19.8 | 20.2 |
| Portfolio investment: assets | 3b9aa | — | — | .... | 7.3 | 1.2 | — | 2.1 | −.1 | 1.2 | −.1 | −.1 | .7 |
| Equity & investment fund shares | 3baaa | — | — | .... | 7.3 | 1.2 | — | 2.1 | −.1 | 1.2 | −.1 | −.1 | .7 |
| Debt securities | 3bbaa | — | — | .... | .... | .... | .... | .... | .... | .... | .... | .... | .... |
| Portfolio investment: liabilities | 3b9la | — | — | .... | .... | .... | .... | .... | .... | .... | .... | .... | .... |
| Equity & investment fund shares . | 3bala | — | — | .... | .... | .... | .... | .... | .... | .... | .... | .... | .... |
| Debt securities | 3bbla | — | — | .... | .... | .... | .... | .... | .... | .... | .... | .... | .... |
| Fin. der.& empl.stk.ops.(ESOs): net. | 3c9na | — | — | .... | .... | .... | .... | .... | .... | .... | .... | .... | .... |
| Fin. der. & ESOs.: assets | 3c9aa | — | — | .... | .... | .... | .... | .... | .... | .... | .... | .... | .... |
| Fin. der. & ESOs.: liabilities | 3c9la | — | — | .... | .... | .... | .... | .... | .... | .... | .... | .... | .... |
| Other investment: assets | 3d9aa | — | 11.7 | † 2.5 | 11.0 | 18.1 | 9.9 | −1.0 | 8.5 | −4.8 | 16.0 | 17.1 | −16.2 |
| Other equity | 3daaa | .... | .... | .... | .... | .... | .... | .... | .... | .... | .... | .... | .... |
| Debt instruments | 3dzaa | — | 11.7 | † 2.5 | 11.0 | 18.1 | 9.9 | −1.0 | 8.5 | −4.8 | 16.0 | 17.1 | −16.2 |
| Other investment: liabilities | 3d9la | −25.1 | −14.6 | † 17.1 | −5.7 | −6.8 | 33.7 | 46.7 | −33.0 | −34.7 | −25.0 | −12.0 | −12.4 |
| Other equity | 3dala | .... | .... | .... | .... | 4.0 | .... | .... | −.5 | −2.2 | −.6 | −1.6 | .... |
| Debt instruments | 3dzla | −25.1 | −14.6 | † 17.1 | −5.7 | −10.8 | 33.7 | 46.7 | −32.5 | −32.5 | −24.4 | −10.4 | −12.4 |
| Curr.+ cap.− finan. acct. balance... | 4y9na | −36.4 | −71.8 | † 31.4 | −4.8 | −19.7 | 36.8 | 115.6 | 127.3 | 114.8 | 57.6 | 11.7 | 58.0 |
| D. Net Errors and Omissions | 409na | −6.5 | 53.4 | † −33.1 | 14.5 | 2.8 | 8.1 | −12.7 | 12.4 | −35.8 | 1.1 | −11.0 | −5.9 |
| E. Reserves and Related Items | 4z9na | −43.0 | −18.4 | † −1.7 | 9.7 | −16.9 | 44.8 | 103.0 | 139.8 | 79.0 | 58.7 | .7 | 52.1 |
| Reserve assets | 3e9aa | −41.4 | −17.5 | † −1.7 | 9.7 | −16.9 | 44.8 | 112.4 | 149.6 | 79.2 | 58.9 | −.4 | 49.4 |
| Credit and loans from the IMF | 3dcla | — | — | † — | — | — | — | 9.5 | 9.8 | .2 | .2 | −1.1 | −2.7 |
| Exceptional financing | 409la | 1.5 | .9 | .... | .... | .... | .... | .... | .... | .... | .... | .... | .... |
| *Excludes components in group E | | | | | | | | | | | | | |
| | | | | | | | | | | | | | |
| **International Investment Position** | | | | | | | *Millions of US Dollars* | | | | | | |
| Assets | 809aa | .... | .... | † 125.4 | 173.8 | 163.2 | 241.7 | 358.5 | 518.2 | 605.7 | 651.5 | 653.7 | 639.5 |
| Direct investment | 8a9aa | .... | .... | † 6.7 | 18.9 | 21.7 | 24.5 | 26.8 | 33.3 | 35.9 | 47.3 | 48.2 | 50.1 |
| Equity & investment fund shares.. | 8aaaa | .... | .... | † 6.7 | 18.9 | 21.7 | 24.5 | 26.8 | 33.3 | 35.9 | 37.3 | 38.8 | 36.8 |
| Debt instruments | 8abaa | .... | .... | .... | .... | .... | .... | .... | .... | .... | 10.0 | 9.4 | 13.3 |
| Portfolio investment | 8b9aa | .... | .... | .... | 10.7 | 12.1 | 12.1 | 14.9 | 14.0 | 16.4 | 16.0 | 15.6 | 14.4 |
| Equity & investment fund shares.. | 8baaa | .... | .... | .... | 10.7 | 12.1 | 12.1 | 14.9 | 14.0 | 16.4 | 16.0 | 15.6 | 14.4 |
| Debt securities | 8bbaa | .... | .... | .... | .... | .... | .... | .... | .... | .... | .... | .... | .... |
| Fin. der.(oth.than reserves) & ESOs | 8c9aa | .... | .... | .... | .... | .... | .... | .... | .... | .... | .... | .... | .... |
| Other investment | 8d9aa | .... | .... | † 14.4 | 23.6 | 39.8 | 59.1 | 51.0 | 58.7 | 53.9 | 60.5 | 76.1 | 55.4 |
| Other equity | 8daaa | .... | .... | .... | .... | .... | .... | .... | .... | .... | .... | .... | .... |
| Debt instruments | 8dzaa | .... | .... | † 14.4 | 23.6 | 39.8 | 59.1 | 51.0 | 58.7 | 53.9 | 60.5 | 76.1 | 55.4 |
| Reserve assets | 8e9aa | .... | .... | † 104.3 | 120.5 | 89.5 | 146.0 | 265.8 | 412.3 | 499.6 | 527.7 | 513.8 | 519.6 |
| Liabilities | 809la | .... | .... | † 381.6 | 463.8 | 513.3 | 597.8 | 826.8 | 981.3 | 906.2 | 940.6 | 947.1 | 661.0 |
| Direct investment | 8a9la | .... | .... | † 186.4 | 271.2 | 332.4 | 378.2 | 551.8 | 732.3 | 689.9 | 759.4 | 781.8 | 522.1 |
| Equity & investment fund shares.. | 8aala | .... | .... | † 147.8 | 210.1 | 257.0 | 289.8 | 367.4 | 467.2 | 382.7 | 359.5 | 317.9 | 411.3 |
| Debt instruments | 8abla | .... | .... | † 38.6 | 61.1 | 75.4 | 88.4 | 184.4 | 265.1 | 307.2 | 399.8 | 464.0 | 110.8 |
| Portfolio investment | 8b9la | .... | .... | .... | .... | .... | .... | .... | .... | .... | .... | .... | .... |
| Equity & investment fund shares.. | 8bala | .... | .... | .... | .... | .... | .... | .... | .... | .... | .... | .... | .... |
| Debt securities | 8bbla | .... | .... | .... | .... | .... | .... | .... | .... | .... | .... | .... | .... |
| Fin. der.(oth.than reserves) & ESOs | 8c9la | .... | .... | .... | .... | .... | .... | .... | .... | .... | .... | .... | .... |
| Other investment | 8d9la | .... | .... | † 195.2 | 192.6 | 181.0 | 219.6 | 275.0 | 249.0 | 216.2 | 181.2 | 165.3 | 138.9 |
| Other equity | 8dala | .... | .... | .... | .... | 4.0 | 4.0 | 4.0 | 4.4 | 2.2 | 1.5 | .... | .... |
| Debt instruments | 8dzla | .... | .... | † 195.2 | 192.6 | 177.0 | 215.6 | 271.0 | 244.6 | 214.0 | 179.7 | 165.3 | 138.9 |
| | | | | | | | *Millions: Midyear Estimates* | | | | | | |
| Population | 99z | .46 | .47 | .48 | .49 | .50 | .51 | .53 | .54 | .55 | .56 | .57 | .58 |

# South Africa   199

| | | 2004 | 2005 | 2006 | 2007 | 2008 | 2009 | 2010 | 2011 | 2012 | 2013 | 2014 | 2015 |
|---|---|---|---|---|---|---|---|---|---|---|---|---|---|
| **Exchange Rates** | | | | | | *Rand per SDR: End of Period* | | | | | | | |
| Principal Rate..................aa=.......... | wa | 8.7434 | 9.0401 | 10.4857 | 10.7615 | 14.3322 | 11.5696 | 10.2129 | 12.5016 | 13.0656 | 16.1544 | 16.7786 | 21.5412 |
| | | | | | | *Rand per US Dollar: End of Period (we) Period Average (wf)* | | | | | | | |
| Principal Rate..................ae=......... | we | 5.6300 | 6.3250 | 6.9700 | 6.8100 | 9.3050 | 7.3800 | 6.6316 | 8.1429 | 8.5012 | 10.4899 | 11.5810 | 15.5450 |
| Principal Rate..................rf=........... | wf | 6.4597 | 6.3593 | 6.7715 | 7.0454 | 8.2612 | 8.4737 | 7.3212 | 7.2611 | 8.2100 | 9.6551 | 10.8527 | 12.7589 |
| | | | | | | *Index Numbers (2010=100): Period Averages* | | | | | | | |
| Principal Rate.............................. | ahx | 113.5 | 115.2 | 108.7 | 103.8 | 89.7 | 87.5 | 100.0 | 101.2 | 89.2 | 75.9 | 67.4 | 57.7 |
| Nominal Effective Exchange Rate..... | nec | 122.6 | 123.0 | 115.6 | 104.2 | 86.5 | 88.2 | 100.0 | 96.3 | 88.3 | 76.2 | 68.4 | 65.7 |
| CPI-Based Real Effect. Ex. Rate........ | rec | 97.6 | 98.9 | 94.9 | 89.3 | 79.4 | 86.6 | 100.0 | 97.9 | 92.6 | 82.8 | 77.6 | 77.2 |
| **Fund Position** | | | | | | *Millions of SDRs: End of Period* | | | | | | | |
| Quota............................................ | 2f.s | 1,868.50 | 1,868.50 | 1,868.50 | 1,868.50 | 1,868.50 | 1,868.50 | 1,868.50 | 1,868.50 | 1,868.50 | 1,868.50 | 1,868.50 | 1,868.50 |
| SDR Holdings................................. | 1b.s | 222.82 | 222.87 | 222.94 | 223.04 | 223.11 | 1,788.16 | 1,788.15 | 1,788.14 | 1,788.14 | 1,788.17 | 1,788.20 | 1,788.20 |
| Reserve Position in the Fund............ | 1c.s | .57 | .69 | .95 | 1.20 | 1.34 | 1.46 | 1.62 | 1.82 | 42.09 | 108.30 | 126.67 | 157.81 |
| Total Fund Cred.&Loans Outstg....... | 2tl | — | — | — | — | — | — | — | — | — | — | — | — |
| SDR Allocations............................. | 1bd | 220.36 | 220.36 | 220.36 | 220.36 | 220.36 | 1,785.42 | 1,785.42 | 1,785.42 | 1,785.42 | 1,785.42 | 1,785.42 | 1,785.42 |
| **International Liquidity** | | | | | | *Millions of US Dollars Unless Otherwise Indicated: End of Period* | | | | | | | |
| Total Reserves minus Gold.............. | 1l.d | 13,141 | 18,579 | 23,057 | 29,589 | 30,584 | 35,237 | 38,175 | 42,595 | 43,995 | 44,864 | 44,267 | 41,620 |
| SDR Holdings............................ | 1b.d | 346 | 319 | 335 | 352 | 344 | 2,803 | 2,754 | 2,745 | 2,748 | 2,754 | 2,591 | 2,478 |
| Reserve Position in the Fund.......... | 1c.d | 1 | 1 | 1 | 2 | 2 | 2 | 2 | 3 | 65 | 167 | 184 | 219 |
| Foreign Exchange........................ | 1d.d | 12,794 | 18,260 | 22,720 | 29,234 | 30,238 | 32,432 | 35,419 | 39,847 | 41,183 | 41,943 | 41,493 | 38,923 |
| Gold (Million Fine Troy Ounces)....... | 1ad | 3.98 | 3.99 | 3.99 | 4.00 | 4.01 | 4.01 | 4.02 | 4.02 | 4.02 | 4.02 | 4.03 | 4.03 |
| Gold (National Valuation)................ | 1and | 1,578 | 2,051 | 2,530 | 3,354 | 3,485 | 4,438 | 5,654 | 6,272 | 6,703 | 4,826 | 4,826 | 4,290 |
| Central Bank: Other Assets.............. | 3..d | 14 | 19 | 14 | 12 | 8 | 10 | 11 | 9 | 8 | 6 | 6 | 4 |
| Central Bank: Other Liabs................ | 4..d | 3,819 | 3,883 | 3,116 | 2,536 | 1,028 | 805 | 600 | 587 | 750 | 712 | 1,080 | 691 |
| Other Depository Corps.: Assets....... | 7a.d | 26,085 | 26,423 | 33,112 | 49,510 | 56,996 | 51,250 | 57,520 | 57,422 | 53,199 | 47,666 | 47,696 | 48,053 |
| Other Depository Corps.: Liabs......... | 7b.d | 11,833 | 12,316 | 16,317 | 35,150 | 48,066 | 42,139 | 46,847 | 40,289 | 41,167 | 32,826 | 41,481 | 40,522 |
| Other Financial Corps.: Assets......... | 7e.d | 29,656 | 32,676 | 34,547 | 33,749 | 27,111 | 36,107 | 43,671 | 46,964 | 52,835 | 59,854 | 62,195 | 56,539 |
| Other Financial Corps.: Liabs............ | 7f.d | 2,005 | 2,491 | 4,593 | 8,643 | 6,188 | 7,670 | 8,231 | 9,043 | 8,916 | 9,177 | 11,869 | 10,033 |
| **Central Bank** | | | | | | *Millions of Rand: End of Period* | | | | | | | |
| Net Foreign Assets............................ | 11n | 59,511 | 104,020 | 154,398 | 204,764 | 304,342 | 266,268 | 267,004 | 371,079 | 401,874 | 485,684 | 528,262 | 667,909 |
| Claims on Nonresidents................. | 11 | 82,941 | 130,595 | 178,425 | 224,414 | 317,068 | 292,866 | 289,216 | 397,056 | 431,560 | 522,010 | 570,722 | 717,287 |
| Liabilities to Nonresidents.............. | 16c | 23,429 | 26,575 | 24,027 | 19,650 | 12,727 | 26,598 | 22,212 | 25,977 | 29,686 | 36,326 | 42,460 | 49,378 |
| Claims on Other Depository Corps.... | 12e | 16,174 | 15,570 | 15,647 | 18,981 | 15,906 | 11,649 | 25,231 | 24,565 | 38,272 | 39,164 | 44,871 | 50,999 |
| Net Claims on Central Government.. | 12an | 21,624 | −17,987 | −51,132 | −83,309 | −158,587 | −106,732 | −109,855 | −204,150 | −246,069 | −318,068 | −352,697 | −483,712 |
| Claims on Central Government...... | 12a | 33,675 | 15,756 | 15,080 | 11,808 | 11,355 | 10,506 | 10,363 | 33,429 | 29,990 | 37,811 | 46,360 | 54,633 |
| Liabilities to Central Government... | 16d | 12,051 | 33,742 | 66,211 | 95,116 | 169,942 | 117,237 | 120,218 | 237,580 | 276,059 | 355,879 | 399,058 | 538,346 |
| Claims on Other Sectors.................. | 12s | 318 | 321 | 334 | 347 | 349 | 363 | 403 | 821 | 1,515 | 1,921 | 1,772 | 1,677 |
| Claims on Other Financial Corps.... | 12g | 14 | 13 | 15 | 14 | 14 | 17 | 26 | 23 | 18 | 18 | 15 | 16 |
| Claims on State & Local Govts....... | 12b | — | — | — | 1 | — | — | — | — | — | 399 | 251 | 62 |
| Claims on Public Nonfin. Corps...... | 12c | 281 | 281 | 281 | 293 | 293 | 299 | 299 | 715 | 1,402 | 1,423 | 1,423 | 1,390 |
| Claims on Private Sector............... | 12d | 23 | 27 | 38 | 40 | 41 | 47 | 78 | 82 | 95 | 82 | 82 | 210 |
| Monetary Base................................. | 14 | 71,179 | 79,554 | 95,948 | 110,029 | 119,560 | 124,292 | 135,853 | 156,551 | 174,103 | 191,139 | 205,184 | 223,630 |
| Currency in Circulation................... | 14a | 48,830 | 54,237 | 63,575 | 68,196 | 72,697 | 77,679 | 82,501 | 101,394 | 112,169 | 119,057 | 131,333 | 137,991 |
| Liabs. to Other Depository Corps.... | 14c | 22,349 | 25,317 | 32,373 | 41,833 | 46,863 | 46,613 | 53,353 | 55,157 | 61,934 | 72,083 | 73,850 | 85,639 |
| Liabilities to Other Sectors............. | 14d | — | — | — | — | — | — | — | — | — | — | — | — |
| Other Liabs. to Other Dep. Corps..... | 14n | 19,803 | 5,327 | 3,619 | 12,064 | 27,039 | 23,722 | 32,017 | 25,910 | 12,005 | 9,414 | 7,627 | 2,317 |
| Dep. & Sec. Excl. f/Monetary Base.... | 14o | 1,569 | 10,764 | 11,539 | 8,403 | 1,796 | 13,402 | 7,750 | 1,871 | 1,600 | 2,256 | 3,052 | 3,487 |
| Deposits Included in Broad Money. | 15 | 1,300 | 2,516 | 1,823 | 1,969 | 1,473 | 2,223 | 2,060 | 1,515 | 1,179 | 1,782 | 2,461 | 2,711 |
| Sec.Ot.th.Shares Incl.in Brd. Money. | 16a | — | — | — | — | — | — | — | — | — | — | — | — |
| Deposits Excl. from Broad Money... | 16b | 269 | 8,247 | 9,716 | 6,435 | 323 | 11,178 | 5,690 | 356 | 421 | 474 | 591 | 776 |
| Sec.Ot.th.Shares Excl.f/Brd.Money.. | 16s | — | — | — | — | — | — | — | — | — | — | — | — |
| Loans............................................. | 16l | — | — | — | — | — | — | — | — | — | — | — | — |
| Financial Derivatives....................... | 16m | — | — | — | — | — | — | — | — | — | — | — | — |
| Shares and Other Equity.................. | 17a | 6,226 | 6,898 | 8,795 | 10,554 | 13,436 | 11,038 | 7,259 | 9,721 | 9,182 | 7,159 | 7,375 | 7,196 |
| Other Items (Net)............................ | 17r | −1,150 | −618 | −654 | −267 | 178 | −905 | −96 | −1,738 | −1,297 | −1,267 | −1,031 | 243 |
| Memo Item: | | | | | | | | | | | | | |
| Total Assets.................................... | 10ra | 134,885 | 163,426 | 210,297 | 256,126 | 346,834 | 318,648 | 326,550 | 466,699 | 507,211 | 606,876 | 670,513 | 830,900 |

|  |  | 2004 | 2005 | 2006 | 2007 | 2008 | 2009 | 2010 | 2011 | 2012 | 2013 | 2014 | 2015 |
|---|---|---|---|---|---|---|---|---|---|---|---|---|---|
| **Other Depository Corporations** |  | *Millions of Rand: End of Period* | | | | | | | | | | | |
| Net Foreign Assets | 21n | 80,241 | 89,295 | 117,062 | 97,814 | 83,100 | 67,241 | 70,777 | 133,745 | 102,230 | 155,710 | 71,976 | 117,474 |
| Claims on Nonresidents | 21 | 146,861 | 167,256 | 230,791 | 337,259 | 530,351 | 378,228 | 381,433 | 448,258 | 451,989 | 500,163 | 552,369 | 749,649 |
| Liabilities to Nonresidents | 26c | 66,620 | 77,961 | 113,729 | 239,445 | 447,251 | 310,986 | 310,656 | 314,513 | 349,758 | 344,454 | 480,393 | 632,175 |
| Claims on Central Bank | 20 | 41,458 | 43,958 | 51,375 | 71,720 | 86,364 | 85,148 | 101,015 | 109,728 | 105,814 | 113,292 | 120,595 | 125,826 |
| Currency | 20a | 9,750 | 10,818 | 13,624 | 14,590 | 15,335 | 15,895 | 17,422 | 25,998 | 31,127 | 32,043 | 37,140 | 36,938 |
| Reserve Deposits and Securities | 20b | 22,268 | 27,094 | 32,472 | 43,391 | 50,535 | 48,852 | 56,228 | 61,620 | 65,606 | 73,934 | 77,164 | 86,425 |
| Other Claims | 20n | 9,440 | 6,047 | 5,279 | 13,739 | 20,494 | 20,401 | 27,364 | 22,110 | 9,081 | 7,315 | 6,291 | 2,463 |
| Net Claims on Central Government | 22an | 37,677 | 27,216 | 12,509 | 33,803 | 107,630 | 161,855 | 161,755 | 187,426 | 221,227 | 202,962 | 244,545 | 284,283 |
| Claims on Central Government | 22a | 99,695 | 93,529 | 99,253 | 106,833 | 169,743 | 215,258 | 243,135 | 299,629 | 326,357 | 329,597 | 385,104 | 414,318 |
| Liabilities to Central Government | 26d | 62,019 | 66,312 | 86,744 | 73,031 | 62,113 | 53,403 | 81,379 | 112,203 | 105,130 | 126,636 | 140,559 | 130,035 |
| Claims on Other Sectors | 22s | 983,282 | 1,173,689 | 1,471,965 | 1,784,710 | 2,050,620 | 2,052,986 | 2,185,816 | 2,307,956 | 2,548,272 | 2,700,014 | 2,940,049 | 3,259,494 |
| Claims on Other Financial Corps | 22g | 56,243 | 77,530 | 99,441 | 108,647 | 197,104 | 136,786 | 195,143 | 209,630 | 262,052 | 268,951 | 322,395 | 428,469 |
| Claims on State & Local Govts | 22b | 1,568 | 4,223 | 3,263 | 4,495 | 11,840 | 13,953 | 22,084 | 22,524 | 20,877 | 21,045 | 21,212 | 19,450 |
| Claims on Public Nonfin. Corps | 22c | 2,512 | 11,633 | 15,013 | 19,952 | 24,918 | 31,608 | 35,315 | 32,247 | 32,260 | 28,631 | 44,580 | 47,968 |
| Claims on Private Sector | 22d | 922,960 | 1,080,303 | 1,354,248 | 1,651,616 | 1,816,758 | 1,870,638 | 1,933,273 | 2,043,555 | 2,233,083 | 2,381,388 | 2,551,862 | 2,763,607 |
| Liabilities to Central Bank | 26g | 14,031 | 12,536 | 13,047 | 12,427 | 11,106 | 7,983 | 16,107 | 22,209 | 24,555 | 25,792 | 39,316 | 50,569 |
| Transf.Dep.Included in Broad Money | 24 | 204,947 | 248,103 | 287,613 | 346,541 | 361,911 | 359,057 | 406,303 | 436,301 | 495,235 | 548,655 | 588,814 | 656,647 |
| Other Dep.Included in Broad Money | 25 | 536,280 | 643,089 | 796,297 | 962,436 | 1,150,864 | 1,154,303 | 1,217,424 | 1,420,874 | 1,475,003 | 1,552,370 | 1,690,421 | 1,853,685 |
| Sec.Ot.th.Shares Incl.in Brd. Money | 26a | 127,948 | 160,681 | 210,483 | 303,768 | 342,591 | 370,544 | 392,113 | 322,641 | 320,980 | 324,044 | 320,973 | 361,181 |
| Deposits Excl. from Broad Money | 26b | — | — | — | — | — | — | — | — | — | — | — | — |
| Sec.Ot.th.Shares Excl.f/Brd.Money | 26s | 3,273 | 2,919 | 4,500 | 2,603 | 57,184 | 68,418 | 75,210 | 90,473 | 170,527 | 173,538 | 188,995 | 215,200 |
| Loans | 26l | 39,690 | 54,926 | 68,305 | 81,010 | 56,352 | 60,346 | 56,930 | 64,017 | 47,085 | 44,784 | 41,440 | 43,841 |
| Financial Derivatives | 26m | — | — | 15,780 | 15,780 | 84,420 | 48,657 | 44,230 | 63,942 | 67,285 | 79,391 | 64,941 | 148,794 |
| Insurance Technical Reserves | 26r | — | — | — | — | — | — | — | — | — | — | — | — |
| Shares and Other Equity | 27a | 125,699 | 134,709 | 166,213 | 203,644 | 178,740 | 202,262 | 226,022 | 253,545 | 292,239 | 312,713 | 332,158 | 364,197 |
| Other Items (Net) | 27r | 90,789 | 77,195 | 90,672 | 59,838 | 84,546 | 95,660 | 85,022 | 64,852 | 84,635 | 110,690 | 110,106 | 92,964 |
| Memo Item: |  |  |  |  |  |  |  |  |  |  |  |  |  |
| Total Assets | 20ra | 1,538,643 | 1,714,681 | 2,108,706 | 2,584,705 | 3,224,829 | 3,032,689 | 3,196,312 | 3,488,131 | 3,746,109 | 3,945,076 | 4,301,716 | 4,957,901 |
| **Depository Corporations** |  | *Millions of Rand: End of Period* | | | | | | | | | | | |
| Net Foreign Assets | 31n | 139,752 | 193,315 | 271,460 | 302,579 | 387,441 | 333,510 | 337,781 | 504,824 | 504,105 | 641,393 | 600,238 | 785,383 |
| Claims on Nonresidents | 31 | 229,802 | 297,851 | 409,216 | 561,673 | 847,419 | 671,094 | 670,649 | 845,314 | 883,549 | 1,022,173 | 1,123,091 | 1,466,937 |
| Liabilities to Nonresidents | 36c | 90,050 | 104,536 | 137,756 | 259,094 | 459,978 | 337,584 | 332,868 | 340,490 | 379,444 | 380,780 | 522,853 | 681,553 |
| Domestic Claims | 32 | 1,042,901 | 1,183,239 | 1,433,617 | 1,735,551 | 2,000,012 | 2,108,473 | 2,238,120 | 2,292,052 | 2,524,945 | 2,586,829 | 2,833,667 | 3,061,742 |
| Net Claims on Central Government | 32an | 59,300 | 9,230 | -38,623 | -49,506 | -50,957 | 55,124 | 51,900 | -16,724 | -24,842 | -115,106 | -108,153 | -199,429 |
| Claims on Central Government | 32a | 133,370 | 109,284 | 114,332 | 118,641 | 181,098 | 225,763 | 253,498 | 333,058 | 356,347 | 367,408 | 431,464 | 468,951 |
| Liabilities to Central Government | 36d | 74,069 | 100,055 | 152,955 | 168,147 | 232,055 | 170,640 | 201,598 | 349,783 | 381,189 | 482,515 | 539,617 | 668,381 |
| Claims on Other Sectors | 32s | 983,601 | 1,174,009 | 1,472,299 | 1,785,058 | 2,050,969 | 2,053,349 | 2,186,219 | 2,308,776 | 2,549,788 | 2,701,935 | 2,941,820 | 3,261,172 |
| Claims on Other Financial Corps | 32g | 56,257 | 77,543 | 99,456 | 108,661 | 197,118 | 136,803 | 195,168 | 209,653 | 262,070 | 268,968 | 322,410 | 428,485 |
| Claims on State & Local Govts | 32b | 1,568 | 4,223 | 3,263 | 4,495 | 11,841 | 13,954 | 22,085 | 22,525 | 20,877 | 21,444 | 21,464 | 19,512 |
| Claims on Public Nonfin. Corps | 32c | 2,792 | 11,913 | 15,294 | 20,245 | 25,211 | 31,907 | 35,615 | 32,961 | 33,663 | 30,054 | 46,003 | 49,358 |
| Claims on Private Sector | 32d | 922,983 | 1,080,330 | 1,354,286 | 1,651,656 | 1,816,799 | 1,870,685 | 1,933,351 | 2,043,637 | 2,233,178 | 2,381,470 | 2,551,944 | 2,763,817 |
| Broad Money Liabilities | 35l | 909,555 | 1,097,809 | 1,346,167 | 1,668,320 | 1,914,200 | 1,947,911 | 2,082,980 | 2,256,727 | 2,373,439 | 2,513,865 | 2,696,862 | 2,975,276 |
| Currency Outside Depository Corps | 34a | 39,080 | 43,419 | 49,951 | 53,606 | 57,362 | 61,784 | 65,079 | 75,396 | 81,042 | 87,014 | 94,193 | 101,053 |
| Transferable Deposits | 34 | 206,247 | 250,620 | 289,436 | 348,510 | 363,384 | 361,281 | 408,363 | 437,816 | 496,413 | 550,437 | 591,275 | 659,359 |
| Other Deposits | 35 | 536,280 | 643,089 | 796,297 | 962,436 | 1,150,864 | 1,154,303 | 1,217,424 | 1,420,874 | 1,475,003 | 1,552,370 | 1,690,421 | 1,853,685 |
| Securities Other than Shares | 36a | 127,948 | 160,681 | 210,483 | 303,768 | 342,591 | 370,544 | 392,113 | 322,641 | 320,980 | 324,044 | 320,973 | 361,181 |
| Deposits Excl. from Broad Money | 36b | 269 | 8,247 | 9,716 | 6,435 | 323 | 11,178 | 5,690 | 356 | 421 | 474 | 591 | 776 |
| Sec.Ot.th.Shares Excl.f/Brd.Money | 36s | 3,273 | 2,919 | 4,500 | 2,603 | 57,184 | 68,418 | 75,210 | 90,473 | 170,527 | 173,538 | 188,995 | 215,200 |
| Loans | 36l | 39,690 | 54,926 | 68,305 | 81,010 | 56,352 | 60,346 | 56,930 | 64,017 | 47,085 | 44,784 | 41,440 | 43,841 |
| Financial Derivatives | 36m | — | — | 15,780 | 15,780 | 84,420 | 48,657 | 44,230 | 63,942 | 67,285 | 79,391 | 64,941 | 148,794 |
| Insurance Technical Reserves | 36r | — | — | — | — | — | — | — | — | — | — | — | — |
| Shares and Other Equity | 37a | 131,925 | 141,607 | 175,008 | 214,199 | 192,176 | 213,301 | 233,281 | 263,265 | 301,421 | 319,872 | 339,533 | 371,393 |
| Other Items (Net) | 37r | 97,941 | 71,047 | 85,661 | 49,784 | 82,798 | 92,171 | 77,579 | 58,096 | 68,872 | 96,297 | 101,543 | 91,846 |
| Broad Money Liabs., Seasonally Adj. | 35l.b | 914,304 | 1,104,210 | 1,352,847 | 1,673,554 | 1,915,337 | 1,945,714 | 2,078,772 | 2,254,248 | 2,375,275 | 2,521,232 | 2,709,056 | 2,990,982 |
| **Other Financial Corporations** |  | *Millions of Rand: End of Period* | | | | | | | | | | | |
| Net Foreign Assets | 41n | 155,673 | 191,071 | 208,779 | 171,018 | 194,685 | 209,867 | 235,009 | 296,019 | 373,145 | 531,757 | 582,825 | 725,532 |
| Claims on Nonresidents | 41 | 166,963 | 206,842 | 240,792 | 229,895 | 252,265 | 266,474 | 289,594 | 366,616 | 448,894 | 628,057 | 720,284 | 882,048 |
| Liabilities to Nonresidents | 46c | 11,290 | 15,771 | 32,014 | 58,878 | 57,581 | 56,607 | 54,585 | 70,597 | 75,749 | 96,301 | 137,459 | 156,517 |
| Claims on Depository Corporations | 40 | 329,272 | 370,954 | 484,966 | 620,923 | 755,302 | 730,381 | 699,226 | 788,689 | 855,364 | 909,689 | 889,666 | 973,617 |
| Net Claims on Central Government | 42an | 387,136 | 402,433 | 408,224 | 396,540 | 402,409 | 453,118 | 520,903 | 532,307 | 656,503 | 763,357 | 885,721 | 905,935 |
| Claims on Central Government | 42a | 417,524 | 441,089 | 457,531 | 456,857 | 475,364 | 534,120 | 617,229 | 645,400 | 795,049 | 927,539 | 1,072,889 | 1,108,348 |
| Liabilities to Central Government | 46d | 30,387 | 38,655 | 49,307 | 60,317 | 72,955 | 81,002 | 96,326 | 113,093 | 138,546 | 164,182 | 187,168 | 202,413 |
| Claims on Other Sectors | 42s | 1,109,310 | 1,412,298 | 1,798,451 | 2,040,737 | 1,773,327 | 2,125,390 | 2,533,007 | 2,571,970 | 2,976,017 | 3,358,502 | 3,652,451 | 3,646,523 |
| Claims on State & Local Govts | 42b | 4,379 | 4,860 | 7,470 | 7,381 | 10,127 | 8,143 | 11,699 | 12,888 | 14,502 | 12,058 | 14,260 | 13,975 |
| Claims on Public Nonfin. Corps | 42c | 153,601 | 222,984 | 257,847 | 307,177 | 255,022 | 328,200 | 360,638 | 381,622 | 428,458 | 445,075 | 437,973 | 409,070 |
| Claims on Private Sector | 42d | 951,329 | 1,184,454 | 1,533,134 | 1,726,179 | 1,508,178 | 1,789,047 | 2,160,670 | 2,177,461 | 2,533,057 | 2,901,368 | 3,200,218 | 3,223,478 |
| Deposits | 46b | 2,809 | 4,520 | 5,117 | 5,960 | 6,704 | 7,568 | 8,536 | 9,509 | 10,255 | 10,918 | 11,877 | 13,351 |
| Securities Other than Shares | 46s | 6,441 | 2,718 | 2,494 | 2,569 | 3,498 | 3,614 | 3,852 | 4,273 | 3,692 | 1,768 | 1,658 | 1,561 |
| Loans | 46l | 49,455 | 61,501 | 98,565 | 97,681 | 112,132 | 123,800 | 143,066 | 158,944 | 204,761 | 225,849 | 268,989 | 312,910 |
| Financial Derivatives | 46m | 9,932 | 6,368 | 14,316 | 9,216 | 11,041 | 2,347 | 2,970 | 4,638 | 8,396 | 10,420 | 10,455 | 14,460 |
| Insurance Technical Reserves | 46r | 1,423,372 | 1,710,452 | 2,069,225 | 2,257,225 | 2,108,754 | 2,223,701 | 2,562,473 | 2,674,415 | 3,161,616 | 3,614,220 | 3,980,497 | 4,048,083 |
| Shares and Other Equity | 47a | 560,874 | 726,324 | 922,451 | 1,024,661 | 1,058,212 | 1,312,060 | 1,490,482 | 1,617,037 | 1,894,767 | 2,265,088 | 2,430,143 | 2,728,469 |
| Other Items (Net) | 47r | -71,489 | -135,127 | -211,749 | -168,092 | -174,619 | -154,334 | -223,234 | -279,831 | -422,458 | -564,957 | -692,957 | -867,226 |
| Memo Item: |  |  |  |  |  |  |  |  |  |  |  |  |  |
| Total Assets | 40ra | 2,272,156 | 2,768,288 | 3,415,389 | 3,867,502 | 3,797,520 | 4,254,613 | 4,815,447 | 5,142,252 | 6,011,534 | 6,921,212 | 7,626,234 | 8,124,721 |

| | | 2004 | 2005 | 2006 | 2007 | 2008 | 2009 | 2010 | 2011 | 2012 | 2013 | 2014 | 2015 |
|---|---|---|---|---|---|---|---|---|---|---|---|---|---|
| **Financial Corporations** | | | | | | *Millions of Rand: End of Period* | | | | | | | |
| Net Foreign Assets..................... | 51n | 295,426 | 384,386 | 480,238 | 473,596 | 582,126 | 543,377 | 572,790 | 800,844 | 877,249 | 1,173,150 | 1,183,063 | 1,510,915 |
| Claims on Nonresidents................ | 51 | 396,765 | 504,693 | 650,008 | 791,568 | 1,099,685 | 937,568 | 960,243 | 1,211,930 | 1,332,443 | 1,650,231 | 1,843,375 | 2,348,985 |
| Liabilities to Nonresidents............. | 56c | 101,340 | 120,306 | 169,770 | 317,972 | 517,559 | 394,191 | 387,453 | 411,087 | 455,193 | 477,081 | 660,312 | 838,070 |
| Domestic Claims............................ | 52 | 2,483,090 | 2,920,428 | 3,540,895 | 4,064,168 | 3,978,629 | 4,550,178 | 5,096,860 | 5,186,676 | 5,895,396 | 6,439,719 | 7,049,429 | 7,185,715 |
| Net Claims on Central Government | 52an | 446,437 | 411,663 | 369,601 | 347,034 | 351,452 | 508,242 | 572,803 | 515,582 | 631,661 | 648,251 | 777,568 | 706,506 |
| Claims on Central Government.... | 52a | 550,893 | 550,373 | 571,864 | 575,499 | 656,462 | 759,883 | 870,727 | 978,458 | 1,151,396 | 1,294,947 | 1,504,353 | 1,577,299 |
| Liabilities to Central Government. | 56d | 104,457 | 138,710 | 202,263 | 228,465 | 305,010 | 251,642 | 297,924 | 462,875 | 519,735 | 646,696 | 726,785 | 870,793 |
| Claims on Other Sectors............... | 52s | 2,036,654 | 2,508,764 | 3,171,294 | 3,717,133 | 3,627,177 | 4,041,936 | 4,524,057 | 4,671,093 | 5,263,735 | 5,791,469 | 6,271,861 | 6,479,210 |
| Claims on State & Local Govts..... | 52b | 5,948 | 9,083 | 10,733 | 11,877 | 21,968 | 22,096 | 33,784 | 35,412 | 35,380 | 33,502 | 35,724 | 33,486 |
| Claims on Public Nonfin. Corps.... | 52c | 156,394 | 234,897 | 273,140 | 327,421 | 280,232 | 360,107 | 396,252 | 414,583 | 462,121 | 475,129 | 483,976 | 458,428 |
| Claims on Private Sector.............. | 52d | 1,874,312 | 2,264,784 | 2,887,420 | 3,377,836 | 3,324,977 | 3,659,733 | 4,094,021 | 4,221,098 | 4,766,234 | 5,282,838 | 5,752,162 | 5,987,295 |
| Currency Outside Financial Corps..... | 54a | 33,401 | 32,731 | 34,030 | 32,393 | 32,434 | 38,829 | 52,572 | 61,257 | 66,113 | 74,872 | 81,117 | 88,957 |
| Deposits...................................... | 55l | 547,499 | 673,635 | 779,041 | 938,117 | 1,068,387 | 1,082,505 | 1,112,875 | 1,248,063 | 1,338,074 | 1,454,088 | 1,598,765 | 1,787,802 |
| Securities Other than Shares........... | 56a | 30,175 | 35,906 | 51,094 | 42,972 | 62,379 | 71,439 | 59,959 | 54,361 | 66,730 | 59,921 | 53,652 | 22,928 |
| Loans......................................... | 56l | 11,528 | 8,036 | 27,469 | 36,234 | 53,767 | 65,088 | 70,224 | 76,317 | 93,955 | 111,944 | 116,941 | 124,136 |
| Financial Derivatives..................... | 56m | | | | | | 49,992 | 30,023 | 11,259 | 19,323 | 18,635 | 40,283 | 31,730 | 101,041 |
| Insurance Technical Reserves.......... | 56r | 1,423,372 | 1,710,452 | 2,069,225 | 2,257,225 | 2,108,754 | 2,223,701 | 2,562,473 | 2,674,415 | 3,161,616 | 3,614,220 | 3,980,497 | 4,048,083 |
| Shares and Other Equity.................. | 57a | 692,799 | 867,932 | 1,097,459 | 1,238,859 | 1,250,388 | 1,525,360 | 1,723,763 | 1,880,303 | 2,196,188 | 2,584,960 | 2,769,677 | 3,099,862 |
| Other Items (Net)........................... | 57r | 39,742 | −23,878 | −37,183 | −8,037 | −65,346 | 56,610 | 76,525 | −26,519 | −168,665 | −327,419 | −399,887 | −576,179 |
| **Monetary Aggregates** | | | | | | *Millions of Rand: End of Period* | | | | | | | |
| Broad Money................................ | 59m | 909,555 | 1,097,809 | 1,346,167 | 1,668,320 | 1,914,200 | 1,947,911 | 2,082,980 | 2,256,727 | 2,373,439 | 2,513,865 | 2,696,862 | 2,975,276 |
| o/w:Currency Issued by Cent.Govt | 59m.a | — | — | — | — | — | — | — | — | — | — | — | — |
| o/w: Dep.in Nonfin. Corporations. | 59m.b | — | — | — | — | — | — | — | — | — | — | — | — |
| o/w:Secs. Issued by Central Govt.. | 59m.c | — | — | — | — | — | — | — | — | — | — | — | — |
| Money (National Definitions) | | | | | | | | | | | | | |
| M0............................................... | 19mc | 71,437 | 79,554 | 95,948 | 110,985 | 119,644 | 126,881 | 135,999 | 158,666 | 176,850 | 193,902 | 209,636 | 225,282 |
| M1A............................................. | 59maa | 244,458 | 291,952 | 337,992 | 400,645 | 419,854 | 421,364 | 472,038 | 512,464 | 577,033 | 636,337 | 683,632 | 758,243 |
| M1............................................... | 59ma | 421,494 | 503,053 | 605,679 | 739,057 | 753,628 | 805,925 | 862,407 | 947,269 | 1,035,142 | 1,132,039 | 1,242,750 | 1,427,839 |
| M2............................................... | 59mb | 818,740 | 963,515 | 1,156,842 | 1,393,528 | 1,561,612 | 1,587,954 | 1,677,211 | 1,798,932 | 1,869,050 | 2,051,308 | 2,228,355 | 2,441,041 |
| M3............................................... | 59mc | 914,150 | 1,101,130 | 1,349,293 | 1,668,320 | 1,914,200 | 1,947,911 | 2,082,980 | 2,256,727 | 2,373,439 | 2,513,865 | 2,696,862 | 2,975,276 |
| M3 Seasonally Adjusted.............. | 59mcc | 910,382 | 1,103,406 | 1,350,994 | 1,682,149 | 1,927,804 | 1,964,664 | 2,090,339 | 2,244,819 | 2,359,181 | 2,498,378 | 2,680,113 | 2,977,693 |
| **Interest Rates** | | | | | | *Percent Per Annum* | | | | | | | |
| Central Bank Policy Rate (EOP)........ | 60 | 7.50 | 7.00 | 9.00 | 11.00 | 11.50 | 7.00 | 5.50 | 5.50 | 5.00 | 5.00 | 5.75 | 6.25 |
| Money Market Rate........................ | 60b | 7.15 | 6.62 | 7.19 | † 9.22 | 11.32 | 8.15 | 6.19 | 5.29 | 5.07 | 4.79 | 5.45 | 5.82 |
| Treasury Bill Rate.......................... | 60c | 7.53 | 6.91 | 7.34 | 9.12 | 10.81 | 7.85 | 6.42 | 5.49 | 5.29 | 5.08 | 5.80 | 6.05 |
| Savings Rate................................. | 60k | 3.32 | 3.26 | 3.63 | 5.37 | † 6.46 | 4.85 | 3.04 | 2.72 | 2.58 | 2.61 | 3.11 | 2.92 |
| Deposit Rate................................. | 60l | 6.55 | 6.04 | 7.14 | 9.15 | † 11.61 | 8.54 | 6.47 | 5.67 | 5.44 | 5.15 | 5.80 | 6.15 |
| Lending Rate................................. | 60p | 11.29 | 10.63 | 11.17 | 13.17 | 15.13 | 11.71 | 9.83 | 9.00 | 8.75 | 8.50 | 9.13 | 9.42 |
| Government Bond Yield.................. | 61 | 9.53 | 8.07 | 7.94 | 7.99 | 9.10 | 8.70 | 8.62 | 8.52 | 7.90 | 7.72 | 8.25 | 8.17 |
| **Prices, Production, Labor** | | | | | | *Index Numbers (2010=100): Period Averages* | | | | | | | |
| Share Prices: All Shares................. | 62 | 78.2 | 103.7 | 146.9 | 195.2 | 181.2 | 98.2 | 100.0 | 109.2 | 120.6 | 141.6 | 164.8 | 168.9 |
| Share Prices: Industrial.................. | 62a | 62.9 | 86.7 | 115.7 | 154.4 | 135.7 | 89.6 | 100.0 | 116.5 | 145.5 | 194.0 | 233.6 | 270.4 |
| Share Prices: Gold Mining.............. | 62b | 170.3 | 156.5 | 240.5 | 225.5 | 183.0 | 128.3 | 100.0 | 110.1 | 97.5 | 56.6 | 50.9 | 42.2 |
| Producer Prices............................. | 63 | 66.6 | 69.0 | 74.3 | 82.4 | † 94.2 | 97.7 | 100.0 | 112.0 | 112.9 | 119.6 | 128.5 | 133.2 |
| Consumer Prices........................... | 64 | 69.3 | 71.6 | 74.9 | 80.3 | † 89.5 | † 95.9 | 100.0 | 105.0 | 110.9 | 117.0 | 124.4 | 130.1 |
| Manufacturing Prod., Seas.Adj........ | 66eyc | 99.1 | 101.9 | 106.7 | 111.2 | † 110.8 | 95.7 | 100.0 | 102.8 | 105.2 | 106.6 | 106.5 | .... |
| Mining Production, Seas Adj........... | 66zxc | 109.8 | 111.2 | 109.8 | 108.8 | 102.6 | 95.8 | † 100.0 | 99.1 | 96.0 | 99.5 | 98.0 | .... |
| Gold Production, Seas Adj......... | 66krc | 179.2 | 156.1 | 143.5 | 134.4 | † 112.7 | 104.7 | 100.0 | 95.5 | 81.7 | 84.4 | 80.2 | .... |
| Mfg. Employment, Seas. Adj........... | 67eyc | 106.6 | 101.3 | 110.9 | 112.7 | 111.0 | 103.5 | 100.0 | 98.6 | 98.3 | † 98.0 | 96.5 | .... |
| Mining Employment, Seas Adj......... | 67zxc | 91.4 | 89.0 | 92.3 | 99.8 | 104.1 | 98.4 | 100.0 | 103.4 | 104.7 | † 101.7 | 98.7 | .... |
| | | | | | | *Number in Thousands: Period Averages* | | | | | | | |
| Labor Force................................... | 67d | 15,989 | 16,766 | 17,341 | 17,338 | † 17,788 | 18,597 | 18,352 | 19,176 | 19,200 | 19,752 | 20,217 | 21,085 |
| Employment.................................. | 67e | 12,044 | 12,769 | 13,419 | 13,468 | † 13,713 | 14,194 | 13,788 | 14,434 | 14,425 | 14,866 | 15,147 | 15,741 |
| Unemployment.............................. | 67c | 3,945 | 3,997 | 3,922 | 3,871 | † 4,075 | 4,403 | 4,564 | 4,742 | 4,775 | 4,886 | 5,070 | 5,344 |
| Unemployment Rate (%)................. | 67r | 24.7 | 23.9 | 22.6 | 22.3 | † 22.9 | 23.7 | 24.9 | 24.7 | 24.9 | 24.7 | 25.1 | 25.4 |
| **Intl. Transactions & Positions** | | | | | | *Millions of Rand* | | | | | | | |
| Exports........................................ | 70 | 296,080 | 328,760 | 396,584 | 490,643 | 692,359 | 523,013 | 596,879 | 703,669 | 717,014 | 807,054 | 990,013 | 1,038,772 |
| Gold Output (Net)....................... | 70kr | 32,830 | 27,023 | 34,470 | 66,740 | 48,519 | 52,773 | 62,371 | 74,835 | 71,048 | 63,887 | 51,297 | 64,479 |
| Imports, c.i.f................................ | 71 | 345,373 | 396,214 | 533,020 | 623,160 | 830,519 | 620,037 | 688,488 | 883,179 | 1,020,819 | 1,031,616 | 1,136,662 | 1,147,311 |
| Imports, f.o.b............................... | 71.v | 304,432 | 349,181 | 461,042 | 561,678 | 777,808 | 541,038 | 585,573 | 724,631 | 832,538 | 977,097 | 1,083,879 | 1,088,005 |
| | | | | | | *2010=100* | | | | | | | |
| Volume of Exports......................... | 72 | 93.8 | 100.0 | .... | .... | .... | .... | .... | .... | .... | .... | .... | .... |
| Volume of Imports......................... | 73 | 90.8 | 100.0 | .... | .... | .... | .... | .... | .... | .... | .... | .... | .... |
| Unit Value of Exports..................... | 74 | 95.3 | 100.0 | .... | .... | .... | .... | .... | .... | .... | .... | .... | .... |
| Unit Value of Imports..................... | 75 | 95.7 | 100.0 | .... | .... | .... | .... | .... | .... | .... | .... | .... | .... |

| | | 2004 | 2005 | 2006 | 2007 | 2008 | 2009 | 2010 | 2011 | 2012 | 2013 | 2014 | 2015 |
|---|---|---|---|---|---|---|---|---|---|---|---|---|---|
| **Balance of Payments** | | | | | | | *Millions of US Dollars* | | | | | | |
| A. Current Account* | 109bx | −6,413.7 | −8,015.4 | −12,075.6 | −16,171.2 | −16,410.9 | −7,906.8 | −5,492.2 | −9,072.7 | −19,678.1 | −21,193.7 | −19,086.5 | −13,647.0 |
| Goods, credit (exports) | 1a9cx | 48,236.9 | 56,261.0 | 66,157.5 | 78,691.6 | 89,030.8 | 70,556.1 | 91,672.3 | 109,507.0 | 100,526.5 | 96,482.5 | 92,478.2 | 81,847.6 |
| Goods, debit (imports) | 1a9dx | 48,518.4 | 56,572.1 | 69,627.0 | 81,262.0 | 90,963.2 | 66,882.0 | 83,362.0 | 102,299.3 | 104,333.0 | 103,625.4 | 98,848.1 | 84,570.0 |
| Balance on goods | 1a9bx | −281.5 | −311.0 | −3,469.5 | −2,570.4 | −1,932.4 | 3,674.1 | 8,310.3 | 7,207.7 | −3,806.5 | −7,142.9 | −6,369.9 | −2,722.4 |
| Services, credit (exports) | 1b9cx | 10,199.1 | 11,828.7 | 13,059.1 | 14,839.6 | 13,998.7 | 13,200.6 | 16,063.0 | 17,346.4 | 17,639.8 | 16,815.2 | 16,837.3 | 15,053.7 |
| Services, debit (imports) | 1b9dx | 10,328.0 | 12,151.0 | 14,144.6 | 16,245.6 | 17,012.6 | 15,397.3 | 19,591.5 | 20,866.3 | 18,914.4 | 18,054.4 | 17,042.1 | 15,531.1 |
| Balance on Goods & Services | 1z9bx | −410.4 | −633.3 | −4,555.0 | −3,976.4 | −4,946.2 | 1,477.4 | 4,781.8 | 3,687.7 | −5,081.1 | −8,382.1 | −6,574.6 | −3,199.8 |
| Primary income: credit | 1c9cx | 3,258.7 | 4,640.3 | 6,078.3 | 6,881.4 | 5,944.1 | 3,988.2 | 4,651.4 | 5,303.9 | 5,937.7 | 6,724.2 | 7,584.0 | 7,900.8 |
| Primary income: debit | 1c9dx | 7,576.5 | 9,569.3 | 11,236.5 | 16,725.1 | 15,075.9 | 10,688.0 | 12,647.3 | 16,092.2 | 16,733.6 | 16,340.5 | 16,919.6 | 15,702.1 |
| Balance on gds, serv. & prim. inc. | 1y9bx | −4,728.2 | −5,562.3 | −9,713.2 | −13,820.2 | −14,078.0 | −5,222.4 | −3,214.2 | −7,100.6 | −15,877.0 | −17,998.4 | −15,910.3 | −11,001.1 |
| Secondary income: credit | 1d9ca | 342.2 | 711.2 | 887.7 | 1,098.6 | 1,376.8 | 1,241.8 | 1,247.2 | 1,540.7 | 1,588.9 | 1,867.7 | 1,872.5 | 1,918.3 |
| Secondary income: debit | 1d9da | 2,027.8 | 3,164.3 | 3,250.1 | 3,449.7 | 3,709.7 | 3,926.2 | 3,525.3 | 3,512.8 | 5,389.9 | 5,063.0 | 5,048.7 | 4,564.3 |
| B. Capital Account* | 209ba | 52.4 | 30.4 | 30.2 | 28.0 | 25.5 | 25.7 | 30.8 | 33.3 | 29.1 | 25.2 | 21.8 | 19.1 |
| Capital account: credit | 209ca | 54.7 | 44.6 | 42.6 | 41.3 | 39.4 | 40.2 | 49.7 | 53.6 | 47.8 | 41.7 | 38.3 | 32.5 |
| Capital account: debit | 209da | 2.3 | 14.1 | 12.4 | 13.4 | 13.9 | 14.5 | 18.9 | 20.3 | 18.6 | 16.4 | 16.6 | 13.4 |
| Balance on current & capital acct. | 129ba | −6,361.3 | −7,985.0 | −12,045.4 | −16,143.3 | −16,385.4 | −7,881.1 | −5,461.5 | −9,039.4 | −19,648.9 | −21,168.4 | −19,064.7 | −13,627.9 |
| C. Financial Account* | 309na | −7,395.2 | −12,612.0 | −16,142.7 | −21,559.9 | −11,995.4 | −18,546.9 | −11,304.3 | −13,760.7 | −21,936.9 | −13,970.0 | −15,412.1 | −10,132.4 |
| Direct investment: assets | 3a9aa | 1,305.4 | 909.4 | 5,928.8 | 2,982.1 | −2,119.6 | 1,311.3 | −161.3 | −153.4 | 2,898.9 | 6,519.9 | 7,692.1 | 5,126.9 |
| Equity & investment fund shares.. | 3aaaa | 1,361.2 | 670.0 | 2,716.0 | 3,334.4 | −1,629.0 | 2,174.1 | 99.8 | 1,985.1 | 4,966.0 | 6,055.3 | 6,202.6 | 4,589.6 |
| Debt instruments | 3abaa | −55.7 | 239.5 | 3,212.8 | −352.3 | −490.6 | −862.8 | −261.1 | −2,138.5 | −2,067.2 | 464.6 | 1,489.4 | 537.4 |
| Direct investment: liabilities | 3a9la | 701.4 | 6,522.1 | 623.3 | 6,586.8 | 9,885.0 | 7,624.5 | 3,693.3 | 4,139.3 | 4,626.0 | 8,232.5 | 5,791.7 | 1,575.2 |
| Equity & investment fund shares . | 3aala | 124.8 | 6,191.5 | −1,556.2 | 1,966.9 | 6,728.5 | 4,956.6 | −4,193.7 | 2,903.4 | 1,671.3 | 2,698.9 | 1,291.7 | −594.8 |
| Debt instruments | 3abla | 576.6 | 330.6 | 2,179.5 | 4,619.9 | 3,156.5 | 2,667.9 | 7,887.0 | 1,235.9 | 2,954.7 | 5,533.6 | 4,500.0 | 2,169.9 |
| Portfolio investment: assets | 3b9aa | 950.3 | 910.7 | 2,231.3 | 3,438.6 | 6,720.1 | 1,745.7 | 4,613.1 | 7,829.0 | 4,184.2 | 1,263.8 | 2,263.0 | 3,887.0 |
| Equity & investment fund shares | 3baaa | 794.8 | 995.6 | 1,626.5 | 1,747.5 | 5,835.4 | 1,288.3 | 3,149.8 | 5,429.4 | 2,677.1 | 1,152.8 | 1,357.3 | 2,357.3 |
| Debt securities | 3bbaa | 155.5 | −84.8 | 604.7 | 1,691.1 | 884.7 | 457.4 | 1,463.4 | 2,399.7 | 1,507.1 | 111.1 | 905.7 | 1,529.7 |
| Portfolio investment: liabilities | 3b9la | 7,309.2 | 5,718.1 | 21,858.7 | 13,681.0 | −7,582.5 | 13,367.7 | 14,386.0 | 12,189.3 | 14,240.0 | 7,231.7 | 6,915.4 | 8,754.3 |
| Equity & investment fund shares . | 3bala | 6,661.1 | 7,230.0 | 14,959.0 | 8,669.9 | −4,707.0 | 9,363.6 | 5,826.0 | −3,768.7 | −679.3 | 1,011.2 | 2,550.6 | 7,335.3 |
| Debt securities | 3bbla | 648.0 | −1,511.9 | 6,899.7 | 5,011.1 | −2,875.5 | 4,004.1 | 8,560.0 | 15,958.1 | 14,919.3 | 6,220.5 | 4,364.9 | 1,419.0 |
| Fin. der.& empl.stk.ops.(ESOs): net. | 3c9na | — | — | — | — | — | — | — | −1,720.3 | −1,821.2 | −800.8 | −1,509.7 | −358.8 |
| Fin. der. & ESOs.: assets | 3c9aa | — | — | — | — | — | — | — | −35,200.2 | −27,865.1 | −20,356.9 | −19,409.0 | −25,397.5 |
| Fin. der. & ESOs.: liabilities | 3c9la | — | — | — | — | — | — | — | −33,479.9 | −26,043.9 | −19,556.1 | −17,899.3 | −25,038.7 |
| Other investment: assets | 3d9aa | 431.7 | 3,621.4 | 6,634.8 | −517.0 | −8,921.5 | −3,101.1 | 3,215.0 | 1,316.2 | −44.3 | −215.4 | 2,373.0 | −3,173.6 |
| Other equity | 3daaa | .... | .... | .... | .... | .... | .... | .... | .... | .... | .... | .... | .... |
| Debt instruments | 3dzaa | 431.7 | 3,621.4 | 6,634.8 | −517.0 | −8,921.5 | −3,101.1 | 3,215.0 | 1,316.2 | −44.3 | −215.4 | 2,373.0 | −3,173.6 |
| Other investment: liabilities | 3d9la | 2,072.2 | 5,813.4 | 8,455.6 | 7,195.8 | 5,372.0 | −2,489.4 | 891.8 | 4,703.6 | 8,288.4 | 5,273.2 | 13,523.4 | 5,284.3 |
| Other equity | 3dala | .... | .... | .... | .... | .... | .... | .... | .... | .... | .... | .... | .... |
| Debt instruments | 3dzla | 2,072.2 | 5,813.4 | 8,455.6 | 7,195.8 | 5,372.0 | −2,489.4 | 891.8 | 4,703.6 | 8,288.4 | 5,273.2 | 13,523.4 | 5,284.3 |
| Curr.+ cap.− finan. acct. balance.. | 4y9na | 1,033.9 | 4,627.0 | 4,097.4 | 5,416.7 | −4,390.0 | 10,665.8 | 5,842.8 | 4,721.3 | 2,287.9 | −7,198.5 | −3,652.6 | −3,495.6 |
| D. Net Errors and Omissions | 409na | 5,290.0 | 1,138.8 | −386.4 | 320.5 | 6,615.5 | −6,494.9 | −2,046.8 | −12.5 | −1,090.1 | 7,697.5 | 5,051.0 | 2,699.8 |
| E. Reserves and Related Items | 4z9na | 6,323.9 | 5,765.8 | 3,711.0 | 5,737.1 | 2,225.5 | 4,170.9 | 3,796.0 | 4,708.8 | 1,197.8 | 499.1 | 1,398.4 | −795.7 |
| Reserve assets | 3e9aa | 6,323.9 | 5,765.8 | 3,711.0 | 5,737.1 | 2,225.5 | 4,170.9 | 3,796.0 | 4,708.8 | 1,197.8 | 499.1 | 1,398.4 | −795.7 |
| Credit and loans from the IMF. | 3dcla | — | — | — | — | — | — | — | — | — | — | — | — |
| Exceptional financing | 409la | — | — | — | — | — | — | — | — | — | — | .... | .... |

*Excludes components in group E

| **International Investment Position** | | | | | | | *Millions of US Dollars* | | | | | | |
|---|---|---|---|---|---|---|---|---|---|---|---|---|---|
| Assets | 809aa | 131,723.1 | 152,741.7 | 180,105.8 | 224,775.4 | 215,226.9 | 267,485.9 | 325,684.4 | 337,341.9 | 375,883.9 | 394,373.8 | 399,916.9 | 402,912.6 |
| Direct investment | 8a9aa | 34,574.2 | 31,037.6 | 41,102.2 | 55,213.7 | 49,438.4 | 70,296.1 | 83,248.5 | 97,050.6 | 111,779.5 | 128,682.0 | 146,023.3 | 162,841.2 |
| Equity & investment fund shares.. | 8aaaa | 31,796.3 | 28,311.9 | 34,557.4 | 48,611.9 | 45,238.3 | 64,589.6 | 76,248.4 | 88,584.0 | 104,183.8 | 121,434.1 | 138,842.1 | 155,976.2 |
| Debt instruments | 8abaa | 2,778.0 | 2,725.7 | 6,544.8 | 6,601.8 | 4,200.1 | 5,706.5 | 7,000.1 | 8,466.5 | 7,595.7 | 7,247.9 | 7,181.3 | 6,865.0 |
| Portfolio investment | 8b9aa | 49,651.2 | 68,244.9 | 75,152.5 | 82,255.1 | 68,589.7 | 101,398.9 | 137,470.3 | 135,522.2 | 159,760.7 | 166,771.8 | 154,864.7 | 143,512.3 |
| Equity & investment fund shares.. | 8baaa | 46,330.9 | 64,315.1 | 70,597.1 | 76,217.3 | 63,107.3 | 95,737.3 | 129,694.6 | 124,089.2 | 146,512.8 | 155,092.0 | 145,802.5 | 134,953.4 |
| Debt securities | 8bbaa | 3,320.2 | 3,929.8 | 4,555.4 | 6,037.7 | 5,482.4 | 5,661.7 | 7,775.6 | 11,433.0 | 13,248.0 | 11,679.8 | 9,062.2 | 8,558.9 |
| Fin. der.(oth.than reserves) & ESOs | 8c9aa | 3,659.5 | 1,793.4 | 2,813.9 | 14,539.5 | 30,533.7 | 22,085.5 | 21,436.3 | 17,756.7 | 15,969.8 | 11,279.6 | 9,984.8 | 14,179.3 |
| Other investment | 8d9aa | 29,120.6 | 31,037.9 | 35,451.9 | 39,826.0 | 32,598.0 | 34,031.6 | 39,702.3 | 38,146.2 | 37,676.9 | 37,952.2 | 39,951.9 | 36,470.8 |
| Other equity | 8daaa | .... | .... | .... | .... | .... | .... | .... | .... | .... | .... | .... | .... |
| Debt instruments | 8dzaa | 29,120.6 | 31,037.9 | 35,451.9 | 39,826.0 | 32,598.0 | 34,031.6 | 39,702.3 | 38,146.2 | 37,676.9 | 37,952.2 | 39,951.9 | 36,470.8 |
| Reserve assets | 8e9aa | 14,717.6 | 20,627.8 | 25,585.3 | 32,941.1 | 34,067.2 | 39,673.9 | 43,826.9 | 48,866.2 | 50,696.9 | 49,688.2 | 49,092.2 | 45,909.0 |
| Liabilities | 809la | 168,841.7 | 207,406.0 | 245,991.2 | 318,788.8 | 232,906.4 | 324,857.1 | 424,512.8 | 380,836.7 | 431,438.9 | 408,963.6 | 426,132.7 | 356,997.4 |
| Direct investment | 8a9la | 80,278.2 | 96,693.3 | 106,929.0 | 131,831.1 | 83,648.8 | 138,750.8 | 179,564.8 | 159,390.1 | 163,510.1 | 152,124.2 | 138,905.0 | 124,946.7 |
| Equity & investment fund shares.. | 8aala | 72,610.7 | 89,013.1 | 97,738.9 | 117,742.6 | 70,187.7 | 119,670.5 | 149,061.9 | 130,960.0 | 134,914.5 | 123,726.3 | 110,373.3 | 101,496.6 |
| Debt instruments | 8abla | 7,667.5 | 7,680.2 | 9,190.1 | 14,088.5 | 13,461.0 | 19,080.4 | 30,502.9 | 28,430.2 | 28,595.7 | 28,397.9 | 28,531.7 | 23,450.0 |
| Portfolio investment | 8b9la | 62,852.9 | 82,837.3 | 102,750.1 | 133,213.2 | 85,668.2 | 126,519.2 | 179,783.3 | 162,989.4 | 203,401.1 | 199,130.1 | 222,366.0 | 168,175.9 |
| Equity & investment fund shares.. | 8bala | 47,448.1 | 67,337.7 | 84,740.6 | 110,112.8 | 63,452.8 | 99,027.0 | 138,097.7 | 111,803.3 | 136,137.7 | 136,279.9 | 158,269.1 | 116,057.1 |
| Debt securities | 8bbla | 15,404.8 | 15,499.6 | 18,009.5 | 23,100.4 | 22,215.5 | 27,492.3 | 41,685.6 | 51,186.1 | 67,263.4 | 62,850.2 | 64,096.8 | 52,118.8 |
| Fin. der.(oth.than reserves) & ESOs | 8c9la | 3,678.3 | 2,040.9 | 3,003.3 | 13,885.5 | 25,914.1 | 20,505.0 | 23,493.1 | 17,813.1 | 15,845.5 | 9,983.4 | 9,949.1 | 12,666.2 |
| Other investment | 8d9la | 22,032.3 | 25,834.5 | 33,308.8 | 39,858.9 | 37,675.3 | 39,082.0 | 41,671.6 | 40,644.2 | 48,682.2 | 47,726.0 | 54,912.7 | 51,208.6 |
| Other equity | 8dala | .... | .... | .... | .... | .... | .... | .... | .... | .... | .... | .... | .... |
| Debt instruments | 8dzla | 22,032.3 | 25,834.5 | 33,308.8 | 39,858.9 | 37,675.3 | 39,082.0 | 41,671.6 | 40,644.2 | 48,682.2 | 47,726.0 | 54,912.7 | 51,208.6 |

# South Africa 199

2016, International Monetary Fund : *International Financial Statistics Yearbook*

|  |  | 2004 | 2005 | 2006 | 2007 | 2008 | 2009 | 2010 | 2011 | 2012 | 2013 | 2014 | 2015 |
|---|---|---|---|---|---|---|---|---|---|---|---|---|---|
| **Government Finance** | | | | | | | | | | | | | |
| **Cash Flow Statement** | | | | | | | | | | | | | |
| **General Government** | | | | | | *Millions of Rand: Fiscal Year Begins April 1* | | | | | | |
| Cash Receipts:Operating Activities... | c1 | 476,424 | 574,993 | 641,781 | 745,928 | 822,299 | 817,530 | 920,364 | 1,022,459 | 1,109,643 | 1,251,854 | 1,388,390 | .... |
| Taxes.............................. | c11 | 383,058 | 450,594 | 525,825 | 608,354 | 661,092 | 642,589 | 725,601 | 803,007 | 877,276 | 975,329 | 1,070,215 | .... |
| Social Contributions...................... | c12 | 8,329 | 9,731 | 10,855 | 12,975 | 14,375 | 15,256 | 15,390 | 15,055 | 16,487 | 23,262 | 25,255 | .... |
| Grants.............................. | c13 | 340 | 244 | 201 | 1,160 | 1,991 | 2,788 | 1,865 | 2,128 | 2,048 | 1,757 | 1,951 | .... |
| Other Receipts........................... | c14 | 84,700 | 114,422 | 104,903 | 123,438 | 144,841 | 156,897 | 177,508 | 202,269 | 213,832 | 251,505 | 290,970 | .... |
| Cash Payments:Operating Activities. | c2 | 474,770 | 538,663 | 583,678 | 648,329 | 754,274 | 859,192 | 945,303 | 1,062,184 | 1,161,020 | 1,270,444 | 1,365,135 | .... |
| Compensation of Employees.......... | c21 | 173,442 | 189,921 | 205,232 | 237,795 | 273,278 | 323,618 | 370,207 | 407,742 | 439,809 | 493,592 | 527,583 | .... |
| Purchases of Goods & Services....... | c22 | 138,781 | 169,824 | 161,714 | 185,245 | 224,153 | 247,948 | 289,255 | 317,971 | 331,154 | 368,638 | 385,733 | .... |
| Interest.............................. | c24 | 50,809 | 53,820 | 54,421 | 56,012 | 58,768 | 62,309 | 72,150 | 82,233 | 94,008 | 110,273 | 124,019 | .... |
| Subsidies.............................. | c25 | 8,553 | 9,557 | 12,143 | 12,808 | 22,371 | 23,861 | 24,567 | 29,695 | 32,342 | 33,649 | 40,315 | .... |
| Grants.............................. | c26 | 13,224 | 13,651 | 24,318 | 24,807 | 29,679 | 26,975 | 17,298 | 21,021 | 40,720 | 41,900 | 49,980 | .... |
| Social Benefits....................... | c27 | 54,291 | 62,688 | 71,190 | 81,313 | 93,269 | 113,706 | 120,668 | 134,878 | 147,998 | 158,858 | 164,967 | .... |
| Other Payments........................... | c28 | 35,670 | 39,200 | 54,659 | 50,347 | 52,756 | 60,775 | 51,158 | 68,642 | 74,989 | 63,534 | 72,538 | .... |
| Net Cash Inflow:Operating Act.[1-2] | ccio | 1,655 | 36,331 | 58,104 | 97,598 | 68,025 | −41,662 | −24,939 | −39,725 | −51,377 | −18,590 | 23,256 | .... |
| Net Cash Outflow:Invest. in NFA...... | c31 | 31,950 | 39,189 | 48,899 | 67,867 | 82,544 | 76,684 | 75,928 | 86,671 | 93,490 | 119,882 | 129,250 | .... |
| Purchases of Nonfinancial Assets... | c31.1 | 32,187 | 39,549 | 49,289 | 68,423 | 83,190 | 77,021 | 76,418 | 87,164 | 94,110 | 120,728 | 130,209 | .... |
| Sales of Nonfinancial Assets.......... | c31.2 | 235 | 360 | 392 | 556 | 646 | 337 | 490 | 493 | 620 | 846 | 959 | .... |
| Cash Surplus/Deficit [1-2-31=1-2M] | ccsd | −30,294 | −2,859 | 9,206 | 29,732 | −14,519 | −118,346 | −100,867 | −126,396 | −144,867 | −138,472 | −105,995 | .... |
| Net Acq. Fin. Assets, excl. Cash...... | c32x | 7,288 | 8,445 | 7,404 | 22,408 | 33,195 | 50,034 | 33,433 | 22,911 | 22,613 | 90,612 | 127,424 | .... |
| Domestic.............................. | c321x | 7,288 | 8,441 | 7,404 | 22,408 | 33,195 | 50,034 | 33,433 | 22,911 | 22,613 | 90,612 | 127,424 | .... |
| Foreign.............................. | c322x | — | 4 | — | — | — | — | — | — | — | — | — | .... |
| Net Incurrence of Liabilities.............. | c33 | 55,076 | 39,534 | 14,963 | 24,353 | 56,831 | 219,785 | 197,714 | 137,447 | 161,544 | 259,085 | 255,553 | .... |
| Domestic.............................. | c331 | 49,241 | 38,565 | 13,019 | 27,856 | 58,091 | 195,433 | 194,532 | 127,735 | 175,534 | 253,352 | 241,718 | .... |
| Foreign.............................. | c332 | 5,835 | 970 | 1,942 | −3,503 | −1,262 | 24,352 | 3,182 | 9,710 | −13,990 | 5,733 | 13,837 | .... |
| Net Cash Inflow, Fin.Act.[-32x+33].. | cnfb | 47,788 | 31,090 | 7,559 | 1,944 | 23,636 | 169,751 | 164,281 | 114,536 | 138,931 | 168,472 | 128,129 | .... |
| Net Change in Stock of Cash........... | cncb | 17,492 | 28,231 | 16,766 | 31,676 | 9,117 | 51,405 | 63,414 | −11,856 | −5,941 | 29,996 | 22,135 | .... |
| Stat. Discrep. [32X-33+NCB-CSD].... | ccsdz | 2 | — | — | — | — | — | — | — | −5 | −5 | — | .... |
| Memo Item:Cash Expenditure[2+31] | c2m | 506,720 | 577,850 | 632,575 | 716,196 | 836,818 | 935,876 | 1,021,231 | 1,148,855 | 1,254,510 | 1,390,325 | 1,494,385 | .... |
| Memo Item: Gross Debt.................. | c63 | .... | .... | .... | .... | .... | .... | .... | .... | .... | .... | .... | |
| **National Accounts** | | | | | | | *Millions of Rand* | | | | | | |
| Househ.Cons.Expend.,incl.NPISHs.... | 96fac | 870,806 | 990,773 | 1,116,315 | 1,264,726 | 1,398,236 | 1,456,089 | 1,575,420 | 1,737,277 | 1,907,247 | 2,057,898 | 2,299,426 | 2,417,293 |
| Government Consumption Expend... | 91fac | 270,300 | 305,733 | 347,928 | 380,214 | 428,852 | 505,469 | 572,188 | 636,446 | 707,031 | 752,781 | 771,641 | 829,070 |
| Gross Fixed Capital Formation......... | 93eac | 225,410 | 263,754 | 324,083 | 406,257 | 524,678 | 531,957 | 521,613 | 559,888 | 604,390 | 654,427 | 769,230 | 826,286 |
| Changes in Inventories.................... | 93iac | 20,989 | 18,367 | 23,912 | 21,974 | −11,958 | −62,069 | −8,561 | 25,067 | 8,161 | 1,092 | 3,578 | 5,760 |
| Exports of Goods and Services........ | 90cac | 372,722 | 430,169 | 530,333 | 634,626 | 809,644 | 657,192 | 727,721 | 854,343 | 891,562 | 1,054,353 | 1,186,640 | 1,233,094 |
| Imports of Goods and Services (-)..... | 98cac | 378,177 | 437,559 | 573,589 | 689,784 | 878,737 | 678,308 | 732,994 | 872,358 | 987,781 | 1,149,542 | 1,257,292 | 1,273,493 |
| Statistical Discrepancy..................... | 99bsc | 13,319 | −164 | −1,560 | −1,847 | 3,424 | −14,361 | 8,882 | 23,598 | 24,585 | 14,360 | 3,578 | .... |
| Gross Domestic Product (GDP)......... | 99bac | 1,395,369 | 1,571,082 | 1,767,422 | 2,016,166 | 2,274,139 | 2,395,969 | 2,664,269 | 2,964,261 | 3,155,195 | 3,385,369 | 3,796,460 | 4,038,010 |
| Net Primary Income from Abroad..... | 98nac | −27,850 | −31,425 | −31,425 | −68,818 | −73,875 | −53,518 | −52,923 | −66,571 | −70,007 | −71,324 | −101,544 | .... |
| Gross National Income (GNI)............ | 99aac | 1,367,519 | 1,509,642 | 1,705,310 | 1,930,773 | 2,181,358 | 2,320,023 | 2,593,072 | 2,883,491 | 3,053,819 | 3,283,379 | 3,694,916 | .... |
| Consumption of Fixed Capital.......... | 99cac | 172,970 | 190,148 | 218,070 | 252,595 | 301,840 | 333,377 | 352,159 | 376,422 | 404,947 | 442,028 | .... | .... |
| GDP Volume 2010 Prices.............. | 99bar | .... | .... | .... | .... | .... | .... | 2,759,622 | 2,828,917 | 2,900,665 | 2,982,851 | 3,034,121 | 3,070,181 |
| GDP Volume (2010=100)............... | 99bvr | 81.4 | 85.6 | 90.4 | 95.5 | 98.9 | 97.2 | † 100.0 | 102.5 | 105.1 | 108.1 | 109.9 | 111.3 |
| GDP Deflator (2010=100)............... | 99bir | 64.4 | 68.9 | 73.3 | 79.3 | 86.3 | 92.5 | 100.0 | 108.5 | 112.7 | 117.6 | 129.6 | 136.2 |
| | | | | | | | *Millions: Midyear Estimates* | | | | | | |
| Population.............................. | 99z | 47.67 | 48.35 | 49.03 | 49.69 | 50.35 | 50.99 | 51.62 | 52.24 | 52.84 | 53.42 | 53.97 | 54.49 |

| | | 2004 | 2005 | 2006 | 2007 | 2008 | 2009 | 2010 | 2011 | 2012 | 2013 | 2014 | 2015 |
|---|---|---|---|---|---|---|---|---|---|---|---|---|---|
| **Exchange Rates** | | | | | | *South Sudanese Pounds per SDR: End of Period* | | | | | | | |
| Official Rate | aa | .... | .... | .... | .... | .... | .... | .... | 4.529 | 4.534 | 4.543 | 4.274 | 23.032 |
| | | | | | *South Sudanese Pounds per US Dollar: End of Period (ae) Period Average (rf)* | | | | | | | | |
| Official Rate | ae | .... | .... | .... | .... | .... | .... | .... | 2.950 | 2.950 | 2.950 | 2.950 | 16.621 |
| Official Rate | rf | .... | .... | .... | .... | .... | .... | .... | 2.989 | 2.950 | 2.950 | 2.950 | 4.089 |
| **Fund Position** | | | | | | *Millions of SDRs: End of Period* | | | | | | | |
| Quota | 2f.s | .... | .... | .... | .... | .... | .... | .... | | 123.00 | 123.00 | 123.00 | 123.00 |
| SDR Holdings | 1b.s | .... | .... | .... | .... | .... | .... | .... | .... | 76.25 | 77.15 | 77.14 | 2.14 |
| Reserve Position in the Fund | 1c.s | .... | .... | .... | .... | .... | .... | .... | .... | 29.52 | 29.52 | 29.52 | — |
| Total Fund Cred.&Loans Outstg | 2tl | .... | .... | .... | .... | .... | .... | .... | .... | — | — | — | — |
| SDR Allocations | 1bd | .... | .... | .... | .... | .... | .... | .... | .... | 105.41 | 105.41 | 105.41 | 105.41 |
| **International Liquidity** | | | | | | *Millions of US Dollars Unless Otherwise Indicated: End of Period* | | | | | | | |
| Total Reserves minus Gold | 1l.d | .... | .... | .... | .... | .... | .... | .... | — | 1,282.09 | 947.81 | 416.81 | 229.88 |
| SDR Holdings | 1b.d | .... | .... | .... | .... | .... | .... | .... | | 117.18 | 118.80 | 111.76 | 2.96 |
| Reserve Position in the Fund | 1c.d | .... | .... | .... | .... | .... | .... | .... | .... | 45.37 | 45.46 | 42.77 | — |
| Foreign Exchange | 1d.d | .... | .... | .... | .... | .... | .... | .... | 1,388.06 | 1,119.53 | 783.54 | 262.28 | 226.92 |
| Gold (Million Fine Troy Ounces) | 1ad | .... | .... | .... | .... | .... | .... | .... | — | — | — | — | — |
| Gold (National Valuation) | 1and | .... | .... | .... | .... | .... | .... | .... | — | — | — | — | — |
| Central Bank: Other Assets | 3..d | .... | .... | .... | .... | .... | .... | .... | 413.03 | — | — | — | — |
| Central Bank: Other Liabs | 4..d | .... | .... | .... | .... | .... | .... | .... | — | — | — | — | — |
| Other Depository Corps.: Assets | 7a.d | .... | .... | .... | .... | .... | .... | .... | 201.05 | 256.24 | 358.72 | 504.32 | 948.04 |
| Other Depository Corps.: Assets | 7b.d | .... | .... | .... | .... | .... | .... | .... | 87.29 | 94.50 | 178.67 | 248.69 | 3,985.56 |
| **Central Bank** | | | | | | *Millions of South Sudanese Pounds: End of Period* | | | | | | | |
| Net Foreign Assets | 11n | .... | .... | .... | .... | .... | .... | .... | 7,185.81 | 3,398.66 | 2,441.89 | 806.34 | 1,662.70 |
| Claims on Nonresidents | 11 | .... | .... | .... | .... | .... | .... | .... | 7,185.81 | 3,398.66 | 2,441.89 | 806.34 | 1,662.70 |
| Liabilities to Nonresidents | 16c | .... | .... | .... | .... | .... | .... | .... | — | — | — | — | — |
| Claims on Other Depository Corps | 12e | .... | .... | .... | .... | .... | .... | .... | — | — | 37.00 | 28.50 | 45.67 |
| Net Claims on Central Government | 12an | .... | .... | .... | .... | .... | .... | .... | −3,444.52 | 580.99 | 2,105.81 | 7,083.60 | 12,290.85 |
| Claims on Central Government | 12a | .... | .... | .... | .... | .... | .... | .... | — | 2,382.86 | 4,459.26 | 8,124.49 | 15,765.57 |
| Liabilities to Central Government | 16d | .... | .... | .... | .... | .... | .... | .... | 3,444.52 | 1,801.87 | 2,353.45 | 1,040.89 | 3,474.72 |
| Claims on Other Sectors | 12s | .... | .... | .... | .... | .... | .... | .... | 6.95 | 7.26 | 42.58 | 40.92 | 40.61 |
| Claims on Other Financial Corps | 12g | .... | .... | .... | .... | .... | .... | .... | — | — | — | — | — |
| Claims on State & Local Govts | 12b | .... | .... | .... | .... | .... | .... | .... | — | — | — | — | — |
| Claims on Public Nonfin. Corps | 12c | .... | .... | .... | .... | .... | .... | .... | — | — | — | — | — |
| Claims on Private Sector | 12d | .... | .... | .... | .... | .... | .... | .... | 6.95 | 7.26 | 42.58 | 40.92 | 40.61 |
| Monetary Base | 14 | .... | .... | .... | .... | .... | .... | .... | 4,749.66 | 5,115.89 | 5,040.38 | 7,491.69 | 19,085.40 |
| Currency in Circulation | 14a | .... | .... | .... | .... | .... | .... | .... | 2,115.39 | 2,184.93 | 2,242.99 | 2,801.50 | 4,771.39 |
| Liabs. to Other Depository Corps | 14c | .... | .... | .... | .... | .... | .... | .... | 1,873.68 | 1,696.04 | 2,248.34 | 4,231.78 | 13,889.59 |
| Liabilities to Other Sectors | 14d | .... | .... | .... | .... | .... | .... | .... | 760.59 | 1,234.92 | 549.05 | 458.41 | 424.42 |
| Other Liabs. to Other Dep. Corps | 14n | .... | .... | .... | .... | .... | .... | .... | — | — | — | — | — |
| Dep. & Sec. Excl. f/Monetary Base | 14o | .... | .... | .... | .... | .... | .... | .... | — | — | — | — | — |
| Deposits Included in Broad Money | 15 | .... | .... | .... | .... | .... | .... | .... | — | — | — | — | — |
| Sec.Ot.th.Shares Incl.in Brd. Money | 16a | .... | .... | .... | .... | .... | .... | .... | — | — | — | — | — |
| Deposits Excl. from Broad Money | 16b | .... | .... | .... | .... | .... | .... | .... | — | — | — | — | — |
| Sec.Ot.th.Shares Excl.f/Brd.Money | 16s | .... | .... | .... | .... | .... | .... | .... | — | — | — | — | — |
| Loans | 16l | .... | .... | .... | .... | .... | .... | .... | — | — | — | — | — |
| Financial Derivatives | 16m | .... | .... | .... | .... | .... | .... | .... | — | — | — | — | — |
| Shares and Other Equity | 17a | .... | .... | .... | .... | .... | .... | .... | −175.61 | 5.17 | 141.40 | 356.52 | −6,010.82 |
| Other Items (Net) | 17r | .... | .... | .... | .... | .... | .... | .... | −825.82 | −1,134.15 | −554.49 | 111.14 | 965.26 |
| Memo Item: | | | | | | | | | | | | | |
| Total Assets | 10ra | .... | .... | .... | .... | .... | .... | .... | 9,064.19 | 6,973.58 | 7,590.90 | 9,124.88 | 16,607.57 |
| **Other Depository Corporations** | | | | | | *Millions of South Sudanese Pounds: End of Period* | | | | | | | |
| Net Foreign Assets | 21n | .... | .... | .... | .... | .... | .... | .... | 335.59 | 477.14 | 531.15 | 754.09 | −8,960.69 |
| Claims on Nonresidents | 21 | .... | .... | .... | .... | .... | .... | .... | 593.11 | 755.91 | 1,058.22 | 1,487.74 | 2,796.72 |
| Liabilities to Nonresidents | 26c | .... | .... | .... | .... | .... | .... | .... | 257.52 | 278.77 | 527.07 | 733.65 | 11,757.41 |
| Claims on Central Bank | 20 | .... | .... | .... | .... | .... | .... | .... | 2,106.19 | 2,114.15 | 2,576.16 | 4,773.11 | 14,639.57 |
| Currency | 20a | .... | .... | .... | .... | .... | .... | .... | 385.87 | 402.73 | 431.22 | 488.25 | 676.95 |
| Reserve Deposits and Securities | 20b | .... | .... | .... | .... | .... | .... | .... | 1,720.32 | 1,711.42 | 2,144.94 | 4,284.86 | 13,962.61 |
| Other Claims | 20n | .... | .... | .... | .... | .... | .... | .... | — | — | — | — | — |
| Net Claims on Central Government | 22an | .... | .... | .... | .... | .... | .... | .... | −85.85 | 952.09 | 992.85 | 1,022.65 | 1,284.94 |
| Claims on Central Government | 22a | .... | .... | .... | .... | .... | .... | .... | — | 1,029.80 | 1,072.55 | 1,101.26 | 1,363.57 |
| Liabilities to Central Government | 26d | .... | .... | .... | .... | .... | .... | .... | 85.85 | 77.71 | 79.70 | 78.61 | 78.63 |
| Claims on Other Sectors | 22s | .... | .... | .... | .... | .... | .... | .... | 250.60 | 423.87 | 613.81 | 704.64 | 955.96 |
| Claims on Other Financial Corps | 22g | .... | .... | .... | .... | .... | .... | .... | — | — | 6.76 | — | — |
| Claims on State & Local Govts | 22b | .... | .... | .... | .... | .... | .... | .... | — | — | .01 | — | — |
| Claims on Public Nonfin. Corps | 22c | .... | .... | .... | .... | .... | .... | .... | 28.88 | 28.76 | 33.30 | — | — |
| Claims on Private Sector | 22d | .... | .... | .... | .... | .... | .... | .... | 221.72 | 395.11 | 573.75 | 704.64 | 955.96 |
| Liabilities to Central Bank | 26g | .... | .... | .... | .... | .... | .... | .... | 41.85 | 25.09 | 25.09 | — | 125.50 |
| Transf.Dep.Included in Broad Money | 24 | .... | .... | .... | .... | .... | .... | .... | 1,950.51 | 2,976.05 | 3,163.35 | 4,092.19 | 9,784.17 |
| Other Dep.Included in Broad Money | 25 | .... | .... | .... | .... | .... | .... | .... | 453.94 | 585.50 | 948.87 | 1,016.74 | 2,762.97 |
| Sec.Ot.th.Shares Incl.in Brd. Money | 26a | .... | .... | .... | .... | .... | .... | .... | — | — | — | — | — |
| Deposits Excl. from Broad Money | 26b | .... | .... | .... | .... | .... | .... | .... | 9.08 | 5.30 | 11.71 | 1,078.58 | 2,004.76 |
| Sec.Ot.th.Shares Excl.f/Brd.Money | 26s | .... | .... | .... | .... | .... | .... | .... | — | — | — | — | — |
| Loans | 26l | .... | .... | .... | .... | .... | .... | .... | — | — | — | — | — |
| Financial Derivatives | 26m | .... | .... | .... | .... | .... | .... | .... | — | — | — | — | — |
| Insurance Technical Reserves | 26r | .... | .... | .... | .... | .... | .... | .... | — | — | — | — | — |
| Shares and Other Equity | 27a | .... | .... | .... | .... | .... | .... | .... | 356.63 | 641.11 | 966.53 | 1,274.65 | 2,858.17 |
| Other Items (Net) | 27r | .... | .... | .... | .... | .... | .... | .... | −205.46 | −265.81 | −401.58 | −207.67 | −9,615.79 |
| Memo Item: | | | | | | | | | | | | | |
| Total Assets | 20ra | .... | .... | .... | .... | .... | .... | .... | 3,448.36 | 4,894.80 | 5,900.65 | 8,599.43 | 30,642.00 |

# South Sudan, Republic of  733

| | | 2004 | 2005 | 2006 | 2007 | 2008 | 2009 | 2010 | 2011 | 2012 | 2013 | 2014 | 2015 |
|---|---|---|---|---|---|---|---|---|---|---|---|---|---|
| **Depository Corporations** | | | | | | *Millions of South Sudanese Pounds: End of Period* | | | | | | | |
| Net Foreign Assets............................ | 31n | .... | .... | .... | .... | .... | .... | .... | 7,521.40 | 3,875.80 | 2,973.04 | 1,560.42 | −7,297.99 |
| Claims on Nonresidents................. | 31 | .... | .... | .... | .... | .... | .... | .... | 7,778.92 | 4,154.58 | 3,500.10 | 2,294.07 | 4,459.42 |
| Liabilities to Nonresidents............. | 36c | .... | .... | .... | .... | .... | .... | .... | 257.52 | 278.77 | 527.07 | 733.65 | 11,757.41 |
| Domestic Claims................................ | 32 | .... | .... | .... | .... | .... | .... | .... | −3,272.83 | 1,964.21 | 3,755.06 | 8,851.81 | 14,572.36 |
| Net Claims on Central Government | 32an | .... | .... | .... | .... | .... | .... | .... | −3,530.37 | 1,533.08 | 3,098.66 | 8,106.25 | 13,575.79 |
| Claims on Central Government..... | 32a | .... | .... | .... | .... | .... | .... | .... | — | 3,412.66 | 5,531.81 | 9,225.75 | 17,129.14 |
| Liabilities to Central Government. | 36d | .... | .... | .... | .... | .... | .... | .... | 3,530.37 | 1,879.58 | 2,433.15 | 1,119.50 | 3,553.35 |
| Claims on Other Sectors................. | 32s | .... | .... | .... | .... | .... | .... | .... | 257.54 | 431.14 | 656.39 | 745.56 | 996.57 |
| Claims on Other Financial Corps.. | 32g | .... | .... | .... | .... | .... | .... | .... | — | — | 6.76 | — | — |
| Claims on State & Local Govts..... | 32b | .... | .... | .... | .... | .... | .... | .... | — | — | .01 | — | — |
| Claims on Public Nonfin. Corps.... | 32c | .... | .... | .... | .... | .... | .... | .... | 28.88 | 28.76 | 33.30 | — | — |
| Claims on Private Sector.............. | 32d | .... | .... | .... | .... | .... | .... | .... | 228.67 | 402.37 | 616.33 | 745.56 | 996.57 |
| Broad Money Liabilities.................... | 35l | .... | .... | .... | .... | .... | .... | .... | 4,894.55 | 6,578.67 | 6,473.05 | 7,880.59 | 17,065.99 |
| Currency Outside Depository Corps | 34a | .... | .... | .... | .... | .... | .... | .... | 1,729.52 | 1,782.20 | 1,811.77 | 2,313.25 | 4,094.44 |
| Transferable Deposits.................... | 34 | .... | .... | .... | .... | .... | .... | .... | 2,711.09 | 4,210.97 | 3,712.41 | 4,550.60 | 10,208.59 |
| Other Deposits.............................. | 35 | .... | .... | .... | .... | .... | .... | .... | 453.94 | 585.50 | 948.87 | 1,016.74 | 2,762.97 |
| Securities Other than Shares.......... | 36a | .... | .... | .... | .... | .... | .... | .... | — | — | — | — | — |
| Deposits Excl. from Broad Money..... | 36b | .... | .... | .... | .... | .... | .... | .... | 9.08 | 5.30 | 11.71 | 1,078.58 | 2,004.76 |
| Sec.Ot.th.Shares Excl.f/Brd.Money..... | 36s | .... | .... | .... | .... | .... | .... | .... | — | — | — | — | — |
| Loans............................................ | 36l | .... | .... | .... | .... | .... | .... | .... | — | — | — | — | — |
| Financial Derivatives........................ | 36m | .... | .... | .... | .... | .... | .... | .... | — | — | — | — | — |
| Insurance Technical Reserves........... | 36r | .... | .... | .... | .... | .... | .... | .... | — | — | — | — | — |
| Shares and Other Equity.................. | 37a | .... | .... | .... | .... | .... | .... | .... | 181.03 | 646.29 | 1,107.93 | 1,631.18 | −3,152.65 |
| Other Items (Net)............................ | 37r | .... | .... | .... | .... | .... | .... | .... | −836.08 | −1,390.24 | −864.59 | −178.11 | −8,643.72 |
| Broad Money Liabs., Seasonally Adj. | 35l.b | .... | .... | .... | .... | .... | .... | .... | 4,428.11 | 5,951.73 | 5,856.17 | 7,129.58 | 15,439.62 |
| **Monetary Aggregates** | | | | | | *Millions of South Sudanese Pounds: End of Period* | | | | | | | |
| Broad Money.................................... | 59m | .... | .... | .... | .... | .... | .... | .... | 4,894.55 | 6,578.67 | 6,473.05 | 7,880.59 | 17,065.99 |
| o/w:Currency Issued by Cent.Govt | 59m.a | .... | .... | .... | .... | .... | .... | .... | — | — | — | — | — |
| o/w: Dep.in Nonfin. Corporations. | 59m.b | .... | .... | .... | .... | .... | .... | .... | — | — | — | — | — |
| o/w:Secs. Issued by Central Govt.. | 59m.c | .... | .... | .... | .... | .... | .... | .... | — | — | — | — | — |
| Money (National Definitions) | | | | | | | | | | | | | |
| Monetary Base........................... | 19ma | .... | .... | .... | .... | .... | .... | .... | 1,729.52 | 1,782.20 | 1,811.77 | 2,313.25 | 4,094.44 |
| M1................................................ | 59ma | .... | .... | .... | .... | .... | .... | .... | 4,749.66 | 5,115.89 | 5,040.38 | 7,491.69 | 19,085.40 |
| M2................................................ | 59mb | .... | .... | .... | .... | .... | .... | .... | 4,894.55 | 6,578.67 | 6,473.05 | 7,880.59 | 17,065.99 |
| **Interest Rates** | | | | | | | *Percent Per Annum* | | | | | | |
| Treasury Bill Rate............................ | 60c | .... | .... | .... | .... | .... | .... | .... | .... | 3.00 | 3.00 | 3.00 | 3.00 |
| Deposit Rate.................................... | 60l | .... | .... | .... | .... | .... | .... | .... | .... | 1.15 | 1.31 | 1.39 | .11 |
| Lending Rate.................................... | 60p | .... | .... | .... | .... | .... | .... | .... | .... | 14.71 | 14.10 | 12.71 | 12.55 |
| **Prices and Production** | | | | | | *Index Numbers (2010=100): Period Averages* | | | | | | | |
| Consumer Prices............................. | 64 | .... | .... | .... | .... | 94.1 | 98.8 | 100.0 | 147.3 | 213.7 | 213.6 | 220.6 | 331.2 |

# South Sudan, Republic of  733

| | | 2004 | 2005 | 2006 | 2007 | 2008 | 2009 | 2010 | 2011 | 2012 | 2013 | 2014 | 2015 |
|---|---|---|---|---|---|---|---|---|---|---|---|---|---|
| **Balance of Payments** | | | | | | *Millions of US Dollars* | | | | | | | |
| A. Current Account* | 109bx | .... | .... | .... | .... | .... | .... | .... | .... | .... | .... | † −935.4 | .... |
| Goods, credit (exports) | 1a9cx | .... | .... | .... | .... | .... | .... | .... | .... | .... | .... | † 3,753.6 | .... |
| Goods, debit (imports) | 1a9dx | .... | .... | .... | .... | .... | .... | .... | .... | .... | .... | † 4,888.8 | .... |
| Balance on goods | 1a9bx | .... | .... | .... | .... | .... | .... | .... | .... | .... | .... | † −1,135.2 | .... |
| Services, credit (exports) | 1b9cx | .... | .... | .... | .... | .... | .... | .... | .... | .... | .... | † 35.8 | .... |
| Services, debit (imports) | 1b9dx | .... | .... | .... | .... | .... | .... | .... | .... | .... | .... | † 502.7 | .... |
| Balance on Goods & Services | 1z9bx | .... | .... | .... | .... | .... | .... | .... | .... | .... | .... | † −1,602.1 | .... |
| Primary income: credit | 1c9cx | .... | .... | .... | .... | .... | .... | .... | .... | .... | .... | † 2.4 | .... |
| Primary income: debit | 1c9dx | .... | .... | .... | .... | .... | .... | .... | .... | .... | .... | † 13.1 | .... |
| Balance on gds, serv. & prim. inc. | 1y9bx | .... | .... | .... | .... | .... | .... | .... | .... | .... | .... | † −1,612.8 | .... |
| Secondary income: credit | 1d9ca | .... | .... | .... | .... | .... | .... | .... | .... | .... | .... | † 897.3 | .... |
| Secondary income: debit | 1d9da | .... | .... | .... | .... | .... | .... | .... | .... | .... | .... | † 219.9 | .... |
| B. Capital Account* | 209ba | .... | .... | .... | .... | .... | .... | .... | .... | .... | .... | † 223.5 | .... |
| Capital account: credit | 209ca | .... | .... | .... | .... | .... | .... | .... | .... | .... | .... | † 227.7 | .... |
| Capital account: debit | 209da | .... | .... | .... | .... | .... | .... | .... | .... | .... | .... | † 4.2 | .... |
| Balance on current & capital acct. | 129ba | .... | .... | .... | .... | .... | .... | .... | .... | .... | .... | † −711.9 | .... |
| C. Financial Account* | 309na | .... | .... | .... | .... | .... | .... | .... | .... | .... | .... | † −135.6 | .... |
| Direct investment: assets | 3a9aa | .... | .... | .... | .... | .... | .... | .... | .... | .... | .... | † −.7 | .... |
| Equity & investment fund shares.. | 3aaaa | .... | .... | .... | .... | .... | .... | .... | .... | .... | .... | † −.7 | .... |
| Debt instruments | 3abaa | .... | .... | .... | .... | .... | .... | .... | .... | .... | .... | .... | .... |
| Direct investment: liabilities | 3a9la | .... | .... | .... | .... | .... | .... | .... | .... | .... | .... | † 1.0 | .... |
| Equity & investment fund shares . | 3aala | .... | .... | .... | .... | .... | .... | .... | .... | .... | .... | † 1.0 | .... |
| Debt instruments | 3abla | .... | .... | .... | .... | .... | .... | .... | .... | .... | .... | .... | .... |
| Portfolio investment: assets | 3b9aa | .... | .... | .... | .... | .... | .... | .... | .... | .... | .... | .... | .... |
| Equity & investment fund shares | 3baaa | .... | .... | .... | .... | .... | .... | .... | .... | .... | .... | .... | .... |
| Debt securities | 3bbaa | .... | .... | .... | .... | .... | .... | .... | .... | .... | .... | .... | .... |
| Portfolio investment: liabilities | 3b9la | .... | .... | .... | .... | .... | .... | .... | .... | .... | .... | .... | .... |
| Equity & investment fund shares . | 3bala | .... | .... | .... | .... | .... | .... | .... | .... | .... | .... | .... | .... |
| Debt securities | 3bbla | .... | .... | .... | .... | .... | .... | .... | .... | .... | .... | .... | .... |
| Fin. der.& empl.stk.ops.(ESOs): net. | 3c9na | .... | .... | .... | .... | .... | .... | .... | .... | .... | .... | .... | .... |
| Fin. der. & ESOs.: assets | 3c9aa | .... | .... | .... | .... | .... | .... | .... | .... | .... | .... | .... | .... |
| Fin. der. & ESOs.: liabilities | 3c9la | .... | .... | .... | .... | .... | .... | .... | .... | .... | .... | .... | .... |
| Other investment: assets | 3d9aa | .... | .... | .... | .... | .... | .... | .... | .... | .... | .... | † −770.6 | .... |
| Other equity | 3daaa | .... | .... | .... | .... | .... | .... | .... | .... | .... | .... | .... | .... |
| Debt instruments | 3dzaa | .... | .... | .... | .... | .... | .... | .... | .... | .... | .... | † −770.6 | .... |
| Other investment: liabilities | 3d9la | .... | .... | .... | .... | .... | .... | .... | .... | .... | .... | † −636.8 | .... |
| Other equity | 3dala | .... | .... | .... | .... | .... | .... | .... | .... | .... | .... | .... | .... |
| Debt instruments | 3dzla | .... | .... | .... | .... | .... | .... | .... | .... | .... | .... | † −636.8 | .... |
| Curr.+ cap.− finan. acct. balance... | 4y9na | .... | .... | .... | .... | .... | .... | .... | .... | .... | .... | † −576.3 | .... |
| D. Net Errors and Omissions | 409na | .... | .... | .... | .... | .... | .... | .... | .... | .... | .... | † 55.0 | .... |
| E. Reserves and Related Items | 4z9na | .... | .... | .... | .... | .... | .... | .... | .... | .... | .... | † −521.3 | .... |
| Reserve assets | 3e9aa | .... | .... | .... | .... | .... | .... | .... | .... | .... | .... | † −521.3 | .... |
| Credit and loans from the IMF | 3dcla | .... | .... | .... | .... | .... | .... | .... | .... | .... | .... | † — | .... |
| Exceptional financing | 409la | .... | .... | .... | .... | .... | .... | .... | .... | .... | .... | .... | .... |

*Excludes components in group E

| | | 2004 | 2005 | 2006 | 2007 | 2008 | 2009 | 2010 | 2011 | 2012 | 2013 | 2014 | 2015 |
|---|---|---|---|---|---|---|---|---|---|---|---|---|---|
| **National Accounts** | | | | | | *Millions of South Sudanese Pounds* | | | | | | | |
| Househ.Cons.Expend.,incl.NPISHs.... | 96f | .... | .... | .... | .... | 11,916 | 13,132 | 15,028 | 20,754 | 30,906 | 31,372 | 32,751 | 49,469 |
| Government Consumption Expend... | 91f | .... | .... | .... | .... | 4,770 | 4,364 | 5,910 | 6,725 | 7,013 | 8,261 | 9,444 | 10,797 |
| Exports of Goods and Services | 90c | .... | .... | .... | .... | 21,472 | 17,040 | 22,270 | 35,208 | 3,096 | 11,458 | 16,502 | 9,837 |
| Gross Fixed Capital Formation | 93e | .... | .... | .... | .... | 4,478 | 3,857 | 3,730 | 5,056 | 3,463 | 4,488 | 4,553 | 5,123 |
| Changes in Inventories | 93i | .... | .... | .... | .... | 43 | −387 | 10 | 7 | 17 | 19 | 77 | 104 |
| Imports of Goods and Services (-) | 98c | .... | .... | .... | .... | 10,159 | 9,754 | 10,698 | 14,467 | 13,835 | 15,200 | 15,945 | 21,487 |
| Gross Domestic Product (GDP) | 99b | .... | .... | .... | .... | 32,521 | 28,252 | 36,251 | 53,284 | 30,659 | 40,397 | 47,381 | 53,844 |
| GDP Volume 2000 Prices | 99b.p | .... | .... | .... | .... | 26,896 | 28,252 | 29,804 | 28,421 | 15,324 | 19,419 | 22,550 | 23,007 |
| GDP Volume (2010=100) | 99bvp | .... | .... | .... | .... | 90.2 | 94.8 | 100.0 | 95.4 | 51.4 | 65.2 | 75.7 | 77.2 |
| GDP Deflator (2010=100) | 99bip | .... | .... | .... | .... | 99.4 | 82.2 | 100.0 | 154.1 | 164.5 | 171.0 | 172.8 | 192.4 |
| | | | | | | *Millions: Midyear Estimates* | | | | | | | |
| **Population** | 99z | 7.784 | 8.100 | 8.446 | 8.815 | 9.209 | 9.623 | 10.056 | 10.510 | 10.981 | 11.454 | 11.911 | 12.340 |

# Spain 184

| | | 2004 | 2005 | 2006 | 2007 | 2008 | 2009 | 2010 | 2011 | 2012 | 2013 | 2014 | 2015 |
|---|---|---|---|---|---|---|---|---|---|---|---|---|---|
| **Exchange Rates** | | | | | | *Euros per SDR: End of Period* | | | | | | | |
| Market Rate............................... | aa | 1.1402 | 1.2116 | 1.1423 | 1.0735 | 1.1068 | 1.0882 | 1.1525 | 1.1865 | 1.1649 | 1.1167 | 1.1933 | 1.2728 |
| | | | | | *Euros per US Dollar: End of Period (ae) Period Average (rf)* | | | | | | | | |
| Market Rate............................... | ae | .7342 | .8477 | .7593 | .6793 | .7185 | .6942 | .7484 | .7729 | .7579 | .7251 | .8237 | .9185 |
| Market Rate............................... | rf | .8054 | .8041 | .7971 | .7306 | .6827 | .7198 | .7550 | .7194 | .7783 | .7532 | .7537 | .9017 |
| | | | | | *Index Numbers (2010=100): Period Averages* | | | | | | | | |
| Nominal Effective Exchange Rate..... | nec | 98.3 | 98.0 | 98.2 | 99.6 | 101.7 | 102.4 | 100.0 | 100.4 | 98.0 | 99.9 | 99.9 | 96.2 |
| CPI-Based Real Effect. Ex. Rate....... | rec | 95.5 | 96.5 | 97.9 | 99.6 | 102.3 | 102.5 | 100.0 | 100.6 | 98.4 | 100.1 | 98.8 | 94.1 |
| ULC-Based Real Effect. Ex. Rate....... | rel | 89.5 | 92.7 | 95.5 | 101.0 | 106.2 | 104.9 | 100.0 | 96.6 | 90.8 | 89.0 | 86.3 | 81.9 |
| **Fund Position** | | | | | | *Millions of SDRs: End of Period* | | | | | | | |
| Quota...................................... | 2f.s | 3,048.90 | 3,048.90 | 3,048.90 | 3,048.90 | 3,048.90 | 3,048.90 | 3,048.90 | 4,023.40 | 4,023.40 | 4,023.40 | 4,023.40 | 4,023.40 |
| SDR Holdings............................. | 1b.s | 213.96 | 232.11 | 222.69 | 233.46 | 144.92 | 2,959.03 | 2,933.13 | 2,664.23 | 2,686.57 | 2,791.42 | 2,710.75 | 2,755.17 |
| Reserve Position in the Fund........... | 1c.s | 1,014.29 | 525.99 | 265.20 | 202.05 | 422.32 | 497.24 | 859.36 | 1,896.15 | 2,068.77 | 1,924.04 | 1,583.49 | 1,119.71 |
| Total Fund Cred.&Loans Outstg........ | 2tl | — | — | — | — | — | — | — | — | — | — | — | — |
| SDR Allocations.......................... | 1bd | 298.81 | 298.81 | 298.81 | 298.81 | 298.81 | 2,827.56 | 2,827.56 | 2,827.56 | 2,827.56 | 2,827.56 | 2,827.56 | 2,827.56 |
| **International Liquidity** | | | | | *Millions of US Dollars Unless Otherwise Indicated: End of Period* | | | | | | | | |
| Total Res.Min.Gold (Eurosys.Def)..... | 1l.d | 12,389 | 9,678 | 10,822 | 11,480 | 12,414 | 18,205 | 19,146 | 32,843 | 35,523 | 35,430 | 39,494 | 44,378 |
| SDR Holdings.............................. | 1b.d | 332 | 332 | 335 | 369 | 223 | 4,639 | 4,517 | 4,090 | 4,129 | 4,299 | 3,927 | 3,818 |
| Reserve Position in the Fund......... | 1c.d | 1,575 | 752 | 399 | 319 | 650 | 780 | 1,323 | 2,911 | 3,180 | 2,963 | 2,294 | 1,552 |
| Foreign Exchange......................... | 1d.d | 10,481 | 8,594 | 10,088 | 10,792 | 11,540 | 12,787 | 13,306 | 25,842 | 28,214 | 28,168 | 32,891 | 38,711 |
| o/w:Fin.Deriv.Rel.to Reserves....... | 1ddd | 20.43 | −24.77 | 167.26 | 67.72 | — | — | — | — | 46.18 | 16.55 | 18.21 | −4.35 |
| Other Reserve Assets.................. | 1e.d | | | | | — | — | — | — | — | — | 381 | 297 |
| Gold (Million Fine Troy Ounces)...... | 1ad | 16.83 | 14.72 | 13.40 | 9.05 | 9.05 | 9.05 | 9.05 | 9.05 | 9.05 | 9.05 | 9.05 | 9.05 |
| Gold (Eurosystem Valuation)............ | 1and | 7,370 | 7,550 | 8,518 | 7,574 | 7,832 | 9,996 | 12,768 | 14,256 | 15,066 | 10,878 | 10,857 | 9,592 |
| Memo:Euro Cl. on Non-EA Res......... | 1dgd | .... | .... | .... | .... | .... | .... | .... | .... | .... | .... | .... | .... |
| Non-Euro Cl. on EA Res.............. | 1dhd | 601 | 2,750 | 1,617 | 3,813 | 14,191 | 114 | −40 | 5,349 | 3,570 | 3,124 | 3,457 | 4,177 |
| Central Bank: Other Assets.............. | 3..d | 72,108 | 66,550 | 105,889 | 100,237 | 94,734 | 90,883 | 75,213 | 78,597 | 62,823 | 52,522 | 43,184 | 56,257 |
| Central Bank: Other Liabs.............. | 4..d | 505 | 460 | 617 | 705 | 700 | 4,813 | 4,889 | 4,833 | 4,533 | 4,554 | 4,727 | 4,009 |
| Other Depository Corps.: Assets....... | 7a.d | 153,239 | 167,654 | 226,887 | 293,578 | 276,017 | 299,486 | 286,034 | 291,120 | 309,791 | 254,135 | 221,504 | 209,307 |
| Other Depository Corps.: Liabs......... | 7b.d | 244,358 | 241,180 | 258,586 | 314,929 | 377,540 | 380,631 | 380,288 | 322,287 | 238,420 | 191,302 | 140,582 | 122,300 |
| **Central Bank** | | | | | | *Millions of Euros: End of Period* | | | | | | | |
| *Euro Area Wide Residency Criterion* | | | | | | | | | | | | | |
| Net Foreign Assets.......................... | 11n.u | 15,208 | 15,878 | 18,389 | 16,925 | 16,146 | 16,584 | 20,456 | 32,776 | 35,045 | 30,296 | 37,489 | 67,028 |
| Claims on Nonresidents................. | 11..u | 15,594 | 16,394 | 19,011 | 17,521 | 16,721 | 19,926 | 24,116 | 36,513 | 38,480 | 33,600 | 41,384 | 70,711 |
| Liabilities to Nonresidents............. | 16c.u | 387 | 516 | 622 | 596 | 575 | 3,342 | 3,660 | 3,737 | 3,436 | 3,303 | 3,895 | 3,683 |
| Claims on Other Depository Corps.... | 12e.u | 24,286 | 37,207 | 32,460 | 83,397 | 107,560 | 101,483 | 77,932 | 192,728 | 383,962 | 215,828 | 165,136 | 160,801 |
| Net Claims on Central Government.. | 12anu | 31,955 | 47,039 | 48,618 | 61,624 | 67,565 | 61,094 | 68,362 | 83,434 | 68,451 | 65,550 | 65,406 | 108,693 |
| Claims on Central Govt................. | 12a.u | 35,433 | 50,796 | 53,006 | 65,818 | 74,646 | 75,516 | 71,995 | 85,531 | 74,758 | 65,961 | 65,421 | 108,793 |
| Liabs. to Central Govt................. | 16d.u | 3,478 | 3,757 | 4,388 | 4,194 | 7,081 | 14,422 | 3,633 | 2,097 | 6,307 | 411 | 15 | 100 |
| Claims on Other Sectors................ | 12s.u | 1,206 | 1,121 | 1,023 | 733 | 931 | 3,933 | 4,547 | 5,223 | 6,080 | 6,971 | 8,734 | 13,982 |
| Claims on Other Financial Corps.... | 12g.u | 52 | 44 | 23 | 733 | 931 | 3,933 | 4,360 | 5,037 | 5,891 | 6,794 | 8,555 | 13,806 |
| Claims on State & Local Govts....... | 12b.u | 1,154 | 1,077 | 1,000 | — | — | — | — | — | — | — | — | — |
| Claims on Public Nonfin. Corps...... | 12c.u | — | — | — | — | — | — | — | — | — | — | — | — |
| Claims on Private Sector............... | 12d.u | — | — | — | — | — | — | 187 | 186 | 189 | 177 | 179 | 176 |
| Monetary Base............................. | 14..u | 78,224 | 87,762 | 99,604 | 139,404 | 147,219 | 145,134 | 128,323 | 155,118 | 180,084 | 142,613 | 140,271 | 157,662 |
| Currency in Circulation................. | 14a.u | 52,701 | 59,356 | 65,929 | 70,920 | 79,438 | 91,741 | 95,502 | 100,710 | 103,323 | 108,074 | 122,000 | 129,246 |
| Liabs. to Other Depository Corps... | 14c.u | 13,091 | 16,531 | 20,559 | 52,321 | 54,315 | 35,089 | 26,964 | 50,934 | 72,115 | 30,784 | 18,186 | 28,329 |
| Liabs. to Other Sectors................. | 14d.u | 12,432 | 11,875 | 13,116 | 16,163 | 13,466 | 18,304 | 5,857 | 3,474 | 4,646 | 3,755 | 85 | 87 |
| Other Liabs. to Other Dep. Corps..... | 14n.u | — | — | — | — | — | — | — | — | — | — | — | — |
| Dep. & Sec. Excl. f/Monetary Base.... | 14o.u | — | — | — | — | — | — | — | — | — | — | — | — |
| Deposits Included in Broad Money. | 15..u | — | — | — | — | — | — | — | — | — | — | — | — |
| Sec.Ot.th.Shares Inc.in.Brd.Money.. | 16a.u | — | — | — | — | — | — | — | — | — | — | — | — |
| Deposits Excl. from Broad Money... | 16b.u | — | — | — | — | — | — | — | — | — | — | — | — |
| Sec.Oh.th.Shares Excl. f/Brd.Money | 16s.u | — | — | — | — | — | — | — | — | — | — | — | — |
| Loans...................................... | 16l.u | — | — | — | — | — | — | — | — | — | — | — | — |
| Financial Derivatives...................... | 16m.u | — | — | — | — | — | — | — | — | — | — | — | — |
| Shares and Other Equity.................. | 17a.u | 7,082 | 10,524 | 10,680 | 11,384 | 13,780 | 15,319 | 17,925 | 21,440 | 24,438 | 21,714 | 27,708 | 32,141 |
| Other Items (Net)........................... | 17r.u | −12,652 | 2,958 | −9,795 | 11,891 | 31,201 | 22,644 | 25,050 | 137,604 | 289,014 | 154,320 | 108,787 | 160,702 |
| *Memorandum Items* | | | | | | | | | | | | | |
| *National Residency Criterion* | | | | | | | | | | | | | |
| Net Foreign Assets.......................... | 11n | 67,059 | 70,500 | 94,464 | 77,164 | 47,054 | 38,185 | 25,591 | −81,572 | −254,823 | −145,326 | −116,719 | −156,551 |
| Claims on Nonresidents................. | 11 | 67,445 | 71,016 | 95,086 | 81,035 | 82,618 | 82,662 | 80,173 | 97,144 | 85,956 | 71,663 | 77,041 | 101,247 |
| Liabilities to Nonresidents............. | 16c | 387 | 516 | 622 | 3,871 | 35,564 | 44,477 | 54,582 | 178,716 | 340,780 | 216,988 | 193,760 | 257,798 |
| Claims on Other Depository Corps.... | 12e | 23,445 | 33,286 | 23,823 | 75,065 | 103,735 | 99,252 | 76,132 | 190,784 | 382,107 | 214,354 | 163,591 | 159,318 |
| Net Claims on Central Government.. | 12an | 12,854 | 13,391 | 10,561 | 10,791 | 9,842 | 5,373 | 18,889 | 29,531 | 27,614 | 33,744 | 36,417 | 84,763 |
| Claims on Central Government...... | 12a | 16,332 | 17,148 | 14,949 | 14,985 | 16,923 | 19,795 | 22,522 | 31,628 | 33,921 | 34,155 | 36,432 | 84,863 |
| Liabilities to Central Government... | 16d | 3,478 | 3,757 | 4,388 | 4,194 | 7,081 | 14,422 | 3,633 | 2,097 | 6,307 | 411 | 15 | 100 |
| Claims on Other Sectors................ | 12s | 1,206 | 1,121 | 1,023 | 733 | 931 | 3,933 | 4,547 | 5,223 | 6,080 | 6,971 | 8,734 | 13,982 |
| Claims on Other Fin. Corps............ | 12g | 52 | 44 | 23 | 733 | 931 | 3,933 | 4,360 | 5,037 | 5,891 | 6,794 | 8,555 | 13,806 |
| Claims on State & Local Govts....... | 12b | 1,154 | 1,077 | 1,000 | — | — | — | — | — | — | — | — | — |
| Claims on Private Sector............... | 12d | — | — | — | — | — | — | 187 | 186 | 189 | 177 | 179 | 176 |
| Liabs.to ODCs, Inc.in Mon.Base....... | 14c | 13,091 | 16,531 | 20,559 | 52,321 | 54,315 | 35,089 | 26,964 | 50,934 | 72,115 | 30,784 | 18,186 | 28,329 |
| Liabs.to Ot.Sectors, Inc.in Mon.Base | 14d | 12,432 | 11,875 | 13,116 | 16,163 | 13,466 | 18,304 | 5,857 | 3,474 | 4,646 | 3,755 | 85 | 87 |
| Liabs.to ODCs,Excl.f/Mon.Base........ | 14n | — | — | — | — | — | — | — | — | — | — | — | — |
| Net Claims on Eurosystem.............. | 12e.s | 32,342 | 17,486 | 29,814 | 1,512 | −30,202 | −35,688 | −45,336 | −169,255 | −331,481 | −207,824 | −183,429 | −247,679 |

# Spain 184

| | | 2004 | 2005 | 2006 | 2007 | 2008 | 2009 | 2010 | 2011 | 2012 | 2013 | 2014 | 2015 |
|---|---|---|---|---|---|---|---|---|---|---|---|---|---|
| **Other Depository Corporations** | | | | | | Millions of Euros: End of Period | | | | | | | |
| Euro Area Wide Residency Criterion | | | | | | | | | | | | | |
| Net Foreign Assets | 21n.u | −66,896 | −62,326 | −24,069 | −14,504 | −72,949 | −56,327 | −70,539 | −24,088 | 54,094 | 45,561 | 66,652 | 79,918 |
| Claims on Nonresidents | 21..u | 112,502 | 142,116 | 172,276 | 199,428 | 198,331 | 207,890 | 214,065 | 224,994 | 234,797 | 184,276 | 182,443 | 192,254 |
| Liabilities to Nonresidents | 26c.u | 179,398 | 204,442 | 196,345 | 213,932 | 271,280 | 264,217 | 284,604 | 249,082 | 180,703 | 138,715 | 115,791 | 112,336 |
| Claims on Eurosystem | 20..u | 20,544 | 24,020 | 28,747 | 60,702 | 63,161 | 43,444 | 34,670 | 58,238 | 79,372 | 37,882 | 25,255 | 35,829 |
| Currency | 20a.u | 7,453 | 7,489 | 8,188 | 8,381 | 8,846 | 8,355 | 7,706 | 7,304 | 7,257 | 7,098 | 7,413 | 7,769 |
| Reserve Deposits and Securities | 20b.u | 13,091 | 16,531 | 20,559 | 52,321 | 54,315 | 35,089 | 26,964 | 50,934 | 72,115 | 30,784 | 17,842 | 28,060 |
| Other Claims | 20n.u | — | — | — | — | — | — | — | — | — | — | — | — |
| Net Claims on Central Government | 22anu | 104,950 | 124,426 | 61,519 | 64,874 | 77,726 | 129,207 | 116,228 | 147,821 | 223,354 | 228,153 | 263,761 | 233,185 |
| Claims on Central Government | 22a.u | 122,310 | 145,601 | 84,559 | 91,606 | 113,398 | 173,339 | 161,689 | 193,762 | 270,216 | 262,764 | 310,344 | 276,044 |
| Liabilities to Central Government | 26d.u | 17,360 | 21,175 | 23,040 | 26,732 | 35,672 | 44,132 | 45,461 | 45,941 | 46,862 | 34,611 | 46,583 | 42,859 |
| Claims on Other Sectors | 22s.u | 1,121,738 | 1,404,981 | 1,790,671 | 2,169,175 | 2,491,078 | 2,484,952 | 2,536,508 | 2,556,288 | 2,398,756 | 2,124,593 | 1,978,530 | 1,859,208 |
| Claims on Other Financial Corps | 22g.u | 65,654 | 78,807 | 145,547 | 285,097 | 503,084 | 521,251 | 572,169 | 638,796 | 636,026 | 500,650 | 493,671 | 445,913 |
| Claims on State & Local Govts | 22b.u | 39,519 | 43,819 | 42,583 | 45,680 | 56,375 | 69,109 | 87,160 | 100,780 | 100,913 | 98,441 | 103,158 | 92,802 |
| Claims on Public Nonfin. Corps | 22c.u | — | — | — | — | — | — | — | — | — | — | — | — |
| Claims on Private Sector | 22d.u | 1,016,565 | 1,282,355 | 1,602,541 | 1,838,398 | 1,931,619 | 1,894,592 | 1,877,179 | 1,816,712 | 1,661,817 | 1,525,502 | 1,381,701 | 1,320,493 |
| Liabilities to Eurosystem | 26g.u | 23,445 | 34,905 | 31,076 | 82,515 | 107,119 | 100,819 | 77,128 | 191,786 | 382,882 | 214,746 | 163,820 | 159,486 |
| Transf.Dep.Included in Broad Money | 24..u | 214,716 | 433,701 | 493,647 | 485,294 | 464,300 | 509,258 | 509,360 | 502,408 | 495,296 | 523,236 | 590,126 | 684,169 |
| Other.Dep.Included in Broad Money | 25..u | 471,046 | 333,975 | 355,677 | 470,225 | 643,138 | 582,826 | 570,154 | 512,399 | 514,199 | 474,871 | 435,021 | 401,163 |
| Sec.Ot.th.Shares Inc.in.Brd. Money | 26a.u | 37,789 | 47,243 | 71,173 | 100,783 | 58,537 | 44,519 | 19,632 | 34,722 | 47,918 | 4,689 | 21,230 | 22,593 |
| Deposits Excl. from Broad Money | 26b.u | 147,609 | 266,276 | 378,880 | 508,243 | 577,247 | 607,376 | 658,794 | 672,618 | 519,427 | 506,840 | 460,270 | 374,669 |
| Sec.Ot.th.Shares Excl.f/Brd. Money | 26s.u | 95,559 | 151,020 | 232,151 | 262,509 | 261,512 | 297,589 | 323,792 | 304,669 | 245,441 | 214,097 | 177,547 | 157,670 |
| Loans | 26l.u | — | — | — | — | — | — | — | — | — | — | — | — |
| Financial Derivatives | 26m.u | — | — | 64,210 | 94,883 | 149,610 | 112,123 | 131,262 | 188,544 | 206,534 | 129,118 | 153,619 | 133,263 |
| Insurance Technical Reserves | 26r.u | — | — | — | — | — | — | — | — | — | — | — | — |
| Shares and Other Equity | 27a.u | 146,625 | 166,603 | 180,986 | 206,287 | 242,447 | 269,789 | 282,530 | 367,140 | 402,865 | 428,249 | 336,116 | 310,433 |
| Other Items (Net) | 27r.u | 43,542 | 57,380 | 49,066 | 69,499 | 55,109 | 76,978 | 44,210 | −36,024 | −58,986 | −59,657 | −3,503 | −35,298 |
| Memorandum Items | | | | | | | | | | | | | |
| Total Assets | 20ra | 1,775,419 | 2,207,727 | 2,526,871 | 3,005,280 | 3,409,439 | 3,446,810 | 3,471,031 | 3,621,172 | 3,581,072 | 3,151,732 | 2,973,063 | 2,828,421 |
| National Residency Criterion | | | | | | | | | | | | | |
| Net Foreign Assets | 21n | −77,454 | −51,307 | −45,081 | −45,558 | −95,783 | −102,670 | −147,948 | −110,754 | 65,336 | 39,057 | 28,993 | 67,922 |
| Claims on Nonresidents | 21 | 252,938 | 333,918 | 341,731 | 417,378 | 421,550 | 420,127 | 373,744 | 386,323 | 407,698 | 349,034 | 355,434 | 373,661 |
| Liabilities to Nonresidents | 26c | 330,392 | 385,225 | 386,812 | 462,936 | 517,333 | 522,797 | 521,692 | 497,077 | 342,362 | 309,977 | 326,441 | 305,739 |
| Net Claims on Central Government | 22an | 74,839 | 65,730 | 46,364 | 47,182 | 60,725 | 103,689 | 104,775 | 136,258 | 214,377 | 215,407 | 238,295 | 199,202 |
| Claims on Central Government | 22a | 92,079 | 86,652 | 69,402 | 73,912 | 96,393 | 147,819 | 150,233 | 181,996 | 256,951 | 249,789 | 281,024 | 240,030 |
| Liabilities to Central Government | 26d | 17,240 | 20,922 | 23,038 | 26,730 | 35,668 | 44,130 | 45,458 | 45,738 | 42,574 | 34,382 | 42,729 | 40,828 |
| Claims on Other Sectors | 22s | 1,088,956 | 1,367,421 | 1,745,923 | 2,100,936 | 2,419,404 | 2,410,194 | 2,476,741 | 2,493,669 | 2,305,406 | 2,037,370 | 1,908,925 | 1,795,514 |
| Claims on Other Fin. Corps | 22g | 53,339 | 63,307 | 130,063 | 249,262 | 464,031 | 481,196 | 544,907 | 608,570 | 574,109 | 444,329 | 457,917 | 417,975 |
| Claims on State & Local Govts | 22b | 38,565 | 43,063 | 42,266 | 45,328 | 55,973 | 68,623 | 86,601 | 100,283 | 100,523 | 98,232 | 103,022 | 92,558 |
| Claims on Private Sector | 22d | 997,052 | 1,261,051 | 1,573,594 | 1,806,346 | 1,899,400 | 1,860,375 | 1,845,233 | 1,784,816 | 1,630,774 | 1,494,809 | 1,347,986 | 1,284,981 |
| Transf.Dep.Included in Broad Money | 24 | 211,561 | 428,800 | 488,500 | 481,229 | 460,513 | 504,842 | 504,352 | 497,185 | 491,432 | 518,152 | 584,510 | 678,206 |
| Other.Dep.Included in Broad Money | 25 | 453,493 | 326,568 | 344,938 | 456,755 | 623,697 | 564,831 | 541,761 | 493,485 | 503,570 | 460,655 | 420,384 | 387,316 |
| Sec.Ot.th.Shares Inc.in.Brd. Money | 26a | 40,243 | 48,253 | 66,159 | 83,262 | 49,349 | 32,784 | 11,089 | 31,924 | 47,501 | 6,482 | 20,370 | 17,904 |
| Deposits Excl. from Broad Money | 26b | 133,437 | 251,241 | 365,717 | 492,687 | 563,994 | 593,091 | 643,995 | 621,875 | 504,404 | 488,841 | 439,447 | 351,053 |
| Sec.Ot.th.Shares Excl.f/Brd. Money | 26s | 109,067 | 169,337 | 253,577 | 283,193 | 277,891 | 311,994 | 334,565 | 313,561 | 250,216 | 218,410 | 182,115 | 161,547 |

**Spain 184**

| | | 2004 | 2005 | 2006 | 2007 | 2008 | 2009 | 2010 | 2011 | 2012 | 2013 | 2014 | 2015 |
|---|---|---|---|---|---|---|---|---|---|---|---|---|---|
| **Depository Corporations** | | | | | | *Millions of Euros: End of Period* | | | | | | | |
| Euro Area Wide Residency Criterion | | | | | | | | | | | | | |
| Net Foreign Assets | 31n.u | −51,688 | −46,448 | −5,680 | 2,421 | −56,803 | −39,743 | −50,083 | 8,688 | 89,139 | 75,857 | 104,141 | 146,946 |
| Claims on Nonresidents | 31..u | 128,096 | 158,510 | 191,287 | 216,949 | 215,052 | 227,816 | 238,181 | 261,507 | 273,277 | 217,876 | 223,827 | 262,965 |
| Liabilities to Nonresidents | 36c.u | 179,785 | 204,958 | 196,967 | 214,528 | 271,855 | 267,559 | 288,264 | 252,819 | 184,139 | 142,018 | 119,686 | 116,019 |
| Domestic Claims | 32..u | 1,259,849 | 1,577,567 | 1,901,831 | 2,296,406 | 2,637,300 | 2,679,186 | 2,725,645 | 2,792,766 | 2,696,641 | 2,425,267 | 2,316,431 | 2,215,068 |
| Net Claims on Central Government | 32anu | 136,905 | 171,465 | 110,137 | 126,498 | 145,291 | 190,301 | 184,590 | 231,255 | 291,805 | 293,703 | 329,167 | 341,878 |
| Claims on Central Government | 32a.u | 157,743 | 196,397 | 137,565 | 157,424 | 188,044 | 248,855 | 233,684 | 279,293 | 344,974 | 328,725 | 375,765 | 384,837 |
| Liabilities to Central Government | 36d.u | 20,838 | 24,932 | 27,428 | 30,926 | 42,753 | 58,554 | 49,094 | 48,038 | 53,169 | 35,022 | 46,598 | 42,959 |
| Claims on Other Sectors | 32s.u | 1,122,944 | 1,406,102 | 1,791,694 | 2,169,908 | 2,492,009 | 2,488,885 | 2,541,055 | 2,561,511 | 2,404,836 | 2,131,564 | 1,987,264 | 1,873,190 |
| Claims on Other Financial Corps | 32g.u | 65,706 | 78,851 | 145,570 | 285,830 | 504,015 | 525,184 | 576,529 | 643,833 | 641,917 | 507,444 | 502,226 | 459,719 |
| Claims on State & Local Govts | 32b.u | 40,673 | 44,896 | 43,583 | 45,680 | 56,375 | 69,109 | 87,160 | 100,780 | 100,913 | 98,441 | 103,158 | 92,802 |
| Claims on Public Nonfin. Corps | 32c.u | — | — | — | — | — | — | — | — | — | — | — | — |
| Claims on Private Sector | 32d.u | 1,016,565 | 1,282,355 | 1,602,541 | 1,838,398 | 1,931,619 | 1,894,592 | 1,877,366 | 1,816,898 | 1,662,006 | 1,525,679 | 1,381,880 | 1,320,669 |
| Broad Money Liabilities | 35l.u | 781,233 | 878,665 | 991,356 | 1,135,005 | 1,250,034 | 1,238,294 | 1,192,800 | 1,146,410 | 1,158,126 | 1,107,528 | 1,161,050 | 1,229,490 |
| Currency Outside Depository Corps | 34a.u | 45,248 | 51,867 | 57,741 | 62,539 | 70,592 | 83,386 | 87,796 | 93,406 | 96,066 | 100,976 | 114,587 | 121,477 |
| Transferable Deposits | 34..u | 227,148 | 445,576 | 506,763 | 501,457 | 477,766 | 527,562 | 515,217 | 505,882 | 499,942 | 526,991 | 590,211 | 684,256 |
| Other Deposits | 35..u | 471,048 | 333,979 | 355,679 | 470,226 | 643,139 | 582,827 | 570,155 | 512,400 | 514,200 | 474,872 | 435,022 | 401,164 |
| Securities Other than Shares | 36a.u | 37,789 | 47,243 | 71,173 | 100,783 | 58,537 | 44,519 | 19,632 | 34,722 | 47,918 | 4,689 | 21,230 | 22,593 |
| Deposits Excl. from Broad Money | 36b.u | 147,609 | 266,276 | 378,880 | 508,243 | 577,247 | 607,376 | 658,794 | 672,618 | 519,427 | 506,840 | 460,270 | 374,669 |
| Sec.Oth.th.Shares Excl.f/Brd. Money. | 36s.u | 95,559 | 151,020 | 232,151 | 262,509 | 261,512 | 297,589 | 323,792 | 304,669 | 245,441 | 214,097 | 177,547 | 157,670 |
| Loans | 36l.u | — | — | — | — | — | — | — | — | — | — | — | — |
| Financial Derivatives | 36m.u | — | — | 64,210 | 94,883 | 149,610 | 112,123 | 131,262 | 188,544 | 206,534 | 129,118 | 153,619 | 133,263 |
| Insurance Technical Reserves | 36r.u | — | — | — | — | — | — | — | — | — | — | — | — |
| Shares and Other Equity | 37a.u | 153,707 | 177,127 | 191,666 | 217,671 | 256,227 | 285,108 | 300,455 | 388,580 | 427,303 | 449,963 | 363,824 | 342,574 |
| Other Items (Net) | 37r.u | 30,049 | 58,036 | 37,887 | 80,508 | 85,869 | 98,958 | 68,456 | 100,638 | 228,948 | 93,581 | 104,312 | 124,358 |
| Broad Money Liabs., Seasonally Adj. | 35lub | 771,541 | 868,656 | 980,943 | 1,124,226 | 1,239,598 | 1,229,166 | 1,184,405 | 1,138,436 | 1,150,879 | 1,101,328 | 1,155,242 | 1,223,659 |
| Memorandum Items | | | | | | | | | | | | | |
| National Residency Criterion | | | | | | | | | | | | | |
| Net Foreign Assets | 31n | −10,395 | 19,193 | 49,383 | 31,606 | −48,729 | −64,485 | −122,357 | −192,326 | −189,487 | −106,269 | −87,726 | −88,629 |
| Claims on Nonresidents | 31 | 320,383 | 404,934 | 436,817 | 498,413 | 504,168 | 502,789 | 453,917 | 483,467 | 493,654 | 420,697 | 432,475 | 474,908 |
| Liabilities to Nonresidents | 36c | 330,779 | 385,741 | 387,434 | 466,807 | 552,897 | 567,274 | 576,274 | 675,793 | 683,142 | 526,965 | 520,201 | 563,537 |
| Domestic Claims | 32 | 1,177,855 | 1,447,663 | 1,803,871 | 2,159,642 | 2,490,902 | 2,523,189 | 2,604,952 | 2,664,681 | 2,553,477 | 2,293,492 | 2,192,371 | 2,093,461 |
| Net Claims on Central Government | 32an | 87,693 | 79,121 | 56,925 | 57,973 | 70,567 | 109,062 | 123,664 | 165,789 | 241,991 | 249,151 | 274,712 | 283,965 |
| Claims on Central Government | 32a | 108,411 | 103,800 | 84,351 | 88,897 | 113,316 | 167,614 | 172,755 | 213,624 | 290,872 | 283,944 | 317,456 | 324,893 |
| Liabilities to Central Government | 36d | 20,718 | 24,679 | 27,426 | 30,924 | 42,749 | 58,552 | 49,091 | 47,835 | 48,881 | 34,793 | 42,744 | 40,928 |
| Claims on Other Sectors | 32s | 1,090,162 | 1,368,542 | 1,746,946 | 2,101,669 | 2,420,335 | 2,414,127 | 2,481,288 | 2,498,892 | 2,311,486 | 2,044,341 | 1,917,659 | 1,809,496 |
| Claims on Other Financial Corps | 32g | 53,391 | 63,351 | 130,086 | 249,995 | 464,962 | 485,129 | 549,267 | 613,607 | 580,000 | 451,123 | 466,472 | 431,781 |
| Claims on State & Local Govts | 32b | 39,719 | 44,140 | 43,266 | 45,328 | 55,973 | 68,623 | 86,601 | 100,283 | 100,523 | 98,232 | 103,022 | 92,558 |
| Claims on Private Sector | 32d | 997,052 | 1,261,051 | 1,573,594 | 1,806,346 | 1,899,400 | 1,860,375 | 1,845,420 | 1,785,002 | 1,630,963 | 1,494,986 | 1,348,165 | 1,285,157 |
| Transf.Dep.Included in Broad Money | 34 | 223,991 | 440,671 | 501,614 | 497,391 | 473,978 | 523,145 | 510,208 | 500,658 | 496,077 | 521,906 | 584,594 | 678,292 |
| Other Dep.Included in Broad Money. | 35 | 453,495 | 326,572 | 344,940 | 456,756 | 623,698 | 564,832 | 541,762 | 493,486 | 503,571 | 460,656 | 420,385 | 387,317 |
| Sec.Ot.th.Shares Inc.in.Brd. Money | 36a | 40,243 | 48,253 | 66,159 | 83,262 | 49,349 | 32,784 | 11,089 | 31,924 | 47,501 | 6,482 | 20,370 | 17,904 |
| Deposits Excl. from Broad Money | 36b | 133,437 | 251,241 | 365,717 | 492,687 | 563,994 | 593,091 | 643,995 | 621,875 | 504,404 | 488,841 | 439,447 | 351,053 |
| Sec.Ot.th.Shares Excl./f.Brd. Money | 36s | 109,067 | 169,337 | 253,577 | 283,193 | 277,891 | 311,994 | 334,565 | 313,561 | 250,216 | 218,410 | 182,115 | 161,547 |
| **Interest Rates** | | | | | | | *Percent Per Annum* | | | | | | |
| Money Market Rate | 60b | 2.04 | 2.09 | 2.83 | 3.85 | 3.85 | .68 | .45 | 1.02 | .27 | .15 | .12 | −.08 |
| Treasury Bill Rate | 60c | 2.17 | 2.19 | 3.26 | 4.07 | 3.71 | 1.00 | 1.69 | 3.04 | 2.66 | 1.17 | .39 | .05 |
| Deposit Rate | | | | | | | | | | | | | |
| Households: Stocks, up to 2 years | 60lhs | 1.84 | 1.86 | 2.37 | 3.43 | 4.39 | 3.41 | 2.43 | 2.76 | 2.71 | 2.37 | 1.49 | .74 |
| New Business, up to 1 year | 60lhn | 1.96 | 2.07 | 2.75 | 3.88 | 4.63 | 2.48 | 2.41 | 2.62 | 2.65 | 1.52 | .85 | .42 |
| Corporations: Stocks, up to 2 years | 60lcs | 2.00 | 2.05 | 2.59 | 3.70 | 4.56 | 2.99 | 2.26 | 2.63 | 2.52 | 2.20 | 1.45 | .92 |
| New Business, up to 1 year | 60lcn | 2.02 | 2.05 | 2.76 | 3.94 | 4.41 | 1.69 | 1.79 | 2.13 | 1.87 | 1.46 | .76 | .34 |
| REPOS, Stocks | 60lcr | 2.00 | 2.06 | 2.69 | 3.72 | 3.81 | .98 | .78 | 1.69 | 2.15 | 1.87 | .65 | .33 |
| Lending Rate | | | | | | | | | | | | | |
| Households: Stocks, up to 1 year | 60phs | 6.57 | 5.79 | 5.81 | 6.60 | 7.41 | 6.96 | 7.22 | 8.09 | 8.30 | 9.34 | 9.44 | 9.42 |
| New Bus., Floating & up to 1 year | 60pns | 8.06 | 7.97 | 8.73 | 9.89 | 11.02 | 10.72 | 7.36 | 5.96 | 6.96 | 6.76 | 6.14 | 4.50 |
| House Purch., Stocks,Over 5 years | 60phm | 3.56 | 3.35 | 3.69 | 4.74 | 5.46 | 4.40 | 2.84 | 2.93 | 2.90 | 2.27 | 2.08 | 1.67 |
| House Purch., New Bus., 5-10 yrs | 60phn | 6.75 | 6.56 | 6.95 | 6.77 | 7.81 | 7.56 | 7.58 | 7.65 | 7.54 | 6.33 | 6.71 | 4.96 |
| Corporations: Stocks, up to 1 year | 60pcs | 3.54 | 3.50 | 4.14 | 5.23 | 5.96 | 3.94 | 3.35 | 4.15 | 4.17 | 3.88 | 3.50 | 2.74 |
| New Bus., Over € 1 mil.,up to 1 yr | 60pcn | 2.84 | 2.87 | 3.71 | 4.89 | 5.25 | 2.44 | 2.16 | 3.02 | 2.74 | 2.72 | 2.69 | 2.01 |
| Government Bond Yield | 61 | 4.10 | 3.39 | 3.79 | 4.31 | 4.37 | 3.98 | 4.25 | 5.44 | 5.85 | 4.56 | 2.72 | 1.74 |
| **Prices, Production, Labor** | | | | | | *Index Numbers (2010=100): Period Averages* | | | | | | | |
| Share Prices (End of Month) | 62.ep | 82.0 | 101.2 | 127.6 | 155.4 | 119.9 | 100.1 | 100.0 | 93.7 | 72.6 | 83.9 | 101.9 | 102.3 |
| Industrial Prices | 63 | 82.0 | 85.8 | 90.5 | 93.7 | 99.8 | 96.4 | 100.0 | 106.9 | 111.0 | 111.7 | 110.5 | 107.9 |
| Consumer Prices | 64 | 86.1 | † 89.0 | 92.1 | 94.7 | 98.5 | 98.2 | 100.0 | 103.2 | 105.7 | 107.2 | 107.1 | 106.5 |
| Harmonized CPI | 64h | 85.7 | 88.6 | 91.7 | 94.3 | 98.2 | 98.0 | 100.0 | 103.0 | 105.6 | 107.2 | 107.0 | 106.3 |
| Wages | 65 | 80.1 | 82.9 | 86.5 | 90.1 | † 94.1 | 99.4 | 100.0 | 102.2 | 102.2 | 104.0 | 102.5 | 95.5 |
| Industrial Production | 66 | 119.0 | 119.8 | 124.5 | 127.0 | 117.8 | 99.2 | 100.0 | 98.6 | 92.3 | 90.7 | 92.0 | 95.0 |
| Employment | 67 | 92.7 | 98.9 | 107.0 | 110.3 | 109.8 | 102.3 | 100.0 | 98.1 | 93.6 | 84.0 | 94.0 | 96.8 |
| | | | | | | *Number in Thousands: Period Averages* | | | | | | | |
| Labor Force | 67d | 20,376 | 20,999 | 21,631 | 22,281 | 22,909 | 23,107 | 23,210 | 23,280 | 23,282 | 23,044 | 22,814 | 22,767 |
| Employment | 67e | 18,019 | 19,068 | 19,793 | 20,437 | 20,316 | 18,957 | 18,574 | 18,271 | 17,477 | 17,002 | 17,211 | 17,718 |
| Unemployment | 67c | 2,234 | 1,934 | 1,841 | † 1,846 | 2,596 | 4,154 | 4,640 | 5,013 | 5,811 | 6,051 | 5,610 | 5,056 |
| Unemployment Rate (%) | 67r | 11.0 | 9.2 | 8.5 | † 8.2 | 11.3 | 17.9 | 19.9 | 21.4 | 24.8 | 26.1 | 24.5 | 22.1 |
| **Intl. Transactions & Positions** | | | | | | | *Millions of Euros* | | | | | | |
| Exports | 70 | 146,458.2 | 153,559.0 | 169,872.0 | 181,478.6 | 188,184.4 | 158,254.3 | 185,799.0 | 214,485.5 | 222,643.9 | 234,239.8 | 240,034.9 | 250,251.3 |
| Imports, c.i.f. | 71 | 207,128.3 | 231,371.6 | 259,559.0 | 280,430.6 | 282,251.3 | 208,436.8 | 238,081.6 | 260,823.2 | 253,401.2 | 251,354.2 | 264,546.7 | 274,415.2 |
| | | | | | | | *2010=100* | | | | | | |
| Volume of Exports | 72 | 84.8 | 85.1 | 90.5 | 94.0 | 96.0 | 86.4 | 100.0 | 110.8 | 111.1 | 117.2 | 122.5 | 126.7 |
| Volume of Imports | 73 | 92.0 | 97.9 | 105.7 | 113.3 | 109.6 | 91.6 | 100.0 | 101.2 | 93.9 | 96.8 | 104.8 | 111.5 |
| Unit Value of Exports | 74 | 92.6 | 96.9 | 101.3 | 103.9 | 105.7 | 98.5 | 100.0 | 104.8 | 107.0 | 106.8 | 105.7 | 106.3 |
| Unit Value of Imports | 75 | 94.6 | 99.3 | 103.3 | 104.1 | 108.5 | 95.6 | 100.0 | 108.5 | 113.5 | 108.6 | 106.1 | 103.4 |

# Spain 184

| | | 2004 | 2005 | 2006 | 2007 | 2008 | 2009 | 2010 | 2011 | 2012 | 2013 | 2014 | 2015 |
|---|---|---|---|---|---|---|---|---|---|---|---|---|---|
| **Balance of Payments** | | | | | | | *Millions of US Dollars* | | | | | | |
| A. Current Account* | 109bx | −59,777.1 | −87,005.5 | −113,748.7 | −143,136.6 | −152,544.9 | −63,720.5 | −56,363.3 | −47,060.3 | −3,420.4 | 20,709.7 | 12,811.8 | 16,657.9 |
| Goods, credit (exports) | 1a9cx | 185,495.6 | 193,553.3 | 211,569.3 | 261,110.9 | 284,228.6 | 228,589.3 | 253,062.8 | 300,392.9 | 288,215.9 | 311,560.7 | 317,058.3 | 277,850.8 |
| Goods, debit (imports) | 1a9dx | 255,177.5 | 281,856.4 | 320,160.4 | 389,205.4 | 413,147.3 | 286,587.1 | 316,344.0 | 362,213.0 | 325,845.1 | 330,498.7 | 346,991.5 | 302,593.0 |
| Balance on goods | 1a9bx | −69,681.9 | −88,303.1 | −108,591.1 | −128,094.6 | −128,918.7 | −57,997.8 | −63,281.2 | −61,820.1 | −37,629.2 | −18,938.0 | −29,933.2 | −24,742.2 |
| Services, credit (exports) | 1b9cx | 84,173.1 | 92,173.9 | 103,448.6 | 119,892.6 | 132,364.8 | 112,723.3 | 112,898.1 | 130,909.9 | 122,217.9 | 126,469.7 | 132,689.7 | 117,928.0 |
| Services, debit (imports) | 1b9dx | 55,540.0 | 61,339.7 | 69,327.0 | 80,417.4 | 88,124.1 | 71,437.6 | 68,276.4 | 71,367.0 | 64,328.1 | 63,242.4 | 68,358.1 | 64,697.9 |
| Balance on Goods & Services | 1z9bx | −41,048.8 | −57,468.9 | −74,469.4 | −88,619.4 | −84,677.9 | −16,712.1 | −18,659.6 | −2,277.2 | 20,260.7 | 44,289.3 | 34,398.4 | 28,488.0 |
| Primary income: credit | 1c9cx | 42,593.8 | 46,931.7 | 67,596.0 | 87,558.2 | 85,957.0 | 71,719.5 | 70,590.4 | 73,453.2 | 63,887.6 | 63,962.7 | 66,763.7 | 57,382.9 |
| Primary income: debit | 1c9dx | 51,719.3 | 63,597.1 | 88,956.3 | 123,858.0 | 131,141.2 | 98,330.3 | 90,437.0 | 99,201.0 | 72,863.7 | 70,110.4 | 72,909.8 | 58,486.5 |
| Balance on gds, serv. & prim. inc. | 1y9bx | −50,174.3 | −74,134.3 | −95,829.8 | −124,919.3 | −129,862.1 | −43,322.9 | −38,506.2 | −28,025.1 | 11,284.6 | 38,141.6 | 28,252.2 | 27,384.4 |
| Secondary income: credit | 1d9ca | 10,626.6 | 11,320.4 | 10,969.7 | 14,592.5 | 15,001.0 | 15,094.7 | 14,605.7 | 17,447.3 | 17,341.0 | 16,994.1 | 17,213.5 | 16,134.8 |
| Secondary income: debit | 1d9da | 20,229.4 | 24,191.6 | 28,888.6 | 32,809.8 | 37,683.8 | 35,492.2 | 32,462.8 | 36,482.5 | 32,046.0 | 34,425.9 | 32,654.0 | 26,861.2 |
| B. Capital Account* | 209ba | 9,606.1 | 9,046.4 | 7,121.3 | 5,912.1 | 6,985.4 | 4,629.1 | 6,500.0 | 5,641.8 | 6,642.3 | 9,018.3 | 5,982.3 | 6,615.8 |
| Capital account: credit | 209ca | 10,260.5 | 9,666.3 | 8,127.0 | 7,059.9 | 8,192.6 | 7,040.9 | 8,542.7 | 7,789.3 | 8,391.6 | 11,470.1 | 6,767.6 | 7,503.2 |
| Capital account: debit | 209da | 654.4 | 619.9 | 1,005.7 | 1,147.8 | 1,207.2 | 2,411.8 | 2,042.7 | 2,147.5 | 1,749.3 | 2,451.8 | 785.3 | 887.3 |
| Balance on current & capital acct. | 129ba | −50,171.1 | −77,959.1 | −106,627.4 | −137,224.5 | −145,559.5 | −59,091.4 | −49,863.3 | −41,418.5 | 3,222.0 | 29,728.0 | 18,794.1 | 23,273.7 |
| C. Financial Account* | 309na | −36,565.9 | −73,518.0 | −107,231.7 | −137,626.4 | −148,691.6 | −80,750.8 | −58,117.2 | −55,032.1 | −815.3 | 46,251.9 | 23,519.9 | 31,133.0 |
| Direct investment: assets | 3a9aa | 62,068.6 | 44,062.9 | 105,301.9 | 146,652.3 | 75,665.6 | 15,896.1 | 37,829.9 | 44,986.8 | −2,516.4 | 25,941.8 | 46,052.1 | 47,373.7 |
| Equity & investment fund shares | 3aaaa | 56,554.5 | 38,486.6 | 101,128.9 | 132,320.6 | 67,288.2 | 12,647.3 | 31,055.6 | 26,361.0 | −1,171.9 | 29,014.8 | 37,479.5 | 37,052.0 |
| Debt instruments | 3abaa | 5,514.1 | 5,576.4 | 4,173.0 | 14,331.7 | 8,377.4 | 3,248.8 | 6,774.4 | 18,625.8 | −1,344.5 | −3,073.0 | 8,572.7 | 10,321.7 |
| Direct investment: liabilities | 3a9la | 25,176.4 | 26,719.8 | 32,990.5 | 73,772.1 | 79,556.7 | 13,478.9 | 41,020.2 | 31,782.6 | 24,915.0 | 45,097.9 | 34,233.0 | 22,062.6 |
| Equity & investment fund shares | 3aala | 17,685.9 | 16,438.5 | 25,363.9 | 49,465.7 | 48,576.6 | 11,145.1 | 37,200.7 | 35,993.8 | 38,126.9 | 41,531.6 | 27,142.8 | 22,942.0 |
| Debt instruments | 3abla | 7,490.4 | 10,281.3 | 7,626.6 | 24,306.4 | 30,980.2 | 2,333.7 | 3,819.5 | −4,211.3 | −13,212.0 | 3,566.3 | 7,090.2 | −879.4 |
| Portfolio investment: assets | 3b9aa | 39,870.9 | 119,731.1 | 12,159.9 | 6,863.0 | −30,070.6 | −1,705.5 | −92,542.7 | −51,489.0 | −12,159.6 | −21,681.3 | 65,648.2 | 96,097.4 |
| Equity & investment fund shares | 3baaa | 15,283.2 | 19,744.7 | 26,954.2 | −9,181.8 | −40,092.6 | 11,614.0 | 12,577.0 | −12,779.4 | 8,365.6 | 19,083.1 | 49,162.4 | 58,844.8 |
| Debt securities | 3bbaa | 24,587.7 | 99,986.4 | −14,794.3 | 16,044.8 | 10,022.0 | −13,319.6 | −105,119.6 | −38,709.6 | −20,525.2 | −40,764.4 | 16,485.8 | 37,252.6 |
| Portfolio investment: liabilities | 3b9la | 141,684.8 | 172,713.0 | 243,889.9 | 124,059.6 | −26,903.8 | 70,081.9 | −46,564.9 | −95,550.1 | −66,531.7 | 38,766.5 | 77,054.2 | 69,899.7 |
| Equity & investment fund shares | 3bala | 10,917.7 | −9,572.9 | −24,005.4 | 15,594.7 | −2,488.9 | 9,059.2 | −4,723.2 | 4,210.7 | 9,822.1 | 9,678.6 | 27,940.4 | 22,858.8 |
| Debt securities | 3bbla | 130,767.1 | 182,285.9 | 267,895.3 | 108,464.9 | −24,415.0 | 61,022.6 | −41,841.6 | −99,760.8 | −76,353.7 | 29,087.9 | 49,113.8 | 47,040.9 |
| Fin. der.& empl.stk.ops.(ESOs): net | 3c9na | −76.7 | −272.8 | −2,526.9 | 5,914.6 | 12,611.0 | 8,272.9 | −11,295.2 | 3,098.3 | −10,800.2 | 1,482.9 | 1,298.4 | −1,575.5 |
| Fin. der. & ESOs: assets | 3c9aa | .... | .... | .... | .... | .... | .... | .... | .... | .... | .... | .... | .... |
| Fin. der. & ESOs.: liabilities | 3c9la | .... | .... | .... | .... | .... | .... | .... | .... | .... | .... | .... | .... |
| Other investment: assets | 3d9aa | 52,656.1 | 42,196.6 | 96,611.6 | 47,975.5 | 26,085.0 | 8,106.7 | 23,185.6 | 47,218.8 | 63,401.2 | −61,265.7 | 27,017.3 | 25,918.6 |
| Other equity | 3daaa | .... | .... | .... | .... | .... | .... | .... | .... | .... | 4,712.6 | 2,990.7 | −379.7 |
| Debt instruments | 3dzaa | 52,656.1 | 42,196.6 | 96,611.6 | 47,975.5 | 26,085.0 | 8,106.7 | 23,185.6 | 47,218.8 | 63,401.2 | −65,978.4 | 24,026.6 | 26,298.4 |
| Other investment: liabilities | 3d9la | 24,223.6 | 79,803.1 | 41,897.8 | 147,199.9 | 180,329.7 | 27,760.2 | 20,839.6 | 162,614.3 | 80,357.0 | −185,638.6 | 5,208.9 | 44,718.9 |
| Other equity | 3dala | .... | .... | .... | .... | .... | .... | .... | .... | .... | 5.9 | 48.2 | −10.4 |
| Debt instruments | 3dzla | 24,223.6 | 79,803.1 | 41,897.8 | 147,199.9 | 180,329.7 | 27,760.2 | 20,839.6 | 162,614.3 | 80,357.0 | −185,644.6 | 5,160.7 | 44,729.3 |
| Curr.+ cap.− finan. acct. balance | 4y9na | −13,605.2 | −4,441.2 | 604.3 | 401.8 | 3,132.1 | 21,659.4 | 8,254.0 | 13,613.5 | 4,037.3 | −16,523.9 | −4,725.8 | −7,859.3 |
| D. Net Errors and Omissions | 409na | 7,192.7 | 2,521.5 | −26.1 | −187.0 | −2,444.6 | −15,689.2 | −7,203.5 | 18.8 | −1,108.9 | 17,211.9 | 9,604.9 | 13,565.5 |
| E. Reserves and Related Items | 4z9na | −6,412.5 | −1,919.6 | 578.2 | 214.9 | 687.5 | 5,970.2 | 1,050.5 | 13,632.4 | 2,928.5 | 688.0 | 4,879.0 | 5,706.2 |
| Reserve assets | 3e9aa | −6,412.5 | −1,919.6 | 578.2 | 214.9 | 687.5 | 5,970.2 | 1,050.5 | 13,632.4 | 2,928.5 | 688.0 | 4,879.0 | 5,706.2 |
| Credit and loans from the IMF | 3dcla | — | — | — | — | — | — | — | — | — | — | | |
| Exceptional financing | 409la | .... | .... | .... | .... | .... | .... | .... | .... | .... | .... | .... | .... |
| *Excludes components in group E | | | | | | | | | | | | | | |

| | | 2004 | 2005 | 2006 | 2007 | 2008 | 2009 | 2010 | 2011 | 2012 | 2013 | 2014 | 2015 |
|---|---|---|---|---|---|---|---|---|---|---|---|---|---|
| **International Investment Position** | | | | | | | *Millions of US Dollars* | | | | | | |
| Assets | 809aa | 1,172,230.5 | 1,247,110.1 | 1,649,304.0 | 1,991,379.0 | 1,894,224.6 | 1,950,456.8 | 1,797,446.1 | 1,785,076.1 | † 1,934,141.6 | 1,868,881.0 | 1,851,541.9 | 1,784,352.8 |
| Direct investment | 8a9aa | 304,810.6 | 320,003.7 | 462,422.3 | 621,192.3 | 631,727.2 | 688,270.0 | 685,816.0 | 678,929.9 | † 706,592.6 | 695,524.7 | 673,233.5 | 620,277.0 |
| Equity & investment fund shares | 8aaaa | 259,752.3 | 279,316.1 | 405,506.4 | 542,195.3 | 548,179.8 | 582,720.8 | 601,685.2 | 592,503.8 | † 594,465.4 | 584,778.3 | 566,278.3 | 510,778.1 |
| Debt instruments | 8abaa | 45,058.4 | 40,687.6 | 56,915.8 | 78,996.9 | 83,547.3 | 105,549.2 | 84,130.8 | 86,426.2 | † 112,127.2 | 110,746.3 | 106,955.2 | 109,498.9 |
| Portfolio investment | 8b9aa | 523,419.2 | 589,701.3 | 681,455.1 | 757,958.5 | 595,299.6 | 641,688.1 | 503,990.3 | 418,066.0 | † 443,297.0 | 473,377.1 | 498,588.5 | 528,408.0 |
| Equity & investment fund shares | 8baaa | 110,302.3 | 129,330.7 | 187,137.3 | 210,239.7 | 94,831.4 | 124,249.0 | 137,724.7 | 113,893.9 | † 137,877.5 | 189,342.8 | 213,072.1 | 243,564.3 |
| Debt securities | 8bbaa | 413,116.9 | 460,370.6 | 494,317.9 | 547,718.8 | 500,468.2 | 517,439.1 | 366,265.6 | 304,172.0 | † 305,419.6 | 284,034.3 | 285,516.4 | 284,843.7 |
| Fin. der.(oth.than reserves) & ESOs | 8c9aa | — | — | 43,425.8 | 65,718.1 | 150,690.9 | 111,572.7 | 127,093.8 | 181,437.5 | † 207,417.2 | 144,930.2 | 146,068.6 | 119,247.9 |
| Other investment | 8d9aa | 324,242.1 | 320,178.4 | 442,660.8 | 527,456.2 | 496,262.4 | 480,725.4 | 448,631.2 | 459,544.5 | † 526,246.0 | 508,742.6 | 483,319.5 | 462,455.3 |
| Other equity | 8daaa | .... | .... | .... | .... | .... | .... | .... | .... | † 17,807.8 | 24,398.2 | 22,825.4 | 19,349.0 |
| Debt instruments | 8dzaa | 324,242.1 | 320,178.4 | 442,660.8 | 527,456.2 | 496,262.4 | 480,725.4 | 448,631.2 | 459,544.5 | † 508,438.3 | 484,344.4 | 460,494.0 | 443,106.3 |
| Reserve assets | 8e9aa | 19,758.6 | 17,226.6 | 19,340.0 | 19,054.0 | 20,244.5 | 28,200.6 | 31,914.8 | 47,098.2 | † 50,588.7 | 46,306.5 | 50,331.9 | 53,964.6 |
| Liabilities | 809la | 1,825,203.6 | 1,893,990.9 | 2,550,170.8 | 3,257,215.2 | 3,140,748.4 | 3,404,348.7 | 3,076,651.1 | 3,058,460.0 | † 3,172,849.8 | 3,236,855.3 | 3,059,578.3 | 2,849,451.3 |
| Direct investment | 8a9la | 495,736.9 | 459,577.0 | 561,951.4 | 710,539.3 | 700,580.1 | 761,860.1 | 728,861.1 | 714,153.9 | † 731,771.2 | 794,217.5 | 736,612.8 | 681,467.1 |
| Equity & investment fund shares | 8aala | 318,195.4 | 295,680.8 | 357,319.4 | 452,356.3 | 446,911.5 | 471,824.3 | 452,494.4 | 453,902.0 | † 459,245.6 | 510,441.3 | 471,528.5 | 442,396.8 |
| Debt instruments | 8abla | 177,541.5 | 163,896.2 | 204,631.9 | 258,183.0 | 253,668.6 | 290,035.8 | 276,366.7 | 260,251.9 | † 272,525.6 | 283,776.3 | 265,084.3 | 239,070.2 |
| Portfolio investment | 8b9la | 766,167.5 | 859,272.5 | 1,270,352.1 | 1,600,084.2 | 1,333,186.1 | 1,538,632.9 | 1,264,344.6 | 1,089,862.3 | † 1,043,821.8 | 1,244,588.5 | 1,228,749.2 | 1,146,300.5 |
| Equity & investment fund shares | 8bala | 249,551.0 | 232,810.4 | 323,564.3 | 415,619.3 | 236,787.8 | 320,705.6 | 241,893.7 | 209,975.5 | † 236,138.2 | 333,542.5 | 332,115.5 | 309,585.8 |
| Debt securities | 8bbla | 516,616.5 | 626,462.2 | 946,787.7 | 1,184,465.0 | 1,096,398.3 | 1,217,927.3 | 1,022,450.9 | 879,886.8 | † 807,683.7 | 911,046.0 | 896,633.6 | 836,714.7 |
| Fin. der.(oth.than reserves) & ESOs | 8c9la | — | — | 56,063.0 | 93,459.3 | 158,691.3 | 113,084.4 | 123,543.8 | 173,919.9 | † 200,924.9 | 137,746.3 | 149,216.3 | 121,162.3 |
| Other investment | 8d9la | 563,299.2 | 575,141.3 | 661,804.4 | 853,132.4 | 948,291.0 | 990,771.3 | 959,901.6 | 1,080,523.9 | † 1,196,331.8 | 1,060,303.0 | 945,000.0 | 900,521.5 |
| Other equity | 8dala | .... | .... | .... | .... | .... | .... | .... | .... | † 736.1 | 981.3 | 706.3 | 81.2 |
| Debt instruments | 8dzla | 563,299.2 | 575,141.3 | 661,804.4 | 853,132.4 | 948,291.0 | 990,771.3 | 959,901.6 | 1,080,523.9 | † 1,195,595.6 | 1,059,321.7 | 944,293.7 | 900,440.3 |

| | | 2004 | 2005 | 2006 | 2007 | 2008 | 2009 | 2010 | 2011 | 2012 | 2013 | 2014 | 2015 |
|---|---|---|---|---|---|---|---|---|---|---|---|---|---|
| **Government Finance Operations Statement General Government** | | | | | | *Millions of Euros: Fiscal Year Ends December 31; Data Reported through Eurostat* | | | | | | | |
| Revenue | a1 | 332,905 | 367,699 | 407,937 | 442,300 | 409,909 | 375,628 | 391,661 | 387,353 | 391,168 | 394,196 | 401,722 | 413,456 |
| Taxes | a11 | 193,521 | 218,998 | 245,400 | 267,610 | 229,579 | 198,109 | 215,266 | 212,419 | 218,696 | 225,128 | 230,398 | 242,265 |
| Social Contributions | a12 | 109,168 | 117,460 | 127,099 | 136,417 | 142,049 | 139,727 | 138,649 | 137,802 | 131,859 | 128,217 | 130,063 | 132,333 |
| Grants | a13 | .... | .... | .... | .... | .... | .... | .... | .... | .... | .... | .... | .... |
| Other Revenue | a14 | .... | .... | .... | .... | .... | .... | .... | .... | .... | .... | .... | .... |
| Expense | a2 | 316,528 | 336,960 | 364,363 | 393,681 | 430,501 | 462,305 | 467,915 | 477,396 | 501,409 | 469,923 | 468,308 | 471,014 |
| Compensation of Employees | a21 | 84,489 | 90,719 | 98,039 | 107,445 | 118,136 | 125,564 | 124,884 | 122,601 | 113,925 | 114,711 | 114,938 | 118,699 |
| Use of Goods & Services | a22 | 38,688 | 43,222 | 47,156 | 54,226 | 59,219 | 61,032 | 61,050 | 61,292 | 58,599 | 54,974 | 54,957 | 56,389 |
| Consumption of Fixed Capital | a23 | 17,735 | 19,450 | 21,277 | 22,874 | 24,414 | 25,130 | 26,770 | 27,364 | 27,898 | 27,832 | 27,775 | 27,952 |
| Interest | a24 | 17,101 | 16,220 | 16,100 | 16,892 | 17,256 | 18,348 | 20,248 | 26,315 | 30,922 | 34,669 | 35,291 | 33,122 |
| Subsidies | a25 | 8,853 | 9,728 | 10,429 | 11,857 | 12,409 | 12,485 | 12,354 | 12,204 | 10,004 | 10,853 | 11,400 | 12,536 |
| Grants | a26 | .... | .... | .... | .... | .... | .... | .... | .... | .... | .... | .... | .... |
| Social Benefits | a27 | 120,741 | 129,936 | 140,143 | 149,786 | 165,992 | 186,763 | 194,251 | 194,720 | 197,042 | 198,812 | 198,747 | 198,800 |
| Other Expense | a28 | .... | .... | .... | .... | .... | .... | .... | .... | .... | .... | .... | .... |
| Gross Operating Balance [1-2+23] | agob | 34,112 | 50,189 | 64,851 | 71,493 | 3,822 | −61,547 | −49,484 | −62,679 | −82,343 | −47,895 | −38,811 | −29,606 |
| Net Operating Balance [1-2] | anob | 16,377 | 30,739 | 43,574 | 48,619 | −20,592 | −86,677 | −76,254 | −90,043 | −110,241 | −75,727 | −66,586 | −57,558 |
| Net Acq. of Nonfinancial Assets | a31 | 16,741 | 19,510 | 21,430 | 26,999 | 28,793 | 31,560 | 25,191 | 12,865 | −1,338 | −4,486 | −5,267 | −2,593 |
| Aquisition of Nonfin. Assets | a31.1 | .... | .... | .... | .... | .... | .... | .... | .... | .... | .... | .... | .... |
| Disposal of Nonfin. Assets | a31.2 | .... | .... | .... | .... | .... | .... | .... | .... | .... | .... | .... | .... |
| Net Lending/Borrowing [1-2-31] | anlb | −364 | 11,229 | 22,144 | 21,620 | −49,385 | −118,237 | −101,445 | −102,908 | −108,903 | −71,241 | −61,319 | −54,965 |
| Net Acq. of Financial Assets | a32 | 11,200 | 21,880 | 31,484 | 22,033 | 13,938 | 24,964 | −15,389 | −1,377 | 17,684 | 2,314 | 12,001 | −16,279 |
| By instrument | | | | | | | | | | | | | |
| Monetary Gold & SDRs | a3201 | — | — | — | — | — | — | — | — | — | — | — | — |
| Currency & Deposits | a3202 | 6,130 | 11,377 | 13,342 | 12,168 | 819 | 17,813 | −24,635 | −17,606 | 7,170 | −13,276 | 10,982 | 1,485 |
| Securities other than Shares | a3203 | 927 | 4,594 | 10,496 | 6,162 | 10,219 | −5,414 | −5,449 | −8,072 | −8,992 | 124 | −1,891 | −3,810 |
| Loans | a3204 | 1,714 | 656 | 2,033 | 2,021 | 2,539 | 8,129 | 6,901 | 12,463 | 9,147 | 4,703 | 700 | −2,875 |
| Shares & Other Equity | a3205 | −444 | 463 | 257 | 503 | 838 | 345 | 8,251 | −477 | 3,488 | 1,769 | 1,112 | −3,708 |
| Insurance Technical Reserves | a3206 | — | — | — | — | — | — | — | — | — | — | — | — |
| Financial Derivatives | a3207 | −123 | −7 | −3 | −9 | 27 | 45 | −31 | 37 | 165 | 177 | — | — |
| Other Accounts Receivable | a3208 | 2,994 | 4,796 | 5,357 | 1,187 | −504 | 4,045 | −425 | 12,278 | 6,704 | 8,818 | 1,099 | −7,371 |
| By debtor | | | | | | | | | | | | | |
| Domestic | a321 | .... | .... | .... | .... | .... | .... | .... | .... | .... | .... | .... | .... |
| Foreign | a322 | .... | .... | .... | .... | .... | .... | .... | .... | .... | .... | .... | .... |
| Net Incurrence of Liabilities | a33 | 11,564 | 10,651 | 9,340 | 413 | 63,323 | 143,201 | 86,056 | 101,532 | 126,587 | 73,556 | 73,320 | 39,521 |
| By instrument | | | | | | | | | | | | | |
| Special Drawing Rights (SDRs) | a3301 | — | — | — | — | — | — | — | — | — | — | — | — |
| Currency & Deposits | a3302 | 236 | 255 | 267 | 243 | 113 | 49 | 116 | 101 | −4 | 15 | 151 | 208 |
| Securities other than Shares | a3303 | 1,648 | 3,979 | −2,941 | −8,286 | 43,663 | 121,334 | 60,781 | 73,917 | 62,510 | 99,322 | 65,328 | 58,997 |
| Loans | a3304 | 7,881 | −12 | 419 | −136 | 13,156 | 12,636 | 18,925 | 16,838 | 88,052 | −20,384 | 8,164 | −20,715 |
| Shares & Other Equity | a3305 | — | — | — | — | — | 2,250 | — | — | — | — | — | — |
| Insurance Technical Reserves | a3306 | — | — | — | — | — | — | — | — | — | — | — | — |
| Financial Derivatives | a3307 | — | — | — | — | — | — | — | — | — | — | — | — |
| Other Accounts Payable | a3308 | 1,800 | 6,428 | 11,595 | 8,591 | 6,392 | 6,933 | 6,235 | 10,676 | −23,971 | −5,397 | −322 | 1,030 |
| By creditor | | | | | | | | | | | | | |
| Domestic | a331 | .... | .... | .... | .... | .... | .... | .... | .... | .... | .... | .... | .... |
| Foreign | a332 | .... | .... | .... | .... | .... | .... | .... | .... | .... | .... | .... | .... |
| Stat. Discrepancy [32-33-NLB] | anlbz | — | — | — | — | — | — | — | −1 | — | −1 | — | −835 |
| Memo Item: Expenditure [2+31] | a2m | 333,269 | 356,470 | 385,793 | 420,680 | 459,294 | 493,865 | 493,106 | 490,261 | 500,071 | 465,437 | 463,041 | 468,421 |
| **Balance Sheet** | | | | | | | | | | | | | |
| Net Worth | a6 | .... | .... | .... | .... | .... | .... | .... | .... | .... | .... | .... | .... |
| Nonfinancial Assets | a61 | .... | .... | .... | .... | .... | .... | .... | .... | .... | .... | .... | .... |
| Financial Assets | a62 | 163,379 | 199,206 | 237,491 | 263,485 | 277,746 | 304,167 | 294,857 | 318,479 | 344,640 | 345,872 | 364,405 | 366,310 |
| By instrument | | | | | | | | | | | | | |
| Monetary Gold & SDRs | a6201 | — | — | — | — | — | — | — | — | — | — | — | — |
| Currency & Deposits | a6202 | 64,228 | 75,605 | 88,948 | 101,116 | 101,935 | 119,749 | 95,114 | 77,523 | 84,693 | 71,418 | 82,400 | 85,455 |
| Securities other than Shares | a6203 | 1,366 | 6,127 | 16,684 | 22,844 | 34,403 | 28,038 | 22,358 | 14,409 | 4,895 | 4,907 | 2,717 | 3,834 |
| Loans | a6204 | 10,953 | 12,145 | 13,790 | 15,483 | 18,194 | 26,247 | 34,023 | 46,574 | 55,637 | 60,179 | 61,210 | 58,634 |
| Shares and Other Equity | a6205 | 60,829 | 74,531 | 81,914 | 86,700 | 86,377 | 89,251 | 102,905 | 127,237 | 139,916 | 141,054 | 148,663 | 156,333 |
| Insurance Technical Reserves | a6206 | — | — | — | — | — | — | — | — | — | — | — | — |
| Financial Derivatives | a6207 | — | — | — | — | — | — | — | — | — | — | — | — |
| Other Accounts Receivable | a6208 | 26,002 | 30,798 | 36,155 | 37,342 | 36,837 | 40,883 | 40,457 | 52,735 | 59,498 | 68,315 | 69,414 | 62,055 |
| By debtor | | | | | | | | | | | | | |
| Domestic | a621 | .... | .... | .... | .... | .... | .... | .... | .... | .... | .... | .... | .... |
| Foreign | a622 | .... | .... | .... | .... | .... | .... | .... | .... | .... | .... | .... | .... |
| Liabilities | a63 | 452,361 | 465,103 | 460,500 | 451,017 | 526,148 | 668,430 | 721,045 | 832,824 | 961,136 | 1,071,571 | 1,227,301 | 1,261,941 |
| By instrument | | | | | | | | | | | | | |
| Special Drawing Rights (SDRs) | a6301 | — | — | — | — | — | — | — | — | — | — | — | — |
| Currency & Deposits | a6302 | 2,543 | 2,798 | 3,064 | 3,307 | 3,420 | 3,468 | 3,584 | 3,685 | 3,681 | 3,696 | 3,847 | 4,056 |
| Securities other than Shares | a6303 | 352,127 | 357,439 | 341,241 | 323,750 | 379,109 | 498,918 | 527,283 | 609,640 | 674,834 | 812,063 | 960,528 | 1,005,058 |
| Loans | a6304 | 66,885 | 66,897 | 67,308 | 66,873 | 79,970 | 92,555 | 111,449 | 129,146 | 217,157 | 196,598 | 204,739 | 194,557 |
| Shares and Other Equity | a6305 | — | — | — | — | — | 2,250 | 2,250 | 2,250 | — | — | — | — |
| Insurance Technical Reserves | a6306 | — | — | — | — | — | — | — | — | — | — | — | — |
| Financial Derivatives | a6307 | — | — | — | — | — | — | — | — | — | — | — | — |
| Other Accounts Payable | a6308 | 30,805 | 37,969 | 48,887 | 57,087 | 63,649 | 71,240 | 76,479 | 88,103 | 65,463 | 59,213 | 58,187 | 58,270 |
| By creditor | | | | | | | | | | | | | |
| Domestic | a631 | .... | .... | .... | .... | .... | .... | .... | .... | .... | .... | .... | .... |
| Foreign | a632 | .... | .... | .... | .... | .... | .... | .... | .... | .... | .... | .... | .... |
| Net Financial Worth [62-63] | a6m2 | −288,982 | −265,897 | −223,009 | −187,532 | −248,402 | −364,263 | −426,188 | −514,345 | −616,496 | −725,699 | −862,896 | −895,631 |
| Memo Item: Debt at Market Value | a6m3 | 452,360 | 465,103 | 460,500 | 451,017 | 526,148 | 666,181 | 718,795 | 830,574 | 961,135 | 1,071,570 | 1,227,301 | 1,261,941 |
| Memo Item: Debt at Face Value | a6m35 | 420,693 | 431,448 | 441,055 | 440,885 | 503,420 | 639,940 | 725,738 | 831,633 | 956,189 | 1,025,254 | 1,091,924 | 1,130,453 |
| Memo Item: Maastricht Debt | a6m36 | 389,888 | 393,479 | 392,168 | 383,798 | 439,771 | 568,700 | 649,259 | 743,530 | 890,726 | 966,041 | 1,033,737 | 1,072,183 |
| Memo Item: Debt at Nominal Value | a6m4 | .... | .... | .... | .... | .... | .... | .... | .... | .... | .... | .... | .... |

# Spain 184

| National Accounts | | 2004 | 2005 | 2006 | 2007 | 2008 | 2009 | 2010 | 2011 | 2012 | 2013 | 2014 | 2015 |
|---|---|---|---|---|---|---|---|---|---|---|---|---|---|
| | | | | | | | *Billions of Euros:* | | | | | | |
| Househ.Cons.Expend.,incl.NPISHs.... | 96f.c | 499 | 537 | 577 | 616 | 634 | 605 | 619 | 623 | 619 | 610 | 625 | 622 |
| Government Consumption Expend... | 91f.c | 148 | 161 | 175 | 191 | 210 | 221 | 222 | 220 | 207 | 204 | 203 | 209 |
| Gross Fixed Capital Formation.......... | 93e.c | 246 | 278 | 313 | 336 | 326 | 262 | 249 | 230 | 208 | 194 | 200 | 220 |
| Changes in Inventories..................... | 93i.c | 2 | 1 | 2 | 3 | 4 | 3 | 6 | 5 | 5 | 5 | 6 | 3 |
| Exports of Goods and Services.......... | 90c.c | 217 | 230 | 251 | 278 | 283 | 245 | 276 | 310 | 320 | 331 | 339 | 358 |
| Imports of Goods and Services (-)..... | 98c.c | 250 | 276 | 310 | 343 | 340 | 257 | 290 | 312 | 303 | 295 | 314 | 331 |
| Gross Domestic Product (GDP)......... | 99b.c | 861 | 931 | 1,008 | 1,081 | 1,116 | 1,079 | 1,081 | 1,075 | 1,055 | 1,049 | 1,058 | 1,081 |
| Net Primary Income from Abroad..... | 98.nc | .... | .... | .... | .... | .... | .... | .... | .... | .... | .... | .... | .... |
| Gross National Income (GNI)........... | 99a | 830 | 896 | 969 | 1,029 | 1,059 | 1,028 | 1,036 | 1,042 | 1,017 | 1,015 | .... | .... |
| Net Current Transf.from Abroad....... | 98t | −5 | −7 | −10 | −10 | −12 | −11 | −10 | −9 | −8 | −8 | .... | .... |
| Gross Nat'l Disposable Inc.(GNDI).... | 99i | 825 | 889 | 959 | 1,019 | 1,047 | 1,017 | 1,023 | 1,016 | 1,009 | 1,006 | .... | .... |
| Gross Saving................................... | 99s | 189 | 201 | 216 | 221 | 212 | 200 | 193 | 181 | 191 | 195 | .... | .... |
| Consumption of Fixed Capital.......... | 99cf | 116 | 128 | 141 | 152 | 161 | 163 | 167 | 168 | 169 | 168 | .... | .... |
| GDP Volume 2010 Ref., Chained..... | 99b.r | 989 | 1,025 | 1,068 | 1,108 | 1,121 | 1,081 | 1,081 | 1,074 | 1,052 | 1,039 | 1,053 | 1,072 |
| GDP Volume (2010=100)............... | 99bvr | 91.5 | 94.9 | 98.8 | 102.5 | 103.7 | 100.0 | 100.0 | 99.4 | 97.3 | 96.1 | 97.4 | 99.1 |
| GDP Deflator (2010=100)............... | 99bir | 87.1 | 90.8 | 94.4 | 97.5 | 99.6 | 99.8 | 100.0 | 100.1 | 100.3 | 101.0 | 100.5 | 100.9 |
| | | | | | | | *Millions: Midyear Estimates* | | | | | | |
| Population................................. | 99z | 43.17 | 43.85 | 44.54 | 45.21 | 45.82 | 46.30 | 46.60 | 46.71 | 46.64 | 46.46 | 46.26 | 46.12 |

# Sri Lanka 524

| | | 2004 | 2005 | 2006 | 2007 | 2008 | 2009 | 2010 | 2011 | 2012 | 2013 | 2014 | 2015 |
|---|---|---|---|---|---|---|---|---|---|---|---|---|---|
| **Exchange Rates** | | | | | | *Rupees per SDR: End of Period* | | | | | | | |
| Market Rate | aa | 162.453 | 145.953 | 162.032 | 171.804 | 174.266 | 179.319 | 170.871 | 174.869 | 195.436 | 201.360 | 189.865 | 199.631 |
| | | | | | | *Rupees per US Dollar: End of Period (ae) Period Average (rf)* | | | | | | | |
| Market Rate | ae | 104.605 | 102.117 | 107.706 | 108.719 | 113.140 | 114.384 | 110.953 | 113.901 | 127.161 | 130.753 | 131.049 | 144.062 |
| Market Rate | rf | 101.194 | 100.498 | 103.914 | 110.623 | 108.334 | 114.945 | 113.064 | 110.565 | 127.603 | 129.069 | 130.565 | 135.857 |
| **Fund Position** | | | | | | *Millions of SDRs: End of Period* | | | | | | | |
| Quota | 2f.s | 413.40 | 413.40 | 413.40 | 413.40 | 413.40 | 413.40 | 413.40 | 413.40 | 413.40 | 413.40 | 413.40 | 413.40 |
| SDR Holdings | 1b.s | .12 | 1.06 | 1.80 | 4.31 | 1.27 | 12.80 | 1.60 | 2.87 | 2.52 | 10.09 | 6.32 | 4.86 |
| Reserve Position in the Fund | 1c.s | 47.86 | 47.86 | 47.86 | 47.86 | 47.86 | 47.86 | 47.86 | 47.86 | 47.86 | 47.86 | 47.86 | 47.86 |
| Total Fund Cred.&Loans Outstg. | 2tl | 189.26 | 266.78 | 162.41 | 158.97 | 109.48 | 460.08 | 851.16 | 1,119.08 | 1,633.32 | 1,334.94 | 861.25 | 499.53 |
| SDR Allocations | 1bd | 70.87 | 70.87 | 70.87 | 70.87 | 70.87 | 395.46 | 395.46 | 395.46 | 395.46 | 395.46 | 395.46 | 395.46 |
| **International Liquidity** | | | | | | *Millions of US Dollars Unless Otherwise Indicated: End of Period* | | | | | | | |
| Total Reserves minus Gold | 1l.d | 2,132 | 2,650 | 2,726 | 3,380 | 2,469 | 4,616 | 6,710 | 6,248 | 6,378 | 6,611 | 7,316 | 6,543 |
| SDR Holdings | 1b.d | — | 2 | 3 | 7 | 2 | 20 | 2 | 4 | 4 | 16 | 9 | 7 |
| Reserve Position in the Fund | 1c.d | 74 | 68 | 72 | 76 | 74 | 75 | 74 | 73 | 74 | 74 | 69 | 66 |
| Foreign Exchange | 1d.d | 2,057 | 2,580 | 2,652 | 3,297 | 2,393 | 4,521 | 6,634 | 6,170 | 6,300 | 6,522 | 7,237 | 6,470 |
| Gold (Million Fine Troy Ounces) | 1ad | .167 | .167 | .167 | .167 | .170 | .678 | .346 | .321 | .438 | .738 | .742 | .716 |
| Gold (National Valuation) | 1and | 73 | 86 | 111 | 129 | 92 | 742 | 487 | 500 | 727 | 884 | 893 | 760 |
| Monetary Authorities: Other Liabs. | 4..d | 409 | 431 | 408 | 514 | 823 | 1,113 | 1,992 | 3,165 | 3,289 | 2,950 | 2,390 | 2,830 |
| Deposit Money Banks: Assets | 7a.d | 1,243 | 1,466 | 1,169 | 1,448 | 1,238 | 1,658 | 1,408 | 1,231 | 1,480 | 1,078 | 1,676 | 2,033 |
| Deposit Money Banks: Liabs. | 7b.d | 1,066 | 1,422 | 1,713 | 2,046 | 1,861 | 1,763 | 2,578 | 3,366 | 4,801 | 5,709 | 6,811 | 8,103 |
| **Monetary Authorities** | | | | | | *Millions of Rupees: End of Period* | | | | | | | |
| Foreign Assets | 11 | 225,223 | 281,106 | 301,334 | 377,525 | 281,310 | 620,388 | 800,087 | 774,684 | 894,521 | 1,012,329 | 1,093,230 | 1,066,994 |
| Claims on Central Government | 12a | 117,630 | 91,345 | 116,523 | 104,291 | 222,875 | 117,331 | 98,377 | 259,165 | 259,965 | 112,091 | 265,691 | 253,864 |
| Claims on Private Sector | 12d | 58 | 36 | 52 | 46 | 43 | 1,168 | 654 | 170 | 280 | 79 | 603 | 108 |
| Claims on Deposit Money Banks | 12e | 2,547 | 5,670 | 4,666 | 4,272 | 16,960 | 3,268 | 4,424 | 21,805 | 28,451 | 14,333 | 4,167 | 1,049 |
| Reserve Money | 14 | 171,852 | 198,852 | 241,211 | 265,833 | 269,656 | 305,863 | 363,594 | 441,302 | 485,048 | 488,997 | 578,217 | 673,855 |
| of which: Currency Outside DMBs | 14a | 99,669 | 114,070 | 135,020 | 147,183 | 155,023 | 181,840 | 216,549 | 242,871 | 251,538 | 264,607 | 329,426 | 388,057 |
| Other Liabilities to DMBs | 14n | 7,213 | 14,107 | 562 | 18 | 13,743 | 6,000 | 18,400 | 14,089 | 7,015 | 84,601 | 328,252 | 105,465 |
| Liabs. of Central Bank: Securities | 16ac | — | — | — | — | — | 78,023 | 95,055 | — | — | — | — | — |
| Restricted Deposits | 16b | 8 | 199 | 7 | 2 | 7 | 3 | 6 | 4 | 4 | 5 | 5 | 3 |
| Foreign Liabilities | 16c | 85,048 | 93,330 | 81,697 | 95,384 | 124,489 | 280,746 | 434,028 | 625,401 | 814,685 | 734,133 | 551,749 | 586,417 |
| Central Government Deposits | 16d | — | — | — | — | — | — | — | — | — | — | — | — |
| Capital Accounts | 17a | 88,897 | 78,605 | 105,510 | 133,648 | 123,208 | 134,271 | 125,823 | 161,247 | 189,034 | 118,638 | 82,517 | 55,219 |
| Other Items (Net) | 17r | −7,559 | −6,936 | −6,413 | −8,751 | −9,915 | −62,752 | −133,364 | −186,151 | −312,771 | −287,018 | −177,025 | −98,945 |
| **Deposit Money Banks** | | | | | | *Millions of Rupees: End of Period* | | | | | | | |
| Reserves | 20 | 70,904 | 87,481 | 107,936 | 119,500 | 115,508 | 123,885 | 146,809 | 200,073 | 235,987 | 226,363 | 251,897 | 303,289 |
| Claims on Mon.Author.:Securities | 20c | — | — | — | — | — | 78,023 | 90,120 | — | — | — | — | — |
| Other Claims on Monetary Author. | 20n | 7,213 | 14,107 | 562 | 18 | 13,743 | 6,000 | 18,400 | 14,089 | 7,015 | 84,601 | 328,252 | 105,465 |
| Foreign Assets | 21 | 129,987 | 149,654 | 125,868 | 157,454 | 140,074 | 189,657 | 156,222 | 140,223 | 188,157 | 140,967 | 219,630 | 292,900 |
| Claims on Central Government | 22a | 124,877 | 188,069 | 277,911 | 311,749 | 379,197 | 551,821 | 581,349 | 621,309 | 839,173 | 1,153,909 | 1,022,930 | 1,497,433 |
| Claims on Nonfin.Pub.Enterprises | 22ca | 41,171 | 9,672 | 24,555 | 42,167 | 46,991 | 73,233 | 144,578 | 198,500 | 292,477 | 365,098 | 446,047 | 522,966 |
| Claims on Cooperatives | 22cb | 1,148 | 1,256 | 1,135 | 1,464 | 1,948 | 1,830 | 1,829 | 2,131 | 2,453 | 1,976 | 1,936 | 1,828 |
| Claims on Private Sector | 22d | 640,162 | 806,893 | 998,324 | 1,190,054 | 1,265,653 | 1,195,034 | 1,491,078 | 2,004,901 | 2,356,009 | 2,532,407 | 2,756,275 | 3,447,792 |
| Demand Deposits | 24 | 88,777 | 116,620 | 124,657 | 119,407 | 122,285 | 154,849 | 190,637 | 195,835 | 198,496 | 219,966 | 282,722 | 326,905 |
| Time and Savings Deposits | 25 | 670,191 | 791,576 | 944,866 | 1,137,426 | 1,245,453 | 1,469,459 | 1,684,216 | 2,053,032 | 2,479,021 | 2,933,275 | 3,263,698 | 3,850,929 |
| Foreign Liabilities | 26c | 111,464 | 145,249 | 184,535 | 222,389 | 210,531 | 201,696 | 286,052 | 383,427 | 610,494 | 746,461 | 892,522 | 1,167,266 |
| Central Government Deposits | 26d | 19,802 | 27,063 | 33,426 | 38,746 | 27,384 | 27,459 | 49,458 | 64,531 | 79,799 | 51,175 | 64,954 | 73,354 |
| Credit from Monetary Authorities | 26g | 6,502 | 9,174 | 9,375 | 8,773 | 7,949 | 7,578 | 10,216 | 10,582 | 9,456 | 8,285 | 7,696 | 8,453 |
| Capital Accounts | 27a | 77,220 | 110,928 | 136,834 | 168,506 | 183,183 | 191,017 | 237,814 | 313,334 | 375,920 | 444,945 | 528,661 | 608,898 |
| Other Items (Net) | 27r | 41,506 | 56,520 | 102,598 | 127,161 | 166,328 | 167,426 | 171,991 | 160,484 | 168,085 | 101,214 | −13,287 | 135,869 |
| **Monetary Survey** | | | | | | *Millions of Rupees: End of Period* | | | | | | | |
| Foreign Assets (Net) | 31n | 158,698 | 192,180 | 160,969 | 217,207 | 86,364 | 327,602 | 236,229 | −93,921 | −342,501 | −327,298 | −131,411 | −393,789 |
| Domestic Credit | 32 | 905,245 | 1,070,207 | 1,385,074 | 1,611,027 | 1,889,322 | 1,912,958 | 2,268,407 | 3,021,713 | 3,670,356 | 4,114,909 | 4,428,552 | 5,650,637 |
| Claims on Central Govt. (Net) | 32an | 222,706 | 252,350 | 361,008 | 377,295 | 574,688 | 641,693 | 630,268 | 815,943 | 1,019,339 | 1,214,824 | 1,223,667 | 1,677,943 |
| Claims on Nonfin.Pub.Enterprises | 32ca | 41,171 | 9,672 | 24,555 | 42,167 | 46,991 | 73,233 | 144,578 | 198,500 | 292,477 | 365,098 | 446,047 | 522,966 |
| Claims on Cooperatives | 32cb | 1,148 | 1,256 | 1,135 | 1,464 | 1,948 | 1,830 | 1,829 | 2,131 | 2,453 | 1,976 | 1,936 | 1,828 |
| Claims on Private Sector | 32d | 640,220 | 806,929 | 998,376 | 1,190,100 | 1,265,695 | 1,196,202 | 1,491,732 | 2,005,139 | 2,356,087 | 2,533,011 | 2,756,901 | 3,447,900 |
| Money | 34 | 189,339 | 231,621 | 261,033 | 268,005 | 278,553 | 339,036 | 410,275 | 440,505 | 450,734 | 484,990 | 612,460 | 715,390 |
| Quasi-Money | 35 | 670,191 | 791,576 | 944,866 | 1,137,426 | 1,245,453 | 1,469,459 | 1,684,216 | 2,053,032 | 2,479,021 | 2,933,275 | 3,263,698 | 3,850,929 |
| Liabs. of Central Bank: Securities | 36ac | — | — | — | — | — | — | 4,935 | — | — | — | — | — |
| Restricted Deposits | 36b | 8 | 199 | 7 | 2 | 7 | 3 | 6 | 4 | 4 | 5 | 5 | 3 |
| Capital Accounts | 37a | 166,117 | 189,533 | 242,344 | 302,154 | 306,391 | 325,287 | 363,637 | 474,581 | 564,954 | 563,583 | 611,178 | 664,118 |
| Other Items (Net) | 37r | 38,289 | 49,458 | 97,794 | 120,645 | 145,281 | 106,775 | 41,568 | −40,331 | −166,859 | −194,241 | −190,201 | 26,408 |
| Money plus Quasi-Money | 35l | 859,529 | 1,023,197 | 1,205,898 | 1,405,432 | 1,524,006 | 1,808,495 | 2,094,491 | 2,493,537 | 2,929,756 | 3,418,264 | 3,876,158 | 4,566,319 |
| **Money (National Definitions)** | | | | | | *Millions of Rupees: End of Period* | | | | | | | |
| Reserve Money | 19mb | .... | .... | .... | .... | 268,425 | 303,537 | 360,511 | 439,504 | 484,362 | 488,586 | 577,912 | 673,432 |
| Narrow Money | 59ma | .... | .... | .... | .... | 277,323 | 336,710 | 407,192 | 438,707 | 450,049 | 484,578 | 612,155 | 714,967 |
| Broad Money | 59mb | .... | .... | .... | .... | 1,282,194 | 1,536,755 | 1,813,000 | 2,192,603 | 2,593,185 | 3,058,793 | 3,460,558 | 4,057,191 |
| **Interest Rates** | | | | | | *Percent Per Annum* | | | | | | | |
| Discount Rate (End of Period) | 60.a | 15.00 | 15.00 | 15.00 | 15.00 | 15.00 | 15.00 | 15.00 | 15.00 | 15.00 | 15.00 | 15.00 | 15.00 |
| Money Market Rate | 60b | 8.87 | 10.15 | 12.89 | 30.88 | 21.22 | 11.67 | 9.02 | 8.15 | 10.11 | 8.76 | 6.62 | 6.35 |
| Treasury Bill Rate | 60c | 7.71 | 9.03 | 10.98 | 16.60 | 18.91 | 12.93 | 8.57 | 7.63 | 12.10 | 10.68 | 6.60 | 6.65 |
| Deposit Rate | 60l | 5.07 | 5.64 | 6.80 | 9.08 | 10.89 | 10.61 | 6.90 | 6.43 | 8.67 | 10.23 | 7.50 | 5.99 |
| Lending Rate | 60p | 9.47 | 10.76 | 12.85 | 17.08 | 18.89 | 15.67 | 10.22 | 9.41 | 13.28 | 12.62 | 7.84 | 6.96 |

| | | 2004 | 2005 | 2006 | 2007 | 2008 | 2009 | 2010 | 2011 | 2012 | 2013 | 2014 | 2015 |
|---|---|---|---|---|---|---|---|---|---|---|---|---|---|
| **Prices and Labor** | | \textit{Index Numbers (2010=100): Period Averages} | | | | | | | | | | | |
| Share Prices (End of Month) | 62.ep | 26.6 | 39.1 | 45.2 | 51.5 | 43.9 | 46.9 | 100.0 | 134.0 | 104.2 | 115.0 | 129.3 | 138.0 |
| Wholesale Prices | 63 | 48.5 | 54.1 | 60.4 | 75.1 | 93.9 | 89.9 | 100.0 | .... | .... | .... | .... | .... |
| Consumer Prices | 64 | 52.2 | † 58.3 | 64.1 | 74.2 | † 91.0 | 94.1 | 100.0 | 106.7 | 114.8 | 122.7 | 126.7 | 127.9 |
| Wages: Agr. Minimum Rates | 65 | 42.0 | 45.9 | 47.1 | 54.7 | 68.7 | 70.6 | 100.0 | .... | .... | .... | .... | .... |
| | | \textit{Number in Thousands: Period Averages} | | | | | | | | | | | |
| Labor Force | 67d | 8,043 | 8,126 | 7,602 | 7,489 | 7,569 | 7,572 | 7,610 | 7,738 | .... | 8,802 | 8,786 | .... |
| Employment | 67e | 7,362 | 7,518 | 7,104 | 7,042 | 7,175 | 7,140 | 7,236 | 7,430 | .... | 8,418 | 8,405 | .... |
| Unemployment | 67c | 680 | 623 | 498 | 447 | 394 | 433 | 375 | 308 | .... | 384 | 381 | .... |
| Unemployment Rate (%) | 67r | 8.5 | 7.7 | 6.5 | 6.0 | 5.2 | 5.7 | 4.9 | 4.0 | .... | 4.4 | 4.3 | .... |
| **Intl. Transactions & Positions** | | \textit{Millions of Rupees} | | | | | | | | | | | |
| Exports | 70 | 583,968 | 638,275 | 716,579 | 856,806 | 881,320 | 813,911 | 937,737 | 1,167,588 | 1,245,531 | 1,342,971 | .... | .... |
| Tea | 70s | 74,898 | 81,483 | 91,667 | 113,565 | 137,599 | 136,171 | 155,376 | .... | .... | .... | .... | .... |
| Imports, c.i.f. | 71 | 808,364 | 888,358 | 1,066,615 | 1,251,136 | 1,510,732 | 1,154,388 | 1,526,604 | 2,241,488 | 2,441,879 | 2,322,677 | .... | .... |
| | | \textit{2010=100} | | | | | | | | | | | |
| Volume of Exports | 72 | 81.3 | 86.6 | 74.5 | 96.5 | 96.9 | 85.0 | 100.0 | .... | .... | .... | .... | .... |
| Tea | 72s | 95.6 | 98.3 | 104.2 | 99.2 | 101.7 | 92.2 | 100.0 | .... | .... | .... | .... | .... |
| Volume of Imports | 73 | 82.4 | 84.8 | 91.0 | 94.5 | 99.3 | 88.3 | 100.0 | .... | .... | .... | .... | .... |
| Unit Value of Exports | 74 | 68.4 | 70.0 | 75.7 | 83.8 | 86.8 | 91.0 | 100.0 | .... | .... | .... | .... | .... |
| Tea | 74s | 50.4 | 53.3 | 56.6 | 73.7 | 87.1 | 95.1 | 100.0 | .... | .... | .... | .... | .... |
| Unit Value of Imports (2000=100) | 75 | .... | .... | 151.5 | 75.9 | 67.0 | 83.0 | .... | .... | .... | .... | .... | .... |
| **Balance of Payments** | | \textit{Millions of US Dollars} | | | | | | | | | | | |
| A. Current Account* | 109bx | −677.2 | −742.7 | −1,598.6 | −1,497.7 | −3,986.2 | −292.0 | −1,127.5 | −4,675.1 | † −4,009.1 | −2,540.6 | −1,987.7 | −2,008.5 |
| Goods, credit (exports) | 1a9cx | 5,757.2 | 6,346.7 | 6,882.6 | 7,639.9 | 8,110.6 | 7,084.5 | 8,625.8 | 10,558.8 | † 9,773.5 | 10,394.3 | 11,130.1 | 10,504.9 |
| Goods, debit (imports) | 1a9dx | 7,199.8 | 7,976.9 | 9,227.6 | 10,166.9 | 12,682.1 | 9,185.9 | 12,105.9 | 18,241.9 | † 19,190.2 | 18,002.8 | 19,416.8 | 18,934.6 |
| Balance on goods | 1a9bx | −1,442.6 | −1,630.1 | −2,345.0 | −2,527.0 | −4,571.5 | −2,101.4 | −3,480.0 | −7,683.1 | † −9,416.7 | −7,608.5 | −8,286.7 | −8,429.7 |
| Services, credit (exports) | 1b9cx | 1,526.6 | 1,540.1 | 1,624.9 | 1,775.0 | 2,002.4 | 1,892.4 | 2,474.2 | 3,083.9 | † 3,799.9 | 4,685.1 | 5,605.0 | 6,396.7 |
| Services, debit (imports) | 1b9dx | 1,907.9 | 2,088.7 | 2,393.6 | 2,601.8 | 3,009.9 | 2,522.5 | 3,112.7 | 4,011.9 | † 2,538.4 | 3,505.2 | 3,724.9 | 4,071.9 |
| Balance on Goods & Services | 1z9bx | −1,823.9 | −2,178.7 | −3,113.7 | −3,353.7 | −5,579.0 | −2,731.5 | −4,118.5 | −8,611.2 | † −8,155.2 | −6,428.7 | −6,406.6 | −6,104.9 |
| Primary income: credit | 1c9cx | 156.7 | 75.9 | 311.6 | 449.1 | 224.9 | 121.7 | 323.3 | 466.6 | † 142.3 | 131.8 | 155.2 | 127.3 |
| Primary income: debit | 1c9dx | 360.3 | 375.4 | 700.0 | 806.9 | 1,197.3 | 609.4 | 940.1 | 1,113.7 | † 1,388.2 | 1,883.2 | 1,963.3 | 2,224.3 |
| Balance on gds, serv. & prim. inc. | 1y9bx | −2,027.4 | −2,478.2 | −3,502.1 | −3,711.5 | −6,551.4 | −3,219.2 | −4,735.3 | −9,258.2 | † −9,401.1 | −8,180.1 | −8,214.7 | −8,201.8 |
| Secondary income: credit | 1d9ca | 1,563.9 | 1,968.5 | 2,161.0 | 2,501.5 | 2,918.0 | 3,330.2 | 4,116.0 | 5,144.8 | † 6,038.3 | 6,427.9 | 7,045.8 | 7,007.0 |
| Secondary income: debit | 1d9da | 213.7 | 232.9 | 257.5 | 287.8 | 352.8 | 403.0 | 508.1 | 561.7 | † 646.3 | 788.4 | 818.7 | 813.7 |
| B. Capital Account* | 209ba | 55.0 | 242.0 | 281.1 | 259.1 | 279.7 | 221.2 | 150.5 | 144.4 | † 130.3 | 70.9 | 58.3 | 46.3 |
| Capital account: credit | 209ca | 55.0 | 242.0 | 281.1 | 259.1 | 279.7 | 221.2 | 150.5 | 144.4 | † 145.8 | 89.6 | 72.8 | 70.7 |
| Capital account: debit | 209da | — | — | — | — | — | — | — | — | † 15.5 | 18.7 | 14.6 | 24.4 |
| Balance on current & capital acct. | 129bx | −622.2 | −500.7 | −1,317.5 | −1,238.7 | −3,706.5 | −70.8 | −977.0 | −4,530.7 | † −3,878.8 | −2,469.7 | −1,929.4 | −1,962.2 |
| C. Financial Account* | 309na | 132.5 | −67.1 | −687.1 | −14.2 | −4.3 | 1,105.4 | 952.0 | −1,727.2 | † −4,243.8 | −4,628.3 | −3,803.9 | −3,127.5 |
| Direct investment: assets | 3a9aa | 5.8 | 38.4 | 29.3 | 55.0 | 61.7 | 20.0 | 42.5 | 60.0 | † 63.9 | 65.1 | 66.8 | 53.3 |
| Equity & investment fund shares | 3aaaa | — | — | — | 55.0 | 61.7 | 20.0 | 42.5 | 60.0 | † 63.9 | 65.1 | 66.8 | 53.3 |
| Debt instruments | 3abaa | 5.8 | 38.4 | 29.3 | .... | .... | .... | .... | .... | .... | .... | .... | .... |
| Direct investment: liabilities | 3a9la | 232.8 | 272.4 | 479.7 | 603.0 | 752.2 | 404.0 | 477.6 | 955.9 | † 941.1 | 932.6 | 893.6 | 681.2 |
| Equity & investment fund shares | 3aala | 222.8 | 272.4 | 479.7 | 444.0 | 542.2 | 173.0 | 239.6 | 251.1 | † 360.1 | 410.4 | 468.6 | 425.7 |
| Debt instruments | 3abla | 10.0 | — | — | 159.0 | 210.0 | 231.0 | 237.9 | 704.8 | † 581.0 | 522.1 | 425.0 | 255.6 |
| Portfolio investment: assets | 3b9aa | −111.3 | −275.9 | −355.0 | −326.0 | 174.4 | 47.4 | −171.9 | — | † −10.0 | — | −.2 | — |
| Equity & investment fund shares | 3baaa | −111.3 | −275.9 | −355.0 | −423.0 | −547.9 | −375.0 | −818.8 | — | .... | .... | .... | .... |
| Debt securities | 3bbaa | — | — | — | 97.0 | 722.3 | 422.4 | 646.9 | — | † −10.0 | — | −.2 | — |
| Portfolio investment: liabilities | 3b9la | −100.4 | −215.5 | −304.0 | −322.0 | −487.9 | −381.5 | −1,048.5 | 828.5 | † 2,116.1 | 2,068.4 | 2,065.0 | 688.9 |
| Equity & investment fund shares | 3bala | −100.4 | −215.5 | −304.0 | −322.0 | −487.9 | −381.5 | −1,048.5 | −171.4 | † 272.4 | 225.7 | 178.1 | −57.7 |
| Debt securities | 3bbla | — | — | — | — | — | — | — | 999.9 | † 1,843.7 | 1,842.8 | 1,887.0 | 746.6 |
| Fin. der.& empl.stk.ops.(ESOs): net. | 3c9na | — | — | — | — | .... | .... | .... | .... | .... | .... | .... | .... |
| Fin. der. & ESOs: assets | 3c9aa | .... | .... | .... | .... | .... | .... | .... | .... | .... | .... | .... | .... |
| Fin. der. & ESOs: liabilities | 3c9la | .... | .... | .... | .... | .... | .... | .... | .... | .... | .... | .... | .... |
| Other investment: assets | 3d9aa | 353.5 | 222.9 | −296.6 | 280.5 | −210.2 | 435.1 | −248.8 | −182.9 | † 362.6 | −191.1 | 972.9 | 553.0 |
| Other equity | 3daaa | .... | .... | .... | .... | .... | .... | .... | .... | .... | .... | .... | .... |
| Debt instruments | 3dzaa | 353.5 | 222.9 | −296.6 | 280.5 | −210.2 | 435.1 | −248.8 | −182.9 | † 362.6 | −191.1 | 972.9 | 553.0 |
| Other investment: liabilities | 3d9la | −17.0 | −4.4 | −110.9 | −257.3 | −234.1 | −625.4 | −759.2 | −180.1 | † 1,603.1 | 1,501.3 | 1,884.8 | 2,363.6 |
| Other equity | 3dala | .... | .... | .... | .... | .... | .... | .... | .... | .... | .... | .... | .... |
| Debt instruments | 3dzla | −17.0 | −4.4 | −110.9 | −257.3 | −234.1 | −625.4 | −759.2 | −180.1 | † 1,603.1 | 1,501.3 | 1,884.8 | 2,363.6 |
| Curr.+ cap.− finan. acct. balance | 4y9na | −754.7 | −433.5 | −630.4 | −1,224.4 | −3,702.2 | −1,176.2 | −1,929.0 | −2,803.4 | † 365.0 | 2,158.6 | 1,874.5 | 1,165.3 |
| D. Net Errors and Omissions | 409na | −180.1 | −64.8 | −86.6 | −149.8 | 734.4 | −127.6 | −852.7 | −268.4 | † −387.9 | −592.5 | 393.2 | −308.6 |
| E. Reserves and Related Items | 4z9na | −934.8 | −498.4 | −717.0 | −1,374.2 | −2,967.8 | −1,303.8 | −2,781.7 | −3,071.8 | † −23.0 | 1,566.1 | 2,267.6 | 856.7 |
| Reserve assets | 3e9aa | −133.5 | 539.8 | 73.0 | 675.2 | −1,111.4 | 3,289.9 | 2,069.1 | −15.2 | † 760.4 | 1,111.7 | 1,548.5 | 350.3 |
| Credit and loans from the IMF | 3dcla | −111.6 | 118.4 | −152.5 | −5.4 | −77.3 | 554.4 | 580.6 | 423.5 | † 783.4 | −454.4 | −719.1 | −506.4 |
| Exceptional financing | 409la | 912.9 | 919.7 | 942.5 | 2,054.8 | 1,933.7 | 4,039.3 | 4,270.2 | 2,633.2 | .... | .... | .... | .... |

*Excludes components in group E

# Sri Lanka   524

| | | 2004 | 2005 | 2006 | 2007 | 2008 | 2009 | 2010 | 2011 | 2012 | 2013 | 2014 | 2015 |
|---|---|---|---|---|---|---|---|---|---|---|---|---|---|
| **International Investment Position** | | | | | | | | *Millions of US Dollars* | | | | | |
| Assets................................. | 809aa | .... | .... | .... | .... | .... | .... | .... | † 8,414.4 | 9,192.2 | 9,455.9 | 11,185.9 | 10,887.3 |
| Direct investment...................... | 8a9aa | .... | .... | .... | .... | .... | .... | .... | † 423.7 | 475.1 | 540.2 | 607.0 | 660.2 |
| Equity & investment fund shares.. | 8aaaa | .... | .... | .... | .... | .... | .... | .... | † 420.4 | 471.8 | 536.9 | 603.7 | 657.0 |
| Debt instruments...................... | 8abaa | .... | .... | .... | .... | .... | .... | .... | † 3.3 | 3.3 | 3.3 | 3.3 | 3.3 |
| Portfolio investment.................. | 8b9aa | .... | .... | .... | .... | .... | .... | .... | † 10.3 | .... | .3 | .1 | .1 |
| Equity & investment fund shares.. | 8baaa | .... | .... | .... | .... | .... | .... | .... | .... | .... | .... | .... | .... |
| Debt securities........................ | 8bbaa | .... | .... | .... | .... | .... | .... | .... | † 10.3 | .... | .3 | .1 | .1 |
| Fin. der.(oth.than reserves) & ESOs | 8c9aa | .... | .... | .... | .... | .... | .... | .... | .... | .... | .... | .... | .... |
| Other investment...................... | 8d9aa | .... | .... | .... | .... | .... | .... | .... | † 1,231.1 | 1,611.2 | 1,420.2 | 2,370.4 | 2,923.3 |
| Other equity.......................... | 8daaa | .... | .... | .... | .... | .... | .... | .... | .... | .... | .... | .... | .... |
| Debt instruments.................... | 8dzaa | .... | .... | .... | .... | .... | .... | .... | † 1,231.1 | 1,611.2 | 1,420.2 | 2,370.4 | 2,923.3 |
| Reserve assets........................ | 8e9aa | .... | .... | .... | .... | .... | .... | .... | † 6,749.3 | 7,105.9 | 7,495.3 | 8,208.4 | 7,303.6 |
| Liabilities............................. | 809la | .... | .... | .... | .... | .... | .... | .... | † 39,429.0 | 45,601.7 | 47,808.5 | 52,811.2 | 53,586.3 |
| Direct investment...................... | 8a9la | .... | .... | .... | .... | .... | .... | .... | † 6,587.4 | 8,086.7 | 8,959.5 | 10,571.8 | 9,971.9 |
| Equity & investment fund shares.. | 8aala | .... | .... | .... | .... | .... | .... | .... | † 5,411.9 | 6,311.0 | 6,859.3 | 8,027.8 | 7,253.3 |
| Debt instruments...................... | 8abla | .... | .... | .... | .... | .... | .... | .... | † 1,175.5 | 1,775.6 | 2,100.2 | 2,544.0 | 2,718.6 |
| Portfolio investment.................. | 8b9la | .... | .... | .... | .... | .... | .... | .... | † 6,442.8 | 9,242.4 | 9,473.2 | 12,664.2 | 12,374.9 |
| Equity & investment fund shares.. | 8bala | .... | .... | .... | .... | .... | .... | .... | † 1,269.3 | 2,187.8 | 1,043.9 | 1,869.3 | 1,536.1 |
| Debt securities........................ | 8bbla | .... | .... | .... | .... | .... | .... | .... | † 5,173.5 | 7,054.6 | 8,429.3 | 10,794.9 | 10,838.8 |
| Fin. der.(oth.than reserves) & ESOs | 8c9la | .... | .... | .... | .... | .... | .... | .... | .... | .... | .... | .... | .... |
| Other investment...................... | 8d9la | .... | .... | .... | .... | .... | .... | .... | † 26,398.8 | 28,272.7 | 29,375.8 | 29,575.1 | 31,239.6 |
| Other equity.......................... | 8dala | .... | .... | .... | .... | .... | .... | .... | .... | .... | .... | .... | .... |
| Debt instruments.................... | 8dzla | .... | .... | .... | .... | .... | .... | .... | † 26,398.8 | 28,272.7 | 29,375.8 | 29,575.1 | 31,239.6 |

## Government Finance
### Cash Flow Statement
### Budgetary Central Government

| | | 2004 | 2005 | 2006 | 2007 | 2008 | 2009 | 2010 | 2011 | 2012 | 2013 | 2014 | 2015 |
|---|---|---|---|---|---|---|---|---|---|---|---|---|---|
| | | | | | | | | *Billions of Rupees: Fiscal Year Ends December 31* | | | | | |
| Cash Receipts:Operating Activities... | c1 | 320.05 | 412.31 | 506.89 | 595.01 | 686.48 | 725.57 | 834.19 | 949.92 | 1,066.70 | 1,153.31 | 1,187.02 | .... |
| Taxes................................... | c11 | 281.55 | 336.83 | 428.38 | 508.95 | 585.62 | 618.93 | 724.75 | 812.61 | 908.91 | 1,005.89 | 1,050.36 | .... |
| Social Contributions...................... | c12 | 3.44 | 4.91 | 6.47 | 8.78 | 6.79 | 11.17 | 11.12 | 12.63 | 11.74 | 15.15 | 14.92 | .... |
| Grants................................... | c13 | 8.68 | 32.64 | 30.07 | 30.51 | 31.22 | 25.92 | 16.91 | 15.14 | 16.07 | 15.86 | 9.42 | .... |
| Other Receipts............................ | c14 | 26.37 | 37.93 | 41.97 | 46.78 | 62.85 | 69.55 | 81.41 | 109.54 | 129.98 | 116.41 | 112.32 | .... |
| Cash Payments:Operating Activities. | c2 | 433.04 | 495.36 | 621.46 | 717.41 | 847.37 | 1,013.40 | 1,080.69 | 1,167.01 | 1,354.54 | 1,406.95 | 1,530.45 | .... |
| Compensation of Employees.......... | c21 | 106.19 | 138.60 | 175.03 | 214.16 | 239.08 | 271.23 | 300.56 | 319.60 | 347.75 | 393.23 | 440.98 | .... |
| Purchases of Goods & Services....... | c22 | 58.34 | 56.26 | 77.99 | 78.47 | 121.25 | 108.50 | 87.73 | 113.53 | 140.09 | 119.40 | 162.65 | .... |
| Interest................................. | c24 | 119.78 | 120.16 | 150.78 | 182.68 | 212.48 | 309.68 | 352.59 | 356.90 | 408.50 | 444.01 | 436.40 | .... |
| Subsidies............................... | c25 | 22.40 | 26.95 | 39.93 | 36.46 | 39.55 | 41.37 | 40.31 | 45.16 | 46.80 | 53.26 | 66.01 | .... |
| Grants................................... | c26 | 6.31 | 11.90 | 20.70 | 20.66 | 21.84 | 24.90 | 26.03 | 29.87 | 26.73 | 201.77 | 207.55 | .... |
| Social Benefits.......................... | c27 | 81.64 | 100.82 | 103.13 | 110.84 | 130.76 | 147.68 | 153.98 | 169.64 | 187.90 | 195.29 | 216.86 | .... |
| Other Payments......................... | c28 | 38.37 | 40.67 | 53.90 | 74.15 | 82.42 | 110.04 | 119.50 | 132.30 | 196.80 | — | — | .... |
| Net Cash Inflow:Operating Act.[1-2] | ccio | −112.99 | −83.06 | −114.58 | −122.40 | −160.89 | −287.84 | −246.50 | −217.09 | −287.85 | −253.64 | −343.43 | .... |
| Net Cash Outflow:Invest. in NFA...... | c31 | 40.34 | 88.06 | 87.70 | 110.97 | 128.83 | 143.51 | 158.25 | 202.11 | 175.73 | 252.54 | 234.70 | .... |
| Purchases of Nonfinancial Assets... | c31.1 | 40.45 | 88.14 | 88.21 | 111.51 | 128.95 | 143.59 | 158.49 | 202.63 | 176.56 | .... | .... | .... |
| Sales of Nonfinancial Assets.......... | c31.2 | .11 | .08 | .51 | .55 | .12 | .08 | .24 | .51 | .83 | .... | .... | .... |
| Cash Surplus/Deficit [1-2-31=1-2M] | ccsd | −153.33 | −171.12 | −202.27 | −233.36 | −289.72 | −431.35 | −404.75 | −419.20 | −463.58 | −506.18 | −578.13 | .... |
| Net Acq. Fin. Assets, excl. Cash....... | c32x | .98 | .26 | 3.47 | 12.68 | 19.81 | 44.94 | 41.03 | 30.46 | 25.39 | .... | .... | .... |
| Domestic................................. | c321x | .98 | .26 | 3.47 | 12.68 | 19.81 | 44.94 | 41.03 | 30.46 | 25.39 | .... | .... | .... |
| Foreign.................................. | c322x | — | — | — | — | — | — | — | — | — | .... | .... | .... |
| Net Incurrence of Liabilities.............. | c33 | 157.63 | 179.04 | 212.56 | 251.43 | 297.98 | 477.53 | 460.45 | 472.29 | 484.36 | 516.09 | 604.92 | .... |
| Domestic................................. | c331 | 120.56 | 131.26 | 170.62 | 150.52 | 302.63 | 246.72 | 216.66 | 253.33 | 197.90 | 392.39 | 392.39 | .... |
| Foreign.................................. | c332 | 37.07 | 47.77 | 41.94 | 100.91 | −4.64 | 230.81 | 243.79 | 218.96 | 286.46 | 123.70 | 212.52 | .... |
| Net Cash Inflow, Fin.Act.[-32x+33].. | cnfb | 156.65 | 178.78 | 209.09 | 238.75 | 278.17 | 432.59 | 419.43 | 441.82 | 458.96 | 506.18 | 591.80 | .... |
| Net Change in Stock of Cash........... | cncb | 3.32 | 7.66 | 6.82 | 5.39 | −11.54 | 1.17 | 14.43 | 22.11 | −4.61 | — | 13.67 | .... |
| Stat. Discrep. [32X-33+NCB-CSD].... | ccsdz | — | — | — | — | — | −.08 | −.24 | −.51 | .01 | — | — | .... |
| Memo Item:Cash Expenditure[2+31] | c2m | 473.38 | 583.42 | 709.16 | 828.37 | 976.20 | 1,156.91 | 1,238.94 | 1,369.12 | 1,530.27 | 1,659.49 | 1,765.15 | .... |
| Memo Item: Gross Debt.................. | c63 | 2,139.53 | 2,222.34 | 2,606.59 | 3,041.69 | .... | .... | 4,591.25 | 5,133.37 | 6,000.11 | 6,793.25 | 7,390.90 | .... |

## National Accounts

| | | 2004 | 2005 | 2006 | 2007 | 2008 | 2009 | 2010 | 2011 | 2012 | 2013 | 2014 | 2015 |
|---|---|---|---|---|---|---|---|---|---|---|---|---|---|
| | | | | | | | | *Millions of Rupees* | | | | | |
| Househ.Cons.Expend.,incl.NPISHs.... | 96f | 1,483,192 | 1,692,765 | 1,988,378 | 2,403,167 | 3,085,296 | 3,116,221 | 3,651,578 | 4,568,393 | 5,274,451 | 5,803,277 | 6,398,345 | .... |
| Government Consumption Expend... | 91f | 264,069 | 321,037 | 451,438 | 546,545 | 713,788 | 851,549 | 872,610 | 967,702 | 1,021,443 | 1,137,291 | 1,317,832 | .... |
| Gross Fixed Capital Formation.......... | 93e | 473,323 | 573,263 | 730,910 | 884,688 | 1,115,310 | 1,147,440 | 1,452,002 | 1,772,515 | 2,189,805 | 2,536,648 | 2,752,263 | .... |
| Changes in Inventories.................... | 93i | 54,693 | 84,756 | 91,330 | 115,632 | 99,938 | 34,009 | 93,498 | 186,968 | 128,448 | 23,566 | 152,724 | .... |
| Exports of Goods and Services......... | 90c | 738,713 | 793,153 | 885,381 | 1,041,935 | 1,095,679 | 1,031,289 | 1,254,021 | 1,508,565 | 1,730,467 | 1,949,158 | 2,185,039 | .... |
| Imports of Goods and Services (-)..... | 98c | 923,149 | 1,012,192 | 1,208,757 | 1,413,278 | 1,699,328 | 1,345,216 | 1,719,605 | 2,460,830 | 2,766,060 | 2,775,711 | 3,021,530 | .... |
| Gross Domestic Product (GDP)......... | 99b | 2,090,841 | 2,452,782 | 2,938,680 | 3,578,688 | 4,410,682 | 4,835,293 | 5,604,104 | 6,543,313 | 7,578,554 | 8,674,230 | 9,784,672 | .... |
| Statistical Discrepancy..................... | 99bs | .... | .... | .... | .... | .... | .... | .... | .... | .... | .... | .... | .... |
| Net Primary Income from Abroad..... | 98.n | −20,732 | −30,049 | −40,424 | −39,054 | −105,032 | −55,795 | −69,776 | −72,041 | −154,889 | −226,086 | −240,065 | .... |
| Gross National Income (GNI)........... | 99a | 2,070,109 | 2,422,733 | 2,898,256 | 3,539,634 | 4,305,650 | 4,779,498 | 5,534,328 | 6,471,272 | 7,423,665 | 8,448,144 | 9,544,608 | .... |
| GDP at Fact.Cost,Vol.'02 Prices........ | 99bap | 1,827,597 | 1,941,671 | 2,090,564 | 2,232,656 | 2,365,501 | 2,449,214 | 2,645,542 | 2,863,691 | 3,045,288 | 3,266,041 | 3,506,664 | .... |
| GDP Volume (2010=100)................ | 99bvp | 69.1 | 73.4 | 79.0 | 84.4 | 89.4 | 92.6 | 100.0 | 108.2 | 115.1 | 123.5 | 132.5 | .... |
| GDP Deflator (2010=100)............... | 99bip | 54.0 | 59.6 | 66.4 | 75.7 | 88.0 | 93.2 | 100.0 | 107.9 | 117.5 | 125.4 | 131.7 | .... |
| | | | | | | | | *Millions: Midyear Estimates* | | | | | |
| **Population**............................... | 99z | 19.74 | 19.95 | 20.14 | 20.30 | 20.45 | 20.60 | 20.76 | 20.93 | 21.10 | 21.27 | 21.45 | .... |

# Sudan 732

| | | 2004 | 2005 | 2006 | 2007 | 2008 | 2009 | 2010 | 2011 | 2012 | 2013 | 2014 | 2015 |
|---|---|---|---|---|---|---|---|---|---|---|---|---|---|
| **Exchange Rates** | | | | | | *Pounds per SDR: End of Period* | | | | | | | |
| Market Rate | aa | 3.892 | 3.295 | 3.029 | 3.244 | 3.364 | 3.511 | 3.823 | 4.110 | 6.810 | 8.772 | 8.653 | 8.442 |
| | | | | | | *Pounds per US Dollar: End of Period (ae) Period Average (rf)* | | | | | | | |
| Market Rate | ae | 2.506 | 2.305 | 2.013 | 2.053 | 2.184 | 2.240 | 2.482 | 2.677 | 4.431 | 5.696 | 5.972 | 6.092 |
| Market Rate | rf | 2.579 | 2.436 | 2.172 | 2.016 | 2.090 | 2.302 | 2.306 | 2.667 | 3.573 | 4.757 | 5.737 | 6.026 |
| **Fund Position** | | | | | | *Millions of SDRs: End of Period* | | | | | | | |
| Quota | 2f.s | 169.70 | 169.70 | 169.70 | 169.70 | 169.70 | 169.70 | 169.70 | 169.70 | 169.70 | 169.70 | 169.70 | 169.70 |
| SDR Holdings | 1b.s | — | .04 | — | — | — | 125.76 | 125.62 | 125.39 | 125.33 | 125.29 | 125.24 | 125.21 |
| Reserve Position in the Fund | 1c.s | .01 | .01 | .01 | .01 | .01 | .01 | .01 | .01 | .01 | .01 | .01 | .01 |
| Total Fund Cred.&Loans Outstg | 2tl | 381.75 | 362.61 | 344.27 | 305.09 | 263.65 | 256.76 | 252.95 | 246.25 | 241.43 | 236.64 | 229.59 | 224.22 |
| SDR Allocations | 1bd | 52.19 | 52.19 | 52.19 | 52.19 | 52.19 | 177.99 | 177.99 | 177.99 | 177.99 | 177.99 | 177.99 | 177.99 |
| **International Liquidity** | | | | | | *Millions of US Dollars Unless Otherwise Indicated: End of Period* | | | | | | | |
| Total Reserves minus Gold | 1l.d | 1,338.0 | 1,868.6 | 1,659.9 | 1,377.9 | 1,399.0 | 1,094.2 | 1,036.2 | 192.5 | 192.6 | 193.0 | 181.5 | 173.5 |
| SDR Holdings | 1b.d | — | .1 | — | — | — | 197.2 | 193.5 | 192.5 | 192.6 | 192.9 | 181.4 | 173.5 |
| Reserve Position in the Fund | 1c.d | — | — | — | — | — | — | — | — | — | — | — | — |
| Foreign Exchange | 1d.d | 1,338.0 | 1,868.5 | 1,659.9 | 1,377.9 | 1,399.0 | 897.0 | 842.8 | — | — | — | — | — |
| Central Bank: Other Assets | 3..d | 51.2 | 68.0 | † 41.1 | 40.6 | 50.9 | 49.7 | 63.6 | 54.6 | 53.7 | 55.5 | 51.0 | 47.7 |
| Central Bank: Other Liabs | 4..d | 1,920.1 | 1,961.0 | † 2,118.7 | 2,105.8 | 2,352.0 | 2,238.9 | 2,482.1 | 2,418.8 | 2,308.9 | 2,590.5 | 2,468.5 | 4,136.7 |
| Other Depository Corps.: Assets | 7a.d | 563.3 | 762.1 | † 883.9 | 1,057.6 | 1,231.9 | 991.7 | 1,444.4 | 929.9 | 1,109.9 | 824.4 | 862.2 | 600.9 |
| Other Depository Corps.: Assets | 7b.d | 72.3 | 120.1 | † 236.5 | 288.0 | 281.3 | 469.9 | 517.5 | 289.9 | 406.8 | 350.5 | 334.4 | 301.7 |
| **Central Bank** | | | | | | *Millions of Pounds: End of Period* | | | | | | | |
| Net Foreign Assets | 11n | −609 | 1,283 | † 33 | −770 | −1,059 | −2,276 | −2,444 | −3,319 | −3,312 | −6,357 | −6,796 | −19,858 |
| Claims on Nonresidents | 11 | 4,204 | 5,804 | † 4,298 | 3,552 | 4,078 | 2,739 | 3,560 | 3,156 | 6,868 | 8,397 | 7,946 | 5,344 |
| Liabilities to Nonresidents | 16c | 4,812 | 4,521 | † 4,266 | 4,322 | 5,137 | 5,015 | 6,004 | 6,475 | 10,180 | 14,755 | 14,742 | 25,202 |
| Claims on Other Depository Corps | 12e | 300 | 350 | † 1,078 | 2,376 | 3,028 | 4,073 | 3,124 | 3,485 | 4,095 | 5,156 | 7,041 | 10,965 |
| Net Claims on Central Government | 12an | 970 | 913 | † 2,777 | 3,824 | 3,481 | 5,162 | 7,769 | 13,256 | 22,530 | 29,641 | 34,753 | 39,898 |
| Claims on Central Government | 12a | 2,486 | 2,664 | † 3,170 | 3,912 | 5,277 | 6,234 | 8,360 | 14,011 | 23,384 | 30,647 | 36,179 | 40,872 |
| Liabilities to Central Government | 16d | 1,515 | 1,751 | † 393 | 87 | 1,796 | 1,072 | 591 | 755 | 854 | 1,006 | 1,426 | 974 |
| Claims on Other Sectors | 12s | 155 | 198 | † 433 | 411 | 468 | 352 | 410 | 456 | 786 | 978 | 894 | 1,170 |
| Claims on Other Financial Corps | 12g | — | — | † 132 | 116 | 39 | 19 | 63 | 58 | 62 | 186 | — | — |
| Claims on State & Local Govts | 12b | — | — | † — | — | — | — | — | — | — | — | — | — |
| Claims on Public Nonfin. Corps | 12c | 155 | 198 | † 301 | 295 | 429 | 333 | 346 | 397 | 724 | 792 | 894 | 1,170 |
| Claims on Private Sector | 12d | — | — | † — | — | — | — | — | — | — | — | — | — |
| Monetary Base | 14 | 4,622 | 6,410 | † 7,819 | 8,849 | 10,845 | 13,909 | 16,570 | 21,067 | 30,445 | 36,498 | 42,344 | 51,864 |
| Currency in Circulation | 14a | 3,197 | 3,982 | † 5,671 | 6,222 | 7,339 | 8,832 | 10,897 | 13,660 | 17,870 | 20,413 | 25,060 | 29,340 |
| Liabs. to Other Depository Corps | 14c | 1,223 | 1,940 | † 1,743 | 2,254 | 2,930 | 4,620 | 4,619 | 5,555 | 9,745 | 12,662 | 16,089 | 19,143 |
| Liabilities to Other Sectors | 14d | 202 | 488 | † 405 | 373 | 576 | 457 | 1,054 | 1,853 | 2,830 | 3,422 | 1,196 | 3,380 |
| Other Liabs. to Other Dep. Corps | 14n | 1 | 173 | † — | — | — | 134 | 190 | 230 | 392 | 677 | 597 | 521 |
| Dep. & Sec. Excl. f/Monetary Base | 14o | — | — | † — | — | — | — | — | — | 5,824 | 14,656 | 13,547 | 12,423 |
| Deposits Included in Broad Money | 15 | — | — | † — | — | — | — | — | — | — | — | — | — |
| Sec.Ot.th.Shares Incl.in Brd. Money | 16a | — | — | † — | — | — | — | — | — | — | — | — | — |
| Deposits Excl. from Broad Money | 16b | — | — | † — | — | — | — | — | — | 5,824 | 14,656 | 13,547 | 12,423 |
| Sec.Ot.th.Shares Excl.f/Brd.Money | 16s | — | — | † — | — | — | — | — | — | — | — | — | — |
| Loans | 16l | — | — | † — | — | — | — | — | — | — | — | — | — |
| Financial Derivatives | 16m | — | — | † — | — | — | — | — | — | — | — | — | — |
| Shares and Other Equity | 17a | −3,468 | −3,144 | † −3,319 | −3,591 | −3,609 | −4,515 | −5,027 | −3,494 | −9,113 | −17,185 | −18,415 | −20,715 |
| Other Items (Net) | 17r | −343 | −696 | † −179 | 583 | −1,319 | −2,217 | −2,875 | −3,926 | −3,450 | −5,230 | −2,182 | −11,917 |
| Memo Item: | | | | | | | | | | | | | |
| Total Assets | 10ra | 7,498.06 | 9,721.38 | † 9,970.95 | 10,906.14 | 16,257.63 | 17,778.28 | 20,002.99 | 26,451.34 | 41,920.17 | 51,811.32 | 57,012.90 | 76,051.26 |
| **Other Depository Corporations** | | | | | | *Millions of Pounds: End of Period* | | | | | | | |
| Net Foreign Assets | 21n | 1,231 | 1,480 | † 1,303 | 1,580 | 2,076 | 1,169 | 2,242 | 1,713 | 3,100 | 2,700 | 3,152 | 1,921 |
| Claims on Nonresidents | 21 | 1,412 | 1,757 | † 1,779 | 2,171 | 2,690 | 2,221 | 3,494 | 2,489 | 4,894 | 4,696 | 5,149 | 3,859 |
| Liabilities to Nonresidents | 26c | 181 | 277 | † 476 | 591 | 614 | 1,053 | 1,252 | 776 | 1,793 | 1,996 | 1,997 | 1,937 |
| Claims on Central Bank | 20 | 1,185 | 1,702 | † 2,097 | 2,936 | 3,453 | 5,750 | 5,870 | 6,879 | 13,223 | 14,529 | 18,986 | 21,915 |
| Currency | 20a | 148 | 221 | † 315 | 582 | 565 | 766 | 829 | 810 | 1,118 | 1,234 | 1,717 | 1,845 |
| Reserve Deposits and Securities | 20b | 1,037 | 1,481 | † 1,782 | 2,354 | 2,742 | 4,733 | 4,760 | 5,640 | 11,847 | 13,158 | 17,174 | 19,974 |
| Other Claims | 20n | — | — | † — | — | 147 | 250 | 281 | 429 | 258 | 137 | 95 | 96 |
| Net Claims on Central Government | 22an | 353 | 637 | † 1,507 | 1,367 | 1,527 | 2,923 | 3,980 | 6,044 | 7,120 | 7,464 | 8,707 | 11,113 |
| Claims on Central Government | 22a | 466 | 880 | † 1,681 | 1,533 | 2,293 | 3,594 | 4,907 | 6,132 | 7,277 | 7,590 | 8,773 | 11,191 |
| Liabilities to Central Government | 26d | 113 | 243 | † 173 | 166 | 766 | 671 | 927 | 88 | 157 | 126 | 67 | 79 |
| Claims on Other Sectors | 22s | 4,364 | 7,000 | † 11,677 | 12,999 | 14,961 | 18,163 | 21,186 | 22,867 | 30,483 | 37,657 | 44,321 | 53,457 |
| Claims on Other Financial Corps | 22g | 6 | 95 | † 261 | 526 | 982 | 627 | 618 | 403 | 312 | 444 | 1,364 | 1,903 |
| Claims on State & Local Govts | 22b | 13 | 6 | † 4 | 26 | — | 76 | 145 | 613 | 758 | 966 | 1,923 | 2,046 |
| Claims on Public Nonfin. Corps | 22c | 134 | 202 | † 552 | 687 | 1,268 | 1,947 | 2,464 | 2,424 | 2,446 | 3,213 | 5,114 | 7,901 |
| Claims on Private Sector | 22d | 4,212 | 6,697 | † 10,859 | 11,759 | 12,711 | 15,513 | 17,959 | 19,427 | 26,966 | 33,034 | 35,920 | 41,606 |
| Liabilities to Central Bank | 26g | 106 | 67 | † 146 | 390 | 790 | 1,657 | 891 | 721 | 1,213 | 1,544 | 2,851 | 4,326 |
| Transf.Dep.Included in Broad Money | 24 | 2,795 | 3,937 | † 5,599 | 6,483 | 7,575 | 9,362 | 11,031 | 12,999 | 17,864 | 20,414 | 24,258 | 29,115 |
| Other Dep.Included in Broad Money | 25 | 3,347 | 5,284 | † 6,447 | 7,228 | 8,021 | 10,520 | 13,715 | 14,522 | 21,304 | 23,416 | 28,920 | 33,951 |
| Sec.Ot.th.Shares Incl.in Brd. Money | 26a | — | — | † — | — | — | — | — | — | — | — | — | — |
| Deposits Excl. from Broad Money | 26b | — | — | † 20 | 30 | 52 | 205 | 114 | 61 | 129 | 78 | 109 | 89 |
| Sec.Ot.th.Shares Excl.f/Brd.Money | 26s | — | — | † — | — | — | — | — | — | — | — | — | — |
| Loans | 26l | 212 | 312 | † 69 | 27 | 54 | 48 | 55 | 36 | 43 | 42 | 43 | 100 |
| Financial Derivatives | 26m | — | — | † — | — | — | — | — | — | — | — | — | — |
| Insurance Technical Reserves | 26r | — | — | † — | — | — | — | — | — | — | — | — | — |
| Shares and Other Equity | 27a | 1,149 | 1,465 | † 3,137 | 4,177 | 4,784 | 6,285 | 7,181 | 8,108 | 10,899 | 12,993 | 14,848 | 16,838 |
| Other Items (Net) | 27r | −476 | −245 | † 1,166 | 547 | 742 | −73 | 292 | 1,056 | 2,475 | 3,862 | 4,136 | 3,986 |
| Memo Item: | | | | | | | | | | | | | |
| Total Assets | 20ra | 10,435.06 | 15,303.10 | † 23,144.28 | 26,197.43 | 30,649.86 | 36,666.89 | 43,107.74 | 46,504.08 | 67,049.56 | 77,479.76 | 92,317.05 | 108,937.57 |

# Sudan 732

| | | 2004 | 2005 | 2006 | 2007 | 2008 | 2009 | 2010 | 2011 | 2012 | 2013 | 2014 | 2015 |
|---|---|---|---|---|---|---|---|---|---|---|---|---|---|
| **Depository Corporations** | | *Millions of Pounds: End of Period* | | | | | | | | | | | |
| Net Foreign Assets............................ | 31n | 622 | 2,763 | † 1,336 | 810 | 1,017 | −1,107 | −202 | −1,605 | −212 | −3,658 | −3,644 | −17,937 |
| Claims on Nonresidents................ | 31 | 5,615 | 7,561 | † 6,078 | 5,723 | 6,768 | 4,960 | 7,054 | 5,646 | 11,762 | 13,093 | 13,095 | 9,203 |
| Liabilities to Nonresidents............. | 36c | 4,994 | 4,798 | † 4,742 | 4,914 | 5,751 | 6,067 | 7,256 | 7,251 | 11,973 | 16,751 | 16,739 | 27,140 |
| Domestic Claims........................... | 32 | 5,842 | 8,748 | † 16,394 | 18,601 | 20,436 | 26,600 | 33,344 | 42,622 | 60,919 | 75,739 | 88,674 | 105,638 |
| Net Claims on Central Government | 32an | 1,324 | 1,550 | † 4,284 | 5,191 | 5,008 | 8,085 | 11,748 | 19,300 | 29,650 | 37,104 | 43,460 | 51,011 |
| Claims on Central Government.... | 32a | 2,952 | 3,544 | † 4,850 | 5,445 | 7,570 | 9,829 | 13,267 | 20,143 | 30,661 | 38,237 | 44,953 | 52,064 |
| Liabilities to Central Government. | 36d | 1,628 | 1,995 | † 566 | 254 | 2,562 | 1,744 | 1,518 | 843 | 1,011 | 1,132 | 1,493 | 1,053 |
| Claims on Other Sectors................. | 32s | 4,519 | 7,198 | † 12,110 | 13,410 | 15,429 | 18,516 | 21,595 | 23,323 | 31,269 | 38,635 | 45,215 | 54,627 |
| Claims on Other Financial Corps.. | 32g | 6 | 95 | † 393 | 642 | 1,021 | 646 | 682 | 462 | 375 | 630 | 1,364 | 1,903 |
| Claims on State & Local Govts..... | 32b | 13 | 6 | † 4 | 26 | — | 76 | 145 | 613 | 758 | 966 | 1,923 | 2,046 |
| Claims on Public Nonfin. Corps.... | 32c | 289 | 399 | † 853 | 982 | 1,696 | 2,280 | 2,810 | 2,821 | 3,170 | 4,004 | 6,008 | 9,071 |
| Claims on Private Sector............. | 32d | 4,212 | 6,697 | † 10,859 | 11,759 | 12,711 | 15,513 | 17,959 | 19,427 | 26,966 | 33,034 | 35,920 | 41,606 |
| Broad Money Liabilities.................... | 35l | 9,392 | 13,470 | † 17,806 | 19,723 | 22,947 | 28,405 | 35,868 | 42,223 | 58,750 | 66,431 | 77,717 | 93,942 |
| Currency Outside Depository Corps | 34a | 3,049 | 3,761 | † 5,355 | 5,640 | 6,775 | 8,066 | 10,068 | 12,850 | 16,751 | 19,178 | 23,343 | 27,495 |
| Transferable Deposits................... | 34 | 2,995 | 4,369 | † 5,959 | 6,816 | 8,125 | 9,718 | 11,999 | 14,126 | 18,495 | 21,035 | 24,638 | 30,443 |
| Other Deposits.............................. | 35 | 3,349 | 5,340 | † 6,492 | 7,268 | 8,047 | 10,621 | 13,800 | 15,247 | 23,504 | 26,217 | 29,736 | 36,004 |
| Securities Other than Shares.......... | 36a | — | — | † — | — | — | — | — | — | — | — | — | — |
| Deposits Excl. from Broad Money..... | 36b | — | — | † 20 | 30 | 52 | 205 | 114 | 61 | 5,953 | 14,734 | 13,656 | 12,512 |
| Sec.Ot.th.Shares Excl.f/Brd.Money.... | 36s | — | — | † — | — | — | — | — | — | — | — | — | — |
| Loans........................................... | 36l | 212 | 312 | † 69 | 27 | 54 | 48 | 55 | 36 | 43 | 42 | 43 | 100 |
| Financial Derivatives...................... | 36m | — | — | † — | — | — | — | — | — | — | — | — | — |
| Insurance Technical Reserves........... | 36r | — | — | † — | — | — | — | — | — | — | — | — | — |
| Shares and Other Equity.................. | 37a | −2,319 | −1,679 | † −182 | 586 | 1,175 | 1,771 | 2,154 | 4,614 | 1,786 | −4,192 | −3,567 | −3,877 |
| Other Items (Net)............................ | 37r | −825 | −592 | † 17 | −956 | −2,774 | −4,935 | −5,048 | −5,917 | −5,825 | −4,934 | −2,819 | −14,977 |
| Broad Money Liabs., Seasonally Adj. | 35l.b | 9,617 | 13,797 | † 17,552 | 19,476 | 22,712 | 28,201 | 35,728 | 42,186 | 58,794 | 66,505 | 78,113 | .... |
| **Monetary Aggregates** | | *Millions of Pounds: End of Period* | | | | | | | | | | | |
| Broad Money.................................. | 59m | .... | .... | 17,806 | 19,723 | 22,947 | 28,405 | 35,868 | 42,223 | 58,750 | 66,431 | 77,717 | 93,942 |
| o/w:Currency Issued by Cent.Govt | 59m.a | .... | .... | — | — | — | — | — | — | — | — | — | — |
| o/w: Dep.in Nonfin. Corporations. | 59m.b | .... | .... | — | — | — | — | — | — | — | — | — | — |
| o/w:Secs. Issued by Central Govt.. | 59m.c | .... | .... | — | — | — | — | — | — | — | — | — | — |
| Money (National Definitions) | | | | | | | | | | | | | |
| M1.............................................. | 59ma | 6,044 | 8,130 | 10,519 | 11,368 | 13,630 | 16,106 | 19,908 | 24,850 | 35,117 | 40,213 | 47,981 | 57,939 |
| M2.............................................. | 59mb | 9,392 | 13,470 | 17,803 | 19,688 | 22,869 | 28,285 | 35,462 | 41,817 | 58,621 | 66,431 | 77,717 | 93,942 |
| **Prices and Labor** | | *Index Numbers (2010=100): Period Averages* | | | | | | | | | | | |
| Consumer Prices............................. | 64 | 55.3 | 60.0 | 64.3 | † 69.4 | 79.4 | 88.3 | 100.0 | 122.1 | 167.8 | 218.0 | 298.5 | 349.0 |
| **Intl. Transactions & Positions** | | *Millions of US Dollars: Fiscal Year Ends June 30 through 1994, Fiscal Year Ends December 31 Thereafter* | | | | | | | | | | | |
| Exports............................................ | 70..d | 3,777.8 | 4,824.3 | 5,656.6 | 8,866.3 | 11,670.5 | 8,257.1 | 11,404.3 | 9,688.8 | 4,066.5 | 7,086.2 | 5,462.5 | 2,985.0 |
| Imports, c.i.f..................................... | 71..d | 4,075.2 | 6,756.8 | 8,073.5 | 8,450.0 | 9,351.5 | 9,690.9 | 10,044.8 | 9,236.0 | 9,230.3 | 9,917.9 | 9,222.1 | 8,584.6 |

# Sudan 732

| | | 2004 | 2005 | 2006 | 2007 | 2008 | 2009 | 2010 | 2011 | 2012 | 2013 | 2014 | 2015 |
|---|---|---|---|---|---|---|---|---|---|---|---|---|---|
| **Balance of Payments** | | | | | | | *Millions of US Dollars* | | | | | | |
| A. Current Account*...................... | 109bx | −870.9 | −2,472.7 | −6,495.9 | −3,597.2 | −3,593.9 | −4,926.6 | † −1,725.4 | −2,652.9 | −6,259.1 | −5,822.1 | −3,545.5 | −5,933.5 |
| Goods, credit (exports)................ | 1a9cx | 3,777.8 | 4,824.3 | 5,656.6 | 8,879.2 | 11,670.5 | 8,257.1 | † 11,404.3 | 10,193.4 | 4,066.5 | 4,789.7 | 4,453.7 | 3,169.0 |
| Goods, debit (imports)................. | 1a9dx | 3,586.2 | 5,946.0 | 7,104.7 | 7,722.4 | 8,229.4 | 8,528.0 | † 8,839.4 | 8,127.6 | 8,122.7 | 8,727.9 | 8,105.9 | 8,367.6 |
| Balance on goods................. | 1a9bx | 191.6 | −1,121.7 | −1,448.1 | 1,156.8 | 3,441.1 | −270.9 | † 2,564.9 | 2,065.9 | −4,056.2 | −3,938.2 | −3,652.2 | −5,198.7 |
| Services, credit (exports)............. | 1b9cx | 44.1 | 147.0 | 273.9 | 510.4 | 417.5 | 324.0 | † 242.1 | 832.7 | 1,058.8 | 1,258.0 | 1,568.1 | 1,767.0 |
| Services, debit (imports)............... | 1b9dx | 1,064.5 | 1,503.0 | 2,525.8 | 2,681.3 | 2,531.8 | 2,100.9 | † 2,532.6 | 2,900.0 | 2,108.8 | 2,029.8 | 2,074.8 | 1,773.9 |
| Balance on Goods & Services...... | 1z9bx | −828.8 | −2,477.7 | −3,700.0 | −1,014.0 | 1,326.8 | −2,047.8 | † 274.5 | −1.4 | −5,106.2 | −4,710.0 | −4,159.0 | −5,205.6 |
| Primary income: credit................ | 1c9cx | 21.8 | 47.9 | 114.4 | 192.9 | 80.5 | 36.7 | † 138.6 | 13.5 | 14.3 | 9.2 | 38.1 | 40.8 |
| Primary income: debit................. | 1c9dx | 1,134.5 | 1,449.8 | 4,110.9 | 3,548.1 | 5,623.9 | 4,131.8 | † 4,305.5 | 3,794.7 | 2,038.7 | 2,809.3 | 986.1 | 1,856.5 |
| Balance on gds, serv. & prim. inc. | 1y9bx | −1,941.5 | −3,879.5 | −7,696.5 | −4,369.2 | −4,216.6 | −6,142.9 | † −3,892.5 | −3,782.5 | −7,130.6 | −7,510.1 | −5,107.0 | −7,021.3 |
| Secondary income: credit............. | 1d9ca | 1,580.2 | 2,023.3 | 2,527.7 | 2,889.9 | 4,261.3 | 3,177.8 | † 3,395.9 | 2,076.2 | 1,526.3 | 2,138.3 | 1,974.3 | 1,458.3 |
| Secondary income: debit.............. | 1d9da | 509.6 | 616.5 | 1,327.0 | 2,117.9 | 3,638.6 | 1,961.5 | † 1,228.8 | 946.6 | 654.7 | 450.3 | 412.8 | 370.5 |
| B. Capital Account*...................... | 209ba | — | 165.3 | 205.3 | 173.2 | 177.5 | 235.9 | † 378.0 | 594.7 | 628.7 | 313.5 | 212.8 | 250.3 |
| Capital account: credit................ | 209ca | — | 165.3 | 205.3 | 173.2 | 177.5 | 235.9 | † 378.0 | 594.7 | 628.7 | 313.5 | 212.8 | 250.3 |
| Capital account: debit................. | 209da | — | — | — | — | — | — | .... | .... | .... | .... | .... | .... |
| Balance on current & capital acct. | 129ba | −870.9 | −2,307.4 | −6,290.5 | −3,423.9 | −3,416.4 | −4,690.6 | † −1,347.3 | −2,058.2 | −5,630.4 | −5,508.5 | −3,332.7 | −5,683.1 |
| C. Financial Account* | 309na | −1,427.8 | −1,990.8 | −5,848.0 | −4,338.9 | −2,495.8 | −4,522.6 | † 69.3 | −977.5 | −1,518.0 | −1,965.4 | −1,542.6 | −4,588.7 |
| Direct investment: assets............. | 3a9aa | — | — | — | — | — | — | .... | .... | .... | .... | .... | .... |
| Equity & investment fund shares.. | 3aaaa | — | — | — | — | — | — | .... | .... | .... | .... | .... | .... |
| Debt instruments....................... | 3abaa | — | — | — | — | — | — | .... | .... | .... | .... | .... | .... |
| Direct investment: liabilities ......... | 3a9la | 1,511.1 | 1,561.7 | 1,841.8 | 1,504.4 | 1,653.1 | 1,726.3 | † 2,063.7 | 1,734.4 | 2,311.5 | 1,687.9 | 1,251.3 | 1,736.8 |
| Equity & investment fund shares . | 3aala | 1,511.1 | −675.5 | −747.3 | −932.0 | −947.4 | −845.9 | † 2,063.7 | 1,734.4 | 2,311.5 | 1,687.9 | 1,251.3 | 1,736.8 |
| Debt instruments....................... | 3abla | — | 2,237.2 | 2,589.1 | 2,436.3 | 2,600.5 | 2,572.2 | .... | .... | .... | .... | .... | .... |
| Portfolio investment: assets .......... | 3b9aa | −19.9 | 31.4 | −21.5 | −39.6 | 30.4 | −20.0 | † 1.4 | −34.9 | 1.2 | 3.7 | −6.2 | 2.8 |
| Equity & investment fund shares | 3baaa | — | 31.4 | −21.5 | −39.6 | 30.4 | −20.0 | † 1.4 | −34.9 | 1.2 | 3.7 | −6.2 | 2.8 |
| Debt securities ......................... | 3bbaa | −19.9 | — | — | — | — | — | .... | .... | .... | .... | .... | .... |
| Portfolio investment: liabilities....... | 3b9la | — | 78.2 | −33.7 | .5 | 72.2 | −.5 | † 7.5 | 12.7 | 2.2 | — | 2.3 | .... |
| Equity & investment fund shares . | 3bala | — | 78.2 | −33.7 | .5 | 72.2 | −.5 | † 7.5 | 12.7 | 2.2 | — | 2.3 | .... |
| Debt securities......................... | 3bbla | — | — | — | — | — | — | .... | .... | .... | .... | .... | .... |
| Fin. der.& empl.stk.ops.(ESOs): net. | 3c9na | — | — | — | — | — | — | .... | .... | .... | .... | .... | .... |
| Fin. der. & ESOs: assets............. | 3c9aa | — | — | — | — | — | — | .... | .... | .... | .... | .... | .... |
| Fin. der. & ESOs.: liabilities......... | 3c9la | — | — | — | — | — | — | .... | .... | .... | .... | .... | .... |
| Other investment: assets.............. | 3d9aa | −598.8 | 1,245.1 | 912.6 | 571.9 | 1,444.6 | 1,310.9 | † 2,522.0 | 1,523.9 | 830.4 | −80.6 | 25.9 | −497.6 |
| Other equity............................. | 3daaa | .... | .... | .... | .... | .... | .... | .... | .... | .... | .... | .... | .... |
| Debt instruments....................... | 3dzaa | −598.8 | 1,245.1 | 912.6 | 571.9 | 1,444.6 | 1,310.9 | † 2,522.0 | 1,523.9 | 830.4 | −80.6 | 25.9 | −497.6 |
| Other investment: liabilities............ | 3d9la | −702.0 | 1,627.5 | 4,930.9 | 3,366.3 | 2,245.5 | 4,087.6 | † 382.8 | 719.4 | 35.9 | 200.6 | 308.7 | 2,357.2 |
| Other equity............................. | 3dala | .... | .... | .... | .... | .... | .... | .... | .... | .... | .... | .... | .... |
| Debt instruments....................... | 3dzla | −702.0 | 1,627.5 | 4,930.9 | 3,366.3 | 2,245.5 | 4,087.6 | † 382.8 | 719.4 | 35.9 | 200.6 | 308.7 | 2,357.2 |
| Curr.+ cap.− finan. acct. balance.. | 4y9na | 556.9 | −316.6 | −442.5 | 915.0 | −920.6 | −168.1 | † −1,416.7 | −1,080.7 | −4,112.4 | −3,543.1 | −1,790.1 | −1,094.4 |
| D. Net Errors and Omissions......... | 409na | 212.1 | 859.0 | 239.2 | −1,160.1 | 991.4 | −187.7 | † −285.2 | −757.6 | 2,322.3 | 1,386.2 | 1,438.3 | −7.0 |
| E. Reserves and Related Items......... | 4z9na | 769.0 | 542.4 | −203.4 | −245.1 | 70.8 | −355.8 | † −1,701.9 | −1,838.3 | −1,790.1 | −2,156.9 | −351.8 | −1,101.4 |
| Reserve assets............................. | 3e9aa | 729.8 | 530.6 | −208.7 | −282.0 | 21.1 | −359.5 | † −27.0 | −686.5 | −24.4 | −17.9 | 8.0 | 42.8 |
| Credit and loans from the IMF...... | 3dcla | −18.0 | −11.8 | −5.3 | −36.9 | −49.6 | −3.7 | † −1.5 | −5.5 | −3.8 | −3.9 | −7.3 | −4.8 |
| Exceptional financing................... | 409la | −21.2 | — | — | — | — | — | † 1,676.4 | 1,157.4 | 1,769.5 | 2,142.9 | 367.0 | 1,149.1 |
| *Excludes components in group E | | | | | | | | | | | | | |

| **International Investment Position** | | | | | | | *Millions of US Dollars* | | | | | | |
|---|---|---|---|---|---|---|---|---|---|---|---|---|---|
| Assets.......................................... | 809aa | 3,377.0 | † 4,171.1 | 4,402.1 | 4,746.1 | 7,124.0 | 7,429.1 | 9,912.7 | 10,744.7 | 4,212.7 | 4,145.6 | 4,183.8 | 3,841.0 |
| Direct investment........................ | 8a9aa | .... | .... | .... | .... | .... | .... | .... | .... | .... | .... | .... | .... |
| Equity & investment fund shares.. | 8aaaa | .... | .... | .... | .... | .... | .... | .... | .... | .... | .... | .... | .... |
| Debt instruments....................... | 8abaa | .... | .... | .... | .... | .... | .... | .... | .... | .... | .... | .... | .... |
| Portfolio investment.................... | 8b9aa | 32.2 | † 76.5 | 66.6 | 77.4 | 110.8 | 92.2 | 93.6 | 90.9 | 92.7 | 96.4 | 90.2 | 93.0 |
| Equity & investment fund shares.. | 8baaa | 32.2 | † 76.5 | 66.6 | 77.4 | 110.8 | 92.2 | 93.6 | 90.9 | 92.7 | 96.4 | 90.2 | 93.0 |
| Debt securities......................... | 8bbaa | .... | .... | .... | .... | .... | .... | .... | .... | .... | .... | .... | .... |
| Fin. der.(oth.than reserves) & ESOs | 8c9aa | .... | .... | .... | .... | .... | .... | .... | .... | .... | .... | .... | .... |
| Other investment........................ | 8d9aa | 2,192.1 | † 2,226.0 | 2,675.6 | 3,290.7 | 5,614.1 | 6,185.2 | 8,697.9 | 10,219.7 | 3,903.0 | 3,849.8 | 3,897.6 | 3,517.1 |
| Other equity............................. | 8daaa | .... | .... | .... | .... | .... | .... | .... | .... | .... | .... | .... | .... |
| Debt instruments....................... | 8dzaa | 2,192.1 | † 2,226.0 | 2,675.6 | 3,290.7 | 5,614.1 | 6,185.2 | 8,697.9 | 10,219.7 | 3,903.0 | 3,849.8 | 3,897.6 | 3,517.1 |
| Reserve assets.......................... | 8e9aa | 1,152.7 | † 1,868.6 | 1,659.9 | 1,377.9 | 1,399.0 | 1,151.7 | 1,121.2 | 434.1 | 216.9 | 199.4 | 196.0 | 230.9 |
| Liabilities.................................... | 809la | 33,926.2 | † 37,229.1 | 42,476.5 | 46,861.0 | 50,371.8 | 55,388.2 | 59,461.4 | 63,077.0 | 67,200.2 | 71,231.4 | 73,044.6 | 78,211.2 |
| Direct investment........................ | 8a9la | 5,999.5 | † 6,901.0 | 8,742.8 | 10,247.2 | 11,900.3 | 13,626.6 | 15,690.3 | 17,424.7 | 19,736.2 | 21,424.0 | 22,675.3 | 24,412.1 |
| Equity & investment fund shares.. | 8aala | 5,379.4 | † 6,901.0 | 8,742.8 | 10,247.2 | 11,900.3 | 13,626.6 | 15,690.3 | 17,424.7 | 19,736.2 | 21,424.0 | 22,675.3 | 24,412.1 |
| Debt instruments....................... | 8abla | 620.1 | .... | .... | .... | .... | .... | .... | .... | .... | .... | .... | .... |
| Portfolio investment.................... | 8b9la | .... | † 148.8 | 156.5 | 197.3 | 269.5 | 271.0 | 278.5 | 291.2 | 293.4 | 293.4 | 293.4 | 293.4 |
| Equity & investment fund shares.. | 8bala | .... | † 148.8 | 156.5 | 197.3 | 269.5 | 271.0 | 278.5 | 291.2 | 293.4 | 293.4 | 293.4 | 293.4 |
| Debt securities......................... | 8bbla | .... | .... | .... | .... | .... | .... | .... | .... | .... | .... | .... | .... |
| Fin. der.(oth.than reserves) & ESOs | 8c9la | .... | .... | .... | .... | .... | .... | .... | .... | .... | .... | .... | .... |
| Other investment........................ | 8d9la | 27,926.7 | † 30,179.3 | 33,577.2 | 36,417.0 | 38,202.0 | 41,490.7 | 43,492.6 | 45,361.1 | 47,170.7 | 49,514.0 | 50,075.9 | 53,505.7 |
| Other equity............................. | 8dala | .... | .... | .... | .... | .... | .... | .... | .... | .... | .... | .... | .... |
| Debt instruments....................... | 8dzla | 27,926.7 | † 30,179.3 | 33,577.2 | 36,417.0 | 38,202.0 | 41,490.7 | 43,492.6 | 45,361.1 | 47,170.7 | 49,514.0 | 50,075.9 | 53,505.7 |

| **National Accounts** | | | | | | *Millions of Pounds: Yr.End.June 30 through '94, December 31 Thereafter* | | | | | | | |
|---|---|---|---|---|---|---|---|---|---|---|---|---|---|
| Gross Domestic Product (GDP)........ | 99b | 68,721 | 85,707 | 98,719 | 114,018 | 127,747 | 148,137 | 162,204 | 186,690 | 243,413 | 294,630 | .... | .... |
| | | | | | | | *Millions: Midyear Estimates* | | | | | | |
| **Population**............................... | 99z | 31.18 | 31.99 | 32.81 | 33.64 | 34.47 | 35.30 | 36.11 | 36.92 | 37.71 | 38.52 | 39.35 | 40.23 |

# Suriname 366

| | | 2004 | 2005 | 2006 | 2007 | 2008 | 2009 | 2010 | 2011 | 2012 | 2013 | 2014 | 2015 |
|---|---|---|---|---|---|---|---|---|---|---|---|---|---|
| **Exchange Rates** | | *Surinamese Dollars per SDR: End of Period* | | | | | | | | | | | |
| Official Rate | aa | 4.2164 | 3.9162 | 4.1296 | 4.3378 | 4.2280 | 4.3033 | 4.2274 | 5.0664 | 5.0718 | 5.0820 | 4.7811 | 5.5429 |
| | | *Surinamese Dollars per US Dollar: End of Period (ae) Period Average (rf)* | | | | | | | | | | | |
| Official Rate | ae | 2.7150 | 2.7400 | 2.7450 | 2.7450 | 2.7450 | 2.7450 | 2.7450 | 3.3000 | 3.3000 | 3.3000 | 3.3000 | 4.0000 |
| Official Rate | rf | 2.7336 | 2.7317 | 2.7438 | 2.7450 | 2.7450 | 2.7450 | 2.7454 | 3.2680 | 3.3000 | 3.3000 | 3.3000 | 3.4167 |
| **Fund Position** | | *Millions of SDRs: End of Period* | | | | | | | | | | | |
| Quota | 2f.s | 92.10 | 92.10 | 92.10 | 92.10 | 92.10 | 92.10 | 92.10 | 92.10 | 92.10 | 92.10 | 92.10 | 92.10 |
| SDR Holdings | 1b.s | 1.21 | 1.06 | .84 | .57 | .36 | 80.67 | 80.65 | 80.62 | 80.61 | 81.28 | 81.27 | 45.27 |
| Reserve Position in the Fund | 1c.s | 6.12 | 6.12 | 6.12 | 6.12 | 6.12 | 6.12 | 6.12 | 6.12 | 6.12 | 6.12 | 6.12 | — |
| Total Fund Cred.&Loans Outstg. | 2tl | — | — | — | — | — | — | — | — | — | — | — | — |
| SDR Allocations | 1bd | 7.75 | 7.75 | 7.75 | 7.75 | 7.75 | 88.09 | 88.09 | 88.09 | 88.09 | 88.09 | 88.09 | 88.09 |
| **International Liquidity** | | *Millions of US Dollars Unless Otherwise Indicated: End of Period* | | | | | | | | | | | |
| Total Reserves minus Gold | 1l.d | 129.40 | 125.78 | 215.52 | 370.08 | 561.93 | 596.60 | 601.73 | 708.36 | 885.11 | 738.41 | 573.29 | 284.66 |
| SDR Holdings | 1b.d | 1.89 | 1.52 | 1.26 | .89 | .56 | 126.46 | 124.20 | 123.77 | 123.89 | 125.17 | 117.75 | 62.73 |
| Reserve Position in the Fund | 1c.d | 9.51 | 8.75 | 9.21 | 9.68 | 9.43 | 9.60 | 9.43 | 9.40 | 9.41 | 9.43 | 8.87 | — |
| Foreign Exchange | 1d.d | 118.00 | 115.50 | † 205.04 | 359.51 | 551.93 | 460.53 | 468.10 | 575.19 | 751.81 | 603.81 | 446.67 | 221.94 |
| Gold (Million Fine Troy Ounces) | 1ad | .021 | .031 | .034 | .040 | .047 | .056 | .063 | .071 | .074 | .034 | .043 | .043 |
| Gold (National Valuation) | 1and | 7.52 | 14.33 | † 21.72 | 33.20 | 40.61 | 60.43 | 89.08 | 108.52 | 123.27 | 40.35 | 51.86 | 45.58 |
| Central Bank: Other Assets | 3..d | .33 | .33 | .38 | .41 | .41 | .42 | .17 | .38 | .40 | 2.37 | 2.34 | 2.08 |
| Central Bank: Other Liabs | 4..d | 3.20 | 3.65 | 3.86 | 3.00 | 2.87 | 3.03 | 2.81 | 2.53 | 3.49 | 3.70 | 3.38 | 137.69 |
| Other Depository Corps.: Assets | 7a.d | 243.67 | 242.53 | 306.89 | 415.35 | 378.49 | 514.12 | 525.23 | 594.80 | 695.70 | 791.45 | 759.63 | 753.04 |
| Other Depository Corps.: Liabs | 7b.d | 8.07 | 10.99 | 35.66 | 56.52 | 53.94 | 49.28 | 52.10 | 50.50 | 55.31 | 76.04 | 103.81 | 98.50 |
| **Central Bank** | | *Thousands of Surinamese Dollars: End of Period* | | | | | | | | | | | |
| Net Foreign Assets | 11n | 325,164 | 400,150 | 683,552 | 1,148,921 | 1,787,628 | 1,707,251 | 1,775,533 | 2,606,119 | 3,058,016 | 2,224,943 | 1,675,040 | 378,261 |
| Claims on Nonresidents | 11 | 366,543 | 440,502 | 726,148 | 1,190,780 | 1,828,267 | 2,094,653 | 2,155,659 | 3,060,770 | 3,516,328 | 2,684,848 | 2,107,361 | 1,417,312 |
| Liabilities to Nonresidents | 16c | 41,378 | 40,352 | 42,596 | 41,859 | 40,639 | 387,402 | 380,126 | 454,651 | 458,311 | 459,905 | 432,321 | 1,039,051 |
| Claims on Other Depository Corps. | 12e | 30,712 | 28,792 | 22,047 | 29,907 | 22,028 | 22,506 | 26,873 | 35,905 | 16,125 | 122,423 | 93,881 | 154,568 |
| Net Claims on Central Government | 12an | 227,590 | 232,552 | 168,963 | 35,647 | −89,251 | 142,192 | 134,802 | −247,099 | −81,501 | 376,576 | 551,804 | 2,217,974 |
| Claims on Central Government | 12a | 310,723 | 312,573 | 278,836 | 200,214 | 164,661 | 583,517 | 427,747 | 488,713 | 400,336 | 1,077,695 | 641,800 | 2,507,569 |
| Liabilities to Central Government | 16d | 83,133 | 80,020 | 109,873 | 164,566 | 253,912 | 441,325 | 292,945 | 735,812 | 481,837 | 701,120 | 89,996 | 289,594 |
| Claims on Other Sectors | 12s | 11,894 | 11,107 | 15,245 | 12,018 | 11,185 | 12,433 | 14,644 | 14,926 | 12,455 | 12,531 | 12,202 | 12,113 |
| Claims on Other Financial Corps. | 12g | 3,596 | 3,466 | 898 | 919 | 741 | 742 | 1,814 | 1,904 | — | — | — | — |
| Claims on State & Local Govts. | 12b | — | — | — | — | — | — | — | — | — | — | — | — |
| Claims on Public Nonfin. Corps. | 12c | 2,675 | 914 | 4,217 | 26 | 26 | 26 | — | — | — | 145 | — | — |
| Claims on Private Sector | 12d | 5,623 | 6,727 | 10,129 | 11,074 | 10,418 | 11,665 | 12,830 | 13,022 | 12,455 | 12,385 | 12,202 | 12,113 |
| Monetary Base | 14 | 528,537 | 570,104 | 759,818 | 992,619 | 1,110,765 | 1,461,323 | 1,662,951 | 1,795,054 | 2,416,979 | 2,401,512 | 2,198,235 | 2,601,763 |
| Currency in Circulation | 14a | 285,632 | 321,960 | 388,838 | 472,413 | 566,816 | 669,703 | 789,356 | 815,921 | 976,733 | 1,026,797 | 1,114,267 | 1,124,286 |
| Liabs. to Other Depository Corps. | 14c | 202,791 | 196,399 | 304,789 | 427,376 | 438,720 | 664,337 | 711,990 | 757,736 | 1,193,403 | 1,318,879 | 996,517 | 1,344,443 |
| Liabilities to Other Sectors | 14d | 40,114 | 51,745 | 66,191 | 92,830 | 105,230 | 127,284 | 161,605 | 221,396 | 246,843 | 55,836 | 87,451 | 133,034 |
| Other Liabs. to Other Dep. Corps. | 14n | — | — | — | — | — | — | — | — | — | — | — | 11,210 |
| Dep. & Sec. Excl. f/Monetary Base | 14o | 2,554 | 10,344 | 27,249 | 45,785 | 388,178 | 124,141 | 22,869 | 60,438 | 116,997 | 2,690 | 2,452 | 2,266 |
| Deposits Included in Broad Money | 15 | 2,554 | 8,727 | 155 | 2,858 | 311,801 | 19,588 | 21,305 | 58,565 | 115,122 | 811 | 584 | — |
| Sec.Ot.th.Shares Incl.in Brd. Money | 16a | — | — | — | — | — | — | — | — | — | — | — | — |
| Deposits Excl. from Broad Money | 16b | — | 1,618 | 27,095 | 42,927 | 76,377 | 104,552 | 1,564 | 1,873 | 1,875 | 1,879 | 1,868 | 2,266 |
| Sec.Ot.th.Shares Excl.f/Brd.Money | 16s | — | — | — | — | — | — | — | — | — | — | — | — |
| Loans | 16l | — | — | — | — | — | — | — | — | — | — | — | — |
| Financial Derivatives | 16m | — | — | — | — | — | — | — | — | — | — | — | — |
| Shares and Other Equity | 17a | 91,161 | 110,939 | 141,988 | 229,278 | 274,191 | 275,204 | 264,297 | 566,649 | 444,157 | 424,392 | 171,529 | 193,930 |
| Other Items (Net) | 17r | −26,892 | −18,786 | −39,249 | −41,188 | −41,544 | 23,714 | 1,735 | −12,289 | 26,963 | −92,121 | −39,289 | −46,253 |
| Memo Item: | | | | | | | | | | | | | |
| Total Assets | 10ra | 754,238 | 837,331 | 1,092,988 | 1,489,626 | 2,099,392 | 2,766,144 | 2,698,170 | 3,686,667 | 4,039,041 | 4,034,627 | 2,978,942 | 4,232,796 |
| **Other Depository Corporations** | | *Thousands of Surinamese Dollars: End of Period* | | | | | | | | | | | |
| Net Foreign Assets | 21n | 639,648 | 634,395 | 744,537 | 984,982 | 890,885 | 1,275,980 | 1,298,736 | 1,796,166 | 2,113,288 | 2,360,865 | 2,164,208 | 2,618,189 |
| Claims on Nonresidents | 21 | 661,553 | 664,519 | 842,426 | 1,140,140 | 1,038,953 | 1,411,261 | 1,441,762 | 1,962,824 | 2,295,805 | 2,611,790 | 2,506,789 | 3,012,178 |
| Liabilities to Nonresidents | 26c | 21,905 | 30,124 | 97,889 | 155,158 | 148,068 | 135,281 | 143,026 | 166,658 | 182,517 | 250,925 | 342,581 | 393,989 |
| Claims on Central Bank | 20 | 246,917 | 244,828 | 358,988 | 503,765 | 548,310 | 805,048 | 836,813 | 812,652 | 1,309,070 | 1,473,595 | 1,197,601 | 1,467,649 |
| Currency | 20a | 38,777 | 43,057 | 47,612 | 64,285 | 102,645 | 101,301 | 120,159 | 130,847 | 145,244 | 160,983 | 213,763 | 173,204 |
| Reserve Deposits and Securities | 20b | 208,140 | 201,771 | 311,376 | 439,480 | 445,665 | 703,747 | 716,654 | 681,805 | 1,163,826 | 1,312,612 | 983,838 | 1,283,181 |
| Other Claims | 20n | — | — | — | — | — | — | — | — | — | — | — | 11,264 |
| Net Claims on Central Government | 22an | 144,048 | 138,192 | 160,282 | 102,755 | 22,367 | −27,631 | 55,707 | −12,464 | 71,391 | 148,183 | 739,003 | 416,801 |
| Claims on Central Government | 22a | 163,577 | 202,235 | 216,146 | 161,688 | 97,117 | 79,625 | 184,718 | 168,112 | 260,139 | 406,375 | 994,453 | 643,432 |
| Liabilities to Central Government | 26d | 19,529 | 64,043 | 55,864 | 58,933 | 74,750 | 107,256 | 129,011 | 180,576 | 188,747 | 258,192 | 255,450 | 226,631 |
| Claims on Other Sectors | 22s | 775,421 | 965,168 | 1,289,575 | 1,749,651 | 2,374,697 | 2,675,831 | 3,021,686 | 3,631,449 | 4,204,406 | 4,969,475 | 5,391,812 | 6,248,322 |
| Claims on Other Financial Corps. | 22g | 11,395 | 10,787 | 15,871 | 26,567 | 39,349 | 50,764 | 58,995 | 100,386 | 130,511 | 138,402 | 157,000 | 189,891 |
| Claims on State & Local Govts. | 22b | — | — | — | — | — | — | — | — | — | — | — | — |
| Claims on Public Nonfin. Corps. | 22c | 8,628 | 14,630 | 23,618 | 12,452 | 31,374 | 40,242 | 94,978 | 125,137 | 110,179 | 120,145 | 105,466 | 162,324 |
| Claims on Private Sector | 22d | 755,398 | 939,751 | 1,250,086 | 1,710,632 | 2,303,974 | 2,584,826 | 2,867,713 | 3,405,926 | 3,963,716 | 4,710,928 | 5,129,346 | 5,896,107 |
| Liabilities to Central Bank | 26g | 19,388 | 25,041 | 20,562 | 27,305 | 88,584 | 162,332 | 135,598 | 30,421 | 97,092 | 134,158 | 92,055 | 165,275 |
| Transf.Dep.Included in Broad Money | 24 | 939,963 | 945,215 | 1,153,119 | 1,461,732 | 1,597,302 | 2,011,919 | 2,224,141 | 2,677,529 | 3,230,712 | 3,579,614 | 3,670,255 | 3,851,316 |
| Other Dep.Included in Broad Money | 25 | 725,334 | 881,962 | 1,203,743 | 1,605,172 | 1,845,898 | 2,246,000 | 2,430,036 | 3,044,157 | 3,689,714 | 4,507,972 | 4,840,616 | 5,682,408 |
| Sec.Ot.th.Shares Incl.in Brd. Money | 26a | — | — | — | — | — | — | — | — | — | — | — | — |
| Deposits Excl. from Broad Money | 26b | — | — | — | — | — | — | — | — | — | — | — | — |
| Sec.Ot.th.Shares Excl.f/Brd.Money | 26s | — | — | — | — | — | — | — | — | — | — | — | — |
| Loans | 26l | — | — | — | — | — | — | — | — | — | — | — | — |
| Financial Derivatives | 26m | — | — | — | — | — | — | — | — | — | — | — | 1,884 |
| Insurance Technical Reserves | 26r | 7,643 | 123 | 1,437 | 2,608 | 3,234 | 5,932 | 7,579 | 9,849 | 13,516 | 18,691 | 21,492 | 24,747 |
| Shares and Other Equity | 27a | 139,898 | 168,866 | 217,373 | 263,357 | 324,540 | 384,964 | 450,512 | 545,460 | 674,877 | 806,468 | 945,435 | 944,258 |
| Other Items (Net) | 27r | −26,192 | −38,624 | −42,853 | −19,022 | −23,299 | −81,919 | −34,924 | −79,614 | −7,756 | −94,786 | −77,230 | 81,073 |
| Memo Item: | | | | | | | | | | | | | |
| Total Assets | 20ra | 2,006,879 | 2,275,843 | 2,954,798 | 3,876,296 | 4,597,443 | 5,406,085 | 5,978,226 | 7,198,814 | 8,747,375 | 10,115,335 | 10,845,442 | 12,291,248 |

# Suriname 366

| | | 2004 | 2005 | 2006 | 2007 | 2008 | 2009 | 2010 | 2011 | 2012 | 2013 | 2014 | 2015 |
|---|---|---|---|---|---|---|---|---|---|---|---|---|---|
| **Depository Corporations** | | *Thousands of Surinamese Dollars: End of Period* | | | | | | | | | | | |
| Net Foreign Assets............. | 31n | 964,812 | 1,034,545 | 1,428,089 | 2,133,902 | 2,678,513 | 2,983,231 | 3,074,269 | 4,402,285 | 5,171,304 | 4,585,808 | 3,839,248 | 2,996,449 |
| Claims on Nonresidents............... | 31 | 1,028,096 | 1,105,021 | 1,568,574 | 2,330,919 | 2,867,220 | 3,505,914 | 3,597,421 | 5,023,594 | 5,812,132 | 5,296,638 | 4,614,150 | 4,429,489 |
| Liabilities to Nonresidents........... | 36c | 63,283 | 70,476 | 140,485 | 197,017 | 188,707 | 522,683 | 523,152 | 621,309 | 640,828 | 710,830 | 774,902 | 1,433,040 |
| Domestic Claims............. | 32 | 1,158,953 | 1,347,020 | 1,634,065 | 1,900,072 | 2,318,998 | 2,802,825 | 3,226,839 | 3,386,812 | 4,206,752 | 5,506,764 | 6,694,821 | 8,895,210 |
| Net Claims on Central Government | 32an | 371,638 | 370,744 | 329,245 | 138,402 | −66,885 | 114,561 | 190,509 | −259,562 | −10,109 | 524,758 | 1,290,806 | 2,634,775 |
| Claims on Central Government.... | 32a | 474,300 | 514,808 | 494,982 | 361,902 | 261,777 | 663,141 | 612,464 | 656,825 | 660,475 | 1,484,070 | 1,636,253 | 3,151,001 |
| Liabilities to Central Government. | 36d | 102,662 | 144,063 | 165,737 | 223,500 | 328,662 | 548,581 | 421,955 | 916,388 | 670,584 | 959,312 | 345,446 | 516,226 |
| Claims on Other Sectors............... | 32s | 787,315 | 976,275 | 1,304,820 | 1,761,669 | 2,385,882 | 2,688,264 | 3,036,330 | 3,646,375 | 4,216,862 | 4,982,005 | 5,404,015 | 6,260,434 |
| Claims on Other Financial Corps.. | 32g | 14,991 | 14,253 | 16,769 | 27,486 | 40,090 | 51,505 | 60,808 | 102,290 | 130,511 | 138,402 | 157,000 | 189,891 |
| Claims on State & Local Govts..... | 32b | — | — | — | — | — | — | — | — | — | — | — | — |
| Claims on Public Nonfin. Corps.... | 32c | 11,303 | 15,544 | 27,835 | 12,478 | 31,400 | 40,268 | 94,978 | 125,137 | 110,179 | 120,290 | 105,466 | 162,324 |
| Claims on Private Sector............. | 32d | 761,021 | 946,478 | 1,260,215 | 1,721,705 | 2,314,393 | 2,596,491 | 2,880,543 | 3,418,948 | 3,976,172 | 4,723,313 | 5,141,548 | 5,908,219 |
| Broad Money Liabilities................... | 35l | 1,954,820 | 2,166,552 | 2,764,435 | 3,570,721 | 4,324,401 | 4,973,192 | 5,506,283 | 6,686,721 | 8,113,880 | 9,010,047 | 9,499,410 | 10,617,840 |
| Currency Outside Depository Corps | 34a | 246,855 | 278,903 | 341,226 | 408,128 | 464,170 | 568,401 | 669,197 | 685,074 | 831,489 | 865,815 | 900,504 | 951,082 |
| Transferable Deposits................... | 34 | 955,405 | 971,523 | 1,179,355 | 1,504,559 | 1,957,885 | 2,087,923 | 2,315,720 | 2,838,076 | 3,459,148 | 3,582,577 | 3,729,128 | 3,953,833 |
| Other Deposits............................ | 35 | 728,532 | 886,581 | 1,211,332 | 1,613,827 | 1,854,873 | 2,255,775 | 2,441,332 | 3,055,615 | 3,701,172 | 4,519,430 | 4,852,074 | 5,693,991 |
| Securities Other than Shares.......... | 36a | 24,029 | 29,545 | 32,521 | 44,207 | 47,473 | 61,094 | 80,034 | 107,955 | 122,071 | 42,225 | 17,704 | 18,934 |
| Deposits Excl. from Broad Money..... | 36b | — | 1,618 | 27,095 | 42,927 | 76,377 | 104,552 | 1,564 | 1,873 | 1,875 | 1,879 | 1,868 | 2,266 |
| Sec.Ot.th.Shares Excl.f/Brd.Money.... | 36s | — | — | — | — | — | — | — | — | — | — | — | — |
| Loans............................................. | 36l | — | — | — | — | — | — | — | — | — | — | — | — |
| Financial Derivatives....................... | 36m | — | — | — | — | — | — | — | — | — | — | — | 1,884 |
| Insurance Technical Reserves........... | 36r | 7,643 | 123 | 1,437 | 2,608 | 3,234 | 5,932 | 7,579 | 9,849 | 13,516 | 18,691 | 21,492 | 24,747 |
| Shares and Other Equity.................. | 37a | 231,059 | 279,805 | 359,362 | 492,636 | 598,731 | 660,168 | 714,809 | 1,112,109 | 1,119,034 | 1,230,860 | 1,116,964 | 1,138,187 |
| Other Items (Net).......................... | 37r | −69,757 | −66,533 | −90,175 | −74,917 | −5,232 | 42,211 | 70,873 | −21,456 | 129,750 | −168,905 | −105,665 | 106,734 |
| Broad Money Liabs., Seasonally Adj. | 35l.b | 1,949,720 | 2,155,100 | 2,744,760 | 3,540,424 | 4,288,724 | 4,931,842 | 5,459,552 | 6,622,643 | 8,021,182 | 8,888,011 | 9,352,286 | 10,444,170 |
| **Monetary Aggregates** | | *Thousands of Surinamese Dollars: End of Period* | | | | | | | | | | | |
| Broad Money.............................. | 59m | 1,975,120 | 2,195,152 | 2,790,935 | 3,594,321 | 4,344,401 | 4,991,192 | 5,524,224 | 6,709,500 | 8,127,824 | 9,027,390 | 9,519,457 | 10,638,421 |
| o/w:Currency Issued by Cent.Govt | 59m.a | 20,300 | 28,600 | 26,500 | 23,600 | 20,000 | 18,000 | 17,941 | 22,779 | 13,944 | 17,343 | 20,047 | 20,581 |
| o/w: Dep.in Nonfin. Corporations. | 59m.b | — | — | — | — | — | — | — | — | — | — | — | — |
| o/w:Secs. Issued by Central Govt.. | 59m.c | — | — | — | — | — | — | — | — | — | — | — | — |
| Money (National Definitions) | | | | | | | | | | | | | |
| M1........................................... | 59ma | 699,500 | 772,600 | 941,200 | 1,177,700 | 1,363,000 | 1,672,000 | † 3,002,858 | 3,546,000 | 4,304,581 | 4,465,735 | 4,649,679 | 4,925,496 |
| M2........................................... | 59mb | 785,800 | 890,300 | 1,094,100 | 1,377,400 | 1,589,200 | 1,993,500 | † 5,524,224 | 6,709,500 | 8,127,824 | 9,027,390 | 9,519,457 | 10,638,421 |
| M3........................................... | 59mc | 1,001,200 | 1,153,400 | 1,419,700 | 1,821,400 | 2,103,200 | 2,682,900 | .... | .... | .... | .... | .... | .... |
| **Interest Rates** | | *Percent per Annum* | | | | | | | | | | | |
| Central Bank Policy Rate (EOP)........ | 60 | 14.00 | 14.00 | 14.00 | 10.00 | 9.00 | 9.00 | 9.00 | 9.00 | 9.00 | 9.00 | 12.50 | 12.50 |
| Deposit Rate................................. | 60l | 8.34 | 7.27 | 6.63 | 6.42 | 6.34 | 6.38 | 6.17 | 6.39 | 6.79 | 7.09 | 7.35 | 7.53 |
| Deposit Rate in USD...................... | 60l.f | .... | 2.60 | 2.80 | 3.10 | 3.00 | 2.90 | 2.74 | 2.60 | 2.60 | 2.80 | 3.30 | 3.80 |
| Deposit Rate in Euros.................... | 60l.u | .... | 1.10 | 1.20 | 1.40 | 1.50 | 1.00 | .94 | .80 | .70 | .70 | .70 | .60 |
| Lending Rate................................. | 60p | 20.44 | 17.40 | 15.64 | 13.77 | 12.20 | 11.65 | 11.59 | 11.76 | 11.74 | 11.98 | 12.28 | 12.62 |
| Lending Rate in USD...................... | 60p.f | .... | 9.73 | 9.71 | 9.71 | 9.52 | 9.48 | 9.40 | 9.52 | 9.52 | 9.70 | 9.65 | 9.55 |
| Lending Rate in Euros.................... | 60p.u | .... | 10.20 | 9.70 | 10.10 | 9.90 | 10.30 | 9.70 | 9.80 | 9.60 | 10.60 | 9.50 | 9.20 |
| **Prices and Labor** | | *Index Numbers (2010=100): Period Averages* | | | | | | | | | | | |
| Consumer Prices............................ | 64 | 62.8 | 69.0 | 76.7 | 81.7 | 93.7 | 93.5 | 100.0 | 117.7 | 123.6 | 126.0 | 130.2 | 139.2 |
| Crude Oil Production....................... | 66aa | .... | .... | 81.8 | 91.6 | 101.8 | 101.1 | 100.0 | 103.4 | 102.4 | 103.2 | 105.8 | 106.8 |
| **Intl. Transactions & Positions** | | *Millions of Surinamese Dollars* | | | | | | | | | | | |
| Exports......................................... | 70 | 1,950.0 | 2,156.3 | 3,082.3 | 3,534.0 | 4,577.5 | 3,823.3 | 5,081.7 | 7,703.5 | 8,775.5 | 7,852.7 | 6,972.1 | 5,369.8 |
| Gold Exports................................. | 70kr | .... | 848.2 | 1,091.3 | 1,307.2 | 1,938.9 | 2,362.8 | 3,142.9 | 4,887.9 | 5,553.9 | 4,792.0 | 3,802.2 | 2,978.8 |
| Oil Product Exports, Val................. | 70ab | .... | .... | 132.08 | 197.77 | 499.96 | 242.14 | 487.24 | 1,103.63 | 1,187.00 | 1,178.81 | 1,067.17 | 508.37 |
| Imports, c.i.f................................. | 71 | 1,615.9 | 2,266.1 | 2,453.3 | 3,049.2 | 4,167.3 | 3,722.8 | 3,788.3 | 5,456.8 | 6,478.9 | 7,064.5 | 6,539.9 | 6,623.9 |
| | | *Index Numbers (2010=100): Period Averages* | | | | | | | | | | | |
| Oil Product Exports, Vol................. | 72ab | .... | .... | 42.077 | 51.485 | 97.636 | 95.601 | 100.000 | 138.252 | 137.776 | 139.509 | 140.912 | 124.197 |
| Gold Exports, Vol........................... | 72kr | .... | 74.653 | 71.132 | 73.021 | 87.570 | 94.387 | 100.000 | 102.434 | 109.488 | 108.117 | 99.328 | 84.279 |

# Suriname 366

| | | 2004 | 2005 | 2006 | 2007 | 2008 | 2009 | 2010 | 2011 | 2012 | 2013 | 2014 | 2015 |
|---|---|---|---|---|---|---|---|---|---|---|---|---|---|
| **Balance of Payments** | | | | | | | *Millions of US Dollars* | | | | | | |
| A. Current Account* | 109bx | .... | −143.6 | 220.6 | 324.5 | 324.7 | 111.3 | 650.8 | 431.3 | 162.4 | −196.0 | −415.5 | −808.1 |
| Goods, credit (exports) | 1a9cx | .... | 1,211.5 | 1,174.5 | 1,359.0 | 1,743.5 | 1,401.8 | 2,084.1 | 2,646.9 | 2,700.3 | 2,416.7 | 2,148.9 | 1,665.8 |
| Goods, debit (imports) | 1a9dx | .... | 1,189.1 | 902.6 | 1,044.8 | 1,406.7 | 1,390.7 | 1,397.9 | 1,679.1 | 1,971.5 | 2,125.6 | 1,965.6 | 1,972.6 |
| Balance on goods | 1a9bx | .... | 22.4 | 271.9 | 314.2 | 336.8 | 11.1 | 686.2 | 967.8 | 728.8 | 291.1 | 183.2 | −306.9 |
| Services, credit (exports) | 1b9cx | .... | 204.1 | 236.6 | 253.4 | 284.2 | 286.7 | 241.4 | 200.8 | 171.5 | 172.2 | 202.7 | 177.4 |
| Services, debit (imports) | 1b9dx | .... | 351.8 | 269.3 | 317.9 | 407.2 | 285.3 | 259.0 | 562.5 | 618.2 | 594.6 | 803.1 | 716.0 |
| Balance on Goods & Services | 1z9bx | .... | −125.3 | 239.2 | 249.7 | 213.8 | 12.5 | 668.6 | 606.1 | 282.1 | −131.3 | −417.2 | −845.5 |
| Primary income: credit | 1c9cx | .... | 24.0 | 25.0 | 43.6 | 42.2 | 29.8 | 26.1 | 16.2 | 27.1 | 27.1 | 21.6 | 14.5 |
| Primary income: debit | 1c9dx | .... | 64.4 | 79.5 | 46.2 | 21.8 | 25.0 | 130.4 | 278.3 | 219.6 | 158.4 | 91.1 | 42.4 |
| Balance on gds, serv. & prim. inc. | 1y9bx | .... | −165.7 | 184.7 | 247.1 | 234.2 | 17.3 | 564.3 | 344.0 | 89.6 | −262.6 | −486.6 | −873.4 |
| Secondary income: credit | 1d9ca | .... | 52.3 | 73.5 | 139.8 | 141.0 | 147.2 | 141.8 | 159.4 | 145.5 | 153.2 | 151.4 | 139.4 |
| Secondary income: debit | 1d9da | .... | 30.2 | 37.6 | 62.4 | 50.5 | 53.2 | 55.3 | 72.1 | 72.8 | 86.6 | 80.2 | 74.1 |
| B. Capital Account* | 209ba | .... | 14.5 | 19.3 | 8.1 | 31.9 | 87.7 | 53.9 | 35.0 | −7.0 | .1 | −.4 | 1.3 |
| Capital account: credit | 209ca | .... | 14.5 | 19.3 | 8.1 | 31.9 | 87.7 | 53.9 | 35.0 | .8 | .1 | .1 | 1.3 |
| Capital account: debit | 209da | .... | — | — | — | — | — | — | — | 7.8 | — | .6 | .1 |
| Balance on current & capital acct. | 129bx | .... | −129.1 | 239.9 | 332.6 | 356.6 | 199.0 | 704.7 | 466.3 | 155.4 | −195.9 | −415.9 | −806.8 |
| C. Financial Account* | 309na | .... | 20.6 | 255.5 | 366.3 | 48.3 | 141.5 | 501.6 | 84.9 | −487.2 | −429.1 | −688.4 | −697.4 |
| Direct investment: assets | 3a9aa | .... | .... | — | — | — | — | — | 72.4 | −3.4 | −.8 | −223.8 | −83.1 |
| Equity & investment fund shares | 3aaaa | .... | .... | — | — | — | — | — | — | −.3 | — | — | — |
| Debt instruments | 3abaa | .... | .... | — | — | — | — | — | 72.4 | −3.1 | −.8 | −223.8 | −83.1 |
| Direct investment: liabilities | 3a9la | .... | 27.9 | −163.4 | −246.7 | −231.4 | −93.4 | −247.7 | 145.3 | 169.4 | 186.8 | −59.9 | 196.7 |
| Equity & investment fund shares | 3aala | .... | .... | — | — | — | — | 8.0 | 121.1 | 49.1 | 100.6 | 151.0 | 157.5 |
| Debt instruments | 3abla | .... | 27.9 | −163.4 | −246.7 | −231.4 | −93.4 | −255.7 | 24.2 | 120.4 | 86.2 | −210.9 | 39.2 |
| Portfolio investment: assets | 3b9aa | .... | .... | — | — | 15.2 | 9.9 | 2.3 | −5.5 | 5.8 | 1.2 | −.6 | 9.5 |
| Equity & investment fund shares | 3baaa | .... | .... | — | — | — | — | — | — | — | .1 | −.1 | — |
| Debt securities | 3bbaa | .... | .... | — | — | 15.2 | 9.9 | 2.3 | −5.5 | 5.8 | 1.1 | −.5 | 9.5 |
| Portfolio investment: liabilities | 3b9la | .... | −2.0 | −.3 | −1.3 | −1.7 | −.9 | −9.7 | — | — | — | — | — |
| Equity & investment fund shares | 3bala | .... | .... | — | — | — | — | — | — | — | — | — | — |
| Debt securities | 3bbla | .... | −2.0 | −.3 | −1.3 | −1.7 | −.9 | −9.7 | — | — | — | — | — |
| Fin. der.& empl.stk.ops.(ESOs): net | 3c9na | .... | .... | — | — | — | — | — | — | — | — | — | — |
| Fin. der. & ESOs: assets | 3c9aa | .... | .... | — | — | — | — | — | — | — | — | — | — |
| Fin. der. & ESOs: liabilities | 3c9la | .... | .... | — | — | — | — | — | — | — | — | — | — |
| Other investment: assets | 3d9aa | .... | 31.9 | 88.6 | 37.2 | −193.5 | 148.9 | 289.2 | 483.2 | −258.7 | −35.7 | −55.9 | −78.0 |
| Other equity | 3daaa | .... | .... | .... | .... | .... | .... | .... | .... | .... | .... | .... | .... |
| Debt instruments | 3dzaa | .... | 31.9 | 88.6 | 37.2 | −193.5 | 148.9 | 289.2 | 483.2 | −258.7 | −35.7 | −55.9 | −78.0 |
| Other investment: liabilities | 3d9la | .... | −14.6 | −3.2 | −81.2 | 6.6 | 111.6 | 47.3 | 319.9 | 61.4 | 207.0 | 468.1 | 349.1 |
| Other equity | 3dala | .... | .... | .... | .... | .... | .... | .... | .... | .... | .... | .... | .... |
| Debt instruments | 3dzla | .... | −14.6 | −3.2 | −81.2 | 6.6 | 111.6 | 47.3 | 319.9 | 61.4 | 207.0 | 468.1 | 349.1 |
| Curr.+ cap.– finan. acct. balance | 4y9na | .... | −149.7 | −15.6 | −33.7 | 308.4 | 57.5 | 203.1 | 381.4 | 642.6 | 233.3 | 272.5 | −109.4 |
| D. Net Errors and Omissions | 409na | .... | 169.4 | 79.5 | 179.8 | −100.0 | −18.9 | −168.1 | −257.3 | −462.4 | −381.0 | −422.7 | −206.7 |
| E. Reserves and Related Items | 4z9na | .... | 19.7 | 63.9 | 146.1 | 208.4 | 38.6 | 35.0 | 124.1 | 180.1 | −147.7 | −150.2 | −316.1 |
| Reserve assets | 3e9aa | .... | 19.7 | 63.9 | 146.1 | 208.4 | 38.6 | 35.0 | 124.1 | 180.1 | −147.7 | −150.2 | −266.1 |
| Credit and loans from the IMF | 3dcla | .... | — | — | — | — | — | — | — | — | — | — | — |
| Exceptional financing | 409la | .... | — | — | — | — | — | — | — | — | — | — | 50.0 |
| *Excludes components in group E | | | | | | | | | | | | | |
| | | | | | | | | | | | | | |
| **International Investment Position** | | | | | | | *Millions of US Dollars* | | | | | | |
| Assets | 809aa | .... | .... | .... | .... | .... | .... | .... | 2,526.7 | 2,462.9 | 2,318.4 | 1,884.5 | 1,438.0 |
| Direct investment | 8a9aa | .... | .... | .... | .... | .... | .... | .... | 500.3 | 496.1 | 495.2 | 271.4 | 188.4 |
| Equity & investment fund shares | 8aaaa | .... | .... | .... | .... | .... | .... | .... | .... | .... | .... | .... | .... |
| Debt instruments | 8abaa | .... | .... | .... | .... | .... | .... | .... | 500.3 | 496.1 | 495.2 | 271.4 | 188.4 |
| Portfolio investment | 8b9aa | .... | .... | .... | .... | .... | .... | .... | 35.3 | 41.1 | 42.4 | 41.8 | 51.2 |
| Equity & investment fund shares | 8baaa | .... | .... | .... | .... | .... | .... | .... | .... | .... | .1 | .1 | — |
| Debt securities | 8bbaa | .... | .... | .... | .... | .... | .... | .... | 35.3 | 41.1 | 42.2 | 41.7 | 51.2 |
| Fin. der.(oth.than reserves) & ESOs | 8c9aa | .... | .... | .... | .... | .... | .... | .... | .... | .... | .... | .... | .... |
| Other investment | 8d9aa | .... | .... | .... | .... | .... | .... | .... | 1,174.1 | 917.3 | 1,002.1 | 946.1 | 868.1 |
| Other equity | 8daaa | .... | .... | .... | .... | .... | .... | .... | .... | .... | .... | .... | .... |
| Debt instruments | 8dzaa | .... | .... | .... | .... | .... | .... | .... | 1,174.1 | 917.3 | 1,002.1 | 946.1 | 868.1 |
| Reserve assets | 8e9aa | .... | .... | .... | .... | .... | .... | .... | 816.9 | 1,008.4 | 778.8 | 625.1 | 330.2 |
| Liabilities | 809la | .... | .... | .... | .... | .... | .... | .... | 2,232.8 | 2,590.7 | 3,026.7 | 3,424.3 | 3,970.4 |
| Direct investment | 8a9la | .... | .... | .... | .... | .... | .... | .... | 1,242.2 | 1,531.5 | 1,726.7 | 1,668.6 | 1,868.1 |
| Equity & investment fund shares | 8aala | .... | .... | .... | .... | .... | .... | .... | 918.0 | 1,082.0 | 1,184.7 | 1,335.8 | 1,493.3 |
| Debt instruments | 8abla | .... | .... | .... | .... | .... | .... | .... | 324.2 | 449.5 | 542.0 | 332.8 | 374.8 |
| Portfolio investment | 8b9la | .... | .... | .... | .... | .... | .... | .... | .... | .... | .... | .... | .... |
| Equity & investment fund shares | 8bala | .... | .... | .... | .... | .... | .... | .... | .... | .... | .... | .... | .... |
| Debt securities | 8bbla | .... | .... | .... | .... | .... | .... | .... | .... | .... | .... | .... | .... |
| Fin. der.(oth.than reserves) & ESOs | 8c9la | .... | .... | .... | .... | .... | .... | .... | .... | .... | .... | .... | .... |
| Other investment | 8d9la | .... | .... | .... | .... | .... | .... | .... | 990.7 | 1,059.2 | 1,300.0 | 1,755.7 | 2,102.3 |
| Other equity | 8dala | .... | .... | .... | .... | .... | .... | .... | .... | .... | .... | .... | .... |
| Debt instruments | 8dzla | .... | .... | .... | .... | .... | .... | .... | 990.7 | 1,059.2 | 1,300.0 | 1,755.7 | 2,102.3 |

# Suriname 366

| | | 2004 | 2005 | 2006 | 2007 | 2008 | 2009 | 2010 | 2011 | 2012 | 2013 | 2014 | 2015 |
|---|---|---|---|---|---|---|---|---|---|---|---|---|---|
| **Government Finance** | | | | | | | | | | | | | |
| **Cash Flow Statement** | | | | | | | | | | | | | |
| **Budgetary Central Government** | | | | | *Millions of Surinamese Dollars: Fiscal Year Ends December 31* | | | | | | | |
| Cash Receipts:Operating Activities... | c1 | 1,106,355 | 1,401,048 | 1,739,999 | 2,367,933 | 2,354,693 | 2,944,643 | 2,606,152 | 3,537,459 | 4,217,380 | .... | .... | .... |
| Taxes........................................ | c11 | 853,107 | 1,006,747 | 1,206,957 | 1,520,749 | 1,682,481 | 1,831,708 | 1,877,709 | 2,666,690 | 3,212,428 | .... | .... | .... |
| Social Contributions...................... | c12 | — | — | — | — | — | — | — | | | .... | .... | .... |
| Grants........................................ | c13 | 58,167 | 86,043 | 159,730 | 423,225 | 243,585 | 354,070 | 149,149 | 115,375 | — | .... | .... | .... |
| Other Receipts............................. | c14 | 195,082 | 308,259 | 373,312 | 423,959 | 428,627 | 758,864 | 579,294 | 755,394 | 1,004,952 | .... | .... | .... |
| Cash Payments:Operating Activities. | c2 | 1,071,483 | 1,282,937 | 1,626,407 | 1,819,217 | 1,987,365 | 2,467,863 | 2,501,718 | 3,019,604 | 3,681,168 | .... | .... | .... |
| Compensation of Employees.......... | c21 | 465,179 | 501,626 | 603,032 | 692,432 | 758,546 | 967,631 | 1,075,123 | 1,208,774 | 1,315,617 | .... | .... | .... |
| Purchases of Goods & Services....... | c22 | 219,344 | 304,638 | 416,658 | 480,766 | 488,006 | 652,250 | 638,699 | 771,969 | 1,246,393 | .... | .... | .... |
| Interest...................................... | c24 | 68,199 | 97,325 | 108,407 | 97,170 | 61,641 | 133,287 | 103,573 | 139,840 | 140,561 | .... | .... | .... |
| Subsidies.................................... | c25 | 260,593 | 293,304 | 338,581 | 391,748 | 435,588 | 499,925 | 535,174 | 783,646 | 978,597 | .... | .... | .... |
| Grants........................................ | c26 | — | — | — | — | — | — | — | — | — | .... | .... | .... |
| Social Benefits............................. | c27 | — | — | — | — | — | — | — | — | — | .... | .... | .... |
| Other Payments........................... | c28 | 58,167 | 86,043 | 159,730 | 157,101 | 243,585 | 214,770 | 149,149 | 115,375 | — | .... | .... | .... |
| Net Cash Inflow:Operating Act.[1-2] | ccio | 34,872 | 118,112 | 113,592 | 548,717 | 367,327 | 476,780 | 104,434 | 517,855 | 536,212 | .... | .... | .... |
| Net Cash Outflow:Invest. in NFA...... | c31 | 97,209 | 152,683 | 145,983 | 197,854 | 222,453 | 391,621 | 353,522 | 631,521 | 728,385 | .... | .... | .... |
| Purchases of Nonfinancial Assets... | c31.1 | 97,209 | 152,683 | 145,983 | 197,854 | 222,453 | 391,621 | 353,522 | 631,521 | 728,385 | .... | .... | .... |
| Sales of Nonfinancial Assets.......... | c31.2 | | | | | | | | | | .... | .... | .... |
| Cash Surplus/Deficit [1-2-31=1-2M] | ccsd | −62,337 | −34,571 | −32,391 | 350,862 | 144,874 | 85,159 | −249,089 | −113,666 | −192,173 | .... | .... | .... |
| Net Acq. Fin. Assets, excl. Cash....... | c32x | 2,435 | — | — | 1,113 | — | — | — | — | — | .... | .... | .... |
| Domestic...................................... | c321x | 2,435 | — | — | 1,113 | — | — | — | — | — | .... | .... | .... |
| Foreign....................................... | c322x | — | — | — | — | — | — | — | — | — | .... | .... | .... |
| Net Incurrence of Liabilities.............. | c33 | 18,882 | 56,040 | −87,234 | −460,877 | −159,571 | 220,949 | 202,818 | 284,516 | 443,471 | .... | .... | .... |
| Domestic...................................... | c331 | 64,479 | 23,962 | −7,334 | −187,977 | −193,371 | 237,249 | 18,318 | −129,084 | 95,871 | .... | .... | .... |
| Foreign....................................... | c332 | −45,597 | 32,078 | −79,900 | −272,900 | 33,800 | −16,300 | 184,500 | 413,600 | 347,600 | .... | .... | .... |
| Net Cash Inflow, Fin.Act.[-32x+33].. | cnfb | 16,447 | 56,040 | −87,234 | −461,990 | −159,571 | 220,949 | 202,818 | 284,516 | 443,471 | .... | .... | .... |
| Net Change in Stock of Cash........... | cncb | −45,891 | 21,469 | −119,625 | −111,128 | −14,697 | 306,107 | −46,270 | 170,851 | 251,298 | .... | .... | .... |
| Stat. Discrep. [32X-33+NCB-CSD].... | ccsdz | — | — | — | — | — | — | — | — | — | .... | .... | .... |
| Memo Item:Cash Expenditure[2+31] | c2m | 1,168,693 | 1,435,619 | 1,772,390 | 2,017,071 | 2,209,818 | 2,859,484 | 2,855,240 | 3,651,125 | 4,409,553 | .... | .... | .... |
| Memo Item: Gross Debt.................. | c63 | .... | .... | .... | .... | .... | .... | .... | .... | | | | |
| **National Accounts** | | | | | | *Millions of Surinamese Dollars* | | | | | | | |
| Househ.Cons.Expend.,incl.NPISHs..... | 96f | .... | .... | 2,870 | 2,968 | 3,893 | 3,907 | 4,308 | .... | .... | .... | .... | .... |
| Government Consumption Expend... | 91f | 916 | 972 | 913 | 816 | 1,057 | 1,402 | 1,598 | .... | .... | .... | .... | .... |
| Gross Capital Formation................. | 93 | 144 | 126 | 2,895 | 3,410 | 4,297 | 5,339 | 4,342 | .... | .... | .... | .... | .... |
| Gross Fixed Capital Formation....... | 93e | 144 | 126 | 2,741 | 3,410 | 4,409 | 5,008 | 4,502 | .... | .... | .... | .... | .... |
| Exports of Goods and Services......... | 90c | 2,331 | 2,767 | 3,801 | 4,363 | 5,519 | 4,694 | 6,302 | .... | .... | .... | .... | .... |
| Imports of Goods and Services (-)..... | 98c | 2,364 | 3,368 | 3,273 | 3,809 | 5,068 | 4,659 | 4,607 | .... | .... | .... | .... | .... |
| Gross Domestic Product (GDP)......... | 99b | 4,058 | 4,899 | 7,206 | 8,061 | 9,698 | 10,683 | 11,943 | .... | .... | .... | .... | .... |
| Net Primary Income from Abroad..... | 98.n | −165 | −50 | −144 | 22 | 58 | 15 | −285 | .... | .... | .... | .... | .... |
| Gross National Income (GNI)............ | 99a | 3,884 | 4,786 | 7,062 | 8,083 | 9,756 | 10,698 | 11,658 | .... | .... | .... | .... | .... |
| GDP Volume 2007 Prices................ | 99b.p | .... | .... | 7,669 | 8,061 | 8,395 | 8,648 | 9,094 | 9,573 | 9,867p | 10,147p | 10,334p | 10,358p |
| GDP Volume (2010=100)................ | 99bvp | 77.7 | 81.2 | † 84.3 | 88.6 | 92.3 | 95.1 | 100.0 | 105.3 | 108.5 | 111.6 | 113.6 | 113.9 |
| GDP Deflator (2010=100)............... | 99bip | 43.7 | 50.5 | 71.5 | 76.1 | 88.0 | 94.1 | 100.0 | .... | .... | .... | .... | .... |
| | | | | | | *Millions: Midyear Estimates* | | | | | | | |
| Population.................................. | 99z | .49 | .49 | .50 | .50 | .51 | .51 | .52 | .52 | .53 | .53 | .54 | .54 |

# Swaziland   734

| | | 2004 | 2005 | 2006 | 2007 | 2008 | 2009 | 2010 | 2011 | 2012 | 2013 | 2014 | 2015 |
|---|---|---|---|---|---|---|---|---|---|---|---|---|---|
| **Exchange Rates** | | | | | | | *Emalangeni per SDR: End of Period* | | | | | | |
| Official Rate.................................. | aa | 8.7434 | 9.0401 | 10.4857 | 10.7615 | 14.3322 | 11.5696 | 10.2129 | 12.5016 | 13.0656 | 16.1544 | 16.7786 | 21.5412 |
| | | | | | *Emalangeni per US Dollar: End of Period (ae) Period Average (rf)* | | | | | | | | |
| Official Rate.................................. | ae | 5.6300 | 6.3250 | 6.9700 | 6.8100 | 9.3050 | 7.3800 | 6.6316 | 8.1429 | 8.5012 | 10.4899 | 11.5810 | 15.5450 |
| Official Rate.................................. | rf | 6.4597 | 6.3593 | 6.7715 | 7.0454 | 8.2612 | 8.4737 | 7.3212 | 7.2611 | 8.2100 | 9.6551 | 10.8527 | 12.7589 |
| **Fund Position** | | | | | | | *Millions of SDRs: End of Period* | | | | | | |
| Quota......................................... | 2f.s | 50.70 | 50.70 | 50.70 | 50.70 | 50.70 | 50.70 | 50.70 | 50.70 | 50.70 | 50.70 | 50.70 | 50.70 |
| SDR Holdings................................. | 1b.s | 2.47 | 2.48 | 2.49 | 2.51 | 2.55 | 44.41 | 44.41 | 44.41 | 44.56 | 48.73 | 48.74 | 48.74 |
| Reserve Position in the Fund............ | 1c.s | 6.56 | 6.56 | 6.56 | 6.56 | 6.56 | 6.56 | 6.56 | 6.56 | 6.56 | 6.56 | 6.56 | 6.56 |
| Total Fund Cred.&Loans Outstg........ | 2tl | — | — | — | — | — | — | — | — | — | — | — | — |
| SDR Allocations............................ | 1bd | 6.43 | 6.43 | 6.43 | 6.43 | 6.43 | 48.28 | 48.28 | 48.28 | 48.28 | 48.28 | 48.28 | 48.28 |
| **International Liquidity** | | | | | | *Millions of US Dollars Unless Otherwise Indicated: End of Period* | | | | | | | |
| Total Reserves minus Gold.............. | 1l.d | 323.56 | 243.90 | 372.53 | 774.19 | 751.94 | 958.87 | 756.34 | 600.51 | 740.96 | 762.54 | 690.76 | 548.00 |
| SDR Holdings................................ | 1b.d | 3.84 | 3.55 | 3.74 | 3.96 | 3.93 | 69.62 | 68.39 | 68.18 | 68.49 | 75.05 | 70.61 | 67.54 |
| Reserve Position in the Fund......... | 1c.d | 10.19 | 9.38 | 9.87 | 10.37 | 10.11 | 10.29 | 10.11 | 10.07 | 10.08 | 10.11 | 9.51 | 9.09 |
| Foreign Exchange......................... | 1d.d | 309.53 | 230.97 | 358.91 | 759.86 | 737.90 | 878.96 | 677.85 | 522.25 | 662.39 | 677.39 | 610.64 | 471.36 |
| Central Bank: Other Assets.............. | 3..d | † 76.04 | 125.42 | 243.53 | 345.78 | 517.22 | 554.24 | 376.99 | 345.81 | 439.90 | 527.49 | 417.33 | 358.27 |
| Central Bank: Other Liabs.............. | 4..d | † 4.32 | 2.57 | 10.17 | 15.33 | 8.76 | 6.10 | 7.05 | 6.60 | 8.40 | 9.62 | 9.24 | 7.83 |
| Other Depository Corps.: Assets....... | 7a.d | † 97.50 | 70.10 | 127.13 | 112.42 | 159.87 | 302.42 | 331.14 | 198.99 | 246.94 | 175.19 | 123.37 | 144.01 |
| Other Depository Corps.: Liabs......... | 7b.d | † 7.30 | 10.90 | 17.82 | 9.99 | 34.62 | 39.97 | 61.34 | 143.95 | 90.13 | 107.94 | 68.48 | 45.13 |
| **Central Bank** | | | | | | *Millions of Emalangeni: End of Period* | | | | | | | |
| Net Foreign Assets........................ | 11n | † 850.58 | 1,522.97 | 2,534.53 | 5,062.12 | 6,886.83 | 5,876.10 | 3,954.14 | 3,576.10 | 4,934.75 | 7,157.53 | 7,078.47 | 7,360.68 |
| Claims on Nonresidents................. | 11 | † 931.16 | 1,597.35 | 2,672.84 | 5,235.75 | 7,062.42 | 6,479.06 | 4,494.18 | 4,233.51 | 5,637.92 | 8,042.99 | 7,995.07 | 8,522.99 |
| Liabilities to Nonresidents............. | 16c | † 80.58 | 74.38 | 138.31 | 173.63 | 175.59 | 602.96 | 540.04 | 657.41 | 703.16 | 885.46 | 916.60 | 1,162.31 |
| Claims on Other Depository Corps.... | 12e | † 1.86 | .73 | 21.87 | 1.88 | 1.87 | 1.86 | 1.86 | 1.86 | .66 | .66 | 1.83 | .65 |
| Net Claims on Central Government.. | 12an | † −508.67 | −1,082.95 | −1,976.59 | −4,048.63 | −5,219.18 | −4,107.09 | −2,322.81 | −1,169.83 | −2,503.52 | −4,355.89 | −4,241.11 | −4,005.34 |
| Claims on Central Government...... | 12a | † 100.23 | 100.57 | 55.12 | 14.74 | — | .78 | .84 | 746.26 | 58.42 | 60.36 | 2.61 | 1.39 |
| Liabilities to Central Government... | 16d | † 608.90 | 1,183.52 | 2,031.71 | 4,063.37 | 5,219.18 | 4,107.87 | 2,323.65 | 1,916.09 | 2,561.94 | 4,416.26 | 4,243.72 | 4,006.73 |
| Claims on Other Sectors................. | 12s | † 12.37 | 8.88 | 20.45 | 7.52 | 9.90 | 12.96 | 24.50 | 20.22 | 21.57 | 20.90 | 23.21 | 26.72 |
| Claims on Other Financial Corps... | 12g | † — | — | — | — | — | 1.66 | 3.17 | 4.82 | 5.44 | 6.84 | 6.04 | 2.25 |
| Claims on State & Local Govts..... | 12b | † — | — | — | — | — | — | — | — | — | — | — | — |
| Claims on Public Nonfin. Corps...... | 12c | † — | — | — | — | — | — | — | — | — | — | — | — |
| Claims on Private Sector............... | 12d | † 12.37 | 8.88 | 20.45 | 7.52 | 9.90 | 11.30 | 21.34 | 15.40 | 16.14 | 14.06 | 17.17 | 24.47 |
| Monetary Base............................. | 14 | † 482.39 | 496.52 | 566.51 | 758.50 | 943.54 | 1,305.05 | 1,171.32 | 1,781.20 | 1,794.27 | 1,901.24 | 1,886.45 | 2,176.53 |
| Currency in Circulation.................. | 14a | † 301.66 | 341.21 | 378.51 | 407.94 | 416.19 | 507.66 | 563.52 | 540.90 | 642.78 | 732.71 | 871.66 | 962.88 |
| Liabs. to Other Depository Corps.... | 14c | † 179.02 | 148.65 | 186.39 | 349.75 | 525.73 | 795.80 | 599.05 | 868.50 | 777.01 | 796.34 | 996.82 | 1,201.08 |
| Liabilities to Other Sectors............. | 14d | † 1.71 | 6.66 | 1.61 | .81 | 1.62 | 1.60 | 8.74 | 371.80 | 374.48 | 372.19 | 17.97 | 12.57 |
| Other Liabs. to Other Dep. Corps..... | 14n | † — | — | — | — | — | — | — | — | — | — | — | — |
| Dep. & Sec. Excl. f/Monetary Base.... | 14o | † — | — | — | — | — | — | — | — | — | — | — | — |
| Deposits Included in Broad Money. | 15 | † — | — | — | — | — | — | — | — | — | — | — | — |
| Sec.Ot.th.Shares Incl.in Brd. Money | 16a | † — | — | — | — | — | — | — | — | — | — | — | — |
| Deposits Excl. from Broad Money... | 16b | † — | — | — | — | — | — | — | — | — | — | — | — |
| Sec.Ot.th.Shares Excl.f/Brd.Money.. | 16s | † — | — | — | — | — | — | — | — | — | — | — | — |
| Loans....................................... | 16l | † — | — | — | — | — | — | — | — | — | — | — | — |
| Financial Derivatives...................... | 16m | † — | — | — | — | — | — | — | — | — | — | — | — |
| Shares and Other Equity................ | 17a | † −70.94 | −12.73 | 85.74 | 386.48 | 951.62 | 568.60 | 524.90 | 824.06 | 957.95 | 1,278.65 | 1,385.01 | 1,907.18 |
| Other Items (Net)........................... | 17r | † −55.30 | −34.15 | −51.99 | −122.10 | −215.74 | −89.82 | −38.52 | −176.91 | −298.76 | −356.69 | −409.05 | −700.97 |
| Memo Item: | | | | | | | | | | | | | |
| Total Assets................................. | 10ra | † 1,533.36 | 2,216.19 | 3,347.67 | 5,918.33 | 7,905.72 | 7,342.96 | 5,259.15 | 5,869.83 | 6,667.40 | 9,229.58 | 9,320.35 | 10,143.52 |
| **Other Depository Corporations** | | | | | | *Millions of Emalangeni: End of Period* | | | | | | | |
| Net Foreign Assets......................... | 21n | † 507.86 | 374.45 | 761.93 | 697.54 | 1,178.13 | 1,934.69 | 1,789.82 | 448.25 | 1,334.72 | 709.08 | 635.27 | 1,537.76 |
| Claims on Nonresidents................. | 21 | † 548.95 | 443.37 | 886.12 | 765.57 | 1,503.75 | 2,229.32 | 2,196.72 | 1,620.39 | 2,101.93 | 1,847.23 | 1,427.91 | 2,239.69 |
| Liabilities to Nonresidents............. | 26c | † 41.08 | 68.91 | 124.19 | 68.03 | 325.61 | 294.63 | 406.90 | 1,172.14 | 767.21 | 1,138.16 | 792.64 | 701.93 |
| Claims on Central Bank.................. | 20 | † 211.71 | 210.55 | 353.61 | 498.97 | 609.05 | 912.92 | 1,133.68 | 1,023.21 | 999.67 | 1,056.07 | 1,295.21 | 1,608.50 |
| Currency.................................... | 20a | † 65.81 | 99.13 | 128.00 | 159.30 | 136.37 | 180.02 | 214.18 | 183.89 | 233.44 | 233.55 | 341.99 | 408.16 |
| Reserve Deposits and Securities..... | 20b | † 145.90 | 111.41 | 225.62 | 283.66 | 328.27 | 441.54 | 397.02 | 817.65 | 766.23 | 822.52 | 953.22 | 1,200.33 |
| Other Claims............................... | 20n | † — | — | — | 56.01 | 144.42 | 291.36 | 522.48 | 21.67 | — | — | — | — |
| Net Claims on Central Government.. | 22an | † 311.37 | 296.09 | 299.68 | 164.28 | −77.05 | −130.75 | 91.24 | 550.95 | 914.18 | 1,347.93 | 1,276.52 | 1,267.81 |
| Claims on Central Government...... | 22a | † 332.49 | 309.37 | 363.49 | 338.89 | 320.68 | 360.92 | 607.81 | 1,007.28 | 1,296.21 | 1,679.81 | 1,591.01 | 1,746.34 |
| Liabilities to Central Government... | 26d | † 21.12 | 13.28 | 63.82 | 174.61 | 397.73 | 491.67 | 516.57 | 456.33 | 382.03 | 331.89 | 314.49 | 478.53 |
| Claims on Other Sectors................. | 22s | † 2,995.73 | 3,610.50 | 4,337.14 | 5,266.74 | 5,740.06 | 6,498.07 | 6,874.61 | 8,258.93 | 8,040.55 | 9,738.27 | 10,848.83 | 11,398.84 |
| Claims on Other Financial Corps.... | 22g | † 188.89 | 74.31 | 55.57 | 45.72 | 161.57 | 175.64 | 514.78 | 229.93 | 201.84 | 260.12 | 480.04 | 543.56 |
| Claims on State & Local Govts....... | 22b | † 4.36 | 5.58 | 5.86 | 4.77 | 10.42 | 14.39 | 13.15 | 22.21 | 21.51 | 51.14 | 24.92 | 69.34 |
| Claims on Public Nonfin. Corps...... | 22c | † 69.74 | 70.01 | 45.99 | 39.67 | 51.28 | 69.70 | 152.52 | 189.24 | 135.37 | 186.75 | 202.37 | 220.65 |
| Claims on Private Sector............... | 22d | † 2,732.73 | 3,460.60 | 4,229.72 | 5,176.58 | 5,516.79 | 6,238.35 | 6,194.15 | 7,817.55 | 7,681.83 | 9,240.26 | 10,141.50 | 10,565.30 |
| Liabilities to Central Bank.............. | 26g | † 34.05 | — | 20.00 | — | — | — | — | — | 1.42 | — | — | — |
| Transf.Dep.Included in Broad Money | 24 | † 843.08 | 1,046.03 | 1,106.01 | 1,417.33 | 1,690.71 | 2,007.75 | 2,180.95 | 2,510.68 | 3,012.28 | 3,900.03 | 3,715.71 | 4,189.83 |
| Other Dep.Included in Broad Money. | 25 | † 2,081.96 | 2,175.15 | 2,982.16 | 3,605.18 | 4,110.81 | 5,376.24 | 5,783.69 | 5,538.91 | 5,861.74 | 6,425.55 | 7,375.30 | 8,461.97 |
| Sec.Ot.th.Shares Incl.in Brd. Money. | 26a | † — | — | — | — | — | — | — | — | — | — | — | — |
| Deposits Excl. from Broad Money..... | 26b | † — | — | — | — | — | — | — | — | — | — | — | — |
| Sec.Ot.th.Shares Excl.f/Brd.Money.... | 26s | † 30.84 | 15.26 | 28.64 | 20.15 | 13.56 | 15.57 | 16.55 | 13.08 | 9.53 | 8.80 | 7.40 | 4.83 |
| Loans....................................... | 26l | † — | — | — | — | — | — | — | — | — | — | — | — |
| Financial Derivatives...................... | 26m | † — | — | — | — | — | — | — | — | — | — | — | — |
| Insurance Technical Reserves.......... | 26r | † — | — | — | — | — | — | — | — | — | — | — | — |
| Shares and Other Equity................ | 27a | † 1,007.35 | 1,106.22 | 1,386.82 | 1,562.93 | 1,705.37 | 1,852.15 | 1,911.49 | 2,058.56 | 2,167.28 | 2,454.56 | 2,866.48 | 3,155.61 |
| Other Items (Net)........................... | 27r | † 29.39 | 148.94 | 228.72 | 21.95 | −70.26 | −36.79 | −3.34 | 160.10 | 236.88 | 62.41 | 90.95 | .68 |
| Memo Item: | | | | | | | | | | | | | |
| Total Assets................................. | 20ra | † 4,502.61 | 4,837.30 | 6,409.46 | 7,296.89 | 8,655.13 | 10,540.79 | 11,277.17 | 12,343.78 | 12,976.53 | 14,998.56 | 15,905.33 | 17,969.13 |

| | | 2004 | 2005 | 2006 | 2007 | 2008 | 2009 | 2010 | 2011 | 2012 | 2013 | 2014 | 2015 |
|---|---|---|---|---|---|---|---|---|---|---|---|---|---|
| **Depository Corporations** | | *Millions of Emalangeni: End of Period* | | | | | | | | | | | |
| Net Foreign Assets.......................... | **31n** | † 1,358.44 | 1,897.43 | 3,296.46 | 5,759.66 | 8,064.96 | 7,810.79 | 5,743.96 | 4,024.35 | 6,269.48 | 7,866.61 | 7,713.74 | 8,898.44 |
| Claims on Nonresidents................ | **31** | † 1,480.11 | 2,040.72 | 3,558.96 | 6,001.32 | 8,566.17 | 8,708.38 | 6,690.89 | 5,853.90 | 7,739.85 | 9,890.22 | 9,422.98 | 10,762.69 |
| Liabilities to Nonresidents............. | **36c** | † 121.66 | 143.29 | 262.49 | 241.66 | 501.21 | 897.59 | 946.93 | 1,829.55 | 1,470.37 | 2,023.62 | 1,709.24 | 1,864.25 |
| Domestic Claims............................. | **32** | † 2,810.79 | 2,832.52 | 2,680.68 | 1,389.91 | 453.73 | 2,273.20 | 4,667.53 | 7,660.27 | 6,472.78 | 6,751.20 | 6,751.20 | 8,688.04 |
| Net Claims on Central Government | **32an** | † −197.31 | −786.86 | −1,676.91 | −3,884.35 | −5,296.23 | −4,237.84 | −2,231.57 | −618.89 | −1,589.34 | −3,007.97 | −2,964.58 | −2,737.53 |
| Claims on Central Government.... | **32a** | † 432.71 | 409.94 | 418.62 | 353.63 | 320.68 | 361.69 | 608.65 | 1,753.54 | 1,354.63 | 1,740.18 | 1,593.63 | 1,747.73 |
| Liabilities to Central Government. | **36d** | † 630.02 | 1,196.80 | 2,095.53 | 4,237.99 | 5,616.91 | 4,599.53 | 2,840.22 | 2,372.42 | 2,943.97 | 4,748.14 | 4,558.21 | 4,485.26 |
| Claims on Other Sectors................ | **32s** | † 3,008.10 | 3,619.38 | 4,357.59 | 5,274.26 | 5,749.96 | 6,511.03 | 6,899.11 | 8,279.15 | 8,062.12 | 9,759.17 | 10,872.04 | 11,425.56 |
| Claims on Other Financial Corps.. | **32g** | † 188.89 | 74.31 | 55.57 | 45.72 | 161.57 | 177.30 | 517.95 | 234.76 | 207.27 | 266.96 | 486.08 | 545.81 |
| Claims on State & Local Govts..... | **32b** | † 4.36 | 5.58 | 5.86 | 4.77 | 10.42 | 14.39 | 13.15 | 22.21 | 21.51 | 51.14 | 24.92 | 69.34 |
| Claims on Public Nonfin. Corps.... | **32c** | † 69.74 | 70.01 | 45.99 | 39.67 | 51.28 | 69.70 | 152.52 | 189.24 | 135.37 | 186.75 | 202.37 | 220.65 |
| Claims on Private Sector............. | **32d** | † 2,745.10 | 3,469.47 | 4,250.17 | 5,184.10 | 5,526.69 | 6,249.65 | 6,215.48 | 7,832.95 | 7,697.97 | 9,254.32 | 10,158.67 | 10,589.77 |
| Broad Money Liabilities................... | **35l** | † 3,162.59 | 3,469.91 | 4,340.30 | 5,271.96 | 6,082.96 | 7,713.23 | 8,322.73 | 8,778.41 | 9,657.84 | 11,196.93 | 11,638.65 | 13,219.08 |
| Currency Outside Depository Corps | **34a** | † 235.85 | 242.08 | 250.51 | 248.64 | 279.82 | 327.63 | 349.35 | 357.01 | 409.34 | 499.17 | 529.67 | 554.72 |
| Transferable Deposits................... | **34** | † 844.79 | 1,052.69 | 1,107.63 | 1,418.14 | 1,692.33 | 2,009.35 | 2,189.70 | 2,524.99 | 3,029.28 | 3,914.68 | 3,733.68 | 4,202.40 |
| Other Deposits.............................. | **35** | † 2,081.96 | 2,175.15 | 2,982.16 | 3,605.18 | 4,110.81 | 5,376.24 | 5,783.69 | 5,896.41 | 6,219.22 | 6,783.08 | 7,375.30 | 8,461.97 |
| Securities Other than Shares.......... | **36a** | † — | — | — | — | — | — | — | — | — | — | — | — |
| Deposits Excl. from Broad Money..... | **36b** | † — | — | — | — | — | — | — | — | — | — | — | — |
| Sec.Ot.th.Shares Excl.f/Brd.Money.... | **36s** | † 30.84 | 15.26 | 28.64 | 20.15 | 13.56 | 15.57 | 16.55 | 13.08 | 9.53 | 8.80 | 7.40 | 4.83 |
| Loans...................... | **36l** | † — | — | — | — | — | — | — | — | — | — | — | — |
| Financial Derivatives....................... | **36m** | † — | — | — | — | — | — | — | — | — | — | — | — |
| Insurance Technical Reserves........... | **36r** | † — | — | — | — | — | — | — | — | — | — | — | — |
| Shares and Other Equity.................. | **37a** | † 936.41 | 1,093.49 | 1,472.56 | 1,949.41 | 2,657.00 | 2,420.75 | 2,436.38 | 2,882.62 | 3,125.23 | 3,733.21 | 4,251.49 | 5,062.79 |
| Other Items (Net)............................ | **37r** | † 39.39 | 151.29 | 135.64 | −91.94 | −234.83 | −65.57 | −364.17 | 10.51 | −50.34 | −321.13 | −276.34 | −700.22 |
| Broad Money Liabs., Seasonally Adj. | **35l.b** | † 3,213.47 | 3,527.08 | 4,415.79 | 5,359.11 | 6,156.01 | 7,743.44 | 8,274.18 | 8,665.59 | 9,478.47 | 10,954.17 | 11,359.36 | 12,897.84 |
| **Monetary Aggregates** | | *Millions of Emalangeni: End of Period* | | | | | | | | | | | |
| Broad Money.............................. | **59m** | 3,162.59 | 3,469.91 | 4,340.30 | 5,271.96 | 6,082.96 | 7,713.23 | 8,322.73 | 8,778.41 | 9,657.84 | 11,196.93 | 11,638.65 | 13,219.08 |
| o/w:Currency Issued by Cent.Govt | **59m.a** | — | — | — | — | — | — | — | — | — | — | — | — |
| o/w: Dep.in Nonfin. Corporations. | **59m.b** | — | — | — | — | — | — | — | — | — | — | — | — |
| o/w:Secs. Issued by Central Govt.. | **59m.c** | — | — | — | — | — | — | — | — | — | — | — | — |
| Money (National Definitions) | | | | | | | | | | | | | |
| M1.......................................... | **59ma** | 1,078.93 | 1,288.10 | 1,356.57 | 1,665.97 | 1,970.53 | 2,335.39 | 2,530.30 | 2,867.69 | 3,421.62 | 4,399.20 | 4,245.38 | 4,744.54 |
| M2.......................................... | **59mb** | 3,162.59 | 3,469.91 | 4,340.34 | 5,271.96 | 6,082.96 | 7,713.23 | 8,322.73 | 8,778.41 | 9,657.84 | 11,196.93 | 11,638.65 | 13,219.08 |
| **Interest Rates** | | *Percent Per Annum* | | | | | | | | | | | |
| Discount Rate (End of Period).......... | **60.a** | 7.50 | 7.00 | 9.00 | 11.00 | 11.00 | 6.50 | 5.50 | 5.50 | 5.00 | 5.00 | 5.25 | 5.75 |
| Money Market Rate........................ | **60b** | 4.12 | 3.47 | 4.40 | 6.67 | 8.17 | 5.40 | 3.85 | 2.85 | 2.47 | 2.08 | 2.14 | 2.27 |
| Treasury Bill Rate........................... | **60c** | 7.94 | 7.08 | 7.54 | 9.03 | 10.77 | 7.93 | 6.60 | 6.07 | 6.87 | 6.31 | 6.43 | 6.44 |
| Savings Rate................................. | **60k** | 3.71 | 3.08 | 3.18 | 4.03 | 4.88 | 2.85 | 1.75 | 2.40 | 2.38 | 2.25 | 2.32 | 2.39 |
| Deposit Rate................................. | **60l** | 4.63 | 4.01 | 4.93 | 7.05 | 8.17 | 5.40 | 3.85 | 2.85 | 2.47 | 2.08 | 2.14 | 2.27 |
| Lending Rate................................. | **60p** | 11.29 | 10.63 | 11.17 | 13.17 | 14.83 | 11.38 | 9.75 | 9.00 | 8.75 | 8.50 | 8.63 | 9.04 |
| **Prices and Labor** | | *Index Numbers (2010=100): Period Averages* | | | | | | | | | | | |
| Consumer Prices............................. | **64** | 66.3 | 69.5 | † 73.1 | 79.0 | 89.1 | 95.7 | 100.0 | † 106.1 | 115.6 | 122.1 | 129.0 | 135.4 |
| **Intl. Transactions & Positions** | | *Millions of Emalangeni* | | | | | | | | | | | |
| Exports............................. | **70** | 12,590.1 | 11,256.0 | 12,121.1 | 13,245.3 | 14,044.1 | 12,286.8 | 11,347.9 | .... | .... | .... | .... | .... |
| Imports, c.i.f................................... | **71** | 12,434.3 | 12,082.7 | 13,001.4 | 12,998.7 | 14,044.1 | 13,557.9 | 12,446.1 | .... | .... | .... | .... | .... |

# Swaziland 734

|  |  | 2004 | 2005 | 2006 | 2007 | 2008 | 2009 | 2010 | 2011 | 2012 | 2013 | 2014 | 2015 |
|---|---|---|---|---|---|---|---|---|---|---|---|---|---|
| **Balance of Payments** | | | | | | | *Millions of US Dollars* | | | | | | |
| A. Current Account* | 109bx | 71.3 | −102.6 | −196.6 | −65.5 | −231.4 | −415.1 | −388.6 | −375.7 | 97.9 | 149.6 | 58.0 | .... |
| Goods, credit (exports) | 1a9cx | 1,791.8 | 1,601.3 | 1,560.6 | 1,625.8 | 1,489.2 | 1,564.9 | 1,805.3 | 1,905.7 | 1,925.8 | 1,860.8 | 1,803.2 | .... |
| Goods, debit (imports) | 1a9dx | 1,640.9 | 1,779.9 | 1,806.3 | 1,934.7 | 1,529.3 | 1,696.1 | 1,953.9 | 1,943.0 | 1,848.0 | 1,691.5 | 1,687.3 | .... |
| Balance on goods | 1a9bx | 150.9 | −178.6 | −245.7 | −308.8 | −40.1 | −131.2 | −148.6 | −37.3 | 77.9 | 169.3 | 115.9 | |
| Services, credit (exports) | 1b9cx | 189.9 | 203.3 | 277.3 | 493.1 | 255.1 | 210.5 | 257.5 | 299.7 | 241.8 | 231.8 | 290.6 | |
| Services, debit (imports) | 1b9dx | 377.9 | 403.1 | 373.6 | 507.5 | 650.9 | 562.9 | 670.9 | 874.9 | 826.3 | 702.3 | 648.8 | |
| Balance on Goods & Services | 1z9bx | −37.1 | −378.4 | −342.1 | −323.3 | −435.9 | −483.5 | −562.0 | −612.5 | −506.6 | −301.1 | −242.2 | |
| Primary income: credit | 1c9cx | 127.5 | 271.3 | 241.7 | 280.8 | 298.0 | 290.8 | 212.5 | 192.3 | 200.5 | 188.2 | 240.7 | |
| Primary income: debit | 1c9dx | 124.9 | 93.0 | 227.7 | 217.0 | 303.2 | 413.4 | 438.6 | 448.0 | 514.3 | 555.2 | 635.6 | |
| Balance on gds, serv. & prim. inc. | 1y9bx | −34.5 | −200.1 | −328.1 | −259.5 | −441.1 | −606.2 | −788.1 | −868.2 | −820.4 | −668.1 | −637.1 | |
| Secondary income: credit | 1d9ca | 370.8 | 339.6 | 366.3 | 403.5 | 417.7 | 404.9 | 482.6 | 580.1 | 1,013.6 | 954.6 | 829.5 | |
| Secondary income: debit | 1d9da | 265.0 | 242.1 | 234.8 | 209.5 | 208.0 | 213.8 | 83.1 | 87.6 | 95.3 | 136.8 | 134.5 | |
| B. Capital Account* | 209ba | — | −3.3 | 22.0 | −35.2 | 39.4 | −3.8 | 14.4 | 20.2 | 113.3 | 26.0 | 78.0 | .... |
| Capital account: credit | 209ca | — | 1.0 | 26.3 | 5.9 | 41.1 | 5.7 | 22.2 | 21.7 | 117.9 | 26.8 | 79.2 | .... |
| Capital account: debit | 209da | — | 4.2 | 4.3 | 41.0 | 1.7 | 9.5 | 7.8 | 1.5 | 4.6 | .7 | 1.3 | .... |
| Balance on current & capital acct. | 129ba | 71.3 | −105.9 | −174.7 | −100.7 | −192.0 | −418.9 | −374.2 | −355.5 | 211.3 | 175.7 | 135.9 | .... |
| C. Financial Account* | 309na | 204.0 | −148.1 | −260.7 | −431.0 | −448.1 | −473.0 | −87.8 | −116.6 | 73.8 | 189.1 | 339.1 | .... |
| Direct investment: assets | 3a9aa | −1.4 | −22.0 | −.6 | 23.2 | −7.9 | 7.0 | 3.9 | −9.0 | −6.4 | .3 | .5 | .... |
| Equity & investment fund shares.. | 3aaaa | — | .1 | −.3 | — | 5.1 | 5.8 | 3.0 | .4 | — | 2.9 | .1 | .... |
| Debt instruments | 3abaa | −1.4 | −22.1 | −.3 | 23.2 | −13.0 | 1.2 | 1.0 | −9.4 | −6.4 | −2.5 | .4 | .... |
| Direct investment: liabilities | 3a9la | 69.6 | −45.9 | 121.0 | 37.5 | 105.7 | 65.7 | 135.7 | 93.2 | 89.7 | 29.4 | 26.6 | .... |
| Equity & investment fund shares . | 3aala | 32.3 | −15.8 | 78.5 | 70.5 | 90.6 | 53.1 | 49.3 | 50.3 | 2.7 | 29.8 | 55.1 | .... |
| Debt instruments | 3abla | 37.3 | −30.0 | 42.5 | −33.0 | 15.1 | 12.6 | 86.4 | 42.9 | 87.0 | −.3 | −28.5 | .... |
| Portfolio investment: assets | 3b9aa | .9 | −3.7 | 9.5 | −4.2 | 75.5 | −122.8 | −49.7 | 103.7 | 13.1 | 236.8 | 2.3 | .... |
| Equity & investment fund shares | 3baaa | −.2 | — | −.2 | .1 | 76.9 | −3.5 | 100.2 | 9.9 | .7 | 215.0 | 50.0 | .... |
| Debt securities | 3bbaa | 1.1 | −3.7 | 9.6 | −4.4 | −1.4 | −119.3 | −149.8 | 93.8 | 12.4 | 21.8 | −47.8 | .... |
| Portfolio investment: liabilities | 3b9la | .3 | .8 | 5.5 | 1.0 | 43.9 | −6.6 | 4.7 | | | | | .... |
| Equity & investment fund shares . | 3bala | .3 | .8 | 5.5 | 1.0 | 43.9 | −6.6 | 4.7 | — | — | — | | .... |
| Debt securities | 3bbla | .... | .... | .... | .... | .... | .... | .... | .... | .... | .... | .... | .... |
| Fin. der.& empl.stk.ops.(ESOs): net. | 3c9na | .... | .... | .... | .... | .... | .... | .... | .... | .... | .... | .... | .... |
| Fin. der. & ESOs.: assets | 3c9aa | .... | .... | .... | .... | .... | .... | .... | .... | .... | .... | .... | .... |
| Fin. der. & ESOs.: liabilities | 3c9la | .... | .... | .... | .... | .... | .... | .... | .... | .... | .... | .... | .... |
| Other investment: assets | 3d9aa | 231.4 | −84.3 | −101.2 | −357.8 | −190.1 | −249.7 | 161.6 | −42.1 | 69.1 | −14.5 | 274.2 | .... |
| Other equity | 3daaa | .... | .... | .... | .... | .... | .... | .... | .... | .... | .... | .... | .... |
| Debt instruments | 3dzaa | 231.4 | −84.3 | −101.2 | −357.8 | −190.1 | −249.7 | 161.6 | −42.1 | 69.1 | −14.5 | 274.2 | .... |
| Other investment: liabilities | 3d9la | −43.0 | 83.1 | 41.8 | 53.7 | 176.0 | 48.4 | 63.3 | 76.1 | −87.6 | 4.1 | −88.7 | .... |
| Other equity | 3dala | .... | .... | .... | .... | .... | .... | .... | .... | .... | .... | .... | .... |
| Debt instruments | 3dzla | −43.0 | 83.1 | 41.8 | 53.7 | 176.0 | 48.4 | 63.3 | 76.1 | −87.6 | 4.1 | −88.7 | .... |
| Curr.+ cap.− finan. acct. balance... | 4y9na | −132.7 | 42.2 | 86.0 | 330.4 | 256.1 | 54.2 | −286.3 | −238.9 | 137.5 | −13.4 | −203.2 | .... |
| D. Net Errors and Omissions | 409na | 167.6 | −41.1 | −235.0 | −695.8 | −36.2 | −55.3 | 55.5 | 108.3 | −29.6 | 103.6 | 75.4 | .... |
| E. Reserves and Related Items | 4z9na | 34.9 | 1.1 | −148.9 | −365.5 | 219.9 | −1.1 | −230.9 | −130.6 | 107.9 | 90.2 | −127.8 | .... |
| Reserve assets | 3e9aa | 34.4 | −.6 | −151.2 | −365.2 | 220.1 | −.3 | −230.6 | −95.0 | 158.8 | 193.2 | −23.5 | .... |
| Credit and loans from the IMF | 3dcla | — | — | — | — | — | — | — | — | — | — | — | .... |
| Exceptional financing | 409la | −.5 | −1.7 | −2.3 | .2 | .2 | .8 | .3 | 35.6 | 50.9 | 103.0 | 104.2 | .... |

*Excludes components in group E

| **International Investment Position** | | | | | | | *Millions of US Dollars* | | | | | | |
|---|---|---|---|---|---|---|---|---|---|---|---|---|---|
| Assets | 809aa | 2,162.2 | 1,981.5 | 2,693.1 | 3,226.8 | 1,585.0 | 3,442.1 | 2,877.0 | 2,619.3 | 2,808.8 | 2,437.9 | 2,590.0 | .... |
| Direct investment | 8a9aa | 110.0 | 75.8 | 68.2 | 92.3 | 22.2 | 31.4 | 90.8 | 103.2 | 91.9 | 35.3 | 28.4 | .... |
| Equity & investment fund shares.. | 8aaaa | 1.7 | 1.6 | 1.2 | 21.0 | 19.4 | 26.4 | 28.0 | 59.7 | 70.4 | 22.1 | 20.2 | .... |
| Debt instruments | 8abaa | 108.3 | 74.1 | 67.0 | 71.3 | 2.9 | 5.0 | 62.8 | 43.4 | 21.5 | 13.2 | 8.2 | .... |
| Portfolio investment | 8b9aa | 17.8 | 12.1 | 20.2 | 16.2 | 8.8 | 1,454.4 | 1,113.8 | 1,114.0 | 1,177.9 | 896.0 | 1,085.8 | .... |
| Equity & investment fund shares.. | 8baaa | 3.1 | 2.8 | 2.4 | 2.5 | .... | 739.0 | 932.8 | 812.2 | 862.8 | 651.6 | 880.2 | .... |
| Debt securities | 8bbaa | 14.7 | 9.3 | 17.8 | 13.7 | 8.8 | 715.5 | 181.0 | 301.8 | 315.1 | 244.4 | 205.6 | .... |
| Fin. der.(oth.than reserves) & ESOs | 8c9aa | .... | .... | .... | .... | .... | .... | .... | .... | .... | .... | .... | .... |
| Other investment | 8d9aa | 1,750.6 | 1,641.1 | 2,221.3 | 2,457.1 | 795.1 | 1,078.3 | 994.8 | 882.1 | 875.8 | 740.4 | 797.6 | .... |
| Other equity | 8daaa | .... | .... | .... | .... | .... | .... | .... | .... | .... | .... | .... | .... |
| Debt instruments | 8dzaa | 1,750.6 | 1,641.1 | 2,221.3 | 2,457.1 | 795.1 | 1,078.3 | 994.8 | 882.1 | 875.8 | 740.4 | 797.6 | .... |
| Reserve assets | 8e9aa | 283.8 | 252.5 | 383.5 | 661.2 | 758.8 | 878.0 | 677.6 | 520.1 | 663.2 | 766.2 | 678.3 | .... |
| Liabilities | 809la | 1,452.2 | 1,304.5 | 1,357.0 | 1,390.2 | 1,083.6 | 1,510.1 | 1,607.3 | 1,582.8 | 1,581.2 | 1,494.6 | 1,240.2 | .... |
| Direct investment | 8a9la | 935.0 | 786.2 | 831.0 | 719.5 | 516.1 | 742.6 | 986.9 | 970.3 | 1,071.8 | 823.7 | 681.8 | .... |
| Equity & investment fund shares.. | 8aala | 616.8 | 533.1 | 560.1 | 570.3 | 312.0 | 571.4 | 684.7 | 552.6 | 511.3 | 497.1 | 546.3 | .... |
| Debt instruments | 8abla | 318.2 | 253.1 | 270.9 | 149.2 | 204.1 | 171.1 | 302.2 | 417.7 | 560.4 | 326.5 | 135.5 | .... |
| Portfolio investment | 8b9la | 1.1 | 1.7 | 6.9 | 1.9 | 44.8 | 2.4 | .1 | 2.0 | 1.8 | .2 | .2 | .... |
| Equity & investment fund shares.. | 8bala | 1.1 | 1.7 | 6.9 | 1.9 | 44.8 | 2.4 | .1 | 2.0 | 1.8 | .2 | .2 | .... |
| Debt securities | 8bbla | .... | .... | .... | .... | .... | .... | .... | .... | .... | .... | .... | .... |
| Fin. der.(oth.than reserves) & ESOs | 8c9la | .... | .... | .... | .... | .... | .... | .... | .... | .... | .... | .... | .... |
| Other investment | 8d9la | 516.2 | 516.7 | 519.1 | 668.8 | 522.7 | 765.1 | 620.3 | 610.6 | 507.6 | 670.7 | 558.1 | .... |
| Other equity | 8dala | .... | .... | .... | .... | .... | .... | .... | .... | .... | .... | .... | .... |
| Debt instruments | 8dzla | 516.2 | 516.7 | 519.1 | 668.8 | 522.7 | 765.1 | 620.3 | 610.6 | 507.6 | 670.7 | 558.1 | .... |

# Swaziland 734

| | | 2004 | 2005 | 2006 | 2007 | 2008 | 2009 | 2010 | 2011 | 2012 | 2013 | 2014 | 2015 |
|---|---|---|---|---|---|---|---|---|---|---|---|---|---|
| **Government Finance** | | | | | | | | | | | | | |
| **Cash Flow Statement** | | | | | | | | | | | | | |
| **Budgetary Central Government** | | | | | *Millions of Emalangeni: Fiscal Year Begins April 1* | | | | | | | |
| Cash Receipts:Operating Activities... | c1 | 4,198.3 | 4,672.5 | 7,182.7 | 7,148.6 | 8,566.9 | 8,142.3 | 5,572.2 | 6,010.4 | 11,584.4 | .... | .... | .... |
| Taxes.......... | c11 | 3,978.9 | 4,451.3 | 6,903.8 | 6,668.1 | 8,112.9 | 7,667.8 | 5,199.7 | 5,707.8 | 11,326.8 | .... | .... | .... |
| Social Contributions............... | c12 | — | — | — | — | — | — | — | — | — | .... | .... | .... |
| Grants............... | c13 | 60.6 | 31.4 | 32.7 | 60.4 | 41.3 | 165.0 | 10.4 | 17.6 | 15.2 | .... | .... | .... |
| Other Receipts............... | c14 | 158.8 | 189.7 | 246.2 | 420.0 | 412.7 | 309.6 | 362.2 | 285.1 | 242.4 | .... | .... | .... |
| Cash Payments:Operating Activities. | c2 | 3,503.7 | 4,220.4 | 4,958.8 | 5,249.1 | 7,085.2 | 7,856.5 | 8,022.6 | 7,778.6 | 8,958.5 | .... | .... | .... |
| Compensation of Employees.......... | c21 | 1,838.9 | 2,218.0 | 2,570.7 | 2,814.1 | 3,519.5 | 3,772.6 | 4,444.6 | 4,406.2 | 4,485.7 | .... | .... | .... |
| Purchases of Goods & Services....... | c22 | 1,154.5 | 1,066.5 | 1,152.5 | 1,312.4 | 1,820.9 | 2,074.4 | 1,657.6 | 1,427.3 | 1,850.1 | .... | .... | .... |
| Interest............... | c24 | 134.1 | 176.8 | 191.4 | 153.1 | 227.1 | 322.0 | 227.5 | 261.0 | 270.1 | .... | .... | .... |
| Subsidies............... | c25 | 37.5 | 93.2 | 47.8 | 45.1 | 76.1 | 153.0 | 43.7 | 41.2 | 114.9 | .... | .... | .... |
| Grants............... | c26 | 193.8 | 599.5 | 813.9 | 843.5 | 1,022.5 | 1,302.1 | 1,397.7 | 1,395.4 | 2,077.5 | .... | .... | .... |
| Social Benefits............... | c27 | 25.6 | 34.0 | 67.6 | 34.4 | 227.1 | 196.0 | 221.9 | 229.9 | 132.5 | .... | .... | .... |
| Other Payments............... | c28 | 119.3 | 32.5 | 114.9 | 46.5 | 192.0 | 36.4 | 29.6 | 17.5 | 27.7 | .... | .... | .... |
| Net Cash Inflow:Operating Act.[1-2] | ccio | 694.6 | 452.0 | 2,223.9 | 1,899.4 | 1,481.7 | 285.9 | −2,450.3 | −1,768.2 | 2,625.8 | .... | .... | .... |
| Net Cash Outflow:Invest. in NFA...... | c31 | 981.3 | 1,307.3 | 1,088.7 | 1,892.0 | 2,032.3 | 2,504.8 | 1,912.7 | 1,010.5 | 1,459.5 | .... | .... | .... |
| Purchases of Nonfinancial Assets... | c31.1 | 981.3 | 1,307.3 | 1,088.7 | 1,892.0 | 2,032.3 | 2,504.8 | 1,912.7 | 1,010.5 | 1,459.5 | .... | .... | .... |
| Sales of Nonfinancial Assets.......... | c31.2 | — | — | — | — | — | — | — | — | — | .... | .... | .... |
| Cash Surplus/Deficit [1-2-31=1-2M] | ccsd | −286.7 | −855.3 | 1,135.2 | 7.4 | −550.7 | −2,218.9 | −4,363.0 | −2,778.7 | 1,166.3 | .... | .... | .... |
| Net Acq. Fin. Assets, excl. Cash..... | c32x | .... | .... | .... | 15.0 | 17.6 | 17.9 | 15.4 | — | 9.5 | .... | .... | .... |
| Domestic............... | c321x | .... | .... | .... | 15.0 | 17.6 | 17.9 | 15.4 | — | 9.5 | .... | .... | .... |
| Foreign............... | c322x | .... | .... | .... | — | — | — | — | — | — | .... | .... | .... |
| Net Incurrence of Liabilities.............. | c33 | .... | .... | .... | 49.1 | −256.9 | −195.3 | 947.0 | 323.9 | 820.7 | .... | .... | .... |
| Domestic............... | c331 | .... | .... | .... | −69.4 | −58.2 | −12.7 | 1,065.7 | 459.9 | 967.7 | .... | .... | .... |
| Foreign............... | c332 | .... | .... | .... | 118.5 | −198.7 | −182.6 | −118.8 | −135.9 | −147.0 | .... | .... | .... |
| Net Cash Inflow, Fin.Act.[-32x+33].. | cnfb | .... | .... | .... | 34.1 | −274.5 | −213.2 | 931.6 | 323.9 | 811.2 | .... | .... | .... |
| Net Change in Stock of Cash........... | cncb | .... | .... | .... | 41.6 | −825.1 | −2,432.1 | −3,431.4 | −2,454.8 | 1,977.5 | .... | .... | .... |
| Stat. Discrep. [32X-33+NCB-CSD].... | ccsdz | .... | .... | .... | | | | | | | .... | .... | .... |
| Memo Item:Cash Expenditure[2+31] | c2m | 4,484.9 | 5,527.7 | 6,047.6 | 7,141.1 | 9,117.5 | 10,361.2 | 9,935.2 | 8,789.1 | 10,418.0 | .... | .... | .... |
| Memo Item: Gross Debt................... | c63 | .... | .... | .... | .... | .... | .... | 4,138.0 | 4,379.5 | 5,168.2 | .... | .... | .... |
| **National Accounts** | | | | | *Millions of Emalangeni: Fiscal Year Ends March 31* | | | | | | | | |
| Househ.Cons.Expend.,incl.NPISHs.... | 96f | 11,282.3 | 12,138.4 | 15,106.5 | 16,017.8 | 21,177.7 | 23,622.0 | .... | .... | .... | .... | .... | .... |
| Government Consumption Expend... | 91f | 2,363.6 | 2,501.0 | 2,771.2 | 3,041.4 | 3,337.9 | 3,663.4 | .... | .... | .... | .... | .... | .... |
| Gross Fixed Capital Formation.......... | 93e | 2,387.8 | 2,471.4 | 2,557.9 | 2,644.4 | 2,756.1 | 2,757.1 | .... | .... | .... | .... | .... | .... |
| Changes in Inventories................... | 93i | — | — | — | .... | .... | .... | .... | .... | .... | .... | .... | .... |
| Exports of Goods and Services......... | 90c | 13,279.9 | 14,307.7 | 15,294.1 | 16,280.5 | 14,808.8 | 14,874.9 | .... | .... | .... | .... | .... | .... |
| Imports of Goods and Services (-)..... | 98c | 13,677.1 | 14,985.4 | 15,771.8 | 16,558.2 | 17,133.6 | 18,129.4 | .... | .... | .... | .... | .... | .... |
| Gross Domestic Product (GDP)........ | 99b | 15,636.4 | 16,433.0 | 19,957.8 | 21,425.9 | 24,947.0 | 26,788.0 | .... | .... | .... | .... | .... | .... |
| Net Primary Income from Abroad..... | 98.n | .... | .... | .... | .... | .... | .... | .... | .... | .... | .... | .... | .... |
| Gross National Income (GNI)........... | 99a | .... | .... | .... | .... | .... | .... | .... | .... | .... | .... | .... | .... |
| Consumption of Fixed Capital.......... | 99cf | .... | .... | .... | .... | .... | .... | .... | .... | .... | .... | .... | .... |
| Net National Income................... | 99e | .... | .... | .... | .... | .... | .... | .... | .... | .... | .... | .... | .... |
| GDP Volume 2000 Prices................. | 99b.p | 11,510.9 | 11,763.2 | 12,096.9 | .... | .... | .... | .... | .... | .... | .... | .... | .... |
| GDP Volume (2005=100)............... | 99bvp | 97.9 | 100.0 | 102.8 | .... | .... | .... | .... | .... | .... | .... | .... | .... |
| GDP Deflator (2005=100)............... | 99bip | 97.2 | 100.0 | 118.1 | .... | .... | .... | .... | .... | .... | .... | .... | .... |
| | | | | | *Millions: Midyear Estimates* | | | | | | | | |
| **Population**............... | 99z | 1.09 | 1.10 | 1.12 | 1.13 | 1.15 | 1.17 | 1.19 | 1.21 | 1.23 | 1.25 | 1.27 | 1.29 |

# Sweden   144

| | | 2004 | 2005 | 2006 | 2007 | 2008 | 2009 | 2010 | 2011 | 2012 | 2013 | 2014 | 2015 |
|---|---|---|---|---|---|---|---|---|---|---|---|---|---|
| **Exchange Rates** | | | | | | *Kronor per SDR: End of Period* | | | | | | | |
| Official Rate...................... | aa | 10.273 | 11.375 | 10.327 | 10.135 | 12.030 | 11.156 | 10.333 | 10.574 | 9.997 | 9.893 | 11.209 | 11.697 |
| | | | | | | *Kronor per US Dollar: End of Period (ae) Period Average (rf)* | | | | | | | |
| Official Rate...................... | ae | 6.6146 | 7.9584 | 6.8644 | 6.4136 | 7.8106 | 7.1165 | 6.7097 | 6.8877 | 6.5045 | 6.4238 | 7.7366 | 8.4408 |
| Official Rate...................... | rf | 7.3489 | 7.4731 | 7.3782 | 6.7588 | 6.5911 | 7.6538 | 7.2075 | 6.4935 | 6.7750 | 6.5140 | 6.8608 | 8.4348 |
| | | | | | | *Kroner per Euro: End of Period (ea) Period Average (eb)* | | | | | | | |
| Euro Rate...................... | ea | 9.0206 | 9.3885 | 9.0404 | 9.4415 | 10.8700 | 10.2520 | 8.9655 | 8.9120 | 8.5820 | 8.8591 | 9.3930 | 9.1895 |
| Euro Rate...................... | eb | 9.1250 | 9.2806 | 9.2533 | 9.2519 | 9.6159 | 10.6200 | 9.5469 | 9.0276 | 8.7067 | 8.6505 | 9.0969 | 9.3545 |
| | | | | | | *Index Numbers (2010=100): Period Averages* | | | | | | | |
| Official Rate...................... | ahx | 98.0 | 96.6 | 97.6 | 106.5 | 110.4 | 94.5 | 100.0 | 110.9 | 106.2 | 110.4 | 105.2 | 85.3 |
| Nominal Effective Exchange Rate..... | nec | 103.7 | 101.4 | 101.7 | 103.5 | 101.7 | 92.7 | 100.0 | 106.2 | 107.2 | 110.4 | 105.7 | 99.4 |
| CPI-Based Real Effect. Ex. Rate...... | rec | 108.9 | 104.7 | 104.1 | 105.6 | 103.5 | 93.4 | 100.0 | 106.2 | 105.7 | 106.9 | 100.9 | 94.1 |
| ULC-Based Real Effect. Ex. Rate...... | rel | 112.6 | 106.6 | 101.2 | 105.6 | 106.8 | 103.5 | 100.0 | 97.0 | 98.4 | 100.4 | 95.5 | 89.3 |
| **Fund Position** | | | | | | *Millions of SDRs: End of Period* | | | | | | | |
| Quota............................. | 2f.s | 2,395.50 | 2,395.50 | 2,395.50 | 2,395.50 | 2,395.50 | 2,395.50 | 2,395.50 | 2,395.50 | 2,395.50 | 2,395.50 | 2,395.50 | 2,395.50 |
| SDR Holdings.................... | 1b.s | 134.80 | 123.47 | 256.70 | 256.69 | 198.72 | 2,290.79 | 2,287.29 | 2,203.04 | 2,136.95 | 2,156.04 | 2,099.44 | 2,166.80 |
| Reserve Position in the Fund........... | 1c.s | 842.47 | 371.96 | 211.10 | 162.46 | 300.80 | 462.70 | 729.50 | 1,130.85 | 1,262.86 | 1,168.40 | 936.42 | 708.15 |
| Total Fund Cred. & Loans Outstg...... | 2tl | — | — | — | — | — | — | — | — | — | — | — | — |
| SDR Allocations...................... | 1bd | 246.53 | 246.53 | 246.53 | 246.53 | 246.53 | 2,248.96 | 2,248.96 | 2,248.96 | 2,248.96 | 2,248.96 | 2,248.96 | 2,248.96 |
| **International Liquidity** | | | | | | *Millions of US Dollars Unless Otherwise Indicated: End of Period* | | | | | | | |
| Total Reserves minus Gold.............. | 1l.d | 22,158 | 22,090 | 24,778 | 27,044 | 25,896 | 42,860 | 42,565 | 44,025 | 45,519 | 60,495 | 57,704 | 53,814 |
| SDR Holdings.................... | 1b.d | 209 | 176 | 386 | 406 | 306 | 3,591 | 3,522 | 3,382 | 3,284 | 3,320 | 3,042 | 3,003 |
| Reserve Position in the Fund.......... | 1c.d | 1,308 | 532 | 318 | 257 | 463 | 725 | 1,123 | 1,736 | 1,941 | 1,799 | 1,357 | 981 |
| Foreign Exchange........................ | 1d.d | 20,640 | 21,382 | 24,074 | 26,382 | 25,127 | 38,543 | 37,919 | 38,907 | 40,294 | 55,375 | 53,306 | 49,830 |
| Gold (Million Fine Troy Ounces)....... | 1ad | 5.961 | 5.414 | 5.096 | 4.784 | 4.405 | 4.042 | 4.042 | 4.042 | 4.042 | 4.042 | 4.042 | 4.042 |
| Gold (National Valuation)............... | 1and | † 2,617 | 2,800 | 3,245 | 3,993 | 3,821 | 4,431 | 5,735 | 6,324 | 6,715 | 4,888 | 4,795 | 4,293 |
| Central Bank: Other Assets............. | 3..d | 2,572.9 | 2,810.0 | 3,573.7 | 3,205.4 | 1,584.1 | 514.3 | 389.4 | 922.5 | 555.6 | 3,163.7 | 2,146.4 | 1,374.8 |
| Central Bank: Other Liabs............... | 4..d | 788.4 | 1,287.8 | 2,035.4 | 1,891.1 | 25,580.4 | 9.8 | 74.5 | 15.4 | 23.8 | 109.9 | 256.2 | 982.3 |
| Other Depository Corps.: Assets....... | 7a.d | 157,436.3 | 161,686.1 | 230,232.4 | 305,113.2 | 300,140.3 | 315,318.3 | 333,417.4 | 371,450.1 | 397,912.4 | 433,098.0 | 389,870.1 | 348,369.8 |
| Other Depository Corps.: Liabs......... | 7b.d | 206,603.6 | 192,077.2 | 258,343.9 | 309,262.7 | 301,784.8 | 297,150.3 | 287,851.3 | 306,139.8 | 304,613.7 | 314,649.1 | 292,968.6 | 243,744.8 |
| **Central Bank** | | | | | | *Billions of Kronor: End of Period* | | | | | | | |
| Net Foreign Assets........................... | 11n | 160.4 | 184.9 | 177.3 | 188.3 | 30.4 | 313.2 | 301.3 | 323.1 | 317.9 | 397.7 | 462.0 | 461.3 |
| Claims on Nonresidents................ | 11 | 168.1 | 197.9 | 193.9 | 202.9 | 233.2 | 338.4 | 325.0 | 346.9 | 340.6 | 420.7 | 489.2 | 495.9 |
| Liabilities to Nonresidents.............. | 16c | 7.7 | 13.1 | 16.5 | 14.6 | 202.8 | 25.2 | 23.7 | 23.9 | 22.6 | 23.0 | 27.2 | 34.6 |
| Claims on Other Depository Corps.... | 12e | 13.6 | 9.6 | 5.4 | 7.2 | 463.1 | 368.8 | .5 | — | — | — | — | — |
| Net Claims on Central Government.. | 12an | — | — | — | — | — | −92.5 | −83.8 | −86.5 | −85.2 | −183.4 | −217.1 | −74.6 |
| Claims on Central Government...... | 12a | — | — | — | — | — | — | — | — | 3.2 | 9.7 | 11.3 | 165.9 |
| Liabilities to Central Government... | 16d | — | — | — | — | — | 92.5 | 83.8 | 86.5 | 88.4 | 193.1 | 228.3 | 240.5 |
| Claims on Other Sectors.................. | 12s | — | .1 | .1 | — | — | — | — | — | — | .3 | .3 | .3 |
| Claims on Other Financial Corps..... | 12g | — | — | — | — | — | — | — | — | — | — | — | — |
| Claims on State & Local Govts....... | 12b | — | — | — | — | — | — | — | — | — | — | — | — |
| Claims on Public Nonfin. Corps...... | 12c | — | — | — | — | — | — | — | — | — | — | — | — |
| Claims on Private Sector............... | 12d | — • | .1 | .1 | — | — | — | — | — | — | .3 | .3 | .3 |
| Monetary Base.......................... | 14 | 109.5 | 111.3 | 112.5 | 114.5 | 319.1 | 281.8 | 110.5 | 117.0 | 122.6 | 107.4 | 98.0 | 144.4 |
| Currency in Circulation.................. | 14a | 108.9 | 111.1 | 112.4 | 114.3 | 112.3 | 110.7 | 105.4 | 100.1 | 96.4 | 85.7 | 83.2 | 73.5 |
| Liabs. to Other Depository Corps.... | 14c | .6 | .3 | .1 | .1 | 206.8 | 171.2 | 5.1 | 16.9 | 26.2 | 21.7 | 14.8 | 70.9 |
| Liabilities to Other Sectors.............. | 14d | — | — | — | — | — | — | — | — | — | — | — | — |
| Other Liabs. to Other Dep. Corps..... | 14n | — | — | — | — | 48.9 | 192.2 | — | — | 3.0 | 25.0 | 35.0 | 143.4 |
| Dep. & Sec. Excl. f/Monetary Base.. | 14o | — | — | — | — | — | — | — | — | — | — | — | — |
| Deposits Included in Broad Money. | 15 | — | — | — | — | — | — | — | — | — | — | — | — |
| Sec.Ot.th.Shares Incl.in Brd. Money | 16a | — | — | — | — | — | — | — | — | — | — | — | — |
| Deposits Excl. from Broad Money... | 16b | — | — | — | — | — | — | — | — | — | — | — | — |
| Sec.Ot.th.Shares Excl.f/Brd.Money.. | 16s | — | — | — | — | — | — | — | — | — | — | — | — |
| Loans.................................... | 16l | — | — | — | — | — | — | — | — | — | — | — | — |
| Financial Derivatives....................... | 16m | — | — | — | — | — | — | — | — | — | — | — | — |
| Shares and Other Equity................. | 17a | 63.5 | 56.8 | 54.8 | 58.2 | 58.7 | 64.0 | 72.4 | 66.8 | 63.2 | 58.3 | 53.0 | 97.5 |
| Other Items (Net)........................... | 17r | 1.0 | 26.4 | 15.6 | 22.8 | 66.8 | 51.4 | 35.1 | 52.8 | 43.9 | 23.9 | 59.2 | 1.7 |

# Sweden 144

| | | 2004 | 2005 | 2006 | 2007 | 2008 | 2009 | 2010 | 2011 | 2012 | 2013 | 2014 | 2015 |
|---|---|---|---|---|---|---|---|---|---|---|---|---|---|
| **Other Depository Corporations** | | | | | | *Billions of Kronor: End of Period* | | | | | | | |
| Net Foreign Assets............ | 21n | −325.2 | −241.9 | −193.0 | −26.6 | −12.8 | 129.3 | 305.7 | 449.8 | 606.9 | 760.9 | 749.7 | 883.1 |
| Claims on Nonresidents......... | 21 | 1,041.4 | 1,286.8 | 1,580.4 | 1,956.9 | 2,344.3 | 2,244.0 | 2,237.1 | 2,558.4 | 2,588.2 | 2,782.1 | 3,016.3 | 2,940.5 |
| Liabilities to Nonresidents...... | 26c | 1,366.6 | 1,528.6 | 1,773.4 | 1,983.5 | 2,357.1 | 2,114.7 | 1,931.4 | 2,108.6 | 1,981.4 | 2,021.2 | 2,266.6 | 2,057.4 |
| Claims on Central Bank........ | 20 | 15.8 | 10.7 | 11.8 | 15.0 | 268.9 | 361.9 | 14.9 | 24.9 | 37.5 | 47.2 | 52.4 | 216.2 |
| Currency...................... | 20a | 10.7 | 10.7 | 11.6 | 13.9 | 12.9 | 10.6 | 9.0 | 8.0 | 8.4 | 3.2 | 2.1 | 1.9 |
| Reserve Deposits and Securities..... | 20b | 5.1 | — | .2 | 1.1 | 207.1 | 159.1 | 5.9 | 16.9 | 26.0 | 18.9 | 15.3 | 70.9 |
| Other Claims.................. | 20n | — | — | — | — | 48.9 | 192.2 | — | — | 3.0 | 25.0 | 35.0 | 143.4 |
| Net Claims on Central Government.. | 22an | 81.3 | 152.7 | 159.5 | 148.4 | 92.7 | 231.5 | 196.0 | 170.9 | 153.9 | 136.6 | 91.2 | 51.6 |
| Claims on Central Government...... | 22a | 88.7 | 171.4 | 187.5 | 171.7 | 145.3 | 256.7 | 214.4 | 192.6 | 175.2 | 155.8 | 174.1 | 115.6 |
| Liabilities to Central Government... | 26d | 7.5 | 18.7 | 28.0 | 23.4 | 52.5 | 25.2 | 18.3 | 21.7 | 21.3 | 19.2 | 82.9 | 64.0 |
| Claims on Other Sectors........... | 22s | 2,965.3 | 3,251.5 | 3,588.1 | 4,129.0 | 5,014.0 | 4,768.4 | 5,057.0 | 5,490.7 | 5,700.1 | 5,673.1 | 6,296.4 | 6,353.5 |
| Claims on Other Financial Corps.... | 22g | 274.8 | 242.6 | 278.8 | 331.4 | 881.1 | 521.0 | 569.6 | 723.6 | 748.8 | 538.4 | 968.5 | 770.1 |
| Claims on State & Local Govts...... | 22b | 100.9 | 103.3 | 106.9 | 112.8 | 116.3 | 106.7 | 109.1 | 144.7 | 156.4 | 149.7 | 162.7 | 193.1 |
| Claims on Public Nonfin. Corps..... | 22c | — | — | — | — | — | — | — | — | — | — | — | — |
| Claims on Private Sector........... | 22d | 2,589.6 | 2,905.7 | 3,202.4 | 3,684.8 | 4,016.6 | 4,140.7 | 4,378.3 | 4,622.4 | 4,795.0 | 4,985.1 | 5,165.2 | 5,390.3 |
| Liabilities to Central Bank........ | 26g | 14.1 | — | 5.6 | 7.2 | 438.4 | 313.0 | .7 | .2 | .6 | 3.3 | .4 | .1 |
| Transf.Dep.Included in Broad Money | 24 | 832.6 | 957.6 | 1,078.0 | 1,174.5 | 1,236.0 | 1,361.1 | 1,464.8 | 1,485.9 | 1,586.3 | 1,746.4 | 1,933.8 | 2,217.8 |
| Other Dep.Included in Broad Money. | 25 | 264.7 | 343.6 | 389.5 | 477.6 | 591.5 | 510.2 | 565.7 | 701.5 | 665.8 | 646.6 | 611.8 | 518.5 |
| Sec.Ot.th.Shares Incl.in Brd.Money.. | 26a | 105.9 | 114.4 | 175.5 | 315.3 | 197.2 | 163.5 | 82.8 | 77.1 | 95.9 | 53.5 | 7.9 | 1.9 |
| Deposits Excl. from Broad Money..... | 26b | 21.3 | 19.2 | 31.4 | 29.5 | 32.0 | 30.1 | 29.8 | 29.7 | 40.7 | 32.6 | 28.4 | 23.2 |
| Sec.Ot.th.Shares Excl.f/Brd.Money.... | 26s | 910.7 | 1,104.2 | 1,193.9 | 1,295.7 | 1,739.8 | 2,165.7 | 2,438.0 | 2,722.5 | 2,820.1 | 3,004.9 | 3,442.9 | 3,620.6 |
| Loans....................... | 26l | — | — | — | — | — | — | — | — | — | — | — | — |
| Financial Derivatives.............. | 26m | 190.8 | 147.9 | 173.3 | 202.8 | 676.3 | 363.1 | 393.4 | 506.2 | 564.4 | 404.5 | 645.2 | 562.3 |
| Insurance Technical Reserves.......... | 26r | — | — | — | — | — | — | — | — | — | — | — | — |
| Shares and Other Equity............. | 27a | 338.6 | 357.5 | 378.2 | 414.9 | 456.0 | 542.9 | 553.1 | 582.0 | 618.8 | 637.4 | 696.6 | 721.3 |
| Other Items (Net)................. | 27r | 58.4 | 128.7 | 141.1 | 348.1 | −4.5 | 41.5 | 45.4 | 31.3 | 105.8 | 88.5 | −181.6 | −160.3 |
| Memo Item: | | | | | | | | | | | | | |
| Total Assets...................... | 20ra | 5,409.5 | 6,189.7 | 7,069.2 | 8,072.0 | 9,864.8 | 9,598.6 | 9,576.5 | 10,164.7 | 10,413.3 | 10,761.1 | 11,725.2 | 11,775.6 |
| **Depository Corporations** | | | | | | *Billions of Kronor: End of Period* | | | | | | | |
| Net Foreign Assets.............. | 31n | −164.8 | −57.0 | −15.6 | 161.7 | 17.6 | 442.5 | 607.0 | 772.9 | 924.8 | 1,158.6 | 1,211.7 | 1,344.5 |
| Claims on Nonresidents......... | 31 | 1,209.5 | 1,484.7 | 1,774.3 | 2,159.8 | 2,577.5 | 2,582.3 | 2,562.2 | 2,905.4 | 2,928.8 | 3,202.8 | 3,505.4 | 3,436.5 |
| Liabilities to Nonresidents......... | 36c | 1,374.3 | 1,541.7 | 1,789.9 | 1,998.1 | 2,559.9 | 2,139.8 | 1,955.1 | 2,132.5 | 2,004.0 | 2,044.2 | 2,293.8 | 2,092.0 |
| Domestic Claims................ | 32 | 3,046.6 | 3,404.3 | 3,747.6 | 4,277.4 | 5,106.7 | 4,907.3 | 5,169.2 | 5,575.0 | 5,768.8 | 5,626.6 | 6,170.8 | 6,330.7 |
| Net Claims on Central Government | 32an | 81.3 | 152.7 | 159.5 | 148.4 | 92.7 | 139.0 | 112.3 | 84.4 | 68.7 | −46.9 | −125.9 | −23.0 |
| Claims on Central Government..... | 32a | 88.7 | 171.4 | 187.5 | 171.7 | 145.3 | 256.7 | 214.4 | 192.6 | 178.4 | 165.5 | 185.4 | 281.5 |
| Liabilities to Central Government. | 36d | 7.5 | 18.7 | 28.0 | 23.4 | 52.5 | 117.7 | 102.1 | 108.2 | 109.7 | 212.3 | 311.3 | 304.5 |
| Claims on Other Sectors............ | 32s | 2,965.3 | 3,251.6 | 3,588.2 | 4,129.0 | 5,014.0 | 4,768.4 | 5,057.0 | 5,490.7 | 5,700.1 | 5,673.5 | 6,296.7 | 6,353.8 |
| Claims on Other Financial Corps.. | 32g | 274.8 | 242.6 | 278.8 | 331.4 | 881.1 | 521.0 | 569.6 | 723.6 | 748.8 | 538.4 | 968.5 | 770.1 |
| Claims on State & Local Govts...... | 32b | 100.9 | 103.3 | 106.9 | 112.8 | 116.3 | 106.7 | 109.1 | 144.7 | 156.4 | 149.7 | 162.7 | 193.1 |
| Claims on Public Nonfin. Corps.... | 32c | — | — | — | — | — | — | — | — | — | — | — | — |
| Claims on Private Sector.......... | 32d | 2,589.6 | 2,905.8 | 3,202.4 | 3,684.8 | 4,016.6 | 4,140.7 | 4,378.3 | 4,622.4 | 4,795.0 | 4,985.4 | 5,165.5 | 5,390.6 |
| Broad Money Liabilities................. | 35l | 1,301.5 | 1,516.0 | 1,743.8 | 2,067.9 | 2,124.1 | 2,134.9 | 2,209.7 | 2,356.6 | 2,436.0 | 2,528.9 | 2,634.6 | 2,809.7 |
| Currency Outside Depository Corps | 34a | 98.2 | 100.4 | 100.8 | 100.5 | 99.4 | 100.1 | 96.4 | * 92.1 | 88.0 | 82.5 | 81.1 | 71.5 |
| Transferable Deposits.................. | 34 | 832.6 | 957.6 | 1,078.0 | 1,174.5 | 1,236.0 | 1,361.1 | 1,464.8 | 1,485.9 | 1,586.3 | 1,746.4 | 1,933.8 | 2,217.8 |
| Other Deposits........................... | 35 | 264.7 | 343.6 | 389.5 | 477.6 | 591.5 | 510.2 | 565.7 | 701.5 | 665.8 | 646.6 | 611.8 | 518.5 |
| Securities Other than Shares.......... | 36a | 105.9 | 114.4 | 175.5 | 315.3 | 197.2 | 163.5 | 82.8 | 77.1 | 95.9 | 53.5 | 7.9 | 1.9 |
| Deposits Excl. from Broad Money..... | 36b | 21.3 | 19.2 | 31.4 | 29.5 | 32.0 | 30.1 | 29.8 | 29.7 | 40.7 | 32.6 | 28.4 | 23.2 |
| Sec.Ot.th.Shares Excl.f/Brd.Money.... | 36s | 910.7 | 1,104.2 | 1,193.9 | 1,295.7 | 1,739.8 | 2,165.7 | 2,438.0 | 2,722.5 | 2,820.1 | 3,004.9 | 3,442.9 | 3,620.6 |
| Loans....................... | 36l | — | — | — | — | — | — | — | — | — | — | — | — |
| Financial Derivatives.............. | 36m | 190.8 | 147.9 | 173.3 | 202.8 | 676.3 | 363.1 | 393.4 | 506.2 | 564.4 | 404.5 | 645.2 | 562.3 |
| Insurance Technical Reserves.......... | 36r | — | — | — | — | — | — | — | — | — | — | — | — |
| Shares and Other Equity............. | 37a | 402.1 | 414.3 | 432.9 | 473.2 | 514.7 | 606.9 | 625.5 | 648.8 | 682.0 | 695.7 | 749.7 | 818.8 |
| Other Items (Net)................. | 37r | 55.4 | 145.7 | 156.7 | 369.9 | 37.3 | 49.2 | 79.9 | 84.2 | 150.5 | 118.5 | −122.4 | −158.5 |
| Broad Money Liabs., Seasonally Adj. | 35l.b | 1,271.7 | 1,481.3 | 1,704.5 | 2,024.2 | 2,083.6 | 2,098.3 | 2,175.8 | 2,323.9 | 2,405.6 | 2,498.6 | 2,604.0 | 2,777.0 |
| **Monetary Aggregates** | | | | | | *Billions of Kronor: End of Period* | | | | | | | |
| Broad Money..................... | 59m | 1,301.5 | 1,516.0 | 1,743.8 | 2,067.9 | 2,124.1 | 2,134.9 | 2,209.7 | 2,356.6 | 2,436.0 | 2,528.9 | 2,634.6 | 2,809.7 |
| o/w:Currency Issued by Cent.Govt | 59m.a | — | — | — | — | — | — | — | — | — | — | — | — |
| o/w: Dep.in Nonfin. Corporations. | 59m.b | — | — | — | — | — | — | — | — | — | — | — | — |
| o/w:Secs. Issued by Central Govt.. | 59m.c | — | — | — | — | — | — | — | — | — | — | — | — |
| Money (National Definitions) | | | | | | | | | | | | | |
| M0............................... | 19mc | 98.20 | 100.37 | 100.76 | 100.46 | 99.41 | 100.07 | 96.39 | 92.25 | 88.00 | 82.36 | 79.64 | 71.54 |
| M1............................... | 59ma | 949.56 | 1,086.67 | 1,219.13 | 1,320.04 | 1,485.30 | 1,628.20 | 1,584.65 | 1,598.57 | 1,692.69 | 1,844.99 | 2,023.84 | 2,289.42 |
| M2............................... | 59mb | 1,167.22 | 1,296.92 | 1,478.88 | 1,640.94 | 1,861.89 | 1,909.10 | 2,010.00 | 2,131.87 | 2,259.05 | 2,387.66 | 2,520.73 | 2,728.92 |
| M3............................... | 59mc | 1,356.73 | 1,531.35 | 1,771.28 | 2,090.17 | 2,258.80 | 2,188.39 | 2,235.25 | 2,378.59 | 2,425.17 | 2,465.92 | 2,592.66 | 2,788.68 |
| **Interest Rates** | | | | | | *Percent Per Annum* | | | | | | | |
| Central Bank Policy Rate (EOP)........ | 60 | 2.00 | 1.50 | 2.50 | 3.50 | 2.00 | .50 | .50 | 1.91 | 1.14 | .75 | — | −.35 |
| Repurchase Rate (End of Period)...... | 60a | 2.00 | 1.50 | 3.00 | 4.00 | 2.00 | .25 | 1.25 | 2.00 | 1.50 | 1.00 | 1.00 | — |
| Money Market Rate...................... | 60b | 2.28 | 1.85 | 2.37 | 3.66 | 4.38 | .77 | .67 | 2.07 | 1.66 | 1.07 | .52 | −.25 |
| Treasury Bill Rate........................ | 60c | 2.11 | 1.72 | 2.33 | 3.55 | 3.91 | .40 | .50 | 1.65 | 1.25 | .93 | .42 | −.29 |
| Deposit Rate (End of Period)........... | 60l | 1.00 | .79 | .... | .... | .... | .... | .... | .... | .... | .... | .... | .... |
| Lending Rate (End of Period)........... | 60p | 4.00 | 3.31 | .... | .... | .... | .... | .... | .... | .... | .... | .... | .... |
| Government Bond Yield................. | 61 | 4.43 | 3.38 | 3.71 | 4.17 | 3.89 | 3.25 | 2.89 | 2.61 | 1.59 | 2.12 | 1.72 | .72 |

# Sweden 144

| Indicator | Code | 2004 | 2005 | 2006 | 2007 | 2008 | 2009 | 2010 | 2011 | 2012 | 2013 | 2014 | 2015 |
|---|---|---|---|---|---|---|---|---|---|---|---|---|---|
| **Prices, Production, Labor** | | | | | | | | | | | | | |
| *Index Numbers (2010=100): Period Averages* | | | | | | | | | | | | | |
| Share Prices (End of Month) | 62.ep | 65.1 | 79.6 | 100.5 | 119.4 | 83.2 | 77.2 | 100.0 | 102.5 | 100.8 | 118.3 | 137.2 | 158.6 |
| Forest Industries (EOP) (2000=100) | 62aep | .... | .... | .... | .... | .... | .... | .... | .... | .... | .... | .... | .... |
| Industrials (EOP) (2000=100) | 62bep | .... | .... | .... | .... | .... | .... | .... | .... | .... | .... | .... | .... |
| Prices: Domestic Supply | 63 | 82.1 | 86.4 | 91.0 | 94.4 | 99.6 | 98.6 | 100.0 | 102.8 | 102.4 | 99.7 | 100.7 | 99.8 |
| Consumer Prices | 64 | 92.3 | 92.7 | 94.0 | 96.0 | 99.3 | 98.9 | 100.0 | 103.0 | 103.9 | 103.8 | 103.6 | 103.6 |
| Harmonized CPI | 64h | 89.5 | 90.3 | 91.6 | 93.1 | 96.3 | 98.1 | 100.0 | 101.4 | 102.3 | 102.8 | 103.0 | 103.7 |
| Wages: Hourly Earnings | 65 | 83.0 | 85.5 | 88.1 | 91.1 | 94.9 | 96.9 | 100.0 | 102.7 | 106.1 | 108.6 | 111.0 | 113.9 |
| Industrial Production | 66 | 104.7 | 107.3 | 110.6 | 114.5 | 111.4 | 91.4 | 100.0 | 105.9 | 103.7 | 98.6 | 94.2 | 96.8 |
| Industrial Employment | 67 | 120.4 | 117.5 | 117.3 | 117.0 | 116.6 | 102.5 | 100.0 | 102.1 | 99.3 | 97.2 | 94.7 | 95.0 |
| *Number in Thousands: Period Averages* | | | | | | | | | | | | | |
| Labor Force | 67d | 4,636 | † 4,613 | 4,687 | 4,750 | 4,797 | 4,799 | 4,827 | 4,887 | 4,909 | 4,963 | 5,005 | 5,044 |
| Employment | 67e | 4,288 | † 4,263 | 4,352 | 4,453 | 4,494 | 4,392 | 4,403 | 4,498 | 4,510 | 4,555 | 4,598 | 4,660 |
| Unemployment | 67c | 246 | † 367 | 336 | 211 | 303 | 407 | 424 | 390 | 402 | 410 | 411 | 387 |
| Unemployment Rate (%) | 67r | 5.5 | † 7.6 | 7.0 | 6.1 | 6.2 | 8.3 | 8.6 | 7.8 | 8.0 | 8.0 | 7.9 | 7.4 |
| **Intl. Transactions & Positions** | | | | | | | | | | | | | |
| *Millions of Kronor* | | | | | | | | | | | | | |
| Exports | 70 | 904,500 | 977,300 | 1,089,400 | 1,139,600 | 1,194,400 | 996,700 | 1,136,000 | 1,214,500 | 1,170,200 | 1,091,600 | 1,112,639 | 1,175,900 |
| Imports, c.i.f. | 71 | 738,900 | 833,800 | 939,500 | 1,034,700 | 1,097,900 | 912,900 | 1,067,100 | 1,133,500 | 1,111,400 | 1,039,900 | 1,092,200 | 1,149,500 |
| *2010=100* | | | | | | | | | | | | | |
| Volume of Exports | 72 | 89.5 | 93.9 | 101.1 | 103.8 | 105.5 | 86.8 | 100.0 | 108.6 | 106.9 | 103.2 | 104.6 | 108.8 |
| Volume of Imports | 73 | 77.5 | 83.2 | 90.2 | 99.6 | 101.3 | 85.0 | 100.0 | 108.0 | 106.8 | 104.3 | 109.6 | 115.5 |
| Export Prices | 76 | 85.3 | 88.9 | 92.5 | 95.9 | 98.6 | 101.2 | 100.0 | 100.0 | 99.1 | 94.4 | 97.1 | 98.4 |
| Import Prices | 76.x | 81.8 | 87.8 | 92.9 | 94.9 | 100.9 | 100.0 | 100.0 | 101.7 | 100.7 | 96.8 | 98.2 | 96.9 |
| **Balance of Payments** | | | | | | | | | | | | | |
| *Millions of US Dollars* | | | | | | | | | | | | | |
| A. Current Account* | 109bx | 24,991.1 | 26,423.0 | 34,677.7 | 43,319.7 | 44,621.9 | 25,192.1 | 29,402.1 | † 34,462.4 | 31,985.7 | 34,862.9 | 30,554.9 | 28,497.3 |
| Goods, credit (exports) | 1a9cx | 126,910.5 | 131,080.4 | 156,218.7 | 180,691.1 | 197,963.6 | 138,540.4 | 148,081.1 | † 177,053.6 | 164,667.1 | 160,091.9 | 160,552.1 | 137,251.2 |
| Goods, debit (imports) | 1a9dx | 98,483.2 | 110,859.3 | 128,791.9 | 153,844.8 | 170,057.7 | 120,294.2 | 128,941.3 | † 156,848.1 | 144,635.8 | 139,055.4 | 141,526.4 | 123,398.0 |
| Balance on goods | 1a9bx | 28,427.3 | 20,221.1 | 27,426.7 | 26,846.3 | 27,905.9 | 18,246.1 | 19,139.8 | † 20,205.5 | 20,031.3 | 21,036.5 | 19,025.7 | 13,853.2 |
| Services, credit (exports) | 1b9cx | 32,051.4 | 41,857.9 | 43,642.0 | 53,793.5 | 59,264.7 | 50,455.2 | 54,405.9 | † 65,189.8 | 64,761.5 | 73,015.1 | 76,325.9 | 71,808.6 |
| Services, debit (imports) | 1b9dx | 31,406.2 | 33,931.8 | 38,964.0 | 46,879.5 | 53,092.7 | 45,225.1 | 47,479.0 | † 54,846.9 | 54,808.8 | 60,684.9 | 65,826.3 | 59,222.1 |
| Balance on Goods & Services | 1c9bx | 29,072.4 | 28,147.2 | 32,104.8 | 33,760.3 | 34,077.8 | 23,476.3 | 26,066.8 | † 30,548.5 | 29,984.0 | 33,367.0 | 29,525.6 | 26,439.6 |
| Primary income: credit | 1c9cx | 31,029.1 | 38,650.4 | 50,724.1 | 69,388.9 | 73,900.8 | 47,413.6 | 56,575.3 | † 63,327.4 | 60,553.4 | 60,107.4 | 60,237.8 | 48,733.4 |
| Primary income: debit | 1c9dx | 30,727.3 | 35,699.5 | 43,273.9 | 55,066.1 | 56,823.8 | 40,197.2 | 46,846.1 | † 52,423.2 | 48,484.3 | 48,877.3 | 49,563.6 | 38,508.0 |
| Balance on gds, serv. & prim. inc. | 1y9bx | 29,374.2 | 31,098.2 | 39,555.0 | 48,083.2 | 51,154.8 | 30,692.7 | 35,796.0 | † 41,452.7 | 42,053.2 | 44,597.1 | 40,199.8 | 36,665.0 |
| Secondary income: credit | 1d9ca | 3,267.4 | 4,864.1 | 5,130.4 | 5,807.1 | 6,216.2 | 4,533.3 | 4,812.7 | † 7,239.7 | 5,575.2 | 6,340.7 | 6,705.7 | 5,386.0 |
| Secondary income: debit | 1d9da | 7,650.5 | 9,539.3 | 10,007.7 | 10,570.6 | 12,749.1 | 10,033.9 | 11,206.5 | † 14,230.0 | 15,642.6 | 16,074.9 | 16,350.7 | 13,553.7 |
| B. Capital Account* | 209ba | 544.9 | 392.3 | −2,556.3 | −456.0 | −772.9 | −519.7 | −662.2 | † −1,264.9 | −910.1 | −1,438.7 | −808.3 | −976.4 |
| Capital account: credit | 209ca | 544.9 | 392.3 | 495.2 | 933.0 | 486.3 | 775.7 | 679.2 | † 648.6 | 649.1 | 366.5 | 411.9 | 471.1 |
| Capital account: debit | 209da | — | — | 3,051.5 | 1,389.0 | 1,259.3 | 1,295.4 | 1,341.4 | † 1,913.4 | 1,559.2 | 1,805.2 | 1,220.2 | 1,447.4 |
| Balance on current & capital acct. | 129ba | 25,536.0 | 26,815.3 | 32,121.3 | 42,863.7 | 43,848.9 | 24,672.3 | 28,740.0 | † 33,197.5 | 31,075.6 | 33,424.2 | 29,746.6 | 27,520.9 |
| C. Financial Account* | 309na | 26,356.4 | 27,016.9 | 34,455.8 | 9,685.4 | −21,941.5 | −7,705.7 | 37,447.2 | † 43,972.3 | 7,999.4 | 3,729.0 | 16,562.9 | 12,498.9 |
| Direct investment: assets | 3a9aa | 27,007.4 | 36,475.6 | 22,013.5 | 53,665.8 | 34,327.7 | 25,535.8 | 23,359.4 | † 23,316.5 | 17,075.6 | 16,856.2 | 5,250.5 | 21,509.4 |
| Equity & investment fund shares | 3aaaa | 15,417.5 | 29,820.0 | 23,320.8 | 48,083.3 | 29,665.3 | 35,779.4 | 20,048.5 | † 24,132.5 | 25,203.7 | 6,650.3 | −9,652.2 | 5,249.8 |
| Debt instruments | 3abaa | 11,589.9 | 6,655.6 | −1,307.3 | 5,582.4 | 4,662.3 | −10,243.5 | 3,310.9 | † −816.0 | −8,128.2 | 10,205.9 | 14,902.7 | 16,259.6 |
| Direct investment: liabilities | 3a9la | 16,816.6 | 20,302.6 | 22,666.0 | 44,410.3 | 41,490.5 | 9,091.1 | 2,287.3 | † 6,973.5 | 4,350.9 | 1,637.7 | −9,122.7 | 15,852.5 |
| Equity & investment fund shares | 3aala | 10,408.3 | 10,610.8 | 14,988.7 | 16,026.6 | 8,945.2 | 15,909.6 | 3,131.5 | † 5,962.7 | 33,991.3 | 16,180.5 | 5,144.9 | 22,477.6 |
| Debt instruments | 3abla | 6,408.3 | 9,691.8 | 7,677.4 | 28,383.6 | 32,545.3 | −6,818.5 | −844.2 | † 1,011.0 | −29,640.3 | −14,542.9 | −14,267.6 | −6,625.2 |
| Portfolio investment: assets | 3b9aa | 25,083.1 | 13,131.9 | 33,460.1 | 49,666.7 | 20,192.0 | 18,704.7 | 18,453.0 | † 9,259.1 | 31,189.0 | 25,193.9 | 29,789.9 | −9,509.7 |
| Equity & investment fund shares | 3baaa | 6,330.3 | −118.4 | 22,156.9 | 8,061.5 | 1,099.4 | 16,288.6 | 7,725.9 | † 5,880.5 | 28,394.3 | 19,333.6 | 9,645.1 | −9,075.4 |
| Debt securities | 3bbaa | 18,752.8 | 13,250.3 | 11,303.2 | 41,605.2 | 19,092.6 | 2,416.1 | 10,727.1 | † 3,378.5 | 2,795.8 | 5,860.4 | 20,145.0 | −434.2 |
| Portfolio investment: liabilities | 3b9la | −60.1 | 13,789.3 | 11,829.9 | 64,637.0 | −7,244.3 | 81,880.1 | 39,843.6 | † 38,071.9 | 47,652.5 | 73,793.4 | 5,799.4 | 2,044.0 |
| Equity & investment fund shares | 3bala | −91.8 | 2,170.2 | −1,460.9 | 4,489.1 | −1,626.3 | 1,372.3 | 5,144.9 | † 2,211.3 | 3,969.5 | 5,099.8 | 2,007.9 | 1,927.2 |
| Debt securities | 3bbla | 31.6 | 11,619.1 | 13,290.7 | 60,147.9 | −5,618.0 | 80,507.8 | 34,698.7 | † 35,860.8 | 43,683.2 | 68,693.5 | 3,791.8 | 116.9 |
| Fin. der.& empl.stk.ops.(ESOs): net | 3c9na | 410.5 | 897.0 | −124.2 | 1,165.3 | −1,520.4 | 2,282.7 | −4,154.5 | † 2,933.1 | −5,327.6 | −9,801.2 | −3,123.7 | −291.9 |
| Fin. der. & ESOs: assets | 3c9aa | −27,604.8 | −29,435.2 | −29,119.5 | −39,248.9 | −79,088.2 | −117,985.0 | −107,366.8 | .... | .... | .... | .... | .... |
| Fin. der. & ESOs: liabilities | 3c9la | −28,015.2 | −30,332.2 | −28,995.2 | −40,414.2 | −77,567.8 | −120,267.7 | −103,212.3 | .... | .... | .... | .... | .... |
| Other investment: assets | 3d9aa | 18,003.9 | 13,473.9 | 50,622.1 | 47,695.7 | 1,381.7 | −14,120.7 | 30,609.9 | † 61,776.6 | 10,503.2 | 30,279.5 | 5,124.9 | −3,770.2 |
| Other equity | 3daaa | .... | .... | .... | .... | .... | .... | .... | † 606.1 | 515.3 | .... | .... | .... |
| Debt instruments | 3dzaa | 18,003.9 | 13,473.9 | 50,622.1 | 47,695.7 | 1,381.7 | −14,120.7 | 30,609.9 | † 61,170.4 | 9,987.9 | 30,279.5 | 5,124.9 | −3,770.2 |
| Other investment: liabilities | 3d9la | 27,392.0 | 2,869.6 | 37,019.8 | 33,460.8 | 42,076.3 | −50,863.1 | −11,310.2 | † 8,267.3 | −6,561.8 | −6,426.1 | 14,149.5 | −17,208.1 |
| Other equity | 3dala | .... | .... | .... | .... | .... | .... | .... | † 75.1 | 27.9 | 30.8 | 219.4 | 521.2 |
| Debt instruments | 3dzla | 27,392.0 | 2,869.6 | 37,019.8 | 33,460.8 | 42,076.3 | −50,863.1 | −11,310.2 | † 8,192.2 | −6,589.8 | −6,457.0 | 13,930.1 | −17,729.3 |
| Curr.+ cap.− finan. acct. balance | 4y9na | −820.5 | −201.7 | −2,334.5 | 33,178.4 | 65,790.5 | 32,378.0 | −8,707.2 | † −10,774.8 | 23,076.2 | 29,695.2 | 13,183.6 | 15,022.0 |
| D. Net Errors and Omissions | 409na | −520.7 | 614.1 | 3,623.2 | −33,625.9 | −64,104.6 | −17,085.4 | 7,531.3 | † 11,421.8 | −22,527.8 | −14,784.2 | −12,697.6 | −13,711.0 |
| E. Reserves and Related Items | 4z9na | −1,341.2 | 412.4 | 1,288.8 | −447.5 | 1,685.9 | 15,292.6 | −1,175.9 | † 647.0 | 548.0 | 14,910.3 | 485.6 | 1,311.0 |
| Reserve assets | 3e9aa | −1,341.2 | 412.4 | 1,288.8 | −447.5 | 1,685.9 | 15,292.6 | −1,175.9 | † 647.0 | 548.0 | 14,910.3 | 485.6 | 1,311.0 |
| Credit and loans from the IMF | 3dcla | — | — | — | — | — | — | — | † — | — | — | — | .... |
| Exceptional financing | 409la | .... | .... | .... | .... | .... | .... | .... | .... | .... | .... | .... | .... |

*Excludes components in group E

# Sweden   144

| International Investment Position | | 2004 | 2005 | 2006 | 2007 | 2008 | 2009 | 2010 | 2011 | 2012 | 2013 | 2014 | 2015 |
|---|---|---|---|---|---|---|---|---|---|---|---|---|---|
| | | | | | | | *Millions of US Dollars* | | | | | | |
| Assets | 809aa | 768,437.9 | 779,224.8 | 1,020,850.8 | 1,294,305.9 | †1,125,036.0 | 1,280,668.3 | 1,400,580.6 | 1,418,798.3 | 1,510,780.5 | 1,654,368.2 | 1,553,601.0 | 1,414,290.4 |
| Direct investment | 8a9aa | 293,150.2 | 284,489.7 | 348,017.9 | 452,368.4 | †437,902.6 | 483,302.7 | 508,955.8 | 508,979.8 | 525,034.8 | 558,712.9 | 481,576.4 | 444,971.1 |
| Equity & investment fund shares | 8aaaa | 196,311.3 | 191,929.4 | 244,285.0 | 312,387.6 | †306,557.0 | 344,158.4 | 365,875.4 | 361,772.9 | 372,663.2 | 389,298.2 | 343,953.9 | 316,859.8 |
| Debt instruments | 8abaa | 96,838.8 | 92,560.3 | 103,732.9 | 139,980.8 | †131,345.6 | 139,144.4 | 143,080.5 | 147,206.9 | 152,371.6 | 169,414.7 | 137,622.5 | 128,111.3 |
| Portfolio investment | 8b9aa | 272,840.7 | 298,026.5 | 396,712.0 | 482,947.0 | †323,183.5 | 430,787.7 | 492,876.9 | 439,397.6 | 492,060.3 | 571,234.3 | 556,797.4 | 512,679.0 |
| Equity & investment fund shares | 8baaa | 179,243.5 | 202,216.4 | 259,638.9 | 311,405.3 | †184,631.3 | 279,632.0 | 333,881.7 | 295,771.4 | 343,159.2 | 416,500.8 | 401,911.3 | 377,711.0 |
| Debt securities | 8bbaa | 93,597.2 | 95,810.1 | 137,073.2 | 171,541.7 | †138,552.2 | 151,155.9 | 158,995.2 | 143,626.2 | 148,901.1 | 154,733.6 | 154,886.1 | 134,968.0 |
| Fin. der.(oth.than reserves) & ESOs | 8c9aa | 33,970.6 | 26,330.9 | 25,365.1 | 34,681.3 | †68,999.4 | 50,666.9 | 52,703.7 | 71,589.8 | 75,007.5 | 52,908.1 | 79,151.4 | 61,357.6 |
| Other investment | 8d9aa | 143,194.6 | 145,368.4 | 222,521.0 | 293,040.6 | †265,135.3 | 268,405.1 | 297,677.7 | 348,534.5 | 366,396.5 | 406,084.4 | 372,896.0 | 337,165.8 |
| Other equity | 8daaa | .... | .... | .... | .... | †6,780.7 | 8,042.2 | 9,116.7 | 9,478.9 | 10,570.8 | 10,596.8 | 8,798.7 | 8,064.6 |
| Debt instruments | 8dzaa | 143,194.6 | 145,368.4 | 222,521.0 | 293,040.6 | †258,354.7 | 260,363.0 | 288,561.0 | 339,055.6 | 355,825.7 | 395,487.6 | 364,097.3 | 329,101.2 |
| Reserve assets | 8e9aa | 25,281.8 | 25,009.2 | 28,234.8 | 31,268.6 | †29,815.2 | 47,505.7 | 48,366.5 | 50,296.8 | 52,281.6 | 65,428.5 | 63,180.5 | 58,116.9 |
| Liabilities | 809la | 868,790.5 | 851,310.0 | 1,076,962.1 | 1,301,902.0 | †1,171,148.7 | 1,333,175.2 | 1,447,910.2 | 1,476,667.8 | 1,608,403.7 | 1,740,282.9 | 1,566,488.7 | 1,421,563.6 |
| Direct investment | 8a9la | 277,246.8 | 248,556.1 | 312,838.0 | 414,703.0 | †393,732.4 | 462,032.5 | 481,720.6 | 478,751.7 | 509,249.9 | 522,554.6 | 418,867.1 | 380,940.3 |
| Equity & investment fund shares | 8aala | 141,841.2 | 125,876.8 | 153,989.3 | 200,939.4 | †175,321.4 | 216,222.7 | 236,867.2 | 238,475.4 | 278,646.9 | 308,612.8 | 244,371.6 | 231,547.7 |
| Debt instruments | 8abla | 135,405.6 | 122,679.3 | 158,848.7 | 213,763.6 | †218,410.9 | 245,809.7 | 244,853.4 | 240,276.3 | 230,603.0 | 213,941.7 | 174,495.5 | 149,392.6 |
| Portfolio investment | 8b9la | 352,191.5 | 376,568.9 | 477,815.4 | 530,331.8 | †381,156.0 | 529,564.4 | 627,660.6 | 637,341.6 | 728,106.8 | 866,291.3 | 797,550.6 | 752,929.9 |
| Equity & investment fund shares | 8bala | 124,104.4 | 141,279.7 | 209,105.5 | 204,057.0 | †86,848.0 | 140,041.7 | 202,626.9 | 170,539.1 | 223,163.3 | 278,344.7 | 262,878.3 | 263,909.0 |
| Debt securities | 8bbla | 228,087.1 | 235,289.3 | 268,709.9 | 326,274.8 | †294,308.0 | 389,522.7 | 425,033.6 | 466,802.6 | 504,943.5 | 587,946.5 | 534,672.3 | 489,020.9 |
| Fin. der.(oth.than reserves) & ESOs | 8c9la | 36,136.6 | 28,284.3 | 26,515.4 | 35,609.6 | †62,501.5 | 41,741.0 | 40,459.6 | 53,613.3 | 58,839.0 | 44,112.5 | 62,589.1 | 46,557.7 |
| Other investment | 8d9la | 203,215.5 | 197,900.6 | 259,793.4 | 321,257.6 | †333,758.8 | 299,837.3 | 298,069.2 | 306,961.3 | 312,208.1 | 307,324.4 | 287,482.0 | 241,135.7 |
| Other equity | 8dala | .... | .... | .... | .... | †819.5 | 990.5 | 1,132.7 | 1,179.6 | 1,241.0 | 1,281.2 | 1,251.2 | 1,662.0 |
| Debt instruments | 8dzla | 203,215.5 | 197,900.6 | 259,793.4 | 321,257.6 | †332,939.3 | 298,846.8 | 296,936.5 | 305,781.7 | 310,967.1 | 306,043.2 | 286,230.8 | 239,473.7 |

| | | 2004 | 2005 | 2006 | 2007 | 2008 | 2009 | 2010 | 2011 | 2012 | 2013 | 2014 | 2015 |
|---|---|---|---|---|---|---|---|---|---|---|---|---|---|

**Government Finance**
**Operations Statement**
**General Government**

*Millions of Kronor: Fiscal Year Ends December 31; Data Reported through Eurostat*

| | | 2004 | 2005 | 2006 | 2007 | 2008 | 2009 | 2010 | 2011 | 2012 | 2013 | 2014 | 2015 |
|---|---|---|---|---|---|---|---|---|---|---|---|---|---|
| Revenue | a1 | 1,489,708 | 1,584,554 | 1,659,040 | 1,747,114 | 1,771,358 | 1,722,534 | 1,800,068 | 1,845,189 | 1,869,571 | 1,922,157 | 1,965,733 | 2,095,896 |
| Taxes | a11 | 1,183,317 | 1,264,157 | 1,337,118 | 1,388,912 | 1,391,883 | 1,352,613 | 1,421,444 | 1,446,943 | 1,458,959 | 1,505,578 | 1,562,782 | 1,676,235 |
| Social Contributions | a12 | 116,733 | 111,323 | 107,109 | 116,221 | 123,298 | 123,761 | 126,700 | 136,485 | 138,236 | 142,202 | 146,906 | 154,525 |
| Grants | a13 | .... | .... | .... | .... | .... | .... | .... | .... | .... | .... | .... | .... |
| Other Revenue | a14 | .... | .... | .... | .... | .... | .... | .... | .... | .... | .... | .... | .... |
| Expense | a2 | 1,461,234 | 1,513,291 | 1,567,603 | 1,610,531 | 1,679,696 | 1,719,006 | 1,765,805 | 1,811,419 | 1,863,687 | 1,934,545 | 1,985,962 | 2,053,579 |
| Compensation of Employees | a21 | 361,548 | 371,099 | 387,547 | 404,801 | 420,216 | 420,882 | 429,604 | 441,946 | 460,586 | 476,349 | 494,187 | 516,508 |
| Use of Goods & Services | a22 | 223,289 | 231,651 | 248,117 | 255,988 | 273,160 | 285,930 | 295,009 | 305,983 | 310,635 | 320,908 | 328,208 | 343,453 |
| Consumption of Fixed Capital | a23 | 90,686 | 94,220 | 98,068 | 102,696 | 109,439 | 113,994 | 116,823 | 120,574 | 125,042 | 127,065 | 130,896 | 135,711 |
| Interest | a24 | 48,006 | 51,301 | 50,788 | 54,877 | 52,847 | 38,086 | 37,441 | 41,372 | 34,093 | 30,601 | 27,147 | 20,201 |
| Subsidies | a25 | 37,920 | 40,715 | 45,211 | 46,546 | 49,337 | 50,597 | 55,412 | 59,750 | 61,974 | 62,900 | 66,586 | 68,702 |
| Grants | a26 | .... | .... | .... | .... | .... | .... | .... | .... | .... | .... | .... | .... |
| Social Benefits | a27 | 499,609 | 511,275 | 527,449 | 534,956 | 555,046 | 591,772 | 605,050 | 612,167 | 640,466 | 671,377 | 686,081 | 711,369 |
| Other Expense | a28 | .... | .... | .... | .... | .... | .... | .... | .... | .... | .... | .... | .... |
| Gross Operating Balance [1-2+23] | agob | 119,160 | 165,483 | 189,505 | 239,279 | 201,101 | 117,522 | 151,086 | 154,344 | 130,926 | 114,677 | 110,667 | 178,028 |
| Net Operating Balance [1-2] | anob | 28,474 | 71,263 | 91,437 | 136,583 | 91,662 | 3,528 | 34,263 | 33,770 | 5,884 | −12,388 | −20,229 | 42,317 |
| Net Acq. of Nonfinancial Assets | a31 | 19,320 | 18,612 | 23,740 | 26,533 | 25,487 | 27,127 | 35,289 | 36,966 | 40,167 | 39,147 | 41,248 | 42,361 |
| Aquisition of Nonfin. Assets | a31.1 | .... | .... | .... | .... | .... | .... | .... | .... | .... | .... | .... | .... |
| Disposal of Nonfin. Assets | a31.2 | .... | .... | .... | .... | .... | .... | .... | .... | .... | .... | .... | .... |
| Net Lending/Borrowing [1-2-31] | anlb | 9,154 | 52,651 | 67,697 | 110,050 | 66,175 | −23,599 | −1,026 | −3,196 | −34,283 | −51,535 | −61,477 | −44 |
| Net Acq. of Financial Assets | a32 | 49,394 | 61,059 | 22,060 | −5,513 | −76,717 | 4,221 | 11,019 | −71,254 | −32,300 | 43,474 | 91,534 | −92,284 |
| By instrument | | | | | | | | | | | | | |
| Monetary Gold & SDRs | a3201 | — | — | — | — | — | — | — | — | — | — | — | — |
| Currency & Deposits | a3202 | 3,794 | 1,034 | 24,590 | −5,035 | 48,739 | −39,265 | −12,077 | 34,215 | −5,780 | −6,475 | 78,791 | −14,148 |
| Securities other than Shares | a3203 | 26,631 | 38,416 | 38,326 | 47,194 | −54,838 | 1,261 | 32,740 | −7,226 | −2,099 | −423 | 57,832 | 8,633 |
| Loans | a3204 | 11,341 | 28,742 | 19,810 | 8,635 | 22,144 | 101,347 | 14,453 | 27,676 | 16,911 | 127,255 | 29,763 | 29,019 |
| Shares & Other Equity | a3205 | 10,900 | −33,484 | −18,299 | −15,289 | −5,348 | 3,039 | −8,907 | −4,907 | 23,622 | −21,561 | −19,065 | −58,815 |
| Insurance Technical Reserves | a3206 | | | | | | | | | | | | |
| Financial Derivatives | a3207 | −14,231 | −8,779 | −37,916 | −63,354 | −67,199 | −79,372 | −52,625 | −91,987 | −64,160 | −78,589 | −68,426 | −97,313 |
| Other Accounts Receivable | a3208 | 10,959 | 35,130 | −4,451 | 22,336 | −20,215 | 17,211 | 37,435 | −29,025 | −794 | 23,267 | 12,639 | 40,340 |
| By debtor | | | | | | | | | | | | | |
| Domestic | a321 | .... | .... | .... | .... | .... | .... | .... | .... | .... | .... | .... | .... |
| Foreign | a322 | .... | .... | .... | .... | .... | .... | .... | .... | .... | .... | .... | .... |
| Net Incurrence of Liabilities | a33 | 28,936 | 21,842 | −44,103 | −125,192 | −143,497 | 26,264 | 17,512 | −63,781 | −3,033 | 88,407 | 150,535 | −95,282 |
| By instrument | | | | | | | | | | | | | |
| Special Drawing Rights (SDRs) | a3301 | — | — | — | — | — | — | — | — | — | — | — | — |
| Currency & Deposits | a3302 | 1,402 | 2,749 | −20,314 | −1,936 | 19,212 | −8,344 | 5,079 | 10,289 | 6,277 | −20,400 | 1,222 | −7,975 |
| Securities other than Shares | a3303 | 23,009 | 19,921 | −45,025 | −111,834 | −66,935 | 60,619 | 51,783 | −54,849 | 27,051 | 106,122 | 105,043 | 58,405 |
| Loans | a3304 | 11,641 | 8,854 | 17,582 | 19,546 | 3,245 | 59,979 | −40,287 | 49,935 | −16,948 | 17,078 | 102,452 | −22,339 |
| Shares & Other Equity | a3305 | | | | | | | | | | | | |
| Insurance Technical Reserves | a3306 | 6,899 | 8,103 | 5,877 | 7,778 | 8,025 | 7,727 | 10,217 | 13,902 | 10,307 | 10,730 | 13,237 | 12,247 |
| Financial Derivatives | a3307 | −4,919 | −29,826 | −14,690 | −45,611 | −116,197 | −87,469 | −31,428 | −73,123 | −47,365 | −37,808 | −72,586 | −127,785 |
| Other Accounts Payable | a3308 | −9,096 | 12,041 | 12,467 | 6,865 | 9,153 | −6,248 | 22,148 | −9,935 | 17,645 | 12,685 | 1,167 | −7,835 |
| By creditor | | | | | | | | | | | | | |
| Domestic | a331 | .... | .... | .... | .... | .... | .... | .... | .... | .... | .... | .... | .... |
| Foreign | a332 | .... | .... | .... | .... | .... | .... | .... | .... | .... | .... | .... | .... |
| Stat. Discrepancy [32-33-NLB] | anlbz | 11,304 | −13,434 | −1,534 | 9,629 | 605 | 1,556 | −5,467 | −4,277 | 5,016 | 6,602 | 2,476 | 3,042 |
| Memo Item: Expenditure [2+31] | a2m | 1,480,554 | 1,531,903 | 1,591,343 | 1,637,064 | 1,705,183 | 1,746,133 | 1,801,094 | 1,848,385 | 1,903,854 | 1,973,692 | 2,027,210 | 2,095,940 |

**Balance Sheet**

| | | 2004 | 2005 | 2006 | 2007 | 2008 | 2009 | 2010 | 2011 | 2012 | 2013 | 2014 | 2015 |
|---|---|---|---|---|---|---|---|---|---|---|---|---|---|
| Net Worth | a6 | .... | .... | .... | .... | .... | .... | .... | .... | .... | .... | .... | .... |
| Nonfinancial Assets | a61 | .... | .... | .... | .... | .... | .... | .... | .... | .... | .... | .... | .... |
| Financial Assets | a62 | 1,614,656 | 1,849,365 | 2,092,798 | 2,200,779 | 2,070,596 | 2,313,304 | 2,444,835 | 2,645,095 | 2,771,270 | 2,926,722 | 3,299,551 | 3,338,933 |
| By instrument | | | | | | | | | | | | | |
| Monetary Gold & SDRs | a6201 | — | — | — | — | — | — | — | — | — | — | — | — |
| Currency & Deposits | a6202 | 47,749 | 51,898 | 80,604 | 73,279 | 120,117 | 80,349 | 66,246 | 100,811 | 97,391 | 91,417 | 173,849 | 159,701 |
| Securities other than Shares | a6203 | 198,462 | 248,244 | 273,456 | 326,196 | 310,158 | 317,445 | 339,679 | 342,651 | 350,658 | 348,834 | 449,252 | 454,867 |
| Loans | a6204 | 311,484 | 339,245 | 360,573 | 379,639 | 400,426 | 494,162 | 497,701 | 526,592 | 546,123 | 669,654 | 733,718 | 782,038 |
| Shares and Other Equity | a6205 | 790,336 | 930,483 | 1,073,271 | 1,115,368 | 922,590 | 1,089,748 | 1,160,795 | 1,326,672 | 1,408,542 | 1,446,912 | 1,559,491 | 1,525,595 |
| Insurance Technical Reserves | a6206 | | | | | | | | | | | | |
| Financial Derivatives | a6207 | 35,133 | 13,910 | 43,760 | 22,734 | 52,447 | 48,957 | 60,966 | 62,241 | 75,373 | 53,588 | 53,733 | 46,884 |
| Other Accounts Receivable | a6208 | 231,492 | 265,585 | 261,134 | 283,563 | 264,858 | 282,643 | 319,448 | 286,128 | 293,183 | 316,317 | 329,508 | 369,848 |
| By debtor | | | | | | | | | | | | | |
| Domestic | a621 | .... | .... | .... | .... | .... | .... | .... | .... | .... | .... | .... | .... |
| Foreign | a622 | .... | .... | .... | .... | .... | .... | .... | .... | .... | .... | .... | .... |
| Liabilities | a63 | 1,764,311 | 1,865,691 | 1,791,667 | 1,728,593 | 1,783,998 | 1,812,773 | 1,842,585 | 1,942,893 | 1,984,838 | 2,132,727 | 2,495,471 | 2,527,230 |
| By instrument | | | | | | | | | | | | | |
| Special Drawing Rights (SDRs) | a6301 | — | — | — | — | — | — | — | — | — | — | — | — |
| Currency & Deposits | a6302 | 50,981 | 54,761 | 42,217 | 41,662 | 61,480 | 53,133 | 55,399 | 65,757 | 71,439 | 51,148 | 53,045 | 45,059 |
| Securities other than Shares | a6303 | 1,250,599 | 1,309,823 | 1,207,293 | 1,088,842 | 1,045,088 | 1,057,772 | 1,095,605 | 1,113,201 | 1,116,783 | 1,215,190 | 1,425,254 | 1,499,772 |
| Loans | a6304 | 142,909 | 150,695 | 181,817 | 209,908 | 214,089 | 274,068 | 234,166 | 290,191 | 278,376 | 304,728 | 407,234 | 384,926 |
| Shares and Other Equity | a6305 | | | | | | | | | | | | |
| Insurance Technical Reserves | a6306 | 182,726 | 196,318 | 204,037 | 214,572 | 227,424 | 243,678 | 251,325 | 280,315 | 299,312 | 325,189 | 339,934 | 354,773 |
| Financial Derivatives | a6307 | 11,655 | 17,006 | 6,748 | 17,186 | 67,000 | 18,960 | 14,778 | 17,416 | 6,636 | 11,479 | 43,764 | 24,289 |
| Other Accounts Payable | a6308 | 125,441 | 137,088 | 149,555 | 156,423 | 168,917 | 165,162 | 191,312 | 176,013 | 212,292 | 224,993 | 226,240 | 218,411 |
| By creditor | | | | | | | | | | | | | |
| Domestic | a631 | .... | .... | .... | .... | .... | .... | .... | .... | .... | .... | .... | .... |
| Foreign | a632 | .... | .... | .... | .... | .... | .... | .... | .... | .... | .... | .... | .... |
| Net Financial Worth [62-63] | a6m2 | −149,655 | −16,326 | 301,131 | 472,186 | 286,598 | 500,531 | 602,250 | 702,202 | 786,432 | 793,995 | 804,080 | 811,703 |
| Memo Item: Debt at Market Value | a6m3 | 1,752,656 | 1,848,685 | 1,784,919 | 1,711,407 | 1,716,949 | 1,793,813 | 1,827,807 | 1,925,477 | 1,978,202 | 2,121,248 | 2,451,707 | 2,502,941 |
| Memo Item: Debt at Face Value | a6m35 | 1,468,602 | 1,538,712 | 1,487,282 | 1,418,695 | 1,417,017 | 1,493,828 | 1,515,847 | 1,526,773 | 1,582,072 | 1,724,338 | 1,980,867 | 2,023,160 |
| Memo Item: Maastricht Debt | a6m36 | 1,343,161 | 1,401,624 | 1,337,727 | 1,262,272 | 1,248,100 | 1,328,666 | 1,324,535 | 1,350,760 | 1,369,780 | 1,499,345 | 1,754,627 | 1,804,749 |
| Memo Item: Debt at Nominal Value | a6m4 | .... | .... | .... | .... | .... | .... | .... | .... | .... | .... | .... | .... |

# Sweden 144

|  |  | 2004 | 2005 | 2006 | 2007 | 2008 | 2009 | 2010 | 2011 | 2012 | 2013 | 2014 | 2015 |
|---|---|---|---|---|---|---|---|---|---|---|---|---|---|
| **National Accounts** |  |  |  |  |  |  | *Billions of Kronor* |  |  |  |  |  |  |
| Househ.Cons.Expend.,incl.NPISHs.... | 96f | 1,286.19 | 1,336.45 | 1,388.68 | 1,462.21 | 1,511.30 | 1,550.39 | 1,634.64 | 1,692.90 | 1,715.03 | 1,759.31 | 1,811.95 | 1,879.32 |
| Government Consumption Expend... | 91f | 701.02 | 722.64 | 761.56 | 793.46 | 833.37 | 860.57 | 886.37 | 920.82 | 954.91 | 992.63 | 1,031.20 | 1,083.77 |
| Gross Fixed Capital Formation.......... | 93e | 605.53 | 643.62 | 712.79 | 787.63 | 823.86 | 733.90 | 783.32 | 829.74 | 834.18 | 842.15 | 921.99 | 1,006.64 |
| Changes in Inventories.................... | 93i | −.81 | −3.89 | .83 | 23.74 | 6.76 | −45.81 | 23.21 | 41.11 | −1.03 | 5.89 | 9.78 | 14.53 |
| Exports of Goods and Services.......... | 90c | 1,218.74 | 1,333.70 | 1,493.45 | 1,591.09 | 1,687.47 | 1,461.82 | 1,625.72 | 1,707.00 | 1,706.92 | 1,651.25 | 1,743.75 | 1,877.99 |
| Imports of Goods and Services (-)..... | 98c | 1,005.55 | 1,125.17 | 1,258.21 | 1,361.08 | 1,475.17 | 1,272.36 | 1,433.26 | 1,534.98 | 1,525.21 | 1,481.31 | 1,600.46 | 1,703.53 |
| Gross Domestic Product (GDP)......... | 99b | 2,805.12 | 2,907.35 | 3,099.08 | 3,297.05 | 3,387.60 | 3,288.51 | 3,519.99 | 3,656.58 | 3,684.80 | 3,769.91 | 3,918.20 | 4,158.73 |
| Net Primary Income from Abroad..... | 98.n | 15.42 | 39.29 | 73.39 | 117.13 | 137.50 | 84.41 | 103.16 | 109.29 | 120.02 | 101.79 | 88.09 | 95.86 |
| Gross National Income (GNI)............ | 99a | 2,820.54 | 2,946.64 | 3,172.47 | 3,414.19 | 3,525.10 | 3,372.92 | 3,623.16 | 3,765.87 | 3,804.82 | 3,871.70 | 4,006.29 | 4,254.59 |
| Net Current Transf.from Abroad....... | 98t | −40.69 | −42.52 | −49.38 | −50.64 | −60.42 | −53.11 | −61.15 | −60.16 | −62.87 | −65.06 | −67.46 | −68.73 |
| Gross Nat'l Disposable Inc.(GNDI).... | 99i | 2,676.10 | 2,794.16 | 3,008.43 | 3,241.93 | 3,335.33 | 3,179.84 | 3,420.49 | 3,562.44 | 3,594.71 | 3,662.22 | . . . . | . . . . |
| Gross Saving.................................. | 99s | 631.95 | 687.12 | 784.26 | 903.12 | 930.82 | 725.29 | 855.57 | 946.05 | 913.28 | . . . . | . . . . | . . . . |
| Consumption of Fixed Capital.......... | 99cf | 330.73 | 344.06 | 363.06 | 385.07 | 416.57 | 437.41 | 446.48 | 458.10 | 471.85 | 486.97 | . . . . | . . . . |
| Net National Income...................... | 99e | 2,386.06 | 2,492.63 | 2,694.75 | 2,907.50 | 2,979.18 | 2,795.54 | 3,035.16 | 3,164.50 | 3,185.73 | 3,240.31 | 3,351.84 | 3,567.15 |
| GDP Vol. Ref., Chained 2015 Prices. | 99b.p | 3,385.74 | 3,481.16 | 3,644.36 | 3,768.45 | 3,747.46 | 3,553.16 | 3,765.96 | 3,866.30 | 3,855.23 | 3,903.08 | 3,991.56 | 4,158.73 |
| GDP Volume (2010=100)............... | 99bvp | 89.9 | 92.4 | 96.8 | 100.1 | 99.5 | 94.3 | 100.0 | 102.7 | 102.4 | 103.6 | 106.0 | 110.4 |
| GDP Deflator (2010=100)............... | 99bip | 88.6 | 89.4 | 91.0 | 93.6 | 96.7 | 99.0 | 100.0 | 101.2 | 102.3 | 103.3 | 105.0 | 107.0 |
|  |  |  |  |  |  | *Millions: Midyear Estimates* |  |  |  |  |  |  |  |
| Population............................... | 99z | 8.98 | 9.03 | 9.09 | 9.15 | 9.23 | 9.30 | 9.38 | 9.46 | 9.54 | 9.62 | 9.70 | 9.78 |

| | | 2004 | 2005 | 2006 | 2007 | 2008 | 2009 | 2010 | 2011 | 2012 | 2013 | 2014 | 2015 |
|---|---|---|---|---|---|---|---|---|---|---|---|---|---|
| **Exchange Rates** | | | | | | *Francs per SDR: End of Period* | | | | | | | |
| Market Rate................................ | aa | 1.7574 | 1.8785 | 1.8358 | 1.7786 | 1.6384 | 1.6155 | 1.4470 | 1.4445 | 1.4087 | 1.3729 | 1.4330 | 1.3748 |
| | | | | | *Francs per US Dollar: End of Period (ae) Period Average (rf)* | | | | | | | | |
| Market Rate................................ | ae | 1.1316 | 1.3143 | 1.2203 | 1.1255 | 1.0637 | 1.0305 | .9396 | .9409 | .9166 | .8915 | .9891 | .9921 |
| Market Rate................................ | rf | 1.2435 | 1.2452 | 1.2538 | 1.2004 | 1.0831 | 1.0881 | 1.0429 | .8880 | .9377 | .9269 | .9162 | .9624 |
| | | | | | *Index Numbers (2010=100): Period Averages* | | | | | | | | |
| Market Rate................................ | ahx | 83.8 | 83.7 | 83.0 | 86.8 | 96.5 | 96.1 | 100.0 | 117.5 | 111.0 | 112.3 | 113.7 | 108.2 |
| Nominal Effective Exchange Rate..... | nec | 88.7 | 88.4 | 87.2 | 85.0 | 89.7 | 93.6 | 100.0 | 112.6 | 112.4 | 112.3 | 114.0 | 125.1 |
| CPI-Based Real Effect. Ex. Rate........ | rec | 94.1 | 93.0 | 90.8 | 87.0 | 91.0 | 94.5 | 100.0 | 109.8 | 106.5 | 104.5 | 104.9 | 113.3 |
| ULC-Based Real Effect. Ex. Rate........ | rel | 88.2 | 88.9 | 88.1 | 86.7 | 90.0 | 94.8 | 100.0 | 114.7 | 115.9 | 116.6 | 119.7 | 133.6 |
| **Fund Position** | | | | | | *Millions of SDRs: End of Period* | | | | | | | |
| Quota....................................... | 2f.s | 3,458.50 | 3,458.50 | 3,458.50 | 3,458.50 | 3,458.50 | 3,458.50 | 3,458.50 | 3,458.50 | 3,458.50 | 3,458.50 | 3,458.50 | 3,458.50 |
| SDR Holdings............................. | 1b.s | 45.50 | 41.86 | 182.72 | 156.92 | 148.93 | 3,439.08 | 3,242.06 | 3,209.31 | 3,028.43 | 3,130.14 | 3,070.05 | 3,403.47 |
| Reserve Position in the Fund........... | 1c.s | 1,153.85 | 571.23 | 302.33 | 227.33 | 441.84 | 761.60 | 740.73 | 2,176.25 | 1,998.34 | 1,673.00 | 1,416.96 | 1,162.73 |
| Total Fund Cred. & Loans Outstg...... | 2tl | — | — | — | — | — | — | — | — | — | — | — | — |
| SDR Allocations.......................... | 1bd | — | — | — | — | — | 3,288.04 | 3,288.04 | 3,288.04 | 3,288.04 | 3,288.04 | 3,288.04 | 3,288.04 |
| **International Liquidity** | | | | | *Millions of US Dollars Unless Otherwise Indicated: End of Period* | | | | | | | | |
| Total Reserves minus Gold.............. | 1l.d | 55,497 | 36,297 | 38,094 | 44,474 | 45,061 | 98,199 | 223,481 | 279,390 | 475,659 | 495,958 | 505,463 | 566,960 |
| SDR Holdings........................ | 1b.d | 71 | 60 | 275 | 248 | 229 | 5,391 | 4,993 | 4,927 | 4,654 | 4,820 | 4,448 | 4,716 |
| Reserve Position in the Fund.......... | 1c.d | 1,792 | 816 | 455 | 359 | 681 | 1,194 | 1,141 | 3,341 | 3,071 | 2,576 | 2,053 | 1,611 |
| Foreign Exchange..................... | 1d.d | 53,634 | 35,421 | 37,364 | 43,867 | 44,151 | 91,614 | 217,347 | 271,122 | 467,933 | 488,561 | 498,962 | 560,632 |
| Gold (Million Fine Troy Ounces)....... | 1ad | 43.54 | 41.48 | 41.48 | 36.82 | 33.44 | 33.44 | 33.44 | 33.44 | 33.44 | 33.44 | 33.44 | 33.44 |
| Gold (National Valuation)............... | 1and | 19,123 | 21,342 | 26,404 | 30,898 | 29,013 | 37,055 | 46,816 | 52,482 | 55,391 | 39,893 | 40,066 | 35,749 |
| Monetary Authorities: Other Liabs.... | 4..d | 291 | † 592 | 400 | 1,608 | 4,240 | 4,764 | 21,807 | 7,528 | 18,646 | 22,040 | 32,693 | 66,612 |
| Deposit Money Banks: Assets........... | 7a.d | 680,718 | 709,244 | 803,014 | 1,116,564 | 834,806 | 739,492 | 756,171 | 761,137 | 757,317 | 867,803 | 788,955 | 733,639 |
| Deposit Money Banks: Liabs............. | 7b.d | 608,308 | 634,711 | 717,630 | 1,044,111 | 810,239 | 752,443 | 769,050 | 841,568 | 901,610 | 924,623 | 834,940 | 841,168 |
| Trustee Accounts: Assets................. | 7k.d | 363,438 | 387,912 | 492,737 | 624,248 | 517,067 | 346,873 | 299,900 | 272,686 | 216,407 | 191,199 | 159,583 | 139,571 |
| Trustee Accounts: Liabilities............. | 7m.d | 306,107 | 324,491 | 406,003 | 517,351 | 430,934 | 288,889 | 252,073 | 231,418 | 183,410 | 162,547 | 136,372 | 119,929 |
| **Monetary Authorities** | | | | | | *Billions of Francs: End of Period* | | | | | | | |
| Foreign Assets........................... | 11 | 84.83 | † 87.29 | 89.50 | 101.88 | 181.70 | 173.79 | 255.03 | 327.46 | 490.91 | 486.43 | 545.72 | 630.65 |
| Claims on Central Government........ | 12a | 9.81 | † 2.38 | 2.05 | 1.66 | 1.55 | 1.46 | 1.30 | 1.30 | 1.31 | 1.05 | 1.29 | 1.31 |
| Claims on State & Local Govt........... | 12b | — | † .92 | .75 | .61 | .36 | .30 | .36 | .39 | .40 | .46 | .52 | .53 |
| Claims on Private Sector................ | 12d | — | † .06 | .04 | .04 | .06 | .43 | .06 | .06 | .05 | .04 | .04 | .05 |
| Claims on Deposit Money Banks...... | 12e | 24.52 | † 17.70 | 18.86 | 22.19 | 14.83 | 9.77 | .86 | 8.70 | 1.73 | 1.73 | 13.14 | 5.41 |
| Claims on Other Banking Insts......... | 12g | — | † .14 | .12 | .07 | 15.30 | 21.05 | 11.87 | 7.72 | 4.45 | .07 | .08 | .08 |
| Reserve Money.......................... | 14 | 48.68 | † 47.22 | 49.90 | 52.93 | 86.35 | 94.96 | 89.45 | 236.45 | 343.62 | 382.90 | 395.60 | 475.20 |
| of which: Currency Outside DMBs.. | 14a | 42.14 | † 41.37 | 43.18 | 44.26 | 49.16 | 49.97 | 51.50 | 55.73 | 61.80 | 65.77 | 67.60 | 72.88 |
| Other Liabilities to DMBs................. | 14n | — | † .01 | — | 5.23 | 54.81 | 26.71 | 105.44 | 10.55 | .02 | — | — | — |
| Time and Savings Deposits.............. | 15 | — | † 3.32 | 1.22 | 1.25 | 10.19 | 9.47 | 7.19 | 34.10 | 75.97 | 35.26 | 42.18 | 28.67 |
| Foreign Liabilities......................... | 16c | .33 | † .78 | .49 | 1.81 | 4.51 | 10.22 | 25.25 | 11.83 | 21.72 | 24.16 | 37.05 | 70.61 |
| Central Government Deposits.......... | 16d | 2.32 | † — | — | — | — | — | — | — | — | — | .05 | .05 |
| Capital Accounts......................... | 17a | 68.84 | † 57.65 | 60.19 | 65.67 | 58.45 | 65.90 | 42.59 | 53.12 | 58.08 | 48.02 | 86.30 | 61.05 |
| Other Items (Net)......................... | 17r | −1.00 | † −.50 | −.47 | −.46 | −.50 | −.45 | −.44 | −.44 | −.55 | −.56 | −.40 | 2.46 |
| **Deposit Money Banks** | | | | | | *Billions of Francs: End of Period* | | | | | | | |
| Reserves.................................. | 20 | 13.17 | 13.60 | 15.32 | 19.51 | 50.89 | 53.86 | 43.45 | 180.36 | 283.74 | 321.82 | 329.96 | 403.48 |
| Foreign Assets........................... | 21 | 770.30 | 932.16 | 979.92 | 1,256.69 | 887.98 | 762.05 | 710.50 | 716.15 | 694.16 | 773.65 | 780.36 | 727.84 |
| Claims on Central Government........ | 22a | 58.71 | 55.14 | 56.23 | 56.28 | 77.29 | 75.40 | 76.95 | 82.85 | 91.57 | 26.30 | 29.35 | 27.59 |
| Claims on Private Sector................ | 22d | 716.75 | 762.34 | 831.56 | 904.82 | 896.16 | 935.43 | 961.35 | 993.73 | 1,044.14 | 1,073.92 | 1,099.05 | 1,114.04 |
| Demand Deposits....................... | 24 | 181.92 | 194.73 | 186.90 | 194.85 | 239.04 | 311.77 | 335.85 | 379.93 | 427.45 | 442.22 | 443.13 | 436.16 |
| Time and Savings Deposits.............. | 25 | 424.82 | 454.16 | 494.21 | 509.31 | 481.41 | 467.91 | 490.74 | 514.92 | 547.52 | 614.84 | 658.11 | 674.26 |
| Bonds.................................... | 26ab | 116.22 | 115.50 | 124.04 | 131.44 | 142.52 | 142.17 | 144.46 | 147.09 | 159.86 | 168.85 | 181.91 | 179.29 |
| Foreign Liabilities......................... | 26c | 688.36 | 834.20 | 875.72 | 1,175.15 | 861.85 | 775.39 | 722.60 | 791.83 | 826.42 | 824.30 | 825.84 | 834.52 |
| Capital Accounts......................... | 27a | 138.79 | 145.08 | 160.66 | 166.50 | 171.95 | 168.23 | 168.22 | 195.18 | 197.98 | 214.50 | 215.46 | 242.14 |
| Other Items (Net)......................... | 27r | 8.82 | 19.56 | 41.48 | 60.04 | 15.56 | −38.73 | −69.60 | −55.86 | −45.62 | −69.03 | −85.73 | −86.91 |
| **Monetary Survey** | | | | | | *Billions of Francs: End of Period* | | | | | | | |
| Foreign Assets (Net)...................... | 31n | 166.44 | † 184.47 | 193.21 | 181.61 | 203.32 | 150.22 | 217.68 | 239.95 | 336.92 | 411.61 | 463.18 | 453.37 |
| Domestic Credit.......................... | 32 | 782.96 | † 820.96 | 890.75 | 963.47 | 990.72 | 1,034.08 | 1,051.88 | 1,086.05 | 1,141.93 | 1,101.85 | 1,130.29 | 1,143.55 |
| Claims on Central Govt. (Net)........ | 32an | 66.20 | † 57.52 | 58.29 | 57.93 | 78.84 | 76.86 | 78.25 | 84.14 | 92.89 | 27.35 | 30.59 | 28.85 |
| Claims on State & Local Govt........ | 32b | — | † .92 | .75 | .61 | .36 | .30 | .36 | .39 | .40 | .46 | .52 | .53 |
| Claims on Private Sector............ | 32d | 716.75 | † 762.39 | 831.59 | 904.86 | 896.21 | 935.86 | 961.41 | 993.79 | 1,044.19 | 1,073.96 | 1,099.10 | 1,114.08 |
| Claims on Other Banking Insts....... | 32g | — | † .14 | .12 | .07 | 15.30 | 21.05 | 11.87 | 7.72 | 4.45 | .07 | .08 | .08 |
| Money................................... | 34 | 224.06 | † 236.10 | 230.08 | 239.11 | 288.20 | 361.73 | 387.35 | 435.66 | 489.25 | 507.98 | 510.72 | 509.04 |
| Quasi-Money............................. | 35 | 424.82 | † 457.48 | 495.43 | 510.56 | 491.60 | 477.38 | 497.92 | 549.02 | 623.49 | 650.10 | 700.28 | 702.93 |
| Bonds.................................... | 36ab | 116.22 | 115.50 | 124.04 | 131.44 | 142.52 | 142.17 | 144.46 | 147.09 | 159.86 | 168.85 | 181.91 | 179.29 |
| Capital Accounts......................... | 37a | 207.62 | † 202.73 | 220.85 | 232.18 | 230.40 | 234.13 | 210.81 | 248.30 | 256.06 | 262.53 | 301.76 | 303.19 |
| Other Items (Net)......................... | 37r | −23.32 | † −6.37 | 13.55 | 31.80 | 41.32 | −31.11 | 29.03 | −54.08 | −49.80 | −76.00 | −101.22 | −91.03 |
| Money plus Quasi-Money................ | 35l | 648.88 | † 693.57 | 725.52 | 749.67 | 779.80 | 839.11 | 885.27 | 984.68 | 1,112.73 | 1,158.09 | 1,211.01 | 1,211.97 |
| **Other Banking Institutions** | | | | | | *Billions of Francs: End of Period* | | | | | | | |
| Foreign Assets........................... | 41..x | 411.27 | 509.83 | 601.29 | 702.59 | 550.00 | 357.45 | 281.79 | 256.57 | 198.36 | 170.45 | 157.84 | 138.47 |
| Domestic Liabilities...................... | 45..x | 64.88 | 83.36 | 105.84 | 120.31 | 91.62 | 59.75 | 44.94 | 38.83 | 30.25 | 25.54 | 22.96 | 19.49 |
| Foreign Liabilities......................... | 46c.x | 346.39 | 426.48 | 495.45 | 582.28 | 458.39 | 297.70 | 236.85 | 217.74 | 168.11 | 144.91 | 134.89 | 118.98 |
| **Money (National Definitions)** | | | | | | *Billions of Francs: End of Period* | | | | | | | |
| Base Money................................ | 19ma | 43.41 | 44.74 | 45.53 | 46.80 | 77.42 | 89.16 | 74.19 | 231.95 | 350.87 | 380.52 | 384.92 | 474.46 |
| Base Money, Season.Adjusted......... | 19mac | 41.66 | 42.96 | 43.70 | 44.88 | 75.23 | 86.87 | 71.79 | 229.69 | 348.54 | 378.08 | 382.73 | 472.45 |
| M1...................................... | 59ma | 276.30 | 290.30 | 278.37 | 271.17 | 328.75 | 396.65 | 432.18 | 483.41 | 538.55 | 554.43 | 566.87 | 559.15 |
| M2...................................... | 59mb | 483.73 | 496.93 | 470.28 | 445.59 | 513.07 | 620.31 | 671.61 | 736.45 | 812.84 | 873.06 | 895.05 | 908.36 |
| M3...................................... | 59mc | 567.03 | 594.87 | 610.61 | 624.22 | 637.70 | 678.44 | 726.27 | 779.99 | 854.86 | 920.68 | 950.30 | 966.56 |
| **Nonbank Financial Institutions** | | | | | | *Billions of Francs: End of Period* | | | | | | | |
| Claims on Priv.Sec.& Local Govt...... | 42d.s | 263.10 | 264.90 | 270.90 | .... | .... | .... | .... | .... | .... | .... | .... | .... |
| Real Estate.............................. | 42h.s | 28.70 | 28.60 | 28.50 | .... | .... | .... | .... | .... | .... | .... | .... | .... |
| Incr.in Total Assets(Within Per.)....... | 49z.s | −8.30 | 10.70 | 1.80 | .... | .... | .... | .... | .... | .... | .... | .... | .... |
| Liquid Liabilities.......................... | 55l | 713.75 | 776.93 | 831.36 | 869.98 | 871.42 | 898.86 | 930.21 | 1,023.51 | 1,142.98 | 1,183.63 | 1,233.97 | 1,231.46 |

|  |  | 2004 | 2005 | 2006 | 2007 | 2008 | 2009 | 2010 | 2011 | 2012 | 2013 | 2014 | 2015 |
|---|---|---|---|---|---|---|---|---|---|---|---|---|---|
| **Interest Rates** |  | *Percent Per Annum* | | | | | | | | | | | |
| Central Bank Policy Rate (EOP)........ | 60 | 1.25 | 1.50 | 2.50 | 3.25 | 1.00 | .75 | .75 | .25 | .25 | .25 | .25 | −.25 |
| Money Market Rate........................ | 60b | .55 | .63 | 1.94 | 2.00 | .01 | .05 | .04 | .07 | −.02 | .01 | −2.00 | −1.00 |
| Treasury Bill Rate.......................... | 60c | .37 | .71 | 1.36 | 2.16 | 1.33 | — | .03 | −.14 | −.31 | −.10 | −.13 | −1.03 |
| Deposit Rate................................. | 60l | .21 | .52 | 1.40 | 2.13 | † .16 | .08 | .08 | .03 | .03 | .03 | .02 | −.18 |
| Lending Rate................................. | 60p | 3.20 | 3.12 | 3.03 | 3.15 | † 3.34 | 2.75 | 2.73 | 2.72 | 2.69 | 2.69 | 2.69 | 2.68 |
| Government Bond Yield.................. | 61 | 2.38 | 1.96 | 2.49 | 3.11 | 2.15 | 1.97 | 1.67 | .74 | .56 | 1.25 | .38 | −.04 |
| **Prices, Production, Labor** |  | *Index Numbers (2010=100): Period Averages* | | | | | | | | | | | |
| Share Prices (End of Month)............ | 62.ep | 84.6 | 98.7 | 124.1 | 140.3 | 107.6 | 88.6 | 100.0 | 94.6 | 96.6 | 119.5 | 132.3 | 137.2 |
| Producer Prices............................. | 63 | 93.8 | 94.6 | 96.6 | 98.9 | 102.2 | 100.1 | † 100.0 | 98.9 | 98.4 | 98.7 | † 97.9 | 94.4 |
| Prices: Home & Imported Goods....... | 63s | 94.6 | 95.6 | 97.9 | 100.5 | 103.8 | 99.8 | † 100.0 | 99.2 | 98.2 | 98.2 | † 97.1 | 91.9 |
| Consumer Prices............................ | 64 | 94.6 | 95.7 | 96.7 | 97.4 | 99.8 | 99.3 | † 100.0 | 100.2 | 99.5 | 99.3 | 99.3 | 98.2 |
| Wages: Hourly Earnings.................. | 65 | 91.7 | 92.6 | 93.7 | 95.2 | 97.1 | 99.2 | † 100.0 | 101.0 | 101.8 | 102.6 | 103.3 | 103.7 |
| Industrial Production...................... | 66 | 81.1 | 83.8 | 91.4 | 100.6 | 102.8 | 96.0 | 100.0 | 103.6 | 106.3 | 107.1 | 108.6 | 105.9 |
| Manufacturing Employment............. | 67ey | 99.1 | 99.5 | 101.5 | 104.6 | 107.5 | 101.3 | 100.0 | 99.9 | 100.0 | 99.0 | 103.7 | 102.9 |
|  |  | *Number in Thousands: Period Averages* | | | | | | | | | | | |
| Labor Force................................... | 67d | 4,137 | 4,159 | 4,220 | 4,413 | 4,499 | 4,568 | 4,588 | 4,716 | 4,776 | 4,837 | 4,887 | 4,963 |
| Employment.................................. | 67e | 4,178 | 4,196 | 4,291 | 3,851 | 4,027 | 4,091 | 4,281 | 4,366 | 4,408 | 4,461 | 4,829 | 4,880 |
| Unemployment.............................. | 67c | 153 | 149 | 132 | 109 | 102 | 146 | 152 | 123 | 126 | 137 | 137 | 143 |
| Unemployment Rate (%)................. | 67r | 4.3 | 3.8 | 3.3 | 2.8 | 2.6 | 3.7 | 3.8 | 3.1 | 2.9 | 3.2 | 3.2 | 3.3 |
| **Intl. Transactions & Positions** |  | *Millions of Francs* | | | | | | | | | | | |
| Exports........................................ | 70 | 146,312 | 156,977 | 177,475 | 197,533 | 206,330 | 180,534 | 193,253 | 197,907 | 200,612 | 201,213 | 208,357 | 202,919 |
| Imports, c.i.f................................. | 71 | 136,987 | 149,094 | 165,410 | 183,578 | 186,883 | 160,187 | 173,685 | 174,388 | 176,781 | 177,642 | 178,605 | 166,392 |
|  |  | *2010=100* | | | | | | | | | | | |
| Volume of Exports......................... | 72.a | 87.7 | 92.4 | 101.1 | 108.1 | 109.3 | 93.1 | 100.0 | 108.2 | 108.8 | 109.1 | 110.8 | 109.8 |
| Volume of Imports......................... | 73.a | 87.1 | 90.2 | 95.1 | 101.4 | 103.0 | 92.2 | 100.0 | 103.1 | 103.5 | 102.5 | 101.8 | 101.7 |
| Unit Value of Exports..................... | 74.a | 86.2 | 87.7 | 90.7 | 94.4 | 97.5 | 100.2 | 100.0 | 94.5 | 95.3 | 95.3 | 97.1 | 95.4 |
| Unit Value of Imports..................... | 75.a | 90.4 | 95.0 | 100.0 | 104.0 | 104.3 | 99.9 | 100.0 | 97.2 | 98.1 | 99.6 | 100.8 | 94.1 |
| Import Prices................................. | 76.x | 99.2 | 100.8 | 104.0 | 107.2 | 110.7 | 102.5 | 100.0 | 98.4 | 96.5 | 95.8 | † 94.1 | 85.5 |
| **Balance of Payments** |  | *Millions of US Dollars* | | | | | | | | | | | |
| A. Current Account*....................... | 109bx | 59,868.3 | 57,530.2 | 64,220.2 | 51,127.2 | 16,854.3 | 44,442.8 | 86,601.4 | 53,265.1 | 68,588.7 | 76,144.6 | 61,538.8 | 75,917.6 |
| Goods, credit (exports).................. | 1a9cx | 142,433.8 | 152,905.1 | 171,283.7 | 205,940.1 | 251,317.0 | 216,880.4 | 277,166.5 | 345,690.9 | 332,682.5 | 373,417.6 | 327,684.6 | 303,472.5 |
| Goods, debit (imports).................. | 1a9dx | 122,051.5 | 141,404.8 | 156,215.0 | 181,439.1 | 222,829.0 | 201,283.6 | 242,654.3 | 316,593.0 | 292,366.6 | 319,669.8 | 273,745.2 | 247,686.0 |
| Balance on goods...................... | 1a9bx | 20,382.0 | 11,500.3 | 15,068.7 | 24,501.0 | 28,487.6 | 15,597.1 | 34,511.8 | 29,097.9 | 40,315.9 | 53,747.8 | 53,939.4 | 55,786.4 |
| Services, credit (exports)............... | 1b9cx | 60,958.3 | 66,297.1 | 71,269.2 | 85,519.9 | 96,679.2 | 92,071.3 | 94,997.9 | 107,846.8 | 109,126.5 | 114,429.8 | 118,426.8 | 109,723.8 |
| Services, debit (imports)............... | 1b9dx | 43,504.0 | 46,759.6 | 48,844.0 | 56,570.4 | 63,926.5 | 65,520.6 | 69,411.2 | 83,003.4 | 86,183.3 | 92,460.1 | 98,324.9 | 92,557.4 |
| Balance on Goods & Services...... | 1z9bx | 37,836.6 | 31,037.7 | 37,493.9 | 53,450.5 | 61,240.8 | 42,147.4 | 60,098.9 | 53,941.3 | 63,259.1 | 75,717.5 | 74,041.3 | 72,952.9 |
| Primary income: credit.................. | 1c9cx | 72,824.2 | 103,633.0 | 111,265.1 | 126,055.9 | 88,904.4 | 95,388.1 | 124,953.4 | 110,287.2 | 120,907.5 | 119,784.8 | 152,177.9 | 128,732.3 |
| Primary income: debit................... | 1c9dx | 46,435.3 | 68,420.0 | 77,871.4 | 122,024.9 | 123,948.8 | 84,626.6 | 89,723.2 | 102,293.1 | 106,874.7 | 106,709.7 | 146,087.1 | 113,444.6 |
| Balance on gds, serv. & prim. inc. | 1y9bx | 64,225.5 | 66,250.7 | 70,887.6 | 57,481.6 | 26,196.4 | 52,908.9 | 95,329.2 | 61,935.4 | 77,291.9 | 88,792.6 | 80,132.2 | 88,240.5 |
| Secondary income: credit.............. | 1d9ca | 15,184.2 | 16,565.8 | 18,841.7 | 24,392.7 | 29,349.6 | 27,749.8 | 25,770.0 | 32,367.3 | 36,240.6 | 36,675.5 | 39,154.7 | 37,346.2 |
| Secondary income: debit............... | 1d9da | 19,541.4 | 25,286.3 | 25,509.2 | 30,747.1 | 38,691.7 | 36,215.9 | 34,497.8 | 41,037.6 | 44,943.8 | 49,323.5 | 57,748.1 | 49,669.1 |
| B. Capital Account*....................... | 209ba | −3,170.2 | −2,297.5 | −4,341.0 | −4,205.1 | −3,512.9 | −3,488.6 | −4,459.6 | −9,489.5 | −2,358.5 | 763.3 | −11,285.6 | −14,831.7 |
| Capital account: credit.................. | 209ca | 406.3 | 470.0 | 267.1 | 404.9 | 1,013.4 | 132.6 | 344.8 | 545.4 | 363.2 | 1,861.0 | 481.3 | 3,884.3 |
| Capital account: debit................... | 209da | 3,576.5 | 2,767.5 | 4,608.2 | 4,610.0 | 4,526.3 | 3,621.3 | 4,804.4 | 10,034.9 | 2,721.7 | 1,097.7 | 11,766.9 | 18,716.0 |
| Balance on current & capital acct. | 129ba | 56,698.1 | 55,232.7 | 59,879.1 | 46,922.1 | 13,341.3 | 40,954.1 | 82,141.8 | 43,775.6 | 66,230.2 | 76,907.9 | 50,253.2 | 61,085.9 |
| C. Financial Account*..................... | 309na | 70,659.7 | 97,549.4 | 70,547.9 | 33,454.7 | −1,848.1 | −46,352.6 | −16,225.4 | −20,725.8 | −91,484.3 | 99,737.0 | 17,981.1 | −33,476.8 |
| Direct investment: assets............. | 3a9aa | 31,313.9 | 54,033.8 | 85,323.5 | 67,278.8 | 30,284.1 | 44,704.1 | 74,105.2 | 43,331.8 | 53,371.0 | 12,559.7 | 7,469.5 | 121,719.4 |
| Equity & investment fund shares.. | 3aaaa | 26,367.0 | 50,558.6 | 71,597.5 | 44,685.4 | 19,553.8 | 33,516.1 | 62,416.3 | 13,113.2 | 52,479.5 | 18,268.1 | −5,470.9 | 85,050.7 |
| Debt instruments...................... | 3abaa | 4,946.9 | 3,475.2 | 13,726.0 | 22,593.4 | 10,730.3 | 11,188.0 | 11,688.9 | 30,218.6 | 891.5 | −5,708.4 | 12,940.4 | 36,668.8 |
| Direct investment: liabilities......... | 3a9la | 7,102.3 | 2,664.9 | 53,760.8 | 48,688.3 | 2,990.9 | 47,658.6 | 17,670.7 | 23,197.9 | 26,287.7 | −24,898.2 | 18,375.4 | 119,713.9 |
| Equity & investment fund shares . | 3aala | 5,153.0 | −2,023.2 | 42,302.8 | 41,474.3 | −951.1 | 43,162.5 | 21,877.1 | 19,012.1 | 4,401.1 | 10,201.0 | 16,897.5 | 68,504.5 |
| Debt instruments...................... | 3abla | 1,949.3 | 4,688.2 | 11,458.0 | 7,214.0 | 3,942.0 | 4,496.0 | −4,206.4 | 4,185.8 | 21,886.5 | −35,099.2 | 1,477.9 | 51,209.4 |
| Portfolio investment: assets......... | 3b9aa | 42,411.9 | 53,263.4 | 47,183.2 | 27,901.7 | 58,114.1 | 34,860.6 | −8,211.1 | −9,015.1 | −4,943.2 | 21,119.4 | 9,743.0 | 39,944.0 |
| Equity & investment fund shares | 3baaa | 11,303.0 | 17,729.0 | 13,761.8 | 5,221.0 | 3,919.1 | 2,311.4 | 6,201.9 | 146.7 | 563.6 | 16,902.0 | 11,278.4 | 27,580.3 |
| Debt securities.......................... | 3bbaa | 31,108.9 | 35,534.4 | 33,421.3 | 22,680.6 | 54,195.0 | 32,549.2 | −14,413.0 | −9,161.8 | −5,506.8 | 4,217.4 | −1,535.4 | 12,363.7 |
| Portfolio investment: liabilities....... | 3b9la | 2,857.6 | 5,636.4 | 3,434.1 | −291.6 | 25,260.5 | 10,039.4 | 23,333.7 | −23,619.8 | 13,231.2 | 3,599.2 | 2,097.7 | −14,597.3 |
| Equity & investment fund shares . | 3bala | −2,789.1 | 3,950.9 | 537.2 | 688.7 | 24,352.3 | 9,241.4 | −7,167.3 | 7,542.9 | 14,553.9 | 3,026.1 | 3,753.4 | −10,932.6 |
| Debt securities.......................... | 3bbla | 5,646.7 | 1,685.5 | 2,896.9 | −980.3 | 908.2 | 797.9 | 30,501.0 | −31,162.6 | −1,322.7 | 573.1 | −1,655.7 | −3,664.7 |
| Fin. der.& empl.stk.ops.(ESOs): net. | 3c9na | .... | 2,450.2 | 757.1 | 923.8 | −3,704.2 | 1,703.7 | 316.2 | −625.2 | −1,582.9 | −875.0 | −111.7 | 1,357.4 |
| Fin. der. & ESOs: assets.............. | 3c9aa | .... | .... | .... | .... | .... | .... | .... | .... | .... | .... | .... | .... |
| Fin. der. & ESOs: liabilities.......... | 3c9la | .... | .... | .... | .... | .... | .... | .... | .... | .... | .... | .... | .... |
| Other investment: assets.............. | 3d9aa | 32,564.0 | 77,112.1 | 49,470.7 | 277,140.7 | −324,549.8 | −123,087.1 | −32,347.4 | 17,010.1 | −20,689.2 | 78,230.6 | −32,333.9 | −30,705.7 |
| Other equity............................. | 3daaa | .... | .... | .... | .... | .... | .... | .... | .... | .... | .... | .... | .... |
| Debt instruments...................... | 3dzaa | 32,564.0 | 77,112.1 | 49,470.7 | 277,140.7 | −324,549.8 | −123,087.1 | −32,347.4 | 17,010.1 | −20,689.2 | 78,230.6 | −32,333.9 | −30,705.7 |
| Other investment: liabilities........... | 3d9la | 25,670.2 | 81,008.8 | 54,991.8 | 291,393.7 | −266,259.1 | −53,164.0 | 9,083.9 | 71,849.2 | 78,121.1 | 32,596.6 | −53,687.2 | 60,675.3 |
| Other equity............................. | 3dala | .... | .... | .... | .... | .... | .... | .... | .... | .... | .... | .... | .... |
| Debt instruments...................... | 3dzla | 25,670.2 | 81,008.8 | 54,991.8 | 291,393.7 | −266,259.1 | −53,164.0 | 9,083.9 | 71,849.2 | 78,121.1 | 32,596.6 | −53,687.2 | 60,675.3 |
| Curr.+ cap.− finan. acct. balance. | 4y9na | −13,961.6 | −42,316.7 | −10,668.8 | 13,467.4 | 15,189.5 | 87,306.8 | 98,367.2 | 64,501.5 | 157,714.5 | −22,829.1 | 32,272.1 | 94,562.7 |
| D. Net Errors and Omissions........... | 409na | 13,654.4 | 24,643.6 | 11,039.3 | −10,004.3 | −11,335.5 | −39,168.9 | 27,015.7 | −9,834.8 | 26,802.6 | 36,822.7 | 3,627.7 | 4,207.6 |
| E. Reserves and Related Items......... | 4z9na | −307.3 | −17,673.0 | 370.6 | 3,462.9 | 3,853.3 | 48,137.1 | 125,382.3 | 54,666.3 | 184,517.1 | 13,993.6 | 35,899.8 | 98,770.3 |
| Reserve assets............................ | 3e9aa | −307.3 | −17,673.0 | 370.6 | 3,462.9 | 3,853.3 | 48,137.1 | 125,382.3 | 54,666.3 | 184,517.1 | 13,993.6 | 35,899.8 | 98,770.3 |
| Credit and loans from the IMF........ | 3dcla | — | — | — | — | — | — | — | — | — | — | — | — |
| Exceptional financing................... | 409la | .... | .... | .... | .... | .... | .... | .... | .... | .... | .... | .... | .... |

*Excludes components in group E

# Switzerland 146

| | | 2004 | 2005 | 2006 | 2007 | 2008 | 2009 | 2010 | 2011 | 2012 | 2013 | 2014 | 2015 |
|---|---|---|---|---|---|---|---|---|---|---|---|---|---|
| **International Investment Position** | | | | | *Millions of US Dollars* | | | | | | | | |
| Assets | 809aa | 2,046,617.3 | 2,130,177.9 | 2,561,228.8 | 3,328,810.0 | 3,053,445.9 | 3,312,485.0 | 3,695,767.3 | 3,834,030.3 | 4,212,525.9 | 4,362,252.8 | 4,264,838.7 | 4,294,187.1 |
| Direct investment | 8a9aa | 458,969.8 | 492,889.2 | 659,384.9 | 824,172.2 | 892,029.0 | 1,067,947.6 | 1,283,706.5 | 1,364,894.2 | 1,473,862.8 | 1,458,782.1 | 1,426,141.7 | 1,498,363.9 |
| Equity & investment fund shares.. | 8aaaa | 378,872.3 | 411,531.2 | 519,100.6 | 624,128.9 | 668,913.8 | 809,947.9 | 988,875.2 | 1,032,914.4 | 1,119,463.3 | 1,096,884.7 | 964,741.4 | 1,003,774.8 |
| Debt instruments | 8abaa | 80,097.6 | 81,357.9 | 140,284.3 | 200,043.3 | 223,115.2 | 258,043.7 | 294,831.3 | 331,979.8 | 354,399.5 | 361,897.5 | 461,400.3 | 494,589.1 |
| Portfolio investment | 8b9aa | 760,237.8 | 765,553.9 | 933,925.9 | 1,129,604.8 | 952,259.0 | 1,118,746.6 | 1,160,184.3 | 1,120,962.8 | 1,225,646.1 | 1,299,104.3 | 1,253,540.9 | 1,232,640.6 |
| Equity & investment fund shares.. | 8baaa | 339,470.0 | 357,349.1 | 421,497.1 | 511,291.8 | 318,468.3 | 398,894.3 | 441,373.9 | 425,985.6 | 485,698.8 | 573,235.6 | 573,582.5 | 577,248.6 |
| Debt securities | 8bbaa | 420,767.7 | 408,204.8 | 512,428.8 | 618,313.0 | 633,790.7 | 719,852.2 | 718,810.4 | 694,977.2 | 739,947.3 | 725,868.7 | 679,958.4 | 655,392.0 |
| Fin. der.(oth.than reserves) & ESOs | 8c9aa | 27,834.9 | 24,398.0 | 37,895.6 | 51,810.0 | 178,211.2 | 123,358.1 | 144,450.7 | 161,271.8 | 139,970.4 | 117,792.8 | 151,091.5 | 118,639.8 |
| Other investment | 8d9aa | 724,941.5 | 789,647.3 | 865,554.4 | 1,247,679.0 | 956,784.8 | 866,858.6 | 838,725.6 | 855,922.9 | 843,885.1 | 951,105.8 | 886,921.3 | 838,433.9 |
| Other equity | 8daaa | 479.0 | 438.1 | 431.6 | 934.0 | 953.2 | 978.9 | 1,207.5 | 950.2 | 1,074.8 | 1,108.8 | 1,021.3 | 1,076.5 |
| Debt instruments | 8dzaa | 724,462.5 | 789,209.2 | 865,122.8 | 1,246,745.0 | 955,831.6 | 865,879.7 | 837,518.2 | 854,972.7 | 842,810.3 | 949,997.0 | 885,900.0 | 837,357.4 |
| Reserve assets | 8e9aa | 74,633.3 | 57,689.5 | 64,468.0 | 75,544.0 | 74,161.9 | 135,530.1 | 268,700.2 | 330,978.5 | 529,161.5 | 535,467.8 | 547,143.3 | 606,108.9 |
| Liabilities | 809la | 1,555,735.6 | 1,677,709.2 | 2,078,084.1 | 2,679,130.8 | 2,431,527.1 | 2,556,286.1 | 2,851,491.6 | 2,953,279.6 | 3,352,698.7 | 3,623,802.6 | 3,574,614.1 | 3,680,656.6 |
| Direct investment | 8a9la | 280,948.2 | 252,731.1 | 382,383.4 | 551,242.8 | 644,907.9 | 733,912.4 | 888,599.1 | 981,450.9 | 1,054,138.6 | 1,085,435.1 | 1,157,001.8 | 1,262,250.0 |
| Equity & investment fund shares.. | 8aala | 218,632.8 | 191,366.9 | 265,570.7 | 387,618.9 | 459,280.5 | 530,305.8 | 642,274.3 | 723,512.4 | 754,839.4 | 805,240.5 | 780,443.4 | 844,859.4 |
| Debt instruments | 8abla | 62,315.4 | 61,364.2 | 116,812.7 | 163,624.0 | 185,627.3 | 203,606.6 | 246,324.8 | 257,938.5 | 299,299.3 | 280,194.6 | 376,558.4 | 417,390.6 |
| Portfolio investment | 8b9la | 520,924.4 | 612,782.9 | 786,004.7 | 818,139.0 | 599,237.9 | 692,792.8 | 775,147.5 | 696,912.4 | 948,489.2 | 1,151,419.6 | 1,156,396.7 | 1,141,266.5 |
| Equity & investment fund shares.. | 8bala | 456,669.3 | 536,489.9 | 684,249.9 | 725,643.8 | 530,284.8 | 629,078.3 | 671,997.0 | 617,584.5 | 850,196.5 | 1,050,440.6 | 1,047,807.4 | 1,032,399.3 |
| Debt securities | 8bbla | 64,255.0 | 76,293.0 | 101,754.8 | 92,495.2 | 68,953.1 | 63,714.5 | 103,150.5 | 79,327.9 | 98,292.7 | 100,979.0 | 108,589.3 | 108,867.3 |
| Fin. der.(oth.than reserves) & ESOs | 8c9la | 30,170.6 | 32,835.7 | 34,347.6 | 50,820.8 | 182,117.0 | 123,897.9 | 143,186.2 | 164,824.4 | 137,560.0 | 112,471.2 | 149,109.9 | 116,103.0 |
| Other investment | 8d9la | 723,692.5 | 779,359.6 | 875,348.4 | 1,258,928.1 | 1,005,264.4 | 1,005,683.0 | 1,044,558.7 | 1,110,092.0 | 1,212,510.8 | 1,274,476.7 | 1,112,105.6 | 1,161,037.1 |
| Other equity | 8dala | .... | .... | .... | .... | .... | .... | .... | .... | .... | .... | .... | .... |
| Debt instruments | 8dzla | 723,692.5 | 779,359.6 | 875,348.4 | 1,258,928.1 | 1,005,264.4 | 1,005,683.0 | 1,044,558.7 | 1,110,092.0 | 1,212,510.8 | 1,274,476.7 | 1,112,105.6 | 1,161,037.1 |

| Government Finance Operations Statement General Government | | | | | | *Millions of Francs: Fiscal Year Ends December 31* | | | | | | | |
|---|---|---|---|---|---|---|---|---|---|---|---|---|---|
| Revenue | a1 | 164,660 | 171,139 | 179,712 | 189,148 | 188,027 | 186,991 | 188,620 | 196,016 | 195,501 | 207,887 | .... | .... |
| Taxes | a11 | 97,669 | 102,248 | 108,324 | 114,604 | 122,610 | 121,188 | 122,366 | 126,121 | 126,155 | 128,141 | .... | .... |
| Social Contributions | a12 | 31,853 | 32,426 | 33,490 | 35,115 | 37,133 | 38,142 | 38,286 | 40,941 | 41,840 | 43,107 | .... | .... |
| Grants | a13 | 108 | 118 | 120 | 105 | 129 | 162 | 157 | 191 | 216 | 244 | .... | .... |
| Other Revenue | a14 | 35,030 | 36,347 | 37,778 | 39,324 | 28,154 | 27,499 | 27,810 | 28,763 | 27,290 | 36,394 | .... | .... |
| Expense | a2 | 168,493 | 172,313 | 173,677 | 180,540 | 177,530 | 182,709 | 186,125 | 193,002 | 195,325 | 208,081 | .... | .... |
| Compensation of Employees | a21 | 48,418 | 49,155 | 49,882 | 52,188 | 42,674 | 43,308 | 44,538 | 45,303 | 46,091 | 47,996 | .... | .... |
| Use of Goods & Services | a22 | 22,935 | 23,500 | 23,753 | 24,383 | 21,975 | 22,555 | 22,018 | 23,158 | 23,708 | 23,583 | .... | .... |
| Consumption of Fixed Capital | a23 | 9,563 | 9,878 | 10,153 | 10,472 | 11,590 | 11,529 | 11,877 | 12,179 | 12,561 | 18,298 | .... | .... |
| Interest | a24 | 6,625 | 6,921 | 7,178 | 6,901 | 6,489 | 5,738 | 5,470 | 5,424 | 5,051 | 3,973 | .... | .... |
| Subsidies | a25 | 19,722 | 19,643 | 19,391 | 21,183 | 24,360 | 23,893 | 19,198 | 19,854 | 21,358 | 19,210 | .... | .... |
| Grants | a26 | 2,387 | 2,470 | 2,419 | 1,532 | 2,991 | 3,018 | 3,201 | 3,292 | 3,444 | 4,030 | .... | .... |
| Social Benefits | a27 | 56,584 | 58,407 | 58,615 | 59,555 | 60,526 | 64,295 | 66,437 | 66,129 | 67,547 | 71,507 | .... | .... |
| Other Expense | a28 | 2,260 | 2,340 | 2,285 | 4,326 | 6,925 | 8,374 | 13,386 | 17,663 | 15,566 | 19,484 | .... | .... |
| Gross Operating Balance [1-2+23] | agob | 5,730 | 8,703 | 16,189 | 19,080 | 22,086 | 15,811 | 14,371 | 15,192 | 12,737 | 18,104 | .... | .... |
| Net Operating Balance [1-2] | anob | –3,834 | –1,175 | 6,036 | 8,608 | 10,497 | 4,282 | 2,494 | 3,013 | 176 | –194 | .... | .... |
| Net Acq. of Nonfinancial Assets | a31 | 2,246 | 1,553 | 1,265 | 1,407 | 75 | 1,397 | 1,456 | 1,201 | 518 | 962 | .... | .... |
| Aquisition of Nonfin. Assets | a31.1 | .... | .... | .... | .... | .... | .... | .... | .... | .... | .... | | |
| Disposal of Nonfin. Assets | a31.2 | .... | .... | .... | .... | .... | .... | .... | .... | .... | .... | | |
| Net Lending/Borrowing [1-2-31] | anlb | –6,080 | –2,727 | 4,771 | 7,202 | 10,422 | 2,885 | 1,039 | 1,812 | –342 | –1,156 | .... | .... |
| Net Acq. of Financial Assets | a32 | 557 | 14,156 | 5,726 | 25,617 | 20,026 | 7,997 | 3,630 | 3,823 | .... | .... | | |
| By instrument | | | | | | | | | | | | | |
| Monetary Gold & SDRs | a3201 | .... | .... | .... | .... | .... | .... | .... | .... | .... | .... | | |
| Currency & Deposits | a3202 | .... | .... | .... | .... | .... | .... | .... | .... | .... | .... | | |
| Securities other than Shares | a3203 | .... | .... | .... | .... | .... | .... | .... | .... | .... | .... | | |
| Loans | a3204 | .... | .... | .... | .... | .... | .... | .... | .... | .... | .... | | |
| Shares & Other Equity | a3205 | .... | .... | .... | .... | .... | .... | .... | .... | .... | .... | | |
| Insurance Technical Reserves | a3206 | .... | .... | .... | .... | .... | .... | .... | .... | .... | .... | | |
| Financial Derivatives | a3207 | .... | .... | .... | .... | .... | .... | .... | .... | .... | .... | | |
| Other Accounts Receivable | a3208 | .... | .... | .... | .... | .... | .... | .... | .... | .... | .... | | |
| By debtor | | | | | | | | | | | | | |
| Domestic | a321 | 582 | 14,167 | 5,726 | 25,644 | 20,037 | 8,009 | 3,630 | 3,819 | .... | .... | | |
| Foreign | a322 | –25 | –12 | — | –27 | –10 | –12 | — | 4 | .... | .... | | |
| Net Incurrence of Liabilities | a33 | 6,637 | 16,883 | 955 | 18,416 | 9,605 | 5,112 | 2,591 | 2,011 | .... | .... | | |
| By instrument | | | | | | | | | | | | | |
| Special Drawing Rights (SDRs) | a3301 | .... | .... | .... | .... | .... | .... | .... | .... | .... | .... | | |
| Currency & Deposits | a3302 | .... | .... | .... | .... | .... | .... | .... | .... | .... | .... | | |
| Securities other than Shares | a3303 | .... | .... | .... | .... | .... | .... | .... | .... | .... | .... | | |
| Loans | a3304 | .... | .... | .... | .... | .... | .... | .... | .... | .... | .... | | |
| Shares & Other Equity | a3305 | .... | .... | .... | .... | .... | .... | .... | .... | .... | .... | | |
| Insurance Technical Reserves | a3306 | .... | .... | .... | .... | .... | .... | .... | .... | .... | .... | | |
| Financial Derivatives | a3307 | .... | .... | .... | .... | .... | .... | .... | .... | .... | .... | | |
| Other Accounts Payable | a3308 | .... | .... | .... | .... | .... | .... | .... | .... | .... | .... | | |
| By creditor | | | | | | | | | | | | | |
| Domestic | a331 | 6,637 | 16,883 | 955 | 18,416 | 9,605 | 5,112 | 2,591 | 2,011 | .... | .... | | |
| Foreign | a332 | — | — | — | — | — | — | — | — | .... | .... | | |
| Stat. Discrepancy [32-33-NLB] | anlbz | — | — | — | — | — | — | — | — | .... | .... | | |
| Memo Item: Expenditure [2+31] | a2m | 170,739 | 173,866 | 174,941 | 181,947 | 177,605 | 184,106 | 187,581 | 194,204 | 195,843 | 209,043 | .... | .... |

| | | 2004 | 2005 | 2006 | 2007 | 2008 | 2009 | 2010 | 2011 | 2012 | 2013 | 2014 | 2015 |
|---|---|---|---|---|---|---|---|---|---|---|---|---|---|
| **Balance Sheet** | | | | | *Millions of Francs: Fiscal Year Ends December 31* | | | | | | | | |
| Net Worth......................................... | a6 | −64,260 | −61,295 | −36,979 | 7,097 | 62,679 | 92,408 | 79,073 | 85,579 | .... | .... | .... | .... |
| Nonfinancial Assets......................... | a61 | 58,630 | 59,166 | 59,544 | 66,204 | 120,540 | 127,872 | 131,013 | 134,148 | 140,240 | 191,968 | .... | .... |
| Financial Assets.............................. | a62 | 202,222 | 215,049 | 219,774 | 241,632 | 229,172 | 238,359 | 224,393 | 237,326 | .... | .... | .... | .... |
| By instrument | | | | | | | | | | | | | |
| Monetary Gold & SDRs................. | a6201 | — | — | — | .... | — | — | — | — | .... | .... | .... | .... |
| Currency & Deposits..................... | a6202 | 15,985 | 31,101 | 28,625 | 29,761 | 25,634 | 32,532 | 31,140 | 32,805 | .... | .... | .... | .... |
| Securities other than Shares.......... | a6203 | 18,621 | 19,954 | 21,476 | 14,515 | 22,513 | 17,452 | 18,195 | 18,908 | .... | .... | .... | .... |
| Loans............................................ | a6204 | 23,475 | 20,452 | 18,053 | 31,756 | 28,401 | 25,394 | 26,341 | 27,734 | .... | .... | .... | .... |
| Shares and Other Equity................ | a6205 | 100,507 | 95,970 | 104,932 | 113,551 | 108,640 | 120,969 | 104,380 | 113,402 | .... | .... | .... | .... |
| Insurance Technical Reserves......... | a6206 | — | — | — | — | — | — | — | — | .... | .... | .... | .... |
| Financial Derivatives..................... | a6207 | 180 | 304 | 388 | 535 | 1,101 | 283 | 827 | 366 | .... | .... | .... | .... |
| Other Accounts Receivable............. | a6208 | 43,454 | 47,268 | 46,300 | 51,514 | 42,883 | 41,730 | 43,510 | 44,111 | .... | .... | .... | .... |
| By debtor | | | | | | | | | | | | | |
| Domestic........................................ | a621 | 191,658 | 198,293 | 201,502 | 216,623 | 212,089 | 220,034 | 205,987 | 219,750 | .... | .... | .... | .... |
| Foreign.......................................... | a622 | 10,563 | 16,757 | 18,272 | 25,009 | 17,084 | 18,325 | 18,405 | 17,577 | .... | .... | .... | .... |
| Liabilities....................................... | a63 | 325,112 | 335,510 | 316,297 | 300,738 | 287,034 | 273,822 | 276,333 | 285,895 | .... | .... | .... | .... |
| By instrument | | | | | | | | | | | | | |
| Special Drawing Rights (SDRs)........ | a6301 | — | — | .... | — | — | — | — | — | .... | .... | .... | .... |
| Currency & Deposits..................... | a6302 | 3,324 | 3,474 | 3,524 | 3,579 | 9,304 | 9,082 | 9,536 | 10,086 | .... | .... | .... | .... |
| Securities other than Shares.......... | a6303 | 151,786 | 156,492 | 144,961 | 134,019 | 136,485 | 123,730 | 123,322 | 132,410 | .... | .... | .... | .... |
| Loans............................................ | a6304 | 113,541 | 111,707 | 102,947 | 100,784 | 94,018 | 91,614 | 92,860 | 92,647 | .... | .... | .... | .... |
| Shares and Other Equity................ | a6305 | — | — | — | — | — | — | — | — | .... | .... | .... | .... |
| Insurance Technical Reserves......... | a6306 | — | — | — | — | — | — | — | — | .... | .... | .... | .... |
| Financial Derivatives..................... | a6307 | 40 | 95 | 117 | 105 | 513 | 575 | 823 | 707 | .... | .... | .... | .... |
| Other Accounts Payable................. | a6308 | 56,420 | 63,742 | 64,748 | 62,252 | 46,715 | 48,822 | 49,792 | 50,046 | .... | .... | .... | .... |
| By creditor | | | | | | | | | | | | | |
| Domestic........................................ | a631 | 249,858 | 244,200 | 226,844 | 208,953 | 214,283 | 203,439 | 231,834 | 235,593 | .... | .... | .... | .... |
| Foreign.......................................... | a632 | 75,253 | 91,310 | 89,454 | 91,785 | 72,751 | 70,383 | 44,499 | 50,302 | .... | .... | .... | .... |
| Net Financial Worth [62-63]............ | a6m2 | −122,890 | −120,461 | −96,523 | −59,107 | −57,862 | −35,463 | −51,941 | −48,569 | .... | .... | .... | .... |
| Memo Item: Debt at Market Value... | a6m3 | 325,072 | 335,415 | 316,180 | 300,633 | 286,521 | 273,247 | 275,510 | 285,188 | .... | .... | .... | .... |
| Memo Item: Debt at Face Value....... | a6m35 | .... | .... | .... | .... | .... | .... | .... | .... | .... | .... | .... | .... |
| Memo Item: Debt at Nominal Value. | a6m4 | .... | .... | .... | .... | .... | .... | .... | .... | .... | .... | .... | .... |
| **National Accounts** | | | | | *Billions of Francs* | | | | | | | | |
| Househ.Cons.Expend.,incl.NPISHs.... | 96f.c | 283.9 | 291.5 | 299.8 | 310.8 | 321.3 | 323.7 | 330.3 | 333.4 | 339.4 | 345.5 | 348.7 | 348.0 |
| Government Consumption Expend... | 91f.c | 56.0 | 57.1 | 58.0 | 59.4 | 60.8 | 64.0 | 64.6 | 66.4 | 68.8 | 69.7 | 70.8 | 72.5 |
| Gross Fixed Capital Formation......... | 93e.c | 119.6 | 124.0 | 131.3 | 140.5 | 144.4 | 133.3 | 138.3 | 144.5 | 147.2 | 148.9 | 151.5 | 151.8 |
| Changes in Inventories.................... | 93i.c | −14.3 | −2.0 | 3.2 | −2.7 | 7.2 | 21.6 | 7.1 | 22.3 | 3.7 | −6.0 | −1.3 | −12.7 |
| Exports of Goods and Services......... | 90c.c | 251.5 | 273.5 | 305.9 | 353.7 | 375.9 | 337.5 | 388.9 | 406.0 | 419.1 | 459.3 | 415.1 | 406.3 |
| Imports of Goods and Services (-)..... | 98c.c | 207.9 | 236.6 | 259.7 | 288.3 | 312.8 | 292.6 | 323.6 | 354.0 | 353.8 | 381.6 | 336.4 | 326.9 |
| Gross Domestic Product (GDP)......... | 99b.c | 488.7 | 507.5 | 538.4 | 573.4 | 596.8 | 587.4 | 605.6 | 618.5 | 624.4 | 635.7 | 648.4 | 639.0 |
| GDP Volume 2010 Ref., Chained..... | 99b.r | 526.5 | 542.7 | 565.0 | 588.4 | 601.4 | 588.7 | 605.6 | 617.1 | 623.9 | 636.0 | 648.7 | .... |
| GDP Volume (2010=100)................ | 99bvr | 86.9 | 89.6 | 93.3 | 97.2 | 99.3 | 97.2 | 100.0 | 101.9 | 103.0 | 105.0 | 107.1 | .... |
| GDP Deflator (2010=100)............... | 99bir | 92.8 | 93.5 | 95.3 | 97.5 | 99.2 | 99.8 | 100.0 | 100.2 | 100.1 | 100.0 | 100.0 | .... |
| | | | | | *Millions: Midyear Estimates* | | | | | | | | |
| Population.................................. | 99z | 7.35 | 7.41 | 7.48 | 7.56 | 7.65 | 7.74 | 7.83 | 7.93 | 8.02 | 8.12 | 8.21 | 8.30 |

# Syrian Arab Republic   463

| | | 2004 | 2005 | 2006 | 2007 | 2008 | 2009 | 2010 | 2011 | 2012 | 2013 | 2014 | 2015 |
|---|---|---|---|---|---|---|---|---|---|---|---|---|---|
| **Exchange Rates** | | | | | *Pounds per SDR: End of Period* | | | | | | | | |
| Principal Rate.................aa= | wa | 17.433 | 16.044 | 16.887 | 17.738 | 17.290 | 17.597 | 17.287 | 17.233 | 17.252 | 17.287 | 16.263 | 15.555 |
| | | | | | | *Pounds per US Dollar: End of Period* | | | | | | | |
| Principal Rate.................ae= | we | 11.225 | 11.225 | 11.225 | 11.225 | 11.225 | 11.225 | 11.225 | 11.225 | 11.225 | 11.225 | 11.225 | 11.225 |
| Secondary Rate.................... | xe | 52.200 | 54.850 | 51.100 | † 48.100 | 46.350 | 45.700 | 46.940 | 55.720 | 77.505 | .... | .... | .... |
| Tertiary Rate...................... | ye | 48.570 | 49.850 | 49.850 | .... | .... | .... | .... | .... | .... | .... | .... | .... |
| **Fund Position** | | | | | | *Millions of SDRs: End of Period* | | | | | | | |
| Quota................................ | 2f.s | 293.60 | 293.60 | 293.60 | 293.60 | 293.60 | 293.60 | 293.60 | 293.60 | 293.60 | 293.60 | 293.60 | 293.60 |
| SDR Holdings..................... | 1b.s | 36.58 | 36.58 | 36.57 | 36.57 | 36.57 | 279.19 | 279.18 | 279.18 | 280.04 | 282.20 | 282.20 | 282.20 |
| Reserve Position in the Fund........... | 1c.s | .01 | .01 | .01 | .01 | .01 | .01 | .01 | .01 | .01 | .01 | .01 | .01 |
| Total Fund Cred.&Loans Outstg....... | 2tl | — | — | — | — | — | — | — | — | | | | |
| SDR Allocations.................... | 1bd | 36.56 | 36.56 | 36.56 | 36.56 | 36.56 | 279.18 | 279.18 | 279.18 | 279.18 | 279.18 | 279.18 | 279.18 |
| **International Liquidity** | | | | | *Millions of US Dollars Unless Otherwise Indicated: End of Period* | | | | | | | | |
| SDR Holdings..................... | 1b.d | 57 | 52 | 55 | 58 | 56 | 438 | 430 | 429 | 430 | 435 | 409 | 391 |
| Reserve Position in the Fund.......... | 1c.d | — | — | — | — | — | — | — | — | | | | |
| Foreign Exchange.................... | 1d.d | .... | 17,295 | 16,412 | 16,955 | 17,006 | 16,960 | 19,035 | .... | .... | .... | .... | .... |
| Gold (Million Fine Troy Ounces)....... | 1ad | .833 | .833 | .833 | .833 | .830 | .830 | .830 | .... | .... | .... | .... | .... |
| Gold (National Valuation)............... | 1and | 29 | 29 | 29 | 39 | 38 | 38 | 54 | .... | .... | .... | .... | .... |
| Central Bank: Other Assets............ | 3..d | — | — | — | — | † 1,516 | 1,876 | 1,934 | 1,962 | .... | .... | .... | .... |
| Central Bank: Other Liabs.............. | 4..d | 450 | 402 | 530 | 1,697 | † 1,688 | 1,636 | 966 | 264 | .... | .... | .... | .... |
| Other Depository Corps.: Assets....... | 7a.d | 55,204 | 56,569 | 52,884 | 47,354 | † 34,143 | 35,537 | 36,124 | 34,365 | .... | .... | .... | .... |
| Other Depository Corps.: Liabs......... | 7b.d | 469 | 1,952 | 824 | 1,203 | † 1,244 | 1,583 | 2,115 | 1,972 | .... | .... | .... | .... |
| **Central Bank** | | | | | *Millions of Pounds: End of Period* | | | | | | | | |
| Net Foreign Assets................... | 11n | 140,221 | 144,153 | 151,123 | 189,276 | † 213,524 | 218,689 | 226,566 | 150,229 | .... | .... | .... | .... |
| Claims on Nonresidents................. | 11 | 145,906 | 149,254 | 157,691 | 208,976 | † 233,110 | 241,973 | 242,238 | 158,002 | .... | .... | .... | .... |
| Liabilities to Nonresidents.............. | 16c | 5,686 | 5,101 | 6,568 | 19,700 | † 19,586 | 23,284 | 15,672 | 7,773 | .... | .... | .... | .... |
| Claims on Other Depository Corps.... | 12e | 144,469 | 143,300 | 155,475 | 161,309 | † 192,975 | 257,166 | 269,074 | 216,829 | .... | .... | .... | .... |
| Net Claims on Central Government.. | 12an | −15,156 | 39,386 | 48,876 | 23,628 | † −37,402 | 21,245 | 39,848 | 377,584 | .... | .... | .... | .... |
| Claims on Central Government.... | 12a | 309,879 | 312,697 | 315,335 | 318,076 | † 318,360 | 318,339 | 318,172 | 644,391 | .... | .... | .... | .... |
| Liabilities to Central Government... | 16d | 325,034 | 273,311 | 266,459 | 294,447 | † 355,761 | 297,094 | 278,324 | 266,807 | .... | .... | .... | .... |
| Claims on Other Sectors.................. | 12s | 106 | 106 | 106 | — | † — | — | — | — | .... | .... | .... | .... |
| Claims on Other Financial Corps.... | 12g | — | — | — | — | † — | — | — | — | .... | .... | .... | .... |
| Claims on State & Local Govts....... | 12b | — | — | — | — | † — | — | — | — | .... | .... | .... | .... |
| Claims on Public Nonfin. Corps...... | 12c | 106 | 106 | 106 | — | † — | — | — | — | .... | .... | .... | .... |
| Claims on Private Sector............... | 12d | — | — | — | — | † — | — | — | — | .... | .... | .... | .... |
| Monetary Base........................... | 14 | 472,826 | 509,241 | 558,545 | 648,706 | † 763,771 | 870,315 | 931,045 | 870,430 | .... | .... | .... | .... |
| Currency in Circulation.................. | 14a | 344,330 | 407,373 | 411,394 | 441,377 | † 492,719 | 520,316 | 577,060 | 663,471 | .... | .... | .... | .... |
| Liabs. to Other Depository Corps.... | 14c | 105,680 | 85,948 | 126,984 | 201,227 | † 258,138 | 327,156 | 329,879 | 169,303 | .... | .... | .... | .... |
| Liabilities to Other Sectors............. | 14d | 22,816 | 15,920 | 20,167 | 6,102 | † 12,915 | 22,842 | 24,107 | 37,656 | .... | .... | .... | .... |
| Other Liabs. to Other Dep. Corps.... | 14n | — | — | — | — | † 1,566 | 2,213 | 3,448 | 4,123 | .... | .... | .... | .... |
| Dep. & Sec. Excl. f/Monetary Base.... | 14o | — | — | — | — | † — | — | — | — | .... | .... | .... | .... |
| Deposits Included in Broad Money. | 15 | — | — | — | — | † — | — | — | — | .... | .... | .... | .... |
| Sec.Ot.th.Shares Incl.in Brd. Money | 16a | — | — | — | — | † — | — | — | — | .... | .... | .... | .... |
| Deposits Excl. from Broad Money... | 16b | — | — | — | — | † — | — | — | — | .... | .... | .... | .... |
| Sec.Ot.th.Shares Excl.f/Brd.Money.. | 16s | — | — | — | — | † — | — | — | — | .... | .... | .... | .... |
| Loans.................................... | 16l | — | — | — | — | † — | — | — | — | .... | .... | .... | .... |
| Financial Derivatives........................ | 16m | — | — | — | — | † — | — | — | — | .... | .... | .... | .... |
| Shares and Other Equity................. | 17a | 80,383 | 98,025 | 100,121 | 10,114 | † 5,027 | 3,100 | 17,785 | 27,572 | .... | .... | .... | .... |
| Other Items (Net)........................... | 17r | −283,569 | −280,327 | −303,086 | −284,606 | † −401,267 | −378,528 | −416,789 | −157,483 | .... | .... | .... | .... |
| Memo Item: | | | | | | | | | | | | | |
| Total Assets................................. | 10ra | 960,779 | 946,332 | 996,261 | 1,034,832 | † 1,153,324 | 1,224,704 | 1,274,625 | 1,206,259 | .... | .... | .... | .... |
| **Other Depository Corporations** | | | | | *Millions of Pounds: End of Period* | | | | | | | | |
| Net Foreign Assets........................... | 21n | 614,392 | 613,073 | 584,371 | 518,047 | † 369,453 | 381,304 | 381,754 | 363,611 | .... | .... | .... | .... |
| Claims on Nonresidents................. | 21 | 619,662 | 634,988 | 593,618 | 531,550 | † 383,422 | 399,078 | 405,489 | 385,744 | .... | .... | .... | .... |
| Liabilities to Nonresidents.............. | 26c | 5,270 | 21,915 | 9,246 | 13,503 | † 13,969 | 17,774 | 23,736 | 22,133 | .... | .... | .... | .... |
| Claims on Central Bank................... | 20 | 117,276 | 109,555 | 134,775 | 218,765 | † 278,778 | 363,610 | 370,876 | 221,841 | .... | .... | .... | .... |
| Currency............................ | 20a | 11,682 | 22,653 | 12,194 | 19,020 | † 23,899 | 39,365 | 36,814 | 37,179 | .... | .... | .... | .... |
| Reserve Deposits and Securities..... | 20b | 105,594 | 86,902 | 122,581 | 199,746 | † 253,852 | 323,236 | 333,028 | 183,444 | .... | .... | .... | .... |
| Other Claims........................... | 20n | — | — | — | — | † 1,028 | 1,010 | 1,034 | 1,218 | .... | .... | .... | .... |
| Net Claims on Central Government.. | 22an | 72,047 | 69,993 | 50,174 | 73,499 | † 83,502 | 47,932 | 63,777 | 80,891 | .... | .... | .... | .... |
| Claims on Central Government...... | 22a | 112,869 | 110,600 | 109,281 | 105,741 | † 111,877 | 86,501 | 99,739 | 111,839 | .... | .... | .... | .... |
| Liabilities to Central Government... | 26d | 40,822 | 40,607 | 59,107 | 32,242 | † 28,376 | 38,569 | 35,963 | 30,948 | .... | .... | .... | .... |
| Claims on Other Sectors.................. | 22s | 330,100 | 421,723 | 473,416 | 633,386 | † 915,835 | 1,029,874 | 1,214,368 | 1,162,070 | .... | .... | .... | .... |
| Claims on Other Financial Corps.... | 22g | — | — | — | 681 | † 1,879 | 2,675 | 2,607 | 2,645 | .... | .... | .... | .... |
| Claims on State & Local Govts....... | 22b | — | — | — | — | † — | — | — | — | .... | .... | .... | .... |
| Claims on Public Nonfin. Corps...... | 22c | 182,450 | 199,303 | 219,659 | 327,862 | † 484,611 | 532,197 | 589,968 | 484,730 | .... | .... | .... | .... |
| Claims on Private Sector............... | 22d | 147,650 | 222,420 | 253,757 | 304,843 | † 429,345 | 495,002 | 621,793 | 674,696 | .... | .... | .... | .... |
| Liabilities to Central Bank............... | 26g | 145,867 | 148,785 | 139,823 | 162,790 | † 181,477 | 258,039 | 277,511 | 230,172 | .... | .... | .... | .... |
| Transf.Dep.Included in Broad Money | 24 | 306,605 | 379,170 | 393,549 | 345,605 | † 456,916 | 484,683 | 586,890 | 458,449 | .... | .... | .... | .... |
| Other Dep.Included in Broad Money. | 25 | 322,658 | 316,941 | 363,733 | 548,881 | † 717,436 | 810,257 | 889,796 | 759,240 | .... | .... | .... | .... |
| Sec.Ot.th.Shares Incl.in Brd. Money. | 26a | — | — | — | — | † — | — | — | — | .... | .... | .... | .... |
| Deposits Excl. from Broad Money..... | 26b | 99,370 | 101,693 | 120,955 | 166,635 | † 17,895 | 22,317 | 26,516 | 26,996 | .... | .... | .... | .... |
| Sec.Ot.th.Shares Excl.f/Brd.Money.... | 26s | — | — | — | — | † 557 | 8 | 9 | 1,542 | .... | .... | .... | .... |
| Loans.................................... | 26l | — | — | — | — | † — | — | 38,467 | 53,532 | .... | .... | .... | .... |
| Financial Derivatives........................ | 26m | — | — | — | — | † — | — | — | — | .... | .... | .... | .... |
| Insurance Technical Reserves.......... | 26r | — | — | — | — | † — | — | — | — | .... | .... | .... | .... |
| Shares and Other Equity.................. | 27a | 53,848 | 73,137 | 194,990 | 208,267 | † 230,821 | 208,008 | 238,296 | 275,863 | .... | .... | .... | .... |
| Other Items (Net)........................... | 27r | 205,467 | 194,618 | 29,686 | 11,518 | † 42,464 | 39,409 | −26,713 | 22,620 | .... | .... | .... | .... |
| Memo Item: | | | | | | | | | | | | | |
| Total Assets................................. | 20ra | 1,250,259 | 1,342,954 | 1,391,730 | 1,593,228 | † 1,777,189 | 1,995,492 | 2,248,633 | 2,006,774 | .... | .... | .... | .... |

| | | 2004 | 2005 | 2006 | 2007 | 2008 | 2009 | 2010 | 2011 | 2012 | 2013 | 2014 | 2015 |
|---|---|---|---|---|---|---|---|---|---|---|---|---|---|
| **Depository Corporations** | | | | | | *Millions of Pounds: End of Period* | | | | | | | |
| Net Foreign Assets | 31n | 754,613 | 757,225 | 735,494 | 707,323 | † 582,977 | 599,993 | 608,320 | 513,840 | .... | .... | .... | .... |
| Claims on Nonresidents | 31 | 765,568 | 784,242 | 751,309 | 740,526 | † 616,532 | 641,051 | 647,727 | 543,746 | .... | .... | .... | .... |
| Liabilities to Nonresidents | 36c | 10,956 | 27,017 | 15,815 | 33,203 | † 33,555 | 41,058 | 39,408 | 29,906 | .... | .... | .... | .... |
| Domestic Claims | 32 | 387,097 | 531,208 | 572,572 | 730,513 | † 961,934 | 1,099,051 | 1,317,992 | 1,620,545 | .... | .... | .... | .... |
| Net Claims on Central Government | 32an | 56,891 | 109,379 | 99,051 | 97,127 | † 46,100 | 69,177 | 103,625 | 458,475 | .... | .... | .... | .... |
| Claims on Central Government.... | 32a | 422,748 | 423,297 | 424,616 | 423,817 | † 430,237 | 404,840 | 417,912 | 756,230 | .... | .... | .... | .... |
| Liabilities to Central Government. | 36d | 365,856 | 313,918 | 325,566 | 326,689 | † 384,137 | 335,663 | 314,287 | 297,755 | .... | .... | .... | .... |
| Claims on Other Sectors | 32s | 330,206 | 421,829 | 473,522 | 633,386 | † 915,835 | 1,029,874 | 1,214,368 | 1,162,070 | .... | .... | .... | .... |
| Claims on Other Financial Corps.. | 32g | — | — | — | 681 | † 1,879 | 2,675 | 2,607 | 2,645 | .... | .... | .... | .... |
| Claims on State & Local Govts..... | 32b | | | | | † — | | | | .... | .... | .... | .... |
| Claims on Public Nonfin. Corps.... | 32c | 182,556 | 199,409 | 219,765 | 327,862 | † 484,611 | 532,197 | 589,968 | 484,730 | .... | .... | .... | .... |
| Claims on Private Sector | 32d | 147,650 | 222,420 | 253,757 | 304,843 | † 429,345 | 495,002 | 621,793 | 674,696 | .... | .... | .... | .... |
| Broad Money Liabilities | 35l | 984,727 | 1,096,751 | 1,176,650 | 1,322,946 | † 1,656,087 | 1,798,734 | 2,041,040 | 1,881,637 | .... | .... | .... | .... |
| Currency Outside Depository Corps | 34a | 332,648 | 384,720 | 399,200 | 422,357 | † 468,820 | 480,952 | 540,246 | 626,292 | .... | .... | .... | .... |
| Transferable Deposits | 34 | 329,421 | 395,090 | 413,716 | 351,707 | † 469,456 | 507,088 | 610,145 | 495,450 | .... | .... | .... | .... |
| Other Deposits | 35 | 322,658 | 316,941 | 363,733 | 548,881 | † 717,811 | 810,695 | 890,649 | 759,896 | .... | .... | .... | .... |
| Securities Other than Shares | 36a | — | — | — | — | † — | — | — | — | .... | .... | .... | .... |
| Deposits Excl. from Broad Money..... | 36b | 99,370 | 101,693 | 120,955 | 166,635 | † 17,895 | 22,317 | 26,516 | 26,996 | .... | .... | .... | .... |
| Sec.Ot.th.Shares Excl.f/Brd.Money.... | 36s | — | — | — | — | † 557 | 8 | 9 | 1,542 | .... | .... | .... | .... |
| Loans | 36l | — | — | — | — | † — | — | 38,467 | 53,532 | .... | .... | .... | .... |
| Financial Derivatives | 36m | — | — | — | — | † — | — | — | — | .... | .... | .... | .... |
| Insurance Technical Reserves | 36r | — | — | — | — | † — | — | — | — | .... | .... | .... | .... |
| Shares and Other Equity | 37a | 134,231 | 171,162 | 295,111 | 218,381 | † 235,849 | 211,108 | 256,081 | 303,435 | .... | .... | .... | .... |
| Other Items (Net) | 37r | −76,618 | −81,178 | −284,649 | −270,126 | † −365,477 | −333,123 | −435,800 | −132,757 | .... | .... | .... | .... |
| Broad Money Liabs., Seasonally Adj. | 35l.b | 973,334 | 1,086,877 | 1,168,515 | 1,315,772 | † 1,647,565 | 1,789,478 | 2,030,537 | 1,871,954 | .... | .... | .... | .... |
| **Monetary Aggregates** | | | | | | *Millions of Pounds: End of Period* | | | | | | | |
| Broad Money | 59m | .... | .... | .... | .... | 1,656,087 | 1,798,734 | 2,041,040 | 1,881,637 | .... | .... | .... | .... |
| o/w:Currency Issued by Cent.Govt | 59m.a | .... | .... | .... | .... | — | — | — | — | .... | .... | .... | .... |
| o/w: Dep.in Nonfin. Corporations. | 59m.b | .... | .... | .... | .... | — | — | — | — | .... | .... | .... | .... |
| o/w: Secs. Issued by Central Govt. | 59m.c | .... | .... | .... | .... | — | — | — | — | .... | .... | .... | .... |
| Money (National Definitions) | | | | | | | | | | | | | |
| M0 | 19mc | 472,836 | 509,251 | 558,564 | 648,714 | 872,528 | 872,528 | 934,493 | 874,553 | .... | .... | .... | .... |
| M1 | 59mak | 610,859 | 697,700 | 687,438 | 687,438 | 828,145 | 904,018 | 1,063,510 | 1,045,091 | .... | .... | .... | .... |
| Quasi Money | 59mal | 462,691 | 502,992 | 623,256 | 623,256 | 827,942 | 894,717 | 977,530 | 836,546 | .... | .... | .... | .... |
| Broad Money | 59mea | 1,073,550 | 1,200,692 | 1,310,694 | 1,310,694 | 1,656,087 | 1,798,734 | 2,041,040 | 1,881,637 | .... | .... | .... | .... |
| **Interest Rates** | | | | | | *Percent Per Annum* | | | | | | | |
| Discount Rate (End of Period) | 60.a | 5.0 | 5.0 | 5.0 | 5.0 | 5.0 | 5.0 | 5.0 | | .... | .... | .... | .... |
| Deposit Rate | 60l | 6.0 | 9.0 | 9.0 | 8.4 | 8.1 | 6.3 | 6.2 | | .... | .... | .... | .... |
| Lending Rate | 60p | 7.5 | 8.0 | 8.0 | 10.2 | 10.2 | 10.0 | 9.9 | | .... | .... | .... | .... |
| **Prices, Production, Labor** | | | | | | *Index Numbers (2010=100): Period Averages* | | | | | | | |
| Share Prices | 62 | .... | .... | .... | .... | .... | .... | 135.2 | | .... | .... | .... | .... |
| Share Prices (EOM) | 62.ep | .... | .... | .... | .... | .... | .... | 132.0 | | .... | .... | .... | .... |
| Wholesale Prices (2005=100) | 63 | 97.3 | † 100.0 | 104.0 | 108.0 | 115.0 | 145.0 | .... | .... | .... | .... | .... | .... |
| Consumer Prices | 64 | 65.6 | 70.3 | † 77.4 | 80.4 | 93.1 | 95.8 | 100.0 | 104.8 | 143.2 | .... | .... | .... |
| Industrial Production (2005=100).... | 66 | 103.4 | 100.0 | 102.2 | 98.9 | 95.5 | 97.8 | | | .... | .... | .... | .... |
| | | | | | | *Number in Thousands: Period Averages* | | | | | | | |
| Labor Force | 67d | 4,948 | 5,106 | 5,293 | 5,400 | 5,432 | 5,442 | 5,531 | 5,816 | .... | .... | .... | .... |
| Employment | 67e | 4,340 | 4,693 | 4,860 | 4,946 | 4,848 | 4,999 | 5,054 | 4,949 | .... | .... | .... | .... |
| Unemployment | 67c | 608 | 413 | 433 | 454 | 594 | 443 | 476 | 866 | .... | .... | .... | .... |
| Unemployment Rate (%) | 67r | 12.3 | 8.1 | 8.2 | 8.4 | 10.9 | 8.1 | 8.6 | 14.9 | .... | .... | .... | .... |
| **Intl. Transactions & Positions** | | | | | | *Millions of Pounds* | | | | | | | |
| Exports | 70 | 82,818 | 97,747 | 122,570 | 129,601 | 172,977 | 121,849 | 157,150 | .... | .... | .... | .... | .... |
| Imports, c.i.f | 71 | 94,415 | 121,928 | 128,956 | 164,504 | 203,226 | 171,644 | 190,264 | .... | .... | .... | .... | .... |

# Syrian Arab Republic   463

| | | 2004 | 2005 | 2006 | 2007 | 2008 | 2009 | 2010 | 2011 | 2012 | 2013 | 2014 | 2015 |
|---|---|---|---|---|---|---|---|---|---|---|---|---|---|
| **Balance of Payments** | | | | | | | *Millions of US Dollars* | | | | | | | |
| A. Current Account* | 109bx | 586.5 | 295.0 | 889.8 | 459.6 | 472.0 | −1,029.5 | −367.4 | .... | .... | .... | .... | .... |
| Goods, credit (exports) | 1a9cx | 7,220.4 | 8,602.0 | 10,244.8 | 11,755.7 | 15,334.0 | 10,883.5 | 12,272.7 | .... | .... | .... | .... | .... |
| Goods, debit (imports) | 1a9dx | 6,957.0 | 8,742.0 | 9,359.0 | 12,276.8 | 16,107.2 | 13,932.6 | 15,875.7 | .... | .... | .... | .... | .... |
| Balance on goods | 1a9bx | 263.4 | −140.0 | 885.8 | −521.1 | −773.2 | −3,049.1 | −3,603.0 | .... | .... | .... | .... | .... |
| Services, credit (exports) | 1b9cx | 2,613.1 | 2,910.0 | 2,924.0 | 3,861.3 | 4,415.3 | 4,798.4 | 7,333.0 | .... | .... | .... | .... | .... |
| Services, debit (imports) | 1b9dx | 2,235.0 | 2,359.0 | 2,520.0 | 3,012.5 | 3,171.2 | 2,734.2 | 3,533.1 | .... | .... | .... | .... | .... |
| Balance on Goods & Services | 1z9bx | 641.5 | 411.0 | 1,289.8 | 327.7 | 470.9 | −984.9 | 197.0 | .... | .... | .... | .... | .... |
| Primary income: credit | 1c9cx | 385.0 | 395.0 | 428.0 | 594.0 | 540.0 | 344.4 | 312.8 | .... | .... | .... | .... | .... |
| Primary income: debit | 1c9dx | 1,114.0 | 1,258.0 | 1,363.0 | 1,283.1 | 1,689.0 | 1,451.1 | 1,826.5 | .... | .... | .... | .... | .... |
| Balance on gds, serv. & prim. inc. | 1y9bx | −87.5 | −452.0 | 354.8 | −361.4 | −678.0 | −2,091.5 | −1,316.7 | .... | .... | .... | .... | .... |
| Secondary income: credit | 1d9ca | 690.0 | 763.0 | 770.0 | 1,040.5 | 1,335.0 | 1,247.4 | 1,449.8 | .... | .... | .... | .... | .... |
| Secondary income: debit | 1d9da | 16.0 | 16.0 | 235.0 | 219.5 | 185.0 | 185.4 | 500.5 | .... | .... | .... | .... | .... |
| B. Capital Account* | 209ba | 18.0 | 18.0 | 18.0 | — | — | 13.0 | 50.1 | .... | .... | .... | .... | .... |
| Capital account: credit | 209ca | 20.0 | 20.0 | 20.0 | — | — | 13.0 | 50.1 | .... | .... | .... | .... | .... |
| Capital account: debit | 209da | 2.0 | 2.0 | 2.0 | — | — | — | — | .... | .... | .... | .... | .... |
| Balance on current & capital acct. | 129ba | 604.5 | 313.0 | 907.8 | 459.6 | 472.0 | −1,016.5 | −317.3 | .... | .... | .... | .... | .... |
| C. Financial Account* | 309na | 97.0 | 162.0 | 332.0 | −715.2 | −737.0 | −1,914.8 | −1,252.0 | .... | .... | .... | .... | .... |
| Direct investment: assets | 3a9aa | — | — | — | — | — | — | — | .... | .... | .... | .... | .... |
| Equity & investment fund shares.. | 3aaaa | — | — | — | — | — | — | — | .... | .... | .... | .... | .... |
| Debt instruments | 3abaa | — | — | — | — | — | — | .... | .... | .... | .... | .... | .... |
| Direct investment: liabilities | 3a9la | 275.0 | 500.0 | 659.0 | 1,242.0 | 1,465.6 | 2,569.5 | 1,469.2 | .... | .... | .... | .... | .... |
| Equity & investment fund shares . | 3aala | 275.0 | 500.0 | 659.0 | 1,242.0 | 1,465.6 | 2,569.5 | 1,469.2 | .... | .... | .... | .... | .... |
| Debt instruments | 3abla | — | — | — | — | — | — | .... | .... | .... | .... | .... | .... |
| Portfolio investment: assets | 3b9aa | — | — | — | — | 55.1 | 241.0 | 192.7 | .... | .... | .... | .... | .... |
| Equity & investment fund shares | 3baaa | — | — | — | — | .4 | .1 | −.4 | .... | .... | .... | .... | .... |
| Debt securities | 3bbaa | — | — | — | — | 54.8 | 240.9 | 193.1 | .... | .... | .... | .... | .... |
| Portfolio investment: liabilities | 3b9la | — | — | — | — | — | — | .... | .... | .... | .... | .... | .... |
| Equity & investment fund shares . | 3bala | — | — | — | — | — | — | .... | .... | .... | .... | .... | .... |
| Debt securities | 3bbla | — | — | — | — | — | — | .... | .... | .... | .... | .... | .... |
| Fin. der.& empl.stk.ops.(ESOs): net. | 3c9na | — | — | — | — | — | — | — | .... | .... | .... | .... | .... |
| Fin. der. & ESOs.: assets | 3c9aa | — | — | — | — | — | — | — | .... | .... | .... | .... | .... |
| Fin. der. & ESOs.: liabilities | 3c9la | — | — | — | — | — | — | — | .... | .... | .... | .... | .... |
| Other investment: assets | 3d9aa | 237.0 | 524.0 | 710.0 | 746.1 | 631.2 | 625.7 | −60.8 | .... | .... | .... | .... | .... |
| Other equity | 3daaa | .... | .... | .... | .... | .... | .... | .... | .... | .... | .... | .... | .... |
| Debt instruments | 3dzaa | 237.0 | 524.0 | 710.0 | 746.1 | 631.2 | 625.7 | −60.8 | .... | .... | .... | .... | .... |
| Other investment: liabilities | 3d9la | −135.0 | −138.0 | −281.0 | 219.4 | −42.3 | 211.9 | −85.3 | .... | .... | .... | .... | .... |
| Other equity | 3dala | .... | .... | .... | .... | .... | .... | .... | .... | .... | .... | .... | .... |
| Debt instruments | 3dzla | −135.0 | −138.0 | −281.0 | 219.4 | −42.3 | 211.9 | −85.3 | .... | .... | .... | .... | .... |
| Curr.+ cap.− finan. acct. balance... | 4y9na | 507.5 | 151.0 | 575.8 | 1,174.8 | 1,208.9 | 898.3 | 934.7 | .... | .... | .... | .... | .... |
| D. Net Errors and Omissions | 409na | −256.4 | −137.0 | −1,487.8 | −631.2 | −1,159.4 | −549.9 | 1,141.7 | .... | .... | .... | .... | .... |
| E. Reserves and Related Items | 4z9na | 251.1 | 14.0 | −912.0 | 543.5 | 49.6 | 348.4 | 2,076.4 | .... | .... | .... | .... | .... |
| Reserve assets | 3e9aa | 256.1 | 18.0 | −882.0 | 543.5 | 49.6 | 348.4 | 2,076.4 | .... | .... | .... | .... | .... |
| Credit and loans from the IMF | 3dcla | — | — | — | — | — | — | — | .... | .... | .... | .... | .... |
| Exceptional financing | 409la | 5.0 | 4.0 | 30.0 | — | — | — | — | .... | .... | .... | .... | .... |

*Excludes components in group E

| **International Investment Position** | | | | | | | *Millions of US Dollars* | | | | | | | |
|---|---|---|---|---|---|---|---|---|---|---|---|---|---|
| Assets | 809aa | .... | .... | .... | 25,140.7 | 25,874.5 | 27,091.9 | 29,292.7 | .... | .... | .... | .... | .... |
| Direct investment | 8a9aa | .... | .... | .... | 4.6 | 4.5 | 4.5 | 4.8 | .... | .... | .... | .... | .... |
| Equity & investment fund shares.. | 8aaaa | .... | .... | .... | 4.6 | 4.5 | 4.5 | 4.8 | .... | .... | .... | .... | .... |
| Debt instruments | 8abaa | .... | .... | .... | .... | .... | .... | .... | .... | .... | .... | .... | .... |
| Portfolio investment | 8b9aa | .... | .... | .... | 96.9 | 152.1 | 393.1 | 585.7 | .... | .... | .... | .... | .... |
| Equity & investment fund shares.. | 8baaa | .... | .... | .... | 14.3 | 14.7 | 14.8 | 14.4 | .... | .... | .... | .... | .... |
| Debt securities | 8bbaa | .... | .... | .... | 82.6 | 137.3 | 378.2 | 571.3 | .... | .... | .... | .... | .... |
| Fin. der.(oth.than reserves) & ESOs | 8c9aa | .... | .... | .... | .... | .... | .... | .... | .... | .... | .... | .... | .... |
| Other investment | 8d9aa | .... | .... | .... | 7,986.6 | 8,617.8 | 9,243.5 | 9,182.7 | .... | .... | .... | .... | .... |
| Other equity | 8daaa | .... | .... | .... | .... | .... | .... | .... | .... | .... | .... | .... | .... |
| Debt instruments | 8dzaa | .... | .... | .... | 7,986.6 | 8,617.8 | 9,243.5 | 9,182.7 | .... | .... | .... | .... | .... |
| Reserve assets | 8e9aa | .... | .... | .... | 17,052.5 | 17,100.2 | 17,450.9 | 19,519.5 | .... | .... | .... | .... | .... |
| Liabilities | 809la | .... | .... | .... | 10,278.4 | 11,701.7 | 14,428.9 | 15,817.8 | .... | .... | .... | .... | .... |
| Direct investment | 8a9la | .... | .... | .... | 4,433.0 | 5,900.0 | 8,469.5 | 9,938.7 | .... | .... | .... | .... | .... |
| Equity & investment fund shares.. | 8aala | .... | .... | .... | 4,433.0 | 5,900.0 | 8,469.5 | 9,938.7 | .... | .... | .... | .... | .... |
| Debt instruments | 8abla | .... | .... | .... | .... | .... | .... | .... | .... | .... | .... | .... | .... |
| Portfolio investment | 8b9la | .... | .... | .... | .... | .... | .... | .... | .... | .... | .... | .... | .... |
| Equity & investment fund shares.. | 8bala | .... | .... | .... | .... | .... | .... | .... | .... | .... | .... | .... | .... |
| Debt securities | 8bbla | .... | .... | .... | .... | .... | .... | .... | .... | .... | .... | .... | .... |
| Fin. der.(oth.than reserves) & ESOs | 8c9la | .... | .... | .... | .... | .... | .... | .... | .... | .... | .... | .... | .... |
| Other investment | 8d9la | .... | .... | .... | 5,845.4 | 5,801.7 | 5,959.3 | 5,879.0 | .... | .... | .... | .... | .... |
| Other equity | 8dala | .... | .... | .... | .... | .... | .... | .... | .... | .... | .... | .... | .... |
| Debt instruments | 8dzla | .... | .... | .... | 5,845.4 | 5,801.7 | 5,959.3 | 5,879.0 | .... | .... | .... | .... | .... |

| | | 2004 | 2005 | 2006 | 2007 | 2008 | 2009 | 2010 | 2011 | 2012 | 2013 | 2014 | 2015 |
|---|---|---|---|---|---|---|---|---|---|---|---|---|---|
| **Government Finance** | | | | | | | | | | | | | |
| **Cash Flow Statement** | | | | | | | | | | | | | |
| **Budgetary Central Government** | | | | | | *Billions of Pounds: Fiscal Year Ends December 31* | | | | | | | |
| Cash Receipts:Operating Activities... | c1 | 342,465 | 356,290 | 434,865 | 458,830 | 490,904 | 600,831 | .... | .... | .... | .... | .... | .... |
| Taxes.......................... | c11 | 207,801 | 208,256 | 248,598 | 286,424 | 348,848 | 362,808 | .... | .... | .... | .... | .... | .... |
| Social Contributions..................... | c12 | — | — | — | — | — | — | .... | .... | .... | .... | .... | .... |
| Grants................................ | c13 | — | — | — | 259 | — | 1 | .... | .... | .... | .... | .... | .... |
| Other Receipts........................... | c14 | 134,664 | 148,034 | 186,267 | 172,147 | 142,056 | 238,022 | .... | .... | .... | .... | .... | .... |
| Cash Payments:Operating Activities. | c2 | 248,498 | 277,044 | 317,213 | 325,697 | 375,327 | 442,180 | .... | .... | .... | .... | .... | .... |
| Compensation of Employees.......... | c21 | 144,122 | 157,039 | 206,966 | 223,173 | 234,708 | 275,232 | .... | .... | .... | .... | .... | .... |
| Purchases of Goods & Services....... | c22 | 19,347 | 21,535 | 22,546 | 24,321 | 27,507 | 30,844 | .... | .... | .... | .... | .... | .... |
| Interest.................................. | c24 | 21,250 | 29,000 | 29,500 | 30,000 | 25,500 | 28,000 | .... | .... | .... | .... | .... | .... |
| Subsidies................................ | c25 | .... | .... | .... | 23,048 | 30,989 | 25,000 | .... | .... | .... | .... | .... | .... |
| Grants................................... | c26 | .... | .... | .... | — | — | — | .... | .... | .... | .... | .... | .... |
| Social Benefits........................... | c27 | .... | .... | .... | 25,155 | 56,623 | 83,104 | .... | .... | .... | .... | .... | .... |
| Other Payments.......................... | c28 | — | — | — | — | — | — | .... | .... | .... | .... | .... | .... |
| Net Cash Inflow:Operating Act.[1-2] | ccio | 93,967 | 79,246 | 117,652 | 133,133 | 115,577 | 158,651 | .... | .... | .... | .... | .... | .... |
| Net Cash Outflow:Invest. in NFA...... | c31 | 156,647 | 154,358 | 176,487 | 194,834 | 173,067 | 212,393 | .... | .... | .... | .... | .... | .... |
| Purchases of Nonfinancial Assets... | c31.1 | 156,647 | 154,358 | 176,487 | 194,834 | 173,067 | 212,393 | .... | .... | .... | .... | .... | .... |
| Sales of Nonfinancial Assets.......... | c31.2 | — | — | — | — | — | — | .... | .... | .... | .... | .... | .... |
| Cash Surplus/Deficit [1-2-31=1-2M] | ccsd | −62,680 | −75,112 | −58,835 | −61,701 | −57,490 | −53,742 | .... | .... | .... | .... | .... | .... |
| Net Acq. Fin. Assets, excl. Cash....... | c32x | — | — | — | — | — | — | .... | .... | .... | .... | .... | .... |
| Domestic............................... | c321x | — | — | — | — | — | — | .... | .... | .... | .... | .... | .... |
| Foreign.................................. | c322x | — | — | — | — | — | — | .... | .... | .... | .... | .... | .... |
| Net Incurrence of Liabilities.............. | c33 | 2,951 | 18,233 | 44,398 | 99,337 | 124,971 | 35,006 | .... | .... | .... | .... | .... | .... |
| Domestic............................... | c331 | −8,621 | 3,464 | 30,239 | 85,218 | 111,776 | 31,006 | .... | .... | .... | .... | .... | .... |
| Foreign.................................. | c332 | 11,572 | 14,769 | 14,159 | 14,119 | 13,195 | 4,000 | .... | .... | .... | .... | .... | .... |
| Net Cash Inflow, Fin.Act.[-32x+33].. | cnfb | 2,951 | 18,233 | 44,398 | 99,337 | 124,971 | 35,006 | .... | .... | .... | .... | .... | .... |
| Net Change in Stock of Cash........... | cncb | −59,729 | −56,879 | −14,437 | 37,636 | 67,481 | .... | .... | .... | .... | .... | .... | .... |
| Stat. Discrep. [32X-33+NCB-CSD].... | ccsdz | — | — | — | — | — | — | .... | .... | .... | .... | .... | .... |
| Memo Item:Cash Expenditure[2+31] | c2m | 405,145 | 431,402 | 493,700 | 520,531 | 548,394 | 654,573 | .... | .... | .... | .... | .... | .... |
| Memo Item: Gross Debt.................. | c63 | .... | .... | .... | .... | .... | .... | .... | .... | .... | .... | .... | .... |
| **National Accounts** | | | | | | *Millions of Pounds* | | | | | | | | |
| Househ.Cons.Expend.,incl.NPISHs.... | 96f | 810,037 | 993,118 | 1,122,666 | 1,192,230 | 1,390,093 | 1,508,579 | .... | .... | .... | .... | .... | .... |
| Government Consumption Expend... | 91f | 197,909 | 206,631 | 194,937 | 248,300 | 274,879 | 301,787 | .... | .... | .... | .... | .... | .... |
| Exports of Goods and Services.......... | 90c | 512,445 | 618,278 | 673,495 | 779,930 | 902,067 | 732,502 | .... | .... | .... | .... | .... | .... |
| Gross Capital Formation.................. | 93 | 274,500 | 346,737 | 371,519 | 412,136 | 408,725 | 451,766 | .... | .... | .... | .... | .... | .... |
| Imports of Goods and Services (-)..... | 98c | 477,186 | 588,876 | 607,587 | 763,573 | 899,045 | 784,658 | .... | .... | .... | .... | .... | .... |
| Gross Domestic Product (GDP)........ | 99b | 1,266,891 | 1,506,440 | 1,704,974 | 2,017,825 | 2,444,220 | 2,519,151 | 2,684,991 | .... | .... | .... | .... | .... |
| Consumption of Fixed Capital........... | 99cf | 49,651 | 59,973 | 69,668 | 80,416 | 97,504 | 99,499 | .... | .... | .... | .... | .... | .... |
| GDP Volume 2000 Prices................ | 99b.p | 1,089,027 | 1,156,714 | 1,215,082 | 1,284,035 | 1,341,516 | 1,422,178 | 1,467,688 | .... | .... | .... | .... | .... |
| GDP Volume (2010=100)............... | 99bvp | 74.2 | 78.8 | 82.8 | 87.5 | 91.4 | 96.9 | 100.0 | .... | .... | .... | .... | .... |
| GDP Deflator (2010=100).............. | 99bip | 63.6 | 71.2 | 76.7 | 85.9 | 99.6 | 96.8 | 100.0 | .... | .... | .... | .... | .... |
| | | | | | | *Millions: Midyear Estimates* | | | | | | | | |
| Population............................... | 99z | 17.67 | 18.13 | 18.73 | 19.43 | 20.10 | 20.57 | 20.72 | 20.50 | 19.98 | 19.32 | 18.77 | 18.50 |

# Tajikistan 923

| | | 2004 | 2005 | 2006 | 2007 | 2008 | 2009 | 2010 | 2011 | 2012 | 2013 | 2014 | 2015 |
|---|---|---|---|---|---|---|---|---|---|---|---|---|---|
| **Exchange Rates** | | | | | | *Somoni per SDR: End of Period* | | | | | | | |
| Official Rate | aa | 4.716 | 4.573 | 5.155 | 5.475 | 5.317 | 6.852 | 6.781 | 7.306 | 7.323 | 7.352 | 7.690 | 9.687 |
| | | | | | | *Somoni per US Dollar: End of Period (ae) Period Average (rf)* | | | | | | | |
| Official Rate | ae | 3.037 | 3.199 | 3.427 | 3.465 | 3.452 | 4.371 | 4.403 | 4.759 | 4.764 | 4.774 | 5.308 | 6.990 |
| Official Rate | rf | 2.971 | 3.117 | 3.298 | 3.442 | 3.431 | 4.143 | 4.379 | 4.610 | 4.738 | 4.764 | 4.938 | 6.163 |
| **Fund Position** | | | | | | *Millions of SDRs: End of Period* | | | | | | | |
| Quota | 2f.s | 87.00 | 87.00 | 87.00 | 87.00 | 87.00 | 87.00 | 87.00 | 87.00 | 87.00 | 87.00 | 87.00 | 87.00 |
| SDR Holdings | 1b.s | .85 | 3.80 | 2.34 | 2.29 | 10.16 | 69.86 | 69.82 | 69.76 | 69.75 | 69.74 | 69.73 | 22.21 |
| Reserve Position in the Fund | 1c.s | — | — | — | — | — | — | — | — | — | — | — | — |
| Total Fund Cred.&Loans Outstg | 2tl | 78.70 | 88.91 | 29.40 | 29.40 | 9.80 | 26.10 | 65.27 | 78.31 | 104.40 | 104.40 | 101.79 | 93.96 |
| SDR Allocations | 1bd | — | — | — | — | — | 82.08 | 82.08 | 82.08 | 82.08 | 82.08 | 82.08 | 82.08 |
| **International Liquidity** | | | | | | *Millions of US Dollars Unless Otherwise Indicated: End of Period* | | | | | | | |
| Total Reserves minus Gold | 1l.d | 157.5 | 168.2 | 175.1 | 40.1 | 103.8 | 174.6 | 324.2 | 289.3 | 297.9 | 460.7 | 177.4 | 64.4 |
| SDR Holdings | 1b.d | 1.3 | 5.4 | 3.5 | 3.6 | 15.7 | 109.5 | 107.5 | 107.1 | 107.2 | 107.4 | 101.0 | 30.8 |
| Reserve Position in the Fund | 1c.d | — | — | — | — | — | — | — | — | — | — | — | — |
| Foreign Exchange | 1d.d | 156.2 | 162.8 | 171.6 | 36.5 | 88.2 | 65.0 | 216.7 | 182.2 | 190.7 | 353.3 | 76.4 | 33.7 |
| Gold (Million Fine Troy Ounces) | 1ad | .03 | .04 | .05 | .05 | .07 | .07 | .06 | .15 | .20 | .17 | .28 | .40 |
| Gold (National Valuation) | 1and | 14.6 | 20.7 | 28.7 | 44.8 | 59.3 | 81.6 | 79.2 | 243.1 | 330.7 | 200.1 | 333.3 | 429.9 |
| Central Bank: Other Assets | 3..d | | | | 1.3 | † 2.8 | 9.0 | 119.2 | 71.0 | 50.2 | 264.3 | 4.3 | .2 |
| Central Bank: Other Liabs | 4..d | .7 | .4 | 10.4 | 35.9 | † 85.7 | 29.7 | 20.7 | 23.7 | 21.8 | 101.3 | 27.2 | 18.0 |
| Other Depository Corps.: Assets | 7a.d | 13.3 | 49.2 | 154.1 | 338.5 | † 137.7 | 171.2 | 160.8 | 192.3 | 262.5 | 254.0 | 206.3 | 250.9 |
| Other Depository Corps.: Liabs | 7b.d | 19.1 | 59.9 | 153.0 | 296.7 | † 254.7 | 172.2 | 183.5 | 317.2 | 339.4 | 508.2 | 608.1 | 517.3 |
| Other Financial Corps.: Assets | 7e.d | .... | .... | .... | .... | 9.2 | 6.7 | 7.4 | 6.1 | 11.0 | 1.5 | 3.1 | .... |
| Other Financial Corps.: Liabs | 7f.d | .... | .... | .... | .... | 86.6 | 38.7 | 40.8 | 58.2 | 99.9 | 22.1 | 24.9 | .... |
| **Central Bank** | | | | | | *Millions of Somoni: End of Period* | | | | | | | |
| Net Foreign Assets | 11n | 191.5 | 223.9 | 545.9 | 21.9 | † 234.6 | 354.0 | 1,009.7 | 1,439.6 | 1,861.1 | 1,685.2 | 1,175.5 | 1,626.0 |
| Claims on Nonresidents | 11 | 564.8 | 631.7 | 733.1 | 307.1 | † 582.6 | 1,225.1 | 2,100.0 | 2,724.1 | 3,330.6 | 3,540.0 | 2,733.7 | 3,456.9 |
| Liabilities to Nonresidents | 16c | 373.3 | 407.8 | 187.2 | 285.3 | † 348.0 | 871.2 | 1,090.3 | 1,284.5 | 1,469.5 | 1,854.8 | 1,558.2 | 1,830.9 |
| Claims on Other Depository Corps. | 12e | 117.8 | 116.8 | 172.5 | 1,022.0 | † 152.6 | 264.6 | 259.1 | 157.1 | 121.6 | 602.1 | 169.3 | 279.0 |
| Net Claims on Central Government | 12an | −190.9 | −219.8 | −315.9 | −456.0 | † −949.0 | −864.5 | −1,461.2 | −855.8 | −342.8 | −193.2 | −665.7 | −1,031.3 |
| Claims on Central Government | 12a | 153.8 | 153.8 | 153.8 | 155.7 | † 154.3 | 154.3 | 154.1 | 274.2 | 1,429.3 | 1,548.8 | 1,609.8 | 1,677.5 |
| Liabilities to Central Government | 16d | 344.7 | 373.6 | 469.7 | 611.7 | † 1,103.2 | 1,018.8 | 1,615.3 | 1,130.1 | 1,772.1 | 1,742.1 | 2,275.5 | 2,708.8 |
| Claims on Other Sectors | 12s | 352.8 | 689.4 | 863.4 | 1,012.9 | † 2,202.5 | 1,427.4 | 154.4 | 152.9 | 328.5 | 458.7 | 453.3 | 560.2 |
| Claims on Other Financial Corps. | 12g | 244.9 | 507.7 | 651.1 | 878.1 | † 2,020.3 | 1,247.2 | — | — | — | — | — | — |
| Claims on State & Local Govts. | 12b | | | | | † — | | | | | | | |
| Claims on Public Nonfin. Corps. | 12c | — | — | — | — | † 10.7 | 13.4 | 9.5 | 11.5 | 4.1 | 4.4 | — | — |
| Claims on Private Sector | 12d | 107.9 | 181.7 | 212.3 | 134.8 | † 171.5 | 166.8 | 144.9 | 141.4 | 324.4 | 454.3 | 453.3 | 560.2 |
| Monetary Base | 14 | 508.9 | 817.6 | 1,017.4 | 1,437.9 | † 1,861.9 | 2,586.9 | 2,992.7 | 3,828.8 | 4,534.0 | 5,362.0 | 6,070.4 | 7,042.8 |
| Currency in Circulation | 14a | 426.8 | 711.5 | 880.1 | 1,115.5 | † 1,565.9 | 2,041.3 | 2,421.4 | 2,988.3 | 3,667.2 | 4,485.4 | 4,759.7 | 5,305.5 |
| Liabs. to Other Depository Corps. | 14c | 69.5 | 103.0 | 134.5 | 263.0 | † 286.5 | 537.9 | 568.2 | 840.3 | 865.4 | 860.4 | 1,244.1 | 1,563.2 |
| Liabilities to Other Sectors | 14d | 12.6 | 3.1 | 2.8 | 59.3 | † 9.5 | 7.7 | 3.1 | .2 | 1.4 | 16.2 | 66.7 | 174.1 |
| Other Liabs. to Other Dep. Corps. | 14n | 2.1 | 27.2 | 4.4 | 10.2 | † — | — | 3.5 | 12.0 | 659.7 | 1,023.2 | 93.2 | 401.0 |
| Dep. & Sec. Excl. f/Monetary Base | 14o | — | — | — | — | † — | — | — | 12.9 | 48.2 | 74.6 | 54.8 | 60.3 |
| Deposits Included in Broad Money. | 15 | — | — | — | — | † — | — | — | — | — | — | — | — |
| Sec.Ot.th.Shares Incl.in Brd. Money | 16a | — | — | — | — | † — | — | — | — | — | — | — | — |
| Deposits Excl. from Broad Money | 16b | — | — | — | — | † — | — | — | — | — | — | — | — |
| Sec.Ot.th.Shares Excl.f/Brd.Money. | 16s | — | — | — | — | † — | — | — | 12.9 | 48.2 | 74.6 | 54.8 | 60.3 |
| Loans | 16l | — | — | — | — | † 71.3 | — | — | — | — | — | — | — |
| Financial Derivatives | 16m | — | — | — | — | † — | — | — | — | — | — | — | — |
| Shares and Other Equity | 17a | 17.7 | 27.6 | 46.1 | 23.9 | † −2,186.9 | −2,669.7 | −2,840.3 | −2,299.0 | −2,679.0 | −3,085.9 | −4,528.0 | −5,432.0 |
| Other Items (Net) | 17r | −57.4 | −62.2 | 197.8 | 128.8 | † 1,894.4 | 1,264.2 | −193.9 | −661.0 | −594.5 | −821.2 | −558.1 | −638.2 |
| Memo Item: | | | | | | | | | | | | | |
| Total Assets | 10ra | 1,624.8 | 2,077.3 | 2,480.3 | 3,269.8 | † 3,949.7 | 3,903.9 | 3,702.0 | 4,837.5 | 6,670.0 | 7,838.0 | 6,431.0 | 7,657.8 |
| **Other Depository Corporations** | | | | | | *Millions of Somoni: End of Period* | | | | | | | |
| Net Foreign Assets | 21n | −17.6 | −34.2 | 3.6 | 145.1 | † −403.6 | −4.6 | −99.9 | −594.4 | −366.4 | −1,213.3 | −2,132.3 | −1,862.0 |
| Claims on Nonresidents | 21 | 40.5 | 157.4 | 527.9 | 1,173.0 | † 475.4 | 748.3 | 707.9 | 915.2 | 1,250.8 | 1,212.7 | 1,095.2 | 1,753.8 |
| Liabilities to Nonresidents | 26c | 58.0 | 191.6 | 524.3 | 1,028.0 | † 879.1 | 752.9 | 807.8 | 1,509.5 | 1,617.2 | 2,426.1 | 3,227.5 | 3,615.8 |
| Claims on Central Bank | 20 | 105.6 | 172.1 | 196.0 | 348.4 | † 439.2 | 934.0 | 1,381.9 | 1,450.6 | 1,816.3 | 1,760.5 | 2,195.1 | 3,123.0 |
| Currency | 20a | 28.2 | 45.4 | 56.4 | 86.9 | † 160.7 | 270.5 | 416.8 | 279.5 | 261.0 | 342.0 | 705.9 | 714.7 |
| Reserve Deposits and Securities | 20b | 71.8 | 100.3 | 136.8 | 253.6 | † 278.3 | 531.7 | 565.1 | 841.7 | 882.4 | 855.8 | 1,240.1 | 1,558.8 |
| Other Claims | 20n | 5.6 | 26.5 | 2.8 | 7.9 | † .2 | 131.8 | 400.1 | 329.4 | 672.8 | 562.7 | 249.1 | 849.5 |
| Net Claims on Central Government | 22an | −25.7 | −34.8 | −37.5 | −85.0 | † −237.0 | −197.7 | −522.7 | −160.0 | −424.1 | −326.6 | −1,151.4 | −1,663.9 |
| Claims on Central Government | 22a | .3 | .3 | .3 | — | † — | — | 78.7 | — | 395.8 | 6.9 | 29.4 | .3 |
| Liabilities to Central Government | 26d | 26.0 | 35.0 | 37.8 | 85.0 | † 237.0 | 276.4 | 522.7 | 555.7 | 430.9 | 356.0 | 1,151.4 | 1,664.2 |
| Claims on Other Sectors | 22s | 290.8 | 502.9 | 775.5 | 1,700.3 | † 2,503.3 | 2,725.5 | 3,435.1 | 4,676.6 | 5,187.9 | 7,730.7 | 10,006.0 | 11,925.0 |
| Claims on Other Financial Corps. | 22g | — | — | — | — | † 18.6 | 70.9 | 88.4 | 72.2 | 53.3 | 33.1 | 40.4 | 86.7 |
| Claims on State & Local Govts. | 22b | | | | | † — | | | | | | | |
| Claims on Public Nonfin. Corps. | 22c | 20.9 | 28.4 | 100.8 | 147.7 | † 131.0 | 125.1 | 354.7 | 326.1 | 749.3 | 914.4 | 902.5 | 1,669.8 |
| Claims on Private Sector | 22d | 269.9 | 474.5 | 674.7 | 1,552.6 | † 2,353.7 | 2,529.5 | 2,992.0 | 4,278.3 | 4,385.2 | 6,783.2 | 9,063.1 | 10,168.5 |
| Liabilities to Central Bank | 26g | 36.2 | 29.3 | 28.3 | 86.9 | † 126.1 | 254.0 | 278.7 | 176.9 | 136.4 | 109.3 | 169.9 | 358.5 |
| Transf.Dep.Included in Broad Money | 24 | 64.1 | 84.4 | 144.7 | 238.3 | † 432.2 | 782.0 | 882.0 | 963.1 | 1,103.1 | 1,160.7 | 1,446.0 | 1,956.3 |
| Other Dep.Included in Broad Money. | 25 | 176.7 | 287.5 | 542.1 | 1,401.1 | † 824.4 | 1,199.0 | 1,568.6 | 2,260.7 | 2,582.0 | 3,171.5 | 3,525.5 | 4,068.5 |
| Sec.Ot.th.Shares Incl.in Brd. Money.. | 26a | | | | | † — | | | | | | | |
| Deposits Excl. from Broad Money | 26b | — | — | — | — | † 71.0 | 194.3 | 234.2 | 451.4 | 625.1 | 713.9 | 1,493.0 | 2,113.1 |
| Sec.Ot.th.Shares Excl.f/Brd.Money | 26s | — | — | — | — | † — | — | — | — | 4.8 | 4.8 | 24.1 | 580.4 |
| Loans | 26l | — | 2.9 | 3.1 | 6.7 | † 1.6 | .6 | .2 | — | — | 1.6 | 43.0 | 126.7 |
| Financial Derivatives | 26m | — | — | — | — | † — | — | .5 | .1 | .4 | 1.6 | 1.5 | — |
| Insurance Technical Reserves | 26r | — | — | — | — | † — | — | — | — | — | — | — | — |
| Shares and Other Equity | 27a | 165.3 | 263.8 | 357.1 | 599.6 | † 948.8 | 1,351.3 | 1,626.7 | 1,919.5 | 2,035.3 | 2,379.7 | 2,002.4 | 1,971.4 |
| Other Items (Net) | 27r | −89.1 | −61.9 | −137.7 | −223.8 | † −102.3 | −323.9 | −396.5 | −398.8 | −273.4 | 408.2 | 212.0 | 347.2 |
| Memo Item: | | | | | | | | | | | | | |
| Total Assets | 20ra | 607.5 | 988.2 | 1,762.3 | 3,676.8 | † 4,099.5 | 5,365.7 | 6,801.4 | 9,584.2 | 10,378.4 | 13,180.3 | 16,237.1 | 20,507.9 |

# Tajikistan   923

| | | 2004 | 2005 | 2006 | 2007 | 2008 | 2009 | 2010 | 2011 | 2012 | 2013 | 2014 | 2015 |
|---|---|---|---|---|---|---|---|---|---|---|---|---|---|
| **Depository Corporations** | | | | | | *Millions of Somoni: End of Period* | | | | | | | |
| Net Foreign Assets | 31n | 174.0 | 189.7 | 549.4 | 166.9 | † −169.0 | 349.4 | 909.8 | 845.2 | 1,494.6 | 471.9 | −956.8 | −235.9 |
| Claims on Nonresidents | 31 | 605.3 | 789.1 | 1,260.9 | 1,480.2 | † 1,058.0 | 1,973.4 | 2,808.0 | 3,639.2 | 4,581.3 | 4,752.7 | 3,828.9 | 5,210.7 |
| Liabilities to Nonresidents | 36c | 431.3 | 599.4 | 711.5 | 1,313.2 | † 1,227.1 | 1,624.1 | 1,898.1 | 2,794.0 | 3,086.7 | 4,280.8 | 4,785.7 | 5,446.6 |
| Domestic Claims | 32 | 427.0 | 937.7 | 1,285.4 | 2,172.2 | † 3,519.8 | 3,090.7 | 1,605.6 | 3,813.7 | 4,749.5 | 7,669.5 | 8,642.2 | 9,789.9 |
| Net Claims on Central Government | 32an | −216.6 | −254.6 | −353.5 | −541.0 | † −1,185.9 | −1,062.3 | −1,983.9 | −1,015.8 | −766.9 | −519.8 | −1,817.1 | −2,695.2 |
| Claims on Central Government | 32a | 154.1 | 154.1 | 154.1 | 155.7 | † 154.3 | 233.0 | 154.1 | 670.0 | 1,436.1 | 1,578.2 | 1,609.8 | 1,677.8 |
| Liabilities to Central Government | 36d | 370.7 | 408.7 | 507.6 | 696.7 | † 1,340.2 | 1,295.3 | 2,138.0 | 1,685.8 | 2,203.0 | 2,098.1 | 3,426.9 | 4,373.0 |
| Claims on Other Sectors | 32s | 643.6 | 1,192.3 | 1,638.9 | 2,713.2 | † 4,705.7 | 4,153.0 | 3,589.5 | 4,829.5 | 5,516.4 | 8,189.3 | 10,459.2 | 12,485.2 |
| Claims on Other Financial Corps.. | 32g | 244.9 | 507.7 | 651.1 | 878.1 | † 2,038.8 | 1,318.1 | 88.4 | 72.2 | 53.3 | 33.1 | 40.4 | 86.7 |
| Claims on State & Local Govts..... | 32b | — | — | — | — | † — | | | | | | | |
| Claims on Public Nonfin. Corps.... | 32c | 20.9 | 28.4 | 100.8 | 147.7 | † 141.7 | 138.5 | 364.1 | 337.6 | 753.4 | 918.7 | 902.5 | 1,669.8 |
| Claims on Private Sector............. | 32d | 377.8 | 656.2 | 886.9 | 1,687.4 | † 2,525.2 | 2,696.3 | 3,136.9 | 4,419.7 | 4,709.6 | 7,237.5 | 9,516.4 | 10,728.7 |
| Broad Money Liabilities............... | 35l | 652.0 | 1,041.1 | 1,513.3 | 2,727.4 | † 2,671.2 | 3,759.4 | 4,458.3 | 5,932.8 | 7,092.7 | 8,491.9 | 9,092.0 | 10,789.7 |
| Currency Outside Depository Corps | 34a | 398.6 | 666.1 | 823.8 | 1,028.7 | † 1,405.2 | 1,770.8 | 2,004.6 | 2,708.8 | 3,406.2 | 4,143.5 | 4,053.8 | 4,590.8 |
| Transferable Deposits.................. | 34 | 65.1 | 84.7 | 145.6 | 239.3 | † 437.2 | 789.6 | 882.4 | 963.2 | 1,104.3 | 1,175.2 | 1,512.2 | 2,129.7 |
| Other Deposits........................... | 35 | 188.3 | 290.3 | 544.0 | 1,459.5 | † 828.8 | 1,199.0 | 1,571.2 | 2,260.8 | 2,582.2 | 3,173.1 | 3,526.0 | 4,069.2 |
| Securities Other than Shares....... | 36a | — | — | — | — | † — | | | | | | | |
| Deposits Excl. from Broad Money..... | 36b | — | — | — | — | † 71.0 | 194.3 | 234.2 | 451.4 | 625.1 | 713.9 | 1,493.0 | 2,113.1 |
| Sec.Ot.th.Shares Excl.f/Brd.Money.... | 36s | — | — | — | — | † — | — | — | 12.9 | 53.0 | 79.4 | 78.9 | 640.7 |
| Loans......................................... | 36l | — | 2.9 | 3.1 | 6.7 | † 73.0 | .6 | .2 | — | — | 1.6 | 43.0 | 126.7 |
| Financial Derivatives................... | 36m | — | — | — | — | † — | — | .5 | .1 | .4 | 1.6 | 1.5 | — |
| Insurance Technical Reserves........... | 36r | — | — | — | — | † — | | | | | | | |
| Shares and Other Equity.................. | 37a | 182.9 | 291.5 | 403.2 | 623.5 | † −1,238.1 | −1,318.4 | −1,213.6 | −379.5 | −643.7 | −706.2 | −2,525.7 | −3,460.6 |
| Other Items (Net)........................ | 37r | −233.9 | −208.1 | −84.8 | −1,018.3 | † 1,773.7 | 804.1 | −964.2 | −1,358.8 | −883.2 | −440.7 | −497.4 | −655.6 |
| Broad Money Liabs., Seasonally Adj. | 35l.b | 620.6 | 974.4 | 1,390.4 | 2,464.7 | † 2,436.6 | 3,457.2 | 4,143.9 | 5,582.3 | 6,720.0 | 8,090.1 | 8,682.0 | .... |
| **Other Financial Corporations** | | | | | | *Millions of Somoni: End of Period* | | | | | | | |
| Net Foreign Assets...................... | 41n | .... | .... | .... | .... | −267.4 | −139.2 | −147.2 | −247.7 | −423.5 | −98.4 | −115.7 | .... |
| Claims on Nonresidents................ | 41 | .... | .... | .... | .... | 31.6 | 29.2 | 32.6 | 29.0 | 52.4 | 7.0 | 16.3 | .... |
| Liabilities to Nonresidents............. | 46c | .... | .... | .... | .... | 299.1 | 168.4 | 179.7 | 276.7 | 475.9 | 105.4 | 132.1 | .... |
| Claims on Depository Corporations.. | 40 | .... | .... | .... | .... | 57.6 | 132.0 | 92.6 | 101.7 | 198.2 | 142.0 | 121.6 | .... |
| Net Claims on Central Government.. | 42an | .... | .... | .... | .... | — | — | — | — | — | — | −.3 | .... |
| Claims on Central Government...... | 42a | .... | .... | .... | .... | — | — | — | — | — | — | — | .... |
| Liabilities to Central Government... | 46d | .... | .... | .... | .... | — | — | — | — | — | — | .3 | .... |
| Claims on Other Sectors.................. | 42s | .... | .... | .... | .... | 2,225.1 | 2,015.4 | 369.7 | 408.2 | 593.0 | 230.6 | 286.3 | .... |
| Claims on State & Local Govts....... | 42b | .... | .... | .... | .... | — | — | — | — | — | — | — | .... |
| Claims on Public Nonfin. Corps...... | 42c | .... | .... | .... | .... | .3 | .2 | 5.5 | 5.4 | 5.3 | 5.2 | 5.1 | .... |
| Claims on Private Sector............... | 42d | .... | .... | .... | .... | 2,224.9 | 2,015.2 | 364.2 | 402.8 | 587.7 | 225.5 | 281.3 | .... |
| Deposits..................................... | 46b | .... | .... | .... | .... | — | — | 3.3 | 1.4 | 4.5 | 3.9 | 4.8 | .... |
| Securities Other than Shares........... | 46s | .... | .... | .... | .... | | | | | | | | |
| Loans......................................... | 46l | .... | .... | .... | .... | 1,784.1 | 1,265.8 | 17.1 | 15.1 | 19.6 | 20.7 | 22.1 | .... |
| Financial Derivatives........................ | 46m | .... | .... | .... | .... | — | — | — | — | — | — | — | .... |
| Insurance Technical Reserves........... | 46r | .... | .... | .... | .... | 8.1 | 6.4 | 50.3 | 40.0 | 42.0 | 43.1 | 49.7 | .... |
| Shares and Other Equity.................. | 47a | .... | .... | .... | .... | 177.2 | 197.5 | 225.1 | 270.9 | 347.1 | 292.7 | 338.9 | .... |
| Other Items (Net)........................... | 47r | .... | .... | .... | .... | 45.9 | 538.4 | 19.4 | −65.2 | −45.6 | −86.2 | −123.6 | .... |
| Memo Item: | | | | | | | | | | | | | |
| Total Assets............................... | 40ra | .... | .... | .... | .... | 2,392.8 | 2,251.2 | 614.8 | 672.5 | 995.4 | 492.8 | 581.8 | .... |
| **Financial Corporations** | | | | | | *Millions of Somoni: End of Period* | | | | | | | |
| Net Foreign Assets...................... | 51n | .... | .... | .... | .... | † −436.4 | 210.2 | 762.7 | 597.5 | 1,071.1 | 373.5 | −1,072.5 | .... |
| Claims on Nonresidents................ | 51 | .... | .... | .... | .... | † 1,089.7 | 2,002.6 | 2,840.5 | 3,668.2 | 4,633.7 | 4,759.7 | 3,845.2 | .... |
| Liabilities to Nonresidents............. | 56c | .... | .... | .... | .... | † 1,526.1 | 1,792.4 | 2,077.9 | 3,070.7 | 3,562.6 | 4,386.2 | 4,917.8 | .... |
| Domestic Claims........................ | 52 | .... | .... | .... | .... | † 3,706.1 | 3,787.9 | 1,886.9 | 4,149.7 | 5,289.2 | 7,867.0 | 8,887.9 | .... |
| Net Claims on Central Government | 52an | .... | .... | .... | .... | † −1,185.9 | −1,062.3 | −1,983.9 | −1,015.8 | −766.9 | −519.8 | −1,817.3 | .... |
| Claims on Central Government..... | 52a | .... | .... | .... | .... | † 154.3 | 233.0 | 154.1 | 670.0 | 1,436.1 | 1,578.2 | 1,609.8 | .... |
| Liabilities to Central Government. | 56d | .... | .... | .... | .... | † 1,340.2 | 1,295.3 | 2,138.0 | 1,685.8 | 2,203.0 | 2,098.1 | 3,427.2 | .... |
| Claims on Other Sectors............... | 52s | .... | .... | .... | .... | † 4,892.0 | 4,850.2 | 3,870.8 | 5,165.5 | 6,056.0 | 8,386.9 | 10,705.2 | .... |
| Claims on State & Local Govts....... | 52b | .... | .... | .... | .... | † — | | | | | | | |
| Claims on Pub. Nonfin. Corps...... | 52c | .... | .... | .... | .... | † 142.0 | 138.7 | 369.7 | 343.0 | 758.8 | 923.9 | 907.6 | .... |
| Claims on Private Sector.............. | 52d | .... | .... | .... | .... | † 4,750.1 | 4,711.5 | 3,501.1 | 4,822.5 | 5,297.3 | 7,463.0 | 9,797.6 | .... |
| Currency Outside Fin. Corporations.. | 54a | .... | .... | .... | .... | 1,403.5 | 1,768.3 | 2,002.5 | 2,706.2 | 3,401.4 | 4,140.1 | 4,050.4 | .... |
| Deposits..................................... | 55l | .... | .... | .... | .... | † 1,253.7 | 2,051.1 | 2,575.9 | 3,528.5 | 4,131.1 | 4,713.0 | 6,314.5 | .... |
| Securities Other than Shares........... | 56a | — | — | — | — | † — | — | — | — | — | — | 3.4 | .... |
| Loans......................................... | 56l | — | — | — | — | † 71.3 | — | — | — | — | 1.6 | 39.2 | .... |
| Financial Derivatives........................ | 56m | — | — | — | — | † — | — | .5 | .1 | .4 | 1.6 | 1.5 | .... |
| Insurance Technical Reserves........... | 56r | — | — | — | — | † 5.8 | 5.0 | 48.5 | 35.6 | 39.8 | 37.0 | 49.4 | .... |
| Shares and Other Equity.................. | 57a | — | — | — | — | † −1,060.9 | −1,120.9 | −988.4 | −108.7 | −296.6 | −413.4 | −2,186.8 | .... |
| Other Items (Net)........................... | 57r | .... | .... | .... | .... | 1,596.3 | 1,294.7 | −989.4 | −1,414.5 | −915.7 | −239.2 | −456.4 | .... |
| **Monetary Aggregates** | | | | | | *Millions of Somoni: End of Period* | | | | | | | |
| Broad Money.............................. | 59m | 652.0 | 1,041.1 | 1,513.3 | 2,727.4 | 2,671.2 | 3,759.4 | 4,458.3 | 5,932.8 | 7,092.7 | 8,491.9 | 9,092.0 | 10,789.7 |
| o/w:Currency Issued by Cent.Govt | 59m.a | — | — | — | — | — | — | — | — | — | — | — | — |
| o/w: Dep.in Nonfin. Corporations | 59m.b | — | — | — | — | — | — | — | — | — | — | — | — |
| o/w: Secs. Issued by Central Govt. | 59m.c | — | — | — | — | — | — | — | — | — | — | — | — |
| Money (National Definitions) | | | | | | | | | | | | | |
| M0............................................. | 19mc | 398.6 | 666.1 | 823.8 | 1,028.7 | 1,405.2 | 1,770.8 | 2,004.6 | 2,708.8 | 3,406.2 | 4,143.5 | 4,053.8 | 4,590.8 |
| M1............................................. | 59ma | 463.7 | 750.8 | 969.4 | 1,267.9 | 1,669.4 | 2,191.8 | 2,525.3 | 3,264.1 | 4,093.1 | 4,788.6 | 4,884.9 | 5,403.3 |
| M2............................................. | 59mb | 495.5 | 807.2 | 1,046.1 | 1,449.7 | 1,908.8 | 2,527.4 | 2,971.7 | 3,861.6 | 4,743.2 | 5,627.1 | 5,825.7 | 6,534.9 |
| M3............................................. | 59mc | 495.5 | 807.2 | 1,046.1 | 1,449.7 | 1,908.8 | 2,527.4 | 2,971.7 | 3,861.6 | 4,743.2 | 5,627.1 | 5,825.7 | 6,534.9 |
| M4............................................. | 59md | 652.0 | 1,041.1 | 1,513.3 | 2,727.4 | 2,671.2 | 3,759.4 | 4,458.3 | 5,932.8 | 7,092.7 | 8,491.9 | 9,092.0 | 10,789.7 |

# Tajikistan   923

| | | 2004 | 2005 | 2006 | 2007 | 2008 | 2009 | 2010 | 2011 | 2012 | 2013 | 2014 | 2015 |
|---|---|---|---|---|---|---|---|---|---|---|---|---|---|
| **Interest Rates** | | | | | | | *Percent Per Annum* | | | | | | |
| Central Bank Policy Rate (EOP)........ | 60 | .... | .... | .... | .... | .... | .... | .... | 23.80 | 18.00 | 17.30 | 18.67 | 17.50 |
| Central Bank Policy Rate (FC) (EOP). | 60..f | .... | .... | .... | .... | .... | .... | .... | 23.80 | 18.00 | 17.30 | 18.67 | 17.50 |
| Refinancing Rate (End of Period)...... | 60.b | 10.00 | 9.00 | 12.00 | 15.00 | 13.50 | 8.00 | 8.25 | 9.80 | 6.50 | 5.50 | 8.00 | 8.00 |
| Central Bank Bill Rate.................... | 60aa | 5.68 | 6.51 | 7.55 | 7.28 | 12.00 | 7.06 | 6.55 | 8.59 | 3.78 | 2.69 | 2.96 | .... |
| Money Market Rate........................ | 60b | 23.88 | 17.33 | 14.03 | 15.63 | 18.03 | 24.19 | 17.59 | 19.56 | 16.49 | 15.63 | 16.49 | .... |
| Money Market Rate (Foreign Curren( | 60b.f | 23.88 | 2.12 | 17.31 | 11.83 | 21.62 | 24.96 | 20.23 | 17.56 | 18.95 | 19.71 | 19.20 | .... |
| Treasury Bill Rate........................... | 60c | .... | .... | .... | .... | .... | 7.00 | 6.72 | 7.40 | 4.96 | .50 | .40 | .... |
| Deposit Rate................................ | 60l | 10.17 | 10.15 | 9.52 | 10.99 | 9.37 | 7.58 | 8.65 | 8.24 | 7.67 | 6.58 | 5.49 | 4.23 |
| Deposit Rate (Foreign Currency)...... | 60l.f | 7.69 | 8.21 | 9.69 | 8.60 | 7.48 | 9.63 | 7.98 | 9.86 | 8.28 | 7.44 | 7.43 | 7.12 |
| Lending Rate................................ | 60p | 20.31 | 23.28 | 24.16 | 22.96 | 23.59 | 22.62 | 23.40 | 22.46 | 21.09 | 24.33 | 24.53 | 25.84 |
| Lending Rate (Foreign Currency)...... | 60p.f | 20.71 | 19.87 | 21.05 | 22.07 | 21.96 | 24.91 | 23.03 | 21.90 | 24.54 | 24.40 | 22.98 | 21.60 |
| **Prices and Labor** | | | | | | | *Percent Change over Previous Period* | | | | | | |
| Wholesale Prices........................... | 63.xx | 1.3 | .5 | 4.0 | 1.3 | −.3 | 3.4 | 2.1 | .... | .... | .... | .... | .... |
| Consumer Prices............................ | 64.xx | 7.1 | 7.1 | 10.0 | 13.1 | 20.5 | 6.4 | 6.4 | 12.4 | 5.8 | 5.0 | 6.1 | 5.7 |
| **Intl. Transactions & Positions** | | | | | | | *Millions of US Dollars* | | | | | | |
| Exports........................................ | 70..d | 914.9 | 909.0 | 1,399.0 | 1,468.0 | 1,409.0 | 1,010.0 | 1,195.0 | 1,257.3 | 1,359.7 | 1,161.8 | 977.3 | 890.6 |
| Imports, c.i.f................................. | 71.vd | 1,191.3 | 1,330.0 | 1,725.0 | 2,547.0 | 3,273.0 | 2,570.0 | 2,657.0 | 3,206.0 | 3,778.0 | 4,151.0 | 4,297.4 | 3,434.9 |
| **Balance of Payments** | | | | | | | *Millions of US Dollars* | | | | | | |
| A. Current Account*...................... | 109bx | −57.0 | −18.9 | −21.4 | −495.1 | 47.6 | −180.3 | −369.6 | −171.3 | −247.6 | −203.1 | † −258.3 | −470.0 |
| Goods, credit (exports)................. | 1a9cx | 1,096.9 | 1,108.1 | 1,511.8 | 1,556.9 | 1,574.9 | 1,038.5 | 459.1 | 593.3 | 825.9 | 574.1 | † 526.8 | 572.0 |
| Goods, debit (imports)................. | 1a9dx | 1,232.4 | 1,430.9 | 1,954.6 | 3,115.0 | 3,699.0 | 2,770.8 | 2,836.3 | 3,568.6 | 4,382.7 | 4,535.5 | † 3,527.9 | 2,824.9 |
| Balance on goods..................... | 1a9bx | −135.5 | −322.8 | −442.8 | −1,558.1 | −2,124.2 | −1,732.3 | −2,377.2 | −2,975.2 | −3,556.8 | −3,961.4 | † −3,001.1 | −2,252.9 |
| Services, credit (exports).............. | 1b9cx | 122.9 | 146.3 | 134.2 | 148.7 | 181.4 | 179.7 | 425.6 | 564.5 | 818.0 | 593.3 | † 309.5 | 252.4 |
| Services, debit (imports).............. | 1b9dx | 212.5 | 251.5 | 394.5 | 592.1 | 455.5 | 291.3 | 528.2 | 670.8 | 890.4 | 861.1 | † 615.3 | 493.8 |
| Balance on Goods & Services....... | 1z9bx | −225.1 | −428.0 | −703.1 | −2,001.5 | −2,398.3 | −1,843.9 | −2,479.8 | −3,081.5 | −3,629.1 | −4,229.2 | † −3,307.0 | −2,494.3 |
| Primary income: credit.................. | 1c9cx | 1.7 | 9.6 | 12.4 | 22.4 | 19.8 | 7.2 | 14.4 | 40.1 | 40.5 | 65.0 | † 2,349.9 | 1,739.3 |
| Primary income: debit................... | 1c9dx | 59.2 | 50.4 | 76.4 | 73.2 | 72.3 | 78.5 | 93.1 | 79.7 | 109.5 | 110.4 | † 166.1 | 213.1 |
| Balance on gds, serv. & prim. inc. | 1y9bx | −282.7 | −468.8 | −767.0 | −2,052.3 | −2,450.8 | −1,915.2 | −2,558.5 | −3,121.1 | −3,698.1 | −4,274.6 | † −1,123.2 | −968.1 |
| Secondary income: credit.............. | 1d9ca | 348.4 | 599.9 | 1,146.0 | 1,794.3 | 2,705.2 | 1,861.8 | 2,420.7 | 3,171.4 | 3,715.2 | 4,304.6 | † 1,158.6 | 670.2 |
| Secondary income: debit............... | 1d9da | 122.8 | 150.0 | 400.4 | 237.1 | 206.8 | 126.9 | 231.8 | 221.6 | 264.7 | 233.1 | † 293.7 | 172.1 |
| B. Capital Account*...................... | 209ba | — | — | — | 32.8 | 39.4 | 120.4 | 68.5 | 49.9 | 71.1 | 26.7 | † 124.0 | 144.0 |
| Capital account: credit................. | 209ca | — | — | — | 32.8 | 39.4 | 120.4 | 68.5 | 49.9 | 71.1 | 26.7 | † 124.0 | 144.0 |
| Capital account: debit.................. | 209da | — | — | — | — | — | — | — | — | — | — | .... | .... |
| Balance on current & capital acct. | 129ba | −57.0 | −18.9 | −21.4 | −462.2 | 87.0 | −59.9 | −301.1 | −121.4 | −176.5 | −176.4 | † −134.3 | −326.0 |
| C. Financial Account*..................... | 309na | −93.4 | −101.5 | −276.0 | −811.3 | 223.5 | −13.6 | −248.3 | −37.1 | −156.1 | −44.5 | † −298.2 | −470.1 |
| Direct investment: assets.............. | 3a9aa | — | — | — | — | — | — | — | — | — | −159.0 | .... | .... |
| Equity & investment fund shares.. | 3aaaa | — | — | — | — | — | — | — | — | — | −31.3 | .... | .... |
| Debt instruments...................... | 3abaa | — | — | — | .... | .... | .... | .... | — | — | −127.7 | .... | .... |
| Direct investment: liabilities .......... | 3a9la | 272.0 | 54.5 | 338.6 | 360.0 | 375.8 | 15.8 | −15.7 | 67.5 | 198.3 | −54.2 | † 309.3 | 391.2 |
| Equity & investment fund shares . | 3aala | 272.0 | 54.5 | 338.6 | 360.0 | 375.8 | 15.8 | 28.9 | 20.0 | 41.4 | −.2 | † 139.4 | 169.4 |
| Debt instruments....................... | 3abla | — | .... | .... | .... | .... | .... | −44.6 | 47.5 | 156.8 | −53.9 | † 169.9 | 221.9 |
| Portfolio investment: assets .......... | 3b9aa | — | — | — | — | — | — | — | — | — | — | † −.4 | — |
| Equity & investment fund shares | 3baaa | — | .... | .... | .... | .... | .... | .... | .... | .... | — | † −.4 | — |
| Debt securities .......................... | 3bbaa | .... | .... | .... | .... | .... | .... | .... | .... | .... | — | † −.4 | — |
| Portfolio investment: liabilities....... | 3b9la | 5.3 | — | — | .2 | .1 | .1 | 6.5 | — | — | — | † 1.4 | — |
| Equity & investment fund shares . | 3bala | — | — | .... | — | — | — | — | — | — | — | † 1.4 | — |
| Debt securities.......................... | 3bbla | 5.3 | — | — | .2 | .1 | .1 | 6.5 | — | — | — | † 1.4 | — |
| Fin. der.& empl.stk.ops.(ESOs): net. | 3c9na | .... | .... | .... | .... | .... | .... | .... | .... | .... | — | — | — |
| Fin. der. & ESOs.: assets.............. | 3c9aa | .... | .... | .... | .... | — | .... | .... | .... | .... | — | — | — |
| Fin. der. & ESOs.: liabilities.......... | 3c9la | .... | .... | .... | .... | — | .... | .... | .... | .... | — | — | — |
| Other investment: assets............... | 3d9aa | 28.4 | 71.3 | 301.9 | 386.7 | 471.9 | −177.7 | 80.2 | 89.3 | 162.3 | 246.5 | † −94.1 | 155.0 |
| Other equity............................. | 3daaa | .... | .... | .... | .... | .... | .... | .... | .... | .... | .... | .... | .... |
| Debt instruments....................... | 3dzaa | 28.4 | 71.3 | 301.9 | 386.7 | 471.9 | −177.7 | 80.2 | 89.3 | 162.3 | 246.5 | † −94.1 | 155.0 |
| Other investment: liabilities........... | 3d9la | −155.5 | 118.3 | 239.2 | 837.8 | −127.4 | −180.0 | 337.7 | 58.9 | 120.1 | 186.2 | † −106.9 | 233.8 |
| Other equity............................. | 3dala | .... | .... | .... | .... | .... | .... | .... | .... | .... | .... | .... | .... |
| Debt instruments....................... | 3dzla | −155.5 | 118.3 | 239.2 | 837.8 | −127.4 | −180.0 | 337.7 | 58.9 | 120.1 | 186.2 | † −106.9 | 233.8 |
| Curr.+ cap.− finan. acct. balance... | 4y9na | 36.4 | 82.6 | 254.6 | 349.1 | −136.5 | −46.3 | −52.8 | −84.3 | −20.3 | −131.9 | † 163.9 | 144.1 |
| D. Net Errors and Omissions............ | 409na | −32.5 | −76.3 | −264.2 | −336.9 | 26.1 | 161.2 | 159.2 | 182.5 | 95.5 | 141.4 | † −249.0 | −114.5 |
| E. Reserves and Related Items.......... | 4z9na | 3.9 | 6.3 | −9.6 | 12.2 | −110.4 | 114.9 | 106.4 | 98.2 | 75.2 | 9.5 | † −85.1 | 29.6 |
| Reserve assets............................. | 3e9aa | 46.2 | 25.6 | 7.1 | 14.5 | −168.8 | 145.7 | 164.8 | 119.0 | 115.2 | 9.5 | † −88.9 | 18.7 |
| Credit and loans from the IMF....... | 3dcla | 16.9 | 15.5 | −86.2 | — | −29.8 | 25.0 | 58.4 | 20.8 | 40.0 | — | † −3.8 | −10.9 |
| Exceptional financing................... | 409la | 25.5 | 3.9 | 103.0 | 2.3 | −28.6 | 5.9 | — | — | — | — | .... | .... |

*Excludes components in group E

# Tajikistan   923

| | | 2004 | 2005 | 2006 | 2007 | 2008 | 2009 | 2010 | 2011 | 2012 | 2013 | 2014 | 2015 |
|---|---|---|---|---|---|---|---|---|---|---|---|---|---|
| **International Investment Position** | | | | | | *Millions of US Dollars* | | | | | | | |
| Assets.............................................. | **809aa** | .... | .... | .... | .... | .... | .... | .... | .... | .... | .... | † 810.8 | 863.4 |
| Direct investment........................... | **8a9aa** | .... | .... | .... | .... | .... | .... | .... | .... | .... | .... | .... | .... |
| Equity & investment fund shares.. | **8aaaa** | .... | .... | .... | .... | .... | .... | .... | .... | .... | .... | .... | .... |
| Debt instruments......................... | **8abaa** | .... | .... | .... | .... | .... | .... | .... | .... | .... | .... | .... | .... |
| Portfolio investment....................... | **8b9aa** | .... | .... | .... | .... | .... | .... | .... | .... | .... | .... | † 1.2 | .9 |
| Equity & investment fund shares.. | **8baaa** | .... | .... | .... | .... | .... | .... | .... | .... | .... | .... | .... | .... |
| Debt securities............................ | **8bbaa** | .... | .... | .... | .... | .... | .... | .... | .... | .... | .... | † 1.2 | .9 |
| Fin. der.(oth.than reserves) & ESOs | **8c9aa** | .... | .... | .... | .... | .... | .... | .... | .... | .... | .... | .... | .... |
| Other investment........................... | **8d9aa** | .... | .... | .... | .... | .... | .... | .... | .... | .... | .... | † 298.9 | 368.2 |
| Other equity................................ | **8daaa** | .... | .... | .... | .... | .... | .... | .... | .... | .... | .... | .... | .... |
| Debt instruments......................... | **8dzaa** | .... | .... | .... | .... | .... | .... | .... | .... | .... | .... | † 298.9 | 368.2 |
| Reserve assets............................... | **8e9aa** | .... | .... | .... | .... | .... | .... | .... | .... | .... | .... | † 510.8 | 494.3 |
| Liabilities......................................... | **809la** | .... | .... | .... | .... | .... | .... | .... | .... | .... | .... | † 5,541.2 | 5,699.4 |
| Direct investment........................... | **8a9la** | .... | .... | .... | .... | .... | .... | .... | .... | .... | .... | † 1,703.9 | 1,991.0 |
| Equity & investment fund shares.. | **8aala** | .... | .... | .... | .... | .... | .... | .... | .... | .... | .... | † 784.2 | 897.4 |
| Debt instruments......................... | **8abla** | .... | .... | .... | .... | .... | .... | .... | .... | .... | .... | † 919.6 | 1,093.6 |
| Portfolio investment....................... | **8b9la** | .... | .... | .... | .... | .... | .... | .... | .... | .... | .... | † 81.5 | 86.1 |
| Equity & investment fund shares.. | **8bala** | .... | .... | .... | .... | .... | .... | .... | .... | .... | .... | † 81.5 | 86.1 |
| Debt securities............................ | **8bbla** | .... | .... | .... | .... | .... | .... | .... | .... | .... | .... | .... | .... |
| Fin. der.(oth.than reserves) & ESOs | **8c9la** | .... | .... | .... | .... | .... | .... | .... | .... | .... | .... | .... | .... |
| Other investment........................... | **8d9la** | .... | .... | .... | .... | .... | .... | .... | .... | .... | .... | † 3,755.8 | 3,622.2 |
| Other equity................................ | **8dala** | .... | .... | .... | .... | .... | .... | .... | .... | .... | .... | .... | .... |
| Debt instruments......................... | **8dzla** | .... | .... | .... | .... | .... | .... | .... | .... | .... | .... | † 3,755.8 | 3,622.2 |
| | | | | | | | | | | | | | |
| **National Accounts** | | | | | | *Millions of Somoni* | | | | | | | |
| Gross Domestic Product (GDP)......... | **99b** | 6,167.2 | 7,206.6 | 9,335.2 | 12,804.4 | 17,706.9 | 20,622.8 | 24,704.7 | 30,069.3 | 36,161.1 | 40,524.5 | 45,605.2 | .... |
| | | | | | | *Millions: Midyear Estimates* | | | | | | | |
| **Population................................** | **99z** | 6.67 | 6.81 | 6.95 | 7.10 | 7.25 | 7.41 | 7.58 | 7.75 | 7.93 | 8.11 | 8.30 | 8.48 |

# Tanzania 738

| | | 2004 | 2005 | 2006 | 2007 | 2008 | 2009 | 2010 | 2011 | 2012 | 2013 | 2014 | 2015 |
|---|---|---|---|---|---|---|---|---|---|---|---|---|---|
| **Exchange Rates** | | | | | | *Shillings per SDR: End of Period* | | | | | | | |
| Official Rate | aa | 1,619.7 | 1,665.8 | 1,898.0 | 1,789.0 | 1,972.0 | 2,080.1 | 2,241.0 | 2,413.0 | 2,415.5 | 2,431.0 | 2,500.3 | 2,977.3 |
| | | | | | | *Shillings per US Dollar: End of Period (ae) Period Average (rf)* | | | | | | | |
| Official Rate | ae | 1,043.0 | 1,165.5 | 1,261.6 | 1,132.1 | 1,280.3 | 1,326.8 | 1,455.2 | 1,571.7 | 1,571.6 | 1,578.6 | 1,725.8 | 2,148.5 |
| Official Rate | rf | 1,089.3 | 1,128.9 | 1,251.9 | 1,245.0 | 1,196.3 | 1,320.3 | 1,409.3 | 1,572.1 | 1,583.0 | 1,600.4 | 1,654.0 | 1,991.4 |
| **Fund Position** | | | | | | *Millions of SDRs: End of Period* | | | | | | | |
| Quota | 2f.s | 198.90 | 198.90 | 198.90 | 198.90 | 198.90 | 198.90 | 198.90 | 198.90 | 198.90 | 198.90 | 198.90 | 198.90 |
| SDR Holdings | 1b.s | .05 | .49 | .04 | .10 | .02 | 158.72 | 158.33 | 156.79 | 154.78 | 152.49 | 134.28 | 90.52 |
| Reserve Position in the Fund | 1c.s | 10.00 | 10.00 | 10.00 | 10.00 | 10.00 | 10.00 | 10.00 | 10.00 | 10.00 | 10.00 | 10.00 | 10.00 |
| Total Fund Cred.&Loans Outstg | 2tl | 272.35 | 239.63 | 8.40 | 11.20 | 11.20 | 210.10 | 229.71 | 228.31 | 226.35 | 298.71 | 280.56 | 236.83 |
| SDR Allocations | 1bd | 31.37 | 31.37 | 31.37 | 31.37 | 31.37 | 190.51 | 190.51 | 190.51 | 190.51 | 190.51 | 190.51 | 190.51 |
| **International Liquidity** | | | | | | *Millions of US Dollars Unless Otherwise Indicated: End of Period* | | | | | | | |
| Total Reserves minus Gold | 1l.d | 2,295.7 | 2,048.8 | 2,259.3 | 2,886.4 | 2,862.9 | 3,470.4 | 3,904.7 | 3,726.2 | 4,052.2 | 4,673.7 | 4,390.4 | 4,072.9 |
| SDR Holdings | 1b.d | .1 | .7 | .1 | .2 | — | 248.8 | 243.8 | 240.7 | 237.9 | 234.8 | 194.5 | 125.4 |
| Reserve Position in the Fund | 1c.d | 15.5 | 14.3 | 15.0 | 15.8 | 15.4 | 15.7 | 15.4 | 15.4 | 15.4 | 15.4 | 14.5 | 13.9 |
| Foreign Exchange | 1d.d | 2,280.1 | 2,033.8 | 2,244.2 | 2,870.4 | 2,847.5 | 3,205.9 | 3,645.4 | 3,470.1 | 3,799.0 | 4,423.5 | 4,181.4 | 3,933.6 |
| Central Bank: Other Assets | 3..d | .8 | 4.0 | 3.4 | 8.1 | 6.8 | 3.7 | 3.6 | .7 | 1.9 | 1.6 | 1.8 | 16.6 |
| Central Bank: Other Liabs | 4..d | 2.2 | 4.5 | 2.8 | 8.0 | 6.7 | 2.7 | 2.6 | .1 | 2.7 | 4.7 | 5.4 | 10.9 |
| Other Depository Corps.: Assets | 7a.d | 589.2 | 680.1 | 867.7 | 833.7 | † 652.0 | 985.8 | 1,060.9 | 1,083.1 | 887.1 | 867.3 | 760.6 | 1,012.1 |
| Other Depository Corps.: Liabs | 7b.d | 28.5 | 55.1 | 78.2 | 274.2 | † 265.7 | 152.4 | 148.5 | 182.8 | 244.0 | 621.0 | 661.3 | 678.9 |
| **Central Bank** | | | | | | *Billions of Shillings: End of Period* | | | | | | | |
| Net Foreign Assets | 11n | 1,912.65 | 1,937.89 | 2,617.68 | 3,041.43 | 3,581.54 | 3,836.30 | 4,760.57 | 4,885.94 | 5,360.38 | 6,183.60 | 6,390.97 | 7,490.73 |
| Claims on Nonresidents | 11 | 2,406.85 | 2,394.62 | 2,696.76 | 3,126.68 | 3,674.13 | 4,664.62 | 5,704.95 | 5,893.50 | 6,371.48 | 7,380.32 | 7,576.41 | 8,786.46 |
| Liabilities to Nonresidents | 16c | 494.20 | 456.73 | 79.08 | 85.25 | 92.59 | 828.32 | 944.38 | 1,007.55 | 1,011.10 | 1,196.71 | 1,185.44 | 1,295.73 |
| Claims on Other Depository Corps | 12e | .10 | 12.24 | 19.65 | 20.40 | 57.53 | 61.71 | 61.75 | 62.73 | 76.38 | 64.23 | 124.95 | 150.11 |
| Net Claims on Central Government | 12an | −793.33 | −766.59 | −1,248.14 | −1,668.44 | −1,480.19 | −965.26 | −929.62 | 6.84 | −180.12 | −500.17 | 354.91 | 1,727.55 |
| Claims on Central Government | 12a | 272.64 | 515.84 | 611.69 | 597.55 | 650.86 | 1,109.52 | 1,095.46 | 1,244.71 | 1,756.61 | 2,053.05 | 2,345.88 | 3,001.71 |
| Liabilities to Central Government | 16d | 1,065.96 | 1,282.42 | 1,859.83 | 2,266.00 | 2,131.05 | 2,074.78 | 2,025.08 | 1,237.87 | 1,936.73 | 2,553.22 | 1,990.97 | 1,274.16 |
| Claims on Other Sectors | 12s | 97.46 | 83.26 | 108.66 | 99.42 | 86.90 | 100.43 | 95.50 | 79.95 | 56.38 | 57.46 | 65.44 | 133.86 |
| Claims on Other Financial Corps | 12g | — | — | — | — | — | — | — | 1.06 | .74 | 1.54 | 1.57 | .36 |
| Claims on State & Local Govts | 12b | — | — | — | — | — | — | — | — | — | — | — | — |
| Claims on Public Nonfin. Corps | 12c | — | — | — | — | — | — | — | — | — | — | — | — |
| Claims on Private Sector | 12d | 97.46 | 83.26 | 108.66 | 99.42 | 86.90 | 100.43 | 95.50 | 78.89 | 55.65 | 55.92 | 63.87 | 133.50 |
| Monetary Base | 14 | 999.99 | 1,284.69 | 1,504.12 | 1,879.05 | 2,276.44 | 3,009.06 | 3,497.85 | 4,111.92 | 4,525.59 | 5,027.78 | 5,909.48 | 6,833.09 |
| Currency in Circulation | 14a | 759.99 | 981.42 | 1,162.88 | 1,354.60 | 1,710.16 | 1,896.84 | 2,298.64 | 2,694.17 | 2,910.00 | 3,324.79 | 3,828.38 | 4,431.83 |
| Liabs. to Other Depository Corps | 14c | 239.99 | 303.27 | 341.25 | 524.44 | 566.28 | 1,112.22 | 1,199.21 | 1,417.75 | 1,615.59 | 1,702.99 | 2,081.10 | 2,401.26 |
| Liabilities to Other Sectors | 14d | — | — | — | — | — | — | — | — | — | — | — | — |
| Other Liabs. to Other Dep. Corps | 14n | 53.88 | 58.33 | 43.95 | 125.37 | 162.14 | 62.02 | 159.76 | 334.31 | 309.85 | 390.04 | 501.39 | 1,024.77 |
| Dep. & Sec. Excl. f/Monetary Base | 14o | 13.28 | 7.72 | 6.53 | 3.79 | 7.38 | 23.29 | 66.00 | 69.72 | 138.26 | 19.96 | 182.09 | 280.63 |
| Deposits Included in Broad Money | 15 | 13.27 | 7.72 | 6.53 | 3.74 | 7.28 | 23.28 | 65.98 | 69.71 | 138.25 | 19.90 | 173.50 | 276.08 |
| Sec.Ot.th.Shares Incl.in Brd. Money | 16a | — | — | — | — | — | — | — | — | — | — | — | — |
| Deposits Excl. from Broad Money | 16b | — | — | — | .06 | .10 | .01 | .01 | .01 | .02 | .05 | 8.59 | 4.55 |
| Sec.Ot.th.Shares Excl.f/Brd.Money | 16s | — | — | — | — | — | — | — | — | — | — | — | — |
| Loans | 16l | — | — | — | — | — | — | — | — | — | — | — | — |
| Financial Derivatives | 16m | — | — | — | — | — | — | — | — | — | — | — | — |
| Shares and Other Equity | 17a | 397.96 | 363.65 | 649.68 | 210.97 | 495.83 | 785.13 | 1,093.18 | 1,159.50 | 1,236.15 | 996.24 | 1,214.74 | 2,112.89 |
| Other Items (Net) | 17r | −248.21 | −447.60 | −706.43 | −726.38 | −696.01 | −846.33 | −828.58 | −639.98 | −896.83 | −628.90 | −871.43 | −749.12 |
| Memo Item: | | | | | | | | | | | | | |
| Total Assets | 10ra | 3,371.17 | 3,818.26 | 4,544.76 | 5,261.58 | 5,823.68 | 7,337.38 | 8,378.39 | 8,844.70 | 9,878.08 | 11,179.22 | 11,857.97 | 13,766.31 |
| **Other Depository Corporations** | | | | | | *Billions of Shillings: End of Period* | | | | | | | |
| Net Foreign Assets | 21n | 584.78 | 728.43 | 996.12 | 633.41 | † 494.61 | 1,094.51 | 1,326.21 | 1,410.44 | 1,010.70 | 388.83 | 171.08 | 715.86 |
| Claims on Nonresidents | 21 | 614.50 | 792.70 | 1,094.78 | 943.78 | † 834.73 | 1,294.60 | 1,542.09 | 1,696.89 | 1,394.14 | 1,369.16 | 1,310.69 | 2,174.45 |
| Liabilities to Nonresidents | 26c | 29.72 | 64.28 | 98.66 | 310.37 | † 340.12 | 200.09 | 215.88 | 286.45 | 383.44 | 980.32 | 1,139.62 | 1,458.59 |
| Claims on Central Bank | 20 | 346.17 | 424.70 | 512.27 | 875.29 | † 961.45 | 1,456.95 | 1,702.41 | 2,174.56 | 2,281.00 | 2,515.08 | 3,034.64 | 4,007.70 |
| Currency | 20a | 65.45 | 91.43 | 128.89 | 192.09 | † 271.52 | 330.09 | 401.50 | 458.34 | 495.21 | 560.83 | 583.65 | 753.34 |
| Reserve Deposits and Securities | 20b | 279.72 | 332.32 | 382.45 | 593.82 | † 629.54 | 1,118.79 | 1,300.91 | 1,716.22 | 1,785.79 | 1,954.25 | 2,450.99 | 3,254.37 |
| Other Claims | 20n | 1.00 | .95 | .92 | 89.39 | † 60.40 | 8.06 | — | — | — | — | — | — |
| Net Claims on Central Government | 22an | 521.20 | 958.66 | 965.51 | 1,348.60 | † 1,145.22 | 1,093.62 | 1,736.28 | 1,464.41 | 2,215.25 | 3,054.73 | 3,296.71 | 3,156.85 |
| Claims on Central Government | 22a | 673.28 | 1,165.22 | 1,195.62 | 1,673.78 | † 1,546.90 | 1,756.24 | 2,435.55 | 2,091.03 | 2,952.03 | 3,847.32 | 4,105.57 | 4,013.82 |
| Liabilities to Central Government | 26d | 152.08 | 206.56 | 230.10 | 325.18 | † 401.68 | 662.62 | 699.27 | 626.62 | 736.78 | 792.59 | 808.86 | 856.97 |
| Claims on Other Sectors | 22s | 1,215.27 | 1,571.02 | 2,201.48 | 3,051.79 | † 4,469.26 | 4,891.46 | 5,896.26 | 7,542.37 | 8,954.00 | 10,335.20 | 12,346.86 | 15,357.77 |
| Claims on Other Financial Corps | 22g | 21.65 | 28.84 | 23.96 | 32.07 | † 223.08 | 249.54 | 259.74 | 331.20 | 269.38 | 446.31 | 498.36 | 596.05 |
| Claims on State & Local Govts | 22b | — | — | — | — | † 3.24 | 4.65 | 9.16 | 23.01 | 33.68 | 29.38 | 83.11 | 48.83 |
| Claims on Public Nonfin. Corps | 22c | — | — | .46 | .05 | † 345.48 | 411.36 | 487.15 | 598.32 | 718.30 | 766.04 | 839.93 | 1,059.72 |
| Claims on Private Sector | 22d | 1,193.62 | 1,542.18 | 2,177.06 | 3,019.68 | † 3,897.42 | 4,225.92 | 5,140.20 | 6,589.84 | 7,932.64 | 9,093.47 | 10,925.46 | 13,653.17 |
| Liabilities to Central Bank | 26g | — | .15 | — | — | † 10.45 | .47 | — | — | 4.20 | .01 | — | — |
| Transf.Dep.Included in Broad Money | 24 | 1,159.95 | 1,574.94 | 1,881.58 | 2,414.69 | † 2,846.12 | 3,266.40 | 4,349.57 | 5,507.59 | 6,387.10 | 6,871.95 | 7,618.25 | 9,342.61 |
| Other Dep.Included in Broad Money | 25 | 1,286.01 | 1,778.08 | 2,242.36 | 2,642.65 | † 3,166.74 | 3,923.72 | 4,699.98 | 5,208.19 | 5,723.41 | 6,450.95 | 7,577.67 | 8,817.44 |
| Sec.Ot.th.Shares Incl.in Brd. Money | 26a | — | — | — | — | † — | — | — | — | — | — | — | — |
| Deposits Excl. from Broad Money | 26b | — | — | — | — | † — | — | — | — | — | — | — | — |
| Sec.Ot.th.Shares Excl.f/Brd.Money | 26s | 49.76 | 7.05 | 6.43 | 8.04 | † 2.12 | 8.20 | 17.14 | 24.78 | 24.80 | 22.43 | 75.09 | 220.14 |
| Loans | 26l | — | — | — | — | † 93.29 | 39.32 | 126.39 | 161.25 | 238.77 | 459.48 | 498.06 | 835.47 |
| Financial Derivatives | 26m | — | — | — | — | † — | — | — | — | — | — | — | — |
| Insurance Technical Reserves | 26r | — | — | — | — | † — | — | — | — | — | — | — | — |
| Shares and Other Equity | 27a | 330.47 | 424.82 | 582.20 | 807.69 | † 1,006.98 | 1,266.11 | 1,521.92 | 1,777.99 | 2,141.84 | 2,544.96 | 2,958.69 | 3,817.14 |
| Other Items (Net) | 27r | −158.77 | −102.22 | −37.19 | 36.03 | † −55.16 | 32.31 | −53.83 | −88.03 | −59.18 | −55.94 | 121.52 | 205.38 |
| Memo Item: | | | | | | | | | | | | | |
| Total Assets | 20ra | 3,352.06 | 4,399.80 | 5,604.01 | 7,296.62 | † 8,775.82 | 10,459.46 | 13,143.41 | 15,207.77 | 17,806.49 | 20,426.27 | 23,436.53 | 28,461.35 |

| | | 2004 | 2005 | 2006 | 2007 | 2008 | 2009 | 2010 | 2011 | 2012 | 2013 | 2014 | 2015 |
|---|---|---|---|---|---|---|---|---|---|---|---|---|---|
| **Depository Corporations** | | | | | | *Billions of Shillings: End of Period* | | | | | | | |
| Net Foreign Assets.......................... | 31n | 2,497.43 | 2,666.31 | 3,613.81 | 3,674.85 | † 4,076.15 | 4,930.81 | 6,086.78 | 6,296.38 | 6,371.08 | 6,572.44 | 6,562.05 | 8,206.59 |
| Claims on Nonresidents................ | 31 | 3,021.35 | 3,187.32 | 3,791.55 | 4,070.46 | † 4,508.87 | 5,959.22 | 7,247.04 | 7,590.38 | 7,765.62 | 8,749.48 | 8,887.10 | 10,960.91 |
| Liabilities to Nonresidents............. | 36c | 523.92 | 521.01 | 177.74 | 395.62 | † 432.72 | 1,028.41 | 1,160.26 | 1,294.00 | 1,394.54 | 2,177.04 | 2,325.05 | 2,754.32 |
| Domestic Claims............................. | 32 | 1,040.60 | 1,846.35 | 2,027.51 | 2,831.37 | † 4,221.20 | 5,120.25 | 6,798.43 | 9,093.57 | 11,045.51 | 12,947.22 | 16,063.92 | 20,376.03 |
| Net Claims on Central Government | 32an | −272.12 | 192.07 | −282.63 | −319.84 | † −334.97 | 128.36 | 806.67 | 1,471.25 | 2,035.13 | 2,554.55 | 3,651.62 | 4,884.40 |
| Claims on Central Government.... | 32a | 945.92 | 1,681.05 | 1,807.30 | 2,271.34 | † 2,197.77 | 2,865.76 | 3,531.01 | 3,335.74 | 4,708.64 | 5,900.37 | 6,451.45 | 7,015.53 |
| Liabilities to Central Government. | 36d | 1,218.04 | 1,488.98 | 2,089.93 | 2,591.18 | † 2,532.73 | 2,737.40 | 2,724.35 | 1,864.49 | 2,673.51 | 3,345.81 | 2,799.83 | 2,131.13 |
| Claims on Other Sectors................. | 32s | 1,312.72 | 1,654.27 | 2,310.14 | 3,151.21 | † 4,556.17 | 4,991.89 | 5,991.77 | 7,622.32 | 9,010.38 | 10,392.66 | 12,412.30 | 15,491.62 |
| Claims on Other Financial Corps.. | 32g | 21.65 | 28.84 | 23.96 | 32.07 | † 223.08 | 249.54 | 259.74 | 332.25 | 270.12 | 447.85 | 499.92 | 596.41 |
| Claims on State & Local Govts..... | 32b | — | — | — | — | † 3.29 | 4.65 | 9.16 | 23.01 | 33.68 | 29.38 | 83.11 | 48.83 |
| Claims on Public Nonfin. Corps.... | 32c | — | — | .46 | .05 | † 345.48 | 411.36 | 487.15 | 598.32 | 718.30 | 766.04 | 839.93 | 1,059.72 |
| Claims on Private Sector............. | 32d | 1,291.08 | 1,625.44 | 2,285.72 | 3,119.09 | † 3,984.32 | 4,326.35 | 5,235.71 | 6,668.74 | 7,988.29 | 9,149.39 | 10,989.34 | 13,786.67 |
| Broad Money Liabilities................... | 35l | 3,153.78 | 4,250.73 | 5,164.46 | 6,223.59 | † 7,458.78 | 8,780.14 | 11,012.66 | 13,021.32 | 14,663.55 | 16,106.77 | 18,614.15 | 22,114.62 |
| Currency Outside Depository Corps | 34a | 694.54 | 889.99 | 1,033.99 | 1,162.51 | † 1,438.64 | 1,566.75 | 1,897.13 | 2,235.83 | 2,414.79 | 2,763.96 | 3,244.72 | 3,678.50 |
| Transferable Deposits................... | 34 | 1,170.11 | 1,579.48 | 1,884.85 | 2,418.27 | † 2,851.11 | 3,288.92 | 4,400.03 | 5,565.55 | 6,453.06 | 6,884.07 | 7,657.78 | 9,501.06 |
| Other Deposits............................. | 35 | 1,289.13 | 1,781.26 | 2,245.62 | 2,642.80 | † 3,169.03 | 3,924.47 | 4,715.50 | 5,219.94 | 5,795.70 | 6,458.74 | 7,711.64 | 8,935.07 |
| Securities Other than Shares.......... | 36a | — | — | — | — | † — | | | | | | | |
| Deposits Excl. from Broad Money..... | 36b | — | — | — | .06 | † .10 | .01 | .01 | .01 | .02 | .05 | 8.59 | 4.55 |
| Sec.Ot.th.Shares Excl.f/Brd.Money.... | 36s | 49.76 | 7.05 | 6.43 | 8.04 | † 2.12 | 8.20 | 17.14 | 24.78 | 24.80 | 22.43 | 75.09 | 220.14 |
| Loans............................................. | 36l | — | — | — | — | † 93.29 | 39.32 | 126.39 | 161.25 | 238.77 | 459.48 | 498.06 | 835.47 |
| Financial Derivatives...................... | 36m | — | — | — | — | † — | — | — | — | — | — | — | — |
| Insurance Technical Reserves.......... | 36r | — | — | — | — | † — | — | — | — | — | — | — | — |
| Shares and Other Equity................. | 37a | 728.43 | 788.47 | 1,231.88 | 1,018.66 | † 1,502.81 | 2,051.24 | 2,615.10 | 2,937.50 | 3,377.99 | 3,541.20 | 4,173.43 | 5,930.03 |
| Other Items (Net)........................... | 37r | −393.93 | −533.58 | −761.45 | −744.14 | † −759.75 | −827.87 | −886.09 | −754.91 | −888.54 | −610.27 | −743.37 | −522.19 |
| Broad Money Liabs., Seasonally Adj. | 35l.b | 3,133.70 | 4,230.93 | 5,147.15 | 6,205.58 | † 7,424.21 | 8,739.85 | 10,966.57 | 12,979.66 | 14,640.52 | 16,103.96 | 18,630.37 | 22,144.93 |
| **Monetary Aggregates** | | | | | | *Billions of Shillings: End of Period* | | | | | | | |
| Broad Money............................... | 59m | 3,153.78 | 4,250.73 | 5,164.46 | 6,223.59 | 7,458.78 | 8,780.14 | 11,012.66 | 13,021.32 | 14,663.55 | 16,106.77 | 18,614.15 | 22,114.62 |
| o/w:Currency Issued by Cent.Govt | 59m.a | — | — | — | — | — | — | — | — | — | — | — | — |
| o/w: Dep.in Nonfin. Corporations. | 59m.b | — | — | — | — | — | — | — | — | — | — | — | — |
| o/w:Secs. Issued by Central Govt.. | 59m.c | — | — | — | — | — | — | — | — | — | — | — | — |
| Money (National Definitions) | | | | | | | | | | | | | |
| M0..................................................... | 19mc | 999.99 | 1,284.69 | 1,504.12 | 1,879.05 | 2,276.44 | 3,009.06 | 3,497.85 | 4,111.92 | 4,525.59 | 5,027.78 | 5,909.48 | 6,833.09 |
| M1..................................................... | 59ma | 1,289.13 | 1,781.26 | 2,245.62 | 2,642.80 | 3,169.03 | 3,924.47 | 4,715.50 | 5,571.99 | 6,538.56 | 7,218.14 | 8,284.16 | 9,575.69 |
| M2..................................................... | 59mb | 1,864.65 | 2,469.47 | 2,918.83 | 3,580.79 | 4,289.75 | 4,855.67 | 6,297.09 | 9,247.94 | 10,724.56 | 11,890.80 | 13,917.04 | 15,779.42 |
| M3..................................................... | 59mc | 3,153.78 | 4,250.73 | 5,164.46 | 6,223.59 | 7,458.78 | 8,780.14 | 11,012.66 | 13,021.32 | 14,663.55 | 16,106.77 | 18,614.15 | 22,114.62 |
| **Interest Rates** | | | | | | *Percent Per Annum* | | | | | | | |
| Discount Rate (End of Period).......... | 60.a | 14.42 | 19.33 | 20.07 | † 16.40 | 15.99 | 3.70 | 7.58 | 12.00 | 12.00 | 16.00 | 16.00 | 16.00 |
| Treasury Bill Rate............................ | 60c | 8.35 | 10.67 | 11.64 | 13.38 | 8.11 | 7.14 | 3.87 | 6.37 | 12.71 | 12.34 | 12.08 | 8.80 |
| Savings Rate.................................... | 60k | 2.44 | 2.61 | 2.61 | 2.58 | 2.69 | 2.70 | 2.70 | 2.55 | 2.90 | 3.03 | 3.16 | 3.50 |
| Deposit Rate.................................... | 60l | 4.20 | 4.73 | 6.73 | 8.68 | 8.25 | 7.97 | 6.57 | 6.78 | 9.51 | 9.82 | 9.86 | 9.90 |
| Lending Rate................................... | 60p | 14.14 | 15.25 | 15.65 | 16.07 | 14.98 | 15.03 | 14.55 | 14.96 | 15.46 | 15.83 | 16.26 | 16.10 |
| **Prices and Production** | | | | | | *Index Numbers (2010=100): Period Averages* | | | | | | | |
| Consumer Prices.............................. | 64 | 63.2 | 66.3 | 71.1 | 76.1 | 84.0 | † 94.2 | 100.0 | 112.7 | 130.7 | 141.0 | 149.7 | † 158.0 |
| Manufacturing Prod. (2005=100)...... | 66ey | 116.5 | 100.0 | .... | .... | .... | .... | .... | .... | .... | .... | .... | .... |
| **Intl. Transactions & Positions** | | | | | | *Millions of Shillings* | | | | | | | |
| Exports............................................. | 70 | 1,597,579 | 1,896,767 | 2,176,987 | 2,510,567 | 3,201,863 | 3,124,061 | 4,988,839 | 6,915,017 | 8,033,236 | .... | .... | .... |
| Imports, c.i.f..................................... | 71 | 2,964,040 | 3,726,104 | 5,335,331 | 6,621,421 | 8,470,083 | 8,309,961 | 10,877,875 | 16,904,699 | 17,832,233 | .... | .... | .... |

# Tanzania 738

| | | 2004 | 2005 | 2006 | 2007 | 2008 | 2009 | 2010 | 2011 | 2012 | 2013 | 2014 | 2015 |
|---|---|---|---|---|---|---|---|---|---|---|---|---|---|
| **Balance of Payments** | | | | | | | *Millions of US Dollars* | | | | | | |
| A. Current Account* | 109bx | −1,065.1 | −1,570.4 | −1,661.8 | −2,341.6 | −3,165.6 | −2,468.3 † −2,210.8 | | −4,381.0 | −3,764.3 | −4,988.0 | −5,017.5 | −3,312.3 |
| Goods, credit (exports) | 1a9cx | 1,481.6 | 1,702.5 | 1,917.6 | 2,226.6 | 3,578.8 | 3,298.1 † 4,324.3 | | 5,097.9 | 5,889.2 | 5,258.1 | 5,321.5 | 5,708.8 |
| Goods, debit (imports) | 1a9dx | 2,482.8 | 2,997.6 | 3,864.1 | 4,860.6 | 7,012.3 | 5,834.1 † 7,165.5 | | 9,827.5 | 10,319.1 | 11,029.1 | 10,917.8 | 9,843.1 |
| Balance on goods | 1a9bx | −1,001.2 | −1,295.1 | −1,946.5 | −2,634.1 | −3,433.5 | −2,536.1 † −2,841.2 | | −4,729.6 | −4,429.9 | −5,771.1 | −5,596.3 | −4,134.2 |
| Services, credit (exports) | 1b9cx | 1,133.6 | 1,269.2 | 1,528.1 | 1,875.7 | 1,998.8 | 1,854.6 † 2,045.7 | | 2,300.3 | 2,786.4 | 3,201.7 | 3,396.0 | 3,748.4 |
| Services, debit (imports) | 1b9dx | 974.7 | 1,207.3 | 1,249.3 | 1,413.7 | 1,661.9 | 1,722.0 † 1,888.9 | | 2,208.1 | 2,358.9 | 2,488.5 | 2,668.7 | 2,685.1 |
| Balance on Goods & Services | 1z9bx | −842.3 | −1,233.2 | −1,667.8 | −2,172.0 | −3,096.6 | −2,403.4 † −2,684.4 | | −4,637.3 | −4,002.4 | −5,057.9 | −4,869.0 | −3,071.0 |
| Primary income: credit | 1c9cx | 81.8 | 80.9 | 80.3 | 107.3 | 122.7 | 161.1 † 160.1 | | 184.2 | 131.1 | 130.1 | 118.4 | 108.7 |
| Primary income: debit | 1c9dx | 311.7 | 436.0 | 103.3 | 389.4 | 437.0 | 458.9 † 737.6 | | 830.0 | 705.1 | 835.8 | 744.2 | 834.5 |
| Balance on gds, serv. & prim. inc. | 1y9bx | −1,072.2 | −1,588.3 | −1,690.7 | −2,454.1 | −3,410.9 | −2,701.1 † −3,261.9 | | −5,283.1 | −4,576.4 | −5,763.6 | −5,494.9 | −3,796.8 |
| Secondary income: credit | 1d9ca | 72.1 | 85.4 | 94.9 | 185.0 | 324.9 | 301.3 † 1,130.2 | | 994.9 | 917.5 | 837.4 | 535.6 | 564.3 |
| Secondary income: debit | 1d9da | 65.0 | 67.5 | 65.9 | 72.5 | 79.6 | 68.4 † 79.0 | | 92.7 | 105.4 | 61.8 | 58.2 | 79.8 |
| B. Capital Account* | 209ba | 459.9 | 393.2 | 5,217.7 | 938.5 | 524.2 | 442.2 † 537.9 | | 690.9 | 777.2 | 712.8 | 535.5 | 421.2 |
| Capital account: credit | 209ca | 459.9 | 393.2 | 5,217.7 | 938.5 | 524.2 | 442.2 † 537.9 | | 690.9 | 777.2 | 712.8 | 535.5 | 421.2 |
| Capital account: debit | 209da | — | — | — | — | — | — | . . . . | . . . . | . . . . | . . . . | . . . . | . . . . |
| Balance on current & capital acct. | 129ba | −605.2 | −1,177.3 | 3,555.9 | −1,403.1 | −2,641.4 | −2,026.1 † −1,672.8 | | −3,690.0 | −2,987.1 | −4,275.2 | −4,482.0 | −2,891.1 |
| C. Financial Account* | 309na | −566.2 | −1,422.3 | −930.2 | −1,392.0 | −2,589.9 | −1,981.2 † −3,060.5 | | −2,843.1 | −3,879.6 | −5,021.0 | −3,897.9 | −3,596.2 |
| Direct investment: assets | 3a9aa | — | — | — | — | — | — | . . . . | . . . . | . . . . | . . . . | . . . . | . . . . |
| Equity & investment fund shares | 3aaaa | — | — | — | — | — | — | . . . . | . . . . | . . . . | . . . . | . . . . | . . . . |
| Debt instruments | 3abaa | — | — | — | — | — | — | . . . . | . . . . | . . . . | . . . . | . . . . | . . . . |
| Direct investment: liabilities | 3a9la | 442.5 | 935.5 | 403.0 | 581.5 | 1,383.3 | 952.6 † 1,813.2 | | 1,229.4 | 1,799.6 | 2,087.3 | 2,044.6 | 1,960.6 |
| Equity & investment fund shares | 3aala | 226.7 | 438.7 | −21.5 | 274.8 | 397.6 | 664.4 † 1,038.2 | | 999.0 | 1,399.0 | 912.5 | 976.4 | 1,017.3 |
| Debt instruments | 3abla | 215.8 | 496.8 | 424.5 | 306.7 | 985.7 | 288.2 † 775.0 | | 230.4 | 400.6 | 1,174.8 | 1,068.1 | 943.3 |
| Portfolio investment: assets | 3b9aa | .1 | −.7 | −.1 | −1.6 | 1.2 | −.4 † .2 | | .7 | −2.5 | 3.3 | 2.4 | −3.8 |
| Equity & investment fund shares | 3baaa | — | — | — | — | — | — † .1 | | — | .2 | — | — | — |
| Debt securities | 3bbaa | .1 | −.7 | −.1 | −1.6 | 1.2 | −.4 † .1 | | .7 | −2.5 | 3.2 | 2.4 | −3.8 |
| Portfolio investment: liabilities | 3b9la | 2.4 | 2.5 | 2.6 | 2.8 | 3.0 | 3.1 † .1 | | 12.0 | 3.6 | 7.8 | 13.9 | 23.8 |
| Equity & investment fund shares | 3bala | 2.4 | 2.5 | 2.6 | 2.8 | 2.9 | 3.0 † 3.2 | | 3.4 | 3.5 | 3.5 | 3.7 | 3.9 |
| Debt instruments | 3bbla | — | — | — | — | .1 | — † −3.1 | | 8.7 | .1 | 4.3 | 10.2 | 20.0 |
| Fin. der.& empl.stk.ops.(ESOs): net | 3c9na | — | — | — | — | — | — | . . . . | . . . . | . . . . | . . . . | . . . . | . . . . |
| Fin. der. & ESOs.: assets | 3c9aa | — | — | — | — | — | — | . . . . | . . . . | . . . . | . . . . | . . . . | . . . . |
| Fin. der. & ESOs.: liabilities | 3c9la | — | — | — | — | — | — | . . . . | . . . . | . . . . | . . . . | . . . . | . . . . |
| Other investment: assets | 3d9aa | −61.2 | −73.8 | 117.5 | −56.7 | −178.6 | 363.3 † 142.0 | | 24.5 | −220.6 | 186.4 | −29.4 | 283.9 |
| Other equity | 3daaa | . . . . | . . . . | . . . . | . . . . | . . . . | . . . . | . . . . | . . . . | . . . . | . . . . | . . . . | . . . . |
| Debt instruments | 3dzaa | −61.2 | −73.8 | 117.5 | −56.7 | −178.6 | 363.3 † 142.0 | | 24.5 | −220.6 | 186.4 | −29.4 | 283.9 |
| Other investment: liabilities | 3d9la | 60.1 | 409.8 | 641.9 | 749.5 | 1,026.3 | 1,388.4 † 1,389.3 | | 1,627.0 | 1,853.4 | 3,115.7 | 1,812.4 | 1,891.9 |
| Other equity | 3dala | . . . . | . . . . | . . . . | . . . . | . . . . | . . . . | . . . . | . . . . | . . . . | . . . . | . . . . | . . . . |
| Debt instruments | 3dzla | 60.1 | 409.8 | 641.9 | 749.5 | 1,026.3 | 1,388.4 † 1,389.3 | | 1,627.0 | 1,853.4 | 3,115.7 | 1,812.4 | 1,891.9 |
| Curr.+ cap.− finan. acct. balance | 4y9na | −39.0 | 245.0 | 4,486.1 | −11.1 | −51.5 | −44.9 † 1,387.7 | | −846.9 | 892.5 | 745.8 | −584.1 | 705.1 |
| D. Net Errors and Omissions | 409na | −94.3 | −839.7 | 377.0 | 322.7 | −428.8 | −241.4 † −1,038.8 | | 686.8 | −597.4 | −222.9 | 327.5 | −936.3 |
| E. Reserves and Related Items | 4z9na | −133.3 | −594.7 | 4,863.1 | 311.7 | −480.2 | −286.4 † 348.9 | | −160.1 | 295.1 | 522.9 | −256.6 | −231.2 |
| Reserve assets | 3e9aa | 307.5 | −251.9 | 126.5 | 419.7 | 108.3 | 680.8 † 377.7 | | −162.3 | 292.1 | 633.5 | −283.2 | −292.2 |
| Credit and loans from the IMF | 3dcla | −32.6 | −48.1 | −334.6 | 4.2 | — | 308.8 † 28.8 | | −2.2 | −3.0 | 110.5 | −26.6 | −61.0 |
| Exceptional financing | 409la | 473.4 | 390.9 | −4,402.0 | 103.9 | 588.5 | 658.4 | . . . . | . . . . | . . . . | . . . . | . . . . | . . . . |

*Excludes components in group E

| **International Investment Position** | | | | | | | *Millions of US Dollars* | | | | | | |
|---|---|---|---|---|---|---|---|---|---|---|---|---|---|
| Assets | 809aa | 3,543.1 | 3,560.7 | 3,809.8 | 4,397.4 | 4,237.3 | 5,317.8 | 5,821.0 | 5,667.1 | 5,751.2 | 6,481.8 | 6,139.1 | 5,988.6 |
| Direct investment | 8a9aa | — | — | — | — | — | — | — | — | — | — | — | — |
| Equity & investment fund shares | 8aaaa | — | — | — | — | — | — | — | — | — | — | — | — |
| Debt instruments | 8abaa | — | — | — | — | — | — | — | — | — | — | — | — |
| Portfolio investment | 8b9aa | 1.3 | 2.1 | 2.2 | 3.8 | 2.0 | 2.9 | 3.0 | 3.7 | 1.2 | 4.4 | 6.8 | 3.0 |
| Equity & investment fund shares | 8baaa | — | — | — | — | — | — | — | — | — | — | — | — |
| Debt securities | 8bbaa | 1.3 | 2.1 | 2.2 | 3.8 | 2.0 | 2.9 | 3.0 | 3.7 | 1.2 | 4.4 | 6.8 | 3.0 |
| Fin. der.(oth.than reserves) & ESOs | 8c9aa | — | — | — | — | — | — | — | — | — | — | — | — |
| Other investment | 8d9aa | 1,234.8 | 1,508.1 | 1,673.6 | 1,639.9 | 1,372.4 | 1,766.7 | 1,896.7 | 1,902.2 | 1,697.7 | 1,803.7 | 1,748.8 | 1,912.6 |
| Other equity | 8daaa | . . . . | . . . . | . . . . | . . . . | . . . . | . . . . | . . . . | . . . . | . . . . | . . . . | . . . . | . . . . |
| Debt instruments | 8dzaa | 1,234.8 | 1,508.1 | 1,673.6 | 1,639.9 | 1,372.4 | 1,766.7 | 1,896.7 | 1,902.2 | 1,697.7 | 1,803.7 | 1,748.8 | 1,912.6 |
| Reserve assets | 8e9aa | 2,306.9 | 2,050.6 | 2,134.1 | 2,753.7 | 2,862.9 | 3,548.2 | 3,921.2 | 3,761.2 | 4,052.4 | 4,673.7 | 4,383.6 | 4,072.9 |
| Liabilities | 809la | 11,616.0 | 11,960.5 | 8,565.9 | 10,767.3 | 12,392.7 | 14,892.0 | 17,467.1 | 19,473.4 | 23,257.8 | 27,744.4 | 31,506.6 | 35,502.0 |
| Direct investment | 8a9la | 3,954.3 | 4,438.8 | 4,827.2 | 5,950.1 | 6,945.6 | 7,898.6 | 9,712.0 | 10,941.4 | 12,740.9 | 14,871.8 | 16,916.3 | 18,876.9 |
| Equity & investment fund shares | 8aala | 2,582.5 | 3,102.5 | 3,170.5 | 4,100.4 | 3,549.5 | 4,214.4 | 5,252.7 | 6,805.4 | 8,622.8 | 9,567.5 | 10,543.9 | 11,561.2 |
| Debt instruments | 8abla | 1,371.8 | 1,336.3 | 1,656.7 | 1,849.7 | 3,396.1 | 3,684.2 | 4,459.3 | 4,136.0 | 4,118.1 | 5,304.3 | 6,372.4 | 7,315.7 |
| Portfolio investment | 8b9la | 53.1 | 20.8 | 42.4 | 62.2 | 20.1 | 22.0 | 19.2 | 27.1 | 21.6 | 29.4 | 53.7 | 93.3 |
| Equity & investment fund shares | 8bala | 44.4 | 13.6 | 25.0 | 30.8 | 11.0 | 12.5 | 12.7 | 12.0 | 6.4 | 9.9 | 23.9 | 43.6 |
| Debt securities | 8bbla | 8.6 | 7.2 | 17.4 | 31.4 | 9.1 | 9.5 | 6.5 | 15.1 | 15.2 | 19.4 | 29.7 | 49.7 |
| Fin. der.(oth.than reserves) & ESOs | 8c9la | — | — | — | — | — | — | — | — | — | — | — | — |
| Other investment | 8d9la | 7,608.6 | 7,500.9 | 3,696.3 | 4,755.0 | 5,427.0 | 6,971.3 | 7,735.9 | 8,504.8 | 10,495.3 | 12,843.2 | 14,536.6 | 16,531.9 |
| Other equity | 8dala | . . . . | . . . . | . . . . | . . . . | . . . . | . . . . | . . . . | . . . . | . . . . | . . . . | . . . . | . . . . |
| Debt instruments | 8dzla | 7,608.6 | 7,500.9 | 3,696.3 | 4,755.0 | 5,427.0 | 6,971.3 | 7,735.9 | 8,504.8 | 10,495.3 | 12,843.2 | 14,536.6 | 16,531.9 |

# Tanzania 738

| | | 2004 | 2005 | 2006 | 2007 | 2008 | 2009 | 2010 | 2011 | 2012 | 2013 | 2014 | 2015 |
|---|---|---|---|---|---|---|---|---|---|---|---|---|---|
| **Government Finance** | | | | | | | | | | | | | |
| **Cash Flow Statement** | | | | | | | | | | | | | |
| **Budgetary Central Government** | | | | | | *Billions of Shillings: Fiscal Year Ends June 30* | | | | | | | |
| Cash Receipts:Operating Activities... | c1 | 2,150.82 | 2,735.98 | 3,078.00 | 3,697.04 | 5,207.78 | 5,550.36 | 6,054.56 | 9,120.87 | 11,424.73 | 11,581.94 | 13,417.51 | .... |
| Taxes............................. | c11 | .... | .... | .... | .... | .... | 4,428.79 | 5,286.42 | 6,501.71 | 7,824.56 | 9,386.88 | 9,899.60 | .... |
| Social Contributions...................... | c12 | .... | .... | .... | .... | .... | — | — | — | — | — | — | .... |
| Grants................................. | c13 | .... | .... | .... | .... | .... | 2,393.26 | 2,322.86 | 2,064.24 | 3,132.45 | 1,472.99 | 2,677.61 | .... |
| Other Receipts............................. | c14 | .... | .... | .... | .... | .... | 216.43 | 284.00 | 554.92 | 467.72 | 722.07 | 840.30 | .... |
| Cash Payments:Operating Activities. | c2 | 2,521.88 | 3,275.56 | 3,914.91 | 4,473.97 | 5,209.00 | 6,811.83 | 8,378.71 | 8,735.77 | 10,823.30 | 13,282.17 | 14,029.82 | .... |
| Compensation of Employees.......... | c21 | .... | .... | .... | .... | .... | 1,159.73 | 1,563.17 | 1,854.90 | 2,228.48 | 2,611.25 | 2,991.90 | .... |
| Purchases of Goods & Services....... | c22 | .... | .... | .... | .... | .... | 866.63 | 1,785.32 | 1,972.15 | 1,929.81 | 2,494.70 | 2,368.83 | .... |
| Interest................................ | c24 | .... | .... | .... | .... | .... | 313.99 | 346.74 | 442.66 | 731.36 | 976.94 | 1,263.78 | .... |
| Subsidies................................. | c25 | .... | .... | .... | .... | .... | — | 2.00 | 1.50 | 1.10 | .97 | 173.83 | .... |
| Grants................................... | c26 | .... | .... | .... | .... | .... | 3,239.82 | 3,804.41 | 4,154.38 | 5,582.96 | 6,720.25 | 6,698.19 | .... |
| Social Benefits.............................. | c27 | .... | .... | .... | .... | .... | 172.54 | 119.29 | 144.71 | 170.40 | 273.01 | 280.38 | .... |
| Other Payments............................ | c28 | .... | .... | .... | .... | .... | 141.95 | 138.71 | 165.48 | 179.18 | 205.06 | 252.92 | .... |
| Net Cash Inflow:Operating Act.[1-2] | ccio | .... | .... | .... | .... | .... | 1,143.82 | 133.63 | 385.10 | 601.42 | -1,700.23 | -612.31 | .... |
| Net Cash Outflow:Invest. in NFA...... | c31 | .... | .... | .... | .... | .... | 1,133.16 | 945.32 | 1,905.72 | 1,498.09 | 588.10 | 390.78 | .... |
| Purchases of Nonfinancial Assets... | c31.1 | .... | .... | .... | .... | .... | 1,133.16 | 945.32 | 1,924.38 | 1,516.35 | .... | .... | .... |
| Sales of Nonfinancial Assets.......... | c31.2 | .... | .... | .... | .... | .... | — | — | — | — | .... | .... | .... |
| Cash Surplus/Deficit [1-2-31=1-2M] | ccsd | -371.06 | -539.58 | -836.92 | -776.93 | -1.22 | -1,261.47 | -2,324.15 | -1,520.62 | -896.67 | -2,288.33 | -1,003.09 | .... |
| Net Acq. Fin. Assets, excl. Cash...... | c32x | .... | .... | .... | .... | .... | -200.55 | 225.25 | 346.44 | 651.92 | .... | .... | .... |
| Domestic................................ | c321x | .... | .... | .... | .... | .... | -194.05 | 205.92 | 336.60 | 574.67 | .... | .... | .... |
| Foreign................................. | c322x | .... | .... | .... | .... | .... | -6.49 | 19.33 | 9.84 | 77.26 | .... | .... | .... |
| Net Incurrence of Liabilities.............. | c33 | 358.82 | 710.41 | 924.41 | 950.38 | 378.41 | 1,202.88 | 2,032.04 | 2,065.36 | 3,630.59 | 3,263.10 | 5,069.84 | .... |
| Domestic................................ | c331 | -39.34 | 144.95 | 363.19 | 238.01 | -351.20 | 258.67 | 567.02 | 369.61 | 717.46 | 847.61 | 1,693.90 | .... |
| Foreign................................. | c332 | 398.16 | 565.46 | 561.22 | 712.37 | 729.61 | 944.20 | 1,465.02 | 1,695.75 | 2,913.12 | 2,415.49 | 3,375.94 | .... |
| Net Cash Inflow, Fin.Act.[-32x+33].. | cnfb | .... | .... | .... | .... | .... | 3,173.93 | 3,712.56 | 2,043.86 | 3,519.08 | 3,243.52 | 5,039.58 | .... |
| Net Change in Stock of Cash.......... | cncb | — | — | — | .... | .... | 3,184.60 | 2,900.87 | -11.47 | 579.68 | 149.37 | -516.18 | .... |
| Stat. Discrep. [32X-33+NCB-CSD]..... | ccsdz | 12.24 | -170.83 | -87.50 | -173.45 | -377.19 | 58.59 | 292.11 | -534.71 | -2,042.73 | -805.82 | -4,552.68 | .... |
| Memo Item:Cash Expenditure[2+31] | c2m | 2,521.88 | 3,275.56 | 3,914.91 | 4,473.97 | 5,209.00 | 6,811.83 | 8,378.71 | 10,641.49 | 12,321.39 | 13,870.27 | 14,420.59 | .... |
| Memo Item: Gross Debt.................. | c63 | .... | .... | .... | .... | .... | .... | .... | .... | .... | .... | .... | .... |
| **National Accounts** | | | | | | *Billions of Shillings* | | | | | | | |
| Housel.Cons.Expend.,incl.NPISHs.... | 96f | 9,352.7 | 10,581.9 | 12,195.2 | 16,426.0 | 20,936.0 | 24,959.0 | 28,652.0 | 34,587.0 | 40,817.0 | 48,815.0 | .... | .... |
| Government Consumption Expend... | 91f | 2,361.7 | 2,804.5 | 3,144.9 | 4,968.0 | 5,276.0 | 6,599.0 | 6,452.0 | 7,294.0 | 9,055.0 | 11,580.0 | .... | .... |
| Gross Fixed Capital Formation.......... | 93e | 3,095.5 | 3,936.7 | 4,883.5 | 8,428.0 | 10,919.0 | 10,893.0 | 12,345.0 | 16,993.0 | 18,806.0 | 20,962.0 | .... | .... |
| Changes in Inventories.................... | 93i | 57.8 | 64.4 | 74.3 | 366.0 | -521.0 | -1,405.0 | -607.0 | 214.0 | -1,276.0 | -300.0 | .... | .... |
| Exports of Goods and Services......... | 90c | 2,745.6 | 3,324.4 | 4,048.0 | 5,065.0 | 6,110.0 | 6,555.0 | 8,218.0 | 10,952.0 | 13,076.0 | 12,524.0 | .... | .... |
| Imports of Goods and Services (-)..... | 98c | 3,641.8 | 4,746.6 | 6,404.6 | 8,482.0 | 10,088.0 | 9,914.0 | 12,769.0 | 19,015.0 | 20,342.0 | 22,045.0 | .... | .... |
| GDP, Production Based.................. | 99bp | 13,971.6 | 15,965.3 | 17,941.3 | 20,948.4 | 24,781.7 | 28,212.6 | 32,293.5 | 37,533.0 | 44,717.7 | 53,174.7 | .... | .... |
| Statistical Discrepancy.................... | 99bs | — | — | — | — | — | — | — | — | — | — | .... | .... |
| Net Primary Income from Abroad..... | 98.n | -4,910.3 | -6,904.0 | -8,879.9 | -11,887.1 | -15,720.3 | -19,151.3 | -23,232.1 | -28,471.6 | -35,656.3 | -44,113.3 | .... | .... |
| Gross National Income (GNI)............ | 99a | .... | .... | .... | .... | .... | .... | .... | .... | .... | .... | .... | .... |
| Net National Income.................... | 99e | 12,413.0 | 14,148.1 | 16,020.9 | 18,798.6 | 22,338.1 | 25,639.8 | 29,518.7 | 34,354.7 | 40,926.2 | 49,439.1 | .... | .... |
| GDP Volume 2007 Prices................. | 99b.p | .... | .... | .... | 26,770.0 | 28,554.0 | 29,656.0 | 31,380.0 | 34,351.0 | 36,090.0 | 39,040.0 | .... | .... |
| GDP Volume (2010=100)............... | 99bvp | 69.5 | 74.6 | 79.6 | †85.3 | 91.0 | 94.5 | 100.0 | 109.5 | 115.0 | 124.4 | .... | .... |
| GDP Deflator (2010=100).............. | 99bip | 47.6 | 50.6 | 53.3 | 74.2 | 84.8 | 94.3 | 100.0 | 110.2 | 123.6 | 136.0 | .... | .... |
| | | | | | | *Millions: Midyear Estimates* | | | | | | | |
| **Population............................** | 99z | 37.94 | 39.07 | 40.26 | 41.52 | 42.84 | 44.22 | 45.65 | 47.12 | 48.65 | 50.21 | 51.82 | 53.47 |

# Thailand 578

| | | 2004 | 2005 | 2006 | 2007 | 2008 | 2009 | 2010 | 2011 | 2012 | 2013 | 2014 | 2015 |
|---|---|---|---|---|---|---|---|---|---|---|---|---|---|
| **Exchange Rates** | | | | | | *Baht per SDR: End of Period* | | | | | | | |
| Official Rate | aa | 60.662 | 58.643 | 54.227 | 53.284 | 53.752 | 52.235 | 46.434 | 48.655 | 47.078 | 50.533 | 47.757 | 50.009 |
| | | | | | | *Baht per US Dollar: End of Period (ae) Period Average (rf)* | | | | | | | |
| Official Rate | ae | 39.061 | 41.030 | 36.045 | 33.718 | 34.898 | 33.320 | 30.151 | 31.691 | 30.632 | 32.814 | 32.963 | 36.089 |
| Official Rate | rf | 40.222 | 40.220 | 37.882 | 34.518 | 33.313 | 34.286 | 31.686 | 30.492 | 31.083 | 30.726 | 32.480 | 34.248 |
| **Fund Position** | | | | | | *Millions of SDRs: End of Period* | | | | | | | |
| Quota | 2f.s | 1,081.90 | 1,081.90 | 1,081.90 | 1,081.90 | 1,081.90 | 1,081.90 | 1,081.90 | 1,440.50 | 1,440.50 | 1,440.50 | 1,440.50 | 1,440.50 |
| SDR Holdings | 1b.s | .66 | .43 | .57 | .12 | 85.23 | 971.48 | 972.00 | 973.32 | 973.82 | 974.14 | 974.59 | 974.78 |
| Reserve Position in the Fund | 1c.s | 106.56 | 131.59 | 95.36 | 70.27 | 137.97 | 230.07 | 245.07 | 452.83 | 471.71 | 523.18 | 536.41 | 450.51 |
| Total Fund Cred.&Loans Outstg | 2tl | — | — | — | — | — | — | — | — | — | — | — | — |
| SDR Allocations | 1bd | 84.65 | 84.65 | 84.65 | 84.65 | 84.65 | 970.27 | 970.27 | 970.27 | 970.27 | 970.27 | 970.27 | 970.27 |
| **International Liquidity** | | | | | *Millions of US Dollars Unless Otherwise Indicated: End of Period* | | | | | | | | |
| Total Reserves minus Gold | 1l.d | 48,664 | 50,691 | 65,291 | 85,221 | 108,661 | 135,483 | 167,530 | 167,389 | 173,328 | 161,328 | 151,253 | 151,266 |
| SDR Holdings | 1b.d | 1 | 1 | 1 | — | 131 | 1,523 | 1,497 | 1,494 | 1,497 | 1,500 | 1,412 | 1,351 |
| Reserve Position in the Fund | 1c.d | 165 | 188 | 143 | 111 | 213 | 361 | 377 | 695 | 725 | 806 | 777 | 624 |
| Foreign Exchange | 1d.d | 48,498 | 50,502 | 65,147 | 85,110 | 108,317 | 133,599 | 165,656 | 165,200 | 171,106 | 159,022 | 149,064 | 149,291 |
| Gold (Million Fine Troy Ounces) | 1ad | 2.700 | 2.700 | 2.700 | 2.700 | 2.700 | 2.700 | 3.200 | 4.900 | 4.900 | 4.900 | 4.900 | 4.900 |
| Gold (National Valuation) | 1and | 1,167 | 1,374 | 1,693 | 2,234 | 2,347 | 2,935 | 4,599 | 7,735 | 8,282 | 5,961 | 5,854 | 5,248 |
| Central Bank: Other Assets | 3..d | 940 | 7,608 | 5,509 | 5,113 | 51 | 60 | 70 | 90 | 689 | 789 | 780 | 862 |
| Central Bank: Other Liabs | 4..d | 1,044 | 8,102 | 6,624 | 6,245 | 525 | 964 | 2,312 | 3,675 | 6,918 | 3,383 | 1,770 | 475 |
| Other Depository Corps.: Assets | 7a.d | 14,509 | 16,308 | 26,162 | 28,183 | 17,820 | 14,711 | 16,240 | 23,349 | 24,661 | 31,025 | 32,945 | 38,965 |
| Other Depository Corps.: Liabs | 7b.d | 10,441 | 9,716 | 10,320 | 9,104 | 10,367 | 13,371 | 22,829 | 23,807 | 38,243 | 44,353 | 41,169 | 35,870 |
| Other Financial Corps.: Assets | 7e.d | .... | .... | .... | 11,365 | 10,519 | 20,982 | 18,408 | 17,862 | 31,388 | 30,983 | 38,880 | 37,616 |
| Other Financial Corps.: Liabs | 7f.d | .... | .... | .... | 293 | 498 | 744 | 3,453 | 4,033 | 7,068 | 10,019 | 11,985 | 11,053 |
| **Central Bank** | | | | | | *Billions of Baht: End of Period* | | | | | | | |
| Net Foreign Assets | 11n | 1,940.7 | 2,118.4 | 2,376.1 | 2,951.1 | 3,872.5 | 4,525.4 | 5,082.3 | 5,440.9 | 5,359.0 | 5,447.1 | 5,262.1 | 5,764.7 |
| Claims on Nonresidents | 11 | 1,986.6 | 2,455.8 | 2,619.4 | 3,166.2 | 3,895.4 | 4,608.2 | 5,196.9 | 5,604.6 | 5,616.6 | 5,607.1 | 5,366.8 | 5,830.3 |
| Liabilities to Nonresidents | 16c | 45.9 | 337.4 | 243.4 | 215.1 | 22.9 | 82.8 | 114.6 | 163.7 | 257.6 | 160.0 | 104.7 | 65.6 |
| Claims on Other Depository Corps. | 12e | 75.7 | 122.6 | 95.4 | 81.9 | 22.4 | 17.8 | 12.5 | — | 203.1 | 198.3 | 165.6 | 135.0 |
| Net Claims on Central Government | 12an | 57.0 | 84.4 | 7.8 | 114.4 | 169.9 | 78.7 | −105.7 | −117.6 | −163.5 | −237.6 | −201.5 | −380.9 |
| Claims on Central Government | 12a | 113.3 | 111.6 | 142.1 | 220.6 | 268.0 | 301.5 | 298.9 | 280.2 | 273.4 | 244.7 | 222.0 | 257.4 |
| Liabilities to Central Government | 16d | 56.3 | 27.2 | 134.3 | 106.2 | 98.1 | 222.8 | 404.6 | 397.7 | 436.8 | 482.3 | 423.5 | 638.3 |
| Claims on Other Sectors | 12s | 260.2 | 259.3 | 218.7 | 91.5 | 65.1 | 52.0 | — | .1 | — | .1 | — | 2.9 |
| Claims on Other Financial Corps. | 12g | 254.3 | 257.5 | 218.6 | 91.5 | 65.1 | 51.9 | — | — | — | — | — | — |
| Claims on State & Local Govts | 12b | — | — | — | — | — | — | — | — | — | — | — | — |
| Claims on Public Nonfin. Corps | 12c | 5.7 | 1.7 | — | — | — | — | — | — | — | — | — | — |
| Claims on Private Sector | 12d | .2 | .1 | .1 | — | — | — | — | .1 | — | .1 | — | 2.9 |
| Monetary Base | 14 | 776.7 | 816.0 | 834.0 | 899.2 | 1,002.2 | 1,064.0 | 1,201.2 | 1,319.5 | 1,447.8 | 1,528.1 | 1,611.5 | 1,651.3 |
| Currency in Circulation | 14a | 714.6 | 753.3 | 773.8 | 842.6 | 924.0 | 1,005.9 | 1,114.5 | 1,248.6 | 1,350.9 | 1,425.3 | 1,503.7 | 1,539.8 |
| Liabs. to Other Depository Corps. | 14c | 55.2 | 59.5 | 56.5 | 52.8 | 63.1 | 54.9 | 83.7 | 67.9 | 92.3 | 99.6 | 105.1 | 108.7 |
| Liabilities to Other Sectors | 14d | 6.9 | 3.3 | 3.7 | 3.8 | 15.1 | 3.1 | 2.9 | 3.1 | 4.6 | 3.2 | 2.7 | 2.7 |
| Other Liabs. to Other Dep. Corps | 14n | 553.4 | 547.3 | 775.0 | 914.7 | 1,531.2 | 1,989.0 | 2,295.6 | 2,473.2 | 2,735.1 | 2,777.5 | 2,878.8 | 2,743.8 |
| Dep. & Sec. Excl. f/Monetary Base | 14o | 51.6 | 310.8 | 375.4 | 703.6 | 681.9 | 831.2 | 1,178.4 | 947.1 | 931.5 | 716.5 | 649.0 | 824.0 |
| Deposits Included in Broad Money | 15 | — | — | — | — | — | — | — | — | — | — | — | — |
| Sec.Ot.th.Shares Incl.in Brd. Money | 16a | — | — | — | — | — | — | — | — | — | — | — | — |
| Deposits Excl. from Broad Money | 16b | — | — | — | — | — | — | — | 2.7 | .1 | — | .1 | 1.1 |
| Sec.Ot.th.Shares Excl.f/Brd.Money | 16s | 51.6 | 310.8 | 375.4 | 703.6 | 681.9 | 831.2 | 1,175.7 | 947.0 | 931.4 | 716.4 | 648.9 | 823.0 |
| Loans | 16l | 1.0 | .6 | 2.4 | 1.3 | 22.0 | 10.8 | — | — | — | — | — | — |
| Financial Derivatives | 16m | — | — | — | — | — | — | — | — | — | — | — | — |
| Shares and Other Equity | 17a | 955.0 | 906.0 | 718.3 | 718.5 | 898.1 | 781.8 | 312.7 | 589.6 | 299.0 | 427.4 | 79.9 | 314.4 |
| Other Items (Net) | 17r | −4.1 | 3.9 | −7.1 | 1.6 | −5.3 | −3.1 | 1.3 | −5.9 | −14.7 | −41.6 | 7.2 | −11.9 |
| Memo Item: | | | | | | | | | | | | | |
| Total Assets | 10ra | 2,504.1 | 3,015.5 | 3,140.6 | 3,627.2 | 4,320.1 | 5,093.0 | 5,633.5 | 6,122.8 | 6,171.7 | 6,157.3 | 5,817.4 | 6,306.7 |
| **Other Depository Corporations** | | | | | | *Billions of Baht: End of Period* | | | | | | | |
| Net Foreign Assets | 21n | 158.9 | 270.5 | 571.0 | 643.3 | 260.1 | 44.6 | −198.4 | −14.5 | −416.0 | −437.3 | −271.4 | 111.7 |
| Claims on Nonresidents | 21 | 566.7 | 669.1 | 943.0 | 950.3 | 621.9 | 490.2 | 488.8 | 740.0 | 755.4 | 1,018.1 | 1,086.0 | 1,406.2 |
| Liabilities to Nonresidents | 26c | 407.9 | 398.6 | 372.0 | 307.0 | 361.8 | 445.5 | 687.2 | 754.5 | 1,171.4 | 1,455.4 | 1,357.1 | 1,294.5 |
| Claims on Central Bank | 20 | 752.0 | 761.4 | 983.9 | 1,162.6 | 1,815.6 | 2,249.0 | 2,609.3 | 2,808.5 | 3,100.1 | 3,176.0 | 3,351.2 | 3,207.5 |
| Currency | 20a | 143.6 | 149.9 | 152.3 | 157.1 | 209.1 | 201.3 | 219.4 | 258.5 | 264.6 | 289.6 | 358.7 | 347.7 |
| Reserve Deposits and Securities | 20b | 51.9 | 59.3 | 58.0 | 52.3 | 62.4 | 54.7 | 220.6 | 100.7 | 106.2 | 117.0 | 140.4 | 139.3 |
| Other Claims | 20n | 556.5 | 552.2 | 773.5 | 953.2 | 1,544.1 | 1,993.0 | 2,169.3 | 2,449.3 | 2,729.3 | 2,769.5 | 2,852.1 | 2,720.4 |
| Net Claims on Central Government | 22an | 205.7 | 138.3 | 90.1 | 18.9 | 35.1 | 214.4 | 262.2 | 319.4 | 516.5 | 473.6 | 602.0 | 802.2 |
| Claims on Central Government | 22a | 660.1 | 658.2 | 656.9 | 610.1 | 650.9 | 825.3 | 896.4 | 910.0 | 1,220.1 | 1,244.7 | 1,469.0 | 1,702.2 |
| Liabilities to Central Government | 26d | 454.4 | 519.9 | 566.8 | 591.2 | 615.8 | 610.9 | 634.2 | 590.5 | 703.6 | 771.1 | 867.0 | 900.0 |
| Claims on Other Sectors | 22s | 7,558.4 | 7,971.3 | 8,231.0 | 8,660.2 | 9,298.9 | 9,670.4 | 10,859.9 | 12,577.6 | 14,366.9 | 15,653.8 | 16,377.4 | 17,135.3 |
| Claims on Other Financial Corps. | 22g | 581.5 | 494.9 | 446.7 | 482.4 | 455.0 | 572.9 | 668.4 | 698.5 | 845.9 | 891.8 | 902.9 | 954.8 |
| Claims on State & Local Govts | 22b | .8 | 1.8 | 2.6 | 3.5 | 5.1 | 5.6 | 18.3 | 18.4 | 22.3 | 24.8 | 22.1 | 18.9 |
| Claims on Public Nonfin. Corps | 22c | 359.7 | 330.2 | 313.0 | 348.1 | 324.9 | 366.2 | 372.2 | 392.2 | 353.9 | 334.2 | 322.0 | 290.6 |
| Claims on Private Sector | 22d | 6,616.4 | 7,144.5 | 7,468.7 | 7,826.2 | 8,513.8 | 8,725.7 | 9,801.1 | 11,468.5 | 13,144.8 | 14,403.0 | 15,130.5 | 15,870.9 |
| Liabilities to Central Bank | 26g | 79.2 | 124.9 | 96.4 | 82.8 | 23.3 | 17.9 | 12.6 | — | 204.5 | 199.9 | 166.9 | 135.8 |
| Transf.Dep.Included in Broad Money | 24 | 225.8 | 256.2 | 254.9 | 276.0 | 273.8 | 327.5 | 362.3 | 375.2 | 457.4 | 469.2 | 479.4 | 524.4 |
| Other Dep.Included in Broad Money | 25 | 6,592.0 | 6,946.3 | 7,458.0 | 7,582.9 | 8,283.1 | 8,726.8 | 9,486.4 | 10,570.3 | 13,001.7 | 14,227.9 | 14,835.0 | 15,576.6 |
| Sec.Ot.th.Shares Incl.in Brd. Money | 26a | 49.5 | 90.4 | 203.9 | 526.7 | 620.0 | 715.7 | 990.0 | 1,575.2 | 366.8 | 173.0 | 291.7 | 197.1 |
| Deposits Excl. from Broad Money | 26b | 2.4 | 2.0 | 2.2 | 2.8 | 2.9 | 5.1 | 2.8 | 5.9 | 9.0 | 9.6 | 7.2 | 7.2 |
| Sec.Ot.th.Shares Excl.f/Brd.Money | 26s | 166.0 | 106.0 | 310.1 | 245.5 | 259.6 | 250.2 | 247.3 | 271.2 | 478.0 | 545.2 | 571.3 | 590.1 |
| Loans | 26l | 145.7 | 200.5 | 87.6 | 104.4 | 137.8 | 197.0 | 172.1 | 256.0 | 98.6 | 81.9 | 82.7 | 81.7 |
| Financial Derivatives | 26m | — | — | — | — | — | — | — | — | — | — | — | — |
| Insurance Technical Reserves | 26r | — | — | — | — | — | — | — | — | — | — | — | — |
| Shares and Other Equity | 27a | 1,165.3 | 1,359.2 | 1,431.0 | 1,541.8 | 1,703.9 | 1,889.4 | 2,153.4 | 2,316.4 | 2,593.7 | 2,873.2 | 3,162.5 | 3,459.4 |
| Other Items (Net) | 27r | 248.9 | 56.2 | 31.8 | 122.0 | 105.3 | 48.9 | 106.2 | 320.7 | 357.8 | 286.1 | 462.9 | 684.2 |
| Memo Item: | | | | | | | | | | | | | |
| Total Assets | 20ra | 10,509.5 | 11,253.7 | 11,982.4 | 12,585.1 | 13,885.1 | 14,954.0 | 17,124.2 | 19,327.8 | 21,938.2 | 24,078.2 | 25,032.3 | 26,269.2 |

# Thailand 578

|  |  | 2004 | 2005 | 2006 | 2007 | 2008 | 2009 | 2010 | 2011 | 2012 | 2013 | 2014 | 2015 |
|---|---|---|---|---|---|---|---|---|---|---|---|---|---|
| **Depository Corporations** | | | | | | | *Billions of Baht: End of Period* | | | | | | |
| Net Foreign Assets | 31n | 2,099.6 | 2,388.9 | 2,947.1 | 3,594.4 | 4,132.6 | 4,570.0 | 4,884.0 | 5,426.4 | 4,943.0 | 5,009.7 | 4,991.0 | 5,876.3 |
| Claims on Nonresidents | 31 | 2,553.3 | 3,124.9 | 3,562.5 | 4,116.4 | 4,517.3 | 5,098.3 | 5,685.7 | 6,344.5 | 6,372.0 | 6,625.1 | 6,452.8 | 7,236.5 |
| Liabilities to Nonresidents | 36c | 453.8 | 736.0 | 615.4 | 522.1 | 384.7 | 528.3 | 801.8 | 918.2 | 1,429.0 | 1,615.4 | 1,461.7 | 1,360.2 |
| Domestic Claims | 32 | 8,081.3 | 8,453.4 | 8,547.6 | 8,885.0 | 9,569.0 | 10,015.5 | 11,016.4 | 12,779.5 | 14,719.9 | 15,889.9 | 16,778.0 | 17,559.5 |
| Net Claims on Central Government | 32an | 262.8 | 222.7 | 97.9 | 133.3 | 205.0 | 293.1 | 156.5 | 201.9 | 353.0 | 236.0 | 400.5 | 421.3 |
| Claims on Central Government | 32a | 773.4 | 769.8 | 799.0 | 830.7 | 918.9 | 1,126.9 | 1,195.3 | 1,190.1 | 1,493.5 | 1,489.3 | 1,691.0 | 1,959.6 |
| Liabilities to Central Government | 36d | 510.6 | 547.1 | 701.1 | 697.4 | 713.8 | 833.7 | 1,038.8 | 988.3 | 1,140.5 | 1,253.3 | 1,290.5 | 1,538.3 |
| Claims on Other Sectors | 32s | 7,818.5 | 8,230.6 | 8,449.7 | 8,751.7 | 9,364.0 | 9,722.4 | 10,859.9 | 12,577.6 | 14,366.9 | 15,653.9 | 16,377.4 | 17,138.2 |
| Claims on Other Financial Corps | 32g | 835.8 | 752.4 | 665.3 | 573.9 | 520.2 | 624.8 | 668.4 | 698.5 | 845.9 | 891.8 | 902.9 | 954.8 |
| Claims on State & Local Govts | 32b | .8 | 1.8 | 2.6 | 3.5 | 5.1 | 5.6 | 18.3 | 18.4 | 22.3 | 24.8 | 22.1 | 18.9 |
| Claims on Public Nonfin. Corps | 32c | 365.3 | 331.8 | 313.0 | 348.1 | 324.9 | 366.2 | 372.2 | 392.2 | 353.9 | 334.2 | 322.0 | 290.6 |
| Claims on Private Sector | 32d | 6,616.6 | 7,144.6 | 7,468.7 | 7,826.2 | 8,513.8 | 8,725.8 | 9,801.1 | 11,468.5 | 13,144.8 | 14,403.1 | 15,130.5 | 15,873.9 |
| Broad Money Liabilities | 35l | 7,445.3 | 7,899.5 | 8,542.0 | 9,074.9 | 9,906.6 | 10,577.6 | 11,736.7 | 13,513.9 | 14,916.8 | 16,009.0 | 16,753.8 | 17,492.9 |
| Currency Outside Depository Corps | 34a | 571.0 | 603.3 | 621.5 | 685.5 | 714.8 | 804.6 | 895.1 | 990.0 | 1,086.3 | 1,135.7 | 1,145.0 | 1,192.1 |
| Transferable Deposits | 34 | 232.7 | 259.5 | 258.6 | 279.8 | 288.9 | 330.6 | 365.2 | 378.3 | 462.0 | 472.4 | 482.1 | 527.1 |
| Other Deposits | 35 | 6,592.0 | 6,946.3 | 7,458.0 | 7,582.9 | 8,283.1 | 8,726.8 | 9,486.4 | 10,570.3 | 13,001.7 | 14,227.9 | 14,835.0 | 15,576.6 |
| Securities Other than Shares | 36a | 49.5 | 90.4 | 203.9 | 526.7 | 620.0 | 715.7 | 990.0 | 1,575.2 | 366.8 | 173.0 | 291.7 | 197.1 |
| Deposits Excl. from Broad Money | 36b | 2.4 | 2.0 | 2.2 | 2.8 | 2.9 | 5.1 | 5.5 | 6.0 | 9.0 | 9.7 | 7.3 | 8.3 |
| Sec.Ot.th.Shares Excl.f/Brd.Money | 36s | 217.5 | 416.8 | 685.5 | 949.1 | 941.5 | 1,081.5 | 1,423.0 | 1,218.2 | 1,409.4 | 1,261.6 | 1,220.2 | 1,413.1 |
| Loans | 36l | 146.7 | 201.1 | 90.0 | 105.7 | 159.8 | 207.8 | 172.1 | 256.0 | 98.6 | 81.9 | 82.7 | 81.7 |
| Financial Derivatives | 36m | — | — | — | — | — | — | — | — | — | — | — | — |
| Insurance Technical Reserves | 36r | — | — | — | — | — | — | — | — | — | — | — | — |
| Shares and Other Equity | 37a | 2,120.3 | 2,265.2 | 2,149.3 | 2,260.2 | 2,602.0 | 2,671.2 | 2,466.1 | 2,906.0 | 2,892.7 | 3,300.5 | 3,242.3 | 3,773.7 |
| Other Items (Net) | 37r | 248.6 | 57.6 | 25.7 | 86.5 | 88.6 | 42.3 | 97.0 | 305.8 | 336.4 | 236.8 | 462.7 | 666.0 |
| Broad Money Liabs., Seasonally Adj. | 35l.b | 7,465.1 | 7,927.8 | 8,569.9 | 9,083.9 | 9,878.6 | 10,514.3 | 11,644.8 | 13,405.7 | 14,799.7 | 15,882.5 | 16,619.6 | 17,350.3 |
| **Other Financial Corporations** | | | | | | | *Billions of Baht: End of Period* | | | | | | |
| Net Foreign Assets | 41n | .... | .... | .... | 373.3 | 349.7 | 674.3 | 450.2 | 438.2 | 745.0 | 687.9 | 886.5 | 958.6 |
| Claims on Nonresidents | 41 | .... | .... | .... | 383.2 | 367.1 | 699.1 | 554.1 | 566.1 | 961.5 | 1,016.7 | 1,281.6 | 1,357.5 |
| Liabilities to Nonresidents | 46c | .... | .... | .... | 9.9 | 17.4 | 24.8 | 103.9 | 127.8 | 216.5 | 328.8 | 395.1 | 398.9 |
| Claims on Depository Corporations | 40 | .... | .... | .... | 1,289.5 | 1,358.0 | 1,401.1 | 1,937.2 | 1,830.7 | 1,898.4 | 1,895.6 | 2,386.3 | 2,208.8 |
| Net Claims on Central Government | 42an | .... | .... | .... | 630.9 | 693.3 | 779.8 | 888.7 | 1,079.3 | 1,250.5 | 1,338.6 | 1,622.0 | 1,905.4 |
| Claims on Central Government | 42a | .... | .... | .... | 630.9 | 693.3 | 779.8 | 889.4 | 1,081.0 | 1,250.5 | 1,338.8 | 1,622.0 | 1,906.2 |
| Liabilities to Central Government | 46d | .... | .... | .... | — | — | — | .7 | 1.8 | — | .2 | — | .9 |
| Claims on Other Sectors | 42s | .... | .... | .... | 2,275.5 | 2,109.1 | 2,217.7 | 3,180.6 | 3,594.8 | 4,132.5 | 4,293.8 | 4,665.5 | 4,963.7 |
| Claims on State & Local Govts | 42b | .... | .... | .... | | | | | | .3 | | | |
| Claims on Public Nonfin. Corps | 42c | .... | .... | .... | 447.9 | 356.9 | 417.2 | 474.4 | 290.9 | 445.1 | 313.0 | 491.3 | 360.3 |
| Claims on Private Sector | 42d | .... | .... | .... | 1,827.6 | 1,752.2 | 1,800.6 | 2,706.3 | 3,303.9 | 3,687.1 | 3,980.8 | 4,174.1 | 4,603.3 |
| Deposits | 46b | .... | .... | .... | | | | | | | | | |
| Securities Other than Shares | 46s | .... | .... | .... | 207.3 | 188.3 | 125.2 | 140.4 | 101.5 | 141.0 | 146.9 | 191.3 | 146.0 |
| Loans | 46l | .... | .... | .... | 75.2 | 40.1 | 41.8 | 442.9 | 497.1 | 636.2 | 755.3 | 666.6 | 717.3 |
| Financial Derivatives | 46m | .... | .... | .... | .2 | 6.4 | 50.8 | 58.4 | 9.3 | 1.3 | 38.5 | 12.7 | 36.6 |
| Insurance Technical Reserves | 46r | .... | .... | .... | 1,468.3 | 1,578.3 | 1,780.8 | 2,021.7 | 2,654.6 | 2,734.2 | 2,785.8 | 3,117.9 | 3,326.3 |
| Shares and Other Equity | 47a | .... | .... | .... | 1,667.3 | 1,620.5 | 1,948.2 | 2,521.6 | 2,791.4 | 3,536.8 | 3,822.8 | 4,938.5 | 5,337.7 |
| Other Items (Net) | 47r | .... | .... | .... | 1,150.8 | 1,076.7 | 1,126.1 | 1,271.6 | 889.1 | 976.8 | 666.6 | 633.3 | 472.7 |
| Memo Item: | | | | | | | | | | | | | |
| Total Assets | 40ra | .... | .... | .... | 5,733.6 | 5,574.7 | 6,022.7 | 7,664.0 | 8,408.4 | 9,689.6 | 10,167.3 | 11,638.3 | 12,144.0 |
| **Financial Corporations** | | | | | | | *Billions of Baht: End of Period* | | | | | | |
| Net Foreign Assets | 51n | .... | .... | .... | 3,967.7 | 4,482.3 | 5,244.3 | 5,334.1 | 5,864.6 | 5,688.0 | 5,697.6 | 5,877.6 | 6,834.9 |
| Claims on Nonresidents | 51 | .... | .... | .... | 4,499.6 | 4,884.4 | 5,797.5 | 6,239.9 | 6,910.6 | 7,333.5 | 7,641.8 | 7,734.4 | 8,594.0 |
| Liabilities to Nonresidents | 56c | .... | .... | .... | 532.0 | 402.0 | 553.1 | 905.7 | 1,046.0 | 1,645.5 | 1,944.2 | 1,856.8 | 1,759.0 |
| Domestic Claims | 52 | .... | .... | .... | 11,217.5 | 11,851.2 | 12,388.2 | 14,417.4 | 16,755.1 | 19,256.9 | 20,630.5 | 22,162.6 | 23,473.7 |
| Net Claims on Central Government | 52an | .... | .... | .... | 764.2 | 898.3 | 1,072.9 | 1,045.2 | 1,281.1 | 1,603.5 | 1,574.6 | 2,022.5 | 2,326.7 |
| Claims on Central Government | 52a | .... | .... | .... | 1,461.7 | 1,612.1 | 1,906.6 | 2,084.7 | 2,271.2 | 2,743.9 | 2,828.2 | 3,313.0 | 3,865.9 |
| Liabilities to Central Government | 56d | .... | .... | .... | 697.4 | 713.8 | 833.7 | 1,039.6 | 990.0 | 1,140.5 | 1,253.5 | 1,290.5 | 1,539.2 |
| Claims on Other Sectors | 52s | .... | .... | .... | 10,453.3 | 10,952.9 | 11,315.3 | 13,372.2 | 15,474.0 | 17,653.5 | 19,055.9 | 20,140.1 | 21,147.1 |
| Claims on State & Local Govts | 52b | .... | .... | .... | 3.5 | 5.1 | 5.6 | 18.3 | 18.4 | 22.6 | 24.8 | 22.1 | 18.9 |
| Claims on Public Nonfin. Corps | 52c | .... | .... | .... | 796.0 | 681.8 | 783.4 | 846.5 | 683.2 | 799.0 | 647.2 | 813.3 | 650.9 |
| Claims on Private Sector | 52d | .... | .... | .... | 9,653.8 | 10,266.0 | 10,526.3 | 12,507.4 | 14,772.4 | 16,831.9 | 18,383.9 | 19,304.7 | 20,477.2 |
| Currency Outside Financial Corps | 54a | .... | .... | .... | 684.9 | 714.1 | 804.0 | 890.5 | 971.8 | 1,082.5 | 1,131.9 | 1,136.4 | 1,183.8 |
| Deposits | 55l | .... | .... | .... | 7,646.6 | 8,283.0 | 8,733.1 | 9,432.8 | 10,497.9 | 12,743.4 | 13,854.0 | 14,328.0 | 15,228.5 |
| Securities Other than Shares | 56a | .... | .... | .... | 837.6 | 955.8 | 1,129.8 | 1,419.4 | 1,532.9 | 811.2 | 536.6 | 610.5 | 507.2 |
| Loans | 56l | .... | .... | .... | 44.6 | 69.3 | 122.0 | 119.8 | 159.4 | 68.4 | 82.2 | 80.3 | 122.4 |
| Financial Derivatives | 56m | .... | .... | .... | — | — | — | — | — | — | — | — | .7 |
| Insurance Technical Reserves | 56r | .... | .... | .... | 1,468.3 | 1,578.3 | 1,780.8 | 2,021.7 | 2,654.6 | 2,734.2 | 2,785.8 | 3,117.9 | 3,326.3 |
| Shares and Other Equity | 57a | .... | .... | .... | 3,927.6 | 4,222.5 | 4,619.4 | 4,987.7 | 5,697.4 | 6,429.5 | 7,123.3 | 8,180.8 | 9,111.4 |
| Other Items (Net) | 57r | .... | .... | .... | 575.6 | 510.6 | 443.6 | 879.6 | 1,105.7 | 1,075.7 | 814.2 | 586.3 | 828.5 |
| **Monetary Aggregates** | | | | | | | *Billions of Baht: End of Period* | | | | | | |
| Broad Money | 59m | 7,472.9 | 7,928.0 | 8,574.5 | 9,110.6 | 9,945.5 | 10,618.3 | 11,780.1 | 13,560.9 | 14,967.6 | 16,063.3 | 16,810.4 | 17,552.8 |
| o/w:Currency Issued by Cent.Govt | 59m.a | 27.6 | 28.4 | 32.5 | 35.7 | 38.7 | 40.7 | 43.3 | 47.0 | 50.9 | 54.3 | 56.6 | 59.9 |
| o/w: Dep.in Nonfin. Corporations | 59m.b | — | — | — | — | — | — | — | — | — | — | — | — |
| o/w:Secs. Issued by Central Govt | 59m.c | — | — | — | — | — | — | — | — | — | — | — | — |
| Money (National Definitions) | | | | | | | | | | | | | |
| Narrow Money | 59mak | 829.9 | 890.2 | 911.5 | 999.9 | 1,041.2 | 1,174.6 | 1,302.4 | 1,414.3 | 1,598.3 | 1,661.3 | 1,681.3 | 1,778.1 |
| Broad Money | 59mea | 7,471.4 | 7,926.9 | 8,573.4 | 9,109.5 | 9,948.7 | 10,617.0 | 11,778.8 | 13,559.9 | 14,966.8 | 16,062.2 | 16,808.0 | 17,551.7 |
| **Interest Rates** | | | | | | | *Percent Per Annum* | | | | | | |
| Central Bank Policy Rate (EOP) | 60 | 2.00 | 4.00 | 5.00 | 3.25 | 2.75 | 1.25 | 2.00 | 3.25 | 2.75 | 2.25 | 2.00 | 1.50 |
| Discount Rate (End of Period) | 60.a | 3.50 | 5.50 | 6.50 | 3.75 | 3.25 | 1.75 | 2.50 | 3.75 | 3.25 | 2.75 | 2.50 | 2.00 |
| Money Market Rate | 60b | 1.23 | 2.62 | 4.64 | 3.75 | 3.28 | 1.21 | 1.25 | 2.80 | 2.89 | 2.54 | 2.00 | 1.59 |
| Treasury Bill Rate | 60c | 1.30 | 2.67 | 4.66 | 3.48 | 3.19 | 1.24 | 1.44 | 2.87 | 2.97 | 2.57 | 2.07 | 1.61 |
| Savings Rate | 60k | .75 | .94 | 4.15 | 1.54 | .75 | .54 | .50 | .80 | .76 | .74 | .77 | .75 |
| Deposit Rate | 60l | 1.00 | 1.88 | 4.44 | 2.88 | 2.48 | 1.04 | 1.01 | 2.28 | 2.80 | 2.88 | 1.96 | 1.42 |
| Lending Rate | 60p | 5.50 | 5.79 | 7.35 | 7.05 | 7.04 | 5.96 | 5.94 | 6.91 | 7.10 | 6.96 | 6.77 | 6.56 |
| Government Bond Yield | 61 | 4.86 | 5.00 | 5.39 | 4.60 | 4.56 | 3.91 | 3.60 | 3.69 | 3.53 | 3.80 | 3.57 | 2.73 |

# Thailand 578

| | | 2004 | 2005 | 2006 | 2007 | 2008 | 2009 | 2010 | 2011 | 2012 | 2013 | 2014 | 2015 |
|---|---|---|---|---|---|---|---|---|---|---|---|---|---|
| **Prices and Labor** | | | | | | *Index Numbers (2010=100): Period Averages* | | | | | | | |
| Share Prices | 62 | 78.4 | 81.7 | 85.0 | 90.6 | 81.2 | 68.7 | 100.0 | 121.3 | 142.3 | 172.6 | 172.3 | 172.6 |
| Producer Prices | 63 | 70.1 | 76.5 | † 81.9 | 84.5 | 95.0 | 91.4 | † 100.0 | 105.5 | 106.6 | 106.9 | 107.0 | 102.6 |
| Consumer Prices | 64 | 82.8 | 86.6 | 90.6 | 92.6 | 97.7 | 96.8 | † 100.0 | 103.8 | 106.9 | 109.3 | 111.3 | 110.3 |
| | | | | | | *Number in Thousands: Period Averages* | | | | | | | |
| Labor Force | 67d | 35,716 | 36,050 | 36,433 | 36,955 | 37,647 | 38,365 | 38,643 | 38,922 | 39,409 | 38,661 | 38,576 | 38,548 |
| Employment | 67e | 34,717 | 35,170 | 35,700 | 36,270 | 36,973 | 37,649 | 38,037 | 38,465 | 38,941 | 38,217 | 38,077 | 38,016 |
| Unemployment | 67c | 741 | 666 | 547 | 501 | 514 | 571 | 402 | 264 | 259 | 282 | 323 | 341 |
| Unemployment Rate (%) | 67r | 2.1 | 1.9 | 1.5 | 1.4 | 1.4 | 1.5 | 1.0 | .7 | .7 | .7 | .8 | .9 |
| **Intl. Transactions & Positions** | | | | | | *Billions of Baht* | | | | | | | |
| Exports | 70 | 3,873.7 | 4,438.7 | 4,937.4 | 5,302.1 | 5,851.4 | 5,194.6 | 6,113.3 | 6,708.0 | 7,078.4 | 6,909.7 | 7,313.1 | 7,227.9 |
| Rice | 70n | 108.3 | 93.0 | 98.2 | 119.2 | 203.2 | 172.2 | 168.2 | 193.8 | 143.0 | 133.8 | 174.9 | 155.9 |
| Rubber | 70l | 137.5 | 148.7 | 205.5 | 194.3 | 223.6 | 146.2 | 249.3 | 382.9 | 270.2 | 249.3 | 193.8 | 170.4 |
| Maize | 70j | 6.0 | 1.7 | 3.6 | 4.0 | 7.7 | 8.6 | 4.9 | 5.6 | 3.4 | 6.6 | 9.6 | 3.7 |
| Tin | 70q | 5.2 | 8.5 | 7.6 | 10.6 | 11.9 | 8.5 | 13.7 | 17.2 | 14.0 | 14.0 | 10.7 | 4.8 |
| Imports, c.i.f. | 71 | 3,801.1 | 4,754.0 | 4,942.9 | 4,870.2 | 5,962.5 | 4,602.0 | 5,856.6 | 6,982.7 | 7,786.1 | 7,657.3 | 7,403.9 | 6,906.5 |
| | | | | | | *2010=100* | | | | | | | |
| Volume of Exports | 72 | 71.4 | 76.7 | 85.3 | 95.3 | 99.9 | 85.7 | 100.0 | 108.3 | 110.9 | 111.3 | 112.1 | 108.2 |
| Rice | 72n | 111.6 | 83.9 | 83.8 | 102.8 | 114.3 | 96.4 | 100.0 | 119.8 | 75.3 | 74.0 | 122.7 | 109.6 |
| Rubber | 72l | 110.5 | 107.8 | 111.9 | 108.5 | 103.6 | 100.2 | 100.0 | 109.6 | 109.7 | 125.7 | 124.7 | 133.7 |
| Maize | 72j | 204.4 | 27.9 | 91.7 | 82.0 | 140.1 | 223.2 | 100.0 | 82.9 | 32.1 | 122.8 | 163.9 | 25.6 |
| Tin | 72q | 69.8 | 126.8 | 106.6 | 99.3 | 90.8 | 88.2 | 100.0 | 98.1 | 97.9 | 96.3 | 68.2 | 38.9 |
| Volume of Imports | 73 | 73.3 | 86.9 | 87.9 | 90.9 | 102.2 | 78.3 | 100.0 | 113.5 | 121.1 | 123.5 | 115.1 | 114.4 |
| Unit Value of Exports | 74 | 89.8 | 95.5 | 95.7 | 91.8 | 99.8 | 100.1 | 100.0 | 106.0 | 109.8 | 106.2 | 110.3 | 103.6 |
| Rice (Unit Value) | 74n | 57.7 | 65.9 | 69.6 | 68.9 | 105.7 | 106.2 | 100.0 | 96.2 | 112.8 | 107.6 | 84.7 | 84.6 |
| Rice (Wholesale Price) | 76n | 59.9 | 70.2 | 69.7 | 69.6 | 141.4 | 122.5 | 100.0 | 102.0 | 109.3 | 96.6 | 84.0 | 78.9 |
| Rubber (Unit Value) | 74l | 49.9 | 55.3 | 73.7 | 71.9 | 86.6 | 58.5 | 100.0 | 140.1 | 98.8 | 79.5 | 62.3 | 51.2 |
| Rubber (Wholesale Price) | 76l | 45.3 | 52.2 | 68.9 | 68.3 | 75.2 | 56.9 | 100.0 | 126.9 | 90.7 | 74.2 | 54.9 | 46.1 |
| Maize (Unit Value) | 74j | 60.0 | 121.3 | 80.4 | 99.5 | 111.9 | 79.2 | 100.0 | 137.2 | 215.6 | 109.7 | 120.2 | 296.4 |
| Tin (Unit Value) | 74q | 54.9 | 49.2 | 51.9 | 77.8 | 95.5 | 70.3 | 100.0 | 128.0 | 104.2 | 106.4 | 114.7 | 89.9 |
| Unit Value of Imports | 75 | 88.0 | 94.4 | 93.5 | 90.1 | 96.1 | 99.1 | 100.0 | 101.7 | 104.3 | 102.6 | 107.4 | 110.6 |
| **Balance of Payments** | | | | | | *Millions of US Dollars* | | | | | | | |
| A. Current Account* | 109bx | 2,759.4 | † −7,646.6 | 2,315.7 | 15,579.5 | 984.3 | 20,660.7 | 9,944.8 | 8,930.8 | −1,458.0 | −5,067.8 | 15,413.5 | 31,604.1 |
| Goods, credit (exports) | 1a9cx | 94,978.7 | † 109,368.5 | 127,929.0 | 151,240.2 | 175,213.6 | 150,787.6 | 191,599.8 | 219,119.3 | 225,703.3 | 225,421.0 | 224,761.7 | 212,136.5 |
| Goods, debit (imports) | 1a9dx | 84,193.5 | † 105,977.0 | 114,264.5 | 124,609.5 | 157,819.9 | 118,180.3 | 161,932.7 | 202,128.5 | 219,015.0 | 218,689.2 | 200,201.0 | 177,493.7 |
| Balance on goods | 1a9bx | 10,785.2 | † 3,391.5 | 13,664.4 | 26,630.7 | 17,393.7 | 32,607.3 | 29,667.2 | 16,990.8 | 6,688.2 | 6,731.8 | 24,560.7 | 34,642.7 |
| Services, credit (exports) | 1b9cx | 19,040.2 | † 19,922.8 | 24,600.2 | 30,108.9 | 33,108.4 | 30,156.7 | 34,326.4 | 41,572.6 | 49,643.0 | 58,642.3 | 55,346.9 | 61,077.0 |
| Services, debit (imports) | 1b9dx | 23,077.1 | † 26,802.6 | 32,604.3 | 38,066.5 | 46,001.7 | 36,514.8 | 45,029.5 | 52,135.7 | 52,986.4 | 54,889.8 | 53,231.4 | 50,958.6 |
| Balance on Goods & Services | 1z9bx | 6,748.3 | † −3,488.3 | 5,660.3 | 18,673.0 | 4,500.3 | 26,249.2 | 18,964.1 | 6,427.8 | 3,344.9 | 10,484.4 | 26,676.2 | 44,761.1 |
| Primary income: credit | 1c9cx | 3,244.0 | † 2,452.8 | 3,331.8 | 5,599.4 | 4,987.0 | 3,854.0 | 5,102.3 | 6,941.2 | 7,610.7 | 6,127.1 | 7,028.4 | 5,556.9 |
| Primary income: debit | 1c9dx | 9,364.4 | † 10,811.5 | 11,367.7 | 14,286.0 | 15,171.0 | 14,789.8 | 20,168.5 | 15,272.8 | 24,629.4 | 32,170.4 | 27,123.0 | 25,938.9 |
| Balance on gds, serv. & prim. inc. | 1y9bx | 627.9 | † −11,847.0 | −2,375.7 | 9,986.5 | −5,683.6 | 15,313.4 | 3,897.9 | −1,903.8 | −13,673.9 | −15,558.8 | 6,581.7 | 24,379.1 |
| Secondary income: credit | 1d9ca | 2,479.4 | † 4,778.4 | 5,319.0 | 6,278.3 | 7,496.8 | 7,140.6 | 7,941.3 | 12,979.5 | 14,623.9 | 13,244.6 | 11,528.8 | 9,951.3 |
| Secondary income: debit | 1d9da | 347.9 | † 578.0 | 627.7 | 685.3 | 828.9 | 1,793.2 | 1,894.5 | 2,144.9 | 2,408.1 | 2,753.6 | 2,697.1 | 2,726.3 |
| B. Capital Account* | 209ba | — | .... | .... | .... | .... | 67.6 | 245.4 | −40.1 | 232.3 | 284.6 | 100.4 | .1 |
| Capital account: credit | 209ca | — | .... | .... | .... | .... | 67.6 | 245.4 | 64.8 | 232.3 | 284.6 | 100.4 | .1 |
| Capital account: debit | 209da | — | .... | .... | .... | .... | .... | .... | 105.0 | .... | .... | .... | .... |
| Balance on current & capital acct. | 129bx | 2,759.4 | † −7,646.6 | 2,315.7 | 15,579.5 | 984.3 | 20,728.3 | 10,190.2 | 8,890.6 | −1,225.7 | −4,783.2 | 15,513.8 | 31,604.1 |
| C. Financial Account* | 309na | −3,664.4 | † −7,863.8 | −7,318.4 | 201.7 | −16,980.5 | −1,404.9 | −23,570.2 | 8,301.0 | −12,727.9 | 2,691.9 | 16,499.7 | 18,066.7 |
| Direct investment: assets | 3a9aa | 76.7 | † 550.0 | 1,043.5 | 1,542.7 | 2,330.2 | 6,006.2 | 8,155.4 | 7,198.1 | 14,222.4 | 12,248.5 | 4,270.3 | 10,551.7 |
| Equity & investment fund shares | 3aaaa | 464.9 | † 714.0 | 1,057.3 | 2,374.8 | 1,287.9 | 3,184.9 | 5,161.4 | 6,393.7 | 5,606.0 | 4,702.5 | 5,119.0 | 6,741.4 |
| Debt instruments | 3abaa | −388.2 | † −164.0 | −13.8 | −832.1 | 1,042.3 | 2,821.4 | 2,994.0 | 804.4 | 8,616.4 | 7,546.0 | −848.7 | 3,810.3 |
| Direct investment: liabilities | 3a9la | 5,860.3 | † 8,222.8 | 8,926.2 | 8,620.8 | 8,566.2 | 6,427.3 | 14,714.9 | 2,468.1 | 12,894.5 | 15,822.1 | 3,718.7 | 8,003.2 |
| Equity & investment fund shares | 3aala | 6,340.8 | † 6,997.4 | 7,694.6 | 8,765.4 | 8,261.0 | 7,140.3 | 15,278.5 | 2,149.8 | 10,809.2 | 10,212.1 | 9,221.2 | 8,769.2 |
| Debt instruments | 3abla | −480.6 | † 1,225.4 | 1,231.5 | −144.5 | 305.3 | −713.0 | −563.6 | 318.3 | 2,085.4 | 5,610.0 | −5,502.5 | −765.9 |
| Portfolio investment: assets | 3b9aa | −1,231.9 | † 1,486.4 | 901.8 | 10,557.5 | −8,587.6 | 10,687.8 | 2,947.6 | −2,261.3 | 6,935.0 | 3,347.4 | 7,351.5 | 5,147.6 |
| Equity & investment fund shares | 3baaa | 243.6 | † 47.2 | 671.8 | 1,877.1 | −1,838.0 | 1,420.4 | 2,055.8 | 464.6 | 731.3 | 2,042.8 | 4,613.4 | 4,139.8 |
| Debt securities | 3bbaa | −1,475.5 | † 1,439.2 | 229.9 | 8,680.4 | −6,749.6 | 9,267.4 | 891.8 | −2,725.9 | 6,203.8 | 1,304.6 | 2,738.1 | 1,007.8 |
| Portfolio investment: liabilities | 3b9la | 1,855.7 | † 8,022.6 | 5,852.6 | 6,632.2 | −8,558.9 | 10,255.3 | 7,809.9 | 3,886.6 | 10,319.3 | −1,473.8 | −4,704.0 | −12,525.1 |
| Equity & investment fund shares | 3bala | 1,319.2 | † 6,268.8 | 5,444.2 | 7,225.5 | −9,419.1 | 9,532.2 | 2,448.9 | 19.5 | 58.0 | −3,351.6 | −5,823.7 | −8,750.0 |
| Debt securities | 3bbla | 536.6 | † 1,753.8 | 408.4 | −593.3 | 860.2 | 723.1 | 5,361.0 | 3,867.2 | 10,261.3 | 1,877.8 | 1,119.6 | −3,775.1 |
| Fin. der.& empl.stk.ops.(ESOs): net | 3c9na | 105.6 | † 525.5 | 893.7 | 178.5 | 173.5 | −183.1 | −143.9 | 610.4 | −540.3 | 341.2 | −429.3 | −906.5 |
| Fin. der. & ESOs: assets | 3c9aa | −10.7 | † −382.1 | 270.5 | −828.4 | −1,685.1 | −2,074.4 | −1,590.1 | −10,041.5 | −9,394.9 | −6,917.6 | −3,828.9 | −7,063.8 |
| Fin. der. & ESOs: liabilities | 3c9la | −116.3 | † −907.6 | −623.2 | −1,007.0 | −1,858.6 | −1,891.4 | −1,446.2 | −10,651.9 | −8,854.6 | −7,258.9 | −3,399.6 | −6,157.3 |
| Other investment: assets | 3d9aa | 1,695.0 | † 5,732.0 | 10,735.0 | 6,943.2 | −12,623.9 | −2,455.7 | 4,381.2 | 9,186.0 | 4,376.1 | 10,946.4 | 7,984.9 | −3,790.8 |
| Other equity | 3daaa | .... | .... | .... | .... | .... | .... | .... | .... | .... | .... | .... | .... |
| Debt instruments | 3dzaa | 1,695.0 | † 5,732.0 | 10,735.0 | 6,943.2 | −12,623.9 | −2,455.7 | 4,381.2 | 9,186.0 | 4,376.1 | 10,946.4 | 7,984.9 | −3,790.8 |
| Other investment: liabilities | 3d9la | −3,406.2 | † −87.7 | 6,113.7 | 3,767.3 | −1,734.7 | −1,222.4 | 16,385.7 | 77.4 | 14,507.2 | 9,843.2 | 3,662.9 | −2,542.8 |
| Other equity | 3dala | .... | .... | .... | .... | .... | .... | .... | .... | .... | .... | .... | .... |
| Debt instruments | 3dzla | −3,406.2 | † −87.7 | 6,113.7 | 3,767.3 | −1,734.7 | −1,222.4 | 16,385.7 | 77.4 | 14,507.2 | 9,843.2 | 3,662.9 | −2,542.8 |
| Curr.+ cap.− finan. acct. balance | 4y9na | 6,423.8 | † 217.2 | 9,634.1 | 15,377.8 | 17,964.7 | 22,133.2 | 33,760.4 | 589.6 | 11,502.2 | −7,475.1 | −985.9 | 13,537.5 |
| D. Net Errors and Omissions | 409na | −710.3 | † 5,199.4 | 3,034.7 | 1,698.9 | 6,475.3 | 1,997.5 | −2,514.8 | 601.0 | −6,266.0 | 2,344.8 | −230.1 | −7,659.2 |
| E. Reserves and Related Items | 4z9na | 5,713.5 | † 5,416.6 | 12,668.8 | 17,076.7 | 24,440.1 | 24,130.7 | 31,245.6 | 1,190.6 | 5,236.2 | −5,130.2 | −1,216.0 | 5,878.3 |
| Reserve assets | 3e9aa | 5,713.5 | † 5,416.6 | 12,668.8 | 17,076.7 | 24,440.1 | 24,130.7 | 31,245.6 | 1,190.6 | 5,236.2 | −5,130.2 | −1,216.0 | 5,878.3 |
| Credit and loans from the IMF | 3dcla | — | † — | — | — | — | — | — | — | — | — | — | — |
| Exceptional financing | 409la | — | .... | .... | .... | .... | .... | .... | .... | .... | .... | .... | .... |

*Excludes components in group E

# Thailand 578

## International Investment Position

Millions of US Dollars

| | | 2004 | 2005 | 2006 | 2007 | 2008 | 2009 | 2010 | 2011 | 2012 | 2013 | 2014 | 2015 |
|---|---|---|---|---|---|---|---|---|---|---|---|---|---|
| Assets | 809aa | 83,820.3 | † 93,657.8 | 123,164.8 | 163,360.0 | 178,500.2 | 218,083.3 | 263,121.6 | 283,961.9 | 316,933.4 | 321,240.2 | 329,693.1 | 336,998.5 |
| Direct investment | 8a9aa | 5,690.0 | † 6,586.7 | 8,756.4 | 9,888.7 | 12,676.6 | 18,034.7 | 24,581.4 | 42,053.9 | 57,063.2 | 66,938.6 | 73,461.4 | 78,679.6 |
| Equity & investment fund shares.. | 8aaaa | 3,569.0 | † 4,450.9 | 6,330.4 | 8,306.5 | 9,989.2 | 12,593.0 | 16,597.1 | 23,795.5 | 30,487.6 | 34,053.5 | 38,014.3 | 43,438.7 |
| Debt instruments | 8abaa | 2,121.0 | † 2,135.8 | 2,426.0 | 1,582.2 | 2,687.4 | 5,441.7 | 7,984.3 | 18,258.5 | 26,575.6 | 32,885.1 | 35,447.1 | 35,241.0 |
| Portfolio investment | 8b9aa | 1,625.0 | † 3,525.1 | 4,831.4 | 15,239.0 | 13,471.3 | 23,431.0 | 22,749.9 | 20,800.3 | 29,279.6 | 29,965.8 | 37,647.5 | 42,276.3 |
| Equity & investment fund shares.. | 8baaa | 694.0 | † 1,016.9 | 1,774.9 | 3,300.1 | 2,183.7 | 3,298.6 | 4,752.6 | 5,826.7 | 7,328.0 | 7,425.1 | 12,153.5 | 16,570.2 |
| Debt securities | 8bbaa | 931.0 | † 2,508.2 | 3,056.4 | 11,938.8 | 11,287.6 | 20,132.4 | 17,997.2 | 14,973.6 | 21,951.5 | 22,540.6 | 25,494.0 | 25,706.1 |
| Fin. der.(oth.than reserves) & ESOs | 8c9aa | 643.0 | † 470.3 | 710.9 | 1,570.6 | 4,594.5 | 3,357.1 | 3,697.9 | 6,573.4 | 4,802.2 | 2,594.0 | 2,856.0 | 3,216.3 |
| Other investment | 8d9aa | 26,031.7 | † 31,010.8 | 41,882.2 | 49,207.4 | 36,750.0 | 34,681.8 | 39,970.9 | 39,346.2 | 44,205.9 | 54,405.5 | 58,615.8 | 56,362.0 |
| Other equity | 8daaa | .... | .... | .... | .... | .... | .... | .... | .... | .... | .... | .... | .... |
| Debt instruments | 8dzaa | 26,031.7 | † 31,010.8 | 41,882.2 | 49,207.4 | 36,750.0 | 34,681.8 | 39,970.9 | 39,346.2 | 44,205.9 | 54,405.5 | 58,615.8 | 56,362.0 |
| Reserve assets | 8e9aa | 49,830.6 | † 52,065.0 | 66,983.9 | 87,454.1 | 111,007.9 | 138,578.6 | 172,121.6 | 175,188.2 | 181,582.4 | 167,336.3 | 157,112.3 | 156,464.3 |
| Liabilities | 809la | 134,786.5 | † 147,493.0 | 178,317.4 | 218,429.2 | 191,917.1 | 222,600.1 | 304,994.3 | 325,008.7 | 398,030.4 | 389,261.2 | 425,268.7 | 378,631.2 |
| Direct investment | 8a9la | 55,149.0 | † 62,832.3 | 80,241.8 | 96,261.3 | 96,643.3 | 110,069.7 | 142,498.2 | 159,342.7 | 180,127.9 | 186,352.8 | 207,854.6 | 186,063.3 |
| Equity & investment fund shares.. | 8aala | 48,536.0 | † 54,614.4 | 70,238.5 | 85,870.8 | 85,871.9 | 98,781.2 | 131,060.0 | 140,750.5 | 159,583.7 | 159,546.3 | 180,064.8 | 168,728.7 |
| Debt instruments | 8abla | 6,613.0 | † 8,217.9 | 10,003.3 | 10,390.5 | 10,771.5 | 11,288.5 | 11,438.2 | 18,592.3 | 20,544.2 | 26,806.4 | 27,789.8 | 17,334.6 |
| Portfolio investment | 8b9la | 32,109.0 | † 39,332.0 | 45,498.3 | 63,459.9 | 33,078.2 | 53,442.4 | 84,591.2 | 87,450.5 | 132,237.2 | 114,382.9 | 133,765.5 | 104,791.3 |
| Equity & investment fund shares.. | 8bala | 26,618.0 | † 32,983.2 | 38,503.8 | 56,936.9 | 25,842.5 | 45,322.7 | 70,318.2 | 70,112.0 | 103,357.4 | 84,578.6 | 101,304.3 | 77,471.5 |
| Debt securities | 8bbla | 5,491.0 | † 6,348.7 | 6,994.6 | 6,522.9 | 7,235.7 | 8,119.7 | 14,273.0 | 17,338.5 | 28,879.8 | 29,804.2 | 32,461.2 | 27,319.8 |
| Fin. der.(oth.than reserves) & ESOs | 8c9la | 843.0 | † 601.1 | 567.1 | 1,206.9 | 4,100.7 | 3,190.7 | 3,058.0 | 9,813.7 | 4,342.5 | 3,204.0 | 3,201.8 | 3,033.4 |
| Other investment | 8d9la | 46,685.5 | † 44,727.6 | 52,010.2 | 57,501.2 | 58,094.9 | 55,897.3 | 74,846.9 | 68,401.8 | 81,322.8 | 85,321.5 | 80,446.8 | 84,743.2 |
| Other equity | 8dala | .... | .... | .... | .... | .... | .... | .... | .... | .... | .... | .... | .... |
| Debt instruments | 8dzla | 46,685.5 | † 44,727.6 | 52,010.2 | 57,501.2 | 58,094.9 | 55,897.3 | 74,846.9 | 68,401.8 | 81,322.8 | 85,321.5 | 80,446.8 | 84,743.2 |

## Government Finance Operations Statement
### Central Government

Billions of Baht: Fiscal Year Ends September 30

| | | 2004 | 2005 | 2006 | 2007 | 2008 | 2009 | 2010 | 2011 | 2012 | 2013 | 2014 | 2015 |
|---|---|---|---|---|---|---|---|---|---|---|---|---|---|
| Revenue | a1 | 1,292.50 | 1,490.93 | 1,644.56 | 1,742.76 | 1,825.93 | 1,694.84 | 1,979.53 | 2,224.57 | 2,337.52 | 2,665.62 | 2,589.50 | 2,836.05 |
| Taxes | a11 | .... | .... | .... | .... | .... | .... | .... | .... | .... | .... | .... | 2,227.55 |
| Social Contributions | a12 | .... | .... | .... | .... | .... | .... | .... | .... | .... | .... | .... | 144.80 |
| Grants | a13 | .... | .... | .... | .... | .... | .... | .... | .... | .... | .... | .... | 1.45 |
| Other Revenue | a14 | .... | .... | .... | .... | .... | .... | .... | .... | .... | .... | .... | 462.25 |
| Expense | a2 | 1,131.99 | .... | .... | .... | .... | .... | .... | .... | .... | 2,499.82 | 2,553.26 | 2,569.74 |
| Compensation of Employees | a21 | .... | .... | .... | .... | .... | .... | .... | .... | .... | .... | .... | 713.08 |
| Use of Goods & Services | a22 | .... | .... | .... | .... | .... | .... | .... | .... | .... | .... | .... | 702.10 |
| Consumption of Fixed Capital | a23 | .... | .... | .... | .... | .... | .... | .... | .... | .... | .... | .... | 110.29 |
| Interest | a24 | .... | .... | .... | .... | .... | .... | .... | .... | .... | .... | .... | 138.74 |
| Subsidies | a25 | .... | .... | .... | .... | .... | .... | .... | .... | .... | .... | .... | 151.24 |
| Grants | a26 | .... | .... | .... | .... | .... | .... | .... | .... | .... | .... | .... | 384.58 |
| Social Benefits | a27 | .... | .... | .... | .... | .... | .... | .... | .... | .... | .... | .... | 302.92 |
| Other Expense | a28 | .... | .... | .... | .... | .... | .... | .... | .... | .... | .... | .... | 66.79 |
| Gross Operating Balance [1-2+23] | agob | 160.51 | .... | .... | .... | .... | .... | .... | .... | .... | 165.79 | 36.24 | 376.60 |
| Net Operating Balance [1-2] | anob | .... | .... | .... | .... | .... | .... | .... | .... | .... | .... | .... | 266.32 |
| Net Acq. of Nonfinancial Assets | a31 | 131.57 | .... | .... | .... | .... | .... | .... | .... | .... | 232.09 | 168.15 | 269.92 |
| Aquisition of Nonfin. Assets | a31.1 | .... | .... | .... | .... | .... | .... | .... | .... | .... | .... | .... | .... |
| Disposal of Nonfin. Assets | a31.2 | .... | .... | .... | .... | .... | .... | .... | .... | .... | .... | .... | .... |
| Net Lending/Borrowing [1-2-31] | anlb | 28.95 | 168.89 | 88.21 | 14.23 | 16.20 | −314.10 | 26.67 | −229.68 | −301.74 | −66.30 | −131.91 | −3.60 |
| Net Acq. of Financial Assets | a32 | 213.94 | −116.57 | 269.53 | 174.56 | 265.29 | 193.98 | 447.98 | 165.95 | 181.35 | 270.20 | 42.64 | 101.00 |
| By instrument | | | | | | | | | | | | | |
| Monetary Gold & SDRs | a3201 | — | — | — | — | — | — | — | — | — | — | — | — |
| Currency & Deposits | a3202 | .... | .... | .... | .... | .... | .... | .... | .... | .... | .... | .... | .... |
| Securities other than Shares | a3203 | .... | .... | .... | .... | .... | .... | .... | .... | .... | .... | .... | .... |
| Loans | a3204 | .... | .... | .... | .... | .... | .... | .... | .... | .... | .... | .... | .... |
| Shares & Other Equity | a3205 | .... | .... | .... | .... | .... | .... | .... | .... | .... | .... | .... | .... |
| Insurance Technical Reserves | a3206 | .... | .... | .... | .... | .... | .... | .... | .... | .... | .... | .... | .... |
| Financial Derivatives | a3207 | .... | .... | .... | .... | .... | .... | .... | .... | .... | .... | .... | .... |
| Other Accounts Receivable | a3208 | .... | .... | .... | .... | .... | .... | .... | .... | .... | .... | .... | .... |
| By debtor | | | | | | | | | | | | | |
| Domestic | a321 | .... | .... | .... | .... | .... | .... | .... | .... | .... | .... | .... | .... |
| Foreign | a322 | .... | .... | .... | .... | .... | .... | .... | .... | .... | .... | .... | .... |
| Net Incurrence of Liabilities | a33 | 185.00 | −285.45 | 181.32 | 160.33 | 249.09 | 508.08 | 420.74 | 395.62 | 483.09 | 336.86 | 169.14 | 104.60 |
| By instrument | | | | | | | | | | | | | |
| Special Drawing Rights (SDRs) | a3301 | .... | .... | .... | .... | .... | .... | .... | .... | .... | .... | .... | .... |
| Currency & Deposits | a3302 | .... | .... | .... | .... | .... | .... | .... | .... | .... | .... | .... | .... |
| Securities other than Shares | a3303 | .... | .... | .... | .... | .... | .... | .... | .... | .... | .... | .... | .... |
| Loans | a3304 | .... | .... | .... | .... | .... | .... | .... | .... | .... | .... | .... | .... |
| Shares & Other Equity | a3305 | .... | .... | .... | .... | .... | .... | .... | .... | .... | .... | .... | .... |
| Insurance Technical Reserves | a3306 | .... | .... | .... | .... | .... | .... | .... | .... | .... | .... | .... | .... |
| Financial Derivatives | a3307 | .... | .... | .... | .... | .... | .... | .... | .... | .... | .... | .... | .... |
| Other Accounts Payable | a3308 | .... | .... | .... | .... | .... | .... | .... | .... | .... | .... | .... | .... |
| By creditor | | | | | | | | | | | | | |
| Domestic | a331 | 203.22 | −221.52 | 218.81 | 244.35 | 289.06 | 514.61 | 429.22 | 405.89 | 478.83 | 197.93 | 127.98 | 116.74 |
| Foreign | a332 | −18.22 | −63.93 | −37.49 | −84.02 | −39.98 | −6.54 | −8.48 | −10.27 | 4.26 | 138.57 | 41.16 | −12.14 |
| Stat. Discrepancy [32-33-NLB] | anlbz | — | — | — | — | — | — | — | — | — | — | — | 3.31 | — |
| Memo Item: Expenditure [2+31] | a2m | 1,263.55 | 1,322.04 | 1,556.35 | 1,728.53 | 1,809.73 | 2,008.93 | 1,952.87 | 2,454.24 | 2,639.26 | 2,731.92 | 2,721.42 | 2,839.65 |
| Memo Item: Debt at Face Value | a6m35 | .... | .... | .... | .... | .... | .... | .... | .... | .... | .... | .... | .... |

# Thailand 578

| National Accounts | | 2004 | 2005 | 2006 | 2007 | 2008 | 2009 | 2010 | 2011 | 2012 | 2013 | 2014 | 2015 |
|---|---|---|---|---|---|---|---|---|---|---|---|---|---|
| | | | | | | | *Billions of Baht* | | | | | | |
| Househ.Cons.Expend.,incl.NPISHs.... | 96f | 3,687.6 | 4,043.7 | 4,379.1 | 4,557.0 | 4,997.7 | 4,993.3 | 5,429.7 | 5,738.2 | 6,535.2 | 6,755.9 | 6,922.6 | 6,974.4 |
| Government Consumption Expend... | 91f | 721.3 | 838.8 | 926.0 | 1,038.8 | 1,128.2 | 1,213.9 | 1,310.0 | 1,399.5 | 2,012.9 | 2,123.6 | 2,235.4 | 2,334.1 |
| Gross Fixed Capital Formation......... | 93e | 1,686.8 | 2,057.0 | 2,204.0 | 2,249.9 | 2,488.9 | 2,181.8 | 2,499.3 | 2,765.5 | 3,335.1 | 3,279.9 | 3,259.5 | 3,375.5 |
| Changes in Inventories.................... | 93i | 75.0 | 188.0 | 15.9 | 4.1 | 131.4 | −261.3 | 121.4 | 34.2 | 127.3 | 267.8 | −98.2 | −108.6 |
| Exports of Goods and Services......... | 90c | 4,587.9 | 5,232.9 | 5,777.6 | 6,259.6 | 6,941.5 | 6,180.1 | 7,203.3 | 8,109.9 | 8,558.3 | 8,730.4 | 9,098.7 | 9,340.7 |
| Imports of Goods and Services (-)..... | 98c | 4,281.9 | 5,338.6 | 5,503.8 | 5,544.5 | 6,692.9 | 5,226.5 | 6,452.5 | 7,629.3 | 8,454.4 | 8,396.7 | 8,230.1 | 7,811.7 |
| Statistical Discrepancy...................... | 99bs | 26.8 | 81.0 | 51.4 | −35.1 | 80.6 | −39.7 | −6.4 | 121.4 | 234.7 | 140.6 | −55.7 | −566.9 |
| Gross Domestic Product (GDP)......... | 99b | 6,503.5 | 7,103.0 | 7,850.2 | 8,529.8 | 9,075.5 | 9,041.6 | 10,104.8 | 10,539.4 | 12,349.0 | 12,901.5 | 13,132.2 | 13,537.5 |
| Net Primary Income from Abroad..... | 98.n | −126.2 | −173.3 | −316.8 | −311.2 | −357.0 | −352.5 | −435.0 | −378.6 | −529.5 | −799.2 | −651.2 | −576.1 |
| Gross National Income (GNI)............ | 99a | 6,377.3 | 6,929.7 | 7,533.4 | 8,218.6 | 8,718.5 | 8,689.0 | 9,669.9 | 10,160.8 | 11,819.5 | 12,102.2 | 12,481.0 | 12,961.4 |
| GDP Volume 1988 Prices................. | 99b.p | 3,678.5 | 3,842.5 | 4,056.6 | 4,256.6 | 4,361.4 | 4,263.1 | 4,596.1 | 4,598.4 | 4,898.2 | 5,038.8 | 5,075.6 | .... |
| GDP Volume (2010=100)................. | 99bvp | 80.0 | 83.6 | 88.3 | 92.6 | 94.9 | 92.8 | 100.0 | 100.1 | † 106.6 | 109.5 | 110.3 | 113.5 |
| GDP Deflator (2010=100)............... | 99bip | 80.4 | 84.1 | 88.0 | 91.1 | 94.6 | 96.5 | 100.0 | 104.2 | 114.7 | 116.7 | 117.8 | 118.1 |
| | | | | | | | *Millions: Midyear Estimates* | | | | | | |
| Population.................................. | 99z | 65.40 | 65.86 | 66.17 | 66.35 | 66.45 | 66.55 | 66.69 | 66.90 | 67.16 | 67.45 | 67.73 | 67.96 |

| | | 2004 | 2005 | 2006 | 2007 | 2008 | 2009 | 2010 | 2011 | 2012 | 2013 | 2014 | 2015 |
|---|---|---|---|---|---|---|---|---|---|---|---|---|---|
| **Exchange Rates** | | *US Dollars per SDR: End of Period* | | | | | | | | | | | |
| Market Rate................................. | aa | 1.5530 | 1.4293 | 1.5044 | 1.5803 | 1.5403 | 1.5677 | 1.5400 | 1.5353 | 1.5369 | 1.5400 | 1.4488 | 1.3857 |
| **Fund Position** | | *Millions of SDRs: End of Period* | | | | | | | | | | | |
| Quota.......................................... | 2f.s | 8.20 | 8.20 | 8.20 | 8.20 | 8.20 | 8.20 | 8.20 | 8.20 | 8.20 | 8.20 | 10.80 | 10.80 |
| SDR Holdings............................ | 1b.s | — | — | — | — | — | 7.73 | 7.73 | 7.73 | 7.75 | 7.75 | 7.10 | 7.10 |
| Reserve Position in the Fund............ | 1c.s | — | — | — | — | — | — | — | — | — | — | .65 | .65 |
| Total Fund Cred.&Loans Outstg........ | 2tl | — | — | — | — | — | — | — | — | — | — | — | — |
| SDR Allocations............................. | 1bd | — | — | — | — | — | 7.73 | 7.73 | 7.73 | 7.73 | 7.73 | 7.73 | 7.73 |
| **International Liquidity** | | *Millions of US Dollars End of Period* | | | | | | | | | | | |
| Total Reserves minus Gold.............. | 1l.d | 182.434 | 153.300 | 83.755 | 230.272 | 210.424 | 249.929 | 406.188 | 461.611 | 883.551 | 686.998 | 311.471 | 437.752 |
| SDR Holdings............................... | 1b.d | — | — | — | — | — | 12.115 | 11.901 | 11.864 | 11.914 | 11.938 | 10.289 | 9.840 |
| Reserve Position in the Fund........ | 1c.d | .002 | .001 | .002 | .002 | .002 | .002 | .002 | .002 | .002 | .002 | .943 | .902 |
| Foreign Exchange..................... | 1d.d | 182.432 | 153.298 | 83.754 | 230.270 | 210.422 | 237.812 | 394.286 | 449.745 | 871.636 | 675.059 | 300.239 | 427.010 |
| Gold (Million Fine Troy Ounces)........ | 1ad | — | — | — | — | — | — | — | — | — | — | — | — |
| Gold (National Valuation)............... | 1and | — | — | — | — | — | — | — | — | — | — | — | — |
| Central Bank: Other Assets............ | 3..d | — | — | — | — | — | — | — | — | — | — | — | — |
| Central Bank: Other Liabs.............. | 4..d | — | — | — | — | — | — | — | — | — | — | — | — |
| Other Depository Corps.: Assets....... | 7a.d | 44 | 52 | 61 | 126 | 211 | 219 | 244 | 295 | 368 | 461 | 521 | 661 |
| Other Depository Corps.: Liabs......... | 7b.d | 43 | 47 | 31 | 38 | 29 | 14 | 16 | 56 | 60 | 65 | 64 | 73 |
| **Central Bank** | | *Millions of US Dollars: End of Period* | | | | | | | | | | | |
| Net Foreign Assets........................ | 11n | 182.446 | 153.300 | 83.755 | 230.272 | 210.424 | 237.814 | 394.287 | 449.741 | 871.622 | 675.105 | 300.279 | 427.149 |
| Claims on Nonresidents............ | 11 | 182.446 | 153.300 | 83.755 | 230.272 | 210.424 | 249.929 | 406.188 | 461.611 | 883.551 | 686.998 | 311.471 | 437.870 |
| Liabilities to Nonresidents.............. | 16c | — | — | — | — | — | 12.115 | 11.901 | 11.870 | 11.929 | 11.893 | 11.192 | 10.720 |
| Claims on Other Depository Corps.... | 12e | 1.278 | 1.593 | .916 | .637 | 42.204 | 2.340 | 23.791 | 23.483 | 71.194 | 72.429 | 71.309 | 74.513 |
| Net Claims on Central Government.. | 12an | −168.641 | −128.540 | −56.332 | −190.182 | −195.672 | −162.538 | −318.264 | −405.965 | −818.979 | −633.827 | −181.394 | −238.085 |
| Claims on Central Government...... | 12a | .002 | .004 | .966 | .199 | 11.625 | 1.147 | 22.380 | 12.980 | .002 | .001 | .001 | .001 |
| Liabilities to Central Government.... | 16d | 168.643 | 128.543 | 57.299 | 190.380 | 207.296 | 163.685 | 340.644 | 418.945 | 818.981 | 633.828 | 181.395 | 238.086 |
| Claims on Other Sectors.................. | 12s | .022 | .023 | .023 | .022 | .051 | .191 | .282 | .764 | 4.219 | 3.670 | 5.608 | 4.113 |
| Claims on Other Financial Corps.... | 12g | — | — | — | — | — | — | — | — | — | — | — | — |
| Claims on State & Local Govts... | 12b | — | — | — | — | — | — | — | — | — | — | — | — |
| Claims on Public Nonfin. Corps...... | 12c | — | — | — | — | — | — | — | — | — | — | — | — |
| Claims on Private Sector............... | 12d | .022 | .023 | .023 | .022 | .051 | .191 | .282 | .764 | 4.219 | 3.670 | 5.608 | 4.113 |
| Monetary Base................................ | 14 | 6.572 | 6.312 | 8.206 | 20.271 | 25.527 | 56.253 | 54.761 | 34.487 | 99.892 | 85.542 | 146.624 | 213.283 |
| Currency in Circulation.................. | 14a | 1.104 | 1.790 | 1.811 | 2.273 | 2.454 | 2.801 | 3.374 | 3.863 | 4.769 | 6.759 | 9.780 | 12.153 |
| Liabs. to Other Depository Corps..... | 14c | 5.468 | 4.522 | 6.395 | 17.998 | 23.074 | 53.451 | 51.387 | 30.624 | 95.123 | 78.784 | 136.844 | 201.130 |
| Liabilities to Other Sectors............. | 14d | — | — | — | — | — | — | — | — | — | — | — | — |
| Other Liabs. to Other Dep. Corps..... | 14n | — | — | — | — | — | — | — | — | — | — | — | — |
| Dep. & Sec. Excl. f/Monetary Base... | 14o | .003 | .009 | .016 | .023 | .031 | .064 | .095 | .128 | .160 | .189 | .226 | .222 |
| Deposits Included in Broad Money.. | 15 | — | — | — | — | — | — | — | — | — | — | — | — |
| Sec.Ot.th.Shares Incl.in Brd. Money | 16a | — | — | — | — | — | — | — | — | — | — | — | — |
| Deposits Excl. from Broad Money... | 16b | .003 | .009 | .016 | .023 | .031 | .064 | .095 | .128 | .160 | .189 | .226 | .222 |
| Sec.Ot.th.Shares Excl.f/Brd.Money.. | 16s | — | — | — | — | — | — | — | — | — | — | — | — |
| Loans........................................... | 16l | — | — | — | — | — | — | — | — | — | — | — | — |
| Financial Derivatives...................... | 16m | — | — | — | — | — | — | — | — | — | — | — | — |
| Shares and Other Equity................ | 17a | 9.036 | 20.871 | 20.228 | 21.099 | 20.330 | 19.961 | 20.082 | 20.454 | 20.867 | 20.877 | 45.452 | 51.235 |
| Other Items (Net)........................... | 17r | −.506 | −.815 | −.088 | −.644 | 11.119 | 1.530 | 25.158 | 12.954 | 7.138 | 10.768 | 3.499 | 2.950 |
| Memo Item: | | | | | | | | | | | | | |
| Total Assets.................................. | 10ra | 197.265 | 168.403 | 99.726 | 245.602 | 279.801 | 268.507 | 466.849 | 513.824 | 974.169 | 778.616 | 407.592 | 536.245 |
| **Other Depository Corporations** | | *Millions of US Dollars: End of Period* | | | | | | | | | | | |
| Net Foreign Assets......................... | 21n | 1.294 | 5.766 | 29.424 | 87.866 | 182.217 | 204.914 | 227.494 | 239.120 | 307.640 | 396.748 | 456.504 | 588.469 |
| Claims on Nonresidents............... | 21 | 44.467 | 52.266 | 60.504 | 125.583 | 211.111 | 218.918 | 243.566 | 294.841 | 367.907 | 461.434 | 520.933 | 661.204 |
| Liabilities to Nonresidents............. | 26c | 43.174 | 46.500 | 31.080 | 37.716 | 28.895 | 14.004 | 16.072 | 55.721 | 60.266 | 64.686 | 64.429 | 72.735 |
| Claims on Central Bank.................. | 20 | 6.049 | 4.417 | 6.393 | 16.558 | 22.394 | 53.451 | 47.831 | 41.328 | 93.554 | 76.749 | 136.203 | 109.481 |
| Currency..................................... | 20a | — | — | — | — | — | — | — | — | — | — | — | — |
| Reserve Deposits and Securities..... | 20b | 6.049 | 4.417 | 6.393 | 16.558 | 22.394 | 53.451 | 47.831 | 41.328 | 93.554 | 76.749 | 136.203 | 109.481 |
| Other Claims............................... | 20n | — | — | — | — | — | — | — | — | — | — | — | — |
| Net Claims on Central Government.. | 22an | −18.180 | −22.769 | −26.853 | −28.447 | −33.836 | −43.656 | −12.750 | −6.654 | −22.249 | −16.960 | −25.772 | −100.833 |
| Claims on Central Government...... | 22a | — | — | — | — | — | — | — | — | — | — | — | — |
| Liabilities to Central Government.... | 26d | 18.180 | 22.769 | 26.853 | 28.447 | 33.836 | 43.656 | 12.750 | 6.654 | 22.249 | 16.960 | 25.772 | 100.833 |
| Claims on Other Sectors................. | 22s | 88.361 | 105.886 | 111.437 | 100.480 | 102.398 | 103.349 | 109.376 | 132.019 | 155.841 | 178.102 | 186.154 | 207.750 |
| Claims on Other Financial Corps.... | 22g | — | — | — | — | — | — | — | — | — | — | — | — |
| Claims on State & Local Govts....... | 22b | — | — | — | — | — | — | — | — | — | — | — | — |
| Claims on Public Nonfin. Corps...... | 22c | — | — | — | — | — | — | — | — | — | — | — | — |
| Claims on Private Sector............... | 22d | 88.361 | 105.886 | 111.437 | 100.480 | 102.398 | 103.349 | 109.376 | 132.019 | 155.841 | 178.102 | 186.154 | 207.750 |
| Liabilities to Central Bank.............. | 26g | 1.349 | 1.592 | .914 | .437 | 40.957 | 2.120 | 23.571 | 23.263 | 57.435 | 63.692 | 70.060 | 74.504 |
| Transf.Dep.Included in Broad Money | 24 | 31.187 | 37.704 | 51.763 | 73.199 | 101.837 | 154.642 | 138.012 | 158.821 | 200.994 | 272.708 | 333.158 | 385.552 |
| Other Dep.Included in Broad Money. | 25 | 33.596 | 38.450 | 46.320 | 68.243 | 88.367 | 110.913 | 153.639 | 159.744 | 201.184 | 220.688 | 256.884 | 244.670 |
| Sec.Ot.th.Shares Incl.in Brd. Money.. | 26a | — | — | — | — | — | — | — | — | — | — | — | — |
| Deposits Excl. from Broad Money..... | 26b | — | — | — | — | — | — | — | — | — | — | .132 | .403 |
| Sec.Ot.th.Shares Excl.f/Brd.Money.... | 26s | — | — | — | — | — | — | — | — | — | — | — | — |
| Loans........................................... | 26l | — | — | — | — | — | — | — | .050 | .194 | .075 | .500 | — |
| Financial Derivatives...................... | 26m | — | — | — | — | — | — | — | — | — | — | — | — |
| Insurance Technical Reserves.......... | 26r | — | — | — | — | — | — | — | — | — | — | — | — |
| Shares and Other Equity................. | 27a | 14.088 | 15.488 | −22.995 | −18.785 | −11.604 | −4.413 | −2.429 | 2.855 | 14.041 | 24.192 | 43.957 | 48.349 |
| Other Items (Net)........................... | 27r | −2.697 | .066 | 44.399 | 53.364 | 53.615 | 54.798 | 59.158 | 61.082 | 60.938 | 53.284 | 48.398 | 51.390 |
| Memo Item: | | | | | | | | | | | | | |
| Total Assets.................................. | 20ra | 145.692 | 169.028 | 185.178 | 249.650 | 344.881 | 386.986 | 414.457 | 483.338 | 634.958 | 743.676 | 884.748 | 1,017.643 |

# Timor-Leste, Dem. Rep. of   537

| | | 2004 | 2005 | 2006 | 2007 | 2008 | 2009 | 2010 | 2011 | 2012 | 2013 | 2014 | 2015 |
|---|---|---|---|---|---|---|---|---|---|---|---|---|---|
| **Depository Corporations** | | | | | | *Millions of US Dollars: End of Period* | | | | | | | |
| Net Foreign Assets............................ | 31n | 183.740 | 159.066 | 113.179 | 318.138 | 392.640 | 442.728 | 621.781 | 688.862 | 1,179.262 | 1,071.853 | 756.783 | 1,015.619 |
| Claims on Nonresidents................. | 31 | 226.913 | 205.566 | 144.259 | 355.854 | 421.535 | 468.847 | 649.755 | 756.452 | 1,251.458 | 1,148.432 | 832.404 | 1,099.074 |
| Liabilities to Nonresidents.............. | 36c | 43.174 | 46.500 | 31.080 | 37.716 | 28.895 | 26.118 | 27.973 | 67.590 | 72.195 | 76.580 | 75.622 | 83.455 |
| Domestic Claims............................ | 32 | −98.438 | −45.399 | 28.275 | −118.127 | −127.059 | −102.653 | −221.356 | −279.836 | −681.169 | −469.015 | −15.404 | −127.055 |
| Net Claims on Central Government | 32an | −186.821 | −151.309 | −83.185 | −218.629 | −229.508 | −206.194 | −331.014 | −412.619 | −841.228 | −650.787 | −207.165 | −338.918 |
| Claims on Central Government.... | 32a | .002 | .004 | .966 | .199 | 11.625 | 1.147 | 22.380 | 12.980 | .002 | .001 | .001 | .001 |
| Liabilities to Central Government. | 36d | 186.823 | 151.313 | 84.152 | 218.827 | 241.133 | 207.341 | 353.394 | 425.599 | 841.230 | 650.788 | 207.167 | 338.919 |
| Claims on Other Sectors................ | 32s | 88.382 | 105.910 | 111.460 | 100.502 | 102.449 | 103.541 | 109.658 | 132.783 | 160.060 | 181.772 | 191.762 | 211.863 |
| Claims on Other Financial Corps.. | 32g | — | — | — | — | — | — | — | — | — | — | — | — |
| Claims on State & Local Govts..... | 32b | — | — | — | — | — | — | — | — | — | — | — | — |
| Claims on Public Nonfin. Corps.... | 32c | — | — | — | — | — | — | — | — | — | — | — | — |
| Claims on Private Sector.............. | 32d | 88.382 | 105.910 | 111.460 | 100.502 | 102.449 | 103.541 | 109.658 | 132.783 | 160.060 | 181.772 | 191.762 | 211.863 |
| Broad Money Liabilities.................... | 35l | 65.887 | 77.944 | 99.894 | 143.714 | 192.658 | 268.356 | 295.025 | 322.428 | 406.947 | 500.154 | 599.822 | 642.375 |
| Currency Outside Depository Corps | 34a | 1.104 | 1.790 | 1.811 | 2.273 | 2.454 | 2.801 | 3.374 | 3.863 | 4.769 | 6.759 | 9.780 | 12.153 |
| Transferable Deposits.................... | 34 | 31.187 | 37.704 | 51.763 | 73.199 | 101.837 | 154.642 | 138.012 | 158.821 | 200.994 | 272.708 | 333.158 | 385.552 |
| Other Deposits............................... | 35 | 33.596 | 38.450 | 46.320 | 68.243 | 88.367 | 110.913 | 153.639 | 159.744 | 201.184 | 220.688 | 256.884 | 244.670 |
| Securities Other than Shares.......... | 36a | — | — | — | — | — | — | — | — | — | — | — | — |
| Deposits Excl. from Broad Money..... | 36b | .003 | .009 | .016 | .023 | .031 | .064 | .095 | .128 | .160 | .189 | .358 | .625 |
| Sec.Ot.th.Shares Excl.f/Brd.Money.... | 36s | — | — | — | — | — | — | — | — | — | — | — | — |
| Loans............................................... | 36l | — | — | — | — | — | — | — | .050 | .194 | .075 | .500 | — |
| Financial Derivatives....................... | 36m | — | — | — | — | — | — | — | — | — | — | — | — |
| Insurance Technical Reserves.......... | 36r | — | — | — | — | — | — | — | — | — | — | — | — |
| Shares and Other Equity................. | 37a | 23.125 | 36.359 | −2.767 | 2.314 | 8.726 | 15.547 | 17.654 | 23.308 | 34.908 | 45.069 | 89.409 | 99.583 |
| Other Items (Net)........................... | 37r | −3.713 | −.645 | 44.311 | 53.961 | 64.167 | 56.108 | 87.652 | 63.112 | 55.886 | 57.351 | 51.290 | 145.980 |
| Broad Money Liabs., Seasonally Adj. | 35l.b | 65.206 | 76.983 | 98.150 | 140.122 | 185.922 | 256.022 | 276.982 | 296.865 | 366.581 | 442.123 | 522.161 | 554.830 |
| **Monetary Aggregates** | | | | | | *Millions of US Dollars: End of Period* | | | | | | | |
| Broad Money................................ | 59m | 65.887 | 77.944 | 99.894 | 143.714 | 192.658 | 268.356 | 295.025 | 322.428 | 406.947 | 500.154 | 599.822 | 642.375 |
| o/w:Currency Issued by Cent.Govt | 59m.a | — | — | — | — | — | — | — | — | — | — | — | — |
| o/w: Dep.in Nonfin. Corporations. | 59m.b | — | — | — | — | — | — | — | — | — | — | — | — |
| o/w:Secs. Issued by Central Govt.. | 59m.c | — | — | — | — | — | — | — | — | — | — | — | — |
| Money (National Definitions) | | | | | | | | | | | | | |
| Narrow Money........................... | 59mak | 32.292 | 39.494 | 53.574 | 75.471 | 104.291 | 157.443 | 141.386 | 162.684 | 205.763 | 279.466 | 342.938 | 397.705 |
| Quasi Money.............................. | 59mal | 33.596 | 38.450 | 46.320 | 68.243 | 88.367 | 110.913 | 153.639 | 159.744 | 201.184 | 220.688 | 256.884 | 244.670 |
| Broad Money............................. | 59mea | 65.887 | 77.944 | 99.894 | 143.714 | 192.658 | 268.356 | 295.025 | 322.428 | 406.947 | 500.154 | 599.822 | 642.375 |
| **Interest Rates** | | | | | | *Percent Per Annum* | | | | | | | |
| Savings Rate.................................... | 60k | .791 | .753 | .651 | .744 | .752 | .752 | .752 | .752 | .752 | .750 | .750 | .750 |
| Deposit Rate.................................... | 60l | .790 | .792 | .796 | .781 | .797 | .831 | .813 | .846 | .905 | .900 | .853 | .777 |
| Lending Rate.................................... | 60p | 15.539 | 16.653 | 16.550 | 15.047 | 13.110 | 11.165 | 11.029 | 11.043 | 12.210 | 12.413 | 12.866 | 13.498 |
| **Prices** | | | | | | *Index Numbers (2010=100): Period Averages* | | | | | | | |
| Consumer Prices.............................. | 64 | 73.6 | 74.4 | 77.3 | 85.3 | 93.0 | 93.7 | 100.0 | 113.5 | † 126.9 | 141.1 | 141.7 | 142.6 |

# Timor-Leste, Dem. Rep. of   537

| Balance of Payments | | 2004 | 2005 | 2006 | 2007 | 2008 | 2009 | 2010 | 2011 | 2012 | 2013 | 2014 | 2015 |
|---|---|---|---|---|---|---|---|---|---|---|---|---|---|
| | | | | | | | *Millions of US Dollars* | | | | | | |
| A. Current Account* | 109bx | .... | .... | 541.0 | 1,177.2 | 2,021.7 | 1,285.0 | 1,671.4 | 2,346.0 | 2,736.0 | 2,390.0 | 1,106.2 | † 238.4 |
| Goods, credit (exports) | 1a9cx | .... | .... | 9.3 | 6.6 | 14.1 | 14.6 | 27.1 | 28.7 | 33.3 | 17.7 | 15.5 | † 18.0 |
| Goods, debit (imports) | 1a9dx | .... | .... | 100.6 | 175.7 | 310.9 | 337.6 | 307.4 | 401.9 | 671.6 | 696.2 | 764.2 | † 652.9 |
| Balance on goods | 1a9bx | .... | .... | −91.4 | −169.0 | −296.9 | −323.0 | −280.4 | −373.3 | −638.4 | −678.5 | −748.8 | † −634.9 |
| Services, credit (exports) | 1b9cx | .... | .... | 34.1 | 62.5 | 44.1 | 51.6 | 67.8 | 72.6 | 69.4 | 70.2 | 74.1 | † 73.0 |
| Services, debit (imports) | 1b9dx | .... | .... | 232.1 | 325.3 | 489.9 | 824.8 | 1,035.3 | 1,463.6 | 989.3 | 508.2 | 451.8 | † 653.4 |
| Balance on Goods & Services | 1z9bx | .... | .... | −289.4 | −431.8 | −742.7 | −1,096.3 | −1,247.9 | −1,764.2 | −1,558.2 | −1,116.5 | −1,126.5 | † −1,215.3 |
| Primary income: credit | 1c9cx | .... | .... | 647.5 | 1,336.3 | 2,416.7 | 1,947.4 | 2,443.1 | 3,586.9 | 3,882.2 | 3,341.3 | 2,153.7 | † 1,307.6 |
| Primary income: debit | 1c9dx | .... | .... | 2.3 | 5.4 | 8.8 | 17.6 | 8.3 | 9.6 | 20.1 | 14.6 | 5.1 | † 17.7 |
| Balance on gds, serv. & prim. inc. | 1y9bx | .... | .... | 355.8 | 899.1 | 1,665.2 | 833.5 | 1,187.0 | 1,813.1 | 2,303.9 | 2,210.2 | 1,022.2 | † 74.7 |
| Secondary income: credit | 1d9ca | .... | .... | 185.6 | 281.2 | 370.6 | 535.5 | 585.9 | 636.3 | 537.7 | 185.6 | 107.8 | † 318.5 |
| Secondary income: debit | 1d9da | .... | .... | .4 | 3.1 | 14.1 | 84.1 | 101.5 | 103.3 | 105.6 | 5.7 | 23.8 | † 154.8 |
| B. Capital Account* | 209ba | .... | .... | 41.6 | 32.2 | 17.2 | 27.3 | 31.3 | 26.2 | 23.4 | 19.5 | −3.3 | † 29.0 |
| Capital account: credit | 209ca | .... | .... | 41.6 | 32.2 | 17.2 | 27.3 | 31.3 | 26.2 | 23.4 | 19.5 | 6.2 | † 29.0 |
| Capital account: debit | 209da | .... | .... | .... | .... | .... | — | — | — | — | — | 9.5 | .... |
| Balance on current & capital acct. | 129ba | .... | .... | 582.5 | 1,209.4 | 2,039.0 | 1,312.3 | 1,702.6 | 2,372.3 | 2,759.4 | 2,409.6 | 1,102.9 | † 267.4 |
| C. Financial Account* | 309na | .... | .... | 649.1 | 1,054.0 | 2,051.6 | 1,272.6 | 1,546.7 | 2,279.9 | 2,249.1 | 2,568.6 | 1,402.4 | † −28.7 |
| Direct investment: assets | 3a9aa | .... | .... | .... | .... | .... | — | 26.0 | −33.0 | 12.7 | 12.7 | 12.7 | † 12.7 |
| Equity & investment fund shares.. | 3aaaa | .... | .... | .... | .... | .... | — | — | — | — | — | — | † — |
| Debt instruments | 3abaa | .... | .... | .... | .... | .... | — | 26.0 | −33.0 | 12.7 | 12.7 | 12.7 | † 12.7 |
| Direct investment: liabilities | 3a9la | .... | .... | 8.5 | 8.7 | 39.7 | 48.0 | 30.3 | 49.1 | 40.4 | 55.9 | 33.9 | † 43.0 |
| Equity & investment fund shares . | 3aala | .... | .... | 8.5 | 7.5 | 39.7 | 49.9 | 28.5 | 47.1 | 38.5 | 49.6 | 33.9 | † 43.0 |
| Debt instruments | 3abla | .... | .... | — | 1.2 | — | −2.0 | 1.8 | 2.0 | 1.9 | 6.2 | — | † — |
| Portfolio investment: assets | 3b9aa | .... | .... | 636.7 | 1,012.1 | 2,003.1 | 1,325.1 | 1,509.0 | 2,406.7 | 2,280.3 | 2,556.4 | 1,384.7 | † −150.8 |
| Equity & investment fund shares | 3baaa | .... | .... | .... | .... | .... | — | — | 281.8 | 2,531.8 | 1,802.2 | 1,091.8 | † −19.9 |
| Debt securities | 3bbaa | .... | .... | 636.7 | 1,012.1 | 2,003.1 | 1,325.1 | 1,227.2 | 2,333.2 | −251.5 | 754.2 | 292.9 | † −130.9 |
| Portfolio investment: liabilities | 3b9la | .... | .... | .... | .... | .... | — | 16.0 | 1.0 | 6.0 | 3.0 | — | .... |
| Equity & investment fund shares . | 3bala | .... | .... | .... | .... | .... | — | — | — | 5.0 | 2.0 | — | .... |
| Debt securities | 3bbla | .... | .... | .... | .... | .... | — | 16.0 | 1.0 | 1.0 | 1.0 | — | .... |
| Fin. der.& empl.stk.ops.(ESOs): net. | 3c9na | .... | .... | .... | .... | .... | — | — | — | — | — | — | .... |
| Fin. der. & ESOs.: assets | 3c9aa | .... | .... | .... | .... | .... | .... | .... | .... | .... | .... | .... | .... |
| Fin. der. & ESOs.: liabilities | 3c9la | .... | .... | .... | .... | .... | .... | .... | .... | .... | .... | .... | .... |
| Other investment: assets | 3d9aa | .... | .... | 5.6 | 56.5 | 97.9 | −8.4 | 60.7 | 13.2 | 2.8 | 70.9 | 60.5 | † 163.5 |
| Other equity | 3daaa | .... | .... | .... | .... | .... | .... | .... | .... | .... | .... | .... | .... |
| Debt instruments | 3dzaa | .... | .... | 5.6 | 56.5 | 97.9 | −8.4 | 60.7 | 13.2 | 2.8 | 70.9 | 60.5 | † 163.5 |
| Other investment: liabilities | 3d9la | .... | .... | −15.3 | 5.9 | 9.8 | −3.8 | 2.6 | 56.9 | .3 | 12.5 | 21.5 | † 11.0 |
| Other equity | 3dala | .... | .... | .... | .... | .... | .... | .... | .... | .... | .... | .... | .... |
| Debt instruments | 3dzla | .... | .... | −15.3 | 5.9 | 9.8 | −3.8 | 2.6 | 56.9 | .3 | 12.5 | 21.5 | † 11.0 |
| Curr.+ cap.− finan. acct. balance | 4y9na | .... | .... | −66.6 | 155.5 | −12.6 | 39.7 | 156.0 | 92.4 | 510.3 | −159.1 | −299.5 | † 296.0 |
| D. Net Errors and Omissions | 409na | .... | .... | −2.9 | −8.9 | −7.3 | −.2 | .5 | −36.9 | −88.4 | −43.2 | −90.1 | † −75.8 |
| E. Reserves and Related Items | 4z9na | .... | .... | −69.5 | 146.5 | −19.8 | 39.5 | 156.5 | 55.5 | 421.9 | −202.3 | −389.6 | † 220.2 |
| Reserve assets | 3e9aa | .... | .... | −69.5 | 146.5 | −19.8 | 39.5 | 156.5 | 55.5 | 421.9 | −196.6 | −373.9 | † 220.2 |
| Credit and loans from the IMF | 3dcla | .... | .... | — | — | — | — | — | — | — | — | — | † — |
| Exceptional financing | 409la | .... | .... | .... | .... | .... | — | — | — | — | 5.7 | 15.7 | .... |

*Excludes components in group E

| International Investment Position | | 2004 | 2005 | 2006 | 2007 | 2008 | 2009 | 2010 | 2011 | 2012 | 2013 | 2014 | 2015 |
|---|---|---|---|---|---|---|---|---|---|---|---|---|---|
| | | | | | | | *Millions of US Dollars* | | | | | | |
| Assets | 809aa | .... | .... | .... | 2,445.6 | 4,638.6 | 5,848.6 | 7,654.6 | 10,201.0 | 13,165.1 | 16,229.4 | 17,472.4 | † 17,418.0 |
| Direct investment | 8a9aa | .... | .... | .... | .... | .... | .... | 94.0 | 61.0 | 73.7 | 86.3 | 86.3 | † 86.3 |
| Equity & investment fund shares.. | 8aaaa | .... | .... | .... | .... | .... | .... | 94.0 | 61.0 | 73.7 | 86.3 | 86.3 | † 86.3 |
| Debt instruments | 8abaa | .... | .... | .... | .... | .... | .... | .... | .... | .... | .... | .... | .... |
| Portfolio investment | 8b9aa | .... | .... | .... | 2,086.0 | 4,196.8 | 5,376.4 | 6,903.8 | 9,311.9 | 11,775.3 | 14,952.1 | 16,538.6 | † 16,217.6 |
| Equity & investment fund shares | 8baaa | .... | .... | .... | .... | .... | .... | .... | 281.8 | 355.2 | 3,034.8 | 5,333.4 | 6,586.6 | † 6,430.5 |

 .... | .... | .... | .... | .... | .... | 281.8 | 355.2 | 3,034.8 | 5,333.4 | 6,586.6 | † 6,430.5

| Equity & investment fund shares | 8baaa | .... | .... | .... | .... | .... | .... | 281.8 | 355.2 | 3,034.8 | 5,333.4 | 6,586.6 | † 6,430.5 |
| Debt securities | 8bbaa | .... | .... | .... | 2,086.0 | 4,196.8 | 5,376.4 | 6,622.0 | 8,956.7 | 8,740.5 | 9,618.7 | 9,952.0 | † 9,787.1 |
| Fin. der.(oth.than reserves) & ESOs | 8c9aa | .... | .... | .... | .... | .... | .... | .... | .... | .... | .... | .... | .... |
| Other investment | 8d9aa | .... | .... | .... | 129.4 | 231.4 | 222.3 | 250.6 | 366.4 | 432.5 | 504.0 | 536.0 | † 676.2 |
| Other equity | 8daaa | .... | .... | .... | .... | .... | .... | .... | .... | .... | .... | .... | .... |
| Debt instruments | 8dzaa | .... | .... | .... | 129.4 | 231.4 | 222.3 | 250.6 | 366.4 | 432.5 | 504.0 | 536.0 | † 676.2 |
| Reserve assets | 8e9aa | .... | .... | .... | 230.3 | 210.4 | 249.9 | 406.2 | 461.6 | 883.6 | 687.0 | 311.5 | † 437.9 |
| Liabilities | 809la | .... | .... | .... | 74.8 | 109.0 | 153.7 | 212.9 | 303.5 | 331.3 | 387.3 | 441.1 | † 511.2 |
| Direct investment | 8a9la | .... | .... | .... | 36.4 | 78.2 | 124.7 | 155.1 | 205.3 | 243.9 | 283.8 | 316.5 | † 350.0 |
| Equity & investment fund shares.. | 8aala | .... | .... | .... | 36.4 | 70.8 | 119.3 | 147.8 | 196.1 | 234.6 | 282.6 | 316.5 | † 350.0 |
| Debt instruments | 8abla | .... | .... | .... | .... | 7.4 | 5.5 | 7.3 | 9.3 | 9.3 | 1.3 | .... | .... |
| Portfolio investment | 8b9la | .... | .... | .... | .... | .... | .... | 27.0 | 21.0 | 7.8 | 6.8 | 6.8 | † 6.8 |
| Equity & investment fund shares.. | 8bala | .... | .... | .... | .... | .... | .... | 11.0 | 6.0 | 4.0 | 3.0 | 3.0 | † 3.0 |
| Debt securities | 8bbla | .... | .... | .... | .... | .... | .... | 16.0 | 15.0 | 3.8 | 3.8 | 3.8 | † 3.8 |
| Fin. der.(oth.than reserves) & ESOs | 8c9la | .... | .... | .... | .... | .... | .... | .... | .... | .... | .... | .... | .... |
| Other investment | 8d9la | .... | .... | .... | 38.4 | 30.8 | 29.0 | 30.8 | 77.2 | 79.7 | 96.8 | 117.9 | † 154.4 |
| Other equity | 8dala | .... | .... | .... | .... | .... | .... | .... | .... | .... | .... | .... | .... |
| Debt instruments | 8dzla | .... | .... | .... | 38.4 | 30.8 | 29.0 | 30.8 | 77.2 | 79.7 | 96.8 | 117.9 | † 154.4 |

# Timor-Leste, Dem. Rep. of   537

| | | 2004 | 2005 | 2006 | 2007 | 2008 | 2009 | 2010 | 2011 | 2012 | 2013 | 2014 | 2015 |
|---|---|---|---|---|---|---|---|---|---|---|---|---|---|
| **Government Finance** | | | | | | | | | | | | | |
| **Cash Flow Statement** | | | | | | | | | | | | | |
| **General Government** | | | | | | | *Millions of US Dollars: Fiscal Year Ends December 31* | | | | | | |
| Cash Receipts:Operating Activities... | c1 | .... | .... | .... | .... | .... | .... | 2,663.8 | 3,856.4 | 4,171.6 | 3,643.7 | .... | .... |
| Taxes...................................... | c11 | .... | .... | .... | .... | .... | .... | 971.6 | 1,412.5 | 1,713.4 | 1,310.1 | .... | .... |
| Social Contributions...................... | c12 | .... | .... | .... | .... | .... | .... | — | | | | .... | .... |
| Grants.......................................... | c13 | .... | .... | .... | .... | .... | .... | 243.6 | 259.7 | 251.8 | 133.1 | .... | .... |
| Other Receipts.............................. | c14 | .... | .... | .... | .... | .... | .... | 1,448.6 | 2,184.3 | 2,206.4 | 2,200.5 | .... | .... |
| Cash Payments:Operating Activities. | c2 | .... | .... | .... | .... | .... | .... | 737.3 | 736.1 | 907.0 | 878.2 | .... | .... |
| Compensation of Employees.......... | c21 | .... | .... | .... | .... | .... | .... | 108.8 | 132.5 | 148.6 | 149.3 | .... | .... |
| Purchases of Goods & Services....... | c22 | .... | .... | .... | .... | .... | .... | 363.1 | 380.1 | 438.1 | 445.1 | .... | .... |
| Interest........................................ | c24 | .... | .... | .... | .... | .... | .... | — | .5 | — | — | .... | .... |
| Subsidies...................................... | c25 | .... | .... | .... | .... | .... | .... | — | — | — | — | .... | .... |
| Grants.......................................... | c26 | .... | .... | .... | .... | .... | .... | — | — | — | — | .... | .... |
| Social Benefits.............................. | c27 | .... | .... | .... | .... | .... | .... | 112.2 | 88.4 | 158.0 | 124.3 | .... | .... |
| Other Payments............................ | c28 | .... | .... | .... | .... | .... | .... | 153.2 | 134.5 | 162.2 | 159.5 | .... | .... |
| Net Cash Inflow:Operating Act.[1-2] | ccio | .... | .... | .... | .... | .... | .... | 1,926.4 | 3,120.3 | 3,264.6 | 2,765.5 | .... | .... |
| Net Cash Outflow:Invest. in NFA...... | c31 | .... | .... | .... | .... | .... | .... | 282.9 | 633.4 | 549.5 | 357.6 | .... | .... |
| Purchases of Nonfinancial Assets... | c31.1 | .... | .... | .... | .... | .... | .... | 282.9 | 633.4 | 549.5 | 357.6 | .... | .... |
| Sales of Nonfinancial Assets.......... | c31.2 | .... | .... | .... | .... | .... | .... | — | — | — | — | .... | .... |
| Cash Surplus/Deficit [1-2-31=1-2M] | ccsd | .... | .... | .... | .... | .... | .... | 1,643.6 | 2,487.0 | 2,715.2 | 2,407.9 | .... | .... |
| Net Acq. Fin. Assets, excl. Cash....... | c32x | .... | .... | .... | .... | .... | .... | 1,508.9 | 2,423.5 | 2,280.3 | 2,991.8 | .... | .... |
| Domestic...................................... | c321x | .... | .... | .... | .... | .... | .... | .... | .... | .... | .... | .... | .... |
| Foreign......................................... | c322x | .... | .... | .... | .... | .... | .... | .... | .... | .... | .... | .... | .... |
| Net Incurrence of Liabilities.............. | c33 | .... | .... | .... | .... | .... | .... | — | — | — | — | .... | .... |
| Domestic...................................... | c331 | .... | .... | .... | .... | .... | .... | — | — | — | — | .... | .... |
| Foreign......................................... | c332 | .... | .... | .... | .... | .... | .... | — | — | — | — | .... | .... |
| Net Cash Inflow, Fin.Act.[-32x+33].. | cnfb | .... | .... | .... | .... | .... | .... | −1,508.9 | −2,423.5 | −2,280.3 | −2,966.2 | .... | .... |
| Net Change in Stock of Cash.......... | cncb | .... | .... | .... | .... | .... | .... | 134.7 | 63.5 | 434.8 | 25.3 | .... | .... |
| Stat. Discrep. [32X-33+NCB-CSD].... | ccsdz | .... | .... | .... | .... | .... | .... | — | — | — | 583.6 | .... | .... |
| Memo Item:Cash Expenditure[2+31] | c2m | .... | .... | .... | .... | .... | .... | 1,020.2 | 1,369.5 | 1,456.4 | 1,235.8 | .... | .... |
| Memo Item: Gross Debt.................. | c63 | .... | .... | .... | .... | .... | .... | .... | .... | .... | .... | | |
| **National Accounts** | | | | | | | *Millions of US Dollars* | | | | | | |
| Househ.Cons.Expend.,incl.NPISHs.... | 96f.d | 429.5 | 423.6 | 388.5 | 468.5 | 510.7 | 568.9 | 636.7 | 723.0 | 906.0 | .... | .... | .... |
| Government Consumption Expend... | 91f.d | 346.6 | 246.8 | 377.6 | 574.7 | 727.8 | 846.8 | 914.3 | 984.0 | 1,089.0 | .... | .... | .... |
| Gross Fixed Capital Formation.......... | 93e.d | 79.7 | 80.9 | 58.9 | 100.5 | 202.2 | 489.4 | 548.7 | 827.0 | 798.0 | .... | .... | .... |
| Changes in Inventories.................... | 93i.d | 1.8 | .6 | .7 | .8 | .8 | .9 | 1.1 | 1.0 | 32.0 | .... | .... | .... |
| Exports of Goods and Services......... | 90c.d | 707.8 | 1,469.5 | 2,735.3 | 2,930.8 | 4,258.6 | 3,066.2 | 3,959.8 | 5,283.0 | 5,187.0 | .... | .... | .... |
| Imports of Goods and Services (-)..... | 98c.d | 486.1 | 420.2 | 737.4 | 1,110.7 | 1,261.7 | 1,673.7 | 1,845.0 | 2,072.0 | 2,400.0 | .... | .... | .... |
| Statistical Discrepancy.................... | 99bsd | −3.6 | 2.3 | 9.0 | 10.0 | 30.2 | −1.6 | −.6 | −20.0 | −34.0 | .... | .... | .... |
| Gross Domestic Product (GDP)......... | 99b.d | 1,079.4 | 1,801.4 | 2,823.7 | 2,964.7 | 4,438.5 | 3,298.5 | 4,215.6 | 5,748.0 | 5,579.0 | .... | .... | .... |
| Net Primary Income from Abroad..... | 98.nd | −391.3 | −967.8 | −1,461.1 | −918.9 | −1,126.0 | −685.3 | −963.1 | .... | .... | .... | .... | .... |
| Gross National Income (GNI)............ | 99a.d | 672.1 | 845.9 | 1,296.0 | 1,955.8 | 3,288.7 | 2,598.1 | 3,167.4 | .... | .... | .... | .... | .... |
| Net Current Transf. from Abroad...... | 98t.d | 196.2 | 110.8 | 245.9 | 404.9 | 480.0 | 465.6 | 521.9 | .... | .... | .... | .... | .... |
| Gross Saving.................................. | 99s.d | 173.6 | 358.3 | 775.8 | 1,328.7 | 2,444.5 | 1,619.3 | 2,115.6 | .... | .... | .... | .... | .... |
| GDP Volume 2010 Prices................ | 99bpd | 1,675.6 | 2,568.3 | 4,113.4 | 4,088.2 | 4,583.0 | 4,275.0 | 4,215.6 | 4,525.1 | .... | .... | .... | .... |
| GDP Volume (2010=100)................ | 99bvp | 39.7 | 60.9 | 97.6 | 97.0 | 108.7 | 101.4 | 100.0 | 107.3 | .... | .... | .... | .... |
| GDP Deflator (2010=100).............. | 99bip | 64.4 | 70.1 | 68.6 | 72.5 | 96.8 | 77.2 | 100.0 | 127.0 | .... | .... | .... | .... |
| | | | | | | *Millions: Midyear Estimates* | | | | | | | |
| **Population**............................... | 99z | .963 | .989 | 1.008 | 1.021 | 1.031 | 1.042 | 1.057 | 1.078 | 1.102 | 1.129 | 1.157 | 1.185 |

| | | 2004 | 2005 | 2006 | 2007 | 2008 | 2009 | 2010 | 2011 | 2012 | 2013 | 2014 | 2015 |
|---|---|---|---|---|---|---|---|---|---|---|---|---|---|
| **Exchange Rates** | | | | | | *CFA Francs per SDR: End of Period* | | | | | | | |
| Official Rate.............. | aa | 747.90 | 794.73 | 749.30 | 704.15 | 725.98 | 713.83 | 756.02 | 778.32 | 764.10 | 732.49 | 782.77 | 834.92 |
| | | | | | | *CFA Francs per US Dollar: End of Period (ae) Period Average (rf)* | | | | | | | |
| Official Rate.............. | ae | 481.58 | 556.04 | 498.07 | 445.59 | 471.34 | 455.34 | 490.91 | 506.96 | 497.16 | 475.64 | 540.28 | 602.51 |
| Official Rate.............. | rf | 528.28 | 527.47 | 522.89 | 479.27 | 447.81 | 472.19 | 495.28 | 471.87 | 510.53 | 494.04 | 494.41 | 591.45 |
| | | | | | | *Index Numbers (2010=100): Period Averages* | | | | | | | |
| Official Rate.............. | ahx | 93.7 | 93.9 | 94.6 | 103.3 | 110.9 | 105.0 | 100.0 | 104.9 | 96.9 | 100.1 | 100.1 | 83.6 |
| Nominal Effective Exchange Rate..... | nec | 100.0 | 98.4 | 97.7 | 100.9 | 104.2 | 104.7 | 100.0 | 101.6 | 98.6 | 102.3 | 106.3 | 99.7 |
| CPI-Based Real Effect. Ex. Rate....... | rec | 99.5 | 100.5 | 98.9 | 99.4 | 104.9 | 106.5 | 100.0 | 100.7 | 96.7 | 98.8 | 100.0 | 92.9 |
| **Fund Position** | | | | | | *Millions of SDRs: End of Period* | | | | | | | |
| Quota........................ | 2f.s | 73.40 | 73.40 | 73.40 | 73.40 | 73.40 | 73.40 | 73.40 | 73.40 | 73.40 | 73.40 | 73.40 | 73.40 |
| SDR Holdings................... | 1b.s | .01 | .01 | .05 | .07 | .08 | 59.24 | 59.35 | 59.30 | 59.28 | 59.28 | 59.26 | 47.65 |
| Reserve Position in the Fund........... | 1c.s | .33 | .33 | .33 | .33 | .33 | .33 | .41 | .45 | .47 | .53 | .55 | .58 |
| Total Fund Cred.&Loans Outstg....... | 2tl | 17.38 | 9.77 | 5.43 | 1.09 | 31.24 | 58.01 | 86.45 | 95.25 | 95.25 | 94.08 | 86.04 | 74.44 |
| SDR Allocations.............. | 1bd | 10.98 | 10.98 | 10.98 | 10.98 | 10.98 | 70.33 | 70.33 | 70.33 | 70.33 | 70.33 | 70.33 | 70.33 |
| **International Liquidity** | | | | | | *Millions of US Dollars Unless Otherwise Indicated: End of Period* | | | | | | | |
| Total Reserves minus Gold.............. | 1l.d | 357.7 | 191.5 | 374.5 | 438.1 | 581.8 | 703.2 | 714.9 | 774.3 | 441.6 | 507.1 | 507.0 | 574.0 |
| SDR Holdings.............. | 1b.d | — | — | .1 | .1 | .1 | 92.9 | 91.4 | 91.0 | 91.1 | 91.3 | 85.9 | 66.0 |
| Reserve Position in the Fund.......... | 1c.d | .5 | .5 | .5 | .5 | .5 | .5 | .6 | .7 | .7 | .8 | .8 | .8 |
| Foreign Exchange.................... | 1d.d | 357.1 | 191.0 | 373.9 | 437.5 | 581.2 | 609.8 | 622.9 | 682.6 | 349.8 | 415.0 | 420.3 | 507.1 |
| Gold (Million Fine Troy Ounces)....... | 1ad | — | — | — | — | — | — | — | — | — | — | — | — |
| Gold (National Valuation).......... | 1and | — | — | — | — | — | — | — | — | — | — | — | .... |
| Monetary Authorities: Other Liabs.... | 4..d | 91.7 | 15.7 | 39.5 | 49.4 | 123.2 | 142.5 | 80.9 | 134.1 | 32.2 | 43.2 | 223.6 | 119.1 |
| Deposit Money Banks: Assets.......... | 7a.d | 174.4 | 165.6 | 183.3 | 192.7 | 240.2 | 303.5 | 345.8 | 446.8 | 718.0 | 847.3 | 781.5 | 859.1 |
| Deposit Money Banks: Liabs............ | 7b.d | 92.5 | 71.0 | 80.8 | 110.6 | 134.1 | 128.9 | 211.3 | 267.5 | 321.3 | 407.4 | 403.7 | 527.5 |
| **Monetary Authorities** | | | | | | *Billions of CFA Francs: End of Period* | | | | | | | |
| Foreign Assets...................... | 11 | 172.2 | 106.5 | 186.5 | 195.2 | 274.2 | 320.2 | 351.0 | 392.5 | 219.5 | 241.2 | 273.9 | 345.8 |
| Claims on Central Government........ | 12a | 35.4 | 26.7 | 20.5 | 13.7 | 32.8 | 88.7 | 108.1 | 115.6 | 111.7 | 105.2 | 93.9 | 79.7 |
| Claims on Deposit Money Banks..... | 12e | — | — | — | .9 | 16.3 | 14.1 | 28.1 | 57.0 | 115.6 | 137.8 | 184.5 | 172.3 |
| Claims on Other Financial Insts....... | 12f | — | — | — | — | — | — | — | — | — | — | — | — |
| Reserve Money........................ | 14 | 112.3 | 90.2 | 139.0 | 155.7 | 188.6 | 208.0 | 272.9 | 328.8 | 265.7 | 271.2 | 255.0 | 377.6 |
| of which: Currency Outside DMBs.. | 14a | 73.4 | 63.1 | 100.1 | 122.0 | 129.2 | 140.3 | 183.3 | 193.8 | 161.3 | 161.7 | 145.8 | 240.5 |
| Foreign Liabilities..................... | 16c | 65.4 | 25.2 | 32.0 | 30.5 | 88.7 | 156.5 | 158.3 | 196.9 | 142.5 | 141.0 | 243.2 | 192.6 |
| Central Government Deposits.......... | 16d | 28.3 | 19.7 | 34.1 | 21.5 | 48.3 | 56.5 | 45.7 | 43.8 | 37.6 | 70.1 | 57.7 | 27.8 |
| Other Items (Net)..................... | 17r | 1.6 | −1.9 | 1.9 | 2.2 | −2.2 | 1.9 | 10.4 | −4.3 | 1.0 | 1.9 | −3.6 | −.2 |
| **Deposit Money Banks** | | | | | | *Billions of CFA Francs: End of Period* | | | | | | | |
| Reserves.............................. | 20 | 34.1 | 24.7 | 33.9 | 27.6 | 56.0 | 63.7 | 90.3 | 127.5 | 94.4 | 87.4 | 108.8 | 119.5 |
| Foreign Assets...................... | 21 | 84.0 | 92.1 | 91.3 | 85.9 | 113.2 | 138.2 | 169.8 | 226.5 | 357.0 | 403.0 | 422.2 | 517.6 |
| Claims on Central Government........ | 22a | 22.9 | 17.1 | 41.1 | 53.3 | 134.0 | 130.4 | 130.2 | 124.7 | 162.5 | 176.5 | 255.2 | 237.8 |
| Claims on Private Sector................ | 22d | 174.1 | 195.1 | 196.2 | 254.7 | 242.9 | 294.7 | 358.5 | 505.6 | 601.7 | 690.2 | 762.1 | 885.6 |
| Claims on Other Financial Insts........ | 22f | — | — | — | — | — | — | — | — | — | — | — | — |
| Demand Deposits.................... | 24 | 117.2 | 121.5 | 147.3 | 150.7 | 200.8 | 224.5 | 227.4 | 293.1 | 352.0 | 338.2 | 397.7 | 427.8 |
| Time Deposits....................... | 25 | 114.1 | 127.2 | 134.8 | 171.1 | 195.5 | 243.8 | 297.7 | 331.0 | 379.0 | 452.6 | 534.3 | 628.7 |
| Foreign Liabilities.................... | 26c | 44.3 | 38.9 | 35.9 | 43.9 | 59.3 | 55.5 | 97.3 | 131.9 | 157.2 | 186.6 | 214.2 | 300.7 |
| Long-Term Foreign Liabilities........... | 26cl | .2 | .6 | 4.4 | 5.4 | 3.9 | 3.2 | 6.5 | 3.7 | 2.6 | 7.1 | 4.0 | 17.2 |
| Central Government Deposits.......... | 26d | 23.5 | 21.6 | 26.2 | 40.8 | 44.7 | 57.1 | 61.3 | 106.1 | 117.6 | 144.9 | 181.3 | 197.3 |
| Credit from Monetary Authorities..... | 26g | — | — | — | .9 | 12.7 | 14.1 | 28.1 | 57.0 | 115.6 | 137.8 | 184.5 | 173.8 |
| Capital Accounts...................... | 27a | 41.8 | 41.3 | 49.2 | 51.7 | 76.6 | 79.3 | 95.7 | 102.3 | 109.0 | 125.1 | 124.9 | 151.8 |
| Other Items (Net)..................... | 27r | −26.1 | −22.3 | −35.3 | −42.9 | −47.3 | −50.5 | −65.2 | −40.7 | −17.4 | −35.2 | −92.4 | −136.7 |
| Treasury Claims: Private Sector....... | 22d.i | .3 | .3 | .2 | .3 | .3 | .3 | .3 | .4 | .1 | .4 | .4 | .3 |
| Post Office: Checking Deposits....... | 24..i | 1.1 | .9 | 1.6 | 3.8 | 5.1 | 7.0 | 7.8 | 8.9 | 10.6 | 14.3 | 14.6 | 16.4 |
| **Monetary Survey** | | | | | | *Billions of CFA Francs: End of Period* | | | | | | | |
| Foreign Assets (Net).................. | 31n | 146.6 | 134.4 | 210.0 | 206.7 | 239.4 | 246.4 | 265.2 | 290.2 | 276.8 | 316.6 | 238.7 | 370.1 |
| Domestic Credit.......................... | 32 | 181.6 | 198.5 | 199.1 | 263.2 | 321.9 | 407.2 | 497.5 | 605.0 | 731.2 | 771.2 | 887.0 | 994.4 |
| Claims on Central Govt. (Net)........ | 32an | 7.2 | 3.2 | 2.6 | 8.1 | 78.6 | 112.2 | 138.8 | 98.9 | 129.4 | 80.6 | 124.4 | 108.4 |
| Claims on Private Sector............ | 32d | 174.4 | 195.3 | 196.4 | 255.1 | 243.3 | 295.0 | 358.8 | 506.0 | 601.8 | 690.6 | 762.6 | 886.0 |
| Claims on Other Financial Insts....... | 32f | — | — | — | — | — | — | — | — | — | — | — | — |
| Money................................ | 34 | 193.3 | 186.4 | 250.2 | 278.4 | 335.9 | 372.9 | 419.4 | 497.8 | 525.4 | 515.4 | 559.8 | 687.1 |
| Quasi-Money......................... | 35 | 114.1 | 127.2 | 134.8 | 171.1 | 195.5 | 243.8 | 297.7 | 331.0 | 379.0 | 452.6 | 534.3 | 628.7 |
| Long-Term Foreign Liabilities........... | 36cl | .2 | .6 | 4.4 | 5.4 | 3.9 | 3.2 | 6.5 | 3.7 | 2.6 | 7.1 | 4.0 | 17.2 |
| Other Items (Net)..................... | 37r | 20.5 | 18.8 | 19.7 | 15.0 | 26.0 | 33.7 | 39.2 | 62.7 | 101.1 | 112.6 | 27.6 | 31.6 |
| Money plus Quasi-Money................. | 35l | 307.4 | 313.6 | 385.0 | 449.5 | 531.4 | 616.7 | 717.0 | 828.8 | 904.3 | 968.0 | 1,094.1 | 1,315.7 |
| **Interest Rates** | | | | | | *Percent Per Annum* | | | | | | | |
| Repurchase Agreement Rate............ | 60.q | 4.00 | 4.00 | 4.25 | 4.25 | 4.75 | 4.25 | 4.25 | 4.25 | 4.00 | 3.50 | 3.50 | 3.50 |
| Deposit Rate........................ | 60l | 3.50 | 3.50 | 3.50 | 3.50 | 3.50 | 3.50 | 3.50 | 3.50 | 3.50 | 3.50 | 3.50 | 3.50 |
| **Prices and Labor** | | | | | | *Index Numbers (2010=100): Period Averages* | | | | | | | |
| Consumer Prices.............................. | 64 | 79.3 | 84.7 | 86.6 | 87.5 | † 95.0 | 98.2 | 100.0 | 103.6 | 106.3 | 108.2 | 108.4 | 110.3 |
| **Intl. Transactions & Positions** | | | | | | *Millions of CFA Francs* | | | | | | | |
| Exports.............................. | 70 | 317,499 | 348,200 | 329,600 | 335,487 | 403,025 | 382,200 | 318,800 | .... | .... | .... | .... | .... |
| Imports, c.i.f........................ | 71 | 464,891 | 559,229 | 567,154 | 592,909 | 675,911 | 919,400 | 492,900 | .... | .... | .... | .... | .... |
| | | | | | | *2010=100* | | | | | | | |
| Export Prices.............................. | 74 | 117.9 | 100.0 | .... | .... | .... | .... | .... | .... | .... | .... | .... | .... |
| Unit Value of Imports....................... | 75 | 85.5 | 100.0 | .... | .... | .... | .... | .... | .... | .... | .... | .... | .... |

# Togo 742

| | | 2004 | 2005 | 2006 | 2007 | 2008 | 2009 | 2010 | 2011 | 2012 | 2013 | 2014 | 2015 |
|---|---|---|---|---|---|---|---|---|---|---|---|---|---|
| **Balance of Payments** | | | | | | | *Millions of US Dollars* | | | | | | |
| A. Current Account* | 109bx | −206.9 | −203.9 | −176.3 | −215.8 | −222.0 | −176.7 | −199.7 | † −301.7 | −294.1 | −568.3 | −457.9 | .... |
| Goods, credit (exports) | 1a9cx | 601.0 | 634.1 | 630.4 | 676.9 | 852.6 | 903.0 | 976.2 | † 1,178.8 | 1,293.3 | 1,522.0 | 1,325.7 | .... |
| Goods, debit (imports) | 1a9dx | 853.2 | 917.4 | 949.1 | 1,072.0 | 1,307.2 | 1,315.2 | 1,424.4 | † 2,019.8 | 1,851.3 | 2,392.5 | 2,212.4 | .... |
| Balance on goods | 1a9bx | −252.2 | −283.3 | −318.7 | −395.1 | −454.6 | −412.1 | −448.2 | † −841.0 | −558.0 | −870.5 | −886.7 | .... |
| Services, credit (exports) | 1b9cx | 150.0 | 176.9 | 200.7 | 236.0 | 283.1 | 293.6 | 320.2 | † 508.8 | 457.7 | 486.0 | 488.9 | .... |
| Services, debit (imports) | 1b9dx | 239.3 | 250.7 | 264.1 | 305.5 | 359.2 | 374.7 | 404.0 | † 473.5 | 442.0 | 471.3 | 426.0 | .... |
| Balance on Goods & Services | 1z9bx | −341.6 | −357.1 | −382.1 | −464.5 | −530.7 | −493.3 | −532.0 | † −805.8 | −542.3 | −855.8 | −823.9 | .... |
| Primary income: credit | 1c9cx | 39.9 | 46.3 | 47.7 | 61.3 | 81.1 | 68.4 | 99.5 | † 391.5 | 253.8 | 310.2 | 326.6 | .... |
| Primary income: debit | 1c9dx | 74.6 | 80.9 | 85.5 | 91.5 | 96.2 | 87.4 | 122.9 | † 157.9 | 247.8 | 284.9 | 280.5 | .... |
| Balance on gds, serv. & prim. inc. | 1y9bx | −376.3 | −391.6 | −419.9 | −494.8 | −545.8 | −512.3 | −555.4 | † −572.2 | −536.3 | −830.6 | −777.8 | .... |
| Secondary income: credit | 1d9ca | 206.8 | 229.3 | 287.8 | 328.5 | 385.2 | 412.9 | 416.7 | † 349.3 | 411.3 | 480.0 | 523.0 | .... |
| Secondary income: debit | 1d9da | 37.4 | 41.5 | 44.1 | 49.5 | 61.4 | 77.2 | 61.0 | † 78.7 | 169.1 | 217.7 | 203.1 | .... |
| B. Capital Account* | 209na | 40.1 | 51.1 | 64.0 | 73.4 | 655.8 | 135.2 | 1,388.1 | † 276.5 | 286.3 | 315.0 | 318.6 | .... |
| Capital account: credit | 209ca | 40.1 | 51.1 | 64.0 | 73.4 | 655.8 | 135.2 | 1,388.1 | † 277.1 | 289.1 | 317.6 | 333.6 | .... |
| Capital account: debit | 209da | — | — | — | — | — | — | — | † .6 | 2.8 | 2.7 | 14.9 | .... |
| Balance on current & capital acct. | 129ba | −166.8 | −152.8 | −112.3 | −142.3 | 433.8 | −41.5 | 1,188.4 | † −25.2 | −7.9 | −253.3 | −139.2 | .... |
| C. Financial Account* | 309na | −291.8 | −30.6 | −250.2 | −150.6 | 744.0 | −86.5 | 1,177.0 | † −106.8 | 344.7 | −306.9 | −228.3 | .... |
| Direct investment: assets | 3a9aa | 8.7 | 4.1 | −.4 | 12.5 | 10.9 | 35.0 | 76.3 | † 1,264.5 | 420.3 | −20.7 | 358.5 | .... |
| Equity & investment fund shares | 3aaaa | 6.6 | 3.3 | .7 | 5.2 | 9.8 | 35.3 | 68.0 | † 1,041.3 | 398.2 | −34.9 | 291.3 | .... |
| Debt instruments | 3abaa | 2.2 | .8 | −1.1 | 7.2 | 1.0 | −.3 | 8.3 | † 223.2 | 22.2 | 14.2 | 67.2 | .... |
| Direct investment: liabilities | 3a9la | 79.8 | 96.0 | 91.3 | 62.3 | 50.7 | 46.1 | 124.9 | † 727.8 | 121.5 | 195.8 | 64.1 | .... |
| Equity & investment fund shares | 3aala | 42.5 | 54.4 | 43.2 | 30.3 | 19.6 | 32.6 | 78.0 | † 44.6 | 109.4 | 79.2 | 107.3 | .... |
| Debt instruments | 3abla | 37.4 | 41.6 | 48.1 | 32.0 | 31.1 | 13.5 | 47.0 | † 683.2 | 12.1 | 116.5 | −43.3 | .... |
| Portfolio investment: assets | 3b9aa | 26.5 | 26.2 | −2.0 | −13.0 | 6.8 | 1.4 | 27.9 | † 212.5 | 27.7 | 60.2 | 193.2 | .... |
| Equity & investment fund shares | 3baaa | 3.9 | 18.0 | −1.0 | −2.1 | −15.1 | 7.0 | −.8 | .... | .... | — | −.6 | .... |
| Debt securities | 3bbaa | 22.5 | 8.2 | −1.0 | −10.9 | 21.9 | −5.7 | 28.6 | † 212.5 | 27.7 | 60.2 | 193.7 | .... |
| Portfolio investment: liabilities | 3b9la | 26.2 | 28.7 | 60.6 | 6.3 | 18.9 | −29.2 | 6.0 | † 84.8 | — | −17.1 | .4 | .... |
| Equity & investment fund shares | 3bala | 14.8 | 16.0 | 10.4 | 6.3 | 1.4 | 2.1 | 4.5 | † — | .... | .... | .... | .... |
| Debt securities | 3bbla | 11.4 | 12.7 | 50.3 | — | 17.5 | −31.3 | 1.5 | † 84.8 | — | −17.1 | .4 | .... |
| Fin. der.& empl.stk.ops.(ESOs): net. | 3c9na | — | −.5 | — | .1 | — | −.1 | — | .... | .... | .... | .... | .... |
| Fin. der. & ESOs.: assets | 3c9aa | — | — | — | .1 | — | −.1 | — | .... | .... | .... | .... | .... |
| Fin. der. & ESOs.: liabilities | 3c9la | — | .5 | — | — | — | — | — | .... | .... | .... | .... | .... |
| Other investment: assets | 3d9aa | −5.7 | 91.3 | 48.9 | −1.1 | −28.4 | 176.8 | −3.1 | † −81.7 | 138.4 | −15.8 | −37.3 | .... |
| Other equity | 3daaa | .... | .... | .... | .... | .... | .... | .... | .... | .... | .... | .... | .... |
| Debt instruments | 3dzaa | −5.7 | 91.3 | 48.9 | −1.1 | −28.4 | 176.8 | −3.1 | † −81.7 | 138.4 | −15.8 | −37.3 | .... |
| Other investment: liabilities | 3d9la | 215.2 | 27.1 | 144.6 | 80.4 | −824.4 | 282.6 | −1,206.9 | † 689.6 | 120.1 | 151.8 | 678.2 | .... |
| Other equity | 3dala | .... | .... | .... | .... | .... | .... | .... | .... | .... | .1 | — | .... |
| Debt instruments | 3dzla | 215.2 | 27.1 | 144.6 | 80.4 | −824.4 | 282.6 | −1,206.9 | † 689.6 | 120.1 | 151.8 | 678.2 | .... |
| Curr.+ cap.− finan. acct. balance | 4y9na | 125.0 | −122.3 | 137.9 | 8.2 | −310.2 | 44.9 | 11.4 | † 81.5 | −352.6 | 53.6 | 89.1 | .... |
| D. Net Errors and Omissions | 409na | 15.8 | 12.0 | 20.0 | 16.5 | 8.0 | 14.1 | 2.5 | † −10.3 | 15.4 | −4.2 | −15.8 | .... |
| E. Reserves and Related Items | 4z9na | 140.8 | −110.2 | 157.8 | 24.7 | −302.2 | 59.0 | 13.9 | † 71.2 | −337.2 | 49.4 | 73.3 | .... |
| Reserve assets | 3e9aa | 124.6 | −121.4 | 151.5 | 18.1 | 176.4 | 100.3 | 57.1 | † 85.3 | −337.2 | 47.6 | 61.2 | .... |
| Credit and loans from the IMF | 3dcla | −16.2 | −11.2 | −6.4 | −6.6 | 47.2 | 41.3 | 43.2 | † 14.0 | — | −1.8 | −12.1 | .... |
| Exceptional financing | 409la | — | — | — | — | 431.4 | — | — | .... | .... | .... | .... | .... |

*Excludes components in group E

| | | 2004 | 2005 | 2006 | 2007 | 2008 | 2009 | 2010 | 2011 | 2012 | 2013 | 2014 | 2015 |
|---|---|---|---|---|---|---|---|---|---|---|---|---|---|
| **International Investment Position** | | | | | | | *Millions of US Dollars* | | | | | | |
| Assets | 809aa | 758.4 | 589.2 | 1,039.4 | 1,207.6 | 1,369.6 | 1,736.2 | 1,747.4 | † 3,893.6 | 4,168.7 | 4,227.8 | 4,815.4 | .... |
| Direct investment | 8a9aa | 33.7 | 31.2 | 33.4 | 46.5 | 128.6 | 165.2 | 202.5 | † 2,225.4 | 2,687.2 | 2,781.6 | 2,993.5 | .... |
| Equity & investment fund shares | 8aaaa | 14.5 | 13.8 | 15.1 | 18.3 | 100.9 | 136.9 | 167.9 | † 1,839.6 | 2,270.3 | 2,506.1 | 2,691.1 | .... |
| Debt instruments | 8abaa | 19.2 | 17.4 | 18.3 | 28.2 | 27.7 | 28.3 | 34.6 | † 385.8 | 416.9 | 275.6 | 302.4 | .... |
| Portfolio investment | 8b9aa | 104.7 | 115.6 | 126.9 | 127.9 | 127.4 | 133.9 | 152.3 | † 318.8 | 332.7 | 281.0 | 570.0 | .... |
| Equity & investment fund shares | 8baaa | 9.7 | 25.5 | 27.4 | 28.4 | 12.5 | 20.2 | 18.0 | † .3 | .4 | .7 | 1.2 | .... |
| Debt securities | 8bbaa | 95.0 | 90.1 | 99.5 | 99.5 | 114.9 | 113.7 | 134.3 | † 318.5 | 332.4 | 280.3 | 568.8 | .... |
| Fin. der.(oth.than reserves) & ESOs | 8c9aa | .... | .... | .... | .... | .... | .... | .... | .... | .... | .... | .... | .... |
| Other investment | 8d9aa | 262.3 | 250.8 | 504.6 | 595.1 | 531.8 | 733.9 | 677.6 | † 575.1 | 707.2 | 658.2 | 744.0 | .... |
| Other equity | 8daaa | .... | .... | .... | .... | .... | .... | .... | .... | .... | .... | .... | .... |
| Debt instruments | 8dzaa | 262.3 | 250.8 | 504.6 | 595.1 | 531.8 | 733.9 | 677.6 | † 575.1 | 707.2 | 658.2 | 744.0 | .... |
| Reserve assets | 8e9aa | 357.7 | 191.5 | 374.5 | 438.1 | 581.8 | 703.2 | 714.9 | † 774.3 | 441.6 | 507.1 | 507.9 | .... |
| Liabilities | 809la | 2,673.3 | 2,506.7 | 3,097.4 | 3,413.9 | 3,095.1 | 3,649.7 | 2,568.2 | † 2,593.7 | 2,918.8 | 3,385.9 | 3,926.9 | .... |
| Direct investment | 8a9la | 207.2 | 263.2 | 389.3 | 498.0 | 524.3 | 586.4 | 642.2 | † 847.6 | 906.2 | 1,121.7 | 999.0 | .... |
| Equity & investment fund shares | 8aala | 157.0 | 185.6 | 252.2 | 310.4 | 317.4 | 358.2 | 383.2 | † 75.6 | 106.5 | 70.9 | 187.9 | .... |
| Debt instruments | 8abla | 50.2 | 77.6 | 137.1 | 187.6 | 206.9 | 228.2 | 259.0 | † 772.0 | 799.7 | 1,050.9 | 811.1 | .... |
| Portfolio investment | 8b9la | 47.0 | 67.9 | 137.4 | 160.3 | 147.7 | 129.9 | 126.6 | † .5 | .5 | 2.4 | 259.6 | .... |
| Equity & investment fund shares | 8bala | 34.3 | 44.9 | 60.9 | 74.9 | 72.1 | 76.8 | 75.8 | † .2 | .2 | .... | .2 | .... |
| Debt securities | 8bbla | 12.7 | 23.0 | 76.4 | 85.4 | 75.6 | 53.1 | 50.8 | † .3 | .3 | 2.4 | 259.3 | .... |
| Fin. der.(oth.than reserves) & ESOs | 8c9la | .... | .... | .... | .... | .... | .... | .... | † — | — | .... | .... | .... |
| Other investment | 8d9la | 2,419.1 | 2,175.7 | 2,570.7 | 2,755.5 | 2,423.1 | 2,933.4 | 1,799.3 | † 1,745.6 | 2,012.0 | 2,261.8 | 2,668.3 | .... |
| Other equity | 8dala | .... | .... | .... | .... | .... | .... | .... | .... | .... | .1 | .1 | .... |
| Debt instruments | 8dzla | 2,419.1 | 2,175.7 | 2,570.7 | 2,755.5 | 2,423.1 | 2,933.4 | 1,799.3 | † 1,745.6 | 2,012.0 | 2,261.8 | 2,668.3 | .... |

| | | 2004 | 2005 | 2006 | 2007 | 2008 | 2009 | 2010 | 2011 | 2012 | 2013 | 2014 | 2015 |
|---|---|---|---|---|---|---|---|---|---|---|---|---|---|
| **Government Finance Operations Statement Budgetary Central Government** | | | | | | *Billions of CFA Francs: Fiscal Year Ends December 31* | | | | | | | |
| Revenue | a1 | 170.1 | 163.5 | 199.3 | 223.7 | 249.9 | 318.0 | 336.4 | 401.2 | 412.3 | 523.3 | .... | .... |
| Taxes | a11 | 156.7 | 154.9 | 170.6 | 195.9 | 211.2 | 229.1 | 246.8 | 291.4 | 327.7 | 403.6 | .... | .... |
| Social Contributions | a12 | — | — | — | — | — | — | — | — | — | — | .... | .... |
| Grants | a13 | 7.8 | — | 16.0 | 20.4 | 29.3 | 64.9 | 62.3 | 84.6 | 40.7 | 73.5 | .... | .... |
| Other Revenue | a14 | 5.6 | 8.6 | 12.7 | 7.4 | 9.4 | 24.1 | 27.4 | 25.2 | 43.9 | 46.2 | .... | .... |
| Expense | a2 | 156.6 | 179.0 | 199.7 | 209.6 | 196.1 | 234.1 | 226.6 | 276.2 | 359.6 | 459.0 | .... | .... |
| Compensation of Employees | a21 | 54.5 | 55.1 | 59.4 | 64.3 | 69.1 | 94.3 | 82.6 | 104.7 | 120.4 | 130.6 | .... | .... |
| Use of Goods & Services | a22 | 44.7 | 86.4 | 47.5 | 52.6 | 40.9 | 56.5 | 59.5 | 63.7 | 96.4 | 129.5 | .... | .... |
| Consumption of Fixed Capital | a23 | .... | .... | .... | .... | .... | .... | .... | .... | .... | — | .... | .... |
| Interest | a24 | 17.9 | 11.6 | 10.5 | 12.4 | 10.8 | 12.8 | 15.1 | 11.6 | 18.6 | 25.7 | .... | .... |
| Subsidies | a25 | .4 | — | 19.2 | 11.6 | 37.0 | 23.9 | — | — | — | 128.2 | .... | .... |
| Grants | a26 | 7.2 | 2.1 | 24.8 | 43.0 | — | 17.2 | 59.6 | 91.0 | 117.8 | 34.3 | .... | .... |
| Social Benefits | a27 | 2.8 | 1.0 | .7 | 1.1 | 1.1 | — | — | — | — | — | .... | .... |
| Other Expense | a28 | 29.2 | 22.8 | 37.6 | 24.6 | 37.1 | 29.4 | 9.7 | 5.3 | 6.4 | 10.7 | .... | .... |
| Gross Operating Balance [1-2+23] | agob | 13.5 | −15.6 | −.5 | 14.1 | 53.7 | 83.9 | 109.8 | 125.1 | 52.6 | 64.2 | .... | .... |
| Net Operating Balance [1-2] | anob | .... | .... | .... | .... | .... | .... | .... | .... | .... | 64.2 | .... | .... |
| Net Acq. of Nonfinancial Assets | a31 | 17.0 | 48.5 | 40.2 | 24.1 | 49.9 | 92.2 | 100.7 | 144.3 | 175.1 | 162.2 | .... | .... |
| Aquisition of Nonfin. Assets | a31.1 | .... | .... | .... | .... | 49.9 | .... | .... | .... | .... | .... | .... | .... |
| Disposal of Nonfin. Assets | a31.2 | .... | .... | .... | .... | — | .... | .... | .... | .... | .... | .... | .... |
| Net Lending/Borrowing [1-2-31] | anlb | −3.4 | −64.0 | −40.6 | −10.0 | 3.8 | −8.3 | 9.1 | −19.2 | −122.4 | −98.0 | .... | .... |
| Net Acq. of Financial Assets | a32 | .... | .... | −3.8 | −21.0 | 38.6 | 17.1 | −3.1 | 35.3 | −1.5 | 23.8 | .... | .... |
| By instrument | | | | | | | | | | | | | |
| Monetary Gold & SDRs | a3201 | .... | .... | — | — | — | — | — | — | — | — | .... | .... |
| Currency & Deposits | a3202 | .... | .... | −17.0 | −9.3 | 30.7 | 20.8 | −7.4 | 34.9 | 1.2 | 47.7 | .... | .... |
| Securities other than Shares | a3203 | .... | .... | 5.5 | — | — | — | — | — | — | — | .... | .... |
| Loans | a3204 | .... | .... | — | — | .3 | −3.7 | — | .4 | .3 | −.4 | .... | .... |
| Shares & Other Equity | a3205 | .... | .... | — | — | 1.2 | — | 4.3 | — | −3.0 | −23.5 | .... | .... |
| Insurance Technical Reserves | a3206 | .... | .... | — | — | — | — | — | — | — | — | .... | .... |
| Financial Derivatives | a3207 | .... | .... | — | — | — | — | — | — | — | — | .... | .... |
| Other Accounts Receivable | a3208 | .... | .... | 7.8 | −11.7 | 6.4 | — | — | — | — | — | .... | .... |
| By debtor | | | | | | | | | | | | | |
| Domestic | a321 | .... | .... | −3.8 | −21.0 | 38.6 | 17.1 | −3.1 | 35.3 | −1.5 | 23.8 | .... | .... |
| Foreign | a322 | .... | .... | — | — | — | — | — | — | — | — | .... | .... |
| Net Incurrence of Liabilities | a33 | .... | .... | 53.7 | 3.1 | 52.1 | 30.4 | −12.2 | 54.5 | 120.9 | 121.8 | .... | .... |
| By instrument | | | | | | | | | | | | | |
| Special Drawing Rights (SDRs) | a3301 | .... | .... | — | — | — | — | — | — | — | — | .... | .... |
| Currency & Deposits | a3302 | .... | .... | 3.9 | −5.4 | 63.8 | −7.2 | 6.4 | — | 18.0 | 10.2 | .... | .... |
| Securities other than Shares | a3303 | .... | .... | 32.5 | 16.8 | −4.3 | −9.1 | 9.5 | 16.7 | 12.5 | 65.0 | .... | .... |
| Loans | a3304 | .... | .... | .7 | 5.1 | 49.6 | 47.7 | 31.4 | 21.5 | 99.4 | 31.1 | .... | .... |
| Shares & Other Equity | a3305 | .... | .... | — | — | — | — | — | — | — | — | .... | .... |
| Insurance Technical Reserves | a3306 | .... | .... | — | — | — | — | — | — | — | — | .... | .... |
| Financial Derivatives | a3307 | .... | .... | — | — | — | — | — | — | — | — | .... | .... |
| Other Accounts Payable | a3308 | .... | .... | 16.6 | −13.5 | −57.0 | −1.0 | −59.4 | 16.3 | −8.9 | 15.6 | .... | .... |
| By creditor | | | | | | | | | | | | | |
| Domestic | a331 | .... | .... | 38.3 | −5.7 | 54.6 | 37.0 | −41.8 | 38.6 | 52.1 | 101.3 | .... | .... |
| Foreign | a332 | .... | .... | 15.4 | 8.7 | −2.5 | −6.6 | 29.6 | 15.9 | 68.8 | 20.5 | .... | .... |
| Stat. Discrepancy [32-33-NLB] | anlbz | — | — | −16.8 | −14.1 | −17.3 | −5.0 | — | — | — | — | .... | .... |
| Memo Item: Expenditure [2+31] | a2m | 173.6 | 227.5 | 239.9 | 233.6 | 246.0 | 326.3 | 327.3 | 420.4 | 534.7 | 621.3 | .... | .... |
| **National Accounts** | | | | | | *Billions of CFA Francs* | | | | | | | |
| Househ.Cons.Expend.,incl.NPISHs | 96f | 924.8 | 975.1 | 1,005.4 | 1,079.4 | 1,245.0 | 1,304.8 | 1,367.3 | 1,607.4 | 1,534.1 | 1,680.0 | 1,970.5 | .... |
| Government Consumption Expend | 91f | 131.5 | 156.4 | 184.3 | 173.7 | 184.6 | 182.0 | 226.8 | 206.2 | 254.7 | 312.5 | 315.0 | .... |
| Gross Fixed Capital Formation | 93e | 179.2 | 193.2 | 220.7 | 225.1 | 266.7 | 321.1 | 359.6 | 309.2 | 476.2 | 493.3 | 526.6 | .... |
| Changes in Inventories | 93i | 136.7 | 66.6 | 18.1 | 19.0 | 23.8 | 14.4 | 6.7 | 30.0 | 1.4 | 1.9 | −13.7 | .... |
| Exports of Goods and Services | 90c | 396.7 | 427.7 | 434.5 | 435.9 | 508.6 | 565.0 | 642.1 | 796.3 | 904.3 | 992.0 | 918.8 | .... |
| Imports of Goods and Services (-) | 98c | 577.2 | 616.1 | 634.4 | 658.6 | 746.2 | 797.9 | 905.5 | 1,176.5 | 1,181.2 | 1,414.8 | 1,454.9 | .... |
| Gross Domestic Product (GDP) | 99b | 1,191.8 | 1,202.9 | 1,228.6 | 1,274.4 | 1,482.4 | 1,589.2 | 1,696.9 | 1,772.6 | 1,989.5 | 2,064.9 | 2,262.3 | .... |
| GDP Volume 2008 Prices | 99b.p | 1,290.1 | 1,306.1 | 1,357.0 | 1,385.3 | 1,482.4 | 1,564.5 | 1,275.7 | 1,337.5 | 1,415.1 | 1,491.0 | 1,578.3 | .... |
| GDP Volume (2000=100) | 99bvp | 101.1 | 102.4 | 106.4 | 108.6 | 116.2 | 122.6 | 100.0 | 104.8 | 110.9 | 116.9 | 123.7 | .... |
| GDP Deflator (2000=100) | 99bip | 69.4 | 69.2 | 68.1 | 69.2 | 75.2 | 76.4 | 100.0 | 99.6 | 105.7 | 104.1 | 107.8 | .... |
| | | | | | | *Millions: Midyear Estimates* | | | | | | | |
| Population | 99z | 5.43 | 5.58 | 5.73 | 5.89 | 6.05 | 6.22 | 6.39 | 6.57 | 6.75 | 6.93 | 7.12 | 7.30 |

# Tonga  866

|  |  | 2004 | 2005 | 2006 | 2007 | 2008 | 2009 | 2010 | 2011 | 2012 | 2013 | 2014 | 2015 |
|---|---|---|---|---|---|---|---|---|---|---|---|---|---|
| **Exchange Rates** |  | | | | | | *Pa'anga per SDR: End of Period* | | | | | | |
| Official Rate | aa | 2.9689 | 2.9439 | 3.0088 | 2.9816 | 3.2863 | 2.9849 | 2.7859 | 2.6493 | 2.6687 | 2.8092 | 2.8303 | 3.0597 |
|  |  | | | *Pa'anga per US Dollar: End of Period (ae) Period Average (rf)* | | | | | | | | | |
| Official Rate | ae | 1.9117 | 2.0597 | 2.0000 | 1.8868 | 2.1336 | 1.9040 | 1.8090 | 1.7256 | 1.7364 | 1.8242 | 1.9535 | 2.2080 |
| Official Rate | rf | 1.9716 | 1.9430 | 2.0259 | 1.9709 | 1.9424 | 2.0345 | 1.9060 | 1.7290 | 1.7195 | 1.7737 | 1.8468 | 2.1058 |
| **Fund Position** |  | | | | | *Millions of SDRs: End of Period* | | | | | | | |
| Quota | 2f.s | 6.90 | 6.90 | 6.90 | 6.90 | 6.90 | 6.90 | 6.90 | 6.90 | 6.90 | 6.90 | 6.90 | 6.90 |
| SDR Holdings | 1b.s | .24 | .28 | .34 | .41 | .48 | 7.07 | 7.08 | 7.09 | 7.09 | 7.09 | 7.09 | 7.09 |
| Reserve Position in the Fund | 1c.s | 1.71 | 1.71 | 1.71 | 1.71 | 1.71 | 1.71 | 1.71 | 1.71 | 1.71 | 1.71 | 1.71 | 1.71 |
| Total Fund Cred.&Loans Outstg | 2tl | — | — | — | — | — | — | — | — | — | — | — | — |
| SDR Allocations | 1bd | — | — | — | — | — | 6.58 | 6.58 | 6.58 | 6.58 | 6.58 | 6.58 | 6.58 |
| **International Liquidity** |  | | | | *Millions of US Dollars Unless Otherwise Indicated: End of Period* | | | | | | | | |
| Total Reserves minus Gold | 1l.d | 55.26 | 46.86 | 47.97 | 65.24 | 69.75 | 95.70 | 104.53 | 143.29 | 152.40 | 155.52 | 158.78 | 156.11 |
| SDR Holdings | 1b.d | .38 | .40 | .51 | .65 | .74 | 11.09 | 10.90 | 10.88 | 10.89 | 10.92 | 10.27 | 9.83 |
| Reserve Position in the Fund | 1c.d | 2.66 | 2.45 | 2.57 | 2.70 | 2.64 | 2.68 | 2.64 | 2.63 | 2.63 | 2.64 | 2.48 | 2.37 |
| Foreign Exchange | 1d.d | 52.23 | 44.01 | 44.89 | 61.88 | 66.38 | 81.93 | 90.99 | 129.79 | 138.88 | 141.97 | 146.03 | 143.91 |
| Central Bank: Other Assets | 3..d | — | — | — | — | — | — | — | — | † .04 | .05 | .60 | .06 |
| Central Bank: Other Liabs | 4..d | 1.18 | 2.80 | 2.24 | 2.82 | 5.75 | 2.38 | 3.48 | 12.10 | † .08 | .02 | .01 | .02 |
| Other Depository Corps.: Assets | 7a.d | 6.61 | 5.50 | 6.16 | 4.83 | 11.93 | 6.38 | 10.11 | 9.66 | † 8.82 | 7.94 | 7.30 | 10.82 |
| Other Depository Corps.: Liabs | 7b.d | 5.67 | 6.29 | 8.01 | 10.85 | 10.54 | 13.11 | 6.97 | 3.13 | † 2.37 | 6.91 | 5.88 | 6.38 |
| **Central Bank** |  | | | | | *Thousands of Pa'anga: End of Period* | | | | | | | |
| Net Foreign Assets | 11n | 92,306 | 81,762 | 81,738 | 110,319 | 113,262 | 137,701 | 154,893 | 190,464 | † 243,497 | 259,862 | 285,426 | 317,352 |
| Claims on Nonresidents | 11 | 94,564 | 87,521 | 86,214 | 115,644 | 125,526 | 161,869 | 179,529 | 228,780 | † 261,199 | 278,503 | 304,080 | 337,529 |
| Liabilities to Nonresidents | 16c | 2,258 | 5,760 | 4,476 | 5,324 | 12,263 | 24,168 | 24,636 | 38,316 | † 17,702 | 18,642 | 18,654 | 20,177 |
| Claims on Other Depository Corps. | 12e | — | — | — | — | — | — | — | — | † 72 | 45 | 57 | 3 |
| Net Claims on Central Government | 12an | −19,730 | −15,327 | −3,748 | −20,389 | −26,168 | −26,560 | −26,491 | −30,388 | † −44,590 | −49,974 | −48,919 | −41,789 |
| Claims on Central Government | 12a | 9,924 | 16,242 | 16,596 | 16,011 | — | — | — | — | † 72 | 45 | 57 | 3 |
| Liabilities to Central Government | 16d | 29,654 | 31,569 | 20,344 | 36,400 | 26,168 | 26,560 | 26,491 | 30,388 | † 44,662 | 50,019 | 48,976 | 41,792 |
| Claims on Other Sectors | 12s | — | — | — | — | — | — | — | — | † 192 | 126 | 910 | 1,546 |
| Claims on Other Financial Corps. | 12g | — | — | — | — | — | — | — | — | † — | — | — | — |
| Claims on State & Local Govts. | 12b | — | — | — | — | — | — | — | — | † — | — | — | — |
| Claims on Public Nonfin. Corps. | 12c | — | — | — | — | — | — | — | — | † — | — | — | — |
| Claims on Private Sector | 12d | — | — | — | — | — | — | — | — | † 192 | 126 | 910 | 1,546 |
| Monetary Base | 14 | 73,509 | 62,579 | 70,370 | 81,234 | 79,869 | 102,431 | 118,176 | 157,134 | † 191,071 | 198,033 | 228,032 | 258,535 |
| Currency in Circulation | 14a | 24,916 | 25,659 | 27,860 | 32,307 | 31,661 | 33,957 | 35,760 | 39,736 | † 44,899 | 47,949 | 56,590 | 68,701 |
| Liabs. to Other Depository Corps. | 14c | 48,594 | 36,919 | 39,223 | 48,928 | 40,226 | 68,474 | 82,416 | 117,398 | † 146,172 | 150,085 | 171,442 | 189,834 |
| Liabilities to Other Sectors | 14d | — | — | 3,287 | — | 7,982 | — | — | — | † — | | | |
| Other Liabs. to Other Dep. Corps. | 14n | — | — | — | — | — | — | — | — | † 84 | 2,096 | 15 | 17 |
| Dep. & Sec. Excl. f/Monetary Base | 14o | — | — | — | — | — | — | — | — | † — | | | |
| Deposits Included in Broad Money. | 15 | — | — | — | — | — | — | — | — | † — | | | |
| Sec.Ot.th.Shares Incl.in Brd.Money | 16a | — | — | — | — | — | — | — | — | † — | | | |
| Deposits Excl. from Broad Money | 16b | — | — | — | — | — | — | — | — | † — | | | |
| Sec.Ot.th.Shares Excl.f/Brd.Money | 16s | — | — | — | — | — | — | — | — | † — | | | |
| Loans | 16l | — | — | — | — | — | — | — | — | † — | | | |
| Financial Derivatives | 16m | — | — | — | — | — | — | — | — | † — | | | |
| Shares and Other Equity | 17a | 5,628 | 10,172 | 13,646 | 15,655 | 15,721 | 19,542 | 20,953 | 12,977 | † 19,986 | 21,225 | 25,991 | 38,571 |
| Other Items (Net) | 17r | −6,562 | −6,317 | −6,026 | −6,959 | −8,495 | −10,833 | −10,727 | −10,036 | † −11,970 | −11,296 | −16,564 | −20,012 |
| Memo Item: |  | | | | | | | | | | | | |
| Total Assets | 10ra | 131,418 | 131,511 | 131,499 | 161,848 | 157,422 | 196,758 | 213,011 | 261,182 | † 294,498 | 311,021 | 344,017 | 381,975 |
| **Other Depository Corporations** |  | | | | | *Thousands of Pa'anga: End of Period* | | | | | | | |
| Net Foreign Assets | 21n | 1,791 | −1,630 | −3,714 | −11,343 | 2,963 | −12,820 | 5,681 | 11,272 | † 11,201 | 1,879 | 2,771 | 9,818 |
| Claims on Nonresidents | 21 | 12,634 | 11,329 | 12,312 | 9,122 | 25,456 | 12,147 | 18,281 | 16,670 | † 15,322 | 14,574 | 14,266 | 23,895 |
| Liabilities to Nonresidents | 26c | 10,843 | 12,959 | 16,026 | 20,465 | 22,493 | 24,967 | 12,600 | 5,398 | † 4,121 | 12,695 | 11,495 | 14,077 |
| Claims on Central Bank | 20 | 55,954 | 41,882 | 48,580 | 59,606 | 57,415 | 77,946 | 90,042 | 128,551 | † 158,314 | 163,721 | 187,684 | 206,751 |
| Currency | 20a | 7,776 | 5,250 | 6,356 | 9,841 | 7,145 | 8,352 | 7,372 | 9,688 | † 11,733 | 10,913 | 12,671 | 15,868 |
| Reserve Deposits and Securities | 20b | 48,178 | 36,632 | 39,224 | 49,765 | 42,270 | 69,594 | 82,670 | 118,863 | † 146,581 | 152,808 | 175,013 | 190,883 |
| Other Claims | 20n | — | — | 3,000 | — | 8,000 | — | — | — | † — | | | |
| Net Claims on Central Government | 22an | −6,802 | −15,132 | −11,064 | −5,521 | −12,053 | −4,349 | 12,492 | −3,784 | † −2,431 | −6,607 | −11,454 | −10,583 |
| Claims on Central Government | 22a | 17,637 | 8,860 | 4,662 | 4,180 | 15,377 | 18,294 | 24,453 | 19,046 | † 19,794 | 17,663 | 19,563 | 19,563 |
| Liabilities to Central Government | 26d | 24,439 | 23,992 | 15,726 | 9,701 | 27,430 | 22,643 | 11,961 | 22,830 | † 22,225 | 24,270 | 31,017 | 30,146 |
| Claims on Other Sectors | 22s | 200,762 | 276,141 | 287,568 | 334,037 | 346,539 | 317,115 | 298,179 | 262,044 | † 259,159 | 275,688 | 296,244 | 334,437 |
| Claims on Other Financial Corps. | 22g | — | — | — | — | — | — | — | — | † 6,345 | 12,449 | 14,169 | 16,433 |
| Claims on State & Local Govts. | 22b | — | — | — | — | — | — | — | — | † — | | | |
| Claims on Public Nonfin. Corps. | 22c | 9,294 | 8,041 | 4,426 | 4,778 | 4,311 | 4,304 | 15,655 | 11,617 | † 14,642 | 35,507 | 43,558 | 45,198 |
| Claims on Private Sector | 22d | 191,468 | 268,100 | 283,142 | 329,259 | 342,228 | 312,811 | 282,524 | 250,427 | † 238,172 | 227,732 | 238,517 | 272,806 |
| Liabilities to Central Bank | 26g | — | — | — | — | — | — | — | — | † — | | 559 | 633 |
| Transf.Dep.Included in Broad Money | 24 | 62,540 | 60,589 | 56,903 | 70,421 | 71,849 | 65,294 | 78,699 | 92,718 | † 112,851 | 134,628 | 141,851 | 172,010 |
| Other Dep.Included in Broad Money. | 25 | 118,464 | 161,020 | 176,667 | 196,567 | 195,143 | 201,396 | 203,751 | 183,278 | † 198,910 | 184,067 | 201,544 | 225,352 |
| Sec.Ot.th.Shares Incl.in Brd.Money | 26a | — | — | — | — | — | — | — | — | † 105 | 100 | 11 | 1 |
| Deposits Excl. from Broad Money | 26b | — | — | — | — | — | — | — | — | † — | | | |
| Sec.Ot.th.Shares Excl.f/Brd.Money | 26s | 19,730 | 15,900 | 16,312 | 20,481 | 19,315 | 20,177 | 23,398 | 25,977 | † — | | | |
| Loans | 26l | 1,126 | 340 | 1,190 | 1,570 | 2,165 | 2,741 | 1,055 | 928 | † — | | | |
| Financial Derivatives | 26m | — | — | — | — | — | — | — | — | † — | | | |
| Insurance Technical Reserves | 26r | — | — | — | — | — | — | — | — | † — | | | |
| Shares and Other Equity | 27a | 49,661 | 57,977 | 65,994 | 82,286 | 93,574 | 75,409 | 83,935 | 91,865 | † 102,315 | 113,287 | 131,965 | 146,752 |
| Other Items (Net) | 27r | 184 | 5,435 | 4,304 | 5,454 | 12,818 | 12,875 | 15,556 | 3,271 | † 12,062 | 2,599 | −685 | −4,325 |
| Memo Item: |  | | | | | | | | | | | | |
| Total Assets | 20ra | 328,550 | 379,259 | 404,772 | 458,533 | 508,034 | 491,105 | 496,941 | 497,470 | † 515,808 | 532,765 | 577,753 | 651,692 |

# Tonga 866

| | | 2004 | 2005 | 2006 | 2007 | 2008 | 2009 | 2010 | 2011 | 2012 | 2013 | 2014 | 2015 |
|---|---|---|---|---|---|---|---|---|---|---|---|---|---|
| **Depository Corporations** | | *Thousands of Pa'anga: End of Period* | | | | | | | | | | | |
| Net Foreign Assets | 31n | 94,097 | 80,132 | 78,024 | 98,976 | 116,225 | 124,881 | 160,574 | 201,736 | † 254,698 | 261,741 | 288,197 | 327,170 |
| Claims on Nonresidents | 31 | 107,198 | 98,850 | 98,526 | 124,766 | 150,982 | 174,016 | 197,810 | 245,450 | † 276,521 | 293,077 | 318,346 | 361,424 |
| Liabilities to Nonresidents | 36c | 13,101 | 18,719 | 20,502 | 25,789 | 34,756 | 49,135 | 37,236 | 43,714 | † 21,823 | 31,337 | 30,149 | 34,254 |
| Domestic Claims | 32 | 174,230 | 245,682 | 272,756 | 308,127 | 308,318 | 286,206 | 284,180 | 227,872 | † 212,330 | 219,233 | 236,781 | 283,611 |
| Net Claims on Central Government | 32an | −26,532 | −30,459 | −14,812 | −25,910 | −38,221 | −30,909 | −13,999 | −34,172 | † −47,021 | −56,581 | −60,373 | −52,372 |
| Claims on Central Government | 32a | 27,561 | 25,102 | 21,258 | 20,191 | 15,377 | 18,294 | 24,453 | 19,046 | † 19,866 | 17,708 | 19,620 | 19,566 |
| Liabilities to Central Government | 36d | 54,093 | 55,561 | 36,070 | 46,101 | 53,598 | 49,203 | 38,452 | 53,218 | † 66,887 | 74,289 | 79,993 | 71,938 |
| Claims on Other Sectors | 32s | 200,762 | 276,141 | 287,568 | 334,037 | 346,539 | 317,115 | 298,179 | 262,044 | † 259,351 | 275,814 | 297,154 | 335,983 |
| Claims on Other Financial Corps | 32g | — | — | — | — | — | — | — | — | † 6,345 | 12,449 | 14,169 | 16,433 |
| Claims on State & Local Govts | 32b | | | | | | | | | † — | | | |
| Claims on Public Nonfin. Corps | 32c | 9,294 | 8,041 | 4,426 | 4,778 | 4,311 | 4,304 | 15,655 | 11,617 | † 14,642 | 35,507 | 43,558 | 45,198 |
| Claims on Private Sector | 32d | 191,468 | 268,100 | 283,142 | 329,259 | 342,228 | 312,811 | 282,524 | 250,427 | † 238,364 | 227,858 | 239,427 | 274,352 |
| Broad Money Liabilities | 35l | 198,144 | 242,018 | 258,362 | 289,454 | 299,490 | 292,295 | 310,838 | 306,044 | † 345,032 | 355,831 | 387,325 | 450,196 |
| Currency Outside Depository Corps | 34a | 17,140 | 20,409 | 21,504 | 22,466 | 24,516 | 25,605 | 28,388 | 30,048 | † 33,166 | 37,036 | 43,919 | 52,833 |
| Transferable Deposits | 34 | 62,540 | 60,589 | 56,903 | 70,421 | 71,849 | 65,294 | 78,699 | 92,718 | † 112,851 | 134,628 | 141,851 | 172,010 |
| Other Deposits | 35 | 118,464 | 161,020 | 176,667 | 196,567 | 195,143 | 201,396 | 203,751 | 183,278 | † 198,910 | 184,067 | 201,544 | 225,352 |
| Securities Other than Shares | 36a | — | — | 3,287 | — | 7,982 | — | — | — | † 105 | 100 | 11 | 1 |
| Deposits Excl. from Broad Money | 36b | — | — | — | — | — | — | — | — | † — | | | |
| Sec.Ot.th.Shares Excl.f/Brd.Money | 36s | 19,730 | 15,900 | 16,312 | 20,481 | 19,315 | 20,177 | 23,398 | 25,977 | † — | — | — | — |
| Loans | 36l | 1,126 | 340 | 1,190 | 1,570 | 2,165 | 2,741 | 1,055 | 928 | † — | — | — | — |
| Financial Derivatives | 36m | — | — | — | — | — | — | — | — | † — | — | — | — |
| Insurance Technical Reserves | 36r | — | — | — | — | — | — | — | — | † — | — | — | — |
| Shares and Other Equity | 37a | 55,289 | 68,149 | 79,640 | 97,941 | 109,295 | 94,951 | 104,888 | 104,842 | † 122,301 | 134,512 | 157,956 | 185,323 |
| Other Items (Net) | 37r | −5,963 | −595 | −4,723 | −2,342 | −5,721 | 922 | 4,575 | −8,230 | † −305 | −9,369 | −20,304 | −24,738 |
| Broad Money Liabs., Seasonally Adj. | 35l.b | 187,642 | 230,587 | 247,978 | 279,652 | 291,205 | 285,696 | 304,842 | 300,540 | † 338,813 | 349,247 | 380,243 | 441,767 |
| **Monetary Aggregates** | | *Thousands of Pa'anga: End of Period* | | | | | | | | | | | |
| Broad Money | 59m | 198,144 | 242,018 | 258,362 | 289,454 | 299,490 | 292,295 | 310,838 | 306,044 | 345,032 | 355,831 | 387,325 | 450,196 |
| o/w:Currency Issued by Cent.Govt | 59m.a | — | — | — | — | — | — | — | — | — | — | — | — |
| o/w: Dep.in Nonfin. Corporations | 59m.b | — | — | — | — | — | — | — | — | — | — | — | — |
| o/w:Secs. Issued by Central Govt | 59m.c | — | — | — | — | — | — | — | — | — | — | — | — |
| Money (National Definitions) | | | | | | | | | | | | | |
| Reserve Money | 19mb | 73,509 | 62,579 | 67,083 | 81,234 | 71,887 | 102,431 | 118,176 | 157,134 | 191,480 | 200,757 | 231,753 | 259,584 |
| M1 | 59ma | 71,694 | 73,442 | 69,862 | 87,654 | 77,025 | 84,809 | 98,358 | 114,852 | 146,017 | 171,664 | 185,920 | 224,843 |
| Quasi-Money | 59mal | 126,450 | 168,576 | 185,212 | 201,800 | 214,483 | 207,486 | 212,480 | 191,192 | 199,015 | 184,167 | 201,555 | 225,353 |
| M2 | 59mb | 198,144 | 242,018 | 255,074 | 289,454 | 291,508 | 292,295 | 310,838 | 306,044 | 345,032 | 355,831 | 387,325 | 450,196 |
| **Interest Rates** | | *Percent Per Annum* | | | | | | | | | | | |
| Deposit Rate | 60l | 5.85 | 5.90 | 6.58 | 6.77 | 6.53 | 5.26 | 4.03 | 3.92 | 2.82 | 2.73 | 2.84 | 3.10 |
| Lending Rate | 60p | 11.59 | 11.38 | 11.97 | 12.16 | 12.46 | 12.47 | 11.54 | 11.37 | 10.03 | 9.66 | 8.95 | 8.33 |
| **Prices and Labor** | | *Index Numbers (2010=100): Period Averages* | | | | | | | | | | | |
| Consumer Prices | 64 | 70.6 | 76.5 | 81.4 | 86.2 | 95.2 | † 96.6 | 100.0 | 106.3 | 107.6 | 108.3 | 111.0 | 109.9 |
| **Intl. Transactions & Positions** | | *Thousands of Pa'anga* | | | | | | | | | | | |
| Exports | 70 | 31,288 | 20,184 | 19,634 | 17,663 | 19,273 | 15,588 | 15,638 | 29,801 | 29,716 | 39,030 | 41,782 | .... |
| Imports, c.i.f. | 71 | 206,380 | 234,512 | 235,693 | 281,032 | 324,445 | 291,926 | 301,754 | 332,210 | 342,742 | 351,628 | 404,122 | .... |

# Tonga   866

| | | 2004 | 2005 | 2006 | 2007 | 2008 | 2009 | 2010 | 2011 | 2012 | 2013 | 2014 | 2015 |
|---|---|---|---|---|---|---|---|---|---|---|---|---|---|
| **Balance of Payments** | | | | | | *Thousands of US Dollars* | | | | | | | |
| A. Current Account* | 109bx | −17,364.8 | −21,289.7 | −48,169.3 | −40,360.6 | −91,306.1 | −98,512.7 | −79,752.7 | † −84,962.1 | −38,759.6 | −32,502.5 | . . . . | . . . . |
| Goods, credit (exports) | 1a9cx | 18,740.5 | 17,145.4 | 8,185.7 | 13,049.2 | 13,053.0 | 9,446.8 | 10,621.0 | † 16,648.5 | 15,487.5 | 16,935.6 | . . . . | . . . . |
| Goods, debit (imports) | 1a9dx | 98,532.8 | 114,474.7 | 132,599.4 | 154,752.2 | 188,483.0 | 188,473.2 | 181,910.6 | † 210,523.0 | 190,709.2 | 186,151.0 | . . . . | . . . . |
| Balance on goods | 1a9bx | −79,792.3 | −97,329.3 | −124,413.6 | −141,703.1 | −175,430.0 | −179,026.4 | −171,289.6 | † −193,874.6 | −175,221.7 | −169,215.4 | . . . . | . . . . |
| Services, credit (exports) | 1b9cx | 23,800.4 | 33,781.3 | 26,113.7 | 30,315.2 | 36,278.5 | 34,018.7 | 45,650.1 | † 55,954.7 | 74,514.6 | 71,800.8 | . . . . | . . . . |
| Services, debit (imports) | 1b9dx | 39,162.7 | 40,063.6 | 37,847.5 | 44,609.5 | 59,010.3 | 50,758.3 | 46,523.0 | † 70,690.3 | 81,016.0 | 92,354.2 | . . . . | . . . . |
| Balance on Goods & Services | 1z9bx | −95,154.6 | −103,611.7 | −136,147.5 | −155,997.4 | −198,161.8 | −195,766.1 | −172,162.5 | † −208,610.1 | −181,723.1 | −189,768.8 | . . . . | . . . . |
| Primary income: credit | 1c9cx | 5,072.7 | 8,052.5 | 8,256.2 | 12,153.3 | 10,748.4 | 10,089.3 | 12,114.6 | † 26,847.5 | 22,918.7 | 23,506.4 | . . . . | . . . . |
| Primary income: debit | 1c9dx | 7,020.0 | 2,267.0 | 3,449.1 | 3,807.5 | 3,704.1 | 6,190.0 | 9,847.0 | † 10,135.1 | 14,242.0 | 14,563.1 | . . . . | . . . . |
| Balance on gds, serv. & prim. inc. | 1y9bx | −97,102.0 | −97,826.3 | −131,340.4 | −147,651.5 | −191,117.5 | −191,866.7 | −169,894.9 | † −191,897.7 | −173,046.4 | −180,825.5 | . . . . | . . . . |
| Secondary income: credit | 1d9ca | 93,813.3 | 90,756.2 | 95,515.4 | 119,202.7 | 113,294.0 | 103,900.3 | 99,440.5 | † 115,034.3 | 145,236.1 | 156,410.6 | . . . . | . . . . |
| Secondary income: debit | 1d9da | 14,076.1 | 14,219.7 | 12,344.3 | 11,911.7 | 13,482.5 | 10,546.3 | 9,298.3 | † 8,098.6 | 10,949.3 | 8,087.5 | . . . . | . . . . |
| B. Capital Account* | 209ba | 11,618.4 | 13,018.5 | 23,921.5 | 19,978.8 | 55,509.4 | 93,284.7 | 33,982.0 | † 57,698.9 | 43,809.8 | 32,866.9 | . . . . | . . . . |
| Capital account: credit | 209ca | 11,638.7 | 13,101.0 | 26,228.0 | 22,901.9 | 58,280.8 | 94,582.6 | 34,197.6 | † 58,996.9 | 45,138.3 | 34,304.9 | . . . . | . . . . |
| Capital account: debit | 209da | 20.3 | 82.5 | 2,306.5 | 2,923.1 | 2,771.4 | 1,297.9 | 215.7 | † 1,298.0 | 1,328.5 | 1,438.1 | . . . . | . . . . |
| Balance on current & capital acct. | 129ba | −5,746.3 | −8,271.3 | −24,247.8 | −20,381.7 | −35,796.7 | −5,228.0 | −45,770.8 | † −27,263.1 | 5,050.3 | 364.4 | . . . . | . . . . |
| C. Financial Account* | 309na | −28,012.3 | −2,838.1 | −11,645.1 | −22,131.4 | −9,058.8 | −17,828.6 | −43,288.0 | † −31,362.5 | −301.0 | −11,477.0 | . . . . | . . . . |
| Direct investment: assets | 3a9aa | — | — | 1,543.3 | 1,466.7 | −477.8 | — | . . . . | . . . . | 1,506.7 | 2,190.3 | . . . . | . . . . |
| Equity & investment fund shares | 3aaaa | — | — | 31.0 | 16.7 | | — | . . . . | . . . . | | | . . . . | . . . . |
| Debt instruments | 3abaa | — | — | 1,512.3 | 1,449.9 | −477.8 | — | . . . . | . . . . | 1,506.7 | 2,190.3 | . . . . | . . . . |
| Direct investment: liabilities | 3a9la | 4,587.0 | 7,204.7 | 11,601.0 | 29,123.5 | 5,949.8 | 424.0 | 8,982.4 | † 3,714.3 | 1,793.7 | 6,666.2 | . . . . | . . . . |
| Equity & investment fund shares | 3aala | 4,587.0 | 7,204.7 | 3,134.7 | 1,596.4 | 168.2 | 7.1 | 8,982.4 | † 3,714.3 | 1,793.7 | 6,666.2 | . . . . | . . . . |
| Debt instruments | 3abla | — | — | 8,466.3 | 27,527.1 | 5,781.6 | 416.9 | . . . . | . . . . | | | . . . . | . . . . |
| Portfolio investment: assets | 3b9aa | . . . . | . . . . | . . . . | . . . . | . . . . | . . . . | . . . . | . . . . | . . . . | . . . . | . . . . | . . . . |
| Equity & investment fund shares | 3baaa | . . . . | . . . . | . . . . | . . . . | . . . . | . . . . | . . . . | . . . . | . . . . | . . . . | . . . . | . . . . |
| Debt securities | 3bbaa | . . . . | . . . . | . . . . | . . . . | . . . . | . . . . | . . . . | . . . . | . . . . | . . . . | . . . . | . . . . |
| Portfolio investment: liabilities | 3b9la | — | — | | | | | . . . . | . . . . | . . . . | . . . . | . . . . | . . . . |
| Equity & investment fund shares | 3bala | — | — | | | | | . . . . | . . . . | . . . . | . . . . | . . . . | . . . . |
| Debt securities | 3bbla | — | — | | | | | . . . . | . . . . | . . . . | . . . . | . . . . | . . . . |
| Fin. der.& empl.stk.ops.(ESOs): net. | 3c9na | — | — | | . . . . | −16,213.6 | 153.7 | . . . . | . . . . | . . . . | . . . . | . . . . | . . . . |
| Fin. der. & ESOs: assets | 3c9aa | — | — | | . . . . | −16,302.0 | −3,208.0 | . . . . | . . . . | . . . . | . . . . | . . . . | . . . . |
| Fin. der. & ESOs: liabilities | 3c9la | — | — | | | −88.4 | −3,361.7 | . . . . | . . . . | . . . . | . . . . | . . . . | . . . . |
| Other investment: assets | 3d9aa | 287.0 | −17.0 | −7,892.6 | −467.6 | −6,220.7 | −11,818.6 | 78.1 | † −970.0 | 801.0 | −1,129.5 | . . . . | . . . . |
| Other equity | 3daaa | . . . . | . . . . | | | | | . . . . | . . . . | | | . . . . | . . . . |
| Debt instruments | 3dzaa | 287.0 | −17.0 | −7,892.6 | −467.6 | −6,220.7 | −11,818.6 | 78.1 | † −970.0 | 801.0 | −1,129.5 | . . . . | . . . . |
| Other investment: liabilities | 3d9la | 23,712.2 | −4,383.6 | −6,305.2 | −5,993.1 | −19,803.0 | 5,739.8 | 34,383.7 | † 26,678.2 | 815.1 | 5,871.5 | . . . . | . . . . |
| Other equity | 3dala | | | | | | | . . . . | . . . . | | | . . . . | . . . . |
| Debt instruments | 3dzla | 23,712.2 | −4,383.6 | −6,305.2 | −5,993.1 | −19,803.0 | 5,739.8 | 34,383.7 | † 26,678.2 | 815.1 | 5,871.5 | . . . . | . . . . |
| Curr.+ cap.− finan. acct. balance | 4y9na | 22,265.9 | −5,433.2 | −12,602.7 | 1,749.7 | −26,737.8 | 12,600.6 | −2,482.8 | † 4,099.3 | 5,351.3 | 11,841.3 | . . . . | . . . . |
| D. Net Errors and Omissions | 409na | −38,370.4 | −11,575.1 | 175,646.6 | 202,405.5 | 251,634.4 | 290,445.3 | −11,573.5 | † 29,407.9 | 9,462.9 | −4,222.6 | . . . . | . . . . |
| E. Reserves and Related Items | 4z9na | −16,104.4 | −17,008.3 | 163,043.8 | 204,155.3 | 224,896.5 | 303,045.9 | −14,056.3 | † 33,507.2 | 14,814.1 | 7,618.8 | . . . . | . . . . |
| Reserve assets | 3e9aa | −16,104.4 | −17,008.3 | 163,043.8 | 204,155.3 | 224,896.5 | 303,045.9 | −14,056.3 | † 33,507.2 | 14,814.1 | 7,618.8 | . . . . | . . . . |
| Credit and loans from the IMF | 3dcla | — | — | — | — | — | — | — | † — | — | — | . . . . | . . . . |
| Exceptional financing | 409la | — | — | . . . . | . . . . | . . . . | . . . . | . . . . | . . . . | . . . . | . . . . | . . . . | . . . . |

*Excludes components in group E

| | | 2004 | 2005 | 2006 | 2007 | 2008 | 2009 | 2010 | 2011 | 2012 | 2013 | 2014 | 2015 |
|---|---|---|---|---|---|---|---|---|---|---|---|---|---|
| **International Investment Position** | | | | | | *Thousands of US Dollars* | | | | | | | |
| Assets | 809aa | . . . . | . . . . | . . . . | . . . . | . . . . | . . . . | † 128,757.5 | 162,221.3 | 183,051.6 | 182,978.8 | . . . . | . . . . |
| Direct investment | 8a9aa | . . . . | . . . . | . . . . | . . . . | . . . . | . . . . | † 6,827.1 | 7,156.8 | 8,609.5 | 10,299.7 | . . . . | . . . . |
| Equity & investment fund shares | 8aaaa | . . . . | . . . . | . . . . | . . . . | . . . . | . . . . | | | | | . . . . | . . . . |
| Debt instruments | 8abaa | . . . . | . . . . | . . . . | . . . . | . . . . | . . . . | † 6,827.1 | 7,156.8 | 8,609.5 | 10,299.7 | . . . . | . . . . |
| Portfolio investment | 8b9aa | . . . . | . . . . | . . . . | . . . . | . . . . | . . . . | . . . . | . . . . | . . . . | . . . . | . . . . | . . . . |
| Equity & investment fund shares | 8baaa | . . . . | . . . . | . . . . | . . . . | . . . . | . . . . | . . . . | . . . . | . . . . | . . . . | . . . . | . . . . |
| Debt securities | 8bbaa | . . . . | . . . . | . . . . | . . . . | . . . . | . . . . | . . . . | . . . . | . . . . | . . . . | . . . . | . . . . |
| Fin. der.(oth.than reserves) & ESOs | 8c9aa | . . . . | . . . . | . . . . | . . . . | . . . . | . . . . | . . . . | . . . . | . . . . | . . . . | . . . . | . . . . |
| Other investment | 8d9aa | . . . . | . . . . | . . . . | . . . . | . . . . | . . . . | † 10,273.8 | 10,592.2 | 12,739.6 | 10,125.7 | . . . . | . . . . |
| Other equity | 8daaa | . . . . | . . . . | . . . . | . . . . | . . . . | . . . . | | | | | . . . . | . . . . |
| Debt instruments | 8dzaa | . . . . | . . . . | . . . . | . . . . | . . . . | . . . . | † 10,273.8 | 10,592.2 | 12,739.6 | 10,125.7 | . . . . | . . . . |
| Reserve assets | 8e9aa | . . . . | . . . . | . . . . | . . . . | . . . . | . . . . | † 111,656.6 | 144,472.4 | 161,702.5 | 162,553.4 | . . . . | . . . . |
| Liabilities | 809la | . . . . | . . . . | . . . . | . . . . | . . . . | . . . . | † 271,032.0 | 304,065.8 | 315,700.5 | 329,697.7 | . . . . | . . . . |
| Direct investment | 8a9la | . . . . | . . . . | . . . . | . . . . | . . . . | . . . . | † 73,775.3 | 75,310.5 | 90,431.2 | 93,180.2 | . . . . | . . . . |
| Equity & investment fund shares | 8aala | . . . . | . . . . | . . . . | . . . . | . . . . | . . . . | † 73,775.3 | 75,310.5 | 90,431.2 | 93,180.2 | . . . . | . . . . |
| Debt instruments | 8abla | . . . . | . . . . | . . . . | . . . . | . . . . | . . . . | | | | | . . . . | . . . . |
| Portfolio investment | 8b9la | . . . . | . . . . | . . . . | . . . . | . . . . | . . . . | . . . . | . . . . | . . . . | . . . . | . . . . | . . . . |
| Equity & investment fund shares | 8bala | . . . . | . . . . | . . . . | . . . . | . . . . | . . . . | . . . . | . . . . | . . . . | . . . . | . . . . | . . . . |
| Debt securities | 8bbla | . . . . | . . . . | . . . . | . . . . | . . . . | . . . . | . . . . | . . . . | . . . . | . . . . | . . . . | . . . . |
| Fin. der.(oth.than reserves) & ESOs | 8c9la | . . . . | . . . . | . . . . | . . . . | . . . . | . . . . | . . . . | . . . . | . . . . | . . . . | . . . . | . . . . |
| Other investment | 8d9la | . . . . | . . . . | . . . . | . . . . | . . . . | . . . . | † 197,256.7 | 228,755.3 | 225,269.3 | 236,517.5 | . . . . | . . . . |
| Other equity | 8dala | . . . . | . . . . | . . . . | . . . . | . . . . | . . . . | | | | | . . . . | . . . . |
| Debt instruments | 8dzla | . . . . | . . . . | . . . . | . . . . | . . . . | . . . . | † 197,256.7 | 228,755.3 | 225,269.3 | 236,517.5 | . . . . | . . . . |

# Tonga 866

| National Accounts | | 2004 | 2005 | 2006 | 2007 | 2008 | 2009 | 2010 | 2011 | 2012 | 2013 | 2014 | 2015 |
|---|---|---|---|---|---|---|---|---|---|---|---|---|---|
| | | *Millions of Pa'anga: Fiscal Year Beginning July 1* | | | | | | | | | | | |
| Househ.Cons.Expend.,incl.NPISHs.... | 96f | 464 | 517 | 554 | 614 | 681 | 693 | 698 | 715 | 751 | .... | .... | .... |
| Government Consumption Expend... | 91f | 76 | 79 | 124 | 109 | 122 | 132 | 129 | 134 | 151 | .... | .... | .... |
| Gross Fixed Capital Formation.......... | 93e | 97 | 112 | 123 | 129 | 136 | 160 | 211 | 224 | 264 | .... | .... | .... |
| Changes in Inventories.................... | 93i | 1 | 2 | 2 | 2 | 2 | 2 | 4 | 56 | 3 | .... | .... | .... |
| Exports of Goods and Services.......... | 90c | 92 | 91 | 85 | 73 | 90 | 93 | 94 | 136 | 142 | .... | .... | .... |
| Imports of Goods and Services (-)..... | 98c | 257 | 296 | 304 | 335 | 383 | 424 | 413 | 477 | 501 | .... | .... | .... |
| Gross Domestic Product (GDP)......... | 99b | 473 | 513 | 594 | 603 | 659 | 664 | 712 | 775 | 799 | .... | .... | .... |
| Net Primary Income from Abroad..... | 98.n | 6 | — | 10 | 14 | 14 | 13 | 8 | 16 | 23 | .... | .... | .... |
| Gross National Income (GNI)............ | 99a | 479 | 512 | 605 | 617 | 674 | 678 | 720 | 791 | 823 | .... | .... | .... |
| GDP Volume 2000/2001 Prices........ | 99b.p | 378 | 383 | 379 | 362 | 369 | 381 | 394 | 405 | 408 | .... | .... | .... |
| GDP Volume (2010=100)............... | 99bvp | 95.9 | 97.4 | 96.4 | 92.0 | 93.7 | 96.8 | 100.0 | 102.9 | 103.8 | .... | .... | .... |
| GDP Deflator (2010=100)............... | 99bip | 69.3 | 73.9 | 86.6 | 92.0 | 98.8 | 96.4 | 100.0 | 105.8 | 108.2 | .... | .... | .... |
| | | *Millions: Midyear Estimates* | | | | | | | | | | | |
| Population................................. | 99z | .10 | .10 | .10 | .10 | .10 | .10 | .10 | .10 | .10 | .11 | .11 | .11 |

| | | 2004 | 2005 | 2006 | 2007 | 2008 | 2009 | 2010 | 2011 | 2012 | 2013 | 2014 | 2015 |
|---|---|---|---|---|---|---|---|---|---|---|---|---|---|
| **Exchange Rates** | | | | | | *TT Dollars per SDR: End of Period* | | | | | | | |
| Market Rate................................ | aa | 9.7838 | 9.0191 | 9.4956 | 10.0207 | 9.7026 | 9.9917 | 9.8922 | 9.8497 | 9.8859 | 9.9584 | 9.2618 | 8.9370 |
| | | | | | *TT Dollars per US Dollar: End of Period (ae) Period Average (rf)* | | | | | | | | |
| Market Rate................................ | ae | 6.2999 | 6.3103 | 6.3119 | 6.3412 | 6.2993 | 6.3735 | 6.4234 | 6.4156 | 6.4323 | 6.4665 | 6.3927 | 6.4493 |
| Market Rate................................ | rf | 6.2990 | 6.2996 | 6.3123 | 6.3280 | 6.2894 | 6.3249 | 6.3755 | 6.4093 | 6.4296 | 6.4426 | 6.4091 | 6.3774 |
| | | | | | *Index Numbers (2010=100): Period Averages* | | | | | | | | |
| Nominal Effective Exchange Rate..... | nec | 104.3 | 103.3 | 102.3 | 100.3 | 99.5 | 102.1 | 100.0 | 97.7 | 99.2 | 99.8 | 101.4 | 108.1 |
| CPI-Based Real Effect. Ex. Rate........ | rec | 74.9 | 76.5 | 79.5 | 81.6 | 86.9 | 94.7 | 100.0 | 99.0 | 107.0 | 111.1 | 117.0 | 129.5 |
| **Fund Position** | | | | | | *Millions of SDRs: End of Period* | | | | | | | |
| Quota................................ | 2f.s | 335.60 | 335.60 | 335.60 | 335.60 | 335.60 | 335.60 | 335.60 | 335.60 | 335.60 | 335.60 | 335.60 | 335.60 |
| SDR Holdings................................ | 1b.s | 1.73 | 2.60 | 2.00 | .56 | .71 | 275.51 | 275.52 | 275.63 | 275.68 | 275.71 | 275.77 | 275.78 |
| Reserve Position in the Fund............ | 1c.s | 111.09 | 49.90 | 34.41 | 22.43 | 39.68 | 60.23 | 72.23 | 104.33 | 110.63 | 122.63 | 124.63 | 104.63 |
| Total Fund Cred.&Loans Outstg........ | 2tl | — | — | — | — | — | — | — | — | — | — | — | — |
| SDR Allocations............................ | 1bd | 46.23 | 46.23 | 46.23 | 46.23 | 46.23 | 321.13 | 321.13 | 321.13 | 321.13 | 321.13 | 321.13 | 321.13 |
| **International Liquidity** | | | | | | *Millions of US Dollars Unless Otherwise Indicated: End of Period* | | | | | | | |
| Total Reserves minus Gold.............. | 1l.d | 3,168.2 | 4,960.8 | 6,585.7 | 6,693.7 | 9,442.6 | 9,177.9 | 9,605.5 | 10,406.0 | 9,794.4 | 10,600.5 | 11,896.7 | 10,315.1 |
| SDR Holdings................................ | 1b.d | 2.7 | 3.7 | 3.0 | .9 | 1.1 | 431.9 | 424.3 | 423.2 | 423.7 | 424.6 | 399.5 | 382.2 |
| Reserve Position in the Fund.......... | 1c.d | 172.5 | 71.3 | 51.8 | 35.4 | 61.1 | 94.4 | 111.2 | 160.2 | 170.0 | 188.9 | 180.6 | 145.0 |
| Foreign Exchange........................ | 1d.d | 2,993.0 | 4,885.8 | 6,530.9 | 6,657.4 | 9,380.4 | 8,651.6 | 9,070.0 | 9,822.7 | 9,200.7 | 9,987.0 | 11,316.6 | 9,788.0 |
| Gold (Million Fine Troy Ounces)........ | 1ad | .061 | .061 | .061 | .061 | .061 | .062 | .062 | .062 | .062 | .062 | .062 | .062 |
| Gold (National Valuation)................ | 1and | 26.8 | 31.4 | 39.0 | 51.2 | 52.9 | 67.9 | 86.7 | 97.4 | 102.9 | 74.1 | 74.0 | 65.8 |
| Central Bank: Other Assets.............. | 3..d | 172.6 | † 510.2 | 337.7 | 171.6 | 458.8 | 842.8 | 1,026.6 | 1,028.0 | 792.9 | 704.9 | 793.6 | 632.1 |
| Central Bank: Other Liabs............... | 4..d | 43.5 | † 395.3 | 274.3 | 100.8 | 258.5 | 780.0 | 1,063.1 | 988.6 | 723.5 | 633.8 | 566.2 | 542.9 |
| Other Depository Corps.: Assets....... | 7a.d | 1,317.5 | † 2,360.6 | 3,215.1 | 3,238.0 | 3,246.2 | 3,277.2 | 2,669.8 | 2,971.9 | 3,382.8 | 3,332.9 | 3,312.5 | 3,730.7 |
| Other Depository Corps.: Liabs........ | 7b.d | 807.5 | † 1,454.7 | 1,328.7 | 1,463.7 | 1,258.5 | 855.9 | 846.0 | 793.3 | 673.3 | 810.7 | 848.1 | 864.7 |
| Other Financial Corps.: Assets......... | 7e.d | .... | .... | .... | .... | .... | .... | 4,738.2 | 5,226.4 | 6,061.1 | 7,109.6 | 7,587.0 | 7,710.8 |
| Other Financial Corps.: Liabs........... | 7f.d | .... | .... | .... | .... | .... | .... | 153.9 | 156.5 | 152.8 | 145.9 | 304.5 | 297.8 |
| **Central Bank** | | | | | | *Millions of TT Dollars: End of Period* | | | | | | | |
| Net Foreign Assets.......................... | 11n | 20,190.2 | † 26,593.1 | 32,189.3 | 42,600.3 | 59,680.0 | 52,900.4 | 55,765.1 | 62,738.9 | 58,474.2 | 64,595.6 | 71,230.8 | 61,985.2 |
| Claims on Nonresidents................ | 11 | 20,916.6 | † 29,504.2 | 34,359.4 | 43,702.9 | 61,757.1 | 61,080.2 | 65,770.6 | 72,244.3 | 66,302.7 | 71,869.4 | 77,824.6 | 68,356.7 |
| Liabilities to Nonresidents.............. | 16c | 726.5 | † 2,911.1 | 2,170.1 | 1,102.6 | 2,077.1 | 8,179.8 | 10,005.5 | 9,505.4 | 7,828.5 | 7,273.8 | 6,593.8 | 6,371.5 |
| Claims on Other Depository Corps.... | 12e | 723.6 | † 332.5 | 321.7 | 169.2 | 12.6 | 12.6 | 12.6 | 12.6 | 12.6 | 12.6 | — | — |
| Net Claims on Central Government.. | 12an | −12,946.8 | † −15,302.7 | −19,518.8 | −26,277.3 | −35,526.9 | −21,712.2 | −21,838.8 | −24,135.7 | −15,814.8 | −18,893.3 | −25,970.3 | −23,011.9 |
| Claims on Central Government..... | 12a | 925.7 | † 9,480.3 | 11,845.2 | 10,262.5 | 12,616.8 | 21,305.0 | 23,149.8 | 26,128.3 | 32,446.0 | 37,512.2 | 42,442.1 | 48,828.5 |
| Liabilities to Central Government... | 16d | 13,872.5 | † 24,782.9 | 31,364.0 | 36,539.8 | 48,143.8 | 43,017.3 | 44,988.6 | 50,264.0 | 48,260.8 | 56,405.5 | 68,412.3 | 71,840.4 |
| Claims on Other Sectors.................. | 12s | 270.0 | † 226.2 | 214.4 | 163.9 | 282.6 | 310.8 | 304.1 | 309.6 | 294.5 | 379.9 | 349.6 | 278.2 |
| Claims on Other Financial Corps.... | 12g | 6.6 | † 181.5 | 170.7 | 134.5 | 255.9 | 281.5 | 281.3 | 286.5 | 272.2 | 358.1 | 319.5 | 219.4 |
| Claims on State & Local Govts....... | 12b | — | † — | — | — | — | — | — | — | — | — | — | — |
| Claims on Public Nonfin. Corps...... | 12c | 245.4 | † — | — | .1 | — | — | — | — | — | — | — | — |
| Claims on Private Sector................ | 12d | 18.0 | † 44.6 | 43.7 | 29.3 | 26.7 | 29.3 | 22.7 | 23.1 | 22.2 | 21.7 | 30.1 | 58.7 |
| Monetary Base................................ | 14 | 5,959.5 | † 8,610.1 | 9,956.9 | 11,177.6 | 15,898.0 | 21,996.9 | 24,870.6 | 28,795.9 | 33,735.4 | 36,852.9 | 37,179.3 | 32,021.5 |
| Currency in Circulation.................. | 14a | 2,554.2 | † 2,991.4 | 3,560.4 | 4,205.4 | 4,486.3 | 4,856.2 | 5,300.6 | 5,938.7 | 6,648.3 | 7,422.1 | 8,350.9 | 9,092.4 |
| Liabs. to Other Depository Corps.... | 14c | 3,231.1 | † 5,043.1 | 6,072.0 | 6,450.8 | 11,019.4 | 14,961.5 | 16,541.2 | 21,428.0 | 22,462.0 | 26,439.0 | 27,219.2 | 22,406.2 |
| Liabilities to Other Sectors.............. | 14d | 174.1 | † 575.5 | 324.4 | 521.4 | 392.2 | 2,179.2 | 3,028.9 | 1,429.2 | 4,625.1 | 2,991.9 | 1,609.1 | 522.9 |
| Other Liabs. to Other Dep. Corps..... | 14n | — | † 8.8 | 12.3 | 7.4 | .1 | 1,795.1 | 1,874.4 | 1,879.0 | 1,878.6 | 1,885.2 | 1,873.9 | 470.5 |
| Dep. & Sec. Excl. f/Monetary Base..... | 14o | — | † 24.5 | 13.3 | 42.8 | 22.4 | 8.0 | 6.6 | 13.4 | 27.0 | 56.1 | 49.1 | 74.8 |
| Deposits Included in Broad Money. | 15 | — | † — | — | — | — | — | — | — | — | — | — | — |
| Sec.Ot.th.Shares Incl.in Brd. Money | 16a | — | † — | — | — | — | — | — | — | — | — | — | — |
| Deposits Excl. from Broad Money... | 16b | — | † 24.5 | 13.3 | 42.8 | 22.4 | 8.0 | 6.6 | 13.4 | 27.0 | 56.1 | 49.1 | 74.8 |
| Sec.Ot.th.Shares Excl.f/Brd.Money.. | 16s | — | † — | — | — | — | — | — | — | — | — | — | — |
| Loans.......................... | 16l | — | † — | — | — | — | — | — | — | — | — | — | — |
| Financial Derivatives........................ | 16m | — | † — | — | — | — | — | — | — | — | — | — | — |
| Shares and Other Equity.................. | 17a | 238.6 | † 1,398.5 | 1,293.6 | 3,929.7 | 3,809.5 | 4,066.1 | 7,429.1 | 8,190.1 | 7,328.8 | 7,538.0 | 6,654.3 | 7,150.7 |
| Other Items (Net)............................ | 17r | 2,039.0 | † 1,807.2 | 1,930.5 | 1,498.5 | 4,718.4 | 3,645.4 | 62.3 | 46.9 | −3.4 | −237.5 | −146.5 | −465.9 |
| Memo Item: | | | | | | | | | | | | | |
| Total Assets.................................. | 10ra | 23,097.2 | † 39,984.2 | 47,137.2 | 55,221.8 | 75,160.0 | 82,702.5 | 92,267.7 | 101,906.4 | 101,892.8 | 112,563.6 | 123,572.4 | 120,649.1 |

| | | 2004 | 2005 | 2006 | 2007 | 2008 | 2009 | 2010 | 2011 | 2012 | 2013 | 2014 | 2015 |
|---|---|---|---|---|---|---|---|---|---|---|---|---|---|
| **Other Depository Corporations** | | | | | | *Millions of TT Dollars: End of Period* | | | | | | | |
| Net Foreign Assets | 21n | 3,212.9 | † 5,716.3 | 11,906.9 | 11,251.0 | 12,521.2 | 15,431.8 | 11,714.9 | 13,976.9 | 17,428.7 | 16,268.6 | 15,754.1 | 18,483.6 |
| Claims on Nonresidents | 21 | 8,300.1 | † 14,895.9 | 20,293.5 | 20,532.6 | 20,448.9 | 20,887.0 | 17,149.4 | 19,066.7 | 21,759.3 | 21,497.4 | 21,175.5 | 24,060.4 |
| Liabilities to Nonresidents | 26c | 5,087.2 | † 9,179.6 | 8,386.6 | 9,281.6 | 7,927.6 | 5,455.1 | 5,434.5 | 5,089.8 | 4,330.6 | 5,228.9 | 5,421.4 | 5,576.8 |
| Claims on Central Bank | 20 | 3,921.5 | † 5,325.6 | 6,613.7 | 7,264.6 | 12,094.3 | 15,464.5 | 16,692.6 | 21,825.4 | 22,232.5 | 26,473.9 | 27,264.7 | 23,644.1 |
| Currency | 20a | 716.8 | † 582.5 | 917.9 | 1,033.9 | 1,064.3 | 1,175.0 | 1,183.2 | 1,429.9 | 1,333.3 | 1,443.5 | 1,559.7 | 1,458.4 |
| Reserve Deposits and Securities | 20b | 3,204.7 | † 4,743.2 | 5,695.8 | 6,230.7 | 11,029.9 | 14,289.5 | 15,509.5 | 20,395.6 | 20,899.3 | 25,030.4 | 25,705.0 | 22,185.7 |
| Other Claims | 20n | — | † — | — | — | — | — | — | — | — | — | — | — |
| Net Claims on Central Government | 22an | 4,440.7 | † 6,045.7 | 3,967.3 | 4,086.4 | 4,428.0 | 9,729.8 | 11,163.0 | 7,708.8 | 14,091.3 | 12,015.3 | 14,958.6 | 13,015.1 |
| Claims on Central Government | 22a | 5,717.8 | † 7,630.5 | 6,255.0 | 6,322.8 | 6,868.3 | 12,388.9 | 14,712.2 | 14,174.9 | 19,089.0 | 18,093.8 | 20,614.7 | 17,610.4 |
| Liabilities to Central Government | 26d | 1,277.1 | † 1,584.8 | 2,287.7 | 2,236.4 | 2,440.3 | 2,659.1 | 3,549.3 | 6,466.2 | 4,997.7 | 6,078.5 | 5,656.1 | 4,595.3 |
| Claims on Other Sectors | 22s | 34,941.4 | † 40,343.6 | 45,346.1 | 52,852.0 | 54,034.3 | 56,382.7 | 55,770.2 | 56,233.1 | 57,434.7 | 59,493.0 | 64,534.4 | 69,161.0 |
| Claims on Other Financial Corps | 22g | 1,956.6 | † 3,296.0 | 4,948.4 | 5,582.7 | 3,505.7 | 6,395.3 | 5,487.0 | 4,300.1 | 4,199.4 | 3,813.9 | 3,464.2 | 2,375.9 |
| Claims on State & Local Govts | 22b | 6.8 | † 26.9 | 155.8 | 331.6 | 359.1 | 328.1 | 345.5 | 330.8 | 257.3 | 26.5 | 89.4 | 6.0 |
| Claims on Public Nonfin. Corps | 22c | 1,240.6 | † 3,344.7 | 2,375.4 | 3,069.9 | 3,380.0 | 6,083.8 | 6,385.6 | 5,778.3 | 5,918.5 | 6,669.6 | 8,708.5 | 11,087.2 |
| Claims on Private Sector | 22d | 31,737.4 | † 33,676.0 | 37,866.5 | 43,867.8 | 46,789.4 | 43,575.5 | 43,552.0 | 45,823.9 | 47,059.5 | 48,983.0 | 52,272.3 | 55,691.9 |
| Liabilities to Central Bank | 26g | 390.4 | † 383.5 | 379.5 | — | 190.8 | | | | | | | |
| Transf.Dep.Included in Broad Money | 24 | 8,766.2 | † 12,023.5 | 13,020.5 | 13,342.9 | 16,237.6 | 22,466.4 | 22,786.4 | 24,104.8 | 32,749.2 | 34,323.3 | 39,391.1 | 36,929.2 |
| Other Dep.Included in Broad Money | 25 | 21,781.2 | † 26,241.5 | 33,402.3 | 38,086.8 | 44,131.7 | 46,930.6 | 46,090.2 | 46,580.2 | 49,896.1 | 52,261.4 | 54,638.9 | 58,504.6 |
| Sec.Ot.th.Shares Incl.in Brd.Money | 26a | — | † — | — | — | — | — | — | — | — | — | — | — |
| Deposits Excl. from Broad Money | 26b | — | † — | — | — | — | — | — | — | — | — | — | — |
| Sec.Ot.th.Shares Excl.f/Brd.Money | 26s | 3,226.2 | † 11,197.3 | 10,997.7 | 11,309.7 | 12,013.4 | 8,492.8 | 6,563.6 | 5,438.2 | 4,068.7 | 3,741.8 | 3,181.2 | 4,076.3 |
| Loans | 26l | — | † 345.4 | 362.6 | 373.2 | 135.6 | 33.2 | 161.2 | — | 15.0 | 85.0 | 10.0 | 90.0 |
| Financial Derivatives | 26m | — | † — | — | — | — | — | — | — | — | — | — | — |
| Insurance Technical Reserves | 26r | — | † — | — | — | — | — | — | — | — | — | — | — |
| Shares and Other Equity | 27a | 10,809.2 | † 11,266.7 | 12,568.1 | 14,116.1 | 16,227.2 | 16,763.2 | 18,065.1 | 18,829.8 | 20,401.0 | 21,587.5 | 21,646.6 | 22,739.5 |
| Other Items (Net) | 27r | 1,543.3 | † –4,026.7 | –2,896.6 | –1,774.7 | –5,667.7 | 2,131.7 | 1,674.1 | 4,791.1 | 4,057.2 | 2,251.8 | 3,644.0 | 1,964.1 |
| Memo Item: | | | | | | | | | | | | | |
| Total Assets | 20ra | 72,532.3 | † 79,595.7 | 89,174.5 | 99,908.8 | 111,238.8 | 115,147.2 | 112,458.5 | 119,133.3 | 128,600.5 | 133,922.9 | 141,916.5 | 142,411.4 |
| **Depository Corporations** | | | | | | *Millions of TT Dollars: End of Period* | | | | | | | |
| Net Foreign Assets | 31n | 23,403.1 | † 32,309.4 | 44,096.2 | 53,851.2 | 72,201.2 | 68,332.2 | 67,480.0 | 76,715.8 | 75,902.9 | 80,864.2 | 86,984.9 | 80,468.8 |
| Claims on Nonresidents | 31 | 29,216.7 | † 44,400.1 | 54,652.9 | 64,235.5 | 82,206.0 | 81,967.2 | 82,920.0 | 91,311.0 | 88,062.0 | 93,366.9 | 99,000.2 | 92,417.0 |
| Liabilities to Nonresidents | 36c | 5,813.6 | † 12,090.7 | 10,556.7 | 10,384.2 | 10,004.8 | 13,635.0 | 15,440.0 | 14,595.2 | 12,159.1 | 12,502.7 | 12,015.3 | 11,948.3 |
| Domestic Claims | 32 | 26,705.3 | † 31,312.8 | 30,009.0 | 30,824.9 | 23,218.0 | 44,711.1 | 45,398.5 | 40,115.7 | 56,005.7 | 52,995.0 | 53,872.3 | 59,442.4 |
| Net Claims on Central Government | 32an | –8,506.1 | † –9,257.0 | –15,551.6 | –22,190.9 | –31,098.9 | –11,982.4 | –10,675.8 | –16,427.0 | –1,723.5 | –6,878.0 | –11,011.7 | –9,996.7 |
| Claims on Central Government | 32a | 6,643.5 | † 17,110.7 | 18,100.2 | 16,585.3 | 19,485.2 | 33,693.9 | 37,862.0 | 40,303.3 | 51,534.9 | 55,606.0 | 63,056.8 | 66,438.9 |
| Liabilities to Central Government | 36d | 15,149.6 | † 26,367.7 | 33,651.7 | 38,776.2 | 50,584.1 | 45,676.3 | 48,537.8 | 56,730.2 | 53,258.4 | 62,484.0 | 74,068.5 | 76,435.7 |
| Claims on Other Sectors | 32s | 35,211.4 | † 40,569.8 | 45,560.5 | 53,015.9 | 54,316.9 | 56,693.5 | 56,074.3 | 56,542.7 | 57,729.2 | 59,872.9 | 64,884.0 | 69,439.2 |
| Claims on Other Financial Corps | 32g | 1,963.1 | † 3,477.5 | 5,119.1 | 5,717.2 | 3,761.6 | 6,676.8 | 5,768.4 | 4,586.6 | 4,471.6 | 4,172.0 | 3,783.7 | 2,595.4 |
| Claims on State & Local Govts | 32b | 6.8 | † 26.9 | 155.8 | 331.6 | 359.1 | 328.1 | 345.5 | 330.8 | 257.3 | 26.5 | 89.4 | 6.0 |
| Claims on Public Nonfin. Corps | 32c | 1,486.1 | † 3,344.7 | 2,375.4 | 3,069.9 | 3,380.0 | 6,083.9 | 6,385.6 | 5,778.3 | 5,918.6 | 6,669.7 | 8,708.5 | 11,087.2 |
| Claims on Private Sector | 32d | 31,755.4 | † 33,720.6 | 37,910.2 | 43,897.1 | 46,816.1 | 43,604.8 | 43,574.8 | 45,847.0 | 47,081.7 | 49,004.7 | 52,302.4 | 55,750.6 |
| Broad Money Liabilities | 35l | 32,558.9 | † 41,249.5 | 49,389.8 | 55,122.6 | 64,183.6 | 75,257.4 | 76,023.0 | 76,623.1 | 92,585.6 | 95,555.2 | 102,430.4 | 103,590.7 |
| Currency Outside Depository Corps | 34a | 1,837.4 | † 2,409.0 | 2,642.5 | 3,171.5 | 3,422.0 | 3,681.2 | 4,117.4 | 4,508.9 | 5,315.1 | 5,978.6 | 6,791.2 | 7,634.1 |
| Transferable Deposits | 34 | 8,940.3 | † 12,497.5 | 13,243.5 | 13,770.8 | 16,528.5 | 24,645.6 | 25,815.6 | 25,534.0 | 37,374.4 | 37,315.1 | 41,000.3 | 37,452.0 |
| Other Deposits | 35 | 21,781.2 | † 26,241.5 | 33,402.3 | 38,086.8 | 44,131.7 | 46,930.6 | 46,090.2 | 46,580.2 | 49,896.1 | 52,261.4 | 54,638.9 | 58,504.6 |
| Securities Other than Shares | 36a | — | † 101.5 | 101.5 | 93.6 | 101.4 | | | | | | | |
| Deposits Excl. from Broad Money | 36b | — | † 24.5 | 13.3 | 42.8 | 22.4 | 8.0 | 6.6 | 13.4 | 27.0 | 56.1 | 49.1 | 74.8 |
| Sec.Ot.th.Shares Excl.f/Brd.Money | 36s | 3,226.2 | † 11,197.3 | 10,997.7 | 11,309.7 | 12,013.4 | 8,492.8 | 6,563.6 | 5,438.2 | 4,068.7 | 3,741.8 | 3,181.2 | 4,076.3 |
| Loans | 36l | — | † 345.4 | 362.6 | 373.2 | 135.6 | 33.2 | 161.2 | — | 15.0 | 85.0 | 10.0 | 90.0 |
| Financial Derivatives | 36m | — | † — | — | — | — | — | — | — | — | — | — | — |
| Insurance Technical Reserves | 36r | — | † — | — | — | — | — | — | — | — | — | — | — |
| Shares and Other Equity | 37a | 11,047.8 | † 12,665.2 | 13,861.7 | 18,045.8 | 20,036.7 | 20,829.3 | 25,494.2 | 27,020.0 | 27,729.9 | 29,125.5 | 28,300.9 | 29,890.2 |
| Other Items (Net) | 37r | 3,275.5 | † –1,859.8 | –519.8 | –217.9 | –972.4 | 8,422.5 | 4,629.9 | 7,736.8 | 7,482.5 | 5,295.5 | 6,885.6 | 2,189.2 |
| Broad Money Liabs., Seasonally Adj. | 35l.b | 32,902.4 | † 40,193.6 | 48,051.6 | 53,542.3 | 62,377.3 | 73,230.0 | 74,184.7 | 75,002.3 | 90,980.4 | 94,111.1 | 100,893.7 | . . . . |
| **Other Financial Corporations** | | | | | | *Millions of TT Dollars: End of Period* | | | | | | | |
| Net Foreign Assets | 41n | . . . . | . . . . | . . . . | . . . . | . . . . | . . . . | 29,447.0 | 32,602.3 | 38,004.4 | 45,031.4 | 46,555.3 | 47,808.5 |
| Claims on Nonresidents | 41 | . . . . | . . . . | . . . . | . . . . | . . . . | . . . . | 30,435.4 | 33,608.5 | 38,987.1 | 45,974.5 | 48,501.6 | 49,729.0 |
| Liabilities to Nonresidents | 46c | . . . . | . . . . | . . . . | . . . . | . . . . | . . . . | 988.5 | 1,006.2 | 982.7 | 943.2 | 1,946.3 | 1,920.5 |
| Claims on Depository Corporations | 40 | . . . . | . . . . | . . . . | . . . . | . . . . | . . . . | 11,476.6 | 11,969.2 | 13,723.3 | 17,077.1 | 17,390.7 | 17,389.7 |
| Net Claims on Central Government | 42an | . . . . | . . . . | . . . . | . . . . | . . . . | . . . . | 11,263.2 | 3,204.0 | 8,549.6 | 12,109.2 | 22,350.0 | 23,228.6 |
| Claims on Central Government | 42a | . . . . | . . . . | . . . . | . . . . | . . . . | . . . . | 13,394.1 | 13,774.4 | 19,418.0 | 23,228.8 | 31,794.2 | 29,266.0 |
| Liabilities to Central Government | 46d | . . . . | . . . . | . . . . | . . . . | . . . . | . . . . | 2,130.9 | 10,570.4 | 10,868.4 | 11,119.6 | 9,444.2 | 6,037.5 |
| Claims on Other Sectors | 42s | . . . . | . . . . | . . . . | . . . . | . . . . | . . . . | 20,636.7 | 23,375.2 | 26,416.2 | 31,292.0 | 30,238.7 | 28,314.8 |
| Claims on State & Local Govts | 42b | . . . . | . . . . | . . . . | . . . . | . . . . | . . . . | 168.1 | 175.0 | 696.1 | 672.1 | 881.8 | 136.6 |
| Claims on Public Nonfin. Corps | 42c | . . . . | . . . . | . . . . | . . . . | . . . . | . . . . | 5,625.9 | 7,090.8 | 7,259.2 | 9,981.0 | 9,909.6 | 9,035.6 |
| Claims on Private Sector | 42d | . . . . | . . . . | . . . . | . . . . | . . . . | . . . . | 14,842.6 | 16,109.4 | 18,460.9 | 20,638.8 | 19,447.3 | 19,142.6 |
| Deposits | 46b | . . . . | . . . . | . . . . | . . . . | . . . . | . . . . | 905.1 | 3,058.3 | 3,198.9 | 3,361.5 | 3,465.2 | 2,391.8 |
| Securities Other than Shares | 46s | . . . . | . . . . | . . . . | . . . . | . . . . | . . . . | — | — | — | — | — | — |
| Loans | 46l | . . . . | . . . . | . . . . | . . . . | . . . . | . . . . | 1,891.4 | 1,564.7 | 1,380.7 | 1,392.7 | 1,643.1 | 1,233.2 |
| Financial Derivatives | 46m | . . . . | . . . . | . . . . | . . . . | . . . . | . . . . | — | — | — | — | — | — |
| Insurance Technical Reserves | 46r | . . . . | . . . . | . . . . | . . . . | . . . . | . . . . | 52,233.2 | 49,968.3 | 55,732.9 | 72,039.5 | 75,110.8 | 75,996.2 |
| Shares and Other Equity | 47a | . . . . | . . . . | . . . . | . . . . | . . . . | . . . . | 18,492.9 | 22,727.1 | 32,515.7 | 36,586.3 | 44,165.0 | 44,937.6 |
| Other Items (Net) | 47r | . . . . | . . . . | . . . . | . . . . | . . . . | . . . . | –698.1 | –6,168.4 | –6,134.2 | –7,864.7 | –7,849.3 | –7,817.2 |
| Memo Item: | | | | | | | | | | | | | |
| Total Assets | 40ra | . . . . | . . . . | . . . . | . . . . | . . . . | . . . . | 86,366.3 | 94,968.8 | 111,673.5 | 132,324.4 | 143,345.7 | 140,436.6 |

| | | 2004 | 2005 | 2006 | 2007 | 2008 | 2009 | 2010 | 2011 | 2012 | 2013 | 2014 | 2015 |
|---|---|---|---|---|---|---|---|---|---|---|---|---|---|
| **Monetary Aggregates** | | | | | | *Millions of TT Dollars: End of Period* | | | | | | | |
| Broad Money...................... | 59m | .... | 41,249.5 | 49,389.8 | 55,122.6 | 64,183.6 | 75,257.4 | 76,023.0 | 76,623.1 | 92,585.6 | 95,555.2 | 102,430.4 | 103,590.7 |
| o/w:Currency Issued by Cent.Govt | 59m.a | .... | — | — | — | — | — | — | — | — | — | — | — |
| o/w: Dep.in Nonfin. Corporations. | 59m.b | .... | — | — | — | — | — | — | — | — | — | — | — |
| o/w: Secs. Issued by Central Govt. | 59m.c | .... | — | — | — | — | — | — | — | — | — | — | — |
| Money (National Definitions) | | | | | | | | | | | | | |
| Base Money (M0)...................... | 19ma | 4,739.9 | 7,097.9 | 8,342.4 | 9,269.3 | 14,038.8 | 18,408.4 | 20,423.4 | 25,767.8 | 27,540.5 | 32,144.6 | 33,727.1 | 29,672.9 |
| M1A............................ | 59maa | 8,377.6 | 12,316.1 | 13,507.9 | 15,122.1 | 16,659.7 | 23,160.3 | 25,283.0 | 31,184.8 | 35,680.9 | 40,123.6 | 47,719.2 | 44,254.0 |
| M1C............................ | 59mab | 17,330.1 | 22,283.4 | 25,031.6 | 28,123.8 | 30,490.3 | 40,862.9 | 45,236.3 | 53,653.2 | 60,429.3 | 67,561.4 | 77,618.7 | 76,140.9 |
| M2............................ | 59mb | 20,841.2 | 28,012.4 | 32,859.9 | 37,309.9 | 42,164.3 | 53,544.4 | 56,217.7 | 64,009.2 | 70,821.2 | 77,034.6 | 87,128.3 | 85,870.5 |
| M2*............................ | 59mba | 27,829.0 | 35,374.7 | 43,365.4 | 49,233.3 | 58,283.2 | 76,474.5 | 75,144.0 | 83,519.3 | 94,279.2 | 98,653.5 | 108,090.1 | 108,120.3 |
| M3............................ | 59mc | 23,908.5 | 29,941.2 | 35,269.4 | 40,034.3 | 45,766.5 | 54,493.6 | 57,396.8 | 65,302.6 | 72,121.1 | 78,643.3 | 89,087.8 | 87,533.9 |
| M3*............................ | 59mca | 34,498.2 | 40,610.4 | 49,459.3 | 55,463.4 | 65,308.0 | 77,578.3 | 77,113.6 | 85,272.4 | 95,901.7 | 100,854.7 | 110,769.0 | 110,367.2 |
| **Interest Rates** | | | | | | *Percent Per Annum* | | | | | | | |
| Discount Rate (End of Period).......... | 60.a | 7.00 | 8.00 | 10.00 | 10.00 | 10.75 | 7.25 | 5.75 | 5.00 | 4.75 | 4.75 | 5.25 | 6.75 |
| Treasury Bill Rate...................... | 60c | 4.77 | 4.86 | 6.07 | 6.91 | 7.01 | 2.69 | .85 | .53 | .37 | .16 | .10 | .47 |
| Savings Rate........................ | 60k | 1.67 | 1.38 | 1.46 | 1.65 | 2.03 | 1.13 | .36 | .25 | .20 | .20 | .20 | .20 |
| Deposit Rate........................ | 60l | 2.79 | 2.20 | 4.79 | 5.90 | 7.37 | 3.42 | 1.51 | 1.50 | 1.50 | 1.50 | 1.50 | 1.50 |
| Deposit Rate (Fgn. Currency)........... | 60l.f | 2.15 | 2.77 | 4.33 | 4.85 | 2.57 | 1.92 | 1.50 | 1.50 | 1.50 | 1.50 | 1.50 | 1.50 |
| Lending Rate...................... | 60p | 9.31 | 9.10 | 10.92 | 11.75 | 12.44 | 11.94 | 9.28 | 7.97 | 7.71 | 7.50 | 7.50 | 8.18 |
| **Prices, Production, Labor** | | | | | | *Index Numbers (2010=100): Period Averages* | | | | | | | |
| Share Prices (End of Month)............ | 62.ep | 112.1 | 137.1 | 114.0 | 114.9 | 125.6 | 97.6 | 100.0 | 115.7 | 127.4 | 138.2 | 142.6 | 141.1 |
| Producer Prices........................ | 63 | 74.2 | 75.9 | 79.4 | 84.9 | 93.3 | 97.4 | 100.0 | 102.8 | 107.1 | 109.1 | 111.3 | .... |
| Consumer Prices........................ | 64 | 60.4 | 64.6 | 70.0 | 75.5 | 84.6 | 90.5 | 100.0 | 105.1 | 114.8 | 120.8 | † 127.7 | 133.6 |
| Industrial Production...................... | 66 | 57.4 | 63.0 | 68.8 | 75.9 | 81.3 | 91.8 | 100.0 | 101.3 | .... | .... | .... | .... |
| Crude Petroleum Production............ | 66aa | 125.5 | 147.1 | 145.3 | 122.2 | 116.7 | 109.1 | 100.0 | 93.6 | 83.4 | 82.6 | .... | .... |
| Total Employment  (2005=100)....... | 67 | 100.0 | 100.0 | .... | .... | .... | .... | .... | .... | .... | .... | .... | .... |
| | | | | | | *Number in Thousands: Period Averages* | | | | | | | |
| Labor Force...................... | 67d | 613 | 624 | 625 | 622 | 627 | 621 | 619 | .... | 646 | .... | .... | .... |
| Employment........................ | 67e | 562 | 574 | 586 | 588 | 598 | 588 | 582 | .... | 597 | .... | .... | .... |
| Unemployment........................ | 67c | 51 | 50 | 39 | 35 | 29 | 33 | 37 | .... | 31 | .... | .... | .... |
| Unemployment Rate (%)................ | 67r | 8.4 | 8.0 | 6.2 | 5.6 | 4.6 | 5.3 | 5.9 | .... | 5.0 | .... | .... | .... |
| **Intl. Transactions & Positions** | | | | | | *Millions of TT Dollars* | | | | | | | |
| Exports............................ | 70 | 41,051.8 | 62,628.1 | 89,348.5 | 84,771.9 | 117,300.6 | 57,720.9 | 64,955.1 | 95,096.5 | .... | .... | .... | .... |
| Imports, c.i.f........................ | 71 | 30,600.6 | 35,869.1 | 40,931.9 | 48,490.6 | 60,324.5 | 43,992.5 | 41,329.3 | 63,948.6 | .... | .... | .... | .... |
| **Balance of Payments** | | | | | | *Millions of US Dollars* | | | | | | | |
| A. Current Account*...................... | 109bx | 1,792.9 | 3,881.3 | 7,124.8 | 5,166.5 | 8,499.0 | 1,632.8 | 4,172.3 | 2,898.6 | .... | .... | .... | .... |
| Goods, credit (exports)................... | 1a9cx | 6,533.3 | 9,981.7 | 14,064.6 | 13,197.7 | 18,620.7 | 9,204.0 | 11,219.3 | 14,913.1 | .... | .... | .... | .... |
| Goods, debit (imports)................... | 1a9dx | 4,877.2 | 5,709.8 | 6,490.8 | 7,662.3 | 9,551.1 | 6,962.6 | 6,481.4 | 9,478.3 | .... | .... | .... | .... |
| Balance on goods................... | 1a9bx | 1,656.1 | 4,271.9 | 7,573.8 | 5,535.4 | 9,069.6 | 2,241.4 | 4,737.9 | 5,434.8 | .... | .... | .... | .... |
| Services, credit (exports)................... | 1b9cx | 850.8 | 896.9 | 814.8 | 923.8 | 936.5 | 764.8 | 874.2 | 5,802.9 | .... | .... | .... | .... |
| Services, debit (imports)................ | 1b9dx | 372.9 | 544.6 | 362.8 | 384.1 | 326.0 | 383.3 | 389.1 | 5,298.3 | .... | .... | .... | .... |
| Balance on Goods & Services....... | 1z9bx | 2,134.0 | 4,624.2 | 8,025.8 | 6,075.1 | 9,680.1 | 2,622.9 | 5,223.0 | 5,939.4 | .... | .... | .... | .... |
| Primary income: credit................... | 1c9cx | 66.2 | 83.8 | 261.9 | 267.1 | 309.9 | 297.6 | 299.7 | 445.5 | .... | .... | .... | .... |
| Primary income: debit................... | 1c9dx | 463.5 | 876.8 | 1,218.1 | 1,235.9 | 1,537.9 | 1,314.7 | 1,379.2 | 3,519.4 | .... | .... | .... | .... |
| Balance on gds, serv. & prim. inc. | 1y9bx | 1,736.7 | 3,831.2 | 7,069.6 | 5,106.3 | 8,452.1 | 1,605.8 | 4,143.5 | 2,865.5 | .... | .... | .... | .... |
| Secondary income: credit.............. | 1d9ca | 98.6 | 102.0 | 104.6 | 121.4 | 108.7 | 137.3 | 108.8 | 145.2 | .... | .... | .... | .... |
| Secondary income: debit.............. | 1d9da | 42.4 | 51.9 | 49.4 | 61.2 | 61.8 | 110.3 | 80.0 | 112.1 | .... | .... | .... | .... |
| B. Capital Account*...................... | 209ba | .... | .... | .... | .... | .... | .... | .... | .... | .... | .... | .... | .... |
| Capital account: credit................... | 209ca | .... | .... | .... | .... | .... | .... | .... | .... | .... | .... | .... | .... |
| Capital account: debit................... | 209da | .... | .... | .... | .... | .... | .... | .... | .... | .... | .... | .... | .... |
| Balance on current & capital acct. | 129ba | 1,792.9 | 3,881.3 | 7,124.8 | 5,166.5 | 8,499.0 | 1,632.8 | 4,172.3 | 2,898.6 | .... | .... | .... | .... |
| C. Financial Account* ................. | 309na | 1,018.3 | 1,509.7 | 5,661.8 | 3,280.5 | 5,890.5 | 2,344.5 | 3,762.5 | 1,076.7 | .... | .... | .... | .... |
| Direct investment: assets.............. | 3a9aa | 25.4 | 341.0 | 370.0 | — | 700.0 | — | — | 1,060.4 | .... | .... | .... | .... |
| Equity & investment fund shares.. | 3aaaa | 25.4 | 341.0 | 370.0 | — | 700.0 | — | — | 1,060.4 | .... | .... | .... | .... |
| Debt instruments..................... | 3abaa | .... | .... | .... | .... | .... | .... | .... | .... | .... | .... | .... | .... |
| Direct investment: liabilities .......... | 3a9la | 998.1 | 939.7 | 882.7 | 830.0 | 2,800.8 | 709.1 | 549.4 | 1,216.1 | .... | .... | .... | .... |
| Equity & investment fund shares . | 3aala | 1,009.8 | 956.1 | 903.0 | 851.0 | 2,816.6 | 721.5 | 560.0 | 1,080.7 | .... | .... | .... | .... |
| Debt instruments...................... | 3abla | −11.7 | −16.4 | −20.3 | −21.0 | −15.8 | −12.4 | −10.6 | 135.4 | .... | .... | .... | .... |
| Portfolio investment: assets .......... | 3b9aa | 690.1 | — | — | — | — | — | — | — | .... | .... | .... | .... |
| Equity & investment fund shares | 3baaa | .... | .... | .... | .... | .... | .... | .... | .... | .... | .... | .... | .... |
| Debt securities .......................... | 3bbaa | 690.1 | — | — | — | — | — | — | — | .... | .... | .... | .... |
| Portfolio investment: liabilities....... | 3b9la | .... | .... | .... | .... | .... | .... | .... | .... | .... | .... | .... | .... |
| Equity & investment fund shares . | 3bala | .... | .... | .... | .... | .... | .... | .... | .... | .... | .... | .... | .... |
| Debt securities........................ | 3bbla | .... | .... | .... | .... | .... | .... | .... | .... | .... | .... | .... | .... |
| Fin. der.& empl.stk.ops.(ESOs): net. | 3c9na | .... | .... | .... | .... | .... | .... | .... | .... | .... | .... | .... | .... |
| Fin. der. & ESOs.: assets.............. | 3c9aa | .... | .... | .... | .... | .... | .... | .... | .... | .... | .... | .... | .... |
| Fin. der. & ESOs.: liabilities.......... | 3c9la | .... | .... | .... | .... | .... | .... | .... | .... | .... | .... | .... | .... |
| Other investment: assets............... | 3d9aa | 326.3 | 390.7 | 980.3 | 39.1 | 1,300.6 | 495.1 | 515.6 | −3,220.3 | .... | .... | .... | .... |
| Other equity....................... | 3daaa | .... | .... | .... | .... | .... | .... | .... | .... | .... | .... | .... | .... |
| Debt instruments...................... | 3dzaa | 326.3 | 390.7 | 980.3 | 39.1 | 1,300.6 | 495.1 | 515.6 | −3,220.3 | .... | .... | .... | .... |
| Other investment: liabilities........... | 3d9la | −974.6 | −1,717.7 | −5,194.2 | −4,071.4 | −6,690.7 | −2,558.5 | −3,796.3 | −4,452.7 | .... | .... | .... | .... |
| Other equity....................... | 3dala | .... | .... | .... | .... | .... | .... | .... | .... | .... | .... | .... | .... |
| Debt instruments...................... | 3dzla | −974.6 | −1,717.7 | −5,194.2 | −4,071.4 | −6,690.7 | −2,558.5 | −3,796.3 | −4,452.7 | .... | .... | .... | .... |
| Curr.+ cap.− finan. acct. balance... | 4y9na | 774.6 | 2,371.6 | 1,463.0 | 1,886.0 | 2,608.5 | −711.8 | 409.8 | 1,821.9 | .... | .... | .... | .... |
| D. Net Errors and Omissions........... | 409na | −268.7 | −984.6 | −367.3 | −365.5 | 123.1 | 37.8 | 26.3 | −1,019.1 | .... | .... | .... | .... |
| E. Reserves and Related Items......... | 4z9na | 505.9 | 1,387.0 | 1,095.7 | 1,520.5 | 2,731.6 | −674.0 | 436.2 | 802.8 | .... | .... | .... | .... |
| Reserve assets............................ | 3e9aa | 505.9 | 1,387.0 | 1,095.7 | 1,520.5 | 2,731.6 | −674.0 | 436.2 | 802.8 | .... | .... | .... | .... |
| Credit and loans from the IMF........ | 3dcla | — | — | — | — | — | — | — | — | .... | .... | .... | .... |
| Exceptional financing.................... | 409la | .... | .... | .... | .... | .... | .... | .... | .... | .... | .... | .... | .... |

*Excludes components in group E

| | | 2004 | 2005 | 2006 | 2007 | 2008 | 2009 | 2010 | 2011 | 2012 | 2013 | 2014 | 2015 |
|---|---|---|---|---|---|---|---|---|---|---|---|---|---|
| **International Investment Position** | | | | | | | *Millions of US Dollars* | | | | | | |
| Assets.......................................... | 809aa | .... | .... | .... | .... | .... | .... | .... | 22,146.7 | .... | .... | .... | .... |
| Direct investment......................... | 8a9aa | .... | .... | .... | .... | .... | .... | .... | 534.9 | .... | .... | .... | .... |
| Equity & investment fund shares.. | 8aaaa | .... | .... | .... | .... | .... | .... | .... | 298.5 | .... | .... | .... | .... |
| Debt instruments..................... | 8abaa | .... | .... | .... | .... | .... | .... | .... | 236.5 | .... | .... | .... | .... |
| Portfolio investment...................... | 8b9aa | .... | .... | .... | .... | .... | .... | .... | 5,508.3 | .... | .... | .... | .... |
| Equity & investment fund shares.. | 8baaa | .... | .... | .... | .... | .... | .... | .... | 1,661.6 | .... | .... | .... | .... |
| Debt securities........................ | 8bbaa | .... | .... | .... | .... | .... | .... | .... | 3,846.6 | .... | .... | .... | .... |
| Fin. der.(oth.than reserves) & ESOs | 8c9aa | .... | .... | .... | .... | .... | .... | .... | 2.3 | .... | .... | .... | .... |
| Other investment.......................... | 8d9aa | .... | .... | .... | .... | .... | .... | .... | 5,843.9 | .... | .... | .... | .... |
| Other equity............................ | 8daaa | .... | .... | .... | .... | .... | .... | .... | .... | .... | .... | .... | .... |
| Debt instruments..................... | 8dzaa | .... | .... | .... | .... | .... | .... | .... | 5,843.9 | .... | .... | .... | .... |
| Reserve assets............................. | 8e9aa | .... | .... | .... | .... | .... | .... | .... | 10,257.3 | .... | .... | .... | .... |
| Liabilities...................................... | 809la | .... | .... | .... | .... | .... | .... | .... | 16,031.8 | .... | .... | .... | .... |
| Direct investment......................... | 8a9la | .... | .... | .... | .... | .... | .... | .... | 3,670.1 | .... | .... | .... | .... |
| Equity & investment fund shares.. | 8aala | .... | .... | .... | .... | .... | .... | .... | 2,071.9 | .... | .... | .... | .... |
| Debt instruments..................... | 8abla | .... | .... | .... | .... | .... | .... | .... | 1,598.2 | .... | .... | .... | .... |
| Portfolio investment...................... | 8b9la | .... | .... | .... | .... | .... | .... | .... | 4,509.8 | .... | .... | .... | .... |
| Equity & investment fund shares.. | 8bala | .... | .... | .... | .... | .... | .... | .... | 2.6 | .... | .... | .... | .... |
| Debt securities........................ | 8bbla | .... | .... | .... | .... | .... | .... | .... | 4,507.2 | .... | .... | .... | .... |
| Fin. der.(oth.than reserves) & ESOs | 8c9la | .... | .... | .... | .... | .... | .... | .... | .... | .... | .... | .... | .... |
| Other investment.......................... | 8d9la | .... | .... | .... | .... | .... | .... | .... | 7,851.9 | .... | .... | .... | .... |
| Other equity............................ | 8dala | .... | .... | .... | .... | .... | .... | .... | .... | .... | .... | .... | .... |
| Debt instruments..................... | 8dzla | .... | .... | .... | .... | .... | .... | .... | 7,851.9 | .... | .... | .... | .... |
| **Government Finance** | | | | | | | | | | | | | |
| **Cash Flow Statement** | | | | | | | | | | | | | |
| **Central Government** | | | | | | *Millions of TT Dollars: Fiscal Year Ends September 30* | | | | | | | |
| Cash Receipts:Operating Activities... | c1 | 20,625.6 | .... | 38,907.0 | 40,034.9 | 56,810.3 | 38,993.5 | 43,632.1 | 47,213.6 | 49,234.5 | 52,258.8 | 57,049.0 | 49,813.4 |
| Taxes..................................... | c11 | 11,740.6 | .... | 13,669.0 | 15,570.5 | 21,422.2 | 17,079.4 | 19,545.4 | 21,222.3 | 23,008.2 | 24,654.5 | 25,758.3 | 25,596.4 |
| Social Contributions...................... | c12 | — | .... | — | — | — | — | — | — | — | — | — | — |
| Grants................................... | c13 | — | .... | — | — | — | — | — | — | — | — | — | — |
| Other Receipts............................. | c14 | 8,885.0 | .... | 25,238.0 | 24,464.4 | 35,388.1 | 21,914.1 | 24,086.7 | 25,991.3 | 26,226.3 | 27,604.3 | 31,290.7 | 24,217.0 |
| Cash Payments:Operating Activities. | c2 | 17,498.5 | .... | 26,384.7 | 29,764.5 | 34,763.0 | 37,052.2 | 37,078.8 | 41,412.6 | 44,486.8 | 48,957.5 | 54,189.0 | 53,431.7 |
| Compensation of Employees.......... | c21 | 3,585.9 | .... | 5,455.6 | 6,221.3 | 6,946.8 | 6,620.4 | 6,711.0 | 7,179.7 | 7,282.2 | 9,170.4 | 8,670.0 | 10,366.4 |
| Purchases of Goods & Services....... | c22 | 2,374.5 | .... | 3,645.3 | 4,064.4 | 4,734.8 | 5,758.3 | 6,244.2 | 6,267.0 | 7,061.5 | 7,180.8 | 8,008.8 | 8,671.2 |
| Interest....................................... | c24 | 2,364.3 | .... | 2,453.3 | 2,698.0 | 2,967.3 | 3,499.9 | 3,290.2 | 2,866.4 | 2,937.1 | 2,808.7 | 3,122.4 | 2,954.7 |
| Subsidies.................................... | c25 | — | .... | 2,213.2 | 2,406.9 | 2,423.0 | 1,939.3 | 1,892.3 | 3,835.4 | 4,231.2 | 2,454.6 | 3,636.6 | 2,514.1 |
| Grants........................................ | c26 | — | .... | 4,442.7 | 4,671.7 | 5,631.7 | 5,200.7 | 5,581.4 | 5,887.7 | 7,127.5 | 7,455.6 | 7,868.1 | 7,886.1 |
| Social Benefits............................. | c27 | — | .... | 4,373.4 | 4,956.5 | 6,908.3 | 6,413.4 | 6,617.2 | 8,128.4 | 8,668.8 | 11,706.9 | 13,459.2 | 13,050.5 |
| Other Payments............................ | c28 | 9,173.8 | .... | 3,801.2 | 4,745.7 | 5,151.1 | 7,620.2 | 6,742.5 | 7,248.0 | 7,178.5 | 8,180.5 | 9,423.9 | 7,988.7 |
| Net Cash Inflow:Operating Act.[1-2] | ccio | 3,127.1 | .... | 12,522.3 | 10,270.4 | 22,047.3 | 1,941.3 | 6,553.3 | 5,801.0 | 4,747.7 | 3,301.3 | 2,860.0 | −3,618.3 |
| Net Cash Outflow:Invest. in NFA...... | c31 | 1,608.8 | .... | 4,611.3 | 7,752.5 | 9,646.9 | 8,362.6 | 6,168.2 | 6,665.5 | 6,944.2 | 7,938.4 | 7,118.3 | 3,395.4 |
| Purchases of Nonfinancial Assets... | c31.1 | 1,612.9 | .... | 4,615.3 | 7,782.0 | 9,684.5 | 8,413.9 | 6,399.2 | 6,952.6 | 6,987.7 | 8,439.8 | 8,434.8 | 8,360.3 |
| Sales of Nonfinancial Assets.......... | c31.2 | 4.1 | .... | 4.0 | 29.5 | 37.6 | 51.3 | 231.0 | 287.1 | 43.5 | 501.4 | 1,316.5 | 4,964.9 |
| Cash Surplus/Deficit [1-2-31=1-2M] | ccsd | 1,518.3 | .... | 7,911.0 | 2,517.9 | 12,400.4 | −6,421.3 | 385.1 | −864.5 | −2,196.5 | −4,637.1 | −4,258.3 | −7,013.7 |
| Net Acq. Fin. Assets, excl. Cash....... | c32x | 8.2 | .... | — | — | — | — | — | — | — | — | — | — |
| Domestic................................... | c321x | 8.2 | .... | — | — | — | — | — | — | — | — | — | — |
| Foreign..................................... | c322x | — | .... | — | — | — | — | — | — | — | — | — | — |
| Net Incurrence of Liabilities............. | c33 | 628.2 | .... | −1,342.0 | 1,958.1 | −813.6 | −1,537.4 | −1,343.9 | −832.0 | 2,525.1 | −3,369.9 | 1,901.7 | 14,782.5 |
| Domestic.................................... | c331 | 907.0 | .... | −1,041.8 | 1,269.8 | −1,055.0 | −121.4 | −1,157.8 | −964.8 | 1,713.1 | −2,806.8 | 1,882.7 | 14,364.5 |
| Foreign...................................... | c332 | −278.8 | .... | −300.2 | 688.3 | 241.4 | −1,416.0 | −186.1 | 132.8 | 812.0 | −563.1 | 19.0 | 418.0 |
| Net Cash Inflow, Fin.Act.[-32x+33].. | cnfb | 620.0 | .... | −1,342.0 | 1,958.1 | −813.6 | −1,537.4 | −1,343.9 | −832.0 | 2,525.1 | −3,369.9 | 1,901.7 | 14,782.5 |
| Net Change in Stock of Cash........... | cncb | 2,138.3 | .... | 6,569.0 | 4,476.0 | 11,586.8 | −7,958.7 | −958.8 | −1,696.5 | 328.6 | −8,007.0 | −2,356.6 | 7,768.8 |
| Stat. Discrep. [32X-33+NCB-CSD].... | ccsdz | — | .... | — | — | — | — | — | — | — | — | — | — |
| Memo Item:Cash Expenditure[2+31] | c2m | 19,107.3 | .... | 30,996.0 | 37,517.0 | 44,409.9 | 45,414.8 | 43,247.0 | 48,078.1 | 51,431.0 | 56,895.9 | 61,307.3 | 56,827.1 |
| Memo Item: Gross Debt.................. | c63 | 19,665.5 | .... | .... | .... | .... | .... | .... | .... | .... | .... | .... | .... |
| **National Accounts** | | | | | | | *Millions of TT Dollars* | | | | | | |
| Househ.Cons.Expend.,incl.NPISHs.... | 96f | 45,424 | 32,675 | 56,339 | 65,691 | 68,668 | .... | .... | .... | .... | .... | .... | .... |
| Government Consumption Expend... | 91f | 9,585 | 11,707 | 12,802 | 14,328 | 16,665 | .... | .... | .... | .... | .... | .... | .... |
| Gross Fixed Capital Formation.......... | 93e | 15,279 | 14,319 | 14,972 | 16,253 | .... | .... | .... | .... | .... | .... | .... | .... |
| Changes in Inventories.................... | 93i | 796 | 430 | 584 | 1,413 | .... | .... | .... | .... | .... | .... | .... | .... |
| Exports of Goods and Services......... | 90c | 45,491 | 66,225 | 79,418 | 88,792 | 111,688 | .... | .... | .... | .... | .... | .... | .... |
| Imports of Goods and Services (-)..... | 98c | 33,023 | 39,257 | 44,597 | 49,051 | 64,324 | .... | .... | .... | .... | .... | .... | .... |
| Gross Domestic Product (GDP)......... | 99b | 83,653 | 100,386 | 115,951 | 136,953 | 175,287 | 121,281 | 131,198 | 150,887 | 149,327 | 157,418 | .... | .... |
| Net Primary Income from Abroad..... | 98.n | −2,492 | −4,762 | −5,878 | −6,072 | −5,652 | .... | .... | .... | .... | .... | .... | .... |
| Gross National Income (GNI)........... | 99a | 81,161 | 95,624 | 116,230 | 131,355 | 146,503 | .... | .... | .... | .... | .... | .... | .... |
| Consumption of Fixed Capital.......... | 99cf | 9,271 | 11,760 | 14,645 | 15,989 | 16,350 | .... | .... | .... | .... | .... | .... | .... |
| GDP Volume 2000 Prices................. | 99b.p | 71,355 | 75,194 | 85,795 | 89,874 | 92,001 | 88,842 | 89,027 | 87,601 | 88,934 | 91,397 | .... | .... |
| GDP Volume (2010=100)............... | 99bvp | 80.1 | 84.5 | 96.4 | 101.0 | 103.3 | 99.8 | 100.0 | 98.4 | 99.9 | 102.7 | .... | .... |
| GDP Deflator (2010=100)............... | 99bip | 79.6 | 90.6 | 91.7 | 103.4 | 129.3 | 92.6 | 100.0 | 116.9 | 113.9 | 116.9 | .... | .... |
| | | | | | | | *Millions: Midyear Estimates* | | | | | | |
| **Population**............................... | 99z | 1.29 | 1.30 | 1.30 | 1.31 | 1.32 | 1.32 | 1.33 | 1.33 | 1.34 | 1.35 | 1.35 | 1.36 |

# Tunisia 744

| | | 2004 | 2005 | 2006 | 2007 | 2008 | 2009 | 2010 | 2011 | 2012 | 2013 | 2014 | 2015 |
|---|---|---|---|---|---|---|---|---|---|---|---|---|---|
| **Exchange Rates** | | | | | | *Dinars per SDR: End of Period* | | | | | | | |
| Market Rate.................................. | aa | 1.8627 | 1.9487 | 1.9514 | 1.9290 | 2.0176 | 2.0651 | 2.2144 | 2.3018 | 2.3831 | 2.5359 | 2.6965 | .... |
| | | | | | *Dinars per US Dollar: End of Period (ae) Period Average (rf)* | | | | | | | | |
| Market Rate.................................. | ae | 1.1994 | 1.3634 | 1.2971 | 1.2207 | 1.3099 | 1.3173 | 1.4379 | 1.4993 | 1.5506 | 1.6467 | 1.8612 | .... |
| Market Rate.................................. | rf | 1.2455 | 1.2974 | 1.3310 | 1.2814 | 1.2321 | 1.3503 | 1.4314 | 1.4078 | 1.5619 | 1.6247 | 1.6977 | 1.9616 |
| | | | | | *Index Numbers (2010=100): Period Averages* | | | | | | | | |
| Nominal Effective Exchange Rate..... | nec | 121.6 | 115.8 | 112.4 | 108.3 | 106.6 | 102.6 | 100.0 | 97.9 | 94.1 | 89.3 | 86.1 | 86.9 |
| CPI-Based Real Effect. Ex. Rate........ | rec | 112.0 | 106.6 | 105.5 | 102.4 | 101.7 | 100.5 | 100.0 | 98.2 | 96.7 | 94.9 | 94.8 | 99.7 |
| **Fund Position** | | | | | | *Millions of SDRs: End of Period* | | | | | | | |
| Quota........................................ | 2f.s | 286.50 | 286.50 | 286.50 | 286.50 | 286.50 | 286.50 | 286.50 | 286.50 | 286.50 | 286.50 | 286.50 | 286.50 |
| SDR Holdings............................... | 1b.s | 6.01 | 1.53 | .86 | 1.25 | 3.38 | 241.80 | 241.78 | 241.84 | 241.87 | 239.43 | 191.40 | 122.83 |
| Reserve Position in the Fund............ | 1c.s | 20.22 | 20.22 | 20.25 | 20.25 | 20.25 | 20.25 | 56.25 | 56.25 | 56.25 | 56.25 | 56.39 | 56.46 |
| Total Fund Cred.&Loans Outstg....... | 2tl | — | — | — | — | — | — | — | — | — | 98.80 | 787.88 | 1,002.75 |
| SDR Allocations............................. | 1bd | 34.24 | 34.24 | 34.24 | 34.24 | 34.24 | 272.78 | 272.78 | 272.78 | 272.78 | 272.78 | 272.78 | 272.78 |
| **International Liquidity** | | | | | *Millions of US Dollars Unless Otherwise Indicated: End of Period* | | | | | | | | |
| Total Reserves minus Gold............... | 1l.d | 3,935.7 | 4,436.7 | 6,773.2 | 7,850.8 | 8,849.3 | 11,057.3 | 9,459.3 | 7,453.5 | 8,357.2 | 7,287.4 | 7,235.1 | .... |
| SDR Holdings............................. | 1b.d | 9.3 | 2.2 | 1.3 | 2.0 | 5.2 | 379.1 | 372.3 | 371.3 | 371.7 | 368.7 | 277.3 | 170.2 |
| Reserve Position in the Fund.......... | 1c.d | 31.4 | 28.9 | 30.5 | 32.0 | 31.2 | 31.7 | 86.6 | 86.4 | 86.4 | 86.6 | 81.7 | 78.2 |
| Foreign Exchange......................... | 1d.d | 3,895.0 | 4,405.6 | 6,741.4 | 7,816.8 | 8,812.9 | 10,646.5 | 9,000.3 | 6,995.9 | 7,899.1 | 6,832.1 | 6,876.1 | .... |
| Gold (Million Fine Troy Ounces)....... | 1ad | .218 | .218 | .218 | .218 | .218 | .218 | .217 | .217 | .217 | .218 | .218 | .... |
| Gold (National Valuation)................ | 1and | 3.7 | 3.2 | 3.4 | 3.4 | 3.4 | 3.3 | 3.3 | 2.9 | 2.8 | 159.9 | 160.1 | .... |
| Deposit Money Banks: Assets........... | 7a.d | 755.3 | 939.4 | 1,074.5 | 1,635.0 | 1,339.8 | 1,730.3 | 1,692.9 | 1,199.0 | 1,411.7 | 1,496.6 | 1,417.1 | 1,454.7 |
| Deposit Money Banks: Liabs............ | 7b.d | 3,942.0 | 3,887.0 | 4,214.3 | 4,907.9 | 4,798.5 | 5,300.3 | 5,165.0 | 4,918.0 | 5,387.9 | 5,681.9 | 5,817.6 | 5,774.9 |
| Other Banking Insts.: Liabilities........ | 7f.d | — | — | — | — | — | — | — | — | — | — | — | — |
| **Monetary Authorities** | | | | | | *Millions of Dinars: End of Period* | | | | | | | |
| Foreign Assets............................... | 11 | 4,814 | 6,030 | 8,802 | 9,684 | 11,740 | 13,943 | 13,667 | 11,287 | 13,415 | 12,663 | 14,262 | 15,042 |
| Claims on Central Government........ | 12a | 71 | 57 | 206 | 75 | 77 | 66 | 51 | 51 | 562 | 888 | 474 | 112 |
| Claims on Private Sector................. | 12d | 25 | 27 | 30 | 30 | 31 | 32 | 33 | 34 | 35 | 39 | 38 | 36 |
| Claims on Deposit Money Banks...... | 12e | 91 | — | 109 | — | — | — | 320 | 3,577 | 2,721 | 3,668 | 3,116 | 4,209 |
| Reserve Money.............................. | 14 | 3,577 | 3,979 | 4,565 | 5,197 | 6,314 | 7,511 | 6,885 | 7,407 | 7,977 | 8,694 | 10,628 | 10,974 |
| of which: Currency Outside DMBs.. | 14a | 2,968 | 3,478 | 3,873 | 4,099 | 4,400 | 5,010 | 5,518 | 6,815 | 6,559 | 7,236 | 8,085 | 8,418 |
| Foreign Liabilities.......................... | 16c | 119 | 208 | 150 | 155 | 131 | 618 | 623 | 788 | 919 | 2,680 | 4,964 | 5,932 |
| Central Government Deposits.......... | 16d | 668 | 693 | 448 | 331 | 403 | 403 | 611 | 656 | 138 | 207 | 625 | 146 |
| Capital Accounts............................ | 17a | 85 | 97 | 94 | 106 | 112 | 99 | 104 | 112 | 149 | 132 | 125 | 122 |
| Other Items (Net)........................... | 17r | 551 | 1,136 | 3,889 | 4,000 | 4,887 | 5,409 | 5,848 | 5,986 | 7,550 | 5,544 | 1,549 | 2,226 |
| **Deposit Money Banks** | | | | | | *Millions of Dinars: End of Period* | | | | | | | |
| Reserves...................................... | 20 | 902 | 1,195 | 1,543 | 2,161 | 3,439 | 3,948 | 2,537 | 2,474 | 3,278 | 3,659 | 2,578 | 2,505 |
| Foreign Assets............................... | 21 | 906 | 1,281 | 1,393 | 1,996 | 1,755 | 2,279 | 2,434 | 1,798 | 2,189 | 2,465 | 2,638 | 2,956 |
| Claims on Central Government........ | 22a | 2,145 | 2,271 | 2,609 | 2,817 | 2,501 | 2,941 | 2,821 | 3,346 | 3,452 | 3,975 | 5,639 | 7,016 |
| Claims on Private Sector................. | 22d | 21,467 | 23,248 | 25,040 | 27,495 | 31,638 | 34,774 | 41,426 | 46,924 | 50,941 | 54,919 | 59,892 | 63,608 |
| Demand Deposits.......................... | 24 | 4,589 | 5,088 | 5,856 | 6,745 | 7,587 | 8,835 | 10,012 | 11,226 | 12,966 | 13,160 | 14,179 | 15,192 |
| Quasi-Monetary Liabilities............... | 25 | 12,151 | 13,275 | 14,674 | 16,539 | 19,278 | 21,427 | 23,961 | 24,524 | 26,838 | 29,124 | 31,322 | 32,240 |
| Foreign Liabilities.......................... | 26c | 2,471 | 3,027 | 3,208 | 4,827 | 5,147 | 5,819 | 6,248 | 6,167 | 7,037 | 7,989 | 9,425 | 10,048 |
| Long-Term Foreign Liabilities........... | 26cl | 2,257 | 2,273 | 2,258 | 1,164 | 1,139 | 1,163 | 1,178 | 1,206 | 1,318 | 1,367 | 1,403 | 1,687 |
| Counterpart Funds......................... | 26e | — | — | — | — | — | — | — | — | — | — | — | — |
| Central Govt. Lending Funds........... | 26f | — | — | — | — | — | — | — | — | — | — | — | — |
| Credit from Monetary Authorities..... | 26g | 93 | 4 | 123 | 17 | 18 | 2 | 311 | 3,570 | 2,749 | 3,697 | 3,130 | 4,223 |
| Capital Accounts............................ | 27a | 3,937 | 4,409 | 4,771 | 5,244 | 5,911 | 6,622 | 7,307 | 8,027 | 9,294 | 10,116 | 12,022 | 13,515 |
| Other Items (Net)........................... | 27r | −78 | −81 | −304 | −66 | 253 | 73 | 200 | −177 | −342 | −437 | −733 | −820 |
| Post Office: Checking Deposits....... | 24..i | 438 | 557 | 592 | 692 | 981 | 1,004 | 896 | 1,562 | 1,133 | 1,226 | 1,246 | 1,974 |
| **Monetary Survey** | | | | | | *Millions of Dinars: End of Period* | | | | | | | |
| Foreign Assets (Net)........................ | 31n | 3,130 | 4,076 | 6,837 | 6,698 | 8,216 | 9,785 | 9,230 | 6,131 | 7,648 | 4,458 | 2,512 | 2,018 |
| Domestic Credit............................. | 32 | 23,478 | 25,467 | 28,028 | 30,777 | 34,825 | 38,413 | 44,615 | 51,261 | 55,985 | 60,839 | 66,665 | 72,600 |
| Claims on Central Govt. (Net)........ | 32an | 1,985 | 2,192 | 2,958 | 3,253 | 3,156 | 3,608 | 3,157 | 4,304 | 5,009 | 5,882 | 6,735 | 8,956 |
| Claims on Private Sector............... | 32d | 21,493 | 23,275 | 25,070 | 27,525 | 31,669 | 34,805 | 41,458 | 46,958 | 50,976 | 54,957 | 59,930 | 63,643 |
| Money......................................... | 34 | 8,036 | 9,140 | 10,339 | 11,579 | 12,991 | 14,874 | 16,454 | 19,658 | 20,756 | 21,774 | 23,606 | 25,633 |
| Quasi-Money................................. | 35 | 12,151 | 13,275 | 14,674 | 16,539 | 19,278 | 21,427 | 23,961 | 24,524 | 26,838 | 29,124 | 31,322 | 32,240 |
| Long-Term Foreign Liabilities........... | 36cl | 2,257 | 2,273 | 2,258 | 1,164 | 1,139 | 1,163 | 1,178 | 1,206 | 1,318 | 1,367 | 1,403 | 1,687 |
| Counterpart Funds......................... | 36e | 270 | 256 | 293 | 503 | 371 | 973 | 1,022 | 963 | 2,568 | 689 | 646 | 2,097 |
| Central Government Lending Funds.. | 36f | — | — | — | — | — | — | — | — | — | — | — | — |
| Other Items (Net)........................... | 37r | 3,894 | 4,600 | 7,300 | 7,690 | 9,263 | 9,762 | 11,230 | 11,041 | 12,154 | 12,343 | 12,199 | 12,961 |
| Money plus Quasi-Money................ | 35l | 20,186 | 22,414 | 25,013 | 28,118 | 32,268 | 36,301 | 40,415 | 44,181 | 47,594 | 50,898 | 54,929 | 57,873 |
| **Other Banking Institutions** | | | | | | *Millions of Dinars: End of Period* | | | | | | | |
| Foreign Assets (Net)........................ | 41n | −44 | −21 | −36 | −55 | −64 | −64 | −75 | −176 | −176 | −148 | −114 | −115 |
| Claims on Central Govt. (Net).......... | 42an | 35 | 4 | 1 | 1 | 1 | 15 | — | — | — | — | — | — |
| Claims on Private Sector................. | 42d | 1,403 | 1,133 | 1,161 | 1,318 | 1,431 | 1,720 | 2,120 | 2,376 | 2,677 | 2,871 | 3,180 | 3,521 |
| Monetary Deposits......................... | 44 | 35 | 9 | 13 | 14 | 16 | 12 | 8 | 20 | 18 | 39 | 7 | 22 |
| Time and Savings Deposits.............. | 45 | 636 | 589 | 576 | 696 | 794 | 1,038 | 1,428 | 1,543 | 1,696 | 1,805 | 2,077 | 2,274 |
| Long-Term Foreign Liabilities........... | 46cl | — | — | — | — | — | — | — | — | — | — | — | — |
| Central Govt. Lending Funds........... | 46f | 202 | 211 | 175 | 148 | 116 | 110 | 107 | 76 | 109 | 96 | 153 | 171 |
| Capital Accounts............................ | 47a | 526 | 302 | 330 | 375 | 359 | 416 | 415 | 477 | 517 | 644 | 661 | 829 |
| Other Items (Net)........................... | 47r | −4 | 4 | 32 | 31 | 81 | 95 | 86 | 82 | 159 | 140 | 170 | 111 |
| **Banking Survey** | | | | | | *Millions of Dinars: End of Period* | | | | | | | |
| Foreign Assets (Net)........................ | 51n | 3,086 | 4,054 | 6,801 | 6,643 | 8,152 | 9,721 | 9,156 | 5,954 | 7,472 | 4,310 | 2,398 | 1,903 |
| Domestic Credit............................. | 52 | 24,916 | 26,603 | 29,190 | 32,096 | 36,256 | 40,148 | 46,735 | 53,637 | 58,662 | 63,710 | 69,845 | 76,121 |
| Claims on Central Govt. (Net)........ | 52an | 2,020 | 2,196 | 2,958 | 3,253 | 3,156 | 3,623 | 3,157 | 4,304 | 5,009 | 5,882 | 6,735 | 8,957 |
| Claims on Private Sector............... | 52d | 22,896 | 24,407 | 26,232 | 28,843 | 33,100 | 36,525 | 43,578 | 49,333 | 53,653 | 57,828 | 63,110 | 67,165 |
| Liquid Liabilities........................... | 55l | 20,857 | 23,012 | 25,602 | 28,828 | 33,079 | 37,351 | 41,852 | 45,745 | 49,309 | 52,742 | 57,012 | 60,169 |
| Long Term Foreign Liabilities........... | 56cl | 2,257 | 2,273 | 2,258 | 1,164 | 1,139 | 1,163 | 1,178 | 1,206 | 1,318 | 1,367 | 1,403 | 1,687 |
| Other Items (Net)........................... | 57r | 4,888 | 5,373 | 8,131 | 8,747 | 10,191 | 11,355 | 12,860 | 12,640 | 15,508 | 13,912 | 13,828 | 16,169 |
| **Interest Rates** | | | | | | *Percent Per Annum* | | | | | | | |
| Money Market Rate....................... | 60b | 5.00 | 5.00 | 5.07 | 5.24 | 5.21 | 4.30 | 4.43 | 4.03 | 3.77 | 4.59 | 4.82 | 4.71 |

# Tunisia 744

| | | 2004 | 2005 | 2006 | 2007 | 2008 | 2009 | 2010 | 2011 | 2012 | 2013 | 2014 | 2015 |
|---|---|---|---|---|---|---|---|---|---|---|---|---|---|
| **Prices, Production, Labor** | | | | | | *Index Numbers (2010=100): Period Averages* | | | | | | | |
| Producer Prices.................... | 63 | 73.5 | 76.6 | 82.0 | 84.8 | 95.1 | 97.0 | 100.0 | 106.4 | 113.3 | 116.7 | † 120.4 | 126.5 |
| Consumer Prices.................... | 64 | 80.0 | 81.6 | † 85.3 | 88.2 | 92.5 | 95.8 | † 100.0 | 103.5 | 108.9 | 115.2 | 120.9 | 126.7 |
| Industrial Production.............. | 66 | 82.8 | 83.5 | 85.8 | 94.1 | 97.2 | 92.8 | 100.0 | 96.3 | 98.3 | 100.0 | † 100.4 | 98.8 |
| Mining Production................. | 66zx | 102.2 | 102.3 | 91.7 | 90.9 | 91.1 | 88.5 | 100.0 | 42.8 | 46.0 | 52.0 | 53.4 | .... |
| Crude Petrol. Prod. (2000=100)...... | 66aa | 91.4 | .... | .... | .... | .... | .... | .... | .... | .... | .... | .... | .... |
| | | | | | | *Number in Thousands: Period Averages* | | | | | | | |
| Labor Force......................... | 67d | 3,329 | † 3,359 | 3,435 | 3,522 | 3,604 | 3,689 | 3,769 | 3,845 | 3,914 | 3,953 | .... | .... |
| Employment......................... | 67e | 2,855 | † 2,929 | 3,005 | 3,085 | 3,155 | 3,199 | 3,277 | 3,140 | 3,234 | 3,327 | .... | 2,424 |
| Unemployment..................... | 67c | 474 | † 433 | 429 | 437 | 447 | 491 | 490 | 705 | 680 | 626 | .... | .... |
| Unemployment Rate (%)............ | 67r | 13.9 | † 12.9 | 12.5 | 12.4 | 12.4 | 13.3 | 13.0 | 18.3 | 17.4 | 15.8 | .... | 15.2 |
| **Intl. Transactions & Positions** | | | | | | *Millions of Dinars* | | | | | | | |
| Exports............................. | 70 | 12,055.0 | 13,607.7 | 15,558.0 | 19,409.8 | 23,637.0 | 19,469.2 | 23,519.0 | 25,092.0 | 26,547.6 | 27,701.1 | 28,406.8 | 27,607.1 |
| Imports, c.i.f......................... | 71 | 15,960.4 | 17,101.6 | 20,003.5 | 24,437.4 | 30,241.2 | 25,877.6 | 31,817.1 | 33,702.0 | 38,182.7 | 39,509.4 | 42,042.5 | 39,654.8 |
| **Balance of Payments** | | | | | | *Millions of US Dollars* | | | | | | | |
| A. Current Account*.................... | 109bx | −441.8 | −299.3 | −619.4 | −916.9 | −1,711.2 | −1,233.7 | −2,104.4 | −3,385.7 | −3,721.4 | −3,878.7 | −4,301.7 | .... |
| Goods, credit (exports)............. | 1a9cx | 10,025.2 | 10,691.3 | 11,738.0 | 15,191.9 | 19,248.5 | 14,481.4 | 16,493.4 | 17,876.3 | 17,071.4 | 17,145.6 | 16,841.3 | .... |
| Goods, debit (imports)............. | 1a9dx | 12,280.4 | 12,594.5 | 14,202.1 | 18,023.5 | 23,193.7 | 18,117.4 | 21,005.4 | 22,623.0 | 23,101.9 | 22,981.1 | 23,402.8 | .... |
| Balance on goods............. | 1a9bx | −2,255.2 | −1,903.2 | −2,464.0 | −2,831.6 | −3,945.2 | −3,636.0 | −4,512.0 | −4,746.7 | −6,030.6 | −5,835.5 | −6,561.5 | .... |
| Services, credit (exports)............. | 1b9cx | 3,477.4 | 3,876.8 | 4,153.0 | 4,772.1 | 5,831.5 | 5,333.9 | 5,631.8 | 4,618.3 | 5,076.7 | 4,830.7 | 4,733.8 | .... |
| Services, debit (imports)............. | 1b9dx | 1,899.7 | 2,106.5 | 2,361.8 | 2,709.9 | 3,252.8 | 2,872.0 | 3,234.4 | 3,177.8 | 3,195.9 | 3,304.3 | 3,400.3 | .... |
| Balance on Goods & Services...... | 1z9bx | −677.5 | −132.9 | −672.8 | −769.4 | −1,366.5 | −1,174.1 | −2,114.6 | −3,306.2 | −4,149.8 | −4,309.1 | −5,228.0 | .... |
| Primary income: credit............. | 1c9cx | 277.1 | 315.9 | 366.6 | 562.7 | 521.5 | 317.6 | 430.5 | 455.4 | 452.5 | 536.7 | 527.5 | .... |
| Primary income: debit.................. | 1c9dx | 1,417.9 | 1,794.5 | 1,755.8 | 2,329.1 | 2,788.6 | 2,328.3 | 2,355.0 | 2,434.0 | 2,173.4 | 2,356.7 | 1,917.5 | .... |
| Balance on gds, serv. & prim. inc. | 1y9bx | −1,818.3 | −1,611.5 | −2,062.0 | −2,535.8 | −3,633.5 | −3,184.8 | −4,039.2 | −5,284.8 | −5,870.8 | −6,129.1 | −6,618.0 | .... |
| Secondary income: credit.............. | 1d9ca | 1,400.8 | 1,339.9 | 1,469.7 | 1,650.4 | 1,948.0 | 1,978.6 | 1,971.9 | 1,946.1 | 2,192.9 | 2,286.1 | 2,362.1 | .... |
| Secondary income: debit.............. | 1d9da | 24.2 | 27.7 | 27.0 | 31.5 | 25.7 | 27.5 | 37.2 | 47.1 | 43.5 | 35.6 | 45.8 | .... |
| B. Capital Account*.................... | 209ba | 107.6 | 127.1 | 144.9 | 165.5 | 78.9 | 164.5 | 82.4 | 183.8 | 448.9 | 114.7 | 286.5 | .... |
| Capital account: credit.................. | 209ca | 113.2 | 128.7 | 149.3 | 167.6 | 81.7 | 168.0 | 90.7 | 189.1 | 453.3 | 120.0 | 295.7 | .... |
| Capital account: debit.................. | 209da | 5.6 | 1.6 | 4.4 | 2.0 | 2.8 | 3.6 | 8.3 | 5.3 | 4.4 | 5.4 | 9.2 | .... |
| Balance on current & capital acct. | 129ba | −334.2 | −172.2 | −474.4 | −751.4 | −1,632.4 | −1,069.3 | −2,022.1 | −3,202.0 | −3,272.4 | −3,764.0 | −4,015.2 | .... |
| C. Financial Account* | 309na | −1,439.2 | −1,136.5 | −2,595.2 | −1,477.2 | −3,185.6 | −2,640.7 | −1,757.1 | −1,435.7 | −4,564.0 | −2,814.9 | −3,865.3 | .... |
| Direct investment: assets............. | 3a9aa | — | — | — | — | — | — | — | — | — | — | — | .... |
| Equity & investment fund shares.. | 3aaaa | | | | | | | | | | | | .... |
| Debt instruments.................. | 3abaa | .... | .... | .... | .... | .... | .... | .... | .... | .... | .... | .... | .... |
| Direct investment: liabilities .......... | 3a9la | 592.1 | 712.7 | 3,239.9 | 1,515.3 | 2,600.7 | 1,525.2 | 1,334.5 | 432.7 | 1,554.3 | 1,058.6 | 1,004.7 | .... |
| Equity & investment fund shares . | 3aala | 595.6 | 715.7 | 3,241.0 | 1,525.6 | 2,609.4 | 1,529.4 | 1,339.0 | 438.6 | 1,560.2 | 1,070.5 | 1,007.3 | .... |
| Debt instruments.................. | 3abla | −3.5 | −3.0 | −1.1 | −10.3 | −8.7 | −4.1 | −4.5 | −6.0 | −6.0 | −11.9 | −2.7 | .... |
| Portfolio investment: assets .......... | 3b9aa | — | — | — | — | — | — | — | — | — | — | — | .... |
| Equity & investment fund shares | 3baaa | — | — | — | — | — | — | — | — | — | — | .... | |
| Debt securities .......................... | 3bbaa | — | — | — | — | — | — | — | — | — | — | .... | |
| Portfolio investment: liabilities........ | 3b9la | 24.1 | 12.1 | 64.8 | 30.0 | −39.0 | −88.6 | −25.9 | −43.8 | −15.4 | 80.0 | 71.9 | .... |
| Equity & investment fund shares . | 3bala | 24.1 | 12.1 | 64.8 | 30.0 | −39.0 | −88.6 | −25.9 | −43.8 | −15.4 | 80.0 | 71.9 | .... |
| Debt securities..................... | 3bbla | .... | .... | .... | .... | .... | .... | .... | .... | .... | .... | .... | |
| Fin. der.& empl.stk.ops.(ESOs): net. | 3c9na | .... | .... | .... | .... | .... | .... | .... | .... | .... | .... | .... | |
| Fin. der. & ESOs.: assets.............. | 3c9aa | .... | .... | .... | .... | .... | .... | .... | .... | .... | .... | .... | |
| Fin. der. & ESOs.: liabilities.......... | 3c9la | .... | .... | .... | .... | .... | .... | .... | .... | .... | .... | .... | |
| Other investment: assets............. | 3d9aa | 204.7 | −17.2 | −19.3 | 238.6 | 25.2 | −5.6 | 240.3 | 18.1 | −114.6 | 59.0 | −97.8 | .... |
| Other equity.......................... | 3daaa | .... | .... | .... | .... | .... | .... | .... | .... | .... | .... | .... | |
| Debt instruments.................. | 3dzaa | 204.7 | −17.2 | −19.3 | 238.6 | 25.2 | −5.6 | 240.3 | 18.1 | −114.6 | 59.0 | −97.8 | .... |
| Other investment: liabilities........... | 3d9la | 1,027.7 | 394.5 | −728.8 | 170.4 | 649.1 | 1,198.5 | 688.8 | 1,064.9 | 2,910.4 | 1,735.3 | 2,691.0 | .... |
| Other equity.......................... | 3dala | .... | .... | .... | .... | .... | .... | .... | .... | .... | .... | .... | |
| Debt instruments....................... | 3dzla | 1,027.7 | 394.5 | −728.8 | 170.4 | 649.1 | 1,198.5 | 688.8 | 1,064.9 | 2,910.4 | 1,735.3 | 2,691.0 | .... |
| Curr.+ cap.− finan. acct. balance... | 4y9na | 1,105.0 | 964.3 | 2,120.8 | 725.8 | 1,553.2 | 1,571.4 | −265.0 | −1,766.3 | 1,291.5 | −949.1 | −149.9 | .... |
| D. Net Errors and Omissions.......... | 409na | −127.8 | −28.3 | −38.4 | −37.1 | 113.6 | 67.4 | 95.2 | 88.6 | 74.6 | 101.4 | 18.1 | .... |
| E. Reserves and Related Items.......... | 4z9na | 977.3 | 936.0 | 2,082.4 | 688.7 | 1,666.8 | 1,638.9 | −169.8 | −1,677.7 | 1,366.1 | −847.7 | −131.7 | .... |
| Reserve assets............................. | 3e9aa | 977.3 | 936.0 | 2,082.4 | 688.7 | 1,666.8 | 1,638.9 | −169.8 | −1,677.7 | 1,366.1 | −698.1 | 917.3 | .... |
| Credit and loans from the IMF........ | 3dcla | — | — | — | — | — | — | — | — | — | 149.7 | 1,049.1 | .... |
| Exceptional financing.................... | 409la | .... | .... | .... | .... | .... | .... | .... | .... | .... | .... | .... | .... |

*Excludes components in group E

2016, International Monetary Fund : *International Financial Statistics Yearbook*

# Tunisia 744

| | | 2004 | 2005 | 2006 | 2007 | 2008 | 2009 | 2010 | 2011 | 2012 | 2013 | 2014 | 2015 |
|---|---|---|---|---|---|---|---|---|---|---|---|---|---|
| **International Investment Position** | | | | | | | *Millions of US Dollars* | | | | | | |
| Assets................................. | 809aa | 6,662.5 | 6,761.6 | 9,255.3 | 10,828.1 | 11,636.4 | 13,239.6 | 12,437.9 | 10,411.3 | 11,353.4 | 10,113.2 | 9,755.2 | .... |
| Direct investment.......................... | 8a9aa | 46.9 | 52.4 | 88.6 | 117.1 | 152.8 | 230.8 | 287.2 | 296.9 | 296.3 | 301.9 | 301.9 | .... |
| Equity & investment fund shares.. | 8aaaa | 46.9 | 52.4 | 88.6 | 117.1 | 152.8 | 230.8 | 287.2 | 296.9 | 296.3 | 301.9 | 301.9 | .... |
| Debt instruments...................... | 8abaa | .... | .... | .... | .... | .... | .... | .... | .... | .... | .... | .... | .... |
| Portfolio investment...................... | 8b9aa | 59.7 | 54.1 | 59.3 | 66.8 | 66.8 | 69.5 | 66.6 | 66.0 | 64.9 | 63.6 | 59.0 | .... |
| Equity & investment fund shares.. | 8baaa | 59.7 | 54.1 | 59.3 | 66.8 | 66.8 | 69.5 | 66.6 | 66.0 | 64.9 | 63.6 | 59.0 | .... |
| Debt securities............................ | 8bbaa | .... | .... | .... | .... | .... | .... | .... | .... | .... | .... | .... | .... |
| Fin. der.(oth.than reserves) & ESOs | 8c9aa | .... | .... | .... | .... | .... | .... | .... | .... | .... | .... | .... | .... |
| Other investment......................... | 8d9aa | 2,542.5 | 2,232.4 | 2,321.6 | 2,711.1 | 2,454.6 | 2,354.8 | 2,396.5 | 2,315.3 | 2,123.3 | 2,057.6 | 1,731.3 | .... |
| Other equity............................ | 8daaa | .... | .... | .... | .... | .... | .... | .... | .... | .... | .... | .... | .... |
| Debt instruments...................... | 8dzaa | 2,542.5 | 2,232.4 | 2,321.6 | 2,711.1 | 2,454.6 | 2,354.8 | 2,396.5 | 2,315.3 | 2,123.3 | 2,057.6 | 1,731.3 | .... |
| Reserve assets........................... | 8e9aa | 4,013.3 | 4,422.8 | 6,785.8 | 7,933.1 | 8,962.2 | 10,584.6 | 9,687.6 | 7,733.0 | 8,868.8 | 7,690.1 | 7,663.0 | .... |
| Liabilities.................................... | 809ll | 38,288.0 | 35,971.1 | 41,846.1 | 48,227.6 | 51,048.9 | 55,505.4 | 55,500.1 | 56,141.3 | 59,735.0 | 61,722.3 | 61,649.8 | .... |
| Direct investment.......................... | 8a9la | 17,843.6 | 16,839.7 | 21,831.7 | 26,193.4 | 28,525.1 | 31,276.6 | 31,363.7 | 31,543.5 | 32,603.9 | 33,001.3 | 31,551.6 | .... |
| Equity & investment fund shares.. | 8aala | 17,636.8 | 16,839.7 | 21,831.7 | 26,193.4 | 28,525.1 | 31,276.6 | 31,363.7 | 31,543.5 | 32,603.9 | 33,001.3 | 31,551.6 | .... |
| Debt instruments...................... | 8abla | 206.8 | | | | | | | | | | | |
| Portfolio investment...................... | 8b9la | 658.5 | 794.3 | 1,169.2 | 1,552.1 | 1,619.0 | 2,085.5 | 2,170.0 | 1,949.0 | 1,822.7 | 1,886.3 | 2,243.7 | .... |
| Equity & investment fund shares.. | 8bala | 658.5 | 794.3 | 1,136.2 | 1,499.2 | 1,566.2 | 2,032.6 | 2,117.2 | 1,896.2 | 1,822.7 | 1,886.3 | 2,243.7 | .... |
| Debt securities............................ | 8bbla | .... | .... | 33.0 | 52.8 | 52.8 | 52.8 | 52.9 | 52.8 | .... | .... | .... | .... |
| Fin. der.(oth.than reserves) & ESOs | 8c9la | .... | .... | .... | .... | .... | .... | .... | .... | .... | .... | .... | .... |
| Other investment......................... | 8d9la | 19,786.0 | 18,337.2 | 18,845.1 | 20,482.1 | 20,904.8 | 22,143.4 | 21,966.4 | 22,648.8 | 25,308.4 | 26,834.8 | 27,854.5 | .... |
| Other equity............................ | 8dala | .... | .... | .... | .... | .... | .... | .... | .... | .... | .... | .... | .... |
| Debt instruments...................... | 8dzla | 19,786.0 | 18,337.2 | 18,845.1 | 20,482.1 | 20,904.8 | 22,143.4 | 21,966.4 | 22,648.8 | 25,308.4 | 26,834.8 | 27,854.5 | .... |
| | | | | | | | | | | | | | |
| **Government Finance** | | | | | | | | | | | | | |
| **Cash Flow Statement** | | | | | | | | | | | | | |
| **Budgetary Central Government** | | | | | | | *Millions of Dinars: Fiscal Year Ends December 31* | | | | | | |
| Cash Receipts:Operating Activities... | c1 | 8,380.2 | 8,907.5 | 9,758.6 | 10,818.7 | 13,266.2 | 13,473.6 | 14,401.3 | 16,050.8 | 16,939.6 | .... | .... | .... |
| Taxes........................................ | c11 | 7,252.0 | 7,904.2 | 8,469.8 | 9,508.1 | 11,330.9 | 11,763.7 | 12,698.6 | 13,667.9 | 14,864.4 | .... | .... | .... |
| Social Contributions...................... | c12 | — | — | — | — | — | — | — | — | — | .... | .... | .... |
| Grants...................................... | c13 | 72.6 | 69.8 | 48.3 | 37.5 | 191.5 | 177.6 | 54.1 | 207.9 | 741.6 | .... | .... | .... |
| Other Receipts........................... | c14 | 1,055.6 | 933.5 | 1,240.5 | 1,273.1 | 1,743.8 | 1,532.3 | 1,648.6 | 2,175.0 | 1,333.6 | .... | .... | .... |
| Cash Payments:Operating Activities. | c2 | 7,694.2 | 8,426.8 | 8,996.5 | 9,913.2 | 11,543.9 | 12,475.6 | 13,223.0 | 17,181.8 | 19,344.8 | .... | .... | .... |
| Compensation of Employees......... | c21 | 3,902.7 | 4,192.6 | 4,501.8 | 4,831.1 | 5,164.1 | 5,602.6 | 6,007.3 | 7,648.1 | 8,616.7 | .... | .... | .... |
| Purchases of Goods & Services....... | c22 | 699.5 | 712.6 | 744.0 | 790.1 | 881.2 | 1,010.1 | 1,058.5 | 1,081.2 | 1,060.7 | .... | .... | .... |
| Interest..................................... | c24 | 989.0 | 1,062.1 | 1,129.8 | 1,181.9 | 1,142.5 | 1,180.1 | 1,152.0 | 1,190.1 | 1,272.1 | .... | .... | .... |
| Subsidies................................... | c25 | 1,021.0 | 1,309.3 | 1,494.1 | 1,846.5 | 2,712.7 | 2,018.3 | 2,125.6 | 3,845.8 | 4,917.2 | .... | .... | .... |
| Grants...................................... | c26 | | | | | | 660.7 | 805.2 | 1,091.7 | 1,160.4 | .... | .... | .... |
| Social Benefits............................ | c27 | — | — | — | — | — | — | — | — | — | .... | .... | .... |
| Other Payments.......................... | c28 | 1,082.0 | 1,150.2 | 1,126.8 | 1,263.6 | 1,643.4 | 2,003.8 | 2,074.4 | 2,324.9 | 2,317.7 | .... | .... | .... |
| Net Cash Inflow:Operating Act.[1-2] | ccio | 686.0 | 480.7 | 762.1 | 905.5 | 1,722.3 | 998.0 | 1,178.3 | −1,131.0 | −2,405.2 | .... | .... | .... |
| Net Cash Outflow:Invest. in NFA...... | c31 | 1,337.4 | 1,253.5 | 1,405.7 | 1,406.3 | 1,529.6 | 1,331.0 | 1,403.6 | 1,224.6 | 1,042.4 | .... | .... | .... |
| Purchases of Nonfinancial Assets... | c31.1 | 1,346.8 | 1,259.3 | 1,412.2 | 1,411.6 | 1,537.5 ₁ | 1,341.1 | 1,418.4 | 1,228.5 | 1,318.9 | .... | .... | .... |
| Sales of Nonfinancial Assets.......... | c31.2 | 9.4 | 5.8 | 6.5 | 5.3 | 7.9 | 10.1 | 14.8 | 3.9 | 276.5 | .... | .... | .... |
| Cash Surplus/Deficit [1-2-31=1-2M] | ccsd | −651.4 | −772.8 | −643.6 | −500.8 | 192.7 | −333.0 | −225.4 | −2,355.6 | −3,447.6 | .... | .... | .... |
| Net Acq. Fin. Assets, excl. Cash...... | c32x | −159.1 | −153.6 | −467.4 | −35.9 | −99.6 | 653.4 | −292.8 | −642.2 | −1,544.3 | .... | .... | .... |
| Domestic.................................. | c321x | −159.1 | −153.6 | −467.4 | −35.9 | −99.6 | 653.4 | −292.8 | −642.2 | −1,544.3 | .... | .... | .... |
| Foreign.................................... | c322x | | | | | | | | | | .... | .... | .... |
| Net Incurrence of Liabilities.............. | c33 | 538.3 | 237.8 | −566.7 | −302.0 | −493.7 | 125.1 | 141.3 | 1,314.2 | 1,912.9 | .... | .... | .... |
| Domestic.................................. | c331 | 331.5 | −78.5 | 380.1 | 126.6 | −624.6 | 150.9 | 371.4 | 914.2 | 592.6 | .... | .... | .... |
| Foreign.................................... | c332 | 206.8 | 316.3 | −946.8 | −428.6 | 130.9 | −25.8 | −230.1 | 400.0 | 1,320.3 | .... | .... | .... |
| Net Cash Inflow, Fin.Act.[-32x+33].. | cnfb | 697.4 | 391.4 | −99.3 | −266.1 | −394.1 | −528.3 | 434.1 | 1,956.4 | 3,457.2 | .... | .... | .... |
| Net Change in Stock of Cash........... | cncb | 46.0 | −381.4 | −742.9 | −766.9 | −201.4 | −861.3 | 208.8 | −399.2 | 9.6 | .... | .... | .... |
| Stat. Discrep. [32X-33+NCB-CSD].... | ccsdz | — | — | — | — | — | — | — | — | — | .... | .... | .... |
| Memo Item:Cash Expenditure[2+31] | c2m | 9,031.6 | 9,680.3 | 10,402.2 | 11,319.5 | 13,073.5 | 13,806.6 | 14,626.6 | 18,406.4 | 20,387.2 | .... | .... | .... |
| Memo Item: Gross Debt................. | c63 | 20,909.7 | 21,949.0 | 22,221.0 | 22,829.2 | 23,926.5 | 25,190.0 | 25,639.6 | 28,779.5 | 31,420.1 | .... | .... | .... |
| **National Accounts** | | | | | | | *Millions of Dinars* | | | | | | |
| Househ.Cons.Expend.,incl.NPISHs.. | 96f | 22,195 | 25,871 | 28,243 | 30,699 | 33,922 | 36,390 | 39,665 | 42,804 | 46,979 | 51,199 | 55,856 | .... |
| Government Consumption Expend... | 91f | 5,405 | 7,084 | 7,645 | 8,298 | 8,917 | 9,680 | 10,478 | 11,609 | 12,818 | 14,010 | 15,116 | .... |
| Gross Fixed Capital Formation......... | 93e | 7,987 | 8,981 | 10,333 | 11,490 | 13,060 | 14,310 | 15,503 | 14,096 | 15,824 | 16,466 | 16,609 | .... |
| Changes in Inventories.................... | 93i | 591 | 96 | 396 | 318 | 998 | 235 | 659 | 798 | 1,373 | 628 | 2,113 | .... |
| Exports of Goods and Services.......... | 90c | 16,440 | 18,810 | 21,060 | 25,470 | 30,760 | 26,428 | 31,210 | 31,299 | 34,154 | 35,293 | 36,328 | .... |
| Imports of Goods and Services (-)..... | 98c | 17,469 | 18,975 | 21,922 | 26,418 | 32,440 | 28,151 | 34,460 | 36,114 | 40,795 | 42,444 | 45,205 | .... |
| Gross Domestic Product (GDP)......... | 99b | 34,934 | 41,871 | 45,756 | 49,857 | 55,270 | 58,890 | 63,055 | 64,492 | 70,354 | 75,152 | 80,816 | .... |
| Net Primary Income from Abroad..... | 98.n | −1,554 | −2,157 | −2,104 | −2,591 | −3,071 | −2,838 | −2,959 | −3,041 | −2,975 | −3,349 | −2,873 | .... |
| Gross National Income (GNI)............ | 99a | 33,380 | 39,714 | 43,652 | 47,266 | 52,148 | 56,052 | 60,096 | 61,451 | 67,380 | 71,803 | 77,944 | .... |
| Net Current Transf.from Abroad....... | 98t | 1,773 | 1,930 | 2,142 | 2,366 | 2,641 | 2,895 | 3,197 | 3,090 | 3,803 | 4,199 | 4,447 | .... |
| Gross Nat'l Disposable Inc.(GNDI).... | 99i | 35,153 | 41,644 | 45,794 | 49,632 | 54,789 | 58,947 | 63,293 | 64,541 | 71,183 | 76,001 | 82,390 | .... |
| GDP Volume 2010 Prices................. | 99b.p | 48,800.0 | 50,500.0 | 53,150.0 | 56,710.0 | 59,120.0 | 60,920.0 | 63,050.0 | 61,850.0 | 64,380.0 | 66,240.0 | 68,040.0 | .... |
| GDP Volume (2010=100)............... | 99bvp | 77.4 | 80.1 | 84.3 | 89.9 | 93.8 | 96.6 | 100.0 | 98.1 | 102.1 | 105.1 | 107.9 | .... |
| GDP Deflator (2010=100)............... | 99bip | 71.6 | 82.9 | 86.1 | 87.9 | 93.5 | 96.7 | 100.0 | 104.3 | 109.3 | 113.4 | 118.8 | .... |
| | | | | | | | *Millions: Midyear Estimates* | | | | | | |
| Population............................... | 99z | 10.02 | 10.10 | 10.20 | 10.30 | 10.41 | 10.52 | 10.64 | 10.76 | 10.88 | 11.01 | 11.13 | 11.25 |

|  |  | 2004 | 2005 | 2006 | 2007 | 2008 | 2009 | 2010 | 2011 | 2012 | 2013 | 2014 | 2015 |
|---|---|---|---|---|---|---|---|---|---|---|---|---|---|
| **Exchange Rates** |  | | | | | *Liras per SDR: End of Period* | | | | | | | |
| Market Rate | aa | 2.0803 | 1.9224 | 2.1197 | 1.8502 | 2.3496 | 2.3373 | 2.3736 | 2.9070 | 2.7386 | 3.2897 | 3.3626 | 4.0328 |
| | | | | | | *Liras per US Dollar: End of Period (ae) Period Average (rf)* | | | | | | | |
| Market Rate | ae | 1.3395 | 1.3451 | 1.4090 | 1.1708 | 1.5255 | 1.4909 | 1.5413 | 1.8935 | 1.7819 | 2.1362 | 2.3210 | 2.9102 |
| Market Rate | rf | 1.4255 | 1.3436 | 1.4285 | 1.3029 | 1.3015 | 1.5500 | 1.5028 | 1.6750 | 1.7960 | 1.9038 | 2.1885 | 2.7200 |
| **Fund Position** |  | | | | | *Millions of SDRs: End of Period* | | | | | | | |
| Quota | 2f.s | 964.00 | 964.00 | 1,191.30 | 1,191.30 | 1,191.30 | 1,191.30 | 1,191.30 | 1,455.80 | 1,455.80 | 1,455.80 | 1,455.80 | 1,455.80 |
| SDR Holdings | 1b.s | 9.02 | 11.07 | 8.13 | 31.59 | 14.95 | 969.14 | 969.93 | 970.71 | 968.81 | 976.89 | 966.15 | 966.12 |
| Reserve Position in the Fund | 1c.s | 112.78 | 112.78 | 112.78 | 112.78 | 112.78 | 112.78 | 112.78 | 112.78 | 112.78 | 112.78 | 112.78 | 112.78 |
| Total Fund Cred.&Loans Outstg | 2tl | 13,848.35 | 10,247.34 | 7,153.70 | 4,529.96 | 5,534.35 | 5,076.34 | 3,653.71 | 1,873.70 | 562.11 | — | — | — |
| SDR Allocations | 1bd | 112.31 | 112.31 | 112.31 | 112.31 | 112.31 | 1,071.33 | 1,071.33 | 1,071.33 | 1,071.33 | 1,071.33 | 1,071.33 | 1,071.33 |
| **International Liquidity** |  | | | | | *Millions of US Dollars Unless Otherwise Indicated: End of Period* | | | | | | | |
| Total Reserves minus Gold | 1l.d | 35,669 | 50,579 | 60,892 | 73,384 | 70,428 | 70,874 | 80,713 | 78,322 | 99,943 | 110,927 | 106,906 | 92,921 |
| SDR Holdings | 1b.d | 14 | 16 | 12 | 50 | 23 | 1,519 | 1,494 | 1,490 | 1,489 | 1,504 | 1,400 | 1,339 |
| Reserve Position in the Fund | 1c.d | 175 | 161 | 170 | 178 | 174 | 177 | 174 | 173 | 173 | 174 | 163 | 156 |
| Foreign Exchange | 1d.d | 35,480 | 50,402 | 60,710 | 73,156 | 70,231 | 69,178 | 79,046 | 76,659 | 98,280 | 109,249 | 105,343 | 91,426 |
| Gold (Million Fine Troy Ounces) | 1ad | 3.733 | 3.733 | 3.733 | 3.733 | 3.733 | 3.733 | 3.733 | 6.280 | 11.563 | 16.710 | 17.011 | 16.574 |
| Gold (National Valuation) | 1and | 1,583 | 1,912 | 2,373 | 3,123 | 3,229 | 4,121 | † 5,258 | 9,888 | 19,235 | 20,077 | 20,401 | 17,606 |
| Central Bank: Other Assets | 3..d | 1,390 | 1,370 | 1,431 | 1,508 | 1,543 | 1,550 | 1,560 | 1,546 | 1,560 | 1,813 | 1,810 | 1,794 |
| Central Bank: Other Liabs | 4..d | 20,973 | 17,601 | 17,563 | 17,363 | 14,699 | 13,763 | 12,198 | 9,882 | 7,606 | 5,736 | 2,924 | 1,710 |
| Other Depository Corps.: Assets | 7a.d | 21,009 | 23,475 | 37,468 | 43,994 | 52,270 | 45,923 | 35,194 | 38,777 | 37,166 | 38,009 | 37,341 | 40,165 |
| Other Depository Corps.: Liabs | 7b.d | 21,344 | 36,193 | 46,127 | 55,819 | 57,327 | 54,472 | 84,981 | 97,274 | 126,795 | 168,745 | 184,736 | 176,259 |
| Other Financial Corps.: Assets | 7e.d | .... | .... | .... | .... | 1,820 | 1,760 | 3,177 | 1,430 | 1,810 | 1,589 | 1,586 | 1,460 |
| Other Financial Corps.: Liabs | 7f.d | .... | .... | .... | .... | 12,136 | 9,011 | 8,178 | 9,473 | 12,361 | 13,978 | 13,642 | 13,215 |
| **Central Bank** |  | | | | | *Millions of Liras: End of Period* | | | | | | | |
| Net Foreign Assets | 11n | −4,751 | 28,566 | 50,620 | 61,954 | 79,051 | 79,702 | 105,123 | 142,318 | 197,122 | 267,698 | 289,016 | 317,291 |
| Claims on Nonresidents | 11 | 52,383 | 72,194 | 90,981 | 90,790 | 114,612 | 115,022 | 135,304 | 169,844 | 215,200 | 283,475 | 299,405 | 326,622 |
| Liabilities to Nonresidents | 16c | 57,135 | 43,628 | 40,362 | 28,836 | 35,562 | 35,320 | 30,181 | 27,527 | 18,078 | 15,777 | 10,389 | 9,331 |
| Claims on Other Depository Corps | 12e | 1,152 | 1,028 | 3,513 | — | 20,275 | 33,957 | 12,704 | 44,285 | 29,881 | 52,315 | 65,751 | 118,168 |
| Net Claims on Central Government | 12an | 16,397 | 4,733 | −1,356 | 361 | −3,177 | −12,135 | −5,049 | −8,679 | −7,086 | −16,901 | −12,247 | −18,621 |
| Claims on Central Government | 12a | 23,294 | 19,539 | 18,879 | 16,997 | 13,712 | 11,064 | 10,422 | 10,697 | 11,189 | 12,152 | 12,456 | 12,653 |
| Liabilities to Central Government | 16d | 6,897 | 14,806 | 20,235 | 16,636 | 16,889 | 23,199 | 15,471 | 19,376 | 18,275 | 29,053 | 24,703 | 31,274 |
| Claims on Other Sectors | 12s | 311 | — | — | — | — | — | — | — | — | — | — | — |
| Claims on Other Financial Corps | 12g | 310 | — | — | — | — | — | — | — | — | — | — | — |
| Claims on State & Local Govts | 12b | — | — | — | — | — | — | — | — | — | — | — | — |
| Claims on Public Nonfin. Corps | 12c | 1 | — | — | — | — | — | — | — | — | — | — | — |
| Claims on Private Sector | 12d | — | — | — | — | — | — | — | — | — | — | — | — |
| Monetary Base | 14 | 33,849 | 47,628 | 61,114 | 66,626 | 85,138 | 85,929 | 105,262 | 146,443 | 190,104 | 263,510 | 296,622 | 352,507 |
| Currency in Circulation | 14a | 13,465 | 19,612 | 26,815 | 27,429 | 31,743 | 38,340 | 48,938 | 55,103 | 60,525 | 74,815 | 85,118 | 103,043 |
| Liabs. to Other Depository Corps | 14c | 20,212 | 27,928 | 34,197 | 39,098 | 53,262 | 46,893 | 56,193 | 91,295 | 128,629 | 188,586 | 211,479 | 249,463 |
| Liabilities to Other Sectors | 14d | 172 | 88 | 102 | 99 | 133 | 695 | 132 | 45 | 950 | 110 | 24 | 1 |
| Other Liabs. to Other Dep. Corps | 14n | 3,561 | 6,014 | 2,418 | 3,913 | 9,940 | 13,700 | 1,102 | 516 | 2,758 | 135 | — | — |
| Dep. & Sec. Excl. f/Monetary Base | 14o | 75 | 74 | 89 | 83 | 76 | 79 | 44 | 45 | 25 | 20 | 871 | 1,463 |
| Deposits Included in Broad Money | 15 | 75 | 74 | 89 | 83 | 76 | 79 | 44 | 45 | 25 | 20 | 871 | 1,463 |
| Sec.Ot.th.Shares Incl.in Brd. Money | 16a | — | — | — | — | — | — | — | — | — | — | — | — |
| Deposits Excl. from Broad Money | 16b | — | — | — | — | — | — | — | — | — | — | — | — |
| Sec.Ot.th.Shares Excl.f/Brd.Money | 16s | — | — | — | — | — | — | — | — | — | — | — | — |
| Loans | 16l | — | — | — | — | — | — | — | — | — | — | — | — |
| Financial Derivatives | 16m | — | — | — | — | — | — | — | — | — | — | — | — |
| Shares and Other Equity | 17a | −1,213 | −1,340 | 2,559 | −1,620 | 11,512 | 11,734 | 11,895 | 33,199 | 25,928 | 36,856 | 42,832 | 60,700 |
| Other Items (Net) | 17r | −23,163 | −18,049 | −13,404 | −6,687 | −10,518 | −9,918 | −5,525 | −2,280 | 1,102 | 2,599 | 2,195 | 2,167 |
| Memo Item: |  | | | | | | | | | | | | |
| Total Assets | 10ra | 77,409 | 93,004 | 113,683 | 108,070 | 148,951 | 160,881 | 159,263 | 226,096 | 257,317 | 349,285 | 379,552 | 460,111 |
| **Other Depository Corporations** |  | | | | | *Millions of Liras: End of Period* | | | | | | | |
| Net Foreign Assets | 21n | −449 | −17,121 | −12,266 | −13,805 | −7,687 | −12,903 | −77,157 | −111,793 | −160,166 | −279,251 | −342,097 | −397,488 |
| Claims on Nonresidents | 21 | 28,142 | 31,603 | 53,073 | 51,363 | 79,450 | 69,313 | 54,542 | 74,107 | 66,416 | 81,188 | 86,667 | 117,311 |
| Liabilities to Nonresidents | 26c | 28,591 | 48,724 | 65,339 | 65,168 | 87,137 | 82,217 | 131,699 | 185,900 | 226,582 | 360,439 | 428,764 | 514,799 |
| Claims on Central Bank | 20 | 23,239 | 35,194 | 38,662 | 43,953 | 64,885 | 64,240 | 62,345 | 96,764 | 140,204 | 198,012 | 221,398 | 260,271 |
| Currency | 20a | 1,154 | 1,838 | 2,934 | 3,072 | 3,190 | 4,495 | 5,315 | 6,512 | 8,505 | 9,812 | 11,159 | 12,900 |
| Reserve Deposits and Securities | 20b | 21,951 | 33,351 | 35,720 | 40,866 | 61,689 | 58,164 | 57,012 | 90,231 | 130,296 | 188,177 | 210,170 | 247,297 |
| Other Claims | 20n | 134 | 6 | 8 | 15 | 6 | 1,581 | 19 | 21 | 1,404 | 24 | 69 | 74 |
| Net Claims on Central Government | 22an | 110,299 | 138,267 | 140,989 | 150,277 | 173,012 | 239,305 | 253,142 | 228,963 | 218,888 | 211,320 | 217,664 | 230,992 |
| Claims on Central Government | 22a | 122,537 | 155,339 | 156,438 | 167,251 | 191,482 | 259,735 | 278,902 | 258,726 | 255,640 | 248,974 | 261,639 | 287,750 |
| Liabilities to Central Government | 26d | 12,238 | 17,072 | 15,449 | 16,975 | 18,470 | 20,430 | 25,760 | 29,764 | 36,752 | 37,654 | 43,975 | 56,757 |
| Claims on Other Sectors | 22s | 104,209 | 153,092 | 207,447 | 264,736 | 329,595 | 373,107 | 516,987 | 678,770 | 806,706 | 1,077,980 | 1,276,928 | 1,533,666 |
| Claims on Other Financial Corps | 22g | 4,673 | 4,647 | 5,203 | 8,517 | 7,735 | 14,215 | 21,023 | 20,164 | 24,588 | 28,888 | 35,218 | 40,794 |
| Claims on State & Local Govts | 22b | 2,481 | 3,094 | 4,150 | 5,532 | 7,943 | 9,232 | 8,855 | 9,567 | 10,722 | 13,962 | 15,330 | 17,620 |
| Claims on Public Nonfin. Corps | 22c | 462 | 971 | 1,355 | 1,983 | 4,099 | 2,122 | 1,364 | 528 | 716 | 869 | 905 | 3,651 |
| Claims on Private Sector | 22d | 96,593 | 144,380 | 196,739 | 248,704 | 309,818 | 347,537 | 485,746 | 648,510 | 770,681 | 1,034,261 | 1,225,474 | 1,471,601 |
| Liabilities to Central Bank | 26g | 1,290 | 1,118 | 3,580 | 74 | 20,459 | 33,827 | 12,713 | 44,564 | 29,859 | 50,836 | 65,569 | 112,852 |
| Transf.Dep.Included in Broad Money | 24 | 34,859 | 63,626 | 65,957 | 71,814 | 75,859 | 95,363 | 113,855 | 132,077 | 143,946 | 173,278 | 194,340 | 230,410 |
| Other Dep.Included in Broad Money | 25 | 145,966 | 181,070 | 230,811 | 273,335 | 356,962 | 390,435 | 457,908 | 519,298 | 568,958 | 687,460 | 760,959 | 881,660 |
| Sec.Ot.th.Shares Incl.in Brd. Money | 26a | — | — | — | — | — | — | 1,113 | 10,338 | 18,492 | 24,532 | 26,469 | 27,380 |
| Deposits Excl. from Broad Money | 26b | 2,868 | — | — | — | — | — | — | — | — | — | — | — |
| Sec.Ot.th.Shares Excl.f/Brd.Money | 26s | — | — | — | — | — | 101 | 100 | 50 | 1,522 | 1,265 | 2,509 | 1,152 |
| Loans | 26l | 1,283 | 196 | 319 | 448 | 274 | 294 | 272 | 1,091 | 1,291 | 2,609 | 12,164 | 12,319 |
| Financial Derivatives | 26m | — | — | — | — | — | 352 | 764 | 381 | 1,292 | 1,226 | 1,553 |
| Insurance Technical Reserves | 26r | — | — | — | — | — | — | — | — | — | — | — | — |
| Shares and Other Equity | 27a | 45,283 | 54,198 | 58,854 | 75,343 | 84,962 | 110,113 | 134,378 | 144,692 | 180,381 | 194,038 | 237,527 | 268,985 |
| Other Items (Net) | 27r | 5,749 | 9,223 | 15,312 | 24,146 | 21,289 | 33,617 | 34,627 | 39,829 | 60,802 | 72,752 | 73,128 | 91,132 |
| Memo Item: |  | | | | | | | | | | | | |
| Total Assets | 20ra | 306,991 | 419,148 | 502,180 | 583,901 | 722,504 | 828,547 | 996,559 | 1,195,911 | 1,357,503 | 1,707,980 | 1,972,431 | 2,338,251 |

| | | 2004 | 2005 | 2006 | 2007 | 2008 | 2009 | 2010 | 2011 | 2012 | 2013 | 2014 | 2015 |
|---|---|---|---|---|---|---|---|---|---|---|---|---|---|
| **Depository Corporations** | | | | | | *Millions of Liras: End of Period* | | | | | | | |
| Net Foreign Assets | 31n | −5,201 | 11,445 | 38,354 | 48,148 | 71,364 | 66,799 | 27,965 | 30,524 | 36,956 | −11,553 | −53,080 | −80,197 |
| Claims on Nonresidents | 31 | 80,525 | 103,797 | 144,055 | 142,152 | 194,063 | 184,336 | 189,846 | 243,951 | 281,616 | 364,663 | 386,072 | 443,933 |
| Liabilities to Nonresidents | 36c | 85,725 | 92,352 | 105,700 | 94,004 | 122,699 | 117,537 | 161,880 | 213,427 | 244,660 | 376,216 | 439,153 | 524,130 |
| Domestic Claims | 32 | 231,215 | 296,092 | 347,079 | 415,374 | 499,431 | 600,277 | 765,081 | 899,053 | 1,018,508 | 1,272,400 | 1,482,344 | 1,746,038 |
| Net Claims on Central Government | 32an | 126,696 | 143,001 | 139,633 | 150,638 | 169,835 | 227,170 | 248,094 | 220,284 | 211,802 | 194,419 | 205,416 | 212,371 |
| Claims on Central Government | 32a | 145,831 | 174,878 | 175,317 | 184,249 | 205,194 | 270,799 | 289,324 | 269,423 | 266,829 | 261,126 | 274,095 | 300,402 |
| Liabilities to Central Government. | 36d | 19,135 | 31,878 | 35,684 | 33,611 | 35,358 | 43,629 | 41,231 | 49,140 | 55,027 | 66,707 | 68,678 | 88,031 |
| Claims on Other Sectors | 32s | 104,519 | 153,092 | 207,447 | 264,736 | 329,595 | 373,107 | 516,987 | 678,770 | 806,706 | 1,077,980 | 1,276,928 | 1,533,666 |
| Claims on Other Financial Corps.. | 32g | 4,983 | 4,647 | 5,203 | 8,517 | 7,735 | 14,215 | 21,023 | 20,164 | 24,588 | 28,888 | 35,218 | 40,794 |
| Claims on State & Local Govts | 32b | 2,481 | 3,094 | 4,150 | 5,532 | 7,943 | 9,232 | 8,855 | 9,567 | 10,722 | 13,962 | 15,330 | 17,620 |
| Claims on Public Nonfin. Corps..... | 32c | 462 | 971 | 1,355 | 1,983 | 4,099 | 2,122 | 1,364 | 528 | 716 | 869 | 905 | 3,651 |
| Claims on Private Sector | 32d | 96,593 | 144,380 | 196,739 | 248,704 | 309,818 | 347,537 | 485,746 | 648,510 | 770,681 | 1,034,261 | 1,225,474 | 1,471,601 |
| Broad Money Liabilities | 35l | 193,383 | 262,633 | 320,839 | 369,689 | 461,584 | 520,417 | 616,674 | 710,395 | 784,392 | 950,402 | 1,056,624 | 1,231,056 |
| Currency Outside Depository Corps | 34a | 12,312 | 17,774 | 23,881 | 24,357 | 28,554 | 33,845 | 43,623 | 48,592 | 52,020 | 65,003 | 73,959 | 90,142 |
| Transferable Deposits | 34 | 35,043 | 63,788 | 66,148 | 71,996 | 76,068 | 95,503 | 114,031 | 132,168 | 144,019 | 173,408 | 195,236 | 231,874 |
| Other Deposits | 35 | 146,029 | 181,070 | 230,811 | 273,335 | 356,962 | 391,069 | 457,908 | 519,298 | 569,861 | 687,460 | 760,959 | 881,660 |
| Securities Other than Shares | 36a | — | — | — | — | — | — | 1,113 | 10,338 | 18,492 | 24,532 | 26,469 | 27,380 |
| Deposits Excl. from Broad Money..... | 36b | 2,868 | | | | | | | | | | | |
| Sec.Ot.th.Shares Excl.f/Brd.Money.... | 36s | — | — | — | — | — | 101 | 100 | 50 | 1,522 | 1,265 | 2,509 | 1,152 |
| Loans | 36l | 1,283 | 196 | 319 | 448 | 274 | 294 | 272 | 1,091 | 1,291 | 2,609 | 12,164 | 12,319 |
| Financial Derivatives | 36m | — | — | — | — | — | — | 352 | 764 | 381 | 1,292 | 1,226 | 1,553 |
| Insurance Technical Reserves | 36r | — | — | — | — | — | — | — | — | — | — | — | — |
| Shares and Other Equity | 37a | 44,070 | 52,859 | 61,413 | 73,723 | 96,475 | 121,846 | 146,273 | 177,891 | 206,309 | 230,894 | 280,359 | 329,685 |
| Other Items (Net) | 37r | −15,589 | −8,150 | 2,863 | 19,662 | 12,462 | 24,418 | 29,375 | 39,388 | 61,569 | 74,392 | 76,382 | 90,076 |
| Broad Money Liabs., Seasonally Adj. | 35l.b | 190,593 | 258,876 | 316,440 | 364,819 | 455,601 | 513,648 | 609,101 | 702,765 | 777,716 | 944,679 | 1,052,362 | 1,227,116 |
| **Other Financial Corporations** | | | | | | *Millions of Liras: End of Period* | | | | | | | |
| Net Foreign Assets | 41n | .... | .... | .... | .... | −15,681 | −10,945 | −7,750 | −15,370 | −18,856 | −26,464 | −27,982 | −34,333 |
| Claims on Nonresidents | 41 | .... | .... | .... | .... | 2,766 | 2,657 | 4,923 | 2,733 | 3,234 | 3,393 | 3,681 | 4,265 |
| Liabilities to Nonresidents | 46c | .... | .... | .... | .... | 18,447 | 13,601 | 12,674 | 18,103 | 22,090 | 29,857 | 31,662 | 38,598 |
| Claims on Depository Corporations.. | 40 | .... | .... | .... | .... | 1,798 | 2,579 | 14,236 | 16,545 | 23,412 | 29,314 | 40,756 | 53,717 |
| Net Claims on Central Government.. | 42an | .... | .... | .... | .... | 2,677 | 4,610 | 13,033 | 9,845 | 10,891 | 11,433 | 14,110 | 16,939 |
| Claims on Central Government | 42a | .... | .... | .... | .... | 2,677 | 4,610 | 13,033 | 9,845 | 10,891 | 11,433 | 14,110 | 16,939 |
| Liabilities to Central Government.... | 46d | .... | .... | .... | .... | — | — | — | — | — | — | — | — |
| Claims on Other Sectors | 42s | .... | .... | .... | .... | 24,878 | 25,633 | 32,256 | 40,697 | 49,128 | 64,406 | 78,712 | 91,258 |
| Claims on State & Local Govts | 42b | .... | .... | .... | .... | 10 | 5 | — | — | — | — | — | 2 |
| Claims on Public Nonfin. Corps | 42c | .... | .... | .... | .... | — | — | — | — | — | — | — | — |
| Claims on Private Sector | 42d | .... | .... | .... | .... | 24,868 | 25,628 | 32,256 | 40,697 | 49,128 | 64,406 | 78,712 | 91,255 |
| Deposits | 46b | .... | .... | .... | .... | — | — | — | — | — | — | — | — |
| Securities Other than Shares | 46s | .... | .... | .... | .... | — | — | — | — | — | — | — | — |
| Loans | 46l | .... | .... | .... | .... | 3,867 | 8,194 | 17,081 | 17,135 | 18,899 | 24,423 | 32,791 | 34,419 |
| Financial Derivatives | 46m | .... | .... | .... | .... | 25 | 56 | 59 | 213 | 55 | 699 | 157 | 255 |
| Insurance Technical Reserves | 46r | .... | .... | .... | .... | — | — | 13,679 | 15,275 | 19,167 | 21,889 | 25,000 | 30,394 |
| Shares and Other Equity | 47a | .... | .... | .... | .... | 9,168 | 13,159 | 25,284 | 24,411 | 30,222 | 34,289 | 47,093 | 59,679 |
| Other Items (Net) | 47r | .... | .... | .... | .... | 613 | 467 | −4,329 | −5,317 | −3,768 | −2,611 | 555 | 2,835 |
| Memo Item: | | | | | | | | | | | | | |
| Total Assets | 40ra | .... | .... | .... | .... | 33,876 | 37,595 | 77,649 | 85,496 | 104,979 | 130,749 | 161,034 | 195,543 |
| **Financial Corporations** | | | | | | *Millions of Liras: End of Period* | | | | | | | |
| Net Foreign Assets | 51n | .... | .... | .... | .... | 55,683 | 55,854 | 20,215 | 15,154 | 18,100 | −38,016 | −81,062 | −114,530 |
| Claims on Nonresidents | 51 | .... | .... | .... | .... | 196,829 | 186,992 | 194,769 | 246,684 | 284,850 | 368,057 | 389,753 | 448,198 |
| Liabilities to Nonresidents | 56c | .... | .... | .... | .... | 141,146 | 131,138 | 174,554 | 231,530 | 266,750 | 406,073 | 470,815 | 562,728 |
| Domestic Claims | 52 | .... | .... | .... | .... | 519,251 | 616,305 | 789,347 | 929,431 | 1,053,939 | 1,319,351 | 1,539,948 | 1,813,440 |
| Net Claims on Central Government | 52an | .... | .... | .... | .... | 172,513 | 231,780 | 261,127 | 230,128 | 222,692 | 205,852 | 219,526 | 229,311 |
| Claims on Central Government.... | 52a | .... | .... | .... | .... | 207,871 | 275,409 | 302,358 | 279,268 | 277,720 | 272,559 | 288,204 | 317,342 |
| Liabilities to Central Government. | 56d | .... | .... | .... | .... | 35,358 | 43,629 | 41,231 | 49,140 | 55,027 | 66,707 | 68,678 | 88,031 |
| Claims on Other Sectors | 52s | .... | .... | .... | .... | 346,738 | 384,525 | 528,220 | 699,303 | 831,246 | 1,113,499 | 1,320,422 | 1,584,130 |
| Claims on State & Local Govts | 52b | .... | .... | .... | .... | 7,952 | 9,237 | 8,855 | 9,568 | 10,722 | 13,963 | 15,330 | 17,623 |
| Claims on Public Nonfin. Corps.... | 52c | .... | .... | .... | .... | 4,099 | 2,122 | 1,364 | 528 | 716 | 869 | 905 | 3,651 |
| Claims on Private Sector | 52d | .... | .... | .... | .... | 334,686 | 373,165 | 518,002 | 689,207 | 819,808 | 1,098,667 | 1,304,186 | 1,562,856 |
| Currency Outside Financial Corps..... | 54a | .... | .... | .... | .... | 28,545 | 33,842 | 43,617 | 48,583 | 52,015 | 64,951 | 73,954 | 90,140 |
| Deposits | 55l | .... | .... | .... | .... | 420,404 | 472,485 | 550,818 | 631,489 | 688,404 | 825,634 | 921,586 | 1,068,802 |
| Securities Other than Shares | 56a | .... | .... | .... | .... | — | — | 1,213 | 10,388 | 20,015 | 25,797 | 28,978 | 28,531 |
| Loans | 56l | .... | .... | .... | .... | 54 | 148 | 138 | 248 | 525 | 48 | 1,156 | 914 |
| Financial Derivatives | 56m | .... | .... | .... | .... | — | — | 329 | 711 | 357 | 1,120 | 1,098 | 1,422 |
| Insurance Technical Reserves | 56r | .... | .... | .... | .... | — | — | 13,679 | 15,275 | 19,167 | 21,889 | 25,000 | 30,394 |
| Shares and Other Equity | 57a | .... | .... | .... | .... | 105,642 | 135,005 | 171,557 | 202,302 | 236,531 | 265,182 | 327,452 | 389,364 |
| Other Items (Net) | 57r | .... | .... | .... | .... | 20,288 | 30,679 | 28,211 | 35,591 | 55,026 | 76,722 | 79,663 | 89,343 |
| **Monetary Aggregates** | | | | | | *Millions of Liras: End of Period* | | | | | | | |
| Broad Money | 59m | 193,518 | 263,121 | 321,466 | 370,411 | 462,361 | 520,894 | 617,503 | 711,388 | 785,531 | 951,693 | 1,058,125 | 1,232,871 |
| o/w:Currency Issued by Cent.Govt | 59m.a | 134 | 488 | 627 | 722 | 778 | 477 | 829 | 994 | 1,139 | 1,291 | 1,502 | 1,815 |
| o/w: Dep.in Nonfin. Corporations. | 59m.b | — | — | — | — | — | — | — | — | — | — | — | — |
| o/w:Secs. Issued by Central Govt.. | 59m.c | — | — | — | — | | | | | | | | |
| Money (National Definitions) | | | | | | *Millions of Liras: End of Period* | | | | | | | |
| Reserve Money | 19mb | 33,625 | 47,779 | 61,227 | 66,765 | 85,231 | 85,433 | 105,936 | 147,356 | 190,247 | 264,734 | 298,283 | 354,557 |
| M1 | 59ma | 28,793 | † 61,991 | 71,771 | 76,351 | 85,476 | 107,347 | 135,191 | 161,213 | 179,935 | 229,376 | 258,294 | 311,647 |
| M2 | 59mb | 108,539 | † 238,801 | 297,735 | 344,377 | 436,380 | 493,061 | 587,261 | 674,410 | 743,043 | 908,011 | 1,015,896 | 1,189,494 |
| M3 | 59mc | 115,839 | † 261,306 | 319,366 | 368,220 | 459,143 | 519,003 | 614,330 | 708,767 | 783,455 | 948,677 | 1,060,143 | 1,232,283 |
| **Interest Rates** | | | | | | *Percent Per Annum* | | | | | | | |
| Central Bank Policy Rate (EOP) | 60 | 18.00 | 13.50 | 17.50 | 15.96 | 15.63 | 6.50 | 1.63 | 5.00 | 5.00 | 3.50 | 7.50 | 7.25 |
| Discount Rate (End of Period) | 60.a | 38.00 | 23.00 | 27.00 | 25.00 | 25.00 | 15.00 | 14.00 | 17.00 | 13.50 | 10.25 | 9.00 | 9.00 |
| Treasury Bill Rate | 60c | 22.08 | 15.49 | 18.37 | 17.65 | .... | .... | .... | .... | .... | .... | | |
| Deposit Rate | 60l | 24.26 | 20.40 | 21.65 | 22.56 | 22.91 | 17.65 | 15.27 | 14.22 | 16.35 | 15.76 | 16.77 | 14.92 |

# Turkey 186

| | | 2004 | 2005 | 2006 | 2007 | 2008 | 2009 | 2010 | 2011 | 2012 | 2013 | 2014 | 2015 |
|---|---|---|---|---|---|---|---|---|---|---|---|---|---|
| **Prices, Production, Labor** | | | | | | *Index Numbers (2010=100): Period Averages* | | | | | | | |
| Share Prices | 62 | 33.5 | 49.4 | 67.0 | 81.2 | 63.2 | 63.1 | 100.0 | 102.1 | 107.2 | 131.1 | 126.5 | 135.7 |
| Producer Prices | 63 | 66.2 | 70.1 | 76.0 | 80.8 | 91.0 | 92.2 | 100.0 | 111.1 | 117.9 | 123.1 | 135.8 | 142.9 |
| Wholesale Prices | 63a | 63.9 | 69.2 | 76.0 | 80.8 | 91.0 | 92.2 | 100.0 | 111.1 | 117.9 | 123.1 | .... | .... |
| Consumer Prices | 64 | 59.8 | † 65.9 | 72.2 | 78.5 | 86.7 | 92.1 | 100.0 | 106.5 | 115.9 | 124.6 | 135.7 | 146.1 |
| Industrial Production | 66 | 81.7 | 86.1 | 92.4 | 98.9 | 98.4 | 88.6 | 100.0 | 110.1 | 112.8 | 116.3 | 120.5 | 124.3 |
| | | | | | | *Number in Thousands: Period Averages* | | | | | | | |
| Labor Force | 67d | 24,188 | † 22,448 | 22,770 | 23,151 | 23,796 | 24,748 | 25,662 | 26,692 | 27,351 | 28,270 | 28,768 | .... |
| Employment | 67e | 21,709 | † 20,074 | 19,885 | 20,219 | 20,634 | 20,698 | 22,003 | 23,450 | 24,171 | 24,856 | 25,257 | 25,886 |
| Unemployment | 67c | 2,479 | † 2,056 | 1,983 | 2,039 | 2,293 | 3,089 | 2,739 | 2,333 | 2,203 | 2,449 | 2,860 | 3,054 |
| Unemployment Rate (%) | 67r | 10.3 | † 9.5 | 9.1 | 9.2 | 10.0 | 13.0 | 11.2 | 9.1 | 8.4 | 9.1 | 10.0 | 10.3 |
| **Intl. Transactions & Positions** | | | | | | *Millions of US Dollars* | | | | | | | |
| Exports | 70..d | 63,167 | 73,476 | 85,535 | 107,272 | 132,027 | 102,143 | 113,883 | 134,907 | 152,462 | 151,803 | 157,614 | 144,047 |
| Imports, c.i.f. | 71..d | 97,540 | 116,774 | 139,576 | 170,063 | 201,964 | 140,928 | 185,544 | 240,842 | 236,545 | 251,661 | 242,177 | 207,191 |
| | | | | | | | *2010=100* | | | | | | |
| Volume of Exports | 72..d | 66.1 | 72.9 | 81.8 | 91.3 | 97.3 | 89.7 | 100.0 | 106.3 | 123.6 | 122.9 | 129.4 | .... |
| Volume of Imports | 73..d | 72.1 | 80.9 | 87.8 | 98.9 | 97.6 | 84.9 | 100.0 | 112.9 | 113.9 | 123.2 | 122.2 | .... |
| Unit Value of Exports/Export Prices | 74..d | 80.7 | 85.6 | 88.6 | 99.8 | 115.3 | 96.7 | 100.0 | 111.5 | 108.4 | 108.5 | 107.0 | .... |
| Unit Value of Imports/Import Prices | 75..d | 75.0 | 80.2 | 87.1 | 95.5 | 114.7 | 92.3 | 100.0 | 114.9 | 111.9 | 110.1 | 107.0 | .... |
| **Balance of Payments** | | | | | | *Millions of US Dollars* | | | | | | | |
| A. Current Account* | 109bx | −14,198.0 | † −20,980.0 | −31,168.0 | −36,949.0 | −39,425.0 | −11,358.0 | −44,616.0 | −74,402.0 | −47,961.0 | −63,608.0 | −43,552.0 | −32,199.0 |
| Goods, credit (exports) | 1a9cx | 68,833.0 | † 78,509.0 | 93,778.0 | 115,379.0 | 140,906.0 | 109,732.0 | 120,992.0 | 142,392.0 | 161,948.0 | 161,789.0 | 168,926.0 | 151,977.0 |
| Goods, debit (imports) | 1a9dx | 91,271.0 | † 111,445.0 | 134,672.0 | 162,210.0 | 193,823.0 | 134,494.0 | 177,317.0 | 231,552.0 | 227,315.0 | 241,706.0 | 232,523.0 | 200,102.0 |
| Balance on goods | 1a9bx | −22,438.0 | † −32,936.0 | −40,894.0 | −46,831.0 | −52,917.0 | −24,762.0 | −56,325.0 | −89,160.0 | −65,367.0 | −79,917.0 | −63,597.0 | −48,125.0 |
| Services, credit (exports) | 1b9cx | 23,085.0 | † 27,822.0 | 26,087.0 | 30,004.0 | 37,109.0 | 35,815.0 | 36,453.0 | 41,258.0 | 43,567.0 | 48,198.0 | 51,856.0 | 46,681.0 |
| Services, debit (imports) | 1b9dx | 10,353.0 | † 11,950.0 | 12,190.0 | 15,915.0 | 18,201.0 | 17,087.0 | 19,704.0 | 20,970.0 | 20,979.0 | 24,518.0 | 25,088.0 | 22,562.0 |
| Balance on Goods & Services | 1z9bx | −9,706.0 | † −17,064.0 | −26,997.0 | −32,742.0 | −34,009.0 | −6,034.0 | −39,576.0 | −68,872.0 | −42,779.0 | −56,237.0 | −36,829.0 | −24,006.0 |
| Primary income: credit | 1c9cx | 2,651.0 | † 4,125.0 | 5,105.0 | 7,271.0 | 7,670.0 | 5,833.0 | 5,197.0 | 4,625.0 | 5,762.0 | 5,289.0 | 4,874.0 | 4,472.0 |
| Primary income: debit | 1c9dx | 8,260.0 | † 9,495.0 | 11,090.0 | 13,549.0 | 15,272.0 | 13,490.0 | 11,712.0 | 11,874.0 | 12,350.0 | 13,866.0 | 13,004.0 | 13,987.0 |
| Balance on gds, serv. & prim. inc. | 1y9bx | −15,315.0 | † −22,434.0 | −32,982.0 | −39,020.0 | −41,611.0 | −13,691.0 | −46,091.0 | −76,121.0 | −49,367.0 | −64,814.0 | −44,959.0 | −33,521.0 |
| Secondary income: credit | 1d9ca | 1,155.0 | † 1,475.0 | 2,241.0 | 2,785.0 | 2,968.0 | 3,034.0 | 2,215.0 | 2,631.0 | 2,465.0 | 2,378.0 | 2,632.0 | 2,473.0 |
| Secondary income: debit | 1d9da | 38.0 | † 21.0 | 427.0 | 714.0 | 782.0 | 701.0 | 740.0 | 912.0 | 1,059.0 | 1,172.0 | 1,225.0 | 1,151.0 |
| B. Capital Account* | 209ba | — | † — | — | −8.0 | −61.0 | −43.0 | −51.0 | −25.0 | −58.0 | −96.0 | −70.0 | −21.0 |
| Capital account: credit | 209ca | — | † — | — | 11.0 | 3.0 | 8.0 | 15.0 | 66.0 | 10.0 | 14.0 | 7.0 | 68.0 |
| Capital account: debit | 209da | — | † — | — | 19.0 | 64.0 | 51.0 | 66.0 | 91.0 | 68.0 | 110.0 | 77.0 | 89.0 |
| Balance on current & capital acct. | 129ba | −14,198.0 | † −20,980.0 | −31,168.0 | −36,957.0 | −39,486.0 | −11,401.0 | −44,667.0 | −74,427.0 | −48,019.0 | −63,704.0 | −43,622.0 | −32,220.0 |
| C. Financial Account* | 309na | −17,702.0 | † −42,685.0 | −42,689.0 | −49,287.0 | −34,761.0 | −9,879.6 | −60,099.0 | −67,146.0 | −71,756.0 | −73,059.0 | −41,594.0 | −10,988.0 |
| Direct investment: assets | 3a9aa | 780.0 | † 1,064.0 | 924.0 | 2,106.0 | 2,549.0 | 1,553.0 | 1,482.0 | 2,370.0 | 4,105.0 | 3,627.0 | 7,047.0 | 5,094.0 |
| Equity & investment fund shares | 3aaaa | 780.0 | † 1,064.0 | 924.0 | 2,106.0 | 2,549.0 | 1,553.0 | 1,464.0 | 2,349.0 | 4,074.0 | 3,114.0 | 4,963.0 | 4,925.0 |
| Debt instruments | 3abaa | — | .... | .... | .... | .... | .... | 18.0 | 21.0 | 31.0 | 513.0 | 2,084.0 | 169.0 |
| Direct investment: liabilities | 3a9la | 2,785.0 | † 10,031.0 | 20,185.0 | 22,047.0 | 19,851.0 | 8,585.0 | 9,099.0 | 16,182.0 | 13,284.0 | 12,384.0 | 12,523.0 | 16,825.0 |
| Equity & investment fund shares | 3aala | 2,435.0 | † 9,975.0 | 19,904.0 | 21,320.0 | 17,650.0 | 7,966.0 | 8,715.0 | 16,158.0 | 12,762.0 | 12,359.0 | 12,636.0 | 15,650.0 |
| Debt instruments | 3abla | 350.0 | † 56.0 | 281.0 | 727.0 | 2,201.0 | 619.0 | 384.0 | 24.0 | 522.0 | 25.0 | −113.0 | 1,175.0 |
| Portfolio investment: assets | 3b9aa | 1,388.0 | † 1,213.0 | 3,987.0 | 1,947.0 | 1,244.0 | 2,711.0 | 3,534.0 | −2,688.0 | −2,657.0 | −2,601.0 | 746.0 | 6,129.0 |
| Equity & investment fund shares | 3baaa | 25.0 | .... | .... | .... | .... | .... | .... | .... | .... | 18.0 | 53.0 | 80.0 |
| Debt securities | 3bbaa | 1,363.0 | † 1,213.0 | 3,987.0 | 1,947.0 | 1,244.0 | 2,711.0 | 3,534.0 | −2,688.0 | −2,657.0 | −2,619.0 | 693.0 | 6,049.0 |
| Portfolio investment: liabilities | 3b9la | 9,411.0 | † 14,670.0 | 11,402.0 | 2,780.0 | −3,770.0 | 2,938.0 | 19,617.0 | 19,516.0 | 38,355.0 | 21,387.0 | 20,850.0 | −9,369.0 |
| Equity & investment fund shares | 3bala | 1,427.0 | † 5,669.0 | 1,939.0 | 5,138.0 | 716.0 | 2,827.0 | 3,468.0 | −985.0 | 6,276.0 | 842.0 | 2,559.0 | −2,395.0 |
| Debt securities | 3bbla | 7,984.0 | † 9,001.0 | 9,463.0 | −2,358.0 | −4,486.0 | 111.0 | 16,149.0 | 20,501.0 | 32,079.0 | 20,545.0 | 18,291.0 | −6,974.0 |
| Fin. der.& empl.stk.ops.(ESOs): net. | 3c9na | — | .... | .... | .... | .... | .... | .... | .... | .... | .... | .... | .... |
| Fin. der. & ESOs.: assets | 3c9aa | — | .... | .... | .... | .... | .... | .... | .... | .... | .... | .... | .... |
| Fin. der. & ESOs.: liabilities | 3c9la | — | .... | .... | .... | .... | .... | .... | .... | .... | .... | .... | .... |
| Other investment: assets | 3d9aa | 6,983.0 | † 573.0 | 13,479.0 | 4,969.0 | 12,056.0 | −10,963.0 | −7,020.0 | −11,197.0 | 703.0 | −2,340.0 | 1,659.0 | 14,781.0 |
| Other equity | 3daaa | .... | † 20.0 | 42.0 | 116.0 | 32.0 | 31.0 | 39.0 | 108.0 | 40.0 | 196.0 | −6.0 | 6.0 |
| Debt instruments | 3dzaa | 6,983.0 | † 553.0 | 13,437.0 | 4,853.0 | 12,024.0 | −10,994.0 | −7,059.0 | −11,305.0 | 663.0 | −2,536.0 | 1,665.0 | 14,775.0 |
| Other investment: liabilities | 3d9la | 14,657.0 | † 20,834.0 | 29,492.0 | 33,482.0 | 34,529.0 | −8,342.4 | 29,379.0 | 19,933.0 | 22,268.0 | 37,974.0 | 17,673.0 | 29,536.0 |
| Other equity | 3dala | .... | .... | .... | .... | .... | .... | .... | .... | .... | .... | .... | .... |
| Debt instruments | 3dzla | 14,657.0 | † 20,834.0 | 29,492.0 | 33,482.0 | 34,529.0 | −8,342.4 | 29,379.0 | 19,933.0 | 22,268.0 | 37,974.0 | 17,673.0 | 29,536.0 |
| Curr.+ cap.− finan. acct. balance | 4y9na | 3,504.0 | † 21,705.0 | 11,521.0 | 12,330.0 | −4,725.0 | −1,521.4 | 15,432.0 | −7,281.0 | 23,737.0 | 9,355.0 | −2,028.0 | −21,232.0 |
| D. Net Errors and Omissions | 409na | 802.7 | † 1,471.2 | −899.6 | −278.0 | 1,959.5 | 2,441.4 | −461.5 | 8,288.6 | −916.6 | 1,419.1 | 1,543.5 | 9,400.9 |
| E. Reserves and Related Items | 4z9na | 4,306.7 | † 23,176.2 | 10,621.4 | 12,052.0 | −2,765.5 | 920.0 | 14,970.5 | 1,007.6 | 22,820.4 | 10,774.1 | −484.5 | −11,831.1 |
| Reserve assets | 3e9aa | 786.7 | † 17,853.8 | 6,102.5 | 8,065.5 | −1,073.7 | 234.7 | 12,810.3 | −1,811.9 | 20,811.1 | 9,923.5 | −484.5 | −11,831.1 |
| Credit and loans from the IMF | 3dcla | −3,520.0 | † −5,322.4 | −4,519.0 | −3,986.5 | 1,691.8 | −685.3 | −2,160.2 | −2,819.5 | −2,009.3 | −850.6 | — | — |
| Exceptional financing | 409la | — | .... | .... | .... | .... | .... | .... | .... | .... | .... | .... | .... |

*Excludes components in group E

# Turkey 186

| | | 2004 | 2005 | 2006 | 2007 | 2008 | 2009 | 2010 | 2011 | 2012 | 2013 | 2014 | 2015 |
|---|---|---|---|---|---|---|---|---|---|---|---|---|---|
| **International Investment Position** | | | | | | | | *Millions of US Dollars* | | | | | |
| Assets........................................... | 809aa | 86,012.4 | 107,154.0 | 144,055.9 | 170,141.1 | 186,429.7 | 182,078.1 | 185,906.4 | 179,667.4 | 214,443.3 | 226,098.1 | 230,014.2 | 219,466.1 |
| Direct investment........................ | 8a9aa | 7,060.0 | 8,315.0 | 8,866.0 | 12,210.0 | 17,846.0 | 23,314.0 | 23,962.0 | 28,294.0 | 31,378.0 | 33,660.0 | 39,933.0 | 45,020.0 |
| Equity & investment fund shares.. | 8aaaa | 7,060.0 | 8,315.0 | 8,866.0 | 12,210.0 | 17,846.0 | 19,923.0 | 20,761.0 | 23,897.0 | 27,513.0 | 29,918.0 | 33,938.0 | 38,863.0 |
| Debt instruments...................... | 8abaa | — | | | | | 3,391.0 | 3,201.0 | 4,397.0 | 3,865.0 | 3,742.0 | 5,995.0 | 6,157.0 |
| Portfolio investment.................... | 8b9aa | 920.0 | 718.0 | 3,111.0 | 2,007.0 | 1,938.0 | 1,907.0 | 2,230.0 | 1,750.0 | 1,320.0 | 1,003.0 | 1,505.0 | 1,572.0 |
| Equity & investment fund shares.. | 8baaa | 108.0 | 89.0 | 150.0 | 77.0 | 58.0 | 219.0 | 372.0 | 279.0 | 324.0 | 362.0 | 493.0 | 596.0 |
| Debt securities........................... | 8bbaa | 812.0 | 629.0 | 2,961.0 | 1,930.0 | 1,880.0 | 1,688.0 | 1,858.0 | 1,471.0 | 996.0 | 641.0 | 1,012.0 | 976.0 |
| Fin. der.(oth.than reserves) & ESOs | 8c9aa | .... | .... | .... | .... | .... | .... | .... | .... | .... | .... | .... | .... |
| Other investment........................ | 8d9aa | 40,389.2 | 45,692.0 | 68,793.0 | 79,485.0 | 92,412.0 | 82,017.0 | 73,732.0 | 61,282.0 | 62,583.0 | 60,431.0 | 61,274.0 | 62,346.0 |
| Other equity........................... | 8daaa | 753.0 | 694.0 | 745.0 | 801.0 | 790.0 | 913.0 | 991.0 | 1,018.0 | 1,071.0 | 1,408.0 | 1,348.0 | 1,311.0 |
| Debt instruments...................... | 8dzaa | 39,636.2 | 44,998.0 | 68,048.0 | 78,684.0 | 91,622.0 | 81,104.0 | 72,741.0 | 60,264.0 | 61,512.0 | 59,023.0 | 59,926.0 | 61,035.0 |
| Reserve assets............................. | 8e9aa | 37,643.1 | 52,429.0 | 63,285.9 | 76,439.1 | 74,233.7 | 74,840.1 | 85,982.4 | 88,341.4 | 119,162.3 | 131,004.1 | 127,302.2 | 110,528.1 |
| Liabilities..................................... | 809la | 214,227.2 | 281,863.6 | 349,787.7 | 484,023.7 | 386,308.0 | 458,317.7 | 547,467.4 | 494,572.8 | 638,455.3 | 621,863.8 | 671,074.2 | 589,710.6 |
| Direct investment........................ | 8a9la | 38,591.0 | 71,322.0 | 95,127.0 | 155,160.0 | 80,462.0 | 144,908.0 | 188,604.0 | 137,249.0 | 190,570.0 | 150,116.0 | 178,029.0 | 145,775.0 |
| Equity & investment fund shares.. | 8aala | 37,175.0 | 69,907.0 | 93,448.0 | 151,929.0 | 75,407.0 | 138,010.0 | 181,171.0 | 130,912.0 | 183,767.0 | 143,475.0 | 171,924.0 | 139,116.0 |
| Debt instruments...................... | 8abla | 1,416.0 | 1,415.0 | 1,679.0 | 3,231.0 | 5,055.0 | 6,898.0 | 7,433.0 | 6,337.0 | 6,803.0 | 6,641.0 | 6,105.0 | 6,659.0 |
| Portfolio investment.................... | 8b9la | 45,751.0 | 72,606.0 | 84,410.0 | 120,629.0 | 68,726.0 | 91,018.0 | 118,195.0 | 109,539.0 | 179,452.0 | 168,456.0 | 192,466.0 | 148,087.0 |
| Equity & investment fund shares.. | 8bala | 16,141.0 | 33,387.0 | 33,816.0 | 64,201.0 | 23,120.0 | 47,080.0 | 61,311.0 | 39,055.0 | 70,501.0 | 52,248.0 | 61,908.0 | 40,210.0 |
| Debt securities........................... | 8bbla | 29,610.0 | 39,219.0 | 50,594.0 | 56,428.0 | 45,606.0 | 43,938.0 | 56,884.0 | 70,484.0 | 108,951.0 | 116,208.0 | 130,558.0 | 107,877.0 |
| Fin. der.(oth.than reserves) & ESOs | 8c9la | .... | .... | .... | .... | .... | .... | .... | .... | .... | .... | .... | .... |
| Other investment........................ | 8d9la | 129,885.2 | 137,935.6 | 170,250.7 | 208,234.7 | 237,120.0 | 222,391.7 | 240,668.4 | 247,784.8 | 268,433.3 | 303,291.8 | 300,579.2 | 295,848.6 |
| Other equity........................... | 8dala | .... | .... | .... | .... | .... | .... | .... | .... | .... | .... | .... | .... |
| Debt instruments...................... | 8dzla | 129,885.2 | 137,935.6 | 170,250.7 | 208,234.7 | 237,120.0 | 222,391.7 | 240,668.4 | 247,784.8 | 268,433.3 | 303,291.8 | 300,579.2 | 295,848.6 |

**Government Finance**
**Operations Statement**
**Budgetary Central Government**

| | | 2004 | 2005 | 2006 | 2007 | 2008 | 2009 | 2010 | 2011 | 2012 | 2013 | 2014 | 2015 |
|---|---|---|---|---|---|---|---|---|---|---|---|---|---|
| | | | | | | *Millions of Liras: Fiscal Year Ends December 31* | | | | | | | |
| Revenue........................................ | a1 | .... | .... | .... | .... | .... | .... | 283,219.2 | 304,281.2 | 341,651.1 | 400,488.4 | 431,880.9 | .... |
| Taxes........................................ | a11 | .... | .... | .... | .... | .... | .... | 231,739.3 | 260,320.1 | 287,324.3 | 335,851.2 | 357,697.3 | .... |
| Social Contributions................... | a12 | .... | .... | .... | .... | .... | .... | 2,304.9 | 2,918.3 | 3,483.6 | 3,819.1 | 4,008.0 | .... |
| Grants....................................... | a13 | .... | .... | .... | .... | .... | .... | 10,714.9 | 242.1 | 5,995.8 | 10,704.2 | 14,223.7 | .... |
| Other Revenue........................... | a14 | .... | .... | .... | .... | .... | .... | 38,460.1 | 40,800.6 | 44,847.4 | 50,113.9 | 55,952.0 | .... |
| Expense....................................... | a2 | .... | .... | .... | .... | .... | .... | 290,713.6 | 301,527.2 | 344,915.8 | 383,533.3 | 427,569.0 | .... |
| Compensation of Employees.......... | a21 | .... | .... | .... | .... | .... | .... | 71,065.0 | 81,616.1 | 99,152.3 | 111,898.5 | 129,192.6 | .... |
| Use of Goods & Services............... | a22 | .... | .... | .... | .... | .... | .... | 26,981.8 | 31,622.2 | 37,922.4 | 45,263.6 | 47,641.0 | .... |
| Consumption of Fixed Capital........ | a23 | .... | .... | .... | .... | .... | .... | 8,004.2 | 11,069.5 | 6,261.9 | 4,702.0 | 7,669.6 | .... |
| Interest...................................... | a24 | .... | .... | .... | .... | .... | .... | 49,410.6 | 44,736.0 | 50,800.4 | 49,459.3 | 49,907.2 | .... |
| Subsidies.................................... | a25 | .... | .... | .... | .... | .... | .... | 8,872.6 | 10,683.0 | 16,230.9 | 16,332.2 | 13,040.2 | .... |
| Grants........................................ | a26 | .... | .... | .... | .... | .... | .... | 64,536.6 | 63,270.0 | 69,624.7 | 81,851.7 | 99,717.8 | .... |
| Social Benefits............................ | a27 | .... | .... | .... | .... | .... | .... | 52,927.9 | 51,520.3 | 57,828.7 | 62,601.8 | 67,294.7 | .... |
| Other Expense............................ | a28 | .... | .... | .... | .... | .... | .... | 8,915.0 | 7,010.1 | 7,094.4 | 11,424.3 | 13,105.9 | .... |
| Gross Operating Balance [1-2+23]... | agob | .... | .... | .... | .... | .... | .... | 509.9 | 13,823.6 | 2,997.1 | 21,657.1 | 11,981.5 | .... |
| Net Operating Balance [1-2]........... | anob | .... | .... | .... | .... | .... | .... | −7,494.4 | 2,754.1 | −3,264.7 | 16,955.1 | 4,311.9 | .... |
| Net Acq. of Nonfinancial Assets....... | a31 | .... | .... | .... | .... | .... | .... | 11,062.1 | 12,457.4 | 24,048.1 | 20,446.5 | 26,213.1 | .... |
| Aquisition of Nonfin. Assets.......... | a31.1 | .... | .... | .... | .... | .... | .... | .... | .... | .... | .... | .... | .... |
| Disposal of Nonfin. Assets............. | a31.2 | .... | .... | .... | .... | .... | .... | .... | .... | .... | .... | .... | .... |
| Net Lending/Borrowing [1-2-31]...... | anlb | .... | .... | .... | .... | .... | .... | −18,556.4 | −9,703.3 | −27,312.8 | −3,491.4 | −21,901.2 | .... |
| Net Acq. of Financial Assets............. | a32 | .... | .... | .... | .... | .... | .... | 17,390.3 | 15,629.4 | 5,794.7 | 26,664.6 | −28,193.5 | .... |
| By instrument | | | | | | | | | | | | | |
| Monetary Gold & SDRs................. | a3201 | .... | .... | .... | .... | .... | .... | — | — | — | — | — | .... |
| Currency & Deposits..................... | a3202 | .... | .... | .... | .... | .... | .... | −3,237.3 | 3,683.2 | −2,739.8 | 6,685.1 | −2,303.5 | .... |
| Securities other than Shares........... | a3203 | .... | .... | .... | .... | .... | .... | 14.6 | — | — | −45.1 | −84.3 | .... |
| Loans........................................ | a3204 | .... | .... | .... | .... | .... | .... | −1,247.5 | −588.4 | −3,592.1 | 6,600.8 | 3,053.9 | .... |
| Shares & Other Equity................... | a3205 | .... | .... | .... | .... | .... | .... | 3,095.5 | 2,922.9 | 6,292.6 | 1,622.8 | −23,877.4 | .... |
| Insurance Technical Reserves.......... | a3206 | .... | .... | .... | .... | .... | .... | | | | | | .... |
| Financial Derivatives..................... | a3207 | .... | .... | .... | .... | .... | .... | — | — | — | — | — | .... |
| Other Accounts Receivable............. | a3208 | .... | .... | .... | .... | .... | .... | 18,765.1 | 9,611.7 | 5,834.0 | 11,801.0 | −4,982.3 | .... |
| By debtor | | | | | | | | | | | | | |
| Domestic.................................... | a321 | .... | .... | .... | .... | .... | .... | 22,387.5 | 16,126.4 | 4,161.4 | 23,848.3 | −28,206.7 | .... |
| Foreign...................................... | a322 | .... | .... | .... | .... | .... | .... | −4,997.1 | −497.0 | 1,633.2 | 2,816.4 | 13.2 | .... |
| Net Incurrence of Liabilities.............. | a33 | .... | .... | .... | .... | .... | .... | 39,538.1 | 29,129.2 | 33,830.2 | 31,429.8 | −6,977.9 | .... |
| By instrument | | | | | | | | | | | | | |
| Special Drawing Rights (SDRs)........ | a3301 | .... | .... | .... | .... | .... | .... | — | — | — | — | — | .... |
| Currency & Deposits..................... | a3302 | .... | .... | .... | .... | .... | .... | 372.1 | −15.5 | 212.4 | 104.9 | 210.8 | .... |
| Securities other than Shares........... | a3303 | .... | .... | .... | .... | .... | .... | 30,089.0 | 30,345.1 | 32,998.2 | 9,153.3 | −2,751.4 | .... |
| Loans........................................ | a3304 | .... | .... | .... | .... | .... | .... | 1,991.2 | −8,255.4 | −3,620.6 | 24,917.5 | −4,870.3 | .... |
| Shares & Other Equity................... | a3305 | .... | .... | .... | .... | .... | .... | | | | | | .... |
| Insurance Technical Reserves.......... | a3306 | .... | .... | .... | .... | .... | .... | — | — | — | — | — | .... |
| Financial Derivatives..................... | a3307 | .... | .... | .... | .... | .... | .... | | | | | | .... |
| Other Accounts Payable................. | a3308 | .... | .... | .... | .... | .... | .... | 7,086.0 | 7,055.0 | 4,240.1 | −2,745.9 | 432.9 | .... |
| By creditor | | | | | | | | | | | | | |
| Domestic.................................... | a331 | .... | .... | .... | .... | .... | .... | 30,588.0 | 26,224.7 | 28,048.3 | 32,643.7 | 16,841.0 | .... |
| Foreign...................................... | a332 | .... | .... | .... | .... | .... | .... | 8,950.2 | 2,904.5 | 5,782.0 | −1,213.9 | −23,818.9 | .... |
| Stat. Discrepancy [32-33-NLB]........ | anlbz | .... | .... | .... | .... | .... | .... | −3,591.4 | −3,796.5 | −722.7 | −1,273.7 | 685.6 | .... |
| Memo Item: Expenditure [2+31]...... | a2m | .... | .... | .... | .... | .... | .... | 301,775.7 | 313,984.5 | 368,963.9 | 403,979.8 | 453,782.1 | .... |

|  |  | 2004 | 2005 | 2006 | 2007 | 2008 | 2009 | 2010 | 2011 | 2012 | 2013 | 2014 | 2015 |
|---|---|---|---|---|---|---|---|---|---|---|---|---|---|
| **National Accounts** |  |  |  |  |  | *Millions of Liras* |  |  |  |  |  |  |  |
| Househ.Cons.Expend.,incl.NPISHs.... | 96f | 398,559 | 465,402 | 534,849 | 601,239 | 663,944 | 680,768 | 787,753 | 923,836 | 994,320 | 1,109,722 | 1,203,897 | 1,341,190 |
| Government Consumption Expend... | 91f | 66,802 | 76,499 | 93,525 | 107,816 | 121,681 | 140,029 | 157,514 | 180,708 | 210,239 | 236,589 | 268,157 | 306,605 |
| Gross Fixed Capital Formation.......... | 93e | 113,717 | 136,475 | 169,045 | 180,598 | 189,094 | 160,718 | 207,816 | 283,163 | 286,949 | 318,580 | 351,725 | 396,604 |
| Changes in Inventories..................... | 93i | −5,320 | −6,756 | −1,334 | −2,961 | 17,949 | −18,427 | 6,708 | 22,528 | −2,808 | 4,948 | 1,262 | −35,006 |
| Exports of Goods and Services......... | 90c | 131,661 | 141,826 | 171,926 | 188,225 | 227,253 | 222,103 | 233,046 | 311,148 | 373,227 | 401,787 | 484,675 | 546,251 |
| Imports of Goods and Services (-)..... | 98c | 146,386 | 164,514 | 209,172 | 231,738 | 269,388 | 232,632 | 294,036 | 423,670 | 446,141 | 504,337 | 562,352 | 602,082 |
| Gross Domestic Product (GDP)........ | 99b | 559,033 | 648,932 | 758,391 | 843,178 | 950,534 | 952,559 | 1,098,799 | 1,297,713 | 1,415,786 | 1,567,289 | 1,747,363 | 1,953,561 |
| GDP Volume 1998 Prices................ | 99b.p | 83,486 | 90,500 | 96,738 | 101,255 | 101,922 | 97,003 | 105,886 | 115,175 | 117,675 | 122,557 | 126,129 | 131,289 |
| GDP Volume (2010=100)................ | 99bvp | 78.8 | 85.5 | 91.4 | 95.6 | 96.3 | 91.6 | 100.0 | 108.8 | 111.1 | 115.7 | 119.1 | 124.0 |
| GDP Deflator (2010=100)................ | 99bip | 64.5 | 69.1 | 75.5 | 80.2 | 89.9 | 94.6 | 100.0 | 108.6 | 115.9 | 123.2 | 133.5 | 143.4 |
|  |  |  |  |  |  | *Millions: Midyear Estimates* |  |  |  |  |  |  |  |
| **Population**............................... | 99z | 66.97 | 67.86 | 68.70 | 69.52 | 70.34 | 71.26 | 72.31 | 73.52 | 74.85 | 76.22 | 77.52 | 78.67 |

# Tuvalu 869

| | | 2004 | 2005 | 2006 | 2007 | 2008 | 2009 | 2010 | 2011 | 2012 | 2013 | 2014 | 2015 |
|---|---|---|---|---|---|---|---|---|---|---|---|---|---|
| **Exchange Rates** | | | | | | *Australian Dollars per SDR: End of Period* | | | | | | | |
| Market Rate | aa | 1.9936 | 1.9480 | 1.9012 | 1.7925 | 2.2233 | 1.7479 | 1.5153 | 1.5117 | 1.4771 | 1.7372 | 1.7664 | 1.8967 |
| | | | | *Australian Dollars per US Dollar: End of Period (ae) Period Average (rf)* | | | | | | | | | |
| Market Rate | ae | 1.2837 | 1.3630 | 1.2637 | 1.1343 | 1.4434 | 1.1150 | .9840 | .9846 | .9611 | 1.1280 | 1.2192 | 1.3687 |
| Market Rate | rf | 1.3598 | 1.3095 | 1.3280 | 1.1951 | 1.1922 | 1.2822 | 1.0902 | .9695 | .9658 | 1.0358 | 1.1094 | 1.3311 |
| **Fund Position** | | | | | | *Millions of SDRs: End of Period* | | | | | | | |
| Quota | 2f.s | .... | .... | .... | .... | — | — | 1.80 | 1.80 | 1.80 | 1.80 | 1.80 | 1.80 |
| SDR Holdings | 1b.s | .... | .... | .... | .... | — | — | 1.26 | 1.26 | 1.26 | 1.26 | 1.26 | 1.26 |
| Reserve Position in the Fund | 1c.s | .... | .... | .... | .... | — | — | .43 | .43 | .43 | .43 | .43 | .43 |
| Total Fund Cred.&Loans Outstg. | 2tl | .... | .... | .... | .... | — | — | — | — | — | — | — | — |
| SDR Allocations | 1bd | .... | .... | .... | .... | — | — | 1.69 | 1.69 | 1.69 | 1.69 | 1.69 | 1.69 |
| **Balance of Payments** | | | | | | *Thousands of US Dollars* | | | | | | | |
| A. Current Account* | 109bx | −7,060.9 | −4,277.8 | 6,549.3 | −4,364.2 | −3,708.6 | −16,906.8 | −14,013.8 | −23,862.2 | 6,428.4 | 6,808.3 | .... | .... |
| Goods, credit (exports) | 1a9cx | 301.5 | 336.8 | 417.9 | 400.8 | 542.7 | 2,574.6 | 10,014.6 | 10,502.8 | 20,616.2 | 16,429.9 | .... | .... |
| Goods, debit (imports) | 1a9dx | 10,079.6 | 10,698.5 | 9,680.4 | 9,760.0 | 9,616.0 | 23,659.0 | 18,410.5 | 21,127.3 | 22,169.8 | 21,476.2 | .... | .... |
| Balance on goods | 1a9bx | −9,778.0 | −10,361.7 | −9,262.5 | −9,359.2 | −9,073.3 | −21,084.4 | −8,395.9 | −10,624.6 | −1,553.5 | −5,046.3 | .... | .... |
| Services, credit (exports) | 1b9cx | 2,414.5 | 2,290.2 | 2,597.3 | 2,865.6 | 3,518.0 | 2,938.7 | 4,045.9 | 4,346.1 | 4,494.4 | 4,138.1 | .... | .... |
| Services, debit (imports) | 1b9dx | 14,668.8 | 9,514.2 | 11,792.0 | 21,863.6 | 29,881.9 | 27,026.9 | 33,836.3 | 44,005.1 | 27,559.7 | 18,019.3 | .... | .... |
| Balance on Goods & Services | 1z9bx | −22,032.4 | −17,585.7 | −18,457.2 | −28,357.3 | −35,437.1 | −45,172.6 | −38,186.4 | −50,283.6 | −24,618.8 | −18,927.5 | .... | .... |
| Primary income: credit | 1c9cx | 8,767.5 | 7,817.9 | 12,796.8 | 13,665.3 | 18,313.4 | 15,286.7 | 13,281.2 | 14,591.2 | 14,173.3 | 23,960.3 | .... | .... |
| Primary income: debit | 1c9dx | 598.7 | 669.8 | 717.3 | 797.0 | 776.1 | 1,227.7 | 2,420.8 | 2,347.2 | 4,653.1 | 3,754.3 | .... | .... |
| Balance on gds, serv. & prim. inc. | 1y9bx | −13,863.6 | −10,437.6 | −6,377.7 | −15,519.0 | −17,899.8 | −31,113.6 | −27,326.0 | −38,039.5 | −15,098.5 | 1,278.6 | .... | .... |
| Secondary income: credit | 1d9ca | 7,695.4 | 7,219.5 | 14,418.1 | 13,019.4 | 16,362.0 | 15,864.7 | 15,332.7 | 16,665.7 | 23,699.7 | 7,983.2 | .... | .... |
| Secondary income: debit | 1d9da | 892.7 | 1,059.7 | 1,491.1 | 1,864.6 | 2,170.7 | 1,657.8 | 2,020.5 | 2,488.4 | 2,172.8 | 2,453.5 | .... | .... |
| B. Capital Account* | 209ba | 6,439.1 | 2,415.6 | 2,675.7 | 11,769.3 | 10,606.9 | 7,287.5 | 8,796.9 | 15,127.6 | 7,467.7 | 4,204.3 | .... | .... |
| Capital account: credit | 209ca | 6,439.1 | 2,415.6 | 2,675.7 | 11,769.3 | 10,606.9 | 7,796.6 | 8,796.9 | 15,127.6 | 7,467.7 | 4,204.3 | .... | .... |
| Capital account: debit | 209da | .... | .... | .... | .... | .... | 509.1 | .... | .... | .... | .... | .... | .... |
| Balance on current & capital acct. | 129ba | −621.8 | −1,862.1 | 9,225.0 | 7,405.1 | 6,898.3 | −9,619.2 | −5,216.8 | −8,734.7 | 13,896.1 | 11,012.6 | .... | .... |
| C. Financial Account* | 309na | 2,681.6 | 1,680.9 | −2,925.1 | −1,127.9 | −2,189.7 | −13,423.8 | 3,432.9 | 4,676.2 | 9,838.5 | −1,775.7 | .... | .... |
| Direct investment: assets | 3a9aa | .... | .... | .... | .... | .... | .... | .... | .... | .... | .... | .... | .... |
| Equity & investment fund shares | 3aaaa | .... | .... | .... | .... | .... | .... | .... | .... | .... | .... | .... | .... |
| Debt instruments | 3abaa | .... | .... | .... | .... | .... | .... | .... | .... | .... | .... | .... | .... |
| Direct investment: liabilities | 3a9la | −11.7 | −11.4 | −10.6 | −11.1 | 1,687.8 | 1,751.1 | 455.2 | −119.1 | 1,325.0 | 336.8 | .... | .... |
| Equity & investment fund shares | 3aala | −11.7 | −11.4 | −10.6 | −11.1 | 1,687.8 | 191.7 | 844.7 | −119.1 | 2,090.4 | 784.7 | .... | .... |
| Debt instruments | 3abla | .... | .... | .... | .... | .... | 1,559.4 | −389.5 | .... | −765.4 | −447.8 | .... | .... |
| Portfolio investment: assets | 3b9aa | 2,353.4 | 1,669.5 | 30.5 | 1,894.1 | 2,248.8 | −2,294.4 | 2,306.4 | 3,759.1 | 7,244.2 | 1,076.9 | .... | .... |
| Equity & investment fund shares | 3baaa | .... | .... | .... | .... | .... | .... | .... | .... | .... | .... | .... | .... |
| Debt securities | 3bbaa | 2,353.4 | 1,669.5 | 30.5 | 1,894.1 | 2,248.8 | −2,294.4 | 2,306.4 | 3,759.1 | 7,244.2 | 1,076.9 | .... | .... |
| Portfolio investment: liabilities | 3b9la | .... | .... | .... | .... | .... | .... | .... | .... | .... | .... | .... | .... |
| Equity & investment fund shares | 3bala | .... | .... | .... | .... | .... | .... | .... | .... | .... | .... | .... | .... |
| Debt securities | 3bbla | .... | .... | .... | .... | .... | .... | .... | .... | .... | .... | .... | .... |
| Fin. der.& empl.stk.ops.(ESOs): net | 3c9na | .... | .... | .... | .... | .... | .... | .... | .... | .... | .... | .... | .... |
| Fin. der. & ESOs.: assets | 3c9aa | .... | .... | .... | .... | .... | .... | .... | .... | .... | .... | .... | .... |
| Fin. der. & ESOs.: liabilities | 3c9la | .... | .... | .... | .... | .... | .... | .... | .... | .... | .... | .... | .... |
| Other investment: assets | 3d9aa | .... | .... | −2,966.1 | −2,563.3 | −2,561.5 | 681.7 | 96.1 | 1,460.6 | 4,879.5 | −6,698.6 | .... | .... |
| Other equity | 3daaa | .... | .... | −2,966.1 | −2,563.3 | −2,565.1 | −803.7 | .... | .... | .... | .... | .... | .... |
| Debt instruments | 3dzaa | .... | .... | — | — | 3.6 | 1,485.4 | 96.1 | 1,460.6 | 4,879.5 | −6,698.6 | .... | .... |
| Other investment: liabilities | 3d9la | −316.5 | .... | .... | 469.7 | 189.2 | 10,060.1 | −1,485.6 | 662.6 | 960.2 | −4,182.8 | .... | .... |
| Other equity | 3dala | .... | .... | .... | .... | .... | .... | .... | .... | .... | .... | .... | .... |
| Debt instruments | 3dzla | −316.5 | .... | .... | 469.7 | 189.2 | 10,060.1 | −1,485.6 | 662.6 | 960.2 | −4,182.8 | .... | .... |
| Curr.+ cap.− finan. acct. balance | 4y9na | −3,303.4 | −3,543.0 | 12,150.0 | 8,533.0 | 9,088.0 | 3,804.6 | −8,649.7 | −13,410.9 | 4,057.6 | 12,788.2 | .... | .... |
| D. Net Errors and Omissions | 409na | 2,844.6 | 2,273.4 | −3,224.9 | −2,948.2 | 663.7 | 1,932.0 | 4,825.7 | 11,694.2 | −2,107.2 | −3,154.6 | .... | .... |
| E. Reserves and Related Items | 4z9na | −458.8 | −1,269.6 | 8,925.2 | 5,584.8 | 9,751.7 | 5,736.6 | −3,824.0 | −1,716.7 | 1,950.3 | 9,633.6 | .... | .... |
| Reserve assets | 3e9aa | −458.8 | −1,269.6 | 8,925.2 | 5,584.8 | 9,751.7 | 5,736.6 | −3,824.0 | −1,716.7 | 1,950.3 | 9,633.6 | .... | .... |
| Credit and loans from the IMF | 3dcla | .... | .... | .... | .... | .... | .... | — | — | — | — | .... | .... |
| Exceptional financing | 409la | .... | .... | .... | .... | .... | .... | .... | .... | .... | .... | .... | .... |

*Excludes components in group E

| | | 2004 | 2005 | 2006 | 2007 | 2008 | 2009 | 2010 | 2011 | 2012 | 2013 | 2014 | 2015 |
|---|---|---|---|---|---|---|---|---|---|---|---|---|---|
| **International Investment Position** | | | | | | *Thousands of US Dollars* | | | | | | | |
| Assets | 809aa | 68,653.4 | 71,469.4 | 89,682.7 | 106,894.7 | 78,960.1 | 110,363.9 | 129,514.7 | 131,648.2 | 152,905.8 | 140,976.4 | .... | .... |
| Direct investment | 8a9aa | .... | .... | .... | .... | .... | .... | .... | .... | .... | .... | .... | .... |
| Equity & investment fund shares | 8aaaa | .... | .... | .... | .... | .... | .... | .... | .... | .... | .... | .... | .... |
| Debt instruments | 8abaa | .... | .... | .... | .... | .... | .... | .... | .... | .... | .... | .... | .... |
| Portfolio investment | 8b9aa | 30,555.6 | 32,864.8 | 38,055.1 | 45,426.5 | 31,384.8 | 42,346.8 | 53,087.5 | 55,208.9 | 64,689.3 | 58,213.8 | .... | .... |
| Equity & investment fund shares | 8baaa | .... | .... | .... | .... | .... | .... | .... | .... | .... | .... | .... | .... |
| Debt securities | 8bbaa | 30,555.6 | 32,864.8 | 38,055.1 | 45,426.5 | 31,384.8 | 42,346.8 | 53,087.5 | 55,208.9 | 64,689.3 | 58,213.8 | .... | .... |
| Fin. der.(oth.than reserves) & ESOs | 8c9aa | .... | .... | .... | .... | .... | .... | .... | .... | .... | .... | .... | .... |
| Other investment | 8d9aa | 31,646.3 | 33,748.1 | 37,052.2 | 42,169.0 | 28,888.8 | 40,331.6 | 49,441.5 | 51,996.6 | 59,606.8 | 49,150.2 | .... | .... |
| Other equity | 8daaa | 31,646.3 | 33,748.1 | 37,052.2 | 42,169.0 | 28,203.2 | 38,073.9 | 46,785.5 | 47,680.0 | 52,450.6 | 47,471.1 | .... | .... |
| Debt instruments | 8dzaa | — | — | — | — | 685.5 | 2,257.7 | 2,656.0 | 4,316.6 | 7,156.2 | 1,679.2 | .... | .... |
| Reserve assets | 8e9aa | 6,451.5 | 4,856.5 | 14,575.4 | 19,299.1 | 18,686.5 | 27,685.5 | 26,985.7 | 24,442.7 | 28,609.7 | 33,612.4 | .... | .... |
| Liabilities | 809la | 194.1 | 7,845.3 | 9,572.0 | 11,133.4 | 10,066.1 | 27,621.5 | 30,271.7 | 30,840.3 | 34,122.9 | 28,105.9 | .... | .... |
| Direct investment | 8a9la | 194.1 | 171.9 | 174.2 | 182.5 | 1,520.4 | 4,120.4 | 5,407.9 | 5,377.1 | 6,877.7 | 6,511.0 | .... | .... |
| Equity & investment fund shares | 8aala | 194.1 | 171.9 | 174.2 | 182.5 | 1,520.4 | 2,091.4 | 3,279.5 | 3,251.6 | 5,422.3 | 5,621.3 | .... | .... |
| Debt instruments | 8abla | .... | .... | .... | .... | .... | 2,029.0 | 2,128.4 | 2,125.4 | 1,455.4 | 889.7 | .... | .... |
| Portfolio investment | 8b9la | .... | .... | .... | .... | .... | .... | .... | .... | .... | .... | .... | .... |
| Equity & investment fund shares | 8bala | .... | .... | .... | .... | .... | .... | .... | .... | .... | .... | .... | .... |
| Debt securities | 8bbla | .... | .... | .... | .... | .... | .... | .... | .... | .... | .... | .... | .... |
| Fin. der.(oth.than reserves) & ESOs | 8c9la | .... | .... | .... | .... | .... | .... | .... | .... | .... | .... | .... | .... |
| Other investment | 8d9la | .... | 7,673.4 | 9,397.7 | 10,950.9 | 8,545.7 | 23,501.0 | 24,863.8 | 25,463.2 | 27,245.2 | 21,594.9 | .... | .... |
| Other equity | 8dala | .... | .... | .... | .... | .... | .... | .... | .... | .... | .... | .... | .... |
| Debt instruments | 8dzla | .... | 7,673.4 | 9,397.7 | 10,950.9 | 8,545.7 | 23,501.0 | 24,863.8 | 25,463.2 | 27,245.2 | 21,594.9 | .... | .... |

|  |  | 2004 | 2005 | 2006 | 2007 | 2008 | 2009 | 2010 | 2011 | 2012 | 2013 | 2014 | 2015 |
|---|---|---|---|---|---|---|---|---|---|---|---|---|---|
| **Exchange Rates** |  | *Shillings per SDR: End of Period* | | | | | | | | | | | |
| Principal Rate | aa | 2,700.0 | 2,596.8 | 2,619.8 | 2,682.2 | 3,002.3 | 2,978.2 | 3,554.9 | 3,824.3 | 4,128.1 | 3,893.1 | 4,017.6 | 4,679.6 |
|  |  | *Shillings per US Dollar: End of Period (ae) Period Average (rf)* | | | | | | | | | | | |
| Principal Rate | ae | 1,738.6 | 1,816.9 | 1,741.4 | 1,697.3 | 1,949.2 | 1,899.7 | 2,308.3 | 2,491.0 | 2,685.9 | 2,528.0 | 2,773.1 | 3,377.0 |
| Principal Rate | rf | 1,810.3 | 1,780.7 | 1,831.5 | 1,723.5 | 1,720.4 | 2,030.5 | 2,177.6 | 2,522.7 | 2,504.6 | 2,586.9 | 2,599.8 | 3,240.6 |
|  |  | *Index Numbers (2010=100): Period Averages* | | | | | | | | | | | |
| Principal Rate | ahx | 120.2 | 122.0 | 118.6 | 126.0 | 126.7 | 107.3 | 100.0 | 86.4 | 86.8 | 84.0 | 83.6 | 67.5 |
| Nominal Effective Exchange Rate | nec | 124.9 | 125.1 | 120.9 | 122.2 | 121.0 | 108.2 | 100.0 | 85.4 | 88.6 | 88.3 | 89.9 | 80.9 |
| CPI-Based Real Effect. Ex. Rate | rec | 97.9 | 102.3 | 102.4 | 105.6 | 109.2 | 107.3 | 100.0 | 95.8 | 109.0 | 110.9 | 114.3 | 105.6 |
| **Fund Position** |  | *Millions of SDRs: End of Period* | | | | | | | | | | | |
| Quota | 2f.s | 180.50 | 180.50 | 180.50 | 180.50 | 180.50 | 180.50 | 180.50 | 180.50 | 180.50 | 180.50 | 180.50 | 180.50 |
| SDR Holdings | 1b.s | .43 | .80 | .06 | .17 | .13 | 143.66 | 143.37 | 142.24 | 141.00 | 139.78 | 48.54 | 47.47 |
| Reserve Position in the Fund | 1c.s | — | — | — | — | — | — | — | — | — | — | — | — |
| Total Fund Cred.&Loans Outstg. | 2tl | 123.32 | 91.73 | 6.00 | 6.00 | 6.00 | 6.00 | 5.80 | 4.80 | 3.60 | 2.40 | 1.20 | .20 |
| SDR Allocations | 1bd | 29.40 | 29.40 | 29.40 | 29.40 | 29.40 | 173.06 | 173.06 | 173.06 | 173.06 | 173.06 | 173.06 | 173.06 |
| **International Liquidity** |  | *Millions of US Dollars Unless Otherwise Indicated: End of Period* | | | | | | | | | | | |
| Total Reserves minus Gold | 1l.d | 1,308.1 | 1,344.2 | 1,810.9 | 2,559.8 | 2,300.5 | 2,994.5 | 2,706.0 | 2,617.5 | 3,167.2 | 3,337.5 | 3,316.4 | 2,908.9 |
| SDR Holdings | 1b.d | .7 | 1.1 | .1 | .3 | .2 | 225.2 | 220.8 | 218.4 | 216.7 | 215.3 | 70.3 | 65.8 |
| Reserve Position in the Fund | 1c.d | — | — | — | — | — | — | — | — | — | — | — | — |
| Foreign Exchange | 1d.d | 1,307.4 | 1,343.1 | 1,810.8 | 2,559.5 | 2,300.3 | 2,769.3 | 2,485.2 | 2,399.1 | 2,950.5 | 3,122.3 | 3,246.0 | 2,843.1 |
| Central Bank: Other Assets | 3..d | 43.1 | 34.9 | 35.3 | 32.9 | 43.3 | 56.3 | 292.3 | 169.4 | 386.3 | 812.4 | 385.8 | 501.6 |
| Central Bank: Other Liabs | 4..d | 2.4 | 1.7 | 1.8 | 1.4 | 1.2 | 1.6 | .1 | .1 | .1 | 241.6 | 9.9 | 75.2 |
| Other Depository Corps.: Assets | 7a.d | 411.2 | 349.5 | 489.2 | 548.6 | 504.6 | 497.0 | 516.1 | 567.6 | 544.6 | 675.9 | 445.7 | 709.5 |
| Other Depository Corps.: Liabs | 7b.d | 66.6 | 64.8 | 110.1 | 190.9 | 238.3 | 295.3 | 343.4 | 329.4 | 463.4 | 732.0 | 706.7 | 701.9 |
| **Central Bank** |  | *Billions of Shillings: End of Period* | | | | | | | | | | | |
| Net Foreign Assets | 11n | 1,911.09 | 2,162.20 | 3,124.85 | 4,335.21 | 4,495.33 | 4,832.91 | 5,772.61 | 5,718.88 | 8,236.48 | 8,652.35 | 9,343.95 | 10,229.99 |
| Claims on Nonresidents | 11 | 2,327.55 | 2,479.81 | 3,220.66 | 4,432.49 | 4,603.95 | 5,369.24 | 6,408.73 | 6,399.38 | 8,966.11 | 9,946.12 | 10,071.44 | 11,294.85 |
| Liabilities to Nonresidents | 16c | 416.46 | 317.61 | 95.80 | 97.28 | 108.61 | 536.34 | 636.12 | 680.50 | 729.62 | 1,293.77 | 727.49 | 1,064.86 |
| Claims on Other Depository Corps. | 12e | 117.81 | 106.42 | 111.04 | 132.92 | 74.01 | 33.82 | 48.02 | 294.25 | 43.58 | 44.02 | 42.45 | 65.38 |
| Net Claims on Central Government | 12an | −623.78 | −825.51 | −1,361.61 | −2,341.65 | −1,931.81 | −2,245.66 | −1,854.17 | −1,589.67 | −2,671.24 | −2,858.47 | −2,325.62 | −1,652.45 |
| Claims on Central Government | 12a | 1,653.29 | 1,609.90 | 1,594.59 | 2,224.71 | 2,792.26 | 2,907.39 | 4,275.01 | 6,021.55 | 7,061.31 | 8,485.93 | 2,473.95 | 2,124.98 |
| Liabilities to Central Government | 16d | 2,277.07 | 2,435.41 | 2,956.21 | 4,566.36 | 4,724.07 | 5,153.04 | 6,129.18 | 7,611.22 | 9,732.55 | 11,344.40 | 4,799.57 | 3,777.43 |
| Claims on Other Sectors | 12s | 100.33 | 62.58 | 74.23 | 76.38 | 68.50 | 42.79 | 43.56 | 63.70 | 68.65 | 54.45 | 67.68 | 80.60 |
| Claims on Other Financial Corps. | 12g | 26.74 | 34.62 | 44.60 | 44.06 | 36.19 | 24.98 | 16.97 | 9.57 | 5.48 | 6.37 | 8.06 | 11.41 |
| Claims on State & Local Govts. | 12b | — | — | — | — | — | — | — | — | — | — | — | — |
| Claims on Public Nonfin. Corps. | 12c | 5.27 | 4.85 | 4.43 | 4.10 | 4.10 | .36 | .36 | .36 | .36 | — | — | — |
| Claims on Private Sector | 12d | 68.32 | 23.10 | 25.20 | 28.22 | 28.21 | 17.45 | 26.24 | 53.76 | 62.81 | 48.07 | 59.62 | 69.19 |
| Monetary Base | 14 | 924.57 | 1,051.21 | 1,226.60 | 1,543.53 | 1,926.96 | 2,181.52 | 2,878.52 | 3,301.31 | 3,976.34 | 4,022.38 | 5,188.54 | 5,707.18 |
| Currency in Circulation | 14a | 696.51 | 832.74 | 1,026.34 | 1,199.98 | 1,487.71 | 1,595.25 | 2,103.79 | 2,487.28 | 2,683.77 | 2,832.08 | 3,320.14 | 3,716.50 |
| Liabs. to Other Depository Corps. | 14c | 228.06 | 218.48 | 200.26 | 343.56 | 439.25 | 586.27 | 774.74 | 814.02 | 1,292.57 | 1,190.29 | 1,868.39 | 1,990.68 |
| Liabilities to Other Sectors | 14d | — | — | — | — | — | — | — | — | — | — | — | — |
| Other Liabs. to Other Dep. Corps. | 14n | 80.61 | 98.42 | 133.38 | 65.08 | 19.70 | 38.03 | 17.67 | 20.33 | 20.47 | 582.92 | 266.90 | 42.79 |
| Dep. & Sec. Excl. f/Monetary Base | 14o | 1.78 | 1.96 | 4.94 | 1.05 | .17 | .05 | .36 | 1.95 | .01 | .08 | .06 | .02 |
| Deposits Included in Broad Money | 15 | — | — | — | — | — | — | — | — | — | — | — | — |
| Sec.Ot.th.Shares Incl.in Brd. Money | 16a | — | — | — | — | — | — | — | — | — | — | — | — |
| Deposits Excl. from Broad Money | 16b | 1.78 | 1.96 | 4.94 | 1.05 | .17 | .05 | .36 | 1.95 | .01 | .08 | .06 | .02 |
| Sec.Ot.th.Shares Excl.f/Brd.Money | 16s | — | — | — | — | — | — | — | — | — | — | — | — |
| Loans | 16l | — | — | — | — | — | — | — | — | — | — | — | — |
| Financial Derivatives | 16m | — | — | — | — | — | — | — | — | — | — | — | — |
| Shares and Other Equity | 17a | 396.26 | 324.89 | 350.94 | 439.54 | 594.59 | 585.70 | 1,312.77 | 1,315.19 | 1,748.80 | 1,502.56 | 2,094.58 | 3,575.24 |
| Other Items (Net) | 17r | 102.23 | 29.22 | 232.64 | 153.65 | 164.61 | −141.44 | −199.31 | −151.61 | −68.12 | −215.59 | −421.61 | −601.71 |
| Memo Item: |  |  |  |  |  |  |  |  |  |  |  |  |  |
| Total Assets | 10ra | 4,827.02 | 4,897.87 | 5,639.31 | 7,558.90 | 8,300.14 | 9,343.42 | 11,149.18 | 13,272.72 | 16,652.28 | 19,152.11 | 13,383.64 | 14,576.92 |
| **Other Depository Corporations** |  | *Billions of Shillings: End of Period* | | | | | | | | | | | |
| Net Foreign Assets | 21n | 599.19 | 517.22 | 660.14 | 607.21 | 519.07 | 383.20 | 398.69 | 593.57 | 218.18 | −141.98 | −723.79 | 25.84 |
| Claims on Nonresidents | 21 | 714.91 | 635.04 | 851.91 | 931.23 | 983.63 | 944.22 | 1,191.27 | 1,414.00 | 1,462.78 | 1,708.58 | 1,235.87 | 2,396.14 |
| Liabilities to Nonresidents | 26c | 115.72 | 117.82 | 191.77 | 324.02 | 464.56 | 561.02 | 792.58 | 820.43 | 1,244.60 | 1,850.56 | 1,959.66 | 2,370.30 |
| Claims on Central Bank | 20 | 391.57 | 454.42 | 476.99 | 474.41 | 695.86 | 879.21 | 1,109.77 | 1,244.69 | 1,779.58 | 2,190.64 | 2,705.76 | 2,570.49 |
| Currency | 20a | 107.90 | 122.51 | 140.47 | 177.65 | 233.19 | 265.50 | 322.09 | 408.83 | 437.90 | 460.47 | 562.58 | 548.57 |
| Reserve Deposits and Securities | 20b | 267.66 | 301.22 | 273.77 | 296.76 | 462.67 | 593.70 | 787.68 | 835.79 | 1,341.62 | 1,185.95 | 1,914.86 | 2,020.84 |
| Other Claims | 20n | 16.00 | 30.69 | 62.75 | — | — | 20.00 | — | .07 | .06 | 544.22 | 228.33 | 1.08 |
| Net Claims on Central Government | 22an | 595.40 | 766.67 | 799.48 | 1,231.71 | 1,378.50 | 1,678.09 | 2,291.03 | 1,829.05 | 2,642.25 | 3,204.48 | 3,909.85 | 3,543.77 |
| Claims on Central Government | 22a | 952.53 | 976.42 | 1,016.04 | 1,400.06 | 1,532.56 | 1,839.38 | 2,532.47 | 2,091.33 | 3,066.61 | 3,656.55 | 4,486.35 | 4,104.05 |
| Liabilities to Central Government | 26d | 357.13 | 209.75 | 216.56 | 168.35 | 154.06 | 161.29 | 241.44 | 262.27 | 424.36 | 452.08 | 576.50 | 560.28 |
| Claims on Other Sectors | 22s | 1,190.81 | 1,382.35 | 1,855.56 | 2,197.23 | 3,454.36 | 4,076.36 | 5,488.03 | 7,285.77 | 8,130.66 | 8,657.50 | 9,856.95 | 11,355.26 |
| Claims on Other Financial Corps. | 22g | 11.66 | 8.10 | 9.09 | 34.75 | 57.07 | 45.60 | 20.12 | 26.70 | 25.47 | 29.73 | 21.58 | 38.36 |
| Claims on State & Local Govts. | 22b | .58 | .39 | 1.73 | .13 | .45 | .01 | 1.19 | .68 | 1.06 | .81 | .62 | 1.81 |
| Claims on Public Nonfin. Corps. | 22c | 9.05 | 14.06 | 29.20 | 22.86 | 19.64 | 52.92 | 28.90 | 42.86 | 39.15 | 46.45 | 50.67 | 31.15 |
| Claims on Private Sector | 22d | 1,169.52 | 1,359.79 | 1,815.54 | 2,139.49 | 3,377.19 | 3,977.83 | 5,437.83 | 7,215.52 | 8,064.98 | 8,580.51 | 9,784.08 | 11,283.94 |
| Liabilities to Central Bank | 26g | 248.77 | 209.70 | 218.50 | 46.36 | 52.14 | 35.66 | 161.46 | 319.67 | 52.75 | 50.30 | 49.02 | 71.86 |
| Transf.Dep.Included in Broad Money | 24 | 1,260.91 | 1,401.35 | 1,631.70 | 2,063.20 | 2,525.60 | 3,071.21 | 4,148.53 | 4,268.57 | 5,101.78 | 5,593.62 | 6,398.38 | 7,024.44 |
| Other Dep.Included in Broad Money | 25 | 797.16 | 989.88 | 1,108.68 | 1,337.26 | 2,005.60 | 2,396.74 | 3,456.28 | 4,203.46 | 4,775.47 | 5,305.31 | 6,130.56 | 6,877.19 |
| Sec.Ot.th.Shares Incl.in Brd. Money | 26a | — | — | — | — | — | — | — | — | — | — | — | — |
| Deposits Excl. from Broad Money | 26b | — | — | — | — | — | — | — | 17.12 | 18.36 | 21.73 | 50.91 | 49.20 |
| Sec.Ot.th.Shares Excl.f/Brd.Money | 26s | — | — | — | — | — | — | 90.63 | 100.95 | 99.52 | 93.06 | 70.51 | 57.77 |
| Loans | 26l | 19.90 | 84.83 | 98.32 | 346.40 | 270.99 | 230.19 | 48.46 | 106.08 | 115.70 | 100.94 | 98.41 | 124.81 |
| Financial Derivatives | 26m | — | — | — | — | — | — | 21.10 | 9.03 | 3.71 | 9.78 | 18.66 | .86 |
| Insurance Technical Reserves | 26r | — | — | — | — | — | — | — | — | — | — | — | — |
| Shares and Other Equity | 27a | 387.20 | 381.06 | 484.29 | 696.74 | 1,155.60 | 1,381.00 | 1,513.65 | 2,022.70 | 2,612.08 | 2,804.98 | 3,279.90 | 3,705.22 |
| Other Items (Net) | 27r | 63.01 | 53.85 | 250.68 | 20.59 | 37.85 | −97.95 | −152.58 | −94.49 | −8.70 | −69.08 | −347.60 | −415.98 |
| Memo Item: |  |  |  |  |  |  |  |  |  |  |  |  |  |
| Total Assets | 20ra | 3,586.98 | 3,900.43 | 4,683.77 | 5,607.73 | 7,596.63 | 8,729.94 | 11,715.32 | 13,882.68 | 16,616.78 | 18,684.56 | 21,156.04 | 23,625.12 |

# Uganda   746

| | | 2004 | 2005 | 2006 | 2007 | 2008 | 2009 | 2010 | 2011 | 2012 | 2013 | 2014 | 2015 |
|---|---|---|---|---|---|---|---|---|---|---|---|---|---|
| **Depository Corporations** | | | | | | *Billions of Shillings: End of Period* | | | | | | | |
| Net Foreign Assets.................... | **31n** | 2,510.27 | 2,679.43 | 3,784.99 | 4,942.42 | 5,014.41 | 5,216.11 | 6,171.30 | 6,312.46 | 8,454.66 | 8,510.37 | 8,620.16 | 10,255.82 |
| Claims on Nonresidents................ | **31** | 3,042.45 | 3,114.85 | 4,072.57 | 5,363.72 | 5,587.58 | 6,313.47 | 7,600.00 | 7,813.38 | 10,428.88 | 11,654.70 | 11,307.30 | 13,690.99 |
| Liabilities to Nonresidents............. | **36c** | 532.18 | 435.43 | 287.58 | 421.30 | 573.17 | 1,097.36 | 1,428.70 | 1,500.93 | 1,974.22 | 3,144.33 | 2,687.15 | 3,435.16 |
| Domestic Claims....................... | **32** | 1,262.76 | 1,386.09 | 1,367.66 | 1,163.67 | 2,969.55 | 3,551.58 | 5,968.45 | 7,588.85 | 8,170.32 | 9,057.95 | 11,508.85 | 13,327.18 |
| Net Claims on Central Government | **32an** | −28.38 | −58.84 | −562.14 | −1,109.94 | −553.31 | −567.57 | 436.86 | 239.38 | −28.99 | 346.00 | 1,584.22 | 1,891.32 |
| Claims on Central Government.... | **32a** | 2,605.82 | 2,586.32 | 2,610.63 | 3,624.77 | 4,324.82 | 4,746.76 | 6,807.48 | 8,112.88 | 10,127.92 | 12,142.48 | 6,960.30 | 6,229.03 |
| Liabilities to Central Government. | **36d** | 2,634.20 | 2,645.16 | 3,172.77 | 4,734.71 | 4,878.13 | 5,314.34 | 6,370.62 | 7,873.50 | 10,156.91 | 11,796.48 | 5,376.07 | 4,337.71 |
| Claims on Other Sectors................ | **32s** | 1,291.14 | 1,444.92 | 1,929.80 | 2,273.61 | 3,522.86 | 4,119.15 | 5,531.59 | 7,349.47 | 8,199.31 | 8,711.95 | 9,924.63 | 11,435.86 |
| Claims on Other Financial Corps.. | **32g** | 38.40 | 42.72 | 53.69 | 78.81 | 93.26 | 70.57 | 37.09 | 36.28 | 30.95 | 36.11 | 29.65 | 49.77 |
| Claims on State & Local Govts..... | **32b** | .58 | .39 | 1.73 | .13 | .45 | .01 | 1.19 | .68 | 1.06 | .81 | .62 | 1.81 |
| Claims on Public Nonfin. Corps.... | **32c** | 14.32 | 18.92 | 33.63 | 26.96 | 23.75 | 53.28 | 29.26 | 43.22 | 39.51 | 46.45 | 50.67 | 31.15 |
| Claims on Private Sector............. | **32d** | 1,237.84 | 1,382.89 | 1,840.74 | 2,167.71 | 3,405.40 | 3,995.28 | 5,464.06 | 7,269.28 | 8,127.79 | 8,628.59 | 9,843.69 | 11,353.13 |
| Broad Money Liabilities.................. | **35l** | 2,646.68 | 3,101.45 | 3,626.25 | 4,422.79 | 5,785.73 | 6,797.70 | 9,386.51 | 10,550.48 | 12,123.13 | 13,270.54 | 15,286.51 | 17,069.55 |
| Currency Outside Depository Corps | **34a** | 588.61 | 710.22 | 885.87 | 1,022.33 | 1,254.52 | 1,329.75 | 1,781.70 | 2,078.45 | 2,245.87 | 2,371.62 | 2,757.57 | 3,167.92 |
| Transferable Deposits.................. | **34** | 1,260.91 | 1,401.35 | 1,631.70 | 2,063.20 | 2,525.60 | 3,071.21 | 4,148.53 | 4,268.57 | 5,101.78 | 5,593.62 | 6,398.38 | 7,024.44 |
| Other Deposits............................. | **35** | 797.16 | 989.88 | 1,108.68 | 1,337.26 | 2,005.60 | 2,396.74 | 3,456.28 | 4,203.46 | 4,775.47 | 5,305.31 | 6,130.56 | 6,877.19 |
| Securities Other than Shares.......... | **36a** | — | — | — | — | — | — | | | | | | |
| Deposits Excl. from Broad Money..... | **36b** | 1.78 | 1.96 | 4.94 | 1.05 | .17 | .05 | .36 | 19.07 | 18.36 | 21.81 | 50.97 | 49.22 |
| Sec.Ot.th.Shares Excl.f/Brd.Money.... | **36s** | — | — | — | — | — | — | 90.63 | 100.95 | 99.52 | 93.06 | 70.51 | 57.77 |
| Loans.......................................... | **36l** | 19.90 | 84.83 | 98.32 | 346.40 | 270.99 | 230.19 | 48.46 | 106.08 | 115.70 | 100.94 | 98.41 | 124.81 |
| Financial Derivatives.................... | **36m** | — | — | — | — | — | — | 21.10 | 9.03 | 3.71 | 9.78 | 18.66 | .86 |
| Insurance Technical Reserves............. | **36r** | — | — | — | — | — | — | | | | | | |
| Shares and Other Equity................. | **37a** | 783.47 | 705.95 | 835.23 | 1,136.28 | 1,750.20 | 1,966.70 | 2,826.42 | 3,337.89 | 4,360.88 | 4,307.54 | 5,374.48 | 7,280.46 |
| Other Items (Net)........................... | **37r** | 321.21 | 171.33 | 587.91 | 199.56 | 176.87 | −226.97 | −233.72 | −222.19 | −96.30 | −235.35 | −770.53 | −999.67 |
| Broad Money Liabs., Seasonally Adj. | **35l.b** | 2,646.86 | 3,092.67 | 3,600.75 | 4,378.10 | 5,719.03 | 6,717.20 | 9,264.91 | 10,408.92 | 11,962.51 | 13,094.33 | 15,080.54 | 16,837.13 |
| **Monetary Aggregates** | | | | | | *Billions of Shillings: End of Period* | | | | | | | |
| Broad Money.............................. | **59m** | 2,646.68 | 3,101.45 | 3,626.25 | 4,422.79 | 5,785.73 | 6,797.70 | 9,386.51 | 10,550.48 | 12,123.13 | 13,270.54 | 15,286.51 | 17,069.55 |
| o/w:Currency Issued by Cent.Govt | **59m.a** | — | — | — | — | — | — | — | — | — | — | — | — |
| o/w: Dep.in Nonfin. Corporations. | **59m.b** | — | — | — | — | — | — | — | — | — | — | — | — |
| o/w: Secs. Issued by Central Govt. | **59m.c** | — | — | — | — | — | — | — | — | — | — | — | — |
| Money (National Definitions) | | | | | | | | | | | | | |
| Base Money.............................. | **19ma** | 924.57 | 1,051.21 | 1,226.60 | 1,543.53 | 1,926.96 | 2,181.52 | 2,878.52 | 3,301.31 | 3,976.34 | 4,022.38 | 5,188.54 | 5,707.18 |
| M1............................................ | **59ma** | 1,328.02 | 1,606.55 | 1,890.27 | 2,287.02 | 2,891.56 | 3,308.00 | 4,393.16 | 4,546.75 | 5,413.53 | 5,736.51 | 6,634.15 | 6,851.67 |
| M2............................................ | **59mb** | 2,000.53 | 2,435.65 | 2,831.42 | 3,388.31 | 4,522.51 | 5,385.08 | 7,249.46 | 7,762.54 | 8,844.41 | 9,583.00 | 11,081.07 | 11,678.20 |
| M2A........................................ | **59mba** | 2,000.53 | 2,435.65 | 2,831.42 | 3,388.31 | 4,522.51 | 5,385.08 | 7,249.46 | 7,762.54 | 8,844.41 | 9,583.00 | 11,081.07 | 11,678.20 |
| M3............................................ | **59mc** | 2,646.68 | 3,101.45 | 3,626.25 | 4,422.79 | 5,785.73 | 6,797.70 | 9,386.51 | 10,550.48 | 12,123.13 | 13,270.54 | 15,286.51 | 17,069.55 |
| **Interest Rates** | | | | | | *Percent Per Annum* | | | | | | | |
| Discount Rate (End of Period).......... | **60.a** | 16.15 | 14.36 | 16.30 | 14.68 | 19.42 | 9.65 | 11.97 | 29.00 | 17.00 | 15.50 | 15.00 | 22.00 |
| Treasury Bill Rate.......................... | **60c** | 9.02 | 8.50 | 8.12 | 9.05 | 9.08 | 7.10 | 5.01 | 14.61 | 15.70 | 9.92 | 10.23 | 15.83 |
| Savings Rate................................ | **60k** | 2.03 | 1.83 | 2.02 | 2.32 | 2.31 | 2.29 | 2.38 | 2.35 | 3.23 | 2.94 | 2.72 | 3.35 |
| Deposit Rate................................ | **60l** | 7.74 | 8.79 | 9.09 | 9.26 | 10.67 | 9.75 | 7.69 | 13.02 | 16.23 | 11.84 | 10.81 | 12.77 |
| Lending Rate................................ | **60p** | 20.60 | 19.65 | 18.70 | 19.11 | 20.45 | 20.96 | 20.17 | 21.83 | 26.31 | 23.25 | 21.53 | 22.60 |
| **Prices** | | | | | | *Index Numbers (2010=100): Period Averages* | | | | | | | |
| Consumer Prices........................... | **64** | 61.5 | 66.7 | † 71.6 | 75.9 | 85.1 | 96.2 | 100.0 | 118.7 | 135.3 | 142.7 | 148.8 | † 156.6 |
| **Intl. Transactions & Positions** | | | | | | *Millions of Shillings* | | | | | | | |
| Exports........................................ | **70** | 1,374,239 | 1,810,955 | 2,175,107 | 3,445,307 | 4,651,150 | 6,066,443 | 6,750,428 | 6,082,239 | 7,167,848 | 7,372,068 | 6,928,948 | 8,704,335 |
| Imports, c.i.f. (Cash Basis)............... | **71** | 3,124,586 | 3,657,731 | 4,683,589 | 6,020,767 | 7,786,486 | 8,624,236 | 10,256,296 | 11,567,072 | 13,087,548 | 12,738,605 | 13,219,685 | 15,377,275 |

# Uganda 746

| | | 2004 | 2005 | 2006 | 2007 | 2008 | 2009 | 2010 | 2011 | 2012 | 2013 | 2014 | 2015 |
|---|---|---|---|---|---|---|---|---|---|---|---|---|---|
| **Balance of Payments** | | | | | | | *Millions of US Dollars* | | | | | | |
| A. Current Account* | 109bx | −60.7 | −12.8 | −363.5 | −619.4 | −1,269.8 | −1,092.3 | −1,659.1 | −2,116.7 | −1,710.8 | −1,845.5 | −2,430.6 | −2,305.5 |
| Goods, credit (exports) | 1a9cx | 759.1 | 1,015.9 | 1,187.6 | 1,776.2 | 2,207.6 | 2,326.6 | 2,164.0 | 2,519.1 | 2,810.5 | 2,828.7 | 2,724.8 | 2,667.2 |
| Goods, debit (imports) | 1a9dx | 1,426.8 | 1,745.6 | 2,215.6 | 2,958.2 | 4,042.8 | 3,835.2 | 4,375.7 | 4,996.7 | 5,261.5 | 4,974.1 | 5,099.6 | 4,911.4 |
| Balance on goods | 1a9bx | −667.6 | −729.7 | −1,027.9 | −1,182.0 | −1,835.1 | −1,508.7 | −2,211.7 | −2,477.6 | −2,451.1 | −2,145.4 | −2,374.8 | −2,244.2 |
| Services, credit (exports) | 1b9cx | 373.2 | 526.2 | 548.0 | 662.9 | 832.1 | 1,027.2 | 1,303.7 | 1,778.5 | 2,117.9 | 2,498.5 | 2,006.8 | 2,180.2 |
| Services, debit (imports) | 1b9dx | 489.6 | 608.8 | 770.5 | 977.2 | 1,257.4 | 1,393.0 | 1,802.7 | 2,434.5 | 2,485.2 | 2,774.3 | 2,705.9 | 2,734.0 |
| Balance on Goods & Services | 1z9bx | −784.0 | −812.4 | −1,250.5 | −1,496.4 | −2,260.4 | −1,874.4 | −2,710.7 | −3,133.6 | −2,818.4 | −2,421.2 | −3,074.0 | −2,797.9 |
| Primary income: credit | 1c9cx | 35.7 | 49.8 | 71.9 | 97.1 | 130.2 | 44.7 | 60.0 | 17.1 | 75.1 | −12.3 | 27.9 | 31.9 |
| Primary income: debit | 1c9dx | 314.2 | 286.9 | 300.4 | 327.9 | 380.0 | 409.9 | 321.5 | 424.2 | 532.9 | 620.0 | 593.1 | 925.5 |
| Balance on gds, serv. & prim. inc. | 1y9bx | −1,062.5 | −1,049.4 | −1,479.0 | −1,727.3 | −2,510.2 | −2,239.7 | −2,972.2 | −3,540.6 | −3,276.2 | −3,053.5 | −3,639.1 | −3,691.5 |
| Secondary income: credit | 1d9ca | 1,143.5 | 1,181.4 | 1,300.9 | 1,311.0 | 1,564.0 | 1,541.2 | 1,563.0 | 1,719.1 | 1,713.1 | 1,415.6 | 1,402.0 | 1,560.9 |
| Secondary income: debit | 1d9da | 141.7 | 144.8 | 185.5 | 203.2 | 323.7 | 393.8 | 250.0 | 295.1 | 147.8 | 207.5 | 193.4 | 174.8 |
| B. Capital Account* | 209ba | — | — | — | — | — | — | — | 12.0 | 21.8 | 80.0 | 94.7 | 108.1 |
| Capital account: credit | 209ca | — | — | — | — | — | — | — | 12.0 | 21.8 | 80.0 | 94.7 | 108.1 |
| Capital account: debit | 209da | .... | .... | .... | .... | .... | .... | .... | .... | .... | .... | .... | .... |
| Balance on current & capital acct. | 129ba | −60.7 | −12.8 | −363.5 | −619.4 | −1,269.8 | −1,092.3 | −1,659.1 | −2,104.6 | −1,689.0 | −1,765.5 | −2,335.9 | −2,197.3 |
| C. Financial Account* | 309na | −500.1 | −565.5 | −745.8 | −1,305.3 | −1,195.1 | −1,502.4 | −1,070.5 | −1,510.8 | −1,622.3 | −1,366.6 | −1,850.0 | −1,492.6 |
| Direct investment: assets | 3a9aa | .... | .... | .... | .... | .... | 28.9 | 37.2 | −11.8 | 46.3 | −47.2 | 27.0 | .3 |
| Equity & investment fund shares.. | 3aaaa | .... | .... | .... | .... | .... | 25.7 | 36.8 | −10.5 | 47.0 | −45.8 | .6 | .3 |
| Debt instruments | 3abaa | .... | .... | .... | .... | .... | 3.1 | .4 | −1.3 | −.7 | −1.4 | 26.4 | — |
| Direct investment: liabilities | 3a9la | 295.4 | 379.8 | 644.3 | 792.3 | 728.9 | 841.6 | 543.9 | 894.3 | 1,205.4 | 1,096.0 | 1,058.6 | 1,057.3 |
| Equity & investment fund shares . | 3aala | 305.9 | 381.2 | 639.8 | 742.1 | 577.6 | 770.6 | 248.0 | 573.0 | 921.7 | 848.2 | 741.4 | 775.3 |
| Debt instruments | 3abla | −10.4 | −1.4 | 4.5 | 50.2 | 151.2 | 71.0 | 295.9 | 321.2 | 283.6 | 247.8 | 317.1 | 282.0 |
| Portfolio investment: assets | 3b9aa | .... | .... | .... | .... | 12.1 | — | — | −2.6 | 8.9 | 194.3 | 147.9 | 164.8 |
| Equity & investment fund shares | 3baaa | .... | .... | .... | .... | 12.1 | — | — | −2.6 | 5.7 | 18.3 | 26.3 | 111.2 |
| Debt securities | 3bbaa | .... | .... | .... | .... | .... | .... | .... | .... | 3.2 | 176.0 | 121.7 | 53.7 |
| Portfolio investment: liabilities | 3b9la | 6.2 | −13.4 | 21.7 | 67.7 | 29.7 | 28.7 | −110.5 | 256.8 | 12.0 | 179.8 | 199.8 | −63.8 |
| Equity & investment fund shares . | 3bala | 24.0 | .... | 19.1 | −23.1 | 13.1 | 131.1 | −70.5 | 105.5 | 14.1 | 94.8 | 4.8 | 3.4 |
| Debt securities | 3bbla | −17.8 | −13.4 | 2.5 | 90.8 | 16.6 | −102.3 | −40.0 | 151.2 | −2.1 | 84.9 | 195.0 | −67.3 |
| Fin. der.& empl.stk.ops.(ESOs): net. | 3c9na | .... | .... | .... | −1.4 | −6.9 | 6.2 | 1.4 | −5.5 | −3.8 | −1.7 | −2.6 | −5.0 |
| Fin. der. & ESOs.: assets | 3c9aa | .... | .... | .... | 7.6 | 25.8 | 21.2 | 10.0 | 14.6 | 14.9 | 7.5 | 10.1 | 14.9 |
| Fin. der. & ESOs.: liabilities | 3c9la | .... | .... | .... | 9.0 | 32.6 | 15.0 | 8.5 | 20.1 | 18.7 | 9.2 | 12.7 | 19.9 |
| Other investment: assets | 3d9aa | −25.0 | −50.0 | 83.5 | 92.3 | −38.7 | 213.3 | 107.1 | −3.1 | 327.6 | 458.8 | −457.8 | 436.2 |
| Other equity | 3daaa | .... | .... | .... | .... | .... | .... | .... | .... | .... | .... | — | — |
| Debt instruments | 3dzaa | −25.0 | −50.0 | 83.5 | 92.3 | −38.7 | 213.3 | 107.1 | −3.1 | 327.6 | 458.8 | −457.8 | 436.2 |
| Other investment: liabilities | 3d9la | 173.4 | 149.1 | 163.4 | 536.3 | 403.1 | 880.4 | 782.9 | 336.7 | 784.0 | 695.0 | 306.1 | 1,095.5 |
| Other equity | 3dala | .... | .... | .... | .... | .... | .... | .... | .... | 29.4 | 4.0 | .6 | −7.3 |
| Debt instruments | 3dzla | 173.4 | 149.1 | 163.4 | 536.3 | 403.1 | 880.4 | 782.9 | 336.7 | 754.6 | 691.0 | 305.5 | 1,102.7 |
| Curr.+ cap.− finan. acct. balance... | 4y9na | 439.4 | 552.7 | 382.3 | 685.8 | −74.7 | 410.1 | −588.6 | −593.8 | −66.7 | −398.9 | −485.9 | −704.7 |
| D. Net Errors and Omissions | 409na | −298.9 | −450.4 | −11.8 | −22.3 | 90.6 | −258.1 | 497.6 | 461.0 | 554.5 | 580.0 | 510.2 | 264.6 |
| E. Reserves and Related Items | 4z9na | 140.5 | 102.2 | 370.5 | 663.5 | 15.9 | 152.0 | −91.1 | −132.9 | 487.9 | 181.1 | 24.3 | −440.1 |
| Reserve assets | 3e9aa | 162.0 | 92.5 | 403.0 | 713.5 | 42.9 | 184.7 | −44.8 | −87.1 | 528.7 | 223.4 | 76.0 | −388.8 |
| Credit and loans from the IMF | 3dcla | −52.7 | −46.2 | −124.0 | — | — | — | −.3 | −1.6 | −1.8 | −1.8 | −1.8 | −1.4 |
| Exceptional financing | 409la | 74.2 | 36.4 | 156.5 | 50.0 | 27.0 | 32.7 | 46.6 | 47.4 | 42.7 | 44.1 | 53.6 | 52.7 |
| *Excludes components in group E | | | | | | | | | | | | | |
| | | | | | | | | | | | | | |
| **International Investment Position** | | | | | | | *Millions of US Dollars* | | | | | | |
| Assets | 809aa | 2,069.8 | 2,013.7 | 2,617.0 | 3,398.5 | 3,085.0 | 3,666.0 | 3,572.1 | 3,453.7 | 4,325.1 | 5,058.6 | 4,848.0 | 5,029.2 |
| Direct investment | 8a9aa | .... | .... | .... | .... | .... | 28.9 | 66.1 | 54.2 | 100.6 | 53.3 | 80.4 | 80.7 |
| Equity & investment fund shares.. | 8aaaa | .... | .... | .... | .... | .... | 25.7 | 62.5 | 52.0 | 99.0 | 53.2 | 53.8 | 54.1 |
| Debt instruments | 8abaa | .... | .... | .... | .... | .... | 3.1 | 3.5 | 2.2 | 1.6 | .1 | 26.6 | 26.6 |
| Portfolio investment | 8b9aa | .... | .... | .... | .... | 12.1 | 12.1 | 12.1 | 9.5 | 18.4 | 212.7 | 360.6 | 525.5 |
| Equity & investment fund shares.. | 8baaa | .... | .... | .... | .... | 12.1 | 12.1 | 12.1 | 9.5 | 15.2 | 33.4 | 59.7 | 170.9 |
| Debt securities | 8bbaa | .... | .... | .... | .... | .... | .... | .... | .... | 3.2 | 179.2 | 300.9 | 354.6 |
| Fin. der.(oth.than reserves) & ESOs | 8c9aa | .... | .... | .... | .... | .... | .... | — | — | .1 | .1 | .6 | .1 |
| Other investment | 8d9aa | 761.7 | 669.4 | 806.1 | 967.7 | 872.2 | 1,118.4 | 1,077.7 | 1,028.4 | 1,295.9 | 1,689.5 | 1,187.8 | 1,533.1 |
| Other equity | 8daaa | .... | .... | .... | .... | .... | .... | .... | .... | .... | .... | .... | .... |
| Debt instruments | 8dzaa | 761.7 | 669.4 | 806.1 | 967.7 | 872.2 | 1,118.4 | 1,077.7 | 1,028.4 | 1,295.9 | 1,689.5 | 1,187.8 | 1,533.1 |
| Reserve assets | 8e9aa | 1,308.1 | 1,344.2 | 1,810.9 | 2,430.9 | 2,200.7 | 2,506.7 | 2,416.2 | 2,361.5 | 2,910.1 | 3,103.0 | 3,218.6 | 2,889.8 |
| Liabilities | 809la | 6,972.7 | 6,934.8 | 4,370.1 | 5,879.1 | 6,959.5 | 8,846.3 | 10,161.0 | 11,645.6 | 13,701.4 | 15,761.1 | 17,007.2 | 18,842.9 |
| Direct investment | 8a9la | 1,644.6 | 2,024.4 | 2,668.6 | 3,460.9 | 4,189.8 | 5,031.4 | 5,575.2 | 6,469.5 | 7,674.9 | 8,770.9 | 9,829.5 | 10,886.8 |
| Equity & investment fund shares.. | 8aala | 1,301.9 | 1,683.1 | 2,322.9 | 3,065.0 | 3,642.7 | 4,413.2 | 4,661.2 | 5,234.3 | 6,156.0 | 7,004.2 | 7,745.6 | 8,520.9 |
| Debt instruments | 8abla | 342.7 | 341.2 | 345.7 | 395.9 | 547.1 | 618.1 | 914.0 | 1,235.3 | 1,518.9 | 1,766.7 | 2,083.9 | 2,365.9 |
| Portfolio investment | 8b9la | 29.1 | 32.8 | 51.6 | 148.3 | 128.9 | 194.9 | 119.6 | 356.0 | 335.4 | 508.3 | 679.9 | 656.3 |
| Equity & investment fund shares.. | 8bala | 24.6 | 24.6 | 43.8 | 70.0 | 37.6 | 153.1 | 103.3 | 179.2 | 205.8 | 274.7 | 334.0 | 324.0 |
| Debt securities | 8bbla | 4.4 | 8.1 | 7.8 | 78.3 | 91.3 | 41.8 | 16.2 | 176.9 | 129.5 | 233.7 | 345.9 | 332.4 |
| Fin. der.(oth.than reserves) & ESOs | 8c9la | .... | .... | .... | .... | .... | .... | .5 | .5 | .... | .2 | 1.0 | 1.9 |
| Other investment | 8d9la | 5,299.0 | 4,877.7 | 1,649.9 | 2,269.8 | 2,640.8 | 3,620.1 | 4,465.6 | 4,819.5 | 5,691.1 | 6,481.7 | 6,496.8 | 7,297.8 |
| Other equity | 8dala | .... | .... | .... | .... | .... | .... | .... | .... | 29.4 | 33.4 | 34.1 | 26.8 |
| Debt instruments | 8dzla | 5,299.0 | 4,877.7 | 1,649.9 | 2,269.8 | 2,640.8 | 3,620.1 | 4,465.6 | 4,819.5 | 5,661.7 | 6,448.2 | 6,462.7 | 7,271.1 |

# Uganda  746

|  |  | 2004 | 2005 | 2006 | 2007 | 2008 | 2009 | 2010 | 2011 | 2012 | 2013 | 2014 | 2015 |
|---|---|---|---|---|---|---|---|---|---|---|---|---|---|
| **Government Finance** | | | | | | | | | | | | | |
| **Cash Flow Statement** | | | | | | | | | | | | | |
| **Budgetary Central Government** | | | | | *Billions of Shillings: Fiscal Year Ends June 30* | | | | | | | |
| Cash Receipts:Operating Activities... | c1 | .... | .... | .... | 3,810.3 | 3,985.4 | 4,671.4 | 5,183.1 | 7,292.5 | 7,763.4 | 8,277.0 | 8,870.3 | 11,044.8 |
| Taxes............................................. | c11 | .... | .... | .... | 2,625.8 | 3,161.1 | 3,662.3 | 4,205.7 | 6,306.9 | 6,528.3 | 7,149.5 | 8,031.0 | 9,892.5 |
| Social Contributions...................... | c12 | .... | .... | .... | — | — | — | — | — | — | — | | |
| Grants........................................... | c13 | .... | .... | .... | 1,087.8 | 738.6 | 884.8 | 863.6 | 890.5 | 1,129.3 | 936.2 | 702.4 | 930.8 |
| Other Receipts.............................. | c14 | .... | .... | .... | 96.7 | 85.7 | 124.3 | 113.9 | 95.1 | 105.9 | 191.4 | 136.9 | 221.5 |
| Cash Payments:Operating Activities. | c2 | .... | .... | .... | 3,487.3 | 3,761.9 | 4,173.6 | 5,694.2 | 7,408.5 | 7,176.9 | 7,454.2 | 8,649.4 | 9,698.4 |
| Compensation of Employees......... | c21 | .... | .... | .... | 416.0 | 472.8 | 589.9 | 706.1 | 985.0 | 1,199.0 | 1,403.2 | 1,564.7 | 1,762.9 |
| Purchases of Goods & Services....... | c22 | .... | .... | .... | 979.9 | 1,050.4 | 1,302.2 | 1,874.1 | 2,715.9 | 2,001.2 | 1,708.9 | 2,124.4 | 2,505.5 |
| Interest......................................... | c24 | .... | .... | .... | 234.0 | 309.4 | 357.9 | 385.1 | 423.5 | 603.3 | 889.7 | 1,081.4 | 1,213.0 |
| Subsidies...................................... | c25 | .... | .... | .... | 220.7 | 87.4 | 92.0 | 87.4 | 184.0 | 186.8 | 29.0 | 35.7 | 68.0 |
| Grants........................................... | c26 | .... | .... | .... | 1,539.0 | 1,747.3 | 1,692.7 | 2,201.1 | 2,644.7 | 2,783.0 | 2,879.3 | 3,227.2 | 3,666.6 |
| Social Benefits.............................. | c27 | .... | .... | .... | 78.6 | 78.5 | 79.0 | 222.4 | 203.2 | 201.1 | 260.3 | 228.7 | 244.2 |
| Other Payments............................ | c28 | .... | .... | .... | 19.2 | 16.0 | 60.0 | 218.1 | 252.1 | 202.6 | 283.7 | 387.4 | 238.2 |
| Net Cash Inflow:Operating Act.[1-2] | ccio | .... | .... | .... | 323.0 | 223.5 | 497.8 | −511.1 | −116.0 | 586.4 | 822.9 | 221.0 | 1,346.2 |
| Net Cash Outflow:Invest. in NFA...... | c31 | .... | .... | .... | 468.9 | 556.1 | 775.3 | 1,091.3 | 1,400.5 | 1,846.9 | 2,595.1 | 2,912.5 | 3,220.3 |
| Purchases of Nonfinancial Assets... | c31.1 | .... | .... | .... | 468.9 | 556.1 | 775.3 | 1,091.3 | 1,400.5 | 1,846.9 | 2,595.1 | 2,912.4 | 3,220.3 |
| Sales of Nonfinancial Assets.......... | c31.2 | .... | .... | .... | — | — | — | — | — | — | — | — | — |
| Cash Surplus/Deficit [1-2-31=1-2M] | ccsd | .... | .... | .... | −145.9 | −332.6 | −277.5 | −1,602.3 | −1,516.5 | −1,260.4 | −1,772.2 | −2,691.5 | −1,874.1 |
| Net Acq. Fin. Assets, excl. Cash....... | c32x | .... | .... | .... | 101.1 | −162.9 | −56.7 | −36.7 | −30.2 | −185.5 | 539.7 | .... | .... |
| Domestic...................................... | c321x | .... | .... | .... | 1,100.3 | 675.3 | 424.3 | 265.5 | 1,682.3 | 2,759.6 | 1,876.9 | | |
| Foreign......................................... | c322x | .... | .... | .... | .... | .... | .... | .... | .... | .... | .... | | |
| Net Incurrence of Liabilities............. | c33 | .... | .... | .... | 1,266.9 | 890.9 | 764.2 | 1,679.7 | 3,347.2 | 3,688.6 | 3,539.9 | −1,892.9 | 615.1 |
| Domestic...................................... | c331 | .... | .... | .... | 366.6 | 539.0 | 207.2 | 921.4 | 2,623.1 | 2,534.7 | 2,122.0 | −2,753.4 | −303.9 |
| Foreign......................................... | c332 | .... | .... | .... | 900.3 | 351.7 | 557.1 | 758.3 | 724.1 | 1,153.9 | 1,417.9 | 860.5 | 919.0 |
| Net Cash Inflow, Fin.Act.[-32x+33].. | cnfb | .... | .... | .... | 1,165.8 | 1,053.6 | 820.9 | 1,716.4 | 3,377.5 | 3,874.1 | 3,000.2 | .... | .... |
| Net Change in Stock of Cash........... | cncb | .... | .... | .... | 1,100.3 | 675.3 | 424.3 | 265.5 | 1,682.3 | 2,759.6 | 1,876.9 | .... | .... |
| Stat. Discrep. [32X-33+NCB-CSD].... | ccsdz | .... | .... | .... | 80.4 | −45.7 | −119.1 | 151.5 | −178.7 | 146.0 | 649.0 | | |
| Memo Item:Cash Expenditure[2+31] | c2m | .... | .... | .... | 3,956.2 | 4,318.0 | 4,949.0 | 6,785.5 | 8,809.0 | 9,023.8 | 10,049.3 | 11,561.8 | 12,918.8 |
| Memo Item: Gross Debt.................. | c63 | .... | .... | .... | .... | .... | .... | .... | .... | | | | |
| **National Accounts** | | | | | *Billions of Shillings* | | | | | | | |
| Househ.Cons.Expend.,incl.NPISHs.... | 96f | 10,290.5 | 11,818.2 | 14,138.9 | 16,439.4 | 18,007.9 | 23,506.8 | 27,856.0 | 32,694.0 | 41,646.0 | 42,617.0 | .... | .... |
| Government Consumption Expend... | 91f | 2,133.4 | 2,326.2 | 2,567.9 | 2,695.0 | 2,746.4 | 3,035.4 | 3,374.0 | 3,839.0 | 4,039.0 | 5,089.0 | .... | .... |
| Gross Fixed Capital Formation.......... | 93e | 3,063.9 | 3,563.5 | 3,810.3 | 4,966.3 | 5,572.7 | 6,532.3 | 8,109.0 | 9,686.0 | 12,211.0 | 13,514.0 | .... | .... |
| Changes in Inventories.................... | 93i | 30.9 | 24.6 | 37.4 | 45.4 | 56.2 | 75.8 | 82.0 | 89.0 | 116.0 | 126.0 | .... | .... |
| Exports of Goods and Services......... | 90c | 1,950.5 | 2,275.9 | 2,781.6 | 3,256.6 | 5,948.0 | 7,263.2 | 7,148.0 | 8,401.0 | 11,643.0 | 12,743.0 | .... | .... |
| Imports of Goods and Services (-)..... | 98c | 3,496.9 | 3,982.9 | 5,163.8 | 6,190.9 | 7,833.8 | 10,312.5 | 11,660.4 | 15,624.0 | 19,483.0 | 18,514.0 | .... | .... |
| Gross Domestic Product (GDP)........ | 99b | 13,972.3 | 16,025.5 | 18,172.3 | 21,211.9 | 24,497.4 | 30,101.0 | 34,908.4 | 39,086.0 | 50,172.0 | 55,574.0 | .... | .... |
| GDP Volume 1997/1998 Prices........ | 99b.p | 11,004.2 | .... | .... | .... | .... | .... | .... | .... | .... | .... | .... | .... |
| GDP Volume 2002 Prices................. | 99b.p | 13,069.8 | 13,897.4 | 15,396.2 | 16,685.2 | 18,145.0 | 19,460.8 | 20,601.4 | 21,977.6 | 22,841.3 | 24,031.0 | .... | .... |
| GDP Volume (2010=100)............... | 99bvp | 63.4 | 67.5 | 74.7 | 81.0 | 88.1 | 94.5 | 100.0 | 106.7 | 110.9 | 116.6 | .... | .... |
| GDP Deflator (2010=100)............... | 99bip | 63.1 | 68.1 | 69.7 | 75.0 | 79.7 | 91.3 | 100.0 | 105.0 | 129.6 | 136.5 | .... | .... |
| | | | | | *Millions: Midyear Estimates* | | | | | | | |
| **Population................................** | 99z | 27.11 | 28.04 | 29.00 | 29.99 | 31.01 | 32.07 | 33.15 | 34.26 | 35.40 | 36.57 | 37.78 | 39.03 |

# Ukraine 926

| | | 2004 | 2005 | 2006 | 2007 | 2008 | 2009 | 2010 | 2011 | 2012 | 2013 | 2014 | 2015 |
|---|---|---|---|---|---|---|---|---|---|---|---|---|---|
| **Exchange Rates** | | | | | | | | | | | | | |
| Official Rate | aa | 8.2393 | 7.2178 | 7.5972 | 7.9803 | 11.8601 | 12.5180 | 12.2613 | 12.2665 | 12.2846 | 12.3092 | 22.8456 | 33.2584 |
| Official Rate | ae | 5.3054 | 5.0500 | 5.0500 | 5.0500 | 7.7000 | 7.9850 | 7.9617 | 7.9898 | 7.9930 | 7.9930 | 15.7686 | 24.0007 |
| Official Rate | rf | 5.3192 | 5.1247 | 5.0500 | 5.0500 | 5.2672 | 7.7912 | 7.9356 | 7.9676 | 7.9910 | 7.9930 | 11.8867 | 21.8447 |
| Nominal Effective Exchange Rate | nec | 154.6 | 157.4 | 158.3 | 147.6 | 137.0 | 102.6 | 100.0 | 98.1 | 104.6 | 105.5 | 77.2 | 50.7 |
| CPI-Based Real Effect. Ex. Rate | rec | 91.7 | 100.9 | 106.1 | 106.5 | 116.1 | 97.4 | 100.0 | 100.3 | 102.8 | 99.6 | 78.3 | 73.7 |
| **Fund Position** | | | | | | | | | | | | | |
| Quota | 2f.s | 1,372.00 | 1,372.00 | 1,372.00 | 1,372.00 | 1,372.00 | 1,372.00 | 1,372.00 | 1,372.00 | 1,372.00 | 1,372.00 | 1,372.00 | 1,372.00 |
| SDR Holdings | 1b.s | .75 | .70 | .99 | 1.78 | 5.59 | 40.55 | 5.17 | 11.66 | 5.98 | 10.36 | 2.58 | 6.37 |
| Reserve Position in the Fund | 1c.s | — | — | — | — | .02 | .02 | .02 | .02 | .02 | .02 | .02 | .02 |
| Total Fund Cred.&Loans Outstg | 2tl | 1,033.68 | 830.85 | 551.88 | 272.90 | 3,057.28 | 7,000.00 | 9,250.00 | 9,250.00 | 7,015.63 | 3,359.38 | 3,941.42 | 7,700.77 |
| SDR Allocations | 1bd | — | — | — | — | — | 1,309.44 | 1,309.44 | 1,309.44 | 1,309.44 | 1,309.44 | 1,309.44 | 1,309.44 |
| **International Liquidity** | | | | | | | | | | | | | |
| Total Reserves minus Gold | 1l.d | 9,490.7 | 18,988.0 | 21,844.6 | 31,786.0 | 30,800.6 | 25,556.9 | 33,327.4 | 30,409.3 | 22,655.8 | 18,775.5 | 6,622.2 | 12,368.1 |
| SDR Holdings | 1b.d | 1.2 | 1.0 | 1.5 | 2.8 | 8.6 | 63.6 | 8.0 | 17.9 | 9.2 | 15.9 | 3.7 | 8.8 |
| Reserve Position in the Fund | 1c.d | | | | | | | | | | | | |
| Foreign Exchange | 1d.d | 9,489.5 | 18,987.0 | 21,843.2 | 31,783.2 | 30,791.9 | 25,493.3 | 33,319.4 | 30,391.4 | 22,646.6 | 18,759.5 | 6,618.5 | 12,359.2 |
| Gold (Million Fine Troy Ounces) | 1ad | .5200 | .7800 | .8100 | .8370 | .8540 | .8680 | .8850 | .9010 | 1.1400 | 1.3600 | .7600 | .8800 |
| Gold (National Valuation) | 1and | 224.1 | 402.5 | 513.5 | 693.1 | 742.7 | 948.2 | 1,249.0 | 1,385.3 | 1,890.4 | 1,640.2 | 911.1 | 931.9 |
| Central Bank: Other Assets | 3..d | 408.4 | 726.4 | 801.6 | 1,281.2 | 1,174.1 | 1,428.0 | 2,046.5 | 1,132.7 | 887.5 | 1,337.0 | 333.0 | 4,580.1 |
| Central Bank: Other Liabs | 4..d | 327.6 | 75.3 | 61.5 | 37.6 | 35.2 | 36.8 | 31.9 | 34.1 | 31.9 | 5.8 | 8.5 | 5,683.3 |
| Other Depository Corps.: Assets | 7a.d | 2,304.2 | 2,832.8 | 4,073.4 | 6,061.4 | 7,494.3 | 10,186.8 | 11,555.2 | 13,235.5 | 16,089.9 | 13,262.1 | 8,156.4 | 7,554.4 |
| Other Depository Corps.: Liabs | 7b.d | 2,247.1 | 5,243.6 | 12,825.7 | 28,612.2 | 36,860.0 | 28,861.7 | 24,828.8 | 23,814.9 | 21,787.8 | 22,434.5 | 14,926.3 | 10,427.3 |
| Other Financial Corps.: Assets | 7e.d | .... | .... | .... | .... | 289.3 | 1,086.4 | 1,461.7 | 898.4 | 1,560.2 | 1,495.3 | 1,085.0 | 859.7 |
| Other Financial Corps.: Liabs | 7f.d | .... | .... | .... | .... | 4.2 | 644.6 | 707.4 | 535.1 | 2,807.6 | 3,037.7 | 2,680.3 | 1,508.0 |
| **Central Bank** | | | | | | | | | | | | | |
| Net Foreign Assets | 11n | 43,573.2 | 94,973.4 | 111,240.0 | 165,325.0 | 209,994.9 | 148,452.5 | 204,589.2 | 182,457.1 | 143,549.3 | 136,165.1 | 54,716.1 | 114,724.6 |
| Claims on Nonresidents | 11 | 53,828.2 | 101,350.6 | 115,743.1 | 167,692.4 | 246,525.8 | 215,393.3 | 281,371.3 | 259,314.8 | 199,414.7 | 167,325.1 | 120,406.5 | 426,838.2 |
| Liabilities to Nonresidents | 16c | 10,255.0 | 6,377.2 | 4,503.1 | 2,367.5 | 36,530.9 | 66,940.8 | 76,782.1 | 76,857.7 | 55,865.4 | 31,160.0 | 65,690.4 | 312,113.5 |
| Claims on Other Depository Corps | 12e | 4,210.4 | 895.1 | 1,579.6 | 1,876.5 | 61,162.3 | 87,515.2 | 74,937.3 | 74,654.0 | 79,187.2 | 80,579.5 | 113,772.8 | 106,443.5 |
| Net Claims on Central Government | 12an | 12,736.4 | −8,148.7 | −8,948.9 | −6,273.7 | 10,753.8 | 55,618.9 | 49,956.1 | 77,427.7 | 115,865.8 | 145,270.6 | 323,714.4 | 362,741.7 |
| Claims on Central Government | 12a | 18,000.8 | 10,315.1 | 9,676.1 | 9,057.8 | 23,673.9 | 57,011.0 | 71,525.8 | 89,650.0 | 117,165.2 | 149,131.0 | 338,111.2 | 413,643.3 |
| Liabilities to Central Government | 16d | 5,264.4 | 18,463.8 | 18,625.0 | 15,331.5 | 12,920.1 | 1,392.1 | 21,569.7 | 12,222.3 | 1,299.3 | 3,860.3 | 14,396.8 | 50,901.6 |
| Claims on Other Sectors | 12s | 281.5 | 279.5 | 350.2 | 347.0 | 701.5 | 1,911.9 | 1,821.8 | 1,999.3 | 5,198.7 | 7,899.6 | 5,598.4 | 2,623.1 |
| Claims on Other Financial Corps | 12g | 23.6 | 23.9 | 44.4 | 45.6 | 107.7 | 1,331.9 | 1,307.8 | 1,509.5 | 4,550.1 | 7,337.8 | 5,123.0 | 2,328.6 |
| Claims on State & Local Govts | 12b | — | — | .2 | — | — | 1.3 | .4 | 1.0 | 1.4 | 1.3 | 3.2 | .7 |
| Claims on Public Nonfin. Corps | 12c | 113.7 | 108.4 | 122.7 | 101.3 | 160.5 | 170.2 | 169.4 | 170.8 | 219.1 | 79.6 | 58.2 | 5.0 |
| Claims on Private Sector | 12d | 144.2 | 147.2 | 182.9 | 200.2 | 433.2 | 408.5 | 344.2 | 317.9 | 428.0 | 480.9 | 414.0 | 288.8 |
| Monetary Base | 14 | 53,763.2 | 82,759.7 | 97,214.2 | 141,901.1 | 186,670.9 | 194,965.3 | 225,691.8 | 239,884.8 | 255,283.4 | 307,138.8 | 333,194.2 | 335,999.6 |
| Currency in Circulation | 14a | 45,669.1 | 65,409.1 | 82,133.3 | 122,470.4 | 167,538.0 | 170,535.8 | 200,092.5 | 209,565.1 | 222,785.7 | 261,870.3 | 304,811.9 | 308,237.4 |
| Liabs. to Other Depository Corps | 14c | 8,017.8 | 17,252.4 | 14,899.0 | 19,049.9 | 18,622.7 | 23,183.1 | 24,404.5 | 29,185.1 | 31,157.5 | 43,963.9 | 27,488.9 | 27,699.0 |
| Liabilities to Other Sectors | 14d | 76.2 | 98.2 | 181.9 | 380.7 | 510.2 | 1,246.3 | 1,194.8 | 1,134.7 | 1,340.2 | 1,304.6 | 894.2 | 63.3 |
| Other Liabs. to Other Dep. Corps | 14n | 1,755.6 | 2,957.6 | 788.1 | 3,485.9 | 3,095.4 | 3,621.7 | 11,366.7 | 7,783.7 | 3,477.5 | 6,630.7 | 20,742.7 | 93,241.3 |
| Dep. & Sec. Excl. f/Monetary Base | 14o | 103.1 | 71.5 | 13.7 | 35.4 | 54.7 | 130.1 | 138.7 | 139.3 | 128.4 | 131.3 | 180.9 | 349.6 |
| Deposits Included in Broad Money | 15 | 102.9 | 71.2 | 13.4 | 35.0 | 54.1 | 129.8 | 138.5 | 139.3 | 128.4 | 131.3 | 177.9 | 349.3 |
| Sec.Ot.th.Shares Incl.in Brd. Money | 16a | — | — | — | — | — | — | — | — | — | — | — | — |
| Deposits Excl. from Broad Money | 16b | .2 | .3 | .3 | .5 | .6 | .3 | .3 | — | — | — | 3.0 | .3 |
| Sec.Ot.th.Shares Excl.f/Brd.Money | 16s | — | — | — | — | — | — | — | — | — | — | — | — |
| Loans | 16l | — | — | — | — | — | — | — | — | — | — | — | — |
| Financial Derivatives | 16m | — | — | — | — | — | — | — | — | — | — | — | — |
| Shares and Other Equity | 17a | 7,653.0 | 3,363.8 | 8,308.9 | 22,096.1 | 97,905.0 | 105,005.1 | 104,002.5 | 98,837.7 | 96,927.6 | 68,121.5 | 142,505.3 | 161,007.0 |
| Other Items (Net) | 17r | −2,473.3 | −1,153.3 | −2,104.0 | −6,243.7 | −5,113.4 | −10,223.7 | −9,895.4 | −10,107.4 | −12,015.7 | −12,107.5 | 1,178.5 | −4,064.7 |
| Memo Item: | | | | | | | | | | | | | |
| Total Assets | 10ra | 90,019.5 | 125,956.4 | 141,237.5 | 198,333.1 | 356,127.8 | 388,256.6 | 456,720.9 | 453,416.1 | 430,107.7 | 433,639.4 | 623,683.1 | 1,008,994.2 |

*Hryvnias per SDR: End of Period* (aa) — *Hryvnias per US Dollar: End of Period (ae) Period Average (rf)* — *Index Numbers (2010=100): Period Averages* (nec, rec) — *Millions of SDRs: End of Period* (Fund Position) — *Millions of US Dollars Unless Otherwise Indicated: End of Period* (International Liquidity) — *Millions of Hryvnias: End of Period* (Central Bank)

# Ukraine   926

| | | 2004 | 2005 | 2006 | 2007 | 2008 | 2009 | 2010 | 2011 | 2012 | 2013 | 2014 | 2015 |
|---|---|---|---|---|---|---|---|---|---|---|---|---|---|
| **Other Depository Corporations** | | *Millions of Hryvnias: End of Period* | | | | | | | | | | | |
| Net Foreign Assets | 21n | 303.4 | −12,174.6 | −44,198.8 | −113,881.5 | −226,115.8 | −149,119.7 | −105,680.0 | −84,527.6 | −45,543.3 | −73,315.1 | −106,751.7 | −68,951.1 |
| Claims on Nonresidents | 21 | 12,224.9 | 14,305.4 | 20,570.8 | 30,609.9 | 57,706.0 | 81,341.2 | 91,999.1 | 105,748.8 | 128,606.3 | 106,004.3 | 128,614.1 | 181,310.3 |
| Liabilities to Nonresidents | 26c | 11,921.5 | 26,480.1 | 64,769.6 | 144,491.4 | 283,821.8 | 230,460.9 | 197,679.1 | 190,276.5 | 174,149.7 | 179,319.3 | 235,365.8 | 250,261.4 |
| Claims on Central Bank | 20 | 11,808.3 | 24,988.1 | 22,614.4 | 33,576.2 | 34,326.1 | 40,394.1 | 52,746.7 | 53,765.9 | 53,649.5 | 74,461.2 | 69,042.5 | 142,425.5 |
| Currency | 20a | 3,324.2 | 5,177.7 | 7,149.7 | 11,351.7 | 12,779.4 | 13,506.4 | 17,102.6 | 16,900.3 | 19,540.7 | 24,093.7 | 21,864.0 | 25,564.5 |
| Reserve Deposits and Securities | 20b | 8,305.1 | 17,381.8 | 15,280.0 | 19,120.0 | 18,767.8 | 23,346.4 | 26,201.8 | 31,321.6 | 33,749.7 | 47,234.8 | 27,554.3 | 27,544.4 |
| Other Claims | 20n | 179.0 | 2,428.6 | 184.7 | 3,104.5 | 2,778.9 | 3,541.3 | 9,442.3 | 5,544.0 | 359.0 | 3,132.7 | 19,624.2 | 89,316.6 |
| Net Claims on Central Government | 22an | 1,779.4 | 2,379.6 | 2,191.8 | 2,744.0 | 13,032.0 | 16,649.6 | 63,259.7 | 67,184.9 | 65,689.0 | 95,984.8 | 115,130.3 | 100,866.8 |
| Claims on Central Government | 22a | 2,710.3 | 3,530.2 | 4,457.2 | 6,304.1 | 18,211.1 | 29,393.9 | 71,437.3 | 73,104.1 | 73,546.2 | 101,260.9 | 121,542.0 | 109,516.3 |
| Liabilities to Central Government | 26d | 930.9 | 1,150.6 | 2,265.4 | 3,560.1 | 5,179.1 | 12,744.2 | 8,177.6 | 5,919.3 | 7,857.2 | 5,276.1 | 6,411.7 | 8,649.5 |
| Claims on Other Sectors | 22s | 94,457.5 | 152,242.0 | 255,038.3 | 443,209.7 | 753,944.9 | 734,993.2 | 745,507.9 | 819,958.5 | 848,839.0 | 956,687.5 | 1,068,260.1 | 1,040,175.9 |
| Claims on Other Financial Corps. | 22g | 1,229.6 | 2,814.9 | 4,351.6 | 10,091.5 | 15,799.6 | 18,131.4 | 18,228.0 | 21,149.7 | 21,406.2 | 25,571.5 | 34,691.9 | 19,226.8 |
| Claims on State & Local Govts. | 22b | 187.5 | 316.7 | 362.8 | 466.7 | 490.0 | 1,905.6 | 1,979.3 | 2,321.5 | 6,763.0 | 6,776.5 | 6,268.9 | 3,533.1 |
| Claims on Public Nonfin. Corps. | 22c | 6,329.0 | 7,123.6 | 9,106.2 | 13,603.9 | 37,694.1 | 44,659.7 | 49,975.1 | 61,253.2 | 64,921.5 | 64,403.3 | 77,990.8 | 82,265.4 |
| Claims on Private Sector | 22d | 86,711.4 | 141,986.8 | 241,217.6 | 419,047.6 | 699,961.3 | 670,296.4 | 675,325.4 | 735,234.1 | 755,748.2 | 859,936.3 | 949,308.4 | 935,150.6 |
| Liabilities to Central Bank | 26g | 4,067.2 | 764.5 | 1,440.8 | 1,738.0 | 60,985.6 | 86,369.0 | 72,782.7 | 73,700.2 | 77,988.6 | 78,930.2 | 110,243.0 | 65,199.2 |
| Transf.Dep.Included in Broad Money | 24 | 31,593.4 | 48,115.5 | 61,136.3 | 90,364.1 | 104,807.2 | 116,785.8 | 147,135.9 | 169,019.4 | 175,484.7 | 196,984.0 | 239,165.9 | 290,944.0 |
| Other Dep.Included in Broad Money. | 25 | 51,366.0 | 84,629.0 | 123,098.0 | 189,374.3 | 252,396.9 | 209,580.6 | 265,381.7 | 318,842.8 | 390,928.0 | 470,040.0 | 432,163.5 | 419,782.1 |
| Sec.Ot.th.Shares Incl.in Brd. Money.. | 26a | 221.6 | 925.3 | 1,650.1 | 4,883.5 | 3,200.2 | 2,526.3 | 1,030.7 | 3,713.7 | 2,072.3 | 2,757.8 | 1,379.1 | 250.4 |
| Deposits Excl. from Broad Money | 26b | 1,192.6 | 1,725.9 | 1,416.6 | 3,535.5 | 1,920.9 | 446.2 | 207.9 | 159.6 | 140.8 | 188.6 | 206.4 | 634.8 |
| Sec.Ot.th.Shares Excl.f/Brd.Money.... | 26s | — | — | — | — | — | — | — | — | — | — | — | — |
| Loans | 26l | 208.4 | 160.2 | 258.7 | 1,037.9 | 1,467.8 | 1,310.1 | 1,053.4 | 1,737.5 | 2,020.9 | 1,493.8 | 2,159.3 | 3,282.3 |
| Financial Derivatives | 26m | — | — | — | — | 290.2 | 24.3 | 18.5 | 13.4 | 66.6 | 13.2 | 73.0 | 24.8 |
| Insurance Technical Reserves | 26r | — | — | — | — | — | — | — | — | — | — | — | — |
| Shares and Other Equity | 27a | 19,832.9 | 28,040.5 | 47,325.3 | 77,431.2 | 135,846.4 | 145,925.4 | 173,969.8 | 190,273.1 | 202,398.6 | 232,102.6 | 213,554.2 | 162,090.0 |
| Other Items (Net) | 27r | −133.4 | 3,074.3 | −680.2 | −2,716.1 | 14,272.0 | 79,949.4 | 94,253.7 | 98,922.0 | 71,533.5 | 71,308.2 | 146,736.8 | 272,309.6 |
| Memo Item: | | | | | | | | | | | | | |
| Total Assets | 20ra | 143,898.1 | 226,080.2 | 357,096.0 | 617,682.8 | 969,263.5 | 1,001,922.1 | 1,087,681.3 | 1,214,803.0 | 1,269,662.9 | 1,412,061.1 | 1,516,116.3 | 1,589,475.6 |
| **Depository Corporations** | | *Millions of Hryvnias: End of Period* | | | | | | | | | | | |
| Net Foreign Assets | 31n | 43,876.6 | 82,798.8 | 67,041.2 | 51,443.4 | −16,120.9 | −667.2 | 98,909.3 | 97,929.5 | 98,006.0 | 62,850.0 | −52,035.6 | 45,773.5 |
| Claims on Nonresidents | 31 | 66,053.1 | 115,656.1 | 136,313.9 | 198,302.3 | 304,231.9 | 296,734.6 | 373,370.5 | 365,063.6 | 328,021.0 | 273,329.4 | 249,020.6 | 608,148.5 |
| Liabilities to Nonresidents | 36c | 22,176.5 | 32,857.3 | 69,272.7 | 146,858.9 | 320,352.7 | 297,401.8 | 274,461.2 | 267,134.2 | 230,015.0 | 210,479.3 | 301,056.2 | 562,375.0 |
| Domestic Claims | 32 | 109,254.9 | 146,752.4 | 248,631.3 | 440,027.1 | 778,432.3 | 809,173.5 | 860,545.5 | 966,570.4 | 1,035,592.5 | 1,205,842.5 | 1,512,703.2 | 1,506,407.5 |
| Net Claims on Central Government | 32an | 14,515.8 | −5,769.1 | −6,757.1 | −3,529.7 | 23,785.9 | 72,268.5 | 113,215.8 | 144,612.6 | 181,554.8 | 241,255.4 | 438,844.7 | 463,608.5 |
| Claims on Central Government | 32a | 20,711.1 | 13,845.3 | 14,133.4 | 15,361.9 | 41,885.0 | 86,404.8 | 142,963.0 | 162,754.2 | 190,711.4 | 250,391.8 | 459,653.2 | 523,159.6 |
| Liabilities to Central Government. | 36d | 6,195.3 | 19,614.4 | 20,890.5 | 18,891.6 | 18,099.1 | 14,136.3 | 29,747.3 | 18,141.6 | 9,156.6 | 9,136.4 | 20,808.5 | 59,551.1 |
| Claims on Other Sectors | 32s | 94,739.1 | 152,521.5 | 255,388.4 | 443,556.8 | 754,646.4 | 736,905.0 | 747,329.7 | 821,957.8 | 854,037.7 | 964,587.1 | 1,073,858.5 | 1,042,799.0 |
| Claims on Other Financial Corps.. | 32g | 1,253.2 | 2,838.8 | 4,396.0 | 10,137.1 | 15,907.3 | 19,463.3 | 19,535.8 | 22,659.2 | 25,956.4 | 32,909.3 | 39,814.9 | 21,555.4 |
| Claims on State & Local Govts. | 32b | 187.5 | 316.7 | 363.0 | 466.8 | 490.0 | 1,906.9 | 1,979.7 | 2,322.6 | 6,764.4 | 6,777.8 | 6,272.1 | 3,533.7 |
| Claims on Public Nonfin. Corps.. | 32c | 6,442.7 | 7,232.0 | 9,228.9 | 13,705.2 | 37,854.6 | 44,829.9 | 50,144.5 | 61,424.0 | 65,140.7 | 64,482.8 | 78,049.0 | 82,270.4 |
| Claims on Private Sector | 32d | 86,855.6 | 142,134.0 | 241,400.5 | 419,247.7 | 700,394.4 | 670,704.9 | 675,669.6 | 735,552.0 | 756,176.3 | 860,417.2 | 949,722.5 | 935,439.5 |
| Broad Money Liabilities | 35l | 125,704.9 | 194,070.5 | 261,063.4 | 396,156.4 | 515,727.1 | 487,298.2 | 597,871.6 | 685,514.6 | 773,198.6 | 908,994.3 | 956,727.7 | 994,062.0 |
| Currency Outside Depository Corps | 34a | 42,344.9 | 60,231.4 | 74,983.6 | 111,118.7 | 154,758.5 | 157,029.4 | 182,989.9 | 192,664.8 | 203,245.0 | 237,776.6 | 282,947.1 | 282,672.8 |
| Transferable Deposits | 34 | 31,772.5 | 48,284.8 | 61,331.6 | 90,779.8 | 105,371.5 | 118,161.9 | 148,462.2 | 170,293.3 | 176,953.3 | 198,419.9 | 240,238.0 | 291,356.6 |
| Other Deposits | 35 | 51,366.0 | 84,629.0 | 123,098.0 | 189,374.3 | 252,396.9 | 209,580.6 | 265,381.7 | 318,842.8 | 390,928.0 | 470,040.0 | 432,163.5 | 419,782.1 |
| Securities Other than Shares | 36a | 221.6 | 925.3 | 1,650.1 | 4,883.5 | 3,200.2 | 2,526.3 | 1,030.7 | 3,713.7 | 2,072.3 | 2,757.8 | 1,379.1 | 250.4 |
| Deposits Excl. from Broad Money | 36b | 1,192.8 | 1,726.3 | 1,416.9 | 3,536.0 | 1,921.6 | 446.6 | 208.1 | 159.6 | 140.8 | 188.6 | 209.4 | 635.1 |
| Sec.Ot.th.Shares Excl.f/Brd.Money.... | 36s | — | — | — | — | — | — | — | — | — | — | — | — |
| Loans | 36l | 208.4 | 160.2 | 258.7 | 1,037.9 | 1,467.8 | 1,310.1 | 1,053.4 | 1,737.5 | 2,020.9 | 1,493.8 | 2,159.3 | 3,282.3 |
| Financial Derivatives | 36m | — | — | — | — | 290.2 | 24.3 | 18.5 | 13.4 | 66.6 | 13.2 | 73.0 | 24.8 |
| Insurance Technical Reserves | 36r | — | — | — | — | — | — | — | — | — | — | — | — |
| Shares and Other Equity | 37a | 27,485.9 | 31,404.3 | 55,634.3 | 99,527.3 | 233,751.4 | 250,930.5 | 277,972.3 | 289,110.8 | 299,326.2 | 300,224.2 | 356,059.5 | 323,097.0 |
| Other Items (Net) | 37r | −1,460.6 | 2,190.0 | −2,700.7 | −8,787.1 | 9,153.3 | 68,496.6 | 82,330.8 | 87,963.9 | 58,845.3 | 57,778.5 | 145,438.6 | 231,079.9 |
| Broad Money Liabs., Seasonally Adj. | 35l.b | 122,266.6 | 187,865.2 | 252,012.9 | 382,631.4 | 500,523.7 | 476,225.9 | 587,977.4 | 677,174.2 | 766,080.3 | 903,096.9 | 952,763.1 | 991,244.7 |
| **Other Financial Corporations** | | *Millions of Hryvnias: End of Period* | | | | | | | | | | | |
| Net Foreign Assets | 41n | .... | .... | .... | .... | 2,195.0 | 3,527.9 | 5,982.3 | 2,902.6 | −9,970.7 | −12,323.3 | −25,157.8 | −15,559.0 |
| Claims on Nonresidents | 41 | .... | .... | .... | .... | 2,227.3 | 8,674.9 | 11,592.3 | 7,178.1 | 12,470.4 | 11,947.8 | 17,110.7 | 20,634.4 |
| Liabilities to Nonresidents | 46c | .... | .... | .... | .... | 32.2 | 5,147.0 | 5,610.0 | 4,275.5 | 22,441.1 | 24,271.2 | 42,268.4 | 36,193.4 |
| Claims on Depository Corporations.. | 40 | .... | .... | .... | .... | 22,035.8 | 18,562.0 | 21,471.3 | 27,107.9 | 25,417.9 | 29,873.5 | 33,686.5 | 34,070.7 |
| Net Claims on Central Government | 42an | .... | .... | .... | .... | 452.2 | 1,229.9 | 2,225.1 | 2,199.3 | 3,379.6 | 3,282.3 | 4,184.6 | 3,757.5 |
| Claims on Central Government | 42a | .... | .... | .... | .... | 597.6 | 1,399.2 | 2,414.4 | 2,444.5 | 3,635.9 | 3,531.1 | 4,609.4 | 4,288.6 |
| Liabilities to Central Government | 46d | .... | .... | .... | .... | 145.5 | 169.4 | 189.3 | 245.3 | 256.3 | 248.8 | 424.8 | 531.1 |
| Claims on Other Sectors | 42s | .... | .... | .... | .... | 137,530.7 | 156,572.6 | 173,227.0 | 188,445.1 | 221,197.5 | 215,978.8 | 244,096.1 | 206,514.4 |
| Claims on State & Local Govts. | 42b | .... | .... | .... | .... | 50.5 | 36.6 | 32.1 | 27.9 | 15.6 | 11.9 | .8 | .7 |
| Claims on Public Nonfin. Corps. | 42c | .... | .... | .... | .... | | | | | | | | 14,269.6 |
| Claims on Private Sector | 42d | .... | .... | .... | .... | 137,480.2 | 156,536.0 | 173,194.8 | 188,417.2 | 221,181.8 | 215,966.9 | 244,095.3 | 192,244.1 |
| Deposits | 46b | .... | .... | .... | .... | 4,254.6 | 3,348.7 | 2,145.9 | 1,298.0 | 1,403.8 | 1,452.4 | 1,090.8 | 950.1 |
| Securities Other than Shares | 46s | .... | .... | .... | .... | 5,519.8 | 7,499.4 | 9,326.9 | 7,174.6 | 16,920.6 | 18,724.9 | 19,616.6 | 11,065.8 |
| Loans | 46l | .... | .... | .... | .... | 9,789.3 | 14,013.9 | 13,430.3 | 16,441.2 | 16,228.8 | 21,351.5 | 26,401.1 | 17,065.4 |
| Financial Derivatives | 46m | .... | .... | .... | .... | 195.5 | 14.7 | 21.9 | 3.4 | 146.6 | 1,389.1 | 171.0 |
| Insurance Technical Reserves | 46r | .... | .... | .... | .... | 8,647.4 | 8,584.4 | 9,470.4 | 12,232.0 | 14,309.2 | 14,946.0 | 16,339.0 | 18,872.3 |
| Shares and Other Equity | 47a | .... | .... | .... | .... | 112,870.6 | 127,318.8 | 161,737.5 | 187,896.7 | 226,324.7 | 249,458.6 | 261,000.1 | 264,229.4 |
| Other Items (Net) | 47r | .... | .... | .... | .... | 20,936.5 | 19,126.9 | 6,780.0 | −4,409.6 | −35,166.0 | −69,268.8 | −69,027.2 | −83,570.4 |
| Memo Item: | | | | | | | | | | | | | |
| Total Assets | 40ra | .... | .... | .... | .... | 205,064.3 | 237,873.8 | 279,937.9 | 311,593.8 | 371,712.4 | 402,887.6 | 469,169.7 | 476,697.8 |

# Ukraine 926

| | | 2004 | 2005 | 2006 | 2007 | 2008 | 2009 | 2010 | 2011 | 2012 | 2013 | 2014 | 2015 |
|---|---|---|---|---|---|---|---|---|---|---|---|---|---|
| **Financial Corporations** | | | | | | *Millions of Hryvnias: End of Period* | | | | | | | |
| Net Foreign Assets | 51n | .... | .... | .... | .... | −13,925.8 | 2,860.7 | 104,891.6 | 100,832.0 | 88,035.3 | 50,526.7 | −77,193.4 | 30,214.6 |
| Claims on Nonresidents | 51 | .... | .... | .... | .... | 306,459.2 | 305,409.5 | 384,962.8 | 372,241.7 | 340,491.4 | 285,277.2 | 266,131.2 | 628,782.9 |
| Liabilities to Nonresidents | 56c | .... | .... | .... | .... | 320,385.0 | 302,548.8 | 280,071.2 | 271,409.7 | 252,456.1 | 234,750.5 | 343,324.6 | 598,568.3 |
| Domestic Claims | 52 | .... | .... | .... | .... | 900,507.8 | 947,512.7 | 1,016,461.7 | 1,134,555.5 | 1,234,213.2 | 1,392,194.3 | 1,721,169.0 | 1,695,124.1 |
| Net Claims on Central Government | 52an | .... | .... | .... | .... | 24,238.0 | 73,498.4 | 115,440.9 | 146,811.9 | 184,934.4 | 244,537.8 | 443,029.3 | 467,366.0 |
| Claims on Central Government | 52a | .... | .... | .... | .... | 42,482.6 | 87,804.0 | 145,377.4 | 165,198.7 | 194,347.3 | 253,922.9 | 464,262.5 | 527,448.2 |
| Liabilities to Central Government | 56d | .... | .... | .... | .... | 18,244.6 | 14,305.7 | 29,936.6 | 18,386.9 | 9,412.9 | 9,385.2 | 21,233.3 | 60,082.2 |
| Claims on Other Sectors | 52s | .... | .... | .... | .... | 876,269.8 | 874,014.3 | 901,020.9 | 987,743.7 | 1,049,278.8 | 1,147,656.6 | 1,278,139.7 | 1,227,758.1 |
| Claims on State & Local Govts | 52b | .... | .... | .... | .... | 540.5 | 1,943.5 | 2,011.9 | 2,350.5 | 6,780.0 | 6,789.7 | 6,272.9 | 3,534.5 |
| Claims on Public Nonfin. Corps | 52c | .... | .... | .... | .... | 37,854.6 | 44,829.9 | 50,144.5 | 61,424.0 | 65,140.7 | 64,482.8 | 78,049.0 | 96,540.0 |
| Claims on Private Sector | 52d | .... | .... | .... | .... | 837,874.6 | 827,241.0 | 848,864.5 | 923,969.2 | 977,358.1 | 1,076,384.1 | 1,193,817.8 | 1,127,683.6 |
| Currency Outside Financial Corps | 54a | .... | .... | .... | .... | 154,622.8 | 156,880.8 | 182,851.5 | 192,448.3 | 202,965.8 | 237,313.7 | 282,495.8 | 282,070.7 |
| Deposits | 55l | .... | .... | .... | .... | 344,639.3 | 315,167.7 | 396,628.3 | 468,400.1 | 548,143.4 | 643,795.0 | 643,585.3 | 683,347.3 |
| Securities Other than Shares | 56a | .... | .... | .... | .... | 5,655.1 | 6,291.3 | 6,680.5 | 5,562.1 | 11,387.9 | 10,213.9 | 10,251.2 | 6,468.3 |
| Loans | 56l | .... | .... | .... | .... | — | — | — | — | — | 2,034.0 | 825.4 | 1,501.0 |
| Financial Derivatives | 56m | .... | .... | .... | .... | 138.9 | 24.2 | 18.2 | 12.1 | 63.7 | 6.9 | 67.2 | 16.6 |
| Insurance Technical Reserves | 56r | .... | .... | .... | .... | 8,647.4 | 8,584.4 | 9,470.4 | 12,232.0 | 14,309.2 | 14,946.0 | 16,339.0 | 18,872.3 |
| Shares and Other Equity | 57a | .... | .... | .... | .... | 346,622.0 | 378,249.3 | 439,709.8 | 477,007.5 | 525,650.9 | 549,682.8 | 617,059.6 | 587,326.4 |
| Other Items (Net) | 57r | .... | .... | .... | .... | 26,256.5 | 85,175.6 | 85,994.6 | 79,725.5 | 19,727.6 | −15,271.3 | 73,352.0 | 145,736.1 |
| **Monetary Aggregates** | | | | | | *Millions of Hryvnias: End of Period* | | | | | | | |
| Broad Money | 59m | 125,704.9 | 194,070.5 | 261,063.4 | 396,156.4 | 515,727.1 | 487,298.2 | 597,871.6 | 685,514.6 | 773,198.6 | 908,994.3 | 956,727.7 | 994,062.0 |
| o/w:Currency Issued by Cent.Govt | 59m.a | — | — | — | — | — | — | — | — | — | — | — | — |
| o/w: Dep.in Nonfin. Corporations. | 59m.b | — | — | — | — | — | — | — | — | — | — | — | — |
| o/w:Secs. Issued by Central Govt | 59m.c | — | — | — | — | — | — | — | — | — | — | — | — |
| Money (National Definitions) | | | | | | | | | | | | | |
| Reserve Money | 19mb | 53,763.0 | 82,759.7 | 97,214.2 | 141,901.1 | 186,670.9 | 194,965.3 | 225,691.8 | 239,884.8 | 255,283.4 | 307,138.8 | 333,194.2 | 335,999.6 |
| M0 | 19mc | 42,345.0 | 60,231.4 | 74,983.6 | 111,118.7 | 154,758.5 | 157,029.4 | 182,989.9 | 192,664.8 | 203,245.0 | 237,776.6 | 282,947.1 | 282,672.8 |
| M1 | 59ma | 67,090.0 | 98,572.6 | 123,275.6 | 181,665.2 | 225,127.2 | 233,748.4 | 289,893.6 | 311,046.6 | 323,225.3 | 383,820.7 | 435,474.7 | 472,217.1 |
| M2 | 59mb | 125,483.0 | 193,145.3 | 259,413.2 | 391,272.9 | 512,526.9 | 484,771.9 | 596,840.8 | 681,800.9 | 771,126.3 | 906,236.5 | 955,348.6 | 993,811.5 |
| M3 | 59mc | 125,801.0 | 194,070.5 | 261,063.4 | 396,156.4 | 515,727.1 | 487,298.2 | 597,871.6 | 685,514.6 | 773,198.6 | 908,994.3 | 956,727.7 | 994,062.0 |
| **Interest Rates** | | | | | | *Percent Per Annum* | | | | | | | |
| Refinancing Rate (End of Period) | 60.b | 9.00 | 9.50 | 8.50 | 8.00 | 12.00 | 10.25 | 7.75 | 7.75 | 7.50 | 6.50 | 14.00 | 22.00 |
| Money Market Rate | 60b | 6.34 | 4.16 | 3.58 | 2.27 | 13.71 | 12.64 | 3.42 | 7.11 | 12.15 | 4.50 | 12.81 | 21.88 |
| Money Market Rate (Fgn. Cur.) | 60b.f | 2.15 | 2.85 | 4.13 | 4.82 | 4.30 | 1.09 | 1.40 | 1.24 | 1.94 | 2.55 | 5.80 | 6.64 |
| Deposit Rate | 60l | 7.80 | 8.57 | 7.57 | 8.12 | 9.95 | 13.76 | 10.56 | 7.90 | 12.96 | 10.78 | 12.10 | 13.01 |
| Deposit Rate (Fgn. Currency) | 60l.f | 6.27 | 6.82 | 5.86 | 5.84 | 5.91 | 8.98 | 7.85 | 5.47 | 5.77 | 5.87 | 6.72 | 6.71 |
| Lending Rate | 60p | 17.40 | 16.17 | 15.17 | 13.90 | 17.49 | 20.86 | 15.87 | 15.95 | 18.39 | 16.65 | 17.72 | 21.82 |
| Lending Rate (Fgn. Currency) | 60p.f | 12.29 | 11.60 | 11.29 | 11.33 | 11.68 | 10.26 | 10.56 | 9.31 | 8.40 | 9.35 | 9.00 | 8.92 |
| **Prices, Production, Labor** | | | | | | *Index Numbers (2010=100): Period Averages* | | | | | | | |
| Share Prices (End of Month) | 62.ep | 18.0 | 40.0 | 51.4 | 117.0 | 83.1 | 52.5 | 100.0 | 103.3 | 51.8 | 38.6 | 50.4 | 41.5 |
| Producer Prices | 63 | 37.5 | 43.7 | 47.9 | 57.3 | † 77.6 | 82.7 | 100.0 | † 119.1 | 123.5 | 123.4 | 144.5 | 196.4 |
| Consumer Prices | 64 | 45.1 | 51.2 | 55.8 | 63.0 | † 78.9 | 91.4 | 100.0 | † 108.0 | 108.6 | 108.3 | 121.5 | 180.6 |
| Industrial Production | 66 | 101.6 | 104.5 | † 110.5 | 118.4 | 112.5 | 89.3 | 100.0 | 108.0 | 107.2 | 102.6 | 92.2 | 80.2 |
| Industrial Employment | 67 | 119.9 | 120.2 | 118.3 | 115.7 | 112.2 | 100.3 | 100.0 | 98.5 | 97.2 | 94.1 | 80.8 | 71.8 |
| | | | | | | *Number in Thousands: Period Averages* | | | | | | | |
| Labor Force | 67d | 22,202 | 22,281 | 22,245 | 22,322 | 22,397 | 22,150 | 22,052 | 22,057 | 22,012 | 21,981 | 19,921 | .... |
| Employment | 67e | 20,296 | 20,680 | 20,730 | 20,905 | 20,972 | 20,192 | 20,266 | 20,324 | 20,354 | 20,404 | 18,073 | 16,443 |
| Unemployment | 67c | 1,907 | 1,601 | 1,515 | 1,418 | 1,425 | 1,959 | 1,786 | 1,733 | 1,657 | 1,577 | 1,848 | .... |
| Unemployment Rate (%) | 67r | 8.6 | 7.2 | 6.8 | 6.4 | 6.4 | 8.8 | 8.1 | 7.9 | 7.5 | 7.2 | 9.3 | 9.1 |
| **Intl. Transactions & Positions** | | | | | | *Millions of US Dollars* | | | | | | | |
| Exports | 70..d | 32,666 | 34,228 | 38,368 | 49,296 | 66,967 | 39,696 | 51,405 | 68,394 | 68,831 | 63,321 | 53,902 | 38,135 |
| Imports, c.i.f. | 71..d | 28,997 | 36,136 | 45,039 | 60,618 | 85,535 | 45,433 | 60,742 | 82,608 | 84,718 | 76,987 | 54,429 | 37,502 |

# Ukraine 926

| | | 2004 | 2005 | 2006 | 2007 | 2008 | 2009 | 2010 | 2011 | 2012 | 2013 | 2014 | 2015 |
|---|---|---|---|---|---|---|---|---|---|---|---|---|---|
| **Balance of Payments** | | | | | | | *Millions of US Dollars* | | | | | | |
| A. Current Account*....................... | 109bx | 6,909.0 | † 2,534.0 | −1,619.0 | −5,251.0 | −12,781.0 | −1,736.0 | −3,016.0 | −10,233.0 | −14,335.0 | −16,518.0 | −4,596.0 | −176.0 |
| Goods, credit (exports)................... | 1a9cx | 30,581.0 | † 32,184.0 | 36,174.0 | 46,168.0 | 63,188.0 | 37,134.0 | 47,299.0 | 62,383.0 | 64,427.0 | 59,106.0 | 50,552.0 | 35,428.0 |
| Goods, debit (imports)................... | 1a9dx | 27,839.0 | † 34,377.0 | 42,220.0 | 57,753.0 | 80,640.0 | 42,477.0 | 56,896.0 | 80,414.0 | 86,273.0 | 81,234.0 | 57,680.0 | 38,737.0 |
| Balance on goods........................ | 1a9bx | 2,742.0 | † −2,193.0 | −6,046.0 | −11,585.0 | −17,452.0 | −5,343.0 | −9,597.0 | −18,031.0 | −21,846.0 | −22,128.0 | −7,128.0 | −3,309.0 |
| Services, credit (exports)................ | 1b9cx | 8,878.0 | † 10,442.0 | 12,181.0 | 15,244.0 | 19,292.0 | 14,946.0 | 18,327.0 | 21,269.0 | 22,089.0 | 22,613.0 | 14,884.0 | 12,369.0 |
| Services, debit (imports)................. | 1b9dx | 6,642.0 | † 7,575.0 | 9,205.0 | 11,790.0 | 16,208.0 | 11,560.0 | 12,712.0 | 13,383.0 | 14,589.0 | 16,119.0 | 12,362.0 | 10,751.0 |
| Balance on Goods & Services....... | 1z9bx | 4,978.0 | † 674.0 | −3,070.0 | −8,131.0 | −14,368.0 | −1,957.0 | −3,982.0 | −10,145.0 | −14,346.0 | −15,634.0 | −4,606.0 | −1,691.0 |
| Primary income: credit................... | 1c9cx | 389.0 | † 758.0 | 1,332.0 | 3,656.0 | 5,419.0 | 4,624.0 | 4,715.0 | 5,485.0 | 7,082.0 | 7,767.0 | 5,503.0 | 4,298.0 |
| Primary income: debit................... | 1c9dx | 1,034.0 | † 1,743.0 | 3,054.0 | 4,315.0 | 6,959.0 | 7,064.0 | 6,724.0 | 9,281.0 | 10,047.0 | 10,800.0 | 7,034.0 | 5,411.0 |
| Balance on gds, serv. & prim. inc. | 1y9bx | 4,333.0 | † −311.0 | −4,792.0 | −8,790.0 | −15,908.0 | −4,397.0 | −5,991.0 | −13,941.0 | −17,311.0 | −18,667.0 | −6,137.0 | −2,804.0 |
| Secondary income: credit.............. | 1d9ca | 2,671.0 | † 3,111.0 | 3,533.0 | 4,147.0 | 4,165.0 | 3,460.0 | 4,042.0 | 4,751.0 | 4,219.0 | 4,129.0 | 3,424.0 | 3,432.0 |
| Secondary income: debit............... | 1d9da | 95.0 | † 266.0 | 360.0 | 608.0 | 1,038.0 | 799.0 | 1,067.0 | 1,043.0 | 1,243.0 | 1,980.0 | 1,883.0 | 804.0 |
| B. Capital Account*...................... | 209ba | 21.0 | † −43.0 | 22.0 | 25.0 | 28.0 | 599.0 | 188.0 | 101.0 | 40.0 | −60.0 | 400.0 | 456.0 |
| Capital account: credit.................. | 209ca | 21.0 | † 14.0 | 22.0 | 25.0 | 28.0 | 616.0 | 247.0 | 209.0 | 108.0 | 201.0 | 421.0 | 471.0 |
| Capital account: debit................... | 209da | — | † 57.0 | .... | .... | .... | 17.0 | 59.0 | 108.0 | 68.0 | 261.0 | 21.0 | 15.0 |
| Balance on current & capital acct. | 129ba | 6,930.0 | † 2,491.0 | −1,597.0 | −5,226.0 | −12,753.0 | −1,137.0 | −2,828.0 | −10,132.0 | −14,295.0 | −16,578.0 | −4,196.0 | 280.0 |
| C. Financial Account* .................. | 309na | 4,521.0 | † −8,126.0 | −3,929.0 | −15,127.0 | −9,164.0 | 10,883.8 | −6,508.0 | −6,706.0 | −8,727.0 | −19,241.0 | 9,644.0 | −696.0 |
| Direct investment: assets.............. | 3a9aa | 4.0 | † 275.0 | −133.0 | 975.0 | 797.0 | 115.0 | 692.0 | 192.0 | 980.0 | 430.0 | 548.0 | 38.0 |
| Equity & investment fund shares.. | 3aaaa | 4.0 | † 275.0 | −8.0 | 975.0 | 797.0 | 115.0 | 692.0 | 192.0 | 1,206.0 | 420.0 | 105.0 | −51.0 |
| Debt instruments........................ | 3abaa | — | .... | −125.0 | .... | .... | .... | .... | .... | −226.0 | 10.0 | 443.0 | 89.0 |
| Direct investment: liabilities .......... | 3a9la | 1,715.0 | † 7,808.0 | 5,604.0 | 10,193.0 | 10,700.0 | 4,769.0 | 6,451.0 | 7,207.0 | 8,175.0 | 4,509.0 | 847.0 | 3,050.0 |
| Equity & investment fund shares . | 3aala | 1,496.0 | † 7,493.0 | 4,539.0 | 8,381.0 | 9,612.0 | 4,456.0 | 5,550.0 | 6,121.0 | 6,248.0 | 3,668.0 | 712.0 | 4,003.0 |
| Debt instruments........................ | 3abla | 219.0 | † 315.0 | 1,065.0 | 1,812.0 | 1,088.0 | 313.0 | 901.0 | 1,086.0 | 1,927.0 | 841.0 | 135.0 | −953.0 |
| Portfolio investment: assets .......... | 3b9aa | 6.0 | † — | 3.0 | 29.0 | −12.0 | 8.0 | 17.0 | 48.0 | 72.0 | −5.0 | −1.0 | 3.0 |
| Equity & investment fund shares | 3baaa | 6.0 | † −4.0 | 2.0 | 21.0 | −10.0 | 6.0 | −4.0 | 8.0 | 23.0 | −11.0 | −1.0 | 3.0 |
| Debt securities........................... | 3bbaa | — | † 4.0 | 1.0 | 8.0 | −2.0 | 2.0 | 21.0 | 40.0 | 49.0 | 6.0 | .... | .... |
| Portfolio investment: liabilities....... | 3b9la | 2,073.0 | † 2,757.0 | 3,586.0 | 5,782.0 | −1,292.0 | −1,525.0 | 4,359.0 | 1,617.0 | 4,761.0 | 8,782.0 | −2,701.0 | 370.0 |
| Equity & investment fund shares . | 3bala | −61.0 | † 82.0 | 322.0 | 715.0 | 388.0 | 105.0 | 290.0 | 519.0 | 516.0 | 1,180.0 | −391.0 | 177.0 |
| Debt securities........................... | 3bbla | 2,134.0 | † 2,675.0 | 3,264.0 | 5,067.0 | −1,680.0 | −1,630.0 | 4,069.0 | 1,098.0 | 4,245.0 | 7,602.0 | −2,310.0 | 193.0 |
| Fin. der.& empl.stk.ops.(ESOs): net | 3c9na | .... | .... | .... | .... | .... | .... | .... | .... | .... | .... | .... | .... |
| Fin. der. & ESOs.: assets............. | 3c9aa | .... | .... | .... | .... | .... | .... | .... | .... | .... | .... | .... | .... |
| Fin. der. & ESOs.: liabilities.......... | 3c9la | .... | .... | .... | .... | .... | .... | .... | .... | .... | .... | .... | .... |
| Other investment: assets.............. | 3d9aa | 12,495.0 | † 7,913.0 | 15,580.0 | 22,838.0 | 22,884.0 | 10,822.0 | 10,748.0 | 9,883.0 | 9,225.0 | −1,720.0 | 1,515.0 | −1,015.0 |
| Other equity............................. | 3daaa | .... | † 5.0 | 3.0 | .... | .... | .... | 5.0 | .... | 7.0 | 1.0 | −4.0 | 12.0 |
| Debt instruments........................ | 3dzaa | 12,495.0 | † 7,908.0 | 15,577.0 | 22,838.0 | 22,884.0 | 10,822.0 | 10,743.0 | 9,883.0 | 9,218.0 | −1,721.0 | 1,519.0 | −1,027.0 |
| Other investment: liabilities........... | 3d9la | 4,196.0 | † 5,749.0 | 10,189.0 | 22,994.0 | 23,425.0 | −3,182.8 | 7,155.0 | 8,005.0 | 6,068.0 | 4,655.0 | −5,728.0 | −3,698.0 |
| Other equity............................. | 3dala | .... | .... | .... | .... | .... | .... | .... | .... | .... | .... | .... | .... |
| Debt instruments........................ | 3dzla | 4,196.0 | † 5,749.0 | 10,189.0 | 22,994.0 | 23,425.0 | −3,182.8 | 7,155.0 | 8,005.0 | 6,068.0 | 4,655.0 | −5,728.0 | −3,698.0 |
| Curr.+ cap.− finan. acct. balance... | 4y9na | 2,409.0 | † 10,617.0 | 2,332.0 | 9,901.0 | −3,589.0 | −12,020.8 | 3,680.0 | −3,426.0 | −5,568.0 | 2,663.0 | −13,840.0 | 976.0 |
| D. Net Errors and Omissions............ | 409na | 114.3 | † 107.5 | 77.3 | −494.6 | 563.8 | 305.9 | 1,364.9 | 972.0 | 1,393.8 | −658.2 | 532.1 | −183.4 |
| E. Reserves and Related Items.......... | 4z9na | 2,523.3 | † 10,724.5 | 2,409.3 | 9,406.4 | −3,025.2 | −11,715.0 | 5,044.9 | −2,454.0 | −4,174.2 | 2,004.8 | −13,307.9 | 792.6 |
| Reserve assets........................... | 3e9aa | 2,225.6 | † 10,425.2 | 1,999.0 | 8,979.1 | 1,080.5 | −5,653.3 | 8,460.7 | −2,454.0 | −7,592.4 | −3,553.5 | −12,413.8 | 6,007.6 |
| Credit and loans from the IMF....... | 3dcla | −297.6 | † −299.3 | −410.3 | −427.3 | 4,105.8 | 6,061.7 | 3,415.8 | — | −3,418.1 | −5,558.2 | 894.1 | 5,215.1 |
| Exceptional financing.................... | 409la | .... | .... | .... | .... | .... | .... | .... | .... | .... | .... | .... | .... |

*Excludes components in group E

| **International Investment Position** | | | | | | | *Millions of US Dollars* | | | | | | |
|---|---|---|---|---|---|---|---|---|---|---|---|---|---|
| Assets............................................. | 809aa | 28,164.2 | 42,712.0 | 57,023.5 | 90,616.8 | 106,595.6 | 112,535.6 | † 133,426.0 | 140,240.9 | 143,852.2 | 138,304.0 | 122,882.8 | 125,094.9 |
| Direct investment......................... | 8a9aa | 198.0 | 468.0 | 344.0 | 6,376.0 | 7,089.0 | 7,298.0 | † 7,958.0 | 8,117.0 | 9,506.0 | 9,912.0 | 10,087.0 | 9,916.0 |
| Equity & investment fund shares.. | 8aaaa | 198.0 | 219.0 | 221.0 | 6,256.0 | 6,971.0 | 7,175.0 | † 7,835.0 | 7,994.0 | 9,228.0 | 9,617.0 | 9,576.0 | 9,444.0 |
| Debt instruments........................ | 8abaa | .... | 249.0 | 123.0 | 120.0 | 118.0 | 123.0 | † 123.0 | 123.0 | 278.0 | 295.0 | 511.0 | 472.0 |
| Portfolio investment...................... | 8b9aa | 36.0 | 56.0 | 63.0 | 103.0 | 49.0 | 79.0 | † 94.0 | 108.0 | 173.0 | 176.0 | 188.0 | 210.0 |
| Equity & investment fund shares.. | 8baaa | 33.0 | 50.0 | 56.0 | 88.0 | 45.0 | 73.0 | † 67.0 | 50.0 | 64.0 | 74.0 | 68.0 | 75.0 |
| Debt securities........................... | 8bbaa | 3.0 | 6.0 | 7.0 | 15.0 | 4.0 | 6.0 | † 27.0 | 58.0 | 109.0 | 102.0 | 120.0 | 135.0 |
| Fin. der.(oth.than reserves) & ESOs | 8c9aa | .... | .... | .... | .... | .... | .... | .... | .... | .... | .... | .... | .... |
| Other investment.......................... | 8d9aa | 18,405.0 | 22,797.0 | 34,360.0 | 51,675.0 | 67,915.0 | 78,654.0 | † 90,798.0 | 100,221.0 | 109,627.0 | 107,800.0 | 105,075.0 | 101,669.0 |
| Other equity............................. | 8daaa | .... | .... | .... | .... | .... | .... | † 147.0 | 147.0 | 148.0 | 156.0 | 142.0 | 144.0 |
| Debt instruments........................ | 8dzaa | 18,405.0 | 22,797.0 | 34,360.0 | 51,675.0 | 67,915.0 | 78,654.0 | † 90,651.0 | 100,074.0 | 109,479.0 | 107,644.0 | 104,933.0 | 101,525.0 |
| Reserve assets............................. | 8e9aa | 9,525.2 | 19,391.0 | 22,256.5 | 32,462.8 | 31,542.6 | 26,504.6 | † 34,576.0 | 31,794.9 | 24,546.2 | 20,416.0 | 7,532.8 | 13,299.9 |
| Liabilities......................................... | 809la | 40,283.3 | 56,869.5 | 76,942.2 | 117,316.3 | 146,795.0 | 152,795.6 | † 172,211.9 | 188,188.6 | 203,300.0 | 215,128.0 | 186,006.5 | 177,233.7 |
| Direct investment......................... | 8a9la | 9,606.0 | 17,209.0 | 23,125.0 | 38,358.0 | 47,081.0 | 52,057.0 | † 57,985.0 | 65,485.0 | 75,189.0 | 79,061.0 | 64,293.0 | 62,161.0 |
| Equity & investment fund shares.. | 8aala | 9,047.0 | 16,375.0 | 21,182.0 | 34,980.0 | 42,748.0 | 46,943.0 | † 52,092.0 | 58,365.0 | 64,744.0 | 67,876.0 | 55,036.0 | 53,599.0 |
| Debt instruments........................ | 8abla | 559.0 | 834.0 | 1,943.0 | 3,378.0 | 4,333.0 | 5,114.0 | † 5,893.0 | 7,120.0 | 10,445.0 | 11,185.0 | 9,257.0 | 8,562.0 |
| Portfolio investment...................... | 8b9la | 6,391.0 | 9,011.0 | 12,861.0 | 18,618.0 | 17,059.0 | 15,567.0 | † 20,085.0 | 21,806.0 | 26,765.0 | 35,956.0 | 33,032.0 | 29,854.0 |
| Equity & investment fund shares.. | 8bala | 589.0 | 876.0 | 1,248.0 | 2,082.0 | 2,304.0 | 2,421.0 | † 2,773.0 | 3,588.0 | 3,930.0 | 5,197.0 | 4,662.0 | 4,871.0 |
| Debt securities........................... | 8bbla | 5,802.0 | 8,135.0 | 11,613.0 | 16,536.0 | 14,755.0 | 13,146.0 | † 17,312.0 | 18,218.0 | 22,835.0 | 30,759.0 | 28,370.0 | 24,983.0 |
| Fin. der.(oth.than reserves) & ESOs | 8c9la | .... | .... | .... | .... | .... | .... | .... | .... | .... | .... | .... | .... |
| Other investment.......................... | 8d9la | 24,286.3 | 30,649.5 | 40,956.2 | 60,340.3 | 82,655.0 | 85,171.6 | † 94,141.9 | 100,897.6 | 101,346.0 | 100,111.0 | 88,681.5 | 85,218.7 |
| Other equity............................. | 8dala | .... | .... | .... | .... | .... | .... | .... | .... | .... | .... | .... | .... |
| Debt instruments........................ | 8dzla | 24,286.3 | 30,649.5 | 40,956.2 | 60,340.3 | 82,655.0 | 85,171.6 | † 94,141.9 | 100,897.6 | 101,346.0 | 100,111.0 | 88,681.5 | 85,218.7 |

# Ukraine   926

| | | 2004 | 2005 | 2006 | 2007 | 2008 | 2009 | 2010 | 2011 | 2012 | 2013 | 2014 | 2015 |
|---|---|---|---|---|---|---|---|---|---|---|---|---|---|
| **Government Finance** | | | | | | | | | | | | | | |
| **Cash Flow Statement** | | | | | | | | | | | | | | |
| **Budgetary Central Government** | | | | | | *Millions of Hryvnias Fiscal Year Ends December 31* | | | | | | | | |
| Cash Receipts:Operating Activities... | c1 | 69,487.1 | 104,605.1 | 132,967.1 | 164,169.3 | 229,597.6 | 208,640.2 | 240,028.3 | 314,099.2 | 344,822.7 | 338,971.5 | 356,196.1 | 534,523.4 |
| Taxes.............................. | c11 | 45,816.0 | 75,590.2 | 96,573.8 | 118,809.6 | 169,541.9 | 149,530.8 | 168,059.8 | 240,694.0 | 257,286.6 | 257,309.2 | 274,446.6 | 402,506.1 |
| Social Contributions..................... | c12 | 2,594.9 | 3,623.0 | 4,862.3 | 6,118.5 | 6,497.7 | — | — | — | — | — | — | — |
| Grants............................... | c13 | 2,011.0 | 1,645.8 | 1,729.4 | 4,456.2 | 7,837.2 | 8,414.3 | 6,930.4 | 3,200.0 | 1,565.2 | 3,138.5 | 7,501.0 | 4,944.4 |
| Other Receipts........................ | c14 | 19,065.2 | 23,746.1 | 29,801.6 | 34,785.0 | 45,720.8 | 50,695.1 | 65,038.1 | 70,205.2 | 85,970.9 | 78,523.8 | 74,248.6 | 127,073.0 |
| Cash Payments:Operating Activities. | c2 | 73,843.8 | 108,895.6 | 132,603.2 | 166,460.0 | 232,303.0 | 237,968.4 | 297,642.7 | 325,635.5 | 386,153.8 | 396,331.5 | 425,638.2 | 565,291.6 |
| Compensation of Employees.......... | c21 | 17,161.1 | 19,383.9 | 24,756.9 | 32,577.6 | 43,380.5 | 45,183.4 | 51,249.2 | 54,464.9 | 59,774.3 | 64,313.7 | 69,283.8 | 79,854.6 |
| Purchases of Goods & Services....... | c22 | 12,032.0 | 18,702.2 | 22,543.9 | 29,245.5 | 38,507.5 | 43,977.6 | 48,986.7 | 56,826.5 | 65,646.9 | 61,325.8 | 65,431.6 | 87,324.1 |
| Interest............................... | c24 | 3,054.2 | 3,265.5 | 3,377.2 | 3,735.8 | 4,418.8 | 9,907.3 | 16,639.5 | 24,591.2 | 25,753.3 | 34,409.3 | 51,018.2 | 86,808.4 |
| Subsidies............................. | c25 | 5,017.0 | 6,873.0 | 10,029.7 | 14,582.2 | 24,814.6 | 18,498.3 | 20,370.5 | 14,468.2 | 20,528.8 | 19,268.8 | 17,111.3 | 10,138.9 |
| Grants................................ | c26 | 23,212.3 | 46,796.2 | 53,145.6 | 70,882.0 | 100,846.9 | 62,298.7 | 142,236.8 | 153,772.1 | 189,749.4 | 199,543.1 | 206,777.8 | 270,501.9 |
| Social Benefits........................ | c27 | 4,532.4 | 7,050.5 | 10,283.0 | 1,661.3 | 8,044.6 | 50,451.1 | 2,814.6 | 2,069.5 | 1,850.6 | 4,745.5 | 5,231.3 | 9,093.6 |
| Other Payments....................... | c28 | 8,834.8 | 6,824.3 | 8,466.9 | 13,775.6 | 12,290.1 | 7,652.1 | 15,345.4 | 19,443.1 | 22,850.5 | 12,725.4 | 10,784.2 | 21,570.0 |
| Net Cash Inflow:Operating Act.[1-2] | ccio | −4,356.7 | −4,290.5 | 363.9 | −2,290.7 | −2,705.4 | −29,328.2 | −57,614.4 | −11,536.3 | −41,331.1 | −57,360.1 | −69,442.0 | −30,768.2 |
| Net Cash Outflow:Invest. in NFA...... | c31 | 4,777.2 | 3,355.2 | 3,950.3 | 6,024.4 | 7,061.8 | 3,408.8 | 5,359.1 | 7,306.3 | 8,296.6 | 6,869.1 | 3,691.5 | 11,448.4 |
| Purchases of Nonfinancial Assets... | c31.1 | 5,627.8 | 4,080.4 | 4,504.8 | 7,794.3 | 9,187.1 | 4,468.8 | 5,946.1 | 7,824.0 | 9,528.1 | 7,124.5 | 4,579.6 | 11,619.8 |
| Sales of Nonfinancial Assets.......... | c31.2 | 850.6 | 725.2 | 554.5 | 1,769.9 | 2,125.3 | 1,060.1 | 587.0 | 517.7 | 1,231.5 | 255.4 | 888.1 | 171.4 |
| Cash Surplus/Deficit [1-2-31=1-2M] | ccsd | −9,133.9 | −7,645.7 | −3,586.4 | −8,315.1 | −9,767.2 | −32,737.0 | −62,973.5 | −18,842.6 | −49,627.7 | −64,229.2 | −73,133.5 | −42,216.6 |
| Net Acq. Fin. Assets, excl. Cash... | c32x | 1,150.9 | 255.6 | −23.3 | 1,378.5 | 20,204.8 | 53,345.6 | 8,451.9 | 26,069.0 | 4,054.1 | 13,697.5 | 127,778.4 | 77,400.5 |
| Domestic......................... | c321x | 1,082.7 | 299.9 | 190.3 | 1,527.7 | 20,204.8 | 53,345.6 | 8,451.9 | 26,069.0 | 4,054.1 | 13,697.5 | 127,778.4 | 77,400.5 |
| Foreign.......................... | c322x | 68.2 | −44.3 | −213.6 | −149.3 | — | — | — | — | — | — | — | — |
| Net Incurrence of Liabilities.............. | c33 | 10,641.1 | 20,218.2 | 2,576.5 | 6,487.5 | 29,630.9 | 90,464.9 | 98,693.8 | 46,507.4 | 36,795.3 | 81,038.8 | 201,833.6 | 117,507.3 |
| Domestic......................... | c331 | 9,972.2 | 19,314.4 | −2,016.5 | 3,664.9 | 25,801.4 | 45,665.0 | 51,435.5 | 32,802.6 | 23,961.1 | 67,109.1 | 159,577.2 | 7,817.1 |
| Foreign.......................... | c332 | 668.9 | 903.8 | 4,593.0 | 2,822.6 | 3,829.5 | 44,799.9 | 47,258.3 | 13,704.8 | 12,834.2 | 13,929.7 | 42,256.4 | 109,690.2 |
| Net Cash Inflow, Fin.Act.[-32x+33].. | cnfb | 9,490.2 | 19,962.6 | 2,599.8 | 5,109.1 | 9,426.1 | 37,119.3 | 90,242.0 | 20,438.4 | 32,741.2 | 67,341.3 | 74,055.2 | 40,106.8 |
| Net Change in Stock of Cash........... | cncb | 356.3 | 12,316.9 | −986.6 | −3,206.0 | −341.1 | 4,382.4 | 27,268.5 | 1,595.8 | −16,886.5 | 3,112.1 | 921.7 | −2,109.8 |
| Stat. Discrep. [32X-33+NCB-CSD].... | ccsdz | — | — | — | — | — | .1 | — | — | — | — | — | — |
| Memo Item:Cash Expenditure[2+31] | c2m | 79,471.5 | 112,975.9 | 137,108.0 | 174,254.3 | 241,490.1 | 241,377.2 | 303,588.8 | 333,459.5 | 394,450.4 | 403,200.6 | 429,329.7 | 576,740.0 |
| Memo Item: Gross Debt.................. | c63 | 85,401.2 | 78,146.6 | 80,548.6 | 88,744.7 | 131,084.9 | 227,195.7 | 323,475.2 | 357,273.4 | 422,534.0 | 491,656.0 | 956,710.1 | .... |
| **National Accounts** | | | | | | *Billions of Hryvnias* | | | | | | | | |
| Househ.Cons.Expend.,incl.NPISHs.... | 96f | 232.1 | 320.2 | 403.5 | 535.9 | 733.4 | 737.0 | 825.3 | 1,016.1 | 1,133.8 | 1,241.6 | 1,316.8 | 1,566.0 |
| Government Consumption Expend... | 91f | 23.5 | 30.5 | 38.3 | 47.6 | 61.8 | 63.7 | 72.3 | 78.1 | 87.4 | 88.1 | 113.2 | 149.6 |
| Gross Fixed Capital Formation.......... | 93e | 80.3 | 100.2 | 138.0 | 204.0 | 257.0 | 173.9 | 184.2 | 229.9 | 267.5 | 247.3 | 224.7 | 263.0 |
| Changes in Inventories.................... | 93i | −4.9 | 2.7 | .7 | 4.7 | 14.4 | −12.3 | 41.1 | 61.8 | 37.5 | 23.6 | −12.1 | 40.3 |
| Exports of Goods and Services......... | 90c | 209.9 | 218.3 | 244.2 | 310.1 | 428.6 | 406.6 | 507.9 | 647.6 | 670.3 | 629.4 | 771.1 | 1,044.5 |
| Imports of Goods and Services (-)..... | 98c | 183.4 | 214.6 | 259.7 | 351.2 | 504.4 | 421.9 | 551.4 | 733.5 | 791.8 | 764.7 | 826.8 | 1,084.0 |
| Gross Domestic Product (GDP)......... | 99b | 357.5 | 457.3 | 565.0 | 751.1 | 990.8 | 947.0 | 1,079.3 | 1,300.0 | 1,404.7 | 1,465.2 | 1,586.9 | 1,979.5 |
| Net Primary Income from Abroad..... | 98.n | −3.4 | −5.0 | −8.7 | −3.3 | −8.7 | −19.0 | −6.1 | −21.8 | −18.6 | −24.9 | −18.1 | −22.5 |
| Gross National Income (GNI)........... | 99a | 341.7 | 436.4 | 535.5 | 717.4 | 939.4 | 894.3 | 1,073.3 | 1,278.2 | 1,386.1 | 1,440.3 | 1,568.8 | 1,956.9 |
| Net Current Transf.from Abroad....... | 98t | 13.7 | 14.8 | 16.4 | 18.4 | 17.0 | 30.3 | 30.1 | 35.8 | 39.1 | 44.8 | 44.8 | 87.2 |
| Gross Nat'l Disposable Inc.(GNDI)..... | 99i | 355.4 | 451.2 | 551.9 | 735.8 | 956.4 | 924.6 | 1,103.4 | 1,313.9 | 1,425.2 | 1,485.1 | 1,613.5 | 2,044.2 |
| Gross Saving................................ | 99s | 109.8 | 113.4 | 127.0 | 177.2 | 197.5 | 151.7 | 205.8 | 219.7 | 204.0 | 155.5 | 183.6 | 328.5 |
| GDP Volume 2007 Ref., Chained..... | 99b.p | 605.3 | 623.5 | 669.9 | 720.7 | 737.3 | 628.5 | 654.6 | 688.6 | 690.7 | 690.4 | .... | .... |
| GDP Volume (2010=100)............... | 99bvp | 92.5 | 95.2 | 102.3 | 110.1 | 112.6 | 96.0 | 100.0 | 105.2 | 105.5 | 105.5 | .... | .... |
| GDP Deflator (2010=100)............... | 99bip | 35.8 | 44.5 | 51.2 | 63.2 | 81.5 | 91.4 | 100.0 | 114.5 | 123.3 | 128.7 | .... | .... |
| | | | | | | *Millions: Midyear Estimates* | | | | | | | | |
| **Population...............................** | 99z | 47.13 | 46.80 | 46.50 | 46.25 | 46.03 | 45.83 | 45.65 | 45.48 | 45.32 | 45.17 | 45.00 | 44.82 |

# United Arab Emirates   466

| | | 2004 | 2005 | 2006 | 2007 | 2008 | 2009 | 2010 | 2011 | 2012 | 2013 | 2014 | 2015 |
|---|---|---|---|---|---|---|---|---|---|---|---|---|---|
| **Exchange Rates** | | | | | *Dirhams per SDR: End of Period* | | | | | | | | |
| Official Rate...................... | aa | 5.7034 | 5.2490 | 5.5249 | 5.8035 | 5.6566 | 5.7573 | 5.6558 | 5.6383 | 5.6443 | 5.6557 | 5.3208 | 5.0891 |
| | | | | | *Dirhams per US Dollar: End of Period (ae) Period Average (rf)* | | | | | | | | |
| Official Rate...................... | ae | 3.6725 | 3.6725 | 3.6725 | 3.6725 | 3.6725 | 3.6725 | 3.6725 | 3.6725 | 3.6725 | 3.6725 | 3.6725 | 3.6725 |
| Official Rate...................... | rf | 3.6725 | 3.6725 | 3.6725 | 3.6725 | 3.6725 | 3.6725 | 3.6725 | 3.6725 | 3.6725 | 3.6725 | 3.6725 | 3.6725 |
| | | | | | *Index Numbers (2010=100): Period Averages* | | | | | | | | |
| Official Rate...................... | ahx | 100.0 | 100.0 | 100.0 | 100.0 | 100.0 | 100.0 | 100.0 | 100.0 | 100.0 | 100.0 | 100.0 | 100.0 |
| Nominal Effective Exchange Rate..... | nec | 104.1 | 103.5 | 103.3 | 98.4 | 96.1 | 100.9 | 100.0 | 96.9 | 101.5 | 106.1 | 110.7 | 122.1 |
| **Fund Position** | | | | | *Millions of SDRs: End of Period* | | | | | | | | |
| Quota................................. | 2f.s | 611.70 | 611.70 | 611.70 | 611.70 | 611.70 | 611.70 | 611.70 | 752.50 | 752.50 | 752.50 | 752.50 | 752.50 |
| SDR Holdings...................... | 1b.s | 3.49 | 6.73 | 8.13 | 8.68 | 11.08 | 541.03 | 541.25 | 541.81 | 542.06 | 542.21 | 542.42 | 542.52 |
| Reserve Position in the Fund........... | 1c.s | 203.16 | 93.04 | 62.02 | 39.97 | 78.42 | 118.42 | 130.42 | 226.02 | 244.62 | 270.62 | 273.62 | 252.62 |
| Total Fund Cred. & Loans Outstg...... | 2tl | — | — | — | — | — | — | — | — | — | — | — | — |
| SDR Allocations.................... | 1bd | 38.74 | 38.74 | 38.74 | 38.74 | 38.74 | 568.41 | 568.41 | 568.41 | 568.41 | 568.41 | 568.41 | 568.41 |
| **International Liquidity** | | | | | *Millions of US Dollars Unless Otherwise Indicated: End of Period* | | | | | | | | |
| Total Reserves minus Gold.............. | 1l.d | 18,529.9 | 21,010.3 | 27,617.4 | 77,238.8 | 31,694.5 | 26,104.2 | 32,785.3 | 37,269.3 | 47,035.2 | 68,202.7 | 78,424.4 | 93,673.7 |
| SDR Holdings..................... | 1b.d | 5.4 | 9.6 | 12.2 | 13.7 | 17.1 | 848.2 | 833.5 | 831.8 | 833.1 | 835.0 | 785.9 | 751.8 |
| Reserve Position in the Fund......... | 1c.d | 315.5 | 133.0 | 93.3 | 63.2 | 120.8 | 185.6 | 200.8 | 347.0 | 376.0 | 416.7 | 396.4 | 350.1 |
| Foreign Exchange................. | 1d.d | 18,209.0 | 20,867.7 | 27,511.9 | 77,161.9 | 31,556.6 | 25,070.4 | 31,750.9 | 36,090.5 | 45,826.1 | 66,950.9 | 77,242.1 | 92,571.8 |
| Gold (Million Fine Troy Ounces)....... | 1ad | — | — | — | — | — | — | — | — | — | — | — | .241 |
| Gold (National Valuation)................ | 1and | — | — | — | — | — | — | — | — | — | — | — | 256.0 |
| Central Bank: Other Liabs.............. | 4..d | 149.2 | 311.0 | 345.3 | 368.1 | 315.3 | 182.7 | 170.2 | 37.6 | 46.3 | 49.0 | 1,353.3 | 1,642.5 |
| Deposit Money Banks: Assets........... | 7a.d | 34,412.8 | 47,659.1 | 63,155.3 | 53,613.6 | 55,380.8 | 56,679.9 | 63,584.2 | 67,767.5 | 83,473.4 | 111,579.0 | 133,942.0 | 135,180.4 |
| Deposit Money Banks: Liabs........... | 7b.d | 11,542.8 | 23,203.5 | 48,383.4 | 87,398.2 | 76,950.0 | 68,369.2 | 73,982.0 | 78,913.0 | 85,876.1 | 111,625.6 | 131,810.2 | 158,021.8 |
| **Monetary Authorities** | | | | | *Millions of Dirhams: End of Period* | | | | | | | | |
| Foreign Assets......................... | 11 | 68,568 | 78,181 | 102,721 | 285,974 | 113,545 | 93,672 | 120,501 | 136,621 | 172,903 | 250,532 | 288,247 | 345,147 |
| Claims on Central Government........ | 12a | — | 2,425 | 625 | — | 55,000 | 106,725 | 106,725 | 98,725 | 90,193 | 55,418 | 51,957 | 51,745 |
| Claims on Nonfin.Pub.Enterprises.... | 12c | — | — | — | — | — | — | — | — | — | — | — | — |
| Claims on Deposit Money Banks...... | 12e | 25 | — | — | — | 23,794 | 6,725 | 1,421 | 1,620 | 2,767 | 3,797 | 1,229 | 495 |
| Claims on Other Financial Insts........ | 12f | — | — | — | — | — | — | — | — | — | — | — | — |
| Reserve Money......................... | 14 | 54,766 | 65,347 | 86,499 | 265,656 | 168,911 | 185,248 | 206,362 | 212,307 | 238,067 | 281,537 | 308,924 | 364,796 |
| of which: Currency Outside DMBs.. | 14a | 15,778 | 17,522 | 21,837 | 25,941 | 36,967 | 37,217 | 38,560 | 41,591 | 45,615 | 50,408 | 59,016 | 58,391 |
| Time, Savings,& Fgn.Currency Dep... | 15 | — | — | — | — | — | — | — | — | — | — | — | — |
| Foreign Liabilities...................... | 16c | 769 | 1,345 | 1,482 | 1,577 | 1,377 | 3,944 | 3,840 | 3,343 | 3,378 | 3,395 | 7,994 | 8,925 |
| Central Government Deposits........... | 16d | 11,578 | 12,444 | 13,825 | 15,989 | 21,150 | 16,459 | 15,915 | 1,723 | 2,356 | 3,199 | 3,364 | 1,600 |
| Capital Accounts....................... | 17a | 1,560 | 1,560 | 1,560 | 1,560 | 1,500 | 1,500 | 1,500 | 17,152 | 18,077 | 21,243 | 19,827 | 20,218 |
| Other Items (Net)....................... | 17r | −79 | −91 | −20 | 1,192 | −599 | −29 | 1,030 | 2,441 | 3,985 | 373 | 1,324 | 1,848 |
| **Deposit Money Banks** | | | | | *Millions of Dirhams: End of Period* | | | | | | | | |
| Reserves................................ | 20 | 38,988 | 47,824 | 64,662 | 239,712 | 131,943 | 148,031 | 167,802 | 170,716 | 192,452 | 231,129 | 249,908 | 306,405 |
| Foreign Assets......................... | 21 | 126,381 | 175,028 | 231,938 | 196,896 | 203,386 | 208,157 | 233,513 | 248,876 | 306,556 | 409,774 | 491,902 | 496,450 |
| Claims on Central Government........ | 22a | 31,776 | 42,055 | 55,183 | 69,379 | 85,181 | 112,530 | 121,868 | 122,931 | 143,425 | 170,357 | 178,108 | 194,077 |
| Claims on Nonfin.Pub.Enterprises..... | 22c | 13,884 | 24,797 | 33,002 | 45,385 | 56,064 | 77,259 | 87,581 | 119,852 | 132,954 | 178,055 | 196,737 | 204,886 |
| Claims on Private Sector.................. | 22d | 204,727 | 290,239 | 385,730 | 530,737 | 777,141 | 786,495 | 792,030 | 819,112 | 832,534 | 859,975 | 959,015 | 1,040,004 |
| Claims on Other Financial Insts........ | 22f | 6,612 | 15,243 | 32,362 | 55,208 | 97,940 | 94,350 | 99,708 | 92,716 | 88,237 | 91,888 | 42,352 | 49,310 |
| Demand Deposits...................... | 24 | 65,040 | 86,927 | 98,183 | 155,723 | 171,171 | 186,265 | 194,401 | 222,505 | 253,558 | 329,142 | 377,116 | 398,543 |
| Time and Savings Deposits.............. | 25 | 167,588 | 219,615 | 279,274 | 384,037 | 466,172 | 517,136 | 553,427 | 561,662 | 563,201 | 677,213 | 704,984 | 748,643 |
| Foreign Liabilities...................... | 26c | 42,391 | 85,215 | 177,688 | 320,970 | 282,599 | 251,086 | 271,699 | 289,808 | 315,380 | 409,945 | 484,073 | 580,335 |
| Central Government Deposits........... | 26d | 51,804 | 79,196 | 93,696 | 114,595 | 203,920 | 192,627 | 183,175 | 174,822 | 219,554 | 176,380 | 206,521 | 177,052 |
| Credit from Monetary Authorities..... | 26g | 25 | 26 | 8 | 2 | 25,260 | 6,776 | 4,314 | 1,484 | 2,567 | 4,215 | 1,311 | 560 |
| Capital Accounts....................... | 27a | 52,463 | 78,132 | 104,089 | 130,882 | 165,569 | 244,031 | 273,038 | 280,791 | 298,814 | 272,176 | 299,144 | 324,816 |
| Other Items (Net)........................ | 27r | 43,057 | 46,075 | 49,939 | 31,108 | 36,964 | 28,901 | 22,448 | 43,131 | 43,084 | 72,107 | 44,873 | 61,183 |
| **Monetary Survey** | | | | | *Millions of Dirhams: End of Period* | | | | | | | | |
| Foreign Assets (Net)........................ | 31n | 151,789 | 166,648 | 155,489 | 160,323 | 32,955 | 46,799 | 78,475 | 92,346 | 160,701 | 246,966 | 288,082 | 252,337 |
| Domestic Credit........................ | 32 | 193,685 | 283,183 | 399,440 | 570,178 | 846,305 | 968,329 | 1,008,868 | 1,076,833 | 1,065,475 | 1,176,150 | 1,218,315 | 1,361,425 |
| Claims on Central Govt. (Net)........ | 32an | −31,606 | −47,160 | −51,713 | −61,205 | −84,889 | 10,169 | 29,503 | 45,111 | 11,708 | 46,196 | 20,180 | 67,170 |
| Claims on Nonfin.Pub.Enterprises.. | 32c | 13,884 | 24,797 | 33,002 | 45,385 | 56,064 | 77,259 | 87,581 | 119,852 | 132,954 | 178,055 | 196,737 | 204,886 |
| Claims on Private Sector........ | 32d | 204,795 | 290,303 | 385,789 | 530,790 | 777,190 | 786,551 | 792,076 | 819,154 | 832,576 | 860,011 | 959,046 | 1,040,059 |
| Claims on Other Financial Insts...... | 32f | 6,612 | 15,243 | 32,362 | 55,208 | 97,940 | 94,350 | 99,708 | 92,716 | 88,237 | 91,888 | 42,352 | 49,310 |
| Money................................. | 34 | 80,818 | 104,449 | 120,020 | 181,664 | 208,138 | 223,482 | 232,961 | 264,096 | 299,173 | 379,550 | 436,132 | 456,934 |
| Quasi-Money........................... | 35 | 167,588 | 219,615 | 279,274 | 384,037 | 466,172 | 517,136 | 553,427 | 561,662 | 563,201 | 677,213 | 704,984 | 748,643 |
| Capital Accounts....................... | 37a | 54,023 | 79,692 | 105,649 | 132,442 | 167,069 | 245,531 | 274,538 | 297,943 | 316,891 | 293,419 | 318,971 | 345,034 |
| Other Items (Net)........................ | 37r | 97,069 | 125,767 | 155,635 | 164,800 | 204,950 | 274,510 | 300,955 | 343,421 | 363,802 | 366,353 | 365,281 | 408,185 |
| Money plus Quasi-Money.................. | 35l | 248,406 | 324,064 | 399,294 | 565,701 | 674,310 | 740,618 | 786,388 | 825,758 | 862,374 | 1,056,763 | 1,141,116 | 1,205,577 |
| **Prices and Production** | | | | | *Index Numbers (2010=100): Period Averages* | | | | | | | | |
| Consumer Prices........................ | 64 | .... | .... | .... | 87.0 | 97.6 | 99.1 | 100.0 | 100.9 | 101.5 | 102.7 | 105.1 | 109.3 |
| Crude Petroleum Production........... | 66aa | 100.3 | 103.8 | 103.8 | 106.3 | 110.1 | 95.6 | 100.0 | 111.9 | 113.6 | 120.1 | 119.6 | 128.1 |
| **Intl. Transactions & Positions** | | | | | *Millions of US Dollars* | | | | | | | | |
| Imports, c.i.f........................... | 71..d | 72,082 | 84,654 | 100,057 | 132,500 | 177,000 | 150,000 | 165,000 | 205,000 | 220,000 | 245,000 | 262,000 | 230,000 |
| **National Accounts** | | | | | *Billions of Dirhams* | | | | | | | | |
| Househ.Cons.Expend.,incl.NPISHs.... | 96f | 338.7 | 386.5 | 469.6 | 584.8 | 710.7 | 506.0 | 617.3 | 665.5 | 612.6 | 646.2 | 700.3 | .... |
| Government Consumption Expend... | 91f | 42.3 | 45.5 | 51.0 | 56.2 | 66.6 | 89.3 | 90.1 | 93.7 | 94.3 | 97.3 | 110.7 | .... |
| Gross Fixed Capital Formation......... | 93e | 101.4 | 121.9 | 143.4 | 223.3 | 259.2 | 269.2 | 262.6 | 277.7 | 309.2 | 321.6 | 348.0 | .... |
| Changes in Inventories................. | 93i | 3.4 | 5.7 | 6.7 | 7.4 | 15.2 | 12.2 | 12.1 | 12.2 | 8.2 | 8.2 | 9.0 | .... |
| Exports of Goods and Services......... | 90c | 345.1 | 448.3 | 559.8 | 685.6 | 913.7 | 741.7 | 827.3 | 1,156.2 | 1,380.1 | 1,441.0 | 1,442.0 | .... |
| Imports of Goods and Services (-)..... | 98c | 288.0 | 344.7 | 414.7 | 610.1 | 806.9 | 687.3 | 759.0 | 925.3 | 1,033.0 | 1,092.3 | 1,143.0 | .... |
| Gross Domestic Product (GDP)........ | 99b | 542.9 | 663.3 | 815.7 | 947.2 | 1,158.6 | 931.2 | 1,050.5 | 1,280.0 | 1,371.4 | 1,422.0 | 1,467.0 | .... |
| GDP Volume 2007 Prices........ | 99b.p | 835.8 | 918.0 | 947.2 | 977.4 | 926.2 | 941.3 | 990.4 | 1,058.6 | 1,104.4 | 1,154.8 | .... | .... |
| GDP Volume (2010=100).............. | 99bvp | 84.4 | 92.7 | 95.6 | 98.7 | 93.5 | 95.1 | 100.0 | 106.9 | 111.5 | 116.6 | .... | .... |
| GDP Deflator (2010=100).............. | 99bip | 61.2 | 68.1 | 81.2 | 91.4 | 117.9 | 93.3 | 100.0 | 114.0 | 117.1 | 116.1 | .... | .... |
| | | | | | *Millions: Midyear Estimates* | | | | | | | | |
| **Population**........................... | 99z | 3.98 | 4.48 | 5.17 | 6.01 | 6.90 | 7.71 | 8.33 | 8.73 | 8.95 | 9.04 | 9.09 | 9.16 |

# United Kingdom  112

|  |  | 2004 | 2005 | 2006 | 2007 | 2008 | 2009 | 2010 | 2011 | 2012 | 2013 | 2014 | 2015 |
|---|---|---|---|---|---|---|---|---|---|---|---|---|---|
| **Exchange Rates** | | | | | | *SDRs per Pound: End of Period* | | | | | | | |
| Market Rate | ac | 1.2436 | 1.2047 | 1.3048 | 1.2678 | .9465 | 1.0330 | 1.0165 | 1.0071 | 1.0267 | 1.0694 | 1.0773 | 1.0694 |
| | | | | *US Dollars per Pound: End of Period (ag) Period Average (rh)* | | | | | | | | | |
| Market Rate | ag | 1.9314 | 1.7219 | 1.9630 | 2.0034 | 1.4578 | 1.6195 | 1.5655 | 1.5461 | 1.5780 | 1.6468 | 1.5608 | 1.4819 |
| Market Rate | rh | 1.8318 | 1.8204 | 1.8426 | 2.0017 | 1.8532 | 1.5645 | 1.5461 | 1.6036 | 1.5853 | 1.5645 | 1.6474 | 1.5290 |
| | | *ECUs per Pound through 1998; Euros per Pound Beginning 1999: End of Period (ec) Period Average (ed)* | | | | | | | | | | | |
| Euro Rate | ec | 1.4180 | 1.4596 | 1.4905 | 1.3609 | 1.0475 | 1.1242 | 1.1716 | 1.1949 | 1.1960 | 1.1941 | 1.2856 | 1.3612 |
| Euro Rate | ed | 1.4753 | 1.4638 | 1.4688 | 1.4625 | 1.2652 | 1.1262 | 1.1674 | 1.1536 | 1.2338 | 1.1783 | 1.2417 | 1.3786 |
| | | *Index Numbers (2010=100): Period Averages* | | | | | | | | | | | |
| Market Rate | ahx | 118.5 | 117.7 | 119.2 | 129.5 | 119.9 | 101.2 | 100.0 | 103.7 | 102.5 | 101.2 | 106.6 | 98.9 |
| Nominal Effective Exchange Rate | nec | 127.3 | 126.1 | 126.9 | 129.0 | 112.6 | 99.4 | 100.0 | 99.2 | 103.5 | 101.0 | 107.3 | 114.4 |
| CPI-Based Real Effect. Ex. Rate | rec | 119.8 | 119.5 | 121.5 | 125.7 | 110.1 | 96.5 | 100.0 | 101.5 | 106.8 | 105.8 | 113.7 | 121.8 |
| ULC-Based Real Effect. Ex. Rate | rel | 113.2 | 113.2 | 116.3 | 118.8 | 101.4 | 93.3 | 100.0 | 100.7 | 104.8 | 101.2 | 106.9 | 114.3 |
| **Fund Position** | | | | | | *Millions of SDRs: End of Period* | | | | | | | |
| Quota | 2f.s | 10,738.50 | 10,738.50 | 10,738.50 | 10,738.50 | 10,738.50 | 10,738.50 | 10,738.50 | 10,738.50 | 10,738.50 | 10,738.50 | 10,738.50 | 10,738.50 |
| SDR Holdings | 1b.s | 211.29 | 200.59 | 263.03 | 227.93 | 290.81 | 9,149.50 | 9,167.60 | 9,504.94 | 9,620.52 | 9,648.08 | 9,621.64 | 9,552.89 |
| Reserve Position in the Fund | 1c.s | 3,562.41 | 1,627.83 | 939.63 | 696.15 | 1,525.76 | 2,125.94 | 3,176.29 | 5,498.11 | 5,766.52 | 5,189.07 | 3,698.14 | 3,028.92 |
| Total Fund Cred.&Loans Outstg. | 2tl | — | — | — | — | — | — | — | — | — | — | — | — |
| SDR Allocations | 1bd | 1,913.07 | 1,913.07 | 1,913.07 | 1,913.07 | 1,913.07 | 10,134.20 | 10,134.20 | 10,134.20 | 10,134.20 | 10,134.20 | 10,134.20 | 10,134.20 |
| **International Liquidity** | | | | | *Billions of US Dollars Unless Otherwise Indicated: End of Period* | | | | | | | | |
| Total Reserves minus Gold | 1l.d | 39.94 | 38.47 | 40.70 | 48.96 | 44.35 | 55.70 | 68.34 | 79.27 | 88.60 | 92.40 | 95.70 | 119.03 |
| SDR Holdings | 1b.d | .33 | .29 | .40 | .36 | .45 | 14.34 | 14.12 | 14.59 | 14.79 | 14.86 | 13.94 | 13.24 |
| Reserve Position in the Fund | 1c.d | 5.53 | 2.33 | 1.41 | 1.10 | 2.35 | 3.33 | 4.89 | 8.44 | 8.86 | 7.99 | 5.36 | 4.20 |
| Foreign Exchange | 1d.d | 34.08 | 35.85 | 38.89 | 47.50 | 41.55 | 38.03 | 49.33 | 56.24 | 64.95 | 69.55 | 76.40 | 101.59 |
| Other Liquid Foreign Assets | 1e.d | 17.80 | 15.54 | 16.78 | 20.44 | 11.76 | 12.90 | 15.66 | 15.19 | 11.96 | 14.33 | 16.76 | 18.51 |
| Gold (Million Fine Troy Ounces) | 1ad | 10.04 | 9.99 | 9.97 | 9.98 | 9.98 | 9.98 | 9.98 | 9.98 | 9.98 | 9.98 | 9.98 | 9.98 |
| Gold (National Valuation) | 1and | 4.40 | 5.13 | 6.34 | 8.34 | 8.63 | 11.01 | 14.07 | 15.27 | 16.53 | 12.02 | 12.03 | 10.59 |
| Banking Insts.: Foreign Assets | 7a.d | 3,643.33 | 3,937.75 | 4,914.15 | .... | .... | .... | .... | .... | .... | .... | .... | .... |
| Banking Insts.: Foreign Liabs | 7b.d | 4,033.35 | 4,251.40 | 5,254.85 | .... | .... | .... | .... | .... | .... | .... | .... | .... |
| **Monetary Authorities** | | | | | | *Billions of Pounds: End of Period* | | | | | | | |
| Foreign Assets | 11 | 12.22 | 14.60 | 15.26 | 14.17 | 39.08 | 16.47 | 17.12 | 14.11 | 9.13 | 10.10 | 11.46 | 13.03 |
| Claims on Central Govt. (Net) | 12an | 14.94 | 13.98 | 14.08 | 14.04 | 28.16 | 188.76 | 206.95 | 281.26 | 396.43 | 374.50 | 406.19 | 399.67 |
| Claims on Private Sector | 12d | 6.17 | 7.07 | 12.23 | 5.59 | 16.26 | 7.26 | 3.67 | 1.33 | 2.14 | .23 | .08 | .26 |
| Reserve Money | 14 | 39.13 | 40.27 | 62.34 | 70.79 | 95.51 | 196.89 | 193.16 | 221.87 | 331.77 | 360.61 | 364.58 | 379.87 |
| of which: Currency Outside DMBs | 14a | 27.99 | 30.24 | 32.39 | 36.64 | 39.26 | 42.73 | 44.69 | 47.19 | 49.45 | 52.71 | 54.85 | 58.81 |
| Foreign Liabilities | 16c | 13.28 | 16.53 | 16.95 | 24.04 | 50.79 | 16.42 | 20.03 | 21.66 | 34.76 | 19.32 | 20.98 | 26.22 |
| Other Items (Net) | 17r | −19.07 | −21.15 | −37.72 | −61.03 | −62.81 | −.82 | 14.55 | 53.17 | 41.17 | 4.90 | 32.17 | 6.88 |
| **Banking Institutions** | | | | | | *Billions of Pounds: End of Period* | | | | | | | |
| Reserves | 20 | 13.00 | 13.38 | 29.73 | 32.25 | 60.79 | 155.35 | 146.19 | 173.26 | 263.70 | 300.95 | 301.80 | 297.50 |
| Foreign Assets | 21 | 1,969.16 | 2,400.57 | 2,645.43 | 3,440.58 | 3,905.22 | 3,349.76 | 3,502.56 | 3,715.09 | 3,446.48 | 3,062.28 | 3,154.24 | 3,049.91 |
| Claims on Central Govt. (Net) | 22an | 8.43 | 7.34 | −11.31 | −19.38 | −23.58 | 16.01 | 71.67 | 102.10 | 79.63 | 107.92 | 127.60 | 127.69 |
| Claims on Official Entities | 22bx | 6.31 | 7.18 | 8.39 | 9.92 | 9.73 | 9.87 | 10.42 | 7.80 | 7.72 | 7.59 | 7.87 | 7.98 |
| Claims on Private Sector | 22d | 1,807.60 | 1,994.87 | 2,256.21 | 2,625.88 | 3,030.30 | 2,973.23 | 2,965.64 | 2,831.16 | 2,752.78 | 2,663.81 | 2,523.85 | 2,507.11 |
| Demand,Time,Savings,Fgn.Cur.Dep. | 25l | 1,399.55 | 1,595.00 | 1,821.98 | 2,110.92 | 2,490.64 | 2,485.53 | 2,584.45 | 2,465.79 | 2,482.88 | 2,532.86 | 2,465.18 | 2,510.18 |
| Foreign Liabilities | 26c | 2,050.27 | 2,421.45 | 2,635.58 | 3,477.42 | 3,968.95 | 3,393.09 | 3,413.04 | 3,539.00 | 3,240.36 | 2,916.56 | 2,908.84 | 2,764.93 |
| Other Items (Net) | 27r | 354.68 | 406.88 | 470.90 | 500.92 | 522.87 | 625.58 | 699.00 | 824.62 | 827.08 | 693.13 | 741.34 | 715.28 |
| **Banking Survey** | | | | | | *Billions of Pounds: End of Period* | | | | | | | |
| Foreign Assets (Net) | 31n | −82.17 | −22.81 | 8.17 | −46.71 | −75.45 | −43.29 | 86.61 | 168.54 | 180.50 | 136.49 | 235.88 | 271.79 |
| Domestic Credit | 32 | 1,843.45 | 2,030.44 | 2,279.59 | 2,636.05 | 3,060.87 | 3,195.13 | 3,258.36 | 3,223.64 | 3,238.70 | 3,154.04 | 3,065.59 | 3,042.71 |
| Claims on Central Govt. (Net) | 32an | 23.37 | 21.31 | 2.77 | −5.34 | 4.58 | 204.77 | 278.62 | 383.35 | 476.06 | 482.42 | 533.78 | 527.36 |
| Claims on Official Entities | 32bx | 6.31 | 7.18 | 8.39 | 9.92 | 9.73 | 9.87 | 10.42 | 7.80 | 7.72 | 7.59 | 7.87 | 7.98 |
| Claims on Private Sector | 32d | 1,813.77 | 2,001.94 | 2,268.43 | 2,631.47 | 3,046.56 | 2,980.49 | 2,969.31 | 2,832.49 | 2,754.92 | 2,664.04 | 2,523.93 | 2,507.37 |
| Money Plus Quasi-Money | 35l | 1,427.54 | 1,625.24 | 1,854.36 | 2,147.56 | 2,529.90 | 2,528.26 | 2,629.13 | 2,512.98 | 2,532.33 | 2,585.56 | 2,520.03 | 2,568.99 |
| Other Items (Net) | 37r | 333.75 | 382.38 | 433.39 | 441.78 | 455.52 | 623.58 | 715.84 | 879.21 | 886.87 | 704.97 | 781.43 | 745.52 |
| **Money (National Definitions)** | | | | | | *Billions of Pounds: End of Period* | | | | | | | |
| M0 | 19mc | 44.46 | 47.09 | .... | .... | .... | .... | .... | .... | .... | .... | .... | .... |
| M4 | 59md | 1,179.20 | 1,328.32 | 1,498.94 | 1,674.88 | 1,937.22 † | 1,539.55 | 1,570.88 | 1,560.72 | 1,640.66 | 1,714.19 | 1,791.36 | 1,864.85 |
| | | | | *Millions of Pounds: Period Change* | | | | | | | | | |
| M0, Seasonally Adjusted | 19mcc | 2,285 | 2,276 | .... | .... | .... | .... | .... | .... | .... | .... | .... | .... |
| M4, Seasonally Adjusted | 59mdc | 95,515 | 149,734 | 165,649 | 189,367 | 257,919 | † 14,578 | 35,664 | 21,445 | 85,286 | 63,626 | 71,203 | 67,994 |
| **Interest Rates** | | | | | | *Percent Per Annum* | | | | | | | |
| Central Bank Policy Rate (EOP) | 60 | 4.75 | 4.50 | 5.00 | 5.50 | 2.00 | .50 | .50 | .50 | .50 | .50 | .50 | .50 |
| Money Market Rate | 60b | 4.29 | 4.70 | 4.77 | 5.67 | 4.68 | .53 | .48 | .52 | .48 | .45 | .41 | .39 |
| Treasury Bill Rate | 60c | 4.43 | 4.55 | 4.65 | 5.52 | 4.30 | .53 | .50 | .49 | .31 | .30 | .38 | .44 |
| Treas. Bill Rate(Bond Equivalent) | 60cs | 4.44 | 4.59 | 4.67 | 5.60 | 4.35 | .54 | .50 | .49 | .31 | .30 | .38 | .44 |
| Eurodollar Rate in London | 60d | 1.58 | 3.53 | 5.16 | 5.28 | 3.20 | .94 | .53 | .42 | .42 | .33 | .28 | .47 |
| Lending Rate | 60p | 4.38 | 4.65 | 4.64 | 5.51 | 4.68 | .64 | .50 | .50 | .50 | .50 | .50 | |
| Govt. Bond Yield: Short-Term | 61a | 4.82 | 4.38 | 4.63 | 5.18 | 4.31 | 2.73 | 2.37 | 1.94 | .85 | 1.25 | 1.72 | 1.24 |
| Govt. Bond Yield: Long-Term | 61 | 4.88 | 4.41 | 4.50 | 5.01 | 4.59 | 3.65 | 3.62 | 3.14 | 1.92 | 2.39 | 2.57 | 1.90 |

# United Kingdom   112

| | | 2004 | 2005 | 2006 | 2007 | 2008 | 2009 | 2010 | 2011 | 2012 | 2013 | 2014 | 2015 |
|---|---|---|---|---|---|---|---|---|---|---|---|---|---|
| **Prices, Production, Labor** | | | | | | *Index Numbers (2010=100): Period Averages* | | | | | | | |
| Share Prices............................. | 62 | 79.9 | 91.9 | 107.4 | 117.4 | 96.9 | 82.6 | 100.0 | 104.8 | 106.0 | 121.7 | 127.0 | 127.6 |
| Share Prices (End of Month)............. | 62.ep | 80.6 | 92.9 | 108.7 | 118.6 | 97.3 | 83.8 | 100.0 | 106.3 | 106.5 | 123.1 | 128.2 | 128.3 |
| FTSE 100................................ | 62a | 82.7 | 94.4 | 108.4 | 117.2 | 98.2 | 83.5 | 100.0 | 104.1 | 105.1 | 118.4 | 122.3 | 120.7 |
| Prices: Manufacturing Output.......... | 63 | 85.4 | 87.0 | 88.8 | 90.8 | 96.9 | 97.4 | 100.0 | 104.8 | 107.0 | 108.4 | 108.4 | 106.6 |
| Consumer Prices........................ | 64 | 85.6 | 87.3 | 89.4 | 91.5 | 94.8 | 96.8 | 100.0 | 104.5 | 107.4 | 110.2 | † 111.8 | 111.8 |
| Retail Prices........................... | 64b | 83.5 | 85.9 | 88.6 | 92.4 | 96.1 | 95.6 | 100.0 | 105.2 | 108.6 | 111.9 | 114.5 | 115.7 |
| Wages: Avg. Monthly Earnings........ | 65..c | 82.2 | 86.0 | 90.1 | 94.5 | 97.8 | 97.7 | 100.0 | 102.4 | 103.8 | 105.0 | 106.2 | 108.9 |
| Industrial Production................... | 66 | 108.7 | 107.9 | 108.6 | 108.9 | 106.1 | 96.9 | 100.0 | 99.4 | 96.7 | 95.9 | 97.2 | 98.4 |
| Employment, Seas. Adj................. | 67..c | 99.7 | 101.1 | 102.2 | 102.9 | 103.4 | 101.1 | 100.0 | 100.2 | 101.8 | 102.9 | 105.8 | 107.8 |
| | | | | | | *Number in Thousands: Period Averages* | | | | | | | |
| Labor Force............................. | 67d | 29,766 | 29,584 | 30,046 | 30,236 | 30,570 | 30,666 | 30,728 | 30,943 | 31,162 | 31,337 | 31,504 | 31,651 |
| Employment............................. | 67e | 28,456 | 28,162 | 28,418 | 28,622 | 28,827 | 28,319 | 28,290 | 28,404 | 28,651 | 28,917 | 29,531 | 29,930 |
| Unemployment........................... | 67c | 1,422 | 1,441 | 1,640 | 1,624 | 1,757 | 2,369 | 2,460 | 2,559 | 2,534 | 2,441 | 1,996 | 1,741 |
| Unemployment Rate (%)................ | 67r | 4.7 | 4.8 | 5.4 | 5.3 | 5.6 | 7.6 | 7.8 | 8.1 | 7.9 | 7.6 | 6.2 | 5.4 |
| **Intl. Transactions & Positions** | | | | | | *Millions of Pounds* | | | | | | | |
| Exports................................. | 70..c | 190,099 | 210,704 | 242,899 | 219,981 | 251,565 | 227,727 | 270,816 | 308,171 | 304,302 | 306,226 | 293,739 | 285,642 |
| Imports, c.i.f........................... | 71..c | 251,177 | 279,853 | 319,741 | 310,516 | 345,826 | 310,660 | 368,226 | 401,713 | 410,800 | 421,457 | 416,882 | 410,670 |
| Exports................................. | 70 | 190,099 | 210,704 | 242,899 | 219,981 | 251,565 | 227,727 | 265,243 | 298,421 | 300,457 | 304,977 | 290,273 | .... |
| Imports, c.i.f........................... | 71 | 251,177 | 279,853 | 319,741 | 310,516 | 345,826 | 310,660 | 363,828 | 398,513 | 409,157 | 412,752 | 403,046 | .... |
| | | | | | | *2010=100* | | | | | | | |
| Volume of Exports...................... | 72..c | 89.7 | † 97.1 | 110.4 | 100.5 | 102.0 | 91.2 | † 100.0 | 106.7 | 105.9 | 105.2 | 106.5 | 110.8 |
| Volume of Imports...................... | 73..c | 89.7 | † 96.4 | 107.2 | 103.9 | 101.9 | 90.0 | † 100.0 | 101.2 | 103.6 | 106.1 | 110.4 | 114.4 |
| Export Prices........................... | 76 | 77.3 | † 80.1 | 81.4 | 81.0 | 92.2 | 93.6 | † 100.0 | 107.9 | 107.8 | 109.0 | 103.1 | 95.5 |
| Import Prices........................... | 76.x | 75.5 | † 78.7 | 81.0 | 81.0 | 92.6 | 94.6 | † 100.0 | 108.5 | 108.7 | 109.1 | 103.5 | 97.6 |
| **Balance of Payments** | | | | | | *Billions of US Dollars* | | | | | | | |
| A. Current Account*.................... | 109bx | −41.7 | −30.1 | −59.9 | −74.8 | −101.1 | −69.4 | −67.6 | −43.7 | −86.4 | −122.2 | −151.9 | −146.9 |
| Goods, credit (exports)................. | 1a9cx | 351.0 | 385.1 | 448.2 | 446.5 | 472.8 | 358.7 | 417.8 | 493.7 | 480.7 | 478.9 | 483.4 | 436.2 |
| Goods, debit (imports)................. | 1a9dx | 464.4 | 512.7 | 593.7 | 627.8 | 649.7 | 493.8 | 568.6 | 643.7 | 648.9 | 659.3 | 685.9 | 627.7 |
| Balance on goods...................... | 1a9bx | −113.4 | −127.6 | −145.5 | −181.3 | −176.9 | −135.1 | −150.7 | −149.9 | −168.3 | −180.5 | −202.5 | −191.5 |
| Services, credit (exports)............... | 1b9cx | 210.0 | 234.8 | 268.8 | 315.7 | 307.7 | 265.0 | 269.3 | 302.9 | 311.9 | 335.9 | 361.7 | 345.4 |
| Services, debit (imports)............... | 1b9dx | 161.1 | 173.5 | 190.1 | 214.1 | 218.2 | 184.1 | 185.3 | 194.9 | 197.2 | 209.2 | 215.8 | 210.0 |
| Balance on Goods & Services....... | 1z9bx | −64.5 | −66.3 | −66.8 | −79.6 | −87.4 | −54.2 | −66.7 | −42.0 | −53.6 | −53.8 | −56.6 | −56.1 |
| Primary income: credit................. | 1c9cx | 266.2 | 358.5 | 467.9 | 624.7 | 546.3 | 280.0 | 275.4 | 327.6 | 275.1 | 237.6 | 237.0 | 203.5 |
| Primary income: debit.................. | 1c9dx | 223.1 | 298.9 | 437.8 | 591.9 | 533.4 | 270.6 | 244.2 | 294.7 | 273.4 | 264.0 | 291.1 | 256.6 |
| Balance on gds, serv. & prim. inc. | 1y9bx | −21.4 | −6.6 | −36.6 | −46.8 | −74.5 | −44.9 | −35.5 | −9.0 | −51.8 | −80.2 | −110.6 | −109.1 |
| Secondary income: credit.............. | 1d9ca | 23.6 | 27.4 | 37.4 | 27.7 | 37.4 | 26.1 | 24.1 | 22.8 | 26.0 | 29.7 | 31.7 | 29.9 |
| Secondary income: debit.............. | 1d9da | 43.9 | 50.9 | 60.7 | 55.7 | 64.0 | 50.7 | 56.1 | 57.4 | 60.6 | 71.7 | 73.0 | 67.6 |
| B. Capital Account*.................... | 209ba | .1 | −1.4 | −2.8 | −.3 | .5 | .6 | — | −.2 | −.5 | −.7 | −2.1 | −1.7 |
| Capital account: credit................. | 209ca | 2.3 | 3.3 | 2.4 | 3.3 | 4.6 | 3.7 | 3.9 | 3.7 | 3.1 | 3.1 | 1.9 | 2.4 |
| Capital account: debit.................. | 209da | 2.2 | 4.7 | 5.2 | 3.6 | 4.1 | 3.1 | 3.8 | 3.8 | 3.7 | 3.9 | 4.0 | 4.1 |
| Balance on current & capital acct. | 129bx | −41.6 | −31.5 | −62.8 | −75.1 | −100.6 | −68.8 | −67.6 | −43.8 | −87.0 | −123.0 | −153.9 | −148.6 |
| C. Financial Account*  ............... | 309na | −25.2 | −22.3 | −51.7 | −56.3 | −66.8 | −54.5 | −57.3 | −37.0 | −82.9 | −116.7 | −177.6 | −175.5 |
| Direct investment: assets.............. | 3a9aa | 128.6 | 159.9 | 142.3 | 370.4 | 356.7 | −48.4 | 54.4 | 80.8 | 12.0 | −29.6 | −88.6 | −43.4 |
| Equity & investment fund shares.. | 3aaaa | 93.9 | 114.8 | 133.0 | 260.5 | 155.3 | 21.2 | 78.5 | 91.9 | 30.4 | −9.4 | −130.9 | 9.1 |
| Debt instruments...................... | 3abaa | 34.7 | 45.1 | 9.2 | 109.9 | 201.4 | −69.6 | −24.0 | −11.0 | −18.3 | −20.2 | 42.3 | −52.5 |
| Direct investment: liabilities .......... | 3a9la | 87.1 | 252.7 | 203.6 | 209.5 | 253.5 | 14.5 | 66.7 | 27.0 | 46.8 | 35.0 | 45.5 | 57.7 |
| Equity & investment fund shares . | 3aala | 57.0 | 157.2 | 134.3 | 206.0 | 110.6 | 66.0 | 74.6 | 32.4 | 46.9 | 54.2 | 44.3 | 58.9 |
| Debt instruments....................... | 3abla | 30.1 | 95.4 | 69.3 | 3.5 | 142.8 | −51.5 | −7.9 | −5.4 | −.1 | −19.2 | 1.1 | −1.2 |
| Portfolio investment: assets .......... | 3b9aa | 269.9 | 291.0 | 268.0 | 196.8 | −180.4 | 280.5 | 159.9 | 20.6 | 207.9 | −7.4 | 11.8 | −22.8 |
| Equity & investment fund shares | 3baaa | 111.5 | 126.5 | 48.8 | 71.7 | −95.2 | 34.6 | 47.9 | −30.1 | 76.8 | −34.9 | −38.9 | −22.4 |
| Debt securities ......................... | 3bbaa | 158.4 | 164.4 | 219.2 | 125.2 | −85.2 | 246.0 | 112.0 | 50.7 | 131.0 | 27.5 | 50.7 | −.4 |
| Portfolio investment: liabilities....... | 3b9la | 266.9 | 377.3 | 370.1 | 413.7 | 253.0 | 323.9 | 136.5 | .4 | −128.3 | 72.6 | 201.5 | 387.8 |
| Equity & investment fund shares . | 3bala | 3.6 | 12.5 | −18.3 | −20.2 | 71.8 | 72.8 | −10.9 | −14.0 | −11.7 | 47.0 | 49.4 | 115.4 |
| Debt securities......................... | 3bbla | 263.3 | 364.8 | 388.3 | 433.9 | 181.2 | 251.0 | 147.3 | 14.3 | −116.5 | 25.6 | 152.1 | 272.4 |
| Fin. der.& empl.stk.ops.(ESOs): net. | 3c9na | 12.0 | −9.1 | −40.4 | 54.0 | 219.2 | −49.1 | −38.5 | 4.3 | −47.3 | 21.9 | −23.5 | −49.9 |
| Fin. der. & ESOs.: assets.............. | 3c9aa | .... | .... | .... | .... | .... | .... | .... | .... | .... | .... | .... | .... |
| Fin. der. & ESOs.: liabilities.......... | 3c9la | .... | .... | .... | .... | .... | .... | .... | .... | .... | .... | .... | .... |
| Other investment: assets............... | 3d9aa | 605.4 | 920.5 | 706.1 | 1,310.9 | −1,080.1 | −529.8 | 362.1 | 167.8 | −370.4 | −326.7 | 191.0 | −107.7 |
| Other equity........................... | 3daaa | .2 | .2 | .6 | .5 | .3 | .4 | .1 | .5 | .2 | 2.3 | .4 | .1 |
| Debt instruments....................... | 3dzaa | 605.2 | 920.4 | 705.5 | 1,310.4 | −1,080.4 | −530.3 | 362.0 | 167.3 | −370.7 | −329.0 | 190.5 | −107.8 |
| Other investment: liabilities.......... | 3d9la | 687.2 | 754.6 | 554.0 | 1,365.2 | −1,124.3 | −630.7 | 392.0 | 283.1 | −33.4 | −332.7 | 21.4 | −494.0 |
| Other equity........................... | 3dala | — | — | — | — | — | — | — | — | — | — | — | — |
| Debt instruments....................... | 3dzla | 687.2 | 754.6 | 554.0 | 1,365.2 | −1,124.3 | −630.7 | 392.0 | 283.1 | −33.4 | −332.7 | 21.4 | −494.0 |
| Curr.+ cap.− finan. acct. balance.. | 4y9na | −16.4 | −9.2 | −11.0 | −18.7 | −33.8 | −14.3 | −10.3 | −6.8 | −4.1 | −6.3 | 23.6 | 26.9 |
| D. Net Errors and Omissions........... | 409na | 16.8 | 10.9 | 9.7 | 21.3 | 30.7 | 23.9 | 20.3 | 17.7 | 15.7 | 13.3 | −13.5 | 4.5 |
| E. Reserves and Related Items.......... | 4z9na | .4 | 1.7 | −1.3 | 2.6 | −3.1 | 9.6 | 10.0 | 10.9 | 11.6 | 7.0 | 10.1 | 31.3 |
| Reserve assets........................ | 3e9aa | .4 | 1.7 | −1.3 | 2.6 | −3.1 | 9.6 | 10.0 | 10.9 | 11.6 | 7.0 | 10.1 | 31.3 |
| Credit and loans from the IMF....... | 3dcla | — | — | — | — | — | — | — | — | — | — | — | — |
| Exceptional financing.................. | 409la | .... | .... | .... | .... | .... | .... | .... | .... | .... | .... | .... | .... |

*Excludes components in group E

| | | 2004 | 2005 | 2006 | 2007 | 2008 | 2009 | 2010 | 2011 | 2012 | 2013 | 2014 | 2015 |
|---|---|---|---|---|---|---|---|---|---|---|---|---|---|
| **International Investment Position** | | | | | | *Billions of US Dollars* | | | | | | | |
| Assets................................ | **809aa** | 9,329.9 | 10,119.8 | 12,397.7 | 15,876.8 | 16,470.4 | 14,247.6 | 15,939.1 | 17,226.6 | 16,614.6 | 15,948.2 | 15,910.1 | 14,686.0 |
| Direct investment.......................... | **8a9aa** | 1,633.7 | 1,580.8 | 1,871.0 | 2,203.1 | 1,988.9 | 1,927.0 | 1,990.9 | 2,005.5 | 2,127.2 | 2,087.3 | 1,915.0 | 2,040.0 |
| Equity & investment fund shares.. | **8aaaa** | 1,253.5 | 1,211.9 | 1,441.5 | 1,680.6 | 1,451.4 | 1,493.3 | 1,570.1 | 1,618.4 | 1,631.3 | 1,537.6 | 1,399.3 | 1,609.1 |
| Debt instruments.......................... | **8abaa** | 380.2 | 368.9 | 429.6 | 522.5 | 537.5 | 433.8 | 420.8 | 387.1 | 496.0 | 549.7 | 515.7 | 430.8 |
| Portfolio investment...................... | **8b9aa** | 2,163.2 | 2,381.6 | 3,054.9 | 3,451.5 | 2,473.6 | 3,114.9 | 3,356.8 | 3,293.9 | 3,704.3 | 4,024.2 | 3,975.0 | 3,812.9 |
| Equity & investment fund shares.. | **8baaa** | 977.6 | 1,163.1 | 1,490.8 | 1,672.7 | 950.9 | 1,270.8 | 1,419.2 | 1,316.7 | 1,575.9 | 1,833.3 | 1,801.9 | 1,707.7 |
| Debt securities............................ | **8bbaa** | 1,185.6 | 1,218.6 | 1,564.0 | 1,778.8 | 1,522.7 | 1,844.0 | 1,937.6 | 1,977.2 | 2,128.4 | 2,190.9 | 2,173.0 | 2,105.2 |
| Fin. der.(oth.than reserves) & ESOs | **8c9aa** | 1,370.1 | 1,412.1 | 1,675.9 | 2,761.0 | 5,889.8 | 3,524.7 | 4,638.3 | 5,593.5 | 4,828.8 | 3,992.5 | 4,414.9 | 3,602.3 |
| Other investment.......................... | **8d9aa** | 4,118.0 | 4,702.2 | 5,750.9 | 7,407.8 | 6,065.2 | 5,616.1 | 5,875.5 | 6,245.9 | 5,856.2 | 5,743.2 | 5,499.6 | 5,101.3 |
| Other equity.............................. | **8daaa** | 4.3 | 4.0 | 5.1 | 5.7 | 4.4 | 5.3 | 5.2 | 5.7 | 6.0 | 8.7 | 8.7 | 8.3 |
| Debt instruments........................ | **8dzaa** | 4,113.7 | 4,698.2 | 5,745.8 | 7,402.1 | 6,060.9 | 5,610.8 | 5,870.2 | 6,240.2 | 5,850.2 | 5,734.5 | 5,490.9 | 5,093.0 |
| Reserve assets.............................. | **8e9aa** | 44.9 | 43.2 | 45.0 | 53.5 | 52.9 | 65.0 | 77.6 | 87.8 | 98.0 | 101.2 | 105.6 | 129.5 |
| Liabilities......................................... | **809la** | 9,618.4 | 10,318.5 | 12,787.1 | 16,236.9 | 16,363.7 | 14,613.9 | 16,137.5 | 17,414.8 | 17,162.9 | 16,350.0 | 16,583.6 | 14,783.9 |
| Direct investment.......................... | **8a9la** | 1,008.4 | 1,182.5 | 1,509.6 | 1,567.5 | 1,367.0 | 1,416.7 | 1,473.4 | 1,525.2 | 1,961.5 | 1,997.4 | 2,146.0 | 1,959.3 |
| Equity & investment fund shares.. | **8aala** | 486.3 | 606.3 | 814.1 | 947.7 | 763.8 | 832.6 | 898.0 | 950.7 | 1,170.8 | 1,262.9 | 1,448.6 | 1,336.1 |
| Debt instruments.......................... | **8abla** | 522.1 | 576.2 | 695.5 | 619.8 | 603.2 | 584.1 | 575.3 | 574.5 | 790.7 | 734.4 | 697.5 | 623.2 |
| Portfolio investment...................... | **8b9la** | 2,431.7 | 2,581.3 | 3,423.9 | 4,054.3 | 2,974.0 | 3,947.7 | 4,016.8 | 3,889.5 | 3,991.8 | 4,083.5 | 4,094.7 | 4,050.4 |
| Equity & investment fund shares.. | **8bala** | 1,110.1 | 1,131.5 | 1,532.8 | 1,675.3 | 882.8 | 1,368.8 | 1,464.6 | 1,285.5 | 1,383.2 | 1,609.3 | 1,584.0 | 1,583.9 |
| Debt securities............................ | **8bbla** | 1,321.6 | 1,449.8 | 1,891.1 | 2,379.0 | 2,091.2 | 2,578.9 | 2,552.2 | 2,604.1 | 2,608.6 | 2,474.3 | 2,510.7 | 2,466.5 |
| Fin. der.(oth.than reserves) & ESOs | **8c9la** | 1,381.0 | 1,431.1 | 1,748.0 | 2,789.2 | 5,707.7 | 3,395.8 | 4,532.2 | 5,496.3 | 4,784.9 | 3,914.0 | 4,380.4 | 3,618.4 |
| Other investment.......................... | **8d9la** | 4,797.4 | 5,123.5 | 6,105.5 | 7,825.9 | 6,315.0 | 5,853.7 | 6,115.2 | 6,503.8 | 6,424.7 | 6,355.1 | 5,962.5 | 5,155.9 |
| Other equity.............................. | **8dala** | — | — | — | — | — | — | — | — | — | — | — | — |
| Debt instruments........................ | **8dzla** | 4,797.4 | 5,123.5 | 6,105.5 | 7,825.9 | 6,315.0 | 5,853.7 | 6,115.2 | 6,503.8 | 6,424.7 | 6,355.1 | 5,962.5 | 5,155.9 |

|  |  | 2004 | 2005 | 2006 | 2007 | 2008 | 2009 | 2010 | 2011 | 2012 | 2013 | 2014 | 2015 |
|---|---|---|---|---|---|---|---|---|---|---|---|---|---|
| **Government Finance Operations Statement General Government** | | | | | | *Millions of Pounds: Fiscal Year Ends December 31; Data Reported through Eurostat* | | | | | | | |
| Revenue | a1 | 485,701 | 521,843 | 562,741 | 591,112 | 631,438 | 577,744 | 608,937 | 635,804 | 641,074 | 682,429 | 695,744 | 724,038 |
| Taxes | a11 | 346,086 | 369,733 | 400,545 | 418,647 | 447,890 | 395,256 | 426,304 | 450,965 | 451,459 | 468,042 | 484,304 | 504,063 |
| Social Contributions | a12 | 98,022 | 105,430 | 111,030 | 116,097 | 122,539 | 120,646 | 123,820 | 128,152 | 131,560 | 134,807 | 138,660 | 145,718 |
| Grants | a13 | .... | .... | .... | .... | .... | .... | .... | .... | .... | .... | .... | .... |
| Other Revenue | a14 | .... | .... | .... | .... | .... | .... | .... | .... | .... | .... | .... | .... |
| Expense | a2 | 516,460 | 567,408 | 587,287 | 619,600 | 683,020 | 710,086 | 733,746 | 738,323 | 760,834 | 763,513 | 779,008 | 788,448 |
| Compensation of Employees | a21 | 133,984 | 144,157 | 152,599 | 157,374 | 161,417 | 166,401 | 172,352 | 171,185 | 171,580 | 167,154 | 170,449 | 172,139 |
| Use of Goods & Services | a22 | 129,599 | 139,221 | 151,743 | 160,200 | 175,681 | 186,993 | 187,622 | 186,630 | 189,040 | 197,332 | 204,941 | 206,713 |
| Consumption of Fixed Capital | a23 | 17,008 | 18,222 | 19,416 | 20,204 | 21,612 | 22,667 | 23,850 | 25,266 | 26,500 | 27,387 | 28,246 | 29,176 |
| Interest | a24 | 24,014 | 26,950 | 28,568 | 32,965 | 34,083 | 28,141 | 45,234 | 51,648 | 48,320 | 49,506 | 48,953 | 43,729 |
| Subsidies | a25 | 6,392 | 7,353 | 8,854 | 9,066 | 9,062 | 9,637 | 9,238 | 8,012 | 9,125 | 9,219 | 9,960 | 11,871 |
| Grants | a26 | | | | | | | | | | | | |
| Social Benefits | a27 | 159,266 | 166,351 | 171,799 | 183,305 | 196,481 | 217,841 | 227,386 | 234,461 | 245,921 | 250,774 | 256,793 | 262,482 |
| Other Expense | a28 | | | | | | | | | | | | |
| Gross Operating Balance [1-2+23] | agob | −13,751 | −27,343 | −5,130 | −8,284 | −29,970 | −109,675 | −100,959 | −77,253 | −93,260 | −53,697 | −55,018 | −35,234 |
| Net Operating Balance [1-2] | anob | −30,759 | −45,565 | −24,546 | −28,488 | −51,582 | −132,342 | −124,809 | −102,519 | −119,760 | −81,084 | −83,264 | −64,410 |
| Net Acq. of Nonfinancial Assets | a31 | 14,235 | 1,385 | 16,368 | 15,832 | 24,590 | 26,815 | 25,234 | 21,504 | 17,787 | 16,460 | 18,917 | 17,811 |
| Aquisition of Nonfin. Assets | a31.1 | .... | .... | .... | .... | .... | .... | .... | .... | .... | .... | .... | .... |
| Disposal of Nonfin. Assets | a31.2 | .... | .... | .... | .... | .... | .... | .... | .... | .... | .... | .... | .... |
| Net Lending/Borrowing [1-2-31] | anlb | −44,994 | −46,950 | −40,914 | −44,320 | −76,172 | −159,157 | −150,043 | −124,023 | −137,547 | −97,544 | −102,181 | −82,221 |
| Net Acq. of Financial Assets | a32 | 2,354 | 5,809 | 10,145 | 7,758 | 68,726 | 56,172 | 2,282 | 9,886 | 11,565 | −25,772 | 12,681 | 332 |
| By instrument | | | | | | | | | | | | | |
| Monetary Gold & SDRs | a3201 | −37 | −8 | 47 | −50 | −24 | 8,522 | 18 | 333 | 111 | 43 | −14 | 55 |
| Currency & Deposits | a3202 | 878 | −951 | 7,548 | 10,855 | 12,050 | 3,309 | −12,984 | 12,037 | 2,886 | 5,390 | 6,326 | −3,913 |
| Securities other than Shares | a3203 | 2,186 | 3,157 | 2,626 | 796 | 5,074 | −7,930 | 6,679 | 7,555 | 1,720 | −3,741 | 6,204 | 16,529 |
| Loans | a3204 | 1,784 | 2,810 | 2,274 | 4,972 | 22,367 | 12,127 | 8,858 | −3,283 | 4,202 | 1,176 | 6,002 | −236 |
| Shares & Other Equity | a3205 | −4,117 | −4,448 | −3,837 | −7,389 | 9,081 | 35,559 | −712 | −1,121 | 1,263 | −29,462 | −8,209 | −13,784 |
| Insurance Technical Reserves | a3206 | 45 | −24 | −11 | 82 | 21 | −144 | −65 | −17 | 13 | −23 | — | −6 |
| Financial Derivatives | a3207 | −173 | 188 | −648 | 37 | 1,151 | 619 | −301 | −123 | 557 | −37 | −888 | −967 |
| Other Accounts Receivable | a3208 | 1,788 | 5,085 | 2,146 | −1,545 | 19,009 | 4,110 | 789 | −5,495 | 813 | 882 | 3,260 | 2,654 |
| By debtor | | | | | | | | | | | | | |
| Domestic | a321 | .... | .... | .... | .... | .... | .... | .... | .... | .... | .... | .... | .... |
| Foreign | a322 | .... | .... | .... | .... | .... | .... | .... | .... | .... | .... | .... | .... |
| Net Incurrence of Liabilities | a33 | 46,413 | 53,155 | 50,075 | 47,674 | 154,347 | 209,921 | 158,802 | 132,440 | 146,733 | 74,828 | 111,660 | 81,367 |
| By instrument | | | | | | | | | | | | | |
| Special Drawing Rights (SDRs) | a3301 | — | — | — | — | — | 8,654 | — | — | — | — | — | — |
| Currency & Deposits | a3302 | 2,740 | 5,853 | 5,423 | 7,939 | 19,328 | 7,024 | −5,036 | 7,934 | −2,528 | −7,301 | 17,852 | 11,802 |
| Securities other than Shares | a3303 | 38,236 | 40,024 | 40,092 | 39,171 | 112,345 | 220,054 | 163,504 | 129,129 | 109,811 | 79,354 | 87,461 | 58,890 |
| Loans | a3304 | 8,299 | 4,719 | −622 | 793 | 9,217 | −29,005 | −1,274 | −1,284 | 1,171 | 412 | 1,299 | 8,815 |
| Shares & Other Equity | a3305 | — | — | — | — | — | — | — | — | — | — | — | — |
| Insurance Technical Reserves | a3306 | 1,176 | 1,310 | 1,479 | 1,585 | 1,530 | 1,540 | 1,809 | 1,841 | 1,914 | 2,037 | 2,037 | 1,972 |
| Financial Derivatives | a3307 | — | — | — | — | — | — | — | — | — | — | — | — |
| Other Accounts Payable | a3308 | −4,038 | 1,249 | 3,703 | −1,814 | 11,927 | 1,654 | −201 | −5,180 | 36,365 | 326 | 3,011 | −112 |
| By creditor | | | | | | | | | | | | | |
| Domestic | a331 | .... | .... | .... | .... | .... | .... | .... | .... | .... | .... | .... | .... |
| Foreign | a332 | .... | .... | .... | .... | .... | .... | .... | .... | .... | .... | .... | .... |
| Stat. Discrepancy [32-33-NLB] | anlbz | 935 | −396 | 984 | 4,404 | −9,449 | 5,408 | −6,477 | 1,469 | 2,379 | −3,056 | 3,202 | 1,186 |
| Memo Item: Expenditure [2+31] | a2m | 530,695 | 568,793 | 603,655 | 635,432 | 707,610 | 736,901 | 758,980 | 759,827 | 778,621 | 779,973 | 797,925 | 806,259 |
| **Balance Sheet** | | | | | | | | | | | | | |
| Net Worth | a6 | .... | .... | .... | .... | .... | .... | .... | .... | .... | .... | .... | .... |
| Nonfinancial Assets | a61 | .... | .... | .... | .... | .... | .... | .... | .... | .... | .... | .... | .... |
| Financial Assets | a62 | 241,205 | 268,686 | 272,973 | 288,379 | 377,334 | 426,784 | 553,558 | 545,395 | 586,325 | 560,215 | 578,023 | 566,219 |
| By instrument | | | | | | | | | | | | | |
| Monetary Gold & SDRs | a6201 | 2,461 | 3,153 | 3,436 | 4,344 | 6,276 | 15,701 | 18,159 | 19,250 | 19,342 | 16,267 | 16,677 | 16,215 |
| Currency & Deposits | a6202 | 30,511 | 29,415 | 36,805 | 47,928 | 62,686 | 65,525 | 64,279 | 75,748 | 77,481 | 79,810 | 81,171 | 73,102 |
| Securities other than Shares | a6203 | 22,315 | 25,471 | 26,069 | 27,820 | 40,567 | 29,958 | 46,866 | 53,852 | 54,070 | 49,115 | 55,022 | 71,291 |
| Loans | a6204 | 25,894 | 28,612 | 30,890 | 36,248 | 58,352 | 70,387 | 148,545 | 145,383 | 149,776 | 149,874 | 154,351 | 152,604 |
| Shares and Other Equity | a6205 | 118,423 | 135,241 | 127,239 | 125,683 | 146,417 | 175,204 | 198,091 | 180,027 | 213,803 | 195,738 | 200,863 | 187,377 |
| Insurance Technical Reserves | a6206 | 807 | 783 | 772 | 854 | 875 | 731 | 701 | 684 | 697 | 674 | 674 | 668 |
| Financial Derivatives | a6207 | 182 | 696 | 787 | −109 | −2,354 | −275 | 2,038 | 2,739 | 3,287 | 2,938 | 2,095 | 1,008 |
| Other Accounts Receivable | a6208 | 40,612 | 45,315 | 46,975 | 45,611 | 64,515 | 69,553 | 74,879 | 67,712 | 67,869 | 65,799 | 67,170 | 63,954 |
| By debtor | | | | | | | | | | | | | |
| Domestic | a621 | .... | .... | .... | .... | .... | .... | .... | .... | .... | .... | .... | .... |
| Foreign | a622 | .... | .... | .... | .... | .... | .... | .... | .... | .... | .... | .... | .... |
| Liabilities | a63 | 642,028 | 700,301 | 732,746 | 778,589 | 996,699 | 1,175,596 | 1,406,562 | 1,683,062 | 1,791,225 | 1,776,533 | 2,059,951 | 2,095,387 |
| By instrument | | | | | | | | | | | | | |
| Special Drawing Rights (SDRs) | a6301 | 1,538 | 1,588 | 1,466 | 1,509 | 2,021 | 9,810 | 10,098 | 10,063 | 9,637 | 9,450 | 9,406 | 9,476 |
| Currency & Deposits | a6302 | 82,397 | 88,189 | 93,581 | 101,520 | 120,846 | 127,872 | 127,904 | 135,982 | 133,761 | 126,593 | 144,404 | 155,651 |
| Securities other than Shares | a6303 | 412,837 | 465,273 | 490,940 | 532,816 | 677,656 | 880,156 | 1,129,345 | 1,391,994 | 1,479,092 | 1,485,168 | 1,747,999 | 1,768,057 |
| Loans | a6304 | 45,156 | 49,036 | 48,498 | 51,911 | 60,672 | 28,314 | 26,693 | 27,924 | 27,496 | 27,818 | 29,663 | 33,623 |
| Shares and Other Equity | a6305 | — | — | — | — | — | — | — | — | — | — | — | — |
| Insurance Technical Reserves | a6306 | 72,755 | 71,134 | 74,133 | 68,619 | 100,873 | 92,038 | 74,174 | 84,975 | 73,378 | 63,253 | 63,138 | 67,263 |
| Financial Derivatives | a6307 | — | 35 | 240 | 173 | 392 | 658 | 2,740 | 3,298 | 2,359 | 1,259 | 1,109 | 1,132 |
| Other Accounts Payable | a6308 | 27,345 | 25,046 | 23,888 | 22,041 | 34,239 | 36,748 | 35,608 | 28,826 | 65,502 | 62,992 | 64,232 | 60,185 |
| By creditor | | | | | | | | | | | | | |
| Domestic | a631 | .... | .... | .... | .... | .... | .... | .... | .... | .... | .... | .... | .... |
| Foreign | a632 | .... | .... | .... | .... | .... | .... | .... | .... | .... | .... | .... | .... |
| Net Financial Worth [62-63] | a6m2 | −400,823 | −431,615 | −459,773 | −490,210 | −619,365 | −748,812 | −853,004 | −1,137,667 | −1,204,900 | −1,216,318 | −1,481,928 | −1,529,168 |
| Memo Item: Debt at Market Value | a6m3 | 642,028 | 700,266 | 732,506 | 778,416 | 996,301 | 1,174,938 | 1,403,822 | 1,679,764 | 1,788,866 | 1,775,274 | 2,058,842 | 2,094,255 |
| Memo Item: Debt at Face Value | a6m35 | 533,362 | 578,606 | 622,412 | 669,741 | 822,563 | 1,022,103 | 1,236,625 | 1,363,071 | 1,495,870 | 1,568,381 | 1,675,829 | 1,732,645 |
| Memo Item: Maastricht Debt | a6m36 | 504,479 | 551,972 | 597,058 | 646,191 | 786,303 | 975,545 | 1,190,919 | 1,324,182 | 1,420,731 | 1,495,939 | 1,602,191 | 1,662,984 |
| Memo Item: Debt at Nominal Value | a6m4 | .... | .... | .... | .... | .... | .... | .... | .... | .... | .... | .... | .... |

| | | 2004 | 2005 | 2006 | 2007 | 2008 | 2009 | 2010 | 2011 | 2012 | 2013 | 2014 | 2015 |
|---|---|---|---|---|---|---|---|---|---|---|---|---|---|
| **National Accounts** | | | | | | | *Billions of Pounds* | | | | | | | |
| Househ.Cons.Expend.,incl.NPISHs.... | **96f.c** | 807.62 | 851.60 | 892.09 | 941.55 | 973.46 | 958.34 | 1,004.15 | 1,039.10 | 1,072.55 | 1,111.46 | 1,156.78 | 1,212.70 |
| Government Consumption Expend... | **91f.c** | 250.75 | 267.75 | 285.16 | 296.65 | 315.93 | 330.07 | 336.58 | 337.29 | 343.88 | 345.19 | 352.48 | 362.33 |
| Gross Fixed Capital Formation.......... | **93e.c** | 227.25 | 238.84 | 254.93 | 273.75 | 272.52 | 239.08 | 250.20 | 260.78 | 268.82 | 282.08 | 307.30 | 322.20 |
| Changes in Inventories.................... | **93i.c** | 4.30 | 3.55 | 5.31 | 7.54 | .54 | −16.04 | 4.29 | 2.75 | 1.77 | 8.90 | 11.89 | −2.42 |
| Exports of Goods and Services......... | **90c.c** | 305.77 | 341.69 | 390.39 | 379.77 | 420.90 | 400.26 | 447.06 | 499.45 | 500.74 | 515.89 | 507.72 | 511.21 |
| Imports of Goods and Services (-)..... | **98c.c** | 341.15 | 376.33 | 423.61 | 420.46 | 465.80 | 428.38 | 484.12 | 523.28 | 535.20 | 549.63 | 541.47 | 547.52 |
| Gross Domestic Product (GDP)......... | **99b.c** | 1,255.19 | 1,326.66 | 1,403.73 | 1,480.96 | 1,518.68 | 1,482.14 | 1,558.37 | 1,617.68 | 1,655.38 | 1,713.12 | 1,791.49 | 1,864.00 |
| Net Primary Income from Abroad..... | **98.nc** | 21.69 | 30.69 | 14.50 | 14.07 | 2.58 | 2.54 | 17.17 | 18.73 | −5.26 | −15.76 | −38.76 | −34.13 |
| Gross National Income (GNI)............ | **99a.c** | 1,276.89 | 1,357.35 | 1,418.23 | 1,495.03 | 1,521.25 | 1,484.68 | 1,575.54 | 1,636.41 | 1,650.12 | 1,697.36 | 1,752.73 | 1,829.87 |
| Net Current Transf.from Abroad....... | **98t.c** | −9.65 | −11.05 | −10.62 | −11.80 | −11.82 | −13.94 | −17.56 | −20.08 | 1.10 | −16.83 | −32.90 | −34.78 |
| Gross Nat'l Disposable Inc.(GNDI).... | **99i.c** | 1,246.60 | 1,304.88 | 1,369.16 | 1,451.28 | 1,498.54 | 1,456.04 | 1,509.35 | 1,548.40 | 1,627.93 | 1,670.20 | 1,727.31 | 1,805.09 |
| Gross Saving................................ | **99s.c** | 216.43 | 221.88 | 234.51 | 263.61 | 254.37 | 218.05 | 219.92 | 241.48 | 215.89 | 215.15 | 225.49 | 234.03 |
| Consumption of Fixed Capital.......... | **99cfc** | 171.15 | 179.14 | 193.23 | 202.58 | 199.65 | 203.46 | 207.52 | 212.99 | 218.75 | 227.38 | 241.25 | 242.27 |
| GDP Volume 2012 Ref., Chained..... | **99b.r** | 1,536.63 | 1,582.68 | 1,624.80 | 1,666.82 | 1,659.04 | 1,589.49 | 1,613.97 | 1,645.81 | 1,665.21 | 1,701.18 | 1,749.71 | 1,790.47 |
| GDP Volume (2010=100)............... | **99bvr** | 95.2 | 98.1 | 100.7 | 103.3 | 102.8 | 98.5 | 100.0 | 102.0 | 103.2 | 105.4 | 108.4 | 110.9 |
| GDP Deflator (2010=100)............... | **99bir** | 84.6 | 86.8 | 89.5 | 92.0 | 94.8 | 96.6 | 100.0 | 101.8 | 103.0 | 104.3 | 106.0 | 107.8 |
| | | | | | | | *Millions: Midyear Estimates* | | | | | | | |
| Population................................ | **99z** | 59.85 | 60.21 | 60.65 | 61.15 | 61.69 | 62.22 | 62.72 | 63.16 | 63.57 | 63.96 | 64.33 | 64.72 |

# United States   111

| | | 2004 | 2005 | 2006 | 2007 | 2008 | 2009 | 2010 | 2011 | 2012 | 2013 | 2014 | 2015 |
|---|---|---|---|---|---|---|---|---|---|---|---|---|---|
| **Exchange Rates** | | | | | | *End of Period (sa and sc) Period Averages (sb and sd)* | | | | | | | |
| US Dollar/SDR Rate..............aa=.... | sa | 1.5530 | 1.4293 | 1.5044 | 1.5803 | 1.5403 | 1.5677 | 1.5400 | 1.5353 | 1.5369 | 1.5400 | 1.4488 | 1.3857 |
| US Dollar/SDR Rate......................... | sb | 1.4810 | 1.4773 | 1.4712 | 1.5306 | 1.5801 | 1.5420 | 1.5257 | 1.5787 | 1.5317 | 1.5196 | 1.5190 | 1.3991 |
| SDR/US Dollar Rate..............ac=.... | sc | .6439 | .6997 | .6647 | .6328 | .6492 | .6379 | .6493 | .6514 | .6507 | .6494 | .6902 | .7216 |
| SDR/US Dollar Rate......................... | sd | .6752 | .6769 | .6797 | .6533 | .6329 | .6485 | .6554 | .6334 | .6529 | .6581 | .6583 | .7147 |
| | | | | | *Dollars per ECU through 1998; Dollars per Euro Beginning 1999:* | | | | | | | | |
| Euro Rate........................................ | ag | 1.3621 | 1.1797 | 1.3170 | 1.4721 | 1.3917 | 1.4406 | 1.3362 | 1.2939 | 1.3194 | 1.3791 | 1.2141 | 1.0887 |
| Euro Rate........................................ | rh | 1.2433 | 1.2458 | 1.2556 | 1.3706 | 1.4717 | 1.3928 | 1.3269 | 1.3914 | 1.2856 | 1.3282 | 1.3288 | 1.1096 |
| | | | | | *Index Numbers (2010=100): Period Averages* | | | | | | | | |
| Nominal Effective Exchange Rate..... | nec | 111.8 | 109.0 | 107.2 | 102.0 | 98.0 | 103.4 | 100.0 | 95.1 | 98.2 | 99.8 | 102.3 | 116.4 |
| CPI-Based Real Effect. Ex. Rate........ | rec | 110.9 | 109.4 | 108.7 | 103.6 | 99.5 | 104.0 | 100.0 | 95.1 | 98.0 | 99.1 | 101.2 | 113.8 |
| ULC-Based Real Effect. Ex. Rate....... | rel | 112.5 | 109.3 | 109.1 | 102.3 | 99.7 | 105.0 | 100.0 | 94.1 | 97.9 | 100.4 | 102.6 | 117.7 |
| **Fund Position** | | | | | | *Billions of SDRs: End of Period* | | | | | | | |
| Quota................................................ | 2f.s | 37,149.3 | 37,149.3 | 37,149.3 | 37,149.3 | 37,149.3 | 37,149.3 | 37,149.3 | 42,122.4 | 42,122.4 | 42,122.4 | 42,122.4 | 42,122.4 |
| Quota................................................ | 2f.s | 37.15 | 37.15 | 37.15 | 37.15 | 37.15 | 37.15 | 37.15 | 42.12 | 42.12 | 42.12 | 42.12 | 42.12 |
| SDR Holdings................................... | 1b.s | 8.77 | 5.74 | 5.90 | 6.00 | 6.06 | 36.88 | 36.90 | 35.79 | 35.82 | 35.83 | 35.85 | 35.86 |
| Reserve Position in the Fund............ | 1c.s | 12.58 | 5.62 | 3.35 | 2.69 | 4.99 | 7.26 | 8.11 | 19.59 | 22.23 | 19.97 | 17.37 | 12.71 |
| Total Fund Cred. & Loans Outstg...... | 2tl | — | — | — | — | — | — | — | — | — | — | — | — |
| SDR Allocations.............................. | 1bd | 4.90 | 4.90 | 4.90 | 4.90 | 4.90 | 35.32 | 35.32 | 35.32 | 35.32 | 35.32 | 35.32 | 35.32 |
| **International Liquidity** | | | | | | *Billions of US Dollars Unless Otherwise Indicated: End of Period* | | | | | | | |
| Total Reserves minus Gold............... | 1l.d | 75.89 | 54.08 | 54.85 | 59.52 | 66.61 | 119.72 | 121.39 | 136.91 | 139.13 | 133.53 | 119.05 | 106.54 |
| SDR Holdings................................ | 1b.d | 13.63 | 8.21 | 8.87 | 9.48 | 9.34 | 57.81 | 56.82 | 54.95 | 55.05 | 55.18 | 51.94 | 49.69 |
| Reserve Position in the Fund......... | 1c.d | 19.54 | 8.04 | 5.04 | 4.24 | 7.68 | 11.39 | 12.49 | 30.08 | 34.16 | 30.75 | 25.16 | 17.61 |
| Foreign Exchange......................... | 1d.d | 42.72 | 37.84 | 40.94 | 45.80 | 49.58 | 50.52 | 52.08 | 51.88 | 49.92 | 47.60 | 41.94 | 39.24 |
| Gold (Million Fine Troy Ounces)....... | 1ad | 261.59 | 261.55 | 261.50 | 261.50 | 261.50 | 261.50 | 261.50 | 261.50 | 261.50 | 261.50 | 261.50 | 261.50 |
| Gold (National Valuation)................ | 1and | 11.04 | 11.04 | 11.04 | 11.04 | 11.04 | 11.04 | 11.04 | 11.04 | 11.04 | 11.04 | 11.04 | 11.04 |
| Central Bank: Other Assets.............. | 3..d | — | — | — | — | — | — | 10.27 | .08 | 99.82 | 8.89 | .27 | .03 | 1.00 |
| Central Bank: Other Liabs................ | 4..d | 30.03 | 30.46 | 32.22 | 40.64 | 89.51 | 72.72 | 62.92 | 89.05 | 106.02 | 159.24 | 304.04 | 503.75 |
| Other Depository Corps.: Assets....... | 7a.d | 1,117.97 | 1,287.14 | 1,635.61 | 2,050.40 | 1,820.03 | 2,296.75 | 2,519.66 | 2,383.95 | 2,316.00 | 2,248.30 | 2,140.59 | 2,080.52 |
| Other Depository Corps.: Liabs........ | 7b.d | 1,228.52 | 1,361.93 | 1,759.56 | 1,887.13 | 2,077.57 | 2,137.24 | 2,268.84 | 2,436.35 | 2,184.47 | 2,485.01 | 2,453.43 | 2,221.92 |
| Other Financial Corps.: Assets......... | 7e.d | 2,485.87 | 2,966.24 | 3,663.46 | 4,394.63 | 2,978.17 | 3,805.56 | 4,467.16 | 4,401.91 | 4,991.40 | 5,517.30 | 5,659.72 | 5,728.98 |
| Other Financial Corps.: Liabs............ | 7f.d | 1,841.70 | 2,189.92 | 2,910.71 | 3,356.90 | 2,727.47 | 2,873.02 | 2,720.26 | 2,665.39 | 2,578.65 | 2,433.84 | 2,478.02 | 2,459.21 |
| **Central Bank** | | | | | | *Billions of US Dollars: End of Period* | | | | | | | |
| Net Foreign Assets............................ | 11n | 49.5 | 27.5 | 26.2 | 22.2 | −18.7 | 13.4 | 15.5 | 104.8 | −.7 | −70.8 | −222.8 | −431.8 |
| Claims on Nonresidents................ | 11 | 87.1 | 64.9 | 65.8 | 70.6 | 78.4 | 141.4 | 132.8 | 248.1 | 159.6 | 142.8 | 132.4 | 120.9 |
| Liabilities to Nonresidents.............. | 16c | 37.6 | 37.5 | 39.6 | 48.4 | 97.1 | 128.1 | 117.3 | 143.3 | 160.3 | 213.6 | 355.2 | 552.7 |
| Claims on Other Dep. Corporations.. | 12e | .1 | .1 | .1 | 24.5 | 636.8 | 165.6 | 45.1 | 9.1 | .6 | .2 | .1 | .6 |
| Net Claims on Central Government... | 12an | 712.1 | 740.0 | 774.5 | 750.1 | 68.7 | 621.8 | 727.2 | 1,579.3 | 1,600.1 | 2,111.7 | 2,281.7 | 2,134.9 |
| Claims on Central Government...... | 12a | 717.8 | 744.2 | 778.9 | 754.6 | 476.0 | 776.6 | 1,016.1 | 1,672.1 | 1,656.9 | 2,208.8 | 2,461.4 | 2,461.6 |
| Liabilities to Central Government... | 16d | 5.7 | 4.2 | 4.5 | 4.5 | 407.3 | 154.8 | 288.9 | 92.8 | 56.8 | 97.1 | 179.8 | 326.7 |
| Claims on Other Sectors................. | 12s | 33.0 | 45.3 | 36.0 | 42.5 | 507.8 | 1,172.5 | 1,232.6 | 976.3 | 1,005.7 | 1,752.6 | 1,976.8 | 1,955.1 |
| Claims on Other Financial Corps... | 12g | 33.0 | 45.3 | 36.0 | 42.5 | 176.1 | 250.2 | 240.5 | 139.1 | 79.1 | 255.7 | 229.4 | 207.6 |
| Claims on State & Local Govt......... | 12b | — | — | — | — | — | — | — | — | — | — | — | — |
| Claims on Pub. Nonfin. Corps........ | 12c | — | — | — | — | — | — | — | — | — | — | — | — |
| Claims on Private Sector................ | 12d | — | — | — | — | 331.7 | 922.3 | 992.1 | 837.3 | 926.6 | 1,496.9 | 1,747.4 | 1,747.5 |
| Monetary Base................................... | 14 | 744.6 | 776.6 | 795.8 | 803.5 | 1,683.2 | 1,941.7 | 1,970.0 | 2,674.7 | 2,680.0 | 3,713.7 | 3,963.6 | 3,611.4 |
| Currency in Circulation.................. | 14a | 722.9 | 759.2 | 782.7 | 791.8 | 849.7 | 889.7 | 943.7 | 1,034.5 | 1,124.6 | 1,195.2 | 1,294.2 | 1,380.8 |
| Liabs. to Other Dep. Corporations.. | 14c | 21.4 | 17.1 | 12.8 | 11.4 | 819.4 | 1,025.3 | 1,025.8 | 1,569.3 | 1,532.7 | 2,450.7 | 2,609.6 | 2,208.7 |
| Liabilities to Other Sectors............. | 14d | .2 | .3 | .3 | .3 | 14.1 | 26.8 | .4 | 70.9 | 22.7 | 67.7 | 59.7 | 21.9 |
| Other Liabs. to Other Dep. Corps.... | 14n | 6.7 | 7.9 | 5.9 | 2.7 | 3.1 | 2.5 | 2.0 | 1.6 | .8 | 1.2 | .7 | .3 |
| Dep. & Sec. Excl. f/Monetary Base... | 14o | — | — | — | — | — | — | — | — | — | — | — | — |
| Deposits Included in Broad Money. | 15 | — | — | — | — | — | — | — | — | — | — | — | — |
| Sec.Ot.th.Shares Incl.in Brd. Money | 16a | — | — | — | — | — | — | — | — | — | — | — | — |
| Deposits Excl. from Broad Money... | 16b | — | — | — | — | — | — | — | — | — | — | — | — |
| Sec.Ot.th.Shares Excl. f/Brd.Money. | 16s | — | — | — | — | — | — | — | — | — | — | — | — |
| Loans................................................ | 16l | — | — | — | — | — | — | — | — | — | — | — | — |
| Financial Derivatives........................ | 16m | — | — | — | — | — | — | — | — | — | — | — | — |
| Shares and Other Equity................... | 17a | 23.3 | 28.0 | 30.7 | 37.1 | 42.5 | 52.1 | 56.6 | 53.8 | 54.7 | 55.0 | 57.1 | 39.5 |
| Other Items (Net)............................. | 17r | 20.1 | .3 | 4.8 | −4.1 | −534.1 | −23.0 | −8.0 | −60.5 | −129.8 | 23.8 | 14.3 | 7.7 |
| Memo Item: | | | | | | | | | | | | | |
| Total Assets...................................... | 10ra | 813.5 | 851.6 | 875.1 | 894.3 | 2,259.3 | 2,237.5 | 2,423.6 | 2,928.6 | 2,908.9 | 4,032.5 | 4,509.5 | 4,486.6 |

| | | 2004 | 2005 | 2006 | 2007 | 2008 | 2009 | 2010 | 2011 | 2012 | 2013 | 2014 | 2015 |
|---|---|---|---|---|---|---|---|---|---|---|---|---|---|
| **Other Depository Corporations** | | *Billions of US Dollars: End of Period* | | | | | | | | | | | |
| Net Foreign Assets | 21n | −110.6 | −74.8 | −123.9 | 163.3 | −257.5 | 159.5 | 250.8 | −52.4 | 131.5 | −236.7 | −312.8 | −141.4 |
| Claims on Nonresidents | 21 | 1,118.0 | 1,287.1 | 1,635.6 | 2,050.4 | 1,820.0 | 2,296.7 | 2,519.7 | 2,383.9 | 2,316.0 | 2,248.3 | 2,140.6 | 2,080.5 |
| Liabilities to Nonresidents | 26c | 1,228.5 | 1,361.9 | 1,759.6 | 1,887.1 | 2,077.6 | 2,137.2 | 2,268.8 | 2,436.3 | 2,184.5 | 2,485.0 | 2,453.4 | 2,221.9 |
| Claims on Central Bank | 20 | 77.5 | 82.7 | 85.7 | 94.2 | 938.8 | 1,077.5 | 1,061.2 | 1,672.3 | 1,616.3 | 2,426.6 | 2,626.8 | 2,293.1 |
| Currency | 20a | 41.5 | 50.1 | 51.7 | 55.0 | 57.7 | 54.9 | 52.7 | 60.8 | 71.1 | 73.6 | 75.7 | 74.2 |
| Reserve Deposits and Securities | 20b | 24.0 | 19.0 | 18.7 | 20.8 | 860.0 | 977.0 | 968.1 | 1,562.3 | 1,491.0 | 2,249.1 | 2,378.0 | 1,977.2 |
| Other Claims | 20n | 11.9 | 13.5 | 15.3 | 18.5 | 21.1 | 45.6 | 40.4 | 49.3 | 54.2 | 103.9 | 173.1 | 241.7 |
| Net Claims on Central Government | 22an | 189.0 | 169.7 | 166.7 | 268.1 | 523.6 | 528.5 | 484.0 | 667.1 | 759.7 | 707.8 | 774.9 | 802.6 |
| Claims on Central Government | 22a | 223.2 | 205.7 | 197.5 | 307.9 | 682.7 | 638.4 | 667.9 | 723.8 | 824.3 | 819.6 | 930.5 | 1,024.9 |
| Liabilities to Central Government | 26d | 34.2 | 36.0 | 30.8 | 39.9 | 159.1 | 109.9 | 183.8 | 56.7 | 64.6 | 111.8 | 155.6 | 222.3 |
| Claims on Other Sectors | 22s | 10,023.1 | 11,015.4 | 12,066.7 | 13,196.0 | 13,893.1 | 12,643.3 | 12,367.8 | 12,509.2 | 12,856.1 | 13,060.7 | 13,627.1 | 14,333.7 |
| Claims on Other Financial Corps | 22g | 3,126.7 | 3,393.1 | 3,704.1 | 4,037.7 | 4,497.1 | 4,291.2 | 3,961.2 | 4,100.2 | 4,129.4 | 4,092.6 | 4,142.9 | 4,205.1 |
| Claims on State & Local Govt | 22b | 380.5 | 417.1 | 466.7 | 563.8 | 600.4 | 698.8 | 670.7 | 682.8 | 729.1 | 755.6 | 754.0 | 791.4 |
| Claims on Pub. Nonfin. Corps | 22c | | | | | | | | | | | | |
| Claims on Private Sector | 22d | 6,515.9 | 7,205.2 | 7,895.9 | 8,594.4 | 8,795.0 | 7,653.3 | 7,735.9 | 7,726.2 | 7,997.5 | 8,212.5 | 8,730.8 | 9,337.3 |
| Liabilities to Central Bank | 26g | 31.4 | 39.5 | 29.3 | 74.5 | 591.9 | 96.6 | .2 | .2 | .1 | .1 | .1 | .1 |
| Transf.Dep.Included in Broad Money | 24 | 726.5 | 695.5 | 646.9 | 641.8 | 636.1 | 853.1 | 861.5 | 1,320.7 | 1,503.4 | 1,641.5 | 1,788.9 | 1,820.5 |
| Other Dep.Included in Broad Money | 25 | 7,297.3 | 8,006.7 | 8,881.6 | 10,085.9 | 10,961.9 | 11,313.1 | 10,923.5 | 11,163.1 | 11,621.1 | 11,996.6 | 12,530.0 | 13,002.7 |
| Sec.Ot.th.Shares Incl.in Brd. Money | 26a | — | — | — | — | — | — | — | — | — | — | — | — |
| Deposits Excl. from Broad Money | 26b | — | — | — | — | — | — | — | — | — | — | — | — |
| Sec.Ot.th.Shares Excl.f/Brd.Money | 26s | 347.2 | 384.5 | 430.7 | 522.7 | 604.7 | 149.3 | 362.8 | 360.4 | 275.7 | 203.4 | 190.6 | 189.4 |
| Loans | 26l | 925.1 | 959.6 | 965.7 | 1,115.8 | 1,036.2 | 976.0 | 841.8 | 755.0 | 742.8 | 759.8 | 809.4 | 843.7 |
| Financial Derivatives | 26m | | | | | | | | | | | | |
| Insurance Technical Reserves | 26r | | | | | | | | | | | | |
| Shares and Other Equity | 27a | 1,166.4 | 1,238.6 | 1,410.5 | 1,557.0 | 1,627.1 | 1,910.3 | 1,924.4 | 2,023.4 | 2,222.9 | 2,276.6 | 2,455.7 | 2,503.1 |
| Other Items (Net) | 27r | −315.0 | −131.4 | −169.6 | −276.2 | −359.9 | −889.6 | −750.5 | −826.5 | −1,002.2 | −919.5 | −1,058.2 | −1,071.4 |
| Memo Item: | | | | | | | | | | | | | |
| Total Assets | 20ra | 14,124.1 | 15,288.7 | 16,932.7 | 19,033.9 | 21,306.4 | 18,520.9 | 18,279.2 | 18,909.1 | 19,222.2 | 20,145.6 | 20,986.6 | 21,322.2 |
| **Depository Corporations** | | *Billions of US Dollars: End of Period* | | | | | | | | | | | |
| Net Foreign Assets | 31n | −61.1 | −47.3 | −97.7 | 185.4 | −276.2 | 172.9 | 266.3 | 52.4 | 130.8 | −307.5 | −535.7 | −573.2 |
| Claims on Nonresidents | 31 | 1,205.1 | 1,352.1 | 1,701.4 | 2,120.9 | 1,898.4 | 2,438.2 | 2,652.5 | 2,632.0 | 2,475.6 | 2,391.1 | 2,273.0 | 2,201.4 |
| Liabilities to Nonresidents | 36c | 1,266.2 | 1,399.4 | 1,799.1 | 1,935.5 | 2,174.6 | 2,265.3 | 2,386.1 | 2,579.6 | 2,344.8 | 2,698.6 | 2,808.6 | 2,774.6 |
| Domestic Claims | 32 | 10,957.1 | 11,970.4 | 13,043.8 | 14,256.6 | 14,993.2 | 14,966.1 | 14,811.7 | 15,732.0 | 16,221.5 | 17,632.8 | 18,661.0 | 19,226.3 |
| Net Claims on Central Government | 32an | 901.0 | 909.7 | 941.1 | 1,018.2 | 592.3 | 1,150.3 | 1,211.3 | 2,246.4 | 2,359.8 | 2,819.5 | 3,056.6 | 2,937.5 |
| Claims on Central Government | 32a | 941.0 | 949.9 | 976.4 | 1,062.5 | 1,158.7 | 1,415.0 | 1,684.0 | 2,395.9 | 2,481.2 | 3,028.4 | 3,392.0 | 3,486.5 |
| Liabilities to Central Government | 36d | 40.0 | 40.2 | 35.3 | 44.4 | 566.4 | 264.7 | 472.7 | 149.4 | 121.4 | 208.9 | 335.4 | 549.0 |
| Claims on Other Sectors | 32s | 10,056.1 | 11,060.7 | 12,102.7 | 13,238.5 | 14,400.9 | 13,815.8 | 13,600.4 | 13,485.6 | 13,861.7 | 14,813.3 | 15,604.4 | 16,288.8 |
| Claims on Other Fin.Corporations | 32g | 3,159.7 | 3,438.4 | 3,740.1 | 4,080.2 | 4,673.8 | 4,541.4 | 4,201.7 | 4,239.3 | 4,208.5 | 4,348.3 | 4,372.3 | 4,412.7 |
| Claims on State & Local Govts | 32b | 380.5 | 417.1 | 466.7 | 563.8 | 600.4 | 698.8 | 670.7 | 682.8 | 729.1 | 755.6 | 754.0 | 791.4 |
| Claims on Pub. Nonfin. Corps | 32c | | | | | | | | | | | | |
| Claims on Private Sector | 32d | 6,515.9 | 7,205.2 | 7,895.9 | 8,594.4 | 9,126.7 | 8,575.6 | 8,728.1 | 8,563.5 | 8,924.1 | 9,709.4 | 10,478.2 | 11,084.8 |
| Broad Money Liabilities | 35l | 8,704.9 | 9,410.6 | 10,259.4 | 11,465.1 | 12,405.4 | 13,029.7 | 12,678.1 | 13,529.4 | 14,201.4 | 14,828.4 | 15,597.7 | 16,151.7 |
| Currency Outside Dep. Corporation | 34a | 681.4 | 709.2 | 731.0 | 736.8 | 792.0 | 834.8 | 891.0 | 973.7 | 1,053.5 | 1,121.6 | 1,218.6 | 1,306.5 |
| Transferable Deposits | 34 | 726.2 | 694.7 | 646.7 | 642.5 | 651.5 | 881.9 | 863.5 | 1,392.7 | 1,526.8 | 1,710.3 | 1,849.1 | 1,842.5 |
| Other Deposits | 35 | 7,297.3 | 8,006.7 | 8,881.6 | 10,085.9 | 10,961.9 | 11,313.1 | 10,923.5 | 11,163.1 | 11,621.1 | 11,996.6 | 12,530.0 | 13,002.7 |
| Securities Other than Shares | 36a | — | — | — | — | — | — | — | — | — | — | — | — |
| Deposits Excluded from Brd. Money | 36b | — | — | — | — | — | — | — | — | — | — | — | — |
| Sec.Ot.th.Shares Excl.f/Brd. Money | 36s | 347.2 | 384.5 | 430.7 | 522.7 | 604.7 | 149.3 | 362.8 | 360.4 | 275.7 | 203.4 | 190.6 | 189.4 |
| Loans | 36l | 925.1 | 959.6 | 965.7 | 1,115.8 | 1,036.2 | 976.0 | 841.8 | 755.0 | 742.8 | 759.8 | 809.4 | 843.7 |
| Financial Derivatives | 36m | | | | | | | | | | | | |
| Insurance Technical Reserves | 36r | — | — | — | — | — | — | — | — | — | — | — | — |
| Shares and Other Equity | 37a | 1,189.7 | 1,266.6 | 1,441.2 | 1,594.1 | 1,669.6 | 1,962.4 | 1,981.0 | 2,077.2 | 2,277.6 | 2,331.6 | 2,512.8 | 2,542.6 |
| Other Items (Net) | 37r | −270.9 | −98.3 | −151.0 | −255.7 | −999.0 | −978.5 | −785.7 | −937.6 | −1,145.0 | −797.9 | −985.2 | −1,074.2 |
| Broad Money Liabs., Seasonally Adj. | 35l.b | 8,677.4 | 9,379.7 | 10,220.6 | 11,414.2 | 12,338.4 | 12,945.8 | 12,579.7 | 13,418.2 | 14,084.9 | 14,713.9 | 15,479.6 | 16,034.7 |
| **Other Financial Corporations** | | *Billions of US Dollars: End of Period* | | | | | | | | | | | |
| Net Foreign Assets | 41n | 644.2 | 776.3 | 752.8 | 1,037.1 | 250.7 | 932.5 | 1,746.9 | 1,736.5 | 2,412.7 | 3,083.5 | 3,181.7 | 3,269.8 |
| Claims on Nonresidents | 41 | 2,485.9 | 2,966.2 | 3,663.5 | 4,394.6 | 2,978.2 | 3,805.6 | 4,467.2 | 4,401.9 | 4,991.4 | 5,517.3 | 5,659.7 | 5,729.0 |
| Liabilities to Nonresidents | 46c | 1,841.7 | 2,189.9 | 2,910.7 | 3,356.9 | 2,727.5 | 2,873.0 | 2,720.3 | 2,665.4 | 2,578.7 | 2,433.8 | 2,478.0 | 2,459.2 |
| Claims on Depository Corporations | 40 | 1,296.1 | 1,310.7 | 1,423.7 | 1,860.1 | 2,378.6 | 3,553.7 | 3,581.8 | 3,637.7 | 3,702.1 | 3,734.3 | 4,001.1 | 4,129.5 |
| Net Claims on Central Government | 42an | 1,485.2 | 1,542.3 | 1,629.7 | 1,707.3 | 2,032.8 | 3,158.2 | 3,559.5 | 4,095.7 | 4,435.1 | 4,585.7 | 4,721.3 | 3,516.5 |
| Claims on Central Government | 42a | 1,517.7 | 1,584.9 | 1,677.8 | 1,752.6 | 2,142.7 | 3,358.6 | 3,719.4 | 4,138.7 | 4,440.2 | 4,590.2 | 4,726.0 | 3,521.3 |
| Liabilities to Central Government | 46d | 32.4 | 42.6 | 48.1 | 45.4 | 109.9 | 200.5 | 160.0 | 42.9 | 5.1 | 4.5 | 4.7 | 4.8 |
| Claims on Other Sectors | 42s | 16,852.9 | 18,251.3 | 20,425.7 | 22,268.3 | 19,552.2 | 20,421.2 | 20,635.2 | 20,393.7 | 21,463.4 | 23,976.9 | 25,137.2 | 25,076.8 |
| Claims on State & Local Govts | 42b | 790.5 | 860.1 | 927.3 | 994.7 | 1,004.2 | 1,102.6 | 1,169.4 | 1,165.9 | 1,257.9 | 1,239.7 | 1,287.6 | 1,338.1 |
| Claims on Pub. Nonfin. Corps | 42c | .2 | .2 | .2 | .3 | .3 | — | — | — | — | — | — | — |
| Claims on Private Sector | 42d | 16,062.1 | 17,391.0 | 19,498.2 | 21,273.3 | 18,547.8 | 19,318.6 | 19,465.8 | 19,227.8 | 20,205.5 | 22,737.3 | 23,849.5 | 23,738.7 |
| Deposits | 46b | 18.4 | 19.2 | 19.0 | 20.9 | 15.5 | | | | | | | |
| Securities Other than Shares | 46s | 3,867.7 | 4,269.7 | 4,560.8 | 5,161.5 | 5,568.3 | 6,094.4 | 5,691.7 | 5,445.9 | 5,268.9 | 5,615.5 | 5,572.8 | 5,600.3 |
| Loans | 46l | 626.1 | 803.0 | 991.2 | 1,213.3 | 1,316.6 | 852.6 | 807.2 | 876.7 | 854.7 | 804.4 | 849.6 | 830.9 |
| Financial Derivatives | 46m | — | — | — | — | — | — | — | — | — | — | — | — |
| Insurance Technical Reserves | 46r | 12,512.1 | 13,416.4 | 14,817.9 | 15,529.0 | 12,567.0 | 16,494.1 | 18,117.1 | 18,616.1 | 19,662.1 | 21,178.8 | 22,046.7 | 22,456.5 |
| Shares and Other Equity | 47a | 6,848.6 | 7,747.5 | 9,059.6 | 9,976.9 | 7,414.8 | 9,988.9 | 11,181.2 | 11,295.7 | 13,456.4 | 16,041.0 | 17,452.6 | 17,810.7 |
| Other Items (Net) | 47r | −3,594.4 | −4,375.2 | −5,216.6 | −5,028.2 | −2,667.7 | −5,364.5 | −6,273.8 | −6,370.7 | −7,228.7 | −8,259.3 | −8,880.5 | −10,705.9 |
| Memo Item: | | | | | | | | | | | | | |
| Total Assets | 40ra | 33,763.2 | 36,757.8 | 41,435.5 | 45,211.7 | 39,712.0 | 50,695.5 | 52,134.6 | 52,524.6 | 56,310.6 | 60,151.4 | 62,661.2 | 61,286.0 |

| | | 2004 | 2005 | 2006 | 2007 | 2008 | 2009 | 2010 | 2011 | 2012 | 2013 | 2014 | 2015 |
|---|---|---|---|---|---|---|---|---|---|---|---|---|---|
| **Financial Corporations** | | | | | | *Billions of US Dollars: End of Period* | | | | | | | |
| Net Foreign Assets | 51n | 583.1 | 729.0 | 655.0 | 1,223.2 | −25.5 | 1,105.4 | 2,013.3 | 1,788.9 | 2,543.6 | 2,775.9 | 2,646.0 | 2,696.6 |
| Claims on Nonresidents | 51 | 3,690.9 | 4,318.3 | 5,364.9 | 6,515.6 | 4,876.6 | 6,243.8 | 7,119.7 | 7,034.0 | 7,467.0 | 7,908.4 | 7,932.7 | 7,930.4 |
| Liabilities to Nonresidents | 56c | 3,107.9 | 3,589.3 | 4,709.9 | 5,292.4 | 4,902.1 | 5,138.3 | 5,106.4 | 5,245.0 | 4,923.4 | 5,132.5 | 5,286.7 | 5,233.8 |
| Domestic Claims | 52 | 26,135.5 | 28,325.5 | 31,359.2 | 34,151.9 | 31,904.4 | 34,004.1 | 34,804.7 | 35,982.2 | 37,911.6 | 41,847.2 | 44,147.2 | 43,406.9 |
| Net Claims on Central Government | 52an | 2,386.3 | 2,452.0 | 2,570.8 | 2,725.4 | 2,625.1 | 4,308.5 | 4,770.7 | 6,342.1 | 6,794.9 | 7,405.2 | 7,777.8 | 6,454.0 |
| Claims on Central Government | 52a | 2,458.7 | 2,534.8 | 2,654.2 | 2,815.2 | 3,301.4 | 4,773.6 | 5,403.4 | 6,534.5 | 6,921.4 | 7,618.7 | 8,118.0 | 7,007.6 |
| Liabilities to Central Government | 56d | 72.4 | 82.8 | 83.3 | 89.7 | 676.3 | 465.2 | 632.7 | 192.4 | 126.5 | 213.5 | 340.1 | 553.8 |
| Claims on Other Sectors | 52s | 23,749.3 | 25,873.6 | 28,788.4 | 31,426.5 | 29,279.3 | 29,695.6 | 30,034.0 | 29,640.0 | 31,116.6 | 34,442.0 | 36,369.3 | 36,953.0 |
| Claims on State & Local Govts | 52b | 1,171.0 | 1,277.2 | 1,394.1 | 1,558.5 | 1,604.6 | 1,801.4 | 1,840.1 | 1,848.7 | 1,987.1 | 1,995.3 | 2,041.6 | 2,129.4 |
| Claims on Pub. Nonfin. Corps | 52c | .2 | .2 | .2 | .3 | .3 | — | — | — | — | — | — | — |
| Claims on Private Sector | 52d | 22,578.1 | 24,596.2 | 27,394.1 | 29,867.8 | 27,674.5 | 27,894.3 | 28,193.9 | 27,791.3 | 29,129.6 | 32,446.7 | 34,327.7 | 34,823.5 |
| Currency Outside Fin. Corporations | 54a | 681.4 | 709.2 | 731.0 | 736.8 | 792.0 | 834.8 | 891.0 | 973.7 | 1,053.5 | 1,121.6 | 1,218.6 | 1,306.5 |
| Deposits | 55l | 7,212.3 | 7,881.3 | 8,634.8 | 9,459.8 | 9,977.6 | 10,257.0 | 10,144.0 | 10,890.6 | 11,568.8 | 12,058.1 | 12,723.2 | 13,271.5 |
| Securities Other than Shares | 56a | 1,644.5 | 1,945.5 | 2,079.6 | 2,571.9 | 2,451.2 | 2,005.3 | 1,897.1 | 1,803.1 | 1,580.6 | 1,318.4 | 1,035.8 | 883.4 |
| Loans | 56l | 223.0 | 247.9 | 275.9 | 230.8 | 155.6 | 119.6 | 118.5 | 113.5 | 110.5 | 99.2 | 100.1 | 101.6 |
| Financial Derivatives | 56m | — | — | — | — | — | — | — | — | — | — | — | — |
| Insurance Technical Reserves | 56r | 12,512.1 | 13,416.4 | 14,817.9 | 15,529.0 | 12,567.0 | 16,494.1 | 18,117.1 | 18,616.1 | 19,662.1 | 21,178.8 | 22,046.7 | 22,456.5 |
| Shares and Other Equity | 57a | 8,038.3 | 9,014.1 | 10,500.8 | 11,571.0 | 9,084.4 | 11,951.3 | 13,162.2 | 13,372.9 | 15,734.0 | 18,372.7 | 19,965.4 | 20,353.3 |
| Other Items (Net) | 57r | −3,592.9 | −4,159.9 | −5,025.8 | −4,724.1 | −3,148.9 | −6,552.6 | −7,512.0 | −7,998.8 | −9,254.4 | −9,525.6 | −10,296.6 | −12,269.4 |
| **Monetary Aggregates** | | | | | | *Billions of US Dollars: End of Period* | | | | | | | |
| Broad Money | 59m | 8,741.4 | 9,447.1 | 10,297.6 | 11,503.8 | 12,444.3 | 13,072.4 | 12,721.6 | 13,573.7 | 14,246.2 | 14,873.9 | 15,644.1 | 16,199.3 |
| o/w:Currency Issued by Cent.Govt | 59m.a | 36.4 | 36.5 | 38.2 | 38.7 | 38.8 | 42.7 | 43.6 | 44.3 | 44.8 | 45.5 | 46.3 | 47.6 |
| o/w: Dep.in Nonfin. Corporations | 59m.b | | | | | | | | | | | | |
| o/w:Secs. Issued by Central Govt | 59m.c | — | — | — | — | — | — | — | — | — | — | — | — |
| Money (National Definitions) | | | | | | | | | | | | | |
| Monetary Base | 19ma | 764.7 | 793.4 | 818.4 | 829.8 | 1,659.2 | 2,022.1 | 2,013.7 | 2,614.5 | 2,674.3 | 3,717.5 | 3,934.5 | 3,835.8 |
| M1 | 59ma | 1,401.0 | 1,396.4 | 1,386.5 | 1,393.2 | 1,630.8 | 1,723.8 | 1,865.3 | 2,207.7 | 2,505.3 | 2,711.0 | 2,981.0 | 3,147.0 |
| M1, Seasonally Adjusted | 59mac | 1,376.4 | 1,374.9 | 1,366.3 | 1,373.6 | 1,602.8 | 1,693.6 | 1,828.3 | 2,161.2 | 2,447.2 | 2,642.1 | 2,914.5 | 3,087.2 |
| M2 | 59mb | 6,436.7 | 6,698.2 | 7,094.2 | 7,521.8 | 8,269.2 | 8,552.3 | 8,848.9 | 9,692.3 | 10,490.9 | 11,068.5 | 11,718.7 | 12,401.5 |
| M2, Seasonally Adjusted | 59mbc | 6,408.6 | 6,674.4 | 7,066.0 | 7,494.7 | 8,248.4 | 8,530.6 | 8,812.2 | 9,639.4 | 10,417.1 | 10,975.2 | 11,629.2 | 12,314.8 |
| M3 | 59mc | 9,482.2 | 10,201.4 | .... | .... | .... | .... | .... | .... | .... | .... | .... | .... |
| M3, Seasonally Adjusted | 59mcc | 9,433.0 | 10,154.0 | .... | .... | .... | .... | .... | .... | .... | .... | .... | .... |
| **Interest Rates** | | | | | | *Percent Per Annum* | | | | | | | |
| Central Bank Policy Rate (EOP) | 60 | 2.25 | 4.25 | 5.25 | 4.25 | .13 | .13 | .13 | .13 | .13 | .13 | .13 | .38 |
| Discount Rate (End of Period) | 60.a | 3.25 | 5.25 | 6.25 | 4.75 | .50 | .50 | .75 | .75 | .75 | .75 | .75 | 1.00 |
| Federal Funds Rate | 60b | 1.35 | 3.21 | 4.96 | 5.02 | 1.93 | .16 | .18 | .10 | .14 | .11 | .09 | .13 |
| Commercial Paper Rate | 60bc | 1.49 | 3.38 | 5.03 | 4.99 | 2.12 | .26 | .23 | .17 | .19 | .11 | .10 | .17 |
| Treasury Bill Rate | 60c | 1.37 | 3.15 | 4.72 | 4.41 | 1.46 | .16 | .13 | .06 | .09 | .06 | .04 | .06 |
| Treas. Bill Rate(Bond Equivalent) | 60cs | 1.39 | 3.21 | 4.85 | 4.45 | 1.37 | .14 | .13 | .05 | .08 | .05 | .03 | .... |
| Certificates of Deposit Rate | 60lc | 1.56 | 3.51 | 5.15 | 5.27 | 2.97 | .56 | .31 | .30 | .28 | .... | .... | .... |
| Lending Rate (Prime Rate) | 60p | 4.34 | 6.19 | 7.96 | 8.05 | 5.09 | 3.25 | 3.25 | 3.25 | 3.25 | 3.25 | 3.25 | 3.26 |
| Mortgage Rate | 60pa | 5.84 | 5.87 | 6.41 | 6.34 | 6.04 | 5.04 | 4.69 | 4.46 | 3.66 | 3.98 | 4.17 | 3.85 |
| Govt. Bond Yield: Med.-Term | 61a | 2.78 | 3.93 | 4.77 | 4.34 | 2.24 | 1.43 | 1.11 | .75 | .38 | .54 | .90 | 1.03 |
| Govt. Bond Yield: Long-Term | 61 | 4.27 | 4.29 | 4.79 | 4.63 | 3.67 | 3.26 | 3.21 | 2.79 | 1.80 | 2.35 | 2.54 | 2.14 |
| **Prices, Production, Labor** | | | | | | *Index Numbers (2010=100): Period Averages* | | | | | | | |
| Share Prices | 62 | 96.8 | 98.9 | 107.0 | 123.5 | 105.5 | 83.2 | 100.0 | 112.2 | 121.6 | 140.7 | 157.3 | 165.0 |
| NASDAQ Composite | 62a | 84.6 | 89.4 | 96.5 | 109.8 | 92.1 | 78.4 | 100.0 | 114.2 | 126.3 | 150.7 | 186.3 | 210.6 |
| S&P Industrials | 62b | 87.3 | 93.5 | 100.3 | 115.5 | 101.6 | 83.1 | 100.0 | 114.2 | 125.5 | 147.8 | 174.0 | 186.2 |
| AMEX Average | 62c | 65.0 | 80.8 | 99.9 | 117.3 | 103.3 | 82.0 | 100.0 | 117.9 | 122.7 | 122.5 | 133.6 | 121.4 |
| Producer Prices | 63 | 79.4 | 85.2 | 89.2 | 93.5 | 102.6 | 93.6 | 100.0 | 108.8 | 109.4 | 110.1 | 111.1 | 103.1 |
| Industrial Goods | 63a | 78.9 | 85.7 | 90.3 | 93.6 | 102.8 | 93.5 | 100.0 | 108.0 | 108.1 | 108.5 | 109.2 | 101.0 |
| Finished Goods | 63b | 82.6 | 86.6 | 89.2 | 92.7 | 98.5 | 96.0 | 100.0 | 106.0 | 108.0 | 109.4 | 111.5 | 107.8 |
| Consumer Goods | 63ba | 80.2 | 84.9 | 87.8 | 91.7 | 98.5 | 94.7 | 100.0 | 107.6 | 109.7 | 111.2 | 113.5 | 108.1 |
| Capital Equipment | 63bb | 89.9 | 91.9 | 93.3 | 95.0 | 97.8 | 99.6 | 100.0 | 101.5 | 103.5 | 104.4 | 105.8 | 107.1 |
| Consumer Prices | 64 | 86.6 | 89.6 | 92.4 | 95.1 | 98.7 | 98.4 | 100.0 | 103.2 | 105.3 | 106.8 | 108.6 | 108.7 |
| Wages: Hourly Earnings(Mfg) | 65ey | 86.8 | 89.0 | 90.3 | 92.8 | 95.4 | 98.0 | 100.0 | 101.7 | 102.5 | 103.7 | 105.1 | 107.0 |
| Industrial Production | 66 | 102.1 | 105.5 | 107.9 | 110.6 | 106.8 | 94.7 | 100.0 | 103.0 | 105.9 | 108.0 | 112.0 | 113.5 |
| Crude Petroleum Production | 66aa | 99.1 | 94.5 | 92.8 | 92.6 | 91.2 | 97.6 | 100.0 | 102.8 | 118.1 | 135.9 | 158.8 | 172.0 |
| Nonagr.Employment, Seas.Adj | 67..c | 100.9 | 102.9 | 104.7 | 105.9 | 105.3 | 100.7 | 100.0 | 101.2 | 103.0 | 104.7 | 106.7 | 108.9 |
| | | | | | | *Number in Thousands: Period Averages* | | | | | | | |
| Labor Force | 67d | 147,401 | 149,321 | 151,428 | 153,125 | 154,287 | 154,143 | 153,889 | 153,616 | 154,975 | 155,389 | 155,922 | 157,129 |
| Employment | 67e | 139,252 | 141,730 | 144,427 | 146,047 | 145,363 | 139,878 | 139,064 | 139,869 | 142,469 | 143,929 | 146,305 | 148,833 |
| Unemployment | 67c | 8,149 | 7,591 | 7,001 | 7,078 | 8,924 | 14,265 | 14,825 | 13,747 | 12,506 | 11,460 | 9,617 | 8,296 |
| Unemployment Rate (%) | 67r | 5.5 | 5.1 | 4.6 | 4.6 | 5.8 | 9.3 | 9.6 | 8.9 | 8.1 | 7.4 | 6.2 | 5.3 |
| **Intl. Transactions & Positions** | | | | | | *Billions of US Dollars* | | | | | | | |
| Exports, f.a.s. | 70 | 818.82 | 901.08 | 1,025.97 | 1,148.20 | 1,287.44 | 1,056.04 | 1,278.49 | 1,480.29 | 1,545.71 | 1,579.05 | 1,623.41 | 1,504.58 |
| Imports, c.i.f. | 71 | 1,525.37 | 1,735.06 | 1,918.08 | 2,020.40 | 2,169.49 | 1,605.30 | 1,969.18 | 2,265.89 | 2,336.52 | 2,329.06 | 2,412.55 | 2,315.30 |
| Imports, f.o.b. | 71.v | 1,469.55 | 1,673.45 | 1,853.94 | 1,956.96 | 2,103.64 | 1,559.62 | 1,913.86 | 2,208.06 | 2,276.30 | 2,268.32 | 2,347.69 | 2,248.23 |
| | | | | | | *2010=100* | | | | | | | |
| Volume of Exports | 72 | 76.1 | 81.2 | 89.3 | 95.3 | 100.7 | 86.6 | 100.0 | 107.2 | 111.5 | 114.4 | 118.2 | 116.9 |
| Volume of Imports | 73 | 96.0 | 101.6 | 107.1 | 108.2 | 104.2 | 87.1 | 100.0 | 103.8 | 106.7 | 107.5 | 112.6 | 120.3 |
| Export Prices | 76 | 84.1 | 86.8 | 89.9 | 94.3 | 100.0 | 95.4 | 100.0 | 108.1 | 108.4 | 108.0 | 107.4 | 100.6 |
| Import Prices | 76.x | 80.7 | 86.7 | 91.0 | 94.8 | 105.7 | 93.6 | 100.0 | 110.9 | 111.2 | 110.0 | 108.8 | 97.7 |

| | | 2004 | 2005 | 2006 | 2007 | 2008 | 2009 | 2010 | 2011 | 2012 | 2013 | 2014 | 2015 |
|---|---|---|---|---|---|---|---|---|---|---|---|---|---|
| **Balance of Payments** | | | | | | | ***Billions of US Dollars*** | | | | | | |
| A. Current Account* | 109bx | −633.8 | −745.4 | −806.7 | −718.6 | −690.8 | −384.0 | −442.0 | −460.4 | −449.7 | −376.8 | −389.5 | −484.1 |
| Goods, credit (exports) | 1a9cx | 823.6 | 913.0 | 1,040.9 | 1,165.2 | 1,308.8 | 1,070.3 | 1,290.3 | 1,499.2 | 1,562.6 | 1,592.0 | 1,632.6 | 1,513.5 |
| Goods, debit (imports) | 1a9dx | 1,488.3 | 1,695.8 | 1,878.2 | 1,986.3 | 2,141.3 | 1,580.0 | 1,939.0 | 2,239.9 | 2,303.7 | 2,294.6 | 2,374.1 | 2,272.8 |
| Balance on goods | 1a9bx | −664.8 | −782.8 | −837.3 | −821.2 | −832.5 | −509.7 | −648.7 | −740.6 | −741.2 | −702.6 | −741.5 | −759.3 |
| Services, credit (exports) | 1b9cx | 338.0 | 373.0 | 416.7 | 488.4 | 532.8 | 512.7 | 563.3 | 627.8 | 656.4 | 687.9 | 710.6 | 710.2 |
| Services, debit (imports) | 1b9dx | 283.1 | 304.5 | 341.2 | 372.6 | 409.1 | 386.8 | 409.3 | 435.8 | 452.0 | 463.7 | 477.4 | 490.6 |
| Balance on Goods & Services | 1z9bx | −609.9 | −714.3 | −761.7 | −705.4 | −708.7 | −383.8 | −494.7 | −548.6 | −536.8 | −478.4 | −508.3 | −539.8 |
| Primary income: credit | 1c9cx | 420.6 | 544.0 | 693.1 | 844.0 | 823.7 | 614.4 | 684.9 | 759.7 | 769.5 | 794.8 | 823.4 | 783.1 |
| Primary income: debit | 1c9dx | 356.5 | 476.4 | 649.8 | 743.4 | 677.6 | 490.8 | 507.3 | 538.8 | 557.3 | 570.2 | 585.4 | 591.8 |
| Balance on gds, serv. & prim. inc. | 1y9bx | −545.8 | −646.6 | −718.4 | −604.8 | −562.6 | −260.2 | −317.0 | −327.7 | −324.6 | −253.9 | −270.3 | −348.4 |
| Secondary income: credit | 1d9ca | 60.2 | 66.0 | 71.4 | 71.9 | 86.6 | 88.5 | 92.3 | 100.8 | 109.6 | 126.6 | 140.0 | 132.0 |
| Secondary income: debit | 1d9da | 148.2 | 164.8 | 159.7 | 185.8 | 214.8 | 212.3 | 217.2 | 233.5 | 234.7 | 249.5 | 259.2 | 267.6 |
| B. Capital Account* | 209ba | 3.0 | 13.1 | −1.8 | .4 | 6.0 | −.1 | −.2 | −1.2 | 6.9 | −.4 | — | — |
| Capital account: credit | 209ca | 3.8 | 15.5 | — | .5 | 6.2 | — | — | — | 7.7 | — | — | — |
| Capital account: debit | 209da | .7 | 2.3 | 1.8 | .1 | .2 | .1 | .2 | 1.2 | .8 | .4 | — | — |
| Balance on current & capital acct. | 129ba | −630.7 | −732.3 | −808.5 | −718.3 | −684.8 | −384.2 | −442.1 | −461.5 | −442.8 | −377.2 | −389.6 | −484.1 |
| C. Financial Account* | 309na | −529.5 | −686.6 | −806.8 | −617.4 | −735.4 | −283.1 | −438.8 | −531.6 | −445.7 | −392.7 | −236.1 | −202.9 |
| Direct investment: assets | 3a9aa | 378.1 | 61.9 | 296.1 | 532.9 | 351.7 | 313.7 | 354.6 | 440.4 | 377.9 | 399.2 | 357.2 | 345.1 |
| Equity & investment fund shares | 3aaaa | 296.2 | 51.6 | 266.3 | 431.4 | 360.1 | 262.1 | 343.0 | 401.5 | 322.6 | 336.9 | 355.6 | 312.9 |
| Debt instruments | 3abaa | 82.0 | 10.3 | 29.7 | 101.6 | −8.4 | 51.7 | 11.5 | 38.9 | 55.3 | 62.3 | 1.6 | 32.3 |
| Direct investment: liabilities | 3a9la | 207.9 | 138.3 | 294.3 | 340.1 | 332.7 | 153.8 | 259.3 | 257.4 | 232.0 | 287.2 | 131.8 | 409.9 |
| Equity & investment fund shares | 3aala | 142.4 | 112.5 | 184.1 | 190.4 | 294.9 | 148.5 | 203.1 | 185.1 | 193.8 | 211.8 | 68.9 | 302.9 |
| Debt instruments | 3abla | 65.4 | 25.9 | 110.1 | 149.6 | 37.9 | 5.3 | 56.2 | 72.4 | 38.2 | 75.4 | 63.0 | 107.0 |
| Portfolio investment: assets | 3b9aa | 192.0 | 267.3 | 493.4 | 380.8 | −284.3 | 375.9 | 199.6 | 85.4 | 238.8 | 476.2 | 538.1 | 186.3 |
| Equity & investment fund shares | 3baaa | 84.8 | 186.7 | 137.3 | 147.8 | −38.6 | 63.7 | 79.2 | 7.0 | 95.8 | 284.3 | 436.5 | 172.5 |
| Debt securities | 3bbaa | 107.2 | 80.6 | 356.0 | 233.0 | −245.7 | 312.2 | 120.5 | 78.4 | 143.0 | 191.9 | 101.5 | 13.8 |
| Portfolio investment: liabilities | 3b9la | 867.3 | 832.0 | 1,126.7 | 1,156.6 | 523.7 | 357.4 | 820.4 | 311.6 | 747.0 | 502.0 | 705.0 | 263.4 |
| Equity & investment fund shares | 3bala | 61.8 | 89.3 | 145.5 | 275.6 | 126.8 | 219.3 | 179.0 | 123.4 | 239.1 | −67.5 | 155.1 | −171.3 |
| Debt securities | 3bbla | 805.6 | 742.8 | 981.3 | 881.0 | 396.9 | 138.0 | 641.5 | 188.3 | 507.9 | 569.5 | 550.0 | 434.6 |
| Fin. der.& empl.stk.ops.(ESOs): net. | 3c9na | .... | .... | −29.7 | −6.2 | 32.9 | −44.8 | −14.1 | −35.0 | 7.1 | 2.2 | −54.4 | −25.4 |
| Fin. der. & ESOs.: assets | 3c9aa | .... | .... | .... | .... | .... | .... | .... | .... | .... | .... | .... | .... |
| Fin. der. & ESOs.: liabilities | 3c9la | .... | .... | .... | .... | .... | .... | .... | .... | .... | .... | .... | .... |
| Other investment: assets | 3d9aa | 495.5 | 257.2 | 549.8 | 658.6 | −381.8 | −609.7 | 407.4 | −45.3 | −453.7 | −228.4 | −99.5 | −282.9 |
| Other equity | 3daaa | .... | .... | .... | .... | .... | .... | .... | .... | .... | .... | .... | .... |
| Debt instruments | 3dzaa | 495.5 | 257.2 | 549.8 | 658.6 | −381.8 | −609.7 | 407.4 | −45.3 | −453.7 | −228.4 | −99.5 | −282.9 |
| Other investment: liabilities | 3d9la | 519.9 | 302.7 | 695.3 | 686.9 | −402.4 | −192.9 | 306.6 | 408.0 | −363.3 | 252.8 | 140.6 | −247.2 |
| Other equity | 3dala | .... | .... | .... | .... | .... | .... | .... | .... | .... | .... | .... | .... |
| Debt instruments | 3dzla | 519.9 | 302.7 | 695.3 | 686.9 | −402.4 | −192.9 | 306.6 | 408.0 | −363.3 | 252.8 | 140.6 | −247.2 |
| Curr.+ cap.− finan. acct. balance. | 4y9na | −101.2 | −45.7 | −1.7 | −100.9 | 50.6 | −101.0 | −3.3 | 70.1 | 2.9 | 15.6 | −153.5 | −281.2 |
| D. Net Errors and Omissions | 409na | 98.4 | 31.6 | −.6 | 101.0 | −45.8 | 153.2 | 5.1 | −54.1 | 1.5 | −18.6 | 149.9 | 274.9 |
| E. Reserves and Related Items | 4z9na | −2.8 | −14.1 | −2.4 | .1 | 4.8 | 52.2 | 1.8 | 16.0 | 4.5 | −3.1 | −3.6 | −6.3 |
| Reserve assets | 3e9aa | −2.8 | −14.1 | −2.4 | .1 | 4.8 | 52.2 | 1.8 | 16.0 | 4.5 | −3.1 | −3.6 | −6.3 |
| Credit and loans from the IMF | 3dcla | — | — | — | — | — | — | — | — | — | — | — | — |
| Exceptional financing | 409la | .... | .... | .... | .... | .... | .... | .... | .... | .... | .... | .... | .... |

*Excludes components in group E

| **International Investment Position** | | | | | | | ***Billions of US Dollars*** | | | | | | |
|---|---|---|---|---|---|---|---|---|---|---|---|---|---|
| Assets | 809aa | 10,589.0 | 13,357.0 | 16,409.9 | 20,704.5 | 19,423.4 | 19,426.5 | 21,767.8 | 22,208.9 | 22,561.9 | 24,159.1 | 24,595.5 | 23,208.3 |
| Direct investment | 8a9aa | 3,746.9 | 4,047.2 | 4,929.9 | 5,857.9 | 3,707.2 | 4,945.3 | 5,486.4 | 5,214.8 | 5,968.5 | 7,117.3 | 7,124.0 | 6,907.9 |
| Equity & investment fund shares | 8aaaa | 3,170.5 | 3,449.3 | 4,294.3 | 5,091.0 | 2,928.1 | 4,097.2 | 4,620.9 | 4,320.1 | 4,983.9 | 6,052.1 | 6,052.0 | 5,787.2 |
| Debt instruments | 8abaa | 576.3 | 597.9 | 635.6 | 767.0 | 779.1 | 848.1 | 865.5 | 894.8 | 984.6 | 1,065.2 | 1,072.0 | 1,120.7 |
| Portfolio investment | 8b9aa | 3,828.3 | 4,629.0 | 6,017.1 | 7,262.0 | 4,320.8 | 6,058.6 | 7,160.4 | 6,871.7 | 7,984.0 | 9,206.5 | 9,572.5 | 9,534.4 |
| Equity & investment fund shares | 8baaa | 2,560.4 | 3,317.7 | 4,329.0 | 5,248.0 | 2,748.4 | 3,995.3 | 4,900.2 | 4,501.4 | 5,321.9 | 6,472.9 | 6,719.7 | 6,753.2 |
| Debt securities | 8bbaa | 1,267.9 | 1,311.3 | 1,688.1 | 2,014.1 | 1,572.4 | 2,063.3 | 2,260.1 | 2,370.3 | 2,662.1 | 2,733.6 | 2,852.8 | 2,781.2 |
| Fin. der.(oth.than reserves) & ESOs | 8c9aa | .... | 1,190.0 | 1,239.0 | 2,559.3 | 6,127.5 | 3,489.8 | 3,652.3 | 4,716.6 | 3,619.8 | 3,019.8 | 3,224.5 | 2,397.6 |
| Other investment | 8d9aa | 2,824.2 | 3,302.8 | 4,004.0 | 4,748.0 | 4,974.2 | 4,529.0 | 4,980.1 | 4,868.7 | 4,417.4 | 4,367.3 | 4,240.2 | 3,984.7 |
| Other equity | 8daaa | .... | .... | .... | .... | .... | .... | .... | .... | .... | .... | .... | .... |
| Debt instruments | 8dzaa | 2,824.2 | 3,302.8 | 4,004.0 | 4,748.0 | 4,974.2 | 4,529.0 | 4,980.1 | 4,868.7 | 4,417.4 | 4,367.3 | 4,240.2 | 3,984.7 |
| Reserve assets | 8e9aa | 189.6 | 188.0 | 219.9 | 277.2 | 293.7 | 403.8 | 488.7 | 537.0 | 572.4 | 448.3 | 434.3 | 383.6 |
| Liabilities | 809la | 12,952.4 | 15,214.9 | 18,218.3 | 21,984.0 | 23,418.7 | 22,054.1 | 24,279.6 | 26,663.9 | 27,079.8 | 29,486.6 | 31,615.2 | 30,565.1 |
| Direct investment | 8a9la | 3,101.5 | 3,227.1 | 3,752.6 | 4,134.2 | 3,091.2 | 3,618.6 | 4,099.1 | 4,199.2 | 4,661.2 | 5,780.6 | 6,228.8 | 6,513.1 |
| Equity & investment fund shares | 8aala | 2,398.7 | 2,483.7 | 2,895.5 | 3,097.5 | 2,000.5 | 2,513.9 | 2,927.8 | 2,968.4 | 3,407.3 | 4,441.0 | 4,839.4 | 4,945.4 |
| Debt instruments | 8abla | 702.7 | 743.4 | 857.1 | 1,036.7 | 1,090.7 | 1,104.7 | 1,171.3 | 1,230.9 | 1,253.9 | 1,339.6 | 1,389.4 | 1,567.7 |
| Portfolio investment | 8b9la | 6,621.2 | 7,337.8 | 8,843.5 | 10,327.0 | 9,475.9 | 10,463.2 | 11,869.3 | 12,647.2 | 13,978.9 | 15,542.5 | 16,917.1 | 16,666.2 |
| Equity & investment fund shares | 8bala | 2,123.3 | 2,304.0 | 2,791.9 | 3,231.7 | 2,132.4 | 2,917.7 | 3,545.8 | 3,841.9 | 4,545.4 | 5,864.6 | 6,665.2 | 6,270.7 |
| Debt securities | 8bbla | 4,498.0 | 5,033.8 | 6,051.6 | 7,095.3 | 7,343.4 | 7,545.6 | 8,323.5 | 8,805.3 | 9,433.5 | 9,677.9 | 10,251.9 | 10,395.5 |
| Fin. der.(oth.than reserves) & ESOs | 8c9la | .... | 1,132.0 | 1,179.2 | 2,487.9 | 5,967.8 | 3,363.4 | 3,541.9 | 4,630.5 | 3,562.0 | 2,942.4 | 3,150.7 | 2,340.5 |
| Other investment | 8d9la | 3,229.7 | 3,517.8 | 4,443.0 | 5,034.9 | 4,883.8 | 4,608.8 | 4,769.3 | 5,186.9 | 4,877.8 | 5,221.1 | 5,318.6 | 5,045.2 |
| Other equity | 8dala | .... | .... | .... | .... | .... | .... | .... | .... | .... | .... | .... | .... |
| Debt instruments | 8dzla | 3,229.7 | 3,517.8 | 4,443.0 | 5,034.9 | 4,883.8 | 4,608.8 | 4,769.3 | 5,186.9 | 4,877.8 | 5,221.1 | 5,318.6 | 5,045.2 |

# United States   111

| | | 2004 | 2005 | 2006 | 2007 | 2008 | 2009 | 2010 | 2011 | 2012 | 2013 | 2014 | 2015 |
|---|---|---|---|---|---|---|---|---|---|---|---|---|---|
| **Government Finance Operations Statement General Government** | | | | | | *Billions of US Dollars: Fiscal Year Ends December 31* | | | | | | | |
| Revenue | a1 | 3,596.5 | 4,013.4 | 4,371.7 | 4,585.4 | 4,510.5 | 4,099.3 | 4,351.3 | 4,556.2 | 4,748.6 | 5,278.1 | 5,453.9 | 5,693.3 |
| Taxes | a11 | 2,228.7 | 2,564.6 | 2,821.7 | 2,960.6 | 2,851.8 | 2,416.7 | 2,598.6 | 2,861.1 | 3,007.6 | 3,251.1 | 3,418.8 | 3,626.8 |
| Social Contributions | a12 | 833.6 | 878.0 | 927.2 | 966.1 | 993.1 | 969.4 | 989.0 | 922.2 | 956.2 | 1,112.0 | 1,164.1 | 1,207.8 |
| Grants | a13 | .5 | .7 | 1.1 | 1.1 | 1.1 | 1.0 | .8 | .9 | .9 | .9 | 1.1 | .7 |
| Other Revenue | a14 | 533.8 | 570.1 | 621.7 | 657.6 | 664.6 | 712.3 | 762.8 | 772.0 | 783.9 | 914.2 | 870.0 | 858.0 |
| Expense | a2 | 4,095.2 | 4,395.0 | 4,623.3 | 4,916.8 | 5,363.6 | 5,737.2 | 5,967.1 | 6,059.3 | 6,070.2 | 6,092.7 | 6,241.3 | 6,403.3 |
| Compensation of Employees | a21 | 1,186.3 | 1,243.4 | 1,300.9 | 1,369.9 | 1,442.2 | 1,491.4 | 1,545.8 | 1,557.5 | 1,564.9 | 1,581.0 | 1,617.8 | 1,656.1 |
| Use of Goods & Services | a22 | 694.5 | 744.7 | 794.4 | 834.2 | 911.1 | 935.3 | 969.3 | 965.4 | 958.9 | 921.8 | 921.2 | 903.4 |
| Consumption of Fixed Capital | a23 | 283.1 | 303.6 | 324.4 | 349.0 | 372.9 | 387.6 | 401.0 | 419.2 | 433.1 | 441.2 | 449.6 | 453.7 |
| Interest | a24 | 417.0 | 456.7 | 493.1 | 530.5 | 515.8 | 543.3 | 573.7 | 617.5 | 625.5 | 618.2 | 623.8 | 631.1 |
| Subsidies | a25 | 46.4 | 60.9 | 51.5 | 54.6 | 52.6 | 58.3 | 55.9 | 60.1 | 58.0 | 59.4 | 57.9 | 58.6 |
| Grants | a26 | 31.7 | 43.5 | 37.0 | 42.7 | 45.8 | 53.2 | 54.2 | 59.3 | 56.4 | 54.7 | 52.8 | 52.8 |
| Social Benefits | a27 | 1,415.2 | 1,502.3 | 1,605.5 | 1,710.8 | 1,935.4 | 2,124.9 | 2,298.3 | 2,327.3 | 2,341.5 | 2,404.3 | 2,506.6 | 2,639.8 |
| Other Expense | a28 | 21.0 | 40.0 | 16.7 | 25.1 | 87.8 | 143.3 | 69.0 | 53.1 | 31.7 | 12.2 | 11.5 | 7.8 |
| Gross Operating Balance [1-2+23] | agob | −215.6 | −78.0 | 72.7 | 17.6 | −480.1 | −1,250.4 | −1,214.8 | −1,083.9 | −888.5 | −373.4 | −337.7 | −256.3 |
| Net Operating Balance [1-2] | anob | −498.6 | −381.6 | −251.7 | −331.4 | −853.1 | −1,637.9 | −1,615.8 | −1,503.1 | −1,321.7 | −814.6 | −787.4 | −710.0 |
| Net Acq. of Nonfinancial Assets | a31 | 176.9 | 174.7 | 178.1 | 203.7 | 201.9 | 209.1 | 203.2 | 163.6 | 125.4 | 93.4 | 85.9 | 68.1 |
| Aquisition of Nonfin. Assets | a31.1 | …. | …. | …. | …. | …. | …. | …. | …. | …. | …. | …. | …. |
| Disposal of Nonfin. Assets | a31.2 | …. | …. | …. | …. | …. | …. | …. | …. | …. | …. | …. | …. |
| Net Lending/Borrowing [1-2-31] | anlb | −675.5 | −556.3 | −429.8 | −535.1 | −1,055.0 | −1,847.1 | −1,819.0 | −1,666.7 | −1,447.0 | −908.0 | −873.2 | −778.1 |
| Net Acq. of Financial Assets | a32 | 135.5 | 175.4 | 136.5 | 163.0 | 450.2 | 160.5 | 311.5 | −177.6 | 143.8 | 226.1 | 205.1 | 339.9 |
| **By instrument** | | | | | | | | | | | | | |
| Monetary Gold & SDRs | a3201 | .4 | −4.5 | .2 | .2 | .1 | 48.2 | — | −1.8 | — | — | — | — |
| Currency & Deposits | a3202 | −30.0 | 20.3 | 17.6 | 58.4 | 341.5 | −139.9 | 150.7 | −207.1 | 24.0 | 91.0 | 80.4 | 107.9 |
| Securities other than Shares | a3203 | 53.6 | 47.2 | 53.4 | 58.9 | 6.5 | 123.5 | 1.0 | −146.3 | −57.1 | −40.1 | −15.9 | 2.4 |
| Loans | a3204 | 24.7 | 16.7 | 28.4 | 32.1 | 21.8 | 173.3 | 144.6 | 131.8 | 144.6 | 125.6 | 128.0 | 136.4 |
| Shares & Other Equity | a3205 | 23.8 | 22.4 | 26.3 | 29.2 | 183.4 | −107.3 | 6.6 | 9.7 | −9.5 | −2.1 | 11.6 | 29.9 |
| Insurance Technical Reserves | a3206 | — | — | — | — | — | — | — | — | — | — | — | — |
| Financial Derivatives | a3207 | — | — | — | — | — | — | — | — | — | — | — | — |
| Other Accounts Receivable | a3208 | 63.1 | 73.4 | 10.5 | −15.7 | −103.1 | 62.7 | 8.6 | 36.1 | 41.8 | 51.6 | .9 | 63.2 |
| **By debtor** | | | | | | | | | | | | | |
| Domestic | a321 | 136.6 | 188.6 | 137.2 | 161.7 | 444.6 | 106.9 | 307.6 | −196.4 | 137.1 | 227.2 | 206.5 | 341.6 |
| Foreign | a322 | −1.1 | −13.2 | −.7 | 1.3 | 5.6 | 53.6 | 3.9 | 18.8 | 6.7 | −1.0 | −1.5 | −1.7 |
| Net Incurrence of Liabilities | a33 | 772.0 | 593.1 | 474.8 | 620.4 | 1,658.3 | 2,016.2 | 2,045.0 | 1,538.1 | 1,551.8 | 1,141.4 | 1,015.0 | 1,062.2 |
| **By instrument** | | | | | | | | | | | | | |
| Special Drawing Rights (SDRs) | a3301 | — | — | — | — | — | 50.6 | — | — | — | — | — | — |
| Currency & Deposits | a3302 | .7 | .8 | .6 | −.7 | −.8 | −.4 | −.3 | — | — | −.4 | −.3 | — |
| Securities other than Shares | a3303 | 537.8 | 381.0 | 260.5 | 338.7 | 1,367.1 | 1,632.6 | 1,705.8 | 1,119.5 | 1,132.0 | 835.7 | 684.7 | 718.8 |
| Loans | a3304 | .3 | .6 | .6 | .7 | .8 | .8 | .9 | .9 | .4 | .5 | .4 | .3 |
| Shares & Other Equity | a3305 | — | — | — | — | — | — | — | — | — | — | — | — |
| Insurance Technical Reserves | a3306 | 186.8 | 140.0 | 167.1 | 216.3 | 230.4 | 347.0 | 292.6 | 356.9 | 376.2 | 247.5 | 271.1 | 280.6 |
| Financial Derivatives | a3307 | — | — | — | — | — | — | — | — | — | — | — | — |
| Other Accounts Payable | a3308 | 46.4 | 70.6 | 46.0 | 65.5 | 60.8 | −14.4 | 46.1 | 60.8 | 43.2 | 58.0 | 59.1 | 62.6 |
| **By creditor** | | | | | | | | | | | | | |
| Domestic | a331 | …. | …. | …. | …. | …. | …. | …. | …. | …. | …. | …. | …. |
| Foreign | a332 | …. | …. | …. | …. | …. | …. | …. | …. | …. | …. | …. | …. |
| Stat. Discrepancy [32-33-NLB] | anlbz | 39.0 | 138.6 | 91.5 | 77.7 | −153.2 | −8.7 | 85.4 | −48.9 | 39.0 | −7.3 | 63.3 | 55.8 |
| Memo Item: Expenditure [2+31] | a2m | 4,272.1 | 4,569.7 | 4,801.5 | 5,120.5 | 5,565.5 | 5,946.4 | 6,170.2 | 6,223.0 | 6,195.6 | 6,186.1 | 6,327.2 | 6,471.4 |
| **Balance Sheet** | | | | | | *Billions of US Dollars: Fiscal Year Ends December 31* | | | | | | | |
| Net Worth | a6 | 498.6 | 849.5 | 1,643.8 | 2,088.1 | 726.4 | −686.2 | −2,070.1 | −3,157.3 | −3,889.5 | −3,746.5 | −3,927.3 | −4,686.5 |
| Nonfinancial Assets | a61 | 7,939.9 | 8,685.5 | 9,587.8 | 10,334.4 | 11,022.5 | 11,085.1 | 11,515.0 | 12,135.4 | 12,521.9 | 12,925.2 | 13,238.8 | 13,288.2 |
| Financial Assets | a62 | 2,294.6 | 2,447.8 | 2,630.1 | 2,842.8 | 3,306.9 | 3,476.1 | 3,790.7 | 3,594.6 | 3,749.6 | 3,990.6 | 4,240.3 | 4,535.9 |
| **By instrument** | | | | | | | | | | | | | |
| Monetary Gold & SDRs | a6201 | 13.6 | 8.2 | 8.9 | 9.5 | 9.3 | 57.8 | 56.8 | 55.0 | 55.1 | 55.2 | 51.9 | 49.7 |
| Currency & Deposits | a6202 | 284.1 | 303.1 | 321.1 | 379.7 | 721.1 | 581.6 | 732.1 | 524.5 | 567.6 | 658.6 | 737.3 | 841.7 |
| Securities other than Shares | a6203 | 657.4 | 704.5 | 757.9 | 816.9 | 823.4 | 946.9 | 947.9 | 801.7 | 744.5 | 704.5 | 688.6 | 691.0 |
| Loans | a6204 | 543.1 | 559.9 | 605.5 | 637.1 | 657.1 | 826.9 | 972.1 | 1,101.6 | 1,244.2 | 1,368.8 | 1,496.2 | 1,632.0 |
| Shares and Other Equity | a6205 | 262.4 | 290.2 | 333.4 | 367.8 | 490.2 | 416.1 | 443.3 | 454.7 | 463.6 | 498.9 | 524.1 | 552.6 |
| Insurance Technical Reserves | a6206 | — | — | — | — | — | — | — | — | — | — | — | — |
| Financial Derivatives | a6207 | — | — | — | — | — | — | — | — | — | — | — | — |
| Other Accounts Receivable | a6208 | 534.0 | 581.8 | 603.3 | 631.9 | 605.7 | 646.8 | 638.5 | 657.2 | 674.6 | 704.6 | 742.2 | 769.0 |
| **By debtor** | | | | | | | | | | | | | |
| Domestic | a621 | 2,195.2 | 2,366.3 | 2,547.5 | 2,756.3 | 3,214.8 | 3,328.7 | 3,640.1 | 3,425.6 | 3,575.0 | 3,818.1 | 4,077.3 | 4,381.8 |
| Foreign | a622 | 99.4 | 81.5 | 82.7 | 86.5 | 92.0 | 147.4 | 150.6 | 168.9 | 174.7 | 172.5 | 163.0 | 154.2 |
| Liabilities | a63 | 9,735.9 | 10,283.8 | 10,574.1 | 11,089.1 | 13,603.0 | 15,247.4 | 17,375.8 | 18,887.3 | 20,161.1 | 20,662.3 | 21,406.3 | 22,510.6 |
| **By instrument** | | | | | | | | | | | | | |
| Special Drawing Rights (SDRs) | a6301 | 9.8 | 9.2 | 9.6 | 9.9 | 9.7 | 60.6 | 59.6 | 59.4 | 59.5 | 59.6 | 56.4 | 54.1 |
| Currency & Deposits | a6302 | 26.7 | 27.5 | 28.1 | 27.4 | 26.6 | 26.2 | 25.9 | 25.9 | 25.9 | 25.6 | 25.3 | 25.3 |
| Securities other than Shares | a6303 | 7,283.9 | 7,651.9 | 7,912.4 | 8,251.0 | 9,618.1 | 11,250.7 | 12,956.4 | 14,075.9 | 15,208.0 | 16,043.7 | 16,728.4 | 17,447.1 |
| Loans | a6304 | 10.0 | 10.6 | 11.2 | 11.9 | 12.7 | 13.5 | 14.4 | 15.3 | 15.7 | 16.2 | 16.6 | 16.9 |
| Shares and Other Equity | a6305 | — | — | — | — | — | — | — | — | — | — | — | — |
| Insurance Technical Reserves | a6306 | 1,780.9 | 1,894.5 | 1,882.6 | 1,992.8 | 3,079.2 | 3,057.4 | 3,437.2 | 3,781.6 | 3,871.9 | 3,480.9 | 3,487.7 | 3,816.8 |
| Financial Derivatives | a6307 | — | — | — | — | — | — | — | — | — | — | — | — |
| Other Accounts Payable | a6308 | 624.6 | 690.0 | 730.2 | 796.0 | 856.6 | 839.0 | 882.3 | 929.1 | 980.1 | 1,036.3 | 1,091.9 | 1,150.4 |
| **By creditor** | | | | | | | | | | | | | |
| Domestic | a631 | …. | …. | …. | …. | …. | …. | …. | …. | …. | …. | …. | …. |
| Foreign | a632 | …. | …. | …. | …. | …. | …. | …. | …. | …. | …. | …. | …. |
| Net Financial Worth [62-63] | a6m2 | −7,441.3 | −7,836.0 | −7,943.9 | −8,246.3 | −10,296.1 | −11,771.3 | −13,585.1 | −15,292.7 | −16,411.5 | −16,671.7 | −17,166.1 | −17,974.7 |
| Memo Item: Debt at Market Value | a6m3 | | | | | | | | | | | | |
| Memo Item: Debt at Face Value | a6m35 | 9,735.9 | 10,283.8 | 10,574.1 | 11,089.1 | 13,603.0 | 15,247.4 | 17,375.8 | 18,887.3 | 20,154.9 | 20,650.0 | 21,395.3 | …. |
| Memo Item: Debt at Nominal Value | a6m4 | …. | …. | …. | …. | …. | …. | …. | …. | …. | …. | …. | …. |

| | | 2004 | 2005 | 2006 | 2007 | 2008 | 2009 | 2010 | 2011 | 2012 | 2013 | 2014 | 2015 |
|---|---|---|---|---|---|---|---|---|---|---|---|---|---|
| **National Accounts** | | | | | | | *Billions of US Dollars* | | | | | | | |
| Househ.Cons.Expend.,incl.NPISHs.... | **96fac** | 8,260.0 | 8,794.1 | 9,304.0 | 9,750.5 | 10,013.7 | 9,847.0 | 10,202.2 | 10,689.3 | 11,050.6 | 11,392.3 | 11,866.0 | 12,271.9 |
| Government Consumption Expend... | **91fac** | 1,868.9 | 1,980.0 | 2,089.9 | 2,209.7 | 2,368.6 | 2,442.1 | 2,522.2 | 2,530.9 | 2,544.2 | 2,521.9 | 2,556.3 | 2,572.0 |
| Gross Fixed Capital Formation.......... | **93eac** | 2,701.3 | 2,981.2 | 3,166.1 | 3,201.4 | 3,091.5 | 2,672.7 | 2,691.1 | 2,836.0 | 3,064.3 | 3,185.6 | 3,378.8 | 3,522.8 |
| Changes in Inventories.................... | **93iac** | 63.9 | 59.6 | 67.0 | 34.5 | −32.0 | −147.6 | 61.5 | 41.8 | 61.8 | 71.8 | 77.1 | 109.3 |
| Exports of Goods and Services......... | **90cac** | 1,181.5 | 1,308.9 | 1,476.3 | 1,664.6 | 1,842.0 | 1,587.7 | 1,852.3 | 2,106.4 | 2,198.2 | 2,263.3 | 2,342.0 | 2,253.4 |
| Imports of Goods and Services (-)..... | **98cac** | 1,800.7 | 2,030.1 | 2,247.3 | 2,383.1 | 2,565.0 | 1,983.2 | 2,365.0 | 2,686.4 | 2,763.8 | 2,771.7 | 2,871.9 | 2,782.3 |
| Gross Domestic Product (GDP)......... | **99bac** | 12,274.9 | 13,093.7 | 13,855.9 | 14,477.6 | 14,718.6 | 14,418.7 | 14,964.4 | 15,517.9 | 16,155.3 | 16,663.2 | 17,348.1 | 17,947.0 |
| Net Primary Income from Abroad..... | **98nac** | 89.1 | 92.6 | 67.6 | 125.6 | 172.0 | 151.1 | 206.0 | 246.7 | 237.6 | 250.4 | 263.1 | 213.6 |
| Gross National Income (GNI)............ | **99aac** | 12,372.7 | 13,221.8 | 14,140.8 | 14,585.7 | 14,791.2 | 14,494.5 | 15,121.1 | 15,802.9 | 16,596.1 | 17,091.2 | 17,823.2 | 18,367.6 |
| Net Current Transf. from Abroad...... | **98tac** | −97.0 | −109.1 | −98.8 | −125.2 | −140.6 | −137.5 | −139.3 | −148.2 | −140.1 | −137.7 | −134.3 | . . . . |
| Gross Saving.................................. | **99sac** | 2,146.7 | 2,338.6 | 2,648.1 | 2,500.3 | 2,268.4 | 2,068.0 | 2,257.5 | 2,434.6 | 2,861.3 | 3,039.2 | 3,266.8 | 3,374.0 |
| Consumption of Fixed Capital.......... | **99cac** | 1,831.7 | 1,981.9 | 2,136.0 | 2,264.4 | 2,363.4 | 2,368.4 | 2,381.6 | 2,450.7 | 2,534.2 | 2,632.8 | 2,746.7 | 2,821.3 |
| GDP Volume 2009 Ref., Chained..... | **99bar** | 13,773.5 | 14,234.3 | 14,613.8 | 14,873.8 | 14,830.4 | 14,418.8 | 14,783.8 | 15,020.6 | 15,354.6 | 15,583.3 | 15,961.7 | 16,348.9 |
| GDP Volume (2010=100)............... | **99bvr** | 93.2 | 96.3 | 98.9 | 100.6 | 100.3 | 97.5 | 100.0 | 101.6 | 103.9 | 105.4 | 108.0 | 110.6 |
| GDP Deflator (2010=100).............. | **99bir** | 88.0 | 90.9 | 93.7 | 96.2 | 98.0 | 98.8 | 100.0 | 102.1 | 103.9 | 105.6 | 107.4 | 108.5 |
| | | | | | | | *Millions: Midyear Estimates* | | | | | | | |
| **Population.................................** | **99z** | 293.53 | 296.14 | 298.86 | 301.66 | 304.47 | 307.23 | 309.88 | 312.39 | 314.80 | 317.14 | 319.45 | 321.77 |

# Uruguay 298

| | | 2004 | 2005 | 2006 | 2007 | 2008 | 2009 | 2010 | 2011 | 2012 | 2013 | 2014 | 2015 |
|---|---|---|---|---|---|---|---|---|---|---|---|---|---|
| **Exchange Rates** | | | | | | *Pesos per SDR: End of Period* | | | | | | | |
| Market Rate.................... | aa | 40.922 | 34.445 | 36.707 | 33.975 | 37.506 | 30.769 | 30.945 | 30.549 | 29.815 | 32.939 | 35.254 | 41.396 |
| | | | | | *Pesos per US Dollar: End of Period (ae) Period Average (rf)* | | | | | | | | |
| Market Rate.................... | ae | 26.350 | 24.100 | 24.400 | 21.500 | 24.350 | 19.627 | 20.094 | 19.898 | 19.399 | 21.389 | 24.333 | 29.873 |
| Market Rate.................... | rf | 28.704 | 24.479 | 24.073 | 23.471 | 20.949 | 22.568 | 20.059 | 19.314 | 20.311 | 20.482 | 23.246 | 27.327 |
| | | | | | *Index Numbers (2010=100): Period Averages* | | | | | | | | |
| Market Rate.................... | ahx | 70.0 | 81.9 | 83.3 | 85.5 | 96.2 | 89.2 | 100.0 | 103.9 | 98.9 | 98.2 | 86.3 | 73.7 |
| Nominal Effective Exchange Rate..... | nec | 76.4 | 86.3 | 86.2 | 84.1 | 91.2 | 90.6 | 100.0 | 100.7 | 101.8 | 105.5 | 100.5 | 100.0 |
| CPI-Based Real Effect. Ex. Rate........ | rec | 69.5 | 78.1 | 79.2 | 79.4 | 87.0 | 89.3 | 100.0 | 102.0 | 105.2 | 112.1 | 110.2 | 114.3 |
| **Fund Position** | | | | | | *Millions of SDRs: End of Period* | | | | | | | |
| Quota.................... | 2f.s | 306.50 | 306.50 | 306.50 | 306.50 | 306.50 | 306.50 | 306.50 | 306.50 | 306.50 | 306.50 | 306.50 | 306.50 |
| SDR Holdings.................... | 1b.s | .78 | 4.37 | .72 | .23 | 2.65 | 245.67 | 245.58 | 245.63 | 245.67 | 245.69 | 245.73 | 245.74 |
| Reserve Position in the Fund........ | 1c.s | — | — | — | — | — | — | 63.02 | 95.32 | 101.12 | 111.12 | 114.32 | 96.32 |
| Total Fund Cred.&Loans Outstg....... | 2tl | 1,728.38 | 1,612.15 | — | — | — | · — | — | — | — | — | — | — |
| SDR Allocations.................... | 1bd | 49.98 | 49.98 | 49.98 | 49.98 | 49.98 | 293.26 | 293.26 | 293.26 | 293.26 | 293.26 | 293.26 | 293.26 |
| **International Liquidity** | | | | | | *Millions of US Dollars Unless Otherwise Indicated: End of Period* | | | | | | | |
| Total Reserves minus Gold.............. | 1l.d | 2,508 | 3,074 | 3,085 | 4,114 | 6,353 | 8,029 | 7,644 | 10,289 | 13,591 | 16,271 | 17,545 | 15,630 |
| SDR Holdings.................... | 1b.d | 1 | 6 | 1 | — | 4 | 385 | 378 | 377 | 378 | 378 | 356 | 341 |
| Reserve Position in the Fund......... | 1c.d | — | — | — | — | — | — | 97 | 146 | 155 | 171 | 166 | 133 |
| Foreign Exchange.................... | 1d.d | 2,507 | 3,068 | 3,084 | 4,114 | 6,349 | 7,644 | 7,168 | 9,765 | 13,058 | 15,721 | 17,023 | 15,156 |
| Gold (Million Fine Troy Ounces)........ | 1ad | .008 | .008 | .008 | .009 | .008 | .008 | .008 | .008 | .008 | .008 | .008 | .003 |
| Gold (National Valuation).............. | 1and | 4 | 4 | 5 | 7 | 7 | 9 | 12 | 13 | 14 | 10 | 10 | 4 |
| Central Bank: Other Assets.............. | 3..d | 365 | 655 | 325 | 1,202 | 998 | 926 | 972 | 855 | 1,047 | 1,031 | 1,065 | 1,033 |
| Central Bank: Other Liabs............. | 4..d | 215 | 89 | 52 | 107 | 268 | 273 | 516 | 382 | 1,084 | 1,403 | 1,456 | 927 |
| Other Depository Corps.: Assets....... | 7a.d | 3,817 | 4,023 | 4,367 | 4,632 | 4,750 | 6,241 | 8,616 | 8,734 | 8,083 | 8,273 | 8,624 | 10,711 |
| Other Depository Corps.: Liabs........ | 7b.d | 1,985 | 2,054 | 2,205 | 2,288 | 3,028 | 3,451 | 3,710 | 3,971 | 4,430 | 5,249 | 5,575 | 5,874 |
| Other Financial Corps.: Assets.......... | 7e.d | 1,777 | 1,733 | 1,651 | 1,768 | 1,877 | 1,934 | 1,911 | 431 | 474 | 449 | 576 | 562 |
| Other Financial Corps.: Liabs........... | 7f.d | 1,665 | 1,554 | 1,564 | 1,671 | 1,792 | 1,846 | 1,818 | 340 | 364 | 332 | 467 | 443 |
| **Central Bank** | | | | | | *Millions of Pesos: End of Period* | | | | | | | |
| Net Foreign Assets.......................... | 11n | −2,632.0 | 30,592.7 | 80,083.6 | 110,507.3 | 170,810.2 | 161,588.3 | 153,908.9 | 205,434.7 | 254,446.1 | 330,590.8 | 407,787.8 | 458,138.0 |
| Claims on Nonresidents................ | 11 | 75,815.7 | 89,988.2 | 83,190.7 | 114,505.6 | 179,213.4 | 175,977.9 | 173,347.0 | 221,998.7 | 284,215.8 | 370,255.0 | 453,551.7 | 497,977.5 |
| Liabilities to Nonresidents.............. | 16c | 78,447.8 | 59,395.5 | 3,107.1 | 3,998.3 | 8,403.1 | 14,389.7 | 19,438.1 | 16,564.0 | 29,769.8 | 39,664.2 | 45,763.8 | 39,839.5 |
| Claims on Other Depository Corps.... | 12e | 1,418.4 | 2,224.5 | 1,000.2 | 802.9 | 1,437.5 | 953.6 | 1,223.4 | 2,785.9 | 3,129.1 | 2,171.7 | 1,257.1 | 2,150.4 |
| Net Claims on Central Government.. | 12an | 69,836.8 | 48,775.7 | 20,027.2 | 1,872.5 | 41,601.2 | 27,328.0 | 62,360.7 | 29,803.8 | 54,883.8 | 87,456.0 | 77,070.2 | 49,596.5 |
| Claims on Central Government...... | 12a | 93,480.7 | 76,289.9 | 38,439.6 | 35,871.0 | 67,174.2 | 63,402.1 | 81,585.2 | 82,145.7 | 103,274.5 | 125,033.1 | 137,827.4 | 141,913.2 |
| Liabilities to Central Government... | 16d | 23,643.9 | 27,514.2 | 18,412.4 | 33,998.5 | 25,573.0 | 36,074.1 | 19,224.5 | 52,341.9 | 48,390.7 | 37,577.1 | 60,757.2 | 92,316.7 |
| Claims on Other Sectors................. | 12s | 7,353.9 | 4,972.6 | 5,569.0 | 3,186.7 | 2,966.5 | 2,555.3 | 2,538.6 | 2,516.3 | 2,482.6 | 2,655.0 | 2,973.7 | 2,822.7 |
| Claims on Other Financial Corps... | 12g | 2,550.9 | 1,096.7 | 2,172.7 | 2,008.2 | 2,051.9 | 1,809.3 | 1,782.9 | 1,763.4 | 1,745.8 | 1,824.3 | 1,924.7 | 1,551.8 |
| Claims on State & Local Govts....... | 12b | 6.8 | 5.5 | 6.4 | 5.8 | 4.7 | 4.2 | 4.1 | 4.1 | 4.2 | 4.7 | 5.1 | 5.9 |
| Claims on Public Nonfin. Corps...... | 12c | 4,397.9 | 3,507.7 | 3,033.8 | 851.3 | 559.6 | 452.2 | 463.0 | 459.0 | 447.0 | 491.6 | 555.8 | 680.2 |
| Claims on Private Sector............... | 12d | 398.3 | 362.7 | 356.1 | 321.4 | 350.3 | 289.6 | 288.6 | 289.7 | 285.6 | 334.4 | 488.0 | 584.8 |
| Monetary Base.............................. | 14 | 15,827.3 | 24,589.9 | 27,111.7 | 31,548.2 | 40,788.3 | 43,425.7 | 50,481.6 | 59,219.0 | 75,033.8 | 84,740.9 | 85,912.3 | 92,066.2 |
| Currency in Circulation.................. | 14a | 14,170.3 | 17,285.0 | 22,064.7 | 24,617.3 | 28,262.6 | 31,980.1 | 38,163.9 | 45,188.7 | 52,876.5 | 59,524.3 | 63,108.8 | 68,004.9 |
| Liabs. to Other Depository Corps.... | 14c | 1,163.6 | 6,380.8 | 4,862.5 | 5,640.0 | 11,640.7 | 10,364.4 | 10,091.7 | 12,945.2 | 18,420.3 | 23,400.4 | 21,799.3 | 23,321.1 |
| Liabilities to Other Sectors............. | 14d | 493.5 | 924.1 | 184.6 | 1,290.9 | 884.9 | 1,081.2 | 2,226.1 | 1,085.1 | 3,737.1 | 1,816.2 | 1,004.1 | 740.2 |
| Other Liabs. to Other Dep. Corps...... | 14n | 48,980.6 | 48,362.5 | 56,290.7 | 59,042.2 | 100,502.9 | 82,856.9 | 75,110.7 | 85,774.3 | 118,704.4 | 152,454.2 | 192,429.0 | 209,514.5 |
| Dep. & Sec. Excl. f/Monetary Base.... | 14o | 20,618.4 | 24,440.3 | 33,904.4 | 44,188.8 | 57,487.7 | 70,159.2 | 88,226.3 | 94,027.4 | 115,591.6 | 167,007.1 | 181,215.4 | 167,426.0 |
| Deposits Included in Broad Money. | 15 | — | — | — | — | — | — | — | — | — | — | — | — |
| Sec.Ot.th.Shares Incl.in Brd. Money | 16a | — | — | — | — | — | — | — | — | — | — | — | — |
| Deposits Excl. from Broad Money... | 16b | 10,068.6 | 10,023.8 | 12,021.5 | 13,811.7 | 19,262.6 | 18,608.0 | 14,982.6 | 18,743.8 | 16,667.2 | 28,779.1 | 36,851.5 | 77,629.1 |
| Sec.Ot.th.Shares Excl.f/Brd.Money.. | 16s | 10,549.7 | 14,416.4 | 21,882.9 | 30,377.1 | 38,225.0 | 51,551.2 | 73,243.7 | 75,283.6 | 98,924.4 | 138,228.0 | 144,363.9 | 89,796.9 |
| Loans.................... | 16l | — | — | — | — | — | — | — | — | — | — | — | — |
| Financial Derivatives........................ | 16m | — | — | — | — | — | — | — | — | 15.4 | — | — | 57.5 |
| Shares and Other Equity................. | 17a | −13,872.9 | −15,479.8 | −14,856.5 | −22,164.2 | 13,745.3 | −7,175.6 | 2,834.8 | −1,434.4 | 2,603.6 | 15,389.5 | 25,723.1 | 40,754.2 |
| Other Items (Net)........................... | 17r | 4,423.8 | 4,652.7 | 4,229.8 | 3,754.4 | 4,291.4 | 3,159.0 | 3,378.2 | 2,954.4 | 2,992.7 | 3,281.8 | 3,809.0 | 2,889.2 |
| Memo Item: | | | | | | | | | | | | | |
| Total Assets.................... | 10ra | 191,413.4 | 184,887.3 | 140,389.3 | 165,712.9 | 263,446.7 | 253,980.4 | 269,592.2 | 320,304.4 | 403,797.7 | 512,009.2 | 608,361.9 | 659,857.1 |

| | | 2004 | 2005 | 2006 | 2007 | 2008 | 2009 | 2010 | 2011 | 2012 | 2013 | 2014 | 2015 |
|---|---|---|---|---|---|---|---|---|---|---|---|---|---|
| **Other Depository Corporations** | | | | | | ***Millions of Pesos: End of Period*** | | | | | | | |
| Net Foreign Assets | 21n | 48,262.3 | 47,452.4 | 52,745.1 | 50,412.3 | 41,932.2 | 54,757.9 | 98,585.1 | 94,783.2 | 70,879.8 | 64,678.1 | 74,201.2 | 144,472.5 |
| Claims on Nonresidents | 21 | 100,574.5 | 96,957.4 | 106,549.9 | 99,596.6 | 115,668.0 | 122,498.8 | 173,125.7 | 173,793.3 | 156,810.7 | 176,942.1 | 209,849.0 | 319,956.1 |
| Liabilities to Nonresidents | 26c | 52,312.3 | 49,505.0 | 53,804.8 | 49,184.3 | 73,735.8 | 67,740.8 | 74,540.5 | 79,010.0 | 85,930.9 | 112,264.1 | 135,647.8 | 175,483.5 |
| Claims on Central Bank | 20 | 49,182.5 | 60,306.7 | 68,688.9 | 72,207.2 | 120,353.7 | 102,037.2 | 95,600.6 | 113,772.8 | 152,604.7 | 192,637.6 | 232,248.8 | 252,368.6 |
| Currency | 20a | 3,366.6 | 3,969.9 | 5,933.9 | 5,724.8 | 6,855.9 | 7,674.1 | 8,647.8 | 10,154.7 | 13,390.0 | 14,449.0 | 15,049.6 | 17,148.7 |
| Reserve Deposits and Securities | 20b | 43,776.3 | 47,857.3 | 49,668.4 | 44,323.2 | 91,967.0 | 61,295.6 | 44,339.0 | 63,563.6 | 98,438.6 | 139,544.8 | 189,803.3 | 220,992.8 |
| Other Claims | 20n | 2,039.6 | 8,479.5 | 13,086.6 | 22,159.2 | 21,530.7 | 33,067.5 | 42,613.8 | 40,054.5 | 40,776.2 | 38,643.8 | 27,395.9 | 14,227.2 |
| Net Claims on Central Government | 22an | 11,392.4 | 2,137.4 | 2,058.6 | –1,492.3 | –6,054.8 | 16,918.9 | 5,888.0 | 19,592.6 | 16,490.5 | 10,474.0 | 20,904.5 | 21,282.3 |
| Claims on Central Government | 22a | 27,011.7 | 23,099.5 | 24,880.8 | 21,723.9 | 21,538.5 | 36,847.7 | 25,203.0 | 34,125.2 | 33,671.4 | 29,701.8 | 41,416.6 | 42,065.8 |
| Liabilities to Central Government | 26d | 15,619.4 | 20,962.2 | 22,822.2 | 23,216.2 | 27,593.3 | 19,928.8 | 19,315.0 | 14,532.7 | 17,181.0 | 19,227.7 | 20,512.1 | 20,783.5 |
| Claims on Other Sectors | 22s | 110,830.1 | 107,222.9 | 121,827.8 | 133,959.2 | 182,981.9 | 153,780.7 | 185,280.9 | 220,065.7 | 253,117.0 | 316,072.4 | 373,202.9 | 456,293.3 |
| Claims on Other Financial Corps | 22g | 9,836.2 | 5,839.1 | 3,630.3 | 1,103.1 | 175.0 | 365.6 | 270.2 | 510.1 | 585.9 | 709.5 | 1,534.6 | 2,051.3 |
| Claims on State & Local Govts | 22b | 2,688.2 | 2,154.5 | 1,835.1 | 1,704.1 | 2,091.8 | 1,421.7 | 1,254.1 | 1,270.3 | 1,467.9 | 1,703.6 | 2,226.1 | 2,434.7 |
| Claims on Public Nonfin. Corps | 22c | 3,660.4 | 4,069.4 | 3,839.3 | 2,837.6 | 3,944.4 | 5,649.4 | 3,931.5 | 4,916.7 | 7,143.1 | 7,748.6 | 10,160.3 | 13,973.4 |
| Claims on Private Sector | 22d | 94,645.3 | 95,159.9 | 112,523.1 | 128,314.4 | 176,770.7 | 146,344.0 | 179,825.1 | 213,368.6 | 243,920.2 | 305,910.7 | 359,281.8 | 437,833.9 |
| Liabilities to Central Bank | 26g | 1,603.0 | 1,307.0 | 1,062.3 | 991.9 | 1,843.5 | 1,298.1 | 1,328.5 | 2,894.5 | 3,949.7 | 2,415.1 | 1,301.5 | 2,227.9 |
| Transf.Dep.Included in Broad Money | 24 | 46,917.3 | 50,515.6 | 59,526.5 | 71,396.3 | 98,369.4 | 96,454.4 | 125,127.7 | 150,780.8 | 163,254.2 | 195,734.5 | 224,675.3 | 271,680.0 |
| Other Dep.Included in Broad Money | 25 | 122,818.6 | 117,739.0 | 130,160.4 | 125,030.3 | 163,164.9 | 155,212.1 | 182,375.3 | 212,955.3 | 231,279.3 | 279,466.0 | 344,862.0 | 439,262.2 |
| Sec.Ot.th.Shares Incl.in Brd. Money | 26a | 11,382.6 | 9,974.8 | 8,853.8 | 6,443.4 | 2,943.3 | 2,117.1 | 1,761.2 | 2,501.1 | 4,650.3 | 5,211.0 | 10,663.5 | 16,601.1 |
| Deposits Excl. from Broad Money | 26b | 5,950.3 | 5,400.6 | 5,347.2 | 4,904.0 | 5,503.1 | 4,336.3 | 4,736.6 | 5,427.9 | 6,764.7 | 7,870.9 | 9,305.9 | 11,417.3 |
| Sec.Ot.th.Shares Excl.f/Brd.Money | 26s | 2,835.9 | 2,017.1 | 1,960.7 | 1,303.7 | 1,106.1 | 767.2 | 1,412.2 | 1,853.1 | 1,953.6 | 1,758.6 | 3,105.8 | 4,780.0 |
| Loans | 26l | 3.5 | 11.9 | 34.1 | .2 | — | — | — | — | — | — | — | — |
| Financial Derivatives | 26m | 538.6 | 561.8 | 550.7 | 860.4 | 1,428.2 | 622.3 | 1,090.3 | 1,036.1 | 885.3 | 2,442.3 | 1,517.6 | 2,890.8 |
| Insurance Technical Reserves | 26r | — | — | — | — | — | — | — | — | — | — | — | — |
| Shares and Other Equity | 27a | 26,419.0 | 25,531.1 | 31,477.8 | 38,128.0 | 44,746.1 | 52,369.6 | 57,701.6 | 60,488.6 | 65,189.3 | 72,518.3 | 84,434.4 | 97,080.0 |
| Other Items (Net) | 27r | 1,198.5 | 4,060.6 | 6,347.1 | 6,028.3 | 20,108.4 | 14,317.5 | 9,821.3 | 10,276.9 | 15,165.8 | 16,445.3 | 20,691.5 | 28,477.5 |
| Memo Item: | | | | | | | | | | | | | |
| Total Assets | 20ra | 335,125.4 | 330,801.3 | 368,290.9 | 373,051.4 | 481,231.9 | 445,789.4 | 513,706.9 | 577,569.7 | 628,560.9 | 751,513.9 | 891,814.3 | 1,110,574.7 |
| **Depository Corporations** | | | | | | ***Millions of Pesos: End of Period*** | | | | | | | |
| Net Foreign Assets | 31n | 45,630.2 | 78,045.1 | 132,828.7 | 160,919.7 | 212,742.4 | 216,346.2 | 252,494.0 | 300,218.0 | 325,325.9 | 395,268.8 | 481,989.1 | 602,610.5 |
| Claims on Nonresidents | 31 | 176,390.2 | 186,945.6 | 189,740.6 | 214,102.2 | 294,881.3 | 298,476.7 | 346,472.6 | 395,792.0 | 441,026.6 | 547,197.1 | 663,400.7 | 817,933.6 |
| Liabilities to Nonresidents | 36c | 130,760.0 | 108,900.5 | 56,912.0 | 53,182.6 | 82,138.9 | 82,130.5 | 93,978.6 | 95,574.0 | 115,700.7 | 151,928.3 | 181,411.6 | 215,323.0 |
| Domestic Claims | 32 | 199,413.3 | 163,108.6 | 149,482.7 | 137,526.1 | 221,495.0 | 200,582.9 | 256,068.2 | 271,978.4 | 326,973.9 | 416,657.4 | 474,151.3 | 529,994.8 |
| Net Claims on Central Government | 32an | 81,229.2 | 50,913.1 | 22,085.8 | 380.2 | 35,546.5 | 44,246.9 | 68,248.7 | 49,396.4 | 71,374.3 | 97,930.0 | 97,974.7 | 70,878.7 |
| Claims on Central Government | 32a | 120,492.5 | 99,389.5 | 63,320.4 | 57,594.9 | 88,712.7 | 100,249.7 | 106,788.2 | 116,270.9 | 136,945.9 | 154,734.9 | 179,244.1 | 183,978.9 |
| Liabilities to Central Government | 36d | 39,263.2 | 48,476.4 | 41,234.6 | 57,214.7 | 53,166.2 | 56,002.9 | 38,539.5 | 66,874.5 | 65,571.7 | 56,804.9 | 81,269.3 | 113,100.2 |
| Claims on Other Sectors | 32s | 118,184.1 | 112,195.6 | 127,396.9 | 137,145.9 | 185,948.5 | 156,336.0 | 187,819.5 | 222,582.0 | 255,599.6 | 318,727.4 | 376,176.6 | 459,116.0 |
| Claims on Other Financial Corps | 32g | 12,387.1 | 6,935.8 | 5,803.0 | 3,111.3 | 2,226.9 | 2,174.8 | 2,053.1 | 2,273.6 | 2,331.6 | 2,533.8 | 3,459.4 | 3,603.1 |
| Claims on State & Local Govts | 32b | 2,695.0 | 2,160.1 | 1,841.5 | 1,709.8 | 2,096.5 | 1,425.9 | 1,258.3 | 1,274.4 | 1,472.1 | 1,708.3 | 2,231.2 | 2,440.6 |
| Claims on Public Nonfin. Corps | 32c | 8,058.3 | 7,577.1 | 6,873.1 | 3,688.9 | 4,504.0 | 6,101.7 | 4,394.5 | 5,375.7 | 7,590.1 | 8,240.2 | 10,716.2 | 14,653.6 |
| Claims on Private Sector | 32d | 95,043.7 | 95,522.7 | 112,879.2 | 128,635.8 | 177,121.0 | 146,633.6 | 180,113.6 | 213,658.3 | 244,205.8 | 306,245.1 | 359,769.9 | 438,418.7 |
| Broad Money Liabilities | 35l | 192,415.7 | 192,468.6 | 214,856.0 | 223,053.4 | 286,769.3 | 279,170.8 | 341,006.3 | 402,356.4 | 442,407.3 | 527,303.0 | 629,264.3 | 779,139.7 |
| Currency Outside Depository Corps | 34a | 10,803.7 | 13,315.1 | 16,130.7 | 18,892.5 | 21,406.7 | 24,306.0 | 29,516.1 | 35,034.1 | 39,486.5 | 45,075.4 | 48,059.3 | 50,856.2 |
| Transferable Deposits | 34 | 47,410.8 | 51,439.7 | 59,711.0 | 71,624.0 | 98,811.7 | 97,072.6 | 126,702.7 | 151,576.9 | 163,838.9 | 196,575.6 | 225,469.5 | 272,369.2 |
| Other Deposits | 35 | 122,818.6 | 117,739.0 | 130,160.4 | 125,875.9 | 163,607.5 | 155,599.1 | 182,433.3 | 213,244.3 | 234,431.7 | 280,441.0 | 345,072.0 | 439,313.2 |
| Securities Other than Shares | 36a | 11,382.6 | 9,974.8 | 8,853.8 | 6,661.0 | 2,943.3 | 2,193.1 | 2,354.2 | 2,501.1 | 4,650.3 | 5,211.0 | 10,663.5 | 16,601.1 |
| Deposits Excl. from Broad Money | 36b | 16,018.9 | 15,424.4 | 17,368.7 | 18,715.7 | 24,765.7 | 22,944.3 | 19,719.2 | 24,171.7 | 23,431.9 | 36,650.0 | 46,157.4 | 89,046.5 |
| Sec.Ot.th.Shares Excl.f/Brd.Money | 36s | 13,385.6 | 16,433.5 | 23,843.6 | 31,680.8 | 39,331.1 | 52,318.4 | 74,655.9 | 77,136.6 | 100,877.9 | 139,986.6 | 147,469.7 | 94,576.8 |
| Loans | 36l | 3.5 | 11.9 | 34.1 | .2 | — | — | — | — | — | — | — | — |
| Financial Derivatives | 36m | 538.6 | 561.8 | 550.7 | 860.4 | 1,428.2 | 622.3 | 1,090.3 | 1,036.1 | 900.7 | 2,442.3 | 1,517.6 | 2,948.3 |
| Insurance Technical Reserves | 36r | — | — | — | — | — | — | — | — | — | — | — | — |
| Shares and Other Equity | 37a | 12,546.1 | 10,051.3 | 16,621.2 | 15,963.9 | 58,491.4 | 45,194.0 | 60,536.3 | 59,054.2 | 67,792.8 | 87,907.8 | 110,157.4 | 137,834.2 |
| Other Items (Net) | 37r | 10,135.1 | 6,202.2 | 9,037.1 | 8,171.3 | 23,451.6 | 16,679.3 | 11,554.2 | 8,441.3 | 16,889.0 | 17,636.5 | 21,574.0 | 29,059.8 |
| Broad Money Liabs., Seasonally Adj. | 35l.b | 191,479.8 | 191,115.4 | 212,941.0 | 220,957.6 | 284,226.9 | 277,187.5 | 339,919.5 | 402,673.1 | 444,748.1 | 532,158.4 | 637,847.3 | 791,639.5 |
| **Other Financial Corporations** | | | | | | ***Millions of Pesos: End of Period*** | | | | | | | |
| Net Foreign Assets | 41n | 2,966.1 | 4,311.2 | 2,106.6 | 2,086.7 | 2,049.9 | 1,724.0 | 1,851.9 | 1,815.6 | 2,133.3 | 2,504.8 | 2,644.5 | 3,569.1 |
| Claims on Nonresidents | 41 | 46,827.8 | 41,757.0 | 40,276.9 | 38,014.3 | 45,693.6 | 37,960.5 | 38,389.8 | 8,572.7 | 9,192.7 | 9,614.2 | 14,012.1 | 16,801.6 |
| Liabilities to Nonresidents | 46c | 43,861.6 | 37,445.7 | 38,170.3 | 35,927.6 | 43,643.7 | 36,236.5 | 36,537.8 | 6,757.1 | 7,059.4 | 7,109.4 | 11,367.6 | 13,232.5 |
| Claims on Depository Corporations | 40 | 121.7 | 87.5 | 86.8 | 83.2 | 80.5 | 68.8 | 97.0 | 177.7 | 171.3 | 103.9 | 47.8 | 33.6 |
| Net Claims on Central Government | 42an | 151.4 | 139.2 | 106.4 | — | — | 20.0 | 20.0 | 1.0 | 1.7 | 2.0 | 2.4 | 3.1 |
| Claims on Central Government | 42a | 151.4 | 139.2 | 106.4 | — | — | 20.0 | 20.0 | 1.0 | 1.7 | 2.0 | 2.4 | 3.1 |
| Liabilities to Central Government | 46d | — | — | — | — | — | — | — | — | — | — | — | — |
| Claims on Other Sectors | 42s | 15.2 | 16.5 | 8.4 | 4.7 | 7.7 | 5.3 | 7.6 | 7.1 | 6.6 | 6.8 | .3 | .3 |
| Claims on State & Local Govts | 42b | — | — | — | — | — | — | — | — | — | — | — | — |
| Claims on Public Nonfin. Corps | 42c | — | — | — | — | — | — | — | — | — | — | — | — |
| Claims on Private Sector | 42d | 15.2 | 16.5 | 8.4 | 4.7 | 7.7 | 5.3 | 7.6 | 7.1 | 6.6 | 6.8 | .3 | .3 |
| Deposits | 46b | — | — | — | — | — | — | — | — | — | — | — | — |
| Securities Other than Shares | 46s | — | — | — | — | — | — | — | — | — | — | — | — |
| Loans | 46l | — | — | — | — | — | — | — | — | — | — | — | — |
| Financial Derivatives | 46m | — | — | — | — | — | — | — | — | — | — | — | — |
| Insurance Technical Reserves | 46r | — | — | — | — | — | — | — | — | — | — | — | — |
| Shares and Other Equity | 47a | 3,215.3 | 4,530.5 | 2,273.8 | 2,128.0 | 2,086.9 | 1,517.8 | 1,559.1 | 1,615.1 | 1,975.7 | 2,142.6 | 1,898.6 | 2,620.3 |
| Other Items (Net) | 47r | 39.2 | 23.9 | 34.4 | 46.6 | 51.3 | 300.3 | 417.4 | 386.3 | 337.3 | 474.8 | 796.5 | 985.9 |
| Memo Item: | | | | | | | | | | | | | |
| Total Assets | 40ra | 47,156.6 | 42,072.5 | 40,551.3 | 38,169.6 | 45,858.4 | 38,117.9 | 38,594.7 | 8,840.4 | 9,445.0 | 9,769.3 | 14,074.6 | 16,853.3 |

| | | 2004 | 2005 | 2006 | 2007 | 2008 | 2009 | 2010 | 2011 | 2012 | 2013 | 2014 | 2015 |
|---|---|---|---|---|---|---|---|---|---|---|---|---|---|
| **Monetary Aggregates** | | | | | | | *Millions of Pesos: End of Period* | | | | | | |
| Broad Money.................................. | 59m | 192,415.7 | 192,468.6 | 214,856.0 | 223,053.4 | 286,769.3 | 279,170.8 | 341,006.3 | 402,356.4 | 442,407.3 | 527,303.0 | 629,264.3 | 779,139.7 |
| o/w:Currency Issued by Cent.Govt | 59m.a | — | — | — | — | — | — | — | — | — | — | — | — |
| o/w: Dep.in Nonfin. Corporations. | 59m.b | — | — | — | — | — | — | — | — | — | — | — | — |
| o/w:Secs. Issued by Central Govt.. | 59m.c | — | — | — | — | — | — | — | — | — | — | — | — |
| Money (National Definitions) | | | | | | | | | | | | | |
| Base Money.............................. | 19ma | 15,827.5 | 24,590.1 | 27,111.9 | 31,548.4 | 40,788.2 | 43,426.1 | 50,482.1 | 59,221.4 | 72,193.0 | 84,741.3 | 85,911.3 | 92,063.3 |
| M1................................................ | 59ma | 22,281.4 | 29,693.0 | 35,711.2 | 47,050.9 | 55,267.0 | 61,816.2 | 79,252.3 | 94,491.7 | 103,202.3 | 116,671.1 | 117,871.9 | 123,945.8 |
| M2................................................ | 59mb | 34,699.9 | 44,124.0 | 53,886.0 | 70,582.5 | 82,767.5 | 95,093.4 | 124,585.1 | 152,153.4 | 167,769.8 | 190,764.0 | 202,944.9 | 221,260.9 |
| **Interest Rates** | | | | | | | *Percent Per Annum* | | | | | | |
| Central Bank Policy Rate (EOP)........ | 60 | . . . . | . . . . | . . . . | . . . . | 7.75 | 6.25 | 6.50 | 8.75 | 9.00 | 9.25 | 9.25 | 9.25 |
| Discount Rate (End of Period)........... | 60.a | 10.00 | 10.00 | 10.00 | 10.00 | 20.00 | 20.00 | 20.00 | 20.00 | 20.00 | 30.00 | 30.00 | 30.00 |
| Discount Rate (Fgn.Cur.) (EOP)........ | 60.af | 12.37 | . . . . | . . . . | . . . . | . . . . | . . . . | . . . . | . . . . | . . . . | . . . . | . . . . | . . . . |
| Money Market Rate........................ | 60b | 3.57 | 1.25 | 1.60 | 4.11 | 9.80 | 8.60 | 6.31 | 7.58 | 8.82 | 10.28 | 10.94 | 11.78 |
| Treasury Bill Rate.......................... | 60c | 14.75 | 4.14 | 4.54 | 7.11 | 10.05 | 11.87 | 9.06 | 8.77 | 9.40 | 11.37 | 14.36 | 13.47 |
| Savings Rate.................................. | 60k | 2.55 | 1.33 | .94 | .84 | .69 | .72 | .71 | .70 | .69 | .53 | .39 | .52 |
| Savings Rate (Fgn. Currency)........... | 60k.f | .45 | .51 | .44 | .24 | .24 | .21 | .19 | .10 | .10 | .08 | .07 | .08 |
| Deposit Rate.................................. | 60l | 6.20 | 2.84 | 1.83 | 2.36 | 3.23 | 4.40 | 4.17 | 4.55 | 4.45 | 4.65 | 4.90 | 5.60 |
| Deposit Rate (Fgn. Currency)........... | 60l.f | 1.03 | 1.28 | 1.73 | 1.87 | 1.17 | 1.24 | .42 | .28 | .22 | .19 | .24 | .21 |
| Lending Rate.................................. | 60p | 23.68 | 13.61 | 9.25 | 8.94 | 12.45 | 15.28 | 10.33 | 9.78 | 11.20 | 12.43 | 15.53 | 15.84 |
| Lending Rate (Fgn. Currency)........... | 60p.f | 7.35 | 6.77 | 7.49 | 7.25 | 6.04 | 6.17 | 5.53 | 5.15 | 4.94 | 4.81 | 4.60 | 4.41 |
| **Prices, Production, Labor** | | | | | | | *Index Numbers (2010=100): Period Averages* | | | | | | |
| Wholesale Prices............................ | 63 | 67.4 | 65.7 | 69.6 | 77.8 | 91.0 | 92.9 | 100.0 | 115.9 | 123.4 | 127.6 | 141.6 | 151.3 |
| Consumer Prices............................ | 64 | 67.4 | 70.5 | 75.1 | 81.1 | 87.5 | 93.7 | † 100.0 | 108.1 | 116.8 | 126.9 | 138.1 | 150.1 |
| Manuf. Prod. (2005=100)................ | 66ey | 89.8 | 100.0 | 108.9 | . . . . | . . . . | . . . . | . . . . | . . . . | . . . . | . . . . | . . . . | . . . . |
| | | | | | | | *Number in Thousands: Period Averages* | | | | | | |
| Labor Force................................... | 67d | 1,242 | 1,269 | 1,581 | . . . . | . . . . | . . . . | . . . . | . . . . | . . . . | . . . . | . . . . | . . . . |
| Employment.................................. | 67e | 1,078 | 1,115 | 1,414 | . . . . | . . . . | . . . . | . . . . | . . . . | . . . . | . . . . | . . . . | . . . . |
| Unemployment.............................. | 67c | 164 | 155 | 167 | . . . . | . . . . | . . . . | . . . . | . . . . | . . . . | . . . . | . . . . | . . . . |
| Unemployment Rate (%)................ | 67r | 13.1 | 12.2 | 10.9 | 9.2 | 7.7 | 7.3 | 7.2 | 6.3 | 6.5 | 6.6 | 6.6 | 7.5 |
| **Intl. Transactions & Positions** | | | | | | | *Millions of US Dollars* | | | | | | |
| Exports......................................... | 70..d | 2,930.8 | 3,404.5 | 3,953.2 | 4,485.2 | 6,420.8 | 5,417.0 | 6,707.1 | 7,997.5 | 8,600.6 | 8,843.6 | 9,475.2 | 7,741.6 |
| Imports, c.i.f.................................. | 71..d | 3,113.6 | 3,878.9 | 4,757.4 | 5,726.1 | 8,943.4 | 6,208.8 | 8,618.9 | 10,623.4 | 10,641.5 | 10,989.6 | 10,900.5 | 9,095.5 |
| **Balance of Payments** | | | | | | | *Millions of US Dollars* | | | | | | |
| A. Current Account*....................... | 109bx | 3.1 | 24.3 | −391.9 | −220.5 | −1,729.0 | −407.5 | −756.4 | −1,341.3 | −2,617.2 | −2,883.2 | −2,677.7 | −1,968.2 |
| Goods, credit (exports).................. | 1a9cx | 3,145.0 | 3,774.1 | 4,399.8 | 5,099.9 | 7,095.5 | 6,391.8 | 8,030.7 | 9,273.7 | 9,915.8 | 10,256.9 | 10,344.0 | 9,066.5 |
| Goods, debit (imports)................... | 1a9dx | 2,992.2 | 3,753.3 | 4,898.5 | 5,645.4 | 8,809.7 | 6,895.7 | 8,557.7 | 10,704.3 | 12,277.1 | 11,608.9 | 11,251.6 | 9,345.5 |
| Balance on goods...................... | 1a9bx | 152.8 | 20.8 | −498.7 | −545.5 | −1,714.2 | −503.9 | −527.0 | −1,430.5 | −2,361.3 | −1,352.0 | −907.6 | −278.9 |
| Services, credit (exports)............... | 1b9cx | 1,111.6 | 1,311.3 | 1,387.4 | 1,833.5 | 2,276.7 | 2,319.7 | 2,688.2 | 3,641.9 | 3,601.0 | 3,481.5 | 3,346.1 | 3,002.3 |
| Services, debit (imports)............... | 1b9dx | 786.1 | 939.5 | 978.7 | 1,130.0 | 1,523.3 | 1,294.9 | 1,530.9 | 2,050.3 | 2,411.5 | 3,240.0 | 3,202.8 | 2,669.4 |
| Balance on Goods & Services....... | 1z9bx | 478.3 | 392.6 | −89.9 | 158.0 | −960.8 | 520.9 | 630.2 | 161.1 | −1,171.8 | −1,110.6 | −764.2 | 53.9 |
| Primary income: credit.................. | 1c9cx | 372.4 | 563.1 | 741.5 | 885.0 | 757.5 | 531.6 | 454.6 | 504.8 | 356.6 | 269.8 | 250.1 | 275.8 |
| Primary income: debit................... | 1c9dx | 960.4 | 1,057.3 | 1,169.8 | 1,400.9 | 1,674.1 | 1,571.6 | 1,955.7 | 2,136.2 | 1,893.0 | 2,150.7 | 2,271.8 | 2,400.2 |
| Balance on gds, serv. & prim. inc. | 1y9bx | −109.7 | −101.5 | −518.2 | −357.9 | −1,877.4 | −519.3 | −870.9 | −1,470.3 | −2,708.3 | −2,991.5 | −2,786.0 | −2,070.5 |
| Secondary income: credit.............. | 1d9ca | 127.2 | 143.1 | 150.0 | 164.6 | 187.7 | 149.6 | 171.5 | 179.6 | 168.2 | 169.5 | 169.0 | 160.9 |
| Secondary income: debit............... | 1d9da | 14.3 | 17.3 | 23.7 | 27.1 | 39.3 | 37.8 | 57.0 | 50.6 | 77.1 | 61.1 | 60.7 | 58.7 |
| B. Capital Account*....................... | 209ba | 5.3 | 3.8 | 6.5 | 3.7 | .2 | — | — | — | 40.0 | 201.2 | 12.0 | 159.0 |
| Capital account: credit.................. | 209ca | 5.3 | 3.8 | 6.5 | 3.7 | .2 | — | — | — | 40.0 | 201.2 | 12.0 | 159.0 |
| Capital account: debit................... | 209da | — | — | — | — | — | — | — | — | — | — | — | — |
| Balance on current & capital acct. | 129ba | 8.4 | 28.1 | −385.4 | −216.7 | −1,728.8 | −407.5 | −756.4 | −1,341.3 | −2,577.2 | −2,682.0 | −2,665.7 | −1,809.2 |
| C. Financial Account* ................. | 309na | 81.9 | −923.6 | −2,935.6 | −1,506.2 | −3,097.6 | −1,182.8 | −1,056.7 | −4,190.3 | −6,246.2 | −4,519.5 | −4,023.2 | −89.8 |
| Direct investment: assets.............. | 3a9aa | 38.1 | 15.5 | 13.8 | 118.7 | 25.4 | 90.4 | −157.7 | 179.2 | 30.2 | 13.3 | 236.6 | 133.8 |
| Equity & investment fund shares.. | 3aaaa | 24.2 | 39.9 | 1.7 | 88.7 | −.6 | 11.9 | −48.1 | −2.8 | 4.6 | 6.4 | 20.2 | 14.3 |
| Debt instruments........................ | 3abaa | 13.9 | −24.4 | 12.2 | 30.0 | 25.9 | 78.5 | −109.6 | 182.0 | 25.6 | 6.9 | 216.4 | 119.5 |
| Direct investment: liabilities .......... | 3a9la | 352.7 | 826.6 | 1,508.4 | 1,358.7 | 2,142.0 | 1,602.6 | 2,191.1 | 2,690.1 | 2,569.2 | 3,040.2 | 2,385.1 | 1,747.7 |
| Equity & investment fund shares . | 3aala | 280.8 | 363.6 | 794.9 | 881.8 | 1,565.4 | 1,446.5 | 2,280.7 | 2,240.8 | 2,441.3 | 2,725.7 | 2,715.0 | 1,607.9 |
| Debt instruments........................ | 3abla | 71.9 | 463.0 | 713.4 | 476.9 | 576.6 | 156.1 | −89.7 | 449.3 | 127.9 | 314.4 | −329.9 | 139.8 |
| Portfolio investment: assets .......... | 3b9aa | 695.7 | −577.7 | 97.2 | −195.2 | 54.8 | 706.7 | 1,340.6 | −1,156.8 | 392.0 | −148.1 | 145.3 | 1,167.6 |
| Equity & investment fund shares | 3baaa | −.9 | −.3 | .2 | .3 | — | 3.2 | 1.9 | 1.1 | −.4 | −3.2 | −.8 | −.8 |
| Debt securities .......................... | 3bbaa | 696.6 | −577.4 | 96.9 | −195.5 | 54.8 | 703.5 | 1,338.7 | −1,157.9 | 392.4 | −144.9 | 146.1 | 1,168.5 |
| Portfolio investment: liabilities....... | 3b9la | 273.4 | 228.2 | 1,783.5 | 955.3 | −503.0 | −114.6 | 658.0 | 819.0 | 2,035.2 | 2,622.0 | 1,270.8 | 900.1 |
| Equity & investment fund shares . | 3bala | 20.1 | −2.4 | −26.6 | 2.3 | −11.7 | −17.9 | — | — | .1 | — | −.3 | −.3 |
| Debt securities .......................... | 3bbla | 253.3 | 230.6 | 1,810.2 | 953.0 | −491.4 | −96.6 | 658.0 | 819.0 | 2,035.1 | 2,622.0 | 1,271.0 | 900.4 |
| Fin. der.& empl.stk.ops.(ESOs): net. | 3c9na | — | — | — | — | — | — | — | — | — | — | — | — |
| Fin. der. & ESOs.: assets............. | 3c9aa | — | — | — | — | — | — | — | — | — | — | — | — |
| Fin. der. & ESOs.: liabilities......... | 3c9la | — | — | — | — | — | — | — | — | — | — | — | — |
| Other investment: assets............... | 3d9aa | 259.7 | 1,112.7 | −1,414.9 | 2,027.5 | −43.4 | 1,465.1 | −352.3 | −894.3 | 118.1 | 1,132.8 | 93.7 | 1,724.1 |
| Other equity............................... | 3daaa | . . . . | . . . . | . . . . | . . . . | . . . . | . . . . | . . . . | . . . . | . . . . | . . . . | . . . . | . . . . |
| Debt instruments........................ | 3dzaa | 259.7 | 1,112.7 | −1,414.9 | 2,027.5 | −43.4 | 1,465.1 | −352.3 | −894.3 | 118.1 | 1,132.8 | 93.7 | 1,724.1 |
| Other investment: liabilities........... | 3d9la | 285.4 | 419.4 | −1,660.3 | 1,143.1 | 1,495.4 | 1,957.0 | −961.8 | −1,190.7 | 2,182.1 | −144.6 | 843.0 | 467.5 |
| Other equity............................... | 3dala | . . . . | . . . . | . . . . | . . . . | . . . . | . . . . | . . . . | . . . . | . . . . | . . . . | . . . . | . . . . |
| Debt instruments........................ | 3dzla | 285.4 | 419.4 | −1,660.3 | 1,143.1 | 1,495.4 | 1,957.0 | −961.8 | −1,190.7 | 2,182.1 | −144.6 | 843.0 | 467.5 |
| Curr.+ cap.− finan. acct. balance... | 4y9na | −73.5 | 951.8 | 2,550.2 | 1,289.5 | 1,368.8 | 775.3 | 300.3 | 2,849.0 | 3,669.0 | 1,837.5 | 1,357.5 | −1,719.4 |
| D. Net Errors and Omissions............ | 409na | 377.9 | −173.4 | −182.8 | −284.1 | 863.5 | 785.4 | −687.4 | −311.3 | −406.2 | 1,063.6 | −20.0 | −90.2 |
| E. Reserves and Related Items.......... | 4z9na | 304.4 | 778.4 | 2,367.4 | 1,005.4 | 2,232.3 | 1,560.6 | −387.1 | 2,537.6 | 3,262.8 | 2,901.1 | 1,337.5 | −1,809.7 |
| Reserve assets............................. | 3e9aa | 454.2 | 620.9 | −15.8 | 1,005.4 | 2,232.3 | 1,586.9 | −361.5 | 2,564.3 | 3,287.2 | 2,923.0 | 1,360.0 | −1,788.0 |
| Credit and loans from the IMF........ | 3dcla | 149.8 | −175.5 | −2,383.2 | — | — | — | — | — | — | — | — | — |
| Exceptional financing.................... | 409la | | 18.0 | — | — | — | 26.2 | 25.6 | 26.7 | 24.4 | 21.9 | 22.5 | 21.7 |

*Excludes components in group E

| | | 2004 | 2005 | 2006 | 2007 | 2008 | 2009 | 2010 | 2011 | 2012 | 2013 | 2014 | 2015 |
|---|---|---|---|---|---|---|---|---|---|---|---|---|---|
| **International Investment Position** | | | | | | *Millions of US Dollars* | | | | | | | |
| Assets............................... | 809aa | 15,383.1 | 17,137.3 | 17,013.2 | 20,324.1 | 22,601.7 | 26,906.3 | 28,778.1 | 29,141.2 | 33,006.5 | 36,368.7 | 38,302.1 | 38,737.4 |
| Direct investment......................... | 8a9aa | 122.8 | 158.8 | 218.4 | 336.6 | 258.3 | 399.1 | 345.3 | 354.4 | 160.0 | 154.9 | 139.2 | 153.5 |
| Equity & investment fund shares.. | 8aaaa | .... | .... | .... | .... | .... | .... | .... | .... | 144.2 | 141.1 | 130.7 | 139.5 |
| Debt instruments....................... | 8abaa | 122.8 | 158.8 | 218.4 | 336.6 | 258.3 | 399.1 | 345.3 | 354.4 | 15.8 | 13.8 | 8.5 | 14.0 |
| Portfolio investment.................... | 8b9aa | 2,448.6 | 1,858.3 | 2,328.8 | 2,321.8 | 2,374.1 | 2,722.8 | 5,433.9 | 4,043.4 | 4,753.9 | 4,455.9 | 4,793.6 | 5,369.2 |
| Equity & investment fund shares.. | 8baaa | .... | .... | .... | .... | .... | .... | .... | .... | 949.4 | 666.6 | 810.1 | 679.8 |
| Debt securities........................... | 8bbaa | 2,448.6 | 1,858.3 | 2,328.8 | 2,321.8 | 2,374.1 | 2,722.8 | 5,433.9 | 4,043.4 | 3,804.6 | 3,789.3 | 3,983.5 | 4,689.4 |
| Fin. der.(oth.than reserves) & ESOs | 8c9aa | .... | .... | .... | .... | .... | .... | .... | .... | .... | .... | .... | .... |
| Other investment........................... | 8d9aa | 10,299.8 | 12,048.8 | 11,368.7 | 13,544.4 | 13,609.1 | 15,796.5 | 15,343.5 | 14,441.5 | 14,488.1 | 15,468.1 | 15,814.6 | 17,580.9 |
| Other equity........................... | 8daaa | .... | .... | .... | .... | .... | .... | .... | .... | .... | .... | .... | .... |
| Debt instruments....................... | 8dzaa | 10,299.8 | 12,048.8 | 11,368.7 | 13,544.4 | 13,609.1 | 15,796.5 | 15,343.5 | 14,441.5 | 14,488.1 | 15,468.1 | 15,814.6 | 17,580.9 |
| Reserve assets........................... | 8e9aa | 2,511.9 | 3,071.4 | 3,097.3 | 4,121.4 | 6,360.2 | 7,987.9 | 7,655.3 | 10,301.9 | 13,604.5 | 16,289.9 | 17,554.7 | 15,633.9 |
| Liabilities.................................. | 809la | 16,989.0 | 18,509.5 | 17,800.4 | 22,432.4 | 24,647.9 | 30,098.0 | 31,251.3 | 33,943.0 | 40,591.3 | 44,808.0 | 48,228.6 | 49,142.5 |
| Direct investment......................... | 8a9la | 2,110.3 | 2,843.7 | 3,898.7 | 6,355.8 | 7,998.1 | 10,668.3 | 12,478.7 | 15,146.7 | 17,426.5 | 19,584.4 | 21,300.9 | 21,651.0 |
| Equity & investment fund shares.. | 8aala | 2,110.3 | 2,843.7 | 3,898.7 | 6,355.8 | 7,998.1 | 9,875.8 | 11,807.4 | 13,994.9 | 16,170.2 | 18,009.7 | 19,916.9 | 20,294.2 |
| Debt instruments....................... | 8abla | .... | .... | .... | .... | .... | 792.5 | 671.3 | 1,151.8 | 1,256.3 | 1,574.8 | 1,384.0 | 1,356.8 |
| Portfolio investment.................... | 8b9la | 3,830.7 | 4,409.9 | 6,435.8 | 7,857.8 | 7,175.8 | 7,812.4 | 7,996.3 | 9,035.4 | 11,056.2 | 13,279.7 | 13,865.8 | 13,996.0 |
| Equity & investment fund shares.. | 8bala | .... | .... | .... | .... | .... | .... | .... | .... | .... | .... | .... | .... |
| Debt securities........................... | 8bbla | 3,830.7 | 4,409.9 | 6,435.8 | 7,857.8 | 7,175.8 | 7,812.4 | 7,996.3 | 9,035.4 | 11,056.2 | 13,279.7 | 13,865.8 | 13,996.0 |
| Fin. der.(oth.than reserves) & ESOs | 8c9la | .... | .... | .... | .... | .... | .... | .... | .... | .... | .... | .... | .... |
| Other investment........................... | 8d9la | 11,048.0 | 11,256.0 | 7,466.0 | 8,218.9 | 9,474.0 | 11,617.2 | 10,776.4 | 9,760.9 | 12,108.7 | 11,943.8 | 13,061.8 | 13,495.4 |
| Other equity........................... | 8dala | .... | .... | .... | .... | .... | .... | .... | .... | .... | .... | .... | .... |
| Debt instruments....................... | 8dzla | 11,048.0 | 11,256.0 | 7,466.0 | 8,218.9 | 9,474.0 | 11,617.2 | 10,776.4 | 9,760.9 | 12,108.7 | 11,943.8 | 13,061.8 | 13,495.4 |
| **Government Finance** | | | | | | | | | | | | | |
| **Cash Flow Statement** | | | | | | | | | | | | | |
| **Central Government** | | | | | | *Millions of Pesos: Fiscal Year Ends December 31* | | | | | | | |
| Cash Receipts:Operating Activities... | c1 | 100,589 | 111,941 | 128,963 | † 145,650 | 168,650 | 208,841 | 241,696 | 278,123 | 312,077 | 366,411 | 384,908 | .... |
| Taxes................................ | c11 | 70,109 | 76,065 | 89,499 | † 100,661 | 116,046 | 133,775 | 152,617 | 176,951 | 195,975 | 224,371 | 247,032 | .... |
| Social Contributions...................... | c12 | 18,846 | 22,918 | 26,535 | † 30,273 | 37,107 | 61,974 | 71,770 | 84,465 | 100,775 | 118,584 | 113,353 | .... |
| Grants................................ | c13 | — | — | — | † — | — | — | — | — | — | — | 398 | .... |
| Other Receipts......................... | c14 | 11,634 | 12,957 | 12,929 | † 14,715 | 15,498 | 13,092 | 17,309 | 16,707 | 15,327 | 23,456 | 24,126 | .... |
| Cash Payments:Operating Activities. | c2 | 104,466 | 112,873 | 126,622 | † 145,570 | 162,874 | 208,163 | 237,738 | 269,761 | 318,026 | 367,722 | 448,455 | .... |
| Compensation of Employees.......... | c21 | 22,771 | 25,211 | 28,448 | † 33,006 | 38,560 | 51,218 | 54,719 | 63,710 | 73,672 | 84,789 | 98,506 | .... |
| Purchases of Goods & Services....... | c22 | 14,812 | 16,306 | 19,503 | † 22,569 | 24,352 | 25,909 | 29,857 | 31,747 | 36,828 | 43,255 | 48,966 | .... |
| Interest...................................... | c24 | 18,646 | 17,947 | 19,881 | † 20,736 | 18,311 | 19,488 | 19,213 | 22,477 | 24,173 | 27,987 | 30,291 | .... |
| Subsidies.................................... | c25 | 9,542 | 10,396 | 10,095 | † 14,666 | 16,359 | 2,462 | 1,828 | 1,869 | 2,930 | 2,926 | 3,308 | .... |
| Grants........................................ | c26 | — | — | — | † — | — | 4,483 | 51 | 84 | — | — | 12,972 | .... |
| Social Benefits............................. | c27 | 38,694 | 43,014 | 48,694 | † 54,593 | 65,292 | 90,913 | 108,624 | 124,432 | 148,210 | 170,624 | 176,304 | .... |
| Other Payments............................ | c28 | — | — | — | † — | — | 13,690 | 23,446 | 25,442 | 32,214 | 38,141 | 39,054 | .... |
| Net Cash Inflow:Operating Act.[1-2] | ccio | −3,877 | −932 | 2,342 | † 80 | 5,776 | 677 | 3,959 | 8,363 | −5,949 | −1,311 | −63,547 | .... |
| Net Cash Outflow:Invest. in NFA...... | c31 | 5,646 | 5,542 | 6,626 | † 8,518 | 11,576 | 11,214 | 11,214 | 13,590 | 15,073 | 16,571 | 18,439 | .... |
| Purchases of Nonfinancial Assets... | c31.1 | 5,646 | 5,542 | 6,626 | .... | .... | .... | .... | .... | .... | .... | .... | .... |
| Sales of Nonfinancial Assets.......... | c31.2 | | | | | | | | | | | | |
| Cash Surplus/Deficit [1-2-31=1-2M] | ccsd | −9,523 | −6,475 | −4,284 | † −8,438 | −5,800 | −10,536 | −7,255 | −5,227 | −21,023 | −17,882 | −81,987 | .... |
| Net Acq. Fin. Assets, excl. Cash....... | c32x | 4,366 | −1,221 | −2,266 | † −1,629 | 1,836 | 18,834 | −1,830 | 2,284 | 4,803 | .... | .... | .... |
| Domestic...................................... | c321x | 4,276 | −972 | −2,266 | † −1,629 | 1,836 | 18,834 | −1,830 | 2,284 | 4,803 | .... | .... | .... |
| Foreign........................................ | c322x | 91 | −249 | — | † — | — | — | — | — | — | .... | .... | .... |
| Net Incurrence of Liabilities.............. | c33 | 4,854 | 16,638 | −6,535 | † 21,698 | 1,238 | 43,927 | −9,578 | 37,673 | 27,906 | 15,512 | 33,661 | .... |
| Domestic...................................... | c331 | −1,848 | 9,724 | 2,294 | † −2,276 | 9,767 | 26,736 | −6,508 | 39,452 | 6,383 | −16,048 | 1,039 | .... |
| Foreign........................................ | c332 | 6,702 | 6,914 | −8,829 | † 23,974 | −8,529 | 17,192 | −3,070 | −1,779 | 21,523 | 31,560 | 32,622 | .... |
| Net Cash Inflow, Fin.Act.[-32x+33].. | cnfb | 487 | 17,859 | −4,269 | † 23,327 | −598 | 25,093 | −7,748 | 35,389 | 23,103 | 7,753 | 39,569 | .... |
| Net Change in Stock of Cash.......... | cncb | −8,603 | 11,547 | −8,221 | † 14,250 | −7,462 | 13,385 | −16,801 | 29,925 | 2,472 | −11,165 | 9,038 | .... |
| Stat. Discrep. [32X-33+NCB-CSD].... | ccsdz | 432 | 163 | 332 | † −639 | −1,064 | −1,172 | −1,797 | −237 | 391 | −1,035 | 51,456 | .... |
| Memo Item:Cash Expenditure[2+31] | c2m | 110,111 | 118,415 | 133,247 | † 154,087 | 174,450 | 219,377 | 248,951 | 283,350 | 333,100 | 384,293 | 466,894 | .... |
| Memo Item: Gross Debt.................. | c63 | 335,594 | 323,500 | 325,354 | † 321,506 | 364,213 | 352,069 | 357,354 | 420,116 | 451,921 | 503,629 | 590,186 | .... |

| | | 2004 | 2005 | 2006 | 2007 | 2008 | 2009 | 2010 | 2011 | 2012 | 2013 | 2014 | 2015 |
|---|---|---|---|---|---|---|---|---|---|---|---|---|---|
| **Balance Sheet** | | | | | | | | | | | | | |
| Net Worth............................ | c6 | .... | .... | .... | .... | .... | .... | .... | .... | .... | .... | .... | .... |
| Nonfinancial Assets................. | c61 | .... | .... | .... | .... | .... | .... | .... | .... | .... | .... | .... | .... |
| Financial Assets..................... | c62 | 57,590 | 64,124 | 54,249 | † 61,997 | 59,277 | 78,341 | 69,875 | 95,971 | 102,810 | 105,197 | 120,752 | .... |
| By instrument | | | | | | | | | | | | | |
| Monetary Gold & SDRs............ | c6201 | — | — | — | — | — | — | — | — | — | — | — | .... |
| Currency & Deposits.............. | c6202 | 30,720 | 41,492 | 34,175 | † 45,753 | 43,397 | 49,432 | 35,396 | 63,068 | 68,303 | 55,117 | 70,877 | .... |
| Securities other than Shares...... | c6203 | 354 | 46 | 41 | † 2 | 1 | 10,923 | 16,394 | 22,718 | 25,743 | 25,917 | 29,719 | .... |
| Loans............................... | c6204 | 26,326 | 22,396 | 20,034 | † 16,243 | 15,879 | 13,153 | 13,206 | 5,497 | 5,016 | 20,415 | 16,218 | .... |
| Shares and Other Equity.......... | c6205 | 190 | 190 | — | † — | — | 4,833 | 4,878 | 4,688 | 3,748 | 3,748 | 3,938 | .... |
| Insurance Technical Reserves...... | c6206 | — | — | — | † — | — | — | — | — | — | — | — | .... |
| Financial Derivatives.............. | c6207 | — | — | — | † — | — | — | — | — | — | — | — | .... |
| Other Accounts Receivable........ | c6208 | .... | .... | .... | .... | .... | .... | .... | .... | .... | .... | .... | .... |
| By debtor | | | | | | | | | | | | | |
| Domestic............................ | c621 | 57,159 | 64,000 | 54,064 | 61,819 | 59,102 | 78,183 | 69,681 | 95,822 | 102,737 | 105,045 | 120,661 | .... |
| Foreign............................. | c622 | 430 | 124 | 185 | † 178 | 175 | 157 | 194 | 149 | 73 | 153 | 90 | .... |
| Liabilities.......................... | c63 | 335,594 | 323,500 | 325,354 | † 321,506 | 364,213 | 352,069 | 357,354 | 420,116 | 451,921 | 503,629 | 590,186 | .... |
| By instrument | | | | | | | | | | | | | |
| Currency & Deposits.............. | c6302 | — | — | — | † — | — | — | — | — | — | — | — | .... |
| Securities other than Shares...... | c6303 | 181,350 | 185,563 | 241,139 | † 247,105 | 272,567 | 252,012 | 262,679 | 320,696 | 357,588 | 413,732 | 491,875 | .... |
| Loans............................... | c6304 | 154,244 | 137,938 | 84,215 | † 74,401 | 91,647 | 100,057 | 94,675 | 99,420 | 94,333 | 89,897 | 98,311 | .... |
| Shares and Other Equity.......... | c6305 | — | — | — | † — | — | — | — | — | — | — | — | .... |
| Insurance Technical Reserves...... | c6306 | — | — | — | † — | — | — | — | — | — | — | — | .... |
| Financial Derivatives.............. | c6307 | — | — | — | † — | — | — | — | — | — | — | — | .... |
| Other Accounts Payable........... | c6308 | .... | .... | .... | .... | .... | .... | .... | .... | .... | .... | .... | .... |
| By creditor | | | | | | | | | | | | | |
| Domestic............................ | c631 | 107,554 | 111,592 | 115,355 | † 107,558 | 131,963 | 143,233 | 144,505 | 194,900 | 201,729 | 198,729 | 224,357 | .... |
| Foreign............................. | c632 | 228,040 | 211,908 | 209,999 | † 213,948 | 232,250 | 208,837 | 212,849 | 225,216 | 250,193 | 304,900 | 365,830 | .... |
| Net Financial Worth [62-63]...... | c6m2 | −278,005 | −259,377 | −271,105 | † −259,509 | −304,936 | −273,729 | −287,479 | −324,145 | −349,111 | −398,431 | −469,435 | .... |
| Memo Item: Debt at Market Value... | c6m3 | .... | .... | .... | .... | .... | .... | .... | .... | .... | .... | .... | .... |
| Memo Item: Debt at Face Value....... | c6m35 | .... | 323,500 | 325,354 | † 321,506 | 364,213 | 352,069 | 357,354 | 420,116 | .... | .... | .... | .... |
| Memo Item: Debt at Nominal Value. | c6m4 | .... | .... | .... | .... | .... | .... | .... | .... | .... | .... | .... | .... |
| **National Accounts** | | | | | | *Millions of Pesos* | | | | | | | |
| Househ.Cons.Expend.,incl.NPISHs.... | 96f | 270,197 | 295,113 | 332,914 | 384,756 | 441,367 | 476,069 | 541,086 | 618,435 | 697,951 | 789,538 | 892,812 | 972,615 |
| Government Consumption Expend... | 91f | 43,233 | 46,478 | 53,192 | 63,080 | 77,694 | 92,486 | 102,189 | 118,207 | 138,209 | 159,339 | 182,232 | 202,664 |
| Gross Fixed Capital Formation......... | 93e | 56,443 | 70,330 | 85,959 | 102,079 | 130,750 | 133,936 | 154,101 | 177,106 | 230,663 | 257,377 | 285,236 | 291,209 |
| Changes in Inventories.................... | 93i | 12,182 | 4,894 | 5,767 | 5,211 | 16,888 | 6,287 | 2,727 | 16,339 | 7,934 | 7,564 | −3,131 | −1,741 |
| Exports of Goods and Services......... | 90c | 126,153 | 129,223 | 142,806 | 159,843 | 192,137 | 193,630 | 212,872 | 244,763 | 269,878 | 275,177 | 313,237 | 325,706 |
| Imports of Goods and Services (-)..... | 98c | 115,358 | 121,018 | 149,294 | 165,500 | 222,685 | 187,885 | 204,897 | 248,494 | 303,425 | 310,664 | 339,878 | 330,013 |
| Gross Domestic Product (GDP)......... | 99b | 392,850 | 425,018 | 471,344 | 549,470 | 636,151 | 714,523 | 808,079 | 926,356 | 1,001,376 | 1,100,202 | 1,232,690 | 1,302,628 |
| Net Primary Income from Abroad..... | 98.n | −16,961 | −12,236 | −10,512 | −12,160 | −18,997 | −23,429 | −30,139 | −31,482 | −31,172 | −38,268 | −46,892 | −58,000 |
| Gross National Income (GNI)........... | 99a | 375,888 | 412,783 | 460,832 | 537,310 | 617,154 | 691,094 | 777,939 | 894,874 | 1,010,039 | 1,140,063 | 1,283,617 | 1,402,439 |
| GDP Volume 1983 Prices.............. | 99b.p | 281,461 | 300,104 | .... | .... | .... | .... | .... | .... | .... | .... | .... | .... |
| GDP Volume 2005 Prices.............. | 99b.p | 395,513 | 425,018 | 442,438 | 471,380 | 505,207 | 526,646 | 567,742 | 597,050 | 618,174 | 646,842 | 667,792 | 674,352 |
| GDP Volume (2010=100).............. | 99bvp | 69.7 | 74.9 | 77.9 | 83.0 | 89.0 | 92.8 | 100.0 | 105.2 | 108.9 | 113.9 | 117.6 | 118.8 |
| GDP Deflator (2010=100).............. | 99bip | 69.8 | 70.3 | 74.8 | 81.9 | 88.5 | 95.3 | 100.0 | 109.0 | 113.8 | 119.5 | 129.7 | 135.7 |
| | | | | | | *Millions: Midyear Estimates* | | | | | | | |
| Population............................ | 99z | 3.32 | 3.33 | 3.33 | 3.34 | 3.35 | 3.36 | 3.37 | 3.39 | 3.40 | 3.41 | 3.42 | 3.43 |

# Vanuatu 846

| | | 2004 | 2005 | 2006 | 2007 | 2008 | 2009 | 2010 | 2011 | 2012 | 2013 | 2014 | 2015 |
|---|---|---|---|---|---|---|---|---|---|---|---|---|---|
| **Exchange Rates** | | *Vatu per SDR: End of Period* | | | | | | | | | | | |
| Official Rate | aa | 165.44 | 160.55 | 160.19 | 157.80 | 173.43 | 153.52 | 143.45 | 143.64 | 140.98 | 149.84 | 148.82 | 153.15 |
| | | *Vatu per US Dollar: End of Period (ae) Period Average (rf)* | | | | | | | | | | | |
| Official Rate | ae | 106.53 | 112.33 | 106.48 | 99.86 | 112.60 | 97.93 | 93.15 | 93.56 | 91.73 | 97.30 | 102.72 | 110.52 |
| Official Rate | rf | 111.79 | 109.25 | 110.64 | 102.44 | 101.33 | 106.74 | 96.91 | 89.47 | 92.64 | 94.54 | 97.07 | 108.99 |
| **Fund Position** | | *Millions of SDRs: End of Period* | | | | | | | | | | | |
| Quota | 2f.s | 17.00 | 17.00 | 17.00 | 17.00 | 17.00 | 17.00 | 17.00 | 17.00 | 17.00 | 17.00 | 17.00 | 17.00 |
| SDR Holdings | 1b.s | .93 | .99 | 1.08 | 1.19 | 1.30 | 1.58 | 1.55 | 1.49 | 1.53 | 1.52 | 1.50 | 1.42 |
| Reserve Position in the Fund | 1c.s | 2.50 | 2.50 | 2.50 | 2.50 | 2.50 | 2.50 | 2.50 | 2.50 | 2.50 | 2.50 | 2.50 | 2.50 |
| Total Fund Cred.&Loans Outstg. | 2tl | — | — | — | — | — | — | — | — | — | — | — | 17.00 |
| SDR Allocations | 1bd | — | — | — | — | — | 16.27 | 16.27 | 16.27 | 16.27 | 16.27 | 16.27 | 16.27 |
| **International Liquidity** | | *Millions of US Dollars Unless Otherwise Indicated: End of Period* | | | | | | | | | | | |
| Total Reserves minus Gold | 1l.d | 61.81 | 67.20 | 104.66 | 119.62 | 115.23 | 148.61 | 161.38 | 173.79 | 182.23 | 179.20 | 184.00 | 269.17 |
| SDR Holdings | 1b.d | 1.44 | 1.42 | 1.63 | 1.89 | 2.00 | 2.48 | 2.39 | 2.29 | 2.35 | 2.33 | 2.18 | 1.97 |
| Reserve Position in the Fund | 1c.d | 3.88 | 3.57 | 3.75 | 3.94 | 3.84 | 3.91 | 3.84 | 3.83 | 3.84 | 3.84 | 3.62 | 3.46 |
| Foreign Exchange | 1d.d | 56.49 | 62.21 | 99.28 | 113.79 | 109.39 | 142.22 | 155.15 | 167.67 | 176.05 | 173.02 | 178.20 | 263.74 |
| Monetary Authorities | 1dad | 56.49 | 62.21 | 99.28 | 113.79 | 109.39 | 142.22 | 155.15 | 167.67 | 176.05 | 173.02 | 178.20 | 263.74 |
| Government | 1dbd | | | | | | | | | | | | |
| Central Bank: Other Assets | 3..d | — | — | — | — | — | — | — | — | — | — | — | — |
| Central Bank: Other Liabs | 4..d | .06 | .44 | .33 | 1.21 | .33 | 2.88 | .45 | .08 | .10 | .04 | .10 | .05 |
| Other Depository Corps.: Assets | 7a.d | 263.41 | 260.65 | 291.18 | 342.13 | 325.89 | 292.94 | 232.82 | 173.14 | 141.26 | 94.64 | † 95.17 | 112.24 |
| Other Depository Corps.: Liabs | 7b.d | 64.76 | 63.58 | 88.02 | 81.86 | 76.66 | 87.21 | 131.25 | 105.46 | 91.62 | 80.86 | † 120.73 | 119.72 |
| **Central Bank** | | *Millions of Vatu: End of Period* | | | | | | | | | | | |
| Net Foreign Assets | 11n | 6,690 | 7,653 | 11,257 | 11,970 | 13,036 | 11,873 | 12,806 | 14,035 | 14,537 | 14,932 | 16,533 | 24,693 |
| Claims on Nonresidents | 11 | 6,697 | 7,702 | 11,293 | 12,091 | 13,073 | 14,652 | 15,181 | 16,379 | 16,839 | 17,373 | 18,964 | 29,794 |
| Liabilities to Nonresidents | 16c | 6 | 49 | 35 | 121 | 37 | 2,779 | 2,375 | 2,344 | 2,302 | 2,441 | 2,431 | 5,100 |
| Claims on Other Depository Corps. | 12e | 22 | 2 | 3 | 17 | 694 | 52 | 38 | 36 | 28 | 63 | — | 7 |
| Net Claims on Central Government | 12an | 821 | −48 | −471 | −486 | −2,039 | −1,782 | −934 | −866 | −910 | 152 | 61 | −4,690 |
| Claims on Central Government | 12a | 1,505 | 1,254 | 1,290 | 1,338 | 655 | 649 | 1,467 | 1,610 | 1,613 | 1,921 | 2,614 | 2,513 |
| Liabilities to Central Government | 16d | 684 | 1,302 | 1,761 | 1,824 | 2,695 | 2,431 | 2,401 | 2,476 | 2,523 | 1,769 | 2,553 | 7,204 |
| Claims on Other Sectors | 12s | 300 | 269 | 281 | 307 | 189 | 157 | 234 | 245 | 211 | 160 | 171 | 221 |
| Claims on Other Financial Corps | 12g | — | — | — | — | — | — | — | — | — | — | — | — |
| Claims on State & Local Govts | 12b | — | — | — | — | — | — | — | — | — | — | — | — |
| Claims on Public Nonfin. Corps | 12c | 17 | 2 | — | — | — | — | — | — | — | — | — | — |
| Claims on Private Sector | 12d | 283 | 267 | 281 | 307 | 189 | 157 | 234 | 245 | 211 | 160 | 171 | 221 |
| Monetary Base | 14 | 5,292 | 5,934 | 7,919 | 8,806 | 9,277 | 9,421 | 11,157 | 11,881 | 12,992 | 15,328 | 16,851 | 20,287 |
| Currency in Circulation | 14a | 2,964 | 3,375 | 3,898 | 4,688 | 5,004 | 5,282 | 5,873 | 6,572 | 6,962 | 6,936 | 7,491 | 8,531 |
| Liabs. to Other Depository Corps. | 14c | 2,328 | 2,559 | 4,020 | 4,118 | 4,273 | 4,139 | 5,283 | 5,309 | 6,030 | 8,392 | 9,359 | 11,756 |
| Liabilities to Other Sectors | 14d | — | — | — | — | — | — | — | — | — | — | — | — |
| Other Liabs. to Other Dep. Corps | 14n | 1,085 | 611 | 1,840 | 1,647 | 1,318 | 1,002 | 1,218 | 1,673 | 833 | 646 | 265 | 496 |
| Dep. & Sec. Excl. f/Monetary Base | 14o | — | — | — | — | — | — | — | — | — | — | — | — |
| Deposits Included in Broad Money | 15 | — | — | — | — | — | — | — | — | — | — | — | — |
| Sec.Ot.th.Shares Incl.in Brd. Money | 16a | — | — | — | — | — | — | — | — | — | — | — | — |
| Deposits Excl. from Broad Money | 16b | — | — | — | — | — | — | — | — | — | — | — | — |
| Sec.Ot.th.Shares Excl.f/Brd.Money | 16s | — | — | — | — | — | — | — | — | — | — | — | — |
| Loans | 16l | — | — | — | — | — | — | — | — | — | — | — | — |
| Financial Derivatives | 16m | — | — | — | — | — | — | — | — | — | — | — | — |
| Shares and Other Equity | 17a | 902 | 895 | 903 | 1,271 | 1,894 | 891 | 672 | 870 | 901 | 141 | 722 | 516 |
| Other Items (Net) | 17r | 554 | 437 | 408 | 82 | −611 | −1,014 | −902 | −975 | −860 | −808 | −1,073 | −1,068 |
| Memo Item: | | | | | | | | | | | | | |
| Total Assets | 10ra | 8,576 | 9,369 | 13,065 | 14,290 | 15,650 | 17,091 | 18,632 | 19,965 | 20,372 | 20,689 | 23,851 | 34,705 |
| **Other Depository Corporations** | | *Millions of Vatu: End of Period* | | | | | | | | | | | |
| Net Foreign Assets | 21n | 21,162 | 22,138 | 21,632 | 25,991 | 28,063 | 20,146 | 9,461 | 6,332 | 4,554 | 1,340 | † −2,625 | −826 |
| Claims on Nonresidents | 21 | 28,061 | 29,279 | 31,005 | 34,166 | 36,695 | 28,687 | 21,687 | 16,199 | 12,958 | 9,208 | † 9,774 | 12,405 |
| Liabilities to Nonresidents | 26c | 6,899 | 7,141 | 9,373 | 8,174 | 8,632 | 8,541 | 12,226 | 9,867 | 8,404 | 7,868 | † 12,399 | 13,231 |
| Claims on Central Bank | 20 | 3,890 | 3,858 | 6,606 | 6,884 | 6,839 | 6,507 | 7,833 | 8,669 | 8,936 | 10,919 | † 11,583 | 14,499 |
| Currency | 20a | 477 | 688 | 745 | 1,119 | 1,248 | 1,365 | 1,332 | 1,686 | 2,073 | 1,881 | † 1,959 | 2,247 |
| Reserve Deposits and Securities | 20b | 2,328 | 2,559 | 4,020 | 4,118 | 4,273 | 4,139 | 5,283 | 5,309 | 6,030 | 8,392 | † 9,359 | 11,756 |
| Other Claims | 20n | 1,085 | 611 | 1,840 | 1,647 | 1,318 | 1,002 | 1,218 | 1,673 | 833 | 646 | † 265 | 496 |
| Net Claims on Central Government | 22an | 650 | 402 | 287 | 156 | −141 | −532 | 154 | 593 | 136 | −867 | † −1,213 | −1,678 |
| Claims on Central Government | 22a | 836 | 859 | 741 | 509 | 530 | 435 | 786 | 1,187 | 787 | 987 | † 593 | 713 |
| Liabilities to Central Government | 26d | 185 | 457 | 454 | 352 | 672 | 966 | 632 | 594 | 651 | 1,855 | † 1,807 | 2,391 |
| Claims on Other Sectors | 22s | 15,989 | 18,585 | 20,445 | 22,944 | 32,853 | 40,978 | 43,806 | 47,988 | 51,260 | 52,636 | † 58,025 | 58,866 |
| Claims on Other Financial Corps | 22g | — | — | — | — | — | — | — | — | — | — | † 50 | 75 |
| Claims on State & Local Govts | 22b | 6 | 13 | 13 | 17 | 13 | 16 | 16 | 34 | 36 | 85 | † 91 | 74 |
| Claims on Public Nonfin. Corps | 22c | 29 | 27 | 81 | 67 | 72 | 107 | 95 | 410 | 371 | 648 | † 1,307 | 1,185 |
| Claims on Private Sector | 22d | 15,953 | 18,545 | 20,351 | 22,860 | 32,768 | 40,854 | 43,695 | 47,544 | 50,853 | 51,903 | † 56,576 | 57,532 |
| Liabilities to Central Bank | 26g | 22 | 2 | 3 | 17 | 694 | 52 | 38 | 36 | 28 | 63 | † — | 7 |
| Transf.Dep.Included in Broad Money | 24 | 10,243 | 11,349 | 12,611 | 14,927 | 16,256 | 18,532 | 17,592 | 17,528 | 17,745 | 21,422 | † 22,669 | 29,184 |
| Other Dep.Included in Broad Money | 25 | 25,415 | 28,523 | 29,788 | 34,409 | 39,861 | 37,697 | 34,407 | 34,874 | 34,296 | 27,296 | † 30,189 | 29,593 |
| Sec.Ot.th.Shares Incl.in Brd. Money | 26a | — | — | — | — | — | — | — | — | — | — | † — | — |
| Deposits Excl. from Broad Money | 26b | — | — | — | — | — | — | — | — | — | — | † — | — |
| Sec.Ot.th.Shares Excl.f/Brd.Money | 26s | — | — | — | — | — | — | — | — | — | — | † — | — |
| Loans | 26l | — | — | — | — | — | — | — | — | — | — | † — | — |
| Financial Derivatives | 26m | — | — | — | — | — | — | — | — | — | — | † — | — |
| Insurance Technical Reserves | 26r | — | — | — | — | — | — | — | — | — | — | † — | — |
| Shares and Other Equity | 27a | 5,889 | 5,436 | 6,801 | 6,472 | 10,576 | 10,517 | 9,865 | 10,585 | 11,591 | 15,144 | † 9,882 | 9,471 |
| Other Items (Net) | 27r | 123 | −327 | −233 | 152 | 228 | 301 | −647 | 558 | 1,226 | 104 | † 3,028 | 2,607 |
| Memo Item: | | | | | | | | | | | | | |
| Total Assets | 20ra | 50,828 | 54,847 | 61,015 | 66,938 | 80,402 | 81,628 | 78,942 | 78,824 | 79,183 | 81,071 | † 84,617 | 91,785 |

| | | 2004 | 2005 | 2006 | 2007 | 2008 | 2009 | 2010 | 2011 | 2012 | 2013 | 2014 | 2015 |
|---|---|---|---|---|---|---|---|---|---|---|---|---|---|
| **Depository Corporations** | | | | | | | | *Millions of Vatu: End of Period* | | | | | |
| Net Foreign Assets............................ | 31n | 27,853 | 29,790 | 32,889 | 37,961 | 41,099 | 32,019 | 22,267 | 20,367 | 19,091 | 16,272 | † 13,908 | 23,867 |
|   Claims on Nonresidents................. | 31 | 34,757 | 36,981 | 42,297 | 46,257 | 49,768 | 43,340 | 36,868 | 32,578 | 29,797 | 26,581 | † 28,738 | 42,199 |
|   Liabilities to Nonresidents............. | 36c | 6,905 | 7,191 | 9,408 | 8,295 | 8,669 | 11,320 | 14,601 | 12,211 | 10,706 | 10,309 | † 14,830 | 18,331 |
| Domestic Claims............................ | 32 | 17,760 | 19,209 | 20,542 | 22,921 | 30,862 | 38,821 | 43,260 | 47,959 | 50,697 | 52,081 | † 57,043 | 52,719 |
|   Net Claims on Central Government | 32an | 1,471 | 354 | −183 | −330 | −2,180 | −2,314 | −780 | −273 | −774 | −715 | † −1,153 | −6,368 |
|     Claims on Central Government.... | 32a | 2,341 | 2,113 | 2,031 | 1,847 | 1,186 | 1,083 | 2,254 | 2,797 | 2,400 | 2,908 | † 3,207 | 3,227 |
|     Liabilities to Central Government. | 36d | 870 | 1,759 | 2,215 | 2,177 | 3,366 | 3,397 | 3,034 | 3,070 | 3,175 | 3,623 | † 4,360 | 9,595 |
|   Claims on Other Sectors................. | 32s | 16,289 | 18,854 | 20,726 | 23,251 | 33,042 | 41,135 | 44,040 | 48,232 | 51,471 | 52,796 | † 58,196 | 59,087 |
|     Claims on Other Financial Corps.. | 32g | — | — | — | — | — | — | — | — | — | — | † 50 | 75 |
|     Claims on State & Local Govts..... | 32b | 6 | 13 | 13 | 17 | 13 | 16 | 16 | 34 | 36 | 85 | † 91 | 74 |
|     Claims on Public Nonfin. Corps.... | 32c | 46 | 28 | 81 | 67 | 72 | 107 | 95 | 410 | 371 | 648 | † 1,307 | 1,185 |
|     Claims on Private Sector.............. | 32d | 16,236 | 18,813 | 20,631 | 23,167 | 32,958 | 41,011 | 43,929 | 47,788 | 51,064 | 52,063 | † 56,747 | 57,753 |
| Broad Money Liabilities................... | 35l | 38,145 | 42,559 | 45,552 | 52,820 | 59,873 | 60,146 | 56,539 | 57,288 | 56,930 | 53,772 | † 58,391 | 65,061 |
|   Currency Outside Depository Corps | 34a | 2,487 | 2,687 | 3,153 | 3,569 | 3,756 | 3,917 | 4,542 | 4,886 | 4,889 | 5,054 | † 5,532 | 6,284 |
|   Transferable Deposits................... | 34 | 10,243 | 11,349 | 12,611 | 14,842 | 16,256 | 18,532 | 17,591 | 17,528 | 17,745 | 21,422 | † 22,669 | 29,184 |
|   Other Deposits............................. | 35 | 25,415 | 28,523 | 29,788 | 34,409 | 39,861 | 37,697 | 34,407 | 34,874 | 34,296 | 27,296 | † 30,189 | 29,593 |
|   Securities Other than Shares.......... | 36a | — | — | — | — | — | — | — | — | — | — | † — | — |
| Deposits Excl. from Broad Money..... | 36b | — | — | — | — | — | — | — | — | — | — | † — | — |
| Sec.Ot.th.Shares Excl.f/Brd.Money.... | 36s | — | — | — | — | — | — | — | — | — | — | † — | — |
| Loans............................................. | 36l | — | — | — | — | — | — | — | — | — | — | † — | — |
| Financial Derivatives...................... | 36m | — | — | — | — | — | — | — | — | — | — | † — | — |
| Insurance Technical Reserves........... | 36r | — | — | — | — | — | — | — | — | — | — | † — | — |
| Shares and Other Equity.................. | 37a | 6,791 | 6,331 | 7,705 | 7,743 | 12,471 | 11,408 | 10,537 | 11,455 | 12,492 | 15,284 | † 10,604 | 9,987 |
| Other Items (Net)........................... | 37r | 677 | 110 | 175 | 319 | −382 | −714 | −1,549 | −417 | 366 | −704 | † 1,955 | 1,538 |
| Broad Money Liabs., Seasonally Adj. | 35l.b | 38,109 | 42,440 | 45,252 | 52,223 | 59,025 | 59,354 | 56,082 | 57,248 | 57,302 | 54,418 | † 58,728 | 65,446 |
| **Monetary Aggregates** | | | | | | | | *Millions of Vatu: End of Period* | | | | | |
|   Broad Money................................ | 59m | 38,145 | 42,559 | 45,552 | 52,820 | 59,873 | 60,146 | 56,539 | 57,288 | 56,930 | 53,772 | 58,391 | 65,061 |
|     o/w:Currency Issued by Cent.Govt | 59m.a | — | — | — | — | — | — | — | — | — | — | — | — |
|     o/w: Dep.in Nonfin. Corporations. | 59m.b | — | — | — | — | — | — | — | — | — | — | — | — |
|     o/w:Secs. Issued by Central Govt.. | 59m.c | — | — | — | — | — | — | — | — | — | — | — | — |
|   Money (National Definitions) | | | | | | | | | | | | | |
|     Reserve Money.......................... | 19mb | 5,292 | 5,934 | 7,919 | 8,806 | 9,277 | 9,421 | 11,157 | 11,881 | 12,992 | 15,328 | 16,851 | 20,287 |
|     M1............................................ | 59ma | 12,730 | 14,036 | 15,764 | 18,496 | 20,012 | 22,448 | 22,133 | 22,413 | 22,634 | 26,476 | 28,202 | 35,468 |
|     M2............................................ | 59mb | 38,145 | 42,559 | 45,552 | 52,905 | 59,873 | 60,146 | 56,540 | 57,288 | 56,930 | 53,772 | 58,391 | 65,061 |
| **Interest Rates** | | | | | | | | *Percent Per Annum* | | | | | |
| Discount Rate (End of Period).......... | 60.a | 6.50 | 6.25 | 6.00 | 6.00 | 6.00 | 6.00 | 6.00 | 6.00 | 6.00 | 5.50 | 5.25 | 1.85 |
| Money Market Rate....................... | 60b | 5.50 | 5.50 | 5.50 | 5.50 | 5.78 | 5.61 | 5.50 | 5.50 | 5.50 | 5.08 | 4.96 | 2.20 |
| Deposit Rate.................................. | 60l | 1.71 | 2.00 | 1.94 | 1.31 | 1.25 | 1.25 | 1.58 | 1.50 | 1.31 | 1.25 | 1.10 | 1.42 |
| Lending Rate.................................. | 60p | 7.61 | 7.47 | 8.25 | 8.16 | 5.29 | 5.50 | 5.50 | 5.50 | 6.05 | 5.00 | 4.69 | 3.63 |
| Government Bond Yield.................. | 61 | 8.50 | 8.50 | 8.50 | 8.58 | 8.50 | 8.45 | 8.24 | 7.91 | 7.64 | 7.82 | 7.81 | 7.80 |
| **Prices** | | | | | | | | *Index Numbers (2010=100): Period Averages* | | | | | |
| Consumer Prices............................ | 64 | 82.9 | 83.9 | 85.6 | 89.0 | 93.3 | 97.3 | 100.0 | 100.9 | 102.2 | 103.7 | 104.5 | 107.1 |
| **Intl. Transactions & Positions** | | | | | | | | *Millions of Vatu* | | | | | |
| Exports.......................................... | 70 | 4,167 | 4,124 | 5,397 | 5,106 | 5,721 | 6,070 | 4,695 | 6,012 | 5,072 | .... | .... | .... |
| Imports, c.i.f.................................. | 71 | 14,306 | 16,295 | 24,039 | 23,503 | 31,667 | 31,086 | 27,510 | 27,256 | 27,453 | .... | .... | .... |

|  |  | 2004 | 2005 | 2006 | 2007 | 2008 | 2009 | 2010 | 2011 | 2012 | 2013 | 2014 | 2015 |
|---|---|---|---|---|---|---|---|---|---|---|---|---|---|
| **Balance of Payments** |  |  |  |  |  | | *Millions of US Dollars* | | | | | | |
| A. Current Account* | 109bx | −41.6 | −52.7 | −50.3 | −53.8 | −176.0 | −12.0 | † −63.7 | −72.1 | −72.0 | −5.2 | 19.5 | .... |
| Goods, credit (exports) | 1a9cx | 38.1 | 38.1 | 37.7 | 33.5 | 41.9 | 55.2 | † 48.8 | 67.3 | 54.7 | 38.5 | 63.4 | .... |
| Goods, debit (imports) | 1a9dx | 113.0 | 131.1 | 147.6 | 176.5 | 317.8 | 187.2 | † 243.8 | 260.0 | 253.2 | 267.5 | 269.3 | .... |
| Balance on goods | 1a9bx | −74.9 | −93.0 | −109.9 | −142.9 | −275.9 | −131.9 | † −195.0 | −192.7 | −198.5 | −228.9 | −206.0 | .... |
| Services, credit (exports) | 1b9cx | 122.3 | 138.8 | 145.8 | 185.9 | 233.6 | 248.3 | † 276.7 | 283.2 | 301.8 | 352.4 | 333.7 | .... |
| Services, debit (imports) | 1b9dx | 65.6 | 73.8 | 71.2 | 75.7 | 134.6 | 108.7 | † 124.6 | 145.0 | 145.9 | 149.1 | 144.9 | .... |
| Balance on Goods & Services | 1z9bx | −18.2 | −27.9 | −35.3 | −32.7 | −176.9 | 7.6 | † −43.0 | −54.5 | −42.7 | −25.6 | −17.2 | .... |
| Primary income: credit | 1c9cx | 27.1 | 27.6 | 31.8 | 36.3 | 38.2 | 27.4 | † 37.5 | 42.5 | 37.2 | 33.6 | 36.4 | .... |
| Primary income: debit | 1c9dx | 45.9 | 53.7 | 51.9 | 61.0 | 40.5 | 49.6 | † 59.0 | 61.5 | 80.3 | 33.9 | 31.5 | .... |
| Balance on gds, serv. & prim. inc. | 1y9bx | −36.9 | −54.0 | −55.4 | −57.4 | −179.1 | −14.6 | † −64.5 | −73.5 | −85.8 | −25.9 | −12.2 | .... |
| Secondary income: credit | 1d9ca | 5.3 | 7.4 | 10.1 | 6.7 | 5.4 | 4.6 | † 4.1 | 3.5 | 16.6 | 25.2 | 37.3 | .... |
| Secondary income: debit | 1d9da | 10.0 | 6.1 | 5.0 | 3.0 | 2.3 | 2.0 | † 3.3 | 2.1 | 2.8 | 4.5 | 5.7 | .... |
| B. Capital Account* | 209bx | 12.8 | 20.1 | 33.7 | 30.0 | 17.0 | 30.4 | † 20.7 | 24.0 | 22.6 | 21.0 | 31.7 | .... |
| Capital account: credit | 209ca | 12.8 | 20.1 | 33.7 | 30.0 | 17.0 | 30.4 | † 20.7 | 24.0 | 22.6 | 21.0 | 31.7 | .... |
| Capital account: debit | 209da | — | — | — | — | — | — | — | .... | .... | .... | .... | .... |
| Balance on current & capital acct. | 129ba | −28.8 | −32.6 | −16.6 | −23.8 | −159.0 | 18.3 | † −43.0 | −48.0 | −49.5 | 15.9 | 51.2 | .... |
| C. Financial Account* | 309na | −48.4 | −37.9 | −33.4 | −15.0 | −5.3 | −42.6 | † −155.5 | −112.8 | −68.7 | −130.9 | −2.9 | .... |
| Direct investment: assets | 3a9aa | .8 | .8 | .7 | .6 | .5 | .1 | † 1.0 | .8 | .4 | .4 | .5 | .... |
| Equity & investment fund shares | 3aaaa | .7 | .7 | .7 | .6 | .6 | .2 | † 1.0 | .8 | .4 | .4 | .5 | .... |
| Debt instruments | 3abaa | .1 | .1 | .1 | — | −.1 | −.1 | .... | .... | .... | .... | .... | .... |
| Direct investment: liabilities | 3a9la | 19.8 | 13.3 | 43.4 | 34.2 | 37.7 | 32.1 | † 63.1 | 61.1 | 60.4 | 59.4 | 13.3 | .... |
| Equity & investment fund shares | 3aala | 17.9 | 13.5 | 43.2 | 31.9 | 29.6 | 23.8 | † 50.6 | 54.5 | 43.1 | 24.5 | 22.2 | .... |
| Debt instruments | 3abla | 2.0 | −.3 | .3 | 2.2 | 8.1 | 8.3 | † 12.5 | 6.6 | 17.2 | 34.9 | −8.9 | .... |
| Portfolio investment: assets | 3b9aa | −.2 | 1.1 | .3 | −1.7 | −3.5 | .9 | † 1.6 | −6.7 | .2 | 17.5 | −10.2 | .... |
| Equity & investment fund shares | 3baaa | .... | .... | .... | .... | .... | .... | .... | .... | .... | .... | .... | .... |
| Debt securities | 3bbaa | −.2 | 1.1 | .3 | −1.7 | −3.5 | .9 | † 1.6 | −6.7 | .2 | 17.5 | −10.2 | .... |
| Portfolio investment: liabilities | 3b9la | — | — | — | — | — | — | .... | .... | .... | .... | .... | .... |
| Equity & investment fund shares | 3bala | .... | .... | .... | .... | .... | — | .... | .... | .... | .... | .... | .... |
| Debt securities | 3bbla | — | — | — | — | — | — | .... | .... | .... | .... | .... | .... |
| Fin. der.& empl.stk.ops.(ESOs): net. | 3c9na | .... | .... | .... | .... | .... | .... | .... | .... | .... | .... | .... | .... |
| Fin. der. & ESOs.: assets | 3c9aa | .... | .... | .... | .... | .... | .... | .... | .... | .... | .... | .... | .... |
| Fin. der. & ESOs.: liabilities | 3c9la | .... | .... | .... | .... | .... | .... | .... | .... | .... | .... | .... | .... |
| Other investment: assets | 3d9aa | 14.8 | −26.6 | 27.5 | −51.3 | 48.9 | −133.1 | † −121.0 | −77.4 | −55.6 | −46.1 | 92.6 | .... |
| Other equity | 3daaa | .... | .... | .... | .... | .... | .... | .... | .... | .... | .... | .... | .... |
| Debt instruments | 3dzaa | 14.8 | −26.6 | 27.5 | −51.3 | 48.9 | −133.1 | † −121.0 | −77.4 | −55.6 | −46.1 | 92.6 | .... |
| Other investment: liabilities | 3d9la | 43.8 | −.1 | 18.4 | −71.5 | 13.4 | −121.7 | † −26.1 | −31.7 | −46.7 | 43.3 | 72.5 | .... |
| Other equity | 3dala | .... | .... | .... | .... | .... | .... | .... | .... | .... | .... | .... | .... |
| Debt instruments | 3dzla | 43.8 | −.1 | 18.4 | −71.5 | 13.4 | −121.7 | † −26.1 | −31.7 | −46.7 | 43.3 | 72.5 | .... |
| Curr.+ cap.− finan. acct. balance | 4y9na | 19.5 | 5.3 | 16.8 | −8.8 | −153.7 | 60.9 | † 112.5 | 64.8 | 19.2 | 146.7 | 54.1 | .... |
| D. Net Errors and Omissions | 409na | −24.5 | −16.6 | −3.9 | −4.3 | 101.2 | −60.8 | † −128.0 | −63.2 | −17.2 | −136.7 | −41.8 | .... |
| E. Reserves and Related Items | 4z9na | −5.0 | −11.3 | 12.9 | −13.2 | −52.5 | .1 | † −15.5 | 1.5 | 2.0 | 10.0 | 12.3 | .... |
| Reserve assets | 3e9aa | 14.9 | 9.0 | 32.6 | 9.0 | 8.3 | 22.4 | † 6.0 | 12.6 | 5.4 | 10.0 | 12.3 | .... |
| Credit and loans from the IMF | 3dcla | — | — | — | — | — | — | † — | .... | .... | .... | — | .... |
| Exceptional financing | 409la | 19.9 | 20.3 | 19.7 | 22.2 | 60.8 | 22.3 | † 21.5 | 11.1 | 3.4 | .... | .... | .... |

*Excludes components in group E

| **International Investment Position** |  |  |  |  |  | | *Millions of US Dollars* | | | | | | |
|---|---|---|---|---|---|---|---|---|---|---|---|---|---|
| Assets | 809aa | 555.0 | 510.4 | 594.8 | 579.0 | 578.8 | 530.7 | † 579.4 | 495.4 | 438.9 | 395.8 | 444.0 | .... |
| Direct investment | 8a9aa | 13.3 | 13.5 | 15.2 | 17.4 | 16.5 | 20.3 | † 22.5 | 23.3 | 24.3 | 23.4 | 22.7 | .... |
| Equity & investment fund shares | 8aaaa | 13.3 | 13.5 | 15.2 | 17.4 | 16.5 | 20.3 | † 22.5 | 23.3 | 24.3 | 23.4 | 22.7 | .... |
| Debt instruments | 8abaa | — | — | — | — | — | — | .... | .... | .... | .... | .... | .... |
| Portfolio investment | 8b9aa | 13.5 | 14.0 | 14.9 | 17.2 | 19.7 | 22.0 | † 15.6 | 12.0 | 12.8 | 15.5 | 4.9 | .... |
| Equity & investment fund shares | 8baaa | .... | .... | .... | .... | .... | .... | .... | .... | .... | .... | .... | .... |
| Debt securities | 8bbaa | 13.5 | 14.0 | 14.9 | 17.2 | 19.7 | 22.0 | † 15.6 | 12.0 | 12.8 | 15.5 | 4.9 | .... |
| Fin. der.(oth.than reserves) & ESOs. | 8c9aa | .... | .... | .... | .... | .... | .... | .... | .... | .... | .... | .... | .... |
| Other investment | 8d9aa | 466.4 | 415.8 | 460.0 | 424.8 | 427.3 | 339.8 | † 379.9 | 286.3 | 219.5 | 177.7 | 232.4 | .... |
| Other equity | 8daaa | .... | .... | .... | .... | .... | .... | .... | .... | .... | .... | .... | .... |
| Debt instruments | 8dzaa | 466.4 | 415.8 | 460.0 | 424.8 | 427.3 | 339.8 | † 379.9 | 286.3 | 219.5 | 177.7 | 232.4 | .... |
| Reserve assets | 8e9aa | 61.8 | 67.2 | 104.7 | 119.6 | 115.2 | 148.6 | † 161.4 | 173.8 | 182.2 | 179.2 | 184.0 | .... |
| Liabilities | 809la | 626.6 | 590.5 | 678.6 | 678.6 | 658.2 | 648.8 | † 829.7 | 875.9 | 897.6 | 889.0 | 893.3 | .... |
| Direct investment | 8a9la | 168.1 | 181.0 | 256.9 | 316.7 | 331.6 | 412.9 | † 454.0 | 519.4 | 608.1 | 554.5 | 508.1 | .... |
| Equity & investment fund shares | 8aala | 147.7 | 160.3 | 232.7 | 289.1 | 307.3 | 382.3 | † 424.0 | 483.7 | 534.0 | 450.2 | 419.8 | .... |
| Debt instruments | 8abla | 20.4 | 20.8 | 24.2 | 27.5 | 24.4 | 30.7 | † 30.0 | 35.8 | 74.1 | 104.3 | 88.3 | .... |
| Portfolio investment | 8b9la | .... | .... | .... | .... | .... | .... | .... | .... | .... | .... | .... | .... |
| Equity & investment fund shares | 8bala | .... | .... | .... | .... | .... | .... | .... | .... | .... | .... | .... | .... |
| Debt securities | 8bbla | .... | .... | .... | .... | .... | .... | .... | .... | .... | .... | .... | .... |
| Fin. der.(oth.than reserves) & ESOs. | 8c9la | .... | .... | .... | .... | .... | .... | .... | .... | .... | .... | .... | .... |
| Other investment | 8d9la | 458.5 | 409.4 | 421.7 | 361.9 | 326.6 | 235.9 | † 375.6 | 356.5 | 289.5 | 334.5 | 385.2 | .... |
| Other equity | 8dala | .... | .... | .... | .... | .... | .... | .... | .... | .... | .... | .... | .... |
| Debt instruments | 8dzla | 458.5 | 409.4 | 421.7 | 361.9 | 326.6 | 235.9 | † 375.6 | 356.5 | 289.5 | 334.5 | 385.2 | .... |

# Vanuatu 846

| | | 2004 | 2005 | 2006 | 2007 | 2008 | 2009 | 2010 | 2011 | 2012 | 2013 | 2014 | 2015 |
|---|---|---|---|---|---|---|---|---|---|---|---|---|---|
| **National Accounts** | | | | | | | *Millions of Vatu* | | | | | | |
| Househ.Cons.Expend.,incl.NPISHs.... | 96f | 28,184 | 28,974 | 30,638 | 32,144 | 34,940 | 38,200 | 42,086 | 43,654 | 45,294 | 47,360 | . . . . | . . . . |
| Government Consumption Expend... | 91f | 5,627 | 5,715 | 6,843 | 8,724 | 9,282 | 10,396 | 11,876 | 11,651 | 11,202 | 11,284 | . . . . | . . . . |
| Gross Fixed Capital Formation......... | 93e | 9,206 | 10,103 | 13,378 | 16,864 | 24,157 | 25,256 | 22,962 | 18,973 | 16,173 | 19,133 | . . . . | . . . . |
| Changes in Inventories.................... | 93i | 276 | 304 | 417 | 536 | 830 | 722 | 576 | 515 | 515 | 515 | . . . . | . . . . |
| Exports of Goods and Services......... | 90c | 18,606 | 19,582 | 20,063 | 21,999 | 27,823 | 31,980 | 31,665 | 31,425 | 35,547 | 36,252 | . . . . | . . . . |
| Imports of Goods and Services (-)..... | 98c | 21,669 | 23,641 | 23,464 | 25,700 | 35,497 | 36,647 | 35,816 | 35,412 | 36,815 | 38,884 | . . . . | . . . . |
| Gross Domestic Product (GDP)......... | 99b | 40,803 | 43,148 | 48,613 | 53,926 | 61,607 | 65,119 | 67,912 | 70,873 | 72,415 | 75,803 | . . . . | . . . . |
| Net Primary Income from Abroad..... | 98.n | −2,086 | −2,835 | −2,241 | −2,834 | −481 | −2,483 | −1,352 | −2,321 | −2,527 | −1,997 | . . . . | . . . . |
| Gross National Income (GNI)............ | 99a | 38,717 | 40,313 | 46,372 | 51,092 | 61,126 | 62,636 | 66,560 | 68,552 | 69,888 | 73,806 | . . . . | . . . . |
| GDP Volume 2006 Prices................. | 99b.p | 42,561 | 44,819 | 48,611 | 51,126 | 54,425 | 56,227 | 57,143 | 57,842 | 58,858 | 60,017 | . . . . | . . . . |
| GDP Volume (2010=100)............... | 99bvp | 74.5 | 78.4 | 85.1 | 89.5 | 95.2 | 98.4 | 100.0 | 101.2 | 103.0 | 105.0 | . . . . | . . . . |
| GDP Deflator (2010=100)............... | 99bip | 80.7 | 81.0 | 84.1 | 88.8 | 95.2 | 97.4 | 100.0 | 103.1 | 103.5 | 106.3 | . . . . | . . . . |
| | | | | | | | *Millions: Midyear Estimates* | | | | | | |
| Population................................. | 99z | .20 | .21 | .21 | .22 | .23 | .23 | .24 | .24 | .25 | .25 | .26 | .26 |

# Venezuela, República Bolivariana de   299

| | | 2004 | 2005 | 2006 | 2007 | 2008 | 2009 | 2010 | 2011 | 2012 | 2013 | 2014 | 2015 |
|---|---|---|---|---|---|---|---|---|---|---|---|---|---|
| **Exchange Rates** | | *Bolivares per SDR: End of Period* | | | | | | | | | | | |
| Official Rate.................................... | aa | 2.979 | 3.069 | 3.230 | 3.393 | 3.307 | 3.366 | 3.994 | 6.585 | 6.592 | 9.678 | 9.105 | 8.708 |
| | | *Bolivares per US Dollar: End of Period (ae) Period Average (rf)* | | | | | | | | | | | |
| Official Rate.................................... | ae | 1.918 | 2.147 | 2.147 | 2.147 | 2.147 | 2.147 | 2.594 | 4.289 | 4.289 | 6.284 | 6.284 | 6.284 |
| Official Rate.................................... | rf | 1.891 | 2.090 | 2.147 | 2.147 | 2.147 | 2.147 | 2.582 | 4.289 | 4.289 | 6.048 | 6.284 | 6.284 |
| | | *Index Numbers (2010=100): Period Averages* | | | | | | | | | | | |
| Market Rate.................................... | ahx | 136.9 | 123.8 | 120.2 | 120.2 | 120.2 | 120.2 | 100.0 | 60.2 | 60.2 | 43.2 | 41.1 | 41.1 |
| Nominal Effective Exchange Rate..... | nec | 151.2 | 132.2 | 126.8 | 121.3 | 117.9 | 123.6 | 100.0 | 58.6 | 60.3 | 43.9 | 42.9 | 48.5 |
| CPI-Based Real Effect. Ex. Rate........ | rec | 53.1 | 52.2 | 55.2 | 60.6 | 74.1 | 98.1 | 100.0 | 71.8 | 86.8 | 84.8 | 128.3 | 302.2 |
| **Fund Position** | | *Millions of SDRs: End of Period* | | | | | | | | | | | |
| Quota............................................. | 2f.s | 2,659.10 | 2,659.10 | 2,659.10 | 2,659.10 | 2,659.10 | 2,659.10 | 2,659.10 | 2,659.10 | 2,659.10 | 2,659.10 | 2,659.10 | 2,659.10 |
| SDR Holdings.................................. | 1b.s | 5.48 | 3.32 | .01 | .90 | 13.84 | 2,239.80 | 2,239.59 | 2,239.28 | 2,239.16 | 2,258.64 | 2,258.57 | 579.63 |
| Reserve Position in the Fund............ | 1c.s | 321.90 | 321.90 | 321.90 | 321.90 | 321.90 | 321.90 | 321.90 | 321.90 | 321.90 | 321.90 | 321.90 | 321.90 |
| Total Fund Cred.&Loans Outstg........ | 2tl | — | — | — | — | — | — | — | — | — | — | — | — |
| SDR Allocations............................... | 1bd | 316.89 | 316.89 | 316.89 | 316.89 | 316.89 | 2,543.26 | 2,543.26 | 2,543.26 | 2,543.26 | 2,543.26 | 2,543.26 | 2,543.26 |
| **International Liquidity** | | *Millions of US Dollars Unless Otherwise Indicated: End of Period* | | | | | | | | | | | |
| Total Reserves minus Gold.............. | 1l.d | 18,375 | 23,919 | 29,417 | 24,196 | 33,098 | 21,703 | 13,137 | 9,930 | 9,900 | 6,038 | 7,457 | 6,324 |
| SDR Holdings................................. | 1b.d | 9 | 5 | — | 1 | 21 | 3,511 | 3,449 | 3,438 | 3,441 | 3,478 | 3,272 | 803 |
| Reserve Position in the Fund.......... | 1c.d | 500 | 460 | 484 | 509 | 496 | 505 | 496 | 494 | 495 | 496 | 466 | 446 |
| Foreign Exchange.......................... | 1d.d | 17,867 | 23,454 | 28,933 | 23,686 | 32,581 | 17,687 | 9,192 | 5,998 | 5,964 | 2,064 | 3,718 | 5,075 |
| Gold (Million Fine Troy Ounces)....... | 1ad | 11.49 | 11.47 | 11.48 | 11.47 | 11.46 | 11.60 | 11.76 | 11.76 | 11.76 | 11.82 | 11.61 | 8.77 |
| Gold (National Valuation)............... | 1and | 5,122 | 5,718 | 7,255 | 9,281 | 9,201 | 13,297 | 16,363 | 19,959 | 19,987 | 15,440 | 14,621 | 10,042 |
| Central Bank: Other Assets............. | 3..d | 3,671 | 3,294 | 2,364 | 2,545 | 3,362 | 3,983 | 4,402 | 4,809 | 4,960 | 4,783 | .... | .... |
| Central Bank: Other Liabs............... | 4..d | 236 | 152 | 147 | 364 | 480 | 237 | 289 | 792 | 1,390 | 1,249 | .... | .... |
| Other Depository Corps.: Assets....... | 7a.d | 1,637 | 1,382 | 3,108 | 3,564 | 2,792 | 2,119 | 3,249 | 2,120 | 2,288 | 2,510 | 2,463 | 1,412 |
| Other Depository Corps.: Liabs........ | 7b.d | 53 | 72 | 316 | 723 | 425 | 498 | 350 | 212 | 413 | 717 | 926 | 801 |
| **Central Bank** | | *Millions of Bolivares: End of Period* | | | | | | | | | | | |
| Net Foreign Assets......................... | 11n | 50,828 | 69,655 | 82,133 | 87,335 | 95,340 | 75,435 | 76,616 | 147,107 | 130,705 | 139,295 | .... | .... |
| Claims on Nonresidents................ | 11 | 52,224 | 70,953 | 83,472 | 89,192 | 97,418 | 84,505 | 87,522 | 167,252 | 153,432 | 171,840 | .... | .... |
| Liabilities to Nonresidents............. | 16c | 1,395 | 1,298 | 1,339 | 1,856 | 2,078 | 9,069 | 10,906 | 20,145 | 22,727 | 32,545 | .... | .... |
| Claims on Other Depository Corps.... | 12e | 1 | 1 | 5 | 6 | 6 | 100 | 2,296 | 2,433 | 2,419 | 2,412 | .... | .... |
| Net Claims on Central Government.. | 12an | −7,371 | 6,452 | 5,030 | 3,131 | 23,562 | 55,013 | 55,206 | 2,328 | 28,188 | −6,410 | .... | .... |
| Claims on Central Government...... | 12a | 997 | 14,891 | 12,957 | 30,555 | 34,528 | 60,008 | 77,385 | 63,978 | 85,868 | 128,913 | .... | .... |
| Liabilities to Central Government... | 16d | 8,368 | 8,439 | 7,926 | 27,424 | 10,966 | 4,996 | 22,179 | 61,650 | 57,681 | 135,323 | .... | .... |
| Claims on Other Sectors.................. | 12s | 162 | 171 | 232 | 307 | 332 | 896 | 26,982 | 106,447 | 190,364 | 448,739 | .... | .... |
| Claims on Other Financial Corps... | 12g | 1 | 1 | 4 | 4 | 4 | 8 | 1,615 | 1,632 | 39 | 55 | .... | .... |
| Claims on State & Local Govts....... | 12b | — | — | — | — | — | — | — | — | — | — | .... | .... |
| Claims on Public Nonfin. Corps...... | 12c | — | — | — | — | — | 443 | 24,783 | 103,453 | 188,226 | 445,539 | .... | .... |
| Claims on Private Sector............... | 12d | 160 | 171 | 228 | 303 | 327 | 446 | 584 | 1,362 | 2,099 | 3,144 | .... | .... |
| Monetary Base............................... | 14 | 17,092 | 23,344 | 44,318 | 65,609 | 83,886 | 104,408 | 128,448 | 192,749 | 275,578 | 461,148 | .... | .... |
| Currency in Circulation.................. | 14a | 7,953 | 10,777 | 15,490 | 20,569 | 28,318 | 36,412 | 46,470 | 58,676 | 92,904 | 147,253 | .... | .... |
| Liabs. to Other Depository Corps.... | 14c | 7,468 | 11,176 | 28,275 | 43,671 | 54,865 | 61,048 | 76,088 | 118,476 | 174,377 | 296,886 | .... | .... |
| Liabilities to Other Sectors............. | 14d | 1,671 | 1,392 | 553 | 1,369 | 703 | 6,948 | 5,890 | 15,597 | 8,297 | 17,008 | .... | .... |
| Other Liabs. to Other Dep. Corps..... | 14n | 7,187 | 30,398 | 34,827 | 12,665 | 23,047 | 7,564 | 8,934 | 9,204 | 21,495 | 51,198 | .... | .... |
| Dep. & Sec. Excl. f/Monetary Base..... | 14o | 501 | 422 | 265 | 200 | 133 | 1,825 | 14,530 | 9,168 | 21,895 | 21,859 | .... | .... |
| Deposits Included in Broad Money. | 15 | — | — | — | — | — | — | — | — | — | — | .... | .... |
| Sec.Ot.th.Shares Incl.in Brd. Money | 16a | — | — | — | — | — | — | — | — | — | — | .... | .... |
| Deposits Excl. from Broad Money... | 16b | 501 | 422 | 265 | 200 | 133 | 1,825 | 14,530 | 9,168 | 21,895 | 21,859 | .... | .... |
| Sec.Ot.th.Shares Excl.f/Brd.Money.. | 16s | — | — | — | — | — | — | — | — | — | — | .... | .... |
| Loans............................................. | 16l | — | — | — | — | — | — | — | — | — | — | .... | .... |
| Financial Derivatives....................... | 16m | — | — | — | — | — | — | — | — | — | — | .... | .... |
| Shares and Other Equity................. | 17a | 12,069 | 14,721 | 8,171 | 13,189 | 13,685 | 18,892 | 9,325 | 35,847 | 27,080 | 43,382 | .... | .... |
| Other Items (Net)............................ | 17r | 6,772 | 7,395 | −180 | −882 | −1,511 | −1,245 | −137 | 11,348 | 5,628 | 6,450 | .... | .... |
| Memo Item: | | | | | | | | | | | | | |
| Total Assets.................................... | 10ra | 54,252 | 86,821 | 105,128 | 129,747 | 142,188 | 155,943 | 207,017 | 358,987 | 450,530 | 777,135 | .... | .... |

# Venezuela, República Bolivariana de   299

| | | 2004 | 2005 | 2006 | 2007 | 2008 | 2009 | 2010 | 2011 | 2012 | 2013 | 2014 | 2015 |
|---|---|---|---|---|---|---|---|---|---|---|---|---|---|
| **Other Depository Corporations** | | | | | | *Millions of Bolivares: End of Period* | | | | | | | |
| Net Foreign Assets | 21n | 3,035 | 2,810 | 5,988 | 6,102 | 5,084 | 3,482 | 7,516 | 8,183 | 8,042 | 11,297 | 9,687 | 3,833 |
| Claims on Nonresidents | 21 | 3,135 | 2,965 | 6,666 | 7,653 | 5,996 | 4,551 | 8,425 | 9,093 | 9,812 | 15,816 | 15,519 | 8,867 |
| Liabilities to Nonresidents | 26c | 101 | 155 | 678 | 1,552 | 912 | 1,069 | 909 | 910 | 1,770 | 4,519 | 5,832 | 5,033 |
| Claims on Central Bank | 20 | 16,045 | 23,728 | 62,986 | 58,460 | 81,522 | 75,860 | 92,816 | 129,533 | 207,206 | 369,004 | 657,266 | 1,281,746 |
| Currency | 20a | 1,482 | 1,902 | 2,696 | 3,634 | 6,658 | 8,011 | 10,131 | 12,482 | 21,202 | 30,247 | 33,577 | 71,515 |
| Reserve Deposits and Securities | 20b | 7,803 | 11,092 | 28,078 | 43,204 | 54,041 | 60,172 | 75,224 | 110,267 | 167,307 | 290,231 | 523,338 | 1,044,111 |
| Other Claims | 20n | 6,761 | 10,734 | 32,212 | 11,622 | 20,823 | 7,677 | 7,461 | 6,784 | 18,698 | 48,526 | 100,351 | 166,120 |
| Net Claims on Central Government | 22an | 5,549 | 3,286 | 12,237 | 4,581 | −3,698 | 13,382 | 23,040 | 57,788 | 113,062 | 184,014 | 156,526 | 99,147 |
| Claims on Central Government | 22a | 9,970 | 10,297 | 24,613 | 21,775 | 16,650 | 35,001 | 50,799 | 94,081 | 163,143 | 270,319 | 338,761 | 388,094 |
| Liabilities to Central Government | 26d | 4,422 | 7,011 | 12,376 | 17,194 | 20,348 | 21,619 | 27,759 | 36,293 | 50,081 | 86,304 | 182,236 | 288,947 |
| Claims on Other Sectors | 22s | 24,032 | 41,039 | 68,653 | 118,739 | 148,062 | 174,219 | 198,491 | 290,308 | 459,001 | 764,459 | 1,334,163 | 2,778,215 |
| Claims on Other Financial Corps | 22g | 623 | 1,025 | 1,767 | 2,901 | 2,499 | 6,580 | 3,703 | 12,121 | 16,774 | 24,100 | 29,314 | 33,369 |
| Claims on State & Local Govts | 22b | — | — | — | — | — | — | 2,397 | — | — | — | — | — |
| Claims on Public Nonfin. Corps | 22c | — | — | — | 5 | 414 | 1,074 | 1,257 | 1,614 | 30,497 | 72,082 | 107,065 | 204,033 |
| Claims on Private Sector | 22d | 23,409 | 40,014 | 66,886 | 115,833 | 145,150 | 166,565 | 191,134 | 276,573 | 411,731 | 668,277 | 1,197,784 | 2,540,813 |
| Liabilities to Central Bank | 26g | 54 | 124 | 12 | 641 | 89 | 547 | 367 | 2,418 | 2,411 | 2,400 | 2,387 | 1,965 |
| Transf.Dep.Included in Broad Money | 24 | 40,260 | 60,737 | 94,555 | 117,306 | 148,598 | 188,899 | 261,289 | 407,086 | 651,124 | 1,033,243 | 1,846,222 | 3,640,898 |
| Other Dep.Included in Broad Money | 25 | 221 | 201 | 12,704 | 19,323 | 23,741 | 26,853 | 15,399 | 15,817 | 13,702 | 19,796 | 47,771 | 90,907 |
| Sec.Ot.th.Shares Incl.in Brd. Money | 26a | 240 | 836 | 3,837 | 11,688 | 19,907 | 13,580 | 8,086 | 3,210 | 3,080 | 942 | 410 | 96 |
| Deposits Excl. from Broad Money | 26b | 1,020 | 1,775 | 3,673 | 6,023 | 7,876 | 12,292 | 14,542 | 22,016 | 57,716 | 59,637 | 88,097 | 108,751 |
| Sec.Ot.th.Shares Excl.f/Brd.Money | 26s | 17 | 12 | 55 | 569 | 49 | 114 | 135 | 99 | 136 | 5 | 1 | 6 |
| Loans | 26l | 478 | 505 | 24,239 | 17,587 | 7,519 | 6,770 | 2,884 | 4,839 | 8,189 | 9,798 | 3,508 | 7,093 |
| Financial Derivatives | 26m | 1 | 18 | 15 | 63 | 44 | 23 | — | — | — | — | — | — |
| Insurance Technical Reserves | 26r | — | — | — | — | — | — | — | — | — | — | — | — |
| Shares and Other Equity | 27a | 7,173 | 9,451 | 12,765 | 17,984 | 24,119 | 24,525 | 33,968 | 49,305 | 73,582 | 120,576 | 180,351 | 336,224 |
| Other Items (Net) | 27r | −803 | −2,797 | −1,993 | −3,303 | −972 | −6,659 | −14,808 | −18,977 | −22,629 | 82,379 | −11,105 | −22,998 |
| Memo Item: | | | | | | | | | | | | | |
| Total Assets | 20ra | 58,849 | 88,067 | 183,422 | 230,144 | 285,827 | 338,522 | 411,810 | 599,116 | 921,762 | 1,539,237 | 2,496,803 | 4,770,747 |
| **Depository Corporations** | | | | | | *Millions of Bolivares: End of Period* | | | | | | | |
| Net Foreign Assets | 31n | 53,863 | 72,465 | 88,121 | 93,437 | 100,424 | 78,917 | 84,132 | 155,290 | 138,747 | 150,592 | .... | .... |
| Claims on Nonresidents | 31 | 55,359 | 73,917 | 90,138 | 96,845 | 103,415 | 89,055 | 95,947 | 176,345 | 163,245 | 187,656 | .... | .... |
| Liabilities to Nonresidents | 36c | 1,496 | 1,452 | 2,017 | 3,408 | 2,991 | 10,138 | 11,815 | 21,055 | 24,497 | 37,064 | .... | .... |
| Domestic Claims | 32 | 22,372 | 50,948 | 86,152 | 126,758 | 168,258 | 243,510 | 303,719 | 456,872 | 790,616 | 1,390,802 | .... | .... |
| Net Claims on Central Government | 32an | −1,822 | 9,738 | 17,267 | 7,712 | 19,864 | 68,395 | 78,246 | 60,116 | 141,250 | 177,605 | .... | .... |
| Claims on Central Government | 32a | 10,967 | 25,188 | 37,570 | 52,331 | 51,178 | 95,009 | 128,183 | 158,059 | 249,011 | 399,232 | .... | .... |
| Liabilities to Central Government | 36d | 12,789 | 15,450 | 20,303 | 44,618 | 31,313 | 26,615 | 49,938 | 97,943 | 107,762 | 221,627 | .... | .... |
| Claims on Other Sectors | 32s | 24,194 | 41,210 | 68,885 | 119,046 | 148,394 | 175,115 | 225,473 | 396,756 | 649,366 | 1,213,198 | .... | .... |
| Claims on Other Financial Corps | 32g | 625 | 1,025 | 1,771 | 2,905 | 2,503 | 6,588 | 5,318 | 13,753 | 16,812 | 24,155 | .... | .... |
| Claims on State & Local Govts | 32b | — | — | — | — | — | — | 2,397 | — | — | — | .... | .... |
| Claims on Public Nonfin. Corps | 32c | — | — | — | 5 | 414 | 1,517 | 26,041 | 105,068 | 218,723 | 517,622 | .... | .... |
| Claims on Private Sector | 32d | 23,569 | 40,185 | 67,114 | 116,136 | 145,477 | 167,010 | 191,717 | 277,935 | 413,830 | 671,421 | .... | .... |
| Broad Money Liabilities | 35l | 48,862 | 72,042 | 124,443 | 166,621 | 214,609 | 264,680 | 327,003 | 487,903 | 747,905 | 1,187,995 | .... | .... |
| Currency Outside Depository Corps | 34a | 6,471 | 8,875 | 12,794 | 16,934 | 21,660 | 28,401 | 36,339 | 46,193 | 71,702 | 117,006 | .... | .... |
| Transferable Deposits | 34 | 41,930 | 62,129 | 95,108 | 118,675 | 149,301 | 195,846 | 267,179 | 422,683 | 659,422 | 1,050,251 | .... | .... |
| Other Deposits | 35 | 221 | 201 | 12,704 | 19,323 | 23,741 | 26,853 | 15,399 | 15,817 | 13,702 | 19,796 | .... | .... |
| Securities Other than Shares | 36a | 240 | 836 | 3,837 | 11,688 | 19,907 | 13,580 | 8,086 | 3,210 | 3,080 | 942 | .... | .... |
| Deposits Excl. from Broad Money | 36b | 1,521 | 2,197 | 3,939 | 6,223 | 8,009 | 14,117 | 29,071 | 31,183 | 79,611 | 81,496 | .... | .... |
| Sec.Ot.th.Shares Excl.f/Brd.Money | 36s | 17 | 12 | 55 | 569 | 49 | 114 | 135 | 99 | 136 | 5 | .... | .... |
| Loans | 36l | 478 | 505 | 24,239 | 17,587 | 7,519 | 6,770 | 2,884 | 4,839 | 8,189 | 9,798 | .... | .... |
| Financial Derivatives | 36m | 1 | 18 | 15 | 63 | 44 | 23 | — | — | — | — | | |
| Insurance Technical Reserves | 36r | — | — | — | — | — | — | — | — | — | — | | |
| Shares and Other Equity | 37a | 19,241 | 24,171 | 20,937 | 31,173 | 37,804 | 43,417 | 43,294 | 85,151 | 100,662 | 163,957 | .... | .... |
| Other Items (Net) | 37r | 6,115 | 24,469 | 646 | −2,041 | 648 | −6,694 | −14,535 | 2,986 | −7,141 | 98,144 | .... | .... |
| Broad Money Liabs., Seasonally Adj. | 35l.b | 46,891 | 68,836 | 118,524 | 158,529 | 204,407 | 252,540 | 312,323 | 465,899 | 713,178 | 1,218,138 | | |
| **Monetary Aggregates** | | | | | | *Millions of Bolivares: End of Period* | | | | | | | |
| Broad Money | 59m | 48,862 | 72,042 | 124,443 | 166,621 | 214,609 | 264,680 | 327,003 | 487,903 | 747,905 | 1,187,995 | | |
| o/w:Currency Issued by Cent.Govt | 59m.a | — | — | — | — | — | — | — | — | — | — | .... | .... |
| o/w: Dep.in Nonfin. Corporations | 59m.b | — | — | — | — | — | — | — | — | — | — | .... | .... |
| o/w:Secs. Issued by Central Govt | 59m.c | — | — | — | — | — | — | — | — | — | — | .... | .... |
| Money (National Definitions) | | | | | | | | | | | | | |
| Base Money | 19ma | 16,524 | 23,087 | 44,818 | 64,179 | 83,593 | 97,563 | 123,051 | 172,751 | 268,356 | 444,894 | 757,994 | 1,600,945 |
| M1 | 59ma | 27,748 | 42,913 | † 104,940 | 130,338 | 166,398 | 202,352 | 272,162 | 426,590 | 697,769 | 1,199,722 | 1,952,748 | 3,932,145 |
| M2 | 59mb | 46,368 | 70,796 | † 144,663 | 176,953 | 217,903 | 249,098 | 296,596 | 446,617 | 714,898 | 1,220,137 | 2,001,241 | 4,015,682 |
| M3 | 59mc | 46,380 | 70,804 | † 144,670 | 176,968 | 217,906 | 249,099 | 296,597 | 446,618 | 714,899 | 1,220,137 | 2,001,241 | 4,015,683 |
| **Interest Rates** | | | | | | *Percent Per Annum* | | | | | | | |
| Discount Rate (End of Period) | 60.a | 28.50 | 28.50 | 28.50 | 28.50 | 33.50 | 29.50 | 29.50 | 29.50 | 29.50 | 29.50 | 29.50 | 29.50 |
| Injection Rate (End of Period) | 60..j | 26.50 | 22.83 | 18.25 | 18.50 | 22.67 | 22.71 | 21.00 | 21.00 | 21.00 | 21.00 | 21.00 | 21.00 |
| Absorption Rate (End of Period) | 60.t | .... | 11.50 | 10.13 | 10.08 | 12.50 | 7.33 | 6.00 | 6.00 | 6.00 | 6.00 | 6.00 | 6.00 |
| Money Market Rate | 60b | 4.38 | 2.62 | 5.26 | 8.72 | 11.09 | 10.03 | 5.36 | 4.93 | .82 | 1.61 | 6.37 | 3.37 |
| Savings Rate | 60k | 4.47 | 6.38 | 6.84 | 7.42 | 13.84 | 13.48 | 12.58 | 12.57 | 12.51 | 12.57 | 13.95 | 13.10 |
| Deposit Rate | 60l | 12.60 | 11.63 | 10.26 | 10.71 | 16.15 | 16.41 | 14.80 | 14.59 | 14.51 | 14.50 | 14.68 | 14.89 |
| Lending Rate | 60p | 18.50 | 16.81 | 15.48 | 17.11 | 22.37 | 19.89 | 18.35 | 17.15 | 16.38 | 15.90 | 17.21 | 19.40 |
| Government Bond Yield | 61 | 15.57 | 12.93 | 7.81 | 9.55 | 14.47 | 12.84 | 15.53 | 17.52 | 16.76 | 15.26 | 16.12 | 15.39 |

| | | 2004 | 2005 | 2006 | 2007 | 2008 | 2009 | 2010 | 2011 | 2012 | 2013 | 2014 | 2015 |
|---|---|---|---|---|---|---|---|---|---|---|---|---|---|
| **Prices, Production, Labor** | | | | | *Index Numbers (2010=100): Period Averages* | | | | | | | | |
| Share Prices (End of Month)............ | 62.ep | 43.7 | 36.9 | 54.9 | 66.2 | 58.0 | 73.3 | 100.0 | 140.7 | 439.1 | 2,201.1 | 4,261.3 | 16,286.7 |
| Industrial Share Prices (End Month).. | 62aep | 48.6 | 41.9 | 60.1 | 59.9 | 66.8 | 89.7 | 100.0 | 137.1 | 403.7 | 891.2 | 1,425.6 | 7,176.2 |
| Prices: Home & Import Goods......... | 63 | 30.8 | 36.4 | 41.2 | 49.1 | 61.1 | 78.9 | 100.0 | 122.1 | 141.4 | 194.4 | 305.7 | 751.6 |
| Prices: Home Goods........................ | 63a | 28.9 | 34.6 | 39.8 | 48.1 | 60.5 | 78.7 | 100.0 | 123.4 | 144.2 | 197.9 | 320.1 | 785.8 |
| Consumer Prices(National).............. | 64 | .... | .... | .... | .... | 61.4 | 78.0 | 100.0 | 126.1 | 152.7 | 214.7 | 348.2 | 772.0 |
| Consumer Prices (Caracas).............. | 64a | † 29.3 | 34.0 | 38.6 | 45.8 | 60.3 | 77.5 | 100.0 | 127.1 | 154.0 | 213.3 | 335.6 | 710.7 |
| | | | | | | *Number in Thousands: Period Averages* | | | | | | | |
| Labor Force.................................... | 67d | 12,067 | 11,972 | 12,187 | 12,366 | 12,587 | 12,933 | 13,111 | 13,248 | 13,490 | 13,833 | 14,176 | 14,172 |
| Employment.................................... | 67e | 10,249 | 10,506 | 10,973 | 11,316 | 11,661 | 11,914 | 11,996 | 12,116 | 12,435 | 12,791 | 13,190 | 13,206 |
| Unemployment................................ | 67c | 1,819 | 1,466 | 1,214 | 1,050 | 926 | 1,019 | 1,115 | 1,132 | 1,055 | 1,042 | 986 | 966 |
| Unemployment Rate (%)................. | 67r | 15.1 | 12.2 | 10.0 | 8.5 | 7.4 | 7.9 | 8.5 | 8.5 | 7.8 | 7.5 | 7.0 | 6.8 |
| **Intl. Transactions & Positions** | | | | | | *Billions of Bolivares:* | | | | | | | |
| Exports.......................................... | 70 | † 75.0 | 116.4 | 140.8 | 148.2 | 204.3 | 123.7 | 169.9 | .... | 418.5 | 542.1 | 481.2 | 318.0 |
| Petroleum................................... | 70a | .... | .... | 104.1 | 110.7 | 187.5 | .... | .... | .... | 402.3 | 539.3 | 451.9 | 221.4 |
| Crude Petroleum....................... | 70aa | .... | .... | 75.1 | 81.9 | 150.3 | .... | .... | .... | 329.1 | 442.2 | 369.7 | 180.4 |
| Imports, c.i.f................................. | 71 | 31.6 | 51.0 | 72.4 | 99.1 | 106.6 | 87.9 | 100.5 | 296.2 | 187.0 | 691.5 | 981.9 | 4,268.4 |
| Imports, f.o.b................................ | 71.v | 28.8 | 46.3 | 65.8 | 90.1 | 96.9 | 79.9 | 91.3 | 269.2 | 170.0 | 628.6 | 892.6 | 3,880.3 |
| | | | | | | *Millions of US Dollars* | | | | | | | |
| Exports.......................................... | 70..d | 33,994 | 51,859 | 59,208 | 69,165 | 95,021 | 57,603 | 65,745 | 92,811 | 97,877 | 88,753 | 74,714 | 37,236 |
| Petroleum.................................... | 70a.d | 26,829 | 38,971 | 47,817 | 51,615 | 87,443 | .... | .... | .... | 93,569 | 85,603 | 71,731 | 35,136 |
| Imports, f.o.b................................ | 71.vd | 15,163 | 21,843 | 30,560 | 41,906 | 45,093 | 36,906 | 30,741 | 34,860 | 39,546 | 42,148 | 40,435 | 36,496 |
| Volume of Exports | | | | | | *2000=100* | | | | | | | |
| Import Prices(Wholesale)................. | 76.x | 38.2 | 43.1 | 46.6 | 53.1 | 63.1 | 80.0 | 100.0 | 120.2 | 130.5 | 181.2 | 250.4 | 619.9 |
| **Balance of Payments** | | | | | | *Millions of US Dollars* | | | | | | | |
| A. Current Account*...................... | 109bx | 15,519.0 | † 25,447.0 | 26,462.0 | 13,464.0 | 31,297.0 | 429.0 | 5,585.0 | 16,342.0 | 2,586.0 | 4,604.0 | 3,598.0 | −20,360.0 |
| Goods, credit (exports)................. | 1a9cx | 39,664.0 | † 55,712.0 | 65,574.0 | 70,193.0 | 96,053.0 | 58,514.0 | 66,883.0 | 93,743.0 | 97,873.0 | 88,749.0 | 74,710.0 | 37,232.0 |
| Goods, debit (imports)................. | 1a9dx | 17,013.0 | † 24,002.0 | 33,547.0 | 47,368.0 | 51,169.0 | 41,584.0 | 41,702.0 | 52,543.0 | 65,917.0 | 57,151.0 | 47,476.0 | 36,464.0 |
| Balance on goods...................... | 1a9bx | 22,651.0 | † 31,710.0 | 32,027.0 | 22,825.0 | 44,884.0 | 16,930.0 | 25,181.0 | 41,200.0 | 31,956.0 | 31,598.0 | 27,234.0 | 768.0 |
| Services, credit (exports)............... | 1b9cx | 1,118.0 | † 1,346.0 | 1,548.0 | 1,869.0 | 2,187.0 | 2,144.0 | 1,848.0 | 1,912.0 | 2,160.0 | 2,216.0 | 1,873.0 | 1,593.0 |
| Services, debit (imports)................ | 1b9dx | 4,505.0 | † 5,345.0 | 5,990.0 | 11,006.0 | 13,274.0 | 13,348.0 | 14,336.0 | 16,890.0 | 19,428.0 | 19,285.0 | 16,916.0 | 14,300.0 |
| Balance on Goods & Services...... | 1z9bx | 19,264.0 | † 27,711.0 | 27,585.0 | 13,688.0 | 33,797.0 | 5,726.0 | 12,693.0 | 26,222.0 | 14,688.0 | 14,529.0 | 12,191.0 | −11,939.0 |
| Primary income: credit.................. | 1c9cx | 2,050.0 | † 4,150.0 | 8,226.0 | 10,140.0 | 7,539.0 | 2,297.0 | 1,750.0 | 2,023.0 | 1,777.0 | 2,223.0 | 1,815.0 | 850.0 |
| Primary income: debit................... | 1c9dx | 5,723.0 | † 6,352.0 | 9,271.0 | 9,625.0 | 9,106.0 | 6,943.0 | 7,958.0 | 11,102.0 | 12,876.0 | 10,930.0 | 10,190.0 | 9,060.0 |
| Balance on gds, serv. & prim. inc. | 1y9bx | 15,591.0 | † 25,509.0 | 26,540.0 | 14,203.0 | 32,230.0 | 1,080.0 | 6,485.0 | 17,143.0 | 3,589.0 | 5,822.0 | 3,816.0 | −20,149.0 |
| Secondary income: credit.............. | 1d9ca | 227.0 | † 258.0 | 309.0 | 617.0 | 799.0 | 1,147.0 | 638.0 | 524.0 | 716.0 | 758.0 | 454.0 | 594.0 |
| Secondary income: debit............... | 1d9da | 299.0 | † 320.0 | 387.0 | 1,356.0 | 1,732.0 | 1,798.0 | 1,538.0 | 1,325.0 | 1,719.0 | 1,976.0 | 672.0 | 805.0 |
| B. Capital Account*...................... | 209ba | — | † — | — | — | — | — | −211.0 | — | — | — | — | −3,980.0 |
| Capital account: credit.................. | 209ca | — | † — | — | — | — | — | — | — | — | — | — | — |
| Capital account: debit.................. | 209da | — | † — | — | — | — | — | 211.0 | — | — | — | — | 3,980.0 |
| Balance on current & capital acct. | 129ba | 15,519.0 | † 25,447.0 | 26,462.0 | 13,464.0 | 31,297.0 | 429.0 | 5,374.0 | 16,342.0 | 2,586.0 | 4,604.0 | 3,598.0 | −24,340.0 |
| C. Financial Account*..................... | 309na | 10,861.0 | † 16,430.0 | 19,347.0 | 18,031.0 | 19,933.0 | 8,429.9 | 9,583.0 | 18,873.0 | 1,310.0 | 5,596.0 | 641.0 | −22,523.0 |
| Direct investment: assets............. | 3a9aa | 625.0 | † 1,028.0 | 2,230.0 | 575.0 | 767.0 | 2,476.0 | 2,501.0 | −255.0 | 3,307.0 | 217.0 | 1,094.0 | 1,054.0 |
| Equity & investment fund shares.. | 3aaaa | 246.0 | † 309.0 | 765.0 | 1.0 | 294.0 | 326.0 | 1,348.0 | −1,723.0 | 1,952.0 | 964.0 | 227.0 | 72.0 |
| Debt instruments...................... | 3abaa | 379.0 | † 719.0 | 1,465.0 | 574.0 | 473.0 | 2,150.0 | 1,153.0 | 1,468.0 | 1,355.0 | −747.0 | 867.0 | 982.0 |
| Direct investment: liabilities ......... | 3a9la | 1,489.0 | † 2,450.0 | 198.0 | 4,358.0 | 2,083.0 | −1,137.0 | 1,583.0 | 5,855.0 | 4,986.0 | 2,145.0 | 390.0 | 3,764.0 |
| Equity & investment fund shares . | 3aala | 2,327.0 | † 2,588.0 | 1,815.0 | 2,515.0 | 2,638.0 | −1,350.0 | 117.0 | 2,988.0 | 2,681.0 | 896.0 | 1,287.0 | 165.0 |
| Debt instruments...................... | 3abla | −838.0 | † −138.0 | −1,617.0 | 1,843.0 | −555.0 | 213.0 | 1,466.0 | 2,867.0 | 2,305.0 | 1,249.0 | −897.0 | 3,599.0 |
| Portfolio investment: assets......... | 3b9aa | 813.0 | † 2,311.0 | 5,966.0 | −458.0 | −4,199.0 | −4,098.0 | −888.0 | 60.0 | 1,275.0 | −1,363.0 | −2,615.0 | −502.0 |
| Equity & investment fund shares | 3baaa | −27.0 | † 227.0 | 25.0 | −37.0 | −287.0 | 48.0 | −52.0 | −22.0 | — | −9.0 | −2.0 | −6.0 |
| Debt securities ......................... | 3bbaa | 840.0 | † 2,084.0 | 5,941.0 | −421.0 | −3,912.0 | −4,146.0 | −836.0 | 82.0 | 1,275.0 | −1,354.0 | −2,613.0 | −496.0 |
| Portfolio investment: liabilities...... | 3b9la | −1,271.0 | † 3,224.0 | −3,982.0 | 4,093.0 | 610.0 | 5,372.0 | 3,143.0 | 2,243.0 | 4,051.0 | −1,955.0 | 402.0 | −3,455.0 |
| Equity & investment fund shares . | 3bala | −170.0 | † 28.0 | 41.0 | 50.0 | 1.0 | 118.0 | 10.0 | 6.0 | −34.0 | −571.0 | 49.0 | 5.0 |
| Debt securities......................... | 3bbla | −1,101.0 | † 3,196.0 | −4,023.0 | 4,043.0 | 609.0 | 5,254.0 | 3,133.0 | 2,237.0 | 4,085.0 | −1,384.0 | 353.0 | −3,460.0 |
| Fin. der.& empl.stk.ops.(ESOs): net. | 3c9na | — | † −22.0 | 1.0 | 5.0 | — | — | — | — | — | — | — | 315.0 |
| Fin. der. & ESOs: assets.............. | 3c9aa | — | † — | — | — | — | — | — | — | — | — | — | 315.0 |
| Fin. der. & ESOs: liabilities.......... | 3c9la | — | † 22.0 | −1.0 | −5.0 | — | — | — | — | — | — | — | .... |
| Other investment: assets................ | 3d9aa | 8,233.0 | † 18,181.0 | 6,341.0 | 30,996.0 | 27,475.0 | 22,353.0 | 23,977.0 | 36,769.0 | 9,867.0 | 8,851.0 | 4,721.0 | −17,780.0 |
| Other equity.............................. | 3daaa | .... | † — | — | — | — | — | — | — | — | — | — | .... |
| Debt instruments...................... | 3dzaa | 8,233.0 | † 18,181.0 | 6,341.0 | 30,996.0 | 27,475.0 | 22,353.0 | 23,977.0 | 36,769.0 | 9,867.0 | 8,851.0 | 4,721.0 | −17,780.0 |
| Other investment: liabilities............ | 3d9la | −1,408.0 | † −606.0 | −1,025.0 | 4,636.0 | 1,417.0 | 8,066.1 | 11,281.0 | 9,603.0 | 4,102.0 | 1,919.0 | 1,767.0 | 5,301.0 |
| Other equity.............................. | 3dala | .... | † — | — | — | — | — | — | — | — | — | — | .... |
| Debt instruments....................... | 3dzla | −1,408.0 | † −606.0 | −1,025.0 | 4,636.0 | 1,417.0 | 8,066.1 | 11,281.0 | 9,603.0 | 4,102.0 | 1,919.0 | 1,767.0 | 5,301.0 |
| Curr.+ cap.− finan. acct. balance... | 4y9na | 4,658.0 | † 9,017.0 | 7,115.0 | −4,567.0 | 11,364.0 | −8,000.9 | −4,209.0 | −2,531.0 | 1,276.0 | −992.0 | 2,957.0 | −1,817.0 |
| D. Net Errors and Omissions............ | 409na | −2,503.2 | † −3,592.2 | −2,211.9 | −789.7 | −1,911.7 | −2,805.6 | −3,730.3 | −1,481.5 | −2,122.2 | −3,418.0 | −3,566.1 | −2,653.1 |
| E. Reserves and Related Items.......... | 4z9na | 2,154.8 | † 5,424.8 | 4,903.1 | −5,356.7 | 9,452.3 | −10,806.5 | −7,939.3 | −4,012.5 | −846.2 | −4,410.0 | −609.1 | −4,470.1 |
| Reserve assets............................... | 3e9aa | 2,154.8 | † 5,424.8 | 4,903.1 | −5,356.7 | 9,452.3 | −10,806.5 | −7,939.3 | −4,012.5 | −846.2 | −4,410.0 | −609.1 | −4,470.1 |
| Credit and loans from the IMF....... | 3dcla | — | † — | — | — | — | — | — | — | — | — | — | — |
| Exceptional financing.................... | 409la | — | .... | .... | .... | .... | .... | .... | .... | .... | .... | .... | .... |

*Excludes components in group E

# Venezuela, República Bolivariana de   299

| | | 2004 | 2005 | 2006 | 2007 | 2008 | 2009 | 2010 | 2011 | 2012 | 2013 | 2014 | 2015 |
|---|---|---|---|---|---|---|---|---|---|---|---|---|---|
| **International Investment Position** | | | | | | *Millions of US Dollars* | | | | | | | |
| Assets................................ | 809aa | 100,258.4 | † 123,281.8 | 146,833.3 | 177,741.1 | 210,250.1 | 225,085.0 | 235,941.8 | 276,108.1 | 288,584.1 | 284,617.0 | 285,351.6 | 258,588.3 |
| Direct investment.......................... | 8a9aa | 10,287.0 | † 10,402.0 | 15,074.0 | 17,538.0 | 17,702.0 | 22,616.0 | 22,511.0 | 25,810.0 | 28,811.0 | 28,277.0 | 28,940.0 | 30,035.0 |
| Equity & investment fund shares.. | 8aaaa | 8,260.0 | † 8,569.0 | 11,349.0 | 12,806.0 | 13,063.0 | 16,539.0 | 17,886.0 | 19,719.0 | 21,511.0 | 21,932.0 | 22,147.0 | 22,216.0 |
| Debt instruments...................... | 8abaa | 2,027.0 | † 1,833.0 | 3,725.0 | 4,732.0 | 4,639.0 | 6,077.0 | 4,625.0 | 6,091.0 | 7,300.0 | 6,345.0 | 6,793.0 | 7,819.0 |
| Portfolio investment................... | 8b9aa | 6,740.0 | † 9,070.0 | 17,650.0 | 17,553.0 | 13,890.0 | 9,408.0 | 8,608.0 | 8,891.0 | 10,189.0 | 8,825.0 | 5,827.0 | 5,270.0 |
| Equity & investment fund shares.. | 8baaa | 519.0 | † 745.0 | 735.0 | 705.0 | 63.0 | 137.0 | 70.0 | 59.0 | 63.0 | 79.0 | 98.0 | 37.0 |
| Debt securities............................ | 8bbaa | 6,221.0 | † 8,325.0 | 16,915.0 | 16,848.0 | 13,827.0 | 9,271.0 | 8,538.0 | 8,832.0 | 10,126.0 | 8,746.0 | 5,729.0 | 5,233.0 |
| Fin. der.(oth.than reserves) & ESOs | 8c9aa | .... | † — | — | — | — | — | — | — | — | — | — | .... |
| Other investment........................ | 8d9aa | 59,024.0 | † 73,442.0 | 76,669.0 | 108,364.0 | 135,531.0 | 157,231.0 | 174,491.0 | 211,515.0 | 219,694.0 | 226,034.0 | 228,503.0 | 206,914.0 |
| Other equity........................... | 8daaa | .... | .... | .... | .... | .... | .... | .... | .... | .... | .... | .... | .... |
| Debt instruments...................... | 8dzaa | 59,024.0 | † 73,442.0 | 76,669.0 | 108,364.0 | 135,531.0 | 157,231.0 | 174,491.0 | 211,515.0 | 219,694.0 | 226,034.0 | 228,503.0 | 206,914.0 |
| Reserve assets........................... | 8e9aa | 24,207.4 | † 30,367.8 | 37,440.3 | 34,286.1 | 43,127.1 | 35,830.0 | 30,331.8 | 29,892.1 | 29,890.1 | 21,481.0 | 22,081.6 | 16,369.3 |
| Liabilities................................ | 809la | 83,834.1 | † 87,554.9 | 88,575.7 | 93,552.8 | 76,485.1 | 94,469.0 | 111,592.7 | 131,138.6 | 150,260.8 | 135,550.6 | 120,981.7 | 124,138.3 |
| Direct investment.......................... | 8a9la | 43,471.0 | † 45,491.0 | 48,350.0 | 48,910.0 | 38,575.0 | 38,385.0 | 39,447.0 | 43,659.0 | 42,600.0 | 34,838.0 | 31,730.0 | 32,182.0 |
| Equity & investment fund shares.. | 8aala | 28,522.0 | † 30,590.0 | 34,152.0 | 32,951.0 | 21,102.0 | 20,195.0 | 21,357.0 | 24,262.0 | 21,272.0 | 13,317.0 | 11,369.0 | 9,442.0 |
| Debt instruments...................... | 8abla | 14,949.0 | † 14,901.0 | 14,198.0 | 15,959.0 | 17,473.0 | 18,190.0 | 18,090.0 | 19,397.0 | 21,328.0 | 21,521.0 | 20,361.0 | 22,740.0 |
| Portfolio investment................... | 8b9la | 22,129.0 | † 24,577.0 | 22,506.0 | 21,773.0 | 13,101.0 | 22,851.0 | 27,121.0 | 32,238.0 | 47,057.0 | 37,575.0 | 24,495.0 | 21,089.0 |
| Equity & investment fund shares.. | 8bala | 1,812.0 | † 1,173.0 | 2,251.0 | 665.0 | 559.0 | 627.0 | 285.0 | 310.0 | 484.0 | 181.0 | 218.0 | 214.0 |
| Debt securities............................ | 8bbla | 20,317.0 | † 23,404.0 | 20,255.0 | 21,108.0 | 12,542.0 | 22,224.0 | 26,836.0 | 31,928.0 | 46,573.0 | 37,394.0 | 24,277.0 | 20,875.0 |
| Fin. der.(oth.than reserves) & ESOs | 8c9la | .... | † 22.0 | 21.0 | 16.0 | 16.0 | 16.0 | 16.0 | 16.0 | 16.0 | 16.0 | 16.0 | .... |
| Other investment........................ | 8d9la | 18,234.1 | † 17,464.9 | 17,698.7 | 22,853.8 | 24,793.1 | 33,217.0 | 45,008.7 | 55,225.6 | 60,587.8 | 63,121.6 | 64,740.7 | 70,867.3 |
| Other equity........................... | 8dala | .... | .... | .... | .... | .... | .... | .... | .... | .... | .... | .... | |
| Debt instruments...................... | 8dzla | 18,234.1 | † 17,464.9 | 17,698.7 | 22,853.8 | 24,793.1 | 33,217.0 | 45,008.7 | 55,225.6 | 60,587.8 | 63,121.6 | 64,740.7 | 70,867.3 |
| | | | | | | | | | | | | | |
| **National Accounts** | | | | | | *Billions of Bolivares:* | | | | | | | |
| Househ.Cons.Expend.,incl.NPISHs..... | 96f | 104.7 | 142.2 | 185.1 | 252.9 | 349.0 | 444.7 | 568.4 | 748.8 | 969.4 | 1,461.8 | 2,282.2 | .... |
| Government Consumption Expend... | 91f | 25.4 | 33.6 | 46.1 | 61.7 | 80.3 | 96.9 | 114.0 | 156.4 | 199.4 | 278.2 | 442.7 | .... |
| Gross Fixed Capital Formation.......... | 93e | 39.0 | 61.7 | 88.0 | 123.8 | 149.8 | 166.4 | 190.0 | 240.7 | 332.2 | 499.0 | 655.5 | .... |
| Changes in Inventories.................... | 93i | 7.4 | 8.2 | 18.1 | 26.3 | 32.0 | 16.0 | 33.4 | 72.5 | 102.8 | 113.4 | 96.6 | .... |
| Exports of Goods and Services......... | 90c | 77.0 | 120.6 | 143.9 | 154.0 | 208.8 | 127.8 | 290.1 | 406.5 | 428.0 | 556.2 | 506.0 | .... |
| Imports of Goods and Services (-)..... | 98c | 40.8 | 62.2 | 87.2 | 124.0 | 142.3 | 144.6 | 179.0 | 267.4 | 396.3 | 662.8 | 951.7 | .... |
| Gross Domestic Product (GDP)........ | 99b | 212.7 | 304.1 | 393.9 | 494.6 | 677.6 | 707.3 | 1,016.8 | 1,357.5 | 1,635.5 | 2,245.8 | 3,031.2 | .... |
| Net Primary Income from Abroad..... | 98.n | −6.7 | −4.7 | −2.3 | 4.3 | .1 | −6.4 | −13.3 | −36.4 | −47.4 | −78.4 | −29.4 | .... |
| Gross National Income (GNI)........... | 99a | 206.1 | 299.5 | 391.8 | 499.8 | 679.1 | 701.5 | 1,004.3 | 1,323.2 | 1,592.2 | 2,174.8 | 2,997.1 | .... |
| Consumption of Fixed Capital.......... | 99cf | 11.5 | 14.8 | 20.2 | 33.5 | 37.8 | 43.7 | 59.8 | 81.9 | 97.4 | 134.6 | 181.1 | .... |
| GDP Volume 1997 Prices................. | 99b.p | 42.2 | 46.5 | 51.1 | 55.6 | 58.5 | 56.7 | 55.8 | 58.1 | 61.4 | 62.2 | 59.8 | .... |
| GDP Volume (2010=100)............... | 99bvp | 75.6 | 83.4 | 91.6 | 99.6 | 104.9 | 101.5 | 100.0 | 104.2 | 110.0 | 111.5 | 107.2 | .... |
| GDP Deflator (2010=100)............... | 99bip | 27.7 | 35.9 | 42.3 | 48.8 | 63.5 | 68.5 | 100.0 | 128.1 | 146.2 | 198.1 | 278.2 | .... |
| | | | | | | | | | | | | | |
| | | | | | | *Millions: Midyear Estimates* | | | | | | | |
| **Population**............................. | 99z | 26.31 | 26.77 | 27.22 | 27.67 | 28.12 | 28.56 | 29.00 | 29.43 | 29.85 | 30.28 | 30.69 | 31.11 |

# Vietnam 582

| | | 2004 | 2005 | 2006 | 2007 | 2008 | 2009 | 2010 | 2011 | 2012 | 2013 | 2014 | 2015 |
|---|---|---|---|---|---|---|---|---|---|---|---|---|---|
| **Exchange Rates** | | | | *Dong per SDR: End of Period* | | | | | | | | | |
| Market Rate.................................. | aa | 24,502 | 22,748 | 24,152 | 25,464 | 26,149 | 28,126 | 29,156 | 31,977 | 32,011 | 32,395 | 30,781 | 30,334 |
| | | | | *Dong per US Dollar: End of Period (ae) Period Average (rf)* | | | | | | | | | |
| Market Rate.................................. | ae | 15,777 | 15,916 | 16,054 | 16,114 | 16,977 | 17,941 | 18,932 | 20,828 | 20,828 | 21,036 | 21,246 | 21,890 |
| Market Rate.................................. | rf | 15,746 | 15,859 | 15,994 | 16,105 | 16,302 | 17,065 | 18,613 | 20,510 | 20,828 | 20,933 | 21,148 | 21,698 |
| **Fund Position** | | | | *Millions of SDRs: End of Period* | | | | | | | | | |
| Quota........................................... | 2f.s | 329.10 | 329.10 | 329.10 | 329.10 | 329.10 | 329.10 | 329.10 | 460.70 | 460.70 | 460.70 | 460.70 | 460.70 |
| SDR Holdings.............................. | 1b.s | .29 | .61 | 1.05 | 4.81 | 5.32 | 267.70 | 267.85 | 268.02 | 268.08 | 268.04 | 267.99 | 267.97 |
| Reserve Position in the Fund............ | 1c.s | .01 | .01 | .01 | .01 | .01 | .01 | .01 | .01 | .01 | .01 | .01 | .01 |
| Total Fund Cred.&Loans Outstg....... | 2tl | 178.56 | 142.32 | 120.06 | 103.50 | 78.66 | 53.82 | 28.98 | 8.28 | — | — | — | — |
| SDR Allocations............................ | 1bd | 47.66 | 47.66 | 47.66 | 47.66 | 47.66 | 314.79 | 314.79 | 314.79 | 314.79 | 314.79 | 314.79 | 314.79 |
| **International Liquidity** | | | | *Millions of US Dollars Unless Otherwise Indicated: End of Period* | | | | | | | | | |
| Total Reserves minus Gold.............. | 1l.d | 7,041.5 | 9,050.6 | 13,384.1 | 23,479.4 | 23,890.3 | 16,447.1 | 12,466.6 | 13,539.1 | 25,573.3 | 25,893.5 | 34,189.4 | 28,250.3 |
| SDR Holdings.............................. | 1b.d | .5 | .9 | 1.6 | 7.6 | 8.2 | 419.7 | 412.5 | 411.5 | 412.0 | 412.8 | 388.3 | 371.3 |
| Reserve Position in the Fund.......... | 1c.d | — | — | — | — | — | — | — | — | — | — | — | — |
| Foreign Exchange......................... | 1d.d | 7,041.0 | 9,049.7 | 13,382.5 | 23,471.8 | 23,882.0 | 16,027.4 | 12,054.1 | 13,127.6 | 25,161.3 | 25,480.7 | 33,801.1 | 27,878.9 |
| Gold (Market Valuation)................. | 1and | 144.6 | 165.9 | 206.9 | 268.3 | 285.7 | 356.1 | 459.6 | 506.4 | 539.5 | 393.7 | 385.8 | 365.6 |
| Monetary Authorities: Other Liabs.... | 4..d | 486.0 | 391.3 | 389.7 | 372.0 | 326.3 | 707.8 | 678.7 | 642.8 | 626.4 | 614.9 | 578.3 | 553.8 |
| Deposit Money Banks: Assets........ | 7a.d | 3,678.7 | 4,469.1 | 6,187.9 | 4,980.5 | 5,234.1 | 7,279.8 | 9,224.2 | 9,487.0 | 10,285.3 | 14,675.2 | 14,673.0 | 19,313.2 |
| Deposit Money Banks: Liabs............ | 7b.d | 1,197.8 | 1,457.7 | 2,044.7 | 3,468.9 | 5,132.3 | 6,873.4 | 9,131.9 | 9,617.9 | 10,641.9 | 11,262.4 | 9,857.3 | 9,215.4 |
| **Monetary Authorities** | | | | *Billions of Dong: End of Period* | | | | | | | | | |
| Foreign Assets............................. | 11 | 113,375 | 146,689 | 218,190 | 382,671 | 410,434 | 301,465 | 244,718 | 292,541 | 543,878 | 561,660 | 742,831 | 634,099 |
| Claims on General Government........ | 12a | 21,005 | 16,952 | 21,507 | 12,915 | 12,708 | 76,068 | 82,224 | 55,180 | 43,111 | 27,585 | 11,121 | 80,450 |
| Claims on Banking Institutions......... | 12e | 14,400 | 11,024 | 8,031 | 15,614 | 12,945 | 50,761 | 127,483 | 152,362 | 45,523 | 28,574 | 40,873 | 75,766 |
| Reserve Money............................. | 14 | 141,165 | 174,505 | 230,756 | 315,712 | 378,989 | 422,253 | 439,622 | 522,809 | 655,511 | 695,653 | 825,687 | 985,307 |
| of which: Currency Outside DMBs.. | 14a | 109,097 | 131,179 | 158,809 | 220,514 | 236,848 | 293,225 | 337,949 | 370,992 | 455,504 | 506,739 | 624,832 | 726,559 |
| Liabs. of Central Bank: Securities..... | 16ac | | | 1,500 | 68,200 | 24,136 | 2 | — | — | 59,404 | 51,791 | 140,827 | — |
| Foreign Liabilities........................ | 16c | 8,835 | 7,311 | 7,407 | 7,208 | 6,786 | 21,552 | 22,027 | 23,453 | 23,124 | 23,133 | 21,977 | 21,671 |
| General Government Deposits.......... | 16d | 9,729 | 9,079 | 28,495 | 42,745 | 36,289 | — | — | — | — | 95 | 3,763 | −2,417 |
| Capital Accounts........................... | 17a | 18,584 | 18,543 | 31,200 | 48,149 | 57,065 | 82,163 | 89,927 | 117,221 | 106,164 | 119,471 | 93,929 | 108,355 |
| Other Items (Net)........................... | 17r | −29,534 | −34,772 | −51,630 | −70,814 | −67,177 | −97,676 | −97,151 | −163,400 | −211,691 | −272,324 | −291,359 | −322,602 |
| **Banking Institutions** | | | | *Billions of Dong: End of Period* | | | | | | | | | |
| Reserves...................................... | 20 | 31,646 | 42,961 | 71,282 | 94,052 | 139,814 | 127,826 | 99,222 | 151,541 | 199,955 | 188,940 | 201,456 | 257,801 |
| Claims on Mon.Author.:Securities.... | 20c | 333 | 499 | 1,500 | 58,914 | 26,883 | 549 | 2,015 | — | 60,857 | 50,953 | 138,737 | — |
| Foreign Assets............................. | 21 | 58,039 | 71,130 | 99,340 | 80,255 | 88,859 | 130,606 | 174,633 | 197,596 | 214,223 | 308,707 | 311,742 | 422,766 |
| Claims on General Government........ | 22a | 43,857 | 70,831 | 83,722 | 109,270 | 152,519 | 158,080 | 201,743 | 258,866 | 364,822 | 480,536 | 608,125 | 674,839 |
| Claims on Rest of the Economy........ | 22d | 420,046 | 552,667 | 693,834 | 1,067,729 | 1,339,263 | 1,869,255 | 2,475,535 | 2,829,890 | 3,077,703 | 3,469,683 | 3,949,676 | 4,692,917 |
| Demand Deposits.......................... | 24 | 88,891 | 110,823 | 133,405 | 214,653 | 196,470 | 271,988 | 287,503 | 315,128 | 384,630 | 482,582 | 574,568 | 688,264 |
| Time and Savings Deposits.............. | 25a | 182,408 | 261,269 | 382,396 | 597,162 | 791,066 | 1,004,770 | 1,466,950 | 1,683,540 | 2,211,874 | 2,691,221 | 3,276,868 | 3,716,613 |
| Foreign Currency Deposits............... | 25b | 115,050 | 145,303 | 166,400 | 221,668 | 289,159 | 340,604 | 385,909 | 404,621 | 403,214 | 514,079 | 546,371 | 640,001 |
| Bonds & Money Mkt. Instruments.... | 26a | 26,530 | 31,048 | 68,378 | 74,421 | 89,464 | 148,271 | 282,438 | 309,571 | 210,231 | 159,385 | 96,429 | 196,967 |
| Restricted Deposits....................... | 26b | 10,369 | 10,782 | 13,284 | 19,826 | 19,122 | 33,589 | 28,436 | 42,108 | 37,415 | 46,687 | 60,148 | 51,205 |
| Foreign Liabilities........................ | 26c | 18,898 | 23,201 | 32,826 | 55,898 | 87,131 | 123,315 | 172,886 | 200,322 | 221,650 | 236,916 | 209,428 | 201,726 |
| General Government Deposits.......... | 26d | 32,201 | 33,656 | 36,177 | 47,084 | 64,448 | 63,355 | 69,534 | 80,068 | 80,741 | 98,554 | 85,189 | 69,190 |
| Credit from Central Bank................ | 26g | 16,679 | 20,943 | 25,436 | 24,571 | 17,560 | 98,822 | 189,640 | 215,921 | 67,141 | 45,401 | 60,727 | 153,564 |
| Capital Accounts.......................... | 27a | 59,411 | 71,920 | 99,827 | 175,697 | 239,779 | 320,162 | 430,718 | 539,384 | 575,321 | 632,536 | 651,877 | 701,726 |
| Other Items (Net).......................... | 27r | 3,482 | 29,143 | −8,450 | −20,759 | −46,862 | −118,560 | −360,865 | −352,770 | −274,657 | −408,541 | −351,870 | −370,933 |
| **Banking Survey** | | | | *Billions of Dong: End of Period* | | | | | | | | | |
| Foreign Assets (Net)...................... | 31n | 143,680 | 187,306 | 277,298 | 399,820 | 405,377 | 287,205 | 224,439 | 266,361 | 513,327 | 610,318 | 823,168 | 833,468 |
| Domestic Credit............................ | 32 | 442,978 | 597,715 | 734,391 | 1,100,085 | 1,403,754 | 2,040,049 | 2,689,967 | 3,063,869 | 3,404,895 | 3,879,154 | 4,479,970 | 5,381,433 |
| Claims on General Govt. (Net)........ | 32an | 22,932 | 45,048 | 40,557 | 32,356 | 64,491 | 170,793 | 214,432 | 233,978 | 327,192 | 409,472 | 530,293 | 688,516 |
| Claims on Rest of the Economy...... | 32d | 420,046 | 552,667 | 693,834 | 1,067,729 | 1,339,263 | 1,869,255 | 2,475,535 | 2,829,890 | 3,077,703 | 3,469,683 | 3,949,676 | 4,692,917 |
| Money......................................... | 34 | 197,989 | 242,002 | 292,215 | 435,168 | 433,318 | 565,213 | 625,451 | 686,120 | 840,134 | 989,321 | 1,199,400 | 1,414,823 |
| Quasi-Money................................ | 35 | 297,459 | 406,572 | 548,796 | 818,830 | 1,080,226 | 1,345,374 | 1,852,859 | 2,088,161 | 2,615,087 | 3,205,300 | 3,823,239 | 4,356,614 |
| Bonds & Money Mkt. Instruments.... | 36a | 26,530 | 31,048 | 68,378 | 74,421 | 89,464 | 148,271 | 282,438 | 309,571 | 210,231 | 159,385 | 96,429 | 196,967 |
| Restricted Deposits........................ | 36b | 10,369 | 10,782 | 13,284 | 19,826 | 19,122 | 33,589 | 28,436 | 42,108 | 37,415 | 46,687 | 60,148 | 51,205 |
| Capital Accounts........................... | 37a | 77,995 | 90,463 | 131,027 | 223,846 | 296,845 | 402,325 | 520,646 | 656,605 | 681,485 | 752,006 | 745,807 | 810,081 |
| Other Items (Net)........................... | 37r | −23,684 | 4,156 | −42,010 | −72,185 | −109,844 | −167,519 | −395,423 | −452,335 | −466,131 | −663,226 | −621,885 | −614,789 |
| Money plus Quasi-Money................. | 35l | 495,447 | 648,574 | 841,011 | 1,253,997 | 1,513,544 | 1,910,587 | 2,478,310 | 2,774,281 | 3,455,221 | 4,194,620 | 5,022,639 | 5,771,436 |
| **Interest Rates** | | | | *Percent Per Annum* | | | | | | | | | |
| Central Bank Policy Rate (EOP)........ | 60 | 5.00 | 5.00 | 6.50 | 6.50 | 10.25 | 8.00 | 9.00 | 15.00 | 9.00 | 7.00 | 6.50 | 6.50 |
| Treasury Bill Rate........................... | 60c | 5.69 | 6.13 | 4.73 | 4.15 | 12.13 | 8.04 | 11.15 | 12.35 | 8.82 | 6.64 | 5.04 | 4.23 |
| Deposit Rate................................. | 60l | 6.17 | 7.15 | 7.63 | 7.49 | 12.73 | 7.91 | 11.19 | 13.99 | 10.50 | 7.14 | 5.76 | 4.75 |
| Lending Rate................................. | 60p | 9.72 | 11.03 | 11.18 | 11.18 | 15.78 | 10.07 | 13.14 | 16.95 | 13.47 | 10.37 | 8.67 | 7.12 |
| **Prices** | | | | *Index Numbers (2010=100): Period Averages* | | | | | | | | | |
| Share Prices (End of Month)............. | 62.ep | 50.2 | 54.3 | 106.3 | 207.8 | 99.3 | 89.1 | 100.0 | 88.9 | 85.1 | 101.0 | 120.1 | 119.3 |
| Consumer Prices............................ | 64 | 55.3 | 59.9 | 64.4 | 69.7 | 85.8 | 91.9 | 100.0 | † 118.7 | 129.5 | 138.0 | † 143.6 | 144.9 |
| **Intl. Transactions & Positions** | | | | *Millions of US Dollars* | | | | | | | | | |
| Exports........................................ | 70..d | 25,984 | 31,726 | 39,606 | 48,313 | 62,685 | 57,096 | 71,658 | 94,518 | 115,458 | 132,478 | 149,565 | 162,061 |
| Imports, c.i.f................................. | 71..d | 31,470 | 36,408 | 44,410 | 60,697 | 80,714 | 69,949 | 83,779 | 104,041 | 115,101 | 131,260 | 148,770 | 162,825 |

|  |  | 2004 | 2005 | 2006 | 2007 | 2008 | 2009 | 2010 | 2011 | 2012 | 2013 | 2014 | 2015 |
|---|---|---|---|---|---|---|---|---|---|---|---|---|---|
| **Balance of Payments** |  |  |  |  |  | *Millions of US Dollars* |  |  |  |  |  |  |  |
| A. Current Account*...................... | 109bx | −957.0 | −560.2 | −163.7 | −6,953.1 | −10,823.0 | −6,608.0 | −4,276.0 | 236.0 | 9,429.0 | † 7,745.0 | 9,359.0 | 906.0 |
| Goods, credit (exports).................. | 1a9cx | 26,485.0 | 32,447.0 | 39,826.0 | 48,561.0 | 62,685.0 | 57,096.0 | 72,237.0 | 96,906.0 | 114,694.0 | † 132,032.0 | 150,217.0 | 162,112.0 |
| Goods, debit (imports)................. | 1a9dx | 28,772.0 | 34,886.2 | 42,601.6 | 58,999.1 | 75,468.0 | 64,703.0 | 77,373.0 | 97,356.0 | 104,781.0 | † 123,319.0 | 138,091.0 | 154,716.0 |
| Balance on goods............ | 1a9bx | −2,287.0 | −2,439.2 | −2,775.6 | −10,438.1 | −12,783.0 | −7,607.0 | −5,136.0 | −450.0 | 9,913.0 | † 8,713.0 | 12,126.0 | 7,396.0 |
| Services, credit (exports)............... | 1b9cx | 3,867.0 | 4,176.0 | 5,100.0 | 6,030.0 | 7,006.0 | 5,766.0 | 7,460.0 | 8,879.0 | 9,620.0 | † 10,711.0 | 10,970.0 | 11,200.0 |
| Services, debit (imports)............... | 1b9dx | 4,739.0 | 4,472.0 | 5,108.2 | 6,785.0 | 7,956.0 | 8,187.0 | 9,921.0 | 11,859.0 | 12,087.0 | † 13,820.0 | 14,500.0 | 15,500.0 |
| Balance on Goods & Services...... | 1z9bx | −3,159.0 | −2,735.2 | −2,783.7 | −11,193.1 | −13,733.0 | −10,028.0 | −7,597.0 | −3,430.0 | 7,446.0 | † 5,604.0 | 8,596.0 | 3,096.0 |
| Primary income: credit.................. | 1c9cx | 188.0 | 364.0 | 668.0 | 1,166.0 | 1,357.0 | 753.0 | 456.0 | 395.0 | 295.0 | † 281.0 | 323.0 | 399.0 |
| Primary income: debit.................. | 1c9dx | 1,079.0 | 1,569.0 | 2,097.0 | 3,356.0 | 5,758.0 | 3,781.0 | 5,020.0 | 5,414.0 | 6,524.0 | † 7,617.0 | 9,167.0 | 10,324.0 |
| Balance on gds, serv. & prim. inc. | 1y9bx | −4,050.0 | −3,940.2 | −4,212.7 | −13,383.1 | −18,134.0 | −13,056.0 | −12,161.0 | −8,449.0 | 1,217.0 | † −1,732.0 | −248.0 | −6,829.0 |
| Secondary income: credit............... | 1d9ca | 3,093.0 | 3,380.0 | 4,049.0 | 6,430.0 | 7,311.0 | 6,448.0 | 7,885.0 | 8,685.0 | 8,212.0 | † 10,027.0 | 10,307.0 | 8,586.0 |
| Secondary income: debit................ | 1d9da | .... | .... | .... | — | .... | — | .... | — | — | † 550.0 | 700.0 | 851.0 |
| B. Capital Account*................. | 209ba | .... | .... | .... | .... | .... | .... | .... | .... | .... | .... | .... | .... |
| Capital account: credit.................. | 209ca | .... | .... | .... | .... | .... | .... | .... | .... | .... | .... | .... | .... |
| Capital account: debit.................. | 209da | .... | .... | .... | .... | .... | .... | .... | .... | .... | .... | .... | .... |
| Balance on current & capital acct. | 129ba | −957.0 | −560.2 | −163.7 | −6,953.1 | −10,823.0 | −6,608.0 | −4,276.0 | 236.0 | 9,429.0 | † 7,745.0 | 9,359.0 | 906.0 |
| C. Financial Account*................ | 309na | −2,807.0 | −3,087.0 | −3,088.0 | −17,730.0 | −12,341.0 | −7,172.2 | −6,201.0 | −6,390.0 | −7,970.0 | † 280.2 | −5,571.3 | −1,575.0 |
| Direct investment: assets.............. | 3a9aa | .... | 65.0 | 85.0 | 184.0 | 300.0 | 700.0 | 900.0 | 950.0 | 1,200.0 | † 1,956.0 | 1,150.0 | 1,100.0 |
| Equity & investment fund shares.. | 3aaaa | .... | .... | .... | .... | .... | .... | .... | .... | .... | .... | .... | .... |
| Debt instruments..................... | 3abaa | .... | .... | .... | .... | .... | .... | .... | .... | .... | .... | .... | .... |
| Direct investment: liabilities .......... | 3a9la | 1,610.0 | 1,954.0 | 2,400.0 | 6,700.0 | 9,579.0 | 7,600.0 | 8,000.0 | 7,430.0 | 8,368.0 | † 8,900.0 | 9,200.0 | 11,800.0 |
| Equity & investment fund shares . | 3aala | .... | 1,204.0 | 1,605.0 | 6,204.5 | 8,960.2 | 6,369.4 | 7,100.7 | 5,941.0 | 6,943.0 | † 6,202.0 | 7,676.3 | 10,313.0 |
| Debt instruments..................... | 3abla | .... | 750.0 | 795.0 | 495.5 | 618.8 | 1,230.6 | 899.3 | 1,489.0 | 1,425.0 | † 2,698.0 | 1,523.7 | 1,487.0 |
| Portfolio investment: assets .......... | 3b9aa | .... | .... | .... | .... | .... | 199.0 | 13.0 | −348.0 | −23.0 | † −80.0 | — | — |
| Equity & investment fund shares | 3baaa | .... | — | .... | .... | .... | .... | 13.0 | −348.0 | −23.0 | † −80.0 | — | — |
| Debt securities ........................... | 3bbaa | .... | — | .... | .... | .... | .... | .... | .... | .... | .... | .... | .... |
| Portfolio investment: liabilities....... | 3b9la | .... | 865.0 | 1,313.0 | 6,243.0 | −578.0 | 128.0 | 2,383.0 | 1,064.0 | 1,263.0 | † 1,386.0 | 93.0 | −65.0 |
| Equity & investment fund shares . | 3bala | .... | 115.0 | 1,313.0 | 6,243.0 | −578.0 | 128.0 | 2,383.0 | 1,064.0 | 1,263.0 | † 1,270.0 | 252.0 | 134.0 |
| Debt securities......................... | 3bbla | .... | 750.0 | .... | .... | .... | .... | .... | .... | — | † 116.0 | −159.0 | −199.0 |
| Fin. der.& empl.stk.ops.(ESOs): net. | 3c9na | .... | .... | .... | .... | .... | .... | .... | .... | .... | .... | .... | .... |
| Fin. der. & ESOs.: assets.............. | 3c9aa | .... | .... | .... | .... | .... | .... | .... | .... | .... | .... | .... | .... |
| Fin. der. & ESOs.: liabilities.......... | 3c9la | .... | .... | .... | .... | .... | .... | .... | .... | .... | .... | .... | .... |
| Other investment: assets............... | 3d9aa | −35.0 | 634.0 | 1,535.0 | −2,623.0 | −677.0 | 4,803.0 | 7,063.0 | 6,402.0 | 6,254.0 | † 12,874.2 | 7,558.7 | 14,237.0 |
| Other equity........................... | 3daaa | .... | .... | .... | .... | .... | .... | .... | .... | .... | .... | .... | .... |
| Debt instruments...................... | 3dzaa | −35.0 | 634.0 | 1,535.0 | −2,623.0 | −677.0 | 4,803.0 | 7,063.0 | 6,402.0 | 6,254.0 | † 12,874.2 | 7,558.7 | 14,237.0 |
| Other investment: liabilities........... | 3d9la | 1,162.0 | 967.0 | 995.0 | 2,348.0 | 2,963.0 | 5,146.2 | 3,794.0 | 4,900.0 | 5,770.0 | † 4,184.0 | 4,987.0 | 5,177.0 |
| Other equity........................... | 3dala | .... | .... | .... | .... | .... | .... | .... | .... | .... | .... | .... | .... |
| Debt instruments...................... | 3dzla | 1,162.0 | 967.0 | 995.0 | 2,348.0 | 2,963.0 | 5,146.2 | 3,794.0 | 4,900.0 | 5,770.0 | † 4,184.0 | 4,987.0 | 5,177.0 |
| Curr.+ cap.− finan. acct. balance... | 4y9na | 1,850.0 | 2,526.8 | 2,924.3 | 10,776.9 | 1,518.0 | 564.2 | 1,925.0 | 6,626.0 | 17,399.0 | † 7,464.8 | 14,930.3 | 2,481.0 |
| D. Net Errors and Omissions............ | 409na | −914.6 | −396.7 | 1,400.2 | −565.3 | −1,044.4 | −9,029.0 | −3,689.8 | −5,475.0 | −5,539.3 | † −6,907.9 | −6,555.4 | −8,513.0 |
| E. Reserves and Related Items.......... | 4z9na | 935.4 | 2,130.2 | 4,324.5 | 10,211.6 | 473.6 | −8,464.8 | −1,764.8 | 1,151.0 | 11,859.7 | † 556.9 | 8,374.9 | −6,032.0 |
| Reserve assets............................... | 3e9aa | 808.3 | 2,076.6 | 4,291.6 | 10,186.0 | 434.2 | −8,503.3 | −1,802.8 | 1,118.4 | 11,847.1 | † 556.9 | 8,374.9 | −6,032.0 |
| Credit and loans from the IMF....... | 3dcla | −73.2 | −53.6 | −32.8 | −25.5 | −39.4 | −38.4 | −37.9 | −32.6 | −12.6 | † — | — | — |
| Exceptional financing.................... | 409la | −54.0 | .... | .... | .... | .... | .... | .... | .... | .... | .... | .... | .... |

*Excludes components in group E

| **Government Finance** |  |  |  |  |  |  |  |  |  |  |  |  |  |
|---|---|---|---|---|---|---|---|---|---|---|---|---|---|
| **Cash Flow Statement** |  |  |  |  |  |  |  |  |  |  |  |  |  |
| **Budgetary Central Government** |  |  |  |  |  | *Billions of Dong: Fiscal Year Ends December 31* |  |  |  |  |  |  |  |
| Cash Receipts:Operating Activities... | c1 | 175,389 | 212,829 | 262,063 | 296,746 | 397,663 | 415,198 | 536,866 | 667,579 | 687,980 | 781,954 | .... | .... |
| Taxes.............................. | c11 | 154,922 | 190,999 | 235,537 | 267,711 | 362,008 | 372,048 | 481,711 | 617,368 | 615,867 | 683,514 | .... | .... |
| Social Contributions...................... | c12 | — | — | — | — | — | — | — | — | — | — | .... | .... |
| Grants............................... | c13 | 2,877 | 3,789 | 7,897 | 6,012 | 9,413 | 7,908 | 11,868 | 12,103 | 10,267 | 11,124 | .... | .... |
| Other Receipts............................ | c14 | 17,590 | 18,041 | 18,629 | 23,023 | 26,242 | 35,242 | 43,287 | 38,108 | 61,846 | 87,316 | .... | .... |
| Cash Payments:Operating Activities. | c2 | 125,607 | 156,250 | 187,332 | 237,620 | 301,751 | 338,993 | 413,966 | 510,945 | 659,230 | 772,863 | .... | .... |
| Compensation of Employees.......... | c21 | .... | .... | .... | .... | .... | .... | .... | .... | .... | .... | .... | .... |
| Purchases of Goods & Services....... | c22 | .... | .... | .... | .... | .... | .... | .... | .... | .... | .... | .... | .... |
| Interest.............................. | c24 | 7,217 | 6,621 | 7,965 | 12,660 | 16,730 | 20,490 | 25,400 | 29,786 | 39,884 | 54,084 | .... | .... |
| Subsidies.............................. | c25 | .... | .... | .... | .... | .... | .... | .... | .... | .... | .... | .... | .... |
| Grants............................... | c26 | .... | .... | .... | .... | .... | .... | .... | .... | .... | .... | .... | .... |
| Social Benefits.......................... | c27 | .... | .... | .... | .... | .... | .... | .... | .... | .... | .... | .... | .... |
| Other Payments.......................... | c28 | .... | .... | .... | .... | .... | .... | .... | .... | .... | .... | .... | .... |
| Net Cash Inflow:Operating Act.[1-2] | ccio | 49,782 | 56,579 | 74,731 | 59,126 | 95,912 | 76,205 | 122,900 | 156,634 | 28,750 | 9,091 | .... | .... |
| Net Cash Outflow:Invest. in NFA...... | c31 | 46,206 | 57,383 | 63,669 | 67,527 | 77,200 | 129,448 | 120,787 | 141,258 | 207,513 | 212,314 | .... | .... |
| Purchases of Nonfinancial Assets... | c31.1 | .... | .... | .... | .... | .... | .... | .... | .... | .... | .... | .... | .... |
| Sales of Nonfinancial Assets.......... | c31.2 | .... | .... | .... | .... | .... | .... | .... | .... | .... | .... | .... | .... |
| Cash Surplus/Deficit [1-2-31=1-2M] | ccsd | 3,576 | −804 | 11,062 | −8,401 | 18,712 | −53,243 | 2,113 | 15,376 | −178,763 | −203,223 | .... | .... |
| Net Acq. Fin. Assets, excl. Cash....... | c32x | .... | .... | .... | .... | .... | .... | .... | .... | .... | .... | .... | .... |
| Domestic............................ | c321x | .... | .... | .... | .... | .... | .... | .... | .... | .... | .... | .... | .... |
| Foreign............................... | c322x | .... | .... | .... | .... | .... | .... | .... | .... | .... | .... | .... | .... |
| Net Incurrence of Liabilities.............. | c33 | .... | .... | .... | .... | .... | .... | .... | .... | .... | .... | .... | .... |
| Domestic............................. | c331 | .... | .... | .... | .... | .... | .... | .... | .... | .... | .... | .... | .... |
| Foreign............................. | c332 | .... | .... | .... | .... | .... | .... | .... | .... | .... | .... | .... | .... |
| Net Cash Inflow, Fin.Act.[-32x+33].. | cnfb | .... | .... | .... | .... | .... | .... | .... | .... | .... | .... | .... | .... |
| Net Change in Stock of Cash........... | cncb | .... | .... | .... | .... | .... | .... | .... | .... | .... | .... | .... | .... |
| Stat. Discrep. [32X-33+NCB-CSD].... | ccsdz | .... | .... | .... | .... | .... | .... | .... | .... | .... | .... | .... | .... |
| Memo Item:Cash Expenditure[2+31] | c2m | 171,813 | 213,633 | 251,001 | 305,147 | 378,951 | 468,441 | 534,753 | 652,203 | 866,743 | 985,177 | .... | .... |
| Memo Item: Gross Debt................. | c63 | .... | .... | .... | .... | .... | .... | .... | .... | .... | .... | .... | .... |

| | | 2004 | 2005 | 2006 | 2007 | 2008 | 2009 | 2010 | 2011 | 2012 | 2013 | 2014 | 2015 |
|---|---|---|---|---|---|---|---|---|---|---|---|---|---|
| **National Accounts** | | | | | | | *Billions of Dong* | | | | | | | |
| Househ.Cons.Expend.,incl.NPISHs.... | 96f | 465,506 | 598,567 | 690,954 | 849,141 | 1,145,361 | 1,239,151 | 1,436,289 | 1,844,377 | 2,093,261 | 2,346,160 | 2,591,337 | . . . . |
| Government Consumption Expend... | 91f | 45,715 | 49,952 | 58,734 | 69,247 | 90,904 | 104,540 | 129,313 | 164,323 | 192,362 | 220,642 | 246,711 | . . . . |
| Gross Fixed Capital Formation.......... | 93e | 237,868 | 285,841 | 332,949 | 437,702 | 513,987 | 612,526 | 704,401 | 745,494 | 785,337 | 847,475 | 938,452 | . . . . |
| Changes in Inventories.................... | 93i | 15,818 | 22,702 | 33,680 | 55,598 | 75,759 | 59,800 | 65,810 | 81,538 | 98,823 | 108,650 | 118,180 | . . . . |
| Exports of Goods and Services.......... | 90c | 470,216 | 582,069 | 717,109 | 879,461 | 1,157,178 | 1,132,688 | 1,535,816 | 2,205,858 | . . . . | . . . . | . . . . | . . . . |
| Imports of Goods and Services (-)..... | 98c | 524,216 | 617,157 | 761,547 | 1,060,763 | 1,383,006 | 1,304,350 | 1,739,363 | 2,312,711 | . . . . | . . . . | . . . . | . . . . |
| Gross Domestic Product (GDP)......... | 99b | 715,307 | 914,001 | 1,061,565 | 1,246,769 | 1,616,047 | 1,809,149 | 2,157,828 | 2,779,880 | 3,245,419 | 3,584,262 | 3,937,856 | . . . . |
| Net Primary Income from Abroad..... | 98.n | −13,401 | −16,779 | −22,810 | −34,963 | −48,083 | −77,928 | −82,250 | −119,804 | −130,192 | −153,594 | −192,341 | . . . . |
| Gross National Income (GNI)............ | 99a | 701,906 | 897,222 | 1,038,755 | 1,211,806 | 1,567,964 | 1,731,221 | 2,075,578 | 2,660,076 | 3,115,227 | 3,430,668 | 3,745,515 | . . . . |
| GDP Volume 2010 Prices................ | 99b.p | . . . . | 1,588,646 | 1,699,501 | 1,820,667 | 1,923,749 | 2,027,591 | 2,157,828 | 2,292,483 | 2,412,778 | 2,543,596 | 2,695,796 | . . . . |
| GDP Volume (2010=100)................ | 99bvp | 67.9 | † 73.6 | 78.8 | 84.4 | 89.2 | 94.0 | 100.0 | 106.2 | 111.8 | 117.9 | 124.9 | . . . . |
| GDP Deflator (2010=100)............... | 99bip | 48.8 | 57.5 | 62.5 | 68.5 | 84.0 | 89.2 | 100.0 | 121.3 | 134.5 | 140.9 | 146.1 | . . . . |
| | | | | | | | *Millions: Midyear Estimates* | | | | | | | |
| Population................................ | 99z | 83.44 | 84.20 | 84.98 | 85.77 | 86.59 | 87.45 | 88.36 | 89.32 | 90.34 | 91.38 | 92.42 | 93.45 |

# WAEMU  759

| | | 2004 | 2005 | 2006 | 2007 | 2008 | 2009 | 2010 | 2011 | 2012 | 2013 | 2014 | 2015 |
|---|---|---|---|---|---|---|---|---|---|---|---|---|---|
| **Exchange Rates** | | | | | | *CFA Francs per SDR: End of Period* | | | | | | | |
| Official Rate.................................. | aa | 747.90 | 794.73 | 749.30 | 704.15 | 725.98 | 713.83 | 756.02 | 778.32 | 764.10 | 732.49 | 782.77 | 834.92 |
| | | | | | *CFA Francs per US Dollar: End of Period (ae) Period Average (rf)* | | | | | | | | |
| Official Rate.................................. | ae | 481.58 | 556.04 | 498.07 | 445.59 | 471.34 | 455.34 | 490.91 | 506.96 | 497.16 | 475.64 | 540.28 | 602.51 |
| Official Rate.................................. | rf | 528.28 | 527.47 | 522.89 | 479.27 | 447.81 | 472.19 | 495.28 | 471.87 | 510.53 | 494.04 | 494.41 | 591.45 |
| **Fund Position** | | | | | | *Millions of SDRs: End of Period* | | | | | | | |
| Quota........................................ | 2f.s | 855.80 | 855.80 | 855.80 | 855.80 | 855.80 | 855.80 | 855.80 | 855.80 | 855.80 | 855.80 | 855.80 | 855.80 |
| SDR Holdings.............................. | 1b.s | 6.41 | 2.48 | 1.26 | .77 | 2.14 | 699.69 | 700.75 | 700.28 | 794.29 | 948.20 | 791.54 | 861.44 |
| Reserve Position in the Fund............ | 1c.s | 29.49 | 29.81 | 30.13 | 30.47 | 30.74 | 31.11 | 31.46 | 31.78 | 32.02 | 32.26 | 32.41 | 32.61 |
| Total Fund Cred.&Loans Outstg....... | 2tl | 655.86 | 535.51 | 175.89 | 191.21 | 309.41 | 554.39 | 665.88 | 885.38 | 1,071.83 | 1,206.99 | 1,333.46 | 1,395.83 |
| SDR Allocations........................... | 1bd | 118.62 | 118.62 | 118.62 | 118.62 | 118.62 | 818.69 | 818.69 | 818.69 | 818.69 | 818.69 | 818.69 | 818.69 |
| **International Liquidity** | | | | | *Millions of US Dollars Unless Otherwise Indicated: End of Period* | | | | | | | | |
| Total Reserves minus Gold.............. | 1l.d | 7,246.2 | 6,193.9 | 7,371.7 | 9,634.7 | 9,324.3 | 12,074.7 | 11,824.7 | 12,111.8 | 12,120.1 | 12,200.5 | 11,505.3 | 11,060.2 |
| SDR Holdings.......................... | 1b.d | 10.0 | 3.5 | 1.9 | 1.2 | 3.3 | 1,096.9 | 1,079.2 | 1,075.1 | 1,220.8 | 1,460.2 | 1,146.8 | 1,193.7 |
| Reserve Position in the Fund.......... | 1c.d | 45.8 | 42.6 | 45.3 | 48.2 | 47.4 | 48.8 | 48.5 | 48.8 | 49.2 | 49.7 | 47.0 | 45.2 |
| Foreign Exchange...................... | 1d.d | 7,190.5 | 6,147.8 | 7,324.4 | 9,585.4 | 9,273.6 | 10,929.1 | 10,697.0 | 10,987.9 | 10,850.1 | 10,690.6 | 10,311.5 | 9,821.3 |
| Gold (Million Fine Troy Ounces)........ | 1ad | 1.173 | 1.173 | 1.173 | 1.173 | 1.173 | 1.173 | 1.173 | 1.173 | 1.173 | 1.173 | 1.173 | . . . . |
| Gold (National Valuation).............. | 1and | 508.3 | 567.4 | 717.8 | . . . . | . . . . | . . . . | . . . . | . . . . | . . . . | . . . . | . . . . | . . . . |
| Monetary Authorities: Other Liabs..... | 4..d | 373.4 | 279.5 | 361.7 | 537.8 | 620.5 | 639.7 | 695.4 | 776.4 | 880.3 | 1,095.7 | 984.9 | 822.8 |
| Deposit Money Banks: Assets.......... | 7a.d | 922.9 | 891.6 | 1,204.7 | 1,363.9 | 1,308.3 | 1,520.5 | 1,509.0 | 1,401.4 | 1,729.6 | 1,578.7 | 1,414.0 | 1,093.9 |
| Deposit Money Banks: Liabs............ | 7b.d | 600.2 | 659.3 | 855.5 | 974.9 | 1,125.2 | 1,245.3 | 1,342.9 | 1,544.2 | 1,627.5 | 1,831.4 | 2,076.8 | 2,265.5 |
| **Monetary Authorities** | | | | | | *Billions of CFA Francs: End of Period* | | | | | | | |
| Foreign Assets............................. | 11 | 3,728 | 3,747 | 4,028 | 4,796 | 5,053 | 6,207 | 6,767 | 7,293 | 7,051 | 6,574 | 7,034 | 7,487 |
| Claims on Central Government........ | 12a | 972 | 869 | 517 | 496 | 560 | 1,163 | 1,227 | 1,413 | 1,516 | 1,540 | 1,568 | 1,602 |
| Claims on Deposit Money Banks...... | 12e | 1 | 11 | 23 | 128 | 365 | 333 | 425 | 722 | 1,045 | 1,723 | 2,561 | 3,291 |
| Claims on Other Financial Insts........ | 12f | 1 | 1 | 2 | 1 | 1 | 2 | 4 | 1 | 5 | 2 | 3 | 2 |
| Reserve Money............................ | 14 | 2,634 | 2,733 | 2,925 | 3,487 | 3,863 | 4,472 | 5,032 | 5,483 | 5,389 | 5,933 | 6,711 | 7,784 |
| of which: Currency Outside DMBs.. | 14a | 1,800 | 2,049 | 2,230 | 2,541 | 2,776 | 3,118 | 3,559 | 3,676 | 3,893 | 4,235 | 4,664 | 5,227 |
| Foreign Liabilities......................... | 16c | 759 | 675 | 401 | 458 | 603 | 1,271 | 1,464 | 1,720 | 1,882 | 2,005 | 2,217 | 2,345 |
| Central Government Deposits........... | 16d | 414 | 329 | 369 | 526 | 574 | 806 | 649 | 837 | 887 | 842 | 1,119 | 1,065 |
| Capital Accounts.......................... | 17a | 1,084 | 1,149 | 951 | 952 | 1,061 | 1,076 | 1,065 | 1,031 | 1,016 | 1,091 | 1,202 | 1,752 |
| Other Items (Net)......................... | 17r | −188 | −258 | −77 | −3 | −122 | 80 | 214 | 358 | 442 | −32 | −83 | −564 |
| **Deposit Money Banks** | | | | | | *Billions of CFA Francs: End of Period* | | | | | | | |
| Reserves.................................... | 20 | 828 | 633 | 648 | 893 | 1,048 | 1,295 | 1,500 | 1,768 | 1,486 | 1,695 | 2,030 | 2,439 |
| Foreign Assets............................. | 21 | 444 | 496 | 600 | 608 | 617 | 692 | 741 | 710 | 860 | 751 | 764 | 659 |
| Claims on Central Government........ | 22a | 851 | 883 | 1,056 | 1,408 | 1,485 | 1,802 | 2,574 | 3,118 | 3,603 | 4,454 | 5,984 | 7,461 |
| Claims on Private Sector................. | 22d | 3,503 | 3,890 | 4,277 | 4,887 | 5,610 | 6,102 | 6,780 | 7,804 | 8,808 | 10,258 | 11,674 | 13,491 |
| Claims on Other Financial Insts........ | 22f | — | — | — | — | — | — | — | — | — | — | — | — |
| Demand Deposits.......................... | 24 | 2,083 | 2,173 | 2,440 | 2,957 | 3,138 | 3,541 | 4,103 | 4,959 | 5,430 | 6,143 | 7,059 | 8,428 |
| Time Deposits............................. | 25 | 1,902 | 2,037 | 2,266 | 2,683 | 3,031 | 3,607 | 4,263 | 4,539 | 5,108 | 5,581 | 6,565 | 7,395 |
| Foreign Liabilities......................... | 26c | 247 | 324 | 366 | 376 | 468 | 505 | 583 | 730 | 758 | 767 | 1,022 | 1,253 |
| Long-Term Foreign Liabilities........... | 26cl | 42 | 43 | 60 | 59 | 62 | 62 | 76 | 53 | 51 | 104 | 100 | 112 |
| Central Government Deposits........... | 26d | 766 | 760 | 790 | 990 | 1,054 | 1,130 | 1,322 | 1,467 | 1,480 | 1,655 | 1,871 | 2,380 |
| Credit from Monetary Authorities..... | 26g | 1 | 10 | 23 | 128 | 357 | 315 | 407 | 686 | 1,005 | 1,700 | 2,494 | 3,266 |
| Capital Accounts.......................... | 27a | 641 | 701 | 788 | 888 | 1,087 | 1,243 | 1,468 | 1,653 | 1,802 | 1,970 | 2,104 | 2,374 |
| Other Items (Net)......................... | 27r | −56 | −145 | −151 | −285 | −438 | −512 | −626 | −685 | −877 | −761 | −762 | −1,157 |
| **Monetary Survey** | | | | | | *Billions of CFA Francs: End of Period* | | | | | | | |
| Foreign Assets (Net)...................... | 31n | 3,166 | 3,244 | 3,861 | 4,570 | 4,598 | 5,123 | 5,461 | 5,554 | 5,271 | 4,552 | 4,559 | 4,549 |
| Domestic Credit........................... | 32 | 4,183 | 4,583 | 4,739 | 5,336 | 6,080 | 7,193 | 8,643 | 10,065 | 11,597 | 13,798 | 16,277 | 19,154 |
| Claims on Central Govt. (Net)........ | 32an | 665 | 674 | 441 | 432 | 453 | 1,077 | 1,842 | 2,251 | 2,777 | 3,529 | 4,584 | 5,645 |
| Claims on Private Sector............... | 32d | 3,517 | 3,908 | 4,296 | 4,903 | 5,626 | 6,114 | 6,796 | 7,813 | 8,815 | 10,266 | 11,690 | 13,507 |
| Claims on Other Financial Insts...... | 32f | 1 | 1 | 2 | 1 | 1 | 2 | 4 | 1 | 5 | 2 | 3 | 2 |
| Money....................................... | 34 | 3,933 | 4,264 | 4,736 | 5,592 | 5,989 | 6,741 | 7,709 | 8,714 | 9,440 | 10,488 | 11,852 | 13,831 |
| Quasi-Money............................... | 35 | 1,902 | 2,037 | 2,266 | 2,683 | 3,031 | 3,607 | 4,263 | 4,539 | 5,108 | 5,581 | 6,565 | 7,395 |
| Long-Term Foreign Liabilities........... | 36cl | 42 | 43 | 60 | 59 | 62 | 62 | 76 | 53 | 51 | 104 | 100 | 112 |
| Capital Accounts.......................... | 37a | 1,725 | 1,850 | 1,739 | 1,841 | 2,148 | 2,318 | 2,532 | 2,684 | 2,818 | 3,061 | 3,305 | 4,126 |
| Other Items (Net)......................... | 37r | −253 | −366 | −202 | −268 | −551 | −413 | −476 | −371 | −549 | −883 | −987 | −1,762 |
| Money plus Quasi-Money................ | 35l | 5,835 | 6,301 | 7,002 | 8,275 | 9,020 | 10,348 | 11,972 | 13,252 | 14,547 | 16,068 | 18,417 | 21,226 |
| **Interest Rates** | | | | | | *Percent Per Annum* | | | | | | | |
| Repurchase Agreement Rate............ | 60.q | 4.00 | 4.00 | 4.25 | 4.25 | 4.75 | 4.25 | 4.25 | 4.25 | 4.00 | 3.50 | 3.50 | 3.50 |
| Deposit Rate................................ | 60l | 3.50 | 3.50 | 3.50 | 3.50 | 3.50 | 3.50 | 3.50 | 3.50 | 3.50 | 3.50 | 3.50 | 3.50 |
| **Prices** | | | | | | *Index Numbers (2010=100): Period Averages* | | | | | | | |
| Share Prices................................ | 62 | 53.8 | 64.9 | 90.0 | 109.9 | 150.9 | 98.7 | 100.0 | 104.6 | 102.7 | 138.4 | 166.0 | 192.8 |
| Share Prices (End of Month)............ | 62.ep | 54.0 | 65.4 | 89.3 | 112.1 | 149.6 | 97.5 | 100.0 | 103.2 | 102.6 | 139.5 | 166.0 | 193.3 |
| BRVM 10................................... | 62a | 53.9 | 71.2 | 104.9 | 110.2 | 148.6 | 92.6 | 100.0 | 105.9 | 101.7 | 133.5 | 152.7 | 170.6 |
| BRVM 10 (End of Month)................ | 62aep | 54.2 | 72.0 | 104.0 | 112.1 | 146.8 | 91.3 | 100.0 | 104.2 | 101.3 | 134.1 | 152.6 | 170.2 |
| Consumer Prices........................... | 64 | 83.8 | 87.4 | 89.4 | 91.5 | †98.3 | 98.7 | 100.0 | 103.9 | 106.3 | 108.0 | 107.8 | 108.9 |
| **National Accounts** | | | | | | *Billions of CFA Francs* | | | | | | | |
| Househ.Cons.Expend.,incl.NPISHs.... | 96f | 16,867.7 | 18,114.6 | 19,134.6 | 20,712.1 | 23,184.8 | 24,226.8 | 25,400.2 | 27,290.7 | 29,614.6 | 31,368.2 | 34,299.2 | . . . . |
| Government Consumption Expend... | 91f | 3,576.8 | 3,734.6 | 3,966.0 | 4,264.5 | 4,371.0 | 4,664.1 | 5,011.5 | 5,108.6 | 5,888.4 | 6,254.9 | 6,816.1 | . . . . |
| Gross Fixed Capital Formation.......... | 93e | 3,578.2 | 3,953.0 | 4,457.3 | 5,047.5 | 5,958.5 | 6,321.3 | 7,164.8 | 7,444.9 | 8,412.0 | 10,516.6 | 11,686.1 | . . . . |
| Changes in Inventories.................... | 93i | 254.9 | 631.2 | −41.3 | 139.0 | 699.7 | −150.1 | 509.6 | −333.2 | 968.7 | 997.3 | 181.9 | . . . . |
| Exports of Goods and Services......... | 90c | 7,294.8 | 8,049.3 | 8,706.7 | 8,587.9 | 9,459.8 | 10,520.2 | 11,969.3 | 13,170.6 | 14,863.0 | 14,834.5 | 14,992.0 | . . . . |
| Imports of Goods and Services (-)..... | 98c | 8,253.0 | 9,514.8 | 9,873.9 | 10,623.2 | 11,911.1 | 12,247.0 | 14,023.6 | 14,866.0 | 17,742.6 | 19,179.2 | 19,965.7 | . . . . |
| Gross Domestic Product (GDP)........ | 99b | 23,319.3 | 24,967.9 | 26,349.4 | 28,127.9 | 31,762.7 | 33,335.4 | 36,031.8 | 37,815.6 | 42,004.2 | 44,792.2 | 48,009.6 | . . . . |
| GDP Volume 2008 Prices................ | 99b.p | 26,402.7 | 27,518.6 | 28,325.5 | 29,235.3 | 31,762.7 | 32,702.9 | 34,115.0 | 34,379.6 | 36,710.0 | 38,886.8 | 41,432.5 | . . . . |
| GDP Volume (2010=100)............... | 99bvp | 77.4 | 80.7 | 83.0 | 85.7 | 93.1 | 95.9 | 100.0 | 100.8 | 107.6 | 114.0 | 121.4 | . . . . |
| GDP Deflator (2010=100).............. | 99bip | 83.6 | 85.9 | 88.1 | 91.1 | 94.7 | 96.5 | 100.0 | 104.1 | 108.3 | 109.1 | 109.7 | . . . . |

|  |  | 2004 | 2005 | 2006 | 2007 | 2008 | 2009 | 2010 | 2011 | 2012 | 2013 | 2014 | 2015 |
|---|---|---|---|---|---|---|---|---|---|---|---|---|---|
| **Exchange Rates** |  | *US Dollars per SDR: End of Period (sa)* | | | | | | | | | | | |
| Market Rate.................................. | sa | 1.5530 | 1.4293 | 1.5044 | 1.5803 | 1.5403 | 1.5677 | 1.5400 | 1.5353 | 1.5369 | 1.5400 | 1.4488 | 1.3857 |
| **International Liquidity** |  | *Millions of US Dollars Unless Otherwise Indicated: End of Period* | | | | | | | | | | | |
| Total Reserves minus Gold.............. | 1l.d | .... | .... | 314.1 | 354.8 | 509.5 | 498.2 | 531.8 | 498.0 | 664.0 | 685.2 | 672.4 | 580.9 |
| Foreign Exchange......................... | 1d.d | .... | .... | 314.1 | 354.8 | 509.5 | 498.2 | 531.8 | 498.0 | 664.0 | 685.2 | 672.4 | 580.9 |
| Central Bank: Other Assets.............. | 3..d | .... | .... | † .9 | 1.3 | 3.1 | 2.8 | 2.9 | 313.1 | 255.1 | 285.4 | 338.4 | 376.7 |
| Central Bank: Other Liabs............... | 4..d | .... | .... | † — | — | — | — | — | — | — | — | — | — |
| Other Depository Corps.: Assets....... | 7a.d | .... | .... | † 2,695.8 | 3,745.0 | 3,971.4 | 4,061.0 | 4,049.1 | 3,796.0 | 3,760.1 | 4,474.9 | 4,433.3 | 4,365.5 |
| Other Depository Corps.: Liabs........ | 7b.d | .... | .... | † 182.8 | 180.6 | 212.9 | 343.6 | 234.3 | 367.1 | 449.0 | 554.6 | 420.0 | 541.9 |
| Other Financial Corps.: Assets.......... | 7e.d | .... | .... | .... | .... | .... | .... | .... | .... | 98.2 | 93.3 | 152.8 | 178.2 |
| Other Financial Corps.: Liabs............ | 7f.d | .... | .... | .... | .... | .... | .... | .... | .... | — | — | 35.7 | 57.4 |
| **Central Bank** |  | *Millions of US Dollars: End of Period* | | | | | | | | | | | |
| Net Foreign Assets........................ | 11n | 401.5 | 375.8 | † 352.8 | 444.4 | 980.1 | 1,027.2 | 936.2 | 811.3 | 919.2 | 970.6 | 1,010.8 | 957.7 |
| Claims on Nonresidents................. | 11 | 401.5 | 375.8 | † 352.8 | 444.4 | 980.1 | 1,027.2 | 936.2 | 811.3 | 919.2 | 970.6 | 1,010.8 | 957.7 |
| Liabilities to Nonresidents.............. | 16c | — | — | † — | — | — | — | — | — | — | — | — | — |
| Claims on Other Depository Corps... | 12e | 158.2 | 201.6 | † 193.4 | 308.3 | 195.9 | 253.9 | 216.7 | 209.3 | 179.4 | 197.6 | 146.2 | 309.2 |
| Net Claims on Central Government.. | 12an | 7.9 | 7.4 | † 6.9 | 6.4 | 5.5 | 4.4 | 3.3 | 3.1 | 2.9 | −63.0 | 2.6 | 2.5 |
| Claims on Central Government...... | 12a | 7.9 | 7.4 | † 6.9 | 6.5 | 5.6 | 4.6 | 3.5 | 3.4 | 3.4 | 3.3 | 3.2 | 3.1 |
| Liabilities to Central Government... | 16d | — | — | † — | .1 | .1 | .2 | .2 | .3 | .4 | 66.3 | .6 | .6 |
| Claims on Other Sectors................. | 12s | — | — | † .3 | .2 | .3 | .8 | .4 | .5 | .7 | 3.7 | 3.3 | 3.5 |
| Claims on Other Financial Corps.... | 12g | — | — | † — | — | — | — | — | — | — | — | — | — |
| Claims on State & Local Govts....... | 12b | — | — | † — | — | — | — | — | — | — | — | — | — |
| Claims on Public Nonfin. Corps...... | 12c | — | — | † — | — | — | — | — | — | — | — | — | — |
| Claims on Private Sector................ | 12d | — | — | † .3 | .2 | .3 | .8 | .4 | .5 | .7 | 3.6 | 3.3 | 3.5 |
| Monetary Base............................... | 14 | 530.0 | 539.6 | † 492.6 | 685.2 | 1,089.6 | 1,188.6 | 1,055.1 | 919.1 | 994.4 | 997.3 | 1,051.8 | 1,165.3 |
| Currency in Circulation.................. | 14a | — | — | † — | — | — | — | — | — | — | — | — | — |
| Liabs. to Other Depository Corps.... | 14c | 530.0 | 539.6 | † 492.3 | 684.8 | 1,089.0 | 1,187.4 | 1,053.8 | 917.1 | 992.1 | 995.0 | 1,030.1 | 1,120.2 |
| Liabilities to Other Sectors............. | 14d | — | — | † .3 | .4 | .6 | 1.2 | 1.4 | 1.9 | 2.4 | 2.3 | 21.7 | 45.1 |
| Other Liabs. to Other Dep. Corps..... | 14n | — | — | † .2 | .2 | .3 | .4 | .4 | .4 | .4 | .6 | 1.1 | 1.5 |
| Dep. & Sec. Excl. f/Monetary Base.... | 14o | — | — | † 2.9 | .1 | 2.1 | 2.4 | 2.4 | .3 | .3 | 1.7 | .3 | .4 |
| Deposits Included in Broad Money. | 15 | — | — | † 2.9 | .1 | 2.1 | 2.2 | 2.2 | — | — | 1.4 | — | — |
| Sec.Ot.th.Shares Incl.in Brd. Money | 16a | — | — | † — | — | — | — | — | — | — | — | — | — |
| Deposits Excl. from Broad Money. | 16b | — | — | † — | — | — | .2 | .2 | .3 | .3 | .3 | .3 | .3 |
| Sec.Ot.th.Shares Excl.f/Brd.Money.. | 16s | — | — | † — | — | — | — | — | — | — | — | — | — |
| Loans............................................ | 16l | — | — | † — | — | — | — | — | — | — | — | — | — |
| Financial Derivatives...................... | 16m | — | — | † — | — | — | — | — | — | — | — | — | — |
| Shares and Other Equity.................. | 17a | 37.0 | 45.7 | † 50.2 | 66.9 | 80.1 | 86.3 | 91.0 | 95.2 | 98.0 | 100.5 | 105.8 | 108.2 |
| Other Items (Net)............................ | 17r | .6 | −.5 | † 7.4 | 7.0 | 9.7 | 8.6 | 7.6 | 9.2 | 9.0 | 8.8 | 3.8 | −2.5 |
| Memo Item: |  |  |  |  |  |  |  |  |  |  |  |  |  |
| Total Assets.................................. | 10ra | .... | .... | † 560.9 | 766.9 | 1,189.8 | 1,292.9 | 1,167.9 | 1,037.4 | 1,117.2 | 1,193.8 | 1,188.5 | 1,306.9 |
| **Other Depository Corporations** |  | *Millions of US Dollars: End of Period* | | | | | | | | | | | |
| Net Foreign Assets........................ | 21n | 2,488.1 | 2,487.3 | † 2,513.0 | 3,564.4 | 3,758.5 | 3,717.4 | 3,814.7 | 3,428.9 | 3,311.1 | 3,920.3 | 4,013.3 | 3,823.6 |
| Claims on Nonresidents................ | 21 | 2,620.9 | 2,665.5 | † 2,695.8 | 3,745.0 | 3,971.4 | 4,061.0 | 4,049.1 | 3,796.0 | 3,760.1 | 4,474.9 | 4,433.3 | 4,365.5 |
| Liabilities to Nonresidents............. | 26c | 132.8 | 178.2 | † 182.8 | 180.6 | 212.9 | 343.6 | 234.3 | 367.1 | 449.0 | 554.6 | 420.0 | 541.9 |
| Claims on Central Bank.................. | 20 | 541.5 | 557.8 | † 521.7 | 703.1 | 1,111.3 | 1,215.9 | 1,074.8 | 940.9 | 998.9 | 997.6 | 1,041.5 | 1,134.1 |
| Currency..................................... | 20a | — | — | † — | — | — | — | — | — | — | — | — | — |
| Reserve Deposits and Securities..... | 20b | 541.5 | 557.8 | † 521.7 | 703.1 | 1,111.3 | 1,215.9 | 1,074.8 | 940.9 | 998.9 | 997.6 | 1,041.5 | 1,134.1 |
| Other Claims............................... | 20n | — | — | † — | — | — | — | — | — | — | — | — | — |
| Net Claims on Central Government.. | 22an | −12.2 | 38.3 | † 180.2 | 43.0 | 49.5 | 214.0 | 287.0 | 661.8 | 929.6 | 841.4 | 626.8 | 967.4 |
| Claims on Central Government...... | 22a | 383.3 | 545.2 | † 455.7 | 404.0 | 517.4 | 627.2 | 821.2 | 1,098.9 | 1,402.9 | 1,372.7 | 1,239.1 | 1,455.0 |
| Liabilities to Central Government... | 26d | 395.5 | 506.9 | † 275.5 | 361.0 | 467.9 | 413.2 | 534.1 | 437.1 | 473.3 | 531.3 | 612.3 | 487.6 |
| Claims on Other Sectors.................. | 22s | 1,105.7 | 1,412.2 | † 1,447.2 | 1,366.7 | 1,312.2 | 1,602.5 | 2,103.4 | 2,586.5 | 2,956.2 | 3,271.3 | 3,828.6 | 4,560.7 |
| Claims on Other Financial Corps.... | 22g | 4.3 | 4.3 | † 9.9 | 11.0 | 11.0 | 13.7 | 19.9 | 17.0 | 16.6 | 10.7 | 8.5 | 7.9 |
| Claims on State & Local Govts....... | 22b | 3.3 | 6.1 | † 5.6 | 8.5 | 5.2 | 1.3 | 1.4 | 1.8 | 4.5 | 1.3 | .7 | 1.1 |
| Claims on Public Nonfin. Corps...... | 22c | 33.9 | 46.2 | † 29.9 | 17.5 | 11.6 | 8.9 | 14.6 | .1 | — | 3.1 | — | — |
| Claims on Private Sector.............. | 22d | 1,064.1 | 1,355.6 | † 1,401.9 | 1,329.7 | 1,284.4 | 1,578.6 | 2,067.5 | 2,567.6 | 2,935.2 | 3,256.3 | 3,819.3 | 4,551.7 |
| Liabilities to Central Bank.............. | 26g | 146.5 | 190.5 | † 179.1 | 245.7 | 157.6 | 208.8 | 160.0 | 178.9 | 173.1 | 190.5 | 134.6 | 299.2 |
| Transf.Dep.Included in Broad Money | 24 | 1,215.9 | 1,325.1 | † 1,327.3 | 1,633.4 | 1,803.9 | 2,139.5 | 2,569.2 | 2,728.5 | 3,467.8 | 3,821.0 | 4,047.0 | 4,444.5 |
| Other Dep.Included in Broad Money. | 25 | 2,282.5 | 2,308.4 | † 2,523.0 | 3,006.3 | 3,444.2 | 3,424.3 | 3,527.2 | 3,611.2 | 3,300.4 | 3,672.6 | 3,966.8 | 4,377.8 |
| Sec.Ot.th.Shares Incl.in Brd. Money.. | 26a | — | 5.4 | † — | — | — | — | — | — | — | — | — | — |
| Deposits Excl. from Broad Money..... | 26b | — | — | † — | — | — | — | — | — | — | — | — | — |
| Sec.Ot.th.Shares Excl.f/Brd.Money.... | 26s | — | — | † — | — | — | — | — | — | — | — | — | — |
| Loans............................................ | 26l | — | — | † — | — | — | — | — | — | — | — | — | — |
| Financial Derivatives...................... | 26m | — | — | † — | — | — | — | — | — | — | — | — | — |
| Insurance Technical Reserves........... | 26r | — | — | † — | — | — | — | — | — | — | — | — | — |
| Shares and Other Equity.................. | 27a | 291.5 | 531.6 | † 596.8 | 685.7 | 807.8 | 967.8 | 1,095.5 | 1,182.0 | 1,257.5 | 1,361.7 | 1,456.9 | 1,454.5 |
| Other Items (Net)............................ | 27r | 186.7 | 134.6 | † 35.9 | 106.1 | 18.0 | 9.3 | −71.8 | −82.5 | −3.0 | −15.1 | −95.2 | −90.2 |
| Memo Item: |  |  |  |  |  |  |  |  |  |  |  |  |  |
| Total Assets................................... | 20ra | .... | .... | † 5,772.1 | 7,003.9 | 7,637.7 | 8,091.5 | 8,797.9 | 9,343.4 | 10,051.9 | 11,194.8 | 11,822.3 | 12,602.3 |

| | | 2004 | 2005 | 2006 | 2007 | 2008 | 2009 | 2010 | 2011 | 2012 | 2013 | 2014 | 2015 |
|---|---|---|---|---|---|---|---|---|---|---|---|---|---|
| **Depository Corporations** | | | | | *Millions of US Dollars: End of Period* | | | | | | | | |
| Net Foreign Assets.......................... | 31n | 2,895.2 | 2,855.8 | † 2,865.7 | 4,008.8 | 4,738.6 | 4,744.5 | 4,751.0 | 4,240.2 | 4,230.3 | 4,890.9 | 5,024.0 | 4,781.3 |
| Claims on Nonresidents................ | 31 | 3,028.0 | 3,033.9 | † 3,048.5 | 4,189.4 | 4,951.5 | 5,088.2 | 4,985.3 | 4,607.2 | 4,679.3 | 5,445.6 | 5,444.0 | 5,323.2 |
| Liabilities to Nonresidents............. | 36c | 132.8 | 178.2 | † 182.8 | 180.6 | 212.9 | 343.6 | 234.3 | 367.1 | 449.0 | 554.6 | 420.0 | 541.9 |
| Domestic Claims............................. | 32 | 1,100.6 | 1,457.3 | † 1,634.6 | 1,416.3 | 1,367.5 | 1,821.7 | 2,394.2 | 3,251.9 | 3,889.4 | 4,053.4 | 4,461.3 | 5,534.1 |
| Net Claims on Central Government | 32an | −5.0 | 45.1 | † 187.1 | 49.3 | 55.0 | 218.4 | 290.3 | 664.9 | 932.6 | 778.4 | 629.4 | 969.9 |
| Claims on Central Government.... | 32a | 390.7 | 552.1 | † 462.6 | 410.4 | 523.0 | 631.8 | 824.7 | 1,102.3 | 1,406.3 | 1,376.0 | 1,242.3 | 1,458.1 |
| Liabilities to Central Government. | 36d | 395.7 | 507.0 | † 275.6 | 361.1 | 468.0 | 413.4 | 534.4 | 437.4 | 473.7 | 597.6 | 612.9 | 488.2 |
| Claims on Other Sectors................. | 32s | 1,105.7 | 1,412.2 | † 1,447.5 | 1,367.0 | 1,312.4 | 1,603.3 | 2,103.9 | 2,587.0 | 2,956.9 | 3,275.0 | 3,831.9 | 4,564.2 |
| Claims on Other Financial Corps.. | 32g | 4.3 | 4.3 | † 9.9 | 11.0 | 11.0 | 13.7 | 19.9 | 17.0 | 16.6 | 10.7 | 8.5 | 7.9 |
| Claims on State & Local Govts..... | 32b | 3.3 | 6.1 | † 5.6 | 8.5 | 5.2 | 1.3 | 1.4 | 1.8 | 4.5 | 1.3 | .7 | 1.1 |
| Claims on Public Nonfin. Corps.. | 32c | 33.9 | 46.2 | † 29.9 | 17.5 | 11.6 | 8.9 | 14.6 | .1 | — | 3.1 | — | — |
| Claims on Private Sector.............. | 32d | 1,064.1 | 1,355.6 | † 1,402.2 | 1,329.9 | 1,284.7 | 1,579.4 | 2,067.9 | 2,568.1 | 2,935.8 | 3,259.9 | 3,822.6 | 4,555.1 |
| Broad Money Liabilities................. | 35l | 3,498.4 | 3,639.0 | † 3,853.6 | 4,640.2 | 5,250.7 | 5,567.2 | 6,099.9 | 6,341.7 | 6,770.6 | 7,497.2 | 8,035.5 | 8,867.5 |
| Currency Outside Depository Corps | 34a | — | — | † — | — | — | — | — | — | — | — | — | — |
| Transferable Deposits.................... | 34 | 1,215.9 | 1,325.1 | † 1,327.4 | 1,633.4 | 1,803.9 | 2,139.6 | 2,569.2 | 2,728.7 | 3,468.7 | 3,821.7 | 4,062.0 | 4,479.3 |
| Other Deposits.............................. | 35 | 2,282.5 | 2,308.4 | † 2,526.2 | 3,006.7 | 3,446.8 | 3,427.6 | 3,530.7 | 3,613.0 | 3,301.9 | 3,675.5 | 3,973.5 | 4,388.2 |
| Securities Other than Shares.......... | 36a | — | 5.4 | † — | — | — | — | — | — | — | — | — | — |
| Deposits Excl. from Broad Money..... | 36b | — | — | † — | — | — | .2 | .2 | .3 | .3 | .3 | .3 | .3 |
| Sec.Ot.th.Shares Excl.f/Brd.Money.... | 36s | — | — | † — | — | — | — | — | — | — | — | — | — |
| Loans............................................. | 36l | — | — | † — | — | — | — | — | — | — | — | — | — |
| Financial Derivatives...................... | 36m | — | — | † — | — | — | — | — | — | — | — | — | — |
| Insurance Technical Reserves.......... | 36r | — | — | † — | — | — | — | — | — | — | — | — | — |
| Shares and Other Equity................. | 37a | 335.8 | 590.4 | † 647.0 | 752.6 | 888.0 | 1,054.1 | 1,186.6 | 1,277.2 | 1,355.5 | 1,462.2 | 1,562.7 | 1,562.7 |
| Other Items (Net).......................... | 37r | 161.6 | 83.7 | † −.3 | 32.3 | −32.7 | −55.3 | −141.5 | −127.0 | −6.7 | −15.4 | −113.3 | −115.2 |
| Broad Money Liabs., Seasonally Adj. | 35l.b | 3,514.3 | 3,647.4 | † 3,850.9 | 4,636.0 | 5,244.5 | 5,555.9 | 6,085.5 | 6,325.5 | 6,759.2 | 7,488.9 | 8,033.6 | 8,867.0 |
| **Other Financial Corporations** | | | | | | *Millions of US Dollars: End of Period* | | | | | | | |
| Net Foreign Assets.......................... | 41n | .... | .... | .... | .... | .... | .... | .... | .... | 98.2 | 93.3 | 117.0 | 120.8 |
| Claims on Nonresidents................ | 41 | .... | .... | .... | .... | .... | .... | .... | .... | 98.2 | 93.3 | 152.8 | 178.2 |
| Liabilities to Nonresidents............. | 46c | .... | .... | .... | .... | .... | .... | .... | .... | — | — | 35.7 | 57.4 |
| Claims on Depository Corporations.. | 40 | .... | .... | .... | .... | .... | .... | .... | .... | 70.3 | 79.9 | 237.8 | 201.1 |
| Net Claims on Central Government... | 42an | .... | .... | .... | .... | .... | .... | .... | .... | 2.6 | 8.4 | 115.3 | 102.3 |
| Claims on Central Government...... | 42a | .... | .... | .... | .... | .... | .... | .... | .... | 16.1 | 17.7 | 123.2 | 105.9 |
| Liabilities to Central Government... | 46d | .... | .... | .... | .... | .... | .... | .... | .... | 13.5 | 9.2 | 7.9 | 3.6 |
| Claims on Other Sectors................. | 42s | .... | .... | .... | .... | .... | .... | .... | .... | 80.0 | 95.6 | 561.4 | 550.5 |
| Claims on State & Local Govts....... | 42b | .... | .... | .... | .... | .... | .... | .... | .... | — | — | — | — |
| Claims on Public Nonfin. Corps... | 42c | .... | .... | .... | .... | .... | .... | .... | .... | — | — | — | — |
| Claims on Private Sector.............. | 42d | .... | .... | .... | .... | .... | .... | .... | .... | 80.0 | 95.6 | 561.4 | 550.5 |
| Deposits......................................... | 46b | .... | .... | .... | .... | .... | .... | .... | .... | — | — | — | — |
| Securities Other than Shares........... | 46s | .... | .... | .... | .... | .... | .... | .... | .... | — | — | — | — |
| Loans............................................. | 46l | .... | .... | .... | .... | .... | .... | .... | .... | — | — | 64.9 | 69.8 |
| Financial Derivatives...................... | 46m | .... | .... | .... | .... | .... | .... | .... | .... | — | — | — | — |
| Insurance Technical Reserves.......... | 46r | .... | .... | .... | .... | .... | .... | .... | .... | 160.3 | 177.9 | 170.1 | 164.2 |
| Shares and Other Equity................. | 47a | .... | .... | .... | .... | .... | .... | .... | .... | 108.9 | 119.8 | 997.0 | 992.0 |
| Other Items (Net)........................... | 47r | .... | .... | .... | .... | .... | .... | .... | .... | −18.1 | −20.4 | −200.4 | −251.2 |
| Memo Item: | | | | | | | | | | | | | |
| Total Assets................................... | 40ra | .... | .... | .... | .... | .... | .... | .... | .... | 352.9 | 380.2 | 1,448.6 | 1,453.6 |
| **Monetary Aggregates** | | | | | | *Millions of US Dollars: End of Period* | | | | | | | |
| Broad Money.................................. | 59m | .... | .... | 3,853.6 | 4,640.2 | 5,250.7 | 5,567.2 | 6,099.9 | 6,341.7 | 6,770.6 | 7,497.2 | 8,035.5 | 8,867.5 |
| o/w:Currency Issued by Cent.Govt | 59m.a | .... | .... | — | — | — | — | — | — | — | — | — | — |
| o/w: Dep.in Nonfin. Corporations. | 59m.b | .... | .... | — | — | — | — | — | — | — | — | — | — |
| o/w:Secs. Issued by Central Govt.. | 59m.c | .... | .... | — | — | — | — | — | — | — | — | — | — |
| Money (National Definitions) | | | | | | | | | | | | | |
| Monetary Base............................ | 19mb | 530.0 | 539.6 | 492.6 | 685.2 | 1,089.6 | 1,188.6 | 1,055.1 | 919.1 | 994.4 | 997.3 | 1,051.8 | 1,165.3 |
| Broad Money (M2)...................... | 59mea | .... | .... | .... | .... | 6,618.9 | 6,898.7 | 7,558.4 | 7,821.6 | 8,581.1 | 9,387.3 | 9,249.4 | 10,153.3 |
| **Interest Rates** | | | | | | *Percent Per Annum* | | | | | | | |
| Deposit Rate................................... | 60l | 1.12 | 2.24 | 2.97 | 3.02 | .81 | .40 | .29 | .53 | .46 | .62 | .83 | .95 |
| Lending Rate.................................. | 60p | 6.92 | 7.34 | 7.73 | 7.98 | 7.19 | 6.19 | 6.24 | 6.79 | 6.97 | 7.52 | 6.41 | 6.80 |
| **Prices and Labor** | | | | | | *Index Numbers (2010=100): Period Averages* | | | | | | | |
| Consumer Prices............................. | 64 | 77.5 | 80.7 | 83.8 | 85.4 | 93.8 | 96.4 | 100.0 | 102.9 | 105.7 | 107.6 | 109.4 | 111.0 |
| | | | | | | *Number in Thousands: Period Averages* | | | | | | | |
| Labor Force.................................... | 67d | 836 | 827 | 872 | .... | .... | 951 | 976 | 1,059 | 1,114 | 1,119 | 1,255 | 1,299 |
| Employment................................... | 67e | 612 | 633 | 667 | .... | .... | 717 | 744 | 837 | 858 | 849 | 917 | 963 |
| Unemployment............................... | 67c | 224 | 194 | 206 | .... | .... | 233 | 232 | 222 | 256 | 270 | 338 | 336 |
| Unemployment Rate (%)................. | 67r | 26.8 | 23.5 | 23.6 | 21.6 | 26.0 | 24.5 | 23.7 | 20.9 | 23.0 | 24.1 | 26.9 | 25.9 |

| | | 2004 | 2005 | 2006 | 2007 | 2008 | 2009 | 2010 | 2011 | 2012 | 2013 | 2014 | 2015 |
|---|---|---|---|---|---|---|---|---|---|---|---|---|---|
| **Balance of Payments** | | | | | | | *Millions of US Dollars* | | | | | | |
| A. Current Account* | 109bx | −1,587.9 | −1,365.3 | −1,233.5 | −418.5 | 380.6 | −1,143.4 | −1,306.9 | −2,069.5 | −1,821.1 | −2,383.7 | −1,386.8 | .... |
| Goods, credit (exports) | 1a9cx | 370.9 | 498.1 | 556.7 | 807.2 | 811.0 | 803.0 | 816.5 | 1,051.1 | 1,133.8 | 1,133.4 | 1,255.9 | .... |
| Goods, debit (imports) | 1a9dx | 2,624.8 | 3,116.6 | 3,223.0 | 3,645.2 | 3,943.1 | 4,176.6 | 4,271.0 | 4,832.1 | 5,270.9 | 5,816.4 | 6,651.7 | .... |
| Balance on goods | 1a9bx | −2,253.9 | −2,618.5 | −2,666.3 | −2,837.9 | −3,132.1 | −3,373.7 | −3,454.5 | −3,781.0 | −4,137.1 | −4,683.0 | −5,395.8 | .... |
| Services, credit (exports) | 1b9cx | 225.9 | 225.2 | 179.6 | 259.0 | 354.0 | 330.3 | 550.8 | 748.3 | 737.3 | 938.5 | 1,042.0 | .... |
| Services, debit (imports) | 1b9dx | 512.6 | 457.4 | 460.3 | 638.9 | 702.2 | 766.6 | 993.3 | 891.0 | 1,029.3 | 987.9 | 1,129.8 | .... |
| Balance on Goods & Services | 1z9bx | −2,540.6 | −2,850.6 | −2,947.1 | −3,217.8 | −3,480.3 | −3,809.9 | −3,897.0 | −3,923.7 | −4,429.1 | −4,732.5 | −5,483.6 | .... |
| Primary income: credit | 1c9cx | 260.1 | 384.0 | 431.1 | 560.4 | 674.6 | 605.2 | 714.1 | 843.7 | 941.4 | 1,263.8 | 1,482.4 | .... |
| Primary income: debit | 1c9dx | 32.0 | 35.1 | 8.5 | 7.8 | 3.2 | 79.6 | 115.0 | 94.2 | 83.9 | 103.5 | 101.1 | .... |
| Balance on gds, serv. & prim. inc. | 1y9bx | −2,312.5 | −2,501.7 | −2,524.4 | −2,665.2 | −2,808.9 | −3,284.3 | −3,297.9 | −3,174.2 | −3,571.6 | −3,572.2 | −4,102.3 | .... |
| Secondary income: credit | 1d9ca | 848.5 | 1,229.6 | 1,395.9 | 2,359.1 | 3,312.6 | 2,336.6 | 2,247.1 | 1,668.8 | 2,331.5 | 1,862.9 | 3,170.3 | .... |
| Secondary income: debit | 1d9da | 123.9 | 93.2 | 105.0 | 112.4 | 123.1 | 195.7 | 256.1 | 564.1 | 581.1 | 674.4 | 454.8 | .... |
| B. Capital Account* | 209ba | 659.7 | 386.1 | 272.2 | 394.8 | 390.9 | 713.0 | 828.1 | 640.0 | 560.2 | 545.7 | 322.5 | .... |
| Capital account: credit | 209ca | 659.7 | 386.1 | 272.2 | 394.8 | 390.9 | 713.0 | 828.1 | 640.0 | 560.2 | 545.7 | 322.5 | .... |
| Capital account: debit | 209da | .... | .... | .... | .... | .... | .... | .... | .... | — | .... | .... | .... |
| Balance on current & capital acct. | 129bx | −928.3 | −979.2 | −961.2 | −23.7 | 771.5 | −430.4 | −478.8 | −1,429.5 | −1,260.9 | −1,838.0 | −1,064.3 | .... |
| C. Financial Account* | 309na | −871.3 | −892.2 | −968.3 | 33.6 | 674.4 | −425.1 | −237.9 | −1,361.9 | −1,100.4 | −1,614.5 | −1,050.6 | .... |
| Direct investment: assets | 3a9aa | −37.4 | 32.2 | 129.4 | 35.2 | −4.3 | 69.3 | 58.1 | −238.5 | 33.7 | −34.5 | −29.6 | .... |
| Equity & investment fund shares | 3aaaa | −37.4 | 32.2 | 129.4 | 35.2 | −4.3 | 69.3 | 84.0 | −246.7 | 30.5 | −50.5 | −29.6 | .... |
| Debt instruments | 3abaa | .... | .... | .... | .... | .... | .... | −25.9 | 8.2 | 3.2 | 16.0 | .... | .... |
| Direct investment: liabilities | 3a9la | 20.5 | 36.2 | 18.6 | 19.6 | 51.5 | 300.5 | 179.9 | 238.8 | 63.0 | 189.6 | 126.5 | .... |
| Equity & investment fund shares . | 3aala | 20.5 | 29.0 | 18.6 | 19.6 | 51.5 | 300.5 | 179.9 | 238.8 | 63.0 | 189.6 | 126.5 | .... |
| Debt instruments | 3abla | .... | 7.2 | .... | .... | .... | .... | .... | .... | — | .... | .... | .... |
| Portfolio investment: assets | 3b9aa | 15.9 | 15.3 | 4.9 | 138.1 | 116.3 | 258.3 | 364.5 | 120.4 | 42.0 | −103.2 | 127.1 | .... |
| Equity & investment fund shares | 3baaa | 11.5 | −8.7 | −6.6 | 107.0 | −48.8 | — | −1.8 | 30.8 | 64.0 | −152.4 | −15.9 | .... |
| Debt securities | 3bbaa | 4.4 | 24.0 | 11.5 | 31.0 | 165.1 | 258.3 | 366.3 | 89.5 | −22.1 | 49.2 | 143.0 | .... |
| Portfolio investment: liabilities | 3b9la | 7.8 | 13.7 | .... | .... | .... | 77.5 | −2.9 | −.7 | 25.8 | 83.6 | 71.7 | .... |
| Equity & investment fund shares . | 3bala | 7.8 | 13.7 | .... | .... | .... | 77.5 | −2.9 | −.7 | 25.8 | 83.6 | 53.3 | .... |
| Debt securities | 3bbla | .... | .... | .... | .... | .... | .... | .... | .... | — | .... | 18.4 | .... |
| Fin. der.& empl.stk.ops.(ESOs): net. | 3c9na | .... | .... | .... | .... | .... | .... | .... | .... | .... | .... | .... | .... |
| Fin. der. & ESOs.: assets | 3c9aa | .... | .... | .... | .... | .... | .... | .... | .... | .... | .... | .... | .... |
| Fin. der. & ESOs.: liabilities | 3c9la | .... | .... | .... | .... | .... | .... | .... | .... | .... | .... | .... | .... |
| Other investment: assets | 3d9aa | −750.7 | −777.5 | −1,085.5 | −139.1 | 622.0 | −192.4 | −641.6 | −736.7 | −1,021.5 | −885.7 | −807.0 | .... |
| Other equity | 3daaa | .... | .... | .... | .... | .... | .... | .... | .... | .... | .... | .... | .... |
| Debt instruments | 3dzaa | −750.7 | −777.5 | −1,085.5 | −139.1 | 622.0 | −192.4 | −641.6 | −736.7 | −1,021.5 | −885.7 | −807.0 | .... |
| Other investment: liabilities | 3d9la | 70.7 | 112.1 | −1.5 | −19.1 | 8.1 | 182.4 | −158.2 | 268.8 | 65.8 | 318.0 | 142.8 | .... |
| Other equity | 3dala | .... | .... | .... | .... | .... | .... | .... | .... | .... | .... | .... | .... |
| Debt instruments | 3dzla | 70.7 | 112.1 | −1.5 | −19.1 | 8.1 | 182.4 | −158.2 | 268.8 | 65.8 | 318.0 | 142.8 | .... |
| Curr.+ cap.− finan. acct. balance.. | 4y9na | −57.0 | −87.0 | 7.0 | −57.4 | 97.1 | −5.3 | −240.9 | −67.6 | −160.5 | −223.5 | −13.7 | .... |
| D. Net Errors and Omissions | 409na | 51.2 | 94.4 | 13.1 | 17.1 | −250.0 | −5.8 | 277.3 | 33.9 | 298.5 | 239.1 | −6.8 | .... |
| E. Reserves and Related Items | 4z9na | −5.9 | 7.4 | 20.1 | −40.3 | −152.9 | −11.1 | 36.4 | −33.7 | 138.0 | 15.6 | −20.5 | .... |
| Reserve assets | 3e9aa | −5.9 | 7.4 | 20.1 | −40.3 | −152.9 | −11.1 | 36.4 | −33.7 | 166.0 | 21.2 | −12.9 | .... |
| Credit and loans from the IMF | 3dcla | .... | .... | .... | .... | .... | .... | .... | .... | .... | .... | .... | .... |
| Exceptional financing | 409la | .... | .... | .... | .... | .... | .... | .... | .... | 28.0 | 5.6 | 7.6 | .... |
| *Excludes components in group E | | | | | | | | | | | | | |

| | | 2004 | 2005 | 2006 | 2007 | 2008 | 2009 | 2010 | 2011 | 2012 | 2013 | 2014 | 2015 |
|---|---|---|---|---|---|---|---|---|---|---|---|---|---|
| **International Investment Position** | | | | | | | *Millions of US Dollars* | | | | | | |
| Assets | 809aa | .... | .... | .... | .... | .... | 5,569.4 | 5,428.0 | 5,237.3 | 5,264.1 | † 5,828.2 | 5,950.0 | .... |
| Direct investment | 8a9aa | .... | .... | .... | .... | .... | 148.9 | 245.9 | 196.1 | 233.9 | † 171.0 | 167.0 | .... |
| Equity & investment fund shares.. | 8aaaa | .... | .... | .... | .... | .... | 148.9 | 240.5 | 190.9 | 231.9 | † 171.0 | 167.0 | .... |
| Debt instruments | 8abaa | .... | .... | .... | .... | .... | — | 5.3 | 5.2 | 2.0 | .... | .... | .... |
| Portfolio investment | 8b9aa | .... | .... | .... | .... | .... | 761.2 | 806.3 | 1,147.5 | 1,030.0 | † 1,005.3 | 1,183.5 | .... |
| Equity & investment fund shares.. | 8baaa | .... | .... | .... | .... | .... | 205.0 | 203.2 | 234.0 | 298.0 | † 145.6 | 132.9 | .... |
| Debt securities | 8bbaa | .... | .... | .... | .... | .... | 556.2 | 603.2 | 913.5 | 732.0 | † 859.8 | 1,050.6 | .... |
| Fin. der.(oth.than reserves) & ESOs | 8c9aa | .... | .... | .... | .... | .... | .... | .... | .... | .... | .... | .... | .... |
| Other investment | 8d9aa | .... | .... | .... | .... | .... | 4,163.8 | 3,845.2 | 3,396.6 | 3,336.2 | † 3,966.6 | 3,927.1 | .... |
| Other equity | 8daaa | .... | .... | .... | .... | .... | .... | .... | .... | .... | .... | .... | .... |
| Debt instruments | 8dzaa | .... | .... | .... | .... | .... | 4,163.8 | 3,845.2 | 3,396.6 | 3,336.2 | † 3,966.6 | 3,927.1 | .... |
| Reserve assets | 8e9aa | .... | .... | .... | .... | .... | 495.4 | 530.6 | 497.0 | 664.0 | † 685.2 | 672.3 | .... |
| Liabilities | 809la | .... | .... | .... | .... | .... | 4,007.7 | 4,142.1 | 4,516.3 | 4,596.7 | † 4,947.6 | 4,715.5 | .... |
| Direct investment | 8a9la | .... | .... | .... | .... | .... | 1,958.7 | 2,180.2 | 2,331.8 | 2,338.2 | † 2,458.6 | 2,453.0 | .... |
| Equity & investment fund shares.. | 8aala | .... | .... | .... | .... | .... | 1,957.2 | 2,147.4 | 2,307.4 | 2,320.2 | † 2,458.6 | 2,453.0 | .... |
| Debt instruments | 8abla | .... | .... | .... | .... | .... | 1.5 | 32.7 | 24.4 | 18.0 | .... | .... | .... |
| Portfolio investment | 8b9la | .... | .... | .... | .... | .... | 614.8 | 611.9 | 611.2 | 675.5 | † 768.2 | 709.6 | .... |
| Equity & investment fund shares.. | 8bala | .... | .... | .... | .... | .... | 614.8 | 611.9 | 611.2 | 675.5 | † 768.2 | 709.6 | .... |
| Debt securities | 8bbla | .... | .... | .... | .... | .... | .... | .... | .... | .... | .... | .... | .... |
| Fin. der.(oth.than reserves) & ESOs | 8c9la | .... | .... | .... | .... | .... | .... | .... | .... | .... | .... | .... | .... |
| Other investment | 8d9la | .... | .... | .... | .... | .... | 1,434.1 | 1,350.1 | 1,573.3 | 1,583.0 | † 1,720.8 | 1,552.8 | .... |
| Other equity | 8dala | .... | .... | .... | .... | .... | .... | .... | .... | .... | .... | .... | .... |
| Debt instruments | 8dzla | .... | .... | .... | .... | .... | 1,434.1 | 1,350.1 | 1,573.3 | 1,583.0 | † 1,720.8 | 1,552.8 | .... |

# West Bank and Gaza   487

| | | 2004 | 2005 | 2006 | 2007 | 2008 | 2009 | 2010 | 2011 | 2012 | 2013 | 2014 | 2015 |
|---|---|---|---|---|---|---|---|---|---|---|---|---|---|
| **Government Finance** | | | | | | | | | | | | | |
| **Operations Statement** | | | | | | | | | | | | | |
| **Budgetary Central Government** | | | | | *Millions of US Dollars: Fiscal Year Ends December 31* | | | | | | | |
| Revenue......................... | a1 | . . . . | . . . . | 1,886.8 | 2,181.0 | 3,596.0 | 3,094.3 | 3,277.5 | 3,134.8 | 2,951.2 | 3,640.6 | 4,032.8 | . . . . |
| Taxes................................ | a11 | . . . . | . . . . | 1,006.6 | 1,048.0 | 1,211.5 | 1,491.4 | 1,816.3 | 1,966.7 | 1,984.3 | 2,164.8 | 2,599.0 | . . . . |
| Social Contributions...................... | a12 | . . . . | . . . . | — | — | — | — | — | — | — | — | — | . . . . |
| Grants................................ | a13 | . . . . | . . . . | 670.2 | 1,012.0 | 1,809.4 | 1,416.5 | 1,288.7 | 1,054.9 | 955.0 | 1,358.2 | 1,231.3 | . . . . |
| Other Revenue.............................. | a14 | . . . . | . . . . | 210.0 | 121.0 | 575.1 | 186.4 | 172.5 | 113.2 | 11.9 | 117.6 | 202.4 | . . . . |
| Expense............................... | a2 | . . . . | . . . . | 2,298.0 | 2,238.0 | 3,036.0 | 3,010.5 | 3,073.5 | 3,153.5 | 3,137.5 | 3,405.7 | 3,725.1 | . . . . |
| Compensation of Employees...... | a21 | . . . . | . . . . | 1,189.3 | 1,443.0 | 2,032.8 | 1,551.4 | 1,738.4 | 1,954.9 | 1,928.8 | 2,080.5 | 2,248.2 | . . . . |
| Use of Goods & Services............... | a22 | . . . . | . . . . | 239.3 | 344.0 | 370.7 | 348.7 | 460.0 | 531.5 | 521.6 | 493.2 | 555.5 | . . . . |
| Consumption of Fixed Capital........ | a23 | . . . . | . . . . | . . . . | . . . . | . . . . | . . . . | . . . . | . . . . | . . . . | . . . . | . . . . | . . . . |
| Interest........................................ | a24 | . . . . | . . . . | 55.2 | 33.0 | 38.6 | 57.2 | 45.4 | 59.6 | 69.0 | 89.3 | 70.0 | . . . . |
| Subsidies...................................... | a25 | . . . . | . . . . | 375.7 | — | 40.3 | — | — | .1 | 8.8 | — | 8.4 | . . . . |
| Grants........................................ | a26 | . . . . | . . . . | — | — | — | 70.9 | 9.2 | 24.8 | 9.6 | 17.9 | 28.8 | . . . . |
| Social Benefits............................... | a27 | . . . . | . . . . | 200.5 | 180.0 | 514.8 | 577.7 | 479.7 | 480.6 | 530.7 | 674.9 | 746.3 | . . . . |
| Other Expense............................... | a28 | . . . . | . . . . | 238.0 | 238.0 | 39.0 | 404.6 | 340.7 | 102.2 | 69.1 | 50.1 | 68.0 | . . . . |
| Gross Operating Balance [1-2+23]... | agob | . . . . | . . . . | −411.2 | −57.0 | 559.8 | 83.8 | 204.0 | −18.7 | −186.3 | 234.9 | 307.6 | . . . . |
| Net Operating Balance [1-2].......... | anob | . . . . | . . . . | . . . . | . . . . | . . . . | . . . . | . . . . | . . . . | . . . . | . . . . | . . . . | . . . . |
| Net Acq. of Nonfinancial Assets....... | a31 | . . . . | . . . . | 12.0 | 9.0 | 74.9 | 49.9 | 27.9 | 205.4 | 133.4 | 114.0 | 143.3 | . . . . |
| Aquisition of Nonfin. Assets........... | a31.1 | . . . . | . . . . | . . . . | . . . . | . . . . | . . . . | . . . . | . . . . | . . . . | . . . . | . . . . | . . . . |
| Disposal of Nonfin. Assets............. | a31.2 | . . . . | . . . . | . . . . | . . . . | . . . . | . . . . | . . . . | . . . . | . . . . | . . . . | . . . . | . . . . |
| Net Lending/Borrowing [1-2-31]...... | anlb | . . . . | . . . . | −423.2 | −66.0 | 485.0 | 34.0 | 176.0 | −224.1 | −319.7 | 120.9 | 164.4 | . . . . |
| Net Acq. of Financial Assets............. | a32 | . . . . | . . . . | 487.5 | −144.0 | 458.2 | 479.6 | 484.0 | 541.0 | 576.3 | 374.3 | 582.8 | . . . . |
| By instrument | | | | | | | | | | | | | |
| Monetary Gold & SDRs................. | a3201 | . . . . | . . . . | — | — | — | — | — | — | — | — | — | . . . . |
| Currency & Deposits...................... | a3202 | . . . . | . . . . | . . . . | 11.0 | — | 56.5 | 210.6 | 358.0 | 18.2 | 94.4 | 312.8 | . . . . |
| Securities other than Shares........... | a3203 | . . . . | . . . . | . . . . | — | — | — | — | — | — | — | — | . . . . |
| Loans.......................................... | a3204 | . . . . | . . . . | . . . . | — | — | — | — | 164.7 | 305.4 | 207.6 | 173.8 | . . . . |
| Shares & Other Equity.................... | a3205 | . . . . | . . . . | . . . . | — | — | — | — | — | — | — | — | . . . . |
| Insurance Technical Reserves......... | a3206 | . . . . | . . . . | . . . . | — | — | — | — | — | — | — | — | . . . . |
| Financial Derivatives..................... | a3207 | . . . . | . . . . | . . . . | — | — | — | — | — | — | — | — | . . . . |
| Other Accounts Receivable............. | a3208 | . . . . | . . . . | . . . . | −155.0 | 458.2 | 423.1 | 273.4 | 18.3 | 252.7 | 72.3 | 96.1 | . . . . |
| By debtor | | | | | | | | | | | | | |
| Domestic.................................... | a321 | . . . . | . . . . | 60.9 | 278.0 | 445.0 | 442.0 | 436.3 | 529.8 | 552.5 | 321.9 | 489.8 | . . . . |
| Foreign....................................... | a322 | . . . . | . . . . | 426.6 | −422.0 | 13.2 | 37.6 | 47.7 | 11.2 | 23.9 | 52.4 | 93.0 | . . . . |
| Net Incurrence of Liabilities.............. | a33 | . . . . | . . . . | 910.6 | −78.0 | −26.7 | 445.9 | 294.3 | 752.2 | 893.5 | 253.4 | 410.0 | . . . . |
| By instrument | | | | | | | | | | | | | |
| Special Drawing Rights (SDRs)....... | a3301 | . . . . | . . . . | . . . . | — | — | — | — | — | — | — | — | . . . . |
| Currency & Deposits...................... | a3302 | . . . . | . . . . | . . . . | — | — | 139.8 | 96.0 | 262.6 | 235.0 | — | — | . . . . |
| Securities other than Shares........... | a3303 | . . . . | . . . . | . . . . | — | — | — | — | — | — | — | — | . . . . |
| Loans.......................................... | a3304 | . . . . | . . . . | . . . . | — | −262.3 | 120.0 | −28.5 | 330.0 | 62.6 | −225.9 | −5.0 | . . . . |
| Shares & Other Equity.................... | a3305 | . . . . | . . . . | . . . . | — | — | — | — | — | — | — | — | . . . . |
| Insurance Technical Reserves......... | a3306 | . . . . | . . . . | . . . . | — | — | — | — | — | — | — | — | . . . . |
| Financial Derivatives..................... | a3307 | . . . . | . . . . | . . . . | — | — | — | — | — | — | — | — | . . . . |
| Other Accounts Payable................. | a3308 | . . . . | . . . . | . . . . | −78.0 | 235.6 | 186.1 | 226.9 | 159.7 | 595.9 | 479.2 | 415.0 | . . . . |
| By creditor | | | | | | | | | | | | | |
| Domestic.................................... | a331 | . . . . | . . . . | 910.6 | −78.0 | −22.6 | 445.9 | 312.3 | 681.1 | 731.0 | 207.4 | 420.3 | . . . . |
| Foreign....................................... | a332 | . . . . | . . . . | — | — | −4.1 | — | −18.0 | 71.2 | 162.5 | 46.0 | −10.3 | . . . . |
| Stat. Discrepancy [32-33-NLB]........ | anlbz | . . . . | . . . . | — | — | — | — | −.3 | 13.7 | 12.9 | 2.6 | — | 8.4 | . . . . |
| Memo Item: Expenditure [2+31]...... | a2m | . . . . | . . . . | 2,310.0 | 2,247.0 | 3,111.1 | 3,060.3 | 3,101.4 | 3,358.9 | 3,270.9 | 3,519.7 | 3,868.4 | . . . . |
| | | | | *Millions: Midyear Estimates* | | | | | | | | | |
| **Population...............................** | 99z | 3.51 | 3.58 | 3.66 | 3.75 | 3.85 | 3.96 | 4.07 | 4.18 | 4.30 | 4.42 | 4.54 | 4.67 |

# Yemen, Republic of   474

| | | 2004 | 2005 | 2006 | 2007 | 2008 | 2009 | 2010 | 2011 | 2012 | 2013 | 2014 | 2015 |
|---|---|---|---|---|---|---|---|---|---|---|---|---|---|
| **Exchange Rates** | | | | | | | *Rial per SDR: End of Period* | | | | | | |
| Market Rate | aa | 288.66 | 278.82 | 298.62 | 315.32 | 308.18 | 325.01 | 329.26 | 328.24 | 330.27 | 330.93 | 311.33 | 297.78 |
| | | | | | | *Rial per US Dollar: End of Period (ae) Period Average (rf)* | | | | | | | |
| Market Rate | ae | 185.87 | 195.08 | 198.50 | 199.54 | 200.08 | 207.32 | 213.80 | 213.80 | 214.89 | 214.89 | 214.89 | 214.89 |
| Market Rate | rf | 184.78 | 191.51 | 197.05 | 198.95 | 199.76 | 202.85 | 219.59 | 213.80 | 214.35 | 214.89 | 214.89 | 214.89 |
| **Fund Position** | | | | | | | *Millions of SDRs: End of Period* | | | | | | |
| Quota | 2f.s | 243.50 | 243.50 | 243.50 | 243.50 | 243.50 | 243.50 | 243.50 | 243.50 | 243.50 | 243.50 | 243.50 | 243.50 |
| SDR Holdings | 1b.s | 33.03 | 13.18 | 4.72 | — | .27 | 200.03 | 182.17 | 165.40 | 165.17 | 163.23 | 152.53 | 76.97 |
| Reserve Position in the Fund | 1c.s | .01 | — | .01 | .01 | .01 | .01 | .01 | .01 | .01 | .01 | .01 | .01 |
| Total Fund Cred.&Loans Outstg | 2tl | 242.25 | 204.50 | 163.67 | 107.08 | 61.88 | 33.50 | 50.54 | 34.79 | 95.67 | 95.67 | 144.42 | 144.42 |
| SDR Allocations | 1bd | 28.74 | 28.74 | 28.74 | 28.74 | 28.74 | 232.25 | 232.25 | 232.25 | 232.25 | 232.25 | 232.25 | 232.25 |
| **International Liquidity** | | | | | | *Millions of US Dollars Unless Otherwise Indicated: End of Period* | | | | | | | |
| Total Reserves minus Gold | 1l.d | 5,664.8 | 6,115.4 | 7,511.5 | 7,715.4 | 8,111.4 | 6,935.6 | 5,868.4 | 4,448.9 | 6,067.6 | 5,284.1 | . . . . | . . . . |
| SDR Holdings | 1b.d | 51.3 | 18.8 | 7.1 | — | .4 | 313.6 | 280.5 | 253.9 | 253.8 | 251.4 | 221.0 | 106.7 |
| Reserve Position in the Fund | 1c.d | — | — | — | — | — | — | — | — | — | — | — | — |
| Foreign Exchange | 1d.d | 5,613.5 | 6,096.6 | 7,504.4 | 7,715.4 | 8,110.9 | 6,622.0 | 5,587.8 | 4,195.0 | 5,813.7 | 5,032.7 | . . . . | . . . . |
| Gold (Million Fine Troy Ounces) | 1ad | .050 | .050 | .050 | .050 | .050 | .050 | .050 | .050 | .050 | .050 | . . . . | . . . . |
| Gold (National Valuation) | 1and | 23.4 | 27.2 | 32.9 | 44.2 | 46.1 | 57.4 | 74.4 | 82.4 | 90.0 | 65.3 | . . . . | . . . . |
| Monetary Authorities: Other Liabs. | 4..d | 139.2 | 144.6 | 150.3 | 159.3 | 164.2 | 167.3 | 174.4 | 181.4 | 1,187.0 | 1,193.2 | . . . . | . . . . |
| Deposit Money Banks: Assets | 7a.d | 888.4 | 875.3 | 1,387.4 | 1,394.5 | 1,542.6 | 2,064.1 | 2,387.0 | 2,233.2 | 2,520.6 | 2,558.7 | . . . . | . . . . |
| Deposit Money Banks: Liabs | 7b.d | 52.6 | 61.5 | 98.3 | 138.6 | 158.2 | 124.6 | 157.1 | 78.8 | 132.6 | 177.6 | . . . . | . . . . |
| **Monetary Authorities** | | | | | | | *Millions of Rial: End of Period* | | | | | | |
| Foreign Assets | 11 | 1,057,038 | 1,198,238 | 1,497,462 | 1,548,246 | 1,632,066 | 1,449,647 | 1,270,308 | 968,533 | 1,322,966 | 1,149,370 | . . . . | . . . . |
| Claims on General Government | 12a | 2,606 | 982 | 3,386 | 418 | 105,921 | 329,668 | 477,489 | 718,984 | 707,901 | 706,002 | . . . . | . . . . |
| Claims on Nonfin.Pub.Enterprises | 12c | 1,767 | 1,854 | 1,656 | 10,261 | 84,917 | 81,138 | 84,996 | 158,365 | 260,023 | 266,139 | . . . . | . . . . |
| Claims on Deposit Money Banks | 12e | — | — | — | — | — | — | — | — | — | — | . . . . | . . . . |
| Reserve Money | 14 | 436,649 | 529,882 | 617,081 | 692,679 | 744,031 | 825,457 | 887,999 | 1,007,802 | 1,147,481 | 1,167,843 | . . . . | . . . . |
| of which: Currency Outside Banks | 14a | 297,939 | 330,620 | 412,520 | 425,840 | 472,225 | 532,372 | 547,284 | 777,376 | 803,336 | 784,768 | . . . . | . . . . |
| Other Liab. to Dep. Money Banks | 14n | 31,440 | 16,630 | 97,540 | 97,045 | 257,019 | | | | 91,890 | | . . . . | . . . . |
| Time, Savings,& Fgn.Currency Dep | 15 | 23,040 | 38,537 | 41,626 | 52,173 | 49,466 | 65,346 | 72,501 | 29,967 | 30,340 | 11,171 | . . . . | . . . . |
| Restricted Deposits | 16b | 41,234 | 48,395 | 38,956 | 42,491 | 67,248 | 76,851 | 73,084 | 46,284 | 62,559 | 61,860 | . . . . | . . . . |
| Foreign Liabilities | 16c | 104,092 | 93,240 | 87,296 | 74,618 | 60,786 | 121,064 | 130,405 | 126,428 | 363,370 | 364,921 | . . . . | . . . . |
| General Government Deposits | 16d | 169,015 | 216,048 | 294,828 | 222,609 | 268,501 | 316,185 | 278,081 | 236,443 | 150,482 | 121,264 | . . . . | . . . . |
| Liabs. to Nonbank Financial Insts | 16j | 56,892 | 57,772 | 62,349 | 65,116 | 67,113 | 76,030 | 65,358 | 59,436 | 57,709 | 17,982 | . . . . | . . . . |
| Capital Accounts | 17a | 172,592 | 191,281 | 268,238 | 313,586 | 261,770 | 327,786 | 318,590 | 310,997 | 326,997 | 330,629 | . . . . | . . . . |
| Other Items (Net) | 17r | 26,458 | 9,289 | −5,410 | −1,393 | 46,970 | 51,735 | 6,774 | 28,525 | 60,062 | 45,839 | . . . . | . . . . |
| **Deposit Money Banks** | | | | | | | *Millions of Rial: End of Period* | | | | | | |
| Reserves | 20 | 112,679 | 152,886 | 152,863 | 208,289 | 215,182 | 232,901 | 275,523 | 174,952 | 276,839 | 321,852 | . . . . | . . . . |
| Other Claims on Monetary Author. | 20n | 31,440 | 16,630 | 97,040 | 97,045 | 256,531 | — | — | — | 91,890 | — | . . . . | . . . . |
| Foreign Assets | 21 | 165,128 | 170,756 | 275,402 | 278,261 | 308,649 | 427,935 | 510,341 | 477,462 | 541,643 | 549,836 | . . . . | . . . . |
| Claims on General Government | 22a | 158,680 | 180,205 | 202,693 | 296,414 | 260,769 | 534,552 | 598,315 | 629,407 | 863,766 | 1,263,072 | . . . . | . . . . |
| Claims on Nonfin.Pub.Enterprises | 22c | 1,943 | 3,179 | 9,242 | 6,855 | 9,609 | 11,033 | 12,810 | 13,716 | 28,231 | 20,519 | . . . . | . . . . |
| Claims on Private Sector | 22d | 183,611 | 222,648 | 259,940 | 352,622 | 414,203 | 394,323 | 426,846 | 354,654 | 352,426 | 489,539 | . . . . | . . . . |
| Demand Deposits | 24 | 69,628 | 69,368 | 99,625 | 130,417 | 151,636 | 165,915 | 175,592 | 162,300 | 231,544 | 261,599 | . . . . | . . . . |
| Time, Savings,& Fgn.Currency Dep | 25 | 485,199 | 547,200 | 696,449 | 851,020 | 987,917 | 1,113,634 | 1,306,594 | 1,151,427 | 1,517,759 | 1,889,437 | . . . . | . . . . |
| Restricted Deposits | 26b | 18,495 | 21,309 | 54,894 | 69,281 | 92,822 | 62,584 | 36,136 | 34,403 | 46,135 | 66,389 | . . . . | . . . . |
| Foreign Liabilities | 26c | 9,774 | 11,995 | 19,508 | 27,647 | 31,649 | 25,827 | 33,586 | 16,847 | 28,496 | 38,163 | . . . . | . . . . |
| General Government Deposits | 26d | 219 | 83 | 76 | 215 | 234 | 332 | 470 | 503 | 4,045 | 7,910 | . . . . | . . . . |
| Credit from Monetary Authorities | 26g | — | 288 | 2 | 48 | 585 | 8 | — | — | 822 | 875 | . . . . | . . . . |
| Capital Accounts | 27a | 48,127 | 62,933 | 88,187 | 117,117 | 157,023 | 178,385 | 214,155 | 216,544 | 245,476 | 274,586 | . . . . | . . . . |
| Other Items (Net) | 27r | 22,040 | 33,129 | 38,439 | 43,743 | 43,077 | 54,059 | 57,301 | 68,167 | 80,521 | 105,859 | . . . . | . . . . |
| **Monetary Survey** | | | | | | | *Millions of Rial: End of Period* | | | | | | |
| Foreign Assets (Net) | 31n | 1,108,302 | 1,263,759 | 1,666,060 | 1,724,242 | 1,848,280 | 1,730,691 | 1,616,657 | 1,302,720 | 1,472,744 | 1,296,122 | . . . . | . . . . |
| Domestic Credit | 32 | 179,373 | 192,737 | 182,013 | 443,747 | 606,685 | 1,034,198 | 1,321,904 | 1,638,180 | 2,057,821 | 2,616,097 | . . . . | . . . . |
| Claims on General Govt. (Net) | 32an | −7,948 | −34,944 | −88,825 | 74,008 | 97,955 | 547,703 | 797,252 | 1,111,445 | 1,417,140 | 1,839,900 | . . . . | . . . . |
| Claims on Nonfin.Pub.Enterprises | 32c | 3,710 | 5,033 | 10,898 | 17,116 | 94,526 | 92,171 | 97,806 | 172,082 | 288,255 | 286,657 | . . . . | . . . . |
| Claims on Private Sector | 32d | 183,611 | 222,648 | 259,940 | 352,622 | 414,203 | 394,323 | 426,846 | 354,654 | 352,426 | 489,539 | . . . . | . . . . |
| Money | 34 | 390,541 | 442,464 | 558,461 | 613,748 | 680,159 | 758,561 | 786,560 | 993,000 | 1,104,820 | 1,116,583 | . . . . | . . . . |
| Quasi-Money | 35 | 508,239 | 585,737 | 738,075 | 903,192 | 1,037,383 | 1,178,979 | 1,379,096 | 1,181,394 | 1,548,099 | 1,900,608 | . . . . | . . . . |
| Restricted Deposits | 36b | 59,729 | 69,704 | 93,849 | 111,772 | 160,070 | 139,435 | 109,220 | 80,687 | 108,694 | 128,250 | . . . . | . . . . |
| Liabs. to Nonbank Financial Insts | 36j | 56,892 | 57,772 | 62,349 | 65,116 | 67,113 | 76,030 | 65,358 | 59,436 | 57,709 | 17,982 | . . . . | . . . . |
| Capital Accounts | 37a | 220,719 | 254,214 | 356,426 | 430,703 | 418,794 | 506,171 | 532,745 | 527,541 | 572,473 | 605,215 | . . . . | . . . . |
| Other Items (Net) | 37r | 51,554 | 46,606 | 38,913 | 43,457 | 91,445 | 105,713 | 65,583 | 98,843 | 138,770 | 143,580 | . . . . | . . . . |
| Money plus Quasi-Money | 35l | 898,781 | 1,028,200 | 1,296,536 | 1,516,940 | 1,717,542 | 1,937,540 | 2,165,656 | 2,174,394 | 2,652,919 | 3,017,191 | . . . . | . . . . |
| **Interest Rates** | | | | | | | *Percent Per Annum* | | | | | | |
| Treasury Bill Rate | 60c | 13.84 | 14.89 | 15.65 | 15.86 | 15.20 | 13.47 | 20.92 | 22.87 | 22.17 | 16.66 | . . . . | . . . . |
| Deposit Rate | 60l | 13.00 | 13.00 | 13.00 | 13.00 | 13.00 | 10.67 | 18.67 | 20.00 | 19.50 | 15.25 | . . . . | . . . . |
| Lending Rate | 60p | 18.50 | 18.00 | 18.00 | 18.00 | 18.00 | 18.00 | 23.83 | 25.00 | 24.50 | 22.08 | . . . . | . . . . |
| **Prices** | | | | | | | *Index Numbers (2010=100): Period Averages* | | | | | | |
| Consumer Prices | 64 | 53.6 | † 60.0 | 66.5 | 71.7 | † 85.3 | 89.9 | 100.0 | 119.5 | 131.4 | 145.8 | 157.6 | . . . . |
| **Intl. Transactions & Positions** | | | | | | | *Millions of Rial* | | | | | | |
| Exports | 70 | 752,497 | 1,073,919 | 1,311,182 | 1,253,196 | 1,514,968 | 1,269,608 | 1,866,515 | . . . . | . . . . | . . . . | . . . . | . . . . |
| Imports, c.i.f | 71 | 736,532 | 1,029,883 | 1,196,812 | 1,693,234 | 2,106,745 | 1,863,116 | 2,130,023 | . . . . | . . . . | . . . . | . . . . | . . . . |

# Yemen, Republic of 474

| | | 2004 | 2005 | 2006 | 2007 | 2008 | 2009 | 2010 | 2011 | 2012 | 2013 | 2014 | 2015 |
|---|---|---|---|---|---|---|---|---|---|---|---|---|---|
| **Balance of Payments** | | | | | | | *Millions of US Dollars* | | | | | | |
| A. Current Account* | 109bx | .... | 624.1 | 205.7 | −1,508.3 | −1,251.3 | −2,527.4 | −1,397.7 | −1,161.2 | −334.6 | −1,530.5 | −842.2 | .... |
| Goods, credit (exports) | 1a9cx | .... | 6,413.2 | 7,316.4 | 7,049.5 | 8,976.9 | 5,881.0 | 7,648.3 | 9,116.7 | 7,808.3 | 7,841.6 | 7,600.9 | .... |
| Goods, debit (imports) | 1a9dx | .... | 4,712.9 | 5,926.1 | 7,490.3 | 9,333.8 | 7,867.8 | 8,472.9 | 8,542.5 | 11,354.5 | 10,755.9 | 10,862.2 | .... |
| Balance on goods | 1a9bx | .... | 1,700.3 | 1,390.3 | −440.7 | −356.9 | −1,986.8 | −824.6 | 574.2 | −3,546.2 | −2,914.3 | −3,261.3 | .... |
| Services, credit (exports) | 1b9cx | .... | 372.1 | 548.8 | 723.8 | 1,205.4 | 1,237.2 | 1,622.2 | 1,267.3 | 1,577.2 | 1,725.6 | 1,706.7 | .... |
| Services, debit (imports) | 1b9dx | .... | 1,241.4 | 1,855.1 | 1,867.1 | 2,347.7 | 2,120.6 | 2,156.1 | 2,165.3 | 2,341.3 | 2,272.2 | 2,532.1 | .... |
| Balance on Goods & Services | 1z9bx | .... | 830.9 | 84.1 | −1,584.0 | −1,499.2 | −2,870.2 | −1,358.5 | −323.8 | −4,310.4 | −3,460.9 | −4,086.8 | .... |
| Primary income: credit | 1c9cx | .... | 178.2 | 316.2 | 384.9 | 321.3 | 115.0 | 54.5 | 53.3 | 29.3 | 24.9 | 27.2 | .... |
| Primary income: debit | 1c9dx | .... | 1,790.7 | 1,550.5 | 1,735.2 | 2,236.6 | 1,287.1 | 1,873.5 | 2,390.7 | 1,510.7 | 1,719.1 | 1,742.4 | .... |
| Balance on gds, serv. & prim. inc. | 1y9bx | .... | −781.5 | −1,150.3 | −2,934.3 | −3,414.5 | −4,042.3 | −3,177.5 | −2,661.2 | −5,791.7 | −5,155.1 | −5,802.0 | .... |
| Secondary income: credit | 1d9ca | .... | 1,458.4 | 1,401.7 | 1,474.5 | 2,223.0 | 1,628.3 | 1,837.5 | 1,549.6 | 5,517.3 | 3,691.6 | 5,016.1 | .... |
| Secondary income: debit | 1d9da | .... | 52.8 | 45.7 | 48.6 | 59.8 | 113.4 | 57.7 | 49.6 | 60.2 | 67.0 | 56.3 | .... |
| B. Capital Account* | 209ba | .... | 202.3 | 94.4 | 94.2 | 19.3 | — | 88.4 | — | .2 | — | — | .... |
| Capital account: credit | 209ca | .... | 202.3 | 94.4 | 94.2 | 19.3 | — | 88.4 | — | .2 | — | — | .... |
| Capital account: debit | 209da | .... | — | — | — | — | — | — | — | — | — | — | .... |
| Balance on current & capital acct. | 129ba | .... | 826.4 | 300.1 | −1,414.1 | −1,232.0 | −2,527.4 | −1,309.3 | −1,161.2 | −334.4 | −1,530.5 | −842.2 | .... |
| C. Financial Account* | 309na | .... | 605.9 | −631.7 | −747.4 | −1,530.0 | 364.1 | 317.4 | 617.6 | −602.0 | 226.6 | 697.8 | .... |
| Direct investment: assets | 3a9aa | .... | .... | — | — | — | — | — | — | — | — | — | .... |
| Equity & investment fund shares.. | 3aaaa | .... | .... | — | — | — | — | — | — | — | — | — | .... |
| Debt instruments | 3abaa | .... | .... | — | — | — | — | — | — | — | — | — | .... |
| Direct investment: liabilities | 3a9la | .... | −302.1 | 1,121.0 | 917.3 | 1,554.6 | 129.2 | 188.6 | −517.8 | −14.2 | −133.6 | −738.0 | .... |
| Equity & investment fund shares . | 3aala | .... | — | — | 40.4 | 40.4 | — | 42.5 | 44.2 | 30.2 | — | — | .... |
| Debt instruments | 3abla | .... | −302.1 | 1,121.0 | 876.9 | 1,514.2 | 129.2 | 146.1 | −562.1 | −44.4 | −133.6 | −738.0 | .... |
| Portfolio investment: assets | 3b9aa | .... | 14.2 | 34.0 | 8.5 | 44.0 | 13.5 | 358.1 | −114.5 | 105.5 | 166.5 | −257.1 | .... |
| Equity & investment fund shares | 3baaa | .... | 14.2 | 34.0 | 8.5 | 44.0 | 13.5 | 358.1 | −114.5 | 105.5 | 166.5 | −257.1 | .... |
| Debt securities | 3bbaa | .... | .... | — | — | — | — | — | — | — | — | — | .... |
| Portfolio investment: liabilities | 3b9la | .... | .... | — | — | — | — | — | — | — | — | — | .... |
| Equity & investment fund shares . | 3bala | .... | .... | — | — | — | — | — | — | — | — | — | .... |
| Debt securities | 3bbla | .... | .... | — | — | — | — | — | — | — | — | — | .... |
| Fin. der.& empl.stk.ops.(ESOs): net | 3c9na | .... | .... | — | — | — | — | — | — | — | — | — | .... |
| Fin. der. & ESOs.: assets | 3c9aa | .... | .... | .... | .... | .... | .... | .... | .... | .... | .... | .... | .... |
| Fin. der. & ESOs.: liabilities | 3c9la | .... | .... | .... | .... | .... | .... | .... | .... | .... | .... | .... | .... |
| Other investment: assets | 3d9aa | .... | 81.6 | 387.1 | 87.8 | −157.1 | 574.9 | −61.3 | −38.4 | 141.1 | −226.8 | −64.0 | .... |
| Other equity | 3daaa | .... | .... | .... | .... | .... | .... | .... | .... | .... | .... | .... | .... |
| Debt instruments | 3dzaa | .... | 81.6 | 387.1 | 87.8 | −157.1 | 574.9 | −61.3 | −38.4 | 141.1 | −226.8 | −64.0 | .... |
| Other investment: liabilities | 3d9la | .... | −208.0 | −68.2 | −73.7 | −137.7 | 95.1 | −209.1 | −252.6 | 862.7 | −153.3 | −280.8 | .... |
| Other equity | 3dala | .... | .... | .... | .... | .... | .... | .... | .... | .... | .... | .... | .... |
| Debt instruments | 3dzla | .... | −208.0 | −68.2 | −73.7 | −137.7 | 95.1 | −209.1 | −252.6 | 862.7 | −153.3 | −280.8 | .... |
| Curr.+ cap.− finan. acct. balance | 4y9na | .... | 220.6 | 931.9 | −666.7 | 298.0 | −2,891.5 | −1,626.7 | −1,778.8 | 267.5 | −1,757.1 | −1,540.0 | .... |
| D. Net Errors and Omissions | 409na | .... | 213.3 | 179.8 | 465.4 | 55.9 | 1,589.6 | 65.7 | −345.0 | 880.8 | 716.8 | 213.8 | .... |
| E. Reserves and Related Items | 4z9na | .... | 433.8 | 1,111.7 | −201.3 | 353.9 | −1,301.9 | −1,561.0 | −2,123.7 | 1,148.3 | −1,040.3 | −1,326.2 | .... |
| Reserve assets | 3e9aa | .... | 713.4 | 1,401.2 | 68.9 | 564.7 | −1,004.0 | −832.3 | −1,411.2 | 1,626.1 | −808.7 | −671.0 | .... |
| Credit and loans from the IMF | 3dcla | .... | −55.8 | −60.1 | −86.8 | −71.7 | −43.5 | 25.5 | −25.0 | 93.9 | — | 73.1 | .... |
| Exceptional financing | 409la | .... | 335.4 | 349.6 | 357.0 | 282.5 | 341.4 | 703.2 | 737.5 | 383.9 | 231.6 | 582.1 | .... |
| *Excludes components in group E | | | | | | | | | | | | | |
| | | | | | | | | | | | | | |
| **International Investment Position** | | | | | | | *Millions of US Dollars* | | | | | | |
| Assets | 809aa | .... | 7,290.4 | 9,121.0 | 9,424.6 | .... | .... | .... | .... | .... | .... | .... | .... |
| Direct investment | 8a9aa | .... | .... | .... | .... | .... | .... | .... | .... | .... | .... | .... | .... |
| Equity & investment fund shares.. | 8aaaa | .... | .... | .... | .... | .... | .... | .... | .... | .... | .... | .... | .... |
| Debt instruments | 8abaa | .... | .... | .... | .... | .... | .... | .... | .... | .... | .... | .... | .... |
| Portfolio investment | 8b9aa | .... | 28.5 | 62.5 | 71.0 | .... | .... | .... | .... | .... | .... | .... | .... |
| Equity & investment fund shares.. | 8baaa | .... | 28.5 | 62.5 | 71.0 | .... | .... | .... | .... | .... | .... | .... | .... |
| Debt securities | 8bbaa | .... | .... | .... | .... | .... | .... | .... | .... | .... | .... | .... | .... |
| Fin. der.(oth.than reserves) & ESOs | 8c9aa | .... | .... | .... | .... | .... | .... | .... | .... | .... | .... | .... | .... |
| Other investment | 8d9aa | .... | 1,119.2 | 1,514.2 | 1,594.0 | .... | .... | .... | .... | .... | .... | .... | .... |
| Other equity | 8daaa | .... | .... | .... | .... | .... | .... | .... | .... | .... | .... | .... | .... |
| Debt instruments | 8dzaa | .... | 1,119.2 | 1,514.2 | 1,594.0 | .... | .... | .... | .... | .... | .... | .... | .... |
| Reserve assets | 8e9aa | .... | 6,142.6 | 7,544.4 | 7,759.6 | .... | .... | .... | .... | .... | .... | .... | .... |
| Liabilities | 809la | .... | 6,221.1 | 7,689.4 | 9,316.4 | .... | .... | .... | .... | .... | .... | .... | .... |
| Direct investment | 8a9la | .... | 803.3 | 1,924.3 | 2,985.1 | .... | .... | .... | .... | .... | .... | .... | .... |
| Equity & investment fund shares.. | 8aala | .... | | | 2,985.1 | .... | .... | .... | .... | .... | .... | .... | .... |
| Debt instruments | 8abla | .... | 803.3 | 1,924.3 | | .... | .... | .... | .... | .... | .... | .... | .... |
| Portfolio investment | 8b9la | .... | .... | .... | .... | .... | .... | .... | .... | .... | .... | .... | .... |
| Equity & investment fund shares.. | 8bala | .... | .... | .... | .... | .... | .... | .... | .... | .... | .... | .... | .... |
| Debt securities | 8bbla | .... | .... | .... | .... | .... | .... | .... | .... | .... | .... | .... | .... |
| Fin. der.(oth.than reserves) & ESOs | 8c9la | .... | .... | .... | .... | .... | .... | .... | .... | .... | .... | .... | .... |
| Other investment | 8d9la | .... | 5,417.8 | 5,765.1 | 6,331.2 | .... | .... | .... | .... | .... | .... | .... | .... |
| Other equity | 8dala | .... | .... | .... | .... | .... | .... | .... | .... | .... | .... | .... | .... |
| Debt instruments | 8dzla | .... | 5,417.8 | 5,765.1 | 6,331.2 | .... | .... | .... | .... | .... | .... | .... | .... |

# Yemen, Republic of 474

| | | 2004 | 2005 | 2006 | 2007 | 2008 | 2009 | 2010 | 2011 | 2012 | 2013 | 2014 | 2015 |
|---|---|---|---|---|---|---|---|---|---|---|---|---|---|
| **Government Finance** | | | | | | | | | | | | | |
| **Cash Flow Statement** | | | | | | | | | | | | | |
| **General Government** | | | | | *Millions of Rials: Fiscal Year Ends December 31* | | | | | | | | |
| Cash Receipts:Operating Activities... | c1 | 811,848 | 1,107,738 | 1,447,005 | 1,428,645 | 1,992,563 | 1,278,678 | 1,778,549 | 1,689,634 | 2,122,868 | 2,093,601 | .... | .... |
| Taxes............................................. | c11 | 240,163 | 284,416 | 266,396 | 315,414 | 371,434 | 405,041 | 451,440 | 518,576 | 515,298 | 531,495 | .... | .... |
| Social Contributions........................ | c12 | — | — | — | — | — | — | — | — | — | — | .... | .... |
| Grants.......................................... | c13 | 18,681 | 13,736 | 15,016 | 14,727 | 14,197 | 20,743 | 22,699 | 324,195 | 208,972 | 101,742 | .... | .... |
| Other Receipts............................... | c14 | 553,004 | 809,586 | 1,165,593 | 1,098,504 | 1,606,932 | 852,894 | 1,304,410 | 846,863 | 1,398,598 | 1,460,364 | .... | .... |
| Cash Payments:Operating Activities. | c2 | 616,830 | 853,646 | 1,062,090 | 1,352,490 | 1,866,499 | 1,476,336 | 1,733,760 | 1,875,647 | 2,327,847 | 2,607,350 | .... | .... |
| Compensation of Employees........ | c21 | 239,497 | 297,209 | 386,849 | 494,553 | 577,981 | 559,057 | 589,873 | 700,851 | 839,613 | 884,725 | .... | .... |
| Purchases of Goods & Services....... | c22 | 90,450 | 108,691 | 147,776 | 202,039 | 192,377 | 221,443 | 247,039 | 193,357 | 257,153 | 252,295 | .... | .... |
| Interest........................................ | c24 | 53,976 | 69,072 | 86,929 | 97,385 | 125,916 | 127,132 | 162,743 | 233,209 | 412,238 | 472,671 | .... | .... |
| Subsidies..................................... | c25 | 152,365 | 286,351 | 309,298 | 407,745 | 765,294 | 446,472 | 616,960 | 541,122 | — | — | .... | .... |
| Grants......................................... | c26 | — | — | — | — | — | 15,739 | 968 | — | — | — | .... | .... |
| Social Benefits............................. | c27 | 17,230 | 18,549 | 22,496 | 24,946 | 29,809 | 106,441 | 116,056 | 29,781 | 623,618 | 810,414 | .... | .... |
| Other Payments........................... | c28 | 63,312 | 73,774 | 108,742 | 125,822 | 175,122 | 52 | 121 | 177,327 | 195,225 | 187,245 | .... | .... |
| Net Cash Inflow:Operating Act.[1-2] | ccio | 195,018 | 254,092 | 384,915 | 76,155 | 126,064 | −197,658 | 44,789 | −186,013 | −204,979 | −513,749 | .... | .... |
| Net Cash Outflow:Invest. in NFA...... | c31 | 209,860 | 249,531 | 271,342 | 309,604 | 299,732 | 284,375 | 259,236 | 126,564 | 189,308 | 198,114 | .... | .... |
| Purchases of Nonfinancial Assets... | c31.1 | 210,164 | 252,634 | 274,015 | 309,976 | 300,420 | 284,740 | 259,340 | 126,702 | 189,404 | 198,229 | .... | .... |
| Sales of Nonfinancial Assets.......... | c31.2 | 304 | 3,103 | 2,673 | 372 | 688 | 365 | 104 | 138 | 96 | 115 | .... | .... |
| Cash Surplus/Deficit [1-2-31=1-2M] | ccsd | −14,842 | 4,561 | 113,573 | −233,449 | −173,668 | −482,033 | −214,447 | −312,577 | −394,287 | −711,863 | .... | .... |
| Net Acq. Fin. Assets, excl. Cash....... | c32x | 40,503 | 62,962 | 67,861 | 71,014 | 54,669 | 68,894 | 53,407 | 18,897 | 97,707 | 44,287 | .... | .... |
| Domestic....................................... | c321x | 40,503 | 62,962 | 67,861 | 71,014 | 54,669 | 68,894 | 53,407 | 18,897 | 97,707 | 44,287 | .... | .... |
| Foreign......................................... | c322x | — | — | — | — | — | — | — | — | — | — | .... | .... |
| Net Incurrence of Liabilities.............. | c33 | 123,978 | 105,299 | 33,061 | 232,383 | 274,248 | 24,580 | −3,333 | 314,935 | 409,574 | 730,797 | .... | .... |
| Domestic....................................... | c331 | 120,315 | 84,892 | 14,237 | 217,448 | 261,608 | — | — | 337,144 | 358,769 | 769,758 | .... | .... |
| Foreign......................................... | c332 | 3,663 | 20,407 | 18,824 | 14,935 | 12,640 | 24,580 | −3,333 | −22,209 | 50,805 | −38,961 | .... | .... |
| Net Cash Inflow, Fin.Act.[-32x+33].. | cnfb | 83,475 | 42,337 | −34,800 | 161,369 | 219,579 | −44,314 | −56,740 | 296,038 | 311,867 | 686,510 | .... | .... |
| Net Change in Stock of Cash........... | cncb | 68,633 | 46,898 | 78,773 | −72,080 | 45,911 | −526,347 | −271,187 | −16,539 | −82,420 | −25,353 | .... | .... |
| Stat. Discrep. [32X-33+NCB-CSD].... | ccsdz | | | | | | | | | | | | |
| Memo Item:Cash Expenditure[2+31] | c2m | 826,690 | 1,103,177 | 1,333,432 | 1,662,094 | 2,166,231 | 1,761,076 | 1,993,100 | 2,002,211 | 2,517,155 | 2,805,464 | | |
| Memo Item: Gross Debt.................. | c63 | .... | .... | .... | .... | .... | .... | .... | .... | .... | .... | .... | .... |
| **National Accounts** | | | | | | *Millions of Rial* | | | | | | | |
| Househ.Cons.Expend.,incl.NPISHs... | 96f | 1,837,198 | 2,093,741 | 2,773,653 | 3,278,958 | 4,018,275 | 4,281,535 | 4,899,780 | 4,573,171 | 5,336,891 | 6,074,983 | .... | .... |
| Government Consumption Expend... | 91f | 334,230 | 415,868 | 585,071 | 757,593 | 819,710 | 826,645 | 886,613 | 972,497 | 1,135,636 | 1,298,755 | .... | .... |
| Gross Fixed Capital Formation......... | 93e | 577,725 | 665,702 | 751,524 | 990,122 | 1,067,345 | 1,142,324 | 1,344,701 | 1,028,337 | 1,249,089 | 1,314,277 | .... | .... |
| Changes in Inventories.................... | 93i | 112,755 | 308,746 | 369,821 | 388,033 | 466,746 | 96,937 | −44,834 | 139,876 | 77,756 | −479,716 | .... | .... |
| Exports of Goods and Services......... | 90c | 932,382 | 1,311,034 | 1,549,130 | 1,544,316 | 2,033,922 | 1,424,381 | 2,034,046 | 2,220,108 | 2,011,876 | 2,120,209 | .... | .... |
| Imports of Goods and Services (-)...... | 98c | 908,710 | 1,148,534 | 1,534,019 | 1,859,117 | 2,333,726 | 1,998,906 | 2,333,491 | 2,289,329 | 2,935,995 | 2,868,808 | .... | .... |
| Gross Domestic Product (GDP)......... | 99b | 2,885,580 | 3,646,557 | 4,495,179 | 5,099,905 | 6,072,272 | 5,772,915 | 6,786,814 | 6,644,660 | 6,875,253 | 7,459,699 | .... | .... |
| Net Primary Income from Abroad..... | 98.n | −235,531 | −295,555 | −229,593 | −254,068 | −360,983 | −219,392 | −376,175 | −476,931 | −259,107 | −324,081 | .... | .... |
| Gross National Income (GNI)........... | 99a | 2,650,049 | 3,351,002 | 4,265,586 | 4,845,838 | 5,711,289 | 5,553,524 | 6,467,728 | 6,237,962 | 6,784,191 | | .... | .... |
| GDP Volume 2000 Prices................. | 99b.p | 2,163,551 | 2,274,736 | 2,380,299 | 2,463,015 | 2,561,890 | 2,667,820 | 2,819,774 | 2,459,809 | 2,509,477 | | .... | .... |
| GDP Volume (2010=100)................ | 99bvp | 76.7 | 80.7 | 84.4 | 87.3 | 90.9 | 94.6 | 100.0 | 87.2 | 89.0 | | .... | .... |
| GDP Deflator (2010=100)............... | 99bip | 55.4 | 66.6 | 78.5 | 86.0 | 98.5 | 89.9 | 100.0 | 112.2 | 113.8 | | .... | .... |
| | | | | | | *Millions: Midyear Estimates* | | | | | | | |
| **Population**................................ | 99z | 19.93 | 20.50 | 21.09 | 21.70 | 22.32 | 22.95 | 23.59 | 24.23 | 24.88 | 25.53 | 26.18 | 26.83 |

# Zambia 754

| | | 2004 | 2005 | 2006 | 2007 | 2008 | 2009 | 2010 | 2011 | 2012 | 2013 | 2014 | 2015 |
|---|---|---|---|---|---|---|---|---|---|---|---|---|---|
| **Exchange Rates** | | | | | *New Kwacha per SDR: End of Period* | | | | | | | | |
| Official Rate.................................. | aa | 7.4099 | 5.0153 | 6.6294 | 6.0758 | 7.4430 | 7.2750 | 7.3862 | 7.8560 | 7.9099 | 8.4894 | 9.2619 | 15.2180 |
| | | | | *New Kwacha per US Dollar: End of Period (ae) Period Average (rf)* | | | | | | | | | |
| Official Rate.................................. | ae | 4.7713 | 3.5090 | 4.4067 | 3.8448 | 4.8323 | 4.6406 | 4.7961 | 5.1170 | 5.1466 | 5.5126 | 6.3928 | 10.9819 |
| Official Rate.................................. | rf | 4.7789 | 4.4635 | 3.6031 | 4.0025 | 3.7457 | 5.0461 | 4.7971 | 4.8607 | 5.1473 | 5.3959 | 6.1528 | 8.6324 |
| | | | | *Index Numbers (2010=100): Period Averages* | | | | | | | | | |
| Official Rate.................................. | ahx | 100.3 | 108.3 | 134.1 | 119.9 | 129.5 | 95.4 | 100.0 | 98.6 | 93.1 | 88.8 | 78.0 | 58.2 |
| Nominal Effective Exchange Rate..... | nec | 103.9 | 109.9 | 136.7 | 118.3 | 128.6 | 99.6 | 100.0 | 94.9 | 94.8 | 94.7 | 86.8 | 73.8 |
| CPI-Based Real Effect. Ex. Rate........ | rec | 64.9 | 79.3 | 103.8 | 95.6 | 110.1 | 94.5 | 100.0 | 97.4 | 100.6 | 104.2 | 100.0 | 90.9 |
| **Fund Position** | | | | | | *Millions of SDRs: End of Period* | | | | | | | |
| Quota................................................ | 2f.s | 489.10 | 489.10 | 489.10 | 489.10 | 489.10 | 489.10 | 489.10 | 489.10 | 489.10 | 489.10 | 489.10 | 489.10 |
| SDR Holdings................................. | 1b.s | 16.00 | 11.00 | 8.87 | 6.17 | 6.87 | 406.73 | 405.98 | 402.40 | 394.60 | 382.84 | 359.66 | 316.15 |
| Reserve Position in the Fund............ | 1c.s | .02 | .02 | .02 | .02 | .02 | .02 | .02 | .02 | .02 | .02 | .02 | .02 |
| Total Fund Cred.&Loans Outstg........ | 2tl | 573.28 | 413.60 | 27.51 | 55.02 | 62.01 | 219.93 | 256.17 | 271.27 | 263.56 | 251.86 | 228.77 | 185.33 |
| SDR Allocations.............................. | 1bd | 68.30 | 68.30 | 68.30 | 68.30 | 68.30 | 469.14 | 469.14 | 469.14 | 469.14 | 469.14 | 469.14 | 469.14 |
| **International Liquidity** | | | | *Millions of US Dollars Unless Otherwise Indicated: End of Period* | | | | | | | | | |
| Total Reserves minus Gold.............. | 1l.d | 337.1 | 559.8 | 719.7 | 1,090.0 | 1,095.6 | 1,892.1 | 2,093.8 | 2,324.0 | 3,042.2 | 2,683.8 | 3,078.4 | 2,967.6 |
| SDR Holdings................................. | 1b.d | 24.8 | 15.7 | 13.3 | 9.7 | 10.6 | 637.6 | 625.2 | 617.8 | 606.5 | 589.6 | 521.1 | 438.1 |
| Reserve Position in the Fund.......... | 1c.d | — | — | — | — | — | — | — | — | — | — | — | — |
| Foreign Exchange......................... | 1d.d | 312.2 | 544.0 | 706.4 | 1,080.2 | 1,085.0 | 1,254.4 | 1,468.5 | 1,706.2 | 2,435.7 | 2,094.2 | 2,557.3 | 2,529.5 |
| Gold (Million Fine Troy Ounces)........ | 1ad | — | — | — | — | — | — | — | — | — | — | — | — |
| Gold (National Valuation)................. | 1and | — | — | — | — | — | — | — | — | — | — | — | — |
| Central Bank: Other Assets.............. | 3..d | 2.2 | 6.7 | .9 | 5.0 | 1.7 | 3.3 | .9 | 2.8 | 6.9 | 1.6 | 4.8 | 2.4 |
| Central Bank: Other Liabs.............. | 4..d | 51.1 | 39.2 | 15.9 | 16.0 | 12.5 | 57.1 | 5.8 | 6.6 | 7.5 | 10.6 | 3.8 | 14.3 |
| Other Depository Corps.: Assets...... | 7a.d | 334.0 | 343.5 | 417.2 | 608.4 | 525.5 | 604.3 | 793.6 | 970.6 | 712.9 | 903.2 | 904.9 | 1,097.2 |
| Other Depository Corps.: Liabs........ | 7b.d | 42.9 | 141.9 | 169.9 | 296.6 | 359.0 | 349.7 | 366.4 | 335.0 | 475.0 | 353.2 | 500.7 | 455.1 |
| Other Financial Corps.: Assets........ | 7e.d | .... | .... | .... | .... | .... | .... | .... | | | | | |
| Other Financial Corps.: Liabs........... | 7f.d | .... | .... | .... | .... | .... | .... | .... | 12.3 | 15.6 | 23.2 | 3.8 | 4.9 |
| **Central Bank** | | | | | *Millions of New Kwacha: End of Period* | | | | | | | | |
| Net Foreign Assets........................ | 11n | −3,497.7 | −1,060.1 | 2,408.6 | 3,353.3 | 4,180.5 | 3,731.5 | 4,641.0 | 6,140.5 | 10,789.0 | 8,630.9 | 12,722.4 | 22,523.9 |
| Claims on Nonresidents.............. | 11 | 1,500.1 | 1,494.2 | 3,113.7 | 4,164.0 | 5,210.7 | 9,009.7 | 10,026.3 | 11,991.1 | 16,623.2 | 14,809.9 | 19,210.7 | 32,640.9 |
| Liabilities to Nonresidents.............. | 16c | 4,997.8 | 2,554.3 | 705.1 | 810.8 | 1,030.2 | 5,278.2 | 5,385.3 | 5,850.6 | 5,834.2 | 6,179.0 | 6,488.3 | 10,117.0 |
| Claims on Other Depository Corps.... | 12e | 209.4 | 223.3 | 244.9 | 189.9 | 144.7 | 141.0 | 335.6 | 163.4 | 153.7 | 160.0 | 159.2 | 420.9 |
| Net Claims on Central Government.. | 12an | 5,743.5 | 3,123.8 | 928.0 | 78.5 | 703.3 | 1,125.7 | 2,233.3 | −218.4 | −2,151.1 | 2,533.9 | 2,437.8 | 5,699.3 |
| Claims on Central Government...... | 12a | 6,563.5 | 4,023.7 | 2,028.3 | 2,035.5 | 2,054.3 | 3,562.8 | 4,602.5 | 4,186.6 | 3,704.1 | 5,417.1 | 5,274.2 | 8,678.7 |
| Liabilities to Central Government... | 16d | 820.0 | 899.9 | 1,100.3 | 1,957.0 | 1,351.0 | 2,437.2 | 2,369.3 | 4,405.0 | 5,855.2 | 2,883.3 | 2,836.3 | 2,979.4 |
| Claims on Other Sectors.................. | 12s | 95.0 | 134.7 | 41.0 | 45.1 | 42.4 | 42.6 | 48.5 | 37.7 | 42.0 | 57.9 | 65.6 | 133.9 |
| Claims on Other Financial Corps.... | 12g | — | — | — | — | — | — | — | — | — | — | — | — |
| Claims on State & Local Govts....... | 12b | — | — | — | — | — | — | — | — | — | — | — | — |
| Claims on Public Nonfin. Corps...... | 12c | 60.9 | 96.3 | — | — | — | — | — | — | — | — | — | — |
| Claims on Private Sector............... | 12d | 34.2 | 38.3 | 41.0 | 45.1 | 42.4 | 42.6 | 48.5 | 37.7 | 42.0 | 57.9 | 65.6 | 133.9 |
| Monetary Base.............................. | 14 | 1,913.4 | 2,280.8 | 3,249.1 | 3,554.9 | 4,605.6 | 4,714.9 | 7,148.0 | 5,531.7 | 8,377.8 | 10,145.3 | 13,301.0 | 16,247.9 |
| Currency in Circulation................. | 14a | 815.5 | 962.0 | 1,224.2 | 1,513.4 | 1,931.9 | 1,999.1 | 2,747.9 | 3,405.7 | 3,839.6 | 4,597.0 | 5,724.1 | 6,446.2 |
| Liabs. to Other Depository Corps.... | 14c | 1,088.7 | 1,307.8 | 2,016.1 | 2,024.4 | 2,655.1 | 2,694.4 | 4,379.4 | 2,106.7 | 4,517.6 | 5,524.8 | 7,556.5 | 9,774.4 |
| Liabilities to Other Sectors............. | 14d | 9.2 | 11.0 | 8.8 | 17.2 | 18.6 | 21.4 | 20.6 | 19.3 | 20.5 | 23.5 | 20.3 | 27.3 |
| Other Liabs. to Other Dep. Corps..... | 14n | 3.9 | .1 | .1 | 9.5 | .2 | .2 | — | — | — | — | — | — |
| Dep. & Sec. Excl. f/Monetary Base..... | 14o | .3 | 5.5 | 1.2 | .3 | .2 | — | — | — | — | — | — | — |
| Deposits Included in Broad Money. | 15 | .3 | .2 | 1.2 | .3 | .2 | — | — | — | — | — | — | — |
| Sec.Ot.th.Shares Incl.in Brd. Money | 16a | — | 5.3 | — | — | — | — | — | — | — | — | — | — |
| Deposits Excl. from Broad Money... | 16b | — | — | — | — | — | — | — | — | — | — | — | — |
| Sec.Ot.th.Shares Excl.f/Brd.Money.. | 16s | — | — | — | — | — | — | — | — | — | — | — | — |
| Loans.............................................. | 16l | — | — | — | — | — | — | — | — | — | — | — | — |
| Financial Derivatives........................ | 16m | — | — | — | — | — | — | — | — | — | — | — | — |
| Shares and Other Equity.................. | 17a | 215.8 | −2.4 | 514.1 | 323.0 | 764.3 | 599.2 | 447.2 | 1,099.4 | 283.7 | 1,198.3 | 1,835.1 | 12,068.1 |
| Other Items (Net)............................ | 17r | 416.8 | 137.7 | −142.0 | −220.9 | −299.4 | −273.5 | −336.8 | −508.0 | 171.6 | 39.0 | 249.0 | 462.1 |
| Memo Item: | | | | | | | | | | | | | |
| Total Assets.................................. | 10ra | 11,758.4 | 9,397.3 | 7,905.6 | 9,786.8 | 10,585.8 | 17,255.3 | 18,915.2 | 20,484.5 | 24,955.7 | 24,890.0 | 29,989.0 | 47,559.4 |

# Zambia 754

| | | 2004 | 2005 | 2006 | 2007 | 2008 | 2009 | 2010 | 2011 | 2012 | 2013 | 2014 | 2015 |
|---|---|---|---|---|---|---|---|---|---|---|---|---|---|
| **Other Depository Corporations** | | | | | | | *Millions of New Kwacha: End of Period* | | | | | | |
| Net Foreign Assets | 21n | 1,388.9 | 707.4 | 1,089.7 | 1,198.7 | 804.2 | 1,181.7 | 2,049.0 | 3,252.4 | 1,224.7 | 3,031.9 | 2,584.0 | 7,050.8 |
| Claims on Nonresidents | 21 | 1,593.8 | 1,205.3 | 1,838.5 | 2,339.2 | 2,539.2 | 2,804.3 | 3,806.1 | 4,966.5 | 3,669.2 | 4,979.1 | 5,784.7 | 12,049.2 |
| Liabilities to Nonresidents | 26c | 204.9 | 497.9 | 748.8 | 1,140.5 | 1,735.0 | 1,622.6 | 1,757.1 | 1,714.1 | 2,444.5 | 1,947.1 | 3,200.7 | 4,998.4 |
| Claims on Central Bank | 20 | 1,111.4 | 1,488.2 | 2,247.3 | 2,294.1 | 3,047.3 | 3,147.5 | 5,011.3 | 2,843.6 | 5,219.0 | 6,537.8 | 9,109.4 | 12,196.7 |
| Currency | 20a | 88.5 | 143.1 | 157.7 | 213.6 | 322.6 | 419.5 | 518.4 | 615.3 | 824.3 | 1,153.8 | 1,535.9 | 1,733.5 |
| Reserve Deposits and Securities | 20b | 1,022.9 | 1,345.1 | 2,089.5 | 2,080.6 | 2,724.7 | 2,728.0 | 4,492.9 | 2,228.3 | 4,394.8 | 5,384.1 | 7,573.5 | 10,463.2 |
| Other Claims | 20n | — | — | — | — | — | — | — | — | — | — | — | — |
| Net Claims on Central Government | 22an | 1,106.0 | 1,390.5 | 1,474.0 | 1,599.3 | 1,182.9 | 2,837.5 | 3,315.1 | 5,418.5 | 5,393.2 | 7,801.3 | 6,743.7 | 5,233.7 |
| Claims on Central Government | 22a | 1,824.6 | 2,104.3 | 2,323.8 | 2,698.5 | 2,517.6 | 4,257.1 | 4,947.8 | 7,703.2 | 8,227.6 | 11,527.7 | 11,228.6 | 9,503.0 |
| Liabilities to Central Government | 26d | 718.7 | 713.8 | 849.7 | 1,099.2 | 1,334.8 | 1,419.6 | 1,632.7 | 2,284.7 | 2,834.3 | 3,726.4 | 4,485.0 | 4,269.3 |
| Claims on Other Sectors | 22s | 2,175.2 | 2,578.8 | 3,979.9 | 5,849.1 | 8,409.3 | 7,970.3 | 9,091.7 | 11,612.6 | 16,455.2 | 18,011.0 | 22,739.6 | 29,360.9 |
| Claims on Other Financial Corps. | 22g | .6 | 16.1 | 46.9 | 59.7 | 91.6 | 57.9 | 75.8 | 85.3 | 78.0 | 135.0 | 201.8 | 275.2 |
| Claims on State & Local Govts | 22b | .5 | 1.2 | 2.5 | 1.8 | 4.0 | 5.1 | 7.3 | 11.9 | 18.6 | 22.8 | 37.0 | 50.4 |
| Claims on Public Nonfin. Corps. | 22c | 113.4 | 133.3 | 216.4 | 372.4 | 146.8 | 208.5 | 115.3 | 98.7 | 693.5 | 235.7 | 231.6 | 285.2 |
| Claims on Private Sector | 22d | 2,060.7 | 2,428.1 | 3,714.1 | 5,415.2 | 8,166.9 | 7,698.8 | 8,893.3 | 11,416.6 | 15,665.1 | 17,617.6 | 22,269.1 | 28,750.1 |
| Liabilities to Central Bank | 26g | 39.4 | 121.7 | 113.2 | 23.7 | 80.0 | 55.6 | 219.2 | 24.9 | 45.3 | 78.5 | 20.3 | 348.1 |
| Transf.Dep.Included in Broad Money | 24 | 3,164.7 | 2,993.9 | 4,698.2 | 5,801.1 | 6,862.5 | 7,495.7 | 10,019.3 | 11,516.4 | 13,230.8 | 15,662.6 | 17,188.2 | 23,968.5 |
| Other Dep.Included in Broad Money | 25 | 1,680.3 | 1,933.9 | 2,527.2 | 3,281.0 | 4,324.5 | 4,700.2 | 5,647.1 | 7,478.8 | 9,432.3 | 11,912.9 | 13,562.4 | 18,553.7 |
| Sec.Ot.th.Shares Incl.in Brd. Money | 26a | .1 | .2 | — | — | — | — | — | — | — | — | — | — |
| Deposits Excl. from Broad Money | 26b | 46.7 | 46.7 | 46.7 | 46.7 | 46.7 | 46.7 | 46.7 | 46.7 | 46.7 | 46.7 | 46.7 | 46.7 |
| Sec.Ot.th.Shares Excl.f/Brd.Money | 26s | — | — | — | — | — | — | — | — | — | — | — | — |
| Loans | 26l | 177.3 | 199.3 | 189.4 | 234.4 | 455.3 | 532.2 | 544.7 | 944.3 | 933.7 | 1,011.3 | 2,083.8 | 2,753.0 |
| Financial Derivatives | 26m | — | — | — | — | — | — | — | — | — | — | — | — |
| Insurance Technical Reserves | 26r | — | — | — | — | — | — | — | — | — | — | — | — |
| Shares and Other Equity | 27a | 638.2 | 931.2 | 1,020.3 | 1,363.4 | 1,698.6 | 1,965.1 | 2,316.7 | 2,841.3 | 4,040.6 | 5,966.3 | 8,109.5 | 8,779.9 |
| Other Items (Net) | 27r | 34.7 | −62.0 | 195.9 | 190.9 | −23.9 | 341.5 | 673.4 | 274.6 | 562.8 | 703.7 | 165.7 | −607.9 |
| Memo Item: | | | | | | | | | | | | | |
| Total Assets | 20ra | 7,408.2 | 8,200.4 | 11,291.7 | 14,621.1 | 18,211.5 | 20,033.3 | 24,807.7 | 29,458.3 | 36,185.6 | 44,160.5 | 53,200.6 | 69,835.0 |
| **Depository Corporations** | | | | | | | *Millions of New Kwacha: End of Period* | | | | | | |
| Net Foreign Assets | 31n | −2,108.8 | −352.7 | 3,498.3 | 4,552.0 | 4,984.7 | 4,913.2 | 6,690.1 | 9,392.9 | 12,013.7 | 11,662.8 | 15,306.4 | 29,574.7 |
| Claims on Nonresidents | 31 | 3,093.9 | 2,699.5 | 4,952.2 | 6,503.3 | 7,749.9 | 11,814.0 | 13,832.4 | 16,957.5 | 20,292.5 | 19,789.0 | 24,995.4 | 44,690.1 |
| Liabilities to Nonresidents | 36c | 5,202.7 | 3,052.2 | 1,453.9 | 1,951.3 | 2,765.2 | 6,900.7 | 7,142.4 | 7,564.7 | 8,278.8 | 8,126.2 | 9,689.0 | 15,115.4 |
| Domestic Claims | 32 | 9,119.7 | 7,227.8 | 6,423.0 | 7,572.1 | 10,337.8 | 11,976.0 | 14,688.6 | 16,850.3 | 19,739.3 | 28,404.0 | 31,986.7 | 40,427.8 |
| Net Claims on Central Government | 32an | 6,849.5 | 4,514.3 | 2,402.0 | 1,677.9 | 1,886.1 | 3,963.1 | 5,548.4 | 5,200.1 | 3,242.1 | 10,335.2 | 9,181.5 | 10,933.0 |
| Claims on Central Government | 32a | 8,388.1 | 6,128.0 | 4,352.1 | 4,734.1 | 4,571.9 | 7,819.9 | 9,550.3 | 11,889.8 | 11,931.7 | 16,944.8 | 16,502.8 | 18,181.7 |
| Liabilities to Central Government | 36d | 1,538.6 | 1,613.6 | 1,950.1 | 3,056.2 | 2,685.8 | 3,856.8 | 4,002.0 | 6,689.7 | 8,689.6 | 6,609.6 | 7,321.3 | 7,248.7 |
| Claims on Other Sectors | 32s | 2,270.2 | 2,713.5 | 4,020.9 | 5,894.2 | 8,451.7 | 8,012.9 | 9,140.2 | 11,650.2 | 16,497.2 | 18,068.9 | 22,805.2 | 29,494.8 |
| Claims on Other Financial Corps. | 32g | .6 | 16.1 | 46.9 | 59.7 | 91.6 | 57.9 | 75.8 | 85.3 | 78.0 | 135.0 | 201.8 | 275.2 |
| Claims on State & Local Govts | 32b | .5 | 1.2 | 2.5 | 1.8 | 4.0 | 5.1 | 7.3 | 11.9 | 18.6 | 22.8 | 37.0 | 50.4 |
| Claims on Public Nonfin. Corps. | 32c | 174.3 | 229.7 | 216.4 | 372.4 | 146.8 | 208.5 | 115.3 | 98.7 | 693.5 | 235.7 | 231.6 | 285.2 |
| Claims on Private Sector | 32d | 2,094.8 | 2,466.4 | 3,755.1 | 5,460.3 | 8,209.3 | 7,741.4 | 8,941.9 | 11,454.3 | 15,707.1 | 17,675.4 | 22,334.8 | 28,884.0 |
| Broad Money Liabilities | 35l | 5,581.6 | 5,763.3 | 8,301.9 | 10,399.5 | 12,815.1 | 13,796.9 | 17,916.5 | 21,804.8 | 25,699.0 | 31,042.2 | 34,959.1 | 47,262.1 |
| Currency Outside Depository Corps | 34a | 727.0 | 818.9 | 1,066.4 | 1,299.8 | 1,609.3 | 1,579.6 | 2,229.5 | 2,790.3 | 3,015.3 | 3,443.2 | 4,188.3 | 4,712.7 |
| Transferable Deposits | 34 | 3,174.0 | 3,004.9 | 4,707.1 | 5,818.3 | 6,881.2 | 7,517.1 | 10,039.9 | 11,535.6 | 13,251.3 | 15,686.1 | 17,208.5 | 23,995.7 |
| Other Deposits | 35 | 1,680.5 | 1,934.1 | 2,528.4 | 3,281.3 | 4,324.6 | 4,700.2 | 5,647.1 | 7,478.8 | 9,432.3 | 11,912.9 | 13,562.4 | 18,553.7 |
| Securities Other than Shares | 36a | .1 | 5.4 | — | — | — | — | — | — | — | — | — | — |
| Deposits Excl. from Broad Money | 36b | 46.7 | 46.7 | 46.7 | 46.7 | 46.7 | 46.7 | 46.7 | 46.7 | 46.7 | 46.7 | 46.7 | 46.7 |
| Sec.Ot.th.Shares Excl.f/Brd.Money | 36s | — | — | — | — | — | — | — | — | — | — | — | — |
| Loans | 36l | 177.3 | 199.3 | 189.4 | 234.4 | 455.3 | 532.2 | 544.7 | 944.3 | 933.7 | 1,011.3 | 2,083.8 | 2,753.0 |
| Financial Derivatives | 36m | — | — | — | — | — | — | — | — | — | — | — | — |
| Insurance Technical Reserves | 36r | — | — | — | — | — | — | — | — | — | — | — | — |
| Shares and Other Equity | 37a | 854.0 | 928.8 | 1,534.4 | 1,686.4 | 2,462.9 | 2,564.4 | 2,763.9 | 3,940.7 | 4,324.2 | 7,164.6 | 9,944.5 | 20,848.0 |
| Other Items (Net) | 37r | 351.3 | −63.0 | −151.1 | −243.0 | −457.5 | −50.9 | 106.8 | −493.5 | 748.8 | 801.9 | 258.9 | −907.3 |
| Broad Money Liabs., Seasonally Adj. | 35l.b | 5,395.1 | 5,562.1 | 8,018.2 | 10,070.9 | 12,469.2 | 13,490.8 | 17,617.9 | 21,528.6 | 25,420.6 | 30,709.7 | 34,583.4 | 46,754.8 |
| **Other Financial Corporations** | | | | | | | *Millions of New Kwacha: End of Period* | | | | | | |
| Net Foreign Assets | 41n | .... | .... | .... | .... | .... | .... | .... | −63.1 | −80.5 | −127.8 | −24.2 | −53.7 |
| Claims on Nonresidents | 41 | .... | .... | .... | .... | .... | .... | .... | — | — | — | — | — |
| Liabilities to Nonresidents | 46c | .... | .... | .... | .... | .... | .... | .... | 63.1 | 80.5 | 127.8 | 24.2 | 53.7 |
| Claims on Depository Corporations | 40 | .... | .... | .... | .... | .... | .... | .... | 1,704.5 | 2,472.5 | 3,297.7 | 4,250.2 | 4,704.3 |
| Net Claims on Central Government | 42an | .... | .... | .... | .... | .... | .... | .... | 2,986.1 | 3,839.6 | 5,033.8 | 5,112.2 | 6,834.6 |
| Claims on Central Government | 42a | .... | .... | .... | .... | .... | .... | .... | 2,986.1 | 3,839.6 | 5,033.8 | 5,112.2 | 6,834.6 |
| Liabilities to Central Government | 46d | .... | .... | .... | .... | .... | .... | .... | — | — | — | — | — |
| Claims on Other Sectors | 42s | .... | .... | .... | .... | .... | .... | .... | 4,292.1 | 5,291.1 | 6,450.2 | 6,213.4 | 7,135.3 |
| Claims on State & Local Govts | 42b | .... | .... | .... | .... | .... | .... | .... | — | — | — | — | — |
| Claims on Pub. Nonfin. Corps | 42c | .... | .... | .... | .... | .... | .... | .... | 132.4 | 179.7 | 189.6 | 1.9 | — |
| Claims on Private Sector | 42d | .... | .... | .... | .... | .... | .... | .... | 4,159.8 | 5,111.4 | 6,260.6 | 6,211.5 | 7,135.3 |
| Deposits | 46b | | | | | | | | — | — | — | — | — |
| Securities Other than Shares | 46s | | | | | | | | — | — | — | — | — |
| Loans | 46l | .... | .... | .... | .... | .... | .... | .... | 584.3 | 987.1 | 1,215.8 | 592.2 | 662.1 |
| Financial Derivatives | 46m | | | | | | | | — | — | 2.7 | 5.0 | 24.3 |
| Insurance Technical Reserves | 46r | .... | .... | .... | .... | .... | .... | .... | 8,619.5 | 10,627.4 | 14,284.9 | 16,457.0 | 20,092.7 |
| Shares and Other Equity | 47a | .... | .... | .... | .... | .... | .... | .... | 842.8 | 999.6 | 1,162.0 | 1,055.1 | 862.8 |
| Other Items (Net) | 47r | .... | .... | .... | .... | .... | .... | .... | −1,127.0 | −1,091.5 | −2,011.6 | −2,557.7 | −3,021.4 |
| Memo Item: | | | | | | | | | | | | | |
| Total Assets | 40ra | .... | .... | .... | .... | .... | .... | .... | 10,591.2 | 13,343.4 | 17,686.1 | 19,480.0 | 23,193.1 |

# Zambia 754

| | | 2004 | 2005 | 2006 | 2007 | 2008 | 2009 | 2010 | 2011 | 2012 | 2013 | 2014 | 2015 |
|---|---|---|---|---|---|---|---|---|---|---|---|---|---|
| **Financial Corporations** | | | | | | *Millions of New Kwacha: End of Period* | | | | | | | |
| Net Foreign Assets............................ | 51n | .... | .... | .... | .... | .... | .... | .... | 9,329.8 | 11,933.2 | 11,535.0 | 15,282.2 | 29,521.0 |
| Claims on Nonresidents................. | 51 | .... | .... | .... | .... | .... | .... | .... | 16,957.5 | 20,292.5 | 19,789.0 | 24,995.4 | 44,690.1 |
| Liabilities to Nonresidents.............. | 56c | .... | .... | .... | .... | .... | .... | .... | 7,627.7 | 8,359.3 | 8,254.0 | 9,713.2 | 15,169.1 |
| Domestic Claims............................. | 52 | .... | .... | .... | .... | .... | .... | .... | 24,043.2 | 28,792.1 | 39,753.0 | 43,110.5 | 54,122.5 |
| Net Claims on Central Government | 52an | .... | .... | .... | .... | .... | .... | .... | 8,186.2 | 7,081.8 | 15,368.9 | 14,293.7 | 17,767.6 |
| Claims on Central Government.... | 52a | .... | .... | .... | .... | .... | .... | .... | 14,875.9 | 15,771.3 | 21,978.6 | 21,615.0 | 25,016.3 |
| Liabilities to Central Government. | 56d | .... | .... | .... | .... | .... | .... | .... | 6,689.7 | 8,689.6 | 6,609.6 | 7,321.3 | 7,248.7 |
| Claims on Other Sectors................ | 52s | .... | .... | .... | .... | .... | .... | .... | 15,857.0 | 21,710.3 | 24,384.1 | 28,816.8 | 36,354.9 |
| Claims on State & Local Govts..... | 52b | .... | .... | .... | .... | .... | .... | .... | 11.9 | 18.6 | 22.8 | 37.0 | 50.4 |
| Claims on Pub. Nonfin. Corps...... | 52c | .... | .... | .... | .... | .... | .... | .... | 231.1 | 873.2 | 425.3 | 233.5 | 285.2 |
| Claims on Private Sector.............. | 52d | .... | | .... | .... | .... | .... | .... | 15,614.0 | 20,818.4 | 23,936.0 | 28,546.2 | 36,019.3 |
| Currency Outside Fin. Corporations.. | 54a | .... | .... | .... | .... | .... | .... | .... | 2,727.4 | 2,890.7 | 3,437.7 | 4,187.9 | 4,711.9 |
| Deposits......................................... | 55l | .... | .... | .... | .... | .... | .... | .... | 18,495.5 | 21,094.5 | 26,267.2 | 29,048.0 | 41,181.8 |
| Securities Other than Shares............ | 56a | .... | .... | .... | .... | .... | .... | .... | — | — | — | — | — |
| Loans............................................. | 56l | .... | .... | .... | .... | .... | .... | .... | 1,198.2 | 1,176.9 | 1,936.8 | 2,603.5 | 3,349.5 |
| Financial Derivatives........................ | 56m | .... | .... | .... | .... | .... | .... | .... | — | — | — | — | — |
| Insurance Technical Reserves........... | 56r | .... | .... | .... | .... | .... | .... | .... | 8,619.5 | 10,627.4 | 14,284.9 | 16,457.0 | 20,092.7 |
| Shares and Other Equity.................. | 57a | .... | .... | .... | .... | .... | .... | .... | 4,783.5 | 5,323.9 | 8,326.6 | 10,999.7 | 21,710.9 |
| Other Items (Net)............................ | 57r | .... | .... | .... | .... | .... | .... | .... | −2,451.1 | −388.6 | −2,965.1 | −4,903.4 | −7,403.1 |
| **Monetary Aggregates** | | | | | | *Millions of New Kwacha: End of Period* | | | | | | | |
| Broad Money................................. | 59m | 5,581.6 | 5,763.3 | 8,301.9 | 10,399.5 | 12,815.1 | 13,796.9 | 17,916.5 | 21,804.8 | 25,699.0 | 31,042.2 | 34,959.1 | 47,262.1 |
| o/w:Currency Issued by Cent.Govt | 59m.a | — | — | — | — | — | — | — | — | — | — | — | — |
| o/w: Dep.in Nonfin. Corporations. | 59m.b | — | — | — | — | — | — | — | — | — | — | — | — |
| o/w:Secs. Issued by Central Govt.. | 59m.c | — | — | — | — | — | — | — | — | — | — | — | — |
| Money (National Definitions) | | | | | | | | | | | | | |
| Monetary Base............................ | 19ma | 1,908.2 | 2,269.4 | 3,276.5 | 3,541.0 | 4,590.3 | 4,695.3 | 7,118.5 | 5,512.4 | 8,357.1 | 10,113.4 | 13,301.0 | 16,247.9 |
| M1.............................................. | 59ma | 1,860.4 | 2,167.1 | 3,340.1 | 3,825.6 | 4,982.5 | 4,961.9 | 6,977.9 | 8,345.1 | 11,254.1 | 13,053.5 | 13,537.1 | 14,147.1 |
| M2.............................................. | 59mb | 5,302.9 | 5,501.5 | 8,134.6 | 9,883.3 | 12,090.8 | 12,991.5 | 17,677.3 | 20,850.4 | 25,031.0 | 29,957.1 | 32,880.1 | 41,061.3 |
| M3.............................................. | 59mc | 5,639.4 | 5,783.8 | 8,344.0 | 10,446.6 | 12,867.6 | 13,844.6 | 18,080.3 | 22,351.9 | 26,178.0 | 31,463.1 | 34,959.1 | 47,262.1 |
| **Interest Rates** | | | | | | *Percent Per Annum* | | | | | | | |
| Discount Rate (End of Period)........... | 60.a | 16.68 | 14.81 | 8.79 | 11.73 | 14.49 | 8.39 | 7.17 | 9.71 | 10.38 | 12.13 | 17.23 | 16.87 |
| Treasury Bill Rate............................. | 60c | 12.60 | 16.32 | 10.37 | 11.95 | 13.47 | 15.39 | 6.28 | 9.55 | 10.13 | 11.44 | 15.36 | 19.02 |
| Savings Rate................................... | 60k | 6.41 | 5.73 | 6.10 | 5.74 | 4.78 | 4.72 | 4.69 | 4.46 | 4.28 | 3.48 | 3.53 | 3.36 |
| Deposit Rate................................... | 60l | 11.51 | 11.19 | 10.33 | 9.22 | 6.55 | 7.09 | 7.40 | 7.02 | 7.00 | 6.49 | 7.88 | 8.99 |
| Lending Rate................................... | 60p | 30.73 | 28.21 | 23.15 | 18.89 | 19.06 | 22.06 | 20.92 | 18.84 | 12.15 | 9.52 | 11.57 | 13.25 |
| **Prices and Production** | | | | | | *Index Numbers (2010=100): Period Averages* | | | | | | | |
| Share Prices (End of Month)............ | 62.ep | 20.1 | 35.4 | 50.8 | 95.7 | 125.9 | 86.4 | 100.0 | 129.0 | 128.2 | 152.9 | 201.2 | 199.4 |
| Consumer Prices.............................. | 64 | 50.6 | 59.9 | 65.3 | 72.3 | 81.3 | 92.2 | † 100.0 | 106.4 | 113.4 | 121.3 | 130.8 | 144.0 |
| **Intl. Transactions & Positions** | | | | | | *Billions of New Kwacha* | | | | | | | |
| Exports............................................ | 70 | 7.5 | 9.6 | 13.4 | 18.4 | 18.7 | 21.4 | 34.5 | 42.9 | 48.2 | 57.2 | 59.6 | 60.4 |
| Imports, c.i.f.................................... | 71 | 10.3 | 11.5 | 11.0 | 15.9 | 18.5 | 18.9 | 25.5 | 35.4 | 45.3 | 54.9 | 58.7 | 73.4 |

# Zambia   754

## Balance of Payments

*Millions of US Dollars*

| | | 2004 | 2005 | 2006 | 2007 | 2008 | 2009 | 2010 | 2011 | 2012 | 2013 | 2014 | 2015 |
|---|---|---|---|---|---|---|---|---|---|---|---|---|---|
| A. Current Account* | 109bx | −488.8 | † −363.2 | 476.2 | −320.6 | −767.5 | 714.1 | 1,376.8 | 958.5 | 1,247.9 | −218.5 | −401.4 | .... |
| Goods, credit (exports) | 1a9cx | 1,844.5 | † 2,278.2 | 3,984.8 | 4,555.6 | 5,013.1 | 4,371.9 | 7,483.5 | 8,753.6 | 9,520.8 | 10,843.4 | 10,220.2 | .... |
| Goods, debit (imports) | 1a9dx | 1,726.9 | † 2,160.7 | 2,635.8 | 3,610.5 | 4,554.3 | 3,413.4 | 4,709.9 | 6,454.2 | 7,925.5 | 9,195.4 | 8,594.8 | .... |
| Balance on goods | 1a9bx | 117.6 | † 117.5 | 1,349.0 | 945.1 | 458.9 | 958.5 | 2,773.6 | 2,299.4 | 1,595.3 | 1,648.0 | 1,625.4 | .... |
| Services, credit (exports) | 1b9cx | 231.8 | † 549.5 | 562.3 | 671.5 | 618.5 | 528.5 | 570.9 | 665.4 | 990.1 | 758.0 | 850.9 | .... |
| Services, debit (imports) | 1b9dx | 447.3 | † 412.2 | 514.0 | 835.0 | 834.7 | 671.8 | 888.1 | 1,093.0 | 1,333.9 | 1,816.2 | 1,644.4 | .... |
| Balance on Goods & Services | 1z9bx | −97.9 | † 254.7 | 1,397.2 | 781.6 | 242.7 | 815.3 | 2,456.3 | 1,871.8 | 1,251.4 | 589.8 | 831.8 | .... |
| Primary income: credit | 1c9cx | 32.0 | † 13.9 | 19.7 | 35.2 | 29.5 | 5.5 | 8.4 | 11.1 | 10.1 | 5.3 | 5.9 | .... |
| Primary income: debit | 1c9dx | 407.4 | † 607.7 | 1,186.7 | 1,521.4 | 1,428.9 | 424.2 | 1,371.4 | 1,168.1 | 343.6 | 1,158.6 | 1,522.5 | .... |
| Balance on gds, serv. & prim. inc. | 1y9bx | −473.3 | † −339.1 | 230.3 | −704.5 | −1,156.6 | 396.6 | 1,093.3 | 714.8 | 917.9 | −563.5 | −684.7 | .... |
| Secondary income: credit | 1d9ca | 48.4 | † 52.9 | 338.7 | 479.8 | 499.4 | 354.6 | 322.6 | 285.2 | 398.0 | 393.4 | 335.7 | .... |
| Secondary income: debit | 1d9da | 63.9 | † 77.0 | 92.7 | 95.9 | 110.3 | 37.0 | 39.2 | 41.5 | 68.0 | 48.4 | 52.3 | .... |
| B. Capital Account* | 209ba | 239.0 | † 287.0 | 229.4 | 222.8 | 230.0 | 237.3 | 149.7 | 151.0 | 223.0 | 277.9 | 51.0 | .... |
| Capital account: credit | 209ca | 239.0 | † 287.0 | 229.4 | 222.8 | 230.0 | 237.3 | 149.7 | 151.0 | 223.0 | 277.9 | 51.0 | .... |
| Capital account: debit | 209da | — | .... | .... | .... | .... | .... | .... | .... | .... | .... | .... | .... |
| Balance on current & capital acct. | 129ba | −249.8 | † −76.2 | 705.6 | −97.8 | −537.5 | 951.5 | 1,526.5 | 1,109.5 | 1,470.9 | 59.4 | −350.4 | .... |
| C. Financial Account* | 309na | −103.2 | † 1,887.9 | 2,192.8 | −327.4 | −392.9 | 602.6 | 1,564.3 | 969.3 | 1,267.9 | 277.2 | −698.5 | .... |
| Direct investment: assets | 3a9aa | −25.0 | .... | .... | .... | .... | 269.6 | 1,095.4 | −1.4 | −701.9 | 409.5 | −976.0 | .... |
| Equity & investment fund shares.. | 3aaaa | −25.0 | .... | .... | .... | .... | .... | .... | .... | .... | .... | .... | .... |
| Debt instruments | 3abaa | .... | .... | .... | .... | .... | 269.6 | 1,095.4 | −1.4 | −701.9 | 409.5 | −976.0 | .... |
| Direct investment: liabilities | 3a9la | 364.0 | † 356.9 | 615.8 | 1,323.9 | 938.6 | 694.8 | 1,729.3 | 1,108.5 | 1,731.5 | 2,099.8 | 1,507.8 | .... |
| Equity & investment fund shares . | 3aala | 321.6 | † 328.8 | 434.4 | 908.0 | 602.8 | 471.6 | 1,227.9 | 941.7 | −24.9 | 369.6 | 726.6 | .... |
| Debt instruments | 3abla | 42.5 | † 28.2 | 181.4 | 415.9 | 335.8 | 223.2 | 501.4 | 166.8 | 1,756.4 | 1,730.2 | 781.2 | .... |
| Portfolio investment: assets | 3b9aa | — | .... | .... | .... | .... | .... | .... | .... | −104.7 | −6.6 | −20.7 | .... |
| Equity & investment fund shares | 3baaa | — | .... | .... | .... | .... | .... | .... | .... | −104.7 | −6.6 | −20.7 | .... |
| Debt securities | 3bbaa | — | .... | .... | .... | .... | .... | .... | .... | .... | .... | .... | .... |
| Portfolio investment: liabilities | 3b9la | −.1 | † 122.4 | 50.4 | 41.8 | −6.1 | −74.9 | 73.6 | 70.7 | 794.6 | 89.9 | 1,184.8 | .... |
| Equity & investment fund shares . | 3bala | −.1 | † 5.3 | 2.0 | 3.8 | −5.7 | −13.1 | 100.5 | 24.6 | −7.4 | 5.5 | 6.1 | .... |
| Debt securities | 3bbla | — | † 117.1 | 48.5 | 38.0 | −.4 | −61.8 | −26.9 | 46.1 | 802.0 | 84.4 | 1,178.7 | .... |
| Fin. der.& empl.stk.ops.(ESOs): net | 3c9na | — | .... | .... | .... | .... | −219.6 | −225.7 | 154.3 | 10.8 | −3.2 | .8 | .... |
| Fin. der. & ESOs.: assets | 3c9aa | — | .... | .... | .... | .... | −127.6 | 76.7 | 34.7 | 13.6 | .3 | 7.0 | .... |
| Fin. der. & ESOs.: liabilities | 3c9la | — | .... | .... | .... | .... | 92.0 | 302.4 | −119.6 | 2.8 | 3.5 | 6.2 | .... |
| Other investment: assets | 3d9aa | 199.7 | † 519.8 | 1,127.6 | 1,615.0 | 453.4 | 1,978.8 | 2,709.5 | 2,301.2 | 5,179.9 | 2,172.9 | 3,300.4 | .... |
| Other equity | 3daaa | .... | .... | .... | .... | .... | .... | .... | .... | .... | .... | .... | .... |
| Debt instruments | 3dzaa | 199.7 | † 519.8 | 1,127.6 | 1,615.0 | 453.4 | 1,978.8 | 2,709.5 | 2,301.2 | 5,179.9 | 2,172.9 | 3,300.4 | .... |
| Other investment: liabilities | 3d9la | −86.2 | † −1,847.4 | −1,731.4 | 576.7 | −86.2 | 806.3 | 212.0 | 305.6 | 590.1 | 105.7 | 310.4 | .... |
| Other equity | 3dala | .... | .... | .... | .... | .... | .... | .... | .... | .... | .... | .... | .... |
| Debt instruments | 3dzla | −86.2 | † −1,847.4 | −1,731.4 | 576.7 | −86.2 | 806.3 | 212.0 | 305.6 | 590.1 | 105.7 | 310.4 | .... |
| Curr.+ cap.– finan. acct. balance... | 4y9na | −146.7 | † −1,964.1 | −1,487.2 | 229.6 | −144.6 | 348.8 | −37.8 | 140.2 | 203.1 | −217.7 | 348.1 | .... |
| D. Net Errors and Omissions | 409na | 173.8 | † −122.1 | −213.3 | −69.8 | −8.0 | −10.9 | −28.6 | −34.0 | −37.3 | −44.9 | −47.2 | .... |
| E. Reserves and Related Items | 4z9na | 27.2 | † −2,086.2 | −1,700.5 | 159.8 | −152.7 | 337.9 | −66.4 | 106.2 | 165.8 | −262.6 | 301.0 | .... |
| Reserve assets | 3e9aa | 64.4 | † 86.6 | 260.8 | 348.2 | 29.7 | 779.7 | 136.9 | 264.7 | 277.9 | −223.4 | 280.6 | .... |
| Credit and loans from the IMF | 3dcla | −6.8 | † −231.4 | −558.4 | 41.8 | 11.3 | 243.3 | 55.1 | 24.2 | −11.8 | −17.8 | −34.4 | .... |
| Exceptional financing | 409la | 44.1 | † 2,404.1 | 2,519.7 | 146.6 | 171.0 | 198.4 | 148.3 | 134.3 | 123.9 | 57.0 | 14.0 | .... |

*Excludes components in group E

## International Investment Position

*Millions of US Dollars*

| | | 2004 | 2005 | 2006 | 2007 | 2008 | 2009 | 2010 | 2011 | 2012 | 2013 | 2014 | 2015 |
|---|---|---|---|---|---|---|---|---|---|---|---|---|---|
| Assets | 809aa | .... | .... | † 2,421.5 | 4,528.1 | 5,997.6 | 8,879.5 | 12,768.7 | 15,279.2 | 20,830.6 | 23,204.3 | 25,725.4 | .... |
| Direct investment | 8a9aa | .... | .... | † 67.7 | 153.4 | 971.5 | 1,279.5 | 2,192.9 | 2,113.7 | 2,220.1 | 2,629.6 | 1,653.6 | .... |
| Equity & investment fund shares.. | 8aaaa | .... | .... | † 1.7 | 2.4 | 5.7 | 5.9 | 5.9 | 5.9 | 63.3 | 182.7 | 182.7 | .... |
| Debt instruments | 8abaa | .... | .... | † 66.0 | 151.0 | 965.8 | 1,273.6 | 2,187.0 | 2,107.8 | 2,156.8 | 2,446.9 | 1,470.9 | .... |
| Portfolio investment | 8b9aa | .... | .... | .... | .... | 40.0 | 40.0 | 108.3 | 108.2 | 92.9 | 86.5 | 65.8 | .... |
| Equity & investment fund shares.. | 8baaa | .... | .... | .... | .... | 40.0 | 40.0 | 108.3 | 108.2 | 92.9 | 86.5 | 65.8 | .... |
| Debt securities | 8bbaa | .... | .... | .... | .... | .... | .... | .... | .... | .... | .... | .... | .... |
| Fin. der.(oth.than reserves) & ESOs | 8c9aa | .... | .... | .... | .... | 127.6 | 5.8 | 86.1 | 2.5 | 2.9 | 3.2 | 10.2 | .... |
| Other investment | 8d9aa | .... | .... | † 1,758.7 | 3,461.8 | 3,917.0 | 5,801.2 | 8,484.8 | 10,885.9 | 16,059.8 | 18,233.8 | 21,534.2 | .... |
| Other equity | 8daaa | .... | .... | .... | .... | .... | .... | .... | .... | .... | .... | .... | .... |
| Debt instruments | 8dzaa | .... | .... | † 1,758.7 | 3,461.8 | 3,917.0 | 5,801.2 | 8,484.8 | 10,885.9 | 16,059.8 | 18,233.8 | 21,534.2 | .... |
| Reserve assets | 8e9aa | .... | .... | † 595.1 | 912.9 | 941.6 | 1,753.0 | 1,896.5 | 2,168.9 | 2,454.9 | 2,251.2 | 2,461.5 | .... |
| Liabilities | 809la | .... | .... | † 8,497.2 | 10,357.1 | 11,665.7 | 13,450.8 | 14,772.0 | 15,980.9 | 20,510.4 | 23,220.3 | 25,059.9 | .... |
| Direct investment | 8a9la | .... | .... | † 5,834.0 | 7,072.0 | 8,222.0 | 8,880.0 | 9,957.0 | 10,917.0 | 12,975.9 | 14,971.7 | 15,822.9 | .... |
| Equity & investment fund shares.. | 8aala | .... | .... | † 3,965.0 | 4,919.0 | 5,523.0 | 5,994.0 | 7,223.0 | 7,851.4 | 7,572.3 | 7,862.3 | 7,932.3 | .... |
| Debt instruments | 8abla | .... | .... | † 1,869.0 | 2,153.0 | 2,699.0 | 2,886.0 | 2,734.0 | 3,065.6 | 5,403.6 | 7,109.4 | 7,890.6 | .... |
| Portfolio investment | 8b9la | .... | .... | † 217.7 | 273.1 | 218.8 | 156.3 | 153.6 | 203.5 | 992.6 | 1,078.5 | 2,263.2 | .... |
| Equity & investment fund shares.. | 8bala | .... | .... | † 53.1 | 56.8 | 51.2 | 38.1 | 37.9 | 65.4 | 67.5 | 68.0 | 74.1 | .... |
| Debt securities | 8bbla | .... | .... | † 164.6 | 216.3 | 167.6 | 118.2 | 115.7 | 138.1 | 925.1 | 1,010.5 | 2,189.2 | .... |
| Fin. der.(oth.than reserves) & ESOs | 8c9la | .... | .... | .... | .... | 20.0 | 112.2 | 136.4 | 5.3 | 6.7 | 13.3 | 14.1 | .... |
| Other investment | 8d9la | .... | .... | † 2,445.5 | 3,012.0 | 3,204.9 | 4,302.4 | 4,525.0 | 4,855.1 | 6,535.2 | 7,156.8 | 6,959.5 | .... |
| Other equity | 8dala | .... | .... | .... | .... | .... | .... | .... | 112.8 | 117.9 | 117.9 | 117.9 | .... |
| Debt instruments | 8dzla | .... | .... | † 2,445.5 | 3,012.0 | 3,204.9 | 4,302.4 | 4,525.0 | 4,742.3 | 6,417.3 | 7,038.9 | 6,841.6 | .... |

2016, International Monetary Fund : *International Financial Statistics Yearbook*

# Zambia 754

| | | 2004 | 2005 | 2006 | 2007 | 2008 | 2009 | 2010 | 2011 | 2012 | 2013 | 2014 | 2015 |
|---|---|---|---|---|---|---|---|---|---|---|---|---|---|
| **National Accounts** | | | | | | *Billions of New Kwacha* | | | | | | | |
| Househ.Cons.Expend.,incl.NPISHs.... | 96f | 17.8 | 20.9 | 23.6 | 25.8 | 30.1 | 37.3 | 44.5 | 52.6 | 60.7 | .... | .... | .... |
| Government Consumption Expend... | 91f | 4.5 | 5.9 | 7.2 | 8.3 | 9.5 | 11.7 | 12.7 | 19.2 | 25.6 | .... | .... | .... |
| Gross Fixed Capital Formation......... | 93e | 6.1 | 7.2 | 8.0 | 9.5 | 10.7 | 12.6 | 16.4 | 21.9 | 26.2 | .... | .... | .... |
| Changes in Inventories.................... | 93i | .3 | .4 | .5 | .6 | .8 | .9 | 1.2 | 1.4 | 1.8 | .... | .... | .... |
| Exports of Goods and Services......... | 90c | 9.8 | 11.1 | 14.8 | 18.9 | 19.4 | 22.6 | 36.3 | 43.2 | 49.7 | .... | .... | .... |
| Imports of Goods and Services (-)..... | 98c | 10.4 | 11.7 | 11.6 | 18.1 | 20.4 | 20.8 | 27.1 | 37.1 | 47.7 | .... | .... | .... |
| Gross Domestic Product (GDP)......... | 99b | 28.1 | 33.7 | 42.5 | 45.1 | 50.1 | 64.4 | 84.0 | 101.2 | 116.3 | 144.7 | 166.5 | .... |
| Net Primary Income from Abroad..... | 98.n | −1.7 | −2.7 | −4.2 | −6.2 | −5.2 | .... | .... | .... | .... | .... | .... | .... |
| Gross National Income (GNI)............ | 99a | 24.3 | 29.3 | 34.4 | 40.2 | 50.2 | .... | .... | .... | .... | .... | .... | .... |
| GDP Volume 1994 Prices................. | 99b.p | 3.0 | 3.2 | 3.4 | 3.6 | 3.8 | 4.0 | 4.3 | 4.6 | 4.9 | 5.3 | .... | .... |
| GDP Volume (2005=100)............... | 99bvp | 94.9 | 100.0 | 106.2 | 112.8 | 119.2 | 126.8 | 136.5 | 145.8 | 156.4 | 166.7 | .... | .... |
| GDP Deflator (2005=100)............... | 99bip | 88.0 | 100.0 | 118.8 | 118.5 | 124.7 | 150.7 | 182.5 | 205.9 | 220.7 | 257.7 | .... | .... |
| | | | | | | *Millions: Midyear Estimates* | | | | | | | |
| Population................................ | 99z | 11.73 | 12.04 | 12.38 | 12.74 | 13.11 | 13.51 | 13.92 | 14.34 | 14.79 | 15.25 | 15.72 | 16.21 |

# Zimbabwe 698

| | | 2004 | 2005 | 2006 | 2007 | 2008 | 2009 | 2010 | 2011 | 2012 | 2013 | 2014 | 2015 |
|---|---|---|---|---|---|---|---|---|---|---|---|---|---|
| **Exchange Rates** | | | | | *Zimbabwe $ per SDR: End of Period* | | | | | | | | |
| Official Rate................................ | aa | 9.2 | 115.4 | 389.5 | 47,407.5 | 7,547,323.0 | .... | .... | .... | .... | .... | .... | .... |
| | | | | | | *Zimbabwe $ per US $* | | | | | | | |
| Official Rate (End of Period)............ | ae | 5.9 | 80.8 | 258.9 | 30,000.0 | 4,900,000.0 | .... | .... | .... | .... | .... | .... | .... |
| Official Rate (Period Average).......... | rf | 5.1 | 22.4 | 164.5 | 9,686.8 | 430,972.7 | .... | .... | .... | .... | .... | .... | .... |
| **Fund Position** | | | | | | *Millions of SDRs: End of Period* | | | | | | | |
| Quota...................................... | 2f.s | 353.40 | 353.40 | 353.40 | 353.40 | 353.40 | 353.40 | 353.40 | 353.40 | 353.40 | 353.40 | 353.40 | 353.40 |
| SDR Holdings.............................. | 1b.s | — | .02 | — | — | — | 230.45 | 164.91 | 164.45 | 93.03 | 92.90 | 92.73 | 92.63 |
| Reserve Position in the Fund.......... | 1c.s | .33 | .33 | .33 | .33 | .33 | .33 | .33 | .33 | .33 | .33 | .33 | .33 |
| Total Fund Cred.&Loans Outstg........ | 2tl | 188.80 | 77.32 | 74.97 | 74.89 | 73.83 | 73.76 | 71.14 | 71.14 | 66.24 | 65.06 | 63.77 | 62.48 |
| SDR Allocations........................... | 1bd | 10.20 | 10.20 | 10.20 | 10.20 | 10.20 | 272.18 | 272.18 | 272.18 | 272.18 | 272.18 | 272.18 | 272.18 |
| **International Liquidity** | | | | | *Millions of US Dollars Unless Otherwise Indicated: End of Period* | | | | | | | | |
| Total Reserves minus Gold.............. | 1l.d | 223.2 | 97.2 | 154.6 | 144.5 | 75.5 | 821.9 | 731.8 | 659.2 | 574.4 | 474.5 | 363.3 | 323.4 |
| SDR Holdings............................. | 1b.d | — | — | — | — | — | 361.3 | 254.0 | 252.5 | 143.0 | 143.1 | 134.3 | 128.4 |
| Reserve Position in the Fund.......... | 1c.d | .5 | .5 | .5 | .5 | .5 | .5 | .5 | .5 | .5 | .5 | .5 | .5 |
| Foreign Exchange....................... | 1d.d | 222.7 | 96.7 | 154.1 | 144.0 | 75.0 | 460.1 | 477.3 | 406.2 | 430.9 | 330.9 | 228.5 | 194.6 |
| Gold (Million Fine Troy Ounces)...... | 1ad | .03 | .... | .... | .02 | .01 | .... | .... | — | — | — | — | .02 |
| Gold (National Valuation)............... | 1and | 1.2 | 11.7 | 11.1 | 9.0 | 3.0 | .... | .... | 1.1 | 1.1 | .5 | .5 | 15.6 |
| Monetary Authorities: Other Liabs.... | 4..d | 282.5 | 239.4 | 265.5 | 395.2 | 543.9 | .... | .... | .... | .... | .... | | |
| Deposit Money Banks: Assets.......... | 7a.d | 142.8 | 174.5 | 235.1 | 536.7 | .... | .... | .... | .... | .... | .... | | |
| Deposit Money Banks: Liabs........... | 7b.d | 100.3 | 48.1 | 53.5 | 83.7 | .... | .... | .... | .... | .... | .... | | |
| Other Banking Insts.: Assets............ | 7e.d | — | — | — | — | .... | .... | .... | .... | .... | .... | | |
| Other Banking Insts.: Liabs.............. | 7f.d | .7 | — | — | — | .... | .... | .... | .... | .... | .... | | |
| **Monetary Authorities** | | *Millions of Zimbabwe Dollars through 2006; Billions in 2007; Quintillions of New Zimbabwe Dollars in 2008: End of Period* | | | | | | | | | | | |
| Claims on Deposit Money Banks...... | 12e | 3,250 | 3,483 | 37,474 | † 13,694 | † — | .... | .... | .... | .... | .... | | |
| Reserve Money........................... | 14 | 2,330 | 12,908 | 299,706 | † 206,774 | † 92,591 | .... | .... | .... | .... | .... | | |
| of which: Currency Outside DMBs.. | 14a | 1,656 | 9,876 | 228,064 | † 73,075 | † — | .... | .... | .... | .... | .... | | |
| Liabs. of Central Bank: Securities..... | 16ac | 732 | 4,927 | 14,131 | † 128 | † — | .... | .... | .... | .... | .... | | |
| Foreign Liabilities........................ | 16c | 3,511 | 29,444 | 101,906 | † 15,891 | † — | .... | .... | .... | .... | .... | | |
| Central Government Deposits........... | 16d | 394 | 3,119 | 72,902 | † 47,283 | † 40,569 | .... | .... | .... | .... | .... | | |
| Capital Accounts.......................... | 17a | −92 | −1,176 | −3,972 | † −484 | † — | .... | .... | .... | .... | .... | | |
| Other Items (Net)......................... | 17r | 648 | −3,291 | −268,572 | † 114,860 | † 496,562 | .... | .... | .... | .... | .... | | |
| **Deposit Money Banks** | | *Millions of Zimbabwe Dollars through 2006; Billions in 2007; Quintillions of New Zimbabwe Dollars in 2008: End of Period* | | | | | | | | | | | |
| Reserves................................... | 20 | 3,904 | 17,414 | 409,523 | † 251,330 | † 176,353 | .... | .... | .... | .... | .... | | |
| Claims on Mon.Author.:Securities.... | 20c | 732 | 4,927 | 14,131 | † 128 | † — | .... | .... | .... | .... | .... | | |
| Foreign Assets............................. | 21 | 848 | 14,092 | 60,860 | † 16,100 | † 1 | .... | .... | .... | .... | .... | | |
| Claims on Central Government........ | 22a | 3,561 | 20,223 | 237,349 | † 147,595 | † 15,659 | .... | .... | .... | .... | .... | | |
| Claims on Local Government........... | 22b | 32 | 74 | 454 | † 72 | † 163 | .... | .... | .... | .... | .... | | |
| Claims on Nonfin.Pub.Enterprises..... | 22c | 435 | 677 | 13,334 | † 9,400 | † — | .... | .... | .... | .... | .... | | |
| Claims on Private Sector................. | 22d | 4,981 | 15,793 | 275,193 | † 255,470 | † 4,801,664 | .... | .... | .... | .... | .... | | |
| Claims on Other Banking Insts......... | 22f | 53 | 96 | 970 | † 375 | † 3,199 | .... | .... | .... | .... | .... | | |
| Claims on Nonbank Financial Insts.... | 22g | 103 | 87 | 15,667 | † 18,823 | † 15,987 | .... | .... | .... | .... | .... | | |
| Demand Deposits......................... | 24 | 5,148 | 34,048 | 404,965 | † 350,999 | † 151,709 | .... | .... | .... | .... | .... | | |
| Time, Savings,& Fgn.Currency Dep... | 25 | 2,377 | 13,678 | 270,556 | † 123,289 | † 50,221 | .... | .... | .... | .... | .... | | |
| Money Market Instruments.............. | 26aa | 381 | 1,517 | 22,972 | † 8,579 | † 430 | .... | .... | .... | .... | .... | | |
| Foreign Liabilities........................ | 26c | 595 | 3,887 | 13,842 | † 2,511 | † 1,726 | .... | .... | .... | .... | .... | | |
| Central Government Deposits........... | 26d | 267 | 1,107 | 8,383 | † 3,354 | † 2,557 | .... | .... | .... | .... | .... | | |
| Credit from Monetary Authorities..... | 26g | 3,460 | 5,644 | 146,578 | † 88,543 | † 17,602 | .... | .... | .... | .... | .... | | |
| Capital Accounts.......................... | 27a | 1,964 | 10,176 | 260,785 | † 198,503 | † 12,869,991 | .... | .... | .... | .... | .... | | |
| Other Items (Net)......................... | 27r | 455 | 3,327 | −100,600 | † −76,484 | † −8,081,209 | .... | .... | .... | .... | .... | | |
| **Monetary Survey** | | *Millions of Zimbabwe Dollars through 2006; Billions in 2007; Quintillions of New Zimbabwe Dollars in 2008: End of Period* | | | | | | | | | | | |
| Foreign Assets (Net)...................... | 31n | −1,624 | −9,860 | −35,620 | † 2,211 | † −1,725 | .... | .... | .... | .... | .... | | |
| Domestic Credit........................... | 32 | 11,142 | 65,793 | 621,042 | † 747,345 | † 5,423,269 | .... | .... | .... | .... | .... | | |
| Claims on Central Govt. (Net)........ | 32an | 5,502 | 44,633 | 204,702 | † 105,078 | † −23,467 | .... | .... | .... | .... | .... | | |
| Claims on Local Government........... | 32b | 32 | 74 | 454 | † 72 | † 163 | .... | .... | .... | .... | .... | | |
| Claims on Nonfin.Pub.Enterprises... | 32c | 435 | 1,666 | 15,416 | † 9,403 | † — | .... | .... | .... | .... | .... | | |
| Claims on Private Sector............... | 32d | 5,017 | 19,237 | 383,832 | † 613,593 | † 5,427,388 | .... | .... | .... | .... | .... | | |
| Claims on Other Banking Insts....... | 32f | 53 | 96 | 970 | † 375 | † 3,199 | .... | .... | .... | .... | .... | | |
| Claims on Nonbank Financial Insts. | 32g | 103 | 87 | 15,667 | † 18,823 | † 15,987 | .... | .... | .... | .... | .... | | |
| Money..................................... | 34 | 6,857 | 44,746 | 636,799 | † 425,445 | † 164,182 | .... | .... | .... | .... | .... | | |
| Quasi-Money.............................. | 35 | 2,377 | 13,678 | 270,556 | † 123,289 | † 50,221 | .... | .... | .... | .... | .... | | |
| Money Market Instruments.............. | 36aa | 381 | 1,517 | 22,972 | † 8,579 | † 430 | .... | .... | .... | .... | .... | | |
| Liabs. of Central Bank:Securities...... | 36ac | — | — | — | † — | † — | .... | .... | .... | .... | .... | | |
| Capital Accounts.......................... | 37a | 1,872 | 8,999 | 256,813 | † 198,019 | † 12,869,991 | .... | .... | .... | .... | .... | | |
| Other Items (Net)......................... | 37r | −1,969 | −13,008 | −601,717 | † −5,777 | † −7,663,279 | .... | .... | .... | .... | .... | | |
| Money plus Quasi-Money............... | 35l | 9,234 | 58,425 | 907,354 | † 548,734 | † 214,403 | .... | .... | .... | .... | .... | | |
| **Other Banking Institutions** | | *Millions of Zimbabwe Dollars through 2006; Billions in 2007; Quintillions of New Zimbabwe Dollars in 2008: End of Period* | | | | | | | | | | | |
| Reserves................................... | 40 | 511 | 2,348 | 31,258 | † 22,594 | † 5,027 | .... | .... | .... | .... | .... | .... | |
| Foreign Assets............................. | 41 | — | — | — | † — | † — | .... | .... | .... | .... | .... | .... | |
| Claims on Central Government........ | 42a | 473 | 4,390 | 41,545 | † 14,781 | † 74 | .... | .... | .... | .... | .... | .... | |
| Claims on Local Government............ | 42b | — | 7 | 20 | † 20 | † — | .... | .... | .... | .... | .... | .... | |
| Claims on Nonfin.Pub.Enterprises..... | 42c | 8 | 3 | — | † — | † — | .... | .... | .... | .... | .... | .... | |
| Claims on Private Sector................. | 42d | 287 | 1,087 | 14,123 | † 107,533 | † 6,466 | .... | .... | .... | .... | .... | .... | |
| Claims on Nonbank Financial Insts... | 42g | 2 | 18 | 17 | † 3,011 | † 81,315 | .... | .... | .... | .... | .... | .... | |
| Time, Savings,& Fgn.Currency Dep... | 45 | 1,106 | 6,834 | 77,915 | † 46,653 | † 6,503 | .... | .... | .... | .... | .... | .... | |
| Money Market Instruments.............. | 46aa | 33 | 14 | — | † — | † — | .... | .... | .... | .... | .... | .... | |
| Foreign Liabilities........................ | 46c | 4 | — | — | † — | † — | .... | .... | .... | .... | .... | .... | |
| Credit from Deposit Money Banks..... | 46h | 13 | — | — | † 319 | † 295 | .... | .... | .... | .... | .... | .... | |
| Capital Accounts.......................... | 47a | 257 | 2,470 | 101,384 | † 78,257 | † 168,025 | .... | .... | .... | .... | .... | .... | |
| Other Items (Net)......................... | 47r | −131 | −1,464 | −92,334 | † 22,710 | † −81,941 | .... | .... | .... | .... | .... | .... | |

# Zimbabwe 698

|  |  | 2004 | 2005 | 2006 | 2007 | 2008 | 2009 | 2010 | 2011 | 2012 | 2013 | 2014 | 2015 |
|---|---|---|---|---|---|---|---|---|---|---|---|---|---|
| **Banking Survey** | | | | | | | | | | | | | |

*Millions of Zimbabwe Dollars through 2006; Billions in 2007; Quintillions of New Zimbabwe Dollars in 2008: End of Period*

| Banking Survey |  | 2004 | 2005 | 2006 | 2007 | 2008 | 2009 | 2010 | 2011 | 2012 | 2013 | 2014 | 2015 |
|---|---|---|---|---|---|---|---|---|---|---|---|---|---|
| Foreign Assets (Net) | 51n | −1,628 | −9,860 | −35,620 | † 2,211 | † −1,725 | .... | .... | .... | .... | .... | .... | .... |
| Domestic Credit | 52 | 11,859 | 71,203 | 675,778 | † 872,315 | † 5,507,925 | .... | .... | .... | .... | .... | .... | .... |
| Claims on Central Govt. (Net) | 52an | 5,975 | 49,024 | 246,248 | † 119,859 | † −23,393 | .... | .... | .... | .... | .... | .... | .... |
| Claims on Local Government | 52b | 32 | 81 | 475 | † 92 | † 163 | .... | .... | .... | .... | .... | .... | .... |
| Claims on Nonfin.Pub.Enterprises | 52c | 444 | 1,669 | 15,417 | † 9,403 | † — | .... | .... | .... | .... | .... | .... | .... |
| Claims on Private Sector | 52d | 5,304 | 20,324 | 397,956 | † 721,126 | † 5,433,853 | .... | .... | .... | .... | .... | .... | .... |
| Claims on Nonbank Financial Insts. | 52g | 104 | 105 | 15,684 | † 21,834 | † 97,302 | .... | .... | .... | .... | .... | .... | .... |
| Liquid Liabilities | 55l | 9,828 | 62,911 | 954,011 | † 572,793 | † 215,879 | .... | .... | .... | .... | .... | .... | .... |
| Money Market Instruments | 56aa | 414 | 1,530 | 22,972 | † 8,579 | † 430 | .... | .... | .... | .... | .... | .... | .... |
| Liabs. of Central Bank:Securities | 56ac | — | — | — | † — | † — | .... | .... | .... | .... | .... | .... | .... |
| Capital Accounts | 57a | 2,129 | 11,470 | 358,197 | † 276,276 | † 13,038,016 | .... | .... | .... | .... | .... | .... | .... |
| Other Items (Net) | 57r | −2,140 | −14,568 | −695,022 | † 16,877 | † −7,748,124 | .... | .... | .... | .... | .... | .... | .... |

**Interest Rates** — *Percent Per Annum*

| Treasury Bill Rate | 60c | 125.68 | 185.11 | 322.36 | 248.77 | .... | .... | .... | .... | .... | .... | .... | .... |
|---|---|---|---|---|---|---|---|---|---|---|---|---|---|
| Deposit Rate | 60l | 103.21 | 91.08 | 203.38 | 121.50 | .... | .... | .... | .... | .... | .... | .... | .... |
| Lending Rate | 60p | 278.92 | 235.68 | 496.46 | 578.96 | .... | .... | .... | .... | .... | .... | .... | .... |

**Prices, Production, Labor** — *Index Numbers (2000=.1): Period Averages*

| Industrial Share Prices | 62a | 4.4 | 41.1 | 1,225.3 | 1,874,222.2 | .... | .... | .... | .... | .... | .... | .... | .... |
|---|---|---|---|---|---|---|---|---|---|---|---|---|---|
| Consumer Prices | 64 | .... | .... | .... | .... | .... | 97.1 | 100.0 | 103.3 | 107.3 | 109.1 | 108.8 | 106.2 |

**Intl. Transactions & Positions** — *Millions of US Dollars*

| Exports | 70..d | 1,887.00 | 1,850.00 | 2,000.00 | 2,400.00 | 2,200.00 | 2,268.90 | 3,199.23 | 3,512.13 | 3,800.00 | 3,551.89 | 3,438.00 | 2,715.70 |
|---|---|---|---|---|---|---|---|---|---|---|---|---|---|
| Imports, c.i.f. | 71..d | 2,203.78 | 2,350.00 | 2,300.00 | 2,550.00 | 2,950.00 | 2,900.00 | 3,800.00 | 4,400.00 | 4,400.00 | 4,300.00 | 4,200.00 | 4,000.00 |

**Government Finance**
**Cash Flow Statement**
**Budgetary Central Government** — *Thousands of US Dollars: Fiscal Year Ends December 31*

| Cash Receipts:Operating Activities | c1 | .... | .... | .... | .... | .... | 944,427 | 2,336,960 | 2,915,262 | 3,490,582 | .... | .... | .... |
|---|---|---|---|---|---|---|---|---|---|---|---|---|---|
| Taxes | c11 | .... | .... | .... | .... | .... | 888,953 | 2,099,453 | 2,528,228 | 3,052,517 | .... | .... | .... |
| Social Contributions | c12 | .... | .... | .... | .... | .... | 819 | 1,355 | 4,107 | 2,150 | .... | .... | .... |
| Grants | c13 | .... | .... | .... | .... | .... | — | — | — | — | .... | .... | .... |
| Other Receipts | c14 | .... | .... | .... | .... | .... | 54,655 | 236,152 | 382,927 | 435,915 | .... | .... | .... |
| Cash Payments:Operating Activities | c2 | .... | .... | .... | .... | .... | 914,918 | 1,941,220 | 2,690,222 | 3,459,224 | .... | .... | .... |
| Compensation of Employees | c21 | .... | .... | .... | .... | .... | 515,383 | 946,522 | 1,544,093 | 2,172,981 | .... | .... | .... |
| Purchases of Goods & Services | c22 | .... | .... | .... | .... | .... | 161,914 | 290,863 | 387,349 | 439,670 | .... | .... | .... |
| Interest | c24 | .... | .... | .... | .... | .... | 21,095 | 30,771 | 34,233 | 21,806 | .... | .... | .... |
| Subsidies | c25 | .... | .... | .... | .... | .... | | | | | .... | .... | .... |
| Grants | c26 | .... | .... | .... | .... | .... | 162,560 | 564,309 | 662,904 | 794,886 | .... | .... | .... |
| Social Benefits | c27 | .... | .... | .... | .... | .... | 31,223 | 108,755 | 61,644 | 29,880 | .... | .... | .... |
| Other Payments | c28 | .... | .... | .... | .... | .... | 22,743 | — | — | — | .... | .... | .... |
| Net Cash Inflow:Operating Act.[1-2] | ccio | .... | .... | .... | .... | .... | 29,508 | 395,741 | 225,040 | 31,358 | .... | .... | .... |
| Net Cash Outflow:Invest. in NFA | c31 | .... | .... | .... | .... | .... | 11,993 | 73,403 | 108,717 | 32,236 | .... | .... | .... |
| Purchases of Nonfinancial Assets | c31.1 | .... | .... | .... | .... | .... | 11,993 | 73,403 | 108,717 | 32,236 | .... | .... | .... |
| Sales of Nonfinancial Assets | c31.2 | .... | .... | .... | .... | .... | | | | | .... | .... | .... |
| Cash Surplus/Deficit [1-2-31=1-2M] | ccsd | .... | .... | .... | .... | .... | 17,516 | 322,338 | 116,323 | −878 | .... | .... | .... |
| Net Acq. Fin. Assets, excl. Cash | c32x | .... | .... | .... | .... | .... | 362,667 | 54,404 | 90,853 | −107 | .... | .... | .... |
| Domestic | c321x | .... | .... | .... | .... | .... | 1,818 | 154,840 | 91,593 | 111,013 | .... | .... | .... |
| Foreign | c322x | .... | .... | .... | .... | .... | 360,849 | −100,436 | −740 | −111,120 | .... | .... | .... |
| Net Incurrence of Liabilities | c33 | .... | .... | .... | .... | .... | 1,561,496 | −24,499 | 74,179 | −94,831 | .... | .... | .... |
| Domestic | c331 | .... | .... | .... | .... | .... | 1,151,320 | −24,499 | 74,179 | −145,759 | .... | .... | .... |
| Foreign | c332 | .... | .... | .... | .... | .... | 410,176 | — | — | 50,928 | .... | .... | .... |
| Net Cash Inflow, Fin.Act.[-32x+33] | cnfb | .... | .... | .... | .... | .... | 1,198,829 | −78,903 | −16,675 | −94,724 | .... | .... | .... |
| Net Change in Stock of Cash | cncb | .... | .... | .... | .... | .... | 133,504 | −27,370 | 77,073 | −60,013 | .... | .... | .... |
| Stat. Discrep. [32X-33+NCB-CSD] | ccsdz | .... | .... | .... | .... | .... | −1,082,841 | −270,805 | −22,575 | 35,589 | .... | .... | .... |
| Memo Item:Cash Expenditure[2+31] | c2m | .... | .... | .... | .... | .... | 926,911 | 2,014,623 | 2,798,939 | 3,491,460 | .... | .... | .... |
| Memo Item: Gross Debt | c63 | .... | .... | .... | .... | .... | | | | | .... | .... | .... |

**National Accounts** — *Millions of Zimbabwe Dollars*

| Househ.Cons.Expend.,incl.NPISHs | 96f | 17,634 | 123,263 | .... | .... | .... | .... | .... | .... | .... | .... | .... | .... |
|---|---|---|---|---|---|---|---|---|---|---|---|---|---|
| Government Consumption Expend | 91f | 5,015 | 5,415 | .... | .... | .... | .... | .... | .... | .... | .... | .... | .... |
| Gross Fixed Capital Formation | 93e | 3,047 | .... | .... | .... | .... | .... | .... | .... | .... | .... | .... | .... |
| Changes in Inventories | 93i | −625 | .... | .... | .... | .... | .... | .... | .... | .... | .... | .... | .... |
| Exports of Goods and Services | 90c | 8,587 | 32,001 | .... | .... | .... | .... | .... | .... | .... | .... | .... | .... |
| Imports of Goods and Services (-) | 98c | 10,481 | 40,653 | .... | .... | .... | .... | .... | .... | .... | .... | .... | .... |
| Gross Domestic Product (GDP) | 99b | 23,802 | 129,533 | .... | .... | .... | .... | .... | .... | .... | .... | .... | .... |
| Net Primary Income from Abroad | 98.n | .... | .... | .... | .... | .... | .... | .... | .... | .... | .... | .... | .... |
| Gross National Income (GNI) | 99a | 14,457 | .... | .... | .... | .... | .... | .... | .... | .... | .... | .... | .... |
| GDP Volume 1990 Prices | 99b.p | 19 | .... | .... | .... | .... | .... | .... | .... | .... | .... | .... | .... |
| GDP Volume (2000=100) | 99bvp | 80.1 | .... | .... | .... | .... | .... | .... | .... | .... | .... | .... | .... |
| GDP Deflator (2000=100) | 99bip | 9,042.0 | .... | .... | .... | .... | .... | .... | .... | .... | .... | .... | .... |

*Millions: Midyear Estimates*

| Population | 99z | 12.87 | 12.98 | 13.13 | 13.30 | 13.50 | 13.72 | 13.97 | 14.26 | 14.57 | 14.90 | 15.25 | 15.60 |
|---|---|---|---|---|---|---|---|---|---|---|---|---|---|

# Notes

# Notes

# Notes

# Notes

# Notes

# Notes

# Notes